1886 LARGE DRAGON COVER OF IMPERIAL CHINA. Estimated Cash Value: US$ 20,000.00

Buying • Selling • Auctions
Specializing In Chinese Philatelics

High prices paid and liberal cash advances made for Chinese philatelics

Selling Chinese Philatelics can be a profitable experience if the right auction company is used by the collector.
Sun Philatelics suggests that those companies that specialize in the sale of Chinese Philatelics, will constantly produce the highest return for the collector.

Sun Philatelics specializes in the sale of Chinese Philatelics at international auctions in Hong Kong & Tokyo, the heart of the market for Chinese & Asian Philatelics. When you are ready to sell, and if you insist on the highest return from your stamp investment, we suggest that you first make contact with Sun Philatelics, proven professionals in the sale of Chinese Philatelics.

Your Chinese stamps and postal history are now commanding some of the highest prices in the philatelic market. Sun Philatelics understands this, and we are committed to seeing that your investment in Chinese stamps brings you the best prices when sold at auction.

We are now taking consignments for our coming auctions to be held in Hong Kong & Tokyo. If you are interested in selling, or if you would like to learn more about how to sell Chinese Philatelics for the best prices, contact Sun Philatelics prior to our next consignment deadline.

You may call us collect, or use our facsimile or telex contacts. (printed below) We also publish a color auction catalogue of Chinese and Asian stamps and philatelics on a quarterly basis. Those collectors interested in selling should request a catalogue, along with a description of your holdings

SUN PHILATELIC AUCTIONS
SAN FRANCISCO • TOKYO • HONG KONG
Auctioneers of Fine Asian Philatelics

Telephone: (415) 822-2006 Fax: (415) 822-6275 Telex: 184150

Liberal cash advances given to consignors of Chinese Philatelics
Immediate cash payments made for private sales

Sun Philatelic Auctions

MAILING ADDRESS: SUN PHILATELIC AUCTIONS POST OFFICE BOX 88-2290, SAN FRANCISCO, CA. 94188-2290. U.S.A.

SCOTT®

1989 Standard Postage Stamp Catalogue

ONE HUNDRED AND FORTY-FIFTH EDITION IN FOUR VOLUMES

VOLUME 2

EUROPEAN COUNTRIES and COLONIES
INDEPENDENT NATIONS of
AFRICA, ASIA, LATIN AMERICA
A - F

PRESIDENT/PUBLISHER	**Wayne Lawrence**
VICE PRESIDENT	**Charles M. Pritchett**
EDITORIAL DIRECTOR	**Richard L. Sine**
EDITOR	**William W. Cummings**
ASSISTANT EDITOR	**William H. Hatton**
PRICING EDITOR	**Martin J. Frankevicz**
NEW ISSUES EDITOR	**Robin A. Denaro**
COMPUTER CONTROL COORDINATOR	**Elaine Cottrel**
EDITORIAL ASSISTANTS	**Joyce A. Cecil** **Mary D. Sturwold**
PRICING ANALYSTS	**David C. Akin** **Roger L. Listwan**
ART/PRODUCTION DIRECTOR	**Edward Heys**
PRODUCTION COORDINATOR	**J. Skinn Apple**
DIRECTOR OF MARKETING & SALES	**Stuart J. Morrissey**
ADVERTISING MANAGER	**David Lodge**

Scott Publishing Co.

911 Vandemark Road, Sidney, Ohio 45365

A division of AMOS PRESS INC., publishers of *Linn's Stamp News, Coin World, Cars & Parts* magazine and *The Sidney Daily News.*

TABLE OF CONTENTS

See Volumes 3 and 4 for nations of Africa, Asia, Europe, Latin America and their affiliated territories, G-Z.

See Volume 1 for United States and Affiliated Territories, United Nations, and British Commonwealth of Nations.

ISBN 0-89487-109-9

Library of Congress Card No. 2-3301

SPECIAL NOTICES

This catalogue lists adhesive postage stamps of the various countries, except for the United States where additional listings cover revenue stamps and postal stationery.

To facilitate identification, the following style of listing is used:

Canada

41	A24	3c	bright vermilion	17.50	30
		a.	3c rose carmine	300.00	6.00

The number (41) in the first column is the index or identification number, the letter and number combination (A24) indicates the design and refers to the illustration having this (A24) designation; next comes the denomination (3c) followed by the color (bright vermilion) or a description of the stamp; the prices are in two columns at the right, the first (17.50) being that of an unused stamp and the last (30) of a canceled one. This is known as a major listing or variety.

Variations from so-called "normal" stamps are listed in small type and designated by lowercase letters of the alphabet. These are called minor varieties. When they immediately follow the major listing in the catalogue the original index and design numbers are understood to be the same. In the preceding example, the minor variety, No. 41a, differs from the major variety, No. 41, only in shade; its design, perforation, etc., remain unchanged.

When year, perforation, watermark or printing method is mentioned, the description applies to all succeeding listings until a change is noted. The heading note "Without Gum" applies only to the set it precedes.

When a stamp is printed in black on colored paper, the color of the paper alone is given in italics.

With stamps printed in two or more colors, the color given first is that of the frame or outer parts of the design starting at the upper left corner. The colors that follow are those of the vignette or inner parts of the design.

For some sets which include both vertical and horizontal format stamps, a single illustration is used, with the various designs and formats described beneath the illustration.

Abbreviations

The most frequently used abbreviations are:

Imperf. = Imperforate. Perf. = Perforated. Wmk. = Watermark. Unwmkd. = Unwatermarked. Litho. = Lithographed. Photo. = Photogravure. Engr. = Engraved. Typo. = Typographed.

When no color is given for an overprint or surcharge, it is understood to be in black. Abbreviations are sometimes used, as (B) or (Bk) Black, (Bl) Blue, (R) Red, (G) Green, etc.

New Issue Listings

Scott's Catalogue Update appears regularly in the *Scott Stamp Monthly* and reports new listings.

Condition

A stamp's condition is a crucial factor of its price. Prices quoted in this catalogue are for stamps with no flaws; all perforations intact; unfaded color; reasonable centering, i.e., no worse than the design not quite touching the perforations on some issues and much closer to perfect centering on more recent issues; and for unused stamps with the major part of original gum intact (unless, of course, the stamp was issued without gum). Exceptional copies often bring higher prices. For some countries, or for specific issues within countries, a note with the listing indicates that prices are for specimens without gum.

Slightly defective stamps which are off-center, heavily canceled, faded, or stained are usually sold at large discounts. Damaged stamps which are torn or mutilated or have serious defects seldom bring more than a small fraction of the price of a fine specimen.

Standards of condition may vary greatly in the stamps of different countries. By way of example, early stamps of the United States, Great Britain, Victoria and Japan were perforated in such a manner as to make most examples appear severely off center. They also normally were heavily canceled. It therefore is difficult to obtain early stamps from these countries, and others, in as fine a condition as stamps from countries where more care was taken during the perforating process and where lighter cancellations were applied.

Pricing Limitations

Each price appearing in this catalogue represents an estimate by Scott Publishing Co. of the current value basis for a specimen of that single stamp (or, where noted, set of stamps) of the condition noted in the first section of this explanation, offered by a retail stamp dealer to a collector. Because this catalogue is issued only once each year, it is impossible for it to reflect the price fluctuations that may occur over the short term. What should remain constant, however, is the relative price (value) of items over the long term.

These prices are not intended to reflect "wholesale" transactions, i.e., between dealers or a collector selling to a dealer. Many factors may affect the differential between an individual price shown in these pages and the actual price of a transaction: individual bargaining, the effect of dealer mark-up and profit margins, condition of the item in question, changes in popularity of the item, temporary change in supply of the item, local custom, unusual postal markings on a used example of the item, unexpected political situations within the country of issue, newly discovered philatelic or other information, or changes in the relative value of that nation's currency against the U.S. dollar.

As a point of philatelic economic fact, the lower the price shown for an item in this catalogue, the greater the percentage of that price which is attributed to dealer mark-up and profit margin. Thus, packets of 1,000 different stamps — all of which have a catalogue price of at least 5 cents — normally sell for considerably less than $50!

Scott Publishing Co. endeavors to obtain more than one judgment of the prices and to incorporate in its pricing the various price factors listed above. There can be no assurance, however, that all of the prices listed are accurate estimate of prices which would be paid in actual transactions. Some of the items listed have not been publicly traded recently. The pricing, therefore, is based on the editor's estimates of the probable prices which the stamp would command if it were offered individually for sale to a collector.

Users of this catalogue should not enter into any transaction solely in reliance on the prices, valuations, or stamp availability information set forth in the catalogue. Persons wishing to further establish the value of a particular stamp or other material may wish to consult with recognized stamp experts (collector or dealer) and review current information or recent development which would affect stamp prices.

Scott Publishing Co. assumes no obligation to revise the prices during the distribution period of this catalogue or to advise users of other factors, such as stamp availability, political and economic conditions, or collecting preferences, all of which may have an immediate positive or negative impact on prices. The publisher endeavors to balance these factors with its general understanding of stamp pricing considerations to avoid unnecessary fluctuations in the prices included in this catalogue:

It should be noted that persons relied upon for pricing information also may deal in stamps and/or may maintain substantial personal stamp collections. They may buy, sell, and deal in stamps for their own account and for the account of others and therefore may have both a direct and indirect interest in the price of the stamps. In some cases, the references to prices may reflect valuations of their personal holdings or stamps in which they deal for themselves and others.

Understanding Pricing Notations

The absence of a price does not necessarily indicate that the stamp is scarce or rare. In the United States listings, a dash in the price column means that the stamp is known in a stated form or variety, but that information is lacking or insufficient for pricing.

The minimum price of a stamp is fixed at 5 cents to cover a dealer's labor and service cost of purchasing that stamp at wholesale and preparing it for resale. As noted above, the sum of these list prices does not properly represent the "value" of a packet of unsorted or unmounted stamps sold in bulk which generally consists of only the lesser valued stamps.

Prices in the "unused" column are for stamps that have been hinged for items of the British area through mid-1953 and for United States items through 1960. Prices for unused stamps after those dates are for unhinged examples. Where prices for a used example of a stamp is considerably higher than for the unused stamp, the price applies to a stamp showing a distinct contemporary postmark of origin.

Beginning with issues of about 1900, and sometimes for earlier issues, prices for sets are provided for most issues of five or more stamps. Unless otherwise noted, the set price excludes minor varieties. The parenthetical number in the set-price line notes the number of stamps in the priced total. Set prices are the sum of the individual prices.

Many countries sell canceled-to-order stamps at a marked reduction of face value. Exceptions which sell or have sold canceled-to-order stamps at full face value include Australia, Netherlands, France, and Switzerland. It is almost impossible to identify such stamps, if the gum has been removed, as the official government canceling devices are used. Postally used copies on cover are worth more than the canceled-to-order stamps with original gum.

How To Order From Your Dealer

It is not necessary to write the full description of a stamp as listed in this catalogue. All that is needed is the name of the country, the index number and whether unused or used. For example. "Japan Scott No. 422 unused" is sufficient to identify the stamp of Japan listed as "422 A206 5y brown."

Addenda And Number Changes

Stamps received too late to be included in the body of the catalogue are listed in the Addenda at the back of this volume.

A list of stamps whose catalogue numbers have been changed from those of the preceding edition appears at the back of this volume.

Examination

Scott Publishing Co. cannot undertake to pass upon genuineness or condition of stamps, due to the time and responsibility involved, but refers collectors to the several expertizing/verification groups which undertake this work. Neither can Scott Publishing Co. undertake to appraise or identify. The Company cannot take responsibility for unsolicited stamps or covers.

INFORMATION FOR COLLECTORS

The anatomy of a stamp can be divided into the following parts: paper, watermark, separation, impression, design and gum.

Paper

Paper is a material composed of a compacted web of cellulose fibers formed into sheets. The fibers most often used for the paper on which stamps are printed are mulberry bark, wood, straw and certain grasses, with linen or cotton rags added for greater strength. These fibers are ground, bleached and boiled until they are reduced to a slushy pulp known as "stuff." Sizing, or weak glue, and coloring matter may be added to the pulp. Thin coatings of pulp are poured on sieve-like frames which allow the water to run off while retaining the matted pulp. When it is almost dry, the appearance of the pulp is converted by mechanical processes. It may be passed through smooth or engraved rollers (dandy rolls) or placed between cloth in a press that flattens and dries the product under pressure, thus forming a sheet of paper.

Stamp paper falls broadly into two types — "wove" and "laid." The differences in appearance are caused by the surface of the frame onto which the pulp is first fed. If the surface is smooth and even, the paper will be of uniform texture throughout, showing no light and dark areas when held up to a light. This is called *Wove Paper.* Early paper making machines poured the pulp on to continuously circulating webs of felt, but modern machines feed the pulp on to a cloth-like screen made of closely interwoven fine wires. This paper, when held up to a light, will show little dots or points, very close together. Technically, it is called "wire wove," but because it is the most common form, it is generally known as "wove paper." Any United States or British stamp printed after 1880 will furnish an example of wire wove paper.

The frames utilized for *Laid Paper* are made of closely spaced parallel wires, with cross wires at wider intervals. Obviously a greater thickness of the pulp will settle between the wires, and the paper, when held up to a light, will show alternate light and dark lines. The spacing and the thickness of the lines may vary, but on any one sheet of paper, they are all alike. (Russia Nos. 31-38.)

If the lines are spaced quite far apart, like the ruling on a writing tablet, the paper is called *Batonne* from the French word meaning a staff. Batonne paper may be either wove or laid. If it is laid, fine laid lines can be seen between the batons. The laid lines, which are actually a form of watermark, may be geometrical figures such as squares, diamonds, rectangles, or wavy lines.

When the lines form little squares, the paper is called *Quadrille.* When they form rectangles instead of squares, the paper is called *Oblong Quadrille.* (Mexico-Guadalajara Nos. 38-41.)

Paper is also classified as thick or thin, hard or soft, and by color if dye was added during production, such as yellowish, greenish, bluish and reddish.

Pelure Paper — An extremely thin, hard and often brittle paper. It is sometimes bluish or grayish. (Serbia No. 170.)

Native Paper — A term applied to the handmade papers on which some of the early stamps of the Indian States were printed. Japanese paper, originally made of mulberry fibers and rice flour, is part of this group. (Japan Nos. 1-18.)

Manila Paper — Often used to make stamped envelopes and wrappers, it is a coarse textured stock, usually smooth on one side and rough on the other. It is made in a variety of colors.

Silk Paper — Introduced by the British in 1847 as a safeguard against counterfeiting, there are scattered bits of colored silk thread in it. Silk-thread paper has continuous threads of colored silk arranged so that one or more threads run through the stamp or postal stationery. (Great Britain Nos. 5-8.)

Granite Paper — Not to be confused with either of the silk papers, it is filled with minute fibers of various colors and lengths in the paper substance. (Austria Nos. 172-175.)

Chalky Paper — Coated with a chalk-like substance to discourage the cleaning and reuse of canceled stamps. As the design is imprinted on the water-soluble coating of the stamp, any attempts to remove a cancellation will destroy the stamp. **Collectors are warned not to soak these stamps in any fluid.** If one is to be removed from envelope paper, a good way is to wet the paper from underneath until the gum dissolves enough to slip the stamp off it. (St. Kitts-Nevis Nos. 89-90.)

India Paper — Originally introduced from China about 1750, it is sometimes referred to as China Paper. It is a thin, opaque paper often used for plate and die proofs by many countries.

Double Paper — In philately this has two distinct meanings. The first, used experimentally as a means to discourage reuse, is two-ply paper, usually of a thick and thin sheet, joined together during the process of manufacture. Any attempt to remove a cancellation would destroy the design which is printed on the thin paper. The second occurs on the rotary press when the printer glues the end of one paper roll onto the next roll to save time in feeding the paper through the press. Stamp designs are printed over the joined paper and if overlooked by inspectors, may get into post-office stocks.

Goldbeater's Skin — Used for the 1886 issue of Prussia, it was made of a tough translucent paper. The design was printed in reverse on the back of the stamp, and the gum applied on top of the printing. It is impossible to remove them from the paper to which they are affixed without destroying the design.

Ribbed Paper — An uneven, corrugated surface made by passing it through ridged rollers. (Exists on some copies of U.S. No. 163.)

Various other substances that have been used for stamp manufacture include aluminum, copper, silver and gold foil, plastic, silk and cotton fabrics. Most of these are considered novelties designed for sale to novice collectors.

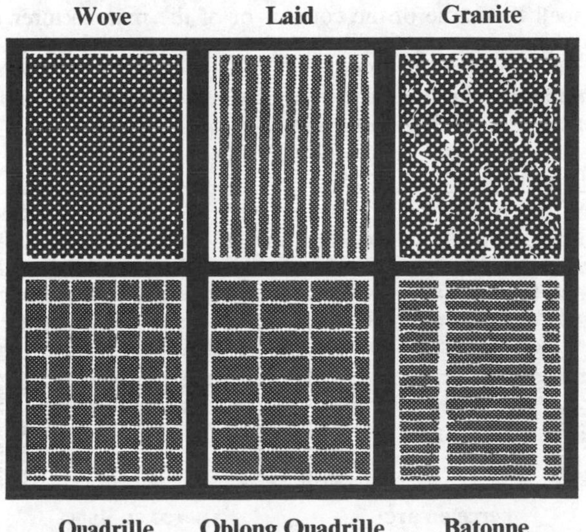

Watermarks

Watermarks are an integral part of the paper as they are formed in the process of manufacture. They consist of small designs such as crowns, stars, anchors, letters, etc. formed of wire or cut from metal that are soldered to the surface of the dandy roll or mold. These pieces of metal (referred to as "bits") impress a design into the paper which may be seen by holding the stamp up to the light. They are more easily seen in a watermark detector, a small black tray. The stamp is placed face down in the tray and dampened with a watermark detection fluid which brings up the watermark in dark lines against a lighter background.

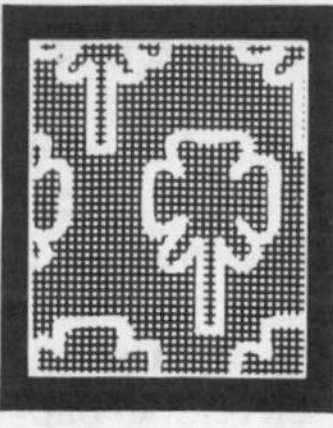

Multiple Watermarks of Crown Agents and Burma

Watermarks of Uruguay, Vatican and Jamaica

WARNING

Some inks used in the photogravure process dissolve in watermark fluids. (See SOLUBLE PRINTING INKS). These are also electric watermark detectors that come with plastic discs of various colors. When the light is turned on the watermark can be seen through the disc that neutralizes the color of the stamp.

Watermarks may be found reversed, inverted, sideways or diagonal, as seen from the back of the stamp, depending on the position of the printing plates or the manner in which paper was fed through the press. On machine-made paper they normally read from right to left. In a "multiple watermark" the design is repeated closely throughout the sheet. In a "sheet watermark" the design appears only once on the sheet, but extends over many stamps. Individual stamps may carry only a small fraction or none of the watermark.

"Marginal watermarks" occur in the margins of sheets or panes of stamps. Outside the border of some papers a large row of letters may spell the name of the country or of the manufacturer of the paper. Careless press feeding may cause parts of these letters to show on stamps of the outer rows. **For easier reference watermarks are numbered in the Scott Catalogue. See numerical index of Watermarks at back of this volume.**

Separation

Separation is the general term used to describe methods of separating stamps. The earliest issues, such as the 1840 Penny Blacks, did not have any means provided for separating and were intended to be cut apart with scissors. These are called imperforate stamps. As many stamps that were first issued imperforate were later issued perforated, care must be observed in buying imperforate stamps to be sure they are really imperforate and not perforated copies that have been trimmed. Although sometimes priced as singles, it is recommended that imperforate varieties of normally perforated stamps be collected in pairs or larger pieces as indisputable evidence of their imperforate character.

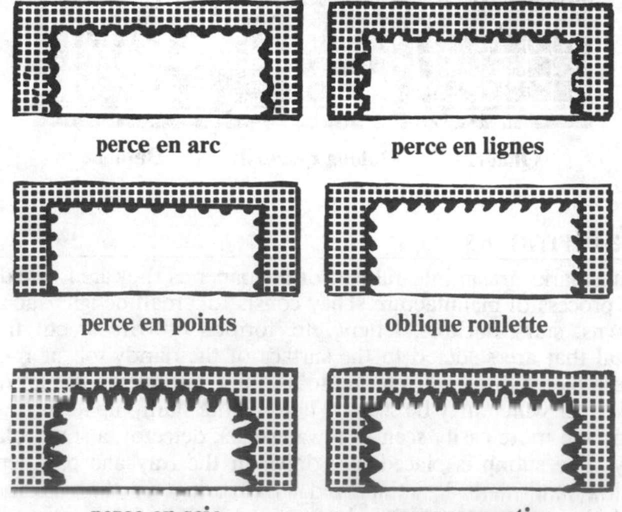

perce en arc **perce en lignes**

perce en points **oblique roulette**

perce en scie **perce serpentin**

Separation is effected by two general methods, rouletting and perforating. In rouletting the paper is cut partly or wholly through, but no paper is removed. In perforating a part of the paper is removed. Rouletting derives its name from the French roulette, a spur-like wheel. As the wheel is rolled over the paper, each point makes a small cut. The number of cuts made in two centimeters determines the gauge of the roulette. This is fully explained under "Perforation."

ROULETTING

The shape and arrangement of the teeth on the wheels varies. French names are usually used to describe the various roulettes:

Perce en lignes: rouletted in lines. The paper receives short, straight cuts in lines. (Mexico No. 500.)

Perce en points: pin-perforated. Round, equidistant holes are pricked through the paper, but no paper is removed, which distinguishes it from a small perforation. (Mexico Nos. 242-256.)

Perce en arc and perce en scie: pierced in an arc or sawtoothed rouletted, forming half circles or small triangles. (Hanover Nos. 25-29.)

Perce en serpentin: serpentine roulette. The cuts form a serpentine or wavy line. (Brunswick Nos. 13-22.)

PERFORATION

The second chief style of separation of stamps, and the one which is in universal use today, is called perforating. By this process the paper between the stamps is cut away in a line of holes, usually round, leaving little bridges of paper between the stamps to hold them together. These little bridges, which project from the stamp when it is torn from the sheet are called the teeth of the perforation. As the size of the perforation is sometimes the only way to differentiate between two otherwise identical stamps, it is necessary to be able to measure and describe them. This is done with a perforation gauge, a ruler-like device that has dots to show how many perforations can be counted in the space of 2 centimeters, the space universally adopted as the length in which perforations are measured. Run your stamp along the gauge until the dots on it fit exactly into the perforations. If the number alongside the dots into which it fits is 11, this means that 11 perforations fit between two centimeters and the stamp is described as "perf. 11." If the gauge of the perforations on the top and bottom of a stamp differs from that on the sides, it is called a "compound perforation." In measuring compound perforations the gauge at the top and bottom is always given first, then the sides. Thus a stamp measures 10½ at top and bottom and 11 at the sides is described as "10½x11." (U.S. No. 1526.)

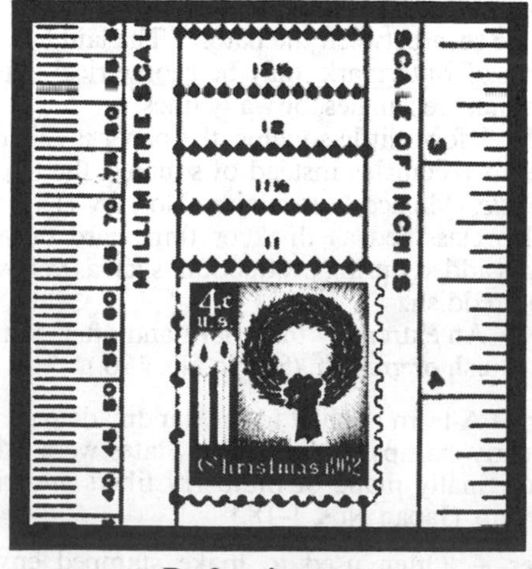

Perforation gauge

A perforation with small holes and teeth close together is called a "fine perforation." One with large holes and teeth far apart is a "coarse perforation." If the holes are jagged rather than clean cut, it is called "rough perforation." Blind perforations are the slight impressions left by the perforating pins if they fail to puncture the paper. Multiples showing blind perfs may command a slight premium over normally perforated stamps.

Printing Processes

ENGRAVING (Intaglio)

Master Die — The initial operation in the engraving process is the making of the master die. The die is a small flat block of soft steel on which the stamp design is recess engraved in reverse.

The original art is reduced photographically to the appropriate size, and serves as a tracing guide for the initial outline of the design. After the engraving is completed, the die is hardened to withstand the stress and pressures of subsequent transfer operations.

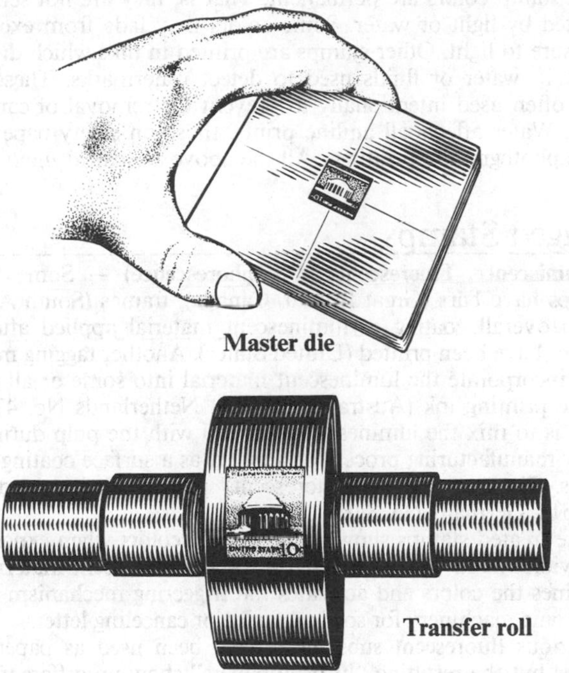

Master die

Transfer roll

Transfer Roll — The next operation is the making of the transfer roll which, as the name implies, is the medium used to transfer the subject from the die to the plate. A blank roll of soft steel, mounted on a mandrel, is placed under the bearers of a transfer press, so as to allow it to roll freely on its axis. The hardened die is placed on the bed of the press and the face of the transfer roll is brought to bear on the die under pressure. The bed is then rocked back and forth under increasing pressure until the soft steel of the roll is forced into every engraved line of the die. The resulting impression on the roll is known as a "relief" of a "relief transfer." When the required number of reliefs are "rocked in," the soft steel transfer roll is also hardened.

A "relief" is the normal reproduction of the design on the die in reverse. A "defective relief" may occur during the "rocking in" process due to a minute piece of foreign material lodging on the die, or other causes. Imperfections in the steel of the transfer roll may result in a breaking away of parts of the design. If the damaged relief is continued in use, it will transfer a repeating defect to the plate. Sometimes reliefs are deliberately altered. "Broken relief" and "altered relief" are terms used to designate these changed conditions.

Plate — The final step in the procedure is the making of the printing plate. A flat piece of soft steel replaces the die on the bed of the transfer press and one of the reliefs on the transfer roll is brought to bear on it. The position on the plate is determined by position dots, which have been lightly marked on the plate in advance. After the position of the relief is determined, pressure is brought to bear and, by following the same method used in making the transfer roll, a transfer is entered. This transfer reproduces

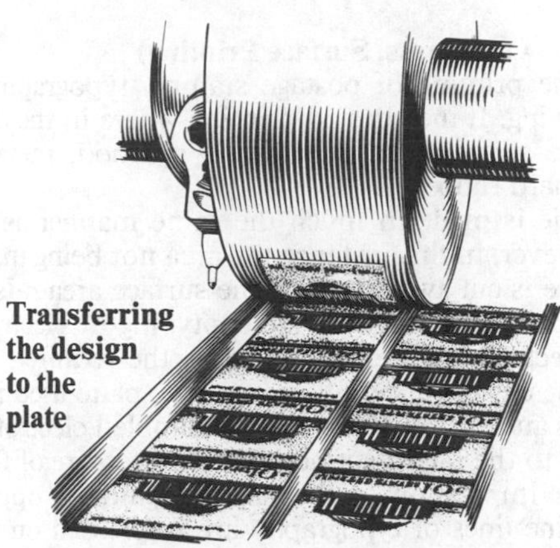

Transferring the design to the plate

in reverse and in detail the design of the relief. As many transfers are entered on the plate as there are to be subjects.

After the required transfers have been entered, the position dots, layout dots and lines, scratches, etc. are generally burnished out. Any required *guide lines, plate numbers* or other *marginal markings* are added. A proof impression is then taken and if "certified" (approved), the plate is machined for fitting to the press, hardened and sent to the plate vault ready for use.

On press, the plate is inked and the surface automatically wiped clean, leaving the ink only in the depressed lines. Damp paper under pressure is forced down into the engraved depressed lines, thereby receiving the ink. Consequently, the lines on engraved stamps are slightly raised; and, conversely, slight depressions occur on the back of the stamp.

The expressions *taille douce,* engraved, line engraved and steel plate all designate substantially the same processes for producing engraved stamps.

Rotary Press — Engraved stamps were printed only with flat plates until 1915, when rotary press printing was introduced. *Rotary press plates,* after being certified, require additional machining. They are curved to fit the press cylinder and "gripper slots" are cut into the back of each plate to receive the "grippers," which hold the plate securely on the press, after which the plate is hardened. Stamps printed from rotary press plates are usually longer or wider than the same stamps printed from flat press plates. The stretching of the plate during the curving process causes this enlargement.

Re-entry — In order to execute a re-entry the transfer roll is reapplied to the plate, usually at some time after it has been put to press. Thus worn-out designs can be resharpened by carefully re-entering the transfer roll. If the transfer roll is not precisely in line with the impression on the plate, the registration will not be true and a double transfer will result. After a plate has been curved for the rotary press, it is impossible to make a re-entry.

Double Transfer — A description of the condition of a transfer on a plate that shows evidence of a duplication of all, or a portion of the design. It is usually the result of the changing of the registration between the transfer roll and the plate during the rocking-in of the original entry.

It is sometimes necessary to remove the original transfer from a plate and repeat the process a second time. If the finished re-transfer shows indications of the original impression due to incomplete erasure, the result is also a double transfer.

Re-engraved — Either the die that has been used to make a plate or the plate itself may have its "temper" drawn (softened) and be re-cut. The resulting impressions from such a re-engraved die or plate may differ slightly from the original issue, and are known as "re-engraved."

Short Transfer — It sometimes happens that the transfer roll is not rocked its entire length in entering a transfer on a plate, with the result that the finished transfer fails to show the complete design. This is known as a "short transfer." (U.S. No. 8, Type III of 1851-56 1c.)

TYPOGRAPHY (Letterpress, Surface Printing)
As related to the printing of postage stamps, typography is the reverse of engraving. It includes all printing where in the design is raised above the surface area, whether it is wood, metal, or in some instances hard rubber.

The master die is made in much the same manner as the engraved die. However, in this instance the area not being utilized as a printing surface is cut away, leaving the surface area raised. The original die is then reproduced by stereoptyping or electrotyping. The resulting electrotypes are assembled in the required number and format of the desired sheet of stamps. The plate used in printing the stamps is an electroplate of these assembled electrotypes.

Ink is applied to the raised surface and the pressure of the press transfers the ink impression to the paper. Again, as opposed to engraving, the fine lines of typography are impressed on the surface of the stamp. When viewed from the back (as on a typewritten page) the corresponding linework will be raised slightly above the surface.

PHOTOGRAVURE (Rotogravure, Heliogravure)
In this process the basic principles of photography are applied to a sensitized metal plate, as opposed to photographic paper. The design is photographically transferred to the plate through a halftone screen, breaking the reproduction into tiny dots. The plate is treated chemically and the dots form depressions of varying depths, depending on the degrees of shade in the design. The depressions in the plate hold the ink, which is lifted out when the paper is pressed against the plate, in a manner similar to that of engraved printing.

LITHOGRAPHY
This process is based on the principle that oil and water will not mix. The design is drawn by hand or transferred from engraving to the surface of a lithographic stone or metal plate in a greasy (oily) ink. The stone (or plate) is wet with an acid fluid, causing it to repel the printing ink in all areas not covered by the greasy ink.

Transfers are made from the original stone or plate by means of transfer paper. A series of duplicate transfers are grouped and these in turn are transferred to the final printing plate.

Photolithography — The application of photographic processes to lithography. This process allows greater flexibility of design, relating to use of halftone screens combined with linework.

Offset — A development of the lithographic process. A rubber-covered blanket cylinder takes up the impression from the inked lithographic plate. From the "blanket" the impression is *offset* or transferred to the paper. Because of its greater flexibility and speed, offset printing has largely displaced lithography. Since the processes and results are almost identical, stamps printed by either method are designated as lithographed.

Sometimes two or even three printing methods are combined in producing stamps.

EMBOSSED (RELIEF) PRINTING
A method in which the design is sunk into the metal of the die and the printing is done against a yielding platen, such as leather or linoleum, which is forced up into the depression of the die, thus forming the design on the paper in relief.

Emblossing may be done without color (Sardinia Nos. 4-6); with color printed around the embossed area (Great Britain No. 5 and most U.S. envelopes); and with color in exact registration with the embossed subject (Canada Nos. 656-657).

INK COLORS
Pigments or dyes, usually of mineral origin, are used in the manufacture of inks or colored papers on which stamps are printed. The tone of any given color may be affected by numerous factors: heavier pressure will cause a more intense color, slight interruptions in the ink feed will cause a lighter tint.

Hand-mixed ink formulas produced under different conditions (humidity, temperature) at different times account for notable color variations in early printings, mostly 19th century, of the same stamp (U.S. Nos. 248-250, 279B, etc.).

Colors may vary in shade because papers of different quality and consistency were used for the same printing. Most pelure papers, for example, show a richer color when compared to wove or laid papers. (Russia No. 181a.)

The very nature of the printing processes can cause a variety of differences in shades or hues of the same stamp. Some of these shades are scarcer than others, and are of particular interest to the advanced collector.

Soluble Printing Inks

WARNING
Most stamp colors are permanent. That is, they are not seriously affected by light or water. Some colors may fade from excessive exposure to light. Other stamps are printed in inks which dissolve easily in water or fluids used to detect watermarks. These inks were often used intentionally to prevent the removal of cancellations. Water affects all aniline prints, those on safety paper, and some photogravure printings. All the above are called *fugitive colors*.

Tagged Stamps

(Luminiscence, Fluorescence, Phosphorescence) — Some tagged stamps have bars (Great Britain, Canada), frames (South Africa), or an overall coating of luminescent material applied after the stamps have been printed (United States). Another tagging method is to incorporate the luminescent material into some or all colors of the printing ink (Australia No. 366, Netherlands No. 478). A third is to mix the luminescent material with the pulp during the paper manufacturing process or apply it as a surface coating afterwards. These are called "fluorescent" papers. (Switzerland Nos. 510-514, Germany No. 848.)

The treated stamps show up in specific colors when exposed to ultraviolet light. The wave length of the luminescent material determines the colors and activates the triggering mechanism of the electronic machinery for sorting, facing or canceling letters.

Various fluorescent substances have been used as paper whiteners, but the resulting "hi-brite papers" show up differently under ultraviolet light and do not trigger the machines. They are not noted in the Catalogue.

Introduced in Great Britain in 1959 on an experimental basis, tagging in its various forms is now used by many countries to expedite the handling of mail. Following Great Britain were Germany ('61); Canada and Denmark ('62); United States, Australia, Netherlands and Switzerland ('63); Belgium and Japan ('66); Sweden and Norway ('67); Italy ('68); Russia ('69); and so forth.

Certain stamps were issued both with and without the luminescent factor. In these instances, the "tagged" variety is listed in the United States, Canada, Great Britain and Switzerland, and is noted in some of the other countries.

Gum

The gum on a stamp's back may be smooth, crinkly, dark, white, colored or tinted, and either obvious or virtually invisible as on Canada No. 453 or Rwanda Nos. 287-294. Most stamp gumming has been carried out with adhesives using gum arabic or dextrine as a base, but certain polymers such as polyvinyl alcohol (PVA) have been used extensively since World War II. The PVA gum which Harrison & Sons of Great Britain introduced in 1968 is dull, slightly yellowish and almost invisible.

Stamps having full *original gum* sell for more than those from which the gum has been removed. Reprints may have gum differing from the originals.

Reprints And Reissues

Reprints – These are impressions of stamps (usually obsolete) made from the original plates or stones. If valid for postage and from obsolete issues, they are called reissues. If they are from current issues, they are *second, third,* etc. *printings.* If designated for a particular purpose, they are called *special printings.*

When reprints are not valid for postage, but made from original dies and plates by authorized persons they are *official reprints* – to distinguish them from *private reprints* made from original plates and dies by private hands. *Official reproductions* or imitations are made from new dies and plates by government authorization.

For the 1876 Centennial, the U.S. government made official imitations of its first postage stamps, which are listed as Nos. 3-4; official reprints of the demonetized pre-1861 issues; re-issued the 1869 stamps and made special printings of the current 1875 denominations. An example of the private reprint is that of the New Haven postmaster's provisional.

Most reprints differ slightly from the original stamp in some characteristic such as gum, paper, perforation, color, watermark (or lack thereof). Sometimes the details have been followed so meticulously that only a student of that stamp can tell the reprint from the original.

Remainders And Canceled To Order

Some countries sell their stock of old stamps when a new issue replaces them. The *remainders* are usually canceled with a punch hole, a heavy line or bar, or a more or less regular cancellation to avoid postal use. The most famous merchant of remainders was Nicholas F. Seebeck, who arranged printing contracts between the Hamilton Bank Note Co., of which he was a director, and several Central and Latin American countries in the 1880's and 1890's. The contracts provided that the plates and all remainders of the yearly issues became the property of Hamilton, and Seebeck saw to it that ample stock remained. The "Seebecks," both remainders and reprints, were standard packet fillers for decades.

Some countries also issue stamps *canceled to order* (CTO), either in sheets with original gum or stuck onto pieces of paper or envelopes and canceled. Such CTO items generally are worth less than postally used stamps. Most can be detected by the presence of gum. However, as the CTO practice goes back at least to 1885, the gum inevitably has been washed off some stamps so they could pass for postally used. The normally applied postmarks usually differ slightly and specialists can tell the difference. When applied individually to envelopes by philatelically minded persons, CTO material is known as *favor canceled* and generally sells at large discounts.

Cinderellas And Facsimilies

Cinderella is a catchall term used by collectors of phantoms, fantasies, bogus items, municipal issues, exhibition seals, local revenues, transportation stamps, labels, poster stamps, etc. Cinderellas are not issued by any national government for postal purposes. Some cinderella collectors include local postage issues, telegraph stamps, essays and proofs, forgeries and counterfeits.

A fantasy is an adhesive created for a nonexisting stamp issuing authority. Fantasy items range from imaginary countries (Kingdom of Sedang or Principality of Trinidad) to nonexisting locals (Winans City Post), or nonexisting transportation lines (McRobish & Co.'s Acapulco-San Francisco Line). On the other hand, if the entity exists and might have issued stamps or did issue other stamps, the items are *bogus* stamps. These would include the Mormon postage stamps of Utah, S. Allan Taylor's Guatemala and Paraguay inventions, the propaganda issues for the South Moluccas and the adhesives of the Page & Keyes local post of Boston.

Both fantasies and bogus issues are sometimes called *phantoms.*

Facsimilies – These are copies or imitations made to represent original stamps, but which do not pretend to be originals. A catalogue illustration is such a facsimile. Illustrations from the Moens catalogue of the last century were occasionally colored and passed as stamps. Since the beginning of stamp collecting, facsimilies have been made for collectors as space fillers or for reference. They often carry the words "facsimile" "falsch" (German), "sanko" or "mozo" (Japanese), or "faux" (French) overprinted on the face or stamped on the back. Naturally, they have only curio value.

Counterfeits Or Forgeries

Postal counterfeits or *postal forgeries* are unauthorized imitations of stamps intended to deprive the post of revenue. They often command higher prices than the genuine stamps they imitate. Sales are illegal and governments can, and do, prosecute.

The first postal forgery was of Spain's 4-cuartos carmine of 1854, No. 25. The forgers lithographed it, though the original was typographed. Apparently they were not satisfied and soon made an engraved forgery which is fairly common, unlike the scarce lithographed counterfeit. Postal forgeries quickly followed in Spain, Austria, Naples, Sardinia and the Roman States.

An infamous counterfeit to defraud the government is the 1-shilling Great Britain "Stock Exchange" forgery of 1872 used on telegrams at the exchange that year. It escaped detection until a stamp dealer noticed it in 1898. Many postal counterfeits are known of U.S. stamps.

Because the governments concerned did not issue them, the *wartime propaganda* stamps of both World Wars may be classed as postal counterfeits. They were put out by other governments or resistance groups.

Philatelic forgeries or *counterfeits* are unauthorized imitations of stamps designed to deceive and defraud collectors. Such spurious items first appeared on the market around 1860 and most old-time collections contain one or more. Many are crude and easily spotted even by the non-specialist, but some can deceive the better-than-average collector.

An important supplier of these early philatelic forgeries was the Hamburg printer, Gebruder Spiro. Many others indulged in this craft including S. Allan Taylor, George Hussey, James Chute, Georges Fourne, Benjamin & Sarpy, Julius Goldner, E. Oneglia and L. H. Mercier. Among the noted 20th century forgers are Francois Fournier, Jean Sperati and the prolific Raoul DeThuin.

Most classic rarities, many medium priced stamps and, in this century, cheap stamps on a wholesale basis destined for beginners' packets, have been fraudulently produced. However, few new philatelic forgeries have appeared in recent decades and virtually no new frauds of valuable classics. Successful imitation of engraved work is virtually impossible.

It has proven far easier to produce a fake by altering a genuine stamp than to duplicate a stamp completely.

Repairs And Fakes

Most collectors will not object to restoration of a stamp or cover, although they will not accept repairs on the same basis. *Restoration* in this sense includes cleaning with a soft eraser or soap and water. It may include the ironing out of a crease or removal of a cellophane tape stain. Removal of old hinges is acceptable. Some collectors believe that freshening of a stamp is valid restoration, whether done by the removal of oxides, "toning," or the effect of wax paper left on stamps shipped to the tropics between such sheets. Regumming may have been acceptable restoration half a century ago, but today it is considered faking. Restored stamps or covers do not normally sell at a discount, and may even change hands at a premium.

Repairs include filling in thin spots, mending tears by reweaving, adding a missing corner or perforation "tooth." Repaired stamps sell at substantial discounts.

Fakes – Genuine stamps altered in some way to make them more desirable and sold without revealing the alterations. According to one major student, 30,000 varieties of fakes were known in the 1950's. The number has grown. The widespread existence of fakes makes it important for collectors to study their philatelic holdings and relevant literature. For the same reason they should buy from reputable dealers who will guarantee their stamps and make full prompt refund should a purchase be declared not genuine by some mutually agreed-upon authority. Because fakes always have some genuine characteristics, it is not always possible to obtain unanimity among expert students regarding specific items. These students may change their opinions as philatelic knowledge increases. More than 80 percent of all fakes on the market today are regummed, reperforated or altered in regard to overprints, surcharges or cancellations.

Stamps can be chemically treated to alter or eliminate colors. For example a pale rose can be recolored into a blue of higher value, or a "missing color" variety created. Designs may be changed by "painting," or a stroke or dot added or bleached out to turn an ordinary variety into a scarce stamp. Part of a stamp can be bleached and reprinted in a different version, achieving an inverted center or frame. Margins can be added or repairs done so deceptively that the stamp moves from the repaired to the fake category.

The fakers have not left the backs of stamps untouched. They may create false watermarks or add fake grills (or press out genuine ones). A thin India paper proof may be glued onto a thicker backing to "create" an issued stamp, or a cardboard proof may be shaved down. Silk threads have been impressed in and stamps have been split so that a rare paper variety, from a cheap stamp, can be applied as a back to falsely identify the stamp. However, the most common back treatment is regumming.

Some operators openly advertise "foolproof" application of "original gum" to stamps that lack it. This is faking, not counterfeiting. As few early stamps have survived without being hinged, the large number of never-hinged examples now offered for sale suggests the extent of regumming that has been and is being done. Regumming may be used to hide repairs and thin spots, but dipping in watermark fluid will often reveal these flaws.

The fakers also tamper with separations. Ingenious ways to add margins are known, and perforated wide-margin stamps may be falsely represented as imperforate when trimmed. Reperforating is commonly done to create scarce coil or perforation varieties and to eliminate the straight-edge stamps found in sheet margin positions of many earlier issues. Custom has made straight edges less desirable and the fakers have obliged by reperforating them so extensively that many are now uncommon if not rare.

Another main field of the faker is that of the overprint, surcharge and cancellation. The forging of rare surcharges or overprints began in the 1880's or 1890's. These forgeries are sometimes difficult to detect, but the better experts have probably identified almost all of them. Only occasionally are the overprints or cancellations removed to create unoverprinted stamps or unused items. The SPECIMEN overprints are sometimes removed — scraping and repainting is one way — to create unoverprinted varieites. Cheap revenues or pen-canceled stamps are used to generate "unused" stamps for further faking by adding other markings. The quartz lamp and a high-powered magnifying glass help in detecting cancellation removals.

The big problem, however, is the addition of overprints, surcharges or cancellations — many quite dangerous. Plating of the stamps or the overprint can be an important detecting method.

Fake postmarks can range from numerous spurious fancy cancellations, to the host of markings applied to transatlantic covers to create rare uses. With the advance of cover collecting and the wide interest in postal history, a fertile new field for fakers arose. Some have tried to create entire covers. Others specialize in adding stamps, tied by fake cancellations, to genuine stampless covers, or replacing cheaper or damaged stamps with more valuable ones. Detailed study of rates and postmarks (including the analysis of "breaks" in each handstamp over a period), ink analysis, etc. will usually unmask the fraud.

Classifications Of Stamps

The various functions of stamps are classified by their names. Postage stamps; air post stamps; postage due stamps for unpaid postage, collected at time of delivery; late fee stamps, a special fee for forwarding a letter after regular mail delivery; registration stamps, fee for keeping special record of letter and ensuring its delivery; special delivery and express stamps, for delivery of letter in advance of regular delivery. With the exception of regular postage, all numbers in the catalogue include a prefix letter denoting the class to which the stamp belongs. (B=Semi-Postal; C=Air Post; E=Special Delivery; J=Postage Due; O=Official; CO=Air Post Official; etc.).

Terminology

BOOKLETS

Many countries have issued stamps in small booklets for the convenience of users. They are usually sold by the post office at a small premium. Booklets have been issued in all sizes and forms, often with advertising on the covers, on the panes of stamps or on the interleaving. The panes may be printed from special plates or made from regular sheets. All panes from booklets issued by the United States and many from those of other countries are straight edged on the bottom and both sides, but perforated between the stamps. Any unit in the pane, either printed or blank, which is not a postage stamp, is called a *label* in the catalogue listings.

CANCELLATIONS

The marks or obliterations put on a stamp by the postal authorities to show that it has done service and is no longer valid for postage. If it is made with a pen, it is called a pen cancellation. When the location of the post office appears in the cancellation, it is called a town cancellation. When it calls attention to a cause or celebration, it is a slogan cancellation. Many other types and styles of cancellations exist, such as duplex, numerals, targets, etc.

COIL STAMPS

Stamps issued in rolls for use in affixing and vending machines. Those of the United States, Canada, etc., are perforated horizontally or vertically only, with the outer edges imperforate. Coil stamps of some countries (Great Britain) are perforated on all four sides.

COVERS

Envelopes, with or without adhesive postage stamps, which have passed through the mail and bear postal or other markings of philatelic interest. Before the introduction of envelopes (1840), people folded letters and wrote the address on the outside. Many people covered their letters with an extra sheet of paper on the outside for the address. Hence the word "cover." Used air letter sheets, stamped envelopes, and other items of postal stationery are also referred to as "covers."

ERRORS

Stamps having some unintentional deviation from the normal. Errors include, but are not limited to, mistakes in color, paper or watermark; inverted centers (or frames), surcharges or overprints, and double impressions. A factually wrong or misspelled inscription, if it appears on all examples of a stamp, is not classified as a philatelic error. (Panama No. J1.)

OVERPRINTED AND SURCHARGED STAMPS

Overprinting is a wording placed on stamps to alter the place of use ("Canal Zone" or U.S. issues); to adapt them for a special purpose ("Porto" on Denmark's 1913-20 regular issues for use as postage dues, Nos. J1-J7); or for a special occasion. (Guatemala Nos. 374-378.)

The term *surcharge* is used when the overprint changes or restates the value (1923 "Inflation Issues" of Germany; Australia No. 580).

Surcharges and overprints may be handstamped, typeset or, occasionally, lithographed or engraved.

PRECANCELS
Stamps canceled by the issuing government before they are sold at the post office. Precanceling is done to expedite the handling of large mailings.

In the United States precancellations generally identify the point of origin. That is, the city and state names (or initials) appear, usually centered by an arrangement of parallel lines.

In France the abbreviation *Affranchts* in a semicircle together with the word *Postes* is the general form. Belgian precancellations are usually a square box in which the name of the city appears. Netherlands' precancellations have the name of the city enclosed between a large and small circle, sometimes called a "life-saver."

Precancellations of other countries usually follow these patterns, but may be any arrangement of bars, boxes and city names.

PROOFS AND ESSAYS
Proofs are impressions taken from an approved die, plate or stone in which the design and color are the same as the stamp issued to the public. Trail color proofs are impressions taken from approved dies, plates or stones in varying colors. An essay is the impression of a design that differs in some way from the stamp as issued.

PROVISIONALS
Stamps issued on short notice and intended for temporary use pending the arrival of regular (definitive) issues. They are usually issued to meet contingencies: changes in government or currency; shortage of necessary postage values, or military occupation.

In the 1840's, postmasters in certain American cities issued stamps that were valid only at specific post offices. Postmasters of the Confederate States also issued stamps with limited validity. These are known as Postmasters' Provisionals.

SE-TENANT
Joined together, referring to an unsevered pair, strip or block of stamps differing in design, denomination or overprint. (U.S. Nos. 1530-1537.)

TETE BECHE
A pair of stamps in which one is upside down in relation to the other. Some of these are the result of intentional sheet arrangement (Morocco Nos. B10-B11). Others occurred when one or more electrotypes were accidentally placed upside down on the plate. (Colombia No. 57a.) Separation of course destroys the tete beche variety.

SPECIMENS
One of the regulations of the Universal Postal Union requires member nations to send samples of all stamps they put into service to the International Bureau in Switzerland. These are then sent to all other member nations as samples of what stamps are valid for postage. Many are overprinted, handstamped or initial-perforated "Specimen," "Canceled" or "Muestra." Some are marked with bars across the denominations (China), punched holes (Czechoslovakia) or back inscriptions (Mongolia).

Stamps distributed to government officials or for publicity purposes, and stamps submitted by private security printers for official approval may also receive such defacements.

These markings prevent postal use, and all such items are generally known as "specimens."

COLOR ABBREVIATIONS

amb	amber
anil	aniline
ap	apple
aqua	aquamarine
az	azure
bis	bister
bl	blue
bld	blood
blk	black
bril	brilliant
brn	brown
brnsh	brownish
brnz	bronze
brt	bright
brnt	burnt
car	carmine
cer	cerise
chlky	chalky
cham	chamois
chnt	chestnut
choc	chocolate
chr	chrome
cit	citron
cl	claret
cob	cobalt
cop	copper
crim	crimson
cr	cream
dk	dark
dl	dull
dp	deep
db	drab
emer	emerald
gldn	golden
grysh	grayish
grn	green
grnsh	greenish
hel	heliotrope
hn	henna
ind	indigo
int	intense
lav	lavender
lem	lemon
lil	lilac
lt	light
mag	magenta
man	manila
mar	maroon
mv	mauve
multi	multicolored
mlky	milky
myr	myrtle
ol	olive
olvn	olivine
org	orange
pck	peacock
pnksh	pinkish
Prus	Prussian
pur	purple
redsh	reddish
res	reseda
ros	rosine
ryl	royal
sal	salmon
saph	sapphire
scar	scarlet
sep	sepia
sien	sienna
sil	silver
sl	slate
stl	steel
turq	turquoise
ultra	ultramarine
ven	venetian
ver	vermilion
vio	violet
yel	yellow
yelsh	yellowish

CATALOGUE COLORS TRANSLATED

ENGLISH	FRENCH	GERMAN	SPANISH	ITALIAN
Apple green	Verte-pomme	Apfelgrun	Verde manzana	Verde mela
Bister	Bistre	Bister	Bistre	Bistro
Black	Noir	Schwarz	Negro	Nero
Blue	Bleu	Blau	Azul	Azzurro
Brick red	Rouge-brique	Ziegelrot	Rojo ladrillo	Rosso di mattone
Bronze	Bronze	Bronze	Bronce	Bronzo
Brown	Brun	Braun	Castano, pardo	Bruno
Buff	Chamois	Samisch	Anteado	Camoscio
Carmine	Carmin	Karmin	Carmin	Carminio
Cerise	Cerise	Kirschrot	Color de ceresa	Color ciliegia
Chalky blue	Bleu terne	Kreideblau	Azul turbio	Azzurro smorto
Chamois	Chamois	Samisch	Anteado	Camoscio
Chestnut	Marron	Kastanienbraun	Castano rojo	Marrone
Chocolate	Chocolat	Schokoladebraun	Chocolate	Cioccolato
Chrome yellow	Jaune-chrome	Chromgelb	Amarillo cromo	Giallo croma
Citron	Citron	Zitronengelb	Cidra	Cedro
Claret	Lie de vin	Weinrot	Rojo vinoso	Vinaccia
Cobalt	Cobalt	Kobaltblau	Cobalto	Cobalto
Copper red	Rouge-cuivre	Kupferrot	Rojo cobre	Rosso di rame
Cream	Creme	Rahmfarbe	Crema	Crema
Crimson	Cramoisi	Karmesin	Carmesi	Cremisi
Emerald	Vert-emeraude	Smaragdgrun	Esmeralda	Smeraldo
Flesh	Chair	Fleischfarben	Carne	Carnicino
Gray	Gris	Grau	Gris	Grigio
Green	Vert	Grun	Verde	Verde
Indigo	Indigo	Indigo	Azul indigo	Indaco
Lake	Lie de vin	Lackfarbe	Laca	Lacca
Lemon	Jaune-citron	Zitronengelb	Limon	Limone
Lilac	Lilas	Lila	Lila	Lilla
Magenta	Magenta	Magentarot	Magenta	Magenta
Mauve	Mauve	Malvenfarbe	Malva	Malva
Milky blue	Bleu laiteux	Milchblau	Azul lechoso	Azzurro di latte
Moss green	Vert mousse	Moosgrun	Verde musgo	Verde muscosa
Multicolored	Polychrome	Mehrfarbig	Multicolores	Policromo
Ocher	Ocre	Ocker	Ocre	Ocra
Olive	Olive	Oliv	Oliva	Oliva
Orange	Orange	Orange	Naranja	Arancio
Pink	Rose	Rosa	Rosa	Rosa
Plum	Prune	Pflaumenfarbe	Color de ciruela	Prugna
Prussian blue	Bleu de Prusse	Preussischblau	Azul de Prusia	Azzurro di Prussia
Purple	Pourpe	Purpur	Purpura	Porpora
Red	Rouge	Rot	Rojo	Rosso
Rose	Rose	Rosa	Rosa	Rosa
Rosine	Rose vif	Lebhaftrosa	Rosa vivo	Rosa vivo
Royal blue	Bleu-roi	Konigsblau	Azul real	Azzurro reale
Rust	Brun-rouille	Rostbraun	Castano oxidado	Castagna
Sage green	Vert-sauge	Salbeigrun	Verde salvia	Verde salvia
Salmon	Saumon	Lachs	Salmon	Salmone
Scarlet	Ecarlate	Scharlach	Escarlata	Scarlatto
Sea green	Vert de mer	Seegrun	Verde mar	Verde mare
Sepia	Sepia	Sepia	Sepia	Seppia
Sienna	Terre de Sienne	Siena	Siena	Siena
Sky blue	Bleu ciel	Himmelblau	Azul celeste	Azzurro cielo
Slate	Ardoise	Schiefer	Pizarra	Ardesia
Steel blue	Bleu acier	Stahlblau	Azul acero	Azzurro acciaio
Straw	Jaune-paille	Strohgelb	Amarillo pajizo	Giallo pallido
Turquoise blue	Bleu-turquoise	Turkisblau	Azul turquesa	Azzurro turchese
Ultramarine	Outremer	Ultramarin	Ultramar	Oltremare
Vermilion	Vermillon	Zinnober	Cinabrio	Vermiglione
Violet	Violet	Violett	Violeta	Violetto
Yellow	Jaune	Gelb	Amarillo	Giallo

CATALOGUE TERMS TRANSLATED

ENGLISH	FRENCH	GERMAN	SPANISH	ITALIAN
Air mail	Poste aerienne	Flugpost	Correo aereo	Posta aerea
Back	Verso	Ruckseitig	Dorso	Dorso
Background	Fond	Hintergrund	Fondo	Sfondo
Bar	Barre	Balken	Barra	Barra
Bisected stamp	Timbre coupe	Halbiert	Partido en dos	Frazionato
Block of four	Bloc de quatre	Viererblock	Bloque de cuatro	Blocco di quattro
Booklet	Carnet	Heftchen	Cuadernillo	Libretto
Bottom	Bas	Unten	Abajo	Basso
Bright	Vif	Lebhaft	Vivo	Vivo
Broken	Interrompu	Unterbrochen	Interrumpido	Interrotto
Cancellation	Obliteration	Entwertung	Matasello	Annullamento
Cancellation to order	Obliteration de complaisance	Gefalligkeitsabstempelung	Matasello de complacencia	Annullamento di compiacenza
Canceled	Annule	Gestempelt	Cancelado	Annullato
Center	Centre du timbre	Mittelstuck	Centro	Centro
Centering	Centrage	Zentrierung	Centrado	Centratura
Chalky paper	Papier couche	Kreidepapier	Papel estucado	Carta gessata
Circle	Cercle	Kreis	Circulo	Circolo
Coat of arms	Armoiries	Wappen	Escudo de armas	Arme
Coil	Rouleau de timbres	Markenrolle	Rollo de sellos	Rollo di francobolli
Color	Couleur	Farbe	Color	Colore
Comb perforation	Dentelure en peigne	Kammzahnung	Dentado de peine	Dentellatura e pettine
Commemorative	Commemoratif	Gedenkausgabe	Conmemorativo	Commemorativo
Corner	Angle	Ecke	Esquina	Angolo
Counterfeit	Faux	Falschung	Falsificacion	Falsificazione
Cover	Lettre	Brief	Carta	Lettera
Crescent	Croissant	Halbmond	Media luna	Luna crescente
Crown	Couronne	Krone	Corona	Corona
Cut square	Coupure	Ausschnitt	Recorte	Ritaglio
Dark	Fonce	Dunkel	Oscuro	Oscuro
Date	Date	Datum	Fecha	Data
Definitive	Definitif	Freimarken	Definitivo	Definitivo
Design	Dessin	Zeichnung	Diseno	Disegno
Die	Matrice	Urstempel	Cuno	Conio
District	District	Bezirk	Destrito	Distretto
Double	Double	Doppelt	Doble	Doppio
Dull	Terne	Trub	Turbio	Smorto
Embossing	Impression en relief	Pragedruck	Impresion en relieve	Rilievo
Engraved	Grave	Graviert	Grabado	Inciso
Error	Erreur	Fehler	Error	Errore
Essay	Essai	Probedruck	Ensayo	Saggio
Figure	Chiffre	Ziffer	Cifra	Cifra
Forerunner	Precurseur	Vorlaufer	Precursor	Precursore
Forgery	Faux	Falschung	Falsificacion	Falsificazione
Frame	Cadre	Rahmen	Marco	Cornice
Genuine	Authentique	Echt	Autentico	Autentico
Glossy paper	Papier glace	Glanzpapier	Papel lustre	Carta patinata
Granite paper	Papier melangre de fils de soie	Faserpapier	Papel con filamentos	Carta con fili de seta
Gum	Gomme	Gummi	Goma	Gomma
Gutter	Interpanneau	Zwischensteg	Espacio blanco entre dos grupos	Interspazio
Half	Moitie	Halfte	Mitad	Meta
Handstamp	Cachet a la main	Handstempel	Matasello manual	Annullamento manuale
Imperforate	Non-dentele	Geschitten	Sin dentar	Non dentellato
Inscription	Inscription	Inschrift	Inscripcion	Dicitura
Inverted	Renverse	Kopfstehend	Invertido	Capovolto
Issue	Emission	Ausgabe	Emision	Emissione
King	Roi	Konig	Rey	Re
Kingdom	Royaume	Konigreich	Reino	Regno
Laid	Verge	Gestrichen	Listado	Vergato
Large	Grand	Gross	Grande	Grosso

ENGLISH	FRENCH	GERMAN	SPANISH	ITALIAN
Late fee stamp	Timbre pour lettres en retard	Verspatungsmarke	Sello para cartas Vetardadas	Francobollo per le lettere in ritardo
Left	Gauche	Links	Izquierda	Sinistro
Light	Clair	Hell	Claro	Chiaro
Line perforation	Dentelure en lignes	Linienzahnung	Dentado en linea	Dentellatura lineare
Lithography	Lithographie	Steindruck	Litografia	Litografia
Lozenges	Losanges	Rauten	Rombos	Losanghe
Margin	Marge	Rand	Borde	Margine
Multiple	Multiple	Mehrfach	Multiple	Multiplo
Narrow	Etroit	Eng	Estrecho	Stretto
Network	Burelage	Netz	Burelage	Rete
Newspaper stamp	Timbre pour journaux	Zeitungsmarke	Sello para periodicos	Francobollo per giornali
Not issued	Non emis	Nicht verausgabt	No emitido	Non emesso
Numeral	Chiffre	Ziffer	Cifra	Numerale
Occupation	Occupation	Besetzung	Occupacion	Occupazione
Official stamp	Timbre de service	Dienstmarke	Sello de servicio	Francobollo servizio
Oval	Ovale	Eiformig	Ovalo	Ovale
Overprint	Surcharge	Aufdruck	Sobrecarga	Soprastampa
Pair	Paire	Paar	Pareja	Coppia
Pale	Pale	Blass	Palido	Pallido
Pane	Panneau	Gruppe	Grupo	Gruppo
Paper	Papier	Papier	Papel	Carta
Parcel post stamp	Timbre pour colis postaux	Paketmarke	Sello para paquete postal	Francobollo per pacchi postali
Pen canceled	Oblitere a plume	Federzugentwertung	Cancelado a pluma	Annullato a penna
Perforated	Dentele	Gezahnt	Dentado	Dentellato
Perforation	Dentelure	Zahnung	Dentar	Dentellatura
Photogravure	Heliogravure	Rastertiefdruck	Fotograbado	Rotocalco
Piece	Fragment	Briefstuck	Fragmento	Frammento
Pin perforation	Perce en points	In Punkten durchstochen	Horadado con alfileres	Perforato a punti
Plate	Planche	Platte	Plancha	Lastra
Postage due stamp	Timbre-taxe	Portomarke	Sello de tasa	Segnatasse
Postage stamp	Timbre-poste	Briefmarke	Sello de correos	Francobollo postale
Postal forgery	Faux pour servir	Postfalschung	Falso por correo	Falso per posta
Postal tax stamp	Timbre surtaxe obligatoire	Zwangszuschlags-marke	Sello de sobretasa obligatorio	Francobollo per sopratassa obligatorio
Postmark	Obliteration postale	Poststempel	Matasello	Bollo
Price	Prix	Preis	Precio	Prezzo
Printing	Impression	Druck	Impresion	Stampa
Private	Prive	Privat	Privado	Privato
Proof	Epreuve	Druckprobe	Prueba de impresion	Prova
Quadrille	Quadrille	Gegittert	Cuadriculado	Quadriglia
Quarter	Un quart	Viertel	Un cuarto	Quarto
Recess printing	Impression en taille douce	Tiefdruck	Grabado	Incisione
Reengraving	Regravure	Neugravierung	Regrabado	Rincisione
Reentry	Double frappe	Nachgravierung	Regrabado	Doppia incisione
Registration stamp	Timbre pour lettre recommandee	Einschreibemarke	Sello de certificado	Francobollo per lettere raccomandate
Reprint	Reimpression	Nachdruck	Reimpresion	Ristampa
Revenue stamp	Timbre fiscal	Stempelmarke	Sello fiscal	Francobollo fiscale
Reversed	Retourne	Umgekehrt	Invertido	Rovesciato
Ribbed	Cannele	Geriffelt	Acanalado	Scanalatura
Right	Droite	Rechts	A la derecha	Destro
Rotary printing	Impresion par cylindre	Walzendruck	Impresion cilindrica	Stampa rotativa
Roulette	Percage	Durchstich	Picadura	Foratura
Rouletted	Perce	Durchstochen	Picado	Forato
Semipostal stamp	Timbre de bienfaisance	Wohltatigkeitsmarke	Sello de beneficencia	Francobollo di beneficenza
Serpentine routlette	Perce en serpentin	Schlangenartiger Durchstich	Picado a serpentina	Perforazione a serpentina
Set	Serie	Satz	Serie	Serie
Set price	Prix de la serie	Satzpreis	Precio por serie	Prezzo per serie

ENGLISH	FRENCH	GERMAN	SPANISH	ITALIAN
Se-tenant	Se-tenant	Zusammendruck	Combinacion	Combinazione
Shade	Nuance	Tonung	Tono	Gradazione di colore
Sheet	Feuille	Bogen	Hoja	Foglio
Side	Cote	Seite	Lado	Lato
Small	Petit	Klein	Pequeno	Piccolo
Souvenir sheet	Bloc commemoratif	Block, gedenkblock	Hojita-bloque conmemorativa	Foglietto commemorativo
Special delivery stamp	Timbre pour expres	Eilmrke	Sello de urgencia	Francobollo per espressi
Specimen	Specimen	Muster	Muestra	Saggio
Strip	Bande	Streifen	Tira	Striscia
Surcharge	Surcharge	Zuschlag	Sobrecarga	Soprastampa
Surtax	Surtaxe	Zuschlag	Sobretasa	Sopratassa
Tete beche	Tete-beche	Kehrdruck	Tete-beche	Tete-beche
Thick	Epais	Dick	Grueso	Spesso
Thin	Mince	Dunn	Delgado	Smilzo
Tinted paper	Papier teinte	Getontes papier	Papel coloreado	Carta colorata
Top	Haut	Oben	Arriba	Alto
Typography	Typographie	Buchdruck	Tipografia	Tipografia
Unused	Neuf	Ungebraucht	Nuevo	Nuovo
Used	Oblitere	Gebraucht	Usado	Usato
War tax stamp	Timbre d'impot de guerre	Kriegssteuermarke	Sello de impuesto de guerra	Francobollo per tassa di guerra
Watermark	Filigrane	Wasserzeichen	Filigrana	Filigrana
Wide	Espace	Weit	Ancho	Largo
With	Avec	Mit	Con	Con
Without	Sans	Ohne	Sin	Senza
Worn	Use	Abgenutzt	Gastado	Usato
Wove paper	Papier ordinarie	Einfaches Papier	Papel avitelado	Carta unita

COLONIES, FORMER COLONIES, OFFICES, TERRITORIES CONTROLLED BY PARENT STATES

Belgium

Belgian Congo
Ruanda-Urundi

Denmark

Danish West Indies
Faroe Islands
Greenland
Iceland

Finland

Aland Islands

France

COLONIES PAST AND PRESENT, CONTROLLED TERRITORIES

Afars & Issas, Territory of
Alaouites
Alexandretta
Algeria
Alsace & Lorraine
Ajouan
Annam & Tonkin
Benin
Cambodia (Khmer)
Cameroun
Castellorizo
Chad
Cilicia
Cochin China
Comoro Islands
Dahomey
Diego Suarez
Djibouti (Somali Coast)
Fezzan
French Congo
French Equatorial Africa
French Guiana
French Guinea
French India
French Morocco
French Polynesia (Oceania)
French Southern & Antarctic Territories
French Sudan
French West Africa
Gabon
Germany
Ghadames
Grand Comoro
Guadeloupe
Indo-China
Inini
Ivory Coast
Laos
Latakia
Lebanon
Madagascar
Martinique
Mauritania
Mayotte
Memel
Middle Congo
Moheli
New Caledonia
New Hebrides
Niger Territory
Nossi-Be
Obock
Reunion
Rouad, Ile
Ste.-Marie de Madagascar
St. Pierre & Miquelon
Senegal
Senegambia & Niger
Somali Coast
Syria
Tahiti
Togo
Tunisia
Ubangi-Shari
Upper Senegal & Niger
Upper Volta
Viet Nam
Wallis & Futuna Islands

POST OFFICES IN FOREIGN COUNTRIES

China
Crete
Egypt
Turkish Empire
Zanzibar

Germany

EARLY STATES

Baden
Bavaria
Bergedorf
Bremen
Brunswick
Hamburg
Hanover
Lubeck
Mecklenburg-Schwerin
Mecklenburg-Strelitz
Oldenburg
Prussia
Saxony
Schleswig-Holstein
Wurttemberg

FORMER COLONIES

Cameroun (Kamerun)
Caroline Islands
German East Africa
German New Guinea
German South-West Africa
Kiauchau
Mariana Islands
Marshall Islands
Samoa
Togo

Italy

EARLY STATES

Modena
Parma
Romagna
Roman States
Sardinia
Tuscany
Two Sicilies
- Naples
- Neapolitan Provinces
- Sicily

FORMER COLONIES, CONTROLLED TERRITORIES, OCCUPATION AREAS

Aegean Islands
- Calimno (Calino)
- Caso
- Cos (Coo)
- Karki (Carchi)
- Leros (Lero)
- Lipso
- Nisiros (Nisiro)
- Patmos (Patmo)
- Piscopi
- Rodi (Rhodes)
- Scarpanto
- Simi
- Stampalia

Castellorizo
Corfu
Cyrenaica
Eritrea
Ethiopia (Abyssinia)
Fiume
Ionian Islands
- Cephalonia
- Ithaca
- Paxos

Italian East Africa
Libya
Oltre Giuba
Saseno
Somalia (Italian Somaliland)
Tripolitania

POST OFFICES IN FOREIGN COUNTRIES "ESTERO"*

Austria
China
- Peking
- Tientsin

Crete
Tripoli
Turkish Empire
- Constantinople
- Durazzo
- Janina

Jerusalem
Salonika
Scutari
Smyrna
Valona

*Stamps overprinted "ESTERO" were used in various parts of the world.

Netherlands

Aruba
Netherlands Antilles (Curacao)
Netherlands Indies
Netherlands New Guinea
Surinam (Dutch Guiana)

Portugal

COLONIES PAST AND PRESENT, CONTROLLED TERRITORIES

Angola
Angra
Azores
Cape Verde
Funchal
Horta
Inhambane
Kionga
Lourenco Marques
Macao
Madeira
Mozambique
Mozambique Co.
Nyassa
Ponta Delgada
Portuguese Africa
Portuguese Congo
Portuguese Guinea
Portuguese India
Quelimane
St. Thomas & Prince Islands
Tete
Timor
Zambezia

Russia

ALLIED TERRITORIES AND REPUBLICS, OCCUPATION AREAS

Armenia
Aunus (Olonets)
Azerbaijan
Batum
Estonia
Far Eastern Republic
Georgia
Karelia
Latvia
Lithuania
North Ingermanland
Ostland
Russian Turkestan
Siberia
South Russia
Tannu Tuva
Transcaucasian Fed. Republics
Ukraine
Wenden (Livonia)
Western Ukraine

Spain

COLONIES PAST AND PRESENT, CONTROLLED TERRITORIES

Aguera, La
Cape Juby
Cuba
Elobey, Annobon & Corisco
Fernando Po
Ifni
Mariana Islands
Philippines
Puerto Rico
Rio de Oro
Rio Muni
Spanish Guinea
Spanish Morocco
Spanish Sahara
Spanish West Africa

POST OFFICES IN FOREIGN COUNTRIES

Morocco
Tangier
Tetuan

ACKNOWLEDGMENTS

The editors thank all those many good friends of Scott who have helped this year or in previous years in the task of revising the *Scott Standard Postage Stamp Catalogue.* They have generously shared their stamp knowledge with others through this medium.

No lists of aides can be complete, and several helpers prefer anonymity. The following men are chiefly those who have undertaken to assist on one or more specific countries:

Bruce W. Ball
Brian M. Bleckwenn
Hamish Bird
Wally A. Bizer
John R. Boker, Jr.
Paul Brenner
George W. Brett
Steven Carol
Herbert E. Conway
Ellery Denison
Pandelis J. Drossos
Daniel S. Franklin
Frank P. Geiger
Henry Gitner
Brian M. Green
Horacio E. Groio
David Gronbeck-Jones
Mihran B. Hagopian
Calvet M. Hahn
John Hain
Leo John Harris
Clifford O. Herrick
Juan J. Holler
Robert L. Huggins
Lewis S. Kaufman
Joseph E. Landry, Jr.
David MacDonnell
Nick Macris
Robert L. Markovits
Robert P. Odenweller
Souren Panirian
Frank E. Patterson III
Gilbert N. Plass
Henrik Pollak
Alex Rendon
Stanley J. Richmond
Michael Rogers
Milo D. Rowell
Otto G. Schaffling
Jacques Schiff
Richard Schwartz
Alfredo M. Seiferheld
F. Burton Sellers
Michael Shamilzadeh
James W. Smith
Sherwood Springer
Willard F. Stanley
Carlos Vieiro
Richard A. Washburn
John M. Wilson

Among the organizations that have helped are:

American Air Mail Society
102 Arbor Road, Cinnaminson, NJ 08077

American Philatelic Society
P.O. Box 8000, State College, PA 16803

American Revenue Association
Bruce Miller, Sec'y, 701 S. First Ave., Suite 332, Arcadia, CA 91006

American Stamp Dealers' Association
5 Dakota Dr., Suite 102, Lake Success, NY 11042

Arabian Philatelic Association
Aramco Box 1929, Dhahran 31311, Saudi Arabia

American Belgian Philatelic Society
8604 So. Yakima Ave., Tacoma, WA 98444

Brazil Philatelic Association
Tony DeBellis, 30 W. 60th St., New York, NY 10023

Bureau Issues Association
4630 Greylock St., Boulder, CO 80301

Canadian Society of Russian Philately
P.O. Box 5722, Station A, Toronto, Ontario, Canada M5W 1P2

Canadian Stamp Dealers' Association
P.O. Box 1123, Adelaide St., P.O., Toronto, Ontario, Canada M5C 2K5

Canal Zone Study Group
Alfred R. Bew, Sec'y., 29 S. South Carolina Ave., Atlantic City, NJ 08401

China Stamp Society
J. Lewis Blackburn, Pres., 21816 8th Place W., Bothell, WA 98011

Confederate Stamp Alliance
Brian M. Green, 110 E. Passaic Ave. #2A, Rutherford, NJ 07070

Costa Rica Collectors, Society of
T. C. Willoughby, 7600 Ridgemont Dr., Newburgh, IN 47630

Croatian Philatelic Society
1512 Lancelot Rd., Borger, TX 79007

Czechoslovak Philately, Society for
87 Carmita Ave., Rutherford, NJ 07070

Eire Philatelic Association
Robert C. Jones, Sec'y., 8 Beach St., Brockton, MA 02402

Estonian Philatelic Society
Rudolf Hamar, Pres., 243 E. 34th St., New York, NY 10016

France & Colonies Philatelic Society
Walter Parshall, Sec'y., 103 Spruce St., Bloomfield, NJ 07003

Germany Philatelic Society
P.O. Box 779, Arnold, MD 21012

Guatemala Collectors, International Society of
Henry B. Madden, Pres., 4003 N. St. Charles St., Baltimore, MD 21218

Hellenic Philatelic Society of America
Dr. Nicholas Asimakopulos, Sec'y., 541 Cedar Hill Ave., Wyckoff, NJ 07481

Indo-China Philatelists, Society of
c/o Paul Blake, Sec., 1466 Hamilton Way, San Jose, CA 95125

Japanese Philately, International Society for
Kenneth Kamholz, Sec'y., P.O. Box 1283, Haddonfield, NJ 08033

Korea Stamp Society, Inc.
Forrest W. Calkins, Sec'y., P.O. Box 1057, Grand Junction, CO 81502

Mexico-Elmhurst Philatelic Society International
Robert Jones, 2350 Bunker Hill Way, Costa Mesa, CA 92626

Oceania Philatelic Society
William Hagan, Pres., 1523 East Meadowbrook Drive, Loveland, OH 45140

Philatelic Foundation
270 Madison Ave., New York, NY 10016

Polonus Philatelic Society
864 N. Ashland Ave., Chicago, IL 60622

Portuguese Philately, International Society for
Nancy M. Gaylord, 1116 Marineway West, North Palm Beach, FL 33408

Rossica, Society of Russian Philately
Norman Epstein, Treas., 33 Crooke Ave., Brooklyn, NY 11226

El Salvador, Associated Collectors of
Robert Fisher, Box 306, Oaks, PA 19456

Scandinavian Collectors Club
Robert B. Brandeberry, 58 W. Salisbury Dr., Wilmington, DE 19809

Turkey & Ottoman Philatelic Society
George Tarnowski, 2050 Spring Valley Rd., Lansdale, PA 19446

United Postal Stationery Society
P.O. Box 48, Redlands, CA 92373

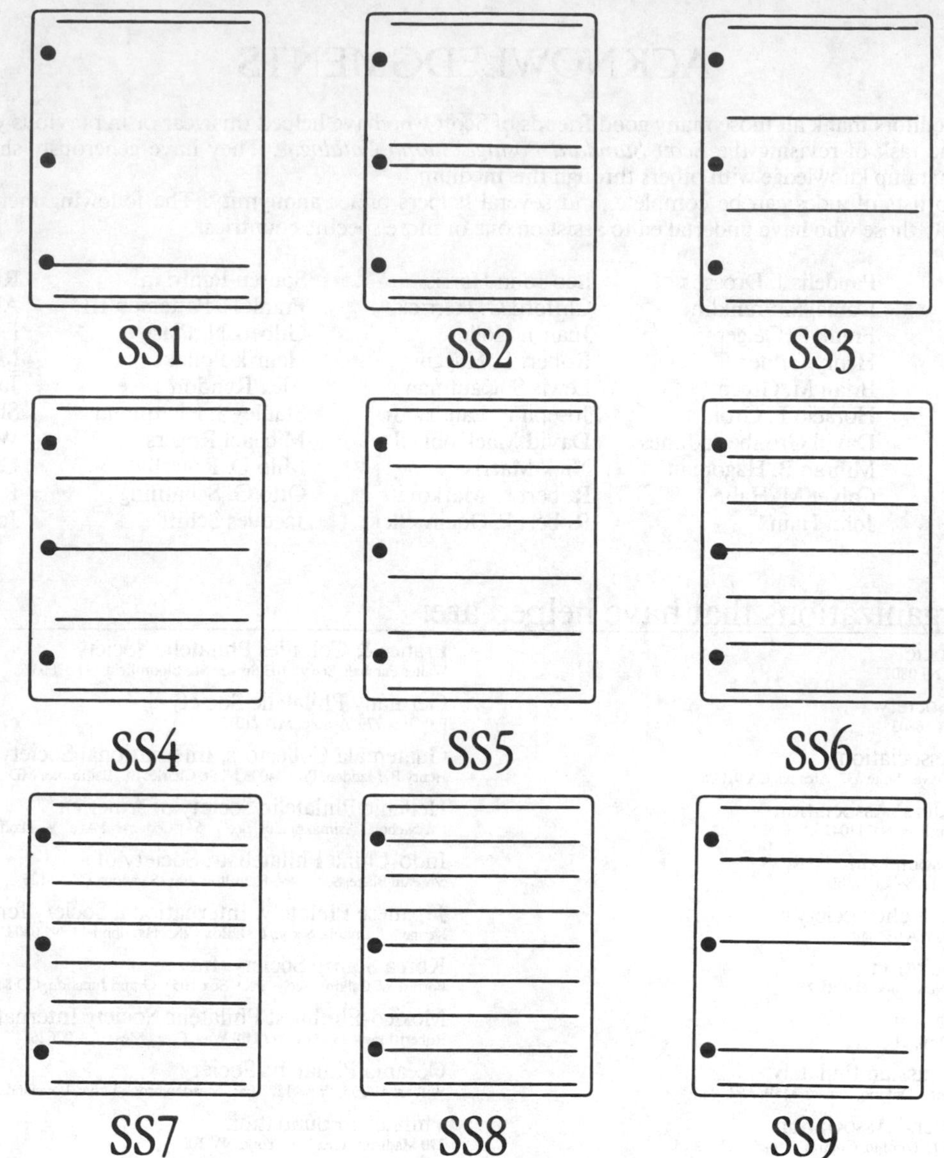

Collect the Scott way with

Scott StockPages

Similar in quality and style to Hagner stock pages.

- 9 different page formats, 8½″ x 11″, hold every size stamp. Available with luxuriously padded three-ring binder and matching slipcase.

COMMON DESIGN TYPES

Pictured in this section are issues where one illustration has been used for a number of countries in the Catalogue. Not included in this section are overprinted stamps or those issues which are illustrated in each country.

EUROPA

Europa Issue, 1956

The design symbolizing the cooperation among the six countries comprising the Coal and Steel Community is illustrated in each country.

- Belgium 496-497
- France 805-806
- Germany 748-749
- Italy 715-716
- Luxembourg 318-320
- Netherlands 368-369

Europa Issue, 1958

"E" and Dove
CD1

European Postal Union at the service of European integration.

1958, Sept. 13

- Belgium 527-528
- France 889 890
- Germany 790-791
- Italy 750-751
- Luxembourg 341-343
- Netherlands 375-376
- Saar 317-318

Europa Issue, 1959

6-Link Endless Chain
CD2

1959, Sept. 19

- Belgium 536-537
- France 929-930
- Germany 805-806
- Italy 791-792
- Luxembourg 354-355
- Netherlands 379-380

Europa Issue, 1960

19-Spoke Wheel
CD3

First anniversary of the establishment of C.E.P.T. (Conference Europeenne des Administrations des Postes et des Telecommunications.)

The spokes symbolize the 19 founding members of the Conference.

1960, Sept.

- Belgium 553-554
- Denmark 379
- Finland 376-377
- France 970-971
- Germany 818-820
- Great Britain 377-378
- Greece 688
- Iceland 327-328
- Ireland 175-176
- Italy 809-810
- Luxembourg 374-375
- Netherlands 385-386
- Norway 387
- Portugal 866-867
- Spain 941-942
- Sweden 562-563
- Switzerland 400-401
- Turkey 1493-1494

Europa Issue, 1961

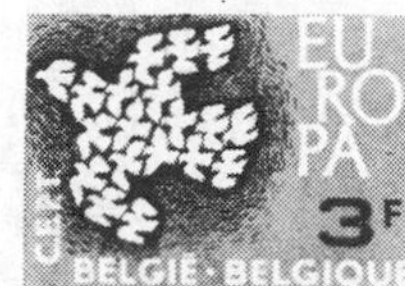

19 Doves Flying as One
CD4

The 19 doves represent the 19 members of the Conference of European Postal and Telecommunications Administrations C.E.P.T.

1961-62

- Belgium 572-573
- Cyprus 201-203
- France 1005-1006
- Germany 844-845
- Great Britain 383-384
- Greece 718-719
- Iceland 340-341
- Italy 845-846
- Luxembourg 382-383
- Netherlands 387-388
- Spain 1010 1011
- Switzerland 410-411
- Turkey 1518-1520

Europa Issue 1962

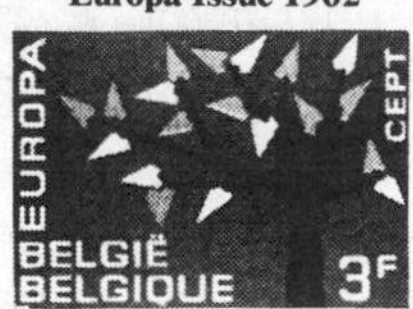

Young Tree with 19 Leaves
CD5

The 19 leaves represent the 19 original members of C.E.P.T.

1962-63

- Belgium 582-583
- Cyprus 219-221
- France 1045-1046
- Germany 852-853
- Greece 739-740
- Iceland 348-349
- Ireland 184-185
- Italy 860-861
- Luxembourg 386-387
- Netherlands 394-395
- Norway 414-415
- Switzerland 416-417
- Turkey 1553-1555

Europa Issue, 1963

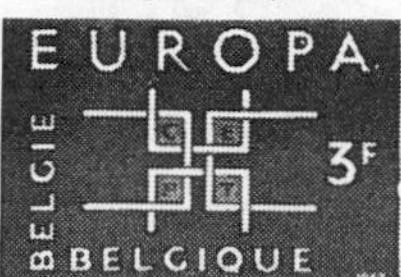

Stylized Links, Symbolizing Unity
CD6

1963, Sept.

- Belgium 598-599
- Cyprus 229-231
- Finland 419
- France 1074-1075
- Germany 867-868
- Greece 768-769
- Iceland 357-358
- Ireland 188-189
- Italy 880-881
- Luxembourg 403-404
- Netherlands 416-417
- Norway 441-442
- Switzerland 429
- Turkey 1602-1603

Europa Issue, 1964

Symbolic Daisy
CD7

5th anniversary of the establishment of C.E.P.T. The 22 petals of the flower symbolize the 22 members of the Conference.

1964, Sept.

- Austria 738
- Belgium 614-615
- Cyprus 244-246
- France 1109-1110
- Germany 897-898
- Greece 801-802
- Iceland 367-368
- Ireland 196-197
- Italy 894-895
- Luxembourg 411-412
- Monaco 590-591
- Netherlands 428-429
- Norway 458
- Portugal 931-933
- Spain 1262-1263
- Switzerland 438-439
- Turkey 1628-1629

Europa Issue, 1965

Leaves and "Fruit"
CD8

1965

- Belgium 636-637
- Cyprus 262-264
- Finland 437
- France 1131-1132
- Germany 934-935
- Greece 833-834
- Iceland 375-376
- Ireland 204-205
- Italy 915-916
- Luxembourg 432-433
- Monaco 616-617
- Netherlands 438-439
- Norway 475-476
- Portugal 958-960
- Switzerland 469
- Turkey 1665-1666

Europa Issue, 1966

Symbolic Sailboat
CD9

1966, Sept.

- Andorra, French 172
- Belgium 675-676
- Cyprus 275-277
- France 1163-1164
- Germany 963-964
- Greece 862-863
- Iceland 384-385
- Ireland 216-217
- Italy 942-943
- Liechtenstein 415
- Luxembourg 440-441
- Monaco 639-640
- Netherlands 441-442
- Norway 496-497
- Portugal 980-982
- Switzerland 477-478
- Turkey 1718-1719

Europa Issue, 1967

Cogwheels
CD10

1967

- Andorra, French 174-175
- Belgium 688-689
- Cyprus 297-299
- France 1178-1179
- Greece 891-892
- Germany 969-970
- Iceland 389-390
- Ireland 232-233
- Italy 951-952
- Liechtenstein 420
- Luxembourg 449-450
- Monaco 669-670
- Netherlands 444-447
- Norway 504-505
- Portugal 994-996
- Spain 1465-1466
- Switzerland 482
- Turkey B120-B121

Europa Issue, 1968

Golden Key with C.E.P.T. Emblem
CD11

1968

- Andorra, French 182-183
- Belgium 705-706
- Cyprus 314-316
- France 1209-1210
- Germany 983-984
- Greece 916-917
- Iceland 395-396
- Ireland 242-243
- Italy 979-980
- Liechtenstein 442
- Luxembourg 466-467
- Monaco 689-691
- Netherlands 452-453
- Portugal 1019-1021
- San Marino 687
- Spain 1526
- Turkey 1775-1776

Europa Issue, 1969

"EUROPA" and "CEPT"
CD12

Tenth anniversary of C.E.P.T.

1969

- Andorra, French 188-189
- Austria 837
- Belgium 718-719
- Cyprus 326-328
- Denmark 458
- Finland 483
- France 1245-1246
- Germany 996-997
- Great Britain 585
- Greece 947-948

Iceland	406-407
Ireland	270-271
Italy	1000-1001
Jugoslavia	1003-1004
Liechtenstein	453
Luxembourg	474-475
Monaco	722-724
Netherlands	475-476
Norway	533-534
Portugal	1038-1040
San Marino	701-702
Spain	1567
Sweden	814-816
Switzerland	500-501
Turkey	1799-1800
Vatican	470-472

Europa Issue, 1970

Interwoven Threads CD13

1970

Andorra, French	196-197
Belgium	741-742
Cyprus	340-342
France	1271-1272
Germany	1018-1019
Greece	985, 987
Iceland	420-421
Ireland	279-281
Italy	1013-1014
Jugoslavia	1024-1025
Liechtenstein	470
Luxembourg	489-490
Monaco	768-770
Netherlands	483-484
Portugal	1060-1062
San Marino	729-730
Spain	1607
Switzerland	515-516
Turkey	1848-1849

Europa Issue, 1971

"Fraternity, Cooperation, Common Effort"—CD14

1971

Andorra, French	205-206
Belgium	803-804
Cyprus	365-367
Finland	504
France	1304
Germany	1064-1065
Greece	1029-1030
Iceland	429-430
Ireland	305-306
Italy	1038-1039
Jugoslavia	1052-1053
Liechtenstein	485
Luxembourg	500-501
Malta	425-427
Monaco	797-799
Netherlands	488-489
Portugal	1094-1096
San Marino	749-750
Spain	1675-1676
Switzerland	531-532
Turkey	1876-1877

Europa Issue, 1972

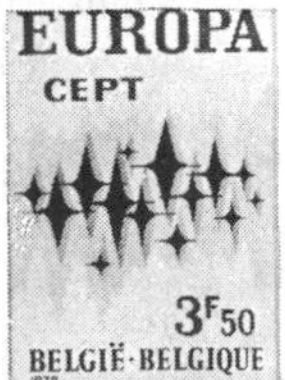

Sparkles, Symbolic of Communications CD15

1972

Andorra, French	210-211
Andorra, Spanish	62
Belgium	825-826
Cyprus	380-382
Finland	512-513
France	1341
Germany	1089-1090
Greece	1049-1050
Iceland	439-440
Ireland	316-317
Italy	1065-1066
Jugoslavia	1100-1101
Liechtenstein	504
Luxembourg	512-513
Malta	450-453
Monaco	831-832
Netherlands	494-495
Portugal	1141-1143
San Marino	771-772
Spain	1718
Switzerland	544-545
Turkey	1907-1908

Europa Issue, 1973

Post Horn and Arrows CD16

1973

Andorra, French	319-320
Andorra, Spanish	76
Belgium	839-840
Cyprus	396-398
Finland	526
France	1367
Germany	1114-1115
Greece	1090-1092
Iceland	447-448
Ireland	329-330
Italy	1108-1109
Jugoslavia	1138-1139
Liechtenstein	528-529
Luxembourg	523-524
Malta	469-471
Monaco	866-867
Netherlands	504-505
Norway	604-605
Portugal	1170-1172
San Marino	802-803
Spain	1753
Switzerland	580-581
Turkey	1935-1936

PORTUGAL & COLONIES

Vasco da Gama Issue

Fleet Departing—CD20

Fleet Arriving at Calicut CD21

Embarking at Rastello—CD22

Muse of History CD23

Flagship San Gabriel, da Gama and Camoens CD24

Archangel Gabriel, the Patron Saint CD25

Flagship San Gabriel CD26

Vasco da Gama CD27

Fourth centenary of Vasco da Gama's discovery of the route to India.

1898

Azores	93-100
Macao	67-74
Madeira	37-44
Portugal	147-154
Port. Africa	1-8
Port. india	189-196
Timor	45-52

Pombal Issue
POSTAL TAX

Marquis de Pombal CD28

Planning Reconstruction of Lisbon, 1755 CD29

Pombal Monument, Lisbon CD30

Sebastiao Jose' de Carvalho e Mello, Marquis de Pombal (1699-1782), statesman, rebuilt Lisbon after earthquake of 1755. Tax was for the erection of Pombal monument. Obligatory on all mail on certain days throughout the year.

1925

Angola	RA1-RA3
Azores	RA9-RA11
Cape Verde	RA1-RA3
Macao	RA1-RA3
Madeira	RA1-RA3
Mozambique	RA1-RA3
Portugal	RA11-RA13
Port. Guinea	RA1-RA3
Port. India	RA1-RA3
St. Thomas & Prince Islands	RA1-RA3
Timor	RA1-RA3

Pombal Issue
POSTAL TAX DUES

Marquis de Pombal CD31

Planning Reconstruction of Lisbon, 1755 CD32

Pombal Monument, Lisbon CD33

1925

Angola	RAJ1-RAJ3
Azores	RAJ2-RAJ4
Cape Verde	RAJ1-RAJ3
Macao	RAJ1-RAJ3
Madeira	RAJ1-RAJ3
Mozambique	RAJ1-RAJ3
Portugal	RAJ2-RAJ4
Port. Guinea	RAJ1-RAJ3
Port. India	RAJ1-RAJ3
St. Thomas & Prince Islands	RAJ1-RAJ3
Timor	RAJ1-RAJ3

Vasco da Gama CD34

Mousinho de Albuquerque CD35

Dam CD36

Prince Henry the Navigator CD37

Affonso de Albuquerque CD38

1938-39

Angola	274-291
Cape Verde	234-251
Macao	289-305
Mozambique	270-287
Port. Guinea	233-250
Port. India	439-453
St. Thomas & Prince Islands	302-319, 323-340
Timor	223-239

Plane over Globe CD39

1938-39

Angola	C1-C9
Cape Verde	C1-C9
Macao	C7-C15
Mozambique	C1-C9
Port. Guinea	C1-C9
Port. India	C1-C8
St. Thomas & Prince Islands	C1-C18
Timor	C1-C9

Lady of Fatima Issue

Our Lady of the Rosary, Fatima, Portugal
CD40

1948-49

Angola	315-318
Cape Verde	266
Macao	336
Mozambique	325-328
Port. Guinea	271
Port. India	480
St. Thomas & Prince Islands	351
Timor	254

A souvenir sheet of 9 stamps was issued in 1951 to mark the extension of the 1950 Holy Year. The sheet contains: Angola No. 316, Cape Verde No. 266, Macao No. 336, Mozambique No. 325, Portuguese Guinea No. 271, Portugese India Nos. 480, 485, St. Thomas & Prince Islands No. 351, Timor No. 254.

The sheet also contains a portrait of Pope Pius XII and is inscribed "Encerramento do Ano Santo, Fatima 1951." It was sold for 11 escudos.

Holy Year Issue

Church Bells and Dove
CD41

Angel Holding Candelabra
CD42

Holy Year, 1950.

1950-51

Angola	331-332
Cape Verde	268-269
Macao	339-340
Mozambique	330-331
Port. Guinea	273-274
Port. India	490-491, 496-503
St. Thomas & Prince Islands	353-354
Timor	258-259

A souvenir sheet of 8 stamps was issued in 1951 to mark the extension of the Holy Year. The sheet contains: Angola No. 331, Cape Verde No. 269, Macao No. 340, Mozambique No. 331, Portuguese Guinea No. 275, Portuguese India No. 490, St. Thomas & Prince Islands No. 354, Timor No. 258, some with colors changed. The sheet contains doves and is inscribed "Encerramento do Ano Santo, Fatima 1951." It was sold for 17 escudos.

Holy Year Conclusion Issue

Our Lady of Fatima
CD43

Conclusion of Holy Year. Sheets contain alternate vertical rows of stamps and labels bearing quotation from Pope Pius XII, different for each colony.

1951

Angola	357
Cape Verde	270
Macao	352
Mozambique	356
Port. Guinea	275
Port. India	506
St. Thomas & Prince Islands	355
Timor	270

Medical Congress Issue

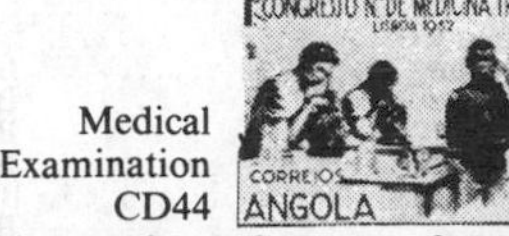

Medical Examination
CD44

First National Congress of Tropical Medicine, Lisbon, 1952.
Each stamp has a different design.

1952

Angola	358
Cape Verde	287
Macao	364
Mozambique	359
Port. Guinea	276
Port. India	516
St. Thomas & Prince Islands	356
Timor	271

POSTAGE DUE STAMPS

CD45

1952

Angola	J37-J42
Cape Verde	J31-J36
Macao	J53-J58
Mozambique	J51-J56
Port. Guinea	J40-J45
Port. India	J47-J52
St. Thomas & Prince Islands	J52-J57
Timor	J31-J36

Sao Paulo Issue

Father Manuel de Nobrega and View of Sao Paulo
CD46

400th anniversary of the founding of Sao Paulo, Brazil.

1954

Angola	385
Cape Verde	297
Macao	382
Mozambique	395
Port. Guinea	291
Port. India	530
St. Thomas & Prince Islands	369
Timor	279

Tropical Medicine Congress Issue

Securidaca Longipedunculata
CD47

Sixth International Congress for Tropical Medicine and Malaria, Lisbon, Sept. 1958.
Each stamp shows a different plant.

1958

Angola	409
Cape Verde	303
Macao	392
Mozambique	404
Port. Guinea	295
Port. India	569
St. Thomas & Prince Islands	371
Timor	289

Sports Issue

Flying
CD48

Each stamp shows a different sport.

1962

Angola	433-438
Cape Verde	320-325
Macao	394-399
Mozambique	424-429
Port. Guinea	299-304
St. Thomas & Prince Islands	374-379
Timor	313-318

Anti-Malaria Issue

Anopheles Funestus and Malaria Eradication Symbol
CD49

World Health Organization drive to eradicate malaria.

1962

Angola	439
Cape Verde	326
Macao	400
Mozambique	430
Port. Guinea	305
St. Thomas & Prince Islands	380
Timor	319

Airline Anniversary Issue

Map of Africa, Super Constellation and Jet Liner
CD50

Tenth anniversary of Transportes Aereos Portugueses (TAP).

1963

Angola	490
Cape Verde	327
Mozambique	434
Port. Guinea	318
St. Thomas & Prince Islands	381

National Overseas Bank Issue

Antonio Teixeira de Sousa
CD51

Centenary of the National Overseas Bank of Portugal.

1964, May 16

Angola	509
Cape Verde	328
Port. Guinea	319
St. Thomas & Prince Islands	382
Timor	320

ITU Issue

ITU Emblem and St. Gabriel
CD52

Centenary of the International Communications Union.

1965, May 17

Angola	511
Cape Verde	329
Macao	402
Mozambique	464
Port. Guinea	320
St. Thomas & Prince Islands	383
Timor	321

National Revolution Issue

St. Paul's Hospital, and Commercial and Industrial School
CD53

40th anniversary of the National Revolution.
Different buildings on each stamp.

1966, May 28

Angola	525
Cape Verde	338
Macao	403
Mozambique	465
Port. Guinea	329
St. Thomas & Prince Islands	392
Timor	322

Navy Club Issue

Mendes Barata and Cruiser Dom Carlos I
CD54

Centenary of Portugal's Navy Club.
Each stamp has a different design.

1967, Jan. 31

Angola	527-528
Cape Verde	339-340
Macao	412-413
Mozambique	478-479
Port. Guinea	330-331
St. Thomas & Prince Islands	393-394
Timor	323-324

Admiral Coutinho Issue

Admiral Gago Coutinho and his First Ship
CD55

Centenary of the birth of Admiral Carlos Viegas Gago Coutinho (1869-1959), explorer and aviation pioneer.
Each stamp has a different design.

1969, Feb. 17

Angola	547
Cape Verde	355
Macao	417
Mozambique	484
Port. Guinea	335
St. Thomas & Prince Islands	397
Timor	335

Administration Reform Issue

Luiz Augusto Rebello da Silva
CD56

Centenary of the administration reforms of the overseas territories.

1969, Sept. 25

Angola	549
Cape Verde	357
Macao	419
Mozambique	491
Port. Guinea	337
St. Thomas & Prince Islands	399
Timor	338

Marshal Carmona Issue

Marshal A.O. Carmona
CD57

Birth centenary of Marshal Antonio Oscar Carmona de Fragoso (1869-1951), President of Portugal.
Each stamp has a different design.

1970, Nov. 15

Angola	563
Cape Verde	359
Macao	422
Mozambique	493
Port. Guinea	340
St. Thomas & Prince Islands	403
Timor	341

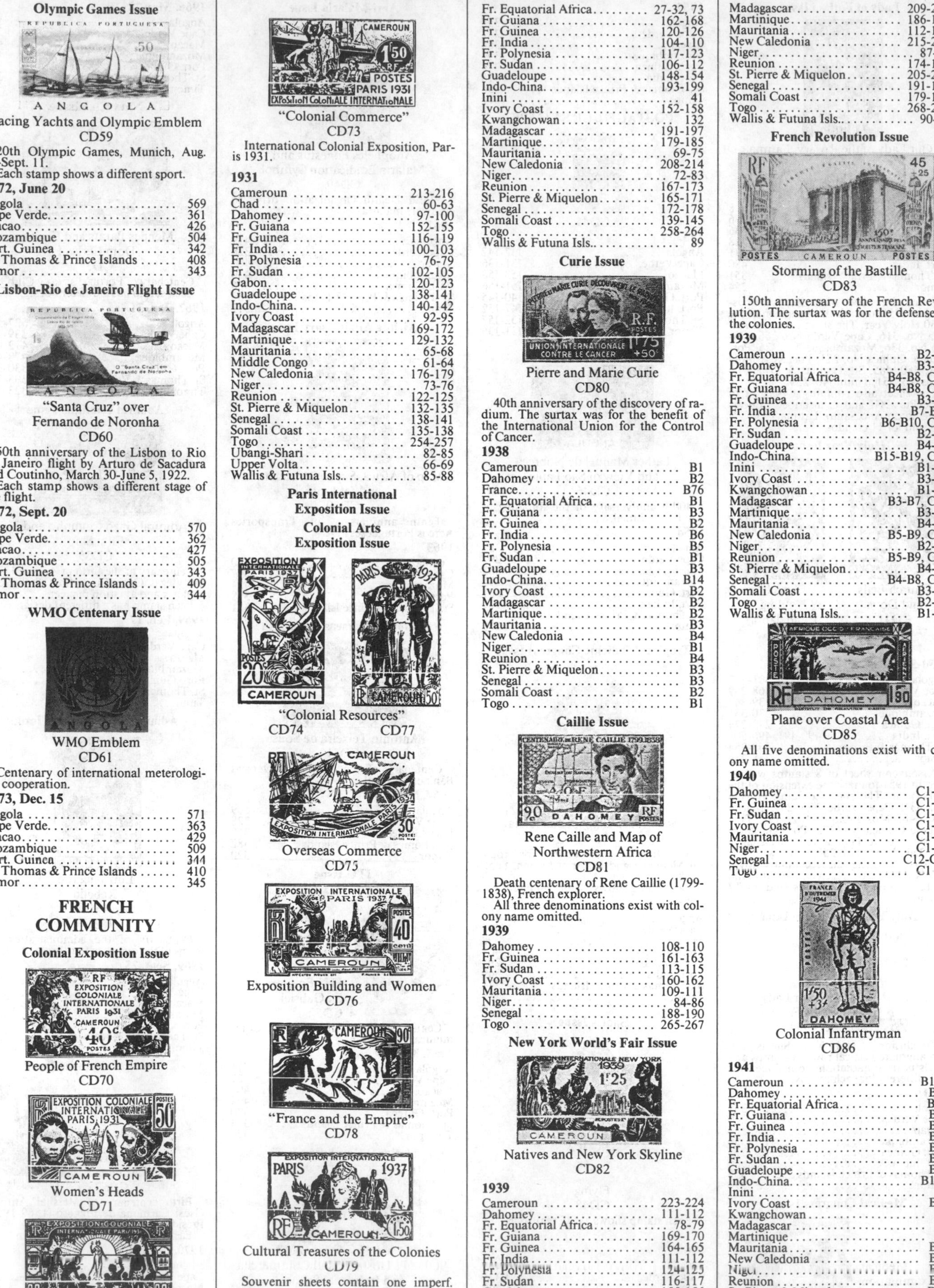

Olympic Games Issue

Racing Yachts and Olympic Emblem
CD59

20th Olympic Games, Munich, Aug. 26-Sept. 11.
Each stamp shows a different sport.

1972, June 20

Angola	569
Cape Verde	361
Macao	426
Mozambique	504
Port. Guinea	342
St. Thomas & Prince Islands	408
Timor	343

Lisbon-Rio de Janeiro Flight Issue

"Santa Cruz" over Fernando de Noronha
CD60

50th anniversary of the Lisbon to Rio de Janeiro flight by Arturo de Sacadura and Coutinho, March 30-June 5, 1922.
Each stamp shows a different stage of the flight.

1972, Sept. 20

Angola	570
Cape Verde	362
Macao	427
Mozambique	505
Port. Guinea	343
St. Thomas & Prince Islands	409
Timor	344

WMO Centenary Issue

WMO Emblem
CD61

Centenary of international meterological cooperation.

1973, Dec. 15

Angola	571
Cape Verde	363
Macao	429
Mozambique	509
Port. Guinea	344
St. Thomas & Prince Islands	410
Timor	345

FRENCH COMMUNITY

Colonial Exposition Issue

People of French Empire
CD70

Women's Heads
CD71

France Showing Way to Civilization
CD72

"Colonial Commerce"
CD73

International Colonial Exposition, Paris 1931.

1931

Cameroun	213-216
Chad	60-63
Dahomey	97-100
Fr. Guiana	152-155
Fr. Guinea	116-119
Fr. India	100-103
Fr. Polynesia	76-79
Fr. Sudan	102-105
Gabon	120-123
Guadeloupe	138-141
Indo-China	140-142
Ivory Coast	92-95
Madagascar	169-172
Martinique	129-132
Mauritania	65-68
Middle Congo	61-64
New Caledonia	176-179
Niger	73-76
Reunion	122-125
St. Pierre & Miquelon	132-135
Senegal	138-141
Somali Coast	135-138
Togo	254-257
Ubangi-Shari	82-85
Upper Volta	66-69
Wallis & Futuna Isls.	85-88

Paris International Exposition Issue
Colonial Arts Exposition Issue

"Colonial Resources"
CD74 CD77

Overseas Commerce
CD75

Exposition Building and Women
CD76

"France and the Empire"
CD78

Cultural Treasures of the Colonies
CD79

Souvenir sheets contain one imperf. stamp.

1937

Cameroun	217-222A
Dahomey	101-107
Fr. Equatorial Africa	27-32, 73
Fr. Guiana	162-168
Fr. Guinea	120-126
Fr. India	104-110
Fr. Polynesia	117-123
Fr. Sudan	106-112
Guadeloupe	148-154
Indo-China	193-199
Inini	41
Ivory Coast	152-158
Kwangchowan	132
Madagascar	191-197
Martinique	179-185
Mauritania	69-75
New Caledonia	208-214
Niger	72-83
Reunion	167-173
St. Pierre & Miquelon	165-171
Senegal	172-178
Somali Coast	139-145
Togo	258-264
Wallis & Futuna Isls.	89

Curie Issue

Pierre and Marie Curie
CD80

40th anniversary of the discovery of radium. The surtax was for the benefit of the International Union for the Control of Cancer.

1938

Cameroun	B1
Dahomey	B2
France	B76
Fr. Equatorial Africa	B1
Fr. Guiana	B3
Fr. Guinea	B2
Fr. India	B6
Fr. Polynesia	B5
Fr. Sudan	B1
Guadeloupe	B3
Indo-China	B14
Ivory Coast	B2
Madagascar	B2
Martinique	B2
Mauritania	B3
New Caledonia	B4
Niger	B1
Reunion	B4
St. Pierre & Miquelon	B3
Senegal	B3
Somali Coast	B2
Togo	B1

Caillie Issue

Rene Caille and Map of Northwestern Africa
CD81

Death centenary of Rene Caillie (1799-1838), French explorer.
All three denominations exist with colony name omitted.

1939

Dahomey	108-110
Fr. Guinea	161-163
Fr. Sudan	113-115
Ivory Coast	160-162
Mauritania	109-111
Niger	84-86
Senegal	188-190
Togo	265-267

New York World's Fair Issue

Natives and New York Skyline
CD82

1939

Cameroun	223-224
Dahomey	111-112
Fr. Equatorial Africa	78-79
Fr. Guiana	169-170
Fr. Guinea	164-165
Fr. India	111-112
Fr. Polynesia	124-125
Fr. Sudan	116-117
Guadeloupe	155-156
Indo-China	203-204
Inini	42-43
Ivory Coast	163-164
Kwangchowan	121-122
Madagascar	209-210
Martinique	186-187
Mauritania	112-113
New Caledonia	215-216
Niger	87-88
Reunion	174-175
St. Pierre & Miquelon	205-206
Senegal	191-192
Somali Coast	179-180
Togo	268-269
Wallis & Futuna Isls.	90-91

French Revolution Issue

Storming of the Bastille
CD83

150th anniversary of the French Revolution. The surtax was for the defense of the colonies.

1939

Cameroun	B2-B6
Dahomey	B3-B7
Fr. Equatorial Africa	B4-B8, CB1
Fr. Guiana	B4-B8, CB1
Fr. Guinea	B3-B7
Fr. India	B7-B11
Fr. Polynesia	B6-B10, CB1
Fr. Sudan	B2-B6
Guadeloupe	B4-B8
Indo-China	B15-B19, CB1
Inini	B1-B5
Ivory Coast	B3-B7
Kwangchowan	B1-B5
Madagascar	B3-B7, CB1
Martinique	B3-B7
Mauritania	B4-B8
New Caledonia	B5-B9, CB1
Niger	B2-B6
Reunion	B5-B9, CB1
St. Pierre & Miquelon	B4-B8
Senegal	B4-B8, CB1
Somali Coast	B3-B7
Togo	B2-B6
Wallis & Futuna Isls.	B1-B5

Plane over Coastal Area
CD85

All five denominations exist with colony name omitted.

1940

Dahomey	C1-C5
Fr. Guinea	C1-C5
Fr. Sudan	C1-C5
Ivory Coast	C1-C5
Mauritania	C1-C5
Niger	C1-C5
Senegal	C12-C16
Togo	C1-C5

Colonial Infantryman
CD86

1941

Cameroun	B13B
Dahomey	B13
Fr. Equatorial Africa	B8B
Fr. Guiana	B10
Fr. Guinea	B13
Fr. India	B13
Fr. Polynesia	B12
Fr. Sudan	B12
Guadeloupe	B10
Indo-China	B19B
Inini	B7
Ivory Coast	B13
Kwangchowan	B7
Madagascar	B9
Martinique	B9
Mauritania	B14
New Caledonia	B11
Niger	B12
Reunion	B11
St. Pierre & Miquelon	B8B
Senegal	B14
Somali Coast	B9
Togo	B10B
Wallis & Futuna Isls.	B7

Cross of Lorraine and Four-motor Plane
CD87

1941-5

Cameroun C1-C7
Fr. Equatorial Africa C17-C23
Fr. Guiana C9-C10
Fr. India C1-C6
Fr. Polynesia C3-C9
Fr. West Africa C1-C3
Guadeloupe C1-C2
Madagascar C37-C43
Martinique C1-C2
New Caledonia C7-C13
Reunion C18-C24
St. Pierre & Miquelon C1-C7
Somali Coast C1-C7

Transport Plane
CD88

Caravan and Plane—CD89

1942

Dahomey C6-C13
Fr. Guinea C6-C13
Fr. Sudan C6-C13
Ivory Coast C6-C13
Mauritania C6-C13
Niger C6-C13
Senegal C17-C25
Togo C6-C13

Red Cross Issue

Marianne
CD90

The surtax was for the French Red Cross and national relief.

1944

Cameroun B28
Fr. Equatorial Africa B38
Fr. Guiana B12
Fr. India B14
Fr. Polynesia B13
Fr. West Africa B1
Guadeloupe B12
Madagascar B15
Martinique B11
New Caledonia B13
Reunion B15
St. Pierre & Miquelon B13
Somali Coast B13
Wallis & Futuna Isls. B9

Eboue Issue

Felix Eboue
CD91

Felix Eboue, first French colonial administrator to proclaim resistance to Germany after French surrender in World War II.

1945

Cameroun 296-297
Fr. Equatorial Africa 156-157
Fr. Guiana 171-172
Fr. India 210-211
Fr. Polynesia 150-151
Fr. West Africa 15-16
Guadeloupe 187-188
Madagascar 259-260
Martinique 196-197
New Caledonia 274-275
Reunion 238-239
St. Pierre & Miquelon 322-323
Somali Coast 238-239

Victory Issue

Victory
CD92

European victory of the Allied Nations in World War II.

1946, May 8

Cameroun C8
Fr. Equatorial Africa C24
Fr. Guiana C11
Fr. India C7
Fr. Polynesia C10
Fr. West Africa C4
Guadeloupe C3
Indo-China C19
Madagascar C44
Martinique C3
New Caledonia C14
Reunion C25
St. Pierre & Miquelon C8
Somali Coast C8
Wallis & Futuna Isls. C1

Chad to Rhine Issue

Leclerc's Departure from Chad
CD93

Battle at Cufra Oasis
CD94

Tanks in Action, Mareth
CD95

Normandy Invasion
CD96

Entering Paris
CD97

Liberation of Strasbourg
CD98

"Chad to the Rhine" march, 1942-44, by Gen. Jacques Leclerc's column, later French 2nd Armored Division.

1946, June 6

Cameroun C9-C14
Fr. Equatorial Africa C25-C30
Fr. Guiana C12-C17
Fr. India C8-C13
Fr. Polynesia C11-C16
Fr. West Africa C5-C10
Guadeloupe C4-C9
Indo-China C20-C25
Madagascar C45-C50
Martinique C4-C9
New Caledonia C15-C20
Reunion C26-C31
St. Pierre & Miquelon C9-C14
Somali Coast C9-C14
Wallis & Futuna Isls. C2-C7

UPU Issue

French Colonials, Globe and Plane
CD99

75th anniversary of the Universal Postal Union.

1949, July 4

Cameroun C29
Fr. Equatorial Africa C34
Fr. India C17
Fr. Polynesia C20
Fr. West Africa C15
Indo-China C26
Madagascar C55
New Caledonia C24
St. Pierre & Miquelon C18
Somali Coast C18
Togo C18
Wallis & Futuna Isls. C10

Tropical Medicine Issue

Doctor Treating Infant
CD100

The surtax was for charitable work.

1950

Cameroun B29
Fr. Equatorial Africa B39
Fr. India B15
Fr. Polynesia B14
Fr. West Africa B3
Madagascar B17
New Caledonia B14
St. Pierre & Miquelon B14
Somali Coast B14
Togo B11

Military Medal Issue

Medal, Early Marine and Colonial Soldier
CD101

Centenary of the creation of the French Military Medal.

1952

Cameroun 332
Comoro Isls. 39
Fr. Equatorial Africa 186
Fr. India 233
Fr. Polynesia 179
Fr. West Africa 57
Madagascar 286
New Caledonia 295
St. Pierre & Miquelon 345
Somali Coast 267
Togo 327
Wallis & Futuna Isls. 149

Liberation Issue

Allied Landing, Victory Sign and Cross of Lorraine
CD102

10th anniversary of the liberation of France.

1954, June 6

Cameroun C32
Comoro Isls. C4
Fr. Equatorial Africa C38
Fr. India C18
Fr. Polynesia C23
Fr. West Africa C17
Madagascar C57
New Caledonia C25
St. Pierre & Miquelon C19
Somali Coast C19
Togo C19
Wallis & Futuna Isls. C11

FIDES Issue

Plowmen
CD103

Efforts of FIDES, the Economic and Social Development Fund for Overseas Possessions (Fonds d' Investissement pour le Developpement Economique et Social).

Each stamp has a different design.

1956

Cameroun 326-329
Comoro Isls. 43
Fr. Polynesia 181
Madagascar 292-295
New Caledonia 303
Somali Coast 268
Togo 331

Flower Issue

Euadania
CD104

Each stamp shows a different flower.

1958-9

Cameroun 333
Comoro Isls. 45
Fr. Equatorial Africa 200-201
Fr. Polynesia 192
Fr. So. & Antarctic Terr. 11
Fr. West Africa 79-83
Madagascar 301-302
New Caledonia 304-305
St. Pierre & Miquelon 357
Somali Coast 270
Togo 348-349
Wallis & Futuna Isls. 152

Human Rights Issue

Sun, Dove and U.N. Emblem
CD105

10th anniversary of the signing of the Universal Declaration of Human Rights.

1958

Comoro Isls. 44
Fr. Equatorial Africa 202
Fr. Polynesia 191
Fr. West Africa 85
Madagascar 300
New Caledonia 306
St. Pierre & Miquelon 356
Somali Coast 274
Wallis & Futuna Isls. 153

C.C.T.A. Issue

Map of Africa and Cogwheels
CD106

10th anniversary of the Commission for Technical Cooperation in Africa south of the Sahara.

1960

- Cameroun 335
- Cent. African Rep. 3
- Chad 66
- Congo, P.R. 90
- Dahomey 138
- Gabon 150
- Ivory Coast 180
- Madagascar 317
- Mali 9
- Mauritania 117
- Niger 104
- Upper Volta 89

Air Afrique Issue, 1961

Modern and Ancient Africa, Map and Planes
CD107

Founding of Air Afrique (African Airlines).

1961-62

- Cameroun C37
- Cent. African Rep. C5
- Chad C7
- Congo, P.R. C5
- Dahomey C17
- Gabon C5
- Ivory Coast C18
- Mauritania C17
- Niger C22
- Senegal C31
- Upper Volta C4

Anti-Malaria Issue

Malaria Eradication Emblem
CD108

World Heatlh Organization drive to eradicate malaria.

1962, Apr. 7

- Cameroun B36
- Cent. African Rep. B1
- Chad B1
- Comoro Isls. B1
- Congo, P.R. B3
- Dahomey B15
- Gabon B4
- Ivory Coast B15
- Madagascar B19
- Mali B1
- Mauritania B16
- Niger B14
- Senegal B16
- Somali Coast B15
- Upper Volta B1

Abidjan Games Issue

Relay Race
CD109

Abidjan Games, Ivory Coast, Dec. 24-31, 1961.
Each stamp shows a different sport.

1962

- Chad 83-84
- Cent. African Rep. 19-20
- Congo, P.R. 103-104
- Gabon 163-164
- Niger 109-111
- Upper Volta 103-105

African and Malagasy Union Issue

Flag of African and Malagasy Union
CD110

First anniversary of the Union.

1962, Sept. 8

- Cameroun 373
- Cent. African Rep. 21
- Chad 85
- Congo, P.R. 105
- Dahomey 155
- Gabon 165
- Ivory Coast 198
- Madagascar 332
- Mauritania 170
- Niger 112
- Senegal 211
- Upper Volta 106

Telstar Issue

Telstar and Globe Showing Andover and Pleumeur-Bodou
CD111

First television connection of the United States and Europe through the Telstar satellite, July 11-12, 1962.

1962-63

- Andorra, French 154
- Comoro Isls. C7
- Fr. Polynesia C29
- Fr. So. & Antarctic Terr. C5
- New Caledonia C33
- Somali Coast C31
- St. Pierre & Miquelon C26
- Wallis & Futuna Isls. C17

Freedom From Hunger Issue

World Map and Wheat Emblem
CD112

United Nations Food and Agriculture Organization's "Freedom from Hunger" campaign.

1963, Mar. 21

- Cameroun B37-B38
- Cent. African Rep. B2
- Chad B2
- Congo, P.R. B4
- Dahomey B16
- Gabon B5
- Ivory Coast B16
- Madagascar B21
- Mauritania B17
- Niger B15
- Senegal B17
- Upper Volta B2

Red Cross Centenary Issue

Centenary Emblem
CD113

Centenary of the International Red Cross.

1963, Sept. 2

- Comoro Isls. 55
- Fr. Polynesia 205
- New Caledonia 328
- St. Pierre & Miquelon 367
- Somali Coast 297
- Wallis & Futuna Isls. 165

African Postal Union Issue

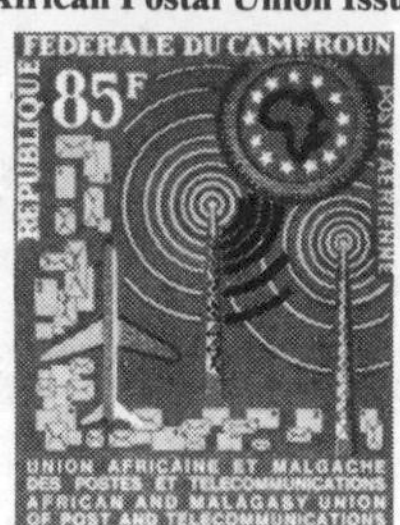

UAMPT Emblem, Radio Masts, Plane and Mali
CD114

Establishment of the African and Malagasy Posts and Telecommunications Union, UAMPT.

1963, Sept. 8

- Cameroun C47
- Cent. African Rep. C10
- Chad C9
- Congo, P.R. C13
- Dahomey C19
- Gabon C13
- Ivory Coast C25
- Madagascar C75
- Mauritania C22
- Niger C27
- Rwanda 36
- Senegal C32
- Upper Volta C9

Air Afrique Issue, 1963

Symbols of Flight
CD115

First anniversary of Air Afrique and inauguration of DC-8 service.

1963, Nov. 19

- Cameroun C48
- Chad C10
- Congo, P.R. C14
- Gabon C18
- Ivory Coast C26
- Mauritania C26
- Niger C35
- Senegal C33

Europafrica Issue

Europe and Africa Linked Together
CD116

Signing of an economic agreement between the European Economic Community and the African and Malagasy Union, Yaounde, Cameroun, July 20, 1963.

1963-64

- Cameroun 402
- Chad C11
- Cent. African Rep. C12
- Congo, P.R. C16
- Gabon C19
- Ivory Coast 217
- Niger C43
- Upper Volta C11

Human Rights Issue

Scales of Justice and Globe
CD117

15th anniversary of the Universal Declaration of Human Rights.

1963, Dec. 10

- Comoro Isls. 58
- Fr. Polynesia 206
- New Caledonia 329
- St. Pierre & Miquelon 368
- Somali Coast 300
- Wallis & Futuna Isls. 166

PHILATEC Issue

Stamp Album, Champs Elysees Palace and Horses of Marly
CD118

"PHILATEC," International Philatelic and Postal Techniques Exhibition, Paris, June 5-21, 1964.

1963-64

- Comoro Isls. 60
- France 1078
- Fr. Polynesia 207
- New Caledonia 341
- St. Pierre & Miquelon 369
- Somali Coast 301
- Wallis & Futuna Isls. 167

Cooperation Issue

Maps of France and Africa and Clasped Hands
CD119

Cooperation between France and the French-speaking countries of Africa and Madagascar.

1964

- Cameroun 409-410
- Cent. African Rep. 39
- Chad 103
- Congo, P.R. 121
- Dahomey 193
- France 1111
- Gabon 175
- Ivory Coast 221
- Madagascar 360
- Mauritania 181
- Niger 143
- Senegal 236
- Togo 495

ITU Issue

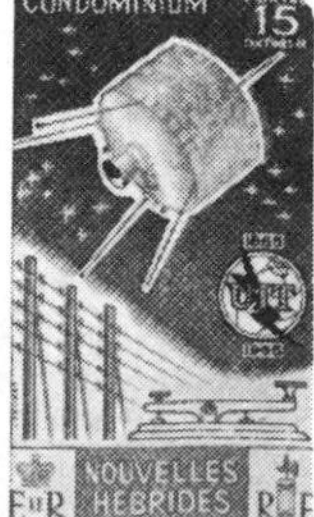

Telegraph, Syncom Satellite and ITU Emblem
CD120

Centenary of the International Telecommunication Union.

1965, May 17

- Comoro Isls. C14
- Fr. Polynesia C33
- Fr. So. & Antarctic Terr. C8
- New Caledonia C40
- New Hebrides 124-125

St. Pierre & Miquelon	C29
Somali Coast	C36
Wallis & Futuna Isls.	C20

French Satellite A-1 Issue

Diamant Rocket and Launching Installation
CD121

Launching of France's first satellite, Nov. 26, 1965.

1965-66	
Comoro Isls.	C15-C16
France	1137-1138
Fr. Polynesia	C40-C41
Fr. So. & Antarctic Terr.	C9-C10
New Caledonia	C44-C45
St. Pierre & Miquelon	C30-C31
Somali Coast	C39-C40
Wallis & Futuna Isls.	C22-C23

French Satellite D-1 Issue

D-1 Satellite in Orbit
CD122

Launching of the D-1 satellite at Hammaguir, Algeria, Feb. 17, 1966.

1966	
Comoro Isls.	C17
France	1148
Fr. Polynesia	C42
Fr. So. & Antarctic Terr.	C11
New Caledonia	C46
St. Pierre & Miquelon	C32
Somali Coast	C49
Wallis & Futuna Isls.	C24

Air Afrique Issue, 1966

Planes and Air Afrique Emblem
CD123

Introduction of DC-8F planes by Air Afrique.

1966	
Cameroun	C79
Cent. African Rep.	C35
Chad	C26
Congo, P.R.	C42
Dahomey	C42
Gabon	C47
Ivory Coast	C32
Mauritania	C57
Niger	C63
Senegal	C47
Togo	C54
Upper Volta	C31

African Postal Union, 1967

Telecommunications Symbols and Map of Africa
CD124

Fifth anniversary of the establishment of the African and Malagasy Union of Posts and Telecommunications, UAMPT.

1967	
Cameroun	C90
Cent. African Rep.	C46
Chad	C37
Congo, P.R.	C57
Dahomey	C61
Gabon	C58
Ivory Coast	C34
Madagascar	C85
Mauritania	C65
Niger	C75
Rwanda	C1-C3
Senegal	C60
Togo	C81
Upper Volta	C50

Monetary Union Issue

Gold Token of the Ashantis, 17-18th Centuries
CD125

Fifth anniversary of the West African Monetary Union.

1967, Nov. 4	
Dahomey	244
Ivory Coast	259
Mauritania	238
Niger	204
Senegal	294
Togo	623
Upper Volta	181

WHO Anniversary Issue

Sun, Flowers and WHO Emblem
CD126

20th anniversary of the World Health Organization.

1968, May 4	
Afars & Issas	317
Comoro Isls.	73
Fr. Polynesia	241-242
Fr. So. & Antarctic Terr.	31
New Caledonia	367
St. Pierre & Miquelon	377
Wallis & Futuna Isls.	169

Human Rights Year Issue

Human Rights Flame
CD127

International Human Rights Year.

1968, Aug. 10	
Afars & Issas	322-323
Comoro Isls.	76
Fr. Polynesia	243-244
Fr. So. & Antarctic Terr.	32
New Caledonia	369
St. Pierre & Miquelon	382
Wallis & Futuna Isls.	170

2nd PHILEXAFRIQUE Issue

Gabon No. 131 and Industrial Plant
CD128

Opening of PHILEXAFRIQUE, Abidjan, Feb. 14.

Each stamp shows a local scene and stamp.

1969, Feb. 14	
Cameroun	C118
Cent. African Rep.	C65
Chad	C48
Congo, P.R.	C77
Dahomey	C94
Gabon	C82
Ivory Coast	C38-C40
Madagascar	C92
Mali	C65
Mauritania	C80
Niger	C104
Senegal	C68
Togo	C104
Upper Volta	C62

Concorde Issue

Concorde in Flight
CD129

First flight of the prototpye Concorde super-sonic plane at Toulouse, Mar. 1, 1969.

1969	
Afars & Issas	C56
Comoro Isls.	C29
France	C42
Fr. Polynesia	C50
Fr. So. & Antarctic Terr.	C18
New Caledonia	C63
St. Pierre & Miquelon	C40
Wallis & Futuna Isls.	C30

Development Bank Issue

Bank Emblem—CD130

Fifth anniversary of the African Development Bank.

1969	
Cameroun	499
Chad	217
Congo, P.R.	181-182
Ivory Coast	281
Mali	127-128
Mauritania	267
Niger	220
Senegal	317-318
Upper Volta	201

ILO Issue

ILO Headquarters, Geneva, and Emblem
CD131

50th anniversary of the International Labor Organization.

1969-70	
Afars & Issas	337
Comoro Isls.	83
Fr. Polynesia	251-252
Fr. So. & Antarctic Terr.	35
New Caledonia	379
St. Pierre & Miquelon	396
Wallis & Futuna Isls.	172

ASECNA Issue

Map of Africa, Plane and Airport
CD132

10th anniversary of the Agency for the Security of Aerial Navigation in Africa and Madagascar (ASECNA, Agence pour la Securite de la Navigation Aerienne en Afrique et a Madagascar).

1969-70	
Cameroun	500
Cent. African Rep.	119
Chad	222
Congo, P.R.	197
Dahomey	269
Gabon	260
Ivory Coast	287
Mali	130
Niger	221
Senegal	321
Upper Volta	204

U.P.U. Headquarters Issue

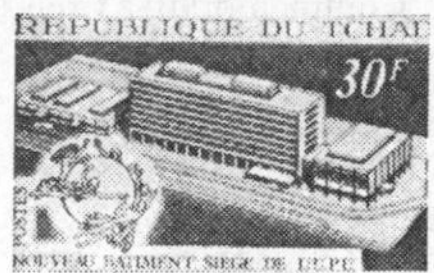

U.P.U. Headquarters and Emblem
CD133

New Universal Postal Union headquarters, Bern, Switzerland.

1970	
Afars & Issas	342
Algeria	443
Cameroun	503-504
Cent. African Rep.	125
Chad	225
Comoro Isls.	84
Congo, P.R.	216
Fr. Polynesia	261-262
Fr. So. & Antarctic Terr.	36
Gabon	258
Ivory Coast	295
Madagascar	444
Mali	134-135
Mauritania	283
New Caledonia	382
Niger	231-232
St. Pierre & Miquelon	397-398
Senegal	328-329
Tunisia	535
Wallis & Futuna Isls.	173

De Gaulle Issue

General de Gaulle 1940
CD134

First anniversary of the death of Charles de Gaulle, (1890-1970), President of France.

1971-72	
Afars & Issas	356-357
Comoro Isls.	104-105
France	1322-1325
Fr. Polynesia	270-271
Fr. So. & Antarctic Terr.	52-53
New Caledonia	393-394
Reunion	377, 380
St. Pierre & Miquelon	417-418
Wallis & Futuna Isls.	177-178

African Postal Union Issue, 1971

Carved Stool, UAMPT Building, Brazzaville, Congo
CD135

10th anniversary of the establishment of the African and Malagasy Posts and Telecommunications Union, UAMPT.

Each stamp has a different native design.

1971, Nov. 13	
Cameroun	C177
Cent. African Rep.	C89
Chad	C94
Congo, P.R.	C136
Dahomey	C146
Gabon	C120
Ivory Coast	C47
Mauritania	C113
Niger	C164
Rwanda	C8
Senegal	C105
Togo	C166
Upper Volta	C97

West African Monetary Union Issue

African Couple, City, Village and Commemorative Coin
CD136

10th anniversary of the West African Monetary Union.

1972, Nov. 2

Dahomey	300
Ivory Coat	331
Mauritania	299
Niger	258
Senegal	374
Togo	825
Upper Volta	280

African Postal Union Issue, 1973

Telecommunications Symbols and Map of Africa
CD137

11th anniversary of the African and Malagasy Posts and Telecommunications Union (UAMPT).

1973, Sept. 12

Cameroun	574
Cent. African Rep.	194
Chad	272
Congo, P.R.	289
Dahomey	311
Gabon	320
Ivory Coast	361
Madagascar	500
Mauritania	304
Niger	287
Rwanda	540
Senegal	393
Togo	849
Upper Volta	285

Philexafrique II—Essen Issue

Buffalo and Dahomey
No. C33
CD138

Wild Ducks and Baden
No. 1
CD139

Designs: Indigenous fauna, local and German stamps.

Types CD138-CD139 printed horizontally and vertically se-tenant in sheets of 10 (2x5). Label between horizontal pairs alternately commemoratives Philexafrique II, Libreville, Gabon, June 1978, and 2nd International Stamp Fair, Essen, Germany, Nov. 1-5.

1978-1979

Benin	C285-C286
Central Africa	C200-C201
Chad	C238-C239
Congo Republic	C245-C246
Djibouti	C121-C122
Gabon	C215-C216
Ivory Coast	C64-C65
Mali	C356-C357
Mauritania	C185-C186
Niger	C291-C292
Rwanda	C12-C13
Senegal	C146-C147
Togo	C363-C364
Upper Volta	C253-C254

HISTORICAL FOOTNOTES

Scouting Year: 75th anniversary of scouting and 125th birth anniversary of its founder, Lord Baden-Powell (1857-1941).

Robert Koch: Centenary of tuberculosis bacillus discovery by Robert Koch (1843-1910), German physician. Awarded 1905 Nobel Prize for physiology and medicine; also discovered cholera bacillus, 1883.

George Washington: 250th birth anniversary of George Washington (1732-1799), first U.S. president.

Charles Darwin: Death centenary of Charles Darwin (1809-1882), British naturalist. Traveled through South America and Australasia, 1831-1836, aboard the Beagle developing his theory of evolution. Published findings in *On the Origin of Species,* 1859.

Norman Rockwell (1894-1978): American illustrator who is best known for his paintings of people in everyday situations. Many of his works have been on the covers of *The Saturday Evening Post, Boy's Life, American Boy* and *St. Nicholas.*

Lewis B. Carroll (1832-1898): English author of the childhood classics *Alice in Wonderland* and *Through the Looking Glass.* He also wrote many works on mathematics under his real name, Charles Lutwidge Dodgson.

World Cup Soccer: The 12th World Cup Soccer Championship was held in Spain from June 13th to July 11th. The series, held every 4 years, opened in Barcelona with Belgium over Argentina before a crowd of 95,000. The 52 games were held in 17 stadiums in 14 cities with 24 participating teams. The final game was played in Madrid with Italy defeating Germany by a score of 3 to 1.

Olympic Games: The 14th Winter Olympic Games were held in Sarajevo, Jugoslavia, Feb. 7-18, 1984. Russia captured 25 medals, though East Germany won the most gold, with 9. The United States Received 4 gold and 4 silver medals, primarily on the surprisingly strong showing of the ski team.

The 23rd Olympic Games were held in Los Angeles, July 28-August 12, 1984, marred by a boycott by Russia and other eastern bloc nations. The boycott was viewed as a retaliatory action against the U.S. led boycott of the 1980 Moscow Olympics. The U.S. gathered 174 medals, 83 of them gold, to lead all participants.

Universal Postal Union Congress: The 19th Universal Postal Union Congress was held in Hamburg, Germany, July 18-July 27, 1984. It was attended by approximately 750 delegates from 166 member countries.

International Stamp Exhibition:
AUSIPEX '84 Melbourne, Australia, Sept. 21-30, 1984.
PHILATELIA '84 Stuttgart, Germany, Oct. 5-7, 1984.
FILACENTO '84 The Hague, Netherlands, Sept. 6-9, 1984.
ITALIA '85 Rome, Italy, Oct. 25-Nov. 3, 1985.

AFARS AND ISSAS,

French Territory of the

LOCATION — East Africa
GOVT. — French Overseas Territory
AREA — 8,880 sq. mi.
POP. — 150,000 (est. 1974)
CAPITAL — Djibouti (Jibuti)

The French overseas territory of Somali Coast was renamed the French Territory of the Afars and Issas in 1967. It became the Djibouti Republic (which see) on June 27, 1977.

100 Centimes = 1 Franc

Imperforates

Most stamps of Afars and Issas exist imperforate in issued and trial colors, and also in small presentation sheets in issued colors.

Grayheaded Kingfisher A48

Designs: 15fr, Oystercatcher. 50fr, Greenshanks. 55fr, Abyssinian roller. 60fr, Ground squirrel (vert.).

1967 Engr. Unwmk. *Perf. 13*

310 A48 10fr brt bl, gray grn & blk 1.75 1.75
311 A48 15fr dk brn, bl, ol & ocher 2.50 2.50
312 A48 50fr blk, sl grn & brn 9.50 6.00
313 A48 55fr vio, brt bl & gray grn 12.00 7.75
314 A48 60fr ocher, brt grn & sl grn 17.50 12.00
Nos. 310-314 (5) 43.25 30.00

Dates of Issue: 10fr, 55fr, Aug. 21; 15fr, 50fr, 60fr, Sept. 25. See No. C50.

Soccer A49

Design: 30fr, Basketball.

1967, Dec. 18 Engr. *Perf. 13*

315 A49 25fr bl, brn & emer 2.25 1.50
316 A49 30fr red lil, Prus bl & brn 3.00 2.75

WHO Anniversary Issue

Common Design Type

1968, May 4 Engr. *Perf. 13*

317 CD126 15fr multi 1.65 1.10

Issued to commemorate the 20th anniversary of the World Health Organization.

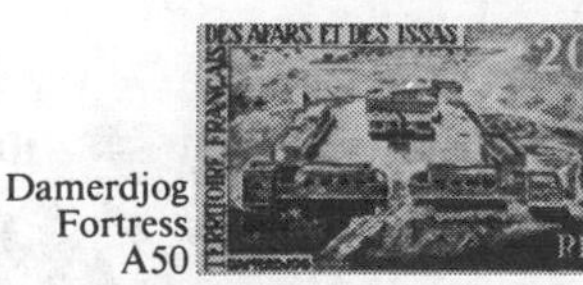

Damerdjog Fortress A50

Administration Buildings: 25fr, Ali Addé. 30fr, Dorra. 40fr, Assamo.

1968, May 17 Engr. *Perf. 13*

318 A50 20fr sl, brn & emer 95 70
319 A50 25fr brt grn, bl & brn 1.10 70
320 A50 30fr brn ol, brn org & sl 1.25 95
321 A50 40fr brn ol, sl & brt grn 2.50 1.90

Common Design Types
Pictured in section at front of book.

Human Rights Year Issue

Common Design Type

1968, Aug. 10 Engr. *Perf. 13*

322 CD127 10fr pur, ver & org 1.00 90
323 CD127 70fr grn, pur & org 2.25 1.75

International Human Rights Year.

Radio-television Station, Djibouti — A52

High Commission Palace, Djibouti — A53

Designs: 2fr, Justice Building. 5fr, Chamber of Deputies. 8fr, Great Mosque. 15fr, Monument of Free French Forces (vert.). 40fr, Djibouti Post Office. 70fr, Residence of Gov. Leonce Lagarde at Obock. No. 332, Djibouti Harbormaster's Building. No. 333, Control tower, Djibouti Airport.

1968-70 Engr. *Perf. 13*

324 A52 1fr dk red, sky bl & ind ('69) 26 18
325 A52 2fr grn, bl & ind ('69) 30 18
326 A52 5fr brn, sky bl & grn ('69) 42 26
327 A52 8fr choc, emer & gray ('69) 48 26
328 A52 15fr grn, sky bl & yel brn ('69) 3.50 2.50
329 A52 40fr grn, brn & sl ('70) 2.25 1.25
330 A53 60fr multi 2.50 2.00
331 A53 70fr dl grn, gray & ol bis ('69) 3.50 2.50
332 A53 85fr multi ('69) 4.75 3.00
333 A52 85fr dk grn, bl & gray ('70) 5.25 3.50
Nos. 324-333 (10) 23.21 15.63

Locust A54

Designs: 50fr, Pest control by helicopter. 55fr, Pest control by plane.

1969, Oct. 6 Engr. *Perf. 13*

334 A54 15fr brn, grn & sl 1.75 1.00
335 A54 50fr dk grn, bl & ol brn 2.50 1.50
336 A54 55fr red brn, bl & brn 3.50 2.50

Campaign against locusts.

ILO Issue

Common Design Type

1969, Nov. 24 Engr. *Perf. 13*

337 CD131 30fr org, gray & lil 2.00 1.25

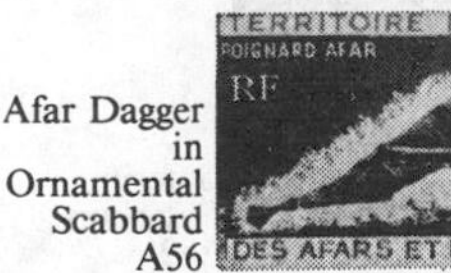

Afar Dagger in Ornamental Scabbard A56

1970, Apr. 3 Engr. *Perf. 13*

338 A56 10fr yel grn, dk grn & org brn 70 42
339 A56 15fr yel grn, bl & org brn 90 42
340 A56 20fr yel grn, red & org brn 1.00 60
341 A56 25fr yel grn, plum & org brn 1.75 60

See No. 364.

U.P.U. Headquarters Issue

Common Design Type

1970, May 20 Engr. *Perf. 13*

342 CD133 25fr brn, brt grn & choc 1.50 90

Trapshooting — A57

Motorboats A58

Designs: 50fr, Steeplechase. 55fr, Sailboat (vert.). 60fr, Equestrians.

1970 Engr. *Perf. 13*

343 A57 30fr dp brn, yel grn & brt bl 2.00 1.40
344 A58 48fr bl & multi 2.25 1.25
345 A58 50fr cop red, bl & pur 2.50 1.75
346 A58 55fr red brn, bl & ol 2.25 1.40
347 A58 60fr ol, blk & red brn 3.50 2.50
Nos. 343-347 (5) 12.50 8.30

Issue dates: 30fr, June 5; 48fr, Oct. 9; 50fr, 60fr, Nov. 6.

Automatic Ferry, Tadjourah A59

1970, Nov. 25

348 A59 48fr bl, brn & grn 2.00 1.10

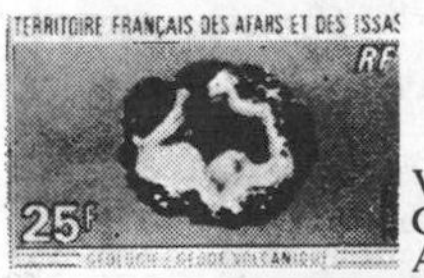

Volcanic Geode A60

Diabase and Chrysolite A61

Designs: 10fr, Doleritic basalt. 15fr, Olivine basalt.

1971 Photo. *Perf. 13*

349 A61 10fr blk & multi 60 52
350 A61 15fr blk & multi 70 52
351 A60 25fr blk, crim & brn 1.75 1.25
352 A61 40fr blk & multi 3.00 2.00

Issue dates: 10fr, Nov. 22; 15fr, Oct. 8; 25fr, Apr. 26; 40fr, Jan. 25.

Manta Ray — A62

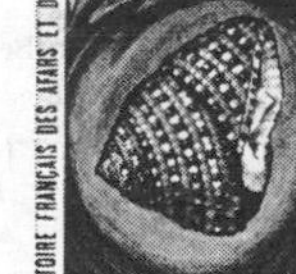

Strawberry Top — A63

Fishes: 5fr, Dolphinfish. 9fr, Smalltooth sawfish.

1971, July 1 Photo. *Perf. 12x12½*

353 A62 4fr grn & multi 85 52
354 A62 5fr bl & multi 85 52
355 A62 9fr red & multi 1.40 1.10

See No. C60.

De Gaulle Issue

Common Design Type

Designs: 60fr, Gen. Charles de Gaulle, 1940. 85fr, Pres. de Gaulle, 1970.

1971, Nov. 9 Engr. *Perf. 13*

356 CD134 60fr dk vio bl & blk 3.00 2.50
357 CD134 85fr dk vio bl & blk 4.00 2.50

1972, Mar. 8 Photo. *Perf. 12½x13*

Shells: 9fr, Cypraea pantherina. 20fr, Bullmouth helmet. 50fr, Ethiopian volute.

358 A63 4fr ol & multi 48 35
359 A63 9fr dk bl & multi 65 52
360 A63 20fr dp grn & multi 1.50 80
361 A63 50fr dp cl & multi 3.00 1.40

Shepherd — A64

Design: 10fr, Dromedary breeding.

1973, Apr. 11 Photo. *Perf. 13*

362 A64 9fr bl & multi 75 45
363 A64 10fr bl & multi 75 45

Afar Dagger — A65

1974, Jan. 29 Engr. *Perf. 13*

364 A65 30fr sl grn & dk brn 1.75 1.00

Flamingos, Lake Abbé — A66

Designs: Flamingos and different views of Lake Abbé.

1974, Feb. 22 Photo. *Perf. 13*

370 A60 5fr multi 42 26
371 A60 15fr multi 70 35
372 A60 50fr multi 2.25 1.10

Soccer Ball — A67

1974, May 24 Engr. *Perf. 13*

373 A67 25fr blk & emer 2.00 1.25

World Cup Soccer Championship, Munich, June 13-July 7.

Letters Around UPU Emblem A68

Oleo Chrysophylla A69

1974, Oct. 9 Engr. *Perf. 13*
374 A68 20fr multi 1.75 90
375 A68 100fr multi 4.25 3.50

Centenary of Universal Postal Union.

1974, Nov. 22 Photo.
376 A69 10fr *shown* 50 40
377 A69 15fr *Ficus species* 75 60
378 A69 20fr *Solanum adoense* 1.75 1.25

Day Primary Forest.

No. 364 Surcharged with New Value and Two Bars in Red

1975, Jan. 1 Engr. *Perf. 13*
379 A65 40fr on 30fr multi 2.50 1.75

Treasury — A70

Design: 25fr, Government buildings.

1975, Jan. 7 Engr. *Perf. 13*
380 A70 8fr bl, gray & red 60 42
381 A70 25fr red, bl & ind 1.10 90

Ranella Spinosa — A71

Sea Shells: No. 382, Darioconus textile. No. 383, Murex palmarosa. 10fr, Conus sumatrensis. 15fr, Cypraea pulchra. No. 386, 45fr, Murex scolopax. No. 387, Cypraea exhusta. 55fr, Cypraea erythraensis. 60fr, Conus taeniatus.

1975-76 Engr. *Perf. 13*
382 A71 5fr bl grn & brn 52 30
383 A71 5fr bl & multi ('76) 40 18
384 A71 10fr lil, blk & brn 60 40
385 A71 15fr bl, ind & brn 1.10 55
386 A71 20fr pur & lt brn 1.75 1.10
387 A71 20fr brt grn & multi ('76) 55 35
388 A71 40fr grn & brn 2.75 1.50
389 A71 45fr grn, bl & bis 2.50 1.50
390 A71 55fr turq & multi ('76) 1.75 1.10
391 A71 60fr buff & sep ('76) 2.75 1.65
Nos. 382-391 (10) 14.67 8.63

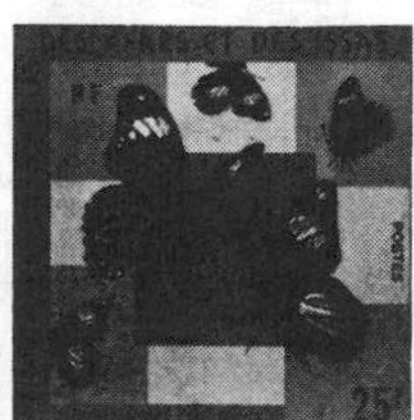
Hypolimnas Misippus A72

Butterflies: 40fr, Papilio nireus. 50fr, Acraea anemosa. 65fr, Holocerina smilax menieri. 70fr, Papilio demodocus. No. 397, Papilio dardanus. No. 398, Balachowsky gonimbrasca. 150fr, Vanessa cardui.

1975-76 Photo. *Perf. 13*
392 A72 25fr emer & multi 1.40 1.10
393 A72 40fr yel & multi 1.65 1.10
394 A72 50fr ultra & multi ('76) 2.00 1.50
395 A72 65fr ol & multi ('76) 2.50 1.50
396 A72 70fr vio & multi 3.50 2.75
397 A72 100fr bl & multi 4.50 2.75
398 A72 100fr Prus bl & multi ('76) 3.50 2.50
399 A72 150fr grn & multi ('76) 4.50 2.75
Nos. 392-399 (8) 23.55 15.95

Prices of premium quality never hinged stamps will be in excess of catalogue price.

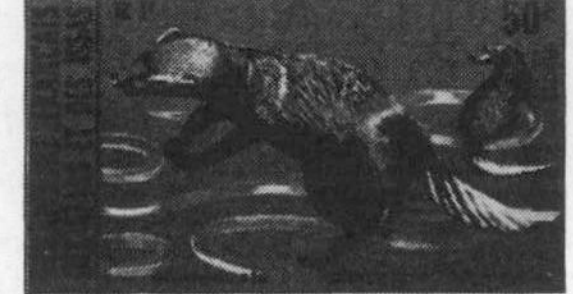
Mongoose — A73

Animals: 10fr, Hyena. No. 401, Catarrhine monkeys (vert.). No. 402, Wild ass (vert.). 30fr, Antelope. 60fr, Porcupines (vert.). 70fr, Skunks. 200fr, Aardvarks.

Perf. 13x12½, 12½x13

1975-76 Photo.
400 A73 10fr lt vio & multi ('76) 42 26
401 A73 15fr yel grn & multi 90 52
402 A73 15fr grn & multi ('76) 60 42
403 A73 30fr bl & multi ('76) 1.00 70
404 A73 50fr dp org & multi 2.50 1.50
405 A73 60fr yel brn & multi 2.75 1.90
406 A73 70fr blk & brn 4.25 2.50
407 A73 200fr bl gray & multi 6.00 4.25
Nos. 400-407 (8) 18.42 12.05

Pin-tailed Whydah — A74

Palms — A75

Birds: 25fr, Rose-ringed parakeet. 50fr, Variable sunbird. 60fr, Purple heron. No. 417, Hammerhead. No. 418, Turtle dove. 300fr, African spoonbill.

1975-76 Photo. *Perf. 12½x13*
413 A74 20fr lil, blk & org 1.00 75
414 A74 25fr car rose & multi ('76) 1.00 40
415 A74 50fr bl & multi 2.00 1.25
416 A74 60fr multi 2.75 1.75
417 A74 100fr lt grn & multi 3.75 2.50
418 A74 100fr lt yel & multi ('76) 2.75 2.00
419 A74 300fr multi ('76) 8.00 5.50
Nos. 413-419 (7) 21.25 14.15

1975, Dec. 19 Engr. *Perf. 13*
421 A75 20fr brt bl & multi 70 42

Satellite and Alexander Graham Bell — A76

1976, Mar. 10 Engr. *Perf. 13*
422 A76 200fr dp bl, org & sl grn 4.75 3.50

Centenary of the first telephone call by Alexander Graham Bell, Mar. 10, 1876.

Basketball A77

Designs: 15fr, Bicycling. 40fr, Soccer. 60fr, Running.

1976, July 7 Litho. *Perf. 12½*
423 A77 10fr lt bl & multi 42 22
424 A77 15fr yel & multi 60 30
425 A77 40fr org red & multi 1.10 70
426 A77 60fr lt grn & multi 1.75 1.10

21st Olympic Games, Montreal, Canada, July 17-Aug. 1.

Turkeyfish — A78

1976, Aug. 10 Photo. *Perf. 13x13½*
428 A78 45fr bl & multi 2.00 1.50

Psammophis Elegans — A79

Design: 70fr, Naja nigricollis (vert.).

Perf. 13x13½, 13½x13

1976, Sept. 27 Photo.
430 A79 70fr ocher & multi 2.50 2.25
431 A79 80fr emer & multi 3.00 2.50

Motorcyclist A80

1977, Jan. 27 Litho. *Perf. 12x12½*
432 A80 200fr multi 5.75 4.00

Moto-Cross motorcycle race.

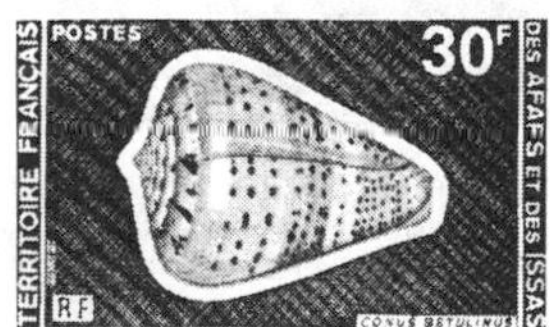

Conus Betulinus — A81

Sea Shells: 5fr, Cyprea tigris. 70fr, Conus striatus. 85fr, Cyprea mauritiana.

1977 Engr. *Perf. 13*
433 A81 5fr multi 60 42
434 A81 30fr multi 80 52
435 A81 70fr multi 2.75 1.75
436 A81 85fr multi 4.50 3.00

Gaterin Gaterinus A82

Design: 65fr, Barracudas.

1977, Apr. 15 Photo. *Perf. 13x12½*
437 A82 15fr multi 80 42
438 A82 65fr multi 2.25 1.25

Stamps of the French Territory of the Afars and Issas were replaced in 1977 by those of the Republic of Djibouti.

AIR POST STAMPS

Tawny Eagles AP16

Parachutists AP17

Unwmk.

1967, Aug. 21 Engr. *Perf. 13*
C50 AP16 200fr multi 17.50 9.50

1968 Engr. *Perf. 13*

Design: 85fr, Water skier and skin diver.

C51 AP17 48fr brn ol, Prus bl & brn 4.00 2.50
C52 AP17 85fr dk brn, ol & Prus bl 5.75 4.00

Issue dates: 48fr. Jan. 5; 85fr, Mar. 15.

Aerial Map of the Territory — AP18

1968, Nov. 15 Engr. *Perf. 13*
C53 AP18 500fr bl, dk brn & ocher 37.50 12.00

Buildings Type of Regular Issue

Designs: 100fr, Cathedral (vert.). 200fr, Sayed Hassan Mosque (vert.).

1969 Engr. *Perf. 13*
C54 A53 100fr grn, sky bl & bis brn 4.00 2.25
C55 A53 200fr lil, bl, brn & blk 8.25 4.75

Issue dates: 100fr, Apr. 4; 200fr, May 8.

Concorde Issue
Common Design Type

1969, Apr. 17
C56 CD129 100fr org red & ol 22.50 15.00

Arta Ionospheric Station — AP19

Japanese Sword Guard, Fish Design — AP20

1970, May 8 Engr. *Perf. 13*
C57 AP19 70fr multi 4.00 3.00

Gold embossed

1970, Sept. 29 *Perf. 12½*

Design: 200fr, Japanese sword guard, horse design.

C58 AP20 100fr gold, yel grn, ultra & brn	10.50	7.00
C59 AP20 200fr gold, car, yel grn & brn	14.00	8.75

EXPO "70 International Exposition, Osaka, Japan, Mar. 15-Sept. 13.

Parrotfish — AP21

1971, July 1 **Photo.** *Perf. 12½*

C60 AP21 30fr blk & multi	3.50	2.50

Djibouti Harbor — AP22

1971, Nov. 26

C61 AP22 100fr bl & multi	4.75	3.25

New Djibouti harbor.

Lichtenstein's Sandgrouse AP23

Running, Olympic Rings AP24

Birds: 49fr, Hoopoe. 66fr, Great snipe. 500fr, Tawny-breasted francolin.

1972 **Photo.** *Perf. 12½x13*

C62 AP23 30fr multi	2.50	2.00
C63 AP23 49fr multi	3.75	3.75
C64 AP23 66fr bl & multi	5.25	3.75
C65 AP23 500fr multi	24.00	12.00

Issue dates: No. C65, Nov. 3, others Apr. 21.

1972, June 8 **Engr.** *Perf. 13*

Designs (Olympic Rings and): 10fr, Basketball. 55fr, Swimming (horiz.). 60fr, Olympic torch and Greek frieze (horiz.).

C66 AP24 5fr pur, bl grn & dk brn	52	35
C67 AP24 10fr dk red, sl grn & dk brn	60	42
C68 AP24 55fr grn, brn & bl	2.25	1.40
C69 AP24 60fr bl grn, dk red & pur	3.00	1.75

20th Olympic Games, Munich, Aug. 26-Sept. 11.

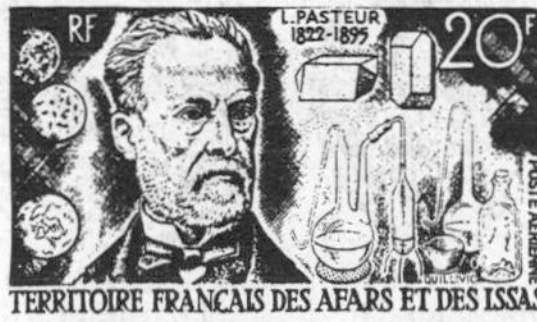

Louis Pasteur — AP25

Design: 100fr, Albert Calmette and C. Guerin.

1972, Oct. 5 **Engr.** *Perf. 13*

C70 AP25 20fr rose car, ol bis & brt grn	1.25	70
C71 AP25 100fr dk brn, brt grn & dl red	4.25	3.25

Pasteur, Calmette, Guerin, chemists and bacteriologists, benefactors of mankind.

Map and Views of Territory — AP26

Design: 200fr, Woman and Mosque of Djibouti (vert.).

1973, Jan. 15 **Photo.** *Perf. 13*

C72 AP26 30fr brn & multi	5.25	4.25
C73 AP26 200fr multi	12.00	9.50

Visit of Pres. Georges Pompidou of France, Jan. 15-17.

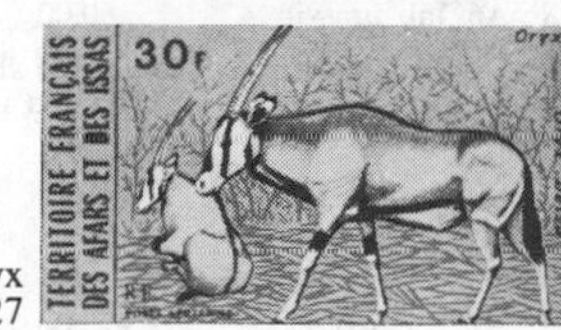

Oryx AP27

Animals: 50fr, Dik-dik. 66fr, Caracal.

1973, Feb. 26 **Photo.** *Perf. 13x12½*

C74 AP27 30fr grn & multi	1.75	1.10
C75 AP27 50fr rose & multi	3.00	1.50
C76 AP27 66fr lil & multi	4.00	3.00

See also Nos. C94-C96.

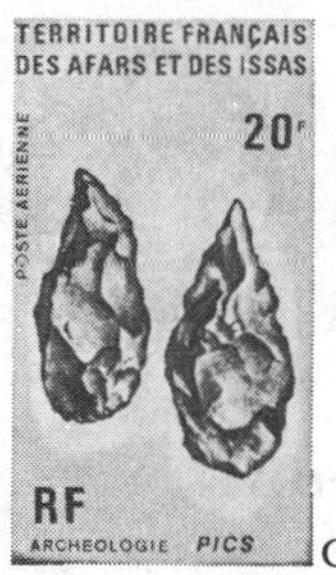

Celts — AP28

Designs: Various pre-historic flint tools. 40fr, 60fr, horizontal.

1973 *Perf. 13*

C77 AP28 20fr yel grn, blk & brn	2.25	1.65
C78 AP28 40fr yel & multi	2.25	1.65
C79 AP28 49fr lil & multi	3.75	2.75
C80 AP28 60fr bl & multi	3.75	2.75

Issue dates: 20fr, 49fr, Mar. 16; 40fr, 60fr, Sept. 7.

Octopus — AP29

Design: 60fr, Dugong.

1973, Mar. 16

C81 AP29 40fr multi	2.25	1.25
C82 AP29 60fr brn & multi	4.00	2.50

Copernicus AP30

Baboons AP31

Designs: 8fr, Nicolaus Copernicus (1473-1534), Polish astronomer. 9fr, William C. Roentgen (1845-1923), physicist, X-ray discoverer. C85, Edward Jenner (1749-1823), physician, discoverer of vaccination. No. C86, Marie Curie (1867-1934), discoverer of radium and polonium. 49fr, Robert Koch (1843-1910), physician and bacteriologist. 50fr, Clement Ader (1841-1925), French aviation pioneer. 55fr, Guglielmo Marconi (1874-13937), Italian electrical engineer, inventor. 85fr, Moliere (1622-1673), French playwright. 100fr, Henri Farman (1874-1937), French aviation pioneer. 150fr, Andre-Marie Ampere (1775-1836), French physicist. 250fr, Michelangelo Buonarroti (1475-1564), Italian sculptor, painter and architect.

1973-75 **Engr.** *Perf. 13*

C83 AP30 8fr blk, dk bis & mar	70	42
C84 AP30 9fr brn, ocher & vio brn	60	42
C85 AP30 10fr car, brn & vio brn	60	42
C86 AP30 10fr red lil, dp cl & bl	70	42
C87 AP30 49fr sl grn, yel grn & vio brn	3.75	2.50
C88 AP30 50fr ol brn, sl grn & bl	2.75	2.00
C89 AP30 55fr multi ('74)	2.50	2.00
C90 AP30 85fr bl, vio & ind	5.25	3.50
C91 AP30 100fr yel grn, vio brn & bl ('74)	4.75	4.00
C92 AP30 150fr multi	4.75	4.00
C93 AP30 250fr blk, grn & brn	8.00	6.00
Nos. C83-C93 (11)	34.35	25.68

Issue dates: 8fr, 85fr, May 9, 1973. 9fr, C85, 49fr, Oct. 12, 1973. 100fr, Jan. 29, 1974. 55fr, Mar. 22, 1974. C86, Aug. 23, 1974. 150fr, July 24, 1975. 250fr, June 26, 1975. 50fr, Sept. 25, 1975.

Perf. 12½x13, 13x12½

1973, Dec. 12 **Photo.**

Designs: 50fr, Genets (horiz.). 66fr, Hares.

C94 AP31 20fr org & multi	1.25	90
C95 AP31 50fr multi	2.50	1.25
C96 AP31 66fr bl & multi	4.00	2.50

Spearfishing — AP32

1974, Apr. 14 **Engr.** *Perf. 13*

C97 AP32 200fr multi	7.75	6.50

No. C97 was prepared for release in Nov. 1972, to commemorate the 3rd Underwater Spearfishing Contest in the Red Sea. Dates have been obliterated with a rectangle and the stamp was not issued without this obliteration.

Rock Carvings, Balho — AP33

1974, Apr. 26

C98 AP33 200fr car & sl	10.00	8.00

Lake Assal — AP34

Designs (Lake Assal): 50fr, Rock formations on shore. 85fr, Crystallized wood.

1974, Oct. 25 **Photo.** *Perf. 13*

C99 AP34 49fr multi	1.50	1.25
C100 AP34 50fr multi	1.90	1.40
C101 AP34 85fr multi	3.50	3.00

Guinea Dove — AP35

1975, May 23 **Photo.** *Perf. 13*

C102 AP35 500fr multi	16.00	8.75

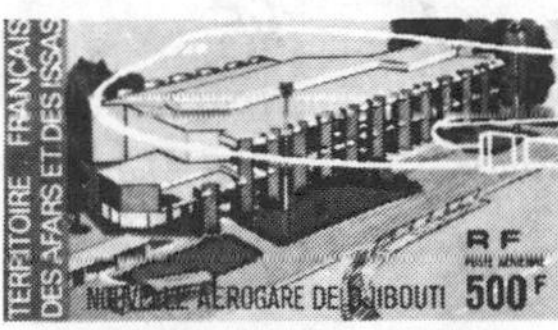

Djibouti Airport — AP36

1977, Mar. 1 **Litho.** *Perf. 12*

C103 AP36 500fr multi	13.00	10.50

Opening of new Djibouti Airport.

Thomas A. Edison and Phonograph — AP37

Design: 75fr, Alexander Volta, electric train, lines and light bulb.

1977, May 5 **Engr.** *Perf. 13*

C104 AP37 55fr multi	3.00	2.00
C105 AP37 75fr multi	4.75	3.50

Famous inventors: Thomas Alva Edison (1847-1931) and Alexander Volta (1745-1827).

POSTAGE DUE STAMPS

Nomad's Milk Jug — D3

Perf. 14x13

1969, Dec. 15 **Engr.** **Unwmk.**

J49 D3 1fr red brn, red lil & sl	10	10

J50	D3	2fr red brn, emer & sl	18	18
J51	D3	5fr red brn, bl & sl	40	40
J52	D3	10fr red brn, brn & sl	90	90

AFGHANISTAN

LOCATION — Central Asia, bounded by Iran, Russian Turkestan, Pakistan, Baluchistan and China.
GOVT. — Republic
AREA — 251,773 sq. mi.
POP. — 17,150,000 (1984 est.)
CAPITAL — Kabul

Afghanistan changed from a constitutional monarchy to a republic in July 1973.

12 Shahi = 6 Sanar = 3 Abasi =
2 Krans = 1 Rupee Kabuli
60 Paisas = 1 Rupee (1921)
100 Pouls = 1 Rupee Afghani (1927)

1871-78 A7 A8

Sanar. Abasi. 6 Shahi.

1871–78 1871 1872

1 Rupee. ½ Rupee.

1874 1876(A8) 1876 (A7)

1 Rupee.

Rupee.

1872 1874 1876 (A8) 1877-78

From 1871 to 1892 and 1898 the Moslem year date appears on the stamp. Numerals as follows:

Until 1891 cancellation consisted of cutting or tearing a piece from the stamps. Such copies should not be considered as damaged.

Prices are for cut square examples of good color. Cut to shape or faded copies sell for much less, particularly Nos. 2-10.

Nos. 2-108 are on laid paper of varying thickness except where wove is noted.

Until 1907 all stamps were issued ungummed.

The tiger's head on types A2 to A11 symbolizes the name of the contemporary amir, Sher (Tiger) Ali.

Kingdom of Kabul

Tiger's Head — A2

(Both circles dotted.)

Dated "1288".

1871 Unwmk. Litho. *Imperf.*

2	A2	1sh black	175.00	35.00
3	A2	1sa black	110.00	30.00
4	A2	1ab black	55.00	30.00

Thirty varieties of the shahi, 10 of the sanar and 5 of the abasi.

Similar designs without the tiger's head in the center are revenues.

A3

(Outer circle dotted.)

Dated "1288".

5	A3	1sh black	250.00	50.00
6	A3	1sa black	110.00	32.50
7	A3	1ab black	55.00	35.00

Five varieties of each.

A4

Dated "1289".

1872

Toned Wove Paper

8	A4	6sh violet	*850.00*	*550.00*
9	A4	1rup violet	*1,100.*	*650.00*

Two varieties of each. Date varies in location. Printed in sheets of 4 (2x2) containing two of each denomination.

Most used copies are smeared with a greasy ink cancel.

A4a

Dated "1290"

1873

White Laid Paper

10	A4a	1sh black	13.00	6.75
a.		Corner ornament missing	*600.00*	*500.00*
b.		Corner ornament retouched	*90.00*	*37.50*

15 varieties. Nos. 10a, 10b are the sixth stamp on the sheet.

A5

1873

11	A5	1sh black	3.25	2.75
11A	A5	1sh violet	*725.00*	

Sixty varieties of each.

1874

Dated "1291".

12	A5	1ab black	55.00	37.50
13	A5	½rup black	30.00	27.50
14	A5	1rup black	35.00	30.00

Five varieties of each.

Nos. 12-14 were printed on the same sheet. Se-tenant varieties exist.

A6 A7

1875

Dated "1292".

15	A6	1sa black	*250.00*	*175.00*
a.		Wide outer circle	*900.00*	
16	A6	1ab black	350.00	250.00
17	A6	1sa brn vio	35.00	35.00
a.		Wide outer circle	*175.00*	
18	A6	1ab brn vio	60.00	37.50

Ten varieties of the sanar, five of the abasi.

Nos. 15-16 and 17-18 were printed in the same sheets. Se-tenant pairs exist.

1876

Dated "1293"

19	A7	1sh black	425.00	225.00
20	A7	1sa black	550.00	300.00
21	A7	1ab black	750.00	300.00
22	A7	½rup black	550.00	300.00
23	A7	1rup black	750.00	300.00
24	A7	1sh violet	550.00	300.00
25	A7	1sa violet	525.00	300.00
26	A7	1ab violet	650.00	300.00
27	A7	½rup violet	135.00	80.00
28	A7	1rup violet	135.00	110.00

12 varieties of the shahi and 3 each of the other values.

A8

1876

Dated "1293".

29	A8	1sh gray	7.50	6.00
30	A8	1sa gray	11.00	6.00
31	A8	1ab gray	22.50	11.00
32	A8	½rup gray	25.00	15.00
33	A8	1rup gray	32.50	15.00
34	A8	1sh ol blk	190.00	
35	A8	1sa ol blk	250.00	
36	A8	1ab ol blk	525.00	
37	A8	½rup ol blk	350.00	
38	A8	1rup ol blk	425.00	
39	A8	1sh green	32.50	5.50
40	A8	1sa green	50.00	23.50
41	A8	1ab green	75.00	52.50
42	A8	½rup green	150.00	60.00
43	A8	1rup green	150.00	120.00
44	A8	1sh ocher	32.50	11.00
45	A8	1sa ocher	50.00	22.50
46	A8	1ab ocher	85.00	40.00
47	A8	½rup ocher	110.00	90.00
48	A8	1rup ocher	190.00	160.00
49	A8	1sh violet	32.50	8.00
50	A8	1sa violet	32.50	11.00
51	A8	1ab violet	50.00	15.00
52	A8	½rup violet	85.00	32.50
53	A8	1rup violet	110.00	50.00

24 varieties of the shahi, 4 of which show denomination written

12 varieties of the sanar, 6 of the abasi and 3 each of the ½ rupee and rupee.

A9

1877

Dated "1294".

54	A9	1sh gray	5.25	3.25
55	A9	1sa gray	8.50	4.25
56	A9	1ab gray	14.00	8.50
57	A9	½rup gray	18.00	18.00
58	A9	1rup gray	18.00	18.00
59	A9	1sh black	14.00	
60	A9	1sa black	27.50	
61	A9	1ab black	62.50	
62	A9	½rup black	67.50	
63	A9	1rup black	67.50	
64	A9	1sh green	6.75	5.00
a.		Wove paper	18.00	
65	A9	1sa green	11.00	5.00
a.		Wove paper	25.00	18.00
66	A9	1ab green	14.00	14.00
a.		Wove paper	40.00	
67	A9	½rup green	20.00	20.00
a.		Wove paper	45.00	45.00
68	A9	1rup green	21.00	21.00
a.		Wove paper	45.00	45.00
69	A9	1sh ocher	5.00	3.00
70	A9	1sa ocher	14.00	5.00
71	A9	1ab ocher	27.50	24.00
72	A9	½rup ocher	45.00	45.00
73	A9	1rup ocher	45.00	45.00
74	A9	1sh violet	5.50	3.00
75	A9	1sa violet	11.00	4.00
76	A9	1ab violet	16.50	11.00
77	A9	½rup violet	27.50	21.00
78	A9	1rup violet	27.50	21.00

25 varieties of the shahi, 8 of the sanar, 3 of the abasi and 2 each of the ½rupee and rupee.

A10 A11

1878

Dated "1295"

79	A10	1sh gray	2.25	2.25
80	A10	1sa gray	2.75	2.75
81	A10	1ab gray	5.50	5.50
82	A10	½rup gray	14.00	11.00
83	A10	1rup gray	14.00	11.00
84	A10	1sh black	4.50	
85	A10	1sa black	4.50	
86	A10	1ab black	15.00	
87	A10	½rup black	30.00	
88	A10	1rup black	30.00	
89	A10	1sh green	32.50	30.00
90	A10	1sa green	4.50	4.50
91	A10	1ab green	16.00	14.00
92	A10	½rup green	32.50	27.50
93	A10	1rup green	32.50	27.50
94	A10	1sh ocher	14.00	4.50
95	A10	1sa ocher	4.50	3.50
96	A10	1ab ocher	16.00	14.00
97	A10	½rup ocher	32.50	32.50
98	A10	1rup ocher	25.00	25.00
99	A10	1sh violet	2.50	2.50
100	A10	1sa violet	2.50	2.50
101	A10	1ab violet	8.00	8.00
102	A10	½rup violet	32.50	27.50
103	A10	1rup violet	32.50	27.50
104	A11	1sh gray	3.00	2.75
105	A11	1sh black	*135.00*	
106	A11	1sh green	2.50	2.50
107	A11	1sh ocher	2.00	2.00
108	A11	1sh violet	3.00	2.75

40 varieties of the shahi, 30 of the sanar, 6 of the abasi and 2 each of the ½ rupee and 1 rupee.

The 1876, 1877 and 1878 issues were printed in separate colors for each main post office on the Peshawar-Kabul-Khulm (Tashkurghan) postal route. Some specialists consider the black printings to be proofs or trial colors.

There are many shades of these colors.

1ab, Type I Diameter 26 mm. — A12

1ab, Type II Diameter 28 mm. — A13

A14

A15

Dated "1298", numerals scattered through design.

Handstamped, in watercolor.

1881-90

Thin White Laid Batonné Paper

109	A12	1ab violet	2.50	1.75
109A	A13	1ab violet	5.00	3.75
110	A12	1ab blk brn	5.00	2.75
111	A12	1ab rose	3.00	3.00
b.		Se-tenant with 111A	25.00	
111A	A13	1ab rose	3.75	3.00
112	A14	2ab violet	2.75	2.25
113	A14	2ab blk brn	7.50	6.00
114	A14	2ab rose	4.50	4.50
115	A15	1rup violet	3.75	2.25
116	A15	1rup blk brn	10.00	10.00
117	A15	1rup rose	4.50	4.50

Thin White Wove Batonné Paper

118	A12	1ab violet	10.00	6.00
119	A12	1ab vermilion	6.25	
120	A12	1ab rose		
121	A14	2ab violet		
122	A14	2ab vermilion	7.50	
122A	A14	2ab blk brn		
123	A15	1rup violet	12.50	
124	A15	1rup vermilion	10.00	
125	A15	1rup blk brn	12.50	

Thin White Laid Batonné Paper

126	A12	1ab brn org	3.75	3.75
126A	A13	1ab brn org (II)	5.00	5.00
127	A12	1ab car lake	3.75	3.75
a.		Laid paper		
128	A14	2ab brn org	3.75	3.75
129	A14	2ab car lake	4.50	4.50
130	A15	1rup brn org	15.00	15.00
131	A15	1rup car lake	6.25	6.25

Yellowish Laid Batonné Paper

132	A12	1ab purple		5.00
133	A12	1ab red	10.00	5.00

1884

Colored Wove Paper

133A	A13	1ab pur, *yel* (II)	27.50	27.50
134	A12	1ab pur, *grn*	30.00	
135	A12	1ab pur, *bl*	47.50	32.50
136	A12	1ab red, *grn*	55.00	
137	A12	1ab red, *yel*	2.50	
139	A12	1ab red, *rose*	8.75	
140	A14	2ab red, *yel*	8.75	
142	A14	2ab red, *rose*	8.00	
143	A15	1rup red, *yel*	10.00	10.00
145	A15	1rup red, *rose*	11.00	11.00

Thin Colored Ribbed Paper

146	A14	2ab red, *yel*	4.50	
147	A15	1rup red, *yel*	12.50	
148	A12	1ab lake, *lil*	6.00	
149	A14	2ab lake, *lil*	7.25	
150	A15	1rup lake, *lil*	6.00	
151	A12	1ab lake, *grn*	3.00	
152	A14	2ab lake, *grn*	6.00	
153	A15	1rup lake, *grn*	6.00	

1886-88

Colored Wove Paper.

155	A12	1ab *magenta*	42.50	
156	A12	1ab cl brn, *org*	30.00	
156A	A12	1ab red, *org*	3.00	
156B	A14	2ab red, *org*	7.00	
156C	A15	1rup red, *org*	5.00	

Laid Batonné Paper.

157	A12	1ab *lavender*	4.00	
158	A12	1ab cl brn, *grn*	10.00	
159	A12	1ab *pink*	27.50	
160	A14	2ab *pink*	50.00	
161	A15	1rup *pink*	30.00	

Laid Paper.

162	A12	1ab *pink*	10.00	
163	A14	2ab *pink*	10.00	
164	A15	1rup *pink*	10.00	
165	A12	1ab brn, *yel*	10.00	
166	A14	2ab brn, *yel*	10.00	
167	A15	1rup brn, *yel*	10.00	
168	A12	1ab bl, *grn*	10.00	
169	A14	2ab bl, *grn*	10.00	
170	A15	1rup bl, *grn*	10.00	

1891

Colored Wove Paper.

175	A12	1ab grn, *rose*	35.00	
176	A15	1rup pur, *grn batonné*	35.00	

Nos. 109-176 fall into three categories:

1. Those regularly issued and in normal postal use from 1881 on, handstamped on thin white laid or wove paper in strip sheets containing 12 or more impressions of the same denomination arranged in two irregular rows, with the impressions often touching or overlappng.

2. The 1884 postal issues provisionally printed on smooth or ribbed colored wove paper as needed to supplement low stocks of the normal white paper stamps.

3. The "special" printings made in a range of colors on several types of laid or wove colored papers, most of which were never used for normal printings. These were produced periodically from 1886 to 1891 to meet philatelic demands. Although nominally valid for postage, most of the special printings were exported directly to fill dealers' orders, and few were ever postally used. Many of the sheets contained all three denominations with impressions separated by ruled lines. Sometimes different colors were used, so se-tenant multiples of denomination or color exist. Many combinations of stamp and paper colors exist besides those listed.

Various shades of each color exist.

Type A12 is known dated "1297".

Counterfeits, lithographed or typographed, are plentiful.

Kingdom of Afghanistan

A16

A17

A18

Dated "1309".

1891 — Pelure Paper — Litho.

177	A16	1ab sl bl	1.25	1.25
a.		Tete beche pair	20.00	
178	A17	2ab sl bl	8.75	7.50
179	A18	1rup sl bl	18.50	15.00

Revenue stamps of similar design exist in various colors.

Nos. 177-179 were printed in panes on the same sheet, so se-tenant gutter pairs exist. Examples in black or red are proofs.

A Mosque Gate and Crossed Cannons (National Seal) — A19

Dated "1310" in Upper Right Corner.

1892

Flimsy Wove Paper

180	A19	1ab *green*	3.00	2.50
181	A19	1ab *orange*	3.75	3.75
182	A19	1ab *yellow*	3.00	2.50
183	A19	1ab *pink*	3.75	2.50
184	A19	1ab *lil rose*	3.75	3.75
185	A19	1ab *blue*	6.25	5.00
186	A19	1ab *salmon*	3.75	3.00
187	A19	1ab *magenta*	3.75	3.75
188	A19	1ab *violet*	3.75	3.75
188A	A19	1ab *scarlet*	3.75	2.50

Many shades exist.

A20

A21

Undated

1894

Flimsy Wove Paper

189	A20	2ab *green*	10.00	10.00
190	A21	1rup *green*	15.00	15.00

24 varieties of the 2 abasi and 12 varieties of the rupee.

Nos. 189-190 and F3 were printed se-tenant in the same sheet. Pairs exist.

A21a

Dated "1316"

1898

Flimsy Wove Paper

191	A21a	2ab *pink*	3.75	
192	A21a	2ab *magenta*	3.75	
193	A21a	2ab *yellow*	1.75	
193A	A21a	2ab *salmon*	4.50	
194	A21a	2ab *green*	2.00	
195	A21a	2ab *purple*	2.50	
195A	A21a	2ab *blue*	35.00	

Nos. 191-195A were not regularly issued. Genuinely used copies are scarce. No. 195A was found in remainder stocks and probably was never released.

A22

A23

A24

1907 — Engr. — *Imperf.*

Medium Wove Paper

196	A22	1ab bl grn	3.75	2.50
a.		emerald	8.50	5.00
197	A22	1ab brt bl	7.50	6.25
198	A23	2ab dp bl	1.85	1.25
199	A24	1rup green	3.00	2.50
a.		bl grn	6.00	6.00

Zigzag Roulette 10

200	A22	1ab green	35.00	25.00
201	A23	2ab blue	50.00	45.00
201A	A24	1rup bl grn	*70.00*	*60.00*

1908 — *Perf. 12*

202	A22	1ab green	6.25	6.25
203	A23	2ab dp bl	1.25	1.25
204	A24	1rup bl grn	3.00	3.00

Twelve varieties of the 1 abasi, 6 of the 2 abasi, 4 of the 1 rupee.

Nos. 196-204 were issued in small sheets containing 3 or 4 panes. Gutter pairs, normal and tete beche, exist.

A25

A26

A27

1909-19 — Typo. — *Perf. 12*

205	A25	1ab ultra	50	35
a.		Imperf., pair	3.00	
206	A25	1ab red ('16)	35	25
a.		Imperf.		
207	A25	1ab rose ('18)	35	25
208	A26	2ab green	75	75
a.		Imperf., pair	7.00	
b.		Horizontal pair, imperf. between		
208C	A26	2ab yel ('16)	1.25	1.25
209	A26	2ab bis ('18-'19)	90	90
210	A27	1rup lil brn	1.50	1.50
a.		red brn	1.50	1.50
211	A27	1rup ol bis ('16)	1.50	1.50
		Nos. 205-211 (8)	7.10	6.75

A28

1913

212	A28	2pa db brn	1.25	1.25
a.		red brn	1.25	1.25

No. 212 is inscribed 'Tiket waraq dak' (Postal card stamps). It was usable only on postcards and not accepted for postage on letters.

Nos. 196-212 sometimes show letters of a papermaker's watermark, "Howard & Jones, London."

Royal Star — A29

1920, Aug. 24 — *Perf. 12*

Size: 39x47mm.

214	A29	10pa rose	18.50	16.00
215	A29	20pa red brn	42.50	25.00
216	A29	30pa green	87.50	87.50

Issued in sheets of two.

1921, Mar.

Size: 22½x28¼mm.

217	A29	10pa rose	50	25
a.		Perf. 11 ('27)	1.00	1.50
218	A29	20pa red brn	1.50	75
219	A29	30pa yel grn	1.50	75
a.		Tete beche pair	7.50	7.50
b.		30pa grn	1.50	75
c.		As "b," Tete beche pair	7.50	7.50

Two types of the 10pa, three of the 20pa.

Crest of King Amanullah — A30

1924, Feb. 26 — *Perf. 12*

220	A30	10pa chocolate	16.00	10.00
a.		Tete beche pair	35.00	30.00

Issued to commemorate the 6th Independence Day.

Printed in sheets of four consisting of two tete beche pairs, and in sheets of two. Two types exist.

Some authorities believe that Nos. Q15-Q16 were issued as regular postage stamps.

Crest of King Amanullah
A32

1925, Feb. 26 *Perf. 12*

Size: 29x37mm.

222	A32 10pa lt brn	15.00	8.75

Issued to commemorate the 7th Independence Day.

Printed in sheets of 8 (two panes of 4).

1926, Feb. 28

Wove Paper

Size: 26x33mm.

224	A32 10pa dk bl	2.00	2.00
a.	Imperf., pair	12.50	12.50
b.	Horizontal pair, imperf. between	15.00	
c.	Vertical pair, imperf. between	12.50	
d.	Laid paper	10.00	7.50

Issued for the 7th anniversary of Independence. Printed in sheets of 4, and in sheets of 8 (two panes of 4). Tete beche gutter pairs exist.

Tughra and Crest of Amanullah — A33

1927, Feb.

225	A33 10pa magenta	6.00	4.25
a.	Vertical pair, imperf. between	20.00	

Dotted Background.

226	A33 10pa magenta	5.50	4.25
a.	Horizontal pair, imperf. between	15.00	

The surface of No. 226 is covered by a net of fine dots.

Nos. 225 and 226 were issued to commemorate the eighth anniversary of Independence. Printed in sheets of 8 (two panes of 4). Tete beche gutter pairs exist.

National Seal — A34

A35

A35a

A36

1927, Oct. *Imperf.*

227	A34 15p pink	35	35
228	A35 30p Prus grn	80	40
229	A36 60p lt bl	1.50	1.50
a.	Tete beche pair	4.50	5.00

1927-30 *Perf. 11, 12*

230	A34 15p pink	35	25
231	A34 15p ultra ('29)	1.00	75
232	A35 30p Prus grn	50	50
233	A35a 30p dp grn ('30)	1.25	1.25
234	A36 60p brt bl	2.50	2.50
a.	Tete beche pair	6.00	6.00
235	A36 60p blk ('29)	2.00	1.00
	Nos. 230-235 (6)	7.60	6.25

Nos. 230, 232 and 234 are usually imperforate on one or two sides.

No. 233 has been redrawn. A narrow border of pearls has been added and "30", in European and Arabic numerals, inserted in the upper spandrels.

Tughra and Crest of Amanullah A37

1928, Feb. 27

236	A37 15p pink	3.75	3.75
a.	Tete beche pair	10.00	10.00
b.	Imperf. vertically, pair	12.50	
c.	Same as "a", imperf. vertically, block of 4		

Issued to commemorate the ninth anniversary of Independence. This stamp is always imperforate on one or two sides.

A 15p blue of somewhat similar design was prepared for the 10th anniversary, but was not issued due to Amanullah's dethronement. Price, $5.

National Seal A38

A39

A40

A41

A42

1928-30 *Perf. 11, 12*

237	A38 2p dl bl	3.75	2.50
a.	Vertical pair, imperf. between		
238	A38 2p lt rose ('30)	25	25
239	A39 10p gray grn	25	15
a.	Tete beche pair	7.50	7.50
b.	Imperf. horizontally, pair	1.00	
c.	Vertical pair, imperf. between	75	
240	10p choc ('30)	1.00	1.00
a.	10p brn pur ('29)	4.50	2.50
241	A40 25p car rose	35	25
242	A40 25p Prus grn ('29)	75	60
243	A41 40p ultra	40	35
a.	Tete beche pair	7.50	7.50
244	A41 40p rose ('29)	1.50	1.25
a.	Tete beche pair	10.00	10.00
b.	Imperf. horizontally, pair	5.00	
245	A42 50p red	40	40
246	A42 50p dk bl ('29)	2.50	2.00
	Nos. 237-246 (10)	11.15	8.75

The sheets of these stamps are often imperforate at the outer margins.

Nos. 237-238 are newspaper stamps.

Independence Monument — A46

Foreign postal stationery (stamped envelopes, postal cards and air letter sheets) lies beyond the scope of this Catalogue, which is limited to adhesive postage stamps.

Wmk. Large Seal in the Sheet.

1931, Aug. Litho. *Perf. 12*

Laid Paper

262	A46 20p red	1.25	75

Issued to commemorate the 13th Independence Day. Issued without gum.

National Assembly Chamber — A47

A48

A50

National Assembly Building A49

National Assembly Chamber A51

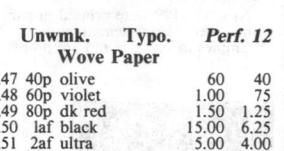

National Assembly Building A52

1932 Unwmk. Typo. *Perf. 12*

Wove Paper

263	A47 40p olive	60	40
264	A48 60p violet	1.00	75
265	A49 80p dk red	1.50	1.25
266	A50 1af black	15.00	6.25
267	A51 2af ultra	5.00	4.00
268	A52 3af gray grn	6.50	5.00
	Nos. 263-268 (6)	29.60	17.65

Issued to commemorate the formation of the National Council. Imperforate or perforated examples of Nos. 263-268 on ungummed chalky paper are proofs.

See also Nos. 304-305.

Mosque at Balkh — A53

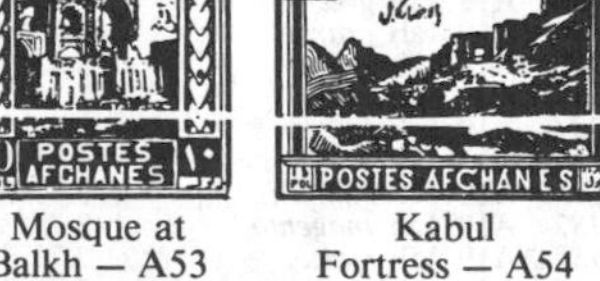

Kabul Fortress — A54

Parliament House, Darul Funun — A55

Parliament House, Darul Funun — A56

Arch of Qalai Bist — A57

Memorial Pillar of Knowledge and Ignorance A58

Independence Monument A59

Minaret at Herat A60

Arch of Paghman — A61

Ruins at Balkh — A62

Minarets of Herat A63

Great Buddha at Bamian A64

1932 Typo. *Perf. 12*

269	A53 10p brown	18	15
270	A54 15p dk brn	30	15
271	A55 20p red	40	25
272	A56 25p dk grn	40	20
273	A57 30p red	60	40
274	A58 40p orange	1.00	50
275	A59 50p blue	1.25	50
a.	Tete beche pair	8.00	
276	A60 60p blue	1.50	75
277	A61 80p violet	2.50	1.50
278	A62 1af dk bl	4.00	85
279	A63 2af dk red vio	4.50	3.00
280	A64 3af claret	6.50	3.75
	Nos. 269-280 (12)	23.13	12.00

Counterfeits of types A53-A65 exist.

See also Nos. 290-295, 298-299, 302-303.

Entwined 2's — A65

Two types:

Type I. Numerals shaded. Size about 21x29mm.

Type II. Numerals unshaded. Size about 21¾x30mm.

1931-38 *Perf. 12, 11x12*

281	A65 2p red brn (I)	8	8
282	A65 2p ol blk (I) ('34)	10	8
283	A65 2p grnsh gray (I) ('34)	25	8
283A	A65 2p blk (II) ('36)	15	8
284	A65 2p sal (II) ('38)	25	8

284A A65 2p rose (I) ('38) 10 10
b. Imperf., pair 75

Imperf

285 A65 2p blk (II) ('37) 25 10
286 A65 2p sal (II) ('38) 10 10
Nos. 281-286 (8) 1.28 70

The newspaper rate was 2 pouls.

Independence Monument — A66

1932, Aug. *Perf. 12*
287 A66 1af dp rose 2.75 2.25

Issued to commemorate the 14th Independence Day.

1929 Liberation Monument, Kabul — A67

1932, Oct. **Typo.**
288 A67 80p red brn 1.25 75

Arch of Paghman A68

1933, Aug.
289 A68 50p lt ultra 1.50 1.50

Issued to commemorate the 15th Independence Day.

Types of 1932 and

Royal Palace, Kabul — A69

Darrah-Shikari Pass, Hindu Kush — A70

1934-38 **Typo.** *Perf. 12*

290 A53 10p dp vio	25	12
291 A54 15p turq grn	30	15
292 A55 20p magenta	35	15
293 A56 25p dp rose	40	25
294 A57 30p orange	60	30
295 A58 40p bl blk	90	40
296 A69 45p dk bl	1.75	1.50
297 A69 45p red ('38)	30	25
298 A59 50p orange	40	25
299 A60 60p purple	60	25
300 A70 75p red	90	50
301 A70 75p dk bl ('38)	90	60
302 A61 80p brn vio	1.50	75
303 A62 1af red vio	2.00	1.50
304 A51 2af gray blk	4.50	3.00
305 A52 3af ultra	6.00	4.50
Nos. 290-305 (16)	21.65	14.47

Nos. 290, 292, 300, 304, 305 exist imperf.

The lack of a price for a listed item does not necessarily indicate rarity.

Independence Monument — A71

1934, Aug. **Litho.**

Without Gum

306 A71 50p pale grn 1.50 1.50
a. Tete beche pair 4.50 4.50

Issued to commemorate the 16th year of Independence. Each sheet of 40 (4x10) included 4 tete beche pairs as lower half of sheet was inverted.

Independence Monument A74

Fireworks Display A75

1935, Aug. 15

Laid Paper

309 A74 50p dk bl 1.50 1.50

Issued in commemoration of the 17th year of Independence.

1936, Aug. 15 *Perf. 12*

Wove Paper

310 A75 50p red vio 1.75 1.50

Issued in commemoration of the 18th year of Independence.

Independence Monument and Nadir Shah — A76

1937
311 A76 50p vio & bis brn 1.25 75
a. Imperf., pair 2.75

Issued in commemoration of the 19th year of Independence.

A77

Mohammed Nadir Shah — A78

1938 *Perf. 11x12*
315 A77 50p brt bl & sep 1.00 1.00
a. Imperf. pair 6.25 3.75

Issued in commemoration of the 20th year of Independence. Issued without gum.

1939 *Perf. 11, 12x11*
317 A78 50p dp sal 1.50 1.00

Issued in commemoration of the 21st year of Independence.

National Arms A79

Parliament House, Darul Funun A80

Royal Palace, Kabul A81

Independence Monument A82

Independence Monument and Nadir Shah — A83

Mohammed Zahir Shah — A84

Mohammed Zahir Shah — A85

Perf. 11, 11x12, 12x11, 12

1939-61 **Typo.**

318 A79 2p int blk	10	10
318A A79 2p brt pink ('61)	25	15
319 A80 10p brt pur	10	10
320 A80 15p brt grn	12	10
321 A80 20p red lil	15	10
322 A81 25p rose red	50	25
322A A81 25p grn ('41)	25	8
323 A81 30p orange	20	15
324 A81 40p dk gray	20	15
325 A82 45p brt car	20	15
326 A82 50p dp org	30	20
327 A82 60p violet	30	20
328 A83 75p ultra	3.00	75
328A A83 75p red vio ('41)	75	30
328C A83 75p brt red ('44)	1.75	1.35
328D A83 75p chnt brn ('49)	2.00	1.65
329 A83 80p chocolate	50	50
a. 80p dl red vio (error)		
330 A84 1af brt red vio	1.50	75
330A A85 1af brt red vio ('44)	2.50	1.50
331 A85 2af dp rose red	2.50	1.35
a. 2af cop red	1.75	50
332 A84 3af dp bl	3.75	1.60
Nos. 318-332 (21)	20.92	11.48

On No. 332 the King faces slightly left. No. 318A issued with and without gum. See Nos. 795A-795B.

Mohammed Nadir Shah — A86

1940, Aug. 23 *Perf. 11*
333 A86 50p gray grn 1.00 85

Issued in commemoration of the 22nd year ofIndependence.

Independence Monument A87

Arch of Paghman A88

1941, Aug. 23 *Perf. 12*
334 A87 15p gray grn 6.50 2.75
335 A88 50p red brn 1.25 85

Issued in commemoration of the 23rd year of Independence.

Sugar Factory, Baghlan — A89

1942, April *Perf. 12*
336 A89 1.25af ultra 2.50 1.75
a. 1.25af bl (shades) 1.50 50

In 1949, a 1.50af brown, type A89, was sold for 3af by the Philatelie Office, Kabul. It was not valid for postage. Price $3.50.

Independence Monument A90

Mohammed Nadir Shah and Arch of Paghman A91

1942, Aug. 23 *Perf. 12*
337 A90 35p brt grn 4.00 3.00
338 A91 125p chlky bl 2.00 1.75

Issued in commemoration of the 24th year of Independence.

Independence Monument and Nadir Shah — A92

Mohammed Nadir Shah — A93

Perf. 11x12, 12x11

1943, Aug. 25 **Typo.** **Unwmk.**
339 A92 35p carmine 15.00 9.00
340 A93 1.25af dk bl 5.00 1.75

25th year of Independence.

Tomb of Gohar Shad, Herat A94

Ruins of Qalai Bist A95

1944, May 1 *Perf. 12, 11x12*
341 A94 35p orange 60 40
342 A95 70p violet 1.20 75
a. 70p rose lil 4.75 1.00

Arch of Paghman — A96

Independence Monument and Mohammed Nadir Shah — A97

1944, Aug. ***Perf. 12***

343 A96 35p crimson 1.00 75
344 A97 1.25af ultra 1.75 1.50

Issued to commemorate the 26th year of Independence.

Independence Monument A98

Mohammed Nadir Shah and Arch of Paghman A99

1945, July

345 A98 35p dp red lil 1.00 90
346 A99 1.25af blue 2.50 2.00

Issued to commemorate the 27th year of Independence.

Mohammed Zahir Shah A100

Independence Monument A101

Mohammed Nadir Shah — A102

1946, July

347 A100 15p emerald 60 45
348 A101 20p dp red lil 90 70
349 A102 125p blue 2.25 2.25

Issued to commemorate the 28th year of Independence.

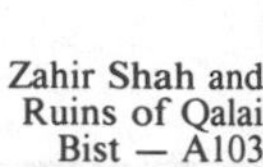

Zahir Shah and Ruins of Qalai Bist — A103

Arch of Paghman A104

Nadir Shah and Independence Monument A105

1947, Aug.

350 A103 15p yel grn 40 20
351 A104 35p plum 50 30
352 A105 125p dp bl 1.85 1.85

Issued to commemorate the 29th year of Independence.

Begging Child A106

A107

1948, May Unwmk. Typo. ***Perf. 12***

353 A106 35p yel grn 4.00 2.75
354 A107 125p gray bl 4.00 3.25

Issued to commemorate Children's Day, May 29, 1948, and valid only on that day. Proceeds were used for Child Welfare.

Arch of Paghman A108

Independence Monument A109

Mohammed Nadir Shah — A110

1948, Aug.

355 A108 15p green 30 20
356 A109 20p magenta 50 25
357 A110 125p dk bl 1.10 90

Issued to commemorate the 30th year of Independence.

United Nations Emblem — A111

1948, Oct. 24

358 A111 125p dk vio bl 10.00 8.50

Issued to commemorate the third anniversary of the formation of the United Nations. Valid one day only. Sheets of 9.

Maiwand Victory Column, Kandahar — A112

Zahir Shah and Ruins of Qalai Bist — A113

Independence Monument and Nadir Shah — A114

1949, Aug. Typo. ***Perf. 12***

359 A112 25p green 35 25
360 A113 35p magenta 50 35
361 A114 1.25af blue 1.25 1.00

Issued to commemorate the 31st year of Independence.

Nadir Shah — A117

1950, Aug.

364 A117 35p red brn 40 40
365 A117 125p blue 1.00 75

Issued to commemorate the 32nd year of Independence.

Medical School and Nadir Shah A119

1950, Dec. 22 Typo. ***Perf. 12***

Size: 38x25mm.

367 A119 35p emerald 75 75

Size: 46x30mm.

368 A119 1.25af dp bl 2.50 2.00
a. 1.25af blk (error) 6.00

Issued to commemorate the 19th anniversary of the founding of Afghanistan's Faculty of Medicine. On sale and valid for use on Dec. 22-28, 1950.

Minaret, Herat A120

Zahir Shah A121

Mosque of Khodja Abu Parsar, Balkh — A122

A123

Zahir Shah — A124

Designs: 20p, Buddha at Bamian. 40p, Ruined arch. 45p, Maiwand Victory Monument. 50p, View of Kandahar. 60p, Ancient tower. 70p, Afghanistan flag. 80p, 1af, Profile of Zahir Shah in uniform.

Photogravure, Engraved, Engraved and Lithographed

Perf. 12, 12½, 13x12½, 13½.

1951, Mar. 21 Unwmk.

Imprint: "Waterlow & Sons Limited, London."

369 A120 10p yel & brn 10 8
370 A120 15p bl & brn 15 8
371 A120 20p black 7.00 3.50
372 A121 25p green 18 10
373 A122 30p cerise 25 12
374 A121 35p violet 25 12
375 A122 40p chnt brn 30 12
376 A120 45p dp bl 25 15
377 A122 50p ol blk 60 18
378 A120 60p black 60 20
379 A122 70p dk grn, blk, red & grn 35 20
380 A123 75p cerise 80 25
381 A123 80p car & blk 85 50
382 A123 1af dp grn & vio 60 50
383 A124 1.25af rose lil & blk *4.00* 50
384 A124 2af ultra 1.40 50
385 A124 3af ultra & blk 3.25 1.25
Nos. 369-385 (17) 20.93 8.35

Nos. 372, 374 and 381 to 385 are engraved, No. 379 is engraved and lithographed.

See also Nos. 445-451, 453, 552A-552D.

Arch of Paghman A125

Nadir Shah and Independence Monument A126

Overprint in Violet

Perf. 13½x13, 13

1951, Aug. 25 **Engr.**

386 A125 35p dk grn & blk 85 50
387 A126 1.25af dp bl 2.10 1.25

Overprint reads "Sol 33 Istiqlal" or "33rd Year of Independence." Overprint measures about 11 mm. wide.

See also Nos. 398-399B, 441-442.

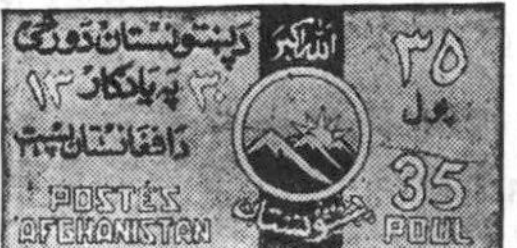

Proposed Flag of Pashtunistan — A127

Design: 1.25af, Flag and Pashtunistan warrior.

1951, Sept. 2 Litho. ***Perf. 11½***

388 A127 35p dl choc 1.25 1.00
389 A127 125p blue 3.00 2.75

Issued to publicize "Free Pashtunistan" Day.

Imperforates

From 1951 to 1958, quantities of nearly all locally-printed stamps were left imperforate and sold by the government at double face. From 1959 until March, 1964, many of the imperforates were sold for more than face value.

Avicenna — A128

1951, Nov. 4 **Typo.** ***Perf. 11½***
390 A128 35p dp cl 75 50
391 A128 125p blue 2.10 1.65

Issued to commemorate the 20th anniversary of the founding of the national Graduate School of Medicine.

A129

Dove and U. N. Symbols — A130

1951, Oct. 24
392 A129 35p magenta 2.00 1.50
393 A130 125p blue 5.00 4.00

Issued to commemorate the 7th anniversary of the formation of the United Nations.

Amir Sher Ali Khan and Tiger Head Stamp — A131

Design: Nos. 395 and 397, Zahir Shah and stamp.

1951, Dec. 23 **Litho.**
394 A131 35p chocolate 50 50
395 A131 35p rose lil 50 50
396 A131 125p ultra 1.00 90
a. Cliche of 35p in plate of 125p 125.00 125.00
397 A131 125p aqua 1.00 90

Issued to commemorate the 76th anniversary of the formation of the Universal Postal Union.

Stamps of 1951 Without Overprint.

Perf. 13½x13, 13

1952, Aug. 24 **Engr.**
398 A125 35p dk grn & blk 2.50 2.50
399 A126 1.25af dp bl 2.50 2.50

Same Overprinted in Violet

399A A125 35p dk grn & blk 90 60
399B A126 1.25af dp bl 2.50 1.50

Nos. 398-399B were issued to commemorate the 34th Independence Day.

Globe — A132

Perf. 11½

1952, Oct. 25 **Unwmk.** **Litho.**
400 A132 35p rose 80 70
401 A132 125p aqua 1.75 1.50

Issued to honor the United Nations.

Symbol of Medicine A134

Tribal Warrior and National Flag A135

1952, Nov. ***Perf. 11½***
403 A134 35p chocolate 60 50
404 A134 125p vio bl 1.75 1.75

Issued to commemorate the 21st anniversary of the national Graduate School of Medicine.

No. 404 is inscribed in French with white letters on a colored background.

1952, Sept. 1 ***Perf. 11***
405 A135 35p red 40 40
406 A135 125p dk bl 85 85

No. 406 is inscribed in French "Pashtunistan Day, 1952."

Flags of Afghanistan and Pashtunistan A139

Badge of Pashtunistan A140

Perf. 10½x11, 11

1953, Sept. 1 **Unwmk.**
411 A139 35p vermilion 30 25
412 A140 125p blue 85 65

Issued to publicize "Free Pashtunistan" Day.

Nadir Shah and Flag Bearer A141

Nadir Shah and Independence Monument A142

1953, Aug. 24 ***Perf. 11***
413 A141 35p green 25 20
414 A142 125p violet 1.00 75

Issued to commemorate the 35th anniversary of Independence.

United Nations Emblem — A143

1953, Oct. 24
415 A143 35p lilac 75 75
416 A143 125p vio bl 1.85 1.50

Issued to publicize United Nations Day, 1953.

Nadir Shah

A144 A145

1953, Nov. 29
417 A144 35p orange 1.00 1.00
418 A145 125p chlky bl 2.25 2.25

Issued to commemorate the 22nd anniversary of the founding of the national Graduate School of Medicine.

Redrawn 35p. Original - Right character in second line of Persian inscription:

٣

Redrawn - Persian character:

٢

125p. Original - Inscribed "XXIII," "MADECINE" and "ANNIVERAIRE"
Redrawn - Inscribed "XXII," "MEDECINE" and "ANNIVERSAIRE"

1953
419 A144 35p dp org 5.00
420 A145 125p chlky bl 6.50

Nadir Shah and Symbols of Independence A146

1954, Aug. **Typo.** ***Perf. 11***
421 A146 35p car rose 50 40
422 A146 125p vio bl 1.50 1.25

Issued to commemorate the 36th year of Independence.

Raising Flag of Pashtunistan A147

1954, Sept. ***Perf. 11½***
423 A147 35p chocolate 50 40
424 A147 125p blue 1.50 1.25

Issued to publicize "Free Pashtunistan" Day.

U.N. Flag and Map — A148

1954, Oct. 24 ***Perf. 11***
425 A148 35p car rose 1.00 1.00
426 A148 125p dk vio bl 3.00 3.00

Issued to commemorate the 9th anniversary of the United Nations.

U. N. Symbols — A149

Design: 125p, U. N. emblem & flags.

1955, June 26 **Litho.** ***Perf. 11***

Size: 26½x36mm.
427 A149 35p dk grn 60 50

Size: 28½x36mm.
428 A149 125p aqua 1.50 1.25

Issued to commemorate the 10th anniversary of the signing of the United Nations charter.

Nadir Shah (center) and Brothers — A150

1929 Civil War Scene and Zahir Shah — A151

Tribal Elders' Council and Pashtun Flag — A152

1955, Aug. **Unwmk.** ***Perf. 11***
429 A150 35p brt prink 40 40
430 A150 35p vio bl 40 40
431 A151 125p rose lil 1.25 1.00
432 A151 125p lt vio 1.25 1.00

Issued to commemorate the 37th anniversary of Independence.

1955, Sept. 5
433 A152 35p org brn 35 35
434 A152 125p yel grn 1.25 1.00

Issued for "Free Pashtunistan" Day.

United Nations Flag A153

Nadir Shah and Independence Monument A154

1955, Oct. 24 **Unwmk.** ***Perf. 11***
435 A153 35p org brn 90 75
436 A153 125p brt ultra 1.85 1.50

Issued to commemorate the tenth anniversary of the United Nations, Oct. 24, 1955.

1956, Aug. **Litho.**
437 A154 35p lt grn 35 30
438 A154 140p lt vio bl 1.35 1.10

Issued to commemorate the 38th year of Independence.

Jesh'n Exhibition Hall — A155

1956, Aug. 25

439 A155 50p chocolate 45 30
440 A155 50p lt vio bl 45 30

International Exposition at Kabul.

Of the 50p face value, only 35p paid postage. The remaining 15p went to the Exposition.

Nos. 398-399 Handstamped in Violet

a — b: 39 em Anv

1957, Aug. Engr. ***Perf. 13½x13, 13***

441 A125 (a) 35p dk grn & blk 60 30
442 A126 (b) 1.25af dp bl 90 75

Arabic overprint on No. 441 measures 19mm. No. 442 overprinted: "39 em Anv". Issued to commemorate the 39th year of independence.

Pashtunistan Flag — A156

1957, Sept. 1 Litho. ***Perf. 11***

443 A156 50p pale lil rose 75 50
444 A156 155p lt vio 1.25 1.00

Issued for "Free Pashtunistan" Day. French inscription on No. 444.

Types of 1951 and

Game of Buzkashi A157

Perf. 12, 12½, 12½x13, 13, 13x12, 13x12½, 13½x14

fPhotogravure, Engraved, Engraved and Lithographed

1957, Nov. 23 Unwmk.

Imprint: "Waterlow & Sons Limited, London."

445 A122 30p brown 22 6
446 A122 40p rose red 32 6
447 A122 50p yellow 48 8
448 A120 60p ultra 55 10
449 A123 75p brt vio 70 10
450 A123 80p vio & brn 75 10
451 A123 1af car & ultra 1.50 20
452 A157 140p ol & dp cl 3.00 75
453 A124 3af org & blk 3.75 75
Nos. 445-453 (9) 11.27 2.20

No. 452 lacks imprint.

Nadir Shah and Flag-bearer A158

1958, Aug. 25 ***Perf. 13½x14***

454 A158 35p dp yel grn 25 20
455 A158 140p brown 60 50

Issued to commemorate the 40th year of Independence.

Exposition Buildings A159

1958, Aug. 23 Litho. ***Perf. 11***

456 A159 35p brt bl grn 25 20
457 A159 140p vermilion 70 60

Issued for the International Exposition at Kabul.

Pres. Celal Bayar of Turkey A160

Flags of U.N. and Afghanistan A161

1958, Sept. 13 Unwmk.

458 A160 50p lt bl 30 20
459 A160 100p brown 50 40

Issued to commemorate the visit of President Celal Bayar of Turkey.

1958, Oct. 24 Photo. ***Perf. 14x13½***

Flags in Original Colors.

460 A161 50p dk gray 75 75
461 A161 100p green 1.50 1.25

Issued for United Nations Day, Oct. 24.

Atomic Energy Encircling the Hemispheres A162

1958, Oct. 20 ***Perf. 13½x14***

462 A162 50p blue 50 50
463 A162 100p dp red lil 85 85

Issued to promote Atoms for Peace.

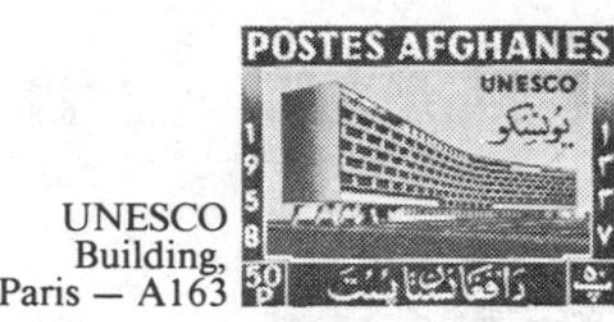

UNESCO Building, Paris — A163

1958, Nov. 3

464 A163 50p dp yel grn 75 60
465 A163 100p brn ol 1.10 90

Issued to commemorate the opening of UNESCO (U.N. Educational, Scientific and Cultural Organization) Headquarters in Paris, Nov. 3.

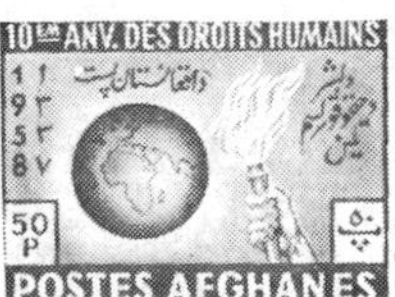

Globe and Torch — A164

Perf. 13½x14

1958, Dec. 10 Unwmk.

466 A164 50p lil rose 50 50
467 A164 100p maroon 1.00 1.00

Issued to commemorate the tenth anniversary of the signing of the Universal Declaration of Human Rights.

Nadir Shah and Flags — A165

1959, Aug. Litho ***Perf. 11 Rough***

468 A165 35p lt ver 30 30
469 A165 165p lt vio 1.00 60

Issued to commemorate the 41st year of Independence.

Uprooted Oak Emblem — A166

1960, Apr. 7 ***Perf. 11***

470 A166 50p dp org 20 15
471 A166 165p blue 50 40

Issued to publicize World Refugee Year, July 1, 1959-June 30, 1960.

Two imperf. souvenir sheets exist. Both contain a 50p and a 165p, type A166, with marginal inscriptions and WRY emblem in maroon. On one sheet the stamps are in the colors of Nos. 470-471 (size 108x81mm.). On the other, the 50p is blue and the 165p is deep orange (size 107x80mm.). Price $6 each.

Buzkashi A167

1960, May 4 ***Perf. 11, Imperf.***

472 A167 25p rose red 35 20
473 A167 50p bluish grn 75 50
a. Cliche of 25p in plate of 50p 20.00 20.00

See also Nos. 549-550A.

Independence Monument — A168

1960, Aug. ***Perf. 11, 12***

474 A168 50p lt bl 15 15
475 A168 175p brt pink 50 50

Issued to commemorate the 42nd Independence Day.

Globe and Flags — A169

1960, Oct. 24 Litho. ***Perf. 11, 12***

476 A169 50p rose lil 30 25
477 A169 175p ultra 1.00 85

Issued to commemorate United Nations Day.

An imperf. souvenir sheet contains one each of Nos. 476-477 with marginal inscriptions ("La Journée des Nations Unies 1960" in French and Persian) and UN emblem in light blue. Size: 127x85½mm. Price $5.

This sheet was surcharged "+20ps" in 1962. Price $8.50.

Teacher Pointing to Globe A170

1960, Oct. 23 ***Perf. 11***

478 A170 50p brt pink 25 18
479 A170 100p brt grn 90 60

Issued to publicize Teacher's Day.

Mohammed Zahir Shah — A171

1960, Oct. 15

480 A171 50p red brn 40 20
481 A171 150p dk car rose 1.25 40

Issued to honor the King on his 46th birthday.

Buzkashi A172

1960, Nov. 9 ***Perf. 11***

482 A172 175p lt red brn 1.50 60

See also Nos. 551-552.

No. 482 Overprinted "1960" and Olympic Rings in Bright Green.

1960, Dec. 24

483 A172 175p red brn 3.25 3.00
a. Souvenir sheet 12.00

Issued to commemorate the 17th Olympic Games, Rome, Aug. 25-Sept. 11.

No. 483a contains one of No. 483, imperf. Bright green marginal inscription. Size: 86x61mm.

Mir Wais — A173

1961, Jan. 5 Unwmk. ***Perf. 10½***

484 A173 50p brt rose lil 30 20
485 A173 175p ultra 75 50
a. Souv. sheet of 2 2.25 2.25

Issued to honor Mir Wais (1665-1708), national leader.

No. 485a contains one each of Nos. 484-485, imperf. Emerald marginal inscription. Size: 108x78mm.

No Postal Need

existed for the 1p to 15p denominations released with commemorative or semipostal sets of 1961-63 (between Nos. 486 and 649, B37 and B65). The lowest denomination actually used for non-philatelic postage

---

Horse, Sheep and Camel A174

Designs: No. 487, 175p, Rock partridge. 10p, 100p, Afghan hound. 15p, 150p, Grain and grasshopper (vert.).

1961, Mar. 29 Photo. ***Perf. 13½x14***

486 A174 2p mar & buff
487 A174 2p ultra & org
488 A174 5p brn & yel
489 A174 10p blk & sal
490 A174 15p bl grn & yel
491 A174 25p blk & pink
492 A174 50p blk & cit
493 A174 100p blk & pink

494 A174 150p grn & yel
495 A174 175p ultra & pink
Nos. 486-495 (10) 3.00

Two souvenir sheets, perf. and imperf., contain two stamps, one each of Nos. 492-493. Black marginal inscriptions, "Journee d'Agriculture 1961" in Persian and French. Size: 111x64mm. Price $2 each.

Afghan Fencing A175

Designs: No. 497, 5p, 25p, 50p, Wrestlers. 10p, 100p, Man with Indian clubs. 15p, 150p, Afghan fencing. 175p, Children skating.

1961, July 6 ***Perf. 13½x14***

496 A175 2p grn & rose lil
497 A175 2p brn & cit
498 A175 5p gray & rose
499 A175 10p bl & bis
500 A175 15p sl bl & dl lil
501 A175 25p blk & dl bl
502 A175 50p sl grn & bis brn
503 A175 100p brn & bl grn
504 A175 150p brn & org yel
505 A175 175p blk & bl
Nos. 496-505 (10) 1.75

Issued for Children's Day.
A souvenir sheet exists, perf. and imperf., containing one each of Nos. 502-503. Size: 111x65mm. Price $3.50 each.

Bande Amir Lakes A176

1961, Aug. 7 Photo. ***Perf. 13½x14***

506 A176 3af brt bl 50 40
507 A176 10af rose cl 1.75 1.50

Nadir Shah — A177

Girl Scout — A178

1961, Aug. 23 ***Perf. 14x13½***

508 A177 50p rose red & blk 50 40
509 A177 175p brt grn & org brn 1.00 80

Issued to commemorate the 43rd Independence Day.
Two souvenir sheets, perf. and imperf., contain one each of Nos. 508-509. Black marginal inscription and control number, flag in black, red & green. Size: 104x74mm. Price, each $2.50.

Perf. 14x13½

1961, July 23 **Unwmk.**

510 A178 50p dp car & dk gray 40 20
511 A178 175p dp grn & rose brn 90 60

Issued for Women's Day.
Two souvenir sheets exist, perf. and imperf., containing one each of Nos. 510-511. Black marginal inscription. Size: 105x75mm. Price $4 each.

Exhibition Hall, Kabul A179

1961, Aug. 23 ***Perf. 13½x14***

512 A179 50p yel brn & yel grn 25 20
513 A179 175p bl & brn 60 40

International Exhibition at Kabul.

Pathan with Pashtunistan Flag — A180

1961, Aug. 31 Photo. ***Perf. 14x13½***

514 A180 50p blk, lil & red 20 18
515 A180 175p brn, grnsh bl & red 50 40

Issued for "Free Pashtunistan Day."
Souvenir sheets exist perf. and imperf. containing one each of Nos. 514-515 with black marginal inscription and flag in red and black. Size: 104x75mm. Price $2 each.

Assembly Building A181

1961, Sept. 10 ***Perf. 12***

516 A181 50p dk gray & brt grn 25 18
517 A181 175p ultra & brn 65 45

Issued to commemorate the anniversary of the founding of the National Assembly.
Souvenir sheets exist, perf. and imperf., containing one each of Nos. 516-517 with black marginal inscription and flower in ultramarine and green. Size: 106x70mm. Price $1 each.

Exterminating Anopheles Mosquito A182

1961, Oct. 5 ***Perf. 13½x14***

518 A182 50p blk & brn lil 70 40
519 A182 175p mar & brt grn 1.50 75

Issued to publicize the Anti-Malaria campaign. Souvenir sheets exist, perf. and imperf., containing one each of Nos. 518-519 with black marginal inscription and mosquito. Size: 110x65mm. Price $5 each.

Zahir Shah — A183

1961, Oct. 15 ***Perf. 13½***

520 A183 50p lil & bl 25 20
521 A183 175p emer & red brn 60 50

Issued to honor King Mohammed Zahir Shah on his 47th birthday.
See also Nos. 609-612.

Pomegranates A184

Fruit: No. 523, 5p, 25p, 50p, Grapes. 10p, 150p, Apples. 15p, 175p, Pomegranates. 100p, Melons.

1961, Oct. 16 ***Perf. 13½x14***

Fruit in Natural Colors.

522 A184 2p black
523 A184 2p green
524 A184 5p lil rose
525 A184 10p lilac
526 A184 15p dk bl
527 A184 25p dl red
528 A184 50p purple
529 A184 100p brt bl
530 A184 150p brown
531 A184 175p ol gray
Nos. 522-531 (10) 2.00

For Afghan Red Crescent Society.
Souvenir sheets exist, perf. and imperf., containing one each of Nos. 528-529 with black marginal inscription and red crescent. Size: 110x65mm. Price $1.75 each.

U.N. Headquarters, N.Y. — A185

1961, Oct. 24 ***Perf. 13½x14***

Vertical Borders in Emerald, Red and Black.

532 A185 1p rose lil
533 A185 2p slate
534 A185 3p brown
535 A185 4p ultra
536 A185 50p rose red
537 A185 75p gray
538 A185 175p brt grn
Nos. 532-538 (7) 1.25

Issued to commemorate the 16th anniversary of the United Nations. Souvenir sheets exist, perf. and imperf., containing one each of Nos. 536-538. Black marginal inscription with U.N. emblem and control number. Size: 114x95mm. Price $2.25 each.

Children Giving Flowers to Teacher — A186

People Raising UNESCO Symbol — A187

Designs: No. 540, 5p, 25p, 50p, Tulips. 10p, 100p, Narcissus. 15p, 150p, Children giving flowers to teacher. 175p, Teacher with children in front of school.

1961, Oct. 26 Photo. ***Perf. 12***

539 A186 2p multi
540 A186 2p multi
541 A186 5p multi
542 A186 10p multi
543 A186 15p multi
544 A186 25p multi
545 A186 50p multi
546 A186 100p multi
547 A186 150p multi
548 A186 175p multi
Nos. 539-548 (10) 2.00

Issued for Teacher's Day.
Souvenir sheets exist, perf. and imperf. containing one each of Nos. 545-546. Gray marginal inscription and black control number. Size: 104x78mm. Price, 2 sheets, $3.

Buzkashi Types of 1960.

1961-72 Litho. ***Perf. 10½, 11***

549 A167 25p violet 10 5
b. 25p brt vio, typo. ('72) 5 5
549A A167 25p cit ('63) 15 5
550 A167 50p blue 30 5
550A A167 50p yel org ('69) 10 5
551 A172 100p citron 40 10
551A A172 150p org ('64) 30 15
552 A172 2af lt grn 1.00 60
Nos. 549-552 (7) 2.35 1.05

Zahir Shah Types of 1951

Photogravure, Engraved, Engraved & Lithographed

1962 ***Perf. 13x12, 13***

Imprint: "Thomas De La Rue & Co. Ltd."

552A A123 75p brt pur 1.50 35
552B A123 1af car & ultra 1.85 42
552C A124 2af blue 2.25 95
552D A124 3af org & blk 5.25 1.40

1962, July 2 Photo. ***Perf. 14x13½***

553 A187 2p rose lil & brn
554 A187 2p ol bis & brn
555 A187 5p dp org & dk grn
556 A187 10p gray & mag
557 A187 15p bl & brn
558 A187 25p org yel & pur
559 A187 50p lt grn & pur
560 A187 75p brt cit & brn
561 A187 100p dp org & brn
Nos. 553-561 (9) 1.40

Issued to commemorate the 15th anniversary of UNESCO (U.N. Educational, Scientific and Cultural Organization). Souvenir sheets exist, perf. and imperf. One contains Nos. 558-559 with purple marginal inscription; the other contains one each of Nos. 560-561 with brown marginal inscription and black control numbers. Size: 99x80mm. Price, $4 each.

Ahmad Shah — A188

Afghan Hound — A189

1962, Feb. 24 Photo. ***Perf. 13½***

562 A188 50p red brn & gray 15 10
563 A188 75p grn & sal 25 20
564 A188 100p cl & bis 40 30

Issued to honor Ahmad Shah (1724-1773), who founded the Afghan kingdom in 1747 and ruled until 1773.

1962, Apr. 21 ***Perf. 14x13½***

Designs: 5p, 75p, Afghan cock. 10p, 100p, Kondjid plant. 15p, 125p, Astrakhan skins.

565 A189 2p rose & brn
566 A189 2p lt grn & brn
567 A189 5p dp rose & cl
568 A189 10p lt grn & sl grn
569 A189 15p bl grn & blk
570 A189 25p bl & brn
571 A189 50p gray & brn
572 A189 75p rose lil & lil
573 A189 100p gray & dl grn
574 A189 125p rose brn & blk
Nos. 565-574 (10) 2.00

Issued for Agriculture Day. Perf. and imperf. souvenir sheets exist. Set of 4 sheets, price $4.

Athletes with Flag and Nadir Shah A190

Woman in National Costume A191

1962, Aug. 23 ***Perf. 12***

575 A190 25p multi 12 5
576 A190 50p multi 18 6
577 A190 150p multi 25 8

44th Independence Day.

1962, Aug. 30 ***Perf. 11½x12***
578 A191 25p lil & brn 12 6
579 A191 50p grn & brn 25 15

Issued for Women's Day. For souvenir sheet see note after No. C16.

Man and Woman with Flag — A192

Malaria Eradication Emblem and Swamp — A193

1962, Aug. 31 **Photo.**
580 A192 25p blk, pale bl & red 12 6
581 A192 50p blk, grn & red 25 12
582 A192 150p blk, pink & red 60 20

Issued for "Free Pashtunistan Day."

1962, Sept. 5 ***Perf. 14x13½***
583 A193 2p dk grn & ol gray
584 A193 2p dk grn & sal
585 A193 5p red brn & ol
586 A193 10p red brn & brt grn
587 A193 15p red brn & gray
588 A193 25p brt bl & bluish grn
589 A193 50p brt bl & rose lil
590 A193 75p blk & bl
591 A193 100p blk & brt pink
592 A193 150p blk & bis brn
593 A193 175p blk & org
Nos. 583-593 (11) 2.25

Issued for the World Health Organization drive to eradicate malaria. Perf. and imperf. souvenir sheets exist. Set of 4 sheets, price $6.50.

National Assembly Building A194

Perf. 10½, 11(100p)
1962, Sept. 10 **Unwmk.** **Litho.**
594 A194 25p lt grn 8 6
595 A194 50p blue 12 8
596 A194 75p rose 15 12
597 A194 100p violet 25 20
598 A194 125p ultra 28 25
Nos. 594-598 (5) 88 71

Establishment of the National Assembly.

Horse Racing — A195

Designs: 2p, Pole vaulting. 3p, Wrestling. 4p, Weight lifting. 5p, Soccer.

1962, Sept. 22 **Photo.** ***Perf. 12***
Black Inscriptions
599 A195 1p lt ol & red brn
600 A195 2p lt grn & red brn
601 A195 3p yel & dk pur
602 A195 4p pale bl & grn
603 A195 5p bluish grn & dk brn
Nos. 599-603, C17-C22 (11) 2.50

Issued to commemorate the 4th Asian Games, Djakarta, Indonesia. Two souvenir sheets exist. A perforated one contains a 125p blue, dark blue and brown stamp in horse racing design. An imperf. one contains a 2af buff, purple and black stamp in soccer design. Both sheets have black control number. Size: 64x90mm. Price, $4.50 each.

Runners A196

Designs: 1p, 2p, Diver (vert.). 4p, Peaches. 5p, Iris (vert.).

Perf. 11½x12, 12x11½
1962, Oct. 2 **Unwmk.**
604 A196 1p rose lil & brn
605 A196 2p bl & brn
606 A196 3p brt bl & lil
607 A196 4p ol gray & multi
608 A196 5p gray & multi
Nos. 604-608, C23-C25 (8) 2.00

Issued for Children's Day.

King Type of 1961, Dated "1962"
1962, Oct. 15 ***Perf. 13½***
Various Frames
609 A183 25p lil rose & brn 8 8
610 A183 50p org brn & grn 15 15
611 A183 75p bl & lake 22 22
612 A183 100p grn & red brn 30 30

Issued to honor King Mohammed Zahir Shah on his 48th birthday.

Grapes A197

Designs: 3p, Pears. 4p, Wistaria. 5p, Blossoms.

1962, Oct. 16 ***Perf. 12***
Fruit and Flowers in Natural Colors; Carmine Crescent
613 A197 1p dp rose
614 A197 2p blue
615 A197 3p lilac
616 A197 4p gray brn
617 A197 5p gray
Nos. 613-617, C26-C28 (8) 1.20

For the Afghan Red Crescent Society.

U.N. Headquarters, N.Y. and Flags of U.N. and Afghanistan — A198

1962, Oct. 24 **Unwmk.**
Flags in Original Colors, Black Inscriptions
618 A198 1p ol bis
619 A198 2p lil rose
620 A198 3p dl vio
621 A198 4p green
622 A198 5p redsh brn
Nos. 618-622, C29-C31 (8) 1.50

Issued for United Nations Day. Souvenir sheets exist. One contains a single 4af ultramarine stamp, perforated; the other, a 4af ocher stamp, imperf. Both sheets have a black marginal inscription and control number. Size: 89x65mm. Price, 2 sheets, $6.50.

Boy Scout — A199

Pole Vault — A200

1962, Oct. 18 **Photo.** ***Perf. 12***
623 A199 1p yel, dk grn & sal
624 A199 2p dl yel, sl & sal
625 A199 3p rose, blk & sal
626 A199 4p multi
Nos. 623-626, C32-C35 (8) 1.75

Issued to honor the Boy Scouts.

1962, Oct. 25 **Unwmk.** ***Perf. 12***

Designs: 3p, High jump. 4p, 5p, Different blossoms.

627 A200 1p lil & dk grn
628 A200 2p yel grn & brn
629 A200 3p bis & vio
630 A200 4p sal pink, grn & ultra
631 A200 5p yel, grn & bl
Nos. 627-631, C36-C37 (7) 1.40

Issued for Teacher's Day.

Rockets A201

1962, Nov. 29
632 A201 50p pale lil & dk bl 60
633 A201 100p lt bl & red brn 1.25

Issued to commemorate the United Nations World Meteorological Day. A souvenir sheet contains one 5af pink and green stamp, green marginal inscription and black control number. Size: 89x65mm. Price $8.

Ansari Mausoleum, Herat — A202

Perf. 13½
1963, Jan. 3 **Unwmk.** **Photo.**
634 A202 50p pur & grn 12 12
635 A202 75p gray & mag 18 18
636 A202 100p org brn & brn 30 30

Issued to honor Khwaja Abdullah Ansari, Sufi, religious leader and poet, on the 900th anniversary of his death.

Sheep A203

Silkworm, Cocoons, Moth and Mulberry Branch A204

1963, March 1 ***Perf. 12***
637 A203 1p grnsh bl & blk
638 A203 2p yel grn & blk
639 A203 3p lil rose & blk
640 A204 4p gray, grn & brn
641 A204 5p red lil, grn & brn
Nos. 637-641, C42-C44 (8) 1.75

Issued for the Day of Agriculture.

Rice — A205

Designs: 3p, Corn. 300p, Wheat emblem.

1963, March 27 **Unwmk.** ***Perf. 14***
642 A205 2p gray, cl & grn 8 8
643 A205 3p grn, yel & ocher 12 12
644 A205 300p dk bl & yel 45 45

Issued for the "Freedom from Hunger" campaign of the U.N. Food and Agriculture Organization.

Meteorological Measuring Instrument A206

Designs: 3p, 10p, Weather station. 4p, 5p, Rockets in space.

1963, May 23 **Photo.** ***Perf. 13½x14***
645 A206 1p dp mag & brn
646 A206 2p brt bl & brn
647 A206 3p red & brn
648 A206 4p org & lil
649 A206 5p grn & dl vio

Imperf
650 A206 10p red brn & grn
Nos. 645-650, C46-C50 (11) 9.50

Issued to commemorate the United Nations Third World Meteorological Day, Mar. 23.

Independence Monument — A207

1963, Aug. 23 **Litho.** ***Perf. 10½***
651 A207 25p lt grn 10 6
652 A207 50p orange 20 15
653 A207 150p rose car 50 35

Issued to commemorate the 45th Independence Day.

Pathans in Forest A208

1963, Aug. 31 **Unwmk.** ***Perf. 10½***
654 A208 25p pale vio 10 6
655 A208 50p sky bl 20 18
656 A208 150p dl red brn 60 50

Issued for "Free Pashtunistan Day."

National Assembly Building A209

1963, Sept. 10 *Perf. 11*

657	A209	25p gray	6	6
658	A209	50p dl red	12	8
659	A209	75p brown	20	15
660	A209	100p olive	30	15
661	A209	125p lilac	40	20
		Nos. 657-661 (5)	1.08	64

Issued to honor the National Assembly.

Balkh Gate A210

1963, Oct. 8

662	A210	3af choc (screened margins)	60	40
a.		white margins	1.50	50

In the original printing (No. 662), a half-tone screen extended across the plate, covering the space between the stamps. A retouch removed the screen between the stamps (No. 662a).

Zahir Shah — A211

Kemal Ataturk — A212

1963, Oct. 15 *Perf. 10½*

663	A211	25p green	10	5
664	A211	50p gray	20	8
665	A211	75p car rose	30	15
666	A211	100p dl redsh brn	40	18

Issued to honor King Mohammed Zahir Shah on his 49th birthday.

1963, Oct. 10 *Perf. 10½*

667	A212	1af blue	15	12
668	A212	3af rose lil	60	50

Issued to commemorate the 25th anniversary of the death of Kemal Ataturk, president of Turkey.

"Tiger's Head" of 1878 — A214

1964, March 22 **Photo.** *Perf. 12*

675	A214	1.25af gold, grn & blk	20	10
676	A214	5af gold, rose car & blk	50	35

Issued to honor philately.

Unisphere and Flags — A215

1964, May 3 *Perf. 13½x14*

677	A215	6af crim, gray & grn	40	30

New York World's Fair, 1964-65.

Hand Holding Torch — A216

1964, May 12 **Photo.** *Perf. 14x13½*

678	A216	3.75af brt bl, org, yel & blk	25	25

Issued to commemorate the first United Nations Seminar on Human Rights in Kabul, May 1964. The denomination in Persian at right erroneously reads "3.25" but the stamp was sold and used as 3.75af.

Kandahar Airport A217

1964, Apr. **Litho.** *Perf. 10½, 11*

679	A217	7.75af dk red brn	60	30
680	A217	9.25af lt grn	75	35
681	A217	10.50af lt grn	75	40
682	A217	13.75af car rose	90	50

Inauguration of Kandahar Airport.

Snow Leopard A218

Designs: 50p, Ibex (vert.). 75p, Head of argali. 5af, Yak.

1964, June 25 **Photo.** *Perf. 12*

683	A218	25p yel & bl	8	8
684	A218	50p dl red & grn	8	8
685	A218	75p Prus bl & lil	8	8
686	A218	5af brt grn & dk brn	30	30

View of Herat — A219

Flag and Map of Afghanistan A220

Design: 75p, Tomb of Queen Gowhar Shad (vert.).

Perf. 13½x14, 14x13½

1964, July 12

687	A219	25p sep & bl	5	5
688	A219	75p dp bl & buff	5	5
689	A220	3af red, blk & grn	30	10

Issued for tourist publicity.

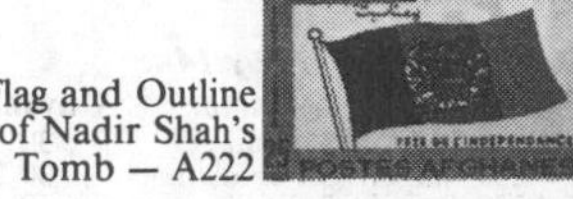

Wrestling A221

Designs: 25p, Hurdling (vert.). 1af, Diving (vert.). 5af, Soccer.

1964, July 26 *Perf. 12*

690	A221	25p ol bis, blk & car	5	5
691	A221	1af bl grn, blk & car	8	8
692	A221	3.75af yel grn, blk & car	35	35
693	A221	5af brn, blk & car	45	45
a.		Souv. sheet of 4	1.10	1.10

Issued to commemorate the 18th Olympic Games, Tokyo, Oct. 10-25, 1964. No. 693a contains 4 imperf. stamps similar to Nos. 690-693, black inscription. Size: 95x95mm. Sold for 15af. The additional 5af went to the Afghanistan Olympic Committee.

Flag and Outline of Nadir Shah's Tomb — A222

1964, Aug. 24 **Photo.**

695	A222	25p gold, bl, blk, red & grn	7	7
696	A222	75p gold, bl, blk, red & grn	10	10

Issued to commemorate Independence Day. The stamps were printed with an erroneous inscription in upper left corner: "33rd year of independence." This was locally obliterated with a typographed gold bar.

Pashtunistan Flag — A223

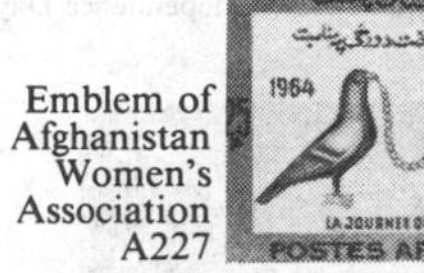

Zahir Shah — A225

1964, Sept. 1 **Unwmk.**

697	A223	100p gold, blk, red, bl & grn	7	7

Issued for "Free Pashtunistan Day."

1964, Oct. 17 *Perf. 14x13½*

699	A225	1.25af gold & yel grn	10	5
700	A225	3.75af gold & rose	20	15
701	A225	50af gold & gray	3.00	2.50

Issued to honor King Mohammed Zahir Shah on his 50th birthday.

Coat of Arms of Afghanistan and U.N. Emblem A226

1964, Oct. 24 *Perf. 13½x14*

702	A226	5af gold, blk & dl bl	30	20

Issued for United Nations Day.

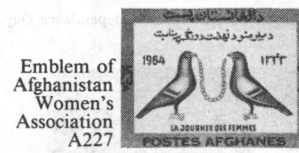

Emblem of Afghanistan Women's Association A227

1964, Nov. 9 **Photo.** **Unwmk.**

703	A227	25p pink, dk bl & emer	5	5
704	A227	75p aqua, dk bl & emer	5	5
705	A227	1af sil, dk bl & emer	10	5

Issued for Women's Day.

Abdul Rahman Jami — A228

1964, Nov. 23 **Litho.** *Perf. 11 Rough*

706	A228	1.50af blk, emer & yel	1.25	

Issued to commemorate the 550th anniversary of the birth of the poet Mowlana Nooruddin Abdul Rahman Jami (1414-1492).

Woodpecker A229

Birds: 3.75af, Black-throated jay (vert.). 5af, Impeyan pheasant (vert.).

Perf. 13½x14, 14x13½

1965, Apr. 20 **Photo.** **Unwmk.**

707	A229	1.25af multi	12	6
708	A229	3.75af multi	30	20
709	A229	5af multi	40	20

ITU Emblem, Old and New Communication Equipment — A230

1965, May 17 *Perf. 13½x14*

710	A230	5af lt bl, blk & red	35	35

Issued to commemorate the centenary of the International Telecommunication Union.

"Red City," Bamian — A231

Designs: 3.75af, Ruins of ancient Bamian city. 5af, Bande Amir, mountain lakes.

1965, May 30 *Perf. 13x13½*

711	A231	1.25af pink & multi	10	10
712	A231	3.75af lt bl & multi	25	25
713	A231	5af yel & multi	40	40

Issued for tourist publicity.

ICY Emblem A232

1965, June 25 *Perf. 13½x13*

714	A232	5af grn, yel, blk, red & vio bl	25	25

International Cooperation Year, 1965.

ARIANA Air Lines Emblem and DC-3 — A233

Designs: 5af, DC-6 at right. 10af, DC-3 on top.

Perf. 13½x14

1965, July 15 **Photo.** **Unwmk.**

715	A233	1.25af brt bl, gray & blk	10	10
716	A233	5af red lil, blk & bl	30	30

717 A233 10af bis, blk, bl gray & grn 75 75
a. Souv. sheet of 3 1.25 1.25

Issued to commemorate the 10th anniversary of Afghan Air Lines, ARIANA. No. 717a contains 3 imperf. stamps similar to Nos. 715-717; blue marginal inscription, black control number. Size: 90x90mm.

Nadir Shah — A234

1965, Aug. 23 ***Perf. 14x13½***
718 A234 1af dl grn, blk & red brn 12 12

For the 47th Independence Day.

Flag of Pashtunistan A235

Perf. 13½x14
1965, Aug. 31 Photo. Unwmk.
719 A235 1af ultra, blk, gold, car & grn 10 10

Issued for "Free Pashtunistan Day."

Zahir Shah Signing Constitution — A236

1965, Sept. 11 ***Perf. 13x13½***
720 A236 1.50af brt grn & blk 25 25

Promulgation of the new Constitution.

Zahir Shah and Oak Leaves — A237

1965, Oct. 14 ***Perf. 14x13½***
721 A237 1.25af blk, ultra & sal 20 15
722 A237 6af blk, lt bl & rose lil 60 50

Issued to honor King Mohammed Zahir Shah on his 51st birthday.

Flags of UN and Afghanistan A238

1965, Oct. 24 ***Perf. 13½x14***
723 A238 5af multi 30 30

Issued for United Nations Day.

Dappled Ground Gecko A239

Designs: 4af, Caucasian agamid (lizard). 8af, Horsfield's tortoise.

Perf. 13½x14
1966, May 10 Photo. Unwmk.
724 A239 3af tan & multi 30 30
725 A239 4af brt grn & multi 30 30
726 A239 8af vio & multi 50 50

Soccer Player and Globe — A240

1966, July 31 Litho. ***Perf. 14x13½***
727 A240 2af rose red & blk 75 25
728 A240 6af vio bl & blk 1.50 35
729 A240 12af bis brn & blk 3.00 75

Issued to commemorate the World Cup Soccer Championship, Wembley, England, July 11-30.

Cotton Flower and Boll — A241

Designs: 5af, Silkworm. 7af, Farmer plowing with oxen.

1966, July 31 ***Perf. 13½x14***
730 A241 1af multi 15 10
731 A241 5af multi 40 30
732 A241 7af multi 60 40

Issued for the Day of Agriculture.

Independence Monument A242

1966, Aug. 23 Photo. ***Perf. 13½x14***
733 A242 1af multi 10 10
734 A242 3af multi 35 25

Issued to commemorate Independence Day.

Flag of Pashtunistan — A243

1966, Aug. 31 Litho. ***Perf. 11 Rough***
735 A243 1af brt bl 25 10

Issued for "Free Pashtunistan Day."

Bagh-i-Bala Park Casino A244

Designs: 2af, Map of Afghanistan. 8af, Tomb of Abd-er-Rahman. The casino on 4af is the former summer palace of Abd-er-Rahman near Kabul.

1966, Oct. 3 Photo. ***Perf. 13½x14***
736 A244 2af red & multi 18 15
737 A244 4af multi 40 30
738 A244 8af multi 65 60
a. Souvenir sheet of 3 1.50 1.50

Issued for tourist publicity. No. 738a contains 3 imperf. stamps similar to Nos. 736-738: light yellow margin with black inscription and control number. Size: 110x80mm.

Zahir Shah — A245

UNESCO Emblem — A246

1966, Oct. 14 ***Perf. 14x13½***
739 A245 1af dk sl grn 20 10
740 A245 5af red brn 50 25

Issued to honor King Mohammed Zahir Shah on his 52nd birthday. See Nos. 760-761.

1967, Mar. 6 Litho. ***Perf. 12***
741 A246 2af multi 75 20
742 A246 6af multi 1.00 20
743 A246 12af multi 2.00 40

Issued to commemorate the 20th anniversary of UNESCO (United Nations Educational, Scientific and Cultural Organization).

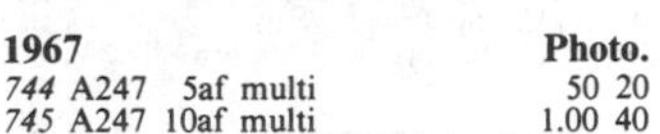

Zahir Shah and U.N. Emblem A247

1967 Photo.
744 A247 5af multi 50 20
745 A247 10af multi 1.00 40

Issued to commemorate the 20th anniversary of the U.N. International Organization for Refugees.

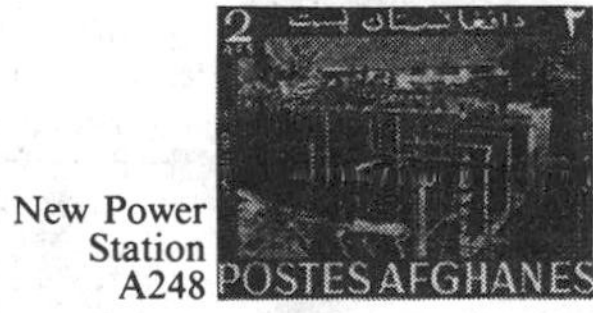

New Power Station A248

Designs: 5af, Carpet (vert.). 8af, Cement factory.

1967, Jan. 7 Photo. ***Perf. 13½x14***
746 A248 2af red lil & ol grn 12 8
747 A248 5af multi 30 25
748 A248 8af blk, dk bl & tan 50 35

Issued to publicize industrial development.

International Tourist Year Emblem A249

Designs: 6af, International Tourist Year emblem and map of Afghanistan.

1967, May 11 Photo. ***Perf. 12***
749 A249 2af yel, blk & lt bl 15 10
750 A249 6af bis brn, blk & lt bl 50 30
a. Souv. sheet of 3 1.00 1.00

Issued for International Tourist Year, 1967. No. 750a contains 2 imperf. stamps similar to Nos. 749-750 with black marginal inscription. Size: 110x70mm. Sold for 10af.

Power Dam, Dorunta A250

Macaque A251

Designs: 6af, Sirobi Dam (vert.). 8af, Reservoir at Jalalabad.

1967, July 2 Photo. ***Perf. 12***
751 A250 1af dk grn & lil 6 6
752 A250 6af red brn & grnsh bl 35 35
753 A250 8af plum & dk bl 50 50

Issued to publicize progress in agriculture through electricity.

1967, July 28 Photo. ***Perf. 12***

Designs: 6af, Striped hyena (horiz.). 12af, Persian gazelles (horiz.).

754 A251 2af dl yel & ind 12 12
755 A251 6af lt grn & sep 35 35
756 A251 12af lt bl & red brn 75 75

Pashtun Dancers — A252

1967, Sept. 1 Photo. ***Perf. 12***
757 A252 2af mag & vio 12 12

Issued for "Free Pashtunistan Day."

Retreat of British at Maiwand A253

Fireworks and U.N. Emblem A254

1967, Aug. 24
758 A253 1af dk brn & org ver 7 7
759 A253 2af dk brn & brt pink 12 12

Issued to commemorate Independence Day.

King Type of 1966.

1967, Oct. 15 Photo. ***Perf. 14x13½***
760 A245 2af brn red 12 10
761 A245 8af dk bl 50 25

Issued to honor King Mohammed Zahir Shah on his 53rd birthday.

1967, Oct. 24 Litho. ***Perf. 12***
762 A254 10af vio bl & multi 65 35

Issued for United Nations Day.

Greco-Roman Wrestlers A255

Said Jamalluddin Afghan A256

Design: 6af, Wrestlers (free style).

1967, Nov. 20 Photo.
763 A255 4af ol grn & rose lil 25 12

764 A255 6af dp car & brn 40 20
a. Souv. sheet of 2 1.10 1.10

Issued to publicize the 1968 Olympic Games. No. 764a contains 2 imperf. stamps similar to Nos. 763-764. Rose lilac marginal inscription and black control number. Size: 100x65mm.

1967, Nov. 27
765 A256 1af magenta 7 7
766 A256 5af brown 35 20

Issued to honor Said Jamalluddin Afghan, politician (1839-1897).

Bronze Vase, 11th-12th Centuries A257

WHO Emblem A258

Design: 7af, Bronze vase, Ghasnavide era, 11th-12th centuries.

1967, Dec. 23 Photo. *Perf. 12*
767 A257 3af lt grn & brn 18 15
768 A257 7af yel & sl grn 42 30
a. Souv. sheet of 2 1.25 1.25

No. 768a contains 2 imperf. stamps similar to Nos. 767-768. Slate green marginal inscription and black control number. Size: 65x100mm.

1968, Apr. 7 Photo. *Perf. 12*
769 A258 2af cit & brt bl 8 8
770 A258 7af rose & brt bl 28 22

Issued to commemorate the 20th anniversary of the World Health Organization.

Karakul A259

1968, May 20 Photo. *Perf. 12*
771 A259 1af yel & blk 6 5
772 A259 6af lt bl & blk 35 20
773 A259 12af ultra & dk brn 70 40

Issued for the Day of Agriculture.

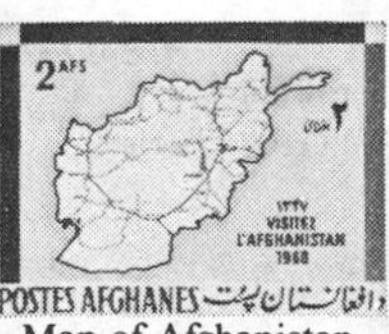

Map of Afghanistan A260

Victory Tower, Ghazni A261

Cinereous Vulture — A262

Design: 16af, Mausoleum, Ghazni.

1968, June 3 *Perf. 13½x14, 12*
774 A260 2af red, blk, lt bl & grn 12 8
775 A261 3af yel, dk brn & lt bl 18 10
776 A261 16af pink & multi 95 50

Issued for tourist publicity.

1968, July 3 *Perf. 12*

Birds: 6af, Eagle owl. 7af, Greater flamingoes.

777 A262 1af sky bl & multi 7 5
778 A262 6af yel & multi 45 20
779 A262 7af multi 50 30

Game of "Pegsticking" A263

Designs: 2af, Olympic flame and rings (vert.). 12af, Buzkashi.

1968, July 20 Photo. *Perf. 12*
780 A263 2af multi 12 7
781 A263 8af org & multi 50 30
782 A263 12af multi 75 45

19th Olympic Games, Mexico City, Oct. 12-27.

Flower-decked Armored Car — A264

1968, Aug. 23
783 A264 6af multi 40 20

Issued to commemorate Independence Day.

Flag of Pashtunistan A265

1968 Aug. 31 Photo. *Perf. 12*
784 A265 3af multi 25 10

Issued for "Free Pashtunistan Day."

Zahir Shah A266

Human Rights Flame A267

1968, Oct. 14 Photo. *Perf. 12*
785 A266 2af ultra 12 6
786 A266 8af brown 45 28

Issued to honor King Mohammed Zahir Shah on his 54th birthday.

1968, Oct. 24
787 A267 1af multi 10 5
788 A267 2af vio, bis & blk 25 6
789 A267 6af vio blk, bis & vio 50 20

Souvenir Sheet

Imperf

790 A267 10af plum, bis & red org 1.00 1.00

Issued for International Human Rights Year. No. 790 contains one stamp. Bister margin with plum inscription and black control number. Size: 100x65mm.

Maolana Djalalodine Balkhi A268

Kushan Mural A269

1968, Nov. 26 Photo. *Perf. 12*
791 A268 4af dk grn & mag 27 12

Maolana Djalalodine Balkhi (1207-1273), historian.

1969, Jan. 2 *Perf. 12*

Design: 3af, Jug shaped like female torso.

792 A269 1af dk grn, mar & yel 10 5
793 A269 3af vio, gray & mar 25 10
a. Souv. sheet of 2 40 40

Issued to publicize the archaeological finds at Bagram, 1st century B.C. to 2nd century A.D.

No. 793a contains 2 imperf. stamps similar to Nos. 792-793. Maroon marginal inscription and black control number. Size: 100x65mm.

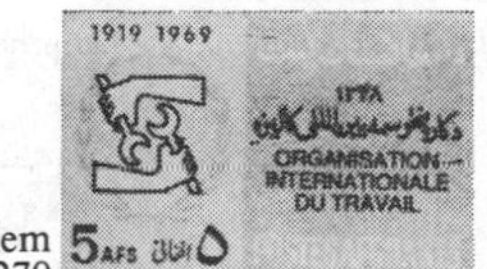

ILO Emblem A270

1969, Mar. 23 Photo. *Perf. 12*
794 A270 5af lt yel, lem & blk 30 18
795 A270 8af lt bl, grnsh bl & blk 50 30

Issued for the 50th anniversary of the International Labor Organization.

Arms Type of 1939

1969, May (?) Typo.
795A A79 100p dk grn 8 5
795B A79 150p dp brn 10 6

Nos. 795A-795B were normally used as newspaper stamps.

Badakhshan Scene A271

Designs: 2af, Map of Afghanistan. 7af, Three men on mules ascending the Pamir Mountains.

1969, July 6 Photo. *Perf. 13½x14*
796 A271 2af ocher & multi 15 6
797 A271 4af multi 25 12
798 A271 7af multi 55 22
a. Souv. sheet of 3 1.10 1.10

Issued for tourist publicity. No. 798a contains 3 imperf. stamps similar to Nos. 796-798. Black marginal inscription and control number. Size: 136x90½mm. Sold for 15af.

Bust, from Hadda Treasure, 3rd-5th Centuries A272

Zahir Shah and Queen Humeira A273

Designs: 5af, Vase and jug. 10af, Statue of crowned woman. 5af and 10af from Bagram treasure, 1st-2nd centuries.

1969, Aug. 3 Photo. *Perf. 14x13½*
799 A272 1af ol grn & gold 5 5
800 A272 5af pur & gold 20 16
801 A272 10af dp bl & gold 40 32

1969, Aug. 23 *Perf. 12*
802 A273 5af gold, dk bl & red brn 35 20
803 A273 10af gold, dp lil & bl grn 65 35

Issued to commemorate Independence Day.

Map of Pashtunistan and Rising Sun — A274

1969, Aug. 31 Typo. *Perf. 10½*
804 A274 2af lt bl & red 12 6

Issued for "Free Pashtunistan Day."

Zahir Shah — A275

1969, Oct. 14 Photo. *Perf. 12*
Portrait in Natural Colors
805 A275 2af dk brn & gold 15 6
806 A275 6af brn & gold 45 20

Issued to honor King Mohammed Zahir Shah on his 55th birthday.

U.N. Emblem and Flag of Afghanistan — A276

1969, Oct. 24 Litho. *Perf. 13½*
807 A276 5af bl & multi 27 16

Issued for United Nations Day.

ITU Emblem — A277

Wild Boar — A278

1969, Nov. 12
808 A277 6af ultra & multi 30 20
809 A277 12af rose & multi 60 35

Issued for World Telecommunications Day.

1969, Dec. 7 Photo. *Perf. 12*

Designs: 1af, Long-tailed porcupine. 8af, Red deer.

810 A278 1af yel & multi 6 5
811 A278 3af bl & multi 18 10
812 A278 8af pink & multi 50 25

Man's First Footprints on Moon, and Earth — A279

1969, Dec. 28 *Perf. 13½x14*

813 A279 1af yel grn & multi 6 5
814 A279 3af yel & multi 17 10
815 A279 6af bl & multi 30 20
816 A279 10af rose & multi 50 32

Moon landing. See note after Algeria No. 427.

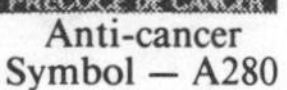

Anti-cancer Symbol — A280

Mirza Abdul Quader Bedel — A281

1970, Apr. 7 **Photo.** *Perf. 14*

817 A280 2af dk grn & rose car 15 6
818 A280 6af dk bl & rose cl 40 20

Issued to publicize the fight against cancer.

1970, May 6 *Perf. 14x13½*

819 A281 5af multi 27 15

Issued for the 250th anniversary of the death of Mirza Abdul Quader Bedel (1643-1720), poet.

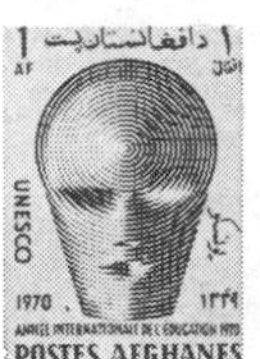

Education Year Emblem A282

Mother and Child A283

1970, June 7 **Photo.** *Perf. 12*

820 A282 1af black 6 5
821 A282 6af dp rose 35 20
822 A282 12af green 75 35

International Education Year 1970.

1970, June 15 *Perf. 13½*

823 A283 6af yel & multi 27 20

Issued for Mother's Day.

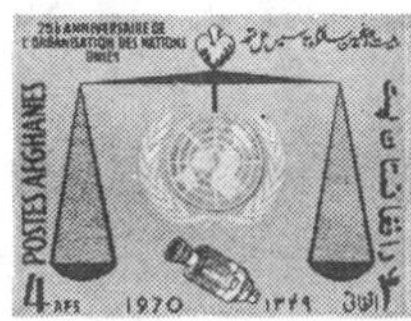

U.N. Emblem, Scales of Justice, Spacecraft A284

1970, June 26

824 A284 4af yel, dk bl & dp bl 20 12
825 A284 6af pink, dk bl & brt bl 35 20

25th anniversary of United Nations.

Mosque of the Amir of the two Swords, Kabul A285

Designs: 2af, Map of Afghanistan. 7af, Arch of Paghman.

1970, July 6 *Perf. 12*

Size: 30½x30½mm.

826 A285 2af lt bl, blk & cit 12 6

Size: 36x26mm.

827 A285 3af pink & multi 18 10
828 A285 7af yel & multi 42 22

Issued for tourist publicity.

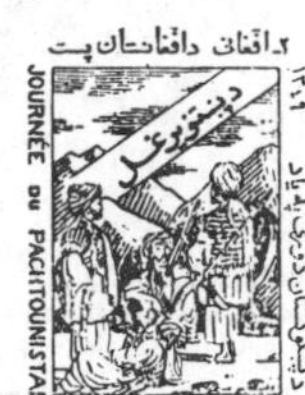

Zahir Shah Reviewing Troops A286

1970, Aug. 23 **Photo.** *Perf. 13½*

829 A286 8af multi 60 25

Issued to commemorate Independence Day.

Pathans — A287

1970, Aug. 31 **Typo.** *Perf. 10½*

830 A287 2af ultra & red 12 6

Issued for "Free Pashtunistan Day."

Quail — A288

Designs: 4af, Golden eagle. 6af, Ring-necked pheasant.

1970, Sept. **Photo.** *Perf. 12*

831 A288 2af multi 8 6
832 A288 4af multi 20 16
833 A288 6af multi 30 25

Zahir Shah A289

Red Crescents A290

1970, Oct. 14 **Photo.** *Perf. 14x13½*

834 A289 3af grn & vio 20 10
835 A289 7af dk bl & vio brn 60 22

Issued to honor King Mohammed Zahir Shah on his 56th birthday.

1970, Oct. 16 **Typo.** *Perf. 10½*

836 A290 2af blk, gold & red 12 6

Issued for the Red Crescent Society.

U. N. Emblem and Charter A291

1970, Oct. 24 **Photo.** *Perf. 14*

837 A291 1af gold & multi 10 5
838 A291 5af gold & multi 20 16

United Nations Day.

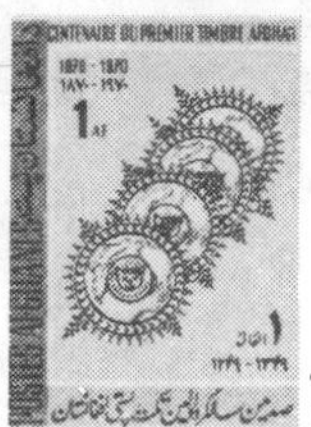

Tiger Heads of 1871 — A292

1970, Nov. 10 *Perf. 12*

839 A292 1af sal, lt grnsh bl & blk 5 5
840 A292 4af lt ultra, yel & blk 16 12
841 A292 12af lil, lt bl & blk 48 35

Issued to commemorate the centenary of the first Afghan postage stamps. The postal service was established in 1870, but the first stamps were issued in May, 1871.

Globe and Waves A293

1971, May 17 **Photo.** *Perf. 13½*

842 A293 12af grn, blk & bl 60 35

3rd World Telecommunications Day.

Callimorpha Principalis A294

Designs: 3af, Epizygaenella species. 5af, Parnassius autocrator.

1971, May 30 *Perf. 13½x14*

843 A294 1af ver & multi 5 5
844 A294 3af yel & multi 20 15
845 A294 5af ultra & multi 30 25

"UNESCO" and Half of Ancient Kushan Statue — A295

1971, June 26 **Photo.** *Perf. 13½*

846 A295 6af ocher & vio 40 20
847 A295 10af lt bl & mar 65 30

UNESCO-sponsored International Kushani Seminar.

Tughra and Independence Monument — A296

1971, Aug. 23

848 A296 7af rose red & multi 40 22
849 A296 9af red org & multi 65 28

Independence Day.

Pashtunistan Square, Kabul — A297

1971, Aug. 31 **Typo.** *Perf. 10½*

850 A297 5af dp rose lil 27 15

"Free Pashtunistan Day."

Zahir Shah — A298

1971, Oct. 14 **Photo.** *Perf. 12½x12*

851 A298 9af lt grn & multi 40 28
852 A298 17af yel & multi 75 55

57th birthday of King Mohammed Zahir Shah.

Map of Afghanistan, Red Crescent, Various Activities — A299

1971, Oct. 16 *Perf. 14x13½*

853 A299 8af lt bl, red, grn & blk 45 25

For Afghan Red Crescent Society.

Equality Year Emblem A300

1971, Oct. 24 *Perf. 12*

854 A300 24af brt bl 1.25 70

International Year Against Racial Discrimination and United Nations Day.

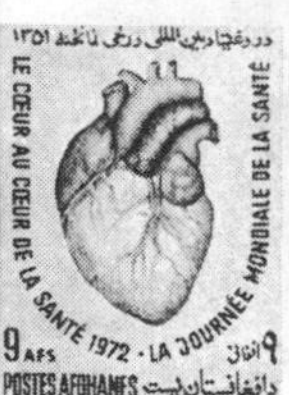
"Your Heart is your Health" — A301

Tulip — A302

1972, Apr. 7 Photo. Perf. 14

855 A301 9af pale yel & multi 36 28
856 A301 12af gray & multi 48 35

World Health Day.

1972, June 5 Photo. Perf. 14

Designs: 10af, Rock partridge (horiz.). 12af, Lynx (horiz.). 18af, Allium stipitatum (flower).

857 A302 7af grn & multi 28 22
858 A302 10af bl & multi 40 32
859 A302 12af lt grn & multi 48 35
860 A302 18af bl grn & multi 72 60

Buddhist Shrine, Hadda A302a

Designs: 7af, Greco-Bactrian animal seal, 250 B.C. 9af, Greco-Oriental temple, Ai-Khanoum, 3rd-2nd centuries B.C.

1972, July 16 Photo. Perf. 12

861 A302a 3af brn & dl bl 12 9
862 A302a 7af rose cl & dl grn 28 22
863 A302a 9af grn & lil 36 30

Tourist publicity.

King and Queen Reviewing Parade — A303

1972, Aug. 23 Photo. Perf. 13½

864 A303 25af gold & multi 4.00 1.00

Independence Day.

Used later with king and queen part removed.

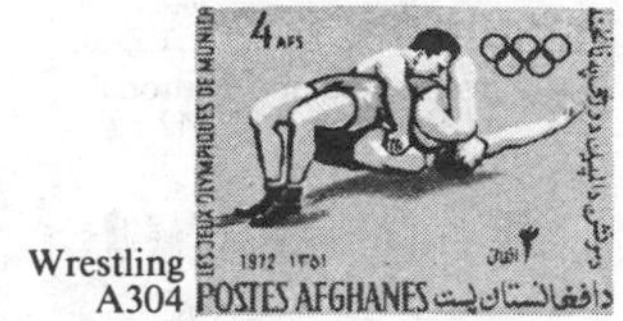
Wrestling A304

Designs: 8af, Like 4af. 10af, 19af, 21af, Wrestling, different hold.

1972, Aug. 26

865 A304 4af ol bis & multi 20 12
866 A304 8af lt bl & multi 40 25
867 A304 10af yel grn & multi 50 32
868 A304 19af multi 90 40
869 A304 21af lil & multi 1.00 45
a. Souv. sheet of 5 3.25 3.25
Nos. 865-869 (5) 3.00 1.54

20th Olympic Games, Munich, Aug. 26-Sept. 11. No. 869a contains 5 imperf. stamps similar to Nos. 865-869. Olive bister marginal inscription and ornament, black control number. Size: 159x110mm. Sold for 60af.

Pathan and View of Tribal Territory — A305

Zahir Shah — A306

1972, Aug. 31 Perf. 12½x12

870 A305 5af ultra & multi 27 15

Pashtunistan day.

1972, Oct. 14 Photo. Perf. 14x13½

871 A306 7af gold, blk & Prus bl 1.50 30
872 A306 14af gold, blk & lt brn 3.00 50

58th birthday of King Mohammed Zahir Shah.

City Destroyed by Earthquake, Refugees — A307

1972, Oct. 16 Perf. 13½

873 A307 7af lt bl, red & blk 40 22

For Afghan Red Crescent Society.

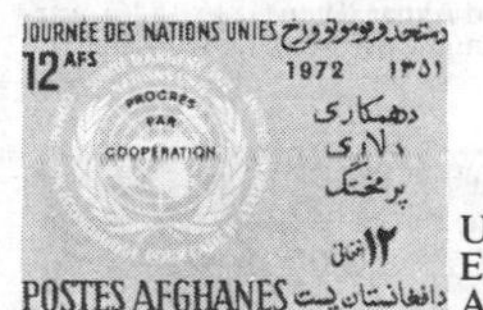
U.N. Emblem A308

1972, Oct. 24

874 A308 12af lt ultra & blk 65 35

United Nations Economic Commission for Asia and the Far East (ECAFE), 25th anniversary.

Ceramics A309

Designs: 9af, Leather coat (vert.). 12af, Metal ware (vert.). 16af, Inlaid artifacts.

1972, Dec. 10 Photo. Perf. 12

875 A309 7af gold & multi 42 22
876 A309 9af gold & multi 55 28
877 A309 12af gold & multi 70 35
878 A309 16af gold & multi 1.00 50
a. Souvenir sheet of 4 2.75 2.75

Handicraft industries. No. 878a contains 4 imperf. stamps similar to Nos. 875-878. Gold marginal inscription and black control number. Size: 109x109mm. Sold for 45af.

WMO and National Emblems — A310

1973, Apr. 3 Photo. Perf. 14

879 A310 7af lt lil & dk grn 42 22
880 A310 14af lt bl & dp cl 85 45

Centenary of international meteorological cooperation.

Abu Rayhan al-Biruni — A311

Family — A312

1973, June 16 Photo. Perf. 13½

881 A311 10af multi 55 32

Millennium of birth (973-1048), philosopher and mathematician.

1973, June 30 Photo. Perf. 13½

882 A312 9af org & red lil 50 30

International Family Planning Federation, 21st anniversary.

Republic

Impeyan Pheasant A313

Birds: 9af, Great crested grebe. 12af, Himalayan snow cock.

1973, July 29 Photo. Perf. 12x12½

883 A313 8af yel & multi 65 25
884 A313 9af bl & multi 90 30
885 A313 12af multi 1.25 35

Stylized Buzkashi Horseman A314

1973, Aug. Perf. 13½

886 A314 8af black 32 25

Tourist publicity.

Fireworks A315

1973, Aug. 23 Photo. Perf. 12

887 A315 12af multi 48 35

55th Independence Day.

Lake Abassine, Pashtunistan Flag — A316

1973, Aug. 31 Perf. 14x13½

888 A316 9af multi 50 30

Pashtunistan Day.

Red Crescent — A317

1973, Oct. 16 Perf. 13½

889 A317 10af red, blk & gold 60 32

Red Crescent Society.

Kemal Ataturk A318

1973, Oct. 28 Litho. Perf. 10½

890 A318 1af blue 6 5
891 A318 7af redsh brn 42 22

50th anniversary of the Turkish Republic.

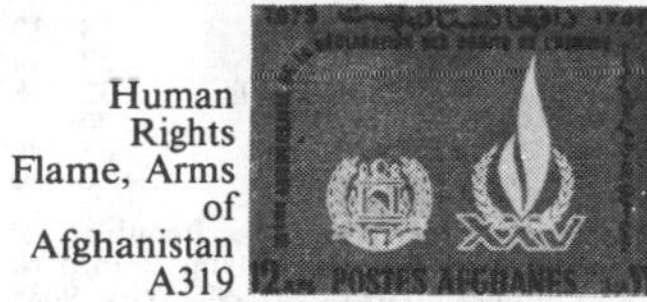
Human Rights Flame, Arms of Afghanistan A319

1973, Dec. 10 Photo. Perf. 12

892 A319 12af sil, blk & lt bl 45 35

25th anniversary of the Universal Declaration of Human Rights.

Asiatic Black Bears A320

1974, Mar. 26 Litho. Perf. 12

893 A320 5af *shown* 18 15
894 A320 7af *Afghan hound* 25 22
895 A320 10af *Persian goat* 35 28
896 A320 12af *Leopard* 45 35
a. Souvenir sheet of 4 1.25 1.25

No. 896a contains 4 imperf. stamps similar to Nos. 893-896. Magenta border and black marginal inscription. Size: 120x100mm.

The indexes in each volume of the Scott Catalogue contain many listings which help to identify stamps.

Worker and Farmer A321

Perf. 13½x12½

1974, May 1 **Photo.**
897 A321 9af rose red & multi 40 25

International Labor Day, May 1.

Independence Monument and Arch — A322

1974, May 27 **Photo.** ***Perf. 12***
898 A322 4af bl & multi 12 10
899 A322 11af gold & multi 35 30

56th Independence Day.

Arms of Afghanistan and Symbol of Cooperation A323

Pres. Mohammad Daoud Khan — A324

Designs: 5af, Flag of Republic of Afghanistan. 15af, Soldiers and coat of arms of the Republic.

1974, July 25 ***Perf. 13½x12½, 14***
Sizes: 4af, 15af, 36x22mm.; 5af, 7af, 36x26, 26x36mm.
900 A323 4af multi 18 10
901 A323 5af multi 22 12
902 A324 7af grn, brn & blk 32 18
a. Souvenir sheet of 2 70 70
903 A323 15af multi 65 40
a. Souvenir sheet of 2 1.00 1.00

First anniversary of the Republic of Afghanistan. No. 902a contains 2 imperf. stamps similar to Nos. 901-902, No. 903a contains 2 imperf. stamps similar to Nos. 900 and 903. Both sheets have yellow margins, black inscriptions and control numbers. Sizes: No. 902a, 99x99mm., No. 903a, 120x80mm.

Lesser Spotted Eagle A325

Birds: 6af, White-fronted goose, ruddy shelduck and gray-lag goose. 11af, European coots and European crane.

1974, Aug. 6 **Photo.** ***Perf. 13½x13***
904 A325 1af car rose & multi 6 5
905 A325 6af bl & multi 40 18
906 A325 11af yel & multi 80 40

Nos. 904-906 printed se-tenant.

A particular stamp may be scarce, but if few collectors want it, its market value may remain relatively low.

Flags of Pashtunistan and Afghanistan A326

1974, Aug. 31 **Photo.** ***Perf. 14***
907 A326 5af multi 27 12

Pashtunistan Day.

Coat of Arms A327

1974, Oct. 9
908 A327 7af gold, grn & blk 22 18

Centenary of Universal Postal Union.

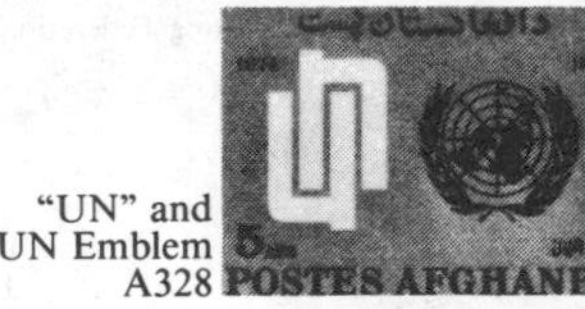

"UN" and UN Emblem A328

1974, Oct. 24 **Photo.** ***Perf. 14***
909 A328 5af lt ultra & dk bl 27 12

United Nations Day.

Minaret of Jam — A329

Buddha, Hadda — A330

Design: 14af, Lady riding griffin, 2nd century, Bagram.

1975, May 5 **Photo.** ***Perf. 13½***
910 A329 7af multi 22 15
911 A330 14af multi 44 30
912 A330 15af multi 48 30
a. Souvenir sheet of 3 1.50 1.50

South Asia Tourism Year 1975.
No. 912a contains 3 imperf. stamps similar to Nos. 910-912. Tourism Year emblem in margin and black control number. Size: 130x90mm.

New Flag of Afghanistan A331

1975, May 27 **Photo.** ***Perf. 12***
913 A331 16af multi 75 35

57th Independence Day.

Celebrating Crowd A332

1975, July 17 **Photo.** ***Perf. 13½***
914 A332 9af bl & multi 42 20
915 A332 12af car & multi 55 28

Second anniversary of the Republic.

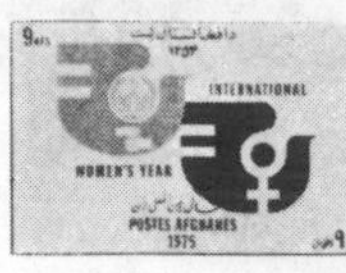

Women's Year Emblems A333

1975, Aug. 24 **Photo.** ***Perf. 12***
916 A333 9af car, lt bl & blk 28 22

International Women's Year 1975.

Pashtunistan Flag, Sun Rising Over Mountains A334

Mohammed Akbar Khan A335

1975, Aug. 31 ***Perf. 13½***
917 A334 10af multi 30 25

Pashtunistan Day.

1976, Feb. 4 **Photo.** ***Perf. 14***
918 A335 15af lt brn & multi 45 35

Mohammed Akbar Khan (1816-1846), warrior son of Amir Dost Mohammed Khan.

Pres. Mohammad Daoud Khan
A336 A337

1974-78 **Photo.** ***Perf. 14***
919 A336 10af multi 70 28
920 A336 16af multi ('78) 2.75 *1.10*
921 A336 19af multi 1.10 55
922 A336 21af multi 1.40 60
923 A336 22af multi ('78) 4.00 *2.25*
924 A336 30af multi ('78) 5.25 *3.00*
925 A337 50af multi('75) 3.00 1.40
926 A337 100af multi('75) 6.00 2.75
Nos. 919-926 (8) 21.35 10.73

Arms of Republic, Independence Monument — A338

1976, June 1 **Photo.** ***Perf. 14***
927 A338 22af bl & multi 65 45

58th Independence Day.

Flag Raising — A339

1976, July 17 **Photo.** ***Perf. 14***
928 A339 30af multi 90 75

Republic Day.

Mountain Peaks and Flag of Pashtunistan A340

1976, Aug. 31 **Photo.** ***Perf. 14***
929 A340 16af multi 48 38

Pashtunistan Day.

Coat of Arms A340a

1976, Sept. **Litho.** ***Perf. 11 Rough***
929A A340a 25p salmon 25 15
930 A340a 50p lt grn 25 15
931 A340a 1af ultra 25 15

Flag and Views on Open Book A341

1977, May 27 **Photo.** ***Perf. 14***
937 A341 20af grn & multi 60 50

59th Independence Day.

Pres. Daoud and National Assembly — A342

President Taking Oath of Office A343

Designs: 10af, Inaugural address. 18af, Promulgation of Constitution.

1977, June 22
938 A342 7af multi 65 45
939 A343 8af multi 70 60
940 A343 10af multi 90 75
941 A342 18af multi 1.65 1.25
a. Souvenir sheet of 4 3.00 3.00

Election of first President and promulgation of Constitution. No. 941a contains 4 imperf. stamps similar to Nos. 938-941. Black marginal inscription and control number. Size: 135x105mm.

Jamalluddin Medal A344

1977, July 6 Photo. *Perf. 14*
942 A344 12af bl, blk & gold 35 30

Sajo Jamalluddin Afghani, reformer, 80th death anniversary.

Afghanistan Flag over Crowd — A345

1977, July 17
943 A345 22af multi 65 55

Dancers, Fountain, Pashtunistan Flag — A346

1977, Aug. 31
944 A346 30af multi 90 75

Pashtunistan Day.

Arms and Carrier Pigeon A346a

1977, Oct. 30 Litho. *Perf. 11*
944A A346a 1af blk & bl 5 5

Members of Parliament Congratulating Pres. Daoud — A347

1978, Feb. 5 Litho. *Perf. 14*
945 A347 20af multi 1.75

Election of first president, first anniversary.

Map of Afghanistan, UPU Emblem A348

1978, Apr. 1 Photo. *Perf. 14*
946 A348 10af grn, blk & gold 30 25

50th anniversary of Afghanistan's membership in Universal Postal Union.

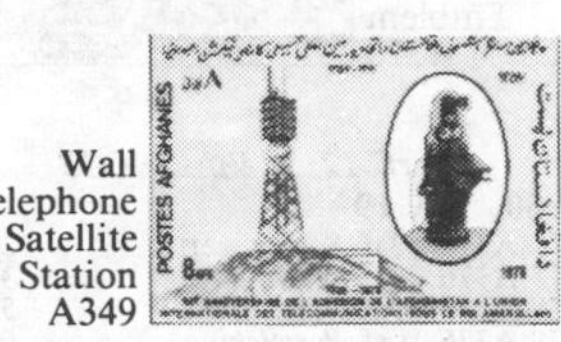

Wall Telephone and Satellite Station A349

1978, Apr. 12
947 A349 8af multi 24 20

50th anniversary of Afghanistan's membership in International Telecommunications Union.

Democratic Republic

Arrows Pointing to Crescent, Cross and Lion — A350

1978, July 6 Litho. *Perf. 11 Rough*
948 A350 3af black 10 6

50th anniversary of Afghani Red Crescent Society.

Khalq Party Emblem A350a

1978, Aug. Litho. *Perf. 11*
948A A350a 1af rose red & gold 5 5
948B A350a 4af rose red & gold 12 8

Arch A351

1978, Aug. 19 *Perf. 14*
949 A351 16af Bamian Buddha 45 40
949A A351 22af shown 65 55
949B A351 30af Hazara Women 1.20 90

Democratic Republic of Afghanistan.

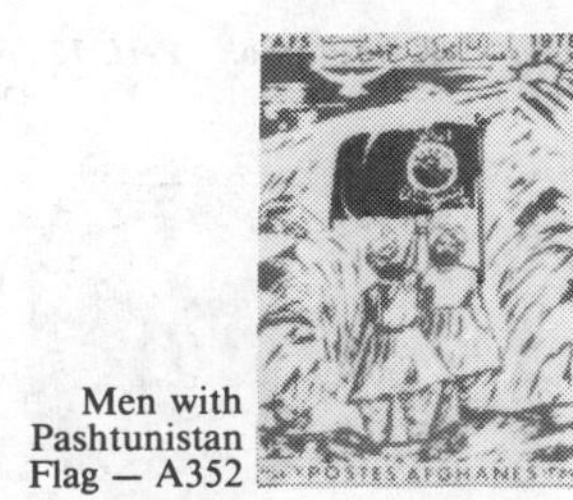

Men with Pashtunistan Flag — A352

Coat of Arms and Emblems — A353

1978, Aug. 31 *Perf. 11 Rough*
950 A352 7af ultra & red 22 16

Pashtunistan Day.

1978, Sept. 8 *Perf. 11*
951 A353 20af rose red 60 50

World Literacy Day.

A354

Perf. 11½ Rough
1978, Oct. 25 Litho.
952 A354 18af lt grn 55 45

Hero of Afghanistan.

Khalq Party Flag — A355

1978, Oct. 19 Photo. *Perf. 11½*
953 A355 8af blk, red & gold 24 20
954 A355 9af blk, red & gold 30 22

"The mail serving the people."

Nour Mohammad Taraki — A356

1979, Jan. 1 Litho. *Perf. 12*
955 A356 12af multi 35 10

Nour Mohammad Taraki, founder of People's Democratic Party of Afghanistan, installation as president.

Woman Breaking Chain — A357

1979, Mar. 8 Litho. *Perf. 11*
956 A357 14af red & ultra *1.50* 50

Women's Day. Inscribed "POSSTES."

Map of Afghanistan, Census Emblem — A358

1979, Mar. 25 Litho. *Perf. 12*
957 A358 3af multi 15 10

First comprehensive population census.

Farmers A359

1979, Mar. 21
958 A359 1af multi 15 10

Agricultural advances.

Pres. Taraki Reading First Issue of Khalq — A360

1979, Apr. 11 *Perf. 12½x12*
959 A360 2af multi 10 8

Khalq, newspaper of People's Democratic Republic of Afghanistan.

Pres. Noor Mohammad Taraki A361

Plaza with Tank Monument and Fountain — A362

House where Revolution Started — A363

Design: 12af, House where 1st Khalq Party Congress was held.

Perf. 12, 12½x12 (A362)
1979, Apr. 27 Litho.
959A A353 50p Taraki, tank 5 5
960 A361 4af multi 12 10
961 A362 5af multi 18 12
962 A363 6af multi 20 18
963 A363 12af multi 40 35
Nos. 959A-963 (5) 85 72

1st anniversary of revolution.

Carpenter and Blacksmith A364

1979, May 1 ***Perf. 12***
964 A364 10af multi 30 25

Int'l Labor Day.

Children, Flag and Map of Afghanistan — A366

1979, June 1 Litho. ***Perf. 12½x12***
966 A366 16af multi 48 40

International Year of the Child.

Doves Circling Asia in Globe A366a

1979 Litho. ***Perf. 11x10½***
966A A366a 2af red & bl 6 5

Armed Afghans, Kabul Memorial and Arch — A367

Pashtunistan Citizens, Flag — A368

1979, Aug. 19 Litho. ***Perf. 12***
967 A367 30af multi 90 75

60th anniv. of independence.

1979, Aug. 31
968 A368 9 af multi 28 22

Pashtunistan Day.

UPU Day — A369

1979, Oct. 9 Litho. ***Perf. 12***
969 A369 15af multi 45 38

Tombstone — A369a

1979, Oct. 25 Litho. ***Perf. 12½x12***
969A A369a 22af multi 65 45

International Women's Day — A370

1980, Mar. 8 Litho. ***Perf. 12***
970 A370 8af multi *1.00*

Farmers' Day — A371

1980, Mar. 21 Litho. ***Perf. 11½x12***
971 A371 2af multi 10 8

Non-smoker and Smoker A372

1980, Apr. 7 ***Perf. 11½***
972 A372 5af multi 15 12

Anti-smoking campaign; World Health Day.

Lenin, 110th Birth Anniversary A373

1980, Apr. 22 ***Perf. 12x12½***
973 A373 12af multi 35 30

People and Fist on Map of Afghanistan A374

1980, Apr. 27 Litho. ***Perf. 12½x12***
974 A374 1af multi 5 5

Saur Revolution, 2nd anniversary.

International Workers' Solidarity Day — A375

1980, May 1
975 A375 9af multi 28 22

Wrestling, Moscow '80 Emblem A376

Perf. 12x12½, 12½x12

1980, July 19
976 A376 3af *Soccer*, vert. 20 8
977 A376 6af *shown* 35 15
978 A376 9af *Buzkashi* 55 22
979 A376 10af *Pegsticking* 60 25

22nd Summer Olympic Games, Moscow, July 19-Aug. 3.

61st Anniversary of Independence — A377

1980, Aug. 19 Litho. ***Perf. 12½x12***
980 A377 3af multi 10 8

Pashtunistan Day — A378

1980, Aug. 30
981 A378 25af multi 80 65

International U.P.U. Day — A379

1980, Oct. 9 Litho. ***Perf. 12½x12***
982 A379 20af multi 60 50

International Women's Day — A381

1981, Mar. 9 Litho. ***Perf. 12½x12***
984 A381 15af multi 45 38

Farmers' Day — A382

1981, Mar. 20 Litho. ***Perf. 12½x12***
985 A382 1af multi 5 5

Bighorn Mountain Sheep (Protected Species) A383

1981, Apr. 4 ***Perf. 12x12½***
986 A383 12af multi 36 30

Saur Revolution, 3rd Anniversary A384

International Workers' Solidarity Day — A385

1981, Apr. 27 ***Perf. 11***
987 A384 50p brown 5 5

1981, May 1 ***Perf. 12½x12***
988 A385 10af multi 30 25

13th World Telecommunications Day — A387

Intl. Children's Day — A388

1981, May 17 Litho. ***Perf. 12½x12***
990 A387 9af multi 28 22

1981, June 1 ***Perf. 12x12½***
991 A388 15af multi 45 38

People's Independence Monument 62nd Anniv. of Independence — A389

1981, Aug. 19
992 A389 4af multi 12 10

Pashtunistan Day — A390

1981, Aug. 31 **Litho.** ***Perf. 12***
992A A390 2af multi 6 5

Intl. Tourism Day — A391

1981, Sept. 27 ***Perf. 12½x12***
993 A391 5af multi 15 12

World Food Day — A392

1981, Oct. 16
995 A392 7af multi 22 15

Asia-Africa Solidarity Meeting A393

1981, Nov. 18 **Litho.** ***Perf. 11***
996 A393 8af blue 24 20

Struggle Against Apartheid A394

1300th Anniv. of Bulgaria A395

1981, Dec. 1 ***Perf. 12½x12***
997 A394 4af multi 12 10

1981, Dec. 9 ***Perf. 12x12½***
998 A395 20af multi 60 50

Buzkashi Game A395a

1980 **Photo.** ***Perf. 14***
998A A395a 50af multi 3.00 1.00
998B A395a 100af multi 5.00 2.00

Intl. Women's Day — A396

1982, Mar. 8 **Litho.** ***Perf. 12***
999 A396 6af multi 18 15

Farmers' Day — A397

1982, Mar. 21
1000 A397 4af multi 12 10

Rhubarb Plant — A398

Saur Revolution, 4th Anniv. — A399

Designs: Various local plants.

1982, Apr. 9 **Litho.** ***Perf. 12***
1001 A398 3af Judas trees 10 8
1002 A398 4af Rose of Sharan 12 10
1003 A398 16af shown 50 40

1982, Apr. 27
1004 A399 1af multi 5 5

George Dimitrov (1882-1947), First Prime Minister of Bulgaria — A400

Intl. Workers' Solidarity Day — A401

1982, Apr. 30
1005 A400 30af multi 90 75

1982, May 1
1006 A401 10af multi 30 25

Storks — A402

1982, May 31
1007 A402 6af shown 20 15
1008 A402 11af Nightingales 35 28

Hedgehogs A403

1982, July 6 **Litho.** ***Perf. 12***
1009 A403 3af shown 10 8
1010 A403 14af Cobra 45 35

See Nos. 1020-1022.

63rd Anniv. of Independence — A404

1982, Aug. 19
1011 A404 20af multi 60 50

Pashtunistan Day — A405

1982, Aug. 31
1012 A405 32af multi 1.00 80

World Tourism Day — A406

1982, Sept. 27 **Litho.** ***Perf. 12***
1013 A406 9af multi 30 22

UPU Day — A407

1982, Oct. 9
1014 A407 4af multi 12 10

World Food Day — A408

1982, Oct. 16
1015 A408 9af multi 30 22

37th Anniv. of UN — A409

1982, Oct. 24
1016 A409 15af multi 45 38

ITU Plenipotentiaries Conference, Nairobi, Sept. — A410

1982, Oct. 26
1017 A410 8af multi 25 20

TB Bacillus Centenary A411

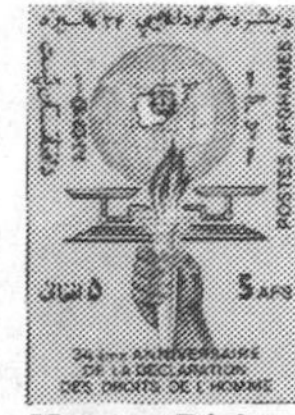

Human Rights Declaration, 34th Anniv. A412

1982, Nov. 24 **Litho.** ***Perf. 12***
1018 A411 7af multi 22 18

1982, Dec. 10
1019 A412 5af multi 15 12

Animal Type of 1982

1982, Dec. 16
1020 A403 2af Lions 6 5
1021 A403 7af Donkeys 22 18
1022 A403 12af Marmots, vert. 36 28

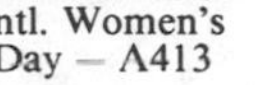

Intl. Women's Day — A413

Mir Alicher Nawai Research Decade — A414

1983, Mar. 8
1023 A413 3af multi 10 8

1983, Mar. 19
1024 A414 22af multi 70 50

Farmers' Day — A415

1983, Mar. 21 **Litho.** ***Perf. 12***
1025 A415 10af multi 30 25

5th Anniv. of Saur Revolution A416

1983, Apr. 27 **Litho.** ***Perf. 12***
1026 A416 15af multi 45 38

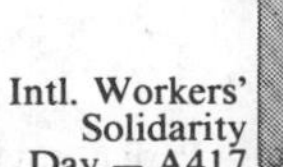

Intl. Workers' Solidarity Day — A417

1983, May 1
1027 A417 2af multi 60 50

World Communications Year — A418

1983, May 17

1028	A418	4af Modes of communication	12	10
1029	A418	11af Building	34	28

Intl. Children's Day — A419

1983, June 1 Litho. *Perf. 12*
1030 A419 25af Multi

2nd Anniv. of National Front — A420

1983, June 15
1031 A420 1af multi

Local Butterflies A421

Various butterflies. 9af, 13af vert.

1983, July 6
1032 A421 9af multi
1033 A421 13af multi
1034 A421 21af multi

Struggle Against Apartheid — A422

1983, Aug. 1 Litho. *Perf. 12*
1035 A422 10 af multi

64th Anniv of Independence — A423

1983, Aug. 19
1036 A423 6 af multi

Parliament House A423a

1983, Sept. Litho. *Perf. 12*
1036A A423a 50af shown
1036B A423a 100af Afghan Woman, Camel

A424

World Tourism Day — A425

1983, Sept. 27 Litho. *Perf. 12*
1037 A424 5af shown
1038 A425 7af shown
1039 A424 12af Golden statues
1040 A425 16af Stone carving

World Communications Year — A426

1983, Oct. 9 Litho. *Perf. 12*
1041 A426 14af Dish antenna, dove
1042 A426 15af shown

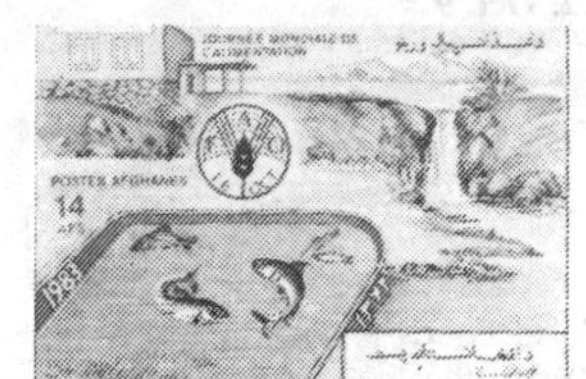
World Food Day — A427

1983, Oct. 16 Litho. *Perf. 12*
1043 A427 14af multi

Boxing A428

1983, Nov. 1 Litho. *Perf. 12*
1044 A428 1af Running
1045 A428 18af shown
1046 A428 21af Wrestling

Pashtunistan Day — A428a

1983, Litho. *Perf. 12*
1046A A428a 3af Pathans Waving Flag

Handicrafts A429

1983, Nov. 22
1047 A429 2af Jewelry
1048 A429 8af Stone ashtrays, dishes
1049 A429 19af Furniture
1050 A429 30af Leather goods

U.N. Declaration of Human Rights, 35th Anniv. A430

1983, Dec. 10 Litho. *Perf. 12*
1051 A430 20af multi

Kabul Polytechnical Institute, 20th Anniv. — A431

1983, Dec. 28 *Perf. 12½x12*
1052 A431 30af multi

1984 Winter Olympics A432

1984, Jan. *Perf. 12*
1053 A432 5af Figure skating
1054 A432 9af Skiing
1055 A432 11af Speed skating
1056 A432 15af Hockey
1057 A432 18af Biathlon
1058 A432 20af Ski jumping
1059 A432 22af Bobsledding

Intl. Women's Day — A433

1984, Mar. 8
1060 A433 4af multi

Farmers' Day A434

Various agricultural scenes.

1984, Mar. 21 Litho. *Perf. 12*

1061	A434	2af multi	5
1062	A434	4af multi	16
1063	A434	7af multi	28
1064	A434	9af multi	36
1065	A434	15af multi	60
1066	A434	18af multi	72
1067	A434	20af multi	80
		Nos. 1061-1067 (7)	2.97

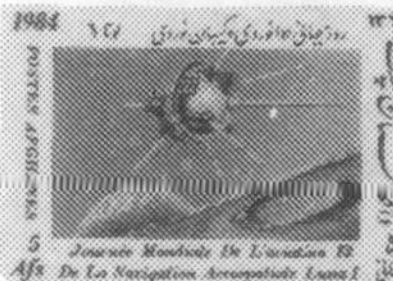
World Aviation Day A435

1984, Apr. 12

1068	A435	5af Luna 1	20
1069	A435	8af Luna 2	32
1070	A435	11af Luna 3	45
1071	A435	17af Apollo 11	68
1072	A435	22af Soyuz 6	90
1073	A435	28af Soyuz 7	1.15
1074	A435	34af Soyuz 6, 7, 8	1.35
		Nos. 1068-1074 (7)	5.05

Souvenir Sheet
Perf. 12x12½

1075 A435 25af S. Koroliov 1.00

No. 1075 contains one stamp (30x41mm.); multicolored margin continues design. Size: 66x88mm.

Saur Revolution, 6th Anniv. A436

1984, Apr. 27 *Perf. 12*
1076 A436 3af multi 12

65th Anniv. of Independence — A437

1984, Aug. 19 Litho. *Perf. 12*
1077 A437 6af multi 24

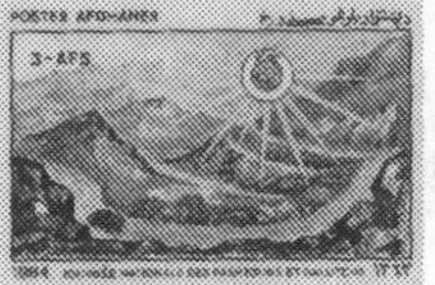
Pashto's and Balutchi's Day A438

1984, Aug. 31
1078 A438 3af Symbolic sun, tribal terr. 12

Wildlife A439

Perf. 12½x12, 12x12½
1984, May 5 Litho.

1079	A439	1af Cape hunting dog, vert.	5
1080	A439	2af Argali sheep, vert.	8
1081	A439	6af Przewalski's horse	22
1082	A439	8af Wild boar, vert.	30
1083	A439	17af Snow leopard	65
1084	A439	19af Tiger	68
1085	A439	22af Indian elephant, vert.	85
		Nos. 1079-1085 (7)	2.83

19th UPU Congress, Hamburg A440

1984, June 18 *Perf. 12x12½*

1086	A440	25af German postman, 17th cent.	1.00
1087	A440	35af Postrider, 16th cent.	1.40
1088	A440	40af Carrier pigeon, letter	1.50

Souvenir Sheet

1089 A440 50af Hamburg No. 3 in black 2.00

No. 1089 contains one stamp (size: 30x40mm); multicolored decorative margin pictures aerial view of Hamburg, Germany, and UPU emblem. Size: 97x67mm.

Natl. Aviation, 40th Anniv. A441

Soviet civil aircraft.

1984, June 29
1090 A441 1af Antonov AN-2 5
1091 A441 4af Ilyushin IL-12 15
1092 A441 9af Tupolev TU-104 35
1093 A441 10af Ilyushin IL-18 40
1094 A441 13af Tupolev TU-134 50
1095 A441 17af Ilyushin IL-62 65
1096 A441 21af Ilyushin IL-28 85
Nos. 1090-1096 (7) 2.95

Ettore Bugatti (1881-1947), Type 43, Italy — A442

Classic automobiles and their designers: 5af, Henry Ford (1863-1947), 1903 Model A, USA. 8af, Rene Panhard (1841-1908), 1899 Landau, France. 11af, Gottlieb Daimler (1834-1900), 1935 Daimler-Benz, Germany. 12af, Carl Benz (1844-1929), 1893 Victoris, Germany. 15af, Armand Peugeot (1848-1915), 1892 Vis-a-Vis, France. 22af, Louis Chevrolet (1879-1941), 1925 Sedan, USA.

1984, June 30
1097 A442 2af multi 8
1098 A442 5af multi 20
1099 A442 8af multi 30
1100 A442 11af multi 42
1101 A442 12af multi 48
1102 A442 15af multi 60
1103 A442 22af multi 85
Nos. 1097-1103 (7) 2.93

Ornamental Arch — A443

World Tourism Day: 2af, Ornamental buckled harness. 5af, Victory Monument and Memorial Arch, Kabul. 9af, Standing sculpture of Afghani ruler and attendants. 10af, Buffalo riders in snow. 19af, Camel driver, tent, camel in caparison. 21af, Horsemen playing buzkashi.

1984, Sept. 27
1104 A443 1af multi 5
1105 A443 2af multi 8
1106 A443 5af multi 20
1107 A443 9af multi 35
1108 A443 10af multi 40
1109 A443 19af multi 75
1110 A443 21af multi 85
Nos. 1104-1110 (7) 2.68

UN World Food Day — A444

Fruit-bearing trees.

1984, Oct. 16
1111 A444 2af multi 8
1112 A444 4af multi 16
1113 A444 6af multi 24
1114 A444 9af multi 35
1115 A444 13af multi 50
1116 A444 15af multi 60
1117 A444 26af multi 1.00
Nos. 1111-1117 (7) 2.93

People's Democratic Party, 20th Anniv. A445

1985, Jan. 1
1118 A445 25af multi 1.00

Farmer's Day A446

1985
1119 A446 1af Oxen 5
1120 A446 3af Mare, foal 12
1121 A446 7af Brown horse 28
1122 A446 8af White horse, vert. 30
1123 A446 15af Sheep, sheepskins 60
1124 A446 16af Shepherd, cattle, sheep 62
1125 A446 25af Family, camels 1.00
Nos. 1119-1125 (7) 2.97

Geologist's Day — A447

1985
1126 A447 4af multi 15

Lenin Leading Red Army, 1917 — A448

Lenin and: 10af, Soviet Workers' Party deputies, Smolny. 15af, Revolutionaries, 1917, Leningrad. 50af, Portrait.

1985 ***Perf. 12x12½***
1127 A448 10af multi 40
1128 A448 15af multi 60
1129 A448 25af multi 1.00

Souvenir Sheet

1130 A448 50af multi 2.00

No. 1130 has red and black margin picturing a scene from the 1917 Revolution, Russia. Size: 90x122mm.

Saur Revolution, 7th Anniv. — A449

1985, Apr. 27
1131 A449 21af multi 85

Berlin-Treptow Soviet War Memorial, Red Army at Siege of Berlin, 1945 — A450

Designs: 9af, Victorious Motherland monument, fireworks over Kremlin. 10af, Caecilienhof, site of Potsdam Treaty signing, flags of Great Britain, USSR and US.

1985, Mar. ***Perf. 12½x12***
1132 A450 6af multi 22
1133 A450 9af multi 35
1134 A450 10af multi 38

End of World War II, defeat of Nazi Germany, 40th anniv.

INTELSAT, 20th Anniv. — A451

Designs: 6af, INTELSAT satellite orbiting Earth. 9af, INTELSAT III. 10af, Rocket launch, Baikanur Space Center, vert.

Perf. 12x12½, 12½x12

1985, Apr. 6 **Litho.**
1135 A451 6af multi 22
1136 A451 9af multi 35
1137 A451 10af multi 40

12th World Youth Festival, Moscow — A452

1985, May 5
1138 A452 7af Olympic stadium, Moscow 28
1139 A452 12af Festival emblem 48
1140 A452 13af Kremlin 50
1141 A452 18af Folk doll, emblem 65

Intl. Child Survival Campaign A453

1985, June 1
1142 A453 1af Weighing child 5
1143 A453 2af Immunization 8
1144 A453 4af Breastfeeding 15
1145 A453 5af Mother, child 20

Flowers A454

1985, July 5
1146 A454 2af Oenothera affinis 8
1147 A454 4af Erythrina crista-galli 15
1148 A454 8af Tillandsia aeranthos 30
1149 A454 13af Vinca major 50
1150 A454 18af Mirabilis jalapa 65
1151 A454 25af Cypella herbertii 1.00
1152 A454 30af Clytostoma callistegioides 1.15
Nos. 1146-1152 (7) 3.83

Souvenir Sheet

Perf. 12½x11½

1153 A454 75af Sesbania punicea, horiz. 3.00

ARGENTINA '85. No. 1153 has multicolored decorative margin continuing the illustration. Size: 79x100mm.

Independence, 66th Anniv. — A455

1985, Aug. 19 ***Perf. 12x12½***
1154 A455 33af Mosque 1.25

Pashto's and Balutchi's Day — A456

1985, Aug. 30
1155 A456 25af multi 1.00

UN Decade for Women A457

1985, Sept. 22
1156 A457 10af Emblems 40

UN 40th Anniv. — A458

Birds — A459

1985, Oct. 24 ***Perf. 12½x12***
1157 A458 22af multi 85

Perf. 12½x12, 12x12½

1985, Oct. 25
1158 A459 2af Jay 8
1159 A459 4af Plover, hummingbird 15
1160 A459 8af Pheasant 30

1161 A459 13af Hoopoe 50
1162 A459 18af Falcon 65
1163 A459 25af Partridge 1.00
1164 A459 30af Pelicans, horiz. 1.15
Nos. 1158-1164 (7) 3.83

Souvenir Sheet

Perf. 12x12½

1165 A459 75af Parakeets 3.00

No. 1165 has multicolored decorative margin continuing the design. Size: 88x119mm.

Mushrooms A460

1985, June 10 Litho. *Perf. 12½x12*

1166 A460 4af Boletus miniatoporus 16
1167 A460 7af Amanita rubescens 28
1168 A460 11af Boletus scaber 45
1169 A460 12af Coprinus atramentarius 48
1170 A460 18af Hypholoma 72
1171 A460 20af Boletus aurantiacus 80
Nos. 1166-1171 (6) 2.89

World Wildlife Fund — A461

1985, Nov. 25

1172 A461 2af Leopard, cubs 8
1173 A461 9af Adult's head 38
1174 A461 11af Adult 45
1175 A461 15af Cub 60

Motorcycle, Cent. — A462

Designs: Different makes and landmarks.

1985, Dec. 16

1176 A462 2af multi 8
1177 A462 4af multi 16
1178 A462 8af multi 32
1179 A462 13af multi 52
1180 A462 18af multi 72
1181 A462 25af multi 1.00
1182 A462 30af multi 1.20
Nos. 1176-1182 (7) 4.00

Souvenir Sheet

Perf. 11½x12½

1183 A462 75af multi 3.00

No. 1183 has multicolored margin continuing the design. Size: 100x80mm.

People's Democratic Party, 21st Anniv. — A463

1986, Jan. 1 ***Perf. 12½x12***

1184 A463 2af multi

27th Soviet Communist Party Congress — A464

1986, Mar. 31

1185 A464 25af Lenin

First Man in Space, 25th Anniv. — A465

Designs: 3af, Spacecraft, 7af, Soviet space achievement medal, vert. 9af, Rocket lift-off, vert. 11af, Yuri Gagarin, military decorations, vert. 13af, Gagarin, cosmonaut. 15af, Gagarin, politician. 17af, Gagarin wearing flight suit, vert.

Perf. 12½x12, 12x12½

1986, Apr. 12 Litho.

1186 A465 3af multi
1187 A465 7af multi
1188 A465 9af multi
1189 A465 11af multi
1190 A465 13af multi
1191 A465 15af multi
1192 A465 17af multi

Loya Jirgah (Grand Assembly) of the People's Democratic Republic, 1st Anniv. A465a

1986, Apr. 23 Litho. *Perf. 12x12½*

1192A A465a 3af multi

Intl. Day of Labor Solidarity — A465b

1986, May 1 ***Perf. 12½x12***

1192B A465b 5af multi

Intl. Red Crescent Day — A465c

1986, May 8 ***Perf. 12x12½***

1192C A465c 7af multi

Intl. Children's Day — A466

1986, June 1 ***Perf. 12***

1193 A466 1af Mother, children, vert.
1194 A466 3af Mother, child, vert.
1195 A466 9af Children, map

World Youth Day A466a

1986, July 31 ***Perf. 12x12½***

1195A A466a 15af multi

Natl. Independence, 68th Anniv. — A466b

1986, Aug. 19

1195B A466b 3af multi

Pashtos' and Baluchis' Day — A467

1986, Aug. 31 ***Perf. 12x12½***

1196 A467 4af multi

Intl. Peace Year — A468

1986, Sept. 30 Photo. *Perf. 12½x12*

1197 A468 12af blk & Prus bl

A469

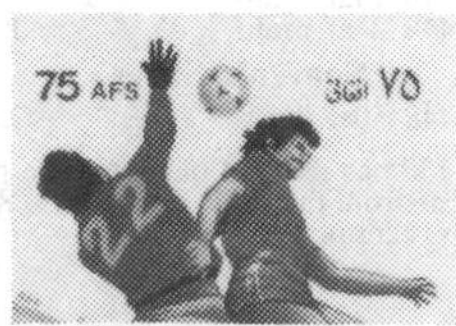
1986 World Cup Soccer Championships, Mexico — A470

Various soccer plays.

1986, Apr. 15 Litho. *Perf. 12*

1198 A469 3af multi, vert
1199 A469 4af multi
1200 A469 7af multi
1201 A469 11af multi, vert.
1202 A469 12af multi
1203 A469 18af multi, vert.
1204 A469 20af multi, vert.

Souvenir Sheet

Perf. 12½x12

1205 A470 75af multi

No. 1205 has multicolored inscribed margin continuing the design. Size: 120x89mm.

Lenin — A471

1986, Apr. 21 ***Perf. 12½x12***

1206 A471 16af multi

Natl. Independence, 67th Anniv. — A473

1986, Aug. 19 Litho. *Perf. 12½x12*

1208 A473 10af multi

Literacy Day — A474

1986, Sept. 18 ***Perf. 12x12½***

1209 A474 2af multi

Dogs A475 Lizards A476

1986, May 19 Litho. *Perf. 12x12½*

1210 A475 5af St. Bernard
1211 A475 7af Collie
1212 A475 8af Pointer
1213 A475 9af Golden retriever
1214 A475 11af German shepherd
1215 A475 15af Bulldog
1216 A475 20af Afghan hound

1986, July 7 *Perf. 12x12½, 12½x12*

1217 A476 3af Cobra
1218 A476 4af shown
1219 A476 5af Praying mantis
1220 A476 8af Beetle
1221 A476 9af Tarantula
1222 A476 10af Python
1223 A476 11af Scorpions

Nos. 1217, 1219, 1221-1223 horiz.

STOCKHOLMIA '86 — A477

Ships.

1986, Aug. 28 *Perf. 12½x12*

1224 A477 4af multi
1225 A477 5af multi
1226 A477 6af multi
1227 A477 7af multi
1228 A477 8af multi
1229 A477 9af multi
1230 A477 11af multi

Reunion of Afghan Tribes under the Supreme Girgah — A479

1986, Sept. 14 *Perf. 12*

1232 A479 3af lt blue, blk & olive gray

Natl. Youth Solidarity — A480

1986, Oct. 25 *Perf. 12½x12*

1233 A480 3af Blk & brt ver

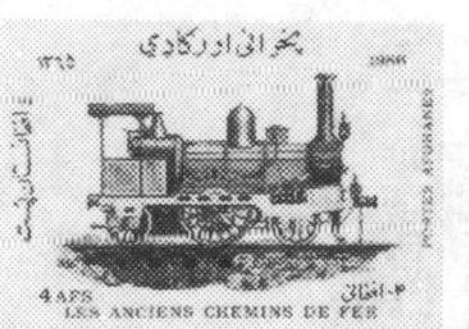

Locomotives — A481

1986, June 21 *Perf. 12½x12*

1234 A481 4af multi
1235 A481 5af multi
1236 A481 6af multi
1237 A481 7af multi
1238 A481 8af multi
1239 A481 9af multi
1240 A481 11af multi

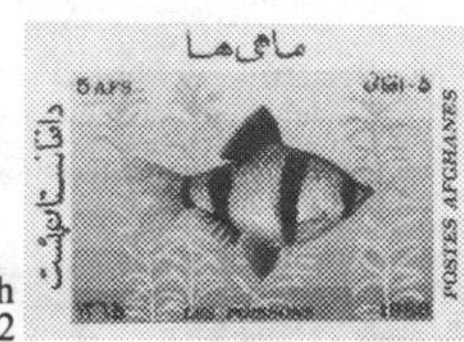

Fish A482

Various fish.

1986, May 25

1241 A482 5af multi
1242 A482 7af multi
1243 A482 8af multi
1244 A482 9af multi
1245 A482 11af multi
1246 A482 15af multi
1247 A482 20af multi

Saur Revolution, 9th Anniv. A483

1987, Apr. 27 *Perf. 12*

1248 A483 3af multi

Natl. Reconciliation — A484

1987, May 27 *Perf. 12x12½*

1249 A484 3af multi

A485

A486

U.N. Child Survival Campaign — A487

1987, June 1 *Perf. 12*

1250 A485 1af multi
1251 A486 5af multi
1252 A487 9af multi

Conference of Clergymen and Ulema, 1st Anniv. A488

1987, June 30

1253 A488 5af multi

Butterflies — A489

1987, July 3

1254 A489 7af multi
1255 A489 9af multi, diff.
1256 A489 10af multi, diff.
1257 A489 12af multi, diff.
1258 A489 15af multi, diff.
1259 A489 22af multi, diff.
1260 A489 25af multi, diff.

10af, 15af and 22af horiz.

1st Election of Local Representatives for State Power and Administration A490

1987, Aug. 11

1261 A490 1af multi

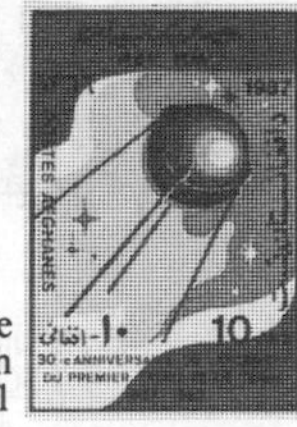

1st Artificial Satellite (Sputnik), 30th Anniv. — A491

1987, Oct. 4 **Litho.** *Perf. 12½x12*

1262 A491 10af Sputnik
1263 A491 15af Rocket launch
1264 A491 25af Soyuz

World Post Day — A492

1987, Oct. 9 *Perf. 12x12½*

1265 A492 22af multi

Intl. Communications and Transport Day — A493

1987, Oct. 24 *Perf. 12½x12*

1266 A493 42af multi

October Revolution in Russia, 70th Anniv. — A494

Mice — A495

1987, Nov. 7

1267 A494 25af Lenin

1987, Dec. 6 *Perf. 12½x12, 12x12½*

Various mice. Nos. 1269-1272 horiz.

1268 A495 2af multi
1269 A495 4af multi, diff.
1270 A495 8af multi, diff.
1271 A495 16af multi, diff.
1272 A495 20af multi, diff.

SEMI-POSTAL STAMPS

No. 373 Surcharged in Violet

a

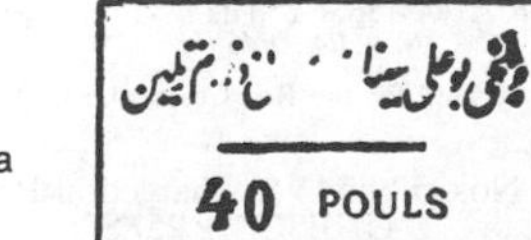

b

MILLIEME ANNIVERSAIRE
DE BOALI SINAI BALKI
125 POULS

1952, July 12 **Unwmk.** *Perf. 12½*

B1	A122(a)	40p + 30p cer	1.85	1.85
B2	A122(b)	125p + 30p cer	3.00	2.50

Issued to commemorate the 1000th anniversary of the birth of Avicenna.

Children at Play — SP1

1955, July 3 **Typo.** *Perf. 11*

B3	SP1	35p + 15p dk grn	60	40
B4	SP1	125p + 25p pur	1.25	1.00

The surtax was for child welfare.

Amir Sher Ali Khan, Tiger Head Stamp and Zahir Shah — SP2

Children at Play — SP3

1955, July 2 **Litho.**

B5	SP2	35p + 15p car	60	40
B6	SP2	125p + 25p pale vio bl	1.25	80

Issued to commemorate the 85th anniversary of the Afghan post.

1956, June 20 **Typo.**

B7	SP3	35p + 15p brt vio bl	40	40
B8	SP3	140p + 15p dk org brn	1.00	1.00

Issued for Children's Day. The surtax was for child welfare. No. B8 inscribed in French.

Pashtunistan Monument, Kabul — SP4

1956, Sept. 1 **Litho.**

B9	SP4	35p + 15p dp vio	25	25
B10	SP4	140p + 15p dk brn	75	75

Issued for "Free Pashtunistan" Day. The surtax aided the "Free Pashtunistan" movement.

No. B9 measures 30½x19½mm.; No. B10, 29x19mm. On sale and valid for use only on Sept. 1-2.

Globe and Sun — SP5

Children on Seesaw — SP6

1956, Oct. 24 *Perf. 11*

B11	SP5	35p + 15p ultra	1.00	85
B12	SP5	140p + 15p red brn	1.85	1.50

Issued for the tenth anniversary of Afghanistan's admission to the United Nations.

1957, June 20 **Unwmk.**

B13	SP6	35p + 15p brt rose	50	30
B14	SP6	140p + 15p ultra	1.25	90

Issued for Children's Day. The surtax was for child welfare.

U. N. Headquarters and Emblems — SP7

1957, Oct. 24 *Perf. 11 Rough*

B15 SP7 35p + 15p red brn 50 30
B16 SP7 140p + 15p lt ultra 1.00 90

Issued for United Nations Day.

Swimming Pool and Children — SP8

1958, June 22 *Perf. 11*

B17 SP8 35p + 15p rose 40 30
B18 SP8 140p + 15p dl red brn 1.00 75

Issued for Children's Day. The surtax was for child welfare.

Pashtunistan Flag — SP9

1958, Aug. 31

B19 SP9 35p + 15p lt bl 25 25
B20 SP9 140p + 15p red brn 75 75

Issued for "Free Pashtunistan Day."

Children Playing Tug of War — SP10

1959, June 23 **Litho.** *Perf. 11*

B21 SP10 35p + 15p brn vio 35 25
B22 SP10 165p + 15p brt pink 1.10 75

Issued for Children's Day. The surtax was for child welfare.

Pathans in Tribal Dance — SP11

1959, Sept. **Unwmk.** *Perf. 11 Rough*

B23 SP11 35p + 15p grn 20 20
B24 SP11 165p + 15p org 75 75

Issued for "Free Pashtunistan Day."

Afghan Cavalryman with U.N. Flag — SP12

1959, Oct. 24 *Perf. 11 Rough*

B25 SP12 35p + 15p org 30 25
B26 SP12 165p + 15p lt bl grn 65 60

Issued for United Nations Day.

Children SP13

1960, Oct. 23 **Litho.**

B27 SP13 75p + 25p lt ultra 33 30
B28 SP13 175p + 25p lt grn 60 45

Issued for Children's Day. The surtax was for child welfare.

Man with Spray Gun — SP14

1960, Sept. 6 *Perf. 11 Rough*

B29 SP14 50p + 50p org 1.25 1.00
B30 SP14 175p + 50p red brn 3.00 2.00

11th anniversary of the WHO malaria control program in Afghanistan.

SP15

1960, Sept. 1 **Unwmk.**

B31 SP15 50p + 50p rose 35 30
B32 SP15 175p + 50p dk bl 85 60

Issued for "Free Pashtunistan Day.'

Ambulance — SP16

1960, Oct. 16 *Perf. 11*

Crescent in Red

B33 SP16 50p + 50p vio 50 25
B34 SP16 175p + 50p bl 1.10 90

Issued for the Red Crescent Society.

Nos. 470-471 Surcharged in Blue or Orange.

1960, Dec. 31 **Litho.** *Perf. 11*

B35 A166 50p + 25p dp org (Bl) 3.00 3.00
B36 A166 165p + 25p bl (O) 3.00 3.00

The souvenir sheets described after No. 471 were surcharged in carmine "+25 Ps" on each stamp. Price $5 each.

See general note after No. 485.

Nos. 496-500 Surcharged UNICEF يونيسف +25PS

1961 **Unwmk.** **Photo.** *Perf. 13½x14*

B37 A175 2p + 25p grn & rose lil
B38 A175 2p + 25p brn & cit
B39 A175 5p + 25p gray & rose
B40 A175 10p + 25p bl & bis
B41 A175 15p + 25p sl bl & dl lil
Nos. B37-B41 (5) 2.25

Issued for the United Nations Children's Fund, UNICEF. The same surcharge was applied to an imperf. souvenir sheet like that noted after No. 505. Price $4.50.

Nos. 522-526 Surcharged "+25PS" and Crescent in Red.

1961, Oct. 16 *Perf. 13½x14*

B42 A184 2p + 25p blk
B43 A184 2p + 25p grn
B44 A184 5p + 25p lil rose
B45 A184 10p + 25p lil
B46 A184 15p + 25p dk bl
Nos. B42-B46 (5) 2.50

Issued for the Red Crescent Society.

Nos. 539-543 Surcharged in Red: "UNESCO + 25PS"

1962 *Perf. 12*

B47 A186 2p + 25p multi
B48 A186 2p + 25p multi
B49 A186 5p + 25p multi
B50 A186 10p + 25p multi
B51 A186 15p + 25p multi
Nos. B47-B51 (5) 1.30

Issued for the United Nations Educational, Scientific and Cultural Organization. The same surcharge was also applied to the souvenir sheets mentioned after No. 548. Price, 2 sheets, $3.50.

Nos. 553-561 Surcharged: "Dag Hammarskjöld +20PS"

1962, Sept. 17 *Perf. 14x13½*

B52 A187 2p + 20p rose lil & brn
B53 A187 2p + 20p ol bis & brn
B54 A187 5p + 20p dp org & dk grn
B55 A187 10p + 20p gray & mag
B56 A187 15p + 20p bl & brn
B57 A187 25p + 20p org yel & pur
B58 A187 50p + 20p lt grn & pur
B59 A187 75p + 20p brt cit & brn
B60 A187 100p + 20p dp org & brn
Nos. B52-B60 (9) 2.25

Issued in memory of Dag Hammarskjold, Secretary General of the United Nations, 1953-61. Perf. and imperf. souvenir sheets exist. Price, 2 sheets, $3.

Nos. 583-593 Surcharged "+15PS"

1963, Mar. 15 *Perf. 14x13½*

B61 A193 2p + 15p dk grn & ol gray
B62 A193 2p + 15p dk grn & sal
B63 A193 5p + 15p red brn & ol
B64 A193 10p + 15p red brn & brt grn
B65 A193 15p + 15p red brn & gray
B66 A193 25p + 15p brt bl & bluish grn
B67 A193 50p + 15p brt bl & rose lil
B68 A193 75p + 15p blk & bl
B69 A193 100p + 15p blk & brt pink
B70 A193 150p + 15p blk & bis brn
B71 A193 175p + 15p blk & org
Nos. B61-B71 (11) 10.00

Issued for the World Health Organization drive to eradicate malaria.

Postally used copies of Nos. B37-B71 are uncommon and command a considerable premium over the prices for unused copies.

Blood Transfusion Kit — SP17

1964, Oct. 18 **Litho.** *Perf. 10½*

B72 SP17 1af + 50p blk & rose 15 10

Issued for the Red Crescent Society and Red Crescent Week, Oct. 18-24.

First Aid Station SP18

1965, Oct. **Photo.** *Perf. 13½x14*

B73 SP18 1.50af + 50p grn, choc & red 25 10

Issued for the Red Crescent Society.

Children Playing SP19

1966, Nov. 28 **Photo.** *Perf. 13½x14*

B74 SP19 1af + 1af yel grn & cl 18 12
B75 SP19 3af + 2af yel & brn 40 30
B76 SP19 7af + 3af rose lil & grn 85 60

Children's Day.

Nadir Shah Presenting Society Charter SP20

1967 **Photo.** *Perf. 13x14*

B77 SP20 2af + 1af red & dk grn 25 15
B78 SP20 5af + 1af lil rose & brn 50 25

Issued for the Red Crescent Society.

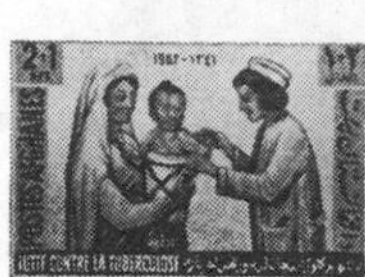

Vaccination SP21

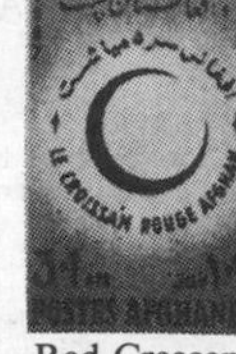

Red Crescent SP22

1967, June 6 **Photo.** *Perf. 12*

B79 SP21 2af + 1af yel & blk 25 10
B80 SP21 5af + 2af pink & brn 50 25

The surtax was for anti-tuberculosis work.

1967, Oct. 18 **Photo.** *Perf. 12*

Crescent in Red

B81 SP22 3af + 1af gray ol & blk 25 15
B82 SP22 5af + 1af dl bl & blk 35 20

Issued for the Red Crescent Society.

Queen Humeira SP23

Red Crescent SP24

1968, June 14 **Photo.** *Perf. 12*

B83 SP23 2af + 2af red brn 25 20
B84 SP23 7af + 2af dl grn 75 50

Issued for Mother's Day.

1968, Oct. 16 **Photo.** *Perf. 12*

B85 SP24 4af + 1af yel, blk & red 45 27

Issued for the Red Crescent Society.

Red Cross, Crescent, Lion and Sun Emblems SP25

Mother and Child SP26

1969, May 5 **Litho.** *Perf. 14x13½*

B86 SP25 3af + 1af multi 30 18
B87 SP25 5af + 1af multi 50 30

Issued to commemorate the 50th anniversary of the League of Red Cross Societies.

1969, June 14 **Photo.** *Perf. 12*

B88 SP26 1af + 1af yel org & brn 18 12

B89 SP26 4af + 1af rose lil & pur 40 27
a. Souv. sheet of 2 1.10 1.10

Issued for Mother's Day. No. B89a contains 2 imperf. stamps similar to Nos. B88-B89. Brown marginal inscription and black control number. Size: 120x80mm. Sold for 10af.

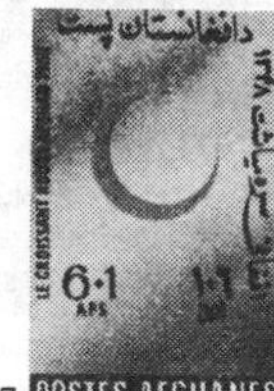

Red Crescent — SP27

1969, Oct. 16 Photo. *Perf. 12*
B90 SP27 6af + 1af multi 55 30

Issued for the Red Crescent Society.

UN and FAO Emblems, Farmer SP28

1973, May 24 Photo. *Perf. 13½*
B91 SP28 14af + 7af grnsh bl & lil 1.10 75

World Food Program, 10th anniversary.

Dome of the Rock, Jerusalem — SP29

1977, Sept. 11 Photo. *Perf. 14*
B92 SP29 12af + 3af multi 45 36

The surtax was for Palestinian families and soldiers.

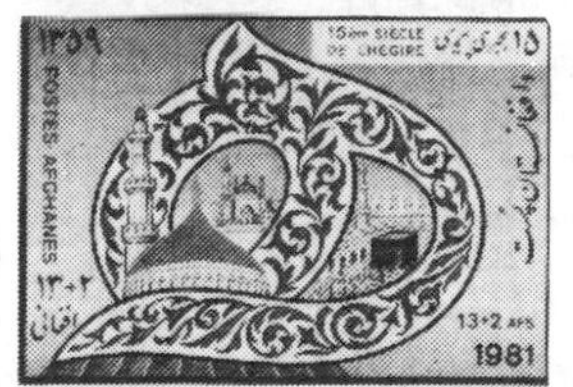

15 cent. (lunar) of Islamic pilgrimage (Hegira) — SP30

1981, Jan. 17 Litho. *Perf. 12½x12*
B93 SP30 13 + 2af multi 45 38

Red Crescent Aid Programs SP31

1981, May 8 *Perf. 12x12½*
B94 SP31 1 + 4af multi 15 12

Intl. Year of the Disabled A392

1981, Oct. 12 *Perf. 12x12½*
B95 SP32 6 + 1af multi 22 15

AIR POST STAMPS

Plane over Kabul AP1

Perf. 12, 12x11, 11

1939, Oct. 1 Typo. Unwmk.

C1 AP1 5af orange 3.00 3.00
a. Imperf. pair ('47) 35.00 35.00
b. Imperf. vertically, pair 30.00
C2 AP1 10af blue 3.00 2.50
a. lt bl 4.00 4.00
b. Imperf. pair ('47) 35.00
c. Imperf. vertically, pair 30.00
C3 AP1 20af emerald 7.00 7.00
a. Imperf. pair ('47) 35.00
b. Imperf. vertically, pair 30.00
c. Imperf. horiz., pair 35.00

These stamps come with clean-cut or rough perforations. Counterfeits exist.

1948, June 14 *Perf. 12x11½.*
C4 AP1 5af emerald 22.50 22.50
C5 AP1 10af red org 22.50 22.50
C6 AP1 20af blue 22.50 22.50

Imperforates exist.

Plane over Palace Grounds, Kabul AP2

1951-54 Engr. *Perf. 13½.*
Imprint: "Waterlow & Sons, Limited, London"

C7 AP2 5af hn brn 2.00 80
C8 AP2 5af dp grn ('54) 1.50 70
C9 AP2 10af gray 6.00 2.00
C10 AP2 20af dk bl 10.00 3.50

1957
C11 AP2 5af ultra 1.25 75
C12 AP2 10af dk vio 2.50 1.50

See also No. C38.

Ariana DC-3 Plane over Hindu Kush — AP3

Perf. 11, Imperf.

1960-63 Litho. Unwmk.
C13 AP3 75p lt vio 30 30
C14 AP3 125p blue 40 45

Perf. 10½, 11
C14A AP3 5af cit ('63) 1.10 1.10

Girl Scout — AP4

1962, Aug. 30 Photo. *Perf. 11½x12*
C15 AP4 100p ocher & brn 60 60
C16 AP4 175p brt yel grn & brn 85 85

Issued for Women's Day. A souvenir sheet exists containing one each of Nos. 578-579 and C15-C16. Brown inscription. Size: 109x105mm. Price $3.

Sports Type of Regular Issue, 1962

Designs: 25p, 50p, Horse racing. 75p, 100p, Wrestling. 150p, Weight lifting. 175p, Soccer.

1962, Sept. 25 Unwmk. *Perf. 12*
Black Inscriptions.

C17 A195 25p rose & red brn
C18 A195 50p gray & red brn
C19 A195 75p pale vio & dk grn
C20 A195 100p gray ol & dk pur
C21 A195 150p rose lil & grn
C22 A195 175p sal & brn
Nos. C17-C22 2.25

4th Asian Games, Djakarta, Indonesia.

Children's Day Type of Regular Issue

Designs: 75p, Runners. 150p, Peaches. 200p, Iris (vert.).

Perf. 11½x12, 12x11½

1962, Oct. 14 Unwmk.
C23 A196 75p lt grn & lil
C24 A196 150p bl & multi
C25 A196 200p ol & multi

Issued for Children's Day. A souvenir sheet contains one each of Nos. C23-C25. Lilac marginal inscription and black control number. Size: 119x90mm. Price $2.50.

Red Crescent Type of Regular Issue

Designs: 25p, Grapes. 50p, Pears. 100p, Wistaria.

1962, Oct. 16 *Perf. 12*
Fruit and Flowers in Natural Colors; Carmine Crescent

C26 A197 25p brown
C27 A197 50p dl grn
C28 A197 100p dk bl gray

Issued for the Afghan Red Crescent Society. Two souvenir sheets exist. One contains a 150p gray brown stamp in blossom design, the other a 200p gray stamp in wistaria design, imperf. Each sheet has marginal inscriptions in color of stamp, and black control number. Size: 89x65mm. Price, each $5.

U.N. Type of Regular Issue

1962, Oct. 24 Photo.
Flags in Original Colors, Black Inscriptions

C29 A198 75p blue
C30 A198 100p lt brn
C31 A198 125p brt grn

Issued for United Nations Day.

Boy Scout Type of Regular Issue

1962, Oct. 25 Unwmk. *Perf. 12*
C32 A199 25p gray, blk, dl grn & sal
C33 A199 50p grn, brn & sal
C34 A199 75p bl grn, red brn & sal
C35 A199 100p bl, sl & sal

Issued to honor the Boy Scouts.

Teacher's Day Type of Regular Issue

Designs: 100p, Pole vault. 150p, High jump.

1962, Oct. 25
C36 A200 100p yel & blk
C37 A200 150p bluish grn & brn

Issued for Teacher's Day. A souvenir sheet contains one 250p pink and slate green stamp in design of 150p. Slate green marginal inscription and black control number. Size: 65x89mm. Price $2.50.

Type of 1951-54

1962 Engr. *Perf. 13½*
Imprint: "Thomas De La Rue & Co. Ltd."

C38 AP2 5af ultra 9.00 1.00

Agriculture Types of Regular Issue

Unwmk.
1963, March 1 Photo. *Perf. 12*
C42 A204 100p dk car, grn & brn
C43 A203 150p ocher & blk
C44 A204 200p ultra, grn & brn

Issued for the Day of Agriculture.

Hands Holding Wheat Emblem AP5

1963, Mar. 27 Photo. *Perf. 14*
C45 AP5 500p lil, lt brn & brn 85 85

Issued for the "Freedom from Hunger" campaign of the U.N. Food and Agriculture Organization.

Two souvenir sheets exist. One contains a 1000p blue green, light brown and brown, type AP5, imperf. Claret marginal inscription. Size: 76x100mm. The other contains a 200p brown and green and 300p ultramarine, yellow and ocher in rice and corn designs, type A205. Green marginal inscription. Size: 100x75mm. Both sheets have black control number. Prices $60 and $2.50.

Meteorological Day Type of Regular Issue

Designs: 100p, 500p, Meteorological measuring instrument. 200p, 400p, Weather station. 300p, Rockets in space.

1963, May 23 *Imperf.*
C46 A206 100p brn & bl

Perf. 13½x14
C47 A206 200p brt grn & lil
C48 A206 300p dk bl & rose
C49 A206 400p bl & dl red brn
C50 A206 500p car rose & gray grn

Issued to commemorate the United Nations Third World Meteorological Day, March 23. Nos. C47 and C50 printed se-tenant.

Two souvenir sheets exist. One contains a 125p red and brown stamp in rocket design. Red marginal inscription. The other contains a 100p blue and dull red brown in "rockets in space" design. Blue marginal inscription. Both sheets have black control number, and measure 100x75mm. Prices $5 and $7.50.

Kabul International Airport AP8

Perf. 12x11

1964, Apr. Unwmk. Photo.
C57 AP8 10af red lil & grn 80 35
C58 AP8 20af dk grn & red lil 1.20 60
a. Perf. 12 ('68) 2.00
C59 AP8 50af dk bl & grnsh bl 3.25 1.50
a. Perf. 12 ('68) 5.00

Inauguration of Kabul Airport Terminal. Nos. C58-C59 are 36mm. wide. Nos. C58a-C59a are 35½mm. wide.

Zahir Shah and Ariana Plane — AP9

Design: 50af, Zahir Shah and Kabul Airport.

1971 Photo. *Perf. 12½x13½*
C60 AP9 50af multi 15.00 12.00
C61 AP9 100af blk, red & grn 8.00 5.00

No C60 was used, starting in 1978, with king's portrait removed.

Demand, as well as supply, determines a stamp's market value. One is as important as the other.

REGISTRATION STAMPS.

R1

Dated "1309"

1891 Unwmk. Litho. *Imperf.*
Pelure Paper.

F1 R1 1r sl bl 2.00
a. Tete beche pair 15.00

R2

Dated "1311".

1893 Thin Wove Paper.

F2 R2 1r *grn* 1.60

Genuinely used copies of Nos. F1-F2 are rare. Counterfeit cancellations exist.

R3

Undated.

1894

F3 R3 2ab *green* 11.00 14.00

12 varieties. See note below Nos. 189-190.

R4

Undated

1898-1900

F4	R4	2ab	*dp rose*	5.50 6.75
F5	R4	2ab	*lil rose*	5.50 6.75
F6	R4	2ab	*magenta*	5.50 6.75
F7	R4	2ab	*salmon*	5.50 6.75
F8	R4	2ab	*orange*	5.50 6.75
F9	R4	2ab	*yellow*	5.50 6.75
F10	R4	2ab	*green*	5.50 6.75
			Nos. F4-F10 (7)	43.75 52.50

Many shades of paper.

Nos. F4-F10 come in two sizes, measured between outer frame lines: 52x36mm., first printing; 46x33mm., second printing. The outer frame line (not pictured) is 3-6mm. from inner frame line.

Used on P.O. receipts.

OFFICIAL STAMPS

(Used only on interior mail.)

Coat of Arms O1

1909 Unwmk. Typo. *Perf. 12*
Wove Paper.

O1 O1 red 1.00 1.00
a. car ('19?) 1.25 1.25

Later printings of No. O1 in scarlet, vermilion, claret, etc., on various types of paper, were issued until 1927.

Coat of Arms — O2

1939-68? Typo. *Perf. 11, 12*

O3	O2	15p emerald	50 25
O4	O2	30p ocher ('40)	75 75
O5	O2	45p dk car	60 50
O6	O2	50p brt car ('68)	40 40
a.		car rose ('55)	75 60
O7	O2	1af brt red vio	1.25 75
		Nos. O3-O7 (5)	3.50 2.65

Size of 50p, 24x31mm. Others 22½x28mm.

1964-65 Litho. *Perf. 11*

O8 O2 50p rose 75 75
a. sal ('65) 1.50 1.50

Stamps of this type are revenues.

PARCEL POST STAMPS

Coat of Arms — PP1

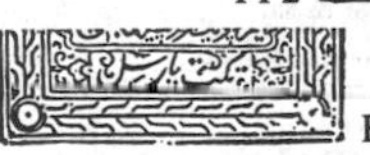
PP2

PP3

PP4

1909 Unwmk. Typo. *Perf. 12.*

Q1	PP1	3sh bister	50 60
a.		Imperf., pair	1.25
Q2	PP2	1kr ol gray	75 1.00
a.		Imperf., pair	2.00
Q3	PP3	1r orange	3.00 2.25
Q4	PP3	1r ol grn	1.25 2.75
Q5	PP4	2r red	3.75 2.50
		Nos. Q1-Q5 (5)	9.25 9.10

1916-18

Q6	PP1	3sh green	1.00 75
Q7	PP2	1kr pale red	1.50 1.25
a.		rose red ('18)	2.00 2.00
Q8	PP3	1r brn org	1.50 1.25
a.		dp brn ('18)	2.50 2.50
Q9	PP4	2r blue	3.00 3.00

Nos. Q1-Q9 sometimes show letters of the papermaker's watermark "HOWARD & JONES LONDON."

Ungummed copies are remainders. They sell for one-third the price of mint examples.

Old Habibia College, near Kabul PP5

1921
Wove Paper.

Q10	PP5	10pa chocolate	1.75 1.75
a.		Tete beche pair	6.25
Q11	PP5	15pa lt brn	2.50 2.50
a.		Tete beche pair	6.25
Q12	PP5	30pa red vio	3.50 2.75
a.		Tete beche pair	8.75
b.		Laid paper	15.00 7.50
Q13	PP5	1r brt bl	5.50 5.50
a.		Tete beche pair	12.00

Stamps of this issue are usually perforated on one or two sides only.

The laid paper of No. Q12b has a papermaker's watermark in the sheet.

PP6

1924-26
Wove Paper

Q15 PP6 5kr ultra ('26) 25.00 15.00
Q16 PP6 5r lilac 8.75 8.75

A 15r rose exists, but is not known to have been placed in use.

PP7

PP8

1928-29 *Perf. 11, 11xImperf.*

Q17	PP7	2r yel org	5.00 4.00
Q18	PP7	2r grn ('29)	4.00 3.50
Q19	PP8	3r dp grn	6.50 6.00
Q20	PP8	3r brn ('29)	6.50 6.00

POSTAL TAX STAMPS

Aliabad Hospital near Kabul PT1

Pierre and Marie Curie — PT2

Perf. 12x11½, 12
1938, Dec. 22 Typo. Unwmk.

RA1 PT1 10p pck grn 1.75 2.75
RA2 PT2 15p dl bl 1.75 2.75

Obligatory on all mail Dec. 22-28, 1938. The money was used for the Aliabad Hospital. See note with CD80.

Begging Child PT3 PT4

1949, May 28 Typo. *Perf. 12*

RA3 PT3 35p red org 2.00 2.00
RA4 PT4 125p ultra 3.00 2.00

United Nations Children's Day, May 28.

Obligatory on all foreign mail on that date. Proceeds were used for child welfare.

Paghman Arch and U. N. Emblem PT5

1949, Oct. 24

RA5 PT5 125p dk bl grn 15.00 11.00

Issued to commemorate the fourth anniversary of the formation of the United Nations. Valid one day only. Issued in sheets of 9 (3x3).

Zahir Shah and Map of Afghanistan — PT6

1950, Mar. 30 Typo.

RA6 PT6 125p bl grn 2.50 1.25

Issued to celebrate the return of Zahir Shah from a trip to Europe for his health. Valid for two weeks. The tax was used for public health purposes.

Hazara Youth — PT7

1950, May 28 Typo. *Perf. 11½*

RA7 PT7 125p dk bl grn 3.00 2.00

The tax was for Child Welfare. Obligatory and valid only on May 28, 1950, on foreign mail.

Ruins of Qalai Bist and Globe PT8

1950, Oct. 24

RA8	PT8 1.25af ultra	6.50	5.00

Issued to commemorate the 5th anniversary of the formation of the United Nations. Proceeds went to Afghanistan's U.N. Projects Committee.

Zahir Shah and Medical Center PT9

1950, Dec. 22 Typo. *Perf. 11½*
Size: 38x25mm.

RA9	PT9	35p carmine	50	50
RA10	PT9	1.25af black	6.00	3.00

The tax was for the national Graduate School of Medicine.

Koochi Girl with Lamb — PT10

Kohistani Boy and Sheep PT11

1951, May 28

RA11	PT10	35p emerald	1.25	1.00
RA12	PT11	1.25af ultra	1.25	1.00

The tax was for Child Welfare.

Distributing Gifts to Children — PT12

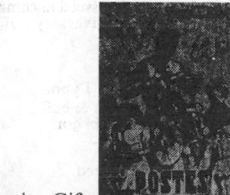
Qandahari Boys Dancing the "Attan" PT13

The only foreign revenue stamps listed in this Catalogue are those authorized for prepayment of postage.

1952, May 28 Litho.

RA13	PT12 35p chocolate	40	40
RA14	PT13 125p violet	1.10	1.10

The tax was for Child Welfare.

Soldier Receiving First Aid — PT14

1952, Oct.

RA15	PT14 10p lt grn	60	45

Stretcher-bearers and Wounded — PT15

Soldier Assisting Wounded — PT16

1953, Oct.

RA16	PT15 10p yel grn & org red	60	50
RA17	PT16 10p vio brn & org red	60	50

Prince Mohammed Nadir — PT17

Map and Young Musicians — PT18

1953, May 28

RA18	PT17 35p org yel	25	20
RA19	PT17 125p chlky bl	75	75

No. RA19 is inscribed in French "Children's Day." The tax was for child welfare.

1954, May 28 Unwmk. *Perf. 11*

RA20	PT18 35p purple	40	20
RA21	PT18 125p ultra	1.50	1.50

No. RA21 is inscribed in French. The tax was for child welfare.

Red Crescent
PT19 PT20

1954, Oct. 17 *Perf. 11½*

RA22	PT19 20p bl & red	35	30

1955, Oct. 18 *Perf. 11*

RA23	PT20 20p dl grn & car	30	25

Zahir Shah and Red Crescent — PT21

1956, Oct. 18

RA24	PT21 20p lt grn & rose car	35	25

Red Crescent Headquarters, Kabul — PT22

1957, Oct. 17

RA25	PT22 20p lt ultra & car	35	25

Map and Crescent PT23

1958, Oct. Unwmk. *Perf. 11*

RA26	PT23 25p yel grn & red	25	20

PT24

1959, Oct. 17 Litho. *Perf. 11*

RA27	PT24 25p lt vio & red	25	15

The tax on Nos. RA15-RA17, RA22-RA27 was for the Red Crescent Society. Use of these stamps was required for one week.

AGUERA, LA

LOCATION — An administrative district in southern Rio de Oro on the northwest coast of Africa.
GOVT. — Spanish possession
AREA — Because of indefinite political boundaries, figures for area and population are not available.
See Spanish Sahara.

100 Centimos = 1 Peseta

Type of 1920 Issue of Rio de Oro Overprinted **LA AGÜERA**

1920 Unwmk. *Perf. 13*

1	A8	1c bl grn	2.00	2.00
2	A8	2c ol brn	2.00	2.00
3	A8	5c dp grn	2.00	2.00
4	A8	10c lt red	2.00	2.00
5	A8	15c yellow	2.00	2.00
6	A8	20c lilac	2.00	2.00
7	A8	25c dp bl	2.00	2.00
8	A8	30c dk brn	2.00	2.00
9	A8	40c pink	2.00	2.00
10	A8	50c brt bl	5.25	4.75
11	A8	1p red brn	9.00	7.75
12	A8	4p dk vio	30.00	25.00
13	A8	10p orange	60.00	55.00
		Nos. 1-13 (13)	122.25	110.50

King Alfonso XIII — A2

1922 Typo.

14	A2	1c turq bl	1.00	1.00
15	A2	2c dk grn	1.00	1.00
16	A2	5c bl grn	1.00	1.00
17	A2	10c red	1.00	1.00
18	A2	15c red brn	1.00	1.00
19	A2	20c yellow	1.00	1.00
20	A2	25c dp bl	1.00	1.00
21	A2	30c dk brn	1.00	1.00
22	A2	40c rose red	1.25	1.25
23	A2	50c red vio	5.00	3.50
24	A2	1p rose	9.00	7.25
25	A2	4p violet	20.00	15.00
26	A2	10p orange	30.00	25.00
		Nos. 14-26 (13)	73.75	60.00

For later issues see Spanish Sahara in Vol. IV.

ALAOUITES

LOCATION — A division of Syria, in Western Asia.
GOVT. — Under French Mandate
AREA — 2,500 sq. mi.
POP. — 278,000 (approx. 1930)
CAPITAL — Latakia

This territory became an independent state in 1924, although still administered under the French Mandate. In 1930 it was renamed Latakia and Syrian stamps overprinted "Lattaquie" superseded the stamps of Alaouites. For these and subsequent issues see Latakia and Syria.

100 Centimes = 1 Piaster

Issued under French Mandate.
Stamps of France Surcharged:

ALAOUITES 0 P. 25 العلوين ١/٤ الغرش — a

ALAOUITES 2 PIASTRES العلوين غروش ٢ — b

1925 Unwmk. *Perf. 14x13½*

1	A16(a)	10c on 2c vio brn	1.50	1.50
2	A22(a)	25c on 5c org	1.00	1.00
3	A20(a)	75c on 15c gray grn	1.90	1.90
4	A22(a)	1p on 20c red brn	1.25	1.25
5	A22(a)	1.25p on 25c bl	1.75	1.75
6	A22(a)	1.50p on 30c red	5.25	5.25
7	A22(b)	2p on 35c vio	1.25	1.25
8	A18(b)	2p on 40c red & pale bl	2.50	2.50
9	A18(b)	2p on 45c grn & bl	5.25	5.25
10	A18(b)	3p on 60c vio & ultra	3.00	3.00
11	A20(b)	3p on 60c lt vio	5.25	5.25
12	A20(b)	4p on 85c ver	90	90
13	A18(b)	5p on 1fr cl & ol grn	3.75	3.75
14	A18(b)	10p on 2fr org & pale bl	4.75	4.75
15	A18(b)	25p on 5fr Bl & buff	6.50	6.50
		Nos. 1-15 (15)	45.80	45.80

Same Surcharges on Stamps of France, 1923-24 (Pasteur)

16	A23(a)	50c on 10c grn	95	95
17	A23(a)	75c on 15c grn	95	95
18	A23(a)	1.50p on 30c red	1.25	1.25
19	A23(b)	2p on 45c red	1.40	1.40
20	A23(b)	2.50p on 50c bl	1.75	1.75
21	A23(b)	4p on 75c bl	2.50	2.50
		Nos. 16-21 (6)	8.80	8.80

Stamps of Syria, 1925, Overprinted in Red, Black or Blue:

ALAOUITES العلوين — c

ALAOUITES العلوين — d

1925, Mar. 1 *Perf. 12½, 13½*

25	A3(c)	10c dk vio (R)	48	48
a.		Dbl. ovpt.	17.50	17.50
26	A4(d)	25c ol blk (R)	90	90
a.		Inverted overprint	10.00	10.00
b.		Blue ovpt.	17.50	17.50

27 A4(d) 50c yel grn	70	70
a. Inverted overprint	8.75	8.75
b. Blue ovpt.	17.50	17.50
c. Red ovpt.	17.50	17.50
28 A4(d) 75c brn org	80	80
a. Inverted overprint	10.00	10.00
29 A5(c) 1p magenta	1.25	1.25
30 A4(d) 1.25p dp grn	90	90
a. Red ovpt.	15.00	15.00
31 A4(d) 1.50p rose red (Bl)	80	80
a. Inverted overprint	10.00	10.00
b. Black ovpt.	17.50	17.50
32 A4(d) 2p dk brn (R)	90	90
a. Blue ovpt.	10.00	10.00
33 A4(d) 2.50p pck bl (R)	1.10	1.10
a. Black ovpt.	10.00	10.00
34 A4(d) 3p org brn	90	90
a. Inverted overprint	10.00	10.00
b. Blue ovpt.	21.00	21.00
35 A4(d) 5p violet	1.00	1.00
a. Red ovpt.	21.00	21.00
36 A4(d) 10p vio brn	1.65	1.65
37 A4(d) 25p ultra (R)	3.50	3.50
Nos. 25-37 (13)	14.88	14.88

Stamps of Syria, 1925, Surcharged in Black or Red:

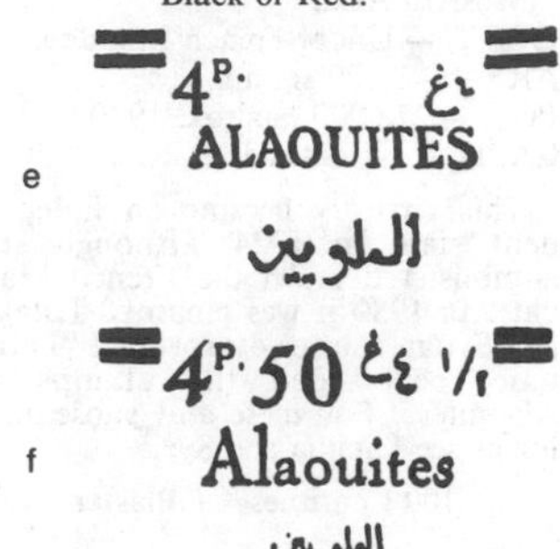

e

f

1926

38 A4(e) 3.50p on 75c brn org	95	80
a. Surcharged on face and back	7.00	7.00
39 A4(e) 4p on 25c ol blk (R)	1.00	80
40 A4(e) 6p on 2.50p pck bl (R)	90	80
41 A4(e) 12p on 1.25p dp grn	90	80
a. Inverted surch.	9.50	9.50
42 A4(e) 20p on 1.25p dp grn	1.50	1.25
43 A4(f) 4.50p on 75c brn org	3.00	1.75
a. Invtd. surch.	10.00	
44 A4(f) 7.50p on 2.50p pck bl	2.25	1.25
45 A4(f) 15p on 25p ultra	4.25	3.00
Nos. 38-45 (8)	14.75	10.45

Syria No. 199 Overprinted Type "c" in Red.

1928

46 A3(c) 5c on 10c dk vio	42	42
a. Double surcharge	13.00	

Syria Nos. 178 and 174 Surcharged in Red.

47 A4 (f) 2p on 1.25p dp grn	8.50	4.75
48 A4 (f) 4p on 25c ol blk	5.25	3.50

4P

ALAOUITES

العلويين

g

49 A4 (g) 4p on 25c ol blk	45.00	40.00
a. Double impression		

AIR POST STAMPS

Nos. 8, 10, 13 & 14 with Additional Overprint in Black

Avion

Perf. 14 x 13½.

1925, Jan. 1 **Unwmk.**

C1 A18 2p red & pale bl	5.00	5.00
a. Overprint reversed	65.00	
C2 A18 3p on 60c vio & ultra	8.00	8.00
a. Overprint reversed	65.00	65.00
C3 A18 5p on 1fr cl & ol grn	5.00	5.00
C4 A18 10p on 2fr org & pale bl	5.00	5.00

AVION

Nos. 32, 34, 35 & 36 With Additional Overprint in Green

1925, Mar. 1 ***Perf. 13½***

C5 A4 2p dk brn	1.50	1.50
C6 A4 3p org brn	1.50	1.50
C7 A4 5p violet	1.50	1.50
C8 A4 10p vio brn	1.50	1.50

Nos. 32, 34, 35 & 36 With Additional Overprint in Red

k

1926, May 1

C9 A4 2p dk brn	2.00	2.00
C10 A4 3p org brn	2.00	2.00
C11 A4 5p violet	2.00	2.00
C12 A4 10p vio brn	2.00	2.00

No. C9 has the type "d" overprint in black.

Double or inverted overprints, types "d' or "k," are known on most of Nos. C9-C12. Price, $8-$10.

The red plane overprint, "k," was also applied to Nos. C5-C8. These are believed to have been essays, and were not regularly issued.

Nos. 27, 29, and 37 With Additional Overprint of Airplane (k) in Red or Black.

1929, June-July

C17 A4 50c yel grn (R)	1.10	1.10
a. Red overprint (k) double	13.00	
b. Red overprint (k) on face and back	13.00	
c. Pair with overprint (k) tête bêche	40.00	
C18 A5 1p mag (Bk)	3.50	3.50
C19 A4 25p ultra (R)	17.50	17.50
a. Overprint (k) inverted	65.00	65.00

Nos. 47 and 45 With Additional Overprint of Airplane (k) in Red.

1929-30

C20 A4 2p on 1.25p dp grn ('30)	1.75	1.75
a. Surcharge inverted	6.00	
b. Double surch.	5.00	
C21 A4 15p on 25p ultra (Bk + R)	27.50	21.00
a. Overprint (k) inverted	50.00	50.00

POSTAGE DUE STAMPS

Postage Due Stamps of France, 1893-1920, Surcharged in Black.

1925 **Unwmk.** ***Perf. 14 x 13½.***

J1 D2 (a) 50c on 10c choc	2.25	2.25
J2 D2 (a) 1p on 20c ol grn	2.25	2.25
J3 D2 (b) 2p on 30c red	2.25	2.25
J4 D2 (b) 3p on 50c vio brn	2.25	2.25
J5 D2 (b) 5p on 1 fr red brn, *straw*	2.25	2.25
Nos. J1-J5 (5)	11.25	11.25

Postage Due Stamps of Syria, 1925, Overprinted in Black, Blue or Red.

1925 ***Perf. 13½***

J6 D5 (d) 50c brn, *yel*	90	90
J7 D6 (c) 1p vio *rose* (Bl)	90	90
a. Blk. overprint	13.00	13.00
b. Double overprint (Bk + Bl)	21.00	21.00
J8 D5 (d) 2p *blue*	1.40	1.40
J9 D5 (d) 3p *red org*	2.00	2.00
J10 D5 (d) 5p *bl grn*	3.00	3.00
Nos. J6-J10 (5)	8.20	8.20

The stamps of Alaouites were superseded in 1930 by those of Latakia.

ALBANIA

LOCATION — Southeastern Europe

GOVT. — Republic

AREA — 11,101 sq. mi.

POP. — 2,750,000 (1982 est.)

CAPITAL — Tirana

After the outbreak of World War I, the country fell into a state of anarchy when the Prince and all members of the International Commission left Albania. Subsequently General Ferrero in command of Italian troops declared Albania an independent country. A constitution was adopted and a republican form of government was instituted which continued until 1928 when, by constitutional amendment, Albania was declared to be a monarchy. The President of the republic, Ahmed Zogu, became king of the new state. Many unlisted varieties or surcharges and lithographed labels are said to have done postal duty in Albania and Epirus during this unsettled period.

In March 1939, Italy invaded Albania. King Zog fled but did not abdicate. The King of Italy acquired the crown.

Germany occupied Albania from September, 1943, until late 1944 when it became an independent state. The People's Republic began in January, 1946.

40 Paras = 1 Piastre = 1 Grossion
100 Centimes = 1 Franc (1917)
100 Qintar = 1 Franc
100 Qintar (Qindarka) = 1 Lek (1947)

Stamps of Turkey Handstamped

Handstamped on Issue of 1908.

Perf. 12, 13½ and Compound.

1913, June **Unwmk.**

1 A19 2½pi vio brn	300.00	250.00

With Additional Overprint in Carmine

2 A19 10pa bl grn	250.00	225.00

The eagle handstamp was applied to other Turkish stamps of 1908: 25pi green and 50 pi red brown. The 5pa ocher, Albania #4, was surcharged "2 paras" These three stamps were retained by officials. Prices, $3,000, $7,500, $500.

Handstamped on Issue of 1909.

4 A21 5pa ocher	125.00	100.00
5 A21 10pa bl grn	100.00	90.00
6 A21 20pa car rose	75.00	60.00
7 A21 1pi ultra	85.00	75.00
8 A21 2pi bl blk	130.00	110.00
10 A21 5pi dk vio	450.00	325.00
11 A21 10pi dl red	1,400.	1,200.

With Additional Overprint in Blue or Carmine

14 A21 20pa car rose (Bl)	225.00	175.00
15 A21 1pi brt bl (C)	575.00	525.00

Handstamped on Newspaper Stamp of 1911

17 A21 2pa ol grn	130.00	120.00

Handstamped on Postage Due Stamp of 1908.

18 A19 1pi *dp rose*	800.00	600.00

No. 18 was used for regular postage.

No. 6 Surcharged With New Value.

19 A21 10pa on 20pa car rose	300.00	275.00

The overprint on Nos. 1 to 19 was handstamped and, as usual, is found inverted, double, etc.

Nos. 6, 7 and 8 exist with the handstamp in red, blue or violet, but these varieties are not known to have been regularly issued.

Excellent counterfeits exist of Nos. 1 to 19.

A1

Posta e Qeverries së Përkohëshme
të Shqipënies
10 para

1913, July ***Imperf.***

Handstamped on White Laid Paper Without Eagle and Value.

20 A1 (1pi) black	135.00	120.00
Cut to shape	60.00	60.00
a. Sewing machine perf.	200.00	175.00

1913, Aug.

Value Typewritten in Violet

With Eagle.

21 A1 10pa violet	5.50	3.50
22 A1 20pa red & blk	5.50	3.75
23 A1 1gr black	5.50	3.50
24 A1 2gr bl & vio	6.50	5.00
25 A1 5gr vio & bl	8.75	7.00
26 A1 10gr blue	9.00	7.00
Nos. 21-26 (6)	40.75	29.75

Nos. 21-26 exist with the eagle inverted or omitted and with numerous errors in the figures of value and the spelling of the word "grosh".

A2

Skanderbeg (George Castriota) — A3

1913, Nov. ***Perf. 11½***

Handstamped on White Laid Paper

Eagle and Value in Black.

27 A2 10pa green	2.25	1.25
b. Eagle and value in grn	20.00	
c. 10pa red (error)	15.00	15.00
d. 10pa vio (error)	15.00	15.00
29 A2 20pa red	2.25	1.25
b. 20pa grn (error)	15.00	15.00
30 A2 30pa violet	2.50	1.65
a. 30pa ultra (error)	15.00	15.00
b. 30pa red (error)	15.00	15.00
31 A2 1gr ultra	3.50	2.25
a. 1gr grn (error)	15.00	15.00
b. 1gr blk (error)	15.00	15.00
c. 1gr vio (error)	15.00	15.00
33 A2 2gr black	5.75	4.50
a. 2gr vio (error)	15.00	15.00
b. 2gr bl (error)	15.00	15.00
Nos. 27-33 (5)	16.25	10.90

The stamps of this issue are known with eagle or value inverted or omitted.

The stamps were issued in commemoration of the first anniversary of Albanian independence.

1913, Dec. **Typo.** ***Perf. 14***

35 A3 2q org brn & buff	65	50
36 A3 5q grn & bl grn	65	50
37 A3 10q rose red	60	40
38 A3 25q dk bl	80	60
39 A3 50q vio & red	1.25	1.00
40 A3 1fr dp brn	6.00	6.00
Nos. 35-40 (6)	9.95	9.00

Nos. 35-40 Handstamped in Black or Violet

7. Mars
1914
RROFTË MBRETI

1914, Mar. 7

41 A3 2q org brn & buff	12.50	10.00
42 A3 5q grn & bl grn (V)	12.50	10.00
43 A3 10q rose red	12.50	10.00
44 A3 25q dk bl (V)	12.50	10.00

45 A3 50q vio & red 12.50 10.00
46 A3 1fr dp brn 12.50 10.00
Nos. 41-46 (6) 75.00 60.00

Issued to celebrate the arrival of Prince Wilhelm zu Wied on Mar. 7, 1914.

Nos. 35-40 Surcharged in Black:

5 • PARA •
a

1 GROSH
b

1914, Apr. 2
47 A3 (a) 5pa on 2q org brn & buff 75 75
a. Inverted surcharge 5.00 5.00
48 A3 (a) 10pa on 5q grn & bl grn 75 75
a. Inverted surcharge 5.00 5.00
49 A3 (a) 20pa on 10q rose red 1.25 1.10
a. Inverted surcharge 5.00 5.00
50 A3 (b) 1gr on 25q bl 1.25 1.10
a. Inverted surcharge 6.00 6.00
51 A3 (b) 2gr on 50q vio & red 1.75 1.50
a. Inverted surcharge 7.50 7.50
52 A3 (b) 5gr on 1fr dp brn 10.00 10.00
b. Invtd. surch. 10.00 10.00
Nos. 47-52 (6) 15.75 15.20

Korce (Korytsa) Issues

A4

1914 Handstamped *Imperf.*
52A A4 10pa vio & red 60.00 50.00
c. 10pa blk & red 85.00 70.00
53 A4 25pa vio & red 60.00 50.00
a. 25pa blk & red 110.00 100.00

Nos. 52A-53a originally were handstamped directly on the cover, so the paper varies. Later they were also produced in sheets; these are rarely found. Nos. 52A-53a were issued by Albanian military authorities.

A5

A6

Typographed and Lithographed

1917 *Perf. 11½*
54 A5 1c dk brn & grn 12.50 10.00
55 A5 2c red & grn 12.50 10.00
56 A5 3c gray grn & grn 12.50 10.00
57 A5 5c grn & blk 9.00 5.00
58 A5 10c rose red & blk 9.00 5.00
59 A5 25c bl & blk 9.00 5.00
60 A5 50c vio & blk 9.00 5.00
61 A5 1fr brn & blk 12.50 10.00
Nos. 54-61 (8) 86.00 60.00

1917-18
62 A6 1c dk brn & grn 4.00 3.25
63 A6 2c red brn & grn 4.00 3.25
a. "CTM" for "CTS" 17.50 17.50
64 A6 3c blk & grn 4.00 3.25
a. "CTM" for "CTS" 17.50 17.50
65 A6 5c grn & blk 4.50 4.50
66 A6 10c dl red & blk 4.50 4.50
67 A6 50c vio & blk 8.50 8.50
68 A6 1fr red brn & blk 15.00 10.00
Nos. 62-68 (7) 44.50 37.25

Counterfeits abound of Nos. 54-68, 80-81.

No. 65 Surcharged in Red

QARKU
I
KORÇËS
25 CTS

1918
80 A6 25c on 5c grn & blk 60.00 50.00

A7

1918
81 A7 25c bl & blk 37.50 30.00

General Issue

A8

A9

Handstamped in Rose or Blue

XV I MCMXIX

1919 *Perf. 12½*
84 A8 (2)q on 2h brn 5.00 4.50
85 A8 5q on 16h grn 5.00 4.50
86 A8 10q on 8h rose (Bl) 5.00 4.50
87 A8 25q on 64h bl 5.00 4.50
88 A9 25q on 64h bl 200.00 *175.00*
89 A8 50q on 32h vio 5.00 4.50
90 A8 1fr on 1.28k org, *bl* 5.00 4.50
Nos. 84-90 (7) 230.00 202.00

Handstamped in Rose or Blue

1919, Jan. 16
91 A8 (2)q on 2h brn 6.50 6.50
92 A8 5q on 16h grn 6.50 6.50
93 A8 10q on 8h rose (Bl) 6.50 6.50
94 A8 25q on 64h bl 35.00 35.00
95 A9 25q on 64h bl 30.00 30.00
96 A8 50q on 32h vio 6.50 6.50
97 A8 1fr on 1.28k org, *bl* 6.50 6.50
Nos. 91-97 (7) 97.50 97.50

Handstamped in Violet

1919
98 A8 (2)q on 2h brn 7.00 7.00
99 A8 5q on 16h grn 7.00 7.00
100 A8 10q on 8h rose 7.00 7.00
101 A8 25q on 64h bl 7.00 7.00
102 A9 25q on 64h bl 30.00 30.00
103 A8 50q on 32h vio 7.00 7.00
104 A8 1fr on 1.28k org, *bl* 7.00 7.00
Nos. 98-104 (7) 72.00 72.00

No. 50 Overprinted in Violet

1919 *Perf. 14*
105 A3 1gr on 25q bl 3.00 *4.00*

A10

A11

1919, June 5 *Perf. 11½, 12½*
106 A10 10q on 2h brn 4.00 4.00
107 A11 15q on 8h rose 4.00 4.00
108 A11 20q on 16h grn 4.00 4.00
109 A10 25q on 64h bl 4.00 4.00
110 A11 50q on 32h vio 4.00 4.00
111 A11 1fr on 96h org 4.00 4.00
112 A10 2fr on 1.60k vio, *buff* 8.00 8.00
Nos. 106-112 (7) 32.00 32.00

Nos. 106-108, 110 exist with inverted surcharge.

A12

A13

Black or Violet Surcharge

1919
113 A12 10q on 8h car 4.00 4.00
114 A12 15q on 8h car (V) 4.00 4.00
115 A13 20q on 16h grn 4.00 4.00
116 A13 25q on 35h vio 4.00 4.00
117 A13 50q on 64h bl 8.50 8.50
118 A13 1fr on 96h org 5.00 5.00
119 A12 2fr on 1.60k vio, *buff* 5.00 5.00
Nos. 113-119 (7) 34.50 34.50

A14

A15

Overprinted in Blue or Black. Without New Value.

1920 *Perf. 12½.*
120 A14 1q gray (Bl) 30.00 35.00
121 A14 10q rose (Bk) 2.50 4.00
a. Double overprint 35.00 *40.00*
122 A14 20q brn (Bl) 15.00 17.50
123 A14 25q bl (Bk) 160.00 *175.00*
124 A14 50q brn vio (Bk) 20.00 25.00
Nos. 120-124 (5) 227.50 256.50

Counterfeit overprints exist of Nos. 120-128.

Surcharged with New Value.

125 A14 2q on 10q rose (R) 4.00 6.00
126 A14 5q on 10q rose (G) 4.00 6.00
127 A14 25q on 10q rose (Bl) 4.00 6.00
128 A14 50q on 10q rose (Br) 4.00 6.00

Stamps of type A14 (Portrait of the Prince zu Wied) were not placed in use without overprint or surcharge.

Post Horn Overprinted in Black.

1920 *Perf. 14x13*
129 A15 2q orange 2.00 2.00
130 A15 5q dp grn 2.75 2.25
131 A15 10q red 7.00 5.50
132 A15 25q lt bl 12.50 7.00
133 A15 50q gray grn 2.00 2.00
134 A15 1fr claret 2.00 2.00
Nos. 129-134 (6) 28.25 20.75

Type A15 was never placed in use without post horn or "Besa" overprint.

Stamps of Type A15 (No Post Horn) Overprinted

1921
135 A15 2q orange 1.75 1.75
136 A15 5q dp grn 2.50 2.50
137 A15 10q red 4.25 4.25
138 A15 25q lt bl 9.00 7.50
139 A15 50q gray grn 3.00 3.00
140 A15 1fr claret 2.50 2.50
Nos. 135-140 (6) 23.00 21.50

Stamps of these types, and with "TAKSE" overprint, were unauthorized and never placed in use.

Gjinokaster A18

Korcha — A19

Designs: 5q, Kanina. 10q, Berati. 25q, Bridge at Vezirit. 50q, Rozafat. 2fr, Dursit.

1923 Typo. *Perf. 12½, 11½*
147 A18 2q orange 70 95
148 A18 5q yel grn 55 30
149 A18 10q carmine 55 30
150 A18 25q dk bl 55 30
151 A18 50q dk grn 55 30
152 A19 1fr dk vio 80 1.10
153 A19 2fr ol grn 2.25 3.00
Nos. 147-153 (7) 5.95 6.25

No. 135 Surcharged

1922 *Perf. 14x13*
154 A15 1q on 2q org 2.00 2.00

Stamps of Type A15 (No Post Horn) Overprinted

1922
156 A15 5q dp grn 3.00 2.75
157 A15 10q red 3.00 2.75

Nos. 147-151 Overprinted (top line in Black; diamond in Violet)

1924, Jan. *Perf. 12½*
158 A18 2q red org 3.00 4.00
159 A18 5q yel grn 3.00 4.00
160 A18 10q carmine 3.00 4.00
161 A18 25q dk bl 3.00 4.00
162 A18 50q dk grn 3.00 4.00
Nos. 158-162 (5) 15.00 20.00

The words "Mbledhje Kushtetuese" are in taller letters on the 25q than on the other values. This issue was to commemorate the opening of the Constituent Assembly.

No. 147 Surcharged

1924
163 A18 1q on 2q red org 75 75

Nos. 163, 147-152 Overprinted

Triumf' i legalitetit
24 Dhetuer 1924

1924
164 A18 1q on 2q org 1.75 1.75
165 A18 2q orange 1.75 1.75
166 A18 5q yel grn 1.75 1.75
167 A18 10q carmine 1.75 1.75
168 A18 25q dk bl 1.75 1.75
169 A18 50q dk grn 1.75 1.75
170 A19 1fr dk vio 1.75 1.75
Nos. 164-170 (7) 12.25 12.25

Issued to celebrate the return of the Government to the Capital after a revolution.

Nos. 163, 147-152 Overprinted

Republika Shqiptare
21 Kallnduer 1925

1925
171 A18 1q on 2q org 1.65 1.65
172 A18 2q orange 1.65 1.65
173 A18 5q yel grn 1.65 1.65
174 A18 10q carmine 1.65 1.65
175 A18 25q dk bl 1.65 1.65
176 A18 50q dk grn 1.65 1.65
177 A19 1fr dk vio 1.65 1.65
Nos. 171-177 (7) 11.55 11.55

Issued in honor of the proclamation of the Republic, Jan. 21, 1925. The date "1921" instead of "1925" occurs once in each sheet of 50.

Nos. 163, 147-153 Overprinted

1925
178 A18 1q on 2q org 65 65
a. Inverted overprint 8.25 8.25
179 A18 2q orange 65 65
180 A18 5q yel grn 65 65
a. Inverted overprint 8.25 8.25
181 A18 10q carmine 65 65
182 A18 25q dk bl 65 65
183 A18 50q dk grn 65 65
184 A19 1fr dk vio 80 80
185 A19 2fr ol grn 80 80
Nos. 178-185 (8) 5.50 5.50

President Ahmed Zogu
A25 A26

1925 *Perf. 13½, 13½x13*
186 A25 1q orange 15 15
187 A25 2q red brn 15 15
188 A25 5q green 15 15
189 A25 10q rose red 15 15
190 A25 15q gray brn 1.75 1.75
191 A25 25q dk bl 15 15
192 A25 50q bl grn 60 60
193 A26 1fr red & ultra 1.10 1.10
194 A26 2fr grn & org 1.10 1.10
195 A26 3fr brn & vio 1.75 1.75
196 A26 5fr vio & blk 4.25 4.25
Nos. 186-196 (11) 11.30 11.30

No. 193 in ultramarine and brown, and No. 194 in gray and brown were not regularly issued. Price, both $15.

Nos. 186-190 Overprinted in Various Colors

1927
197 A25 1q org (V) 50 50
198 A25 2q red brn (G) 20 20
199 A25 5q grn (R) 1.00 20
200 A25 10q rose red (Bl) 20 10
201 A25 15q gray brn (G) 10.00 10.00
202 A25 25q dk bl (R) 20 10
203 A25 50q bl grn (Bl) 20 10
204 A26 1fr red & ultra (Bk) 20 20
205 A26 2fr grn & org (Bk) 20 20
206 A26 3fr brn & vio (Bk) 75 75
207 A26 5fr vio & blk (Bk) 1.25 1.25
Nos. 197-207 (11) 14.70 13.60

No. 200 exists perf. 11.

Nos. 200, 202 Surcharged in Black or Red.

= 5 =

1928
208 A25 1q on 10q rose red 45 30
a. Inverted surcharge 5.00 5.00
209 A25 5q on 25q dk bl (R) 45 30
a. Inverted surcharge 5.00 5.00

King Zog I
A27 A28

Black Overprint.

1928 *Perf. 14 x 13½.*
210 A27 1q org brn 2.50 2.50
211 A27 2q slate 2.50 2.50
212 A27 5q bl grn 2.50 2.50
213 A27 10q rose red 2.50 2.50
214 A27 15q bister 13.50 13.50
215 A27 25q dp bl 2.00 2.00
216 A27 50q lil rose 2.50 2.50

Red Overprint.
Perf. 13½x14.
217 A28 1fr bl & sl 2.75 2.75
Nos. 210-217 (8) 30.75 30.75

A29 A30

Black or Red Overprint.

1928 *Perf. 14 x 13½.*
218 A29 1q org brn 8.50 8.50
219 A29 2q sl (R) 8.50 8.50
220 A29 5q bl grn 7.00 7.00
221 A29 10q rose red 4.50 4.50
222 A29 15q bister 5.00 5.00
223 A29 25q dp bl (R) 5.00 5.00
224 A29 50q lil rose 5.50 5.50

Perf. 13½ x 14.
225 A30 1fr bl & sl (R) 8.00 8.00
226 A30 2fr grn & sl (R) 9.50 9.50
Nos. 218-226 (9) 61.50 61.50

Issued in commemoration of the proclamation of Ahmed Zogu as King of Albania.

A31 A32

Black Overprint.

1928 *Perf. 14 x 13½.*
227 A31 1q org brn 40 40
228 A31 2q slate 20 20
229 A31 5q bl grn 1.75 20
230 A31 10q rose red 20 15
231 A31 15q bister 12.50 8.00
232 A31 25q dp bl 25 15
233 A31 50q lil rose 25 15

Perf. 13½x14.
234 A32 1fr bl & sl 50 75
235 A32 2fr grn & sl 60 75
236 A32 3fr dk red & ol bis 1.25 1.25
237 A32 5fr dl vio & gray 2.50 2.25
Nos. 227-237 (11) 20.40 14.25

The overprint reads "Kingdom of Albania".

Mbr. Shqiptare

Nos. 203, 202, 200 Surcharged in Black

■ 5 ■

1929 *Perf. 13½ x 13, 11½*
238 A25 1q on 50q bl grn 40 40
239 A25 5q on 25q dk bl 40 40
240 A25 15q on 10q rose red 65 60

RROFT-MBRETI

Nos. 186-189, 191-194 Overprinted in Black or Red

8X1929.

1929 *Perf. 11½, 13½.*
241 A25 1q orange 4.00 4.00
242 A25 2q red brn 4.00 4.00
243 A25 5q green 4.00 4.00
244 A25 10q rose red 4.00 4.00
245 A25 25q dk bl 4.00 4.00
246 A25 50q bl grn (R) 4.50 4.50
247 A26 1fr red & ultra 7.00 7.00
248 A26 2fr grn & org 8.50 8.50
Nos. 241-248 (8) 40.00 40.00

Issued to commemorate the 34th birthday of King Zog. The overprint reads "Long live the King."

Lake Butrinto
A33

King Zog I
A34

Zog Bridge
A35

Ruin at Zog Manor
A36

Wmk.220

Wmk. Double Headed Eagle. (220)
1930, Sept. 1 Photo. *Perf. 14, 14½*
250 A33 1q slate 15 10
251 A33 2q org red 15 10
252 A34 5q yel grn 15 10
253 A34 10q carmine 15 10
254 A34 15q dk brn 20 20
255 A34 25q dk ultra 25 20
256 A33 50q sl grn 35 30
257 A35 1fr violet 90 90
258 A35 2fr indigo 1.00 1.00
259 A36 3fr gray grn 2.25 2.25
260 A36 5fr org brn 3.50 3.50
Nos. 250-260 (11) 9.05 8.75

2nd anniversary of accession of King Zog I.

Nos. 250-259 Overprinted in Black

1 1
9 9
2 3
4=24Dhetuer=4

1934, Dec. 24
261 A33 1q slate 2.00 2.00
262 A33 2q org red 2.00 2.00
263 A34 5q yel grn 2.00 2.00
264 A34 10q carmine 2.00 2.00
265 A34 15q dk brn 2.00 2.00
266 A34 25q dk ultra 2.00 2.00
267 A33 50q sl grn 2.00 2.00
268 A35 1fr violet 4.50 4.50
269 A35 2fr indigo 9.00 9.00
270 A36 3fr gray grn 12.50 12.50
Nos. 261-270 (10) 40.00 40.00

Tenth anniversary of the Constitution.

Allegory of Death of Skanderbeg
A37

Albanian Eagle in Turkish Shackles
A38

Designs: 5q, 25q, 40q, 2fr, Eagle with wings spread.

1937 Unwmk. *Perf. 14*
271 A37 1q brn vio 20 20
272 A38 2q brown 20 20
273 A38 5q lt grn 30 30
274 A37 10q ol brn 40 40
275 A38 15q rose red 50 50
276 A38 25q blue 90 90
277 A37 50q dp grn 1.25 1.25
278 A38 1fr violet 2.25 2.25
279 A38 2fr org brn 5.50 5.50
Nos. 271-279 (9) 11.50 11.50

Souvenir Sheet.
280 Sheet of three 14.00 16.00
a. A37 20q red vio 2.75 3.25
b. A38 30q ol brn 2.75 3.25
c. A38 40q red 2.75 3.25

Nos. 271-280 commemorate the 25th anniversary of independence from Turkey, proclaimed Nov. 26, 1912. No. 280 measures 138x140mm.

Queen Geraldine and King Zog — A40

1938 *Perf. 14*
281 A40 1q sl vio 15 15
282 A40 2q red brn 15 15
283 A40 5q green 15 15
284 A40 10q ol brn 25 30
285 A40 15q rose red 35 50
286 A40 25q blue 60 75
287 A40 50q Prus grn 1.75 2.00
288 A40 1fr purple 3.75 4.00
Nos. 281-288 (8) 7.15 8.00

Souvenir Sheet.
289 A40 Sheet of four 17.50 20.00
a. 20q dk red vio 1.75 1.75
b. 30q brn ol 1.75 1.75

Nos. 281-289 were issued to commemorate the wedding of King Zog and Countess Geraldine Apponyi, April 27, 1938. Souvenir sheet measures 110½x139mm.

Catalogue prices for unused stamps up to mid-1953 are for hinged copies matching the condition specified in this volume's introduction.

Queen Geraldine
A42

National Emblems
A43

King Zog I — A44

1938

No.	Type	Description		
290	A42	1q dp red vio	15	20
291	A43	2q red org	15	20
292	A42	5q dp grn	15	20
293	A44	10q red brn	15	20
294	A42	15q dp rose	45	45
295	A44	25q dp bl	60	75
296	A43	50q gray blk	1.50	1.75
297	A44	1fr sl grn	5.00	5.50
		Nos. 290-297 (8)	8.15	9.25

Souvenir Sheet.

No.	Type	Description		
298		Sheet of three	17.50	20.00
b.	A43	20q Prus grn	2.25	2.25
c.	A44	30q dp vio	2.25	2.25

Nos. 290-298 were issued to commemorate the 10th anniversary of royal rule. They were on sale for three days (Aug. 30-31, Sept. 1) only, during which their use was required on all mail.

No. 298 has marginal inscriptions in Prussian green. Size: 110x65mm. The 15q deep rose (type A42) is identical with No. 294.

Issued under Italian Dominion.

Nos. 250-260 Overprinted in Black

Mbledhja Kushtetuëse 12-IV-1939 XVII

1939 Wmk. 220 *Perf. 14*

No.	Type	Description		
299	A33	1q slate	10	10
300	A33	2q org red	15	15
301	A34	5q yel grn	15	15
302	A34	10q carmine	20	20
303	A34	15q dk brn	20	20
304	A34	25q dk ultra	30	30
305	A33	50q sl grn	40	40
306	A35	1fr violet	75	75
307	A35	2fr indigo	1.00	1.00
308	A36	3fr gray grn	2.25	2.25
309	A36	5fr org brn	3.00	3.00
		Nos. 299-309 (11)	8.50	8.50

Issued in commemoration of the resolution adopted by the National Assembly, April 12, 1939, offering the Albanian Crown to Italy.

Native Costumes
A46 A47 A48

King Victor Emmanuel III
A49 A50

Native Costume
A51

Monastery
A52

Designs: 2fr, Bridge at Vezirit. 3fr, Ancient Columns. 5fr, Amphitheater.

1939 Unwmk. Photo. *Perf. 14*

No.	Type	Description		
310	A46	1q bl gray	12	12
311	A47	2q ol grn	10	10
312	A48	3q gldn brn	10	10
313	A49	5q green	10	10
314	A50	10q brown	15	10
315	A50	15q crimson	20	15
316	A50	25q sapphire	30	20
317	A50	30q brt vio	40	25
318	A51	50q dl pur	50	25
319	A49	65q red brn	75	75
320	A52	1fr myr grn	1.00	1.00
321	A52	2fr brn lake	2.25	2.25
322	A52	3fr brn blk	4.50	4.50
323	A52	5fr gray vio	8.75	8.75
		Nos. 310-323 (14)	19.22	18.62

King Victor Emmanuel III — A56

1942 Photo.

No.	Type	Description		
324	A56	5q green	12	12
325	A56	10q brown	12	12
326	A56	15q rose red	12	12
327	A56	25q blue	20	20
328	A56	65q red brn	30	30
329	A56	1fr myr grn	60	60
330	A56	2fr gray vio	1.25	1.25
		Nos. 324-330 (7)	2.71	2.71

Issued to commemorate the third anniversary of the conquest of Albania by Italy.

No. 311 Surcharged in Black **1 QIND**

No.	Type	Description		
331	A47	1q on 2q ol grn	40	40

Issued under German Administration

Stamps of 1939 Overprinted in Carmine or Brown **14 Shtator 1943**

1943

No.	Type	Description		
332	A47	2q ol grn	1.25	2.00
333	A48	3q gldn brn	1.25	2.00
334	A49	5q green	1.25	2.00
335	A50	10q brown	1.25	2.00
336	A50	15q crim (Br)	1.25	2.00
337	A50	25q sapphire	1.25	2.00
338	A50	30q brt vio	1.25	2.00
339	A49	65q red brn	1.50	3.50
340	A52	1fr myr grn	9.00	15.00
341	A52	2fr brn lake	12.00	*30.00*
342	A52	3fr brn blk	52.50	*80.00*

Surcharged with New Values.

No.	Type	Description		
343	A48	1q on 3q gldn brn	1.25	2.00
344	A49	50q on 65q red brn	1.50	3.50
		Nos. 332-344 (13)	86.50	148.00

Proclamation of Albanian independence. The overprint "14 Shtator 1943" on Nos. 324 to 328 is private and fraudulent.

Independent State

Nos. 312 to 317 and 319 to 321 Surcharged with New Value and Bars in Black or Carmine, and **QEVERIJA DEMOKRAT. E SHQIPERISE 22-X-1944**

1945

No.	Type	Description		
345	A48	30q on 3q gldn brn	2.75	2.75
346	A49	40q on 5q grn	2.75	2.75
347	A50	50q on 10q brn	2.75	2.75
348	A50	60q on 15q crim	2.75	2.75
349	A50	80q on 25q saph (C)	2.75	2.75
350	A50	1fr on 30q brt vio	2.75	2.75
351	A49	2fr on 65q red brn	2.75	2.75
352	A52	3fr on 1fr myr grn	2.75	2.75
353	A52	5fr on 2fr brn lake	2.75	2.75
		Nos. 345-353 (9)	24.75	24.75

"DEMOKRATIKE" is not abbreviated on Nos. 352 and 353.

Nos. 250, 251, 256 and 258 Surcharged in Black or Carmine, and

1945 Wmk. 220

No.	Type	Description		
354	A33	30q on 1q sl	60	60
355	A33	60q on 1q sl	70	70
356	A33	80q on 1q sl	80	80
357	A33	1fr on 1q sl	1.25	1.25
358	A33	2fr on 2q org red	1.75	1.75
359	A33	3fr on 50q sl grn	4.25	4.25
360	A35	5fr on 2fr ind	5.50	6.00
		Nos. 354-360 (7)	14.85	15.35

Albanian National Army of Liberation, second anniversary.

The surcharge on No. 360 is condensed to fit the size of the stamp.

Country House, Labinot — A57

Designs: 40q, 60q, Bridge at Berat. 1fr, 3fr, Permet.

Unwmk.

1945, Nov. 28 Typo. *Perf. 11*

No.	Type	Description		
361	A57	20q bluish grn	25	25
362	A57	30q dp org	50	50
363	A57	40q brown	50	50
364	A57	60q red vio	75	75
365	A57	1fr rose red	1.50	1.50
366	A57	3fr dk bl	7.50	7.50
		Nos. 361-366 (6)	11.00	11.00

Counterfeits exist. See note after No. B33.

Nos. 361 to 366 Overprinted in Black

ASAMBLEJA KUSHTETUESE
10 KALLHUER 1946

1946

No.	Type	Description		
367	A57	20q bluish grn	75	75
368	A57	30q dp org	75	75
369	A57	40q brown	1.25	1.25
370	A57	60q red vio	2.25	2.25
371	A57	1fr rose red	6.00	6.00
372	A57	3fr dk bl	9.50	9.50
		Nos. 367-372 (6)	20.50	20.50

Issued to commemorate the convocation of the Constitutional Assembly, January 10, 1946.

People's Republic

Nos. 361 to 366 Overprinted in Black

REPUBLIKA POPULLORE E SHQIPERISE

1946

No.	Type	Description		
373	A57	20q bluish grn	75	75
374	A57	30q dp org	1.25	1.25
375	A57	40q brown	1.75	1.75
376	A57	60q red vio	2.75	2.75
377	A57	1fr rose red	5.00	5.00
378	A57	3fr dk bl	8.50	8.50
		Nos. 373-378 (6)	20.00	20.00

Issued to commemorate the proclamation of the Albanian People's Republic.

Globe, Dove and Olive Branch — A60

Perf. 11½, Imperf.

1946, Mar. 8 Typo.

Denomination in Black.

No.	Type	Description		
379	A60	20q lil & dl red	15	15
380	A60	40q dp lil & dl red	25	25
381	A60	50q vio & dl red	40	40
382	A60	1fr lt bl & red	60	60
383	A60	2fr dk bl & red	1.25	1.25
		Nos. 379-383 (5)	2.65	2.65

International Women's Congress.

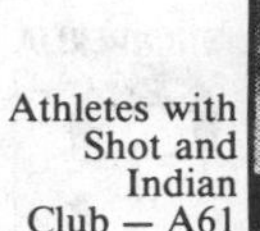

Athletes with Shot and Indian Club — A61

Perf. 11½

1946, Oct. 6 Litho. Unwmk.

No.	Type	Description		
384	A61	1q grnsh blk	8.00	8.00
385	A61	2q green	8.00	8.00
386	A61	5q brown	8.00	8.00
387	A61	10q crimson	8.00	8.00
388	A61	20q ultra	8.00	8.00
389	A61	40q rose vio	8.00	8.00
390	A61	1fr dp org	12.50	12.50
		Nos. 384-390 (7)	60.50	60.50

Balkan Games, Tirana, Oct. 6-13.

Qemal Stafa — A62

1947, May 5 *Perf. 12½x11½*

No.	Type	Description		
391	A62	20q brn & yel brn	1.75	1.75
392	A62	28q dk bl & bl	1.75	1.75
393	A62	40q brn blk & gray brn	3.00	3.00
a.		Souvenir sheet	6.50	6.50

Nos. 391 to 393a commemorate the 5th anniversary of the death of Qemal Stafa, May 5, 1942. No. 393a contains one each of Nos. 391-393 imperf. with illustrations above and below the stamps.

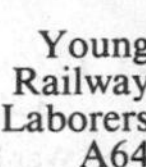

Young Railway Laborers
A64

1947, May 16 *Perf. 11½*

No.	Type	Description		
395	A64	1q brn blk & gray brn	1.00	50
396	A64	4q dk grn & grn	1.00	50
397	A64	10q blk brn & bis brn	1.00	50
398	A64	15q dk red & red	1.25	50
399	A64	20q ind & bl gray	1.75	75
400	A64	28q dk bl & bl	2.50	75
401	A64	40q brn vio & rose vio	6.50	3.50
402	A64	68q dk brn & org brn	10.00	6.50
		Nos. 395-402 (8)	25.00	13.50

Issued to publicize the construction of the Durres Elbasan Railway by Albanian youths.

Citizens Led by Hasim Zeneli — A65

Enver Hoxha and Vasil Shanto — A66

Inauguration of Vithkuq Brigade A67

Vojo Kushi — A68

1947, July 10 **Litho.**

403 A65 16q brn org & red brn 2.00 2.00
404 A66 20q org brn & dk brn 2.00 2.00
405 A67 28q bl & dk bl 2.25 2.25
406 A68 40q lil & dk brn 3.25 3.25

Issued to commemorate the 4th anniversary of the formation of Albania's army, July 10, 1943.

Conference Building Ruins, Peza — A69

Disabled Soldiers — A70

1947, Sept. 16

407 A69 2l red vio 2.50 2.00
408 A69 2.50l dp bl 2.50 2.00

Issued to commemorate the 5th anniversary of the Peza Conference, September 16, 1942.

1947, Nov. 17 ***Perf. 12½x11½***

408A A70 1l red 3.50 3.50

Issued to publicize the Disabled War Veterans Congress, November 14-20, 1947.

A71

A73

Designs: 2l, Banquet. 2.50l, Peasants rejoicing.

Perf. 11½x12½, 12½x11½

1947, Nov. 17 **Unwmk.**

409 A71 1.50l dl vio 2.75 2.75
410 A71 2l brown 2.75 2.75
411 A71 2.50l blue 2.75 2.75
412 A73 3l rose red 2.75 2.75

Issued to commemorate the 1st anniversary of the agrarian reform law of November 17, 1946.

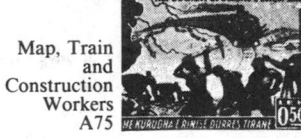

Burning Farm Buildings A74

Designs: 2.50l, Trench scene. 5l, Firing line. 8l, Winter advance. 12l, Infantry column.

1947, Nov. 29 ***Perf. 11½x12½***

Inscribed: "29-XI-1944-1947 Pervjetori I IIIte Iclirimit."

413 A74 1.50l red 2.00 2.00
414 A74 2.50l rose brn 2.50 2.50
415 A74 5l blue 3.00 3.00
416 A74 8l purple 5.00 5.00
417 A74 12l brown 7.50 7.50
Nos. 413-417 (5) 20.00 20.00

Issued to commemorate the third anniversary of Albania's liberation.

Nos. 373 to 378 Surcharged with New Value and Bars in Black.

1948, Feb. 22 ***Perf. 11***

418 A57 50q on 30q dp org 30 30
419 A57 1l on 20q bluish grn 60 60
420 A57 2.50l on 60q red vio 1.25 1.25
421 A57 3l on 1fr rose red 1.75 1.75
422 A57 5l on 3fr dk bl 2.75 2.75
423 A57 12l on 40q brn 6.00 6.00
Nos. 418-423 (6) 12.65 12.65

The two bars consist of four type squares each set close together.

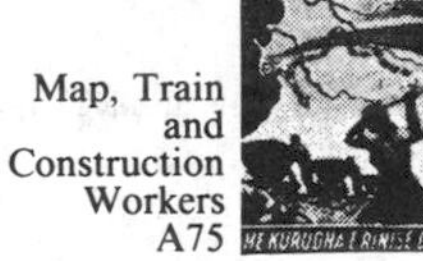

Map, Train and Construction Workers A75

1948, June 1 **Litho.** ***Perf. 11½***

424 A75 50q dk car rose 1.25 60
425 A75 1l lt grn & blk 1.50 60
426 A75 1.50l dp rose 1.50 60
427 A75 2.50l org brn & dk brn 1.50 60
428 A75 5l dl bl 2.50 1.25
429 A75 8l sal & dk brn 5.50 2.50
430 A75 12l red vio & dk vio 7.75 2.75
431 A75 20l ol gray 15.00 6.00
Nos. 424-431 (8) 36.50 14.90

Issued to publicize the construction of the Durres-Tirana Railway.

Marching Soldiers A76

Design: 8l, Battle scene.

1948, July 10

432 A76 2.50l yel brn 75 75
433 A76 5l dk bl 1.00 1.00
434 A76 8l vio gray 2.00 2.00

Issued to commemorate the 5th anniversary of the formation of Albania's army.

Bricklayer, Flag, Globe and "Industry" A77

Map and Soldier A78

1949, May 1 **Photo.** ***Perf. 12½x12***

435 A77 2.50l ol brn 25 25
436 A77 5l blue 65 65
437 A77 8l vio brn 1.00 1.00

Issued to publicize Labor Day, May 1, 1949.

1949, July 10 **Unwmk.**

438 A78 2.50l brown 35 35
439 A78 5l lt ultra 50 50
440 A78 8l brn org 1.25 1.25

Issued to commemorate the 6th anniversary of the formation of Albania's army.

Enver Hoxha A79

Albanian Citizen and Spasski Tower, Kremlin A80

1949, Oct. 16 **Engr.** ***Perf. 12½***

441 A79 50q purple 7 5
442 A79 1l dl grn 7 5
443 A79 1.50l car lake 15 5
444 A79 2.50l brown 30 5
445 A79 5l vio bl 60 15
446 A79 8l sepia 1.00 75
447 A79 12l rose lil 2.25 1.25
448 A79 20l gray bl 4.50 2.00
Nos. 441-448 (8) 8.94 4.35

1949, Sept. 10 **Photo.** ***Perf. 12½x12***

449 A80 2.50l org brn 45 45
450 A80 5l dp ultra 90 90

Albanian-Soviet friendship.

Albanian Soldier and Flag — A81

Battle Scene — A82

1949, Nov. 29 **Unwmk.** ***Perf. 12***

451 A81 2.50l brown 20 20
452 A82 3l dk red 30 40
453 A81 5l violet 45 55
454 A82 8l black 1.50 1.50

Fifth anniversary of Albania's liberation.

Joseph V. Stalin — A83

Symbols of UPU and Postal Transport — A84

1949, Dec. 21

455 A83 2.50l dk brn 25 30
456 A83 5l vio bl 65 75
457 A83 8l rose brn 1.10 1.25

Issued to commemorate the 70th anniversary of the birth of Joseph V. Stalin.

Canceled to Order

Beginning in 1950, Albania sold some issues in sheets canceled to order. Prices in second column when much less than unused are for "CTO" copies. Postally used stamps are valued at slightly less than, or the same as, unused.

1950, July 1 **Photo.** ***Perf. 12x12½***

458 A84 5l blue 1.25 1.25
459 A84 8l rose brn 1.75 1.75
460 A84 12l sepia 2.25 2.25

Issued to commemorate the 75th anniversary (in 1949) of the formation of the Universal Postal Union.

Sami Frasheri A85

Arms and Albanian Flags A86

Authors: 2.50l, Andon Zako. 3l, Naim Frasheri. 5l, Kostandin Kristoforidhi.

1950, Nov. 5 ***Perf. 14***

461 A85 2l dk grn 25 15
462 A85 2.50l red brn 35 20
463 A85 3l brn car 50 25
464 A85 5l dp bl 75 60

Issued to commemorate the "Jubilee of the Writers of the Renaissance."

1951, Jan. 11 **Engr.** ***Perf. 14x13½***

465 A86 2.50l brn car 50 25
466 A86 5l dp bl 1.00 50
467 A86 8l sepia 1.50 1.00

Issued to commemorate the 5th anniversary of the formation of the Albanian People's Republic.

Skanderbeg A87

Enver Hoxha and Congress of Permet A88

1951, Mar. 1

468 A87 2.50l brown 40 25
469 A87 5l violet 85 50
470 A87 8l ol bis 1.50 1.00

Issued to commemorate the 483rd anniversary of the death of George Castriota (Skanderbeg).

1951, May 24 **Photo.** ***Perf. 12***

471 A88 2.50l dk brn 30 20
472 A88 3l rose brn 45 30
473 A88 5l vio bl 75 50
474 A88 8l rose lil 1.25 80

Congress of Permet, 7th anniversary.

Condition is the all-important factor of price. Prices quoted are for stamps in fine condition.

Child and Globe — A89 Weighing Baby — A90

1951, July 16

475 A89	2l green	45	30
476 A90	2.50l brown	60	40
477 A90	3l red	85	50
478 A89	5l blue	1.25	80

Issued to publicize International Children's Day, June 1, 1951.

Enver Hoxha and Birthplace of Albanian Communist Party — A91

1951, Nov. 8 Photo. *Perf. 14*

479 A91	2.50l ol brn	25	25
480 A91	3l rose brn	35	35
481 A91	5l dk sl bl	60	60
482 A91	8l black	85	85

Issued to commemorate the 10th anniversary of the founding of Albania's Communist Party.

Battle Scene — A92

Designs: 5l, Schoolgirl, "Agriculture and Industry." 8l, Four portraits.

1951, Nov. 28 *Perf. 12x12½*

483 A92	2.50l brown	30	15
484 A92	5l blue	50	40
485 A92	8l brn car	1.00	75

Issued to commemorate the 10th anniversary of the formation of the Albanian Communist Youth Organization.

Albanian Heroes (Haxhija, Lezhe, Giyebegej, Mezi and Dedej) — A93

1950, Dec. 25 Unwmk. *Perf. 14*

Various Portraits

486 A93	2l dk grn	40	20
487 A93	2.50l purple	50	25
488 A93	3l scarlet	55	35
489 A93	5l brt bl	95	50
490 A93	8l ol brn	2.25	1.50
	Nos. 486-490 (5)	4.65	2.80

Issued to commemorate the 6th anniversary of Albania's liberation. Nos. 486-489 each show five "Heroes of the People"; No. 490 shows two (Stafa and Shanto).

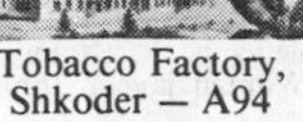

Tobacco Factory, Shkoder — A94 Composite, Lenin Hydroelectric Plant — A95

Designs: 1l, Canal. 2.50l, Textile factory. 3l, "8 November" Cannery. 5l, Motion Picture Studio, Tirana. 8l, Stalin Textile Mill, Tirana. 20l, Central Hydroelectric Dam.

1953, Aug. 1 *Perf. 12x12½, 12½x12*

491 A94	50q red brn	5	5
492 A94	1l dl grn	10	5
493 A94	2.50l brown	40	5
494 A94	3l rose brn	55	10
495 A94	5l blue	85	12
496 A94	8l brn ol	1.40	25
497 A94	12l dp plum	2.25	50
498 A94	20l sl bl	4.00	75
	Nos. 491-498 (8)	9.60	1.87

Liberation Scene — A96

1954, Nov. 29 *Perf. 12x12½*

499 A96	50q brn vio	9	5
500 A96	1l ol grn	20	5
501 A96	2.50l yel brn	45	10
502 A96	3l car rose	60	25
503 A96	5l gray bl	75	25
504 A96	8l rose brn	1.50	85
	Nos. 499-504 (6)	3.59	1.55

10th anniversary of Albania's liberation.

School — A97

Pandeli Sotiri, Petro Nini Luarasi, Nuci Naci — A98

1956, Feb. 23 Unwmk.

505 A97	2l rose vio	20	6
506 A98	2.50l lt grn	30	12
507 A98	5l ultra	60	30
508 A97	10l brt grnsh bl	1.35	50

Issued to commemorate the 70th anniversary of the opening of the first Albanian school.

Flags — A99

Designs: 5l, Labor Party headquarters, Tirana. 8l, Marx and Lenin.

1957, June 1 Engr. *Perf. 11½x11*

509 A99	2.50l brown	25	10
510 A99	5l lt vio bl	50	20
511 A99	8l rose lil	1.10	30

Issued to commemorate the 15th anniversary of the founding of Albania's Labor Party.

Congress Emblem A100

1957, Oct. 4 Unwmk. *Perf. 11½*

512 A100	2.50l gray brn	25	8
513 A100	3l rose red	35	10
514 A100	5l dk bl	45	15
515 A100	8l green	90	30

Issued to publicize the fourth International Trade Union Congress, Leipzig, Oct. 4-15.

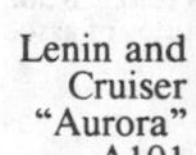

Lenin and Cruiser "Aurora" A101

1957, Nov. 7 Litho. *Perf. 10½*

516 A101	2.50l vio brn	20	12
517 A101	5l vio bl	45	22
518 A101	8l gray	60	40

Issued to commemorate the 40th anniversary of the Russian Revolution.

Albanian Fighter Holding Flag A102 Naum Veqilharxhj A103

1957, Nov. 28 *Perf. 10½*

519 A102	1.50l magenta	20	6
520 A102	2.50l brown	35	10
521 A102	5l blue	65	25
522 A102	8l green	1.10	40

Issued to commemorate the 45th anniversary of the proclamation of independence.

1958, Feb. 1 Unwmk.

523 A103	2.50l dk brn	25	12
524 A103	5l vio bl	50	20
525 A103	8l rose lil	90	40

Issued to commemorate the 160th anniversary of the birth of Naum Veqilharxhj, patriot and writer.

Luigi Gurakuqi A104 Soldiers A105

1958, Apr. 15 Photo. *Perf. 10½*

526 A104	1.50l dk grn	15	5
527 A104	2.50l brown	25	10
528 A104	5l blue	45	20
529 A104	8l sepia	90	30

Issued to commemorate the transfer of the ashes of Luigi Gurakuqi.

1958, July 10 Litho.

Design: 2.50l, 11l, Airman, sailor, soldier and tank.

530 A105	1.50l bl grn	12	5
531 A105	2.50l dk red brn	20	6
532 A105	8l rose red	60	20
533 A105	11l brt bl	90	30

15th anniversary of Albanian army.

Cerciz Topulli and Mihal Grameno A106 Buildings and Tree A107

1958, July 1

534 A106	2.50l dk ol bis	20	8
535 A107	3l green	25	10
536 A106	5l blue	45	18
537 A107	8l red brn	70	30

50th anniversary, Battle of Mashkullore.

Ancient Amphitheater and Goddess of Butrinto A108

1959, Jan. 25 Litho. *Perf. 10½*

538 A108	2.50l redsh brn	30	6
539 A108	6.50l lt bl grn	75	25
540 A108	11l dk bl	1.25	50

Cultural Monuments Week.

Frederic Joliot-Curie and World Peace Congress Emblem A109 Basketball A110

1959, July 1 Unwmk.

541 A109	1.50l car rose	75	20
542 A109	2.50l rose vio	1.35	30
543 A109	11l blue	3.75	1.50

Issued to commemorate the 10th anniversary of the World Peace Movement.

1959, Nov. 20 *Perf. 10½*

Sports: 2.50l, Soccer. 5l, Runner. 11l, Man and woman runners with torch and flags.

544 A110	1.50l brt vio	20	8
545 A110	2.50l emerald	25	15
546 A110	5l car rose	60	25
547 A110	11l ultra	1.75	75

Issued to publicize the first Albanian Spartacist Games.

Fighter and Flags A111 Mother and Child, U.N. Emblem A112

1959, Nov. 29

Designs: 2.50l, Miner with drill standing guard. 3l, Farm woman with sheaf of grain. 6.50l, Man and woman in laboratory.

548 A111	1.50l brt car	25	5
549 A111	2.50l red brn	35	5
550 A111	3l brt bl grn	45	10
551 A111	6.50l brt red	90	30
a.	Souvenir sheet	5.50	5.50

15th anniversary of Albania's liberation.

No. 551a contains one each of Nos. 548-551, imperf. and all in bright carmine. Inscribed ribbon frame of sheet and frame lines for each stamp are blue green. Size: 144x97mm.

1959, Dec. 5 Unwmk.

552 A112	5l lt grnsh bl	1.65	60
a.	Miniature sheet	4.00	4.00

Issued to commemorate the 10th anniversary (in 1958) of the signing of the Universal Declaration of Human Rights.

No. 552a contains one imperf. stamp similar to No. 552; ornamental border. Size: 74½x66mm.

Woman with Olive Branch
A113

Alexander Moissi
A114

1960, Mar. 8 Litho. *Perf. 10½*

553 A113 2.50l chocolate 30 12
554 A113 11l rose car 1.25 40

Issued to commemorate the 50th anniversary of International Women's Day, March 8.

1960, Apr. 20

555 A114 3l dp brn 20 10
556 A114 11l Prus grn 75 30

80th anniversary of the birth of Alexander Moissi (Moisiu) (1880-1935), German actor.

Lenin
A115

School Building
A116

1960, Apr. 22

557 A115 4l Prus bl 70 8
558 A115 11l lake 1.50 20

90th anniversary of birth of Lenin.

1960, May 30 Litho. *Perf. 10½*

559 A116 5l green 75 30
560 A116 6.50l plum 75 30

Issued to commemorate the 50th anniversary of the first Albanian secondary school.

Soldier on Guard Duty
A117

Liberation Monument, Tirana, Family and Policeman
A118

1960, May 12 Unwmk. *Perf. 10½*

561 A117 1.50l car rose 20 8
562 A117 11l Prus bl 1.25 30

15th anniversary of the Frontier Guards.

1960, May 14

563 A118 1.50l green 20 5
564 A118 8.50l brown 1.25 30

15th anniversary of the People's Police.

Congress Site
A119

Pashko Vasa
A120

1960, Mar. 25

565 A119 2.50l sepia 15 10
566 A119 7.50l dl bl 60 25

40th anniversary, Congress of Louchnia.

1960, May 5

Designs: 1.50l, Jani Vreto. 6.50l, Sami Frasheri. 11l, Page of statutes of association.

567 A120 1l gray ol 15 5
568 A120 1.50l brown 25 5
569 A120 6.50l blue 50 12
570 A120 11l rose red 1.00 25

Issued to commemorate the 80th anniversary (in 1959) of the Association of Albanian Authors.

Albanian Fighter and Cannon
A121

TU-104 Plane, Clock Tower, Tirana, and Kremlin, Moscow
A122

1960, Aug. 2 Litho. *Perf. 10½*

571 A121 1.50l ol brn 20 5
572 A121 2.50l maroon 25 10
573 A121 5l dk bl 60 20

Issued to commemorate the 40th anniversary of the Battle of Viona (against Italian troops.)

1960, Aug. 18

574 A122 1l redsh brn 35 12
575 A122 7.50l brt grnsh bl 1.25 50
576 A122 11.50l gray 2.25 90

Issued to commemorate the 2nd anniversary of TU-104 flights, Moscow-Tirana.

Rising Sun and Federation Emblem
A123

Ali Kelmendi
A124

1960, Nov. 10 Unwmk. *Perf. 10½*

577 A123 1.50l ultra 15 6
578 A123 8.50l red 60 20

Issued to commemorate the 15th anniversary of the International Youth Federation.

1960, Dec. 5 Litho. *Perf. 10½*

579 A124 1.50l pale gray grn 20 6
580 A124 11l dl rose lake 55 20

Issued to honor Ali Kelmendi, communist leader, on his 60th birthday.

Flags of Russia and Albania and Clasped Hands
A125

Marx and Lenin
A126

1961, Jan. 10 Unwmk. *Perf. 10½*

581 A125 2l violet 20 6
582 A125 8l dl red brn 55 20

Issued to commemorate the 15th anniversary of the Albanian-Soviet Friendship Society.

1961, Feb. 13 Litho.

583 A126 2l rose red 20 6
584 A126 8l vio bl 70 20

Fourth Communist Party Congress.

Man from Shkoder
A127

Otter
A128

1961, Apr. 28 *Perf. 10½*

Costumes: 1.50l, Woman from Shkoder. 6.50l, Man from Lume. 11l, Woman from Mirdite.

585 A127 1l slate 25 5
586 A127 1.50l dl cl 35 6
587 A127 6.50l ultra 1.25 25
588 A127 11l red 2.00 50

1961, June 25 Unwmk. *Perf. 10½*

Designs: 6.50l, Badger. 11l, Brown bear.

589 A128 2.50l grysh bl 90 25
590 A128 6.50l bl grn 2.00 60
591 A128 11l dk red brn 3.50 1.00

Dalmatian Pelicans
A129

Cyclamen
A130

Birds: 7.50l, Gray herons. 11l, Little egret.

1961, Sept. 30 *Perf. 14*

592 A129 1.50l rose car, *pnksh* 75 20
593 A129 7.50l vio, *bluish* 1.50 40
594 A129 11l red brn, *pnksh* 2.00 60

1961, Oct. 27 Litho.

Designs: 8l, Forsythia. 11l, Lily.

595 A130 1.50l brt bl & lil rose 60 15
596 A130 8l red lil & org 1.10 35
597 A130 11l brt grn & car rose 1.50 60

Milosh G. Nikolla
A131

Flag with Marx and Lenin
A132

1961, Oct. 30 *Perf. 14*

598 A131 50q vio brn 15 6
599 A131 8.50l Prus grn 60 25

Issued to commemorate the 50th anniversary of the birth of Milosh Gjergi Nikolla, poet.

1961, Nov. 8

600 A132 2.50l vermilion 30 10
601 A132 7.50l dl red brn 60 30

Issued to commemorate the 20th anniversary of the founding of Albania's Communist Party.

Worker, Farm Woman and Emblem
A133

Yuri Gagarin and Vostok 1
A134

1961, Nov. 23 Unwmk. *Perf. 14*

602 A133 2.50l vio bl 30 12
603 A133 7.50l rose cl 60 35

Issued to commemorate the 20th anniversary of the Albanian Workers' Party.

1962, Feb. 15 Unwmk. *Perf. 14*

604 A134 50q blue 35 7
605 A134 4l red lil 1.50 20
606 A134 11l dk sl grn 3.00 90

Issued to commemorate the first manned space flight, made by Yuri A. Gagarin, Soviet astronaut, Apr. 12, 1961.

Nos. 604-606 were overprinted with an over-all yellow tint and with "POSTA AJRORE" (Air Mail) in maroon in 1962. Price, set $50.

Petro Nini Luarasi
A135

Malaria Eradication Emblem
A136

1962, Feb. 28 Litho.

607 A135 50q Prus bl 20 5
608 A135 8.50l ol gray 1.20 25

Issued to commemorate the 50th anniversary (in 1961) of the death of Petro Nini Luarasi, Albanian patriot.

1962, Apr. 30 Unwmk. *Perf. 14*

609 A136 1.50l brt grn 15 6
610 A136 2.50l brn red 15 8
611 A136 10l red lil 50 25
612 A136 11l blue 75 35

Issued for the World Health Organization drive to eradicate malaria.

A souvenir sheet, issued both perf. and imperf., contains one each of Nos. 609-612, with blue marginal inscription and U.N. emblem. Size: 88x106½mm. Price $10 each. Nos. 609-612 imperf., price, set $10.

Camomile
A137

Woman Diver
A138

1962, May 10

Medicinal Plants: 8l, Linden. 11.50l, Garden sage.

613 A137 50q gray vio, yel & grn 20 7
614 A137 8l gray, yel & grn 75 25
615 A137 11.50l bis, grn & pur 1.75 50

Price, imperf. set $10.

1962, May 31 *Perf. 14*

Designs: 2.50l, Pole vault. 3l, Mt. Fuji and torch (horiz.). 9l, Woman javelin thrower. 10l, Shot putting.

616 A138 50q brt grnsh bl & blk 15 5

617 A138 2.50l gldn brn & sep 20 7
618 A138 3l bl & gray 40 8
619 A138 9l rose car & dk brn 1.10 25
620 A138 10l ol & blk 1.25 30
Nos. 616-620 (5) 3.10 75

1964 Olympic Games, Tokyo. Price, imperf. set $25. A 15l (like 3l) exists in souv. sheet, perf. and imperf.

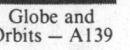

Globe and Orbits — A139

Dog Laika and Sputnik 2 — A140

Designs: 1.50l, Rocket to the sun. 20l, Lunik 3 photographing far side of the moon.

1962, June **Unwmk.** ***Perf. 14***

621 A139 50q vio & org 20 5
622 A140 1l bl grn & brn 35 10
623 A140 1.50l yel & ver 50 15
624 A139 20l mag & bl 3.50 1.00

Russian space explorations.

Nos. 621-624 exist imperforate in changed colors.

Two miniature sheets exist (101x77mm.), each containing one 14-lek picturing Sputnik 1. The perforated 14-lek is yellow and brown; the imperf. red and brown. Marginal design in blue and black.

Soccer Game, Map of South America A141

Design: 2.50l, 15l, Soccer game and globe as ball.

1962, July **Litho.**

625 A141 1l org & dk pur 10 5
626 A141 2.50l emer & bluish grn 20 5
627 A141 6.50l lt brn & pink 60 10
628 A141 15l bluish grn & mar 1.05 40

Issued to commemorate the World Soccer Championships, Chile, May 30-June 17.

Nos. 625-628 exist imperforate in changed colors.

Two miniature sheets exist (67x49mm.), each containing a single 20-lek in design similar to A141. The perforated sheet is brown and green; the imperforate sheet, brown and orange.

Map of Europe and Albania A142

Woman of Dardhe A143

Designs: 1l, 2.50l, Map of Adriatic Sea and Albania and Roman statue.

1962, Aug.

630 A142 50q multi 30 30
631 A142 1l ultra & red 75 75
632 A142 2.50l bl & red 2.25 2.25
633 A142 11l multi 4.50 4.50

Issued for tourist propaganda. Imperforates in changed colors exist.

Miniature sheets containing a 7l and 8l stamp, perf. and imperf., exist.

1962, Sept.

Regional Costumes: 1l, Man from Devoll. 2.50l, Woman from Lunxheri. 14l, Man from Gjirokaster.

635 A143 50q car, bl & pur 7 5
636 A143 1l red brn & ocher 10 5
637 A143 2.50l vio, yel grn & blk 35 15
638 A143 14l red brn & pale grn 1.25 50

Price, imperf. set $10.

Chamois A144

Ismail Qemali A145

Animals: 1l, Lynx (horiz.). 1.50l, Wild boar (horiz.). 15l, 20l, Roe deer.

1962, Oct. 24 **Unwmk.** ***Perf. 14***

639 A144 50q sl grn & dk pur 40 5
640 A144 1l org & blk 70 10
641 A144 1.50l red brn & blk 1.00 12
642 A144 15l yel ol & red brn 5.00 1.00

Miniature Sheet

643 A144 20l yel ol & red brn 12.50 12.50

No. 643 measures 71½x89mm. Imperfs. in changed colors, price #639-642 $10, #643 $15.

1962, Dec. 28 **Litho.**

Designs: 1l, Albania eagle. 16l, Eagle over fortress formed by "RPSH."

644 A145 1l red & red brn 15 5
645 A145 3l org brn & blk 30 10
646 A145 16l dk car rose & blk 1.85 70

50th anniv. of independence. Imperfs. in changed colors, price, set $10.

Monument of October Revolution A146

Henri Dunant, Cross, Globe and Nurse A147

Design: 10l, Lenin statue.

1963, Jan. 5 **Unwmk.** ***Perf. 14***

647 A146 5l yel & dl vio 25 10
648 A146 10l red org & blk 65 25

Issued to commemorate the 45th anniversary of the October Revolution (Russia, 1917).

1963, Jan 25 **Unwmk.** ***Perf. 14***

649 A147 1.50l rose lake, red & blk 20 5
650 A147 2.50l lt bl, red & blk 30 15
651 A147 6l emer, red & blk 70 30
652 A147 10l dl yel, red & blk 1.25 50

Issued to commemorate the centenary of the Geneva Conference, which led to the establishment of the International Red Cross in 1864. Imperfs. in changed colors, price, set $10.

Stalin and Battle of Stalingrad A148

Andrian G. Nikolayev A149

1963, Feb. 2

653 A148 8l dk grn & sl 2.00 50

Issued to commemorate the 20th anniversary of the Battle of Stalingrad. See No. C67.

1963, Feb. 28 **Litho.**

Designs: 7.50l, Vostoks 3 and 4 and globe (horiz.). 20l, Pavel R. Popovich. 25l, Nikolayev, Popovich and globe with trajectories.

654 A149 2.50l vio bl & sep 35 5
655 A149 7.50l lt bl & blk 70 15
656 A149 20l vio & sep 2.10 75

Miniature Sheet

657 A149 25l vio bl & sep 12.00 12.00

Issued to commemorate the first group space flight of Vostoks 3 and 4, Aug. 11-15, 1962. No. 657 measures 88x73mm. Imperfs. in changed colors, price #654-656 $10, #657 $12.

"Albania" Decorating Police Officer — A150

Polyphylla Fullo — A151

1963, Mar. 20 **Unwmk.** ***Perf. 14***

658 A150 2.50l crim, mag & blk 35 10
659 A150 7.50l org ver, dk red & blk 1.25 25

20th anniversary of the security police.

1963, Mar. 20

Beetles: 1.50l, Lucanus cervus. 8l, Procerus gigas. 10l, Cicindela Albanica.

660 A151 50q ol grn & brn 15 5
661 A151 1.50l bl & brn 35 10
662 A151 8l dl rose & blk vio 1.60 70
663 A151 10l brt cit & blk 1.90 85

1913 Stamp and Postmark A152

Design: 10l, Stamps of 1913, 1937 and 1962.

1963, May 5

664 A152 5l yel, buff, bl & blk 70 25
665 A152 10l car rose, grn & blk 1.35 45

50th anniversary of Albanian stamps.

Boxer — A153

Crested Grebe — A154

Designs: 3l, Basketball baskets. 5, 1, Volleyball. 6l, Bicyclists. 9l, Gymnast. 15l, Hands holding torch, and map of Japan.

1963, May 25 ***Perf. 13½***

666 A153 2l yel, blk & red brn 20 5
667 A153 3l ocher, brn & bl 30 10
668 A153 5l gray bl, red brn & brn 50 15
669 A153 6l gray, dk gray & grn 70 25
670 A153 9l rose, red brn & bl 1.40 30
Nos. 666-670 (5) 3.10 85

Miniature Sheet

671 A153 15l lt bl, car, blk & brn 6.75 6.75

Issued to publicize the 1964 Olympic Games in Tokyo. No. 671 contains one stamp (31x49mm.) with ocher border. Size: 60x80mm. Price, imperfs. #666-670 $5, #671 $6.

1963, Apr. 20 **Litho.** ***Perf. 14***

Birds: 3l, Golden eagle. 6.50l, Gray partridges. 11l, Capercaillie.

672 A154 50q multi 15 7
673 A154 3l multi 60 20
674 A154 6.50l multi 1.40 45
675 A154 11l multi 2.25 70

Soldier and Building A155

Designs: 2.50l, Soldier with pack, ship and plane. 5l, Soldier in battle. 6l, Soldier and bulldozer.

1963, July 10 **Unwmk.** ***Perf. 12***

676 A155 1.50l brick red, yel & blk 15 5
677 A155 2.50l bl, ocher & brn 20 6
678 A155 5l bluish grn, gray & blk 45 20
679 A155 6l red brn, buff & bl 60 35

Albanian army, 20th anniversary.

Maj. Yuri A. Gagarin A156

Designs: 5l, Maj. Gherman Titov. 7l, Maj. Andrian G. Nikolayev. 11l, Lt. Col. Pavel R. Popovich. 14l, Lt. Col. Valeri Bykovski. 20l, Lt. Valentina Tereshkova.

1963, July 30

Portraits in Yellow and Black

680 A156 3l brt pur 35 10
681 A156 5l dl bl 50 15
682 A156 7l gray 70 15
683 A156 11l dp cl 1.20 35
684 A156 14l bl grn 1.75 55
685 A156 20l ultra 2.50 1.00
Nos. 680-685 (6) 7.00 2.30

Man's conquest of space. Price, imperf. set $12.50.

Volleyball A157

Sports: 3l, Weight lifting. 5l, Soccer. 7l, Boxing. 8l, Rowing.

1963, Aug. 31 ***Perf. 12x12½***

686 A157 2l cit, red & blk 15 5
687 A157 3l dk red, bis & blk 25 8
688 A157 5l emer, org & blk 45 15
689 A157 7l dp pink, emer & blk 55 25
690 A157 8l dp bl, dp pink & blk 1.05 30
Nos. 686-690 (5) 2.45 83

European championships. Imperfs. in changed colors, price set $10.

Papilio Podalirius A158

1963, Sept. 29 **Litho.**

Various Butterflies and Moths in Natural Colors

691 A158 1l red 15 5

692 A158 2l blue 30 10
693 A158 4l dl lil 50 25
694 A158 5l pale grn 90 40
695 A158 8l bister 1.10 55
696 A158 10l lt bl 1.65 70
Nos. 691-696 (6) 4.60 2.05

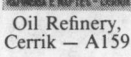

Oil Refinery, Cerrik — A159

Flag and Shield — A160

Designs: 2.50l, Food processing plant, Tirana (horiz.). 30l, Fruit canning plant. 50l, Tannery (horiz.).

1963, Nov. 15 Unwmk. *Perf. 14*
697 A159 2.50l rose red, *pnksh* 25 8
698 A159 20l sl grn,*grnsh* 85 20
699 A159 30l dl pur,*grysh* 2.00 50
700 A159 50l ocher,*yel* 2.25 75

Industrial development in Albania.

1963, Nov. 24 *Perf. 12½x12*
701 A160 2l grnsh bl, blk, ocher & red 35 6
702 A160 8l bl, blk, ocher & red 1.00 65

1st Congress of Army Aid Assn.

Chinese, Caucasian and Negro Men A161

1963, Dec. 10 *Perf. 12x11½*
703 A161 3l bis & blk 35 15
704 A161 5l bis & ultra 60 25
705 A161 7l bis & vio 1.00 40

Issued to commemorate the 15th anniversary of the Universal Declaration of Human Rights.

Slalom Ascent A162

Lenin A163

Designs: 50q, Bobsled (horiz.). 6.50l, Ice hockey (horiz.). 12.50l, Women's figure skating. No. 709A, Ski jumper.

1963, Dec. 25 *Perf. 14*
706 A162 50q grnsh bl & blk 15 5
707 A162 2.50l red, gray & blk 30 6
708 A162 6.50l yel, blk & gray 80 20
709 A162 12.50l red, blk & yel grn 1.75 50

Miniature Sheet

709A A162 12.50l multi 4.50 4.50

Issued to publicize the 9th Winter Olympic Games, Innsbruck, Jan. 29-Feb. 9, 1964. Size of No. 709A: 56x75mm. Imperfs. in changed colors, price #706-709 $12.50, #709A $15.

1964, Jan. 21 *Perf. 12½x12*
710 A163 5l gray & bis 30 12
711 A163 10l gray & ocher 60 30

40th anniversary, death of Lenin.

A little time given to the study of the arrangement of the Scott Catalogue can make it easier to use effectively.

Hurdling A164

Sturgeon A165

Designs: 3l, Track (horiz.). 6.50l, Rifle shooting (horiz.). 8l, Basketball.

Perf. 12½x12, 12x12½

1964, Jan. 30 Litho.
712 A164 2.50l pale vio & ultra 20 10
713 A164 3l lt grn & red brn 30 15
714 A164 6.50l bl & cl 60 25
715 A164 8l lt bl & ocher 85 30

Issued to commemorate the 1st Games of the New Emerging Forces, GANEFO, Jakarta, Indonesia, Nov. 10-22, 1963.

1964, Feb. 26 Unwmk. *Perf. 14*

Designs: Various fish.

716 A165 50q *shown* 10 5
717 A165 1l *Gilthead* 10 5
718 A165 1.50l *Striped mullet* 25 10
719 A165 2.50l *Carp* 40 15
720 A165 6.50l *Mackerel* 1.10 40
721 A165 10l *Lake Ohrid trout* 1.90 50
Nos. 716-721 (6) 3.85 1.25

Red Squirrel A166

Designs: Wild animals.

1964, March 28 *Perf. 12½x12*
722 A166 1l *shown* 10 5
723 A166 1.50l *Beech marten* 15 5
724 A166 2l *Red fox* 30 5
725 A166 2.50l *Hedgehog* 35 10
726 A166 3l *Hare* 40 15
727 A166 5l *Jackal* 70 25
728 A166 7l *Wildcat* 1.00 35
729 A166 8l *Wolf* 1.25 50
Nos. 722-729 (8) 4.25 1.50

Lighting Olympic Torch — A167

Designs: 5l, Torch and globes. 7l, 15l, Olympic flag and Mt. Fuji. 10l, National Stadium, Tokyo.

1964, May 18 *Perf. 12x12½*
730 A167 3l lt yel grn, yel & buff 20 6
731 A167 5l red & vio bl 35 10
732 A167 7l lt bl, ultra & yel 50 20
733 A167 10l org, bl & vio 70 30

Miniature Sheet

734 A167 15l lt bl, ultra & org 6.50 6.50

Issued to publicize the 18th Olympic Games, Tokyo, October 10-25, 1964. No. 734 contains one stamp (49x62mm.) with orange border. Size: 80x90mm. Imperfs. in changed colors, price #730-733 $6.50, #734 $9.

Partisans — A168

Designs: 5l, Arms of Albania. 8l, Enver Hoxha.

Perf. 12½x12

1964, May 24 Litho. Unwmk.
735 A168 2l org, red & blk 15 6
736 A168 5l multi 35 10
737 A168 8l red brn, blk & red 70 20

Issued to commemorate the 20th anniversary of the National Anti-Fascist Congress of Liberation, Permet, May 24, 1944. The label attached to each stamp, without perforations between, carries a quotation from the 1944 Congress.

Albanian Flag and Revolutionists A169

Full Moon A170

Perf. 12½x12

1964, June 10 Litho. Unwmk.
738 A169 2.50l red & gray 10 10
739 A169 7.50l lil rose & gray 35 20

Issued to commemorate the 40th anniversary of the Albanian revolution of 1924.

1964, June 27 *Perf. 12x12½*

Designs: 5l, New moon. 8l, Half moon. 11l, Waning moon. 15l, Far side of moon.

740 A170 1l pur & yel 15 5
741 A170 5l vio & yel 40 15
742 A170 8l bl & yel 70 30
743 A170 11l grn & yel 1.05 45

Miniature Sheet

Perf. 12 on 2 sides

744 A170 15l ultra & yel 7.00 7.00

No. 744 contains one stamp (35x36mm.) with bister border, perforated at top and bottom. Size: 66½x79mm. Imperfs. in changed colors, price #740-743 $7, #744 $9.

No. 733 with Added Inscription: "Rimini 25-VI-64"

1964 *Perf. 12x12½*
745 A167 10l org, bl & vio 2.10 2.10

Issued to commemorate the "Toward Tokyo 1964" Philatelic Exhibition at Rimini, Italy, June 25-July 6.

Wren — A171

Birds: 1l, Penduline titmouse. 2.50l, Green woodpecker. 3l, Tree creeper. 4l, Nuthatch. 5l, Great titmouse. 6l, Goldfinch. 18l, Oriole.

1964, July 31 *Perf. 12x12½*
746 A171 50q multi 10 5
747 A171 1l org & multi 10 5
748 A171 2.50l multi 20 3
749 A171 3l bl & multi 30 7
750 A171 4l yel & multi 40 10
751 A171 5l bl & multi 50 15

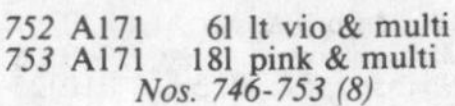
752 A171 6l lt vio & multi 70 30
753 A171 18l pink & multi 2.10 85
Nos. 746-753 (8) 4.40 1.62

Running and Gymnastics A172

Sport: 2l, Weight lifting, judo. 3l, Equestrian, bicycling. 4l, Soccer, water polo. 5l, Wrestling, boxing. 6l, Pentathlon, hockey. 7l, Swimming, sailing. 8l, Basketball, volleyball. 9l, Rowing, canoeing. 10l, Fencing, pistol shooting. 20l, Three winners.

Perf. 12x12½

1964, Sept. 25 Litho. Unwmk.
754 A172 1l lt bl, rose & emer 10 5
755 A172 2l bis brn, bluish grn & vio 10 5
756 A172 3l vio, red org & ol bis 25 5
757 A172 4l grnsh bl, ol & ultra 25 10
758 A172 5l grnsh bl, car & pale lil 40 15
759 A172 6l dk bl, org & lt bl 45 20
760 A172 7l dk bl, lt ol & org 50 20
761 A172 8l emer, gray & yel 70 30
762 A172 9l bl, yel & lil rose 85 40
763 A172 10l brt grn, org brn & yel grn 2.10 65
Nos. 754-763 (10) 5.70 2.15

Miniature Sheet

Perf. 12

764 A172 20l vio & lem 8.00 8.00

Issued to commemorate the 18th Olympic Games, Tokyo, Oct. 10-25. No. 764 contains one stamp (41x68mm.) with violet border. Size: 55x82mm. Imperfs. in changed colors, price #754-763 $10, #764 $8.

Arms of People's Republic of China — A173

Mao Tse-tung and Flag A174

1964, Oct. 1 *Perf. 11½x12, 12x11½*
765 A173 7l blk, red & yel 65 30
766 A174 8l blk, red & yel 1.0040

Issued to commemorate the 15th anniversary of the People's Republic of China.

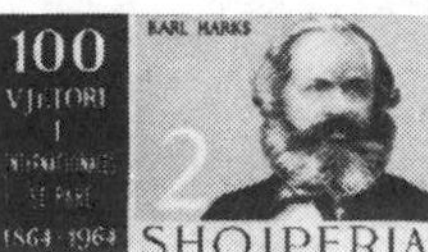

Karl Marx A175

Jeronim de Rada A176

Designs: 5l, St. Martin's Hall, London. 8l, Friedrich Engels.

1964, Nov. 5 *Perf. 12x11½*
767 A175 2l red, lt vio & blk 38 10
768 A175 5l gray bl 85 20
769 A175 8l ocher, blk & red 1.65 35

Centenary of First Socialist International.

1964, Nov. 15 *Perf. 12½x11½*

770	A176	7l sl grn	65	30
771	A176	8l dl vio	85	35

Issued to commemorate the 150th anniversary of the birth of Jeronim de Rada, poet.

Arms of Albania — A177

Factories A178

Designs: 3l, Combine harvester. 4l, Woman chemist. 10l, Hands holding Constitution, hammer and sickle.

Perf. 11½x12, 12x11½

1964, Nov. 29

772	A177	1l multi	20	5
773	A178	2l red, yel & vio bl	28	6
774	A178	3l red, yel & brn	50	8
775	A178	4l red, yel & gray grn	60	15
776	A177	10l red, bl & blk	1.00	45
		Nos. 772-776 (5)	2.58	79

20th anniversary of liberation.

Planet Mercury — A179

Planets: 2l, Venus and rocket. 3l, Earth, moon and rocket. 4l, Mars and rocket. 5l, Jupiter. 6l, Saturn. 7l, Uranus. 8l, Neptune. 9l, Pluto. 15l, Solar system and rocket.

1964, Dec. 15 *Perf. 12x12½*

777	A179	1l yel & pur	10	5
778	A179	2l multi	15	5
779	A179	3l multi	25	5
780	A179	4l multi	30	15
781	A179	5l yel, dk pur & brn	45	15
782	A179	6l lt grn, vio brn & yel	70	20
783	A179	7l yel & grn	80	25
784	A179	8l yel & vio	1.00	30
785	A179	9l lt grn, yel & blk	1.35	50
		Nos. 777-785 (9)	5.10	1.70

Miniature Sheet

Perf. 12 on 2 sides

786	A179	15l car, bl, yel & grn	10.00	10.00

No. 786 contains one stamp (62x51mm.) with yellow marginal inscription, perforated at top and bottom. Size: 87x72mm. Imperfs. in changed colors, price #777-785 $10, #786 $10.

European Chestnut A180

Symbols of Industry A181

1965, Jan. 25 *Perf. 11½x12*

787	A180	1l *shown*	10	5
788	A180	2l *Medlars*	15	5
789	A180	3l *Persimmon*	30	10
790	A180	4l *Pomegranate*	35	15
791	A180	5l *Quince*	50	20
792	A180	10l *Orange*	1.00	35
		Nos. 787-792 (6)	2.40	90

1965, Feb. 20

Designs: 5l, Books, triangle and compass. 8l, Beach, trees and hotel.

793	A181	2l blk, car rose & pink	50	40
794	A181	5l yel, gray & blk	1.00	85
795	A181	8l blk, vio bl & lt bl	1.75	1.60

Issued to commemorate the 20th anniversary of professional trade associations.

Water Buffalo A182

Various designs: Water buffalo.

1965, Mar. *Perf. 12x11½*

796	A182	1l lt yel grn, yel & brn blk	20	5
797	A182	2l lt bl, dk gray & blk	45	10
798	A182	3l yel, brn & grn	60	15
799	A182	7l brt grn, yel & brn blk	1.40	35
800	A182	12l pale lil, dk brn & ind	2.25	65
		Nos. 796-800 (5)	4.90	1.30

Mountain View, Valbona — A183

Views: 1.50l, Seashore. 3l, Glacier and peak (vert.). 4l, Gorge (vert.). 5l, Mountain peaks. 9l, Lake and hills.

1965, Mar. **Litho.** *Perf. 12*

801	A183	1.50l multi	75	20
802	A183	2.50l multi	1.10	30
803	A183	3l multi	1.40	35
804	A183	4l multi	1.75	50
805	A183	5l multi	2.50	70
806	A183	9l multi	4.00	1.00
		Nos. 801-806 (6)	11.50	3.05

Frontier Guard A184

Small-bore Rifle Shooting, Prone A185

1965, Apr. 25 **Unwmk.**

807	A184	2.50l lt bl & multi	75	15
808	A184	12.50l l ultra & multi	3.25	90

20th anniversary of the Frontier Guards.

1965, May 10

Designs: 2l, Rifle shooting, standing. 3l, Target over map of Europe, showing Bucharest. 4l, Pistol shooting. 15l, Rifle shooting, kneeling.

809	A185	1l lil, car rose, blk & brn	10	5
810	A185	2l bl, blk, brn & vio bl	25	5
811	A185	3l pink & car rose	30	15
812	A185	4l bis, blk & vio brn	40	15
813	A185	15l brt grn, brn & vio brn	1.40	50
		Nos. 809-813 (5)	2.45	90

Issued to commemorate the European Shooting Championships, Bucharest.

ITU Emblem, Old and New Communications Equipment A186

Col. Pavel Belyayev A187

1965, May 17 *Perf. 12½x12*

814	A186	2.50l brt grn, blk & lil rose	50	10
815	A186	12.50l vio, blk & brt bl	3.00	45

Issued to commemorate the centenary of the International Telecommunication Union.

1965, June 15 *Perf. 12*

Designs: 2l, Voskhod II. 6.50l, Lt. Col. Alexei Leonov. 20l, Leonov floating in space.

816	A187	1.50l lt bl & brn	10	5
817	A187	2l dk bl, lt vio & lt ultra	15	5
818	A187	6.50l lil & brn	60	20
819	A187	20l chlky bl, yel & blk	1.75	45

Miniature Sheet

Perf. 12 on 2 sides

820	A187	20l brt bl, org & blk	7.00	7.00

Issued to commemorate the space flight of Voskhod II and the first man walking in space, Lt. Col. Alexei Leonov. No. 820 contains one stamp (size: 51x59½mm.), orange border, perforated at top and bottom; size: 72x85mm. Imperf., brt grn background, price $7.

Marx and Lenin — A188

1965, June 21 *Perf. 12*

821	A188	2.50l dk brn, red & yel	50	15
822	A188	7.50l sl grn, org ver & buff	1.25	35

Issued to commemorate the 6th Conference of Postal Ministers of Communist Countries, Peking, June 21-July 15.

Mother and Child — A189

Designs: 2l, Pioneers. 3l, Boy and girl at play (horiz.). 4l, Child on beach. 15l, Girl with book.

Perf. 12½x12, 12x12½

1965, June 29 **Litho.** **Unwmk.**

823	A189	1l brt bl, rose lil & blk	10	5
824	A189	2l sal, vio & blk	20	10
825	A189	3l grn, org & vio	30	10
826	A189	4l multi	40	15
827	A189	15l lil rose, brn & ocher	1.25	50
		Nos. 823-827 (5)	2.25	90

Issued for International Children's Day.

Statue of Magistrate A190

Fuchsia A191

1965, July 20 *Perf. 12*

Designs: 1l, Amphora. 2l, Illyrian armor. 3l, Mosaic (horiz.). 15l, Torso, Apollo statue.

828	A190	1l lt ol, org & brn	10	5
829	A190	2l gray grn, grn & brn	20	5
830	A190	3l tan, brn, car & lil	35	10
831	A190	4l grn, bis & brn	50	20
832	A190	15l gray & pale cl	1.25	65
		Nos. 828-832 (5)	2.40	1.05

1965, Aug. 11 *Perf. 12½x12*

Flowers: 2l, Cyclamen. 3l, Tiger lily. 3.50l, Iris. 4l, Dahlia. 4.50l, Hydrangea. 5l, Rose. 7l, Tulips.

833	A191	1l multi	10	5
834	A191	2l multi	15	5
835	A191	3l multi	25	10
836	A191	3.50l multi	30	15
837	A191	4l multi	35	15
838	A191	4.50l multi	40	15
839	A191	5l multi	50	20
840	A191	7l multi	90	30
		Nos. 833-840 (8)	2.95	1.15

Nos. 698-700 Surcharged New Value and Two Bars

1965, Aug. 16 *Perf. 14*

841	A159	5q on 30l dl pur, *grysh*	12	10
842	A159	15q on 30l dl pur, *grysh*	30	12
843	A159	25q on 50l ocher, *yel*	45	12
844	A159	80q on 50l ocher, *yel*	90	30
845	A159	1.10l on 20l sl grn, *grnsh*	1.35	45
846	A159	2l on 20l sl grn, *grnsh*	2.75	90
		Nos. 841-846 (6)	5.87	1.99

White Stork — A192

"Homecoming," by Bukurosh Sejdini — A193

Migratory Birds: 20q, Cuckoo. 30q, Hoopoe. 40q, European bee-eater. 50q, European nightjar. 1.50l, Quail.

1965, Aug. 31 *Perf. 12*

847	A192	10q yel, blk & gray	10	5
848	A192	20q brt pink, blk & dk bl	20	10
849	A192	30q vio, blk & bis	30	15
850	A192	40q emer, blk yel & org	65	20
851	A192	50q ultra, brn & red brn	75	30
852	A192	1.50l bis, red brn & dp org	2.10	1.00
		Nos. 847-852 (6)	4.10	1.80

1965, Sept. 26 **Litho.** *Perf. 12x12½*

853	A193	25q ol blk	90	20
854	A193	65q bl blk	2.10	40
855	A193	1.10l black	3.00	75

Second war veterans' meeting.

The first price column gives the catalogue value of an unused stamp, the second that of a used stamp.

Hunter and Capercaillie A194

Oleander A195

Hunting: 20q, Deer. 30q, Pheasant. 40q, Mallards. 50q, Boar. 1l, Rabbit.

1965, Oct. 6 Litho. Unwmk.

856	A194	10q	gray & multi	12	5
857	A194	20q	lt grn, red brn & dk brn	20	10
858	A194	30q	bl & multi	40	18
859	A194	40q	rose lil & grn	60	20
860	A194	50q	lt vio bl, blk & brn	70	25
861	A194	1l	cit, ol & brn	2.10	55
			Nos. 856-861 (6)	4.12	1.33

1965, Oct. 26 *Perf. 12½x12*

Flowers: 20q, Forget-me-nots. 30q, Pink. 40q, White water lily. 50q, Bird's foot. 1l, Corn poppy.

862	A195	10q	brt bl, grn & car rose	20	5
863	A195	20q	org red, bl, brn & grn	24	10
864	A195	30q	vio, car rose & grn	50	12
865	A195	40q	emer, yel & blk	70	18
866	A195	50q	org brn, yel & grn	80	20
867	A195	1l	yel grn, blk & rose red	1.75	70
			Nos. 862-867 (6)	4.19	1.35

Hotel Turizmi, Fier — A196

Freighter "Teuta" — A197

Buildings: 10q, Hotel, Peshkopi. 15q, Sanatorium, Tirana. 25q, Rest home, Pogradec. 65q, Partisan Sports Arena, Tirana. 80q, Rest home, Mali Dajt. 1.10l, Culture House, Tirana. 1.60l, Hotel Adriatik, Durres. 2l, Migjeni Theater, Shkoder. 3l, Alexander Moissi House of Culture, Durres.

1965, Oct. *Perf. 12x12½*

868	A196	5q	bl & blk	5	5
869	A196	10q	ocher & blk	6	5
870	A196	15q	dl grn & blk	10	5
871	A196	25q	vio & blk	18	10
872	A196	65q	lt brn & blk	65	12
873	A196	80q	yel grn & blk	80	20
874	A196	1.10l	lil & blk	1.25	30
875	A196	1.60l	lt vio bl & blk	1.60	50
876	A196	2l	dl rose & blk	2.25	70
877	A196	3l	gray & blk	3.75	1.00
			Nos. 868-877 (10)	10.69	3.07

1965, Nov. 16

Ships: 20q, Raft. 30q, Sailing ship, 19th century. 40q, Sailing ship, 18th century. 50q, Freighter "Vlora." 1l, Illyric galleys.

878	A197	10q	brt grn & dk grn	10	5
879	A197	20q	ol bis & dk grn	20	10
880	A197	30q	lt & dp ultra	35	12
881	A197	40q	vio & dp vio	60	18
882	A197	50q	pink & dk red	75	20
883	A197	1l	bis & brn	1.50	45
			Nos. 878-883 (6)	3.50	1.10

Brown Bear A198

Basketball and Players A199

Designs: Various Albanian bears. 50q, 55q, 60q, horizontal.

1965, Dec. 7 *Perf. 11½x12*

884	A198	10q	bis & dk brn	28	5
885	A198	20q	pale brn & dk brn	38	10
886	A198	30q	bis, dk brn & car	60	12
887	A198	35q	pale brn & dk brn	75	15
888	A198	40q	bis & dk brn	1.10	18
889	A198	50q	bis & dk brn	1.40	20
890	A198	55q	bis & dk brn	1.40	30
891	A198	60q	pale brn, dk brn & car	1.50	45
			Nos. 884-891 (8)	7.41	1.55

1965, Dec. 15 Litho. *Perf. 12½x12*

Designs: 10q, Games' emblem (map of Albania and basket). 30q, 50q, Players with ball (diff. designs). 1.40l, Basketball medal on ribbon.

892	A199	10q	bl, yel & car	18	5
893	A199	20q	rose lil, lt brn & blk	30	6
894	A199	30q	bis, lt brn, red & blk	40	12
895	A199	50q	lt grn, lt brn & blk	90	20
896	A199	1.40l	rose, blk, brn & yel	1.75	70
			Nos. 892-896 (5)	3.53	1.13

Issued to commemorate the Seventh Balkan Basketball Championships, Tirana, Dec. 15-19.

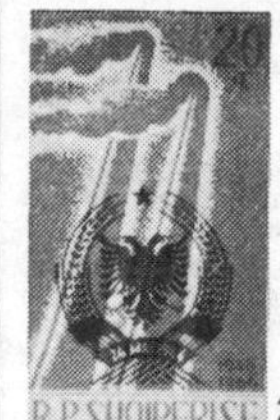

Arms of Republic and Smokestacks — A200

Designs (Arms and): 10q, Book. 30q, Wheat. 60q, Book, hammer and sickle. 80q, Factories.

1966, Jan. 11 Litho. *Perf. 11½x12*
Coat of Arms in Gold

897	A200	10q	crim & brn	10	5
898	A200	20q	bl & vio bl	12	5
899	A200	30q	org yel & brn	25	7
900	A200	60q	yel grn & brt grn	40	20
901	A200	80q	crim & brn	90	25
			Nos. 897-901 (5)	1.77	62

Issued to commemorate the 20th anniversary of the Albanian People's Republic.

Cow — A201

Perf. 12½x12, 12x12½
1966, Feb. 25

902	A201	10q	*shown*	16	6
903	A201	20q	*Pig*	26	10
904	A201	30q	*Ewe & lamb*	40	12
905	A201	35q	*Ram*	55	18
906	A201	40q	*Dog*	80	20
907	A201	50q	*Cat*, vert.	90	20
908	A201	55q	*Horse*, vert.	1.10	30
909	A201	60q	*Ass*, vert.	1.40	35
			Nos. 902-909 (8)	5.57	1.51

Soccer Player and Map of Uruguay A202

Andon Zako Cajupi A203

Designs: 5q, Globe in form of soccer ball. 15q, Player and map of Italy. 20q, Goalkeeper and map of France. 25q, Player and map of Brazil. 30q, Player and map of Switzerland. 35q, Player and map of Sweden. 40q, Player and map of Chile. 50q, Player and map of Great Britain. 70q, World Championship cup and ball.

1966, March 20 Litho. *Perf. 12*

910	A202	5q	gray & dp org	10	5
911	A202	10q	lt brn, bl & vio	12	5
912	A202	15q	cit, dk bl & brt bl	20	5
913	A202	20q	org, vio bl & brt bl	30	10
914	A202	25q	sal & sep	35	10
915	A202	30q	lt yel grn & brn	40	18
916	A202	35q	lt ultra & emer	45	20
917	A202	40q	pink & brn	70	20
918	A202	50q	pale grn, mag & rose red	70	25
919	A202	70q	gray, brn, yel & blk	90	40
			Nos. 910-919 (10)	4.22	1.58

Issued to publicize the World Cup Soccer Championship, Wembley, England, July 11-30.

1966, March 27 Unwmk.

920	A203	40q	bluish blk	30	12
921	A203	1.10l	dk grn	90	25

Issued to commemorate the centenary of the birth of the poet Andon Zako Cajupi.

Painted Lady — A204

WHO Headquarters, Geneva, and Emblem — A205

Designs: 20q, Blue dragonfly. 30q, Cloudless sulphur butterfly. 35q, 40q, Splendid dragonfly. 50q, Machaon swallow-tail. 55q, Sulphur butterfly. 60q, Whitemarbled butterfly.

1966, Apr. 21 Litho. *Perf. 11½x12*

922	A204	10q	multi	10	6
923	A204	20q	yel & multi	18	6
924	A204	30q	yel & multi	30	10
925	A204	35q	sky bl & multi	35	12
926	A204	40q	multi	40	15
927	A204	50q	rose & multi	55	20
928	A204	55q	multi	60	20
929	A204	60q	multi	1.00	25
			Nos. 922-929 (8)	3.48	1.14

Perf. 12x12½, 12½x12
1966, May 3 Litho.

Designs (WHO Emblem and): 35q, Ambulance and stretcher bearers (vert.). 60q, Albanian mother and nurse weighing infant (vert.). 80q, X-ray machine and hospital.

930	A205	25q	lt bl & blk	30	5
931	A205	35q	sal & ultra	60	10
932	A205	60q	lt grn, bl & red	90	18
933	A205	80q	yel, bl, grn & lt brn	1.35	35

Issued to commemorate the inauguration of the World Health Organization Headquarters, Geneva.

Bird's Foot Starfish — A206

Designs: 25q, Starfish. 35q, Brittle star. 45q, But-thorn starfish. 50q, Starfish. 60q, Sea cucumber. 70q, Sea urchin.

1966, May 10 *Perf. 12x12½*

934	A206	15q	multi	20	5
935	A206	25q	multi	35	8
936	A206	35q	multi	50	10
937	A206	45q	multi	70	15
938	A206	50q	multi	85	18
939	A206	60q	multi	1.00	20
940	A206	70q	multi	1.40	35
			Nos. 934-940 (7)	5.00	1.11

Luna 10 — A207

Designs: 30q, 80q, Trajectory of Luna 10, earth and moon.

1966, June 10 *Perf. 12x12½*

941	A207	20q	bl, yel & blk	30	10
942	A207	30q	yel grn, blk & bl	45	15
943	A207	70q	vio, yel & blk	90	25
944	A207	80q	yel, vio, grn & blk	1.25	25

Issued to commemorate the launching of the first artificial moon satellite, Luna 10, April 3, 1966.

Jules Rimet Cup and Soccer A208

Designs: Various scenes of soccer play.

1966, July 12 Litho. *Perf. 12x12½*
Black Inscriptions

945	A208	10q	ocher & lil	10	5
946	A208	20q	lt bl & cit	15	6
947	A208	30q	brick red & Prus bl	25	10
948	A208	35q	lt ultra & rose	35	15
949	A208	40q	yel grn & lt red brn	40	15
950	A208	50q	lt red brn & yel grn	65	18
951	A208	55q	rose lil & yel grn	70	20
952	A208	60q	dp rose & ocher	1.35	35
			Nos. 945-952 (8)	3.95	1.24

Issued to commemorate the World Cup Soccer Championship, Wembley, England, July 11-30.

Water Level Map of Albania — A209

Designs: 30q, Water measure and fields. 70q, Turbine and pylon. 80q, Hydrological decade emblem.

1966, July *Perf. 12½x12*

953	A209	20q	brick red, blk & org	18	10
954	A209	30q	emer, blk & lt brn	25	12
955	A209	70q	brt vio & blk	65	30
956	A209	80q	brt bl, org, yel & blk	70	35

Issued to publicize the Hydrological Decade (UNESCO), 1965-74.

Greek Turtle — A210

Designs: 15q, Grass snake. 25q, European pond turtle. 30q, Wall lizard. 35q, Wall gecko. 45q, Emerald lizard. 50q, Slowworm. 90q, Horned viper (or sand viper).

1966, Aug. 10 Litho. *Perf. 12½x12*

957 A210 10q gray & multi 10 5
958 A210 15q yel & multi 20 10
959 A210 25q ultra & multi 30 15
960 A210 30q multi 40 18
961 A210 35q multi 55 20
962 A210 45q multi 65 25
963 A210 50q org & multi 75 30
964 A210 90q lil & multi 1.65 55
Nos. 957-964 (8) 4.60 1.78

Persian Cat A211

Cats: 10q, Siamese (vert.). 15q, European tabby (vert.). 25q, Black kitten. 60q, 65q, 80q, Various Persians.

Perf. 12x12½, 12½x12

1966, Sept. 20 Litho.

965 A211 10q multi 14 5
966 A211 15q blk, sep & car 25 6
967 A211 25q blk, dk & lt brn 35 12
968 A211 45q blk, org & yel 70 20
969 A211 60q blk, brn & yel 90 25
970 A211 65q multi 1.00 25
971 A211 80q blk, gray & yel 1.75 35
Nos. 965-971 (7) 5.09 1.28

Pjeter Budi — A212

1966, Oct. 5 *Perf. 12x12½*

972 A212 25q buff & sl grn 20 10
973 A212 1.75l gray & dl cl 1.35 65

Issued to honor Pjeter Budi, writer.

UNESCO Emblem A213

Designs (UNESCO Emblem and): 15q, Open book, rose and school. 25q, Male folk dancers. 1.55l, Jug, column and old building.

1966, Oct. 20 Litho. *Perf. 12*

974 A213 5q lt gray & multi 12 5
975 A213 15q dp bl & multi 25 10
976 A213 25q gray & multi 50 18
977 A213 1.55l multi 2.25 60

Issued to commemorate the 20th anniversary of UNESCO (United Nations Educational, Scientific and Cultural Organization).

Prices of premium quality never hinged stamps will be in excess of catalogue price.

Hand Holding Book with Pictures of Marx, Engels, Lenin and Stalin A214

Hammer and Sickle, Party Emblem in Sunburst A215

Designs: 25q, Map of Albania, hammer and sickle, symbols of agriculture and industry. 65q, Symbolic grain and factories. 95q, Fists holding rifle, spade, axe, sickle and book.

1966, Nov. 1 Litho. *Perf. 11½x12*

978 A214 15q ver & gold 18 5
979 A214 25q multi 25 8
980 A214 65q brn, brn org & gold 65 20
981 A214 95q yel & multi 90 45

Issued to commemorate the 5th Congress of the Albanian Communist Party.

1966, Nov. 8

Designs: 25q, Partisan and sunburst. 65q, Steel worker and blast furnace. 95q, Combine harvester, factories, and pylon.

982 A215 15q org & multi 18 5
983 A215 25q red & multi 25 8
984 A215 65q multi 65 20
985 A215 95q bl & multi 90 45

Issued to commemorate the 25th anniversary of the founding of the Albanian Workers Party.

Russian Wolfhound — A216

Dogs: 15q, Sheep dog. 25q, English setter. 45q, English springer spaniel. 60q, Bulldog. 65q, Saint Bernard. 80q, Dachshund.

1966 Litho. *Perf. 12½x12*

986 A216 10q grn & multi 22 6
987 A216 15q multi 30 10
988 A216 25q lil & multi 42 15
989 A216 45q rose & multi 90 45
990 A216 60q brn & multi 1.10 50
991 A216 65q ultra & multi 1.25 55
992 A216 80q bl grn & multi 1.75 65
Nos. 986-992 (7) 5.94 2.46

Ndre Mjeda A217

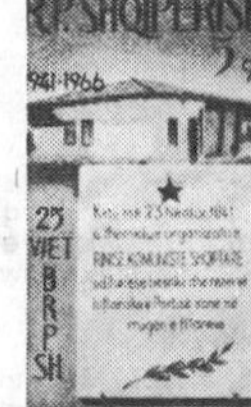

Proclamation A218

1966 *Perf. 12½x12*

993 A217 25q brt bl & dk brn 45 10
994 A217 1.75l brt grn & dk brn 1.75 65

Birth Centenary of the priest Ndre Mjeda.

1966 *Perf. 11½x12, 12x11½*

Designs: 10q, Banner, man and woman holding gun and axe (horiz.). 1.85l, man with axe and banner and partisan with gun.

995 A218 5q lt brn, red & blk 5 5
996 A218 10q red, blk, gray & bl 18 5
997 A218 1.85l red, blk & sal 1.35 45

Issued to commemorate the 25th anniversary of the Albanian Communist Party.

Golden Eagle — A219

Birds of Prey: 15q, European sea eagle. 25q, Griffon vulture. 40q, Common sparrowhawk. 50q, Osprey. 70q, Egyptian vulture. 90q, Kestrel.

1966, Dec. 20 Litho. *Perf. 11½x12*

998 A219 10q gray & multi 12 5
999 A219 15q multi 18 10
1000 A219 25q cit & multi 35 18
1001 A219 40q multi 55 25
1002 A219 50q multi 65 30
1003 A219 70q yel & multi 90 45
1004 A219 90q multi 1.25 65
Nos. 998-1004 (7) 4.00 1.98

Hake A220

Fish: 15q, Red mullet. 25q, Opah. 40q, Atlantic wolf fish. 65q, Lumpfish. 80q, Swordfish. 1.15l, Shorthorn sculpin.

1967, Jan. Photo. *Perf. 12x11½*

Fish in Natural Colors

1005 A220 10q blue 14 5
1006 A220 15q lt yel grn 24 5
1007 A220 25q Prus bl 30 10
1008 A220 40q emerald 75 18
1009 A220 65q brt bl grn 85 25
1010 A220 80q blue 1.25 35
1011 A220 1.15l brt grn 1.65 60
Nos. 1005-1011 (7) 5.18 1.58

White Pelican A221

Designs: Various groups of pelicans.

1967, Feb. 22 Litho. *Perf. 12*

1012 A221 10q pink & multi 10 5
1013 A221 15q pink & multi 15 6
1014 A221 25q pink & multi 40 10
1015 A221 50q pink & multi 70 20
1016 A221 2l pink & multi 2.75 1.00
Nos. 1012-1016 (5) 4.10 1.41

Camellia A222

Flowers: 10q, Chrysanthemum. 15q, Hollyhock. 25q, Flowering Maple. 35q, Peony. 65q, Gladiolus. 80q, Freesia. 1.15l, Carnation.

Unwmk.

1967, Apr. 12 Litho. *Perf. 12*

Flowers in Natural Colors

1017 A222 5q pale brn 10 5
1018 A222 10q lt lil 10 5
1019 A222 15q gray 15 6
1020 A222 25q ultra 25 10
1021 A222 35q lt bl 45 10
1022 A222 65q lt bl grn 70 20
1023 A222 80q lt bluish gray 1.00 35
1024 A222 1.15l dl yel 1.35 65
Nos. 1017-1024 (8) 4.10 1.56

Congress Emblem and Power Station — A223

1967, Apr. 24 Litho. *Perf. 12*

1025 A223 25q gray lil, sep & brt rose 25 10
1026 A223 1.75l gray, blk & brt rose 2.00 55

Issued to commemorate the Congress of the Union of Professional Workers, Tirana, Apr. 24.

Rose — A224

Various Roses in Natural Colors

1967, May 15 *Perf. 12x12½*

1027 A224 5q bl gray 5 5
1028 A224 10q brt bl 7 5
1029 A224 15q rose vio 10 5
1030 A224 25q lemon 30 5
1031 A224 35q brt grnsh bl 40 10
1032 A224 65q gray 70 20
1033 A224 80q brown 90 30
1034 A224 1.65l gray grn 2.00 55
Nos. 1027-1034 (8) 4.52 1.35

Seashore, Bregdet Borsh — A225

Views: 15q, Buthrotum (vert.). 25q, Shore, Fshati Piqeras. 45q, Shore, Bregdet. 50q, Shore, Bregdet Himare. 65q, Ship, Sarande (Santi Quaranta). 80q, Shore, Dhermi. 1l, Sunset, Bregdet (vert.).

Perf. 12x12½, 12½x12

1967, June 10

1035 A225 15q multi 10 5
1036 A225 20q multi 15 6
1037 A225 25q multi 18 10
1038 A225 45q multi 45 15
1039 A225 50q multi 50 20
1040 A225 65q multi 70 25
1041 A225 80q multi 75 30
1042 A225 1l multi 1.00 45
Nos. 1035-1042 (8) 3.83 1.56

Fawn A226

Roe Deer: 20q, Stag (vert.). 25q, Doe (vert.). 30q, Young stag and doe. 35q, Doe and fawn. 40q, Young stag (vert.). 65q, Stag and doe (vert.). 70q, Running stag and does.

Perf. 12½x12, 12x12½

1967, July 20 **Litho.**

1043 A226 15q yel grn, gldn brn & blk 25 5
1044 A226 20q lt bl, org brn & blk 25 6
1045 A226 25q yel, org brn & blk 38 8
1046 A226 30q vio bl, ol bis & blk 45 10
1047 A226 35q pink, dk red brn & blk 55 10
1048 A226 40q lt vio, bis brn & blk 70 10
1049 A226 65q yel, org brn & blk 1.10 30
1050 A226 70q grnsh bl, org brn & blk 1.10 35
Nos. 1043-1050 (8) 4.78 1.14

Man and Woman from Madhe A227

Fighters and Newspaper — A228

Regional Costumes: 20q, Woman from Zadrimes. 25q, Dancer and drummer, Kukesit. 45q, Woman spinner, Dardhes. 50q, Farm couple, Myseqese. 65q, Dancer with tambourine, Tirana. 80q, Man and woman, Dropullit. 1l, Piper, Laberise.

1967, Aug. 25 *Perf. 12*

1051 A227 15q tan & multi 10 6
1052 A227 20q lt yel grn 20 10
1053 A227 25q multi 20 10
1054 A227 45q sky bl & multi 40 25
1055 A227 50q lem & multi 60 30
1056 A227 65q pink & multi 70 45
1057 A227 80q multi 90 50
1058 A227 1l gray & multi 1.25 65
Nos. 1051-1058 (8) 4.35 2.41

1967, Aug. 25 *Perf. 12½x12*

Designs: 75q, Printing plant, newspapers and microphone. 2l, People holding newspaper.

1059 A228 25q multi 30 8
1060 A228 75q pink & multi 70 18
1061 A228 2l multi 1.75 50

Issued for the Day of the Press.

Street Scene, by Kolé Idromeno — A229

Hakmarrja Battalion, by Sali Shijaku — A230

Designs: 20q, David, fresco by Onufri, 16th century (vert.). 45q, Woman's head, ancient mosaic (vert.). 50q, Men on horseback from 16th century icon (vert.). 65q, Farm Women, by Zef Shoshi. 80q, Street Scene, by Vangjush Mio. 1l, Bride, by Kolé Idromeno (vert.).

Perf. 12, 12x12½, (A230)

1967, Oct. 25 **Litho.**

1062 A229 15q multi 25 8
1063 A229 20q multi 30 8
1064 A230 25q multi 35 10
1065 A229 45q multi 75 12
1066 A229 50q multi 85 14
1067 A230 65q multi 1.00 18
1068 A230 80q multi 1.25 30
1069 A230 1l multi 1.75 40
Nos. 1062-1069 (8) 6.50 1.40

Lenin at Storming of Winter Palace A231

Rabbit A232

Designs: 15q, Lenin and Stalin (horiz.). 50q, Lenin and Stalin addressing meeting. 1.10l, Storming of the Winter Palace (horiz.).

1967, Nov. 7 *Perf. 12*

1070 A231 15q red & multi 15 5
1071 A231 25q sl grn & blk 25 10
1072 A231 50q brn, blk & brn vio 40 15
1073 A231 1.10l lil, gray & blk 1.25 30

Issued to commemorate the 50th anniversary of the Russian October Revolution.

1967, Nov. 25

Designs: Various hares and rabbits. The 15q, 25q, 35q, 40q and 1l are horizontal.

1074 A232 15q org & multi 10 5
1075 A232 20q brt yel & multi 10 5
1076 A232 25q lt brn & multi 12 5
1077 A232 35q multi 18 8
1078 A232 40q yel & multi 30 8
1079 A232 50q pink & multi 35 15
1080 A232 65q multi 65 30
1081 A232 1l lil & multi 95 45
Nos. 1074-1081 (8) 2.75 1.21

University, Torch and Book — A233

1967 **Litho.** *Perf. 12*

1082 A233 25q multi 25 5
1083 A233 1.75l multi 1.60 40

Issued to commemorate the 10th anniversary of the founding of the State University, Tirana.

Coat of Arms and Soldiers A234

Designs: 65q, Arms, Factory, grain, flag, gun and radio tower. 1.20l, Arms and hand holding torch.

1967 *Perf. 12x11½*

1084 A234 15q multi 15 5
1085 A234 65q multi 65 15
1086 A234 1.20l multi 1.10 20

25th anniversary of the Democratic Front.

Turkey — A235

Designs: 20q, Duck. 25q, Hen. 45q, Rooster. 50q, Guinea fowl. 65q, Goose (horiz.). 80q, Mallard (horiz.). 1l, Chicks (horiz.).

Perf. 12x12½, 12½x12

1967, Nov. 25 **Photo.**

1087 A235 15q gold & multi 10 5
1088 A235 20q gold & multi 10 5
1089 A235 25q gold & multi 12 6
1090 A235 45q gold & multi 20 10
1091 A235 50q gold & multi 30 10
1092 A235 65q gold & multi 40 20
1093 A235 80q gold & multi 70 30
1094 A235 1l gold & multi 90 40
Nos. 1087-1094 (8) 2.82 1.26

Skanderbeg A236

Designs: 10q, Arms of Skanderbeg. 25q, Helmet and sword. 30q, Kruje Castle. 35q, Petreles Castle. 65q, Berati Castle. 80q, Skanderbeg addressing national chiefs. 90q, Battle of Albulenes.

1967, Dec. 10 **Litho.** *Perf. 12x12½*

Medallion in Bister and Dark Brown

1095 A236 10q gold & vio 6 5
1096 A236 15q gold & rose car 8 5
1097 A236 25q gold & vio bl 13 6
1098 A236 30q gold & dk bl 15 9
1099 A236 35q gold & mar 20 12
1100 A236 65q gold & grn 35 18
1101 A236 80q gold & gray brn 60 20
1102 A236 90q gold & ultra 1.00 25
Nos. 1095-1102 (8) 2.57 1.00

Issued to commemorate the 500th anniversary of the death of Skanderbeg (George Castriota), national hero.

Ice Hockey — A237

Designs: 15q, 2l, Winter Olympics emblem. 30q, Women's figure skating. 50q, Slalom. 80q, Downhill skiing. 1l, Ski jump.

1967-68

1103 A237 15q multi 6 5
1104 A237 25q multi 10 5
1105 A237 30q multi 15 6
1106 A237 50q multi 30 12
1107 A237 80q multi 60 20
1108 A237 1l multi 85 30
Nos. 1103-1108 (6) 2.06 78

Miniature Sheet

Imperf

1109 A237 2l red, gray & brt bl ('68) 6.00 6.00

Issued to publicize the 10th Winter Olympic Games, Grenoble, France, Feb. 6-18. Size of No. 1109: 55x66mm.

Nos. 1103-1108 issued Dec. 29, 1967.

Skanderbeg Monument, Kruje — A238

Designs: 10q, Skanderbeg monument, Tirana. 15q, Skanderbeg portrait, Uffizi Galleries, Florence. 25q, engraved portrait of Gen. Tanush Topia. 35q, Portrait of Gen. Gjergj Arianti (horiz.). 65q, Portrait bust of Skanderbeg by O. Paskali. 80q, Title page of "The Life of Skanderbeg." 90q, Skanderbeg battling the Turks, painting by S. Rrota (horiz.).

Perf. 12x12½, 12½x12

1968, Jan. 17 **Litho.**

1110 A238 10q multi 15 5
1111 A238 15q multi 25 5
1112 A238 25q blk, yel & lt bl 35 5
1113 A238 30q multi 40 5
1114 A238 35q lt vio, pink & blk 60 10
1115 A238 65q multi 1.00 15
1116 A238 80q pink, blk & yel 1.25 20
1117 A238 90q beige & multi 1.75 25
Nos. 1110-1117 (8) 5.75 90

Issued to commemorate the 500th anniversary of the death of Skanderbeg (George Castriota), national hero.

Carnation A239

1968, Feb. 15 *Perf. 12*

Various Carnations in Natural Colors

1118 A239 15q green 8 5
1119 A239 20q dk brn 10 5
1120 A239 25q brt bl 12 5
1121 A239 50q gray ol 20 10
1122 A239 80q bluish gray 55 20
1123 A239 1.10l vio gray 75 30
Nos. 1118-1123 (6) 1.80 75

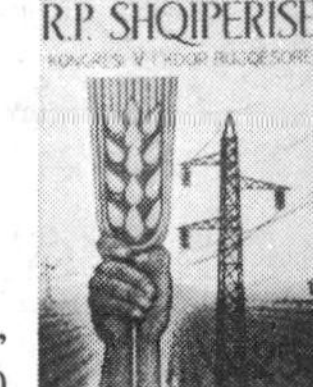

"Electrification" A240

Designs: 65q, Farm tractor (horiz.). 1.10l, Cow and herd.

1968, Mar. 5 **Litho.** *Perf. 12*

1124 A240 25q multi 20 5
1125 A240 65q multi 60 10
1126 A240 1.10l multi 85 25

Fifth Farm Cooperatives Congress.

Goat A241

Designs: Various goats. 15q, 20q and 25q are vertical.

Perf. 12x12½, 12½x12

1968, Mar. 25

1127 A241 15q multi 10 5
1128 A241 20q multi 10 5
1129 A241 25q multi 15 5
1130 A241 30q multi 18 5
1131 A241 40q multi 25 8
1132 A241 50q multi 30 10
1133 A241 80q multi 50 20
1134 A241 1.40l multi 1.25 40
Nos. 1127-1134 (8) 2.83 98

Zef N. Jubani A242

Physician and Hospital A243

1968, Mar. 30 *Perf. 12*

1135 A242 25q yel & choc 20 10
1136 A242 1.75l lt vio & blk 85 35

Issued to commemorate the sesquicentennial of the birth of Zef N. Jubani, writer and scholar.

Perf. 12½x12, 12x12½

1968, Apr. 7 **Litho.**

Designs (World Health Organization Emblem and): 65q, Hospital and microscope (horiz.). 1.10l, Mother feeding child.

1137 A243 25q grn & cl 20 6
1138 A243 65q blk, yel & bl 60 15
1139 A243 1.10l blk & dp org 90 25

Issued to commemorate the 20th anniversary of the World Health Organization.

Scientist A244

Women: 15q, Militia member. 60q, Farm worker. 1l, Factory worker.

1968, Apr. 14 *Perf. 12*

1140 A244 15q ver & dk red 15 5
1141 A244 25q bl grn & grn 20 10
1142 A244 60q dl yel & brn 35 18
1143 A244 1l lt vio & vio 85 35

Issued to commemorate the 25th anniversary of the Albanian Women's Organization.

Karl Marx — A245

Designs: 25q, Marx lecturing to students. 65q, "Das Kapital," "Communist Manifesto" and marching crowd. 95q, Full-face portrait.

1968, May 5 **Litho.** *Perf. 12*

1144 A245 15q gray, dk bl & bis 15 6
1145 A245 25q brn vio, dk brn & dl yel 30 10
1146 A245 65q gray, blk, brn & car 80 25
1147 A245 95q gray, ocher & blk 1.25 50

Karl Marx, 150th birth anniversary.

Heliopsis A246

Flowers: 20q, Red flax. 25q, Orchid. 30q, Gloxinia. 40q, Turk's-cap lily. 80q, Amaryllis. 1.40l, Red magnolia.

1968, May 10 *Perf. 12x12½*

1148 A246 15q gold & multi 6 5
1149 A246 20q gold & multi 8 5
1150 A246 25q gold & multi 10 5
1151 A246 30q gold & multi 15 5
1152 A246 40q gold & multi 40 10
1153 A246 80q gold & multi 50 10
1154 A246 1.40l gold & multi 75 30
Nos. 1148-1154 (7) 2.04 70

Proclamation of Prizren A247

Designs: 25q, Abdyl Frasheri. 40q, House in Prizren.

1968, June 10 **Litho.** *Perf. 12*

1155 A247 25q emer & blk 20 5
1156 A247 40q multi 45 10
1157 A247 85q yel & multi 85 25

Issued to commemorate the 90th anniversary of the League of Prizren against the Turks.

Shepherd, by A. Kushi — A248

Paintings from Tirana Art Gallery: 20q, View of Tirana, by V. Mio (horiz.). 25q, Mountaineer, by G. Madhi. 40q, Refugees, by A. Buza. 80q, Guerrillas of Shahin Matrakut, by S. Xega. 1.50l, Portrait of an Old Man, by S. Papadhimitri. 1.70l, View of Scutari, by S. Rrota. 2.50l, Woman in Scutari Costume, by Z. Colombi.

1968, June 20 *Perf. 12x12½*

1158 A248 15q gold & multi 10 5
1159 A248 20q gold & multi 12 5
1160 A248 25q gold & multi 15 6
1161 A248 40q gold & multi 30 10
1162 A248 80q gold & multi 50 10
1163 A248 1.50l gold & multi 90 25
1164 A248 1.70l gold & multi 1.00 50
Nos. 1158-1164 (7) 3.07 1.11

Miniature Sheet

Perf. 12½xImperf.

1165 A248 2.50l multi 2.50 1.00

No. 1165 contains one stamp with picture frame in margin. Size of stamp: 50x71mm.; size of sheet: 89x113mm.

Soldier and Guns — A249

Designs: 25q, Sailor and warships. 65q, Aviator and planes (vert.). 95q, Militiamen and woman.

1968, July 10 **Litho.** *Perf. 12*

1166 A249 15q multi 15 5
1167 A249 25q multi 25 10
1168 A249 65q multi 65 15
1169 A249 95q multi 1.20 25

25th anniversary of the People's Army.

Squid A250

Designs: 20q, Crayfish. 25q, Whelk. 50q, Crab. 70q, Spiny lobster. 80q, Shore crab. 90q, Norway lobster.

1968, Aug. 20

1170 A250 15q multi 10 5
1171 A250 20q multi 10 5
1172 A250 25q multi 15 5
1173 A250 50q multi 25 10
1174 A250 70q multi 40 25
1175 A250 80q multi 50 30
1176 A250 90q multi 75 35
Nos. 1170-1176 (7) 2.25 1.15

Women's Relay Race — A251

Sport: 20q, Running. 25q, Women's discus. 30q, Equestrian. 40q, High jump. 50q, Women's hurdling. 80q, Soccer. 1.40l, Woman diver. 2l, Olympic stadium.

1968, Sept. 23 **Photo.** *Perf. 12*

1177 A251 15q multi 8 5
1178 A251 20q multi 12 5
1179 A251 25q multi 15 5
1180 A251 30q multi 25 5
1181 A251 40q multi 30 10
1182 A251 50q multi 45 10
1183 A251 80q multi 70 20
1184 A251 1.40l multi 1.25 45
Nos. 1174-1184 (8) 3.30 1.05

Souvenir Sheet

Perf. 12½ Horizontally

1185 A251 2l multi 3.00 1.00

Issued to publicize the 19th Olympic Games, Mexico City, Oct. 12-27. No. 1185 contains one rectangular stamp, size: 64x54mm. Sheet has ocher marginal inscription. Size: 90x82mm. Price of imperfs., #1177-1184 $6, #1185 $5.

Enver Hoxha — A252

1968, Oct. 16 **Litho.** *Perf. 12*

1186 A252 25q bl gray 25 12
1187 A252 35q rose brn 40 18
1188 A252 80q violet 70 35
1189 A252 1.10l brown 90 50

Souvenir Sheet

Imperf

1190 A252 1.50l rose red, bl vio & gold *55.00 55.00*

Issued for the 60th birthday of Enver Hoxha, First Secretary of the Central Committee of the Communist Party of Albania. No. 1190 contains portrait (size: 45x55mm.) with name of country, denomination and commemorative inscription in margin. Size: 79x90mm.

Book and Pupils A253

1968, Nov. 14 **Photo.**

1191 A253 15q mar & sl grn 20 10
1192 A253 85q gray ol & sep 1.30 25

Issued to commemorate the 60th anniversary of the Congress of Monastir, Nov. 14-22, 1908, which adopted a unified Albanian alphabet.

Waxwing — A254

Birds: 20q, Rose-colored starling. 25q, Kingfishers. 50q, Long-tailed tits. 80q, Wallcreeper. 1.10l, Bearded tit.

1968, Nov. 15 **Litho.**

Birds in Natural Colors

1193 A254 15q lt bl & blk 10 5
1194 A254 20q bis & blk 15 5
1195 A254 25q pink & blk 25 10
1196 A254 50q lt yel grn & blk 30 15
1197 A254 80q bis brn & blk 65 25
1198 A254 1.10l pale grn & blk 85 30
Nos. 1193-1198 (6) 2.30 90

Mao Tse-tung — A255

1968, Dec. 26 **Litho.** *Perf. 12½x12*

1199 A255 25q gold, red & blk 25 15
1200 A255 1.75l gold, red & blk 1.25 30

Issued to commemorate the 75th birthday of Mao Tse-tung, Chairman of the Communist Party of the People's Republic of China.

Adem Reka and Crane — A256

Portraits: 10q, Pjeter Lleshi and power lines. 15q, Mohammed Shehu and Myrteza Kepi. 25q, Shkurte Vata and women railroad workers. 65q, Agron Elezi, frontier guard. 80q, Ismet Bruçaj and mountain road. 1.30l, Fuat Cela, blind revolutionary.

1969, Feb. 10 **Litho.** *Perf. 12x12½*

1201 A256 5q multi 5 5
1202 A256 10q multi 6 5
1203 A256 15q multi 10 5
1204 A256 25q multi 12 6
1205 A256 65q multi 35 10

1206	A256	80q	multi	60	15
1207	A256	1.30l	multi	1.00	30
			Nos. 1201-1207 (7)	2.28	76

Issued to honor a contemporary heroine and heroes.

Meteorological Instruments A257

Designs: 25q, Water gauge. 1.60l, Radar, balloon and isobars.

1969, Feb. 25 ***Perf. 12***

1208	A257	15q	multi	15	5
1209	A257	25q	ultra, org & blk	25	10
1210	A257	1.60l	rose vio, yel & blk	1.35	35

Issued to commemorate the 20th anniversary of Albanian hydrometeorology.

Partisans, 1944, by F. Haxmiu — A258

Paintings: 5q, Student Revolutionists, by P. Mele (vert.). 65q, Steel Mill, by C. Ceka. 80q, Reconstruction, by V. Kilica. 1.10l, Harvest, by N. Jonuzi. 1.15l, Terraced Landscape, by S. Kaceli. 2l, Partisans' Meeting.

Perf. 12x12½, 12½x12

1969, Apr. 25 **Litho.**

Size: 31½x41½mm.

1211	A258	5q	buff & multi	5	5

Size: 51½x30½mm.

1212	A258	25q	buff & multi	10	6

Size: 40½x32mm.

1213	A258	65q	buff & multi	25	10

Size: 51½x30½mm.

1214	A258	80q	buff & multi	35	15
1215	A258	1.10l	buff & multi	55	20
1216	A258	1.15l	buff & multi	70	25
			Nos. 1211-1216 (6)	2.00	81

Miniature Sheet

Imperf

Size: 111x90mm.

1217	A258	2l	ocher & multi	1.50	90

Leonardo da Vinci, Self-portrait A259

Designs (after Leonardo da Vinci): 35q, Lilies. 40q, Design for a flying machine (horiz.). 1l, Portrait of Beatrice. No. 1222, Portrait of a Noblewoman. No. 1223, Mona Lisa.

Perf. 12x12½, 12½x12

1969, May 2 **Litho.**

1218	A259	25q	gold & sep	15	5
1219	A259	35q	gold & sep	25	10
1220	A259	40q	gold & sep	30	10
1221	A259	1l	gold & multi	80	20
1222	A259	2l	gold & sep	1.50	55
			Nos. 1218-1222 (5)	3.00	1.00

Miniature Sheet

Imperf

1223	A259	2l	gold & multi	3.00	2.25

Issued to commemorate the 450th anniversary of the death of Leonardo da Vinci (1452-1519), painter, sculptor, architect and engineer. Size of No. 1223: 64x95mm.

First Congress Meeting Place A260

Designs: 1l, Albanian coat of arms. 2.25l, Two partisans with guns and flag.

1969, May 24 ***Perf. 12***

1224	A260	25q	lt grn, blk & red	25	15
1225	A260	2.25l	multi	1.75	1.10

Souvenir Sheet

1226	A260	1l	gold, bl, blk & red	*22.50*	*15.00*

25th anniversary of the First Anti-Fascist Congress of Permet, May 24, 1944.

No. 1226 contains one stamp; blue, black and red decorative margin. Size: 94½x100mm.

Albanian Violet — A261

Designs: Violets and Pansies.

1969, June 30 **Litho.** ***Perf. 12x12½***

1227	A261	5q	gold & multi	5	5
1228	A261	10q	gold & multi	10	5
1229	A261	15q	gold & multi	10	5
1230	A261	20q	gold & multi	15	10
1231	A261	25q	gold & multi	25	10
1232	A261	80q	gold & multi	40	30
1233	A261	1.95l	gold & multi	1.00	65
			Nos. 1227-1233 (7)	2.05	1.30

Plum, Fruit and Blossoms A262

Designs: Blossoms and Fruits.

1969, Aug. 10 **Litho.** ***Perf. 12***

1234	A262	10q	*shown*	5	5
1235	A262	15q	*Lemon*	10	5
1236	A262	25q	Pomegranate	15	5
1237	A262	50q	*Cherry*	30	10
1238	A262	80q	*Peach*	50	20
1239	A262	1.20l	*Apple*	90	35
			Nos. 1234-1239 (6)	2.00	80

Basketball — A263

Designs: 10q, 80q, 2.20l, Various views of basketball game. 25q, Hand aiming ball at basket and map of Europe (horiz.).

1969, Sept. 15 **Litho.** ***Perf. 12***

1240	A263	10q	multi	7	5
1241	A263	15q	buff & multi	10	5
1242	A263	25q	bl & multi	25	7
1243	A263	80q	multi	60	15
1244	A263	2.20l	multi	1.50	45
			Nos. 1240-1244 (5)	2.52	77

Issued to publicize the 16th European Basketball Championships, Naples, Italy, Sept. 27-Oct. 5.

Runner A264

Designs: 5q, Games' emblem. 10q, Woman gymnast. 20q, Pistol shooting. 25q, Swimmer at start. 80q, Bicyclist. 95q, Soccer.

1969, Sept. 30

1245	A264	5q	multi	5	5
1246	A264	10q	multi	8	5
1247	A264	15q	multi	10	5
1248	A264	20q	multi	18	6
1249	A264	25q	multi	25	8
1250	A264	80q	multi	55	18
1251	A264	95q	multi	85	25
			Nos. 1245-1251 (7)	2.06	72

Second National Spartakiad.

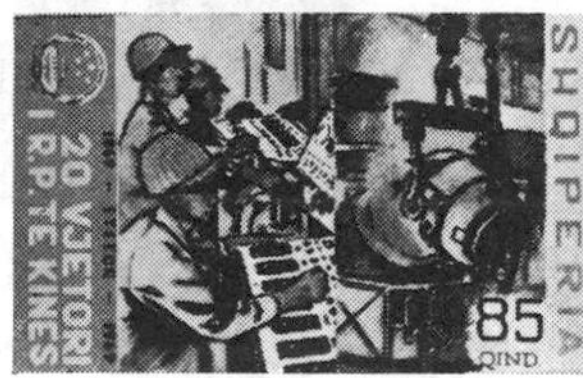

Electronic Technicians, Steel Ladle — A265

Designs: 25q, Mao Tse-tung with microphones (vert.). 1.40l, Children holding Mao's red book (vert.).

1969, Oct. 1 **Litho.** ***Perf. 12***

1252	A265	25q	multi	20	5
1253	A265	85q	multi	50	15
1254	A265	1.40l	multi	80	30

Issued to commemorate the 20th anniversary of the People's Republic of China.

Enver Hoxha A266

Designs: 80q, Pages from Berat resolution. 1.45l, Partisans with flag.

1969, Oct. 20 **Litho.** ***Perf. 12***

1255	A266	25q	multi	20	5
1256	A266	80q	gray & multi	50	15
1257	A266	1.45l	ocher & multi	80	30

Issued to commemorate the 25th anniversary of the second reunion of the National Antifascist Liberation Council, Berat.

Soldiers — A267

Designs: 30q, Oil refinery. 35q, Combine harvester. 45q, Hydroelectric station and dam. 55q, Militia woman, man and soldier. 1.10l, Dancers and musicians.

1969, Nov. 29

1258	A267	25q	multi	10	5
1259	A267	30q	multi	10	5
1260	A267	35q	multi	10	5
1261	A267	45q	multi	15	10
1262	A267	55q	multi	35	10
1263	A267	1.10l	multi	75	15
			Nos. 1258-1263 (6)	1.55	50

Issued to commemorate the 25th anniversary of the socialist republic.

Joseph V. Stalin — A268

1969, Dec. 21 **Litho.** ***Perf. 12***

1264	A268	15q	lilac	6	5
1265	A268	25q	sl bl	10	5
1266	A268	1l	brown	40	15
1267	A268	1.10l	vio bl	70	20

Issued to commemorate the 90th anniversary of the birth of Joseph V. Stalin (1879-1953), Russian political leader.

Head of Woman — A269

Greco-Roman Mosaics: 25q, Geometrical floor design (horiz.). 80q, Bird and tree (horiz.). 1.10l, Floor with birds and grapes (horiz.). 1.20l, Fragment with corn within oval design.

1969, Dec. 25 ***Perf. 12½x12***

1268	A269	15q	gold & multi	10	5
1269	A269	25q	gold & multi	15	5
1270	A269	80q	gold & multi	40	10
1271	A269	1.10l	gold & multi	60	20
1272	A269	1.20l	gold & multi	80	35
			Nos. 1268-1272 (5)	2.05	75

Cancellation of 1920 — A270

Design: 25q, Proclamation and congress site.

1970, Jan. 21 Litho. *Perf. 12*

1273	A270	25q	red, gray & blk	15	6
1274	A270	1.25l	dk grn, yel & blk	85	15

Congress of Louchnia, 50th anniversary.

Worker, Student and Flag
A271

1970, Feb. 11 *Perf. 12½x12*

1275	A271	25q	red & multi	15	5
1276	A271	1.75l	red & multi	85	30

Issued to commemorate the 25th anniversary of vocational organizations in Albania.

Turk's-cap Lily
A272

Lilies: 5q, Cernum (vert.). 15q, Madonna (vert.). 25q, Royal (vert.). 1.10l, Tiger. 1.15l, Albanian.

Perf. 11½x12, 12x11½

1970, Mar. 10 Litho.

1277	A272	5q	multi	5	5
1278	A272	15q	multi	8	5
1279	A272	25q	multi	15	5
1280	A272	80q	multi	40	12
1281	A272	1.10l	multi	60	20
1282	A272	1.15l	multi	75	30
			Nos. 1277-1282 (6)	2.03	77

Lenin
A273

Designs (Lenin): 5q, Portrait (vert.). 25q, As volunteer construction worker. 95q, Addressing crowd. 1.10l, Saluting (vert.).

1970, Apr. 22 Litho. *Perf. 12*

Red, Black & Silver

1283	A273	5q	5	5
1284	A273	15q	7	5
1285	A273	25q	14	5
1286	A273	95q	40	10
1287	A273	1.10l	65	20
		Nos. 1283-1287 (5)	1.31	45

Centenary of birth of Lenin (1870-1924).

Frontier Guard
A274

1970, Apr. 25

1288	A274	25q	multi	15	5
1289	A274	1.25l	multi	85	25

25th anniversary of Frontier Guards.

Soccer Players — A275

Designs: 5q, Jules Rimet Cup and globes. 10q, Aztec Stadium, Mexico City. 25q, Defending goal. 65q, 80q, No. 1296, Two soccer players in various plays. No. 1297, Mexican horseman and volcano Popocatepetl.

1970, May 15 Litho. *Perf. 12½x12*

1290	A275	5q	multi	5	5
1291	A275	10q	multi	5	5
1292	A275	15q	multi	10	5
1293	A275	25q	lt grn & multi	15	6
1294	A275	65q	pink & multi	32	10
1295	A275	80q	lt bl & multi	50	18
1296	A275	2l	yel & multi	1.35	30
			Nos. 1290-1296 (7)	2.52	79

Souvenir Sheet

Perf. 12x Imperf.

1297	A275	2l	multi	2.00	1.00

Issued to publicize the World Soccer Championships for the Jules Rimet Cup, Mexico City, May 31-June 21, 1970. No. 1297 contains one large horizontal stamp, decorative border and inscription. Size: 81x74mm. Nos. 1290-1297 exist imperf.

U.P.U. Headquarters and Monument, Bern — A276

1970, May 30 Litho. *Perf. 12½x12*

1298	A276	25q	ultra, gray & blk	15	5
1299	A276	1.10l	org, buff & blk	60	25
1300	A276	1.15l	grn, gray & blk	80	30

Issued to commemorate the inauguration of the new Universal Postal Union Headquarters in Bern.

Bird and Grapes Mosaic
A277

Mosaics, 5th-6th centuries, excavated near Pogradec: 10q, Waterfowl and grapes. 20q, Bird and tree stump. 25q, Bird and leaves. 65q, Fish. 2.25l, Peacock (vert.).

Perf. 12½x12, 12x12½

1970, July 10

1301	A277	5q	multi	5	5
1302	A277	10q	multi	10	5
1303	A277	20q	multi	15	5
1304	A277	25q	multi	20	8
1305	A277	65q	multi	35	15
1306	A277	2.25l	multi	1.25	40
			Nos. 1301-1306 (6)	2.10	78

Fruit Harvest and Dancers
A278

Designs: 25q, Contour-plowed fields and conference table. 80q, Cattle and newspapers. 1.30l, Wheat harvest.

1970, Aug. 28 Litho. *Perf. 12x11½*

1307	A278	15q	brt vio & blk	10	5
1308	A278	25q	dp bl & blk	15	5
1309	A278	80q	dp brn & blk	40	10
1310	A278	1.30l	org brn & blk	60	20

Issued to commemorate the 25th anniversary of the agrarian reform law.

Attacking Partisans — A279

Designs: 25q, Partisans with horses and flag. 1.60l, Partisans.

1970, Sept. 3 *Perf. 12*

1311	A279	15q	org brn & blk	5	5
1312	A279	25q	brn, yel & blk	10	6
1313	A279	1.60l	dp grn & blk	85	35

50th anniversary of liberation of Vlona.

Miners, by Nexhmedin Zajmi — A280

Paintings from the National Gallery, Tirana: 5q, Bringing in the Harvest, by Isuf Sulovari (vert.). 15q, The Activists, by Dhimitraq Trebicka (vert.). 65q, Instruction of Partisans, by Hasan Nallbani. 95q, Architectural Planning, by Vilson Kilica. No. 1319, Woman Machinist, by Zef Shoshi (vert.). No. 1320, Partisan Destroying Tank, by Sali Shijaku (vert.).

Perf. 12½x12, 12x12½

1970, Sept. 25 Litho.

1314	A280	5q	multi	5	5
1315	A280	15q	multi	6	5
1316	A280	25q	multi	15	5
1317	A280	65q	multi	20	8
1318	A280	95q	multi	35	15
1319	A280	2l	multi	1.20	40
			Nos. 1314-1319 (6)	2.01	78

Miniature Sheet

Imperf

1320	A280	2l	multi	1.50	1.25

Size of No. 1320: 66x93½mm.

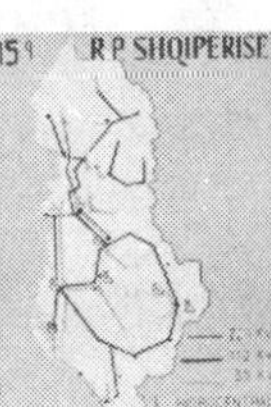

Electrification Map of Albania — A281

Designs: 25q, Light bulb, hammer and sickle emblem, map of Albania and power graph. 80q, Linemen at work. 1.10l, Use of electricity on the farm, in home and business.

1970, Oct. 25 Litho. *Perf. 12*

1321	A281	15q	multi	10	5
1322	A281	25q	multi	10	5
1323	A281	80q	multi	50	10
1324	A281	1.10l	multi	70	15

Issued to publicize the completion of Albanian village electrification.

Friedrich Engels — A282

Designs: 1.10l, Engels as young man. 1.15l, Engels addressing crowd.

1970, Nov. 28 Litho. *Perf. 12x12½*

1325	A282	25q	bis & dk bl	20	5
1326	A282	1.10l	bis & dp cl	60	20
1327	A282	1.15l	bis & dk ol grn	70	25

Issued to commemorate the 150th anniversary of the birth of Friedrich Engels (1820-1895), German socialist, collaborator with Karl Marx.

Ludwig van Beethoven — A283

Designs: 5q, Birthplace, Bonn. 25q, 65q, 1.10l, various portraits. 1.80l, Scene from Fidelio (horiz.).

1970, Dec. 16 Litho. *Perf. 12*

1328	A283	5q	dp plum & gold	5	5
1329	A283	15q	brt rose lil & sil	5	5
1330	A283	25q	grn & gold	10	5
1331	A283	65q	mag & sil	30	10
1332	A283	1.10l	dk bl & gold	60	22
1333	A283	1.80l	blk & sil	1.25	45
			Nos. 1328-1333 (6)	2.35	92

Bicentenary of the birth of Ludwig van Beethoven (1770-1827), composer.

Coat of Arms
A284

Designs: 25q, Proclamation. 80q, Enver Hoxha reading proclamation. 1.30l, Young people and proclamation.

1971, Jan. 11 Litho. *Perf. 12*

1334	A284	15q	lt bl, gold, blk & red	10	5
1335	A284	25q	rose lil, blk, gold & gray	15	5
1336	A284	80q	emer, blk & gold	45	12
1337	A284	1.30l	yel org, blk & gold	70	30

Declaration of the Republic, 25th anniversary.

"Liberty"
A285

Black Men
A286

Designs: 50q, Women's brigade. 65q, Street battle (horiz.). 1.10l, Execution (horiz.).

Perf. 12x11½, 11½x12

1971, March 18 Litho.

1338	A285	25q	dk bl & bl	13	5
1339	A285	50q	sl grn	25	7
1340	A285	65q	dk brn & chnt	35	15
1341	A285	1.10l	purple	55	20

Centenary of the Paris Commune.

1971, March 21 *Perf. 12x12½*

Designs: 1.10l, Men of 3 races. 1.15l, Black protest.

1342	A286	25q	blk & bis brn	12	5
1343	A286	1.10l	blk & rose car	45	15
1344	A286	1.15l	blk & ver	55	20

International year against racial discrimination.

Tulip — A287

Horseman, by Dürer — A288

Designs: Various tulips.

1971, March 25

1345	A287	5q multi	5	5
1346	A287	10q yel & multi	5	5
1347	A287	15q pink & multi	6	5
1348	A287	20q lt bl & multi	8	5
1349	A287	25q multi	18	6
1350	A287	80q multi	35	10
1351	A287	1l multi	50	18
1352	A287	1.45l cit & multi	75	25
		Nos. 1345-1352 (8)	2.02	79

Perf. 11½x12, 12x11½

1971, May 15 Litho.

Art Works by Dürer: 15q, Three peasants. 25q, Dancing peasant couple. 45q, The bagpiper. 65q, View of Kalkrebut (horiz.). 2.40l, View of Trent (horiz.). 2.50l, Self-portrait.

1353	A288	10q blk & pale grn	5	5
1354	A288	15q blk & pale lil	10	5
1355	A288	25q blk & pale bl	15	5
1356	A288	45q blk & pale rose	20	7
1357	A288	65q blk & multi	30	18
1358	A288	2.40l blk & multi	1.25	40
		Nos. 1353-1358 (6)	2.05	80

Miniature Sheet

Imperf

1359	A288	2.50l multi	1.50	1.00

500th anniversary of the birth of Albrecht Dürer (1471-1528), German painter and engraver. Size of No. 1359: 93x90mm.

Satellite Orbiting Globe — A289

Designs: 1.20l, Government Building, Tirana, and Red Star emblem. 2.20l, like 60q, 2.50l, Flag of People's Republic of China forming trajectory around globe.

1971, June 10 Litho. *Perf. 12x12½*

1360	A289	60q pur & multi	40	15
1361	A289	1.20l ver & multi	1.00	25
1362	A289	2.20l grn & multi	1.60	45

Imperf

1363	A289	2.50l vio blk & multi	2.50	90

Space developments of People's Republic of China. Size of No. 1363: 64x112mm.

Mao Tse-tung — A290

Designs: 1.05l, House where Communist Party was founded (horiz.). 1.20l, Peking crowd with placards (horiz.).

1971, July 1 *Perf. 12x12½, 12½x12*

1364	A290	25q sil & multi	18	5
1365	A290	1.05l sil & multi	55	15
1366	A290	1.20l sil & multi	70	25

50th anniversary of Chinese Communist Party.

Crested Titmouse — A291

1971, Aug. 15 Litho. *Perf. 12½x12*

1367	A291	5q *shown*	5	5
1368	A291	10q *European serin*	6	5
1369	A291	15q *Linnet*	8	5
1370	A291	25q *Firecrest*	10	6
1371	A291	45q *Rock thrush*	30	12
1372	A291	60q *Blue tit*	45	25
1373	A291	2.40l *Chaffinch*	1.50	60
		Nos. 1367-1373 (7)	2.54	1.18

Printed se-tenant in blocks of 8 (2x4) including a label showing bird's nest. The label is se-tenant horizontally with the 5q, and vertically with the 10q.

Olympic Rings and Running — A292

Designs (Olympic Rings and): 10q, Hurdles. 15q, Canoeing. 25q, Gymnastics. 80q, Fencing. 1.05l, Soccer. 2l, Runner at finish line. 3.60l, Diving, women's.

1971, Sept. 15

1374	A292	5q grn & multi	5	5
1375	A292	10q multi	6	5
1376	A292	15q bl & multi	8	5
1377	A292	25q vio & multi	10	10
1378	A292	80q lil & multi	30	15
1379	A292	1.05l multi	40	20
1380	A292	3.60l multi	2.00	65
		Nos. 1374-1380 (7)	2.99	1.25

Souvenir Sheet

Imperf

1381	A292	2l brt bl & multi	1.50	1.00

20th Olympic Games, Munich, Aug. 26-Sept. 10, 1972. No. 1381 contains one stamp, gray margin with brown inscription. Olympic rings and deep orange and silver flame emblem. Size: 68x82mm.

Workers with Flags A293

Designs: 1.05l, Party Headquarters, Tirana, and Red Star. 1.20l, Rifle, star, flag and "VI" (vert.).

1971, Nov. 1 *Perf. 12*

1382	A293	25q gold, sil, red & bl	15	5
1383	A293	1.05l gold, sil, red & bl	50	14
1384	A293	1.20l gold, sil, red & blk	60	25

6th Congress of Workers' Party.

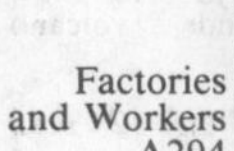

Factories and Workers A294

Designs: 80q, "XXX" and flag (vert.). 1.55l, Enver Hoxha and flags.

1971, Nov. 8

1385	A294	15q gold, sil, lil & yel	10	5
1386	A294	80q gold, sil & red	40	12
1387	A294	1.55l gold, sil, red & brn	75	30

30th anniversary of Workers' Party.

Construction Work, by M. Fushekati — A295

Albanian Paintings: 5q, Young Man, by R. Kuci (vert.). 25q, Partisan, by D. Jukniu (vert.). 80q, Fliers, by S. Kristo. 1.20l, Girl in Forest, by A. Sadikaj. 1.55l, Warriors with Spears and Shields, by S. Kamberi. 2l, Freedom Fighter, by I. Lulani.

Perf. 12x12½, 12½x12

1971, Nov. 20

1388	A295	5q gold & multi	5	5
1389	A295	15q gold & multi	7	5
1390	A295	25q gold & multi	11	5
1391	A295	80q gold & multi	30	10
1392	A295	1.20l gold & multi	65	22
1393	A295	1.55l gold & multi	85	30
		Nos. 1388-1393 (6)	2.03	77

Miniature Sheet

Imperf

1394	A295	2l gold & multi	1.50	90

Contemporary Albanian paintings. Size of No. 1394: 87x67½mm.

Young Workers Emblem — A296

1971, Nov. 23 *Perf. 12x12½*

1395	A296	15q lt bl & multi	10	5
1396	A296	1.35l grnsh gray & multi	70	25

30th anniversary of the Albanian Young Workers' Union.

"Halili and Hajria" Ballet — A297

Scenes from "Halili and Hajria" Ballet: 10q, Brother and sister. 15q, Hajria before Sultan Suleiman. 50q, Hajria and husband. 80q, Execution of Halili. 1.40l, Hajria killing her husband.

1971, Dec. 27 *Perf. 12½x12*

1397	A297	5q sil & multi	5	5
1398	A297	10q sil & multi	8	5
1399	A297	15q sil & multi	7	5
1400	A297	50q sil & multi	35	10
1401	A297	80q sil & multi	55	15
1402	A297	1.40l sil & multi	90	40
		Nos. 1397-1402 (6)	2.00	80

Albanian ballet Halili and Hajria after drama by Kol Jakova.

Biathlon and Olympic Rings — A298

Designs (Olympic Rings and): 10q, Sledding. 15q, Ice hockey. 20q, Bobsledding. 50q, Speed skating. 1l, Slalom. 2l, Ski jump. 2.50l, Figure skating, pairs.

1972, Feb. 10

1403	A298	5q lt ol & multi	5	5
1404	A298	10q lt vio & multi	6	5
1405	A298	15q multi	7	5
1406	A298	20q pink & multi	10	5
1407	A298	50q lt bl & multi	25	10
1408	A298	1l ocher & multi	60	25
1409	A298	2l lil & multi	1.25	45
		Nos. 1403-1409 (7)	2.38	1.00

Souvenir Sheet

Imperf

1410	A298	2.50l bl & multi	1.75	75

11th Winter Olympic Games, Sapporo, Japan, Feb. 3-13. No. 1410 contains one stamp. Blue, ultramarine and silver margin with inscription. Size: 71x90mm.

Wild Strawberries A299

Wild Fruits and Nuts: 10q, Blackberries. 15q, Hazelnuts. 20q, Walnuts. 25q, Strawberry-tree fruit. 30q, Dogwood berries. 2.40l, Rowan berries.

1972, Mar. 20 Litho. *Perf. 12*

1411	A299	5q lt grn & multi	5	5
1412	A299	10q yel & multi	6	5
1413	A299	15q lt vio & multi	10	5
1414	A299	20q pink & multi	15	5
1415	A299	25q multi	20	15
1416	A299	30q multi	30	15
1417	A299	2.40l multi	1.50	55
		Nos. 1411-1417 (7)	2.36	1.05

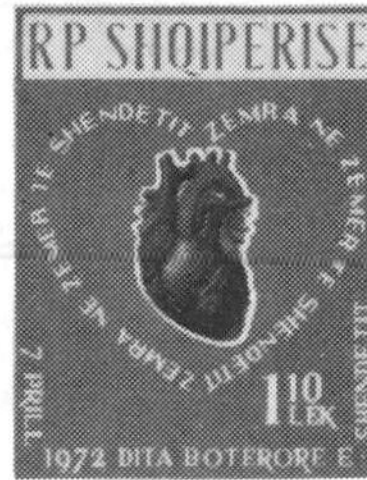

"Your Heart is your Health" A300

Worker and Student A301

Design: 1.20l, Cardiac patient and electrocardiogram.

1972, Apr. 7 *Perf. 12x12½*

1418	A300	1.10l multi	60	20
1419	A300	1.20l rose & multi	75	30

World Health Day 1972.

Perf. 11½x12½

1972, Apr. 24 Litho.

Design: 2.05l, Assembly Hall, dancers and emblem.

1420	A301	25q multi	15	5
1421	A301	2.05l bl & multi	1.00	45

7th Trade Union Congress, May 8.

Canceled-to-order stamps are often from remainders. Most collectors of canceled stamps prefer postally used specimens.

Qemal Stafa A302

Designs: 15q, Memorial flame. 25q, Monument "Spirit of Defiance" (vert.).

1972, May 5 *Perf. 12½x12, 12x12½*

1422	A302	15q gray & multi	7	5
1423	A302	25q sal rose, blk & gray	15	8
1424	A302	1.90l dl yel & blk	1.10	30

30th anniversary of the murder of Qemal Stafa and of Martyrs' Day.

Camellia A303

Designs: Various camellias.

1972, May 10 *Perf. 12x12½*

Flowers in Natural Colors

1425	A303	5q lt bl & blk	5	5
1426	A303	10q cit & blk	6	5
1427	A303	15q grnsh gray & blk	7	5
1428	A303	25q pale sal & blk	10	5
1429	A303	45q gray & blk	20	10
1430	A303	50q sal pink & blk	35	15
1431	A303	2.50l bluish gray & blk	1.50	85
		Nos. 1425-1431 (7)	2.33	1.30

High Jump — A304

Designs (Olympic and Motion Emblems and): 10q, Running. 15q, Shot put. 20q, Bicycling. 25q, Pole vault. 50q, Hurdles, women's. 75q, Hockey. 2l, Swimming. 2.50l, Diving, women's.

1972, June 30 Litho. *Perf. 12½x12*

1432	A304	5q multi	5	5
1433	A304	10q lt brn & multi	5	5
1434	A304	15q lt lil & multi	7	5
1435	A304	20q multi	8	5
1436	A304	25q lt vio & multi	10	6
1437	A304	50q lt grn & multi	25	10
1438	A304	75q multi	50	15
1439	A304	2l multi	95	30
		Nos. 1432-1439 (8)	2.05	81

Miniature Sheet

Imperf

1440	A304	2.50l multi	2.00	1.10

20th Olympic Games, Munich, Aug. 26-Sept. 11. Nos. 1432-1439 each issued in sheets of 8 stamps and one label (3x3) showing Olympic rings in gold. Size of No. 1440: 70x87mm.

Autobus A305

Designs: 25q, Electric train. 80q, Ocean liner Tirana. 1.05l, Automobile. 1.20l, Trailer truck.

1972, July 25 Litho. *Perf. 12*

1441	A305	15q org brn & multi	10	5
1442	A305	25q gray & multi	8	5
1443	A305	80q dp grn & multi	40	8
1444	A305	1.05l multi	55	15
1445	A305	1.20l multi	70	18
		Nos. 1441-1445 (5)	1.83	51

Arm Wrestling A306

Folk Games: 10q, Piggyback ball game. 15q, Women's jumping. 25q, Rope game (srum). 90q, Leapfrog. 2l, Women throwing pitchers.

1972, Aug. 18

1446	A306	5q multi	5	5
1447	A306	10q lt bl & multi	5	5
1448	A306	15q rose & multi	10	5
1449	A306	25q lt bl & multi	15	5
1450	A306	90q ocher & multi	50	15
1451	A306	2l lt grn & multi	95	30
		Nos. 1446-1451 (6)	1.80	65

1st National Festival of People's Games.

Mastheads — A307

Designs: 25q, Printing press. 1.90l, Workers reading paper.

1972, Aug. 25

1452	A307	15q lt bl & blk	10	5
1453	A307	25q red, grn & blk	15	5
1454	A307	1.90l lt vio & blk	1.00	35

30th Press Day.

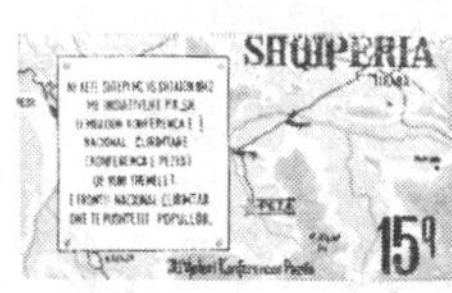

Map of Peza Area, Memorial Tablet A308

1972, Sept. 16

1455	A308	15q *shown*	10	5
1456	A308	25q *Guerrillas with flag*	15	5
1457	A308	1.90l *Peza Conference memorial*	1.00	35

30th anniversary, Conference of Peza.

Partisans, by Sotir Capo — A309

Paintings: 10q, Woman, by Ismail Lulani (vert.). 15q, "Communists," by Lec Shkreli (vert.). 20q, View of Nendorit, 1941, by Sali Shijaku (vert.). 50q, Woman with Sheaf, by Zef Shoshi (vert.). 1l, Landscape with Children, by Dhimitraq Trebicka. 2l, Women on Bicycles, by Vilson Kilica. 2.30l, Folk Dance, by Abdurrahim Buza.

Perf. 12½x12, 12x12½

1972, Sept. 25 **Litho.**

1458	A309	5q gold & multi	5	5
1459	A309	10q gold & multi	5	5
1460	A309	15q gold & multi	7	5
1461	A309	20q gold & multi	10	5
1462	A309	50q gold & multi	25	10
1463	A309	1l gold & multi	50	20
1464	A309	2l gold & multi	1.10	50
		Nos. 1458-1464 (7)	2.12	1.00

Miniature Sheet

Imperf

1465	A309	2.30l gold & multi	1.50	1.00

No. 1465 contains one stamp (41x68mm.); silver margin. Size: 55x82mm.

Congress Emblem — A310

Design: 2.05l, Young worker with banner.

1972, Oct. 23 Litho. *Perf. 12*

1466	A310	25q sil, red & gold	10	5
1467	A310	2.05l sil & multi	1.00	45

Union of Working Youth, 6th Congress.

Hammer and Sickle A311

Ismail Qemali A312

Design: 1.20l, Lenin as orator.

1972, Nov. 7 Litho. *Perf. 11½x12*

1468	A311	1.10l multi	60	25
1469	A311	1.20l multi	65	30

55th anniversary of the Russian October Revolution.

Perf. 12x11½, 11½x12

1972, Nov. 29

Designs: 15q, Albanian fighters (horiz.). 65q, Rally (horiz.). 1.25l, Coat of arms.

1470	A312	15q red, brt bl & blk	10	5
1471	A312	25q yel, blk & red	15	5
1472	A312	65q red, sal & blk	35	10
1473	A312	1.25l dl red & blk	70	25

60th anniv. of independence.

Cock, Mosaic A313

Mosaics, 2nd-5th centuries, excavated near Buthrotium and Apollonia: 10q, Bird (vert.). 15q, Partridges (vert.). 25q, Warrior's legs. 45q, Nymph riding dolphin (vert.). 50q, Fish (vert.). 2.50l, Warrior with helmet.

Perf. 12½x12, 12x12½

1972, Dec. 10

1474	A313	5q sil & multi	5	5
1475	A313	10q sil & multi	5	5
1476	A313	15q sil & multi	10	6
1477	A313	25q sil & multi	14	8
1478	A313	45q sil & multi	25	9
1479	A313	50q sil & multi	30	10
1480	A313	2.50l sil & multi	1.40	50
		Nos. 1474-1480 (7)	2.29	93

Nicolaus Copernicus A314

Designs: 10q, 25q, 80q, 1.20l, Various portraits of Copernicus. 1.60l, Heliocentric solar system.

1973, Feb. 19 Litho. *Perf. 12x12½*

1481	A314	5q lil rose & multi	5	5
1482	A314	10q dl ol & multi	5	5
1483	A314	25q multi	15	7
1484	A314	80q lt vio & multi	50	15
1485	A314	1.20l bl & multi	75	30
1486	A314	1.60l gray & multi	1.00	40
		Nos. 1481-1486 (6)	2.50	1.02

500th anniversary of the birth of Nicolaus Copernicus (1473-1543), Polish astronomer.

Flowering Cactus — A315

Designs: Various flowering cacti.

1973, Mar. 25 Litho. *Perf. 12*

1487	A315	10q multi	5	5
1488	A315	15q multi	7	5
1489	A315	20q beige & multi	7	5
1490	A315	25q gray & multi	10	5
1491	A315	30q beige & multi	15	6
1492	A315	65q gray & multi	40	10
1493	A315	80q multi	50	15
1494	A315	2l multi	1.25	35
		Nos. 1487-1494 (8)	2.59	86

Nos. 1487-1494 printed se-tenant.

Guard and Factories A316

Design: 1.80l, Guard and guards with prisoner.

1973, Mar. 20 Litho. *Perf. 12½x12*

1495	A316	25q ultra & blk	18	10
1496	A316	1.80l dk red & multi	85	60

30th anniversary of the State Security Branch.

Common Tern A317

Sea Birds: 15q, White-winged black terns (vert.). 25q, Black-headed gull (vert.). 45q, Great black-headed gull. 80q, Slender-billed gull (vert.). 2.40l, Sandwich terns.

Perf. 12½x12, 12x12½

1973, Apr. 30

1497	A317	5q gold & multi	5	5
1498	A317	15q gold & multi	8	5
1499	A317	25q gold & multi	15	5
1500	A317	45q gold & multi	20	10

1501 A317 80q gold & multi 45 25
1502 A317 2.40l gold & multi 1.35 55
Nos. 1497-1502 (6) 2.28 1.05

Letters, 1913 Cancellation and Post Horn — A318

Design: 1.80l, Mailman and 1913 cancelation.

1973, May, 5 Litho. *Perf. 12x11½*
1503 A318 25q red & multi 20 10
1504 A318 1.80l red & multi 1.25 75

60th anniversary of Albanian stamps.

Farmer, Worker, Soldier A319

Design: 25q, Woman and factory (vert.).

1973, June 4 *Perf. 12*
1505 A319 25q car rose 20 10
1506 A319 1.80l yel, dp org & blk 1.00 50

7th Congress of Albanian Women's Union.

Creation of General Staff, by G. Madhi — A320

Designs: 40q, "August 1949," sculpture by Sh. Haderi (vert.). 60q, "Generation after Generation," sculpture by H. Dule (vert.). 80q, "Defend Revolutionary Victories," by M. Fushekati.

1973, July 10 Litho. *Perf. 12½x12*
1507 A320 25q gold & multi 25 10
1508 A320 40q gold & multi 40 15
1509 A320 60q gold & multi 60 25
1510 A320 80q gold & multi 75 30

30th anniversary of the People's Army.

"Electrification," by S. Hysa — A321

Albanian Paintings: 10q, Woman Textile Worker, by N. Nallbani. 15q, Gymnasts, by M. Fushekati. 50q, Aviator, by F. Stamo. 80q, Fascist Prisoner, by A. Lakuriqi. 1.20l, Workers with Banner, by P. Mele. 1.30l, Farm Woman, by Zef Shoshi. 2.05l, Battle of Tenda, by F. Haxhiu. 10q, 50q, 80q, 1.20l, 1.30l, vertical.

Perf. 12½x12, 12x12½
1973, Aug. 10
1511 A321 5q gold & multi 5 5
1512 A321 10q gold & multi 7 5
1513 A321 15q gold & multi 10 5
1514 A321 50q gold & multi 30 10
1515 A321 80q gold & multi 60 12
1516 A321 1.20l gold & multi 90 15
1517 A321 1.30l gold & multi 1.00 25
Nos. 1511-1517 (7) 3.02 77

Souvenir Sheet
Imperf
1518 A321 2.05l multi 1.50 75

No. 1518 contains one stamp; light yellow margin. Size: 98x62mm.

Mary Magdalene, by Caravaggio A322

Paintings by Michelangelo da Caravaggio: 10q, The Lute Player (horiz.). 15q, Self-portrait. 50q, Boy Carrying Fruit and Flowers. 80q, Still Life (horiz.). 1.20l, Narcissus. 1.30l, Boy Peeling Apple. 2.05l, Man with Feathered Hat.

Perf. 12x12½, 12½x12
1973, Sept. 28
1519 A322 5q gold & multi 5 5
1520 A322 10q gold & multi 5 5
1521 A322 15q gold, blk & gray 7 5
1522 A322 50q gold & multi 18 5
1523 A322 80q gold & multi 40 10
1524 A322 1.20l gold & multi 60 30
1525 A322 1.30l gold & multi 70 30
Nos. 1519-1525 (7) 2.05 90

Souvenir Sheet
Imperf
1526 A322 2.05l multi 2.00 75

400th anniversary of the birth of Michelangelo da Caravaggio (Merisi; 1573?-1609), Italian painter. No. 1526 contains one stamp (63x73mm.); gray marginal inscription. Size: 81x99mm.

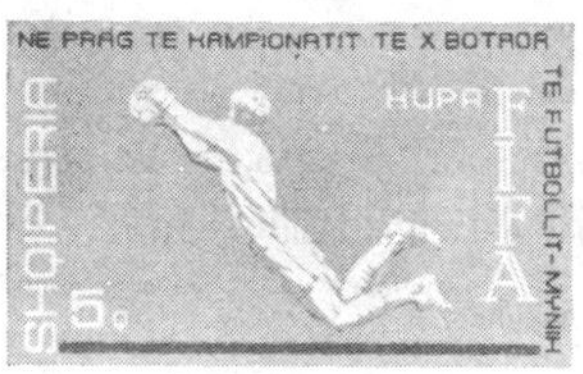

Soccer — A323

Designs: 5q-1.25l, Various soccer scenes. 2.05l, Ball in goal and list of cities where championships were held.

1973, Oct. 30 Litho. *Perf. 12½x12*
1527 A323 5q multi 5 5
1528 A323 10q multi 5 5
1529 A323 15q multi 7 5
1530 A323 20q multi 10 5
1531 A323 25q multi 15 5
1532 A323 90q multi 60 10
1533 A323 1.20l multi 80 20
1534 A323 1.25l multi 1.00 25
Nos. 1527-1534 (8) 2.82 80

Minature Sheet
Imperf
1535 A323 2.05l multi 2.00 75

World Soccer Cup, Munich 1974. Size of No. 1535: 82x54mm.

Weight Lifter — A324

Designs: Various stages of weight lifting. 1.20l, 1.60l, horizontal.

1973, Oct. 30 Litho. *Perf. 12*
1536 A324 5q multi 6 5
1537 A324 10q multi 6 5
1538 A324 25q multi 15 5
1539 A324 90q multi 45 18
1540 A324 1.20l multi 35 10
1541 A324 1.60l multi 75 15
Nos. 1536-1541 (6) 1.82 58

Weight Lifting Championships, Havana, Cuba.

Ballet — A325

Harvester Combine — A326

Perf. 12½x12, 12x12½
1973-74 Litho.

Designs: 5q, Cement factory, Kavaje. 10q, Ali Kelmendi truck factory and tank cars (horiz.). 25q, "Communication." 35q, Skiers and hotel (horiz.). 60q, Resort (horiz.). 80q, Mountain lake. 1l, Mao Tse-tung textile mill. 1.20l, Steel workers. 2.40l, Welder and pipe. 3l, Skanderbeg Monument, Tirana. 5l, Roman arches, Durres.

1543 A325 5q gold & multi 5 5
1544 A325 10q gold & multi 5 5
1545 A325 15q gold & multi 7 5
1545A A326 20q gold & multi 12 5
1546 A326 25q gold & multi 20 5
1547 A326 35q gold & multi 20 7
1548 A326 60q gold & multi 30 10
1549 A326 80q gold & multi 45 17
1549A A326 1l gold & multi 38 10
1549B A326 1.20l gold & multi 65 15
1549C A326 2.40l gold & multi 1.40 40
1550 A326 3l gold & multi 1.65 40
1551 A326 5l gold & multi 2.50 75
Nos. 1543-1551 (13) 8.02 2.39

Issue dates: Nos. 1545-1546, 1549-1550, Dec. 5, 1973; others in 1974.

Mao Tse-tung — A327

Design: 1.20l, Mao Tse-tung addressing crowd.

1973, Dec. 26 *Perf. 12*
1552 A327 85q gold, red & sep 45 10
1553 A327 1.20l gold, red & sep 65 15

80th birthday of Mao Tse-tung.

Old Man and Dog, by Gericault — A328

Paintings by Jean Louis André Theodore Gericault: 10q, Horse's Head. 15q, Male Model. 25q, Head of Black Man. 1.20l, Self-portrait. 2.05l, Raft of the Medusa (horiz.). 2.20l, Battle of the Giants.

Perf. 12x12½, 12½x12
1974, Jan. 18 Litho.
1554 A328 10q gold & multi 5 5
1555 A328 15q gold & multi 7 5
1556 A328 20q gold & multi 10 5
1557 A328 25q gold & blk 15 5
1558 A328 1.20l gold & multi 55 15
1559 A328 2.20l gold & multi 1.10 40
Nos. 1554-1559 (6) 2.02 75

Souvenir Sheet
Imperf
1560 A328 2.05l gold & multi 1.35 55

No. 1560 contains one stamp (87x78mm.). Sheet has gold margin and inscription. Size: 100x78mm.

Lenin, by Pandi Mele — A329

Designs: 25q, Lenin with Sailors on Cruiser Aurora, by Dhimitraq Trebicka (horiz.). 1.20l, Lenin, by Vilson Kilica.

Perf. 12½x12, 12x12½
1974, Jan. 21
1561 A329 25q gold & multi 15 5
1562 A329 60q gold & multi 35 10
1563 A329 1.20l gold & multi 75 25

50th anniversary of the death of Lenin (1870-1924).

Swimming Duck, Mosaic — A330

Designs: Mosaics from the 5th-6th Centuries A.D., excavated near Buthrotium, Pogradec and Apollonia.

1974, Feb. 20 Litho. *Perf. 12½x12*
1564 A330 5q *shown* 5 5
1565 A330 10q *Bird and flower* 5 5
1566 A330 15q *Vase and grapes* 7 5
1567 A330 25q *Duck* 15 5
1568 A330 40q *Donkey and bird* 25 6
1569 A330 2.50l *Sea horse* 1.25 35
Nos. 1564-1569 (6) 1.82 61

Soccer — A331

Designs: Various scenes from soccer. 2.05l, World Soccer Cup and names of participating countries.

1974, Apr. 25 Litho. *Perf. 12½x12*
1570 A331 10q gold & multi 5 5
1571 A331 15q gold & multi 7 5
1572 A331 20q gold & multi 8 5
1573 A331 25q gold & multi 15 5
1574 A331 40q gold & multi 25 6
1575 A331 80q gold & multi 50 15
1576 A331 1l gold & multi 75 25
1577 A331 1.20l gold & multi 1.00 35
Nos. 1570-1577 (8) 2.85 1.01

Souvenir Sheet
Imperf
1578 A331 2.05l gold & multi 2.25 90

World Cup Soccer Championship, Munich, June 13-July 7. No. 1578 contains one stamp (60x60mm.) with simulated perforations. Size: 72x75mm. Nos. 1570-1577 exist imperf, No. 1578 with simulated perfs omitted.

Arms of Albania, Soldier — A332

Design: 1.80l, Soldier and front page of 1944 Congress Book.

1974, May 24 Litho. *Perf. 12*

No.	Type	Value	Description	Unused	Used
1579	A332	25q	multi	11	5
1580	A332	1.80l	multi	75	25

30th anniversary of the First Anti-Fascist Liberation Congress of Permet.

Bittersweet A333

Designs: Medicinal Plants. 40q, 80q, 2.20l, horizontal.

1974, May 5 *Perf. 12x12½*

No.	Type	Value	Description	Unused	Used
1581	A333	10q	*shown*	5	5
1582	A333	15q	*Arbutus*	7	5
1583	A333	20q	*Lilies of the valley*	8	5
1584	A333	25q	*Autumn crocus*	11	5
1585	A333	40q	*Borage*	15	6
1586	A333	80q	*Soapwort*	45	15
1587	A333	2.20l	*Gentian*	1.00	40
			Nos. 1581-1587 (7)	1.91	81

Revolutionaries with Albanian Flag — A334

Design: 1.80l, Portraits of 5 revolutionaries (vert.).

Perf. 12½x12, 12x12½

1974, June 10

No.	Type	Value	Description	Unused	Used
1588	A334	25q	red, blk & lil	11	5
1589	A334	1.80l	yel, red & blk	70	25

50th anniversary Albanian Bourgeois Democratic Revolution.

European Redwing — A335

Designs: Songbirds; Nos. 1597-1600 vertical.

Perf. 12½x12, 12x12½

1974, July 15 Litho.

No.	Type	Value	Description	Unused	Used
1594	A335	10q	*shown*	5	5
1595	A335	15q	*European robin*	7	5
1596	A335	20q	*Greenfinch*	5	5
1597	A335	25q	*Bullfinch*	8	5
1598	A335	40q	*Hawfinch*	20	6
1599	A335	80q	*Blackcap*	50	20
1600	A335	2.20l	*Nightingale*	1.10	45
			Nos. 1594-1600 (7)	2.05	91

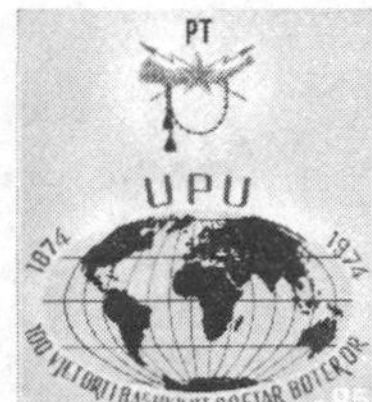

Globe — A336

Designs: 1.20l, UPU emblem. 2.05l, Jet over globe.

1974, Aug. 25 Litho. *Perf. 12x12½*

No.	Type	Value	Description	Unused	Used
1601	A336	85q	grn & multi	45	15
1602	A336	1.20l	vio & ol grn	65	20

Miniature Sheet

Imperf

No.	Type	Value	Description	Unused	Used
1603	A336	2.05l	bl & multi	12.00	12.00

Centenary of Universal Postal Union. No. 1603 contains one stamp, gold margin. Size: 77x78mm.

Widows, by Sali Shijaku — A337

Albanian Paintings: 15q, Drillers, by Danish Jukniu (vert.). 20q, Workers with Blueprints, by Clirim Ceka. 25q, Call to Action, by Spiro Kristo (vert.). 40q, Winter Battle, by Sabaudin Xhaferi. 80q, Comrades, by Clirim Ceka (vert.). 1l, Aiding the Partisans, by Guri Madhi. 1.20l, Teacher with Pupils, by Kleo Nini Brezat. 2.05l, Comrades in Arms, by Guri Madhi.

Perf. 12½x12, 12x12½

1974, Sept. 25

No.	Type	Value	Description	Unused	Used
1604	A337	10q	sil & multi	5	5
1605	A337	15q	sil & multi	7	5
1606	A337	20q	sil & multi	8	5
1607	A337	25q	sil & multi	11	5
1608	A337	40q	sil & multi	20	6
1609	A337	80q	sil & multi	35	12
1610	A337	1l	sil & multi	45	15
1611	A337	1.20l	sil & multi	50	25
			Nos. 1604-1611 (8)	1.81	78

Miniature Sheet

Imperf

No.	Type	Value	Description	Unused	Used
1612	A337	2.05l	sil & multi	1.25	50

No. 1612 contains one stamp. Size: 86x77mm.

Crowd on Tien An Men Square A338

Design: 1.20l, Mao Tse-tung (vert.).

1974, Oct. 1 *Perf. 12*

No.	Type	Value	Description	Unused	Used
1613	A338	85q	gold & multi	42	12
1614	A338	1.20l	gold & multi	60	20

25th anniversary of the proclamation of the People's Republic of China.

Women's Volleyball A339

Designs (Spartakiad Medal and): 15q, Women hurdlers. 20q, Women gymnasts. 25q, Mass exercises in Stadium. 40q, Weight lifter. 80q, Wrestlers. 1l, Military rifle drill. 1.20l, Soccer.

1974, Oct. 9 *Perf. 12x12½*

No.	Type	Value	Description	Unused	Used
1615	A339	10q	multi	5	5
1616	A339	15q	multi	7	5
1617	A339	20q	multi	8	5
1618	A339	25q	gray & multi	11	5
1619	A339	40q	multi	15	6
1620	A339	80q	multi	40	12
1621	A339	1l	multi	45	15
1622	A339	1.20l	tan & multi	50	20
			Nos. 1615-1622 (8)	1.81	73

National Spartakiad, Oct. 9-17.

View of Berat — A340

Designs: 80q, Enver Hoxha addressing Congress, bas-relief (horiz.). 1l, Hoxha and leaders leaving Congress Hall.

Perf. 12x12½, 12½x12

1974, Oct. 20 Litho.

No.	Type	Value	Description	Unused	Used
1623	A340	25q	rose car & blk	15	5
1624	A340	80q	yel, brn & blk	30	12
1625	A340	1l	dp lil & blk	45	15

30th anniversary of 2nd Congress of Berat.

Anniversary Emblem, Factory Guards — A341

Designs (Anniversary Emblem and): 35q, Chemical industry. 50q, Agriculture. 80q, Arts. 1l, Atomic diagram and computer. 1.20l, Youth education. 2.05l, Anniversary emblem: Crowd and History Book.

1974, Nov. 29 Litho. *Perf. 12½x12*

No.	Type	Value	Description	Unused	Used
1626	A341	25q	grn & multi	5	5
1627	A341	35q	ultra & multi	12	7
1628	A341	50q	brn & multi	22	10
1629	A341	80q	multi	40	12
1630	A341	1l	vio & multi	45	15
1631	A341	1.20l	multi	50	20
			Nos. 1626-1631 (6)	1.74	69

Miniature Sheet

Imperf

No.	Type	Value	Description	Unused	Used
1632	A341	2.05l	gold & multi	1.50	60

30th anniversary of liberation from Fascism. No. 1632 contains one stamp. Size: 80x69mm.

Artemis, from Apolloni A342

1974, Dec. 25 Photo. *Perf. 12x12½*

Silver & Multicolored

No.	Type	Value	Description	Unused	Used
1633	A342	10q	*shown*	5	5
1634	A342	15q	*Zeus statue*	8	5
1635	A342	20q	*Poseidon statue*	8	5
1636	A342	25q	*Illyrian helmet*	8	5
1637	A342	40q	*Amphora*	15	6
1638	A342	80q	*Agrippa*	40	10
1639	A342	1l	*Demosthenes*	45	12
1640	A342	1.20l	*Head of Bilia*	55	20
			Nos. 1633-1640 (8)	1.84	68

Miniature Sheet

Imperf

No.	Type	Value	Description	Unused	Used
1641	A342	2.05l	*Artemis & amphora*	1.50	60

Archaeological discoveries in Albania. No. 1641 contains one stamp. Size: 95x95mm.

Workers and Factories A343

Design: 25q, Handshake, tools and book (vert.).

1975, Feb. 11 Litho. *Perf. 12*

No.	Type	Value	Description	Unused	Used
1642	A343	25q	brn & multi	8	5
1643	A343	1.80l	yel & multi	75	30

Albanian Trade Unions, 30th anniversary.

Chicory A344

1975, Feb. 15

Gray and Multicolored

No.	Type	Value	Description	Unused	Used
1644	A344	5q	*shown*	5	5
1645	A344	10q	*Houseleek*	5	5
1646	A344	15q	*Columbine*	7	5
1647	A344	20q	*Anemone*	8	5
1648	A344	25q	*Hibiscus*	10	5
1649	A344	30q	*Gentian*	10	6
1650	A344	35q	*Hollyhock*	12	6
1651	A344	2.70l	*Iris*	1.20	40
			Nos. 1644-1651 (8)	1.77	77

Protected flowers.

Jesus, from Doni Madonna A345

Works by Michelangelo: 10q, Slave, sculpture. 15q, Head of Dawn, sculpture. 20q, Awakening Giant, sculpture. 25q, Cumaenian Sybil, Sistine Chapel. 30q, Lorenzo di Medici, sculpture. 1.20l, David, sculpture. 2.05l, Self-portrait. 3.90l, Delphic Sybil, Sistine Chapel.

1975, Mar. 20 Litho. *Perf. 12x12½*

No.	Type	Value	Description	Unused	Used
1652	A345	5q	gold & multi	5	5
1653	A345	10q	gold & multi	5	5
1654	A345	15q	gold & multi	7	5
1655	A345	20q	gold & multi	8	5
1656	A345	25q	gold & multi	8	5
1657	A345	30q	gold & multi	10	6
1658	A345	1.20l	gold & multi	40	20
1659	A345	3.90l	gold & multi	1.75	60
			Nos. 1652-1659 (8)	2.58	1.11

Miniature Sheet

Imperf

No.	Type	Value	Description	Unused	Used
1660	A345	2.05l	gold & multi	1.25	60

500th birth anniversary of Michelangelo Buonarroti (1475-1564), Italian sculptor, painter and architect. Size of No. 1660: 76x85mm.

Two-wheeled Cart — A346

Albanian Transportation of the Past: 5q, Horseback rider. 15q, Lake ferry. 20q, Coastal three-master. 25q, Phaeton. 3.35l, Early automobile on bridge.

1975, Apr. 15 Litho. *Perf. 12½x12*

1661	A346	5q bl grn & multi	5	5
1662	A346	10q ol & multi	5	5
1663	A346	15q lil & multi	7	5
1664	A346	20q multi	8	5
1665	A346	25q multi	15	6
1666	A346	3.35l ocher & multi	1.40	50
		Nos. 1661-1666 (6)	1.80	76

Guard at Frontier Stone — A347

Guardsman and Militia — A348

1975, Apr. 25 *Perf. 12*

1667	A347	25q multi	11	5
1668	A348	1.80l multi	75	25

30th anniversary of Frontier Guards.

Posting Illegal Poster — A349

Designs: 60q, Partisans in battle. 1.20l, Partisan killing German soldier, and Albanian coat of arms.

1975, May 9 *Perf. 12½x12*

1669	A349	25q multi	11	5
1670	A349	60q multi	20	10
1671	A349	1.20l red & multi	50	25

30th anniversary of victory over Fascism.

European Widgeons — A350

Waterfowl: 10q, Red-crested pochards. 15q, White-fronted goose. 20q, Northern pintails. 25q, Red-breasted merganser. 30q, Eider ducks. 35q, Whooper swan. 2.70l, Shovelers.

1975, June 15 Litho. *Perf. 12*

1672	A350	5q brt bl & multi	5	5
1673	A350	10q yel grn & multi	5	5
1674	A350	15q brt rose lil & multi	7	5
1675	A350	20q bl grn & multi	8	5
1676	A350	25q multi	10	5
1677	A350	30q multi	10	6
1678	A350	35q org & multi	12	6
1679	A350	2.70l multi	1.35	40
		Nos. 1672-1679 (8)	1.92	77

Shyqyri Kanapari, by Musa Qarri — A351

Albanian Paintings: 10q, Woman Saving Children in Sea, by Agim Faja. 15q, "November 28, 1912" (revolution), by Petrit Ceno (horiz.). 20q, "Workers Unite," by Sali Shijaku. 25q, The Partisan Shota Galica, by Ismail Lulani. 30q, Victorious Resistance Fighters, 1943, by Nestor Jonuzi. 80q, Partisan Couple in Front of Red Flag, by Vilson Halimi. 2.05l, Dancing Procession, by Abdurahim Buza. 2.25l, Republic Day Celebration, by Fatmir Haxhiu (horiz.).

Perf. 12x12½, 12½x12

1975, July 15 Litho.

1680	A351	5q gold & multi	5	5
1681	A351	10q gold & multi	5	5
1682	A351	15q gold & multi	7	5
1683	A351	20q gold & multi	10	5
1684	A351	25q gold & multi	10	5
1685	A351	30q gold & multi	17	6
1686	A351	80q gold & multi	30	10
1687	A351	2.25l gold & multi	1.00	35
		Nos. 1680-1687 (8)	1.84	76

Miniature Sheet

Imperf

1688	A351	2.05l gold & multi	1.10	60

No. 1688 contains one stamp. Size: 67x98mm. Nos. 1680-1687 issued in sheets of 8 stamps and gold center label showing palette and easel.

Farmer Holding Reform Law — A352

Design: 2l, Produce and farm machinery.

1975, Aug. 28 *Perf. 12*

1689	A352	15q multi	7	5
1690	A352	2l multi	75	35

Agrarian reform, 30th anniversary.

Alcynonium Palmatum A353

Corals: 10q, Paramuricea chamaeleon. 20q, Coralium rubrum. 25q, Eunicella covalini. 3.70l, Cladocora cespitosa.

1975, Sept. 25 Litho. *Perf. 12*

1691	A353	5q bl, ol & blk	5	5
1692	A353	10q bl & multi	5	5
1693	A353	20q bl & multi	10	5
1694	A353	25q bl & blk	18	6
1695	A353	3.70l bl & blk	1.50	60
		Nos. 1691-1695 (5)	1.88	81

Bicycling A354

Designs (Montreal Olympic Games Emblem and): 10q, Canoeing. 15q, Fieldball. 20q, Basketball. 25q, Water polo. 30q, Hockey. 1.20l, Pole vault. 2.05l, Fencing. 2.15l, Montreal Olympic Games emblem and various sports.

1975, Oct. 20 Litho. *Perf. 12½*

1696	A354	5q multi	5	5
1697	A354	10q multi	5	5
1698	A354	15q multi	7	5
1699	A354	20q multi	8	5
1700	A354	25q multi	12	6
1701	A354	30q multi	12	8
1702	A354	1.20l multi	45	20
1703	A354	2.05l multi	95	30
		Nos. 1696-1703 (8)	1.89	84

Miniature Sheet

Imperf

1704	A354	2.15l org & multi	3.00	2.50

21st Olympic Games, Montreal, July 18-Aug. 8, 1976. Size of No. 1704: 72x76mm. Nos. 1696-1703 exist imperf.

Power Lines Leading to Village — A355

Designs: 25q, Transformers and insulators. 80q, Dam and power station. 85q, Television set, power lines, grain and cogwheel.

1975, Oct. 25 *Perf. 12x12½*

1705	A355	15q ultra & yel	7	5
1706	A355	25q brt vio & pink	11	5
1707	A355	80q lt grn & gray	35	10
1708	A355	85q ocher & brn	35	15

General electrification, 5th anniversary.

Child, Rabbit and Teddy Bear Planting Tree — A356

Fairy Tales: 10q, Mother fox. 15q, Ducks in school. 20q, Little pigs building house. 25q, Animals watching television. 30q, Rabbit and bear at work. 35q, Working and playing ants. 2.70l, Wolf in sheep's clothes.

1975, Dec. 25 Litho. *Perf. 12½x12*

1709	A356	5q blk & multi	5	5
1710	A356	10q blk & multi	5	5
1711	A356	15q blk & multi	7	5
1712	A356	20q blk & multi	8	5
1713	A356	25q blk & multi	10	5
1714	A356	30q blk & multi	10	6
1715	A356	35q blk & multi	20	6
1716	A356	2.70l blk & multi	1.25	35
		Nos. 1709-1716 (8)	1.90	72

Arms, People, Factories A357

Design: 1.90l, Arms, government building, celebrating crowd.

1976, Jan. 11 Litho. *Perf. 12*

1717	A357	25q gold & multi	10	5
1718	A357	1.90l gold & multi	70	30

30th anniversary of proclamation of Albanian People's Republic.

Ice Hockey, Olympic Games' Emblem — A358

Designs: 10q, Speed skating. 15q, Biathlon. 50q, Ski jump. 1.20l, Slalom. 2.15l, Figure skating, pairs. 2.30l, One-man bobsled.

1976, Feb. 4

1719	A358	5q sil & multi	5	5
1720	A358	10q sil & multi	5	5
1721	A358	15q sil & multi	7	5
1722	A358	50q sil & multi	20	10
1723	A358	1.20l sil & multi	45	15
1724	A358	2.30l sil & multi	1.10	40
		Nos. 1719-1724 (6)	1.92	80

Miniature Sheet

Perf. 12 on 2 sides x imperf.

1725	A358	2.15l sil & multi	1.25	1.00

12th Winter Olympic Games, Innsbruck, Austria, Feb. 4-15. Size of No. 1725 66x79mm.

Meadow Saffron — A359

Medicinal Plants: 10q, Deadly night-shade. 15q, Yellow gentian. 20q, Horse chestnut. 70q, Shield fern. 80q, Marsh mallow. 2.30l, Thorn apple.

1976, Apr. 10 Litho. *Perf. 12x12½*

1726	A359	5q blk & multi	5	5
1727	A359	10q blk & multi	5	5
1728	A359	15q blk & multi	7	5
1729	A359	20q blk & multi	8	5
1730	A359	70q blk & multi	20	10
1731	A359	80q blk & multi	40	12
1732	A359	2.30l blk & multi	1.10	35
		Nos. 1726-1732 (7)	1.95	77

Bowl and Spoon — A360

Designs: 15q, Flask (vert.). 20q, Carved handles (vert.). 25q, Pistol and dagger. 80q,

Wall hanging (vert.). 1.20l, Earrings and belt buckle. 1.40l, Jugs (vert.).

1976 Litho. *Perf. 12½x12, 12x12½*

1733	A360	10q lil & multi	5	5
1734	A360	15q gray & multi	7	5
1735	A360	20q multi	8	5
1736	A360	25q car & multi	12	5
1737	A360	80q yel & multi	35	12
1738	A360	1.20l multi	50	15
1739	A360	1.40l tan & multi	65	25
		Nos. 1733-1739 (7)	1.82	72

National Ethnographic Conference, Tirana, June 28.

Founding of Cooperatives, by Zef Shoshi — A361

Paintings: 10q, Going to Work, by Agim Zajmi (vert.). 25q, Crowd Listening to Loudspeaker, by Vilson Kilica. 40q, Woman Welder, by Sabaudin Xhaferi (vert.). 50q, Factory, by Isuf Sulovari (vert.). 1.20l, 1942 Revolt, by Lec Shkreli (vert.). 1.60l, Coming Home from Work, by Agron Dine. 2.05l, Honoring a Young Pioneer, by Andon Lakuriqi.

Perf. 12½x12, 12x12½

1976, Aug. 8 Litho.

1740	A361	5q gold & multi	5	5
1741	A361	10q gold & multi	5	5
1742	A361	25q gold & multi	11	5
1743	A361	40q gold & multi	15	8
1744	A361	50q gold & multi	15	10
1745	A361	1.20l gold & multi	54	15
1746	A361	1.60l gold & multi	75	30
		Nos. 1740-1746 (7)	1.80	78

Miniature Sheet

Perf. 12 on 2 sides x imperf.

1747	A361	2.05l gold & multi	1.00	50

Size of No. 1747: 92x79mm.

Red Flag, Agricultural Symbols A362

Enver Hoxha, Partisans and Albanian Flag A363

Design: 1.20l, Red flag and raised pickax.

1976, Nov. 1

1748	A362	25q multi	12	5
1749	A362	1.20l multi	50	20

7th Workers Party Congress.

1976, Oct. 28 *Perf. 12x12½*

Design: 1.90l, Demonstrators with Albanian flag.

1750	A363	25q multi	12	5
1751	A363	1.90l multi	80	30

35th anniversary of anti-Fascist demonstrations.

Attacking Partisans, Meeting House — A364

Designs (Red Flag and): 25q, Partisans, pickax and gun. 80q, Workers, soldiers, pickax and gun. 1.20l, Agriculture and industry. 1.70l, Dancers, symbols of science and art.

1976, Nov. 8 Litho. *Perf. 12x12½*

1752	A364	15q gold & multi	6	5
1753	A364	25q gold & multi	12	5
1754	A364	80q gold & multi	25	10
1755	A364	1.20l gold & multi	45	15
1756	A364	1.70l gold & multi	90	20
		Nos. 1752-1756 (5)	1.78	55

35th anniversary of 1st Workers Party Congress.

Young Workers and Track A365

Design: 1.25l, Young soldiers and Albanian flag.

1976, Nov. 23 *Perf. 12*

1757	A365	80q yel & multi	35	12
1758	A365	1.25l car & multi	50	25

Union of Young Communists, 35th anniversary.

"Cuca e Maleve" Ballet A366

Designs: Scenes from ballet "Mountain Girl."

1976, Dec. 14 *Perf. 12*

1759	A366	10q gold & multi	6	5
1760	A366	15q gold & multi	10	5
1761	A366	20q gold & multi	12	5
1762	A366	25q gold & multi	15	5
1763	A366	80q gold & multi	45	12
1764	A366	1.20l gold & multi	60	20
1765	A366	1.40l gold & multi	80	25
		Nos. 1759-1765 (7)	2.28	77

Miniature Sheet

Perf. 12 on 2 sides x imperf.

1766	A366	2.05l gold & multi	1.40	50

Size of No. 1766: 77x68mm.

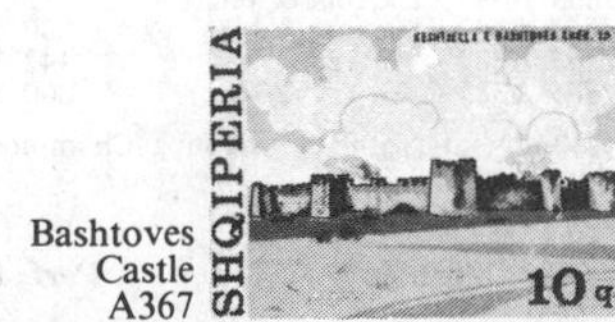

Bashtoves Castle A367

Albanian Castles: 15q, Gjirokastres. 20q, Ali Pash Tepelenes. 25q, Petreles. 80q, Beratit. 1.20l, Durresit. 1.40l, Krujes.

1976, Dec. 30 Litho. *Perf. 12*

1767	A367	10q blk & dl bl	5	5
1768	A367	15q blk & grn	8	5
1769	A367	20q blk & gray	10	5
1770	A367	25q blk & brn	12	5
1771	A367	80q blk & rose	30	12
1772	A367	1.20l blk & vio	35	20
1773	A367	1.40l blk & brn red	70	20
		Nos. 1767-1773 (7)	1.70	72

Skanderbeg's Shield and Spear — A368

Skanderbeg's Weapons: 80q, Helmet, sword and scabbard. 1l, Halberd, quiver with arrows, crossbow and spear.

1977, Jan. 28 Litho. *Perf. 12*

1774	A368	15q sil & multi	35	8
1775	A368	80q sil & multi	1.40	40
1776	A368	1l sil & multi	2.00	50

Skanderbeg (1403-1468), national hero.

Ilia Oiqi, Messenger in Storm — A369

Polyvinylchloride Plant, Vlore — A370

Modern Heroes: 10q, Ilia Dashi, sailor in battle. 25q, Fran Ndue Ivanaj, fisherman in storm. 80q, Zeliha Allmetaj, woman rescuing child. 1l, Ylli Zaimi, rescuing goats from flood. 1.90l, Isuf Plloci, fighting forest fire.

1977, Feb. 28 Litho. *Perf. 12x12½*

1777	A369	5q brn & multi	5	5
1778	A369	10q ultra & multi	5	5
1779	A369	25q bl & multi	10	5
1780	A369	80q ocher & multi	40	10
1781	A369	1l brn & multi	60	15
1782	A369	1.90l brn & multi	1.10	25
		Nos. 1777-1782 (6)	2.30	65

1977, Mar. 29 Litho. *Perf. 12½x12*

Designs: 25q, Naphtha fractioning plant, Ballsh. 65q, Hydroelectric station and dam, Fjerzes. 1l, Metallurgical plant and blast furance, Elbasan.

1783	A370	15q sil & multi	5	5
1784	A370	25q sil & multi	15	5
1785	A370	65q sil & multi	35	12
1786	A370	1l sil & multi	55	20

6th Five-year plan.

Qerime Halil Galica — A371

Victory Monument, Tirana — A372

Design: 1.25l, Qerime Halil Galica "Shota" and father Azem Galica.

1977, Apr. 20 Litho. *Perf. 12*

1787	A371	80q dk red	30	12
1788	A371	1.25l gray bl	50	20

"Shota" Galica, communist fighter.

1977, May 5 Litho. *Perf. 12*

Designs (Red Star and): 80q, Clenched fist, Albanian flag. 1.20l, Bust of Qemal Stafa and poppies.

1789	A372	25q multi	12	5
1790	A372	80q multi	35	12
1791	A372	1.20l multi	55	20

35th anniversary of Martyrs' Day.

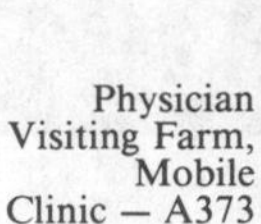

Physician Visiting Farm, Mobile Clinic — A373

Designs: 10q, Cowherd and cattle ranch. 20q, Militia woman helping with harvest, rifle and combine. 80q, Modern village, highway and power lines. 2.95l, Tractor and greenhouses.

1977, June 18

1792	A373	5q multi	5	5
1793	A373	10q multi	5	5
1794	A373	20q multi	10	5
1795	A373	80q multi	30	12
1796	A373	2.95l multi	1.80	50
		Nos. 1792-1796 (5)	2.30	77

"Socialist transformation of the villages."

Armed Workers, Flag and Factory — A374

Design: 1.80l, Workers with proclamation and flags.

1977, June 20

1797	A374	25q multi	12	5
1798	A374	1.80l multi	75	25

9th Labor Unions Congress.

Kerchief Dance — A375

Designs: Various folk dances.

1977, Aug. 20 Litho. *Perf. 12*

1799	A375	5q multi	5	5
1800	A375	10q multi	5	5
1801	A375	15q multi	8	5
1802	A375	25q multi	8	5
1803	A375	80q multi	30	12
1804	A375	1.20l multi	60	20
1805	A375	1.55l multi	75	25
		Nos. 1799-1805 (7)	1.91	77

Miniature Sheet

Perf. 12 on 2 sides x imperf.

1806	A375	2.05l multi	1.00	50

Size of No. 1806: 56x74mm.

See Nos. 1836-1840, 1884-1888.

Attack A376

Designs: 25q, Enver Hoxha addressing Army. 80q, Volunteers and riflemen. 1l, Volunteers, hydrofoil patrolboat and MiG planes. 1.90l, Volunteers and Albanian flag.

1977, July 10 Litho. *Perf. 12*

1807	A376	15q gold & multi	5	5
1808	A376	25q gold & multi	8	5
1809	A376	80q gold & multi	30	12
1810	A376	1l gold & multi	45	12
1811	A376	1.90l gold & multi	90	25
		Nos. 1807-1811 (5)	1.78	59

"One People-One Army."

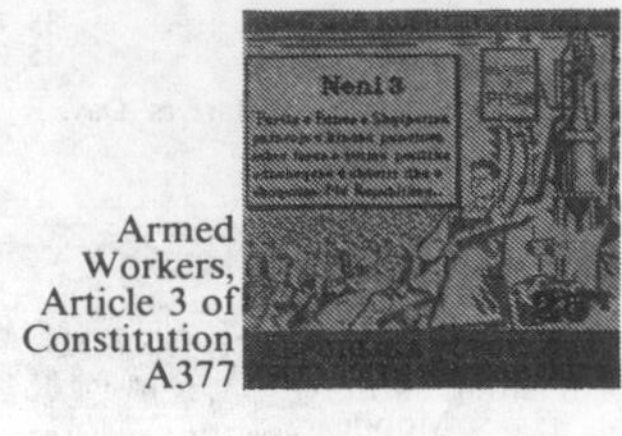

Armed Workers, Article 3 of Constitution A377

Design: 1.20l, Symbols of farming and fertilizer industry, Article 25 of Constitution.

1977, Oct.
1812 A377 25q red, gold & blk 15 5
1813 A377 1.20l red, gold & blk 55 20

New Constitution.

Picnic — A378

Film Frames: 15q, Telephone lineman in winter. 25q, Two men and a woman. 80q, Workers. 1.20l, Boys playing in street. 1.60l, Harvest.

1977, Oct. 25 Litho. *Perf. 12½x12*
1814 A378 10q bl grn 5 5
1815 A378 15q multi 5 5
1816 A378 25q black 8 5
1817 A378 80q multi 35 12
1818 A378 1.20l dp cl 60 15
1819 A378 1.60l multi 75 25
Nos. 1814-1819 (6) 1.88 67

Albanian films.

Farm Workers in Field, by V. Mio A379

Paintings by V. Mio: 10q, Landscape in Snow. 15q, Grazing Sheep under Walnut Tree in Spring. 25q, Street in Korce. 80q, Horseback Riders on Mountain Pass. 1l, Boats on Shore. 1.75l, Tractors Plowing Fields. 2.05l, Self-portrait.

1977, Dec. 25 Litho. *Perf. 12½x12*
1820 A379 5q gold & multi 5 5
1821 A379 10q gold & multi 5 5
1822 A379 15q gold & multi 8 5
1823 A379 25q gold & multi 8 5
1824 A379 80q gold & multi 35 12
1825 A379 1l gold & multi 40 15
1826 A379 1.75l gold & multi 70 20
Nos. 1820-1826 (7) 1.71 67

Miniature Sheet

Imperf.; Perf. 12 Horiz. between Vignette and Value Panel.

1827 A379 2.05l gold & multi 90 40

Size of No. 1827: 66x101mm.

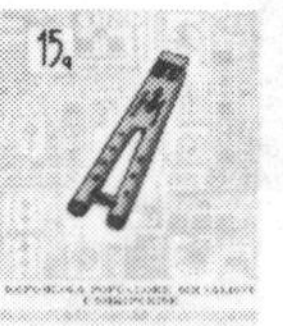

Pan Flute — A380

Albanian Flag, Monument and People — A381

Folk Musical Instruments: 20q, Single-string goat's-head fiddle. 80q, Woodwind. 1.20l, Drum. 1.70l, Bagpipe. Background shows various woven folk patterns.

1978, Jan. 20 *Perf. 12x12½*
1828 A380 15q multi 8 5
1829 A380 25q multi 12 5
1830 A380 80q multi 35 12
1831 A380 1.20l multi 55 15
1832 A380 1.70l multi 75 20
Nos. 1828-1832 (5) 1.85 57

1978 *Perf. 12½x12, 12x12½*

Designs: 25q, Ismail Qemali and fighters (horiz.). 1.65l, People dancing around Albanian flag (horiz.).

1833 A381 15q multi 8 5
1834 A381 25q multi 12 5
1835 A381 1.65l multi 75 25

65th anniversary of independence.

Folk Dancing Type of 1977

Designs: Various dances.

1978, Feb. 15 Litho. *Perf. 12*
1836 A375 5q multi 5 5
1837 A375 25q multi 8 5
1838 A375 80q multi 30 12
1839 A375 1l multi 45 15
1840 A375 2.30l multi 90 30
Nos. 1836-1840 (5) 1.78 67

Nos. 1836-1840 have white background around dancers, Nos. 1799-1805 have pinkish shadows.

Tractor Drivers, by Dhimitraq Trebicka A382

Working Class Paintings: 80q, Steeplejack, by Spiro Kristo. 85q, "A Point in the Discussion," by Skender Milori. 90q, Oil rig crew, by Anesti Cini (vert.). 1.60l, Metal workers, by Ramadan Karanxha. 2.20l, Political discussion, by Sotiraq Sholla.

1978, Mar. 25 Litho. *Perf. 12*
1841 A382 25q multi 8 5
1842 A382 80q multi 30 12
1843 A382 85q multi 30 12
1844 A382 90q multi 35 16
1845 A382 1.60l multi 75 25
Nos. 1841-1845 (5) 1.78 70

Miniature Sheet

Perf. 12 on 2 sides x imperf.

1846 A382 2.20l multi 1.00 40

Size of No. 1846: 72x98mm.

Woman with Rifle and Pickax A383

Design: 1.95l, Farm and Militia women, industrial plant.

1978, June 1 Litho. *Perf. 12*
1847 A383 25q gold & red 12 5
1848 A383 1.95l gold & red 75 25

8th Congress of Women's Union.

Children and Flowers — A384

Designs: 10q, Children with rifle, ax, book and flags. 25q, Dancing children in folk costume. 1.80l, Children in school.

1978, June 1 Litho.
1849 A384 5q multi 5 5
1850 A384 10q multi 5 5
1851 A384 25q multi 12 5
1852 A384 1.80l multi 75 25

International Children's Day.

Spirit of Skanderbeg as Conqueror A385

Designs: 10q, Battle at Mostar Bridge. 80q, Marchers and Albanian flag. 1.20l, Riflemen in winter battle. 1.65l, Abdyl Frasheri (1839-1892). 2.20l, Rifles, scroll and pen, League building. 2.60l, League headquarters, Prizren.

1978, June 10 Litho. *Perf. 12*
1853 A385 10q multi 5 5
1854 A385 25q multi 8 5
1855 A385 80q multi 25 12
1856 A385 1.20l multi 50 15
1857 A385 1.65l multi 75 20
1858 A385 2.60l multi 90 35
Nos. 1853-1858 (6) 2.53 92

Miniature Sheet

Perf. 12 on 2 sides x imperf.

1859 A385 2.20l multi 1.00 40

Centenary of League of Prizren. Size of No. 1859: 74x69mm.

Guerrillas and Flag, 1943 — A386

Designs: 25q, Soldier, sailor, airman, militiaman (horiz.). 1.90l, Members of armed forces, civil guards, and Young Pioneers.

1978, July 10 *Perf. 11½x12½*
1860 A386 5q multi 5 5
1861 A386 25q multi 12 5
1862 A386 1.90l multi 1.00 25

35th anniversary of People's Army.

Woman with Machine Carbine A387

Kerchief Dance A388

Designs: 25q, Man with target rifle (horiz.). 95q, Man shooting with telescopic sights (horiz.). 2.40l, Woman target shooting with pistol.

Perf. 12½x12, 12x12½

1978, Sept. 20 Litho.
1863 A387 25q blk & yel 12 5
1864 A387 80q org & blk 30 12
1865 A387 95q red & blk 42 14
1866 A387 2.40l car & blk 1.00 30

32nd National Rifle-shooting Championships, Sept. 20.

1978, Oct. 6 *Perf. 12*

Designs: 15q, Musicians. 25q, Fiddler with single-stringed instrument. 80q, Dancers, men. 1.20l, Saber dance. 1.90l, Singers, women.

1867 A388 10q multi 5 5
1868 A388 15q multi 8 5
1869 A388 25q multi 12 5
1870 A388 80q multi 25 12
1871 A388 1.20l multi 50 15
1872 A388 1.90l multi 80 25
Nos. 1867-1872 (6) 1.80 67

National Folklore Festival.

No. 1736 Surcharged with New Value, 2 Bars and "RICCIONE 78"

1978 Litho. *Perf. 12½x12*
1873 A360 3.30l on 25q multi 4.00 1.50

Riccione 78 Philatelic Exhibition.

Enver Hoxha — A389

1978, Oct. 16 Litho. *Perf. 12x12½*
1874 A389 80q red & multi 30 12
1875 A389 1.20l red & multi 45 15
1876 A389 3.40l red & multi 90 25

Miniature Sheet

Perf. 12½ on 2 sides x imperf.

1877 A389 2.20l red & multi 85 40

70th birthday of Enver Hoxha, First Secretary of Central Committee of the Communist Party of Albania. Size of No. 1877: 67x88½mm.

Woman and Wheat — A390

Designs: 25q, Woman with egg crates. 80q, Shepherd and sheep. 2.60l, Milkmaid and cows.

1978, Dec. 15 *Perf. 12x12½*
1878 A390 15q multi 10 5
1879 A390 25q multi 15 5
1880 A390 80q multi 40 12
1881 A390 2.60l multi 1.10 50

Dora d'Istria — A391

Tower House — A392

Design: 1.10l, Full portrait of Dora d"Istria, author; birth sesquicentennial.

1979, Jan. 22 Litho. *Perf. 12*
1882 A391 80q lt grn & blk 45 12
1883 A391 1.10l vio brn & blk 55 18

Costume Type of 1977

Designs: Various folk dances.

1979, Feb. 25
1884 A375 15q multi 8 5
1885 A375 25q multi 12 5
1886 A375 80q multi 45 12
1887 A375 1.20l multi 60 18
1888 A375 1.40l multi 85 30
Nos. 1884-1888 (5) 2.10 70

Nos. 1884-1888 have white background. Denomination in upper left on No. 1885, in upper right on No. 1802; lower left on No. 1886, upper left on No. 1803.

1979, Mar. 20

Traditional Houses: 15q, Stone gallery house (horiz.). 80q, House with wooden galleries (horiz.). 1.20l, Galleried tower house. 1.40l, 1.90l, Tower houses (diff.).

1889 A392 15q multi 8 5
1890 A392 25q multi 12 5
1891 A392 80q multi 45 12
1892 A392 1.20l multi 60 18
1893 A392 1.40l multi 85 30
Nos. 1889-1893 (5) 2.10 70

Miniature Sheet
Perf. 12 on 2 sides x imperf.
1894 A392 1.90l multi 1.00 50
Size of No. 1894: 62x75mm.

Soldier, Factories, Wheat A393

Design: 1.65l, Soldiers, workers and coat of arms.

1979, May 14 Litho. *Perf. 12*
1895 A393 25q multi 18 5
1896 A393 1.65l multi 80 25

Congress of Permet, 35th anniversary.

R P S E SHQIPERISE Albanian Flag — A394

1979, June 4
1897 A394 25q multi 18 5
1898 A394 1.65l multi 80 25

5th Congress of Albanian Democratic Front.

Vasil Shanto A395

Alexander Moissi — A396

1979
1899 A395 15q multi 8 5
1900 A395 25q multi 12 8
1901 A395 60q multi 35 10
1902 A395 80q multi 45 12
1903 A395 90q multi 45 15
1904 A396 1.10l multi 60 18
Nos. 1899-1904 (6) 2.05 68

Vasil Shanto (1913-1944) and Qemal Stafa (1921-1942), Anti-Fascist fighters; Alexander Moissi (1880-1935), actor.

Winter Campaign, by Arben Basha — A397

Paintings of Military Scenes by: 25q, Ismail Lulani. 80q, Myrteza Fushekati. 1.20l, Muhamet Deliu. 1.40l, Jorgji Gjikopulli. 1.90l, Fatmir Haxhiu.

1979, Oct. Litho. *Perf. 12½x12*
1905 A397 15q multi 8 5
1906 A397 25q multi 12 8
1907 A397 80q multi 35 12
1908 A397 1.20l multi 60 18
1909 A397 1.40l multi 65 30
Nos. 1905-1909 (5) 1.80 73

Miniature Sheet
Perf. 12 on 2 sides x imperf.
1910 A397 1.90l multi 1.00 50
Size of No. 1910: 78x103mm.

Athletes Surrounding Flag A398

Literary Society Headquarters A399

1979, Oct. 1 Litho. *Perf. 12*
1911 A398 15q *shown* 8 5
1912 A398 25q *Shooting* 12 5
1913 A398 80q *Dancing* 35 12
1914 A398 1.20l *Soccer* 65 18
1915 A398 1.40l *High jump* 85 30
Nos. 1911-1915 (5) 2.05 70

Liberation Spartakiad, 35th anniversary.

1979, Oct. 12

Albanian Literary Society Centenary: 25q, Seal and charter. 80q, Founder. 1.55l, 1879 Headquarters. 1.90l, Founders.

1916 A399 25q multi 15 5
1917 A399 80q multi 40 12
1918 A399 1.20l multi 55 18
1919 A399 1.55l multi 75 25

Miniature Sheet
Perf. 12½ on 2 sides x imperf.
1920 A399 1.90l multi 1.00 50
Size of No. 1920: 78½x66mm.

Congress Statute, Coat of Arms — A400

1979, Oct. 20 Photo. *Perf. 12x12½*
1921 A400 25q multi 18 5
1922 A400 1.65l multi 80 30

2nd Congress of Berat, 35th anniversary.

Children Entering School, Books — A401

1979 Litho. *Perf. 12½x12*
1923 A401 5q shown 5 5
1924 A401 10q Communications 5 5
1925 A401 15q Steel workers 12 5
1926 A401 20q Dancers, instruments 12 5
1927 A401 25q Newspapers, radio, television 18 5
1928 A401 60q Textile worker 35 15
1929 A401 80q Armed forces 50 20
1930 A401 1.20l Industry 70 30
1931 A401 1.60l transportation 90 45
1932 A401 2.40l Agriculture 1.30 60
1932A A401 3l Medicine 1.70 85
Nos. 1923-1932A (11) 5.97 2.80

Workers and Factory A402

Worker, Red Flag and: 80q, Hand holding sickle and rifle. 1.20l, Red star and open book. 1.55l, Open book and cogwheel.

1979, Nov. 29
1933 A402 25q multi 12 5
1934 A402 80q multi 35 10
1935 A402 1.20l multi 55 18
1936 A402 1.55l multi 65 20

35th anniversary of independence.

Joseph Stalin — A403

Design: 1.10l, Stalin on dais (horiz.).

1979, Dec. 21 Litho. *Perf. 12*
1937 A403 80q red & dk bl 40 12
1938 A403 1.10l red & dk bl 55 20

Joseph Stalin (1879-1953), birth centenary.

Fireplace and Pottery, Korcar A404

Home Furnishings: 80q, Cupboard bed, dagger, pistol, ammunition pouch, Shkodar. 1.20l, Stool, pot, chair, Mirdit. 1.35l, Chimney, dagger, jacket, Gjirokastro.

1980, Feb. 27 Litho. *Perf. 12*
1939 A404 25q multi 10 5
1940 A404 80q multi 35 12
1941 A404 1.20l multi 55 20
1942 A404 1.35l multi 60 30

Pipe, Painted Flask A405

1980, Mar. 4
1943 A405 25q *shown* 10 5
1944 A405 80q *Leather handbags* 35 12
1945 A405 1.20l *Carved eagle, embroidered rug* 55 20
1946 A405 1.35l *Lace* 60 30

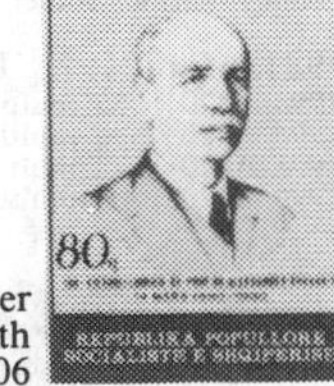
Prof. Aleksander Xhuvanit Birth Centenary — A406

1980, Mar. 14
1947 A406 80q multi 35 12
1948 A406 1l multi 45 18

Revolutionaries on Horseback — A407

Insurrection at Kosove, 70th Anniversary: 1l, Battle scene.

1980, Apr. 4
1949 A407 80q red & blk 35 12
1950 A407 1l red & blk 45 18

Soldiers and Workers Laboring to Aid the Stricken Populations, by D. Jukinui and I. Lulani — A408

1980, Apr. 15 Litho. *Perf. 12½*
1951 A408 80q lt bl & multi 35 12
1952 A408 1l lt bl grn & multi 45 18

Lenin, 110th Birth Anniversary A409

1980, Apr. 22
1953 A409 80q multi 35 12
1954 A409 1l multi 45 18

Misto Mame and Ali Demi, War Martyrs A410

War Martyrs: 80q, Sadik Staveleci, Vojo Kusji, Hoxhi Martini. 1.20l, Bule Naipi, Persefoni Kokedhima. 1.35l, Ndoc Deda, Hydajet Lezha, Naim Gyylbegu, Ndoc Mazi, Ahmed Haxha.

1980, May 5
1955 A410 25q multi 12 5
1956 A410 80q multi 35 12
1957 A410 1.20l multi 50 20
1958 A410 1.35l multi 60 30

See Nos. 2025-2028, 2064-2067, 2122-2125, 2171-2174, 2207-2209.

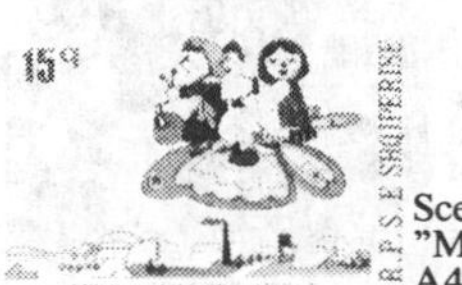

Scene from "Mirela" A411

1980, June 7
1959 A411 15q *shown* 8 5
1960 A411 25q *The Scribbler* 10 5
1961 A411 80q *Circus Bears* 35 12
1962 A411 2.40l *Waterdrops* 1.00 45

Scott's editorial staff cannot undertake to identify, authenticate or appraise stamps and postal markings.

Carrying Iron Castings in the Enver Hoxha Tractor Combine, by S. Shijaku and M. Fushekati — A412

Paintings (Gallery of Figurative Paintings, Tirana): 80q, The Welder, by Harilla Dhima. 1.20l, Steel Erectors, by Petro Kokushta. 1.35l, Pandeli Lena, 1.80l Communists, by Vilson Kilica.

1980, July 22

1963 A412 25q multi 12 5
1964 A412 80q multi 35 12
1965 A412 1.20l multi 50 20
1966 A412 1.35l multi 65 30

Souvenir Sheet

1967 A412 1.80l multi 85 60

Gate, Parchment Miniature, 11th Cent. — A413

Bas reliefs of the Middle Ages: 80q, Eagle, 13th cent. 1.20l, Heraldic lion, 14th cent. 1.35l, Pheasant, 14th cent.

1980, Sept. 27 Litho. ***Perf. 12***

1968 A413 25q gold & blk 12 5
1969 A413 80q gold & blk 35 15
1970 A413 1.20l gold & blk 55 20
1971 A413 1.35l gold & blk 70 30

Divjaka National Park — A414

1980, Nov. 6 **Photo.**

1972 A414 80q shown 35 15
1973 A414 1.20l Lura 55 30
1974 A414 1.60l Thethi 75 35

Park Type of 1980

Souvenir Sheet

1980, Nov. 6 Photo. ***Perf. 12½***

1975 A414 1.80l Llogara Park 90 90

No. 1975 has multicolored decorative margin. Size: 90x90mm.

Citizens, Flag and Arms of Albania A415

1981, Jan. 11 Litho. ***Perf. 12***

1976 A415 80q shown 35 15
1977 A415 1l People's Party Headquarters, Tirana 50 25

35th anniversary of the Republic.

Child's Bed — A416

1981, Mar. 20 Litho. ***Perf. 12***

1978 A416 25q shown 12 5
1979 A416 80q Wooden bucket, brass bottle 40 25
1980 A416 1.20l Shoes 60 30
1981 A416 1.35l Jugs 65 35

Soldiers Fighting with Rifles — A417

1981, Apr. 20

1982 A417 80q shown 40 25
1983 A417 1l Sword combat 55 30

Souvenir Sheet

Perf. 12½ Vert.

1984 A417 1.80l Soldier with pistol 90 90

Battle of Shtimje centenary. No. 1984 contains one stamp; purple margin shows battle scene. Size: 85x68mm.

House Interior, Labara A418

1981, Feb. 25 Litho. ***Perf. 12***

1985 A418 25q shown 12 5
1986 A418 80q Labara, diff. 40 25
1987 A418 1.20l Mat 60 30
1988 A418 1.35l Dibres 65 35

Boys Riding Unicycles — A419

Designs: Children's circus.

1981, June ***Perf. 12***

1989 A419 15q multi 8 5
1990 A419 25q multi 12 5
1991 A419 80q multi 40 25
1992 A419 2.40l multi 1.20 70

Soccer Players A420

1982 World Cup Soccer Elimination Games: Various soccer players.

1981, Mar. 31 Litho. ***Perf. 12***

1993 A420 25q multi 25 25
1994 A420 80q multi 2.00 60
1995 A420 1.20l multi 3.00 95
1996 A420 1.35l multi 3.50 1.20

Allies, by S. Hysa A421

Paintings: 80q, Warriors, by A. Buza. 1.20l, Rallying to the Flag, Dec. 1911, by A. Zajmi (vert.). 1.35l, My Flag is My Heart, by L. Cefa (vert.). 1.80l, Circling the Flag in a Common Cause, by N. Vasia.

1981, July 10 ***Perf. 12½x12***

1997 A421 25q multi 15 5
1998 A421 80q multi 50 25
1999 A421 1.20l multi 70 35
2000 A421 1.35l multi 75 40

Souvenir Sheet

2001 A421 1.80l multi 1.20 1.10

No. 2001 contains one stamp (55x55mm.); multicolored margin. Size: 82x109mm.

Rifleman A422

1981, Aug. 30 ***Perf. 12***

2002 A422 25q shown 15 5
2003 A422 80q Weight lifting 50 25
2004 A422 1.20l Volleyball 70 35
2005 A422 1.35l Soccer 80 40

Albanian Workers' Party, 8th Congress A423

1981, Nov. 1

2006 A423 80q Flag, star 40 25
2007 A423 1l Flag, hammer and sickle 55 30

Albanian Workers' Party, 40th Anniv. — A424

Communist Youth Org., 40th Anniv. — A425

1981, Nov. 8

2008 A424 80q Symbols of industrialization 40 25
2009 A424 2.80l Fist, emblem 1.50 80

Souvenir Sheet

2010 A424 1.80l Enver Hoxha, Memoirs 1.00 1.00

Size of No. 2010: 79x99mm.

1981, Nov. 23

2011 A425 80q Star, ax, map 40 25
2012 A425 1l Flags, star 55 30

War Martyrs Type of 1980

Portraits: 25q, Perlat Rexhepi (1919-1942) and Branko Kadia (1921-1942). 80q, Xheladin Beqiri (1908-1944) and Hajdar Dushi (1916-1944). 1.20l, Koci Bako (1905-1941), Vasil Laci (1923-1941) and Mujo Ulqinaku (1898-1939). 1.35l, Mine Peza (1875-1942) and Zoja Cure (1920-1944).

1981, May 5 Litho. ***Perf. 12***

2012A A410 25q sil & multi 25 12
2012B A410 80q gold & multi 80 40
2012C A410 1.20l sil & multi 1.15 55
2012D A410 1.35l gold & multi 1.25 62

Fan S. Noli, Writer, Birth Centenary A426

Traditional House, Bulqize A427

1982, Jan. 6 Litho. ***Perf. 12***

2013 A426 80q lt ol grn & gold 40 25
2014 A426 1.10l lt red brn & gold 55 30

1982, Feb. ***Perf. 12½x12***

2015 A427 25q shown 40 25
2016 A427 80q Lebush 40 25
2017 A427 1.20l Bicaj 65 35
2018 A427 1.55l Klos 90 55

TB Bacillus Centenary A428

1982, Mar. 24 ***Perf. 12***

2019 A428 80q Globe 50 25
2020 A428 1.10l Koch 70 35

Albanian League House, Prizren, by K. Buza — A429

Kosova Landscapes: 25q, Castle at Prizrenit, by G. Madhi. 1.20l, Mountain Gorge at Rogove, by K. Buza. 1.55l, Street of the Hadhji at Zekes, by G. Madhi. 25q, 1.20l, 1.55l vert.

Perf. 12x12½, 12½x12

1982, Apr. 15 **Litho.**

2021 A429 25q multi 15 5
2022 A429 80q multi 40 18
2023 A429 1.20l multi 60 25
2024 A429 1.55l multi 80 35

War Martyr Type of 1980

Designs: 25q, Hibe Palikuqi, Liri Gero. 80q, Mihal Duri, Kajo Karafili. 1.20l, Fato Dudumi, Margarita Tutulani, Shejnaze Juka. 1.55l, Memo Meto, Gjok Doci.

1982, May ***Perf. 12***

2025 A410 25q multi 15 5
2026 A410 80q multi 40 25
2027 A410 1.20l multi 65 35
2028 A410 1.55l multi 90 55

Loading Freighter — A430

Children's Paintings.

1982, June 15 ***Perf. 12½x12***

2029 A430 15q shown 10 5
2030 A430 80q Forest 40 25
2031 A430 1.20l City 65 35
2032 A430 1.65l Park 95 55

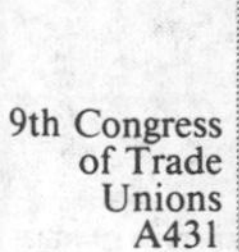

9th Congress of Trade Unions A431

1982, June 6 **Litho.** ***Perf. 12***
2033 A431 80q Workers, factories 40 18
2034 A431 1.10l Emblem, flag 55 22

Alpine Village Festival, by Danish Jukniu A432

Industrial Development Paintings: 80q, Hydroelectric Station Builders, by Ali Miruku. 1.20l, Steel Workers, by Clirim Ceka. 1.55l, Oil drillers, by Pandeli Lena. 1.90l, Trapping the Furnace, by Jorgji Gjikopulli.

1982, July ***Perf. 12½***
2035 A432 25q multi 12 5
2036 A432 80q multi 40 18
2037 A432 1.20l multi 60 25
2038 A432 1.55l multi 80 35

Souvenir Sheet

2039 A432 1.90l multi 1.25 50

No. 2039 contains one stamp (54x48mm., perf. 12); silver and black margin. Size: 76x91mm.

40th Anniv. of Democratic Front A433

1982, Sept. 16 ***Perf. 12***
2040 A433 80q Glory to the Heroes of Peza Monument 40 18
2041 A433 1.10l Marchers 55 22

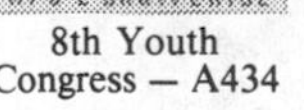

8th Youth Congress — A434

Handmade Shoulder Bags — A435

1982, Oct. 4
2042 A434 80q multi 40 18
2043 A434 1.10l multi 55 22

1982, Nov.
2044 A435 25q Rug, horiz. 12 5
2045 A435 80q shown 40 18
2046 A435 1.20l Wooden pots, bowls, horiz. 60 25
2047 A435 1.55l Jug 80 35

70th Anniv. of Independence — A436

1982, Nov. 28
2048 A436 20q Ishamil Qemali 10 5
2049 A436 1.20l Partisans 60 25
2050 A436 2.40l Partisans, diff. 1.20 50

Souvenir Sheet

2051 A436 1.90l Independence Monument, Tirana 1.25 50

Size of No. 2051: 91x88mm.

Dhermi Beach A437

1982, Dec. 20
2052 A437 25q shown 12 5
2053 A437 80q Sarande 40 18
2054 A437 1.20l Ksamil 60 25
2055 A437 1.55l Lukove 80 35

Handkerchief Dancers — A438

Folkdancers.

1983, Feb. 20 **Litho.** ***Perf. 12***
2056 A438 25q shown 12 5
2057 A438 80q With kerchief, drum 40 18
2058 A438 1.20l With guitar, flute, tambourine 60 25
2059 A438 1.55l Women 80 35

Karl Marx (1818-1883) A439

1983, Mar. 14 **Litho.** ***Perf. 12***
2060 A439 80q multi 40 18
2061 A439 1.10l multi 55 22

Energy Development A440

1983, Apr. 20
2062 A440 80q Electricity generation 40 18
2063 A440 1.10l Gas & oil production 55 22

War Martyr Type of 1980

Designs: 25q, Asim Zeneli (1916-1943), Nazmi Rushiti (1919-1942). 80q, Shyqyri Ishmi (1922-1942), Shyqyri Alimerko (1923-1943), Myzafer Asqeriu (1918-1942). 1.20l, Qybra Sokoli (1924-1944), Qeriba Derri (1905-1944), Ylbere Bilibashi (1928-1944). 1.55l, Themo Vasi (1915-1943), Abaz Shehu (1905-1942).

1983, May 5 **Litho.** ***Perf. 12***
2064 A410 25q multi 12 5
2065 A410 80q multi 40 18
2066 A410 1.20l multi 60 25
2067 A410 1.55l multi 80 35

Women's Union, 9th Congress A441

1983, June 1 **Litho.** ***Perf. 12x12½***
2068 A441 80q red & gold 40 18
2069 A441 1.10l bl & gold 55 22

Bicycling A442

1983, June 20 ***Perf. 12***
2070 A442 25q shown 12 5
2071 A442 80q Chess 40 18
2072 A442 1.20l Gymnastics 60 25
2073 A442 1.55l Wrestling 80 35

40th Anniv. of People's Army — A443

1983, July 10
2074 A443 20q Armed services 10 5
2075 A443 1.20l Soldier, gun barrels 60 25
2076 A443 2.40l Factory guard, crowd 1.20 50

Sunny Day, by Myrteza Fushekati A444

Paintings: 80q, Messenger of the Grasp, by Niko Progi. 1.20l, 29 November 1944, by Harilla Dhimo. 1.55l, Fireworks, by Pandi Mele. 1.90l, Partisan Assault, by Sali Shijaku and M. Fushekati.

1983, Aug. 28 **Litho.** ***Perf. 12½x12***
2077 A444 25q multi 12 5
2078 A444 80q multi 40 18
2079 A444 1.20l multi 60 25
2080 A444 1.55l multi 80 35

Souvenir Sheet

Perf. 12

2081 A444 1.90l multi 1.00 50

Size of No. 2081: 112x76mm.

Gjirokaster Folklore Festival — A445

Folkdances.

1983, Oct. 6 **Litho.** ***Perf. 12***
2082 A445 25q Sword dance 12 5
2083 A445 80q Kerchief dance 40 18
2084 A445 1.20l Shepherd flautists 60 25
2085 A445 1.55l Garland dance 80 35

World Communications Year — A446

1983, Nov. 10
2086 A446 60q multi 30 12
2087 A446 1.20l multi 60 25

75th Birthday of Enver Hoxha — A447

1983, Oct. 16 **Litho.** ***Perf. 12½***
2088 A447 80q multi 40 18
2089 A447 1.20l multi 60 25
2090 A447 1.80l multi 90 38

Souvenir Sheet

Perf. 12

2091 A447 1.90l multi 1.00 50

Size of No. 2091: 77x100mm.

The Right to a Joint Triumph, by J. Keraj A448

Era of Skanderbeg in Figurative Art: 80q, The Heroic Center of the Battle of Krujes, by N. Bakalli. 1.20l, The Rights of the Enemy after our Triumph, by N. Progri. 1.55l, The Discussion at Lezhes, by B. Ahmeti. 1.90l, Victory over the Turks, by G. Madhi.

1983, Dec. 10 ***Perf. 12½x12***
2092 A448 25q multi 12 5
2093 A448 80q multi 40 18
2094 A448 1.20l multi 60 25
2095 A448 1.55l multi 80 35

Souvenir Sheet

Perf. 12

2096 A448 1.90l multi 1.25 50

Size of No. 2096: 79x92mm.

Greco-Roman Ruins of Illyris — A449

1983, Dec. 28 ***Perf. 12***
2097 A449 80q Amphitheater, Buthroxtum 40 18
2098 A449 1.20l Colonnade, Apollonium 60 25
2099 A449 1.80l Vaulted gallery, amphitheater at Epidamnus 90 38

Foreign postal stationery (stamped envelopes, postal cards and air letter sheets) lies beyond the scope of this Catalogue, which is limited to adhesive postage stamps.

Archeological Discoveries A450

Designs: Apollo, 3rd cent. 25q, Tombstone, Korce, 3rd cent. 80q, Apollo, diff. 1st cent. 1.10 l, Earthenware pot (child's head), Tren, 1st cent. 1.20 l, Man's head, Dyrrah, 2.20 l, Eros with Dolphin, statue Bronze Dyrrah, 3rd cent.

1984, Feb. 25 *Perf. 12x12½*

2100 A450 15q multi 8 5
2101 A450 25q multi 12 5
2102 A450 80q multi 40 18
2103 A450 1.10l multi 55 22
2104 A450 1.20l multi 60 25
2105 A450 2.20l multi 1.10 50
Nos. 2100-2105 (6) 2.85 1.25

Clock Towers — A451

1984, Mar. 30 **Litho.** *Perf. 12*

2106 A451 15q Gjirokaster 8 5
2107 A451 25q Kavaje 12 5
2108 A451 80q Elbasan 40 18
2109 A451 1.10l Tirana 55 22
2110 A451 1.20l Peqin 60 25
2111 A451 2.20l Kruje 1.10 50
Nos. 2106-2111 (6) 2.85 1.25

40th Anniv. of Liberation A452

1984, Apr. 20 **Litho.** *Perf. 12*

2112 A452 15q Student & microscope 8 5
2113 A452 25q Guerrilla with flag 12 5
2114 A452 80q Children with flag 40 18
2115 A452 1.10l Soldier 55 22
2116 A452 1.20l Workers with flag 60 25
2117 A452 2.20l Militia at dam 1.10 50
Nos. 2112-2117 (6) 2.85 1.25

Children — A453

1984, May **Litho.** *Perf. 12*

2118 A453 15q Children reading 8 5
2119 A453 25q Young pioneers 12 5
2120 A453 60q Gardening 30 14
2121 A453 2.80l Kite flying 1.40 60

War Martyr Type of 1980

Designs: 15q, Manush Almani, Mustafa Matohiti, Kastriot Muco. 25q, Zaho Koka, Reshit Collaku, Maliq Muco. 1.20l, Lefter Talo, Tom Kola, Fuat Babani. 2.20l, Myslysm Shyri, Dervish Hexali, Skender Caci.

1984, May 5 **Litho.** *Perf. 12*

2122 A410 15q multi 8 5
2123 A410 25q multi 12 5
2124 A410 1.20l multi 65 30
2125 A410 2.20l multi 1.25 60

40th Anniv. of Permet Congress — A454

1984, May 24 **Litho.** *Perf. 12*

2126 A454 80q Enver Hoxha 45 20
2127 A454 1.10l Resistance fighter 65 30

European Soccer Championships A455

1984, June 12 **Litho.** *Perf. 12*

2128 A455 15q Goalkeeper 12 6
2129 A455 25q Referee 20 10
2130 A455 1.20l Map of Europe 90 45
2131 A455 2.20l Field diagram 1.75 90

Freedom Came, by Myrteza Fushekati A456

Paintings, Tirana Gallery of Figurative Art: 25q, Morning, by Zamir Mati, vert. 80q, My Darling, by Agim Zajmi, vert. 2.60l, For the Partisans, by Arben Basha. 1.90l, Eagle, by Zamir Mati, vert.

1984, June 12 *Perf. 12½*

2132 A456 15q multi 12 6
2133 A456 25q multi 20 10
2134 A456 80q multi 60 30
2135 A456 2.60l multi 2.00 1.00

Souvenir Sheet

Perf. 12 Horiz.

2136 A456 1.90l multi 1.50 75

Size: 80x96mm.

Flora — A457

1984, Aug. 20 **Litho.** *Perf. 12*

2137 A457 15q Moraceae L. 15 8
2138 A457 25q Plantaginaceae L. 25 12
2139 A457 1.20 l Hypericaceae L. 1.15 58
2140 A457 2.20 l Leontopodium alpinum 2.10 1.05

AUSIPEX '84, Melbourne, Sept. 21-30 — A458

1984, Sept. 21 **Litho.** *Perf. 12 Horiz.*

2141 A458 1.90l Sword dancers, emblem 1.50 75

No. 2141 has gray inscribed margin. Size: 72x101mm.

Forestry, Logging, UNFAO Emblem — A459

1984, Sept. 25 *Perf. 12*

2142 A459 15q Beech trees, transport 12 6
2143 A459 25q Pine forest, logging cable 20 10
2144 A459 1.20l Firs, sawmill 90 45
2145 A459 2.20l Forester clearing woods 1.75 90

EURPHILA '84, Rome — A460

1984, Oct. 13 *Perf. 12½*

2146 A460 1.20l View of Gjirokaster 90 45

5th National Spartakiad A461

1984, Oct. 19 *Perf. 12*

2147 A461 15q Soccer 12 6
2148 A461 25q Women's track & field 20 10
2149 A461 80q Weight lifting 60 30
2150 A461 2.20l Pistol shooting 1.75 90

Souvenir Sheet

Perf. 12 Horiz.

2151 A461 1.90l Opening ceremony, red flags 1.50 75

No. 2151 has orange inscribed margin. Size: 70x90mm.

November 29 Revolution, 40th Anniv. A462

1984, Nov. 29 *Perf. 12*

2152 A462 80q Industrial reconstruction 60 30
2153 A462 1.10l Natl. flag, partisans 80 40

Souvenir Sheet

Perf. 12 Horiz.

2154 A462 1.90l Gen. Enver Hoxha reading 1944 declaration 1.50 75

No. 2154 has grayish margin. Size: 69x90mm.

Archaeological Discoveries from Illyria — A463

1985, Feb. 25 *Perf. 12x12½*

2155 A463 15q Iron Age water container 16 8
2156 A463 80q Terra-cotta woman's head, 6th-7th century B.C. 78 40
2157 A463 1.20l Aphrodite, bust, 3rd century B.C. 1.15 55
2158 A463 1.70l Nike, A.D. 1st-2nd century bronze statue 1.75 85

Hysni Kapo (1915-1980), Natl. Labor Party Leader — A464

1985, Mar. 4 *Perf. 12*

2159 A464 90q red & blk 85 42
2160 A464 1.10l chlky bl & blk 1.10 55

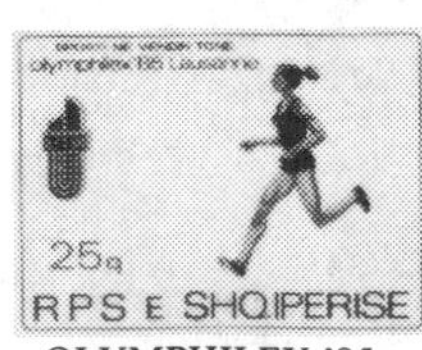

OLYMPHILEX '85, Lausanne — A465

1985, Mar. 18

2161 A465 25q Women's track & field 25 12
2162 A465 60q Weight lifting 58 30
2163 A465 1.20l Soccer 1.15 55
2164 A465 1.50l Women's pistol shooting 1.25 65

The lack of a price for a listed item does not necessarily indicate rarity.

Johann Sebastian Bach — A466

1985, Mar. 31

2165	A466	80q	Portrait, manuscript	78	40
2166	A466	1.20l	Eisenach, birthplace	1.15	55

Gen. Enver Hoxha (1908-1985) A467

1985, Apr. ***Perf. 12½***

2167	A467	80q	multi	78	40

Souvenir Sheet

Imperf

2168	A467	1.90l	multi	2.00	1.00

No. 2168 has gold and black inscribed margin. Size: 67x91mm.

Natl. Frontier Guards, 40th Anniv. A468

1985, Apr. 25 ***Perf. 12***

2169	A468	25q	Guardsman, family	25	12
2170	A468	80q	At frontier post	78	40

War Martyrs Type of 1980

Cameo portraits: 25q, Mitro Xhani (1916-1944), Nimete Progonati (1929-1944), Kozma Nushi (1909-1944). 40q, Ajet Xhindoli (1922-1943), Mustafa Kacaci (1903-1944), Estref Caka Osaja (1919-1944). 60q, Celo Sinani (1929-1944), Lt. Ambro Andoni (1920-1944), Meleq Gosnishti (1913-1944). 1.20l, Thodhori Mastora (1920-1944), Fejzi Micoli (1919-1945), Hysen Cino (1920-1944).

1985, May 5

2171	A410	25q	multi	25	12
2172	A410	40q	multi	40	20
2173	A410	60q	multi	58	30
2174	A410	1.20l	multi	1.15	55

Victory over Fascism A469

Designs: 25q, Rifle, red flag, inscribed May 9. 80q, Hand holding rifle, globe, broken swastika.

1985, May 9

2175	A469	25q	multi	25	12
2176	A469	80q	multi	78	40

End of World War II, 40th anniv.

Primary School, by Thoma Malo A470

Paintings, Tirana Gallery of Figurative Art: 80q, The Heroes, by Hysen Devolli, vert. 90q, In Our Days, by Angjelin Dodmasej, vert. 1.20l, Going Off to Sow, by Ksenofon Dilo. 1.90l, Foundry Workers, by Mikel Gurashi.

1985, June 25 ***Perf. 12½***

2177	A470	25q	multi	25	12
2178	A470	80q	multi	78	40
2179	A470	90q	multi	85	42
2180	A470	1.20l	multi	1.15	55

Souvenir Sheet

Perf. 12 Horiz.

2181	A470	1.90l	multi	2.00	1.00

No. 2181 has gray inscribed margin. Size: 75x90mm.

Basketball Championships, Spain — A471

Fruits — A472

Various plays.

1985, July 20 Litho. ***Perf. 12***

2182	A471	25q	dl bl & blk	22	10
2183	A471	80q	dl grn & blk	78	40
2184	A471	1.20l	dl vio & blk	1.15	58
2185	A471	1.60l	dl rose & blk	1.50	75

1985, Aug. 20

2186	A472	25q	Oranges	22	10
2187	A472	80q	Plums	78	40
2188	A472	1.20l	Apples	1.15	58
2189	A472	1.60l	Cherries	1.50	75

Architecture A473

1985, Sept. 20

2190	A473	25q	Kruja	22	10
2191	A473	80q	Gjirokastra	78	40
2192	A473	1.20l	Berati	1.15	58
2193	A473	1.60l	Shkodera	1.50	75

Natl. Folk Theater Festival — A474

Various scenes from folk plays.

1985, Oct. 6

2194	A474	25q	multi	22	10
2195	A474	80q	multi	78	40
2196	A474	1.20l	multi	1.15	58
2197	A474	1.60l	multi	1.50	75

Size: 56x82mm.

Imperf

2198	A474	1.90l	multi	1.75	88
			Nos. 2194-2198 (5)	5.40	2.71

Socialist People's Republic, 40th Anniv. — A475

1986, Jan. 11 Litho. ***Perf. 12½***

2199	A475	25q	Natl. crest, vert.	25	12
2200	A475	80q	Proclamation, 1946	78	40

Enver Hoxha Hydro-electric Power Station, Koman — A476

Designs: 25q, Dam, River Drin, Melgun. 80q, Bust of Enver Hoxha, dam power house.

1986, Feb. 20 ***Perf. 12***

2201	A476	25q	multi	25	12
2202	A476	80q	multi	78	40

Flowers — A477

1986, Mar. 20 Litho. ***Perf. 12***

2203	A477	25q	Gymnospermium shqipetarum	22	10
2204	A477	1.20l	Leucojum valentinum	1.15	58

Nos. 2203-2204 printed se-tenant. Sold only in booklets of 2; exists imperf.

A478

Famous Men — A479

Designs: 25q, Maxim Gorky (1868-1936), Russian author. 80q, Andre Marie Ampere (1775-1836), French physicist. 1.20l, James Watt (1736-1819), English inventor of modern steam engine. 2.40l, Franz Liszt (1811-1886), Hungarian composer.

1986, Apr. 20

2205			Strip of 4	4.40	2.20
a.	A478	25q	dl red brn	25	12
b.	A478	80q	dl vio	78	40
c.	A478	1.20l	bl grn	1.15	58
d.	A478	2.40l	dl lil rose	2.20	1.10

Size: 88x72mm.

Imperf

2206	A479	1.90l	multi	1.75	88

No. 2206 has central area picturing Gorky, Ampere, Watt and Liszt, perf. 12½.

War Martyrs Type of 1980

Portraits: 25q, Ramiz Aranitasi (1923-1943), Inajete Dumi (1924-1944) and Laze Nuro Ferraj (1897-1944). 80q, Dine Kalenja (1919-1944), Kozma Naska (1921-1944), Met Hasa (1929-1944) and Fahri Ramadani (1920-1944). 1.20l, Hiqmet Buzi (1927-1944), Bajram Tushe (1922-1942), Mumin Selami (1923-1942) and Hajrdfin Bylyshi (1923-1942).

1986, May 5 ***Perf. 12***

2207	A410	25q	multi	25	12
2208	A410	80q	multi	78	40
2209	A410	1.20l	multi	1.15	55

A480

1986 World Cup Soccer Championships, Mexico — A481

1986, May 31 Litho. ***Perf. 12***

2210	A480	25q	Globe, world cup	22	10
2211	A480	1.20l	Player, soccer ball	1.15	58

Size: 97x64mm.

Imperf

2212	A481	1.90l	multi	1.75	88

No. 2212 has central label, perf. 12½.

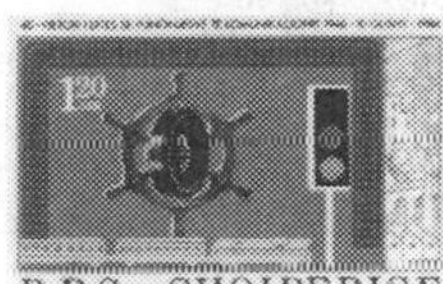

Transportation Workers' Day, 40th Anniv. — A482

1986, Aug. 10 Litho. ***Perf. 12***

2213	A482	1.20l	multi	1.15	58

Prominent Albanians A483

Designs: 30q, Naim Frasheri (1846-1900), poet. 60q, Ndre Mjeda (1866-1937), poet. 90q, Petro Nini Luarasi (1865-1911), poet, journalist. 1 l, Andon Zako Cajupi (1866-1930), poet. 1.20 l, Millosh Gjergj Nikolla Migjeni (1911-1938), novelist. 2.60 l, Urani Rumbo (1884-1936), educator.

1986, Sept. 20 Litho. ***Perf. 12***

2214	A483	30q	multi	30	15
2215	A483	60q	multi	58	30
2216	A483	90q	multi	88	45
2217	A483	1 l	multi	95	48
2218	A483	1.20 l	multi	1.15	58
2219	A483	2.60 l	multi	2.50	1.25
			Nos. 2214-2219 (6)	6.36	3.21

Albanian Workers' Party, 9th Congress, Tirana A484

1986, Nov. 3 Litho. *Perf. 12*

2220	A484	30q multi	30	25

Albanian Workers' Party, 45th Anniv. — A485

Designs: 30q, Handstamp, signature of Hoxha. 1.20 l, Marx, Engels, Lenin and Stalin, party building.

1986, Nov. 8

2221	A485	30q multi	30	15
2222	A485	1.20 l multi	1.15	58

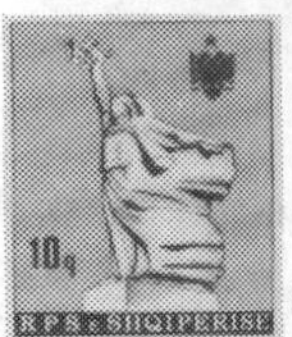

Statue of Mother Albania — A486

1986, Nov. 29 *Perf. 12x12½*

2223	A486	10q	Peacock blue	10	5
2224	A486	20q	henna brn	20	10
2225	A487	30q	ver	30	15
2226	A487	50q	dark olive bister	50	25
2227	A487	60q	lt olive grn	58	30
2228	A487	80q	rose	78	40
2229	A487	90q	ultra	88	45
2230	A487	1.20 l	grn	1.15	58
2231	A487	1.60 l	red vio	1.50	75
2232	A487	2.20 l	myrtle grn	2.10	1.05
2233	A487	3 l	brn org	2.75	1.40
2234	A487	6 l	yel bister	5.50	2.25
			Nos. 2223-2234 (12)	16.34	7.73

Artifacts A487

Designs: 30q, Head of Aesoulapius, 5th cent. B.C. Byllis, marble. 80q, Aphrodite, 3rd cent. B.C., Fier, terracotta. 1 l, Pan, 3rd-2nd cent, B.C., Byllis, bronze. 1.20 l, Jupiter, A.D. 2nd cent., Tirana, limestone.

1987, Feb. 20

2235	A487	30q multi	30	15
2236	A487	80q multi	78	40
2237	A487	1 l multi	95	48
2238	A487	1.20 l multi	1.15	58

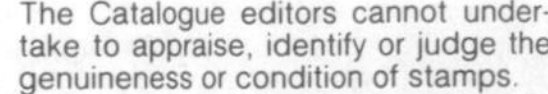
The Catalogue editors cannot undertake to appraise, identify or judge the genuineness or condition of stamps.

1st Albanian School, Cent. — A488

Gun, quill pen, book of the alphabet and: 30q, Monument, vert. 80q, School, Korca. 1.20 l, Students.

1987, Mar. 7 *Perf. 12*

2239	A488	30q multi	30	15
2240	A488	80q multi	75	38
2241	A488	1.20 l multi	1.15	58

Famous Men — A489

1987, Apr. 20

Designs: 30q, Victor Hugo (1802-1885), French author. 80q, Galileo Galilei (1564-1642), Italian mathematician, philosopher. 90q, Charles Darwin (1808-1882), British biologist. 1.30 l, Miguel Cervantes (1547-1616), Spanish novelist.

2242	A489	30q dull vio, pale dull vio & blk	30	15
2243	A489	80q buff, org brn & blk	75	38
2244	A489	90q dull blue, slate blue & blk	88	45
2245	A489	1.30 l lt olive grn, pale lt olive green & blk	1.25	80

World Food Day — A490

1987, May 20

2246	A490	30q Forsythia europaea	30	15
2247	A490	90q Moltkia doerfleri	88	45
2248	A490	2.10 l Wulfenia baldacii	2.00	1.00

10th Trade Unions Congress — A491

1987, June 25

2249	A491	1.20 l multi	1.15	58

Sowing, by Bujar Asllani — A492

Paintings in the Eponymous Museum, Tirana: 30q, The Sustenance of Industry, by Myrteza Fushekati, vert. 80q, The Gifted Partisan, by Skender Kokobobo, vert. 1.20 l, At the Forging Block, by Clirim Ceka.

Perf. 12x12½, 12½x12

1987, July 20 Litho.

2250	A492	30q multi	30	15
2251	A492	80q multi	80	40
2252	A492	1 l shown	1.00	50
2253	A492	1.20 l multi	1.20	60

A493

OLYMPHILEX '87, Rome, Aug. 29-Sept. 6 — A494

1987, Aug. 29 Litho. *Perf. 12½*

2254	A493	30q Hammer throw	30	15
2255	A493	90q Running	90	45
2256	A493	1.10 l Shot put	1.15	58

Size: 85x60mm.

2257	A494	1.90 l Runner, globe	2.00	1.00

Famous Men A495

Designs: 30q, Themistokli Germenji (1871-1917), author, politician. 80q, Bajram Curri (1862-1925), founder of the Albanian League. 90q, Aleks Stavre Drenova (1872-1947), poet. 1.30 l, Gjerasim D. Qiriazi (1861-1894), teacher, journalist.

1987, Sept. 30 *Perf. 12*

2258	A495	30q golden brn, dark red & sepia	30	15
2259	A495	80q rose claret, dark red & sepia	80	40
2260	A495	90q vio, dark red & blk	90	45
2261	A495	1.30 l grn, dark red & blk	1.30	65

SEMI-POSTAL STAMPS

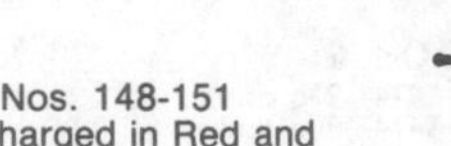

Nos. 148-151 Surcharged in Red and Black

1924

B1	A18	5q + 5q yel grn	4.00	5.00
B2	A18	10q + 5q car	4.00	5.00
B3	A18	25q + 5q dk bl	4.00	5.00
B4	A18	50q + 5q dk grn	4.00	5.00

Nos. B1 to B4 with Additional Surcharge in Red and Black

+ 5 qind.

1924

B5	A18	5q + 5q + 5q yel grn	4.00	5.00
B6	A18	10q + 5q + 5q car	4.00	5.00
B7	A18	25q + 5q + 5q dk bl	4.00	5.00
B8	A18	50q + 5q + 5q dk grn	4.00	5.00

Issued under Italian Dominion.

Nurse and Child — SP1

1943 Unwmk. Photo. *Perf. 14*

B9	SP1	5q + 5q dk grn	10	15
B10	SP1	10q + 10q ol brn	10	15
B11	SP1	15q + 10q rose red	15	20
B12	SP1	25q + 15q saph	20	25
B13	SP1	30q + 20q vio	25	30
B14	SP1	50q + 25q dk org	30	35
B15	SP1	65q + 30q grnsh blk	45	50
B16	SP1	1fr + 40q chnt	1.00	1.10
		Nos. B9-B16 (8)	2.55	3.00

The surtax was for the control of tuberculosis.

Issued under German Administration.

War Victims SP2

1944

B17	SP2	5q + 5(q) dp grn	3.00	4.00
B18	SP2	10q + 5(q) dp brn	3.00	4.00
B19	SP2	15q + 5(q) car lake	3.00	4.00
B20	SP2	25q + 10(q) dp bl	3.00	4.00
B21	SP2	1fr + 50q dk ol	3.00	4.00
B22	SP2	2fr + 1(fr) pur	3.00	4.00
B23	SP2	3fr + 1.50(fr) dk org	3.00	4.00
		Nos. B17-B23 (7)	21.00	28.00

The surtax was for victims of World War II.

Independent State

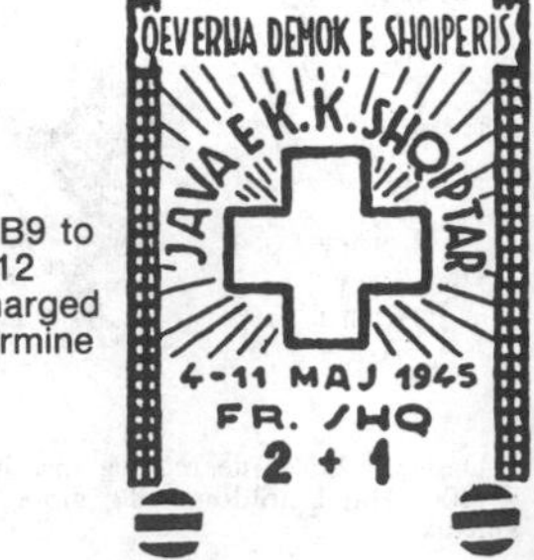

Nos. B9 to B12 Surcharged in Carmine

1945 Unwmk. *Perf. 14.*

B24	SP1	30q + 15q on 5q + 5q	1.75	1.75
B25	SP1	50q + 25q on 10q + 10q	1.75	1.75
B26	SP1	1fr + 50q on 15q + 10q	5.25	5.25
B27	SP1	2fr + 1fr on 25q + 15q	9.00	9.00

The surtax was for the Albanian Red Cross.

People's Republic

Nos. 361 to 366 Overprinted in Red (cross) and Surcharged in Black

KONGRESI
K.K.SH.
24-25-11-46
+0.10

1946 *Perf. 11*

B28 A57 20q + 10q bluish grn 7.00 7.00
B29 A57 30q + 15q dp org 7.00 7.00
B30 A57 40q + 20q brn 7.00 7.00
B31 A57 60q + 30q red vio 7.00 7.00
B32 A57 1fr + 50q rose red 7.00 7.00
B33 A57 3fr + 1.50fr dk bl 7.00 7.00
Nos. B28-B33 (6) 42.00 42.00

To honor and benefit the Congress of the Albanian Red Cross.

Counterfeits: lithographed, dull gum. Genuine: typographed, shiny gum.

First Aid and Red Cross — SP3

Designs: 25q+5q, Nurse carrying child on stretcher. 65q+25q, Symbolic blood transfusion. 80q+40q, Mother and child.

1967, Dec. 1 Litho. *Perf. 11½x12*

B34 SP3 15q + 5q blk, red & brn 90 70
B35 SP3 25q + 5q multi 1.00 90
B36 SP3 65q + 25q multi 3.00 1.00
B37 SP3 80q + 40q multi 5.00 2.25

6th congress of the Albanian Red Cross.

AIR POST STAMPS

Airplane Crossing Mountains — AP1

Wmk.125

Wmk. Lozenges. (125)

1925, May 30 Typo. *Perf. 14*

C1 AP1 5q green 60 60
C2 AP1 10q rose red 60 60
C3 AP1 25q dp bl 65 65
C4 AP1 50q dk grn 1.25 1.25
C5 AP1 1fr dk vio & blk 2.25 2.25
C6 AP1 2fr ol grn & vio 3.50 3.50
C7 AP1 3fr brn org & dk grn 6.25 6.25
Nos. C1-C7 (7) 15.10 15.10

Nos. C1-C7 exist imperforate but are not known to have been regularly issued in that condition.

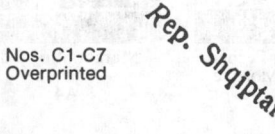

Nos. C1-C7 Overprinted

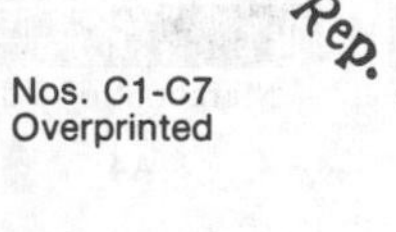

1927, Jan. 18

C8 AP1 5q green 4.50 4.50
a. Double overprint, one inverted 40.00
C9 AP1 10q rose red 4.50 4.50
a. Inverted overprint 40.00
b. Double overprint, one inverted 40.00
C10 AP1 25q dp bl 2.25 2.25
C11 AP1 50q dk grn 2.25 2.25
a. Inverted overprint 40.00
C12 AP1 1fr dk vio & blk 2.25 2.25
a. Inverted overprint 40.00
b. Double overprint 40.00
C13 AP1 2fr ol grn & vio 2.25 2.25
C14 AP1 3fr brn org & dk grn 4.00 4.00
Nos. C8-C14 (7) 22.00 22.00

Nos. C1-C7 Overprinted

REP. SHQYPTARE
Fluturim' i I-ar
Vlonë--Brindisi
21. IV. 1928

1928, Apr. 21

C15 AP1 5q green 1.50 1.50
a. Inverted overprint 30.00
C16 AP1 10q rose red 1.50 1.50
C17 AP1 25q dp bl 1.50 1.50
C18 AP1 50q dk grn 1.50 1.50
C19 AP1 1fr dk vio & blk 22.50 22.50
C20 AP1 2fr ol grn & vio 22.50 22.50
C21 AP1 3fr brn org & dk grn 22.50 22.50
Nos. C15-C21 (7) 73.50 73.50

First flight across the Adriatic, Valona to Brindisi, Apr. 21, 1928.

The variety "SHQYRTARE" occurs once in the sheet for each value. Price 3 times normal.

Nos. C1-C7 Overprinted in Red Brown

Mbr. Shqiptare

1929, Dec. 1

C22 AP1 5q green 4.00 4.00
C23 AP1 10q rose red 4.00 4.00
C24 AP1 25q dp bl 4.00 4.00
C25 AP1 50q dk grn 13.00 15.00
C26 AP1 1fr dk vio & blk 160.00 175.00
C27 AP1 2fr ol grn 160.00 175.00
C28 AP1 3fr brn org & dk grn 160.00 175.00
Nos. C22-C28 (7) 505.00 552.00

Excellent counterfeits exist of Nos. C22 to C28.

King Zog and Airplane over Tirana AP2

AP3

1930, Oct. 8 Photo. Unwmk.

C29 AP2 5q yel grn 30 30
C30 AP2 15q rose red 40 40
C31 AP2 20q sl bl 60 60
C32 AP2 50q ol grn 75 75
C33 AP3 1fr dk bl 1.75 1.75
C34 AP3 2fr ol brn 6.00 6.00
C35 AP3 3fr purple 7.50 7.50
Nos. C29-C35 (7) 17.30 17.30

Nos. C29-C35 Overprinted

6 KORRIK 1931

1931, July 6

C36 AP2 5q yel grn 2.00 2.00
a. Double overprint 100.00
C37 AP2 15q rose red 2.00 2.00
C38 AP2 20q sl bl 2.00 2.00
C39 AP2 50q ol grn 2.00 2.00
C40 AP3 1fr dk bl 15.00 15.00
C41 AP3 2fr ol brn 15.00 15.00
C42 AP3 3fr purple 15.00 15.00
a. Inverted overprint 250.00
Nos. C36-C42 (7) 53.00 53.00

Issued in connection with the first air post flight from Tirana to Rome.

Only a very small part of this issue was sold to the public. Most of the stamps were given to the Aviation Company to help provide funds for conducting the service.

Issued under Italian Dominion.

Nos. C29-C30 Overprinted in Black

Mbledhja
Kushtetuëse
12-IV-1939
XVII

1939, Apr. 19 Unwmk. *Perf. 14.*

C43 AP2 5q yel grn 75 75
C44 AP2 15q rose red 75 75

No. C32 With Additional Surcharge

C45 AP2 20q on 50q ol grn 1.50 1.50
a. Inverted ovpt.

See note after No. 309.

King Victor Emmanuel III and Plane over Mountains AP4

1939, Aug. 4 Photo.

C46 AP4 20q brown 7.00 3.50

Shepherds AP5

Map of Albania Showing Air Routes — AP6

Designs: 20q, Victor Emmanuel III and harbor view. 50q, Woman and river valley. 1fr, Bridge at Vezirit. 2fr, Ruins. 3fr, Women waving to plane.

1940, Mar. Unwmk.

C47 AP5 5q green 20 20
C48 AP6 15q rose red 20 20
C49 AP5 20q dp bl 20 20
C50 AP6 50q brown 50 50
C51 AP5 1fr myr grn 1.00 1.10
C52 AP6 2fr brn blk 3.00 3.50
C53 AP6 3fr rose vio 9.00 10.00
Nos. C47-C53 (7) 14.10 15.70

People's Republic

Vuno-Himare AP12

Designs (Albanian towns): 1l and 10l, Rozafat-Shkoder. 2l and 20l, Keshtjelle-Butrinto.

1950, Dec. 15 Engr. *Perf. 12½x12*

C54 AP12 50q gray blk 10 5
C55 AP12 1l red brn 15 7
C56 AP12 2l ultra 35 12
C57 AP12 5l dp grn 80 25
C58 AP12 10l dp bl 1.75 1.00
C59 AP12 20l purple 5.00 2.25
Nos. C54-C59 (6) 8.15 3.74

Nos. C56-C58 Surcharged with New Value and Bars in Red or Black

1952-53

C60 AP12 50q on 2l (R) 50.00 50.00
C61 AP12 50q on 5l ('53) 7.00 4.00
C62 AP12 2.50l on 5l (R) 100.00 100.00
C63 AP12 2.50l on 10l ('53) 8.00 4.00

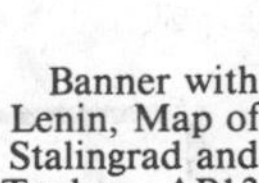

Banner with Lenin, Map of Stalingrad and Tanks — AP13

1963, Feb. 2 Litho. *Perf. 14*

C67 AP13 7l grn & dp car 2.00 80

20th anniversary, Battle of Stalingrad.

Sputnik and Sun AP14

Designs: 3l, Lunik 4. 5l, Lunik 3 photographing far side of the Moon. 8l, Venus space probe. 12l, Mars 1.

1963, Oct. 31 Unwmk. *Perf. 12*

C68 AP14 2l org, yel & blk 25 10
C69 AP14 3l multi 30 10
C70 AP14 5l rose lil, yel & blk 70 40
C71 AP14 8l dl vio, yel & dp car 1.10 55
C72 AP14 12l bl & org 2.50 1.25
Nos. C68-72 (5) 4.85 2.40

Russian interplanetary explorations.

Nos. C68 and C71 Overprinted: "Riccione 23-8-1964"

1964, Aug. 23

C73 AP14 2l org, yel & blk 4.50 4.50
C74 AP14 8l dl vio, yel & dp car 7.00 7.00

Issued to commemorate the International Space Exhibition in Riccione, Italy.

Plane over Berat AP15

Designs (Plane over): 40q, Gjirokaster. 60q, Sarande. 90q, Dürres. 1.20l, Kruje. 2.40l, Boga. 4.05l, Tirana.

1975, Nov. 25 Litho. *Perf. 12*

C75 AP15 20q multi 10 5
C76 AP15 40q multi 10 8
C77 AP15 60q multi 15 8
C78 AP15 90q multi 30 15
C79 AP15 1.20l multi 50 15
C80 AP15 2.40l multi 1.15 40
C81 AP15 4.05l multi 1.75 90
Nos. C75-C81 (7) 4.05 1.81

SPECIAL DELIVERY STAMPS

Issued under Italian Dominion.

King Victor Emmanuel III — SD1

1940 Unwmk. Photo. *Perf. 14.*

E1 SD1 25q brt vio 40 40
E2 SD1 50q red org 1.35 1.60

Issued under German Administration.

No. E1 Overprinted in Carmine

14
Shtator
1943

1943

E3 SD1 25q brt vio 15.00 17.50

Proclamation of Albanian independence.

POSTAGE DUE STAMPS

Nos. 35-39 Handstamped in Various Colors

1914 **Unwmk.** ***Perf. 14.***

No.	Type	Description	Unused	Used
J1	A3	2q org brn & buff	2.00	1.20
J2	A3	5q green	2.00	1.50
J3	A3	10q rose red	2.75	1.50
J4	A3	25q dk bl	3.25	2.00
J5	A3	50q vio & red	4.00	2.75
		Nos. J1-J5 (5)	14.00	8.95

The two parts of the overprint are handstamped separately. Stamps exist with one or both handstamps inverted, double, omitted or in wrong color.

Nos. 48-51 Overprinted in Black TAKSË

1914

No.	Type	Description	Unused	Used
J6	A3 (a)	10pa on 5q grn	2.50	2.50
J7	A3 (a)	20pa on 10q rose red	2.50	2.50
J8	A3 (b)	1gr on 25q bl	2.50	2.50
J9	A3 (b)	2gr on 50q vio & red	2.50	2.50

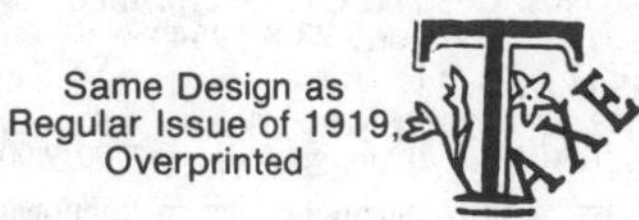

Same Design as Regular Issue of 1919, Overprinted

1919 ***Perf. 11½, 12½***

No.	Type	Description	Unused	Used
J10	A8	(4)q on 4h rose	6.00	6.00
J11	A8	(10)q on 10k red, *grn*	6.00	6.00
J12	A8	20q on 2k org,*gray*	6.00	6.00
J13	A8	50q on 5k brn,*yel*	6.00	6.00

Fortress at Scutari — D3

D5

Post Horn Overprinted in Black.

1920 ***Perf. 14 x 13.***

No.	Type	Description	Unused	Used
J14	D3	4q ol grn	40	50
J15	D3	10q rose red	40	50
J16	D3	20q bis brn	40	50
J17	D3	50q black	70	80

1922 ***Perf. 12½, 11½***

Background of Red Wavy Lines.

No.	Type	Description	Unused	Used
J23	D5	4q *red*	85	1.10
J24	D5	10q *red*	85	1.10
J25	D5	20q *red*	85	1.10
J26	D5	50q *red*	85	1.10

Same Overprinted in White Republika Shqiptare

1925

No.	Type	Description	Unused	Used
J27	D5	4q *red*	85	1.10
J28	D5	10q *red*	85	1.10
J29	D5	20q *red*	85	1.10
J30	D5	50q *red*	85	1.10

The 10q with overprint in gold was a trial printing. It was not put in use.

D7

Coat of Arms — D8

Overprinted "QINDAR" in Red.

1926 ***Perf. 13½ x 13***

No.	Type	Description	Unused	Used
J31	D7	10q dk bl	15	25
J32	D7	20q green	30	50
J33	D7	30q red brn	50	75
J34	D7	50q dk brn	75	1.25

Wmk. Double Headed Eagle. (220)

1930 **Photo.** ***Perf. 14, 14½***

No.	Type	Description	Unused	Used
J35	D8	10q dk bl	5.00	5.00
J36	D8	20q rose red	1.25	1.25
J37	D8	30q violet	1.25	1.25
J38	D8	50q dk grn	1.50	1.50

Nos. J36-J38 exist with overprint '14 Shtator 1943" (see Nos. 332-344) which is private and fraudulent on these stamps.

No. 253 Overprinted Taksë

1936 ***Perf. 14***

No.	Type	Description	Unused	Used
J39	A34	10q carmine	6.00	8.00

Issued under Italian Dominion.

Coat of Arms — D9

1940 **Unwmk.** **Photo.** ***Perf. 14.***

No.	Type	Description	Unused	Used
J40	D9	4q red org	8.00	8.00
J41	D9	10q brt vio	2.50	2.50
J42	D9	20q brown	2.50	2.50
J43	D9	30q dk bl	3.00	3.00
J44	D9	50q car rose	6.00	6.00
		Nos. J40-J44 (5)	22.00	22.00

ALEXANDRETTA

LOCATION — A political territory in northern Syria, bordering on Turkey.
GOVT. — A former French mandate.
AREA — 10,000 sq. mi. (approx.)
POP. — 270,000 (approx.)

Included in the Syrian territory mandated to France under the Versailles Treaty, the name was changed to Hatay in 1938. The following year France returned the territory to Turkey in exchange for certain concessions. See Hatay.

100 Centimes = 1 Piastre

Stamps of Syria, 1930-36, Overprinted or Surcharged in Black or Red:

Sandjak d'Alexandrette
a

SANDJAK D'ALEXANDRETTE
b

Sandjak d'Alexandrette
c

d

POSTES Sandjak d'Alexandrette 12P.50
e

1938 **Unwmk.** ***Perf. 12x12½, 13½.***

No.	Type	Description	Unused	Used
1	A6 (a)	10c vio brn	52	52
2	A6 (a)	20c brn org	52	52
3	A9 (b)	50c vio (R)	52	52
4	A10 (b)	1p bis brn	70	70
5	A9 (b)	2p dk vio (R)	95	95
6	A13 (b)	3p yel grn (R)	2.00	2.00
7	A10 (b)	4p yel org	2.25	2.25
8	A16 (b)	6p grnsh blk (R)	2.50	2.50
9	A18 (b)	25p vio brn	7.00	7.00

Perf. 13½

No.	Type	Description	Unused	Used
10	A15 (c)	75c org red	70	70
11	A10 (d)	2.50p on 4p yel org	1.40	1.40
12	AP2 (e)	12.50p on 15p org red	3.75	3.75
		Nos. 1-12 (12)	22.81	22.81

Nos. 4, 7, 10-12 Overprinted in Black

1938, Dec.

No.	Type	Description	Unused	Used
13	A15	75c org red	37.50	37.50
14	A10	1p bis brn	24.00	22.50
15	A10	2.50p on 4p yel org	15.00	13.00
16	A10	4p yel org	19.00	17.00
17	AP2	12.50p on 15p org red	37.50	37.50
		Nos. 13-17 (5)	133.00	127.50

Death of Kemal Ataturk, president of Turkey.

AIR POST STAMPS

Air Post Stamps of Syria, 1937, Overprinted Type "b' in Red or Black

1938 **Unwmk.** ***Perf. 13.***

No.	Type	Description	Unused	Used
C1	AP14	½p dk vio (R)	65	65
C2	AP15	1p blk (R)	65	65
C3	AP14	2p bl grn (R)	1.65	1.65
C4	AP15	3p dp ultra	2.00	2.00
C5	AP14	5p rose lake	5.00	5.00
C6	AP15	10p red brn	5.50	5.50
C7	AP14	15p lake brn	6.50	6.50
C8	AP15	25p dk bl (R)	8.25	8.25
		Nos. C1-C8 (8)	30.20	30.20

POSTAGE DUE STAMPS

Postage Due Stamps of Syria, 1925-31, Overprinted Type "b" in Black or Red

1938 **Unwmk.** ***Perf. 13½.***

No.	Type	Description	Unused	Used
J1	D5	50c brn, *yel*	1.25	1.25
J2	D6	1p vio, *rose*	1.75	1.75
J3	D5	2p *bl* (R)	2.50	2.50
J4	D5	3p *red org*	4.75	4.75
J5	D5	5p *bl grn* (R)	7.75	7.75
J6	D7	8p *gray bl* (R)	7.75	7.75
		Nos. J1-J6 (6)	25.75	25.75

On No. J2, the overprint is vertical, reading up. On the other denominations, it is horizontal.

Stamps of Alexandretta were discontinued in 1938 and replaced by those of Hatay.

ALGERIA

LOCATION — North Africa
GOVT. — Republic
AREA — 919,595 sq. mi.
POP. — 21,463,000 (1984 est.)
CAPITAL — Algiers

The former French colony of Algeria became an integral part of France on Sept. 1, 1958, when French stamps replaced Algerian stamps. Algeria became an independent country July 3, 1962.

100 Centimes = 1 Franc
100 Centimes = 1 Dinar (1964)

Stamps of France Overprinted in Red, Blue or Black:

ALGÉRIE
a

ALGÉRIE
b

ALGÉRIE
c

ALGÉRIE
d

1924-26 **Unwmk.** ***Perf. 14x13½***

No.	Type	Description	Unused	Used
1	A16 (a)	1c dk gray (R)	5	5
2	A16 (a)	2c vio brn	5	5
3	A16 (a)	3c orange	5	5
4	A16 (a)	4c yel brn (Bl)	10	10
5	A22 (a)	5c org (Bl)	14	14
6	A16 (a)	5c grn ('25)	26	26
7	A23 (a)	10c green	8	6
b.		Booklet pane of 10	3.00	
8	A22 (a)	10c grn ('25)	45	15
9	A20 (a)	15c sl grn	15	6
10	A23 (a)	15c grn ('25)	18	18
11	A22 (a)	15c red brn (Bl) ('26)	20	10
12	A22 (a)	20c red brn (Bl)	6	5
13	A22 (a)	25c bl (R)	6	5
a.		Booklet pane of 10	5.75	
14	A23 (a)	30c red (Bl)	22	22
15	A22 (a)	30c cer ('25)	45	22
16	A22 (a)	30c lt bl (R) ('25)	6	5
a.		Booklet pane of 10	4.00	
17	A22 (a)	35c violet	26	8
18	A18 (b)	40c red & pale bl	30	18
19	A22 (a)	40c ol brn (R) ('25)	85	38
20	A18 (b)	45c grn & bl (R)	40	22
21	A23 (a)	45c red (Bl) ('25)	30	18
22	A23 (a)	50c bl (R)	30	6
23	A20 (a)	60c lt vio	30	10
a.		Inverted overprint	475.00	
24	A20 (a)	65c rose (Bl)	30	10
25	A23 (a)	75c bl (R)	38	22
a.		Double overprint	125.00	
26	A20 (a)	80c ver ('26)	80	30
27	A20 (a)	85c ver (Bl)	45	22
28	A18 (b)	1fr cl & ol grn	1.25	25
29	A22 (a)	1.05fr ver ('26)	1.10	45
30	A18 (c)	2fr org & pale bl	75	50
31	A18 (b)	3fr vio & bl ('26)	5.00	90
32	A18 (d)	5fr bl & buff (R)	10.00	5.50
		Nos. 1-32 (32)	25.30	11.43

No. 15 was issued precanceled only. Prices for precanceled stamps in first column are for those which have not been through the post and have original gum. Prices in second column are for postally used, gumless stamps.

Street in Kasbah, Algiers
A1

Mosque of Sidi Abd-er-Rahman
A2

La Pêcherie Mosque
A3

Marabout of Sidi Yacoub
A4

1926-39 **Typo.** ***Perf. 14x13½***

No.	Type	Description	Unused	Used
33	A1	1c olive	18	18
34	A1	2c red brn	6	5
35	A1	3c orange	25	25
36	A1	5c bl grn	5	5
37	A1	10c brt vio	5	5
a.		Booklet pane of 10	4.75	
38	A2	15c org brn	8	6
39	A2	20c green	5	5
40	A2	20c dp rose	18	5

No.	Type	Description	Unused	Used
41	A2	25c bl grn	25	25
42	A2	25c bl ('27)	50	6
43	A2	25c vio bl ('39)	5	5
44	A2	30c blue	35	22
45	A2	30c bl grn ('27)	1.10	45
46	A2	35c dp vio	1.25	1.00
47	A2	40c ol grn	5	5
a.		Booklet pane of 10	4.00	
48	A3	45c vio brn	35	30
49	A3	50c blue	35	22
a.		Booklet pane of 10	5.25	
50	A3	50c dk red ('30)	10	5
a.		Booklet pane of 10	7.00	
51	A3	60c yel grn	18	5
52	A3	65c blk brn ('27)	1.75	1.25
53	A1	65c ultra ('38)	30	5
a.		Booklet pane of 10	2.75	
54	A3	75c carmine	42	35
55	A3	75c bl ('29)	3.75	26
56	A3	80c org red	55	38
57	A3	90c red ('27)	5.25	4.00
58	A4	1fr gray grn & red brn	80	26
59	A3	1.05fr lt brn	75	40
60	A3	1.10fr mag ('27)	7.00	2.75
61	A4	1.25fr dk bl & ultra	1.50	1.25
62	A4	1.50fr dk bl & ultra ('27)	2.50	22
63	A4	2fr Prus bl & blk brn	2.75	26
64	A4	3fr vio & org	4.00	1.00
65	A4	5fr red & vio	7.50	3.00
66	A4	10fr ol brn & rose ('27)	47.50	30.00
67	A4	20fr vio & grn ('27)	8.50	6.00
		Nos. 33-67 (35)	100.25	54.87

Type A4, 50c blue and rose red, inscribed "CENTENAIRE-ALGERIE" is France No. 255.

Stamps of 1926 Surcharged with New Values.

1927

No.	Type	Description	Unused	Used
68	A2	10c on 35c dp vio	10	10
69	A2	25c on 30c bl	6	6
70	A2	30c on 25c bl grn	16	8
71	A3	65c on 60c yel grn	90	70
72	A3	90c on 80c org red	48	40
73	A3	1.10fr on 1.05fr lt brn	48	32
74	A4	1.50fr on 1.25fr dk bl & ultra	1.75	90
		Nos. 68-74 (7)	3.93	2.56

Bars cancel the old value on Nos. 68, 69, 73 and 74.

No. 4 Surcharged **5c**

1927

75 A16 5c on 4c yel brn *1.50* 50

Bay of Algiers A5

1930, May 4 Engr. *Perf. 11, 12½*

78 A5 10fr red brn 14.00 13.00
a. Imperf. (pair) 47.50

Centenary of Algeria and for International Philatelic Exhibition of North Africa, May, 1930.

One copy of No. 78 was sold with each 10fr admission.

Travel across the Sahara — A6

Arch of Triumph, Lambese A7

Admiralty Building, Algiers — A8

Kings' Tombs near Touggourt A9

El-Kebir Mosque, Algiers A10

Oued River at Colomb-Bechar A11

View of Ghardaia A12

Sidi Bon Medine Cemetery at Tlemcen — A13

1936-41 Engr. *Perf. 13*

No.	Type	Description	Unused	Used
79	A6	1c ultra	5	5
80	A11	2c dk vio	5	5
81	A7	3c dk bl grn	15	15
82	A12	5c red vio	6	6
83	A8	10c emerald	6	5
84	A9	15c red	6	5
85	A13	20c dk bl grn	6	5
86	A10	25c rose vio	60	6
87	A12	30c yel grn	52	8
88	A9	40c brn vio	6	6
89	A13	45c dp ultra	1.25	70
90	A8	50c red	70	5
91	A6	65c red brn	4.50	3.00
92	A6	65c rose car ('37)	60	5
93	A6	70c red brn ('39)	8	8
94	A11	75c sl bl	35	10
95	A7	90c hn brn	1.25	85
96	A10	1fr brown	35	5
97	A8	1.25fr lt vio	60	35
98	A8	1.25fr car rose ('39)	50	18
99	A11	1.50fr turq bl	1.75	35
99A	A11	1.50fr rose ('40)	60	22
100	A12	1.75fr hn brn	20	6
101	A7	2fr dk brn	25	8
102	A6	2.25fr yel grn	15.00	12.00
103	A11	2.50fr dk ultra ('41)	52	50
104	A13	3fr magenta	50	14
105	A10	3.50fr pck bl	3.50	2.75
106	A8	5fr sl bl	55	18
107	A11	10fr hn brn	60	35
108	A9	20fr turq bl	1.10	60
		Nos. 79-108 (31)	36.42	23.30

See also Nos. 124-125, 162.

Nos. 82 and 100 with surcharge "E. F. M. 30frs" (Emergency Field Message) were used in 1943 to pay cable tolls for U. S. and Canadian servicemen.

Algerian Pavilion — A14

1937 *Perf. 13*

109 A14 40c brt grn 65 52
110 A14 50c rose car 40 14
111 A14 1.50fr blue 90 40
112 A14 1.75fr brn blk 1.00 75

Paris International Exposition.

Constantine in 1837 — A15

1937

113 A15 65c dp rose 48 22
114 A15 1fr brown 4.75 70
115 A15 1.75fr bl grn 40 30
116 A15 2.15fr red vio 26 22

Issued in commemoration of the centenary of the taking of Constantine by the French.

Ruins of a Roman Villa — A16

1938

117 A16 30c green 70 48
118 A16 65c ultra 5 5
119 A16 75c rose vio 80 55
120 A16 3fr car rose 2.00 2.00
121 A16 5fr yel brn 3.25 3.25
Nos. 117-121 (5) 6.80 6.33

Centenary of Philippeville.

No. 90 Surcharged in Black

0,25

1938

122 A8 25c on 50c red 6 6
a. Dbl. surch. 40.00 35.00
b. Invtd. surch. 26.00 22.50

Types of 1936.

1939

Numerals of Value on Colorless Background.

124 A7 90c hn brn 8 5
125 A10 2.25fr bl grn 26 30

American Export Liner Unloading Cargo — A17

1939

126 A17 20c green 1.00 70
127 A17 40c red vio 1.00 70
128 A17 90c brn blk 52 35
129 A17 1.25fr rose 3.50 1.25
130 A17 2.25fr ultra 1.00 90
Nos. 126-130 (5) 7.02 3.90

New York World's Fair.

Type of 1926, Surcharged in Black

Two types of surcharge:
I. Bars 6mm.
II. Bars 7mm.

1939-40 *Perf. 14x13½*

131 A1 1fr on 90c crim (I) 12 5
a. Booklet pane of 10
b. Dbl. surcharge (I) 52.50
c. Invtd. surcharge (I) 35.00
d. Pair, one without surch. (I) *1,200.*
e. Type II ('40) 2.25 22
f. Invtd. surcharge (II) 40.00
g. Pair, one without surch. (II) *1,200.*

View of Algiers — A18

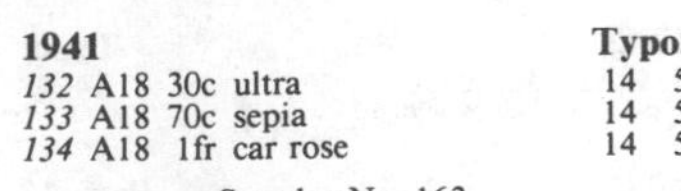

1941 Typo.

132 A18 30c ultra 14 5
133 A18 70c sepia 14 5
134 A18 1fr car rose 14 5

See also No. 163.

Marshal Pétain
A19 A20

1941 Engr. *Perf. 13*

135 A19 1fr dk bl 35 25

No. 53 Surcharged in Black with New Value and Bars.

1941 *Perf. 14x13½*

136 A1 50c on 65c ultra 40 6
a. Booklet pane of 10
b. Inverted surch. 32.50
c. Pair, one without surch. 77.50

1942 *Perf. 14x13*

137 A20 1.50fr org red 15 8

Four other denominations of type A20 exist (4fr, 5fr, 10fr, 20fr), but were not placed in use.

Arms of Constantine A21

Arms of Oran A22

Arms of Algiers — A23

Engraver's Name at Lower Left.

1942-43 Photo. *Perf. 12.*

No.	Type	Description	Unused	Used
138	A21	40c dk vio ('43)	15	15
139	A22	60c rose ('43)	8	8
140	A21	1.20fr yel grn ('43)	12	10
141	A23	1.50fr car rose	8	8
142	A22	2fr sapphire	28	8
143	A21	2.40fr rose ('43)	10	8
144	A23	3fr sapphire	28	8
145	A21	4fr bl ('43)	15	15
146	A22	5fr yel grn ('43)	10	10
		Nos. 138-146 (9)	1.34	90

Imperforates

Nearly all of Algeria Nos. 138-285, B39-B96, C1-C12 and CB1-CB3 exist imperforate. See note after France No. 395.

Without Engraver's Name.

1942-45 Typo. *Perf. 14x13½*

No.	Type	Description	Unused	Used
147	A23	10c dl brn vio ('45)	6	6
148	A22	30c dp bl grn ('45)	8	8
149	A21	40c dl brn vio ('45)	6	6
150	A22	60c rose ('45)	8	8
151	A21	70c dp bl ('45)	8	6
152	A23	80c dk bl grn ('43)	35	35
153	A21	1.20fr dp bl grn ('45)	8	8
154	A23	1.50fr brt rose ('43)	6	6
155	A22	2fr dp bl ('45)	8	6
156	A21	2.40fr rose ('45)	35	35
157	A23	3fr dp bl ('45)	10	8
158	A22	4.50fr brn vio	18	18
		Nos. 147-158 (12)	1.56	1.50

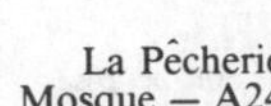

La Pêcherie Mosque — A24

1942 **Typo.**
159 A24 50c dl red 14 5
a. Booklet pane of 10 4.00

1942 **Photo.** ***Perf. 12***
160 A24 40c gray grn 14 8
161 A24 50c red 14 8

Types of 1936-41, Without "RF"

1942 **Engr.** ***Perf. 13***
162 A11 1.50fr rose 14 5

Typo. ***Perf. 14x13½.***
163 A18 30c ultra 14 6

"One Aim Alone - Victory"
A25 A26

1943 **Litho.** ***Perf. 12***
164 A25 1.50fr dp rose 14 5
165 A26 1.50fr dk bl 14 5

Type of 1942-3 Surcharged with New Value in Black.

1943 **Photo.**
166 A22 2fr on 5fr red org 14 8
a. Surcharge omitted 190.00

Summer Palace, Algiers
A27

1944, Dec. 1 **Litho.**
167 A27 15fr slate 1.00 1.00
168 A27 20fr lt bl grn 90 45
169 A27 50fr dk car 60 50
170 A27 100fr dp bl 1.70 1.50
171 A27 200fr dl bis brn 2.75 1.75
Nos. 167-171 (5) 6.95 5.20

Marianne
A28

Gallic Cock
A29

1944-45
172 A28 10c gray 5 5
173 A28 30c red vio 5 5
174 A29 40c rose car ('45) 14 14
175 A28 50c red 6 5
176 A28 80c emerald 6 6
177 A29 1fr grn ('45) 6 5
178 A28 1.20fr rose lil 8 6
179 A28 1.50fr dk bl 5 5
a. Dbl impression 30.00
180 A29 2fr red 6 5
a. Double impression 35.00
181 A29 2fr dk brn ('45) 6 5
182 A28 2.40fr rose red 8 6
183 A28 3fr purple 8 5
184 A29 4fr ultra ('45) 8 6
185 A28 4.50fr ol blk 35 35
186 A29 10fr grnsh blk ('45) 55 40
Nos. 172-186 (15) 1.81 1.53

No. 38 Surcharged in Black **0f.30**

1944 ***Perf. 14 x 13½.***
187 A2 30c on 15c org brn 18 6
a. Inverted surch. 14.00 6.00

This stamp exists precanceled only. See note below No. 32.

No. 154 Surcharged "RF" and New Value.

1945
190 A2350c on 1.50fr brt rose 14 5
a. Inverted surch. 22.50

Stamps of France, 1944, Overprinted in Black — a **ALGÉRIE**

1945-46
191 A99 80c yel grn 5 5
192 A99 1fr grnsh bl 8 6
193 A99 1.20fr violet 14 14
194 A99 2fr vio brn 35 14
195 A99 2.40fr car rose 35 14
196 A99 3fr orange 35 14
Nos. 191-196 (6) 1.32 67

Same Overprint on Stamps of France, 1945-47, in Black, Red or Carmine.

1945-47
197 A145 40c lil rose 6 6
198 A145 50c vio bl (R) 6 6
199 A146 60c brt ultra (R) 35 14
200 A146 1fr rose red ('47) 6 5
201 A146 1.50fr rose lil ('47) 6 5
202 A147 2fr myr grn (R) ('46) 6 5
203 A147 3fr dp rose 5 5
204 A147 4.50fr ultra (C) ('47) 80 14
205 A147 5fr lt grn ('46) 6 5
206 A147 10fr ultra 42 40
Nos. 197-206 (10) 1.98 1.05

Same Overprint on France No. 383 and New Value Surcharged in Black

1946
207 A99 2fr on 1.50fr hn brn 6 5
a. Without "2F" 160.00

Same Overprint on France Nos. 562 and 564, in Carmine or Blue.

1947
208 A153 10c dp ultra & blk (C) 5 5
209 A155 50c brn, yel & red (Bl) 35 35

Arms of Constantine
A30

Arms of Algiers
A31

Arms of Oran — A32

Perf. 14x13½

1947-49 **Unwmk.** **Typo.**
210 A30 10c dk grn & brt red 5 5
211 A31 50c blk & org 6 5
212 A32 1fr ultra & yel 5 5
213 A30 1.30fr blk & grnsh bl 80 52
214 A31 1.50fr pur & org yel 5 5
215 A32 2fr blk & brt grn 6 5
216 A30 2.50fr blk & brt red 52 42
217 A31 3fr vio brn & grn 14 5
218 A32 3.50fr lt grn & rose lil 14 8
219 A30 4fr dk brn & brt grn 14 14
220 A31 4.50fr ultra & scar 6 5
221 A31 5fr blk & grnsh bl 25 5
222 A32 6fr brn & scar 35 12
223 A32 8fr choc & ultra ('48) 26 6
224 A30 10fr car & choc ('48) 48 5
225 A31 15fr blk & red ('49) 52 5
Nos. 210-225 (16) 3.93 1.84

See also Nos. 274-280, 285.

Peoples of the World
A33

1949, Oct. 24 **Engr.** ***Perf. 13***
226 A33 5fr green 1.75 1.40
227 A33 15fr scarlet 1.75 1.40
228 A33 25fr ultra 3.75 3.75

Issued to commemorate the 75th anniversary of the formation of the Universal Postal Union.

Grapes
A34

Apollo of Cherchell
A35

Designs: 25fr, Dates. 40fr, Oranges and lemons.

1950, Feb. 25
229 A34 20fr vio brn, grn & cl 1.00 35
230 A34 25fr dk brn, dk grn & brn org 1.25 70
231 A34 40fr brn, grn, red org & org 3.00 1.00

1952 **Unwmk.** ***Perf. 13***

Designs: 12fr, 18fr, Isis statue, Cherchell. 15fr, 20fr, Child with eagle.

240 A35 10fr gray blk 35 5
241 A35 12fr org brn 52 8
242 A35 15fr dp bl 35 6
243 A35 18fr rose red 52 35
244 A35 20fr dp grn 52 18
245 A35 30fr dp bl 95 52
Nos. 240-245 (6) 3.21 1.24

War Memorial, Algiers
A38

Fossilized Nautilus
A39

Phonolite Dike — A40

1952, Apr. 11
246 A38 12fr dk grn 70 52

Issued to honor the French Africa Army.

1952, Aug. 11
247 A39 15fr brt crim 1.25 90
248 A40 30fr dp ultra 1.40 1.00

Issued to publicize the 19th International Geological Congress, Algiers, Sept. 8-15, 1952.

French and Algerian Soldiers and Camel — A41

1952, Nov. 30
249 A41 12fr chnt brn 1.25 90

Issued to commemorate the 50th anniversary of the establishment of the Sahara Companies.

Eugène Millon
A42

François C. Maillot
A43

Oranges
A44

Portrait: 50fr, Alphonse Laveran.

Unwmk.

1954, Jan. 4 **Engr.** ***Perf. 13***
250 A42 25fr dk grn & choc 1.75 26
251 A43 40fr org brn & brn car 2.25 90
252 A42 50fr ultra & ind 2.25 35

Military Health Service.

1954, May 8
253 A44 15fr ind & bl 90 60

Issued to publicize the third International Congress on Agronomy, Algiers, 1954.

Type of France, 1954 Overprinted type "a" in Black.

Unwmk.

1954, June 6 **Engr.** ***Perf. 13***
254 A240 15fr rose car 70 70

Liberation of France, 10th anniversary.

Darguinah Hydroelectric Works
A45

Patio of Bardo Museum
A46

1954, June 19
255 A45 15fr lil rose 90 70

Issued to commemorate the opening of Darguinah hydroelectric works.

1954 **Typo.** ***Perf. 14x13½***
257 A46 12fr red brn & brn org 30 14
258 A46 15fr dk bl & bl 35 5

See also Nos. 267-271.

Type of France, 1954, Overprinted type "a" in Carmine.

1954 **Engr.** ***Perf. 13***
260 A247 12fr dk grn 80 70

Issued to commemorate the 150th anniversary of the first Legion of Honor awards at Camp de Boulogne.

St. Augustine — A47

1954, Nov. 11
261 A47 15fr chocolate 70 70

Issued to commemorate the 1600th anniversary of the birth of St. Augustine.

The indexes in each volume of the Scott Catalogue contain many listings which help to identify stamps.

Aesculapius Statue and El Kattar Hospital, Algiers
A48

1955, Apr. 3 **Unwmk.** ***Perf. 13***
262 A48 15fr red 60 52

Issued to publicize the 30th French Congress of Medicine, Algiers, April 3-6, 1955.

Chenua Mountain and View of Tipasa
A49

1955, May 31
263 A49 50fr brn car 95 26

Issued to commemorate the 2000th anniversary of the founding of Tipasa.

Type of France, 1955 Overprinted type "a" in Red

1955, June 13
264 A251 30fr dp ultra 90 70

Issued to commemorate the 50th anniversary of the founding of Rotary International.

Marianne
A50

Great Kabylia Mountains
A51

Perf. 14x13½
1955, Oct. 3 **Typo.** **Unwmk.**
265 A50 15fr carmine 35 5

See also No. 284.

1955, Dec. 17 **Engr.** ***Perf. 13***
266 A51 100fr ind & ultra 3.00 35

Bardo Type of 1954, "Postes" and "Algerie" in White.
Perf. 14x13½

1955-57 **Unwmk.** **Typo.**
267 A46 10fr dk brn & lt brn 22 5
268 A46 12fr red brn & brn org ('56) 18 5
269 A46 18fr crim & ver ('57) 70 26
270 A46 20fr grn & yel grn ('57) 52 42
271 A46 25fr pur & brt pur 60 8
Nos. 267-271 (5) 2.22 86

Marshal Franchet d'Esperey
A52

1956, May 25 **Engr.** ***Perf. 13***
272 A52 15fr saph & ind 90 90

Birth centenary of Marshal Franchet d'Esperey.

Marshal Jacques Leclerc
A53

1956, Nov. 29
273 A53 15fr red brn & sep 70 70

Issued to commemorate the death of Marshal Leclerc.

Type of 1947-49 and

Arms of Bône — A54

Designs: 2fr, Arms of Tizi-Quzou. 3fr, Arms of Mostaganem. 5fr, Arms of Tlemcen. 10fr, Arms of Setif. 12fr, Arms of Orleansville.

1956-58 **Typo.** ***Perf. 14x13½***
274 A54 1fr grn & ver 5 5
275 A54 2fr ver & ultra ('58) 52 40
276 A54 3fr ultra & emer ('58) 60 22
277 A54 5fr ultra & yel 26 18
278 A31 6fr red & grn ('57) 70 52
279 A54 10fr dp cl & emer ('58) 70 52
280 A54 12fr ultra & red ('58) 70 52
Nos. 274-280 (7) 3.53 2.41

Nos. 275 and 279 are inscribed "Republique Francaise." See also No. 285.

View of Oran — A55

1956-58 **Engr.** ***Perf. 13.***
281 A55 30fr dl pur 70 26
282 A55 35fr car rose ('58) 1.00 70

Electric Train Crossing Bridge
A56

1957, Mar. 25
283 A56 40fr dk bl grn & emer 90 26

Marianne Type of 1955 Inscribed "Algerie" Vertically.
Perf. 14x13½

1957, Dec. 2 **Typo.** **Unwmk.**
284 A50 20fr ultra 60 8

Arms Type of 1947-49 Inscribed "Republique Francaise"

1958, July
285 A31 6fr red & grn 15.00 15.00

Independent State

France Nos. 939, 968, 945-946 and 1013 Overprinted "EA" and Bars, Handstamped or Typographed, in Black or Red

1962, July 2
286 A336 10c brt grn 35 26
a. Typo. ovpt. 60 42
287 A349 25c lake & gray 42 26
a. Handstamped ovpt. 52 26
288 A339 45c brt vio & ol gray 5.25 4.00
a. Handstamped ovpt. 22.50 16.00
289 A339 50c sl grn & lt cl 7.50 4.00
a. Handstamped ovpt. 25.00 17.00
290 A372 1fr dk bl, sl & bis 2.50 1.50
a. Handstamped ovpt. 3.50 2.00
Nos. 286-290 (5) 16.02 10.02

Post offices were authorized to overprint their stock of these 5 French stamps. The size of the letters was specified as 3x6mm. each, but various sizes were used. The post offices had permission to make their own rubber stamps. Typography, pen or pencil were also used. Many types exist. Colors of handstamped overprints include black, red, blue, violet. "EA" stands for Etat Algerien.

Mosque, Tlemcen — A57

Roman Gates of Lodi, Medea
A58

Designs: 5c, Kerrata Gorge. 10c, Dam at Foum el Gherza. 95c, Oil field, Hassi Messaoud.

1962, Nov. 1 **Engr.** ***Perf. 13***
291 A57 5c Prus grn, grn & choc 18 8
292 A58 10c ol blk & dk bl 22 8
293 A57 25c sl grn, brn & ver 60 8
294 A57 95c dk bl, blk & bis 2.25 80
295 A58 1fr grn & blk 2.25 1.75
Nos. 291-295 (5) 5.50 2.79

The designs of Nos. 291-295 are similar to French issues of 1959-61 with "Republique Algerienne" replacing "Republique Francaise."

Flag, Rifle, Olive Branch — A59

Design: Nos. 300-303, Broken chain and rifle added to design A59.

1963, Jan. 6 **Litho.** ***Perf. 12½***
Flag in Green and Red
296 A59 5c bis brn 18 14
297 A59 10c blue 26 14
298 A59 25c vermilion 1.90 5
299 A59 95c violet 1.75 90
300 A59 1fr green 1.50 26
301 A59 2fr brown 4.00 90
302 A59 5fr lilac 6.00 2.50
303 A59 10fr gray 22.50 14.00
Nos. 296-303 (8) 38.09 18.89

Nos. 296-299 commemorate the successful revolution and Nos. 300-303 commemorate the return of peace.

Men of Various Races, Wheat Emblem and Globe — A60

1963, Mar. 21 **Engr.** ***Perf. 13***
304 A60 25c mar, dl grn & yel 42 35

Issued for the "Freedom from Hunger" campaign of the U.N. Food and Agriculture Organization.

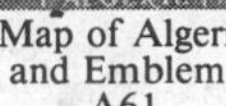

Map of Algeria and Emblems
A61

Physicians from 13th Century Manuscript
A62

1963, July 5 **Unwmk.** ***Perf. 13***
305 A61 25c bl, dk brn, grn & red 60 35

Issued to commemorate the first aniiversary of Algeria's independence.

1963, July 29 **Engr.**
306 A62 25c brn red, grn & bis 1.40 52

Issued to commemorate the Second Congress of the Union of Arab physicians.

Orange and Blossom
A63

Scales and Scroll
A64

1963 ***Perf. 14x13***
307 A63 8c gray grn & org 75 20
308 A63 20c sl & org red 1.00 35
309 A63 40c grnsh bl & org 1.25 60
310 A63 55c ol grn & org red 2.25 1.00

Nos. 307-310 issued precanceled only. See note below No. 32.

1963, Oct. 13 **Unwmk.** ***Perf. 13***
311 A64 25c blk, grn & rose red 65 40

Issued to honor the new constitution.

Guerrilla Fighters
A65

Centenary Emblem
A66

1963, Nov. 1
312 A65 25c dk brn, yel grn & car 65 38

9th anniversary of Algerian revolution.

1963, Dec. 8 **Photo.** ***Perf. 12***
313 A66 25c lt vio bl, yel & dk red 80 42

Centenary of International Red Cross.

UNESCO Emblem, Scales and Globe
A67

Workers
A68

1963, Dec. 16 **Unwmk.** ***Perf. 12***
314 A67 25c lt bl & blk 70 30

Issued to commemorate the 15th anniversary of the Universal Declaration of Human Rights.

1964, May 1 **Engr.** ***Perf. 13***
315 A68 50c dl red, red org & bl 1.25 48

Issued for the Labor Festival.

Map of Africa and Flags — A69

1964, May 25 **Unwmk.** ***Perf. 13***
316 A69 45c bl, org & car 90 40

Issued for Africa Day on the first anniversary of the Addis Ababa charter on African unity.

A particular stamp may be scarce, but if few collectors want it, its market value may remain relatively low.

Ramses II Battling the Hittites (from Abu Simbel) — A70

Design: 30c, Two statues of Ramses II.

1964, June 28 Engr. *Perf. 13*

317 A70 20c choc, red & vio bl 80 48
318 A70 30c brn, red & grnsh bl 95 55

Issued to publicize the UNESCO world campaign to save historic monuments in Nubia.

Tractors — A71

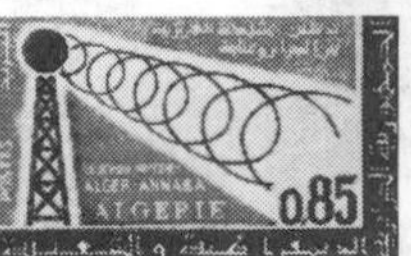

Communications Tower — A72

Designs: 5c, 25c, 85c, Tractors. 10c, 30c, 65c, Men working with lathe. 12c, 15c, 45c, Electronics center and atom symbol. 20c, 50c, 95c, Draftsman and bricklayer.

1964-65 Typo. *Perf. 14x13½*

319 A71 5c red lil 6 6
320 A71 10c brown 12 6
321 A71 12c emer ('65) 45 10
322 A71 15c dk bl ('65) 30 12
323 A71 20c yellow 50 15
324 A71 25c red 60 6
325 A71 30c pur ('65) 50 6
326 A71 45c rose car 60 22
327 A71 50c ultra 75 10
328 A71 65c orange 1.00 22
329 A71 85c green 1.75 28
330 A71 95c car rose 2.00 35
Nos. 319-330 (12) 8.63 1.78

1964, Aug. 30 Engr. *Perf. 13*

331 A72 85c bl, blk & red brn 1.90 75

Inauguration of the Hertzian cable telephone line Algiers-Annaba.

Industrial and Agricultural Symbols A73

Gas Flames and Pipes A74

1964, Sept. 26 Typo. *Perf. 13½x14*

332 A73 25c lt ultra, yel & red 1.00 50

Issued to publicize the first International Fair at Algiers, Sept. 26-Oct. 11.

1964, Sept. 27

333 A74 30c vio, bl & yel 55 40

Issued to commemorate the opening of the Arzew natural gas liquification plant.

Planting Trees A75

Children and UNICEF Emblem A76

1964, Nov. 29 Unwmk.

334 A75 25c sl grn, yel & car 42 30

National reforestation campaign.

1964, Dec. 13 *Perf. 13½x14*

335 A76 15c pink, vio bl & lt grn 40 30

Issued for Children's Day.

Decorated Camel Saddle — A77

1965, May 29 Typo. *Perf. 13½x14*

336 A77 20c blk, red, emer & brn 35 22

Handicrafts of Sahara.

ICY Emblem A78

1965, Aug. 29 Engr. *Perf. 13*

337 A78 30c blk, mar & bl grn 90 48
338 A78 60c blk, brt bl & bl grn 1.25 55

International Cooperation Year, 1965.

ITU Emblem A79

1965, Sept. 19

339 A79 60c pur, emer & buff 90 55
340 A79 95c dk brn, mar & buff 1.25 65

Issued to commemorate the centenary of the International Telecommunication Union.

Musicians A80

Miniatures by Mohammed Racim: 60c, Two female musicians. 5d, Algerian princess and antelope.

1965, Dec. 27 Photo. *Perf. 11½*

341 A80 30c multi 1.00 70
342 A80 60c multi 1.50 1.00
343 A80 5d multi 11.00 7.00

Bulls, Painted in 6000 B.C. — A81

Wall Paintings from Tassili-N-Ajjer, c. 6000 B.C.: No. 345, Shepherd (vert.). 2d, Fleeing ostriches. 3d, Two girls (vert.).

1966, Jan. 29 Photo. *Perf. 11½*

344 A81 1d brn, bis & red brn 3.50 2.50
345 A81 1d gray, blk, ocher & dk brn 3.50 2.50
346 A81 2d brn, ocher & red brn 8.25 4.25
347 A81 3d buff, blk, ocher & brn red 10.00 6.00

See also Nos. 365-368.

Pottery — A82

Handicrafts from Great Kabylia: 50c, Weaving, woman at loom (horiz.). 70c, Jewelry.

1966, Feb. 26 Engr. *Perf. 13*

348 A82 40c Prus bl, brn red & blk 42 35
349 A82 50c dk red, ol & ocher 55 42
350 A82 70c vio bl, blk & red 1.00 60

Weather Balloon, Compass Rose and Anemometer — A83

1966, Mar. 23 Engr. Unwmk.

351 A83 1d cl, brt bl & grn 1.25 55

World Meteorological Day

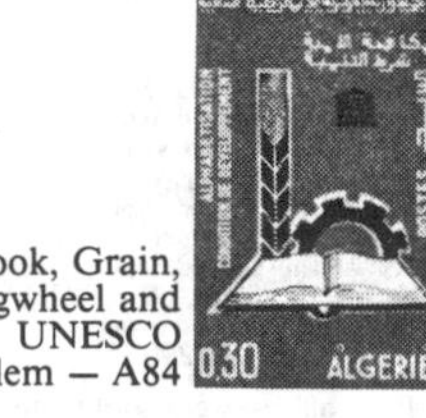

Book, Grain, Cogwheel and UNESCO Emblem — A84

Design: 60c, Grain, cogwheel, book and UNESCO emblem.

1966, May 2 Typo. *Perf. 13x14*

352 A84 30c yel bis & blk 35 30
353 A84 60c dk red, gray & blk 60 35

Literacy as basis for development.

WHO Headquarters, Geneva — A85

1966, May 30 Engr. *Perf. 13*

354 A85 30c multi 48 35
355 A85 60c multi 85 42

Issued to commemorate the inauguration of the World Health Organization Headquarters, Geneva.

Algerian Scout Emblem A86

Arab Jamboree Emblem A87

1966, July 23 Photo. *Perf. 12x12½*

356 A86 30c multi 75 35
357 A87 1d multi 2.00 70

No. 356 commemorates the 30th anniversary of the Algerian Mohammedan Boy Scouts. No. 357, the 7th Arab Boy Scout Jamboree, held at Good Daim, Libya, Aug. 12.

Map of Palestine and Victims A88

Abd-el-Kader A89

1966, Sept. 26 Typo. *Perf. 10½*

358 A88 30c red & blk 1.00 35

Deir Yassin Massacre, Apr. 9, 1948.

1966, Nov. 2 Photo. *Perf. 11½*

359 A89 30c multi 50 14
360 A89 95c multi 1.50 40

Issued to commemorate the transfer from Damascus to Algiers of the ashes of Abd-el-Kader (1807?-1883), Emir of Mascara. See also Nos. 382-387.

UNESCO Emblem — A90

1966, Nov. 19 Typo. *Perf. 10½*

361 A90 1d multi 1.50 52

Issued to commemorate the 20th anniversary of UNESCO (United Nations Educational, Scientific and Cultural Organization).

Horseman A91

Miniatures by Mohammed Racim: 1.50d, Woman at her toilette. 2d, The pirate Barbarossa in front of the Admiralty.

1966, Dec. 17 Photo. Perf. 11½
Granite Paper

362 A91 1d multi 3.50 1.75
363 A91 1.50d multi 5.00 2.50
364 A91 2d multi 8.00 4.25

Wall Paintings Type of 1966

Wall Paintings from Tassili-N-Ajjer, c.6000 B.C.: 1d, Cow. No. 366, Antelope. No. 367, Archers. 3d, Warrior (vert.).

1967, Jan. 28 Photo. Perf. 11½

365 A81 1d brn, bis & dl vio 3.50 2.25
366 A81 2d brn, ocher & red brn 5.75 4.00
367 A81 2d brn, yel & red brn 5.75 4.00
368 A81 3d blk, gray, yel & red brn 9.50 5.75

Bardo Museum A92

La Kalaa Minaret — A93

Design: 1.30d, Ruins at Sedrata.

1967, Feb. 27 Photo. Perf. 13

369 A92 35c multi 35 26
370 A93 95c multi 90 55
371 A92 1.30d multi 1.50 80

Moretti and International Tourist Year Emblem A94

Design: 70c, Tuareg riding camel, Tassili, and Tourist Year Emblem (vert.).

1967, Apr. 29 Litho. Perf. 14

372 A94 40c multi 75 35
373 A94 70c multi 1.50 52

International Tourist Year, 1967.

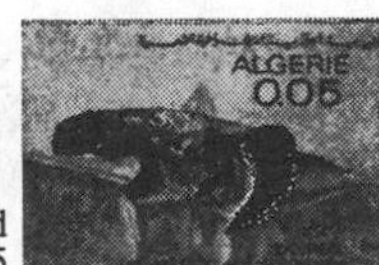

Spiny-tailed Agamid — A95

Designs: 20c, Ostrich (vert.). 40c, Slender-horned gazelle (vert.). 70c, Fennec.

1967, June 24 Photo. Perf. 11½

374 A95 5c bis & blk 45 36
375 A95 20c ocher, blk & pink 90 60
376 A95 40c ol bis, blk & red brn 1.50 80
377 A95 70c gray, blk & dp org 2.75 1.40

Dancers — A96

Typographed and Engraved
1967, July 4 Perf. 10½

378 A96 50c gray vio, yel & blk 75 48

National Youth Festival.

Map of the Mediterranean and Sport Scenes — A97

1967, Sept. 2 Typo. Perf. 10½

379 A97 30c blk, red & bl 42 30

Issued to publicize the 5th Mediterranean Games, Tunis, Sept. 8-17.

Skiers — A98

Olympic Emblem and Sports A99

1967, Oct. 21 Engr. Perf. 13

380 A98 30c brt bl & ultra 60 40
381 A99 95c brn org, pur & brt grn 1.50 1.00

Issued to publicize the 10th Winter Olympic Games, Grenoble, Feb. 6-18, 1968.

Abd-el-Kader Type of 1966

Lithographed, Photogravure
1967-71 Perf. 13½, 11½

382 A89 5c dl pur ('68) 5 5
383 A89 10c green 1.00 30
383A A89 10c sl grn (litho., '69) 14 5
383B A89 25c org ('71) 26 8
384 A89 30c blk ('68) 40 6
385 A89 30c lt vio ('68) 50 25
386 A89 50c rose cl 1.00 26
387 A89 70c vio bl 1.25 35
Nos. 382-387 (8) 4.60 1.40

The 10c (No. 383), 50c and 70c are on granite paper, photogravure, and were issued Nov. 13, 1967. The 5c, 10c (No. 383A), 25c and both 30c are lithographed and perf. 13½; others, perf. 11½.

The three 1967 stamps (No. 383, 50c, 70c) have numerals thin, narrow and close together; the Arabic inscription at lower right is 2mm. high. The five lithographed stamps are redrawn, with numerals thicker and spaced more widely; Arabic at lower right 3mm. high.

Boy Scouts Holding Jamboree Emblem A100

1967, Dec. 23 Engr. Perf. 13

388 A100 1d multi 1.50 85

Issued to commemorate the 12th Boy Scout World Jamboree, Farragut State Park, Idaho, Aug. 1-9.

No. 324 Surcharged

1967 Typo. Perf. 14x13½

389 A71 30c on 25c red 75 30

Mandolin — A101

Musical Instruments: 40c, Lute. 1.30d, Rebec.

1968, Feb. 17 Photo. Perf. 12½x13

390 A101 30c dk brn, ocher & lt bl 52 35
391 A101 40c multi 60 40
392 A101 1.30d multi 2.00 1.00

Nememcha Rug — A102

Algerian Rugs: 70c, Guergour. 95c, Djebel-Amour. 1.30d, Kalaa.

1968, Apr. 13 Photo. Perf. 11½

393 A102 30c multi 70 42
394 A102 70c multi 1.40 80
395 A102 95c multi 2.25 1.25
396 A102 1.30d multi 2.50 1.50

Human Rights Flame A103

1968, May 18 Typo. Perf. 10½

397 A103 40c bl, red & yel 60 42

International Human Rights Year, 1968.

WHO Emblem A104

1968, May 18

398 A104 70c blk, lt bl & yel 80 42

Issued for the 20th anniversary of the World Health Organization.

Welder A105

Athletes, Olympic Flame and Rings A106

1968, June 15 Engr. Perf. 13

399 A105 30c gray, brn & ultra 40 26

Algerian emigration to Europe.

Perf. 12½x13, 13x12½
1968, July 4 Photo.

Designs: 50c, Soccer player. 1d, Mexican pyramid, emblem, Olympic flame, rings and athletes (horiz.).

400 A106 30c grn, red & yel 52 42
401 A106 50c rose car & multi 90 48
402 A106 1d dk grn, org, brn & red 1.65 1.00

Issued to publicize the 19th Olympic Games, Mexico City, Oct. 12-27.

Scouts and Emblem A107

Barbary Sheep A108

1968, July 4 Perf. 13

403 A107 30c multi 75 26

Issued to publicize the 8th Arab Boy Scout Jamboree, Algiers, 1968.

1968, Oct. 19 Photo. Perf. 11½

Design: 1d, Red deer.

404 A108 40c red brn, bis & blk 70 38
405 A108 1d lt & dk ol grn & brn 1.90 85

Hunting Scenes, Djemila A109

"Industry" A110

Design: 95c, Neptune's chariot, Timgad (horiz.). Both designs are from Roman mosaics.

Perf. 12½x13, 13x12½
1968, Nov. 23 Photo.

406 A109 40c gray & multi 52 35
407 A109 95c gray & multi 1.25 70

1968, Dec. 14 Perf. 11½

Designs: No. 409, Miner with drill. 95c, "Energy" (circle and rays).

408 A110 30c dp org & sil 42 26
409 A110 30c brn & multi 42 26
410 A110 95c sil, red & blk 1.25 52

Issued to publicize industrial development.

Opuntia Ficus Indica — A111

Flowers: 40c, Carnations. 70c, Roses. 95c, Bird-of-paradise flower.

1969, Jan. Photo. Perf. 11½
Flowers in Natural Colors

411 A111 25c pink & blk 42 30
412 A111 40c yel & blk 60 40

413 A111 70c gray & blk 1.10 52
414 A111 95c brt bl & blk 1.75 90

See also Nos. 496-499.

Irrigation Dam at Djorf Torba-Oued Guir — A112

Design: 1.50d, Truck on Highway No. 51 and camel caravan.

1969, Feb. 22 Photo. *Perf. 11½*
415 A112 30c multi 42 26
416 A112 1.50d multi 2.25 1.00

Public works in the Sahara.

Mail Coach A113

1969, Mar. 22 Photo. *Perf. 11½*
417 A113 1d multi 1.75 90

Issued for Stamp Day, 1969.

Capitol, Timgad — A114

Design: 1d, Septimius Temple, Djemila (horiz.).

1969, Apr. 5 Photo. *Perf. 13x12½*
418 A114 30c gray & multi 52 26
419 A114 1d gray & multi 1.25 52

Second Timgad Festival, Apr. 4-8.

ILO Emblem A115

Arabian Saddle A116

1969, May 24 Photo. *Perf. 11½*
420 A115 95c dp car, yel & blk 1.40 55

50th anniversary of the International Labor Organization.

1969, June 28 Photo. *Perf. 12x12½*

Algerian Handicrafts: 30c, Bookcase. 60c, Decorated copper plate. Granite Paper

421 A116 30c multi 42 30
422 A116 60c multi 80 38
423 A116 1d multi 1.40 70

No. 321 Surcharged

1969 Typo. *Perf. 14x13½*
424 A71 20c on 12c emer 35 18

Pan-African Culture Festival Emblem — A117

African Development Bank Emblem — A118

1969, July 19 Photo. *Perf. 12½*
425 A117 30c multi 38 26

Issued to commemorate the First Pan-African Culture Festival, Algiers, July 21-Aug. 1.

1969, Aug. 23 Typo. *Perf. 10½*
426 A118 30c dl bl, yel & blk 38 30

Issued to commemorate the 5th anniversary of the African Development Bank.

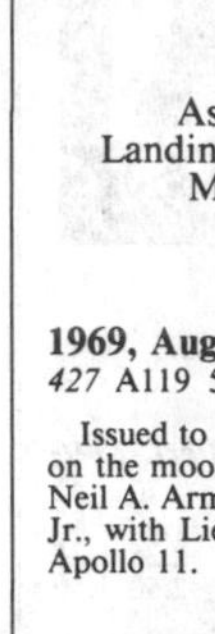
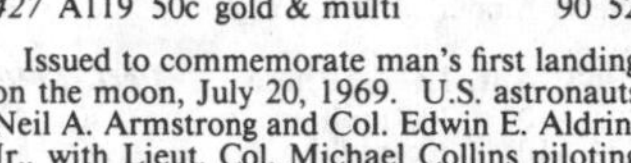

Astronauts and Landing Module on Moon — A119

Perf. 12½x11½
1969, Aug. 23 Photo.
427 A119 50c gold & multi 90 52

Issued to commemorate man's first landing on the moon, July 20, 1969. U.S. astronauts Neil A. Armstrong and Col. Edwin E. Aldrin, Jr., with Lieut. Col. Michael Collins piloting Apollo 11.

Algerian Women, by Dinet — A120

Design: 1.50d, The Watchmen, by Etienne Dinet.

1969, Nov. 29 Photo. *Perf. 14½*
428 A120 1d multi 2.25 1.10
429 A120 1.50d multi 3.25 1.75

Mother and Child — A121

1969, Dec. 27 Photo. *Perf. 11½*
430 A121 30c multi 60 42

Issued to promote mother and child protection.

Agricultural Growth Chart, Tractor and Dam A122

Designs: 30c, Transportation and development. 50c, Abstract symbols of industrialization.

1970, Jan. 31 Photo. *Perf. 12½*
Size: 37x23mm.
431 A122 25c dk brn, yel & org 26 22

Litho. *Perf. 14*
Size: 49x23mm.
432 A122 30c bl & multi 42 26

Photo. *Perf. 12½*
Size: 37x23mm.
433 A122 50c rose lil & blk 52 30

Issued to publicize the Four-Year Development Plan.

Old and New Mail Delivery A123

Spiny Lobster A124

1970, Feb. 28 Photo. *Perf. 11½*
Granite Paper
434 A123 30c multi 42 26

Issued for Stamp Day.

1970, Mar. 28

Designs: 40c, Mollusks. 75c, Retepora cellulosa. 1d, Red coral.

435 A124 30c ocher & multi 42 26
436 A124 40c multi 52 35
437 A124 75c ultra & multi 1.00 52
438 A124 1d lt bl & multi 1.50 70

Oranges, EXPO '70 Emblem A125

Designs (EXPO '70 Emblem and): 60c, Algerian pavilion. 70c, Grapes.

1970, Apr. 25 Photo. *Perf. 12½x12*
439 A125 30c lt bl, grn & org 42 22
440 A125 60c multi 52 26
441 A125 70c multi 80 48

EXPO '70 International Exhibition, Osaka, Japan, Mar. 15-Sept. 13, 1970.

Olives, Oil Bottle — A126

Saber — A127

1970, May 16 Photo. *Perf. 12½x12*
442 A126 1d yel & multi 1.25 70

Olive Year, 1969-1970.

U.P.U. Headquarters Issue
Common Design Type
1970, May 30 *Perf. 13*
Size: 36x26mm.
443 CD133 75c multi 80 42

1970, June 27 Photo. *Perf. 12½*

Designs: 40c, Guns, 18th century (horiz.). 1d, Pistol, 18th century (horiz.).

444 A127 40c yel & multi 70 42
445 A127 75c red & multi 1.00 80
446 A127 1d multi 1.75 1.00

Map of Arab Countries and Arab League Flag — A128

Typographed and Engraved
1970, July 25 *Perf. 10½*
447 A128 30c grn, ocher & lt bl 35 22

25th anniversary of the Arab League.

Lenin — A129

1970, Aug. 29 Litho. *Perf. 11½x12*
448 A129 30c brn & buff 30 22

Issued to commemorate the centenary of the birth of Lenin (1870-1924), Russian communist leader.

Exhibition Hall and Algiers Fair Emblem — A130

1970, Sept. 11 Engr. *Perf. 14x13½*
449 A130 60c lt ol grn 52 30

New Exhibition Hall for Algiers International Fair.

Demand, as well as supply, determines a stamp's market value. One is as important as the other.

Education Year Emblem, Blackboard, Atom Symbol — A131

Koran Page — A132

1970, Oct. 24 Photo. *Perf. 14*

450 A131 30c pink, blk, gold & lt bl 35 26
451 A132 3d multi 3.00 2.25

Issued for International Education Year.

Common Design Types pictured in section at front of book.

Great Mosque, Tlemcen A133

Design: 40c, Ketchaoua Mosque, Algiers (vert.). 1d, Mosque, Sidi-Okba (vert.).

1970-71 Litho. *Perf. 14*

456 A133 30c multi 35 22
457 A133 40c sep & lem ('71) 38 18
458 A133 1d multi 1.00 42

Symbols of the Arts — A134

1970, Dec. 26 Photo. *Perf. 13x12½*

459 A134 1d grn, lt grn & org 1.00 52

Main Post Office, Algiers A135

1971, Jan. 23 *Perf. 11½*

460 A135 30c multi 48 30

Stamp Day, 1971.

Hurdling A136

Designs: 40c, Vaulting (vert.). 75c, Basketball (vert.).

1971, Mar. 7 Photo. *Perf. 11½*

461 A136 20c lt bl & sl 38 22
462 A136 40c lt ol grn & sl 55 40
463 A136 75c sal pink & sl 95 60

Mediterranean Games, Izmir, Turkey, Oct. 1971.

Symbolic Head — A137

1971, March 27 *Perf. 12½*

464 A137 60c car rose, blk & sil 55 30

International year against racial discrimination.

Emblem and Technicians A138

1971, Apr. 24 Photo. *Perf. 12½x12*

465 A138 70c cl, org & bluish blk 65 35

Founding of the Institute of Technology.

Woman from Aures — A139

Regional Costumes: 70c, Man from Oran. 80c, Man from Algiers. 90c, Woman from Amour Mountains.

1971, Oct. 16 *Perf. 11½*

466 A139 50c gold & multi 1.25 52
467 A139 70c gold & multi 1.50 70
468 A139 80c gold & multi 2.00 90
469 A139 90c gold & multi 2.25 1.00

See Nos. 485-488, 534-537.

UNICEF Emblem, Birds and Plants — A140

1971, Dec. 6 *Perf. 11½*

470 A140 60c multi 70 48

25th anniversary of United Nations International Children's Fund (UNICEF).

Lion of St. Mark A141

Design: 1.15d, Bridge of Sighs, Venice (vert.).

1972, Jan. 24 Litho. *Perf. 12*

471 A141 80c multi 90 60
472 A141 1.15d multi 1.50 95

UNESCO campaign to save Venice.

Javelin A142

Book and Book Year Emblem A143

Designs: 25c, Bicycling (horiz.). 60c, Wrestling. 1d, Gymnast on rings.

1972, Mar. 25 Photo. *Perf. 11½*

473 A142 25c mar & multi 38 22
474 A142 40c ocher & multi 48 30
475 A142 60c ultra & multi 70 42
476 A142 1d rose & multi 1.25 60

20th Olympic Games, Munich, Aug. 26-Sept. 11.

1972, Apr. 15

477 A143 1.15d bis, brn & red 90 60

International Book Year 1972.

Mailmen A144

Jasmine A145

1972, Apr. 22

478 A144 40c gray & multi 38 22

Stamp Day 1972.

1972, May 27

Flowers: 60c, Violets. 1.15d, Tuberose.
Flowers in Natural Colors

479 A145 50c brn & pale sal 60 42
480 A145 60c vio & gray 70 52
481 A145 1.15d lt bl & Prus bl 1.50 80

Olympic Stadium, Cheraga A146

1972, June 10

482 A146 50c gray, choc & grn 52 35

New Day, Algerian Flag — A147

1972, July 5

483 A147 1d grn & multi 1.00 65

10th anniversary of independence.

Festival Emblem — A148

Mailing a Letter — A149

1972, July 5 Litho. *Perf. 10½*

484 A148 40c grn, dk brn & org 35 18

First Arab Youth Festival, Algiers, July 5-11.

Costume Type of 1971

Regional Costumes: 50c, Woman from Hoggar. 60c, Kabyle woman. 70c, Man from Mzab. 90c, Woman from Tlemcen.

1972, Nov. 18 Photo. *Perf. 11½*

485 A139 50c gold & multi 1.00 70
486 A139 60c gold & multi 1.00 70
487 A139 70c gold & multi 1.25 90
488 A139 90c gold & multi 1.50 1.25

1973, Jan. 20 Photo. *Perf. 11*

489 A149 40c org & multi 40 22

Stamp Day.

Ho Chi Minh, Map of Viet Nam — A150

1973, Feb. 17 Photo. *Perf. 11½*

490 A150 40c multi 40 22

To honor the people of Viet Nam.

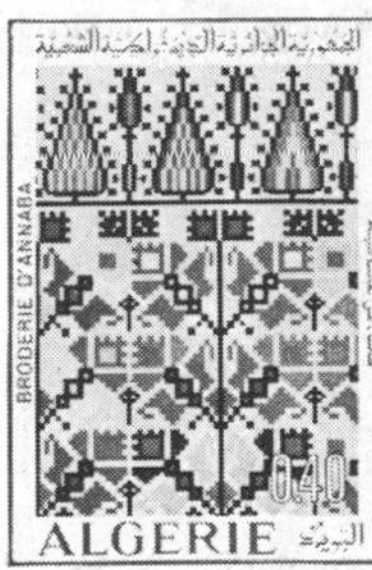

Embroidery from Annaba A151

Designs: 60c, Tree of Life pattern from Algiers. 80c, Constantine embroidery.

1973, Feb. 24

491 A151 40c gray & multi 60 40
492 A151 60c bl and multi 90 55
493 A151 80c dk red, gold & blk 1.10 80

Stylized Globe and Wheat — A152

1973, Mar. 26 Photo. *Perf. 11½*

494 A152 1.15d brt rose lil, org & grn 80 42

World Food Program, 10th anniversary.

Soldier and Flag A153

1973, Apr. 23 Photo. *Perf. 14x13½*
495 A153 40c multi 35 22

Honoring the National Service.

Flower Type of 1969

Flowers: 30c, Opuntia ficus indica. 40c, Roses. 1d, Carnations. 1.15d, Bird-of-paradise flower.

1973, May 21 Photo. *Perf. 11½*
Flowers in Natural Colors

496 A111	30c pink & blk	35	26
497 A111	40c gray & blk	42	30
498 A111	1d yel & multi	1.10	60
499 A111	1.15d multi	1.50	75

OAU Emblem — A154

1973, May 28 Photo. *Perf. 12½x13*
500 A154 40c multi 40 26

Organization for African Unity, 10th anniversary.

Desert and Fruitful Land, Farmer and Family — A155

1973, June 18 *Perf. 11½*
501 A155 40c gold & multi 52 35

Agricultural revolution.

Map of Africa, Scout Emblem — A156

1973, July 16 Litho. *Perf. 10½*
502 A156 80c purple 90 42

24th Boy Scout World Conference (1st in Africa), Nairobi, Kenya, July 16-21.

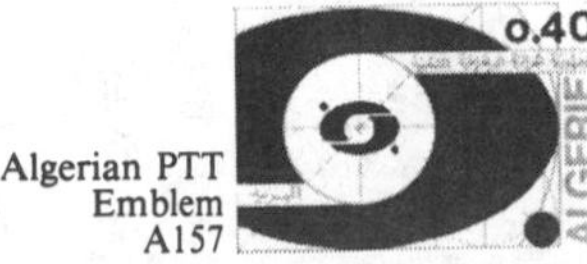

Algerian PTT Emblem A157

1973, Aug. 6 *Perf. 14*
503 A157 40c bl & org 35 22

Adoption of new emblem for Post, Telegraph and Telephone System.

Conference Emblem — A158

Perf. 13½x12½
1973, Sept. 5 Photo.
504 A158 40c dp rose & multi 35 26
505 A158 80c bl grn & multi 70 35

4th Summit Conference of Non-aligned Nations, Algiers, Sept. 5-9.

Port of Skikda A159

1973, Sept. 29 Photo. *Perf. 11½*
506 A159 80c ocher, blk & ultra 70 40

New port of Skikda.

Young Workers — A160

1973, Oct. 22 Photo. *Perf. 13*
507 A160 40c multi 35 22

Voluntary work service.

Arms of Algiers A161

1973, Dec. 22 Photo. *Perf. 13*
508 A161 2d gold & multi 2.50 1.75

Millennium of Algiers.

Infant — A162

1974, Jan. 7 Litho. *Perf. 10½x11*
509 A162 80c org & multi 90 52

Fight against tuberculosis.

Man and Woman, Industry and Transportation — A163

1974, Feb. 18 Photo. *Perf. 11½*
510 A163 80c multi 70 30

Four-year plan.

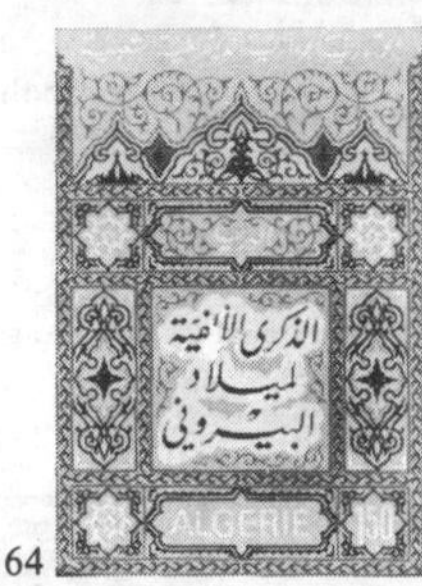

A164

1974, Feb. 25 Photo. *Perf. 11½*
511 A164 1.50d multi 1.75 1.00

Millennium of the birth of abu-al-Rayhan al-Biruni (973-1048), philosopher and mathematician.

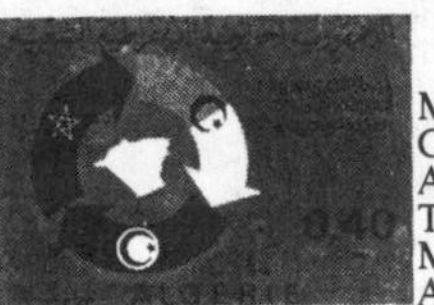

Map and Colors of Algeria, Tunisia, Morocco A165

1974, Mar. 4 Photo. *Perf. 13*
512 A165 40c gold & multi 40 30

Maghreb Committee for Coordination of Posts and Telecommunications.

Hand Holding Rifle A166

Mother and Children A167

1974, Mar. 25 *Perf. 11½*
513 A166 80c red & blk 52 30

Solidarity with the struggle of the people of South Africa.

1974, Apr. 8 *Perf. 13½*
514 A167 85c multi 65 35

Honoring Algerian mothers.

Village A168

Designs: 80c, Harvest. 90c, Tractor and sun. Designs after children's drawings.

1974, June 15
Size: 45x26mm.
515 A168 70c multi 60 26

Size: 48x33mm.
516 A168 80c multi 70 42
517 A168 90c multi 90 65

Nos. 498-499 Overprinted "FLORALIES/1974"

1974, June 22 Photo. *Perf. 11½*
518 A111 1d multi 95 52
519 A111 1.15d multi 1.10 60

1974 Flower Show.

Stamp Vending Machine — A169

1974, Oct. 7 Photo. *Perf. 13*
520 A169 80c multi 65 30

Stamp Day 1974.

UPU Emblem and Globe A170

1974, Oct. 14 *Perf. 14*
521 A170 80c multi 75 42

Centenary of Universal Postal Union.

"Revolution" — A171

Soldiers and Mountains A172

Raising New Flag A173

Design: 1d, Algerian struggle for independence (people, sun and fields).

1974, Nov. 4 Photo. *Perf. 14*
522 A171 40c multi 40 26
523 A172 70c multi 55 35
524 A173 95c multi 70 35
525 A171 1d multi 90 42

20th anniversary of the start of the revolution.

The only foreign revenue stamps listed in this Catalogue are those authorized for prepayment of postage.

"Horizon 1980" — A174

Ewer and Basin — A175

1974, Nov. 23 Photo. *Perf. 13*

526 A174 95c ocher, dk red & blk	80	40

10-year development plan, 1971-1980.

1974, Dec. 21 *Perf. 11½*

Designs: 60c, Coffee pot. 95c, Sugar bowl. 1d, Bath tub.

527 A175 50c pink & multi	42	30
528 A175 60c pale yel & multi	52	40
529 A175 95c cit & multi	90	52
530 A175 1d ultra & multi	1.00	70

17th century Algerian copperware.

No. 497 Surcharged with New Value and Heavy Bar

1975, Jan. 4

531 A111 50c on 40c multi	52	30

Mediterranean Games' Emblem — A176

1975, Jan. 27 *Perf. 13½*

532 A176 50c pur, yel & grn	42	26
533 A176 1d org, bl & mar	90	35

Mediterranean Games, Algiers, 1975.

Costume Type of 1971

Regional Costumes: No. 534, Woman from Hoggar. No. 535, Woman from Algiers. No. 536, Woman from Oran. No. 537, Man from Tlemcen.

1975, Feb. 22 Photo. *Perf. 11½*

534 A139 1d gold & multi	1.25	90
535 A139 1d gold & multi	1.25	90
536 A139 1d gold & multi	1.25	90
537 A139 1d gold & multi	1.25	90

Map of Arab Countries, ALO Emblem A177

1975, Mar. 10 Litho. *Perf. 10½x11*

538 A177 50c red brn	40	18

Arab Labor Organization, 10th anniversary.

Blood Transfusion A178

1975, Mar. 15 *Perf. 14*

539 A178 50c car rose & multi	48	26

Blood donation and transfusions.

Catalogue prices for unused stamps up to mid-1953 are for hinged copies matching the condition specified in this volume's introduction.

Post Office, Al-Kantara A179

Policeman and Map of Algeria A180

1975, May 10 Photo. *Perf. 11½*
Granite Paper

540 A179 50c multi	40	18

Stamp Day 1975.

1975, June 1 Photo. *Perf. 13*

541 A180 50c multi	75	25

National Security and 10th National Police Day.

Ground Receiving Station A181

Designs: 1d, Map of Algeria with locations of radar sites, transmission mast and satellite. 1.20d, Main and subsidiary stations.

1975, June 28 Photo. *Perf. 13*

542 A181 50c bl & multi	42	22
543 A181 1d bl & multi	80	30
544 A181 1.20d bl & multi	95	35

National satellite telecommunications network.

Revolutionary with Flag — A182

1975, Aug. 20 Photo. *Perf. 11½*

545 A182 1d multi	75	40

August 20th Revolutionary Movement (Skikda), 20th anniversary.

Swimming and Games' Emblem A183

Perf. 13x13½, 13½x13

1975, Aug. 23 Photo.

546 A183 25c *shown*	22	18
547 A183 50c *Wrestling and map*	40	26
548 A183 70c *Soccer* (vert.)	70	35
549 A183 1d *Running* (vert.)	80	40
550 A183 1.20d *Handball* (vert.)	1.10	55
a. Souvenir sheet of 5	6.75	6.75
Nos. 546-550 (5)	3.22	1.74

7th Mediterranean Games, Algiers, Aug. 23-Sept. 6.

No. 550a contains one each of Nos. 546-550, perf. 13, buff margin with marginal inscription and ornament in blue and maroon. Size: 135x135mm. Sold for 4.50d. Exists imperf.; same price.

Setif, Guelma, Kherrata — A184

1975 Litho. *Perf. 13½x14*

551 A184 5c org & blk	10	5
552 A184 10c emer & brn	14	5
553 A184 25c dl bl & blk	18	6
554 A184 30c lem & blk	22	8
555 A184 50c brt grn & blk	35	8
556 A184 70c fawn & blk	52	18
557 A184 1d ver & blk	75	40
Nos. 551-557 (7)	2.26	90

30th anniv. of victory in World War II.
Issue dates: 50c, 1d, Nov. 3; others, Dec. 17.

Map of Maghreb and APU Emblem A185

1975, Nov. 20 Photo. *Perf. 11½*

558 A185 1d multi	80	42

10th Congress of Arab Postal Union, Algiers.

Mosaic, Bey Constantine's Palace — A186

Dey-Alger Palace — A187

Design: 2d, Prayer niche, Medersa Sidi-Boumediene, Tlemcen.

1975, Dec. 22

559 A186 1d lt bl & multi	90	35
560 A186 2d buff & multi	1.75	90
561 A187 2.50d buff & blk	2.50	1.25

Famous buildings.

Al-Azhar University A188

Perf. 11½x12½

1975, Dec. 29 Litho.

562 A188 2d multi	1.75	90

Millennium of Al-Azhar University.

Red-billed Firefinch — A189

Birds: 1.40d, Black-headed bush shrike (horiz.). 2d, Blue tit. 2.50d, Blackbellied sandgrouse (horiz.).

1976, Jan. 24 Photo. *Perf. 11½*

563 A189 50c multi	52	26
564 A189 1.40d multi	1.25	80
565 A189 2d multi	1.75	1.00
566 A189 2.50d multi	2.25	1.40

See Nos. 595-598.

Telephones 1876 and 1976 — A190

Map of Africa with Angola and its Flag — A191

1976, Feb. 23 Photo. *Perf. 13½x13*

567 A190 1.40d rose, dk & lt bl	95	55

Centenary of first telephone call by Alexander Graham Bell, Mar. 10, 1876.

1976, Feb. 23 *Perf. 11½*

568 A191 50c brn & multi	40	22

Algeria's solidarity with the People's Republic of Angola.

Sahraoui Flag and Child, Map of former Spanish Sahara — A192

1976, Mar. 15 Photo. *Perf. 11½*

569 A192 50c multi	40	22

Algeria's solidarity with Sahraoui Arab Democratic Republic, former Spanish Sahara.

Mailman — A193

1976, Mar. 22

570 A193 1.40d multi	95	48

Stamp Day 1976.

Microscope, Slide with TB Bacilli, Patients A194

1976, Apr. 26 *Perf. 13x13½*

571 A194 50c multi 42 22

Fight against tuberculosis.

"Setif, Guelma, Kherrata" — A195

1976, May 24 Photo. *Perf. 13½x13*

572 A195 50c bl & yel 50 8

a. Booklet pane of 6 4.50

b. Booklet pane of 10 6.00

No. 572 was issued in booklet only.

Ram's Head over Landscape — A196

1976, June 17 Photo. *Perf. 11½*

573 A196 50c multi 42 26

Livestock breeding.

People Holding Torch, Map of Algeria — A197

Palestine Map and Flag — A198

1976, June 29 Photo. *Perf. 14x13½*

574 A197 50c multi 42 18

National Charter.

1976, July 12 *Perf. 11½*

Granite Paper

575 A198 50c multi 1.50 50

Solidarity with the Palestinians.

Map of Africa — A199

1976, Oct. 3 Litho. *Perf. 10½x11*

576 A199 2d dk bl & multi 1.50 75

2nd Pan-African Commercial Fair, Algiers.

Certain countries cancel stamps in full sheets and sell them (usually with gum) for less than face value. Dealers generally sell "CTO".

Blind Brushmaker A200

The Blind, by Dinet A201

1976, Oct. 23 Photo. *Perf. 14½*

577 A200 1.20d bl & multi 1.00 52

578 A201 1.40d gold & multi 1.40 70

Rehabilitation of the blind.

"Constitution 1976" — A202

1976, Nov. 19 Photo. *Perf. 11½*

579 A202 2d multi 1.50 80

New Constitution.

Soldiers Planting Seedlings — A203

1976, Nov. 25 Litho. *Perf. 12*

580 A203 1.40d multi 1.10 52

Green barrier against the Sahara.

Ornamental Border and Inscription A204

1976, Dec. 18 Photo. *Perf. 11½*

Granite Paper

581 A204 2d multi 1.50 80

Re-election of Pres. Houari Boumediene.

Map with Charge Zones and Dials A205

People and Buildings A206

1977, Jan. 22 *Perf. 13*

582 A205 40c sil & multi 40 22

Inauguration of automatic national and international telephone service.

1977, Jan. 29 Photo. *Perf. 11½*

583 A206 60c on 50c multi 52 26

2nd General Population and Buildings Census. No. 583 was not issued without the typographed red brown surcharge, date, and bars.

Sahara Museum, Uargla — A207

1977, Feb. 12 Litho. *Perf. 14*

584 A207 60c multi 52 30

El-Kantara Gorge — A208

Perf. 12½x13½

1977, Feb. 19 **Photo.**

585 A208 20c grn & yel 8 6

a. Booklet pane of 7 (3 #585, 4 #586 + label) 3.50

b. Booklet pane of 7 (5 #585, 2 #587 + label) 5.00

586 A208 60c brt lil & yel 26 14

587 A208 1d brn & yel 60 22

National Assembly — A209

1977, Feb. 27 *Perf. 11½*

588 A209 2d multi 1.40 70

People and Flag — A210

Soldier and Flag — A211

Perf. 13½, 11½ (3d)

1977, Mar. 12 **Photo.**

589 A210 2d multi 1.40 65

590 A211 3d multi 2.00 1.00

Solidarity with the peoples of Zimbabwe (Rhodesia), 2d; Namibia, 3d.

Winter, Roman Mosaic A212

The Seasons from Roman Villa, 2nd century A.D.: 1.40d, Fall. 2d, Summer. 3d, Spring.

1977, Apr. 21 Photo. *Perf. 11½*

Granite Paper

591 A212 1.20d multi 1.00 52

592 A212 1.40d multi 1.25 52

593 A212 2d multi 1.75 1.00

594 A212 3d multi 14.00 14.00

a. Souv. sheet of 4, perf. imperf. 10.00 10.00

No. 594a contains one each of Nos. 591-594; gray marginal inscription. Size: 101x145mm. Sold for 8d.

Bird Type of 1976

Birds: 60c, Tristram's warbler. 1.40d, Moussier's redstart (horiz.). 2d, Temminck's horned lark (horiz.). 3d, Eurasian hoopoe.

1977, May 21 Photo. *Perf. 11½*

595 A189 60c multi 75 35

596 A189 1.40d multi 1.25 60

597 A189 2d multi 2.00 1.00

598 A189 3d multi 3.00 1.75

Horseman — A213

Design: 5d, Attacking horsemen (horiz.).

1977, June 25 Photo. *Perf. 11½*

599 A213 2d multi 1.90 1.00

600 A213 5d multi 4.25 2.50

Flag Colors, Games Emblem — A214

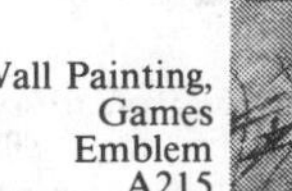

Wall Painting, Games Emblem A215

1977, Sept. 24 Photo. *Perf. 11½*

601 A214 60c multi 52 35

602 A215 1.40d multi 1.25 70

3rd African Games, Algiers 1978.

Village and Tractor A216

1977, Nov. 12 *Perf. 14x13*
603 A216 1.40d multi 1.00 52

Socialist agricultural village.

Almohades Dirham, 12th Century — A217

Ancient Coins: 1.40d, Almohades coin, 12th century. 2d, Almoravides dinar, 11th century.

1977, Dec. 17 **Photo.** *Perf. 11 ½*
604 A217 60c ultra, sil & blk 52 35
605 A217 1.40d grn, gold & brn 1.25 52
606 A217 2d red brn, gold & brn 1.75 1.00

Cherry Blossoms — A218

Flowering Trees: 1.20d, Peach. 1.30d, Almond. 1.40d, Apple.

1978, Feb. 11 **Photo.** *Perf. 11 ½*
607 A218 60c multi 42 26
608 A218 1.20d multi 90 52
609 A218 1.30d multi 90 52
610 A218 1.40d multi 95 60

No. 555 Surcharged with New Value and Bar

1978, Feb. 11 **Litho.** *Perf. 13 ½x14*
611 A184 60c on 50c 75 25

Children with Traffic Signs and Car — A219

1978, Apr. 29 **Photo.** *Perf. 11 ½*
612 A219 60c multi 42 22

Road safety and protection of children.

Sports and Games Emblems A220

Designs (Games Emblem and): 60c, Rower (vert.). 1.20d, Flag colors. 1.30d, Fireworks (vert.). 1.40d, Map of Africa and dancers (vert.).

1978, July 13 **Photo.** *Perf. 11 ½*
613 A220 40c multi 26 18
614 A220 60c multi 42 26
615 A220 1.20d multi 90 42
616 A220 1.30d multi 90 52
617 A220 1.40d multi 1.00 52
Nos. 613-617 (5) 3.48 1.90

3rd African Games, Algiers, July 13-28.

TB Patient Returning to Family — A221

1978, Oct. 5 **Photo.** *Perf. 13 ½x14*
618 A221 60c multi 50 25

Anti-tuberculosis campaign.

Holy Kaaba — A222

1978, Oct. 28 **Photo.** *Perf. 11 ½*
619 A222 60c multi 42 18

Pilgrimage to Mecca.

National Servicemen Building Road — A223

1978, Nov. 4
620 A223 60c multi 42 22

African Unity Road from El Goleah to In Salah, inauguration.

Fibula — A224

Jewelry: 1.35d, Pendant. 1.40d, Ankle ring.

1978, Dec. 21 **Photo.** *Perf. 12x11 ½*
621 A224 1.20d multi 90 42
622 A224 1.35d multi 1.00 42
623 A224 1.40d multi 1.10 70

Pres. Boumediène — A225

1979, Jan. 7 **Photo.** *Perf. 12x11 ½*
624 A225 60c grn, red & brn 42 14

Houari Boumediene, president of Algeria 1965-1978.

Torch and Books A226

1979, Jan. 27 **Photo.** *Perf. 11 ½*
625 A226 60c multi 42 26

National Front of Liberation Party Congress.

Pres. Boumediène — A227

1979, Feb. 4 **Photo.** *Perf. 11 ½*
626 A227 1.40d multi 1.00 42

Forty days after death of Pres. Houari Boumediene.

Proclamation of New President — A228

1979, Feb. 10
627 A228 2d multi 1.40 52

Election of Pres. Chadli Bendjedid.

Sheik Abdul-Hamid Ben Badis (1889-1940) A229

1979, Apr. 18 **Photo.** *Perf. 11 ½*
628 A229 60c multi 42 22

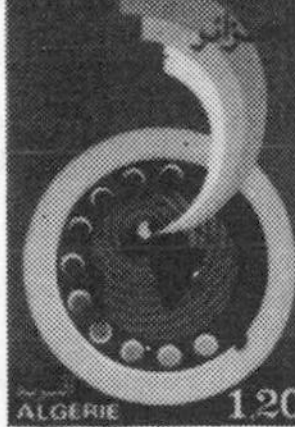

Telephone Dial, Map of Africa — A230

1979, May 19 **Photo.** *Perf. 13 ½x14*

Design: 1.40d, Symbolic Morse key and waves.

629 A230 1.20d multi 80 35
630 A230 1.40d multi 95 35

Telecom '79 Exhibition, Geneva, Sept. 20-26.

Harvest, IYC Emblem A231

Design: 1.40d, Dancers and IYC emblem (vert.).

Perf. 11 ½x11, 11x11 ½

1979, June 21
631 A231 60c multi 42 18
632 A231 1.40d multi 95 52

International Year of the Child.

Nuthatch — A232

1979, Oct. 20 **Photo.** *Perf. 11 ½*
633 A232 1.40d multi 1.00 42

Flag, Soldiers and Workers A233

Design: 3d, Revolutionaries and emblem.

1979, Nov. 1 **Photo.** *Perf. 12 ½*
634 A233 1.40d multi 90 35

Size: 37x48mm.

Perf. 11 ½

635 A233 3d multi 3.00 1.00

November 1 revolution, 25th anniversary.

Hegira, 1500 Anniv. A234

1979, Dec. 2 **Photo.** *Perf. 11 ½*
636 A234 3d multi 1.90 95

Camels, Lion, Men and Slave — A235

Dionysian Procession (Setif Mosaic): 1.35d, Elephants, tigers and women. Men in tiger-drawn cart. Nos. 637-639 se-tenant in continuous design.

1980, Feb. 16 Photo. *Perf. 11½*
Granite Paper

637 A235 1.20d multi 80 35
638 A235 1.35d multi 90 52
639 A235 1.40d multi 95 70

Science Day — A236

1980, Apr. 19 Photo. *Perf. 12*

640 A236 60c multi 42 18

Dam and Workers A237

1980, June 17 Photo. *Perf. 11½*

641 A237 60c multi 42 22

Extraordinary Congress of the National Liberation Front Party.

Olympic Sports, Moscow '80 Emblem A238

1980, June 28

642 A238 50c Flame, rings, vert. 35 18
643 A238 1.40d *shown* 95 52

22nd Summer Olympic Games, Moscow, July 19-Aug. 3.

20th Anniversary of OPEC — A239

Condition is the all-important factor of price. Prices quoted are for stamps in fine condition.

Perf. 11x10½, 10½x11

1980, Sept. 15 Engr.

644 A239 60c *Men holding OPEC emblem, vert.* 42 18
645 A239 1.40d *shown* 95 52

Aures Valley A240

1980, Sept. 25 Litho. *Perf. 13½x14*

646 A240 50c *shown* 35 18
647 A240 1d *El Oued Oasis* 60 26
648 A240 1.40d *Tassili Rocks* 90 35
649 A240 2d *View of Algiers* 1.40 60

World Tourism Conference, Manila, Sept. 27.

Avicenna (980-1037), Philosopher and Physician A241

1980, Oct. 25 Photo. *Perf. 12*

650 A241 2d multi 1.75 70

Ruins of El Asnam A242

1980, Nov. 13 Photo. *Perf. 12*

651 A242 3d multi 1.90 70

Earthquake relief.

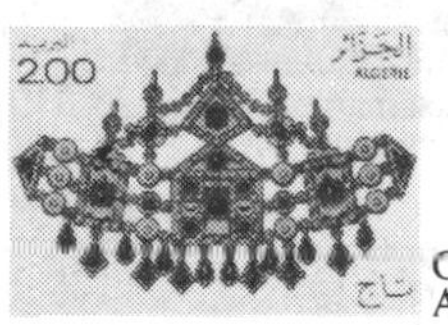

Crown A243

1980, Dec. 20 Photo. *Perf. 12*
Granite Paper

652 A243 60c *Necklace*, vert. 42 26
653 A243 1.40d *Earrings, bracelet*, vert. 90 42
654 A243 2d *shown* 1.25 70

See Nos. 705-707.

1980-1984 Five-Year Plan — A244

1981, Jan. 29 Litho. *Perf. 14*

655 A244 60c multi 40 8

Basket Weaving — A245

1981, Feb. 19 Photo. *Perf. 12½*
Granite Paper

656 A245 40c shown 30 18
657 A245 60c Rug weaving 40 22
658 A245 1d Coppersmith 60 26
659 A245 1.40d Jeweler 90 48

Cedar Tree — A246

Arbor Day: 1.40d, Cypress tree (vert.).

1981, Mar. 19 Photo. *Perf. 12*
Granite Paper

660 A246 60c multi 45 14
661 A246 1.40d multi 85 48

Mohamed Bachir el Ibrahimi (1869-1965) A247

Children Going to School — A248

1981, Apr. 16
Granite Paper

662 A247 60c multi 40 18
663 A248 60c multi 40 8

Science Day.

12th International Hydatidological Congress, Algiers — A249

1981, Apr. 23 *Perf. 14x13½*

664 A249 2d multi 1.25 48

13th World Telecommunications Day — A250

1981, May 14 Photo. *Perf. 14x13½*

665 A250 1.40d multi 90 30

Disabled People and Hand Offering Flower — A251

Perf. 12½x13, 13x12½

1981, June 20 Litho.

666 A251 1.20d Symbolic globe, vert. 80 26
667 A251 1.40d shown 90 26

Intl. Year of the Disabled.

Papilio Machaon A252

1981, Aug. 20 Photo. *Perf. 11½*
Granite Paper

668 A252 60c shown 40 18
669 A252 1.20d Rhodocera rhamni 80 30
670 A252 1.40d Charaxes jasius 90 40
671 A252 2d Papilio podalirius 1.25 52

Monk Seal — A253

1981, Sept. 17 *Perf. 14x13½*

672 A253 60c shown 40 18
673 A253 1.40d Macaque 90 52

World Food Day — A254

Cave Drawings of Tassili — A255

1981, Oct. 16 Photo. *Perf. 14x14½*

674 A254 2d multi 1.25 52

1981, Nov. 21 *Perf. 11½*

Designs: Various cave drawings. 1.60d, 2d horiz.

675 A255 60c multi 40 22
676 A255 1d multi 60 26
677 A255 1.60d multi 1.00 48
678 A255 2d multi 1.25 60

A little time given to the study of the arrangement of the Scott Catalogue can make it easier to use effectively.

Galley, 17-18th Cent. A256

1981, Dec. 17 Photo. *Perf. 11½*

679 A256 60c shown 40 26
680 A256 1.60d Ship, diff. 1.00 52

1982 World Cup Soccer A257

Designs: Various soccer players.

Perf. 13x12½x 12½x13

1982, Feb. 25 Litho.

681 A257 80c multi, vert. 52 22
682 A257 2.80d multi 1.75 75

TB Bacillus Centenary A258

1982, Mar. 20 Photo. *Perf. 14½x14*

683 A258 80c multi 52 22

Painted Stand A259

1982, Apr. 24 Photo. *Perf. 11½*

Granite Paper

684 A259 80c Mirror, vert. 52 26
685 A259 2d shown 1.25 60

Size: 48x33mm.

686 A259 2.40d Chest 1.50 80

Djamaael Djadid Mosque, Algiers — A260

1982, May 15 Litho. *Perf. 14*

687 A260 80c shown 52 22
688 A260 2.40d Sidi Boumediene Mosque, Tlemcen 1.40 70
689 A260 3d Garden of Dey, Algiers 1.90 85

Callitris Articulata A261

Independence, 20th Anniv. A262

Designs: Medicinal plants.

1982, May 27 Photo. *Perf. 11½*

Granite Paper

690 A261 50c shown 30 18
691 A261 80c Artemisia herba-alba 40 22
692 A261 1d Ricinus communis 70 30
693 A261 2.40d Thymus fontanesii 1.40 70

1982, July 5

Granite Paper

694 A262 50c Riflemen 30 18
695 A262 80c Soldiers, horiz. 48 26
696 A262 2d Symbols, citizens, horiz. 1.25 70

Souvenir Sheet

697 A262 5d Emblem 3.00 3.00

No. 697 contains one stamp (32x39mm.); green and red decorative margin. Size: 75x83mm.

Soummam Congress A263

1982, Aug. 20 Litho.

698 A263 80c Congress building 52 18

Scouting Year — A264

1982, Oct. 21 Photo.

Granite Paper

699 A264 2.80d multi 1.75 70

Palestinian Child — A265

Chlamydotis Undulata — A266

1982, Nov. 25 Litho. *Perf. 10½*

700 A265 1.60d multi 2.50 50

Perf. 15x14, 14x15

1982, Dec. 23 Photo.

Protected birds. 50c, 2d horiz.

701 A266 50c Geronticus eremita 50 18
702 A266 80c shown 75 26
703 A266 2d Aguila rapax 1.50 60
704 A266 2.40d Gypaetus barbatus 2.00 70

Jewelry Type of 1980

1983, Feb. 10 *Perf. 11½*

Granite Paper

705 A243 50c Picture frame 30 18
706 A243 1d Flaska 60 42
707 A243 2d Brooch, horiz. 1.25 70

Intl. Arbor Day — A267

1983, Mar. 17 Photo.

Granite Paper

708 A267 80c Abies numidica, vert. 48 22
709 A267 2.80d Acacia raddiana 1.75 90

Minerals — A268

Various minerals. 70c, 80c vert.

Perf. 12x12½, 12½x12

1983, Apr. 21 Photo.

Granite Paper

710 A268 70c multi 42 18
711 A268 80c multi 48 26
712 A268 1.20d multi 75 52
713 A268 2.40d multi 1.40 90

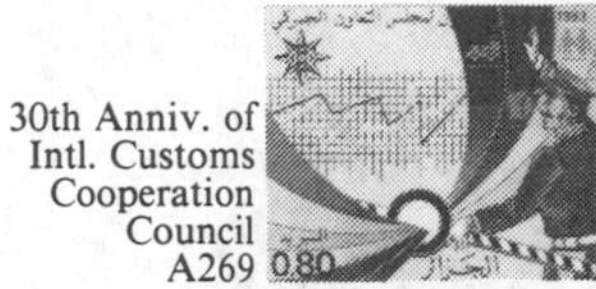

30th Anniv. of Intl. Customs Cooperation Council A269

1983, May 14 Photo. *Perf. 11½*

Granite Paper

714 A269 80c multi 52 26

Emir Abdelkader Death Centenary — A270

1983, May 22 Photo. *Perf. 12*

Granite Paper

715 A270 4d multi 2.50 1.10

Local Mushrooms — A271

1983, July 21 *Perf. 14x15*

716 A271 50c Amanita muscaria 30 18
717 A271 80c Amanita phalloides 48 26
718 A271 1.40d Pleurotus eryngii 80 52
719 A271 2.80d Tefezia leonis 1.50 90

ibn-Khaldun, Historian, Philosopher — A272

1983, Sept. 1 Photo. *Perf. 11½*

720 A272 80c multi 52 22

World Communications Year — A273

Perf. 11½x12½

1983, Sept. 22 Litho.

721 A273 80c Post Office, Algiers 52 22
722 A273 2.40d Telephone, circuit box 1.40 55

Goat and Tassili Mountains A274

1983, Oct. 20 Litho. *Perf. 12½x13*

723 A274 50c shown 30 18
724 A274 80c Tuaregs in native costume 48 26
725 A274 2.40d Animals, rock painting 1.40 60
726 A274 2.80d Rock formation 1.50 90

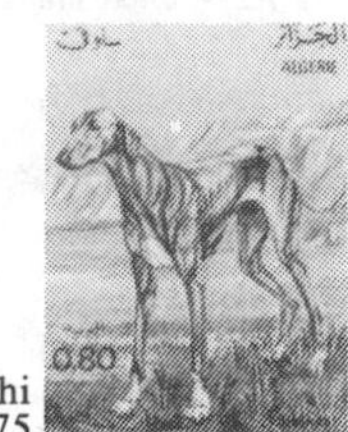

Sloughi Dog — A275

Perf. 14x14½, 14½x14

1983, Nov. 24 Photo.

727 A275 80c Sloughi, vert. 48 26
728 A275 2.40d shown 1.40 90

Natl. Liberation Party, 5th Congress — A276

1983, Dec. 19 Photo. *Perf. 11½*

729 A276 80c Symbols of development 52 35

Souvenir Sheet

730 A276 5d Emblem 3.00 3.00

No. 730 contains one stamp (32x38mm.); multicolored decorative margin. Size: 75x83mm.

View of Oran, 1830 — A277

1984, Jan. 26 Litho. *Perf. 14*

731 A277 10c shown 5 5
732 A277 1d Sidi Abderahman and Taalibi Mosques 60 26
733 A277 2d Bejaia, 1830 1.25 52
734 A277 4d Constantine, 1830 2.50 90

See Nos. 745-747.

Pottery A278

Perf. 11½x12, 12x11½

1984, Feb. 23 **Photo.**

Granite Paper

735	A278	80c	Jug, vert.	52	35
736	A278	1d	Platter	60	35
737	A278	2d	Oil lamp, vert.	1.25	70
738	A278	2.40d	Pitcher	1.50	90

Fountains of Old Algiers — A279

Various fountains.

1984, Mar. 22 **Photo.** *Perf. 11½*

Granite Paper

739	A279	50c	multi	30	22
740	A279	80c	multi	55	30
741	A279	2.40d	multi	1.50	90

1984 Summer Olympics — A280

1984, May 19 **Photo.** *Perf. 11½*

Granite Paper

742	A280	1d	multi	70	42

Brown Stallion A281

1984, June 14 **Photo.** *Perf. 11½*

Granite Paper

743	A281	80c	shown	52	26
744	A281	2.40d	White mare	1.50	90

View Type of 1984

1984 **Litho.** *Perf. 14*

745	A277	5c	Mustapha Pacha	5	5
746	A277	20c	Bab Azzoun	14	5
746A	A277	30c	Algiers	14	6
746B	A277	40c	Kolea	18	8
746C	A277	50c	Algiers	22	10
747	A277	70c	Mostaganem	48	22
			Nos. 745-747 (6)	1.21	56

Issue dates: Nos. 745, 746, 747, July 19. Nos. 746A-746C, Oct. 20.

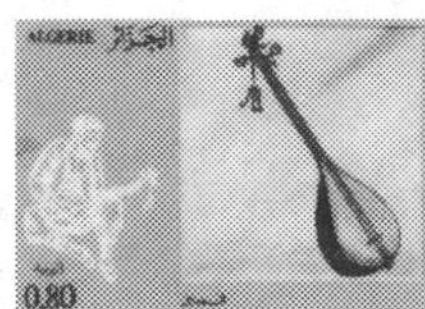

Lute A282

Native musical instruments.

1984, Sept. 22 **Litho.** *Perf. 15x14*

748	A282	80c	shown	32	16
749	A282	1d	Drum	40	20
750	A282	2.40d	Fiddle	1.00	50
751	A282	2.80d	Bagpipe	1.15	55

The first price column gives the catalogue value of an unused stamp, the second that of a used stamp.

30th Anniv. of Algerian Revolution — A284

1984, Nov. 3 **Photo.** *Perf. 11½x12*

757	A284	80c	Partisans	32	16

Souvenir Sheet

758	A284	5d	Algerian flags, vert.	2.00	1.00

Size: 75x82mm.

M'Zab Valley A285

Perf. 15x14, 14x15

1984, Dec. 15 **Photo.**

759	A285	80c	Map of valley	32	16
760	A285	2.40d	Town of M'Zab, vert.	96	48

18th and 19th Century Metalware — A286

1985, Jan. 26 **Photo.** *Perf. 11½*

761	A286	80c	Coffee pot	32	16
762	A286	2d	Bowl, horiz.	78	40
763	A286	2.40d	Covered bowl	96	48

Fish A287

1985, Feb. 23 **Photo.** *Perf. 15x14*

764	A287	50c	Thunnus thynnus	20	10
765	A287	80c	Sparus aurata	30	15
766	A287	2.40d	Epinephelus guaza	90	45
767	A287	2.80d	Mustelus mustelus	1.00	50

National Games — A288

1985, Mar. 28 *Perf. 11½x12*

Granite Paper

768	A288	80c	Doves, emblem	30	15

Environmental Conservation — A289

1985, Apr. 25 *Perf. 13½*

769	A289	80c	Stylized trees	30	15
770	A289	1.40d	Stylized waves	55	28

The Casbah — A290

Perf. 13½x12½ on 3 or 4 Sides

1985, June 1

773	A290	20c	dk bl & buff	8	5
777	A290	80c	sage grn & buff	30	15
779	A290	2.40d	chnt & buff	90	45
a.			Bklt. pane of 5 (20c, 3 80c, 2.40d) + label	2.00	65

Issued only in booklet panes.

UN, 40th Anniv. — A291

1985, June 26 **Photo.** *Perf. 14*

784	A291	1d	Dove, emblem, 40	40	20

Natl. Youth Festival — A292

1985, July 5 **Litho.** *Perf. 13½*

785	A292	80c	multi	30	15

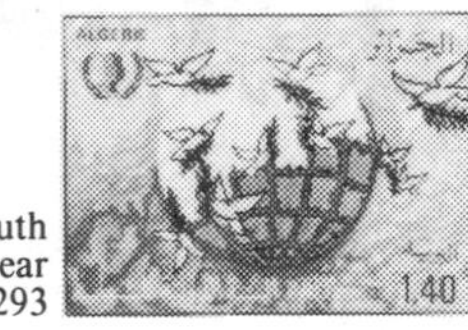

Intl. Youth Year A293

1985, July 5

786	A293	80c	Silhouette, globe, emblem, vert.	30	15
787	A293	1.40d	Doves, globe	55	28

World Map, OPEC — A294

1985, Sept. 14 **Photo.** *Perf. 12½x13*

788	A294	80c	multi	30	15

Organization of Petroleum Exporting Countries, 25th anniv.

Family Planning A295

El-Meniaa Township A296

1985, Oct. 3 **Litho.** *Perf. 14*

789	A295	80c	Mother and sons	30	15
790	A295	1.40d	Weighing infant	55	28
791	A295	1.70d	Breast-feeding	68	35

1985, Oct. 24 **Engr.** *Perf. 13*

792	A296	80c	Chetaibi Bay, horiz.	30	15
793	A296	2d	shown	78	40
794	A296	2.40d	Bou Noura Town, horiz.	95	48

The Palm Grove, by N. Dinet — A297

1985, Nov. 21 **Photo.** *Perf. 11½x12*

Granite Paper

795	A297	2d	multi	78	40
796	A297	3d	multi, diff.	1.15	58

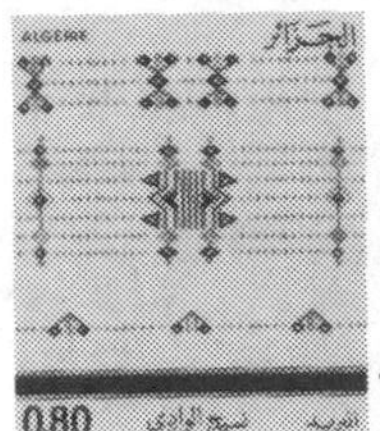

Tapestries A298

Various designs.

1985, Dec. 19

Granite Paper

797	A298	80c	multi	30	15
798	A298	1.40d	multi	55	28
799	A298	2.40d	multi	95	48
800	A298	2.80d	multi	1.10	55

Wildcats A299

Perf. 12x11½, 11½x12

1986, Jan. 23

Granite Paper

801	A299	80c	Felis margarita	30	15
802	A299	1d	Felis caracal	40	20
803	A299	2d	Felis sylvestris	78	40
804	A299	2.40d	Felis serval, vert.	95	48

UN Child Survival Campaign A300

Algerian General Worker's Union, 30th Anniv. A301

1986, Feb. 13 Litho. *Perf. 13½*
805 A300 80c Oral vaccine 30 15
806 A300 1.40d Mother, child, sun 55 28
807 A300 1.70d Three children 68 35

1986, Feb. 24 *Perf. 12½*
Granite Paper
808 A301 2d multi 78 40

National Charter A302

Natl. Day of the Disabled A303

1986, Mar. 6 Photo. *Perf. 11½*
Granite Paper
809 A302 4d multi 1.60 80

1986, Mar. 15 *Perf. 12½x13*
810 A303 80c multi 30 15

Anti-Tuberculosis Campaign — A304

1986 World Cup Soccer Championships, Mexico — A305

1986, Apr. 17 Litho. *Perf. 14x15*
811 A304 80c multi 30 15

1986, Apr. 24 *Perf. 14*
812 A305 2d Soccer ball, sombrero 78 40
813 A305 2.40d Soccer players 95 48

Inner Courtyards — A306

1986, May 15 Photo. *Perf. 11½*
Granite Paper
814 A306 80c multi 30 15
815 A306 2.40d multi, diff. 95 48
816 A306 3d multi, diff. 1.20 60

Blood Donation Campaign — A307

1986, June 26 Litho. *Perf. 13½*
817 A307 80c multi 32 16

Southern District Radio Communication Inauguration A308

1986, July *Perf. 13*
818 A308 60c multi 24 12

Mosque Gateways A309

1986, Sept. 27 Photo. *Perf. 12x11½*
Granite Paper
819 A309 2d Door 78 40
820 A309 2.40d Ornamental arch 95 48

Intl. Peace Year — A310

Perf. 13½x14½
1986, Oct. 16 Photo.
821 A310 2.40d multi 95 48

Folk Dancing A311

1986, Nov. 22 Litho. *Perf. 14x13½*
822 A311 80c Woman, scarf 32 16
823 A311 2.40d Woman, diff. 95 48
824 A311 2.80d Man, sword 1.10 55

Flowers — A312

1986, Dec. 18 Photo. *Perf. 14*
825 A312 80c Narcissus tazetta 32 16
826 A312 1.40d Iris unguicularis 55 28
827 A312 2.40d Capparis spinosa 95 48
828 A312 2.80d Gladiolus segetum 1.10 55

Abstract Paintings by Mohammed Issia Khem A313

Perf. 11½x12, 12x11½
1987, Jan. 29 Litho.
829 A313 2d Man and woman, vert. 1.00 50
830 A313 5d Man and books 2.50 1.25

Jewelry from Aures A314

1987, Feb. 27 Photo. *Perf. 12*
Granite Paper
831 A314 1d Earrings 50 25
832 A314 1.80d Bracelets 90 45
833 A314 2.90d Nose rings 1.50 75
834 A314 3.30d Necklace 1.65 85

Nos. 831-833 vert.

Petroglyphs, Atlas — A315

1987, Mar. 26 Litho. *Perf. 12x11½*
Granite Paper
835 A315 1d Man and woman 52 25
836 A315 2.90d Goat 1.50 75
837 A315 3.30d Horse, bull 1.65 85

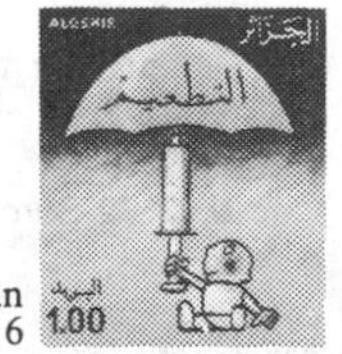
Syringe as an Umbrella — A316

1987, Apr. 7 *Perf. 11½*
Granite Paper
838 A316 1d multi 52 25

Child Immunization Campaign, World Health Day.

Volunteers A317

1987, Apr. 23 *Perf. 10½*
839 A317 1d multi 52 25

Third General Census — A318

1987, May 21 *Perf. 13½*
840 A318 1d multi 52 25

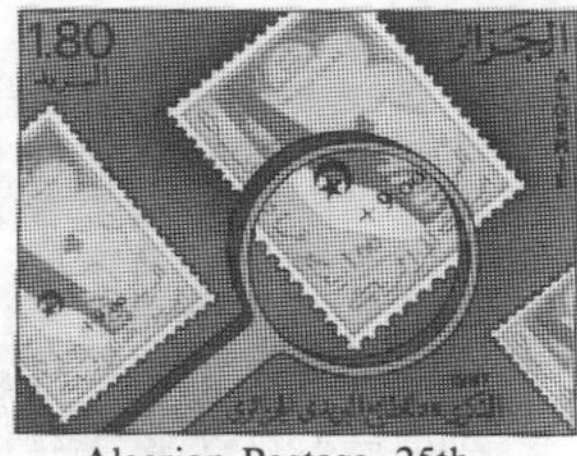
Algerian Postage, 25th Anniv. — A319

Design: War Orphans' Fund label (1fr + 9fr) of 1962.

1987, July 5 Photo. *Perf. 11½x12*
Granite Paper
841 A319 1.80d multi 95 48

A320

A321

1987, July 5
Granite Paper
842 A320 1d multi 52 25
Souvenir Sheet
843 A321 5d multi 2.50 2.50

Natl. independence, 25th anniv. No. 843 has inscribed decorative margin. Size: 75x83mm.

Amateur Theater Festival, Mostaganem A322

1987, July 20 *Perf. 12x11½*
Granite Paper
844 A322 1d Actors on stage 52 25
845 A322 1.80d Theater 95 48

Nos. 844-845 se-tenant in continuous design.

Mediterranean Games, Latakia — A323

1987, Aug. 6 *Perf. 13x12½, 12½x13*

846 A323 1d Discus 52 25
847 A323 2.90d Tennis, vert. 1.50 75
848 A323 3.30d Team handball 1.75 88

Birds — A324

1987 **Litho.** *Perf. 13½*

849 A324 1d Phoenicopterus ruber roseus 52 25
850 A324 1.80d Porphyrio porphyrio 95 48
851 A324 2.50d Elanus caeruleus 1.30 65
852 A324 2.90d Milvus milvus 1.50 75

Agriculture A325

Perf. 10½x11, 11x10½

1987, Nov. 26 **Litho.**

853 A325 1d Planting 50 25
854 A325 1d Reservoir 50 25
855 A325 1d Harvesting crop, vert. 50 25
856 A325 1d Produce, vert. 50 25

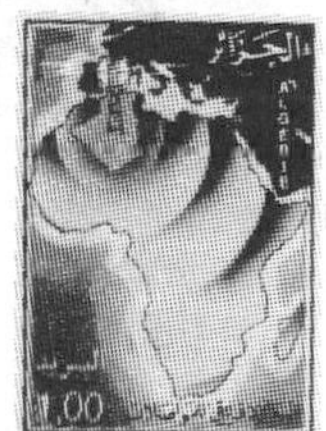

African Telecommunications Day — A326

1987, Dec. 7 *Perf. 10½*

857 A326 1d multi 50 25

SEMI-POSTAL STAMPS

Regular Issue of 1926 Surcharged in Black or Red

+10c

1927 **Unwmk.** *Perf. 14x13½.*

B1 A1 5c +5c bl grn 50 50
B2 A1 10c +10c lil 50 50
B3 A2 15c +15c org brn 50 50
B4 A2 20c +20c car rose 50 50
B5 A2 25c +25c bl grn 50 50
B6 A2 30c +30c lt bl 50 50
B7 A2 35c +35c dp vio 50 50
B8 A2 40c +40c ol grn 50 50
B9 A3 50c +50c dp bl (R) 50 50
  a. Dbl. surch. 165.00 165.00
B10 A3 80c +80c red org 50 50
B11 A4 1fr +1fr gray grn & red brn 50 50
B12 A4 2fr +2fr Prus bl & blk brn 17.00 17.00
B13 A4 5fr +5fr red & vio 25.00 25.00
  Nos. B1-B13 (13) 47.50 47.50

The surtax was for the benefit of wounded soldiers. Government officials speculated in this issue.

Railroad Terminal, Oran — SP1

Ruins at Djemila SP2

Mosque of Sidi Abd-er-Rahman SP3

Designs: 10c+10c, Rummel Gorge, Constantine. 15c+15c, Admiralty Buildings, Algiers. 25c+25c, View of Algiers. 30c+30c, Trajan's Arch, Timgad. 40c+40c, Temple of the North, Djemila. 75c+75c Mansourah Minaret, Tlemcen. 1f+1f, View of Ghardaia. 1.50f+1.50f, View of Tolga. 2f+2f, Tuareg warriors. 3f+3f, Kasbah, Algiers.

1930 **Engr.** *Perf. 12½.*

B14 SP1 5c +5c org 7.00 7.00
B15 SP1 10c +10c ol grn 7.00 7.00
B16 SP1 15c +15c dk brn 7.00 7.00
B17 SP1 25c +25c blk 7.00 7.00
B18 SP1 30c +30c dk red 7.00 7.00
B19 SP1 40c +40c ap grn 7.00 7.00
B20 SP2 50c +50c ultra 7.00 7.00
B21 SP2 75c +75c red pur 7.00 7.00
B22 SP2 1fr +1fr org red 7.00 7.00
B23 SP2 1.50fr +1.50fr dp ultra 7.00 7.00
B24 SP2 2fr +2fr dk car 7.00 7.00
B25 SP2 3fr +3fr dk grn 7.00 7.00
B26 SP3 5fr +5fr grn & car 13.00 13.00
  a. Center inverted 475.00
  Nos. B14-B26 (13) 97.00 97.00

Issued in connection with the celebration of the centenary of the French occupation of Algeria. The surtax on the stamps was given to the funds for the celebration.

Nos. B14-B26 exist imperf. Price, set in pairs, $350.

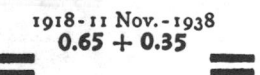

1918-11 Nov.-1938
0.65 + 0.35

No. 102 Surcharged in Red

1938 *Perf. 13.*

B27 A6 65c +35c on 2.25fr yel grn 55 55

20th anniversary of Armistice.

René Caillié, Charles Lavigerie and Henri Duveyrier SP14

1939 **Engr.**

B28 SP14 30c +20c dk bl grn 90 90
B29 SP14 90c +60c car rose 90 90
B30 SP14 2.25fr +75c ultra 9.00 9.00
B31 SP14 5fr +5fr brn blk 18.00 18.00

Pioneers of the Sahara.

French and Algerian Soldiers SP15

1940 **Photo.** *Perf. 12*

B32 SP15 1fr +1fr bl & car 60 60
B33 SP15 1fr +2fr brn rose & blk 60 60
B34 SP15 1fr +4fr dp grn & red 90 90
B35 SP15 1fr +9fr brn & car 1.40 1.40

The surtax was used to assist the families of mobilized men.

Type of Regular Issue, 1941 Surcharged in Carmine

+4f

1941 **Engr.** *Perf. 13.*

B36 A19 1fr +4fr blk 26 26

No. 135 Surcharged in Carmine

SECOURS
NATIONAL
+4f

B37 A19 1fr +4fr dk bl 26 26

The surtax was for National Relief.

No. 124 Surcharged in Black "+60c"

1942

B38 A7 90c +60c hn brn 10 6
  a. Double surch. 80.00

The surtax was used for National Relief. The stamp could also be used as 1.50 francs for postage.

Mother and Child — SP16

1943, Dec. 1 **Litho.** *Perf. 12*

B39 SP16 50c +4.50fr brt pink 60 48
B40 SP16 1.50fr +8.50fr lt grn 60 48
B41 SP16 3fr +12fr dp bl 60 48
B42 SP16 5fr +15fr vio brn 60 48

The surtax was for the benefit of soldiers and prisoners of war.

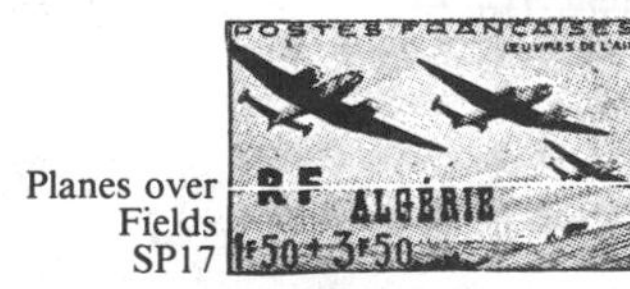

Planes over Fields SP17

Unwmk.

1945, July 2 **Engr.** *Perf. 13*

B43 SP17 1.50fr +3.50fr lt ultra, red org & blk 30 30

The surtax was for the benefit of Algerian airmen and their families.

France No. B192 Overprinted in Black — a

ALGÉRIE

1945

B44 SP146 4fr +6fr dk vio brn 30 30

The surtax was for war victims of the P.T.T.

Overprinted in Blue on Type of France, 1945.

1945, Oct. 15

B45 SP150 2fr +3fr dk brn 52 52

For Stamp Day.

Overprinted in Blue on Type of France, 1946.

1946, June 29

B46 SP160 3fr +2fr red 70 70

For Stamp Day.

Children Playing by Stream SP18

Girl SP19

Athlete SP20

Repatriated Prisoner and Bay of Algiers SP21

1946, Oct. 2 **Engr.** *Perf. 13*

B47 SP18 3fr +17fr dk grn 1.00 1.00
B48 SP19 4fr +21fr red 1.00 1.00
B49 SP20 8fr +27fr rose lil 4.00 4.00
B50 SP21 10fr +35fr dk bl 1.10 1.10

Type of France, 1947, Overprinted type "a" in Carmine.

1947, Mar. 15

B51 SP172 4.50fr +5.50fr dp ultra 50 50

For Stamp Day.

Same on Type of France, 1947, Surcharged Like No. B36 in Carmine.

1947, Nov. 13

B52 A173 5fr +10fr dk Prus grn 52 52

Type of France, 1948, Overprinted in Dark Green — f

ALGÉRIE

1948, Mar. 6

B53 SP176 6fr +4fr dk grn 60 60

For Stamp Day.

Type of France, 1948, Overprinted type "a" in Blue and New Value.

1948, May

B54 A176 6fr +4fr red 45 45

Battleship Richelieu and the Admiralty, Algiers SP22

Aircraft Carrier Arromanches SP23

Unwmk.

1949, Jan. 15 **Engr.** *Perf. 13*

B55 SP22 10fr +15fr dp bl 5.75 5.75
B56 SP23 18fr +22fr red 5.75 5.75

The surtax was for naval charities.

Type of France, 1949, Overprinted in Blue — g ALGÉRIE

1949, Mar. 26
B57 SP180 15fr +5fr lil rose 1.25 1.25

For Stamp Day, Mar. 26-27.

Type of France, 1950, Overprinted type "f" in Green.

1950, Mar. 11
B58 SP183 12fr +3fr blk brn 1.40 1.40

For Stamp Day, Mar. 11-12.

Foreign Legionary — SP24

1950, Apr. 30
B59 SP24 15fr +5fr dk grn 1.50 1.50

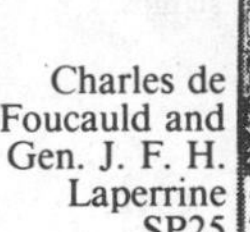

Charles de Foucauld and Gen. J. F. H. Laperrine SP25

1950, Aug. 21 **Unwmk.** ***Perf. 13***
B60 SP25 25fr +5fr brn ol & brn blk 4.25 4.25

50th anniversary of the presence of the French in the Sahara.

Emir Abd-el-Kader and Marshal T. R. Bugeaud SP26

1950, Aug. 21
B61 SP26 40fr +10fr dk brn & blk brn 4.25 4.25

Unveiling of a monument to Emir Abd-el-Kader at Cacheron.

Col. Colonna d'Ornano and Fine Arts Museum, Algiers SP27

1951, Jan. 11
B62 SP27 15fr +5fr blk brn, vio brn & red brn 90 90

Issued to commemorate the tenth anniversary of the death of Col. Colonna d'Ornano.

Type of France, 1951, Overprinted type "a" in Black.

1951, Mar. 10
B63 SP186 12fr +3fr brn 1.25 1.25

For Stamp Day.

Type of France, 1952, Overprinted type "g" in Dark Blue.

1952, Mar. 8 **Unwmk.** ***Perf. 13***
B64 SP190 12fr +3fr dk bl 2.00 2.00

For Stamp Day.

Canceled-to-order stamps are often from remainders. Most collectors of canceled stamps prefer postally used specimens.

French Military Medal — SP28

Unwmk.

1952, July 5 **Engr.** ***Perf. 13***
B65 SP28 15fr +5fr grn, yel & brn 2.00 2.00

Issued to commemorate the centenary of the creation of the French Military Medal.

Type of France 1952, Surcharged type "g" and Surtax in Black

1952, Sept. 15
B66 A222 30fr +5fr dp ultra 1.75 1.75

Issued to commemorate the 10th anniversary of the defense of Bir-Hakeim.

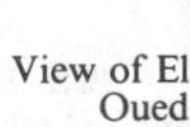

View of El Oued SP29

Design: 12fr+3fr, View of Bou-Noura.

1952, Nov. 15 **Engr.**
B67 SP29 8fr +2fr ultra & red 1.75 1.75
B68 SP29 12fr +3fr red 2.50 2.50

The surtax was for the Red Cross.

Type of France, 1953, Overprinted type "a" in Black.

1953, Mar. 14 **Engr.**
B69 SP193 12fr +3fr pur 1.50 1.40

For Stamp Day. Surtax for Red Cross.

Victory of Cythera — SP30

Unwmk.

1953, Dec. 18 **Engr.** ***Perf. 13***
B70 SP30 15fr +5fr blk brn & brn 90 90

The surtax was for army welfare work.

Type of France, 1954, Overprinted type "a" in Black.

1954, Mar. 20 **Unwmk.** ***Perf. 13***
B71 SP196 12fr +3fr scar 1.00 1.00

For Stamp Day.

Soldiers and Flags SP31

Foreign Legionary SP32

1954, Mar. 27
B72 SP31 15fr +5fr dk brn 52 52

The surtax was for old soldiers.

1954, Apr. 30
B73 SP32 15fr +5fr dk grn 1.40 1.40

The surtax was for the welfare fund of the Foreign Legion.

Nurses and Verdun Hospital, Algiers — SP33

Design: 15fr+5fr, J. H. Dunant & ruins at Djemila.

1954, Oct. 30
B74 SP33 12fr +3fr ind & red 3.00 3.00
B75 SP33 15fr +5fr pur & red 3.50 3.50

The surtax was for the Red Cross.

Earthquake Victims and Ruins SP34

First Aid SP35

Designs: 15fr+5fr, As No. B76, 20fr+7fr, As No. B78. 25fr+8fr & 30fr+10fr, Removing wounded.

1954, Dec. 5
B76 SP34 12fr +4fr dk vio brn 1.90 1.90
B77 SP34 15fr +5fr dp bl 1.90 1.90
B78 SP35 18fr +6fr lil rose 2.25 2.25
B79 SP35 20fr +7fr vio 2.25 2.25
B80 SP35 25fr +8fr rose brn 2.50 2.50
B81 SP35 30fr +10fr brt bl grn 2.50 2.50
Nos. B76-B81 (6) 13.30 13.30

The surtax was for victims of the Orleansville earthquake disaster of September 1954.

Type of France, 1955, Overprinted type "a" in Black.

1955, Mar. 19
B82 SP199 12fr +3fr dp ultra 1.25 1.25

For Stamp Day, Mar. 19-20.

Women and Children SP36

Cancer Victim SP37

1955, Nov. 5
B83 SP36 15fr +5fr bl & ind 70 70

The tax was for war victims.

1956, Mar. 3 **Unwmk.** ***Perf. 13***
B84 SP37 15fr +5fr dk brn 70 70

The surtax was for the Algerian Cancer Society. The male figure in the design is Rodin's "Age of Bronze."

Type of France, 1956, Overprinted type "a" in Black.

1956, Mar.
B85 SP202 12fr +3fr red 70 70

For Stamp Day, Mar. 17-18.

Foreign Legion Rest Home SP38

1956, Apr. 29
B86 SP38 15fr +5fr dk bl grn 1.50 1.50

Issued in honor of the French Foreign Legion.

Type of France, 1957, Overprinted type "f" in Black

1957, Mar. 16 **Engr.** ***Perf. 13***
B87 SP204 12fr +3fr dl pur 1.00 1.00

For Stamp Day and to honor the Maritime Postal Service.

Fennec SP39

Design: 15fr+5fr, Stork flying over roofs.

1957, Apr. 6
B88 SP39 12fr +3fr red brn & red 5.75 5.75
B89 SP39 15fr +5fr sep & red 5.75 5.75

The surtax was for the Red Cross.

Type of Regular Issue, 1956 Surcharged in Dark Blue — 18 JUIN 1940 + 5F

1957, June 18
B90 A53 15fr +5fr scar & rose red 90 90

Issued to commemorate the 17th anniversary of General de Gaulle's appeal for a Free France.

The Giaour, by Delacroix — SP40

On the Banks of the Oued, by Fromentin SP41

Design: 35fr+10fr, Dancer, by Chasseriau.

Unwmk.

1957, Nov. 30 **Engr.** ***Perf. 13***
B91 SP40 15fr +5fr dk car 5.25 5.25
B92 SP41 20fr +5fr grn 5.25 5.25
B93 SP40 35fr +10fr dk bl 5.25 5.25

The surtax was for army welfare organizations.

Type of France Overprinted type "f" in Blue.

1958, Mar. 15 **Unwmk.** ***Perf. 13***
B94 SP206 15fr +5fr org brn 1.00 1.00

For Stamp Day.

Prices of premium quality never hinged stamps will be in excess of catalogue price.

Bird-of-Paradise Flower — SP42

Arms and Marshal's Baton — SP43

1958, June 14 **Engr.** ***Perf. 13***

B95	SP42	20fr +5fr grn, org & vio	2.50	2.50

The surtax was for Child Welfare.

1958, July 20

B96	SP43	20fr +5fr ultra, car & grn	1.50	1.50

Issued for the Marshal de Lattre Foundation.

Independent State

Clasped Hands, Wheat and Olive Branch SP44

Burning Books SP45

1963, May 27 **Unwmk.** ***Perf. 13***

B97	SP44	50c +20c sl grn, brt grn & car	1.25	90

The surtax was for the National Solidarity Fund.

1965, June 7 **Engr.** ***Perf. 13***

B98	SP45	20c +5c ol grn, red & blk	52	38

Issued to commemorate the burning of the Library of Algiers, June 7, 1962.

Soldiers and Woman Comforting Wounded Soldier — SP46

1966, Aug. 20 **Photo.** ***Perf. 11½***

B99	SP46	30c +10c multi	1.50	90
B100	SP46	95c +10c multi	2.50	1.50

Issued for the Day of the Moudjahid (Moslem volunteers).

Red Crescent, Boy and Girl — SP47

Allenstein stamps can be mounted in Scott's Germany Part II Album.

1967, May 27 **Litho.** ***Perf. 14***

B101	SP47	30c +10c brt grn, brn & car	70	52

Algerian Red Crescent Society.

Flood Victims — SP48

Design: 95c+25c, Rescuing flood victims.

1969, Nov. 15 **Typo.** ***Perf. 10½***

B102	SP48	30c +10c dl bl, sal & blk	70	52

Litho.

B103	SP48	95c +25c multi	1.50	1.00

Red Crescent Flag — SP49

1971, May 17 **Engr.** ***Perf. 10½***

B104	SP49	30c +10c sl grn & car	52	42

Algerian Red Crescent Society.

AIR POST STAMPS

Plane over Algiers Harbor AP1

Two types of 20fr:
Type I. Monogram "F" without serifs. "POSTE" indented 3mm.
Type II. Monogram "F" with serifs. "POSTE" indented 4½mm.

Perf. 13.

1946, June 20 **Unwmk.** **Engr.**

C1	AP1	5fr red	6	5
C2	AP1	10fr dp bl	6	5
C3	AP1	15fr dp grn	52	5
C4	AP1	20fr brn (II)	26	5
C4A	AP1	20fr brn (I)	125.00	85.00
C5	AP1	25fr violet	60	14
C6	AP1	40fr gray blk	70	14
		Nos. C1-C4,C5-C6 (6)	2.20	48

No. C1 Surcharged in Black — 10 %

1947, Jan. 18

C7	AP1	(4.50fr) on 5fr red	5	5

Storks over Mosque — AP2

Plane over Village AP3

1949-53

C8	AP2	50fr green	3.00	42
C9	AP3	100fr brown	2.50	42
C10	AP2	200fr brt red	6.00	4.25
C11	AP3	500fr ultra ('53)	21.00	15.00

Beni Bahdel Dam — AP4

1957, July 1 **Unwmk.** ***Perf. 13***

C12	AP4	200fr dk red	5.25	1.25

Caravelle over Ghardaia — AP5

Designs: 2d, Caravelle over El Oued. 5d, Caravelle over Tipasa.

1967-68 **Engr.** ***Perf. 13***

C13	AP5	1d lil, org brn & emer	1.25	60
C14	AP5	2d brt bl, org brn & emer	3.00	1.50
C15	AP5	5d brt bl, grn & org brn ('68)	7.75	3.50

Plane over Casbah, Algiers — AP6

Designs: 3d, Plane over Oran. 4d, Plane over Rhumel Gorge.

1971-72 **Photo.** ***Perf. 12½***

C16	AP6	2d grysh blk & multi	1.90	1.00
C17	AP6	3d vio & blk ('72)	3.00	1.75
C18	AP6	4d blk & multi ('72)	4.00	2.25

Issue dates: 2d, June 12, 1971; 3d, 4d, Feb. 28, 1972.

Storks and Plane — AP7

1979, Mar. 24 **Photo.** ***Perf. 11½***

C19	AP7	10d multi	6.00	2.50

AIR POST SEMI-POSTAL STAMPS

No. C2 Surcharged in Carmine

✝ 18 Juin 1940 +10Fr.

1947, June 18 ***Perf. 13.***

CB1	AP1	10fr +10fr dp bl	60	60

Issued to commemorate the 7th anniversary of Gen. Charles de Gaulle's speech in London, June 18, 1940.

No. C1 Surcharged in Blue

✝ 18 JUIN 1940 +10 Fr.

1948, June 18

CB2	AP1	5fr +10fr red	60	60

Issued to commemorate the 8th anniversary of Gen. Charles de Gaulle's speech in London, June 18, 1940.

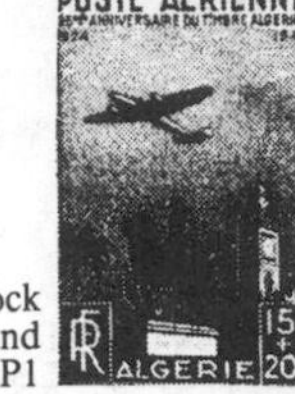

Monument, Clock Tower and Plane — SPAP1

1949, Nov. 10 **Engr.** **Unwmk.**

CB3	SPAP1	15fr +20fr dk brn	3.75	3.75

Issued to commemorate the 25th anniversary of Algeria's first postage stamps.

POSTAGE DUE STAMPS

D1

D2

Perf. 14x13½.

1926-27 **Typo.** **Unwmk.**

J1	D1	5c lt bl	5	5
J2	D1	10c dk brn	5	5
J3	D1	20c ol grn	26	22
J4	D1	25c car rose	52	52
J5	D1	30c rose red	26	22
J6	D1	45c bl grn	75	75
J7	D1	50c brn vio	5	5
J8	D1	60c grn ('27)	1.90	55
J9	D1	1fr red brn, *straw*	18	18
J10	D1	2fr lil rose ('27)	26	26
J11	D1	3fr dp bl ('27)	26	22
		Nos. J1-J11 (11)	4.54	3.07

1926-27

J12	D2	1c ol grn	5	5
J13	D2	10c violet	60	26
J14	D2	30c bister	52	30
J15	D2	60c dl red	35	30
J16	D2	1fr brt vio ('27)	14.00	2.50
J17	D2	2fr lt bl ('27)	10.00	1.00
		Nos. J12-J17 (6)	25.52	4.41

See note below France No. J51.

Stamps of 1926 Surcharged with New Values.

1927

J18	D1	60c on 20c ol grn	1.25	42
J19	D1	2fr on 45c bl grn	1.50	1.00
J20	D1	3fr on 25c car rose	70	42

Recouvrement Stamps of 1926 Surcharged

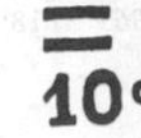

1927-32

J21	D2	10c on 30c bis ('32)	3.50	2.25
J22	D2	1fr on 1c ol grn	1.00	90
J23	D2	1fr on 60c dl red ('32)	16.00	35
J24	D2	2fr on 10c vio	9.50	9.50

Type of 1926, Without "R F"

1942 **Typo.** ***Perf. 14x13½***

J25	D1	30c dk red	6	6
J26	D1	2fr magenta	26	26

Type of 1926 Surcharged in Red

T
0.50

1944 *Perf. 14x13½.*
J27 A2 50c on 20c yel grn 18 14
a. Inverted surch. 5.25
b. Double surch. 14.00

No. J27 was issued precanceled only. See note after No. 32.

Type of 1926.

1944 **Litho.** ***Perf. 12.***
J28 D1 1.50fr brt rose lil 42 35
J29 D1 2fr grnsh bl 42 35
J30 D1 5fr rose car 42 30

Type of 1926

1947 **Typo.** ***Perf. 14x13½***
J32 D1 5fr green 90 70

France Nos. J80-J81 Overprinted in Carmine or Black

ALGÉRIE

1947
J33 D5 10c sep (C) 18 14
J34 D5 30c brt red vio 18 14

D3

1947-55 **Unwmk.** **Engr.** ***Perf. 14x13***
J35 D3 20c red 18 18
J36 D3 60c ultra 35 30
J37 D3 1fr dk org brn 5 5
J38 D3 1.50fr dl grn 60 55
J39 D3 2fr red 5 5
J40 D3 3fr violet 10 10
J41 D3 5fr ultra ('49) 18 14
J42 D3 6fr black 30 26
J43 D3 10fr lil rose 30 18
J44 D3 15fr ol grn ('55) 70 70
J45 D3 20fr brt grn 35 18
J46 D3 30fr red org ('55) 60 55
J47 D3 50fr ind ('51) 1.40 1.40
J48 D3 100fr brt bl ('53) 6.00 5.00
Nos. J35-J48 (14) 11.16 9.64

Independent State

France Nos. J93-J97 Overprinted "EA" in Black like Nos. 286-290

Perf. 14x13½

1962, July 2 **Typo.** **Unwmk.**

Handstamped Overprint

J49 D6 5c brt pink 3.50 2.50
J50 D6 10c red org 3.50 1.90
J51 D6 20c ol bis 3.50 1.90
J52 D6 50c dk grn 4.50 4.25
J53 D6 1fr dp grn 6.50 6.00
Nos. J49-J53 (5) 21.50 16.55

Typographed Overprint

J49a D6 5c brt pink 9.00 9.00
J50a D6 10c red org 9.00 9.00
J51a D6 20c ol bis 8.00 8.00
J52a D6 50c dk grn 21.00 21.00
J53a D6 1fr dp grn 37.50 37.50
Nos. J49A-J53A (5) 84.50 84.50

See note after No. 290.

Scales
D4

Grain
D5

1963, June 25 ***Perf. 14x13½***
J54 D4 5c car rose & blk 10 5
J55 D4 10c ol & car 22 8
J56 D4 20c ultra & blk 35 14
J57 D4 50c bis brn & grn 1.00 52
J58 D4 1fr lil & org 1.75 1.00
Nos. J54-J58 (5) 3.42 1.79

No. J58 Surcharged with New Value and 3 Bars

1968, Mar. 28 **Typo.** ***Perf. 14x13½***
J59 D4 60c on 1fr lil & org 60 42

1972, Oct. 21 **Litho.** ***Perf. 13½x14***
J60 D5 10c bister 6 6
J61 D5 20c dp brn 10 6
J62 D5 40c orange 30 12
J63 D5 50c dk vio bl 32 14
J64 D5 80c dk ol gray 55 20
J65 D5 1d green 65 38
J66 D5 2d blue 1.40 65
Nos. J60-J66 (7) 3.38 1.61

NEWSPAPER STAMPS

Nos. 1 and 33 Surcharged in Red

1
—
2
centime

1924-26 **Unwmk.** ***Perf. 14x13½***
P1 A16 ½c on 1c dk gray 5 5
a. Triple surcharge 87.50
P2 A1 ½c on 1c ol ('26) 14 14

ALLENSTEIN

LOCATION — In East Prussia
AREA — 4,457 sq. mi.
POP. — 540,000 (estimated 1920)
CAPITAL — Allenstein

Allenstein, a district of East Prussia, held a plebiscite in 1920 under the Versailles Treaty, voting to join Germany rather than Poland. Later that year, Allenstein became part of the German Republic.

100 Pfennig = 1 Mark

Stamps of Germany, 1906-20, Overprinted

PLÉBISCITE
OLSZTYN
ALLENSTEIN

Perf. 14, 14½, 14x14½, 14½x14

1920 **Wmk. 125**
1 A16 5pf green 25 25
2 A16 10pf carmine 25 25
3 A22 15pf dk vio 25 25
4 A22 15pf vio brn 8.00 7.00
5 A16 20pf bl vio 25 25
6 A16 30pf org & blk, *buff* 38 38
7 A16 40pf lake & blk 28 28
8 A16 50pf pur & blk, *buff* 30 30
9 A16 75pf grn & blk 30 28
10 A17 1m car rose 1.00 1.00
a. Double ovpt. 500.00 825.00
11 A17 1.25m green 85 85
a. Double ovpt. 650.00 1,400.
12 A17 1.50m yel brn 85 85
13 A21 2.50m lil rose 1.00 2.25
14 A19 3m blk vio 2.00 2.00
a. Double ovpt. 450.00 1,250.
b. Inverted overprint 500.00 825.00
Nos. 1-14 (14) 15.96 16.19

Overprinted

15 A16 5pf green 25 38
16 A16 10pf carmine 25 38
17 A22 15pf dk vio 25 25
18 A22 15pf vio brn 35.00 37.50
19 A16 20pf bl vio 25 25
20 A16 30pf org & blk, *buff* 38 38
21 A16 40pf lake & blk 38 38
22 A16 50pf pur & blk, *buff* 25 25
23 A16 75pf grn & blk 25 25
24 A17 1m car rose 85 85
a. Inverted overprint 750.00 1,000.
25 A17 1.25m green 85 85
26 A17 1.50m yel brn 85 85
27 A21 2.50m lil rose 1.25 2.25
28 A19 3m blk vio 1.50 1.50
a. Inverted overprint 400.00 750.00
b. Double ovpt. 375.00 600.00
Nos. 15-28 (14) 42.56 46.32

The 40pf carmine rose (Germany No. 124) exists with this oval overprint, but it is doubtful whether it was regularly issued. Price $400.

ANDORRA

LOCATION — On the southern slope of the Pyrenees Mountains between France and Spain.
GOVT. — Co-principality
AREA — 179 sq. mi.
POP. — 26,500 (1976)
CAPITAL — Andorre-la-Vieille

Andorra is subject to the joint control of France and the Spanish Bishop of Urgel and pays annual tribute to both. The country has no monetary unit of its own, the peseta and franc both being in general use.

100 Centimos = 1 Peseta
100 Centimes = 1 Franc

SPANISH ADMINISTRATION

Stamps of Spain, 1922-26, Overprinted in Red or Black

:-: CORREOS :-:

ANDORRA

Perf. 14, 13½x12½, 12½x11½.

1928 **Unwmk.**
1 A49 2c ol grn 30 20

Control Numbers on Back

2 A49 5c car rose (Bk) 40 30
3 A49 10c green 40 30
4 A49 15c sl bl 2.00 2.00
5 A49 20c violet 2.00 2.00
6 A49 25c rose red (Bk) 2.00 2.00
7 A49 30c blk brn 10.00 7.00
8 A49 40c dp bl 10.00 5.00
9 A49 50c org (Bk) 10.00 7.25
10 A49a 1p bl blk 12.00 10.00
11 A49a 4p lake (Bk) 85.00 70.00
12 A49a 10p brn (Bk) 140.00 100.00
Nos. 1-12 (12) 274.10 206.05

Counterfeit overprints exist.

La Vall
A1

St. Juan de Caselles
A2

St. Julia de Loria
A3

St. Coloma
A4

General Council — A5

1929 **Engr.** ***Perf. 14, 11½***
13 A1 2c ol grn 1.00 30
a. Perf. 11½ 6.00 60

Control Numbers on Back

14 A2 5c car lake 2.25 40
a. Perf. 11½ 6.50 1.75
15 A3 10c yel grn 2.25 1.50
a. Perf. 11½ 12.00 2.25
16 A4 15c sl grn 2.25 1.50
a. Perf. 11½ 40.00 27.50
17 A3 20c violet 2.25 1.50
a. Perf. 11½ 12.00 6.75
18 A4 25c car rose 5.50 2.25
a. Perf. 11½ 12.00 6.75
19 A1 30c ol brn 100.00 65.00
a. Perf. 11½ 100.00 75.00
20 A2 40c dk bl 4.50 1.00
a. Perf. 11½ 20.00 15.00
21 A3 50c dp org 4.50 1.50
22 A5 1p slate 9.50 5.00
a. Perf. 11½ 50.00 27.50
b. Perf. 11½, control # omitted 2,750.
23 A5 4p dp rose 62.50 35.00
24 A5 10p bis brn 70.00 50.00
Nos. 13-24 (12) 266.50 164.95

Nos. 13-24, 26, 28, 32 exist imperforate.

Without Control Numbers.

1936-43 ***Perf. 11½x11***
25 A1 2c red brn ('37) 1.65 70
26 A2 5c dk brn 1.65 70
27 A3 10c bl grn 8.25 1.50
a. 10c yel grn 85.00 24.00
28 A4 15c grn ('37) 5.00 1.50
29 A3 20c violet 5.00 1.50
30 A4 25c dp rose ('37) 1.90 1.50
31 A1 30c carmine 3.50 1.50
31A A2 40c dk bl 550.00 30.00
32 A1 45c rose red ('37) 1.50 70
33 A3 50c dp org 7.00 2.75
34 A1 60c dp bl ('37) 4.00 1.50
35 A5 4p dp rose ('43) 26.00 24.00
36 A5 10p bis brn ('43) 37.50 24.00
Nos. 25-36 (13) 652.95 91.85

Edelweiss
A6

Provost
A7

Coat of Arms — A8

Plaza of Ordino — A9

Chapel of Meritxell
A10

Map
A11

1948-53 **Unwmk.** **Photo.** ***Perf. 12½***
37 A6 2c dk ol grn ('51) 50 30
38 A6 5c dp org ('53) 50 30
39 A6 10c dp bl ('53) 50 30

Engr. ***Perf. 9½x10***
40 A7 20c brn vio 12.50 1.00
41 A7 25c org, perf. 12½ ('53) 7.50 65
42 A8 30c dk sl grn 12.50 1.70
43 A9 50c dp grn 15.00 2.25
44 A10 75c dk bl 20.00 2.25
45 A9 90c dp car rose 10.00 2.25
46 A10 1p brt org ver 15.00 2.25
47 A8 1.35p dk bl vio 10.00 2.50

Perf. 10.
48 A11 4p ultra ('53) 15.00 5.00
49 A11 10p dk vio brn ('51) 30.00 11.00
Nos. 37-49 (13) 149.00 31.75

Bridge of St. Anthony — A12

Madonna of Meritxell, 8th Century — A13

Designs: 70c, Aynos pasture. 1p, View of Canillo. 2p, St. Coloma. 2.50p, Arms of Andorra. 3p, Old Andorra (horiz.). 5p, View of Ordino (horiz.).

1963-64 Unwmk. Engr. *Perf. 13*

50 A12 25c dk gray & sep 25 6
51 A12 70c dk sl grn & brn blk 25 6
52 A12 1p sl & dl pur 40 6
53 A12 2p vio & dl pur 40 6
54 A12 2.50p rose cl ('64) 1.00 60
55 A12 3p blk & grnsh gray ('64) 1.75 60
56 A12 5p dk brn & choc ('64) 2.00 1.10
57 A13 6p sep & car ('64) 3.25 1.10
Nos. 50-57 (8) 9.30 3.64

Narcissus — A14

Encamp Valley — A15

Flowers: 1p, Pinks. 5p, Jonquils. 10p, Hellebore.

1966, June 10 Engr. *Perf. 13*

58 A14 50c sl bl & vio bl 10 10
59 A14 1p brn & cl 25 10
60 A14 5p brt grn & sl bl 1.50 60
61 A14 10p dk vio & blk 3.25 75

Europa Issue 1972

Common Design Type

1972, May 2 Photo. *Perf. 13*

Size: 25½x38mm.

62 CD15 8p dk grn & multi 225.00 150.00

1972, July 4 Photo. *Perf. 13*

Designs: 1.50p, Massana (village). 2p, Skiing on De La Casa Pass. 5p, Pessons Lake (horiz.).

63 A15 1p multi 25 10
64 A15 1.50p multi 80 45
65 A15 2p multi 1.90 45
66 A15 5p multi 2.50 80

Tourist publicity.

Butterfly Stroke A16

Design: 2p, Volleyball (vert.).

1972, Oct. Photo. *Perf. 13*

67 A16 2p lt bl & multi 60 30
68 A16 5p multi 70 40

20th Olympic Games, Munich, Aug. 26-Sept. 11.

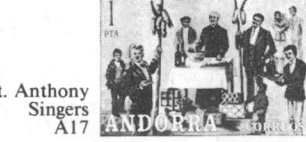

St. Anthony Singers A17

1972, Dec. 5 Photo. *Perf. 13*

69 A17 1p *shown* 20 6
70 A17 1.50p *Les Caramelles (boys' choir)* 20 6
71 A17 2p *Nativity scene* 15 10
72 A17 5p *Man holding giant cigar* (vert.) 90 15
73 A17 8p *Hermit of Meritxell* (vert.) 1.10 45
74 A17 15p *Marratxa dancers* 2.75 65
Nos. 69-74 (5) 5.10 1.41

Andorran customs. No. 71 is for Christmas 1972.

Common Design Types pictured in section at front of book.

Europa Issue 1973

Common Design Type and

Symbol of Unity A18

1973, Apr. 30 Photo. *Perf. 13*

75 A18 2p ultra, red & blk 40 20

Size: 37x25mm.

76 CD16 8p tan, red & blk 1.65 55

Nativity — A19

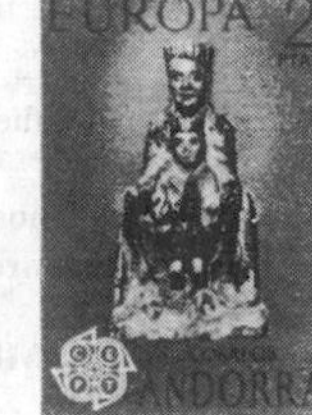

Virgin of Ordino — A20

Design: 5p, Adoration of the Kings. Designs are from altar panels of Meritxell Parish Church.

1973, Dec. 14 Photo. *Perf. 13*

77 A19 2p multi 25 20
78 A19 5p multi 1.00 40

Christmas 1973.

Europa Issue 1974

1974, Apr. 29 Photo. *Perf. 13*

Design: 8p, Les Banyes Cross.

79 A20 2p multi 1.25 30
80 A20 8p sl & brt bl 3.75 1.00

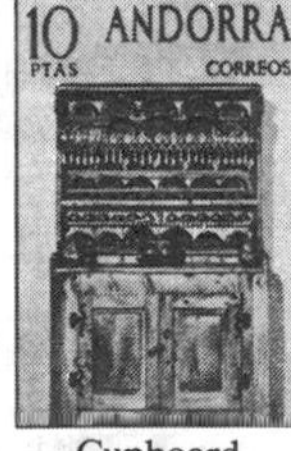

Cupboard A21

Crowns of Virgin and Child of Roser A22

1974, July 30 Photo. *Perf. 13*

81 A21 10p multi 1.65 60
82 A22 25p dk red & multi 4.00 1.50

UPU Monument, Bern — A23

1974, Oct. Photo. *Perf. 13*

83 A23 15p multi 2.00 75

Centenary of Universal Postal Union.

Andorra, Spanish Administration, stamps can be mounted in Scott's annual Spain and Spanish Andorra Supplement.

Nativity A24

Design: 5p, Adoration of the Kings.

1974, Dec. 4 Photo. *Perf. 13*

84 A24 2p multi 60 20
85 A24 5p multi 2.25 45

Christmas 1974.

Mail Delivery, Andorra, 19th Century — A25

12th Century Painting, Ordino Church — A26

1975, Apr. 4 Photo. *Perf. 13*

86 A25 3p multi 45 18

Espana 75 International Philatelic Exhibition, Madrid, Apr. 4-13.

1975, Apr. 28 Photo. *Perf. 13*

Design: 12p, Christ in Glory, 12th century Romanesque painting, Ordino church.

87 A26 3p multi 1.75 40
88 A26 12p multi 3.25 65

Urgel Cathedral and Document — A27

1975, Oct. 4 Photo. *Perf. 13*

89 A27 7p multi 2.25 1.10

Millennium of consecration of Urgel Cathedral, and Literary Festival 1975.

Nativity, Ordino A28

Design: 7p, Adoration of the Kings, Ordino.

1975, Dec. 3 Photo. *Perf. 13*

90 A28 3p multi 45 20
91 A28 7p multi 65 35

Christmas 1975.

Caldron and CEPT Emblem A29

Slalom and Montreal Olympic Emblem A30

Europa Issue 1976

Design: 12p, Chest and CEPT emblem (horiz.).

1976, May 3 Photo. *Perf. 13*

92 A29 3p bis & multi 50 15
93 A29 12p yel & multi 1.50 40

1976, July 9 Photo. *Perf. 13*

Design: 15p, One-man canoe and Montreal Olympic emblem (horiz.).

94 A30 7p multi 35 15
95 A30 15p multi 85 40

21st Olympic Games, Montreal, Canada, July 17-Aug. 1.

Nativity A31

Design: 25p, Adoration of the Kings. Wall paintings in La Massana Church.

1976, Dec. 7 Photo. *Perf. 13*

96 A31 3p multi 25 10
97 A31 25p multi 1.00 45

Christmas 1976.

Europa Issue 1977

View of Ansalonge — A32

Design: 12p, Xuclar, valley and mountains.

1977, May 2 Litho. *Perf. 13*

98 A32 3p multi 25 15
99 A32 12p multi 80 35

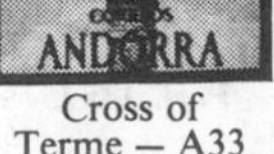

Cross of Terme — A33

Map of Post Offices — A34

Design: 12p, Church of St. Miguel d'Engolasters.

1977, Dec. 2 Photo. *Perf. 13x12½*

100 A33 3p multi 15 30
101 A33 12p multi 1.10 65

Christmas 1977.

Souvenir Sheet

Designs: 10p, Mail delivery. 20p, Post Office, 1928. 25p, Andorran coat of arms.

1978, Mar. 31 Photo. *Perf. 13x13½*

102	Sheet of 4	1.00 1.00
a.	A34 5p multi	10 6
b.	A34 10p multi	20 15
c.	A34 20p multi	30 30
d.	A34 25p multi	35 35

Spanish postal service in Andorra, 50th anniversary. No. 102 has black marginal inscription. Size: 105x149mm.

Europa Issue 1978

La Vall — A35

Design: 12p, St. Juan de Caselles.

1978, May 2 *Perf. 13*

103 A35 5p multi 25 10
104 A35 12p multi 60 30

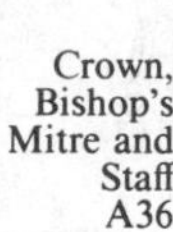

Crown, Bishop's Mitre and Staff A36

1978, Sept. 24 Photo. *Perf. 13*

105 A36 5p brn, car & yel 65 20

700th anniversary of the signing of treaty establishing Co-Principality of Andorra.

Holy Family — A37

Design: 25p, Adoration of the Kings. Both designs after frescoes in the Church of St. Mary d'Encamp.

1978, Dec. 5 Photo. *Perf. 13*

106 A37 5p multi 15 10
107 A37 25p multi 65 40

Christmas 1978.

Young Woman — A38

Designs: 5p, Young man. 12p, Bridegroom and bride riding mule.

1978, Feb. 14 Photo. *Perf. 13*

108 A38 3p multi 10 6
109 A38 5p multi 15 6
110 A38 12p multi 35 20

> The Catalogue editors cannot undertake to appraise, identify or judge the genuineness or condition of stamps.

Europa Issue 1979

Old Mail Truck A39

Design: 12p, Stampless covers of 1846 and 1854.

1979, Apr. 30 Engr. *Perf. 13*

111 A39 5p yel grn & dk bl 30 10
112 A39 12p dk red & vio 70 30

Children Holding Hands A40

1979, Oct. 18 Photo. *Perf. 13*

113 A40 19p multi 70 35

International Year of the Child.

St. Coloma's Church — A41

Design: 25p, Agnus Dei roundel, St. Coloma's Church.

1979, Nov. 28 Photo. *Perf. 13½*

114 A41 8p multi 25 8
115 A41 25p multi 55 35

Christmas 1979.

Bishop Pere d'Arg A42

Bishops of Urgel: 5p, Josep Caixal. 13p, Joan Benlloch.

1979, Dec. 27 Engr.

116 A42 1p dk bl & brn 5 5
117 A42 5p rose lake & pur 10 6
118 A42 13p brn & dk grn 25 15

Europa Issue 1980

Antoni Fiter I. Rosell, Magistrate — A43

Design: 19p, Francesc Cairat I. Freixes, magistrate.

1980, Apr Photo. *Perf. 13x13½*

119 A43 8p bis, blk & brn 12 10
120 A43 19p it grn & blk 35 18

Boxing, Moscow '80 Emblem A44

1980 Photo. *Perf. 13½x13*

121 A44 5p *Downhill skiing* 10 6
122 A44 8p *shown* 12 10
123 A44 50p *Target shooting* 70 40

12th Winter Olympic Games, Lake Placid, N.Y., Feb. 12-24 (5p); 22nd Summer Olympic Games, Moscow, July 19-Aug. 3.

Nativity A45

1980 Litho. *Perf. 13*

124 A45 10p *Nativity,* vert. 15 10
125 A45 22p *shown* 40 20

Christmas 1980.

Europa Issue 1981

Children Dancing at Santa Anna Feast A46

Design: 30p, Going to church on Aplec de la Verge de Canolich Day.

1981, May 7 Photo. *Perf. 13*

126 A46 12p multi 20 10
127 A46 30p multi 45 25

50th Anniv. of Police Force A47

1981, July 2 Photo. *Perf. 13½x13*

128 A47 30p multi 45 20

Intl. Year of the Disabled A48

1981, Oct. 8 Photo. *Perf. 13½*

129 A48 50p multi 75 30

Christmas 1981 — A49

Designs: Encamp Church retable.

1981, Dec. 3 Photo. *Perf. 13½*

130 A49 12p Nativity 18 10
131 A49 30p Adoration 45 20

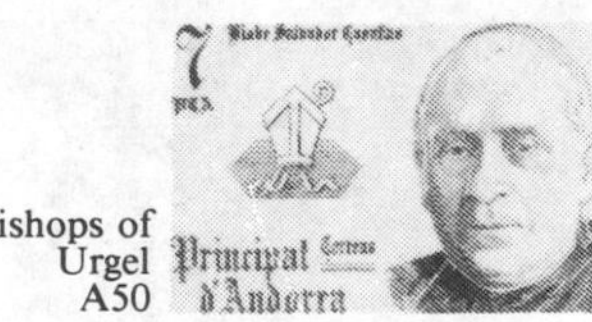

Bishops of Urgel A50

1981, Dec. 12 Engr. *Perf. 13½*

132 A50 7p Salvador Casanas 10 6
133 A50 20p Josep de Boltas 30 12

Natl. Arms — A51

1982, Feb. 17 Photo. *Perf. 13x13½*

134 A51 1p brt pink 5 5
135 A51 3p bis brn 10 6
136 A51 7p red org 10 10
137 A51 12p lake 18 10
138 A51 15p ultra 25 10
139 A51 20p bl grn 30 10
140 A51 30p crim rose 45 15

1982, July Engr. *Perf. 13x12½*
Size: 25½x30½mm

141 A51 50p dk grn 75 25
142 A51 100p dk bl 1.50 50
Nos. 134-142 (9) 3.68 1.41

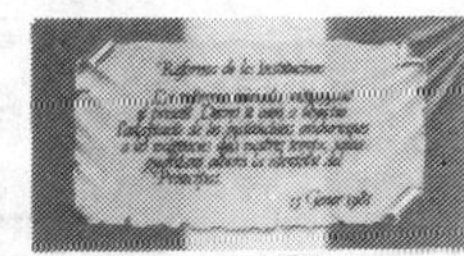

Europa 1982 — A52

1982, May 12 Photo. *Perf. 13*

143 A52 14p New Reforms, 1866, vert. 20 10
144 A52 33p Reform of Institutions, 1981 50 25

1982 World Cup — A53

Designs: Various soccer players.

1982, June 13 Photo. *Perf. 13x13½*

145 A53 14p multi 75 75
146 A53 33p multi 1.50 1.50

Centenary of Permanent Spanish and French Delegations — A54

Anniversaries: 14p, 50th anniv. of Andorran stamps. 23p, St. Francis of Assisi (1182-1226). 33p, Anyos Pro-Vicarial District membership centenary (Relacio sobre la Vall de Andorra titlepage).

1982, Sept. 7 Engr. *Perf. 13*

147 A54 9p dk bl & brn 15 10
148 A54 14p blk & grn 55 25
149 A54 23p dk bl & brn 35 15
150 A54 33p blk & ol grn 1.00 50

Christmas 1982 — A55

Designs: 14p, Madonna and Child, Andorra la Vella Church (vert.). 33p, El Tio de Nadal (children in traditional costumes striking hollow tree).

Perf. 13x13½, 13½x13

1982, Dec. 9 **Photo.**
151 A55 14p multi 20 10
152 A55 33p multi 50 25

Europa 1983 A56

1983, June 7 **Photo.** ***Perf. 13***
153 A56 16p La Cortinada Church, architect, 12th cent. 25
154 A56 38p Water mill, 16th cent. 60 30

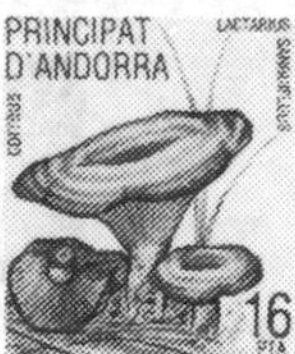

Local Mushrooms — A57

1983, July 20 **Photo.** ***Perf. 13x12½***
155 A57 16p Lactarius sanguifluus 25 8

See Nos. 165, 169, 172.

Universal Suffrage, 50th Anniv. A58

Photogravure and Engraved

1983, Sept. 6 ***Perf. 13***
156 A58 10p multi 15 8

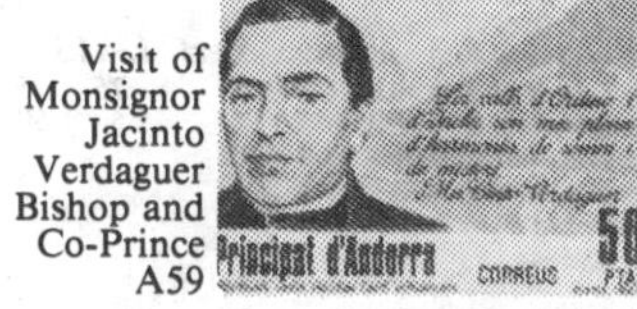

Visit of Monsignor Jacinto Verdaguer Bishop and Co-Prince A59

Photogravure and Engraved

1983, Sept. 6 ***Perf. 13***
157 A59 50p multi 75 35

Christmas 1983 — A60

Unidentified saint, Romanesque fresco, Church of San Cerni de Nagol.

1983, Nov. 24 **Photo.** ***Perf. 13½***
158 A60 16p multi 25 8

Joan J. Laguarda Fenollera, Bishop of Urgel, 1902-06 A61

1983, Dec. 7 **Engr.** ***Perf. 13***
159 A61 26p red & brn 40 15

1984 Winter Olympics A62

1984, Feb. 17 **Litho.** ***Perf. 13½x14***
160 A62 16p Ski jumping 25 8

ESPANA '84 — A63

1984, Apr. 27 **Photo.** ***Perf. 13***
161 A63 26p Emblems 40 15

Europa (1959-84) A64

1984, May 5 **Engr.**
162 A64 16p brown 25 8
163 A64 38p blue 60 30

1984 Summer Olympics A65

1984, Aug. 9 **Litho.** ***Perf. 13½x14***
164 A65 40p Running 60 30

Mushroom Type of 1983

1984, Sept. 27 **Photo.** ***Perf. 13x12½***
165 A57 11p Morchella esculenta *1.00* 25

Christmas 1984 A66

1984, Dec. 6 **Photo.** ***Perf. 13½***
166 A66 17p Nativity carving 25 10

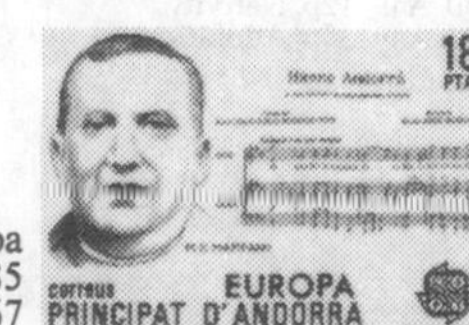

Europa 1985 A67

Designs: 18p, Mossen Enric Arfany, composer, natl. hymn score. 45p, Musician Playing Viol, Romanesque fresco detail, La Cortinada Church, vert.

1985, May 3 **Engr.** ***Perf. 13½***
167 A67 18p dk vio, grn & choc 30 10
168 A67 45p grn & choc 70 20

Mushroom Type of 1983

Perf. 13½x12½

1985, Sept. 19 **Photo.**
169 A57 30p Gyromitra esculenta 45 15

Pal Village — A68

1985, Nov. 7 **Engr.** ***Perf. 13½***
170 A68 17p brt ultra & dk bl 25 10

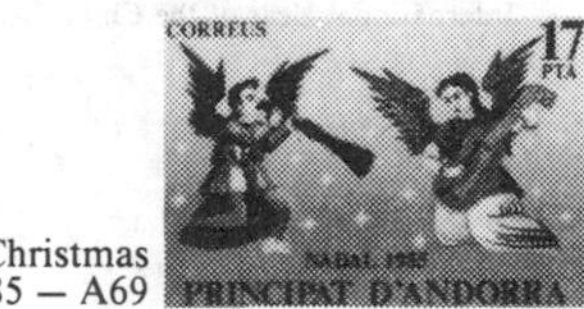

Christmas 1985 — A69

Fresco: Angels Playing Trumpet and Psaltery, St. Bartholomew Chapel.

1985, Dec. 11 **Photo.** ***Perf. 13½x13***
171 A69 17p multi 25 10

Mushroom Type of 1983

Perf. 13½x12½

1986, Apr. 10 **Photo.**
172 A57 30p Marasmius oreades 45 15

Europa 1986 — A70

1986, May 5 **Engr.** ***Perf. 13***
173 A70 17p Water 25 10
174 A70 45p Soil and air 70 20

Co-Princes of Andorra A71

Design: Justi Guitart, Bishop of Urgel, 1920-1940, and miter.

1986, Sept. 11 **Engr.** ***Perf. 13½***
175 A71 35p yel brn & int blue 60 30

Santa Roma de Les Bons Church Bell — A72

1986, Dec. 11 **Litho.** ***Perf. 14***
176 A72 19p multi 30 15

Christmas.

Contemporary Natl. Coat of Arms — A73

1987, Mar. 27 **Photo.** ***Perf. 14***
177 A73 48p multi 78 40

Visit of the co-princes: the Bishop of Urgel and president of France, September 26, 1986.

Europa 1987 A74

Modern architecture: 19p, Meritxell Sanctuary interior. 48p, Sanctuary exterior, vert.

1987, May 15 **Engr.** ***Perf. 14x13½***
178 A74 19p dark blue & brn 30 15
179 A74 48p dark blue & brn 78 40

Souvenir Sheet

1992 Summer Olympics, Barcelona A75

Designs: 20p, House of the Valleys. 50p, Bell tower, Chapel of the Archangel Michael, and torch-bearer.

1987, July 20 **Photo.** ***Perf. 14***
180 Sheet of 2 3.00 3.00
a. A75 20p multi 85 85
b. A75 50p multi 2.15 2.15

No. 180 has black inscribed margin containing control number. Size: 123x86mm.

Local Muschrooms — A76

1987, Sept. 11 ***Perf. 13½x12½***
181 A76 100p Boletus edulis 1.70 85

Christmas A77

Design: Detail from a Catalan manuscript, De Nativitat, by R. Llull.

1987, Nov. 18 Litho. *Perf. 14*

No.	Type	Description	Unused	Used
182	A77	20p multi	38	38

AIR POST STAMPS

AP1

Perf. 11.

1951, June 27 Unwmk. Engr.

No.	Type	Description	Unused	Used
C1	AP1	1p dk vio brn	30.00	3.50

Jaime Sansa Nequi, Episcopal Church Official — AP2

Lithographed and Engraved

1983, Oct. 20 *Perf. 13*

No.	Type	Description	Unused	Used
C2	AP2	20p brn & bis brn	30	20

Pyrenees Art Center — AP3

1984, Oct. 25 Photo. *Perf. 13*

No.	Type	Description	Unused	Used
C3	AP3	20p multi	30	20

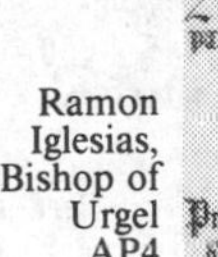

Ramon Iglesias, Bishop of Urgel AP4

1985, June 13 Engr. *Perf. 13½*

No.	Type	Description	Unused	Used
C4	AP4	20p org brn & yel brn	30	15

SPECIAL DELIVERY STAMPS

Special Delivery Stamp of Spain, 1905 Overprinted

CORREOS

ANDORRA

1982 Unwmk. *Perf. 14.*

Without Control Number on Back

No.	Type	Description	Unused	Used
E1	SD1	20c red	62.50	42.50

With Control Number on Back

No.	Type	Description	Unused	Used
E2	SD1	20c pale red	32.50	17.50

Eagle over Mountain Pass — SD2

Arms and Squirrel — SD3

1929 *Perf. 14*

With Control Number on Back

No.	Type	Description	Unused	Used
E3	SD2	20c scarlet	19.00	8.00
a.		Perf. 11½	450.00	

1937 *Perf. 11½x11.*

Without Control Number on Back

No.	Type	Description	Unused	Used
E4	SD2	20c red	6.75	4.00

1949 Unwmk. Engr. *Perf. 10x9½*

No.	Type	Description	Unused	Used
E5	SD3	25c red	7.00	4.00

FRENCH ADMINISTRATION

Stamps and Types of France, 1900-1929, Overprinted **ANDORRE**

1931 Unwmk. *Perf. 14x13½*

No.	Type	Description	Unused	Used
1	A16	1c gray	50	50
a.		Double ovpt.	1,000.	1,000.
2	A16	2c red brn	60	60
3	A16	3c orange	60	60
4	A16	5c green	95	95
5	A16	10c lilac	1.40	1.40
6	A22	15c red brn	2.75	2.75
7	A22	20c red vio	4.00	4.00
8	A22	25c yel brn	4.00	4.00
9	A22	30c green	4.00	4.00
10	A22	40c ultra	6.75	6.75
11	A20	45c lt vio	7.50	7.50
12	A20	50c vermilion	6.25	6.25
13	A20	65c gray grn	9.50	9.50
14	A20	75c rose lil	13.00	13.00
15	A22	90c red	17.00	17.00
16	A20	1fr dl bl	18.00	18.00
17	A22	1.50fr lt bl	24.00	24.00

Overprinted **ANDORRE**

No.	Type	Description	Unused	Used
18	A18	2fr org & pale bl	17.00	17.00
19	A18	3fr brt vio & rose	60.00	60.00
20	A18	5fr dk bl & buff	95.00	95.00
21	A18	10fr grn & red	200.00	200.00
22	A18	20fr mag & grn	250.00	250.00
		Nos. 1-22 (22)	742.80	742.80

See No. P1 for ½c on 1c gray.

Nos. 9, 15 and 17 were not issued in France without overprint.

Chapel of Meritxell A50

Bridge of St. Anthony A51

St. Miguel d'Engolasters A52

Gorge of St. Julia A53

Old Andorra A54

1932-43 Engr. *Perf. 13*

No.	Type	Description	Unused	Used
23	A50	1c gray blk	45	38
24	A50	2c violet	65	65
25	A50	3c brown	45	35
26	A50	5c bl grn	65	50
27	A51	10c dl lil	1.00	85
28	A50	15c dp red	1.40	1.40
29	A51	20c lt rose	9.50	7.00
30	A52	25c brown	3.50	3.50
31	A51	25c brn car ('37)	6.75	9.50
32	A51	30c emerald	2.75	2.50
33	A51	40c ultra	7.50	6.50
34	A51	40c brn blk ('39)	1.00	90
35	A51	45c lt red	9.00	7.00
36	A51	45c bl grn ('39)	4.25	3.75
37	A52	50c lil rose	9.50	7.00
38	A51	50c lt vio ('39)	4.25	3.75
38A	A51	50c grn ('40)	2.00	2.00
39	A51	55c lt vio ('38)	14.00	8.50
40	A51	60c yel brn ('38)	90	75
41	A52	65c yel grn	40.00	37.50
42	A51	65c bl ('38)	10.00	8.00
43	A51	70c red ('39)	2.00	1.50
44	A52	75c violet	4.75	4.00
45	A51	75c ultra ('39)	3.75	3.25
46	A51	80c grn ('38)	19.00	14.00
46A	A53	80c bl grn ('40)	40	45
47	A53	90c dp rose	4.75	3.00
48	A53	90c dk grn ('39)	3.25	3.25
49	A53	1fr bl grn	14.00	8.50
50	A53	1fr scar ('38)	19.00	14.00
51	A53	1fr dp ultra ('39)	38	38
51A	A53	1.20fr brt vio ('42)	38	35
52	A50	1.25fr rose car ('33)	35.00	21.00
52A	A50	1.25fr rose ('38)	4.25	2.00
52B	A53	1.30fr sep ('40)	38	35
53	A54	1.50fr ultra	12.50	11.00
53A	A53	1.50fr crim ('40)	38	35
54	A53	1.75fr vio ('33)	100.00	75.00
55	A53	1.75fr dk bl ('38)	35.00	25.00
56	A53	2fr red vio	5.50	5.00
56A	A50	2fr rose red ('40)	1.40	1.00
56B	A50	2fr dk bl grn ('42)	40	30
57	A50	2.15fr dk vio ('38)	42.50	32.50
58	A50	2.25fr ultra ('39)	6.00	4.50
58A	A50	2.40fr red ('42)	38	30
59	A50	2.50fr gray blk ('39)	6.00	4.50
59A	A50	2.50fr dp ultra ('40)	2.00	1.90
60	A53	3fr org brn	5.50	5.00
60A	A50	3fr red brn ('40)	45	38
60B	A50	4fr sl bl ('42)	45	38
60C	A50	4.50fr dp vio ('42)	1.25	1.25
61	A54	5fr brown	60	45
62	A54	10fr violet	70	60
62B	A54	15fr dp ultra ('42)	75	55
63	A54	20fr rose lake	75	60
63A	A51	50fr turq bl ('43)	1.50	75
		Nos. 23-63A (56)	464.80	359.62

A 20c ultra exists. Price $12,500.

No. 37 Surcharged with Bars and New Value in Black.

1935

No.	Type	Description	Unused	Used
64	A52	20c on 50c lil rose	15.00	12.00
a.		Double surcharge	950.00	

Coat of Arms A55 A56

1936-42 *Perf. 14x13*

No.	Type	Description	Unused	Used
65	A55	1c blk ('37)	12	12
66	A55	2c blue	12	12
67	A55	3c brown	12	12
68	A55	5c rose lil	12	12
69	A55	10c ultra ('37)	12	12
70	A55	15c red vio	80	80
71	A55	20c emer ('37)	12	12
72	A55	30c cop red ('38)	38	38
72A	A55	30c blk brn ('42)	22	22
73	A55	35c Prus grn ('38)	40.00	40.00
74	A55	40c cop red ('42)	22	22
75	A55	50c Prus grn ('42)	22	22
76	A55	60c turq bl ('42)	22	22
77	A55	70c vio ('42)	22	22
		Nos. 65-77 (14)	43.00	43.00

1944

No.	Type	Description	Unused	Used
78	A56	10c violet	5	5
79	A56	30c dp mag	5	5
80	A56	40c dl bl	15	15
81	A56	50c org red	6	6
82	A56	60c black	6	6
83	A56	70c brt red vio	6	6
84	A56	80c bl grn	15	15
		Nos. 78-84 (7)	58	58

See also No. 114.

St. Jean de Caselles A57

La Maison des Vallees A58

Old Andorra A59

Provost A60

1944-47 *Perf. 13*

No.	Type	Description	Unused	Used
85	A57	1fr brn vio	18	15
86	A57	1.20fr blue	15	15
87	A57	1.50fr red	18	15
88	A57	2fr dk bl grn	15	15
89	A58	2.40fr rose red	22	18
90	A58	2.50fr rose red ('46)	1.25	50
91	A58	3fr sepia	15	15
92	A58	4fr ultra	18	15
93	A59	4.50fr brn blk	18	15
94	A58	4.50fr dk bl grn ('47)	4.00	3.50
95	A59	5fr ultra	22	18
96	A59	5fr Prus grn ('46)	40	30
97	A59	6fr rose car ('45)	30	15
98	A59	10fr Prus grn	15	12
99	A59	10fr ultra ('46)	18	12
100	A60	15fr rose lil	38	25
101	A60	20fr dp bl	55	45
102	A60	25fr lt rose red ('46)	1.40	1.10
103	A60	40fr dk grn ('46)	1.40	1.10
104	A60	50fr sepia	1.40	1.10
		Nos. 85-104 (20)	13.02	10.10

1948-49

No.	Type	Description	Unused	Used
105	A58	4fr lt bl grn	70	70
106	A59	6fr vio brn	35	35
107	A59	8fr indigo	1.00	1.00
108	A59	12fr brt red	75	75
109	A59	12fr bl grn ('49)	90	75
110	A59	15fr crim ('49)	45	45
111	A60	18fr dp bl	2.50	1.50
112	A60	20fr dk vio	2.00	1.65
113	A60	25fr ultra ('49)	1.40	1.10
		Nos. 105-113 (9)	10.05	8.25

1949-51 *Perf. 14x13, 13*

No.	Type	Description	Unused	Used
114	A56	1fr dp bl	60	55
115	A57	3fr red ('51)	4.50	3.25
116	A57	4fr sepia	2.00	2.00
117	A58	5fr emerald	2.25	1.65
118	A58	5fr pur ('51)	2.25	1.40
119	A58	6fr bl grn ('51)	2.00	1.65
120	A58	8fr brown	60	60
121	A59	15fr blk brn ('51)	2.00	1.65
122	A59	18fr rose red ('51)	11.00	7.25
123	A60	30fr ultra ('51)	17.50	7.50
		Nos. 114-123 (10)	44.70	27.50

Les Escaldres Spa — A61

St. Coloma Belfry A62

Designs: 15fr, 18fr, 20fr, 25fr, Gothic cross. 30fr, 35fr, 40fr, 50fr, 65fr, 70fr, 75fr, Village of Les Bons.

1955-58 Unwmk. Engr. *Perf. 13*

No.	Type	Description	Unused	Used
124	A61	1fr dk gray bl	18	15
125	A61	2fr dp grn	18	15
126	A61	3fr red	18	15
127	A61	5fr chocolate	18	15
128	A62	6fr dk bl grn	45	38
129	A62	8fr rose brn	45	45
130	A62	10fr brt vio	70	55
131	A62	12fr indigo	75	60
132	A61	15fr red	1.00	85
133	A61	18fr bl grn	1.00	85
134	A61	20fr dp pur	1.65	1.50
135	A61	25fr sepia	2.00	1.50
136	A62	30fr dp bl	24.00	16.00
137	A62	35fr Prus bl ('57)	9.00	6.75
138	A62	40fr dk grn	25.00	18.00
139	A62	50fr cerise	3.00	2.25
140	A62	65fr pur ('58)	8.50	5.75
141	A62	70fr chnt ('57)	6.00	5.75
142	A62	75fr vio bl	40.00	32.50
		Nos. 124-142 (19)	124.22	94.28

Coat of Arms — A63

Gothic Cross, Meritxell A64

Designs: 65c, 85c, 1fr, Pond of Engolasters. 30c, 45c, 50c, as 25c.

1961, June 19 Typo. *Perf. 14x13*

No.	Type	Description	Unused	Used
143	A63	5c brt grn & blk	5	5
144	A63	10c red, pink & blk	5	5
145	A63	15c bl & blk	6	6
146	A63	20c yel & brn	10	10

Engr. *Perf. 13*

No.	Type	Description	Unused	Used
147	A64	25c vio, bl & grn	22	22
148	A64	30c mar, ol grn & brn	38	38
149	A64	45c ind, bl & grn	13.00	8.00
150	A64	50c pur, lt brn & ol grn	1.40	1.40
151	A64	65c bl, ol & brn	16.00	12.00
152	A64	85c rose lil, vio bl & brn	16.00	12.00
153	A64	1fr grnsh bl, ind & brn	1.25	90
		Nos. 143-153 (11)	48.51	35.16

See also Nos. 161-166A.

Imperforates

Most stamps of Andorra, French Administration, from 1961 onward exist imperforate in issued and trial colors, and also in small presentation sheets in issued colors.

Telstar and Globe Showing Andover and Pleumeur-Bodou — A65

1962, Sept. 29 Engr.

No.	Type	Description	Unused	Used
154	A65	50c ultra & pur	1.90	1.90

Issued to commemorate the first television connection of the United States and Europe through the Telstar satellite, July 11-12.

"La Sardane" A66

Charlemagne Crossing Andorra — A67

Design: 1fr, Louis le Debonnaire giving founding charter.

1963, June 22 Unwmk. *Perf. 13*

No.	Type	Description	Unused	Used
155	A66	20c lil rose, cl & ol grn	4.50	4.50
156	A67	50c sl grn & dk car rose	7.50	7.50
157	A67	1fr red brn, ultra & dk grn	12.00	12.00

Old Andorra Church and Champs-Elysees Palace — A68

1964, Jan. 20 Engr.

No.	Type	Description	Unused	Used
158	A68	25c blk, grn & vio brn	1.40	90

Issued to publicize "PHILATEC," International Philatelic and Postal Techniques Exhibition, Paris, June 5-21, 1964.

Bishop of Urgel and Seigneur of Caboet Confirming Co-Principality, 1288 — A69

Design: 60c, Napoleon re-establishing Co-principality, 1806.

1964, Apr. 25 Engr. *Perf. 13*

No.	Type	Description	Unused	Used
159	A69	60c dk brn, red brn & sl grn	16.00	16.00
160	A69	1fr brt bl, org brn & blk	16.00	16.00

Arms Type of 1961

1964, May 16 Typo. *Perf. 14x13*

No.	Type	Description	Unused	Used
161	A63	1c dk bl & gray	10	10
162	A63	2c blk & org	5	5
163	A63	12c pur, emer & yel	30	30
164	A63	18c blk, lil & pink	30	30

Scenic Type of 1961

Designs: 40c, 45c, Gothic Cross, Meritxell. 60c, 90c, Pond of Engolasters.

1965-71 Engr. *Perf. 13*

No.	Type	Description	Unused	Used
165	A64	40c dk brn, org brn & sl grn	50	50
165A	A64	45c vio bl, ol bis & sl ('70)	1.00	75
166	A64	60c org brn & dk brn	60	60
166A	A64	90c ultra, bl grn & bis ('71)	50	50

Syncom Satellite over Pleumeur-Bodou Station — A70

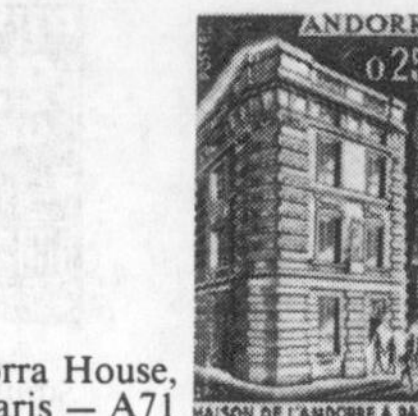

Andorra House, Paris — A71

1965, May 17 Unwmk.

No.	Type	Description	Unused	Used
167	A70	60c dp car, lil & bl	5.25	4.50

Issued to commemorate the centenary of the International Telecommunication Union.

1965, June 5

No.	Type	Description	Unused	Used
168	A71	25c dk bl, org brn & ol gray	1.00	85

Ski Lift — A72

Design: 25c, Chair lift (vert.).

1966, Apr. 2 Engr. *Perf. 13*

No.	Type	Description	Unused	Used
169	A72	25c brt bl, grn & dk brn	1.25	1.00
170	A72	40c mag, brt ultra & sep	1.75	1.50

Winter sports in Andorra.

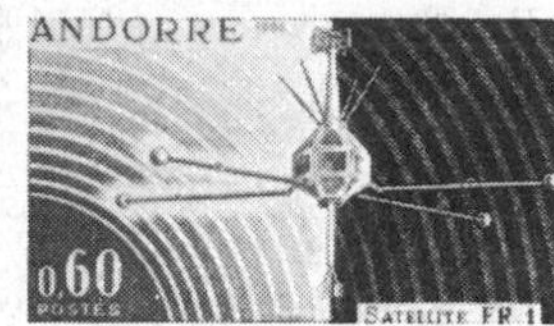

FR-1 Satellite — A73

1966, May 7 *Perf. 13*

No.	Type	Description	Unused	Used
171	A73	60c brt bl, grn & dk grn	1.90	1.90

Issued to commemorate the launching of the scientific satellite FR-1, Dec. 6, 1965.

Europa Issue, 1966

Common Design Type

1966, Sept. 24 Engr. *Perf. 13*

Size: 21½x35½mm.

No.	Type	Description	Unused	Used
172	CD9	60c brown	3.75	3.25

Folk Dancers, Sculpture by Josep Viladomat A74

Telephone Encircling the Globe A75

1967, Apr. 29 Engr. *Perf. 13*

No.	Type	Description	Unused	Used
173	A74	30c ol grn, dp grn & sl	60	45

Issued to commemorate the centenary (in 1966) of the New Reform, which reaffirmed and strengthened political freedom in Andorra.

Europa Issue, 1967

Common Design Type

1967, Apr. 29

Size: 22x36mm.

No.	Type	Description	Unused	Used
174	CD10	30c bluish blk & lt bl	2.25	1.90
175	CD10	60c dk red & brt pink	3.75	2.75

1967, Apr. 29

No.	Type	Description	Unused	Used
176	A75	60c dk car, vio & blk	1.40	1.10

Automatic telephone service.

Injured Father at Home A76

1967, Sept. 23 Engr. *Perf. 13*

No.	Type	Description	Unused	Used
177	A76	2.30fr ocher, dk red brn & brn red		8.00

Introduction of Social Security System.

Jesus in Garden of Gethsemane A77

Designs (from 16th century frescoes in La Maison des Vallees): 30c, The Kiss of Judas. 60c, The Descent from the Cross (Pieta).

1967, Sept. 23

No.	Type	Description	Unused	Used
178	A77	25c blk & red brn	70	55
179	A77	30c pur & red lil	1.00	75
180	A77	60c ind & Prus bl	1.75	1.10

See also Nos. 185-187.

Downhill Skier — A78

1968, Jan. 27 Engr. *Perf. 13*

No.	Type	Description	Unused	Used
181	A78	40c org, ver & red lil	90	75

Issued to publicize the 10th Winter Olympic Games, Grenoble, France, Feb. 6-18.

Europa Issue, 1968

Common Design Type

1968, Apr. 27 Engr. *Perf. 13*

Size: 36x22mm.

No.	Type	Description	Unused	Used
182	CD11	30c gray & brt bl	4.75	3.75
183	CD11	60c brn & lil	6.25	4.75

High Jump — A79

1968, Oct. 12 Engr. *Perf. 13*

No.	Type	Description	Unused	Used
184	A79	40c brt bl & brn	1.40	1.25

Issued to commemorate the 19th Olympic Games, Mexico City, Oct. 12-27.

Fresco Type of 1967

Designs (from 16th century frescoes in La Maison des Vallees): 25c, The Scourging of Christ. 30c, Christ Carrying the Cross. 60c, The Crucifixion. (All horizontal.)

1968, Oct. 12

No.	Type	Description	Unused	Used
185	A77	25c dk grn & gray grn	75	75
186	A77	30c dk brn & lil	1.25	1.25
187	A77	60c dk car & vio brn	1.75	1.75

Europa Issue, 1969
Common Design Type

1969, Apr. 26 **Engr.** ***Perf. 13***
188 CD12 40c rose car, gray & dl bl 4.00 3.25
189 CD12 70c ind, dl red & ol 6.50 4.75

Issued to commemorate the 10th anniversary of the Conference of European Postal and Telecommunications Administrations.

Kayak on Isere River A80

Drops of Water and Diamond A80a

1969, Aug. 2 **Engr.** ***Perf. 13***
190 A80 70c dk sl grn, ultra & ind 1.75 1.75

Issued to commemorate the International Canoe and Kayak Championships, Bourg-Saint-Maurice, Savoy, July 31-Aug. 6.

1969, Sept. 27 **Engr.** ***Perf. 13***
191 A80a 70c blk, dp ultra & grnsh bl 3.00 3.00

European Water Charter.

St. John, the Woman and the Dragon A81

The Revelation (From the Altar of St. John, Caselles): 40c, St. John Hearing Voice from Heaven on Patmos. 70c, St. John and the Seven Candlesticks.

1969, Oct. 18
192 A81 30c brn, dp pur & brn red 80 80
193 A81 40c gray, dk brn & brn ol 1.25 1.25
194 A81 70c dk red, mar & brt rose lil 2.25 2.25

See also Nos. 199-201, 207-209, 214-216.

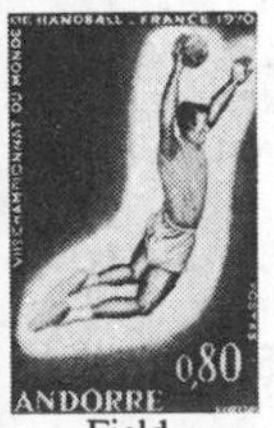

Field Ball — A82

Shot Put — A83

1970, Feb. 21 **Engr.** ***Perf. 13***
195 A82 80c multi 2.00 1.50

Issued to publicize the 7th International Field Ball Games, France, Feb. 26-Mar. 8.

Europa Issue, 1970
Common Design Type

1970, May 2 **Engr.** ***Perf. 13***
Size: 36x22mm.
196 CD13 40c orange 2.50 1.90
197 CD13 80c vio bl 3.50 2.75

1970, Sept. 11 **Engr.** ***Perf. 13***
198 A83 80c bl & dk brn 1.50 1.25

Issued to publicize the First European Junior Athletic Championships, Colombes, France, Sept. 11-13.

Altar Type of 1969

The Revelation (from the Altar of St. John, Caselles): 30c, St. John recording angel's message. 40c, Angel erecting column symbolizing faithful in heaven. 80c, St. John's trial in kettle of boiling oil.

1970, Oct. 24
199 A81 30c dp car, dk brn & brt pur 1.00 1.00
200 A81 40c vio & sl grn 1.25 1.25
201 A81 80c ol, dk bl & car rose 2.25 2.25

Ice Skating A84

1971, Feb. 20 **Engr.** ***Perf. 13***
202 A84 80c dk red, red lil & pur 3.00 2.25

World Figure Skating Championships, Lyons, France, Feb. 23-28.

Capercaillie — A85

Design: No. 204, Brown bear.

1971, Apr. 24 **Photo.** ***Perf. 13***
203 A85 80c multi 3.00 1.75

Engr.
204 A85 80c bl, grn & brn 3.00 1.75

Nature Protection.

Europa Issue, 1971
Common Design Type

1971, May 8 **Engr.** ***Perf. 13***
Size: 35½x22mm.
205 CD14 50c rose red 3.00 2.25
206 CD14 80c lt bl grn 4.25 3.00

Altar Type of 1969

The Revelation (from the Altar of St. John, Caselles): 30c, St. John preaching, Rev. 1:3. 50c, "The Sign of the Beast . . ." Rev. 16:1-2. 90c, The Woman, Rev. 17:1.

1971, Sept. 18
207 A81 30c dl grn, ol & brt grn 1.10 1.10
208 A81 50c rose car, org & ol brn 1.40 1.40
209 A81 90c blk, dk pur & bl 2.50 2.50

Europa Issue 1972
Common Design Type

1972, Apr. 29 **Photo.** ***Perf. 13***
Size: 21½x37mm.
210 CD15 50c brt mag & multi 3.00 2.75
211 CD15 90c multi 4.00 3.25

Golden Eagle — A86

1972, May 27 **Engr.**
212 A86 60c dk grn, ol & plum 2.00 1.65

Nature protection.

Shooting A87

1972, July 8
213 A87 1fr dk pur 2.00 1.65

20th Olympic Games, Munich, Aug. 26-Sept. 11.

Altar Type of 1969

The Revelation (from the Altar of St. John, Caselles): 30c, St. John, bishop and servant. 50c, Resurrection of Lazarus. 90c, Angel with lance and nails.

1972, Sept. 16 **Engr.** ***Perf. 13***
214 A81 30c dk ol, gray & red lil 90 90
215 A81 50c vio bl & sl 1.40 1.40
216 A81 90c dk Prus bl & sl grn 2.25 2.25

De Gaulle as Coprince of Andorra — A88

Design: 90c, De Gaulle in front of Maison des Vallees.

1972, Oct. 23 **Engr.** ***Perf. 13***
217 A88 50c vio bl 1.50 1.50
218 A88 90c dk car 2.25 2.25

5th anniversary of the visit of Charles de Gaulle to Andorra. Nos. 217-218 printed se-tenant in sheets of 10 stamps and 5 labels showing Andorran coat of arms and commemorative inscription.

Europa Issue 1973
Common Design Type

1973, Apr. 28 **Photo.** ***Perf. 13***
Size: 36x22mm.
219 CD16 50c vio & multi 3.00 2.75
220 CD16 90c dk red & multi 4.00 3.00

Virgin of Canolich A89

1973, June 16 **Engr.** ***Perf. 13***
221 A89 1fr ol, Prus bl & vio 2.00 2.00

Lily — A90

Designs: 45c, Iris. 50c, Columbine. 65c, Tobacco. No. 226, Pinks. No. 227, Narcissuses.

1973-74 **Photo.** ***Perf. 13***
222 A90 30c car rose & multi 50 50
223 A90 45c yel grn & multi 28 28
224 A90 50c buff & multi 1.65 1.65
225 A90 65c gray & multi 45 45
226 A90 90c ultra & multi 1.10 1.10
227 A90 90c grnsh bl & multi 90 90
Nos. 222-227 (6) 4.88 4.88

See Nos. 238-240.

Blue Titmouse — A91

Designs: 60c, Citril finch and mistletoe. 80c, Eurasian bullfinch. 1fr, Lesser spotted woodpecker.

1973-74 **Photo.** ***Perf. 13***
228 A91 60c buff & multi 1.65 1.40
229 A91 80c gray & multi 1.65 1.40
230 A91 90c gray & multi 1.40 1.10
231 A91 1fr yel grn & multi 2.00 1.50

Nature protection.

Europa Issue 1974

Virgin of Pal — A92

Design: 90c, Virgin of Santa Coloma. Statues are polychrome 12th century carvings by rural artists.

1974, Apr. 27 **Engr.** ***Perf. 13***
232 A92 50c multi 4.00 3.00
233 A92 90c multi 5.50 4.00

Arms of Andorra and Cahors Bridge — A93

Mail Box, Chutes and Globe — A94

1974, Aug. 24 **Engr.** ***Perf. 13***
234 A93 1fr bl, vio & org 1.40 90

First anniversary of meeting of the co-princes of Andorra: Pres. Georges Pompidou of France and Msgr. Juan Marti Alanis, Bishop of Urgel.

1974, Oct. 5 **Engr.** ***Perf. 13***
235 A94 1.20fr multi 1.65 1.40

Centenary of Universal Postal Union.

Europa Issue 1975

Coronation of St. Marti, 16th Century — A95

Design: 80c, Crucifixion, 16th century (vert.).

Perf. 11½x13, 13x11½

1975, Apr. 26 **Photo.**
236 A95 80c gold & multi 5.00 4.00
237 A95 1.20fr gold & multi 5.75 4.00

Flower Type of 1973

Designs: 60c, Gentian. 80c, Anemone. 1.20fr, Autumn crocus.

1975, May 10 **Photo.** ***Perf. 13***
238 A90 60c ol & multi 35 35
239 A90 80c brt rose & multi 80 80
240 A90 1.20fr grn & multi 85 85

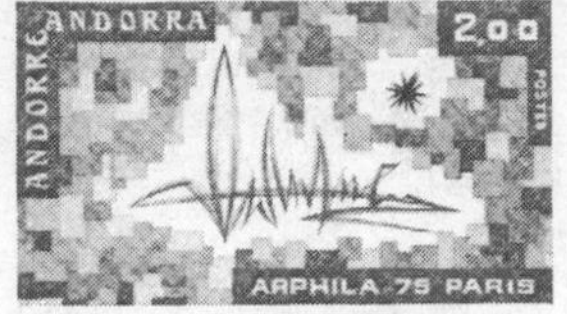

Abstract Design — A96

1975, June 7 **Engr.** ***Perf. 13***
241 A96 2fr bl, mag & emer 2.25 2.25

ARPHILA 75 International Philatelic Exhibition, Paris, June 6-16.

Pres. Georges Pompidou — A97

1975, Aug. 23 **Engr.** ***Perf. 13***
242 A97 80c vio bl & blk 1.00 1.00

Georges Pompidou (1911-1974), president of France and co-prince of Andorra (1969-1974).

Costume and IWY Emblem — A98

1975, Nov. 8 **Engr.** ***Perf. 13***
243 A98 1.20fr multi 1.40 1.25

International Women's Year.

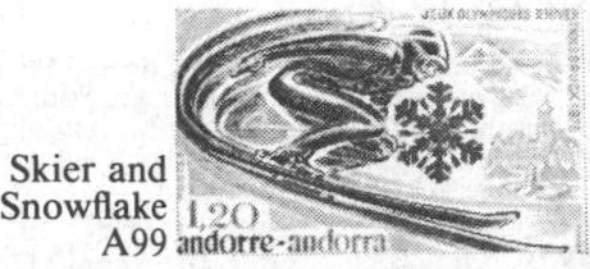

Skier and Snowflake A99

1976, Jan. 31 **Engr.** ***Perf. 13***
244 A99 1.20fr multi 1.40 1.25

12th Winter Olympic Games, Innsbruck, Austria, Feb. 4-15.

Telephone and Satellite — A100

1976, Mar. 20 **Engr.** ***Perf. 13***
245 A100 1fr multi 1.00 1.00

Centenary of first telephone call by Alexander Graham Bell, Mar. 10, 1976.

Europa Issue 1976

Catalan Forge A101

Design: 1.20fr, Lacemaker.

1976, May 8 **Engr.** ***Perf. 13***
246 A101 80c multi 1.10 90
247 A101 1.20fr multi 1.50 1.40

Thomas Jefferson A102

Trapshooting A103

1976, July 3 **Engr.** ***Perf. 13***
248 A102 1.20fr multi 1.40 1.25

American Bicentennial.

1976, July 17 **Engr.** ***Perf. 13***
249 A103 2fr multi 2.00 1.65

21st Olympic Games, Montreal, Canada, July 17-Aug. 1.

Meritxell Sanctuary and Old Chapel — A104

1976, Sept. 4 **Engr.** ***Perf. 13***
250 A104 1fr multi 1.25 1.00

Dedication of rebuilt Meritxell Church, Sept. 8, 1976.

Apollo A105

Ermine A106

Design: 1.40fr, Morio butterfly.

1976, Oct. 16 **Photo.** ***Perf. 13***
251 A105 80c blk & multi 1.00 90
252 A105 1.40fr sal & multi 1.50 1.25

Nature protection.

1977, Apr. 2 **Photo.** ***Perf. 13***
253 A106 1fr vio bl, gray & blk 1.40 1.10

Nature protection.

St. Jean de Caselles A107

Manual Digest, 1748, Arms of Andorra A108

Europa Issue 1977

Design: 1.40fr, Sant Vicens Castle.

1977, Apr. 30 **Engr.** ***Perf. 13***
254 A107 1fr multi 1.25 90
255 A107 1.40fr multi 1.75 1.40

1977, June 11 **Engr.** ***Perf. 13***
256 A108 80c grn, bl & brn 80 70

Establishment of Institute of Andorran Studies.

St. Romanus of Caesarea A109

1977, July 23 **Engr.** ***Perf. 12½x13***
257 A109 2fr multi 1.50 1.25

Design from altarpiece in Church of St. Roma de les Bons.

General Council Chamber A110

Guillem d'Areny Plandolit — A111

1977, Sept. 24 **Engr.** ***Perf. 13***
258 A110 1.10fr multi 1.40 1.10
259 A111 2fr car & dk brn 1.65 1.10

Andorran heritage. Guillem d'Areny Plandolit started Andorran reform movement in 1866.

Squirrel A112

Flag and Valira River Bridge A113

1978, Mar. 18 **Engr.** ***Perf. 13***
260 A112 1fr multi 85 65

1978, Apr. 8
261 A113 80c multi 60 55

700th anniversary of the signing of the treaty establishing the Co-Principality of Andorra.

Europa Issue 1978

Pal Church A114

Design: 1.40fr, Charlemagne's Castle, Charlemagne on horseback (vert.).

1978, Apr. 29 **Engr.** ***Perf. 13***
262 A114 1fr multi 1.25 1.00
263 A114 1.40fr multi 1.75 1.50

Virgin of Sispony A115

1978, May 20 **Engr.** ***Perf. 12x13***
264 A115 2fr multi 1.50 1.25

Visura Tribunal A116

1978, June 24 **Engr.** ***Perf. 13***
265 A116 1.20fr multi 1.00 75

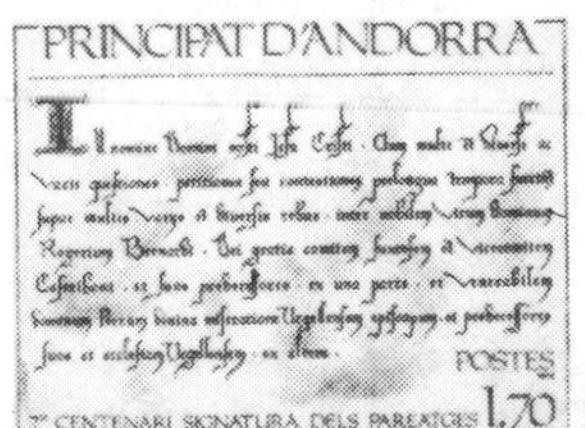

Preamble of 1278 Treaty — A117

1978, Sept. 2 **Engr.** ***Perf. 13x12½***
266 A117 1.70fr multi 1.00 75

700th anniversary of the signing of treaty establishing Co-Principality of Andorra.

Pyrenean Chamois A118

White Partridges A119

1979, Mar. 26 Engr. *Perf. 13*
267 A118 1fr multi 60 40

1979, Apr. 9 Photo. *Perf. 13*
268 A119 1.20fr multi 90 70

Nature protection. See Nos. 288-289.

Europa Issue 1979

French Mailman, 1900 — A120

Design: 1.70fr, First French post office in Andorra.

1979, Apr. 28 Engr. *Perf. 13*
269 A120 1.20fr multi 1.40 1.10
270 A120 1.70fr multi 2.00 1.50

Falcon, Pre-Roman Painting A121

1979, June 2 Engr. *Perf. 12½x13*
271 A121 2fr multi 1.25 90

Child with Lambs, Church, IYC Emblem — A122

1979, July 7 Photo. *Perf. 13*
272 A122 1.70fr multi 1.00 75

International Year of the Child.

Bas-relief, Trobada Monument A123

1979, Sept. 29 Engr. *Perf. 13*
273 A123 2fr multi 1.25 90

700th anniversary of Co-Principality of Andorra

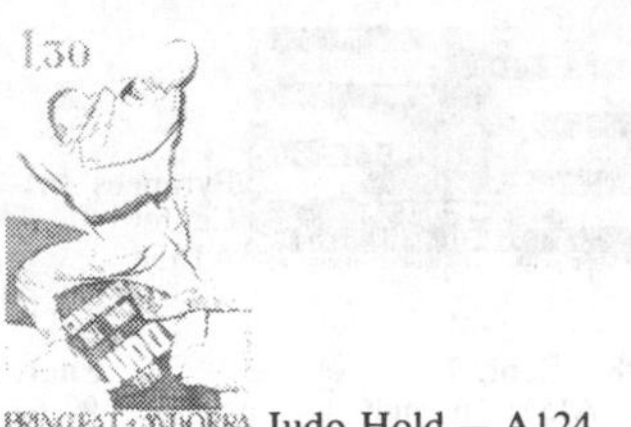

Judo Hold — A124

1979, Nov. 24 Engr. *Perf. 13*
274 A124 1.30fr multi 85 60

World Judo Championships, Paris, Dec. 1979.

Farm House, Cortinada — A125

1980, Jan. 26 Engr. *Perf. 13*
275 A125 1.10fr multi 60 55

Cross-Country Skiing — A126

1980, Feb. 9
276 A126 1.80fr ultra & lil rose 2.00 1.25

13th Winter Olympic Games, Lake Placid, N.Y., Feb. 12-24.

World Bicycling Championships A128

1980, Aug. 30 Engr. *Perf. 13*
278 A128 1.20fr multi 45 38

Europa Issue 1980

Charlemagne (742-814) — A129

Design: 1.80fr, Napoleon I (1769-1821).

1980, Apr. 26 Engr. *Perf. 13*
279 A129 1.30fr multi 65 45
280 A129 1.80fr gray grn & brn 1.00 70

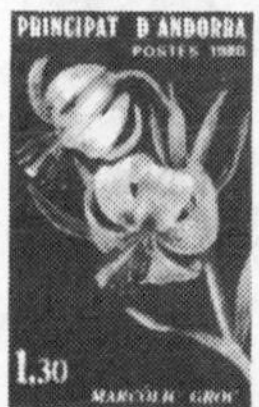

Pyrenees Lily — A130

1980 Photo.
281 A130 1.10fr *Dog-toothed violet* 60 38
282 A130 1.30fr *shown* 65 45

Nature protection. Issue dates: 1.10fr, June 21, 1.30fr, May 17.

De La Vall House, 400th Anniversary of Restoration A131

1980, Sept. 6 Engr.
283 A131 1.40fr multi 50 38

Angel, Church of St. Cerni de Nagol, Pre-Romanesque Fresco — A132

1980, Oct. 27 *Perf. 13x12½*
284 A132 2fr multi 1.25 90

Bordes de Mereig Mountain Village A133

1981, Mar. 21 Engr. *Perf. 13*
285 A133 1.40fr bl gray & dk brn 50 40

Europa Issue 1981

Ball de l'Ossa, Winter Game A134

1981, May 16 Engr.
286 A134 1.40fr shown 65 45
287 A134 2fr El Contrapas dance 80 60

Bird Type of 1979

1981, June 20 Photo.
288 A119 1.20fr Phylloscopus bonelli 45 30
289 A119 1.40fr Tichodroma muraria 55 38

World Fencing Championship, Clermont-Ferrand, July 2-13 — A135

1981, July 4 Engr.
290 A135 2fr bl & blk 75 50

St. Martin, 12th Cent. Tapestry — A136

1981, Sept. 5 Engr. *Perf. 12x13*
291 A136 3fr multi 1.25 90

Intl. Drinking Water Decade A137

Intl. Year of the Disabled A138

1981, Oct. 17 *Perf. 13*
292 A137 1.60fr multi 55 40

1981, Nov. 7
293 A138 2.30fr multi 70 60

Europa 1982 — A139

1982, May 8 Engr. *Perf. 13*
294 A139 1.60fr Creation of Andorran govt., 1982 55 40
295 A139 2.30fr Land Council, 1419 80 55

1982 World Cup — A140

Designs: Various soccer players. Nos. 296-297 se-tenant with label showing natl. arms.

1982, June 12 Engr. *Perf. 13*
296 A140 1.60fr red & dk brn 60 45
297 A140 2.60fr red & dk brn 90 65

Souvenir Sheet

No. 52 — A141

1982, Aug. 21 Engr.
298 A141 5fr blk & rose car 2.00 2.00

First Andorran Stamp Exhibition, Aug. 21-Sept. 19. Black marginal inscription. Size: 143x93mm.

Horse, Roman Wall Painting — A142

1982, Sept. 4 Photo. *Perf. 13x12½*
299 A142 3fr multi 1.10 90

Wild Cat — A143

1982, Oct. 9 **Engr.** ***Perf. 13***
300 A143 1.80fr shown 75 50
301 A143 2.60fr Pine trees 1.10 65

TB Bacillus Centenary A144

St. Thomas Aquinas (1225-1274) A145

1982, Nov. 13
302 A144 2.10fr Koch, lungs 60 50

1982, Dec. 4
303 A145 2fr multi 75 60

Manned Flight Bicentenary A146

1983, Feb. 26 **Engr.**
304 A146 2fr multi 75 60

Nature Protection A147

1983, Apr. 16 **Engr.** ***Perf. 13***
305 A147 1fr Birch trees 40 22
306 A147 1.50fr Trout 55 38

Europa 1983 A148

Catalane Gold Works.

1983, May 7 **Engr.** ***Perf. 13***
307 A148 1.80fr Exterior 60 45
308 A148 2.60fr Interior 80 60

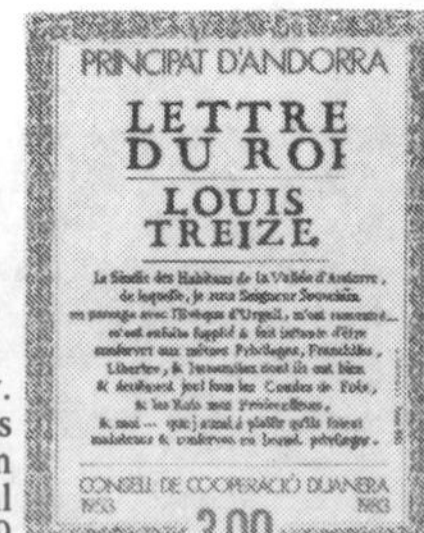

30th Anniv. of Customs Cooperation Council A149

1983, May 14
309 A149 3fr Letter to King Louis XIII 1.10 80

First Arms of Valleys of Andorra A150

1983, Sept. 3 **Engr.** ***Perf. 13***
310 A150 5c ol grn & red 5 5
311 A150 10c grn & ol grn 5 5
312 A150 20c brt pur & red 5 5
313 A150 30c brn vio & red 6 5
314 A150 40c dk bl & ultra 10 6
315 A150 50c gray & red 12 6
316 A150 1fr dp mag 30 18
317 A150 2fr org red & red brn 55 35
318 A150 5fr dk brn & red 1.40 85
Nos. 310-318 (9) 2.68 1.70

See Nos. 332-335.

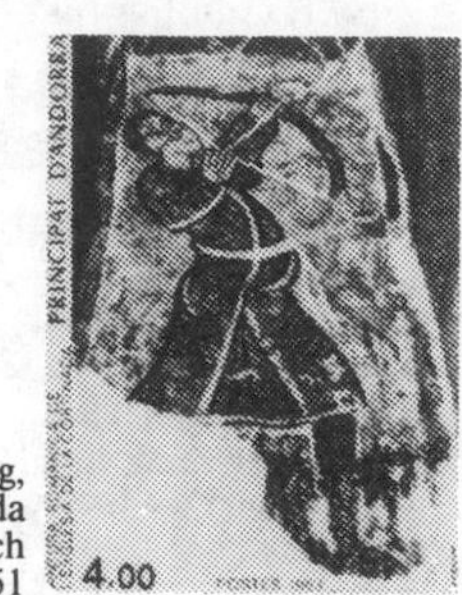

Painting, Cortinada Church A151

1983, Sept. 24 ***Perf. 12x13***
319 A151 4fr multi 1.40 1.00

Plandolit House — A152

1983, Oct. 15 **Photo.** ***Perf. 13***
320 A152 1.60fr dp ultra & brn 50 38

1984 Winter Olympics A153

1984, Feb. 18 **Engr.**
321 A153 2.80fr multi 90 70

Pyrennes Region Work Community (Labor Org.) A154

1984, Apr. 28 **Engr.** ***Perf. 13***
322 A154 3fr brt bl & sep 90 65

Europa (1959-84) A155

1984, May 5 **Engr.**
323 A155 2fr brt grn 60 38
324 A155 2.80fr rose car 90 60

Nature Protection Type of 1983

1984, July 7 **Engr.** ***Perf. 13***
325 A147 1.70fr Chestnut Tree 50 30
326 A147 2.10fr Walnut Tree 60 38

Pyranees Art Center A155a

1984, Sept. 7 **Engr.**
327 A155a 3fr multi 90 60

Romanesque Fresco, Church of St. Cerni de Nagol — A156

1984, Nov. 17 ***Perf. 12x13***
328 A156 5fr multi 1.65 1.10

First Arms Type of 1983

1987, Mar. 28 **Engr.** ***Perf. 13***
329 A1501.90fr emer ('87) 65 12
330 A1502.20fr red org ('87) 75 15
a. Bklt. pane of 8 (2 No. 329, 6 No. 330) 5.80

Nos. 329-330 issued in booklets only.

Arms Type of 1983

1984-86 ***Perf. 13***
332 A150 3fr bl grn & red brn 75 45
333 A150 4fr brt org & brn ('86) 1.15 85
334 A150 10fr brn org & blk ('85) 2.50 1.50
334A A150 15fr grn & dk grn ('86) 4.25 3.25
335 A150 20fr brt bl & red brn 5.25 3.00

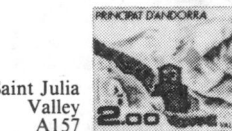

Saint Julia Valley A157

1985, Apr. 13 **Engr.**
336 A157 2fr multi 55 45

Europa 1985 — A158

1985, May 4 **Engr.**
337 A158 2.10fr Le Val D'Andorre 60 45
338 A158 3fr Instruments 80 65

Intl. Youth Year — A159

1985, June 8 **Engr.**
339 A159 3fr multi 80 60

Wildlife Conservation A160

1985, Aug. 3 **Photo.**
340 A160 1.80fr Anas platyrhynchos 50 38
341 A160 2.20fr Carduelis carduelis 60 45

Two Saints, Medieval Fresco in St. Cerni de Nagol Church A161

1985, Sept. 14 **Engr.** ***Perf. 12½x13***
342 A161 5fr multi 1.40 1.10

Postal Museum Inauguration A162

1986, Mar. 22 **Engr.** ***Perf. 13***
343 A162 2.20fr like No. 269 62 12

Europa 1986 A163

1986, May 3 **Engr.** ***Perf. 13***
344 A163 2.20fr Ansalonga 62 12
345 A163 3.20fr Isard 80 16

1986 World Cup Soccer Championships, Mexico — A164

1986, June 14
346 A164 3fr multi 75 15

Angonella Lake A165

1986, June 28
347 A165 2.20fr multi 62 12

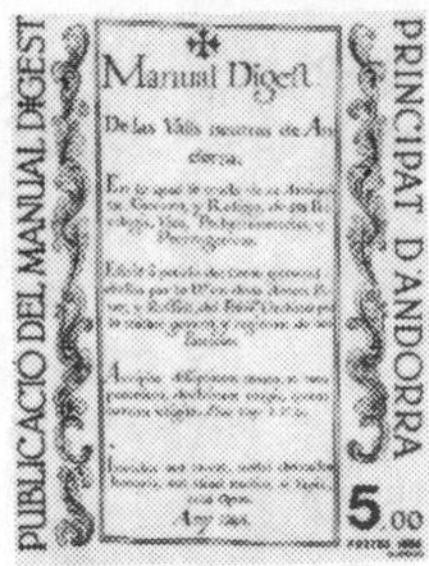

Manual Digest Frontispiece, 1748 — A166

1986, Sept. 6 **Engr.**
348 A166 5fr chnt brn, gray ol & blk 1.55 30

Intl. Peace Year — A167

1986, Sept. 29
349 A167 1.90fr bl gray & grnsh bl 58 12

St. Vicenc D'Enclar — A168

1986, Oct. 18 **Engr.** ***Perf. 13½x13***
350 A168 1.90fr dl gray vio, gray grn & ol brn 60 12

Contemporary Natl. Coat of Arms — A169

1987, Mar. 27 **Litho.** ***Perf. 12½x13***
351 A169 2.20fr multi 75 15

Visit of the French co-prince.

Europa 1987 A170

1987, May 2 **Engr.** ***Perf. 13***
352 A170 2.20fr Meritxell Sanctuary 75 15
353 A170 3.40fr Pleta D'Ordino 1.15 24

Ransol Village — A171

1987, June 13 **Photo.**
354 A171 1.90fr multi 62 12

Nature A172

1987, July 4
355 A172 1.90fr Cavall rogenc 62 12
356 A172 2.20fr Graellsia isabellae 72 15

Aryalsu, Romanesque Painting, La Cortinada Church A173

Litho. & Engr.
1987, Sept. 5 ***Perf. 12½x13***
357 A173 5fr multi 1.70 35

Hiker Looking at Map A174

1987, Sept. 19 **Engr.** ***Perf. 13***
358 A174 2fr olive, grn & dark brn vio 68 14

Medieval Iron Key, La Cortinada A175

1987, Oct. 17 **Litho.**
359 A175 3fr multi 1.00 20

SEMI-POSTAL STAMP

Virgin of St. Coloma — SP1

Unwmk.
1964, July 25 **Engr.** ***Perf. 13***
B1 SP1 25c + 10c multi 30.00 30.00

The surtax was for the Red Cross.

Angola stamps can be mounted in Scott's annual Portugal Supplement.

AIR POST STAMPS

Chamois AP1

Unwmk.
1950, Feb. 20 **Engr.** ***Perf. 13***
C1 AP1 100fr indigo 55.00 35.00

East Branch of Valira River — AP2

1955-57
C2 AP2 100fr dk grn 7.00 5.50
C3 AP2 200fr cerise 14.00 11.00
C4 AP2 500fr dp bl ('57) 77.50 55.00

D'Inclès Valley AP3

1961, June 19 **Unwmk.** ***Perf. 13***
C5 AP3 2fr red, ol gray & cl 90 75
C6 AP3 3fr bl, mar & sl grn 1.40 1.40
C7 AP3 5fr rose lil & red org 2.25 2.00

1964, Apr. 25
C8 AP3 10fr bl grn & sl grn 4.50 4.25

POSTAGE DUE STAMPS.

Postage Due Stamps of France, 1893-1931, Overprinted

ANDORRE

On Stamps of 1893-1926

1931-33 **Unwmk.** ***Perf. 14x13½***
J1 D2 5c blue 1.50 1.50
J2 D2 10c brown 1.50 1.50
J3 D2 30c rose red 45 45
J4 D2 50c vio brn 1.50 1.50
J5 D2 60c green 15.00 15.00
J6 D2 1fr red brn, *straw* 75 75
J7 D2 2fr brt vio 9.00 9.00
J8 D2 3fr magenta 1.75 1.75
Nos. J1-J8 (8) 31.45 31.45

On Stamps of 1927-31
J9 D4 1c ol grn 1.50 1.50
J10 D4 10c rose 3.25 3.25
J11 D4 60c red 20.00 20.00
J12 D4 1fr Prus grn ('32) 80.00 80.00
J13 D4 1.20fr on 2fr bl 60.00 60.00
J14 D4 2fr ol brn ('33) 135.00 135.00
J15 D4 5fr on 1fr vio 75.00 75.00
Nos. J9-J15 (7) 374.75 374.75

D5 D6

1935-41 **Typo.**
J16 D5 1c gray grn 2.00 1.50
J17 D6 5c lt bl ('37) 6.00 5.50
J18 D6 10c brn ('41) 4.75 5.50
J19 D6 2fr vio ('41) 6.75 4.00
J20 D6 5fr red org ('41) 8.50 4.00
Nos. J16-J20 (5) 28.00 20.50

Wheat Sheaves — D7

1943-46 ***Perf. 14x13½***
J21 D7 10c sepia 60 60
J22 D7 30c brt red vio 90 90
J23 D7 50c bl grn 1.10 1.10
J24 D7 1fr brt ultra 50 50
J25 D7 1.50fr rose red 3.50 3.50
J26 D7 2fr turq bl 90 90
J27 D7 3fr brn org 1.65 1.65
J28 D7 4fr dp vio ('45) 2.75 2.75
J29 D7 5fr brt pink 2.75 2.75
J30 D7 10fr red org ('45) 3.50 3.50
J31 D7 20fr ol brn ('46) 3.75 3.75
Nos. J21-J31 (11) 21.90 21.90

Inscribed: "Timbre Taxe."

1946-53
J32 D7 10c sep ('46) 90 90
J33 D7 1fr ultra 60 60
J34 D7 2fr turq bl 75 75
J35 D7 3fr org brn 1.65 1.65
J36 D7 4fr violet 2.25 2.25
J37 D7 5fr brt pink 1.40 1.40
J38 D7 10fr red org 2.25 2.25
J39 D7 20fr ol brn 5.00 5.00
J40 D7 50fr dk grn ('50) 13.00 13.00
J41 D7 100fr dp grn ('53) 70.00 70.00
Nos. J32-J41 (10) 97.80 97.80

Inscribed: "Timbre Taxe."

1961, June 19 ***Perf. 14x13½***
J42 D7 5c rose pink 3.25 3.25
J43 D7 10c red org 6.75 6.75
J44 D7 20c olive 10.00 10.00
J45 D7 50c dk sl grn 16.00 16.00

Flower Type of France, 1964

Designs: 5c, Centaury. 10c, Gentian. 15c, Corn poppy. 20c, Violets. 30c, Forget-me-not. 40c, Columbine. 50c, Clover.

1964-71 **Typo.** ***Perf. 14x13½***
J46 D7 5c car rose, red & grn ('65) 5 5
J47 D7 10c car rose, brt bl & grn ('65) 6 6
J48 D7 15c brn, grn & red 6 6
J49 D7 20c dk grn, grn & vio ('71) 8 8
J50 D7 30c brn, ultra & grn 12 12
J51 D7 40c dk grn, scar & yel ('71) 15 15
J52 D7 50c vio bl, car & grn ('65) 22 22
Nos. J46-J52 (7) 74 74

Wildflowers & Berries — D9

1985, Oct. 21 **Engr.** ***Perf. 13***
J53 D9 10c Holly 5 5
J54 D9 20c Blueberries 5 5
J55 D9 30c Raspberries 8 8
J56 D9 40c Bilberries 12 12
J57 D9 50c Blackberries 15 15
J58 D9 1fr Broom 30 30
J59 D9 2fr Rosehips 60 38
J60 D9 3fr Nightshade 90 58
J61 D9 4fr Nabiu 1.25 75
J62 D9 5fr Strawberries 1.50 95
Nos. J53-J62 (10) 5.00 3.41

NEWSPAPER STAMP.

France No. P7 Overprinted

ANDORRE

1931 **Unwmk.** ***Perf. 14x13½***
P1 A16 ½c on 1c gray 80 80

ANGOLA

LOCATION — Southwestern Africa between Congo and South-West Africa.
GOVT. — Republic
AREA — 481,351 sq. mi.
POP. — 7,108,000 (1983 est.)

CAPITAL — Luanda

Angola was a Portuguese overseas territory until it became independent November 11, 1975, as the People's Republic of Angola.

1000 Reis = 1 Milreis
100 Centavos = 1 Escudo (1913, 1954)
100 Centavos = 1 Angolar (1932)
10 Lweys = 1 Kwanza (1977)

Portuguese Crown — A1

Perf. 12½, 13½.

1870-77 Typo. Unwmk.

1 A1 5r black 2.00 1.75
 a. Perf. 13½ 10.00 5.00
2 A1 10r yellow 20.00 10.00
3 A1 20r bister 2.75 1.90
 a. Perf. 13½ 100.00 75.00
4 A1 25r red 12.00 4.00
 a. 25r rose 12.00 4.00
 b. Laid paper
 c. 25r rose, perf. 14 165.00 100.00
 d. Perf. 13½ 24.00 12.00
5 A1 40r bl ('77) 150.00 90.00
6 A1 50r green 50.00 14.00
 a. Perf. 13½ 275.00 100.00
7 A1 100r lilac 2.25 2.00
 a. Perf. 12½ 10.00 6.00
8 A1 200r org ('77) 3.00 2.00
 a. Perf. 12½ 4.50 2.50
9 A1 300r choc ('77) 3.75 3.00
 a. Perf. 12½ 12.00 5.50

1881-85

10 A1 10r grn ('83) 4.50 2.25
 a. Perf. 12½ 17.50 3.50
11 A1 20r car rose ('85) 11.00 8.50
 a. Cliche of 40r in plate of 20r 750.00
12 A1 25r vio ('85) 7.00 3.00
 a. Perf. 13½ 7.00 4.00
13 A1 40r buff ('82) 5.50 3.25
 a. Perf. 12½ 6.00 3.25
15 A1 50r blue 25.00 2.50
 a. Perf. 13½ 30.00 2.50

Two types of numerals are found on No. 2 and Nos. 11 to 15.

The error, No. 11a, was discovered before the stamps were issued. All copies were cancelled by a blue pencil mark.

In perf. 12½, Nos. 1-4, 4a and 6, as well as 7a, were printed in 1870 on thicker paper and 1875 on normal paper. Stamps of the earlier printing sell for 2 to 15 times more than those of the 1875 printing.

Some reprints of the 1870-85 issues are on a smooth white chalky paper, ungummed and perf. 13½. Price each, $1.50.

Other reprints of these issues are on thin white paper with shiny white gum and clear-cut perf. 13½. Price each, $2.50.

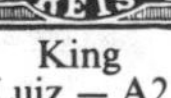
King Luiz — A2

King Carlos — A3

1886 Embossed *Perf. 12½*

16 A2 5r black 7.00 5.00
 a. Perf. 13½ 17.50 13.00
17 A2 10r green 7.00 4.50
 a. Perf. 13½ 20.00 11.00
18 A2 20r rose 15.00 9.50
 a. Perf. 13½ 19.00 10.00
19 A2 25r red vio 11.00 2.00
20 A2 40r chocolate 12.00 6.00
21 A2 50r blue 16.00 3.00
22 A2 100r yel brn 22.50 9.00
23 A2 200r gray vio 27.50 12.50
24 A2 300r orange 30.00 14.00

Reprints of 5, 20 & 100r have cleancut perf. 13½. Price, each $3.

Perf. 11½, 12½, 13½.

1893-94 Typo.

25 A3 5r yellow 1.40 1.15
26 A3 10r redsh vio 3.00 1.30
27 A3 15r chocolate 4.00 1.90
28 A3 20r lavender 4.25 2.00
29 A3 25r green 1.75 1.15
 a. Perf. 12½ 4.25 1.65
30 A3 50r lt bl 3.75 1.65
 a. Perf. 13½ 7.50 4.25
31 A3 75r carmine 7.50 4.25
 a. Perf. 11½ 9.50 7.50
32 A3 80r lt grn 9.00 5.50
33 A3 100r brn, *buff* 10.50 5.50
 a. Perf. 11½ 75.00 50.00
34 A3 150r car, *rose* 18.00 12.00
35 A3 200r dk bl, *lt bl* 22.50 15.00
36 A3 300r dk bl, *sal* 22.50 15.00

No. P1 Surcharged in Blue

CORREIOS DE ANGOLA
25
REIS

1894, Aug.

37 N1 25r on 2½r brn 90.00 60.00

King Carlos — A5

1898-1903 *Perf. 11½*

Name and Value in Black except 500r

38 A5 2½r gray 25 20
39 A5 5r orange 25 20
40 A5 10r yel grn 25 20
41 A5 15r vio brn 2.25 1.10
42 A5 15r gray grn ('03) 1.00 75
43 A5 20r gray vio 40 30
44 A5 25r sea grn 1.50 60
45 A5 25r car ('03) 50 20
46 A5 50r blue 2.00 55
47 A5 50r brn ('03) 6.00 3.00
48 A5 65r dl bl ('03) 7.00 6.50
49 A5 75r rose 7.00 2.50
50 A5 75r red vio ('03) 2.00 1.40
51 A5 80r violet 8.00 2.75
52 A5 100r dk bl, *bl* 1.40 1.00
53 A5 115r org brn, *pink* ('03) 8.00 5.00
54 A5 130r brn, *straw* ('03) 8.00 5.00
55 A5 150r brn, *straw* 8.00 4.25
56 A5 200r red vio, *pink* 3.50 1.50
57 A5 300r dk bl, *rose* 4.25 4.00
58 A5 400r dl bl, *straw* ('03) 3.25 2.50
59 A5 500r blk & red, *bl* ('01) 4.50 4.00
60 A5 700r vio, *yelsh* ('01) 22.50 15.00
 Nos. 38-60 (23) 101.80 62.50

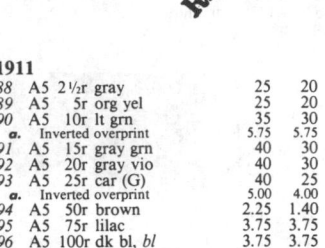

Stamps of 1886-94 Surcharged in Black or Red

Two types of surcharge:
I. 3mm. between numeral and REIS.
II. 4½mm. spacing.

1902 *Perf. 12½*

61 A2 65r on 40r choc 7.00 4.00
62 A2 65r on 300r org, I 7.00 4.00
 a. Type II 50.00 27.50
63 A2 115r on 10r grn 5.75 4.00
 a. Inverted surcharge
 b. Perf. 13½ 27.50 25.00
64 A2 115r on 200r gray vio 5.50 3.50
65 A2 130r on 50r bl 8.75 6.50
66 A2 130r on 100r brn 4.75 3.25
67 A2 400r on 20r rose 50.00 32.50
 a. Perf. 13½ 60.00 42.50
68 A2 400r on 25r vio 11.00 7.50
69 A2 400r on 5r blk (R) 10.50 9.00
 a. Double surcharge
 Nos. 61-69 (9) 110.25 74.25

Perf. 11½, 12½, 13½.

70 A3 65r on 5r yel, I 6.00 4.00
 a. Type II 15.00 15.00
71 A3 65r on 10r red vio, I 5.00 3.50
 a. Type II 20.00 8.00
 b. Perf. 11½, type I 13.50 8.00
 c. Perf. 11½, type II 5.25 3.75
72 A3 65r on 20r lav 6.00 4.00
 a. Type II 10.00 9.00
73 65r on 25r grn 4.50 3.50
 a. Perf. 11½ 14.00 11.00
74 A3 115r on 80r lt grn 8.00 6.25
75 A3 115r on 100r brn, *buff* 8.00 5.00
 a. Perf. 13½ 14.00 10.00
76 A3 115r on 150r car, *rose* 12.00 8.00
 a. Perf. 13½ 15.00 9.00
77 A3 130r on 15r choc 4.25 3.00
78 A3 130r on 75r car 4.75 3.50
 a. Perf. 13½ 22.50 17.50
79 A3 130r on 300r dk bl, *sal* 12.50 9.00
80 A3 400r on 50r lt bl 5.00 4.00
81 A3 400r on 200r bl, *bl* 5.00 4.50
 a. Perf. 13½ 32.50 13.50
82 N1 400r on 2½r brn 1.10 1.10
 a. Type II 3.75 3.50
 Nos. 70-82 (13) 82.10 59.35

Reprints of Nos. 65, 67, 68 and 69 have clean-cut perforation 13½. Price $2.50 each.

Stamps of 1898 Overprinted — a

PROVISORIO

1902 *Perf. 11½*

83 A5 15r brown 1.50 90
84 A5 25r sea grn 1.25 50
85 A5 50r blue 2.25 1.25
86 A5 75r rose 4.25 3.00

No. 48 Surcharged in Black

50 RÉIS

1905

87 A5 50r on 65r dl bl 3.50 2.00

Stamps of 1898-1903 Overprinted in Carmine or Green — b

1911

88 A5 2½r gray 25 20
89 A5 5r org yel 25 20
90 A5 10r lt grn 35 30
 a. Inverted overprint 5.75 5.75
91 A5 15r gray grn 40 30
92 A5 20r gray vio 40 30
93 A5 25r car (G) 40 25
 a. Inverted overprint 5.00 4.00
94 A5 50r brown 2.25 1.40
95 A5 75r lilac 3.75 3.75
96 A5 100r dk bl, *bl* 3.75 3.75
97 A5 115r org brn, *pink* 1.40 90
98 A5 130r brn, *straw* 1.40 90
99 A5 200r red lil, *pnksh* 1.40 90
100 A5 400r dl bl, *straw* 2.00 1.00
101 A5 500r blk & red, *bl* 1.75 1.00
102 A5 700r vio, *yelsh* 2.00 1.10
 Nos. 88-102 (15) 21.75 16.25

King Manuel II — A6

Ceres — A7

Overprinted in Carmine or Green.

1912 *Perf. 11½x12.*

103 A6 2½r violet 35 50
104 A6 5r black 40 60
105 A6 10r gray grn 55 45
106 A6 20r car (G) 55 45
107 A6 25r vio brn 55 45
108 A6 50r dk bl 90 75
109 A6 75r bis brn 1.00 1.50
110 A6 100r brn, *lt grn* 2.50 1.10
111 A6 200r dk grn, *sal* 1.75 1.10
112 A6 300r *azure* 1.75 1.10
 Nos. 103-112 (10) 10.30 8.00

No. 91 Surcharged with New Values as

5

1912, June *Perf. 11½*

113 A5 2½r on 15r gray grn 3.50 3.50
114 A5 5r on 15r gray grn 2.75 2.25
115 A5 10r on 15r gray grn 2.75 2.25

Inverted and double surcharges of Nos. 113-115 were made intentionally.

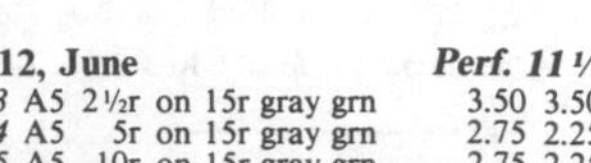

Catalogue prices for unused stamps up to mid-1953 are for hinged copies matching the condition specified in this volume's introduction.

Nos. 86 and 50 Surcharged "25" in Black and Overprinted in Violet — c

1912

116 A5 25r on 75r rose 65.00 40.00
117 A5 25r on 75r red vio 4.00 2.25
 a. "REUPBLICA" 40.00 37.50
 b. "25" omitted 40.00 37.50
 c. "REPUBLICA" omitted 40.00 37.50

Perf. 12x11½, 15x14.

1914-26 Typo.

Name and Value in Black.

118 A7 ¼c ol brn 12 25
 a. Inscriptions inverted 3.00
119 A7 ½c black 12 25
120 A7 1c bl grn 12 25
121 A7 1c yel grn ('22) 12 12
122 A7 1½c lil brn 12 12
123 A7 2c carmine 12 12
124 A7 2c gray ('25) 40 90
125 A7 2½c lt vio 12 12
126 A7 3c org ('22) 12 90
127 A7 4c dl rose ('22) 12 12
128 A7 4½c gray ('22) 12 90
130 A7 5c blue 12 12
131 A7 6c lil ('22) 12 12
132 A7 7c ultra ('22) 12 12
133 A7 7½c yel brn 12 12
134 A7 8c slate 12 12
135 A7 10c org brn 30 12
136 A7 12c ol brn ('22) 55 35
137 A7 12c dp grn ('25) 30 15
138 A7 15c plum 30 25
139 A7 15c brn rose ('22) 17 15
140 A7 20c yel grn 35 15
141 A7 24c ultra ('25) 1.75 65
142 A7 25c choc ('25) 1.75 65
143 A7 30c brn, *grn* 2.00 2.00
144 A7 30c gray grn ('22) 1.00 10
145 A7 40c brn, *pink* 2.75 2.00
146 A7 40c turq bl ('22) 90 12
147 A7 50c org, *sal* 9.00 5.00
148 A7 50c lt vio ('25) 1.50 15
149 A7 60c dk bl ('22) 80 15
150 A7 60c dp rose ('26) 75.00 60.00
151 A7 80c pink ('22) 2.00 15
152 A7 1e grn, *bl* 4.50 3.50
153 A7 1e rose ('22) 2.25 15
154 A7 1e dp bl ('25) 2.00 1.50
155 A7 2e dk vio ('22) 2.00 65
156 A7 5e buff ('25) 7.50 3.50
157 A7 10e pink ('25) 17.50 11.00
158 A7 20e pale turq ('25) 75.00 40.00
 Nos. 118-158 (40) 213.37 137.09

Two kinds of chalky-surfaced paper, ordinary and coated, were used for Nos. 118-120, 122-123, 130, 133-135, 138 and 140. Those on coated paper sell unused for 10 to 40 times the prices listed; used for about 5 to 20 times.

Stamps of 1898-1903 Overprinted type "c" in Red or Green
On Stamps of 1898-1903.

1914 *Perf. 11½, 12.*

159 A5 10r yel grn (R) 4.25 3.25
160 A5 15r gray grn (R) 4.25 3.25
161 A5 20r gray vio (G) 1.00 75
163 A5 75r red vio (G) 75 60
164 A5 100r bl, *bl* (R) 2.00 2.00
165 A5 115r org brn, *pink* (R) 30.00
167 A5 200r red vio, *pnksh* (G) 1.40 75
169 A5 400r dl bl, *straw* (R) 25.00 17.00
170 A5 500r blk & red, *bl* (R) 3.75 3.25
171 A5 700r vio, *yelsh* (G) 13.00 12.00

Inverted and double surcharges were made intentionally. No. 165 was not regularly issued.

Perf. 11½, 12½, 13½.
On Provisional Stamps of 1902.

172 A2 115r on 10r grn (R) 11.00 8.25
 a. Perf. 13½ 12.50 12.50
173 A2 115r on 200r gray vio (R) 11.00 10.00
174 A2 130r on 50r bl (R) 14.00 12.00
175 A3 115r on 80r lt grn (R) 150.00 125.00
176 A3 115r on 100r brn, *buff* (R) 200.00 175.00
177 A3 115r on 150r car, *rose* (G) 175.00 150.00
178 A3 130r on 75r car (G) 2.75 2.50
179 A3 130r on 300r dk bl, *sal* (R) 4.75 3.50
 a. Perf. 12½ 10.00 6.50
180 N1 400r on 2½r brn (R) 40 40
 a. Perf. 11½ 2.50 2.00
 Nos. 172-180 (9) 568.90 486.65

On Stamps of 1902.

Overprinted PROVISORIO

Perf. 11½, 12.

181 A5 50r bl (R) 1.35 90
a. "Republica" double
182 A5 75r rose (G) 3.50 2.75
a. "Republica" inverted

On Stamp of 1905.

183 A5 50r on 65r dl bl (R) 3.50 2.75
a. "Republica" inverted
b. "Republica" double

Vasco da Gama Issue of Various Portuguese Colonies

Common Design Types CD20-CD27 Surcharged

REPUBLICA
ANGOLA
¼ C.

On Stamps of Macao.

1913 *Perf. 12½ to 16.*

184 ¼c on ½a bl grn 2.00 2.00
185 ½c on 1a red 1.65 1.65
186 1c on 2a red vio 1.65 1.65
187 2½c on 4a yel grn 1.40 1.40
188 5c on 8a dk bl 1.40 1.40
189 7½c on 12a vio brn 3.50 3.50
190 10c on 16a bis brn 1.90 1.90
191 15c on 24a bis 1.90 1.90
Nos. 184-191 (8) 15.40 15.40

On Stamps of Portuguese Africa.

Perf. 14 to 15.

192 ¼c on 2½r bl grn 90 90
193 ½c on 5r red 90 90
194 1c on 10r red vio 90 90
195 2½c on 25r yel grn 90 90
196 5c on 50r dk bl 90 90
197 7½c on 75r vio brn 3.50 3.50
198 10c on 100r bis brn 1.40 1.40
199 15c on 150r bis 2.25 2.25
Nos. 192-199 (8) 11.65 11.65

On Stamps of Timor

200 ¼c on ½a bl grn 2.00 2.00
201 ½c on 1a red 2.00 2.00
202 1c on 2a red vio 2.00 2.00
203 2½c on 4a yel grn 1.90 1.90
204 5c on 8a dk bl 1.90 1.90
205 7½c on 12a vio brn 3.25 3.25
206 10c on 16a bis brn 2.00 2.00
207 15c on 24a bis 2.00 2.00
Nos. 200-207 (8) 17.05 17.05

Provisional Issue of 1902 Overprinted in Carmine

REPUBLICA

1915 *Perf. 11½, 12½, 13½.*

208 A2 115r on 10r grn 1.50 *2.00*
209 A2 115r on 200r gray vio 1.40 *1.75*
210 A2 130r on 100r brn 1.10 *1.75*
211 A3 115r on 80r lt grn 1.65 *2.00*
212 A3 115r on 100r brn, *buff* 1.25 *1.75*
a. Perf. 11½ 22.50 *22.50*
213 A3 115r on 150r car, *rose* 2.25 *3.00*
214 A3 130r on 15r choc 1.00 *1.75*
a. Perf. 12½ 6.00 4.50
215 A3 130r on 75r car 2.25 *2.75*
216 A3 130r on 300r dk bl, *sal* 1.75 *2.75*
Nos. 208-216 (9) 14.15 19.50

Stamps of 1911-14 Surcharged in Black:

½ C.

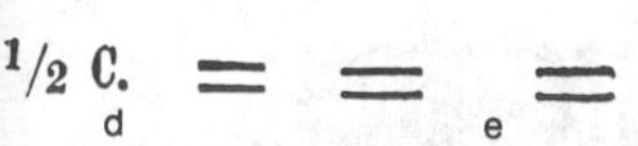

On Stamps of 1911.

1919 *Perf. 11½*

217 A5 (d) ½c on 75r red lil 2.00 *2.50*
218 A5 (d) 2½c on 100r bl, *grysh* 2.25 *2.75*

On Stamps of 1912.

Perf. 11½x12.

219 A6 (e) ½c on 75r bis brn 1.00 *1.00*
220 A6 (e) 2½c on 100r brn, *lt grn* 1.25 60

On Stamps of 1914.

221 A5 (d) ½c on 75r red lil 1.00 60
222 A5 (d) 2½c on 100r bl, *grysh* 1.10 90

Inverted and double surcharges were made for sale to collectors.

Nos. 163, 98 and Type of 1914 Surcharged with New Values and Bars in Black.

1921

223 A5 (c) 00.5c on 75c red vio *175.00 175.00*
224 A5 (b) 4c on 130r brn, *straw* (#98) 1.10 *1.10*
225 A5 (c) 4c on 130r brn, *straw* 4.00 3.00
a. Surch. omitted 150.00

Nos. 109 and 108 Surcharged with New Values and Bars in Black.

226 A6 00.5c on 75c bis brn 1.10 90
227 A6 1c on 50r dk bl 1.10 80

Nos. 133 and 138 Surcharged with New Values and Bars in Black.

228 A7 00.5c on 7½c yel brn 1.10 90
229 A7 04c on 15c plum 1.10 90

Nos. 81-82 Surcharged

República
40 C.

1925 *Perf. 12½*

234 A3 40c on 400r on 200r bl, *bl* 85 55
a. Perf. 13½ 5.00 3.50
235 N1 40c on 400c on 2½r brn 50 45
a. Perf. 13½ 50 45

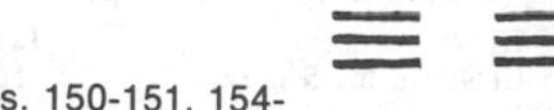

Nos. 150-151, 154-155 Surcharged

70 C.

1931 *Perf. 11½.*

236 A7 50c on 60c dp rose 1.40 1.20
237 A7 70c on 80c pink 2.75 1.50
238 A7 70c on 1e dp bl 2.25 1.75
239 A7 1.40e on 2e dk vio 1.50 1.25

Ceres — A14

Wmk.232

Wmk. Maltese Cross. (232)

1932-46 **Typo.** *Perf. 12x11½*

243 A14 1c bis brn 12 12
244 A14 5c dk brn 12 12
245 A14 10c dp vio 12 12
246 A14 15c black 12 12
247 A14 20c gray 12 12
248 A14 30c myr grn 12 12
249 A14 35c yel grn ('46) 4.50 1.50
250 A14 40c dp org 12 12
251 A14 45c lt bl 1.00 60
252 A14 50c lt brn 12 12
253 A14 60c ol grn 45 20
254 A14 70c org brn 45 25
255 A14 80c emerald 40 15
256 A14 85c rose 3.00 3.00
257 A14 1a claret 80 18
258 A14 1.40a dk bl 6.75 1.65
258A A14 1.75a dk bl ('46) 9.00 1.75
259 A14 2a dl vio 2.50 30
260 A14 5a pale yel grn 4.50 75
261 A14 10a ol bis 12.00 1.40
262 A14 20a orange 30.00 3.00
Nos. 243-262 (21) 76.31 15.69

Stamps of 1932 Surcharged with New Value and Bars.

5½mm. between bars and new value.

1934

263 A14 10c on 45c lt bl 2.00 1.10
264 A14 20c on 85c rose 1.65 1.10
265 A14 30c on 1.40a dk bl 1.65 1.10
266 A14 70c on 2a dl vio 2.25 1.75
267 A14 80c on 5a pale yel grn 3.50 1.50

See also Nos. 294A-300.

Nos. J26, J30 Surcharged in Black

CORREIOS
5
CENTAVOS

1935 **Unwmk.** *Perf. 11½*

268 D2 5c on 6c lt brn 1.40 90
269 D2 30c on 50c gray 1.40 90
270 D2 40c on 50c gray 1.40 90

No. 255 Surcharged in Black

0,15 Cent.

1938 **Wmk. 232** *Perf. 12x11½*

271 A14 5c on 80c emer 50 *90*
272 A14 10c on 80c emer 75 *2.00*
273 A14 15c on 80c emer 1.00 *3.50*

Vasco da Gama Issue

Common Design Types

Engraved; Name and Value Typographed in Black.

Perf. 13½x13

1938, July 26 **Unwmk.**

274 CD34 1c gray grn 12 12
275 CD34 5c org brn 12 12
276 CD34 10c dk car 12 12
277 CD34 15c dk vio brn 25 12
278 CD34 20c slate 28 12
279 CD35 30c rose vio 40 12
280 CD35 35c brt grn 55 30
281 CD35 40c brown 40 25
282 CD35 50c brt red vio 40 25
283 CD36 60c gray blk 50 25
284 CD36 70c brn vio 45 25
285 CD36 80c orange 45 25
286 CD36 1a red 45 25
287 CD37 1.75a blue 1.25 45
288 CD37 2a brn car 2.25 45
289 CD37 5a ol grn 6.75 45
290 CD38 10a bl vio 15.00 90
291 CD38 20a red brn 30.00 1.65
Nos. 274-291 (18) 59.74 6.42

Marble Column and Portuguese Arms with Cross — A20

1938, July 29 *Perf. 12½*

292 A20 80c bl grn 2.00 1.90
293 A20 1.75a dp bl 17.50 3.50
294 A20 20a dk red brn 42.50 22.50

Issued to commemorate the visit of the President of Portugal to this colony in 1938.

Common Design Types pictured in section at front of book.

Stamps of 1932 Surcharged with New Value and Bars.

8mm. between bars and new value.

1941-45 **Wmk. 232** *Perf. 12x11½.*

294A A14 5c on 80c emer ('45) 30 235
295 A14 10c on 45c lt bl 1.00 60
296 A14 15c on 45c lt bl 1.50 60
297 A14 20c on 85c rose 1.00 60
298 A14 35c on 85c rose 1.00 60
299 A14 50c on 1.40a dk bl 1.00 60
300 A14 60c on 1a cl 5.50 4.00
Nos. 294A-300 (7) 11.30 9.35

Nos. 285 to 287 Surcharged with New Values and Bars in Black or Red.

1945 **Unwmk.** *Perf. 13½x13.*

301 CD36 5c on 80c org 40 30
302 CD36 50c on 1a red 60 30
303 CD37 50c on 1.75a bl (R) 40 30
304 CD37 50c on 1.75a bl 60 30

Sao Miguel Fort, Luanda — A21

John IV — A22

Designs: 10c, Our Lady of Nazareth Church, Luanda. 50c, Salvador Correia de Sa e Bene vides. 1a, Surrender of Luanda. 1.75a, Diogo Cao. 2a, Manuel Cerveira Pereira. 5a, Stone Cliffs, Yelala. 10a, Paulo Dias de Novais. 20a, Massangano Fort.

Perf. 14½

1948, May **Unwmk.** **Litho.**

305 A21 5c dk vio 12 12
306 A21 10c dk brn 40 30
307 A22 30c bl grn 20 20
308 A22 50c vio brn 20 10
309 A21 1a carmine 50 20
310 A22 1.75a sl bl 1.00 30
311 A22 2a green 1.00 30
312 A21 5a gray blk 3.00 50
313 A22 10a rose lil 6.00 55
314 A21 20a gray bl 12.00 1.65
a. Sheet of ten 60.00 60.00
Nos. 305-314 (10) 24.42 4.22

Issued to commemorate the 300th anniversary of the restoration of Angola to Portugal.

No. 314a measures 225x162mm. and contains one each of Nos. 305-314 with marginal inscriptions in gray. The sheet sold for 42.50 angolars.

Lady of Fatima Issue

Common Design Type

1948, Dec.

315 CD40 50c carmine 1.25 1.00
316 CD40 3a ultra 4.50 2.75
317 CD40 6a red org 22.50 6.50
318 CD40 9a dp cl 45.00 9.00

Issued to honor Our Lady of the Rosary at Fatima, Portugal.

Chiumbe River — A24

Black Rocks — A25

Designs: 50c, View of Luanda. 2.50a, Sa da Bandeira. 3.50a, Mocamedes. 15a, Cubal River. 50a, Duke of Bragança Falls.

1949 **Unwmk.** *Perf. 13½*

319 A24 20c dk sl bl 30 20
320 A25 40c blk brn 30 15
321 A24 50c rose brn 30 15
322 A24 2.50a bl vio 1.80 40
323 A24 3.50a sl gray 1.80 40
323A A24 15a dk grn 20.00 2.00
324 A24 50a dp grn 135.00 5.50
Nos. 319-324 (7) 159.50 8.80

Angola stamps can be mounted in Scott's annual Portugal Supplement.

Sailing Vessel
A26

U. P. U.
Symbols
A27

1949, Aug. *Perf. 14*

325	A26	1a	chocolate	6.00	50
326	A26	4a	dk Prus grn	20.00	1.25

Centenary of founding of Mocamedes.

1949, Oct.

327	A27	4a	dk grn & lt grn	6.00	2.25

Issued to commemorate the 75th anniversary of the formation of the Universal Postal Union.

Stamp of 1870 — A28

1950, Apr. 2 *Perf. 11½x12*

328	A28	50c	yel grn	1.00	35
329	A28	1a	fawn	1.00	40
330	A28	4a	black	4.00	1.10

Angola's first philatelic exhibition, marking the 80th anniversary of Angola's first stamps.

A sheet of three, perf. 11½, contains one each of Nos. 328, 329 (inverted) and 330, and sold for 6.50 angolars. Size: 119x80 mm. All copies carry an oval exhibition cancellation.

Holy Year Issue
Common Design Types

1950, May *Perf. 13x13½*

331	CD41	1a	dl rose vio	50	15
332	CD42	4a	black	4.50	50

Issued to commemorate the Holy Year, 1950.

Dark Chanting Goshawk
A31

European Bee Eater
A32

Designs: 10c, Racquet-tailed roller. 15c, Bataleur eagle. 50c, Giant kingfisher. 1a, Yellow-fronted barbet. 1.50a, Openbill (stork). 2a, Southern ground hornbill. 2.50a, African skimmer. 3a, Shikra. 3.50a, Denham's bustard. 4a, African golden oriole. 4.50a, Long-tailed shrike. 5a, Red-shouldered glossy starling. 6a, Sharp-tailed glossy starling. 7a, Red-shouldered widow bird. 10a, Half-colored kingfisher. 12.50a, White-crowned shrike. 15a, White-winged babbling starling. 20a, Yellow-billed hornbill. 25a, Amethyst starling. 30a, Orange-breasted shrike. 40a, Secretary bird. 50a, Rosy-faced lovebird.

Photogravure and Lithographed
1951 **Unwmk.** *Perf. 11½*
Birds in Natural Colors.

333	A31	5c	lt bl	15	*1.00*
334	A32	10c	aqua	15	15
335	A32	15c	sal pink	30	*2.00*
336	A32	20c	pale yel	50	45
337	A31	50c	gray bl	30	20
338	A31	1a	lilac	30	20
339	A31	1.50a	gray buff	42	20
340	A31	2a	cream	42	20
341	A32	2.50a	gray	12	30
342	A32	3a	lem yel	38	35
343	A31	3.50a	lt gray	38	35
344	A31	4a	rose buff	60	35
345	A32	4.50a	rose lil	60	40
346	A31	5a	green	3.25	40
347	A31	6a	blue	3.25	1.10
348	A31	7a	orange	3.25	1.50
349	A31	10a	lil rose	27.50	2.25
350	A32	12.50a	sl gray	3.75	3.50
351	A31	15a	pale ol	3.75	3.50
352	A31	20a	pale bis brn	42.50	9.00
353	A31	25a	lil rose	14.00	5.00
354	A32	30a	pale sal	14.00	6.00
355	A31	40a	yellow	22.50	7.50
356	A31	50a	turquoise	65.00	27.50
			Nos. 333-356 (24)	207.67	73.40

Holy Year Extension Issue.
Common Design Type

1951, Oct. **Litho.** *Perf. 14*

357	CD43	4a	orange	2.00	75

Issued to publicize the extension of the Holy Year into 1951.

Sheets contain alternate vertical rows of stamps and labels bearing quotations from Pope Pius XII or the Patriarch Cardinal of Lisbon.

Medical Congress Issue.
Common Design Type

Design: Medical examination

1952, June *Perf. 13½*

358	CD44	1a	vio bl & brn blk	60	30

Issued to publicize the first National Congress of Tropical Medicine, Lisbon, 1952.

Head of Christ — A35

1952, Oct. **Unwmk.** *Perf. 13*

359	A35	10c	dk bl & buff	10	5
360	A35	50c	dk ol grn & ol gray	40	12
361	A35	2a	rose vio & cr	2.50	30

Issued to commemorate the Exhibition of Sacred Missionary Art held at Lisbon in 1951.

Leopard
A36

Sable Antelope
A37

Animals: 20c, Elephant. 30c, Eland. 40c, African crocodile. 50c, Impala. 1a, Mountain zebra. 1.50a, Sitatunga. 2a, Black rhinoceros. 2.30a, Gemsbok. 2.50a, Lion. 3a, Buffalo. 3.50a, Springbok. 4a, Brindled gnu. 5a, Hartebeest. 7a, Wart hog. 10a, Defassa waterbuck. 12.50a, Hippopotamus. 15a, Greater kudu. 20a, Giraffe.

1953, Aug. 15 *Perf. 12½*

362	A36	5c	multi	10	10
363	A37	10c	multi	10	10
364	A37	20c	multi	10	10
365	A37	30c	multi	10	10
366	A36	40c	multi	10	10
367	A37	50c	multi	10	10
368	A37	1a	multi	35	10
369	A37	1.50a	multi	25	10
370	A36	2a	multi	30	15
371	A37	2.30a	multi	40	15
372	A37	2.50a	multi	50	10
373	A36	3a	multi	50	15
374	A37	3.50a	multi	30	12
375	A37	4a	multi	12.00	40
376	A37	5a	multi	55	20
377	A37	7a	multi	1.25	40
378	A37	10a	multi	2.00	35
379	A37	12.50a	multi	4.25	1.50
380	A37	15a	multi	4.25	2.00
381	A37	20a	multi	5.25	60
			Nos. 362-381 (20)	32.75	6.92

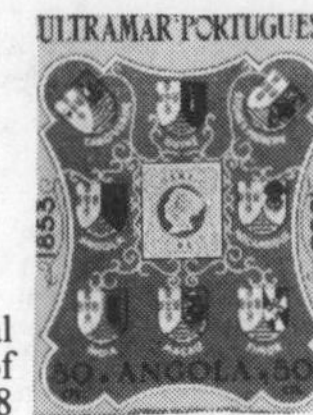

Stamp of Portugal and Arms of Colonies — A38

1953, Nov. **Photo.** *Perf. 13*
Stamp and Arms Multicolored.

382	A38	50c	gray & dk gray	85	50

Issued to commemorate the centenary of Portugal's first postage stamps.

Map and Plane — A39

Typographed and Lithographed
1954, May 27 *Perf. 13½*

383	A39	35c	dk grn, ol, bl grn & red	15	15
384	A39	4.50e	blk, dl vio, aqua & red	1.10	45

Issued to publicize the visit of Pres. Francisco H C. Lopes.

Sao Paulo Issue
Common Design Type

1954 **Litho.**

385	CD46	1e	bis & gray	50	30

Issued to commemorate the 400th anniversary of the founding of Sao Paulo.

Map of Angola — A41

Artur de Paiva — A42

1955, Aug. **Unwmk.** *Perf. 13½*
Blue Outline, Red Highways, Black Inscriptions

386	A41	5c	gray & pale grn	6	6
387	A41	20c	gray, lt bl & sal	7	6
388	A41	50c	brn buff, pale grn & lt bl	15	6
389	A41	1e	gray, lt bl grn, & org yel	20	6
390	A41	2.30e	brn buff, aqua & yel	55	30
391	A41	4e	bis, pale grn & lt bl	1.75	20
392	A41	10e	lil, aqua & cit	1.65	20
393	A41	20e	ol grn & pale grn	3.00	40
			Nos. 386-393 (8)	7.43	1.34

1956, Oct. 9 *Perf. 13½x12½*

394	A42	1e	blk, dk bl & ocher	30	20

Issued to commemorate the centenary of the birth of Col. Artur de Paiva.

Man of Malange
A43

José M. Antunes
A44

Various Costumes in Multicolor; Inscriptions in Black Brown.

1957, Jan. 1 **Photo.** *Perf. 11½*
Granite Paper.

395	A43	5c	gray	5	5
396	A43	10c	org yel	7	6
397	A43	15c	lt bl grn	12	8
398	A43	20c	pale rose vio	12	8
399	A43	30c	brt rose	12	8
400	A43	40c	bl gray	12	8
401	A43	50c	pale ol	12	8
402	A43	80c	lt vio	20	20
403	A43	1.50e	buff	1.50	20
404	A43	2.50e	lt yel grn	1.75	18
405	A43	4e	salmon	50	18
406	A43	10e	sal pink	1.25	40
			Nos. 395-406 (12)	5.92	1.67

1957, April *Perf. 13½*

407	A44	1e	aqua & brn	80	30

Issued to commemorate the centenary of the birth of Father Jose Maria Antunes.

Fair Emblem, Globe and Arms — A45

1958, July **Litho.** *Perf. 12x11½*

408	A45	1.50e	multi	40	25

World's Fair, Brussels, Apr. 17-Oct. 19.

Tropical Medicine Congress Issue
Common Design Type

Design: Securidaca longipedunculata.

1958, Dec. 15 *Perf. 13½*

409	CD47	2.50e	multi	1.90	1.10

Issued to publicize the 6th International Congress for Tropical Medicine and Malaria, Lisbon, Sept. 1958.

Medicine Man — A47

Welwitschia Mirabilis — A48

Designs: 1.50e, Early government doctor. 2.50e, Modern medical team.

1958, Dec. 18 *Perf. 11½x12*

410	A47	1e	bl blk & brn	30	15
411	A47	1.50e	gray, blk & brn	80	35
412	A47	2.50e	multi	1.50	60

Issued to commemorate the 75th anniversary of the Maria Pia Hospital, Luanda.

1959, Oct. 1 **Litho.** *Perf. 14½*
Various Views of Plant and Various Frames.

413	A48	1.50e	lt brn, grn & blk	80	70
414	A48	2.50e	multi	1.20	55
415	A48	5e	multi	1.60	90
416	A48	10e	multi	4.50	1.50

Centenary of discovery of Welwitschia mirabilis, desert plant.

Map of West Africa, c. 1540, by Jorge Reinel — A49

1960, June 25 *Perf. 13½*

417	A49	2.50e	multi	30	20

Issued to commemorate the 500th anniversary of the death of Prince Henry the Navigator.

Angola stamps can be mounted in Scott's annual Portugal Supplement.

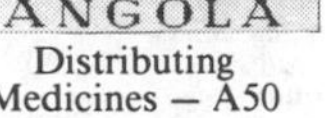

Distributing Medicines — A50

Girl of Angola — A51

1960, Oct. Litho. *Perf. 14½*

418	A50 2.50e multi		45	25

Issued to commemorate the 10th anniversary of the Commission for Technical Co-operation in Africa South of the Sahara (C.C.T.A.).

1961, Nov. 30 Unwmk. *Perf. 13*

Portraits of Angolese Women in Natural Colors

419	A51	10c	blk, yel grn & grn	8	5
420	A51	15c	blk, gray bl & lil	8	8
421	A51	30c	blk, yel & dk bl	10	10
422	A51	40c	blk, gray & dk red	5	5
423	A51	60c	blk, sal & ol	8	8
424	A51	1.50e	blk, bl & red	20	5
425	A51	2e	blk, lil & bis	90	15
426	A51	2.50e	blk, yel & brn	1.25	15
427	A51	3e	blk, pink & ol	3.00	30
428	A51	4e	blk, gray grn & brn	1.40	30
429	A51	5e	blk, lt bl & car	1.10	30
430	A51	7.50e	blk, dl yel & brn	1.40	70
431	A51	10e	blk, ocher & grn	1.10	40
432	A51	15e	blk, beigc & grn	1.00	60
432A	A51	25e	blk, rose & red brn	2.50	1.00
432B	A51	50e	blk, gray & vio bl	4.00	1.50
			Nos. 419-432B (16)	18.24	5.81

Sports Issue

Common Design Type

Sports: 50c, Flying. 1e, Rowing. 1.50e, Water polo. 2.50e, Hammer throwing. 4.50e, High jump. 15e, Weight lifting.

1962, Jan. 18 *Perf. 13½*

Multicolored Design

433	CD48	50c	lt bl	15	10
434	CD48	1e	ol bis	1.10	20
435	CD48	1.50e	salmon	50	15
436	CD48	2.50e	lt brn	60	15
437	CD48	4.50e	pale bl	50	40
438	CD48	15e	yellow	2.25	1.00
			Nos. 433-438 (6)	5.10	2.00

Anti-Malaria Issue

Common Design Type

Design: Anopheles funestus.

1962, April Litho. *Perf. 13½*

439	CD49 2.50e multi	90	50

Issued for the World Health Organization drive to eradicate malaria.

Gen. Norton de Matos — A54

1962, Aug. 8 Unwmk. *Perf. 14½*

440	A54 2.50e multi	45	20

Issued to commemorate the 50th anniversary of the founding of Nova Lisboa.

Locusts — A56

1963, June 2 Litho. *Perf. 14*

447	A56 2.50e multi	60	30

Issued to commemorate the 15th anniversary of the International Anti-Locust Organization.

Arms of Luanda A57

Vila de Santo Antonio do Zaire — A58

Coats of Arms (Provinces and Cities): 10c, Massangano. 15c, Sanza-Pombo. 25c, Ambriz. 30c, Muxima. 40c, Ambrizete. 50c, Carmona. 60c, Catete. 70c, Quibaxe. No. 458, Maquelo do Zombo. 1e, Salazar. 1.20e, Bembe. No. 461, Caxito. 1.50e, Malanje. 1.80e, Dondo. No. 465, Damba. 2e, Henrique de Carvalho. 2.50e, Moçamedes. 3e, Novo Redondo. 3.50e, S. Salvador do Congo. 4e, Cuimba. 5e, Luso. 6.50e, Negage. 7e, Quitexe. 7.50e, S. Filipe de Benguela. 8e, Mucaba. 9e, 31 de Janeiro. 10e, Lobito. 11e, Nova Caipemba. 12.50e, Gabela. 14e, Songo. 15e Sa" da Bandeira. 17e, Quimbele. 17.50e, Silva Porto. 20e, Nova Lisboa. 22.50e, Cabinda. 25e, Noqui. 30e, Serpa Pinto. 35e, Santa Cruz. 50e, General Freire.

1963 *Perf. 13½*

Arms in Original Colors; Red and Violet Blue Inscriptions.

448	A57	5c	tan	10	10
449	A57	10c	lt bl	10	10
450	A58	15c	salmon	10	10
451	A58	20c	olive	10	10
452	A58	25c	lt bl	12	10
453	A57	30c	buff	10	10
454	A58	40c	gray	12	10
455	A57	50c	lt grn	10	10
456	A58	60c	brt yel	18	12
457	A58	70c	dl rose	18	12
458	A57	1e	pale lil	45	10
459	A58	1e	dl yel	30	10
460	A58	1.20e	rose	15	10
461	A57	1.50e	pale sal	90	10
462	A58	1.50e	lt grn	60	12
463	A58	1.80e	yel ol	35	20
464	A57	2e	lt yel grn	45	10
465	A57	2.50e	lt gray	2.25	15
466	A58	2.50e	dl bl	2.00	18
467	A57	3e	yel ol	65	12
468	A57	3.50e	gray	75	15
469	A58	4e	citron	55	20
470	A57	5e	citron	60	35
471	A58	6.50e	tan	60	40
472	A58	7e	rose lil	65	40
473	A57	7.50e	pale lil	85	45
474	A58	8e	lt aqua	70	45
475	A58	9e	yellow	90	45
476	A57	10e	dp sal	1.10	55
477	A58	11e	dl yel grn	1.10	85
478	A57	12.50e	pale bl	1.40	70
479	A58	14e	lt gray	1.40	70
480	A57	15e	lt bl	1.50	70
481	A58	17e	pale bl	1.65	1.10
482	A57	17.50e	dl yel	2.25	1.50
483	A57	20e	lt aqua	2.25	1.10
484	A57	22.50e	gray	2.25	1.50
485	A58	25e	citron	2.25	1.10
486	A57	30e	yellow	3.00	1.90
487	A58	35e	grysh bl	3.00	2.25
488	A58	50e	dp yel	4.50	1.90
			Nos. 448-488 (41)	42.55	21.01

Pres. Américo Rodrigues Thomaz — A59

1963, Sept. 16 Litho.

489	A59 2.50e multi	50	20

Visit of the President of Portugal.

Airline Anniversary Issue

Common Design Type

1963, Oct. 5 Unwmk. *Perf. 14½*

490	CD50 1e lt bl & multi	40	20

Issued to commemorate the 10th anniversary of Transportes Aéreos Portugueses.

Cathedral of Sá da Bandeira A61

Malange Cathedral A62

Churches: 20c, Landana. 30c, Luanda Cathedral. 40c, Gabela. 50c, St. Martin's Chapel, Baia dos Tigres. 1.50e, St. Peter, Chibia. 2e, Church of Our Lady, Benguela. 2.50e, Church of Jesus, Luanda. 3e, Camabatela. 3.50e, Mission, Cabinda. 4e, Vila Folgares. 4.50e, Church of Our Lady, Lobito. 5e, Church of Cabinda. 7.50e, Cacuso Church, Malange. 10e, Lubango Mission. 12.50e, Huila Mission. 15e, Church of Our Lady, Luanda Island.

1953, Nov. 1 Litho.

Multicolored Design and Inscription

491	A61	10c	gray bl	10	10
492	A61	20c	pink	10	10
493	A61	30c	lt bl	10	10
494	A61	40c	tan	10	10
495	A61	50c	lt grn	10	10
496	A62	1e	buff	12	10
497	A61	1.50e	lt vio bl	15	10
498	A62	2e	pale rose	18	10
499	A61	2.50e	gray	25	10
500	A62	3e	buff	28	10
501	A61	3.50e	olive	33	12
502	A62	4e	buff	35	30
503	A62	4.50e	pale bl	42	35
504	A61	5e	tan	45	35
505	A62	7.50e	gray	70	50
506	A61	10e	dl yel	90	60
507	A62	12.50e	bister	1.20	90
508	A62	15e	pale gray vio	2.00	1.10
			Nos. 491-508 (18)	7.83	5.22

National Overseas Bank Issue

Common Design Type

Design: Antonio Teixeira de Sousa.

1964, May 16 *Perf. 13½*

509	CD51 2.50e multi	60	35

Issued to commemorate the centenary of the National Overseas Bank of Portugal.

Commerce Building and Arms of Chamber of Commerce A64

1964, Nov. Litho. *Perf. 12*

510	A64 1e multi	20	10

Luanda Chamber of Commerce centenary.

ITU Issue

Common Design Type

1965, May 17 Unwmk. *Perf. 14½*

511	CD52 2.50e gray & multi	1.10	40

Issued to commemorate the centenary of the International Telecommunication Union.

> Certain countries cancel stamps in full sheets and sell them (usually with gum) for less than face value. Dealers generally sell "CTO".

Plane over Luanda Airport — A65

Harquebusier, 1539 — A66

1965, Dec. 3 Litho. *Perf. 13*

512	A65 2.50e multi	35	20

Issued to commemorate the 25th anniversary of DTA, Direccao dos Transportes Aereos.

1966, Feb. 25 Litho. *Perf. 14½*

Designs: 50c, Harquebusier, 1539. 1e, Harquebusier, 1640. 1.50e, Infantry officer, 1777. 2e, Standard bearer, infantry, 1777. 2.50e, Infantry soldier, 1777. 3e, Cavalry officer, 1783. 4e, Cavalry soldier, 1783. 4.50e, Infantry officer, 1807. 5e, Infantry soldier, 1807. 6e, Cavalry officer, 1807. 8e, Cavalry soldier, 1807. 9e, Infantry soldier, 1873.

513	A66	50c	multi	15	15
514	A66	1e	multi	18	18
515	A66	1.50e	multi	15	15
516	A66	2e	multi	18	18
517	A66	2.50e	multi	30	15
518	A66	3e	multi	30	15
519	A66	4e	multi	40	30
520	A66	4.50e	multi	40	30
521	A66	5e	multi	65	20
522	A66	6e	multi	75	40
523	A66	8e	multi	1.10	55
524	A66	9e	multi	1.40	55
			Nos. 513-524 (12)	5.96	3.26

National Revolution Issue

Common Design Type

Design: St. Paul's Hospital and Commercial and Industrial School.

1966, May 28 Litho. *Perf. 12*

525	CD53 1e multi	30	15

40th anniversary, National Revolution.

Emblem of Holy Ghost Society — A68

1966 Litho. *Perf. 13*

526	A68 1e bl & multi	20	10

Centenary of the Holy Ghost Society.

Navy Club Issue

Common Design Type

Designs: 1e, Mendes Barata and cruiser Dom Carlos I. 2.50e, Capt. Augusto de Castilho and corvette Mindelo.

1967, Jan. 31 Litho. *Perf. 13*

527	CD54 1e multi	50	20
528	CD54 2.50e multi	1.00	25

Centenary of Portugal's Navy Club.

Fatima Basilica — A70

Angola Map, Manuel Cerveira Pereira — A71

1967, May 13 Litho. *Perf. 12½x13*
529 A70 50c multi 15 15

Issued to commemorate the 50th anniversary of the apparition of the Virgin Mary to three shepherd children at Fatima.

1967, Aug. 15 Litho. *Perf. 12½x13*
530 A71 50c multi 18 15

Issued to commemorate the 350th anniversary of the founding of Benguela.

Administration Building, Carmona — A72

1967 Litho. *Perf. 12*
531 A72 1e multi 15 15

Issued to commemorate the 50th anniversary of the founding of Carmona.

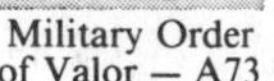

Military Order of Valor — A73

Our Lady of Hope — A74

Designs: 50c, Ribbon of the Three Orders. 1.50e, Military Order of Avis. 2e, Military Order of Christ. 2.50e, Military Order of St. John of Espada. 3e, Order of the Empire. 4e, Order of Prince Henry. 5e, Order of Benemerencia. 10e, Order of Public Instruction. 20e, Order for Industrial and Agricultural Merit.

1967, Oct. 31 *Perf. 14*
532 A73 50c lt gray & multi 10 6
533 A73 1e lt grn & multi 10 6
534 A73 1.50e yel & multi 12 6
535 A73 2e multi 18 6
536 A73 2.50e multi 20 10
537 A73 3e lt ol & multi 28 10
538 A73 4e gray & multi 30 10
539 A73 5e multi 40 10
540 A73 10e lil & multi 60 40
541 A73 20e lt bl & multi 1.50 80
Nos. 532-541 (10) 3.78 1.84

Cabral Issue

Designs: 1e, Belmonte Castle (horiz.). 1.50e, St. Jerome's Convent. 2.50e, Cabral's Armada.

1968, Apr. 22 Litho. *Perf. 14*
542 A74 50c yel & multi 10 10
543 A74 1e gray & multi 40 10
544 A74 1.50e lt bl & multi 60 10
545 A74 2.50e buff & multi 90 20

Issued to commemorate the 500th anniversary of the birth of Pedro Alvares Cabral, navigator who took possession of Brazil for Portugal.

Francisco Inocencio de Souza Coutinho — A75

1969, Jan. 7 Litho. *Perf. 14*
546 A75 2e multi 40 30

Issued to commemorate the 200th anniversary of the founding of Novo Redondo.

Admiral Coutinho Issue
Common Design Type

Design: Adm. Gago Coutinho and his first ship.

1969, Feb. 17 Litho. *Perf. 14*
547 CD55 2.50e multi 45 20

Compass Rose A77

Portal of St. Jeronimo's Monastery A79

1969, Aug. 29 Litho. *Perf. 14*
548 A77 1e multi 20 20

Issued to commemorate the 500th anniversary of the birth of Vasco da Gama (1469-1524), navigator.

Administration Reform Issue
Common Design Type

1969, Sept. 25 Litho. *Perf. 14*
549 CD56 1.50e multi 20 20

Issued to commemorate the centenary of the administration reforms of the overseas territories.

1969, Dec. 1 Litho. *Perf. 14*
550 A79 3e multi 30 20

Issued to commemorate the 500th anniversary of the birth of King Manuel I.

Angolasaurus Bocagei — A80

Fossils and Minerals: 1e, Ferrometeorite. 1.50e, Dioptase crystals. 2e, Gondwanidium. 2.50e, Diamonds. 3e, Estromatolite. 3.50e, Procarcharodon megalodon. 4e, Microceratodus angolensis. 4.50e, Moscovite. 5e, Barite. 6e, Nostoceras. 10e, Rotula orbiculus angolensis.

1970, Oct. 31 Litho. *Perf. 13*
551 A80 50c tan & multi 15 10
552 A80 1e multi 20 10
553 A80 1.50e multi 25 10
554 A80 2e multi 30 10
555 A80 2.50e lt gray & multi 30 10
556 A80 3e multi 30 10
557 A80 3.50e bl & multi 40 20
558 A80 4e lt gray & multi 40 20
559 A80 4.50e gray & multi 40 20
560 A80 5e gray & multi 40 20
561 A80 6e pink & multi 75 30
562 A80 10e lt bl & multi 1.00 50
Nos. 551-562 (12) 4.85 2.20

Marshal Carmona Issue
Common Design Type

1970, Nov. 15 *Perf. 14*
563 CD57 2.50e multi 35 15

Birth centenary of Marshal Antonio Oscar Carmona de Fragoso (1869-1951), President of Portugal.

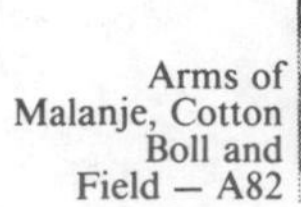

Arms of Malanje, Cotton Boll and Field — A82

1970, Nov. 20 *Perf. 13*
564 A82 2.50e multi 35 20

Centenary of the municipality of Malanje.

Mail Ships and Angola No. 1 — A83

Designs: 4.50e, Steam locomotive and Angola No. 4.

1970, Dec. 1 *Perf. 13½*
565 A83 1.50e multi 45 20
566 A83 4.50e multi 1.00 35

Centenary of stamps of Angola. See No. C36.

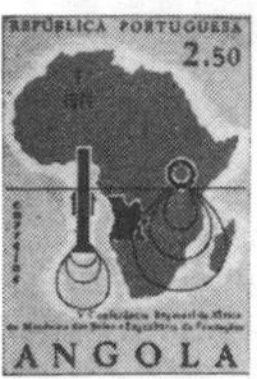

Map of Africa, Diagram of Seismic Tests — A84

Galleon on Congo River — A85

1971, Aug. 22 Litho. *Perf. 13*
567 A84 2.50e multi 20 10

5th Regional Conference of Soil and Foundation Engineers, Luanda, Aug. 22-Sept. 5.

1972, May 25 Litho. *Perf. 13*
568 A85 1e emer & multi 20 15

4th centenary of the publication of The Lusiads by Luiz Camoens.

Olympic Games Issue
Common Design Type

1972, June 20 *Perf. 14x13½*
569 CD59 50c multi 20 15

20th Olympic Games, Munich, Aug. 26-Sept. 11.

Lisbon-Rio de Janeiro Flight Issue
Common Design Type

1972, Sept. 20 Litho. *Perf. 13½*
570 CD60 1e multi 20 15

WMO Centenary Issue
Common Design Type

1973, Dec. 15 Litho. *Perf. 13*
571 CD61 1e dk gray & multi 20 15

Centenary of international meteorological cooperation.

Radar Station A89

1974, June 25 Litho. *Perf. 13*
572 A89 2e multi 35 20

Establishment of satellite communications network via Intelsat among Portugal, Angola and Mozambique.

Harpa Doris — A90

Designs: Sea shells.

1974, Oct. 25 Litho. *Perf. 12x12½*
573 A90 25c *shown* 12 12
574 A90 30c *Murex melanamathos* 12 12

575 A90 50c *Venus foliaceo lamellosa* 12 12
576 A90 70c *Lathyrus filosus* 12 12
577 A90 1e *Cymbium cisium* 12 12
578 A90 1.50e *Cassis tesselata* 20 15
579 A90 2e *Cypraea stercoraria* 20 12
580 A90 2.50e *Conus prometheus* 20 20
581 A90 3e *Strombus latus* 20 20
582 A90 3.50e *Tympanotonus fuscatus* 20 20
583 A90 4e *Cardium costatum* 30 20
584 A90 5e *Natica fulminea* 30 20
585 A90 6e *Lyropecten nodosus* 40 20
586 A90 7e *Tonna galea* 50 20
587 A90 10e *Donax rugosus* 60 30
588 A90 25e *Cymatium trigonum* 1.75 40
589 A90 30e *Olivancilaria acuminata* 2.50 50
590 A90 35e *Semifusus morio* 2.75 60
591 A90 40e *Clavatula lineata* 3.00 1.10
592 A90 50e *Solarium granulatum* 4.00 1.65
Nos. 573-592 (20) 17.70 6.82

No. 386 Overprinted in Blue: "1974 / FILATELIA / JUVENIL"

1974, Dec. 21 Litho. *Perf. 13½*
593 A41 5c multi 20 20

Youth philately.

Republic

Star and Hand Holding Rifle — A91

1975, Nov. 11 Litho. *Perf. 13x13½*
594 A91 1.50e red & multi 20 20

Independence in 1975.

Diquiche Mask — A92

Design: 3e, Bui ou Congolo mask.

1976, Feb. 6 *Perf. 13½*
595 A92 50c lt bl & multi 10 10
596 A92 3e multi 30 10

Workers — A93

President Agostinho Neto — A94

1976, May 1 Litho. *Perf. 12*
597 A93 1e red & multi 20 20

International Workers' Day.

No. 392 Overprinted Bar and: "DIA DO SELO / 15 Junho 1976 / REP. POPULAR / DE"

1976, June 15 Litho. *Perf. 13½*
598 A41 10e multi 60 40

Stamp Day.

1976, Nov. 11 Litho. *Perf. 13*
599 A94 50c yel & dk brn 10 10
600 A94 2e lt gray & plum 20 10
601 A94 3e gray & ind 20 10
602 A94 5e buff & brn 30 10

603 A94 10e tan & sep 60 20
a. Souvenir sheet 3.00 2.00
Nos. 599-603 (5) 1.40 60

First anniversary of independence. No. 603a contains one imperf. stamp. Gold margin with brown inscription. Size: 60x75mm.

Nos. 393, 588-589, 592 Overprinted with Bar over Republica Portuguesa and: "REPUBLICA POPULAR DE"

1977, Feb. 9 ***Perf. 13½, 12x12½***
604 A41 20e multi 1.25 40
605 A90 25e multi 1.50 50
606 A90 30e multi 2.00 60
607 A90 50e multi 3.00 1.00

Overprint in 3 lines on No. 604, in 2 lines on others.

No. 438 Overprinted with Bar over Republica Portuguesa and: "S. Silvestre / 1976 / Rep. Popular / de"

1976, Dec. 31 ***Perf. 13½***
608 CD48 15e multi 90 40

Child and WHO Emblem — A95

Map of Africa, Flag of Angola — A96

1977 **Litho.** ***Perf. 10½***
609 A95 2.50k blk & lt bl 20 10

Campaign for vaccination against poliomyelitis.

1977 **Photo.**
610 A96 6k blk, red & bl 30 20

First congress of Popular Movement for the Liberation of Angola.

Anti-Apartheid Emblem — A97

1979, July **Litho.** ***Perf. 13½***
611 A97 1k multi 15 15

Anti-Apartheid Year.

Human Rights Emblem A98

Child Flowers, Globe, IYC Emblem A99

1979 **Litho.** ***Perf. 13½***
612 A98 2.50k multi 20 10

Declaration of Human Rights, 30th anniversary. in 1975.

1980, Aug. **Litho.** ***Perf. 14x14½***
613 A99 3.50k multi 20 10

International Year of the Child (1979).

Running, Moscow '80 Emblem A100

5th Anniv. of Independence A101

1980 **Litho.** ***Perf. 13½***
614 A100 9k shown 50 20
615 A100 12k Swimming, horiz. 60 30

22nd Summer Olympic Games, Moscow, July 19-Aug. 3.

1980
616 A101 5.50k multi 20 20

Nos. 572, 566 Overprinted with Bar and: "REPUBLICA POPULAR / DE"

1980 **Litho.** ***Perf. 13½x13***
616A A89 2e multi (bar only) 20
616B A83 4.50e multi 45

See No. C37.

Nos. 577-580, 582-591 Overprinted with Black Bar over "Republica Portuguesa"

1981, Sept. **Litho.** ***Perf. 12x12½***
617 A90 1e multi
618 A90 1.50e multi
619 A90 2e multi
620 A90 2.50e multi
621 A90 3.50e multi
622 A90 4e multi
623 A90 5e multi
624 A90 6e multi
625 A90 7e multi
626 A90 10e multi
627 A90 25e multi
628 A90 30e multi
629 A90 35e multi
630 A90 40e multi
Nos. 617-630 (14) 10.00 5.50

Man Walking with Canes, Tchibinda Ilunga Statue — A102

1981, Sept. **Litho.** ***Perf. 13½***
631 A102 9k multi 50 30

Turipex '81 tourism exhibition.

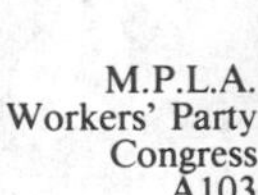

M.P.L.A. Workers' Party Congress A103

1981 **Litho.** ***Perf. 14***
632 A103 50l Millet 10 10
633 A103 5k Coffee 30 20
634 A103 7.50k Sunflowers 40 20
635 A103 13.50k Cotton 60 30
636 A103 14k Oil 70 40
637 A103 16k Diamonds 70 40
Nos. 632-637 (6) 2.80 1.60

People's Power A104

Natl. Heroes' Day A105

1981
638 A104 40k lt bl & blk 2.00 60

1981 ***Perf. 14x13½***
639 A105 4.50k Former Pres. Neto 20 10
640 A105 50k Neto, diff. 2.25 1.00

Soweto Uprising, 5th Anniv. A106

1981
641 A106 4.50k multi 30 10

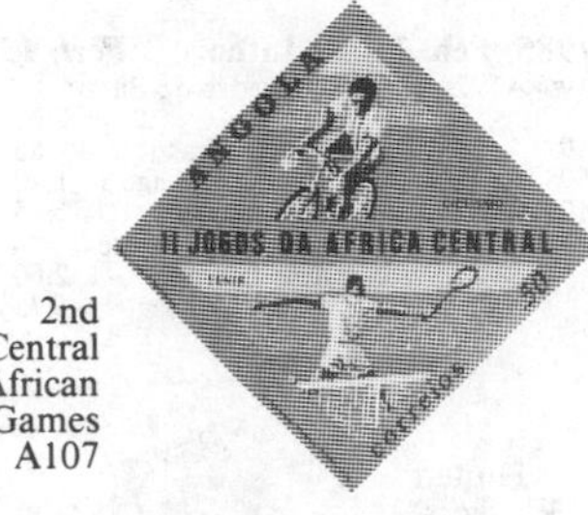

2nd Central African Games A107

1981 **Litho.** ***Perf. 13½***
642 A107 50l Bicycling, tennis 20 10
643 A107 5k Judo, boxing 30 20
644 A107 6k Basketball, volleyball 35 22
645 A107 10k Handball, soccer 60 40

Souvenir Sheet

Imperf

646 A107 15k multi 1.00

Size of No. 646: 112x130mm.

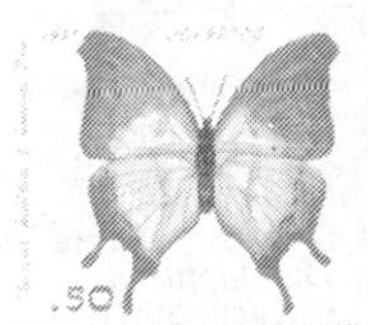

Charaxes Kahldeni A108

1982, Feb. 26 **Litho.** ***Perf. 13½***
647 A108 50l shown 10 10
648 A108 1k Abantis zambesiaca 10 10
649 A108 5k Catacroptera cloanthe 30 20
650 A108 9k Myrina ficedula, vert. 60 20
651 A108 10k Colotis danae 60 20
652 A108 15k Acraea acrita 80 40
653 A108 100k Precis hierta 4.00 2.00
a. 30k Souvenir sheet 3.00 1.50
Nos. 647-653 (7) 6.50 3.20

No. 653a contains Nos. 647-653 (imperf.); blue and black margin. Size: 155x105mm.

5th Anniv. of U.N. Membership — A109

Designs: 5.50k, The Silence of the Night, by Musseque Catambor. 7.50k, Cotton picking, Catete.

1982, Sept. 22 **Litho.**
654 A109 5.50k multi 30 20
655 A109 7.50k multi 40 20

20th Anniv. of Engineering Laboratory A110

1982, Dec. 21 **Litho.** ***Perf. 14***
656 A110 9k Lab 40 20
657 A110 13k Worker, vert. 60 30
658 A110 100k Equipment, vert. 5.00 2.00

Local Flowers A111

1983, Feb. 18 ***Perf. 13½***
659 A111 5k Dichrostachys glomerata 20 20
660 A111 12k Amblygonocarpus obtusangulus 60 20
661 A111 50k Albizzia versicolor 3.00 1.00

Women's Org., First Congress A112

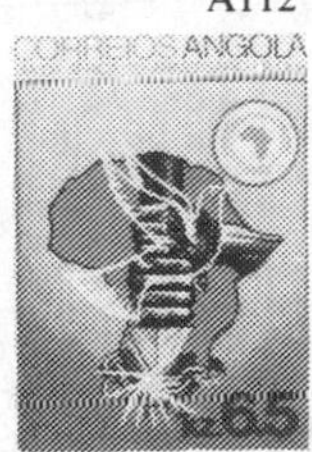

Africa Day — A113

1983 **Litho.** ***Perf. 13½***
662 A112 20k multi 1.20

1983, June 30 ***Perf. 13***
663 A113 6.5k multi 40

BRASILIANA '83 Stamp Exhibition, Rio de Janeiro, July 29-Aug. 7 — A115

Crop-eating insects.

1983, July 29 **Litho.** ***Perf. 13***
666 A115 4.5k Antestiopsis lineaticollis 28
667 A115 6.5k Stephanoderes hampei ferr. 40
668 A115 10k Zonocerus variegatus 62

25th Anniv. of Economic Commission for Africa — A116

1983, Aug. 2
669 A116 10k Map, emblem 62

185th Anniv. of Post Office A117

1983, Dec. 7 Litho. *Perf. 13½*
670 A117 50l Mail collection, vert. 5
671 A117 3.5k Unloading mail plane 22
672 A117 5k Sorting mail 32
673 A117 15k Mailing letter, vert. 92
674 A117 30k Post office box delivery 1.85
a. Miniature sheet of 3 6.25
Nos. 670-674 (5) 3.36

No. 674a contains Nos. 671-672, 674. Size: 142x78mm. Sold for 100k.

Local Butterflies A118

1984, Jan. 20 Litho. *Perf. 13½*
675 A118 50l Parasa karschi 5
676 A118 1k Diaphone angolensis 6
677 A118 3.5k Choeropasis jucunda 22
678 A118 6.5k Hespagarista rendalli 40
679 A118 15k Euchromia guineensis 92
680 A118 17.5k Mazuca roseistriga 1.10
681 A118 20k Utetheisa callima 1.25
Nos. 675-681 (7) 4.00

First Natl. Worker's Union Congress, Apr. 11-16 — A119

1984, Apr. 11 Litho. *Perf. 13½*
682 A119 30k multi 1.85

Local Birds — A120

1984, Oct. 24 Litho. *Perf. 13½*
683 A120 10.50k Bucorvos leadbeateri 70
684 A120 14k Gypohicax angolensis 85
685 A120 16k Ardea goliath 95
686 A120 19.50k Pelicanus onocrotalus 1.20
687 A120 22k Platelea alba 1.30
688 A120 26k Balearica pavonnia 1.55
Nos. 683-688 (6) 6.55

Local Animals A121

1984, Nov. 12
689 A121 1k Tragelephus strepsicerus 6
690 A121 4k Antidorcos marsupialis angolerusis 24
691 A121 5k Pan troglodytes 30
692 A121 10k Sycerus caffer 60
693 A121 15k Hippotragus niger variani 90
694 A121 20k Orycteropus afer 1.20
695 A121 25k Crocuta crocuta 1.50
Nos. 689-695 (7) 4.80

Angolese Monuments A122

1985, Feb. 21 Litho. *Perf. 13½*
696 A122 5k San Pedro da Barra 35
697 A122 12.5k Nova Oeiras 85
698 A122 18k M'Banza Kongo 1.20
699 A122 26k Massangano 1.75
700 A122 39k Escravatura Museum 2.60
Nos. 696-700 (5) 6.75

United Workers' Party, 25th Anniv. A123

1985, May Litho. *Perf. 12*
701 A123 77k XXV, red flags 2.25

Printed in sheets of 5.

Southern African Development Council, 5th Anniv. — A124

1985, May
702 A124 1k Flags 5
703 A124 11k Oil drilling platform, Cabinda 35
704 A124 57k Conference 1.65
a. Strip of 3, #702-704 2.05

Medicinal Plants — A125

Lithographed and Typographed

1985, July 5 *Perf. 11*
705 A125 1k Lonchocarpus sericeus 5
706 A125 4k Gossypium 12
707 A125 11k Cassia occidentalis 35
708 A125 25.50k Gloriosa superba 75
709 A125 55k Cochlospermum angolensis 1.60
Nos. 705-709 (5) 2.87

ARGENTINA '85 exhibition.

5th Natl. Heroes Day — A126

Natl. flag and: 10.50k, Portrait of Agostinho Neto, party leader. 36.50k, Neto working.

1985 Litho. *Perf. 13½*
710 A126 10.50k multi 30
711 A126 36.50k multi 1.05

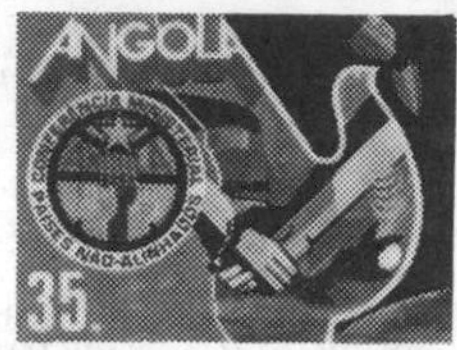

Ministerial Conference of Non-Aligned Countries, Luanda — A127

1985, Sept. 4 Photo. *Perf. 11*
712 A127 35k multi 2.25

UN, 40th Anniv. A128

1985, Oct. 29 Litho. *Perf. 11*
713 A128 12.50k multi 85

Industry and Natural Resources A129

1985, Nov. 11
714 A129 50l Cement Factory 5
715 A129 5k Logging 32
716 A129 7k Quartz 45
717 A129 10k Iron mine 65
a. Souvenir sheet of 4, #714-717, imperf. 1.50

Natl. independence, 10th anniv.
No. 717a has multicolored margin picturing natl. crest, family, industry, aircraft and historical data. Size: 210x124mm.

2nd Natl. Workers' Party Congress (MPLA) A130

1985, Nov. 28 *Perf. 13½*
718 A130 20k multi 1.25

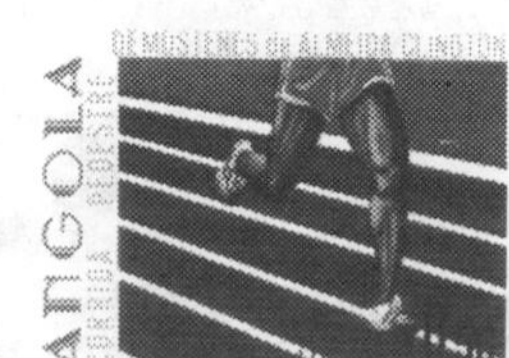

Demostenes de Almeida Clington Races, 30th Anniv. — A131

Various runners.

1985, Dec. 13
719 A131 50l multi 5
720 A131 5k multi 32
721 A131 6.50k multi 42
722 A131 10k multi 65

1986 World Cup Soccer Championships, Mexico — A132

Map, soccer field and various plays.

1986, May 6 Litho. *Perf. 11½x11*
723 A132 50l multi 5
724 A132 3.50k multi 22
725 A132 5k multi 32
726 A132 7k multi 45
727 A132 10k multi 65
728 A132 18k multi 1.29
Nos. 723-728 (6) 2.98

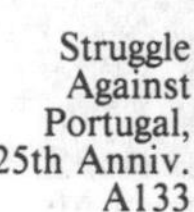

Struggle Against Portugal, 25th Anniv. A133

1986, May 6 *Perf. 11x11½*
729 A133 15k multi 1.00

First Man in Space, 25th Anniv. A134

1986, Aug. 21 Litho. *Perf. 11x11½*
730 A134 50l Skylab, US 5
731 A134 1k Spacecraft 6
732 A134 5k A. Leonov spacewalking 32
733 A134 10k Lunokhod on Moon 65
734 A134 13k Apollo-Soyuz linkup 88
Nos. 730-734 (5) 1.96

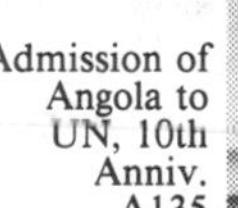

Admission of Angola to UN, 10th Anniv. A135

1986, Dec. 1 Litho. *Perf. 11x11½*
735 A135 22k multi 1.40

Liberation Movement, 30th Anniv. — A136

Angolese at work, fighting and: No. 736a, "1956." No. 736b, Congress emblem, "1980." No. 736c, Labor Party emblem, "1985."

1986, Dec. 3 *Perf. 11½x11*
736 A136 Strip of 3 1.00
a.-c. 5k, any single 30

Agostinho Neto University, 10th Anniv. A137

1986, Dec. 30 Litho. *Perf. 11x11½*
737 A137 50l Mathematics 5
738 A137 1k Law 8
739 A137 10k Medicine 70

Tribal Hairstyles — A138

1987, Apr. 15 Litho. *Perf. 11½x11*
740 A138 1k Ouioca 5 5
741 A138 1.50k Luanda 6 6
742 A138 5k Humbe 18 18
743 A138 7k Muila 25 25
744 A138 20k Muila, diff. 72 72
745 A138 30k Dilolo 1.10 1.10
Nos. 740-745 (6) 2.36 2.36

Landscapes A139
V.I. Lenin A140

Perf. 11½x12, 12x11½
1987, July 7 Litho.
746 A139 50 l Pambala Shore 5 5
747 A139 1.50k Dala Waterfalls 6 6
748 A139 3.50k Black Stones 12 12
749 A139 5k Cuango River 20 20
750 A139 10k Launda coast 36 36
751 A139 20k Hills of Leba 75 75
Nos. 746-751 (6) 1.54 1.54

Nos. 746-747, 749 and 751 horiz.

1987, Nov. 25 *Perf. 12x12½*
752 A140 15k multi 58 58

October Revolution, Russia, 70th anniv.

AIR POST STAMPS

Common Design Type
Perf. 13½x13.
1938, July 26 Engr. Unwmk.
Name and Value in Black.
C1 CD39 10c scarlet 25 25
C2 CD39 20c purple 40 25
C3 CD39 50c orange 25 25
C4 CD39 1a ultra 40 25
C5 CD39 2a lil brn 1.00 25
C6 CD39 3a dk grn 2.50 40
C7 CD39 5a red brn 4.00 55
C8 CD39 9a rose car 5.50 1.60
C9 CD39 10a magenta 7.50 1.75
Nos. C1-C9 (9) 21.80 5.55

No. C7 exists with overprint "Exposicao Internacional de Nova York, 1939-1940" and Trylon and Perisphere.

AP2

1947, Aug. Litho. *Perf. 10½*
C10 AP2 1a red brn 7.50 2.50
C11 AP2 2a yel grn 7.50 2.50
C12 AP2 3a orange 9.00 2.50
C13 AP2 3.50a orange 15.00 6.00
C14 AP2 5a ol grn 110.00 7.50
C15 AP2 6a rose 110.00 10.00
C16 AP2 9a red 275.00 150.00
C17 AP2 10a green 225.00 50.00
C18 AP2 20a blue 225.00 50.00
C19 AP2 50a black 350.00 175.00
C20 AP2 100a yellow 600.00 500.00
Nos. C10-C20 (11) 1,934. 956.00

Planes Circling Globe — AP3

1949, May 1 Photo. *Perf. 11½*
C21 AP3 1a hn brn 25 10
C22 AP3 2a red brn 60 12
C23 AP3 3a plum 1.00 25
C24 AP3 6a dl grn 3.00 60
C25 AP3 9a vio brn 4.50 1.50
Nos. C21-C25 (5) 9.35 2.57

Cambambe Dam — AP4

Designs: 1.50e, Oil refinery (vert.). 3e, Salazar Dam. 4e, Capt. Teofilo Duarte Dam. 4.50e, Craveiro Lopes Dam. 5e, Cuango Dam. 6e, Quanza River Bridge. 7e, Capt. Teofilo Duarte Bridge. 8.50e, Oliveira Salazar Bridge. 12.50e, Capt. Silva Carvalho Bridge.

Perf. 11½x12, 12x11½
1965, July 12 Litho. Unwmk.
C26 AP4 1.50e multi 1.50 10
C27 AP4 2.50e multi 90 10
C28 AP4 3e multi 1.50 20
C29 AP4 4e multi 60 20
C30 AP4 4.50e multi 60 25
C31 AP4 5e multi 1.00 30
C32 AP4 6e multi 1.00 30
C33 AP4 7e multi 1.50 30
C34 AP4 8.50e multi 2.00 85
C35 AP4 12.50e multi 2.25 1.00
Nos. C26-C35 (10) 12.85 3.60

Stamp Centenary Type of Regular Issue

Design: 2.50e, Boeing 707 jet and Angola No. 2.

1970, Dec. 1 Litho. *Perf. 13½*
C36 A83 2.50e multi 55 20
a. Souvenir sheet of 3 3.00 3.00

Centenary of stamps of Angola.
No. C36a contains one each of No. 565-566, C36. Margin shows Duke of Bragança Waterfall, with commemorative inscription. Size: 150x105mm. Sold for 15e.

No. C36 Overprinted with Bar and: "REPUBLICA POPULAR / DE"

1980 Litho. *Perf. 13½*
C37 A83 2.50e multi 25

POSTAGE DUE STAMPS

D1

D2

1904 Unwmk. Typo. *Perf. 11½x12.*
J1 D1 5r yel grn 30 25
J2 D1 10r slate 30 25
J3 D1 20r yel brn 50 45
J4 D1 30r orange 60 50
J5 D1 50r gray brn 60 50
J6 D1 60r red brn 6.00 2.75
J7 D1 100r lilac 2.50 2.00
J8 D1 130r dl bl 2.50 2.00
J9 D1 200r carmine 6.00 3.00
J10 D1 500r gray vio 6.00 3.00
Nos. J1-J10 (10) 25.30 14.70

Postage Due Stamps of 1904 Overprinted in Carmine or Green

1911
J11 D1 5r yel grn 30 30
J12 D1 10r slate 30 30
J13 D1 20r yel brn 30 30
J14 D1 30r orange 45 45
J15 D1 50r gray brn 45 45
J16 D1 60r red brn 90 90
J17 D1 100r lilac 90 90
J18 D1 130r dl bl 90 90
J19 D1 200r car (G) 90 90
J20 D1 500r gray vio 1.10 1.10
Nos. J11-J20 (10) 6.50 6.50

1921 *Perf. 11½*
J21 D2 ½c yel grn 12 12
J22 D2 1c slate 12 12
J23 D2 2c org brn 12 12
J24 D2 3c orange 12 12
J25 D2 5c gray brn 12 12
J26 D2 6c lt brn 12 12
J27 D2 10c red vio 12 12
J28 D2 13c dl bl 30 30
J29 D2 20c carmine 30 30
J30 D2 50c gray 30 30
Nos. J21-J30 (10) 1.74 1.74

Stamps of 1932 Surcharged in Black

= =
PORTEADO
10
Centavos

1948 Wmk. 232 *Perf. 12x11½.*
J31 A14 10c on 20c gray 20 20
J32 A14 20c on 30c myr grn 20 20
J33 A14 30c on 50c lt brn 40 30
J34 A14 40c on 1a cl 45 45
J35 A14 50c on 2a dl vio 80 45
J36 A14 1a on 5a pale yel grn 1.10 90
Nos. J31-J36 (6) 3.15 2.50

Common Design Type
Photogravure and Typographed
1952 Unwmk. *Perf. 14.*
Numeral in Red, Frame Multicolored.
J37 CD45 10c red brn 15 15
J38 CD45 30c ol grn 15 15
J39 CD45 50c chocolate 15 15
J40 CD45 1a dk vio bl 15 15
J41 CD45 2a red brn 30 30
J42 CD45 5a blk brn 50 50
Nos. J37-J42 (6) 1.40 1.40

NEWSPAPER STAMP

N1

Perf. 11½, 12½, 13½.
1893 Typo. Unwmk.
P1 N1 2½r brown 1.50 1.10

No. P1 was also used for ordinary postage.

POSTAL TAX STAMPS

Pombal Issue.
Common Design Types
1925 Unwmk. *Perf. 12½.*
RA1 CD28 15c lil & blk 50 40
RA2 CD29 15c lil & blk 50 40
RA3 CD30 15c lil & blk 50 40

"Charity" PT1

Coat of Arms PT2

1929 Litho. *Perf. 11.*
Without Gum
RA4 PT1 50c dk bl 4.00 1.10

1939 Without Gum. *Perf. 10½.*
RA5 PT2 50c turq grn 2.75 20
RA6 PT2 1a red 4.00 2.00

A 1.50a, type PT2, was issued for fiscal use.

Old Man PT3

Mother and Child PT4

Designs: 1e, Boy. 1.50e, Girl.

Imprint: "Foto-Lito-E.G.A.-Luanda"
1955 Unwmk. *Perf. 13*
Heads in dark brown.
RA7 PT3 50c dk ocher 20 15
RA8 PT3 1e org ver 75 30
RA9 PT3 1.50e brt yel grn 55 25

A 2.50e, type PT3 showing an old woman, was issued for revenue use.
See also Nos. RA16, RA19-RA21, RA25-RA27.

No. RA7 Surcharged with New Values and two Bars in Red or Black.
1957-58
Head in dark brown.
RA11 PT3 10c on 50c dk ocher (R) 40 25
RA12 PT3 10c on 50c dk ocher ('58) 30 20
RA13 PT3 30c on 50c dk ocher 35 25

1959 Litho. *Perf. 13*

Design: 30c, Boy and girl.

RA14 PT4 10c org & blk 20 20
RA15 PT4 30c sl & blk 20 20

Type of 1955 Redrawn

Design: 1e, Boy.

1961, Nov. *Perf. 13*
RA16 PT3 1e sal pink & dk brn 30 30

Denomination in italics.

Yellow, White and Black Men — PT5

1962 Typo. *Perf. 10½*
Without Gum
RA17 PT5 50c multi 1.00 1.00
RA18 PT5 1e multi 50 50

Issued for the Provincial Settlement Committee (Junta Provincial do Povoamento). The tax was used to promote Portuguese settlement in Angola, and to raise educational and living standards of recent immigrants.
See also No. RAJ4. Denominations higher than 2e were used for revenue purposes.

Head Type of 1955
Without Imprint

Designs: 50c, Old man. 1e, Boy. 1.50e, Girl.

1964-65 Litho. *Perf. 11½*

Heads in dark brown

RA19	PT3	50c orange7	22	15
RA20	PT3	1e dl red org ('65)	30	15
RA21	PT3	1.50e yel grn ('65)	40	25

No. RA20 is second redrawing of 1e, with bolder lettering and denomination in gothic. Space between "Assistencia" and denomination on RA19-RA21 is ½mm.; on 1955 issue space is 2mm.

Map of Angola, Industrial and Farm Workers — PT6

1965 Litho. *Perf. 13*

RA22	PT6	50c multi	50	25
RA23	PT6	1e multi	65	40

See also No. RAJ5.

Head Type of 1955

Imprint: "I.N.A." or "INA" (1e)

1966

Heads in dark brown

RA25	PT3	50c dl org	15	15
RA26	PT3	1e dl brick red	25	15
RA27	PT3	1.50e lt yel grn	25	20

Woman Planting Tree — PT7

Designs: 1e, Workers. 2e, Produce.

1972 Litho. *Perf. 13*

RA28	PT7	50c gray & pink	10	10
RA29	PT7	1e grn & blk	20	20
RA30	PT7	2e brn & blk	30	30

POSTAL TAX DUE STAMPS

Pombal Issue.

Common Design Types

1925 Unwmk. *Perf. 12½.*

RAJ1	CD31	30c lil & blk	75	*1.25*
RAJ2	CD32	30c lil & blk	75	*1.25*
RAJ3	CD33	30c lil & blk	75	*1.25*

See note after Portugal No. RAJ4.

Three-Men Type of Postal Tax Stamps, 1962.

1962 Typo. *Perf. 10½*

Without Gum

RAJ4	PT5	2e multi	80	*1.00*

See note after Nos. RA17-RA18.

Type of Postal Tax Stamps, 1965

1965 Litho. *Perf. 13*

RAJ5	PT6	2e multi	35	*1.00*

ANGRA

LOCATION — An administrative district of the Azores, consisting of the islands of Terceira, Sao Jorge and Graciosa.

GOVT. — A district of Portugal.

AREA — 275 sq. mi.

POP. — 70,000 (approx.)

CAPITAL — Angra do Heroismo

1000 Reis = 1 Milreis

King Carlos

A1 A2

Perf. 11½, 12½, 13½.

1892-93 Typo. Unwmk.

1	A1	5r yellow	2.00	1.25
a.		Perf. 11½	6.00	3.00
2	A1	10r redsh vio	2.75	1.75
3	A1	15r chocolate	3.25	2.25
4	A1	20r lavender	3.50	2.25
a.		Perf. 13½	7.50	2.50
5	A1	25r green	2.50	35
a.		Perf. 12½	6.50	75
7	A1	50r blue	5.25	2.25
a.		Perf. 13½	8.50	5.00
8	A1	75r carmine	9.00	4.25
9	A1	80r yel grn	10.00	6.50
10	A1	100r brn, *yel*, perf. 13½ ('93)	35.00	17.50
a.		Perf. 12½	125.00	100.00
11	A1	150r car, *rose* ('93)	40.00	30.00
12	A1	200r dk bl, *bl* ('93)	40.00	30.00
13	A1	300r dk bl, *sal* ('93)	40.00	30.00

Reprints of 50r, 150r, 200r and 300r, made in 1900, are perf. 11½ and ungummed. Price, each $7.50. Reprints of all values, made in 1905, have shiny white gum and clean-cut perf. 13½. Price, each $1.

1897-1905 *Perf. 11½*

Name and Value in Black except Nos. 26 and 35.

14	A2	2½r gray	35	25
15	A2	5r orange	35	25
a.		Diagonal half used as 2½r on cover		*12.50*
16	A2	10r yel grn	35	25
17	A2	15r brown	6.50	2.75
18	A2	15r gray grn ('99)	1.25	70
19	A2	20r gray vio	1.25	45
20	A2	25r sea grn	1.50	50
a.		Imperf., pair	12.50	
21	A2	25r car rose ('99)	90	25
22	A2	50r dk bl	2.50	90
23	A2	50r ultra ('05)	9.00	7.50
24	A2	65r sl bl ('98)	45	30
25	A2	75r rose	1.50	75
26	A2	75r gray brn & car, *straw* ('05)	9.50	8.00
27	A2	80r violet	55	45
28	A2	100r dk bl, *bl*	1.50	60
29	A2	115r org brn, *pink* ('98)	1.10	90
30	A2	130r gray brn, *straw* ('98)	1.10	90
31	A2	150r lt brn, *straw*	1.00	75
32	A2	180r sl, *pnksh* ('98)	1.60	1.25
33	A2	200r red vio, *pnksh*	3.00	2.25
34	A2	300r bl, *rose*	5.50	4.00
35	A2	500r blk & red, *bl*	11.00	8.00
a.		Perf. 12½	22.50	14.00
		Nos. 14-35 (22)	61.75	41.95

Azores stamps were used in Angra from 1906 to 1931, when they were superseded by those of Portugal.

ANJOUAN

LOCATION — One of the Comoro Islands in the Mozambique Channel between Madagascar and Mozambique.

GOVT. — Former French colony.

AREA — 89 sq. mi.

POP. — 20,000 (approx. 1912).

CAPITAL — Mossamondu.

See Comoro Islands.

100 Centimes = 1 Franc

Navigation and Commerce — A1

Perf. 14x13½.

1892-1907 Typo. Unwmk.

Name of Colony in Blue or Carmine.

1	A1	1c *blue*	1.00	1.00
2	A1	2c brn, *buff*	1.50	1.40
3	A1	4c cl, *lav*	1.75	1.50
4	A1	5c grn, *grnsh*	3.75	2.75
5	A1	10c *lavender*	3.75	3.00
6	A1	10c red ('00)	10.00	8.00
7	A1	15c bl, quadrille paper	4.75	3.75
8	A1	15c gray, *lt gray* ('00)	7.50	6.00
9	A1	20c red, *grn*	4.75	3.75
10	A1	25c *rose*	5.50	4.50
11	A1	25c bl ('00)	8.25	8.25
12	A1	30c brn, *bis*	11.00	9.00
13	A1	35c *yel* ('06)	6.00	4.50
14	A1	40c red, *straw*	18.00	15.00
15	A1	45c *gray grn* ('07)	85.00	75.00
16	A1	50c car, *rose*	22.50	15.00
17	A1	50c brn, *az* ('00)	15.00	10.00
18	A1	75c vio, *org*	20.00	15.00
19	A1	1fr brnz grn, *straw*	45.00	45.00
		Nos. 1-19 (19)	275.00	232.40

Issues of 1892-1907 Surcharged in Black or Carmine

05 10

1912

20	A1	5c on 2c brn, *buff*	50	50
21	A1	5c on 4c cl, *lav* (C)	50	50
22	A1	5c on 15c bl (C)	50	50
23	A1	5c on 20c red, *grn*	50	50
24	A1	5c on 25c *rose* (C)	50	50
25	A1	5c on 30c brn, *bis* (C)	50	50
26	A1	10c on 40c red, *straw*	75	75
27	A1	10c on 45c *gray grn* (C)	1.00	1.00
28	A1	10c on 50c car, *rose*	1.75	1.75
29	A1	10c on 75c vio, *org*	1.25	1.25
30	A1	10c on 1fr brnz grn, *straw*	1.50	1.50
		Nos. 20-30 (11)	9.25	9.25

Nos. 21-23, 30 exist in pairs, one without surcharge. Price, $225 each.

Two spacings between the surcharged numerals are found on Nos. 20 to 30.

Nos. 20 to 30 were available for use in Madagascar and the entire Comoro archipelago.

The stamps of Anjouan were superseded by those of Madagascar, and in 1950 by those of Comoro Islands.

ANNAM AND TONKIN

LOCATION — In French Indo-China bordering on the China Sea on the east and Siam on the west.

GOVT. — French Protectorate

AREA — 97,503 sq. mi.

POP. — 14,124,000 (approx. 1890)

CAPITAL — Annam: Hue; Tonkin: Hanoi

For administrative purposes, the Protectorates of Annam, Tonkin, Cambodia, Laos and the Colony of Cochin-China were grouped together and were known as French Indo-China.

100 Centimes = 1 Franc

Stamps of French Colonies, 1881-86 Surcharged in Black:

A & T 1 A & T 5

1888 Unwmk. *Perf. 14x13½.*

1	A9	1c on 2c brn, *buff*	24.00	21.00
a.		Inverted surch.	82.50	82.50
2	A9	1c on 4c cl, *lav*	17.50	16.00
a.		Inverted surch.	82.50	82.50
3	A9	5c on 10c *lav*	19.00	17.50
a.		Inverted surch.	82.50	82.50

Hyphen between "A" and "T"

7	A9	1c on 2c brn, *buff*	225.00	225.00
8	A9	1c on 4c cl, *lav*	350.00	325.00
9	A9	5c on 10c *lav*	175.00	175.00

A 5c on 2c was prepared but not issued.

In these surcharges there are different types of numerals and letters.

These stamps were superseded in 1892 by those of Indo-China.

ARGENTINA

LOCATION — In South America

GOVT. — Republic

AREA — 1,084,120 sq. mi.

POP. — 27,949,480 (1980)

CAPITAL — Buenos Aires

100 Centavos = 1 Peso

100 Centavos = 1 Austral

Argentine Confederation

Symbolical of the Argentine Confederation

A1 A2

Unwmk.

1858, May 1 Litho. *Imperf.*

1	A1	5c red	2.25	12.50
a.		Colon after "5"	1.75	*15.00*
b.		Colon after "V"	1.75	*15.00*
2	A1	10c green	3.25	*75.00*
a.		Half used as 5c on cover		*275.00*
3	A1	15c blue	22.50	*200.00*
a.		One-third used as 5c on cover		*5,000.*

1860, Jan.

4	A2	5c red	3.25	*100.00*
4A	A2	10c green	8.00	
4B	A2	15c blue	37.50	

Nos. 4A and 4B were never placed in use. There are nine varieties of Nos. 1, 2 and 3, sixteen of No. 4 and eight of Nos. 4A and 4B. Forged cancellations are plentiful.

> **Prices for Unused**
>
> Unused prices for Nos. 5-15, 17-67 are for copies without gum. Copies with original gum command higher prices. From No. 68 onward, unused prices are for stamps with original gum.

Argentine Republic

Seal of the Republic — A3

Broad "C" in "CENTAVOS", Accent on "U" of "REPUBLICA".

1862, Jan. 11

5	A3	5c rose	65.00	60.00
a.		rose lil	125.00	50.00
6	A3	10c green	250.00	110.00
b.		Diagonal half used as 5c on cover		*6,000.*
7	A3	15c blue	500.00	400.00
a.		Without accent on "U"	*8,000.*	*4,000.*
b.		Tete beche pair	*50,000.*	*30,000.*
i.		15c ultra	600.00	450.00

Broad "C" in "CENTAVOS", No Accent on "U"

1863

7C	A3	5c rose	30.00	35.00
d.		5c rose lil	150.00	165.00
e.		Worn plate	300.00	75.00
7F	A3	10c yel grn	500.00	250.00
g.		10c ol grn	*900.00*	350.00

Narrow "C" in "CENTAVOS", No Accent on "U"

1864

7H	A3	5c rose red	300.00	50.00

The so-called reprints of 10c and 15c are counterfeits. They have narrow "C" and straight lines in shield. Nos. 7C and 7H have been extensively counterfeited.

Rivadavia Issue

Bernardino Rivadavia
A4 A5

Rivadavia — A6

Wmk.84

Wmk. RA in Italics (84)

1864-67 **Engr.** ***Imperf.***

Clear Impressions

8 A4 5c brn rose *1,800.* *250.00*
a. 5c org red ('67) *2,500.* *200.00*
9 A5 10c green *3,000.* *1,500.*
10 A6 15c blue *10,000.* *4,000.*

Perf. 11½

Dull to Worn Impressions

11 A4 5c brn rose ('65) 45.00 20.00
11B A4 5c lake 125.00 30.00
12 A5 10c green 100.00 40.00
a. Diagonal half used as 5c on cover *1,000.*
13 A6 15c blue 175.00 110.00

1867-72 **Unwmk.** ***Imperf.***

14 A4 5c car ('72) 300.00 100.00
15 A4 5c rose 300.00 125.00
15A A5 10c green *6,000.* *6,000.*
16 A6 15c blue *3,000.* *3,000.*

Nos. 15A-16 issued without gum.

1867 ***Perf. 11½.***

17 A4 5c carmine 500.00 225.00

Nos. 14, 15 and 17 exist with part of papermaker's wmk. "LACROIX FRERES".

Rivadavia
A7

Manuel Belgrano
A8

José de San Martin — A9

Groundwork of Horizontal Lines

1867-68 ***Perf. 12***

18 A7 5c vermilion 300.00 15.00
18A A8 10c green 45.00 7.50
b. Diagonal half used as 5c on cover *750.00*
19 A9 15c blue 75.00 22.50

Groundwork of Crossed Lines

20 A7 5c vermilion 15.00 1.00
21 A9 15c blue 150.00 17.50

See also Nos. 27, 33-34, 39 and types A19, A33, A34, A37.

Gen. Antonio G. Balcarce
A10

Mariano Moreno
A11

Carlos Maria de Alvear
A12

Gervasio Antonio Posadas
A13

Cornelio Saavedra — A14

1873

22 A10 1c purple 5.50 3.50
a. 1c gray vio 9.00 3.50
23 A11 4c brown 8.50 55
a. 4c red brn 25.00 3.00
24 A12 30c orange 150.00 25.00
25 A13 60c black 150.00 8.00
26 A14 90c blue 35.00 4.00

1873

Laid Paper

27 A8 10c green 225.00 25.00

A15

A16

Surcharged in Black

1877, Feb.

Wove Paper

30 A15 1c on 5c ver 75.00 25.00
a. Inverted surcharge 500.00 300.00
31 A15 2c on 5c ver 150.00 100.00
a. Inverted surcharge 1,000. 750.00
32 A16 8c on 10c grn 175.00 50.00
b. Inverted surcharge 750.00 600.00

Forgeries of these surcharges include the inverted and double varieties.

1876-77 ***Rouletted***

33 A7 5c vermilion 225.00 100.00
34 A7 8c lake ('77) 35.00 50

Belgrano
A17

Dalmacio Velez Sarsfield
A18

San Martin — A19

1878 ***Rouletted***

35 A17 16c green 12.50 2.00
36 A18 20c blue 15.00 5.00
37 A19 24c blue 27.50 4.50

See No. 56.

Vicente Lopez
A20

Alvear
A21

1877-80 ***Perf. 12***

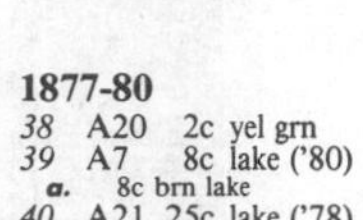

38 A20 2c yel grn 6.50 1.50
39 A7 8c lake ('80) 6.50 50
a. 8c brn lake *40.00* 50
40 A21 25c lake ('78) 35.00 10.00

A22

A23

Surcharged in Black

1882

41 A22 ½c on 5c ver 1.50 1.50
a. Double surcharge 35.00 20.00
b. Inverted surcharge 25.00 20.00
c. "PROVISORIO" omitted 50.00 50.00
d. Fraction omitted 35.00
e. "PROVISOBIO" 12.50 12.50
f. Pair, one without surcharge 125.00

Perforated across Middle of Stamp

42 A22 ½c on 5c ver 2.50 2.50
a. "PROVISORIQ" 15.00 12.50

The "½ (PROVISORIO)" surcharge on Nos. 41-42 is found in two types: I. Small "P" and narrow "V." II. Large "P" and wider "V."

1882 **Typo.** ***Perf. 12***

43 A23 ½c brown 2.25 1.25
a. Imperf., pair 35.00 35.00
44 A23 1c red, perf. 14 4.50 1.35
a. Perf. 12 12.50 6.00
45 A23 12c ultra 90.00 15.00
a. Perf. 14 65.00 15.00

Perf. 14

46 A23 12c grnsh bl 160.00 20.00

No. 21 Surcharged in Red:

a

1 C
1884

b

1884 **Engr.** ***Perf. 12***

47 A9 (a) ½c on 15c bl 3.00 2.00
a. Groundwork of horizontal lines 90.00 70.00
b. Inverted surcharge 20.00 15.00
48 A9 (b) 1c on 15c bl 15.00 12.00
a. Groundwork of horizontal lines 9.00 7.00
b. Inverted surcharge 60.00 50.00
c. Double surcharge 22.50 20.00
d. Triple surch. 450.00

Nos. 20-21 Surcharged in Black

CUATRO
Centavos
1884

c

49 A7 (a) ½c on 5c ver 3.25 2.50
a. Inverted surcharge 125.00 100.00
b. Date omitted 45.00
c. Pair, one without surcharge 160.00
50 A9 (a) ½c on 15c bl 10.00 8.00
a. Groundwork of horizontal lines 35.00 25.00
b. Inverted surcharge 35.00 30.00
51 A7 (c) 4c on 5c ver 12.50 8.00
a. Inverted surcharge 20.00 15.00
b. Double surcharge 350.00 225.00
c. Pair, one without surcharge but with "4" in manuscript 275.00 150.00

A29

1884-85 **Engr.** ***Perf. 12***

52 A29 ½c red brn 1.50 60
a. Imperf., pair 65.00
53 A29 1c rose red 7.50 60
a. Imperf., pair 65.00
54 A29 12c grnsh bl ('85) 35.00 2.00
a. 12c dp bl 35.00 2.00
b. Imperf., pair 65.00

San Martin Type of 1878

1887 **Engr.**

56 A19 24c blue 25.00 2.00

Justo José de Urquiza
A30

Lopez
A31

Miguel Juárez Celman
A32

Rivadavia (Large head)
A33

Rivadavia (Small head)
A34

Domingo F. Sarmiento
A35

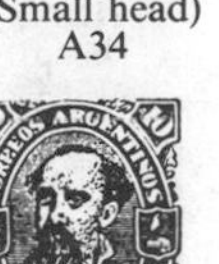

Nicolás Avellaneda
A36

San Martin
A37

Julio A. Roca
A37a

Belgrano
A37b

Manuel Dorrego
A38

Moreno
A39

Bartolomé Mitre — A40

CINCO CENTAVOS.
Type I. A33. Shows collar on left side only.
Type II. A34. Shows collar on both sides. Lozenges in background larger and clearer than in Type I.

1888-90 Litho. *Perf. 11½*

No.	Design	Description	Unused	Used
57	A30	½c blue	85	75
a.		Imperf. pair	50.00	35.00
58	A31	2c yel grn	15.00	10.00
a.		Imperf., pair	40.00	
59	A32	3c bl grn	2.25	1.00
a.		Imperf., pair	25.00	17.50
b.		Imperf. vert., pair	35.00	
c.		Horizontal pair, imperf. between	40.00	
d.		Vertical pair, imperf. between	15.00	
60	A33	5c car, type I	17.50	3.00
61	A34	5c car, type II	12.50	1.00
a.		Imperf., pair		*75.00*
b.		Vertical pair, imperf. between	50.00	
62	A35	6c red	35.00	25.00
a.		Imperf., pair	*40.00*	
b.		Vertical pair, imperf. between	50.00	
c.		Perf. 12	75.00	60.00
63	A36	10c brown	25.00	1.75
a.		Imperf. pair	*40.00*	
64	A37	15c orange	25.00	2.75
c.		Imperf., pair		*150.00*
64A	A37a	20c green	20.00	2.00
64B	A37b	25c purple	25.00	2.75
65	A38	30c chocolate	35.00	4.00
a.		Imperf., pair	*200.00*	*150.00*
66	A39	40c sl, perf. 12	35.00	5.00
a.		Perf. 11½	85.00	22.50
67	A40	50c blue	130.00	13.50
		Nos. 57-67 (13)	378.10	72.50

In this issue there are several varieties of each value, the difference between them being in the relative position of the head to the frame.

Urquiza
A41

Velez
Sarsfield
A42

Miguel
Juarez
Celman
A43

Rivadavia
(Large
head)
A44

Sarmiento
A45

Juan
Bautista
Alberdi
A46

1888-89 Engr. *Perf. 11½, 11½x12*

No.	Design	Description	Unused	Used
68	A41	½c ultra	50	15
a.		Imperf. horiz., pair	25.00	15.00
b.		Imperf., pair	25.00	15.00
69	A42	1c brown	1.50	30
a.		Imperf. horiz., pair	25.00	
b.		Vertical pair, imperf. between	25.00	
c.		Imperf. pair	25.00	
70	A43	3c bl grn	3.75	75
71	A44	5c rose	5.00	20
a.		Imperf., pair	35.00	25.00
72	A45	6c bl blk	2.50	1.00
b.		Perf. 11½x12	15.00	4.00
73	A46	12c blue	7.50	2.00
a.		Imperf., pair	20.00	
b.		bluish paper	5.00	1.25
c.		Perf. 11½	12.50	5.00
		Nos. 68-73 (6)	20.75	4.40

Nos. 69-70 exist with papermakers' watermarks.
See also Nos. 77 and 89.

Jose Maria
Paz
A48

Santiago
Derqui
A49

Rivadavia
(Small head)
A50

Avellaneda
A51

Moreno
A53

Mitre
A54

Posadas — A55

A56

1890 Engr. *Perf. 11½*

No.	Design	Description	Unused	Used
75	A48	¼c green	20	10
76	A49	2c violet	1.50	30
a.		2c pur	1.50	30
b.		2c sl	2.25	50
c.		Horizontal pair, imperf. between	22.50	
d.		Imperf., pair	27.50	
e.		Perf. 11½x12	6.00	50
77	A50	5c carmine	3.25	12
a.		Imperf., pair	60.00	30.00
b.		Perf. 11½x12	3.25	60
78	A51	10c brown	3.00	40
b.		Imperf., pair		150.00
80	A53	40c ol grn	7.00	1.25
a.		Imperf., pair	30.00	
81	A54	50c orange	7.00	1.25
a.		Imperf., pair	45.00	
b.		Perf. 11½x12	7.50	1.75
82	A55	60c black	22.50	4.00
a.		Imperf., pair	50.00	50.00
		Nos. 75-82 (7)	44.45	7.42

Type A50 differs from type A44 in having the head smaller, the letters of "Cinco Centavos" not as tall, and the curved ornaments at sides close to the first and last letters of "Republica Argentina".

Black or Red Lithographed Surcharge

1890 *Perf. 11½x12*

No.	Design	Description	Unused	Used
83	A56	¼c on 12c bl (Blk)	60	50
a.		Perf. 11½	50.00	30.00
84	A56	¼c on 12c bl (R)	60	50
a.		Double surcharge	75.00	75.00
b.		Perf. 11½	10.00	3.00

Rivadavia
A57

José de San
Martin
A58

Gregorio
Araoz de
Lamadrid
A59

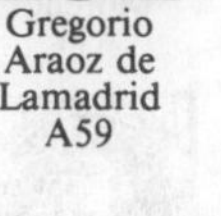
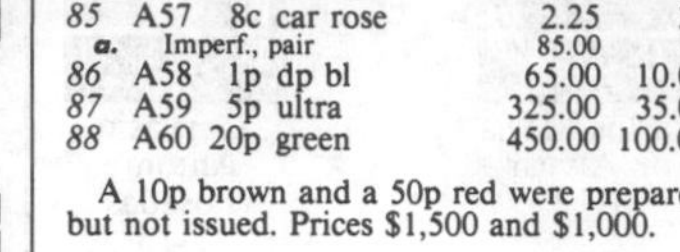
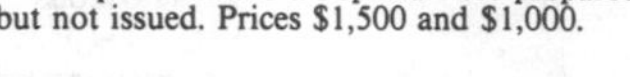
Admiral
Guillermo
Brown
A60

1891 Engr. *Perf. 11½*

No.	Design	Description	Unused	Used
85	A57	8c car rose	2.25	35
a.		Imperf., pair	85.00	
86	A58	1p dp bl	65.00	10.00
87	A59	5p ultra	325.00	35.00
88	A60	20p green	450.00	100.00

A 10p brown and a 50p red were prepared but not issued. Prices $1,500 and $1,000.

Vélez Sarsfield — A61

1890 *Perf. 11½*

No.	Design	Description	Unused	Used
89	A61	1c brown	1.50	40

Type A61 is a re-engraving of A42. The figure "1" in each upper corner has a short horizontal serif instead of a long one pointing downward. In type A61 the first and last letters of "Correos y Telegrafos" are closer to the curved ornaments below than in type A42. Background is of horizontal lines (cross-hatching on No. 69).

"Santa Maria," "Nina" and "Pinta" — A62

Wmk.85

Wmk.86

The Small Sun (85) is 4½mm. in diameter and the Large Sun (86) 6mm.

Wmk. Small Sun (85)

1892, Oct. 12 *Perf. 11½*

No.	Design	Description	Unused	Used
90	A62	2c lt bl	10.00	5.00
a.		Dbl. impression	275.00	
91	A62	5c dk bl	14.00	7.00

Discovery of America, 400th anniv. Counterfeits of Nos. 90-91 are litho.

Rivadavia
A63

Belgrano
A64

San Martin — A65

Perf. 11½, 12 and Compound

1892-95 Wmk. 85

No.	Design	Description	Unused	Used
92	A63	½c dl bl	30	10
a.		½c brt ultra	35.00	10.00
b.		Imperf., pair	40.00	
93	A63	1c brown	60	8
a.		Imperf., pair	40.00	
94	A63	2c green	60	8
a.		Imperf., pair	17.50	
95	A63	3c org ('95)	1.50	10
96	A63	5c carmine	2.00	5
a.		Imperf., pair	17.50	17.50
b.		5c grn (error)	300.00	225.00
98	A64	10c car rose	9.00	12
a.		Imperf., pair	45.00	
99	A64	12c dp bl ('93)	9.00	40
a.		Imperf., pair	45.00	
100	A64	16c gray	16.50	1.00
a.		Imperf., pair	45.00	
101	A64	24c gray brn	16.50	1.00
a.		Imperf., pair	45.00	
b.		Perf. 12	35.00	10.00
102	A64	50c bl grn	24.00	1.00
a.		Imperf., pair	35.00	
b.		Perf. 12	35.00	4.00
103	A65	1p lake ('93)	15.00	1.35
a.		1p red brn	25.00	7.00
b.		Imperf., pair	50.00	
104	A65	2p dk grn	35.00	3.50
a.		Perf. 12	110.00	40.00
105	A65	5p dk bl	60.00	4.00
a.		Imperf., pair	100.00	
		Nos. 92-105 (13)	190.00	12.78

Part-perforate varieties of Nos. 92-98 include vert. or horiz. pairs imperf. between and pairs imperf. vert. or horiz. Price $6-$35.

The high values of this and succeeding issues are frequently punched with the word "INUTILIZADO," parts of the letters showing on each stamp. These punched stamps sell for only a small fraction of the catalogue prices.

Reprints of No. 96b have white gum. The original stamp has yellowish gum. Price $125.

1896-97 Wmk. Large Sun. (86)

No.	Design	Description	Unused	Used
106	A63	½c slate	50	10
a.		½c gray bl	50	10
b.		½c ind	50	10
107	A63	1c brown	60	5
108	A63	2c yel grn	1.00	5
109	A63	3c orange	1.00	10
110	A63	5c carmine	1.00	5
a.		Imperf., pair	30.00	
111	A64	10c car rose	10.00	5
112	A64	12c dp bl	5.00	5
a.		Imperf., pair	*45.00*	
113	A64	16c gray	15.00	85
114	A64	24c gray brn	17.50	2.25
a.		Imperf., pair	25.00	
115	A64	30c org ('97)	16.00	85
116	A64	50c bl grn	16.00	85
117	A64	80c dl vio	22.50	1.10
118	A65	1p lake	35.00	1.10
119	A65	1p20c blk ('97)	17.50	4.00
120	A65	2p dk grn	25.00	10.00
121	A65	5p dk bl	125.00	10.00
a.		Perf. 12	275.00	70.00
		Nos. 106-121 (16)	308.60	31.45

Allegory, Liberty Seated
A66 A67

Perf. 11½, 12 and Compound

1899-1903

No.	Design	Description	Unused	Used
122	A66	½c yel brn	12	5
a.		Imperf., pair	25.00	
123	A66	1c green	30	5
a.		Imperf., pair	35.00	
124	A66	2c slate	30	5
a.		Imperf., pair	9.00	5.00
125	A66	3c org ('01)	1.00	30
a.		Imperf., pair	140.00	85.00
126	A66	4c yel ('03)	2.00	35
127	A66	5c car rose	30	5
a.		Imperf., pair	7.50	6.00
128	A66	6c blk ('03)	1.10	40
a.		Imperf., pair	45.00	
129	A66	10c dk grn	2.00	5
a.		Imperf., pair	45.00	
130	A66	12c dl bl	1.50	60
131	A66	12c ol grn ('01)	1.50	50
132	A66	15c sea grn ('01)	4.00	25
a.		Imperf., pair	45.00	
132B	A66	15c dl bl ('01)	3.00	30
133	A66	16c orange	11.00	8.00
134	A66	20c claret	3.00	15
135	A66	24c violet	5.00	1.50
136	A66	30c rose	11.00	85
137	A66	30c ver ('01)	5.50	30
a.		30c scar	75.00	4.00
138	A66	50c brt bl	7.00	35
139	A67	1p bl & blk, perf. 11½	20.00	1.50
a.		Center inverted	*2,250.*	*800.00*
b.		Perf. 12	275.00	80.00

140 A67 5p org & blk 85.00 20.00
Punch cancellation 1.25
a. Center inverted 2,500.
141 A67 10p grn & blk 75.00 20.00
Punch cancellation 1.25
a. Center invtd. 3,500.
Punch cancellation 1,100.
142 A67 20p red & blk 300.00 60.00
Punch cancellation 60
a. Center inverted (punch canc.) 2,000.
Nos. 122-142 (22) 539.62 115.60

Part-perforate varieties of Nos. 122-129 include vert. or horiz. pairs imperf. between and pairs imperf. vert. or horiz. Price 50 cents to $10.

River Port of Rosario A68

1902, Oct. 26 ***Perf. 11½, 11½x12***
143 A68 5c dp bl 7.00 3.00
a. Imperf., pair 120.00

Completion of port facilities at Rosario.

San Martin
A69 A70

Perf. 13½, 13½x12½
1908-09 **Typo.**
144 A69 ½c violet 20 10
145 A69 1c brnsh buff 30 10
146 A69 2c chocolate 90 10
147 A69 3c green 1.10 50
148 A69 4c redsh vio 2.25 50
149 A69 5c carmine 50 10
150 A69 6c ol bis 1.25 40
151 A69 10c gray grn 2.50 15
152 A69 12c yel buff 65 60
153 A69 12c dk bl ('09) 2.00 20
154 A69 15c ap grn 2.75 1.35
155 A69 20c ultra 2.00 15
156 A69 24c red brn 5.00 1.00
157 A69 30c dl rose 8.00 1.00
158 A69 50c black 7.50 70
159 A70 1p sl bl & pink 17.50 2.75
Nos. 144-159 (16) 54.40 9.70

The 1c in blue was not issued. Price $250.
Wmk. 86 appears on ½, 1, 6, 20, 24 and 50c. Other values have similar wmk. with wavy rays.
Stamps lacking wmk. are from outer rows printed on sheet margin.

Centenary of the Republic Issue

Pyramid of May — A71

Nicolás Rodríguez Pena and Hipolito Vieytes — A72

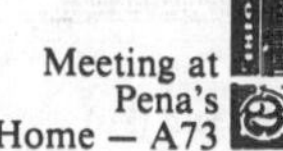

Meeting at Pena's Home — A73

Designs: 3c, Miguel de Azcuénaga (1754-1833) and Father Manuel M. Alberti (1763-1811). 4c, Viceroy's house and Fort Buenos Aires. 5c, Cornelio Saavedra (1759-1829). 10c, Antonio Luis Beruti (1772-1842) and French distributing badges. 12c, Congress building. 20c, Juan Jose Castelli (1764-1812) and Domingo Matheu (1765-1831). 24c, First council. 30c, Manuel Belgrano (1770-1820) and Juan Larrea (1782-1847). 50c, First meeting of republican government, May 25, 1810. 1p, Mariano Moreno (1778-1811) and Juan Jose Paso (1758-1833). 5p, Oath of the Junta. 10p, Centenary Monument. 20p, Jose Francisco de San Martin (1778-1850).

Inscribed "1810 1910"
Various Frames

1910, May 1 **Engr.** ***Perf. 11½***
160 A71 ½c bl & gray bl 60 20
a. Center inverted 800.00
161 A72 1c bl grn & blk 60 15
a. Center inverted 800.00
b. Horiz. pair, imperf. between 80.00
162 A73 2c ol & gray 45 10
a. Center inverted 950.00
163 A72 3c green 1.25 25
164 A73 4c dk bl & grn 1.25 40
a. Center inverted 450.00
165 A71 5c carmine 1.00 5
166 A73 10c yel brn & blk 3.00 35
167 A73 12c brt bl 2.50 40
a. Center inverted 800.00
168 A72 20c gray brn & blk 4.00 60
169 A73 24c org brn & bl 3.00 1.50
170 A72 30c lil & blk 3.00 1.10
171 A71 50c car & blk 8.00 1.50
a. Center inverted 800.00
172 A72 1p brt bl 17.50 6.00
173 A73 5p org & vio 135.00 50.00
Punch cancel 4.00
a. Center inverted 800.00
174 A71 10p org & blk 175.00 110.00
Punch cancel 5.00
175 A71 20p dp bl & ind 275.00 150.00
Punch cancel 7.50
Nos. 160-175 (16) 631.15 322.60

Domingo F. Sarmiento A87

Agriculture A88

1911, May 15 **Typo.** ***Perf. 13½***
176 A87 5c gray brn & blk 1.25 60

Issued to commemorate the centenary of the birth of Domingo Faustino Sarmiento (1811-88), president of Argentina, 1868-74.

Wmk. 86, without Face
1911 **Engr.** ***Perf. 12.***
Size: 19x25mm.
177 A88 5c vermilion 60 10
178 A88 12c dp bl 7.50 30

Wmk. 86, with Face
1911 **Typo.** ***Perf. 13½x12½***
Size: 18x23mm.
179 A88 ½c violet 15 8
180 A88 1c brn ocher 20 8
181 A88 2c chocolate 30 6
a. Perf. 13½ 7.50 3.00
b. Imperf., pair 45.00
182 A88 3c green 75 15
183 A88 4c brn vio 60 35
184 A88 10c gray grn 90 10
185 A88 20c ultra 7.50 1.50
186 A88 24c red brn 9.00 5.00
187 A88 30c claret 3.00 85
188 A88 50c black 15.00 1.50
Nos. 179-188 (10) 37.40 9.67

The 5c dull red is a proof. In this issue Wmk. 86 comes: straight rays (4c, 20c, 24c) and wavy rays (2c). All other values exist with both forms.

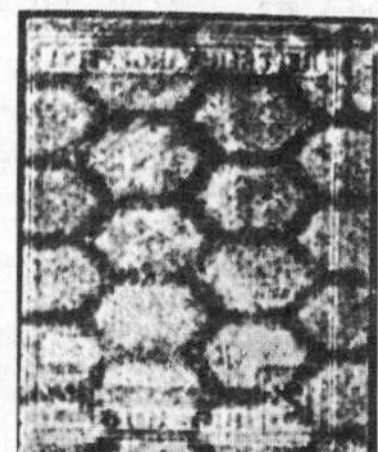
Wmk.87

Wmk. Honeycomb (87) (Horizontal or Vertical)

1912-14 ***Perf. 13½x12½***
189 A88 ½c violet 30 10
a. Perf. 13½ 1.50 50
190 A88 1c ocher 30 10
a. Perf. 13½ 1.50 50
191 A88 2c chocolate 60 6
a. Perf. 13½ 1.50 30
192 A88 3c green 1.10 30
a. Perf. 13½ 65.00 30.00
193 A88 4c brn vio 1.10 30
a. Perf. 13½ 3.00 1.25
194 A88 5c red 30 5
a. Perf. 13½ 60 10
195 A88 10c dp grn 2.50 15
196 A88 12c dp bl 2.50 5
a. Perf. 13½ 6.00 1.50
197 A88 20c ultra 15.00 1.25
a. Perf. 13½ 9.00 1.25
198 A88 24c red brn 6.00 3.00
199 A88 30c claret 15.00 1.10
200 A88 50c black 9.00 1.10
Nos. 189-200 (12) 53.70 7.56

See Nos. 208-212.

A89

1912-13 ***Perf. 13½***
201 A89 1p dl bl & rose 11.00 1.75
Punch cancel 25
202 A89 5p sl & ol grn 35.00 10.00
Punch cancel 50
203 A89 10p vio & bl 135.00 16.50
Punch cancel 1.25
204 A89 20p bl & cl 325.00 100.00
Punch cancel 1.75

1915 **Unwmk.** ***Perf. 13½x12½***
208 A88 1c ocher 75 12
209 A88 2c chocolate 75 8
212 A88 5c red 60 7

Only these denominations were printed on paper without watermark.
Other stamps of the series are known unwatermarked but they are from the outer rows of sheets the other parts of which are watermarked.

Francisco Narciso de Laprida A90

Declaration of Independence A91

José de San Martin
A92 A92a

Perf. 13½, 13½x12½
1916, July 9 **Litho.** **Wmk. 87**
215 A90 ½c violet 30 6
216 A90 1c buff 40 8

Perf. 13½x12½
217 A90 2c chocolate 30 10
218 A90 3c green 75 15
219 A90 4c red vio 1.10 15

Perf. 13½
220 A91 5c red 50 5
a. Imperf., pair 65.00
221 A91 10c gray grn 2.00 15
222 A92 12c blue 1.10 20
223 A92 20c ultra 1.10 25
224 A92 24c red brn 3.00 1.25
225 A92 30c claret 3.00 60
226 A92 50c gray blk 6.00 75
227 A92a 1p sl bl & red 15.00 6.00
Punch cancel 60
a. Imperf., pair 400.00
228 A92a 5p blk & gray grn 175.00 75.00
Punch cancel 6.00
229 A92a 10p vio & bl 175.00 135.00
Punch cancel 4.00
230 A92a 20p dl bl & cl 275.00 120.00
Punch cancel 1.50
a. Imperf., pair 800.00
Nos. 215-230 (16) 659.55 339.79

Issued to commemorate the centenary of Argentina's declaration of independence of Spain, July 9, 1816.
The watermark is either vertical or horizontal on Nos. 215-220, 222; only vertical on No. 221, and only horizontal on Nos. 223-230.

A93

A94

A94a

1917 ***Perf. 13½, 13½x12½***
231 A93 ½c violet 30 6
232 A93 1c buff 30 6
233 A93 2c brown 30 5
234 A93 3c lt grn 1.00 10
235 A93 4c red vio 1.00 50
236 A93 5c red 30 5
a. Imperf., pair 20.00
237 A93 10c gray grn 2.00 10

Perf. 13½
238 A94 12c blue 1.25 10
239 A94 20c ultra 2.00 30
240 A94 24c red brn 6.50 3.00
241 A94 30c claret 6.50 85
242 A94 50c gray blk 6.00 90
243 A94a 1p sl bl & red 6.00 60
244 A94a 5p blk & gray grn 25.00 4.00
Punch cancel 1.00
245 A94a 10p vio & bl 60.00 16.00
Punch cancel 60
246 A94a 20p dl bl & cl 135.00 25.00
Punch cancel 60
a. Center inverted 1,500. 1,100.
Nos. 231-246 (16) 253.45 51.67

The watermark is either vertical or horizontal on Nos. 231-236, 238; only vertical on No. 237, and only horizontal on Nos. 239-246.

Juan Gregorio Pujol — A95

1918, June 15 **Litho.** ***Perf. 13½***
247 A95 5c bis & gray 1.25 30

Issued to commemorate the centenary of the birth of Juan G. Pujol (1817-61), lawyer and legislator.

Perf. 13½, 13½x12½
1918-19 **Unwmk.**
248 A93 ½c violet 20 10
249 A93 1c buff 20 6
a. Imperf., pair 25.00
250 A93 2c brown 25 5
251 A93 3c lt grn 45 10
252 A93 4c red vio 45 15
253 A93 5c red 25 5
254 A93 10c gray grn 2.00 5

Perf. 13½
255 A94 12c blue 2.00 8
256 A94 20c ultra 3.00 8
257 A94 24c red brn 3.50 85
258 A94 30c claret 4.25 50
259 A94 50c gray blk 10.00 45
Nos. 248-259 (12) 26.55 2.52

The stamps of this issue sometimes show letters of papermakers' watermarks.
There were two printings, in 1918 and 1923, using different ink and paper.

Wmk.88

Wmk. Multiple Suns (88)

1920 *Perf. 13½, 13½x12½*

264 A93 ½c violet 30 10
265 A93 1c buff 40 6
266 A93 2c brown 40 8
267 A93 3c green 2.25 60
268 A93 4c red vio 3.00 1.50
269 A93 5c red 60 5
270 A93 10c gray grn 5.00 12

Perf. 13½

271 A94 12c blue 2.75 15
272 A94 20c ultra 4.00 15
274 A94 30c claret 12.50 1.25
275 A94 50c gray blk 7.50 1.75
Nos. 264-275 (11) 38.70 5.81

See Nos. 292-300, 304-307A, 310-314, 318, 322.

Belgrano's Mausoleum A96

Creation of Argentine Flag A97

Gen. Manuel Belgrano — A98

1920, June 18 *Perf. 13½*

280 A96 2c red 75 25
a. Perf. 13½x12½ 75 25
281 A97 5c rose & bl 75 10
282 A98 12c grn & bl 1.50 1.10

Issued to commemorate the centenary of the death of Manuel Belgrano (1770-1820), Argentine general, patriot and diplomat.

Gen. Justo Jose de Urquiza A99

Bartolome Mitre A100

1920, Nov. 11

283 A99 5c gray bl 45 20

Issued to honor Gen. Justo José de Urquiza (1801-1870), president of Argentina, 1854-1860. See also No. 303.

1921, June 26 **Unwmk.**

284 A100 2c vio brn 50 25
285 A100 5c lt bl 50 20

Issued to commemorate the centenary of the birth of Bartolomé Mitre (1821-1906), president of Argentina, 1862-65.

Allegory, Pan-America — A101

1921, Aug. 25 *Perf. 13½*

286 A101 3c violet 1.10 40
287 A101 5c blue 1.50 20
288 A101 10c vio brn 2.75 50
289 A101 12c rose 4.00 1.00

Argentina stamps through 1975 can be mounted in Scott's Argentina Album.

Inscribed "Buenos Aires-Agosto de 1921" A102

Inscribed "Republica Argentina" A103

1921, Oct. *Perf. 13½x12½*

290 A102 5c rose 50 8
a. Perf. 13½ 2.25 8
291 A103 5c rose 2.75 6
a. Perf. 13½ 4.00 6

Issued to commemorate the first Pan-American Postal Congress, held at Buenos Aires, August, 1921.
See Nos. 308-309, 319.

Wmk.89

In this watermark the face of the sun is 7mm. in diameter, the rays are heavier than in the large sun watermark of 1896-1911 and the watermarks are placed close together, so that parts of several frequently appear on one stamp. This paper was intended to be used for fiscal stamps and is usually referred to as "fiscal sun paper".

Perf. 13½, 13½x12½

1920 **Wmk. Large Sun (89)**

292 A93 ½c violet 2.50 1.00
293 A93 1c buff 7.00 1.00
294 A93 2c brown 4.00 1.00
297 A93 5c red 5.50 60
298 A93 10c gray grn 5.50 60

Perf. 13½

299 A94 12c blue *3,500.* 150.00
300 A94 20c ultra 20.00 1.50
Nos. 292-298,300 (6) 44.50 5.70

1920

303 A99 5c gray bl 450.00 300.00

Wmk.90

In 1928 the watermark R. A. in Sun (90) was slightly modified, making the diameter of the Sun 9mm. instead of 10mm. Several types of this watermark exist.

Perf. 13½, 13½x12½

1922-23 **Wmk. RA in Sun (90)**

304 A93 ½c violet 25 10
305 A93 1c buff 25 5
306 A93 2c brown 25 5
307 A93 3c green 75 50
307A A93 4c red vio 6.00 1.50
308 A102 5c rose 3.75 20
309 A103 5c red 2.50 10
310 A93 10c gray grn 7.50 50

Perf. 13½

311 A94 12c blue 1.10 20
312 A94 20c ultra 2.00 10
313 A94 24c red brn 15.00 7.00
314 A94 30c claret 9.00 75
Nos. 304-314 (12) 48.35 11.05

Paper with Gray Overprint RA in Sun

Perf. 13½, 13½x12½

1922-23 **Unwmk.**

318 A93 2c brown 4.00 1.25
319 A103 5c red 2.50 35

Perf. 13½

322 A94 20c ultra 25.00 1.75

San Martin
A104 A105

With Period after Value

1923, May **Litho.** **Wmk. 90**

323 A104 ½c red vio 40 30
324 A104 1c buff 60 15
325 A104 2c dk brn 60 6
326 A104 3c lt grn 60 35
327 A104 4c red brn 60 30
328 A104 5c red 60 5
329 A104 10c dl grn 5.00 15
330 A104 12c dp bl 75 15
331 A104 20c ultra 2.00 8
332 A104 24c lt brn 5.00 2.75
333 A104 30c claret 15.00 85
334 A104 50c black 7.50 60

Without Period after Value

Wmk. Honeycomb (87)

Perf. 13½

335 A105 1p bl & red 7.50 20
336 A105 5p gray lil & grn 30.00 3.00
Punch cancel 75
337 A105 10p cl & bl 100.00 17.50
Punch cancel 1.25
338 A105 20p sl & brn lake 150.00 45.00
Punch cancel 70
a. Center inverted
Nos. 323-338 (16) 326.15 71.49

Nos. 335 to 338 and 353 to 356 cancelled with round or oval killers in purple (revenue cancellations) sell for one-fifth to one-half the price of postally used copies.

Design of 1923
Without Period after Value

Perf. 13½, 13½x12½

1923-31 **Wmk. RA in Sun (90)**

340 A104 ½c red vio 12 5
341 A104 1c buff 12 5
342 A104 2c dk brn 12 5
343 A104 3c green 20 5
a. Imperf., pair 15.00
b. Typo. 2.00 40
344 A104 4c red brn 75 5
345 A104 5c red 12 5
a. Typo. 3.75 75
346 A104 10c dl grn 50 5
a. Typo. 6.00 30
347 A104 12c dp bl 90 10
a. Typo. 12.50 2.25
348 A104 20c ultra 1.25 5
a. Typo. 50.00 2.50
349 A104 24c lt brn 3.00 1.50
350 A104 25c purple 1.50 5
a. Typo. 30.00 1.10
351 A104 30c claret 3.00 10
a. Typo. 22.50 60
352 A104 50c black 3.00 10
353 A105 1p bl & red 3.75 10
354 A105 5p dk vio & grn 27.50 1.00
Punch cancel 30
355 A105 10p cl & bl 60.00 5.00
Punch cancel 35
356 A105 20p sl & lake 90.00 15.00
Punch cancel 35
Nos. 340-356 (17) 195.83 23.35

There were two printings of many of the stamps of type A104: lithographed (1923-24), clear impression, and typographed (1931-33), rough impression with heavy shading about the eyes and nose. The typographed stamps were issued only in coils. Nos. 343 and 346 are known without watermark.

Nos. 341-345, 347-349, 351 (litho.) may be found in pairs, one with period.

See note after No. 338. See Nos. 362-368.

Rivadavia — A106

1926, Feb. 8 *Perf. 13½*

357 A106 5c rose 75 20

Issued in commemoration of the centenary of the Presidency of Bernardino Rivadavia.

Rivadavia A108

San Martin A109

General Post Office, 1926 — A110

General Post Office, 1826 — A111

1926, July 1 *Perf. 13½x12½*

358 A108 3c gray grn 25 10
359 A109 5c red 25 8

Perf. 13½

360 A110 12c dp bl 1.50 30
361 A111 25c chocolate 2.75 15
a. "1326" for "1826" 9.00 1.25

Centenary of the Post Office.

Wmk.205

The letters "A. P." in the watermark are the initials of "AHORRO POSTAL". This paper was formerly used exclusively for Postal Savings stamps.

Type of 1923-31 Issue
Without Period after Value

Wmk. AP in Oval (205)

1927 *Perf. 13½x12½*

362 A104 ½c red vio 40 30
a. Pelure paper 3.00 2.50
363 A104 1c buff 40 30
364 A104 2c dk brn 40 15
a. Pelure paper 60 30
365 A104 5c red 50 15
a. Period after value 6.00 3.00
b. Pelure paper 75 35
366 A104 10c dl grn 7.50 3.00
367 A104 20c ultra 30.00 3.00

Perf. 13½

368 A105 1p bl & red 60.00 9.00
Nos. 362-368 (7) 99.20 15.90

Arms of Argentina and Brazil — A112

Wmk. RA in Sun (90)

1928, Aug. 27 *Perf. 12½x13*

369 A112 5c rose red 1.50 50
370 A112 12c dp bl 3.00 1.00

Commemorative of the centenary of peace between the Empire of Brazil and the United Provinces of the Rio de la Plata.

Canceled-to-order stamps are often from remainders. Most collectors of canceled stamps prefer postally used specimens.

Allegory, Discovery of the New World
A113

"Spain" and "Argentina"
A114

"America" Offering Laurels to Columbus — A115

1929, Oct. 12 **Litho.** ***Perf. 13½***

371	A113	2c lil brn	1.50	30
372	A114	5c lt red	1.50	12
373	A115	12c dl bl	3.50	1.10

Issued to commemorate the 437th anniversary of the discovery of America by Columbus.

Spirit of Victory Attending Insurgents
A116

March of the Victorious Insurgents
A117

Perf. 13½x12½ (A116), 12½x13 (A117)

1930

374	A116	½c vio gray	30	20
375	A116	1c myr grn	40	20
376	A117	2c dl vio	50	10
377	A116	3c green	75	35
378	A116	4c violet	60	35
379	A116	5c rose red	30	10
380	A116	10c gray blk	1.75	50
381	A117	12c dl bl	1.25	35
382	A117	20c ocher	1.25	30
383	A117	24c red brn	5.00	2.25
384	A117	25c green	6.00	2.25
385	A117	30c dp vio	10.00	3.00
386	A117	50c black	15.00	4.00
387	A117	1p sl bl & red	25.00	15.00
388	A117	2p blk & org	50.00	15.00
389	A117	5p dl grn & blk	150.00	60.00
390	A117	10p dp red brn & dl bl	200.00	60.00
391	A117	20p yel grn & dl bl	575.00	135.00
392	A117	50p dk grn & vio	1,350.	750.00
		Nos. 374-392 (19)	2,393.	1,048.

Issued to commemorate the Revolution of 1930.

Nos. 387-392 with oval (parcel post) cancellation sell for less.

1931 ***Perf. 12½x13***

393	A117	½c red vio	20	15
394	A117	1c gray blk	1.50	60
395	A117	3c green	75	35
396	A117	4c red brn	60	30
397	A117	5c red	20	5
a.		Plane omitted, top left corner	5.00	2.50
398	A117	10c dl grn	1.50	40
		Nos. 393-398 (6)	4.75	1.85

Issued to commemorate the Revolution of 1930.

Stamps of 1924-25 Overprinted in Red or Green

-6-
Septiembre
1930 - 1931

1931, Sept. 6 ***Perf. 13½, 13½x12½***

399	A104	3c grn (R)	35	35
400	A104	10c dl grn (R)	1.00	1.00
401	A104	30c cl (G)	5.50	3.50
402	A104	50c blk (R)	5.50	3.50

Overprinted in Blue

1930
Septiembre
6
1931

403	A105	1p bl & red	6.50	3.50
404	A105	5p dk vio & grn	120.00	32.50

No. 388 Overprinted in Blue

6 Septiembre 1931

Perf. 12½x13

405	A117	2p blk & org	22.50	12.50
		Nos. 399-405 (7)	161.35	56.85

Issued in commemoration of the first anniversary of the Revolution of 1930.

Refrigeration Compressor — A118

Perf. 13½x12½

1932, Aug. 29 **Litho.**

406	A118	3c green	75	40
407	A118	10c scarlet	2.50	25
408	A118	12c gray bl	6.00	1.50

Issued to commemorate the sixth International Refrigeration Congress.

Port of La Plata — A119

President Julio A. Roca — A120

Municipal Palace — A121

Cathedral of La Plata — A122

Dardo Rocha — A123

Perf. 13½x13, 13x13½ (10c)

1933, Jan.

409	A119	3c grn & dk brn	60	40
410	A120	10c org & dk vio	90	30
411	A121	15c dk bl & dp bl	6.00	3.00
412	A122	20c vio & yel brn	3.00	1.50
413	A123	30c dk grn & vio brn	25.00	8.50
		Nos. 409-413 (5)	35.50	13.70

Issued in commemoration of the 50th anniversary of the founding of the city of La Plata, November 19th, 1882.

Christ of the Andes — A124

Buenos Aires Cathedral
A125

1934, Oct. 1 ***Perf. 13x13½, 13½x13***

414	A124	10c rose & brn	1.25	35
415	A125	15c dk bl	2.50	85

Issued to commemorate the 32nd International Eucharistic Congress, Oct. 10-14, 1934.

"Liberty" with Arms of Brazil and Argentina
A126

Symbolical of "Peace" and "Friendship"
A127

1935, May 15 ***Perf. 13x13½***

416	A126	10c red	1.50	40
417	A127	15c blue	3.00	80

Visit of Pres. Getulio Vargas of Brazil.

Belgrano
A128

Sarmiento
A129

Urquiza
A130

Louis Braille
A131

San Martin
A132

Brown
A133

Moreno
A134

Alberdi
A135

Nicolas Avellaneda
A136

Rivadavia
A137

Mitre
A138

Bull (Cattle Breeding)
A139

Martin Güemes
A140

Agriculture
A141

Merino Sheep (Wool)
A142

Sugar Cane
A143

Oil Well (Petroleum)
A144

Map of South America
A145 A146

Fruit
A147

Iguacu Falls (Scenic Wonders)
A148

Grapes (Vineyards)
A149

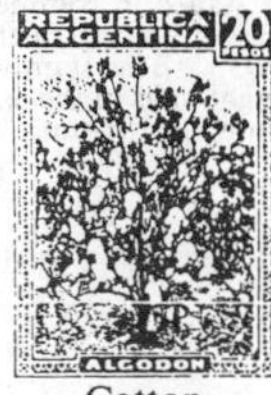

Cotton
A150

Two types of A140:
Type I - Inscribed Juan Martin Guemes.
Type II - Inscribed Martin Güemes.

Perf. 13, 13½x13, 13x13½
Wmk. RA in Sun (90)

1935-51 **Litho.**

418	A128	½c red vio	12	5

419	A129	1c buff	12	5
a.		Typo.	12	5
420	A130	2c dk brn	20	5
421	A131	2½c blk ('39)	12	6
422	A132	3c green	20	5
423	A132	3c lt gray ('39)	12	5
424	A134	3c lt gray ('46)	20	6
425	A133	4c lt gray	20	5
426	A133	4c sage grn ('39)	20	5
427	A134	5c yel brn	2.50	5
a.		Tete beche pair, typo.	8.00	4.00
b.		Booklet pane of 8, typo.		
c.		Booklet pane of 4, typo.		
d.		Typo.	20	5
428	A135	6c ol grn	40	5
429	A136	8c org ('39)	20	8
430	A137	10c car, typo.	50	5
431	A137	10c brn ('42)	20	5
a.		Typo.	75	5
432	A138	12c brown	35	10
433	A138	12c red ('39)	15	5
434	A139	15c sl bl ('36)	1.50	5
435	A139	15c pale ultra ('39)	90	5
436	A140	15c lt gray bl (II) ('42)	65.00	2.50
437	A140	20c lt ultra (I)	1.00	6
438	A140	20c lt ultra (II) ('36)	60	5
439	A140	20c bl gray (II) ('39)	60	5
439A	A139	20c dk bl & pale bl, 22x33mm ('42)	1.50	5
440	A139	20c bl ('51)	20	5
a.		Typo.	20	5
441	A141	25c car ('36)	40	5
442	A142	30c org brn ('36)	90	5
443	A143	40c dk vio ('36)	75	5
444	A144	50c red & org ('36)	60	5
445	A145	1p brn blk & lt bl ('36)	32.50	1.25
446	A146	1p brn blk & lt bl ('37)	12.50	30
a.		Chalky paper	75.00	1.50
447	A147	2p brn lake & dk ultra ('36)	1.50	20
448	A148	5p ind & ol grn ('36)	11.00	50
449	A149	10p brn lake & blk	60.00	3.50
450	A150	20p bl grn & brn ('36)	85.00	12.00
		Nos. 418-450 (34)	282.23	21.71

See Nos. 485-500, 523-540, 659, 668.

No. 439A exists with attached label showing medallion. Price $75 unused, $40 used.

Souvenir Sheet

A151

Without Period after Value

1935, Oct. 17 Litho. *Imperf.*

452	A151	10c dl grn, sheet of four	90.00	50.00
a.		Single stamp	12.00	7.00

Issued in commemoration of the Philatelic Exhibition at Buenos Aires, October 17-24, 1935. The stamps were on sale during the eight days of the exhibition only. Sheets measure 83x101mm.

Plaque — A152

1936, Dec. 1 *Perf. 13x13½*

453 A152 10c rose 90 30

Issued in commemoration of the Inter-American Conference for Peace.

Domingo Faustino Sarmiento A153

"Presidente Sarmiento" A154

1938, Sept. 5

454	A153	3c sage grn	30	10
455	A153	5c red	30	5
456	A153	15c dp bl	1.00	25
457	A153	50c orange	3.00	1.10

Issued in commemoration of the 50th anniversary of the death of Domingo Faustino Sarmiento, president, educator and author.

1939, Mar. 16

458 A154 5c grnsh bl 60 25

Issued in commemoration of the final voyage of the training ship "Presidente Sarmiento."

Allegory of the Universal Postal Union — A155

Post Office, Buenos Aires A156

Coat of Arms A157

Iguacu Falls — A158

Bonete Hill, Nahuel Huapi Park A159

Allegory of Modern Communications A160

Argentina, Land of Promise A161

Lake Frias, Nahuel Huapi Park A162

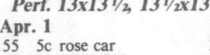

Perf. 13x13½, 13½x13

1939, Apr. 1 Photo.

459	A155	5c rose car	30	10
460	A156	15c grnsh blk	75	30
461	A157	20c brt bl	75	25
462	A158	25c dp bl grn	1.50	75
463	A159	50c brown	3.00	1.25
464	A160	1p brn vio	3.50	1.50
465	A161	2p magenta	16.00	10.00
466	A162	5p purple	65.00	30.00
		Nos. 459-466 (8)	90.80	44.35

Universal Postal Union, 11th Congress.

Souvenir Sheets

A163

A164

1939, May 12 *Imperf.*

467	A163	Sheet of four	10.00	7.00
a.		5c rose car (A155)	1.75	1.25
b.		20c brt bl (A157)	1.75	1.25
c.		25c dp bl grn (A158)	1.75	1.25
d.		50c brn (A159)	1.75	1.25
468	A164	Sheet of four	10.00	7.00

Issued in four forms:

a.	Unsevered horizontal pair of sheets, Type A163 at left, Type A164 at right	25.00	25.00
b.	Unsevered vertical pair of sheets, Type A163 at top, Type A164 at bottom	25.00	25.00
c.	Unsevered block of four sheets, Type A163 at left, Type A164 at right	90.00	90.00
d.	Unsevered block of four sheets, Type A163 at top, Type A164 at bottom	90.00	90.00

Issued in commemoration of the 11th Congress of the Universal Postal Union and the Argentina International Philatelic Exposition (C.Y.T.R.A.).

No. 468 contains one each of Nos. 467a-467d.

Size: No. 468a, 190x95mm. No. 468b, 95x190mm.

Family and New House — A165

Perf. 13½x13

1939, Oct. 2 Litho. Wmk. 90

469 A165 5c bluish grn 45 10

Issued to commemorate the first Pan-American Housing Congress.

Bird Carrying Record A166

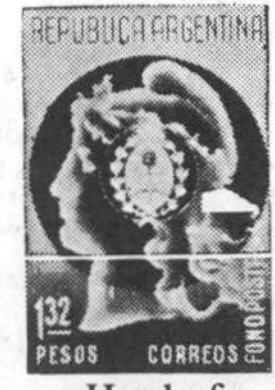

Head of Liberty and Arms of Argentina A167

Record and Winged Letter — A168

1939, Dec. 11 Photo. *Perf. 13*

470	A166	1.18p indigo	27.50	15.00
471	A167	1.32p brt bl	27.50	15.00
472	A168	1.50p dk brn	95.00	60.00

These stamps were issued for the recording and mailing of flexible phonograph records.

Map of the Americas — A169

1940, Apr. 14 *Perf. 13x13½*

473 A169 15c ultra 75 20

Issued to commemorate the 50th anniversary of the Pan American Union.

Souvenir Sheet

Reproductions of Early Argentine Stamps — A170

Wmk. RA in Sun (90)

1940, May 25 Litho. *Imperf.*

474	A170	Sheet of five	17.50	10.00
a.		5c dk bl *(Corrientes)*	2.00	1.25
b.		5c red *(Argentine Republic)*	2.00	1.25
c.		5c dk bl *(Cordoba)*	2.00	1.25
d.		5c red *(Argentine Republic)*	2.00	1.25
e.		10c dk bl *(Buenos Aires)*	2.00	1.25

Issued in sheets measuring 111x116mm., in commemoration of the 100th anniversary of the first postage stamp.

General Domingo French and Colonel Antonio Beruti — A171

1941, Feb. 20 *Perf. 13½x13*

475 A171 5c dk gray bl & lt bl 60 10

Issued in honor of General French and Colonel Beruti, patriots.

Marco M. de Avellaneda A172

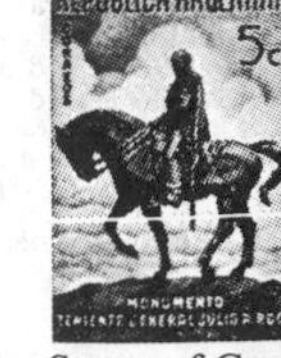

Statue of Gen. Julio Roca A173

1941, Oct. 3 *Perf. 13x13½*

476 A172 5c dl sl bl 60 10

Issued in commemoration of the centenary of the death of Marco M. de Avellaneda, (1814-41), Army leader and martyr.

1941, Oct. 19 Photo. Wmk. 90

477 A173 5c dk ol grn 60 10

Issued to commemorate the dedication of a monument to Lt. Gen. Julio Argentino Roca (1843-1914).

Carlos Pellegrini and Bank of the Nation A174

1941, Oct. 26 *Perf. 13½x13*

478	A174	5c brn car	60	10

Issued to commemorate the 50th anniversary of the founding of the Bank of the Nation.

Gen. Juan Lavalle — A175

1941, Dec. 5 *Perf. 13x13½*

479	A175	5c brt bl	60	10

Issued to commemorate the centenary of the death of Gen. Juan Galo de Lavalle (1797-1841).

National Postal Savings Bank — A176

1942, Apr. 5 Litho. *Perf. 13½x13*

480	A176	1c pale ol	25	10

José Manuel Estrada — A177

1942, July 13 *Perf. 13x13½*

481	A177	5c brn vio	60	10

Issued to commemorate the centenary of the birth of José Estrada (1842-1894), writer and diplomat.

No. 481 exists with label, showing medallion, attached. The pair sells for 15 times the price of the single stamp.

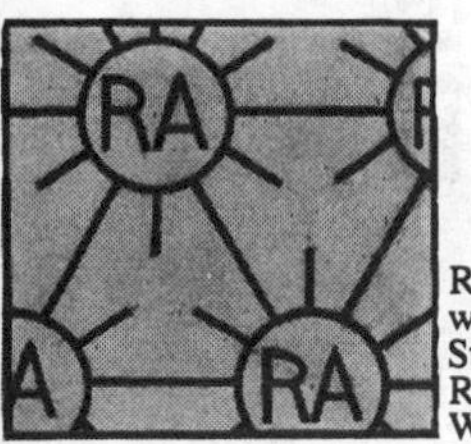

RA in Sun with Straight Rays Wmk.288

Types of 1935-51

Perf. 13, 13x13½, 13½x13

1942-50 Litho. Wmk. 288

485	A128	½c brn vio	7.50	1.25
486	A129	1c buff ('50)	12	5
487	A130	2c dk brn ('50)	12	5
488	A132	3c lt gray	25.00	1.50
489	A134	3c lt gray ('49)	25	5
490	A137	10c red brn ('49)	30	5
491	A138	12c red	30	10
492	A140	15c lt gray bl (II)	45	5
493	A139	20c dk sl bl & pale bl	2.00	5
494	A141	25c dl rose ('49)	90	10
495	A142	30c org brn ('49)	2.00	6
496	A143	40c vio ('49)	12.50	20
497	A144	50c red & org ('49)	12.50	30
498	A146	1p brn blk & lt bl	10.00	30
499	A147	2p brn lake & bl ('49)	20.00	1.00
500	A148	5p ind & ol grn ('49)	80.00	6.00
		Nos. 485-500 (16)	173.94	11.11

No. 493 measures 22x33 mm.

Post Office, Buenos Aires A178

Proposed Columbus Lighthouse A179

Inscribed: "Correos y Telegrafos".

1942, Oct. 5 Litho. *Perf. 13*

503	A178	35c lt ultra	5.00	6

See also Nos. 541-543.

1942, Oct. 12 Wmk. 288

504	A179	15c dl bl	4.00	10

Wmk. 90

505	A179	15c dl bl	100.00	7.00

Nos. 504-505 were issued to commemorate the 450th anniversary of the discovery of America by Columbus.

José C. Paz — A180

Books and Argentine Flag — A181

1942, Dec. 15 Wmk. 288

506	A180	5c dk gray	60	5

Issued in commemoration of the centenary of the birth of José C. Paz, stateman and founder of the newspaper La Prensa.

1943, Apr. 1 Litho. *Perf. 13*

507	A181	5c dl bl	25	5

Issued to commemorate the first Book Fair of Argentina.

Arms of Argentina Inscribed "Honesty, Justice, Duty" — A182

1943-50 Wmk. 288 *Perf. 13*

Size: 20x26mm.

508	A182	5c red ('50)	3.50	5

Wmk. 90

509	A182	5c red	30	5
a.		5c dl red, unsurfaced paper	5.00	8
510	A182	15c green	1.00	15

Perf. 13x13½

Size: 22x33mm.

511	A182	20c dk bl	1.50	15

Issued to commemorate the change of political organization on June 4, 1943.

Independence House, Tucuman A183

Liberty Head and Savings Bank A184

1943-51 Wmk. 90 *Perf. 13*

512	A183	5c bl grn	1.20	8

Wmk. 288

513	A183	5c bl grn ('51)	50	8

Issued to commemorate the restoration of Independence House.

1943, Oct. 25 Wmk. 90

514	A184	5c vio brn	25	5

Wmk. 288

515	A184	5c vio brn	55.00	3.00

Issued to commemorate the first conference of National Postal Savings.

Port of Buenos Aires in 1800 — A185

1943, Dec. 11 Wmk. 90

516	A185	5c gray blk	25	5

Day of Exports.

Warship, Merchant Ship and Sailboat A186

Arms of Argentine Republic A187

1944, Jan. 31 *Perf. 13*

517	A186	5c blue	25	6

Issued to commemorate Sea Week.

1944, June 4

518	A187	5c dl bl	15	6

Issued to commemorate the first anniversary of the change of political organization in Argentina.

St. Gabriel A188

Cross at Palermo A189

1944, Oct. 11

519	A188	3c yel grn	25	8
520	A189	5c dp rose	25	8

Fourth national Eucharistic Congress.

Allegory of Savings A190

Reservists A191

1944, Oct. 24

521	A190	5c gray	15	5

Issued to commemorate the 20th anniversary of the National Savings Bank.

1944, Dec. 1

522	A191	5c blue	15	5

Day of the Reservists.

Types of 1935-51

Perf. 13x13½, 13½x13

1945-47 Litho. Unwmk.

523	A128	½c brn vio ('46)	12	5
524	A129	1c yel brn	12	5
525	A130	2c sepia	15	5
526	A132	3c lt gray *(San Martin)*	70	5
527	A134	3c lt gray *(Moreno)* ('46)	25	5
528	A135	6c ol grn ('47)	30	15
529	A137	10c brn ('46)	2.00	5
530	A140	15c lt gray bl (II)	1.25	5
531	A139	20c dk sl bl & pale bl	2.00	5
532	A141	25c dl rose	75	5
533	A142	30c org brn	60	5
534	A143	40c violet	2.00	12
535	A144	50c red & org	2.00	5
536	A146	1p brn blk & lt bl	2.75	10
537	A147	2p brn lake & bl	15.00	35
538	A148	5p ind & ol grn ('46)	75.00	4.00
539	A149	10p dp cl & int blk	9.25	1.50
540	A150	20p bl grn & brn ('46)	9.50	1.50
		Nos. 523-540 (18)	123.74	8.27

No. 531 measures 22x33mm.

Post Office Type Inscribed: "Correos y Telecommunicaciones"

1945 Unwmk. *Perf. 13x13½*

541	A178	35c lt ultra	2.00	5

Wmk. 90

542	A178	35c lt ultra	2.00	5

Wmk. 288

543	A178	35c lt ultra	60	5

Bernardino Rivadavia A192 A193

Mausoleum of Rivadavia A194

Perf. 13½x13

1945, Sept. 1 Litho. Unwmk.

544	A192	3c bl grn	20	6
545	A193	5c rose	20	5
546	A194	20c blue	50	6

Issued to commemorate the centenary of the death of Bernardino Rivadavia, Argentina's first president.

No. 546 exists with mute label attached. The pair sells for four times the price of the single stamp.

General José de San Martin A195

Monument to Army of the Andes, Mendoza A196

1945-46 Wmk. 90 Typo. or Litho.

547	A195	5c car	15	6
a.		Litho. ('46)	20	6

Wmk. 288

548	A195	5c car, litho.	175.00	30.00

Unwmk.

549	A195	5c car ('46)	75	5
a.		Litho. ('46)	30	5

1946, Jan. 14 Litho. *Perf. 13½x13*

550	A196	5c vio brn	15	5

Issued to honor the Unknown Soldier of the War for Independence.

Franklin D. Roosevelt — A197

Liberty Administering Presidential Oath — A198

1946, Apr. 12
551 A197 5c sl blk 20 8

Issued in memory of Franklin D. Roosevelt.

1946, June 4 ***Perf. 13x13½***
552 A198 5c blue 15 5

Issued to commemorate the inauguration of President Juan D. Perón, June 4, 1946.

Argentina Receiving Popular Acclaim A199

1946, Oct. 17 ***Perf. 13½x13***
553 A199 5c rose vio 30 10
554 A199 10c bl grn 45 15
555 A199 15c dk bl 90 20
556 A199 50c red brn 1.25 40
557 A199 1p car rose 2.50 1.10
Nos. 553-557 (5) 5.40 1.95

First anniversary of the political organization change of Oct. 17, 1945.

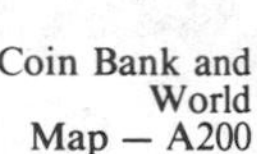

Coin Bank and World Map — A200

1946, Oct. 31 **Unwmk.**
558 A200 30c dk rose cat & pink 1.00 15

Issued to commemorate the Universal Day of Savings, October 31, 1946.

Argentine Industry A201

International Bridge Connecting Argentina and Brazil A202

1946, Dec. 6 ***Perf. 13x13½***
559 A201 5c vio brn 15 5

Day of Argentine Industry, Dec. 6.

1947, May 21 Litho. ***Perf. 13½x13***
560 A202 5c green 15 5

Issued to commemorate the opening of the Argentina-Brazil International Bridge, May 21, 1947.

Map of Argentine Antarctic Claims A203

Justice A204

1947-49 Unwmk. ***Perf. 13x13½***
561 A203 5c vio & lil 60 6
562 A203 20c dk car rose & rose 1.25 10

Wmk. 90
563 A203 20c dk car rose & rose 3.00 20

Wmk. 288
564 A203 20c dk car rose & rose ('49) 3.50 20

Issued to note the 43rd anniversary of the first Argentine Antarctic mail.

1947, June 4 **Unwmk.**
565 A204 5c brn vio & pale yel 15 5

Issued to commemorate the 1st anniversary of the Perón government.

Icarus Falling — A205

1947, Sept. 25 ***Perf. 13½x13***
566 A205 15c red vio 25 8

Aviation Week.

Training Ship Presidente Sarmiento — A206

1947, Oct. 5 ***Perf. 13x13½***
567 A206 5c blue 30 15

Issued to commemorate the 50th anniversary of the launching of the Argentine training frigate "Presidente Sarmiento".

Cervantes and Characters from Don Quixote A207

Perf. 13½x13
1947, Oct. 12 Photo. Wmk. 90
568 A207 5c ol grn 20 5

Issued to commemorate the 400th anniversary of the birth of Miguel de Cervantes Saavedra, playwright and poet.

Gen. José de San Martin A208

Perf. 13½x13
1947-49 Unwmk. Litho.
569 A208 5c dl grn 15 6

Wmk. 288
570 A208 5c dl grn ('49) 25 5

Issued to commemorate the transfer of the remains of Gen. José de San Martin's parents.

School Children A209

Statue of Araucanian Indian A210

1947-49 Unwmk. ***Perf. 13x13½***
571 A209 5c green 15 5

Wmk. 90
574 A209 20c brown 50 10

Wmk. 288
575 A209 5c green 50 5

Argentine School Crusade for World Peace.

1948, May 21 **Wmk. 90**
576 A210 25c yel brn 50 10

American Indian Day, Apr. 19.

Cap of Liberty A211

Manual Stop Signal A212

1948, July 16
577 A211 5c ultra 15 5

Issued to commemorate the 5th anniversary of the Revolution of June 4, 1943.

1948, July 22
578 A212 5c choc & yel 15 5

Traffic Safety Day, June 10.

Post Horn and Oak Leaves A213

Argentine Farmers A214

1948, July 22 **Unwmk.**
579 A213 5c lil rose 15 5

Issued to commemorate the 200th anniversary of the establishment of regular postal service on the Plata River.

Perf. 13x13½
1948, Sept. 20 **Wmk. 288**
580 A214 10c red brn 25 6

Agriculture Day, Sept. 8, 1948.

Liberty and Symbols of Progress — A215

Wmk.287

Wmk. Double Circle and Letters in Sheet (287)

1948, Nov. 23 Photo. ***Perf. 13x13½***
581 A215 25c red brn 30 6

Issued to commemorate the third anniversary of President Juan D. Peron's return to power, October 17, 1945.

Souvenir Sheets

A216

Designs: 15c, Mail coach. 45c, Buenos Aires in 18th century. 55c, First train, 1857. 85c, Sailing ship, 1767.

1948, Dec. 21 Unwmk. ***Imperf.***
582 A216 Sheet of four 4.00 3.00
a. 15c dk grn 60 60
b. 45c org brn 60 60
c. 55c lil brn 60 60
d. 85c ultra 60 60

A217

Designs: 85c, Domingo de Basavilibaso (1709-75). 1.05p, Postrider. 1.20p, Sailing ship, 1798. 1.90p, Courier in the Andes, 1772.

583 A217 Sheet of four 22.50 14.00
a. 85c brn 5.00 3.00
b. 1.05p dk grn 5.00 3.00
c. 1.20p dk bl 5.00 3.00
d. 1.90p red brn 5.00 3.00

Issued in sheets measuring 143x101mm. (No. 582) and 101x143mm. (No. 583) to commemorate the 200th anniversary of the establishment of regular postal service on the Plata River.

Prices of premium quality never hinged stamps will be in excess of catalogue price.

Winged Wheel — A218

Perf. 13½x13

1949, Mar. 1 **Wmk. 288**

584	A218	10c blue	40	5

Nationalization of the railroads, first anniversary.

Liberty A219

1949, June 20 **Engr.** **Wmk. 90**

585	A219	1p red & red vio	75	15

Ratification of the Constitution of 1949.

Allegory of the U.P.U. A220

1949, Nov. 19

586	A220	25c dk grn & yel grn	40	10

Issued to commemorate the 75th anniversary of the formation of the Universal Postal Union.

Gen. José de San Martin — A221

San Martin at Boulogne sur Mer A222

Mausoleum of San Martin — A223

Designs: 20c, 50c, 75c, Different Portraits of San Martin. 1p, House where San Martin died.

Inscribed: "Centenario de la Muerte del General Don José de San Martin 1850-1950."

Engr., Photo. (25c, 1p, 2p)

1950, Aug. 17 **Wmk. 90** ***Perf. 13½***

587	A221	10c ind & dk pur	20	5
588	A221	20c red brn & dk brn	20	6
589	A222	25c brown	25	8
590	A221	50c dk grn & ind	75	12
591	A221	75c choc & dk grn	75	18
a.		Souv. sheet of 4	2.25	1.40
592	A222	1p dk grn	1.50	30
593	A223	2p dp red lil	1.25	50
		Nos. 587-593 (7)	4.90	1.29

Issued to commemorate the centenary of the death of General José de San Martin. No. 591a measures 120x150mm. and contains one each of Nos. 587, 588, 590 and 591, imperf., with marginal inscriptions and ornamental border in brown.

Map Showing Antarctic Claims — A224

1951, May 21 **Litho.** ***Perf. 13x13½***

594	A224	1p choc & lt bl	1.25	10

Pegasus and Train A225

Communications Symbols — A226

Design: 25c, Ship and dolphin.

1951, Oct. 17 **Photo.** ***Perf. 13½***

595	A225	5c dk brn	20	5
596	A225	25c Prus grn	40	12
597	A226	40c rose brn	45	15

Close of Argentine Five Year Plan.

Woman Voter and "Argentina" A227

1951, Dec. 14 ***Perf. 13½x13***

598	A227	10c brn vio	15	6

Granting of women's suffrage.

Eva Perón

A228 A229

Litho. or Engraved (#605)

1952, Aug. 26 **Wmk. 90** ***Perf. 13***

599	A228	1c org brn	12	5
600	A228	5c gray	12	5
601	A228	10c rose lil	12	5
602	A228	20c rose pink	12	5
603	A228	25c dl grn	12	8
604	A228	40c dl vio	20	5
605	A228	45c dp bl	25	10
606	A228	50c dl brn	25	10

Photo.

607	A229	1p dk brn	45	10
608	A229	1.50p dp grn	2.50	15
609	A229	2p brt car	75	15
610	A229	3p indigo	1.25	20
		Nos. 599-610 (12)	6.25	1.13

Inscribed: "Eva Perón"

1952-53 ***Perf. 13x13½***

611	A229	1p dk brn	90	5
612	A229	1.50p dp grn	90	5
613	A229	2p brt car ('53)	2.00	15
614	A229	3p indigo	2.75	20

Engr.

Perf. 13½x13

Size: 30x40mm.

615	A229	5p red brn	2.75	60
616	A228	10p red	7.50	2.50
617	A229	20p green	20.00	7.00
618	A228	50p ultra	30.00	17.50
		Nos. 611-618 (8)	66.80	28.05

Indian Funeral Urn — A230

1953, Aug. 28 **Photo.** ***Perf. 13x13½***

619	A230	50c bl grn	25	10

Issued to commemorate the 400th anniversary of the founding of Santiago del Estero.

Rescue Ship "Uruguay" A231

1953, Oct. 8 ***Perf. 13½***

620	A231	50c ultra	1.50	12

Issued to commemorate the 50th anniversary of the rescue of the Antarctic expedition of Otto C. Nordenskjold.

Planting Argentine Flag in the Antarctic A232

1954, Jan. 20 **Engr.** ***Perf. 13½x13***

621	A232	1.45p blue	2.25	15

Issued to commemorate the 50th anniversary of Argentina's first antarctic post office and the establishing of the La Hoy radio post office in the South Orkneys.

Wired Communications A233

Television A234

Design: 3p, Radio.

Perf. 13x13½, 13½x13

1954, Apr. **Photo.** **Wmk. 90**

622	A233	1.50p vio brn	60	25
623	A233	3p vio bl	2.00	50
624	A234	5p carmine	2.50	1.00

Issued to publicize the International Plenipotentiary Conference of Telecommunications, Buenos Aires, 1952.

Pediment, Buenos Aires Stock Exchange A235

1954, July 13 ***Perf. 13½x13***

625	A235	1p dk grn	50	10

Issued to commemorate the centenary of the establishment of the Buenos Aires Stock Exchange.

Eva Perón — A236

1954 **Wmk. 90**

626	A236	3p dp car rose	2.00	30

Wmk. 288

627	A236	3p dp car rose	250.00	50.00

Issued to commemorate the second anniversary of the death of Eva Perón.

José de San Martin A237

Wheat A238

Industry A238a

Eva Perón Foundation Building A239

Cliffs of Humahuaca — A240

Gen. José de San Martin — A241

Designs: 50c, Buenos Aires harbor. 1p, Cattle ranch (Ganaderia). 3p, Nihuil Dam. 5p, Iguassu Falls (vert.). 20p, Mt. Fitz Roy (vert.).

Engraved (#632, 638-642), Photogravure (#634-637)
Perf. 13½, 13x13½ (80c), 13½x13 (#639, 641-642)

1954-59 Wmk. 90

628	A237	20c brt red, typo.	12	5
629	A237	20c red, litho. ('55)	90	5
630	A237	40c red, litho. ('56)	25	5
631	A237	40c brt red, typo. ('55)	40	5
632	A239	50c bl ('56)	15	5
633	A239	50c bl, litho. ('59)	25	5
634	A238	80c brown	35	5
635	A239	1p brn ('58)	40	5
636	A238a	1.50p ultra ('58)	30	7
637	A239	2p dk rose lake	50	6
638	A239	3p vio brn ('56)	50	6
639	A240	5p gray grn ('55)	8.00	6
a.		Perf. 13½	10.00	6
640	A240	10p yel grn ('55)	6.00	8
641	A240	20p dl vio ('55)	12.00	15
a.		Perf. 13½	15.00	15
642	A241	50p ultra & ind ('55)	12.00	15
a.		Perf. 13½	12.00	15
		Nos. 628-642 (15)	42.12	1.03

See Nos. 699-700. For similar designs inscribed "Republica Argentina" see Nos. 823-827, 890, 935, 937, 940, 990, 995, 1039, 1044, 1048.

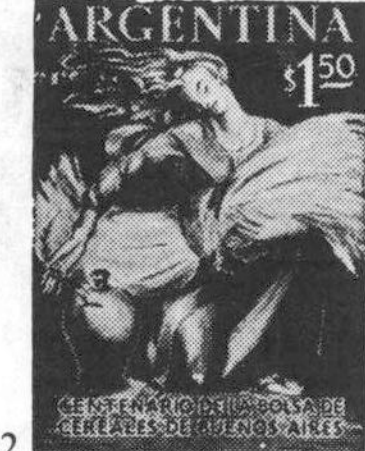

Allegory — A242

1954, Aug. 26 Typo. *Perf. 13½*
643 A242 1.50p sl blk 1.00 10

Issued to commemorate the centenary of the establishment of the Buenos Aires Grain Exchange.

Clasped Hands and Congress Medal — A243

1955, Mar. 21 Photo. *Perf. 13½x13*
644 A243 3p red brn 1.25 15

Issued to publicize the National Productivity and Social Welfare Congress.

Allegory of Aviation A244

Argentina Breaking Chains A245

1955, June 18 Wmk. 90 *Perf. 13½*
645 A244 1.50p ol gray 1.00 8

Issued to commemorate the 25th anniversary of commercial aviation in Argentina.

1955, Oct. 16 Litho.
647 A245 1.50p ol grn 50 6

Liberation Revolution of Sept. 16, 1955.

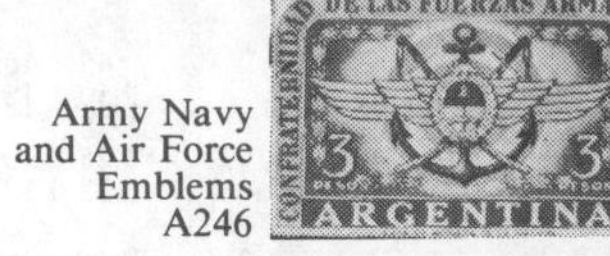

Army Navy and Air Force Emblems A246

Perf. 13½x13
1955, Dec. 31 Photo. Wmk. 90
648 A246 3p blue 75 10

"Brotherhood of the Armed Forces."

Justo José de Urquiza — A247

1956, Feb. 3 *Perf. 13½*
649 A247 1.50p green 50 6

Battle of Caseros, 104th anniversary.

Coin and Die — A248

1956, July 28 Engr. *Perf. 13½x13*
650 A248 2p gray brn & redsh brn 50 10

75th anniversary of the Argentine Mint.

1856 Stamp of Corrientes A249

Juan G. Pujol — A250

Design: 2.40p, Stamp of 1860-78.

1956, Aug. 21
651 A249 40c dk grn & bl 25 10
652 A249 2.40p brn & lil rose 50 12

Photo.
653 A250 4.40p brt bl 1.10 30
a. Souvenir sheet 3.75 3.25

Centenary of Argentine postage stamps.

No. 653a commemorates both the Argentine stamp centenary and the Philatelic Exhibition for the Centenary of Corrientes Stamps, Oct. 12-21. It is imperf. and contains one each of Nos. 651-653, with the 4.40p in photogravure and the other two stamps and border lithographed. Colors of 40c and 2.40p differ slightly from engraved stamps. Marginal inscriptions, coats of arms and scroll work in dull purple. Size: 146x170mm.

Felling Trees, La Pampa A251

Mate Herb and Gourd, Misiones A252

Design: 1p, Cotton plant and harvest, Chaco.

1956, Sept. 1 *Perf. 13½*
654 A251 50c ultra 12 5
655 A251 1p magenta 30 6
656 A252 1.50p green 40 8

Issued to commemorate the elevation of the territories of La Pampa, Chaco and Misiones to provinces.

"Liberty" A253

Florentino Ameghino A254

Perf. 13½
1956, Sept. 15 Wmk. 90 Photo.
657 A253 2.40p lil rose 50 10

Issued to commemorate the first anniversary of the Revolution of Liberation.

1956, Nov. 30
658 A254 2.40p brown 40 5

Issued to honor Florentino Ameghino (1854-1911), anthropologist.

Adm. Brown Type of 1935-51
1956 Litho. *Perf. 13*

Two types:
I. Bust touches upper frame line of name panel at bottom.
II. White line separates bust from frame line.

Size: 19½-20½x26-27mm.

659 A133 20c dl pur (I) 30 5
a. Type II 30 5
b. Size 19½x25¼ mm (I) 25 5

Benjamin Franklin A255

1956, Dec. 22 Photo. *Perf. 13½*
660 A255 40c int bl 50 8

Issued to commemorate the 250th anniversary of the birth of Benjamin Franklin.

Frigate "Hercules" A256

Guillermo Brown A257

1957, Mar. 2
661 A256 40c brt bl 15 6
662 A257 2.40p gray blk 60 15

Issued to commemorate the centenary of the death of Admiral Guillermo (William) Brown (1777-1857), founder of the Argentine navy.

Roque Saenz Pena — A258

Church of Santo Domingo, 1807 — A259

1957, Apr. 1
663 A258 4.40p grnsh gray 60 12

Issued to honor Roque Saenz Peña (1851-1914), president in 1910-1914.

1957, July 6 Wmk. 90
664 A259 40c brt bl grn 15 7

Issued to commemorate the 150th anniversary of the defense of Buenos Aires.

"La Portena" A260

1957, Aug. 31 Wmk. 90 *Perf. 13½*
665 A260 40c pale brn 30 15

Centenary of Argentine railroads.

Esteban Echeverria A261

"Liberty" A262

1957, Sept. 2 *Perf. 13x13½*
666 A261 2p claret 30 5

Esteban Echeverria (1805-1851), poet.

1957, Sept. 28 *Perf. 13½*
667 A262 40c car rose 12 6

Constitutional reform convention.

Portrait Type of 1935-51

Portrait: 5c, Jose Hernandez.

1957, Oct. 28 Litho. *Perf. 13½*
Seze: 16½x22mm.
668 A128 5c buff 15 6

Oil Derrick and Hands Holding Oil — A263

Perf. 13½
1957, Dec. 21 Wmk. 90 Photo.
669 A263 40c brt bl 30 15

Issued to commemorate the 50th anniversary of the national oil industry.

Museum, La Plata — A264

1958, Jan. 11
670 A264 40c dk gray 20 10

City of La Plata, 75th anniversary.

Locomotive and Arms of Argentina and Bolivia — A265

Map of Argentine-Bolivian Boundary and Plane — A266

1958, Apr. 19 Wmk. 90 *Perf. 13½*
671 A265 40c sl & dp car 40 15
672 A266 1p dk brn 40 15

Issued to celebrate Argentine-Bolivian friendship. No. 671 commemorates the opening of the Jacuiba-Santa Cruz railroad; No. 672, the exchange of presidential visits.

Symbols of the Republic A267

Flag Monument A268

Engraved and Photogravure
1958, Apr. 30 Wmk. 90
673 A267 40c multi 15 5
674 A267 1p multi 25 6
675 A267 2p multi 40 12

Transmission of Presidential power.

1958, June 21 Litho. Wmk. 90
676 A268 40c bl & vio bl 15 6

Issued to commemorate the first anniversary of the Flag Monument of Rosario.

Map of Antarctica A269

Stamp of Cordoba and Mail Coach A270

1958, July 12 *Perf. 13½*
677 A269 40c car rose & blk 80 30

International Geophysical Year, 1957-58.

1958, Oct. 18
678 A270 40c pale bl & sl 20 10

Centenary of Cordoba postage stamps. See Nos. C72-C73.

"Slave" by Michelangelo and U. N. Emblem — A271

Engraved and Lithographed
1959, Mar. 14 Wmk. 90 *Perf. 13½*
679 A271 40c vio brn & gray 20 10

Issued to commemorate the tenth anniversary (in 1958) of the signing of the Universal Declaration of Human Rights.

Orchids and Globe — A272

1959, May 23 Photo. *Perf. 13½*
680 A272 1p dl cl 30 15

1st International Horticulture Exposition.

Pope Pius XII A273

William Harvey A274

1959, June 20 Engr. *Perf. 13½*
681 A273 1p yel & blk 30 15

Issued in memory of Pope Pius XII, 1876-1958.

1959, Aug. 8 Litho. Wmk. 90

Portraits: 1p, Claude Bernard. 1.50p, Ivan P. Pavlov.

682 A274 50c green 15 8
683 A274 1p dk red 20 12
684 A274 1.50p brown 40 10

Issued to publicize the 21st International Congress of Physiological Sciences, Buenos Aires.

Type of 1958 and

Domestic Horse A275

José de San Martin A276

Tierra del Fuego — A277

Inca Bridge, Mendoza A278

Ski Jumper A279

Mar del Plata A280

Designs: 10c, Cayman. 20c, Llama. 50c, Puma. No. 690, Sunflower. 3p, Zapata Slope, Catamarca. 12p, 23p, 25p, Red Quebracho tree. 20p, Nahuel Huapi Lake. 22p, "Industry" (cogwheel and factory).

Two overall paper sizes for 1p, 5p:
I. 27x37½mm. or 37½x27mm.
II. 27x39mm. or 39x27mm.

Perf. 13x13½
1959-70 Litho. Wmk. 90

685 A275 10c sl grn 10 5
686 A275 20c dl red brn ('61) 10 5
687 A275 50c bis, litho. ('60) 10 5
688 A275 50c bis, typo. ('60) 30 5
689 A275 1p rose red 10 5

Perf. 13½

690 A278 1p brn, photogravure, paper I ('61) 10 5
a. Paper II ('69) 30 5
690B A278 1p brn, litho., paper I 1.00 5
691 A276 2p rose red, litho. ('61) 40 6
692 A276 2p red, typo. (19½x26mm) ('61) 50 5
a. Redrawn (19½x25mm) 7.50 5
693 A277 3p dk bl, photo. ('60) 25 5
694 A276 4p red, typo ('62) 30 5
694A A276 4p red, litho. ('62) 60 5
695 A277 5p gray brn, photo., paper I 60 5
a. 5p dk brn, paper II ('70) 10.00 5
695A A276 8p ver, litho. ('65) 2.00 6
695B A276 8p red, typo. ('65) 50 5
695C A276 10p ver, litho. ('66) 1.00 8
695D A276 10p red, typo. ('66) 75 6

Photo.

696 A278 10p lt red brn ('60) 75 9
697 A278 12p dk brn vio ('62) 1.25 5
697A A278 12p dk brn, litho. ('64) 12.50 10
698 A278 20p Prus grn ('60) 4.50 8
698A A276 20p red, typo. ('67) 40 5
699 A238a 22p ultra ('62) 2.50 8
700 A238a 22p ultra, litho. ('62) 37.50 10
701 A278 23p grn ('65) 7.50 6
702 A278 25p dp vio ('66) 2.00 6
703 A278 25p pur, litho. ('66) 10.00 6
704 A279 100p bl ('61) 8.00 15
705 A280 300p dp vio ('62) 4.50 20
Nos. 685-705 (29) 100.10 1.99

See Nos. 882-887, 889, 892, 923-925, 928-930, 938, 987-989, 991.

The 300p remained on sale as a 3p stamp after the 1970 currency exchange.

Symbolic Sailboat A281

Child Playing with Doll A282

1959, Oct. 3 Litho. *Perf. 13½*
706 A281 1p blk, red & bl 20 10

Red Cross sanitary education campaign.

1959, Oct. 17
707 A282 1p red & blk 20 10

Issued for Mother's Day, 1959.

Buenos Aires 1p Stamp of 1859 — A283

1959, Nov. 21 Wmk. 90 *Perf. 13½*
708 A283 1p gray & dk bl 20 10

Issued for the Day of Philately.

Bartolomé Mitre and Justo José de Urquiza A284

1959, Dec. 12 Photo. *Perf. 13½*
709 A284 1p purple 20 10

Treaty of San Jose de Flores, centenary.

WRY Emblem A285

Abraham Lincoln A286

1960, Apr. 7 Litho. Wmk. 90
710 A285 1p bis & car 15 10
711 A285 4.20p ap grn & dp cl 45 30

World Refugee Year, July 1, 1959-June 30, 1960. See No. B25.

1960, Apr. 14 Photo. *Perf. 13½*
712 A286 5p ultra 60 25

Issued to commemorate the sesquicentennial (in 1959) of the birth of Abraham Lincoln.

Cornelio Saavedra and Cabildo, Buenos Aires — A287

"Cabildo" and: 2p, Juan José Paso. 4.20p, Manuel Alberti and Miguel Azcuénaga. 10.70p, Juan Larrea and Domingo Matheu.

Perf. 13½
1960, May 28 Wmk. 90 Photo.
713 A287 1p rose lil 15 5

714 A287 2p bluish grn 15 6
715 A287 4.20p gray & grn 35 15
716 A287 10.70p gray & ultra 65 30
Nos. 713-716,C75-C76 (6) 1.95 81

150th anniversary of the May Revolution. Souvenir sheets are Nos. C75a and C76a.

Luis Maria Drago A288

Juan Bautista Alberdi A289

1960, July 8
717 A288 4.20p brown 30 10

Issued to commemorate the centenary of the birth of Dr. Luis Maria Drago, statesman and jurist.

1960, Sept. 10 Wmk. 90 *Perf. 13½*
718 A289 1p green 20 10

Issued to commemorate the 150th anniversary of the birth of Juan Bautista Alberdi, statesman and philosopher.

Map of Argentina and Antarctic Sector — A290

Caravel and Emblem — A291

1960, Sept. 24 Litho. *Perf. 13½*
719 A290 5p violet 1.25 30

National census of 1960.

1960, Oct. 1 Photo.
720 A291 1p dk ol grn 20 6
721 A291 5p brown 70 18

Issued to commemorate the 8th Congress of the Postal Union of the Americas and Spain. See Nos. C78-C79.

Virgin of Lujan, Patroness of Argentina A292

Argentine Boy Scout Emblem A293

1960, Nov. 12 Wmk. 90 *Perf. 13½*
722 A292 1p dk bl 15 8

First Inter-American Marian Congress.

1961, Jan. 17 Litho.
723 A293 1p car rose & blk 40 20

International Patrol Encampment of the Boy Scouts, Buenos Aires.

Argentina stamps through 1975 can be mounted in Scott's Argentina Album.

"Shipment of Cereals," by Quinquela Martin A294

1961, Feb. 11 Photo. *Perf. 13½*
724 A294 1p red brn 40 15

Export drive: "To export is to advance."

Naval Battle of San Nicolas A295

Emperor Trajan Statue — A297

Mariano Moreno by Juan de Dios Rivera A296

1961, Mar. 2 *Perf. 13½*
725 A295 2p gray 40 15

Issued to commemorate the 150th anniversary of the naval battle of San Nicolas.

1961, Mar. 25 *Perf. 13½*
726 A296 2p blue 20 6

Issued to commemorate the 150th anniversary of the death of Mariano Moreno (1778-1811), writer, politician, member of the 1810 Junta.

1961, Apr. 11
727 A297 2p sl grn 20 8

Issued to commemorate the visit of Pres. Giovanni Gronchi of Italy to Argentina, April 1961.

Rabindranath Tagore — A298

1961, May 13 Photo. *Perf. 13½*
728 A298 2p pur, *grysh* 20 6

Issued to commemorate the centenary of the birth of Rabindranath Tagore, Indian poet.

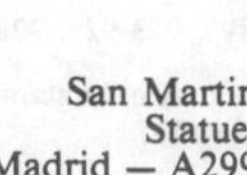

San Martin Statue, Madrid — A299

1961, May 24 Wmk. 90
729 A299 1p ol gray 20 6

Issued to commemorate the unveiling of a statue of General José de San Martin in Madrid.

Manuel Belgrano A300

1961, June 17 *Perf. 13½*
730 A300 2p vio bl 20 6

Issued to commemorate the erection of a monument by Hector Rocha, to General Manuel Belgrano in Buenos Aires.

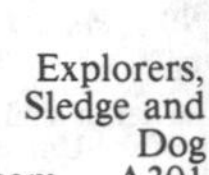

Explorers, Sledge and Dog Team — A301

1961, Aug. 19 Photo. Wmk. 90
731 A301 2p black 1.00 30

Issued to commemorate the 10th anniversary of the General San Martin Base, Argentine Antarctic.

Spanish Conquistador and Sword — A302

Sarmiento Statue by Rodin, Buenos Aires — A303

1961, Aug. 19 Litho.
732 A302 2p red & blk 20 8

First city of Jujuy, 400th anniversary.

1961, Sept. 9 Photo.
733 A303 2p violet 20 8

Issued to commemorate the 150th anniversary of the birth of Domingo Faustino Sarmiento (1811-1888), political leader and writer.

Symbol of World Town Planning A304

1961, Nov. 25 Litho. *Perf. 13½*
734 A304 2p ultra & yel 20 8

World Town Planning Day, Nov. 8.

Manuel Belgrano Statue, Buenos Aires A305

Grenadier, Flag and Regimental Emblem A306

1962, Feb. 24 Photo.
735 A305 2p Prus bl 20 10

150th anniversary of the Argentine flag.

Perf. 13½
1962, March 31 Wmk. 90
736 A306 2p car rose 20 10

Issued to commemorate the 150th anniversary of the San Martin Grenadier Guards regiment.

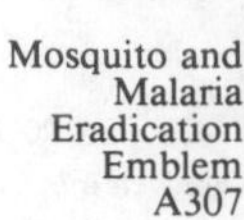

Mosquito and Malaria Eradication Emblem A307

1962, Apr. 7 Litho.
737 A307 2p ver & blk 20 10

Issued for the World Health Organization drive to eradicate malaria.

Church of the Virgin of Lujan — A308

Bust of Juan Jufre — A309

1962, May 12 *Perf. 13½*
738 A308 2p org brn & blk 20 8

Issued to commemorate the 75th anniversary of the pontifical coronation of the Virgin of Lujan.

1962, June 23 Photo.
739 A309 2p Prus bl 20 8

Issued to commemorate the fourth centenary of the founding of San Juan.

"Soaring into Space" A310

Juan Vucetich A311

1962, Aug. 18 Litho. *Perf. 13½*
740 A310 2p mar, blk & bl 20 8

Argentine Air Force, 50th anniversary.

1962, Oct. 6 Photo. Wmk. 90
741 A311 2p green 20 8

Issued to honor Juan Vucetich (1864-1925), inventor of the Argentine system of fingerprinting.

Domingo F. Sarmiento A312

February 20th Monument, Salta A313

Design: 4p, José Hernandez.

1962-66 Photo. *Perf. 13½*
742 A312 2p dp grn 90 5

Litho.
742A A312 2p lt grn ('64) 75 5
Photo.
742B A312 4p dl red ('65) 60 5
Litho.
742C A312 4p rose red ('66) 60 5

See No. 817-819.

1963, Feb. 23 Photo. Wmk. 90
743 A313 2p dk grn 20 8

Issued to commemorate the 150th anniversary of the Battle of Salta, War of Independence.

Gear Wheels — A314

1963, Mar. 16 Litho. *Perf. 13½*
744 A314 4p gray, blk & brt rose 20 8

Issued to commemorate the 75th anniversary of the Argentine Industrial Union.

National College, Buenos Aires — A315

Child Draining Cup — A316

1963, Mar. 16 Wmk. 90
745 A315 4p dl org & blk 25 8

Issued to commemorate the centenary of the National College of Buenos Aires.

1963, Apr. 6
746 A316 4p multi 20 8

Issued for the "Freedom from Hunger" campaign of the U.N. Food and Agriculture Organization.

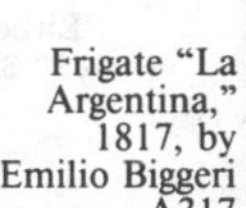

Frigate "La Argentina," 1817, by Emilio Biggeri A317

1963, May 18 Photo.
747 A317 4p bluish grn 40 20

Issued for Navy Day, May 17.

Seat of 1813 Assembly and Official Seal — A318

1963, July 13 Litho. *Perf. 13½*
748 A318 4p lt bl & blk 20 8

150th anniversary of the 1813 Assembly.

Battle of San Lorenzo, 1813 A319

1963, Aug. 24
749 A319 4p grn & blk, *grnsh* 25 8

Issued to commemorate the sesquicentennial of the Battle of San Lorenzo.

Queen Nefertari Offering Papyrus Flowers, Abu Simbel A320

1963, Sept. 14 *Perf. 13½*
750 A320 4p ocher, blk & bl grn 40 20

Campaign to save the historic monuments in Nubia.

Government House, Buenos Aires — A321

1963, Oct. 12 Wmk. 90 *Perf. 13½*
751 A321 5p rose & brn 20 8

Inauguration of President Arturo Illia.

"Science" A322

Francisco de las Carreras, Supreme Court Justice A323

1963, Oct. 16 Litho.
752 A322 4p org brn, bl & blk 20 8

Issued to publicize the 10th Latin-American Neurosurgery Congress.

1963, Nov. 23 Photo. *Perf. 13½*
753 A323 5p bluish grn 20 8

Centenary of judicial power.

Blackboards A324

1963, Nov. 23 Litho.
754 A324 5p red, blk & bl 20 8

Issued to publicize "Teachers for America" through the Alliance for Progress program.

Kemal Atatürk A325

"Payador" by Juan Carlos Castagnino A326

1963, Dec. 28 Photo. *Perf. 13½*
755 A325 12p dk gray 40 15

Issued to commemorate the 25th anniversary of the death of Kemal Atatürk, president of Turkey.

1964, Jan. 25 Litho.
756 A326 4p ultra, blk & lt bl 40 20

Fourth National Folklore Festival.

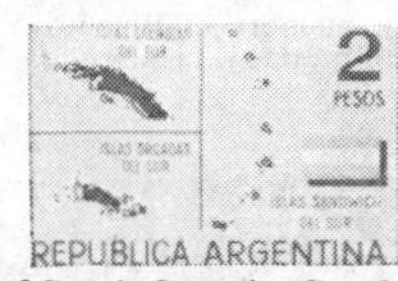

Maps of South Georgia, South Orkney and South Sandwich Islands A327

Design: 4p, Map of Argentina and Antarctic claims (vert.).

1964, Feb. 22 Wmk. 90 *Perf. 13½*
Size: 33x22mm.
757 A327 2p lt & dk bl & bis 2.00 40
Size: 30x40mm.
758 A327 4p lt & dk bl & ol grn 3.00 50

Issued to commemorate the 60th anniversary of Argentina's claim to Antarctic territories. See No. C92.

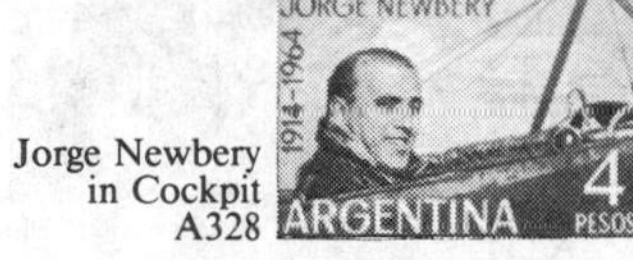

Jorge Newbery in Cockpit A328

1964, Feb. 23 Photo.
759 A328 4p dp grn 20 8

Issued to commemorate the 50th anniversary of the death of Jorge Newbery, aviator.

John F. Kennedy — A329

José Brochero by Jose Cuello — A330

1964, Apr. 14 Engr. Wmk. 90
760 A329 4p cl & dk bl 50 10

Issued in memory of President John F. Kennedy (1917-63).

1964, May 9 Photo. *Perf. 13½*
761 A330 4p lt sep 20 8

Issued to commemorate the 50th anniversary of the death of Father José Gabriel Brochero.

Soldier of Patricios Regiment A331

Pope John XXIII — A332

1964, May 29 Litho. Wmk. 90
762 A331 4p blk, ultra & red 60 30

Issued for Army Day. Later Army Day stamps, inscribed "Republica Argentina," are of type A340a.

1964, June 27 Engr.
763 A332 4p org & blk 30 20

Issued in memory of Pope John XXIII.

University of Cordoba Arms — A333

Pigeons and U.N. Building, N.Y. — A334

1964, Aug. 22 Litho. Wmk. 90
764 A333 4p blk, ultra & yel 20 10

Issued to commemorate the 350th anniversary of the University of Cordoba.

1964, Oct. 24 *Perf. 13½*
765 A334 4p dk bl & lt bl 20 10

Issued for United Nations Day.

Joaquin V. Gonzalez A335

Julio Argentino Roca A336

1964, Nov. 14 Photo.
766 A335 4p dk rose car 20 10

Issued to commemorate the centenary (in 1963) of the birth of Joaquin V. Gonzalez, writer.

1964, Dec. 12 *Perf. 13½*
767 A336 4p vio bl 20 10

Issued to commemorate the 50th anniversary of the death of General Julio A. Roca, (1843-1914), president of Argentina, (1880-86, 1898-1904).

Market at Montserrat Square, by Carlos Morel — A337

Scott's editorial staff cannot undertake to identify, authenticate or appraise stamps and postal markings.

1964, Dec. 19 **Photo.**
768 A337 4p sepia 50 30

Issued to honor the 19th century Argentine painter Carlos Morel.

Icebreaker General San Martin — A338

Girl with Piggy Bank — A339

Design: 2p, General Belgrano Base, Antarctica.

1965 ***Perf. 13½***
769 A338 2p dl pur 70 20
770 A338 4p ultra 80 20

Issued to publicize the national territory of Tierra del Fuego, Antarctic and South Atlantic Isles.
Issue dates: 4p, Feb. 27; 2p, June 5.

1965, Apr. 3 **Litho.**
771 A339 4p red org & blk 15 10

Issued to commemorate the 50th anniversary of the National Postal Savings Bank.

Sun and Globe — A340

1965, May 29
772 A340 4p blk, org & dl bl 40 20

Issued for the International Quiet Sun Year, 1964-65. See Nos. C98-C99.

Hussar of Pueyrredon Regiment A340a

Ricardo Rojas (1882-1957) A341

1965, June 5 **Wmk. 90** ***Perf. 13½***
773 A340a 8p dp ultra, blk & red 80 30

Issued for Army Day. See Nos. 796, 838, 857, 893, 944, 958, 974, 1145.

1965, June 26 **Photo.**

Portraits: No. 775, Ricardo Guiraldes (1886-1927). No. 776, Enrique Larreta (1873-1961). No. 777, Leopoldo Lugones (1874-1938). No. 778, Roberto J. Payro (1867-1928).

774 A341 8p brown 50 20
775 A341 8p brown 50 20
776 A341 8p brown 50 20
777 A341 8p brown 50 20
778 A341 8p brown 50 20
Nos. 774-778 (5) 2.50 1.00

Issued to honor Argentine writers. Printed se-tenant in sheets of 100 (10x10); 2 horizontal rows of each design with Guiraldes in top rows and Rojas in bottom rows.

Foreign postal stationery (stamped envelopes, postal cards and air letter sheets) lies beyond the scope of this Catalogue, which is limited to adhesive postage stamps.

Hipolito Yrigoyen A342

1965, July 3 **Litho.**
779 A342 8p pink & blk 30 20

Issued in memory of Hipolito Yrigoyen (1852-1933), president of Argentina 1916-22 and 1928-30.

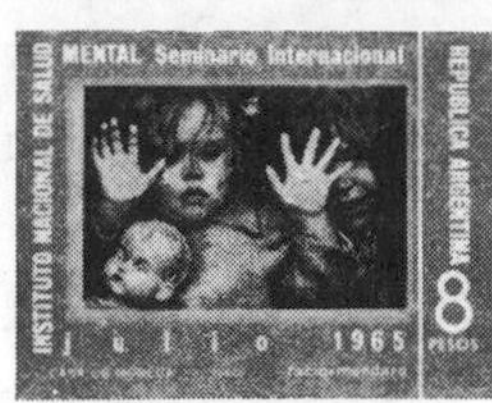
Children Looking Through Window — A343

1965, July 24 **Photo.**
780 A343 8p sal & blk 30 10

International Seminar on Mental Health.

Child's Funerary Urn and 16th Century Map A344

1965, Aug. 7 **Litho.**
781 A344 8p lt grn, dk red, brn & ocher 40 20

City of San Miguel de Tucuman, 400th anniversary.

Cardinal Cagliero A345

Dante Alighieri A346

1965, Aug. 21 **Photo.**
782 A345 8p violet 30 10

Issued to honor Juan Cardinal Cagliero (1839-1926), missionary to Argentina and Bishop of Magida.

1965, Sept. 16 **Wmk. 90** ***Perf. 13½***
783 A346 8p lt ultra 40 20

Issued to commemorate the 700th anniversary of the birth of Dante Alighieri (1265-1321), Italian poet.

Clipper "Mimosa" and Map of Patagonia A347

1965, Sept. 25 **Litho.**
784 A347 8p red & blk 40 20

Issued to commemorate the centenary of Welsh colonization of Chubut, and the founding of the city of Rawson.

Map of Buenos Aires, Cock and Compass Emblem of Federal Police — A348

1965, Oct. 30 **Photo.** ***Perf. 13½***
785 A348 8p car rose 40 20

Issued for Federal Police Day.

Child's Drawing of Children A349

1965, Nov. 6 **Litho.** **Wmk. 90**
786 A349 8p lt yel grn & blk 40 20

Public education law, 81st anniversary.

Church of St. Francis, Catamarca A350

Ruben Dario A351

1965, Dec. 8
787 A350 8p org yel & red brn 30 10

Issued to honor Brother Mamerto de la Asuncion Esquiu, preacher, teacher and official of 1885 Provincial Constitutional Convention.

Litho. and Photo.

1965, Dec. 22 ***Perf. 13½***
788 A351 15p bl vio, *gray* 30 15

Issued to honor Ruben Dario (pen name of Felix Ruben Garcia Sarmiento, 1867-1916), Nicaraguan poet, newspaper correspondent and diplomat.

"The Orange Seller" A352

Pueyrredon Paintings: No. 790, "Stop at the Grocery Store." No. 791, "Landscape at San Fernando" (sailboats). No. 792, "Bathing Horses at River Plata."

1966, Jan. 29 **Photo.** ***Perf. 13½***
789 A352 8p bluish grn 1.00 45
790 A352 8p bluish grn 1.00 45
791 A352 8p bluish grn 1.00 45
792 A352 8p bluish grn 1.00 45

Issued to honor Prilidiano Pueyrredon (1823-1870), painter. Nos. 789-792 are printed in one sheet of 40 stamps and 20 labels.

Sun Yat-sen, Flags of Argentina and China — A353

Perf. 13½

1966, March 12 **Wmk. 90**
793 A353 8p dk red brn 1.00 30

Issued to commemorate the centenary of the birth of Dr. Sun Yat-sen (1866-1925), founder of the Republic of China.

Souvenir Sheet

Rivadavia Issue of 1864 — A354

Wmk. 90

1966, Apr. 20 **Litho.** ***Imperf.***
794 A354 Sheet of three 1.50 1.50
a. 4p gray & red brn 15 15
b. 5p gray & grn 20 20
c. 8p gray & dk bl 25 25

Issued to commemorate the Second Rio de la Plata Stamp Show, Buenos Aires, March 16-24. No. 794 shows flags of Argentina and Uruguay in margin. Marginal inscriptions in gray and red brown, flags in blue and border in green. Size of stamps: 33x43mm. Size of sheet: 140x99mm.

People of Various Races and WHO Emblem A355

1966, Apr. 23 ***Perf. 13½***
795 A355 8p brn & blk 40 20

Issued to commemorate the opening of the World Health Organization Headquarters, Geneva.

Soldier Type of 1965

Design: 8p, Cavalryman, Guemes Infernal Regiment.

1966, May 28 **Litho.**
796 A340a 8p multi 80 30

Issued for Army Day.

Coat of Arms — A356

Designs (all 10p): Arms of Buenos Aires, Federal Capital, Catamarca, Cordoba, Corrientes, Chaco, Chubut, Entre Rios, Formosa, Jujuy, La Pampa, La Rioja, Mendoza, Misiones, Neuquen, Salta, San Juan, San Luis, Santa Cruz, Santa Fe, Santiago del Estero, Tucuman; maps of Rio Negro, and of Tierra del Fuego, Antarctica and South Atlantic Islands.

1966, July 30 **Wmk. 90** ***Perf. 13½***
797 A356 10p blk & multi 1.50 1.00
a. Sheet of 25 40.00

Issued to commemorate the 150th anniversary of Argentina's Declaration of Independence.

Sheets of 25 (5x5) contain 25 different designs with commemorative inscription and border in sheet margin.

Three Crosses, Caritas Emblem A357

1966, Sept. 10 Litho. Perf. 13½
798 A357 10p ol grn, blk & lt bl 30 8

Caritas, charity organization.

Hilario Ascasubi (1807-75) — A358

Portraits: No. 800, Estanislao del Campo (1834-80). No. 801, Miguel Cane (1851-1905). No. 802, Lucio V. Lopez (1848-94). No. 803, Rafael Obligado (1851-1920). No. 804, Luis Agote (1868-1954), M.D. No. 805, Juan B. Ambrosetti (1865-1917), naturalist and archaeologist. No. 806, Miguel Lillo (1862-1931), botanist and chemist. No. 807, Francisco P. Moreno (1852-1919), naturalist and paleontologist. No. 808, Francisco J. Muñiz (1795-1871), physician.

1966 Photo. Wmk. 90

799	A358	10p dk bl grn	60	30
800	A358	10p dk bl grn	60	30
801	A358	10p dk bl grn	60	30
802	A358	10p dk bl grn	60	30
803	A358	10p dk bl grn	60	30
804	A358	10p dp vio	60	30
805	A358	10p dp vio	60	30
806	A358	10p dp vio	60	30
807	A358	10p dp vio	60	30
808	A358	10p dp vio	60	30
		Nos. 799-808 (10)	6.00	3.00

Nos. 799-803 issued Sept. 17 to honor Argentine writers. Printed se-tenant in sheets of 100 (10x10); 2 horizontal rows of each portrait with Ascasubi in top two rows and Obligado in bottom rows. Nos. 804-808 issued Oct. 22 to honor Argentine scientists; 2 horizontal rows of each portrait with Agote in top two rows and Muñiz in bottom rows. Scientists set has value at upper left, frame line with rounded corners.

Anchor — A359

1966, Oct. 8 Litho.
809 A359 4p multi 30 20

Argentine merchant marine.

Flags and Map of the Americas — A360

Argentine National Bank — A361

1966, Oct. 29 Perf. 13½
810 A360 10p gray & multi 30 20

7th Conference of American Armies.

1966, Nov. 5 Photo.
811 A361 10p brt bl grn 25 8

Issued to commemorate the 75th anniversary of the Argentine National Bank.

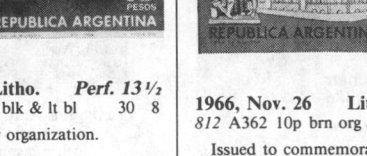

La Salle Monument and College, Buenos Aires A362

1966, Nov. 26 Litho. Perf. 13½
812 A362 10p brn org & blk 25 8

Issued to commemorate the 75th anniversary of the Colegio de la Salle, Buenos Aires, and to honor Saint Jean Baptiste de la Salle (1651-1719), educator.

Map of Argentine Antarctica and Expedition Route — A363

1966, Dec. 10 Wmk. 90
813 A363 10p multi 1.00 40

Issued to commemorate the 1965 Argentine Antarctic expedition, which planted the Argentine flag on the South Pole. See No. 851.

Juan Martin de Pueyrredon A364

Gen. Juan de Las Heras A365

1966, Dec. 17 Photo. Perf. 13½
814 A364 10p dl red brn 25 10

Issued to honor Juan Martin de Pueyrredon (1777-1850), Governor of Cordoba and of the United Provinces of the River Plata.

1966, Dec. 17 Engr.
815 A365 10p black 25 10

Issued to honor Gen. Juan Gregorio de Las Heras (1780-1866), Peruvian field marshal and aide-de-camp to San Martin.

Inscribed "Republica Argentina" Types of 1955-61 and

Guillermo Brown — A366

Trout Leaping in National Park — A366a

Designs: 6p, José Hernandez. 50p, Gen. Jose de San Martin. 500p, Red deer in forest.

Two overall paper sizes for 6p, 50p (No. 827) and 90p:
I. 27x37½mm.
II. 27x39mm.

Perf. 13½
1965-68 Wmk. 90 Photo.

817	A366	6p rose red, litho, paper I ('67)	1.75	8
818	A366	6p rose red, photo. ('67)	3.25	8
819	A366	6p brn, 15x22mm ('68)	10	6
823	A238a	43p dk car rose	9.00	10
824	A238a	45p brn, photo ('66)	6.00	10
825	A238a	45p brn, litho ('67)	10.00	20
826	A241	50p dk bl, 29x40 mm	10.00	18
827	A241	50p dk bl, 22x31½ mm, paper I ('67)	6.75	8
a.		Paper II	3.75	8
828	A366	90p ol bis, paper I ('67)	4.50	15
a.		Paper II	18.00	15

Engr.

829	A495	500p yel grn ('66)	2.00	40
829A	A366a	1,000p vio bl ('68)	8.00	1.50
		Nos. 817-829A (11)	61.35	2.93

The 500p and 1,000p remained on sale as 5p and 10p stamps after the 1970 currency exchange.
See Nos. 888, 891, 939, 941, 992, 1031, 1040, 1045-1047.

Pre-Columbian Pottery — A367

1967, Feb. 18 Litho. Perf. 13½
830 A367 10p multi 40 20

Issued to commemorate the 20th anniversary of UNESCO (United Nations Educational, Scientific and Cultural Organization).

"The Meal" by Fernando Fader A368

1967, Feb. 25 Photo. Wmk. 90
831 A368 10p red brn 40 20

Issued in memory of the Argentine painter Fernando Fader (1882-1935).

Col. Juana Azurduy de Padilla (1781-1862), Soldier — A369

Schooner "Invencible," 1811 — A370

Famous Women: No. 833, Juana Manuela Gorriti, writer. No. 834, Cecilia Grierson (1858-1934), physician. No. 835, Juana Paula Manso (1819-75), writer and educator. No. 836, Alfonsina Storni (1892-1938), writer and educator.

1967, May 13 Photo. Perf. 13½

832	A369	6p dk brn	40	20
833	A369	6p dk brn	40	20
834	A369	6p dk brn	40	20
835	A369	6p dk brn	40	20
836	A369	6p dk brn	40	20
		Nos. 832-836 (5)	2.00	1.00

Issued to honor famous Argentine women. Printed se-tenant in sheets of 100 (10x10); 2 horizontal rows of each portrait with Azurduy in two top rows and Storni in bottom rows.

1967, May 20 Litho.
837 A370 20p multi 1.25 40

Issued for Navy Day.

Soldier Type of 1965

Design: 20p, Highlander (Arribeños Corps).

1967, May 27
838 A340a 20p multi 1.00 40

Issued for Army Day.

Souvenir Sheet

Manuel Belgrano and JoseArtigas — A371

1967, June 22 Imperf.

839	A371	Souv. sheet of 2	60	60
a.		6p gray & brn	15	15
b.		22p brn & gray	35	35

Third Rio de la Plata Stamp Show, Montevideo, Uruguay, June 18-25. Gray marginal inscription. Size: 56x42mm.

Peace Dove and Valise A372

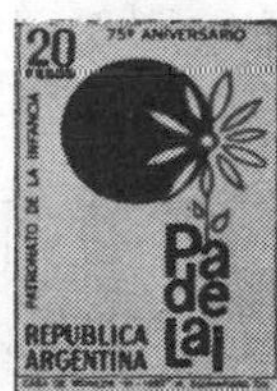

PADELAI Emblem A373

1967, Aug. 5 Litho. Perf. 13½
840 A372 20p multi 30 10

Issued for International Tourist Year 1967.

1967, Aug. 12 Litho.
841 A373 20p multi 30 10

Issued to commemorate the 75th anniversary of the Children's Welfare Association (Patronato de la Infancia-PADELAI).

Stagecoach and Modern City — A374

1967, Sept. 23 Wmk. 90 Perf. 13½
842 A374 20p rose, yel & blk 35 10

Centenary of Villa Maria, Cordoba.

The lack of a price for a listed item does not necessarily indicate rarity.

San Martin by Ibarra — A375

"Battle of Chacabuco" by P. Subercaseaux — A376

1967, Sept. 30 **Litho.**
843 A375 20p blk brn & pale yel 80 10

Engr.

844 A376 40p bl blk 1.25 24

Battle of Chacabuco, 150th anniversary.

Exhibition Rooms — A377

1967, Oct. 11 **Photo.**
845 A377 20p bl gray 30 10

Issued to commemorate the 10th anniversary of the Government House Museum.

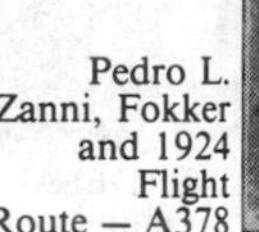

Pedro L. Zanni, Fokker and 1924 Flight Route — A378

1967, Oct. 21 **Litho.** ***Perf. 13½***
846 A378 20p multi 40 20

Issued for Aviation Week and to commemorate the 1924 flight of the Fokker seaplane "Province of Buenos Aires" from Amsterdam, Netherlands, to Osaka, Japan.

Training Ship General Brown, by Emilio Biggeri A379

1967, Oct. 28 **Wmk. 90**
847 A379 20p multi 1.25 40

Issued to honor the Military Naval School.

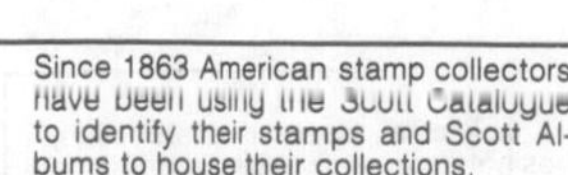

Ovidio Lagos and Front Page — A380

St. Barbara — A381

1967, Nov. 11 **Photo.**
848 A380 20p sepia 20 10

Centenary of La Capital, Rosario newspaper.

1967, Dec. 2 ***Perf. 13½***
849 A381 20p rose red 40 20

Issued to honor St. Barbara, patron saint of artillerymen.

Portrait of his Wife, by Eduardo Sivori — A382

1968, Jan. 27 **Photo.** ***Perf. 13½***
850 A382 20p bl grn 40 20

Issued to commemorate the 50th anniversary of the death of Eduardo Sivori (1847-1918), painter.

Antarctic Type of 1966 and

Admiral Brown Scientific Station A383

Planes over Map of Antarctica A384

Design: 6p, Map showing radio-postal stations 1966-67.

1968, Feb. 17 **Litho.** **Wmk. 90**
851 A363 6p multi 75 30
852 A383 20p multi 1.00 40
853 A384 40p multi 1.75 50

Issued to publicize Argentine research projects in Argentine Antarctica.

The Annunciation, by Leonardo da Vinci — A385

Man in Wheelchair and Factory — A386

1968, Mar. 23 **Photo.** ***Perf. 13½***
854 A385 20p lil rose 30 10

Issued for the Day of the Army Communications System and its patron saint, Gabriel.

1968, Mar. 23 **Litho.**
855 A386 20p grn & blk 30 10

Day of Rehabilitation of the Handicapped.

Children and WHO Emblem — A387

1968, May 11 **Wmk. 90** ***Perf. 13½***
856 A387 20p dk vio bl & ver 30 10

Issued for the 20th anniversary of the World Health Organization.

Soldier Type of 1965

Design: 20p, Uniform of First Artillery Regiment "General Iriarte."

1968, June 8 **Litho.**
857 A340a 20p multi 1.25 40

Issued for Army Day.

Frigate "Libertad," Painting by Emilio Biggeri — A388

1968, June 15 **Wmk. 90**
858 A388 20p multi 1.25 40

Issued for Navy Day.

Guillermo Rawson and Old Hospital A389

1968, July 20 **Photo.** ***Perf. 13½***
859 A389 6p ol bis 20 10

Issued to commemorate the centenary of Rawson Hospital, Buenos Aires.

Student Directing Traffic for Schoolmates A390

1968, Aug. 10 **Litho.** ***Perf. 13½***
860 A390 20p lt bl, blk, buff & car 20 10

Traffic safety and education.

O'Higgins Joining San Martin at Battle of Maipu, by P. Subercaseaux — A391

1968, Aug. 15 **Engr.**
861 A391 40p bluish blk 90 40

Sesquicentennial of the Battle of Maipu.

Osvaldo Magnasco — A392

1968, Sept. 7 **Photo.** ***Perf. 13½***
862 A392 20p brown 30 10

Issued to honor Osvaldo Magnasco (1864-1920), lawyer, Professor of Law and Minister of Justice.

Grandmother's Birthday, by Patricia Lynch — A393

The Sea, by Edgardo Gomez — A394

1968, Sept. 21 **Litho.**
863 A393 20p multi 30 10
864 A394 20p multi 30 10

The designs were chosen in a competition among kindergarten and elementary school children.

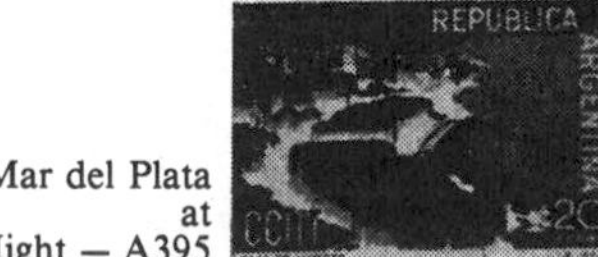

Mar del Plata at Night — A395

1968, Oct. 19 **Litho.** ***Perf. 13½***
865 A395 20p blk, ocher & bl 35 10

Issued to publicize the 4th Plenary Assembly of the International Telegraph and Telephone Consultative Committee, Mar del Plata, Sept. 23-Oct. 25. See Nos. C113, C114.

Frontier Gendarme A396

Patrol Boat A397

1968, Oct. 26

866 A396 20p multi 40 20
867 A397 20p bl, vio bl & blk 40 20

No. 866 honors the Gendarmery; No. 867 the Coast Guard.

Aaron de Anchorena and Pampero Balloon A398

1968, Nov. 2 **Photo.**

868 A398 20p bl & multi 40 20

22nd Aeronautics and Space Week.

St. Martin of Tours, by Alfredo Guido — A399

1968, Nov. 9 **Litho.**

869 A399 20p lil & dk brn 30 10

Issued to honor St. Martin of Tours, patron saint of Buenos Aires.

Municipal Bank Emblem A400

1968, Nov. 16

870 A400 20p multi 30 10

Issued to commemorate the 90th anniversary of the Buenos Aires Municipal Bank.

Anniversary Emblem A401

1968, Dec. 14 **Wmk. 90** ***Perf. 13½***

871 A401 20p car rose & dk grn 30 10

Issued to commemorate the 25th anniversary of ALPI (Fight Against Polio Association).

Shovel and State Coal Fields Emblem A402

Pouring Ladle and Army Manufacturing Emblem A403

1968, Dec. 21 **Litho.**

872 A402 20p org, bl & blk 30 10
873 A403 20p dl vio, dl yel & blk 30 10

Issued to publicize the National Coal and Steel industry at the Rio Turbio coal fields and the Zapla blast furnaces.

Woman Potter, by Ramon Gomez Cornet — A404

1968, Dec. 21 **Photo.** ***Perf. 13½***

874 A404 20p car rose 60 40

Centenary of the Witcomb Gallery.

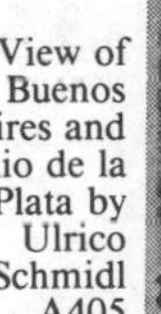

View of Buenos Aires and Rio de la Plata by Ulrico Schmidl A405

1969, Feb. 8 **Litho.** **Wmk. 90**

875 A405 20p yel, blk & ver 60 40

Issued to honor Ulrico Schmidl (c. 1462-1554) who wrote "Journey to the Rio de la Plata and Paraguay."

Types of 1955-67

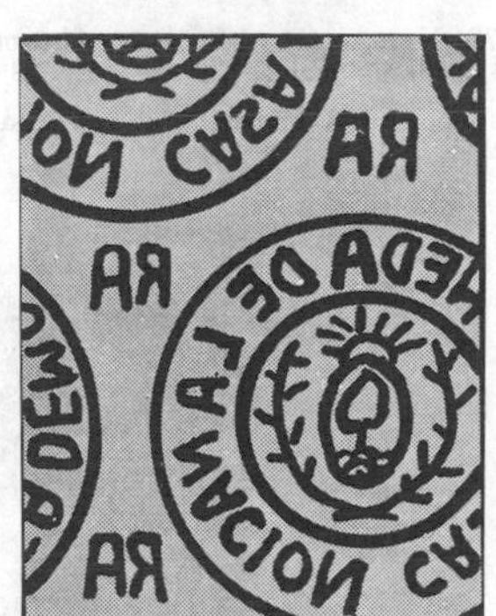

Argentine Arms, "Casa de Moneda de la Nacion" & "RA" Multiple — Wmk.365

Designs: 50c, Puma. 1p, Sunflower. 3p, Zapata Slope, Catamarca. 5p, Tierra del Fuego. 6p, José Hernandez. 10p, Inca Bridge, Mendoza. 50p, José de San Martin. 90p, Guillermo Brown. 100p, Ski jumper.

Photo.; Litho. (50c, 3p, 10p)

1969-70 **Wmk. 365** ***Perf. 13½***

882 A275 50c bis ('70) 1.00 8
883 A277 5p brown 1.50 12
884 A279 100p blue 37.50 1.00

Unwmk.

885 A278 1p brn ('70) 90 8

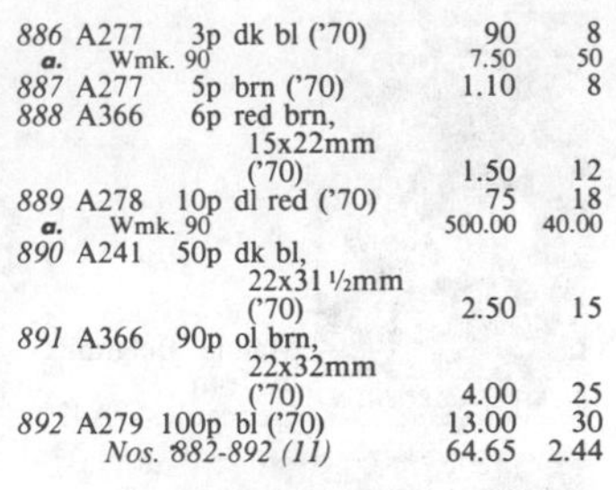

886 A277 3p dk bl ('70) 90 8
a. Wmk. 90 7.50 50
887 A277 5p brn ('70) 1.10 8
888 A366 6p red brn, 15x22mm ('70) 1.50 12
889 A278 10p dl red ('70) 75 18
a. Wmk. 90 500.00 40.00
890 A241 50p dk bl, 22x31½mm ('70) 2.50 15
891 A366 90p ol brn, 22x32mm ('70) 4.00 25
892 A279 100p bl ('70) 13.00 30
Nos. 882-892 (11) 64.65 2.44

Soldier Type of 1965

Design: 20p, Sapper (gastador) of Buenos Aires Province, 1856.

Wmk. 365

1969, May 31 **Litho.** ***Perf. 13½***

893 A340a 20p multi 1.25 40

Issued for Army Day.

Frigate Hercules, by Emilio Biggeri — A406

1969, May 31

894 A406 20p multi 1.25 40

Issued for Navy Day.

"All Men are Equal" A407

ILO Emblem A408

1969, June 28 **Wmk. 90**

895 A407 20p blk & ocher 30 10

International Human Rights Year.

1969, June 28 **Litho.** **Wmk. 365**

896 A408 20p lt grn & multi 30 10

Issued to commemorate the 50th anniversary of the International Labor Organization.

Pedro N. Arata (1849-1922), Chemist A409

Radar Antenna, Balcarce Station and Satellite A410

Portraits: No. 898, Miguel Fernandez (1883-1950), zoologist. No. 899, Angel P. Gallardo (1867-1934), biologist. No. 900, Cristobal M. Hicken (1875-1933), botanist. No. 901, Eduardo Ladislao Holmberg, M.D. (1852-1937), natural scientist.

1969, Aug. 9 **Wmk. 365** ***Perf. 13½***

Red Brown Design on Orange Yellow Background

897 A409 6p *(Arata)* 60 10
898 A409 6p *(Fernandez)* 60 10
899 A409 6p *(Gallardo)* 60 10
900 A409 6p *(Hicken)* 60 10
901 A409 6p *(Holmberg)* 60 10
Nos. 897-901 (5) 3.00 50

Argentine scientists. See No. 778 note.

1969, Aug. 23 **Wmk. 99**

902 A410 20p yel & blk 40 20

Issued to publicize communications by satellite through International Telecommunications Satellite Consortium (INTELSAT). See No. C115.

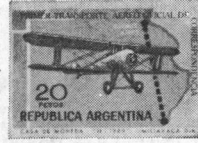

Nieuport 28, Flight Route and Map of Buenos Aires Province A411

1969, Sept. 13 **Litho.** **Wmk. 90**

903 A411 20p multi 40 20

Issued to commemorate the 50th anniversary of the first Argentine airmail service from El Palomar to Mar del Plata, flown Feb. 23-24, 1919, by Capt. Pedro L. Zanni.

Military College Gate and Emblem A412

1969, Oct. 4 **Wmk. 365** ***Perf. 13½***

904 A412 20p multi 40 20

Issued to commemorate the centenary of the National Military College, El Palomar (Greater Buenos Aires).

Gen. Angel Pacheco A413

La Farola, Logotype of La Prensa A414

1969, Nov. 8 **Photo.** **Wmk. 365**

905 A413 20p dp grn 30 10

Issued to commemorate the centenary of the death of Gen. Angel Pacheco (1795-1869).

1969, Nov. 8 **Litho.** ***Perf. 13½***

Design: No. 907, Bartolomé Mitre and La Nacion logotype.

906 A414 20p org, yel & blk 1.00 30
907 A414 20p brt grn & blk 1.00 30

Centenary of newspapers La Prensa and La Nacion.

Julian Aguirre A415

Musicians: No. 909, Felipe Boero. No. 910, Constantino Gaito. No. 911, Carlos Lopez Buchardo. No. 912, Alberto Williams.

Wmk. 365

1969, Dec. 6 Photo. Perf. 13½

Dark Green Design on Light Blue Background

908 A415 6p *(Aguirre)*	80	30
909 A415 6p *(Boero)*	80	30
910 A415 6p *(Gaito)*	80	30
911 A415 6p *(Buchardo)*	80	30
912 A415 6p *(Williams)*	80	30
Nos. 908-912 (5)	4.00	1.50

Argentine musicians. See No. 778 note.

Lt. Benjamin Matienzo and Nieuport Plane A416

1969, Dec. 13 Litho.
913 A416 20p multi 90 40

23rd Aeronautics and Space Week.

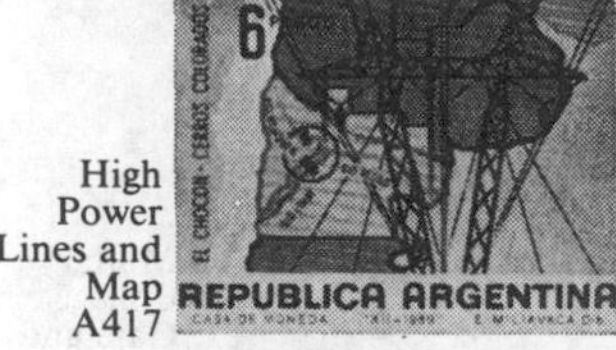

High Power Lines and Map A417

Design: 20p, Map of Santa Fe Province and schematic view of tunnel.

1969, Dec. 13
914 A417 6p multi 70 10
915 A417 20p multi 1.50 20

Issued to publicize the completion of development projects. The 6p commemorates the hydroelectric dams on the Limay and Neuquen Rivers, the 20p the tunnel under the Rio Grance from Sante Fe to Parana.

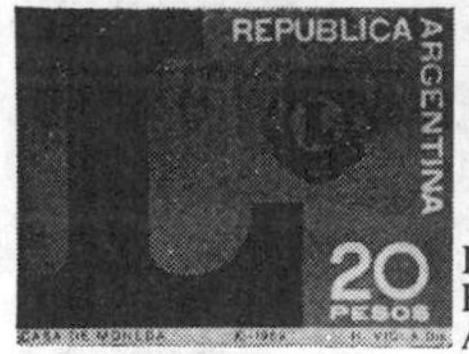

Lions Emblem A418

1969, Dec. 20 Wmk. 365 Perf. 13½
916 A418 20p blk, emer & org 1.00 40

Issued to commemorate the 50th anniversary of the Argentine Lions International Club.

Madonna and Child, by Raul Soldi — A419

1969, Dec. 27 Litho.
917 A419 20p multi 1.00 40

Christmas 1969.

Argentina stamps through 1975 can be mounted in Scott's Argentina Album.

Manuel Belgrano, by Jean Gericault — A420

The Creation of the Flag, Bas-relief by José Fioravanti — A421

Perf. 13½

1970, July 4 Unwmk. Photo.
918 A420 20c dp brn 50 20

Litho. Perf. 12½
919 A421 50c bis, blk & bl 1.25 50

Issued to commemorate the sesquicentennial of the death of Gen. Manuel Belgrano (1770-1820), Argentine patriot.

San José Palace A422

1970, Aug. 9 Litho. Perf. 13½
920 A422 20c yel grn & multi 30 10

Issued to commemorate the centenary of the death of Gen. Justo José de Urquiza (1801-1870), president of Argentina, 1854-60.

Schooner "Juliet" A423

1970, Aug. 8 Unwmk.
921 A423 20c multi 1.25 40

Issued for Navy Day.

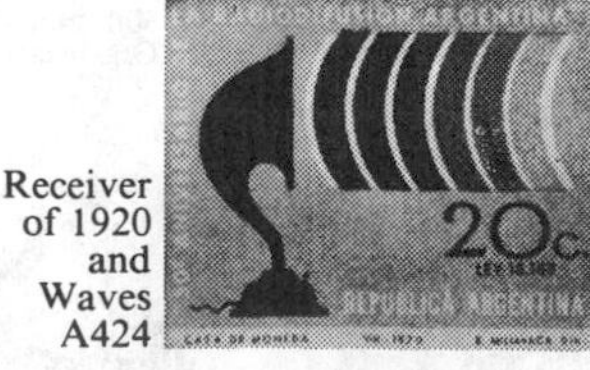

Receiver of 1920 and Waves A424

1970, Aug. 29
922 A424 20c lt bl & multi 40 20

Issued to commemorate the 50th anniversary of Argentine broadcasting.

Types of 1955-67 Inscribed "Republica Argentina" and Types A425, A426

Manuel Belgrano A425

Lujan Basilica A426

Designs: 1c, Sunflower. 3c, Zapata Slope, Catamarca. 5c, Tierra del Fuego. 8c, No. 931, Belgrano. 10c, Inca Bridge, Mendoza. 25c, 50c, 70c, Jose de San Martin. 65c, 90c, 1.20p, San Martin. 1p, Ski jumper. 1.15p, 1.80p, Adm. Brown.

1970-73 Photo. Unwmk. Perf. 13½

923 A278	1c dk grn ('71)	20	5
924 A277	3c car rose ('71)	20	5
925 A277	5c bl ('71)	20	5
926 A425	6c dp bl	20	5
927 A425	8c grn ('72)	20	5
928 A278	10c dl red ('71)	60	6
929 A278	10c brn, litho. ('71)	80	6
930 A278	10c org brn ('72)	70	5
931 A425	10c brn ('73)	30	5
932 A426	18c yel & dk brn, litho ('73)	30	5
933 A425	25c brn ('71)	50	5
934 A425	50c scar ('72)	2.00	5
935 A241	65c brn, 22x31½mm, paper II ('71)	1.00	5
936 A425	70c dk bl ('73)	50	5
937 A241	90c emer, 22x31½ mm ('72)	5.00	5
938 A279	1p brn, 22½x29½ mm ('71)	3.00	5
939 A366	1.15p dk bl, 22½x32 mm ('71)	1.75	5
940 A241	1.20p org, 22x31½ mm ('73)	1.75	5
941 A366	1.80p brn ('73)	1.75	5
	Nos. 923-941 (19)	20.95	97

The imprint "Casa de Moneda de la Nacion" (in capitals) appears on 3c, 5c, Nos. 928-929; 65c, 90c, 1p, 1.20p.

On type A425 only the 6c is inscribed "Ley 18.188" below denomination.

Fluorescent paper was used in printing the 25c, 50c, and 70c. The 3c, 8c, No. 931 and 65c were issued on both ordinary and fluorescent paper.

See Nos. 987-996, 1032-1038, 1042-1043, 1089-1107.

Soldier Type of 1965

Design: 20c, Galloping messenger of Field Army, 1879.

1970, Oct. 17 Litho. Perf. 13½
944 A340a 20c multi 1.25 40

Dome of Cathedral of Cordoba — A430

1970, Nov. 7 Unwmk.
945 A430 50c gray & blk 1.25 20

Bishopric of Tucuman, 400th anniversary. See No. C131.

People Around U.N. Emblem — A431

1970, Nov. 7
946 A431 20c tan & multi 30 10

25th anniversary of the United Nations.

State Mint and Medal A432

1970, Nov. 28 Unwmk. Perf. 13½
947 A432 20c gold, grn & blk 30 10

Inauguration of the State Mint Building, 25th anniversary.

St. John Bosco and Dean Funes College A433

1970, Dec. 19 Litho.
948 A433 20c ol & blk 30 10

Honoring the work of the Salesian Order in Patagonia.

Nativity, by Horacio Gramajo Gutierrez — A434

1970, Dec. 19
949 A434 20c multi 80 40

Christmas 1970.

Argentine Flag, Map of Argentine Antarctica A435

1971, Feb. 20 Litho. Perf. 13½
950 A435 20c multi 2.00 60

Fifth anniversary of Argentine South Pole Expedition.

Phosphorescent Sorting Code and Albert Einstein — A436

1971, Apr. 30 Unwmk. Perf. 13½
951 A436 25c multi 80 40

Electronics in postal development.

Symbolic Road Crossing A437

1971, May 29 Litho.
952 A437 25c bl & blk 40 20

Inter-American Regional Meeting of the International Federation of Roads, Buenos Aires, March 28-31.

Elias Alippi — A438

Actors: No. 954, Juan Aurelio Casacuberta. No. 955, Angelina Pagano. No. 956, Roberto Casaux. No. 957, Florencio Parravicini. See No. 778 note.

1971, May 29 **Litho.**

Black Design on Pale Rose Background

953 A438 15c *(Alippi)* 50 10
954 A438 15c *(Casacuberta)* 50 10
955 A438 15c *(Pagano)* 50 10
956 A438 15c *(Casaux)* 50 10
957 A438 15c *(Parravicini)* 50 10
Nos. 953-957 (5) 2.50 50

Soldier Type of 1965

Design: 25c, Artilleryman, 1826.

1971, July 3 **Unwmk.** ***Perf. 13½***
958 A340a 25c multi 2.00 60

Army Day, May 29.

Bilander "Carmen," by Emilio Biggeri A439

1971, July 3
959 A439 25c multi 1.75 20

Navy Day

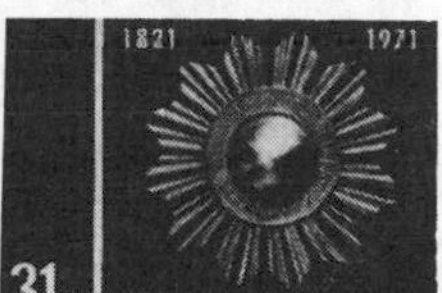
Peruvian Order of the Sun A440

1971, Aug. 28
960 A440 31c multi 50 10

Sesquicentennial of Peru's independence.

Güemes in Battle, by Lorenzo Gigli A441

Design: No. 962, Death of Güemes, by Antonio Alice.

1971, Aug. 28

Size: 39x29mm.
961 A441 25c multi 75 40

Size: 84x29mm.
962 A441 25c multi 75 40

Sesquicentennial of the death of Martin Miguel de Güemes, leader in Gaucho War, Governor and Captain General of Salta Province.

The Catalogue editors cannot undertake to appraise, identify or judge the genuineness or condition of stamps.

Stylized Tulip — A442

1971, Sept. 18
963 A442 25c tan & multi 35 10

3rd International and 8th National Horticultural Exhibition.

Father Antonio Saenz, by Juan Gut — A443

1971, Sept. 18
964 A433 25c gray & multi 35 10

Sesquicentennial of University of Buenos Aires, and to honor Father Antonio Saenz, first Chancellor and Rector.

Fabricaciones Militares Emblem — A444

1971, Oct. 16 **Unwmk.** ***Perf. 13½***
965 A444 25c brn, gold, bl & blk 35 10

30th anniversary of military armament works.

Cars and Trucks A445

Design: 65c, Tree converted into paper.

1971, Oct. 16
966 A445 25c dl bl & multi 85 20
967 A445 65c grn & multi 2.00 60

Nationalized industries. See No. C134.

Luis C. Candelaria and his Plane, 1918 A446

1971, Nov. 27
968 A446 25c multi 40 20

25th Aeronautics and Space Week.

Observatory and Nebula of Magellan — A447

1971, Nov. 27
969 A447 25c multi 40 20

Centenary of Cordoba Astronomical Observatory.

Christ in Majesty — A448

1971, Dec. 18 **Litho.**
970 A448 25c blk & multi 40 20

Christmas 1971. Design is from a tapestry by Horacio Butler in Basilica of St. Francis, Buenos Aires.

Mother and Child, by J. C. Castagnino A449

1972, May 6 **Unwmk.** ***Perf. 13½***
971 A449 25c fawn & blk 40 20

25th anniversary (in 1971) of the International United Nations Children's Fund (UNICEF).

Mailman's Bag A450

1972, Sept. 2 **Litho.** ***Perf. 13½***
972 A450 25c lem & multi 20 8

Bicentenary of appointment of first Argentine mailman.

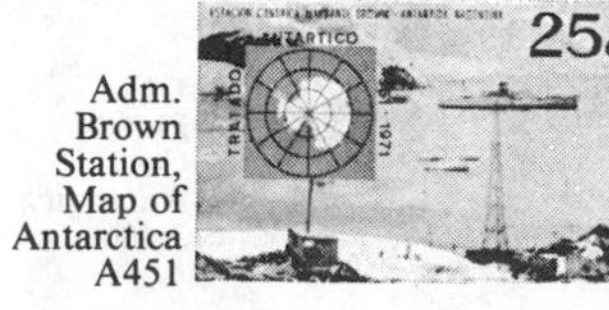
Adm. Brown Station, Map of Antarctica A451

1972, Sept. 2
973 A451 25c bl & multi 1.00 40

10th anniversary (in 1971) of Antarctic Treaty.

Soldier Type of 1965

Design: 25c, Sergeant, Negro and Mulatto Corps, 1806-1807.

1972, Sept. 23
974 A340a 25c multi 1.25 40

Army Day, May 29.

Brigantine "Santisima Trinidad" A452

1972, Sept. 23
975 A452 25c multi 1.25 40

Navy Day. See No. 1006.

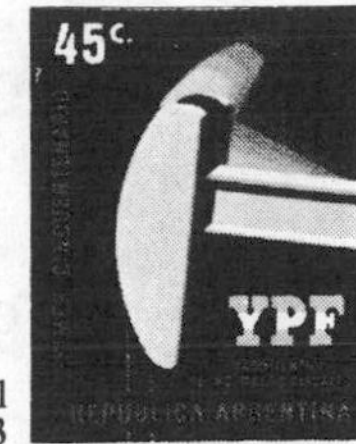
Oil Pump — A453

1972, Sept. 30 **Litho.** ***Perf. 13½***
976 A453 45c blk & multi 1.50 15

50th anniversary of the organization of the state oil fields (Yacimientos Petroliferos Fiscales).

Sounding Balloon — A454

1972, Sept. 30
977 A454 25c blk, bl & ocher 40 20

Centenary of National Meteorological Service.

Trees and Globe — A455

1972, Oct. 14 ***Perf. 13x13½***
978 A455 25c bl, blk & lt bl 1.10 15

7th World Forestry Congress, Buenos Aires, Oct. 4-18.

Arms of Naval School, Frigate "Presidente Sarmiento" — A456

1972, Oct. 14
979 A456 25c gold & multi 1.00 40

Centenary of Military Naval School.

Early Balloon and Plane, Antonio de Marchi — A457

Bartolomé Mitre — A458

1972, Nov. 4 *Perf. 13½*
980 A457 25c multi 40 20

Aeronautics and Space Week, and in honor of Baron Antonio de Marchi (1875-1934), aviation pioneer.

1972, Nov. 4 **Engr.**
981 A458 25c dk bl 20 8

Pres. Bartolome Mitre (1821-1906), writer, historian, soldier.

Flower and Heart — A459

1972, Dec. 2 **Litho.** *Perf. 13½*
982 A459 90c lt bl, ultra & blk 80 40

"Your heart is your health," World Health Day.

"Martin Fierro," by Juan C. Castignano A460

"Spirit of the Gaucho," by Vicente Forte — A461

1972, Dec. 2 **Litho.** *Perf. 13½*
983 A460 50c multi 50 25
984 A461 90c multi 1.00 40

International Book Year 1972, and to commemorate the centenary of publication of the poem, Martin Fierro, by José Hernandez (1834-1886).

Iguassu Falls and Tourist Year Emblem — A462

1972, Dec. 16 *Perf. 13x13½*
985 A462 45c multi 45 12

Tourism Year of the Americas.

King, Wood Carving, 18th Century — A463

1972, Dec. 16 *Perf. 13½*
986 A463 50c multi 80 40

Christmas 1972.

Types of 1955-73 Inscribed "Republica Argentina" and

Moon Valley, San Juan Province — A463a

Designs: 1c, Sunflower. 5c, Tierra del Fuego. 10c, Inca Bridge, Mendoza. 50c, Lujan Basilica. 65c, 22.50p, San Martin. 1p, Ski jumper. 1.15p, 4.50p, Guillermo Brown. 1.80p, Manuel Belgrano.

Litho.; Photo. (1c, 65c, 1p)
Perf. 13½, 12½ (1.80p)

1972-75 **Wmk. 365**

987	A278	1c dk grn	25	5
988	A277	5c dk bl	25	5
989	A278	10c bis brn	25	5
989A	A426	50c dl pur ('75)	25	5
990	A241	65c gray brn	5.00	10
991	A279	1p brown	2.00	6
992	A366	1.15p dk gray bl	2.00	6
993	A425	1.80p bl ('75)	25	5
994	A366	4.50p grn ('75)	1.00	6
995	A241	22.50p vio bl ('75)	2.00	10
996	A463a	50p multi ('75)	4.00	50
		Nos. 987-996 (11)	17.25	1.13

Paper size of 1c is 27½x39mm.; others of 1972, 37x27, 27x37mm.
Size of 22.50p, 50p: 26½x38½mm.
See No. 1050.

Cock (Symbolic of Police) — A464

First Coin of Bank of Buenos Aires — A465

1973, Feb. 3 **Litho.** **Unwmk.**
997 A464 50c lt grn & multi 40 20

Sesquicentennial of Federal Police of Argentina.

1973, Feb. 3 *Perf. 13½*
998 A465 50c pur, yel & brn 20 10

Sesquicentennial of the Bank of Buenos Aires Province.

DC-3 Planes Over Antarctica A466

1973, Apr. 28 **Litho.** *Perf. 13½*
999 A466 50c lt bl & multi 2.00 60

10th anniversary of Argentina's first flight to the South Pole.

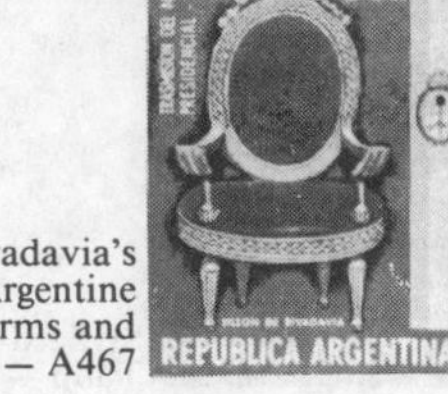

Rivadavia's Chair, Argentine Arms and Colors — A467

1973, May 19 **Litho.** *Perf. 13½*
1000 A467 50c multi 35 12

Inauguration of Pres. Hector J. Campora, May 25, 1973.

San Martin, by Gil de Castro — A468

San Martin and Bolivar A469

1973, July 7 **Litho.** *Perf. 13½*
1001 A468 50c lt grn & multi 45 10
1002 A469 50c yel & multi 45 10

Gen. San Martin's farewell to the people of Peru and his meeting with Simon Bolivar at Guayaquil July 26-27, 1822.

Eva Perón A470

1973, July 26 **Litho.** *Perf. 13½*
1003 A470 70c blk, org & bl 30 10

Maria Eva Duarte de Peron (1919-1952), political leader.

House of Viceroy Sobremonte, by Hortensia de Virgilion — A471

1973, July 28 *Perf. 13x13½*
1004 A471 50c bl & multi 30 10

400th anniversary of the city of Cordoba.

Woman, by Lino Spilimbergo A472

New and Old Telephones A473

1973, Aug. 28 **Litho.** *Perf. 13½*
1005 A472 70c multi 1.10 10

Philatelists' Day. See Nos. B60-B61.

Ship Type of 1972

Design: 70c, Frigate "La Argentina."

1973, Oct. 27 **Litho.** *Perf. 13½*
1006 A452 70c multi 90 40

Navy Day.

1973, Oct. 27
1007 A473 70c brt bl & multi 60 30

25th anniversary of national telecommunications system.

Plume Made of Flags of Participants A474

1973, Nov. 3 *Perf. 13½*
1008 A474 70c yel bis & multi 35 10

12th Congress of Latin Notaries, Buenos Aires.

No. 940 Overprinted

TRANSMISION DEL MANDO PRESIDENCIAL
12 OCTUBRE 1973

1973, Nov. 30 **Photo.**
1010 A241 1.20p orange 1.10 20

Assumption of presidency by Juan Peron, Oct. 12.

Virgin and Child, Window, La Plata Cathedral A476

Design: 1.20p, Nativity, by Bruno Venier, b. 1914.

1973, Dec. 15 **Litho.** *Perf. 13½*
1011 A476 70c gray & multi 50 25
1012 A476 1.20p blk & multi 1.00 50

Christmas 1973.

The Lama, by Juan Batlle Planas — A477

Paintings: 50c, Houses in Boca District, by Eugenio Daneri (horiz.). 90c, The Blue Grotto, by Emilio Pettoruti (horiz.)

1974, Feb. 9 **Litho.** *Perf. 13½*
1013 A477 50c multi 40 20

1014 A477 70c multi 50 30
1015 A477 90c multi 90 40

Argentine painters. See No. B64.

Mar del Plata A478

1974, Feb. 9
1016 A478 70c multi 40 20

Centenary of Mar del Plata.

Weather Symbols A479

Justo Santa Maria de Oro A480

1974, Mar. 23 Litho. *Perf. 13½*
1017 A479 1.20p multi 50 20

Centenary of international meteorological cooperation.

1974, Mar. 23
1018 A480 70c multi 30 10

Bicentenary of the birth of Brother Justo Santa Maria de Oro (1772-1836), theologian, patriot, first Argentine bishop.

Belisario Roldan — A481

1974, June 29 Photo. Unwmk.
1019 A481 70c bl & brn 30 20

Birth centenary of Belisario Roldan (1873-1922), writer.

Poster with Names of OAS Members A482

1974, June 29 Litho.
1020 A482 1.38p multi 25 15

25th anniversary of the Organization of American States.

ENCOTEL Emblem — A483

1974, Aug. 10 Litho. *Perf. 13*
1021 A483 1.20p bl, gold & blk 60 15

ENCOTEL, National Post and Telegraph Press.

Flags of Argentina, Bolivia, Brazil, Paraguay, Uruguay — A484

1974, Aug. 16 *Perf. 13½*
1022 A484 1.38p multi 30 20

6th Meeting of Foreign Ministers of Rio de la Plata Basin Countries.

El Chocon Hydroelectric Complex, Limay River — A485

Somisa Steel Mill, San Nicolas — A486

Gen. Belgrano Bridge, Chaco-Corrientes — A487

Perf. 13½, 13x13½ (4.50p)
1974, Sept. 14
1023 A485 70c multi 50 25
1024 A486 1.20p multi 75 50
1025 A487 4.50p multi 3.00 75

Development projects.

Brigantine Belgrano, by Emilio Biggeri A488

1974, Oct. 26 Litho. *Perf. 13½*
1026 A488 1.20p multi 1.00 40

Departure into exile in Chile of General San Martin, Sept. 22, 1822.

Alberto R. Mascias and Bleriot Plane — A489

1974, Oct. 26 Unwmk.
1027 A489 1.20p multi 80 40

Air Force Day, Aug. 10, and to honor Alberto Roque Garcias (1878-1951), aviation pioneer.

Exists with wmk. 365.

Hussar, 1812, by Eleodoro Marenco A490

1974, Oct. 26
1028 A490 1.20p multi 80 40

Army Day.

Post Horn and Flags A491

1974, Nov. 23 Unwmk. *Perf. 13½*
1029 A491 2.65p multi 1.25 15

Centenary of Universal Postal Union. Exists with wmk. 365.

Franciscan Monastery A492

1974, Nov. 23 Litho.
1030 A492 1.20p multi 60 15

400th anniversary, city of Santa Fe.

Trout Type of 1968

1974 Engr. Unwmk.
1031 A366a 1000p vio bl 5.00 1.00

Due to a shortage of 10p stamps a quantity of this 1,000p was released for use as 10p.

Types of 1954-73 Inscribed "Republica Argentina" and

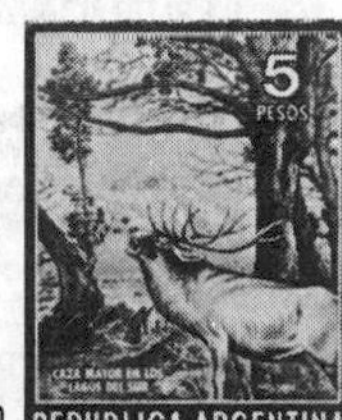

Red Deer in Forest — A495

Congress Building A497

Designs: 30c, 60c, 1.80p, Manuel Belgrano. 50c, Lujan Basilica. No. 1036, 2p, 6p, San Martin (16x22½mm.). 2.70p, 7.50p, 22.50p, San Martin (22x31½mm.). 4.50p, 13.50p, Guillermo Brown. 10p, Leaping trout.

1974-75 Unwmk. Photo. *Perf. 13½*
1032 A425 30c brn vio 15 5
1033 A426 50c blk & brn red ('75) 15 5
1034 A426 50c bis & bl ('75) 15 5
1035 A425 60c ocher ('75) 15 5
1036 A425 1.20p red 45 5
1037 A425 1.80p dp bl ('75) 20 5
1038 A425 2p dk pur ('75) 30 5
1039 A241 2.70p dk bl 22x31½mm 35 5
1040 A366 4.50p green 1.30 5
1041 A495 5p yel grn 60 5
1042 A425 6p red org ('75) 30 5
1043 A425 6p emer ('75) 30 5
1044 A241 7.50p grn, 22x31½ mm ('75) 1.25 6
1045 A366a 10p vio bl 1.50 6
1046 A366 13.50p scar, 16x22½ mm ('75) 1.25 6
1047 A366 13.50p scar, 22x31½ mm ('75) 1.25 8
1048 A241 22.50p dp bl, 22x31½ mm ('75) 1.10 10
1049 A497 30p yel & dk red brn 1.75 12
1050 A463a 50p multi ('76) 2.25 15
Nos. 1032-1050 (19) 14.75 1.23

Fluorescent paper was used in printing No. 1036, 2p, Nos. 1044 and 1047. The 30p was issued on both ordinary and fluorescent paper.

See also No. 829.

Miniature Sheet

A498

1974, Dec. 7 Litho. *Perf. 13½*
1052 A498 Sheet of 6 5.00 4.00
a. 1p *Mariano Necochea* 35
b. 1.20p *Jose de San Martin* 35
c. 1.70p *Manuel Isidoro Suarez* 50
d. 1.90p *Juan Pascual Pringles* 60
e. 2.70p *Latin American flags* 90
f. 4.50p *Jose Felix Bogado* 1.50

Sesquicentennial of Battles of Junin and Ayacucho. No. 1052 has black control number. Size: 140x132mm.

Dove, by Vito Campanella — A499

St. Anne, by Raul Soldi — A500

1974, Dec. 21 Litho. *Perf. 13½*
1053 A499 1.20p multi 80 30
1054 A500 2.65p multi 1.25 50

Christmas 1974.

The indexes in each volume of the Scott Catalogue contain many listings which help to identify stamps.

Boy Looking at Stamp — A501

1974, Dec. 21

No.	Type	Value	Color	Unused	Used
1055	A501	1.70p	blk & yel	50	18

World Youth Philately Year.

Space Monsters, by Raquel Forner A502

Design: 4.50p, Dream, by Emilio Centurion.

1975, Feb. 22 Litho. *Perf. 13½*

No.	Type	Value	Color	Unused	Used
1056	A502	2.70p	multi	1.40	40
1057	A502	4.50p	multi	2.75	60

Argentine modern art.

Indian Woman and Cathedral, Catamarca — A503

Designs: No. 1059, Carved chancel and street scene. No. 1060, Grazing cattle and monastery yard. No. 1061, Painted pottery and power station. No. 1062, Farm cart and colonial mansion. No. 1063, Perito Moreno glacier and spinning mill. No. 1064, Lake Lapataia and scientific surveyor. No. 1065, Los Alerces National Park and oil derrick.

1975 Litho. Unwmk. *Perf. 13½*

No.	Type	Value	Design	Unused	Used
1058	A503	1.20p	*shown*	35	25
1059	A503	1.20p	*Jujuy*	35	25
1060	A503	1.20p	*Salta*	35	25
1061	A503	1.20p	*Santiago del Estero*	35	25
1062	A503	1.20p	*Tucuman*	35	25
1063	A503	6p	*Santa Cruz*	75	25
1064	A503	6p	*Tierra del Fuego*	75	25
1065	A503	6p	*Chubut*	75	25
	Nos. 1058-1065 (8)			4.00	2.00

Tourist publicity.
Issue dates: 1.20p, Mar. 8; 6p, Dec. 20.

"We Have Been Inoculated" A504

1975, Apr. 26 Unwmk. *Perf. 13½*

No.	Type	Value	Color	Unused	Used
1066	A504	2p	multi	60	30

Children's inoculation campaign (child's painting).

A particular stamp may be scarce, but if few collectors want it, its market value may remain relatively low.

Hugo A. Acuña and South Orkney Station — A505

Designs: No. 1068, Francisco P. Moreno and Lake Nahuel Huapi. No. 1069, Lt. Col. Luis Piedra Buena and cutter, Luisito. No. 1070, Ensign José M. Sobral and Snow Hill House. No. 1071, Capt. Carlos M. Moyano and Cerro del Toro (mountain).

1975, June 28 Litho. *Perf. 13*

No.	Type	Value	Color	Unused	Used
1067	A505	2p	grnsh bl & multi	40	20
1068	A505	2p	yel grn & multi	40	20
1069	A505	2p	lt vio & multi	40	20
1070	A505	2p	gray bl & multi	40	20
1071	A505	2p	pale grn & multi	40	20
	Nos. 1067-1071 (5)			2.00	1.00

Pioneers of Antarctica.

Frigate "25 de Mayo" A506

1975, Sept. 27 Unwmk. *Perf. 13½*

No.	Type	Value	Color	Unused	Used
1072	A506	6p	multi	60	30

Navy Day 1975.

Eduardo Bradley and Balloon — A507

1975, Sept. 27 Wmk. 365

No.	Type	Value	Color	Unused	Used
1073	A507	6p	multi	60	30

Air Force Day.

Declaration of Independence, by Juan M. Blanes — A508

1975, Oct. 25

No.	Type	Value	Color	Unused	Used
1074	A508	6p	multi	45	12

Sesquicentennial of Uruguay's declaration of independence.

Flame A509

1975, Oct. 17 Unwmk.

No.	Type	Value	Color	Unused	Used
1075	A509	6p	gray & multi	45	12

Loyalty Day, 30th anniversary of Pres. Peron's accession to power.

Nos. 886, 891 and 932 Surcharged

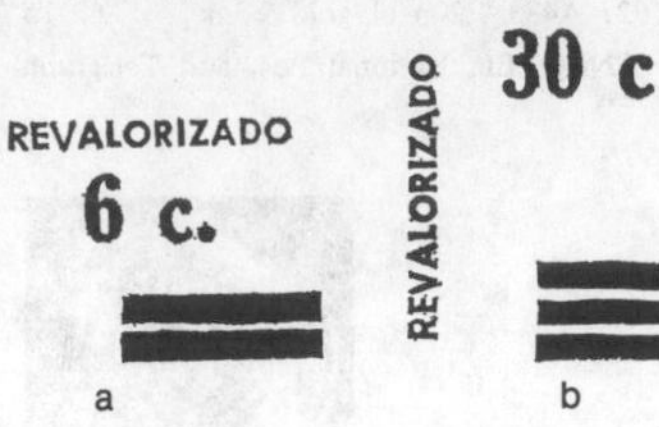

c

REVALORIZADO
5 pesos

1975 Lithographed, Photogravure

No.	Type	Value	Color	Unused	Used
1076	A277	6c	on 3p	20	10
1077	A366	30c	on 90p	20	10
1078	A426	5p	on 18c	60	30

Issue dates: 6c, Oct. 30; 30c, Nov. 20; 5p, Oct. 24. The 6c also exists on No. 886a.

International Bridge, Flags of Argentina and Uruguay — A510

1975, Oct. 25 Litho. Wmk. 365

No.	Type	Value	Color	Unused	Used
1081	A510	6p	multi	60	30

Opening of bridge connecting Colon, Argentina, and Paysandu, Uruguay.

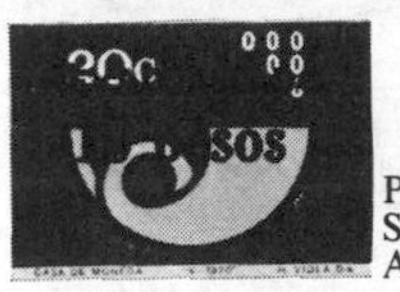

Post Horn, Surcharged A511

1975, Nov. 8

No.	Type	Value	Color	Unused	Used
1082	A511	10p	on 20c multi	75	20

Introduction of postal code. Not issued without surcharge.

Nurse Holding Infant A512

1975, Dec. 13 Litho. *Perf. 13½*

No.	Type	Value	Color	Unused	Used
1083	A512	6p	multi	75	20

Children's Hospital, centenary.

Nativity, Nueva Pompeya Church — A513

1975, Dec. 13 Litho. Unwmk.

No.	Type	Value	Color	Unused	Used
1084	A513	6p	multi	50	30

Christmas 1975.

Types of 1970-75 and

Church of St. Francis, Salta — A515

Designs: 3p, No. 1099, 60p, 90p, Manuel Belgrano. 12p, 15p, 20p, 30p, No. 1100, 100p, 110p, 120p, 130p, San Martin. 15p, 70p, Guillermo Brown. 300p, Moon Valley (lower inscriptions italic). 500p, Adm. Brown Station, Antarctica.

1976-78 Photo. Unwmk. *Perf. 13½*

No.	Type	Value	Color	Unused	Used
1089	A425	3p	slate	20	10
1090	A425	12p	rose red	30	10
1091	A425	12p	rose red, litho.	30	10
1092	A425	12p	emer, litho.	30	10
1093	A425	12p	emer ('77)	30	10
1094	A425	15p	rose red	30	10
1095	A425	15p	vio bl ('77)	30	10
1097	A425	20p	rose red ('77)	50	10
1098	A425	30p	rose red ('77)	50	14
1099	A425	40p	dp grn	75	20
1100	A425	40p	rose red ('77)	50	15
1101	A425	60p	dk bl ('77)	1.00	28
1102	A425	70p	dk bl ('77)	1.25	30
1103	A425	90p	emer ('77)	1.50	40
1104	A425	100p	red	1.10	35
1105	A425	110p	rose red ('78)	75	25
1106	A425	120p	rose red ('78)	85	30
1107	A425	130p	rose red ('78)	1.00	35

Litho.
Perf. 13½
Unwmk.

No.	Type	Value	Color	Unused	Used
1108	A463a	300p	multi	5.00	2.25
1109	A515	500p	multi ('77)	12.00	2.00
1110	A515	1000p	multi ('77)	15.00	3.00
	Nos. 1089-1110 (21)			43.70	10.77

Nos. 1091 and 1092 are perf. 12½x13; wmkd. 365.

Fluorescent paper was used in printing both 12p rose red, 15p rose red, 20p, 30p, 40p rose red, 100p, 110p, 120p, 130p. No. 1099 and the 300p were issued on both ordinary and fluorescent paper.

300p and 500p exist with wmk. 365.

Numeral — A516

1976 Photo. Unwmk. *Perf. 13½*

No.	Type	Value	Color	Unused	Used
1112	A516	12c	gray & blk	5	5
1113	A516	50c	gray & grn	10	5
1114	A516	1p	red & blk	10	5
1115	A516	4p	bl & blk	20	5
1116	A516	5p	org & blk	20	5
1117	A516	5p	org & blk, litho.	20	5
1118	A516	6p	dp brn & blk	20	5
1119	A516	10p	gray & vio bl	30	5
1120	A516	27p	lt grn & blk	75	8
1121	A516	27p	lt grn & blk, litho.	75	8
1122	A516	30p	lt bl & blk	1.25	10
1123	A516	45p	yel & blk	1.25	15
1124	A516	45p	yel & blk, litho.	1.25	15
1125	A516	50p	dl grn & blk	1.75	18
1126	A516	100p	brt grn & red	2.25	35
	Nos. 1112-1126 (15)			10.60	1.49

Litho. stamps are perf. 13x12½; wmkd. 365.

The 1p, 6p, 10p, 50p and No. 1116 were issued on both ordinary and fluorescent paper.

Jet and Airlines Emblem — A517

Perf. 13x13½

1976, Apr. 24 Litho. Unwmk.

No.	Type	Value	Color	Unused	Used
1130	A517	30p	bl, lt bl & dk bl	1.50	20

Argentine Airlines, 25th anniversary.

Frigate Heroina and Map of Falkland Islands — A518

1976, Apr. 26
1131 A518 6p multi 1.50 60

Argentina's claim to Falkland Islands.

Louis Braille — A519

Wmk. 365

1976, May 22 Engr. *Perf. 13½*
1132 A519 19.70 dp bl 45 15

Sesquicentennial of the invention of the Braille system of writing for the blind by Louis Braille (1809-1852).

Private, 7th Infantry Regiment A520

1976, May 29 Litho. Unwmk.
1133 A520 12p multi 60 30

Army Day.

Schooner Rio de la Plata, by Emilio Biggeri A521

1976, June 19
1134 A521 12p multi 60 30

Navy Day.

Dr. Bernardo Houssay A522

Nobel Prize Winners: 15p, Luis F. Leloir, chemistry, 1970. 20p, Carlos Saavedra Lamas, peace, 1936. Bernardo Houssay, medicine and physiology, 1947.

1976, Aug. 14 Litho. *Perf. 13½*
1135 A522 10p org & blk 35 20
1136 A522 15p yel & blk 50 25
1137 A522 20p ocher & blk 75 35

Argentine Nobel Prize winners.

Demand, as well as supply, determines a stamp's market value. One is as important as the other.

Rio de la Plata International Bridge — A523

1976, Sept. 18 Litho. *Perf. 13½*
1138 A523 12p multi 40 20

Inauguration of International Bridge connecting Puerte Unzue, Argentina, and Fray Bentos, Uruguay.

Pipelines and Cooling Tower, Gen. Mosconi Plant A524

1976, Nov. 20 Litho. *Perf. 13½*
1139 A524 28p multi 60 30

Pablo Teodoro Fels and Bleriot Monoplane, 1910 — A525

1976, Nov. 20
1140 A525 15p multi 40 20

Air Force Day.

Nativity A526

1976, Dec. 18 Litho. *Perf. 13½*
1141 A526 20p multi 80 40

Christmas 1976. Painting by Edith Chiapetto.

Water Conference Emblem — A527

1977, Mar. 19 Litho. *Perf. 13½*
1142 A527 70p multi 1.00 35

U.N. Water Conference, Mar del Plata, Mar. 14-25.

Delmacio Velez Sarsfield A528

1977, Mar. 19 Engr.
1143 A528 50p blk & red brn 1.00 40

Dalmacio Velez Sarsfield (1800-1875), author of Argentine civil code.

100 PESOS
150º ANIV.
DEL CORREO
NACIONAL DEL
URUGUAY

Red Deer Type of 1974 Surcharged

1977, July 30 Photo. *Perf. 13½*
1144 A495 100p on 5p brn 2.00 60

Sesquicentennial of Uruguayan postal service. Not issued without surcharge.

Soldier, 16th Lancers — A529

1977, July 30
1145 A529 30p multi 60 30

Army Day.

Schooner Sarandi, by Emilio Biggeri A530

1977, July 30
1146 A530 30p multi 60 30

Navy Day.

Soccer Games' Emblem — A531

Design: 70p, Argentina '78 emblem, flags and soccer field.

1977, May 14
1147 A531 30p multi 65 30
1148 A531 70p multi 1.40 70

11th World Cup Soccer Championship, Argentina, June 1-25, 1978.

The Visit, by Horacio Butler A532

Consecration, by Miguel P. Caride — A533

1977, Mar. 26 Litho.
1149 A532 50p multi 85 40
1150 A533 70p multi 1.10 60

Argentine artists.

Sierra de la Ventana — A534

Views: No. 1152, Civic Center, Santa Rosa. No. 1153, Skiers, San Martin de los Andes. No. 1154, Boat on Lake Fonck, Rio Negro.

1977, Oct. 8 Litho. *Perf. 13x13½*
1151 A534 30p multi 50 25
1152 A534 30p multi 50 25
1153 A534 30p multi 50 25
1154 A534 30p multi 50 25

Guillermo Brown, by R. del Villar — A535

1977, Oct. 8 *Perf. 13½*
1155 A535 30p multi 50 30

Adm. Guillermo Brown (1777-1857), leader in fight for independence, bicentenary of birth.

Jet A536

Double-decker, 1926 — A537

1977 Litho. *Perf. 13½*
1156 A536 30p multi 35 15
1157 A537 40p multi 45 20

50th anniversary of military plane production (30p); Air Force Day (40p).
Issue dates: 30p, Dec. 3; 40p, Nov. 26.

Adoration of the Kings — A538

1977, Dec. 17

1158	A538	100p multi	1.50	40

Christmas 1977.

Historic City Hall, Buenos Aires — A539

Chapel of Rio Grande Museum, Tierra del Fuego — A540

Designs: 5p, 20p, La Plata Museum. 10p, Independence Hall, Tucuman. 40p, City Hall, Salta (vert.). No. 1165, City Hall, Buenos Aires. 100p, Columbus Theater, Buenos Aires. 200p, flag Monument, Rosario. 280p, 300p, Chapel of Rio Grande Museum, Tierra del Fuego. 480p, 520p, 800, Ruins of Jesuit Mission Church of San Ignacio, Misiones. 500p, Candonga Chapel, Cordoba. 1000p, G.P.O., Buenos Aires. 2000p, Civic Center, Bariloche, Rio Negro.

Three types of 10p: I. Nine vertical window bars; small imprint "E. MILIAVACA Dib." II. Nine bars; large imprint "E. MILIAVACA DIB." III. Redrawn; 5 bars; large imprint.

1977-81 Photo. Unwmk. *Perf. 13½*
Size: 32x21mm., 21x32mm.

1159	A540	5p gray & blk ('78)	5	5
1160	A540	10p lt ultra & blk, I ('78)	5	5
a.		Type II ('78)	5	5
1161	A540	10p lt bl & blk, III ('79)	5	5
1162	A540	20p cit & blk, litho. ('78)	5	5
1163	A540	40p gray bl & blk ('78)	30	5
1164	A539	50p yel & blk	35	15
1165	A540	50p cit & blk ('79)	20	5
1166	A540	100p org & blk, litho. ('78)	45	10
a.		Wmk. 365	120.00	30.00
1167	A540	100p red org & blk, photo. ('79)	5	5
1168	A540	100p turq & blk ('81)	5	5
1169	A539	200p lt bl & blk ('79)	60	30
1170	A540	280p rose & blk	17.50	20
1171	A540	300p lem & blk ('78)	1.25	15
1172	A540	480p org & blk ('78)	2.25	30
1173	A540	500p yel grn & blk ('78)	2.25	25
1174	A540	520p org & blk ('78)	2.25	30
1175	A540	800p rose lil & blk ('79)	2.75	40
1176	A540	1000p lem bis & blk ('79)	3.00	50
1177	A540	1000p gold & blk, 40x29mm ('78)	5.00	50
1178	A540	2000p multi ('80)	2.80	50
		Nos. 1159-1178 (20)	41.25	4.05

Nos. 1161, 1163, 1165, 1167, 1169, 1171, 1173, 1176 and 1177 were issued on both ordinary and fluorescent paper. No. 1174 was issued only on fluorescent paper. All others were issued only on ordinary paper.

The only foreign revenue stamps listed in this Catalogue are those authorized for prepayment of postage.

Soccer Games' Emblem A544

1978, Feb. 10 Photo. *Perf. 13½*

1179	A544	200p yel grn & bl	1.25	40

11th World Cup Soccer Championship, Argentina, June 1-25. Exists with wmk. 365.

View of El Rio, Rosario — A545

Designs (Argentina '78 Emblem and): 100p, Rio Tercero Dam, Cordoba. 150p, Cordillera Mountains, Mendoza. 200p, City Center, Mar del Plata. 300p, View of Buenos Aires.

1978, May 6 Litho. *Perf. 13*

1180	A545	50p multi	25	20
1181	A545	100p multi	50	20
1182	A545	150p multi	75	25
1183	A545	200p multi	75	35
1184	A545	300p multi	1.75	50
		Nos. 1180-1184 (5)	4.00	1.50

Sites of 11th World Cup Soccer Championship, June 1-25.

Children — A546

1978, May 20

1185	A546	100p multi	50	20

50th anniversary of Children's Institute.

Labor Day, by B. Quinquela Martin — A547

Design: No. 1187, Woman's torso, sculpture by Orlando Pierri.

1978, May 20 *Perf. 13½*

1186	A547	100p multi	50	20
1187	A547	100p multi	50	20

Argentina, Hungary, France, Italy and Emblem — A548

Stadium A549

Teams and Argentina '78 Emblem: 200p, Poland, Fed. Rep. of Germany, Tunisia, Mexico. 300p, Austria, Spain, Sweden, Brazil. 400p, Netherlands, Iran, Peru, Scotland.

1978 Litho. *Perf. 13*

1188	A548	100p multi	45	10
1189	A548	200p multi	90	10
1190	A548	300p multi	1.35	15
1191	A548	400p multi	1.75	25

Souvenir Sheet
Lithographed and Engraved
Perf. 13½

1192	A549	700p buff & blk	3.50	2.00

11th World Cup Soccer Championship, Argentina, June 1-25. No. 1192 contains one stamp; blue and black margin shows sports and communications emblems. Size: 89x60mm. Issue dates, Nos. 1188-1191, June 6, No. 1192, June 3.

Stadium Type of 1978 Inscribed in Red: "ARGENTINA / CAMPEON"
Lithographed and Engraved
1978, Sept. 2 *Perf. 13½*

1193	A549	1000p bulf, blk & red	4.50	2.00

Argentina's victory in 1978 Soccer Championship. No. 1193 has margin similar to No. 1192 with Rimet Cup emblem added in red. Size: 89x60mm.

Young Tree Nourished by Old Trunk, U.N. Emblem — A550

1978 Sept. 2 Litho.

1194	A550	100p multi	50	30

Technical Cooperation among Developing Countries Conference, Buenos Aires, Sept. 1978.

Emblems of Buenos Aires and Bank — A551

1978, Sept. 16

1195	A551	100p multi	50	30

Bank of City of Buenos Aires, centenary.

General Savio and Steel Production — A552

1978, Sept. 16

1196	A552	100p multi	50	30

Gen. Manuel N. Savio (1892-1948), general manager of military heavy industry, 30th death anniversary.

San Martin — A553

1978, Oct. Engr.

1197	A553	2000p grnsh blk	9.00	1.50

1979 Wmk. 365

1198	A553	2000p grnsh blk	6.00	50

Gen Jose de San Martin (1778-1850), soldier and statesman. See No. 1292.

Globe and Argentine Flag — A554

Chessboard, Queen and Pawn — A555

1978, Oct. 7 Litho. *Perf. 13½*

1199	A554	200p multi	1.00	40

12th International Cancer Congress, Buenos Aires, Oct. 5-11.

1978, Oct. 7

1200	A555	200p multi	3.00	1.00

23rd National Chess Olympics, Buenos Aires, Oct. 25-Nov. 12.

Correct Positioning of Stamps A557

Design: 50p, Use correct postal code number.

1978 Photo. *Perf. 13½*

1201	A557	20p ultra	20	10
1203	A557	50p carmine	30	10

No. 1201 issued on both ordinary and fluorescent paper.

Numeral — A558

A559

1978 Photo. *Perf. 13½*

1204	A558	150p bl & ultra	45	10
1205	A558	180p bl & ultra	55	15
1206	A558	200p bl & ultra	40	12

1207 A559 240p ol bis & bl ('79) 48 16
1208 A559 260p blk & lt bl ('79) 52 18
1209 A559 290p blk & lt bl ('79) 58 18
1210 A559 310p mag & bl ('79) 62 22
1211 A559 350p ver & bl ('79) 70 25
1212 A559 450p ultra & bl 65 22
1213 A559 600p grn & bl ('80) 85 30
1214 A559 700p blk & bl ('80) 85 30
1215 A559 800p red & bl ('81) 80 10
1216 A559 1100p gray & bl ('81) 1.10 10
1217 A559 1500p blk & bl ('81) 45 10
1218 A559 1700p grn & bl ('82) 55 10
Nos. 1204-1218 (15) 9.55 2.58

No. 1204 issued on fluorescent and ordinary paper. No. 1206 issued only on fluorescent paper.

Balsa "24" A561

Ships: 200p, Tug Legador. 300p, River Parana tug No. 34. 400p, Passenger ship Ciudad de Parana.

1978, Nov. 4 Litho. *Perf. 13½*
1220 A561 100p multi 30 5
1221 A561 200p multi 60 5
1222 A561 300p multi 90 10
1223 A561 400p multi 1.20 15

20th anniversary of national river fleet. Nos. 1220 and 1223, 1221-1222 printed se-tenant in sheets of 50. Issued on fluorescent paper.

View and Arms of Bahia Blanca A562

1978, Nov. 25 Litho. *Perf. 13½*
1224 A562 20p multi 60 10

Sesquicentennial of Bahia Blanca.

"Spain," (Queen Isabella and Columbus) by Arturo Dresco — A563

1978, Nov. 25
1225 A563 300p multi 4.00 25

Visit of King Juan Carlos and Queen Sofia of Spain to Argentina, Nov. 26.

Virgin and Child, San Isidro Cathedral A564

1978, Dec. 16
1226 A564 200p gold & multi 80 40

Christmas 1978.

Slope at Chacabuco, by Pedro Subercaseaux — A565

Painting: 1000p, The Embrace of Maipu (San Martin and O'Higgins), by Pedro Subercaseaux (vert.).

1978, Dec. 16 Litho. *Perf. 13½*
1227 A565 500p multi 1.50 40
1228 A565 1000p multi 3.00 60

José de San Martin, 200th birth anniversary.

Adolfo Alsina A566

Design: No. 1230, Mariano Moreno.

1979, Jan. 20
1229 A566 200p lt bl & blk 75 20
1230 A566 200p yel red & blk 75 20

Adolfo Alsina (1828-1877), political leader, vice-president; Mariano Moreno (1778-1811), lawyer, educator, political leader.

Argentina No. 37 and UPU Emblem A567

1979, Jan. 20
1231 A567 200p multi 40 14

Centenary of Argentina's UPU membership.

Still-life, by Carcova A568

Painting: 300p, The Laundresses, by Faustino Brughetti.

1979, Mar. 3
1232 A568 200p multi 75 15
1233 A568 300p multi 1.00 25

Ernesto de la Carcova (1866-1927) and Faustino Brughetti (1877-1956), Argentine painters.

Balcarce Earth Station — A569

1979, Mar. 3
1234 A569 200p multi 1.00 30

Third Inter-American Telecommunications Conference, Buenos Aires, March 5-9.

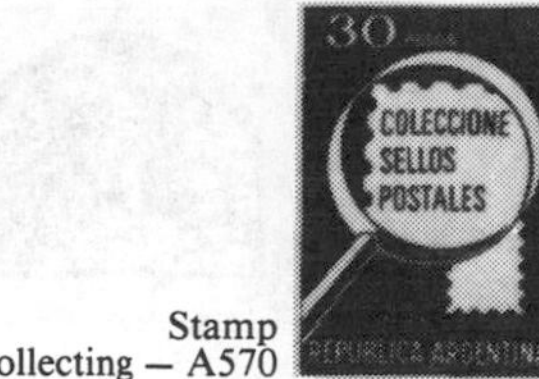

Stamp Collecting — A570

1979
1235 A570 30p brt grn 20 10

Printed on ordinary and fluorescent paper.

European Olive — A571

Laurel and Regimental Emblem — A572

Designs: 200p, Tea. 300p, Sorghum. 400p, Common flax.

1979, June 2 Litho. *Perf. 13½*
1236 A571 100p multi 40 20
1237 A571 200p multi 80 40
1238 A571 300p multi 1.25 60
1239 A571 400p multi 1.65 80

1979, June 9
1240 A572 200p gold & multi 60 30

Founding of Subteniente Berdina Village in memory of Sub-lieutenant Rodolfo Hernan Berdina, killed by terrorists in 1975.

"75" and Automobile Club Emblem — A573

1979, June 9
1241 A573 200p gold & multi 60 30

Argentine Automobile Club, 75th anniversary.

Exchange Building and Emblem A574

1979, June 9
1242 A574 200p bl, blk & gold 60 30

Grain Exchange, 125th anniversary.

Cavalry Officer, 1817 — A575

1979, July 7 Litho. *Perf. 13½*
1243 A575 200p multi 1.25 30

Army Day.

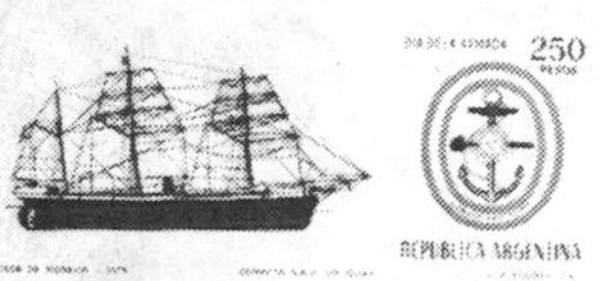

Corvette Uruguay and Navy Emblem — A576

Design: No. 1245, Hydrographic service ship and emblem.

1979 *Perf. 13*
1244 A576 250p multi 1.25 40
1245 A576 250p multi 1.25 40

Navy Day (No. 1244); Centenary of Naval Hydrographic Service (No. 1245). Issue dates: No. 1244, July 28; No. 1245, July 7.

Tree and Man — A577

1979, July 28 *Perf. 13½*
1246 A577 250p multi 80 30

Protection of the Environment Day, June 5.

"Spad" Flying over Andes, and Vicente Almandos Almonacid A578

1979, Aug. 4
1247 A578 250p multi 1.00 30

Air Force Day.

Gen. Julio A. Roca Occupying Rio Negro, by Juan M. Blanes — A579

1979, Aug. 4
1248 A579 250p multi 1.00 30

Conquest of Rio Negro Desert, centenary.

Rowland Hill — A580

1979, Sept. 29 Litho. *Perf. 13½*

1249 A580 300p gray red & blk 80 30

Sir Rowland Hill (1795-1879), originator of penny postage.

Viedma Navarez Monument A581

1979, Sept. 29

1250 A581 300p multi 80 30

Viedma and Carmen de Patagones towns, bicentenary.

Pope Paul VI — A582

Design: No. 1252, Pope John Paul I.

1979, Oct. 27 Engr. *Perf. 13½*

1251 A582 500p black 1.50 40

1252 A582 500p sepia 1.50 40

No. 1169 Overprinted in Red: "75 ANIV. / SOCIEDAD/ FILATELICA / DE ROSARIO"

1979, Nov. 10 Photo. *Perf. 13½*

1253 A539 200p lt bl & blk 1.00 30

Rosario Philatelic Society, 75th anniversary.

Frontier Resettlement A583

1979, Nov. 10 Litho.

1254 A583 300p multi 1.00 40

Military Geographic Institute Centenary A584

1979, Dec. 1 Litho. *Perf. 13½*

1255 A584 300p multi 1.00 40

Christmas 1979 A585

1979, Dec.

1256 A585 300p multi 80 30

General Mosconi Birth Centenary — A586

1979, Dec. 15 Engr. *Perf. 13½*

1257 A586 1000p blk & bl 2.50 40

Rotary Emblem and Globe A587

1979, Dec. 29 Litho.

1258 A587 300p multi 3.00 60

Rotary International, 75th anniversary.

Child and IYC Emblem — A588

Family, by Pablo Menicucci A589

1979, Dec. 29

1259 A588 500p lt bl & sep 1.00 20

1260 A589 1000p multi 2.00 30

International Year of the Child.

Microphone, Waves, ITU Emblem — A590

1980, Mar. 22 Litho. *Perf. 13x13½*

1261 A590 500p multi 1.50 40

Regional Administrative Conference on Broadcasting by Hectometric Waves for Area 2, Buenos Aires, Mar. 10-29.

Catalogue prices for unused stamps up to mid-1953 are for hinged copies matching the condition specified in this volume's introduction.

Guillermo Brown — A591

1980 Engr. *Perf. 13½*

1262 A591 5000p black 7.00 15

See No. 1372.

Argentine Red Cross Centenary — A592

1980, Apr. 19 Litho. *Perf. 13½*

1263 A592 500p multi 80 30

OAS Emblem A593

1980, Apr. 19

1264 A593 500p multi 80 30

Day of the Americas, Apr. 14.

Dish Antennae, Balcarce — A594

Lithographed and Engraved

1980, Apr. 26

1265 A594 300p *shown* 60 30

1266 A594 300p *Hydroelectric Station, Salto Grande* 60 30

1267 A594 300p *Bridge, Zarate-Brazo Largo* 60 30

Capt. Hipolito Bouchard, Frigate "Argentina" — A595

1980, May 31 Litho. *Perf. 13x13½*

1268 A595 500p multi 1.00 40

Navy Day.

"Villarino," San Martin, by Theodore Gericault — A596

1980, May 31

1269 A596 500p multi 1.00 40

Return of the remains of Gen. Jose de San Martin to Argentina, centenary.

Buenos Aires Gazette, 1810, Signature A597

1980, June 7 *Perf. 13½*

1270 A597 500p multi 80 30

Journalism Day.

Coaches in Victoria Square — A598

1980 June 14

1271 Block of 14 10.00 3.50

a. A598 500p any single 70 25

Buenos Aires, 400th anniversary. No. 1271 shows ceramic mural of Victoria Square by Rodolfo Franco in continuous design. See No. 1285.

Gen. Pedro Aramburu A599

1980, July 12 Litho. *Perf. 13½*

1272 A599 500p yel & blk 80 30

Gen. Pedro Eugenio Aramburu (1903-1970), provisional president, 1955.

Army Day A600

1980, July 12

1273 A600 500p multi 1.25 40

Gen. Juan Gregorio de Las Heras (1780-1866), Hero of 1817 War of Independence — A601

Grandees of Argentina Bicentenary: No. 1275, Bernardino Rivadavia (1780-1845), stateman and president. No. 1276, Brig. Gen José Matias Zapiola (1780-1874), naval commander and statesman.

1980, Aug. 2 Litho. ***Perf. 13½***
1274 A601 500p tan & blk 80 30
1275 A601 500p multi 80 30
1276 A601 500p lt lil & blk 80 30

Avro "Gosport" Biplane, Maj. Francisco de Artega — A602

1980, Aug. 16 ***Perf. 13***
1277 A602 500p multi 1.00 30

Air Force Day. Artega (1882-1930) was first director of Military Aircraft Factory where Avro "Gosport" was built (1927).

University of La Plata, 75th Anniversary — A603

1980, Aug. 16 ***Perf. 13½***
1278 A603 500p multi 80 30

Souvenir Sheets

Emperor Penguin — A604

South Orkneys Argentine Base
A605 A606

1980 Sept. 27 Litho. ***Perf. 13½***
1279 Sheet of 12 15.00 10.00
a. A604 500p *shown* 1.00 75
b. A604 500p *Bearded penguin* 1.00 75
c. A604 500p *Adelie penguins* 1.00 75
d. A604 500p *Papua penguins* 1.00 75
e. A604 500p *Sea elephants* 1.00 75
f. A605 500p *shown* 1.00 75
g. A606 500p *shown* 1.00 75
h. A604 500p *Fur seals* 1.00 75
i. A604 500p *Giant petrels* 1.00 75
j. A604 500p *Blue-eyed cormorants* 1.00 75
k. A604 500p *Stormy petrel* 1.00 75
m. A604 500p *Antarctic doves* 1.00 75
1280 Sheet of 12 15.00 10.00
a. A605 500p *Puerto Soledad* 70 30
b. A606 500p *Different view* 70 30

75th anniversary of Argentina's presence in the South Orkneys and 150th anniversary of political and military command in the Falkland Islands. Nos. 1279-1280 each contain 12 stamps (4x3) with landscape designs in center of sheets. Silhouettes of Argentine exploration ships in margins. Size: 150x173mm. No. 1280 contains Nos. 1279a-1279e, 1279h-1279m, 1280a-1280b.

Certain countries cancel stamps in full sheets and sell them (usually with gum) for less than face value. Dealers generally sell "CTO".

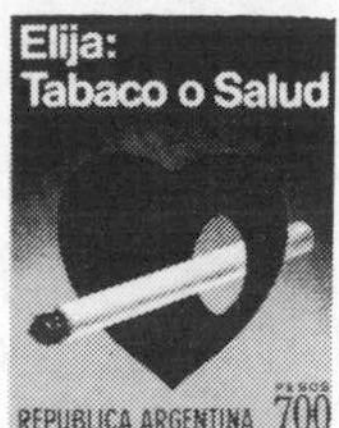

Anti-smoking Campaign A608

1980, Oct. 11
1282 A608 700p multi 1.25 30

National Census — A609

1980, Sept.
1283 A609 500p blk & bl 1.50 30

Madonna and Child (Congress Emblem) A610

1980, Oct. 1 Litho.
1284 A610 700p multi 1.00 15

National Marian Congress, Mendoza, Oct. 8-12

Mural Type of 1980

1980, Oct. 25
1285 Block of 14 10.00 3.50
a. A598 500p, any single 70 25

Buenos Aires, 400th anniversary/Buenos Aires '80 Stamp Exhibition, Oct. 24-Nov. 2. No. 1285 shows ceramic mural Arte bajo la Cuidad by Alfredo Guido in continuous design.

Technical Military Academy, 50th Anniversary A611

Amateur Radio Operation A612

1980, Nov. 1
1286 A611 700p multi 1.00 15

1980, Nov. 1
1287 A612 700p multi 1.00 15

Medal — A613

Lujan Cathedral Floor Plan — A614

1980, Nov. 29 Litho. ***Perf. 13½***
1288 A613 700p multi 1.00 15
1289 A614 700p ol & brn 1.00 15

Christmas 1980. 150th anniversary of apparition of Holy Virgin to St. Catherine Laboure, Paris (No. 1288), 350th anniversary of apparition at Lujan.

150th Death Anniversary of Simon Bolivar A615

1980, Dec. 13
1290 A615 700p multi 1.00 15

Soccer Gold Cup Championship, Montevideo, 1980 — A616

1981, Jan. 3 Litho.
1291 A616 1000p multi 1.40 15

San Martin Type of 1978

1981, Jan. 20 Engr. ***Perf. 13½***
1292 A553 10,000p dk bl 9.00 20

Landscape in Lujan, by Marcos Tiglio A617

Paintings: No. 1304, Expansion of Light along a Straight Line, by Miguel Angel Vidal (vert.).

1981, Apr. 11 Litho.
1303 A617 1000p multi 1.25 30
1304 A617 1000p multi 1.25 30

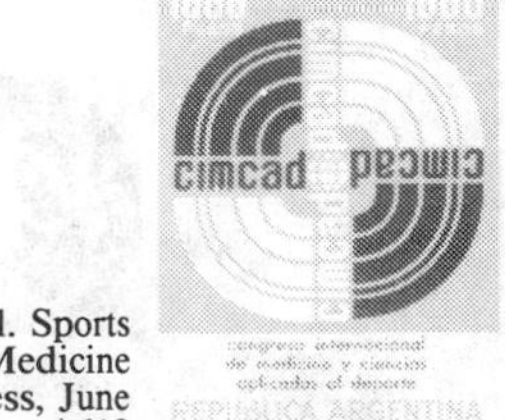

Intl. Sports Medicine Congress, June 7-12 — A618

1981, June 6 Litho. ***Perf. 13½***
1305 A618 1000p bl & dk brn 1.00 15

Esperanza Base, Antarctica — A619

Cargo Plane, Map of Vice-Commodore Marambio Island — A620

Perf. 13½, 13x13½(No. 1308)

1981, June 13
1306 A619 1000p shown 2.00 75
1307 A619 2000p Almirante Irizar 3.50 1.00
1308 A620 2000p shown 3.50 1.50

Antarctic Treaty 20th anniv.

Antique Pistols (Military Club Centenary) A621

1981, June 27 ***Perf. 13½***
1309 A621 1000p Club building 1.00 15
1310 A621 2000p shown 1.00 15

Gen. Juan A. Alvarez de Arenales (1770-1831) A622

Famous Men: No. 1312, Felix G. Frias (1816-1881), writer. No. 1313, Jose E. Uriburu (1831-1914), statesman.

1981, Aug. 8 Litho. ***Perf. 13½***
1311 A622 1000p multi 1.00 15
1312 A622 1000p multi 1.00 15
1313 A622 1000p multi 1.00 15

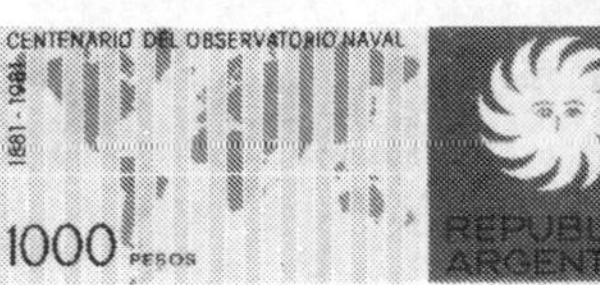

Naval Observatory Centenary — A623

1981, Aug. 15 Litho. ***Perf. 13x13½***
1314 A623 1000p multi 1.25 40

No. 1176 Overprinted in Red: "50 ANIV. DE LA ASOCIACION / FILATELICA Y NUMISMATICA / DE BAHIA BLANCA"

1981, Aug. 15 Photo. ***Perf. 13½***
1315 A540 1000p lem & blk 3.00 40

50th anniv. of Bahia Blanca Philatelic and Numismatic Society.

St. Cayetano, Stained-glass Window, Buenos Aires — A624

1981, Sept. 5 Litho. ***Perf. 13½***
1316 A624 1000p multi 1.00 15

St. Cayetano, founder of Teatino Order, 500th birth anniv.

Pablo Castaibert (1883-1909) and his Monoplane (Air Force Day) — A625

1981, Sept. 5 *Perf. 13x13½*
1317 A625 1000p multi 1.00 15

Intl. Year of the Disabled A626

1981, Sept. 10 *Perf. 13½*
1318 A626 1000p multi 1.00 15

22nd Latin-American Steelmakers' Congress, Buenos Aires, Sept. 21-23 — A627

1981, Sept. 19
1319 A627 1000p multi 1.00 15

Army Regiment No. 1 (Patricios), 175th Anniv. — A628

1981, Oct. 10 Litho. *Perf. 13½*
1320 A628 1500p Natl. arms 70 15
1321 A628 1500p shown 70 15

Nos. 1320-1321 se-tenant.

San Martin as Artillery Captain in Battle of Bailen, 1808 — A629

1981, Oct. 5
1322 Sheet of 8 4.00 1.50
a.-d. A629 1000p multi 30 15
e.-h. A629 1500p multi 45 15

Espamer '81 Intl. Stamp Exhibition (Americas, Spain, Portugal), Buenos Aires, Nov. 13-22. No. 1322 has multicolored margin. Size: 136x212mm.

Anti-indiscriminate Whaling — A630

Espamer '81 Emblem and Ship — A631

1981, Oct. 5
1323 A630 1000p multi 4.00 60

1981
1324 A631 1300p multi 1.00 30

No. 1324 Overprinted in Blue: "CURSO SUPERIOR DE ORGANIZACIONES DE FILATELICOS-UPAE-BUENOS AIRES-1981"

1981, Nov. 7 Photo. *Perf. 13½*
1325 A631 1300p multi 2.00 30

Postal Administration philatelic training course.

Soccer Players — A632

Designs: Soccer players.

1981, Nov. 13 **Litho.**
1326 Sheet of 4 + 2 labels 10.00 6.00
a. A632 1000p multi 30 20
b. A632 3000p multi 90 30
c. A632 5000p multi 1.50 50
d. A632 15000p multi 4.50 1.50

Espamer '81. No. 1326 has black marginal inscription and control number. Size: 137x130mm.

"Peso" Coin Centenary A633

1981, Nov. 21
1327 A633 2000p Patacon, 1881 60 15
1328 A633 3000p Argentine Oro, 1881 90 15

Christmas 1981 — A634

1981, Dec. 12
1329 A634 1500p multi 1.50 40

Traffic Safety A635

1981, Dec. 19 **Litho.**
1330 A635 1000p Observe traffic lights, vert. 1.00 50
1331 A635 2000p Drive carefully, vert. 1.00 50
1332 A635 3000p Cross at white lines 1.50 50
1333 A635 4000p Don't shine headlights 2.00 50

Francisco Luis Bernardez, Ciuda Laura — A636

Writers and title pages from their works: 2000p, Lucio V. Mansilla, Excursion a los indios ranqueles. 3000p, Conrado Nale Roxlo, El Grillo. 4000p, Victoria Ocampo, Sur.

1982, Mar. 20 **Litho.**
1334 A636 1000p shown 90 30
1335 A636 2000p multi 1.25 30
1336 A636 3000p multi 1.75 40
1337 A636 4000p multi 2.50 40

No. 1218 Overprinted: "LAS / MALVINAS / SON/ ARGENTINAS"

1982, Apr. 17 Photo. *Perf. 13½*
1338 A559 1700p grn & bl 75 30

Argentina's claim on Falkland Islds.

Robert Koch — A637

American Airforces Commanders' 22nd Conference A638

1982, Apr. 17 Litho. Wmk. 365
1339 A637 2000p multi 80 40

TB bacillus centenary and 25th Intl. Tuberculosis Conference.

1982, Apr. 17
1340 A638 2000p multi 1.00 40

Stone Carving, City Founder's Signature (Don Hernando de Lerma) A639

1982, Apr. 17
1341 A639 2000p multi 1.00 40

Souvenir Sheet

1342 A639 5000p multi 3.00 3.00

City of Salta, 400th anniv. No. 1342 contains one stamp (43x30mm.); multicolored margin shows map. Size: 89x60mm.

Naval Center Centenary — A640

1982, Apr. 24 *Perf. 13x13½*
1343 A640 2000p multi 1.00 40

Chorisia Speciosa — A641

1982 Unwmk. Photo. *Perf. 13½*
1344 A641 200p Zinnia peruviana 5 5
1345 A641 300p Ipomoea purpurea 5 5
1346 A641 400p Tillandsia aeranthos 5 5
1347 A641 500p shown 8 5
1348 A641 800p Oncidium bifolium 12 5
1349 A641 1000p Erythrina crista-galli 15 8
1350 A641 2000p Jacaranda mimosifolia 30 8
1351 A641 3000p Bauhinia candicans 45 15
1352 A641 5000p Tecoma stans 75 20
1353 A641 10,000p Tabebuia ipe 1.50 30
1354 A641 20,000p Passiflora coerulea 3.00 50
1355 A641 30,000p Aristolochia littoralis 4.50 75
1356 A641 50,000p Oxalis en-neaphylla 7.50 1.00
Nos. 1344-1356 (13) 18.50 3.31

Nos. 1344-1346, 1348-1350 issued on fluorescent paper. Nos. 1353-1356 issued on ordinary paper. Others issued on both fluorescent and ordinary paper.

See Nos. 1429-1442, 1515-1530.

10th Death Anniv. of Gen. Juan C. Sanchez A641a

1982, May 29 Litho. Wmk. 365
1364 A641a 5000p grn & blk 1.25 40

Luis Venet, First Commander — A641b

1982, June 12
1365 A641b 5000p org & blk 1.75 75

Size: 83x28mm.

1366 A641b 5000p Map 1.25 48

153rd Anniv. of Malvinas Political and Military Command District.

Visit of Pope John Paul II — A641c

1982, June 12
1367 A641c 5000p multi 2.50 80

Organ Grinder, by Aldo Severi (b. 1928) — A641d

Design: 3000p, Still Life, by Santiago Cogorno (b. 1915).

1982, July 3 **Wmk. 365**
1368 A641d 2000p shown 40 30
1369 A641d 3000p multi 60 30

Guillermo Brown Type of 1980 and:

Jose de San Martin A641e

Litho. and Engr.
1982 **Unwmk.** ***Perf. 13½***
1372 A591 30000p blk & bl 4.00 75
1376 A641e 50000p sep & car 8.00 1.00

Issue dates: 30,000p, June; 50,000p, July.

Scouting Year A641f

Wmk. 365
1982, Aug. 7 **Litho.** ***Perf. 13½***
1380 A641f 5000p multi 2.50 30

Alconafta Fuel Campaign A641g

1982, Aug. 7 **Wmk. 365**
1381 A641g 2000p multi 45 10

No. 1351 Overprinted: "50 ANIVERSARIO SOCIEDAD FILATELICA DE TUCUMAN"

1982, Aug. 7 **Photo.** **Unwmk.**
1382 A641 5000p multi 2.00 1.50

Rio III Central Nuclear Power Plant, Cordoba A642

Wmk. 365
1982, Sept. 4 **Litho.** ***Perf. 13½***
1383 A642 2000p shown 50 10
1384 A642 2000p Control room 50 10

Namibia Day — A643

1982, Sept. 4
1385 A643 5000p Map 1.25 15

Formosa Cathedral A644

Churches and Cathedrals of the Northeast: 2000p, Our Lady of Itati, Corrientes (vert.). 3000p, Resistencia Cathedral, Chaco (vert.). 10,000p, St. Ignatius Church ruins, Misiones.

1982, Sept. 18 **Wmk. 365** **Engr.**
1386 A644 2000p dk grn & blk 35 20
1387 A644 3000p dk brn & brn 50 20
1388 A644 5000p dk bl & brn 85 30
1389 A644 10,000p dp org & blk 1.65 50

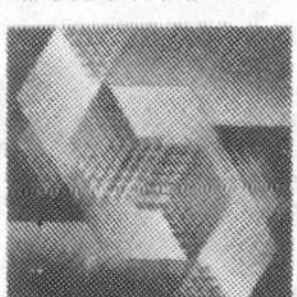

Tension Sideral, by Mario Alberto Agatiello — A645

Sculpture (Espamer '81 and Juvenex '82 Exhibitions): 3000p, Sugerencia II, by Eduardo Mac Entyre. 5000p, Storm, by Carlos Silva.

1982, Oct. 2 **Litho.** ***Perf. 13½***
1390 A645 2000p multi 40 15
1391 A645 3000p multi 75 20
1392 A645 5000p multi 1.00 30

Sante Fe Bridge A646

Lithographed and Engraved
1982, Oct. 16
1393 A646 2000p bl & blk 75 10

2nd Southern Cross Games, Santa Fe and Rosario, Nov. 26-Dec. 5.

10th World Men's Volleyball Championship — A647

1982, Oct. 16 **Litho.** **Wmk. 365**
1394 A647 2000p multi 40 20
1395 A647 5000p multi 80 30

Los Andes Newspaper Centenary A648

Design: Army of the Andes Monument, Hill of Glory, Mendoza.

1982, Oct. 30
1396 A648 5000p multi 80 30

50th Anniv. of Natl. Roads, Administration A649

1982, Oct. 30 **Wmk. 365**
1397 A649 5000p Signs 80 30

La Plata City Centenary A650

1982, Nov. 20 **Litho.**
1398 A650 5000p Cathedral 90 15
1399 A650 5000p City Hall 90 15
1400 Sheet of 6 2.75 1.25
a. A650 2500p Cathedral, diff. 35 10
b. A650 2500p Head, top 35 10
c. A650 2500p Observatory 35 10
d. A650 2500p City Hall, diff. 35 10
e. A650 2500p Head, bottom 35 10
f. A650 2500p University 35 10

No. 1400 has black control number. Size: 120x115mm.

Well, Natl. Hydrocarbon Congress Emblem — A651

1982, Nov. 20
1401 A651 5000p multi 1.00 40

75th Anniv. of Oil Discovery, Comodoro Rivadavia.

Jockey Club of Buenos Aires Centenary — A652

Christmas 1982 — A653

Design: No. 1403, Carlos Pellegrini, first president.

1982, Dec. 4 **Litho.**
1402 A652 5000p Emblem 75 15
1403 A652 5000p multi 75 15

1982, Dec. 18 ***Perf. 13½***
1404 A653 3000p St. Vincent de Paul 2.50 10

Size: 29x38mm.
1405 A653 5000p St. Francis of Assisi 2.00 15

Pedro B. Palacios (1854-1917), Writer — A654

Writers: 2000p, Leopoldo Marechal (1900-1970). 3000p, Delfina Bunge de Galvez (1881-1952). 4000p, Manuel Galvez (1882-1962). 5000p, Evaristo Carriego (1883-1912). Se-tenant.

1983, Mar. 26 **Litho.** ***Perf. 13½***
1406 A654 1000p multi 15 10
1407 A654 2000p multi 30 10
1408 A654 3000p multi 45 15
1409 A654 4000p multi 60 20
1410 A654 5000p multi 75 25
Nos. 1406-1410 (5) 2.25 80

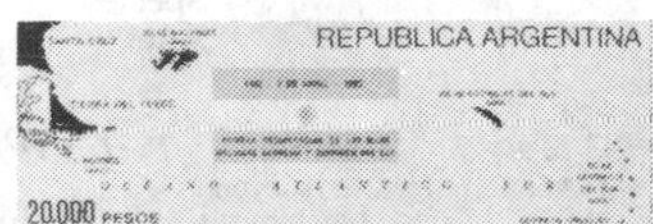

Recovery of the Malvinas — A655

1983, Apr. 9 **Litho.** ***Perf. 13½***
1411 A655 20,000p Map, flag 1.00 50

Telecommunications Systems — A656

1983, Apr. 16 **Wmk. 365**
1412 A656 5000p SITRAM 1.50 10
1413 A656 5000p RED ARPAC 1.50 10

Naval League Emblem — A657

Allegory, by Victor Rebuffo — A658

1983, May 14 Litho. *Perf. 13½*
1414 A657 5000p multi 60 10

Navy Day and 50th anniv. of Naval League.

1983, May 14
1415 A658 5000p multi 60 10

Natl. Arts Fund, 25th Anniv.

75th Anniv. of Colon Opera House, Buenos Aires — A659

1983, May 28 Wmk. 365
1416 A659 5000p Main hall 1.00 10
1417 A659 10000p Stage 1.50 15

Protected Species A660

1983, July 2 Litho. *Perf. 13½*
1418 A660 1p Chrysocyon brachyurus 50 10
1419 A660 1.50p Ozotocerus bezoarticus 75 15
1420 A660 2p Myrmecophaga tridactyla 90 20
1421 A660 2.50p Leo onca 1.00 25

City of Catamarca, 300th Anniv. — A661

Mamerto Esquiu (1826-1883) A662

Foundation of the City of Catamarca, by Luis Varela Lezana (1900-1982).

1983, July 16 Litho. *Perf. 13½*
1422 A661 1p multi 45 10

1983, July 16
1423 A662 1p multi 45 10

Bolivar, by Herrera Toro — A663

Bolivar, Engraving by Kepper — A664

Perf. 13 (A663), 13½ (A664)
1983 Unwmk.
1424 A663 1p multi 45 10
1425 A664 2p black 90 15
1426 A664 10p San Martin 4.50 2.25

Issue dates: 1p, 2p, July 23. 10p, Aug. 20.
See Nos. 1457-1462B.

Gen. Toribio de Luzuriaga (1782-1842) A665

1983, Aug. 20 Litho. *Perf. 13½*
1427 A665 1p multi 45 10

50th Anniv. of San Martin National Institute A666

1983, Aug. 20 Engr. Unwmk.
1428 A666 2p sepia 90 25

Flower Type of 1982 in New Currency

1983-85 Photo. *Perf. 13½*
1429 A641 5c like #1347 5 5
1430 A641 10c like #1349 5 5
1431 A641 20c like #1350 5 5
1432 A641 30c like #1351 5 5
1433 A641 40c Eichhornia crassipes 6 5
1434 A641 50c like #1352 8 5
1435 A641 1p like #1353 14 5
1435A A641 1.80p Mutisia retusa 15 6
1436 A641 2p like #1354 28 10
1437 A641 3p like #1355 42 15
1438 A641 5p like #1356 70 25
1439 A641 10p Alstroemeria aurantiaca 1.40 1.00
1440 A641 20p like #1345 ('84) 70 20
1441 A641 30p Embothrium coccineum 4.25 3.00
1442 A641 50p like #1346 ('84) 1.40 50
1443 A641 100p Oncidium bifolium ('84) 2.00 60
1443A A641 300p Cassia carnaval ('85) 1.00 30
Nos. 1429-1443A (17) 12.78 6.51

Issue Dates: 20p, Aug. 27. 50p, Oct. 19. 100p, Dec. 300p, June 15.

Nos. 1429, 1433, 1435A issued on fluorescent paper. Nos. 1443, 1443A issued on ordinary paper. Others issued on both ordinary and fluorescent paper.

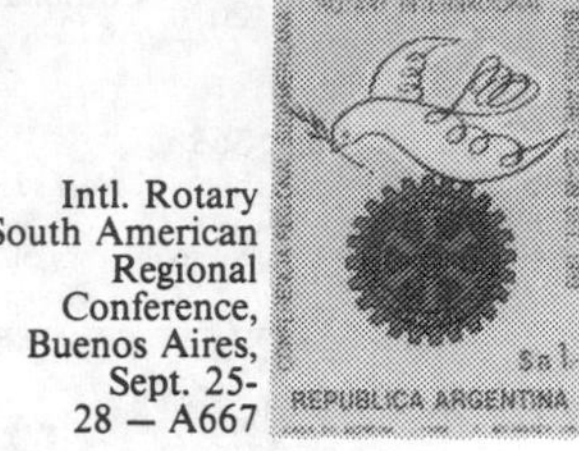

Intl. Rotary South American Regional Conference, Buenos Aires, Sept. 25-28 — A667

1983, Sept. 24 Litho.
1444 A667 1p multi 90 40

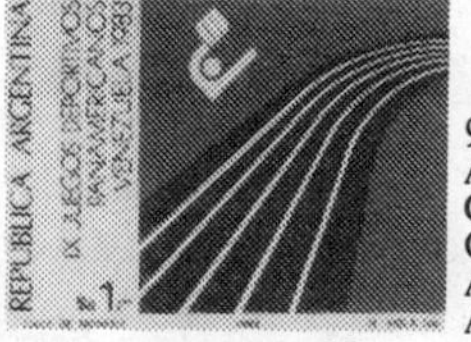

9th Pan American Games, Caracas, Aug. 13-28 A668

1983, Sept. 24
1445 A668 1p Track 45 20
1446 A668 2p Emblem 90 40

World Communications Year — A669

1983, Oct. 8 *Perf. 13½*
1447 A669 2p multi 75 30

Squash Peddler by Antonio Berni (1905-1981) A670

Designs: 2p, Figure in Yellow by Luis Seoane (1910-1979).

1983, Oct. 15 *Perf. 13½*
1448 A670 1p multi 45 15
1449 A670 2p multi 75 30

World Communications Year — A671

Designs: 1p, Wagon, 18th cent. 2p, Post chaise, 19th cent. 4p, Steam locomotive, 1857. 5p, Tramway, 1910.

1983, Nov. 19 Litho. *Perf. 13½*
1450 A671 1p multi 20 10
1451 A671 2p multi 35 20
1452 A671 4p multi 75 30
1453 A671 5p multi 95 40

World Communications Year — A672

Return to Elected Government A673

1983, Nov. 26 Litho. *Perf. 12½x12*
1454 A672 2p General Post Office 60 25

1983, Dec. 10 Photo. *Perf. 13½*
1455 A673 2p Coin, 1813 45 25

Eudyptes crestatus A674

Designs: b., Diomedea exulans. c., Diomedea melanophris. d., Eudyptes chrysolophus. e., Luis Piedra Buena. f., Carlos Maria Moyano. g., Luis Py. h., Augusto Lasserre. i., Phoebetria palpebrata. j., Hydrurga leptonyx. k., Lobodon carcinophagus. l., Leptonychotes weddelli.

1983, Dec. 10 Litho.
1456 Sheet of 12 6.00 3.00
a.-l. A674 2p any single 45 20

Southern pioneers and fauna. Margin depicts various airplanes and emblems.

Bolivar Type of 1983

Famous men: 10p, Angel J. Carranza (1834-1899), historian. No. 1458, 500p, Guillermo Brown. No. 1459, Estanislao del Campo (1834-1880), poet. 30p, Jose Hernandez (1834-1886), author. 40p, Vicente Lopez y Planes (1784-1856), poet and patriot. 50p, Gen. Jose de San Martin (1778-1850), statesman. 200p, Gen. Manuel Belgrano (1770-1820), patriot.

Lithographed and Engraved

1983-85 *Perf. 13½*
1457 A664 10p pale bl & dk bl ('85) 6 5
1458 A664 20p dk bl & blk 3.50 1.75
1459 A664 20p dl brn ol & ol blk ('85) 12 5
1460 A664 30p pale bl & bluish blk ('85) 18 8
1461 A664 40p lt bl grn & blk ('85) 24 10
1462 A664 50p Prus & choc ('85) 1.50 30
1462A A664 200p int bl & blk ('85) 4.00 1.25
1462B A664 500p brn & int bl ('85) 2.00 40
Nos. 1457-1462B (8) 11.60 3.98

Issue dates: 10p, No. 1459, 30p, 40p, Mar. 23. 50p, Apr. 23. 200p, Nov. 2.

Christmas 1983 A675

Nativity Scenes: 2p, Tapestry, by Silke. 3p, Stained-glass window, San Carlos de Bariloche's Wayn Church (vert.).

1983, Dec. 17 Litho. Perf. 13½
1463 A675 2p multi 45 22
1464 A675 3p multi 80 40

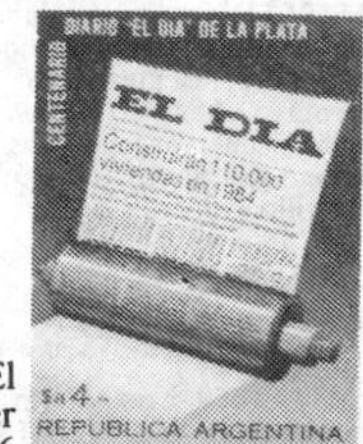
Centenary of El Dia Newspaper A676

1984, Mar. 24 Litho.
1465 A676 4p Masthead, printing roll 55 28

Alejandro Carbo Teachers' College Centenary — A677

1984, June 2 Litho. Perf. 13½
1466 A677 10p Building 60 30

1984 Olympics A678

Designs: No. 1468, Weightlifting, discus, shot put. No. 1469, Javelin, fencing. No. 1470, Bicycling, swimming.

1984, July 28 Litho. Perf. 13½
1467 A678 5p shown 30 15
1468 A678 5p multi 30 15
1469 A678 10p multi 60 30
1470 A678 10p multi 60 30

Rosario Stock Exchange Centenary A679

1984, Aug. 11
1471 A679 10p multi 60 30

A little time given to the study of the arrangement of the Scott Catalogue can make it easier to use effectively.

Wheat A680

1984, Aug. 11
1472 A680 10p shown 60 30
1473 A680 10p Corn 60 30
1474 A680 10p Sunflower 60 30

18th FAO Regional Conference for Latin America and Caribbean (No. 1472); 3rd Natl. Corn Congress (No. 1473); World Food Day (No. 1474).

Wildlife Protection A681

1984, Sept. 22 Litho. Perf. 13½
1475 A681 20p Hippocamelus bisulcus 50 18
1476 A681 20p Vicugna vicugna 50 18
1477 A681 20p Aburria jacutinga 50 18
1478 A681 20p Mergus octosetaceus 50 18
1479 A681 20p Podiceps gallardoi 50 18
Nos. 1475-1479 (5) 2.50 90

First Latin American Theater Festival, Cordoba, Oct. — A682

1984, Oct. 13 Litho. Perf. 13½
1480 A682 20p Mask 24 12

Intl. Eucharistic Congress, 50th Anniv. A683

Design: Apostles' Communion, by Fra Angelico.

1984, Oct. 13
1481 A683 20p multi 30 12

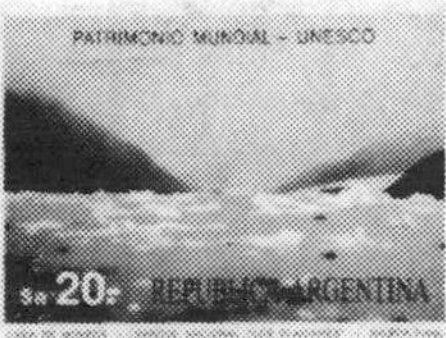
Glaciares Natl. Park (UNESCO World Heritage List) A684

1984, Nov. 17 Litho.
1482 A684 20p Sea 30 12
1483 A684 30p Glacier 50 18

City of Puerto Deseado Centenary A685

1984, Nov. 17 Perf. 13½
1484 A685 20p shown 50 12
1485 A685 20p Ushuaia centenary 50 12

Childrens' Paintings, Christmas 1984 A686

1984, Dec. 1 Litho. Perf. 13½
1486 A686 20p Diego Aguero 50 20
1487 A686 30p Leandro Ruiz 60 22
1488 A686 50p Maria Castillo, vert. 90 22

No. 1439 Overprinted with the Philatelic Center emblem and: "1934-50th Anniversary-1984"

1984, Dec. 1 Photo. Perf. 13½
1489 A641 10p multi 26 22

50th anniversary of the Buenos Aires Philatelic Center.

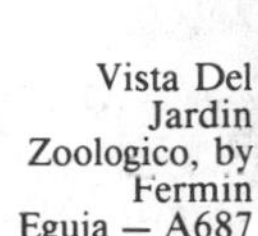

Vista Del Jardin Zoologico, by Fermin Eguia — A687

Paintings: No. 1491, El Congreso Iluminado, by Francisco Travieso. No. 1492, Galpones (La Boca), by Marcos Borio.

1984, Dec. 15 Perf. 13½
1490 A687 20p multi 40 20
1491 A687 20p multi, vert. 40 20
1492 A687 20p multi, vert. 40 20

Gen. Martin Miguel de Guemes (1785-1821) — A688

1985, Mar. 23 Litho. Perf. 13½
1493 A688 30p multi 40 16

ARGENTINA '85 Exhibition — A689

First airmail service from: 20p, Buenos Aires to Montevideo, 1917. 40p, Cordoba to Villa Dolores, 1925. 60p, Bahia Blanca to Comodoro Rivadavia, 1929. 80p, Argentina to Germany, 1934. 100p, naval service to the Antarctic, 1952.

1985, Apr. 27
1494 A689 20p Bleriot Gnome 25 12
1495 A689 40p Junker F-13L 50 16
1496 A689 60p Latte 25 75 30
1497 A689 80p L.Z. 127 Graf Zeppelin 1.00 45
1498 A689 100p Consolidated PBY Catalina 1.25 60
Nos. 1494-1498 (5) 3.75 1.63

Central Bank, 50th Anniv. A690

1985, June 1
1499 A690 80p Bank Bldg., Buenos Aires 90 30

Jose A. Ferreyra (1889-1943), Director of Munequitas Portenas — A691

Famous directors and their films: No. 1501, Leopoldo Torre Nilsson (1924-1978), scene from Martin Fierro.

1985, June 1
1500 A691 100p shown 1.00 30
1501 A691 100p multi 1.00 30

Carlos Gardel (1890-1935), Entertainer A692

Paintings: No. 1502, Gardel playing the guitar on stage, by Carlos Alonso (b. 1929). No. 1503, Gardel in a wide-brimmed hat, by Hermegildo Sabat (b. 1933). No. 1504, Portrait of Gardel in an ornamental frame, by Aldo Severi (b. 1928) and Martiniano Arce (b. 1939).

1985, June 15
1502 A692 200p multi 1.25 60
1503 A692 200p multi 1.25 60
1504 A692 200p multi 1.25 60

The Arrival, by Pedro Figari A693

Oil paintings (details): 30c, The Wagon Square, by C. B. de Quiros. No. 1507, A Halt on the Plains, by Prilidiano Pueyrredon.

1985, July 6 Litho. Perf. 13½
1505 A693 20c multi 1.25 30
1506 A693 30c multi 1.50 30

Souvenir Sheet

Perf. 12

1507 Sheet of 2 3.00
a. A693 20c Pilgrims, vert. 32
b. A693 30c Wagon 48

ARGENTINA '85. No. 1507 contains 2 stamps (size: 30x40mm); multicolored margin continue the painting and is inscribed in silver with the exhibition and Inter-American Philatelic Federation emblems. Size: 146x74mm.

Buenos Aires to Montevideo, 1917 Teodoro Fels Flight A694

Historic flight covers: No. 1508, Shown. No. 1509, Villa Dolores to Cordoba, 1925. No. 1510, Buenos Aires to France, 1929 St. Exupery flight. No. 1511, Buenos Aires to Bremerhaven, 1934 Graf Zeppelin flight. No. 1512, First Antarctic flight, 1952.

1985, July 13 *Perf. 12x12½*

1508	A694 10c emer & multi		50	15
1509	A694 10c ultra & multi		50	15
1510	A694 10c lt choc & multi		50	15
1511	A694 10c chnt & multi		50	15
1512	A694 10c ap grn & multi		50	15
	Nos. 1508-1512 (5)		2.50	75

ARGENTINA '85.

Illuminated Fruit, by Fortunato Lacamera (1887-1951) — A695

Paintings: 20c, Woman with Bird, by Juan del Prete, vert.

1985, Sept. 7 *Perf. 13½*

1513	A695 20c multi	1.25	45
1514	A695 30c multi	1.50	45

Flower Types of 1982-85

1985-87 Photo. *Perf. 13½*

1514A	A641	½c like No. 1356	5	
1514B	A641	1c like No. 1439	5	
1514C	A641	2c like No. 1345	10	
1515	A641	3c like No. 1441	15	8
1516	A641	5c like No. 1346	25	8
1517	A641	10c like No. 1348	40	12
1518	A641	20c like No. 1347	80	
1519	A641	30c like No. 1443A	1.20	
1520	A641	50c like No. 1344	2.00	40
1522	A641	1a Begonia micranthera var. hieronymi	4.00	75
1528	A641	5a Gymnocaylcium bruchii ('87)	7.50	

Size: 15x23mm.

1529	A641	8½clike No. 1349	35	
		Nos. 1514A-1529 (12)	16.85	

Issue dates: ½c, 1c, Dec. 16. 2c, 8½c, 30c, Sept. 18. 3c, 5c, 10c, 50c, 1a, Sept. 7. 20c, Oct. 17. 5a, Mar. 21, 1987.

No. 1435 Surcharged

1986, Dec. Photo. *Perf. 13½*

1530	A641 10c on 1p No. 1435	15

Folk Musical Instruments A699

1985, Sept. 14 Litho. *Perf. 13½*

1531	A699 20c Frame drum	75	30
1532	A699 20c Long flute	75	30
1533	A699 20c Jew's harp	75	30
1534	A699 20c Pan flutes	75	30
1535	A699 20c Musical bow	75	30
	Nos. 1531-1535 (5)	3.75	1.50

The first price column gives the catalogue value of an unused stamp, the second that of a used stamp.

Juan Bautista Alberdi (1810-1884), Historian, Politician A700

Famous men: Nicolas Avellaneda (1836-1885), President in 1874. 30c, Fr. Luis Beltran (1784-1827), military and naval engineer. 40c, Ricardo Levene (1885-1959), historian, author.

1985, Oct. 5

1536	A700 10c multi	30	12
1537	A700 20c multi	60	30
1538	A700 30c multi	90	45
1539	A700 40c multi	1.50	60

Skaters A701

Deception, by J. H. Rivoira — A702

1985, Oct. 19 Litho. *Perf. 13½*

1540	A701 20c multi	32	30
1541	A702 30c multi	48	45

Size: 147x75mm.

Imperf

1542	A693 1a multi	1.75	

IYY. No. 1542 is inscribed in silver with the UN 40th anniversary and IYY emblems.

Provincial Views — A703

Designs: No. 1543, Rock Window, Buenos Aires. No. 1544, Forclaz Windmill, Entre Rios. No. 1545, Lake Potrero de los Funes, San Luis. No. 1546, Mission church, northeast province. No. 1547, Penguin colony, Punta Tombo, Chubut. No. 1548, Water Mirrors, Cordoba.

1985, Nov. 23 *Perf. 13½*

1543	A703 10c multi	16	15
1544	A703 10c multi	16	15
1545	A703 10c multi	16	15
1546	A703 10c multi	16	15
1547	A703 10c multi	16	15
1548	A703 10c multi	16	15
	Nos. 1543-1548 (6)	96	90

Christmas 1985 — A704

Designs: 10c, Birth of Our Lord, by Carlos Cortes. 20c, Christmas, by Hector Viola.

1985, Dec. 7

1549	A704 10c multi	16	12
1550	A704 20c multi	32	30

Natl. Campaign for the Prevention of Blindness — A705

1985, Dec. 7

1551	A705 10c multi	16	12

Rio Gallegos City, Cent. — A716

1985, Dec. 21 Litho. *Perf. 13½*

1552	A716 10c Church	20	15

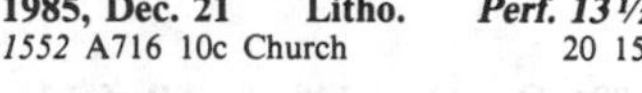

Natl. Grape Harvest Festival, 50th Anniv. A717

1986, Mar. 15

1553	A717 10c multi	20	15

Historical Architecture in Buenos Aires — A718

Designs: No. 1554, Valentin Alsina House, Italian Period, 1860-1870. No. 1555, House on Cerrito Street, French influence, 1880-1900. No. 1556, House on the Avenida de Mayo y Santiago del Estero, Art Nouveau, 1900-1910. No. 1557, Customs Building, academic architecture, 1900-1915. No. 1558, Isaac Fernandez Blanco Museum, house of architect Martin Noel, national restoration, 1910-1930. Nos. 1554-1556 vert.

1986, Apr. 19

1554	A718 20c multi	40	30
1555	A718 20c multi	40	30
1556	A718 20c multi	40	30
1557	A718 20c multi	40	30
1558	A718 20c multi	40	30
	Nos. 1554-1558 (5)	2.00	1.50

Antarctic Bases, Pioneers and Fauna — A719

Designs: No. 1559a, Base, Jubany. No. 1559b, Arctocephalus gazella. No. 1559c, Otaria byronia. No. 1559d, Gen. Belgrano Base. No. 1559e, Daption capensis. No. 1559f, Diomedia melanophris. No. 1559g, Apterodytes patagonica. No. 1559h, Macronectes giganteus. No. 1559i, Hugo Alberto Acuna (1885-1953). No. 1559j, Spheniscus magellanicus. No. 1559k, Gallinago gallinage. No. 1559l, Capt. Agustin del Castillo (1855-1889).

1986, May 31

1559	Sheet of 12	2.50	3.50
a.-l.	A719 10c, any single	20	25

No. 1559 has margin picturing Antarctic postmarks. Size: 150x180mm.

Famous People — A720

Statuary, Buenos Aires — A721

Designs: No. 1560, Dr. Alicia Moreau de Justo, human rights activist. No. 1561, Dr. Emilio Ravignani (1886-1954), historian. No. 1562, Indira Gandhi (1917-1984), prime minister of India.

1986, July 5 Litho. *Perf. 13½*

1560	A720 10c multi	18	15
1561	A720 10c multi	18	15
1562	A720 30c multi	55	45

1986, July 5

Designs: 20c, Fountain of the Nereids, by Dolores Lola Mora (1866-1936). 30c, Lamenting at Work, by Rogelio Yrurtia (1879-1950), horiz.

1563	A721 20c multi	35	30
1564	A721 30c multi	55	45

Famous Men — A722

Designs: No. 1565, Francisco N. Laprida (1786-1829), politician. No. 1566, Estanislao Lopez (1786-1838), brigadier general. No. 1567, Francisco Ramirez (1786-1821), general.

1986, Aug. 9 Litho. *Perf. 13*

1565	A722 20c dl yel, brn & blk	35	30

1566	A722 20c dl yel, brn & blk	35	30
1567	A722 20c dl yel, brn & blk	35	30

Fr. Ceferino Namuncura (1886-1905) A723

1986, Aug. 30 ***Perf. 13½***

1568	A723 20c multi	35	30

Miniature Sheets

Natl. Team Victory, 1986 World Cup Soccer Championships, Mexico — A724

Designs: No. 1569a-1569d, Team. Nos. 1569e-1569h, Shot on goal. Nos. 1570a-1570d, Action close-up. Nos. 1570e-1570h, Diego Maradona holding soccer cup.

1986, Nov. 8 **Litho.** ***Perf. 13½***

1569	Sheet of 8	9.20	12.00
a.-h.	A724 75c, any single	1.15	1.50
1570	Sheet of 8	9.20	12.00
a.-h.	A724 75c, any single	1.15	1.50

Nos. 1569-1570 have bright blue and black margins inscribed with final scores. Sizes: 120x171mm.

San Francisco (Cordoba), Cent. — A725

1986, Nov. 8

1571	A725 20c Municipal Building	32	30

Trelew City (Chubut), Cent. A726

1986, Nov. 22 **Litho.** ***Perf. 13½***

1572	A726 20c Old railroad station, 1865	30	30

Mutualism Day — A727

1986, Nov. 22

1573	A727 20c multi	30	30

Christmas — A728

Designs: 20c, Naif retable, by Aniko Szabo (b. 1945). 30c, Everyone's Tree, by Franca Delacqua (b. 1947).

1986, Dec. 13 **Litho.** ***Perf. 13½***

1574	A728 20c multi	30
1575	A728 30c multi	45

Santa Rosa de Lima, 400th Birth Anniv. — A729

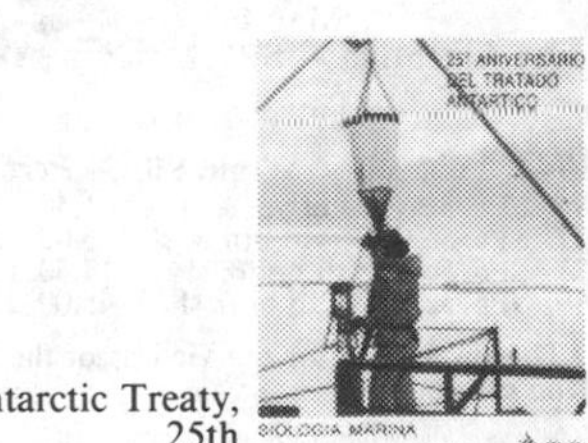

Rio Cuarto Municipal Building — A730

1986, Dec. 13

1576	A729 50c multi	75

1986, Dec. 20

Design: No. 1578, Court Building, Cordoba.

1577	A730 20c shown	30
1578	A730 20c multi	30

Rio Cuarto City, bicent. Court Building, Cordoba, 50th anniv.

Antarctic Treaty, 25th Anniv. — A731

1987, Mar. 7 **Litho.** ***Perf. 13½***

1579	A731 20c Marine biologist	30
1580	A731 30c Ornithologist	45

Souvenir Sheet

Perf. 12

1581	Sheet of 2	75
a.	A731 20c like No. 1579	30
b.	A731 30c like No. 1580	45

No. 1581 contains 2 stamps (size: 40x50mm); multicolored margin pictures penguin and offspring. Size: 160x90mm.

Natl. Mortgage Bank, Cent. A732

1987, Mar. 21 ***Perf. 13½***

1582	A732 20c multi	30

Natl. Cooperative Associations Movement — A733

1987, Mar. 21

1583	A733 20c multi	30

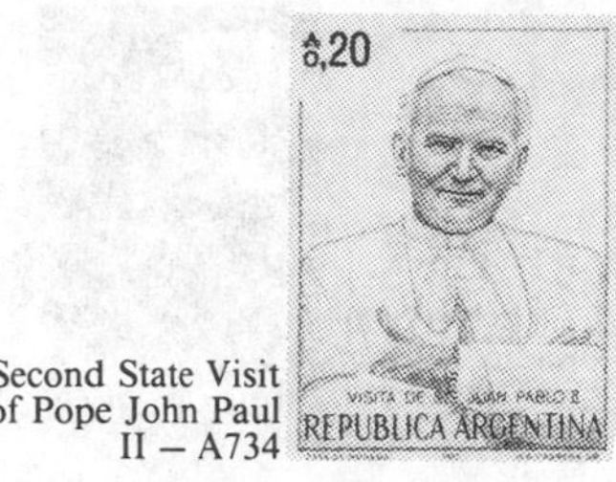

Second State Visit of Pope John Paul II — A734

Engr., Litho. (No. 1585)

1987, Apr. 4 ***Perf. 13½***

1584	A734 20c shown	30
1585	A734 80c Papal blessing	1.20

Souvenir Sheet

1586	A734 1a like 20c	1.50

No. 1586 contains one stamp (size: 40x50mm, perf. 12); multicolored margin pictures papal arms, Purmamarca Church in Jujuy and Santa Rosa de Lima. Size: 161x89mm.

Intl. Peace Year A735

Designs: 30c, Pigeon, abstract sculpture by Victor Kaniuka.

1987, Apr. 11 **Litho.**

1587	A735 20c multi	30
1588	A735 30c multi	45

Low Handicap World Polo Championships A736

Design: Polo Players, painting by Alejandro Moy.

1987, Apr. 11

1589	A736 20c multi	30

Miniature Sheet

ICOM '86 — A737

Designs: a. Emblem. b. Family crest, National History Museum, Buenos Aires. c. St. Bartholomew, Enrique Larreta Museum of Spanish Art, Buenos Aires. d. Zoomorphic club, Patagonian Museum, San Carlos de Bariloche. e. Supplication, anthropomorphic sculpture, Natural Sciences Museum, La Plata. f, Wrought iron lattice from the house of J. Urquiza, president of the Confederation of Argentina, Entre Rios History Museum, Parana. g. St. Joseph, 18th cent. wood figurine, Northern History Museum, Salta. h. Funerary urn, Provincial Archaeological Museum, Santiago del Estero.

1987, May 30

1590	Sheet of 8	3.05
a.-h.	A737 25c any single	38

14th General Conference of the Intl. Council of Museums. Size of No. 1590: 165x120mm.

Natl. College of Monserrat, Cordoba, 300th Anniv. — A738

1987, July 4 ***Imperf.***

1591	A738 1a multi	1.10

Monserrat '87 Philatelic Exposition.

Fight Drug Abuse A739

Design: The Proportions of Man, by da Vinci.

1987, Aug. 15 ***Perf. 13½***

1592	A739 30c multi	35

Famous Men A740

Portraits and quotations: 20c, Jorge Luis Borges (1899-1986), writer. 30c, Armando Discepolo (1887-1971), playwright. 50c, Carlos A. Pueyrredon (1887-1962), professor, Legion of Honor laureate.

1987, Aug. 15

1593	A740 20c multi	22
1594	A740 30c multi	35
1595	A740 50c multi	55

Canceled-to-order stamps are often from remainders. Most collectors of canceled stamps prefer postally used specimens.

The Sower, by Julio Vanzo A743

1987, Sept. 12
1598 A743 30c multi 35

Argentine Agrarian Federation, 75th anniv.

10th Pan American Games, Indianapolis, Aug. 7-25 — A744

1987, Sept. 26
1599 A744 20c Basketball 22
1600 A744 30c Rowing 35
1601 A744 50c Yachting 55

Children Playing Doctor, WHO Emblem A745

1987, Oct. 7
1602 A745 30c multi 35

Vaccinate every child campaign.

Heroes of the Revolution A746

Signing of the San Nicolas Accord, 1852, by Rafael del Villar A747

Independence anniversaries and historic events: No. 1603, Maj.-Col. Ignacio Alvarez Thomas (1787-1857). No. 1604, Col. Manuel Crispulo Bernabe Dorrego (1787-1829). No. 1606, 18th cent. Spanish map of the Falkland Isls., administered by Jacinto de Altolaguirre.

1987, Oct. 17
1603 A746 25c shown 28
1604 A746 25c multi 28
1605 A747 50c shown 55
1606 A747 50c multi 55

Museum established in the House of the San Nicholas Accord, 50th anniv. (No. 1605); Jacinto de Altolaguirre (1754-1787), governor the Malvinas Isls. for the King of Spain (No. 1606).

Celedonio Galvan Moreno, 1st Director A748

1987, Nov. 21
1607 A748 50c multi 55

Postas Argentinas magazine, 50th anniv.

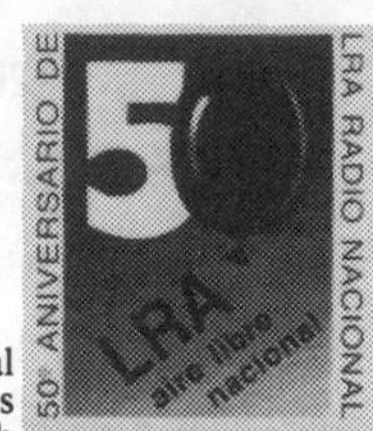

LRA National Radio, Buenos Aires, 50th Anniv. — A749

1987, Nov. 21
1608 A749 50c multi 55

Natl. Philatelic Society, Cent. A750

1987, Nov. 21
1609 A750 1a Jose Marco del Pont 1.10

Christmas A751

Tapestries: 50c, *Navidad*, by Alisia Frega. 1a, *Vitral*, by Silvina Trigos.

1987, Dec. 5
1610 A751 50c multi 55
1611 A751 1a multi 1.10

Natl. Parks — A752

1987, Dec. 19 ***Perf.***
1612 A752 50c Baritu 55
1613 A752 50c Nahuel Huapi 55
1614 A752 50c Rio Pilcomayo 55
1615 A752 50c Tierra del Fuego 55
1616 A752 50c Iguazu 55
Nos. 1612-1616 (5) 2.75

SEMI-POSTAL STAMPS

Samuel F. B. Morse — SP1

Globe — SP2

Landing of Columbus — SP5

Designs: 10c+5c, Alexander Graham Bell. 25c+15c, Rowland Hill.

Wmk. RA in Sun (90)

1944, Jan. 5 Litho. *Perf. 13*
B1 SP1 3c +2c lt vio & sl bl 60 35
B2 SP2 5c +5c dl red & sl bl 1.25 30
B3 SP1 10c +5c org & sl bl 2.50 90
B4 SP1 25c +15c red brn & sl bl 3.25 1.50
B5 SP5 1p +50c lt grn & sl bl 16.00 12.00
Nos. B1-B5 (5) 23.60 15.05

The surtax was for the Postal Employees Benefit Association.

Map of Argentina — SP6

1944, Feb. 17 Wmk. 90 *Perf. 13*
B6 SP6 5c +10c ol yel & sl 1.50 75
B7 SP6 5c +50c vio brn & sl 6.00 3.00
B8 SP6 5c +1p dl org & sl 17.50 12.50
B9 SP6 5c +20p dp bl & sl 45.00 25.00

The surtax was for the victims of the San Juan earthquake.

Souvenir Sheets

National Anthem and Flag — SP7

1944, July 17 *Imperf.*
B10 SP7 5c +1p vio brn & lt bl 3.00 3.00
B11 SP7 5c +50p bl blk & lt bl 400.00 350.00

The sheets measure 75x110mm. The surtax was for the needy in the provinces of La Rioja and Catamarca.

Stamp Designing — SP8

1950, Aug. 26 Photo. *Perf. 13½*
B12 SP8 10c +10c vio 40 40

Issued to publicize the Argentine International Philatelic Exhibition, 1950.

See Nos. CB1-CB5 and note after No. CB5.

Poliomyelitis Victim — SP9

1956, Apr. 14 *Perf. 13½x13*
B13 SP9 20c +30c sl 40 15

The surtax was for the poliomyelitis fund. Head in design is from Correggio's "Antiope," Louvre.

Stamp of 1858 and Mail Coach on Raft — SP10

Designs: 2.40p+1.20p, Album, magnifying glass and stamp of 1858. 4.40p+2.20p, Government seat of Confederation, Parana.

1958, Mar. 29 Litho. *Perf. 13½*
B14 SP10 40c +20c brt grn & dl pur 50 35
B15 SP10 2.40p +1.20p ol gray & bl 60 40
B16 SP10 4.40p +2.20p lt bl & dp cl 90 60
Nos. B14-B16,CB8-CB12 (8) 8.80 7.05

The surtax was for the International Centennial Philatelic Exhibition, Parana, Entre Rios, April 19-27.

View of Flooded Land — SP11

1958, Oct. 4 Photo. *Perf. 13½*
B17 SP11 40c +20c brn 15 10

The surtax was for flood victims in the Buenos Aires district. See Nos. CB13-CB14.

Child Receiving Blood — SP12

Runner — SP13

1958, Dec. 20 Litho. Wmk. 90
B18 SP12 1p +50c blk & rose red 20 15

The surtax went to the Anti-Leukemia Foundation.

1959, Sept. 5 *Perf. 13½*

Designs: 50c+20c, Basketball players (vert.). 1p+50c, Boxers (vert.).

B19 SP13 20c +10c emer & blk 30 25
B20 SP13 50c +20c yel & blk 20 20
B21 SP13 1p +50c mar & blk 25 25
Nos. B19-B21,CB15-CB16 (5) 2.25 1.85

Issued to commemorate the third Pan American Games, Chicago, Aug. 27-Sept. 7, 1959.

Condor — SP14

Birds: 50c+20c, Fork-tailed flycatchers. 1p+50c, Magellanic woodpecker.

1960, Feb. 6
B22 SP14 20c +10c dk bl 12 10
B23 SP14 50c +20c dp vio bl 20 12
B24 SP14 1p +50c brn & buff 30 15
Nos. B22-B24,CB17-CB18 (5) 1.62 1.12

The surtax was for child welfare work. See Nos. B30, CB29.

Souvenir Sheet

Uprooted Oak Emblem — SP15

1960, Apr. 7 Wmk. 90 *Imperf.*
B25 SP15 Sheet of two 1.75 1.75
a. 1p+50c bis & car 75 75
b. 4.20p+2.10p ap grn & dp cl 75 75

Issued to publicize World Refugee Year, July 1, 1959-June 30, 1960. No. B25 measures 112x84mm. with deep claret marginal inscription.
The surtax was for aid to refugees.

Jacaranda — SP16

Flowers: 1p+1p, Passionflower. 3p+3p, Orchid. 5p+5p, Tabebuia.

1960, Dec. 3 Photo. *Perf. 13½*
B26 SP16 50c +50c dp bl 12 8
B27 SP16 1p +1p bluish grn 20 12
B28 SP16 3p +3p hn brn 45 30
B29 SP16 5p +5p dk brn 75 50

Issued to publicize "TEMEX 61" (International Thematic Exposition).

Type of 1960

Bird: 4.20p+2.10p, Blue-eyed shag.

1961, Feb. 25 Wmk. 90 *Perf. 13½*
B30 SP14 4.20p +2.10p chnt brn 75 50

The surtax was for child welfare work. See No. CB29.

Nos. B26-B29 Overprinted in Black, Brown, Blue or Red: "14 DE ABRIL DIA DE LAS AMERICAS"

1961, Apr. 15
B31 SP16 50c +50c dp bl 12 12
B32 SP16 1p +1p bluish grn (Brn) 20 15
B33 SP16 3p +3p hn brn (Bl) 45 35
B34 SP16 5p +5p dk brn (R) 75 60

Day of the Americas, Apr. 14.

Cathedral, Cordoba — SP17

Stamp of 1862 — SP18

Flight into Egypt, by Ana Maria Moncalvo — SP19

Design: 10p+10p, Cathedral, Buenos Aires.

Perf. 13½

1961, Oct. 21 Wmk. 90 Photo.
B35 SP17 2p +2p rose cl 30 20
B36 SP18 3p +3p grn 45 25
B37 SP17 10p +10p brt bl 1.25 75
a. Souvenir sheet of 3 2.25 1.50

Issued to publicize the 1962 International Stamp Exhibition.
No. B37a contains three imperf. stamps similar to Nos. B35-B37 in dark blue. Violet brown marginal inscription. Size: 85x86mm.

1961, Dec. 16 Litho.
B38 SP19 2p +1p lil & blk brn 20 12
B39 SP19 10p +5p lt cl & dp cl 75 20

The surtax was for child welfare.

Chalk-browed Mockingbird SP20

Soccer SP21

Design: 12p+6p, Rufous-collared sparrow.

1962, Dec. 29 *Perf. 13½*
B40 SP20 4p +2p bis, brn & bl grn 1.50 1.00
B41 SP20 12p +6p gray, yel, grn & brn 2.50 1.75

The surtax was for child welfare. See Nos. B44, B47, B48-B50, CB32, CB35-CB36.

1963, May 18 *Perf. 13½*

Design: 12p+6p, Horsemanship.

B42 SP21 4p +2p brt pink, grn & blk 30 15
B43 SP21 12p +6p sal, dk car & blk 65 50
a. Dark car (jacket) omitted

Issued to commemorate the 4th Pan American Games, Sao Paulo. See also No. CB31.

Bird Type of 1962

Design: Vermilion flycatcher.

1963, Dec. 21 Litho.
B44 SP20 4p +2p blk, red, org & grn 1.00 50

The surtax was for child welfare. See No. CB32.

Fencers — SP22

Design: 4p+2p, National Stadium, Tokyo (horiz.).

1964, July 18 Wmk. 90 *Perf. 13½*
B45 SP22 4p +2p red, ocher & brn 25 20
B46 SP22 12p +6p bl grn & blk 60 50

Issued to publicize the 18th Olympic Games, Tokyo, Oct. 10-25, 1964. See No. CB33.

Bird Type of 1962

Design: Red-crested cardinal.

1964, Dec. 23 Litho.
B47 SP20 4p +2p dk bl, red & grn 1.00 50

The surtax was for child welfare. See No. CB35.

Bird Type of 1962
Inscribed "R. ARGENTINA"

Designs: 8p+4p, Lapwing. 10p+5p, Scarlet-headed marshbird (horiz.). 20p+10p, Amazon kingfisher.

1966-67 *Perf. 13½*
B48 SP20 8p +4p blk, ol, brt grn & red 1.00 50
B49 SP20 10p +5p blk, bl, org & grn ('67) 1.00 75
B50 SP20 20p +10p blk, yel, bl & pink ('67) 60 50

The surtax was for child welfare.
Issue dates: 8p+4p, Mar. 26, 1966. 10p+5p, Jan. 14, 1967. 20p+10p, Dec. 23, 1967.
See Nos. CB36, CB38-CB39.

Grandmother's Birthday, by Patricia Lynch; Lions Emblem — SP23

Perf. 12½x13½

1968, Dec. 14 Litho. Wmk. 90
B51 SP23 40p + 20p multi 60 50

Issued to publicize the First Lions International Benevolent Philatelic Exhibition. The surtax was for the Children's Hospital Benevolent Fund.

White-faced Tree Duck — SP24

1969, Sept. 20 Wmk. 365 *Perf. 13½*
B52 SP24 20p + 10p multi 60 50

The surtax was for child welfare. See No. CB40.

Slender-tailed Woodstar (Hummingbird) SP25

1970, May 9 Wmk. 365 *Perf. 13½*
B53 SP25 20c + 10c multi 70 60

The surtax was for child welfare. See Nos. CB41, B56-B59, B62-B63.

Dolphinfish — SP26

1971, Feb. 20 Unwmk. *Perf. 12½*
Size: 75x15mm.
B54 SP26 20c + 10c multi 70 60

The surtax was for child welfare. See No. CB42.

Children with Stamps, by Mariette Lydis — SP27

1971, Dec. 18 Litho. *Perf. 13½*
B55 SP27 1p + 50p multi 75 50

2nd Lions International Solidarity Stamp Exhibition.

Bird Type of 1970

Birds: 25c+10c, Saffron finch. 65c+30c, Rufous-bellied thrush (horiz.).

1972, May 6 Unwmk. *Perf. 13½*
B56 SP25 25c + 10c multi 50 30
B57 SP25 26c + 30c multi 70 50

Surtax was for child welfare.

Bird Type of 1970

Birds: 50c+25c, Southern screamer (chaja). 90c+45c, Saffron-cowled blackbird (horiz.).

1973, Apr. 28
B58 SP25 50c + 25c multi 60 50
B59 SP25 90c + 45c multi 90 75

Surtax was for child welfare.

Painting Type of Regular Issue

Designs: 15c+15c, Still Life, by Alfredo Guttero (horiz.). 90c+90c, Nude, by Miguel C. Victorica (horiz.).

1973, Aug. 28 Litho. *Perf. 13½*
B60 A472 15c + 15c multi 40 25
B61 A472 90c + 90c multi 1.40 1.00

Philatelists' Day.

Bird Type of 1970

Birds: 70c+30c, Blue seed-eater. 1.20p+60c, Hooded siskin.

1974, May 11 Litho. *Perf. 13½*
B62 SP25 70c + 30c multi 70 50
B63 SP25 1.20p + 60c multi 1.10 60

Surtax was for child welfare.

Painting Type of 1974

Design: 70c+30c, The Lama, by Juan Batlle Planas.

1974, May 11 Litho. *Perf. 13½*

B64	A477	70c + 30c multi	40	30

PRENFIL-74 UPU, International Exhibition of Philatelic Periodicals, Buenos Aires, Oct. 1-12.

Plushcrested Jay — SP28

Designs: 13p+6.50p, Golden-collared macaw. 20p+10p, Begonia. 40p+20p, Teasel.

1976, June 12 Litho. *Perf. 13½*

B65	SP28	7p + 3.50p multi	30	20
B66	SP28	13p + 6.50p multi	50	30
B67	SP28	20p + 10p multi	75	50
B68	SP28	40p + 20p multi	1.50	75

Argentine philately.

Telegraph, Communications Satellite — SP29

Designs: 20p+10p, Old and new mail trucks. 60p+30p, Old, new packet boats. 70p+35p, Biplane and jet.

1977, July 16 Litho. *Perf. 13½*

B69	SP29	10p + 5p multi	35	25
B70	SP29	20p + 10p multi	60	75
B71	SP29	60p + 30p multi	1.25	1.00
B72	SP29	70p + 35p multi	1.50	1.00

Surtax was for Argentine philately.
No. B70 exists with wmk. 365.

Church of St. Francis Type, 1977, Inscribed: "EXPOSICION ARGENTINA '77"

1977, Aug. 27

B73	A515	160p + 80p multi	3.50	3.00

Surtax was for Argentina '77 Philatelic Exhibition. Issued in sheets of 4.

No. B73 Overprinted with Soccer Cup Emblem

1978, Feb. 4 Litho. *Perf. 13½*

B74	A515	160p + 80p multi	7.50	7.00
a.		Souvenir sheet of 4	30.00	28.00

11th World Cup Soccer Championship, Argentina, June 1-25.
No. B74a contains 4 No. B74, light blue margin with black inscription. Size: 103x133mm.

Spinus Magellanicus SP30

Birds: 100p+100p, Variable seedeater. 150p+150p, Yellow thrush. 200p+200p, Pyrocephalus rubineus. 500p+500p, Great kiskadee.

1978, Aug. 5 Litho. *Perf. 13½*

B75	SP30	50p + 50p multi	1.50	1.00
B76	SP30	100p + 100p multi	1.75	1.50
B77	SP30	150p + 150p multi	2.25	2.00
B78	SP30	200p + 200p multi	3.00	3.00
B79	SP30	500p + 500p multi	14.00	12.00
		Nos. B75-B79 (5)	22.50	19.50

ARGENTINA '78, Inter-American Philatelic Exhibition, Buenos Aires, Oct. 27-Nov. 5. Nos. B75-B79 issued in sheets of 4 with marginal inscriptions commemorating Exhibition and 1978 Soccer Championship.

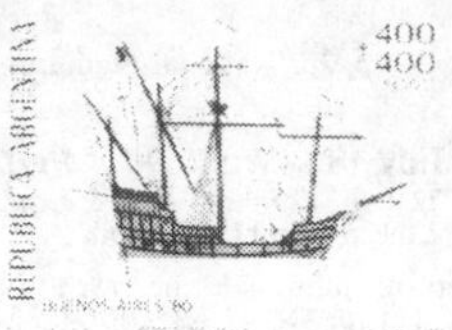

Caravel "Magdalena," 16th Century — SP31

Sailing Ships: 500+500p, Three master "Rio de la Plata," 17th century. 600+600p, Corvette "Descubierta," 18th century. 1500+1500p, Naval Academy yacht "A.R.A. Fortuna," 1979.

1979, Sept. 8 Litho. *Perf. 13½*

B80	SP31	400p + 400p multi	6.00	4.00
B81	SP31	500p + 500p multi	7.50	5.00
B82	SP31	600p + 600p multi	9.00	6.00
B83	SP31	1500p + 1500p multi	22.50	15.00

Buenos Aires '80, International Philatelic Exhibition, Buenos Aires, Oct. 24-Nov. 2, 1980. Issued in sheets of 4.

Purmamarca Church — SP32

Churches: 200p + 100p, Molinos. 300p + 150p, Animana. 400p + 200p, San Jose de Lules.

1979, Nov. 3 Litho. *Perf. 13½*

B84	SP32	100p + 50p multi	40	15
B85	SP32	200p + 100p multi	75	20
B86	SP32	300p + 150p multi	1.00	30
B87	SP32	400p + 200p multi	1.50	40

Buenos Aires No. 3, Exhibition and Society Emblems — SP33

Argentine Stamps: 750p+750p, type A580. 1000p+1000p, No. 91. 2000p+2000p, type A588.

1979, Dec. 15 Litho. *Perf. 13½*

B88	SP33	250p + 250p multi	1.40	1.10
B89	SP33	750p + 750p multi	3.50	2.75
B90	SP33	1000p + 1000p multi	4.75	3.75
B91	SP33	2000p + 2000p multi	9.50	7.75

PRENFIL '80, International Philatelic Literature and Publications Exhibition, Buenos Aires, Nov. 7-16, 1980. Multicolored margins show Exhibition and Society emblems. Size: 89x60mm.

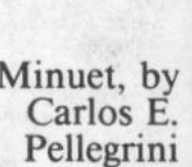

Minuet, by Carlos E. Pellegrini SP34

Paintings: 700p+350p, Media Cana, by Carlos Morel. 800p+400p, Cielito, by Pellegrini. 1000p+500p, El Gato, by Juan Leon Palliere.

1981, July 11 Litho. *Perf. 13½*

B92	SP34	500 + 250p multi	1.00	50
B93	SP34	700 + 350p multi	1.50	1.00
B94	SP34	800 + 400p multi	1.50	1.25
B95	SP34	1000 + 500p multi	2.00	1.75

Espamer '81 Intl. Stamp Exhibition (Americas, Spain, Portugal), Buenos Aires, Nov. 13-22.

Canal, by Beatrix Bongliani (b. 1933) — SP35

Tapestries: 1000p+500p, Shadows, by Silvia Sieburger (vert.). 2000p+1000p, Interpretation of a Rectangle, by Silke R. de Haupt (vert.). 4000p+2000p, Tilcara, by Tana Sachs.

1982, July 31 Litho. *Perf. 13½*

B96	SP35	1000 + 500p multi	25	25
B97	SP35	2000 + 1000p multi	50	50
B98	SP35	3000 + 1500p multi	75	75
B99	SP35	4000 + 2000p multi	1.00	1.00

Boy Playing Marbles — SP36

1983, July 2 Litho. *Perf. 13½*

B100	SP36	20c + 10c shown	10	10
B101	SP36	30c + 15c Jumping rope	50	25
B102	SP36	50c + 25c Hopscotch	50	30
B103	SP36	1p + 50c Flying kites	90	75
B104	SP36	2p + 1p Spinning top	1.00	1.00
		Nos. B100-B104 (5)	3.00	2.40

Surtax was for natl. philatelic associations.
See Nos. B106-B110.

Compass, 15th Cent. — SP37

ARGENTINA '85 Intl. Stamp Show: b., Arms of Spain, Argentina. c., Columbus' arms. d.-f., Columbus' arrival at San Salvador Island. Nos. B105d-B105f in continuous design; ships shown on singles range in size, left to right, from small to large. Surtax was for exhibition.

1984, Apr. 28 Litho. *Perf. 13½*

B105		Block of 6	4.50	4.50
a.-f.	SP37	5p + 2.50p, any single	65	32

Children's Game Type of 1983

1984, July 7 Litho. *Perf. 13½*

B106	SP36	2p + 1p Blind Man's Buff	25	20
B107	SP36	3p + 1.50p The Loop	50	40
B108	SP36	4p + 2p Leap Frog	60	50
B109	SP36	5p + 2.50p Rolling the loop	75	60
B110	SP36	6p + 3p Ball Mold	90	75
		Nos. B106-B110 (5)	3.00	2.45

Butterflies — SP38

1985, Nov. 9 Litho. *Perf. 13½*

B111	SP38	5c + 2c Rothschildia jacobaeae	10	10
B112	SP38	10c + 5c Heliconius erato phyllis	24	24
B113	SP38	20c + 10c Precis evarete hilaris	48	48
B114	SP38	25c + 13c Cyanopepla pretiosa	60	60
B115	SP38	40c + 20c Papilio androgeus	95	95
		Nos. B111-B115 (5)	2.37	2.37

Children's Drawings — SP39

1986, Aug. 30 Litho.

B116	SP39	5c + 2c N. Pastor	10	10
B117	SP39	10c + 5c T. Valleistein	24	24
B118	SP39	20c + 10c J.M. Flores	48	48
B119	SP39	25c + 13c M.E. Pezzuto	60	60
B120	SP39	40c + 20c E. Diehl	95	95
		Nos. B116-B120 (5)	2.37	2.37

Surtax for natl. philatelic associations.

Miniature Sheets

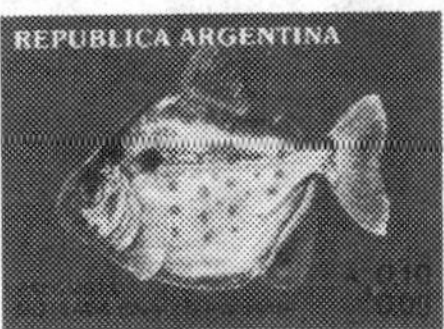

Fresh-water Fish — SP40

Designs: No. B121a, Metynnis maculatus. No. B121b, Cynolebias nigripinnis. No. B121c, Leporinus solarii. No. B121d, Aphyocharax rathbuni. No. B121e, Corydoras aeneus. No. B121f, Thoracocharax securis. No. B121g, Cynolebias melanotaenia. No. B121h, Cichlasoma facetum. Bo. B122a, Tetragonopterus argenteus. No. B122b, Hemigrammus caudovittatus. No. B122c, Astyanax bimaculatus. No. B122d, Gymnocorymbus ternetzi. No. B122e, Hoplias malabaricus. No. B122f, Aphyocharax rubripinnis. No. B122g, Apistogramma agassizi. No. B122h, Pyrrhulina rachoviana.

1987, June 27

B121		Sheet of 8	2.00	
a.-h.	SP40	10c +5c, any single	25	
B122		Sheet of 8	4.00	
a.-h.	SP40	20c +10c, any single	50	

Size of Nos. B121-B122: 125x180mm.

AIR POST STAMPS

Airplane Circles the Globe — AP1

Eagle — AP2

Wings Cross the Sea — AP3

Condor on Mountain Crag — AP4

Perforations of Nos. C1-C37 vary from clean-cut to rough and uneven, with many skipped perfs.

Perf. 13x13½, 13½x13
Wmk. RA in Sun (90)

1928, Mar. 1 **Litho.**

C1	AP1	5c lt red	1.65	75
C2	AP1	10c Prus bl	3.25	1.25
C3	AP2	15c lt brn	3.25	1.25
C4	AP1	18c lil gray	4.50	3.50
a.		18c brn lil	5.00	3.50
b.		Double impression	500.00	
C5	AP2	20c ultra	3.25	1.25
C6	AP2	24c dp bl	5.50	4.00
C7	AP3	25c brt vio	5.50	2.00
C8	AP3	30c rose red	7.75	1.50
C9	AP4	35c rose	5.50	1.50
C10	AP1	36c bis brn	3.50	2.00
C11	AP4	50c gray blk	5.50	75
C12	AP2	54c chocolate	5.50	3.00
C13	AP2	72c yel grn	6.25	3.00
a.		Double impression	400.00	
C14	AP3	90c dk brn	12.00	2.75
C15	AP3	1p sl bl & red	15.00	1.00
C16	AP3	1.08p rose & dk bl	22.50	7.00
C17	AP4	1.26p dl vio & grn	30.00	12.00
C18	AP4	1.80p bl & lil rose	30.00	12.00
C19	AP4	3.60p gray & bl	60.00	30.00
		Nos. C1-C19 (19)	230.40	90.50

The watermark on No. C4a is larger than on the other stamps of this set, measuring 10 mm. across Sun.

Zeppelin First Flight

Air Post Stamps of 1928 Overprinted in Blue

1930, May

C20	AP2	20c ultra	16.00	10.00
C21	AP4	50c gray blk	32.50	20.00
a.		Invtd. ovpt.	750.00	
C22	AP3	1p sl bl & red	35.00	20.00
a.		Invtd. ovpt.	1,100.	
C23	AP4	1.80p bl & lil rose	90.00	50.00
C24	AP4	3.60p gray & bl	250.00	150.00
		Nos. C20-C24 (5)	423.50	250.00

Overprinted in Green

C25	AP2	20c ultra	15.00	10.00
C26	AP4	50c gray blk	20.00	12.50
C27	AP3	90c dk brn	15.00	10.00
C28	AP3	1p sl bl & red	35.00	20.00
C29	AP4	1.80p bl & lil rose	1,100.	750.00
a.		Thick paper	1,200.	
		Nos. C25-C29 (5)	1,185.	802.50

Air Post Stamps of 1928 Overprinted in Red

1930
6
Septiembre
-1931-

1931

C30	AP1	18c lil gray	3.00	1.50
C31	AP2	72c yel grn	21.00	13.00

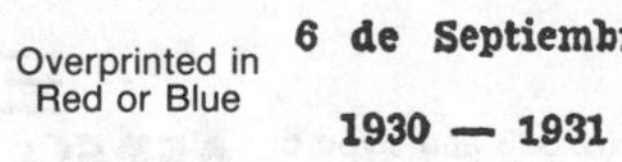

C32	AP3	90c dk brn	21.00	13.00
C33	AP4	1.80p bl & lil rose (Bl)	42.50	27.50
C34	AP4	3.60p gray & bl	85.00	50.00
		Nos. C30-C34 (5)	172.50	105.00

Issued in commemoration of the first anniversary of the Revolution of 1930.

Zeppelin Issue

Air Post Stamps of 1928 Overprinted in Blue or Red

GRAF
ZEPPELIN
1932

1932, Aug. 4

C35	AP1	5c lt red (Bl)	4.00	2.50
C36	AP1	18c lil gray (R)	15.00	13.00
a.		18c brn lil (R)	150.00	85.00

Overprinted

GRAF ZEPPELIN
1932

C37	AP3	90c dk brn (R)	45.00	37.50

Plane and Letter — AP5

Mercury AP6

Plane in Flight AP7

Perf. 13½x13, 13x13½
Wmk. RA in Sun (90)

1940, Oct. 23 **Photo.**

C38	AP5	30c dp org	8.50	15
C39	AP6	50c dk brn	12.50	25
C40	AP5	1p carmine	2.50	10
C41	AP7	1.25p dp grn	75	15
C42	AP5	2.50p brt bl	2.00	25
		Nos. C38-C42 (5)	26.25	90

Plane and Letter — AP8

Mercury and Plane — AP9

Perf. 13½x13, 13x13½

1942, Oct. 6 **Litho.** **Wmk. 90**

C43	AP8	30c orange	25	5
C44	AP9	50c dl brn & buff	60	5

See Nos. C49-C52, C57, C61.

Plane over Iguaçu Falls AP10

Plane over the Andes AP11

Perf. 13½x13

1946, June 10 **Unwmk.**

C45	AP10	15c dl red brn	40	8
C46	AP11	25c gray grn	25	8

See Nos. C53-C54.

Allegory of Flight AP12

Astrolabe — AP13

Perf. 13½x13, 13x13½.

1946, Sept. 25 **Litho.** **Unwmk.**
Surface-Tinted Paper

C47	AP12	15c sl grn, *pale grn*	90	25
C48	AP13	60c vio brn, *ocher*	90	40

Types of 1942

1946-48 **Unwmk.** ***Perf. 13½x13***

C49	AP8	30c orange	2.25	10
C50	AP9	50c dl brn & buff	4.00	25
C51	AP8	1p car ('47)	2.00	20
C52	AP8	2.50p brt bl ('48)	9.00	1.25

Types of 1946

1948 **Wmk. 90**

C53	AP10	15c dl red brn	20	10
C54	AP11	25c gray grn	40	10

Atlas (National Museum, Naples) — AP14

Map of Argentine Republic, Globe and Caliper AP15

Perf. 13½x13, 13x13½

1948-49 **Photo.** **Wmk. 288**

C55	AP14	45c dk brn ('49)	50	25
C56	AP15	70c dk grn	75	35

Issued to commemorate the 4th Pan-American Reunion of Cartographers, Buenos Aires, October-November, 1948.

Mercury Type of 1942

1949 **Litho.** ***Perf. 13x13½***

C57	AP9	50c dl brn & buff	60	18

Marksmanship Trophy — AP16

1949, Nov. 4 **Photo.**

C58	AP16	75c brown	1.10	30

World Rifle Championship, 1949.

Douglas DC-3 and Condor AP17

Perf. 13x13½

1951, June 20 **Wmk. 90**

C59	AP17	20c dk ol grn	20	8

10th anniversary of the State air lines.

Douglas DC-6 and Condor — AP18

1951, Oct. 17 ***Perf. 13½***

C60	AP18	20c blue	20	9

End of Argentine 5-year Plan.

Plane-Letter Type of 1942

1951 **Litho.** ***Perf. 13½x13***

C61	AP8	1p carmine	50	18

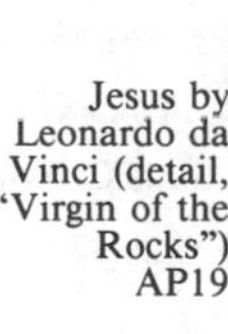

Jesus by Leonardo da Vinci (detail, "Virgin of the Rocks") AP19

Perf. 13½x13

1956, Sept. 29 **Photo.** **Wmk. 90**

C62	AP19	1p dl pur	50	20

Issued to express the gratitude of the children of Argentina to the people of the world for their help against poliomyelitis.

Battle of Montevideo AP20

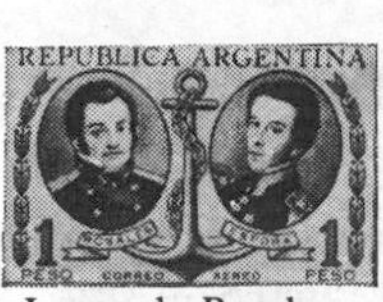

Leonardo Rosales and Tomas Espora AP21

Guillermo Brown AP22

Map of Americas and Arms of Buenos Aires — AP23

1957, March 2 ***Perf. 13½***

C63	AP20	60c bl gray	20	10

C64 AP21 1p brt pink 20 10
C65 AP22 2p brown 35 15

Issued to commemorate the centenary of the death of Admiral Guillermo Brown, founder of the Argentine navy.

1957, Aug. 16
C66 AP23 2p rose vio 60 25

Issued to publicize the Inter-American Economic Conference in Buenos Aires.

Modern Locomotive AP24

1957, Aug. 31 Wmk. 90 *Perf. 13½*
C67 AP24 60c gray 15 8

Centenary of Argentine railroads.

Globe, Flag and Compass Rose — AP25

Design: 2p, Key.

1957, Sept. 14
C68 AP25 1p redsh brn 25 10
C69 AP25 2p Prus bl 40 12

Issued to publicize the 1957 International Congress for Tourism.

Birds Carrying Letters AP26

1957, Nov. 6
C70 AP26 1p brt bl 20 8

Issued for Letter Writing Week, Oct. 6-12.

Early Plane — AP27

1958, May 31 *Perf. 13½*
C71 AP27 2p maroon 25 18

Issued to commemorate the 50th anniversary of the Argentine Aviation Club.

Stamp of 1858 and "The Post of Santa Fe" — AP28

Design: 80c, Stamp of Buenos Aires and view of the Plaza de la Aduana.

1958 Litho. *Perf. 13½*
C72 AP28 80c pale bis & sl bl 25 10
C73 AP28 1p red org & dk bl 30 18

Issued to commemorate the centenary of the first postage stamps of Buenos Aires and the Argentine Confederation.
Issue dates: 80c, Oct. 18; 1p, Aug. 23.

Comet Jet over World Map AP29

1959, May 16 *Perf. 13½*
C74 AP 5p blk & ol 40 10

Issued to commemorate the inauguration of jet flights by Argentine Airlines.

Type of Regular Issue, 1960.

"Cabildo" and: 1.80p, Mariano Moreno. 5p, Manuel Belgrano and Juan Jose Castelli.

Perf. 13½
1960, May 28 Wmk. 90 Photo.
C75 A287 1.80p red brn 20 10
a. Souvenir sheet of 3 1.00 60
C76 A287 5p buff & pur 45 15
a. Souvenir sheet of 3 2.00 1.25

Issued to commemorate the 150th anniversary of the May Revolution.
Souvenir sheets are imperf. No. C75a contains one No. C75 and 1p and 2p resembling Nos. 713-714; stamps in reddish brown, marginal inscriptions in green. No. C76a contains one No. C76 and 4.20p and 10.70p resembling Nos. 715-716; stamps are in green, marginal inscriptions in reddish brown. Sheet size: 152x106mm.

Symbolic of New Provinces — AP30

1960, July 8 Litho.
C77 AP30 1.80p dp car & bl 20 10

Issued to commemorate the elevation of the territories of Chubut, Formosa, Neuquen, Rio Negro and Santa Cruz to provinces.

Type of Regular Issue, 1960
1960, Oct. 1 Photo. *Perf. 13½*
C78 A291 1.80p rose lil 25 10
C79 A291 10.70p brt grnsh bl 60 25

Issued to commemorate the 8th Congress of the Postal Union of the Americas and Spain.

UNESCO Emblem AP31

1962, July 14 Litho.
C80 AP31 13p ocher & brn 60 40

Issued to commemorate the 15th anniversary of UNESCO (U.N. Educational, Scientific and Cultural Organization).

Mail Coach — AP32

1962, Oct. 6 Wmk. 90 *Perf. 13½*
C81 AP32 5.60p gray brn & blk 30 15

Mailman's Day, Sept. 14, 1962.

No. 695 and Type of 1959 Surcharged in Green

AEREO 5 60 PESOS

1962, Oct. 31 Photo.
C82 A277 5.60p on 5p brn 40 20
C83 A277 18p on 5p brn, *grnsh* 1.50 30

UPAE Emblem AP33

Skylark AP34

1962, Nov. 24 Photo. *Perf. 13½*
C84 AP33 5.60p dk bl 25 15

Issued to commemorate the 50th anniversary of the founding of the Postal Union of the Americas and Spain, UPAE.

1963, Feb. 9 Litho.

Design: 11p, Super Albatros.

C85 AP34 5.60p bl & blk 25 15
C86 AP34 11p bl, blk & red 45 20

9th World Gliding Championships.

Symbolic Plane — AP35

1963-65 Wmk. 90 *Perf. 13½*
C87 AP35 5.60p dk pur, car & brt grn 50 20
C88 AP35 7p blk & bis ('64) 75 15
C88A AP35 7p blk & bis ('65) 6.00 75
C89 AP35 11p blk, dk pur & grn 75 35
C90 AP35 18p dk pur, red & vio bl 1.50 50
C91 AP35 21p brn, red & gray 2.00 75
Nos. C87-C91 (6) 11.50 2.70

"Argentina" reads down on No. C88, up on No. C88A. See Nos. C101-C104, C108-C111, C123-C126, C135-C141.

Type of Regular Issue, 1964

Design: 18p, Map of Falkland Islands (Islas Malvinas).

1964, Feb. 22 *Perf. 13½*
Size: 33x22mm.
C92 A327 18p lt & dk bl & ol grn 2.50 1.00

Issued to commemorate the 60th anniversary of Argentina's claim to Antarctic territories.

U.P.U. Monument, Bern, and U.N. Emblem — AP36

1964, May 23 Engr. *Perf. 13½*
C93 AP36 18p red & dk brn 75 30

Issued to commemorate the 15th Universal Postal Union Congress, Vienna, Austria, May-June 1964.

Discovery of America, Florentine Woodcut — AP37

1964, Oct. 10 Litho.
C94 AP37 13p tan & blk 45 25

Issued for the Day of the Race, Columbus Day.

Lt. Matienzo Base, Antarctica AP38

1965, Feb. 27 Photo. *Perf. 13½*
C95 AP38 11p sal pink 75 20

Issued to publicize the national territory of Tierra del Fuego, Antarctic and South Atlantic Isles.

No. C88A Overprinted in Silver: "PRIMERS / JORNADAS FILATELICAS / RIOPLATENSES"
1965, Mar. 17 Litho.
C96 AP35 7p blk & bis 30 20

Issued to commemorate the First Rio de la Plata Stamp Show, sponsored jointly by the Argentine and Uruguayan Philatelic Associations, Montevideo, March 19-28.

ITU Emblem AP39

Ascending Rocket AP40

1965, May 11 Wmk. 90 *Perf. 13½*
C97 AP39 18p sl, blk & red 60 30

Issued to commemorate the centenary of the International Telecommunication Union.

1965, May 29 Photo. *Perf. 13½*

Design: 50p, Earth with trajectories and magnetic field (horiz.).

C98 AP40 18p vermilion 60 30
C99 AP40 50p dp vio bl 1.50 65

Issued to commemorate the 6th Symposium on Space Research, held in Buenos Aires, and to honor the National Commission of Space Research.

Type of 1963-65 Inscribed "Republica Argentina" Reading Down
1965, Oct. 13 Litho. Wmk. 90
C101 AP35 12p dk car rose & brn 2.00 30
C102 AP35 15p vio bl & dk red 1.25 40
C103 AP35 27.50p dk bl grn & gray 2.00 60
C104 AP35 30.50p dk brn & dk bl 3.00 75

Argentine Antarctica Map and Centaur Rocket — AP41

1966, Feb. 19 *Perf. 13½*
C105 AP41 27.50p bl, blk & dp org 1.50 1.00

Issued to commemorate the launchings of sounding balloons and of a Gamma Centaur rocket in Antarctica during February, 1965.

Sea Gull and Southern Cross AP42

1966, May 14 *Perf. 13½*
C106 AP42 12p Prus bl, blk & red 40 20

Issued to commemorate the 50th anniversary of the Naval Aviation School.

Blériot Plane Flown by Fels, 1917 — AP43

1967, Sept. 2 **Litho.** *Perf. 13½*
C107 AP43 26p ol, bl & blk 40 15

Issued to commemorate the flight by Theodore Fels from Buenos Aires to Montevideo, Sept. 2, 1917, allegedly the first International airmail flight.

Type of 1963-65 Inscribed "Republica Argentina" Reading Down

1967, Dec. 20 *Perf. 13½*
C108 AP35 26p brown 1.00 35
C109 AP35 40p violet 7.00 50
C110 AP35 68p bl grn 5.00 75
C111 AP35 78p ultra 2.00 1.00

Vito Dumas and Ketch "Legh II" AP44

1968, July 27 **Litho.** **Wmk. 90**
C112 AP44 68p bl, blk, red & vio bl 1.00 50

Issued to commemorate Vito Dumas's one-man voyage around the world in 1943.

Type of Regular Issue and

Assembly Emblem AP45

Design: 40p, Globe and map of South America.

1968, Oct. 19 **Litho.** *Perf. 13½*
C113 A395 40p brt pink, lt bl & blk 60 25
C114 AP45 68p bl, lt bl, gold & blk 1.00 40

Issued to publicize the 4th Plenary Assembly of the International Telegraph and Telephone Consultative Committee, Mar del Plata, Sept. 23-Oct. 25.

Radar Antenna, Balcarce Station — AP46

Perf. 13½
1969, Aug. 23 **Wmk. 90** **Photo.**
C115 AP46 40p bl gray 1.00 30

Issued to publicize communications by satellite through International Telecommunications Consortium (INTELSAT).

Atucha Nuclear Center AP47

1969, Dec. 13 **Litho.** **Wmk. 365**
C116 AP47 26p bl & multi 2.00 1.00

Completion of Atucha Nuclear Center.

Type of 1963-65 Inscribed "Republica Argentina" Reading Down

1969-71 *Perf. 13½*
C123 AP35 40p violet 7.50 50
C124 AP35 68p dk bl grn ('70) 2.50 75

Unwmk.
C125 AP35 26p yel brn ('71) 50 25
C126 AP35 40p vio ('71) 4.00 50

Old Fire Engine and Fire Brigade Emblem AP48

1970, Aug. 8 **Litho.** **Unwmk.**
C128 AP48 40c grn & multi 80 40

Centenary of the Fire Brigade.

Education Year Emblem — AP49

1970, Aug. 29 *Perf. 13½*
C129 AP49 68c bl & blk 60 25

Issued for International Education Year.

Fleet Leaving Valparaiso, by Antonio Abel AP50

1970, Oct. 17 **Litho.** *Perf. 13½*
C130 AP50 26c multi 1.25 30

Issued to commemorate the 150th anniversary of the departure for Peru of the liberation fleet from Valparaiso, Chile.

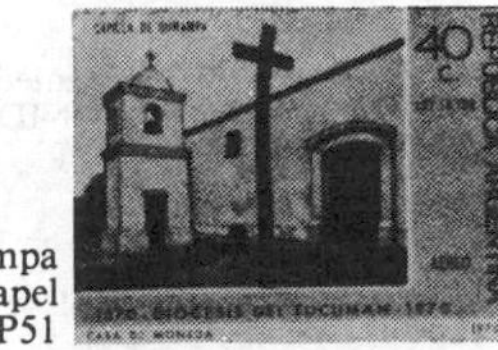

Sumampa Chapel AP51

1970, Nov. 7 **Photo.**
C131 AP51 40c multi 1.50 40

Bishopric of Tucuman, 400th anniversary.

Buenos Aires Planetarium — AP52

1970, Nov. 28 **Litho.** *Perf. 13½*
C132 AP52 40c multi 90 40

Jorge Newbery and Morane Saulnier Plane AP53

1970, Dec. 19
C133 AP53 26c bl, blk, yel & grn 60 25

24th Aeronautics and Space Week.

Industries Type of Regular Issue

Design: 31c, Refinery.

1971, Oct. 16 **Litho.** *Perf. 13½*
C134 A445 31c red, blk & yel 1.00 40

Nationalized industries.

Type of 1963-65 Inscribed "Republica Argentina" Reading Down

1971-74 **Unwmk.**
C135 AP35 45c brown 5.00 10
C136 AP35 68c red 75 10
C137 AP35 70c vio bl ('73) 1.25 10
C138 AP35 90c emer ('73) 3.00 15
C139 AP35 1.70p bl ('74) 75 35
C140 AP35 1.95p emer ('74) 75 40
C141 AP35 2.65p dp cl ('74) 75 50
Nos. C135-C141 (7) 12.25 1.70

Fluorescent paper was used for Nos. C135-C136, C138-C141. The 70c was issued on both ordinary and fluorescent paper.

Don Quixote, Drawing by Ignacio Zuloaga — AP54

1975, Apr. 26 **Photo.** *Perf. 13½*
C145 AP54 2.75p yel, blk & red 80 40

Day of the Race and for Espana 75 International Philatelic Exhibition, Madrid, Apr. 4-13.

No. C87 Surcharged **100 PESOS**

1975, Sept. 15 **Litho.** **Wmk. 90**
C146 AP35 9.20p on 5.60p 1.25 25
C147 AP35 19.70p on 5.60p 1.75 50
C148 AP35 100p on 5.60p 8.00 3.00

No. C87 Surcharged **REVALORIZADO 920 PESOS**

1975, Oct. 15
C149 AP35 9.20p on 5.60p 1.00 30
C150 AP35 19.70p on 5.60p 1.75 70

AIR POST SEMI-POSTAL STAMPS

Stamp Engraving SPAP1

Designs: 70c+70c, Proofing stamp die. 1p+1p, Sheet of stamps. 2.50p+2.50p, The letter. 5p+5p, Gen. San Martin.

Perf. 13½
1950, Aug. 26 **Wmk. 90** **Photo.**
CB1 SPAP1 45c + 45c vio bl 60 40
CB2 SPAP1 70c + 70c dk brn 90 60
a. Souvenir sheet of 3 5.00 5.00
CB3 SPAP1 1p + 1p cer 2.50 2.50
CB4 SPAP1 2.50p + 2.50p ol gray 14.00 10.00
CB5 SPAP1 5p + 5p dl grn 15.00 12.00
Nos. CB1-CB5 (5) 33.00 25.50

Issued to publicize the Argentine International Philatelic Exhibition, 1950.

No. CB2a measures 120x150mm., and contains one each of Nos. B12, CB1 and CB2, imperf., with marginal inscriptions and ornamental border in olive green.

Pieta by Michelangelo SPAP2

1951, Dec. 22 *Perf. 13½x13*
CB6 SPAP2 2.45p +7.55p grnsh blk 30.00 20.00

The surtax was for the Eva Perón Foundation.

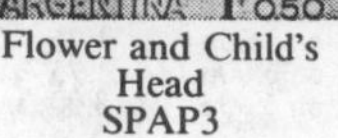

Flower and Child's Head
SPAP3

Stamp of 1858
SPAP4

1958, Mar. 15 *Perf. 13½*
CB7 SPAP3 1p +50c dp cl 35 35

Surtax for National Council for Children.

1958, Mar. 29 Litho. Wmk. 90
CB8 SPAP4 1p + 50c gray ol & bl 60 50
CB9 SPAP4 2p + 1p rose lil & vio 80 65
CB10 SPAP4 3p + 1.50p grn & brn 90 80
CB11 SPAP4 5p + 2.50p gray ol & car rose 1.50 1.25
CB12 SPAP4 10p + 5p gray ol & brn 3.00 2.50
Nos. CB8-CB12 (5) 6.80 5.70

The surtax was for the International Centennial Philatelic Exhibition, Buenos Aires, April 19-27.

Type of Semi-Postal Issue, 1958

Designs: 1p+50c, Flooded area. 5p+2.50p, House and truck under water.

1958, Oct. 4 Photo. *Perf. 13½*
CB13 SP11 1p + 50c dl pur 30 25
CB14 SP11 5p + 2.50p grnsh bl 1.00 90

The surtax was for victims of a flood in the Buenos Aires district.

Type of Semi-Postal Issue, 1959

Designs: 2p+1p, Rowing. 3p+1.50p, Woman diver.

1959, Sept. 5 Litho. *Perf. 13½*
CB15 SP13 2p + 1p brt bl & blk 60 40
CB16 SP13 3p + 1.50p ol & blk 90 75

Issued to commemorate the third Pan American Games, Chicago, Aug. 27-Sept. 7, 1959.

Type of Semi-Postal Issue, 1960

Birds: 2p+1p, Rufous tinamou. 3p+1.50p, Rhea.

1960, Feb. 6 *Perf. 13½*
CB17 SP14 2p + 1p rose car & sal 40 25
CB18 SP14 3p + 1.50p sl grn 60 50

The surtax was for child welfare work.
See No. CB29.

Buenos Aires Market Place, 1810
SPAP5

Seibo, National Flower
SPAP6

Designs: 6p+3p, Oxcart water carrier. 10.70p+5.30p, Settlers landing. 20p+10p, The Fort.

1960, Aug. 20 Photo. Wmk. 90
CB19 SPAP5 2 + 1p rose brn 25 12
CB20 SPAP5 6 + 3p gray 50 35
CB21 SPAP5 10.70 + 5.30p bl 90 50
CB22 SPAP5 20 + 10p bluish grn 1.50 1.25

Issued to publicize the Inter-American Philatelic Exhibition EFIMAYO 1960, Buenos Aires, Oct. 12-24, held to commemorate the sesquicentennial of the May Revolution of 1910.

1960, Sept. 10 *Perf. 13½*

Design: 10.70p+5.30p, Copihue, Chile's national flower.

CB23 SPAP6 6 + 3p lil rose 50 40
CB24 SPAP6 10.70 + 5.30p ver 75 60

The surtax was for earthquake victims in Chile.

Nos. CB19-CB22 Overprinted: "DIA DE LAS NACIONES UNIDAS 24 DE OCTUBRE"

1960, Oct. 8
CB25 SPAP5 2 + 1p rose brn 35 25
CB26 SPAP5 6 + 3p gray 60 50
CB27 SPAP5 10.70 + 5.30p bl 80 75
CB28 SPAP5 20 + 10p bluish grn 1.50 1.35

United Nations Day, Oct. 24, 1960.

Type of Semi-Postal Issue, 1960

Design: Emperor penguins.

1961, Feb. 25 Photo. Wmk. 90
CB29 SP14 1.80p + 90c gray 40 30

The surtax was for child welfare work.

Stamp of 1862
SPAP7

Crutch, Olympic Torch and Rings
SPAP8

1962, May 19 Litho.
CB30 SPAP7 6.50p + 6.50p Prus bl & grnsh bl 90 80

Issued to publicize the opening of the "Argentina 62" Philatelic Exhibition, Buenos Aires, May 19-29.

Type of Semi-Postal Issue, 1963

Design: 11p+5p, Bicycling.

1963, May 18 Wmk. 90 *Perf. 13½*
CB31 SP21 11p + 5p grn, red & blk 70 60

Issued to commemorate the 4th Pan American Games, Sao Paulo, Brazil.

Type of Semi-Postal Issue, 1962

Design: 11p+5p, Great kiskadee.

1963, Dec. 21 *Perf. 13½*
CB32 SP20 11p + 5p dk brn, brn, yel & grn 1.25 1.00

The surtax was for child welfare.

Type of Semi-Postal Issue, 1964

Design: 11p+5p, Sailboat.

1964, July 18 Litho.
CB33 SP22 11p + 5p brt bl & blk 75 75

Issued to publicize the 18th Olympic Games, Tokyo, Oct. 10-25, 1964.

1964, Sept. 19 Litho. *Perf. 13½*
CB34 SPAP8 18p + 9p bluish grn, blk, red & yel 80 80

Issued to publicize the 13th "Olympic" games for the handicapped, Tokyo, 1964.

Bird Type of Semi-Postal Issue, 1962

Design: Chilean swallow.

1964, Dec. 23 Litho. Wmk. 90
CB35 SP20 18p + 9p brn, dk bl & grn 1.50 1.25

The surtax was for child welfare.

Bird Type of Semi-Postal Issue, 1962, Inscribed "R. ARGENTINA"

Design: Rufous ovenbird.

1966, Mar. 26 *Perf. 13½*
CB36 SP20 27.50p + 12.50p bl, ocher, yel & grn 1.50 1.25

The surtax was for child welfare.

Coat of Arms – SPAP9

1966, June 25 Litho. *Perf. 13½*
CB37 SPAP9 10p + 10p yel & multi 2.50 2.00

Issued to publicize the ARGENTINA '66 Philatelic Exhibition held in connection with the sesquicentennial celebration of the Declaration of Independence, Buenos Aires, July 16-23. The surtax was for the Exhibition. Issued in sheets of 4.

Bird Type of Semi-Postal Issue, 1962, Inscribed "R. ARGENTINA"

Designs: 15p+7p, Blue and yellow tanager. 26p+13p, Toco toucan.

1967 Litho. Wmk. 90
CB38 SP20 15p + 7p blk, bl, grn & yel 1.50 1.25
CB39 SP20 26p + 13p blk, org, yel & bl 90 70

The surtax was for child welfare.
Issue dates: 15p+7p, Jan. 14. 26p+13p, Dec. 23.

Bird Type of Semi-Postal Issue, 1969

Design: 26p+13p, Lineated woodpecker.

1969, Sept. 20 Wmk. 365 *Perf. 13½*
CB40 SP24 26p + 13p multi 60 50

The surtax was for child welfare.

Bird Type of Semi-Postal Issue, 1970

Design: 40c+20c, Chilean flamingo.

1970, May 9 Litho. Wmk. 365
CB41 SP25 40c + 20c multi 70 60

The surtax was for child welfare.

Fish Type of Semi-Postal Issue, 1971

Design: Pejerrey (atherinidae family).

1971, Feb. 20 Unwmk. *Perf. 12½*
Size: 75x15mm.
CB42 SP26 40c + 20c lt bl & multi 50 40

The surtax was for child welfare.

OFFICIAL STAMPS

Regular Issues Overprinted in Black

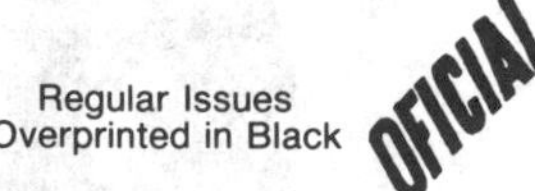

1884-87 Unwmk. *Perf. 12, 14*
O1 A29 ½c brown 9.00 6.00
a. Inverted overprint 9.00 6.00
O2 A23 1c red 5.50 4.00
a. Invtd. ovpt., perf. 14 50.00 37.50
b. Perf. 12 55.00 40.00
c. As "a," perf. 12 35.00 35.00
O3 A29 1c red 60 40
a. Inverted overprint 1.25 85
b. Double overprint 30.00 30.00
O4 A20 2c green 60 40
a. Inverted overprint 55.00 27.50
b. Double overprint 30.00 30.00
O5 A11 4c brown 60 40
a. Inverted overprint 40.00 27.50
O6 A7 8c lake 60 40
a. Inverted overprint 55.00 55.00
O7 A8 10c green 55.00 27.50
O8 A23 12c ultra (#45) 4.00 3.00
a. Perf. 14 55.00 55.00
O9 A29 12c grnsh bl 90 75
a. Inverted overprint 110.00 90.00
O10 A19 24c blue 1.25 90
a. Inverted overprint 4.00 2.50
O11 A21 25c lake 11.00 7.00
O12 A12 30c orange 22.50 15.00
O13 A13 60c black 15.00 9.00
a. Inverted overprint 55.00 35.00
O14 A14 90c blue 11.00 6.50
a. Inverted overprint 45.00 35.00
b. Double overprint 45.00
Nos. O1-O14 (14) 137.55 81.25

1884 ***Rouletted***
O15 A17 16c green 2.00 1.00
a. Double overprint 15.00 15.00
b. Inverted overprint 110.00
O16 A18 20c blue 9.00 6.50
a. Inverted overprint 55.00 37.50
O17 A19 24c blue 1.25 1.10
a. Inverted overprint 4.00 3.50
b. Double ovpt., one inverted 27.50

Overprinted Diagonally in Red

1885 *Perf. 12*
O18 A20 2c green 2.00 1.00
a. Inverted overprint 45.00 27.50
O19 A11 4c brown 2.00 1.25
a. Inverted overprint 45.00 27.50
b. Double overprint 45.00 45.00
O20 A13 60c black 25.00 15.00
O21 A14 90c blue 275.00 150.00

1885 ***Rouletted***
O22 A19 24c blue 20.00 11.00

On all of these stamps, the overprint is found reading both upwards and downwards.
Counterfeits exist of No. O21 overprint and others.

Regular Issues Handstamped Horizontally in Black **OFICIAL**

1884 *Perf. 12, 14*
O23 A23 1c red 70.00 25.00
a. Perf. 12 225.00 125.00
O24 A20 2c green 225.00 175.00
a. Diagonal ovpt. 35.00 20.00
O25 A11 4c brown 15.00 11.00
O26 A7 8c lake 15.00 11.00
O27 A23 12c ultra 40.00 25.00

Overprinted Diagonally

O28 A19 24c bl, rouletted 30.00 20.00
O29 A13 60c black 20.00 10.00

Counterfeit overprints exist.

Liberty Head – O1

1901, Dec. 1 Engr. *Perf. 11½*
O31 O1 1c gray 30 20
O32 O1 2c org brn 45 25
O33 O1 5c red 60 25
O34 O1 10c dk grn 70 30
O35 O1 30c dk bl 4.50 1.10
O36 O1 50c orange 2.50 75
Nos. O31-O36 (6) 9.05 2.85

Regular Stamps of 1935-51 Overprinted in Black

c **SERVICIO OFICIAL**

Perf. 13x13½, 13½x13, 13
1938-54 Wmk. RA in Sun (90)
O37 A129 1c buff ('40) 10 5
O38 A130 2c dk brn ('40) 10 5
O39 A132 3c grn ('39) 12 5
O40 A132 3c lt gray ('39) 10 5
O41 A134 5c yel brn 10 5
O42 A195 5c car ('53) 12 5
O43 A137 10c carmine 10 5
O44 A137 10c brn ('39) 10 5
O45 A140 15c lt gray bl, type II ('47) 12 5
O46 A139 15c sl bl 35 5
O47 A139 15c pale ultra ('39) 12 5
O48 A139 20c bl ('53) 30 5
O49 A141 25c carmine 12 5
a. Overprint 11mm 20 5
O49B A143 40c dk vio 75 8
O50 A144 50c red & org 10 5
a. Overprint 11mm 25 5
O51 A146 1p brn blk & lt bl ('40) 20 5
a. Overprint 11mm

O52 A224 1p choc & lt bl ('51) 20 8
a. Overprint 11mm 20 8
O53 A147 2p brn lake & dk ultra (ovpt. 11mm) ('54) 75 8
Nos. O37-O53 (18) 3.85 99

Overprinted in Black on Stamps and Types of 1945-47

Perf. 13x13½, 13½x13

1945-46 Unwmk.

O54 A130 2c sepia 1.25 30
O55 A134 3c lt gray 1.25 20
O56 A134 5c yel brn 30 5
O57 A195 5c dp car 8 5
O58 A137 10c brown 8 5
a. Double overprint
O59 A140 15c lt gray bl, type II 12 5
O61 A141 25c dl rose 12 5
O62 A144 50c red & org 30 5
O63 A146 1p brn blk & lt bl 12 5
O64 A147 2p brn lake & bl 12 5
O65 A148 5p ind & ol grn 12 6
O66 A149 10p dp cl & int blk 25 8
O67 A150 20p bl grn & brn 50 20
Nos. O54-O67 (13) 4.61 1.24

Overprinted in Black on Stamps and Types of 1942-50

Perf. 13, 13x13½

1944-51 Wmk. 288

O73 A134 3c lt gray 1.50 40
O74 A134 5c yel brn 25 6
O75 A137 10c red brn 10 5
O76 A140 15c lt gray bl, type II 25 5
O77 A144 50c red & org (overprint 11 mm) 2.25 40
O78 A146 1p brn blk & lt bl (overprint 11mm) 2.25 30
Nos. O73-O78 (6) 6.60 1.26

Regular Issue of 1952 Overprinted in Black

d SERVICIO OFICIAL

1953 Wmk. 90 *Perf. 13*

O79 A228 5c gray 8 5
O80 A228 10c rose lil 8 5
O81 A228 20c rose pink 8 5
O82 A228 25c dl grn 12 5
O83 A228 40c dl vio 8 5
O84 A228 45c dp bl 20 5
O85 A228 50c dl brn 12 5

Nos. 611-617 Overprinted Type "e" in Blue

SERVICIO OFICIAL e SERVICIO OFICIAL f

Perf. 13x13½, 13½x13

O86 A229 1p dk brn 15 6
O87 A229 1.50p dp grn 30 8
O88 A229 2p brt car 20 10
O89 A229 3p indigo 60 20

Size: 30x40mm.

O90 A229 5p red brn 60 35
O91 A228 10p red 3.00 1.50
O92 A229 20p green 32.50 15.00
Nos. O79-O92 (14) 38.11 17.64

No. 612 Overprinted Type "f" in Blue

O93 A229 1.50p dp grn 1.00 15

Regular Issues of 1954-59 Variously Overprinted in Black or Blue

S. OFICIAL g SERVICIO OFICIAL h

Perf. 13½, 13x13½, 13½x13

1955-61 Litho. Wmk. 90

O94 A237(c) 20c red (#629) 12 5
O95 A237(d) 20c red (#629) 10 5
O96 A237(d) 40c red, ovpt. 15mm (#630) 12 5

Engr.

O97 A239(g) 50c bl (#632) ('58) 10 5

Photo.

O98 A239(h) 1p brn (#635) ('59) 10 5
O99 A239(e) 1p brn (Bl,#635) ('59) 10 5
O100 A239(e) 1p brn (Bk,#635) ('60) 10 5

Engr.

O101 A239(h) 3p vio brn (#638) ('58) 12 5
O102 A240(h) 5p gray grn (#639) ('57) 30 8
O103 A240(e) 10p yel grn (#640) ('58) 50 15
O104 A240(f) 20p dl vio (#641) ('59) 90 30
O105 A240(h) 20p dl vio (#641) ('58) 90 25
O106 A241(e) 50p ultra & ind (#642) ('61) 1.25 15
Nos. O94-O106 (13) 4.71 1.33

The overprints on Nos. O99-O100 and O103-O104 are horizontal; that on No. O109 is vertical. On No. O106 overprint measures 23mm.

No. 659 Overprinted Type "d"

1957 Wmk. 90 Litho. *Perf. 13*

O108 A133 20c dl pur (ovpt. 15mm) 10 5

Nos. 666, 658 and 663 Variously Overprinted

1957 Photo. *Perf. 13x13½, 13½*

O109 A261(g) 2p claret 20 5
O110 A254(e) 2.40p brown 20 5
O111 A258(c) 4.40p grnsh gray 25 8

Nos. 668, 685-687, 690-691, 693-705, 742, 742C and Types of 1959-65 Overprinted in black, Blue or Red Types "e," "g," or

S. OFICIAL i S. OFICIAL j

S. OFICIAL k S. OFICIAL m

S. OFICIAL n

Lithographed; Photogravure

1960-68 *Perf. 13x13½, 13½*

O112 A128(g) 5c buff (vert. ovpt.) ('62) 10 5
O113 A275(j) 10c sl grn ('62) 8 5
O114 A275(j) 20c dl red brn ('62) 8 5
O115 A275(i) 50c bister 8 5
O116 A278(k) 1p brn ('62) 12 5
O117 A278(j) 1p brn, photo. (vert. ovpt.) ('65) 20 5
O117A A278(j) 1p brn, litho., (down)('68) 20 7
O118 A276(j) 2p rose red ('62) 12 5
O119 A312(m) 2p dp grn (down) ('64) 25 8
O120 A312(j) 2p brt grn (up) ('66) 12 5
O121 A312(j) 2p grn litho. (down) ('67) 25 8
O122 A277(e) 3p dk bl (horiz.) ('61) 20 7
O123 A277(j) 3p dk bl ('67) 20 7
O124 A276(j) 4p red, litho. ('63) 20 5
O125 A312(j) 4p rose red, litho. (down) ('65) 20 5
O126 A277(e) 5p brn (Bl) (horiz.) 25 8
O127 A277(e) 5p brn (Bk) (horiz.) ('61) 25 8
O128 A277(j) 5p sep ('66) 15 5
O129 A277(e) 5p sep (horiz. ovpt.) ('67) 15 5
O130 A276(j) 8p red ('65) 20 8
O131 A278(i) 10p lt red brn 50 10
O132 A276(j) 10p ver ('66) 20 5
O133 A278(j) 10p brn car (up) ('66) 20 5
O134 A278(m) 12p dk brn vio ('64) 40 5
O135 A278(k) 20p Prus grn ('61) 60 10
O136 A278(j) 20p Prus grn (up) ('66) 45 6
O137 A276(j) 20p red, litho. ('67) 40 6
O138 A276(m) 20p red, litho. ('67) 25 5
O139 A278(j) 23p grn (vert. ovpt.) ('65) 60 10
O140 A278(j) 25p dp vio, photo. (R) (up) ('66) 60 6
O141 A278(j) 25p pur, litho. (R) (down) ('67) 60 10
O142 A241(n) 50p dk bl ('66) 1.25 10
O143 A279(m) 100p bl (horiz. ovpt.) ('64) 1.25 25
O144 A279(m) 100p bl (up) ('65) 1.25 25
O145 A280(m) 300p dp vio ('66) 2.50 50

The "m" overprint measures 15½mm. on 2p; 14½mm. on 12p, 100p and 300p; 13mm. on 20p.

Nos. 699, 818, 823-825, 827-829, and Type of 1962 Overprinted in Black or Red Types "j," "m," or "o"

o SERVICIO OFICIAL

Inscribed: "Republica Argentina"

Lithographed, Photogravure, Engraved

1964-67 Wmk. 90 *Perf. 13½*

O149 A312(j) 6p rose red (down) ('67) 30 5
O153 A238a(m) 22p ultra ('64) 60 6
O154 A238a(j) 43p dk car rose (down) 85 6
O155 A238a(j) 45p brn, photo. (up) ('66) 85 6
O156 A238a(j) 45p brn, litho. (up) ('67) 1.25 15
O157 A241(j) 50p dk bl (up) (R) ('67) 2.50 15
O158 A366(j) 90p ol bis (up) ('67) 3.00 15
O162 A279(o) 500p yel grn ('67) 4.00 75

Type of 1959-67 Overprinted Type "j"

1969 Litho. Wmk. 365 *Perf. 13½*

O163 A276 20p vermilion 25 10

OFFICIAL DEPARTMENT STAMPS

Regular issues of 1911-37 Overprinted in Black

Ministry of Agriculture

M. A. (Type I) **M. A.** (Type II)

1913-37

On Stamp of 1911

OD1 A88 2c #181 10 5

On Stamps of 1912-14

OD2 A88 1c #190 10 5
OD3 A88 2c #191 15 6
OD4 A88 5c #194 30 5
OD5 A88 12c #196 10 5

On Stamps of 1915-16

OD6 A88 1c #208 15 12
OD7 A88 2c #209 10 6
OD8 A88 5c #212 10 6
OD9 A91 5c #220 10 5

On Stamp of 1917

OD10 A94 12c #238 30 5

On Stamps of 1918-19

OD11 A93 1c #249 10 5
OD12 A93 2c #250 10 5
OD13 A93 5c #253 10 5
OD14 A94 12c #255 10 5
OD15 A94 20c #256 15 10

On Stamps of 1920

OD16 A93 1c #265 30 20
OD17 A93 2c #266 50 20
OD18 A93 5c #269 20 5

On Stamps of 1922-23

OD19 A94 12c #311 75 25
OD20 A94 20c #312 20.00

On Stamps of 1923

OD21 A104 1c #324 5 5
OD22 A104 2c #325 25 10
OD23 A104 5c #328 5 5
OD24 A104 12c #330 5 5
OD25 A104 20c #331 5 5

On Stamps of 1923-31

OD26 A104 1c #341 5 5
OD27 A104 2c #342, I 5 5
a. Type II 1.20 60
OD28 A104 3c #343 10 5
OD29 A104 5c #345, II 5 5
a. Type I 10 5
OD30 A104 10c #346, II 5 5
a. Type I 10 5
OD31 A104 12c #347 10 5
OD32 A104 20c #348, I 15 5
a. Type II 15 5
OD33 A104 30c #351 15 5

On Stamp of 1926

OD34 A110 12c #360 5 5

Type II

On Stamps of 1935-37

OD35 A129 1c #419 5 5
OD36 A130 2c #420 5 5
OD37 A132 3c #422 5 5
OD38 A134 5c #427 5 5
OD39 A137 10c #430 5 5
OD40 A139 15c #434 30 5
OD41 A140 20c #437 20 6
OD42 A140 20c #438 10 5
OD43 A141 25c #441 20 5
OD44 A142 30c #442 15 5
OD45 A145 1p #445 2.00 1.00
OD46 A146 1p #446 25 10

Ministry of War

M. G. (Type I) **M. G.** (Type II)

On Stamp of 1911

OD47 A88 2c #181 10 5

On Stamps of 1912-14

OD48 A88 1c #190 10 5
OD49 A88 2c #191 75 5
OD50 A88 5c #194 10 5
OD51 A88 12c #196 10 5

On Stamps of 1915-16

OD52 A88 1c #208 6.00 60
OD53 A88 2c #209 50 10
OD54 A88 5c #212 60 5
OD55 A91 5c #220 75 15
OD56 A92 12c #222 75 25

On Stamps of 1917

OD57 A93 1c #232 20 5
OD58 A93 2c #233 30 5
OD59 A93 5c #236 30 5
OD60 A94 12c #238 45 5

On Stamps of 1918-19

OD61 A93 1c #249 15 5
OD62 A93 2c #250 10 5
OD63 A93 5c #253 10 5
OD64 A94 12c #255 30 5
OD65 A94 20c #256 90 5

On Stamps of 1920

OD66 A93 2c #266 30 5
OD67 A93 5c #269 30 5
OD68 A94 12c #271 25 5

On Stamp of 1920

OD69 A94 12c #299 1.50 15

On Stamps of 1922-23

OD70 A93 1c #305 60 10
OD71 A93 2c #306 1.25 30
OD72 A103 5c #309 60 5
OD73 A94 20c #312 20 5

On Stamp of 1922-23

OD74 A93 2c #318 3.50 50

On Stamps of 1923

OD75 A104 1c #324 10 5
OD76 A104 2c #325 10 5
OD77 A104 5c #328 10 5
OD78 A104 12c #330 10 5
OD79 A104 20c #331 75 5

On Stamps of 1923-31

OD80 A104 1c #341 1.00 30
OD81 A104 2c #342 15 5
OD82 A104 3c #343, I 5 5
a. Type II 30 5
OD83 A104 5c #345, I 5 5
a. Type II 15 5
OD84 A104 10c #346, II 5 5
a. Type I 45 5
OD85 A104 20c #348, I 10 5
a. Type II 30 5
OD86 A104 30c #351, II 15 5
a. Type I 90 10
OD87 A105 1p #353 1.25 20

On Stamp of 1926

OD88 A109 5c #359 45 5

Type II

On Stamps of 1935-37

OD89 A129 1c #419 5 5
OD90 A130 2c #420 5 5
OD91 A132 3c #422 5 5
OD92 A134 5c #427 6 5
OD93 A137 10c #430 10 5
OD94 A139 15c #434 15 5

OD95 A140 20c #437 75 5
OD96 A140 20c #438 15 5
OD97 A141 25c #441 10 5
OD98 A142 30c #442 10 5
OD99 A144 50c #444 15 5
OD100 A145 1p #445 80 20
OD101 A146 1p #446 25 10

Ministry of Finance

M. H. (Type I) — M. H. (Type II)

Type I

On Stamp of 1911

OD102 A88 2c #181 10 5

On Stamps of 1912-14

OD103 A88 1c #190 10 5
OD104 A88 2c #191 10 5
OD105 A88 5c #194 10 5
OD106 A88 12c #196 10 5

On Stamps of 1915-16

OD107 A88 2c #209 10 6
OD108 A88 5c #212 10 5
OD109 A91 5c #220 10 5

On Stamps of 1917

OD110 A93 2c #233 10 5
OD111 A93 5c #236 90 5
OD112 A94 12c #238 10 5

On Stamps of 1918-19

OD113 A93 2c #250 20.00
OD114 A93 5c #253 10 5
OD115 A94 12c #255 30 5
OD116 A94 20c #256 30 5

On Stamps of 1920

OD117 A93 1c #265 60 30
OD118 A93 2c #266 90 30
OD119 A93 5c #269 20 5
OD120 A94 12c #271 45 10

On Stamp of 1922-23

OD121 A94 20c #312 10.00 2.00

On Stamps of 1923

OD122 A104 1c #324 60 30
OD123 A104 2c #325 5 5
OD124 A104 5c #328 5 5
OD125 A104 12c #330 5 5
OD126 A104 20c #331 5 5

On Stamps of 1923-31

OD127 A104 3c #343 6.00 1.00
OD128 A104 5c #345 5 5
OD129 A104 10c #346 5 5
OD130 A104 12c #347 6.00 3.00
OD131 A104 20c #348, I 10 5
a. Type II 25 5
OD132 A104 30c #351 15 5
OD133 A105 1p #353 30 15

On Stamp of 1926

OD134 A110 12c #360 10.00 10.00

Type II

On Stamps of 1935-37

OD135 A129 1c #419 5 5
OD136 A130 2c #420 5 5
OD137 A132 3c #422 5 5
OD138 A134 5c #427 5 5
OD139 A137 10c #430 10 5
OD140 A139 15c #434 30 5
OD141 A140 20c #437 15 5
OD142 A140 20c #438 10 5
OD143 A142 30c #442 10 5
OD144 A145 1p #445 1.20 40
OD145 A146 1p #446 25 5

Ministry of the Interior

M. I. (Type I) — M. I. (Type II)

Type I

On Stamp of 1911

OD146 A88 2c #181 25 5

On Stamps of 1912-14

OD147 A88 1c #190 10 5
OD148 A88 2c #191 10 5
OD149 A88 5c #194 10 5
OD150 A88 12c #196 10 5

On Stamps of 1915-17

OD151 A88 2c #209 75 30
OD152 A88 5c #212 60 10
OD153 A91 5c #220 45 10
OD154 A93 5c #236 1.20 10

On Stamps of 1918-19

OD155 A93 2c #250 10 5
OD156 A93 5c #253 10 5

On Stamps of 1920

OD157 A93 1c #265 3.00 75
OD158 A93 5c #269 60 25

On Stamps of 1922-23

OD159 A93 2c #306 10.00 10.00
OD160 A103 5c #309 2.50 75
OD161 A94 12c #311 75 25
OD162 A94 20c #312 75 25

On Stamps of 1923

OD163 A104 1c #324 5 5
OD164 A104 2c #325 5 5
OD165 A104 5c #328 5 5
OD166 A104 12c #330 1.50 1.50
OD167 A104 20c #331 50 5

On Stamps of 1923-31

OD168 A104 1c #341 5 5
OD169 A104 2c #342 5 5
OD170 A104 3c #343, II 5 5
a. Type I 90 20
OD171 A104 5c #345, I 5 5
a. Type II 5 5
OD172 A104 10c #346 5 5
OD173 A104 12c #347 30 5
OD174 A104 20c #348, II 5 5
a. Type I 60 5
OD175 A104 30c #351 5 15

Type II

On Stamps of 1935-37

OD176 A129 1c #419 5 5
OD177 A130 2c #420 5 5
OD178 A132 3c #422 5 5
OD178A A134 5c #427 5 5
OD179 A137 10c #430 5 5
OD180 A139 15c #434 20 5
OD181 A140 20c #437 60 5
OD182 A140 20c #438 10 5
OD182A A142 30c #442 10 5
OD182B A145 1p #445 1.20 50
OD182C A146 1p #446 25 10

Ministry of Justice and Instruction

M. J. I. (Type I) — M. J. I. (Type II)

Type I

On Stamp of 1911

OD183 A88 2c #181 90 5

On Stamps of 1912-14

OD184 A88 1c #190 1.20 5
OD185 A88 2c #191 75 15
OD186 A88 5c #194 30 5
OD187 A88 12c #196 30 5

On Stamps of 1915-17

OD188 A88 1c #208 20 5
OD189 A88 2c #209 20 5
OD190 A88 5c #212 75 10
OD191 A91 5c #220 15 5
OD192 A92 12c #222 50 5

On Stamps of 1917

OD193 A93 1c #232 20 5
OD194 A93 2c #233 60 5
OD195 A93 5c #236 20 5
OD196 A94 12c #238 17.50 5.00

On Stamps of 1918-19

OD197 A93 1c #249 10 5
OD198 A93 2c #250 10 5
OD199 A93 5c #253 10 5
OD200 A94 12c #255 20 5
OD201 A94 20c #256 40 5

On Stamps of 1920

OD202 A93 1c #265 15 5
OD203 A93 2c #266 10 5
OD204 A93 5c #269 10 5
OD205 A94 12c #271 25 5

On Stamps of 1922-23

OD206 A93 1c #305 15 5
OD207 A93 2c #306 1.20 30
OD208 A103 5c #309 15 5
OD209 A94 12c #311 7.50 1.20
OD210 A94 20c #312 1.20 20

On Stamp of 1922-23

OD211 A93 2c #318 2.00 2.00

On Stamps of 1923

OD212 A104 1c #324 10 5
OD213 A104 2c #325 5 5
OD214 A104 5c #328 10 5
OD215 A104 12c #330 10 5
OD216 A104 20c #331 30 5

On Stamps of 1923-31

OD217 A104 ½c #340 1.50 50
OD218 A104 1c #341, I 5 5
a. Type II 5 5
OD219 A104 2c #342 5 5
OD220 A104 3c #343, I 5 5
a. Type II 5 5
OD221 A104 5c #345, I 5 5
a. Type II 5 5
OD222 A104 10c #346, II 5 5
a. Type I 20 5
OD223 A104 12c #347, I 5 5
a. Type II 30 15
OD224 A104 20c #348, I 5 5
a. Type II 5 5
OD225 A104 30c #351 5 5
OD226 A105 1p #353 30 50

On Stamps of 1926

OD227 A109 5c #359 10 5
OD228 A110 12c #360 15 5

Type II

On Stamps of 1935-37

OD229 A129 1c #419 5 5
OD230 A130 2c #420 5 5
OD231 A132 3c #422 5 5
OD232 A134 5c #427 6 5
OD233 A137 10c #430 5 5
OD234 A139 15c #434 30 5
OD234A A140 20c #437 10 5
OD234B A140 20c #438 15 5
OD234C A141 25c #441 10 5
OD234D A142 30c #442 10 5
OD234E A145 1p #445 60 30
OD234F A146 1p #446 15 10

Ministry of Marine

M. M. (Type I) — M. M. (Type II)

Type I

On Stamp of 1911

OD235 A88 2c #181 20 5

On Stamps of 1912-14

OD236 A88 1c #190 10 5
OD237 A88 2c #191 10 5
OD238 A88 5c #194 2.00 10
OD239 A88 12c #196 15 5

On Stamps of 1915-16

OD240 A88 2c #209 50 5
OD241 A88 5c #212 30 5

On Stamps of 1917

OD242 A93 1c #232 10 5
OD243 A93 2c #233 10 5
OD244 A93 5c #236 10 5

On Stamps of 1918-19

OD245 A93 1c #249 10 5
OD246 A93 2c #250 10 5
OD247 A93 5c #253 20 5
OD248 A94 12c #255 20 10
OD249 A94 20c #256 2.50 25

On Stamps of 1920

OD250 A93 1c #265 10 5
OD251 A93 2c #266 15 5
OD252 A93 5c #269 20 5

On Stamps of 1922-23

OD253 A103 5c #309 60 10
OD254 A94 12c #311 7.50 7.50
OD255 A94 20c #312 6.00 1.00

On Stamps of 1923

OD256 A104 1c #324 5 5
OD257 A104 2c #325 10 5
OD258 A104 5c #328 25 5
OD259 A104 12c #330 50 15
OD260 A104 20c #331 50 5

On Stamps of 1923-31

OD261 A104 1c #341 60 15
OD262 A104 2c #342 15 5
OD263 A104 3c #343 45 15
OD264 A104 5c #345, I 10 5
a. Type II 45 5
OD265 A104 10c #346 45 5
OD266 A104 20c #348, II 45 5
a. Type I 60 5
OD267 A104 30c #351 90 5
OD268 A105 1p #353 9.00 2.00

On Stamp of 1926

OD269 A109 5c #359 50 5

Type II

On Stamps of 1935-37

OD270 A129 1c #419 5 5
OD271 A130 2c #420 5 5
OD272 A132 3c #422 5 5
OD273 A134 5c #427 5 5
OD274 A137 10c #430 20 5
OD275 A139 15c #434 20 5
OD276 A140 20c #437 30 5
OD277 A140 20c #438 20 5
OD278 A142 30c #442 20 5
OD279 A145 1p #445 2.50 60
OD280 A146 1p #446 60 15

Ministry of Public Works

M. O. P. (Type I) — M. O. P. (Type II)

Type I

On Stamp of 1911

OD281 A88 2c #181 30 5

On Stamps of 1912-14

OD282 A88 1c #190 30 5
OD283 A88 5c #194 15 5
OD284 A88 12c #196 1.50 25

On Stamps of 1916-19

OD285 A91 5c #220 12.00 75
OD286 A94 12c #238 20.00
OD287 A94 20c #256 20.00

On Stamps of 1920

OD288 A93 2c #266 5.00 2.00
OD289 A93 5c #269 1.50 10
OD290 A94 12c #271 18.00 5.00

On Stamps of 1923

OD291 A104 1c #324 30 10
OD292 A104 2c #325 30 5
OD293 A104 5c #328 30 5
OD294 A104 12c #330 50 10
OD295 A104 20c #331 75 10

On Stamps of 1923-31

OD296 A104 1c #341 5 5
OD297 A104 2c #342 5 5
OD298 A104 3c #343 5 5
OD299 A104 5c #345, I 5 5
a. Type II 5 5
OD300 A104 10c #346 5 5
OD301 A104 12c #347 7.50 90
OD302 A104 20c #348, I 5 5
a. Type II 1.80 50
OD303 A104 30c #351 30 5
OD304 A105 1p #353 18.00 5.00

On Stamp of 1926

OD305 A109 5c #359 50 5

Type II

On Stamps of 1935-37

OD306 A129 1c #419 5 5
OD307 A130 2c #420 5 5
OD308 A132 3c #422 5 5
OD309 A134 5c #427 5 5
OD310 A137 10c #430 30 5
OD311 A139 15c #434 45 5
OD312 A140 20c #437 60 6
OD313 A140 20c #438 10 5
OD314 A142 30c #442 10 5
OD315 A144 50c #444 10 5
OD316 A145 1p #445 1.20 40
OD317 A146 1p #446 25 10

Ministry of Foreign Affairs and Religion

M. R. C. (Type I) — M. R. C. (Type II)

Type I

On Stamp of 1911

OD318 A88 2c #181 7.50 1.25

On Stamps of 1912-14

OD319 A88 1c #190 10 5
OD320 A88 2c #191 10 5
OD321 A88 5c #194 30 5
OD322 A88 12c #196 1.50 25

On Stamps of 1915-19

OD323 A88 5c #212 30 5
OD324 A91 5c #220 15 5
OD325 A94 20c #256 1.50 50

On Stamps of 1920

OD326 A93 1c #265 30 10
OD327 A93 5c #269 10 5

On Stamps of 1922-23

OD328 A93 2c #306 10.00 4.00
OD329 A103 5c #309 25.00
OD330 A93 10c #311 20.00

On Stamps of 1923

OD331 A104 1c #324 5 5
OD332 A104 2c #325 5 5
OD333 A104 5c #328 5 5
OD334 A104 12c #330 10 5
OD335 A104 20c #331 15 5

On Stamps of 1923-31

OD336 A104 ½c #340 75 30
OD337 A104 1c #341 6 5
OD338 A104 2c #342 6 5
OD339 A104 3c #343 5 5
OD340 A104 5c #345 5 5
OD341 A104 10c #346, II 5 5
a. Type I 1.20 5
OD342 A104 12c #347 5 5
OD343 A104 20c #348, I 5 5
a. Type II 15 5
OD344 A104 30c #351, I 15 5
a. Type II 15 5
OD345 A105 1p #353 30 10

On Stamp of 1926

OD346 A110 12c #360 10 5

Type II

On Stamps of 1935-37

OD347 A129 1c #419 5 5
OD348 A130 2c #420 5 5
OD349 A132 3c #422 5 5
OD350 A134 5c #427 5 5
OD351 A137 10c #430 10 5
OD352 A139 15c #434 10 5
OD353 A140 20c #437 10 5
OD354 A140 20c #438 10 5
OD355 A142 30c #442 10 5
OD356 A145 1p #445 1.50 60
OD357 A146 1p #446 75 35

BUENOS AIRES

The central point of the Argentine struggle for independence. At intervals

Buenos Aires maintained an independent government but after 1862 became a province of the Argentine Republic.

8 REALES = 1 PESO

Prices of Buenos Aires Nos. 1-8 vary according to condition. Quotations are for fine copies. Very fine to superb specimens sell at much higher prices, and inferior or poor copies sell at reduced prices, depending on the condition of the individual specimen.

Steamship — A1

1858 Unwmk. Typo. *Imperf.*

1	A1	1 (in) pesos lt brn	500.00	*350.00*
2	A1	2 (dos) pesos bl	250.00	190.00
3	A1	3 (tres) pesos grn	1,600.	*1,000.*
a.		3p dk grn	2,000.	*1,250.*
4	A1	4 (cuatro) pesos ver	5,500.	*3,000.*
5	A1	5 (cinco) pesos org	5,000.	*2,000.*
a.		5p ocher	5,000.	*2,000.*
b.		5p ol yel	5,000.	*2,000.*

Issue dates: Nos. 2-5, Apr. 29, 1858. No. 1, Oct. 26, 1858.

1858, Oct. 26

6	A1	4 (cuatro) reales brn	350.00	300.00
a.		4r gray brn	350.00	300.00
b.		4r yel brn	350.00	300.00

1859, Jan. 1

7	A1	1 (in) pesos bl	225.00	150.00
a.		1p ind	300.00	175.00
b.		Impression on reverse of stamp in bl	2,500.	
c.		Double impression	300.00	225.00
d.		Tete beche pair		*50,000.*
8	A1	1 (to) pesos bl	500.00	400.00

Nos. 1, 2, 3 and 7 have been reprinted on very thick, hand-made paper. The same four stamps and No. 8 have been reprinted on thin, hard, white wove paper.

Counterfeits of Nos. 1-8 are plentiful.

Liberty Head — A2

1859, Sept. 3

9	A2	4r grn, *bluish*	275.00	150.00
10	A2	1p blue	50.00	27.50
11	A2	2p vermilion	400.00	200.00
a.		2p red	400.00	200.00

Both clear and rough impressions of these stamps may be found. They have generally been called Paris and Local prints, respectively, but the opinion now obtains that the differences are due to the impression and that they do not represent separate issues.

Many shades exist of Nos. 1-11.

1862, Oct. 4

12	A2	1p rose	175.00	75.00
13	A2	2p blue	500.00	125.00

All three values have been reprinted in black, brownish black, blue and red brown on thin hard white paper. The 4r has also been reprinted in green on bluish paper.

CORDOBA

A province in the central part of the Argentine Republic.

100 CENTAVOS = 1 PESO

Arms of Cordoba — A1

Unwmk.

1858, Oct. 28 Litho. *Imperf.*

Laid Paper

1	A1	5c blue	125.00
2	A1	10c black	*2,500.*

Cordoba stamps were printed on laid paper, but stamps from edges of the sheets sometimes do not show any laid lines and appear to be on wove paper. Counterfeits are plentiful.

CORRIENTES

The northeast province of the Argentine Republic.

1 Real M(oneda) C(orriente) = 12½ Centavos M. C. = 50 Centavos
100 Centavos Fuertes = 1 Peso Fuerte

Ceres

A1 A2

1856, Aug. 21 Unwmk. *Imperf.*

1	A1	1r *blue*	125.00	400.00

1860, Feb. 8

Pen Stroke Through "Un Real"

2	A1	(3c) *blue*	500.00	750.00

1860-78

3	A2	(3c) *blue*	12.50	40.00
4	A2	(2c) *yel grn* ('64)	50.00	60.00
a.		(2c) *bl grn*	125.00	150.00
5	A2	(2c) *yel* ('67)	10.00	25.00
6	A2	(3c) *dk bl* ('71)	4.00	25.00
7	A2	(3c) *lil rose* ('75)		
a.		(3c) *rose red* ('76)		
8	A2	(3c) *red vio* ('78)	60.00	50.00

Pen cancels sell for much less.

Printed from settings of eight varieties, three or four impressions constituting a sheet. Some impressions were printed inverted and tete beche pairs may be cut from adjacent impressions.

From Jan. 1st to Feb. 24th, 1864, No. 4 was used as a 5 centavos stamp but copies so used can only be distinguished when they bear dated cancellations.

The reprints show numerous spots and small defects which are not found on the originals. They are printed on gray blue, dull blue, gray green, dull orange and light magenta papers.

ARMENIA

LOCATION — In southern Russia bounded by Georgia, Azerbaijan, Persia and Turkey.
GOVT. — A Soviet Socialist Republic
AREA — 11,945 sq. mi.
POP. — 1,214,391 (1923)
CAPITAL — Erevan

With Azerbaijan and Georgia, Armenia made up the Transcaucasian Federation of Soviet Republics.

Stamps of Armenia were replaced in 1923 by those of Transcaucasian Federated Republics.

100 Kopecks = 1 Ruble

Counterfeits abound of all overprinted and surcharged stamps.

National Republic.

Russian Stamps of 1902-19 Handstamped

Thirteen types exist of both framed and unframed overprints. The device is the Armenian "H," initial of Hayasdan (Armenia). Inverted and double overprints are found.

Surcharged K 60 K

Type I. Without periods.
Type II. Periods after first "K" and "60".

Black Surcharge.

1919 Unwmk. *Perf. 14, 14½x15.*

1	A14	60k on 1k org (II)	35	40
a.		Imperf. (I)	25	30
b.		Imperf. (II)	25	30

Violet Surcharge.

2	A14	60k on 1k org (II)	45	50

Handstamped in Violet — a

Perf. 14, 14½x15, 13½.

6	A15	4k carmine	75	75
7	A14	5k claret	3.50	4.00
a.		Imperf.	2.25	2.50
9	A14	10k on 7k lt bl	1.75	2.00
10	A11	15k red brn & bl	40	40
11	A8	20k bl & car	1.25	1.50
13	A11	35k red brn & grn	75	75
14	A8	50k vio & grn	60	60
15	A14	60k on 1k org (II)	3.00	3.50
a.		Imperf. (I)	2.50	2.75
b.		Imperf. (II)	14.00	15.00
18	A13	5r dk bl, grn & pale bl	6.00	7.00
a.		Imperf.	1.50	1.50
19	A12	7r dk grn & pink	2.00	2.25
20	A13	10r scar, yel & gray	2.00	2.25

Handstamped in Black.

Perf. 14, 14½x15, 13½.

31	A14	2k green	6.50	7.00
a.		Imperf.	25	25
32	A14	3k red	4.00	4.00
a.		Imperf.	25	25
33	A15	4k carmine	15	20
34	A14	5k claret	25	30
a.		Imperf.	2.00	2.00
36	A15	10k dk bl	1.50	1.00
37	A14	10k on 7k lt bl	10	15
38	A11	15k red brn & bl	10	15
a.		Imperf.	2.00	2.00
39	A8	20k bl & car	15	20
40	A11	25k grn & gray vio	15	20
41	A11	35k red brn & grn	10	15
42	A8	50k vio & grn	10	15
43	A14	60k on 1k org (II)	4.00	4.00
43A	A11	70k brn & org	30	35
b.		Imperf.	25	30
44	A9	1r pale brn, dk brn & org	70	75
a.		Imperf.	40	50
45	A12	3½r mar & lt grn	1.50	1.25
a.		Imperf.	75	85
46	A13	5r dk bl, grn & pale bl	75	85
a.		Imperf.	1.25	1.25
47	A12	7r dk grn & pink	1.75	1.75
48	A13	10r scar, yel & gray	1.50	1.50

Wmk. Wavy Lines. (168)

1920 *Imperf.*

Vertically Laid Paper.

60	A13	5r dk bl, grn & pale bl	30.00

Handstamped in Violet — c

Perf. 14, 14½x15, 13½.

Unwmk.

Wove Paper.

62	A14	2k green	8.00	8.00
a.		Imperf.	50	50
63	A14	3k red	5.00	4.50
a.		Imperf.	25	25
64	A15	4k carmine	60	60
65	A14	5k claret	60	60
a.		Imperf.	1.00	1.00
67	A15	10k dk bl	1.50	1.25
68	A14	10k on 7k lt bl	1.50	1.00
69	A11	15k red brn & bl	50	50
70	A8	20k bl & car	60	60
71	A11	25k grn & gray vio	50	50
72	A11	35k red brn & grn	40	40
73	A8	50k vio & grn	30	30
74	A14	60k on 1k org (II)	4.00	3.00
a.		Imperf. (I)	2.50	2.50
b.		Imperf. (II)	3.00	3.00
75	A9	1r pale brn, dk brn & org	1.00	1.00
a.		Imperf.	75	75
76	A12	3½r mar & lt grn	1.50	1.50
a.		Imperf.	1.00	1.00
77	A13	5r dk bl, grn & pale bl	3.00	3.00
a.		Imperf.	1.50	1.50
78	A12	7r dk grn & pink	3.00	2.50
79	A13	10r scar, yel & gray	3.00	2.50

Imperf

85	A11	70k brn & org	3.00	3.00

Handstamped in Black.

Perf. 14, 14½x15, 13½.

90	A14	1k orange	7.50	6.50
a.		Imperf.	9.00	9.00
91	A14	2k green	6.00	5.00
a.		Imperf.	10	10
92	A14	3k red	6.00	5.00
a.		Imperf.	25	25
93	A15	4k carmine	20	20
94	A14	5k claret	10	10
a.		Imperf.	1.00	1.00
95	A14	7k lt bl	7.00	6.00
96	A15	10k dk bl	1.50	1.25
97	A14	10k on 7k lt bl	20	10
98	A11	15k red brn & bl	20	12
99	A8	20k bl & car	20	12
100	A11	25k grn & gray vio	40	25
101	A11	35k red brn & grn	20	15
102	A8	50k vio & grn	20	12
102A	A14	60k on 1k org (II)	4.00	2.00
b.		Imperf. (I)	40	40
c.		Imperf. (II)	60	60
103	A9	1r pale brn, dk brn & org	50	50
a.		Imperf.	35	35
104	A12	3½r mar & lt grn	75	75
a.		Imperf.	50	50
105	A13	5r dk bl, grn & pale bl	1.00	1.00
a.		Imperf.	1.25	1.25
106	A12	7r dk grn & pink	1.00	1.00
107	A13	10r scar, yel & gray	1.00	1.00

Imperf

113	A11	70k brn & org	40	40

Handstamped in Violet or Black:

f g

Violet Surcharge.

1920 *Perf. 14, 14½x15*

120	A14 (f)	3r on 3k red	4.00	4.00
a.		Imperf.	1.25	1.25
121	A14 (f)	5r on 3k red	6.00	5.00
122	A15 (f)	5r on 4k car	4.00	3.50
123	A14 (f)	5r on 5k cl	4.00	3.00
a.		Imperf.	2.50	2.50
124	A15 (f)	5r on 10k dk bl	4.00	3.50
125	A14 (f)	5r on 10k on 7k lt bl	4.00	3.00
126	A8 (f)	5r on 20k bl & car		

Imperf

127	A14 (f)	5r on 2k grn	12.50	12.50
128	A11 (f)	5r on 35k red brn & grn	12.50	12.50

Black Surcharge.

Perf. 14 to 15 and Compound, 13½

130	A14 (g)	1r on 1k org	15	15
a.		Imperf.	25	25
131	A14 (f)	3r on 3k red	15	8
a.		Imperf.	8	8
132	A15 (f)	3r on 4k car	5.00	5.00
133	A14 (f)	5r on 2k grn	1.00	1.00
a.		Imperf.	15	12
134	A14 (f)	5r on 3k red	2.50	2.50
a.		Imperf.	2.50	2.50
135	A15 (f)	5r on 4k car	60	60
a.		Imperf.	7.50	7.50
136	A14 (f)	5r on 5k cl	12	12
a.		Imperf.	25	25
137	A14 (f)	5r on 7k lt bl	1.00	1.00
138	A15 (f)	5r on 10k dk bl	12	12
139	A14 (f)	5r on 10k on 7k lt bl	12	12
140	A11 (f)	5r on 14k bl & rose	3.50	3.50

141 A11 (f) 5r on 15k red brn & bl 20 20
a. Imperf. 4.00 4.00
142 A8 (f) 5r on 20k bl & car 20 20
a. Imperf. 4.00 4.00
143 A11 (f) 5r on 20k on 14k bl & rose 5.00 5.00
144 A11 (f) 5r on 25k grn & gray vio 5.00 5.00
145 A14 (g) 10r on 1k org *175.00* *175.00*
a. Imperf. 1.25 1.25
146 A14 (g) 10r on 3k red *90.00* *90.00*
147 A14 (g) 10r on 5k cl 6.00 6.00
a. Imperf. 8.00
148 A8 (f) 10r on 20k bl & car 6.00 6.00
148A A11 (f) 10r on 25k grn & gray vio 2.50 2.50
149 A11 (g) 10r on 25k grn & gray vio 2.00 2.00
a. Imperf. 12.00 12.00
150 A11 (g) 10r on 35k red brn & grn 25 25
151 A8 (f) 10r on 50k brn vio & grn 2.50 2.50
152 A8 (g) 10r on 50k brn vio & grn 65 65
152A A11 (g) 10r on 70k brn & org *100.00* *100.00*
b. Imperf. 4.50 4.50
152C A8 (g) 25r on 20k bl & car 1.50 1.50
153 A11 (g) 25r on 25k grn & gray vio 1.25 1.25
154 A11 (g) 25r on 35k red brn & grn 1.25 1.25
a. Imperf. 6.00 6.00
155 A8 (g) 25r on 50k vio & grn 1.75 1.75
a. Imperf. 3.00 3.00
156 A11 (g) 25r on 70k brn & org 3.00 3.00
a. Imperf. 3.00 3.00
157 A9 (g) 50r on 1r pale brn, dk brn & org 2.00 2.00
a. Imperf. 50 50
158 A13 (g) 50r on 5r dk bl, grn & lt bl 4.00 4.00
a. Imperf. 4.00 4.00
159 A12 (g) 100r on 3½r mar & lt grn 3.50 3.50
a. Imperf. 3.50 3.50
160 A13 (g) 100r on 5r dk bl, grn & pale bl 3.50 3.50
a. Imperf. 3.50 3.50
161 A12 (g) 100r on 7r dk grn & pink 4.00 4.00
a. Imperf. 16.00 16.00
162 A13 (g) 100r on 10r scar, yel & gray 3.50 3.50

Wmk. Wavy Lines. (168)
Perf. 11½.
Vertically Laid Paper.

163 A12 (g) 100r on 3½r blk & gray 15.00 15.00
164 A12 (g) 100r on 7r blk & yel 12.50 12.50

1920 Unwmk. *Imperf.*
Wove Paper.

166 A14 (g) 1r on 60k on 1k org (I) 4.00 4.00
168 A14 (f) 5r on 1k org 12.50 12.50
173 A11 (f) 5r on 35k red brn & grn 4.00 4.00
177 A11 (g) 50r on 70k brn & org 4.00 4.00
179 A12 (g) 50r on 3½r mar & lt grn 3.00 3.00
181 A9 (g) 100r on 1r pale brn, dk brn & org 6.00 6.00

Romanov Issues Surcharged Types "f" or "g".
On Stamps of 1913.

1920 ***Perf. 13½***

184 A16 (g) 1r on 1k brn org 4.00 4.00
185 A18 (f) 3r on 3k rose red 3.50 3.50
186 A19 (f) 5r on 4k dl red 3.50 3.50
187 A22 (f) 5r on 14k bl grn 20.00 20.00
187A A19 (g) 10r on 4k dl red 22.50
187B A26 (g) 10r on 35k gray vio & dk grn
187C A19 (g) 25r on 4k dl red 4.50 4.50
188 A26 (g) 25r on 35k gray vio & dk grn 4.50 4.50
189 A28 (g) 25r on 70k yel grn & brn 4.50 4.50
190 A31 (f) 50r on 3r dk vio 3.50 3.50
190A A16 (g) 100r on 1k brn org 75.00 75.00
190B A17 (g) 100r on 2k grn 75.00 75.00
191 A30 (g) 100r on 2r brn 17.50 17.50
192 A31 (g) 100r on 3r dk vio 17.50 17.50

On Stamps of 1915.
Thin Cardboard.
Inscriptions on Back.
Perf. 12.

193 A21 (g) 100r on 10k bl 5.00
194 A23 (g) 100r on 15k brn 5.00
195 A24 (g) 100r on 20k ol grn 5.00

On Stamps of 1916.
Perf. 13½.

196 A20 (f) 5r on 10k on 7k brn 3.50 3.50
197 A22 (f) 5r on 20k on 14k bl grn 5.50 5.50

Surcharged Type "f" or "g" over type "c", Type "c" in Violet.
Perf. 14, 14½x15, 13½.

200 A15 (f) 5r on 4k car 1.75 1.75
201 A15 (f) 5r on 10k dk bl 1.75 1.75
202 A11 (f) 5r on 15k red brn & bl 3.50 3.50
203 A8 (f) 5r on 20k bl & car 3.00 3.00
204 A11 (g) 10r on 25k grn & gray vio 3.00 3.00
205 A11 (g) 10r on 35k red brn & grn 5.00 5.00
205A A8 (g) 10r on 50k brn vio & grn 6.00 6.00
206 A8 (f) 25r on 50k brn vio & grn *75.00* *75.00*
207 A49 (g) 50r on 1r pale brn, dk brn & org 50.00 50.00
a. Imperf. 6.00 6.00
207B A12 (g) 100r on 3½r mar & lt grn 15.00
207C A12 (g) 100r on 7r dk grn & pink 15.00

Imperf

208 A14 (f) 5r on 2k grn 9.00 9.00
209 A14 (f) 5r on 5k cl 2.50 2.50
210 A11 (g) 25r on 70k brn & org 9.00 9.00
211 A13 (g) 100r on 5r dk bl, grn & pale bl 1.25 1.25

Type "c" in Black.
Perf. 14, 14½x15, 13½.

212 A14 (f) 5r on 7k lt bl *100.00* *100.00*
213 A14 (f) 5r on 10k on 7k lt bl 1.75 1.75
214 A11 (g) 5r on 15k red brn & bl 70 70
215 A8 (f) 5r on 20k bl & car 50 50
215A A11 (g) 10r on 5r on 25k grn & gray vio 7.50 7.50
216 A11 (g) 10r on 35k red brn & grn 75 75
217 A8 (g) 10r on 50k brn vio & grn 1.25 1.25
217A A9 (g) 50r on 1r pale brn, dk brn & org 1.50 1.50
a. Imperf. 1.75 1.75
217C A12 (g) 100r on 3½r mar & lt grn 2.50 2.50
218 A13 (g) 100r on 5r dk bl, grn & pale bl 3.50 3.50
a. Imperf. 3.00 3.00
219 A12 (f) 100r on 7r dk grn & pink 5.00 5.00
219A A13 (f) 100r on 10r scar, yel & gray 5.00 5.00

Imperf

220 A14 (g) 1r on 60k on 1k org (I) 8.00 8.00
221 A14 (f) 5r on 2k grn 1.00 1.00
222 A14 (f) 5r on 5k cl 5.00 5.00
223 A11 (g) 10r on 70k brn & org 3.50 3.50
224 A11 (g) 25r on 70k brn & org 3.00 3.00

Surcharged Type "f" or "g" over type "a".
Type "a" in Violet.
Imperf

231 A9 (g) 50r on 1r pale brn, dk brn & org *60.00* *60.00*
232 A13 (g) 100r on 5r dk bl, grn & pale bl 17.50

Type "a" in Black.
Perf. 14, 14½x15, 13½.

233 A8 (f) 5r on 20k bl & car 1.00 1.00
233A A11 (g) 10r on 25k grn & gray vio *75.00* *75.00*
234 A11 (g) 10r on 35k red brn & grn 1.25 1.25
235 A12 (g) 100r on 3½r mar & lt grn 2.00 2.00
a. Imperf. 2.50 2.50

Imperf

237 A14 (g) 5r on 2k grn 50.00 50.00
237A A11 (g) 10r on 70k brn & org

Surcharged Type "a" and New Value.
Type "a" in Violet.
Perf. 14, 14½x15.

238 A11 10r on 15k red brn & bl 1.00 1.00

Type "a" in Black.

239 A8 5r on 20k bl & car 1.75 1.75
239A A8 10r on 20k bl & car 5.00 5.00
239B A8 10r on 50k brn red & grn 10.00

Imperf

240 A12 100r on 3½r mar & lt grn 3.00 3.00

Surcharged Type "c" and New Value.
Type "c" in Black.

1920 ***Perf. 14, 14½x15, 13½***

241 A15 5r on 4k red 3.00 3.00
242 A11 5r on 15k red brn & bl 1.75 1.75
243 A8 10r on 20k bl & car 3.00 3.00
243A A11 10r on 25k grn & gray vio 1.25 1.25
244 A11 10r on 35k red brn & grn 1.00 1.00
a. With additional surcharge "5r" 2.00 2.00
245 A12 100r on 3½r mar & lt grn 2.00 2.00

Imperf

247 A14 3r on 3k red 8.00 8.00
248 A14 5r on 2k grn 50 50
249 A9 50r on 1r pale brn, dk brn & org 1.50 1.50

Type "c" in Violet.

249A A14 5r on 2k grn 10.00

Postal Savings Stamps Surcharged.

A1

A2

A3

Wmk.171

Wmk. Diamonds. (171)
Perf. 14½x15.

250 A1 60k on 1k red & buff 17.50 17.50
251 A2 1r on 1k red & buff 8.50 8.50
252 A3 5r on 5k grn & buff 12.00 12.00
253 A3 5r on 10k brn & buff 12.00 12.00

Russian Semi-Postal Stamps of 1914-18 Surcharged with Armenian Monogram and New Values like Regular Issues.
On Stamps of 1914.
Perf. 11½, 12½, 13½.
Unwmk.

225 SP5 25r on 1k red brn & dk grn *straw* 70.00 75.00
256 SP6 25r on 3k mar & gray grn, *pink* 50.00 60.00
257 SP7 50r on 7 dk brn & dk grn, *buff* 14.00 15.00
258 SP5 100r on 1k red brn & dk grn, *straw* 5.50 6.00
259 SP6 100r on 3k mar & gray grn, *pink* 5.50 6.00
260 SP7 100r on 7k dk brn & dk grn, *buff* 5.50 6.00

On Stamps of 1915-19.

261 SP5 25r on 1k org brn & gray 60.00 80.00
262 SP6 25r on 3k car & gray 50.00 50.00
263 SP8 50r on 10k dk bl & brn 17.50 20.00
264 SP5 100r on 1k org brn & gray 5.50 6.00
265 SP8 100r on 10k dk bl & brn 5.50 6.00

These surcharged semi-postal stamps were used for ordinary postage.

A set of 10 stamps in the above designs, and in a third design showing a woman quilling, was prepared in 1920, but not issued. Price of set, $4. Exist with "SPECIMEN" overprint and imperf. Counterfeits exist.

Armenia stamps can be mounted in Scott's Soviet Republics Part I Album.

Soviet Socialist Republic.

Hammer and Sickle — A7

Mythological Monster — A8

Symbols of Soviet Republics on Designs from old Armenian Manuscripts A9

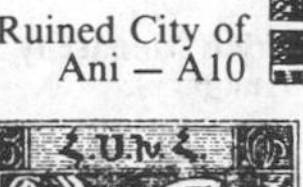

Ruined City of Ani — A10

Mythological Monster — A11

Armenian Soldier — A12

Mythological Monster — A13

Soviet Symbols, Armenian Designs — A14

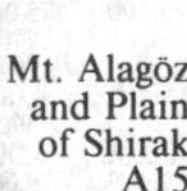

Mt. Alagöz and Plain of Shirak A15

Fisherman on River Aras — A16

Post Office in Erevan and Mt. Ararat A17

Armenia stamps can be mounted in Scott's Soviet Republics Part I Album.

Ruin in City of Ani — A18

Street in Erevan — A19

Lake Gökcha and Sevan Monastery — A20

Mythological Subject from old Armenian Monument — A21

Mt. Ararat A22

1921 Unwmk. *Perf. 11½, Imperf.*

278	A7	1r	gray grn	20	
279	A8	2r	sl gray	20	
280	A9	3r	carmine	20	
281	A10	5r	dk brn	20	
282	A11	25r	gray	20	15
283	A12	50r	red	10	
284	A13	100r	orange	10	
285	A14	250r	dk bl	10	
286	A15	500r	brn vio	10	
287	A16	1000r	sea grn	20	
288	A17	2000r	bister	25	
289	A18	5000r	dk brn	25	
290	A19	10,000r	dl red	25	
291	A20	15,000r	sl bl	25	
292	A21	20,000r	lake	25	
293	A22	25,000r	gray bl	50	
294	A22	25,000r	brn ol	4.00	
		Nos. 278-294 (17)		7.35	

Except the 25r, Nos. 278-294 were not regularly issued and used. Counterfeits exist.

Russian Stamps of 1909-17 Surcharged

Wove Paper
Lozenges of Varnish on Face

1921, August *Perf. 13½*

295	A9	5000r on 1r pale brn, dk brn & org	3.50	
296	A12	5000r on 3½r mar & lt grn	3.50	
297	A13	5000r on 5r dk bl, grn & pale bl	3.50	
298	A12	5000r on 7r dk grn & pink	3.50	
299	A13	5000r on 10r scar, yel & gray	3.50	
		Nos. 295-299 (5)	17.50	

Nos. 295-299 were not officially issued. Counterfeits abound.

Mt. Ararat and Soviet Star
A23 A24

Soviet Symbols — A25

Crane — A26

Peasant — A27

Harpy — A28

Peasant Sowing — A29

Soviet Symbols — A30

Forging — A31

Plowing A32

1922 *Perf. 11½.*

300	A23	50r	grn & red	20
301	A24	300r	sl bl & buff	25
302	A25	400r	bl & pink	25
303	A26	500r	vio & pale lil	25
304	A27	1000r	dl bl & pale bl	25
305	A28	2000r	blk & gray	40
306	A29	3000r	blk & grn	40
307	A30	4000r	blk & lt brn	40
308	A31	5000r	blk & dl red	30
309	A32	10,000r	blk & pale rose	30
a.		Tete beche pair		15.00
		Nos. 300-309 (10)		3.00

Nos. 300 to 309 were not placed in use without surcharge.

Stamps of types A23 to A32, printed in other colors than Nos. 300 to 309, are essays.

Stamps of Preceding Issue with Handstamped Surcharge of New Values in Rose, Violet or Black

1922-23

310	A23	10,000 on 50r grn & red (R)	8.00	8.00
311	A23	10,000 on 50r grn & red (V)	2.50	2.50
312	A23	10,000 on 50r grn & red (Bk)	75	75
313	A24	15,000 on 300r sl bl & buff (R)	12.00	12.00
314	A24	15,000 on 300r sl bl & buff (V)	2.50	2.50
315	A24	15,000 on 300r sl bl & buff (Bk)	1.25	1.25
316	A25	25,000 on 400r bl & pink (V)	2.50	2.50
317	A25	25,000 on 400r bl & pink (Bk)	50	50
318	A26	30,000 on 500r vio & pale lil (R)	15.00	15.00
319	A26	30,000 on 500r vio & pale lil (V)	1.25	1.25
320	A26	30,000 on 500r vio & pale lil (Bk)	75	75
321	A27	50,000 on 1000r dl bl & pale bl (R)	12.00	12.00
322	A27	50,000 on 1000r dl bl & pale bl (V)	5.00	5.00
323	A27	50,000 on 1000r dl bl & pale bl (Bk)	1.25	1.25
324	A29	75,000 on 3000r blk & grn (Bk)	1.50	1.50
325	A28	100,000 on 2000r blk & gray (R)	16.00	16.00
326	A28	100,000 on 2000r blk & gray (V)	5.00	5.00
327	A28	100,000 on 2000r blk & gray (Bk)	1.25	1.25
328	A30	200,000 on 4000r blk & lt brn (V)	1.25	1.25
329	A30	200,000 on 4000r blk & lt brn (Bk)	1.25	1.25
330	A31	300,000 on 5000r blk & dl red (V)	8.50	8.50
331	A31	300,000 on 5000r blk & dl red (Bk)	1.00	1.00
332	A32	500,000 on 10,000r blk & pale rose (V)	5.00	5.00
333	A32	500,000 on 10,000r blk & pale rose (Bk)	1.00	1.00
		Nos. 310-333 (24)	107.00	107.00

Goose — A33

Armenian Village Scene A34

Armenian Woman at Well — A35

Mt. Ararat — A36

Mt. Ararat
A37

New Values in Gold Kopecks, Handstamped Surcharge in Black.

1922 *Imperf.*

334 A33 1(k) on 250r rose 3.00 3.00
335 A33 1(k) on 250r gray 6.00 6.00
336 A34 2(k) on 500r rose 2.50 2.50
337 A34 3(k) on 500r gray 2.00 2.00
338 A35 4(k) on 1000r rose 2.00 2.00
339 A35 4(k) on 1000r gray 3.50 3.50
340 A36 5(k) on 2000r gray 2.00 2.00
341 A36 10(k) on 2000r rose 2.00 2.00
342 A37 15(k) on 5000r rose 12.00 12.00
343 A37 20(k) on 5000r gray 2.00 2.00
Nos. 334-343 (10) 37.00 37.00

Nos. 334-343 were issued for postal tax purposes.

Nos. 334-343 exist without surcharge but are not known to have been issued in that condition. Counterfeits exist of both sets.

Regular Issue of 1921 Handstamped with New Values in Black or Red. Short, Thick Numerals.

1922-23 *Imperf.*

347 A8 2(k) on 2r sl gray (R) 17.50 17.50
350 A11 4(k) on 25r gray (R) 6.00 6.00
353 A13 10(k) on 100r org (R) 12.50 12.50
354 A14 15(k) on 250r dk bl 1.00 1.00
355 A15 20(k) on 500r brn vio 1.50 1.50
a. With "k" written in red 2.00 2.00
357 A22 50(k) on 25,000r bl (R) 20.00 20.00
358 A22 50(k) on 25,000r brn ol (R) 15.00 15.00
359 A22 50(k) on 25,000r brn ol
Nos. 347-358 (7) 73.50 73.50

Perf. 11½.

360 A7 1(k) on 1r gray grn 10.00 10.00
a. Imperf. 3.00 3.00
361 A7 1(k) on 1r gray grn (R) 6.00 6.00
a. Imperf. 10.00 10.00
362 A8 2(k) on 2r sl gray 15.00 15.00
a. Imperf. 6.00 6.00
363 A15 2(k) on 500r brn vio 3.50 3.50
a. Imperf. 3.00 3.00
364 A15 2(k) on 500r brn vio (R) 15.00 15.00
365 A11 4(k) on 25r gray 12.00 12.00
a. Imperf. 6.00 6.00
366 A12 5(k) on 50r red 4.00 4.00
a. Imperf. 3.00 3.00
367 A13 10(k) on 100r org 3.50 3.50
a. Imperf. 3.50 3.50
368 A21 35(k) on 20,000r cl 15.00 15.00
a. With "k" written in vio 15.00 15.00
b. Imperf. 6.00 6.00
c. As "a," imperf. 6.00 6.00
d. With "kop" written in vio, imperf.
Nos. 360-368 (9) 84.00 84.00

Manuscript Surcharge in Red.

Perf. 11½.

371 A14 1k on 250r dk bl 4.00 4.00

Handstamped in Black or Red.

Tall, Thin Numerals.

Imperf

377 A11 4(k) on 25r gray (R) 7.00 7.00
379 A13 10(k) on 100r org 4.00 4.00
380 A15 20(k) on 500r brn vio 10.00 10.00
381 A22 50k on 25,000r bl 1.50 1.50
a. Surcharged "50" only 25.00 25.00
382 A22 50k on 25,000r bl (R) 20.00 20.00
382A A22 50k on 25,000r brn ol 40.00 40.00
Nos. 377-382A (6) 82.50 82.50

On Nos. 381, 382 and 382A the letter "k" forms part of the surcharge.

Perf. 11½.

383 A7 1(k) on 1r gray grn (R) 5.00 5.00
a. Imperf.
384 A14 1(k) on 250r dk bl 3.00 3.00
385 A15 2(k) on 500r brn vio 3.75 3.75
a. Imperf. 4.00 4.00
386 A15 2(k) on 500r brn vio (R) 8.00 8.00
387 A9 3(k) on 3r rose 10.00 10.00
a. Imperf. 10.00 10.00
388 A21 3(k) on 20,000r cl 30.00 30.00
a. Imperf. 5.00 5.00
389 A11 4(k) on 25r gray 4.00 4.00
a. Imperf. 7.00 7.00
390 A12 5(k) on 50r red 3.00 3.00
a. Imperf. 2.00 2.00
Nos. 383-390 (8) 66.75 66.75

ARUBA

Traditional House — A1

1986-87 **Litho.** ***Perf. 14x13***

1 A1 5c shown 5 5
3 A1 15c King William III Tower 12 12
4 A1 20c Loading crane 18 18
4A A1 25c Lighthouse 30 30
5 A1 30c Snake 22 22
6 A1 35c Owl 26 26
7 A1 45c Shell 38 38
8 A1 55c Frog 68 68
9 A1 60c Water skier 45 45
10 A1 65c Net fishing 48 48
12 A1 75c Music box 65 65
13 A1 85c Pre-Columbian bisque pot 1.05 1.05
13A A1 90c Bulb cactus 1.10 1.10
14 A1 100c Grain 85 85
15 A1 150c Watapana tree 1.15 1.15
16 A1 250c Aloe plant 1.85 1.85
Nos. 1-16 (16) 9.77 9.77

Issue dates: 5c, 30c, 60c, 150c, Jan. 1. 15c, 35c, 65c, 250c, Feb. 5. 20c, 45c, 75c, 100c, Apr. 7, 1987. 25c, 55c, 85c, 90c, July 17, 1987.

Independence A2

1986, Jan. 1 ***Perf. 14x13, 13x14***

18 A2 25c Map 20 20
19 A2 45c Coat of arms, vert. 35 35
20 A2 55c Natl. anthem, vert. 42 42
21 A2 100c Flag 75 75

Intl. Peace Year — A3

1986, Aug. 29 ***Perf. 14x13***

22 A3 60c shown 45 45
23 A3 100c Barbed wire 75 75

Princess Juliana and Prince Bernhard, 50th Wedding Anniv. — A4

State Visit of Queen Beatrix and Prince Claus of the Netherlands A5

1987, Jan. 7 **Photo.** ***Perf. 13x14***

24 A4 135c multi 1.25 1.25

1987, Feb. 16 ***Perf. 14x13***

25 A5 55c shown 48 48
26 A5 60c Prince William-Alexander 50 50

Tourism — A6

1987, June 25 **Litho.**

27 A6 60c Beach and sea 90 90
28 A6 100c Rock and cacti 1.50 1.50

SEMI-POSTAL STAMPS

Solidarity SP1

1986, May 7 **Litho.** ***Perf. 14x13***

B1 SP1 30c + 10c shown 30 30
B2 SP1 35c + 15c Three ropes 38 38
B3 SP1 60c + 25c One rope 65 65

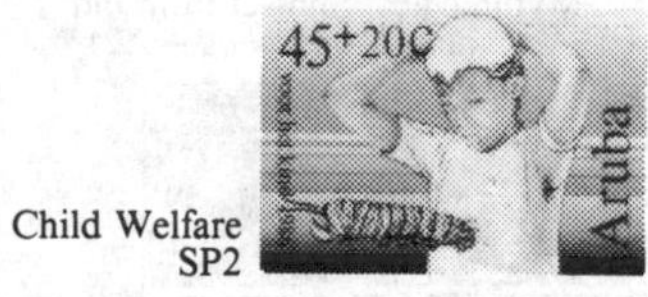

Child Welfare SP2

1986, Oct. 29 **Litho.** ***Perf. 14x13***

B4 SP2 45c + 20c Boy, caterpillar 55 55
B5 SP2 70c + 25c Boy, cocoon 80 80
B6 SP2 100c + 40c Girl, butterfly 1.20 1.20

Christmas SP3

1987, Oct. 27 **Litho.** ***Perf. 14x13***

B7 SP3 25c +10c Boy on beach 42 42
B8 SP3 45c +20c Drawing Christmas tree 80 80
B9 SP3 70c +30c Child, creche figures 1.25 1.25

Surtax for the benefit of child welfare organizations.

AUSTRIA

LOCATION — Central Europe
GOVT. — Republic
AREA — 32,376 sq. mi.
POP. — 7,555,338 (1981)
CAPITAL — Vienna

Before 1867 Austria was an absolute monarchy, which included Hungary and Lombardy-Venetia. In 1867 the Astro-Hungarian Monarchy was established, with Austria and Hungary as equal partners. After World War I, in 1918, the different nationalities established their own states and only the German-speaking parts remained, forming a republic under the name "Deutschosterreich" (German Austria), which name was shortly again changed to "Austria." In 1938 German forces occupied Austria, which became part of the German Reich. After the liberation by Allied troops in 1945, an independent republic was re-established.

60 Kreuzer = 1 Gulden
100 Neu-Kreuzer = 1 Gulden (1858)
100 Heller = 1 Krone (1899)
100 Groschen = 1 Schilling (1925)

Prices of early Austrian stamps vary according to condition. Quotations for Nos. 1-5, P1-P7 and PR1-PR4 are for fine copies. Very fine to superb specimens sell at much higher prices, and inferior or poor copies sell at reduced prices, depending on the condition of the individual specimen.

Prices for unused stamps of 1850-80 issues are for copies in fine condition with original gum. Specimens without gum sell for about one-third of the figures quoted.

Issues of the Austrian Monarchy (including Hungary).

Coat of Arms — A1

Wmk. K. K. H. M. in Sheet or Unwmk.

1850 **Typo.** ***Imperf.***

Thin to Thick Paper.

The stamps of this issue were at first printed on a rough hand-made paper, varying in thickness and having a watermark in script letters K. K. H. M., the initials of Kaiserlich Königliches Handels-Ministerium (Imperial and Royal Ministry of Commerce), vertically in the gutter between the panes. Parts of these letters show on margin stamps in the sheet. From 1854 a thick, smooth machine-made paper without watermark was used. NINE KREUZER.

Type I. The top of "9" is about on a level with "Kreuzer" and not near the top of the label.

Type IA. Similar to type I but with 1¼mm. instead of ½mm. space between "9" and "Kreuzer."

Type II. The top of "9" is much higher than the top of the word "Kreuzer" and nearly touches the top of the label.

1 A1 1kr yellow 850.00 70.00
a. Printed on both sides *1,750.* 160.00
b. 1kr org *1,400.* 65.00
c. 1kr brn org *2,500.* 400.00
2 A1 2kr black 950.00 65.00
a. Ribbed paper *1,750.*
b. 2kr gray blk *1,300.* 80.00
3 A1 3kr red 400.00 3.00
a. Ribbed paper *2,000.* 75.00
b. Laid paper *10,000.*
c. Printed on both sides *10,000.*
4 A1 6kr brown 450.00 4.00
a. Ribbed paper *1,500.*
5 A1 9kr bl, type II 900.00 4.00
a. 9kr bl, type I *1,600.* 9.00
b. 9kr bl, type IA *1,350.*
c. Laid paper, type II *10,000.*
d. Printed on both sides, type II *11,000.*

In 1852-54, Nos. 1 to 5, rouletted 14, were used in Tokay. A 12kr blue exists, but was not issued.

The reprints are printed in brighter colors, some on paper watermarked "Briefmarken" in the sheet.

Emperor Franz Josef
A2 A3 A4

A5 A6

1858-59 Embossed *Perf. 14½.*

Two Types of Each Value.

Type I. Loops of the bow at the back of the head broken, except the 2kr. In the 2kr, the "2" has a flat foot, thinning to the right.

Type II. Loops complete. Wreath projects further at top of head. In the 2kr, the "2" has a more curved foot of uniform thickness, with a shading line in the upper and lower curves.

6	A2	2kr yel, type II	550.00	25.00
a.		2kr yel, type I	1,250.	225.00
b.		2kr org, type II	1,250.	225.00
7	A3	3kr blk, type II	1,750.	150.00
a.		3kr blk, type I	750.00	140.00
8	A3	3kr grn, type II ('59)	500.00	87.50
9	A4	5kr red, type II	175.00	90
a.		5kr red, type I	250.00	7.50
10	A5	10kr brn, type II	450.00	2.25
a.		10kr brn, type I	450.00	19.00
11	A6	15kr bl, type II	350.00	1.50
a.		Type I	800.00	12.00

The reprints are of type II and are perforated 10½, 11, 12, 12½ and 13. There are also imperforate reprints of Nos. 6 to 8.

Emperor Franz Josef — A7

Coat of Arms — A8

1860-61 Embossed *Perf. 14*

12	A7	2kr yellow	325.00	17.50
13	A7	3kr green	300.00	12.50
14	A7	5kr red	175.00	90
15	A7	10kr brown	250.00	2.00
16	A7	15kr blue	200.00	1.00

The reprints are perforated 9, 9½, 10, 10½, 11, 11½, 12, 12½, 13 and 13½. There are also imperforate reprints of the 2 and 3kr.

1863

17	A8	2kr yellow	450.00	75.00
18	A8	3kr green	350.00	65.00
19	A8	5kr rose	200.00	5.00
20	A8	10kr blue	700.00	6.00
21	A8	15kr yel brn	800.00	8.50

Wmk.91

Wmk. "BRIEF-MARKEN" in Double-lined Capitals Across the Middle of the Sheet (91), or, before July 1864, Unwmkd.

1863-64 *Perf. 9½*

22	A8	2kr yel ('64)	125.00	7.50
23	A8	3kr grn ('64)	125.00	6.50
24	A8	5kr rose	45.00	25
25	A8	10kr blue	100.00	1.75
26	A8	15kr yel brn	110.00	1.25

The reprints are perforated 10½, 11½, 13 and 13½. There are also imperforate reprints of the 2 and 3kr.

Issues of Austro-Hungarian Monarchy

From 1867 to 1871 the independent postal administrations of Austria and Hungary used the same stamps.

Emperor Franz Josef
A9 A10

5 kr:

Type I. In arabesques in lower left corner, the small ornament at left of the curve nearest the figure "5" is short and has three points at bottom.

Type II. The ornament is prolonged within the curve and has two points at bottom. The corresponding ornament at top of the lower left corner does not touch the curve (1872).

Type III. Similar to type II but the top ornament is joined to the curve (1881). Two different printing methods were used for the 1867-74 issues. The first produced stamps on which the hair and whiskers were coarse and thick, from the second they were fine and clear.

1867-72 Wmk. 91 Typo. *Perf. 9½*

Coarse Print.

27	A9	2kr yellow	110.00	2.00
28	A9	3kr green	110.00	2.25
29	A9	5kr rose, type I	70.00	10
a.		5kr rose, type II	65.00	13
b.		Perf. 10½, type II	125.00	
c.		Cliche of 3kr in plate of 5kr		*30,000.*
30	A9	10kr blue	135.00	2.00
31	A9	15kr brown	150.00	4.50
32	A9	25kr lilac	20.00	15.00
a.		25kr gray lil	20.00	15.00
b.		25kr brn vio	110.00	32.50

Perf. 12.

33	A10	50kr lt brn	30.00	*62.50*
a.		50kr pale red brn	120.00	75.00
b.		50kr brnsh rose	400.00	150.00
c.		Pair, imperf. btwn., vert. or horizontal	500.00	*1,000.*

Issues for Austria only.

1874-80 *Perf. 9½*

Fine Print.

34	A9	2kr yel ('76)	11.00	90
a.		Perf. 9	175.00	22.50
b.		Perf. 10½	45.00	4.25
c.		Perf. 12	250.00	85.00
d.		Perf. 13	190.00	150.00
35	A9	3kr grn ('76)	32.50	1.10
a.		Perf. 9	160.00	20.00
b.		Perf. 10½	45.00	2.50
c.		Perf. 12	190.00	9.00
d.		Perf. 13	150.00	22.50
36	A9	5kr rose, type III	3.00	6
a.		Perf. 9	75.00	3.50
b.		Perf. 10½	11.00	75
c.		Perf. 12	60.00	2.50
d.		Perf. 13	90.00	10.00
37	A9	10kr bl ('75)	75.00	25
a.		Perf. 9	300.00	22.50
b.		Perf. 10½	80.00	2.50
c.		Perf. 12	375.00	100.00
d.		Perf. 13	190.00	80.00
38	A9	15kr brn ('77)	7.00	4.00
a.		Perf. 9	375.00	70.00
b.		Perf. 10½	190.00	20.00
c.		Perf. 12	600.00	110.00
d.		Perf. 13	350.00	200.00
39	A9	25kr gray lil ('78)	2.00	*80.00*
40	A10	50kr brn, perf. 12 ('80)	12.50	*65.00*
a.		Perf. 13	15.00	*75.00*
b.		Perf. 10½x12	300.00	

Various compound perforations exist.

A11

Inscriptions in Black

Perf. 9, 9½, 10, 10½, 11½, 12, 12½

1883

41	A11	2kr brown	6.00	50
42	A11	3kr green	6.00	35
43	A11	5kr rose	10.00	5
a.		Vertical pair, imperf. between	300.00	400.00
44	A11	10kr blue	6.00	40
45	A11	20kr gray	60.00	6.00
46	A11	50kr red lil	350.00	62.50

The last printings of Nos. 41 to 46 are watermarked "ZEITUNGS-MARKEN" instead of "BRIEF-MARKEN."

The 5kr has been reprinted in a dull red rose, perforated 10½.

Emperor Franz Josef
A12 A13

Perf. 9 to 13½, also Compound.

1890-96 Unwmk.

Granite Paper.

Numerals in black, Nos. 51 to 61.

51	A12	1kr dk gray	2.25	10
a.		Pair, imperf. between	300.00	500.00
52	A12	2kr lt brn	40	5
53	A12	3kr gray grn	50	5
a.		Pair, imperf. between	325.00	500.00
54	A12	5kr rose	40	5
a.		Pair, imperf. between	300.00	400.00
55	A12	10kr ultra	70	6
a.		Pair, imperf. between	375.00	550.00
56	A12	12kr claret	2.75	25
57	A12	15kr lilac	1.75	25
a.		Pair, imperf. between	375.00	550.00
58	A12	20kr ol grn	35.00	2.50
59	A12	24kr gray bl	3.50	85
a.		Pair, imperf. between	400.00	550.00
60	A12	30kr dk brn	3.00	40
61	A12	50kr violet	12.50	7.50

Engr.

62	A13	1gld dk bl	2.25	2.75
63	A13	1gld pale lil ('96)	55.00	3.75
64	A13	2gld carmine	5.00	10.00
65	A13	2gld gray grn ('96)	30.00	30.00

Nearly all values of the 1890-1907 issues are found with numerals missing in one or more corners, some with numerals printed on the back.

A14

Perf. 9 to 13½, also Compound.

1891 Typo.

Numerals in black.

66	A14	20kr ol grn	1.50	12
67	A14	24kr gray bl	3.00	60
68	A14	30kr brown	1.50	12
a.		Pair, imperf. between	425.00	600.00
b.		Perf. 9	175.00	35.00
69	A14	50kr violet	2.00	35

A15 A16

A17

A18

Perf. 10½ to 13½ and Compound.

1899

Without Varnish Bars.

Numerals in black, Nos. 70 to 82.

70 A15 1h lilac 1.10 7
b. Imperf. 75.00 100.00
c. Perf. 10½ 20.00 5.50
d. Numerals inverted 550.00 750.00
71 A15 2h dk gray 3.75 25
72 A15 3h bis brn 5.00 6
b. "3" in lower right corner sideways *1,100.*
73 A15 5h bl grn 12.50 5
c. Perf. 10½ 17.50 5.00
74 A15 6h orange 60 5
75 A16 10h rose 8.00 5
b. Perf. 10½ 400.00 100.00
76 A16 20h brown 1.00 10
77 A16 25h ultra 75.00 20
78 A16 30h red vio 27.50 2.75
b. Horizontal pair, imperf. between 375.00
80 A17 40h green 45.00 3.25
81 A17 50h gray bl 32.50 4.25
b. All four "50's" parallel *1,500.*
82 A17 60h brown 55.00 1.25
b. Horizontal pair, imperf. between 375.00
c. Perf. 10½ 65.00 1.50

Engr.

83 A18 1k car rose 3.00 12
a. 1k car 7.50 12
b. Vertical pair, imperf. between 375.00 400.00
84 A18 2k gray lil 70.00 50
a. Vertical pair, imperf. between 500.00 550.00
85 A18 4k gray grn 7.50 7.00

1901

With Varnish Bars.

70a A15 1h lilac 1.75 30
71a A15 2h dk gray 1.75 20
72a A15 3h bis brn 60 5
73a A15 5h bl grn 30 5
74a A15 6h orange 30 5
75a A16 10h rose 40 5
76a A16 20h brown 1.25 6
77a A16 25h ultra 1.50 12
78a A16 30h red vio 1.50 1.00
79 A17 35h green 1.50 25
80a A17 40h green 2.75 5.00
81a A17 50h gray bl 7.00 7.50
82a A17 60h brown 3.50 60
Nos. 70a-78a,79,80a-82a (13) 24.10 15.23

The diagonal yellow bars of varnish were printed across the face to prevent cleaning.

A19

A20

A21

Perf. 12½ to 13½ and Compound.

1905-07 **Typo.**

Colored Numerals.

Without Varnish Bars.

86 A19 1h lilac 18 20
87 A19 2h dk gray 25 10
88 A19 3h bis brn 28 8
89 A19 5h dk bl grn 12.50 8
90 A19 5h yel grn ('06) 50 5
91 A19 6h dp org 50 8
92 A20 10h car ('06) 75 5
93 A20 12h vio ('07) 1.50 50
94 A20 20h brn ('06) 2.75 10
95 A20 25h ultra ('06) 4.00 30
96 A20 30h red vio ('06) 7.50 25

Black Numerals.

97 A20 10h carmine 9.00 8
98 A20 20h brown 50.00 1.25
99 A20 25h ultra 50.00 3.00
100 A20 30h red vio 50.00 3.00

White Numerals.

101 A21 35h green 3.00 30
102 A21 40h dp vio 3.00 1.00
103 A21 50h dl bl 3.75 4.50
104 A21 60h yel brn 3.75 50
105 A21 72h rose 3.75 1.75
Nos. 86-105 (20) 206.96 17.17

1904

With Varnish Bars

86a A19 1h lilac 75 55
87a A19 2h dk gray 2.75 55
88a A19 3h bis brn 2.75 8
89a A19 5h dk bl grn 6.50 12
91a A19 6h dp org 10.00 40
97a A20 10h carmine 3.75 5
98a A20 20h brown 52.50 75
99a A20 25h ultra 60.00 75
100a A20 30h red vio 65.00 1.40
101a A21 35h green 55.00 60
102a A21 40h dp vio 52.50 5.00
103a A21 50h dl bl 50.00 7.50
104a A21 60h yel brn 50.00 1.25
105a A21 72h rose 1.50 90
Nos. 86a-105a (14) 413.00 19.90

Stamps of the 1901, 1904 and 1905 issues perf. 9 or 10½, also compound with 12½, were not sold at any post office, but were supplied only to some high-ranking officials. This applies also to the contemporary issues of Austrian Offices Abroad.

Emperor Karl VI – A22

Emperor Franz Josef – A23

Schönbrunn Castle – A24

Emperor Franz Josef – A25

Designs: 2h, Empress Maria Theresa. 3h, Emperor Joseph II. 5h, 10h, 25h, Emperor Franz Josef. 6h, Emperor Leopold II. 12h, Emperor Franz I. 20h, Emperor Ferdinand I. 30h, Franz Josef as youth. 35h, Franz Josef in middle age. 60h, Franz Josef on horseback. 1k, Franz Josef in royal robes. 5k, Hofburg, Vienna.

1908-13 **Typo.** ***Perf. 12½.***

110 A22 1h gray blk 50 10
111 A22 2h bl vio ('13) 35 10
a. 2h vio 50 8
112 A22 3h magenta 22 10
113 A22 5h yel grn 22 5
a. Booklet pane of 6 30.00
114 A22 6h buff 90 65
a. 6h ocher ('13) 1.75 1.60
b. 6h org brn ('13) 1.75 1.60
115 A22 10h rose 22 5
a. Booklet pane of 6 110.00
116 A22 12h scarlet 1.75 45
117 A22 20h chocolate 2.75 22
118 A22 25h ultra ('13) 1.60 15
a. 25h dp bl 2.75 28
119 A22 30h ol grn 5.50 28
120 A22 35h slate 4.00 28

Engr.

121 A23 50h dk grn 90 28
a. Pair, imperf. btwn., vert. or horizontal 300.00 325.00
122 A23 60h dp car 50 12
a. Pair, imperf. btwn., vert. or horizontal 375.00 400.00
123 A23 72h dk brn ('13) 2.25 28
124 A23 1k purple 16.00 28
a. Pair, imperf. btwn., vert. or horizontal 300.00 325.00
125 A24 2k lake & ol grn 22.50 55
126 A24 5k bis & dk vio 40.00 5.50
127 A25 10k bl, bis & dp brn 225.00 72.50
Nos. 110-127 (18) 325.16 81.94

Issued in commemoration of the 60th year of the reign of Emperor Franz Josef for permanent use.

The 1 to 35h inclusive exist on both ordinary and chalk-surfaced paper.

All values exist imperforate. They were not sold at any post office, but presented to a number of high government officials. This applies also to all imperforate stamps of later issues, including semi-postals, etc., and those of the Austrian Offices Abroad.

Forgeries of No. 127 exist.

Birthday Jubilee Issue.

Similar to 1908 Issue, but designs enlarged by labels at top and bottom bearing dates "1830" and "1910".

1910 **Typo.**

128 A22 1h gray blk 4.25 3.75
129 A22 2h violet 5.25 5.75
130 A22 3h magenta 5.25 5.75
131 A22 5h yel grn 22 22
132 A22 6h buff 2.25 1.90
133 A22 10h rose 22 22
134 A22 12h scarlet 3.00 3.00
135 A22 20h chocolate 4.25 4.75
136 A22 25h dp bl 90 90
137 A22 30h ol grn 4.25 4.50
138 A22 35h slate 4.25 4.50

Engr.

139 A23 50h dk grn 4.50 5.75
140 A23 60h dp car 4.50 5.75
141 A23 1k purple 4.75 7.75
142 A24 2k lake & ol grn 125.00 140.00
143 A24 5k bis & dk vio 100.00 150.00
144 A25 10k bl, bis & dp brn 200.00 225.00
Nos. 128-144 (17) 472.84 569.49

Issued in celebration of the eightieth birthday of Emperor Franz Josef.

All values exist imperforate.

Forgeries of Nos. 142 to 144 exist.

Austrian Crown – A37

Emperor Franz Josef – A38

Coat of Arms
A39 A40

1916-18 **Typo.**

145 A37 3h brt vio 5 5
146 A37 5h lt grn 5 5
a. Bklt. pane of 6 20.00
b. Booklet pane of 4 + 2 labels 35.00
147 A37 6h dp org 28 65
148 A37 10h magenta 5 5
a. Bklt. pane of 6 35.00
149 A37 12h lt bl 45 1.40
150 A38 15h rose red 60 5
a. Booklet pane of 6 20.00
151 A38 20h chocolate 5.25 12
152 A38 25h blue 8.00 65
153 A38 30h slate 7.25 90
154 A39 40h ol grn 18 5
155 A39 50h bl grn 28 5
156 A39 60h dp bl 22 5
157 A39 80h org brn 18 5
158 A39 90h red vio 18 6
159 A39 1k car, *yel* ('18) 45 8

Engr.

160 A40 2k dk bl 65 22
161 A40 3k claret 7.50 1.10
162 A40 4k dp grn 1.40 2.25
163 A40 10k dp vio 27.50 42.50
Nos. 145-163 (19) 60.52 50.33

Stamps of type A38 have two varieties of the frame. Stamps of type A40 have various decorations about the shield.

Nos. 145-163 exist imperf. Price, set $425.

1917

Ordinary Paper

164 A40 2k lt bl 90 45
165 A40 3k car rose 11.00 90
166 A40 4k yel grn 1.40 1.40
167 A40 10k violet 125.00 65.00

Nos. 164-167 exist imperf. Price, set $325.

See Nos. 172-175 (granite paper).

Emperor Karl I — A42

1917-18 **Typo.**

168 A42 15h dl red 5 5
a. Booklet pane of 6 20.00
169 A42 20h dk grn ('18) 8 5
a. 20h grn ('17) 75 8
170 A42 25h blue 20 5
171 A42 30h dl vio 15 5

Nos. 168-171 exist imperf. Price, set $50.

1918-19 **Engr.**

Granite Paper.

172 A40 2k lt bl 12 65
a. Perf. 11½ 550.00 450.00
173 A40 3k car rose 30 1.50
174 A40 4k yel grn ('19) 5.25 13.00
175 A40 10k dp vio ('19) 6.25 11.00

Issues of the Republic.

Austrian Stamps of 1916-18 Overprinted

1918-19 **Unwmk.** ***Perf. 12½.***

181 A37 3h brt vio 5 5
182 A37 5h lt grn 5 5
183 A37 6h dp org 8 32
184 A37 10h magenta 5 5
185 A37 12h lt bl 15 55
186 A42 15h dl red 8 55
187 A42 20h dp grn 6 5
188 A42 25h blue 15 8
189 A42 30h dl vio 10 8
190 A39 40h ol grn 10 12
191 A39 50h dp grn 45 55
192 A39 60h dp bl 35 55
193 A39 80h org brn 8 15
a. Inverted overprint 275.00 275.00
194 A39 90h red vio 12 15
195 A39 1k car, *yel* 15 15

Granite Paper.

196 A40 2k lt bl 8 8
a. Pair, imperf. between 275.00 275.00
b. Perf. 11½ 11.00 6.75
197 A40 3k car rose 18 50
198 A40 4k yel grn 1.40 1.75
a. Perf. 11½ 15.00 13.00
199 A40 10k dp vio 10.50 13.00
Nos. 181-199 (19) 14.18 18.78

Nos. 181, 182, 184, 187 to 191, 194, 197 and 199 exist imperforate.

Post Horn A43

Coat of Arms A44

Allegory of New Republic — A45

1919-20 **Typo.** ***Perf. 12½.***

Ordinary Paper.

200 A43 3h gray 5 12
201 A44 5h yel grn 5 5
202 A44 5h gray ('20) 5 5
203 A43 6h orange 10 32
204 A44 10h dp rose 5 5
205 A44 10h red ('20) 5 5
a. Thick grysh paper ('20) 5 5
206 A43 12h grnsh bl 6 40
207 A43 15h bis ('20) 22 65
a. Thick grysh paper ('20) 5 5
208 A45 20h dk grn 5 5
a. 20h yel grn 5 5
b. As "a," thick grysh paper ('20) 45 1.25
209 A44 25h blue 5 5
210 A43 25h vio ('20) 5 5
211 A45 30h dk brn 5 5
212 A45 40h violet 5 12
213 A45 40h lake ('20) 5 5
214 A44 45h ol grn 18 45
215 A45 50h dk bl 6 5
a. Thick grysh paper ('20) 8 15
216 A43 60h ol grn ('20) 5 8
217 A44 1k car, *yel* 5 8
218 A44 1k lt bl ('20) 5 6
Nos. 200-218 (19) 1.32 2.78

All values exist imperf. (For regularly issued imperfs, see Nos. 227-235).

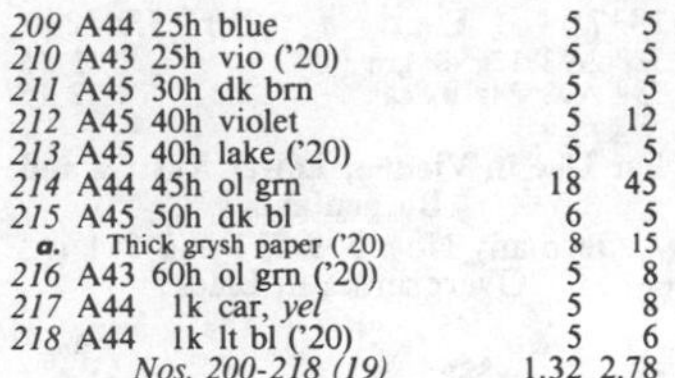

Parliament Building A46

1919-20 **Engr.** ***Perf. 12½, 11½***

Granite Paper.

219 A46 2k ver & blk 25 45
a. Center inverted 3,250.
220 A46 2½k ol bis ('20) 6 20
221 A46 3k bl & blk brn 6 12
222 A46 4k car & blk 6 12
a. Center invert. 1,850. 1,600.
223 A46 5k blk ('20) 8 12
a. Perf. 11½x12½ 37.50 52.50
224 A46 7½k plum 8 32
a. Perf. 11½ 100.00 135.00
b. Perf. 11½x12½ 87.50 135.00
225 A46 10k ol grn & blk brn 20 45
a. Perf. 11½x12½ 75.00 100.00
b. Perf. 11½ 16.00 27.50
226 A46 20k lil & red ('20) 8 55
a. Center invert. 8,500. 7,000.
b. Perf. 11½ 45.00 75.00
Nos. 219-226 (8) 87 2.33

A number of values exist imperforate between. Prices, $300 to $400 a pair.

See No. 248.

1920 **Typo.** ***Imperf.***

Ordinary Paper.

227 A44 5h yel grn 8 30
228 A44 5h gray 5 5
229 A44 10h dp rose 5 5
230 A44 10h red 5 5
231 A43 15h bister 5 10
232 A43 25h violet 5 5
233 A45 30h dk brn 5 5
234 A45 40h violet 5 7
235 A43 60h ol grn 5 12
Nos. 227-235 (9) 48 89

Arms
A47 A48

1920-21 **Typo.** ***Perf. 12½***

Ordinary Paper.

238 A47 80h rose 5 5
239 A47 1k blk brn 5 5
241 A47 1½k grn ('21) 6 10
242 A47 2k blue 5 5
243 A48 3k yel grn & dk grn ('21) 5 5
244 A48 4k red & cl ('21) 6 5
245 A48 5k vio & cl ('21) 6 6
246 A48 7½k yel & brn ('21) 6 6
247 A48 10k ultra & bl ('21) 5 8
Nos. 238-247 (9) 49 55

Nos. 238-245, 247 exist on white paper of good quality and on thick grayish paper of inferior quality; No. 246 only on white paper.

1921 **Engr.**

248 A46 50k dk vio,*yel* 30 90
a. Perf. 11½ 40.00 67.50

Symbols of Agriculture A49

Symbols of Labor and Industry A50

1922-24 **Typo.** ***Perf. 12½***

250 A49 ½k ol bis 5 65
251 A50 1k brown 5 5
252 A50 2k cob bl 5 18
253 A49 2½k org brn 5 8
254 A50 4k dl vio 5 80
255 A50 5k gray grn 5 8
256 A49 7½k gray vio 5 8
257 A50 10k claret 5 8
258 A49 12½k gray grn 5 8
259 A49 15k bluish grn 5 15
260 A49 20k dk bl 5 8
261 A49 25k claret 5 8
262 A50 30k pale gray 5 15
263 A50 45k pale red 5 15
264 A50 50k org brn 5 8
265 A50 60k yel grn 5 8
266 A50 75k ultra 5 8
267 A50 80k yellow 5 8
268 A49 100k gray 5 8
269 A49 120k brown 5 8
270 A49 150k orange 5 8
271 A49 160k lt grn 5 8
272 A49 180k red 5 8
273 A49 200k pink 5 8
274 A49 240k dk vio 5 8
275 A49 300k lt bl 6 8
276 A49 400k dp grn 1.00 12
a. 400k gray grn 1.00 28
277 A49 500k yellow 5 8
278 A49 600k slate 5 8
279 A49 700k brn ('24) 50 8
280 A49 800k vio ('24) 1.00 3.25
281 A50 1000k vio ('23) 50 22
282 A50 1200k car rose ('23) 25 55
283 A50 1500k org ('24) 1.50 12
284 A50 1600k sl ('23) 2.25 3.00
285 A50 2000k dp bl ('23) 4.50 55
286 A50 3000k lt bl ('23) 14.00 1.10
287 A50 4000k dk bl,*bl* ('24) 5.75 2.75
Nos. 250-287 (38) 32.66 15.55

Nos. 250-287 exist imperf. Price, set $700.

Symbols of Art and Science — A51

1922-24 **Engr.** ***Perf. 12½***

288 A51 20k dk brn 8 8
a. Perf. 11½ 1.25 1.40
289 A51 25k blue 8 6
a. Perf. 11½ 1.25 1.40
290 A51 50k brn red 6 8
a. Perf. 11½ 3.75 4.50
291 A51 100k dp grn 8 8
a. Perf. 11½ 7.50 8.00
292 A51 200k dk bio 5 8
a. Perf. 11½ 10.00 15.00
293 A51 500k dp org 12 90
294 A51 1000k blk vio,*yel* 5 6
a. Perf. 11½ 120.00 200.00
295 A51 2000k ol grn*yel* 12 8
296 A51 3000k cl brn ('23) 9.50 65
297 A51 5000k gray blk ('23) 2.50 1.75

Granite Paper.

298 A51 10,000k red brn ('24) 3.50 4.50
Nos. 288-298 (11) 16.14 8.32

On Nos. 281 to 287 and Nos. 291 to 298 "kronen" is abbreviated to "k" and transposed with the numerals.

Nos. 288-298 exist imperf. Price, set $425.

Numeral A52

Fields Crossed by Telegraph Wires A53

White-Shouldered Eagle — A54

Church of Minorite Friars — A55

1925-27 **Typo.** ***Perf. 12***

303 A52 1g dk gray 20 5
304 A52 2g claret 30 5
305 A52 3g scarlet 35 5
306 A52 4g grnsh bl ('27) 90 5
307 A52 5g brn org 1.90 5
308 A52 6g ultra 1.10 5
309 A52 7g chocolate 2.00 5
310 A52 8g yel grn 8.00 5
311 A53 10g orange 28 5
313 A53 15g red lil 28 5
314 A53 16g dk bl 28 5
315 A53 18g ol grn 65 32
316 A54 20g dk vio 38 5
317 A54 24g carmine 50 32
318 A54 30g dk brn 45 5
319 A54 40g ultra 65 8
320 A54 45g yel brn 90 8
321 A54 50g gray 1.10 15
322 A54 80g turq bl 4.00 3.75

Perf. 12½

Engr.

323 A55 1s dp grn 17.50 32
a. 1s lt grn 75.00 1.40
324 A55 2s brn rose 8.00 9.00
Nos. 303-324 (21) 49.72 14.67

Nos. 303-305 and 307-324 exist imperf. Price, set $400.

Güssing — A56

National Library, Vienna — A57

Designs: 15g, Hochosterwitz. 16g, 20g, Durnstein. 18g, Traunsee. 24g, Salzburg. 30g, Seewiesen. 40g, Innsbruck. 50g, Worthersee. 60g, Hohenems. 2s, St. Stephen's Cathedral, Vienna.

1929-30 **Typo.** ***Perf. 12½***

Size: 25½x21½mm

326 A56 10g brn org 1.10 5
327 A56 10g bis ('30) 1.10 5
328 A56 15g vio brn 75 1.50
329 A56 16g dk gray 25 10
330 A56 18g bl grn 55 55
331 A56 20g dk gray ('30) 55 5
332 A56 24g maroon 5.25 7.50
333 A56 24g lake ('30) 9.50 55
334 A56 30g dk vio 5.50 12
335 A56 40g dk bl 10.50 20
336 A56 50g gray vio ('30) 40.00 22
337 A56 60g ol grn 30.00 32

Engr.

Size: 21x26mm.

338 A57 1s blk brn 6.75 28
339 A57 2s dk grn 12.00 8.00
Nos. 326-339 (14) 123.80 19.49

Type of 1929-30 Issue.

Designs: 12g, Traunsee. 64g, Hohenems.

1932 ***Perf. 12***

Size: 21 x 16½ mm.

340 A56 10g ol brn 1.10 5
341 A56 12g bl grn 1.75 5
342 A56 18g bl grn 85 2.75
343 A56 20g dk gray 1.40 5
344 A56 24g car rose 6.75 5
345 A56 24g dl vio 5.50 5
346 A56 30g dk vio 21.00 6
347 A56 30g car rose 5.00 10
348 A56 40g dk bl 25.00 90
349 A56 40g dk vio 7.25 35
350 A56 50g gray vio 30.00 35
351 A56 50g dl bl 8.25 35
352 A56 60g gray grn 65.00 2.25
353 A56 64g gray grn 10.00 22
Nos. 340-353 (14) 188.85 7.58

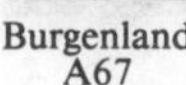

Burgenland A67 — Tyrol A68

Designs (costumes of various districts): 3g, Burgenland. 4g, 5g, Carinthia. 6g, 8g, Lower Austria. 12g, 20g, Upper Austria. 24g, 25g, Salzburg. 30g, 35g, Styria. 45g, Tyrol. 60g, Vorarlberg bridal couple. 64g, Vorarlberg. 1s, Viennese family. 2s, Military.

1934-35 Typo. *Perf. 12*

354 A67	1g dk vio		5	5
355 A67	3g scarlet		5	5
356 A67	4g ol grn		8	6
357 A67	5g red vio		8	5
358 A67	6g ultra		28	25
359 A67	8g green		15	5
360 A67	12g dk brn		15	5
361 A67	20g yel brn		18	5
362 A67	24g grnsh bl		18	5
363 A67	25g violet		28	15
364 A67	30g maroon		25	5
365 A67	35g rose car		42	40

Perf. 12½

366 A68	40g sl gray	50	12
367 A68	45g brn red	42	12
368 A68	60g ultra	75	22
369 A68	64g brown	95	8
370 A68	1s dp vio	80	45
371 A68	2s dl grn	40.00	62.50

Designs Redrawn

Perf. 12 (6g), 12½ (2s)

372 A67	6g ultra ('35)	20	12
373 A68	2s emer ('35)	3.25	6.00
	Nos. 354-373 (20)	49.02	70.87

The design of No. 358 looks as though the man's ears were on backwards, while No. 372 appears correctly.

On No. 373 there are seven feathers on each side of the eagle instead of five.

Nos. 354-373 exist imperf. Price, set $500.

Dollfuss Mourning Issue.

Engelbert Dollfuss — A85

1934 Engr. *Perf. 12½*

374 A85 24g grnsh blk 65 35

1935

375 A85 24g indigo 1.25 1.00

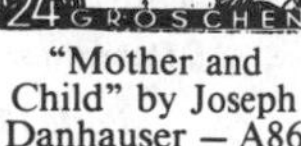

"Mother and Child" by Joseph Danhauser — A86

"Madonna and Child", after Painting by Albrecht Dürer — A87

1935, May 1

376 A86 24g dk bl 65 28

Issued for Mother's Day.

Nos. 376-377 exist imperf. Price, each $225.

1936, May 5 Photo.

377 A87 24g vio bl 28 35

Issued for Mother's Day.

Catalogue prices for unused stamps up to mid-1953 are for hinged copies matching the condition specified in this volume's introduction.

Farm Workers — A88

Design: 5s, Factory workers.

1936, June Engr. *Perf. 12½*

378 A88	3s red org	15.00	20.00
379 A88	5s brn blk	30.00	55.00

Nos. 378-379 exist imperf. Price, set $225.

Engelbert Dollfuss — A90 — Mother and Child — A91

1936, July 25

380 A90 10s dk bl 750.00 850.00

Second anniversary of death of Engelbert Dollfuss, chancellor. Exists imperf. Price, $2,250.

1937, May 5 Photo. *Perf. 12*

381 A91 24g hn brn 32 28

Issued for Mother's Day. Exists imperf. Price, $160.

S. S. Maria Anna — A92

Steamships: 24g, Uranus, 64g, Oesterreich.

1937, June 9

382 A92	12g red brn	80	30
383 A92	24g dp bl	80	30
384 A92	64g dk grn	80	1.00

Centenary of steamship service on Danube River.

Exist imperf. Price, set $160.

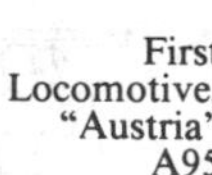

First Locomotive, "Austria" A95

Designs: 25g, Modern steam locomotive. 35g, Modern electric train.

1937, Nov. 22

385 A95	12g blk brn	10	8
386 A95	25g dk vio	50	90
387 A95	35g brn red	1.25	1.40

Centenary of Austrian railways. Exist imperf. Price, set $135

Rose and Zodiac Signs — A98

1937 Engr. *Perf. 13x12½.*

388 A98	12g dk grn	12	15
389 A98	24g dk car	12	15

For Use in Vienna, Lower Austria and Burgenland.

Germany Nos. 509-511 and 511B Overprinted in Black

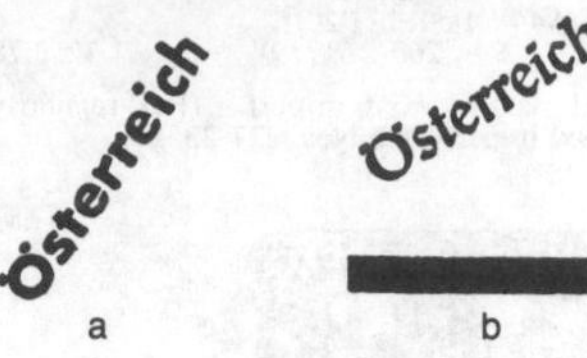

a — b

1945 Unwmk. *Perf. 14.*

390 A115 (a)	5(pf) dp yel grn	5	6
391 A115 (b)	6(pf) purple	6	15
392 A115 (a)	8(pf) red	5	6
393 A115 (b)	12(pf) carmine	6	15

Nos. 390-393 exist with overprint inverted or double.

Germany No. 507, the 3pf, with overprint "a" was prepared, not issued, but sold to collectors after the definitive Republic issue had been placed in use. Price $75.

German Semi-Postal Stamps, Nos. B207, B209, B210 and B283 Surcharged in Black

c — ÖSTERREICH 5 Pf.

d — ÖSTERREICH 8 Pf.

1945 *Perf. 14, 14x13½, 13½x14*

394 SP181 (c)	5pf on 12pf + 88pf grn	75	1.50
395 SP184 (d)	6pf on 6pf + 14pf ultra & dp brn	4.00	9.00
396 SP242 (d)	8pf on 42pf + 108pf brn	75	1.50
397 SP183 (d)	12pf on 3pf + 7pf dl bl	75	1.50

The surcharges are spaced to fit the stamps.

Stamps of Germany, Nos. 509 to 511, 511B, 519 and 529 Overprinted

e — f

1945 Typo. *Perf. 14*

Size: 18½x22½mm.

398 A115 (e)	5(pf) dp yel grn	40	70
399 A115 (f)	5(pf) dp yel grn	7.50	*13.00*
400 A115 (e)	6(pf) purple	22	*45*
401 A115 (e)	8(pf) red	22	*45*
402 A115 (e)	12(pf) carmine	35	*60*

Engr.

Size: 21½x26mm.

403 A115 (e)	30(pf) ol grn	6.00	*11.00*
a.	Thin bar at bottom	20.00	*25.00*
404 A118 (e)	42(pf) brt grn	12.00	*40.00*
a.	Thin bar at bottom	22.50	27.50
	Nos. 398-404 (7)	26.69	66.20

On Nos. 403a and 404a, the bottom bar of the overprint is 2½mm. wide, and, as the overprint was applied in two operations, "Osterreich" is usually not exactly centered in its diagonal slot. On Nos. 403 and 404, the bottom bar is 3mm. wide, and "Osterreich" is always well centered.

Germany Nos. 524-527 (the 1m, 2m, 3m and 5m), overprinted with vertical bars and "Osterreich" similar to "e" and "f", were prepared, not issued, but sold to collectors after the definitive Republic issue had been placed in use. Price for set $175.

For Use in Styria.

Stamps of Germany Nos. 506 to 511, 511A, 511B, 514 to 523 and 529 Overprinted in Black

Österreich

1945 Unwmk. Typo. *Perf. 14*

Size: 18½x22½mm.

405 A115	1(pf) gray blk	1.50	4.50
406 A115	3(pf) lt brn	1.25	4.50
407 A115	4(pf) slate	5.50	15.00
408 A115	5(pf) dp yel grn	1.10	3.00
409 A115	6(pf) purple	22	45
410 A115	8(pf) red	80	2.50
411 A115	10(pf) dk brn	1.50	5.00
412 A115	12(pf) carmine	22	45

Engr.

413 A115	15(pf) brn lake	80	2.75
414 A115	16(pf) pck grn	9.50	27.50
415 A115	20(pf) blue	2.75	8.00
416 A115	24(pf) org brn	9.50	27.50

Size: 22½x26mm.

417 A115	25(pf) brt ultra	1.10	4.00
418 A115	30(pf) ol grn	1.10	3.00
419 A115	40(pf) brt red vio	1.25	3.50
420 A118	42(pf) brt grn	1.50	5.25
421 A115	50(pf) myr grn	1.50	5.25
422 A115	60(pf) dk red brn	2.75	7.25
423 A115	80(pf) indigo	2.00	5.75
	Nos. 405-423 (19)	45.84	135.15

Overprinted on Nos. 524 to 527.

Perf. 12½, 14.

424 A116	1m dk sl grn	8.00	*30.00*
a.	Perf. 12½	160.00	
425 A116	2m violet	7.00	*30.00*
a.	Perf. 14	18.00	*67.50*
426 A116	3m cop red	16.00	*72.50*
a.	Perf. 14	185.00	
427 A116	5m dk bl	175.00	*750.00*
a.	Perf. 14	*850.00*	

On the preceding four stamps the innermost vertical lines are 10½mm. apart; on the pfennig values 6½mm. apart.

Germany Nos. 524 to 527 Overprinted in Black

Österreich

Perf. 14

428 A116	1m dk sl grn	9.00	*27.50*
429 A116	2m violet	9.00	*30.00*

Perf. 12½

430 A116	3m cop red	18.00	*57.50*
431 A116	5m dk bl	125.00	*400.00*
a.	Perf. 14	*900.00*	

On the preceding four stamps, "Osterreich" is thinner, measuring 16mm. On the previous set of 23 values it measures 18mm.

Counterfeits exist of Nos. 424-431 overprints.

For Use in Vienna, Lower Austria and Burgenland.

Coat of Arms

A99 — A100

Typographed or Lithographed

1945, July 3 Unwmk. *Perf. 14x13½*

Size: 21x25mm.

432 A99 3(pf) brown 5 5
433 A99 4(pf) slate 5 12
434 A99 5(pf) dk grn 5 5
435 A99 6(pf) dp vio 5 5
436 A99 8(pf) org brn 5 5
437 A99 10(pf) dp brn 5 8
438 A99 12(pf) rose car 5 5
439 A99 15(pf) org red 5 12
440 A99 16(pf) dl bl grn 5 32

Perf. 14.

Size: 24x28½mm.

441 A99 20(pf) lt bl 5 8
442 A99 24(pf) orange 5 18
443 A99 25(pf) dk bl 5 8
444 A99 30(pf) dp gray grn 5 5
445 A99 38(pf) ultra 5 5
446 A99 40(pf) brt red vio 5 8
447 A99 42(pf) sage grn 5 5
448 A99 50(pf) bl grn 5 *45*
449 A99 60(pf) maroon 5 15
450 A99 80(pf) dl lil 6 15

Engr. *Perf. 14x13½*

451 A100 1(m) dk grn 6 *45*
452 A100 2(m) dk pur 8 *45*
453 A100 3(m) dk vio 12 *45*
454 A100 5(m) brn red 15 *45*
Nos. 432-454 (23) 1.37 4.01

Nos. 432, 433, 437, 439, 440, 443, 446, 448 and 449 are typographed. Nos. 434, 435, 441 and 442 are lithographed; the other values exist both ways.

For General Use.

Lermoos, Winter Scene A101

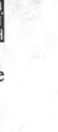

The Prater Woods, Vienna A105

Hochosterwitz, Carinthia A106

Lake Constance A110

Dürnstein, Lower Austria A124

Designs: 4g, Eisenerz surface mine. 5g, Leopoldsberg, near Vienna. 6g, Hohensalzburg, Salzburg Province. 12g, Wolfgang See, near Salzburg. 15g, Forchtenstein Castle, Burgenland. 16g, Gesäuse Valley. 24g, Höldrichs Mill, Lower Austria. 25g, Oetz Valley Outlet, Tyrol. 30g, Neusiedler Lake, Burgenland. 35g, Belvedere Palace, Vienna. 38g, Langbath Lake. 40g, Mariazell, Styria. 42g, Traunkirchen. 45g, Hartenstein Castle. 50g, Silvretta Mountains, Vorarlberg. 60g, Railroad viaducts near Semmering. 70g, Waterfall of Bad-Gastein, Salzburg. 80g, Kaiser Mountains, Tyrol. 90g, Wayside Shrine, Tragöss, Styria. 2s, St. Christof am Arlberg, Tyrol. 3s, Heiligenblut, Carinthia. 5s, Schönbrunn, Vienna.

Perf. 14x13½

1945-46 Photo. Unwmk.

455 A101 3g sapphire 5 5
456 A101 4g dp org ('46) 5 5
457 A101 5g dk car rose 5 5
458 A101 6g dk sl grn 5 5
459 A105 8g gldn brn 5 5
460 A106 10g dk grn 5 5
461 A106 12g dk brn 5 5
462 A106 15g dk sl bl ('46) 5 8
463 A106 16g chnt brn ('46) 5 5

Perf. 13½x14

464 A110 20g dp ultra ('46) 5 5
465 A110 24g dp yel grn ('46) 5 5
466 A110 25g gray blk ('46) 5 8

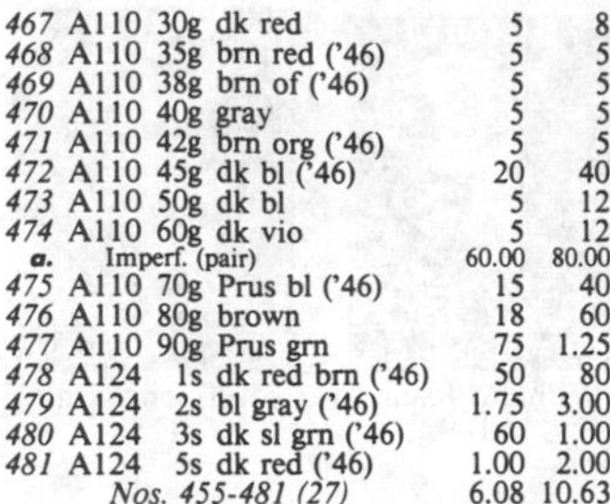

467 A110 30g dk red 5 8
468 A110 35g brn red ('46) 5 5
469 A110 38g brn of ('46) 5 5
470 A110 40g gray 5 5
471 A110 42g brn org ('46) 5 5
472 A110 45g dk bl ('46) 20 40
473 A110 50g dk bl 5 12
474 A110 60g dk vio 5 12
a. Imperf. (pair) 60.00 80.00
475 A110 70g Prus bl ('46) 15 40
476 A110 80g brown 18 60
477 A110 90g Prus grn 75 1.25
478 A124 1s dk red brn ('46) 50 80
479 A124 2s bl gray ('46) 1.75 3.00
480 A124 3s dk sl grn ('46) 60 1.00
481 A124 5s dk red ('46) 1.00 2.00
Nos. 455-481 (27) 6.08 10.63

See also Nos. 486-488, 496-515.

No. 461 Overprinted in Carmine

1946, Sept. 26

482 A106 12g dk brn 10 20

Issued to commemorate the meeting of the Society for Cultural and Economic Relations with the Soviet Union, Vienna, September 26 to 29, 1946.

City Hall Park, Vienna A128

Hochosterwitz, Carinthia A129

Perf. 14x13½

1946-47 Photo. Unwmk.

483 A128 8g dp plum 5 5
484 A128 8g ol brn 5 5
a. 8g dk ol grn 5 5
485 A129 10g dk brn vio ('47) 5 5

Perf. 13½x14

486 A110 30g bl gray ('47) 5 20
487 A110 50g brn vio ('47) 22 40
488 A110 60g vio bl ('47) 1.50 1.75
Nos. 483-488 (6) 1.92 2.50

See also No. 502.

Franz Grillparzer A130

Franz Schubert A131

1947 Engr. *Perf. 14x13½.*

489 A130 18g chocolate 5 8

Photo.

490 A130 18g dk vio brn 8 10

Issued to commemorate the 75th anniversary of the death of Franz Grillparzer, dramatic poet.

A second printing of No. 490 on thicker paper has a darker frame and clearer delineation of the portrait.

1947, Mar. 31 Engr.

491 A131 12g dk grn 6 10

Issued to commemorate the 150th anniversary of the birth of Franz Schubert, musician and composer.

Nos. 469 and 463 Surcharged in Brown

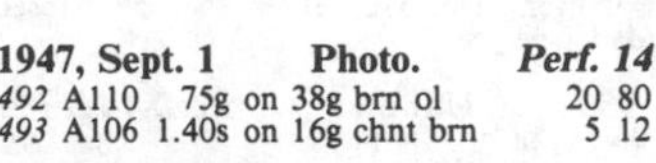

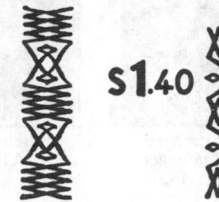

1947, Sept. 1 Photo. *Perf. 14*

492 A110 75g on 38g brn ol 20 80
493 A106 1.40s on 16g chnt brn 5 12

The surcharge on No. 493 varies from brown to black brown.

Symbols of Global Telegraphic Communication A132

1947, Nov. 5 Engr. *Perf. 14x13½*

495 A132 40g dk vio 5 15

Centenary of the telegraph in Austria.

Scenic Type of 1946.

1946, Aug. Photo. *Perf. 13½x14*

496 A124 1s dk brn 65 40
497 A124 2s dk bl 3.25 2.50
498 A124 3s dk sl grn 1.00 70
499 A124 5s dk red 16.00 8.00

On Nos. 478 to 481 the upper and lower panels show a screen effect. On Nos. 496 to 499 the panels appear to be solid color.

Scenic Types of 1945-46.

1947-48 Photo. *Perf. 14x13½*

500 A101 3g brt red 5 5
501 A101 5g brt red 5 5
502 A129 10g brt red 8 5
503 A106 15g brt red ('48) 80 80

Perf. 13½x14

504 A110 20g brt red 25 5
505 A110 30g brt red 40 20
506 A110 40g brt red 40 5
507 A110 50g brt red 55 5
508 A110 60g brt red ('48) 3.50 1.65
509 A110 70g brt red ('48) 1.90 8
510 A110 80g brt red ('48) 1.90 12
511 A110 90g brt red ('48) 2.00 40
512 A124 1s dk vio 40 5
513 A124 2s dk vio 55 20
514 A124 3s dk vio ('48) 4.75 1.25
515 A124 5s dk vio ('48) 5.75 1.60
Nos. 500-515 (16) 23.33 6.65

Carl Michael Ziehrer — A133

Designs: No. 517, Adalbert Stifter. No. 518, Anton Bruckner. 60g, Friedrich von Amerling.

1948-49 Engr.

516 A133 20g dl grn 25 15
517 A133 40g chocolate 3.75 3.50
518 A133 40g dk grn ('49) 3.75 5.25
519 A133 60g rose brn 50 35

Issued to commemorate anniversaries of the death of Carl Michael Ziehrer (1843-1922), composer; Adalbert Stifter (1805-1868), novelist; Friedrich von Amerling (1803-1887), painter, and the birth of Anton Bruckner (1824-1896), composer.

Vorarlberg, Montafon Valley A134

Costume of Vienna, 1850 A135

Designs (Austrian Costumes): 3g, Tyrol, Inn Valley. 5g, Salzburg, Pinzgau. 10g, Styria, Salzkammergut. 15g, Burgenland, Lutzmannsburg. 25g, Vienna, 1850. 30g, Salzburg, Pongau. 40g, Vienna, 1840. 45g, Carinthia, Lesach Valley. 50g, Vorarlberg, Bregenzer Forest. 60g, Carinthia, Lavant Valley. 70g, Lower Austria, Wachau. 75g, Styria, Salzkammergut. 80g, Styria, Enns Valley. 90g, Central Styria. 1s, Tyrol, Puster Valley. 1.20s, Lower Austria, Vienna Woods. 1.40s, Upper Austria, Inn District. 1.45s, Wilten. 1.50s, Vienna, 1853. 1.60s, Vienna, 1830. 1.70s, East Tyrol, Kals. 2s, Upper Austria. 2.20s, Ischl, 1820. 2.40s, Kitzbuhel. 2.50s, Upper Steiermark, 1850. 2.70s, Little Walser Valley. 3s, Burgenland. 3.50s, Lower Austria, 1850. 4.50s, Gail Valley. 5s, Ziller Valley. 7s, Steiermark, Sulm Valley.

Perf. 14x13½

1948-52 Unwmk. Photo.

520 A134 3g gray ('50) 38 60
521 A134 5g dk grn ('49) 5 5
522 A134 10g dp bl 5 5
523 A134 15g brown 38 5
524 A134 20g yel grn 8 5
525 A134 25g brn ('49) 8 5
526 A134 30g dk car rose 1.65 5
527 A134 30g dk vio ('50) 38 5
528 A134 40g violet 1.65 5
529 A134 40g grn ('49) 12 5
530 A134 45g vio bl 1.50 40
531 A134 50g org brn ('49) 38 5
532 A134 60g scarlet 12 5
533 A134 70g brt bl grn ('49) 12 5
534 A134 75g blue 2.50 40
535 A134 80g car rose ('49) 25 5
536 A134 90g brn vio ('49) 15.00 32
537 A134 1s ultra 2.75 5
538 A134 1s rose red ('50) 42.50 12
539 A134 1s dk grn ('51) 12 5
540 A134 1.20s vio ('49) 25 6
541 A134 1.40s brown 1.65 20
542 A134 1.45s dk car ('51) 75 10
543 A134 1.50s ultra ('51) 38 5
544 A134 1.60s org red ('49) 12 5
545 A134 1.70s vio bl ('50) 1.65 80
546 A134 2s bl grn 25 5
547 A134 2.20s sl ('52) 3.25 5
548 A134 2.40s bl ('51) 65 12
549 A134 2.50s brn ('52) 3.00 25
550 A134 2.70s dk brn ('51) 30 50
551 A134 3s brn car ('49) 1.25 5
552 A134 3.50s dl grn ('51) 6.50 5
553 A134 4.50s brn vio ('51) 38 50
554 A134 5s dk red vio 65 8
555 A134 7s ol ('52) 1.00 6

Engr.

556 A135 10s gray ('50) 17.50 4.00
Nos. 520-556 (37) 109.59 9.56

In 1958-59, 21 denominations of this set were printed on white paper, differing from the previous grayish paper with yellowish gum.

Pres. Karl Renner — A136

1948, Nov. 12 *Perf. 14x13½*

557 A136 1s dp bl 1.90 1.75

Issued to commemorate the 30th anniversary of the founding of the Austrian Republic. See also Nos. 573, 636.

Franz Gruber and Josef Mohr
A137

1948, Dec. 18 *Perf. 13½x14*
558 A137 60g red brn 3.75 6.25

Issued to commemorate the 130th anniversary of the hymn "Silent Night, Holy Night."

Symbolical of Child Welfare
A138

Johann Strauss, the Younger
A139

1949, May 14 Photo. *Perf. 14x13½*
559 A138 1s brt bl 10.00 1.90

Issued to commemorate the first year of activity of the United Nations International Children's Emergency Fund in Austria.

1949 **Engr.**

Designs: 30g, Johann Strauss, the elder. No. 561, Johann Strauss, the younger. No. 562, Karl Millöcker.

560 A139 30g vio brn 1.90 2.75
561 A139 1s dk bl 2.50 1.65
562 A139 1s dk bl 10.00 11.00

Issued to commemorate the centenary of the death of Johann Strauss, the elder (1804-1849), and the 50th anniversary of the deaths of Johann Strauss, the younger (1825-1899), and Karl Millöcker (1842-1899), composers. See also No. 574.

Esperanto Star, Olive Branches
A140

St. Gebhard
A141

1949, June 25 **Photo.**
563 A140 20g bl grn 90 80

Austrian Esperanto Congress at Graz.

1949, Aug. 6 **Engr.**
564 A141 30g dk vio 1.50 2.00

Issued to commemorate the millenary of the birth of St. Gebhard (949-995), Bishop of Vorarlberg.

Letter, Roses and Post Horn — A142

Designs: 60g, Plaque. 1s, "Austria," wings and monogram.

1949, Oct. 8 *Perf. 13½x14*
565 A142 40g dk grn 2.75 2.75
566 A142 60g dk car 2.75 2.75
567 A142 1s dk vio bl 4.75 8.00

Issued to commemorate the 75th anniversary of the formation of the Universal Postal Union.

Moritz Michael Daffinger
A143

Andreas Hofer
A144

Designs: 30g, Alexander Girardi. No. 569, Daffinger. No. 570, Hofer. No. 571, Josef Madersperger.

1950 Unwmk. *Perf. 14x13½*
568 A144 30g dk bl 95 95
569 A143 60g red brn 4.50 4.50
570 A144 60g dk vio 7.75 8.25
571 A144 60g purple 3.50 2.75

Issued to commemorate the centenary of the birth of Alexander Girardi (1850-1918), actor; the death centenary of Moritz Michael Daffinger (1790-1849), painter; the 140th anniversary of the death of Andreas Hofer (1767-1810), patriot, and the death centenary of Josef Madersperger (1768-1850), inventor.

Austrian Stamp of 1850 — A146

1950, May 20 *Perf. 14½*
572 A146 1s *straw* 1.25 1.40

Centenary of Austrian postage stamps.

Renner Type of 1948, Frame and Inscriptions Altered.

1951, Mar. 3
573 A136 1s *straw* 1.40 18

Issued in memory of Pres. Karl Renner, 1870-1950.

Strauss Type of 1949.

Portrait: 60g, Joseph Lanner.

1951, Apr. 12
574 A139 60g dk bl grn 2.75 1.75

Issued to commemorate the 150th anniversary of the birth of Joseph Lanner, composer.

Martin Johann Schmidt — A147

Boy Scout Emblem — A148

1951, June 28 Engr. *Perf. 14x13½*
575 A147 1sh brn red 3.50 3.00

Issued to commemorate the 150th anniversary of the death of Martin Johann Schmidt, painter.

Engraved and Lithographed

1951, Aug. 3
576 A148 1sh dk grn, ocher & pink 2.75 4.50

Issued in connection with the 7th World Scout Jamboree, Bad Ischl-St. Wolfgang, Aug. 3-13, 1951.

Wilhelm Kienzl
A149

Josef Schrammel
A150

Design: 1s, Karl von Ghega.

1951-52 Engr. Unwmk.
577 A149 1s dp grn ('52) 4.25 1.65
578 A149 1.50s indigo 2.00 1.40
579 A150 1.50s vio bl ('52) 4.25 1.65

Issued to commemorate the 150th anniversary of the birth of Karl von Ghega (1802-1860), civil engineer; the 10th anniversary of the death of Wilhelm Kienzl (1857-1941), composer, and the birth centenary of Josef Schrammel (1852-1895), composer. See also No. 582.

Breakfast Pavilion, Schönbrunn
A151

1952, May 24 *Perf. 13½x14*
580 A151 1.50s dk grn 3.75 1.75

Issued to commemorate the 200th anniversary of the founding of the Vienna Zoological Gardens.

Globe as Dot Over "i" — A152

School Girl — A153

1952, July 1 *Perf. 14x13½*
581 A152 1.50s dk bl 4.00 1.00

Issued to publicize the formation of the International Union of Socialist Youth Camp, Vienna, July 1-10, 1952.

Type Similar to A150.

Portrait: 1s, Nikolaus Lenau.

1952, Aug. 13
582 A150 1s dp grn 4.25 1.65

Issued to commemorate the 150th anniversary of the birth of Nikolaus Lenau, pseudonym of Nikolaus Franz Niembsch von Strehlenau (1802-1850), poet.

1952, Sept. 6
583 A153 2.40s dp vio bl 6.75 3.00

Issued to stimulate letter-writing between Austrian and foreign school children.

Hugo Wolf — A154

Pres. Theodor Körner — A155

1953, Feb. 21 Engr. *Perf. 14x13½*
587 A154 1.50s dk bl 4.50 1.10

Issued to commemorate the 50th anniversary of the death of Hugo Wolf, composer.

1953, Apr. 24
588 A155 1.50s dk vio bl 4.00 1.10

Issued to commemorate the 80th birthday of Pres. Theodor Körner. See also Nos. 591, 614.

State Theater, Linz, and Masks
A156

1953, Oct. 17 *Perf. 13½x14*
589 A156 1.50s dk gray 9.00 2.25

Issued to commemorate the 150th anniversary of the founding of the State Theater at Linz.

Child and Christmas Tree
A157

Karl von Rokitansky
A158

1953, Nov. 30 *Perf. 14x13½*
590 A157 1s dk grn 1.10 22

See also No. 597.

Type Similar to A155.

Portrait: 1.50s, Moritz von Schwind.

1954, Jan. 21 *Perf. 14x13½*
591 A155 1.50s purple 7.50 1.75

Issued to commemorate the 150th anniversary of the birth of Moritz von Schwind, painter.

1954, Feb. 19
592 A158 1.50s purple 11.00 2.25

Issued to commemorate the 150th anniversary of the birth of Karl von Rokitansky, physician. See also No. 595.

Esperanto Star and Wreath
A159

Engraved and Photogravure

1954, June 5 *Perf. 13½x14*
593 A159 1s dk brn & emer 3.00 22

Issued to commemorate the 50th anniversary of the Esperanto movement in Austria.

Johann Michael Rottmayr — A160

1954, Aug. 4 Engr. ***Perf. 14x13½***
594 A160 1s dk bl grn 7.50 2.50

300th birth anniversary of Johann Michael Rottmayr von Rosenbrunn, painter.

Type Similar to A158

Portrait: 1.50s, Carl Auer von Welsbach.

595 A158 1.50s vio bl 20.00 2.25

25th death anniversary of Carl Auer von Welsbach (1858-1929), chemist.

Organ, St. Florian Monastery and Cherub – A161

1954, Oct. 2 **Unwmk.**
596 A161 1s brown 2.25 28

Issued to publicize the second International Congress for Catholic Church Music, Vienna, October 4-10, 1954.

Christmas Type of 1953

1954, Nov. 30
597 A157 1s dk bl 2.25 40

Arms of Austria and Official Publication A162

1954, Dec. 18 **Engr.**
598 A162 1s sal & blk 1.75 22

Issued to commemorate the 150th anniversary of the founding of Austria's State Printing Plant and the 250th year of publication of the government newspaper, Wiener Zeitung.

Parliament Building A163

Designs: 1s, Western railroad station, Vienna. 1.45s, Letters forming flag. 1.50s, Public housing, Vienna. 2.40s, Limberg dam.

1955, Apr. 27 ***Perf. 13½x14***
599 A163 70g rose vio 90 22
600 A163 1s dp ultra 3.25 22
601 A163 1.45s scarlet 5.25 2.25
602 A163 1.50s brown 11.00 22
603 A163 2.40s dk bl grn 5.25 4.75
Nos. 599-603 (5) 25.65 7.66

Issued to commemorate the 10th anniversary of Austria's liberation.

Type of 1945 Overprinted in Blue **STAATSVERTRAG 1955**

1955, May 15 ***Perf. 14x13½***
604 A100 2(s) bl gray 1.25 35

Issued to commemorate the signing of the state treaty with the United States, France, Great Britain and Russia, May 15, 1955.

Workers of Three Races Climbing Globe A164

1955, May 20 ***Perf. 13½x14***
605 A164 1s indigo 1.25 2.50

Issued to publicize the 4th congress of the International Confederation of Free Trade Unions, Vienna, May 1955.

Burgtheater, Vienna A165

Design: 2.40s, Opera House, Vienna.

1955, July 25
606 A165 1.50s lt sep 2.25 22
607 A165 2.40s dk bl 3.00 2.00

Issued to celebrate the re-opening of the Burgtheater and Opera House in Vienna.

Symbolic of Austria's Desire to Join the U.N. – A166

1955, Oct. 24 **Unwmk.**
608 A166 2.40s green 8.75 2.00

Tenth anniversary of U.N.

Wolfgang Amadeus Mozart – A167

Symbolic of Austria's Joining the U. N. – A168

1956, Jan. 21 ***Perf. 14x13½***
609 A167 2.40s sl bl 2.75 85

Issued to commemorate the 200th anniversary of the birth of Wolfgang Amadeus Mozart, composer.

1956, Feb. 20
610 A168 2.40s chocolate 9.00 1.75

Issued to commemorate Austria's admission to the U.N.

Globe Showing Energy of the Earth A169

1956, May 8 ***Perf. 13½x14***
611 A169 2.40s dp bl 7.50 2.25

Issued to publicize the Fifth International Power Conference, Vienna, June 17-23, 1956.

Map of Europe and City Maps – A170

J. B. Fischer von Erlach – A171

Photogravure and Typographed

1956, June 8 ***Perf. 14x13½***
612 A170 1.45s lt grn blk & red 1.50 85

Issued to publicize the 23rd International Housing and Town Planning Congress, Vienna, July 22-28.

1956, July 20 **Engr.**
613 A171 1.50s brown 1.25 1.75

Issued to commemorate the 300th anniversary of the birth of Johann Bernhard Fischer von Erlach, architect.

Körner Type of 1953.

1957, Jan. 11
614 A155 1.50s gray blk 1.25 1.90

Issued to commemorate the death of Pres. Theodor Körner.

Dr. Julius Wagner-Jauregg A172

Anton Wildgans A173

1957, Mar. 7 ***Perf. 14x13½***
615 A172 2.40s brn vio 2.25 2.00

Issued to commemorate the centenary of the birth of Dr. Julius Wagner-Jauregg, psychiatrist.

1957, May 3 **Unwmk.**
616 A173 1s vio bl 35 25

Issued to commemorate the 25th anniversary of the death of Anton Wildgans, poet.

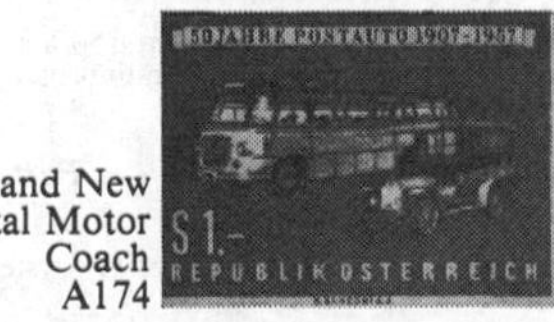

Old and New Postal Motor Coach A174

1957, June 14 ***Perf. 13½x14***
617 A174 1s *yellow* 35 25

Issued to commemorate the 50th anniversary of Austrian Postal Motor Coach Service.

Gasherbrum II and Glacier A175

1957, July 27
618 A175 1.50s gray bl 35 20

Issued in honor of the Austrian Karakorum Expedition, which climbed Mount Gasherbrum II on July 7, 1956.

Mariazell – A176

Heidenreichstein Castle – A177

Designs: 20g, Farmhouse at Mörbisch. 50g, Heiligenstadt, Vienna. 1.40s, County seat, Klagenfurt. 1.50s, Rabenhof Building, Erdberg, Vienna. 1.80s, The Mint, Hall, Tyrol. 2s, Christkindl Church. 3.40s, Steiner Gate, Krems. 4s, Vienna Gate, Hainburg. 4.50s, Schwechat Airport, Vienna. 5.50s, Chur Gate, Feldkirch. 6s, County seat, Graz. 6.40s, "Golden Roof," Innsbruck.

1957-61 Litho. ***Perf. 14x13½***

Size: 20x25mm.

618A A176 20g vio blk ('61) 5 5
619 A176 50g bluish blk ('59) 5 5

Engr.

620 A176 1s chocolate 1.00 12

Typo.

621 A176 1s chocolate 1.40 8

Litho.

622 A176 1s choc ('59) 70 5
622A A176 1.40s brt grnsh bl ('60) 25 5
623 A176 1.50s rose lake ('58) 40 5
624 A176 1.80s brt ultra ('60) 25 5
625 A176 2s dl bl ('58) 4.75 5
626 A176 3.40s yel grn ('60) 70 80
627 A176 4s brt red lil ('60) 60 5
627A A176 4.50s dl grn ('60) 80 50
628 A176 5.50s grnsh gray ('60) 45 20
629 A176 6s brt vio ('60) 80 5
629A A176 6.40s brt bl ('60) 75 90

Engr.

Size: 22x28mm.

630 A177 10s dk bl grn 2.50 45
Nos. 618A-630 (16) 15.45 3.50

Of the three 1s stamps above, Nos. 620 and 621 have two names in imprint (designer H. Strohofer, engraver G. Wimmer). No. 622 has only Strohofer's name.

Prices for Nos. 618A-624, 626-630 are for stamps on white paper. Most denominations also come on grayish paper with yellowish gum.

See also Nos. 688-702.

1960-65 Photo. ***Perf. 14½x14***

Size: 17x21mm.

630A A176 50g sl ('64) 6 5

Size: 18x21½ mm.

630B A176 1s chocolate 12 8

Size: 17x21mm.

630C A176 1.50s dk car ('65) 18 12

Nos. 630A-630C issued in sheets and coils.

Graukogel, Badgastein – A180

1958, Feb. 1 Engr. ***Perf. 14x13½***
631 A180 1.50s dk bl 22 10

Alpine championships of the International Ski Federation, Badgastein, Feb. 2-7.

Plane over Map of Austria A181

1958, Mar. 27 ***Perf. 13½x14***
632 A181 4s red 45 25

Re-opening of Austrian Airlines.

Lombardy-Venetia stamps can be mounted in Scott's Austria Album.

Mother and Daughter
A182

Walther von der Vogelweide
A183

1958, May 8 Unwmk. *Perf. 14x13½*
633 A182 1.50s dk bl 25 12

Issued for Mother's Day, 1958.

Lithographed and Engraved

1958, July 17
634 A183 1.50s multi 25 12

Issued to commemorate the 3rd Austrian Song Festival, Vienna, July 17-20.

Oswald Redlich — A184

Giant "E" on Map — A185

1958, Sept. 17 Engr.
635 A184 2.40s ultra 50 28

Issued to commemorate the centenary of the birth of Prof. Oswald Redlich (1858-1944), historian.

Renner Type of 1948.

1958, Nov. 12
636 A136 1.50s dp grn 35 35

Issued to commemorate the 40th anniversary of the founding of the Austrian Republic.

1959, Mar. 9
637 A185 2.40s emerald 25 32

Issued to promote the idea of a United Europe.

Cigarette Machine and Trademark of Tobacco Monopoly
A186

Archduke Johann
A187

1959, May 8 Unwmk. *Perf. 13½*
638 A186 2.40s dk ol bis 25 25

Issued to commemorate the 175th anniversary of the establishment of the Austrian tobacco monopoly.

1959, May 11 *Perf. 14x13½*
639 A187 1.50s dp grn 25 18

Issued to commemorate the centenary of the death of Archduke Johann of Austria, military leader and humanitarian.

Foreign postal stationery (stamped envelopes, postal cards and air letter sheets) lies beyond the scope of this Catalogue, which is limited to adhesive postage stamps.

Capercaillie
A188

Joseph Haydn
A189

Animals: 1.50s, Roe buck. 2.40s, Wild boar. 3.50s, Red deer, doe and fawn.

1959, May 20 Engr.
640 A188 1s rose vio 25 20
641 A188 1.50s bl vio 60 12
642 A188 2.40s dk bl grn 45 65
643 A188 3.50s dk brn 30 28

Issued to publicize the Congress of the International Hunting Council, Vienna, May 20-24.

1959, May 30 Unwmk.
644 A189 1.50s vio brn 45 18

Issued to commemorate the sesquicentennial of the death of Joseph Haydn, composer.

Coat of Arms, Tyrol
A190

Antenna, Zugspitze
A191

1959, June 13 *Perf. 14x13½*
645 A190 1.50s rose red 25 12

Issued to commemorate the 150th anniversary of the fight for the liberation of Tyrol.

1959, June 19 *Perf. 13½*
646 A191 2.40s dk bl grn 25 20

Inauguration of Austria's relay system.

Field Ball Player
A192

Orchestral Instruments
A193

Designs: 1s, Runner. 1.80s, Gymnast on vaulting horse. 2s, Woman hurdler. 2.20s, Hammer thrower.

1959-70 Engr. *Perf. 14x13½*
647 A192 1s lilac 18 20
648 A192 1.50s bl grn 50 25
648A A192 1.80s car ('62) 45 40
648B A192 2s rose lake ('70) 25 18
648C A192 2.20s bluish blk ('67) 25 18
Nos. 647-648C (5) 1.63 1.21

Lithographed and Engraved

1959, Aug. 19 *Perf. 14x13½*
649 A193 2.40s dl bl & blk 30 28

Issued to publicize the 1959 world tour of the Vienna Philharmonic Orchestra.

Family Fleeing over Mountains
A194

1960, Apr. 7 Engr. *Perf. 13½x14*
650 A194 3s Prus grn 90 45

Issued to publicize World Refugee Year, July 1, 1959-June 30, 1960.

President Adolf Schärf — A195

1960, Apr. 20 *Perf. 14x13½*
651 A195 1.50s gray ol 90 28

Issued to honor President Adolf Scharf on his 70th birthday.

Young Hikers and Hostel
A196

1960, May 20 *Perf. 13½x14*
652 A196 1s car rose 30 25

Issued to publicize youth hiking and the youth hostel movement.

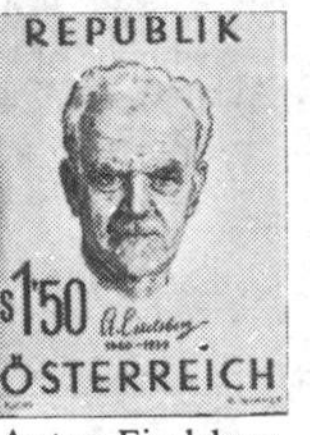

Anton Eiselsberg
A197

Gustav Mahler
A198

Lithographed and Engraved

1960, June 20 *Perf. 14x13½*
653 A197 1.50s buff & dk brn 95 28

Issued to commemorate the centenary of the birth of Dr. Anton Eiselsberg, surgeon.

1960, July 7 Engr.
654 A198 1.50s chocolate 95 28

Issued to commemorate the centenary of the birth of Gustav Mahler, composer.

Jakob Prandtauer, Melk Abbey — A199

Gross Glockner Mountain Road — A200

1960, July 16 Unwmk.
655 A199 1.50s red brn 95 28

Issued to commemorate the 300th anniversary of the birth of Jakob Prandtauer, architect.

1960, Aug. 3
656 A200 1.80s dk bl 85 80

Issued to commemorate the 25th anniversary of the opening of the Gross Glockner Mountain Road.

Europa Issue, 1960

Ionic Capital — A201

1960, Aug. 29 *Perf. 14x13½*
657 A201 3s black 1.90 1.25

Issued to promote the idea of a united Europe.

Griffen, Carinthia
A202

1960, Oct. 10 Engr. *Perf. 13½x14*
658 A202 1.50s sl grn 45 20

Issued to commemorate the 40th anniversary of the plebiscite which kept Carinthia with Austria.

Flame and Broken Chain — A203

1961, May 8 Unwmk. *Perf. 14x13½*
659 A203 1.50s scarlet 45 18

Issued to honor the victims in Austria's fight for freedom.

First Austrian Mail Plane, 1918 — A204

1961, May 15 *Perf. 13½x14*
660 A204 5s vio bl 95 50

Issued to publicize the Airmail Philatelic Exhibition, LUPOSTA 1961, Vienna, May, 1961.

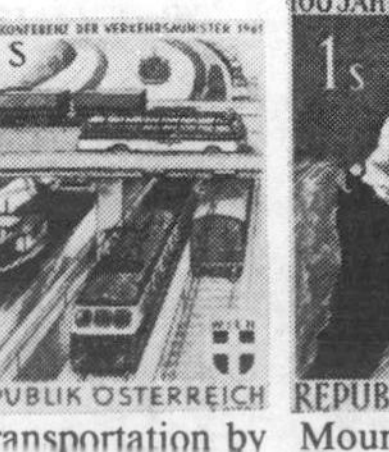

Transportation by Road, Rail and Waterway
A205

Mountain Mower, by Albin Egger-Lienz
A206

Engraved and Typographed

1961, May 29 *Perf. 13½*
661 A205 3s rose red & ol 60 50

Issued to commemorate the 13th European Conference of Transportation ministers, Vienna, May 29-31.

1961, June 12 Engr. *Perf. 13½x14*

Designs: 1.50s, The Kiss, by August von Pettenkofen. 3s, Girl, by Anton Romako. 5s, Ariadne's Triumph, by Hans Makart.

Inscriptions in Red Brown

662 A206 1s rose lake 20 20
663 A206 1.50s dl vio 32 32
664 A206 3s ol grn 1.10 1.10
665 A206 5s bl vio 60 60

Issued to commemorate the centenary of the Society of Creative Artists, Künstlerhaus, Vienna.

Sonnblick Mountain and Observatory A207

Mercury and Globe A208

1961, Sept. 1 *Perf. 14x13½*
666 A207 1.80s vio bl 55 45

Issued to commemorate the 75th anniversary of the establishment of the Sonnblick meteorological observatory.

1961, Sept. 18
667 A208 3s black 1.00 70

Issued to publicize the International Banking Congress, Vienna, Sept. 1961. English inscription listing United Nations financial groups.

Coal Mine Shaft — A209

Designs: 1.50s, Generator. 1.80s, Iron blast furnace. 3s, Pouring steel. 5s, Oil refinery.

1961, Sept. 15 Engr. *Perf. 14x13½*
668 A209 1s black 20 18
669 A209 1.50s green 32 28
670 A209 1.80s dk car rose 65 60
671 A209 3s brt lil 90 80
672 A209 5s blue 1.10 1.10
Nos. 668-672 (5) 3.17 2.96

15th anniversary of nationalized industry.

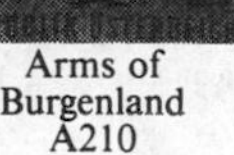

Arms of Burgenland A210

Franz Liszt A211

Engraved and Lithographed

1961, Oct. 9
673 A210 1.50s blk, yel & dk red 50 25

Issued to commemorate the 40th anniversary of Burgenland's joining the Austrian Republic.

1961, Oct. 20 **Engr.**
674 A211 3s dk brn 80 65

Issued to commemorate the 150th anniversary of the birth of Franz Liszt, composer.

Parliament A212

1961, Dec. 18 *Perf. 13½x14*
675 A212 1s brown 28 18

Issued to commemorate the 200th anniversary of the Austrian Bureau of Budget.

Kaprun-Mooserboden Reservoir — A213

Hydroelectric Power Plants: 1.50s, Ybbs-Persenbeug dam and locks. 1.80s, Lünersee dam and reservoir. 3s, Grossraming dam. 4s, Bisamberg transformer plant. 6.40s, St. Andrä power plant.

1962, March 26 **Unwmk.**
676 A213 1s vio bl 20 20
677 A213 1.50s red lil 32 32
678 A213 1.80s green 50 50
679 A213 3s brown 50 50
680 A213 4s rose red 50 50
681 A213 6.40s gray 1.60 1.60
Nos. 676-681 (6) 3.62 3.62

Issued to commemorate the 15th anniversary of the nationalization of the electric power industry.

Johann Nestroy A214

Friedrich Gauermann A215

1962, May 25 *Perf. 14x13½*
682 A214 1s violet 28 20

Issued to commemorate the centenary of the death of Johann Nepomuk Nestroy, Viennese playwright, author and actor.

1962, July 6 **Engr.**
683 A214 1.50s int bl 28 18

Issued to commemorate the centenary of the death of Friedrich Gauermann (1807-1862), landscape painter.

Scout Emblem and Handshake — A216

1962, Oct. 5
684 A216 1.50s dk grn 50 28

Issued to commemorate the 50th anniversary of Austria's Boy Scouts.

Lowlands Forest A217

Designs: 1.50s, Deciduous forest. 3s, Fir and larch forest.

1962, Oct. 12 *Perf. 13½x14*
685 A217 1s grnsh gray 20 20
686 A217 1.50s redsh brn 32 32
687 A217 3s dk sl grn 1.10 1.10

Buildings Types of 1957-61

Designs: 30g, City Hall, Vienna. 40g, Porcia Castle, Spittal on the Drau. 60g, Tanners' Tower, Wels. 70g, Residenz Fountain, Salzburg. 80g, Old farmhouse, Pinzgau. 1s, Romanesque columns, Millstatt Abbey. 1.20s, Kornmesser House, Bruck on the Mur. 1.30s, Schatten Castle, Feldkirch, Vorarlberg. 2s, Dragon Fountain, Klagenfurt. 2.20s, Beethoven House, Vienna. 2.50s, Danube Bridge, Linz. 3s, Swiss Gate, Vienna. 3.50s, Esterhazy Palace, Eisenstadt. 8s, City Hall, Steyr. 20s, Melk Abbey

1962-70 Litho. *Perf. 14x13½*
Size: 20x25mm.

688 A176 30g grnsh gray 50 5
689 A176 40g rose red 12 5
690 A176 60g vio brn 32 5
691 A176 70g dk bl 25 5
692 A176 80g yel brn 32 5
693 A176 1s brn ('70) 20 5
694 A176 1.20s red lil 40 5
695 A176 1.30s grn ('67) 15 5
696 A176 2s dk bl ('68) 25 5
697 A176 2.20s green 1.40 5
698 A176 2.50s violet 80 12
699 A176 3s brt bl 70 5
700 A176 3.50s rose car 80 6
701 A176 8s cl ('65) 1.00 20

Engr. *Perf. 13½*
Size: 28x36½mm.

702 A177 20s rose cl ('63) 2.40 50
Nos. 688-702 (15) 9.61 1.43

Prices for Nos. 688-702 are for stamps on white paper. Some denominations also come on grayish paper with yellowish gum.

Electric Locomotive and Train of 1837 — A218

Lithographed and Engraved

1962, Nov. 9 *Perf. 13½x14*
703 A218 3s buff & blk 1.00 70

125th anniversary of Austrian railroads.

Postilions and Postal Clerk, 1863 — A219

Hermann Bahr — A220

1963, May 7 Photo. *Perf. 14x13½*
704 A219 3s dk brn & cit 90 70

Issued to commemorate the centenary of the first International Postal Conference, Paris, 1863.

Lithographed and Envraved

1963, July 19 *Perf. 14x13½*
705 A220 1.50s bl & blk 32 12

Centenary of birth of Hermann Bahr, poet.

St. Florian Statue, Kefermarkt, Contemporary and Old Fire Engines — A221

1963, Aug. 30 **Unwmk.**
706 A221 1.50s brt rose & blk 32 12

Issued to commemorate the centenary of the Austrian volunteer fire brigades.

Factory, Flag and "ÖGB" on Map of Austria A222

1963, Sept. 23 Litho. *Perf. 13½x14*
707 A222 1.50s gray, red & dk brn 32 12

Issued to commemorate the 5th Congress of the Austrian Trade Union Federation (ÖGB), Sept. 23-28.

Arms of Austria and Tyrol A223

1963, Sept. 27 **Unwmk.**
708 A223 1.50s tan, blk, red & yel 32 12

Issued to commemorate the 600th anniversary of Tyrol's union with Austria.

Prince Eugene of Savoy A224

Centenary Emblem A225

1963, Oct. 18 Engr. *Perf. 14x13½*
709 A224 1.50s violet 32 12

Issued to commemorate the 300th anniversary of the birth of Prince Eugene of Savoy (1663-1736), Austrian general.

Engraved and Photogravure

1963, Oct. 25 **Unwmk.**
710 A225 3s blk, sil & red 60 35

Issued to commemorate the centenary of the founding of the International Red Cross.

The lack of a price for a listed item does not necessarily indicate rarity.

Slalom
A226

Sports: 1.20s, Biathlon (skier with rifle). 1.50s, Ski jump. 1.80s, Women's figure skating. 2.20s, Ice hockey. 3s, Tobogganing. 4s, Bobsledding.

Photogravure and Engraved

1963, Nov. 11 *Perf. 13½x14*

Inscriptions in Gold; Athletes in Black

711 A226 1s lt gray 12 12
712 A226 1.20s lt bl 16 16
713 A226 1.50s gray 20 20
714 A226 1.80s pale lil 25 25
715 A226 2.20s lt grn 40 40
716 A226 3s gray 32 32
717 A226 4s grysh bl 60 60
Nos. 711-717 (7) 2.05 2.05

Issued to publicize the 9th Winter Olympic Games, Innsbruck, Jan. 29-Feb. 9, 1964.

Baroque Crèche by Josef Thaddäus Stammel — A227

1963, Nov. 29 Engr. *Perf. 14x13½*

718 A227 2s dk Prus grn 30 15

Nasturtium
A228

Flowers: 1.50s, Peony. 1.80s, Clematis. 2.20s, Dahlia. 3s, Morning glory. 4s, Hollyhock.

Unwmk.

1964, Apr. 17 Litho. *Perf. 14*

Gray Background

719 A228 1s yel, grn & dk red 12 12
720 A228 1.50s pink, grn & yel 20 20
721 A228 1.80s lil, grn & yel 25 25
722 A228 2.20s car, grn & yel 32 32
723 A228 3s bl, grn & yel 38 38
724 A228 4s grn, yel & pink 50 50
Nos. 719-724 (6) 1.77 1.77

Issued to publicize the Vienna International Garden Show, Apr. 16-Oct. 11.

St. Mary Magdalene and Apostle
A229

Pallas Athena and National Council Chamber
A230

1964, May 21 Engr. *Perf. 13½*

725 A229 1.50s bluish blk 28 20

Issued to publicize Romanesque art in Austria. The 12th century stained-glass window is from the Weitensfeld Church, the bust of the Apostle from the portal of St. Stephen's Cathedral, Vienna.

Engraved and Lithographed

1964, May 25 *Perf. 14x13½*

726 A230 1.80s blk & emer 35 25

Issued to commemorate the second Parliamentary and Scientific Conference, Vienna.

The Kiss, by Gustav Klimt
A231

1964, June 5 Litho. *Perf. 13½*

727 A231 3s multi 60 40

Issued to commemorate the re-opening of the Vienna Secession, a museum devoted to early 20th century art (art nouveau).

Brother of Mercy and Patient — A232

Perf. 14x13½

1964, June 11 Engr. Unwmk.

728 A232 1.50s dk bl 28 18

Issued to commemorate the 350th anniversary of the Brothers of Mercy in Austria.

"Bringing the News of Victory at Kunersdorf" by Bernardo Bellotto — A233

"The Post in Art". 1.20s, Changing Horses at Relay Station, by Julius Hörmann. 1.50s, The Honeymoon Trip, by Moritz von Schwind. 1.80s, After the Rain, by Ignaz Raffalt. 2.20s, Mailcoach in the Mountains, by Adam Klein. 3s, Changing Horses at Bavarian Border, by Friedrich Gauermann. 4s, Postal Sleigh (Truck) in the Mountains, by Adalbert Pilch. 6.40s, Saalbach Post Office, by Adalbert Pilch.

1964, June 15 *Perf. 13½x14*

729 A233 1s rose cl 8 8
730 A233 1.20s sepia 20 20
731 A233 1.50s vio bl 18 18
732 A233 1.80s brt vio 20 20
733 A233 2.20s black 25 25
734 A233 3s dl car rose 40 40
735 A233 4s sl grn 50 50
736 A233 6.40s dl cl 1.10 1.10
Nos. 729-736 (8) 2.91 2.91

Issued to commemorate the 15th Universal Postal Union Congress, Vienna, May-June 1964.

Workers — A234

1964, Sept. 4 *Perf. 14x13½*

737 A234 1s black 20 12

Centenary of Austrian Labor Movement.

Europa Issue, 1964

Common Design Type

Unwmk.

1964, Sept. 14 Litho. *Perf. 12*

Size: 21x36mm.

738 CD7 3s dk bl 35 28

Emblem of Radio Austria and Transistor Radio Panel
A235

1964, Oct. 1 Photo. *Perf. 13½*

739 A235 1s blk brn & red 20 12

Forty years of Radio Austria.

Old Printing Press — A236

Lithographed and Engraved

1964, Oct. 12 *Perf. 14x13½*

740 A236 1.50s tan & blk 20 12

Issued to publicize the 6th Congress of the International Graphic Federation, Vienna, Oct. 12-17.

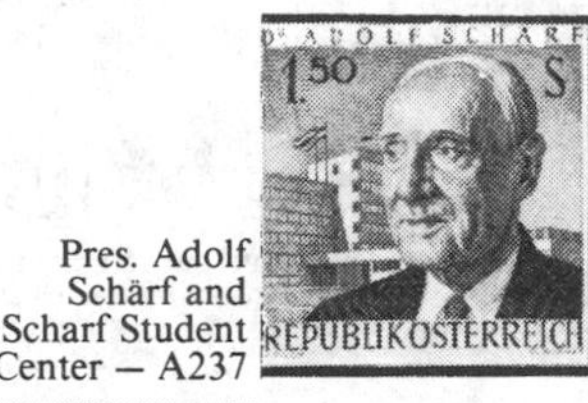

Pres. Adolf Schärf and Schärf Student Center — A237

Ruins and New Buildings — A238

Typographed and Engraved

1965, Apr. 20 *Perf. 12*

741 A237 1.50s bluish blk 32 20

Issued in memory of Dr. Adolf Schärf (1890-1965), President of Austria (1957-65).

1965, Apr. 27 Engr. *Perf. 14x13½*

742 A238 1.80s car lake 25 15

Twenty years of reconstruction.

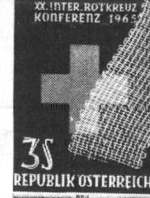

Oldest Seal of Vienna University
A239

St. George, 16th Century Wood Sculpture
A240

Photogravure and Engraved

1965, May 10 *Perf. 14x13½*

743 A239 3s gold & red 40 28

Issued to commemorate the 600th anniversary of the founding of the University of Vienna.

1965, May 17 **Engr.**

744 A240 1.80s bluish blk 28 25

Issued to publicize the art of the Danube Art School, 1490-1540, in connection with an art exhibition, May-Oct. 1965. The stamp background shows an engraving by Albrecht Altdorfer.

ITU Emblem, Telegraph Key and TV Antenna
A241

Ferdinand Raimund
A242

1965, May 17 **Unwmk.**

745 A241 3s vio bl 35 28

Issued to commemorate the centenary of the International Telecommunication Union.

1965 Engr. *Perf. 14x13½*

Portraits: No. 746, Ignaz Philipp Semmelweis. No. 747, Bertha von Suttner. No. 749, Ferdinand Georg Waldmüller.

746 A242 1.50s violet 25 12
747 A242 1.50s bluish blk 25 15
748 A242 3s dk brn 45 25
749 A242 3s grnsh blk 45 30

No. 746 commemorates the centenary of the death of Dr. Ignaz Philipp Semmelweis (1818-65), who discovered the cause of puerperal fever and introduced antisepsis into obstetrics. No. 747, the 60th anniversary of the awarding of the Nobel Prize for Peace to Bertha von Suttner (1843-1914), pacifist and author. No. 748, the 175th anniversary of the birth of Ferdinand Raimund (1790-1836), actor and playwright. No. 749, the centenary of the death of Ferdinand Georg Waldmüller (1793-1865), painter.

Issue dates: No. 746, Aug. 13; No. 747, Dec. 1; No. 748, June 1; No. 749, Aug. 23.

Dancers with Tambourines
A243

Red Cross and Strip of Gauze
A244

Design: 1.50s, Male gymnasts with practice bars.

Photogravure and Engraved

1965, July 20

750 A243 1.50s gray & blk 20 15
751 A243 3s bis & blk 40 32

Issued to commemorate the Fourth Gymnaestrada, international athletic meet, Vienna, July 20-24.

1965, Oct. 1 Litho. *Perf. 14x13½*

752 A244 3s blk & red 35 25

Issued to publicize the 20th International Red Cross Conference, Vienna.

Austrian Flag and Eagle with Mural Crown — A245

Austrian Flag, U.N. Headquarters and Emblem — A246

Photogravure and Engraved

1965, Oct. 7
753 A245 1.50s gold, red & blk 20 18

Issued to commemorate the 50th anniversary of the Union of Austrian Towns.

Lithographed and Engraved

1965, Oct. 25 Unwmk. *Perf. 12*
754 A246 3s blk, brt bl & red 60 30

Issued to commemorate the 10th anniversary of Austria's admission to the United Nations.

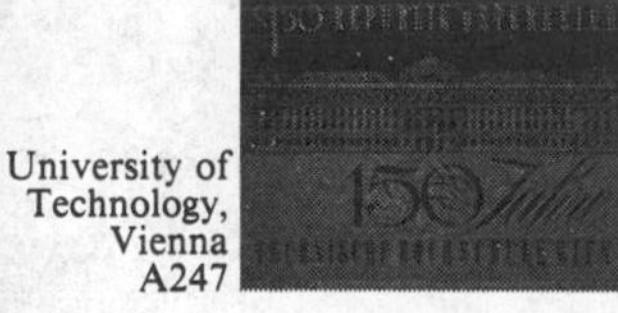
University of Technology, Vienna A247

1965, Nov. 8 Engr. *Perf. 13½x14*
755 A247 1.50s violet 20 15

Issued to commemorate the 150th anniversary of the founding of the Vienna University of Technology.

Map of Austria with Postal Zone Numbers — A248

1966, Jan. 14 Photo. *Perf. 12*
756 A248 1.50s yel, red & blk 20 8

Issued to publicize the introduction of postal zone numbers, Jan. 1, 1966.

PTT Building, Emblem and Churches of Sts. Maria Rotunda and Barbara A249

Maria von Ebner Eschenbach A250

Lithographed and Engraved

1966, March 4 *Perf. 14x13½*
757 A249 1.50s *dl yel* 20 10

Issued to commemorate the centenary of the headquarters of the Post and Telegraph Administration.

1966, March 11 Engr.
758 A250 3s plum 35 20

Issued to commemorate the 50th anniversary of the death of Maria von Ebner Eschenbach (1830-1916), novelist and poet.

Ferris Wheel, Prater — A251

1966, Apr. 19 Engr. *Perf. 14x13½*
759 A251 1.50s sl grn 20 15

Issued to commemorate the 200th anniversary of the opening of the Prater (park), Vienna, to the public by Emperor Joseph II.

Josef Hoffmann A252

Unwmk.

1966, May 6 Engr. *Perf. 12*
760 A252 3s dk brn 35 20

Issued to commemorate the tenth anniversary of the death of Josef Hoffmann (1870-1956), architect.

Arms of Wiener Neustadt — A253

Photogravure and Engraved

1966, May 27 *Perf. 14*
761 A253 1.50s gray & multi 20 15

Issued to publicize the Wiener Neustadt Art Exhibition, centered around the time and person of Emperor Frederick III (1440-1493).

Austrian Eagle and Emblem of National Bank A254

1966, May 27 *Perf. 14*
762 A254 3s gray grn, dk brn & dk grn 35 20

Issued to commemorate the 150th anniversary of the Austrian National Bank.

Puppy A255

Lithographed and Engraved

1966, June 16 *Perf. 12*
763 A255 1.80s yel & blk 20 12

Issued to commemorate the 120th anniversary of the Vienna Humane Society.

Columbine A256

Alpine Flowers: 1.80s, Turk's cap. 2.20s, Wulfenia carinthiaca. 3s, Globeflowers. 4s, Fire lily. 5s, Pasqueflower.

Perf. 13½

1966, Aug. 17 Unwmk. Litho.

Flowers in Natural Colors

764	A256	1.50s dk bl	15	15
765	A256	1.80s dk bl	20	20
766	A256	2.20s dk bl	32	32
767	A256	3s dk bl	50	50
768	A256	4s dk bl	55	55
769	A256	5s dk bl	55	55
		Nos. 764-769 (6)	2.27	2.27

Fair Building A257

1966, Aug. 26 Engr. *Perf. 13½x13*
770 A257 3s vio bl 35 20

First International Fair at Wels.

Peter Anich, Map, Globe and Books — A258

Sick Worker and Health Emblem — A259

1966, Sept. 1 *Perf. 14x13½*
771 A258 1.80s black 20 12

Issued to commemorate the 200th anniversary of the death of Peter Anich (1723-1766), Tirolean cartographer and farmer.

Engraved and Lithographed

1966, Sept. 19
772 A259 3s blk & ver 35 20

Issued to publicize the 15th Occupational Medicine Congress, Vienna, Sept. 19-24.

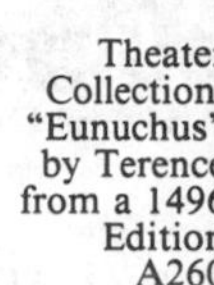

Theater Collection: "Eunuchus" by Terence from a 1496 Edition A260

Designs: 1.80s, Map Collection: Title page of Geographia Blavania (Cronus, Hercules and celestial sphere). 2.20s, Picture Archive and Portrait Collection: View of Old Vienna after a watercolor by Anton Stutzinger. 3s, Manuscript Collection: Illustration from the 15th century "Livre du Cuer d'Amours Espris" of the Duke René d'Anjou.

Photogravure and Engraved

1966, Sept. 28 *Perf. 13½x14*

773	A260	1.50s multi	12	12
774	A260	1.80s multi	20	20
775	A260	2.20s multi	25	25
776	A260	3s multi	28	28

Austrian National Library.

Young Girl — A261

Lithographed and Engraved

1966, Oct. 3 *Perf. 14x13½*
777 A261 3s lt bl & blk 35 20

Issued to commemorate the 10th anniversary of the "Save the Child" society.

Strawberries A262

Coat of Arms of University of Linz A263

Fruit: 1s, Grapes. 1.50s, Apple. 1.80s, Blackberries. 2.20s, Apricots. 3s, Cherries.

1966, Nov. 25 Photo. *Perf. 13½x13*

778	A262	50g multi	20	20
779	A262	1s multi	18	18
780	A262	1.50s multi	18	18
781	A262	1.80s multi	28	28
782	A262	2.20s multi	28	28
783	A262	3s multi	35	35
		Nos. 778-783 (6)	1.47	1.47

Photogravure and Engraved

1966, Dec. 9 *Perf. 14x13½*
784 A263 3s gray, blk, red, sil & gold 35 20

Issued to commemorate the inauguration of the Universary of Linz, Oct. 8, 1966.

Ice Skater, 1866 — A264

Ballet Dancer — A265

Photogravure and Engraved

1967, Feb. 3 *Perf. 14x13½*
785 A264 3s pale bl & dk bl 35 20

Centenary of Vienna Ice Skating Club.

1967, Feb. 15 Engr. *Perf. 11½x12*
786 A265 3s dp cl 35 20
a. Perf. 12 1.50 1.50

Issued to commemorate the centenary of the "Blue Danube" waltz by Johann Strauss.

Karl Schönherr — A266

1967, Feb. 24 Engr. *Perf. 14x13½*
787 A266 3s gray brn 35 20

Issued to commemorate the centenary of the birth of Dr. Karl Schönherr (1867-1943), poet, playwright and physician.

Ice Hockey Goalkeeper A267

Photogravure and Engraved
1967, March 17 *Perf. 13½x14*
788 A267 3s pale grn & dk bl 35 20

Issued to publicize the Ice Hockey Championships, Vienna, March 18-29.

Violin, Organ and Laurel — A268

1967, Mar. 28 Engr. *Perf. 13½*
789 A268 3.50s indigo 45 20

Issued to commemorate the 125th anniversary of the Vienna Philharmonic Orchestra.

Motherhood, Watercolor by Peter Fendi — A269

Unwmk.
1967, Apr. 28 Litho. *Perf. 14*
790 A269 2s multi 25 15

Issued for Mother's Day, 1967.

Gothic Mantle Madonna A270

1967, May 19 Engr. *Perf. 13½x14*
791 A270 3s slate 35 20

Issued to publicize the art exhibition "Austrian Gothic," Krems, 1967. The Gothic wood carving is from Frauenstein in Upper Austria.

The Catalogue editors cannot undertake to appraise, identify or judge the genuineness or condition of stamps.

Medieval Gold Cross A271

Swan, Tapestry by Oscar Kokoschka A272

Lithographed and Engraved
1967, June 9 *Perf. 13½*
792 A271 3.50s Prus grn & multi 40 25

Issued to publicize the Salzburg Treasure Chamber in connection with an exhibition at Salzburg Cathedral, June 12-Sept. 15.

1967, June 9 Photo.
793 A272 2s multi 25 15

Issued to publicize the Nibelungen District Art Exhibition, Pöchlarn, celebrating the 700th anniversary of Pöchlarn as a city. The design is from the border of the Amor and Psyche tapestry at the Salzburg Festival Theater.

View and Arms of Vienna A273

Engraved and Photogravure
1967, June 12 *Perf. 13x13½*
794 A273 3s blk & red 35 20

Issued to publicize the 10th Europa Talks, "Science and Society in Europe," Vienna, June 13-17.

Prize Bull "Mucki" A274

1967, Aug. 28 Engr. *Perf. 13½*
795 A274 2s dp cl 25 15

Issued to commemorate the centenary of the Ried Festival and the Agricultural Fair.

Potato Beetle A275

Engraved and Photogravure
1967, Aug. 29 *Perf. 13½x14*
796 A275 3s blk & multi 35 20

Issued to publicize the 6th International Congress for Plant Protection, Vienna.

First Locomotive Used on Brenner Pass — A276

1967, Sept. 23 Photo. *Perf. 12*
797 A276 3.50s tan & sl grn 45 25

Centenary of railroad over Brenner Pass.

Christ in Glory — A277

1967, Oct. 9 *Perf. 13½*
798 A277 2s multi 25 15

Issued to commemorate the restoration of the Romanesque (11th century) frescoes in the Lambach monastery church.

Main Gate to Fair, Prater, Vienna A278

1967, Oct. 24 Photo. *Perf. 13½x14*
799 A278 2s choc & buff 25 15

Issued to publicize the Congress of International Trade Fairs, Vienna, Oct., 1967.

Medal Showing Minerva and Art Symbols A279

Frankfurt Medal for Reformation, 1717 A280

Lithographed and Engraved
1967, Oct. 25 *Perf. 13½*
800 A279 2s dk brn, dk bl & yel 25 15

Issued to commemorate the 275th anniversary of the Vienna Academy of Fine Arts. The medal was designed by Georg Raphael Donner (1693-1741) and is awarded as an artist's prize.

1967, Oct. 31 Engr. *Perf. 14x13½*
801 A280 3.50s bl blk 40 25

450th anniversary of the Reformation.

Mountain Range and Stone Pines — A281

1967, Nov. 7 *Perf. 13½*
802 A281 3.50s green 40 25

Centenary of academic study of forestry.

Land Survey Monument, 1770 — A282

St. Leopold, Window, Heiligenkreuz Abbey — A283

1967, Nov. 7 Photo.
803 A282 2s ol blk 25 15

150th anniversary of official land records.

Engraved and Photogravure
1967, Nov. 15
804 A283 1.80s multi 25 15

Issued in memory of Margrave Leopold III (1075-1136), patron saint of Austria.

Tragic Mask and Violin — A284

Nativity from 15th Century Altar — A285

1967, Nov. 17 *Perf. 13½*
805 A284 3.50s bluish lil & blk 40 25

Issued to commemorate the 150th anniversary of the Academy of Music and Dramatic Art.

1967, Nov. 27 Engr. *Perf. 14x13½*
806 A285 2s green 25 15

Christmas 1967.
The design shows the late Gothic carved center panel of the altar in St. John's Chapel in Nonnberg Convent, Salzburg.

Innsbruck Stadium, Alps and FISU Emblem — A286

Camillo Sitte — A287

1968, Jan. 22 Engr. *Perf. 13½*
807 A286 2s dk bl 25 15

Issued to publicize the Winter University Games under the auspices of FISU (Federation Internationale du Sport Universitaire), Innsbruck, Jan. 21-28.

1968, Apr. 17 *Perf. 13½*
808 A287 2s blk brn 25 15

Issued to commemorate the 125th anniversary of the birth of Camillo Sitte (1843-1903), architect and city planner.

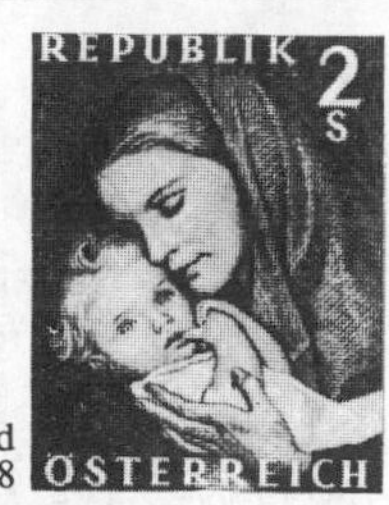

Mother and Child — A288

Cup and Serpent Emblem — A289

1968, May 7
809 A288 2s sl grn 25 15

Issued for Mother's Day, 1968.

1968, May 7 **Photo.**
810 A289 3.50s dp plum, gray & gold 40 25

Bicentenary of the Veterinary College.

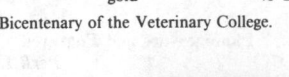

Bride with Lace Veil — A290

1968, May 24 **Engr.** ***Perf. 12***
811 A290 3.50s bl blk 40 25

Issued to commemorate the centenary of the embroidery industry of Vorarlberg.

Horse Race A291

1968, June 4 ***Perf. 13½***
812 A291 3.50s sepia 40 28

Issued to commemorate the centenary of horse racing at Freudenau, Vienna.

Dr. Karl Landsteiner A292

Peter Rosegger A293

1968, June 14 ***Perf. 14x13½***
813 A292 3.50s dk bl 40 28

Issued to commemorate the centenary of the birth of Dr. Karl Landsteiner (1868-1943), pathologist, discoverer of the four main human blood types.

1968, June 26
814 A293 2s sl grn 25 15

Issued to commemorate the 50th anniversary of the death of Peter Rosegger (1843-1918), poet and writer.

Angelica Kauffmann, Self-portrait A294

Bronze Statue of Young Man, 1st Century B.C. A295

1968, July 15 **Engr.** ***Perf. 14x13½***
815 A294 2s int blk 25 15

Issued to publicize the art exhibitions "Angelica Kauffmann and her Contemporaries," Bregenz, July 28-Oct. 13, 1968, and Vienna, Oct. 22, 1968-January 6, 1969.

Lithographed and Engraved

1968, July 15
816 A295 2s grnsh gray & blk 25 15

Issued to publicize 20 years of excavations on Magdalene Mountain, Carinthia.

Bishop, Romanesque Bas-relief — A296

1968, Sept. 20 **Engr.** ***Perf. 14x13½***
817 A296 2s bl gray 25 15

Issued to commemorate the 750th anniversary of the Graz-Seckau Bishopric.

Koloman Moser — A297

Human Rights Flame — A298

Engraved and Photogravure

1968, Oct. 18 ***Perf. 12***
818 A297 2s blk brn & ver 25 15

Issued to commemorate the 50th anniversary of the death of Koloman Moser (1868-1918), stamp designer and painter.

1968, Oct. 18 **Photo.** ***Perf. 14x13½***
819 A298 1.50s gray, dp car & dk grn 40 15

International Human Rights Year.

Pres. Karl Renner and States' Arms — A299

Designs: No. 821, Coats of arms of Austria and Austrian states. No. 822, Article I of Austrian Constitution and States' coats of arms.

Engraved and Photogravure

1968, Nov. 11 ***Perf. 13½***
820 A299 2s blk & multi 40 40
821 A299 2s blk & multi 40 40
822 A299 2s blk & multi 40 40

50th anniversary of Republic of Austria.

Crèche, Memorial Chapel, Oberndorf-Salzburg A300

1968, Nov. 29 **Engr.** ***Perf. 14x13½***
823 A300 2s sl grn 25 15

Christmas 1968. 150th anniversary of "Silent Night, Holy Night."

Angels, from Last Judgment by Troger (Röhrenbach-Greillenstein Chapel) — A301

Baroque Frescoes: No. 825, Vanquished Demons, by Paul Troger, Altenburg Abbey. No. 826, Sts. Peter and Paul, by Troger, Melk Abbey. No. 827, The Glorification of Mary, by Franz Anton Maulpertsch, Maria Treu Church, Vienna. No. 828, St. Leopold Carried into Heaven, by Maulpertsch, Ebenfurth Castle Chapel. No. 829, Symbolic figures from The Triumph of Apollo, by Maulpertsch, Halbthurn Castle.

Engraved and Photogravure

1968, Dec. 11 ***Perf. 13½x14***
824 A301 2s multi 32 32
825 A301 2s multi 32 32
826 A301 2s multi 32 32
827 A301 2s multi 32 32
828 A301 2s multi 32 32
829 A301 2s multi 32 32
Nos. 824-829 (6) 1.92 1.92

St. Stephen — A302

Statues in St. Stephen's Cathedral, Vienna: No. 831, St. Paul. No. 832, Mantle Madonna. No. 833, St. Christopher. No. 834, St. George and the Dragon. No. 835, St. Sebastian.

1969, Jan. 28 **Engr.** ***Perf. 13½***
830 A302 2s black 32 32
831 A302 2s rose cl 32 32
832 A302 2s gray vio 32 32
833 A302 2s sl bl 32 32
834 A302 2s sl grn 32 32
835 A302 2s dk red brn 32 32
Nos. 830-835 (6) 1.92 1.92

500th anniversary of Diocese of Vienna.

Parliament and Pallas Athena Fountain, Vienna A303

1969, Apr. 8 **Engr.** ***Perf. 13½***
836 A303 2s grnsh blk 25 15

Issued to publicize the Interparliamentary Union Conference, Vienna, Apr. 7-13.

Europa Issue, 1969

Common Design Type

1969, Apr. 28 **Photo.** ***Perf. 12***
837 CD12 2s gray grn, brick red & bl 25 15

Council of Europe Emblem A304

1969, May 5
838 A304 3.50s gray, ultra, blk & yel 50 32

20th anniversary of Council of Europe.

Frontier Guards — A305

Engraved and Photogravure

1969, May 14 ***Perf. 12***
839 A305 2s sep & red 25 15

Honor to Austrian Federal Army.

Don Giovanni, by Mozart — A306

Gothic Armor of Maximilian I — A307

1969, May 23 ***Perf. 13½***
840 A306 Sheet of 8, gold, red & brn blk 3.75 3.75
- *a.* 2s *Don Giovanni, Mozart* 30 00
- *b.* 2s *Magic Flute, Mozart* 30 30
- *c.* 2s *Fidelio, Beethoven* 30 30
- *d.* 2s *Lohengrin, Wagner* 30 30
- *e.* 2s *Don Carlos, Verdi* 30 30
- *f.* 2s *Carmen, Bizet* 30 30
- *g.* 2s *Rosencavalier, Richard Strauss* 30 30
- *h.* 2s *Swan Lake, Ballet by Tchaikovsky* 30 30

Centenary of Vienna Opera House.

No. 840 contains 8 stamps arranged around gold and red center label showing Opera House. Printed in sheets containing 4 Nos. 840 with wide gutters between.

1969, June 4 **Engr.**
841 A307 2s bluish blk 25 15

Issued to publicize the Emperor Maximilian I Exhibition, Innsbruck, May 30-Oct. 5.

Oldest Municipal Seal of Vienna — A308

Girl's Head and Village House — A309

1969, June 16 Photo. *Perf. 13½*

842 A308 2s tan, red & blk	25	15

Issued to publicize the 19th Congress of the International Organization of Municipalities, Vienna, June 1969.

Engraved and Photogravure

1969, June 16 *Perf. 13½x14*

843 A309 2s yel grn & sep	25	15

Issued to publicize the 20th anniversary of the Children's Village Movement in Austria (SOS Villages).

Hands Holding Wrench, and U.N. Emblem A310

Austria's Flag and Shield Circling the World A311

1969, Aug. 22 Photo. *Perf. 13x13½*

844 A310 2s dp grn	25	15

Issued to commemorate the 50th anniversary of the International Labor Organization.

Engraved and Lithographed

1969, Aug. 22 *Perf. 14x13½*

845 A311 3.50s sl & red	40	25

Issued to publicize 1969 as the Year of Austrians Living Abroad.

Young Hare, by Dürer — A312

Etchings: No. 847, El Cid Killing a Bull, by Francisco de Goya. No. 848, Madonna with the Pomegranate, by Raphael. No. 849, The Painter, by Peter Brueghel. No. 850, Rubens' Son Nicolas, by Rubens. No. 851, Self-portrait, by Rembrandt. No. 852, Lady Reading, by Francois Guerin. No. 853, Wife of the Artist, by Egon Schiele.

Engraved and Photogravure

1969, Sept. 26 *Perf. 13½*

Gray Frame, Buff Background

846 A312 2s blk & brn	32	32
847 A312 2s black	32	32
848 A312 2s black	32	32
849 A312 2s black	32	32
850 A312 2s blk & sal	32	32
851 A312 2s black	32	32
852 A312 2s blk & sal	32	32
853 A312 2s black	32	32
Nos. 846-853 (8)	2.56	2.56

Bicentenary of the etching collection in the Albertina, Vienna.

President Franz Jonas — A313

1969, Oct. 3

854 A313 2s gray & vio bl	25	15

Issued to commemorate the 70th birthday of Franz Jonas, president of Austria.

Post Horn, Globe and Lightning A314

1969, Oct. 17 *Perf. 13½x14*

855 A314 2s multi	25	15

Issued to commemorate the 50th anniversary of the Union of Postal and Telegraph employees.

Savings Box, about 1450 A315

Madonna, by Albin Egger-Lienz A316

1969, Oct. 31 Photo. *Perf. 13x13½*

856 A315 2s sil & sl grn	25	15

Issued to publicize the importance of savings.

Engraved and Photogravure

1969, Nov. 24 *Perf. 12*

857 A316 2s dp cl & pale yel	25	15

Christmas 1969.

Josef Schöffel A317

St. Klemens M. Hofbauer A318

1970, Feb. 6 Engr. *Perf. 14x13½*

858 A317 2s dl pur	25	15

Issued to commemorate the 60th anniversary of the death of Josef Schöffel, (1832-1910), who saved the Vienna Woods.

Engraved and Photogravure

1970, Mar. 13 *Perf. 14x13½*

859 A318 2s dk brn & lt tan	25	15

Issued to commemorate the 150th anniversary of the death of St. Klemens Maria Hofbauer (1751-1820); Redemptorist preacher in Poland and Austria, canonized in 1909.

Chancellor Leopold Figl A319

Belvedere Palace, Vienna A320

1970, Apr. 27 Engr. *Perf. 13½*

860 A319 2s dk ol gray	30	15
861 A320 2s dk rose brn	30	15

25th anniversary of Second Republic.

Krimml Waterfalls A321

1970, May 19 Engr. *Perf. 13½*

862 A321 2s sl grn	25	15

Issued for the European Nature Conservation Year, 1970.

St. Leopold on Oldest Seal of Innsbruck University A322

Lithographed and Engraved

1970, June 5 *Perf. 13½*

863 A322 2s red & blk	25	15

Issued to commemorate the 300th anniversary of the founding of the Leopold Franzens University in Innsbruck.

Organ, Great Hall, Music Academy — A323

Photogravure and Engraved

1970, June 5 *Perf. 14*

864 A323 2s gold & dp cl	25	15

Issued to commemorate the centenary of the Vienna Music Academy Building.

Tower Clock, 1450-1550 A324

The Beggar Student, by Carl Millöcker A325

Old Clocks from Vienna Horological Museum: No. 866, Lyre clock, 1790-1815. No. 867, Pendant clock 1600-1650. No. 868, Pendant watch, 1800-1830. No. 869, Bracket clock, 1720-1760. No. 870, French column clock, 1820-1850.

1970

865 A324 1.50s buff & sep	25	25
866 A324 1.50s grnsh & grn	25	25
867 A324 2s pale & dk bl	32	32
868 A324 2s pale rose & lake	32	32
869 A324 3.50s buff & brn	60	60
870 A324 3.50s pale lil & brn vio	60	60
Nos. 865-870 (6)	2.34	2.34

Issue dates: Nos. 865, 867, 869, June 22. Others, Oct. 23.

Photogravure and Engraved

1970 *Perf. 13½*

Operettas: No. 872, Fledermaus, by Johann Strauss. No. 873, The Dream Waltz, by Oscar Strauss. No. 874, The Bird Seller, by Carl Zeller. No. 875, The Merry Widow, by Franz Lehar. No. 876, Two Hearts in Three-quarter Time, by Robert Stolz.

871 A325 1.50s pale grn & grn	25	25
872 A325 1.50s yel & vio bl	25	25
873 A325 2s pale rose & vio brn	32	32
874 A325 2s pale grn & sep	32	32
875 A325 3.50s pale bl & ind	60	60
876 A325 3.50s beige & sl	60	60
Nos. 871-876 (6)	2.34	2.34

Issue dates: Nos. 871, 873, 875, July 3. Others Sept. 11.

Bregenz Festival Stage — A326

1970, July 23 Photo.

877 A326 3.50s dk bl & buff	40	32

25th anniversary of Bregenz Festival.

Salzburg Festival Emblem — A327

1970, July 27 *Perf. 14*

878 A327 3.50s blk, red, gold & gray	40	32

50th anniversary of Salzburg Festival.

St. John, by Thomas Schwanthaler
A328

1970, Aug. 31 **Engr.**
879 A328 3.50s dk gray 40 32

Issued to publicize the 13th General Assembly of the World Veterans Federation, Aug. 28-Sept. 4. The head of St. John is from a sculpture showing the Agony in the Garden in the chapel of the Parish Church in Ried. It is attributed to Thomas Schwanthaler (1634-1702).

Thomas Koschat — A329

1970, Sept. 16 ***Perf. 14x13½***
880 A329 2s chocolate 25 15

Issued to commemorate the 125th anniversary of the birth of Thomas Koschat (1845-1914), Carinthian composer of songs.

Mountain Scene
A330

1970, Sept. 16 **Photo.** ***Perf. 14x13½***
881 A330 2s vio bl & pink 25 15

Issued to publicize hiking and mountaineering in Austria.

Alfred Cossmann
A331

Arms of Carinthia
A332

1970, Oct. 2 **Engr.** ***Perf. 14x13½***
882 A331 2s dk brn 25 15

Issued to commemorate the centenary of the birth of Alfred Cossmann (1870-1951), engraver.

Photogravure and Engraved
1970, Oct. 2 ***Perf. 14***
883 A332 2s ol, red, gold, blk & sil 25 15

Carinthian plebiscite, 50th anniversary.

U.N. Emblem — A333

1970, Oct. 23 **Litho.** ***Perf. 14x13½***
884 A333 3.50s lt bl & blk 50 32

25th anniversary of the United Nations.

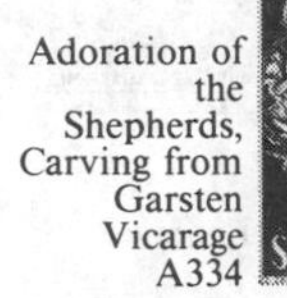

Adoration of the Shepherds, Carving from Garsten Vicarage
A334

1970, Nov. 27 **Engr.** ***Perf. 13½x14***
885 A334 2s dk vio bl 25 15

Christmas 1970.

Karl Renner
A335

Beethoven, by Georg Waldmüller
A336

1970, Dec. 14 **Engr.** ***Perf. 14x13½***
886 A335 2s dp cl 25 15

Centenary of the birth of Karl Renner (1870-1950), President of Austria.

Photogravure and Engraved
1970, Dec. 16 ***Perf. 13½***
887 A336 3.50s blk & buff 40 32

Bicentenary of the birth of Ludwig van Beethoven (1770-1827), composer.

Enrica Handel-Mazzetti
A337

1971, Jan. 11 **Engr.** ***Perf. 14x13½***
888 A337 2s sepia 25 15

Centenary of the birth of Enrica von Handel-Mazzetti (1871-1955), novelist and poet.

"Watch Out for Children!"
A338

1971, Feb. 18 **Photo.** ***Perf. 13½***
889 A338 2s blk, red brn & brt grn 32 15

Traffic safety.

Saltcellar, by Benvenuto Cellini
A339

Art Treasures: 1.50s, Covered vessel, made of prase, gold and precious stones, Florentine, 1580. 2s, Emperor Joseph I, ivory statue by Matthias Steinle, 1693.

Photogravure and Engraved
1971, March 22 ***Perf. 14***
890 A339 1.50s gray & sl grn 25 25
891 A339 2s gray & dp plum 32 32
892 A339 3.50s gray, blk & bis 60 60

Emblem of Austrian Wholesalers' Organization
A340

1971, Apr. 16 **Photo.** ***Perf. 13½***
893 A340 3.50s multi 40 32

International Chamber of Commerce, 23rd Congress, Vienna, Apr. 17-23.

Jacopo de Strada, by Titian — A341

Seal of Paulus of Franchenfordia, 1380 — A342

Paintings in Vienna Museum: 2s, Village Feast, by Peter Brueghel, the Elder. 3.50s, Young Venetian Woman, by Albrecht Dürer.

1971, May 6 **Engr.** ***Perf. 13½***
894 A341 1.50s rose lake 25 25
895 A341 2s grnsh blk 32 32
896 A341 3.5s dp brn 60 60

Photogravure and Engraved
1971, May 6 ***Perf. 13½x14***
897 A342 3.50s dk brn & bis 40 32

Congress commemorating the centenary of the Austrian Notaries' Statute, May 5-8.

St. Matthew
A343

August Neilreich
A344

1971, May 27 ***Perf. 12½x13½***
898 A343 2s brt rose lil & brn 25 15

Exhibition of "1000 Years of Art in Krems." The statue of St. Matthew is from the Lentl Altar, created about 1520 by the Master of the Pulkau Altar.

1971, June 1 **Engr.** ***Perf. 14x13½***
899 A344 2s brown 25 15

Centenary of the death of August Neilreich (1803-1871), botanist.

Singer with Lyre — A345

Photogravure and Engraved
1971, July 1 ***Perf. 13½x14***
900 A345 4s lt bl, vio bl & gold 55 40

International Choir Festival, Vienna, July 1-4.

Coat of Arms of Kitzbuhel — A346

1971, Aug. 23 ***Perf. 14***
901 A346 2.50s gold & multi 28 20

700th anniversary of the town of Kitzbuhel.

Vienna Stock Exchange — A347

1971, Sept. 1 **Engr.** ***Perf. 13½x14***
902 A347 4s redsh brn 45 28

Bicentenary of the Vienna Stock Exchange.

First and Latest Exhibition Halls
A348

1971, Sept. 6 **Photo.** ***Perf. 13½x13***
903 A348 2.50s dp rose lil 32 20

50th anniversary of Vienna International Fair.

Trade Union Emblem
A349

Arms of Burgenland
A350

1971, Sept. 20 ***Perf. 14x13½***
904 A349 2s gray, buff & red 25 15

25th anniversary of Austrian Trade Union Association.

1971, Oct. 1
905 A350 2s dk bl, gold, red & blk 25 15

50th anniversary of Burgenland's joining Austria.

Marcus Car — A351

Photogravure and Engraved

1971, Oct. 1 *Perf. 14*
906 A351 4s pale grn & blk 45 32

75th anniversary of the Austrian Automobile, Motorcycle and Touring Club.

Europa Bridge — A352

1971, Oct. 8 Engr. *Perf. 14x13½*
907 A352 4s vio bl 45 32

Opening of highway over Brenner Pass.

Styria's Iron Mountain A353

Designs: 2s, Austrian Nitrogen Products, Ltd., Linz. 4s, United Austrian Iron and Steel Works, Ltd. (VÖEST), Linz Harbor.

1971, Oct. 15 *Perf. 13½*
908 A353 1.50s redsh brn 25 25
909 A353 2s bluish blk 35 32
910 A353 4s dk sl grn 55 50

25 years of nationalized industry.

High-speed Train on Semmering A354

Trout Fisherman A355

1971, Oct. 21 *Perf. 14*
911 A354 2s claret 25 15

Inter-city rapid train service.

1971, Nov. 15 *Perf. 13½*
912 A355 2s dk red brn 25 15

Erich Tschermak-Seysenegg A356

Infant Jesus as Savior, by Dürer A357

Photogravure and Engraved

1971, Nov. 15 *Perf. 14x13½*
913 A356 2s pale ol & dk pur 25 15

Centenary of the birth of Dr. Erich Tschermak-Seysenegg (1871-1962), botanist.

1971, Nov. 26 *Perf. 13½*
914 A357 2s gold & multi 25 15

Christmas 1971.

Franz Grillparzer, by Moritz Daffinger A358

Fountain, Main Square, Friesach A359

Lithographed and Engraved

1972, Jan. 21 *Perf. 14x13½*
915 A358 2s buff, gold & blk 25 15

Death centenary of Franz Grillparzer (1791-1872), dramatic poet.

1972, Feb. 23 Engr. *Perf. 14x13½*

Designs: 2s, Fountain, Heiligenkreuz Abbey. 2.50s, Leopold Fountain, Innsbruck.

916 A359 1.50s rose lil 25 20
917 A359 2s brown 32 28
918 A359 2.50s olive 40 40

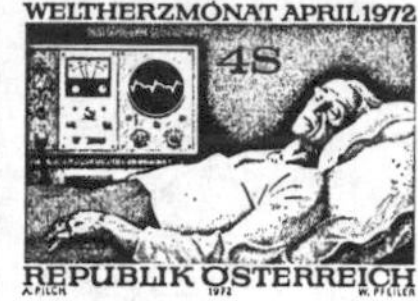
Cardiac Patient and Monitor A360

1972, Apr. 11 *Perf. 13½x14*
919 A360 4s vio brn 45 38

World Health Day 1972.

St. Michael's Gate, Royal Palace, Vienna — A361

1972, Apr. 11 *Perf. 14x13½*
920 A361 4s vio bl 45 38

Conference of European Post and Telecommunications Ministers, Vienna, Apr. 11-14.

Sculpture, Gurk Cathedral A362

Photogravure and Engraved

1972, May 5 *Perf. 14*
921 A362 2s gold & dk brn vio 25 15

900th anniversary of Gurk (Carinthia) Diocese. The design is after the central column supporting the sarcophagus of St. Hemma in Gurk Cathedral.

City Hall, Congress Emblem A363

Lithographed and Engraved

1972, May 23
922 A363 4s red, blk & yel 45 32

9th International Congress of Public and Cooperative Economy, Vienna, May 23-25.

Power Line in Carnic Alps — A364

Designs: 2.50s, Power Station, Simmering. 4s, Zemm Power Station (lake in Zillertaler Alps).

1972, June 28 *Perf. 13½x14*
923 A364 70g gray & vio 8 8
924 A364 2.50s gray & red brn 32 32
925 A364 4s gray & sl 45 45

25 years of nationalization of the power industry.

Runner with Olympic Torch — A365

St. Hermes, by Conrad Laib — A366

Engraved and Photogravure

1972, Aug. 21 *Perf. 14x13½*
926 A365 2s sep & red 25 15

Olympic torch relay from Olympia, Greece, to Munich, Germany, passing through Austria.

1972, Aug. 21 **Engr.**
927 A366 2s vio brn 25 15

Exhibition of Late Gothic Art, Salzburg.

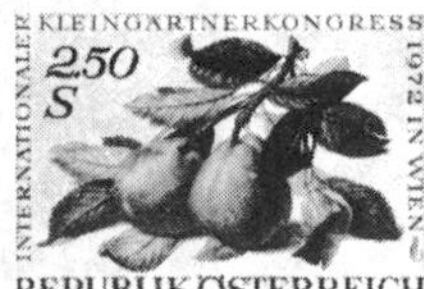
Pears A367

1972, Sept. *Perf. 14*
928 A367 2.50s dk bl & multi 28 20

World Congress of small plot Gardeners, Vienna, Sept. 7-10.

Souvenir Sheet

Spanish Walk — A368

1972, Sept. 12 *Perf. 13½*
929 A368 Sheet of 6, gold, car & dk brn 3.00 3.00
a. 2s *Spanish walk* 32 32
b. 2s *Piaffe* 32 32
c. 2.50s *Levade* 40 40
d. 2.50s *On long rein* 40 40
e. 4s *Capriole* 65 65
f. 4s *Courbette* 65 65

400th anniversary of the Spanish Riding School in Vienna. Gold and carmine margin. Size: 135x180mm.

Arms of University of Agriculture A369

Church and Old University A370

Photogravure and Engraved

1972, Oct. 17 *Perf. 14x13½*
930 A369 2s blk & multi 25 15

Centenary of the University of Agriculture, Vienna.

1972, Nov. 7 **Engr.**
931 A370 4s red brn 45 32

350th anniversary of the Paris Lodron University, Salzburg.

Carl Michael Ziehrer — A371

1972, Nov. 14
932 A371 2s rose cl 25 15

50th anniversary of the death of Carl Michael Ziehrer (1843-1922), composer.

Virgin and Child, Wood. 1420-30 A372

Photogravure and Engraved

1972, Dec. 1 *Perf. 13½*
933 A372 2s ol & choc 25 15

Christmas 1972.

Racing Sleigh, 1750 A373

Designs: 2s, Coronation landau, 1824. 2.50s, Imperial state coach, 1763.

1972, Dec. 12
934 A373 1.50s pale gray & brn 25 25
935 A373 2s pale gray & sl grn 32 32
936 A373 2.50s pale gray & plum 40 40

Collection of historic state coaches and carriages in Schönbrunn Palace.

Map of Austrian Telephone System — A374

1972, Dec. 14 Photo. *Perf. 14*
937 A374 2s yel & blk 25 15

Completion of automation of Austrian telephone system.

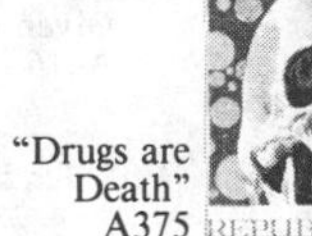
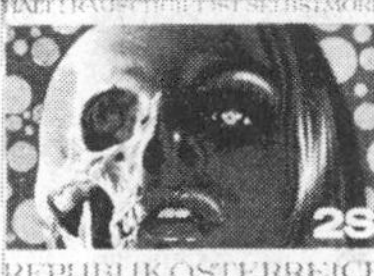

"Drugs are Death" A375

1973, Jan. 26 Photo. *Perf. 13½x14*
938 A375 2s scar & multi 2.00 75

Fight against drug abuse.

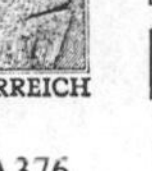

Alfons Petzold — A376

Theodor Körner — A377

1973, Jan. 26 Engr. *Perf. 14x13½*
939 A376 2s redsh brn 25 15

50th anniversary of the death of Alfons Petzold (1882-1923), poet.

Photogravure and Engraved

1973, Apr. 24 *Perf. 14x13½*
940 A377 2s gray & dp cl 25 15

Centenary of the birth of Theodor Korner (1873-1957), President of Austria.

Douglas DC-9 — A378

1973, May 14 *Perf. 13½x14*
941 A378 2s vio bl & rose red 25 15

Austrian aviation anniversaries: First international airmail service Vienna to Kiev, Mar. 31, 1918, 55th anniversary; Austrian Aviation Corporation, 50th anniversary; Austrian Airlines, 15th anniversary.

Otto Loewi A379

"Support" A380

1973, June 4 Engr. *Perf. 14x13½*
942 A379 4s dp vio 50 32

Centenary of the birth of Otto Loewi (1873-1961), pharmacologist, winner of 1936 Nobel prize.

1973, June 25
943 A380 2s dk bl 25 15

Federation of Austrian Social Insurance Institutes, 25th anniversary.

Europa Issue 1973

Post Horn and Telephone A381

1973, July 9 Photo. *Perf. 14*
944 A381 2.50s ocher, blk & yel 28 20

Dornbirn Fair Emblem A382

1973, July 27 *Perf. 13½x14*
945 A382 2s multi 25 15

Dornbirn Trade Fair, 25th anniversary.

Hurdles — A383

Leo Slezak — A384

1973, Aug. 13 Engr. *Perf. 14x13½*
946 A383 4s gray ol 50 32

23rd International Military Pentathlon Championships, Wiener Neustadt, Aug. 13-18.

1973, Aug. 17 *Perf. 14*
947 A384 4s dk brn 50 32

Centenary of the birth of Leo Slezak (1873-1946), operatic tenor.

Gate, Vienna Hofburg, and ISI Emblem — A385

Photogravure and Engraved

1973, Aug. 20 *Perf. 14x13½*
948 A385 2s gray, dk brn & ver 25 15

39th Congress of International Statistical Institute, Vienna, Aug. 20-30.

Tegetthoff off Franz Josef Land, by Julius Prayer A386

1973, Aug. 30 Engr. *Perf. 13½x14*
949 A386 2.50s Prus grn 28 20

Centenary of the discovery of Franz Josef Land by an Austrian North Pole expedition.

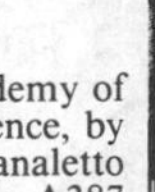

Academy of Science, by Canaletto A387

1973, Sept. 4
950 A387 2.50s violet 28 20

Centenary of international meteorological cooperation.

Arms of Viennese Tanners A388

Max Reinhardt A389

Photogravure and Engraved

1973, Sept. 4 *Perf. 14*
951 A388 4s red & multi 50 32

13th Congress of the International Union of Leather Chemists' Societies, Vienna, Sept. 1-7.

1973, Sept. 7 Engr. *Perf. 13x13½*
952 A389 2s rose mag 25 15

Centenary of the birth of Max Reinhardt (1873-1943), theatrical director and stage manager.

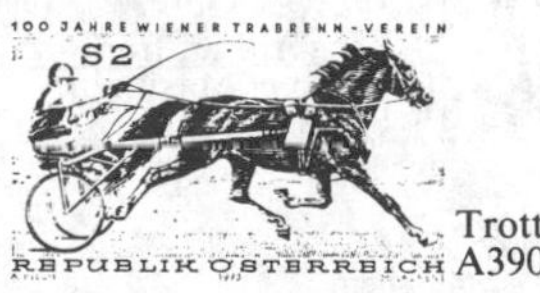

Trotter A390

1973, Sept. 28 *Perf. 13½*
953 A390 2s green 25 15

Centenary of Vienna Trotting Association.

Ferdinand Hanusch A391

1973, Sept. 28 *Perf. 14x13½*
954 A391 2s rose brn 25 15

50th anniversary of the death of Ferdinand Hanusch (1866-1923), secretary of state.

Police Radio Operator A392

1973, Oct. 2 *Perf. 13½x14*
955 A392 4s vio bl 50 32

50th anniversary of International Criminal Police Organization (INTERPOL).

Josef Petzval's Photographic Lens — A393

Lithographed and Engraved

1973, Oct. 8 *Perf. 14*
956 A393 2.50s bl & multi 28 20

EUROPHOT Photographic Congress, Vienna.

Emperor's Spring, Hell Valley A394

Photogravure and Engraved

1973, Oct. 23 *Perf. 13½x14*
957 A394 2s sep, bl & red 25 15

Centenary of Vienna's first mountain spring water supply system.

Almsee, Upper Austria — A395

Hofburg and Prince Eugene Statue, Vienna — A395a

Designs: 50g, Farmhouses, Zillertal, Tirol. 1s, Kahlenbergerdorf. 1.50s, Bludenz, Vorarlberg. 2s, Inn Bridge, Alt Finstermunz. 2.50s, Murau, Styria. 3s, Bischofsmütze, Salzburg. 3.50s, Easter Church, Oberwart. 4.50s, Windmill, Retz. 5s, Aggstein Castle, Lower Austria. 6s, Lindauer Hut, Vorarlberg. 6.50s, Holy Cross Church, Villach, Carinthia. 7s, Falkenstein Castle, Carinthia. 7.50s, Hohensalzburg. 8s, Votive column, Reiteregg, Styria. 10s, Lake Neusiedl, Burgenland. 11s, Old Town, Enns. 16s, Openair Museum, Bad Tatzmannsdorf. 20s, Myra waterfalls.

Photogravure and Engraved

1973-78 *Perf. 13½x14*

Size: 23x29mm.

No.	Design	Value	Color	Unused	Used
958	A395	50g	gray & sl grn ('75)	6	5
959	A395	1s	brn & dk brn ('75)	10	5
960	A395	1.50s	rose & brn ('74)	15	5
961	A395	2s	gray bl & dk bl ('74)	22	5
962	A395	2.50s	vio & dp vio ('74)	28	5
963	A395	3s	lt ultra & vio bl ('74)	35	5
963A	A395	3.50s	dl org & brn ('78)	40	8
964	A395	4s	brt lil & pur	45	5
965	A395	4.50s	brt grn & bl grn ('76)	50	8
966	A395	5s	lil & vio	55	5
967	A395	6s	dp rose & dk vio ('75)	65	8
968	A395	6.50s	bl grn & ind ('77)	70	12
969	A395	7s	sage grn & sl grn	75	8
970	A395	7.50s	lil rose & cl ('77)	80	20
971	A395	8s	dl red & dp brn ('76)	90	15
972	A395	10s	gray grn & dk grn	1.10	15
973	A395	11s	ver & dk car ('76)	1.25	12
974	A395	16s	ocher & blk ('77)	1.75	50

975	A395	20s ol bis & ol grn ('77)	2.25 1.00
976	A395a	50s gray vio & vio bl ('75)	5.50 2.00
		Nos. 958-976 (20)	18.71 4.96

See Nos. 1100-1109.

Nativity — A396

Fritz Pregl — A397

1973, Nov. 30 ***Perf. 14***
977 A396 2s multi 25 15

Christmas 1973. Design from 14th century stained-glass window.

1973, Dec. 12 Engr. ***Perf. 14x13½***
978 A397 4s dp bl 50 32

50th anniversary of the awarding of the Nobel prize for chemistry to Fritz Pregl (1869-1930).

Telex Machine A398

Hugo Hofmannsthal A399

1974, Jan. 14 Photo. ***Perf. 14x13½***
979 A398 2.50s ultra 28 20

50th anniversary of Radio Austria.

1974, Feb. 1 Engr. ***Perf. 14***
980 A399 4s vio bl 50 32

Centenary of the birth of Hugo Hofmannsthal (1874-1929), poet and playwright.

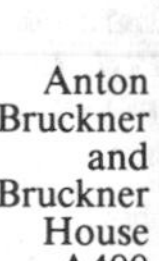

Anton Bruckner and Bruckner House A400

1974, Mar. 22 Engr. ***Perf. 14***
981 A400 4s brown 50 32

Founding of Anton Bruckner House (concert hall), Linz, and sesquicentennial of the birth of Anton Bruckner (1824-1896), composer.

Vegetables A401

Photogravure and Engraved

1974, Apr. 18 ***Perf. 14***
982 A401 2s *shown* 28 20
983 A401 2.50s *Fruits* 33 30
984 A401 4s *Flowers* 50 50

International Garden Show, Vienna, Apr. 18-Oct. 14.

Seal of Judenburg A402

Karl Kraus A403

1974, Apr. 24 Photo. ***Perf. 14x13½***
985 A402 2s plum & multi 25 15

750th anniversary of Judenburg.

1974, Apr. 6 **Engr.**
986 A403 4s dk red 50 32

Centenary of the birth of Karl Kraus (1874-1936), poet and satirist.

St. Michael, by Thomas Schwanthaler A404

King Arthur, from Tomb of Maximilian I — A405

1974, May 3
987 A404 2.50s sl grn 28 20

Exhibition of the works by the Schwanthaler Family of sculptors, (1633-1848), Reichersberg am Inn, May 3-Oct. 13.

Europa Issue 1974

1974, May 8 ***Perf. 13½***
988 A405 2.50s ocher & sl bl 28 20

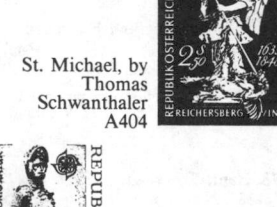

De-Dion-Bouton Motor Tricycle — A406

Photogravure and Engraved

1974, May 17 ***Perf. 14x13½***
989 A406 2s gray & vio brn 25 15

75th anniversary of the Austrian Automobile Association.

Satyr's Head, Terracotta A407

1974, May 22 ***Perf. 13½x14***
990 A407 2s org brn, gold & blk 25 15

Exhibition, "Renaissance in Austria," Schallaburg Castle, May 22-Nov. 14.

Road Transport Union Emblem A408

F. A. Maulbertsch, Self-portrait A409

1974, May 24 Photo. ***Perf. 14x13½***
991 A408 4s dp org & blk 50 32

14th Congress of the International Road Transport Union, Innsbruck.

1974, June 7 Engr. ***Perf. 14x13½***
992 A409 2s vio brn 25 15

250th anniversary of the birth of Franz Anton Maulbertsch (1724-1796), painter.

Gendarmes, 1824 and 1974 — A410

1974, June 7 Photo. ***Perf. 13½x14***
993 A410 2s red & multi 25 15

125th anniversary of Austrian gendarmery.

Fencing A411

Photogravure and Engraved

1974, June 14 ***Perf. 13½***
994 A411 2.50s red org & blk 28 20

Transportation Symbols A412

St. Virgil, Sculpture from Nonntal Church A413

1974, June 18 Photo. ***Perf. 14x13½***
995 A412 4s lt ultra & multi 50 32

European Conference of Transportation Ministers, Vienna, June 18-21.

1974, June 28 Engr. ***Perf. 13½x14***
996 A413 2s vio bl 25 15

1200th anniversary of the consecration of the Cathedral of Salzburg by Scotch-Irish Bishop Feirgil (St. Virgil). Salzburg was a center of Christianization in the 8th century.

Franz Jonas and Austrian Eagle — A414

1974, June 28
997 A414 2s black 25 15

Franz Jonas (1899-1974), President of Austria 1965-1974.

Franz Stelzhamer A415

Diver A416

1974, July 12 Engr. ***Perf. 14x13½***
998 A415 2s indigo 25 15

Death centenary of Franz Stelzhamer (1802-1874), poet who wrote in Upper Austrian vernacular.

Photogravure and Engraved

1974, Aug. 16 ***Perf. 13x13½***
999 A416 4s bl & sep 50 32

13th European Swimming, Diving and Water Polo Championships, Vienna, Aug. 18-25.

Ferdinand Ritter von Hebra — A417

1974, Sept. 10 Engr. ***Perf. 14x13½***
1000 A417 4s brown 50 32

30th Meeting of the Association of German-speaking Dermatologists, Graz, Sept. 10-14. Dr. von Hebra (1816-1880) was a founder of modern dermatology.

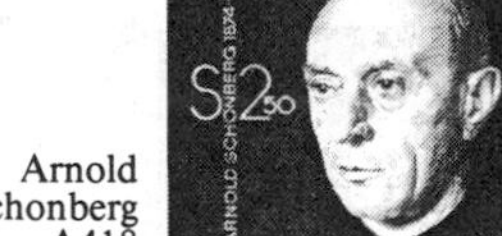

Arnold Schonberg A418

1974, Sept. 13 ***Perf. 13½x14***
1001 A418 2.50s purple 28 20

Centenary of the birth of Arnold Schönberg (1874-1951), composer.

Radio Station, Salzburg A419

1974, Oct. 1 Photo. ***Perf. 13½x14***
1002 A419 2s multi 25 15

50th anniversary of Austrian broadcasting.

Edmund Eysler — A420

1974, Oct. 4 Engr. *Perf. 14x13½*
1003 A420 2s dk ol 25 15

25th death anniversary of Edmund Eysler (1874-1949), composer.

Mailman, Mail Coach and Train, UPU Emblem A421

Design: 4s, Mailman, jet, truck, 1974, and UPU emblem.

1974, Oct. 9 Photo. *Perf. 13½*
1004 A421 2s dp cl & lil 25 15
1005 A421 4s dk bl & gray 50 32

Centenary of Universal Postal Union.

Gauntlet Protecting Rose — A422

1974, Oct. 23 Photo. *Perf. 13½x14*
1006 A422 2s multi 25 15

Environment protection.

Austrian Sports Pool Emblem A423

1974, Oct. 23 Photo. *Perf. 13½x14*
1007 A423 70g multi 8 6

Austrian Sports Pool (lottery), 25th anniversary.

Carl Ditters von Dittersdorf A424

Virgin and Child, Wood, c. 1600 A425

1974, Oct. 24 Engr. *Perf. 14x13½*
1008 A424 2s Prus grn 25 15

175th death anniversary of Carl Ditters von Dittersdorf (1739-1799), composer.

Photogravure and Engraved

1974, Nov. 29
1009 A425 2s brn & gold 25 15

Christmas 1974.

Franz Schmidt — A426

St. Christopher A427

1974, Dec. 18
1010 A426 4s gray & blk 50 32

Birth centenary of Franz Schmidt (1874-1939), composer.

Photogravure and Engraved

1975, Jan. 24 *Perf. 13½*
1011 A427 2.50s gray & brn 28 20

European Architectural Heritage Year. The design shows part of a wooden figure from central panel of the retable in the Kefermarkt Church, 1490-1497.

Safety Belt and Skeleton Arms — A428

Stained Glass Window, Vienna City Hall — A429

1975, Apr. 1 Photo. *Perf. 14x13½*
1012 A428 70g vio & multi 8 6

Introduction of obligatory use of automobile safety belts.

1975, Apr. 2 *Perf. 14*
1013 A429 2.50s multi 28 20

11th meeting of the Council of European Municipalities, Vienna, Apr. 2-5.

Austria as Mediator — A430 Forest — A431

1975, May 2 Litho. *Perf. 14*
1014 A430 2s blk & bis 25 15

30th anniversary of the Second Republic of Austria.

1975, May 6 Engr.
1015 A431 2s green 25 15

National forests, 50th anniversary.

High Priest, by Michael Pacher A432

Gosaukamm Funicular A433

Europa Issue 1975

Photogravure and Engraved

1975, May 27 *Perf. 14x13½*
1016 A432 2.50s blk & multi 28 20

Design is detail from painting "The Marriage of Joseph and Mary," by Michael Pacher (c. 1450-1500).

1975, June 23 *Perf. 14x13½*
1017 A433 2s sl & red 25 15

4th International Funicular Congress, Vienna, June 23-27.

Josef Misson and Mühlbach am Manhartsberg A434

1975, June 27 *Perf. 13½x14*
1018 A434 2s choc & redsh brn 25 15

Death centenary of Josef Misson (1803-1875), poet who wrote in Lower Austrian vernacular.

Setting Sun and "P" — A435

1975, Aug. 27 Litho. *Perf. 14x13½*
1019 A435 1.50s org, blk & bl 20 12

Austrian Association of Pensioners 25th anniversary meeting, Vienna, Aug. 1975.

Ferdinand Porsche A436

Photogravure and Engraved

1975, Sept. 3 *Perf. 13½x14*
1020 A436 1.50s gray & pur 20 12

Ferdinand Porsche (1875-1951), engineer, developer of Porsche and Volkswagen cars, birth centenary.

Leo Fall — A437

1975, Sept. 16 Engr. *Perf. 14x13½*
1021 A437 2s violet 25 15

Leo Fall (1873-1925), composer, 50th death anniversary.

The indexes in each volume of the Scott Catalogue contain many listings which help to identify stamps.

Judo Throw — A438

Heinrich Angeli — A439

1975, Oct. 20 Photo. *Perf. 14x13½*
1022 A438 2.50s gold & multi 28 20

10th World Judo Championships, Vienna, Oct. 20-26.

1975, Oct. 21 Engr. *Perf. 14x13½*
1023 A439 2s rose lake 25 15

Heinrich Angeli (1840-1925), painter, 50th death anniversary.

Johann Strauss and Dancers A440

Photogravure and Engraved

1975, Oct. 24 *Perf. 13½x14*
1024 A440 4s ocher & sep 50 32

Johann Strauss (1825-1899), composer, 150th birth anniversary.

Stylized Musician Playing a Viol — A441

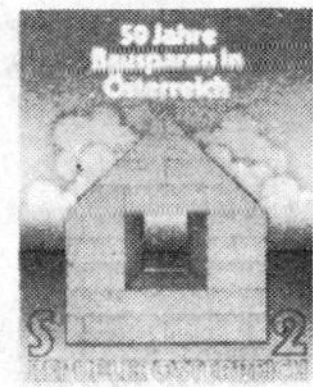

Symbolic House — A442

1975, Oct. 30 *Perf. 14x13½*
1025 A441 2.50s sil & vio bl 28 20

Vienna Symphony Orchestra, 75th anniversary.

1975, Oct. 31 Photo.
1026 A442 2s multi 25 15

Austrian building savings societies, 50th anniversary.

Fan with "Hanswurst" Scene, 18th Century A443

1975, Nov. 14 Photo. *Perf. 13½x14*
1027 A443 1.50s grn & multi 20 12

Salzburg Theater bicentenary.

Virgin and Child, from 15th Century Altar A444

"The Spiral Tree," by Hundertwasser A445

Photogravure and Engraved

1975, Nov. 28 *Perf. 13x13½*

1028 A444 2s gold & dl pur 25 15

Christmas 1975.

Photogravure, Engraved and Typographed

1975, Dec. 11 *Perf. 13½x14*

1029 A445 4s multi 50 40

Austrian modern art. Friedenstreich Hundertwasser is the pseudonym of Friedrich Stowasser (b. 1928).

Old Burgtheater A446

Design: No. 1030b, Grand staircase, new Burgtheater.

Perf. 14 (pane), 13½x14 (stamps)

1976, Apr. 8 **Engr.**

1030 Pane of 2 + label 1.20 1.20
 a. A446 3s vio bl 40 40
 b. A446 3s dp brn 40 40

Bicentenary of Vienna Burgtheater. Printed in sheets of 5 panes. Label (head of Pan) and commemorative inscription in vermilion. Size: 130x60mm.

Dr. Robert Barany — A447

Photogravure and Engraved

1976, Apr. 22 *Perf. 14x13½*

1031 A447 3s bl & brn 35 25

Robert Barany (1876-1936), winner of Nobel Prize for Medicine, 1914, birth centenary.

Ammonite A448

1976, Apr. 30 Photo. *Perf. 13½x14*

1032 A448 3s red & multi 35 25

Vienna Museum of Natural History, Centenary Exhibition.

Carinthian Dukes' Coronation Chair — A449

Siege of Linz, 17th Century Etching — A450

Photogravure and Engraved

1976, May 6 *Perf. 14x13½*

1033 A449 3s grnsh blk & org 35 25

Millennium of Carintnia.

1976, May 14

1034 A450 4s blk & gray grn 50 32

Upper Austrian Peasants' War, 350th anniversary.

Skittles A451

1976, May 14 *Perf. 13½x14*

1035 A451 4s blk & org 50 32

11th World Skittles Championships, Vienna.

Duke Heinrich II, Stained-glass Window — A452

1976, May 14 *Perf. 14*

1036 A452 3s multi 35 25

Babenberg Exhibition, Lilienfeld.

St. Wolfgang, from Pacher Altar — A453

1976, May 26 Engr. *Perf. 13½*

1037 A453 6s brt vio 70 50

International Art Exhibition at St. Wolfgang.

Europa Issue 1976

Tassilo Cup, Kremsmunster, 777 — A454

Photogravure and Engraved

1976, Aug. 13 *Perf. 14x13½*

1038 A454 4s ultra & multi 50 32

Timber Fair Emblem — A455

Constantin Economo, M.D. — A456

1976, Aug. 13 **Photo.**

1039 A455 3s grn & multi 35 25

25 years of Austrian Timber Fair, Klagenfurt.

1976, Aug. 23 **Engr.**

1040 A456 3s dk red brn 35 25

Dr. Constantin Economo (1876-1931); neurologist.

Administrative Court, by Salomon Klein — A457

1976, Oct. 25 Engr. *Perf. 13½x14*

1041 A457 6s dp brn 70 50

Austrian Central Administrative Court, centenary.

Souvenir Sheet

Arms of Lower Austria — A458

Designs: Coats of Arms of Austrian Provinces.

Photogravure and Engraved

1976, Oct. 25 *Perf. 14*

1042 A458 Sheet of 9, multi 3.00 3.00
 a. 2s *shown* 30 30
 b. 2s *Upper Austria* 30 30
 c. 2s *Styria* 30 30
 d. 2s *Carinthia* 30 30
 e. 2s *Tyrol* 30 30
 f. 2s *Vorarlberg* 30 30
 g. 2s *Salzburg* 30 30
 h. 2s *Burgenland* 30 30
 i. 2s *Vienna* 30 30

Millennium of Austria. Austrian coat of arms, red border and black inscription in margin. Size: 135x180mm.

"Cancer" A459

1976, Nov. 17 Photo. *Perf. 14x13½*

1043 A459 2.50s multi 28 20

Fight against cancer.

A particular stamp may be scarce, but if few collectors want it, its market value may remain relatively low.

UN Emblem and Bridge — A460

1976, Nov. 17

1044 A460 3s bl & gold 40 25

UN Industrial Development Organization (UNIDO), 10th anniversary.

Punched Tape, Map of Europe — A461

1976, Nov. 17 *Perf. 14*

1045 A461 1.50s multi 15 12

Austrian Press Agency (APA), 30th anniversary.

Viktor Kaplan, Kaplan Turbine A462

Photogravure and Engraved

1976, Nov. 26 *Perf. 13½x14*

1046 A462 2.50s multi 28 20

Viktor Kaplan (1876-1934), inventor of Kaplan turbine, birth centenary.

Nativity, by Konrad von Friesach, c. 1450 A463

1976, Nov. 26 *Perf. 13½*

1047 A463 3s multi 32 25

Christmas 1976.

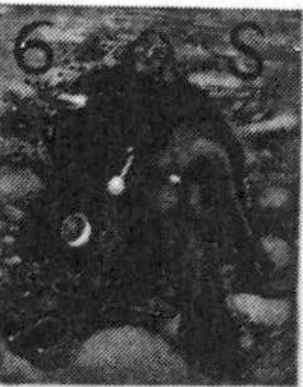

Augustin, the Piper — A464

Photogravure and Engraved

1976, Dec. 29 *Perf. 13½*

1048 A464 6s multi 65 40

Modern Austrian art.

Rainer Maria Rilke (1875-1926), Poet A465

Vienna City Synagogue A466

1976, Dec. 29 Engr. *Perf. 14x13½*
1049 A465 3s dp vio 30 20

1976, Dec. 29 Photo. *Perf. 13½*
1050 A466 1.50s multi 15 10

Sesquicentennial of Vienna City Synagogue.

Nikolaus Joseph Jacquin — A467

1977, Feb. 16 Engr. *Perf. 14x13½*
1051 A467 4s chocolate 40 32

Nikolaus Joseph von Jacquin (1727-1817), botanist.

Oswald von Wolkenstein A468

Photogravure and Engraved
1977, Feb. 16 *Perf. 14*
1052 A468 3s multi 30 20

Oswald von Wolkenstein (1377-1445), poet, 600th birth anniversary.

Handball A469

1977, Feb. 25 Photo. *Perf. 13½x14*
1053 A469 1.50s multi 15 10

World Indoor Handball Championships, Austria, Feb. 5-Mar. 6.

Alfred Kubin — A470

1977, Apr. 12 Engr. *Perf. 14x13½*
1054 A470 6s dk vio bl 70 40

Alfred Kubin (1877-1959), illustrator and writer, birth centenary.

Great Spire, St. Stephen's Cathedral A471

Designs: 3s, Heathen Tower and Frederick's Gable. 4s, Interior view with Albertinian Choir.

1977, Apr. 22 Engr. *Perf. 13½*
1055 A471 2.50s dk brn 32 15
1056 A471 3s dk bl 35 35
1057 A471 4s rose lake 50 40

Restoration and re-opening of St. Stephen's Cathedral, Vienna, 25th anniversary.

Fritz Hermanovsky-Orlando — A472

Photogravure and Engraved
1977, Apr. 29 *Perf. 13½x14*
1058 A472 6s Prus grn & gold 70 40

Fritz Hermanovsky-Orlando (1877-1954), poet and artist, birth centenary.

IAEA Emblem A473

Arms of Schwanenstadt A474

1977, May 2 Photo. *Perf. 14*
1059 A473 3s brt bl, lt bl & gold 35 20

International Atomic Energy Agency (IAEA), 20th anniversary.

1977, June 10 Photo. *Perf. 14x13½*
1060 A474 3s dk brn & multi 35 20

350th anniversary of the town Schwanenstadt.

Europa Issue 1977

Attersee, Upper Austria — A475

1977, June 10 Engr. *Perf. 14*
1061 A475 6s ol grn 65 50

Globe, by Vincenzo Coronelli, 1688 — A476

Photogravure and Engraved
1977, June 29 *Perf. 14*
1062 A476 3s blk & buff 30 25

5th International Symposium of the Coronelli World Federation of Friends of the Globe, Austria, June 29-July 3.

Kayak Race — A477

1977, July 15 Photo. *Perf. 13½x14*
1063 A477 4s multi 40 28

3rd Kayak Slalom White Water Race on Lieser River, Spittal.

The Good Samaritan, by Francesco Bassano — A478

Photogravure and Engraved
1977, Sept. 16
1064 A478 1.50s brn & red 20 12

Workers' Good Samaritan Organization, 50th anniversary.

Papermakers' Coat of Arms — A479

Man with Austrian Flag Lifting Barbed Wire — A480

1977, Oct. 10 *Perf. 14x13½*
1065 A479 3s multi 30 20

17th Conference of the European Committee of Pulp and Paper Technology (EUCEPA), Vienna.

1977, Nov. 3 *Perf. 14*
1066 A480 2.50s sl & red 30 20

Honoring the martyrs for Austria's freedom.

"Austria," First Steam Locomotive in Austria — A481

Designs: 2.50s, Steam locomotive 214. 3s, Electric locomotive 1044.

Photogravure and Engraved
1977, Nov. 17 *Perf. 13½*
1067 A481 1.50s multi 15 12
1068 A481 2.50s multi 28 15
1069 A481 3s multi 35 32

140th anniversary of Austrian railroads.

Virgin and Child, Wood Statue, Mariastein, Tyrol — A482

1977, Nov. 25 *Perf. 14x13½*
1070 A482 3s multi 32 15

Christmas 1977.

The Danube Maiden, by Wolfgang Hutter — A483

1977, Dec. 2 *Perf. 13½x14*
1071 A483 6s multi 65 28

Modern Austrian art.

Egon Friedell A484

Photogravure and Engraved
1978, Jan. 23
1072 A484 3s lt bl & blk 35 25

Egon Friedell (1878-1938), writer and historian.

Subway Train — A485

1978, Feb. 24 Photo. *Perf. 13½x14*
1073 A485 3s multi 35 25

New Vienna subway system.

Biathlon Competition A486

Photogravure and Engraved
1978, Feb. 28
1074 A486 4s multi 45 32

Biathlon World Championships, Hochfilzen, Tyrol, Feb. 28-Mar. 5.

Leopold Kunschak A487

1978, Mar. 13 Engr. ***Perf. 14x13½***
1075 A487 3s vio bl 32 22

Leopold Kunschak (1871-1953), political leader, 25th death anniversary.

Coyote, Aztec Feather Shield A488

1978, Mar. 13 Photo. ***Perf. 13½x14***
1076 A488 3s multi 32 22

Ethnographical Museum, 50th anniversary exhibition.

Alpine Farm, Woodcut by Suitbert Lobisser — A489

1978, Mar. 23 Engr. ***Perf. 13½***
1077 A489 3s dk brn,*buff* 32 22

Suitbert Lobisser (1878-1943), graphic artist, birth centenary.

Capercaillie, Hunting Bag, 1730, and Rifle, 1655 — A490

Photogravure and Engraved

1978, Apr. 28 ***Perf. 13½***
1078 A490 6s multi 70 50

International Hunting Exhibition, Marchegg.

Europa Issue 1978

Riegersburg, Styria — A491

1978, May 3 Engr.
1079 A491 6s dp rose lil 70 50

Parliament, Vienna, and Map of Europe — A492

Admont Pietà, c. 1410 — A493

1978, May 3 Photo. ***Perf. 14x13½***
1080 A492 4s multi 45 30

3rd Interparliamentary Conference for European Cooperation and Security, Vienna.

Photogravure and Engraved

1978, May 26
1081 A493 2.50s ocher & blk 25 15

Gothic Art in Styria Exhibition, St. Lambrecht, 1978.

Ort Castle, Gmunden — A494

1978, June 9
1082 A494 3s multi 32 25

700th anniversary of Gmunden City.

Child with Flowers and Fruit — A495

Lehar and his Home, Bad Ischl — A496

Photogravure and Engraved

1978, June 30 ***Perf. 14x13½***
1083 A495 6s gold & multi 70 50

25 years of Social Tourism.

1978, July 14 Engr. ***Perf. 14x13½***
1084 A496 6s slate 65 45

International Lehar Congress, Bad Ischl. Franz Lehar (1870-1948), operetta composer.

Congress Emblem A497

1978, Aug. 21 Photo. ***Perf. 13½x14***
1085 A497 1.50s blk, red & yel 20 12

Congress of International Federation of Building Construction and Wood Workers, Vienna, Aug. 20-24.

Ottokar of Bohemia and Rudolf of Hapsburg A498

Photogravure and Engraved

1978, Aug. 25
1086 A498 3s multi 35 25

Battle of Durnkrut and Jedenspeigen (Marchfeld), which established Hapsburg rule in Austria, 700th anniversary.

First Documentary Reference to Villach, "ad pontem uillah" — A499

1978, Sept. 8 Litho. ***Perf. 13½x14***
1087 A499 3s multi 35 25

1100th anniversary of Villach, Carinthia.

Seal of Graz, 1440 — A500

Emperor Maximilian Fishing — A501

Photogravure and Engraved

1978, Sept. 13 ***Perf. 14x13½***
1088 A500 4s multi 50 35

850th anniversary of Graz.

1978, Sept. 15 ***Perf. 14x13½***
1089 A501 4s multi 50 32

World Fishing Championships, Vienna, Sept. 1978.

"Aid to the Handicapped" — A502

1978, Oct. 2 Photo. ***Perf. 13½x14***
1090 A502 6s org brn & blk 65 45

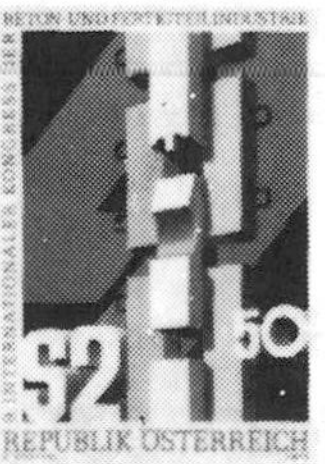

Symbolic Column — A503

1978, Oct. 9 Photo. ***Perf. 13½***
1091 A503 2.50s org, blk & gray 30 22

9th International Congress of Concrete and Prefabrication Industries, Vienna, Oct. 8-13.

Grace, by Albin Egger-Lienz A504

1978, Oct. 27 ***Perf. 13½x14***
1092 A504 6s multi 65 45

European Family Congress, Vienna, Oct. 26-29.

Lise Meitner and Atom Symbol — A505

1978, Nov. 7 Engr. ***Perf. 14x13½***
1093 A505 6s dk vio 65 45

Lise Meitner (1878-1968), physicist.

Viktor Adler, by Anton Hanak A506

Photogravure and Engraved

1978, Nov. 10 ***Perf. 13½x14***
1094 A506 3s ver & blk 35 25

Viktor Adler (1852-1918), leader of Social Democratic Party, 60th death anniversary.

Franz Schubert, by Josef Kriehuber A507

Virgin and Child, Wilhering Church A508

1978, Nov. 17 Engr. ***Perf. 14***
1095 A507 6s redsh brn 70 50

Franz Schubert (1797-1828), composer.

Photogravure and Engraved

1978, Dec. 1 ***Perf. 12½x13½***
1096 A508 3s multi 35 25

Christmas 1978.

Archduke Johann Shelter, Grossglockner — A509

1978, Dec. 6 ***Perf. 13½x14***
1097 A509 1.50s gold & dk vio bl 20 12

Austrian Alpine Club, centenary.

Adam, by Rudolf Hausner — A510

Bound Hands — A511

1978, Dec. 6 Photo. ***Perf. 13½x14***
1098 A510 6s multi 70 50

Modern Austrian art.

1978, Dec. 6 ***Perf. 14x13½***
1099 A511 6s dp cl 65 45

30th anniversary of Universal Declaration of Human Rights.

Type of 1973

Designs: 20g, Freistadt, Upper Austria. 3s, Bishofsmutze, Salzburg. 4.20s, Hirschegg, Kleinwalsertal. 5.50s, Peace Chapel, Stoderzinken. 5.60s, Riezlern, Kleinwalsertal. 9s, Asten Carinthia. 12s, Kufstein Fortress. 14s, Weiszsee, Salzburg.

Sizes: 20g, 27x33mm. 3s, 17x21mm. 4.20s, 5.50s, 5.60s, 9s, 12s, 14s, 23x29mm.

Photogravure and Engraved

1978-84 ***Perf. 13½x14***
1100 A395 20g vio bl & dk bl ('80) 5 5
1102 A395 3s lt ultra & vio bl 35 20
1104 A395 4.20s blk & grysh bl ('79) 45 20
1105 A395 5.50s lil & pur ('82) 60 28
1106 A395 5.60s yel grn & ol grn ('82) 60 30
1107 A395 9s red ('85) 1.00 70
1108 A395 12s ocher & vio brn ('80) 1.35 25
1109 A395 14s lt grn & grn ('82) 1.65 32
Nos. 1100-1109 (8) 6.05 2.30

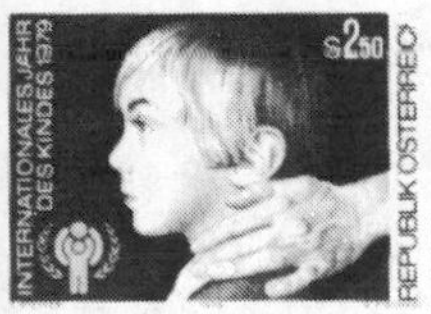

Child and IYC Emblem A512

Photogravure and Engraved

1979, Jan. 16 ***Perf. 14***
1110 A512 2.50s dk bl, blk & brn 25 20

International Year of the Child.

CCIR Emblem A513

1979, Jan. 16 Photo. ***Perf. 13½x14***
1111 A513 6s multi 65 45

International Radio Consultative Committee (CCIR) of the International Telecommunications Union, 50th anniversary.

Air Rifle, Air Pistol and Club Emblem A514

Photogravure and Engraved

1979, Mar. 7 ***Perf. 13½***
1112 A514 6s multi 65 45

Centenary of Austrian Shooting Club, and European Air Rifle and Air Pistol Championships, Graz.

Figure Skater — A515

1979, Mar. 7 Photo. ***Perf. 14x13½***
1113 A515 4s multi 45 35

World Ice Skating Championships, Vienna.

Steamer Franz I — A516

Designs: 2.50s, Tugboat Linz. 3s, Passenger ship Theodor Körner.

1979, Mar. 13 Engr. ***Perf. 13½***
1114 A516 1.50s vio bl 20 15
1115 A516 2.50s sepia 28 20
1116 A516 3s magenta 32 28

First Danube Steamship Company, 150th anniversary.

Fashion Design, by Theo Zasche, 1900 — A517

Photogravure and Engraved

1979, Mar. 26 ***Perf. 13x13½***
1117 A517 2.50s multi 30 20

50th International Fashion Week, Vienna.

Wiener Neustadt Cathedral A518

1979, Mar. 27 Engr. ***Perf. 13½***
1118 A518 4s vio bl 50 35

Cathedral of Wiener Neustadt, 700th anniversary.

Teacher and Pupils, by Franz A. Zauner — A519

Population Chart and Barock Angel — A520

Photogravure and Engraved

1979, Mar. 30 ***Perf. 14x13½***
1119 A519 2.50s multi 30 20

Education of the deaf in Austria, 200th anniversary.

1979, Apr. 6
1120 A520 2.50s multi 30 20

Austrian Central Statistical Bureau, 150th anniversary.

Laurenz Koschier A521

Diesel Motor A522

Europa Issue, 1979

1979, May 4
1121 A521 6s ocher & pur 65 45

1979, May 4 **Photo.**
1122 A522 4s multi 45 32

13th CIMAC Congress (International Organization for Internal Combustion Machines).

Arms of Ried, Schärding and Braunau — A523

Photogravure and Engraved

1979, June 1 ***Perf. 14x13½***
1123 A523 3s multi 32 20

200th anniversary of Innviertel District.

Flood and City A524

1979, June 1 ***Perf. 13½x14***
1124 A524 2.50s multi 30 20

Control and eliminate water polution.

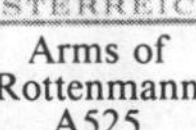

Arms of Rottenmann A525

Jodok Fink A526

Photogravure and Engraved

1979, June 22 ***Perf. 14x13½***
1125 A525 3s multi 32 22

700th anniversary of Rottenmann.

1979, June 29 Engr. ***Perf. 14***
1126 A526 3s brn car 32 22

Jodok Fink (1853-1929), governor of Vorarlberg.

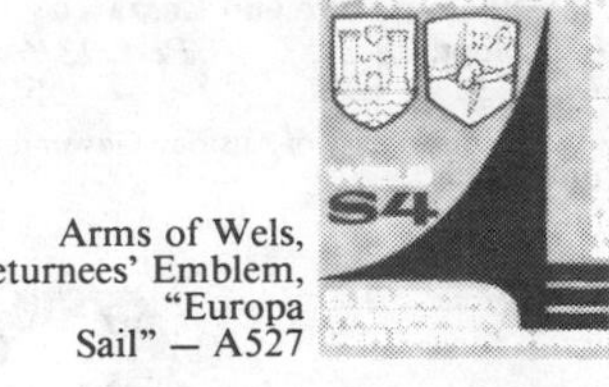

Arms of Wels, Returnees' Emblem, "Europa Sail" — A527

1979, July 6 Photo. ***Perf. 14x13½***
1127 A527 4s yel grn & blk 45 32

5th European Meeting of the International Confederation of Former Prisoners of War, Wels, July 6-8.

Symbolic Flower, Conference Emblem — A528

1979, Aug. 20 Litho. ***Perf. 14x13½***
1128 A528 4s turq bl 45 32

U.N. Conference for Science and Technology, Vienna, Aug. 20-31.

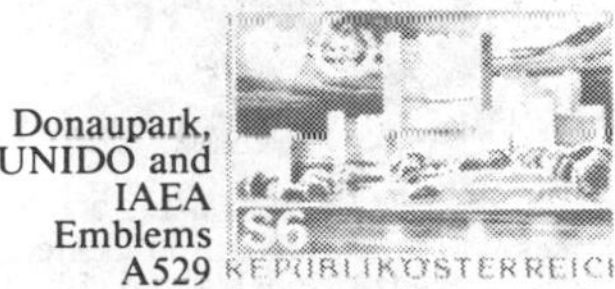

Donaupark, UNIDO and IAEA Emblems A529

1979, Aug. 24 Engr. ***Perf. 13½x14***
1129 A529 6s grysh bl 65 45

Opening of the Donaupark International Center in Vienna, seat of the United Nations Industrial Development Organization (UNIDO) and the International Atomic Energy Agency (IAEA).

Diseased Eye and Blood Vessels A530

1979, Sept. 10 Photo. ***Perf. 14***
1130 A530 2.50s multi 35 25

10th World Congress of International Diabetes Federation, Vienna, Sept. 9-14.

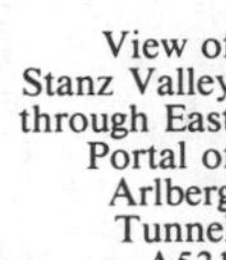

View of Stanz Valley through East Portal of Arlberg Tunnel A531

Photogravure and Engraved

1979, Sept. 14
1131 A531 4s multi 45 30

16th World Road Congress, Vienna, Sept. 16-21.

Steam Printing Press A532

Photogravure and Engraved

1979, Sept. 18 *Perf. 13½x14*

1132 A532 3s multi 32 20

175th anniversary of Austrian Government Printing Office.

Richard Zsigmondy — A533

1979, Sept. 21 Engr. *Perf. 14x13½*

1133 A533 6s multi 65 50

Richard Zsigmondy (1865-1929), chemist.

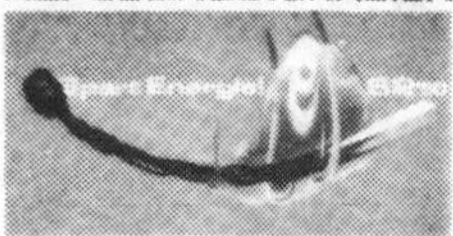

"Save Energy" A534

1979, Oct. 1 Photo. *Perf. 14x13½*

1134 A534 2.50s multi 28 20

Festival and Convention Center, Bregenz (Model) — A535

1979, Oct. 1 Engr. *Perf. 14*

1135 A535 2.50s purple 28 20

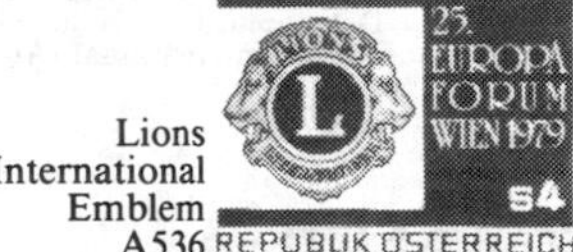

Lions International Emblem A536

Photogravure and Engraved

1979, Oct. 11

1136 A536 4s multi 45 30

25th Lions Europa Forum, Vienna, Oct. 11-13.

Wilhelm Exner — A537

Photogravure and Engraved

1979, Oct. 19 *Perf. 13½x14*

1137 A537 2.50s vio brn & blk 28 20

Centenary of Technological Handicraft Museum, founded by Wilhelm Exner.

The Compassionate Christ, by Hans Fronius — A538

1979, Oct. 23 Litho. *Perf. 13½x14*

1138 A538 4s ol & ol blk 45 32

Modern Austrian art.

Locomotive and Arms — A539

1979, Oct. 24 Photo. *Perf. 13½x14*

1139 A539 2.50s multi 30 25

Centenary of Raab-Odenburg-Ebenfurt railroad.

August Musger — A540

Photogravure and Engraved

1979, Oct. 30 *Perf. 14x13½*

1140 A540 2.50s bl gray & blk 30 20

August Musger (1868-1929), developer of slow-motion film technic.

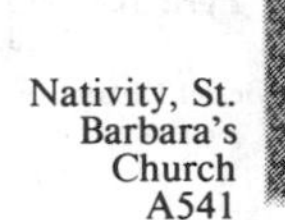

Nativity, St. Barbara's Church A541

Photogravure and Engraved

1979, Nov. 30 *Perf. 13½x14*

1141 A541 4s multi 45 32

Christmas 1979.

Arms of Baden — A542

Photogravure and Engraved

1980, Jan. 25 *Perf. 14*

1142 A542 4s multi 45 32

Baden, 500th anniversary.

Fight Rheumatism A543

1980, Feb. 21 *Perf. 13½*

1143 A543 2.50s red & aqua 30 20

Austrian Exports — A544

Austrian Red Cross Centenary A545

Rudolph Kirchschlager A546

1980, Feb. 21 Photo. *Perf. 14x13½*

1144 A544 4s dk bl & red 45 32

1980, Mar. 14 Photo. *Perf. 13½x14*

1145 A545 2.50s multi 30 20

Photogravure and Engraved

1980, Mar. 20 *Perf. 14x13½*

1146 A546 4s sep & red 45 32

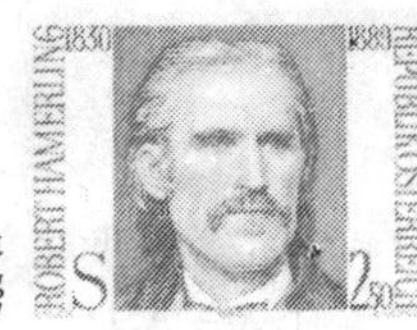

Robert Hamerling A547

1980, Mar. 24 Engr. *Perf. 13½x14*

1147 A547 2.50s ol grn 28 20

Robert Hamerling (1830-1889), poet.

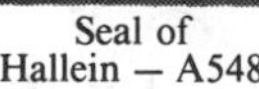

Seal of Hallein — A548

Maria Theresa, by Andreas Moller — A549

Photogravure and Engraved

1980, Apr. 30 *Perf. 14x13½*

1148 A548 4s red & blk 45 32

Hallein, 750th anniversary.

1980, May 13 Engr. *Perf. 13½*

1149 A549 2.50s vio brn 28 28

1150 A549 4s dk bl 45 45

1151 A549 6s rose lake 65 65

Empress Maria Theresa (1717-1780) Paintings by: 4s, Martin van Meytens. 6s, Josef Ducreux.

Flags of Austria and Four Powers — A550

1980, May 14 Photo. *Perf. 13½x14*

1152 A550 4s multi 45 32

State Treaty, 25th anniversary.

St. Benedict, by Meinrad Guggenbichler A551

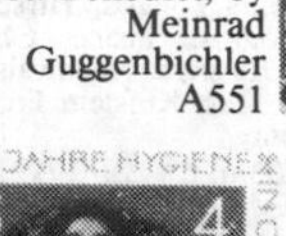

Hygeia by Gustav Klimt — A552

1980, May 16 Engr. *Perf. 14½*

1153 A551 2.50s ol grn 28 20

Congress of Benedictine Order of Austria.

1980, May 20 Photo. *Perf. 14*

1154 A552 4s multi 45 32

175th anniversary of academic teaching of hygiene.

Aflenz Ground Satellite Receiving Station Inauguration A553

1980, May 30 Photo. *Perf. 14*

1155 A553 6s multi 65 45

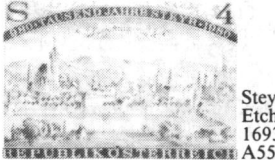

Steyr, Etching, 1693 A554

Photogravure and Engraved

1980, June 4 *Perf. 13½*

1156 A554 4s multi 45 32

Millennium of Steyr.

Worker, Oil Drill Head — A555

1980, June 12
1157 A555 2.50s multi 28 20

Austrian oil production, 25th anniversary.

Seal of Innsbruck, 1267 — A556

1980, June 23 ***Perf. 13½x14½***
1158 A556 2.50s multi 28 20

Innsbruck, 800th anniversary.

Duke's Hat — A557

Leo Ascher (1880-1942), composer A558

Bible Illustration, Book of Genesis — A559

Perf. 14½x13½

1980, June 23 **Photo.**
1159 A557 4s multi 45 32

800th anniversary of Styria as a Duchy.

1980, Aug. 18 **Engr.** ***Perf. 14***
1160 A558 3s dk pur 32 28

1980, Aug. 25 ***Perf. 13½***
1161 A559 4s multi 45 35

10th International Congress of the Organization for Old Testament Studies.

Europa Issue 1980

Robert Stolz — A560

1980, Aug. 25 **Engr.** ***Perf. 14x13½***
1162 A560 6s red brn 65 45

Robert Stolz (1880-1975), composer.

Old and Modern Bridges A561

1980, Sept. 1 **Photo.** ***Perf. 13½***
1163 A561 4s multi 45 35

11th Congress of the International Association for Bridge and Structural Engineering, Vienna.

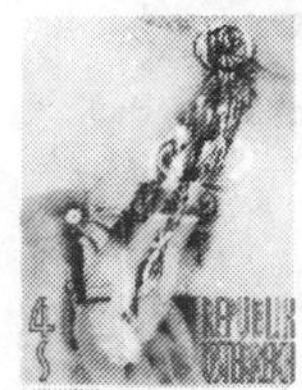

Moon Figure, by Karl Brandstätter A562

Customs Service, Sesquicentennial A563

Photogravure and Engraved

1980, Oct. 10 ***Perf. 14x13½***
1164 A562 4s multi 45 35

1980, Oct. 13 **Photo.**
1165 A563 2.50s multi 28 20

Gazette Masthead, 1810 A564

1980, Oct. 23 **Photo.** ***Perf. 13½***
1166 A564 2.50s multi 28 20

Official Gazette of Linz, 350th anniversary.

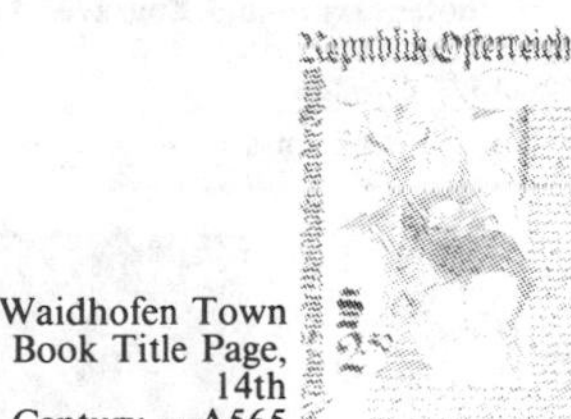

Waidhofen Town Book Title Page, 14th Century — A565

Photogravure and Engraved

1980, Oct. 24 ***Perf. 14***
1167 A565 2.50s multi 28 20

Waidhofen on Thaya, 750th anniversary.

Federal Austrian Army, 25th Anniversary A566

1980, Oct. 24 **Photo.** ***Perf. 13½x14***
1168 A566 2.50s grnsh blk & red 28 20

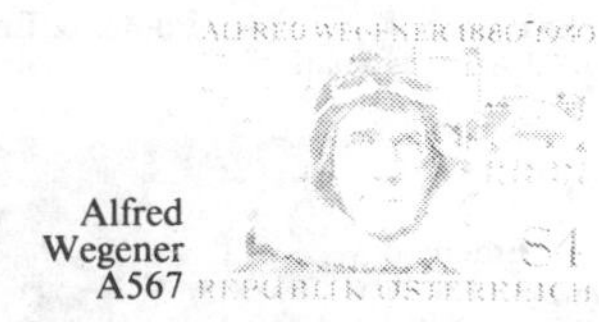

Alfred Wegener A567

1980, Oct. 31 **Engr.**
1169 A567 4s vio bl 45 35

Alfred Wegener (1880-1930), scientist, discovered theory of continental drift.

Robert Musil (1880-1942), Poet — A568

1980, Nov. 6 ***Perf. 14x13½***
1170 A568 4s dk red brn 45 35

Nativity, Stained Glass Window, Klagenfurt — A569

Photogravure and Engraved

1980, Nov. 28 ***Perf. 13½***
1171 A569 4s multi 45 35

Christmas 1980.

25th Anniversary of Social Security A570

1981, Jan. 19 **Litho.** ***Perf. 13½x14***
1172 A570 2.50s multi 28 20

Niebelungen Saga, 1926, by Wilhelm Dachauer A571

Machinist in Wheelchair A572

1981, Apr. 6 **Engr.** ***Perf. 14x13½***
1173 A571 3s sepia 35 25

Wilhelm Dachauer (1881-1951), artist and engraver.

Photogravure and Engraved

1981, Apr. 6
1174 A572 6s multi 65 50

Rehabilitation International, 3rd European Regional Conference.

Sigmund Freud — A573

Congress, Vienna — A574

1981, May 6 **Engr.**
1175 A573 3s rose vio 35 25

Sigmund Freud (1856-1939), psychoanalyst.

1981, May 11 **Photo.**
1176 A574 4s multi 45 35

Azzo (Founder of House of Kuenringer) and his Followers, Bear-skin Manuscript A575

Photogravure and Engraved

1981, May 15
1177 A575 3s multi 35 25

Kuenringer Exhibition, Zwettl Monastery.

Europa Issue 1981

Maypole — A576

1981, May 22 **Photo.**
1178 A576 6s multi 65 50

Telephone Service Centenary A577

Photogravure and Engraved

1981 May 29 ***Perf. 13½x14***
1179 A577 4s multi 45 35

Seibersdorf Research Center, 25th Anniv. — A578

1981, June 29 **Photo.** ***Perf. 13½***
1180 A578 4s multi 45 35

The Frog King (Child's Drawing) A579

1981, June 29 ***Perf. 13½x14***
1181 A579 3s multi 35 25

Town Hall and Town Seal of 1250 — A580

Photogravure and Engraved

1981, July 17 ***Perf. 13½x14***
1182 A580 4s multi 45 35

St. Veit and der Glan, 800th anniv.

Johann Florian Heller (1813-1871), Pioneer of Urinalysis — A581

1981, Aug. 31 ***Perf. 14x13½***
1183 A581 6s red brn 65 50

11th Intl. Clinical Chemistry Congress.

Ludwig Boltzmann (1844-1906), Physicist A582

Scale A583

1981, Sept. 4 Engr. ***Perf. 14x13½***
1184 A582 3s dk grn 35 25

Photogravure and Engraved

1981, Sept. 7 ***Perf. 14***
1185 A583 6s multi 65 50

Intl. Pharmaceutical Federation World Congress, Vienna, Sept. 6-11.

Otto Bauer, Politician, Birth Centenary A584

Escher's Impossible Cube A585

1981, Sept. 7 Photo. ***Perf. 14x13½***
1186 A584 4s multi 45 35

1981, Sept. 14
1187 A585 4s dk bl & brt bl 45 35

10th Intl. Mathematicians' Congress, Innsbruck.

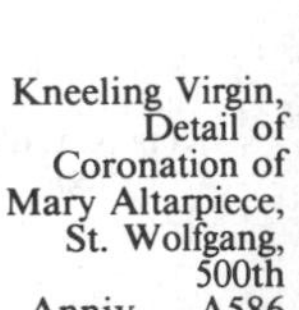

Kneeling Virgin, Detail of Coronation of Mary Altarpiece, St. Wolfgang, 500th Anniv. — A586

1981, Sept. 25 Engr. ***Perf. 14x13½***
1188 A586 3s dk bl 35 25

South-East Fair, Graz, 75th Anniv. A587

1981, Sept. 25 Photo. ***Perf. 13½x14***
1189 A587 4s multi 45 35

Holy Trinity, 12th Cent. Byzantine Miniature A588

1981, Oct. 5
1190 A588 6s multi 65 50

16th Intl. Byzantine Congress.

Hans Kelsen (1881-1973), Co-author of Federal Constitution A589

1981, Oct. 9 **Engr.**
1191 A589 3s dk car 35 25

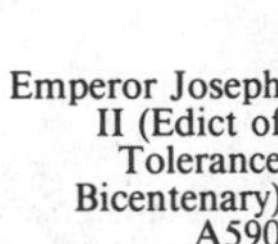

Emperor Joseph II (Edict of Tolerance Bicentenary) A590

Photogravure and Engraved

1981, Oct. 9 ***Perf. 14***
1192 A590 4s multi 45 35

World Food Day A591

1981, Oct. 16 Photo. ***Perf. 13½***
1193 A591 6s multi 65 50

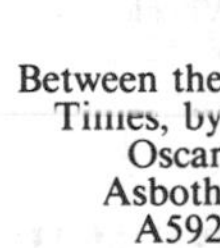

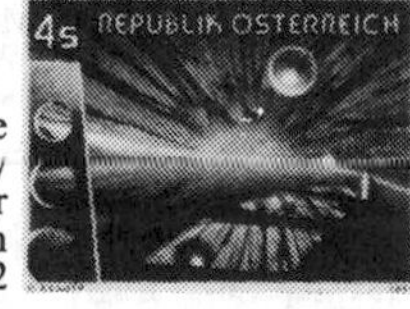

Between the Times, by Oscar Asboth A592

1981, Oct. 22 Litho. ***Perf. 13½x14***
1194 A592 4s multi 45 35

Intl. Catholic Workers' Day — A593

Photogravure and Engraved

1981, Oct. 23 ***Perf. 14x13½***
1195 A593 3s multi 35 25

Baron Josef Hammer-Purgstall, Founder of Oriental Studies, 125th Death Anniv. — A594

Photogravure and Engraved

1981, Nov. 23 ***Perf. 14***
1196 A594 3s multi 35 25

Julius Raab (1891-1964), Politician A595

1981, Nov. 27 Engr. ***Perf. 13½***
1197 A595 6s rose lake 65 50

Nativity, Corn Straw Figures A596

Photogravure and Engraved

1981, Nov. 27
1198 A596 4s multi 45 32

Christmas 1981.

Stefan Zweig (1881-1942), Poet — A597

1981, Nov. 27 Engr. ***Perf. 14x13½***
1199 A597 4s dl vio 45 32

800th Anniv. of St. Nikola on the Danube — A598

1981, Dec. 4 **Photo. & Engr.**
1200 A598 4s multi 45 32

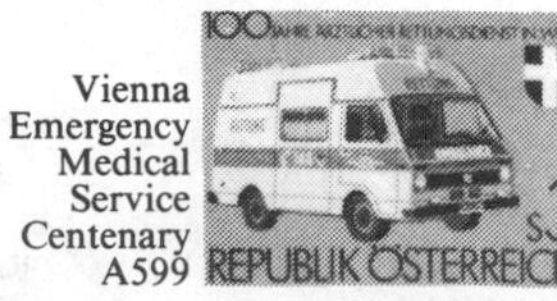

Vienna Emergency Medical Service Centenary A599

1981, Dec. 9 Photo. ***Perf. 13½x14***
1201 A599 3s multi 35 25

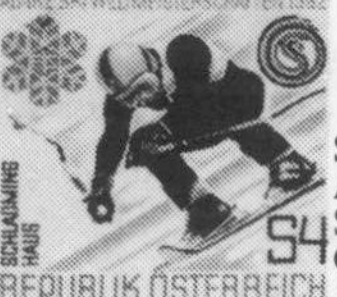

Schladming-Haus Alpine World Skiing Championship A600

1982, Jan. 27 ***Perf. 14***
1202 A600 4s multi 45 32

Dorotheum (State Auction Gallery), 275th Anniv. — A601

Water Rescue Service, 25th Anniv. — A602

Photogravure and Engraved

1982, Mar. 12 ***Perf. 14***
1203 A601 4s multi 45 32

1982, Mar. 19 Photo. ***Perf. 14x13½***
1204 A602 5s multi 60 40

St. Severin — A603

Intl. Kneipp Hydropathy Congress, Vienna — A604

Photogravure and Engraved

1982, Apr. 23 ***Perf. 14x13½***
1205 A603 3s multi 35 25

St. Severin and the End of the Roman Era exhibition.

1982, May 4 ***Perf. 14***
1206 A604 4s multi 45 32

Arms of Printers' Guild A605

Urine Analysis, Canone di Avicenna Manuscript A606

1982, May 7
1207 A605 4s multi 50 32

Printing in Austria, 500th anniv.

1982, May 12 **Photo.**
1208 A606 6s multi 65 50

5th European Urology Society Congress, Vienna.

800th Birth Anniv. of St. Francis of Assisi — A607

Haydn and His Time Exhibition, Rohrau — A608

Photogravure and Engraved

1982, May 14
1209 A607 3s multi 35 25

1982, May 19 **Engr.** ***Perf. 13½***
1210 A608 3s ol grn 35 25

25th World Milk Day — A609

800th Anniv of Gfohl (Market Town) — A610

1982, May 25 **Photo.** ***Perf. 14x13½***
1211 A609 7s multi 75 55

Photogravure and Engraved

1982, May 28 ***Perf. 14***
1212 A610 4s multi 45 32

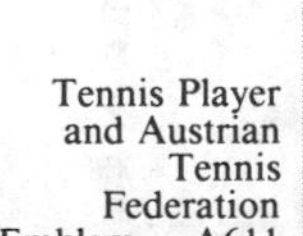

Tennis Player and Austrian Tennis Federation Emblem — A611

1982, June 11
1213 A611 3s multi 35 25

900th Anniv. of City of Langenlois A612

Photogravure and Engraved

1982, June 11 ***Perf. 13½x14***
1214 A612 4s multi 45 32

The only foreign revenue stamps listed in this Catalogue are those authorized for prepayment of postage.

800th Anniv. of City of Weiz — A613

1982, June 18 **Photo.** ***Perf. 14x13½***
1215 A613 4s Arms 45 32

Ignaz Seipel (1876-1932), Statesman A614

1982, July 30 **Engr.** ***Perf. 14x13½***
1216 A614 3s brn vio 35 25

Europa Issue 1982

Sesquicentennial of Linz-Freistadt-Budweis Horse-drawn Railroad — A615

1982, July 30 ***Perf. 13½***
1217 A615 6s brown 65 50

Mail Bus Service, 75th Anniv. — A616

Rocket Lift-off — A617

1982, Aug. 6 **Photo.** ***Perf. 14x13½***
1218 A616 4s multi 45 32

1982, Aug. 9 ***Perf. 14***
1219 A617 4s multi 45 32

2nd UN Conference on Peaceful Uses of Outer Space, Vienna, Aug. 9-21.

Geodesists' Day — A618

Photogravure and Engraved

1982, Sept. 1 ***Perf. 13½x14***
1220 A618 3s Tower, Office of Standards 35 25

Protection of Endangered Species — A619

1982, Sept. 9 ***Perf. 14***
1221 A619 3s Bustard 35 25
1222 A619 4s Beaver 45 32
1223 A619 6s Capercaillie 65 50

10th Anniv. of Intl. Institute for Applied Systems Anaysis, Vienna A620

1982, Oct. 4 **Photo.**
1224 A620 3s Laxenburg Castle 35 25

St. Apollonia (Patron Saint of Dentists) A621

Photogravure and Engraved

1982, Oct. 11
1225 A621 4s multi 45 32

70th Annual World Congress of Dentists.

Emmerich Kalman (1882-1953), Composer A622

1982, Oct. 22 **Engr.** ***Perf. 13½***
1226 A622 3s dk bl 35 25

Max Mell (1882-1971), Poet — A623

Christmas 1982 — A624

1982, Nov. 10 **Photo.** ***Perf. 14x13½***
1227 A623 3s multi 35 25

Photogravure and Engraved

1982, Nov. 25 ***Perf. 13½***

Design: Christmas crib, Damuls Church, Vorarlberg, 1630.

1228 A624 4s multi 45 32

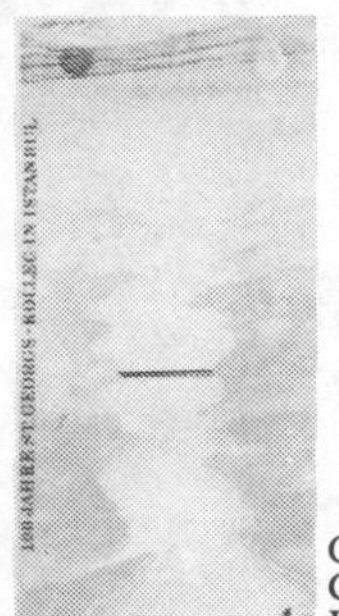

Centenary of St. George's College, Istanbul — A625

1982, Nov. 26 **Litho.** ***Perf. 14***
1229 A625 4s Bosporus 45 32

Portrait of a Girl, by Ernst Fuchs — A626

Photogravure and Engraved

1982, Dec. 10
1230 A626 4s multi 45 32

Postal Savings Bank Centenary A627

Photogravure and Engraved

1983, Jan. 12 ***Perf. 14***
1231 A627 4s Bank 45 32

Hildegard Burjan (1883-1933), Founder of Caritas Socialis A628

1983, Jan. 28 **Engr.**
1232 A628 4s rose lake 45 32

World Communications Year — A629

75th Anniv. Children's Friends Org. — A630

1983, Feb. 18 **Photo.** ***Perf. 13½x14***
1233 A629 7s multi 75 55

Photogravure and Engraved

1983, Feb. 23 *Perf. 14x13½*
1234 A630 4s multi 45 32

Josef Matthias Hauer (1883-1959), Composer A631

1983, Mar. 18 Engr. *Perf. 14*
1235 A631 3s dp lil rose 35 25

25th Anniv. of Austrian Airlines A632

1983, Mar. 31 Photo. *Perf. 13½x14*
1236 A632 6s multi 65 50

Work Inspection Centenary A633

1983, Apr. 8 Photo. *Perf. 13½*
1237 A633 4s multi 45 32

Upper Austria Millennium Provincial Exhibition — A634

1983, Apr. 28 Photo. *Perf. 13½*
1238 A634 3s Wels Castle, by Matthaus Merian 35 25

Gottweig Monastery, 900th Anniv. A635

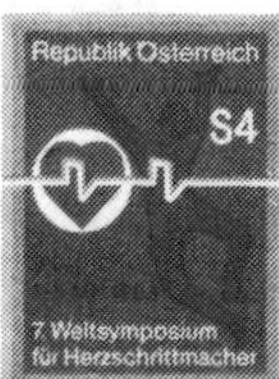

7th World Pacemakers' Symposium A636

Photogravure and Engraved

1983, Apr. 29 *Perf. 13½*
1239 A635 3s multi 35 25

1983, Apr. 29 Photo. *Perf. 14x13½*
1240 A636 4s multi 45 32

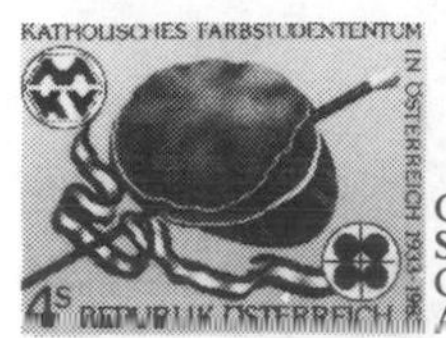

Catholic Students' Org. A637

1983, May 20 Photo. *Perf. 14*
1241 A637 4s multi 45 32

800th Anniv. of City of Weitra A638

Photogravure and Engraved

1983, May 20 *Perf. 13½*
1242 A638 4s multi 45 32

Granting of Town Rights to Hohenems, 650th Anniv. — A639

1983, May 27 Photo. *Perf. 14*
1243 A639 4s multi 45 32

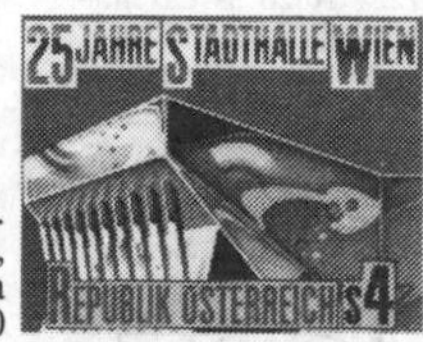

25th Anniv. of Stadthall, Vienna A640

1983, June 24 Photo. *Perf. 14*
1244 A640 4s multi 45 32

Europa 1983 — A641

Design: Viktor Franz Hess (1883-1964), 1936 Nobel Prize winner in physics.

1983, June 24 Engr. *Perf. 14x13½*
1245 A641 6s dk grn 65 50

Kiwanis Intl. Convention, Vienna, July 3-6 — A642

1983, July 1 Photo. *Perf. 13½*
1246 A642 5s multi 55 40

7th World Congress of Psychiatry, Vienna — A643

1983, July 11 Photo. *Perf. 14*
1247 A643 4s Emblem, St. Stephen's Cathedral 45 32

Baron Carl von Hasenauer (1833-1894), Architect A644

1983, July 20 Engr. *Perf. 13½x14*
1248 A644 3s Natural History Museum, Vienna 35 25

27th Intl. Chamber of Commerce Professional Competition, Linz — A645

1983, Aug. 16 **Photo.**
1249 A645 4s Chamber building 45 32

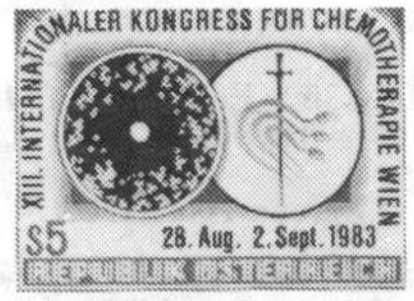

13th Intl. Chemotherapy Congress, Vienna, Aug. 28-Sept. 2 — A646

1983, Aug. 26
1250 A646 5s Penicillin test on cancer 55 40

Catholics' Day — A647

Visit of Pope John Paul II — A648

1983, Sept. 9 Photo. *Perf. 14x13½*
1251 A647 3s multi 32 25

Photogravure and Engraved

1983, Sept. 9 *Perf. 13½*
1252 A648 6s multi 65 50

Souvenir Sheet

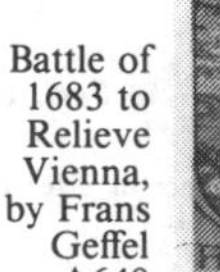

Battle of 1683 to Relieve Vienna, by Frans Geffel A649

1983, Sept. 9 *Perf. 14*
1253 A649 6s multi 65 65

300th anniv. of Vienna's rescue from Turkey. Size: 90x70mm.

Vienna Rathaus Centenary — A650

1983, Sept. 23 *Perf. 13½x14*
1254 A650 4s multi 45 32

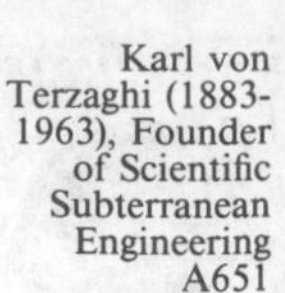

Karl von Terzaghi (1883-1963), Founder of Scientific Subterranean Engineering A651

1983, Oct. 3 **Engr.**
1255 A651 3s dk bl 35 25

10th Trade Unions Federal Congress, Oct. 3-8 A652

1983, Oct. 3 Photo. *Perf. 13½*
1256 A652 3s blk & red 35 25

Evening Sun in Burgenland, by Gottfried Kumpf — A653

Photogravure and Engraved

1983, Oct. 7 *Perf. 13½x14*
1257 A653 4s multi 45 32

Modling-Hinterbruhl Electric Railroad Centenary — A654

1983, Oct. 21 **Photo.**
1258 A654 3s multi 35 25

Provincial Museum of Upper Austria Sesquicentennial — A655

Photogravure and Engraved

1983, Nov. 4
1259 A655 4s Francisco-Carolinum Museum 45 32

Creche, St. Andreas Parish Church, Kitzbuhel A656

Photogravure and Engraved

1983, Nov. 25 *Perf. 14*
1260 A656 4s multi 45 32

Christmas 1983.

Parliament Bldg. Vienna, 100th Anniv. — A657

1983, Dec. 2 **Engr.**
1261 A657 4s sl bl 45 32

Altar Picture, St. Nikola/Pram Church — A658

1983, Dec. 6 **Photo.** ***Perf. 14x13½***
1262 A658 3s multi 35 25

Wolfgang Pauli (1900-58), Physicist, Nobel Prize Winner — A659

Perf. 14½x13½

1983, Dec. 15 **Engr.**
1263 A659 6s dk red brn 65 50

Gregor Mendel (1822-1884), Genetics Founder — A660

Photogravure and Engraved

1984, Jan. 5 ***Perf. 13½***
1264 A660 4s multi 45 32

Anton Hanak (1875-1934), Sculptor — A661

1984, Jan. 5
1265 A661 3s red brn & blk 35 25

50th Anniv. of 1934 Uprising — A662

1984, Feb. 10 **Photo.** ***Perf. 14***
1266 A662 4.50s Memorial, Woellersdorf 50 38

900th Anniv. of Reichersberg Monastery A663

Photogravure and Engraved

1984, Apr. 25 ***Perf. 14x13½***
1267 A663 3.50s Wernher von Reichersberg family, bas-relief, 15th cent. 40 28

Tobacco Monopoly Bicentenary A665

Photogravure and Engraved

1984, May 4 ***Perf. 13½***
1269 A665 4.50s Cigar wrapper, tobacco plant 50 38

1200th Anniv. of Kostendorf Municipality A666

1984, May 4
1270 A666 4.50s View, arms 50 38

Automobile Engineers World Congress A667

1984, May 4 **Photo.** ***Perf. 13½x14***
1271 A667 5s Wheel bearing cross-section 60 40

Europa (1959-84) A668

1984, May 4 ***Perf. 13½***
1272 A668 6s multi 65 50

Archduke Johann (1782-1859) by S. von Carolsfeld A669

Aragonite A670

Photogravure and Engraved

1984, May 11 ***Perf. 14***
1273 A669 4.50s multi 50 38

1984, May 11 ***Perf. 13½***
1274 A670 3.50s multi 40 28

Ore and Iron Provincial Exhibition.

Era of Emperor Francis Joseph Exhibition A671

Design: Cover of Viribus Unitis, publ. by Max Herzig, 1898.

1984, May 18
1275 A671 3.50s red & gold 40 28

City of Vocklabruck, 850th Anniv. — A672

Dionysius, Virinum Mosaic — A673

Photogravure and Engraved

1984, May 30 ***Perf. 14x13½***
1276 A672 4.50s Tower, arms 50 38

1984, June 1 ***Perf. 13½***
1277 A673 3.50s multi 40 28

Museum of Carinthia centenary.

Erosion Prevention Systems Centenary A674

1984, June 5 **Engr.** ***Perf. 14***
1278 A674 4.50s Stone reinforcement wall 50 38

Tyrol Provincial Celebration, 1809-1984 — A675

Art Exhibition: Meeting of Imperial Troops with South Tyrolean Reserves under Andreas Hofer near Sterzing in April 1809, by Ludwig Schnorr von Carolsfeld, 1830.

Photogravure and Engraved

1984, June 5 ***Perf. 14x13½***
1279 A675 3.50s multi 40 38

Ralph Benatzky (1884-1957), Composer — A676

1984, June 5 **Engr.**
1280 A676 4s vio brn 45 32

Christian von Ehrenfels (1859-1932), Philosopher A677

1984, June 22 **Photo.** ***Perf. 14***
1281 A677 3.50s multi 40 28

25th Anniv. of Minimundus (Model City) — A678

1984, June 22 ***Perf. 13½x14***
1282 A678 4s Eiffel Tower, Tower of Pisa, ferris wheel 45 32

Blockheide Eibenstein Nature Park A679

1984 **Photogravure and Engraved**
1283 A679 4s shown 45 32
1284 A679 4s Lake Neusiedl 45 32

Issue dates: No. 1283, June 29; No. 1284, Aug. 13. See Nos. 1349-1352.

Monasteries and Abbeys — A679a

Designs: 3.50s, Geras Monastery, Lower Austria. 4s, Stams. 4.50s, Schagl. 5s, Benedictine Abbey of St. Paul Levanttal. 6s, Rein-Hohenfurth.

Photogravure and Engraved

1984-85 ***Perf. 14***

1285	A679a	3.50s multi	40	28
1286	A679a	4s multi	40	30
1287	A679a	4.50s multi	50	38
1288	A679a	5s multi	50	38
1288A	A679a	6s multi	60	45
		Nos. 1285-1288A (5)	2.40	1.79

Issue dates: 3.50s. Apr. 27; 4s, Sept. 28; 4.50s, May 18; 5s, Sept. 27, 1985; 6s, Oct. 4. See Nos. 1361-1364.

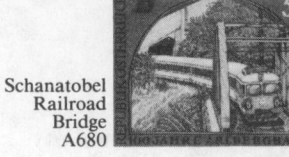

Schanatobel Railroad Bridge A680

Railroad Anniversaries: 3.50s, Arlberg centenary. 4.50s, Tauern, 75th.

1984, July 6 ***Perf. 14***
1289 A680 3.50s shown 40 28
1290 A680 4.50s Falkenstein Bridge 50 38

Balloon Flight in Austria Bicentenary A681

1984, July 6 **Photo.**
1291 A681 6s Johan Stuwer's balloon 65 50

Intl. Lawyers' Congress, Vienna — A682

Photogravure and Engraved

1984, Aug. 31
1292 A682 7s Vienna Palace of Justice, emblem 80 60

7th European Anatomy Congress, Innsbruck, Sept. 3-7 — A683

1984, Sept. 3 **Photo.**
1293 A683 6s Josef Hyrtl, anatomist 65 50

Window, by Karl Korab — A684

1984, Oct. 12
1294 A684 4s multi 45 32

Johannes of Gmunden, Mathematician, 600th Birth Anniv. — A685

1984, Oct. 18
1295 A685 3.50s Clock (Immset Uhr), 1555 40 28

Concordia Press Club, 125th Anniv. — A686

1984, Nov. 9 **Photo.** ***Perf. 13½***
1296 A686 4.50s Quill 50 38

Fanny Eissler, Dancer, Birth Centenary — A687

1984, Nov. 23 **Photo. & Engr.**
1297 A687 4s multi 45 38

Christmas 1984 A688

Design: Christ is Born, Aggsbacher Altar, Herzogenburg Monastery.

Photogravure and Engraved

1984, Nov. 30 ***Perf. 14***
1298 A688 4.50s multi 45 30

Karl Franzens University, Graz, 400th Anniv. — A689

Photogravure and Engraved

1985, Jan. 4 ***Perf. 14x13½***
1299 A689 3.50s Seal 32 22

Dr. Lorenz Bohler, Surgeon, Birth Cent. — A690

1985, Jan. 15 **Engr.**
1300 A690 4.50s dk rose lake 40 28

Nordic Events, Ski Championships, Seefeld — A691

1985, Jan. 17 **Photo.** ***Perf. 13½***
1301 A691 4s Ski jumper, cross country racer 35 25

Linz Diocese Bicentenary A692

1985, Jan. 25
1302 A692 4.50s Linz Cathedral interior 40 28

Alban Berg (1885-1935), Composer — A693

1985, Feb. 8 **Engr.**
1303 A693 6s bluish blk 52 35

Vocational Training Inst., 25th Anniv. A694

1985, Feb. 15 **Photo.** ***Perf. 13½x14***
1304 A694 4.50s multi 40 28

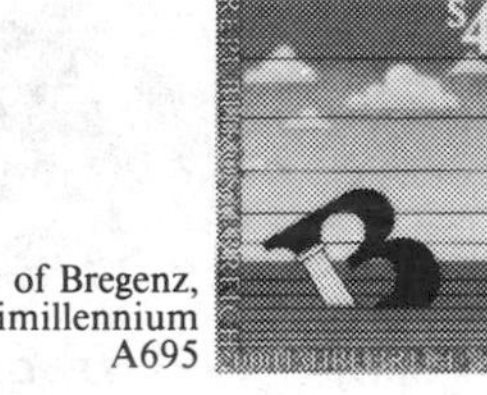

City of Bregenz, Bimillennium A695

1985, Feb. 22 ***Perf. 14x13½***
1305 A695 4s multi 35 25

Austrian Registration Labels Cent. — A696

1985, Mar. 15 ***Perf. 13½x14***
1306 A696 4.50s Label. 1885 40 28

Josef Stefan (1835-1893), Physicist A697

Photogravure and Engraved

1985, Mar. 22 ***Perf. 14x13½***
1307 A697 6s buff, dl red brn & dk brn 52 36

St. Leopold Exhibition, Klosterneuberg A698

Design: St. Leopold, 16th-17th century embroidery.

1985, Mar. 29
1308 A698 3.50s multi 32 22

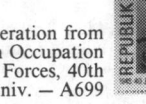

Liberation from German Occupation Forces, 40th Anniv. — A699

1985, Apr. 26 **Photo.**
1309 A699 4.50s multi 42 28

Painter Franz von Defregger (1835-1921) A700

1985, Apr. 26
1310 A700 3.50s Fairy tale teller 32 22

Europa 1985 — A701

Design: Composer Johann Joseph Fux (1660-1741), violin and trombone.

Photogravure and Engraved

1985, May 3 ***Perf. 13½***
1311 A701 6s lil gray & dk brn 52 35

Boheimkirchen (Market Town) Millennium — A702

1985, May 10 ***Perf. 14***
1312 A702 4.50s View, coat of arms 40 28

Austria stamps can be mounted in Scott's annually supplemented Austria Album.

European Free Trade Assoc., 25th Anniv. — A703

Design: Mercury staff, flags of member and affiliate nations.

1985, May 10 Photo. *Perf. 13½*
1313 A703 4s multi 35 25

St. Polten Diocese Bicentenary A704

Design: Episcopal residence gate, Polten diocese arms.

Photogravure and Engraved

1985, May 15
1314 A704 4.50s multi 40 28

The Gumpp Family of Builders, Innsbruck — A705

Perf. 14½x13½

1985, May 17 Photo.
1315 A705 3.50s multi 35 25

Garsten Market Town Millennium A706

Design: 17th century engraving by George Matthaus Fischer (1628-1696).

Photogravure and Engraved

1985, June 7 *Perf. 13½x14*
1316 A706 4.50s multi 45 32

UN 40th Anniv. A707

Perf. 13½x14½

1985, June 26 Photo.
1317 A707 4s multi 40 30

Austrian membership, 30th anniv.

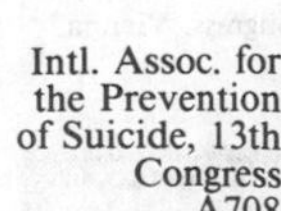

Intl. Assoc. for the Prevention of Suicide, 13th Congress A708

Photogravure and Engraved

1985, June 28 *Perf. 14*
1318 A708 5s brn, lt ap grn & yel 50 38

Souvenir Sheet

Year of the Forest A709

1985, June 28 *Perf. 13½*
1319 A709 6s Healthy and damaged woodland 60 45

No. 1319 has multicolored margin continuing the design. Size: 90x71mm.

Bad Ischl Festival, 25th Anniv. A710

Design: Kurhaus, Bad Ischl operetta activities emblem.

1985, July 5 *Perf. 14*
1320 A710 3.50s multi 35 25

Intl. Competition of Fire Brigades, Vocklabruck A711

1985, July 18 Photo. *Perf. 14x13½*
1321 A711 4.50s Fireman, emblem 45 32

Grossglockner Alpine Motorway, 50th Anniv. — A712

Photogravure and Engraved

1985, Aug. 2 *Perf. 13½*
1322 A712 4s View of Fuschertorl 40 30

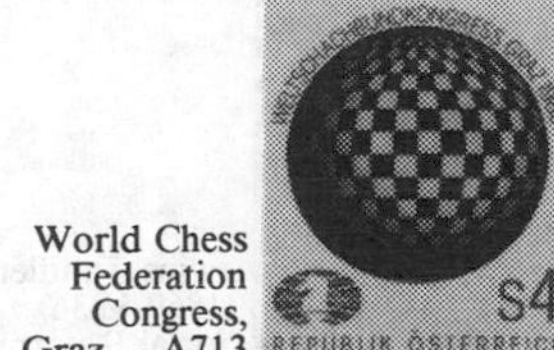

World Chess Federation Congress, Graz — A713

1985, Aug. 28 Photo. *Perf. 13½*
1323 A713 4s Checkered globe, emblem 40 30

The Legendary Foundation of Konigstetten by Charlemagne, by Auguste Stephan, c. 1870 — A714

Photogravure and Engraved

1985, Aug. 30 *Perf. 14*
1324 A714 4.50s multi 45 32

Konigstetten millennium.

Hofkirchen-Taufkirchen-Weibern Municipalities, 1200th Anniv. — A715

Photogravure and Engraved

1985, Aug. 30 *Perf. 13½x14*
1325 A715 4.50s View of Weiburn, municipal arms 45 32

Dr. Adam Politzer (1835-1923), Physician A716

1985, Sept. 12 Engr. *Perf. 14*
1326 A716 3.50s bl vio 35 25

Politzer pioneered aural therapy for auditory disorders.

Intl. Assoc. of Forwarding Agents, World Congress, Vienna A717

1985, Oct. 7 Photo. *Perf. 13½*
1327 A717 6s multi 60 45

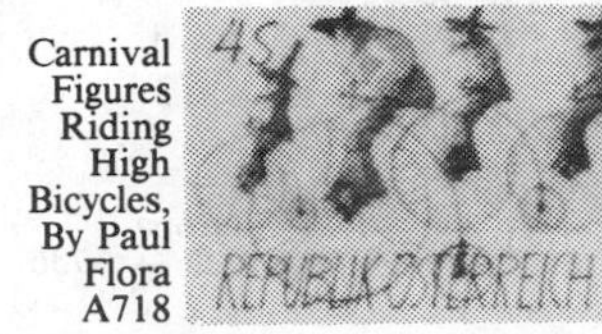

Carnival Figures Riding High Bicycles, By Paul Flora A718

Photogravure and Engraved

1985, Oct. 25 *Perf. 14*
1328 A718 4s multi 45 32

St. Martin on Horseback A719

1985, Nov. 8 Photo.
1329 A719 4.50s multi 50 38

Eisenstadt Diocese, 25th anniv.

Creche, Marble Bas-relief, Salzburg — A720

Photogravure and Engraved

1985, Nov. 29 *Perf. 13½*
1330 A720 4.50s gold, dl vio & buff 50 38

Christmas 1985.

Hanns Horbiger (1860-1931), Inventor — A721

1985, Nov. 29 *Perf. 14*
1331 A721 3.50s gold & sep 40 30

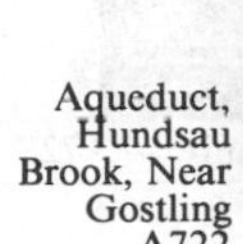

Aqueduct, Hundsau Brook, Near Gostling A722

1985, Nov. 29 *Perf. 13½x14½*
1332 A722 3.50s red, bluish blk & brt ultra 40 30

Vienna Aqueduct, 75th anniv.

Chateau de la Muette, Paris Headquarters A723

1985, Dec. 13
1333 A723 4s sep, rose lil & gold 48 35

Org. for Economic Cooperation and Development, 25th anniv.

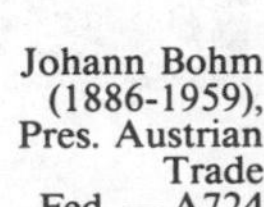

Johann Bohm (1886-1959), Pres. Austrian Trade Fed. — A724

1986, Jan. 24 Photo. *Perf. 14*
1334 A724 4.50s blk, ver & grayish blk 52 38

Intl. Peace Year — A725

Perf. 13½x14½

1986, Jan. 24 **Photo.**
1335 A725 6s multi 70 52

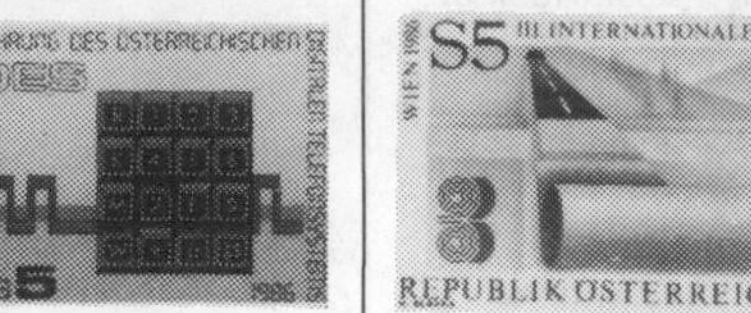

Digital Telephone Service Introduction A726

3rd Intl. Geotextile Congress, Vienna A732

1986, Jan. 29 **Photo.**
1336 A726 5s Push-button keyboard 60 45

Johann Georg Albrechtsberger (b. 1736), Composer — A727

Photogravure and Engraved

1986, Jan. 31 ***Perf. 13½x14½***
1337 A727 3.50s Klosterneuberg organ 42 32

Korneuberg, 850th Anniv. — A728

1986, Feb. 7 **Photo.** ***Perf. 14***
1338 A728 5s multi 60 45

Self-portrait, by Oskar Kokoschka (b.1886) — A729

Perf. 14½x13½

1986, Feb. 28 **Photo.**
1339 A729 4s multi 50 38

Admission to Council of Europe, 30th Anniv. — A730

1986, Feb. 28 **Photo.** ***Perf. 13x13½***
1340 A730 6s multi 75 58

Clemens Holzmeister (b. 1886), Architect, Salzburg Festival Theater, 1926 — A731

Photogravure and Engraved

1986, Mar. 27 ***Perf. 13½***
1341 A731 4s sep & redsh brn 52 40

1986, Apr. 7 **Photo.** ***Perf. 13½x14½***
1342 A732 5s multi 62 48

Prince Eugen and Schlosshof Castle — A733

Photo. & Engr.

1986, Apr. 21 ***Perf. 14***
1343 A733 4s multi 52 40

Prince Eugen Exhibition, Schlosshof and Niederweiden.

St. Florian Monastery, Upper Austria A734

1986, Apr. 24
1344 A734 4s multi 52 40

The World of Baroque provincial exhibition, St. Florian.

Herberstein Castle, Arms of Styria A735

1986, May 2 ***Perf. 13½x14½***
1345 A735 4s multi 52 40

Europa 1986 — A736

1986, May 2 ***Perf. 13½***
1346 A736 6s Pasque flower 80 60

Wagner, Scene from Opera Lohengrin — A737

1986, May 21
1347 A737 4s multi 52 40

Intl. Richard Wagner Congress, Vienna.

Antimonite A738

1986, May 23 ***Perf. 13½x14½***
1348 A738 4s multi 52 40

Burgenland Provincial Minerals Exhibition.

Scenery Type of 1984

Photogravure and Engraved

1986-87 ***Perf. 14***
1349 A679 5s Martinswall, Tyrol 65 50
1350 A679 5s Tschauko Falls, Carinthia 65 50
1351 A679 5s Dachstein Ice Caves ('87) 82 62
1352 A679 5s Gauertal, Montafon ('87) 80 60

Issue dates: No. 1351, June 11. No. 1352, Aug. 21.

Waidhofen on Ybbs Township, 800th Anniv. A739

1986, June 20 **Photo.** ***Perf. 13½***
1355 A739 4s multi 52 40

Salzburg Local Railway, Cent. A740

1986, Aug. 8 **Photo.** ***Perf. 14***
1356 A740 4s multi 55 42

Georgenberg Treaty, 800th Anniv. — A741

Design: Seals, Dukes Leopold of Austria, Otakar of Styria, and Georgenberg Church.

Photogravure and Engraved

1986, Aug. 14
1357 A741 5s multi 68 52

Julius Tandler (1869-1936), Social Reformer A742

1986, Aug. 22
1358 A742 4s multi 55 42

Sonnblick Observatory, Cent. — A743

Photogravure and Engraved

1986, Aug. 27 ***Perf. 13½x14½***
1359 A743 4s Observatory, 1886 55 42

European Assoc. for Anesthesiology, 7th Congress — A744

Design: Discovery of mandrake root.

1986, Aug. 27 ***Perf. 14½x13½***
1360 A744 5s multi 68 52

Monasteries and Abbeys Type of 1984

Designs: 5.50s, St. Gerold's Provostry, Vorarlberg. 7s, Loretto Monastery, Burgenland. 7.50s, Dominican Convent, Vienna.

Photogravure and Engraved

1986-87 ***Perf. 14***
1361 A679a 5.50s brt vio, vio & buff 78 60
1363 A679a 7s brt blue, blue blk & cream 1.15 88
1364 A679a 7.50s gold brn, redsh brn & buff 1.10 85

Issue dates: 5.50s, Sept. 12. 7s, Aug. 14, 1987. 7.50s, Oct. 3.

Otto Stoessl (d. 1936), Writer — A745

Photogravure and Engraved

1986, Sept. 3 ***Perf. 14***
1366 A745 4s multi 55 42

Vienna Fire Brigade, 300th Anniv. — A746

1986, Sept. 3 **Photo.**
1367 A746 4s Fireman, 1686 55 42

Intl. Conference on Oriental Carpets, Vienna, Budapest A747

Design: Silk Viennese hunting tapestry.

Photogravure and Engraved

1986, Sept. 3 ***Perf. 14***
1368 A747 5s multi 68 52

Minister at Pulpit — A748

Photogravure and Engraved

1986, Oct. 10 *Perf. 14*
1369 A748 5s vio, blk & gray 72 55

Protestant Act, 25th anniv., and Protestant Patent of Franz Josef I ensuring religious equality, 125th anniv.

Disintegration, by Walter Schmogner A749

1986, Oct. 17 *Perf. 13½x14*
1370 A749 4s multi 58 45

Franz Liszt, Composer, and Birthplace, Burgenland A750

1986, Oct. 17 *Perf. 13½*
1371 A750 5s grn & sep 72 55

Souvenir Sheet

European Security Conference, Vienna — A751

1986, Nov. 4 *Perf. 13½x14*
1372 A751 6s Vienna 88 65

No. 1372 has multicolored margin continuing the design.

Strettweg Cart, 7th Cent. B.C. A752

Photogravure and Engraved

1986, Nov. 26 *Perf. 14*
1373 A752 4s multi 58 45

Joanneum Styrian Land Museum, 175th anniv.

Catalogue prices for unused stamps up to mid-1953 are for hinged copies matching the condition specified in this volume's introduction.

Christmas A753

Design: The Little Crib, bas-relief by Schwanthaler (1740-1810), Schlierbach Monastery.

1986, Nov. 28
1374 A753 5s gold & rose lake 72 55

Federal Chamber of Commerce, 40th Anniv. — A754

1986, Dec. 2 **Photo.**
1375 A754 5s multi 72 55

Industry A755

1986-87 *Perf. 14*
1376 A755 4s Steel workers 58 45
1377 A755 4s Office worker, computer 65 50

Dates of issue: No. 1376, Dec. 4, 1986. No 1377, Oct. 5, 1987.

The Educated Eye, by Arnulf Rainer — A756

1987, Jan. 13 Photo. *Perf. 13½x14*
1386 A756 5s multi 72 55

Adult education in Vienna, cent.

The Large Blue Madonna, by Anton Faistauer (1887-1970) A757

Paintings: 6s, Self-portrait, 1922, by A. Paris Gutersloh (1887-1973).

1987, Jan. 29 *Perf. 14*
1387 A757 4s multi 58 45
1388 A757 6s multi 88 65

Europa 1987 — A758

Photo. & Engr.

1987, Apr. 6 *Perf. 13½x14*
1389 A758 6s Hundertwasser House 95 55

World Ice Hockey Championships, Vienna — A759

Perf. 13½x14½

1987, Apr. 17 **Photo.**
1390 A759 5s multi 80 60

Opening of the Austria Center, Vienna A760

1987, Apr. 22
1391 A760 5s multi 80 60

Salzburg City Charter, 700th Anniv. A761

1987, Apr. 24
1392 A761 5s multi 80 60

Factory, 1920 — A762

Equal Rights for Men and Women — A763

Photo. & Engr.

1987, Apr. 29 *Perf. 14*
1393 A762 4s dull brn red, blk & steel blue 65 48

Work-Men-Machines, provincial exhibition, Upper Austria.

1987, Apr. 29 Photo. *Perf. 13½*
1394 A763 5s multi 80 60

Adele Block-Bauer I, Abstract by Gustav Klimt — A764

Photo. & Engr.

1987, May 8 *Perf. 13½*
1395 A764 4s multi 65 48

The Era of Emperor Franz Joseph, provincial exhibition, Lower Austria.

Arthur Schnitzler (1862-1931), Poet — A765

1987, May 15 *Perf. 14½x13½*
1396 A765 6s multi 1.00 75

Von Raitenau, View of Salzburg A766

1987, May 15 *Perf. 14*
1397 A766 4s multi 65 48

Prince Archbishop Wolf Dietrich von Raitenau, patron of baroque architecture in Salzburg, provincial exhibition.

Lustenau, 1100th Anniv. — A767

Design: Lace, municipal coat of arms.

1987, May 22
1398 A767 5s multi 82 62

Souvenir Sheet

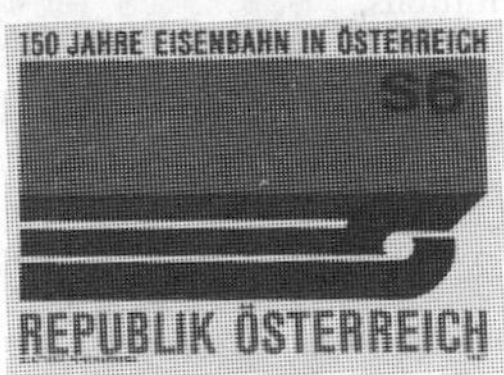
Austrian Railways Sesquicentenary — A768

1987, June 5 Photo. *Perf. 13½*
1399 A768 6s multi 1.00 75

No. 1399 has inscribed margin picturing steam and electric trains. Size: 90x70mm.

8th Intl. Congress of Engravers, Vienna A769

Photo. & Engr.

1987, June 17 ***Perf. 14***
1400 A769 5s gray, gray brn & dull rose 82 62

Dr. Karl Josef Bayer (1847-1904), Chemist — A770

Shipping Achensee, Cent. — A771

1987, June 22 ***Perf. 14x13½***
1401 A770 5s multi 80 60

Eighth Intl. Light Metals Congress, June 22-26, Leoben and Vienna; Bayer Technique for producing aluminum oxide from bauxite, cent.

1987, June 26 **Photo.**
1402 A771 4s multi 65 50

Ombudsmen's Office, 10th Anniv. — A772

Dr. Erwin Schrodinger (1887-1961), 1933 Nobel Laureate in Physics — A773

1987, July 1
1403 A772 5s Palais Rottal, Vienna 80 60

1987, Aug. 11 **Photo. & Engr.**
1404 A773 5s dull olive bister, choc & buff 80 60

Freistadt Exhibitions, 125th Anniv. A774

1987, Aug. 11 ***Perf. 14x14½***
1405 A774 5s multi 80 60

Certain countries cancel stamps in full sheets and sell them (usually with gum) for less than face value. Dealers generally sell "CTO".

Arbing, 850th Anniv. — A775

1987, Aug. 21 ***Perf. 13½***
1406 A775 5s multi 80 60

1987 World Cycling Championships, Villach to Vienna — A776

1987, Aug. 25 ***Perf. 14***
1407 A776 5s multi 80 60

World Congress of Savings Banks, Vienna A777

Perf. 13½x14½

1987, Sept. 9 **Photo.**
1408 A777 5s multi 80 60

Johann Michael Haydn (1737-1806), Composer A778

Perf. 13½x14½

1987, Sept. 14 **Engr.**
1409 A778 4s dull violet 65 50

Paul Hofhaymer (1459-1537), Composer A779

Photo. & Engr.

1987, Sept. 11 ***Perf. 14***
1410 A779 4s gold, blk & ultra 65 50

Bearded Vulture — A780

1987, Sept. 25
1411 A780 4s multi 65 50

Innsbruck Zoo, 25th anniv.

Baumgottinnen, by Arnulf Neuwirth — A781

1987, Oct. 9 ***Perf. 14x13½***
1412 A781 5s multi 80 60

Modern Art.

Gambling Monopoly, 200th Anniv. — A782

Perf. 14½x13½

1987, Oct. 30 **Photo.**
1413 A782 5s Lottery drum 80 60

Christoph Willibald Gluck (1714-1787), Composer A784

Photo. & Engr.

1987, Nov. 13 ***Perf. 14***
1415 A784 5s cream & blk 88 65

Oskar Helmer (b. 1887), Politician — A785

1987, Nov. 13
1416 A785 4s multi 70 52

Christmas A786

Joseph Mohr (1792-1848), clergyman, poet, and Franz Gruber (1787-1863), organist, choir director, authors of *Silent Night, Holy Night.*

1987, Nov. 27
1417 A786 5s multi 88 65

Intl. Education Congress of Salesian Fathers — A787

Photo. & Engr.

1988, Jan. 5 ***Perf. 13½***
1418 A787 5s St. John Bosco, children 88 65

Ernst Mach (1838-1916), Physicist — A788

Perf. 14½x13½

1988, Feb. 10 **Photo. & Engr.**
1419 A788 6s multi 1.05 78

Village with Bridge (1904), by Franz von Zulow (1883-1963), Painter — A789

1988, Feb. 10 **Photo.** ***Perf. 14½x14***
1420 A789 4s multi 70 52

SEMI-POSTAL STAMPS

Issues of the Monarchy

Emperor Franz Josef — SP1

Perf. 12½

1914, Oct. 4 **Typo.** **Unwmk.**
B1 SP1 5h green 10 8
B2 SP1 10h rose 15 15

Nos. B1-B2 were sold at an advance of 2h each over face value. Exist imperf.; price, set $80.

The Firing Step — SP2

Designs: 5h+2h, Cavalry. 10h+2h, Siege gun. 20h+3h, Battleship. 35h+3h, Airplane.

1915, May 1
B3 SP2 3h + 1h vio brn 15 45
B4 SP2 5h + 2h grn 5 5
B5 SP2 10h + 2h dp rose 5 5
B6 SP2 20h + 3h Prus bl 25 1.10
B7 SP2 35h + 3h ultra 2.50 1.65
Nos. B3-B7 (5) 3.00 3.30

Exist imperf. Price, set $135.

Issues of the Republic

Types of Austria, 1919-20, Overprinted in Black

Kärnten
Abstimmung

1920, Sept. 16 *Perf. 12½*

B11	A44	5h gray, *yel*	25	45
B12	A44	10h red, *pink*	50	80
B13	A43	15h bis, *yel*	25	45
B14	A45	20h dk grn, *bl*	25	45
B15	A43	25h vio, *pink*	25	45
B16	A45	30h brn, *buff*	80	1.40
B17	A45	40h car, *yel*	40	65
B18	A45	50h dk bl, *bl*	40	65
B19	A43	60h ol grn, *az*	95	1.65
B20	A47	80h red	25	45
B21	A47	1k org brn	30	52
B22	A47	2k pale bl	25	45

Granite Paper

Imperf

B23	A46	2½k brn red	35	60
B24	A46	3k dk bl & grn	35	60
B25	A46	4k car & vio	52	95
B26	A46	5k blue	65	1.10
B27	A46	7½k yel grn	65	1.10
B28	A46	10k gray grn & red	65	1.10
B29	A46	20k lil & org	65	1.10
		Nos. B11-B29 (19)	8.67	14.92

Carinthia Plebiscite. Sold at three times face value for the benefit of the Plebiscite Propaganda Fund.

Nos. B11-B19 exist imperf. Price, set $175.

Types of Regular Issues of 1919-21 Overprinted

Hochwasser
1920

1921, Mar. 1 *Perf. 12½*

B30	A44	5h gray, *yel*	20	30
B31	A44	10h org brn	20	30
B32	A43	15h gray	20	30
B33	A45	20h grn, *yel*	20	30
B34	A43	25h bl, *yel*	20	30
B35	A45	30h vio, *bl*	20	30
B36	A45	40h org brn, *pink*	24	45
B37	A45	50h grn, *bl*	75	1.75
B38	A43	60h lil, *yel*	20	30
B39	A47	80h pale bl	20	30
B40	A47	1k red org, *bl*	50	1.10
B41	A47	1½k grn, *yel*	24	30
B42	A47	2k lil brn	24	30

Overprinted

Hochwasser
1920

B43	A46	2½k lt bl	24	30
B44	A46	3k ol grn & brn red	24	30
B45	A46	4k lil & org	60	1.25
B46	A46	5k ol grn	35	60
B47	A46	7½k brn red	35	60
B48	A46	10k bl & ol grn	45	1.00
B49	A46	20k car rose & vio	55	1.10
		Nos. B30-B49 (20)	6.35	11.45

Nos. B30-B49 were sold at three times face value, the excess going to help flood victims. Exists imperf. Price, set $250.

Franz Joseph Haydn — SP9

View of Bregenz — SP16

Musicians: 5k, Mozart. 7½k, Beethoven. 10k, Schubert. 25k, Anton Bruckner. 50k, Johann Strauss (son). 100k, Hugo Wolf.

Perf. 11½, 12½

1922, Apr. 24 **Engr.**

B50	SP9	2½k brown	5.25	4.50
B51	SP9	5k dk bl	1.10	1.25
B52	SP9	7½k black	1.25	2.00
a.		Perf. 11½	87.50	125.00
B53	SP9	10k dk vio	2.00	2.25
B54	SP9	25k dk grn	2.50	3.00
B55	SP9	50k claret	1.65	2.75
B56	SP9	100k brn ol	6.00	6.00
		Nos. B50-B56 (7)	19.75	21.75

These stamps were sold at 10 times face value, the excess being given to needy musicians.

All values exist imperf. on both regular and handmade papers. Price, set $350.

A 1969 souvenir sheet without postal validity contains reprints of the 5k in black, 7½k in claret and 50k in dark blue, each overprinted "NEUDRUCK" in black at top. It was issued for the Vienna State Opera Centenary Exhibition.

1923, May 22 *Perf. 12½*

Designs: 120k, Mirabelle Gardens, Salzburg. 160k, Church at Eisenstadt. 180k, Assembly House, Klagenfurt. 200k, "Golden Roof," Innsbruck. 240k, Main Square, Linz. 400k, Castle Hill, Graz. 600k, Abbey at Melk. 1000k, Upper Belvedere, Vienna.

Various Frames

B57	SP16	100k dk grn	3.00	3.00
B58	SP16	120k dp bl	3.00	3.00
B59	SP16	160k dk vio	3.00	3.00
B60	SP16	180k red vio	3.00	3.00
B61	SP16	200k lake	3.00	3.00
B62	SP16	240k red brn	3.00	3.00
B63	SP16	400k dk brn	3.00	3.00
B64	SP16	600k ol brn	3.00	3.00
B65	SP16	1000k black	3.00	3.00
		Nos. B57-B65 (9)	27.00	27.00

Nos. B57-B65 were sold at five times face value, the excess going to needy artists.

All values exist imperf. on both regular and handmade papers. Price, set $375.

Feebleness SP25

Siegfried Slays the Dragon SP30

Designs: 300k+900k, Aid to industry. 500k+1500k, Orphans and widow. 600k+1800k, Indigent old man. 1000k+3000k, Alleviation of hunger.

1924, Sept. 6 **Photo.**

B66	SP25	100k + 300k yel grn	3.50	2.75
B67	SP25	300k + 900k red brn	5.00	6.00
B68	SP25	500k + 1500k brn vio	5.00	6.00
B69	SP25	600k + 1800k pck bl	5.00	6.00
B70	SP25	1000k + 3000k brn org	8.50	9.50
		Nos. B66-B70 (5)	27.00	30.25

The surtax was for child welfare and antituberculosis work. Set exists imperf. Price, $350.

1926, Mar. 8 **Engr.**

Designs: 8g+2g, Gunther's voyage to Iceland. 15g+5g, Brunhild accusing Kriemhild. 20g+5g, Nymphs telling Hagen the future. 24g+6g, Rudiger von Bechelaren welcomes the Nibelungen. 40g+10g, Dietrich von Bern vanquishes Hagen.

B71	SP30	3g + 2g ol blk	95	35
B72	SP30	8g + 2g ind	20	35
B73	SP30	15g + 5g dk cl	20	35
B74	SP30	20g + 5g ol grn	40	60
B75	SP30	24g + 6g dk vio	40	60
B76	SP30	40g + 10g red brn	2.75	3.50
		Nos. B71-B76 (6)	4.90	5.75

Nibelungen issue.

The surtax was for child welfare. Set exists imperf. Price, $350.

President Michael Hainisch SP36

President Wilhelm Miklas SP37

1928, Nov. 5

B77	SP36	10g dk brn	3.50	6.00
B78	SP36	15g red brn	3.50	6.00
B79	SP36	30g black	3.50	6.00
B80	SP36	40g indigo	3.50	6.00

Tenth anniversary of Austrian Republic. Sold at double face value, the premium aiding war orphans and children of war invalids.

Set exists imperf. Price $300.

1930, Oct. 4

B81	SP37	10g lt brn	6.75	8.75
B82	SP37	20g red	6.75	8.75
B83	SP37	30g brn vio	6.75	8.75
B84	SP37	40g indigo	6.75	8.75
B85	SP37	50g dk grn	6.75	8.75
B86	SP37	1s blk brn	6.75	8.75
		Nos. B81-B86 (6)	40.50	52.50

Nos. B81-B86 were sold at double face value. The excess aided the anti-tuberculosis campaign and the building of sanatoria in Carinthia.

Set exists imperf. Price, $425.

Regular Issue of 1929-30 Overprinted in Various Colors

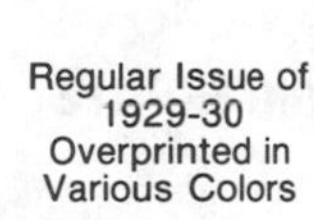

1931, June 20

B87	A56	10g bis (Bl)	37.50	35.00
B88	A56	20g dk gray (R)	37.50	35.00
B89	A56	30g dk vio (Gl)	37.50	35.00
B90	A56	40g dk bl (Gl)	37.50	35.00
B91	A56	50g gray vio (O)	37.50	35.00
B92	A57	1s blk brn (Bk)	37.50	35.00
		Nos. B87-B92 (6)	225.00	210.00

Rotary convention, Vienna.

Nos. B87 to B92 were sold at double their face values. The excess was added to the beneficent funds of Rotary International.

Exists imperf. Price, set $900.

Ferdinand Raimund — SP38

Poets: 20g, Franz Grillparzer. 30g, Johann Nestroy. 40g, Adalbert Stifter. 50g, Ludwig Anzengruber. 1s, Peter Rosegger.

1931, Sept. 12

B93	SP38	10g dk vio	12.50	17.00
B94	SP38	20g gray blk	12.50	17.00
B95	SP38	30g org red	12.50	17.00
B96	SP38	40g dl bl	12.50	17.00
B97	SP38	50g gray grn	12.50	17.00
B98	SP38	1s yel brn	12.50	17.00
		Nos. B93-B98 (6)	75.00	102.00

Nos. B93-B98 were sold at double face value. The surtax aided unemployed young people.

Set exists imperf. Price, $625.

Chancellor Ignaz Seipel SP44

Ferdinand Georg Waldmüller SP45

1932, Oct. 12 *Perf. 13*

B99	SP44	50g ultra	6.50	12.50

Msgr. Ignaz Seipel, Chancellor of Austria, 1922-29. Sold at double face value, the excess aiding wounded veterans of World War I.

Exists imperf. Price, $225.

1932, Nov. 21

Artists: 24g, Moritz von Schwind. 30g, Rudolf von Alt. 40g, Hans Makart. 64g, Gustav Klimt. 1s, Albin Egger-Lienz.

B100	SP45	12g sl grn	13.00	20.00
B101	SP45	24g dp vio	13.00	20.00
B102	SP45	30g dk red	13.00	20.00
B103	SP45	40g dk gray	13.00	20.00
B104	SP45	64g dk brn	13.00	20.00
B105	SP45	1s claret	13.00	20.00
		Nos. B100-B105 (6)	78.00	120.00

Nos. B100 to B105 were sold at double their face values. The surtax was for the assistance of charitable institutions.

Set exists imperf. Price, $725.

Mountain Climbing SP51

Designs: 24g, Ski gliding. 30g, Walking on skis. 50g, Ski jumping.

1933, Jan. 9 **Photo.** *Perf. 12½*

B106	SP51	12g dk grn	7.50	9.50
B107	SP51	24g dk vio	62.50	87.50
B108	SP51	30g brn red	15.00	16.00
B109	SP51	50g dk bl	62.50	87.50

Issued in connection with a meeting of the International Ski Federation at Innsbruck, Feb. 8-13, 1933.

These stamps were sold at double their face value. The surtax was for the benefit of "Youth in Distress."

Nos. B106-B109 exist imperf. Price $1,500.

Vienna Philatelic Exhibition Issue

Stagecoach, after Painting by Moritz von Schwind — SP55

1933, June 23 **Engr.** *Perf. 12½*

Ordinary Paper

B110	SP55	50g dp ultra	100.00	150.00
a.		Granite paper	225.00	375.00

Sheets of 25.

Nos. B110 and B110a exist imperf. Prices four times those of perf. stamps.

Souvenir Sheet

SP55a

Perf. 12
Granite Paper

B111 SP55a 50g dp ultra, sheet of 4 — 1,650. 2,750.
a. Single stamp — 275.00 450.00

Issued in connection with the International Philatelic Exhibition at Vienna in 1933. In addition to the postal value of 50g the stamp was sold at a premium of 50g for charity and of 1s60g for the admission fee to the exhibition.

Size of No. B111: 126x103mm.

The 50g dark red in souvenir sheet, with dark blue overprint ("NEUDRUCK WIPA 1965"), had no postal validity.

St. Stephen's Cathedral in 1683
SP56

Marco d'Aviano, Papal Legate
SP57

Designs: 30g, Count Ernst Rudiger von Starhemberg. 40g, John III Sobieski, King of Poland. 50g, Karl V, Duke of Lorraine. 64g, Burgomaster Johann Andreas von Liebenberg.

1933, Sept. 6 Photo. *Perf. 12½*

B112 SP56 12g dk grn 18.00 22.50
B113 SP57 24g dk vio 16.00 20.00
B114 SP57 30g brn red 16.00 20.00
B115 SP57 40g bl blk 22.50 32.50
B116 SP57 50g dk bl 16.00 20.00
B117 SP57 64g ol brn 22.50 30.00
Nos. B112-B117 (6) 111.00 145.00

Issued in commemoration of the 250th anniversary of the deliverance of Vienna from the Turks and in connection with the Pan-German Catholic Congress on September 6th, 1933.

The stamps were sold at double their face value, the excess being for the aid of Catholic works of charity.

Set exists imperf. Price, $900.

Types of Regular Issue of 1925-30 Surcharged:

+2g Winterhilfe *a*
WINTERHILFE +6g *b*
+50g WINTERHILFE *c*

1933, Dec. 15

B118 A52 (a) 5g + 2g ol grn 28 60
B119 A56 (b) 12g + 3g lt bl 28 60
B120 A56 (b) 24g + 6g brn org 28 60
B121 A57 (c) 1s + 50g org red 30.00 40.00

Winterhelp. Exists imperf. Price, set $175.

Anton Pilgram — SP62

Architects: 24g, J. B. Fischer von Erlach. 30g, Jakob Prandtauer. 40g, A. von Siccardsburg & E. van der Null. 60g, Heinrich von Ferstel. 64g, Otto Wagner.

1934, Dec. 2 Engr. *Perf. 12½*
Thick Yellowish Paper

B122 SP62 12gr (+ 12gr) blk 7.50 10.50
B123 SP62 24gr (+ 24gr) dl vio 7.50 10.50
B124 SP62 30gr (+ 30gr) car 7.50 10.50
B125 SP62 40gr (+ 40gr) brn 7.50 10.50
B126 SP62 60gr (+ 60gr) bl 7.50 10.50
B127 SP62 64gr (+ 64gr) dl grn 7.50 10.50
Nos. B122-B127 (6) 45.00 63.00

Exist imperf. Price, set $550.

Nos. B124-B126 exist in horiz. pairs imperf. between. Price, each $275.

The surtax on this and the following issues was devoted to general charity.

Types of Regular Issue of 1934 Surcharged in Black:

+50g

Winterhilfe +2g a
WINTERHILFE b

1935, Nov. 11 *Perf. 12, 12½*

B128 A67 (a) 5g + 2g emer 50 90
B129 A67 (a) 12g + 3g bl 50 90
B130 A67 (a) 24g + 6g lt brn 50 90
B131 A68 (b) 1s + 50g ver 17.00 37.50

Winterhelp. Set exists imperf. Price, $150.

Prince Eugene of Savoy
SP68

Slalom Turn
SP74

Military Leaders: 24g, Field Marshal Laudon. 30g, Archduke Karl. 40g, Field Marshal Josef Radetzky. 60g, Admiral Wilhelm Tegetthoff. 64g, Field Marshal Franz Conrad Hotzendorff.

1935, Dec. 1 *Perf. 12½*

B132 SP68 12g (+ 12g) brn 7.50 10.50
B133 SP68 24g (+ 24g) dk grn 7.50 10.50
B134 SP68 30g (+ 30g) cl 7.50 10.50
B135 SP68 40g (+ 40g) sl 7.50 10.50
B136 SP68 60g (+ 60g) dp ultra 7.50 10.50
B137 SP68 64g (+ 64g) dk vio 7.50 10.50
Nos. B132-B137 (6) 45.00 63.00

Set exists imperf. Price, $475.

1936, Feb. 20 Photo.

Designs: 24g, Jumper taking off. 35g, Slalom turn. 60g, Innsbruck view.

B138 SP74 12g (+ 12g) Prus grn 3.00 3.25
B139 SP74 24g (+ 24g) dp vio 5.00 5.00
B140 SP74 35g (+ 35g) rose car 24.00 35.00
B141 SP74 60g (+ 60g) saph 24.00 37.50

Ski concourse issue. Set exists imperf. Price, $525.

St. Martin of Tours — SP78

Designs: 12g+3g, Medical clinic. 24g+6g, St. Elizabeth of Hungary. 1s+1s, "Flame of Charity."

1936, Nov. 2

B142 SP78 5g + 2g dp grn 35 45
B143 SP78 12g + 3g dp vio 35 45
B144 SP78 24g + 6g dp bl 35 45
B145 SP78 1s + 1s dk car 6.50 12.00

Winterhelp. Set exists imperf. Price, $175.

Josef Ressel
SP82

Nurse and Infant
SP88

Inventors: 24g, Karl von Ghega. 30g, Josef Werndl. 40g, Carl Auer von Welsbach. 60g, Robert von Lieben. 64g, Viktor Kaplan.

1936, Dec. 6 Engr.

B146 SP82 12g (+ 12g) dk brn 2.50 4.00
B147 SP82 24g (+ 24g) dk vio 2.50 4.00
B148 SP82 30g (+ 30g) dp cl 2.50 4.00
B149 SP82 40g (+ 40g) gray vio 2.50 4.00
B150 SP82 60g (+ 60g) vio bl 2.50 4.00
B151 SP82 64g (+ 64g) dk sl grn 2.50 4.00
Nos. B146-B151 (6) 15.00 24.00

Exists imperf. Price, set $375.

1937, Oct. 18 Photo.

Designs: 12g+3g, Mother and child. 24g+6g, Nursing the aged. 1s+1s, Sister of Mercy with patient.

B152 SP88 5g + 2g dk grn 15 28
B153 SP88 12g + 3g dk brn 15 28
B154 SP88 24g + 6g dk bl 15 28
B155 SP88 1s + 1s dk car 3.75 6.00

Winterhelp. Set exists imperf. Price, $135.

Gerhard van Swieten
SP92

The Dawn of Peace
SP101

Physicians: 8g, Leopold Auenbrugger von Auenbrugg. 12g, Karl von Rokitansky. 20g, Joseph Skoda. 24g, Ferdinand von Hebra. 30g, Ferdinand von Arlt. 40g, Joseph Hyrtl. 60g, Theodor Billroth. 64g, Theodor Meynert.

1937, Dec. 5 Engr. *Perf. 12½*

B156 SP92 5g + (5g) choc 1.65 3.50
B157 SP92 8g + (8g) dk red 1.65 3.50
B158 SP92 12g + (12g) brn blk 1.65 3.50
B159 SP92 20g + (20g) dk grn 1.65 3.50
B160 SP92 24g + (24g) dk vio 1.65 3.50
B161 SP92 30g + (30g) brn car 1.65 3.50
B162 SP92 40g + (40g) dp ol grn 1.65 3.50
B163 SP92 60g + (60g) ind 1.65 3.50
B164 SP92 64g + (64g) brn vio 1.65 3.50
Nos. B156-B164 (9) 14.85 31.50

Set exists imperf. Price, $450.

Unwmk.

1945, Sept. 10 Photo. *Perf. 14*

B165 SP101 1s + 10s dk grn 60 1.40

No. 467 Surcharged in Black

1946, June 25

B166 A110 30g + 20g dk red 2.25 4.50

First anniversary of United Nations.

Pres. Karl Renner
SP102

1946 Engr. *Perf. 13½x14.*

B167 SP102 1s + 1s dk sl grn 1.65 3.50
B168 SP102 2s + 2s dk bl vio 1.65 3.50
B169 SP102 3s + 3s dk pur 1.65 3.50
B170 SP102 5s + 5s dk vio brn 1.65 3.50

See Nos. B185-B188.

Nazi Sword Piercing Austria
SP103

Sweeping Away Fascist Symbols
SP104

Designs: 8g + 6g, St. Stephen's Cathedral in Flames. 12g+12g, Pleading hand in concentration camp. 30g + 30g, Hand choking Nazi serpent. 42g + 42g, Hammer breaking Nazi pillar. 1s + 1s, Oath of allegiance. 2s + 2s, Austrian eagle and burning swastika.

Unwmk.

1946, Sept. 16 Photo. *Perf. 14*

B171 SP103 5g + 3(g) dk brn 32 60
B172 SP104 6g + 4(g) dk sl grn 25 50
B173 SP104 8g + 6(g) org red 25 50
B174 SP104 12g + 12(g) sl blk 25 50
B175 SP104 30g + 30(g) vio 25 50
B176 SP104 42g + 42(g) dl brn 25 50
B177 SP104 1s + 1s dk red 32 60
B178 SP104 2s + 2s dk car rose 45 60
Nos. B171-B178 (8) 2.34 4.30

Issued as anti-fascist propaganda.

Race Horse with Foal — SP111

1946, Oct. 20 Engr. *Perf. 13½x14*
Various Race Horses

B179 SP111 16g + 16g rose brn 1.25 2.75
B180 SP111 24g + 24g dk pur 1.25 2.75
B181 SP111 60g + 60g dk grn 1.25 2.75
B182 SP111 1s + 1s dk bl gray 1.25 2.75
B183 SP111 2s + 2s yel brn 1.25 2.75
Nos. B179-B183 (5) 6.25 13.75

Austria Prize race, Vienna.

St. Ruprecht's Church, Vienna — SP116

1946, Oct. 30 ***Perf. 14x13½***

B184 SP116 30g + 70g dk red 32 60

Issued to commemorate the 950th anniversary of the founding of Austria. The surtax aided the Stamp Day celebration.

Souvenir Sheets

President Karl Renner — SP117

1946, Sept. 5 ***Imperf.***

B185 SP117 1s + 1s dk sl grn 400.00 900.00
a. Single stamp 40.00 95.00
B186 SP117 2s + 2s dk bl vio 400.00 900.00
a. Single stamp 40.00 95.00
B187 SP117 3s + 3s dk pur 400.00 900.00
a. Single stamp 40.00 95.00
B188 SP117 5s + 5s dk vio brn 400.00 900.00
a. Single stamp 40.00 95.00

First anniversary of Austria's liberation. Sheets of 8. Size: 180x153mm.

Statue of Rudolf IV the Founder SP118

Reaping Wheat SP128

Designs: 5g+20g, Tomb of Frederick III. 6g+24g, Main pulpit. 8g+32g, Statue of St. Stephen. 10g+40g, Madonna of the Domestics statue. 12g+48g, High altar. 30g+1.20s, Organ, destroyed in 1945. 50g+1.80s, Anton Pilgram statue. 1s+5s, Cathedral from northeast. 2s+10s, Southwest corner of cathedral.

1946, Dec. 12 **Engr.** ***Perf. 14x13½***

B189 SP118 3g + 12g brn 15 38
B190 SP118 5g + 20g dk vio brn 15 38
B191 SP118 6g + 24g dk bl 15 38
B192 SP118 8g + 32g dk grn 15 38
B193 SP118 10g + 40g dp bl 25 42
B194 SP118 12g + 48g dk vio 30 55
B195 SP118 30g + 1.20s car 75 1.25
B196 SP118 50g + 1.80s dk bl 80 1.50
B197 SP118 1s + 5s brn vio 1.10 2.00
B198 SP118 2s + 10s vio brn 2.25 4.00
Nos. B189-B198 (10) 6.05 11.24

The surtax aided reconstruction of St. Stephen's Cathedral, Vienna.

1947, Mar. 23 ***Perf. 14x13½***

Designs: 8g+2g, Log raft. 10g+5g, Cement factory. 12g+8g, Coal mine. 18g+12g, Oil derricks. 30g+10g, Textile machinery. 35g+15g, Iron furnace. 60g+20g, Electric power lines.

B199 SP128 3g + 2g yel brn 20 30
B200 SP128 8g + 2g dk bl grn 20 30
B201 SP128 10g + 5g sl blk 20 30
B202 SP128 12g + 8g dk pur 20 30
B203 SP128 18g + 12g ol grn 20 30
B204 SP128 30g + 10g dp cl 20 30
B205 SP128 35g + 15g crim 20 30
B206 SP128 60g + 20g dk bl 20 30
Nos. B199-B206 (8) 1.60 2.40

Vienna International Sample Fair, 1947.

Race Horse and Jockey SP136

1947, June 29 ***Perf. 13½x14***

B207 SP136 60g + 20g dp bl, *pale pink* 10 20

Cup of Corvinus SP137

Prisoner of War SP147

Designs: 8g+2g, Statue of Providence, Vienna. 10g+5g, Abbey at Melk. 12g+8g, Picture of a Woman, by Kriehuber. 18g+12g, Children at the Window, by Waldmuller. 20g+10g, Entrance, Upper Belvedere Palace. 30g+10g, Nymph Egeria, Schönbrunn Castle. 35g+15g, National Library, Vienna. 48g+12g, "Workshop of a Printer of Engravings," by Schmutzer. 60g+20g, Girl with Straw Hat, by Amerling.

1947, June 20 ***Perf. 14x13½***

B208 SP137 3g + 2g brn 15 30
B209 SP137 8g + 2g dk bl grn 15 30
B210 SP137 10g + 5g dp cl 15 30
B211 SP137 12g + 8g dk pur 15 30
B212 SP137 18g + 12g gldn brn 15 30
B213 SP137 20g + 10g sep 15 30
B214 SP137 30g + 10g dk yel grn 15 30
B215 SP137 35g + 15g dp car 15 30
B216 SP137 48g + 12g dk brn vio 15 30
B217 SP137 60g + 20g dp bl 15 30
Nos. B208-B217 (10) 1.50 3.00

1947, Aug. 30

Designs: 12g+8g, Prisoners' Mail, 18g+12g, Prison camp visitor. 35g+15g, Family reunion. 60g+20g, "Industry" beckoning. 1s+40g, Sower.

B218 SP147 8g + 2(g) dk grn 12 20
B219 SP147 12g + 8(g) dk vio brn 12 20
B220 SP147 18g + 12(g) blk brn 12 20
B221 SP147 35g + 15(g) rose brn 12 20
B222 SP147 60g + 20(g) dp bl 12 20
B223 SP147 1s + 40(g) redsh brn 12 20
Nos. B218-B223 (6) 72 1.20

Olympic Flame and Emblem SP153

Laabenbach Bridge Neulengbach SP154

1948, Jan. 16 **Engr.**

B224 SP153 1s + 50g dk bl 28 35

The surtax was used to help defray expenses of Austria's 1948 Olympics team.

1948, Feb. 18 ***Perf. 14x13½***

Designs: 20g+10g, Dam, Vermunt Lake. 30g+10g, Danube Port, Vienna. 40g+20g, Mining, Erzberg. 45g+20g, Tracks, Southern Railway Station, Vienna. 60g+30g, Communal housing project, Vienna. 75g+35g, Gas Works, Vienna. 80g+40g, Oil refinery. 1s+50g, Gesäuse Highway, Styria. 1.40s+70g, Parliament Building, Vienna.

B225 SP154 10g + 5g sl blk 12 25
B226 SP154 20g + 10g lil 12 25
B227 SP154 30g + 10g dl grn 38 50
B228 SP154 40g + 20g ol brn 10 18
B229 SP154 45g + 20g dk bl 5 8
B230 SP154 60g + 30g dk red 5 8
B231 SP154 75g + 35g dk vio brn 5 8
B232 SP154 80g + 40g vio brn 5 8
B233 SP154 1s + 50g dp bl 8 15
B234 SP154 1.40s + 70g dp car 28 50
Nos. B225-B234 (10) 1.28 2.15

The surtax was for the Reconstruction Fund.

Violet — SP155

Designs: 20g+10g, Anemone. 30g+10g, Crocus. 40g+20g, Yellow primrose. 45g+20g, Pasqueflower. 60g+30g, Rhododendron. 75g+35g, Dogrose. 80g+40g, Cyclamen. 1s+50g, Alpine Gentian. 1.40s+70g, Edelweiss.

Engraved and Typographed

1948, May 14 **Unwmk.**

B235 SP155 10g + 5g multi 22 18
B236 SP155 20g + 10g multi 10 8
B237 SP155 30g + 10g multi 1.65 2.75
B238 SP155 40g + 20g multi 35 32
B239 SP155 45g + 20g multi 10 8
B240 SP155 60g + 30g multi 10 12
B241 SP155 75g + 35g multi 10 12
B242 SP155 80g + 40g multi 20 25
B243 SP155 1s + 50g multi 25 40
B244 SP155 1.40s + 70g multi 45 70
Nos. B235-B244 (10) 3.52 5.00

Hans Makart — SP156

St. Rupert — SP157

Designs: 20g+10g, Künstlerhaus, Vienna. 40g+20g, Carl Kundmann. 50g+25g, A. S. von Siccardsburg. 60g+30g, Hans Cannon. 1s+50g, William Unger. 1.40s+70g, Friedrich von Schmidt.

1948, June 15 **Engr.**

B245 SP156 20g + 10g dp yel grn 3.50 7.25
B246 SP156 30g + 15g dk brn 1.65 2.75
B247 SP156 40g + 20g ind 1.65 2.75
B248 SP156 50g + 25g dk vio 2.00 4.00
B249 SP156 60g + 30g dk red 2.00 4.00
B250 SP156 1s + 50g dk bl 3.50 7.25
B251 SP156 1.40s + 70g red brn 4.75 10.00
Nos. B245-B251 (7) 19.05 38.00

Issued to commemorate the 80th anniversary of the Kunstlerhaus, home of the leading Austrian Artists Association.

1948, Aug. 6 ***Perf. 14x13½***

Designs: 30g+15g, Cathedral and Fountain. 40g+20g, Facade of Cathedral. 50g+25g, Cathedral from South. 60g+30g, Abbey of St. Peter. 80g+40g, Inside Cathedral. 1s+50g, Salzburg Cathedral and Castle. 1.40s+70g, Madonna by Michael Pacher.

B252 SP157 20g + 10g dp grn 4.50 6.25
B253 SP157 30g + 15g red brn 1.90 3.00
B254 SP157 40g + 20g sl blk 1.50 2.25
B255 SP157 50g + 25g choc 30 50
B256 SP157 60g + 30g dk red 30 50
B257 SP157 80g + 40g dk brn vio 30 50
B258 SP157 1s + 50g dp bl 55 60
B259 SP157 1.40s + 70g dk grn 1.00 1.25
Nos. B252-B259 (8) 10.35 14.85

The surtax was to aid in the reconstruction of Salzburg Cathedral.

Easter — SP158

Arms of Austria, 1230 — SP159

Designs: 60g+20g, St. Nicholas Day. 1s+25g, Birthday. 1.40s+35g, Christmas.

1949, Apr. 13 **Unwmk.**

Inscribed: "Gluckliche Kindheit".

B260 SP158 40g + 10g brn vio 10.50 16.00
B261 SP158 60g + 20g brn red 10.50 16.00
B262 SP158 1s + 25g dp ultra 10.50 16.00
B263 SP158 1.40s + 35g dk grn 10.50 16.00

The surtax was for Child Welfare.

Engraved and Photogravure

1949, Aug. 17

Designs: 60g+15g, Arms, 1450. 1s+25g, Arms, 1600. 1.60s+40g, Arms, 1945.

B264 SP159 40g + 10g yel brn & yel 4.00 7.00

Engraved and Typographed

B265 SP159 60g + 15g brn car & sal 4.00 7.00
B266 SP159 1s + 25g dp bl & ver 4.00 7.00
B267 SP159 1.60s + 40g dp grn & sal 4.00 7.00

The surtax was for returned prisoners of war.

Laurel Branch, Stamps and Magnifier — SP160

1949, Dec. 3 **Engr.**

B268 SP160 60g + 15g dk red 2.00 2.25

Stamp Day, Dec. 3-4.

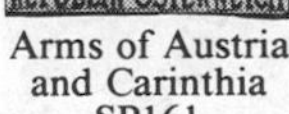
Arms of Austria and Carinthia SP161

Carinthian with Austrian Flag SP162

Design: 1.70s+40g, Casting ballot.

1950, Oct. 10 **Photo.** ***Perf. 14x13½***

B269 SP161 60g + 15g bl grn & choc 17.50 22.50
B270 SP162 1s + 25g red org & red 22.50 25.00
B271 SP162 1.70s + 40g dp bl & grnsh bl 27.50 32.50

Issued to mark the 30th anniversary of the plebiscite in Carinthia.

Collector Examining Cover — SP163

Miner and Mine — SP164

1950, Dec. 2 **Engr.**
B272 SP163 60g + 15g bl grn 5.25 5.75

Stamp Day.

1951, Mar. 10 **Unwmk.**

Designs: 60g+15g, Mason holding brick and trowel. 1s+25g, Bridge builder with hook and chain. 1.70s+40g, Electrician, pole and insulators.

B273	SP164	40g + 10g dk brn	8.50	15.00
B274	SP164	60g + 15g dk grn	8.50	15.00
B275	SP164	1s + 25g red brn	8.50	15.00
B276	SP164	1.70s + 40g vio bl	8.50	15.00

Issued to publicize Austrian reconstruction.

Laurel Branch and Olympic Circles SP165

1952, Jan. 26 ***Perf. 13½x14***
B277 SP165 2.40s + 60g grnsh blk 10.50 20.00

The surtax was used to help defray expenses of Austria's athletes in the 1952 Olympic Games.

Cupid as Postman — SP166

1952, Mar. 10 ***Perf. 14x13½***
B278 SP166 1.50s + 35g dk brn car 12.00 20.00

Stamp Day.

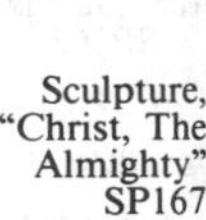

Sculpture, "Christ, The Almighty" SP167

1952, Sept. 6 ***Perf. 13½x14***
B279 SP167 1s + 25g grnsh gray 6.00 9.50

Issued to publicize the Austrian Catholic Convention, Vienna, Sept. 11-14, 1952.

Type of 1945-46 Overprinted in Gold

1953, Aug. 29 **Unwmk.**
B280 A124 1s + 25g on 5s dl bl 2.25 3.00

Issued to commemorate the 60th anniversary of labor unions in Austria.

Bummerlhaus Steyr SP168

Globe and Philatelic Accessories SP169

Designs: 1s+25g, Johannes Kepler. 1.50s+40g, Lutheran Bible, 1st edition. 2.40s+60g, Theophil von Hansen. 3s+75g, Reconstructed Lutheran School, Vienna.

1953, Nov. 5 **Engr.** ***Perf. 14x13½***

B281	SP168	70g + 15g vio brn	20	32
B282	SP168	1s + 25g dk gray bl	20	32
B283	SP168	1.50s + 40g choc	60	90
B284	SP168	2.40s + 60g dk grn	2.00	3.00
B285	SP168	3s + 75g dk pur	4.75	7.75
		Nos. B281-B285 (5)	7.75	12.29

The surtax was used toward reconstruction of the Lutheran School, Vienna.

1953, Dec. 5
B286 SP169 1s + 25g choc 4.50 6.00

Stamp Day.

Type of 1945-46 with Denomination Replaced by Asterisks

Surcharged in Brown

LAWINENOPFER 1954

1s + 20g

1954, Feb. 19 ***Perf. 13½x14***
B287 A124 1s + 20g bl gray 15 8

The surtax was used for aid to avalanche victims.

Patient Under Sun Lamp — SP170

Designs: 70g+15g, Physician using microscope. 1s+25g, Mother and children. 1.45s+35g, Operating room. 1.50s+35g, Baby on scale. 2.40s+60g, Nurse.

1954 **Engr.** ***Perf. 14x13½.***

B288	SP170	30g + 10g pur	90	1.25
B289	SP170	70g + 15g dk brn	15	18
B290	SP170	1s + 25g dk bl	20	25
B291	SP170	1.45s + 35g dk bl grn	28	35
B292	SP170	1.50s + 35g dk red	3.50	4.75
B293	SP170	2.40s + 60g dk red brn	4.25	6.50
		Nos. B288-B293 (6)	9.28	13.28

The surtax was for social welfare.

Early Vienna-Ulm Ferryboat SP171

1954, Dec. 4 ***Perf. 13½x14***
B294 SP171 1s + 25g dk gray grn 3.75 6.00

Stamp Day.

"Industry" Welcoming Returned Prisoner of War — SP172

1955, June 29
B295 SP172 1s + 25g red brn 1.50 2.50

The surtax was for returned prisoners of war and relatives of prisoners not yet released.

Collector Looking at Album — SP173

Ornamental Shield and Letter — SP174

1955, Dec. 3 ***Perf. 14x13½***
B296 SP173 1s + 25g vio brn 2.25 4.00

Issued for the Day of the Stamp. The surtax was for the promotion of Austrian philately.

1956, Dec. 1 **Engr.**
B297 SP174 1s + 25g scar 1.90 3.75

Stamp Day. See note after No. B296.

Arms of Austria, 1945 — SP175

Engraved and Typographed

1956, Dec. 21 ***Perf. 14x13½***
B298 SP175 1.50s + 50g on 1.60s + 40g gray & red 28 40

The surtax was for Hungarian refugees.

New Post Office, Linz 2 — SP176

1957, Nov. 30 **Engr.** ***Perf. 13½x14***
B299 SP176 1s + 25g dk sl grn 2.25 3.75

Stamp Day. See note after No. B296.

1958, Dec. 6

Design: 2.40s+60g, Post office, Kitzbuhel.

B300 SP176 2.40s + 60g bl 45 1.10

Stamp Day. See note after B296. See No. B303.

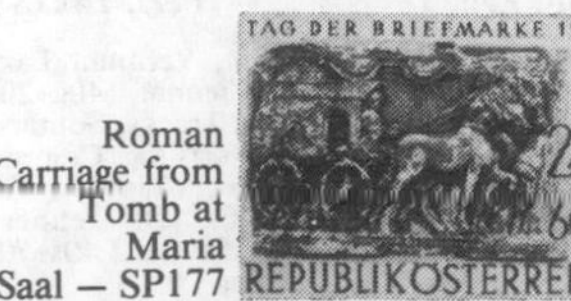
Roman Carriage from Tomb at Maria Saal — SP177

Lithographed and Engraved

1959, Dec. 5 ***Perf. 13½x14***
B301 SP177 2.40s + 60g pale lil & blk 40 90

Stamp Day.

Progressive Die Proof under Magnifying Glass SP178

1960, Dec. 2 **Engr.** ***Perf. 13½x14***
B302 SP178 3s + 70g vio brn 1.10 1.10

Stamp Day.

P. O. Type of 1957

Design: 3s+70g, Post Office, Rust.

1961, Dec. 1 ***Perf. 13½***
B303 SP176 3s + 70g dk bl grn 1.10 1.10

Stamp Day. See note after No. B296.

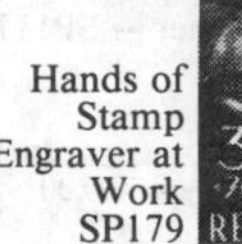

Hands of Stamp Engraver at Work SP179

1962, Nov. 30 ***Perf. 13½x14***
B304 SP179 3s + 70g dl pur 1.50 1.50

Stamp Day.

Railroad Exit, Post Office Vienna 101 — SP180

Lithographed and Engraved

1963, Nov. 29 **Unwmk.**
B305 SP180 3s + 70g tan & blk 75 75

Stamp Day.

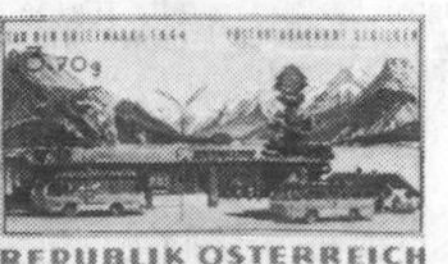
View of Vienna, North SP181

Designs: Various view of Vienna with compass indicating direction.

1964, July 20 **Litho.** ***Perf. 13½x14***

B306	SP181	1.50s + 30g ("N")	18	18
B307	SP181	1.50s + 30g ("NO")	18	18
B308	SP181	1.50s + 30g ("O")	18	18
B309	SP181	1.50s + 30g ("SO")	18	18
B310	SP181	1.50s + 30g ("S")	18	18
B311	SP181	1.50s + 30g ("SW")	18	18
B312	SP181	1.50s + 30g ("W")	18	18
B313	SP181	1.50s + 30g ("NW")	18	18
		Nos. B306-B313 (8)	1.44	1.44

Issued to publicize the Vienna International Philatelic Exhibition (WIPA 1965).

Post Bus Terminal, St. Gilgen, Wolfgangsee — SP182

1964, Dec. 4 Unwmk. *Perf. 13½*
B314 SP182 3s + 70g multi 45 45

Stamp Day.

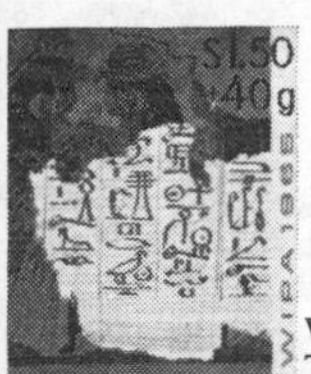
Wall Painting, Tomb at Thebes — SP183

Development of Writing: 1.80s+50g, Cuneiform writing on stone tablet and man's head from Assyrian palace. 2.20s+60g, Wax tablet with Latin writing, Corinthian column. 3s+80g, Gothic writing on sealed letter, Gothic window from Munster Cathedral. 4s+1s, Letter with seal and postmark and upright desk. 5s+1.20s, Typewriter.

Lithographed and Engraved
1965, June 4 *Perf. 14x13½*

B315	SP183	1.50s + 40g dp rose & blk	12	12
B316	SP183	1.80s + 50g yel & blk	20	20
B317	SP183	2.20s + 60g pale vio & blk	40	40
B318	SP183	3s + 80g ap grn & blk	25	25
B319	SP183	4s + 1s lt bl & blk	55	55
B320	SP183	5s + 1.20s brt grn & blk	75	75
		Nos. B315-B320 (6)	2.27	2.27

Issued to commemorate the Vienna International Philatelic Exhibition, WIPA, June 4-13.

Mailman Distributing Mail SP184

Perf. 13½x14
1965, Dec. 3 Engr. Unwmk.
B321 SP184 3s + 70g bl grn 45 45

Stamp Day.

Letter Carrier, 16th Century SP185

Letter Carrier, 16th Century Playing Card SP186

Lithographed and Engraved
1966, Dec. 2 Unwmk. *Perf. 13½*
B322 SP185 3s + 70g multi 45 40

Stamp Day. Design is from Ambras Heroes" Book, Austrian National Library.

Engraved and Photogravure
1967, Dec. 1 *Perf. 13x13½*
B323 SP186 3.50s + 80g multi 50 50

Stamp Day.

Austria stamps can be mounted in Scott's annually supplemented Austria Album.

Mercury, Bas-relief from Purkersdorf SP187

Unken Post Station Sign, 1710 SP188

1968, Nov. 29 Engr. *Perf. 13½*
B324 SP187 3.50s + 80g sl grn 45 45

Stamp Day.

Engraved and Photogravure
1969, Dec. 5 *Perf. 12*
B325 SP188 3.50s + 80g tan, red & blk 40 40

Stamp Day. Design is from a watercolor by Friedrich Zeller.

Saddle, Bag, Harness and Post Horn — SP189

Engraved and Lithographed
1970, Dec. 4 *Perf. 13½x14*
B326 SP189 3.50s + 80g gray blk & yel 50 40

Stamp Day.

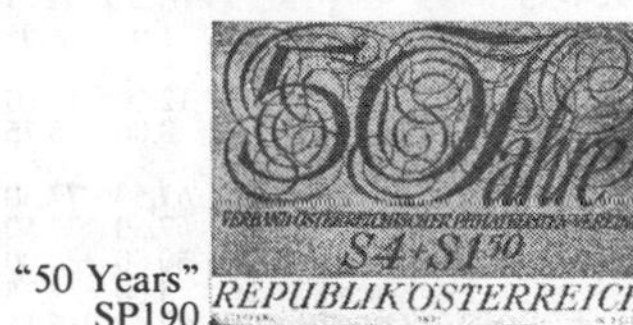
"50 Years" SP190

Engraved and Photogravure
1971, Dec. 3 *Perf. 13½*
B327 SP190 4s + 1.50s gold & red brn 65 65

50th anniversary of the Federation of Austrian Philatelic Societies.

Local Post Carrier SP191

Gabriel, by Lorenz Luchsperger, 15th Century SP192

1972, Dec. 1 Engr. *Perf. 14x13½*
B328 SP191 4s + 1s ol grn 65 65

Stamp Day.

1973, Nov. 30
B329 SP192 4s + 1s mar 60 60

Stamp Day.

Mail Coach Leaving Old PTT Building — SP193

1974, Nov. 29 Engr. *Perf. 14x13½*
B330 SP193 4s + 2s vio bl 70 70

Stamp Day.

Alpine Skiing, Women's SP194

Designs (Innsbruck Winter Olympic Games Emblem and): 1.50s+70g, Ice hockey. 2s+90g, Ski jump. 4s+1.90s, Bobsledding.

1975, Mar. 14 Photo. *Perf. 13½x14*

B331	SP194	1s + 50g multi	25	25
B332	SP194	1.50s + 70g multi	32	32
B333	SP194	2s + 90g multi	40	40
B334	SP194	4s + 1.90s multi	80	80

1975, Nov. 14

Designs (Innsbruck Winter Olympic Games Emblem and): 70g+30g, Figure skating, pair. 2s+1s, Cross-country skiing. 2.50s+1s, Luge. 4s+2s, Biathlon.

B335	SP194	70g + 30g multi	18	18
B336	SP194	2s + 1s multi	35	35
B337	SP194	2.50s + 1s multi	40	40
B338	SP194	4s + 2s multi	75	75

12th Winter Olympic Games, Innsbruck, Feb. 4-15, 1976.

Austria Nos. 5, 250, 455 — SP195

Photogravure and Engraved
1975, Nov. 28 *Perf. 14*
B339 SP195 4s + 2s multi 75 75

Stamp Day and 125th anniversary of Austrian stamps.

Postilion's Gala Hat and Horn SP196

1976, Dec. 3 *Perf. 13½x14*
B340 SP196 6s + 2s blk & lt vio 90 90

Stamp Day 1976.

Emanuel Herrmann SP197

Condition is the all-important factor of price. Prices quoted are for stamps in fine condition.

1977, Dec. 2 *Perf. 14x13½*
B341 SP197 6s + 2s multi 90 90

Stamp Day 1977. Emanuel Herrmann (1839-1902), economist, invented postal card. Austria issued first postal card in 1869.

Post Bus, 1913 SP198

1978, Dec. 1 Photo. *Perf. 13½x14*
B342 SP198 10s + 5s multi 1.75 1.75

Stamp Day 1978.

Heroes' Square, Vienna SP199

Photogravure and Engraved
1979, Nov. 30 *Perf. 13½*
B343 SP199 16s + 8s multi 2.75 2.75

No. B343 Inscribed "2. Phase"

Photogravure and Engraved
1980, Nov. 21 *Perf. 13½*
B344 SP199 16s + 8s multi 2.75 2.75

WIPA 1981 Philatelic Exhibition, Vienna, May 22-31, 1981.

Souvenir Sheet
Photogravure and Engraved
1981, Feb. 20 *Perf. 13½*
B345 SP199 16s + 8s multi 3.25 3.25

WIPA 1981 Philatelic Exhibition, Vienna, May 22-31. No. B345 contains one stamp (without inscription); black and red margin. Size: 90x72mm.

Stamp Day 1982 SP200

Photogravure and Engraved
1982, Nov. 26
B346 SP200 6s + 3s Mainz-Weber mailbox, 1870 1.00 1.00

Stamp Day 1983 — SP201

Photogravure and Engraved
1983, Oct. 21 *Perf. 14*
B347 SP201 6s + 3s Boy examining cover 1.00 1.00

See Nos. B349-B352.

World Winter Games for the Handicapped — SP202

1984, Jan. 5 Photo. *Perf. 13½x13*

No.	Type	Description	Unused	Used
B348	SP202	4s + 2s Downhill skier	65	65

Stamp Day Type of 1983

Design: 6s+3s, Seschemnofer III burial chamber detail, pyramid of Cheops, Gizeh.

Photogravure and Engraved

1984, Nov. 30 *Perf. 13½*

No.	Type	Description	Unused	Used
B349	SP201	6s + 3s multi	1.10	1.10

Stamp Day Type of 1983

Design: 6s+3s, Roman messenger on horseback.

Photogravure and Engraved

1985, Nov. 28 *Perf. 14*

No.	Type	Description	Unused	Used
B350	SP201	6s + 3s multi	1.00	75

Stamp Day Type of 1983

Design: Nuremberg messenger, 16th cent.

1986, Nov. 28 *Perf. 14*

No.	Type	Description	Unused	Used
B351	SP201	6s + 3s multi	1.30	1.00

Stamp Day Type of 1983

Design: *The Postmaster* (detail), 1841, lithograph by Carl Schuster.

Photo. & Engr.

1987, Nov. 19 *Perf. 14*

No.	Type	Description	Unused	Used
B352	SP201	6s +3s multi	1.55	1.15

4th World Winter Sports Championships for the Disabled, Innsbruck — SP203

1988, Jan. 5 Photo. *Perf. 13½*

No.	Type	Description	Unused	Used
B353	SP203	5s + 2.50s multi	1.30	98

AIR POST STAMPS

Issues of the Monarchy

FLUGPOST

Types of Regular Issue of 1916 Surcharged

2·50 K 2·50

1918, Mar. 30 Unwmk. *Perf. 12½*

No.	Type	Description	Unused	Used
C1	A40	1.50k on 2k lil	2.50	3.00
C2	A40	2.50k on 3k ocher	11.00	20.00
a.		Inverted surcharge	*1,500.*	
b.		Perf. 11½	325.00	225.00
c.		Perf. 12½x11½	27.50	37.50

Overprinted FLUGPOST

No.	Type	Description	Unused	Used
C3	A40	4k gray	6.75	10.00

Set exists imperf. Price, $500.

Nos. C1-C3 also exist without surcharge or overprint. Price, set perf., $900; imperf., $750.

Nos. C1-C3 were printed on grayish and on white paper.

A 7k on 10k red brown was prepared but not regularly issued. Price, perf. or imperf., $600.

Issues of the Republic

Hawk — AP1 Wilhelm Kress — AP2

1922-24 Typo. *Perf. 12½*

No.	Type	Description	Unused	Used
C4	AP1	300k claret	35	1.25
C5	AP1	400k grn ('24)	5.50	10.00
C6	AP1	600k bister	10	60
C7	AP1	900k brn org	10	60

Engr.

No.	Type	Description	Unused	Used
C8	AP2	1200k brn vio	10	60
C9	AP2	2400k slate	10	60
C10	AP2	3000k dp brn ('23)	2.00	2.75
C11	AP2	4800k dk bl ('23)	2.50	3.25
		Nos. C4-C11 (8)	10.75	19.65

Set exists imperf. Price, $900.

Plane and Pilot's Head — AP3 Airplane Passing Crane — AP4

1925-30 Typo. *Perf. 12½*

No.	Type	Description	Unused	Used
C12	AP3	2g gray brn	55	1.00
C13	AP3	5g red	30	25
a.		Horiz. pair, imperf. between	275.00	
C14	AP3	6g dk bl	1.10	1.50
C15	AP3	8g yel grn	1.25	1.65
C16	AP3	10g dp org ('26)	1.25	1.65
a.		Horiz. pair, imperf. between	300.00	
C17	AP3	15g red vio ('26)	60	90
a.		Horiz. pair, imperf. between	375.00	
C18	AP3	20g org brn ('30)	12.00	4.00
C19	AP3	25g blk vio ('30)	3.00	6.00
C20	AP3	30g bis ('26)	7.75	6.00
C21	AP3	50g bl gray ('26)	13.00	10.50
C22	AP3	80g dk grn ('30)	1.50	4.00

Photo.

No.	Type	Description	Unused	Used
C23	AP4	10g org red	1.10	2.50
a.		Horiz. pair, imperf. btwn.	300.00	
C24	AP4	15g claret	75	1.25
C25	AP4	30g brn vio	95	2.50
C26	AP4	50g gray blk	95	2.75
C27	AP4	1s dp bl	2.25	3.75
C28	AP4	2s dk grn	1.65	3.75
a.		Vertical pair, imperf. between	275.00	
C29	AP4	3s red brn ('26)	42.50	35.00
C30	AP4	5s ind ('26)	12.50	22.50

Size: 25½x32mm.

No.	Type	Description	Unused	Used
C31	AP4	10s blk brn, *gray* ('26)	10.50	17.00
		Nos. C12-C31 (20)	115.45	128.45

Exists imperf. Price, set $1,100.

Airplane over Güssing Castle — AP5 Airplane over the Danube — AP6

Designs (each includes plane): 10g, Maria-Worth. 15g, Durnstein. 20g, Hallstatt. 25g, Salzburg. 30g, Upper Dachstein and Schladminger Glacier. 40g, Lake Wetter. 50g, Arlberg. 60g, St. Stephen's Cathedral. 80g, Church of the Minorites. 2s, Railroad viaduct, Carinthia. 3s, Gross Glockner mountain. 5s, Aerial railway. 10s, Seaplane and yachts.

1935, Aug. 16 Engr. *Perf. 12½*

No.	Type	Description	Unused	Used
C32	AP5	5g rose vio	12	18
C33	AP5	10g red org	12	18
C34	AP5	15g yel grn	70	55
C35	AP5	20g gray bl	15	32
C36	AP5	25g vio brn	15	32
C37	AP5	30g brn org	18	38
C38	AP5	40g gray grn	18	38
C39	AP5	50g lt sl bl	18	38
C40	AP5	60g blk brn	40	65
C41	AP5	80g lt brn	40	65
C42	AP6	1s rose red	40	90
C43	AP6	2s ol grn	1.75	4.50
C44	AP6	3s yel brn	7.75	13.00
C45	AP6	5s dk grn	4.50	13.00
C46	AP6	10s sl bl	32.50	72.50
		Nos. C32-C46 (15)	49.48	107.89

Set exists imperf. Price, $425.

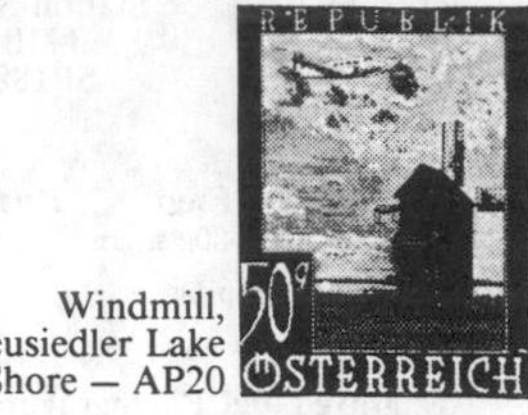

Windmill, Neusiedler Lake Shore — AP20

Designs: 1s, Roman arch, Carnuntum. 2s, Town Hall, Gmund. 3s, Schieder Lake, Hinterstoder. 4s, Praegraten, Eastern Tyrol. 5s, Torsäule, Salzburg. 10s, St. Charles Church, Vienna.

1947 Unwmk. *Perf. 14x13½*

No.	Type	Description	Unused	Used
C47	AP20	50g blk brn	12	28
C48	AP20	1s dk brn vio	25	35
C49	AP20	2s dk grn	28	45
C50	AP20	3s chocolate	1.65	3.00
C51	AP20	4s dk grn	1.10	2.00
C52	AP20	5s dk bl	1.10	2.00
C53	AP20	10s dk bl	55	1.25
		Nos. C47-C53 (7)	5.05	9.33

Rooks AP27

Birds: 1s, Barn swallows. 2s, Blackheaded gulls. 3s, Great cormorants. 5s, Buzzard. 10s, Gray heron. 20s, Golden eagle.

1950-53 *Perf. 13½x14*

No.	Type	Description	Unused	Used
C54	AP27	60g dk bl vio	1.90	1.65
C55	AP27	1s dk vio bl ('53)	12.00	19.00
C56	AP27	2s dk bl	8.00	5.75
C57	AP27	3s dk sl grn ('53)	67.50	77.50
C58	AP27	5s red brn ('53)	67.50	77.50
C59	AP27	10s gray vio ('53)	30.00	30.00
C60	AP27	20s brn blk ('52)	5.50	4.75
		Nos. C54-C60 (7)	192.40	216.15

Value at lower left on Nos. C59 and C60. No. C60 exists imperf.

Etrich "Dove" AP28

Designs: 3.50s, Twin-engine jet airliner. 5s, Four-engine jet airliner.

1968, May 31 Engr. *Perf. 13½x14*

No.	Type	Description	Unused	Used
C61	AP28	2s ol bis	32	32
C62	AP28	3.50s sl grn	55	55
C63	AP28	5s dk bl	80	80

Issued to publicize IFA WIEN 1968 (International Air Post Exhibition), Vienna, May 30-June 4.

POSTAGE DUE STAMPS

Issues of the Monarchy

D1

D2

Wmk. ZEITUNGS-MARKEN (91)

1894-95 Typo. *Perf. 10 to 13½*

No.	Type	Description	Unused	Used
J1	D1	1kr brown	2.00	1.25
a.		Perf. 13½	20.00	6.00
J2	D1	2kr brn ('95)	3.75	1.25
a.		Pair, imperf. btwn.	200.00	225.00
J3	D1	3kr brown	3.25	25
J4	D1	5kr brown	2.75	35
a.		Perf. 13½	14.00	6.50
b.		Pair, imperf. btwn.	175.00	200.00
J5	D1	6kr brn ('95)	3.00	3.00
J6	D1	7kr brn ('95)	85	1.65
a.		Pair, imperf. btwn.	225.00	250.00
J7	D1	10kr brown	5.00	35
J8	D1	20kr brown	80	2.00
J9	D1	50kr brown	37.50	30.00
		Nos. J1-J9 (9)	58.90	40.10

See Nos. J204-J231.

1899-1900 *Imperf.*

No.	Type	Description	Unused	Used
J10	D2	1h brown	25	40
J11	D2	2h brown	25	40
J12	D2	3h brn ('00)	25	30
J13	D2	4h brown	4.00	1.10
J14	D2	5h brn ('00)	3.50	30
J15	D2	6h brown	35	1.40
J16	D2	10h brown	25	30
J17	D2	12h brown	50	2.75
J18	D2	15h brown	50	1.40
J19	D2	20h brown	22.50	75
J20	D2	40h brown	1.00	2.75
J21	D2	100h brown	5.00	2.25
		Nos. J10-J21 (12)	38.35	14.10

Perf. 10½, 12½, 13½ and Compound.

No.	Type	Description	Unused	Used
J22	D2	1h brown	70	25
J23	D2	2h brown	55	20
J24	D2	3h brn ('00)	50	12
J25	D2	4h brown	50	12
J26	D2	5h brn ('00)	35	12
J27	D2	6h brown	35	12
J28	D2	10h brown	50	10
J29	D2	12h brown	55	40
J30	D2	15h brown	90	40
J31	D2	20h brown	60	30
J32	D2	40h brown	1.00	90
J33	D2	100h brown	25.00	1.40
		Nos. J22-J33 (12)	31.50	4.43

Nos. J10 to J33 exist on unwatermarked paper.

D3

1908-13 Unwmk. *Perf. 12½*

No.	Type	Description	Unused	Used
J34	D3	1h carmine	1.25	1.25
J35	D3	2h carmine	50	50
J36	D3	4h carmine	50	25
J37	D3	6h carmine	50	25
J38	D3	10h carmine	50	25
J39	D3	14h car ('13)	3.75	1.50
J40	D3	20h carmine	4.50	25
J41	D3	25h car ('10)	9.00	2.50
J42	D3	30h carmine	5.50	25
J43	D3	50h carmine	6.50	35
J44	D3	100h carmine	14.00	40
		Nos. J34-J44 (11)	46.50	7.75

All values exist on ordinary paper, Nos. J34 to J38, J40 and J42 to J44 on chalky paper and Nos. J34 to J38, J40 and J44 on thin ordinary paper. All values exist imperforate.

1911

No.	Type	Description	Unused	Used
J45	D3	5k violet	35.00	10.00
J46	D3	10k violet	190.00	5.00

A little time given to the study of the arrangement of the Scott Catalogue can make it easier to use effectively.

Regular Issue of 1908 Overprinted or Surcharged in Carmine or Black:

PORTO
15 15

a b

1916

J47 A22 1h gray (C) 8 8
a. Pair, one without overprint 150.00
J48 A22 15h on 2h vio (Bk) 25 35

D4

D5

1916

J49 D4 5h rose red 12 8
J50 D4 10h rose red 12 8
J51 D4 15h rose red 12 8
J52 D4 20h rose red 12 8
J53 D4 25h rose red 50 40
J54 D4 30h rose red 20 12
J55 D4 40h rose red 25 12
J56 D4 50h rose red 1.25 1.25
J57 D5 1k ultra 40 12
a. Horizontal pair, imperf. btwn. 450.00 450.00
J58 D5 5k ultra 1.65 1.75
J59 D5 10k ultra 1.65 1.25
Nos. J49-J59 (11) 6.38 5.33

Exists imperf. Price, set $115.

Type of Regular Issue of 1916 Surcharged

PORTO
15 ✱ 15

1917

J60 A38 10h on 24h bl 2.00 35
J61 A38 15h on 36h vio 30 20
J62 A38 20h on 54h org 30 35
J63 A38 50h on 42h choc 30 20

All values of this issue are known imperforate, also without surcharge, perforated and imperforate.

Issues of the Republic

Postage Due Stamps of 1916 Overprinted

1919

J64 D4 5h rose red 20 25
a. Inverted ovpt. 275.00 275.00
J65 D4 10h rose red 20 25
J66 D4 15h rose red 25 50
J67 D4 20h rose red 45 38
J68 D4 25h rose red 8.50 20.00
J69 D4 30h rose red 25 25
J70 D4 40h rose red 25 38
J71 D4 50h rose red 50 1.25
J72 D5 1k ultra 7.50 7.00
J73 D5 5k ultra 10.00 7.00
J74 D5 10k ultra 11.00 5.00
Nos. J64-J74 (11) 39.10 42.26

Nos. J64, J65, J67 and J70 exist imperforate.

D6

D7

1920-21 *Perf. 12½*

J75 D6 5h brt red 8 22
J76 D6 10h brt red 5 6
J77 D6 15h brt red 5 45
J78 D6 20h brt red 5 8
J79 D6 25h brt red 10 45
J80 D6 30h brt red 5 12
J81 D6 40h brt red 5 8
J82 D6 50h brt red 5 12
J83 D6 80h brt red 5 12
J84 D7 1k ultra 5 12
J85 D7 1½k ultra ('21) 5 12
J86 D7 2k ultra ('21) 5 10
J87 D7 3k ultra ('21) 5 20
J88 D7 4k ultra ('21) 5 20
J89 D7 5k ultra 5 12
J90 D7 8k ultra ('21) 5 20
J91 D7 10k ultra 5 12
J92 D7 20k ultra ('21) 15 60
Nos. J75-J92 (18) 1.08 3.48

Nos. J84 to J92 exist on white paper and on grayish white paper. They also exist imperf.; price, set $120

Imperf

J93 D6 5h brt red 10 30
J94 D6 10h brt red 5 8
J95 D6 15h brt red 5 38
J96 D6 20h brt red 5 8
J97 D6 25h brt red 5 45
J98 D6 30h brt red 5 18
J99 D6 40h brt red 5 12
J100 D6 50h brt red 5 32
J101 D6 80h brt red 5 18
Nos. J93-J101 (9) 50 2.09

No. 207a Surcharged in Dark Blue

Nachmarke
7½K

1921 *Perf. 12½*

J102 A43 7½k on 15h bis 5 18
a. Inverted surch. 250.00 250.00

D8

1922

J103 D8 1k redsh buff 5 18
J104 D8 2k redsh buff 5 18
J105 D8 4k redsh buff 5 25
J106 D8 5k redsh buff 5 18
J107 D8 7½k redsh buff 5 20
J108 D8 10k bl grn 5 18
J109 D8 15k bl grn 6 25
J110 D8 20k bl grn 6 20
J111 D8 25k bl grn 6 25
J112 D8 40k bl grn 6 18
J113 D8 50k bl grn 6 40
Nos. J103-J113 (11) 60 2.45

D9

D10

1922-24

J114 D9 10k cob bl 5 18
J115 D9 15k cob bl 6 20
J116 D9 20k cob bl 5 18
J117 D9 50k cob bl 6 28
J118 D10 100k plum 5 5
J119 D10 150k plum 5 12
J120 D10 200k plum 5 5
J121 D10 400k plum 6 6
J122 D10 600k plum ('23) 6 18
J123 D10 800k plum 6 5
J124 D10 1,000k plum ('23) 5 6
J125 D10 1,200k plum ('23) 45 1.40
J126 D10 1,500k plum ('24) 10 15
J127 D10 1,800k plum ('24) 1.50 4.50
J128 D10 2,000k plum ('23) 20 40
J129 D10 3,000k plum ('24) 5.75 8.00
J130 D10 4,000k plum ('24) 4.00 10.00
J131 D10 6,000k plum ('24) 4.00 16.00
Nos. J114-J131 (18) 16.60 41.86

Price, #J103-J131 imperf, $350.

D11

D12

1925-34 *Perf. 12½*

J132 D11 1g red 6 6
J133 D11 2g red 6 6
J134 D11 3g red 6 12
J135 D11 4g red 6 10
J136 D11 5g red ('27) 6 6
J137 D11 6g red 25 50
J138 D11 8g red 25 25
J139 D11 10g dk bl 15 6
J140 D11 12g dk bl 15 12
J141 D11 14g dk bl ('27) 25 12
J142 D11 15g dk bl 15 12
J143 D11 16g dk bl ('29) 40 20
J144 D11 18g dk bl ('34) 1.40 4.50
J145 D11 20g dk bl 15 12
J146 D11 23g dk bl 75 20
J147 D11 24g dk bl ('32) 1.25 12
J148 D11 28g dk bl ('27) 55 30
J149 D11 30g dk bl 25 18
J150 D11 31g dk bl ('29) 1.00 25
J151 D11 35g dk bl ('30) 65 20
J152 D11 39g dk bl ('32) 1.10 12
J153 D11 40g dk bl 1.10 2.25
J154 D11 60g dk bl 75 1.25
J155 D12 1s dk grn 4.25 1.25
J156 D12 2s dk grn 32.50 4.50
J157 D12 5s dk grn 100.00 37.50
J158 D12 10s dk grn 50.00 5.25
Nos. J132-J158 (27) 197.60 59.76

Issues of 1925-27 (21 values) imperf, price, set $650.

Coat of Arms
D13 D14

1935

J159 D13 1g red 12 18
J160 D13 2g red 12 18
J161 D13 3g red 12 18
J162 D13 5g red 18 12
J163 D13 10g blue 18 5
J164 D13 12g blue 18 5
J165 D13 15g blue 25 60
J166 D13 20g blue 18 12
J167 D13 24g blue 20 5
J168 D13 30g blue 25 12
J169 D13 39g blue 32 6
J170 D13 60g blue 60 1.65
J171 D14 1s green 1.00 60
J172 D14 2s green 1.50 80
J173 D14 5s green 4.00 1.65
J174 D14 10s green 6.00 90
Nos. J159-J174 (16) 15.20 7.31

On Nos. J163-J170, background lines are horizontal.

Nos. J159-J174 exist imperf. Price, set $125.

Coat of Arms
D15 D16

1945 **Unwmk.** **Typo.** *Perf. 10½*

J175 D15 1g vermilion 5 10
J176 D15 2g vermilion 5 10
J177 D15 3g vermilion 5 10
J178 D15 5g vermilion 5 5
J179 D15 10g vermilion 5 5
J180 D15 12g vermilion 5 10
J181 D15 20g vermilion 5 12
J182 D15 24g vermilion 5 5
J183 D15 30g vermilion 5 12
J184 D15 60g vermilion 5 18
J185 D15 1s violet 5 35
J186 D15 2s violet 6 45
J187 D15 5s violet 6 20
J188 D15 10s violet 6 20
Nos. J175-J188 (14) 73 2.17

Occupation Stamps of the Allied Military Government Overprinted in Black

PORTO

1946 *Perf. 11.*

J189 OS1 3g dp org 5 12
J190 OS1 5g brt grn 5 5
J191 OS1 6g red vio 5 10
J192 OS1 8g rose pink 5 5
J193 OS1 10g lt gray 5 20
J194 OS1 12g pale buff brn 5 5
J195 OS1 15g rose red 5 20
J196 OS1 20g cop brn 5 8
J197 OS1 25g dp bl 5 10
J198 OS1 30g brt vio 5 5
J199 OS1 40g lt ultra 5 6
J200 OS1 60g lt ol grn 5 8
J201 OS1 1s dk vio 8 18
J202 OS1 2s yellow 18 28
J203 OS1 5s dp ultra 18 28
Nos. J189-J203 (15) 1.04 1.88

Nos. J189-J203 were issued by the Renner Government. Inverted overprints exist on about half of the denominations.

Type of 1894-95
Inscribed "Republik Osterreich"

1947 **Typo.** *Perf. 14*

J204 D1 1g chocolate 5 5
J205 D1 2g chocolate 5 5
J206 D1 3g chocolate 5 5
J207 D1 5g chocolate 5 5
J208 D1 8g chocolate 5 5
J209 D1 10g chocolate 5 5
J210 D1 12g chocolate 5 5
J211 D1 15g chocolate 5 5
J212 D1 16g chocolate 15 40
J213 D1 17g chocolate 15 40
J214 D1 18g chocolate 15 40
J215 D1 20g chocolate 32 6
J216 D1 24g chocolate 20 30
J217 D1 30g chocolate 12 25
J218 D1 36g chocolate 32 60
J219 D1 40g chocolate 6 8
J220 D1 42g chocolate 30 60
J221 D1 48g chocolate 35 60
J222 D1 50g chocolate 40 12
J223 D1 60g chocolate 12 15
J224 D1 70g chocolate 6 15
J225 D1 80g chocolate 2.50 1.65
J226 D1 1s blue 12 12
J227 D1 1.15s blue 1.65 28
J228 D1 1.20s blue 2.00 1.00
J229 D1 2s blue 25 40
J230 D1 5s blue 25 40
J231 D1 10s blue 30 40
Nos. J204-J231 (28) 10.17 8.76

1949-57

J232 D16 1g carmine 12 6
J233 D16 2g carmine 12 6
J234 D16 4g car ('51) 50 12
J235 D16 5g carmine 1.25 25
J236 D16 8g car ('51) 1.50 1.20
J237 D16 10g carmine 10 5
J238 D16 20g carmine 10 5
J239 D16 30g carmine 10 5
J240 D16 40g carmine 8 5
J241 D16 50g carmine 10 5
J242 D16 60g car ('50) 4.25 12
J243 D16 63g car ('57) 2.50 3.25
J244 D16 70g carmine 10 5
J245 D16 80g carmine 8 8
J246 D16 90g car ('50) 12 12
J247 D16 1s purple 12 5
J248 D16 1.20s purple 18 8
J249 D16 1.35s purple 15 8
J250 D16 1.40s pur ('51) 25 20
J251 D16 1.50s pur ('53) 12 5
J252 D16 1.65s pur ('50) 20 12
J253 D16 1.70s purple 20 12
J254 D16 2s purple 18 5
J255 D16 2.50s pur ('51) 25 6
J256 D16 3s pur ('51) 50 6
J257 D16 4s pur ('51) 50 40
J258 D16 5s purple 90 20
J259 D16 10s purple 1.50 20
Nos. J232-J259 (28) 16.07 7.23

D17

1985-86 **Photo.** *Perf. 14*
Background Color

J260 D17 10g brt yel ('86) 5 5
J261 D17 20g pink ('86) 5 5
J262 D17 50g orange ('86) 8 6
J263 D17 1s lt bl ('86) 14 10

No.	Type	Description	Unused	Used
J264	D17	2s pale brn ('86)	28	20
J265	D17	3s vio ('86)	40	30
J266	D17	5s ocher	58	42
		Nos. J260-J266 (7)	1.58	1.18

MILITARY STAMPS

Issues of the Austro-Hungarian Military Authorities for the Occupied Territories in World War I

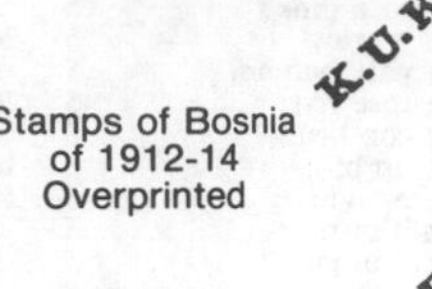
Stamps of Bosnia of 1912-14 Overprinted

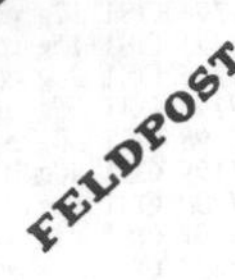

1915 Unwmk. *Perf. 12½*

No.	Type	Description	Unused	Used
M1	A23	1h ol grn	18	25
M2	A23	2h brt bl	18	25
M3	A23	3h claret	18	25
M4	A23	5h green	10	12
M5	A23	6h dk gray	18	25
M6	A23	10h rose car	10	12
M7	A23	12h dp ol grn	28	40
M8	A23	20h org brn	40	48
M9	A23	25h ultra	40	40
M10	A23	30h org red	3.50	*6.00*
M11	A24	35h myr grn	3.00	*4.75*
M12	A24	40h dk vio	3.00	*4.75*
M13	A24	45h ol brn	3.25	*5.25*
M14	A24	50h sl bl	3.00	*4.75*
M15	A24	60h brn vio	45	60
M16	A24	72h dk bl	3.00	*4.75*
M17	A25	1k brn vio, *straw*	3.50	*6.00*
M18	A25	2k dk gray, *bl*	3.50	*4.75*
M19	A26	3k car, *grn*	22.50	32.50
M20	A26	5k dk vio, *gray*	22.50	32.50
M21	A25	10k dk ultra, *gray*	150.00	180.00
		Nos. M1-M21 (21)	223.20	289.12

Exists imperf. Price, set $400.

Nos. M1-M21 also exist with overprint double, inverted and in red. These varieties were made by order of an official but were not regularly issued.

Emperor Franz Josef
M1 M2

Perf. 11½, 12½ and Compound

1915-17 Engr.

No.	Type	Description	Unused	Used
M22	M1	1h ol grn	10	10
M23	M1	2h dl bl	12	10
M24	M1	3h claret	10	10
M25	M1	5h green	10	10
a.		Perf. 11½	40.00	*45.00*
b.		Perf. 11½x12½	50.00	*75.00*
c.		Perf. 12½x11½	80.00	*100.00*
M26	M1	6h dk gray	10	10
M27	M1	10h rose car	12	10
M28	M1	10h gray bl ('17)	12	10
M29	M1	12h dp ol grn	12	15
M30	M1	15h car rose ('17)	6	6
a.		Perf. 11½	8.00	7.25
M31	M1	20h org brn	35	15
M32	M1	20h ol grn ('17)	35	15
M33	M1	25h ultra	18	12
M34	M1	30h vermilion	18	15
M35	M1	35h dk grn	32	40
M36	M1	40h dk vio	32	40
M37	M1	45h ol brn	30	40
M38	M1	50h myr grn	30	25
M39	M1	60h brn vio	30	40
M40	M1	72h dk bl	30	40
M41	M1	80h org brn ('17)	18	20
M42	M1	90h mag ('17)	90	90
M43	M2	1k brn vio, *straw*	1.65	2.00
M44	M2	2k dk gray, *bl*	1.40	80
M45	M2	3k car, *grn*	1.00	1.10
M46	M2	4k dk vio, *gray* ('17)	1.00	1.10
M47	M2	5k dk vio, *gray*	21.00	24.00
M48	M2	10k dk ultra, *gray*	3.00	6.00
		Nos. M22-M48 (27)	33.97	39.83

Nos. M22-M48 exist imperf. Price, set $90.

The first price column gives the catalogue value of an unused stamp, the second that of a used stamp.

Emperor Karl I
M3 M4

1917-18 *Perf. 12½*

No.	Type	Description	Unused	Used
M49	M3	1h grnsh bl ('18)	6	5
a.		Perf. 11½	3.50	4.00
M50	M3	2h red org ('18)	6	5
M51	M3	3h ol gray	6	5
a.		Perf. 11½, 11½x12½	12.50	15.00
M52	M3	5h ol grn	6	5
M53	M3	6h violet	8	5
M54	M3	10h org brn	6	5
M55	M3	12h blue	6	6
a.		Perf. 11½	2.75	3.00
M56	M3	15h brt rose	6	5
M57	M3	20h red brn	8	5
M58	M3	25h ultra	40	40
M59	M3	30h slate	10	5
M60	M3	40h ol bis	10	8
a.		Perf. 11½	1.40	1.50
M61	M3	50h dp grn	10	5
a.		Perf. 11½	4.50	6.00
M62	M3	60h car rose	10	10
M63	M3	80h dl bl	8	5
M64	M3	90h dk vio	45	55
M65	M4	2k rose, *straw*	10	5
a.		Perf. 11½	2.25	3.00
M66	M4	3k grn, *bl*	1.10	1.10
M67	M4	4k rose, *grn*	18.00	14.00
a.		Perf. 11½	27.50	35.00
M68	M4	10k dl vio, *gray*	2.75	4.00
a.		Perf. 11½	11.00	16.00
		Nos. M49-M68 (20)	23.86	20.89

Nos. M49-M68 exist imperf. Price, set $45.
See No. M82.

Emperor Karl I — M5

1918 Typo. *Perf. 12½*

No.	Type	Description	Unused	Used
M69	M5	1h grnsh bl	17.00	
M70	M5	2h orange	8.50	
M71	M5	3h ol gray	6.75	
M72	M5	5h yel grn	28	
M73	M5	10h dk brn	28	
M74	M5	20h red	65	
M75	M5	25h blue	65	
M76	M5	30h bister	65.00	
M77	M5	45h dk sl	65.00	
M78	M5	50h dp grn	42.50	
M79	M5	60h violet	82.50	
M80	M5	80h rose	42.50	
M81	M5	90h brn vio	1.65	

Engr.

No.	Type	Description	Unused	Used
M82	M4	1k ol bis, *bl*	28	
		Nos. M69-M82 (14)	333.54	

Nos. M69-M82 were on sale at the Vienna post office for a few days before the Armistice signing. They were never issued at the Army Post Offices. They exist imperf.; price, set $700.

MILITARY SEMI-POSTAL STAMPS

Emperor Karl I — MSP7

Empress Zita — MSP8

1918 Unwmk. Typo. *Perf. 12½x13*

No.	Type	Description	Unused	Used
MB1	MSP7	10h gray grn	22	28
MB2	MSP8	20h magenta	22	28
MB3	MSP7	45h blue	22	28

These stamps were sold at a premium of 10h each over face value. The surtax was for "Karl's Fund."

Nos. MB1-MB3 exist imperf. Price, set $10.

MILITARY NEWSPAPER STAMPS

Mercury — MN1

1916 Unwmk. Typo. *Perf. 12½*

No.	Type	Description	Unused	Used
MP1	MN1	2h blue	5	5
a.		Perf. 11½	1.75	1.00
b.		Perf. 12½x11½	125.00	*125.00*
MP2	MN1	6h orange	70	60
MP3	MN1	10h carmine	90	60
MP4	MN1	20h brown	50	55
a.		Perf. 11½	2.00	1.25

Exists imperf. Price, set $47.50.

NEWSPAPER STAMPS

From 1851 to 1866, the Austrian Newspaper Stamps were also used in Lombardy-Venetia.

Prices for unused stamps 1851-67 are for fine copies with original gum. Specimens without gum sell for about a third of the figures quoted.

Issues of the Monarchy

Mercury — N1

Two Types.

Type I. The "G" of "Zeitungs" has no crossbar.

Type II. The "G" of "Zeitungs" has a crossbar.

1851-56 Unwmk. Typo. *Imperf.*
Machine-made Paper

No.	Type	Description	Unused	Used
P1	N1	(0.6kr) bl, type II	160.00	80.00
a.		bl, type I	185.00	150.00
b.		Ribbed paper	400.00	160.00
P2	N1	(6kr) yel, type I	*12,500.*	*11,000.*
P3	N1	(30kr) rose, type I	*17,500.*	*10,000.*
P4	N1	(6kr) scar, type II ('56)	*37,500.*	*40,000.*

From 1852 No. P3 and from 1856 No. P2 were used as 0.6 kreuzer values.

Pale shades of Nos. P2 and P3 sell at considerably lower prices.

Originals of Nos. P2 and P3 are usually in pale colors and poorly printed. Prices are for stamps clearly printed and in bright colors. Numerous reprints of Nos. P1 to P4 were made between 1866 and 1904. Those of Nos. P2 and P3 are always well printed and in much deeper colors. All reprints are in type I, but occasionally show faint traces of a crossbar on "G" of "ZEITUNGS."

N2

N3

Two Types of the 1858-59 Issue

Type I. Loops of the bow at the back of the head broken.

Type II. Loops complete. Wreath projects further at top of head.

1858-59 Embossed

No.	Type	Description	Unused	Used
P5	N2	(1kr) bl, type I	400.00	525.00
P6	N2	(1kr) lil, type II ('59)	625.00	175.00

1861

No.	Type	Description	Unused	Used
P7	N3	(1kr) gray	150.00	100.00
a.		(1kr) gray lil	350.00	100.00
b.		(1kr) dp lil	1,600.	450.00

The embossing on the reprints of the 1858-59 and 1861 issues is not as sharp as on the originals.

N4

Wmk. 91, or, before July 1864, Unwmkd.

1863

No.	Type	Description	Unused	Used
P8	N4	(1.05kr) gray	30.00	10.00
a.		Tete beche pair	*20,000.*	
b.		(1.05kr) gray lil	60.00	17.50

The embossing of the reprints is not as sharp as on the originals.

Mercury
N5 N6

1867-73 Typo. Wmk. 91
Coarse Print

Three Types.

Type I. Helmet not defined at back, more or less blurred. Two thick short lines in front of wing of helmet. Shadow on front of face not separated from hair.

Type II. Helmet distinctly defined. Four thin short lines in front of wing. Shadow on front of face clearly defined from hair.

Type III. Outer white circle around head is open at top (closed on types I and II). Greek border at top and bottom is wider than on types I and II.

No.	Type	Description	Unused	Used
P9	N5	(1kr) vio, type I	55.00	1.75
a.		(1kr) vio, type II ('73)	210.00	15.00

1874-76
Fine Print

No.	Type	Description	Unused	Used
P9B	N5	(1kr) vio, type III ('76)	40	22
c.		(1kr) gray lil, type I ('76)	160.00	22.50
d.		(1kr) vio, type II	40.00	4.00
e.		Double impression, type III		225.00

Stamps of this issue, except No. P9Bc, exist in many shades, from gray to lilac brown and deep violet. Stamps in type III exist also privately perforated or rouletted.

1880

No.	Type	Description	Unused	Used
P10	N6	½kr green	8.00	90

Nos. P9B and P10 also exist on thicker paper without sheet watermark and No. P10 exists with unofficial perforation.

N7

1899 Unwmk. *Imperf.*
Without Varnish Bars

No.	Type	Description	Unused	Used
P11	N7	2h dk bl	25	5
P12	N7	6h orange	3.25	1.40
P13	N7	10h brown	1.50	1.40
P14	N7	20h rose	2.00	2.00

1901
With Varnish Bars

No.	Type	Description	Unused	Used
P11a	N7	2h dk bl	1.00	30
P12a	N7	6h orange	14.00	15.00
P13a	N7	10h brown	12.50	12.50
P14a	N7	20h rose	25.00	30.00

Nos. P11 to P14 were re-issued in 1905.

Mercury
N8 N9

1908 *Imperf.*
P15 N8 2h dk bl 1.75 8
a. Tete beche pair 375.00 375.00
P16 N8 6h orange 2.50 40
P17 N8 10h carmine 2.50 40
P18 N8 20h brown 2.50 30

All values are found on chalky, regular and thin ordinary paper. They exist privately perforated.

1916 *Imperf.*
P19 N9 2h brown 5 5
P20 N9 4h green 20 50
P21 N9 6h dk bl 25 1.00
P22 N9 10h orange 25 50
P23 N9 30h claret 30 50
Nos. P19-P23 (5) 1.05 2.55

Issues of the Republic

Newspaper Stamps of 1916 Overprinted

1919
P24 N9 2h brown 5 5
P25 N9 4h green 8 *90*
P26 N9 6h dk bl 8 *1.40*
P27 N9 10h orange 25 *90*
P28 N9 30h claret 12 *1.40*
Nos. P24-P28 (5) 58 4.65

Mercury
N10 N11

1920-21 *Imperf.*
P29 N10 2h violet 5 5
P30 N10 4h brown 5 6
P31 N10 5h slate 5 6
P32 N10 6h turq bl 5 6
P33 N10 8h green 5 6
P34 N10 9h yel ('21) 5 6
P35 N10 10h red 5 6
P36 N10 12h blue 5 12
P37 N10 15h lil ('21) 5 8
P38 N10 18h bl grn ('21) 5 8
P39 N10 20h orange 5 12
P40 N10 30h yel brn ('21) 5 5
P41 N10 45h grn ('21) 5 18
P42 N10 60h claret 5 28
P43 N10 72h choc ('21) 5 45
P44 N10 90h vio ('21) 10 45
P45 N10 1.20k red ('21) 8 45
P46 N10 2.40k yel grn ('21) 8 45
P47 N10 3k gray ('21) 10 45
Nos. P29-P47 (19) 1.11 3.57

Nos. P37-P40, P42, P44 and P47 exist also on thick gray paper.

1921-22
P48 N11 45h gray 6 10
P49 N11 75h brn org ('22) 6 15
P50 N11 1.50k ol bis ('22) 6 22
P51 N11 1.80k gray bl ('22) 6 22
P52 N11 2.25k lt brn 6 22
P53 N11 3k dl grn ('22) 6 45
P54 N11 6k cl ('22) 6 45
P55 N11 7.50k bister 18 45
Nos. P48-P55 (8) 60 2.26

Nos. P24-P55 exist privately perforated.

Canceled-to-order stamps are often from remainders. Most collectors of canceled stamps prefer postally used specimens.

NEWSPAPER TAX STAMPS

Prices for unused stamps 1853-59 are for copies in fine condition with gum. Specimens without gum sell for about one-third of the figures quoted.

Issues of the Monarchy

NT1 NT2

1853 Unwmk. Typo. *Imperf.*
PR1 NT1 2kr green 2,100. 80.00

The reprints are in finer print than the more coarsely printed originals, and on a smooth toned paper.

Wmk. 91, or, before July 1864, Unwmkd.

1858-59

Two Types.
Type I. The banderol on the Crown of the left eagle touches the beak of the eagle.
Type II. The banderol does not touch the beak.

PR2 NT2 1kr bl, type II ('59) 50.00 9.00
a. 1kr bl, type I 700.00 150.00
b. Printed on both sides, type II
PR3 NT2 2kr brn, type II ('59) 25.00 7.50
a. 2kr red brn, type II 400.00 150.00
PR4 NT2 4kr brn, type I 350.00 *1,200.*

Nos. PR2a, PR3a, and PR4 were printed only on unwatermarked paper. Nos. PR2 and PR3 exist on unwatermarked and watermarked paper.
Nos. PR2 and PR3 exist in coarse and (after 1874) in fine print, like the contemporary postage stamps.

The reprints of the 4kr brown are of type II and on a smooth toned paper.

NT3 NT4

1877 **Redrawn**
PR5 NT3 1kr blue 15.00 1.25
a. 1kr pale ultra *1,200.*
PR6 NT3 2kr brown 15.00 1.50

In the redrawn stamps the shield is larger and the vertical bar has eight lines above the white square and nine below, instead of five.
Nos. PR5 and PR6 exist also watermarked "WECHSEL" instead of "ZEITUNGS-MARKEN".

1890
PR7 NT4 1kr brown 12.50 80
PR8 NT4 2kr green 14.00 1.50

Nos. PR5 to PR8 exist with private perforation.

NT5

Wmk. "STEMPEL-MARKEN" in Double-lined Capitals, across the Sheet (91)
Perf. 13, 12½

PR9 NT5 25kr carmine 125.00 160.00

Nos. PR1 to PR9 did not pay postage, but were a fiscal tax, collected by the postal authorities on newspapers.

SPECIAL HANDLING STAMPS

(For Printed Matter Only.)

Issues of the Monarchy

Mercury
SH1

1916 Unwmk. *Perf. 12½*
QE1 SH1 2h cl, *yel* 45 60
QE2 SH1 5h dp grn, *yel* 45 60

SH2

1917 *Perf. 12½*
QE3 SH2 2h cl, *yel* 18 20
a. Pair, imperf. between 300.00 300.00
b. Perf. 11½x12½ 62.50 87.50
c. Perf. 12½x11½ 87.50 125.00
d. Perf. 11½ 1.75 2.50
QE4 SH2 5h dp grn, *yel* 18 20
a. Pair, imperf. between 275.00 275.00
b. Perf. 11½x12½ 62.50 87.50
c. Perf. 12½x11½ 87.50 125.00
d. Perf. 11½ 1.75 2.50

Nos. QE1-QE4 exist imperforate.

Issues of the Republic

Nos. QE3 and QE4 Overprinted

1919
QE5 SH2 2h cl, *yel* 5 25
a. Inverted overprint 325.00
b. Perf. 11½x12½ 6.00 10.00
c. Perf. 12½x11½ 80.00 110.00
d. Perf. 11½ 40 1.25
QE6 SH2 5h dp grn, *yel* 5 35
a. Perf. 11½x12½ 2.50 4.50
b. Perf. 12½x11½ 30.00 45.00
c. Perf. 11½ 30 85

Nos. QE5 and QE6 exist imperforate.

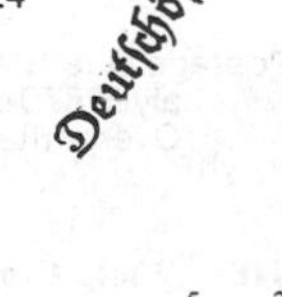

SH3

Dark Blue Surcharge

1921
QE7 SH3 50h on 2h cl, *yel* 6 8

SH4

1922 *Perf. 12½*
QE8 SH4 50h lil, *yel* 6 18

Nos. QE5 to QE8 exist in vertical pairs, imperforate between. No. QE8 exists imperforate.

OCCUPATION STAMPS

Issued under Italian Occupation.

Issued in Trieste.

Austrian Stamps of 1916-18 Overprinted

Regno d'Italia
Venezia Giulia
3. XI. 18.

1918 Unwmk. *Perf. 12½.*
N1 A37 3h brt vio 30 38
a. Double overprint 13.00 16.00
b. Inverted ovpt. 13.00 16.00
N2 A37 5h lt grn 20 38
a. Inverted ovpt. 13.00 16.00
b. "3.XI." omitted 13.00 13.00
c. Double overprint 16.00
N3 A37 6h dp org 38 48
N4 A37 10h magenta 30 38
a. Inverted overprint 9.00 11.00
N5 A37 12h lt bl 95 1.25
a. Double overprint 13.00 16.00
N6 A42 15h dl red 30 38
a. Inverted ovpt. 11.00 15.00
b. Double overprint 13.00 16.00
c. "3.XI." omitted 13.00 13.00
N7 A42 20h dk grn 30 38
a. Inverted ovpt. 9.00 11.00
b. "3.XI." omitted 13.00 15.00
c. Double overprint 26.00
N8 A42 25h dp bl 2.50 3.25
a. Inverted ovpt. 37.50 45.00
b. "3.XI." omitted 75.00 75.00
N9 A42 30h dl vio 75 1.00
N10 A39 40h ol grn 26.00 32.50
N11 A39 50h dk grn 1.10 1.50
N12 A39 60h dp bl 1.90 2.50
N13 A39 80h org brn 1.10 1.50
a. Inverted overprint
N14 A39 1k car, *yel* 1.10 1.50
a. Double ovpt. 26.00 26.00
N15 A40 2k lt bl 45.00 55.00
N16 A40 4k ycl grn 100.00 130.00

Handstamped.

N17 A40 10k dp vio *10,000. 12,000.*

Granite Paper.

N18 A40 2k lt bl
N19 A40 3k car rose 75.00 92.50

Some authorities question the authenticity of No. N18. Counterfeits of Nos. N10, N15-N19 are plentiful.

Italian Stamps of 1901-18 Overprinted

Venezia
Giulia

Wmk. Crown. (140)
Perf. 14.

N20 A42 1c brown 30 75
a. Inverted overprint 6.00 9.00
N21 A43 2c org brn 30 75
a. Inverted overprint 4.50 *6.75*
N22 A48 5c green 15 55
a. Inverted overprint 9.00 *13.00*
b. Double overprint 26.00
N23 A48 10c claret 15 55
a. Inverted overprint 13.00 *18.00*
b. Double overprint 26.00
N24 A50 20c brn org 18 55
a. Inverted overprint 18.00 *27.50*
b. Double overprint 26.00 *37.50*
N25 A49 25c blue 22 55
a. Double overprint *75.00*
b. Invtd. overprint 26.00 *37.50*
N26 A49 40c brown 1.50 *3.75*
a. Inverted overprint *65.00*
N27 A45 45c ol grn 38 90
a. Inverted overprint 26.00 *37.50*
N28 A49 50c violet 55 *1.40*
N29 A49 60c brn car 6.00 *15.00*
N30 A46 1l brn & grn 2.50 *6.25*
Nos. N20-N30 (11) 12.23 31.00

Italian Stamps of 1901-18 Surcharged

Venezia
Giulia
5 Heller

N31 A48 5h on 5c grn 22 48
a. "5" omitted 18.00 *27.50*
b. Inverted surch. 22.50 *32.50*
N32 A50 20h on 20c brn org 22 45
a. Double surcharge 22.50 *32.50*

Issued in the Trentino.

Austrian Stamps of 1916-18 Overprinted

Regno d Italia
Trentino
3 nov 1918

1918 Unwmk. *Perf. 12½*

N33 A37 3h brt vio 90 1.25
 a. Double ovpt. 26.00 *37.50*
 b. Inverted ovpt. 22.50 *30.00*
N34 A37 5h lt grn 55 80
 a. "8 nov. 1918" *1,000.*
 b. Inverted ovpt. 22.50 *30.00*
N35 A37 6h dp org 24.00 32.50
N36 A37 10h magenta 75 1.10
 a. "8 nov. 1918" 30.00 40.00
N37 A37 12h lt bl 75.00 110.00
N38 A42 15h dl red 2.00 3.00
N39 A42 20h dk grn 30 45
 a. "8 nov. 1918" 45.00 *60.00*
 b. Double ovpt. 26.00 37.50
 c. Inverted ovpt. 9.00 11.00
N40 A42 25h dp bl 16.00 24.00
N41 A42 30h dl vio 3.75 5.50
N42 A39 40h ol grn 24.00 32.50
N43 A39 50h dk grn 9.00 13.00
 a. Inverted ovpt. 37.50 47.50
N44 A39 60h dp bl 16.00 24.00
 a. Double ovpt. 45.00 *60.00*
N45 A39 80h org brn 26.00 37.50
N46 A39 90h red vio 375.00 550.00
N47 A39 1k car, *yel* 26.00 37.50
N48 A40 2k lt bl 115.00 170.00
N49 A40 4k yel grn *500.00 925.00*
N50 A40 10k dp vio *33,000.*

Granite Paper.

N51 A40 2k lt bl *185.00*

Counterfeits of Nos. N33-N51 are plentiful.

Italian Stamps of 1901-18 Overprinted — Venezia Tridentina

Wmk. Crown. (140)
Perf. 14.

N52 A42 1c brown 38 90
 a. Inverted overprint 11.00 16.00
N53 A43 2c org brn 38 90
 a. Inverted overprint 11.00 16.00
N54 A48 5c green 38 90
 a. Inverted overprint 11.00 16.00
 b. Double overprint 15.00 22.50
N55 A48 10c claret 38 90
 a. Inverted overprint 15.00 22.50
 b. Double overprint 15.00 22.50
N56 A50 20c brn org 38 90
 a. Inverted overprint 15.00 22.50
N57 A49 40c brown 7.50 19.00
N58 A45 45c ol grn 4.50 11.00
 a. Double overprint 47.50 *75.00*
N59 A49 50c violet 4.50 11.00
N60 A46 1l brn & grn 4.50 11.00
 a. Double overprint 47.50 *75.00*
 Nos. N52-N60 (9) 22.90 56.50

Italian Stamps of 1906-18 Surcharged — Venezia Tridentina 5 Heller

N61 A48 5h on 5c grn 18 50
N62 A48 10h on 10c cl 18 50
 a. Inverted overprint 19.00 *26.00*
N63 A50 20h on 20c brn org 18 50
 a. Double surcharge 19.00 *26.00*

General Issue.

Italian Stamps of 1901-18 Surcharged — 5 centesimi di corona

1919

N64 A42 1c on 1c brn 15 38
 a. Inverted surcharge 3.75 5.50
N65 A43 2c on 2c org brn 15 38
 a. Double surcharge 67.50
 b. Inverted surcharge 1.90 3.00
N66 A48 5c on 5c grn 15 38
 a. Inverted surcharge 9.00 13.00
 b. Double surcharge 18.00 18.00
N67 A48 10c on 10c cl 15 38
 a. Inverted surcharge 9.00 13.00
 b. Double surcharge 18.00 *27.50*
N68 A50 20c on 20c brn org 15 38
 a. Double surcharge 26.00 *37.50*
N69 A49 25c on 25c bl 15 38
 a. Double surcharge 26.00 26.00
N70 A49 40c on 40c brn 15 38
 a. "ccrona" 30.00 *45.00*
N71 A45 45c on 45c ol grn 15 38
 a. Inverted surcharge 26.00 37.50
N72 A49 50c on 50c vio 15 38
N73 A49 60c on 60c brn car 15 38
 a. "00" for "60" 30.00 *45.00*

Surcharged: — 1 corona

N74 A46 1 cor on 1l brn & grn 15 38
 Nos. N64-N74 (11) 1.65 4.18

Surcharges similar to these but differing in style or arrangement of type were used in Dalmatia.

SPECIAL DELIVERY STAMPS

Issued in Trieste.

Special Delivery Stamp of Italy of 1903 Overprinted — Venezia Giulia

1918 Wmk. Crown. (140) *Perf. 14.*

NE1 SD1 25c rose red 4.50 11.00
 a. Invtd. ovpt. 30.00 45.00

General Issue.

Special Delivery Stamps of Italy of 1903-09 Surcharged — 25 centesimi di corona

1919

NE2 SD1 25c on 25c rose 18 38
 a. Double surcharge 15.00 *22.50*
NE3 SD2 30c on 30c bl & rose 26 75

POSTAGE DUE STAMPS

Issued in Trieste.

Postage Due Stamps of Italy, 1870-94, Overprinted — Venezia Giulia

1918 Wmk. Crown. (140) *Perf. 14.*

NJ1 D3 5c buff & mag 15 55
 a. Inverted overprint 3.75 5.50
 b. Double overprint 45.00
NJ2 D3 10c buff & mag 15 55
 a. Inverted overprint 13.00 *19.00*
NJ3 D3 20c buff & mag 22 55
 a. Double overprint 45.00
 b. Inverted overprint 13.00 *19.00*
NJ4 D3 30c buff & mag 38 90
NJ5 D3 40c buff & mag 3.75 9.25
 a. Inverted overprint 67.50 *100.00*
NJ6 D3 50c buff & mag 9.00 22.50
 a. Inverted overprint 67.50 *100.00*
NJ7 D3 1l bl & mag 24.00 60.00
 Nos. NJ1-NJ7 (7) 20.60 8.10

General Issue.

Postage Due Stamps of Italy, 1870-1903 Surcharged — 5 centesimi di corona

1919

NJ8 D3 5c on 5c buff & mag 18 55
 a. Inverted overprint 3.75 5.50
NJ9 D3 10c on 10c buff & mag 18 55
 a. Center and surcharge invtd. 18.00 *27.00*
NJ10 D3 20c on 20c buff & mag 22 55
 a. Double overprint 37.50 *55.00*
NJ11 D3 30c on 30c buff & mag 22 55
NJ12 D3 40c on 40c buff & mag 22 55
NJ13 D3 50c on 50c buff & mag 22 55

Surcharged — una corona

NJ14 D3 1 cor on 1l bl & mag 22 55
NJ15 D3 2 cor on 2l bl & mag 8.25 20.00
NJ16 D3 5 cor on 5l bl & mag 8.25 20.00
 Nos. NJ8-NJ16 (9) 47.15 36.20

A. M. G. ISSUE FOR AUSTRIA

Issued jointly by the Allied Military Government of the United States and Great Britain, for civilian use in areas under American, British and French occupation. (Upper Austria, Salzburg, Tyrol, Vorarlberg, Styria and Carinthia).

OS1

1945 Unwmk. Litho. *Perf. 11.*

4N1 OS1 1g aqua 6 12
4N2 OS1 3g dp org 5 5
4N3 OS1 4g buff 5 5
4N4 OS1 5g brt grn 5 5
4N5 OS1 6g red vio 5 5
4N6 OS1 8g rose pink 5 5
4N7 OS1 10g lt gray 5 8
4N8 OS1 12g pale buff brn 5 5
4N9 OS1 15g rose red 5 5
4N10 OS1 20g cop brn 5 5
4N11 OS1 25g dp bl 5 6
4N12 OS1 30g brt vio 5 5
4N13 OS1 40g lt ultra 5 8
4N14 OS1 60g lt ol grn 5 18
4N15 OS1 1s dk vio 5 28
4N16 OS1 2s yellow 12 30
4N17 OS1 5s dp ultra 25 45
 Nos. 4N1-4N17 (17) 1.13 2.00

AUSTRIAN OFFICES ABROAD

These stamps were on sale and usable at all Austrian post-offices in Crete and in the Turkishp Empire.

100 CENTIMES = 1 FRANC

OFFICES IN CRETE

Used prices are italicized for stamps often found with false cancellations.

Stamps of Austria of 1899-1901 Issue, Surcharged in Black:

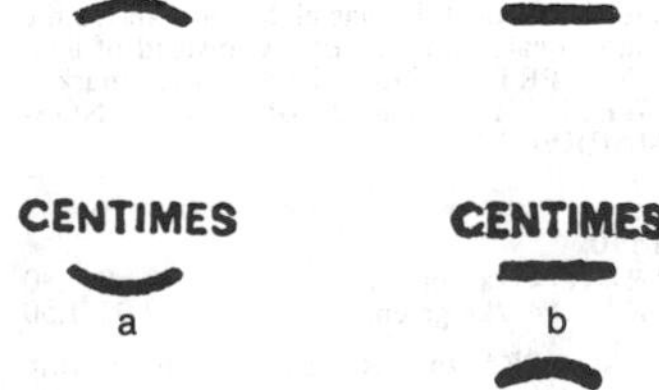

a b

c d

1903-04 Unwmk. *Perf. 12½, 13½*
Granite Paper.
With Varnish Bars
(On Nos. 73a, 75a, 77a, 81a)

1 A15 (a) 5c on 5h bl grn 1.90 2.75
2 A16 (b) 10c on 10h rose 90 *3.00*
3 A16 (b) 25c on 25h ultra 32.50 22.50
4 A17 (c) 50c on 50h gray bl 5.75 *45.00*

Without Varnish Bars
(On Nos. 83, 83a, 84, 85)

5 A18 (d) 1fr on 1k car rose 2.75 *47.50*
 a. 1fr on 1k car 5.00
 b. Horiz. or vert. pair, imperf. between 225.00
6 A18 (d) 2fr on 2k gray lil ('04) 10.00 *165.00*
7 A18 (d) 4fr on 4k gray grn ('04) 11.00 *250.00*

Surcharged on Austrian Stamps of 1904-05.

1905

Without Varnish Bars
(On Nos. 89, 97)

8 A19 (a) 5c on 5h bl grn 40.00 20.00
9 A20 (b) 10c on 10h car 1.10 *5.75*

With Varnish Bars.
(On Nos. 89a, 97a, 99a, 103a)

8a A19 (a) 5c on 5h bl grn 4.50 4.50
9a A20 (b) 10c on 10h car 22.50 14.00
10 A20 (b) 25c on 25h ultra 90 *45.00*
11 A21 (b) 50c on 50h dl bl 1.25 *185.00*

Surcharged on Austrian Stamps and Type of 1906-07.

1907 *Perf. 12½, 13½.*

Without Varnish Bars

12 A19 (a) 5c on 5h yel grn (#90) 1.10 *3.75*
13 A20 (b) 10c on 10h car (#92) 1.40 *11.00*
14 A20 (b) 15c on 15h vio 1.75 *16.50*

A5

A6

1908 Typo. *Perf. 12½*

15 A5 5c grn, *yel* 38 28
16 A5 10c scar, *rose* 45 45
17 A5 15c brn, *buff* 50 *3.00*
18 A5 25c dp bl, *bl* 9.50 3.00

Engr.

19 A6 50c lake, *yel* 2.00 *20.00*
20 A6 1fr brn, *gray* 2.75 *30.00*
 a. Vert pair, imperf. btwn. 225.00
 Nos. 15-20 (6) 15.58 56.73

Nos. 15 to 18 are on paper colored on the surface only. All values exist imperforate.

Issued to commemorate the sixtieth year of the reign of Emperor Franz Josef, for permanent use.

Paper Colored Through.

1914 Typo.

21 A5 10c rose, *rose* 1.75 *650.00*
22 A5 25c ultra, *bl* 75 *72.50*

Nos. 21 and 22 exist imperforate.

OFFICES IN THE TURKISH EMPIRE

From 1863 to 1867 the stamps of Lombardy-Venetia (Nos. 15 to 24) were used at the Austrian Offices in the Turkish Empire.

100 SOLDI = 1 FLORIN
40 PARAS = 1 PIASTRE

Prices for unused stamps are for copies with gum. Specimens without gum sell for about one-third the figures quoted.

Used prices are italicized for stamps often found with false cancellations.

Foreign postal stationery (stamped envelopes, postal cards and air letter sheets) lies beyond the scope of this Catalogue, which is limited to adhesive postage stamps.

A1

A2

Two different printing methods were used, as in the 1867-74 issues of Austria. They may be distinguished by the coarse or fine lines of the hair and whiskers.

Wmk. "BRIEF-MARKEN" in Double-lined Capitals, across the Sheet. (91)

1867 Coarse Print. Typo. *Perf. 9½.*

1 A1 2sld orange 1.10 *14.00*
a. 2sld yel 50.00 25.00
2 A1 3sld green 72.50 22.50
a. 3sld dk grn 85.00 28.50
3 A1 5sld red 72.50 10.00
a. 5sld car 80.00 14.00
4 A1 10sld blue 72.50 1.25
a. 10sld lt bl 80.00 2.25
b. 10sld dk bl 80.00 2.50
5 A1 15sld brown 11.00 4.50
a. 15sld dk brn 37.50 13.00
b. 15sld redsh brn 13.00 9.50
6 A1 25sld gray lil 9.00 *22.50*
a. 25sld brn vio 11.00 *25.00*
7 A2 50sld brn, perf. 10½ 1.10 *37.50*
a. Perf. 12 80.00 52.50
b. Perf. 13 265.00
k. Perf. 9 or 10½x9 22.50 *45.00*
l. 50sld pale red brn, perf. 12 45.00 47.50
m. Vertical pair, imperf. between 350.00 *800.00*
n. Horiz. pair, imperf. btwn. 400.00 *900.00*

Perf. 9, 9½, 10½ and Compound.
1876-83

Fine Print.

7C A1 2sld yel ('83) 18 *1,200.*
7D A1 3sld grn ('78) 1.10 *16.00*
7E A1 5sld red ('78) 38 *15.00*
7F A1 10sld blue 60.00 75
7I A1 15sld org brn ('81) 5.25 *90.00*
7J A1 25sld gray lil ('83) 55 *180.00*

The 10 soldi has been reprinted in deep dull blue, perforated 10½.

A3

1883 *Perf. 9½, 10, 10½.*

8 A3 2sld brown 18 *72.50*
9 A3 3sld green 90 *9.50*
10 A3 5sld rose 18 *5.50*
11 A3 10sld blue 75 38
12 A3 20sld gray 2.00 *3.75*
13 A3 50sld red lil 2.00 *9.00*

A4

A5

10 PARAS ON 3 SOLDI:

Type I. Surcharge 16½mm. across. "PARA" about ½mm. above bottom of "10". 2mm. space between "10" and "P"; 1½mm. between "A" and "10". Perf. 9½ only.

Type II. Surcharge 15¼ to 16mm. across. "PARA" on same line with figures or slightly higher or lower. 1½mm. space between "10" and "P"; 1mm. between "A" and "10". Perf. 9½ and 10.

1886 *Perf. 9½ and 10*

14 A4 10pa on 3sld grn, type II 28 *3.75*
a. 10pa on 3sld grn, type I 250.00 300.00
b. Inverted surcharge, type I *2,250.*

1888

15 A5 10pa on 3kr grn 3.75 4.50
a. "O1 PARA 1O" *500.00*
16 A5 20pa on 5kr rose 75 *5.00*
17 A5 1pi on 10kr bl 47.50 1.10
a. Perf. 13½ 160.00
b. Double surcharge 160.00
18 A5 2pi on 20kr gray 1.75 2.75
19 A5 5pi on 50kr vio 2.75 *13.00*

A6

1890-92 Unwmk. *Perf. 9 to 13½*

Granite Paper.

20 A6 8pa on 2kr brn ('92) 18 20
a. Perf. 9½ 3.75 2.25
21 A6 10pa on 3kr grn 75 18
a. Pair, imperf. between 90.00
22 A6 20pa on 5kr rose 18 18
23 A6 1pi on 10kr ultra 38 8
24 A6 2pi on 20kr ol grn 11.00 *18.50*
25 A6 5pi on 50kr vio 14.00 *45.00*

See note after Austria No. 65 on missing numerals, etc.

A7

A8

1891 *Perf. 9 to 13½*

26 A7 2pi on 20kr ol grn 5.25 32
a. Perf. 9½ 90.00 14.00
27 A7 5pi on 50kr vio 3.75 2.00

There are two types of the surcharge on No. 26.

1892 *Perf. 10½, 11½*

28 A8 10pi on 1gld bl 14.00 18.00
29 A8 20pi on 2gld car 14.00 22.50
a. Double surcharge

1896 *Perf. 10½, 11½, 12½*

30 A8 10pi on 1gld pale lil 14.00 18.00
31 A8 20pi on 2gld gray grn 45.00 45.00

A9

A10

A11

A12

Perf. 10½, 12½, 13½ and Compound.

1900

Without Varnish Bars

32 A9 10pa on 5h bl grn 4.50 1.00
33 A10 20pa on 10h rose 4.50 1.00
b. Perf. 12½x10½ 265.00 32.50
34 A10 1pi on 25h ultra 4.50 18
35 A11 2pi on 50h gray bl 9.50 1.40
36 A12 5pi on 1k car rose 1.40 18
a. 5pi on 1k car 1.75 70
b. Horiz. or vert. pair, imperf. between 135.00
37 A12 10pi on 2k gray lil 3.75 2.25
a. Horizontal pair, imperf. between
38 A12 20pi on 4k gray grn 2.85 *5.00*
Nos. 32-38 (7) 31.00 11.01

In the surcharge on Nos. 37 and 38 "piaster" is printed "PIAST."

1901

With Varnish Bars.

32a A9 10pa on 5h bl grn 2.85 1.50
33a A10 20pa on 10h rose 2.85 *72.50*
34a A10 1pi on 25h ultra 2.25 32
35a A11 2pi on 50h gray bl 4.50 1.40

Lombardy-Venetia stamps can be mounted in Scott's Austria Album.

A13

A14

A15

1906 *Perf. 12½ to 13½*

Without Varnish Bars.

39 A13 10pa dk grn 15.00 1.10
40 A14 20pa rose 95 38
41 A14 1pi ultra 38 18
42 A15 2pi gray bl 1.10 50

1903 With Varnish Bars.

39a A13 10pa dk grn 6.00 90
40a A14 20pa rose 2.75 38
41a A14 1pi ultra 2.25 18
42a A15 2pi gray bl 130.00 1.10

1907

Without Varnish Bars.

43 A13 10pa yel grn 38 *1.50*
45 A14 30pa violet 65 *2.50*

A16

A17

1908 Typo. *Perf. 12½.*

46 A16 10pa grn, *yel* 18 10
47 A16 20pa scar, *rose* 28 15
48 A16 30pa brn, *buff* 40 55
49 A16 1pi dp bl, *bl* 16.00 6
50 A16 60pa vio, *bluish* 75 3.00

Engr.

51 A17 2pi lake, *yel* 45 10
52 A17 5pi brn, *gray* 65 55
53 A17 10pi grn, *yel* 1.10 1.40
54 A17 20pi bl, *gray* 2.00 3.00
Nos. 46-54 (9) 21.81 8.91

Nos. 46 to 50 are on paper colored on the surface only. Issued in commemoration of the sixtieth year of the reign of Empror Franz Josef I for permanent use. All values exist imperforate.

1913-14 Typo.

Paper Colored Through.

57 A16 20pa rose, *rose* ('14) 1.10 *225.00*
58 A16 1pi ultra, *bl* 45 40

Nos. 57 and 58 exist imperforate.

POSTAGE DUE STAMPS.

D1

D2

Black Surcharge.

1902 Unwmk. *Perf. 12½, 13½*

J1 D1 10pa on 5h grn 1.65 2.75
J2 D1 20pa on 10h grn 1.65 2.50
J3 D1 1pi on 20h grn 2.75 3.75
J4 D1 2pi on 40h grn 2.75 2.75
J5 D1 5pi on 100h grn 4.00 1.65
Nos. J1-J5 (5) 12.8013.40

Shades of Nos. J1 to J5 exist, varying from yellowish green to dark green.

1908 Typo. *Perf. 12½.*

J6 D2 ¼pi green 3.75 6.50
J7 D2 ½pi green 1.75 *4.50*
J8 D2 1pi green 2.50 *6.50*
J9 D2 1½pi green 75 *8.00*
J10 D2 2pi green 2.75 *10.00*
J11 D2 5pi green 2.75 *6.50*
J12 D2 10pi green 22.50 *100.00*
J13 D2 20pi green 18.50 *125.00*
J14 D2 30pi green 14.00 9.00
Nos. J6-J14 (9) 69.25 276.00

Nos. J6 to J14 exist in distinct shades of green and on thick chalky, regular and thin ordinary paper. All values exist imperforate.

LOMBARDY-VENETIA

Formerly a kingdom in the north of Italy forming part of the Austrian Empire. Milan and Venice were the two principal cities. Lombardy was annexed to Sardinia in 1859, and Venetia to the kingdom of Italy in 1866.

100 Centesimi = 1 Lira
100 Soldi = 1 Florin (1858)

Prices of the earliest Lombardy-Venetia stamps vary according to condition. Quotations for Nos. 1-6, PR1-PR3 are for fine copies. Very fine to superb specimens sell at much higher prices, and inferior or poor copies sell at reduced prices, depending on the condition of the individual specimen.

Prices for unused stamps are for fine copies with gum. Specimens without gum sell for about one-quarter of the prices quoted.

Coat of Arms — A1

15 CENTESIMI:

Type I. "5" of "15" is on a level with the "1."

Type II. "5" is a trifle sideways and is higher than the "1." 45 CENTESIMI:

Type I. Lower part of "45" is lower than "Centes."

Type II. Lower part of "45" is on a level with lower part of "Centes."

Wmk. K. K. H. M. in Sheet or Unwmkd.

1850 Typo. *Imperf.*

Thick to Thin Paper

1 A1 5c buff 900.00 60.00
a. Printed on both sides *6,000.* 150.00
b. 5c yel *4,500.* 400.00
c. 5c org 750.00 90.00
d. 5c lem yel *800.00*
3 A1 10c black 1,300. 65.00
a. 10c gray blk 1,400. 75.00
4 A1 15c pale red, type II 275.00 2.25
b. 15c red, type I *1,400.* 12.50
c. Ribbed paper, type II *12,500.* 200.00
d. Ribbed paper, type I *7,500.* 65.00
e. Laid paper, type II *4,000.*
5 A1 30c brown 1,100. 4.25
a. Ribbed paper 3,000. 32.50
6 A1 45c bl, type II *3,250.* 7.50
a. 45c bl, type I *5,500.* 15.00
b. Ribbed paper, type I *12,500.* 135.00

The note about the paper of the 1850 issue of Austria will also apply here. No. 1 and its minor varieties exist only on hand-made paper.

The reprints are in brighter colors.

A2

A3

A4

A5

A6

Two Types of Each Value.

Type I. Loops of the bow at the back of the head broken.

Type II. Loops complete. Wreath projects further at top of head.

1858-62 Embossed *Perf. 14½*

No.	Type	Description	Unused	Used
7	A2	2s yel, type II	325.00	55.00
a.		2s yel, type I	900.00	300.00
8	A3	3s blk, type II	1,300.	85.00
a.		3s blk, type I	675.00	175.00
b.		Perf. 16, type I		400.00
c.		Perf. 15x16 or 16x15, type I	*1,200.*	350.00
9	A3	3s grn, type II ('62)	250.00	50.00
10	A4	5s red, type II	135.00	2.25
a.		5s red, type I	225.00	8.50
b.		Printed on both sides, type II		*2,250.*
11	A5	10s brn, type II	625.00	9.00
a.		10s brn, type I	180.00	30.00
12	A6	15s bl, type II	650.00	11.00
a.		15s bl, type I	900.00	50.00

The reprints are of type II and are perforated 10½, 11, 11½, 12, 12½ and 13. There are also imperforate reprints of Nos. 7, 8 and 9.

A7

A8

1861-62 *Perf. 14*

No.	Type	Description	Unused	Used
13	A7	5s red	725.00	2.25
14	A7	10s brn ('62)	675.00	15.00

The reprints are perforated 9, 9½, 10½, 11, 12, 12½ and 13. There are also imperforate reprints of the 2 and 3s.

The 2, 3 and 15s of this type exist only as reprints.

1863

No.	Type	Description	Unused	Used
15	A8	2s yellow	75.00	95.00
16	A8	3s green	550.00	60.00
17	A8	5s rose	550.00	9.00
18	A8	10s blue	1,350.	50.00
19	A8	15s yel brn	1,000.	85.00

Wmk. "BRIEF-MARKEN" in Double-lined Capitals across the Sheet (91)

1864-65 *Perf. 9½.*

No.	Type	Description	Unused	Used
20	A8	2s yel ('65)	75.00	*175.00*
21	A8	3s green	12.50	10.00
22	A8	5s rose	1.50	1.25
23	A8	10s blue	12.50	4.25
24	A8	15s yel brn	17.50	17.50

The reprints are perforated 10 ½ and 13. There are also imperforate reprints of the 2s and 3s.

NEWSPAPER TAX STAMPS.

From 1853 to 1858 the Austrian Newspaper Tax Stamp 2kr green (No. PR1) was also used in Lombardy-Venetia, at the value of 10 centesimi.

NT1

Type I. The banderol of the left eagle touches the beak of the eagle.

Type II. The banderol does not touch the beak.

1858-59 Unwmk. Typo. *Imperf.*

No.	Type	Description	Unused	Used
PR1	NT1	1kr blk, type I ('59)	900.00	*3,250.*
PR2	NT1	2kr red, type II ('59)	180.00	55.00
PR3	NT1	4kr red, type I	*40,000.*	*3,000.*

No. PR2 exists also with watermark "ZEITUNGS-MARKEN" (91).

The reprints are on a smooth toned paper and are all of type II.

AZERBAIJAN

(Azerbaidjan)

LOCATION — Southernmost part of Russia in Eastern Europe. Bounded by Georgia, Dagestan, Caspian Sea, Persia and Armenia.
GOVT. — A Soviet Socialist Republic.
AREA — 32,686 sq. mi.
POP. — 2,096,973 (1923)
CAPITAL — Baku

100 Kopecks = 1 Ruble

National Republic.

Standard Bearer A1

Farmer at Sunset A2

Baku — A3

Temple of Eternal Fires — A4

1919 Unwmk. Litho. *Imperf.*

No.	Type	Description	Unused	Used
1	A1	10k multi	15	20
2	A1	20k multi	15	20
3	A2	40k grn, yel & blk	15	20
4	A2	60k red, yel & blk	15	20
5	A2	1r bl, yel & blk	25	35
6	A3	2r red, bis & blk	25	35
7	A3	5r bl, bis & blk	35	60
8	A3	10r ol grn, bis & blk	50	70
9	A4	25r bl, red & blk	90	1.10
10	A4	50r ol grn, red & blk	1.00	1.25
		Nos. 1-10 (10)	3.85	5.15

The two printings of Nos. 1-10 are distinguished by the grayish or thin white paper. Both have yellowish gum.

Soviet Socialist Republic.

Symbols of Labor — A5

Oil Well — A6

Bibi Eibatt Oil Field — A7

Khan's Palace, Baku — A8

Globe and Workers A9

Maiden's Tower, Baku A10

Goukasoff House A11

Blacksmiths A12

Hall of Judgment, Baku — A13

1922

No.	Type	Description	Unused	Used
15	A5	1r gray grn	20	35
16	A6	2r ol blk	20	35
17	A7	5r gray brn	20	35
18	A8	10r gray	50	65
19	A9	25r org brn	20	40
20	A10	50r violet	20	40
21	A11	100r dl red	35	50
22	A12	150r blue	35	50
23	A9	250r vio & buff	35	50
24	A13	400r dk bl	35	50
25	A12	500r gray vio & blk	35	50
26	A13	1000r dk bl & rose	35	50
27	A8	2000r bl & blk	35	50
28	A7	3000r brn & bl	35	50
a.		Tete beche pair	14.00	15.00
29	A11	5000r *ol grn*	60	75
		Nos. 15-29 (15)	4.90	7.25

Counterfeits exist of Nos. 1-29.

Stamps of 1922 Handstamped from Metal Dies in a Numbering Machine

15000

1922

No.	Type	Description	Unused	Used
32	A5	10.000r on 1r gray grn	7.00	7.50
33	A7	15.000r on 5r gray brn	9.50	10.00
34	A9	33.000r on 250r vio & buff	3.50	3.50
35	A7	50.000r on 3.000r brn & bl	5.00	5.00
36	A8	66.000r on 2.000r bl & blk	10.00	9.00
		Nos. 32-36 (5)	35.00	35.00

Same Surcharges on Regular Issue and Semi-Postal Stamps of 1922.

1922-23

No.	Type	Description	Unused	Used
36A	A7	500r on 5r gray brn	80.00	90.00
37	A6	1.000r on 2r ol blk	12.50	12.50
38	A8	2.000r on 10r gray	4.00	4.00
39	A8	5.000r on 2.000r bl & blk	2.25	2.25
40	A11	15.000r on 5.000r *ol grn*	9.00	9.00
41	A5	20.000r on 1r gray grn	10.00	10.00
42	SP1	25.000r on 500r bl & pale bl	32.50	
43	A7	50.000r on 5r gray brn	15.00	15.00
44	SP2	50.000r on 1.000r brn & bis	32.50	
45	A11	50.000r on 5.000r *ol grn*	4.50	3.50
45A	A8	60.000r on 2.000r bl & blk	15.00	18.00
46	A11	70.000r on 5.000r *ol grn*	24.00	24.00
47	A6	100.000r on 2r ol blk	12.00	12.00
48	A8	200.000r on 10r gray	5.00	5.00
49	A9	200.000r on 25r org brn	19.00	19.00
50	A7	300.000r on 3.000r brn & bl	5.00	5.00
51	A8	500.000r on 2.000r bl & blk	11.00	10.00
		Revalued.		
52	A7	500r on 15.000r on 5r gray brn	37.50	*70.00*
53	A11	15.000r on 70.000r on 5.000r *ol grn*	37.50	*70.00*
54	A7	300.000r on 50.000r on 3.000r brn & bl	60.00	*70.00*
55	A8	500.000r on 66.000r on 2.000r bl & blk	67.50	*100.00*

The surcharged semi-postal stamps were used for regular postage.

Same Surcharges on Stamps of 1919.

No.	Type	Description	Unused	Used
57	A1	25.000r on 10k grn, bl, red & blk	60	90
58	A1	50.000r on 20k bl, red, grn & blk	60	90
59	A2	75.000r on 40k grn, yel & blk	1.65	2.25
60	A2	100.000r on 60k red, yel & blk	60	85
61	A2	200.000r on 1r bl, yel & blk	60	85
62	A3	300.000r on 2r red, bis & blk	75	1.00
63	A3	500.000r on 5r bl, bis & blk	90	1.00
64	A2	750.000r on 40k grn, yel & blk	3.00	2.50
		Nos. 57-64 (8)	8.70	10.25

Handstamped from Settings of Rubber Type in Black or Violet

100000 b **200.000** c

On Stamps of 1922.

No.	Type	Description	Unused	Used
65	A6 (b)	100.000r on 2r ol blk	12.00	12.00
66	A8 (b)	200.000r on 10r gray	20.00	17.00
67	A8 (b)	200.000r on 10r gray (V)	14.00	15.00
68	A9 (b)	200,000r on 25r org brn (V)	12.00	11.00
a.		blk surch.	30.00	32.50
69	A7 (c)	300.000r on 3.000r brn & bl (V)	27.50	27.50
70	A8 (c)	500.000r on 2.000r bl & blk (V)	22.50	22.50
a.		Black surch.	30.00	32.50
71	A11 (b)	1.500.000r on 5.000r *ol grn*	17.30	15.00
72	A11 (b)	1.500.000r on 5.000r *ol grn* (V)	17.50	15.00

On Stamps of 1919.

No.	Type	Description	Unused	Used
75	A1 (b)	50.000r on 20k bl, red, grn & blk	75	
76	A2 (b)	75.000r on 40k grn, yel & blk	50	
77	A2 (b)	100.000r on 60k red, yel & blk	1.00	
78	A2 (b)	200.000r on 1r bl, yel & blk	25	25
79	A3 (b)	300.000r on 2r red, bis & blk	75	
80	A3 (b)	500,000r on 5r bl, bis & blk	1.00	

Inverted and double surcharges of Nos. 32-80 sell for twice the normal price.

Counterfeits exist of Nos. 32-80.

Azerbaijan stamps can be mounted in Scott's Soviet Republics Part I Album.

Baku Province.

Regular and Semi-Postal Stamps of 1922 Handstamped in Violet or Black

БАКИНСКОИ П. К.

The overprint reads "Bakinskoi P(ochtovoy) K(ontory)," meaning Baku Post Office.

1922		Unwmk.	*Imperf.*
300	A5	1r gray grn	20.00
301	A7	5r gray brn	20.00
302	A12	150r blue	6.00
303	A9	250r vio & buff	9.00
304	A13	400r dk bl	8.00
305	SP1	500r bl & pale bl	9.00
306	SP2	1000r brn & bis	12.00
307	A8	2000r bl & blk	12.00
308	A7	3000r brn & bl	20.00
309	A11	5000r *ol grn*	20.00
		Nos. 300-309 (10)	136.00

Stamps of 1922 Handstamped in Violet

БАКИНСКАГО Г-П-Т.О.№1

Overprint reads: Baku Post, Telegraph Office No. 1.

1924

Overprint 24x2mm.

312	A12	150r blue	9.00
313	A9	250r vio & buff	9.00
314	A13	400r dk bl	9.00
317	A8	2000r bl & blk	10.00
318	A7	3000r brn & bl	10.00
319	A11	5000r *ol grn*	10.00

Overprint 30x3½mm.

323	A12	150r blue	9.00
324	A9	250r vio & buff	9.00
325	A13	400r dk bl	9.00
328	A8	2000r bl & blk	9.00
329	A7	3000r brn & bl	10.00
330	A11	5000r *ol grn*	9.00

Overprinted on Nos. 32-33, 35.

331	A5	10,000r on 1r gray grn	32.50
332	A7	15,000r on 5r gray brn	32.50
333	A7	50,000r on 3000r brn & bl	37.50
		Nos. 312-333 (15)	214.50

The overprinted semipostal stamps were used for regular postage.

This handstamp on Nos. 17, B1-B2 in size 24x2mm., and on Nos. 15, 17, B1-B2 in size 30x3½mm., was of private origin and not officially issued.

SEMI-POSTAL STAMPS

Carrying Food to Sufferers SP1

1922		Unwmk.	*Imperf.*
B1	SP1	500r bl & pale bl	50 75

Widow and Orphans — SP2

B2	SP2	1000r brn & bis	1.00 1.50

Counterfeits exist.

Azerbaijan stamps can be mounted in Scott's Soviet Republics Part I Album.

Russian stamps of 1909-18 were privately overprinted as above in red, blue or black by a group of Entente officers working with Russian soldiers returning from Persia. Azerbaijan was not occupied by the Allies. There is evidence that existing covers (some seemingly postmarked at Baku, dated Oct. 19, 1917, and at Tabriz, Russian Consulate, Apr. 25, 1917) are fakes.

AZORES

LOCATION — A group of islands in the North Atlantic Ocean, due west of Portugal.
GOVT. — Integral part of Portugal, former colony.
AREA — 922 sq. mi.
POP. — 253,935 (1930)
CAPITAL — Ponta Delgada

Azores stamps were supplanted by those of Portugal in 1931.

1000 Reis = 1 Milreis
100 Centavos = 1 Escudo (1912)

Prices of early Azores stamps vary according to condition. Quotations for Nos. 1-37 are for fine copies. Very fine to superb specimens sell at much higher prices, and inferior or poor copies sell at reduced prices, depending on the condition of the individual specimen.

Stamps of Portugal Overprinted in Black or Carmine

a AÇORES

A second type of this overprint has a broad "O" and open "S".

1868		Unwmk.	*Imperf.*	
1	A14	5r black	*1,750.*	*750.00*
2	A14	10r yellow	*4,000.*	*2,000.*
3	A14	20r bister	170.00	65.00
4	A14	50r green	175.00	70.00
5	A14	80r orange	175.00	75.00
6	A14	100r lilac	175.00	75.00

The reprints are on thick chalky white wove paper, ungummed, and on thin white paper with shiny white gum. Price $7.50 each.

1868-70 ***Perf. 12½.***

5 REIS:

Type I. The "5" at the right is 1mm. from end of label.

Type II. The "5" is 1½mm. from end of label.

7	A14	5r blk (C)	45.00	30.00
8	A14	10r yellow	60.00	50.00
a.		Inverted overprint	*100.00*	*100.00*
9	A14	20r bister	50.00	37.50
10	A14	25r rose	45.00	6.00
a.		Inverted overprint	*75.00*	*75.00*
11	A14	50r green	150.00	120.00
12	A14	80r orange	150.00	120.00
13	A14	100r lilac	150.00	120.00
14	A14	120r blue	90.00	60.00
15	A14	240r violet	375.00	275.00

The reprints are on thick chalky white paper ungummed and perforated 13, and on thin white paper with shiny white gum and perforated 13½. Price $6 each.

1871-75 ***Perf. 12½, 13½***

21	A15	5r blk (C)	8.50	6.00
a.		Inverted overprint	*50.00*	*50.00*
23	A15	10r yellow	14.00	10.00
a.		Inverted overprint	*50.00*	*50.00*
24	A15	20r bister	15.00	12.00
25	A15	25r rose	10.00	2.25
a.		Inverted overprint	*50.00*	*50.00*
b.		Double overprint	*50.00*	
c.		Perf. 14	140.00	40.00
d.		Double impression of stamp		
26	A15	50r green	45.00	15.00
27	A15	80r orange	60.00	37.50
28	A15	100r lilac	45.00	22.50
a.		Perf. 14	150.00	90.00
29	A15	120r blue	95.00	60.00
a.		Inverted overprint	*150.00*	*125.00*
30	A15	240r violet	675.00	500.00

The reprints are of the second type. They are on thick chalky white paper ungummed and perforated 13, also on thin white paper with shiny white gum and perforated 13½. Price $4 each.

Overprinted in Black

b AÇORES

1875-80

15 REIS:

Type I. The figures of value, 1 and 5, at the right in upper label are close together.

Type II. The figures of value at the right in upper label are spaced.

31	A15	10r bl grn	90.00	75.00
32	A15	10r yel grn	52.50	37.50
33	A15	15r lil brn	9.00	7.50
a.		Inverted overprint	*50.00*	*50.00*
34	A15	50r blue	80.00	37.50
35	A15	150r blue	100.00	80.00
36	A15	150r yellow	120.00	100.00
37	A15	300r violet	37.50	30.00

The reprints have the same papers, gum and perforations as those of the preceding issue. Price $4 each.

Black Overprint.

1880 ***Perf. 11½, 12½ and 13½.***

38	A17	25r gray	60.00	12.50
39	A18	25r red lil	15.00	5.00
a.		25r gray	15.00	5.00
b.		Dbl. ovpt.		

Overprinted in Carmine or Black

1881-82

40	A16	5r blk (C)	10.00	4.50
41	A23	25r brn ('82)	13.50	2.75
a.		Double overprint		
42	A19	50r blue	75.00	20.00

Reprints of Nos. 38, 39, 39a, 40 and 42 have the same papers, gum and perforations as those of preceding issues. Price $1.50 each.

Overprinted in Red or Black

c AÇORES

1882-85

15, 20 REIS

Type I. The figures of value are some distance apart and close to the end of the label.

Type II. The figures are closer together and farther from the end of the label. On the 15 reis this is particularly apparent in the upper right figures.

43	A16	5r blk (R)	9.50	5.50
44	A21	5r slate	4.50	1.25
a.		Dbl. ovpt.		
c.		Inverted overprint		
45	A15	10r green	37.50	30.00
a.		Inverted overprint		
46	A22	10r green	9.00	4.00
a.		Dbl. ovpt.		
47	A15	15r lil brn	22.50	13.50
a.		15r red brn	22.50	13.50
b.		Inverted overprint		
48	A15	20r bister	40.00	30.00
a.		Inverted overprint		
49	A15	20r carmine	60.00	45.00
a.		Double overprint		
50	A23	25r brown	10.00	2.25
51	A15	50r blue	375.00	300.00
52	A24	50r blue	12.00	2.25
a.		Double overprint		
53	A15	80r orange	37.50	30.00
a.		80r yel	30.00	18.00
b.		Double overprint		
54	A15	100r lilac	22.50	15.00
55	A15	150r blue	375.00	300.00
56	A15	150r yellow	25.00	15.00
57	A15	300r violet	37.50	30.00

Reprints of the 1882-85 issues have the same papers, gum and perforations as those of preceding issues. Price $3 each.

Red Overprint.

58	A21	5r slate	7.50	2.25
59	A24a	500r black	100.00	90.00
60	A15	1000r black	45.00	40.00

1887 **Black Overprint.**

61	A25	20r pink	12.00	6.00
a.		Inverted overprint		
b.		Dbl. ovpt.		
62	A26	25r lil rose	12.00	1.25
a.		Inverted overprint		
b.		Double overprint, one inverted		
63	A26	25r red vio	12.00	1.25
a.		Dbl. ovpt.		
64	A24a	500r red vio	75.00	45.00
a.		Perf. 13½	125.00	90.00

Nos. 58 to 64 inclusive have been reprinted on thin white paper with shiny white gum and perforated 13½. Price $2 each.

Prince Henry the Navigator Issue.

Portugal Nos. 97-109 Overprinted AÇORES

1894 ***Perf. 14.***

65	A46	5r org yel	2.25	1.50
a.		Inverted overprint	13.50	11.00
66	A46	10r vio rose	2.25	1.50
a.		Dbl. ovpt.	18.50	
b.		Inverted overprint	15.00	11.00
67	A46	15r brown	2.75	1.50
68	A46	20r violet	2.75	1.50
a.		Double overprint	16.50	
69	A47	25r green	2.75	1.50
a.		Double overprint	13.50	13.50
b.		Inverted overprint	13.50	13.50
70	A47	50r blue	6.00	3.00
71	A47	75r dp car	10.00	6.00
72	A47	80r yel grn	12.00	6.00
73	A47	100r lt brn, *pale buff*	10.00	4.50
a.		Dbl. ovpt.	22.50	
74	A48	150r lt car, *pale rose*	15.00	11.00
75	A48	300r dk bl, *sal buff*	22.50	13.50
76	A48	500r brn vio, *pale lil*	37.50	20.00
77	A48	1000r gray blk, *yelsh*	75.00	37.50
a.		Double overprint		
		Nos. 65-77 (13)	200.75	109.00

St. Anthony of Padua Issue.

Portugal Nos. 132-146 Overprinted in Red or Black AÇORES

1895 ***Perf. 12***

78	A50	2½r blk (R)	2.25	2.00
79	A51	5r brn yel	4.50	2.00
80	A51	10r red lil	4.50	3.00
81	A51	15r red brn	5.25	3.00
82	A51	20r gray lil	5.25	3.00
83	A51	25r grn & vio	4.50	3.25
84	A52	50r bl & brn	15.00	7.50
85	A52	75r rose & brn	22.50	20.00
86	A52	80r lt grn & brn	37.50	22.50
87	A52	100r choc & blk	25.00	20.00
88	A53	150r vio rose & bis	60.00	55.00
89	A53	200r bl & bis	70.00	50.00
90	A53	300r sl & bis	90.00	60.00
91	A53	500r vio brn & grn	125.00	90.00
92	A53	1000r vio & grn	250.00	175.00
		Nos. 78-92 (15)	721.25	516.25

Issued in commemoration of the seventh centenary of the birth of Saint Anthony of Padua.

Vasco da Gama Issue.

Common Design Types

1898 ***Perf. 14, 15.***

93	CD20	2½r bl grn	1.25	75
94	CD21	5r red	1.40	90
a.		Horizontal pair, imperf. between		
95	CD22	10r gray lil	2.50	1.50
96	CD23	25r yel grn	2.25	90
97	CD24	50r dk bl	4.50	3.50
98	CD25	75r vio brn	10.00	6.00
99	CD26	100r bis brn	10.00	5.50
100	CD27	150r bister	15.00	7.50
		Nos. 93-100 (8)	46.90	26.55

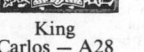

King Carlos — A28

King Manuel II — A29

1906 **Typo.** ***Perf. 11½x12***

101	A28	2½r gray	20	15
a.		Inverted overprint	13.50	13.50
102	A28	5r org yel	20	15
a.		Inverted overprint	13.50	13.50
103	A28	10r yel grn	20	15
104	A28	20r gray vio	50	25
105	A28	25r carmine	25	15
106	A28	50r ultra	3.00	2.50
107	A28	75r brn, *straw*	60	75
108	A28	100r dk bl, *bl*	60	*1.00*
109	A28	200r red lil, *pnksh*	90	*1.25*

110 A28 300r dk bl, *rose* 1.60 *1.60*
111 A28 500r blk, *bl* 2.25 1.50
Nos. 101-111 (11) 10.30 9.45

"Acores" and letters and figures in the corners are in red on the 2½, 10, 20, 75 and 500r and in black on the other values.

1910 ***Perf. 14x15***

112 A29 2½r violet 20 15
113 A29 5r black 25 20
114 A29 10r dk grn 35 30
115 A29 15r lil brn 60 55
116 A29 20r carmine 55 50
117 A29 25r vio brn 25 15
a. Perf. 11½ 1.50 1.00
118 A29 50r blue 1.25 75
a. Booklet pane of 6
119 A29 75r bis brn 2.25 1.50
120 A29 80r slate 2.25 1.50
121 A29 100r brn, *lt grn* 2.75 2.25
122 A29 200r grn, *sal* 2.75 2.25
123 A29 300r *blue* 4.50 3.00
124 A29 500r ol & brn 6.50 5.00
125 A29 1000r bl & blk 11.00 8.00
Nos. 112-125 (14) 35.45 26.10

The errors of color 10r black, 15r dark green, 25r black and 50r carmine were not regularly issued.

Stamps of 1910 Overprinted in Carmine or Green

1910

126 A29 2½r violet 15 10
a. Inverted overprint 2.00 2.00
127 A29 5r black 25 15
a. Inverted overprint 2.00 2.00
128 A29 10r dk grn 25 20
a. Inverted overprint 2.00 2.00
129 A29 15r lil brn 1.00 80
a. Inverted overprint 2.00 2.00
130 A29 20r car (G) 1.25 1.00
a. Inverted overprint 3.00 3.00
b. Double overprint 3.00 3.00
131 A29 25r vio brn 20 15
a. Perf. 11½ 30.00 25.00
132 A29 50r blue 75 60
133 A29 75r bis brn 40 25
a. Double overprint 2.00 2.00
134 A29 80r slate 55 35
135 A29 100r brn, *grn* 40 30
136 A29 200r grn, *sal* 40 75
137 A29 300r *blue* 1.40 1.40
138 A29 500r ol & brn 1.65 *2.25*
139 A29 1000r bl & blk 3.00 *3.50*
Nos. 126-139 (14) 11.65 11.80

Vasco da Gama Issue Overprinted or Surcharged in Black:

REPUBLICA

REPUBLICA
d

REIS 15 REIS
e
REPUBLICA

f

1$000

1911 ***Perf. 14, 15***

141 CD20 (d) 2½r bl grn 40 35
142 CD21 (e) 15r on 5r red 25 25
143 CD23 (d) 25r yel grn 50 30
144 CD24 (d) 50r dk bl 1.25 85
145 CD25 (d) 75r vio brn 75 75
146 CD27 (e) 80r on 150r bis 75 75
147 CD26 (d) 100r yel brn 75 75
a. Dbl. surch. 10.00 10.00
148 CD22 (f) 1000r on 10r lil 9.00 6.00
Nos. 141-148 (8) 13.65 10.00

Postage Due Stamps of Portugal Overprinted or Surcharged in Black "ACORES" and

REPUBLICA

REPUBLICA
g

R$ 300 R$
h

1911 ***Perf. 12***

149 D1 (g) 5r black 50 40
a. Half used as 2½r on cover
150 D1 (g) 10r magenta 1.50 80
a. "Acores" double 7.50 7.50
151 D1 (g) 20r orange 2.00 1.75
152 D1 (g) 200r brn, *buff* 8.00 5.50
a. "Acores" inverted
153 D1 (h) 300r on 50r sl 8.00 5.50
154 D1 (h) 500r on 100r car, *pink* 8.00 5.50
Nos. 149-154 (6) 28.00 19.45

Ceres — A30

Ceres Issue of Portugal Overprinted "ACORES" in Black or Carmine

With Imprint.

1912-31 ***Perf. 12x11½, 15x14***

155 A30 ¼c ol brn 10 10
a. Inverted overprint 2.00
156 A30 ½c blk (C) 10 10
157 A30 1c dp grn 70 40
a. Inverted overprint 4.50
158 A30 1c dp brn ('18) 12 5
a. Inverted overprint
159 A30 1½c choc ('13) 60 50
a. Inverted overprint 3.00
160 A30 1½c dp grn ('18) 25 15
a. Inverted overprint
161 A30 2c carmine 35 25
a. Inverted overprint 4.50
162 A30 2c org ('18) 20 10
a. Inverted overprint 11.00
163 A30 2½c violet 30 15
164 A30 3c rose ('18) 20 10
165 A30 3c dl ultra ('25) 20 15
166 A30 3½c lt grn ('18) 25 10
167 A30 4c lt grn ('19) 15 6
168 A30 4c org ('30) 30 25
169 A30 5c dp bl 30 15
170 A30 5c yel brn ('18) 30 20
171 A30 5c ol brn ('23) 15 8
172 A30 5c blk brn ('30) 3.50 3.00
173 A30 6c dl rose ('20) 25 15
174 A30 6c choc ('25) 25 15
175 A30 6c red brn ('31) 25 *1.00*
176 A30 7½c yel brn 4.00 1.50
177 A30 7½c dp bl ('18) 75 50
178 A30 8c sl ('13) 35 25
179 A30 8c bl grn ('22) 30 20
180 A30 8c org ('25) 60 30
181 A30 10c org brn 35 10
182 A30 12c bl gray ('20) 1.25 90
183 A30 12c dp grn ('22) 55 40
184 A30 13½c chlky bl ('20) 1.25 *3.00*
185 A30 14c dk bl, *yel* ('20) 4.00 *5.00*
186 A30 15c plum ('13) 75 25
187 A30 15c blk (R) ('23) 50 50
188 A30 16c brt ultra ('24) 1.00 30
189 A30 16c dp bl ('30) 1.50 *2.00*
190 A30 20c vio brn, *grn* ('13) 8.50 4.00
191 A30 20c choc ('20) 75 25
192 A30 20c dp grn ('23) 1.00 1.00
a. Double overprint
193 A30 20c gray ('24) 60 25
194 A30 24c grnsh bl ('21) 60 25
195 A30 25c sal ('23) 35 20
196 A30 30c brn, *pink* ('13) 45.00 30.00
197 A30 30c brn, *yel* ('19) 2.75 2.75
198 A30 30c gray brn ('21) 1.00 80
199 A30 32c dp grn ('25) 1.75 1.25
200 A30 36c red ('21) 50 25
201 A30 40c dp bl ('23) 50 25
202 A30 40c blk brn ('24) 25 10
203 A30 40c brt grn ('30) 1.75 50
204 A30 48c brt rose ('24) 1.75 1.25
205 A30 48c dl pink ('31) 2.00 1.50
206 A30 50c org, *sal* ('13) 5.00 1.25
207 A30 50c yel ('23) 1.50 1.25
208 A30 50c bis ('30) 3.00 2.25
209 A30 60c red brn ('31) 2.50 1.75
210 A30 60c bl ('21) 1.10 90
211 A30 64c pale ultra ('24) 1.75 1.25
212 A30 64c brn rose ('31) 15.00 10.00
213 A30 75c dl rose ('23) 5.00 5.00
214 A30 75c car rose ('30) 2.00 1.50
215 A30 80c dl rose ('21) 1.50 85
216 A30 80c vio ('24) 1.50 1.00
217 A30 80c dk grn ('31) 2.00 1.50
218 A30 90c chlky bl ('21) 1.50 85
219 A30 96c dp rose ('26) 8.50 4.00
220 A30 1e dp grn, *bl* 5.50 2.00
221 A30 1e vio ('21) 1.50 85
222 A30 1e gray vio ('24) 2.00 1.25
223 A30 1e brn lake ('30) 24.00 17.50
224 A30 1.10e yel brn ('21) 1.50 1.50
225 A30 1.20e yel grn ('21) 1.75 1.25
226 A30 1.20e buff ('24) 4.50 2.25
227 A30 1.25e dk bl ('30) 1.75 85
228 A30 1.50e blk vio ('23) 3.25 2.25
229 A30 1.50e lil ('25) 3.50 2.25
230 A30 1.60e dp bl ('25) 3.50 2.25
231 A30 2e sl grn ('21) 5.00 2.50
232 A30 2.40e ap grn ('26) 30.00 17.50
233 A30 3e lil pink ('26) 30.00 17.50
234 A30 3.20e gray grn ('25) 10.00 5.00
235 A30 5e emer ('24) 14.00 7.00
236 A30 10e pink ('24) 27.50 11.00
237 A30 20e pale turq ('25) 75.00 50.00
Nos. 155-237 (83) 391.12 245.29

Castello-Branco Issue.

Stamps of Portugal, 1925, Overprinted in Black or Red — AÇORES

1925 ***Perf. 12½.***

238 A73 2c orange 20 20
239 A73 3c green 20 20
240 A73 4c ultra (R) 20 20
241 A73 5c scarlet 20 20
242 A74 10c pale bl 20 20
243 A74 16c red org 30 30
244 A75 25c car rose 30 30
245 A74 32c green 50 50
246 A75 40c grn & blk (R) 30 30
247 A74 48c red brn 1.00 1.00
248 A76 50c bl grn 1.00 1.00
249 A76 64c org brn 1.00 1.00
250 A76 75c gray blk (R) 1.25 1.25
251 A75 80c brown 1.25 1.25
252 A76 96c car rose 1.50 1.50
253 A77 1.50e dk bl, *bl* (R) 1.50 1.10
254 A75 1.60e ind (R) 1.50 1.10
255 A77 2e dk grn, *grn* (R) 2.00 2.00
256 A77 2.40e red, *org* 2.50 2.25
257 A77 3.20e *grn* (R) 3.75 3.00
Nos. 238-257 (20) 20.65 18.85

First Independence Issue.

Stamps of Portugal, 1926, Overprinted in Red — AÇÔRES

1926 ***Perf. 14, 14½***

Center in Black.

258 A79 2c orange 30 30
259 A80 3c ultra 30 30
260 A79 4c yel grn 30 30
261 A80 5c blk brn 30 30
262 A79 6c ocher 30 30
263 A80 15c dk grn 60 60
264 A81 20c dl vio 60 60
265 A82 25c scarlet 60 60
266 A81 32c dp grn 60 60
267 A82 40c yel brn 60 60
268 A82 50c ol bis 1.25 1.25
269 A82 75c red brn 1.25 1.25
270 A83 1e blk vio 2.00 2.00
271 A84 4.50e ol grn 4.50 4.50
Nos. 258-271 (14) 13.50 13.50

The use of these stamps instead of those of the regular issue was obligatory on Aug. 13th and 14th Nov. 30th and Dec. 1st, 1926.

Second Independence Issue.

Stamps of Portugal, 1927, Overprinted in Red — AÇÔRES

1927

Center in Black.

272 A86 2c lt brn 30 30
273 A87 3c ultra 30 30
274 A86 4c orange 30 30
275 A88 5c dk brn 30 30
276 A89 6c org brn 30 30
277 A87 15c blk brn 30 30
278 A86 25c gray 1.25 1.25
279 A89 32c bl grn 1.25 1.25
280 A90 40c yel grn 1.25 1.25
281 A90 96c red 3.00 3.00
282 A88 1.60e myr grn 3.00 3.00
283 A91 4.50e bister 5.50 5.50
Nos. 272-283 (12) 17.05 17.05

Third Independence Issue.

Stamps of Portugal, 1928, Overprinted in Red — AÇÔRES

1928

Center in Black.

284 A93 2c lt bl 30 30
285 A94 3c lt grn 30 30
286 A95 4c lake 30 30
287 A96 5c ol grn 30 30
288 A97 6c org brn 30 30
289 A94 15c slate 50 50
290 A95 16c dk vio 85 85
291 A93 25c ultra 85 85
292 A97 32c dk grn 85 85
293 A96 40c ol brn 85 85
294 A95 50c red org 1.50 1.50
295 A94 80c lt gray 1.50 1.50
296 A97 96c carmine 2.25 2.25
297 A96 1e claret 2.25 2.25
298 A93 1.60e dk bl 2.25 2.25
299 A98 4.50e yellow 5.00 5.00
Nos. 284-299 (16) 20.15 20.15

A31

A32

1929-30 ***Perf. 12x11½, 15x14***

300 A31 4c on 25c pink ('30) 40 40
301 A31 4c on 60c dp bl 40 40
302 A31 10c on 25c pink 60 40
303 A31 12c on 25c pink 60 40
304 A31 15c on 25c pink 75 60
305 A31 20c on 25c pink 1.00 85
306 A31 40c on 1.10e yel brn 3.25 2.75
Nos. 300-306 (7) 7.00 5.80

Black or Red Overprint.

1930 ***Perf. 14.***

Without Imprint at Foot.

307 A32 4c orange 50 40
308 A32 5c dp brn 2.00 1.25
309 A32 10c vermilion 1.00 70
310 A32 15c blk (R) 1.00 70
311 A32 40c brt grn 1.00 70
312 A32 80c violet 14.00 11.00
313 A32 1.60e dk bl 2.25 1.25
Nos. 307-313 (7) 21.75 16.00

POSTAGE DUE STAMPS

D2

D3

Portugal Nos. J7-J13 Overprinted in Black

1904 **Unwmk.** ***Perf. 12***

J1 D2 5r brown 50 50
J2 D2 10r orange 50 50
J3 D2 20r lilac 1.00 1.00
J4 D2 30r gray grn 1.00 1.00
a. Double overprint
J5 D2 40r gray vio 1.75 1.75
J6 D2 50r carmine 2.00 2.00
J7 D2 100r dl bl 3.50 3.50
Nos. J1-J7 (7) 10.25 10.25

Same Overprinted in Carmine or Green (Portugal Nos. J14-J20)

1911

J8 D2 5r brown 25 25
J9 D2 10r orange 25 25
J10 D2 20r lilac 25 25
J11 D2 30r gray grn 25 25
J12 D2 40r gray vio 50 50
J13 D2 50r car (G) 2.50 2.50
J14 D2 100r dl bl 1.50 1.50
Nos. J8-J14 (7) 5.50 5.50

Portugal Nos. J21-J27 Overprinted in Black

1918

J15 D3 ½c brown	15	15
a. Inverted overprint	50	50
b. Double overprint	50	50
J16 D3 1c orange	15	15
a. Inverted overprint	50	50
b. Double overprint	50	50
J17 D3 2c red lil	15	15
a. Inverted overprint	1.00	1.00
b. Double overprint	1.00	1.00
J18 D3 3c green	15	15
a. Inverted overprint	1.00	1.00
b. Double overprint	1.00	1.00
J19 D3 4c gray	15	15
a. Inverted overprint	1.00	1.00
b. Double overprint	1.00	1.00
J20 D3 5c rose	15	15
b. Double overprint	1.00	1.00
J21 D3 10c dk bl	25	25
Nos. J15-J21 (7)	1.15	1.15

Stamps and Type of Portugal Postage Dues, 1921-27, Overprinted in Black

1922-24 ***Perf. 11½x12.***

J30 D3 ½c gray grn ('23)	15	15
J31 D3 1c gray grn ('23)	15	15
J32 D3 2c gray grn ('23)	15	15
J33 D3 3c gray grn ('24)	40	40
J34 D3 8c gray grn ('24)	25	25
J35 D3 10c gray grn ('24)	25	25
J36 D3 12c gray grn ('24)	25	25
J37 D3 16c gray grn ('24)	25	25
J38 D3 20c gray grn	60	60
J39 D3 24c gray grn	25	25
J40 D3 32c gray grn ('24)	25	25
J41 D3 36c gray grn	25	25
J42 D3 40c gray grn ('24)	60	60
J43 D3 48c gray grn ('24)	35	35
J44 D3 50c gray grn	60	60
J45 D3 60c gray grn	40	40
J46 D3 72c gray grn	40	40
J47 D3 80c gray grn ('24)	1.75	1.75
J48 D3 1.20e gray grn	1.75	1.75
Nos. J30-J48 (19)	9.05	9.05

NEWSPAPER STAMPS

N1

N2

N3

Newspaper Stamps of Portugal Overprinted in Black or Red

Perf. 11½, 12½ and 13½.

1876-88 **Unwmk.**

P1 N1 2½r olive	5.50	2.25
a. Inverted overprint		
P2 N2 2½r ol ('82)	4.00	1.25
a. Inverted overprint		
b. Double overprint		
P3 N3 2r blk ('85)	2.00	1.25
a. Inverted overprint		
b. Double overprint, one inverted		
P4 N2 2½r bis ('82)	4.00	1.00
a. Double overprint		
P5 N3 2r blk (R) ('88)	6.50	4.50

Reprints of the newspaper stamps have the same papers, gum and perforations as reprints of the regular issues. Price $2 each.

PARCEL POST STAMPS

Mercury and Commerce PP1

Portugal Nos. Q1-Q17 Overprinted in Black or Red.

1921-22 **Unwmk.** ***Perf. 12.***

Q1 PP1 1c lil brn	20	18
a. Inverted overprint	50	50
Q2 PP1 2c orange	20	18
a. Inverted overprint	50	50
Q3 PP1 5c lt brn	20	18
a. Inverted overprint	1.00	1.00
b. Double overprint	1.00	1.00
Q4 PP1 10c red brn	35	30
a. Inverted overprint	1.00	1.00
b. Double overprint	1.00	1.00
Q5 PP1 20c gray bl	35	30
a. Inverted overprint	1.00	1.00
b. Double overprint	1.00	1.00
Q6 PP1 40c carmine	35	35
a. Double overprint	1.50	1.50
Q7 PP1 50c blk (R)	70	70
Q8 PP1 60c dk bl (R)	70	70
Q9 PP1 70c gray brn	1.75	1.50
a. Double overprint		
Q10 PP1 80c ultra	1.75	1.50
Q11 PP1 90c lt vio	1.75	1.50
Q12 PP1 1e lt grn	1.75	1.50
Q13 PP1 2e pale lil	2.50	2.50
Q14 PP1 3e olive	3.00	3.00
Q15 PP1 4e ultra	5.00	5.00
Q16 PP1 5e gray	5.00	5.00
Q17 PP1 10e chocolate	15.00	15.00
Nos. Q1-Q7 (7)	2.35	2.19

POSTAL TAX STAMPS

for the delivery of postal matter on certain days in the year. The money derived from their sale is applied to works of public charity.

Nos. 114 and 157 Overprinted in Carmine **ASSISTENCIA**

1911-13 **Unwmk.** ***Perf. 14x15***

RA1 A29 10r dk grn	65	50

The 20r of this type was for use on telegrams.

Perf. 15x14

RA2 A30 1c dp grn	1.50	1.50

The 2c of this type was for use on telegrams.

Charity Sheltering Poor — PT1

Postal Tax Stamp of Portugal Overprinted in Black.

1915 ***Perf. 12.***

RA3 PT1 1c carmine	15	12

The 2c of this type was for use on telegrams.

Postal Tax Stamp of 1915 Surcharged **15 ctvs.**

1924

RA4 PT1 15c on 1c rose	50	*1.00*

Comrades of the Great War Issue.

Postal Tax Stamps of Portugal, 1925, Overprinted **AÇORES**

1925 ***Perf. 11.***

RA5 PT3 10c brown	35	35
RA6 PT3 10c green	35	35
RA7 PT3 10c rose	35	35
RA8 PT3 10c ultra	35	35

The use of Nos. RA5-RA11 in addition to the regular postage was compulsory on certain days. If the tax represented by these stamps was not prepaid, it was collected by means of Postal Tax Due Stamps.

Pombal Issue.
Common Design Types

1925 ***Perf. 12½.***

RA9 CD28 20c dp grn & blk	45	35
RA10 CD29 20c dp grn & blk	45	35
RA11 CD30 20c dp grn & blk	45	35

POSTAL TAX DUE STAMPS

Postal Tax Due Stamp of Portugal Overprinted **AÇORES**

1925 **Unwmk.** ***Perf. 11x11½.***

RAJ1 PTD1 20c brn org	50	50

See note after No. RA8.

Pombal Issue.
Common Design Types

1925 ***Perf. 12½.***

RAJ2 CD31 40c dp grn & blk	75	*1.25*
RAJ3 CD32 40c dp grn & blk	75	*1.25*
RAJ4 CD33 40c dp grn & blk	75	*1.25*

See note after No. RA8.

See Portugal for later issues.

BELGIAN CONGO

LOCATION — Central Africa
GOVT. — Belgian colony
AREA — 902,082 sq. mi. (estimated)
POP. — 12,660,000 (1956)
CAPITAL — Leopoldville

Congo was an independent state, founded by Leopold II of Belgium, until 1908 when it was annexed to Belgium as a colony. In 1960 it became the independent Republic of the Congo. See Congo Democratic Republic and Zaire.

100 Centimes = 1 Franc

Independent State

King Leopold II
A1 A2 A3

1886 **Unwmk.** **Typo.** ***Perf. 15.***

1 A1 5c green	11.00	20.00
2 A1 10c rose	4.50	5.00
3 A2 25c blue	55.00	42.50
4 A3 50c ol grn	7.50	6.25
5 A1 5fr lilac	375.00	250.00
a. Perf. 14	750.00	

King Leopold II — A4

1887-94

6 A4 5c grn ('89)	75	75
7 A4 10c rose ('89)	1.25	1.10
8 A4 25c bl ('89)	1.00	90
9 A4 50c brown	57.50	18.00
10 A4 50c gray ('94)	2.50	*15.00*
11 A4 5fr violet	875.00	375.00
12 A4 5fr gray ('92)	125.00	100.00
13 A4 10fr buff ('91)	350.00	225.00

The 25fr and 50fr in gray were not issued. Prices $22.50, $21.

Port Matadi — A5

River Scene on the Congo, Stanley Falls — A6

Inkissi Falls — A7

Railroad Bridge on M'pozo River — A8

Hunting Elephants A9

Bangala Chief and Wife — A10

1894-1901 **Engr.** ***Perf. 12½ to 15***

14 A5 5c pale bl & blk	15.00	14.00
15 A5 5c red brn & blk ('95)	3.50	1.50
16 A5 5c grn & blk ('00)	2.25	50
17 A6 10c red brn & blk	15.00	14.00
18 A6 10c grnsh bl & blk ('95)	1.25	1.25
a. Center invtd.	*1,500.*	*1,900.*
19 A6 10c car & blk ('00)	3.00	50
20 A7 25c yel org & blk	3.75	2.25
21 A7 25c lt bl & blk ('00)	3.25	1.25
22 A8 50c grn & blk	1.40	1.25
23 A8 50c ol & blk ('00)	3.25	65
24 A9 1fr lil & blk	24.00	11.00
a. 1fr rose lil & blk	150.00	17.50
25 A9 1fr car & blk ('01)	175.00	2.00
26 A10 5fr lake & blk	37.50	14.00
Nos. 14-26 (13)	288.15	64.15

Climbing Oil Palms — A11

Congo Canoe — A12

1896

27 A11 15c ocher & blk	3.75	50
28 A12 40c bluish grn & blk	4.00	2.75

Congo Village — A13

River Steamer on the Congo — A14

1898

29 A13 3.50fr red & blk	125.00	62.50
30 A14 10fr yel grn & blk	87.50	17.50
a. Center invtd.		
b. Perf. 12	450.00	17.50
c. Perf. 12x14	325.00	125.00

Belgian Congo

Overprinted CONGO BELGE

1908

31 A5 5c grn & blk 7.50 7.50
a. Handstamped 2.50 1.75
32 A6 10c car & blk 12.50 12.50
a. Handstamped 2.50 1.75
33 A11 15c ocher & blk 6.50 3.50
a. Handstamped 5.00 2.75
34 A7 25c lt bl & blk 5.00 3.50
a. Handstamped 7.50 3.25
35 A12 40c bluish grn & blk 2.25 2.25
a. Handstamped 7.50 5.25
36 A8 50c ol & blk 4.25 2.50
a. Handstamped 4.00 2.50
37 A9 1fr car & blk 21.00 2.50
a. Handstamped 25.00 2.00
38 A13 3.50fr red & blk 20.00 12.50
a. Handstamped 150.00 75.00
39 A10 5fr car & blk 37.50 20.00
a. Handstamped 57.50 25.00
40 A14 10fr yel grn & blk 87.50 17.50
a. Perf. 14 250.00 150.00
b. Handstamped 110.00 27.50
c. Handstamped, perf. 14 300.00 175.00
Nos. 31-40 (10) 204.00 84.25

Most of the above handstamps are also found inverted and double.

Port Matadi — A15

River Scene on the Congo, Stanley Falls — A16

Climbing Oil Palms — A17

Railroad Bridge on M'pozo River — A18

1909 *Perf. 14*

41 A15 5c grn & blk 75 75
42 A16 10c car & blk 65 50
43 A17 15c ocher & blk 21.00 12.00
44 A18 50c ol & blk 3.25 2.50

Port Matadi — A19

River Scene on the Congo, Stanley Falls — A20

Climbing Oil Palms — A21

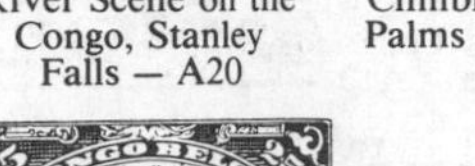

Inkissi Falls — A22

Congo Canoe — A23

Railroad Bridge on M'pozo River — A24

Hunting Elephants A25

Congo Village A26

Bangala Chief and Wife — A27

River Steamer on the Congo — A28

1910-15 **Engr.** *Perf. 14, 15*

45 A19 5c grn & blk 1.25 28
46 A20 10c car & blk 70 25
47 A21 15c ocher & blk 70 25
48 A21 15c grn & blk ('15) 38 25
a. Bklt pane of 10 12.50
49 A22 25c bl & blk 1.75 38
50 A23 40c bluish grn & blk 2.25 2.25
51 A23 40c brn red & blk ('15) 4.50 2.25
52 A24 50c ol & blk 3.75 2.00
53 A24 50c brn lake & blk ('15) 7.00 2.25
54 A25 1fr car & blk 3.50 2.75
55 A25 1fr ol bis & blk ('15) 2.25 90
56 A26 3fr red & blk 17.50 13.00
57 A27 5fr car & blk 20.00 17.50
58 A27 5fr ocher & blk ('15) 1.90 90
59 A28 10fr grn & blk 19.00 16.00
Nos. 45-59 (15) 86.43 61.21

Nos. 48, 51, 53, 55 and 58 exist imperforate.

Port Matadi A29

Stanley Falls, Congo River — A30

Inkissi Falls — A31

TEN CENTIMES.

Type I. Large white space at top of picture and two small white spots at lower edge. Vignette does not fill frame.

Type II. Vignette completely fills frame.

1915

60 A29 5c grn & blk 25 20
a. Booklet pane of 10 8.75
61 A30 10c car & blk (II) 30 20
a. 10c car & blk (I) 30 20
d. Booklet pane of 10 (II) 12.50
62 A31 25c bl & blk 1.40 38
a. Booklet pane of 10 62.50

Nos. 60 to 62 exist imperforate.

Stamps of 1910 Issue Surcharged in Red or Black

1921

64 A23 5c on 40c bluish grn & blk (R) 30 30
65 A19 10c on 5c grn & blk (R) 30 30
66 A24 15c on 50c ol & blk (R) 30 30
67 A21 25c on 15c ocher & blk (R) 1.90 1.40
68 A20 30c on 10c car & blk 30 30
69 A22 50c on 25c bl & blk (R) 1.75 1.25
Nos. 64-69 (6) 4.85 3.85

The position of the new value and the bars varies on Nos. 64 to 69.

Overprinted **1921**

1921

70 A25 1fr car & blk 1.10 1.10
a. Double overprint 17.50
71 A26 3fr red & blk 3.25 3.25
72 A27 5fr car & blk 6.25 6.25
73 A28 10fr grn & blk (R) 5.00 3.75

Belgian Surcharges

Stamps of 1915 Surcharged in Black or Red **·10c**

1922

74 A24 5c on 50c brn lake & blk 50 45
75 A29 10c on 5c grn & blk (R) 50 38
76 A23 25c on 40c brn red & blk (R) 2.50 45
77 A30 30c on 10c car & blk (II) 28 25
a. 30c on 10c car & blk (I) 28 25
b. Double surcharge 6.00 6.00
78 A31 50c on 25c bl & blk (R) 60 38
Nos. 74-78 (5) 4.38 1.91

No. 74 has the surcharge at each side.

Nos. 74-78 were issued only in sheets of 50. Blocks of 10 (5x2), so-called "booklet panes," are believed to be from the sheets of 50.

Congo Surcharges

Nos. 60, 51 Surcharged in Red or Black:

10 c.

a

b

25 c.

1922

80 A29 (a) 10c on 5c grn & blk (R) 75 75
a. Invtd. surch 20.00 20.00
b. Double surcharge 6.00
c. Double surcharge, one inverted 40.00
d. Pair, one without surcharge 45.00
e. On No. 45 150.00 150.00
81 A23 (b) 25c on 40c brn red & blk 1.00 50
a. Inverted surcharge 20.00 20.00
b. Double surcharge 7.00
c. "25c" double
d. 25c on 5c, No. 60 110.00 110.00

Nos. 55, 58 Surcharged with vertical bars over original values **10 c.**

1922

84 A25 10c on 1fr ol bis & blk (R) 75 75
a. Double surcharge 15.00
b. Inverted surcharge 20.00 20.00
85 A27 25c on 5fr ocher & blk 2.00 2.00

Nos. 68, 77 Handstamped **0,25**

86 A20 25c on 30c on 10c car & blk 10.00 10.00
87 A30 25c on 30c on 10c car & blk (II) 10.00 10.00

Nos. 86-87 exist with handstamp surcharge inverted.

Ubangi Woman — A32

Watusi Cattle — A44

Designs: 10c, Baluba woman. 15c, Babuende woman. No. 90, 40c, 1.25fr, 1.50fr, 1.75fr. Ubangi man. 25c, Basketmaking. 30c, 35c, Nos. 101, 102, Carving wood. 50c, Archer. Nos. 92, 100, Weaving. 1fr, Making pottery. 3fr, Working rubber. 5fr, Making palm oil. 10fr, African elephant.

1923-27 **Engr.** *Perf. 12*

88 A32 5c yellow 20 12
89 A32 10c green 20 12
90 A32 15c ol brn 20 12
91 A32 20c ol grn ('24) 18 12
92 A44 20c grn ('26) 20 15
93 A44 25c red brn 30 12
94 A44 30c rose red ('24) 75 90
95 A44 30c ol grn ('25) 20 15
96 A44 35c grn ('27) 50 50
97 A32 40c vio ('25) 20 15
98 A44 50c gray bl 30 22
99 A44 50c buff ('25) 35 12
100 A44 75c red org 42 42
101 A44 75c gray bl ('25) 45 28
102 A44 75c sal red ('26) 25 15
103 A44 1fr bis brn 55 22
104 A44 1fr dl bl ('25) 45 12
105 A44 1fr rose red ('27) 75 15
106 A32 1.25fr dl bl ('26) 38 28
107 A32 1.50fr dl bl ('26) 38 22
108 A32 1.75fr dl bl ('27) 3.75 2.85
109 A44 3fr gray brn ('24) 4.50 1.40
110 A44 5fr gray ('24) 9.25 4.00
111 A44 10fr gray blk ('24) 21.00 6.25

1925-26 *Perf. 12*

112 A44 45c dk vio ('26) 45 38
113 A44 60c car rose 45 22
Nos. 88-113 (26) 46.61 19.73

No. 107 Surcharged **175**

1927, June 14

114 A32 1.75fr on 1.50fr dl bl 50 38

Sir Henry Morton Stanley — A45

1928, June 30 *Perf. 14*

115 A45 5c gray blk 8 8
116 A45 10c dp vio 12 12
117 A45 20c org red 22 22
118 A45 35c green 80 65
119 A45 40c red brn 32 20
120 A45 60c blk brn 32 20
121 A45 1fr carmine 32 12
122 A45 1.60fr dk gray 3.50 3.00

123 A45 1.75fr dp bl 1.40 90
124 A45 2fr dk brn 1.00 38
125 A45 2.75fr red vio 4.00 45
126 A45 3.50fr rose lake 1.25 75
127 A45 5fr sl grn 1.00 30
128 A45 10fr vio bl 1.40 75
129 A45 20fr claret 5.00 2.75
Nos. 115-129 (15) 20.73 10.87

Issued in memory of Sir Henry M. Stanley (1841-1904), explorer.

Stamps of 1928 Surcharged in Red, Blue or Black

1F25

1931, Jan. 15

130 A45 40c on 35c grn (R) 70 55
131 A45 1.25fr on 1fr car (Bl) 55 15
132 A45 2fr on 1.60fr dk gray (R) 1.10 38
133 A45 2fr on 1.75fr dp bl (R) 1.00 35
134 A45 3.25fr on 2.75fr red vio (Bk) 3.00 2.25
135 A45 3.25fr on 3.50fr rose lake (Bk) 3.75 2.50

Stamps of 1923-27 Surcharged in Red

50c

Perf. 12½, 12

136 A44 40c on 35c grn 4.00 3.75
137 A44 50c on 45c dk vio 2.50 1.40

Surcharged 2

138 A32 2(fr) on 1.75fr dl bl 10.00 9.00
Nos. 130-138 (9) 26.60 20.33

View of Sankuru River — A46

Flute Players — A50

Designs: 15c, Kivu Kraal. 20c, Sankuru River rapids. 25c, Uele hut. 50c, Musicians of Lake Leopold II. 60c, Batetelas drummers. 75c, Mangbetu woman. 1fr, Domesticated elephant of Api. 1.25fr, Mangbetu chief. 1.50fr, 2fr, Village of Mondimbi. 2.50fr, 3.25fr, Okapi. 4fr, Canoes at Stanleyville. 5fr, Woman preparing cassava. 10fr, Baluba chief. 20fr, Young woman of Irumu.

1931-37 Engr. Perf. 11½

139 A46 10c gray brn ('32) 8 8
140 A46 15c gray ('32) 8 8
141 A46 20c brn lil ('32) 8 8
142 A46 25c dp bl ('32) 8 8
143 A50 40c dp grn ('32) 25 25
144 A46 50c vio ('32) 8 8
b. Booklet pane of 8 7.50
145 A50 60c vio brn ('32) 15 12
146 A50 75c rose ('32) 12 12
b. Booklet pane of 8 1.65
147 A50 1fr rose red ('32) 20 12
148 A50 1.25fr red brn 18 12
b. Booklet pane of 8 1.65
149 A46 1.50fr dk ol gray ('37) 20 15
b. Booklet pane of 8 7.50
150 A46 2fr ultra ('32) 25 15
151 A46 2.50fr dp bl ('37) 45 18
b. Bklt pane of 8 11.00
152 A46 3.25fr gray blk ('32) 70 40
153 A46 4fr dl vio ('32) 30 20
154 A50 5fr dp vio ('32) 70 30
155 A50 10fr red ('32) 75 50
156 A50 20fr blk brn ('32) 1.90 1.50
Nos. 139-156 (18) 6.55 4.51

No. 109 Surcharged in Red

3F25

1932, Mar. 15 Perf. 12

157 A44 3.25fr on 3fr gray brn 3.50 2.50

King Albert Memorial Issue

King Albert — A62

1934, May 7 Photo. Perf. 11½

158 A62 1.50fr black 1.00 25

Leopold I, Leopold II, Albert I, Leopold III — A63

1935, Aug. 15 Engr. Perf. 12½x12

159 A63 50c green 90 65
160 A63 1.25fr dk car 90 22
161 A63 1.50fr brn vio 90 15
162 A63 2.40fr brn org 3.00 2.50
163 A63 2.50fr lt bl 2.50 1.00
164 A63 4fr brt vio 3.00 1.50
165 A63 5fr blk brn 3.00 1.75
Nos. 159-165 (7) 14.20 7.77

Issued to commemorate the 50th anniversary of the founding of Congo Free State.

Molindi River A64

Bamboos A65

Suza River — A66

Rutshuru River — A67

Karisimbi A68

Mitumba Forest — A69

1937-38 Photo. Perf. 11½

166 A64 5c pur & blk 8 8
167 A65 90c car & brn 70 55
168 A66 1.50fr dp red brn & blk 18 12
169 A67 2.40fr ol blk & brn 30 20
170 A68 2.50fr dp ultra & blk 45 22
171 A69 4.50fr dk grn & brn 45 20
172 A69 4.50fr car & sep 35 35
Nos. 166-172 (7) 2.51 1.72

National Parks.

No. 172 was issued in sheets of four measuring 140x111mm. It was sold by subscription, the subscription closing Oct. 20, 1937. Price, $1.60.

Nos. 166-171 were issued Mar. 1, 1938.

King Albert Memorial, Leopoldville — A70

1941, Feb. 7 Litho. Perf. 11

173 A70 10c lt gray 30 28
174 A70 15c brn vio 30 28
175 A70 25c lt bl 38 30
176 A70 50c lt vio 30 28
177 A70 75c rose pink 1.25 50
178 A70 1.25fr gray 30 30
179 A70 1.75fr orange 1.00 80
180 A70 2.50fr carmine 60 20
181 A70 2.75fr vio bl 1.25 1.00
182 A70 5fr lt ol grn 2.50 2.50
183 A70 10fr rose red 3.75 3.75
Nos. 173-183 (11) 11.93 10.19

Exist imperforate.

Stamps of 1938-41 Surcharged in Blue or Black

5 c.

75 c.

a

b

1941-42 Perf. 11½, 11

184 A66 (a) 5c on 1.50fr dp red brn & blk (Bl) 12 12
a. Inverted surcharge 15.00 15.00
185 A70 (b) 75c on 1.75fr org (Bk) ('42) 50 50
a. Inverted surcharge 15.00 15.00
186 A67 (a) 2.50(fr) on 2.40fr ol blk & brn (Bk) ('42) 1.25 1.00
a. Double surcharge 30.00 30.00
b. Inverted surcharge 15.00 15.00

Oil Palms

A71 A72

Congo Woman — A73

Leopard A74

Askari — A75

Okapi — A76

Inscribed "Congo Belge Belgisch Congo"

1942, May 23 Engr. Perf. 12½

187 A71 5c red 6 6
188 A72 10c ol grn 8 6
189 A72 15c brn car 8 6
190 A72 20c dp ultra 8 6
191 A72 25c brn vio 8 6
192 A72 30c blue 8 8
193 A72 50c dp grn 8 8
194 A72 60c chestnut 10 10
195 A73 75c dl lil & blk 12 10
196 A73 1fr dk brn & blk 15 10
197 A73 1.25fr rose red & blk 15 12
198 A74 1.75fr dk gray brn 75 55
199 A74 2fr ocher 75 18
200 A74 2.50fr carmine 75 10
201 A75 3.50fr dk ol grn 30 12
202 A75 5fr orange 55 20
203 A75 6fr brt ultra 50 12
204 A75 7fr black 50 12
205 A75 10fr dp brn 65 12
206 A76 20fr plum & blk 4.00 95
Nos. 187-206 (20) 9.81 3.34

Same Inscribed "Belgisch Congo Congo Belge"

207 A72 10c ol grn 8 6
208 A72 15c brn car 8 6
209 A72 20c dp ultra 8 6
210 A72 25c brn vio 8 6
211 A72 30c blue 8 8
212 A72 50c dp grn 8 8
213 A72 60c chestnut 10 10
214 A73 75c dl lil & blk 12 10
215 A73 1fr dk brn & blk 15 10
216 A73 1.25fr rose red & blk 15 12
217 A74 1.75fr dk gray brn 75 55
218 A74 2fr ocher 75 18
219 A74 2.50fr carmine 75 10
220 A75 3.50fr dk ol grn 30 12
221 A75 5fr orange 55 20
222 A75 6fr brt ultra 50 12
223 A75 7fr black 50 12
224 A75 10fr dp brn 65 12
225 A76 20fr plum & blk 4.00 95
Nos. 207-225 (19) 9.75 3.28

Miniature sheets of Nos. 193, 194, 197, 200, 211, 214, 217 and 219 were printed in 1944 by the Belgian Government in London and given to the Belgian political review, Message, which distributed them to its subscribers, one a month. Price per sheet, about $12.50.

Remainders of these eight miniature sheets received marginal overprints in various colors in 1950, specifying a surtax of 100fr per sheet and paying tribute to the Universal Postal Union. These sheets, together with four of Ruanda-Urundi, were sold by the Committee of Cultural Works (and not at post offices) in sets of 12 for 1,217.15 francs. Set price, about $150.

Nos. 187 to 227 exist imperforate but had no franking value.

Congo Woman — A77

Askari — A78

1943, Jan. 1

226 A77 50fr ultra & blk 5.00 65
227 A78 100fr car & blk 6.50 1.00

Slaves and Arab Guards
A79

Auguste Lambermont
A80

Design: 10fr, Leopold II.

Perf. 13x11½, 12½x12

1947 **Engr.** **Unwmk.**

228 A79 1.25fr blk brn 25 10
229 A80 3.50fr dk bl 38 12
230 A80 10fr red org 75 22

Issued to commemorate the 50th anniversary of the abolition of slavery in Belgian Congo. See also Nos. 261-262.

Baluba Carving of Former King — A82

Carved Figures and Masks of Baluba Tribe: 10c, 50c, 2fr, "Ndoha," figure of tribal king. 15c, 70c, 1.20fr, 2.50fr, "Tshimanyi," an idol. 20c, 75c, 1.60fr, 3.50fr, "Buangakokoma," statue of kneeling beggar. 25c, 1fr, 2.40fr, 5fr, "Mbuta," sacred double cup, carved with two faces, Man and Woman. 40c, 1.25fr, 6fr, 8fr, "Ngadimuashi," female mask. 1.50fr, 3fr, 10fr, 50fr, "Buadi-Muadi," mask with squared features. 6.50fr, 20fr, 100fr, "Mbowa," executioner's mask with buffalo horns.

1947-50 ***Perf. 12½***

231 A82 10c dp org ('48) 12 8
232 A82 15c ultra ('48) 12 8
233 A82 20c brt bl ('48) 12 10
234 A82 25c rose car ('48) 25 12
235 A82 40c vio ('48) 15 8
236 A82 50c ol brn 15 8
237 A82 70c yel grn ('48) 12 10
238 A82 75c mag ('48) 15 10
239 A82 1fr yel org & dk vio 1.25 8
240 A82 1.20fr gray & brn ('50) 15 12
241 A82 1.25fr lt bl grn & mag ('48) 25 18
242 A82 1.50fr ol & mag ('50) 8.00 2.25
243 A82 1.60fr bl gray & brt bl ('50) 20 18
244 A82 2fr org & mag ('48) 18 8
245 A82 2.40fr bl grn & dk grn ('50) 25 18
246 A82 2.50fr brn red & bl grn 15 8
247 A82 3fr lt ultra & ind ('49) 3.75 8
248 A82 3.50fr lt bl & blk ('48) 2.75 25
249 A82 5fr bis & mag ('48) 50 10
250 A82 6fr brn org & ind ('48) 65 10
251 A82 6.50fr red org & red brn ('49) 1.25 10
252 A82 8fr gray bl & dk grn ('50) 65 25
253 A82 10fr pale vio & red brn ('48) 2.00 12
254 A82 20fr red org & vio brn ('48) 1.00 10
255 A82 50fr dp org & blk ('48) 2.50 30
256 A82 100fr crim & blk brn ('48) 3.75 60
Nos. 231-256 (26) 30.41 5.89

Railroad Train and Map — A83

1948, July 1 **Unwmk.** ***Perf. 13½***

257 A83 2.50fr dp bl & grn 85 25

50th anniversary of railway service in the Congo.

Globe and Ship
A84

1949, Nov. 21 ***Perf. 11½***

Granite Paper

258 A84 4fr vio bl 75 25

Issued to commemorate the 75th anniversary of the formation of the Universal Postal Union.

Allegorical Figure and Map — A85

1950, Aug. 12 ***Perf. 12x12½***

259 A85 3fr bl & ind 1.50 25
260 A85 6.50fr car rose & blk brn 1.75 38

Issued to commemorate the 50th anniversary of the establishment of Katanga Province.

Portrait Type of 1947

Designs: 1.50fr, Cardinal Lavigerie. 3fr, Baron Dhanis.

Perf. 12½x12

1951, June 25 **Unwmk.**

261 A80 1.50fr purple 2.00 38
262 A80 3fr blk brn 2.00 10

Littonia — A86

Flowers: 10c, Dissotis. 15c, Protea. 20c, Vellozia. 40c, Ipomoea. 50c, Angraecum. 60c, Euphorbia. 75c, Ochna. 1fr, Hibiscus. 1.25fr, Protea. 1.50fr, Schrizoglossum. 2fr, Ansellia. 3fr, Costus. 4fr, Nymphaea. 5fr, Thunbergia. 6.50fr, Thonningia. 7fr, Gerbera. 8fr, Gloriosa. 10fr, Silene. 20fr, Aristolochia. 50fr, Eulophia. 100fr, Crytosepalum.

1952-53 **Photo.** ***Perf. 11½***

Granite Paper

Flowers in Natural Colors

Size: 21x25½mm.

263 A86 10c dp plum & ocher 5 5
264 A86 15c red & yel grn 5 5
265 A86 20c grn & gray 5 5
266 A86 25c dk grn & dl org 5 5
267 A86 40c grn & sal 18 15
268 A86 50c dk car & aqua 8 5
269 A86 60c bl grn & pink 8 5
270 A86 75c dp plum & gray 8 5
271 A86 1fr car & yel 8 5
272 A86 1.25fr dk grn & bl ('53) 65 50
273 A86 1.50fr vio & ap grn 15 5
274 A86 2fr ol grn & buff 25 5
275 A86 3fr ol grn & pink 25 5
276 A86 4fr choc & lil 30 5
277 A86 5fr dp plum & lt bl grn 45 5
278 A86 6.50fr dk car & lil 55 5
279 A86 7fr dk grn & fawn 55 5
280 A86 8fr grn & lt yel ('53) 90 15
281 A86 10fr dp plum & pale ol ('53) 1.65 5
282 A86 20fr vio bl & dl sal 1.40 5

Size: 22x32mm.

283 A86 50fr dp plum & gray bl ('53) 7.00 50
284 A86 100fr grn & buff ('53) 11.00 1.10
Nos. 263-284 (22) 25.80 3.25

Nos. 264, 269 and 270 with additional surcharges are varieties of Congo Democratic Republic Nos. 324, 327 and 328.

St. Francis Xavier — A86a

1953, Jan. 5 **Engr.** ***Perf. 12½x13***

285 A86a 1.50fr ultra & gray blk 75 60

Issued to commemorate the 400th anniversary of the death of St. Francis Xavier.

Canoe on Lake Kivu — A87

1953, Jan. 5 ***Perf. 14***

286 A87 3fr car & blk 1.50 30
287 A87 7fr dp bl & brn org 1.65 45

Issued to publicize the Kivu Festival, 1953.

Royal Colonial Institute Jubilee Medal
A88

Design: 6.50fr, Same with altered background and transposed inscriptions.

1954, Dec. 27 **Photo.** ***Perf. 13½***

288 A88 4.50fr ind & gray 1.40 45
289 A88 6.50fr dk grn & brn 1.10 18

Issued to commemorate the 25th anniversary of the founding of the Belgian Royal Colonial Institute.

King Baudouin and Tropical Scene
A89

Designs: King and various views.

Inscribed "Congo Belge--Belgisch Congo"

Engraved; Portrait Photogravure

1955, Feb. 15 **Unwmk.** ***Perf. 11½***

Portrait in Black

290 A89 1.50fr rose car 90 38
291 A89 3fr green 32 12
292 A89 4.50fr ultra 42 15
293 A89 6.50fr dp cl 65 12

Inscribed "Belgisch Congo-Congo Belge"

294 A89 1.50fr rose car 42 28
295 A89 3fr green 32 8
296 A89 4.50fr ultra 42 15
297 A89 6.50fr dp cl 65 12
Nos. 290-297 (8) 4.10 1.40

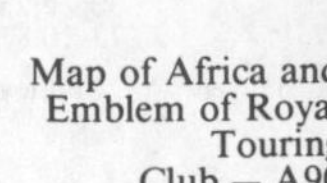

Map of Africa and Emblem of Royal Touring Club — A90

1955, July 26 **Engr.** ***Perf. 11½***

Inscription in French

298 A90 6.50fr vio bl 3.25 50

Inscription in Flemish

299 A90 6.50fr vio bl 3.25 50

5th International Congress of African Tourism, Elisabethville, July 26-Aug. 4. Nos. 298-299 printed in alternate rows.

Kings of Belgium
A91

1958, July 1 **Unwmk.** ***Perf. 12½***

300 A91 1fr rose vio 25 8
301 A91 1.50fr ultra 25 8
302 A91 3fr rose car 25 8
303 A91 5fr green 80 55
304 A91 6.50fr brn red 50 10
305 A91 10fr dl vio 70 15
Nos. 300-305 (6) 2.75 1.04

Issued to commemorate the 50th anniversary of Belgium's annexation of Congo.

Roan Antelope
A92

Black Buffaloes
A93

Animals: 20c, White rhinoceros. 40c, Giraffe. 50c, Thick-tailed bushbaby. 1fr, Gorilla. 2fr, Black-and-white colobus (monkey). 3fr, Elephants. 5fr, Okapis. 6.50fr, Impala. 8fr, Giant pangolin. 10fr, Eland and zebras.

1959 **Photo.** ***Perf. 11½***

Granite Paper

306 A92 10c bl & brn 5 5
307 A93 20c red org & sl 5 5
308 A92 40c brn & bl 8 8
309 A93 50c brt ultra, red & sep 8 8
310 A92 1fr brn, grn & blk 10 8
311 A93 1.50fr blk & org yel 12 8
312 A92 2fr crim, blk & brn 15 8
313 A93 3fr blk, gray & lil rose 25 10
314 A92 5fr brn, dk brn & brt grn 40 18
315 A93 6.50fr bl, brn & org yel 45 10
316 A92 8fr org brn, ol bis & lil 50 30
317 A93 10fr multi 60 15
Nos. 306-317 (12) 2.83 1.33

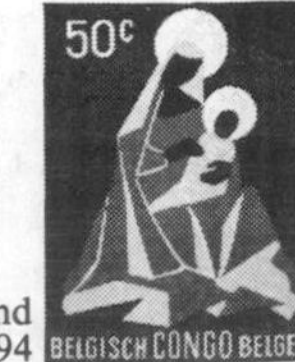

Madonna and Child — A94

1959, Dec. 1 **Unwmk.** ***Perf. 11½***

318 A94 50c gldn brn, ocher & red brn 10 6

319	A94	1fr dk bl, pur & red brn	10	8
320	A94	2fr gray, brt bl & red brn	18	12

Map of Africa and Symbolic Honeycomb A95

1960, Feb. 19 Unwmk. Perf. 11½

Inscription in French

321	A95	3fr gray & red	25	15

Inscription in Flemish

322	A95	3fr gray & red	25	15

Issued to commemorate the 10th anniversary of the Commission for Technical Cooperation in Africa South of the Sahara. (C. C. T. A.)

Succeeding issues are listed under Congo Democratic Republic.

SEMI-POSTAL STAMPS

Types of 1910-15 Issues Surcharged in Red **+ 10c**

1918, May 15 Unwmk. Perf. 14, 15

B1	A29	5c + 10c grn & bl	30	38
B2	A30	10c + 15c car & bl (I)	30	38
B3	A21	15c + 20c bl grn & bl	30	38
B4	A31	25c + 25c dp bl & pale bl	38	38
B5	A23	40c + 40c brn red & bl	50	65
B6	A24	50c + 50c brn lake & bl	50	65
B7	A25	1fr + 1fr ol bis & bl	1.90	2.25
B8	A27	5fr + 5fr ocher & bl	11.50	12.00
B9	A28	10fr + 10fr grn & bl	90.00	90.00
		Nos. B1-B9 (9)	105.68	107.07

The position of the cross and the added value varies on the different stamps.

Nos. B1 to B9 exist imperforate.

SP1

Design: No. B11 inscribed "Belgisch Congo."

1925 Perf. 12½.

B10	SP1	25c + 25c car & blk	25	25
B11	SP1	25c + 25c car & blk	25	25

Colonial campaigns in 1914-1918.

The stamps with French and Flemish inscriptions alternate in the sheet.

The surtax helped erect at Kinshasa a monument to those who died in World War I.

Nurse Weighing Child — SP3

First Aid Station SP5

Designs: 20c+10c, Missionary and Child. 60c+30c, Congo hospital. 1fr+50c, Dispensary service. 1.75fr+75c, Convalescent area. 3.50fr+1.50fr, Instruction on bathing infant. 5fr+2.50fr, Operating room. 10fr+5fr, Students.

1930, Jan. 16 Engr. Perf. 11½

B12	SP3	10c + 5c ver	55	55
B13	SP3	20c + 10c dp brn	70	70
B14	SP5	35c + 15c dp grn	1.25	1.25
B15	SP5	60c + 30c dl vio	1.50	1.50
B16	SP3	1fr + 50c dk car	2.25	2.25
B17	SP5	1.75fr + 75c dp bl	3.25	3.25
B18	SP5	3.50fr + 1.50fr rose lake	6.25	6.25
B19	SP5	5fr + 2.50fr red brn	6.00	6.00
B20	SP5	10fr + 5fr gray blk	6.25	6.25
		Nos. B12-B20 (9)	28.00	28.00

The surtax on these stamps was intended to aid welfare work among the natives, especially the children.

Nos. 161, 163 Surcharged "+50c" in Blue or Red.

1936, May 15 Perf. 12½x12

B21	A63	1.50fr + 50c brn vio (Bl)	2.50	2.50
B22	A63	2.50fr + 50c lt bl (R)	2.50	2.50

The surtax was for the benefit of the King Albert Memorial Fund.

Queen Astrid with Congolese Children — SP12

1936, Aug. 29 Photo. Perf. 12½

B23	SP12	1.25fr + 5c dk brn	75	65
B24	SP12	1.50fr + 10c dl rose	75	65
B25	SP12	2.50fr + 25c dk bl	90	90

Issued in memory of Queen Astrid. The surtax was for the aid of the National League for Protection of Native Children.

Souvenir Sheet

SP13

1938, Oct. 3 Perf. 11½

B26	SP13	Sheet of six	10.50	10.50
a.	A64	5c ultra & lt brn	1.75	1.75
b.	A65	90c ultra & lt brn	1.75	1.75
c.	A66	1.50fr ultra & lt brn	1.75	1.75
d.	A67	2.40fr ultra & lt brn	1.75	1.75
e.	A68	2.50fr ultra & lt brn	1.75	1.75
f.	A69	4.50fr ultra & lt brn	1.75	1.75

Issued in sheets measuring 139x122mm. The star is printed in yellow. Issued in commemoration of the International Tourist Congress. A surtax of 3.15fr was for the benefit of the Congo Tourist Service.

Marabou Storks and Vultures — SP14

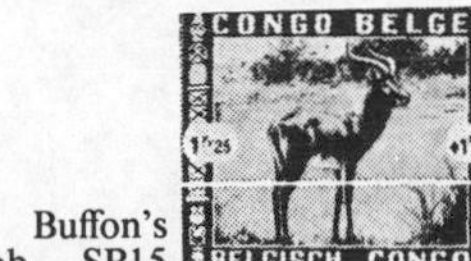

Buffon's Kob — SP15

Designs: 1.50fr+1.50fr, Pygmy chimpanzees. 4.50fr+4.50fr, Dwarf crocodiles. 5fr+5fr, Lioness.

1939 Photo. Perf. 14

B27	SP14	1fr + 1fr dp cl	5.00	5.00
B28	SP15	1.25fr + 1.25fr car	5.00	5.00
B29	SP15	1.50fr + 1.50fr brt pur	7.50	7.50
B30	SP14	4.50fr + 4.50fr sl grn	5.00	5.00
B31	SP15	5fr + 5fr brn	5.50	5.50
		Nos. B27-B31 (5)	28.00	28.00

The surtax was for the Leopoldville Zoological Gardens.

Nos. B27-B31 were sold in full sets by subscription.

Lion of Belgium and Inscription "Belgium Shall Rise Again" — SP19

1942, Feb. 17 Engr. Perf. 12½

B32	SP19	10fr + 40fr brt grn	1.40	1.40
B33	SP19	10fr + 40fr vio bl	1.40	1.40

Nos. 193, 216, 198 and 220 Surcharged in Red

a: Au profit de la Croix Rouge + 50 Fr. Ten voordeele van het Roode Kruis

b: Ten voordeele van het Roode Kruis + 100 Fr. Au profit de la Croix Rouge

c: Au profit de la Croix Rouge + 100 Fr. Ten voordeele van het Roode Kruis

1945

B34	A72 (a)	50c + 50fr dp grn	2.50	2.50
B35	A73 (b)	1.25fr + 100fr rose red & blk	2.50	2.50
B36	A74 (c)	1.75fr + 100fr dk gray brn	2.50	2.75
B37	A75 (b)	3.50fr + 100fr dk ol grn	2.50	2.75

The surtax was for the Red Cross.

Nos. B34-B37 were sold in full sets by subscription.

Mozart at Age 7 — SP20

Queen Elisabeth and Sonata by Mozart — SP21

Perf. 11½

1956, Oct. 10 Unwmk. Engr.

B38	SP20	4.50fr + 1.50fr brt lil	1.50	1.50
B39	SP21	6.50fr + 2.50fr ultra	2.50	2.50

Issued to commemorate the 200th anniversary of the birth of Wolfgang Amadeus Mozart.

The surtax was for the Pro-Mozart Committee.

Nurse and Children — SP22

Designs: 4.50fr+50c, Patient receiving injection. 6.50fr+40c, Patient being bandaged.

1957, Dec. 10 Photo. Perf. 13x10½

Cross in Carmine

B40	SP22	3fr + 50c dk bl	1.10	1.10
B41	SP22	4.50fr + 50c dk grn	1.00	1.00
B42	SP22	6.50fr + 50c red brn	1.25	1.25

The surtax was for the Red Cross.

High Jumper SP23

Sports: 1.50fr+50c, Hurdlers. 2fr+1fr, Soccer. 3fr+1.25fr, Javelin thrower. 6.50fr+3.50fr, Discus thrower.

1960, May 2 Unwmk. Perf. 13½

B43	SP23	50c + 25c ultra & red	12	12
B44	SP23	1.50fr + 50c car & grn	22	22
B45	SP23	2fr + 1fr grn & ver	22	22
B46	SP23	3fr + 1.25fr rose cl & bl	95	95
B47	SP23	6.50fr + 3.50fr red brn & car	1.25	1.25
		Nos. B43-B47 (5)	2.76	2.76

Issued to commemorate the 17th Olympic Games, Rome, Aug. 25-Sept. 11. The surtax was for the youth of Congo.

AIR POST STAMPS

Wharf on Congo River AP1

Congo "Country Store" AP2

View of Congo River AP3

Stronghold in the Interior — AP4

Unwmk.

1920, July 1 **Engr.** ***Perf. 12***

C1 AP1 50c org & blk 25 15
C2 AP2 1fr dl vio & blk 25 12
C3 AP3 2fr bl & blk 80 30
C4 AP4 5fr grn & blk 1.50 70

Kraal AP5

Porters on Safari AP6

1930, Apr. 2

C5 AP5 15fr dk brn & blk 3.50 1.25
C6 AP6 30fr brn vio & blk 4.00 1.25

Fokker F VII over Congo — AP7

1934, Jan. 22 ***Perf. 13½x14***

C7 AP7 50c gray blk 20 20
C8 AP7 1fr dk car 30 20
a. Bklt pane of 8 7.00
C9 AP7 1.50fr green 20 15
C10 AP7 3fr brown 30 15
C11 AP7 4.50fr brt ultra 45 15
a. Bklt pane of 8 15.00
C12 AP7 5fr red brn 35 15
C13 AP7 15fr brn vio 70 45
C14 AP7 30fr red org 1.25 1.10
C15 AP7 50fr violet 3.75 1.75
Nos. C7-C15 (9) 7.50 4.30

The 1fr, 3fr, 4.50fr, 5fr and 15fr exist imperf.

No. C10 Surcharged in Blue with New Value and Bars

1936, Mar. 25

C16 AP7 3.50fr on 3fr brn 25 15

No. C9 Surcharged in Black

50 c.

1942, Apr. 27

C17 AP7 50c on 1.50fr grn 30 30
a. Inverted surcharge 7.50 7.50

POSTAGE DUE STAMPS

In 1908-23 regular postage stamps handstamped "TAXES" or "TAXE," usually boxed, were used in lieu of postage due stamps.

D1

D2

Perf. 14, 14½

1923-29 **Typo.** **Unwmk.**

J1 D1 5c blk brn 18 18
J2 D1 10c rose red 20 18
J3 D1 15c violet 25 20
J4 D1 30c green 40 38
J5 D1 50c ultra 55 50
J6 D1 50c bl ('29) 55 50
J7 D1 1fr gray 65 45
Nos. J1-J7 (7) 2.78 2.39

1943 ***Perf. 14x14½***

J8 D2 10c ol grn 6 6
J9 D2 20c dk ultra 6 6
J10 D2 50c green 15 15
J11 D2 1fr dk brn 18 18
J12 D2 2fr yel org 22 22
Nos. J8-J12 (5) 67 67

1943 ***Perf. 12½***

J8a D2 10c ol grn 25 25
J9a D2 20c dk ultra 25 25
J10a D2 50c green 25 25
J11a D2 1fr dk brn 38 38
J12a D2 2fr yel org 38 38
Nos. J8a-J12a (5) 1.51 1.51

D3

1957 **Engr.** ***Perf. 11½***

J13 D3 10c ol brn 6 6
J14 D3 20c claret 10 10
J15 D3 50c green 15 15
J16 D3 1fr lt bl 30 30
J17 D3 2fr vermilion 45 40
J18 D3 4fr purple 60 55
J19 D3 6fr vio bl 85 70
Nos. J13-J19 (7) 2.51 2.26

PARCEL POST STAMPS

PP1

PP2

PP3

Handstamped Surcharges on Nos. 5, 11-12

1887-93 **Unwmk.** ***Perf. 15***

Blue-Black Surcharge

Q1 PP1 3.50fr on 5fr lil 750.00 500.00

Black Surcharge

Q3 PP2 3.50fr on 5fr vio 700.00 375.00
Q4 PP3 3.50fr on 5fr vio ('88) 500.00 300.00
a. bl surcharge 500.00 300.00
Q6 PP3 3.50fr on 5fr gray ('93) 95.00 62.50

Nos. Q1, Q3-Q4, Q4a and Q6 are known with inverted surcharge, No. Q1 with double surcharge and No. Q6 in pair with unsurcharged stamp. Most of these handstamp varieties sell for more than the normal surcharges.

BELGIUM

LOCATION — Western Europe, bordering the North Sea.
GOVT. — Constitutional Monarchy
AREA — 11,778 sq. mi.
POP. — 9,853,000 (est. 1983)
CAPITAL — Brussels

100 Centimes = 1 Franc

Prices of early Belgian stamps vary according to condition. Quotations for Nos. 1-12 are for fine copies. Very fine to superb specimens sell at much higher prices, and inferior or poor copies sell at reduced prices, depending on the condition of the individual specimen.

Prices for unused stamps of 1849-1863 issues are for copies with original gum. Copies without gum sell for one third of the figures quoted, or less.

King Leopold I
A1 A2

Wmk. 96 (No Frame)

Wmk. Two "L's" Framed. (96)

1849 **Engr.** ***Imperf.***

1 A1 10c brown *2,250.* 100.00
a. 10c red brn *3,500.* 300.00
2 A1 20c blue *3,250.* 90.00
a. 20c mlky bl *3,750.* 225.00

The reprints are on thick and thin wove and thick laid paper unwatermarked.

A souvenir sheet containing reproductions of the 10c, 20c and 40c of 1849-51 with black burelage on back was issued Oct. 17, 1949, for the centenary of the first Belgian stamps. It was sold at BEPITEC 1949, an international stamp exhibition at Brussels, and was not valid. Size: 139x90mm.

1849-50

3 A2 10c brn ('50) *2,000.* 100.00
4 A2 20c bl ('50) *2,250.* 77.50
5 A2 40c car rose *2,000.* 325.00

Nos. 3-5 on thin paper are as priced. Copies on thick paper sell for 5 to 12 percent more.

Wmk. Two "L's" Without Frame. (96)

1851-54

6 A2 10c brown 1,100. 13.00
a. Ribbed paper ('54) 1,300. 57.50
7 A2 20c blue 1,100. 13.00
a. Ribbed paper ('54) 1,300. 57.50
8 A2 40c car rose *2,200.* 90.00
a. Ribbed paper ('54) *2,600.* 250.00

Nos. 6-8 were printed on thin and thick paper. Nos. 6-7 on thick paper, unused, sell for 7 to 10 percent more.

1858-61 **Unwmk.**

9 A2 1c grn ('61) *250.00* 200.00
a. Laid paper
10 A2 10c brown 500.00 13.00
11 A2 20c blue 500.00 13.00
12 A2 40c car rose *2,500.* 90.00

Nos. 9 and 13 were valid for postage on newspapers and printed matter only.

Reprints of Nos. 9 to 12 are on thin wove paper. The colors are brighter than those of the originals. They were made from the dies and show lines outside the stamps.

Perf. 12½, 12½x13, 12½x13½, 14½

1863

No.	Type	Description	Unused	Used
13	A2	1c green	52.50	45.00
14	A2	10c brown	75.00	2.25
15	A2	20c blue	80.00	2.25
16	A2	40c car rose	525.00	22.50

King Leopold I
A3 A3a

A4 A4a

A5

London Print.

1865 **Typo.** ***Perf. 14***

No.	Type	Description	Unused	Used
17	A5	1fr pale vio	900.00	135.00

Brussels Print.
Thick or Thin Paper.

1865-66 ***Perf. 15, 14½x14***

No.	Type	Description	Unused	Used
18	A3	10c sl ('66)	110.00	1.25
a.		Pair, imperf. between		175.00
19	A3a	20c bl ('66)	135.00	1.25
a.		20c lil bl	135.00	1.40
20	A4	30c brown	275.00	9.00
a.		Pair, imperf. between	900.00	
21	A4a	40c rose ('66)	400.00	18.00
22	A5	1fr violet	1,000.	135.00

Nos. 18 to 22 on thin paper are perf. 14½x14; on thick paper, perf. 15.

The reprints are on thin paper, imperforate and ungummed.

Coat of Arms — A6

1866-67 ***Imperf.***

No.	Type	Description	Unused	Used
23	A6	1c gray	250.00	200.00

Perf. 15, 14½x14

No.	Type	Description	Unused	Used
24	A6	1c gray	37.50	16.00
25	A6	2c bl ('67)	135.00	90.00
a.		2c ultra	150.00	110.00
26	A6	5c brown	135.00	90.00

Nos. 23-26 were valid for postage on newspapers and printed matter only.

Nos. 24 to 26 on thin paper are perf. 14½ x 14; on thick paper, perf. 15.

Reprints of Nos. 24 to 26 are on thin paper, imperforate and ungummed.

King Leopold II
A7 A8

A9 A10

A11 A12

1869-70 ***Perf. 15***

No.	Type	Description	Unused	Used
28	A7	1c green	12.00	45
29	A7	2c ultra ('70)	16.00	45
30	A7	5c buff ('70)	57.50	65
31	A7	8c lil ('70)	90.00	62.50
32	A8	10c green	30.00	45
33	A9	20c lt ultra ('70)	125.00	90
34	A10	30c buff ('70)	100.00	5.50
35	A11	40c brt rose ('70)	125.00	5.75
36	A12	1fr dl lil ('70)	300.00	20.00
a.		1fr rose lil	325.00	22.50

The frames and inscriptions of Nos. 30, 31 and 42 differ slightly from the illustration.

Minor "broken letter" varieties exist on several values.

Imperf. varieties of 1869-1912 (between Nos. 28-105) are without gum.

See also Nos. 40-43, 49-51, 55.

A13 A14

A15

1875-78

No.	Type	Description	Unused	Used
37	A13	25c ol bis	80.00	1.40
a.		25c ocher	80.00	1.40
38	A14	50c gray	300.00	8.00
a.		50c gray blk	500.00	67.50
39	A15	5fr pale brn ('78)	3,750.	1,000.
		Roller cancel		450.00
a.		5fr dp red brn	2,100.	1,000.

Printed in Aniline Colors.

1881 ***Perf. 14, 15***

No.	Type	Description	Unused	Used
40	A7	1c gray grn	11.00	45
41	A7	2c lt ultra	17.50	85
42	A7	5c org buff	57.50	65
a.		5c red org	57.50	65
43	A8	10c gray grn	45.00	45
44	A13	25c ol bis	80.00	1.40
		Nos. 40-44 (5)	211.00	3.80

King Leopold II
A16 A17

A18 A19

1883

No.	Type	Description	Unused	Used
45	A16	10c carmine	40.00	1.75
46	A17	20c gray	175.00	4.50
47	A18	25c blue	350.00	32.50
		Roller cancel		12.50
48	A19	50c violet	300.00	35.00
		Roller cancel		12.50

A20 A21

A22

1884-85 ***Perf. 14***

No.	Type	Description	Unused	Used
49	A7	1c ol grn	13.00	65
50	A7	1c gray	5.25	8
51	A7	5c green	27.50	15
52	A20	10c rose, *bluish*	9.00	10
a.		grysh paper	10.00	35
c.		yelsh paper	100.00	20.00
53	A21	25c bl, *pink* ('85)	16.00	55
54	A22	1fr brn, *grnsh*	1,000.	13.00

The frame and inscription of No. 51 differ slightly from the illustration. See note after No. 36.

A23 A24

A25 A26

1886-91

No.	Type	Description	Unused	Used
55	A7	2c pur brn ('88)	13.00	55
56	A23	20c ol, *grnsh*	160.00	70
57	A24	35c vio brn,*brnsh* ('91)	30.00	3.00
58	A25	50c bis, *yelsh*	16.00	2.25
59	A26	2fr vio, *pale lil*	150.00	30.00
		Roller cancel		6.00

Coat of Arms A27 King Leopold A28

1893-1900

No.	Type	Description	Unused	Used
60	A27	1c gray	1.40	10
61	A27	2c yellow	1.75	1.40
a.		Wmkd. coat of arms in sheet ('95)		
62	A27	2c vio brn ('94)	2.25	25
63	A27	2c red brn ('98)	4.25	25
64	A27	5c yel grn	6.75	15
65	A28	10c org brn	6.75	15
66	A28	10c brt rose ('00)	4.50	15
67	A28	20c ol grn	30.00	50
68	A28	25c ultra	27.50	50
a.		No ball to "5" in upper left corner	45.00	16.00
69	A28	35c vio brn	50.00	1.25
a.		35c brn	57.50	1.65
70	A28	50c bister	85.00	11.00
71	A28	50c gray ('97)	75.00	2.50
72	A28	1fr car, *lt grn*	100.00	15.00
73	A28	1fr org ('00)	140.00	6.75
74	A28	2fr lil, *rose*	150.00	110.00
75	A28	2fr lil ('00)	200.00	18.00

Prices quoted for Nos. 60-107, B1-B24 are for stamps with label attached. Stamps without label sell for about half.

Antwerp Exhibition Issue.

Arms of Antwerp — A29

1894

76	A29	5c grn, *rose*	4.50	2.75
77	A29	10c car, *bluish*	4.00	1.10
78	A29	25c bl, *rose*	65	65

Brussels Exhibition Issue.

St. Michael and Satan
A30 A31

1896-97 *Perf. 14x14 ½.*

79	A30	5c dp vio	90	45
80	A31	10c org brn	8.50	3.00
81	A31	10c lil brn	65	35

Coat of Arms A32 King Leopold II A33

King Leopold II
A34 A35

A36 A37

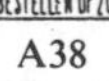

A38 A39

Two types of 1c:
I. Periods after "Dimanche" and "Zondag" in label.
II. No period after "Dimanche". Period often missing after "Zondag".

1905-07 *Perf. 14.*

82	A32	1c gray (I) ('07)	90	22
a.		Type II ('08)	90	25
83	A32	2c red brn ('07)	6.00	2.25
84	A32	5c grn ('07)	6.00	22
85	A33	10c dl rose	2.25	20
86	A34	20c ol grn	16.00	90
87	A35	25c ultra	13.00	75
a.		25c dl bl	13.00	75
88	A36	35c pur brn	25.00	1.90
89	A37	50c bluish gray	65.00	2.50
90	A38	1fr yellow	85.00	8.00
91	A39	2fr violet	85.00	22.50
		Bar cancellation		4.00
		Nos. 82-91 (10)	304.15	39.44

Numeral A40

Coat of Arms A41

Lion of Belgium A42

King Albert I A43

A44

1912

92	A40	1c orange	22	10
93	A41	2c org brn	45	45
94	A42	5c green	35	10
95	A43	10c red	1.10	35
96	A43	20c ol grn	8.50	1.40
97	A43	35c bis brn	1.25	65
98	A43	40c green	13.00	7.25
99	A43	50c gray	1.25	90
100	A43	1fr orange	6.00	4.50
101	A43	2fr violet	14.00	13.00
102	A44	5fr plum	90.00	20.00
		Nos. 92-102 (11)	136.12	48.70

A45

1912-13

Larger Head

103	A45	10c red	55	22
a.		Without engraver's name	25	15
104	A45	20c ol grn ('13)	75	50
a.		Without engraver's name	1.10	1.10
105	A45	25c ultra	4.25	1.90
a.		Without engraver's name	35	45
107	A45	40c grn ('13)	90	75

King Albert I — A46

Cloth Hall of Ypres — A47

Bridge of Dinant — A48

Library of Louvain A49

Scheldt River at Antwerp A50

Anti-slavery Campaign in the Congo — A51

King Albert I at Furnes A52

Kings of Belgium Leopold I, Albert I, Leopold II — A53

1915-20 **Typo.** *Perf. 14, 14½*

108	A46	1c orange	18	5
109	A46	2c chocolate	18	5
110	A46	3c gray blk ('20)	25	6
111	A46	5c green	45	5
112	A46	10c carmine	90	5
113	A46	15c purple	1.10	6
114	A46	20c red vio	1.10	5
115	A46	25c blue	1.25	22

Engr.

116	A47	35c brn org & blk	90	22
117	A48	40c grn & blk	1.40	22
a.		Vertical pair, imperf. between		
118	A49	50c car rose & blk	4.50	22
119	A50	1fr violet	18.00	40
120	A51	2fr slate	21.00	1.75
121	A52	5fr dp bl	200.00	85.00
		Telegraph or railroad cancel		65.00
122	A53	10fr brown	21.00	20.00
		Nos. 108-122 (15)	272.21	108.40

Two types each of the 1c, 10c and 20c; three of the 2c and 15c; four of the 5c, differing in the top left corner.

Nos. 108 to 120 and 122 exist imperforate. See also No. 138.

Perron of Liege (Fountain) A54

King Albert in Trench Helmet A55

1919 *Perf. 11½*

123	A54	25c dp bl	2.00	20
a.		Sheet of ten	*11,000.*	*11,000.*

Perf. 11, 11½, 11½x11, 11x11½.

1919

Size: 18½x22mm.

124	A55	1c lil brn	8	8
125	A55	2c olive	8	8

Size: 23x26mm.

126	A55	5c green	28	22
127	A55	10c carmine	15	8
128	A55	15c gray vio	22	15
129	A55	20c ol blk	70	85
130	A55	25c dp bl	85	90
131	A55	35c bis brn	1.25	1.10
132	A55	40c red	2.00	2.00
133	A55	50c red brn	5.00	5.00
134	A55	1fr lt org	30.00	30.00
135	A55	2fr violet	325.00	300.00

Size: 28x33½mm.

136	A55	5fr car lake	100.00	100.00
137	A55	10fr claret	110.00	110.00
		Nos. 124-137 (14)	575.61	550.46

Type of 1915 Inscribed: "FRANK" instead of "FRANKEN"

1919, Dec. *Perf. 14, 15*

138	A52	5fr dp bl	2.25	1.25

Town Hall at Termonde
A56 A57

1920 *Perf. 11½*

139	A56	65c cl & blk	1.75	30
a.		Center inverted	*30,000.*	

Semi-Postal Stamps of 1920 Surcharged in Red or Black

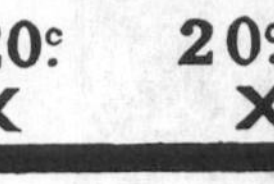

1921 *Perf. 12*

140	SP6	20c on 5c dp grn (R)	1.00	38
a.		Invtd. surcharge	250.00	250.00
141	SP7	20c on 10c car	70	38
b.		Invtd. surcharge	250.00	250.00
142	SP8	20c on 15c dk brn (R)	75	38
a.		Invtd. surcharge	250.00	250.00

Red Surcharge.

143	A57	55c on 65c cl & blk	1.75	60
a.		Pair, one without surcharge	3.00	1.25

A58

A59

1922-27 **Typo.** *Perf. 14*

144	A58	1c orange	8	5
145	A58	2c ol ('26)	10	10
146	A58	3c fawn	8	5
147	A58	5c gray	8	5
148	A58	10c bl grn	12	5
149	A58	15c plum ('23)	12	8
150	A58	20c blk brn	30	6
151	A58	25c dl vio	22	8
152	A58	30c vermilion	70	10
153	A58	30c rose ('25)	55	8
154	A58	35c red brn	45	12
155	A58	35c bl grn ('27)	80	30
156	A58	40c rose	70	12
157	A58	50c bis ('25)	70	8
158	A58	60c ol brn ('27)	3.00	5
159	A58	1.25fr dp bl ('26)	85	60
160	A58	1.50fr brt bl ('26)	2.25	22
161	A58	1.75fr ultra ('27)	1.50	12
a.		Tete beche pair	18.00	9.00
c.		Bklt. pane of 4 + 2 labels	57.50	
		Nos. 144-161 (18)	12.60	2.31

See also Nos. 185-190.

Perf. 11½, 11½x11, 11½x12, 11½x12½.

1921-25 **Engr.**

162	A59	50c dl bl	45	5
163	A59	75c scar ('22)	22	15
164	A59	75c ultra ('24)	55	12
165	A59	1fr blk brn ('22)	1.10	12
166	A59	1fr dk bl ('25)	75	12
167	A59	2fr dk grn ('22)	90	30
168	A59	5fr brn vio ('23)	15.00	19.00
169	A59	10fr mag ('22)	10.00	2.50
		Nos. 162-169 (8)	28.97	22.36

No. 162 measures 18x20 ¾ m m. and was printed in sheets of 100.

Philatelic Exhibition Issue.

1921, May 26 *Perf. 11½*

170	A59	50c dk bl	3.50	3.50
a.		Sheet of 25	225.00	175.00

No. 170 measures 17 ½x21¼mm., was printed in sheets of 25 and sold at the Philatelic Exhibition at Brussels.

Philatelic Exhibition Issue.
Souvenir Sheet.

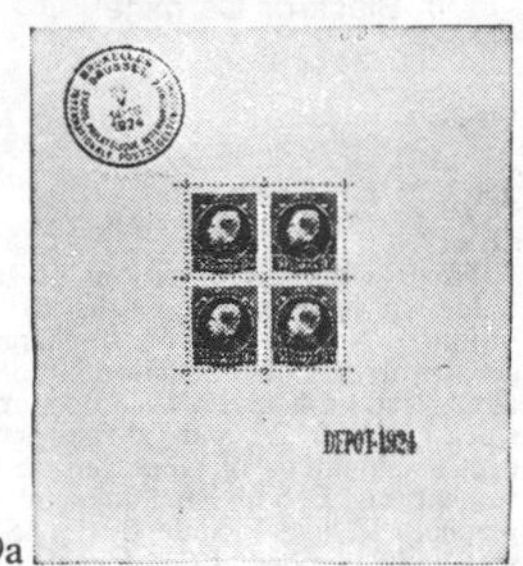

A59a

1924, May 24 *Perf. 11½*
171 A59a 5fr red brn, sheet of 4 100.00 110.00
a. Single stamp (A59) 15.00 15.00

Sold only at the International Philatelic Exhibition, Brussels. Sheet size: 130x145mm.

Kings Leopold I and Albert I — A60

1925 *Perf. 14*
172 A60 10c dp grn 10.50 8.50
173 A60 15c dl vio 6.25 6.25
174 A60 20c red brn 6.25 6.25
175 A60 25c grnsh blk 6.25 6.25
176 A60 30c vermilion 6.25 6.25
177 A60 35c lt bl 6.25 6.25
178 A60 40c brnsh blk 6.25 6.25
179 A60 50c yel brn 6.25 6.25
180 A60 75c dk bl 6.25 6.25
181 A60 1fr dk vio 10.50 9.25
182 A60 2fr ultra 6.25 6.25
183 A60 5fr bl blk 6.25 6.25
184 A60 10fr dp rose 10.50 11.00
Nos. 172-184 (13) 94.00 91.25

75th anniversary of Belgian postage stamps.
Nos. 172-184 were sold only in sets and only by The Administration of Posts, not at post offices.

A61

1926-27 Typo.
185 A61 75c dk vio 90 65
186 A61 1fr pale yel 80 22
187 A61 1fr rose red ('27) 1.10 12
a. Tete beche pair 10.00 6.00
c. Bklt pane 4 + 2 labels 30.00
188 A61 2fr Prus bl 3.00 12
189 A61 5fr emer ('27) 22.50 90
190 A61 10fr dk brn ('27) 50.00 2.50
Nos. 185-190 (6) 78.30 4.51

Stamps of 1921-27 Surcharged in Carmine, Red or Blue ≡ 1F75 ≡

1927
191 A58 3c on 2c ol (C) 6 12
192 A58 10c on 15c plum (R) 12 10
193 A58 35c on 40c rose (Bl) 50 12
194 A58 1.75fr on 1.50fr brt bl (C) 2.50 80

Nos. 153, 185 and 159 Surcharged in Black

1929, Jan. 1
195 A58 5c on 30c rose 12 10
196 A61 5c on 75c dk vio 30 30
197 A58 5c on 1.25fr dp bl 12 12

The surcharge on Nos. 195 to 197 is a precancelation which alters the value of the stamp to which it is applied.
Prices for precanceled stamps in first column are for those which have not been through the post and have original gum. Prices in second column are for postally used, gumless stamps.

A63

A64

1929-32 Typo. *Perf. 14*
198 A63 1c orange 8 10
199 A63 2c emer ('31) 35 35
200 A63 3c red brn 8 5
201 A63 5c slate 12 5
a. Tete beche pair 1.65 1.35
c. Bklt pane of 4 + 2 labels 11.00
202 A63 10c ol grn 12 5
a. Tete beche pair 90 80
c. Bklt pane of 4 + 2 labels 6.00
203 A63 20c brt vio 1.50 10
204 A63 25c rose red 70 5
a. Tete beche pair 4.00 3.25
c. Bklt pane of 4 + 2 labels 11.00
205 A63 35c green 1.00 12
a. Tete beche pair 6.00 5.00
c. Bklt pane of 4 + 2 labels 13.00
206 A63 40c red vio ('30) 45 5
a. Tete beche pair 5.75 4.25
c. Bklt pane of 4 + 2 labels 13.00
207 A63 50c dp bl 80 5
a. Tete beche pair 4.75 3.50
c. Bklt pane of 4 + 2 labels 11.00
208 A63 60c rose ('30) 1.75 20
a. Tete beche pair 16.00 13.00
c. Bklt pane of 4 + 2 labels 40.00
209 A63 70c org brn ('30) 1.10 5
a. Tete beche pair 11.00 9.00
c. Bklt pane of 4 + 2 labels 30.00
210 A63 75c dk bl ('30) 2.75 10
a. Tete beche pair 16.50 15.00
211 A63 75c dp brn ('32) 13.00 5
a. Tete beche pair 57.50 40.00
b. Bklt pane of 4 + 2 labels 135.00
Nos. 198-211 (14) 23.80 1.37

1929, Jan. 25 Engr. *Perf. 14½, 14*
212 A64 10fr dk brn 14.00 4.50
213 A64 20fr dk grn 90.00 6.00
214 A64 50fr red vio 8.50 6.00
a. Perf. 14½ 20.00 20.00
215 A64 100fr rose lake 11.50 11.50
a. Perf. 14½ 27.50 27.50

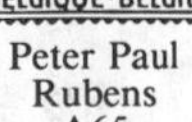

Peter Paul Rubens
A65

Zenobe Gramme
A66

1930, Apr. 26 Photo. *Perf. 12½x12*
216 A65 35c bl grn 65 25
217 A66 35c bl grn 65 25

No. 216 issued for the Antwerp Exhibition, No. 217 the Liege Exhibition.

King Leopold I, by Jacques de Winne
A67

King Leopold II, by Joseph Lempoels
A68

Design: 1.75fr, King Albert I.

1930, July 1 Engr. *Perf. 11½*
218 A67 60c brn vio 30 12
219 A68 1fr carmine 1.50 1.50
220 A68 1.75fr dk bl 3.75 3.75

Centenary of Belgian independence.

Antwerp Exhibition Issue.
Souvenir Sheet.

Arms of Antwerp
A70

1930, Aug. 9 *Perf. 11½*
221 A70 Sheet of one 150.00 200.00
a. 4fr dk grn & gray grn 40.00 60.00

Issued in sheets of one stamp measuring 142x141 mm. Inscription in lower margin "ATELIER DU TIMBRE-1930-ZEGELFABRIEK." Each purchaser of a ticket to the Antwerp Philatelic Exhibition, August 9th to 15th, 1930, was allowed to purchase one of the exhibition stamps. The ticket cost 6 francs.

Nos. 218-220 Overprinted in Blue or Red **B. I. T. OCT. 1930**

1930, Oct.
222 A67 60c brn vio (Bl) 1.75 1.50
223 A68 1fr car (Bl) 8.25 7.50
224 A68 1.75fr dk bl (R) 14.00 14.00

Issued to commemorate the 50th meeting of the administrative council of the International Labor Bureau at Brussels.
The names of the painters and the initials of the engraver have been added at the foot of these stamps.

Stamps of 1929-30 Surcharged in Blue or Black:

≡ 2c ≡
a

b

1931, Feb. 20 *Perf. 14*
225 A63 (a) 2c on 3c red brn (Bl) 12 10
226 A63 (b) 10c on 60c rose (Bk) 90 22

The surcharge on No. 226 is a precancelation which alters the denomination. See note after No. 197.

King Albert
A71 A71a

1931, June 15 Photo.
227 A71 1fr brn car 85 12

1932, June 1
228 A71a 75c bis brn 60 5
a. Tete betche pair 21.00 21.00
c. Bklt pane 4 + 2 labels 27.50

See also No. 257.

A72

1931-32 Engr.
229 A72 1.25fr gray blk 85 35
230 A72 1.50fr brn vio 1.10 30
231 A72 1.75fr dp bl 85 12
232 A72 2fr red brn 1.10 12
233 A72 2.45fr dp vio 1.50 30
234 A72 2.50fr blk brn ('32) 11.50 35
235 A72 5fr dp grn 12.50 90
236 A72 10fr claret 30.00 11.00
Nos. 229-236 (8) 59.40 13.44

Nos. 206 and 209 Surcharged as No. 226, but dated "1932."

1932, Jan. 1
240 A63 10c on 40c red vio 5.25 50
241 A63 10c on 70c org brn 4.00 25

The surcharge on Nos. 240 and 241 is a precancelation which alters the value of the stamps. See note after No. 197.

Gleaner
A73

Mercury
A74

1932, June 1 Typo. *Perf. 13½x14*
245 A73 2c pale grn 20 45
246 A74 5c dp org 20 10
247 A73 10c ol grn 38 5
a. Tete beche pair 8.50 6.75
c. Bklt pane 4 + 2 labels 15.00
248 A74 20c brt vio 80 12
249 A73 25c dp red 80 5
a. Tete beche pair 6.75 6.00
c. Bklt pane 4 + 2 labels 15.00
250 A74 35c dp grn 3.00 10
Nos. 245-250 (6) 5.38 87

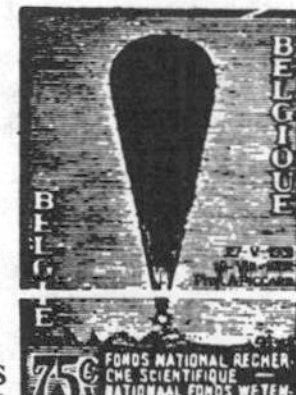

Auguste Piccard's Balloon — A75

1932, Nov. 26 Engr. *Perf. 11½*
251 A75 75c red brn 3.50 30
252 A75 1.75fr dk bl 8.00 1.75
253 A75 2.50fr dk vio 10.50 8.50

Issued in commemoration of Prof. Auguste Piccard's two ascents to the stratosphere.

Nos. 206 and 209 Surcharged as No. 226, but dated "1933."

1933, Nov. *Perf. 14*
254 A63 10c on 40c red vio 22.50 7.00
255 A63 10c on 70c org brn 18.00 2.50

No. 206 Surcharged as No. 226, but dated "1934."

1934, Feb.
256 A63 10c on 40c red vio 13.00 2.50

The surcharge on Nos. 254 to 256 is a precancelation which alters the value of the stamps. See note after No. 197.
Regummed copies of Nos. 254-256 abound.

King Albert Memorial Issue.
Type of 1932 with Black Margins.

1934, Mar. 10 Photo.
257 A71a 75c black 45 8

Certain countries cancel stamps in full sheets and sell them (usually with gum) for less than face value. Dealers generally sell "CTO".

Brussels International Exhibition of 1935.

Congo Pavilion — A76

Designs: 1fr, Brussels pavilion. 1.50fr, "Old Brussels." 1.75fr, Belgian pavilion.

1934, July 1 *Perf. 14x13½*

258	A76	35c green	1.00	10
259	A76	1fr dk car	1.40	25
260	A76	1.50fr brown	3.50	1.10
261	A76	1.75fr blue	8.00	20

King Leopold III
A80 A81

1934-1935 *Perf. 13½x14.*

262	A80	70c ol blk ('35)	45	5
a.		Tete beche pair	2.25	1.25
c.		Bklt pane 4 + 2 labels	7.50	
263	A80	75c brown	90	15

Perf. 14x13½

264	A81	1fr rose car ('35)	4.50	45

Coat of Arms — A82

1935-48 **Typo.** *Perf. 14.*

265	A82	2c grn ('37)	10	5
266	A82	5c orange	10	5
267	A82	10c ol bis	10	5
a.		Tete beche pair	35	30
b.		Bklt pane 4 + 2 labels	6.00	
268	A82	15c dk vio	10	5
269	A82	20c lilac	10	5
270	A82	25c car rose	10	5
a.		Tete beche pair	80	60
c.		Bklt pane 4 + 2 labels	6.00	
271	A82	25c yel org ('46)	25	5
272	A82	30c brown	28	5
273	A82	35c green	12	5
a.		Tete beche pair	35	30
c.		Bklt pane 4 + 2 labels	4.00	
274	A82	40c red vio ('38)	60	5
275	A82	50c blue	28	5
276	A82	60c sl ('41)	18	5
277	A82	65c red lil ('46)	75	5
278	A82	70c lt bl grn ('45)	38	5
279	A82	75c lil rose ('45)	80	5
280	A82	80c grn ('48)	9.00	45
281	A82	90c dl vio ('46)	80	5
282	A82	1fr red brn ('45)	80	5
		Nos. 265-282 (18)	14.84	1.30

Several stamps of type A82 exist in various shades.

Nos. 265, 361 were privately overprinted and surcharged "+10FR." by the Association Belgo-Americaine for the dedication of the Bastogne Memorial, July 16, 1950. The overprint is in six types.

King Leopold III
A83 A83a

Perf. 14, 14x13½, 11½

1936-51 **Photo.**

Size: 17½x21¾ mm.

283	A83	70c brown	55	5
a.		Tete beche pair	2.75	2.00
c.		Bklt pane 4 + 2 labels	10.00	

Size: 20¾x24 mm.

284	A83a	1fr rose car	60	8
285	A83a	1.20fr dk brn ('51)	1.40	5
286	A83a	1.50fr brt red vio ('43)	45	12
287	A83a	1.75fr dp ultra ('43)	20	18
288	A83a	1.75fr dk car ('50)	75	5
289	A83a	2fr dk pur ('43)	90	85
290	A83a	2.25fr grnsh blk ('43)	45	8
291	A83a	2.50fr org red ('51)	4.25	10
292	A83a	3.25fr chnt ('43)	22	5
293	A83a	5fr dp grn ('43)	1.75	40
		Nos. 283-293 (11)	11.52	2.01

Nos. 287-288, 290-291, 293 inscribed "Belgie-Belgique."

King Leopold III
A84 A85

1936-51 **Engr.** *Perf. 14x13½*

294	A84	1.50fr rose lil	90	10
295	A84	1.75fr dl bl	45	5
296	A84	2fr dl vio	90	10
297	A84	2.25fr gray vio ('41)	45	12
298	A84	2.45fr black	45.00	45
299	A84	2.50fr ol blk ('40)	4.50	25
300	A84	3.25fr org brn ('41)	45	12
301	A84	5fr dl grn	3.25	35
302	A84	10fr dk vio brn	1.40	5
303	A84	20fr vermilion	2.75	15

Perf. 11½

304	A84	3fr yel brn ('51)	2.00	5
305	A84	4fr bl, *bluish* ('50)	8.75	10
a.		White paper	19.00	5
306	A84	6fr brt rose car ('51)	8.75	8
307	A84	10fr brn vio ('51)	90	5
308	A84	20fr red ('51)	2.25	6
		Nos. 294-308 (15)	82.70	2.08

See No. 1159.

No. 206 Surcharged as No. 226, but dated "1937."

1937 **Unwmk.** *Perf. 14.*

309	A63	10c on 40c red vio	45	35

The surcharge is a precancelation which alters the value of the stamp. See note after No. 197.

1938-41 **Photo.** *Perf. 13½x14*

310	A85	75c ol gray	80	5
a.		Tete beche pair	3.00	1.65
c.		Bklt pane 4 + 2 labels	9.00	
311	A85	1fr rose pink ('41)	15	5
a.		Tete beche pair	45	30
b.		Booklet pane of 6	3.00	
c.		Bklt pane 4 + 2 labels	3.00	

Nos. 272, 274, 283, 310, 299, 298 Surcharged in Blue, Black, Carmine or Red

= =
10
c
= = 10c.
a b
c ≡ 2F25

1938-42

312	A82 (a)	10c on 30c brn (Bl)	18	12
313	A82 (a)	10c on 40c red vio (Bl)	18	12
314	A83 (b)	10c on 70c brn (Bk)	22	15
315	A85 (b)	50c on 75c ol gray (C)	45	20
316	A84 (c)	2.25fr on 2.50fr ol blk (C)	1.10	90
317	A84 (c)	2.50fr on 2.45fr blk (R)	22.50	35
		Nos. 312-317 (6)	24.63	1.84

Issue date: No. 317, Oct. 31, 1938.

Basilica and Bell Tower — A86
Water Exhibition Buildings — A87

Designs: 1.50fr, Albert Canal and Park. 1.75fr, Eygenbilsen Cut in Albert Canal.

Perf. 14x13½, 13½x14

1938, Oct. 31

318	A86	35c dk bl grn	15	15
319	A87	1fr rose red	90	18
320	A87	1.50fr vio brn	2.25	70
321	A87	1.75fr ultra	2.50	22

Publicity for the International Water Exhibition, Liege, 1939.

Lion Rampant — A90
King Leopold III with Crown and V — A91

1944 **Unwmk.** **Photo.** *Perf. 12½.*

Inscribed: "Belgique-Belgie".

322	A90	5c chocolate	8	5
323	A90	10c green	8	5
324	A90	25c lt bl	8	5
325	A90	35c brown	8	5
326	A90	50c lt bl grn	12	5
327	A90	75c purple	12	12
328	A90	1fr vermilion	8	5
329	A90	1.25fr chestnut	15	22
330	A90	1.50fr orange	40	50
331	A90	1.75fr brt ultra	12	5
332	A90	2fr aqua	3.25	2.50
333	A90	2.75fr dp mag	18	12
334	A90	3fr claret	65	85
335	A90	3.50fr sl blk	65	85
336	A90	5fr dk ol	5.75	6.25
337	A90	10fr black	1.10	1.40
		Nos. 322-337 (16)	12.89	13.16

Inscribed: "Belgie-Belgique".

338	A90	5c chocolate	8	5
339	A90	10c green	8	5
340	A90	25c lt bl	8	5
341	A90	35c brown	8	5
342	A90	50c lt bl grn	12	5
343	A90	75c purple	12	12
344	A90	1fr vermilion	8	5
345	A90	1.25fr chestnut	16	22
346	A90	1.50fr orange	35	50
347	A90	1.75fr brt ultra	15	5
348	A90	2fr aqua	2.25	2.25
349	A90	2.75fr dp mag	20	12
350	A90	3fr claret	75	85
351	A90	3.50fr sl blk	75	85
352	A90	5fr dk ol	6.25	5.50
353	A90	10fr black	1.10	1.40
		Nos. 338-353 (16)	12.60	12.16

1944-57 *Perf. 14x13½*

354	A91	1fr brt rose red	35	6
355	A91	1.50fr magenta	50	6
356	A91	1.75fr dp ultra	50	55
357	A91	2fr dp vio	1.50	8
358	A91	2.25fr grnsh blk	55	65
559	A91	3.25fr chnt brn	75	5
360	A91	5fr dk bl grn	3.00	5
a.		Perf. 11½ ('57)	45.00	10
		Nos. 354-360 (7)	7.15	1.50

Nos. 355, 357, 359 inscribed "Belgique-Belgie."

Stamps of 1935-41 Overprinted in Red

1944 *Perf. 14.*

361	A82	2c pale grn	6	5
362	A82	15c indigo	6	6
363	A82	20c brt vio	10	6
364	A82	60c slate	20	15

See note following No. 282.

Nos. 355, 357, and 360 Surcharged Typographically in Black or Carmine

–10%

1946 *Perf. 14x13½.*

365	A91	On 1.50fr mag	75	10
366	A91	On 2fr dp vio (C)	2.75	65
367	A91	On 5fr dk bl grn (C)	3.75	40

To provide denominations created by a reduction in postal rates, the Government produced Nos. 365-367 by surcharging typographically. Also, each post office was authorized on May 20, 1946, to surcharge its stock of 1.50fr, 2fr and 5fr stamps "-10 percent." Hundreds of types and sizes of this surcharge exist, both hand-stamped and typographed. These include the "1,35", "1,80" and "4,50" applied at Ghislenghien.

M. S. Prince Baudouin — A92

Designs: 2.25fr, S. S. Marie Henriette. 3.15fr, S. S. Diamant.

Perf. 14x13½, 13½x14.

1946, June 15 **Photo.** **Unwmk.**

368	A92	1.35fr brt bluish grn	18	6
369	A92	2.25fr sl grn	45	18
370	A92	3.15fr sl blk	45	25

Centenary of the steamship line between Ostend and Dover.

No. 368 exists in two sizes: 21¼x18¼mm and 21x17mm. Nos. 369-370 are 24½x20mm.

Capt. Adrien de Gerlache — A95
Belgica and Explorers — A96

1947, June *Perf. 14x13½, 11½*

371	A95	1.35fr crim rose	25	6
372	A96	2.25fr gray blk	1.50	1.40

Issued to commemorate the 50th anniversary of Capt. Adrien de Gerlache's Antarctic Expedition.

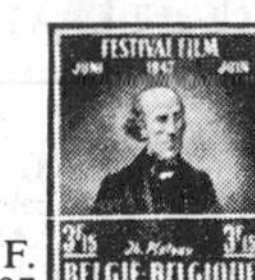

Joseph A. F. Plateau — A97

1947, June *Perf. 14x13½*

373	A97	3.15fr dp bl	60	15

Issued to mark the World Film and Fine Arts Festival, Brussels, June, 1947.

Chemical Industry — A98
Industrial Arts — A99

Agriculture — A100

Communications Center — A101

Textile Industry — A102

Iron Manufacture A103

Photogravure (#374-376, 378), Typographed (#377, 380), Engraved

1948	**Unwmk.**		*Perf. 11½*	
374	A98	60c bl grn	50	15
375	A98	1.20fr brown	1.25	10
376	A99	1.35fr red brn	50	5
377	A100	1.75fr brt red	85	6
378	A99	1.75fr dk gray grn	65	5
379	A101	2.25fr gray bl	1.10	1.10
380	A100	2.50fr dk car rose	4.00	12
381	A101	3fr brt red vio	5.50	18
382	A102	3.15fr dp bl	1.10	15
383	A102	4fr brt ultra	4.75	12
384	A103	6fr bl grn	8.00	12
385	A103	6.30fr brt red vio	2.25	2.50
		Nos. 374-385 (12)	30.45	4.70

King Leopold I — A104

1949, July 1	**Engr.**		*Perf. 14x13½*	
386	A104	90c dk grn	75	60
387	A104	1.75fr brown	60	15
388	A104	3fr red	2.25	3.00
389	A104	4fr dp bl	3.25	1.25

Issued to commemorate the centenary of Belgium's first postage stamps.

See note on souvenir sheet below No. 2.

Stamps of 1935-45 Precanceled and Surcharged in Black

1949			*Perf. 14*	
390	A82	5c on 15c dk vio	8	10
391	A82	5c on 30c brn	8	10
392	A82	5c on 40c red vio	8	10
393	A82	20c on 70c lt bl grn	20	25
394	A82	20c on 75c lil rose	12	10

Similar Surcharge and Precancellation in Black on Nos. B455-B458.

14x13½.

395	SP251	10c on 65 + 35 rose red	3.25	5.75
396	SP251	40c on 90c + 60c gray	90	1.65
397	SP251	80c on 1.35fr + 1.15fr hn brn	60	90
398	SP251	1.20fr on 3.15 + 1.85 brt bl	2.00	2.75
		Nos. 390-398 (9)	7.31	11.70

The surcharges on Nos. 390-398 are combined with the precancellations. See note after No. 197.

St. Mary Magdalene, from Painting by Gerard David — A105

1949, July 15	**Photo.**		*Perf. 11*	
399	A105	1.75fr dk brn	75	35

Issued to publicize the Gerard David Exhibition at Bruges, 1949.

Allegory of U.P.U. A106

1949, Oct. 1	**Engr.**		*Perf. 11½*	
400	A106	4fr dp bl	3.75	3.25

Issued to commemorate the 75th anniversary of the formation of the Universal Postal Union.

Symbolical of Pension Fund A107

Lion Rampant A108

Perf. 11½

1950, May 1	**Unwmk.**		**Photo.**	
401	A107	1.75fr dk brn	50	25

Issued to commemorate the centenary of the foundation of the General Pension Fund.

1951, Feb. 15	**Engr.**		*Perf. 11½*	
402	A108	20c blue	25	8

1951-75	**Typo.**		*Perf. 13½x14*	
		Size: 17½x21mm		
403	A108	2c org brn ('60)	10	5
404	A108	3c brt lil ('60)	10	5
405	A108	5c pale vio	12	5
406	A108	5c brt pink ('74)	15	5
407	A108	10c red org	8	5
408	A108	15c brt pink ('59)	10	5
409	A108	20c claret	5	5
410	A108	25c green	1.50	22
411	A108	25c lt bl grn ('66)	15	5
412	A108	30c gray grn ('57)	12	5
413	A108	40c brn ol	12	5
414	A108	50c ultra	5	5
a.		50c lt bl	12	5
415	A108	60c lil rose	5	5
416	A108	65c vio brn	15.00	55
417	A108	75c bluish lil	30	5
418	A108	80c emerald	1.00	5
419	A108	90c dp bl	1.25	12
420	A108	1fr rose	12	5
421	A108	2fr emer ('73)	30	5
422	A108	2.50fr brn ('70)	30	8
423	A108	3fr brt pink ('70)	30	5
424	A108	4fr brt rose lil ('74)	30	5
425	A108	4.50fr bl ('74)	45	5
426	A108	5fr brt lil ('75)	30	5
		Size: 17x20½mm		
427	A108	1.50fr dk sl grn ('69)	15	10
		Perf. 13½x13		
428	A108	2fr emer ('68)	25	5
		Photo. *Perf. 11½*		
		Size: 20½x24mm		
429	A108	50c lt bl ('61)	1.00	15
430	A108	60c lil rose ('66)	2.25	2.00
431	A108	1fr car rose ('59)	15	5
		Perf. 13½x12½		
		Size: 17½x22mm		
432	A108	50c lt bl ('75)	15	5
a.		Booklet pane of 4 (#432, 784 and 2 #785) + labels	1.00	
b.		Booklet pane of 4 (#432 and 3 #787) + labels	1.35	
433	A108	1fr rose ('69)	9.00	1.50
434	A108	2fr emer ('72)	60	30
e.		Booklet pane of 6 (4 #434 + 2 #475)	5.50	
f.		Booklet pane of 5 (#434, 4 #476 + label)	8.00	
		Nos. 403-434 (32)	35.86	6.17

Counterfeits exist of No. 416. Nos. 429, 431 also issued in coils with black control number on back of every fifth stamp. Nos. 432-434 issued in booklet panes only. No. 432 has one straightedge, and stamps in the pane are tete-beche. Each pane has 2 labels showing Belgian postal emblem and a large selvage with postal code instructions.

Nos. 433-434 have 1 or 2 straight-edges. Panes have a large selvage with inscription or map of Belgium showing postal zones.

Francois de Tassis (Franz von Taxis) — A109

Portraits: 1.75fr, Jean-Baptiste of Thurn & Taxis. 2fr, Baron Leonard I. 2.50fr, Count Lamoral I. 3fr, Count Leonard II. 4fr, Count Lamoral II. 5fr, Prince Eugene Alexander. 5.75fr, Prince Anselme Francois. 8fr, Prince Alexander Ferdinand. 10fr, Prince Charles Anselme. 20fr, Prince Charles Alexander.

Inscribed: "Congres 1952 U.P.U." etc.

1952, May 14	**Engr.**		*Perf. 11½*	
		Laid Paper.		
435	A109	80c ol grn	75	90
436	A109	1.75fr red org	75	30
437	A109	2fr vio brn	1.50	50
438	A109	2.50fr carmine	2.00	1.50
439	A109	3fr ol bis	1.90	90
440	A109	4fr ultra	2.75	75
441	A109	5fr red brn	3.75	1.65
442	A109	5.75fr bl vio	6.25	2.00
443	A109	8fr gray	9.75	2.50
444	A109	10fr rose vio	17.00	4.00
445	A109	20fr brown	42.50	21.00
		Nos. 435-445 (11)	88.90	36.00

Issued on the occasion of the 13th Universal Postal Union Congress, Brussels, 1952. See No. B514.

A110

King Baudouin — A111

1952-58	**Engr.**		*Perf. 11½*	
		Size: 21x24mm		
446	A110	1.50fr gray	55	8
447	A110	2fr crimson	42	5
448	A110	4fr ultra	3.50	30
		Size: 24½x35mm		
449	A110	50fr gray brn	1.75	30
a.		50fr vio brn	20.00	90
450	A110	100fr rose red ('58)	5.00	35

1953-72	**Photo.**		*Perf. 11½*	
451	A111	1.50fr gray	25	5
452	A111	2fr rose car	6.75	5
453	A111	2fr green	25	5
454	A111	2.50fr red brn ('57)	60	5
a.		2.50fr org brn ('70)	45	5
455	A111	3fr rose lil ('58)	38	5
456	A111	3.50fr brt yel grn ('58)	75	5
457	A111	4fr brt ultra	50	5
458	A111	4.50fr dk red brn ('62)	3.00	5
459	A111	5fr vio ('57)	1.25	5
460	A111	6fr dp pink ('58)	75	5
461	A111	6.50fr gray ('60)	60.00	17.00
462	A111	7fr bl ('60)	90	5
463	A111	7.50fr grysh brn ('58)	42.50	20.00
464	A111	8fr bluish gray ('58)	1.25	8
465	A111	8.50fr cl ('58)	15.00	45
466	A111	9fr gray ('58)	45.00	1.10
467	A111	12fr lt bl grn ('66)	90	15
468	A111	30fr red org ('58)	5.50	15
		Redrawn		
469	A111	2.50fr org brn ('71)	35	7
470	A111	4.50fr brn ('72)	2.25	90
471	A111	7fr bl ('71)	60	12
		Perf. 13½x12½		
		Size: 17½x22mm.		
472	A111	1.50fr gray ('70)	60	45
b.		Bklt pane of 10	8.50	
c.		Bklt. pane of 6 (3 #472 + 3 #475)	20.00	
473	A111	2.50fr org brn ('70)	9.00	9.00
h.		Bklt. pane of 6 (#473 + 5 #475)	22.50	
474	A111	3fr lil rose ('69)	60	15
a.		Bklt pane of 5 + label	35.00	
b.		Bklt pane of 8 (2 #433 + 6 #474)	25.00	
475	A111	3.50fr brt yel grn ('70)	60	35
476	A111	4.50fr dl red brn ('72)	75	60
		Nos. 446-476 (31)	211.50	52.20

Nos. 451, 453, 454a, 455, 456, 458 also issued in coils with black control number on back of every fifth stamp. These coils, except for No. 451, are on luminescent paper.

On Nos. 469-471, the 2, 4 and 7 are 3mm high. The background around the head is white. On Nos. 454, 458, 462 the 2, 4 and 7 are 2½mm high and the background is tinted.

Nos. 472-476 issued in booklets only and have 1 or 2 straight-edges. All panes have a large selvage with inscription or map.

Luminescent Paper

Stamps issued on both ordinary and luminescent paper include: Nos. 307-308, 430-431, 449-451, 453-460, 462, 464, 467-468, 472, 643-644, 650-651, 837, Q385, Q410.

Stamps issued only on luminescent paper include: Nos. 433, 454a, 472b, 473-474, 649, 652-658, 664-670, 679-682, 688-690, 694-696, 698-703, 705-711, 713-726, 729-747, 751-754, 756-757, 759, 761-762, 764, 766, 769, 772, 774, 778, 789, 791-793, 795, 797-799, 801-807, 809-811, 814-818, 820-834, 836, 838-848.

See note after No. 857.

Nos. 396 and 398 Surcharged and Precanceled in Black

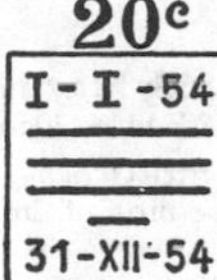

1954, Jan. 1	**Unwmk.**		*Perf. 13½x14*	
477	A108	20c on 65c vio brn	1.75	65
478	A108	20c on 90c dp bl	1.75	45

The surcharge is combined with the precancellation. See note after No. 197.

Map and Rotary Emblem A112

Designs: 80c, Mermaid and Mercury holding emblem. 4fr, Rotary emblem and two globes.

1954, Sept. 10	**Engr.**		*Perf. 11½*	
479	A112	20c red	25	25
480	A112	80c dk grn	65	50
481	A112	4fr ultra	1.40	75

5th regional conf. of Rotary International at Ostend. No. 481 for Rotary 50th Anniv. (in 1955).

A souv. sheet containing one each, imperf., was sold for 500 francs. It was not valid for postage.

The Rabot and Begonia — A113

Designs: 2.50fr, The Oudeburg and azalea. 4fr, "Three Towers" and orchid.

1955, Feb. 15 **Photo.**

482 A113	80c brt car	75	55
483 A113	2.50fr blk brn	4.50	5.50
484 A113	4fr dk rose brn	4.00	1.75

Issued to publicize the Ghent International Flower Exhibition, 1955.

Homage to Charles V as a Child, by Albrecht de Vriendt A114

Charles V, by Titian A115

Design: 4fr, Abdication of Charles V, by Louis Gallait.

1955, Mar. 25 Unwmk. ***Perf. 11½***

485 A114	20c rose red	18	25
486 A115	2fr dk gray grn	1.65	10
487 A114	4fr blue	4.50	1.65

Issued to publicize the Charles V Exhibition, Ghent, 1955.

Emile Verhaeren, by Montald Constant — A116

1955, May 11 **Engr.**

488 A116	20c dk gray	18	8

Issued to commemorate the centenary of the birth of Emile Verhaeren, poet.

Allegory of Textile Manufacture A117

1955, May 11

489 A117	2fr vio brn	1.25	18

Issued to publicize the second International Textile Exhibition, Brussels, June 1955.

"The Foolish Virgin" by Rik Wouters A118

"Departure of Volunteers from Liege, 1830" by Charles Soubre A119

1955, June 10

490 A118	1.20fr ol grn	1.00	1.10
491 A118	2fr violet	1.50	15

Issued to publicize the third biennial exhibition of sculpture, Antwerp, June 11-Sept. 10, 1955.

1955, Sept. 10 **Photo.**

492 A119	20c grnsh sl	18	25
493 A119	2fr chocolate	90	22

Issued to publicize the exhibition "The Romantic Movement in Liege Province," Sept. 10-Oct. 31, 1955; and to mark the 125th anniversary of Belgium's independence from the Netherlands.

Pelican Giving Blood to Young A120

Buildings of Tournai, Ghent and Antwerp A121

1956, Jan. 14 **Engr.**

494 A120	2fr brt car	55	18

Issued in honor of the blood donor service of the Belgian Red Cross.

1956, July 14 **Photo.**

495 A121	2fr brt ultra	38	18

Issued to publicize the Scheldt exhibition (Scaldis) at Tournai, Ghent and Antwerp, July-Sept. 1956.

Europa Issue.

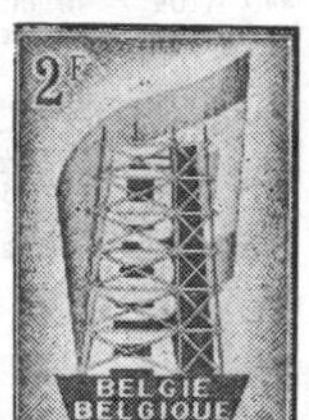
"Rebuilding Europe" — A122

1956, Sept. 15 **Engr.**

496 A122	2fr lt grn	1.75	15
497 A122	4fr purple	8.00	1.00

Issued to symbolize the cooperation among the six countries comprising the Coal and Steel Community.

Train on Map of Belgium and Luxembourg A123

1956, Sept. 29

498 A123	2fr dk bl	60	18

Issued to mark the electrification of the Brussels-Luxembourg railroad.

Edouard Anseele A124

"The Atom" and Exposition Emblem A125

1956, Oct. 27

499 A124	20c vio brn	12	6

Issued to commemorate the centenary of the birth of Edouard Anseele, statesman, and in connection with an exhibition held in his honor at Ghent.

1957-58 **Unwmk.**

500 A125	2fr car rose	45	12
501 A125	2.50fr grn ('58)	60	18
502 A125	4fr brt vio bl	1.50	38
503 A125	5fr cl ('58)	1.25	1.00

Issued to publicize the 1958 World's Fair at Brussels.

Emperor Maximilian I Receiving Letter — A126

1957, May 19

504 A126	2fr claret	55	15

Issued for the Day of the Stamp, May 19, 1957.

Sikorsky S-58 Helicopter A127

1957, June 15

505 A127	4fr gray grn & brt bl	90	80

Issued to publicize the 100,000th passenger carried by Sabena helicopter service, June 15, 1957.

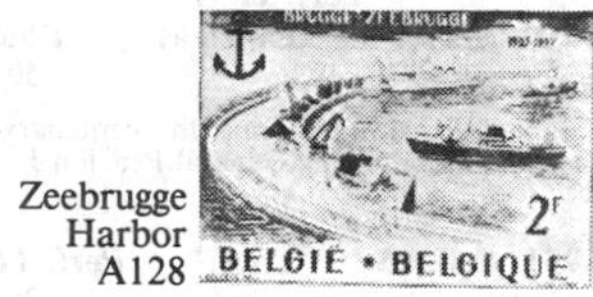
Zeebrugge Harbor A128

1957, July 6

506 A128	2fr dk bl	55	15

Issued to commemorate the 50th anniversary of the completion of the port of Zeebrugge-Bruges.

Leopold I Entering Brussels, 1831 — A129

Leopold I Arriving at Belgian Border A130

1957, July 17 **Photo.**

507 A129	20c dk gray grn	8	12
508 A130	2fr lilac	75	30

Issued to commemorate the 126th anniversary of the arrival in Belgium of King Leopold I.

Boy Scout and Girl Scout Emblems A131

Design: 4fr, Robert Lord Baden-Powell, painted by David Jaggers (vert.).

Perf. 11½

1957, July 29 **Unwmk.** **Engr.**

509 A131	80c gray	38	25
510 A131	4fr lt grn	1.50	75

Issued to commemorate the centenary of the birth of Lord Baden-Powell, founder of the Boy Scout movement.

"Kneeling Woman" by Lehmbruck A132

"United Europe" A133

1957, Aug. 20 **Photo.**

511 A132	2.50fr dk bl grn	1.50	2.00

Issued to commemorate the fourth Biennial Exposition of Sculpture, Antwerp, May 25-Sept. 15.

Europa Issue, 1957.

1957, Sept. 16 **Engr.** ***Perf. 11½***

512 A133	2fr dk vio brn	1.25	25
513 A133	4fr dk bl	2.50	75

Issued to publicize a united Europe for peace and prosperity.

Queen Elisabeth Assisting at Operation, by Allard L'Olivier A134

Perf. 11½

1957, Nov. 23 **Unwmk.** **Engr.**

514 A134	30c rose lil	15	10

Issued to commemorate the 50th anniversary of the founding of the Edith Cavell-Marie Depage and St. Camille schools of nursing.

Post Horn and Historic Postal Insignia A135

1958, Mar. 16 **Photo.** ***Perf. 11½***

515 A135	2.50fr gray	30	15

Postal Museum Day.

United Nations Issue

International Labor Organization A136

Allegory of U. N. — A137

Designs: 1fr, Food and Agriculture Organization. 2fr, World Bank. 2.50fr, UNESCO. 3fr, U. N. Pavilion. 5fr, International Telecommunication Union. 8fr, International Monetary Fund. 11fr, World Health Organization. 20fr, U. P. U.

Perf. 11½

1958, Apr. 17 Unwmk. Engr.

516 A136 50c gray 80 1.40
517 A136 1fr claret 25 45
518 A137 1.50fr dp ultra 25 45
519 A137 2fr gray brn 75 1.25
520 A136 2.50fr ol grn 25 45
521 A136 3fr grnsh bl 75 1.25
522 A137 5fr rose lil 50 90
523 A136 8fr red brn 90 1.65
524 A136 11fr dl lil 1.10 2.00
525 A136 20fr car rose 1.50 2.50
Nos. 516-525 (10) 7.05 12.30

World's Fair, Brussels, Apr. 17-Oct. 19. See Nos. C15-C20.

Postally valid only from the UN pavilion at the Brussels Fair. Proceeds went toward financing the UN exhibits.

Eugène Ysaye A138

1958, Sept. 1

526 A138 30c dk bl & plum 12 8

Issued to commemorate the centenary of the birth of Eugene Ysaye (1858-1931), violinist and composer.

Europa Issue, 1958

Common Design Type

1958, Sept. 13 Photo.

Size: 24½x35mm.

527 CD1 2.50fr brt red & bl 22 6
528 CD1 5fr brt bl & red 38 45

Issued to show the European Postal Union at the service of European integration.

Infant and U. N. Emblem A140

Charles V and Jean-Baptiste of Thurn and Taxis A141

1958, Dec. 10 Engr.

529 A140 2.50fr bl gray 38 10

Issued to commemorate the tenth anniversary of the signing of the Universal Declaration of Human Rights.

1959, Mar. 15 Unwmk.

530 A141 2.50fr green 60 15

Issued for the Day of the Stamp. Design from painting by J.-E. van den Bussche.

NATO Emblem A142

City Hall, Audenarde A143

1959, Apr. 3 Photo. *Perf. 11½*

531 A142 2.50fr dp red & dk bl 60 15
532 A142 5fr emer & dk bl 1.65 1.90

Issued to commemorate the 10th anniversary of the North Atlantic Treaty Organization.

See No. 720.

1959, Aug. 17 Engr.

533 A143 2.50fr dp cl 45 6

Pope Adrian VI, by Jan van Scorel — A144

1959, Aug. 31 *Perf. 11½*

534 A144 2.50fr dk red 30 10
535 A144 5fr Prus bl 85 85

Issued to commemorate the 500th anniversary of the birth of Pope Adrian VI.

Europa Issue, 1959

Common Design Type

1959, Sept. 19 Photo.

Size: 24 x 35½mm.

536 CD2 2.50fr dk red 20 12
537 CD2 5fr brt grnsh bl 45 55

No. 536 inscribed Belgie-Belgique.

Boeing 707 — A146

Engraved and Photogravure

1959, Dec. 1 *Perf. 11½*

538 A146 6fr dk bl gray & car 1.90 1.25

Issued to commemorate the inauguration of jet flights by Sabena Airlines.

Countess of Taxis — A147

Indian Azalea — A148

1960, Mar. 21 Engr. *Perf. 11½*

539 A147 3fr dk bl 1.50 15

Issued to honor Alexandrine de Rye, Countess of Taxis, Grand Mistress of the Netherlands Posts, 1628-1645, and to publicize the day of the stamp, March 21, 1960. The painting of the Countess is by Nicholas van der Eggermans.

1960, Mar. 28 Unwmk.

Flowers: 3fr, Begonia. 6fr, Anthurium and bromelia.

540 A148 40c dl vio & dp car 32 15
541 A148 3fr emer, red & org yel 1.25 15
542 A148 6fr dk bl, grn & brt red 1.40 1.25

Issued to publicize the 24th Ghent International Flower Exhibition, Apr. 23-May 2, 1960.

Steel Workers, by Constantin Meunier — A149

Design: 3fr, The sower, field and dock workers, from "Monument to Labor," Brussels, by Constantin Meunier (horiz.).

Engraved and Photogravure

1960, Apr. 30 *Perf. 11½*

543 A149 40c cl & brt red 28 15
544 A149 3fr brn & brt red 1.65 55

Issued to commemorate the 75th anniversary of the Socialist Party of Belgium.

Congo River Boat Pilot — A150

Designs: 40c, Medical team. 1fr, Planting tree. 2fr, Sculptors. 2.50fr, Shot put. 3fr, Congolese officials. 6fr, Congolese and Belgian girls playing with doll. 8fr, Boy pointing on globe to independent Congo.

1960, June 30 Photo. *Perf. 11½*

Size: 35x24mm.

545 A150 10c brt red 45 15
546 A150 40c rose cl 65 20
547 A150 1fr brt lil 1.25 90
548 A150 2fr gray grn 1.40 1.10
549 A150 2.50fr blue 1.25 90
550 A150 3fr dk bl gray 1.50 60

Size: 51x35mm.

551 A150 6fr vio bl 4.50 2.25
552 A150 8fr dk brn 7.50 5.00
Nos. 545-552 (8) 18.50 11.10

Independence of Congo.

Europa Issue, 1960

Common Design Type

1960, Sept. 17

Size: 35x24½mm.

553 CD3 3fr claret 1.00 15
554 CD3 6fr gray 2.00 65

Children Examining Stamp and Globe A152

H. J. W. Frère-Orban A153

1960, Oct. 1 Photo. *Perf. 11½*

555 A152 40c bis & blk + label 18 15

Issued to promote stamp collecting among children. Issued in sheets of 30 with alternating label. Label shows post horn and inscription in Flemish and French.

Engraved and Photogravure

1960, Oct. 17 Unwmk.

Portrait in Brown

556 A153 10c org yel 15 15
557 A153 40c bl grn 15 15
558 A153 1.50fr brt vio 1.10 1.10
559 A153 3fr red 1.65 15

Centenary of Communal Credit Society.

Common Design Types pictured in section at front of book.

King Baudouin and Queen Fabiola A154

1960, Dec. 13 Photo. *Perf. 11½*

Portraits in Dark Brown

560 A154 40c green 15 15
561 A154 3fr red lil 45 15
562 A154 6fr dl bl 2.00 1.00

Issued to commemorate the wedding of King Baudouin and Dona Fabiola de Mora y Aragon, Dec. 15, 1960.

Nos. 412, 414 Surcharged

1961-68 Typo. *Perf. 13½x14*

563 A108 15c on 30c gray grn 35 8
564 A108 15c on 50c bl ('68) 15 5
565 A108 20c on 30c gray grn 35 15

No. 412 Surcharged and Precanceled

1961

566 A108 15c on 30c gray grn 1.50 12
567 A108 20c on 30c gray grn 3.25 2.25

The surcharges are combined with the precancellations. See note after No. 197.

Nicolaus Rockox, by Anthony Van Dyck — A155

Seal of Jan Bode, Alderman of Antwerp, 1264 — A156

Engraved and Photogravure

1961, Mar. 18 *Perf. 11½*

568 A155 3fr bis, blk & brn 45 15

Issued to commemorate the 400th anniversary of the birth of Nicolaus Rockox, mayor of Antwerp.

1961, Apr. 16 Photo.

569 A156 3fr buff & brn 45 15

Issued for Stamp Day, April 16.

Senate Building, Brussels, Laurel and Sword A157

Engraved and Photogravure

1961, Sept. 14 Unwmk. ***Perf. 11½***

570 A157 3fr brn & Prus grn 30 12
571 A157 6fr dk brn & dk car 1.75 1.75

Issued to commemorate the 50th Conference of the Interparliamentary Union, Brussels, Sept. 14-22.

Europa Issue, 1961
Common Design Type

1961, Sept. 16 Photo.
Size: 35x25½mm.

572 CD4 3fr yel grn & dk grn 20 10
573 CD4 6fr org brn & blk 30 25

Atomic Reactor Plant, BR2, Mol — A159

Designs: 3fr, Atomic Reactor BR3 (vert.). 6fr, Atomic Reactor plant BR3.

1961, Nov. 8 Unwmk. ***Perf. 11½***

574 A159 40c dk bl grn 15 10
575 A159 3fr red lil 20 6
576 A159 6fr brt bl 40 30

Issued to publicize the atomic nuclear research center at Mol.

Horta Museum — A160

1962, Feb. 15 Engr.

577 A160 3fr red brn 30 10

Issued to honor Baron Victor Horta (1861-1947), architect.

Postrider, 16th Century A161

Engraved and Photogravure

1962, March 25 ***Perf. 11½***
Chalky Paper

578 A161 3fr brn & sl grn 30 15

Stamp Day. See No. 677.

Gerard Mercator A162

Bro. Alexis-Marie Gochet A163

Engraved and Photogravure

1962, Apr. 14 Unwmk.

579 A162 3fr sep & gray 30 15

Issued to commemorate the 450th anniversary of the birth of Mercator (Gerhard Kremer, 1512-1594), geographer and map maker.

1962, May 19 Engr. ***Perf. 11½***

Portrait: 3fr, Canon Pierre-Joseph Triest.

580 A163 2fr dk bl 30 18
581 A163 3fr gldn brn 30 10

Issued to honor Brother Alexis-Marie Gochet (1835-1910), geographer and educator, and Canon Pierre-Joseph Triest (1760-1836), educator and founder of hospitals and orphanages.

Europa Issue, 1962
Common Design Type

1962, Sept. 15 Photo.
Size: 35x24mm.

582 CD5 3fr dp car, cit & blk 30 10
583 CD5 6fr ol, cit & blk 45 45

Hand with Barbed Wire and Freed Hand — A165

Engraved and Photogravure

1962, Sept. 16

584 A165 40c lt bl & blk 15 6

Issued in memory of concentration camp victims.

Adam, by Michelangelo, Broken Chain and U.N. Emblem A166

1962, Nov. 24 ***Perf. 11½***

585 A166 3fr gray & blk 30 15
586 A166 6fr lt redsh brn & dk brn 60 45

Issued to publicize the U.N. Declaration of Human Rights.

Henri Pirenne — A167

1963, Jan. 15 Engr.

587 A167 3fr ultra 30 15

Issued to commemorate the centenary of the birth of Henri Pirenne (1862-1935), historian.

Swordsmen and Ghent Belfry A168

Designs: 3fr, Modern fencers. 6fr, Arms of the Royal and Knightly Guild of St. Michael (vert.).

Engraved and Photogravure

1963, Mar. 23 Unwmk. ***Perf. 11½***

588 A168 1fr brn red & pale bl 15 15
589 A168 3fr dk vio & yel grn 25 10
590 A168 6fr gray, blk, red, bl & gold 45 45

Issued to commemorate the 350th anniversary of the granting of a charter to the Ghent guild of fencers.

Stagecoach A169

1963, Apr. 7

591 A169 3fr gray & ocher 30 10

Stamp Day. See No. 678.

Hotel des Postes, Paris, Stagecoach and Stamp, 1863 A170

Perf. 11½

1963, May 7 Unwmk. Engr.

592 A170 6fr dk brn, gray & yel grn 45 45

Issued to commemorate the centenary of the first International Postal Conference, Paris, 1863.

"Peace," Child in Rye Field — A171

Engraved and Photogravure

1963, May 8

593 A171 3fr grn, blk, yel & brn 20 12
594 A171 6fr buff, blk, brn & org 40 30

Issued to publicize the May 8th Movement for Peace. (On May 8, 1945, World War II ended in Europe).

Allegory and Shields of 17 Member Nations A172

1963, June 13 Unwmk. ***Perf. 11½***

595 A172 6fr bl & blk 45 35

10th anniversary of the Conference of European Transport Ministers.

Seal of Union of Belgian Towns — A173

1963, June 17

596 A173 6fr grn, red, blk & gold 45 45

50th anniversary of the International Union of Municipalities.

Caravelle over Brussels National Airport A174

Photogravure and Engraved

1963, Sept. 1 Unwmk. ***Perf. 11½***

597 A174 3fr grn & gray 30 15

40th anniversary of SABENA airline.

Europa Issue, 1963
Common Design Type

1963, Sept. 14 Photo.
Size: 35x24mm.

598 CD6 3fr blk, dl red & lt brn 90 12
599 CD6 6fr blk, lt bl & lt brn 2.50 50

Jules Destree A176

Design: No. 601, Henry Van de Velde.

Perf. 11½

1963, Nov. 16 Unwmk. Engr.

600 A176 1fr rose lil 15 12
601 A176 1fr green 15 12

Issued to commemorate the centenary of the birth of Jules Destree (1863-1936), statesman and founder of the Royal Academy of French Language and Literature (No. 600), and of Henry Van de Velde (1863-1957), architect (No. 601).

No. 600 incorrectly inscribed "1864."

Development of the Mail, Bas-relief A177

Engraved and Photogravure

1963, Nov. 23

602 A177 50c dl red, sl & blk 15 7

50th anniversary of the establishment of postal checking service.

Dr. Armauer G. Hansen A178

Designs: 2fr, Leprosarium. 5fr, Father Joseph Damien.

1964, Jan. 25 Unwmk. ***Perf. 11½***

603 A178 1fr brn org & blk 15 15
604 A178 2fr brn org & blk 30 15
605 A178 5fr brn org & blk 45 35
a. Souvenir sheet of 3 1.90 1.90

Fight against leprosy. No. 605a contains one each of Nos. 603-605. Size: 137x97mm. Sold for 12fr.

Andreas Vesalius — A179

Jules Boulvin A180

Design: 2fr, Henri Jaspar.

Engraved and Photogravure

1964, March 2 Unwmk. ***Perf. 11½***

606 A179 50c pale grn & blk 15 7
607 A180 1fr pale grn & blk 15 10
608 A180 2fr pale grn & blk 25 15

Issued to commemorate 400th anniversary of the death of Andreas Vesalius (1514-64), anatomist (50c); honor Jules Boulvin (1855-1920), mechanical engineer (1fr) and to commemorate the 25th anniversary of the death of Henri Jaspar (1870-1939), statesman and lawyer (2fr).

Postilion of Liège, 1830-40 — A181

1964, Apr. 5 Engr. *Perf. 11½*

609 A181 3fr black 30 6

Issued for Stamp Day 1964.

Arms of Ostend A182

1964, May 16 Photo.

610 A182 3fr ultra, ver, gold & blk 30 6

Millennium of Ostend.

Flame, Hammer and Globe — A183

Designs: 1fr, "SI" and globe. 2fr, Flame over wavy lines.

1964, July 18 Unwmk. *Perf. 11½*

611 A183 50c dk bl & red 15 10
612 A183 1fr dk bl & red 15 12
613 A183 2fr dk bl & red 15 15

Issued to commemorate the centenary of the First Socialist International, founded in London, Sept. 28, 1864.

Europa Issue, 1964
Common Design Type

1964, Sept. 12 Photo. *Perf. 11½*
Size: 24x35½mm.

614 CD7 3fr yel grn, dk car & gray 30 15
615 CD7 6fr car rose, yel grn & bl 45 45

Benelux Issue

King Baudouin, Queen Juliana and Grand Duchess Charlotte — A185

1964, Oct. 12

616 A185 3fr ol, lt grn & mar 30 10

Issued to commemorate the 20th anniversary of the customs union of Belgium, Netherlands and Luxembourg.

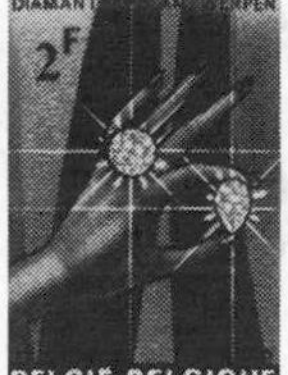

Hand, Round and Pear-shaped Diamonds A186

Symbols of Textile Industry A187

1965, Jan. 23 Unwmk. *Perf. 11½*

617 A186 2fr ultra, dp car & blk 15 15

Issued to publicize the Diamond Exhibition "Diamantexpo," Antwerp, July 10-28, 1965.

1965, Jan. 25 Photo.

618 A187 1fr bl, red & blk 18 18

Issued to publicize the eighth textile industry exhibition "Textirama," Ghent, Jan. 29-Feb. 2, 1965.

Vriesia A188

Paul Hymans A189

Designs: 2fr, Echinocactus. 3fr, Stapelia.

Engraved and Photogravure

1965, Feb. 13

619 A188 1fr multi 15 15
620 A188 2fr multi 15 15
621 A188 3fr multi 15 15
a. Souv. sheet of 3 1.75 1.75

Issued to publicize the 25th Ghent International Flower Exhibition, Apr. 24-May 3, 1965.

No. 621a contains one each of Nos. 619-621, and was issued Apr. 26. It carries the UNRWA and Belgian Postal emblems in the margin. Sold for 20fr.

1965, Feb. 24 Engr. *Perf. 11½*

622 A189 1fr dl pur 15 7

Issued to commemorate the centenary of the birth of Paul Hymans (1865-1941), Belgian Foreign Minister and first president of the League of Nations.

Peter Paul Rubens A190

Sir Rowland Hill as Philatelist A191

Portraits: 2fr, Frans Snyders. 3fr, Adam van Noort. 6fr, Anthony Van Dyck. 8fr, Jacob Jordaens.

Photogravure and Engraved

1965, Mar. 15

Portraits in Sepia

623 A190 1fr car rose 15 15
624 A190 2fr bl grn 15 15
625 A190 3fr plum 15 15
626 A190 6fr dp car 30 15
627 A190 8fr dk bl 45 45
Nos. 623-627 (5) 1.20 1.05

Issued to commemorate the founding of the General Savings and Pensions Bank.

1965, Mar. 27 Engr. *Perf. 11½*

628 A191 50c bl grn 15 7

Issued to publicize youth philately. The design is from a mural by J. E. Van den Bussche in the General Post Office, Brussels.

Postmaster, c. 1833 — A192

Telephone, Globe and Teletype Paper — A193

Staircase, Affligem Abbey — A194

1965, Apr. 26 Unwmk. *Perf. 11½*

629 A192 3fr emerald 25 7

Issued for Stamp Day.

1965, May 8 Photo.

630 A193 2fr dl pur & blk 15 15

Issued to commemorate the centenary of the International Telecommunication Union.

1965, May 27 Engr.

631 A194 1fr gray bl 15 10

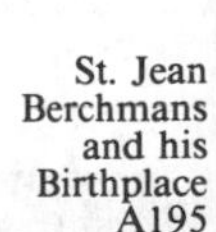

St. Jean Berchmans and his Birthplace A195

Engraved and Photogravure

1965, May 27

632 A195 2fr dk brn & red brn 15 12

Issued to honor St. Jean Berchmans (1599-1621), Jesuit "Saint of the Daily Life."

TOC H Lamp and Arms of Poperinge A196

Farmer with Tractor A197

1965, June 19 Photo. *Perf. 11½*

633 A196 3fr ol bis, blk & car 25 7

Issued to commemorate the 50th anniversary of the founding of Talbot House in Poperinge, which served British soldiers in World War I, and where the TOC H Movement began (Christian Social Service; TOC H is army code for Poperinge Center).

Engraved and Photogravure

1965, July 17 Unwmk. *Perf. 11½*

Design: 3fr, Farmer with horse-drawn roller.

634 A197 50c bl, ol, bis brn & blk 15 10
635 A197 3fr bl, ol grn, ol & blk 22 10

Issued to commemorate the 75th anniversary of the Belgian Farmers' Association (Boerenbond).

Europa Issue, 1965
Common Design Type

1965, Sept. 25 *Perf. 11½*
Size: 35½x24mm.

636 CD8 1fr dl rose & blk 15 12
637 CD8 3fr grnsh gray & blk 18 12

King Leopold I — A199

Joseph Lebeau — A200

1965, Nov. 13 Engr.

638 A199 3fr sepia 30 10
639 A199 6fr brt vio 45 45

Issued to commemorate the centenary of the death of King Leopold I (1790-1865). The designs of the vignettes are similar to the 30c and 1fr of 1865.

1965, Nov. 13 Photo.

640 A200 1fr multi 15 12

Issued to commemorate the centenary of the death of Joseph Lebeau (1794-1865), Foreign Minister.

Tourist Issue

Grapes and Houses, Hoeilaart A201

Bridge and Castle, Huy A202

Designs: No. 643, British War Memorial, Ypres. No. 644, Castle Spontin. No. 645, City Hall, Louvain. No. 646, Ourthe Valley. No. 647, Romanesque Cathedral, gothic fountain, Nivalles. No. 648, Water mill, Kasterlee. No. 649, City Hall, Cloth Guild and Statue of Margarethe of Austria, Malines. No. 650, Town Hall, Lier. No. 651, Castle Bouillon. No. 652, Fountain and Kursaal Spa. No. 653, Windmill, Bokrijk. No. 654, Mountain road, Vielsalm. No. 655, View of Furnes. No. 656, City Hall and Belfry, Mons. No. 657, St. Martin's Church, Aalst. No. 658, Abbey and fountain, St. Hubert.

1965-71 Engr. *Perf. 11½*

641 A201 50c vio bl, lt bl & yel grn 15 7
642 A202 50c sl grn, lt bl & red brn 15 7
643 A202 1fr grn, lt bl, sal & brn 15 5
644 A202 1fr ind, lt bl & ol 15 5
645 A201 1fr brt rose lil, lt bl & blk 15 7
646 A202 1fr blk, grnsh bl & ol 15 8
647 A201 1.50fr sl, sky bl & bis 15 10

648 A202 1.50fr blk, bl & ol 15 10
649 A202 1.50fr dk bl & buff 18 8
650 A201 2fr brn, lt bl & ind 18 8
651 A202 2fr dk brn, grn & ocher 18 8
652 A202 2fr bl, brt grn & blk 15 10
653 A202 2fr blk, lt bl & yel 15 10
654 A202 2fr blk, lt bl & yel grn 15 12
655 A202 2fr car, lt bl & dk brn 15 12
656 A201 2.50fr vio, buff & blk 18 8
657 A201 2.50fr vio, lt bl, blk & ol 25 8
658 A201 2.50fr vio bl & yel 25 8
Nos. 641-658 (18) 3.02 1.51

Issue dates: Nos. 641-642, Nov. 13, 1965; Nos. 643-644, July 15, 1967; Nos. 645-646, Dec. 16, 1968; Nos. 647-648, July 6, 1970; Nos. 649, 656, Dec. 11, 1971; Nos. 650-651, Nov. 11, 1966; Nos. 652-653, June 24, 1968; Nos. 654-655, Sept. 6, 1969; Nos. 657-658, Sept. 11, 1971.

Queen Elisabeth Type of Semi-Postal Issue, 1956

1965, Dec. 23 Photo. *Perf. 11½*
659 SP305 3fr dk gray 30 12

Issued in memory of Queen Elisabeth (1876-1965).

A dark frame has been added in design of No. 659; 1956 date has been changed to 1965; inscription in bottom panel is Koningin Elisabeth Reine Elisabeth 3F.

"Peace on Earth" A203

Arms of Pope Paul VI A204

Rural Mailman, 19th Century A205

Design: 1fr, "Looking toward a Better Future" (family, new buildings, sun and landscape).

1966, Feb. 12 Photo. *Perf. 11½*
660 A203 50c multi 15 10
661 A203 1fr ocher, blk & bl 15 12
662 A204 3fr gray, gold, car & blk 18 15

Issued to commemorate the 75th anniversary of the encyclical by Pope Leo XIII "Rerum Novarum," which proclaimed the general principles for the organization of modern industrial society.

1966, Apr. 17 Photo. Unwmk.
663 A205 3fr blk, dl yel & pale lil 18 7

Issued for Stamp Day 1966.

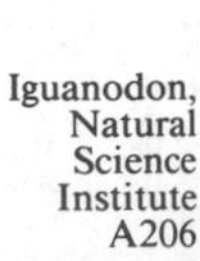

Iguanodon, Natural Science Institute A206

Arend-Roland Comet, Observatory — A207

Designs: No. 665, Ancestral head and spiral pattern, Kasai; Central Africa Museum. No. 666, Snowflakes, Meteorological Institute. No. 667, Seal of Charles V, Royal Archives. No. 668, Medieval scholar, Royal Library. 8fr, Satellite and rocket, Space Aeronautics Institute.

Engraved and Photogravure
1966, May 28
664 A206 1fr grn & blk 15 10
665 A206 2fr gray, blk & brn org 15 12
666 A206 2fr bl, blk & yel 15 12
667 A207 3fr dp rose, blk & gold 15 10
668 A207 3fr multi 15 10
669 A207 6fr ultra, yel & blk 35 18
670 A207 8fr multi 45 45
Nos. 664-670 (7) 1.55 1.17

Issued to publicize the national scientific heritage.

Atom Symbol and Retort — A208

August Kekulé, Benzene Ring — A209

Engraved and Photogravure
1966, July 9 Unwmk. *Perf. 11½*
671 A208 6fr gray, blk & red 22 18

Issued to publicize the European chemical plant, EUROCHEMIC, at Mol.

1966, July 9
672 A209 3fr brt bl & blk 18 12

Issued to honor August Friedrich Kekule (1829-96), chemistry professor at University of Ghent (1858-67).

No. 663 Overprinted with Red and Blue Emblem

1966, July 11 Photo.
673 A205 3fr multi 18 12

Issued to commemorate the 19th International P.T.T. Congress (Postal, Telegraph and Telephone Administrations), Brussels, July 11-15.

Rik Wouters, Self-portrait — A210

1966, Sept. 6 Photo. *Perf. 11½*
674 A210 60c multi 18 12

Issued to commemorate the 50th anniversary of the death of Rik Wouters (1882-1916), painter.

Europa Issue, 1966
Common Design Type
1966, Sept. 24 Engr. *Perf. 11½*
Size: 24x34mm.
675 CD9 3fr brt grn 25 15
676 CD9 6fr brt rose lil 60 50

Types of 1962-1963 Overprinted in Black and Red

Engraved and Photogravure
1966, Nov. 11
677 A161 60c sep & grnsh gray 15 10
678 A169 3fr sep & pale bis 18 10

75th anniversary, Royal Federation of Philatelic Circles of Belgium. Overprint shows emblem of International Philatelic Federation (F.I.P.).

Lions Emblem — A214

Engraved and Photogravure
1967, Jan. 14 *Perf. 11½*
679 A214 3fr gray, blk & bl 18 12
680 A214 6fr lt grn, blk & vio 45 25

Issued to commemorate the 50th anniversary of the founding of the International Association of Lions Clubs.

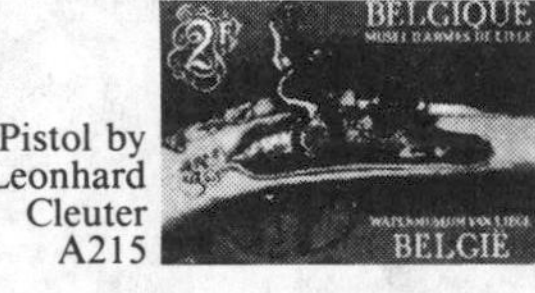

Pistol by Leonhard Cleuter A215

1967, Feb. 11 Photo.
681 A215 2fr dp car, blk & cr 15 10

Fire Arms Museum in Liege.

International Tourist Year Emblem A216

1967, Feb. 11
682 A216 6fr ver, ultra & blk 35 18

International Tourist Year, 1967.

Birches and Trientalis A217

Design: No. 684, Dunes, beach grass, privet and blue thistles.

1967, Mar. 11 Photo. *Perf. 11½*
683 A217 1fr multi 15 8
684 A217 1fr multi 15 8

Issued to publicize the nature preserves at Hautes Fagnes and Westhoek.

Paul E. Janson — A218

1967, Apr. 15 Engr. *Perf. 11½*
685 A218 10fr blue 60 30

Issued in memory of Paul Emile Janson (1872-1944), lawyer and statesman.

Postilion A219

Photogravure and Engraved
1967, Apr. 16
686 A219 3fr rose red & cl 18 10

Issued for Stamp Day, 1967.

Inscribed: "FITCE"
Engraved and Photogravure
1967, June 24 *Perf. 11½*
687 A219 10fr ultra, sep & emer 60 45

Issued to commemorate the meeting of the Federation of Common Market Telecommunications Engineers, Brussels, July 3-8.

Europa Issue, 1967
Common Design Type
1967, May 2 Photo.
Size: 24x35mm.
688 CD10 3fr blk, lt bl & red 30 12
689 CD10 6fr blk, grnsh gray & yel 55 45

Flax, Shuttle and Mills — A221

1967, June 3 Photo. *Perf. 11½*
690 A221 6fr tan & multi 35 25

Belgian linen industry.

Old Kursaal, Ostend — A222

Engraved and Photogravure
1967, June 3
691 A222 2fr dk brn, lt bl & yel 15 12

700th anniversary of Ostend as a city.

Caesar Crossing Rubicon, 15th Century Tapestry — A223

Design: No. 693, Emperor Maximilian Killing a Boar, 16th cent. tapestry.

1967, Sept. 2 Photo. *Perf. 11½*
692 A223 1fr multi 15 12
693 A223 1fr multi 15 12

Issued for the Charles Plisnier and Lodewijk de Raet Foundations.

Arms of University of Ghent — A224

Princess Margaret of York — A225

Design: No. 651, Arms of University of Liege.

Engraved and Photogravure

1967, Sept. 30 *Perf. 11½*
694 A224 3fr gray & multi 18 10
695 A224 3fr gray & multi 18 10

Issued to commemorate the 150th anniversaries of the Universities of Ghent and Liege.

1967, Sept. 30 **Photo.**
696 A225 6fr multi 35 30

British Week, Sept. 28-Oct. 2.

"Virga Jesse," Hasselt — A226

1967, Nov. 11 **Engr.** *Perf. 11½*
697 A226 1fr sl bl 15 12

Christmas, 1967.

Hand Guarding Worker — A227

Military Mailman, 1916, by James Thiriar — A228

1968, Feb. 3 **Photo.** *Perf. 11½*
698 A227 3fr multi 18 7

Issued to publicize industrial safety.

Engraved and Photogravure

1968, Mar. 17 *Perf. 11½*
699 A228 3fr sep, lt bl & brn 18 7

Issued for Stamp Day, 1968.

View of Grammont and Seal of Baudouin VI — A229

Stamp of 1866, No. 23 — A230

Historic Sites: 3fr, Theux-Franchimont tortress, sword and seal. 6fr, Neolithic cave and artifacts, Spiennes. 10fr, Roman oil lamp and St. Medard's Church, Wervik.

1968, Apr. 13 **Photo.** *Perf. 11½*
700 A229 2fr bl, blk, lil & rose 20 20
701 A229 3fr org, blk & car 20 12
702 A229 6fr ultra, ind & bis 45 25
703 A229 10fr tan, blk, yel & gray 75 50

1968, Apr. 13 **Engr.** *Perf. 13*
704 A230 1fr black 15 10

Centenary of the Malines Stamp Printery.

Europa Issue, 1968
Common Design Type

1968, Apr. 27 **Photo.** *Perf. 11½*
Size: 35x24mm.
705 CD11 3fr dl grn, gold & blk 18 12
706 CD11 6fr car, sil & blk 60 42

St. Laurent Abbey, Liège — A232

Designs: 3fr, Gothic Church, Lissewegheh. No. 709. Barges in Zandvliet locks. No. 710, Ship in Neuzen lock, Ghent Canal. 10fr, Ronquieres canal ship lift.

Engraved and Photogravure

1968, Sept. 7 *Perf. 11½*
707 A232 2fr ultra, gray ol & sep 20 20
708 A232 3fr ol bis, gray & sep 20 10
709 A232 6fr ind, brt bl & sep 45 25
710 A232 6fr blk, grnsh bl & ol 35 25
711 A232 10fr bis, brt bl & sep 75 50
Nos. 707-711 (5) 1.95 1.30

No. 710 issued Dec. 14 for opening of lock at Neuzen, Netherlands.

Christmas Candle — A233

Engraved and Photogravure

1968, Dec. 7 *Perf. 11½*
712 A233 1fr multi 15 7

Christmas, 1968.

St. Albertus Magnus — A234

1969, Feb. 15 **Engr.** *Perf. 11½*
713 A234 2fr sepia 15 12

The Church of St. Paul in Antwerp (16th century) was destroyed by fire in Apr. 1968.

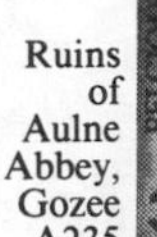

Ruins of Aulne Abbey, Gozee A235

Engraved and Photogravure

1969, Feb. 15
714 A235 3fr brt pink & blk 18 10

Aulne Abbey was destroyed in 1794 during the French Revolution.

The Travelers, Roman Sculpture A236

Broodjes Chapel, Antwerp A237

1969, Mar. 15 **Engr.** *Perf. 11½*
715 A236 2fr vio brn 15 10

2,000th anniversary of city of Arlon.

Engraved and Photogravure

1969, Mar. 15
716 A237 3fr gray & blk 18 10

Issued to commemorate the 150th anniversary of public education in Antwerp.

Post Office Train — A238

1969, Apr. 13 **Photo.** *Perf. 11½*
717 A238 3fr multi 18 7

Issued for Stamp Day.

Europa Issue, 1969
Common Design Type

1969, Apr. 26
Size: 35x24mm.
718 CD12 3fr lt grn, brn & blk 30 12
719 CD12 6fr sal, rose car & blk 45 45

NATO Type of 1959 Redrawn and Dated "1949-1969"

1969, May 31 **Photo.** *Perf. 11½*
720 A142 6fr org brn & ultra 38 38

20th anniv. of NATO. No. 720 inscribed Belgique-Belgie and OTAN-NAVO.

Construction Workers, by F. Leger A240

Bicyclist A241

1969, May 31
721 A240 3fr multi 18 7

Issued to commemorate the 50th anniversary of the International Labor Organization.

1969, July 5 **Photo.** *Perf. 11½*
722 A241 6fr rose & multi 35 30

Issued to publicize the World Bicycling Road Championships, Terlaemen to Zolder, Aug. 10.

Ribbon in Benelux Colors — A242

1969, Sept. 6 **Photo.** *Perf. 11½*
723 A242 3fr blk, red, ultra & yel 25 10

Issued to commemorate the 25th anniversary of the signing of the customs union of Belgium, Netherlands and Luxembourg.

Annevoie Garden and Pascali Rose — A243

Design: No. 690, Lochristi Garden and begonia.

1969, Sept. 6
724 A243 2fr multi 15 12
725 A243 2fr multi 15 12

Armstrong, Collins, Aldrin and Map Showing Tranquillity Base — A245

1969, Sept. 20 **Photo.**
726 A245 6fr black 35 30

See note after Algeria No. 427. See also No. B846.

Wounded Veteran A246

Mailman A247

1969, Oct. 11 **Engr.** *Perf. 11½*
727 A246 1fr bl gray 15 7

Issued to publicize the national war veterans' aid organization (O.N.I.G.). The design is similar to type SP10.

1969, Oct. 18 **Photo.**
728 A247 1fr dp rose & multi 15 7

Issued to publicize youth philately. Design by Danielle Saintenoy, 14.

Kennedy Tunnel Under the Schelde, Antwerp A248

Design: 6fr, Three highways crossing near Loncin.

1969, Nov. 8 Engr. ***Perf. 11½***

729 A248 3fr multi 25 12
730 A248 6fr multi 32 32

Issued to publicize the John F. Kennedy Tunnel under the Schelde and the Walloon auto route and interchange near Loncin.

Henry Carton de Wiart, by Gaston Geleyn — A249

1969, Nov. 8

731 A249 6fr sepia 35 25

Issued to commemorate the centenary of the birth of Count Henry Carton de Wiart (1869-1951), statesman.

The Census at Bethlehem (detail), by Peter Brueghel A250

1969, Dec. 13 Photo.

732 A250 1.50fr multi 15 7

Christmas, 1969.

Symbols of Bank's Activity, 100fr Coin — A251

Engraved and Photogravure

1969, Dec. 13

733 A251 3.50fr lt ultra, blk & sil 20 7

Issued to commemorate the 50th anniversary of the Industrial Credit Bank (Societe nationale de credit à l'industrie).

Camellia A252

Beeches in Botanical Garden A253

Flowers: 2.50fr, Water lily. 3.50fr, Azalea.

1970, Jan. 31 Photo. ***Perf. 11½***

734 A252 1.50fr multi 15 10
735 A252 2.50fr multi 30 30
736 A252 3.50fr multi 30 12
a. Souvenir sheet of 3 2.75 2.75

Ghent Int'l Flower Exhibition.

No. 736a contains one each of Nos. 734-736, and was issued Apr. 25. It carries gray UN and UN Refugees emblems in margin. Size: 121x90mm. Sold for 25fr.

Engraved and Photogravure

1970, Mar. 7 ***Perf. 11½***

Design: 7fr, Birches.

737 A253 3.50fr yel & multi 30 10
738 A253 7fr grn & multi 45 45

European Nature Conservation Year.

Mailman A254

1970, Apr. 4 Photo.

739 A254 1.50fr multi 15 7

Issued for Youth Stamp Day.

New UPU Headquarters and Monument, Bern — A255

Engraved and Photogravure

1970, Apr. 12

740 A255 3.50fr grn & lt grn 30 8

Issued to commemorate the opening of the new Universal Postal Union Headquarters, Bern.

Europa Issue, 1970

Common Design Type

1970, May 1 Photo. ***Perf. 11½***

Size: 35x24mm.

741 CD13 3.50fr rose cl, yel & blk 30 15
742 CD13 7fr ultra, pink & blk 60 45

Cooperative Alliance Emblem — A257

1970, June 27 Photo. ***Perf. 11½***

743 A257 7fr blk & org 45 18

Issued to commemorate the 75th anniversary of the International Cooperative Alliance.

Ship in Ghent Terneuzen Lock, Zelzate A258

Design: No. 745, Clock Tower, Virton (vert.).

Engraved and Photogravure

1970, June 27

744 A258 2.50fr ind & lt bl 18 15
745 A258 2.50fr dk pur & ocher 18 15

King Baudouin — A259

1970-80 Engr. ***Perf. 11½***

746 A259 1.75fr grn ('71) 30 15
747 A259 2.25fr gray grn ('72) 45 15
748 A259 2.50fr gray grn ('74) 20 5
749 A259 3fr emer ('73) 3.75 3.00
750 A259 3.25fr vio brn ('75) 25 5
751 A259 3.50fr org brn 30 5
752 A259 3.50fr brn ('71) 30 5
753 A259 4fr bl ('72) 45 5
754 A259 4.50fr brn ('72) 30 5
755 A259 4.50fr grnsh bl ('74) 30 5
756 A259 5fr lil ('72) 30 6
757 A259 6fr rose car ('72) 35 12
758 A259 6.50fr vio blk (74) 45 6
759 A259 7fr ver ('71) 45 8
760 A259 7.50fr brt pink ('75) 45 5
761 A259 8fr blk ('72) 45 6
762 A259 9fr ol bis ('71) 75 8
763 A259 9fr red brn ('80) 55 6
764 A259 10fr rose car ('71) 60 8
765 A259 11fr gray ('76) 65 15
766 A259 12fr Prus bl ('72) 75 10
767 A259 13fr sl ('75) 90 6
768 A259 14fr gray grn ('76) 85 15
769 A259 15fr lt vio ('71) 90 10
770 A259 16fr grn ('77) 90 8
771 A259 17fr dl mag ('75) 1.00 15
772 A259 18fr stl bl ('71) 1.25 20
773 A259 18fr grnsh bl ('80) 1.10 12
774 A259 20fr vio bl ('71) 1.25 10
775 A259 22fr blk ('74) 1.75 1.75
776 A259 22fr lt grn ('79) 1.40 15
777 A259 25fr lil ('75) 1.50 15
778 A259 30fr ocher ('72) 2.00 15
779 A259 35fr emer ('80) 2.00 30
780 A259 40fr dk bl ('77) 2.50 15
781 A259 45fr brn ('80) 2.75 30

Perf. 12½x13½

Photo.

Size: 22x17mm

782 A259 3fr emer ('73) 3.75 3.50
a. Booklet pane of 4 (#782 and 3 #783) + labels 10.00
783 A259 4fr bl ('73) 90 90
784 A259 4.50fr grnsh bl ('75) 50 45
785 A259 5fr lil ('73) 30 15
a. Booklet pane of 4 + labels 2.75
786 A259 6fr car ('78) 35 25
787 A259 6.50fr dl pur ('75) 55 30
788 A259 8fr gray ('78) 45 18
Nos. 746-788 (43) 41.20 14.19

No. 751 issued Sept. 7, 1970, King Baudouin's 40th birthday, and is inscribed "1930-1970." Dates are omitted on other stamps of type A259.

Nos. 754, 756 also issued in coils in 1973 and Nos. 757, 761 in 1978, with black control number on back of every fifth stamp.

Nos. 782-788 issued in booklets only. Nos. 782, 784 have one straight-edge, Nos. 786, 788 have two. The rest have one or two. Stamps in the panes are tete-beche. Each pane has two labels showing Belgian Postal emblem with a large selvage with postal code instructions. Nos. 786, 788 not luminescent.

See Nos. 432a, 432b, 977a, 977b.

U.N. Headquarters, N.Y. — A260

Fair Emblem — A261

Engraved and Photogravure

1970, Sept. 12

789 A260 7fr dk brn & Prus bl 45 25

25th anniversary of the United Nations.

1970, Sept. 19

790 A261 1.50fr bis, org & brn 15 7

Issued to publicize the 25th International Fair at Ghent, Sept. 12-27.

Queen Fabiola — A262

The Mason, by Georges Minne — A263

1970, Sept. 19

791 A262 3.50fr lt bl & blk 20 7

Issued to publicize the Queen Fabiola Foundation for Mental Health.

Engraved and Photogravure

1970, Oct. 17 ***Perf. 11½***

792 A263 3.50fr dl yel & sep 20 7

Issued to commemorate the 50th anniversary of the National Housing Society.

Man, Woman and City — A264

1970, Oct. 17 Photo.

793 A264 2.50fr blk & multi 15 15

Issued to commemorate the 25th anniversary of the Social Security System.

Madonna with the Grapes, by Jean Gossaert — A265

1970, Nov. 14 Engr. ***Perf. 11½***

794 A265 1.50fr dk brn 15 7

Christmas 1970.

Arms of Eupen, Malmedy and Saint-Vith A266

Engraved and Photogravure

1970, Dec. 12 ***Perf. 11½***

795 A266 7fr sep & dk brn 45 18

The 50th anniversary of the return of the districts of Eupen, Malmedy and Saint-Vith.

Automatic Telephone — A267

"Auto" A268

Touring Club Emblem — A269

1971, Jan. 16 Photo. ***Perf. 11½***

796 A267 1.50fr multi 15 7

Automatization of Belgian telephone system.

1971, Jan. 16
797 A268 2.50fr car & blk 15 15

Fiftieth Automobile Show, Brussels, Jan. 19-31.

1971, Feb. 13
798 A269 3.50fr ultra & multi 25 7

Belgian Touring Club, 75th anniversary.

Tournai Cathedral A270

1971, Feb. 13 **Engr.**
799 A270 7fr brt bl 45 30

Cathedral of Tournal, 8th centenary.

"The Letter Box," by T. Lobrichon — A271

1971, March 13 **Engr.** ***Perf. 11½***
800 A271 1.50fr dk brn 15 8

Youth philately.

Albert I, Jules Destrée and Academy — A272

Engraved and Photogravure

1971, Apr. 17 ***Perf. 11½***
801 A272 7fr gray & blk 45 30

50th anniversary of the founding of the Royal Academy of Language and French Literature.

Mailman — A273

1971, Apr. 25
802 A273 3.50fr multi 25 7

Stamp Day.

Europa Issue, 1971
Common Design Type

1971, May 1 **Photo.**
Size: 35x24mm.
803 CD14 3.50fr ol & blk 30 10
804 CD14 7fr dk ol grn & blk 45 15

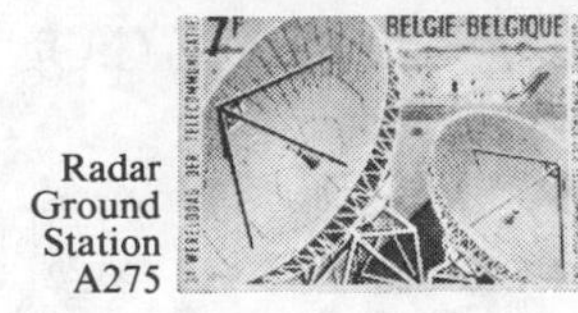

Radar Ground Station A275

1971, May 15 **Photo.** ***Perf. 11½***
805 A275 7fr multi 45 25

3rd World Telecommunications Day.

Antarctic Explorer, Ship and Penguins — A276

1971, June 19 **Photo.** ***Perf. 11½***
806 A276 10fr multi 75 75

Tenth anniversary of the Antarctic Treaty pledging peaceful uses of and scientific cooperation in Antarctica.

Orval Abbey — A277

1971, June 26 **Engr.** ***Perf. 11½***
807 A277 2.50fr chocolate 15 12

9th centenary of the Abbey of Notre Dame, Orval.

Georges Hubin — A278

Engraved and Photogravure

1971, June 26
808 A278 1.50fr vio bl & blk 15 12

Georges Hubin (1863-1947), socialist leader and Minister of State.

Mr. and Mrs. Goliath, the Giants of Ath — A279

View of Ghent A280

1971, Aug. 7 **Photo.**
809 A279 2.50fr multi 15 12

Engr.
810 A280 2.50fr gray brn 15 15

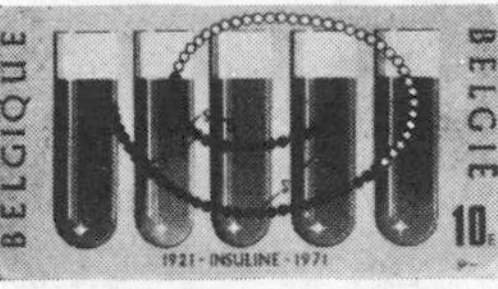

Test Tubes and Insulin Molecular Diagram — A281

1971, Aug. 7 **Photo.**
811 A281 10fr lt gray & multi 60 45

50th anniversary of the discovery of insulin.

Family and "50" — A283

1971, Sept. 11 **Photo.**
812 A283 1.50fr grn & multi 15 12

50th anniversary of the Belgian Large Families League.

Achaemenidaen Tomb, Buzpar, and Persian Coat of Arms — A284

Engraved and Photogravure

1971, Oct. 2 ***Perf. 11½***
813 A284 7fr multi 45 25

2500th anniversary of the founding of the Persian empire by Cyrus the Great.

Dr. Jules Bordet A285

Flight into Egypt, Anonymous A286

Portrait: No. 815, Stijn Streuvels.

1971, Oct. 2 **Engr.**
814 A285 3.50fr sl grn 25 8
815 A285 3.50fr dk brn 25 8

No. 814 honors Dr. Jules Bordet (1870-1945), serologist and immunologist; No. 815, Stijn Streuvels (1871-1945), novelist whose pen name was Frank Lateur.

1971, Nov. 13 **Photo.**
816 A286 1.50fr multi 15 12

Christmas 1971.

Federation Emblem A287

Book Year Emblem A288

1971, Nov. 13
817 A287 3.50fr blk, ultra & gold 25 10

25th anniversary of the Federation of Belgian Industries (FIB).

1972, Feb. 19
818 A288 7fr bis, blk & bl 45 30

International Book Year 1972.

Coins of Belgium and Luxembourg A289

Engraved and Photogravure

1972, Feb. 19
819 A289 1.50fr org blk & sil 15 12

Economic Union of Belgium and Luxembourg, 50th anniversary.

Traffic Signal and Road Signs — A290

1972, Feb. 19 **Photo.**
820 A290 3.50fr bl & multi 25 10

Via Secura (road safety), 25th anniversary.

Belgica '72 Emblem A291

1972, Mar. 27
821 A291 3.50fr choc, bl & lil 25 7

International Philatelic Exhibition, Brussels, June 24-July 9.

"Your Heart is your Health" A292

Auguste Vermeylen A293

1972, Mar. 27
822 A292 7fr blk, gray, red & bl 45 30

World Health Day.

1972, Mar. 27
823 A293 2.50fr multi 15 12

Centenary of the birth of Auguste Vermeylen (1872-1945), Flemish writer and educator. Portrait by Isidore Opsomer.

Astronaut on Moon — A294

1972, Apr. 23
824 A294 3.50fr multi 25 12

Stamp Day 1972.

Europa Issue 1972
Common Design Type

1972, Apr. 29
Size: 24x35mm.
825 CD15 3.50fr lt bl & multi 30 10
826 CD15 7fr rose & multi 60 45

"Freedom of the Press" — A296

1972, May 13 Photo. *Perf. 11½*
827 A296 2.50fr org brn, buff & blk 15 12

50th anniversary of the BELGA news information agency and 25th Congress of the International Federation of Newspaper Editors (F.I.E.J.), Brussels, May 15-19.

Freight Cars with Automatic Coupling A297

1972, June 3
828 A297 7fr bl & multi 45 30

International Railroad Union, 50th anniversary.

View of Couvin — A298

Design: No. 830, Aldeneik Church, Maaseik (vert.).

1972, June 24 Engr. *Perf. 13½x14*
829 A298 2.50fr bl, vio brn & sl grn 30 30
830 A298 2.50fr dk brn & bl 30 30

Beatrice, by Gustave de Smet — A299

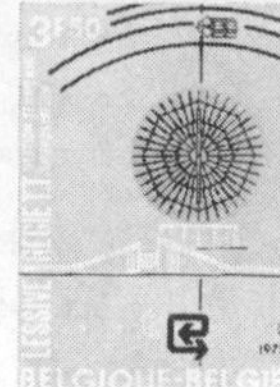

Radar Station, Intelsat 4 — A300

1972, Sept. 9 Photo. *Perf. 11½*
831 A299 3fr multi 18 12

Youth philately.

1972, Sept. 16
832 A300 3.50fr lt bl, sil & blk 25 10

Opening of the Lessive satellite earth station.

Frans Masereel, Self-portrait A301

Adoration of the Kings, by Felix Timmermans A302

1972, Oct. 21
833 A301 4.50fr lt ol & blk 30 6

Frans Masereel (1889-1972), wood engraver.

1972, Nov. 11 Photo. *Perf. 11½*
834 A302 3.50fr blk & multi 25 12

Christmas 1972.

Maria Theresa, Anonymous A303

1972, Dec. 16 Photo. *Perf. 11½*
835 A303 2fr multi 15 15

200th anniversary of the Belgian Academy of Science, Literature and Art, founded by Empress Maria Theresa.

WMO Emblem, Meteorological Institute, Ukkel — A304

1973, Mar. 24 Photo. *Perf. 11½*
836 A304 9fr bl & multi 60 30

Centenary of international meteorological cooperation.

"Fire" A305

Man and WHO Emblem A306

1973, Mar. 24
837 A305 2fr multi 15 12

National industrial fire prevention campaign.

1973, Apr. 7
838 A306 8fr dk red, ocher & blk 45 35

25th anniversary of World Health Organization.

Europa Issue 1973
Common Design Type

1973, Apr. 28
Size: 35x24mm.
839 CD16 4.50fr org brn, vio bl & yel 25 10
840 CD16 8fr ol, dk bl & yel 60 45

Thurn and Taxis Courier — A308

Arrows Circling Globe — A309

Engraved and Photogravure

1973, Apr. 28 *Perf. 11½*
841 A308 4.50fr blk & red brn 30 7

Stamp Day.

1973, May 12 Photo.
842 A309 3.50fr dp ocher & multi 25 7

5th International Telecommunications Day.

Workers' Sports Exhibition Poster, Ghent, 1913 — A310

1973, May 12
843 A310 4.50fr multi 30 12

60th anniversary of the International Workers' Sports Movement.

Fair Emblem A311

1973, May 12 Photo. *Perf. 11½*
844 A311 4.50fr multi 30 10

25th International Fair, Liege, May 12-27.

DC-10 and 1923 Biplane over Brussels Airport — A312

Design: 10fr, Tips biplane, 1908.

Engraved and Photogravure

1973, May 19
845 A312 8fr gray bl, blk & ultra 45 35
846 A312 10fr grn, lt bl & blk 75 60

50th anniversary of SABENA, Belgian airline (No. 845) and 25th anniversary of the "Vieilles Tiges" Belgian flying pioneers' society (No. 846).

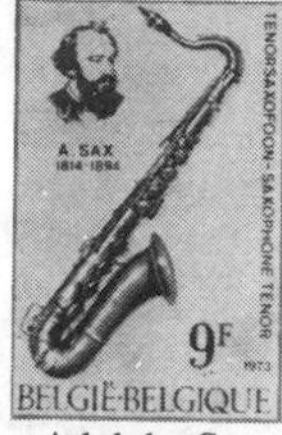

Adolphe Sax and Tenor Saxophone A313

Fresco from Bathhouse, Ostend A314

1973, Sept. 15 Photo.
847 A313 9fr grn, blk & bl 60 30

Adolphe Sax (1814-1894), inventor of saxophone.

1973, Sept. 15
848 A314 4.50fr multi 30 10

Year of the Spa.

St. Nicholas Church, Eupen A315

Charley, by Henri Evenepoel A316

Designs: No. 850, Town Hall, Leau. No. 851, Aarshot Church. No. 852, Chiman Castle. No. 853, Gemmenich Border: Belgium, Germany, Netherlands. No. 854, St. Monan and church, Nassogne. No. 855, Church tower, Dottignes. No. 856, Grand-Place, Sint-Truiden.

1973-75 Engr. *Perf. 13*
849 A315 2fr plum, sep & lt vio 18 12
850 A315 3fr blk, lt bl & mar 45 12
851 A315 3fr brn blk & yel 28 12
852 A315 4fr grnsh blk & grnsh bl 30 12
853 A315 4fr grnsh blk & bl 35 15
854 A315 4fr grnsh blk & bl 35 15
855 A315 4.50fr multi 45 18
856 A315 5fr multi 45 15
Nos. 849-856 (8) 2.81 1.11

Nos. 851, 855 not luminescent. Nos. 850, 852-854, 856 horiz.

1973, Oct. 13 Photo. *Perf. 11½*
857 A316 3fr multi 18 15

Youth philately.

Luminescent Paper
Starting with No. 858, all stamps are on luminescent paper unless otherwise noted.

Jean-Baptiste Moens A317

Engraved and Photogravure
1973, Oct. 13
858 A317 10fr gray & multi 60 30

50th anniversary of the Belgian Stamp Dealers' Association. Printed in sheets of 12 stamps and 12 labels showing association emblem.

Adoration of the Shepherds, by Hugo van der Goes A318

Louis Pierard, by M. I. Ianchelevici A319

1973, Nov. 17 Engr. *Perf. 11½*
859 A318 4fr blue 25 12

Christmas 1973.

Engraved and Photogravure
1973, Nov. 17
860 A319 4fr ver & buff 25 12

Louis Pierard (1886-1952), journalist, member of Parliament.

Highway, Automobile Club Emblem A320

1973, Nov. 17 Photo.
861 A320 5fr yel & multi 30 12

50th anniversary of the Vlaamse Automobile Club.

Early Microphone, Emblem of Radio Belgium — A321

Engraved and Photogravure
1973, Nov. 24
862 A321 4fr bl & blk 25 12

50th anniversary of Radio Belgium.

Felicien Rops, Self-portrait A323

Engraved and Photogravure
1973, Dec. 8 *Perf. 11½*
863 A323 7fr tan & blk 45 25

Felicien Rops (1833-1898), painter and engraver.

King Albert — A324

Sun, Bird, Flowers and Girl — A325

1974, Feb. 16 Photo. *Perf. 11½*
864 A324 4fr Prus grn & blk 30 12

King Albert, 1875-1934.

1974, Mar. 25 Photo. *Perf. 11½*
865 A325 3fr vio & multi 30 12

Protection of the environment.

NATO Emblem A326

1974, Apr. 20 Photo. *Perf. 11½*
866 A326 10fr dp to lt bl 60 35

25th anniversary of the signing of the North Atlantic Treaty.

Hubert Krains A327

"Destroyed City," by Ossip Zadkine A328

Engraved and Photogravure
1974, Apr. 27 *Perf. 11½*
867 A327 5fr blk & gray 30 8

Stamp Day.

Europa Issue 1974

1974, May 4

Design: 10fr, Solidarity, by Georges Minne.

868 A328 5fr blk & red 35 10
869 A328 10fr blk & ultra 90 45

Children A329

1974, May 18 Photo. *Perf. 11½*
870 A329 4fr lt bl & multi 28 15

10th Lay Youth Festival.

Planetarium, Brussels A330

Soleilmont Abbey Ruins — A331

Engr. and Photo.
1974, June 22 *Perf. 11½*

Designs: 4fr, Pillory, Braine-le-Chateau. 7fr, Fountain, Ghent (procession symbolic of Chamber of Rhetoric). 10fr, Belfry, Bruges (vert.).

871	A330	3fr sky bl & blk	20	10
872	A330	4fr lil rose & blk	30	10
873	A331	5fr lt grn & blk	45	12
874	A331	7fr dl yel & blk	60	35
875	A330	10fr blk, bl & brn	75	25
		Nos. 871-875 (5)	2.30	92

Historic buildings and monuments.

"BENELUX" A332

1974, Sept. 7 Photo. *Perf. 11½*
876 A332 5fr bl grn, dk grn & lt bl 30 8

30th anniversary of the signing of the customs union of Belgium, Netherlands and Luxembourg.

Jan Vekemans, by Cornelis de Vos — A333

1974, Sept. 14
877 A333 3fr multi 18 12

Youth philately.

Leon Tresignies, Willebroek Canal Bridge A334

Engraved and Photogravure
1974, Sept. 28
878 A334 4fr brn & ol grn 25 12

60th death anniversary of Corporal Leon Tresignies (1886-1914), hero of World War I.

Montgomery Blair, UPU Emblem A335

Design: 10fr, Heinrich von Stephan and UPU emblem.

Engraved and Photogravure
1974, Oct. 5 *Perf. 11½*
879 A335 5fr grn & blk 35 12
880 A335 10fr brick red & blk 75 50

Centenary of Universal Postal Union.

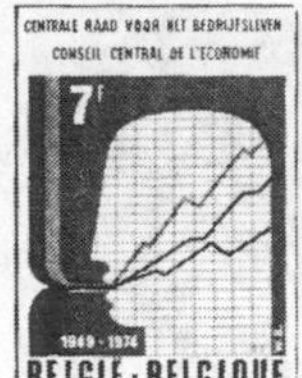
Symbolic Chart — A336

1974, Oct. 12 Photo. *Perf. 11½*
881 A336 7fr multi 45 30

Central Economic Council, 25th anniversary.

Rotary Emblem A337

1974, Oct. 19
882 A337 10fr multi 60 30

Rotary International of Belgium.

Wild Boar (Regiment's Emblem) — A338

1974, Oct. 26
883 A338 3fr multi 25 15

Granting of the colors to the Ardennes Chasseurs Regiment, 40th anniversary.

Angel, by Van Eyck Brothers — A341

1974, Nov. 16 *Perf. 11½*
884 A341 4fr rose lil 28 15

Christmas 1974. The Angel shown is from the triptyque "The Mystical Lamb" in the Saint-Bavon Cathedral, Ghent.

Adolphe Quetelet, by J. Odevaere — A342

Engraved and Photogravure
1974, Dec. 14
885 A342 10fr blk & buff 60 30

Death centenary of Adolphe Quetelet (1796-1874), statistician, astronomer and Secretary of Royal Academy of Brussels.

Condition is the all-important factor of price. Prices quoted are for stamps in fine condition.

Themabelga Emblem A343

Neoregelia Carolinae A344

1975, Feb. 15 Photo. ***Perf. 11½***
912 A343 6.50fr grn, blk & org 35 10

Themabelga, International Thematic Stamp Exhibition, Brussels, Dec. 13-21, 1975.

1975, Feb. 22

Flowers: 5fr, Coltsfoot. 6.50fr, Azalea.

913 A344 4.50fr multi 25 15

Photogravure and Engraved

914 A344 5fr multi 28 20
915 A344 6.50fr multi 35 15

Ghent International Flower Exhibition, Apr. 26-May 5.

School Emblem, Man Leading Boy — A345

Engraved and Photogravure

1975, Mar. 15 ***Perf. 11½***
916 A345 4.50fr blk & multi 30 8

Centenary of the founding of the Charles Buls Normal School for Boys, Brussels.

Davids Foundation Emblem A346

1975, Mar. 22 Photo.
917 A346 5fr yel & multi 30 6

Centenary of the Davids Foundation, a Catholic organization for the promotion of Flemish through education and books.

King Albert — A347

Mailman, 1840, by James Thiriar — A348

Engraved and Photogravure

1975, Apr. 5
918 A347 10fr blk & mar 60 35

King Albert (1875-1934), birth centenary.

1975, Apr. 19 Engr. ***Perf. 11½***
919 A348 6.50fr dl mag 45 8

Stamp Day 1975.

St. John, from Last Supper, by Bouts A349

Concentration Camp Symbols A350

Europa Issue 1975

Design: 10fr, Woman's Head, detail from "Trial by Fire," by Dirk Bouts.

Engraved and Photogravure

1975, Apr. 26
920 A349 6.50fr blk, grn & bl 45 18
921 A349 10fr blk, ocher & red 75 42

1975, May 3 Photo.

Design: "B" denoted political prisoners, "KG" prisoners of war.

922 A350 4.50fr multi 30 12

Liberation of concentration camps, 30th anniversary.

Hospice of St. John, Bruges A351

Church of St. Loup, Namur — A352

Design: 10fr, Martyrs' Square, Brussels.

1975, May 12 Engr. ***Perf. 11½***
926 A351 4.50fr dp rose lil 30 28
927 A352 5fr sl grn 30 18
928 A351 10fr brt bl 60 30

European Architectural Heritage Year.

Library, Louvain University, Ryckmans and Cerfaux A355

1975, June 7 Photo. ***Perf. 11½***
931 A355 10fr dl bl & sep 60 30

25th anniversary of Louvain Bible Colloquium, founded by Professors Gonzague Ryckmans (1887-1969) and Lucien Cerfaux (1883-1968).

"Metamorphose" by Pol Mara — A356

Marie Popelin, Palace of Justice, Brussels — A357

1975, June 14
932 A356 7fr multi 45 30

Queen Fabiola Mental Health Foundation.

Engraved and Photogravure

1975, June 21
933 A357 6.50fr grn & cl 45 10

International Women's Year 1975. Marie Popelin (1846-1913), first Belgian woman doctor of law.

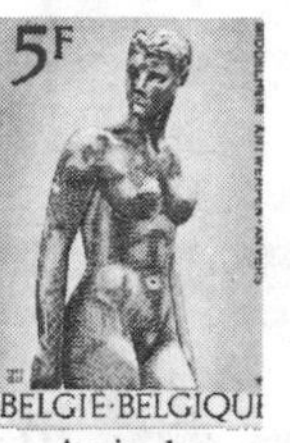
Assia, by Charles Despiau A358

Cornelia Vekemans, by Cornelis de Vos A359

Engraved and Photogravure

1975, Sept. 6 ***Perf. 11½***
934 A358 5fr yel grn & blk 30 12

Middelheim Outdoor Museum, 25th anniversary.

1975, Sept. 20 Photo.
935 A359 4.50fr multi 30 12

Youth philately.

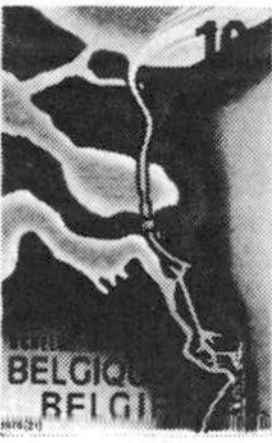
Map of Schelde-Rhine Canal A360

1975, Sept. 20
936 A360 10fr multi 60 30

Opening of connection between the Schelde and Rhine, Sept. 23, 1975.

National Bank, W. F. Orban, Founder A361

Photogravure and Engraved

1975, Oct. 11 ***Perf. 12½x13***
937 A361 25fr multi 1.50 45

National Bank of Belgium, 125th anniversary.

Edmond Thieffry and Plane, 1925 — A362

1975, Oct. 18 ***Perf. 11½***
938 A362 7fr blk & lil 45 30

First flight Brussels to Kinshasa, Congo, 50th anniversary.

"Seat of Wisdom" St. Peter's, Louvain — A363

Engraved and Photogravure

1975, Nov. 8 ***Perf. 11½***
939 A363 6.50fr bl, blk & grn 45 8

University of Louvain, 550th anniversary.

Angels, by Rogier van der Weyden A364

1975, Nov. 15
940 A364 5fr multi 30 12

Christmas 1975.

Willemsfonds Emblem A365

American Bicentennial Emblem A366

1976, Feb. 21 Photo. ***Perf. 11½***
941 A365 5fr multi 30 10

125th anniversary of the Willems Foundation, which supports Flemish language and literature.

1976, Mar. 13 Photo. ***Perf. 11½***
942 A366 14fr gold, red, bl & blk 90 45

American Bicentennial. No. 942 printed checkerwise in sheets of 30 stamps and 30 gold and black labels which show medal with 1626 seal of New York. Black engraved inscription on labels commemorates arrival of first Walloon settlers in Nieu Nederland.

Cardinal Mercier — A367

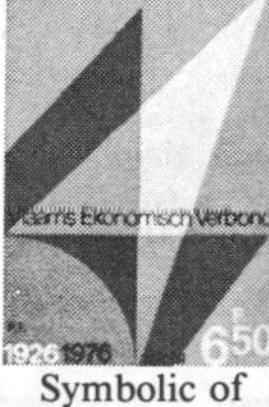
Symbolic of V.E.V. — A368

1976, Mar. 20 Engr.
943 A367 4.50fr brt rose lil 30 12

Desire Joseph Cardinal Mercier (1851-1926), professor at Louvain University, spiritual and patriotic leader during World War I, 50th death anniversary.

1976, Apr. 3 Photo. *Perf. 11½*

944	A368 6.50fr multi	45	6

Flemish Economic Organization (Viaams Ekonomisch Verbond), 50th anniversary.

General Post Office, Brussels A369

1976, Apr. 24 Engr. *Perf. 11½*

945	A369 6.50fr sepia	45	6

Stamp Day.

Europa Issue 1976

Potter's Hands A370

Design: 6.50fr, Basket maker (vert.).

1976, May 8 Photo.

946	A370 6.50fr multi	60	12
947	A370 14fr multi	90	50

Truck on Road A371

1976, May 8

948	A371 14fr blk, yel & red	90	45

15th International Road Union Congress, Brussels, May 9-13.

Queen Elisabeth — A372

1976, May 24 *Perf. 11½*

949	A372 14fr green	90	45

Queen Elisabeth (1876-1965), birth centenary.

Ardennes Draft Horses A373

1976, June 19

950	A373 5fr multi	35	12

Ardennes Draft Horses Association, 50th anniversary.

Souvenir Sheets

King Baudouin — A374

1976, June 26

951	A374 Sheet of 3	4.50	4.50
a.	4.50fr gray	1.40	1.40
b.	6.50fr ocher	1.40	1.40
c.	10fr brick red	1.40	1.40
952	A374 Sheet of 2	6.25	6.25
a.	20fr yel grn	1.75	1.75
b.	30fr Prus bl	1.75	1.75

25th anniversary of the reign of King Baudouin. Nos. 951-952 have silver marginal inscriptions. Size: 110x82mm. No. 951 sold for 30fr, No. 952 for 70fr. The surtax went to a new foundation for the improvement of living conditions in honor of the King.

Electric Train and Society Emblem — A375

1976, Sept. 11 Photo. *Perf. 11½*

953	A375 6.50fr multi	45	8

National Belgian Railroad Society, 50th anniversary.

William of Nassau, Prince of Orange — A376

1976, Sept. 11 Engr.

954	A376 10fr sl grn	60	30

400th anniversary of the pacification of Ghent.

New Subway Train — A377

1976, Sept. 18 Photo.

955	A377 6.50fr multi	45	8

Opening of first line of Brussels subway.

Young Musician, by W. C. Duyster — A378

1976, Oct. 2 Photo. *Perf. 11½*

956	A378 4.50fr multi	30	15

Young musicians and youth philately.

Charles Bernard — A379

St. Jerome in the Mountains, by Le Patinier — A380

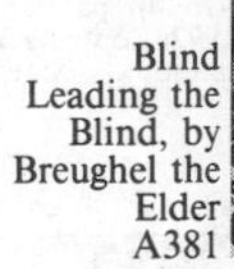

Blind Leading the Blind, by Breughel the Elder A381

Design: No. 958, Fernand Victor Toussaint van Boelaere.

1976, Oct. 16 Engr.

957	A379 5fr violet	25	25
958	A379 5fr red brn & sep	25	25
959	A380 6.50fr dk brn	40	8
960	A381 6.50fr sl grn	40	8

Charles Bernard (1875-1961), Frenchspeaking journalist; Toussaint van Boelaere (1875-1947), Flemish journalist; No. 959, Charles Plisnier Belgian-French Cultural Society. No. 960, Assoc. for Language Promotion.

Remouchamps Caves — A382

Hunnegem Priory, Gramont, and Madonna A383

Designs: No. 963, River Lys and St. Martin's Church. No. 964, Ham-sur-Heure Castle.

1976, Oct. 23 Engr. *Perf. 13*

961	A382 4.50fr multi	24	20
962	A383 4.50fr multi	24	20
963	A383 5fr multi	35	20
964	A383 5fr multi	35	20

Tourism. Nos. 961-962 are not luminescent.

Nativity, by Master of Flemalle — A384

1976, Nov. 20 *Perf. 11½*

965	A384 5fr violet	30	25

Christmas 1976.

Rubens' Monogram — A385

Photogravure and Engraved

1977, Feb. 12 *Perf. 11½*

966	A385 6.50fr lil & blk	45	6

Peter Paul Rubens (1577-1640), painter, 400th birth anniversary.

Heraldic Lion — A386

1977-85 Typo. *Perf. 13½x14*

Size: 17x20mm.

967	A386	50c brn ('80)	15	5
a.		org brn ('85)	5	5
968	A386	1fr brt lil	15	5
a.		brt rose lil ('84)	6	5
969	A386	1.50fr gray ('78)	15	5
970	A386	2fr yel ('78)	15	5
970A	A386	2.50fr yel brn ('81)	15	5
971	A386	2.75fr Prus bl ('80)	30	10
972	A386	3fr vio ('78)	30	5
a.		dl vio ('84)	18	5
973	A386	4fr red brn ('80)	25	6
a.		rose brn ('85)	25	6
974	A386	4.50fr lt ultra	30	5
975	A386	5fr grn ('80)	30	8
a.		emer grn ('84)	20	8
976	A386	6fr dl red brn	35	5
a.		lt red brn ('85)	35	5
		Nos. 967-976 (11)	2.55	64

Perf. 13½x12½, 12½x13½

1978, Aug. Photo.

Size: 17x22mm, 22x17mm.

977	A386 1fr brt lil	15	5
a.	Booklet pane of 4 (#977-978 and 2 #786)	1.50	
b.	Booklet pane of 4 (#977, 979 and 2 #788)	2.00	
978	A386 2fr yellow	30	30
979	A386 3fr violet	45	45

See Nos. 1084-1088. Nos. 977-979 issued in booklets only and have one straight-edge. Each pane has 2 labels showing Belgian Postal emblem, also a large selvage with zip code instructions. No. 977-979 not luminescent.

Anniversary Emblem A387

1977, Mar. 14 Photo. *Perf. 11½*

982	A387 6.50fr sil & multi	45	6

Royal Belgian Association of Civil and Agricultural Engineers, 50th anniversary.

Birds and Lions Emblem A388

1977, Mar. 28

983	A388 14fr multi	90	45

Belgian District No. 112 of Lions International, 25th anniversary.

A little time given to the study of the arrangement of the Scott Catalogue can make it easier to use effectively.

Pillar Box, 1852 — A389

1977, Apr. 23 **Engr.**
984 A389 6.50fr sl grn 45 6

Stamp Day 1977.

Europa Issue 1977

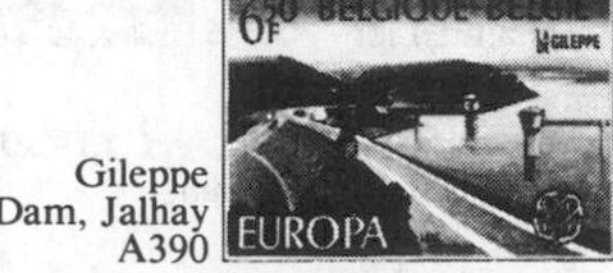

Gileppe Dam, Jalhay A390

Design: 14fr, War Memorial, Yser at Nieuport.

1977, May 7 **Photo.** ***Perf. 11½***
985 A390 6.50fr multi 50 10
986 A390 14fr multi 1.10 15

Mars and Mercury Association Emblem — A391

1977, May 14
987 A391 5fr multi 30 18

Mars and Mercury Association of Reserve and Retired Officers, 50th anniversary.

Prince de Hornes Coat of Arms A392

Conversion of St. Hubertus A394

Battle of the Golden Spur, from Oxford Chest A393

Design: 6.50fr, Froissart writing book.

1977, June 11 **Engr.** ***Perf. 11½***
988 A392 4.50fr violet 28 12
989 A393 5fr red 32 20
990 A394 6.50fr dk brn 35 6
991 A394 14fr sl grn 70 45

300th anniversary of the Principality of Overijse (4.50fr); 675th anniversary of the Battle of the Golden Spur (5f); 600th anniversary of publication of first volume of the Chronicles of Jehan Froissart (6.50fr); 1250th anniversary of the death of St. Hubertus (14fr).

Rubens, Self-portrait — A395

1977, June 25 **Photo.**
992 A395 5fr multi 30 18
a. Souvenir sheet of 3 1.25 1.25

Peter Paul Rubens (1577-1640), painter, 400th birth anniversary. No. 992a contains 3 No. 992; decorative margin. Size: 100x152mm. Sold for 20fr.

Open Book, from The Lamb of God, by Van Eyck Brothers — A396

1977, Sept. 3 **Photo.** ***Perf. 11½***
993 A396 10fr multi 60 30

International Federation of Library Associations (IFLA), 50th Anniversary Congress, Brussels, Sept. 5-10.

Gymnast and Soccer Player — A397

Designs: 6.50fr, Fencers in wheelchairs (horiz.). 10fr, Basketball players. 14fr, Hockey players.

1977, Sept. 10
994 A397 4.50fr multi 30 12
995 A397 6.50fr multi 45 6
996 A397 10fr multi 60 30
997 A397 14fr multi 90 45

Workers' Gymnastics and Sports Center, 50th anniversary (4.50fr); sport for the Handicapped (6.50fr); 20th European Basketball Championships (10fr); First World Hockey Cup (14fr).

Europalia 77 Emblem — A398

1977, Sept. 17
998 A398 5fr gray & multi 30 18

5th Europalia Arts Festival, featuring German Federal Republic, Belgium, Oct.-Nov. 1977.

The Egg Farmer, by Gustave De Smet — A399

Engraved and Photogravure
1977, Oct. 8
999 A399 4.50fr bis & blk 30 12

Publicity for Belgian eggs.

Mother and Daughter with Album, by Constant Cap — A400

1977, Oct. 15 **Engr.**
1000 A400 4.50fr dk brn 30 12

Youth Philately.

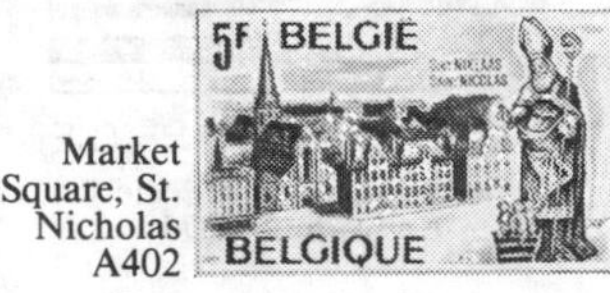

Bailiff's House, Gembloux — A401

Market Square, St. Nicholas A402

Designs: No. 1002, St. Aldegonde Church and Cultural Center. No. 1004, Statue and bridge, Liege.

1977, Oct. 22
1001 A401 4.50fr multi 30 15
1002 A401 4.50fr multi 30 15
1003 A402 5fr multi 30 25
1004 A402 5fr multi 30 25

Tourism. Nos. 1001-1004 are not luminescent.
See Nos. 1017-1018, 1037-1040.

Nativity, by Rogier van der Weyden — A403

1977, Nov. 11 **Engr.**
1005 A403 5fr rose red 30 15

Christmas 1977.

Symbols of Transportation and Map — A404

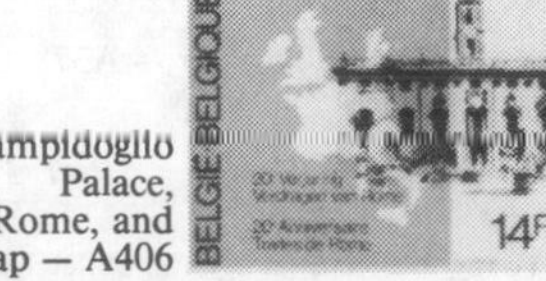

Parliament of Europe, Strasbourg, and Emblem — A405

Campidoglio Palace, Rome, and Map — A406

Design: No. 1009, Paul-Henri Spaak and map of 19 European member countries.

1978, Mar. 18 **Photo.** ***Perf. 11½***
1006 A404 10fr bl & multi 55 22
1007 A405 10fr bl & multi 1.10 22
1008 A406 14fr bl & multi 65 65
1009 A406 14fr bl & multi 65 65

European Action: 25th anniversary of the European Transport Ministers' Conference; 1st general elections for European Parliament; 20th anniversary of the signing of the Treaty of Rome; Paul Henri Spaak (1899-1972), Belgian statesman who worked for the establishment of European Community.

Grimbergen Abbey — A407

1978, Apr. 1 **Engr.**
1010 A407 4.50fr red brn 30 12

850th anniversary of the Premonstratensian Abbey at Grimbergen.

Emblem — A408

No. 39 with First Day Cancel — A409

1978, Apr. 8 **Photo.**
1011 A408 8fr multi 45 6

Ostend Chamber of Commerce and Industry, 175th anniversary.

1978, Apr. 15
1012 A409 8fr multi 45 6

Stamp Day.

Europa Issue

Pont des Trous, Tournai A410

Design: 8fr, Antwerp Cathedral, by Vaclav Hollar (vert.).

Photogravure and Engraved
1978, May 6 ***Perf. 11½***
1013 A410 8fr multi 60 8
1014 A410 14fr multi 90 35

Virgin of Ghent, Porcelain Plaque A411

Paul Pastur Workers' University, Charleroi A412

1978, Sept. 16 Photo. *Perf. 11½*

1015 A411 6fr multi 42 15
1016 A412 8fr multi 55 6

Municipal education in Ghent, 150th anniversary; Paul Pastur Workers' University, Charleroi, 75th anniversary. Nos. 1015-1016 are not luminescent.

Types of 1977 and

Tourist Guide, Brussels A413

Designs: No. 1017, Jonathas House, Enghien. No. 1018, View of Wetteren and couple in local costume. No. 1020, Prince Carnival, Eupen-St. Vith.

Photogravure and Engraved

1978, Sept. 25

1017 A401 4.50fr multi 24 15
1018 A402 4.50fr multi 24 15
1019 A413 6fr multi 35 15
1020 A413 6fr multi 35 15

Tourism. Nos. 1017-1020 are not luminescent.

Emblem A414

1978, Oct. 7 Photo.

1021 A414 8fr red & blk 45 8

Royal Flemish Engineer's Organization, 50th anniversary.

Young Philatelist A415

1978, Oct. 14 Engr. *Perf. 11½*

1022 A415 4.50fr dk vio 30 8

Youth philately.

Nativity, Notre Dame, Huy — A416

1978, Nov. 18 Engr. *Perf. 11½*

1023 A416 6fr black 35 15

Christmas 1978.

Tyll Eulenspiegel, Lay Action Emblem A417

European Parliament Emblem A418

1979, Mar. 3 Photo. *Perf. 11½*

1024 A417 4.50fr multi 30 6

10th anniversary of Lay Action Centers.

1979, Mar. 3

1025 A418 8fr multi 50 12

European Parliament, first direct elections, June 7-10.

St. Michael Banishing Lucifer — A419

Photogravure and Engraved

1979, Mar. 17

1026 A419 4.50fr rose red & blk 30 12
1027 A419 8fr brt grn & blk 45 15

Millennium of Brussels.

NATO Emblem and Monument A420

1979, Mar. 31 Photo.

1028 A420 3fr multi 90 45

North Atlantic Treaty Organization, 30th anniversary.

Prisoner's Head — A421

Photogravure and Engraved

1979, Apr. 7

1029 A421 6fr org & blk 35 12

25th anniversary of the National Political Prisoners' Monument at Breendonk.

Belgium No. Q2 — A422

1979, Apr. 21 Photo. *Perf. 11½*

1030 A422 8fr multi 45 12

Stamp Day 1979.

Europa Issue 1979

Mail Coach and Truck A423

Design: 14fr, Chappe's heliograph, Intelsat satellite and dish antenna.

Photogravure and Engraved

1979, Apr. 28 *Perf. 11½*

1031 A423 8fr multi 45 15
1032 A423 14fr multi 90 40

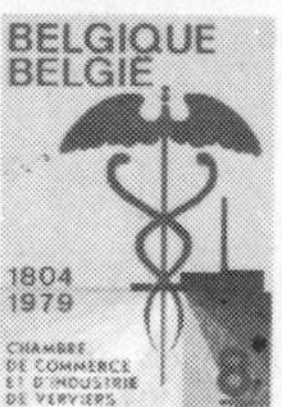

Chamber of Commerce Emblem — A424

1979, May 19 Photo. *Perf. 11½*

1033 A424 8fr multi 45 12

Verviers Chamber of Commerce and Industry, 175th anniversary.

"50" Emblem A425

1979, June 9 Photo. *Perf. 11½*

1034 A425 4.50fr gold & ultra 28 6

National Fund for Professional Credit, 50th anniversary.

Merchants, Roman Bas-relief A426

1979, June 9

1035 A426 10fr multi 60 25

Belgian Chamber of Trade and Commerce, 50th anniversary.

"Tintin" as Philatelist A427

1979, Sept. 29 Photo. *Perf. 11½*

1036 A427 8fr multi 50 20

Youth philately.

Tourism Types of 1977

Designs: No. 1037, Belfry, Thuin. No. 1038, Royal Museum of Central Africa, Tervuren. No. 1039, St. Nicholas Church and cattle, Ciney. No. 1040, St. John's Church and statue of Our Lady, Poperinge.

Perf. 11½ (#1037, 1039), 13 (#1038, 1040)

Photogravure and Engraved

1979, Oct. 22

1037 A401 5fr multi 25 8
1038 A402 5fr multi 25 8
1039 A401 6fr multi 38 18
1040 A402 6fr multi 38 18

Francois Auguste Gevaert A429

Piano, String Instruments A430

Design: 6fr, Emmanuel Durlet.

Photogravure and Engraved

1979, Nov. 3 *Perf. 11½*

1041 A429 5fr brown 35 8
1042 A429 6fr brown 42 10
1043 A430 14fr brown 90 35

Francois Auguste Gevaert (1828-1908), musicologist and composer; Emmanuel Durlet (1893-1977), pianist; Queen Elisabeth Musical Chapel Foundation, 40th anniversary.

Virgin and Child, Notre Dame, Foy — A431

Photogravure and Engraved

1979, Nov. 24

1044 A431 6fr lt grnsh bl 35 10

Christmas 1979.

Independence, 150th Anniversary — A432

1980, Jan. 26 Photo. *Perf. 11½*

1045 A432 9fr purple 60 15

Frans van Cauwelaert A433

Spring Flowers A434

1980, Feb. 25 Engr.

1046 A433 5fr gray 30 8

Frans van Cauwelaert (1880-1961), Minister of State.

1980, Mar. 10 Photo.

1047 A434 5fr *shown* 30 8
1048 A434 6.50fr *Summer flowers* 40 10
1049 A434 9fr *Autumn flowers* 55 15

Ghent Flower Show, Apr. 19-27.

Telephone and Telegraph Administration, 50th Anniversary — A435

1980, Apr. 14 Photo. *Perf. 11½*

1050 A435 10fr multi 60 30

Belgium No. C4 — A436

1980, Apr. 21
1051 A436 9fr multi 55 15

Stamp Day.

Europa Issue 1980

St. Benedict, by Hans Memling — A437

Design: 14fr, Margaret of Austria (1480-1530).

1980, Apr. 28
1052 A437 9fr multi 55 15
1053 A437 14fr multi 85 30

Palais des Nations, Brussels — A438

1980, May 10 Photo. *Perf. 11½*
1054 A438 5fr multi 30 10

4th Interparliamentary Conference for European Cooperation and Security, Brussels, May 12-18.

Golden Carriage, 1780, Mons A439

Design: No. 1056, Canal landscape, Damme.

1980, May 17
1055 A439 6.50fr multi 40 25
1056 A439 6.50fr multi 40 25

Tourism.

Souvenir Sheet

Royal Mint Theater, Brussels — A440

Photogravure and Engraved
1980, May 31 *Perf. 11½*
1057 A440 50fr black 4.50 4.50

150th anniversary of independence. Multicolored decorative margin; sold for 75fr. Size: 100½x151mm.

King Baudouin, 50th Birthday — A441

1980, Sept. 6 Photo. *Perf. 11½*
1058 A441 9fr rose cl 55 15

View of Chiny A442

Portal and Court, Diest — A443

1980 Engr. *Perf. 13*
1059 A442 5fr multi 30 10
1060 A443 5fr multi 30 10

Tourism. Nos. 1059-1060 are not luminescent. Issue dates: No. 1059, Sept. 27; No. 1060, Dec. 13. See Nos. 1072-1075.

Emblem of Belgian Heart League A444

1980, Oct. 4 Photo. *Perf. 11½*
1061 A444 14fr bl & mag 85 40

Heart Week, Oct. 20-25.

Rodenbach Statue, Roulers — A445

1980, Oct. 11
1062 A445 9fr multi 60 15

Albrecht Rodenbach (1856-1880), poet.

Youth Philately — A446

1980, Oct. 27 Photo. *Perf. 11½*
1063 A446 5fr multi 30 10

National Broadcasting Service, 50th Anniversary — A447

1980, Nov. 10
1064 A447 10fr gray & blk 60 30

Garland and Nativity, by Daniel Seghers, 17th Century A448

1980, Nov. 17
1065 A448 6.50fr multi 40 12

Christmas 1980.

Baron de Gerlache, by F.J. Navez — A449

Leopold I, By Geefs — A450

Design: 9fr, Baron de Stassart, by F.J. Navez.

1981, Mar. 16 Photo. *Perf. 11½*
1066 A449 6fr multi 35 18
1067 A449 9fr multi 55 12

Photogravure and Engraved
1068 A450 50fr multi 3.00 75

Sesquicentennial of Chamber of Deputies, Senate and Dynasty.

Europa Issue 1981

Tchantchès and Op-Signoorke, Puppets — A451

Photogravure and Engraved
1981, May 4 *Perf. 11½*
1069 A451 9fr shown 55 12
1070 A451 14fr d'Artagnan and Woltje 90 45

Impression of M.A. de Cock (Founder of Post Museum) — A452

1901, May 18 Photo.
1071 A452 9fr multi 55 12

Stamp Day.

Tourism Types of 1980

Designs: No. 1072, Virgin and Child statue, Our Lady's Church, Tongre-Notre Dame. No. 1073, Egmont Castle, Zottegem. No. 1074, Eau d'Heure River. No. 1075, Tongerlo Abbey, Antwerp.

1981, June 15 Engr. *Perf. 11½*
1072 A442 6fr multi 45 18
1073 A442 6fr multi 45 25
1074 A443 6.50fr multi 45 25
1075 A443 6.50fr multi 45 25

Soccer Player A453

E. Remouchamps, Founder A454

1981, Sept. 5 Photo. *Perf. 11½*
1076 A453 6fr multi 35 18

Soccer in Belgium centenary; Royal Antwerp Soccer Club.

Photogravure and Engraved
1981, Sept. 5
1077 A454 6.50fr multi 40 18

Walloon Language and Literature Club 125th anniv.

Audit Office Sesquicentennial — A455

1981, Sept. 12 Engr.
1078 A455 10fr tan & dk brn 60 30

French Horn — A456

1981, Sept. 12 Photo.
1079 A456 6.50fr multi 40 18

Vredekring (Peace Circle) Band of Antwerp centenary.

Souvenir Sheet

Pieta, by Ben Genaux — A457

1981, Sept. 19 Photo. *Perf. 11½*
1080 A457 20fr multi 1.75 1.75

Mining disaster at Marcinelle, 25th anniv. Red brown and black margin shows mine fire. Size: 150x100mm. Sold for 30fr.

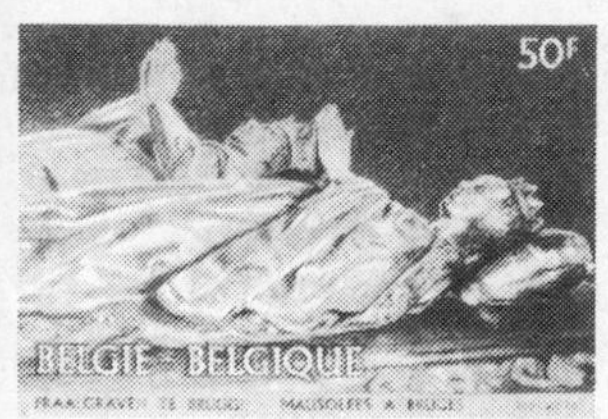

Mausoleum of Marie of Burgundy and Charles the Bold, Bruges — A458

Photogravure and Engraved

1981, Oct. 10

1081 A458 50fr multi 3.00 75

Youth Philately — A459

1981, Oct. 24 **Photo.**

1082 A459 6fr multi 35 18

Type of 1977 and

A459a

A460

King Baudouin A460a

Photo. and Engr.; Photo.

1980-86 ***Perf. 13½x14, 11½***

No.	Type	Value	Description	Unused	Used
1084	A386	65c	brt rose	5	5
1085	A386	1fr	on 5fr grn ('82)	5	5
1086	A386	7fr	brt rose ('82)	42	5
1087	A386	8fr	grnsh bl ('83)	45	6
1088	A386	9fr	dl org ('85)	38	8
1089	A459a	10fr	bl ('82)	60	10
1090	A459a	11fr	dl red ('83)	65	8
1091	A459a	12fr	grn ('84)	70	6
1092	A459a	13fr	scar ('86)	60	6
1093	A459a	15fr	red org ('84)	90	20
1094	A459a	20fr	dk bl ('84)	1.10	28
1095	A459a	22fr	lil ('84)	1.25	30
1096	A459a	23fr	gray grn ('85)	75	55
1097	A459a	30fr	brn ('84)	1.50	40
1098	A459a	40fr	red org ('84)	2.00	55
1099	A460	50fr	lt grnsh bl & bl	2.50	30
1100	A460a	50fr	tan & dk brn ('84)	2.50	60
1101	A460	65fr	pale lil & blk ('81)	3.50	90
1102	A460	100fr	lt bis brn & dk bl ('81)	5.00	1.25
1103	A460a	100fr	lt bl & dk bl ('84)	5.00	1.25
			Nos. 1084-1103 (20)	29.90	7.17

See Nos. 1231-1234.

Max Waller, Movement Founder A461

The Spirit Drinkers, by Gustave van de Woestyne A462

Fernand Severin, Poet, 50th Death Anniv. — A463

Jan van Ruusbroec, Flemish Mystic, 500th Birth Anniv. — A464

Thought and Man TV Series, 25th Anniv. A465

Nativity, 16th Cent. Engraving A466

1981, Nov. 7

No.	Type	Value	Description	Unused	Used
1104	A461	6fr	multi	35	18
1105	A462	6.50fr	multi	40	25
1106	A463	9fr	multi	55	15
1107	A464	10fr	multi	90	30
1108	A465	14fr	multi	85	45
			Nos. 1104-1108 (5)	3.05	1.33

La Jeune Belgique cultural movement centenary (6fr).

1981, Nov. 21

1109 A466 6.50fr multi 40 18

Christmas 1981.

Royal Conservatory of Music Sesquicentennial — A467

Design: 9fr, Judiciary sesquicentennial.

1982, Jan. 25 **Photo.** ***Perf. 11½***

1110 A467 6.50fr multi 40 18
1111 A467 9fr multi 55 8

Galaxy and Microscope — A468

1982, Mar. 1

1112 A468 6fr Cyclatron 35 18
1113 A468 14fr shown 85 45
1114 A468 50fr Koch 3.00 90

Radio-isotope production, Natl. Radio-elements Institute, Fleurus (6fr); Royal Belgian Observatory (14fr); centenary of TB bacillus discovery (50fr).

Joseph Lemaire (1882-1966), Minister of State — A469

1982, Apr. 17 **Photo.** ***Perf. 11½***

1115 A469 6.50fr multi 40 18

Europa 1982 — A470

1982, May 1

1116 A470 10fr Universal suffrage 60 8
1117 A470 17fr Edict of Tolerance, 1781 1.00 45

Stamp Day — A471

Photogravure and Engraved

1982, May 22 ***Perf. 11½***

1118 A471 10fr multi 60 8

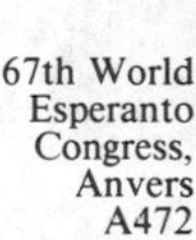

67th World Esperanto Congress, Anvers A472

1982, June 7 **Photo.** ***Perf. 11½***

1119 A472 12fr Tower of Babel 75 35

Tourism Type of 1980

Designs: No. 1120, Tower of Gosselies. No. 1121, Zwijveke Abbey, Dendermonde. No. 1122, Stavelot Abbey. No. 1123, Villers-la-Ville Abbey ruins. No. 1124, Geraardsbergen Abbey entrance. No. 1125, Beveren Pillory.

Photogravure and Engraved

1982, June 21

No.	Type	Value	Description	Unused	Used
1120	A443	7fr	lt bl & blk	42	6
1121	A443	7fr	lt grn & blk	42	6
1122	A442	7.50fr	tan & dk brn	45	30
1123	A442	7.50fr	lt vio & pur	45	30
1124	A443	7.50fr	sl & blk	45	30
1125	A443	7.50fr	beige & blk	45	30
			Nos. 1120-1125 (6)	2.64	1.32

Self Portrait, by L.P. Boon (b. 1912) A473

Abraham Hans, Writer (1882-1932) A474

Designs: 10fr, Adoration of the Shepherds, by Hugo van der Goes (1440-1482). 12fr, The King on His Throne, carving by M. de Ghelderode (1898-1962). 17fr, Madonna and Child, by Pieter Paulus (1881-1959).

1982, Sept. 13 **Photo.** ***Perf. 11½***

No.	Type	Value	Description	Unused	Used
1126	A473	7fr	multi	45	6
1127	A473	10fr	multi	60	6
1128	A473	12fr	multi	75	45
1129	A473	17fr	multi	1.00	45

1982, Sept. 27

1130 A474 17fr multi 1.00 45

Youth Philately and Scouting A475

1982, Oct. 2 **Photo.** ***Perf. 11½***

1131 A475 7fr multi 45 6

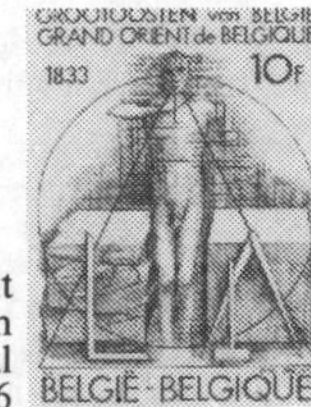

Grand Orient Lodge of Belgium Sesquicentennial A476

Photogravure and Engraved

1982, Oct. 16

1132 A476 10fr Man taking oath 60 6

Cardinal Joseph Cardijn (1882-1967) A477

1982, Nov. 13 **Photo.**

1133 A477 10fr multi 60 6

St. Francis of Assisi (1182-1226) — A478

1982, Nov. 27

1134 A478 20fr multi 1.25 45

Horse-drawn Trolley A479

1983, Feb. 12 **Photo.** ***Perf. 11½***

1135 A479 7.50fr shown 45 25
1136 A479 10fr Electric trolley 60 15
1137 A479 50fr Trolley, diff. 3.00 60

Intl. Fed. for Periodical Press, 24th World Congress, Brussels, May 11-13 A480

1983, Mar. 19 Photo. *Perf. 11½*
1138 A480 20fr multi 1.25 30

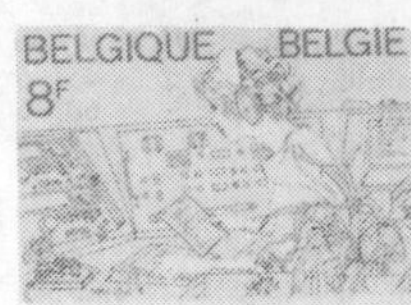
Homage to Women A481

1983, Apr. 16
1139 A481 8fr Operator 60 5
1140 A481 11fr Homemaker 75 8
1141 A481 20fr Executive 1.25 25

Stamp Day — A482

1983, Apr. 23
1142 A482 11fr multi 65 8

Procession of the Precious Blood, Bruges A483

1983, Apr. 30 Photo. *Perf. 11½*
1143 A483 8fr multi 50 5

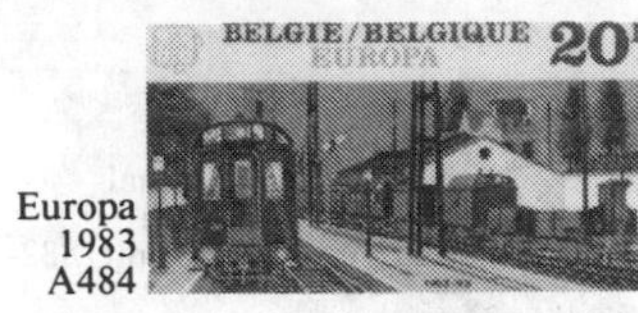
Europa 1983 A484

Paintings by P. Delvaux. 11fr vert.

1983, May 14
1144 A484 11fr Common Man 65 8
1145 A484 20fr Night Train 1.25 45

Manned Flight Bicentenary A485

1983, June 11 Photo. *Perf. 11½*
1146 A485 11fr Balloon over city 65 10
1147 A485 22fr Country 1.40 45

Our Lady's Church, Hastiere A486

1983, June 25
1148 A486 8fr shown 45 18
1149 A486 8fr Landen 45 18
1150 A486 8fr Park, Mouscron 45 18
1151 A486 8fr Wijnendale Castle, Torhout 45 18

Tineke Festival, Heule — A487

1983, Sept. 10 Photo.
1152 A487 8fr multi 45 8

Enterprise Year Emblem A488

1983, Sept. 24
1153 A488 11fr multi 65 12

European year for small and medium-sized enterprises and craft industry.

Youth Philately — A489

1983, Oct. 10 Photo. *Perf. 11½*
1154 A489 8fr multi 45 8

Belgian Exports A490

1983, Oct. 24 *Perf. 11½*
1155 A490 10fr Diamond industry 60 10
1156 A490 10fr Metallurgy 60 10
1157 A490 10fr Textile industry 60 10

See Nos. 1161-1164

Hendrik Conscience, Novelist (1812-1883) — A491

1983, Nov. 7
1158 A491 20fr multi 1.25 25

Leopold III Type of 1936

1983, Dec. 12 Engr. *Perf. 12x11½*
1159 A84 11fr black 65 12

Leopold III memorial (1901-1983), King 1934-1951.

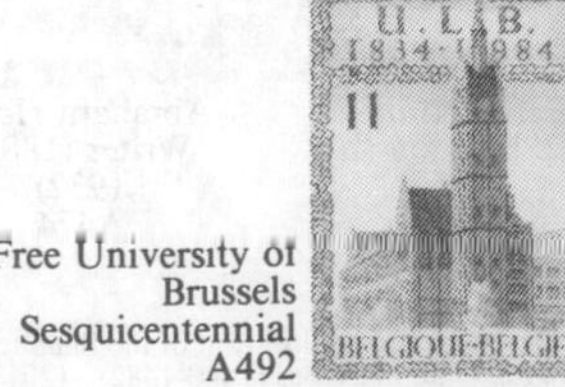
Free University of Brussels Sesquicentennial A492

Photogravure and Engraved

1984, Jan. 14 *Perf. 11½*
1160 A492 11fr multi 65 12

Exports Type of 1983

1984, Jan. 28 Photo.
1161 A490 11fr Chemicals 65 12
1162 A490 11fr Food 65 12
1163 A490 11fr Transportation equipment 65 12
1164 A490 11fr Technology 65 12

50th Death Anniv. of King Albert I — A494

Photogravure and Engraved

1984, Feb. 11
1165 A494 8fr tan & dk brn 45 10

Souvenir Sheet

Archery — A495

1984, Mar. 3 Photo.
1166 Sheet of 2 2.25 2.25
a. A495 10fr shown 60 60
b. A495 24fr Dressage 1.75 1.75

1984 Olympics. See Nos. B1029-B1030. Size: 125x90mm.

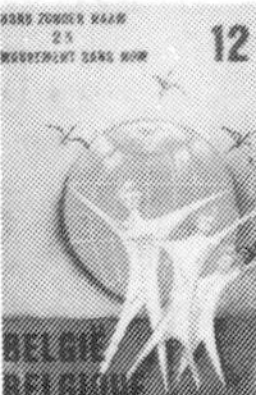
Family, Globe, Birds A496

St. John Roscho Canonization A497

1984, Mar. 24 Photo. *Perf. 11½*
1167 A496 12fr multi 70 14

"Movement without a Name" peace org.

1984, Apr. 7
1168 A497 8fr multi 45 10

Europa (1959-84) A498

1984, May 5 Photo. *Perf. 11½*
1169 A498 12fr blk & red 75 14
1170 A498 22fr blk & ultra 1.40 30

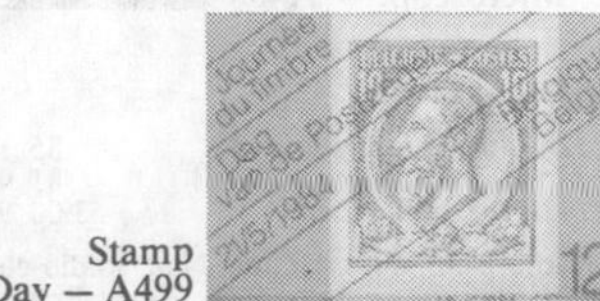
Stamp Day — A499

1984, May 19
1171 A499 12fr No. 52 70 14

2nd European Parliament Elections A500

1984, May 26
1172 A500 12fr multi 70 14

Royal Military School, 150th Anniv. — A501

1984, June 9 Photo. *Perf. 11½*
1173 A501 22fr Hat 1.40 30

Notre-Dame de la Chappelle, Brussels A502

Churches: No. 1175, St. Martin's, Montignyle-Tilleul. No. 1176, Tielt (vert.).

Photogravure and Engraved
Perf. 11½x12, 12x11½

1984, June 23
1174 A502 10fr multi 60 14
1175 A502 10fr multi 60 14
1176 A502 10fr multi 60 14

50th Anniv. of Chirojeugd (Christian Youth Movement) A503

1984, Sept. 15 Photo. *Perf. 11½*
1177 A503 10fr Emblem 60 14

Affligem Abbey A504

Photogravure and Engraved

1984, Oct. 6
1178 A504 8fr Averbode, vert. 48 30
1179 A504 22fr Chimay, vert. 1.40 30
1180 A504 24fr Rochefort, vert. 1.50 45
1181 A504 50fr shown 3.00 60

Youth Philately A505

1984, Oct. 20 Photo.
1182 A505 8fr Postman smurf 45 12

Arthur Meulemans (1884-1966), Composer — A506

Photogravure and Engraved

1984, Nov. 17

1183 A506 12fr multi 75 14

St. Norbert, 850th Death Anniv. — A507

Photogravure and Engraved

1985, Jan. 14

1184 A507 22fr sep & beige 90 30

Europalia '85 — A508

1985, Jan. 21 **Photo.**

1185 A508 12fr Virgin with Lion 40 14

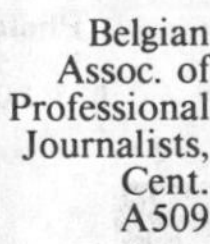

Belgian Assoc. of Professional Journalists, Cent. A509

1985, Feb. 11 **Photo.**

1186 A509 9fr multi 30 10

Ghent Flower Festival, Orchids — A510

Photogravure and Engraved

1985, Mar. 18 ***Perf. 11½***

1187 A510 12fr Vanda coerules 40 14
1188 A510 12fr Phalaenopsis 40 14
1189 A510 12fr Suphrolaelio cattlea riffe 40 14

Visit of Pope John-Paul II — A511

1985, Apr. 1 **Photo.**

1190 A511 12fr multi 40 14

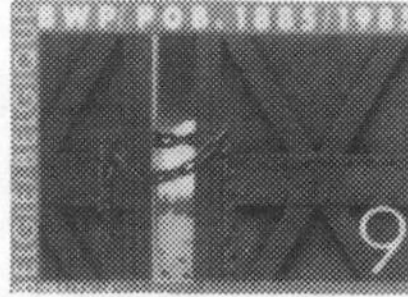

Belgian Worker's Party Cent. A512

1985, Apr. 15 **Photo.**

1191 A512 9fr Chained factory gate 30 10
1192 A512 12fr Broken wall, red flag 40 14

Jean de Bast (1883-1975), Engraver A513

Stamp Day.

1985, Apr. 22 **Engr.**

1193 A513 12fr bl blk 40 14

Public Transportation Year — A514

Design: 9fr, Steam tram locomotive Type 18, 1896. 12fr, Locomotive Elephant and tender, 1835. 23fr, Type 23 tank engine, 1904. 24fr, Type I Pacific locomotive, 1935. 50fr, Type 27 electric locomotive, 1975.

1985, May 6 **Photo.**

1194 A514 9fr multi 30 10
1195 A514 12fr multi 40 14
1196 A514 23fr multi 75 25
1197 A514 24fr multi 80 28

Souvenir Sheet

1198 A514 50fr multi 1.75 1.00

No. 1198 has multicolored margin continuing design. Size 150x100mm.

Europa 1985 — A515

1985, May 13 **Photo.**

1199 A515 12fr Cesar Franck at organ, 1887 40 14
1200 A515 23fr Folk figures 75 25

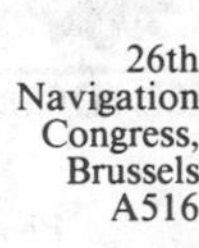

26th Navigation Congress, Brussels A516

1985, June 10 **Photo.** ***Perf. 11½***

1201 A516 23fr Zeebruge Harbor 78 25
1202 A516 23fr Projected lock at Strepy-Thieu 78 25

St. Martin's Church, Marcinelle A517

Tourism: No. 1203, Church of the Assumption of Our Lady, Avernas-le-Baudouin (vert.). No. 1204, Church of the Old Beguinage, Tongres (vert.). No. 1206, Private residence, Puyenbroeck.

1985, June 24 ***Perf. 11½***

1203 A517 12fr multi 40 12
1204 A517 12fr multi 40 12
1205 A517 12fr multi 40 12
1206 A517 12fr multi 40 12

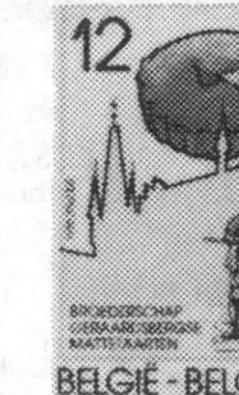

Queen Astrid (1905-1935) A518

Baking Pies for the Mattetart of Geraardsbergen A519

1985, Sept. 2 ***Perf. 11½***

1207 A518 12fr brown 42 14

1985, Sept. 16

Folk events: 24fr, Children dancing, centenary of the St. Lambert de Hermalle-Argenteau Le Rouges youth organization.

1208 A519 12fr multi 42 14
1209 A519 24fr multi 85 28

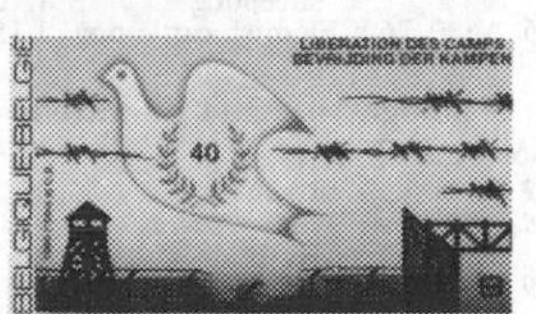

Liberation from German Occupation, 40th Anniv. — A520

Allegories. 9fr, Dove, liberation of concentration camps. 23fr, Battle of Ardennes. 24fr, Destroyer, liberation of the River Scheldt estuary.

1985, Sept. 30 **Photo.** ***Perf. 11½***

1210 A520 9fr multi 35 25
1211 A520 23fr multi 85 65
1212 A520 24fr multi 90 68

Ernest Claes (1885-1968), Author A521

1985, Oct. 7

1213 A521 9fr Portrait, book character 35 25

Intl. Youth Year — A522

1985, Oct. 21

1214 A522 9fr Nude in repose, angel 35 25

King Baudouin & Queen Fabiola, 25th Wedding Anniv. — A523

1985, Dec. 9

1215 A523 12fr multi 48 38

Birds — A524

1985-87 **Typo.** ***Perf. 11½***

1218 A524 3fr Hawkfinch 10 5
1219 A524 3.50fr Robin 18 5
1219A A524 7fr Blue tit ('87) 40 5
1220 A524 8fr Kingfisher 40 8
1221 A524 9fr Goldfinch 30 6
Nos. 1218-1221 (5) 1.38 29

Issue dates: 7fr, Sept. 7, others, Sept. 30.

King Type of 1981

1986 **Photo.** ***Perf. 11½***

1231 A459a 24fr dk grysh grn 1.10 85
1234 A460a 200fr sage grn & dl gray grn 9.50 7.00

Congo Stamp Cent. — A525

1986, Jan. 27 **Photo.** ***Perf. 11½***

1236 A525 10fr Belgian Congo No. 3 42 14

See Zaire No. 1230.

Carnival Cities of Aalst and Binche A526

Folklore: masks, giants.

1986, Feb. 3

1237 A526 9fr Aalst Belfry 38 12
1238 A526 12fr Binche Gilles 50 18

Intl. Peace Year — A527

1986, Mar. 10

1239 A527 23fr Emblem, dove 1.00 35

Stamp Day — A528

1986, Apr. 21 **Photo.** ***Perf. 11½***

1240 A528 13fr Artifacts 55 42

Europa 1986 — A529

1986, May 5
1241 A529 13fr Fish 55 42
1242 A529 24fr Flora 1.10 85

Dogs — A530

St. Ludger's Church, Zele — A531

1986, May 26 Photo. *Perf. 11½*
1243 A530 9fr Malines sheepdog 40 30
1244 A530 13fr Tervueren sheepdog 58 45
1245 A530 24fr Groenendael sheepdog 1.10 82
1246 A530 26fr Flemish cattle dog 1.15 85

Photogravure and Engraved

1986, June 30
1247 A531 9fr shown 40 30
1248 A531 9fr Waver Town Hall 40 30
1249 A531 13fr Nederzwalm Canal, horiz. 58 45
1250 A531 13fr Chapel of Our Lady of the Dunes, Bredene 58 45
1251 A531 13fr Licot Castle, Viroinval, horiz. 58 45
1252 A531 13fr Eynenbourg Castle, La Calamine, horiz. 58 45
Nos. 1247-1252 (6) 3.12 2.40

Youth Philately A532

1986, Sept. 1 Photo. *Perf. 11½*
1253 A532 9fr dl ol grn, blk & dk red 42 32

Cartoon Exhibition, Knokke.

Famous Men — A533

Designs: 9fr, Constant Permeke, painter, sculptor. 13fr, Baron Michel-Edmond de Selys Longchamps, scientist. 24fr, Felix Timmermans, writer. 26fr, Maurice Careme, poet.

1986, Sept. 29
1254 A533 9fr multi 42 32
1255 A533 13fr multi 60 45
1256 A533 24fr multi 1.10 82
1257 A533 26fr multi 1.20 90

Royal Academy for Dutch Language and Literature, Cent. A534

1986, Oct. 6 Engr.
1258 A534 9fr dark blue 42 32

Natl. Beer Industry A535

Perf. 12½x11½

1986, Oct. 13 Photo.
1259 A535 13fr Glass, barley, hops 65 50

Provincial Law and Councils, 150th Anniv. A536

1986, Oct. 27 *Perf. 11½*
1260 A536 13fr Stylized map 65 50

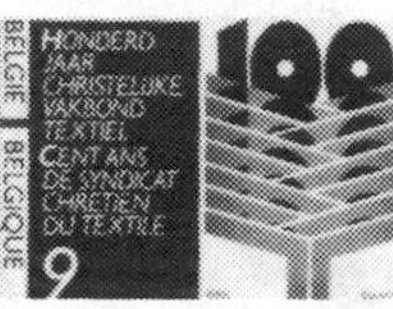

Christian Trade Union, Cent. A537

1986, Dec. 13 Photo. *Perf. 11½*
1261 A537 9fr shown 45 35
1262 A537 13fr design reversed 65 50

Flanders Technology Intl. — A538

1987, Mar. 2 Photo.
1263 A538 13fr multi 65 50

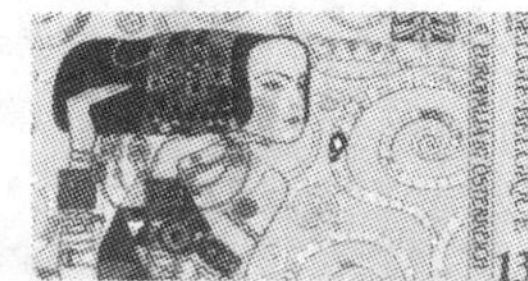

EUROPALIA '87, Austrian Cultural Events — A539

Design: Woman, detail of a fresco by Gustav Klimt, Palais Stoclet, Brussels.

1987, Apr. 4 Photo. *Perf. 11½*
1264 A539 13fr multi 65 50

Stamp Day 1987 — A540

Portrait: Jakob Wiener (1815-1899), 1st engraver of Belgian stamps.

1987, Apr. 11 Photo. & Engr.
1265 A540 13fr lt greenish blue & sage grn 65 50

Folklore A541

1987, Apr. 25 Photo.
1266 A541 9fr Penitents procession, Veurne 45 35
1267 A541 13fr Play of John and Alice, Wavre 65 50

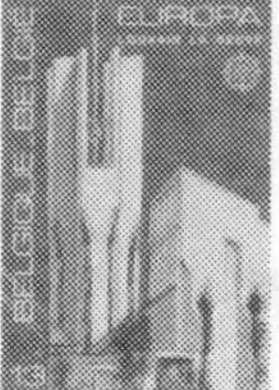

Europa 1987 — A542

Modern architecture: 13fr, Louvain-la-Neuve Church. 24fr, Regional Housing Assoc. Tower, St. Maartensdal at Louvain.

1987, May 9 Photo.
1268 A542 13fr multi 72 55
1269 A542 24fr multi 1.35 1.00

Statue of Andre-Ernest Gretry (1741-1813), French Composer — A543

1987, May 23
1270 A543 24fr multi 1.35 1.00

Wallonie Royal Opera, Liege, 20th anniv.

Tourism — A544

Designs: No. 1271, Statues of Jan Breydel and Pieter de Conin, Bruges. No. 1272, Boondael Chapel, Brussels. No. 1273, Windmill, Keerbergen. No. 1274, St. Christopher's Church, Racour. No. 1275, Virelles Lake, Chimay.

1987, June 13
1271 A544 13fr multi 77 55
1272 A544 13fr multi 77 55
1273 A544 13fr multi 77 55
1274 A544 13fr multi 77 55
1275 A544 13fr multi 77 55
Nos. 1271-1275 (5) 3.85 2.75

Royal Belgian Rowing Assoc., Cent. — A545

European Vollyball Championships
A546

1987, Sept. 5

1276 A545 9fr multi 50 38
1277 A546 13fr multi 72 55

Foreign Trade Year
A547

1987, Sept. 12

1278 A547 13fr multi 72 55

Belgian Social Reform, Cent.
A548

1987, Sept. 19

1279 A548 26fr Leisure, by P. Paulus 1.45 1.10

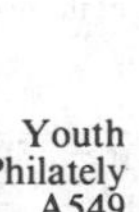

Youth Philately
A549

1987, Oct. 3

1280 A549 9fr multi 50 38

Newspaper Centennials
A550

1987, Dec. 12

1281 A550 9fr Le Soir 55 42
1282 A550 9fr Hett Lattste Nieuws, vert. 55 42

The Sea — A551

Designs: a. Lighthouse, trawler, rider and mount. b. Trawler, youths playing volleyball on beach. c. Cruise ship, sailboat, beach and cabana. d. Shore, birds.

1988, Feb. 6 **Photo.** ***Perf. 11 ½***

1283 Strip of 4 2.50 1.80
a.-d. A551 10fr any single 62 45

No. 1283 printed se-tenant with label picturing mermaid or Neptune. Stamps printed in a continuous design.

Belgium stamps can be mounted in Scott's annual Belgium Supplement.

SEMI-POSTAL STAMPS

St. Martin of Tours Dividing His Cloak with a Beggar
SP1 SP2

Unwmk.

1910, June 1 **Typo.** ***Perf. 14***

B1 SP1 1c gray 1.25 1.25
B2 SP1 2c pur brn 9.25 9.25
B3 SP1 5c pck bl 2.50 2.50
B4 SP1 10c brn red 2.50 2.50
B5 SP2 1c gray grn 2.50 2.50
B6 SP2 2c vio brn 7.25 7.25
B7 SP2 5c pck bl 2.50 2.50
B8 SP2 10c carmine 2.50 2.50
Nos. B1-B8 (8) 30.25 30.25

Overprinted "1911" in Black.

1911, Apr. 1

B9 SP1 1c gray 16.00 10.50
a. Inverted overprint
B10 SP1 2c pur brn 37.50 35.00
B11 SP1 5c pck bl 4.00 3.00
B12 SP1 10c brn red 4.00 3.00
B13 SP2 1c gray grn 30.00 27.50
B14 SP2 2c vio brn 27.50 21.00
B15 SP2 5c pck bl 4.00 3.00
B16 SP2 10c carmine 4.00 3.00
Nos. B9-B16 (8) 127.00 106.00

Overprinted "CHARLEROI-1911"

1911, June

B17 SP1 1c gray 4.00 4.00
B18 SP1 2c pur brn 14.00 13.00
B19 SP1 5c pck bl 6.50 6.00
B20 SP1 10c brn red 6.00 5.25
B21 SP2 1c gray grn 4.00 4.00
B22 SP2 2c vio brn 13.00 12.00
B23 SP2 5c pck bl 5.25 4.75
B24 SP2 10c carmine 4.00 4.00
Nos. B17-B24 (8) 56.75 53.00

Nos. B1-B24 were sold at double face value, except the 10c denominations which were sold for 15c. The surtax benefited the national anti-tuberculosis organization.

SP3

Merode Monument SP4

King Albert I SP5

1914, Oct. 3 **Litho.**

B25	SP3	5c grn & red	1.50	1.75
B26	SP3	10c red	45	45
B27	SP3	20c vio & red	10.00	11.00

1914, Oct. 3

B28	SP4	5c grn & red	5.00	5.00
B29	SP4	10c red	5.00	5.00
B30	SP4	20c vio & red	47.50	47.50

Counterfeits of Nos. B25-B30 abound.

1915, Jan. 1 ***Perf. 12, 14***

B31	SP5	5c grn & red	4.50	2.25
a.		Perf. 12x14	14.00	8.50
B32	SP5	10c rose & red	8.50	4.50
B33	SP5	20c vio & red	22.50	11.00
a.		Perf. 14x12	400.00	325.00
b.		Perf. 12	75.00	35.00

Nos. B25-B33 were sold at double face value. The surtax benefited the Red Cross.

Types of Regular Issue of 1915 Surcharged in Red:

✚ a 1 c ✚ 35c b c ✚ 1F

1918, Jan. 15 **Typo.** ***Perf. 14***

B34	A46 (a)	1c + 1c dp org	40	40
B35	A46 (a)	2c + 2c brn	50	50
B36	A46 (a)	5c + 5c bl grn	1.10	1.10
B37	A46 (a)	10c + 10c red	2.00	2.00
B38	A46 (a)	15c + 15c brt vio	3.00	3.00
B39	A46 (a)	20c + 20c plum	6.25	6.25
B40	A46 (a)	25c + 25c ultra	6.50	6.50

Engr.

B41	A47 (b)	35c + 35c lt vio & blk	9.25	9.25
B42	A48 (b)	40c + 40c dl red & blk	9.25	9.25
B43	A49 (b)	50c + 50c turq bl & blk	11.00	11.00
B44	A50 (c)	1f + 1f bluish sl	32.50	32.50
B45	A51 (c)	2f + 2f dp gray grn	85.00	85.00
B46	A52 (c)	5f + 5f brn	225.00	225.00
B47	A53 (c)	10f + 10f dp bl	450.00	450.00
		Nos. B34-B47 (14)	841.75	841.75

Discus Thrower SP6

Racing Chariot SP7

Runner — SP8

1920, May 20 **Engr.** ***Perf. 12***

B48	SP6	5c + 5c dp grn	2.25	2.50
B49	SP7	10c + 5c car	2.25	2.50
B50	SP8	15c + 15c dk brn	4.50	1.25

Issued to commemorate the 7th International Olympic Games of 1920. The surtax was to benefit wounded soldiers. Imperforates exist.

Allegory: Asking Alms from the Crown SP9

Wounded Veteran SP10

1922, May 20

B51	SP9	20c + 20c brn	1.90	1.50

1923, July 5

B52	SP10	20c + 20c sl gray	2.50	2.50

The surtax on Nos. B51-B52 was to aid wounded veterans.

SP11

SP12

St. Martin, by Van Dyck
SP13 SP14

1925, Dec. 15 **Typo.** ***Perf. 14***

B53	SP11	15c + 15c dl vio & red	45	22
B54	SP11	30c + 5c gray & red	28	12
B55	SP11	1fr + 10c chlky bl & red	1.25	1.50

The surtax on Nos. B53-B55 benefited the National Anti-Tuberculosis League.

1926, Feb. 10

B56	SP12	30c + 30c bluish grn (red surch.)	50	55
B57	SP13	1fr + 1fr lt bl	7.25	7.25
B58	SP14	1fr + 1fr lt bl	1.10	1.25

The surtax on Nos. B56-B58 aided victims of the Meuse flood.

Lion and Cross of Lorraine SP15

Queen Elisabeth and King Albert SP16

1926, Dec. 6 **Typo.** ***Perf. 14***

B59	SP15	5c + 5c dk brn	28	22
B60	SP15	20c + 5c red brn	50	45
B61	SP15	50c + 5c dl vio	32	22

Engr. ***Perf. 11½***

B62	SP16	1.50fr + 25c dk bl	85	85
B63	SP16	5fr + 1fr rose red	7.25	7.25
		Nos. B59-B63 (5)	9.20	8.99

The surtax on Nos. B59-B63 was used to benefit tubercular war veterans.

Boat Adrift — SP17

1927, Dec. 15 **Engr.** ***Perf. 11½, 14***

B64	SP17	25c + 10c dk brn	85	85
B65	SP17	35c + 10c yel grn	85	85
B66	SP17	60c + 10c dp vio	65	45
B67	SP17	1.75fr + 25c dk bl	1.75	2.50
B68	SP17	5fr + 1fr plum	5.25	5.75
		Nos. B64-B68 (5)	9.35	10.40

The surtax on these stamps was divided among several charitable associations.

Ogives of Orval Abbey — SP18

Monk Carving Capital of Column — SP19

Ruins of Orval Abbey SP20

Design: 60c+15c, 1.75fr+25c, 3fr+1fr, Countess Matilda recovering her ring.

1928, Sept. 15 **Photo.** ***Perf. 11½***

B69	SP18	5c + 5c red & gold	28	50
B70	SP18	25c + 5c dk vio & gold	55	1.10

Engr.

B71	SP19	35c + 10c dp grn	1.25	1.75
B72	SP19	60c + 15c red brn	1.75	80
B73	SP19	1.75fr + 25c dk bl	4.00	4.00
B74	SP19	2fr + 40c dp vio	15.00	11.50
B75	SP19	3fr + 1fr red	17.00	14.00

Perf. 14.

B76	SP20	5fr + 5fr rose lake	17.00	18.00
B77	SP20	10fr + 10fr ol grn	17.00	20.00
		Nos. B69-B77 (9)	73.83	71.65

The surtax on these stamps was to be used toward the restoration of the ruined Abbey of Orval.

St. Waudru, Mons — SP22

St. Rombaut, Malines — SP23

Designs: 25c + 15c, Cathedral of Tournai. 60c + 15c, St. Bavon, Ghent. 1.75fr + 25c, St. Gudule, Brussels. 5fr + 5fr, Louvain Library.

1928, Dec. 1 **Photo.** ***Perf. 14, 11½***

B78	SP22	5c + 5c car	20	22
B79	SP22	25c + 15c ol brn	38	45

Engr.

B80	SP23	35c + 10c dp grn	1.25	1.40
B81	SP23	60c + 15c red brn	50	30
B82	SP23	1.75fr + 25c vio bl	8.50	8.25
B83	SP23	5fr + 5fr red vio	16.00	18.00
		Nos. B78-B83 (6)	26.83	28.62

The surtax was for anti-tuberculosis work.

Orval Abbey Stamps of 1928 Overprinted in Blue or Red

1929, Aug. 19

B84	SP18	5c + 5c red & gold	85.00	85.00
B85	SP18	25c + 5c dk vio & gold (R)	85.00	85.00
B86	SP19	35c + 10c dp grn (R)	85.00	85.00
B87	SP19	60c + 15c red brn	85.00	85.00
B88	SP19	1.75fr + 25c dk bl (R)	85.00	85.00
B89	SP19	2fr + 40c dp vio (R)	85.00	85.00
B90	SP19	3fr + 1fr red	85.00	85.00
B91	SP20	5fr + 5fr rose lake	85.00	85.00
B92	SP20	10fr + 10fr dk brn (R)	85.00	85.00
		Nos. B84-B92 (9)	765.00	765.00

Issued in commemoration of the laying of the first stone toward the restoration of the ruined Abbey of Orval. Forgeries of the overprint exist.

Waterfall at Coo — SP28

Bayard Rock, Dinant — SP29

Designs: 35c+10c, Menin Gate, Ypres. 60c+15c, Promenade d'Orleans, Spa. 1.75fr+25c, Antwerp Harbor. 5fr+5fr, Quai Vert, Bruges.

1929, Dec. 2 **Engr.** ***Perf. 11½, 14***

B93	SP28	5c + 5c red brn	20	22

B94 SP29 25c + 15c gray blk 65 60
B95 SP28 35c + 10c grn 70 90
B96 SP28 60c + 15c rose lake 50 45
B97 SP28 1.75fr + 25c dp bl 4.00 4.25
B98 SP29 5fr + 5fr dl vio 25.00 25.00
Nos. B93-B98 (6) 31.05 31.42

Bornhem SP34

Beloeil SP35

Gaesbeek SP36

Designs: 25c + 15c, Wynendaele. 70c + 15c, Oydonck. 1fr + 25c, Ghent. 1.75fr + 25c, Bouillon.

1930, Dec. 1 Photo. *Perf. 14*
B99 SP34 10c + 5c vio 22 30
B100 SP34 25c + 15c ol brn 60 60

Engr.
B101 SP35 40c + 10c brn vio 70 90
B102 SP35 70c + 15c gray blk 45 45
B103 SP35 1fr + 25c rose lake 3.00 3.00
B104 SP35 1.75fr + 25c dp bl 3.50 2.25
B105 SP36 5fr + 5fr gray grn 21.00 27.50
Nos. B99-B105 (7) 29.47 35.00

Prince Leopold SP41

Queen Elisabeth SP42

Philatelic Exhibition Issue.
Souvenir Sheet.

1931, July 18 Photo. *Perf. 14*
B106 SP41 2.45fr + 55c car brn 110.00 110.00

Issued in sheets measuring 122x159mm. Sold exclusively at the Brussels Philatelic Exhibition, July 18th to 21st, 1931. The surtax was for the Veterans' Relief Fund.

1931, Dec. 1 Engr.
B107 SP42 10c + 5c red brn 28 50
B108 SP42 25c + 15c dk vio 1.00 1.10
B109 SP42 50c + 10c dk grn 90 85
B110 SP42 75c + 15c blk brn 80 60
B111 SP42 1fr + 25c rose lake 6.25 5.25
B112 SP42 1.75fr + 25c ultra 4.50 3.50
B113 SP42 5fr + 5fr brn vio 50.00 50.00
Nos. B107-B113 (7) 63.73 61.80

The surtax was for the National Anti-Tuberculosis League.

Desire Cardinal Mercier SP43

Mercier Protecting Children and Aged at Malines SP44

Mercier as Professor at Louvain University — SP45

Mercier in Full Canonicals, Giving His Blessing SP46

1932, June 10 Photo. *Perf. 14½x14*
B114 SP43 10c + 10c dk vio 65 65
B115 SP43 50c + 30c brt vio 2.25 2.50
B116 SP43 75c + 25c ol brn 2.25 2.00
B117 SP43 1fr + 2fr brn red 6.25 6.00

Engr. *Perf. 11½.*
B118 SP44 1.75fr + 75c dp bl 72.50 85.00
B119 SP45 2.50fr + 2.50fr dk brn 72.50 75.00
B120 SP44 3fr + 4.50fr dl grn 72.50 75.00
B121 SP45 5fr + 20fr vio brn 85.00 85.00
B122 SP46 10fr + 40fr brn lake 200.00 225.00
Nos. B114-B122 (9) 513.90 556.15

Issued in commemoration of Cardinal Mercier and to obtain funds to erect a monument to his memory.

Belgian Infantryman SP47

Sanatorium at Waterloo SP48

1932, Aug. 4 *Perf. 14½x14*
B123 SP47 75c + 3.25fr red brn 47.50 47.50
B124 SP47 1.75fr + 4.25fr dk bl 47.50 47.50

Issued in commemoration of the Belgian soldiers who fought in World War I and to obtain funds to erect a national monument to their glory.

1932, Dec. 1 Photo. *Perf. 13½x14*
B125 SP48 10c + 5c dk vio 25 90
B126 SP48 25c + 15c red vio 90 1.25
B127 SP48 50c + 10c red brn 90 1.25
B128 SP48 75c + 15c ol brn 90 80
B129 SP48 1fr + 25c dp red 12.00 11.00
B130 SP48 1.75fr + 25c dp bl 9.50 9.50
B131 SP48 5fr + 5fr gray grn 77.50 90.00
Nos. B125-B131 (7) 101.95 114.70

The surtax was for the assistance of the National Anti-Tuberculosis Society at Waterloo.

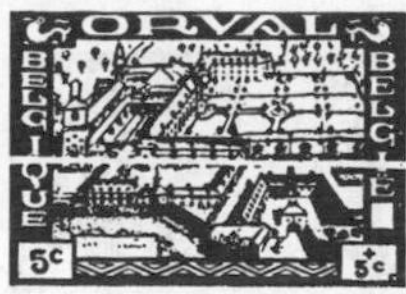

View of Old Abbey SP49

Ruins of Old Abbey — SP50

Count de Chiny Presenting First Abbey to Countess Matilda SP56

Restoration of Abbey in XVI and XVII Centuries SP57

Abbey in XVIII Century, Maria Theresa and Charles V — SP58

Madonna and Arms of Seven Abbeys SP60

Designs: 25c + 15c, Guests, courtyard, 50c + 25c, Transept. 75c + 50c, Bell Tower. 1fr + 1.25fr, Fountain. 1.25fr + 1.75fr, Cloisters. 5fr + 20fr, Duke of Brabant placing first stone of new abbey.

1933, Oct. 15 *Perf. 14*
B132 SP49 5c + 5c dl grn 45.00 50.00
B133 SP50 10c + 15c ol grn 40.00 45.00
B134 SP49 25c + 15c dk brn 40.00 45.00
B135 SP50 50c + 25c red brn 40.00 45.00
B136 SP50 75c + 50c dp grn 40.00 45.00
B137 SP50 1fr + 1.25fr cop red 40.00 45.00
B138 SP49 1.25fr + 1.75fr gray blk 40.00 45.00
B139 SP56 1.75fr + 2.75fr bl 50.00 50.00
B140 SP57 2fr + 3fr mag 50.00 50.00
B141 SP58 2.50fr + 5fr dl brn 50.00 50.00
B142 SP56 5fr + 20fr vio 50.00 50.00

Perf. 11½.
B143 SP60 10fr + 40fr bl 325.00 275.00
Nos. B132-B143 (12) 810.00 795.00

The surtax was for a fund to aid in the restoration of Orval Abbey. Counterfeits exist.

"Tuberculosis Society" SP61

Peter Benoit SP62

1933, Dec. 1 Engr. *Perf. 14x13½*
B144 SP61 10c + 5c blk 65 1.00
B145 SP61 25c + 15c vio 2.50 2.75
B146 SP61 50c + 10c red brn 2.25 2.50
B147 SP61 75c + 15c blk brn 8.50 70
B148 SP61 1fr + 25c cl 10.00 12.00
B149 SP61 1.75fr + 25c vio bl 12.00 10.50
B150 SP61 5fr + 5fr lil 110.00 125.00
Nos. B144-B150 (7) 145.90 154.45

The surtax was for anti-tuberculosis work.

1934, June 1 Photo.
B151 SP62 75c + 25c ol brn 6.00 6.00

The surtax was to raise funds for the Peter Benoit Memorial.

King Leopold III
SP63 SP64

1934, Sept. 15
B152 SP63 75c + 25c ol blk 21.00 20.00
a. Sheet of 20 850.00 850.00
B153 SP64 1fr + 25c red vio 20.00 18.00
a. Sheet of 20 850.00 850.00

The surtax aided the National War Veterans' Fund. Sold for 4.50fr a set at the Exhibition of War Postmarks 1914-18, held at Brussels by the Royal Philatelic Club of Veterans. The price included an exhibition ticket. Sold at Brussels post office Sept. 18-22. No. B152 printed in sheets of 20 (4x5) and 100 (10x10). No. B153 printed in sheets of 20 (4x5) and 150 (10x15).

1934, Sept. 24
B154 SP63 75c + 25c vio 1.50 1.50
B155 SP64 1fr + 25c red brn 8.25 8.50

The surtax aided the National War Veterans' Fund. No. B154 printed in sheets of 100 (10x10); No. B155 in sheets of 150 (10x15). These stamps remained in use one year.

Crusader SP65

1934, Nov. 17 Engr. *Perf. 13½x14*
B156 SP65 10c + 5c blk & red 1.00 45
B157 SP65 25c + 15c brn & red 1.65 1.50
B158 SP65 50c + 10c dl grn & red 1.65 1.50
B159 SP65 75c + 15c vio brn & red 80 45
B160 SP65 1fr + 25c rose & red 8.50 9.25
B161 SP65 1.75fr + 25c ultra & red 7.25 7.50
B162 SP65 5fr + 5fr brn vio & red 100.00 100.00
Nos. B156-B162 (7) 120.85 120.65

The surtax was for anti-tuberculosis work.

Foreign postal stationery (stamped envelopes, postal cards and air letter sheets) lies beyond the scope of this Catalogue, which is limited to adhesive postage stamps.

Prince Baudouin, Princess Josephine and Prince Albert
SP66

1935, Apr. 10 **Photo.**
B163 SP66 35c + 15c dk grn 85 90
B164 SP66 70c + 30c red brn 85 70
B165 SP66 1.75fr + 50c dk bl 3.00 4.00

Surtax was for Child Welfare Society.

Brussels Exhibition Issue.

Stagecoach
SP67

1935, Apr. 27
B166 SP67 10c + 10c ol blk 65 90
B167 SP67 25c + 25c bis brn 2.25 2.25
B168 SP67 35c + 25c dk grn 3.00 3.00

Nos. B166-B168 were printed in sheets of 10. Price, set of 3, $175.

Franz von Taxis
SP68

Queen Astrid
SP69

Souvenir Sheet.

1935, May 25 **Engr.** ***Perf. 14***
B169 SP68 5fr + 5fr grnsh blk 125.00 125.00

Issued in sheets measuring 91 ½ x 117 mm., containing one stamp.
Nos. B166-B169 were issued for the Brussels Philatelic Exhibition (SITEB).

Queen Astrid Memorial Issue.

1935, Dec. 1 **Photo.** ***Perf. 11½***
Borders in Black.
B170 SP69 10c + 5c ol blk 12 18
B171 SP69 25c + 15c brn 15 35
B172 SP69 35c + 5c dk grn 22 30
B173 SP69 50c + 10c rose lil 80 65
B174 SP69 70c + 5c gray blk 12 18
B175 SP69 1fr + 25c red 1.10 90
B176 SP69 1.75fr + 25c bl 2.50 2.00
B177 SP69 2.45fr + 55c dk vio 3.00 3.50
Nos. B170-B177 (8) 8.01 8.06

The surtax was divided among several charitable organizations.

Borgerhout Philatelic Exhibition Issue.
Souvenir Sheet.

Town Hall, Borgerhout
SP70

1936, Oct. 3
B178 SP70 70c + 30c pur brn 45.00 45.00

Issued in sheets, measuring 115x126 mm., containing one stamp.

Town Hall and Belfry of Charleroi
SP71

Prince Baudouin
SP72

Charleroi Youth Exhibition.
Souvenir Sheet.

1936, Oct. 18 **Engr.**
B179 SP71 2.45fr + 55c gray bl 45.00 40.00

Issued in sheets, measuring 95x120 mm., containing one stamp.

1936, Dec. 1 **Photo.** ***Perf. 14x13½***
B180 SP72 10c + 5c dk brn 12 22
B181 SP72 25c + 5c vio 28 35
B182 SP72 35c + 5c dk grn 28 35
B183 SP72 50c + 5c vio brn 40 45
B184 SP72 70c + 5c ol grn 28 22
B185 SP72 1fr + 25c cer 90 60
B186 SP72 1.75fr + 25c ultra 1.50 90
B187 SP72 2.45fr + 2.55fr vio rose 4.00 5.25
Nos. B180-B187 (8) 7.76 8.34

The surtax was for the assistance of the National Anti-Tuberculosis Society.

1937, Jan. 10
B188 SP72 2.45fr + 2.55fr sl 1.25 1.50

Issued in commemoration of International Stamp Day. The surtax was for the benefit of the Brussels Postal Museum, the Royal Belgian Philatelic Federation and the Anti-Tuberculosis Society.

Queen Astrid and Prince Baudouin
SP73

Queen Mother Elisabeth
SP74

1937, Apr. 15 ***Perf. 11½***
B189 SP73 10c + 5c mag 12 20
B190 SP73 25c + 5c ol blk 28 35
B191 SP73 35c + 5c dk grn 28 35
B192 SP73 50c + 5c vio 70 75
B193 SP73 70c + 5c sl 28 40
B194 SP73 1fr + 25c dk car 90 90
B195 SP73 1.75fr + 25c dp ultra 1.50 1.50
B196 SP73 2.45fr + 1.55fr dk brn 3.75 3.25
Nos. B189-B196 (8) 7.81 7.70

The surtax was to raise funds for Public Utility Works.

SP74a

1937, Sept. 15 ***Perf. 14x13½***
B197 SP74 70c + 5c int blk 45 45
B198 SP74 1.75fr + 25c brt ultra 1.10 1.10

Souvenir Sheet.
Perf. 11½.
B199 SP74a Sheet of 4 27.50 22.50
a. 1.50fr+2.50fr red brn 6.50 5.50
b. 2.45fr+3.55fr red vio 5.25 3.50

Nos. B197-B199 were issued for the benefit of the Queen Elisabeth Music Foundation in connection with the Eugene Ysaye international competition.
No. B199 contains two se-tenant pairs of Nos. B199a and B199b. Size: 111x145mm. On sale one day, Sept. 15, at Brussels.

Princess Josephine-Charlotte
SP75

1937, Dec. 1 ***Perf. 14x13½***
B200 SP75 10c + 5c sl grn 12 20
B201 SP75 25c + 5c lt brn 25 22
B202 SP75 35c + 5c yel grn 25 22
B203 SP75 50c + 5c ol gray 50 45
B204 SP75 70c + 5c brn red 18 22
B205 SP75 1fr + 25c red 90 70
B206 SP75 1.75fr + 25c vio bl 1.00 90
B207 SP75 2.45fr + 2.55fr mag 4.00 4.25
Nos. B200-B207 (8) 7.20 7.16

King Albert Memorial Issue
Souvenir Sheet

King Albert Memorial — SP76

1938, Feb. 17 ***Perf. 11½***
B208 SP76 2.45fr + 7.55fr brn vio 11.00 11.00

Issued in connection with the dedication of the monument to King Albert. Sheet size: 143x115mm.

King Leopold III in Military Plane
SP77

1938, Mar. 15
B209 SP77 10c + 5c car brn 22 40
B210 SP77 35c + 5c dp grn 42 1.10
B211 SP77 70c + 5c gray blk 85 60
B212 SP77 1.75fr + 25c ultra 2.00 1.75
B213 SP77 2.45fr + 2.55fr pur 4.25 3.75
Nos. B209-B213 (5) 7.74 7.60

The surtax was for the benefit of the National Fund for Aeronautical Propaganda.

Basilica of Koekelberg
SP78

Interior View of the Basilica of Koekelberg — SP79

1938, June 1 **Photo.**
B214 SP78 10c + 5c lt brn 12 22
B215 SP78 35c + 5c grn 22 22
B216 SP78 70c + 5c gray grn 22 22
B217 SP78 1fr + 25c car 85 70
B218 SP78 1.75fr + 25c ultra 85 85
B219 SP78 2.45fr + 2.55fr brn vio 3.50 4.50

Engr.
B220 SP79 5fr + 5fr dl grn 14.00 13.00
Nos. B214-B220 (7) 19.76 19.71

The surtax was for a fund to aid in completing the National Basilica of the Sacred Heart at Koekelberg.
Nos. B214, B216 and B218 are different views of the exterior of the Basilica.

Souvenir Sheet

Interior of Koekelberg Basilica — SP80

1938, July 21 **Engr.** ***Perf. 14***
B221 SP80 5fr + 5fr lt vio 12.00 10.50

Sheet size 94x120mm.

Stamps of 1938 Surcharged in Black:

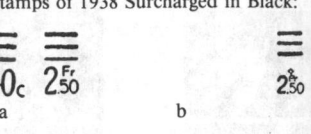

40c 2Fr50 — a
2Fr50 — b

1938, Nov. 10 ***Perf. 11½***
B222 SP78 (a) 40c on 35c+5c grn 38 45
B223 SP78 (a) 75c on 70c+5c gray grn 50 65
B224 SP78 (b) 2.50fr +2.50fr on 2.45fr + 2.55fr 5.25 6.00

Prince Albert of Liege — SP81

1938, Dec. 10 **Photo.** ***Perf. 14x13½***
B225 SP81 10c + 5c brn 12 22
B226 SP81 30c + 5c mag 25 35
B227 SP81 40c + 5c ol gray 25 35
B228 SP81 75c + 5c sl grn 20 22
B229 SP81 1fr + 25c dk car 65 90
B230 SP81 1.75fr + 25c ultra 65 90
B231 SP81 2.50fr + 2.50fr dp grn 4.00 6.50
B232 SP81 5fr + 5fr brn lake 13.00 10.00
Nos. B225-B232 (8) 19.12 19.44

Henri Dunant
SP82

Florence Nightingale
SP83

Queen Mother Elisabeth and Royal Children — SP84

King Leopold and Royal Children SP85

Queen Astrid — SP86

Queen Mother Elisabeth and Wounded Soldier — SP87

1939, Apr. 1 Photo. *Perf. 11½*

The Cross is Printed in Carmine.

B233	SP82	10c + 5c brn	12	22
B234	SP83	30c + 5c brn car	35	35
B235	SP84	40c + 5c ol gray	25	35
B236	SP85	75c + 5c sl blk	50	22
B237	SP84	1fr + 25c brt rose	2.25	1.25
B238	SP85	1.75fr + 25c brt ultra	70	1.00
B239	SP86	2.50fr + 2.50fr dl vio	1.50	2.00
B240	SP87	5fr + 5fr gray grn	5.00	6.50
		Nos. B233-B240 (8)	10.67	11.89

75th anniversary of the founding of the International Red Cross Society.

Rubens' House, Antwerp SP88

"Albert and Nicolas Rubens" — SP89

Arcade, Rubens' House SP90

"Helena Fourment and Her Children" SP91

Rubens and Isabelle Brandt SP92

Peter Paul Rubens — SP93

"The Velvet Hat" — SP94

"Descent from the Cross" SP95

1939, July 1

B241	SP88	10c + 5c brn	10	22
B242	SP89	40c + 5c brn car	35	35
B243	SP90	75c + 5c ol blk	70	60
B244	SP91	1fr + 25c rose	2.00	1.75
B245	SP92	1.50fr + 25c sep	2.00	1.75
B246	SP93	1.75fr + 25c dp ultra	2.75	2.00
B247	SP94	2.50fr + 2.50fr red vio	11.00	12.50
B248	SP95	5fr + 5fr sl gray	16.00	16.00
		Nos. B241-B248 (8)	34.90	35.17

Issued to honor Peter Paul Rubens. The surtax was used to restore Rubens' home in Antwerp.

"Martin van Nieuwenhove" by Hans Memling — SP96

1939, July 1

B249	SP96	75c + 75c ol blk	2.75	2.75

Issued in honor of Hans Memling, (1430?-1495), Flemish painter.

Twelfth Century Monks at Work — SP97

Reconstructed Tower Seen through Cloister — SP98

Monks Laboring in the Fields SP99

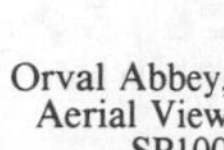

Orval Abbey, Aerial View SP100

Bishop Heylen of Namur, Madonna and Abbot General Smets of the Trappists — SP101

King Albert I and King Leopold III and Shrine — SP102

1939, July 20

B250	SP97	75c + 75c ol blk	2.75	3.00
B251	SP98	1fr + 1fr rose red	1.75	1.75
B252	SP99	1.50fr + 1.50fr dl brn	1.75	1.75
B253	SP100	1.75fr + 1.75fr saph	1.75	1.75
B254	SP101	2.50fr + 2.50fr brt red vio	8.00	7.25
B255	SP102	5fr + 5fr brn car	8.00	8.00
		Nos. B250-B255 (6)	24.00	23.50

The surtax was used for the restoration of the Abbey of Orval.

Belfry at Bruges SP103

Belfry at Furnes SP104

Designs (Belfries): 30c + 5c, Thuin. 40c + 5c, Lierre. 75c + 5c, Mons. 1.75fr+25c, Namur. 2.50fr + 2.50fr, Alost. 5fr + 5fr, Tournai.

1939, Dec. 1 Photo. *Perf. 14x13½*

B256	SP103	10c + 5c ol gray	12	22
B257	SP103	30c + 5c brn org	25	35
B258	SP103	40c + 5c brt red vio	40	45
B259	SP103	75c + 5c ol blk	20	22

Engr.

B260	SP104	1fr + 25c rose car	1.00	1.10
B261	SP104	1.75fr + 25c dk bl	1.00	1.10
B262	SP104	2.50fr + 2.50fr dp red brn	7.50	7.50
B263	SP104	5fr + 5fr pur	10.00	10.50
		Nos. B256-B263 (8)	20.47	21.44

Arms of Mons SP111

Arms of Ghent SP112

Designs (Coats of Arms): 40c + 10c, Arel. 50c + 10c, Bruges. 75c + 15c, Namur. 1fr + 25c, Hasselt. 1.75fr. + 50c, Brussels. 2.50fr + 2.50fr, Antwerp. 5fr + 5fr, Liege.

1940-41 Typo. *Perf. 14x13½*

B264	SP111	10c + 5c multi ('41)	18	22
B265	SP112	30c + 5c multi	28	22
B266	SP111	40c + 10c multi	28	22
B267	SP112	50c + 10c multi	28	22
B268	SP111	75c + 15c multi	18	22
B269	SP112	1fr + 25c multi ('41)	40	45
B270	SP111	1.75fr + 50c multi ('41)	60	55
B271	SP112	2.50fr + 2.50fr multi ('41)	1.75	1.75
B272	SP111	5fr + 5fr multi ('41)	2.25	2.25
		Nos. B264-B272 (9)	6.20	6.10

Surtax for winter relief.

See No. B279.

Queen Elisabeth Music Chapel SP120

Bust of Prince Albert of Liège — SP121

1940, Nov. Photo. *Perf. 11½*

B273	SP120	75c + 75c sl	1.75	1.75
B274	SP120	1fr + 1fr rose red	1.10	1.00
B275	SP121	1.50fr + 1.50fr Prus grn	1.25	1.65
B276	SP121	1.75fr + 1.75fr ultra	1.25	1.65
B277	SP120	2.50fr + 2.50fr brn org	2.50	1.75
B278	SP121	5fr + 5fr red vio	3.00	3.00
		Nos. B273-B278 (6)	10.85	10.80

The surtax was for the Queen Elisabeth Music Foundation. Nos. B273-B278 were not authorized for postal use, but were sold to advance subscribers either mint or canceled to order. See also Nos. B317-B318.

Arms Types of 1940-41

Souvenir Sheets.

Perf. 14x13½, Imperf.

1941, May Typo.

Cross and City Name in Carmine.

Arms in Color of Stamp

B279		Sheet of 9	10.00	11.00
a.	SP111	10c+5c sl	85	90
b.	SP112	30c+5c emer	85	90
c.	SP111	40c+10c choc	85	90
d.	SP112	50c+10c lt vio	85	90
e.	SP111	75c+15c dl pur	85	90
f.	SP112	1fr+25c car	85	90
g.	SP111	1.75fr+50c dl bl	85	90
h.	SP112	2.50fr+2.50fr ol gray	85	90
i.	SP111	5fr+5fr dl vio	3.00	3.25

The sheets measure 106x148 mm. The surtax was used for relief work.

Painting
SP123

Sculpture
SP124

Monks Studying Plans of Orval Abbey — SP128

Designs: 40c+60c, 2fr+3.50fr, Monk carrying candle. 50c+65c, 1.75fr+2.50fr, Monk praying. 75c+1fr, 3fr+5fr, Two monks singing.

1941, June **Photo.** ***Perf. 11½***

B281	SP123	10c + 15c brn org	45	50
B282	SP124	30c + 30c ol gray	45	50
B283	SP124	40c + 60c dp brn	45	50
B284	SP124	50c + 65c vio	45	50
B285	SP124	75c + 1fr brt red vio	45	50
B286	SP124	1fr + 1.50fr rose red	45	50
B287	SP123	1.25fr + 1.75fr dp yel grn	45	50
B288	SP123	1.75fr + 2.50fr dp ultra	45	50
B289	SP123	2fr + 3.50fr red vio	45	50
B290	SP124	2.50fr + 4.50fr dl red brn	45	50
B291	SP124	3fr + 5fr dk ol grn	45	50
B292	SP128	5fr + 10fr grnsh blk	1.50	1.50
		Nos. B281-B292 (12)	6.45	7.00

The surtax was used for the restoration of the Abbey of Orval.

Maria Theresa
SP129

Charles the Bold
SP130

Portraits (in various frames): 35c+5c, Charles of Lorraine. 50c+10c, Margaret of Parma. 60c+10c, Charles V. 1fr+15c, Johanna of Castile. 1.50fr+1fr, Philip the Good. 1.75fr+1.75fr, Margaret of Austria. 3.25fr+3.25fr, Archduke Albert. 5fr+5fr, Archduchess Isabella.

1941-42 **Photo.**

B293	SP129	10c + 5c ol blk	18	22
B294	SP129	35c + 5c dl grn	18	22
B295	SP129	50c + 10c brn	18	22
B296	SP129	60c + 10c pur	18	22
B297	SP129	1fr + 15c brt car rose	18	22
B298	SP129	1.50fr + 1fr red vio	35	30
B299	SP129	1.75fr + 1.75fr ryl bl	35	30
B300	SP130	2.25fr + 2.25fr dl red brn	45	42
B301	SP129	3.25fr + 3.25fr lt brn	60	60
B302	SP129	5fr + 5fr sl grn	65	65
		Nos. B293-B302 (10)	3.30	3.37

Souvenir Sheet.

Archduke Albert and Archduchess Isabella — SP139

B302A	SP139	Sheet of 2 ('42)	4.50	4.50
b.		3.25fr+6.75fr turq bl	2.00	2.00
c.		5fr+10fr dk car	2.00	2.00

The sheets measure 77x59mm.
The surtax was for the benefit of National Social Service Work among soldiers' families.

Souvenir Sheets.

Monks Studying Plans of Orval Abbey — SP140

1941, Oct. **Photo.** ***Perf. 11½***
Inscribed "Belgie-Belgique".

B303	SP140	5fr + 15fr ultra	6.50	9.00

Imperf.
Inscribed "Belgique-Belgie"

B304	SP140	5fr + 15fr ultra	6.50	9.00

The sheets measure 185x165 mm. and are inscribed in black, gold and ultramarine.
The surtax was for the restoration of Orval Abbey.
No. B304 exists perforated.
In 1942 these sheets were privately trimmed and overprinted "1142 1942" and ornament.

St. Martin Statue, Church of Dinant
SP141

Lennik, Saint-Quentin
SP142

St. Martin's Church, Saint-Trond
SP146

Designs (Statues of St. Martin): 50c+10c, 3.25fr+3.25fr, Beck, Limburg. 60c+10c, 2.25fr+2.25fr, Dave on the Meuse. 1.75fr+50c, Hal, Brabant.

1941-42 **Photo.** ***Perf. 11½***

B305	SP141	10c + 5c chnt	15	22
B306	SP142	35c + 5c dk bl grn	15	22
B307	SP142	50c + 10c vio	15	22
B308	SP142	60c + 10c dp brn	15	22
B309	SP142	1fr + 15c car	15	22
B310	SP141	1.50fr + 25c sl grn	30	35
B311	SP142	1.75fr + 50c dk ultra	35	42
B312	SP142	2.25fr + 2.25fr red vio	35	42
B313	SP142	3.25fr + 3.25fr brn vio	35	42
B314	SP146	5fr + 5fr dk ol grn	55	60
		Nos. B305-B314 (10)	2.65	3.31

Souvenir Sheets.
Inscribed "Belgie-Belgique".

B315	SP146	5fr + 20fr vio brn ('42)	11.00	11.00

Imperf.
Inscribed "Belgique-Belgie"

B316	SP146	5fr + 20fr vio brn ('42)	9.00	9.00

Nos. B315-B316 contain one stamp each. Size: 105x139mm.
In 1956, the Bureau Europeen de la Jeunesse et de l'Enfance privately overprinted Nos. B315-B316: "Congres Europeen de l'education 7-12 Mai 1956," in dark red and dark green respectively. A black bar obliterates "Winterhulp-Secours d'Hiver."

Souvenir Sheets.

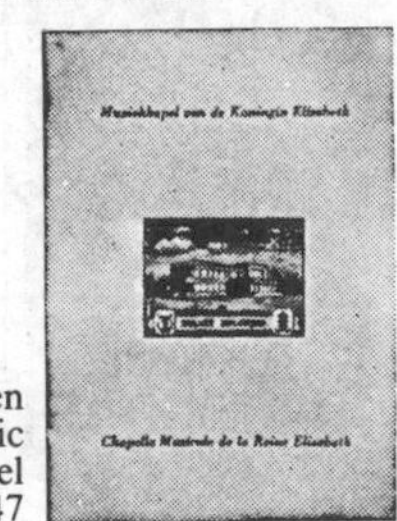
Queen Elisabeth Music Chapel
SP147

1941, Dec. 1 **Photo.** ***Perf. 11½***
Inscribed "Belgique-Belgie".

B317	SP147	10fr + 15fr ol blk	2.00	3.50

Imperf.
Inscribed "Belgie-Belique".

B318	SP147	10fr + 15fr ol blk	2.00	3.50

Issued in sheets measuring 105x139mm.
The surtax was for the Queen Elisabeth Music Foundation. These sheets were perforated with the monogram of Queen Elisabeth in 1942.
In 1954 Nos. B317-B318 were overprinted to commemorate the birth centenary of Edgar Tinel, composer. Inscriptions in French, border in brown on No. B317; inscriptions in Flemish, border in green on No. B318. These overprinted sheets were not postally valid.

Jean Bollandus
SP148

Christophe Plantin
SP156

Designs: 35c+5c, Andreas Vesalius. 50c+10c, Simon Stevinus. 60c+10c, Jean Van Helmont. 1fr+15c, Rembert Dodoens. 1.75fr+50c, Gerardus Mercator. 3.25fr+3.25fr, Abraham Ortelius. 5fr+5fr, Justus Lipsius.

1942, May 15 **Photo.** ***Perf. 14x13½***

B319	SP148	10c + 5c dl brn	12	18
B320	SP148	35c + 5c gray grn	20	22
B321	SP148	50c + 10c fawn	20	22
B322	SP148	60c + 10c grnsh blk	20	22

Engr.

B323	SP148	1fr + 15c brt rose	25	32
B324	SP148	1.75fr + 50c dl bl	38	32
B325	SP148	3.25fr + 3.25fr lil rose	38	32
B326	SP148	5fr + 5fr vio	42	45

Perf. 13½x14.

B327	SP156	10fr + 30fr red org	1.75	1.90
		Nos. B319-B327 (9)	3.90	4.15

The surtax was used to help fight tuberculosis.
No. B327 was sold by subscription at the Brussels Post Office, July 1-10, 1942.

Belgian Prisoner — SP158

1942, Oct. 1 ***Perf. 11½***

B331	SP158	5fr + 45fr ol gray	6.50	6.50

The surtax was for prisoners of war. Price includes a brown label, inscribed "1942 POUR NOS PRISONNIERS/VOOR ONZE GEVANGENEN," which alternates with the stamps in the sheet.

SP159

SP162

SP164

SP168

Various Statues of St. Martin

1942-43

B332	SP159	10c + 5c org	12	8
B333	SP159	35c + 5c dk bl grn	15	15
B334	SP159	50c + 10c dp brn	18	18
B335	SP162	60c + 10c blk	20	20
B336	SP159	1fr + 15c brt rose	25	22
B337	SP164	1.50fr + 25c grnsh blk	30	30
B338	SP164	1.75fr + 50c dk bl	35	35
B339	SP162	2.25fr + 2.25fr brn	50	42
B340	SP162	3.25fr + 3.25fr brt red vio	55	52
B341	SP168	5fr + 10fr hn brn	85	70
B342	SP168	10fr + 20fr rose brn & vio brn ('43)	1.10	1.10

Inscribed "Belgique-Belgie".

B343	SP168	10fr + 20fr gldn brn & vio brn ('43)	1.10	1.10
		Nos. B332-B343 (12)	5.65	5.32

The surtax was for winter relief.

Issue dates: Nos. B332-B341, Nov. 12, 1942. Nos. B342-B343, Apr. 3, 1943.

Prisoners of War — SP170

Design: No. B345, Two prisoners with package from home.

1943, May Photo. *Perf. 11½*

B344	SP170	1fr + 30fr ver	2.75	3.00
B345	SP170	1fr + 30fr brn rose	2.75	3.00

The surtax was used for prisoners of war.

Roof Tiler SP172

Coppersmith SP173

Designs: (Statues in Petit Sablon Park, Brussels). 35c+5c, Blacksmith. 60c+10c, Gunsmith. 1fr+15c, Armsmith. 1.75fr+75c, Goldsmith. 3.25fr+3.25fr, Fishdealer. 5fr+25fr, Watchmaker.

1943, June 1

B346	SP172	10c + 5c chnt brn	12	14
B347	SP172	35c + 5c grn	14	15
B348	SP173	50c + 10c dk brn	15	18
B349	SP173	60c + 10c sl	16	20
B350	SP173	1fr + 15c dl rose brn	20	30
B351	SP173	1.75fr + 75c ultra	32	40
B352	SP173	3.25fr + 3.25fr brt red vio	52	65
B353	SP173	5fr + 25fr dk pur	85	90
		Nos. B346-B353 (8)	2.46	2.92

The surtax was for the control of tuberculosis.

"O" — SP180

"ORVAL" — SP185

Designs: 60c+1.90fr, "R." 1fr+3fr, "V." 1.75fr+5.25fr, "A." 3.25fr+16.75fr, "L."

1943, Oct. 9

B354	SP180	50c + 1fr ol blk	70	80
B355	SP180	60c + 1.90fr dl vio	40	35
B356	SP180	1fr + 3fr rose brn	40	35
B357	SP180	1.75fr + 5.25fr dk bl	40	35
B358	SP180	3.25fr + 16.75fr dk bl grn	55	60
B359	SP185	5fr + 30fr dp brn	1.00	1.00
		Nos. B354-B359 (6)	3.45	3.45

The surtax aided restoration of Orval Abbey.

St. Leonard Church, Leau — SP186

St. Martin Church, Courtrai SP190

Basilica of St. Martin, Angre SP191

Notre Dame, Hal — SP193

St. Martin SP194

Designs: 35c+5c, St. Martin Church, Dion-le-Val. 50c+15c, St. Martin Church, Alost. 60c+20c, St. Martin Church, Liege. 3.25fr+11.75fr, St. Martin Church, Loppem. No. B369, St. Martin, beggar and Meuse landscape.

1943-44

B360	SP186	10c + 5c dp brn	18	22
B361	SP186	35c + 5c dk bl grn	38	45
B362	SP186	50c + 15c ol blk	45	55
B363	SP186	60c + 20c brt red vio	55	65
B364	SP190	1fr + 1fr rose brn	65	65
B365	SP191	1.75fr + 4.25fr dp ultra	1.50	1.00
B366	SP186	3.25fr + 11.75fr red lil	1.50	1.15
B367	SP193	5fr + 25fr dk bl	2.00	2.00
B368	SP194	10fr + 30fr gray grn ('44)	1.50	1.50
B369	SP194	10fr + 30fr blk brn ('44)	1.50	1.50
		Nos. B360-B369 (10)	10.21	9.67

Surtax for winter relief.

"Daedalus and Icarus" SP196

Sir Anthony Van Dyck, Self-portrait SP200

Paintings by Van Dyck: 50c+2.50fr. "The Good Samaritan." 60c+3.40fr, Detail of "Christ Healing the Paralytic." 1fr+5fr, "Madonna and Child." 5fr+30fr, "St. Sebastian."

1944, Apr. 16 Photo. *Perf. 11½*
Crosses in Carmine.

B370	SP196	35c + 1.65fr dk sl grn	30	30
B371	SP196	50c + 2.50fr grnsh blk	30	30
B372	SP196	60c + 3.40fr blk brn	30	30
B373	SP196	1fr + 5fr dk car	45	45
B374	SP200	1.75fr + 8.25fr int bl	55	60
B375	SP196	5fr + 30fr cop brn	55	60
		Nos. B370-B375 (6)	2.45	2.55

The surtax was for the Belgian Red Cross.

Jan van Eyck SP202

Godfrey of Bouillon SP203

Designs: 50c+25c, Jacob van Maerlant. 60c+40c, Jean Joses de Dinant. 1fr+50c, Jacob van Artevelde. 1.75fr+4.25fr, Charles Joseph de Ligne. 2.25fr+8.25fr, Andre Gretry. 3.25fr+11.25fr, Jan Moretus-Plantin. 5fr+35fr, Jan van Ruysbroeck.

1944, May 31

B376	SP203	10c + 15c dk pur	30	30
B377	SP203	35c + 15c grn	30	30
B378	SP203	50c + 25c chnt brn	30	30
B379	SP203	60c + 40c ol blk	30	30
B380	SP203	1fr + 50c rose brn	30	30
B381	SP203	1.75fr + 4.25fr ultra	30	30
B382	SP203	2.25fr + 8.25fr grnsh blk	75	75
B383	SP203	3.25fr + 11.25fr dk brn	30	30
B384	SP203	5fr + 35fr sl bl	60	90
		Nos. B376-B384 (9)	3.45	3.75

The surtax was for prisoners of war.

Sons of Aymon Astride Bayard SP211

Brabo Slaying the Giant Antigoon SP212

Till Eulenspiegel Singing to Nele SP214

Designs: 50c+10c, St. Hubert converted by stag with crucifix. 1fr+15fr, St. George slaying the dragon. 1.75fr+5.25fr, Genevieve of Brabant with son and roe-deer. 3.25fr+11.75fr, Tchantches wrestling with the Saracen. 5fr+25fr, St. Gertrude rescuing the knight with the cards.

1944, June 25

B385	SP211	10c + 5c choc	12	20
B386	SP212	35c + 5c dk bl grn	12	20
B387	SP211	50c + 10c dl vio	12	20
B388	SP214	60c + 10c blk brn	12	20
B389	SP214	1fr + 15c rose brn	12	20
B390	SP214	1.75fr + 5.25fr ultra	22	40
B391	SP211	3.25fr + 11.75fr grnsh blk	32	60
B392	SP211	5fr + 25fr dk bl	45	80
		Nos. B385-B392 (8)	1.59	2.80

The surtax was for the control of tuberculosis.

Nos. B385-B389 were overprinted "Breendonk+10fr." in 1946 by the Union Royale Philatelique for an exhibition at Brussels. They had no postal validity.

Union of the Flemish and Walloon Peoples in their Sorrow — SP219

Union in Reconstruction — SP220

Perf. 11½
1945, May 1 Unwmk. Photo.

B395	SP219	1fr + 30fr car	70	1.25
B396	SP220	1¾fr + 30fr brt ultra	70	1.25

1945, July 21
Size: 34½x23½mm.

B397	SP219	1fr + 9fr scar	25	45
B398	SP220	1fr + 9fr car rose	25	45

The surtax was for the postal employees' relief fund.

Prisoner of War — SP221

Reunion SP222

Awaiting Execution SP223

Symbolical Figures "Recovery of Freedom" SP225

Design: 70c+30c, 3.50fr+3.50fr, Member of Resistance Movement.

1945, Sept. 10

B399	SP221	10c + 15c org	8	12
B400	SP222	20c + 20c dp pur	8	12
B401	SP223	60c + 25c sep	8	12
B402	SP221	70c + 30c dp yel grn	10	12
B403	SP221	75c + 50c org brn	10	18
B404	SP222	1fr + 75c brt bl grn	18	22
B405	SP223	1.50fr + 1fr brt red	18	22
B406	SP221	3.50fr + 3.50fr brt bl	85	1.10
B407	SP225	5fr + 40fr brn	70	1.00
		Nos. B399-B407 (9)	2.35	3.20

The inscriptions are transposed on Nos. B403-B406.

The surtax was for the benefit of prisoners of war, displaced persons, families of executed victims and members of the Resistance Movement.

Arms of West Flanders — SP226

Arms of Provinces: 20c+20c, Luxembourg. 60c+25c, East Flanders. 70c+30c, Namur. 75c+50c, Limburg. 1fr+75c, Hainaut. 1.50fr+1fr, Antwerp. 3.50fr+1.50fr, Liege. 5fr+45fr, Brabant.

1945, Dec. 1

No.	Type	Description	Unused	Used
B408	SP226	10c + 15c sl blk & sl gray	8	12
B409	SP226	20c + 20c rose car & rose	10	18
B410	SP226	60c + 25c dk brn & pale brn	10	18
B411	SP226	70c + 30c dk grn & lt grn	10	18
B412	SP226	75c + 50c org brn & pale org brn	18	30
B413	SP226	1fr + 75c pur & lt pur	10	18
B414	SP226	1.50fr + 1fr car & rose	10	18
B415	SP226	3.50fr + 1.50fr dp bl & gray bl	20	35
B416	SP226	5fr + 45fr dp mag & cer	1.50	2.75
		Nos. B408-B416 (9)	2.46	4.42

The surtax was for tuberculosis prevention.

Father Joseph Damien — SP227

Leper Colony, Molokai Island, Hawaii SP228

Father Damien Comforting Leper — SP229

Perf. 11½

1946, July 15 Unwmk. Photo.

No.	Type	Description	Unused	Used
B417	SP227	65c + 75c dk bl	60	90
B418	SP228	1.35fr + 2fr brn	60	90
B419	SP229	1.75fr + 18fr rose brn	90	1.50

The surtax was for the erection of a museum in Louvain.

Symbols of Wisdom and Patriotism — SP230

François Bovesse SP231

"In Memoriam" SP232

1946, July 15

No.	Type	Description	Unused	Used
B420	SP230	65c + 75c vio	60	90
B421	SP231	1.35fr + 2fr dk org brn	70	1.10
B422	SP232	1.75fr + 18fr car rose	1.10	1.50

The surtax was for the erection of a "House of the Fine Arts" at Namur.

Emile Vandervelde SP233

Vandervelde, Laborer and Family SP234

Sower — SP235

1946, July 15

No.	Type	Description	Unused	Used
B423	SP233	65c + 75c dk sl grn	65	90
B424	SP234	1.35fr + 2fr dk vio bl	70	1.10
B425	SP235	1.75fr + 18fr dp car	1.10	1.50
		Nos. B417-B425 (9)	6.95	10.30

The surtax was for the Emile Vanderveide Institute, to promote social, economic and cultural activities.

Pepin of Herstal SP236

Arms of Malines SP241

Designs: 1fr+50c, Charlemagne. 1.50fr+1fr, Godfrey of Bouillon. 3.50fr+1.50fr, Robert of Jerusalem. Nos. B430-B431, Baldwin of Constantinople.

1946, Sept. 15 Engr. ***Perf. 11½x11***

No.	Type	Description	Unused	Used
B426	SP236	75c + 25c grn	40	50
B427	SP236	1fr + 50c vio	60	70
B428	SP236	1.50fr + 1fr plum	70	90
B429	SP236	3.50fr + 1.50fr brt bl	85	1.10
B430	SP236	5fr + 45fr red vio	7.25	10.00
B431	SP236	5fr + 45fr red org	9.25	11.00
		Nos. B420-B431 (6)	19.05	24.20

The surtax on Nos. B426-B429 was for the benefit of former prisoners of war, displaced persons, the families of executed patriots, and former members of the Resistance Movement.

The surtax on Nos. B430-B431 was divided among several welfare, national celebration and educational organizations.

Issue dates: Nos. B426-B429, Apr. 15; No. B430, Sept. 15; No. B431, Nov. 15.

See also Nos. B437-B441, B465-B466, B472-B476.

1946, Dec. 2 ***Perf. 11½***

Designs (Coats of Arms): 90c+60c, Dinant. 1.35fr+1.15fr, Ostend. 3.15fr+1.85fr, Verviers. 4.50fr+45.50fr, Louvain.

No.	Type	Description	Unused	Used
B432	SP241	65c + 35c rose car	38	45
B433	SP241	90c + 60c lem	38	45
B434	SP241	1.35fr + 1.15fr dp grn	38	45
B435	SP241	3.15fr + 1.85fr bl	1.00	70
B436	SP241	4.50fr + 45.50fr dk vio brn	9.25	11.50
		Nos. B432-B436 (5)	11.39	13.55

The surtax was for anti-tuberculosis work. See also Nos. B442-B446.

Type of 1946.

Designs: 65c+35c, John II, Duke of Brabant. 90c+60c, Count Philip of Alsace. 1.35fr+1.15fr, William the Good. 3.15fr+1.85fr, Bishop Notger of Liege. 20fr+20fr, Philip the Noble.

1947, Sept. 25 Engr. ***Perf. 11½x11***

No.	Type	Description	Unused	Used
B437	SP236	65c + 35c Prus grn	30	85
B438	SP236	90c + 60c yel grn	50	1.10
B439	SP236	1.35fr + 1.15fr car	70	1.50
B440	SP236	3.15fr + 1.85fr ultra	1.00	3.00
B441	SP236	20fr + 20fr red vio	27.50	35.00
		Nos. B437-B441 (5)	30.00	41.45

The surtax was for victims of World War II.

Arms Type of 1946 Dated "1947"

Coats of Arms: 65c+35c, Nivelles. 90c+60c, St. Trond. 1.35fr+1.15fr, Charleroi. 3.15fr+1.85fr, St. Nicolas. 20fr+20fr, Bouillon.

1947, Dec. 15 ***Perf. 11½***

No.	Type	Description	Unused	Used
B442	SP241	65c + 35c org	55	60
B443	SP241	90c + 60c dp cl	42	65
B444	SP241	1.35fr + 1.15fr dk brn	65	70
B445	SP241	3.15fr + 1.85fr dp bl	1.50	1.75
B446	SP241	20fr + 20fr dk grn	12.00	13.00
		Nos. B442-B446 (5)	15.12	16.70

The surtax was for anti-tuberculosis work.

St. Benedict and King Totila — SP247

Achel Abbey SP248

Designs: 3.15fr+2.85fr, St. Benedict, legislator and builder. 10fr+10fr, Death of St. Benedict.

1948, Apr. 5 Photo.

No.	Type	Description	Unused	Used
B447	SP247	65c + 65c red brn	85	70
B448	SP248	1.35fr + 1.35fr gray	1.10	70
B449	SP247	3.15fr + 2.85fr dp ultra	1.65	2.25
B450	SP247	10fr + 10fr brt red vio	8.50	12.00

The surtax was to aid the Abbey of the Trappist Fathers at Achel.

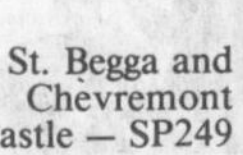

St. Begga and Chevremont Castle — SP249

Chevremont Basilica and Convent SP250

Designs: 3.15fr+2.85fr, Madonna of Chevremont and Chapel. 10fr+10fr, Madonna of Mt. Carmel.

1948, Apr. 5 Unwmk.

No.	Type	Description	Unused	Used
B451	SP249	65c + 65c bl grn	85	70
B452	SP250	1.35fr + 1.35fr dk car rose	1.10	70
B453	SP249	3.15fr + 2.85fr dp bl	1.65	2.25
B454	SP249	10fr + 10fr dp brn	8.25	12.00

The surtax was to aid the Basilica of the Carmelite Fathers of Chevremont.

Anseele Monument Showing French Inscription — SP251

Designs: 90c + 60c, View of Ghent. 1.35fr+1.15fr, Van Artevelde monument, Ghent. 3.15fr+1.85fr. Anseele Monument, Flemish inscription.

1948, June 21 ***Perf. 14x13½***

No.	Type	Description	Unused	Used
B455	SP251	65c + 35c rose red	1.40	1.50
B456	SP251	90c + 60c gray	2.00	2.50
B457	SP251	1.35fr + 1.15fr hn brn	1.00	2.00
B458	SP251	3.15fr + 1.85fr brt bl	4.50	4.75
a.		Souvenir sheet of 4	35.00	47.50

Issued to honor Edouard Anseele, statesman, founder of the Belgian Socialist Party.

No. B458a contains one each of Nos. B455-B458. Size: 144x81mm. Sold for 50fr.

Statue "The Unloader" SP252

Underground Fighter SP253

1948, Sept. 4 ***Perf. 11½x11***

No.	Type	Description	Unused	Used
B460	SP252	10fr + 10fr gray grn	18.00	21.00
B461	SP253	10fr + 10fr red brn	11.00	13.00

The surtax was used toward erection of monuments at Antwerp and Liege.

Portrait Type of 1946 and SP254

Double Barred Cross — SP254

Designs: 4fr+3.25fr, Isabella of Austria. 20fr+20fr, Archduke Albert of Austria.

1948, Dec. 15 Photo. *Perf. 13½x14*

B462	SP254	20c + 5c dk sl grn	25	22
B463	SP254	1.20fr + 30c mag	65	1.00
B464	SP254	1.75fr + 25c red	85	90

Engr. *Perf. 11½x11*

B465	SP236	4fr + 3.25fr ultra	5.00	6.00
B466	SP236	20fr + 20fr Prus grn	22.50	27.50
		Nos. B462-B466 (5)	29.25	35.62

The surtax was divided among several charities.

Souvenir Sheets

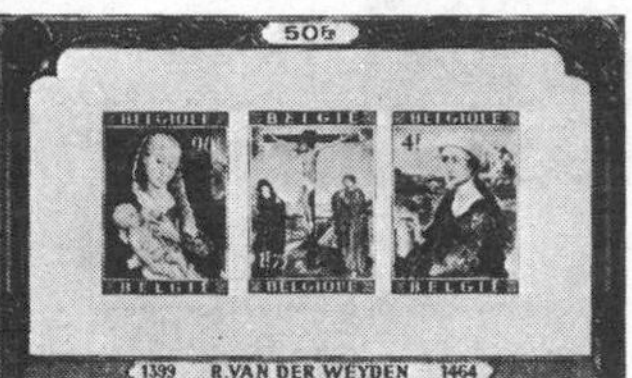

Rogier van der Weyden Paintings — SP255

Paintings by van der Weyden (No. B466A): 90c, Virgin and Child. 1.75fr, Christ on the Cross. 4fr, Mary Magdalene.

Paintings by Jordaens (No. B466B): 90c, Woman Reading. 1.75fr, The Flutist. 4fr, Old Woman Reading Letter.

1949, Apr. 1 Photo. *Perf. 11½*

B466A	SP255	Sheet of 3	65.00	100.00
c.		90c dp brn	20.00	30.00
d.		1.75fr dp rose lil	20.00	30.00
e.		4fr dk vio bl	20.00	30.00
B466B	SP255	Sheet of 3	65.00	100.00
f.		90c dk vio	20.00	30.00
g.		1.75fr red	20.00	30.00
h.		4fr bl	20.00	30.00

The surtax went to various cultural and philanthropic organizations. Nos. B466A and B466B have dark brown and orange decorative border. Size: 140x90½mm. Sheets sold for 50fr each.

Guido Gezelle — SP256

1949, Nov. 15 Photo. *Perf. 14x13½*

B467	SP256	1.75fr + 75c dk Prus grn	2.50	3.25

Issued to commemorate the 50th anniversary of the death of Guido Gezelle, poet. The surtax was for the Guido Gezelle Museum, Bruges.

Portrait Type of 1946 and

Arnica — SP257

Designs: 65c+10c, Sand grass. 90c+10c, Wood myrtle. 1.20fr+30c, Field poppy. 1.75fr+25c, Philip the Good. 3fr+1.50fr, Charles V. 4fr+2fr, Maria-Christina. 6fr+3fr, Charles of Lorraine. 8fr+4fr, Maria-Theresa.

1949, Dec. 20 Typo. *Perf. 13½x14*

B468	SP257	20c + 5c multi	25	65
B469	SP257	65c + 10c multi	65	1.25
B470	SP257	90c + 10c multi	1.00	1.65
B471	SP257	1.20fr + 30c multi	1.25	2.00

Engr. *Perf. 11½x11*

B472	SP236	1.75fr + 25c red org	75	90
B473	SP236	3fr + 1.50fr dp cl	4.00	7.50
B474	SP236	4fr + 2fr ultra	5.00	8.50
B475	SP236	6fr + 3fr choc	8.25	12.00
B476	SP236	8fr + 4fr dl grn	8.25	10.00
		Nos. B468-B476 (9)	29.40	44.45

The surtax was apportioned among several welfare organizations.

Arms of Belgium and Great Britain SP258

British Memorial SP260

Design: 2.50fr+50c, British tanks at Hertain.

Perf. 13½x14, 11½

1950, Mar. 15 Engr.

B477	SP258	80c + 20c grn	85	90
B478	SP258	2.50fr + 50c red	3.25	3.50
B479	SP260	4fr + 2fr dp bl	6.00	6.00

Issued to commemorate the 6th anniversary of the liberation of Belgian territory by the British army.

Hurdling SP261

Relay Race SP262

Designs: 90c+10c, Javelin throwing. 4fr+2fr, Pole vault. 8fr+4fr, Foot race. Inscribed: "Heysel 1950"

Perf. 14x13½, 13½x14.

1950, July 1 Engr. Unwmk.

B480	SP261	20c + 5c brt grn	50	90
B481	SP261	90c + 10c vio brn	2.00	2.25
B482	SP262	1.75fr + 25c car	2.50	2.25
a.		Souvenir sheet	25.00	32.50
B483	SP261	4fr + 2fr lt bl	20.00	22.50
B484	SP261	8fr + 4fr dp grn	22.50	27.50
		Nos. B480-B484 (5)	47.50	55.40

Issued to publicize the European Athletic Games, Brussels, August 1950.

No. B482a measures 89 x 68½ mm., and contains a single copy of No. B482 with inscriptions typographed in black in upper and lower margins.

The margins of No. B482a were trimmed in April, 1951, and an overprint ("25 Francs pour le Fonds Sportif-25e Fofre Internationale Bruxelles") was added in red in French and in black in Flemish by a private committee. These pairs of altered sheets were sold at the Brussels Fair.

Gentian SP263

Sijsele Sanatorium SP264

Tombeek Sanatorium — SP265

Designs: 65c+10c, Cotton Grass. 90c+10c, Foxglove. 1.20fr+30c, Limonia. 4fr+2fr, Jauche Sanatorium.

1950, Dec. 20 Typo. *Perf. 14x13½*

Cross in Red.

B485	SP263	20c + 5c mar, bl & emer	50	45
B486	SP263	65c + 10c brn, buff & emer	1.00	85
B487	SP263	90c + 10c bluish grn, dp mag & yel grn	1.10	1.10
B488	SP263	1.20fr + 30c vio bl, bl & grn	1.50	1.75

Engr. *Perf. 11½.*

B489	SP264	1.75fr + 25c car	1.10	1.10
B490	SP264	4fr + 2fr bl	7.50	6.00
B491	SP265	8fr + 4fr bl grn	12.00	14.00
		Nos. B485-B491 (7)	24.70	25.25

The surtax was for tuberculosis prevention and other charitable purposes.

Chemist — SP266

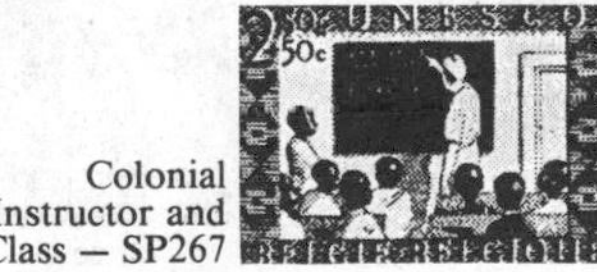

Colonial Instructor and Class — SP267

Allegory of Peace — SP268

1951, Mar. 27 Unwmk.

B492	SP266	80c + 20c grn	85	1.50
B493	SP267	2.50fr + 50c vio brn	6.00	7.25
B494	SP268	4fr + 2fr dp bl	6.50	8.75

The surtax was for the reconstruction fund of the United Nations Educational, Scientific and Cultural Organization.

Monument to Political Prisoners SP269

Fort of Breendonk SP270

Design: 8fr+4fr, Monument: profile of figure on pedestal.

1951, Aug. 20 Photo. *Perf. 11½*

B495	SP269	1.75fr + 25c blk brn	1.10	1.50
B496	SP270	4fr + 2fr bl & sl gray	10.50	13.00
B497	SP269	8fr + 4fr dk bl grn	13.00	16.00

The surtax was for the erection of a national monument.

Queen Elisabeth — SP271

1951, Sept. 22

B498	SP271	90c + 10c grnsh gray	85	90
B499	SP271	1.75fr + 25c plum	1.10	1.50
B500	SP271	3fr + 1fr grn	10.00	10.00
B501	SP271	4fr + 2fr gray bl	11.00	13.00
B502	SP271	8fr + 4fr sep	14.00	15.00
		Nos. B498-B502 (5)	36.95	40.40

The surtax was for the Queen Elisabeth Medical Foundation.

Cross, Sun Rays and Dragon SP272

Beersel Castle SP273

Horst Castle — SP274

Castles: 4fr+2fr, Lavaux St. Anne. 8fr+4fr, Veves.

1951, Dec. 17 Engr. Unwmk.

B503	SP272	20c + 5c red	12	22
B504	SP272	65c + 10c dp ultra	45	60
B505	SP272	90c + 10c sep	50	85
B506	SP272	1.20fr + 30c rose vio	65	90
B507	SP273	1.75fr + 75c red brn	85	1.10
B508	SP274	3fr + 1fr yel grn	6.00	6.00
B509	SP273	4fr + 2fr bl	7.50	7.25
B510	SP274	8fr + 4fr gray	10.50	10.00
		Nos. B503-B510 (8)	26.57	26.92

The surtax was for anti-tuberculosis work.

See Nos. B523-B526, B547-B550.

Main Altar SP275

Basilica of the Sacred Heart Koekelberg SP276

The first price column gives the catalogue value of an unused stamp, the second that of a used stamp.

Procession Bearing Relics of St. Albert of Louvain — SP277

1952, Mar. 1 **Photo.** ***Perf. 11½***

B511 SP275 1.75fr + 25c blk brn 85 1.10
B512 SP276 4fr + 2fr ind 6.50 8.00

Engr.

B513 SP277 8fr + 4fr vio brn 8.25 10.50
a. Souv. sheet 85.00 90.00

Nos. B513a measures 122x72mm., and contains one each of Nos. B511-B513, with inscriptions in indigo and black brown. Sold for 30fr.

Issued to commemorate the 25th anniversary of the Cardinalate of J. E. Van Roey, Primate of Belgium. The surtax was for the Basilica.

Beaulieu Castle, Malines SP278

August Vermeylen SP279

1952, May 14 **Engr.**
Laid Paper.

B514 SP278 40fr + 10fr lt grnsh bl 100.00 125.00

Issued on the occasion of the 13th Universal Postal Union Congress, Brussels, 1952.

Perf. 11½
1952, Oct. 24 **Unwmk.** **Photo.**

Portraits: 80c+40c, Karel Van de Woestijne. 90c+45c, Charles de Coster. 1.75fr+75c, M. Maeterlinck. 4fr+2fr, Emile Verhaeren. 8fr+4fr, Hendrik Conscience.

B515 SP279 65c + 30c pur 85 1.00
B516 SP279 80c + 40c dk grn 1.65 1.25
B517 SP279 90c + 45c sep 1.25 1.65
B518 SP279 1.75fr + 75c cer 1.65 1.75
B519 SP279 4fr + 2fr bl vio 13.00 18.00
B520 SP279 8fr + 4fr dk brn 13.00 22.50
Nos. B515-B520 (6) 31.40 46.15

1952, Nov. 15

Portraits: 4fr, Emile Verhaeren. 8fr, Hendrik Conscience.

B521 SP279 4fr (+ 9fr) bl 60.00 85.00
B522 SP279 8fr (+ 9fr) dk car rose 60.00 85.00

On Nos. B521-B522, the denomination is repeated at either side of the stamp. The surtax is expressed on se-tenant labels bearing quotations of Verhaeren (in French) and Conscience (in Flemish).

A 9-line black overprint was privately applied to these labels: "Conference Internationale de la Musique Bruxelles UNESCO International Music Conference Brussels 1953*"

Price is for stamp with label.

Type of 1951 Dated "1952," and

Arms of Malmedy — SP281

Castle Ruins, Burgreuland SP282

Designs: 4fr+2fr, Vesdre Dam, Eupen. 8fr+4fr, St. Vitus, patron saint of Saint-Vith.

1952, Dec. 15 **Engr.**

B523 SP272 20c + 5c red brn 25 45
B524 SP272 80c + 20c grn 50 70
B525 SP272 1.20fr + 30c lil rose 1.00 1.10
B526 SP272 1.50fr + 50c ol brn 1.00 1.10
B527 SP281 2fr + 75c car 1.65 2.55
B528 SP282 3fr + 1.50fr choc 7.50 10.00
B529 SP281 4fr + 2fr bl 6.50 8.75
B530 SP281 8fr + 4fr vio brn 11.00 13.00
Nos. B523-B530 (8) 29.40 37.65

The surtax on Nos. B523-B530 was for anti-tuberculosis and other charitable works.

Walthère Dewe SP283

Princess Josephine-Charlotte SP284

1953, Feb. 16 **Photo.**

B531 SP283 2fr + 1fr brn car 1.75 2.00

The surtax was for the construction of a memorial to Walthère Dewe, Underground leader in World War II.

1953, Mar. 14 **Cross in Red**

B532 SP284 80c + 20c ol grn 65 90
B533 SP284 1.20fr + 30c brn 85 1.10
B534 SP284 2fr + 50c rose lake 65 1.50
a. Bklt pane of 8 90.00 90.00
B535 SP284 2.50fr + 50c crim 7.50 8.00
B536 SP284 4fr + 1fr brt bl 5.00 6.50
B537 SP284 5fr + 2fr sl grn 6.00 8.00
Nos. B532-B537 (6) 20.65 26.00

The surtax was for the Belgian Red Cross.

The selvage of No. B534a is inscribed in French or Dutch. The price is for the French.

Boats at Dock SP285

Canceled-to-order stamps are often from remainders. Most collectors of canceled stamps prefer postally used specimens.

Bridge and Citadel, Namur SP286

Allegory SP287

Designs: 1.20fr+30c, Bridge at Bouillon. 2fr+50c, Antwerp waterfront. 4fr+2fr, Wharf at Ghent. 8fr+4fr, Meuse River at Freyr.

1953, June 22 **Unwmk.** ***Perf. 11½***

B538 SP285 80c + 20c grn 50 90
B539 SP285 1.20fr + 30c redsh brn 1.00 1.50
B540 SP285 2fr + 50c sep 1.25 2.00
B541 SP286 2.50fr + 50c dp mag 6.00 8.50
B542 SP286 4fr + 2fr vio bl 9.25 8.50
B543 SP286 8fr + 4fr gray blk 11.00 8.50
Nos. B538-B543 (6) 29.00 29.90

The surtax was used to promote tourism in the Ardenne-Meuse region and for various cultural works.

1953, Oct. 26 **Engr.**

B544 SP287 80c + 20c grn 2.50 3.00
B545 SP287 2.50fr + 1fr rose car 22.50 30.00
B546 SP287 4fr + 1.50fr bl 27.50 37.50

The surtax was for the European Bureau of Childhood and Youth.

Type of 1951 Dated "1953," and

Ernest Malvoz — SP288

Robert Koch SP289

Portraits: 3fr+1.50fr, Carlo Forlanini. 4fr+2fr, Leon Charles Albert Calmette.

1953, Dec. 15

B547 SP272 20c + 5c bl 25 45
B548 SP272 80c + 20c rose vio 65 60
B549 SP272 1.20fr + 30c choc 70 90
B550 SP272 1.50fr + 50c dk gray 1.00 1.10
B551 SP288 2fr + 75c dk grn 1.75 1.75
B552 SP288 3fr + 1.50fr dk red 7.50 8.50
B553 SP288 4fr + 2fr ultra 6.50 7.25
B554 SP289 8fr + 4fr choc 10.00 10.50
Nos. B547-B554 (8) 28.35 31.05

The surtax was for anti-tuberculosis and other charitable works.

King Albert I Statue — SP290

Albert I Monument, Namur SP291

Design: 9fr+4.50fr, Cliffs of Marche-les-Dames.

1954, Feb. 17 **Photo.**

B555 SP290 2fr + 50c chnt brn 1.25 1.75
B556 SP291 4fr + 2fr bl 7.50 10.00
B557 SP290 9fr + 4.50fr ol blk 10.00 11.00

Issued to commemorate the 20th anniversary of the death of King Albert I. The surtax aided in the erection of the monument pictured on B556.

Political Prisoners' Monument — SP292

Camp and Fort, Breendonk SP293

Design: 9fr+4.50fr, Political prisoners' monument (profile).

1954, Apr. 1 **Unwmk.** ***Perf. 11½***

B558 SP292 2fr + 1fr red 6.50 7.25
B559 SP293 4fr + 2fr dk brn 14.00 18.00
B560 SP292 9fr + 4.50fr ol grn 16.00 18.00

The surtax was used toward the creation of a monument to political prisoners.

Gatehouse and Gateway SP294

Nuns in Courtyard — SP295

Our Lady of the Vine SP296

Designs: 2fr+1fr, Swans in stream. 7fr+3.50fr Nuns at well. 8fr+4fr, Statue above door.

1954, May 15

B561 SP294 80c + 20c dk bl grn 70 1.10
B562 SP294 2fr + 1fr crim 6.50 1.50
B563 SP295 4fr + 2fr vio 9.25 10.50

B564 SP295 7fr + 3.50fr lil rose 20.00 25.00
B565 SP295 8fr + 4fr brn 18.00 22.50
B566 SP296 9fr + 4.50fr gray bl 30.00 30.00
Nos. B561-B566 (6) 84.45 90.60

The surtax was for the Friends of the Beguinage of Bruges.

Child's Head
SP297

"The Blind Man and the Paralytic," by Antoine Carte
SP298

1954, Dec. 1 **Engr.**

B567 SP297 20c + 5c dk grn 38 55
B568 SP297 80c + 20c dk gray 65 90
B569 SP297 1.20fr + 30c org brn 1.00 1.10
B570 SP297 1.50fr + 50c pur 1.25 1.75
B571 SP298 2fr + 75c rose car 5.00 3.75
B572 SP298 4fr + 1fr brt bl 11.00 10.50
Nos. B567-B572 (6) 19.28 18.55

The surtax was for anti-tuberculosis work.

Ernest Solvay
SP299

Jean-Jacques Dony — SP300

Portraits: 1.20fr+30c, Egide Walschaerts. 25fr+50c, Leo H. Baekeland. 3fr+1fr, Jean-Etienne Lenoir. 4fr+2fr, Emile Fourcault and Emile Gobbe.

Perf. 11½

1955, Oct. 22 **Unwmk.** **Photo.**

B573 SP299 20c + 5c brn & dk brn 25 45
B574 SP300 80c + 20c vio 65 60
B575 SP299 1.20fr + 30c ind 70 90
B576 SP300 2fr + 50c dp car 2.50 3.00
B577 SP300 3fr + 1fr dk grn 7.50 7.25
B578 SP299 4fr + 2fr brn 7.50 7.25
Nos. B573-B578 (6) 19.10 19.45

Issued in honor of Belgian scientists.
The surtax was for the benefit of various cultural organizations.

"The Joys of Spring" by E. Canneel
SP301

Einar Holböll
SP302

Portraits: 4fr+2fr, John D. Rockefeller. 8fr+4fr, Sir Robert W. Philip.

1955, Dec. 5 **Unwmk.** ***Perf. 11½***

B579 SP301 20c + 5c red lil 35 30
B580 SP301 80c + 20c grn 50 60
B581 SP301 1.20fr + 30c redsh brn 65 90
B582 SP301 1.50fr + 50c vio bl 70 1.10
B583 SP302 2fr + 50c car 4.50 4.50
B584 SP302 4fr + 2fr ultra 9.25 11.00
B585 SP302 8fr + 4fr ol gray 11.00 13.00
Nos. B579-B585 (7) 26.95 31.40

The surtax was for anti-tuberculosis work.

Palace of Charles of Lorraine — SP303

Queen Elisabeth and Sonata by Mozart — SP304

Design: 2fr+1fr, Mozart at age 7.

1956, Mar. 5 **Engr.**

B586 SP303 80c + 20c stl bl 60 1.40
B587 SP303 2fr + 1fr rose lake 2.50 4.25
B588 SP304 4fr + 2fr dl pur 4.00 5.25

Issued to commemorate the 200th anniversary of the birth of Wolfgang Amadeus Mozart, composer.
The surtax was for the benefit of the Pro-Mozart Committee in Belgium.

Queen Elisabeth — SP305

1956, Aug. 16 **Photo.**

B589 SP305 80c + 20c sl grn 70 1.40
B590 SP305 2fr + 1fr dp plum 2.00 2.25
B591 SP305 4fr + 2fr brn 2.75 3.50

Issued in honor of the 80th birthday of Queen Elisabeth. The surtax went to the Queen Elisabeth Foundation. See also No. 607.

Ship with Cross
SP306

Infant on Scales
SP307

Rehabilitation
SP308

Design: 4fr+2fr, X-Ray examination.

1956, Dec. 17 **Engr.**

B592 SP306 20c + 5c redsh brn 25 35
B593 SP306 80c + 20c grn 50 70
B594 SP306 1.20fr + 30c dl lil 60 65
B595 SP306 1.5fr + 50c lt sl bl 65 1.00
B596 SP307 2fr + 50c ol grn 1.65 1.75
B597 SP307 4fr + 2fr dl pur 7.50 7.25
B598 SP308 8fr + 4fr dp car 7.50 8.25
Nos. B592-B598 (7) 18.65 19.95

The surtax was for anti-tuberculosis work.

Charles Plisnier and Albrecht Rodenbach
SP309

Portraits: 80c+20c, Emiel Vliebergh and Maurice Wilmotte. 1.20fr+30c, Paul Pastur and Julius Hoste. 2fr+50c, Lodewijk de Raet and Jules Destree. 3fr+1fr, Constantin Meunier and Constant Permeke. 4fr+2fr, Lieven Gevaert and Edouard Empain.

Perf. 11½

1957, June 8 **Unwmk.** **Photo.**

B599 SP309 20c + 5c brt vio 25 35
B600 SP309 80c + 20c lt red brn 38 45
B601 SP309 1.20f + 30c blk brn 45 60
B602 SP309 2fr + 50c cl 1.10 1.10
B603 SP309 3fr + 1fr dk ol grn 1.65 2.25
B604 SP309 4fr + 2fr vio bl 2.25 3.25
Nos. B599-B604 (6) 6.08 8.00

The surtax was for the benefit of various cultural organizations.

Dogs and Antarctic Camp
SP310

1957, Oct. 18 **Engr.** ***Perf. 11½***

B605 SP310 5fr + 2.50fr gray, org & vio brn 2.00 3.75
a. Sheet of four 75.00 110.00
b. bl, sl and red brn 22.50 40.00

Surtax for Belgian Antarctic Expedition, 1957-58.
No. B605a contains 4 No. B605b. Inscribed "Expedition Antarctique Belge 1957-1958" in French and Flemish. Size: 115x83mm.

Gen. Patton's Grave and Flag
SP311

Gen. George S. Patton, Jr. — SP312

Designs: 2.50fr+50c, Memorial, Bastogne. 3fr+1fr, Gen. Patton decorating Brig. Gen. Anthony C. McAuliffe. 6fr+3fr, Tanks of 1918 and 1944.

1957, Oct. 28 **Photo.**
Size: 36x25mm., 25x36mm.

B606 SP311 1fr + 50c dk gray 85 1.10
B607 SP311 2.50fr + 50c ol grn 1.10 1.75
B608 SP311 3fr + 1fr red brn 1.65 2.25
B609 SP312 5fr + 2.50fr grysh bl 4.00 6.00

Size: 53x35mm.

B610 SP311 6fr + 3fr pale brn car 6.00 8.00
Nos. B606-B610 (5) 13.60 19.10

The surtax was for the General Patton Memorial Committee and Patriotic Societies.

Adolphe Max — SP313

1957, Nov. 10 **Engr.**

B611 SP313 2.50fr + 1fr ultra 1.65 3.25

18th anniversary of the death of Adolphe Max, mayor of Brussels. The surtax was for the national "Adolphe Max" fund.

"Chinels," Fosses
SP314

"Op Signoorken," Malines
SP315

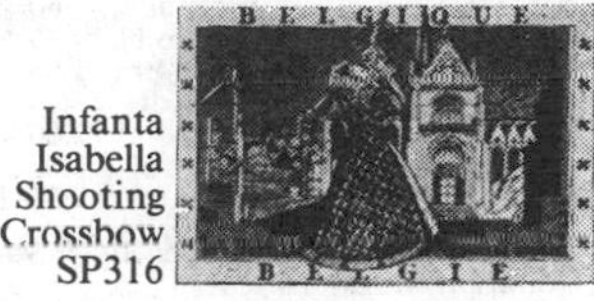

Infanta Isabella Shooting Crossbow
SP316

Legends: 1.50fr+50c, St. Remacle and the wolf. 2fr+1fr, Longman and the pea soup. 5fr+2fr, The Virgin with Inkwell (vert.). 6fr+2.50fr, "Gilles" (clowns), Binche.

Engraved and Photogravure

1957, Dec. 14

B612 SP314 30c + 20c pur & org yel 22 45
B613 SP315 1fr + 50c brn & lt bl 40 45
B614 SP314 1.50fr + 50c gray & red 85 70
B615 SP315 2fr + 1fr gray & brt grn 1.00 1.50
B616 SP316 2.50fr + 1fr bl grn & lil 1.10 1.25
B617 SP316 5fr + 2fr bl & dk gray 3.00 3.25
B618 SP316 6fr + 2.50fr vio brn & red org 4.00 4.50
Nos. B612-B618 (7) 10.57 12.10

The surtax was for anti-tuberculosis work.
See also Nos. B631-B637.

Benelux Gate
SP317

Designs: 1fr+50c, Civil Engineering Pavilion. 1.50fr+50c, Ruanda-Urundi Pavilion. 2.50fr+1fr, Belgium 1900. 3fr+1.50fr, Atomium. 5fr+3fr, Telexpo Pavilion.

Perf. 11½

1958, Apr. 15 **Unwmk.** **Engr.**
Size: 35½x24½mm.

B619 SP317 30c + 20c brn red, vio bl & sep 12 12
B620 SP317 1fr + 50c gray bl, dk brn & emer 12 18
B621 SP317 1.50fr + 50c grnsh bl, pur & cit 25 35
B622 SP317 2.50fr + 1fr ultra, red & brn red 38 65

B623 SP317 3fr + 1.50fr gray, car & lt ultra 85 70

Size: 49x33mm.

B624 SP317 5fr + 3fr gray, ultra & red lil 1.00 70
Nos. B619-B624 (6) 2.72 2.70

World's Fair, Brussels, Apr. 17-Oct. 19.

Marguerite van Eyck by Jan van Eyck — SP318

Christ Carrying Cross, by Hieronymus Bosch SP319

Paintings: 1.50fr+50c, St. Donatien, Jan Gossart. 2.50fr+1fr, Self-portrait, Lambert Lombard. 3fr+150fr, The Rower, James Ensor. 5fr+3fr, Henriette, Henri Evenepoel.

1958, Oct. 30 Photo. *Perf. 11½*
Various Frames in Ocher and Brown.

B625 SP318 30c + 20c dk ol grn 22 45
B626 SP319 1fr + 50c mar 60 1.00
B627 SP318 1.50fr + 50c vio bl 85 1.10
B628 SP318 2.50fr + 1fr dk brn 1.65 2.00
B629 SP319 3fr + 1.50fr dl red 2.00 3.00
B630 SP318 5fr + 3fr brt bl 4.00 7.25
Nos. B625-B630 (6) 9.32 14.80

The surtax was for the benefit of various cultural organizations.

Type of 1957.

Legends: 40c+10c, Elizabeth, Countess of Hoogstraten. 1fr+50c, Jean de Nivelles. 1.50fr+50c, St. Evermare play, Russon. 2fr+1fr, The Penitents of Furnes. 2.50fr+1fr, Manger and "Pax." 5fr+2fr, Sambre-Meuse procession. 6fr+2.50fr, Our Lady of Peace and "Pax" (vert.).

Engraved and Photogravure
1958, Dec. 6 Unwmk. *Perf. 11½*

B631 SP314 40c + 10 ultra & brt grn 25 30
B632 SP315 1fr + 50 gray brn & org 35 40
B633 SP315 1.50fr + 50c cl & brt grn 50 55
B634 SP314 2fr + 1fr brn & red 63 70
B635 SP316 2.50fr + 1fr vio brn & bl grn 2.00 2.75
B636 SP316 5fr + 2fr cl & bl 3.00 4.25
B637 SP316 6fr + 2.50fr bl & rose red 4.00 6.25
Nos. B631-B637 (7) 10.75 15.20

The surtax was for anti-tuberculosis work.

"Europe of the Heart" SP320

1959, Feb. 25 Photo. Unwmk.

B638 SP320 1fr + 50c red lil 75 65
B639 SP320 2.50fr + 1fr dk grn 1.25 1.75
B640 SP320 5fr + 2.50fr dp brn 1.75 2.25

The surtax was for aid for displaced persons.

Allegory of Blood Transfusion SP321

Henri Dunant and Battlefield at Solferino — SP322

Design: 2.50fr+1fr, 3fr+1.50fr, Red Cross, broken sword and drop of blood (horiz.).

1959, June 10 Photo. *Perf. 11½*

B641 SP321 40c + 10c bl gray & car 35 45
B642 SP321 1fr + 50c brn & car 60 65
B643 SP321 1.50fr + 50c dl vio & car 70 90
B644 SP321 2.50fr + 1fr sl grn & car 1.00 1.65
B645 SP321 3fr + 1.50fr vio bl & car 2.50 3.50
B646 SP322 5fr + 3fr dk brn & car 4.00 4.75
Nos. B641-B646 (6) 9.15 11.90

Issued to commemorate the centenary of the International Red Cross idea. The surtax was for the Red Cross and patriotic organizations.

Philip the Good — SP323

Arms of Philip the Good SP324

Designs: 1fr+50c, Charles the Bold. 1.50fr+50c, Emperor Maximilian of Austria. 2.50fr+1fr, Philip the Fair. 3fr+1.50fr, Charles V. Portraits from miniatures by Simon Bening (c. 1483-1561).

1959, July 4 Engr.

B647 SP323 40c + 10c multi 35 45
B648 SP323 1fr + 50c multi 60 65
B649 SP323 1.50fr + 50c multi 70 90
B650 SP323 2.50fr + 1fr multi 1.00 1.65
B651 SP323 3fr + 1.50fr multi 2.50 3.50
B652 SP324 5fr + 3fr multi 4.00 4.50
Nos. B647-B652 (6) 9.15 11.65

The surtax was for the Royal Library, Brussels.

Portraits show Grand Masters of the Order of the Golden Fleece.

Whale, Antwerp SP325

Carnival, Stavelot SP326

Designs: 1fr+50c, Dragon, Mons. 2fr+50c, Prince Carnival, Eupen. 3fr+1fr, Jester and cats, Ypres. 6fr+2fr, Holy Family (horiz.). 7fr+3fr, Madonna, Liege (horiz.).

Engraved and Photogravure
1959, Dec. 5 *Perf. 11½*

B653 SP325 40c + 10c cit, Prus bl & red 38 45
B654 SP325 1fr + 50c ol & grn 60 65
B655 SP325 2fr + 50c lt brn, org & cl 45 45
B656 SP326 2.50fr + 1fr gray, pur & ultra 65 65
B657 SP326 3fr + 1fr gray, mar & yel 1.50 1.25
B658 SP326 6fr + 2fr ol, brt bl & hn brn 2.75 3.00
B659 SP326 7fr + 3fr chlky bl & org yel 4.00 4.25
Nos. B653-B659 (7) 10.33 10.70

The surtax was for anti-tuberculosis work.

Child Refugee — SP327

Designs: 3fr+1.50fr, Man. 6fr+3fr, Woman.

1960, Apr. 7 Engr.

B660 SP327 40c + 10c rose cl 15 15
B661 SP327 3fr + 1.50fr gray brn 60 60
B662 SP327 6fr + 3fr dk bl 1.65 1.50
a. Souv. sheet of 3 45.00 45.00

Issued to publicize World Refugee Year, July 1, 1959-June 30, 1960.

No. B662a contains one each of Nos. B660-B662 with colors changed: 40c+10c, dull purple; 3fr+1.50fr, red brown; 6fr+3fr, henna brown. Black marginal inscription and uprooted oak emblem. Size: 121x92mm.

Parachutists and Plane SP328

Designs: 2fr+50c, 2.50fr+1fr, Parachutists coming in for landing (vert.) 3fr+1fr, 6fr+2fr, Parachutist walking with parachute.

Photogravure and Engraved
1960, June 13 *Perf. 11½*

B663 SP328 40c + 10c lt ultra & blk 15 15
B664 SP328 1fr + 50c bl & blk 75 75
B665 SP328 2fr + 50c bl, blk & ol 1.90 1.40
B666 SP328 2.50fr + 1fr grnsh bl, blk & gray ol 2.50 2.50
B667 SP328 3fr + 1fr bl, blk & sl grn 2.50 2.50
B668 SP328 6fr + 2fr lt vio bl, blk & ol 4.75 4.50
Nos. B663-B668 (6) 12.55 11.80

The surtax was for various patriotic and cultural organizations.

Mother and Child, Planes and Rainbow SP329

Designs: 40c+10c, Brussels Airport, planes and rainbow. 6fr+3fr, Rainbow connecting Congo and Belgium, and planes (vert.)

Perf. 11½
1960, Aug. 3 Unwmk. Photo.
Size: 35x24mm.

B669 SP329 40c + 10c grnsh bl 15 15
B670 SP329 3fr + 1.50fr brt red 3.50 3.25

Size: 35x52mm.

B671 SP329 6fr + 3fr vio 5.25 4.00

The surtax was for refugees from Congo.

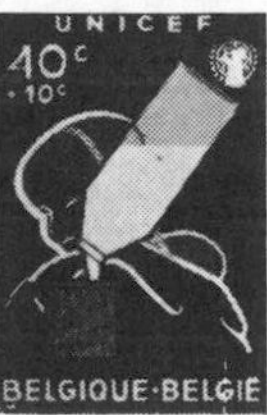

Infant, Milk Bottle and Mug — SP330

Designs: 1fr+50c, Nurse and children of 3 races. 2fr+50c, Refugee woman carrying gift clothes. 2.50fr+1fr, Negro nurse weighing infant. 3fr+1fr, Children of various races dancing. 6fr+2fr, Refugee boys.

Photogravure and Engraved
1960, Oct. 8 *Perf. 11½*

B672 SP330 40c + 10c gldn brn, yel & bl grn 15 15
B673 SP330 1fr + 50c ol gray, mar & sl 1.25 80
B674 SP330 2fr + 50c vio, pale brn & brt grn 1.40 1.10
B675 SP330 2.50fr + 1fr dk red, sep & lt bl 1.75 1.40
B676 SP330 3fr + 1fr bl grn, red org & dl vio 95 95
B677 SP330 6fr + 2fr ultra, emer & brn 3.50 3.25
Nos. B672-B677 (6) 9.00 7.65

Issued for the United Nations Children's Fund, UNICEF.

Tapestry SP331

Belgian handicrafts: 1fr+50c, Cut crystal vases (vert.). 2fr+50c, Lace (vert.). 2.50fr+1fr, Metal plate & jug. 3fr+1fr, Diamonds. 6fr+2fr, Ceramics.

Photogravure and Engraved
1960, Dec. 5 *Perf. 11½*

B678 SP331 40c + 10c bl, bis & brn 15 15
B679 SP331 1fr + 50c ind & org brn 1.10 1.10
B680 SP331 2fr + 50c dk red brn, blk & cit 1.90 1.65
B681 SP331 2.50fr + 1fr choc & yel 2.50 2.50
B682 SP331 3fr + 1fr org brn, blk & ultra 1.25 1.25

B683 SP331 6fr + 2fr dp blk & yel 5.00 4.00
Nos. B678-B683 (6) 11.90 10.65

The surtax was for anti-tuberculosis work.

Jacob Kats and Abbe Nicolas Pietkin SP332

Portraits: 1fr+50c, Albert Mockel and J. F. Willems. 2fr+50c, Jan van Rijswijck and Xavier M. Neujean. 2.50fr+1fr, Joseph Demarteau and A. Van de Perre. 3fr+1fr, Canon Jan-Baptist David and Albert du Bois. 6fr+2fr, Henri Vieuxtemps and Willem de Mol.

Photogravure and Engraved

1961, Apr. 22 Unwmk. *Perf. 11½*

Portraits in Gray Brown

B684 SP332 40c + 10c ver & mar 15 15
B685 SP332 1fr + 50c bis brn & mar 1.25 1.10
B686 SP332 2fr + 50c yel & crim 1.75 1.50
B687 SP332 2.50fr + 1fr pale cit & dk grn 2.50 1.75
B688 SP332 3fr + 1fr lt & dk bl 2.50 2.50
B689 SP332 6fr + 2fr lil & ultra 4.50 4.50
Nos. B684-B689 (6) 12.65 11.50

The surtax was for the benefit of various cultural organizations.

White Rhinoceros SP333

Antonius Cardinal Perrenot de Granvelle SP334

Animals: 1fr+50c, Przewalski horses. 2fr+50c, Okapi. 2.50fr+1fr, Giraffe (horiz.). 3fr+1fr, Lesser panda (horiz.). 6fr+2fr, European elk (horiz.).

Perf. 11½

1961, June 5 Unwmk. Photo.

B690 SP333 40c + 10c bis brn & dk brn 15 15
B691 SP333 1fr + 50c gray & brn 1.25 1.25
B692 SP333 2fr + 50c dp rose & blk 1.75 1.65
B693 SP333 2.50fr + 1fr red org & brn 1.50 1.25
B694 SP333 3fr + 1fr org & brn 1.25 1.25
B695 SP333 6fr + 2fr bl & bis brn 3.25 1.90
Nos. B690-B695 (6) 9.15 7.45

The surtax was for various philanthropic organizations.

1961, July 29 Engr.

Designs: 3fr+1.50fr, Arms of Cardinal de Granvelle. 6fr+3fr, Tower and crosier, symbolic of collaboration between Malines and the Archbishopric.

B696 SP334 40c + 10c mag, car & brn 15 15
B697 SP334 3fr + 1.50fr multi 1.20 90
B698 SP334 6fr + 3fr mag pur & bis 2.50 2.25

Issued to commemorate the 400th anniversary of Malines as an Archbishopric.

Prices of premium quality never hinged stamps will be in excess of catalogue price.

Mother and Child by Pierre Paulus SP335

Castle of the Counts of Male SP336

Plaintings: 1fr+50c, Mother Love, François-Joseph Navez. 2fr+50c, Motherhood, Constant Permeke. 2.50fr+1fr, Madonna and Child, Rogier van der Weyden. 3fr+1fr, Madonna with Apple, Hans Memling. 6fr+2fr, Madonna of the Forget-me-not, Peter Paul Rubens.

1961, Dec. 2 Photo. *Perf. 11½*

Gold Frame

B699 SP335 40c + 10c dp brn 15 15
B700 SP335 1fr + 50c brt bl 60 45
B701 SP335 2fr + 50c rose red 90 70
B702 SP335 2.50fr + 1fr mag 1.40 1.10
B703 SP335 3fr + 1fr vio bl 1.50 1.25
B704 SP335 6fr + 2fr dk sl grn 2.75 2.25
Nos. B699-B704 (6) 7.30 5.90

The surtax was for anti-tuberculosis work.

1962, Mar. 12 Engr. *Perf. 11½*

Designs: 90c+10c, Royal library (horiz.). 1fr+50c, Church of Our Lady, Tongres. 2fr+50c, Collegiate Church, Soignies (horiz.). 2.50fr+1fr, Church of Our Lady, Malines. 3fr+1fr, St. Denis Abbey, Broqueroi. 6fr+2fr, Cloth Hall, Ypres (horiz.).

B705 SP336 40c + 10c brt grn 15 15
B706 SP336 90c + 10c lil rose 30 30
B707 SP336 1fr + 50c dl vio 60 60
B708 SP336 2fr + 50c vio 85 85
B709 SP336 2.50fr + 1fr red brn 1.50 1.25
B710 SP336 3fr + 1fr bl grn 1.50 1.25
B711 SP336 6fr + 2fr car rose 2.00 1.90
Nos. B705-B711 (7) 6.90 6.30

The surtax was for various cultural and philanthropic organizations.

Andean Cock of the Rock — SP337

Handicapped Child — SP338

Birds: 1fr+50c, Red lory. 2fr+50c, Guinea touraco. 2.50fr+1fr, Keel-billed toucan. 3fr+1fr, Great bird of paradise. 6fr+2fr, Congolese peacock.

Engraved and Photogravure

1962, June 23 Unwmk. *Perf. 11½*

Birds in Natural Colors

B712 SP337 40c + 10c bl 15 15
B713 SP337 1fr + 50c ultra & car 60 50
B714 SP337 2fr + 50c blk & car rose 70 60
B715 SP337 2.50fr + 1fr grnsh bl & ver 80 70
B716 SP337 3fr + 1fr red brn & grn 1.75 1.40
B717 SP337 6fr + 2fr red & ultra 3.00 2.75
Nos. B712-B717 (6) 7.00 6.10

The surtax was for various philanthropic organizations.

Perf. 11½

1962, Sept. 22 Unwmk. Photo.

Handicapped Children: 40c+10c, Reading Braille. 2fr+50c, Deaf-mute girl with earphones and electronic equipment (horiz.). 2.50fr+1fr, Child with ball (cerebral palsy). 3fr+1fr, Girl with crutches (polio). 6fr+2fr, Sitting boys playing ball (horiz.).

B718 SP338 40c + 10c choc 15 15
B719 SP338 1fr + 50c rose red 50 45
B720 SP338 2fr + 50c brt lil 95 85
B721 SP338 2.50fr + 1fr dl grn 1.10 95
B722 SP338 3fr + 1fr dk bl 1.40 1.25
B723 SP338 6fr + 2fr dk brn 2.50 2.00
Nos. B718-B723 (6) 6.60 5.65

The surtax was for various institutions for handicapped children.

Queen Louise-Marie SP339

Belgian Queens: No. B725, like No. B724 with "ML" initials. 1fr+50c, Marie-Henriette. 2fr+1fr, Elisabeth. 3fr+1.50fr, Astrid. 8fr+2.50fr, Fabiola.

Photogravure and Engraved

1962, Dec. 8 *Perf. 11½*

B724 SP339 40c + 10c gray, blk & gold ("L") 15 15
B725 SP339 40c + 10c gray, blk & gold ("ML") 15 15
B726 SP339 1fr + 50c gray, blk & gold 75 75
B727 SP339 2fr + 1fr gray, blk & gold 1.25 1.25
B728 SP339 3fr + 1.50fr gray, blk & gold 1.50 1.25
B729 SP339 8fr + 2.50fr gray, blk & gold 2.25 1.65
Nos. B724-B729 (6) 6.05 5.20

The surtax was for anti-tuberculosis work.

British War Memorial (Porte de Menin), Ypres SP340

1962, Dec. 26 Engr. *Perf. 11½*

B730 SP340 1fr + 50c blk, grn, bl & red brn 75 75

Millennium of the city of Ypres. Issued in sheets of eight.

Peace Bell Ringing over Globe SP341

The Sower by Brueghel SP342

Engraved and Photogravure

1963, Feb. 18 Unwmk. *Perf. 11½*

B731 SP341 3fr + 1.50fr blk, bl, org & grn 1.75 1.75
a. Sheet of 4 9.00 9.00
B732 SP341 6fr + 3fr blk, brn & org 1.10 1.10

The surtax was for the installation of the Peace Bell (Bourdon de la Paix) at Koekelberg Basilica and for the benefit of various cultural organizations.

No. B731 was issued in sheets of 4. The sheet is inscribed "Bourdon de la Paix," repeated in Flemish, and measures 85x115mm. No. B732 was issued in sheets of 30.

1963, Mar. 21 *Perf. 11½*

Designs: 3fr+1fr, The Harvest, by Brueghel (horiz.). 6fr+2fr, "Bread," by Anton Carte (horiz.).

B733 SP342 2fr + 1fr grn, ocher & blk 20 20
B734 SP342 3fr + 1fr red lil, ocher & blk 52 45
B735 SP342 6fr + 2fr red brn, cit & blk 75 60

Issued for the "Freedom from Hunger" campaign of the U.N. Food and Agriculture Organization.

Speed Racing — SP343

Designs: 2fr+1fr, Bicyclists at check point (horiz.). 3fr+1.50fr, Team racing (horiz.). 6fr+3fr, Pace setters.

Perf. 11½

1963, July 13 Unwmk. Engr.

B736 SP343 1fr + 50c multi 15 15
B737 SP343 2fr + 1fr bl, car, blk & ol gray 30 30
B738 SP343 3fr + 1.50fr multi 50 50
B739 SP343 6fr + 3fr multi 75 75

Issued to commemorate the 80th anniversary of the founding of the Belgian Bicycle League. The surtax was for athletes at the 1964 Olympic Games.

Princess Paola with Princess Astrid — SP344

Prince Albert and Family — SP345

Designs: 40c+10c, Prince Philippe. 2fr+50c, Princess Astrid. 2.50fr+1fr, Princess Paola. 6fr+2fr, Prince Albert.

1963, Sept. 28 Photo.

Cross in Red

B740 SP344 40c + 10c dk car rose & buff 15 15
B741 SP344 1fr + 50c sl & buff 35 35
B742 SP344 2fr + 50c dk car rose & buff 45 45
B743 SP344 2.50fr + 1fr brt bl & buff 55 55
B744 SP345 3fr + 1fr gray brn & buff 55 55
B745 SP345 3fr + 1fr sl grn & buff 1.65 1.65
a. Bklt pane of 8 55.00 55.00
B746 SP344 6fr + 2fr sl & buff 95 95
Nos. B740-B746 (7) 4.65 4.65

Issued to commemorate the centenary of the International Red Cross. No. B745 issued only in booklet panes of 8, which are in two forms: French and Flemish inscriptions in top and bottom margins transposed.

Daughter of Balthazar Gerbier, Painted by Rubens — SP346

Jesus, St. John and Cherubs by Rubens SP347

Portraits (Rubens' sons): 1fr+40c, Nicolas, 2 yrs. old. 2fr+50c, Franz. 2.50fr+1fr, Nicolas, 6 yrs. old. 3fr+1fr, Albert.

Photogravure and Engraved

1963, Dec. 7 Unwmk. *Perf. 11½*

B747	SP346	50c + 10c buff, gray & dk brn	15	15
B748	SP346	1fr + 40c buff, red brn & dk brn	15	15
B749	SP346	2fr + 50c buff, vio brn & dk brn	30	30
B750	SP346	2.50fr + 1fr buff, grn & dk brn	60	60
B751	SP346	3fr + 1fr buff, red brn & dk brn	50	50
B752	SP347	6fr + 2fr buff & gray	70	70
		Nos. B747-B752 (6)	2.40	2.40

The surtax was for anti-tuberculosis work. See also No. B771.

John Quincy Adams and Lord Gambier Signing Treaty of Ghent, by Amedee Forestier — SP348

1964, May 16 Photo. *Perf. 11½*

B753	SP348	6fr + 3fr dk bl	75	75

Issued to commemorate the 150th anniversary of the signing of the Treaty of Ghent between the United States and Great Britain, Dec. 24, 1814.

Philip van Marnix — SP349

Portraits: 3fr+1.50fr, Ida de Bure Calvin. 6fr+3fr, Jacob Jordaens.

1964, May 30 Engr.

B754	SP349	1fr + 50c bl gray	15	15
B755	SP349	3fr + 1.50fr rose pink	25	25
B756	SP349	6fr + 3fr redsh brn	45	45

Issued to honor Protestantism in Belgium. The surtax was for the erection of a Protestant church.

Foot Soldier, 1918 SP350

Battle of Bastogne SP351

Designs: 2fr+1fr, Flag bearer, Guides Regiment, 1914. 3fr+1.50fr, Trumpeter of the Grenadiers and drummers, 1914.

1964, Aug. 1 Photo. *Perf. 11½*

B757	SP350	1fr + 50c multi	15	15
B758	SP350	2fr + 1fr multi	30	30
B759	SP350	3fr + 1.50fr multi	30	30

Issued to commemorate the 50th anniversary of the German aggression against Belgium in 1914. The surtax aided patriotic undertakings.

1964, Aug. 1 Unwmk.

Design: 6fr+3fr, Liberation of the estuary of the Escaut.

B760	SP351	3fr + 1fr multi	30	30
B761	SP351	6fr + 3fr multi	45	45

Issued to commemorate Belgium's Resistance and liberation of World War II. The surtax was to help found an International Student Center at Antwerp and to aid cultural undertakings.

Souvenir Sheets

Rogier van der Weyden Paintings — SP352

Descent From the Cross — SP353

Designs: 1fr, Philip the Good. 2fr, Portrait of a Lady. 3fr, Man with Arrow.

1964, Sept. 19 Photo. *Perf. 11½*

B762	SP352	Sheet of 3	4.50	4.50
a.		1fr multi	1.10	1.10
b.		2fr multi	1.10	1.10
c.		3fr multi	1.10	1.10

Engr.

B763	SP353	8fr red brn, sheet of 1	4.50	4.50

Issued to commemorate the 5th centenary of the death of the painter Rogier van der Weyden (Roger de La Pasture, 1400-1464). The surtax went to various cultural organizations. Sheets have gray brown frames and marginal inscriptions. Size of sheets: 153x114mm. Size of stamps: 24x36mm. (Nos. B762a,b,c); 54x35mm. (No. B763). No. B762 sold for 14fr, No. B763 for 16fr.

Ancient View of the Pand SP354

Design: 3fr+1fr, Present view of the Pand from Lys River.

1964, Oct. 10 Photo.

B764	SP354	2fr + 1fr blk, grnsh bl & ultra	30	30
B765	SP354	3fr + 1fr lil rose, bl & dk brn	30	30

The surtax was for the restoration of the Pand Dominican Abbey in Ghent.

Type of 1963 and

Child of Charles I, Painted by Van Dyck — SP355

Designs: 1fr+40c, William of Orange with his bride, by Van Dyck. 2fr+1fr, Portrait of a small boy with dogs by Erasmus Quellin and Jan Fyt. 3fr+1fr, Alexander Farnese by Antonio Moro. 4fr+2fr, William II, Prince of Orange by Van Dyck. 6fr+3fr, Artist's children by Cornelis De Vos.

1964, Dec. 5 Engr. *Perf. 11½*

B766	SP355	50c + 10c rose cl	15	15
B767	SP355	1fr + 40c car rose	15	15
B768	SP355	2fr + 1fr vio brn	25	25
B769	SP355	3fr + 1fr gray	25	25
B770	SP355	4fr + 2fr vio bl	38	38
B771	SP347	6fr + 3fr brt pur	38	38
		Nos. B766-B771 (6)	1.56	1.56

The surtax was for anti-tuberculosis work.

Liberator, Shaking Prisoner's Hand, Concentration Camp — SP356

Designs: 1fr+50c, Prisoner's hand reaching for the sun. 3fr+1.50fr, Searchlights and tank breaking down barbed wire (horiz.). 8fr+5fr, Rose growing amid the ruins (horiz.).

Engraved and Photogravure

1965, May 8 Unwmk. *Perf. 11½*

B772	SP356	50c + 50c tan, blk & buff	15	15
B773	SP356	1fr + 50c multi	15	15
B774	SP356	3fr + 1.50fr dl lil & blk	25	25
B775	SP356	8fr + 5fr multi	45	45

Issued to commemorate the 20th anniversary of the liberation of the concentration camps for political prisoners and prisoners of war.

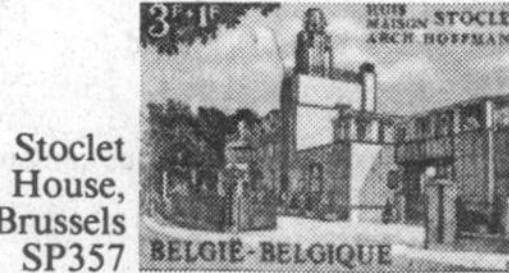
Stoclet House, Brussels SP357

Stoclet House: 6fr+3fr, Hall with marble foundation (vert.). 8fr+4fr, View of house from garden.

1965, June 21

B776	SP357	3fr + 1fr sl & tan	30	30
B777	SP357	6fr + 3fr sep	45	45
B778	SP357	8fr + 4fr vio brn & tan	60	60

Issued to commemorate the 95th anniversary of the birth of the Austrian architect Josef Hoffmann (1870-1956), builder of the art nouveau residence of Adolphe Stoclet, engineer and financier.

Jackson's Chameleon SP358

Animals from Antwerp Zoo: 2fr+1fr, Common iguanas. 3fr+1.50fr, African monitor. 6fr+3fr, Komodo monitor. 8fr+4fr, Nile softshell turtle.

1965, Oct. 16 Photo. *Perf. 11½*

B779	SP358	1fr + 50c multi	15	15
B780	SP358	2fr + 1fr multi	20	20
B781	SP358	3fr + 1.50fr multi	28	28
B782	SP358	6fr + 3fr multi	55	55

Miniature Sheet

B783	SP358	8fr + 4fr multi	2.25	2.25

The surtax was for various cultural and philanthropic organizations. No. B783 contains one stamp (52x35mm.) and has gray animal border. Size: 117x95mm.

Boatmen's and Archers' Guild Halls SP359

Buildings on Grand-Place, Brussels: 1fr+40c, Brewers' Hall. 2fr+1fr, "King of Spain." 3fr+1.50fr, "Dukes of Brabant." 10fr+4.50fr, Tower of City Hall and St. Michael.

1965, Dec. 4 Engr. *Perf. 11½*

Size: 35x24mm.

B784	SP359	50c + 10c ultra	15	15
B785	SP359	1fr + 40c bl grn	18	18
B786	SP359	2fr + 1fr rose cl	22	22
B787	SP359	3fr + 1.50fr vio	25	25

Size: 24x44mm.

B788	SP359	10fr + 4.50fr sep & gray	40	40
		Nos. B784-B788 (5)	1.20	1.20

The surtax was for anti-tuberculosis work.

Souvenir Sheets

Queen Elisabeth — SP360

Design: No. B790, Types of 1931 and 1956.

1966, Apr. 16 Photo. *Perf. 11½*

B789	SP360	Sheet of 2	2.00	2.00
a.		SP74 3fr dk brn & gray grn	80	80
b.		SP87 3fr dk brn, yel grn & gold	80	80

B790 SP360 Sheet of 2 2.00 2.00
 a. SP42 3fr dk brn & dl bl 80 80
 b. SP304 3fr dk brn & gray 80 80

The surtax went to various cultural organizations.

Each sheet contains two stamps plus label with the Queen's initial; sold for 20fr. Dark brown marginal inscription. Size: 81½x115mm.

Luminescent Paper was used in printing Nos. B789-B790, B801-B806, B808-B809, B811-B823, B825-B831, B833-B835, B837-B840, B842-B846, B848-B850, B852-B854, B856-B863, and from B865 onward unless otherwise noted.

Diver — SP361

Design: 10fr+4fr, Swimmer at start.

1966, May 9 **Engr.**

B791 SP361 60c + 40c Prus grn, ol & org brn 15 15
B792 SP361 10fr + 4fr ol grn, org brn & mag 55 55

Issued to publicize the importance of swimming instruction.

Minorites' Convent, Liège — SP362

Designs: 1fr+50c, Val-Dieu Abbey, Aubel. 2fr+1fr, View and seal of Huy. 10fr+4.50fr, Statue of Ambiorix by Jules Bertin, and tower, Tongeren.

1966, Aug. 27 **Engr.** ***Perf. 11½***

B793 SP362 60c + 40c bl, vio brn & org brn 10 10
B794 SP362 1fr + 50c vio brn, bl & grnsh bl 15 15
B795 SP362 2fr + 1fr car rose, vio brn & org brn 18 18
B796 SP362 10fr + 4.50fr brt grn, vio brn & sl bl 70 70

The surtax was for various patriotic and cultural organizations.

Surveyor and Dog Team SP363

Designs: 3fr+1.50fr, Adrien de Gerlache and "Belgica." 6fr+3fr, Surveyor, weather balloon and ship. 10fr+5fr, Penguins and "Magga Dan" (ship used for 1964, 1965 and 1966 expeditions).

1966, Oct. 8 **Engr.** ***Perf. 11½***

B797 SP363 1fr + 50c bl grn 15 15
B798 SP363 3fr + 1.50fr pale vio 25 25
B799 SP363 6fr + 3fr dk car 45 45

Souvenir Sheet

Engraved and Photogravure

B800 SP363 10fr + 5fr dk gray, sky bl & dk red 90 90

Issued to publicize Belgian Antarctic expeditions. No. B800 contains one stamp (52x35mm.); inscriptions, map of Antarctica and observation post in margin. Size: 130x95mm.

Boy with Ball and Dog — SP364

Designs: 2fr+1fr, Girl skipping rope. 3fr+1.50fr, Girl and boy blowing soap bubbles. 6fr+3fr, Girl and boy rolling hoops (horiz.). 8fr+3.50fr, Four children at play and cat (horiz.).

Engraved and Photogravure

1966, Dec. 3 ***Perf. 11½***

B801 SP364 1fr + 1fr pink & blk 15 15
B802 SP364 2fr + 1fr lt bluish grn & blk 18 18
B803 SP364 3fr + 1.50fr lt vio & blk 22 22
B804 SP364 6fr + 3fr pale sal & dk brn 35 35
B805 SP364 8fr + 3.50fr lt yel grn & dk brn 42 42
 Nos. B801-B805 (5) 1.32 1.32

The surtax was for anti-tuberculosis work.

Souvenir Sheet

Refugees — SP365

Designs: 1fr, Boy receiving clothes. 2fr, Tibetan children. 3fr, African mother and children.

1967, Mar. 11 **Photo.** ***Perf. 11½***

B806 SP365 Sheet of 3 1.50 1.50
 a. 1fr blk & yel 35 35
 b. 2fr blk & bl 35 35
 c. 3fr blk & org 50 50

Issued to help refugees around the world. Sheet has black border with Belgian P.T.T. and U.N. Refugee emblems. Size: 110x76mm. Sold for 20fr.

Robert Schuman — SP366

Kongolo Memorial, Gentinnes SP367

Colonial Brotherhood Emblem — SP368

1967, June 24 **Engr.** ***Perf. 11½***

B807 SP366 2fr + 1fr gray bl 40 40

Engraved and Photogravure

B808 SP367 5fr + 2fr brn & ol 45 45
B809 SP368 10fr + 5fr multi 70 60

Issued to commemorate respectively: Robert Schuman (1886-1963), French statesman, one of the founders of European Steel and Coal Community, first president of European Parliament (2fr+1fr); Kongolo Memorial, erected in memory of missionary and civilian victims in the Congo (5fr+2fr); a memorial for African Troops, Brussels (10fr+5fr).

Preaching Fool from "Praise of Folly" by Erasmus SP369

Erasmus, by Quentin Massys SP370

Designs: 2fr+1fr, Exhorting Fool from Praise of Folly. 5fr+2fr, Thomas More's Family, by Hans Holbein (horiz.). 6fr+3fr, Pierre Gilles (Aegidius), by Quentin Massys.

Photogravure and Engraved (SP369); Photogravure (SP370)

1967, Sept. 2 **Unwmk.** ***Perf. 11***

B810 SP369 1fr + 50c tan, blk, bl & car 15 15
B811 SP369 2fr + 1fr tan, blk & car 18 18
B812 SP370 3fr + 1.50fr multi 20 20
B813 SP369 5fr + 2fr tan, blk & car 28 28
B814 SP370 6fr + 3fr multi 35 35
 Nos. B810-B814 (5) 1.16 1.16

Issued to commemorate Erasmus (1466(?)-1536), Dutch scholar and his era.

Souvenir Sheet

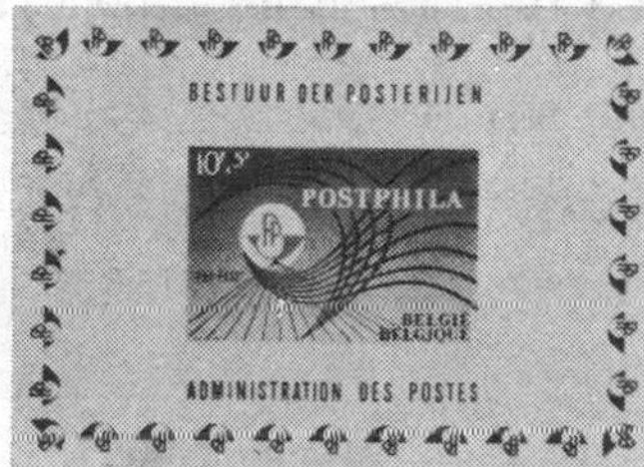

Pro-Post Association Emblem — SP371

Engraved and Photogravure

1967, Oct. 21 ***Perf. 11½***

B815 SP371 10fr + 5fr multi 1.00 1.00

Issued to publicize the POSTPHILA Philatelic Exhibition, Brussels, Oct. 21-29. No. B815 has black marginal inscription and ornaments. Size: 112x77mm.

Detail from Brueghel's "Children's Games" — SP372

Designs: Various Children's Games. Singles of Nos. B816-B821 arranged in 2 rows of 3 show complete painting by Pieter Brueghel.

1967, Dec. 9 **Photo.** ***Perf. 11½***

B816 SP372 1fr + 50c multi 15 15
B817 SP372 2fr + 50c multi 20 20
B818 SP372 3fr + 1fr multi 20 20
B819 SP372 6fr + 3fr multi 32 32
B820 SP372 10fr + 4fr multi 45 45
B821 SP372 13fr + 6fr multi 65 65
 Nos. B816-B821 (6) 1.97 1.97

Queen Fabiola Holding Refugee Child from Congo — SP373

Design: 6fr+3fr, Queen Elisabeth and Dr. Depage.

1968, Apr. 27 **Photo.** ***Perf. 11½***

Cross in Red

B822 SP373 6fr + 3fr sep & gray 40 40
B823 SP373 10fr + 5fr sep & gray 75 75

The surtax was for the Red Cross.

Woman Gymnast and Calendar Stone SP374

Yachting and "The Swimmer" by Andrien SP375

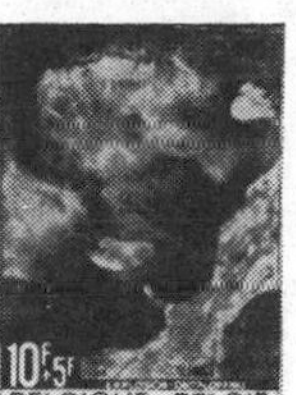

"Explosion" SP376

Designs: 2fr+1fr, Weight lifter and Mayan motif. 3fr+1.50fr, Hurdler, colossus of Tula and animal head from Kukulkan. 6fr+2fr, Bicyclists and Chichen Itza Temple.

Engraved and Photogravure

1968, May 27 ***Perf. 11½***

B824 SP374 1fr + 50c multi 15 15
B825 SP374 2fr + 1fr multi 18 18
B826 SP374 3fr + 1.50fr multi 20 20
B827 SP374 6fr + 2fr multi 32 32

Photo.

B828 SP375 13fr+ 5fr multi 75 75
 Nos. B824-B828 (5) 1.60 1.60

Issued to publicize the 19th Olympic Games, Mexico City, Oct. 12-27.

1968, June 22 **Photo.**

Designs (Paintings by Pol Mara): 12fr+5fr, "Fire." 13fr+5fr, "Tornado."

B829 SP376 10fr + 5fr multi 50 50
B830 SP376 12fr + 5fr multi 80 80
B831 SP376 13fr + 5fr multi 90 90

The surtax was for disaster victims.

Undulate Triggerfish SP377

Tropical Fish: 3fr+1.50fr, Angelfish. 6fr+3fr, Turkeyfish (Pterois volitans). 10fr+5fr, Orange butterflyfish.

Engraved and Photogravure

1968, Oct. 19 ***Perf. 11½***

B832	SP377	1fr + 50c multi	18	18
B833	SP377	3fr + 1.50fr multi	25	25
B834	SP377	6fr + 3fr multi	45	45
B835	SP377	10fr + 5fr multi	65	65

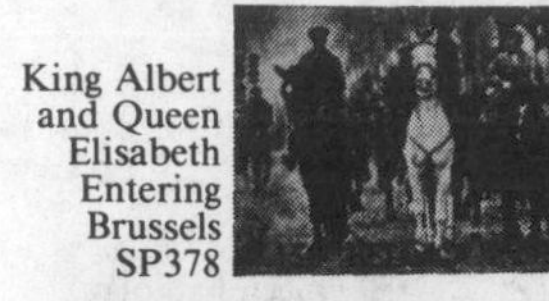

King Albert and Queen Elisabeth Entering Brussels SP378

Tomb of the Unknown Soldier and Eternal Flame, Brussels — SP379

Designs: 1fr+50c, King Albert, Queen Elisabeth and Crown Prince Leopold on balcony, Bruges (vert.). 6fr+3fr, King and Queen entering Liege.

1968, Nov. 9 **Photo.** ***Perf. 11½***

B836	SP378	1fr + 50c multi	15	15
B837	SP378	3fr + 1.50fr multi	25	25
B838	SP378	6fr + 3fr multi	45	45

Engraved and Photogravure

B839	SP379	10fr + 5fr multi	60	60

Issued to commemorate the 50th anniversary of the victory in World War I.

Souvenir Sheet

The Painter and the Amateur, by Peter Brueghel — SP380

1969, May 10 **Engr.** ***Perf. 11½***

B840	SP380	10fr + 5fr sep	1.75	1.75

Issued to publicize the POSTPHILA 1969 Philatelic Exhibition, Brussels, May 10-18. Size of stamp: 40x47mm.; size of sheet: 90x123mm.

Huts, by Ivanka D. Pancheva, Bulgaria SP381

Msgr. Victor Scheppers SP382

Children's Drawings and UNICEF Emblem: 3fr+1.50fr, "My Art" (Santa Claus), by Claes Patric, Belgium. 6fr+3fr, "In the Sun" (young boy), by Helena Rejchlova, Czechoslovakia. 10fr+5fr, "Out for a Walk" by Phillis Sporn, USA (horiz.).

1969, May 31 **Photo.** ***Perf. 11½***

B841	SP381	1fr + 50c multi	15	15
B842	SP381	3fr + 1.50fr multi	20	20
B843	SP381	6fr + 3fr multi	45	45
B844	SP381	10fr + 5fr multi	65	65

The surtax was for philanthropic purposes.

1969, July 5 **Engr.**

B845	SP382	6fr + 3fr rose cl	45	45

Issued to commemorate Msgr. Victor Scheppers (1802-77), prison reformer and founder of the Brothers of Mechlin (Scheppers).

Moon Landing Type of 1969

Design: 20fr+10fr, Armstrong, Collins and Aldrin and moon with Tranquillity Base (vert.). Souvenir Sheet

1969, Sept. 20 **Photo.** ***Perf. 11½***

B846	A245	20fr + 10fr ind	4.50	4.50

See note after No. 693. No. B846 contains one stamp. Margin has commemorative inscription and picture of Armstrong stepping on moon. Size: 94x129mm.

Heads from Alexander the Great Tapestry, 15th Century — SP383

Designs from Tapestries: 3fr+1.50fr, Fiddler from "The Feast," c. 1700. 10fr+4fr, Head of beggar from "The Healing of the Paralytic," 16th century.

1969, Sept. 20

B847	SP383	1fr + 50c multi	15	15
B848	SP383	3fr + 1.50fr multi	30	30
B849	SP383	10fr + 4fr multi	75	75

The surtax was for philanthropic purposes.

Bearded Antwerp Bantam SP384

Engr. and Photo.

1969, Nov. 8 ***Perf. 11½***

B850	SP384	10fr + 5fr multi	80	80

Angel Playing Lute — SP385

Designs from Stained Glass Windows: 1.50fr+50c, Angel with trumpet, St. Waudru's, Mons. 7fr+3fr, Angel with viol, St. Jacques', Liege. 9fr+4fr, King with bagpipes, Royal Art Museum, Brussels.

1969, Dec. 13 **Photo.**

Size: 24x35mm.

B851	SP385	1.50fr + 50c multi	18	18
B852	SP385	3.50fr + 1.50fr multi	25	25
B853	SP385	7fr + 3fr multi	45	45

Size: 35x52mm.

B854	SP386	9fr + 4fr multi	70	70

The surtax was for philanthropic purposes.

Farm and Windmill, Open-air Museum, Bokrijk SP386

Belgian Museums: 3.50fr+1.50fr, Stage Coach Inn, Courcelles. 7fr+3fr, "The Thresher of Trevires," Gallo-Roman sculpture, Gaumais Museum, Virton. 9fr+4fr, "The Sovereigns," by Henry Moore, Middelheim Museum, Antwerp.

Engraved and Photogravure

1970, May 30 ***Perf. 11½***

B855	SP386	1.50fr + 50c multi	20	20
B856	SP386	3.50fr + 1.50fr multi	35	35
B857	SP386	7fr + 3fr multi	45	45
B858	SP386	9fr + 4fr multi	55	55

The surtax went to various culture organizations.

"Resistance" SP387

Design: 7fr+3fr, "Liberation of Camps." The designs were originally used as book covers.

1970, July 4 **Photo.** ***Perf. 11½***

B859	SP387	3.50fr + 1.50fr blk, gray grn & dp car	25	25
B860	SP387	7fr + 3fr blk, lil & dp car	50	50

Issued to honor the Resistance Movement and to commemorate the 25th anniversary of the liberation of concentration camps.

Fishing Rod and Reel SP388

Design: 9fr+4fr, Hockey stick and puck (vert.).

Engraved and Photogravure

1970, Sept. 19 ***Perf. 11½***

B861	SP388	3.50fr + 1.50fr multi	35	35
B862	SP388	9fr + 4fr brt grn & multi	60	60

Souvenir Sheet

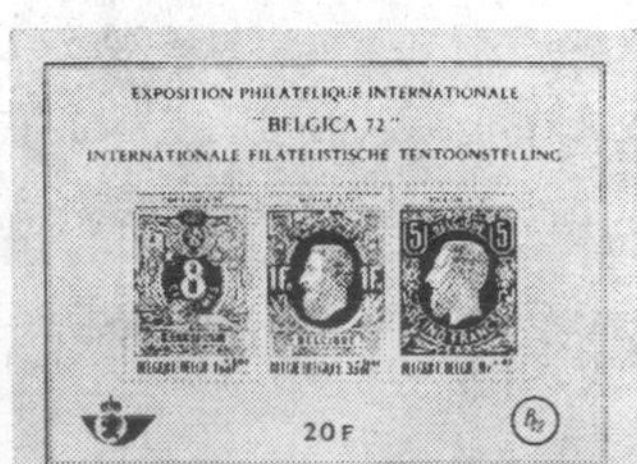

Belgium Nos. 31, 36 and 39 — SP389

Engraved and Photogravure

1970, Oct. 10 ***Perf. 11½***

B863	SP389	sheet of 3	5.50	5.50
a.		1.50fr + 50c blk & dl lil	1.65	1.65
b.		3.50fr + 1.50fr blk & lil	1.65	1.65
c.		9fr + 4fr blk & red brn	1.65	1.65

Issued to publicize BELGICA 72 International Philatelic Exhibition, Brussels, June 24-July 9. No. B863 has black marginal inscription and lilac frame. Size: 130x97mm.

Camille Huysmans (1871-1968) SP390

"Anxious City" (Detail) by Paul Delvaux SP391

Portraits: 3.50fr+1.50fr, Joseph Cardinal Cardijn (1882-1967). 7fr+3fr, Maria Baers (1883-1959). 9fr+4fr, Paul Pastur (1866-1938).

Engraved and Photogravure

1970, Nov. 14 ***Perf. 11½***

Portraits in Sepia

B864	SP390	1.50fr + 50c car rose	15	15
B865	SP390	3.50fr + 1.50fr lil	25	25
B866	SP390	7fr + 3fr grn	50	50
B867	SP390	9fr + 4fr bl	60	60

1970, Dec. 12 **Photo.**

Design: 7fr+3fr, "The Memory," by René Magritte.

B868	SP391	3.50fr + 1.50fr multi	25	25
B869	SP391	7fr + 3fr multi	50	50

Notre Dame du Vivier, Marche-les-Dames — SP392

Design: 7fr+3fr, Turnhout Beguinage and Beguine.

1971, March 13 ***Perf. 11½***

B870	SP392	3.50fr + 1.50 multi	25	25
B871	SP392	7fr + 3fr multi	50	50

The surtax was for philanthropic purposes.

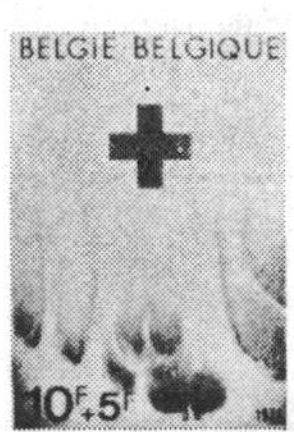

Red Cross — SP393

1971, May 22 **Photo.** ***Perf. 11½***

B872	SP393	10fr + 5fr crim & blk	75	75

Belgian Red Cross.

Discobolus and Munich Cathedral SP394

Festival of Flanders SP395

Engraved and Photogravure

1971, June 19 *Perf. 11½*

B873 SP394 7fr + 3fr bl & blk 60 60

Publicity for the 20th Summer Olympic Games, Munich 1972.

1971, Sept. 11 Photo. *Perf. 11½*

Design: 7fr+3fr, Wallonia Festival.

B874 SP395 3.50fr + 1.50fr multi 25 25
B875 SP395 7fr + 3fr multi 50 50

Attre Palace — SP396

Steen Palace, Elewijt — SP397

Design: 10fr+5fr, Royal Palace, Brussels.

1971, Oct. 23 **Engr.**

B876 SP396 3.50fr + 1.50fr sl grn 45 45
B877 SP397 7fr + 3fr red brn 75 75
B878 SP396 10fr + 5fr vio bl 1.10 1.10

Surtax was for BELGICA 72, International Philatelic Exposition.

Ox Fly — SP398

Insects: 1.50fr+50c, Luna moth (vert.). 7fr+3fr, Wasp, polistes gallicus. 9fr+4fr, Tiger beetle (vert.).

1971, Dec. 11 Photo. *Perf. 11½*

B879 SP398 1.50fr + 50c multi 30 30
B880 SP398 3.50fr + 1.50fr multi 30 30
B881 SP398 7fr + 3fr multi 60 60
B882 SP398 9fr + 4fr multi 90 90

Surtax was for philanthropic purposes.

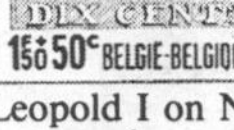
Leopold I on No. 1 SP399

Epilepsy Emblem SP400

Designs: 2fr+1fr, Leopold I on No. 5. 2.50fr+1fr, Leopold II on No. 45. 3.50fr+1.50fr, Leopold II on No. 48. 6fr+3fr, Albert I on No. 135. 7fr+3fr, Albert I on No. 214. 10fr+5fr, Albert I on No. 231. 15fr+7.50fr, Leopold III on No. 290. 20fr+10fr, King Baudouin on No. 718.

Engraved and Photogravure

1972, June 24 *Perf. 11½*

"B" in Gold

B883 SP399 1.50fr + 50c brn & blk 25 25
B884 SP399 2fr + 1fr brick red & brn 25 25
B885 SP399 2.50 + 1fr car & blk 38 38
B886 SP399 3.50fr + 1.50fr vio & blk 60 60
B887 SP399 6fr + 3fr rose lil & blk 95 95
B888 SP399 7fr + 3fr rose car & blk 1.25 1.25
B889 SP399 10fr + 5fr sl bl & blk 1.50 1.50
B890 SP399 15fr + 7fr gray grn & bl grn 2.00 2.00
B891 SP399 20fr + 10fr red brn & brn 3.25 3.25
Nos. B883-B891 (9) 10.43 10.43

Belgica 72, International Philatelic Exhibition, Brussels, June 24-July 9. Nos. B883-B891 issued in sheets of 10 and of 20 (2 tete beche sheets with gutter between). Belgica 72 emblem in stamp color and gray blue border and inscription in margin. Sold in complete sets.

1972, Sept. 9 Photo. *Perf. 11½*

B892 SP400 10fr + 5fr multi 75 75

The surtax was for the William Lennox Center for epilepsy research and treatment.

Gray Lag Goose — SP401

Designs: 4.50fr+2fr, Lapwing. 8fr+4fr, Stork. 9fr+4.50fr, Kestrel (horiz.).

1972, Dec. 16 Photo. *Perf. 11½*

B893 SP401 2fr + 1fr multi 25 25
B894 SP401 4.50fr + 2fr multi 38 38
B895 SP401 8fr + 4fr multi 75 75
B896 SP401 9fr + 4.50fr multi 75 75

Bijloke Abbey, Ghent — SP402

Designs: 4.50fr+2fr, St. Ursmer Collegiate Church, Lobbes. 8fr+4fr, Park Abbey, Heverle. 9fr+4.50fr, Abbey, Floreffe.

1973, Mar. 24 Engr. *Perf. 11½*

B897 SP402 2fr + 1fr sl grn 20 20
B898 SP402 4.50fr + 2fr brn 30 30
B899 SP402 8fr + 4fr rose lil 60 60
B900 SP402 9fr + 4.50fr brt bl 75 75

Basketball SP403

Photogravure and Engraved

1973, Apr. 7

B901 SP403 10fr + 5fr multi 75 75

First World Basketball Championships of the Handicapped, Bruges, Apr. 16-21.

Dirk Martens' Printing Press SP404

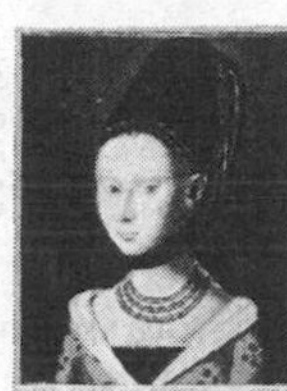
Lady Talbot, by Petrus Christus SP405

Hadrian and Marcus Aurelius Coins SP406

Council of Malines, by Coussaert — SP407

Designs: 3.50fr+1.50fr, Head of Amon and Tutankhamen's cartouche. 10fr+5fr, Three-master of Ostend Merchant Company.

Photogravure and Engraved; Photogravure (B906)

1973, June 23 *Perf. 11½*

B902 SP404 2fr + 1fr multi 25 25
B903 SP404 3.50fr + 1.50fr multi 25 25
B904 SP405 4.50fr + 2fr multi 35 35
B905 SP406 8fr + 4fr multi 1.00 1.00
B906 SP407 9fr + 4.50fr multi 1.40 1.40
B907 SP407 10fr + 5fr multi 2.50 2.50
Nos. B902-B907 (6) 5.75 5.75

Historical Anniversaries: 500th anniversary or first book printed in Belgium (B902); 50th anniversary of Queen Elisabeth Egyptological Foundation (B903); 500th anniversary of death of painter Petrus Christus (B904); Discovery of Roman treasure at Luttre-Liberchies (B905); 500th anniversary of Great Council of Malines (B906); 250th anniversary of the Ostend Merchant Company (B907).

No. B902 is not luminescent.

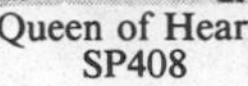
Queen of Hearts SP408

Symbol of Blood Donations SP409

Old Playing Cards: No. B909, King of Clubs. No. B910, Jack of Diamonds. No. B911, King of Spades.

1973, Dec. 8 Photo. *Perf. 11½*

B908 SP408 5 + 2.50fr multi 55 55
B909 SP408 5 + 2.50fr multi 55 55
B910 SP408 5 + 2.50fr multi 55 55
B911 SP408 5 + 2.50fr multi 55 55

Surtax was for philanthropic purposes. Nos. B908-B911 printed se-tenant in sheets of 24 (4x6).

1974, Feb. 23 Photo. *Perf. 11½*

Design: 10fr+5fr, Traffic lights, Red Cross (symbolic of road accidents).

B912 SP409 4fr + 2fr multi 38 438
B913 SP409 10fr + 5fr multi 85 85

The Red Cross as blood collector and aid to accident victims.

Armand Jamar, Self-portrait SP410

Van Gogh, Self-portrait and House at Cuesmes SP411

Designs: 5fr+2.50fr, Anton Bergmann and view of Lierre. 7fr+3.50fr, Henri Vieuxtemps and view of Verviers. 10fr+5fr, James Ensor, self-portrait, and masks.

1974, Apr. 6 Photo. *Perf. 11½*

Size: 24x35mm.

B914 SP410 4fr + 2fr multi 30 30
B915 SP410 5fr + 2.50fr multi 40 40
B916 SP410 7fr + 3.50fr multi 50 50

Size: 35x52mm.

B917 SP410 10fr + 5fr multi 85 85

1974, Sept. 21 Photo. *Perf. 11½*

B918 SP411 10fr + 5fr multi 75 75

Opening of Vincent van Gogh House at Cuesmes, where he worked as teacher.

Gentian — SP412

Badger SP413

Spotted Cat's Ear — SP414

Design: 7fr+3.50fr, Beetle.

1974, Dec. 8 Photo. *Perf. 11½*

B919 SP412 4fr + 2fr multi 40 40
B920 SP413 5fr + 2.50fr multi 45 45
B921 SP413 7fr + 3.50fr multi 60 60
B922 SP414 10fr +5fr multi 90 90

Foreign postal stationery (stamped envelopes, postal cards and air letter sheets) lies beyond the scope of this Catalogue, which is limited to adhesive postage stamps.

Pesaro Palace, Venice SP415

St. Bavon Abbey, Ghent SP416

Virgin and Child, by Michelangelo SP417

1975, Apr. 12 Engr. *Perf. 11½*

B923	SP415	650fr + 2.50fr brn	45	45
B924	SP416	10fr + 4.50 vio brn	80	80
B925	SP417	15fr + 6.50fr brt bl	1.10	1.10

Surtax was for various cultural organizations.

Frans Hemerijckx and Leprosarium, Kasai SP418

1975, Sept. 13 Photo. *Perf. 11½*

B926	SP418	20fr + 10fr multi	1.50	1.50

Dr. Frans Hemerijckx (1902-1969), tropical medicine and leprosy expert.

Emile Moyson — SP419

Hand Reading Braille SP420

Beheading of St. Dympna — SP420a

Design: 6.50fr+3fr, Dr. Ferdinand Augustin Snellaert.

1975, Nov. 22 Engr. *Perf. 11½*

B927	SP419	4.50fr + 2fr lil	35	35
B928	SP419	6.50fr + 3fr grn	50	50

Engraved and Photogravure

B929	SP420	10fr + 5fr multi	70	70

Photo.

B930	SP420a	13fr + 6fr multi	1.00	1.00

Emile Moyson (1838-1868), freedom fighter for the rights of Flemings and Walloons; Dr. Snellaert (1809-1872), physician and Flemish patriot; Louis Braille (1809-1852), sesquicentennial of invention of Braille system of writing for the blind; St. Dympna, patron saint of Geel, famous for treatment of mentally ill.

The Cheese Vendor — SP421

Designs (THEMABELGA Emblem and): No. B932, Potato vendor. No. B933, Basket carrier. No. B934, Shrimp fisherman with horse (horiz.). No. B935, Knife grinder (horiz.). No. B936, Milk vendor with dog cart (horiz.).

Engraved and Photogravure

1975, Dec. 13 *Perf. 11½*

B931	SP421	4.50fr + 1.50fr multi	25	25
B932	SP421	6.50fr + 3fr multi	50	50
B933	SP421	6.50fr + 3fr multi	50	50
B934	SP421	10fr + 5fr multi	75	75
B935	SP421	10fr + 5fr multi	75	75
B936	SP421	30fr + 15fr multi	2.25	2.25
		Nos. B931-B936 (6)	5.00	5.00

THEMABELGA International Topical Philatelic Exhibition, Brussels, Dec. 13-21. Issued in sheets of 10 (5x2).

Blackface Fund Collector — SP422

1976, Feb. 14 Photo. *Perf. 11½*

B937	SP422	10fr + 5fr multi	75	75

Centenary of the "Conservatoire Africain" philanthropic society, and to publicize the Princess Paola creches.

Swimming and Olympic Emblem SP423

Designs (Montreal Olympic Games Emblem and): 5fr+2fr, Running (vert.). 6.50fr+2.50fr, Equestrian.

1976, Apr. 10 Photo. *Perf. 11½*

B938	SP423	4.50fr + 1.50fr multi	25	25
B939	SP423	5fr + 2fr multi	35	35
B940	SP423	6.50fr + 2.50fr multi	60	60

21st Olympic Games, Montreal, Canada, July 17-Aug. 1.

Queen Elisabeth Playing Violin SP424

Perf. 11½

1976, May 1 Engr. Photo.

B941	SP424	14fr + 6fr blk & cl	1.10	1.10

Queen Elisabeth International Music Competition, 25th anniversary.

Souvenir Sheet

Jan Olieslagers, Bleriot Monoplane, Aero Club Emblem — SP425

Engraved and Photogravure

1976, June 12 *Perf. 11½*

B942	SP425	25fr + 10fr multi	3.00	3.00

Royal Belgian Aero Club, 75th anniversary, and Jan Olieslagers (1883-1942), aviation pioneer. No. B942 has blue marginal decorations and black inscription. Size: 83x116mm.

Adoration of the Shepherds (detail), by Rubens SP426

Dwarf, by Velazquez SP427

Rubens Paintings (Details): 4.50fr, Descent from the Cross. No. B945, The Virgin with the Parrot. No. B946, Adoration of the Kings. No. B947, Last Communion of St. Francis. 30fr+15fr, Virgin and Child.

1976, Sept. 4 Photo. *Perf. 11½*

Size: 30x52mm.

B943	SP426	4.50fr + 1.50fr multi	35	35

Size: 24x35mm.

B944	SP426	6.50fr + 3fr multi	55	55
B945	SP426	6.50fr + 3fr multi	55	55
B946	SP426	10fr + 5fr multi	80	80
B947	SP426	10fr + 5fr multi	80	80

Size: 30x52mm.

B948	SP426	30fr + 15fr multi	1.65	1.65
		Nos. B943-B948 (6)	4.70	4.70

Peter Paul Rubens (1577-1640), Flemish painter, 400th birth anniversary.

1976, Nov. 6 Photo. *Perf. 11½*

B949	SP427	14fr + 6fr multi	1.25	1.25

Surtax was for the National Association for the Mentally Handicapped.

Dr. Albert Hustin SP428

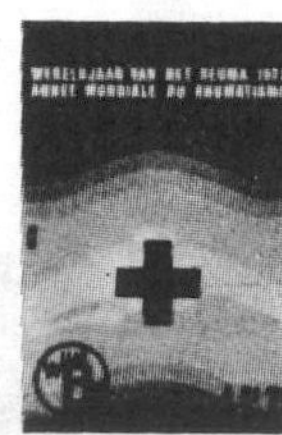
Red Cross and Rheumatism Year Emblem SP429

1977, Feb. 19 Photo. *Perf. 11½*

B950	SP428	6.50fr + 2.50 multi	50	50
B951	SP428	14fr + 7fr multi	1.00	1.00

Belgian Red Cross.

Bordet Atheneum, Empress Maria Theresa SP430

Conductor and Orchestra, by E. Tytgat SP431

Lucien Van Obbergh, Stage SP432

Humanistic Society Emblem SP433

Camille Lemonnier SP434

Design: No. B953, Marie-Therese College, Herve, and coat of arms.

1977, Mar. 21 Photo. *Perf. 11½*

B952	SP430	4.50fr + 1fr multi	35	35
B953	SP430	4.50fr + 1fr multi	35	35
B954	SP431	5fr + 2fr multi	40	40
B955	SP432	6.50fr + 2fr multi	55	55
B956	SP433	6.50fr + 2fr blk & red	55	55

Engr.

B957	SP434	10fr + 5fr sl bl	80	80
		Nos. B952-B957 (6)	3.00	3.00

Bicentenaries of the Jules Bordet Atheneum, Brussels, and the Marie-Therese College, Herve (Nos. B952-B953); 50th anniversaries of the Brussels Philharmonic Society, and Artists' Union (Nos. B954-B955); 25th anniversary of the Flemish Humanistic Organization (No. B956); 75th anniversary of the French-speaking Belgian writers' organization (No. B957).

Young Soccer Players — SP435

1977, Apr. 18 Photo.

B958	SP435	10fr + 5fr multi	75	75

30th International Junior Soccer Tournament.

Albert-Edouard Janssen, Financier — SP436

Famous Men: No. B960, Joseph Wauters (1875-1929), editor of Le Peuple, and newspaper. No. B961, Jean Capart (1877-1947), Egyptologist, and hieroglyph. No. B962, August de Boeck (1865-1937), composer, and score.

1977, Dec. 3 Engr. *Perf. 11½*

B959	SP436	5fr + 2.50fr brn	30	30
B960	SP436	5fr + 2.50fr red	30	30
B961	SP436	10fr + 5fr mag	60	60
B962	SP436	10fr + 5fr bl gray	60	60

Abandoned Child SP437

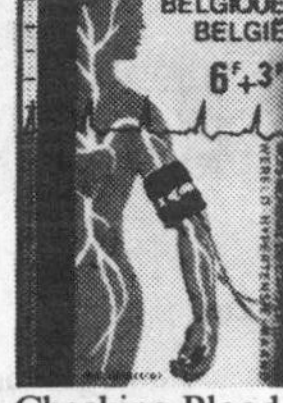
Checking Blood Pressure SP438

De Mick Sanatorium, Brasschaat — SP439

1978, Feb. 18 Photo. *Perf. 11½*

B963	SP437	4.50fr + 1.50fr multi	25	25
B964	SP438	6fr + 3fr multi	50	50
B965	SP439	10fr + 5fr multi	75	75

Help for abandoned children (No. B963); fight against hypertension (No. B964); fight against tuberculosis (No. B965).

Actors and Theater SP440

Karel van de Woestijne SP441

Designs: No. B967, Harquebusier, Harquebusier Palace and coat of arms. 10fr+5fr, John of Austria and his signature.

Engraved and Photogravure

1978, June 17 *Perf. 11½*

B966	SP440	6fr + 3fr multi	50	50
B967	SP440	6fr + 3fr multi	50	50

Engr.

B968	SP441	8fr + 4fr blk	60	60
B969	SP441	10fr + 5fr blk	75	75

Centenary of Royal Flemish Theater, Brussels (No. B966); 400th anniversary of Harquebusiers' Guild of Vise, Liege (No. B967); Karel van de Woestijne (1878-1929), poet (No. B968); 400th anniversary of signing of Perpetual Edict by John of Austria (No. B969).

The lack of a price for a listed item does not necessarily indicate rarity.

Lake Placid '80 and Belgian Olympic Emblems — SP442

Designs (Moscow '80 Emblem and): 8fr+3.50fr, Kremlin Towers and Belgian Olympic Committee emblem. 7fr+3fr, Runners from Greek vase, Lake Placid '80 emblem and Olympic rings. 14fr+6fr, Olympic flame, Lake Placid '80 and Belgian emblems, Olympic rings.

1978, Nov. 4 Photo. *Perf. 11½*

B970	SP442	6fr + 2.50fr multi	45	45
B971	SP442	8fr + 3.50fr multi	65	65

Souvenir Sheet

B972	Sheet of 2	2.00	2.00
a.	SP442 7fr + 3fr multi	80	80
b.	SP442 14fr + 6fr multi	1.25	1.25

Surtax was for 1980 Olympic Games. No. B972 has marginal inscription, Olympic Flame and Rings in blue and brown. Size: 150x100mm.

Great Synagogue, Brussels — SP443

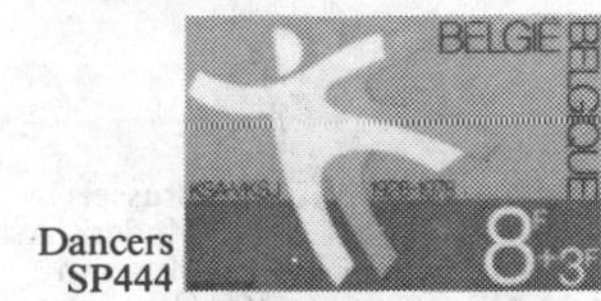
Dancers SP444

Father Pire, African Village SP445

1978, Dec. 2 Engr. *Perf. 11½*

B973	SP443	6fr + 2fr sep	75	75

Photo.

B974	SP444	8fr + 3fr multi	60	60
B975	SP445	14fr + 7fr multi	1.10	1.10

Centenary of Great Synagogue of Brussels; Flemish Catholic Youth Action Organization, 50th anniversary; Nobel Peace Prize awarded to Father Dominique Pire for his "Heart Open to the World" movement, 20th anniversary.

Young People Giving First Aid — SP446

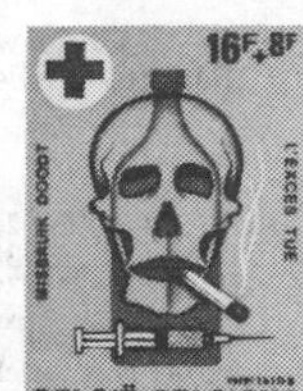
Skull with Bottle, Cigarette, Syringe — SP447

1979, Feb. 10 Photo. *Perf. 11½*

B976	SP446	8fr + 3fr multi	60	60
B977	SP447	16fr + 8fr multi	1.40	1.40

Belgian Red Cross.

Beatrice Soetkens with Statue of Virgin Mary — SP448

Details from Tapestries, 1516-1518, Showing Legend of Our Lady of Sand: 8fr+3fr, Francois de Tassis accepting letter from Emperor Frederick III (beginning of postal service). 14fr+7fr, Arrival of statue, Francois de Tassis and Philip the Fair. No. B981, Statue carried in procession by future Emperor Charles V and his brother Ferdinand. No. B982, Ship carrying Beatrice Soetkens with statue to Brussels (horiz.).

1979, May 5 Photo. *Perf. 11½*

B978	SP448	6fr + 2fr multi	40	40
B979	SP448	8fr + 3fr multi	60	60
B980	SP448	14fr + 7fr multi	1.00	1.00
B981	SP448	20fr + 10fr multi	1.65	1.65

Souvenir Sheet

B982	SP448	20fr + 10fr multi	1.40	1.40

The surtax was for festivities in connection with the millennium of Brussels. No. B982 has multicolored margin showing entire tapestry with burghers receiving letter from kneeling messenger. Size: 100x150mm.

Notre Dame Abbey, Brussels SP449

Designs: 8fr+3fr, Beauvoorde Castle. 14fr+7fr, First issue of "Courrier de L'Escaut" and Barthelemy Dumortier, founder. 20fr+10fr, Shrine of St. Hermes, Renaix.

Engraved and Photogravure

1979, Sept. 15 *Perf. 11½*

B983	SP449	6fr + 2fr multi	50	50
B984	SP449	8fr + 3fr multi	60	60
B985	SP449	14fr + 7fr multi	90	90
B986	SP449	20fr + 10fr multi	1.65	1.65

50th anniversary of restoration of Notre Dame de la Cambre Abbey; historic Beauvoorde Castle, 15th century; sesquicentennial of the regional newspaper "Le Courrier de L'Escaut;" 850th anniversary of the consecration of the Collegiate Church of St. Hermes, Renaix.

Grand-Hornu Coal Mine — SP450

1979, Oct. 22 Engr. *Perf. 11½*

B987	SP450	10fr + 5fr blk	70	70

Henry Heyman SP451

Veterans Organization Medal SP452

Boy and IYC Emblem SP453

1979, Dec. 8 Photo. *Perf. 11½*

B988	SP451	8fr + 3fr multi	60	60
B989	SP452	10fr + 5fr multi	80	80
B990	SP453	16fr + 8fr multi	1.10	1.10

Henri Heyman (1879-1958), Minister of State; Disabled Veterans' Organization, 50th anniversary; International Year of the Child.

Ivo Van Damme, Olympic Rings — SP454

1980, May 3 Photo. *Perf. 11½*

B991	SP454	20fr + 10fr multi	1.40	1.40

Ivo Van Damme (1954-1976), silver medalist, 800-meter race, Montreal Olympics, 1976. Surtax was for Van Damme Memorial Foundation.

Queen Louis, King Leopold I — SP455

150th Anniversary of Independence (Queens and Kings): 9fr+3fr, Marie Henriette. Leopold II. 14fr+6fr, Elisabeth, Albert I. 17fr+8fr, Astrid, Leopold III. 25fr+10fr, Fabiola, Baudouin.

Photogravure and Engraved

1980, May 31 *Perf. 11½*

B992	SP455	6.50 + 1.50fr multi	40	40
B993	SP455	9 + 3fr multi	60	60
B994	SP455	14 + 6fr multi	1.00	1.00
B995	SP455	17 + 8fr multi	1.40	1.40
B996	SP455	25 + 10fr multi	1.75	1.75
		Nos. B992-B996 (5)	5.15	5.15

Miner, by Constantine Meunier SP456

Seal of Bishop Notger, First Prince-Bishop — SP457

Designs: 9fr+3fr, Brewer, 16th century, from St. Lambert's reliquary (vert.). 25fr+10fr, Virgin and Child, 13th century, St. John's Collegiate Church, Liege.

1980, Sept. 13 Photo. *Perf. 11½*

B997	SP456	9 + 3fr multi	55	55
B998	SP456	17 + 6fr multi	1.10	1.10
B999	SP456	25 + 10fr multi	1.75	1.75

Souvenir Sheet

B1000 SP457 20 + 10fr multi 2.00 2.00

Millennium of the Principality of Liege. No. B1000 has gray and brown margin showing baptism of Centurion Cornelius from baptismal font in St. Bartholomew's Church, Liege. Size: 150x100mm.

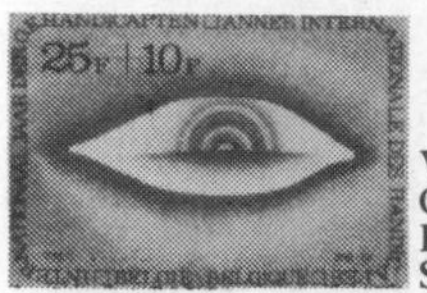

Visual and Oral Handicaps SP458

International Year of the Disabled: 10fr+5fr, Cerebral handicap (vert.).

1981, Feb. 9 Photo. *Perf. 11 1/2*

B1001 SP458 10 + 5fr multi 70 70
B1002 SP458 25 + 10fr multi 1.65 1.65

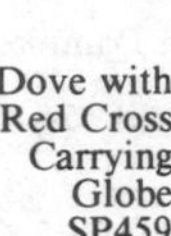

Dove with Red Cross Carrying Globe SP459

Design: 10fr+5fr, Atomic model (vert.).

1981, Apr. 6 Photo. *Perf. 11 1/2*

B1003 SP459 10 + 5fr multi 70 70
B1004 SP459 25 + 10fr multi 1.65 1.65

Red Cross and: 15th International Radiology Congress, Brussels, June 24-July 1 (No. B1003); international disaster relief (No. B1004).

Ovide Decroly SP460

1981, June 1 Photo. *Perf. 11 1/2*

B1005 SP460 35 + 15fr multi 2.25 2.25

Ovide Decroly (1871-1932), developer of educational psychology.

Mounted Police Officer — SP461

Anniversaries: 9fr+4fr, Gendarmerie (State Police Force), 150th. 20fr+7fr, Carabineers Regiment, 150th. 40fr+20fr, Guides Regiment.

1981, Dec. 7 Photo. *Perf. 11 1/2*

B1006 SP461 9 + 4fr multi 60 60
B1007 SP461 20 + 7fr multi 1.25 1.25
B1008 SP461 40 + 20fr multi 2.75 2.75

Billiards — SP462

1982, Mar. 29 Photo. *Perf. 11 1/2*

B1009 SP462 6 + 2fr shown 35 35
B1010 SP462 9 + 4fr Cycling 55 55
B1011 SP462 10 + 5fr Soccer 65 65
B1012 SP462 50 + 14fr Yachting 2.65 2.65

Souvenir Sheet

B1013	Sheet of 4		4.25	4.25
a.	SP462 25fr like #B1009		1.20	1.20
b.	SP462 25fr like #B1010		1.20	1.20
c.	SP462 25fr like #B1011		1.20	1.20
d.	SP462 25fr like #B1012		1.20	1.20

No. B1013 shows designs in changed colors. Size: 105x100mm.

Christmas SP463

1982, Nov. 6

B1014 SP463 10 + 1fr multi 60 45

Surtax was for tuberculosis research.

Belgica '82 Intl. Stamp Exhibition, Brussels, Dec. 11-19 SP464

Messengers (Prints). Nos. B1016-B1018 vert.

Photogravure and Engraved

1982, Dec. 11 *Perf. 11 1/2*

B1015 SP464 7 + 2fr multi 35 35
B1016 SP464 7.50 + 2.50fr multi 40 40
B1017 SP464 10 + 3fr multi 50 50
B1018 SP464 17 + 7fr multi 95 95
B1019 SP464 20 + 9fr multi 1.10 1.10
B1020 SP464 25 + 10fr multi 1.40 1.40
Nos. B1015-B1020 (6) 4.70 4.70

Souvenir Sheet

B1021 SP464 50 + 25fr multi 3.00 3.00

No. B1021 contains one stamp (48x37mm.); multicolored margin continues design. Size: 125x90mm.

50th Anniv. of Catholic Charities — SP465

1983, Jan. 22 Photo. *Perf. 11 1/2*

B1022 SP465 10 + 2fr multi 50 50

Mountain Climbing — SP466

1983, Mar. 7 Photo.

B1023 SP466 12 + 3fr shown 60 60
B1024 SP466 20 + 5fr Hiking 1.00 1.00

Surtax was for Red Cross.

Madonna by Jef Wauters — SP467

1983, Nov. 21 Photo. *Perf. 11 1/2*

B1025 SP467 11 + 1fr multi 45 45

Rifles Uniform — SP468

1983, Dec. 5 Photo. *Perf. 11 1/2*

B1026 SP468 8 + 2fr shown 38 38
B1027 SP468 11 + 2fr Lancers uniform 50 50
B1028 SP468 50 + 12fr Grenadiers uniform 2.25 2.25

Type of 1984

1984, Mar. 3 Photo. *Perf. 11 1/2*

B1029 A495 8 + 2fr Judo, horiz. 40 40
B1030 A495 12 + 3fr Wind surfing 60 60

50th Anniv. of Natl. Lottery SP469

1984, Mar. 31 Photo. *Perf. 11 1/2*

B1031 SP469 12 + 3fr multi 60 60

Brussels Modern Art Museum Opening SP470

Paintings: 8fr+2fr, Les Masques Singuliers, by James Ensor. 12fr+3fr, Empire des Lumieres, by Rene Magritte. 22fr+5fr, The End, by Jan Cox. 50fr+13fr, Rhythm No. 6, by Jo Delahaut.

1984, Sept. 1 Photo.

B1032 SP470 8 + 2fr multi 40 40
B1033 SP470 12 + 3fr multi 60 60
B1034 SP470 22 + 5fr multi 1.10 1.10
B1035 SP470 50 + 13fr multi 2.50 2.50

Child with Parents — SP471

1984, Nov. 3 Photo.

B1036 SP471 10 +2fr shown 48 48
B1037 SP471 12 +3fr Siblings 60 60
B1038 SP471 15 +3fr Merry-go-round 72 72

Surtax was for children's programs.

Christmas 1984 SP472

1984, Dec. 1

B1039 SP472 12 + 1fr Three Kings 52 52

Belgian Red Cross Blood Transfusion Service, 50th Anniv. — SP473

1985, Mar. 4 Photo. *Perf. 11 1/2*

B1040 SP473 9 + 2fr Tree 38 38
B1041 SP473 23 + 5fr Hearts 90 90

Surtax was for the Belgian Red Cross.

Solidarity SP474

Castles.

Photogravure and Engraved

1985, Nov. 4

B1042 SP474 9 + 2fr Trazegnies 42 42
B1043 SP474 12 + 3fr Laarne 58 58
B1044 SP474 23 + 5fr Turnhout 1.00 1.00
B1045 SP474 50 + 12fr Colonster 2.50 2.50

Christmas 1985, New Year 1986 — SP475

Painting: Miniature from the Book of Hours, by Jean duc de Berry.

1985, Nov. 25 Photo.

B1046 SP475 12 + 1fr multi 50 50

King Baudouin Foundation SP476

1986, Mar. 24 Photo.

B1047 SP476 12 + 3fr Emblem 65 65

Surtax for the foundation.

Madonna SP477

Paintings by Hubert van Eyck (c. 1370-1426).

1986, Apr. 7 Photo. *Perf. 11 1/2*

B1048 SP477 9 + 2fr shown 48 48
B1049 SP477 13 + 3fr Christ in Majesty 68 68
B1050 SP477 24 + 6fr St. John the Baptist 1.25 1.25

Souvenir Sheet

Adoration of the Mystic Lamb, St. Bavon Cathedral Altarpiece, Ghent SP478

B1051 SP478 50 + 12fr shown 2.75 2.75

Surtax for cultural organizations. No. B1051 has multicolored margin continuing design. Size: 93x150mm.

Antique Automobiles SP479

1986, Nov. 3 Photo.

B1052 SP479 9 + 2fr Lenoir, 1863 55 55
B1053 SP479 13 + 3fr Pipe de Tourisme, 1911 80 80
B1054 SP479 24 + 6fr Minerva 22 HP, 1930 1.50 1.50
B1055 SP479 26 + 6fr FN 8 Cylinder, 1931 1.60 1.60

Christmas 1986, New Year 1987 SP480

1986, Nov. 24 Photo.

B1056 SP480 13 + 1fr Village in winter 68 68

Natl. Red Cross – SP482

European Conservation Year – SP483

Nobel Prize winners for physiology (1938) and medicine (1974): No. B1058, Corneille Heymans (1892-1968). No. B1059, A. Claude (1899-1983).

Photogravure and Engraved

1987, Feb. 16 *Perf. 11 1/2*

B1058 SP482 13 + 3fr 88 88
B1059 SP482 24 + 6fr 1.65 1.65

1987, Mar. 16 Photo.

B1060 SP483 9 + 2fr Bee orchid 60 60
B1061 SP483 24 + 6fr Horseshoe bat 1.65 1.65
B1062 SP483 26 + 6fr Peregrine falcon 1.75 1.75

Castles – SP484

Photo. & Engr.

1987, Oct. 17 *Perf. 11 1/2*

B1063 SP484 9 +2fr Rixensart 60 60
B1064 SP484 13 +3fr Westerlo 90 90
B1065 SP484 26 +5fr Fallais 1.75 1.75
B1066 SP484 50 12fr Gaasbeek 3.50 3.50

Christmas 1987 – SP485

White and Yellow Cross of Belgium, 50th Anniv. – SP486

Painting: Holy Family, by Rev. Father Lens.

1987, Nov. 14 Photo.

B1067 SP485 13 +1fr multi 85 85

1987, Dec. 5

B1068 SP486 9 +2fr multi 68 68

AIR POST STAMPS

Fokker FVII/3m over Ostend AP1

Designs: 1.50fr, Plane over St. Hubert. 2fr, over Namur. 5fr, over Brussels.

Perf. 11 1/2

1930, Apr. 30 Unwmk. Photo.

C1 AP1 50c blue 50 45
C2 AP1 1.50fr blk brn 2.75 3.00
C3 AP1 2fr dp grn 2.50 65
C4 AP1 5fr brn lake 2.25 1.10

1930, Dec. 5

C5 AP1 5fr dk vio 37.50 37.50

Issued for use on a mail carrying flight from Brussels to Leopoldville, Belgian Congo, starting Dec. 7.

Nos. C1-C5 exist imperforate.

Nos. C2 and C4 Surcharged in Carmine or Blue

1Fr 1Fr

X X

1935, May 23

C6 AP1 1fr on 1.50fr blk brn (C) 60 60
C7 AP1 4fr on 5fr brn lake (Bl) 8.50 5.25

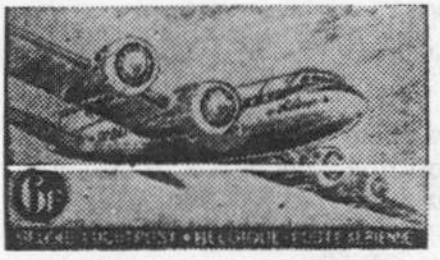
DC-4 Skymaster, Sabena Airline AP5

1946-54 Engr. *Perf. 11 1/2*

C8 AP5 6fr blue 50 32
C9 AP5 8.50fr vio brn 65 45
C10 AP5 50fr yel grn 3.25 75
a. Perf. 12x11 1/2 ('54) 160.00 1.10
C11 AP5 100fr gray 5.25 1.00
a. Perf. 12x11 1/2 ('54) 90.00 1.50

The French and Flemish inscriptions are transposed on Nos. C9 and C11.

Evolution of Postal Transportation – AP6

1949, July 1

C12 AP6 50fr dk brn 17.50 20.00

Centenary of Belgian postage stamps.

Glider AP7

Design: 7fr, "Tipsy" plane.

1951, June 18 Photo. *Perf. 13 1/2*

C12A AP7 Strip of 2 + label 55.00 60.00
b. 6fr dk bl 20.00 25.00
c. 7fr car rose 20.00 25.00

For the 50th anniversary of the Aero Club of Belgium. The label is inscribed "1901-1951 + 37FR. BELGIE BELGIQUE" and carries the club emblem. The strip sold for 50fr.

1951, July 25 *Perf. 13 1/2*

C13 AP7 6fr sepia 2.50 15
C14 AP7 7fr Prus grn 2.00 95

United Nations Issue

Types of Regular Issue, 1958

Designs: 5fr, International Civil Aviation Organization. 6fr, World Meteorological Organization. 7.50fr, Protection of Refugees. 8fr, General Agreement on Tariffs and Trade. 9fr, UNICEF. 10fr, Atomic Energy Agency.

Perf. 11 1/2

1958, Apr. 17 Unwmk. Engr.

C15 A137 5fr dl bl 32 55
C16 A136 6fr yel grn 55 1.00
C17 A137 7.50fr lilac 32 55
C18 A136 8fr sepia 32 55
C19 A137 9fr carmine 75 1.40
C20 A136 10fr redsh brn 1.00 1.65
Nos. C15-C20 (6) 3.26 5.70

World's Fair, Brussels, Apr. 17-Oct. 19. See note after No. 476.

AIR POST SEMI-POSTAL STAMPS

American Soldier in Combat – SPAP1

Perf. 11x11 1/2

1946, June 15 Unwmk. Engr.

CB1 SPAP1 17.50fr + 62.50fr dl brn 1.10 1.75
CB2 SPAP1 17.50fr + 62.50fr dl gray grn 1.10 1.75

The French and Flemish inscriptions are transposed on No. CB2. The surtax was to erect an American memorial at Bastogne.

An overprint, "Hommage a Roosevelt", was privately applied to Nos. CB1 and CB2 in 1947 by the Association Belgo-Americaine.

In 1950 another private overprint was applied, in red, to Nos. CB1-2. It consists of "16-12-1944, 25-1-1945, Dedication July 16, 1950" and outlines of the American eagle emblem and the Bastogne Memorial. Similar overprints were applied to Nos. 265 and 345.

Flight Allegory SPAP2

1946, Sept. 7 *Perf. 11 1/2*

CB3 SPAP2 2fr + 8fr brt vio 60 1.00

The surtax was for the benefit of aviation.

Nos. B417-B425 Surcharged in Various Arrangements in Red or Dark Blue

POSTE AERIENNE
LUCHTPOST
1F +2F

LUCHTPOST
POSTE AERIENNE
1F +2F

Type I. Top line "POSTE AERIENNE."
Type II. Top line "LUCHTPOST."

1947, May 18 Photo. *Perf. 11 1/2*

CB4 SP227 1fr + 2fr on 65c + 75c dk bl (R) 1.00 1.40
a. Type II 1.00 1.40
CB5 SP228 1.50fr + 2.50 on 1.35 + 2 brn (Bl) 1.00 1.40
a. Type II 1.00 1.40
CB6 SP229 2fr + 45fr on 1.75fr + 18fr rose brn (Bl) 1.00 1.40
a. Type II 1.00 1.40
CB7 SP230 1fr + 2fr on 65c + 75c vio (R) 1.00 1.40
a. Type II 1.00 1.40
CB8 SP231 1.50fr + 2.50fr on 1.35fr + 2fr dk org brn (Bl) 1.00 1.40
a. Type II 1.00 1.40
CB9 SP232 2fr + 45fr on 1.75fr + 18fr car rose (Bl) 1.00 1.40
a. Type II 1.00 1.40
CB10 SP233 1fr + 2fr on 65c + 75c dk sl grn (R) 1.00 1.40
a. Type II 1.00 1.40
CB11 SP234 1.50fr + 2.50fr on 1.35fr + 2fr dk vio bl (R) 1.00 1.40
a. Type II 1.00 1.40
CB12 SP235 2fr + 45fr on 1.75fr + 18fr dp car (Bl) 1.00 1.40
a. Type II 1.00 1.40
Nos. CB4-CB12,CB4a-CB12a (18) 18.00 25.20

In 1948 Nos. CB4-CB12 and CB4a-CB12a were punched with the letters "IMABA," and the inscription "Imaba du 21 au 29 aout 1948" was applied to the backs. Price $20.

Helicopter Leaving Airport
SPAP3

1950, Aug. 7
CB13 SPAP3 7fr + 3fr bl 6.75 9.50

The surtax was for the National Aeronautical Committee.

SPECIAL DELIVERY STAMPS

From 1874 to 1903 certain hexagonal telegraph stamps were used as special delivery stamps.

Town Hall, Brussels — SD1

Eupen — SD2

Designs: 2.35fr, Street in Ghent. 3.50fr, Bishop's Palace, Liege. 5.25fr, Notre Dame Cathedral, Antwerp.

1929 Unwmk. Photo. *Perf. 11½.*
E1 SD1 1.75fr dk bl 80 32
E2 SD1 2.35fr carmine 1.50 45
E3 SD1 3.50fr dk vio 4.00 6.50
E4 SD1 5.25fr ol grn 4.00 4.75

1931
E5 SD2 2.45fr dk grn 11.00 1.75
Nos. E1-E5 (5) 21.30 13.77

No. E5 Surcharged in Red

1932
E6 SD2 2.50fr on 2.45fr dk grn 13.00 1.65

POSTAGE DUE STAMPS

D1

D2

1870 Unwmk. Typo. *Perf. 15.*
J1 D1 10c green 5.50 2.25
a. Half used as 5c on piece 6.75
J2 D1 20c ultra 25.00 3.50

1895-09 *Perf. 14.*
J3 D2 5c yel grn 22 22
J4 D2 10c org brn 6.75 1.75
J5 D2 10c car ('00) 22 22
J6 D2 20c ol grn 22 22
J7 D2 30c pale bl ('09) 45 35
J8 D2 50c yel brn 15.00 5.50
J9 D2 50c gray ('00) 90 65
J10 D2 1fr carmine 32.50 17.50
J11 D2 1fr ocher ('00) 11.00 7.25
Nos. J3-J11 (9) 67.26 33.66

1916 Redrawn
J12 D2 5c bl grn 9.00 4.50
J13 D2 10c carmine 9.00 3.50
J14 D2 20c dp gray grn 22.50 11.50
J15 D2 30c brt bl 3.50 2.75
J16 D2 50c gray 45.00 37.50
Nos. J12-J16 (5) 89.00 59.75

In the redrawn stamps the lions have a heavy, colored outline. There is a thick vertical line at the outer edge of the design on each side.

D3

D4

1919 *Perf. 14*
J17 D3 5c green 55 40
J18 D3 10c carmine 1.25 35
J19 D3 20c gray grn 10.00 1.00
J20 D3 30c brt bl 2.00 30
J21 D3 50c gray 4.00 40
Nos. J17-J21 (5) 17.80 2.45

1922-32
J22 D4 5c dk gray 12 12
J23 D4 10c green 15 12
J24 D4 20c dp brn 18 15
J25 D4 30c ver ('24) 32 15
a. 30c rose red 1.10 65
J26 D4 40c red brn ('25) 32 18
J27 D4 50c ultra 2.75 18
J28 D4 70c red brn ('29) 40 18
J29 D4 1fr vio ('25) 65 18
J30 D4 1fr rose lil ('32) 55 18
J31 D4 1.20fr ol grn ('29) 95 65
J32 D4 1.50fr ol grn ('32) 95 65
J33 D4 2fr vio ('29) 1.10 28
J34 D4 3.50fr dp bl ('29) 1.40 32
Nos. J22-J34 (13) 9.84 3.34

1934-46 *Perf. 14x13½.*
J35 D4 35c grn ('35) 55 65
J36 D4 50c slate 32 18
J37 D4 60c car ('38) 55 40
J38 D4 80c sl ('38) 45 28
J39 D4 1.40fr gray ('35) 95 60
J39A D4 3fr org brn ('46) 1.65 90
J39B D4 7fr brt red vio ('46) 3.25 4.50
Nos. J35-J39B (7) 7.72 7.51

See also Nos. J54-J61.

D5

D6

1945 Typo. *Perf. 12½*
Inscribed "TE BETALEN" at Top.
J40 D5 10c gray ol 10 15
J41 D5 20c ultra 10 15
J42 D5 30c carmine 8 10
J43 D5 40c blk vio 8 10
J44 D5 50c dl bl grn 10 10
J45 D5 1fr sepia 15 10
J46 D5 2fr red org 18 15

Inscribed "A PAYER" at Top.
J47 D5 10c gray ol 10 15
J48 D5 20c ultra 10 15
J49 D5 30c carmine 8 10
J50 D5 40c blk vio 8 10
J51 D5 50c dl bl grn 10 10
J52 D5 1fr sepia 15 10
J53 D5 2fr red org 18 15
Nos. J40-J53 (14) 1.58 1.70

Type of 1922-32.

1949 Typo. *Perf. 14x13½.*
J54 D4 65c emerald 6.25 8.00
J55 D4 1.80fr red 11.00 11.00
J56 D4 5fr red brn 3.00 65
J57 D4 8fr lil rose 7.50 10.00
J58 D4 10fr dk vio 6.25 8.00
Nos. J54-J58 (5) 34.00 37.65

1953
J59 D4 1.60fr lil rose 7.50 11.00
J60 D4 2.40fr gray lil 6.50 3.00
J61 D4 4fr dp bl 7.50 1.75

1966-70 Photo.
J62 D6 1fr brt pink 8 5
J63 D6 2fr bl grn 10 10
J64 D6 3fr blue 15 13
J65 D6 5fr purple 28 25
J66 D6 6fr bis brn 32 32
J67 D6 7fr red org ('70) 45 38
J68 D6 20fr sl grn 1.75 1.40
Nos. J62-J68 (7) 3.13 2.63

Type of 1966
1985, Mar. 25 Photo. *Perf. 14½x14*
J69 D6 3fr greenish blue 15 12
J70 D6 4fr green 20 15
J71 D6 8fr pale gray 40 30
J72 D6 9fr rose lake 45 35
J73 D6 10fr lt red brn 50 38
Nos. J69-J73 (5) 1.70 1.30

Type of 1966

1987 Photo. *Perf. 14½x14*
J74 D6 1fr lil rose 5 5
J75 D6 5fr lt vio 25 18
J76 D6 7fr brt org 35 28

Printed on coated paper. No. J71 also exists reprinted on coated paper and issued with Nos. J74-J76.

MILITARY STAMPS

King Baudouin
M1 M2

Unwmk.
1967, July 17 Photo. *Perf. 11*
M1 M1 1.50fr grnsh gray 75 45

1971-75 Engr. *Perf. 11½*
M2 M2 1.75fr green 2.25 1.10
M3 M2 2.25fr gray grn ('72) 2.00 75
M4 M2 2.50fr gray grn ('74) 75 65
M5 M2 3.25fr vio brn ('75) 60 32

Nos. M1-M3 are luminescent, Nos. M4-M5 are not.

MILITARY PARCEL POST STAMP

Type of Parcel Post Stamp of 1938 Surcharged with New Value and "M" in Blue.

1939 Unwmk. *Perf. 13½*
MQ1 PP19 3fr on 5.50fr cop red 45 20

OFFICIAL STAMPS

For franking the official correspondence of the Administration of the Belgian National Railways.

Regular Issue of 1921-27 Overprinted in Black

1929-30 Unwmk. *Perf. 14.*
O1 A58 5c gray 22 30
O2 A58 10c bl grn 32 55
O3 A58 35c bl grn 45 45
O4 A58 60c ol grn 50 40
O5 A58 1.50fr brt bl 9.00 9.00
O6 A58 1.75fr ultra ('30) 2.00 3.00
Nos. O1-O6 (6) 12.49 13.70

Same Overprint, in Red or Black, on Regular Issues of 1929-30.

1929-31
O7 A63 5c sl (R) 22 40
O8 A63 10c ol grn (R) 45 50
O9 A63 25c rose red (Bk) 1.25 1.10
O10 A63 35c dp grn (R) 1.65 65
O11 A63 40c red vio (Bk) 1.10 55
O12 A63 50c dp bl (R) ('31) 70 40
O13 A63 60c rose (Bk) 6.00 7.50
O14 A63 70c org brn (Bk) 4.00 1.40
O15 A63 75c blk vio (R) ('31) 3.50 1.10
Nos. O7-O15 (9) 18.87 13.60

Overprinted on Regular Issue of 1932.

1932
O16 A73 10c ol grn (R) 75 90
O17 A74 35c dp grn 13.00 1.10
O18 A71a 75c bis brn (R) 2.25 40

Overprinted on No. 262 in Red.

1935 *Perf. 13½x14*
O19 A80 70c ol blk 2.75 40

Regular Stamps of 1935-36 Overprinted in Red.

1936-38 *Perf. 13½, 13½x14, 14.*
O20 A82 10c ol bis 18 35
O21 A82 35c green 28 40
O22 A82 50c dk bl 55 35
O23 A83 70c brown 1.75 75

Overprinted in Black or Red on Regular Issue of 1938.
Perf. 13½x14.
O24 A82 40c red vio (Bk) 35 35
O25 A85 75c ol gray (R) 80 30
Nos. O20-O25 (6) 3.91 2.50

Regular Issues of 1935-41 Overprinted in Red or Dark Blue

1941-44 *Perf. 14, 14x13½, 13½x14.*
O26 A82 10c ol bis 12 15
a. Inverted overprint 40.00
O27 A82 40c red vio 55 75
O28 A82 50c dk bl 12 15
a. Inverted overprint
O29 A83a 1fr rose car (Bl) 45 35
O30 A85 1fr rose pink (Bl) 10 12
O31 A83a 2.25fr grnsh blk ('44) 28 50
O32 A84 2.25fr gray vio 45 70
Nos. O26-O32 (7) 2.07 2.72

Nos. O21, O23 and O25 Surcharged with New Values in Black or Red.

1942
O33 A82 10c on 35c grn 18 32
O34 A83 50c on 70c brn 15 18
O35 A85 50c on 75c ol gray (R) 15 18

O1

O2

1946-48 Unwmk. *Perf. 14.*
O36 O1 10c ol bis 20 20
O37 O1 20c brt vio 1.75 75
O38 O1 50c dk bl 25 22
O39 O1 65c red lil ('48) 2.75 1.10
O40 O1 75c lil rose 20 30
O41 O1 90c brn vio 3.50 50
Nos. O36-O41 (6) 8.65 3.07

Types A99, A101 and A102 with "B" Emblem Added to Design

1948 *Perf. 11½.*
O42 A99 1.35fr red brn 2.50 1.10
O43 A99 1.75fr dk gray grn 3.00 38
O44 A101 3fr brt red vio 16.00 5.25
O45 A102 3.15fr dp bl 6.75 11.00
O46 A102 4fr brt ultra 12.50 21.00
Nos. O42-O46 (5) 40.75 38.73

1953-66 Typo. *Perf. 13½x14*
O47 O2 10c orange 65 85
O48 O2 20c red lil 75 60
O49 O2 30c gray grn ('58) 75 1.00
O50 O2 40c ol gray 50 40
O51 O2 50c lt bl 70 50
O51A O2 60c lil rose ('66) 1.10 90
O52 O2 65c red lil 27.50 42.50
O53 O2 80c emerald 1.50 85
O54 O2 90c dp bl 3.00 1.25
O55 O2 1fr rose 38 40
Nos. O47-O55 (10) 36.83 49.25

King Baudouin
O3 O4

1954-70 Photo. *Perf. 11½*
O56 O3 1.50fr gray 1.00 38
O57 O3 2fr rose red 37.50 75

O58 O3 2fr bl grn ('59) 75 30
O59 O3 2.50fr red brn ('58) 24.00 75
O60 O3 3fr red lil ('58) 2.00 60
O61 O3 3.50fr yel grn ('70) 1.10 60
O62 O3 4fr brt bl 2.25 1.00
O63 O3 6fr car rose ('58) 5.00 1.65
Nos. O56-O63 (8) 73.60 6.03

Type of 1953-66 Redrawn

1970-75 Typo. *Perf. 13½x14*
O66 O2 1.50fr grnsh gray ('75) 18 10
O68 O2 2.50fr brown 18 10

1971-73 Engr. *Perf. 11½*
O71 O4 3.50fr org brn ('73) 1.75 1.25
O72 O4 4.50fr brn ('73) 1.10 90
O73 O4 7fr red 45 40
O74 O4 15fr violet 90 90

Nos. O71-O74 are on luminescent paper.

1974-80
O75 O4 3fr yel grn 5.75 1.75
O76 O4 4fr blue 2.25 1.10
O77 O4 4.50fr grnsh bl ('75) 65 38
O78 O4 5fr lilac 30 30
O79 O4 6fr car ('78) 40 40
O80 O4 6.50fr blk ('76) 65 60
O81 O4 8fr bluish blk ('78) 50 45
O82 O4 9fr lt red brn ('80) 50 45
O83 O4 10fr rose car 55 50
O84 O4 25fr lil ('76) 1.40 1.40
O85 O4 30fr org brn ('78) 1.90 1.75
Nos. O75-O85 (11) 14.85 9.08

Heraldic Lion — O5

1977-82 Typo. *Perf. 13½x14*
O87 O5 50c brn ('82) 5 5
O92 O5 1fr lil ('82) 8 8
O94 O5 2fr org ('82) 12 8
O95 O5 4fr red brn 30 25
O96 O5 5fr grn ('80) 35 28
Nos. O87-O96 (5) 90 74

NEWSPAPER STAMPS

Parcel Post Stamps of 1923-27 Overprinted

JOURNAUX
DAGBLADEN
1928

Perf. 14½ x 14, 14 x 14½.
1928 Unwmk.
P1 PP12 10c vermilion 18 30
P2 PP12 20c turq bl 22 30
P3 PP12 40c ol grn 22 30
P4 PP12 60c orange 45 60
P5 PP12 70c dk brn 28 30
P6 PP12 80c violet 35 50
P7 PP12 90c slate 1.50 1.40
P8 PP13 1fr brt bl 55 40
a. 1fr ultra 8.00 3.75
P10 PP13 2fr ol grn 1.00 42
P11 PP13 3fr org red 1.10 60
P12 PP13 4fr rose 1.40 80
P13 PP13 5fr violet 1.40 75
P14 PP13 6fr bis brn 2.75 1.25
P15 PP13 7fr orange 3.25 1.65
P16 PP13 8fr dk brn 3.75 2.00
P17 PP13 9fr red vio 6.75 2.25
P18 PP13 10fr bl grn 5.75 2.00
P19 PP13 20fr magenta 10.00 5.00
Nos. P1-P8,P10-P19 (18) 40.90 20.82

Parcel Post Stamps of 1923-28 Overprinted

JOURNAUX
DAGBLADEN

1929-31
P20 PP12 10c vermilion 28 25
P21 PP12 20c turq bl 28 25
P22 PP12 40c ol grn 35 30
a. Inverted overprint
P23 PP12 60c orange 45 50
P24 PP12 70c dk brn 55 30
P25 PP12 80c violet 65 35
P26 PP12 90c gray 1.75 1.40
P27 PP13 1fr ultra 60 38
a. 1fr brt bl 3.00 70
P28 PP13 1.10fr org brn ('31) 9.00 2.00
P29 PP13 1.50fr gray vio ('31) 9.00 2.75
P30 PP13 2fr ol grn 1.75 38
P31 PP13 2.10fr sl gray ('31) 32.50 13.00
P32 PP13 3fr org red 2.00 60
P33 PP13 4fr rose 2.00 1.00
P34 PP13 5fr violet 3.00 80
P35 PP13 6fr bis brn 3.50 1.40
P36 PP13 7fr orange 3.75 1.40
P37 PP13 8fr dk brn 3.75 1.50
P38 PP13 9fr red vio 5.00 2.25
P39 PP13 10fr bl grn 3.75 1.50
P40 PP13 20fr magenta 12.50 6.50
Nos. P20-P40 (21) 96.41 38.81

PARCEL POST AND RAILWAY STAMPS

Prices for used stamps are for copies with railway cancellations. Stamps with postal cancellations sell for twice as much.

Coat of Arms — PP1

1879-82 Unwmk. Typo. *Perf. 14*
Q1 PP1 10c vio brn 42.50 2.75
Q2 PP1 20c blue 140.00 12.50
Q3 PP1 25c grn ('81) 175.00 7.00
Q4 PP1 50c carmine 1,200. 5.25
Q5 PP1 80c yellow 1,250. 37.50
Q6 PP1 1fr gray ('82) 125.00 9.50

Used copies of Nos. Q1-Q6 with pinholes, a normal state, sell for half price.

PP2

Most of the stamps of 1882-1902 (Nos. Q7 to Q28) are without watermark. Twice in each sheet of 100 stamps they have one of three watermarks: (1) A winged wheel and "Chemins de Fer de l'Etat Belge", (2) Coat of Arms of Belgium and "Royaume de Belgique", (3) Larger Coat of Arms, without inscription.

1882-94 *Perf. 15x14½*
Q7 PP2 10c brn ('86) 14.00 90
Q8 PP2 15c gray ('94) 12.00 9.00
Q9 PP2 20c bl ('86) 60.00 3.00
a. 20c ultra ('90) 55.00 3.00
Q10 PP2 25c yel grn ('91) 52.50 3.50
a. 25c bl grn ('87) 62.50 3.50
Q11 PP2 50c carmine 60.00 45
Q12 PP2 80c brnsh buff 52.50 65
Q13 PP2 80c lemon 65.00 2.75
Q14 PP2 1fr lavender 325.00 2.75
Q15 PP2 2fr yel buff ('94) 215.00 47.50

Counterfeits exist.

PP3

Name of engraver below frame.

1895-97
Numerals in Black, except 1fr, 2fr.
Q16 PP3 10c red brn ('96) 10.00 40
Q17 PP3 15c gray 9.50 7.25
Q18 PP3 20c blue 20.00 90
Q19 PP3 25c green 20.00 1.25
Q20 PP3 50c carmine 22.50 40
Q21 PP3 60c vio ('96) 37.50 55
Q22 PP3 80c ol yel ('96) 32.50 55
Q23 PP3 1fr lil brn 140.00 90
Q24 PP3 2fr yel buff ('97) 150.00 4.50

Counterfeits exist.

1902
Numerals in Black.
Q25 PP3 30c orange 22.50 1.40
Q26 PP3 40c green 25.00 1.40
Q27 PP3 70c blue 40.00 70
a. Numerals omitted 1,000.
Q28 PP3 90c red 47.50 90

Winged Wheel — PP4

Without engraver's name.

1902-14 *Perf. 15*
Q29 PP3 10c yel brn & sl 18 12
Q30 PP3 15c sl & vio 28 15
Q31 PP3 20c ultra & yel brn 18 12
Q32 PP3 25c yel grn & red 28 15
Q33 PP3 30c org & bl grn 28 15
Q34 PP3 35c bis & bl grn ('12) 50 30
Q35 PP3 40c bl grn & vio 28 15
Q36 PP3 50c pale rose & vio 18 12
Q37 PP3 55c lil brn & ultra ('14) 50 30
Q38 PP3 60c vio & red 28 15
Q39 PP3 70c bl & red 22 12
Q40 PP3 80c lem & vio brn 18 12
Q41 PP3 90c red & yel grn 28 15
Q42 PP4 1fr vio brn & org 28 15
Q43 PP4 1.10fr rose & blk ('06) 30 20
Q44 PP4 2fr ocher & bl grn 30 20
Q45 PP4 3fr blk & ultra 50 30
Q46 PP4 4fr yel grn & red ('13) 1.90 1.10
Q47 PP4 5fr org & bl grn ('13) 80 80
Q48 PP4 10fr ol yel & brn vio ('13) 1.40 85
Nos. Q29-Q48 (20) 9.10 5.70

Exist imperforate.

Regular Issues of 1912-13 Handstamped in Violet

1915
Q49 A42 5c green 120.00 120.00
Q50 A43 10c red 700.00 700.00
Q51 A45 10c red 120.00 120.00
a. With engraver's name 450.00 450.00
Q52 A43 20c ol grn *1,100. 1,100.*
Q53 A45 20c ol grn 140.00 140.00
a. With engraver's name 450.00 450.00
Q54 A45 25c ultra 140.00 140.00
a. With engraver's name 450.00 450.00
Q55 A43 35c bis brn 200.00 200.00
Q55A A43 40c green *1,600. 1,600.*
Q56 A45 40c green 140.00 140.00
Q57 A43 50c gray 165.00 165.00
Q58 A43 1fr orange 210.00 210.00
Q59 A43 2fr violet *1,200. 1,200.*
Q60 A44 5fr plum *2,350. 2,350.*

Excellent forgeries of this overprint exist.

PP5

Locomotive PP6

1916 Litho. *Perf. 13½*
Q61 PP5 10c pale bl 90 28
Q62 PP5 15c ol grn 1.10 55
Q63 PP5 20c red 1.65 55
Q64 PP5 25c lt brn 1.65 55
Q65 PP5 30c lilac 1.10 45
Q66 PP5 35c gray 1.10 45
Q67 PP5 40c org yel 2.25 1.40
Q68 PP5 50c bister 2.00 45
Q69 PP5 55c brown 2.25 2.00
Q70 PP5 60c gray vio 1.65 45
Q71 PP5 70c green 1.65 45
Q72 PP5 80c red brn 1.65 45
Q73 PP5 90c blue 1.65 45
Q74 PP6 1fr gray 1.65 45
Q75 PP6 1.10fr ultra *(Franken)* 25.00 25.00
Q76 PP6 2fr red 18.00 45
Q77 PP6 3fr violet 18.50 45
Q78 PP6 4fr emerald 30.00 90
Q79 PP6 5fr brown 30.00 1.40
Q80 PP6 10fr orange 30.00 90
Nos. Q61-Q80 (20) 173.75 38.03

Type of 1916 Inscribed "FRANK" instead of "FRANKEN"

1920
Q81 PP6 1.10fr ultra 2.00 45

PP7

PP8

1920 *Perf. 14.*
Q82 PP7 10c bl grn 1.25 40
Q83 PP7 15c ol grn 1.50 1.25
Q84 PP7 20c red 1.50 40
Q85 PP7 25c gray brn 2.00 1.00
Q86 PP7 30c red vio 12.50 10.00
Q87 PP7 40c pale org 8.50 80
Q88 PP7 50c bister 6.00 60
Q89 PP7 55c pale brn 4.75 2.00
Q90 PP7 60c dk vio 7.50 1.00
Q91 PP7 70c green 11.00 1.65
Q92 PP7 80c red brn 32.50 1.40
Q93 PP7 90c dl bl 6.00 60
Q94 PP8 1fr gray 57.50 1.00
Q95 PP8 1.10fr ultra 16.00 3.25
Q96 PP8 1.20fr dk grn 12.50 50
Q97 PP8 1.40fr blk brn 7.25 50
Q98 PP8 2fr vermilion 62.50 80
Q99 PP8 3fr red vio 75.00 1.25
Q100 PP8 4fr yel grn 75.00 75
Q101 PP8 5fr bis brn 75.00 75
Q102 PP8 10fr brn org 75.00 75
Nos. Q82-Q102 (21) 550.75 30.65

PP9

PP10

Types PP7 and PP9 differ in the position of the wheel and the tablet above it.
Types PP8 and PP10 differ in the bars below "FR".
There are many other variations in the designs.

1920-21 Typo.
Q103 PP9 10c carmine 45 25
Q104 PP9 15c yel grn 42 25
Q105 PP9 20c bl grn 1.10 35
Q106 PP9 25c ultra 1.00 35
Q107 PP9 30c chocolate 1.25 35
Q108 PP9 35c org brn 1.40 45
Q109 PP9 40c orange 1.65 25
Q110 PP9 50c rose 1.65 25
Q111 PP9 55c yel ('21) 3.50 1.75
Q112 PP9 60c dl rose 1.65 25
Q113 PP9 70c emerald 3.25 30
Q114 PP9 80c violet 3.00 20
Q115 PP9 90c lemon 14.00 15.00
Q116 PP9 90c claret 6.75 60
Q117 PP10 1fr buff 7.00 50
Q118 PP10 1fr red brn 6.00 40
Q119 PP10 1.10fr ultra 2.25 75
Q120 PP10 1.20fr orange 3.00 20
Q121 PP10 1.40fr yellow 12.50 1.50
Q122 PP10 1.60fr turq bl 21.00 50
Q123 PP10 1.60fr emerald 50.00 50
Q124 PP10 2fr pale rose 24.00 30
Q125 PP10 3fr dp rose 21.00 30
Q126 PP10 4fr emerald 21.00 40
Q127 PP10 5fr lt vio 18.00 35
Q128 PP10 10fr lemon 115.00 3.75
Q129 PP10 10fr dk brn 19.00 28
Q130 PP10 15fr dp rose ('21) 19.00 35
Q131 PP10 20fr dk bl ('21) 275.00 2.50
Nos. Q103-Q131 (29) 654.82 33.18

PP11

1922 Engr. *Perf. 11½.*

No.	Type	Description	Unused	Used
Q132	PP11	2fr black	4.00	15
Q133	PP11	3fr brown	40.00	28
Q134	PP11	4fr green	10.00	18
Q135	PP11	5r claret	10.00	18
Q136	PP11	10fr yel brn	11.50	25
Q137	PP11	15fr rose red	11.50	35
Q138	PP11	20fr blue	70.00	38
		Nos. Q132-Q138 (7)	157.00	1.77

PP12

PP13

Perf. 14x13½, 13½x14

1923-40 Typo.

No.	Type	Description	Unused	Used
Q139	PP12	5c red brn	28	35
Q140	PP12	10c vermilion	15	12
Q141	PP12	15c ultra	32	45
Q142	PP12	20c turq bl	15	10
Q143	PP12	30c brn vio ('27)	32	15
Q144	PP12	40c ol grn	28	10
Q145	PP12	50c mag ('27)	28	5
Q146	PP12	60c orange	32	15
Q147	PP12	70c dk brn ('24)	20	5
Q148	PP12	80c violet	28	10
Q149	PP12	90c sl ('27)	1.50	18
Q150	PP13	1fr ultra	42	5
Q151	PP13	1fr brt bl ('28)	85	10
Q152	PP13	1.10fr orange	4.25	18
Q153	PP13	1.50fr turq bl	4.75	35
Q154	PP13	1.70fr dp brn ('31)	1.10	25
Q155	PP13	1.80fr claret	8.00	25
Q156	PP13	2fr ol grn ('24)	40	25
Q157	PP13	2.10fr gray grn	8.50	38
Q158	PP13	2.40fr dp vio	8.50	55
Q159	PP13	2.70fr gray ('24)	17.00	25
Q160	PP13	3fr org red	65	12
Q161	PP13	3.30fr brn ('24)	18.00	38
Q162	PP13	4fr rose ('24)	85	15
Q163	PP13	5fr vio ('24)	1.25	15
Q163A	PP13	5fr brn vio ('40)	65	55
Q164	PP13	6fr bis brn ('27)	75	10
Q165	PP13	7fr org ('27)	1.25	10
Q166	PP13	8fr dp brn ('27)	1.10	12
Q167	PP13	9fr red vio ('27)	3.00	15
Q168	PP13	10fr bl grn ('27)	1.25	12
Q168A	PP13	10fr blk ('40)	3.50	4.00
Q169	PP13	20fr mag ('27)	2.75	12
Q170	PP13	30fr turq grn ('31)	8.75	25
Q171	PP13	40fr gray ('31)	60.00	45
Q172	PP13	50fr bis ('27)	13.00	30
		Nos. Q139-Q172 (36)	174.60	11.47

See Nos. Q239-Q262. Stamps overprinted "Bagages Reisgoed" are revenues.

PP14

1924

Green Surcharge.

No.	Type	Description	Unused	Used
Q173	PP14	2.30fr on 2.40fr vio	4.50	25
a.		Inverted surcharge	57.50	

Type of Regular Issue of 1926-27 Overprinted

1928 *Perf. 14.*

No.	Type	Description	Unused	Used
Q174	A61	4fr buff	6.50	90
Q175	A61	5fr bister	6.50	1.10

Central P.O., Brussels PP15

1929-30 Engr. *Perf. 11½*

No.	Type	Description	Unused	Used
Q176	PP15	3fr blk brn	1.75	22
Q177	PP15	4fr gray	1.75	15
Q178	PP15	5fr carmine	1.75	15
Q179	PP15	6fr vio brn ('30)	27.50	30.00

No. Q179 Surcharged in Blue

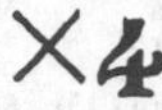
×4 4×

1933

No.	Type	Description	Unused	Used
Q180	PP15	4(fr) on 6fr vio brn	27.50	28

Modern Locomotive PP16

1934 Photo. *Perf. 13½x14*

No.	Type	Description	Unused	Used
Q181	PP16	3fr dk grn	4.50	2.25
Q182	PP16	4fr red vio	1.40	12
Q183	PP16	5fr dp rose	5.00	12

Modern Railroad Train — PP17

Old Railroad Train — PP18

1935 Engr. *Perf. 14x13½, 13½x14*

No.	Type	Description	Unused	Used
Q184	PP17	10c rose car	30	18
Q185	PP17	20c violet	38	15
Q186	PP17	30c blk brn	50	50
Q187	PP17	40c dk bl	60	20
Q188	PP17	50c org red	65	15
Q189	PP17	60c green	75	25
Q190	PP17	70c ultra	85	20
Q191	PP17	80c ol blk	75	25
Q192	PP17	90c rose lake	1.00	70
Q193	PP18	1fr brn vio	1.00	15
Q194	PP18	2fr gray blk	2.00	20
Q195	PP18	3fr red org	2.25	25
Q196	PP18	4fr vio brn	2.75	25
Q197	PP18	5fr plum	3.00	20
Q198	PP18	6fr dp grn	3.50	25
Q199	PP18	7fr dp vio	4.00	20
Q200	PP18	8fr ol blk	5.25	30
Q201	PP18	9fr dk bl	6.00	25
Q202	PP18	10fr car lake	6.00	20
Q203	PP18	20fr green	27.50	30
Q204	PP18	30fr violet	87.50	1.50
Q205	PP18	40fr blk brn	87.50	2.25
Q206	PP18	50fr rose car	100.00	1.75
Q207	PP18	100fr ultra	225.00	30.00
		Nos. Q184-Q207 (24)	569.03	40.63

Centenary of Belgian State Railway.

Winged Wheel — PP19

Surcharge in Red or Blue.

1938 Photo. *Perf. 13½*

No.	Type	Description	Unused	Used
Q208	PP19	5fr on 3.50fr dk grn (R)	10.00	65
Q209	PP19	5fr on 4.50fr rose vio (Bl)	22	10
Q210	PP19	6fr on 5.50fr cop red (Bl)	50	15
a.		Half used as 3fr on piece		2.25

See also Nos. MQ1, Q297-Q299.

Symbolizing Unity Achieved Through Railroads PP20

1939 Engr. *Perf. 13½x14*

No.	Type	Description	Unused	Used
Q211	PP20	20c redsh brn	3.00	3.25
Q212	PP20	50c vio bl	3.00	3.25
Q213	PP20	2fr rose red	3.00	3.25
Q214	PP20	9fr sl grn	3.00	3.25
Q215	PP20	10fr dk vio	3.00	3.25
		Nos. Q211-Q215 (5)	15.00	16.25

Issued in commemoration of the Railroad Exposition and Congress held at Brussels.

Parcel Post Stamps of 1925-27 Overprinted in Blue or Carmine

Perf. 14½x14, 14x14½.

1940 Unwmk.

No.	Type	Description	Unused	Used
Q216	PP12	10c vermilion	12	10
Q217	PP12	20c turq bl (C)	12	10
Q218	PP12	30c brn vio	15	10
Q219	PP12	40c ol grn (C)	12	12
Q220	PP12	50c magenta	12	10
Q221	PP12	60c orange	25	30
Q222	PP12	70c dk brn	18	20
Q223	PP12	80c vio (C)	20	25
Q224	PP12	90c sl (C)	28	30
Q225	PP13	1fr ultra (C)	28	25
Q226	PP13	2fr ol grn (C)	28	25
Q227	PP13	3fr org red	28	25
Q228	PP13	4fr rose	28	25
Q229	PP13	5fr vio (C)	28	25
Q230	PP13	6fr bis brn	40	32
Q231	PP13	7fr orange	40	25
Q232	PP13	8fr dp brn	40	25
Q233	PP13	9fr red vio	40	25
Q234	PP13	10fr bl grn (C)	40	30
Q235	PP13	20fr magenta	70	30
Q236	PP13	30fr turq grn (C)	1.25	1.00
Q237	PP13	40fr gray (C)	1.75	2.50
Q238	PP13	50fr bister	2.00	1.25
		Nos. Q216-Q238 (23)	10.64	9.24

Types of 1923-40.

1941

No.	Type	Description	Unused	Used
Q239	PP12	10c dl ol	12	10
Q240	PP12	20c lt vio	12	10
Q241	PP12	30c fawn	12	10
Q242	PP12	40c dl bl	12	15
Q243	PP12	50c lt grn	12	5
Q244	PP12	60c gray	14	15
Q245	PP12	70c chlky grn	14	15
Q246	PP12	80c orange	18	25
Q247	PP12	90c rose lil	18	25
Q248	PP13	1fr lt yel grn	18	20
Q249	PP13	2fr vio brn	30	20
Q250	PP13	3fr slate	35	20
Q251	PP13	4fr dl ol	42	20
Q252	PP13	5fr rose lil	55	20
Q253	PP13	5fr black	80	35
Q254	PP13	6fr org ver	75	30
Q255	PP13	7fr lilac	75	15
Q256	PP13	8fr chlky grn	75	20
Q257	PP13	9fr blue	90	15
Q258	PP13	10fr rose lil	90	15
Q259	PP13	20fr mlky bl	2.00	15
Q260	PP13	30fr orange	4.75	35
Q261	PP13	40fr rose	5.50	40
Q262	PP13	50fr brt red vio	7.00	25
		Nos. Q239-Q262 (24)	27.14	4.75

Adjusting Tie Plates — PP21

Engineer at Throttle — PP22

Freight Station Interior — PP23

Signal and Electric Train — PP24

1942 Engr. *Perf. 14x13½*

No.	Type	Description	Unused	Used
Q263	PP21	9.20fr red org	60	80
Q264	PP22	12.30fr dp grn	60	85
Q265	PP23	14.30fr dk car	85	1.25

Perf. 11½.

No.	Type	Description	Unused	Used
Q266	PP24	100fr ultra	16.00	24.00

Engineer at Throttle PP25

Adjusting Tie Plates PP26

Freight Station Interior — PP27

1945-46 Photo. Unwmk.

No.	Type	Description	Unused	Used
Q267	PP25	10c ol blk ('46)	20	5
Q268	PP25	20c dp vio	20	5
Q269	PP25	30c chnt brn ('46)	20	12
Q270	PP25	40c dp bl ('46)	20	10
Q271	PP25	50c pck grn	20	6
Q272	PP25	60c blk ('46)	22	15
Q273	PP25	70c emer ('46)	30	25
Q274	PP25	80c orange	50	20
Q275	PP25	90c brn vio ('46)	30	25
Q276	PP26	1fr bl grn ('46)	20	12
Q277	PP26	2fr blk brn	22	10
Q278	PP26	3fr grnsh blk ('46)	1.25	20
Q279	PP26	4fr dk bl	30	20
Q280	PP26	5fr sepia	30	5
Q281	PP26	6fr dk ol grn ('46)	1.50	15
Q282	PP26	7fr dk vio ('46)	50	18
Q283	PP26	8fr red org	50	10
Q284	PP26	9fr dp bl ('46)	65	7
Q285	PP27	10fr dk red ('46)	2.25	15
Q286	PP27	10fr sep ('46)	1.10	25
Q287	PP27	20fr dk yel grn ('46)	50	5
Q288	PP27	30fr dp vio	75	5
Q289	PP27	40fr rose pink	65	5
Q290	PP27	50fr brt bl ('46)	8.00	12
		Nos. Q267-Q290 (24)	20.99	3.07

Mercury — PP28

1945-46 *Perf. 13½x13*

No.	Type	Description	Unused	Used
Q291	PP28	3fr emer ('46)	45	25
Q292	PP28	5fr ultra	12	18
Q293	PP28	6fr red	18	12

Inscribed "Belgique-Belgie".

Q294 PP28 3fr emer ('46) 45 25
Q295 PP28 5fr ultra 12 18
Q296 PP28 6fr red 18 12
Nos. Q291-Q296 (6) 1.50 1.10

Winged Wheel Type of 1938.
Carmine Surcharge.

1946 ***Perf. 13½x14***

Q297 PP19 8fr on 5.50fr brn 65 15
Q298 PP19 10fr on 5.50fr dk bl 75 25
Q299 PP19 12fr on 5.50fr vio 1.10 25

Railway Crossing PP29

1947 **Engr.** ***Perf. 12½***

Q300 PP29 100fr dk grn 8.50 25

Crossbowman with Train — PP30

1947 **Photo.** ***Perf. 11½***

Q301 PP30 8fr dk ol brn 75 25
Q302 PP30 10fr gray & bl 90 30
Q303 PP30 12fr dk vio 1.40 50

Surcharged with New Value and Bars in Carmine.

1948

Q304 PP30 9fr on 8fr dk ol brn 75 25
Q305 PP30 11fr on 10fr gray & bl 90 40
Q306 PP30 13.50fr on 12fr dk vio 1.40 40

Delivery of Parcel — PP31

1948

Q307 PP31 9fr chocolate 4.25 12
Q308 PP31 11fr brn car 4.50 12
Q309 PP31 13.50fr gray 6.50 35

Locomotive of 1835 PP32

Various Locomotives.
Lathe Work in Frame Differs.

1949 **Engr.** ***Perf. 12½***

Q310 PP32 ½fr dk brn 30 12
Q311 PP32 1fr car rose 40 12
Q312 PP32 2fr dp ultra 45 15
Q313 PP32 3fr dp mag 90 12
Q314 PP32 4fr bl grn 1.10 15
Q315 PP32 5fr org red 1.10 15
Q316 PP32 6fr brn vio 1.40 18
Q317 PP32 7fr yel grn 1.75 12
Q318 PP32 8fr grnsh bl 2.00 15
Q319 PP32 9fr yel brn 2.75 18
Q320 PP32 10fr citron 3.50 12
Q321 PP32 20fr orange 5.75 12
Q322 PP32 30fr blue 8.00 12
Q323 PP32 40fr lil rose 10.50 18
Q324 PP32 50fr violet 11.00 25
Q325 PP32 100fr red 32.50 18
Nos. Q310-Q325 (16) 83.40 2.41

See also No. Q337.

Engraved; Center Typographed

Q326 PP32 10fr car rose & blk 4.50 70

1949 **Engr.**

Design: Electric locomotive.

Q327 PP32 60fr blk brn 15.00 25

Opening of Charleroi-Brussels electric railway line, Oct. 15, 1949.

Mailing Parcel Post — PP33

Sorting PP34

Loading PP35

1950-52 ***Perf. 12, 12½***

Q328 PP33 11fr red org 4.00 40
Q329 PP33 12fr red vio ('51) 10.00 1.10
Q330 PP34 13fr dk bl grn 3.50 20
Q331 PP34 15fr ultra ('51) 9.50 30
Q332 PP35 16fr gray 3.75 20
Q333 PP35 17fr brn ('52) 5.00 40
Q334 PP35 18fr brt car ('51) 8.50 40
Q335 PP35 20fr brn org ('52) 5.00 45
Nos. Q328-Q335 (8) 49.25 3.45

Mercury and Winged Wheel — PP36

1951

Q336 PP36 25fr dk bl 9.00 8.00

Issued to commemorate the 25th anniversary of the founding of the National Society of Belgian Railroads.

Type of 1949.

1952 **Unwmk.** ***Perf. 11½***

Design: Electric locomotive.

Q337 PP32 300fr red vio 75.00 65

Nos. Q331, Q328 and Q334 Surcharged with New Value and "X" in Red, Blue or Green.

1953 ***Perf. 12.***

Q338 PP34 13fr on 15fr ultra (R) 32.50 1.40
Q339 PP33 17fr on 11fr red org (Bl) 20.00 1.10
Q340 PP35 20fr on 18fr brt car (G) 16.50 1.50

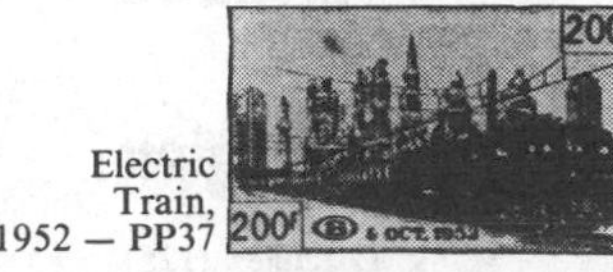

Electric Train, 1952 — PP37

1953 **Engr.**

Q341 PP37 200fr dk yel grn & vio brn 110.00 3.25
Q342 PP37 200fr dk grn 90.00 80

No. Q341 was issued to commemorate the opening of the railway link connecting Brussels North and South Stations, Oct. 4, 1952.

New North Station, Brussels — PP38

Chapelle Station, Brussels PP39

Designs: No. Q348, 15fr, Congress Station. 10fr, 20fr, 30fr, 40fr, 50fr, South Station. 100fr, 200fr, 300fr, Central Station.

1953-57 **Unwmk.** ***Perf. 11½***

Q343 PP38 1fr bister 38 5
Q344 PP38 2fr slate 50 8
Q345 PP38 3fr bl grn 65 5
Q346 PP38 4fr orange 1.00 5
Q347 PP38 5fr red brn 1.00 5
Q348 PP38 5fr dk red brn 7.00 25
Q349 PP38 6fr rose vio 1.20 5
Q350 PP38 7fr brt grn 1.20 5
Q351 PP38 8fr rose red 1.50 5
Q352 PP38 9fr brt grnsh bl 2.00 5
Q353 PP38 10fr lt grn 2.00 5
Q354 PP38 15fr dl red 8.75 10
Q355 PP38 20fr blue 3.25 5
Q356 PP38 30fr purple 5.00 5
Q357 PP38 40fr brt pur 6.25 5
Q358 PP38 50fr lil rose 7.50 5
Q359 PP39 60fr brt pur 15.00 12
Q360 PP39 80fr brn vio 18.00 15
Q361 PP39 100fr emerald 17.50 10
Q361A PP39 200fr brt vio bl 40.00 1.25
Q361B PP39 300fr lil rose 62.50 1.65
Nos. Q343-Q361B (21) 202.18 4.35

Issue dates: No. Q347, 20fr and 30fr, 1953; 80fr, 1955; 200fr, 1956; 300fr, 1957. Rest of set, 1954.

See Nos. Q407, Q431-Q432.

Electric Train — PP40

Mercury and Winged Wheel — PP41

1954

Q362 PP40 13fr chocolate 7.00 15
Q363 PP40 18fr dk bl 8.00 12
Q364 PP40 21fr lil rose 9.00 50

Nos. Q362-Q364 Surcharged with New Value and "X" in Blue, Red or Green.

1956

Q365 PP40 14fr on 13fr choc (B) 7.00 15
Q366 PP40 19fr on 18fr dk bl (R) 7.50 25
Q367 PP40 22fr on 21fr lil rose (G) 8.00 45

1957 **Engr.** ***Perf. 11½***

Q368 PP41 14fr brt grn 6.75 25
Q369 PP41 19fr ol gray 7.75 35
Q370 PP41 22fr car rose 8.00 60

Nos. Q369-Q370 Surcharged with New Value and "X" in Pink or Green.

1959

Q371 PP41 20fr on 19fr ol gray (P) 12.50 38
Q372 PP41 20fr on 22fr car rose (G) 14.00 60

Old North Station, Brussels PP42

1959 **Engr.** ***Perf. 11½***

Q373 PP42 20fr ol grn 10.00 38

See also No. Q381.

Diesel and Electric Locomotives and Association Emblem PP43

1960 **Unwmk.** ***Perf. 11½***

Q374 PP43 20fr red 62.50 47.50
Q375 PP43 50fr dk bl 62.50 40.00
Q376 PP43 60fr red lil 62.50 40.00
Q377 PP43 70fr emerald 62.50 40.00

Issued to commemorate the 75th anniversary of the International Association of Railway Congresses.

No. Q373 Surcharged with New Value and "X" in Red.

1961

Q378 PP42 24fr on 20fr ol grn 80.00 38

South Station, Brussels — PP44

1962 **Unwmk.** ***Perf. 11½***

Q379 PP44 24fr dl red 9.00 38

No. Q379 Surcharged with New Value and "X" in Light Green.

1963

Q380 PP44 26fr on 24fr dl red 7.50 38

Type of 1959

Design: 26fr, Central Station, Antwerp.

1963 **Engr.** ***Perf. 11½***

Q381 PP42 26fr blue 8.00 75

No. Q381 Surcharged in Red

1964, Apr. 20

Q382 PP42 28fr on 26fr bl 8.00 50

Type of 1959.

Design: 28fr, St. Peter's Station, Ghent.

1965 **Engr.** ***Perf. 11½***

Q383 PP42 28fr red lil 8.00 1.25

Nos. Q383 Surcharged with New Value and "X" in Green

1966

Q384 PP42 35fr on 28fr red lil 8.00 1.00

Arlon Railroad Station PP45

Perf. 11½

1967, Aug. **Unwmk.** **Engr.**

Q385 PP45 25fr bister 11.00 30
Q386 PP45 30fr bl grn 5.75 38
Q387 PP45 35fr dp bl 7.75 65

Electric Train — PP46

Designs: 2fr, 3fr, 4fr, 5fr, 6fr, 7fr, 8fr, 9fr, like 1fr. 10fr, 20fr, 30fr, 40fr, Train going right. 50fr, 60fr, 70fr, 80fr, 90fr, Train going left. 100fr, 200fr, 300fr, Diesel train.

1968-73 Engr. *Perf. 11½*

No.	Type	Description	Unused	Used
Q388	PP46	1fr ol bis	6	5
Q389	PP46	2fr slate	12	5
Q390	PP46	3fr bl grn	18	5
Q391	PP46	4fr orange	25	6
Q392	PP46	5fr brown	30	8
Q393	PP46	6fr plum	40	5
Q394	PP46	7fr brt grn	45	8
Q395	PP46	8fr carmine	50	8
Q396	PP46	9fr blue	55	8
Q397	PP46	10fr green	60	5
Q398	PP46	20fr dk bl	1.10	5
Q399	PP46	30fr dk pur	1.65	5
Q400	PP46	40fr brt lil	2.00	5
Q401	PP46	50fr brt pink	2.50	5
Q402	PP46	60fr brt vio	3.00	8
Q402A	PP46	70fr dp bis ('73)	4.00	1.00
Q403	PP46	80fr dk brn	4.00	25
Q403A	PP46	90fr yel grn ('73)	5.50	1.25
Q404	PP46	100fr emerald	5.75	45
Q405	PP46	200fr vio bl	12.50	80
Q406	PP46	300fr lil rose	27.50	1.25
		Nos. Q388-Q406 (21)	72.91	5.91

Types of 1953-68

Designs: 10fr, Congress Station, Brussels. 40fr, Arlon Station. 500fr, Electric train going left.

1968, June Engr. *Perf. 11½*

No.	Type	Description	Unused	Used
Q407	PP38	10fr gray	75	10
Q408	PP45	40fr vermilion	27.50	40
Q409	PP46	500fr yellow	30.00	2.25

Nos. Q385, Q387 and Q408 Surcharged with New Value and "X"

1970, Dec.

No.	Type	Description	Unused	Used
Q410	PP45	37fr on 25fr bis	55.00	3.50
Q411	PP45	48fr on 35fr dp bl	16.00	5.50
Q412	PP45	53fr on 40fr ver	18.00	6.75

Ostend Station PP47

1971, March Engr. *Perf. 11½*

No.	Type	Description	Unused	Used
Q413	PP47	32fr bis & blk	2.25	90
Q414	PP47	37fr gray & blk	2.75	1.25
Q415	PP47	42fr bl & blk	3.00	1.40
Q416	PP47	44fr brt rose & blk	3.50	1.50
Q417	PP47	46fr vio & blk	3.50	1.50
Q418	PP47	50fr brick red & blk	4.00	1.65
Q419	PP47	52fr sep & blk	4.00	1.65
Q420	PP47	54fr yel grn & blk	4.50	1.75
Q421	PP47	61fr grnsh bl & blk	4.50	2.00
		Nos. Q413-Q421 (9)	32.00	13.60

Nos. Q413-Q416, Q419-Q421 Surcharged with New Value and "X"

1971, Dec. 15

Denomination in Black

No.	Type	Description	Unused	Used
Q422	PP47	34fr on 32fr bis	2.00	80
Q423	PP47	40fr on 37fr gray	2.50	1.00
Q424	PP47	47fr on 44fr brt rose	2.75	1.10
Q425	PP47	53fr on 42fr bl	3.25	1.25
Q426	PP47	56fr on 52fr sep	3.50	1.40
Q427	PP47	59fr on 54fr yel grn	4.00	1.40
Q428	PP47	66fr on 61fr grnsh bl	5.00	1.65
		Nos. Q422-Q428 (7)	23.00	8.60

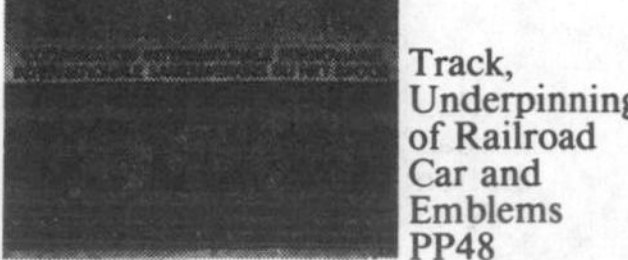
Track, Underpinning of Railroad Car and Emblems PP48

1972, Mar. Photo.

No.	Type	Description	Unused	Used
Q429	PP48	100fr emer, red & blk	13.00	2.75

Centenary of International Railroad Union.

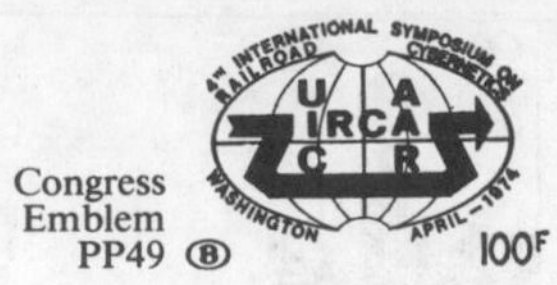

Congress Emblem PP49

1974, Apr. Photo. *Perf. 11½*

No.	Type	Description	Unused	Used
Q430	PP49	100fr yel, blk & red	12.00	2.00

4th International Symposium on Railroad Cybernetics, Washington, D.C., Apr. 1974.

Type of 1953-1957

1975, June 1 Engr. *Perf. 11½*

No.	Type	Description	Unused	Used
Q431	PP38	20fr emerald	1.40	80
Q432	PP38	50fr blue	3.50	2.00

Railroad Tracks PP50

1976, June 10 Photo. *Perf. 11½*

No.	Type	Description	Unused	Used
Q433	PP50	20fr ultra & multi	5.00	1.00
Q434	PP50	50fr brt grn & multi	3.00	2.25
Q435	PP50	100fr dp org & multi	6.75	4.75
Q436	PP50	150fr brt lil & multi	10.00	8.00

Railroad Station — PP51

1977 Photo. *Perf. 11½*

No.	Type	Description	Unused	Used
Q437	PP51	1000fr multi	55.00	*45.00*

Freight Car — PP52

Designs: 2fr, 3fr, 4fr, 5fr, 6fr, 7fr, 8fr, 9fr, Freight car. 10fr, 20fr, 30fr, 40fr, Hopper car. 50fr, 60fr, 70fr, 80fr, 90fr, Maintenance car. 100fr, 200fr, 300fr, 500fr, Liquid fuel car.

1980, Dec. 16 Engr. *Perf. 11½*

No.	Type	Description	Unused	Used
Q438	PP52	1fr bis brn & blk	6	5
Q439	PP52	2fr cl & blk	12	5
Q440	PP52	3fr brt bl & blk	15	5
Q441	PP52	4fr grnsh blk & blk	22	6
Q442	PP52	5fr sep & blk	28	10
Q443	PP52	6fr dp org & blk	30	12
Q444	PP52	7fr pur & blk	38	14
Q445	PP52	8fr black	42	14
Q446	PP52	9fr grn & blk	45	15
Q447	PP52	10fr yel bis & blk	50	20
Q448	PP52	20fr grnsh bl & blk	1.10	40
Q449	PP52	30fr bis & blk	1.65	60
Q450	PP52	40fr lt lil & blk	2.00	80
Q451	PP52	50fr dk brn & blk	2.65	1.00
Q452	PP52	60fr ol & blk	3.00	1.20
Q453	PP52	70fr vio bl & blk	3.75	1.40
Q454	PP52	80fr vio brn & blk	4.25	1.60
Q455	PP52	90fr lil rose & blk	4.75	1.80
Q456	PP52	100fr crim rose & blk	5.25	2.00
Q457	PP52	200fr brn & blk	10.00	4.00
Q458	PP52	300fr ol gray & blk	15.00	6.00
Q459	PP52	500fr dl pur & blk	26.00	10.00
		Nos. Q438-Q459 (22)	82.28	31.86

Train in Station — PP53

1982 Engr. *Perf. 11½*

No.	Type	Description	Unused	Used
Q460	PP53	10fr red & blk	45	20
Q461	PP53	20fr grn & blk	90	40
Q462	PP53	50fr sep & blk	2.50	1.00
Q463	PP53	100fr bl & blk	5.00	2.00

BB-150 Electric Locomotive — PP54

1985, May 3 Photo. *Perf. 11½*

No.	Type	Description	Unused	Used
Q464	PP54	250fr shown	8.00	6.00
Q465	PP54	500fr BB-120 electric locomotive	16.00	12.00

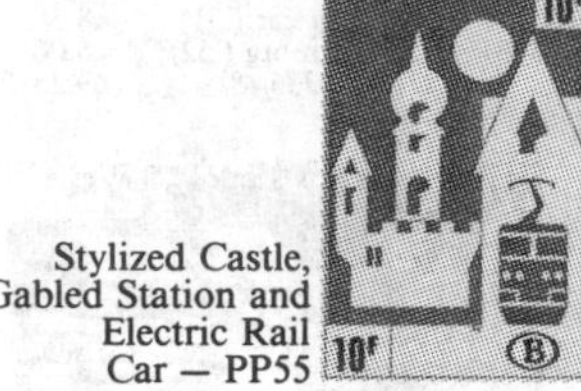

Stylized Castle, Gabled Station and Electric Rail Car — PP55

1987, Oct. 12 Engr. *Perf. 11½*

No.	Type	Description	Unused	Used
Q466	PP55	10fr dark red & blk	50	38
Q467	PP55	20fr dark grn & blk	1.00	75
Q468	PP55	50fr dark brn & blk	2.50	1.90
Q469	PP55	100fr dark lil & blk	5.00	3.75
Q470	PP55	150fr dark olive bister & blk	7.50	5.65
		Nos. Q466-Q470 (5)	16.50	12.43

ISSUED UNDER GERMAN OCCUPATION

German Stamps of 1906-11 Surcharged

a: Belgien 3 Centimes

b: * 1Fr.25C. * Belgien

Wmk. Lozenges. (125)

1914-15 *Perf. 14, 14½.*

No.	Type	Description	Unused	Used
1	A16 (a)	3c on 3pf brn	35	28
2	A16 (a)	5c on 5pf grn	30	22
3	A16 (a)	10c on 10pf car	45	22
4	A16 (a)	25c on 20pf ultra	55	40
5	A16 (a)	50c on 40pf lake & blk	2.25	1.75
6	A16 (a)	75c on 60pf mag	90	1.20
7	A16 (a)	1fr on 80pf lake & blk, *rose*	2.50	2.00
8	A17 (b)	1fr 25c on 1m car	22.50	17.50
9	A21 (b)	2fr 50c on 2m gray bl	20.00	22.50
		Nos. N1-N9 (9)	49.80	46.07

German Stamps of 1906-18 Surcharged

c: Belgien 3 Cent.

d: Belgien 1F.

e: * 1F.25Cent. * Belgien

1916-18

No.	Type	Description	Unused	Used
10	A22 (c)	2c on 2pf db	22	22
11	A16 (c)	3c on 3pf brn	28	18
12	A16 (c)	5c on 5pf grn	28	22
13	A22 (c)	8c on 7½pf org	45	45
14	A16 (c)	10c on 10pf car	22	18
15	A22 (c)	15c on 15pf yel brn	50	25
16	A22 (c)	15c on 15pf dk vio	50	45
17	A16 (c)	20c on 25pf org & blk, *yel*	28	28
18	A16 (c)	25c on 20pf ultra	28	18
a.		25c on 20pf bl	35	22
19	A16 (c)	40c on 30pf org & blk, *buff*	30	28
20	A16 (c)	50c on 40pf lake & blk	28	28
21	A16 (c)	75c on 60pf mag	50	*14.00*
22	A16 (d)	1f on 80pf lake & blk, *rose*	1.65	*4.00*
23	A17 (e)	1f 25c on 1m car	2.75	2.75
24	A21 (e)	2f 50c on 2m gray bl	24.00	24.00
a.		2f50c on 1m car (error)		*4,500*
25	A20(e)	6f 25c on 5m sl & car	32.50	40.00
		Nos. N10-N25 (16)	64.99	87.72

A similar series of stamps without "Belgien" was used in parts of Belgium and France while occupied by German forces. See France Nos. N15-N26.

BENIN

French Colony

LOCATION — West Coast of Africa
GOVT. — Republic
AREA — 43,483 sq. mi.
POP. — 3,832,000 (est. 1984)
CAPITAL — Porto Novo

In 1895 the French possessions known as Benin were incorporated into the colony of Dahomey and postage stamps of Dahomey superseded those of Benin. Dahomey took the name Benin when it became a republic in 1975.

100 Centimes = 1 Franc

Handstamped on Stamps of French Colonies

BÉNIN

1892 Unwmk. *Perf. 14x13½.*

Black Overprint.

No.	Type	Description	Unused	Used
1	A9	1c *bluish*	110.00	90.00
2	A9	2c brn, *buff*	90.00	80.00
3	A9	4c cl, *lav*	32.50	27.50
4	A9	5c grn, *grnsh*	10.00	8.50
5	A9	10c *lavender*	50.00	40.00
6	A9	15c blue	20.00	8.00
7	A9	20c red, *grn*	125.00	140.00
8	A9	25c *rose*	65.00	37.50
9	A9	30c brn, *yelsh*	125.00	100.00
10	A9	35c *orange*	125.00	100.00
11	A9	40c red, *straw*	100.00	90.00
12	A9	75c car, *rose*	250.00	200.00
13	A9	1fr brnz grn, *straw*	275.00	225.00

Red Overprint.

No.	Type	Description	Unused	Used
14	A9	15c blue	62.50	52.50

Blue Overprint.

15 A9 5c grn, *grnsh* 1,750. 475.00
15A A9 15c blue 1,750. 475.00

Nos. 1-13 all exist with overprint inverted, and several with it double. These sell for slightly more than normal stamps. The overprints of Nos. 1-15A are of four types, three without accent mark on "E." They exist diagonal.

Counterfeits exist of Nos. 1-19.

Additional Surcharge Red or Black

40

1892

16 A9 01c on 5c grn, *grnsh* 200.00 150.00
17 A9 40c on 15c bl 140.00 47.50
18 A9 75c on 15c bl 625.00 425.00
19 A9 75c on 15c bl (Bk) 2,500. 1,900.

Navigation and Commerce
A3 A4

1893 **Typo.**

Name of Colony in Blue or Carmine.

20 A3 1c *bluish* 1.75 1.50
21 A3 2c brn, *buff* 2.25 1.90
22 A3 4c cl, *lav* 2.50 1.90
23 A3 5c grn, *grnsh* 3.00 2.25
24 A3 10c *lavender* 3.00 2.50
25 A3 15c bl, quadrille paper 15.00 10.00
26 A3 20c red, *grn* 9.00 5.00
27 A3 25c *rose* 22.50 10.00
28 A3 30c brn, *bis* 10.00 7.75
29 A3 40c red, *straw* 2.75 1.90
30 A3 50c car, *rose* 2.50 1.90
31 A3 75c vio, *org* 5.50 4.25
32 A3 1fr brnz grn, *straw* 35.00 30.00
Nos. 20-32 (13) 114.75 80.85

1894

33 A4 1c *bluish* 1.65 1.25
34 A4 2c brn, *buff* 1.65 1.25
35 A4 4c cl, *lav* 1.65 1.25
36 A4 5c grn, *grnsh* 2.00 1.25
37 A4 10c *lavender* 3.00 2.25
38 A4 15c bl, quadrille paper 4.50 2.25
39 A4 20c red, *grn* 4.75 3.25
40 A4 25c *rose* 5.00 2.50
41 A4 30c brn, *bis* 3.25 2.50
42 A4 40c red, *straw* 10.00 6.00
43 A4 50c car, *rose* 12.00 6.50
44 A4 75c vio, *org* 8.00 6.00
45 A4 1fr brnz grn, *straw* 1.90 1.90
Nos. 33-45 (13) 59.35 38.15

PEOPLE'S REPUBLIC OF BENIN

LOCATION — West Coast of Africa
GOVT. — Republic
AREA — 43,483 sq. mi.
POP. — 3,290,000 (est. 1977)
CAPITAL — Porto-Novo

The Republic of Dahomey proclaimed itself the People's Republic of Benin on Nov. 30, 1975. See Dahomey for stamps issued before then.

Allamanda Cathartica — A83

Flag Bearers, Arms of Benin — A84

Flowers: 35fr, Ixora coccinea. 45fr, Hibiscus. 60fr, Phaemeria magnifica.

Unwmk.

1975, Dec. 8 **Photo.** ***Perf. 13***

342 A83 10fr lil & multi 15 10
343 A83 35fr gray & multi 35 20
344 A83 45fr multi 50 35
345 A83 60fr bl & multi 60 45

1976, Apr. 30 **Litho.** ***Perf. 12***

Designs: 60fr, Speaker, wall with "PRPB," flag and arms of Benin. 100fr, Flag and arms of Benin.

346 A84 50fr ocher & multi 40 30
347 A84 60fr ocher & multi 45 30
348 A84 100fr multi 80 60

Proclamation of the People's Republic of Benin, Nov. 30, 1975.

A. G. Bell, Satellite and 1876 Telephone — A85

1976, July 9 **Litho.** ***Perf. 13***

349 A85 200fr lil, red & brn 1.65 70

Centenary of first telephone call by Alexander Graham Bell, Mar. 10, 1876.

Dahomey Nos. 277-278 Surcharged

1976, July 19 **Photo.** ***Perf. 12½x13***

350 A57 50fr on 1fr multi 40 18
351 A57 60fr on 2fr multi 50 20

Scouts Cooking — A86

Design: 70fr, Three Scouts.

1976, Aug. 16 **Litho.** ***Perf. 12½x13***

352 A86 50fr blk, lil & brn 40 30
353 A86 70fr blk, ol & red brn 55 40

African Jamboree, Nigeria 1976.

Blood Bank, Cotonou — A87

Designs: 50fr, Accident and first aid station. 60fr, Blood donation.

1976, Sept. 24 **Litho.** ***Perf. 13***

354 A87 5fr multi 5 5
355 A87 50fr multi 40 30
356 A87 60fr multi 50 35

National Blood Donors Day.

Manioc — A88

Designs: 50fr, Corn. 60fr, Cacao. 150fr, Cotton.

1976, Oct. 4 **Litho.** ***Perf. 13x12½***

357 A88 20fr multi 15 10
358 A88 50fr multi 40 30
359 A88 60fr multi 45 30
360 A88 150fr multi 1.25 90

National Agricultural production campaign.

Classroom — A89

1976, Oct. 25

361 A89 50fr multi 40 30

Third anniversary of KPARO newspaper, used in local language studies.

Roan Antelope — A90

Flags, Wall, Broken Chains — A91

Designs: 30fr, Buffalo. 50fr, Hippopotamus (horiz.). 70fr, Lion.

1976, Nov. 8 **Photo.**

362 A90 10fr multi 10 6
363 A90 30fr multi 25 18
364 A90 50fr multi 40 30
365 A90 70fr multi 55 35

Penjari National Park.

1976, Nov. 30 **Litho.** ***Perf. 12½***

Design: 150fr, Corn, raised hands with weapons.

366 A91 40fr multi 30 20
367 A91 150fr multi 1.20 90

First anniversary of proclamation of the People's Republic of Benin.

Table Tennis, Map of Africa (Games' Emblem) — A92

Design: 50fr, Stadium, Cotonou.

1976, Dec. 26 **Litho.** ***Perf. 13***

368 A92 10fr multi 10 6
369 A92 50fr multi 40 30

West African University Games, Cotonou, Dec. 26-31.

Europafrica Issue

Planes over Africa and Europe — A93

1977, May 13 **Litho.** ***Perf. 13***

370 A93 200fr multi 1.60 1.20

Snake — A94

Designs: 3fr, Tortoise. 5fr, Zebus. 10fr, Cats.

1977, June 13 **Litho.** ***Perf. 13x13½***

371 A94 2fr multi 10 5
372 A94 3fr multi 10 5
373 A94 5fr multi 10 5
374 A94 10fr multi 25 6

Patients at Clinic — A95

1977, Aug. 2 **Litho.** ***Perf. 12½***

375 A95 100fr multi 85 60

World Rheumatism Year.

Karate, Map of Africa — A96

Designs: 100fr, Javelin, map of Africa, Benin flag (horiz.). 150fr, Hurdles.

1977, Aug. 30 **Litho.** ***Perf. 12½***

376 A96 90fr multi 70 55
377 A96 100fr multi 85 60
378 A96 150fr multi 1.25 90
a. Souvenir sheet of 3 2.75 2.75

2nd West African Games, Lagos, Nigeria. No. 378a contains one each of Nos. 376-378; black marginal inscription. Size: 143x92mm.

Chairman Mao A97

Lister and Vaporizer A98

1977, Sept. 9 Litho. ***Perf. 13x12½***

379 A97 100fr multi 85 60

Chairman Mao Tse-tung (1893-1976), Chinese communist leader, first death anniversary.

1977, Sept. 20 Engr. ***Perf. 13***

Design: 150fr, Scalpels and flames, symbols of antisepsis, and Red Cross.

380 A98 150fr multi 1.20 90
381 A98 210fr multi 1.75 1.25

Joseph Lister (1827-1912), surgeon, founder of antiseptic surgery, birth sesquicentennial.

Guelede Mask, Ethnographic Museum, Porto Novo — A99

Designs: 50fr, Jar, symbol of unity, emblem of King Ghezo, Historical Museum, Abomey (vert.). 210fr, Abomey Museum.

1977, Oct. 17 ***Perf. 13***

382 A99 50fr red & multi 40 30
383 A99 60fr blk, bl & bis 50 35
384 A99 210fr multi 1.75 1.25

Atacora Falls — A100

Mother and Child, Owl of Wisdom — A101

Designs: 60fr, Pile houses, Ganvie (horiz.). 150fr, Round huts, Savalou.

1977, Oct. 24 Litho. ***Perf. 12½***

385 A100 50fr multi 40 30
386 A100 60fr multi 50 35
387 A100 150fr multi 1.25 90
a. Souvenir sheet of 3 2.80 2.80

Tourist publicity. No. 387a contains one each of Nos. 385-387; black marginal inscription. Size: 143x91mm.

Perf. 12½x13, 13x12½

1977, Dec. 3 **Photo.**

Design: 150fr, Chopping down magical tree (horiz.).

388 A101 60fr multi 50 35
389 A101 150fr multi 1.25 90

Campaign against witchcraft.

Battle Scene — A102

1978, Jan. 16 Litho. ***Perf. 12½***

390 A102 50fr multi 50 28

Victory of people of Benin over imperialist forces.

Map, People and Houses of Benin — A103

1978, Feb. 1

391 A103 50fr multi 50 28

General population and dwellings census.

Alexander Fleming, Microscope and Penicillin — A104

1978, Mar. 12 Litho. ***Perf. 13***

392 A104 300fr multi 3.00 1.65

Alexander Fleming (1881-1955), 50th anniversary of discovery of penicillin.

Abdoulaye Issa, Weapons and Fighters A105

1978, Apr. 1 ***Perf. 12½x13***

393 A105 100fr red, blk & gold 1.00 55

First anniversary of death of Abdoulaye Issa and National Day of Benin's Youth.

El Hadj Omar and Horseback Rider — A106

Design: 90fr, L'Almamy Samory Toure (1830-1900) and horseback riders.

1978, Apr. 10 ***Perf. 13x12½***

394 A106 90fr red & multi 90 50
395 A106 100fr multi 1.00 55

African heroes of resistance against colonialism.

ITU Emblem, Satellite, Landscape — A107

1978, May 17 Litho. ***Perf. 13***

396 A107 100fr multi 1.00 55

10th World Telecommunications Day.

Soccer Player, Stadium, Argentina '78 Emblem — A108

Designs (Argentina '78 Emblem and): 300fr, Soccer players and ball (vert.). 500fr, Soccer player, globe with ball on map.

1978, June 1 Litho. ***Perf. 12½***

397 A108 200fr multi 2.00 1.10
398 A108 300fr multi 3.00 1.65
399 A108 500fr multi 5.00 2.75
a. Souvenir sheet of 3 11.00 11.00

11th World Cup Soccer Championship, Argentina, June 1-25. No. 399a contains 3 stamps similar to Nos. 397-399 in changed colors; red marginal inscription and blue border. Size: 190x120mm.

Nos. 397-399a Overprinted in Red Brown:

a. FINALE / ARGENTINE: 3 / HOLLANDE: 1

b. CHAMPION / 1978 / ARGENTINE

c. 3e BRESIL / 4e ITALIE

1978, June 25 Litho. ***Perf. 12½***

400 A108 (a) 200fr multi 2.00 1.10
401 A108 (b) 300fr multi 3.00 1.65
402 A108 (c) 500fr multi 5.00 2.75
a. Souvenir sheet of 3 11.00 11.00

Argentina's victory in 1978 Soccer Championship.

Games' Flag over Africa, Basketball Players — A109

Designs (Games' Emblem and): 60fr, Map of Africa and volleyball players. 80fr, Map of Benin and bicyclists.

1978, July 13 ***Perf. 13x12½***

403 A109 50fr lt bl & multi 50 28
404 A109 60fr ultra & multi 60 35
405 A109 80fr multi 80 50
a. Souvenir sheet of 3 2.00 2.00

3rd African Games, Algiers, July 13-28. No. 405a contains 3 stamps in changed colors similar to Nos. 403-405; rose lilac and black margin. Size: 208-80mm.

Martin Luther King, Jr. — A110

1978, July 30 ***Perf. 12½***

406 A110 300fr multi 3.00 1.65

Martin Luther King, Jr. (1929-1968), American civil rights leader.

Kanna Taxi, Oueme A111

Designs: 60fr, Leatherworker and goods. 70fr, Drummer and tom-toms. 100fr, Metalworker and calabashes.

1978, Aug. 26

407 A111 50fr multi 50 28
408 A111 60fr multi 60 35
409 A111 70fr multi 70 42
410 A111 100fr multi 1.00 55

Getting to know Benin through its provinces.

Map of Italy and Exhibition Poster — A112

1978, Aug. 26 Litho. ***Perf. 13***

411 A112 200fr multi 2.00 1.10

Riccione 1978 Philatelic Exhibition.

Turkeys — A113

Poultry: 20fr, Ducks. 50fr, Chicken. 60fr, Guinea fowl.

1978 Oct. 5 Photo. ***Perf. 12½x13***

412 A113 10fr multi 10 10
413 A113 20fr multi 20 20
414 A113 50fr multi 50 50
415 A113 60fr multi 60 60

Poultry breeding.

Royal Messenger, UPU Emblem A114

Designs (UPU Emblem and): 60fr, Boatsman, ship and car (vert.). 90fr, Special messenger and plane (vert.).

Perf. 13x12½, 12½x13

1978, Oct. 16

416 A114 50fr multi 50 50
417 A114 60fr multi 60 60
418 A114 90fr multi 90 90

Centenary of change of "General Postal Union" to "Universal Postal Union."

Raoul Follereau A115

1978, Dec. 17 Litho. *Perf. 12½*
419 A115 200fr multi 2.00 2.00

Raoul Follereau (1903-1977), apostle to the lepers and educator of the blind.

IYC Emblem A116

Designs: 20fr, Globe as balloon carrying children. 50fr, Children of various races surrounding globe.

1979, Feb. 20 Litho. *Perf. 12x13*
420 A116 10fr multi 10 10
421 A116 20fr multi 20 20
422 A116 50fr multi 50 50

International Year of the Child.

Hydrangea — A117

Flowers: 25fr, Assangokan. 30fr, Geranium. 40fr, Water lilies (horiz.).

Perf. 13x12½, 12½x13
1979, Feb. 28 Litho.
423 A117 20fr multi 20 20
424 A117 25fr multi 25 25
425 A117 30fr multi 30 30
426 A117 40fr multi 40 40

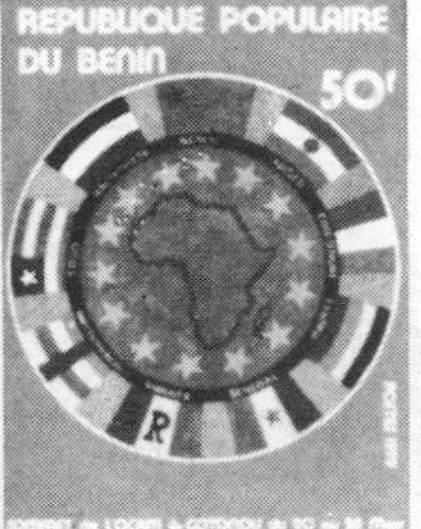

Emblem: Map of Africa and Members' Flags A118

Designs: 60fr, Map of Benin and flags. 80fr, OCAM flag and map of Africa showing member states.

1979, Mar. 20 Litho. *Perf. 12x13*
427 A118 50fr multi 50 50
428 A118 60fr multi 60 60
429 A118 80fr multi 80 80

OCAM Summit Conference, Cotonou, Mar. 20-28.

Tower, Waves, Satellite, ITU Emblem A119

1979, May 17 Litho. *Perf. 12½*
430 A119 50fr multi 50 50

World Telecommunications Day.

Bank Building and Sculpture — A120

1979, May 26 Litho.
431 A120 50fr multi 50 50

Opening of Headquarters of West African Savings Bank in Dakar.

Guelede Mask, Abomey Tapestry, Malaconotus Bird — A121

Design: 50fr, Jet, canoe, satellite, UPU and exhibition emblems.

1979, June 8 Litho. *Perf. 13*
432 A121 15fr multi 15 15

Engr.
433 A121 50fr multi 50 50

Philexafrique II, Libreville, Gabon, June 8-17. Nos. 432, 433 each printed in sheets of 10 with 5 labels showing exhibition emblem.

Nos. 427-429 Overprinted: "26 au 28 juin 1979" and Dots

1979, June 26
434 A118 50fr multi 50 50
435 A118 60fr multi 60 60
436 A118 80fr multi 80 80

2nd OCAM Summit Conference, June 26-28.

Olympic Flame and Emblems A122

Pre-Olympic Year: 50fr, High jump.

1979, July 1 Litho.
437 A122 10fr multi 10 10
438 A122 50fr multi 50 50

Antelope A123

Animals: 10fr, Giraffes, map of Benin (vert.) 20fr, Chimpanzee 50fr, Elephants, map of Benin (vert).

1979, Oct. 1 Litho. *Perf. 13*
439 A123 5fr multi 5 5
440 A123 10fr multi 10 10
441 A123 20fr multi 20 20
442 A123 50fr multi 50 50

Map of Africa, Emblem and Jet — A124

1979, Dec. 12 Litho. *Perf. 12½*
443 A124 50fr multi 50 50
444 A124 60fr multi 60 60

ASECNA (Air Safety Board), 20th anniversary.

Mail Services A125

Design: 50fr, Post Office and headquarters (vert.).

1979, Dec. 19 Litho. *Perf. 13*
445 A125 50fr multi 50 50
446 A125 60fr multi 60 60

Office of Posts and Telecommunications, 20th anniversary.

Lenin and Globe — A126

1980, Apr. 22 Litho. *Perf. 12½*
447 A126 50fr *shown* 40 40
448 A126 150fr *Lenin in library* 1.25 1.25

Lenin, 110th birth anniversary.

Cotonou Club Emblem A127

Galileo, Astrolabe A128

1980, Feb. 23 Litho. *Perf. 12½*
449 A127 90fr *shown* 90 90
450 A127 200fr *Rotary emblem on globe* horiz 2.00

Rotary International, 75th anniversary.

1980, Apr. 2
451 A128 70fr *shown* 70 70
452 A128 100fr *Copernicus, solar system* 1.00 1.00

Discovery of Pluto, 50th anniversary.

Abu Simbel, UNESCO Emblem — A129

1980, Apr. 15 *Perf. 13*
453 A129 50fr *Column*, vert. 50 50
454 A129 60fr *Ramses II*, vert. 60 60
455 A129 150fr *shown* 1.50 1.50

UNESCO campaign to save Nubian monuments, 20th anniversary.

Monument, Martyrs' Square, Cotonou A130

Designs: Various monuments in Martyrs' Square. Cotonou. 60fr, 70fr, 100fr, horiz.

1980, May 2 *Perf. 12½x13, 13x12½*
456 A130 50fr multi 50 50
457 A130 60fr multi 60 60
458 A130 70fr multi 70 70
459 A130 100fr multi 1.00 1.00

Tinbo A131

Musical Instruments: 5fr, Assan (vert.). 15fr, Tam-tam sato (vert.). 20fr, Kora. 30fr, Gangan. 50fr, Sinhoun.

1980, May 20 *Perf. 12½*
460 A131 5fr multi 5 5
461 A131 10fr multi 10 10
462 A131 15fr multi 15 15
463 A131 20fr multi 20 20
464 A131 30fr multi 30 30
465 A131 50fr multi 50 50
Nos. 460-465 (6) 1.30 1.30

First Non-stop Flight, Paris-New York — A132

1980, June 2 Litho. *Perf. 12½*
466 A132 90fr *shown* 90 90
467 A132 100fr *Dieudonne Coste, Maurice Bellonte* 1.00 1.00

Lunokhod I on the Moon — A133

1980, June 15 **Engr.** ***Perf. 13***

468 A133 90fr multi 90 90

Lunokhod I Soviet unmanned moon mission, 10th anniversary. See No. C290.

Olympic Flame and Mischa, Moscow '80 Emblem — A134

1980, July 16 **Litho.** ***Perf. 12½***

469 A134 50fr *shown* 60 60
470 A134 60fr *Equestrian*, vert. 70 70
471 A134 70fr *Judo* 80 80
472 A134 200fr *Flag, sports, globe*, vert. 2.25 2.25
473 A134 300fr *Weight lifting*, vert. 3.50 3.50
Nos. 469-473 (5) 7.85 7.85

22nd Summer Olympic Games, Moscow, July 19-Aug. 3.

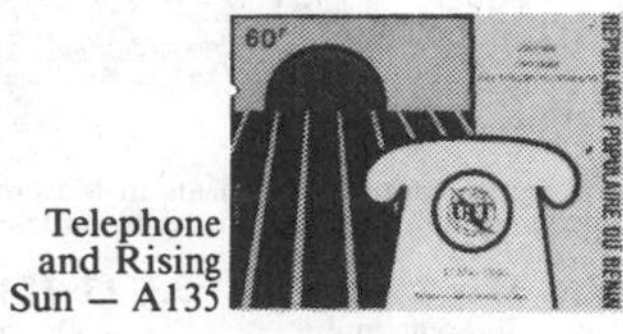

Telephone and Rising Sun — A135

World Telecommunications Day: 50fr, Farmer on telephone (vert.).

1980, May 17 **Litho.** ***Perf. 12½***

474 A135 50fr multi 50 50
475 A135 60fr multi 60 60

Cotonou West African Community Village A136

Designs: Views of Cotonou.

1980, July 26 ***Perf. 13x13½***

476 A136 50fr multi 50 50
477 A136 60fr multi 60 60
478 A136 70fr multi 70 70

Agbadja Dancers — A137

Designs: Dancers and musicians.

1980, Aug. 1 ***Perf. 12½***

479 A137 30fr multi 30 30
480 A137 50fr multi 50 50
481 A137 66fr multi 60 60

Fisherman A138

Philippines under Magnifier A139

Designs: 5fr, Throwing net. 15fr, Canoe and shore fishing. 20fr, Basket traps. 50fr, Hauling net. 60fr, River fishing. All horiz.

1980, Sept. 1

482 A138 5fr multi 5 5
483 A138 10fr multi 10 10
484 A138 15fr multi 15 15
485 A138 20fr multi 20 20
486 A138 50fr multi 50 50
487 A138 60fr multi 60 60
Nos. 482-487 (6) 1.60 1.60

Perf. 13x13½, 13½x13

1980, Sept. 27

World Tourism Conference, Manila, Sept. 27: 60fr, Emblem on flag, hand pointing to Manila on globe (horiz.).

488 A139 50fr multi 50 50
489 A139 60fr multi 60 60

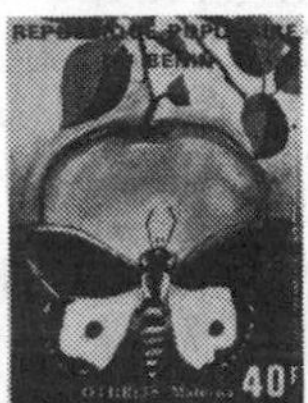

Othreis Materna — A140

1980, Oct. 1 ***Perf. 12½***

490 A140 40fr shown 40 40
491 A140 50fr Othreis fullonia 50 50
492 A140 200fr Oryctes sp. 2.00 2.00

African Postal Union, 5th Anniversary A141

Clasped Hands Breaking Chain, UN Emblem A142

1980, Oct. 24 **Photo.** ***Perf. 13½***

493 A141 75fr multi 75 75

1980, Nov. 4 ***Perf. 12½x13***

494 A142 30fr shown 30 30
495 A142 50fr Freed prisoner 50 50
496 A142 60fr Man holding torch 60 60

Declaration of human rights, 30th anniversary.

Self-portrait, by Vincent van Gogh, 1888 — A143

1980, Dec. 1 **Litho.** ***Perf. 13***

497 A143 100fr shown 1.00 1.00
498 A143 300fr Facteur Roulin 3.00 3.00

Vincent Van Gogh (1853-1890), artist.

Offenbach and Scene from Orpheus in the Underworld — A144

1980, Dec. 15 **Engr.**

499 A144 50fr shown 60 60
500 A144 60fr Paris Life 70 70

Jacques Offenbach (1819-1880), composer.

Kepler and Satellites — A145

1980, Dec. 20

501 A145 50fr Kepler, diagram, vert. 50 50
502 A145 60fr shown 60 60

Johannes Kepler (1571-1630), astronomer, 350th death anniversary.

Intl. Year of the Disabled — A146

1981, Apr. 10 **Litho.** ***Perf. 12½***

503 A146 115fr multi 1.15 1.15

20th Anniv. of Manned Space Flight — A147

1981, May 30 ***Perf. 13***

504 A147 500fr multi 5.00 5.00

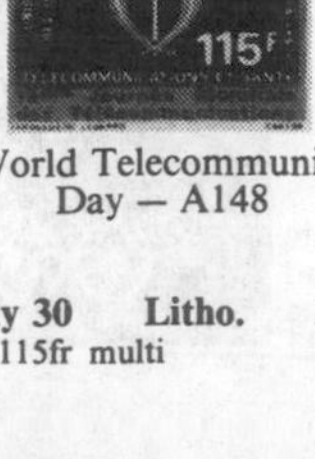

13th World Telecommunications Day — A148

1981, May 30 **Litho.** ***Perf. 12½***

505 A148 115fr multi 1.15 1.15

Amaryllis A149

1981, June 20 ***Perf. 12½***

506 A149 10fr shown 10 10
507 A149 20fr Eischornia crassipes, vert. 20 20
508 A149 80fr Parkia biglobosa, vert. 80 80

Benin Sheraton Hotel A150

1981, July

509 A150 100fr multi 1.00 1.00

Guinea Pig — A151

1981, July 31 ***Perf. 13x13½***

510 A151 5fr shown 5 5
511 A151 60fr Cat 60 60
512 A151 80fr Dogs 80 80

World UPU Day — A152

1981, Oct. 9 **Engr.** ***Perf. 13***

513 A152 100fr red brn & blk 1.00 1.00

25th Intl. Letter Writing Week, Oct. 6-12 — A153

1981, Oct. 15

514 A153 100fr dk bl & pur 1.00 1.00

West African Economic Community A154

1981, Nov. 20 **Litho.** ***Perf. 12½***

515 A154 60fr multi 60 60

West African Rice Development Assoc. 10th Anniv. A155

1981, Dec. 10 ***Perf. 13x13½***
516 A155 60fr multi 60 60

TB Bacillus Centenary A156

1982, Mar. 1 Litho. ***Perf. 13***
517 A156 115fr multi 1.75 1.75

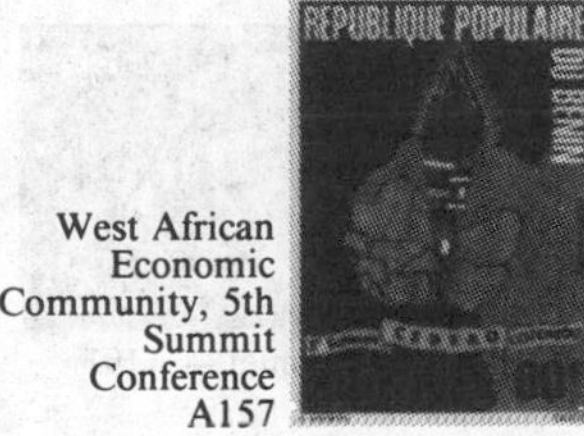
West African Economic Community, 5th Summit Conference A157

1982, May 27 ***Perf. 12½***
518 A157 60fr multi 60 60

1982 World Cup — A158

1982, June 1 ***Perf. 13***
519 A158 90fr Players 1.00 1.00
520 A158 300fr Flags on leg 3.25 3.25

France No. B349 Magnified, Map of France — A159

1982, June 11
521 A159 90fr multi 90 90

PHILEXFRANCE '82 Stamp Exhibition, Paris, June 11-21.

George Washington — A160

1982, Mar. 10 Litho. ***Perf. 14***
522 A160 200fr Washington, flag, map 2.00 2.00

Nos. 519-520 Overprinted with Finalists Names.

1982, Aug. 16 ***Perf. 12½***
523 A158 90fr multi 90 90
524 A158 300fr multi 3.00 3.00

Italy's victory in 1982 World Cup.

Bluethroat A161

1982, Sept. 1 ***Perf. 14x14½, 14½x14***
525 A161 5fr Daoelo gigas, vert. 5 5
526 A161 10fr shown 15 15
527 A161 15fr Swallow, vert. 20 20
528 A161 20fr Kingfisher, weaver bird, vert. 25 25
529 A161 30fr Great sedge warbler 40 40
530 A161 60fr Common warbler 75 75
531 A161 80fr Owl, vert. 95 95
532 A161 100fr Cockatoo, vert. 1.25 1.25
Nos. 525-532 (8) 4.00 4.00

ITU Plenipotentiaries Conference, Nairobi, Sept. — A162

1982, Sept. 26 ***Perf. 13***
533 A162 200fr Map 2.00 2.00

13th World UPU Day — A163

1982, Oct. 9 Engr. ***Perf. 13***
534 A163 100fr Monument 1.00 1.00

Nos. 482, 510, 411 Overprinted in Red or Blue:
#535 "Croix Rouge / 8 Mai 1982"
#536 "UAPT 1982"
#537 "RICCIONE 1982"

Perf. 13, 12½, 13x13½

1982, Nov. Litho.
535 A138 60fr on 5fr multi 60 60
536 A151 60fr on 5fr multi 60 60
537 A112 200fr multi (Bl) 2.00 2.00

Visit of French Pres. Francois Mitterand A164

1983, Jan. 15 Litho. ***Perf. 12½x13***
538 A164 90fr multi 90 90

Nos. 458, 476, 508-509, 512 Surcharged.

Perf. 13x12½, 13x13½, 12½

1983 Litho.
539 A130 60fr on 70fr multi 60 60
540 A136 60fr on 50fr multi 60 60
541 A150 60fr on 100fr multi 60 60
542 A149 75fr on 80fr multi 75 75
543 A151 75fr on 80fr multi 75 75
Nos. 539-543 (5) 3.30 3.30

Seme Oil Rig — A165

1983, Apr. 28 Litho. ***Perf. 13x12½***
544 A165 125fr multi 1.25 1.25

World Communications Year — A166

1983, May 17 Litho. ***Perf. 13***
545 A166 185fr multi 1.85 1.85

Riccione '83, Stamp Show — A167

1983, Aug. 27 Litho. ***Perf. 13***
546 A167 500fr multi 5.00 5.00

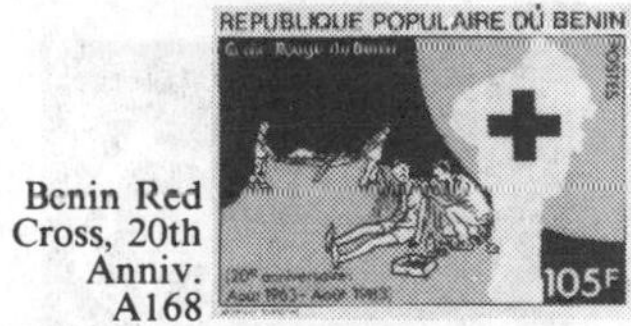
Benin Red Cross, 20th Anniv. A168

1983, Sept. 5 Photo. ***Perf. 13***
547 A168 105fr multi 1.05 1.05

Handicrafts A169

Designs: 75fr, Handcarved lion chairs and table. 90fr, Natural tree table and stools. 200fr, Monkeys holding jar.

1983, Sept. 18 Litho. ***Perf. 13***
548 A169 75fr multi 60 60
549 A169 90fr multi 75 75
550 A169 200fr multi 1.65 1.65

14th UPU Day — A170

1983, Oct. 9 Engr. ***Perf. 13***
551 A170 125fr multi 1.25 1.25

Religious Movements A171

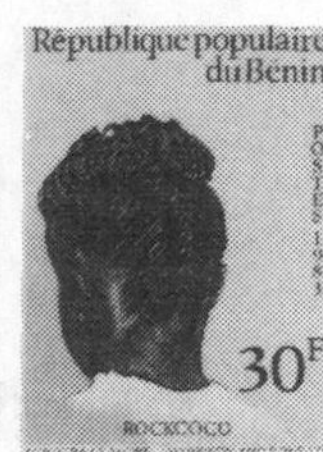
Plaited Hair Styles A172

1983, Oct. 31 Litho. ***Perf. 14x15***
552 A171 75fr Zangbeto 50 50
553 A171 75fr Egoun 50 50

1983, Nov. 14
554 A172 30fr Rockcoco 20 20
555 A172 75fr Serpent 50 50
556 A172 90fr Songas 60 60

Types of 1976-81 Surcharged.

1983, Nov.
557 A139 5fr on 50fr #486 5 5
558 A153 10fr on 100fr #514 8 8
559 A134 15fr on 200fr #472 10 10
560 A98 15fr on 210fr #381 10 10
561 A134 25fr on 70fr #471 18 18
562 A99 25fr on 210fr #384 18 18
563 A151 75fr on 5fr #510 50 50
564 A132 75fr on 100fr #467 50 50
565 A88 75fr on 150fr #360 50 50
566 A88 75fr on 150fr #380 50 50
Nos. 557-566 (10) 2.69 2.69

Alfred Nobel (1833-96) A173

1983, Dec. 19 Litho. ***Perf. 15x14***
567 A173 300fr multi 2.00 2.00

Council of Unity — A174

1984, May 29 Litho. ***Perf. 12***
568 A174 75fr multi 50 50
569 A174 90fr multi 60 60

1984 UPU Congress A175

1984, June 18 Litho. ***Perf. 13***
570 A175 90fr multi 60 60

Abomey Calavi Earth Station A176

1984, June 29 Litho. ***Perf. 12½x13***
571 A176 75fr Satellite dish 50 50

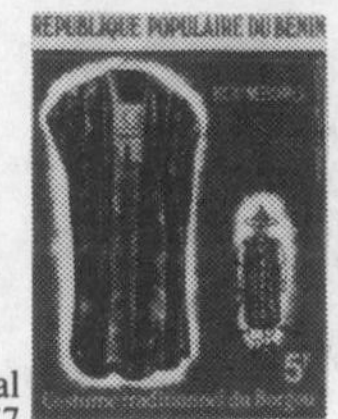
Traditional costumes — A177

1984, July 2 Litho. *Perf. 13½x13*
572 A177 5fr Koumboro 5 5
573 A177 10fr Taka 5 5
574 A177 20fr Toko 10 10

Nos. 389, 498, 503-505, 517, 522, 533, 547, 550 and 551 Surcharged.

1984, Sept.
575 A170 5fr on 125fr multi 5 5
576 A101 5fr on 150fr multi 5 5
577 A160 10fr on 200fr multi 8 8
578 A169 10fr on 200fr multi 8 8
579 A143 15fr on 300fr multi 10 10
580 A147 40fr on 500fr multi 20 20
581 A168 75fr on 105fr multi 50 50
582 A146 75fr on 115fr multi 50 50
583 A148 75fr on 115fr multi 50 50
584 A156 75fr on 115fr multi 50 50
585 A162 75fr on 200fr multi 50 50
Nos. 575-585 (11) 3.06 3.06

World Food Day A178

Dinosaurs A179

1984, Oct. 16 Litho. *Perf. 12½*
586 A178 100fr Malnourished child 45 45

1984, Dec. 14 Litho. *Perf. 13½*
587 A179 75fr Anatosaurus 35 35
588 A179 90fr Brontosaurus 40 40

Cultural & Technical Cooperation Agency, 15th Anniv. — A180

1985, Mar. 20 Litho. *Perf. 13*
589 A180 300fr Emblem, globe, hands, book 1.30 1.30

Stamps of 1977-82 Surcharged.

1985, Mar.
590 A92 75fr on 200fr No. 370 30 30
591 A108 75fr on 200fr No. 397 30 30
592 A110 75fr on 300fr No. 406 30 30
593 A108 75fr on 300fr No. 398 30 30
594 A158 90fr on 300fr No. 520 38 38
595 A108 90fr on 500fr No. 399 38 38
596 A108 90fr on 500fr No. 402 38 38
Nos. 590-596 (7) 2.34 2.34

Traditional Dances A181

1985, June Litho. *Perf. 15x14½*
597 A181 75fr Teke, Borgou Tribe 30 30
598 A181 100fr Tipen'ti, L'Atacora Tribe 42 42

Intl. Youth Year — A182

1985, July 16 *Perf. 13½*
599 A182 150fr multi 70 70

1986 World Cup Soccer Championships, Mexico — A183

1985, July 22 *Perf. 13x12½*
600 A183 200fr multi 90 90

Dahomey No. 336 Ovptd. "REPUBLIQUE POPULAIRE DU BENIN" and Surcharged with Black Bars and New Value.

1985, Aug. *Perf. 12½*
601 A78 15fr on 40fr multi 2828

ASECNA Airlines, 25th Anniv. — A184

1985, Sept. 16 *Perf. 13*
602 A184 150fr multi 70 70

UN 40th Anniv. A185

1985, Oct. 24 *Perf. 12½*
603 A185 250fr multi 1.40 1.40

Benin UN membership, 25th anniv.

ITALIA '85, Rome A186

1985, Oct. 25 *Perf. 13½*
604 A186 200fr multi 1.101.10

PHILEXAFRICA '85, Lome — A187

1985, Nov. 16 *Perf. 13*
605 A187 250fr No. 569, labor emblem 1.40 1.40
606 A187 250fr No. C252, Gabon No. 365, magnified stamp 1.40 1.40

Nos. 605-606 printed se-tenant with center label picturing map of Africa or UAPT emblem.

Audubon Birth Bicent. A188

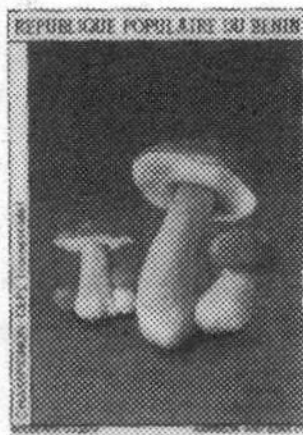
Mushrooms and Toadstools A189

1985, Oct. 17 Litho. *Perf. 14x15*
607 A188 150fr Skua gull 82 82
608 A188 300fr Oyster catcher 1.65 1.65

1985, Oct. 17
609 A189 35fr Boletus edible 20 20
610 A189 40fr Amanite phalloide 22 22
611 A189 100fr Brown chanterelle 55 55

Stamps Inscribed Dahomey Surcharged and Ovptd. with 2 Black Bars and "Populaire Republique du Benin" in 3 lines.

1986, Mar. Photo.
612 A83 75fr on 35fr #343 40 40
613 A57 90fr on 70fr #282 50 50
614 A60 90fr on 140fr #292 50 50

African Parliamentary Union, 10th Anniv. — A190

1986, May 8 Litho. *Perf. 13x12½*
615 A190 100fr multi 55 55

9th Conference, Cotonou, May 8-10.

Halley's Comet — A191

1986, May 30 *Perf. 12½x12*
616 A191 205fr multi 1.10 1.10

Stamps Inscribed Dahomey Surcharged with Bar, "Republique/Populaire/du Benin" and New Value.

Engraved, Photogravure

1986, June *Perf. 13*
617 A58 100fr on 40fr #283 55 55
618 A83 150fr on 45fr #344 82 82

1986 World Cup Soccer Championships, Mexico — A192

1986, June 29 Litho.
619 A192 500fr multi 2.75 2.75

Fight against Desert Encroachment — A193

1986, July 16 *Perf. 13½*
620 A193 150fr multi 82 82

Amazon A194

Flowers A195

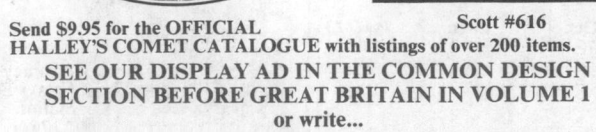

1986, Aug. 1 Engr. *Perf. 13*
622 A194 100fr brt bl 60 60
624 A194 150fr violet 90 90

Perf. 13x12½, 12½x13

1986, Sept. 1 Litho.
631 A195 100fr Haemanthus 65 65
632 A195 205fr Hemerocalle, horiz. 1.40 1.40

Butterflies — A196

Designs: No. 633, Day peacock, little tortoiseshell, morio. No. 634, Aurora, machaon and fair lady.

1986, Sept. 15
633 A196 150fr multi 90 90
634 A196 150fr multi 90 90

Statue of Liberty, Cent. A197

King Behanzin A198

1986, Oct. 28 Litho. *Perf. 12½*
635 A197 250fr multi 1.40 1.40

1986, Oct. 30 *Perf. 13½*
636 A198 440fr multi 2.50 2.50

Behanzin, leader of resistance movement against French occupation (1886-1894).

Brazilian Cultural Week, Cotonou — A200

1987, Jan. 17 *Perf. 12½*
638 A200 150fr multi 88 88

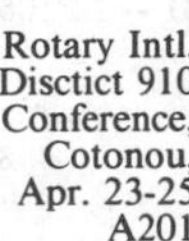

Rotary Intl. Disctict 910 Conference, Cotonou, Apr. 23-25 A201

1987, Apr. 23 Litho. *Perf. 13½*
639 A201 300fr Center for the Blind, Cotonou 1.75 1.75

Automobile Cent. — A202

Modern car and: 150fr, Steam tricycle, by De Dion-Bouton and Trepardoux, 1887. 300fr, Gas-driven Victoria, by Daimler, 1886.

1987, July 1 *Perf. 12½*
640 A202 150fr multi 88 88
641 A202 300fr multi 1.75 1.75

Snake Temple Baptism — A203

1987, July 20 *Perf. 13½*
642 A203 100fr multi 55 55

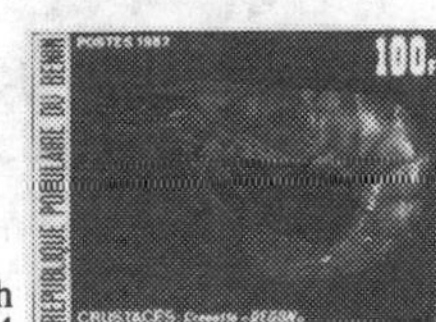

Shellfish A204

1987, July 24 *Perf. 12½*
643 A204 100fr crayfish 55 55
644 A204 150fr crab 90 90

Cure Leprosy — A205

1987, Sept. 4 *Perf. 13*
645 A205 200fr G. Hansen, R. Follereau 1.10 1.10

AIR POST STAMPS

People's Republic

Nativity, by Aert van Leyden — AP84

Paintings: 85fr, Adoration of the Kings, by Rubens (vert.). 140fr, Adoration of the Shepherds, by Charles Lebrun. 300fr, The Virgin with the Blue Diadem, by Raphael (vert.).

1975, Dec. 19 Litho. *Perf. 13*
C240 AP84 40fr gold & multi 40 15
C241 AP84 85fr gold & muli 85 30
C242 AP84 140fr gold & multi 1.20 50
C243 AP84 300fr gold & multi 2.75 1.25

Christmas 1975.

Slalom, Innsbruck Olympic Emblem — AP85

Designs (Innsbruck Olympic Games Emblem and): 150fr, Bobsledding (vert.). 300fr, Figure skating, pairs.

1976, June 28 Litho. *Perf. 12½*
C244 AP85 60fr multi 50 20
C245 AP85 150fr multi 1.25 50
C246 AP85 300fr multi 2.50 1.10

12th Winter Olympic Games, Innsbruck, Austria, Feb. 4-15.

Dahomey Nos. C235-C237 Overprinted: "POPULAIRE / DU BENIN" and Bars, with Surcharge Added on Nos. C236-C237

1976, July 4 Engr. *Perf. 13*
C247 AP82 135fr multi 1.10 50
C248 AP82 210fr on 300fr multi 1.75 70
C249 AP82 380fr on 500fr multi 3.00 1.30

The overprint includes a bar covering "DU DAHOMEY" in shades of brown; "POPULAIRE DU BENIN" is blue on Nos. C247-C248, red on No. C249. The surcharge and bars over old value are blue on No. C248, red, brown on No. C249.

Long Jump AP86

Designs (Olympic Rings and): 150fr, Basketball (vert.). 200fr, Hurdles.

1976, July 16 Photo. *Perf. 13*
C250 AP86 60fr multi 50 20
C251 AP86 150fr multi 1.25 50
C252 AP86 200fr multi 1.65 70
a. Souvenir sheet of 3 3.50 3.50

21st Olympic Games, Montreal, Canada, July 17-Aug 1. No. C252a contains one each of Nos. C250-C252; brown marginal inscription. Size: 150x120mm.

Konrad Adenauer and Cologne Cathedral — AP87

Design: 90fr, Konrad Adenauer (vert.).

1976, Aug. 27 Engr. *Perf. 13*
C253 AP87 90fr multi 70 30
C254 AP87 250fr multi 2.00 80

Konrad Adenauer (1876-1967), German Chancellor, birth centenary.

Children's Heads and Flying Fish (Dahomey Type A32) — AP88

Design: 210fr, Lion cub's head and Benin type A3 (vert.).

1976, Sept. 13
C255 AP88 60fr Prus bl & vio bl 50 20
C256 AP88 210fr multi 1.65 70

JUVAROUEN 76, International Youth Philatelic Exhibition, Rouen, France, Apr. 25-May 2.

Apollo 14 Emblem and Blast-off — AP89

Design: 270fr, Landing craft and man on moon.

1976, Oct. 18 Engr. *Perf. 13*
C257 AP89 130fr multi 1.00 45
C258 AP89 270fr multi 2.25 95

Apollo 14 Moon Mission, 5th anniversary.

Annunciation, by Master of Jativa — AP90

Paintings: 60fr, Nativity, by Gerard David. 270fr, Adoration of the Kings, Dutch School. 300fr, Flight into Egypt, by Gentile Fabriano (horiz.).

1976, Dec. 20 Litho. *Perf. 12½*
C259 AP90 50fr gold & multi 40 25
C260 AP90 60fr gold & multi 50 35
C261 AP90 270fr gold & multi 2.25 95
C262 AP90 300fr gold & multi 2.50 1.50

Christmas 1976.

Gamblers and Lottery Emblem — AP91

1977, Mar. 13 Litho. *Perf. 13*
C263 AP91 50fr multi 40 30

National lottery, 10th anniversary.

Sassenage Castle, Grenoble — AP92

1977, May 16 *Perf. 12½*

C264 AP92 200fr multi 1.25 90

10th anniversary of International French Language Council.

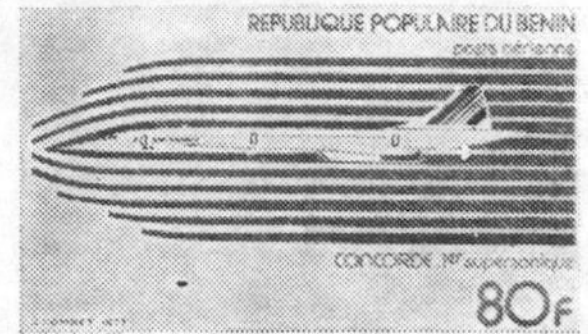

Concorde, Supersonic Plane — AP93

Designs: 150fr, Zeppelin. 300fr, Charles A. Lindbergh and Spirit of St. Louis. 500fr, Charles Nungesser and François Coli, French aviators lost over Atlantic, 1927.

1977, July 25 **Engr.** *Perf. 13*

C265 AP93 80fr ultra & red 65 50
C266 AP93 150fr multi 1.25 90
C267 AP93 300fr multi 2.50 1.80
C268 AP93 500fr multi 4.00 3.00

Aviation history.

Soccer Player — AP94

Design: 200fr, Soccer players and Games' emblem.

1977, July 28 **Litho.** *Perf. 12½x12*

C269 AP94 60fr multi 50 30
C270 AP94 200fr multi 1.65 1.20

World Soccer Cup elimination games.

Miss Haverfield, by Gainsborough — AP95

Designs: 150fr, Self-portrait, by Rubens. 200fr, Anguish, man's head by Da Vinci.

1977, Oct. 3 **Engr.** *Perf. 13*

C271 AP95 100fr sl grn & mar 80 60
C272 AP95 150fr red brn & dk brn 1.25 90
C273 AP95 200fr brn & red 1.65 1.20

Birth anniversaries: Thomas Gainsborough (1727-1788); Peter Paul Rubens (1577-1640); Leonardo da Vinci (1452-1519).

No. C265 Overprinted: "1er VOL COMMERCIAL / 22.11.77 PARIS NEW-YORK"

1977, Nov. 22 **Engr.** *Perf. 13*

C274 AP93 80fr ultra & red 65 50

Concorde, first commercial flight, Paris to New York.

Viking on Mars — AP96

Designs: 150fr, Isaac Newton, apple globe, stars. 200fr, Vladimir M. Komarov, spacecraft and earth. 500fr, Dog Laika, rocket and space.

1977, Nov. 28 **Engr.** *Perf. 13*

C275 AP96 100fr multi 80 60
C276 AP96 150fr multi 1.25 90
C277 AP96 200fr multi 1.65 1.20
C278 AP96 500fr multi 4.00 3.00

Operation Viking on Mars; 250th death anniversary of Isaac Newton (1642-1727); 10th death anniversary of Russian cosmonaut Vladimir M. Komarov; 20th anniversary of first living creature in space.

Monument, Red Star Place, Cotonou AP97

Lithographed; Gold Embossed

1977 Nov. 30 *Perf. 12½*

C279 AP97 500fr multi 4.00 2.50

Suzanne Fourment, by Rubens AP98

Design: 380fr, Nicholas Rubens, By Rubens.

1977, Dec. 12 **Engr.** *Perf. 13*

C280 AP98 200fr multi 1.65 1.20
C281 AP98 380fr cl & ocher 3.00 2.10

Peter Paul Rubens (1577-1640), 400th birth anniversary.

Parthenon and UNESCO Emblem — AP99

Designs: 70fr, Acropolis and frieze showing Pan-Athenaic procession (vert.). 250fr, Parthenon and frieze showing horsemen (vert.).

1978, Sept. 22 **Litho.** *Perf. 12½x12*

C282 AP99 70fr multi 70 40
C283 AP99 250fr multi 2.50 1.50
C284 AP99 500fr multi 5.00 3.00

Save the Parthenon in Athens campaign.

Philexafrique II—Essen Issue

Common Design Types

Designs: No. C285, Buffalo and Dahomey No. C33. No. C286, Wild ducks and Baden No. 1.

1978, Nov. 1 **Litho.** *Perf. 12½*

C285 CD138 100fr multi 1.00 60
C286 CD139 100fr multi 1.00 60

Nos. C285-C286 printed se-tenant.

Wilbur and Orville Wright and Flyer — AP100

1978, Dec. 28 **Engr.** *Perf. 13*

C287 AP100 500fr multi 5.00 3.00

75th anniversary of 1st powered flight.

Cook's Ships, Hawaii, World Map — AP101

Design: 50fr, Battle at Kowrowa.

1979, June 1 **Engr.** *Perf. 13*

C288 AP101 20fr multi 30 30
C289 AP101 50fr multi 70 70

Capt. James Cook (1728-1779), explorer, death bicentenary.

Lunokhod Type of 1980

1980, June 15 **Engr.** *Perf. 13*

Size: 27x48mm.

C290 A133 210fr multi 2.10 2.10

Soccer Players — AP102

1981, Mar. 31 **Litho.** *Perf. 13*

C291 AP102 200fr Ball, globe 2.00 2.00
C292 AP102 500fr shown 5.00 5.00

ESPANA '82 World Soccer Cup eliminations.

Prince Charles and Lady Diana, London Bridge — AP103

1981, July 29 **Litho.** *Perf. 12½*

C293 AP103 500fr multi 5.00 5.00

Royal wedding.

Three Musicians, by Pablo Picasso (1881-1973) — AP104

Perf. 12½x13, 13x12½

1981, Nov. 2 **Litho.**

C294 AP104 300fr Dance, vert. 3.00 3.00
C295 AP104 500fr shown 5.00 5.00

1300th Anniv. of Bulgaria — AP105

1981, Dec. 2 **Litho.** *Perf. 13*

C296 AP105 100fr multi 1.50 1.50

Visit of Pope John Paul II — AP106

1982, Feb. 17 **Litho.** *Perf. 13*

C297 AP106 80fr multi 80 80

20th Anniv. of John Glenn's Flight — AP107

The indexes in each volume of the Scott Catalogue contain many listings which help to identify stamps.

1982, Feb. 21 Litho. *Perf. 13*
C298 AP107 500fr multi 5.00 5.00

Scouting Year AP108

1982, June 1 *Perf. 12½*
C299 AP108 105fr multi 1.05 1.05

Nos. C256, C275 Surcharged.

1982, Nov. Engr. *Perf. 13*
C300 AP88 50fr on 210fr multi 50 50
C301 AP96 50fr on 100fr multi 50 50

Monet in Boat, by Claude Monet (1832-1883) — AP109

1982, Dec. 6 Litho. *Perf. 13x12½*
C302 AP109 300fr multi 3.00 3.00

Christmas 1982 AP110

Virgin and Child Paintings.

1982, Dec. 20 *Perf. 12½x13*
C303 AP110 200fr Matthias Grunewald 2.00 2.00
C304 AP110 300fr Correggio 3.00 3.00

No. C290 Surcharged.

1983 Engr. *Perf. 13*
C305 A133 75fr on 210fr multi 75 75

Bangkok '83 Stamp Exhibition AP111

1983, Aug. 4 Photo. *Perf. 13*
C306 AP111 300fr multi 3.00 3.00

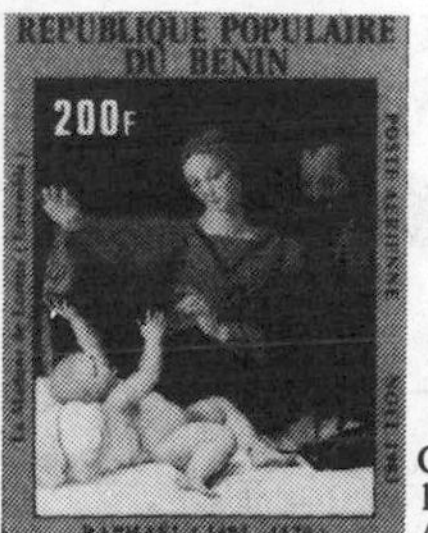

Christmas 1983 AP112

1983, Dec. 26 Litho. *Perf. 12½x13*
C307 AP112 200fr Loretto Madonna, by Raphael 1.00 1.00

Types of 1976-82 Surcharged.

1983, Nov.
C308 AP94 10fr on 200fr #C270 8 8
C309 AP95 15fr on 200fr #C273 10 10
C310 AP90 15fr on 270fr #C261 10 10
C311 AP98 20fr on 200fr #C280 15 15
C312 AP89 25fr on 270fr #C258 18 18
C313 AP98 25fr on 380fr #C281 18 18
C314 AP96 30fr on 200fr #C277 20 20
C315 AP107 40fr on 500fr #C298 30 30
C316 AP93 75fr on 150fr #C266 55 55
C317 AP95 75fr on 150fr #C272 55 55
Nos. C308-C317 (10) 2.39 2.39

Summer Olympics — AP113

1984, July 16 Litho. *Perf. 13x13½*
C318 AP113 300fr Sam the Eagle, mascot 1.50 1.50

Nos. C262, C293-C294, C299, C302-C303, C306-C307 Surcharged.

1984, Sept.
C319 AP112 15fr on 200fr multi 8 8
C320 AP104 15fr on 300fr multi 8 8
C321 AP90 25fr on 300fr multi 14 14
C322 AP111 25fr on 300fr multi 14 14
C323 AP103 40fr on 500fr multi 20 20
C324 AP108 75fr on 105fr multi 38 38
C325 AP110 90fr on 200fr multi 45 45
C326 AP109 90fr on 300fr multi 45 45
Nos. C319-C326 (8) 1.92 1.92

Christmas 1984 AP114

1984, Dec. 17 Litho. *Perf. 12½x13*
C327 AP114 500fr Virgin and Child, by Murillo 2.25 2.25

Ships — AP115

1984, Dec. 28 Litho. *Perf. 13*
C328 AP115 90fr Sidon merchant ship 45 45
C329 AP115 125fr Wavertree, vert. 55 55

Benin-S.O.M. Postal Convention AP116

1985, Apr. 15 Litho. *Perf. 13½*
C330 AP116 75fr Benin arms 32 32
C331 AP116 75fr Sovereign Order of Malta 32 32

Se-tenant.

PHILEXAFRICA III, Lome — AP117

1985, June 24 *Perf. 13*
C332 AP117 200fr Oil platform 85 85
C333 AP117 200fr Soccer players 85 85

Nos. C332-C333 printed se-tenant with center labels picturing the conference emblem or a map of Africa showing Lome.

Stamps of 1977-82 Surcharged.

1985, Mar.
C334 AP92 75fr on 200fr No. C264 30 30
C335 AP102 75fr on 200fr No. C291 30 30
C336 AP93 75fr on 300fr No. C267 30 30
C337 AP110 75fr on 300fr No. C304 30 30
C338 AP99 90fr on 500fr No. C284 38 38
C339 AP100 90fr on 500fr No. C287 38 38
C340 AP104 90fr on 500fr No. C295 38 38
Nos. C334-C340 (7) 2.34 2.34

Dahomey Stamps of 1971-75 Ovptd. "REPUBLIQUE POPULAIRE DU BENIN" or "POPULAIRE DU BENIN" and Surcharged with Black Bar and New Value.

1985, Aug.
C341 AP83 25fr on 40fr No. C238 12 12
C342 AP49 40fr No. C142 18 18
C343 AP56 75fr on 85fr No. C164 30 30
C344 AP60 75fr on 100fr No. C173 30 30
C345 AP64 75fr on 125fr No. C186 30 30
C346 AP56 90fr on 20fr No. C163 38 38
C347 A61 90fr on 150fr No. C153 38 38
C348 AP49 90fr on 200fr No. C143 38 38
C349 AP76 90fr on 200fr No. C221 38 38
C350 AP76 150fr No. C220 70 70
Nos. C341-C350 (10) 3.42 3.42

Christmas — AP118

1985, Dec. 20 Litho. *Perf. 13x12½*
C351 AP118 500fr multi 2.75 2.75

Stamps of Dahomey Surcharged and Ovptd. with 2 BlackBars and "Republique Populaire du Benin" in 3 lines.

1986, Mar. Photo.
C352 AP33 75fr on 70fr #C84 40 40
C353 AP14 75fr on 100fr #C34 40 40
C354 AP15 75fr on 200fr #C35 40 40
C355 AP15 90fr on 250fr #C36 50 50

Stamps of Dahomey Ovptd. or Surcharged with One or Two Bars, "Republique/Populaire/du Benin"

1986, June Photo. *Perf. 12½*
C356 AP45 100fr #C131 55 55
C357 AP14 150fr on 500fr #C37 82 82

Christmas — AP119

1986, Dec. 24 Litho. *Perf. 13x12½*
C358 AP119 300fr multi 1.75 1.75

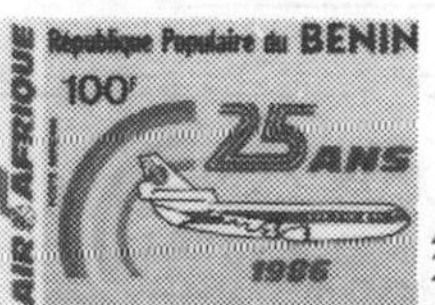

Air Africa, 25th Anniv. AP120

1986, Dec. 30 *Perf. 12½*
C359 AP120 100fr multi 58 58

Intl. Agricultural Development Fund (FIDA), 10th Anniv. — AP121

1987, Dec. 14 Litho. *Perf. 13½*
C360 AP121 500fr multi 3.50 3.50

POSTAGE DUE STAMPS

French Colony

Handstamped in Black on Postage Due Stamps of French Colonies

BENIN

1894 Unwmk. *Imperf.*
J1 D1 5c black 100.00 45.00
J2 D1 10c black 100.00 45.00
J3 D1 20c black 100.00 45.00
J4 D1 30c black 100.00 45.00

Nos. J1-J4 exist with overprint in various positions.

PEOPLE'S REPUBLIC

Pineapples D6

Mail Delivery D7

Designs: 20fr, Cashew (vert.). 40fr, Oranges. 50fr, Akee. 80fr, Mail delivery by boat.

1978, Sept. 5 Photo. *Perf. 13*
J44 D6 10fr multi 12 10
J45 D6 20fr multi 18 15
J46 D6 40fr multi 38 25
J47 D6 50fr multi 55 38

Engr.
J48 D7 60fr multi 42 35
J49 D7 80fr multi 55 42
Nos. J44-J49 (6) 2.20 1.65

PARCEL POST STAMPS

Nos. 448, 459, 473 Overprinted "Colis Postaux"

Perf. 12½, 13x12½

1982, Nov. Litho.
Q8 A126 100fr on 150fr multi 60 30
Q9 A130 100fr multi 60 30
Q10 A134 300fr multi 1.75 90

BHUTAN

LOCATION — Eastern Himalayas
GOVT. — Kingdom
AREA — 18,000 sq. mi.
POP. — 1,250,000 (est. 1983)
CAPITAL — Thimphu

100 Chetrum = 1 Ngultrum or Rupee

Postal Runner — A1

Designs: 3ch, 70ch, Archer. 5ch, 1.30nu, Yak. 15ch, Map of Bhutan, portrait of Druk Gyalpo (Dragon King) Ugyen Wangchuk (1867-1902) and Paro Dzong (fortress-monastery). 33ch, Postal runner. All horiz. except 2ch and 33ch.

Perf. 14x14½, 14½x14

1962 Litho. Unwmk.
1 A1 2ch red & gray 5 5
2 A1 3ch red & ultra 15 15
3 A1 5ch grn & brn 60 60
4 A1 15ch red, blk & org yel 8 8
5 A1 33ch bl grn & lil 15 15
6 A1 70ch dp ultra & lt bl 45 45
7 A1 1.30nu bl & blk 1.25 1.25
Nos. 1-7 (7) 2.73 2.73

Nos. 1-7 were issued for inland use in April, 1962, and became valid for international mail on Oct. 10, 1962.

Refugee Year Emblem and Arms of Bhutan A2

1962, Oct. 10 *Perf. 14½x14*
8 A2 1nu dk bl & dk car rose 60 60
9 A2 2nu yel grn & red lil 1.50 1.50

World Refugee Year.

Equipment of Ancient Warrior A3

Boy Filling Grain Box and Wheat Emblem A4

1963 Unwmk. *Perf. 14x14½*
10 A3 33ch multi 20 20
11 A3 70ch multi 40 40
12 A3 1.30nu multi 90 90

Bhutan's membership in Colombo Plan.

1963, Sept. 17 *Perf. 13½x14*
13 A4 20ch lt bl, yel & red brn 25 25
14 A4 1.50nu rose lil, bl & red brn 1.00 1.00

Issued for the "Freedom from Hunger" Campaign of the U.N. Food and Agriculture Organization.

Masked Dancer — A5

Various Bhutanese Dancers (Five Designs; 2ch, 5ch, 20ch, 1nu, 1.30nu vertical)

1964, Mar. *Perf. 14½x14, 14x14½*
15 A5 2ch bl grn & brn 5 5
16 A5 3ch lt vio & blk 7 7
17 A5 5ch lt ultra & dk bl 7 7
18 A5 20ch yel & red 8 8
19 A5 33ch gray & blk 15 15
20 A5 70ch emer & blk 35 35
21 A5 1nu cit & red 60 60
22 A5 1.30nu bis & dk bl 70 70
23 A5 2nu org & blk 1.10 1.10
Nos. 15-23 (9) 3.17 3.17

Stone Throwing — A6

Sport: 5ch, 33ch, Boxing. 1nu, 3nu, Archery. 2nu, Soccer.

1964, Oct. 10 Litho. *Perf. 14½*
24 A6 2ch emer & multi 5 5
25 A6 5ch org & multi 7 7
26 A6 15ch brt cit & multi 8 8
27 A6 33ch rose lil & multi 15 15
28 A6 1nu multi 50 50
29 A6 2nu rose lil & multi 80 80
30 A6 3nu lt bl & multi 1.25 1.25
Nos. 24-30 (7) 2.90 2.90

Issued to commemorate the 18th Olympic Games, Tokyo, Oct. 10-25. See No. B4.
Nos. 24-30 exist imperf. Price $4.

Flags of the World at Half-mast — A7

1964, Nov. 22 Unwmk. *Perf. 14½*
Flags in Original Colors
31 A7 33ch stl gray 20 20
32 A7 1nu silver 75 75
33 A7 3nu gold 1.75 1.75
a. Souv. sheets per. 13½, imperf. 4.25 4.25

Issued in memory of those who died in the service of their country. Nos. 31-33 exist imperf.
No. 33a contains 2 stamps similar to Nos. 32-33 with flag of Bhutan and gold inscription in margin. Size: 83x118mm.

Primrose — A8

Flowers: 5ch, 33ch, Gentian. 50ch, 1nu, Rhododendron. 75ch, 2nu, Peony.

1964, Dec. Litho. *Perf. 13*
34 A8 2ch lt bl, vio bl & grn 5 5
35 A8 5ch vio, grn & yel 6 6
36 A8 15ch yel, vio & grn 10 10
37 A8 33ch gray, vio bl & grn 15 15
38 A8 50ch lt gray, grn & car 25 25
39 A8 75ch lt grn, yel & brn 40 40
40 A8 1nu pink, grn & dk gray 45 45
41 A8 2nu sep, yel & grn 95 95
Nos. 34-41 (8) 2.41 2.41

Nos. 5, 40, 32, 41 and 33 Overprinted: "WINSTON CHURCHILL 1874-1965"

1965, Feb. 27
42 A1 33ch bl grn & lil 25 25
43 A8 1nu pink, grn & dk gray 65 65
44 A7 1nu sil & multi 65 65
45 A8 2nu sep, yel & grn 1.10 1.10
46 A7 3nu gold & multi 1.50 1.50
Nos. 42-46 (5) 4.15 4.15

Issued in memory of Sir Winston Churchill (1874-1965), British statesman. The overprint is in three lines on Nos. 42-43 and 45; in two lines on Nos. 43 and 46.
Nos. 44 and 46 exist imperf. Price, both, $4.50.

Skyscraper, Pagoda and World's Fair Emblem — A9

Designs: 10ch, 2nu, Pieta by Michelangelo and statue of Khmer Buddha. 20ch, Skyline of New York and Bhutanese village. 33ch, George Washington Bridge, N. Y., and foot bridge, Bhutan.

1965, Apr. 21 Litho. *Perf. 14½*
47 A9 1ch bl & multi 5 5
48 A9 10ch grn & multi 8 8
49 A9 20ch rose lil & multi 12 12
50 A9 33ch bis & multi 18 18
51 A9 1.50nu bis & multi 75 75
52 A9 2nu multi 1.00 1.00
a. Souv. sheets perf. 13½, imperf. 3.00 3.00
Nos. 47-52 (6) 2.18 2.18

Nos. 47-52 exist imperf.; price $3.50.
No. 52a contains two stamps similar to Nos. 51-52. World's Fair emblems in margin in bister and inscription in black. Size: 118½x86½mm.

Telstar, Short-wave Radio and ITU Emblem — A10

Designs (ITU Emblem and): 2nu, Telstar and Morse key. 3nu, Syncom and ear phones.

1966, March 2 Litho. *Perf. 14½*
53 A10 35ch multi 15 15
54 A10 2nu multi 70 70
55 A10 3nu multi 1.00 1.00

Issued to commemorate the centenary (in 1965) of the International Telecommunication Union. Souvenir sheets exist containing two stamps similar to Nos. 54-55, perf. 13½ and imperf. Dark blue margin with white inscription and pictures of satellites in space. Size: 119x78mm. Price, 2 sheets, $5.

Leopard — A11

Animals: 1ch, 4nu, Asiatic black bear. 4ch, 2nu, Pigmy hog. 8ch, 75ch, Tiger. 10ch, 1.50nu, Dhole (Asiatic hunting dog). 1nu, 5nu, Takin (goat).

1966 Litho. *Perf. 13*
56 A11 1ch yel & blk 10 10
57 A11 2ch pale grn & blk 10 10
58 A11 4ch lt cit & blk 10 10
59 A11 8ch lt bl & blk 10 10
60 A11 10ch lt lil & blk 10 10
61 A11 75ch lt yel grn & blk 30 30
62 A11 1nu lt grn & blk 75 75
63 A11 1.50nu lt bl grn & blk 60 60
64 A11 2nu dl org & blk 75 75
65 A11 3nu bluish lil & blk 1.10 1.10
66 A11 4nu lt grn & blk 1.50 1.50
67 A11 5nu pink & blk 2.00 2.00
Nos. 56-67 (12) 7.50 7.50

Issue dates: Nos. 56-60, 62, March 28; Nos. 61, 63-67, Apr. 26.

Nos. 6-9, 20-23 Surcharged

10 CH

1965(?) *Perf. 14½x14, 14x14½*
68 A2 5ch on 1nu dk bl & dk car rose
69 A2 5ch on 2nu yel grn & red lil
70 A5 10ch on 70ch multi
71 A5 10ch on 2nu multi
72 A1 15ch on 70ch dp ultra & lt bl
73 A1 15ch on 1.30nu bl & blk
74 A5 20ch on 1nu multi
75 A5 20ch on 1.30nu multi
Nos. 68-75 (8) 110.

The surcharges on Nos. 68-69 contain two bars at left and right obliterating the denomination on both sides of the design. Four bars on Nos. 72-73.

Simtokha Dzong A12

A particular stamp may be scarce, but if few collectors want it, its market value may remain relatively low.

Tashichho Dzong — A13

Daga Dzong A14

Designs: 5ch, Rinpung Dzong. 50ch, Tongsa Dzong. 1nu, Lhuntsi Dzong.

Perf. 14½x14 (A12), 13½ (A13, A14)

1966-70 Photo.

76	A12	5ch org brn ('67)	12	8
77	A13	10ch dk grn & rose vio ('68)	12	8
78	A12	15ch brown	12	8
79	A12	20ch green	20	20
80	A13	50ch bl grn ('68)	30	20
81	A14	75ch dk bl & ol gray ('70)	30	30
82	A14	1nu dk vio & vio bl ('70)	40	40
		Nos. 76-82 (7)	1.56	1.34

Sizes: 5ch, 15ch, 20ch, 37x20½mm. 10ch, 53½x28½mm. 50ch, 35½x25½mm.

Certain unlisted issues of Bhutan, starting in 1966, are mentioned and briefly described in "For the Record" at the back of this volume.

Mahatma Gandhi — A14a

1969, Oct. 2 Litho. *Perf. 13x13½*

83	A14a	20ch lt bl & brn	60	60
84	A14a	2nu lem & brn ol	1.50	1.50

Mohandas K. Gandhi (1869-1948), leader in India's struggle for independence, birth centenary.

Various Forms of Mail Transport, UPU Headquarters, Bern — A14b

1970, Feb. 25 Photo. *Perf. 13½*

85	A14b	3ch ol grn & gold	15	15
86	A14b	10ch red brn & gold	15	15
87	A14b	20ch Prus bl & gold	20	20
88	A14b	2.50nu dp mag & gold	1.00	1.00

New Headquarters of Universal Postal Union, Bern, Switzerland.
Exist imperf. Price $4.

Wangdiphodrang Dzong and Bridge — A15

1971-73 Photo. *Perf. 13½*

89	A15	2ch gray ('73)	5	5
90	A15	3ch dp red lil ('73)	5	5
91	A15	4ch vio ('73)	5	5
92	A15	5ch dk grn	15	15
93	A15	10ch org brn	15	15
94	A15	15ch dp bl	15	15
95	A15	20ch dp plum	15	15
		Nos. 89-95 (7)	75	75

U.N. Emblem and Bhutan Flag — A16

Designs (Bhutan Flag and): 10ch, U.N. Headquarters, New York. 20ch, Security Council Chamber and mural by Per Krohg. 3nu, General Assembly Hall.

1971, Sept. 21 Photo. *Perf. 13½*

96	A16	5ch gold, bl & multi	5	5
97	A16	10ch gold & multi	5	5
98	A16	20ch gold & multi	6	6
99	A16	3nu gold & multi	85	85
		Nos. 96-99,C1-C3 (7)	1.81	1.81

Bhutan's admission to the United Nations. Exist imperf.

Boy Scout Crossing Stream in Rope Sling — A17

Designs (Emblem and Boy Scouts): 20ch, 2nu, mountaineering. 50ch, 6nu, reading map. 75ch, as 10ch.

1971, Nov. 30 Litho. *Perf. 13½*

143	A17	10ch gold & multi	5	5
144	A17	20ch gold & multi	7	7
145	A17	50ch gold & multi	17	17
146	A17	75ch sil & multi	25	25
147	A17	2nu sil & multi	65	65
148	A17	6nu sil & multi	2.00	2.00
a.		Souvenir sheet of 2	2.75	2.75
		Nos. 143-148 (6)	3.19	3.19

60th anniversary of the Boy Scouts. No. 148a contains one each of Nos. 147-148 and 2 labels. Silver fleur-de-lis pattern on labels and margin. Size: 92½x92½mm. Exist imperf.

Nos. 87-90 Overprinted in Gold

UNHCR
UNRWA
1971

1971, Dec. 23

149	A16	5ch gold & multi	5	5
150	A16	10ch gold & multi	5	5
151	A16	20ch gold & multi	7	7
152	A16	3nu gold & multi	1.00	1.00
		Nos. 149-152,C4-C6 (7)	1.85	1.85

World Refugee Year. Exist imperf.

Book Year Emblem A17a

1972, May 15 Photo. *Perf. 13½x13*

153	A17a	2ch multi	8	8
154	A17a	3ch multi	8	8
155	A17a	5ch multi	12	8
156	A17a	20ch multi	25	10

International Book Year.

King Jigme Singye Wangchuk and Royal Crest — A18

Designs (King and): 25ch, 90ch, Flag of Bhutan. 1.25nu, Wheel with 8 good luck signs. 2nu, 4nu, Punakha Dzong, former winter capital. 3nu, 5nu, Crown. 5ch, same as 10ch.

1974, June 2 Litho. *Perf. 13½*

157	A18	10ch mar & multi	5	5
158	A18	25ch gold & multi	10	10
159	A18	1.25nu multi	45	45
160	A18	2nu gold & multi	70	70
161	A18	3nu multi	1.00	1.00
		Nos. 157-161 (5)	2.30	2.30

Souvenir Sheets

Perf. 13½, Imperf.

162	A18	Sheet of 2	2.00	2.00
a.		5ch mar & multi	5	
b.		5nu red org & multi	1.70	
163	A18	Sheet of 2	2.00	2.00
a.		90ch gold & multi	45	
b.		4nu gold & multi	1.40	

Coronation of King Jigme Singye Wangchuk, June 2, 1974. Nos. 162-163 have maroon and multicolored borders with picture of the king wearing peacock crown. Size: 177x127mm.

Mailman on Horseback A19

Old and New Locomotives A20

Designs (UPU Emblem, Carrier Pigeon and): 3ch, Sailing and steam ships. 4ch, Old biplane and jet. 25ch, Mail runner and jeep.

1974, Oct. 9 Litho. *Perf. 14½*

164	A19	1ch grn & multi	5	5
165	A20	2ch lil & multi	5	5
166	A20	3ch ocher & multi	5	5
167	A20	4ch yel grn & multi	5	5
168	A20	25ch sal & multi	10	10
		Nos. 164-168,C7-C9 (8)	3.65	3.65

Centenary of Universal Postal Union. Issued in sheets of 50 and sheets of 5 plus label with multicolored margin. Exist imperf.

Family and WPY Emblem — A21

1974, Dec. 17 *Perf. 13½*

169	A21	25ch bl & multi	6	6
170	A21	50ch org & multi	12	12
171	A21	90ch ver & multi	22	22
172	A21	2.50nu brn & multi	60	60
a.		Souv. sheet, 10nu	3.50	3.50

Sephisa Chandra — A22

Designs: Indigenous butterflies.

1975, Sept. Litho. *Perf. 14½*

173	A22	1ch *shown*	5	5
174	A22	2ch *Lethe kansa*	5	5
175	A22	3ch *Neope bhadra*	5	5
176	A22	4ch *Euthalia duda*	5	5
177	A22	5ch *Vindula erota*	5	5
178	A22	10ch *Bhutanitis Lidderdale*	5	5
179	A22	3nu *Limenitis zayla*	90	90
180	A22	5nu *Delis thysbe*	2.00	2.00
		Nos. 173-180 (8)	3.20	3.20

Souvenir Sheet

Perf. 13

181	A22	10nu *Dabasa gyas*	3.75	3.75

No. 181 contains one stamp; Bhutanese landscape in multicolored margin. Size: 115x90mm.

Apollo and Apollo-Soyuz Emblem — A23

Design: No. 183, Soyuz and emblem.

1975, Oct. Litho. *Perf. 14x13½*

182	A23	10nu multi	3.50	3.50
183	A23	10nu multi	3.50	3.50
a.		Souvenir sheet of 2, 15nu	12.00	12.00

Apollo Soyuz link-up in space, July 17. Nos. 182-183 printed se-tenant in sheets of 10. No. 183a contains two 15nu stamps similar to Nos 182-183; light green margin with U.S. and U.S.S.R. flags and Apollo-Soyuz emblem. Size: 130x90mm. Exist imperf.

Jewelry A24

Designs: 2ch, Coffee pot, bell and sugar cup. 3ch, Container and drinking horn. 4ch, Pendants and box cover. 5ch, Painter. 15ch, Silversmith. 20ch, Wood carver with tools. 1.50nu, Mat maker. 5nu, 10nu, Printer.

1975, Nov. *Perf. 14½*

184	A24	1ch multi	5	5
185	A24	2ch multi	5	5
186	A24	3ch multi	5	5
187	A24	4ch multi	5	5
188	A24	5ch multi	5	5
189	A24	15ch multi	5	5
190	A24	20ch multi	6	6
191	A24	1.50nu multi	45	45
192	A24	10nu multi	3.00	3.00
		Nos. 184-192 (9)	3.81	3.81

Souvenir Sheet

Perf. 13

193	A24	5nu multi	1.50	1.50

Handicrafts and craftsmen. No. 193 contains one stamp; multicolored margin with black inscription. Size: 105x80mm.

King Jigme Singye Wangchuk A25

Designs: 25ch, 90ch, 1nu, 2nu, 4nu, like 15ch. 1.30nu, 3nu, 5nu, Coat of arms. Sizes (Diameter): 15ch, 1nu, 1.30nu, 38mm. 25ch, 2nu, 3nu, 49mm. 90ch, 4nu, 5nu, 63mm.

Lithographed, Embossed on Gold Foil

1975, Nov. 11 ***Imperf.***

No.	Type	Description	Unused	Used
194	A25	15ch emerald	5	5
195	A25	25ch emerald	8	8
196	A25	90ch emerald	28	28
197	A25	1nu brt car	30	30
198	A25	1.30nu brt car	35	35
199	A25	2nu brt car	50	50
200	A25	3nu brt car	80	80
201	A25	4nu brt car	1.20	1.20
202	A25	5nu brt car	1.50	1.50
		Nos. 194-202 (9)	5.06	5.06

King Jigme Singye Wangchuk's 20th birthday.

Rhododendron Cinnabarinum A28

Designs (Rhododendron): 2ch, Campanulatum. 3ch, Fortunei. 4ch, Red arboreum. 5ch, Pink arboreum. 1nu, Falconeri. 3nu, Hodgsonii. 5nu, Keysii. 10nu, Cinnabarinum.

1976, Feb. 15 Litho. ***Perf. 15***

No.	Type	Description	Unused	Used
203	A28	1ch rose & multi	5	5
204	A28	2ch lt grn & multi	5	5
205	A28	3ch gray & multi	5	5
206	A28	4ch lil & multi	5	5
207	A28	5ch ol gray & multi	5	5
208	A28	1nu brn org & multi	30	24
209	A28	3nu ultra & multi	90	72
210	A28	5nu gray & multi	1.50	1.20
		Nos. 203-210 (8)	2.95	2.41

Souvenir Sheet

Perf. 13½

No.	Type	Description	Unused	Used
211	A28	10numulti	3.50	3.50

No. 211 contains one stamp; multicolored margin showing rhododendrons around pool. Size: 105x80mm.

Slalom and Olympic Games Emblem — A29

Designs (Olympic Games Emblem and): 2ch, 4-men bobsled. 3ch, Ice hockey. 4ch, Cross-country skiing. 5ch, Figure skating, women's. 2nu, Downhill skiing. 4nu, Speed skating. 6nu, Ski jump. 10nu, Figure skating, pairs.

1976, Mar. 29 Litho. ***Perf. 13½***

No.	Type	Description	Unused	Used
212	A29	1ch multi	5	5
213	A29	2ch multi	5	5
214	A29	3ch multi	5	5
215	A29	4ch multi	5	5
216	A29	5ch multi	5	5
217	A29	2nu multi	50	45
218	A29	4nu multi	1.20	90
219	A29	10nu multi	3.00	2.25
		Nos. 212-219 (8)	4.95	3.85

Souvenir Sheet

No.	Type	Description	Unused	Used
220	A29	6nu multi	2.00	2.00

12th Winter Olympic Games, Innsbruck, Austria, Feb. 4-15. No. 220 has orange and brown margin showing ski jump. Size: 78x104mm.

Orchid A30

Designs: Various orchids.

1976, June Litho. ***Perf. 14½***

No.	Type	Description	Unused	Used
221	A30	1ch multi	5	5
222	A30	2ch multi	5	5
223	A30	3ch multi	5	5
224	A30	4ch multi	5	5
225	A30	5ch multi	5	5
226	A30	2nu multi	60	45
227	A30	4nu multi	1.20	90
228	A30	6nu multi	1.80	1.50
		Nos. 221-228 (8)	3.85	3.10

Souvenir Sheet

Perf. 13½

No.	Type	Description	Unused	Used
229	A30	10numulti	3.25	3.00

No. 229 contains one stamp; multicolored margin with orchid design. Size: 106x80mm.

Double Carp Design A31

Designs: Various symbolic designs and Colombo Plan emblem.

1976, July 1 Litho. ***Perf. 14½***

No.	Type	Description	Unused	Used
230	A31	3ch red & multi	5	5
231	A31	4ch ver & multi	5	5
232	A31	5ch multi	5	5
233	A31	25ch bl & multi	20	15
234	A31	1.25nu multi	38	30
335	A31	2nu yel & multi	60	48
236	A31	2.50nu vio & multi	75	60
237	A31	3nu multi	90	72
		Nos. 230-237 (8)	2.98	2.40

Colombo Plan, 25th anniversary.

Bandaranaike Conference Hall — A32

1976, Aug. 16 Litho. ***Perf. 13½***

No.	Type	Description	Unused	Used
238	A32	1.25nu multi	45	30
239	A32	2.50nu multi	85	60

5th Summit Conference of Non-aligned Countries, Colombo, Sri Lanka, Aug. 9-19.

Queen Elizabeth II — A33

Liberty Bell — A34

Spirit of St. Louis — A35

Bhutanese Archer, Olympic Rings — A36

Designs: No. 242, Alexander Graham Bell. No. 245, LZ 3 Zeppelin docking, 1907. No. 246, Alfred B. Nobel.

1978, Nov. 15 Litho. ***Perf. 14½***

No.	Type	Description	Unused	Used
240	A33	20nu multi	6.00	6.00
241	A34	20nu multi	6.00	6.00
242	A33	20nu multi	6.00	6.00
243	A35	20nu multi	6.00	6.00
244	A36	20nu multi	6.00	6.00
245	A35	20nu multi	6.00	6.00
246	A33	20nu multi	6.00	6.00
		Nos. 240-246 (7)	42.00	42.00

Commemoration: 25th anniversary of coronation of Queen Elizabeth II; American Bicentennial; centenary of first telephone call by Alexander Graham Bell; Charles A. Lindbergh crossing the Atlantic, 50th anniversary; Olympic Games; 75th anniversary of the Zeppelin; 75th anniversary of Nobel Prize. Seven souvenir sheets exist, each 25nu, commemorating same events with different designs. Size: 103x80mm.

Issues of 1967-1976 Surcharged with New Value and Bars

Perforations and Printing as Before

1978

No.	Type	Description	Unused	Used
252	A16	25ch on 3nu (#99)		
253	A17	25ch on 6nu (#148)		
254	A21	25ch on 2.50nu (#172)		
255	A22	25ch on 3nu (#179)		
256	A22	25ch on 5nu (#180)		
257	A23	25ch on 10nu (#182)		
258	A23	25ch on 10nu (#183)		
259	A24	25ch on 10nu (#192)		
260	A28	25ch on 5nu (#210)		
261	A29	25ch on 4nu (#218)		
262	A29	25ch on 10nu (#219)		
263	A30	25ch on 4nu (#227)		
264	A30	25ch on 6nu (#228)		
265	A31	25ch on 2.50nu (#236)		
266		25ch on 5nu *Girl Scout*		
267		25ch on 3nu *INDIPEX*		
268		25ch on 4nu *Dog*		
269		25ch on 8nu *Dogs*		
		Nos. 252-269, C11-C18	37.50	37.50

Nos. 266-269 on unlisted issues (see For the Record).

Mother and Child, IYC Emblem — A37

IYC Emblem and: 5nu, Mother and two children. 10nu, Boys with blackboards and stylus.

1979, June Litho. ***Perf. 14x13½***

No.	Type	Description	Unused	Used
289	A37	2nu multi	65	50
290	A37	5nu multi	1.60	1.25
291	A37	10nu multi	3.00	2.50
a.		Souvenir sheet of 3	5.50	4.50

International Year of the Child. No. 291a contains Nos. 289-291, perf. 15x13½, and label; olive green decorative margin. Size: 130x103mm.

Conference Emblem and Dove — A38

Design: 10nu, Emblem and Bhutanese symbols.

1979, Sept. 3 Litho. ***Perf. 14x13½***

No.	Type	Description	Unused	Used
292	A38	25ch multi	8	6
293	A38	10nu multi	3.25	2.50

6th Non-Aligned Summit Conference, Havana, August 1979.

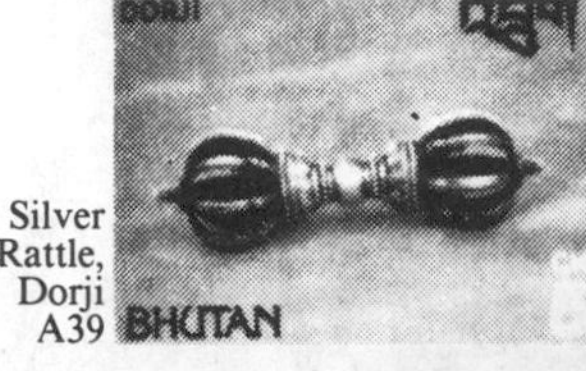

Silver Rattle, Dorji A39

Antiques: 10ch, Silver handell, Dilbu (vert.). 15ch, Cylindrical jar, Jadum (vert.). 25ch, Ornamental teapot, Jamjee. 1nu, Leather container, Kem (vert.). 1.25nu, Brass teapot, Jamjee. 1.70nu, Vessel with elephant-head legs, Sangphor (vert.). 2nu, Teapot with ornamental spout, Jamjee (vert.). 3nu, Metal pot on claw-shaped feet, Yangtho (vert.). 4nu, Dish inlaid with precious stones, Battha. 5nu, Metal circular flask, Chhap (vert.).

1979, Dec. 17 Photo. ***Perf. 14***

No.	Type	Description	Unused	Used
294	A39	5ch multi	5	5
295	A39	10ch multi	5	5
296	A39	15ch multi	5	5
297	A39	25ch multi	8	6
298	A39	1nu multi	30	25
299	A39	1.25nu multi	35	32
300	A39	1.70nu multi	45	45
301	A39	2nu multi	60	50
302	A39	3nu multi	80	75
303	A39	4nu multi	1.10	1.00
304	A39	5nu multi	1.50	1.25
		Nos. 294-304 (11)	5.33	4.73

Hill, Rinpiang Dzong — A40

Hill Statue, Stamps of Bhutan and: 2nu, Dzong. 5nu, Ounsti Dzong. 10nu, Lingzi Dzong, Gt. Britain Type 81. 20nu, Rope bridge, Penny Black.

1980, May 6 Litho. ***Perf. 14x13½***

No.	Type	Description	Unused	Used
305	A40	1nu multi	30	25
306	A40	2nu multi	60	50
307	A40	5nu multi	1.60	1.25
308	A40	10nu multi	3.00	2.50

Souvenir Sheet

No.	Type	Description	Unused	Used
309	A40	20nu multi	6.50	5.00

Sir Rowland Hill (1795-1879), originator of penny postage. No. 309 has multicolored margin showing postal runner and Hill. Size: 102x103mm.

Kichu Lhakhang Monastery, Phari — A41

Guru Padma Sambhava's Birthday: Monasteries.

1981, July 11 Litho. *Perf. 14*

310 A41 1nu Dungtse, Phari (vert.) 32 25
311 A41 2nu shown 65 50
312 A41 2.25nu Kurjey 75 55
313 A41 3nu Tangu, Thimphu 1.00 75
314 A41 4nu Cheri, Thimphu 1.30 1.00
315 A41 5nu Chorten, Kora 1.65 1.25
316 A41 7nu Tak-Tsang, Phari (vert.) 2.30 1.75
Nos. 310-316 (7) 7.97 6.05

Prince Charles and Lady Diana — A42

1981, Sept. 10 Litho. *Perf. 14½*

317 A42 1nu St. Paul's Cathedral 32 25
318 A42 5nu like #317 1.65 1.25
319 A42 20nu shown 6.50 5.00
320 A42 25nu like #319 8.25 6.00

Souvenir Sheet

321 A42 20nu Wedding procession 6.50 5.00

Royal wedding. Nos. 318-319 issued in sheets of 5 plus label. No. 321 has multicolored decorative margin. Size: 69x91mm.

Orange-bellied Chloropsis — A43

1982, Apr. 19 Litho. *Perf. 14*

322 A43 2nu shown 65 50
323 A43 3nu Monal pheasant 1.00 75
324 A43 5nu Ward's trogon 1.65 1.25
325 A43 10nu Mrs. Gould's sunbird 3.25 2.50

Souvenir Sheet

326 A43 25nu Maroon oriole 9.00 6.75

No. 326 has multicolored margin showing birds, map. Size: 95x101mm.

1982 World Cup — A44

Designs: Various soccer players.

1982, June 25 Litho. *Perf. 14½x14*

327 A44 1nu multi 30 25
328 A44 2nu multi 65 50
329 A44 3nu multi 1.00 75
330 A44 20nu multi 6.50 5.00

Souvenir Sheets

331 A44 25nu multi 8.50 6.25

Nos. 331 have multicolored margins continuing design and listing finalists (Algeria, etc. or Hungary, etc.). Sizes: 80x118mm.

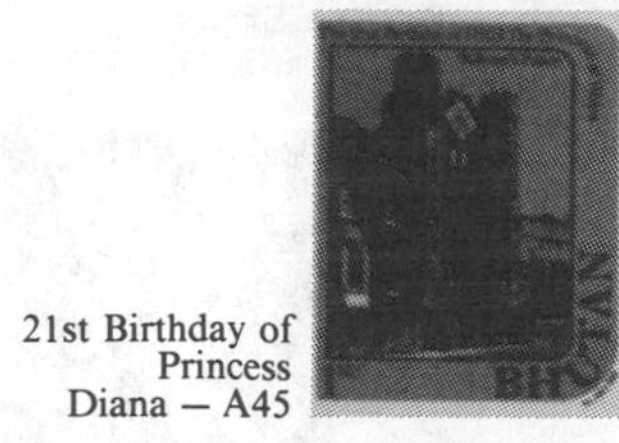

21st Birthday of Princess Diana — A45

1982, Aug.

332 A45 1nu St. James' Palace 32 30
332A A45 10nu Diana, Charles 3.25 2.50
332B A45 15nu Windsor Castle 5.00 5.50
333 A45 25nu Wedding 8.50 6.25

Souvenir Sheet

334 A45 20nu Diana 6.50 5.00

No. 334 has multicolored margin showing family tree, Franklin Roosevelt. Size: 104x75mm.

10nu, 15 nu issued only in sheets of 5 plus label.

Scouting Year A46

1982, Aug. 23 Litho. *Perf. 14*

335 A46 3nu Baden-Powell, vert. 1.00 75
336 A46 5nu Eating around fire 1.65 1.25
337 A46 15nu Reading map 5.00 3.75
338 A46 20nu Pitching tents 6.75 5.00

Souvenir Sheet

339 A46 25nu Mountain climbing 9.00 6.75

No. 339 has multicolored margin continuing design. Size: 91x70mm.

Rama and Cubs with Mowgli — A47

Designs: Scenes from Walt Disney's The Jungle Book.

1982, Sept. 1 *Perf. 11*

340 A47 1ch multi 5 5
341 A47 2ch multi 5 5
342 A47 3ch multi 5 5
343 A47 4ch multi 5 5
344 A47 5ch multi 5 5
345 A47 10ch multi 5 5
346 A47 30ch multi 10 8
347 A47 2nu multi 50 40
348 A47 20nu multi 5.50 4.25
Nos. 340-348 (9) 6.40 5.03

Souvenir Sheets

Perf. 13½

349 A47 20nu Baloo and Mowgli in forest 5.25 4.00
350 A47 20nu Baloo and Mowgli floating 5.25 4.00

Nos. 349-350 have multicolored margins. Size: 127x102mm.

George Washington Surveying — A48

1982, Nov. 15 Litho. *Perf. 15*

351 A48 50ch shown 16 12
352 A48 1nu FDR, Harvard 32 25
353 A48 2nu Washington at Valley Forge 65 50
354 A48 3nu FDR, family 1.00 75
355 A48 4nu Washington, Battle of Monmouth 1.30 1.00
356 A48 5nu FDR, White House 1.65 1.25
357 A48 15nu Washington, Mt. Vernon 5.00 3.75
358 A48 20nu FDR, Churchill, Stalin 6.50 5.00
Nos. 351-358 (8) 16.58 12.62

Souvenir Sheets

359 A48 25nu Washington, vert. 8.25 6.25
360 A48 25nu FDR, vert. 8.25 6.25

George Washington (1732-1799) and Franklin D. Roosevelt (1882-1945). Size of Nos. 359-360: 103x73mm.

Nos. 332-334 Overprinted: "ROYAL BABY / 21.6.82"

1982, Nov. 19 *Perf. 14½x14*

361 A45 1nu multi 32 32
361A A45 10nu multi 3.25 2.50
361B A45 15nu multi 5.00 4.00
362 A45 25nu multi 8.50 6.25

Souvenir Sheet

363 A45 20nu multi 7.00 5.50

Birth of Prince William of Wales, June 21.

500th Birth Anniv. of Raphael A51

Portraits.

1983, Mar. 23 *Perf. 13½*

375 A51 1nu Angelo Doni 32 25
376 A51 4nu Maddalena Doni 1.30 1.00
377 A51 5nu Baldassare Castiglione 1.65 1.25
378 A51 20nu La Donna Velata 6.50 5.00

Souvenir Sheets

379 A51 25nu Expulsion of Heliodorus 8.25 6.25
380 A51 25nu Mass of Bolsena 8.25 6.25

Nos. 148, 184 and Issues of 1972-73 Overprinted: "Druk Air"

Lithographed (30ch), Photogravure

1983, Feb. 11 *Perf. 14½ (30ch), 13½*

381 A24 30ch on 1ch multi 10 8
382 5nu multi INDIPEX 1.90 1.25
383 A17 6nu multi 2.25 1.50
384 7nu multi, olympics 2.50 1.75
385 8nu multi, dogs 2.75 2.00
Nos. 381-385 (5) 9.50 6.58

Druk Air Service inauguration. Overprint of 8nu all caps. Nos. 382, 384 air mail.

Manned Flight Bicentenary A52

1983, Aug. 15 Litho. *Perf. 15*

386 A52 50ch Dornier Wal 16 12
387 A52 3nu Savoia-Marchetti S-66 1.00 75
388 A52 10nu Hawker Osprey 3.25 2.50
389 A52 20nu Ville de Paris 6.50 5.00

Souvenir Sheet

390 A52 25nu Balloon Captif 6.50 4.75

Buddhist Symbols — A53

1983, Aug. 11 Litho. *Perf. 13½*

391 A53 25ch Sacred vase 8 6
392 A53 50ch Five Sensory Symbols 16 12
393 A53 2nu Seven Treasures 50 40
394 A53 3nu Five Sensory Organs 80 60
395 A53 8nu Five Fleshes 2.00 1.50
396 A53 9nu Sacrificial cake 2.50 1.75
a. Souvenir sheet of 6 6.00 4.75
Nos. 391-396 (6) 6.04 4.43

Size of Nos. 393, 396: 45x40mm. No. 396a contains Nos. 391-396. Size: 180x135mm.

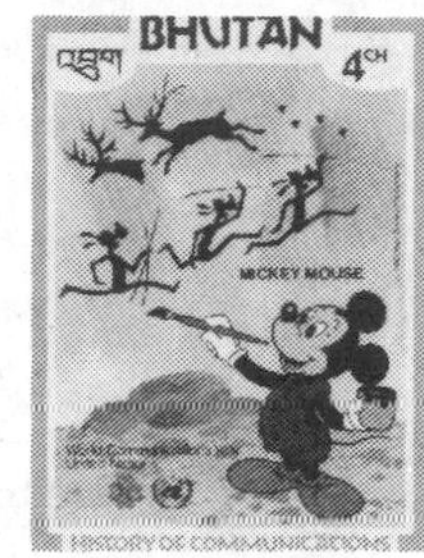

World Communications Year (1983) — A54

Various Disney characters and history of communications.

1984, Apr. 10 Litho. *Perf. 14½x14*

397 A54 4ch multi 5 5
398 A54 5ch multi 5 5
399 A54 10ch multi 5 5
400 A54 20ch multi 6 5
401 A54 25ch multi 8 6
402 A54 50ch multi 16 12
403 A54 1nu multi 32 25
404 A54 5nu multi 1.25 95
405 A54 20nu multi 4.75 3.75
Nos. 397-405 (9) 6.77 5.33

Souvenir Sheets

Perf. 14x14½

406 A54 20nu Donald Duck on phone, horiz. 5.25 4.00
407 A54 20nu Mickey Mouse on TV 5.25 4.00

Nos. 406-407 have multicolored margin continuing design. Size: 128x103mm.

1984 Winter Olympics — A55

1984, Apr. *Perf. 14*

408 A55 50ch Skiing 16 12
409 A55 1nu Cross-country skiing 32 25
410 A55 3nu Speed skating 75 55
411 A55 20nu Bobsledding 4.75 3.75

Souvenir Sheet

412 A55 25nu Hockey 6.50 4.50

Golden Langur
A56

Locomotives
A57

1984, June 1 Litho. *Perf. 14½*

413 A56 50ch shown 10 8
414 A56 1nu Group in tree, horiz. 20 15
415 A56 2nu Family, horiz. 40 30
416 A56 4nu Group walking 80 60

Souvenir Sheets

417 A56 20nu Snow leopard 4.50 3.00
418 A56 25nu Yak 4.50 3.00
419 A56 25nu Blue sheep, horiz. 4.50 3.00

Size: 122x88mm, 88x122mm.

1984, July 16

420 A57 50ch Sans Pareil, 1829 10 8
421 A57 1nu Planet, 1830 20 15
422 A57 3nu Experiment, 1832 60 45
423 A57 4nu Black Hawk, 1835 80 60
424 A57 5.50nu Jenny Lind, 1847 1.10 85
425 A57 8nu Semmering-Bavaria, 1851 1.60 1.25
426 A57 10nu Great Northern #1, 1870 2.00 1.50
427 A57 25nu German Natl. Tinder, 1880 5.00 3.75
Nos. 420-427 (8) 11.40 8.63

Souvenir Sheets

428 A57 20nu Darjeeling Himalayan Railway, 1984 4.00 3.00
429 A57 20nu Sondermann Freight, 1896 4.00 3.00
430 A57 20nu Crampton's locomotive, 1846 4.00 3.00
431 A57 20nu Erzsebet, 1870 4.00 3.00

Nos. 424-427 horiz. Sizes (Nos. 428-431): 93x65mm.

Classic Cars
A58

1984, Aug. 29 Litho. *Perf. 14*

432 A58 50ch Riley Sprite, 1936 10 8
433 A58 1nu Lanchester, 1919 20 15
434 A58 3nu Itala, 1907 65 45
435 A58 4nu Morris Oxford Bullnose, 1913 90 60
436 A58 5.50nu Lagonda LG6, 1939 1.25 85
437 A58 6nu Wolseley, 1903 1.40 90
438 A58 8nu Buick Super, 1952 1.75 1.20
439 A58 20nu Maybach Zeppelin, 1933 4.50 3.00
Nos. 432-439 (8) 10.75 7.23

Souvenir Sheets

440 A58 25nu Simplex, 1912 5.00 3.25
441 A58 25nu Renault, 1901 5.00 3.25

Nos. 440-441 have multicolored margins showing flowers. Size: 126x99mm.

Summer Olympic Games — A59

1984, Oct. 27 Litho.

442 A59 15ch Women's archery 5 5
443 A59 25ch Men's archery 5 5
444 A59 2nu Table tennis 40 30
445 A59 2.25nu Basketball 45 35
446 A59 5.50nu Boxing 1.10 85
447 A59 6nu Running 1.20 90
448 A59 8nu Tennis 1.60 1.20
Nos. 442-448 (7) 4.85 3.70

Souvenir Sheet

449 A59 25nu Archery 4.50 3.25

No. 449 shows Himalayas in margin. Size: 116x83mm.

Nos. 335-339 Surcharged with New Values and Bars in Black or Silver.

1984, Oct. Litho. *Perf. 14*

450 A46 10 nu on 3 nu multi 2.00 1.50
451 A46 10 nu on 5 nu multi 2.00 1.50
452 A46 10 nu on 15 nu multi 2.00 1.50
453 A46 10 nu on 20 nu multi 2.00 1.50

Souvenir Sheet

454 A46 20 nu on 25 nu multi 3.75 3.00

Nos. 332, 332A, 332B, 333-334 Surcharged with New Values and Bars.

1984, Oct.

455 A45 5 nu on 1 nu multi 90 68
456 A45 5 nu on 10 nu multi 90 68
457 A45 5 nu on 15 nu multi 90 68
458 A45 40 nu on 25 nu multi 7.25 5.25

Souvenir Sheet

459 A45 25 nu on 20 nu multi 4.50 3.50

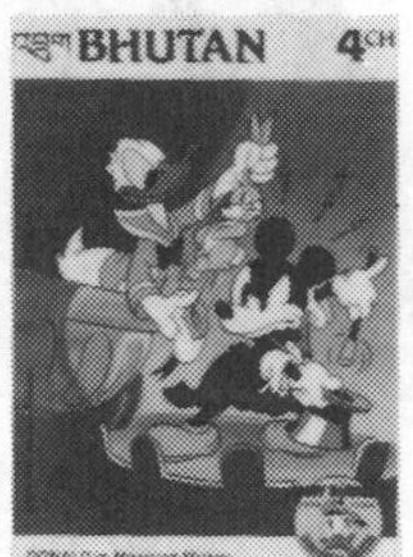

50th Anniv. of Donald Duck — A60

1984, Dec. 10 Litho. *Perf. 13½x14*

460 A60 4ch Magician Mickey 5 5
461 A60 5ch Slide, Donald, Slide 5 5
462 A60 10ch Donald's Golf Game 5 5
463 A60 20ch Mr. Duck Steps Out 5 5
464 A60 25ch Lion Around 5 5
465 A60 50ch Alpine Climbers 10 8
466 A60 1nu Flying Jalopy 25 15
467 A60 5nu Frank Duck 1.10 75
468 A60 20nu Good Scouts 4.50 3.25
Nos. 460-468 (9) 6.20 4.48

Souvenir Sheets

469 A60 20nu Three Caballeros 4.50 3.25
470 A60 20nu Sea Scouts 4.50 3.25

Size: 128x102mm.

Nos. 317-321 Surcharged with New Values and Bars.

1984, Oct. Litho. *Perf. 14½*

471 A42 10 nu on 1 nu multi 2.00 1.50
472 A42 10 nu on 5 nu multi 2.00 1.50
473 A42 10 nu on 20 nu multi 2.00 1.50
474 A42 10 nu on 25 nu multi 2.00 1.50

Souvenir Sheet

475 A42 25 nu on 20 nu multi 5.00 4.00

Nos. 361, 361A, 361B, 362-363 Surcharged with New Values and Bars.

1984, Oct. *Perf. 14½x14*

476 A45 5 nu on 1 nu multi
477 A45 5 nu on 10 nu multi
478 A45 5 nu on 15 nu multi
479 A45 40 nu on 25 nu multi

Souvenir Sheet

480 A45 25 nu on 20 nu multi

Nos. 327-331 Surcharged with New Values and Bars in Black or Silver.

1984, Dec.

481 A44 5 nu on 1 nu multi 90 68
482 A44 5 nu on 2 nu multi 90 68
483 A44 5 nu on 3 nu multi 90 68
484 A44 5 nu on 20 nu multi 90 68

Souvenir Sheets

485 A44 20 nu on 25 nu multi 3.50 2.75

Mask Dance of the Judgement of Death — A61

1984, Dec. *Perf. 13½*

486 A61 5 ch Shinje Choegyel 5 5
487 A61 35 ch Raksh Lango 6 5
488 A61 50 ch Druelgo 10 8
489 A61 2.50 nu Pago 45 35
490 A61 3 nu Telgo 55 42
491 A61 4 nu Due Nakcung 75 58
492 A61 5 nu Lha Karpo 90 68
a. Souvenir sheet of 4, #486-487, 491-492 1.75 1.40
493 A61 5.50 nu Nyalbum 1.00 75
494 A61 6 nu Khimda Pelkyi 1.10 85
Nos. 486-494 (9) 4.96 3.81

No. 492a has multicolored margin containing inscriptions. Size: 91x136mm.

Monasteries
A62

1984, Dec. 1 Litho. *Perf. 12*

495 A62 10ch Domkhar 5 5
496 A62 25ch Shemgang 5 5
497 A62 50ch Chapcha 8 8
498 A62 1nu Tashigang 14 14
499 A62 2nu Pungthang Chhug 28 28
500 A62 5nu Dechhenphoda 70 70
Nos. 495-500 (6) 1.30 1.30

Veteran's War Memorial Building, San Francisco
A63

1985, Oct. 24 Litho. *Perf. 14*

502 A63 50ch Flags of Bhutan, U.N., vert. 9 6
503 A63 15nu Headquarters, New York, vert. 2.75 2.00
504 A63 20nu shown 3.75 2.75

Souvenir Sheet

505 A63 25nu UN Human Rights Declaration 4.25 3.00

UN, 40th anniv. No. 505 has bright blue and black margin picturing the emblems of the UN agencies. Size: 65x80mm.

Audubon Birth Bicentenary — A64

Illustrations of North American bird species by Audubon.

1985

506 A64 50ch Anas breweri 9 6
507 A64 1nu Lagopus lagopus 18 14
508 A64 2nu Charadrius montanus 35 25
509 A64 3nu Cavia stellata 52 40
510 A64 4nu Canachites canadensis 70 52
511 A64 5nu Mergus cucullatus 85 62
512 A64 15nu Olor buccinator 2.50 1.75
513 A64 20nu Bucephala clangula 3.50 2.50
Nos. 506-513 (8) 8.69 6.24

Souvenir Sheets

514 A64 25nu Accipiter striatus 4.75 3.25
515 A64 25nu Parus bicolor 4.75 3.25

Nos. 507, 510-511, 514 Nov. 15. Nos. 506, 508-509, 513, 515 Dec. 6. Nos. 514-515 have multicolored margins continuing the illustrations. Sizes: 75x105mm.

A Tramp Abroad, by Mark Twain (1835-1910)
A65

Walt Disney animated characters.

1985, Nov. 15

516 A65 50ch multi 9 6
517 A65 2nu multi 35 25
518 A65 5nu multi 85 62
519 A65 9nu multi 1.50 1.15
520 A65 20nu multi 3.50 2.50
Nos. 516-520 (5) 6.29 4.58

Souvenir Sheet

521 A65 25nu Goofy, Mickey Mouse 4.25 3.00

Intl. Youth Year. No. 521 has multicolored decorative margin continuing design and picturing Donald Duck and Hirschhorn Castle. Size: 126x101mm.

Rapunzel, by Jacob and Wilhelm Grimm
A66

Walt Disney animated characters.

1985, Nov. 15

522 A66 1nu multi 18 14
523 A66 4nu multi 70 52
524 A66 7nu multi 1.25 95
525 A66 8nu multi 1.40 1.05
526 A66 15nu multi 2.50 1.75
Nos. 522-526 (5) 6.03 4.41

No. 525 printed in sheets of 8.

Souvenir Sheet

527 A66 25nu multi 4.25 3.00

No. 527 has multicolored margin continuing the design. Size: 127x101mm.

First South Asian Regional Cooperation Summit, Dec. 7-8, Dacca, Bangladesh
A67

1985, Dec. 8 *Perf. 14*

528 A67 50ch multi 9 6
529 A67 5nu multi 85 62

Seven Precious Attributes of the Universal King — A68

1986, Feb. 12 Litho. *Perf. 13x12½*

530 A68 30ch Wheel 5 5
531 A68 50ch Gem 8 8
532 A68 1.25nu Queen 18 18
533 A68 2nu Minister 28 28
534 A68 4nu Elephant 55 55
535 A68 6nu Horse 85 85
536 A68 8nu General 1.15 1.15
Nos. 530-536 (7) 3.14 3.14

Nos. 442-443, 445-449 Ovptd. with Medal, Winners' Names and Countries. No. 449 Ovptd. for Men's and Women's Events.

1986, May 5 Litho. *Perf. 14*

537 A59 15ch Hyang Soon Seo, So. Korea 5 5
538 A59 25ch Darrell Pace, US 5 5
539 A59 2.25nu US 32 32
540 A59 5.50nu Mark Breland, US 78 78
541 A59 6nu Daley Thompson, Britain 85 85
542 A59 8nu Stefan Edberg, Sweden 1.15 1.15
Nos. 537-542 (6) 3.20 3.20

Souvenir Sheets

543 A59 25nu Hyang Soon Seo 3.50 3.50
544 A59 25nu Darrel Pace 3.50 3.50

Kilkhor Mandalas, Deities — A69

Religious art: 10ch, 1nu, Phurpa, ritual dagger. 25ch, 3nu, Amitayus in wrath. 50ch, 5nu, Overpowering Deities. 75ch, 7nu, Great Wrathful One, Guru Rinpoche.

1986, June 17 *Perf. 13½*

545 A69 10ch multi 5 5
546 A69 25ch multi 5 5
547 A69 50ch multi 8 8
548 A69 75ch multi 12 12
549 A69 1nu multi 14 14
550 A69 3nu multi 42 42
551 A69 5nu multi 70 70
552 A69 7nu multi 1.00 1.00
Nos. 545-552 (8) 2.56 2.56

Nos. 525, 519, 526, 520, 521 and 527 Ovptd. with AMERIPEX '86 Emblem.

1986, June 16 Litho. *Perf. 14*

553 A66 8nu multi 1.40 1.05
554 A65 9nu multi 1.50 1.15
555 A66 15nu multi 2.50 1.75
556 A65 20nu multi 3.50 2.50

Souvenir Sheets

557 A65 25nu #521 4.25 3.00
558 A66 25nu #527 4.25 3.00

Nos. 335-330 Ovptd. '75th ANNIVERSARY / GIRL GUIDES.'

1986, July 23 Litho. *Perf. 1*

559 A46 3nu multi 50 35
560 A46 5nu multi 85 58
561 A46 15nu multi 2.50 1.75
562 A46 20nu multi 3.50 2.50

Souvenir Sheet

563 A46 25nu multi 4.25 3.00

A70

A71

Halley's Comet A72

Designs: 50ch, Babylonian tablet fragments, 2349 B.C. sighting. 1nu, 17th cent. print, A.D. 66 sighting. 2nu, French silhouette art, 1835 sighting. 3nu, Bayeux Tapestry, 1066 sighting. 4nu, Woodblock, 684 sighting. 5nu, Illustration from Bybel Printen, 1650. 15nu, 1456 Sighting, Cancer constellation. 20nu, Delft plate, 1910 sighting. No. 572, Comet over Himalayas. No. 573, Comet over domed temple Dug-gye Jong.

1986, Nov. 4 Litho. *Perf. 15*

564 A70 50ch multi 10 8
565 A70 1nu multi 18 14
566 A71 2nu multi 35 28
567 A70 3nu multi 50 35
568 A70 4nu multi 68 52
569 A71 5nu multi 85 65
570 A70 15nu multi 2.50 2.00
571 A70 20nu multi 3.50 2.50
Nos. 564-571 (8) 8.66 6.52

Souvenir Sheets

572 A72 25nu multi 4.25 3.00
573 A72 25nu multi 4.25 3.00

Nos. 572-573 have multicolored margins continuing the designs. Sizes: 110x80mm.

A73

Statue of Liberty, Cent. — A74

Statue and ships: 50ch, Mircea, Romania. 1nu, Shalom, Israel. 2nu, Leonardo da Vinci, Italy. 3nu, Libertad, Argentina. 4nu, France, France. 5nu, SS United States, US. 15nu, Queen Elizabeth II, England. 20nu, Europa, West Germany. No. 582, Statue. No. 583, Statue, World Trade Center.

1986, Nov. 4

574 A73 50ch multi 10 8
575 A73 1nu multi 18 14
576 A73 2nu multi 35 28
577 A73 3nu multi 50 35
578 A73 4nu multi 68 52
579 A73 5nu multi 85 65
580 A73 15nu multi 2.50 1.90
581 A73 20nu multi 3.40 2.50
Nos. 574-581 (8) 8.56 6.42

Souvenir Sheets

582 A74 25nu multi 4.25 3.00
583 A74 25nu multi, diff. 4.25 3.00

Nos. 582-583 have multicolored margins continuing the designs picturing Nippon Maru, Japan (#582), and flat-bottom boats, Netherlands (#583). Size: 114x83mm.

Discovery of America, 500th Anniv. — A75

1987, May 25 Litho. *Perf. 14*

584 A75 20ch Santa Maria 5 5
585 A75 25ch Queen Isabella 5 5
586 A75 50ch Ship, flying fish 15 12
587 A75 1nu Columbus's coat of arms 25 18
588 A75 2nu Christopher Columbus 50 38
589 A75 3nu Landing in the New World 75 55
a. Miniature sheet of 6, Nos. 584-589 1.75 1.75
Nos. 584-589 (6) 1.75 1.33

Souvenir Sheet

590 A75 20ch Pineapple 5 5
591 A75 25ch Indian hammock 5 5
592 A75 50ch Tobacco plant 15 12
593 A75 1nu Flamingo 25 18
594 A75 2nu Navigator, astrolabe, 15th cent. 50 38
595 A75 3nu Lizard 75 55
596 A75 5nu Iguana 1.25 95

Nos. 590-596 have multicolored margins picturing various maps or scenes showing the wilderness of the New World, 15th cent. Sizes: 97x66mm.

CAPEX '87 — A76

Locomotives.

1987, June 15

597 A76 50ch Canadian Natl. U1-f 10 8
598 A76 1nu Via Rail L.R.C. 18 14
599 A76 2nu Canadian Natl. GM GF-30t 35 28
600 A76 3nu Canadian Natl. 4-8-4 50 35
601 A76 8nu Canadian Pacific 4-6-2 1.35 1.00
602 A76 10nu Via Express passenger train 1.75 1.30
603 A76 15nu Canadian Nat. Turbotrain 2.50 1.90
604 A76 20nu Canadian Pacific Diesel-Electric Express 3.25 2.50
Nos. 597-604 (8) 9.98 7.55

Souvenir Sheet

605 A76 25nu Royal Hudson 4-6-4 4.25 3.00
606 A76 25nu Canadian Natl. 4-8-4, diff. 4.25 3.00

Nos. 605-606 have inscribed multicolored margins continuing the designs. Sizes: 102x76mm.

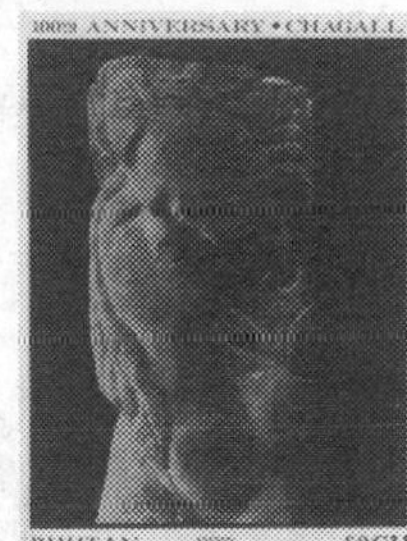

Two Faces, Sculpture by Marc Chagall (1887-1984) A77

Paintings: 1nu, At the Barber's. 2nu, Old Jew with Torah. 3nu, Red Maternity. 4nu, Eve of Yom Kippur. 5nu, The Old Musician. 6nu, The Rabbi of Vitebsk. 7nu, Couple at Dusk. 9nu, The Artistes. 10nu, Moses Breaking the Tablets of the Law. 12nu, Bouquet with Flying Lovers. 20nu, In the Sky of the Opera. No. 619, Romeo and Juliet. No. 620, Magician of Paris. No. 621, Maternity. No. 622, The Carnival for Aleko: Scene II. No. 623, Visit to the Grandparents. No. 624, The Smolensk Newspaper. No. 625, The Concert. No. 626, Composition with Goat. No. 627, Still Life. No. 628, The Red Gateway. No. 629, Cow with Parasol. No. 630, Russian Village.

1987, Dec. 17 Litho. *Perf. 14*

607 A77 50ch multi 8 6
608 A77 1nu multi 16 12
609 A77 2nu multi 32 24
610 A77 3nu multi 48 35
611 A77 4nu multi 65 48
612 A77 5nu multi 80 60
613 A77 6nu multi 95 72
614 A77 7nu multi 1.15 88
615 A77 9nu multi 1.45 1.10
616 A77 10nu multi 1.60 1.20
617 A77 12nu multi 1.90 1.45
618 A77 20nu multi 3.20 2.40

Size: 110x95mm.

Imperf.

619 A77 25nu multi 4.00 3.00
620 A77 25nu multi 4.00 3.00
621 A77 25nu multi 4.00 3.00
622 A77 25nu multi 4.00 3.00
623 A77 25nu multi 4.00 3.00
624 A77 25nu multi 4.00 3.00
625 A77 25nu multi 4.00 3.00
626 A77 25nu multi 4.00 3.00
627 A77 25nu multi 4.00 3.00
628 A77 25nu multi 4.00 3.00
629 A77 25nu multi 4.00 3.00
630 A77 25nu multi 4.00 3.00
Nos. 607-630 (24) 60.74 45.60

SEMI-POSTAL STAMPS

Nos. 10-12 Surcharged

+ 50 ch

Perf. 14x14½

1964, March Litho. Unwmk.

B1 A3 33ch + 50ch multi 3.75 3.75
B2 A3 70ch + 50ch multi 3.75 3.75
B3 A3 1.30nu + 50ch multi 3.75 3.75

Issued to commemorate the 9th Winter Olympic Games, Innsbruck, Jan. 29-Feb. 9, 1964.

Olympic Games Type of Regular Issue, 1964

Designs: 1nu+50ch, Archery. 2nu+50ch, Soccer.

Souvenir Sheet

1964, Oct. 10 *Perf. 13½, Imperf.*

B4 A6 Sheet of 2 6.00 6.00
a. 1nu + 50ch multi 75 75
b. 2nu + 50ch multi 1.75 1.75

18th Olympic Games, Tokyo, Oct. 10-25. No. B4 has multicolored border. Size: 86x117½mm.

AIR POST STAMPS

U.N. Type of Regular Issue

Designs (Bhutan Flag and): 2.50nu, U.N. Headquarters, New York. 5nu, Security Council Chamber and mural by Per Krohg. 6nu, General Assembly Hall.

1971, Sept. 21 Photo. *Perf. 13½*

C1 A16 2.50nu sil & multi 75 75
C2 A16 5nu sil & multi 1.50 1.50
C3 A16 6nu sil & multi 2.00 2.00

Bhutan's admission to the United Nations. Exist imperf.

Nos. C1-C3 Overprinted in Gold: "UNHCR / UNRWA / 1971" Like Nos. 153-156

1971, Dec. 23 Litho. *Perf. 13½*

C4 A16 2.50nu sil & multi 80 80
C5 A16 5nu sil & multi 1.60 1.60
C6 A16 6nu sil & multi 2.00 2.00

World Refugee Year. Exist imperf.

UPU Types of 1974

Designs (UPU Emblem, Carrier Pigeon and): 1nu, Mail runner and jeep. 1.40nu, 10nu, Old and new locomotives. 2nu, Old biplane and jet.

1974, Oct. 9 Litho. *Perf. 14½*

C7 A19 1nu sal & multi 35 35
C8 A20 1.40nu lil & multi 55 55
C9 A20 2nu multi 70 70

Souvenir Sheet

Perf. 13

C10 A20 10nu lil & multi 3.75 3.75

Centenary of Universal Postal Union. No. C10 contains one stamp; yellow and multicolored margin with UPU emblem and black inscription. Size: 91x78mm. Nos. C7-C9 were issued in sheets of 50 and sheets of 5 plus label with multicolored margin. Exist imperf.

Issues of 1968-1974 Surcharged 25ch and Bars

Perforations and Printing as Before

1978

No.	Type	Description
C11	A16	25ch on 5nu (# C2)
C12	A16	25ch on 6nu (# C3)
C13	A20	25ch on 1.40nu (# C8)
C14	A20	25ch on 2nu (# C9)
C15		25ch on 4nu *Mythological creature*
C16		25ch on 10nu *Mythological creature*
C17		25ch on 5nu *INDIPEX*
C18		25ch on 6nu *INDIPEX*

Nos. C15-C18 on unlisted issues (see For the Record).

BOLIVIA

LOCATION — Central South America, separated from the Pacific Ocean by Chile and Peru.
GOVT. — Republic
AREA — 424,165 sq. mi.
POP. — 6,252,250 (est. 1984)
CAPITAL — Sucre (La Paz is the actual seat of government).

100 Centavos = 1 Boliviano
100 Centavos = 1 Peso Boliviano (1963)

On February 21st, 1863, the Bolivian Government decreed contracts for carrying the mails should be let to the highest bidder, the service to commence on the day the bid was accepted, and stamps used for the payment of postage. On March 18th, 1863, the contract was awarded to Sr. Justiniano Garcia and was in effect until April 29th, 1863, when it was rescinded by the government. Stamps in the form illustrated above were prepared in denominations of ½, 1, 2 and 4 reales. All values exist in black and in blue. It is said that used copies exist on covers, but the authenticity of these covers remains to be established.

Condor — A1

A2

A3

72 varieties of each of the 5c, 78 varieties of the 10c, 30 varieties of each of the 50c and 100c.

The plate of the 5c stamps was entirely reengraved four times and retouched at least six times. Various states of the plate have distinguishing characteristics, each of which is typical of most, though not all the stamps in a sheet. These characteristics (usually termed types) are found in the shading lines at the right side of the globe. (a.): vertical and diagonal lines; (b.): diagonal lines only; (c.): diagonal and horizontal with traces of vertical lines; (d): diagonal and horizontal lines; (e.): horizontal lines only; (f.): no lines except the curved ones forming the outlines of the globe.

1867-68 Unwmk. Engr. *Imperf.*

No.	Type	Description	Unused	Used
1	A1	5c bl grn (b)	7.00	*20.00*
a.		5c bl grn (a)	7.00	*20.00*
b.		5c dp grn (a)	7.00	*20.00*
c.		5c ol grn, thick paper (a)	50.00	40.00
d.		5c yel grn, thick paper (a)	125.00	125.00
e.		5c yel grn, thick paper (b)	125.00	125.00
f.		5c yel grn, thin paper (a, b)	5.00	7.00
2	A1	5c grn (d)	6.00	11.00
a.		5c grn (c)	7.00	11.00
b.		5c grn (e)	6.00	11.00
c.		5c grn (f)	6.00	11.00
3	A1	5c vio ('68)	400.00	275.00
a.		5c rose lil ('68)	400.00	275.00
4	A3	10c brown	450.00	275.00
5	A2	50c orange	27.50	
6	A2	50c bl ('68)	*475.00*	
a.		50c dk bl ('68)	*475.00*	
7	A3	100c blue	85.00	
8	A3	100c grn ('68)	200.00	
a.		100c pale bl grn ('68)	200.00	

Used prices are for postally canceled copies. Pen cancellations usually indicate that the stamps have been used fiscally and such stamps sell for about one-fifth as much as those with postal cancellations.

Nos. 2-8 have been reprinted.

Coat of Arms
A4 A5

1868-69 *Perf. 12*

Nine Stars

No.	Type	Description	Unused	Used
10	A4	5c green	25.00	12.50
11	A4	10c vermilion	35.00	12.50
12	A4	50c blue	60.00	35.00
13	A4	100c orange	60.00	40.00
14	A4	500c black	525.00	450.00

Eleven Stars

No.	Type	Description	Unused	Used
15	A5	5c green	12.50	7.50
16	A5	10c vermilion	17.50	12.50
a.		Half used as 5c as cover		600.00
17	A5	50c blue	45.00	20.00
18	A5	100c dp org	40.00	20.00
19	A5	500c black	*2,000.*	*2,000.*

Arms and "The Law" — A6

1878 Various Frames. *Perf. 12*

No.	Type	Description	Unused	Used
20	A6	5c ultra	12.50	5.00
21	A6	10c orange	10.00	4.00
a.		Half used as 5c on cover		75.00
22	A6	20c green	30.00	5.00
a.		Half used as 10c on cover		250.00
23	A6	50c dl car	150.00	15.00

Numerals Upright
(11 Stars)-A7 (9 Stars)-A8

1887 *Rouletted*

No.	Type	Description	Unused	Used
24	A7	1c rose	3.00	1.25
25	A7	2c violet	3.00	1.25
26	A5	5c blue	10.00	2.00
27	A5	10c orange	10.00	2.00

1890 *Perf. 12*

No.	Type	Description	Unused	Used
28	A8	1c rose	2.75	1.50
29	A8	2c violet	6.00	2.00
30	A4	5c blue	3.50	1.50
31	A4	10c orange	7.50	1.75
32	A4	20c dk grn	17.50	2.50
33	A4	50c red	7.50	2.50
34	A4	100c yellow	17.50	6.00
		Nos. 28-34 (7)	62.25	17.75

1893 Litho. *Perf. 11.*

No.	Type	Description	Unused	Used
35	A8	1c rose	5.00	2.00
a.		Imperf. pair	50.00	
b.		Imperf. vert., pair	30.00	
c.		Horizontal pair, imperf. between	50.00	
36	A8	2c violet	5.00	2.00
a.		Block of 4 imperf. vert. and horiz. through center	75.00	
b.		Horizontal pair, imperf. between	40.00	
37	A7	5c blue	7.00	2.00
a.		Imperf. horiz., pair	40.00	
b.		Horizontal pair imperf. between	50.00	
38	A8	10c orange	20.00	3.00
a.		Horizontal pair, imperf. between	75.00	
39	A8	20c dk grn	65.00	20.00
a.		Imperf. pair, vert. or horiz.	200.00	
b.		Pair, imperf. btwn., vert. or horiz.	200.00	
		Nos. 35-39 (5)	102.00	29.00

Coat of Arms — A9

1894 Unwmk. Engr. *Perf. 14, 14½.*

Thin Paper.

No.	Type	Description	Unused	Used
40	A9	1c bister	2.00	1.00
41	A9	2c red org	2.00	1.00
42	A9	5c green	2.00	1.00
43	A9	10c yel brn	2.00	1.00
44	A9	20c dk bl	6.00	2.50
45	A9	50c claret	15.00	3.50
46	A9	100c brn rose	35.00	12.50
		Nos. 40-46 (7)	64.00	22.50

Stamps of type A9 on thick paper were surreptitiously printed in Paris on the order of an official and without government authorization. Some of these stamps were substituted for part of a shipment of stamps on thin paper, which had been printed in London on government order. When the thick paper stamps reached Bolivia they were at first repudiated but afterwards were allowed to do postal duty. A large quantity of the thick paper stamps were fraudulently cancelled in Paris with a cancellation of heavy bars forming an oval.

To be legitimate, copies of the thick paper stamps must have been bought at post offices in Bolivia, or must have genuine cancellations of Bolivia.

The 10c blue on thick paper is not known to have been issued.

President Tomas Frias
A10

President José M. Linares
A11

Pedro Domingo Murillo
A12

Bernardo Monteagudo
A13

Gen. José Ballivian
A14

Gen. Antonio José de Sucre
A15

Simon Bolivar — A16

Coat of Arms — A17

1897 Litho. *Perf. 12*

No.	Type	Description	Unused	Used
47	A10	1c pale yel grn	2.00	1.2
a.		Imperf. horiz. pair	75.00	
b.		Vertical pair, imperf. between	75.00	
48	A11	2c red	3.50	2.5
49	A12	5c dk grn	3.50	1.2
a.		Horizontal pair, imperf. between	75.00	
50	A13	10c brn vio	3.50	1.2
a.		Vertical pair, imperf. between	75.00	
51	A14	20c lake & blk	8.00	1.5
a.		Imperf., pair		225.0
52	A15	50c orange	8.00	3.0
53	A16	1b Prus bl	8.00	7.5
54	A17	2b red, yel, grn & blk	45.00	60.0
		Nos. 47-54 (8)	81.50	78.2

Excellent forgeries of No. 54 exist.

Nos. 40-44 Handstamped in Violet or Blue

E.F.
1899

1899 *Perf. 14½*

No.	Type	Description	Unused	Used
55	A9	1c yel bis	25.00	25.0
56	A9	2c red org	30.00	30.0
57	A9	5c green	20.00	20.0
58	A9	10c yel brn	25.00	20.0
59	A9	20c dk bl	40.00	40.0
		Nos. 55-59 (5)	140.00	135.0

The handstamp is found inverted, double etc. Forgeries of this handstamp are plentiful. "E.F." stands for Estado Federal.

The 50c and 100c (Nos. 45-46) with similar handstamp are considered bogus.

Antonio José de Sucre — A18

Perf. 11½, 12

1899 Engr. Thin Paper

No.	Type	Description	Unused	Used
62	A18	1c gray bl	2.25	1.0
63	A18	2c brnsh red	1.50	1.0
64	A18	5c dk grn	6.00	2.0
65	A18	10c yel org	2.25	1.5
66	A18	20c rose pink	3.00	1.0
67	A18	50c bis brn	6.00	2.5
68	A18	1b gray vio	2.50	2.0
		Nos. 62-68 (7)	23.50	11.0

1901

No.	Type	Description	Unused	Used
69	A18	5c dk red	2.50	1.0

Col. Adolfo Ballivian
A19

Eliodoro Camacho
A20

President Narciso Campero
A21

José Ballivian
A22

Gen. Andrés Santa Cruz — A23

Coat of Arms — A24

1901-02 **Engr.**

70 A19 1c claret 50 25
71 A20 2c green 60 35
73 A21 5c scarlet 60 40
74 A22 10c blue 1.50 25
75 A23 20c vio & blk 80 25
76 A24 2b brown 4.50 4.00
Nos. 70-71,73-76 (6) 8.50 5.50

1904 **Litho.**

77 A19 1c claret 3.00 1.00

In No. 70 the panel above "CENTAVO" is shaded with continuous lines. In No. 77 the shading is of dots.

See also Nos. 103-105, 107, 110.

Coat of Arms of Dept. of La Paz A25

Murillo A26

José Miguel Lanza A27

Ismael Montes A28

1909 **Litho.** ***Perf. 11***

78 A25 5c bl & blk 14.00 6.50
79 A26 10c grn & blk 14.00 6.50
80 A27 20c org & blk 14.00 6.50
81 A28 2b red & blk 14.00 6.50

Centenary of Revolution of July, 1809.

Nos. 78-81 exist imperf. and tete beche.
Nos. 79-81 exist with center inverted.

Miguel Betanzos A29

Col. Ignacio Warnes A30

Murillo A31

Monteagudo A32

Esteban Arce – A33

Antonio José de Sucre – A34

Simon Bolivar A35

Manuel Belgrano A36

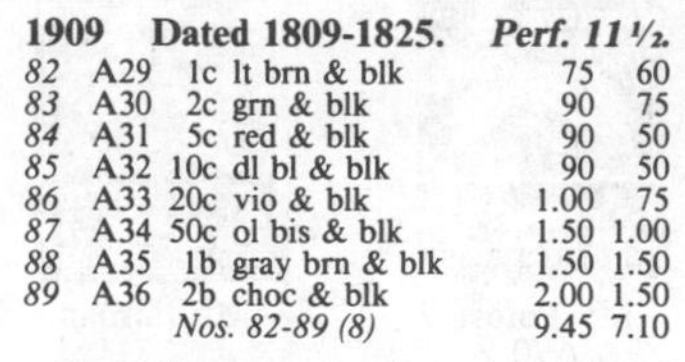

1909 Dated 1809-1825. ***Perf. 11½.***

82 A29 1c lt brn & blk 75 60
83 A30 2c grn & blk 90 75
84 A31 5c red & blk 90 50
85 A32 10c dl bl & blk 90 50
86 A33 20c vio & blk 1.00 75
87 A34 50c ol bis & blk 1.50 1.00
88 A35 1b gray brn & blk 1.50 1.50
89 A36 2b choc & blk 2.00 1.50
Nos. 82-89 (8) 9.45 7.10

Issued in commemoration of the War of Independence, 1809-1825.

Warnes A37

Betanzos A38

Arce – A39

Dated 1910-1825.

1910 ***Perf. 13x13½.***

92 A37 5c grn & blk 40 20
a. Imperf., pair 5.00
93 A38 10c cl & ind 40 20
a. Imperf., pair 7.50
94 A39 20c dl bl & ind 85 50
a. Imperf., pair 5.00

Issued in commemoration of the War of Independence.

Nos. 92-94 may be found with parts of a papermaker's watermark: "A I & Co/ EXTRA STRONG/9303."

Nos. 71 and 75 Surcharged in Black

1911 ***Perf. 11½, 12.***

95 A20 5c on 2c grn 60 30
a. Inverted surcharge 7.00 7.00
b. Double surcharge
c. Period after "1911" 5.00 1.25
d. Blue surcharge 100.00 75.00
96 A23 5c on 20c vio & blk 22.50 22.50
a. Inverted surch. 45.00 45.00

No. 83 Handstamp Surcharged in Green

97 A30 20c on 2c grn & blk *1,300.*

This provisional was issued by local authorities at Villa Bella, a town on the Brazilian border. The 20c surcharge was applied after the stamp had been affixed to the cover. Excellent forgeries of No. 96-97 exist.

"Justice"
A40 A41

1912

Black or Dark Blue Overprint.

98 A40 2c grn (Bk) 60 40
a. Inverted overprint 7.50
99 A41 10c ver (Bl) 1.25 70
a. Inverted overprint 7.50

A42 A43

Red or Black Overprint.

Engr.

100 A42 5c org (R) 50 50
a. Inverted overprint 6.00
b. Pair, one without overprint 15.00
c. Black overprint 75.00

Red or Black Surcharge.

101 A43 10c on 1c bl (R) 50 25
a. Inverted surch. 7.50
b. Double surch. 7.50
c. Double surcharge, one inverted 8.50
d. Black surcharge 150.00 150.00

Revenue Stamp Surcharged "CORREOS / 10 Cts. / - 1917 -" in Red

1917 **Litho.**

102 10c on 1c bl *1,800. 1,750.*

Design similar to type A43.

Frias A45

Sucre A46

Bolivar – A47

1913 **Engr.** ***Perf. 12.***

103 A19 1c car rose 50 40
104 A20 2c vermilion 50 30
105 A21 5c green 60 20
106 A45 8c yellow 1.00 90
107 A22 10c gray 1.00 40
108 A46 50c dl vio 2.00 1.00
109 A47 1b sl bl 3.50 2.00
110 A24 2b black 7.00 4.00
Nos. 103-110 (8) 16.10 9.20

Monolith of Tiahuanacu A48

Mt. Potosi A49

Lake Titicaca – A50

Mt. Illimani – A51

Legislature Building – A53

FIVE CENTAVOS.

Type I. Numerals have background of vertical lines. Clouds formed of dots.

Type II. Numerals on white background. Clouds near the mountain formed of wavy lines.

1916-17 **Litho.** ***Perf. 11½.***

111 A48 ½c brown 30 30
a. Imperf. vert., pair 7.50
112 A49 1c gray grn 35 20
a. Imperf., pair 2.50
113 A50 2c car & blk 35 20
a. Imperf., pair 2.50
b. Imperf. horiz.
c. Center inverted 25.00 22.50
d. Imperf., center inverted 27.50
114 A51 5c dk bl (I) 75 35
a. Imperf., pair 2.50
b. Imperf. horiz., pair 5.00
c. Imperf. vert., pair 5.00
115 A51 5c dk bl (II) 75 15
a. Imperf., pair 3.50
116 A53 10c org & bl 1.25 15
a. Imperf., pair 5.00
b. No period after "Legislativo" 1.25 25
c. Center inverted 75.00 75.00
d. Vertical pair, imperf. between 7.50
Nos. 111-116 (6) 3.75 1.35

Coat of Arms
A54 A55

Printed by the American Bank Note Co.

1919-20 **Engr.** ***Perf. 12.***

118 A54 1c carmine 35 35
119 A54 2c dk vio 6.00 4.00
120 A54 5c dk grn 50 15
121 A54 10c vermilion 50 15
122 A54 20c dk bl 2.00 50
123 A54 22c lt bl 1.25 1.25
124 A54 24c purple 1.25 75
125 A54 50c orange 6.00 1.00
126 A55 1b red brn 7.50 2.00
127 A55 2b blk brn 12.50 7.50
Nos. 118-127 (10) 37.85 17.65

Printed by Perkins, Bacon & Co., Ltd.

Types of 1919-20 Issue.

1923-27 **Re-engraved.** ***Perf. 13½.***

128 A54 1c car ('27) 25 15
129 A54 2c dk vio 35 20
130 A54 5c dp grn 1.00 15
131 A54 10c vermilion 22.50 20.00
132 A54 20c sl bl 2.00 35
135 A54 50c orange 4.00 1.00
136 A55 1b red brn 1.00 50
137 A55 2b blk brn 75 50
Nos. 128-137 (8) 31.85 22.85

The stamps of 1919-20 are perf. 12, those of 1923 are perf. 13½. The two issues may thus be readily distinguished. There are many differences in the designs of the two issues but they are too minute to be illustrated or described.

See also Nos. 144-146.

Stamps of 1919-20 Surcharged in Blue, Black or Red

Habilitada
15 cts.

1924 ***Perf. 12.***

138 A54 5c on 1c car (Bl) 50 35
a. Inverted surcharge 7.50 7.50
b. Double surcharge 7.50 7.50
139 A54 15c on 10c ver (Bk) 1.00 60
a. Inverted surcharge 10.00 10.00
140 A54 15c on 22c lt bl (Bk) 1.00 50
a. Inverted surcharge 9.00 9.00
b. Double surcharge, one inverted
c. Red surcharge 35.00

Same Surcharge on No. 131.

Perf. 13½

142 A54 15c on 10c ver (Bk) 50 40
a. Inverted surch. 10.00 10.00

No. 121 Surcharged

Habilitada
15 cts.

Perf. 12.

143 A54 15c on 10c ver (Bk) 60 50
a. Inverted surch. 10.00 10.00
b. Double surcharge 8.50 8.50
Nos. 138-143 (5) 3.60 2.35

Printed by Waterlow & Sons.
Type of 1919-20 Issue.

Second Re-engraving.

1925 **Unwmk.** ***Perf. 12½***

144 A54 5c dp grn 75 35

145 A54 15c ultra 75 20
146 A54 20c dk bl 50 20

These stamps may be identified by the perforation.

Miner — A56

Condor Looking Toward the Sea — A57

Designs: 2c, Sower. 5c, Torch of Eternal Freedom. 10c, National flower (kantuta). 15c, Pres. Bautista Saavedra. 50c, Liberty head. 1b, Archer on horse. 2b, Mercury. 5b, Gen. A. J. de Sucre.

1925 Engr. *Perf. 14.*

150	A56	1c dk grn	1.50	1.00
151	A56	2c rose	1.50	1.00
152	A56	5c red, *grn*	1.50	50
153	A56	10c car, *yel*	1.75	1.00
154	A56	15c red brn	1.00	50
155	A57	25c ultra	1.25	75
156	A56	50c dp vio	1.25	75
157	A56	1b red	2.25	2.00
158	A57	2b orange	3.50	3.00
159	A56	5b blk brn	4.00	3.00
		Nos. 150-159 (10)	19.50	13.50

Issued to commemorate the centenary of the Republic.

Stamps of 1919-27 Surcharged in Blue, Black or Red

1927
5
CENTAVOS

1927

160	A54	5c on 1c car (Bl)	1.50	1.25
a.		Inverted surcharge	6.00	6.00
b.		Black surcharge	30.00	30.00

Perf. 12.

162	A54	10c on 24c pur (Bk)	1.50	1.25
a.		Inverted surcharge	40.00	40.00
b.		Red surcharge	30.00	30.00

Coat of Arms — A66

Printed by Waterlow & Sons.

1927 Litho. *Perf. 13½.*

165	A66	2c yellow	50	35
166	A66	3c pink	60	50
167	A66	4c red brn	60	50
168	A66	20c lt ol grn	90	35
169	A66	25c dp bl	90	50
170	A66	30c violet	90	75
171	A66	40c orange	2.00	75
172	A66	50c dp brn	2.00	75
173	A55	1b red	2.25	75
174	A55	2b plum	3.50	1.00
175	A55	3b ol grn	3.50	2.50
176	A55	4b claret	5.00	3.00
177	A55	5b bis brn	6.00	2.00
		Nos. 165-177 (13)	28.65	13.70

Canceled-to-order stamps are often from remainders. Most collectors of canceled stamps prefer postally used specimens.

Type of 1927 Issue Overprinted

Octubre

1927

1927

178	A66	5c dk grn	35	25
179	A66	10c slate	50	25
180	A66	15c carmine	75	50

Stamps of 1919-27 Surcharged

15 cts.
1928

1928 *Perf. 12, 12½, 13½*

Red Surcharge.

181	A54	15c on 20c dk bl (No. 122)	10.00	10.00
182	A54	15c on 20c sl bl (No. 132)	10.00	10.00
a.		Black surcharge	35.00	
183	A54	15c on 20c dk bl (No. 146)	250.00	250.00

Black Surcharge.

184	A54	15c on 24c pur (No. 124)	2.00	1.50
a.		Inverted surcharge	5.00	5.00
b.		Blue surcharge	55.00	
185	A54	15c on 50c org (No. 125)	65.00	65.00
186	A54	15c on 50c org (No. 135)	1.50	1.00
		Nos. 181-186 (6)	338.50	337.50

Condor A67

Hernando Siles A68

Map of Bolivia — A69

Printed by Perkins, Bacon & Co., Ltd.

1928 Engr. *Perf. 13½.*

189	A67	5c green	50	10
190	A68	10c slate	50	10
191	A69	15c car lake	1.00	15

Stamps of 1913-17 Surcharged in Various Colors

0.03
Centavos
R.S. 21-4
1930

1930 *Perf. 12, 11½.*

193	A20	1c on 2c ver (Bl)	1.00	1.00
a.		"0.10" for "0.01"	15.00	15.00
194	A50	3c on 2c car & blk (Br)	1.25	1.00
195	A48	25c on ½c brn (Bk)	1.00	75
196	A50	25c on 2c car & blk (V)	1.00	75

The lines of the surcharges were spaced to fit the various shapes of the stamps. The surcharges exist inverted, double, etc.

Trial printings were made of the surcharges on Nos. 193 and 194 in black and on No. 196 in brown.

Mt. Potosi A70

Mt. Illimani A71

Eduardo Abaroa A72

Map of Bolivia A73

Sucre — A74

Bolívar — A75

1931 Engr. *Perf. 14.*

197	A70	2c green	60	50
198	A71	5c lt bl	50	25
199	A72	10c red org	60	25
200	A73	15c violet	1.00	25
201	A73	35c carmine	2.00	1.00
202	A73	45c orange	2.00	1.00
203	A74	50c gray	1.00	75
204	A75	1b brown	2.00	2.00
		Nos. 197-204 (8)	9.70	6.00

See also Nos. 207, 241.

Symbols of 1930 Revolution — A76

1931 Litho. *Perf. 11.*

205	A76	15c scarlet	3.00	50
a.		Pair, imperf. between		
206	A76	50c brt vio	1.00	75
a.		Pair, imperf. between	10.00	

Revolution of June 25, 1930.

Map Type of 1931. Without Imprint.

1932 Litho.

207	A73	15c violet	1.50	40

Stamps of 1927-31 Surcharged

Habilitada
A 15 Cts.
D. S. 13-7.1933

1933 *Perf. 13½, 14.*

208	A66	5c on 1b red	60	30
a.		Without period after "Cts"	1.25	1.25
209	A73	15c on 35c car	30	30
210	A73	15c on 45c org	30	30
a.		Inverted surcharge	3.00	3.00
211	A66	15c on 50c dp brn	60	25
212	A66	25c on 40c org	60	20
		Nos. 208-212 (5)	2.40	1.35

The hyphens in "13-7-33" occur in three positions.

Coat of Arms — A77

1933 Engr. *Perf. 12*

213	A77	2c bl grn	35	20
214	A77	5c blue	25	15
215	A77	10c red	60	40
216	A77	15c dp vio	35	20
217	A77	25c dk bl	90	60
		Nos. 213-217 (5)	2.45	1.55

Mariano Baptista A78

Map of Bolivia A79

1935

218	A78	15c dl vio	75	30

1935

219	A79	2c dk bl	35	25
220	A79	3c yellow	35	25
221	A79	5c vermilion	35	20
222	A79	5c bl grn	35	20
223	A79	10c blk brn	35	20
224	A79	15c dp rose	40	20
225	A79	15c ultra	40	20
226	A79	20c yel grn	50	25
227	A79	25c lt bl	50	20
228	A79	30c dp rose	90	35
229	A79	40c orange	90	30
230	A79	50c gray vio	90	20
231	A79	1b yellow	90	60
232	A79	2b ol brn	2.00	1.25
		Nos. 219-232 (14)	9.15	4.65

Regular Stamps of 1925-33 Surcharged in Black

Comuni-
caciones
D. S.
25-2-37
0.05

1937 *Perf. 11, 12, 13½.*

233	A77	5c on 2c bl grn	30	30
234	A77	15c on 25c dk bl	40	40
235	A77	30c on 25c dk bl	60	60
236	A55	45c on 1b red brn	75	75
237	A55	1b on 2b plum	90	90
a.		"1" missing	5.00	5.00
238	A77	2b on 25c dk bl	90	90

"Comunicaciones" on one line.

239	A76	3b on 50c brt vio	1.25	1.25
a.		"3" of value missing	6.00	6.00
240	A76	5b on 50c brt vio	2.00	2.00
		Nos. 233-240 (8)	7.10	7.10

President Siles — A80

1937 Unwmk. *Perf. 14*

241	A80	1c yel brn	40	35

Native School — A81

Oil Wells — A82

Modern Factories A83

Torch of Knowledge A84

Map of the Sucre-Camiri R. R. — A85

Allegory of Free Education A86

Allegorical Figure of Learning A87

Symbols of Industry A88

Modern Agriculture A89

1938	**Litho.**	***Perf. 10½, 11.***		
242 A81	2c dl red		50	35
243 A82	10c pink		60	35
244 A83	15c yel grn		75	40
245 A84	30c yellow		1.00	50
246 A85	45c rose red		1.25	1.00
247 A86	60c dk vio		1.25	50
248 A87	75c dl bl		1.50	50
249 A88	1b lt brn		2.00	50
250 A89	2b bistcr		2.50	1.00
	Nos. 242-250 (9)		11.35	5.10

Llamas — A90

Vicuna — A91

Coat of Arms A92

Cocoi Herons A93

Chinchilla A94

Toco Toucan A95

Condor — A96

Jaguar — A97

1939, Jan. 21	***Perf. 10½, 11½x10½***		
251 A90	2c green	75	50
252 A90	4c fawn	75	50
253 A90	5c red vio	75	40
254 A91	10c black	75	50
255 A91	15c emerald	75	60
256 A91	20c dk sl grn	75	40
257 A92	25c lemon	75	40
258 A92	30c dk bl	75	50
259 A93	40c vermilion	1.50	50
260 A93	45c gray	1.50	50
261 A94	60c rose red	1.75	1.00
262 A94	75c sl bl	1.75	1.00
263 A95	90c orange	2.50	1.00
264 A95	1b blue	3.00	1.00
265 A96	2b rose lake	4.00	1.00
266 A96	3b dk vio	5.00	1.50
267 A97	4b brn org	6.00	2.00
268 A97	5b gray brn	7.50	2.50
	Nos. 251-268 (18)	40.50	15.80

Imperforate counterfeits of some values exist.

Flags of 21 American Republics — A98

1940, Apr.	**Litho.**	***Perf. 10½***	
269 A98	9b multi	3.00	2.50

Pan American Union, 150th anniversary.

Statue of Murillo A99

Urns of Murillo and Sagarnaga A100

Dream of Murillo A101

Pedro Domingo Murillo A102

1941, Apr. 15			
270 A99	10c dl vio brn	15	10
271 A100	15c lt grn	25	15
a.	Imperf. (pair)	5.00	
272 A101	45c car rose	25	20
a.	Double impression		
273 A102	1.05b dk ultra	50	25

Issued to commemorate the 130th anniversary of the death (by execution) of Pedro Domingo Murillo (1759-1810), patriot.

First Stamp of Bolivia and 1941 Airmail Stamp — A103

1942, Oct.	**Litho.**	***Perf. 13½***	
274 A103	5c pink	1.00	75
275 A103	10c orange	1.00	75
276 A103	20c yel grn	2.00	1.00
277 A103	40c car rose	2.50	1.25
278 A103	90c ultra	5.00	1.50
279 A103	1b violet	6.00	3.00
280 A103	10b ol bis	20.00	12.50
	Nos. 274-280 (7)	37.50	20.75

Issued in commemoration of the first School Philatelic Exposition held in La Paz, October, 1941.

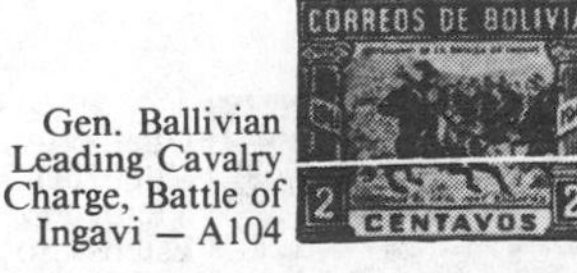
Gen. Ballivian Leading Cavalry Charge, Battle of Ingavi — A104

1943	**Photo.**	***Perf. 12½***	
281 A104	2c lt bl grn	15	10
282 A104	3c orange	15	10
283 A104	25c dp plum	25	15
284 A104	45c ultra	35	20
285 A104	3b scarlet	75	50
286 A104	4b brt rose lil	1.00	60
287 A104	5b blk brn	1.50	90
	Nos. 281-287 (7)	4.15	2.55

Souvenir Sheets.

Perf. 13, Imperf.

288 A104	Sheet of 4	3.00	2.50
289 A104	Sheet of 3	9.00	7.50

Centenary of the Battle of Ingavi, 1841. No. 288 contains 4 stamps similar to Nos. 281-284, No. 289 three stamps similar to Nos. 285-287: black marginal inscriptions. Size: 139x100mm.

Potosí A107

Quechisla A108

Miner — A109

Dam A110

Mine Interior A111

Chaquiri Dam A112

Entrance to Pulacayo Mine A113

1943	**Engr.**	***Perf. 12½.***	
290 A107	15c red brn	35	25
291 A108	45c vio bl	35	25
292 A109	1.25b brt rose vio	50	40
293 A110	1.50b emerald	50	40
294 A111	2b brn blk	60	50
295 A112	2.10b lt bl	75	60
296 A113	3b red org	1.00	90
	Nos. 290-296 (7)	4.05	3.30

General José Ballivian and Cathedral at Trinidad A114

1943, Nov. 18			
297 A114	5c dk grn & brn	15	15
298 A114	10c dl pur & brn	20	20
299 A114	30c rose red & brn	25	25
300 A114	45c brt ultra & brn	35	35
301 A114	2.10b dp org & brn	50	50
	Nos. 297-301,C91-C95 (10)	3.25	2.80

Department of Beni centenary.

"Honor, Work, Law" A115

"United for the Country" A116

1944	**Litho.**	***Perf. 13½***	
302 A115	20c orange	10	10
303 A115	90c ultra	15	10
304 A116	1b brt red vio	20	15
305 A116	2.40b dl brn	30	20

1945			
306 A115	20c green	5	5
307 A115	90c dp rose	15	10
	Nos. 302-307,C96-C99 (10)	2.05	1.25

Nos. 302-307 were issued to commemorate the Revolution of Dec. 20, 1943.

Leopold Benedetto Vincenti, Joseph Ignacio de Sanjines and Bars of Anthem A117

1946, Aug. 21	**Litho.**	***Perf. 10½***	
308 A117	5c rose vio & blk	20	15
309 A117	10c ultra & blk	20	15
310 A117	15c bl grn & blk	20	15
311 A117	30c ver & brn	25	20
a.	Souvenir sheet	1.25	1.25
312 A117	90c dk bl & brn	25	20
313 A117	2b blk & brn	60	25
a.	Souvenir sheet	2.50	2.50
	Nos. 308-313 (6)	1.70	1.10

Issued to commemorate the centenary of the adoption of Bolivia's national anthem.

Nos. 311a and 313a measure 86x136½mm., contain respectively one each of Nos. 311 and 313, and are imperforate. The price of each sheet included a surtax of 4 bolivianos.

Nos. 248 and 262 Surcharged in Carmine, Black or Orange

1947, Mar. 12	***Perf. 10½, 11***		
314 A87	1.40b on 75c dl bl (C)	20	8
315 A94	1.40b on 75c sl bl (Bk)	20	8
316 A94	1.40b on 75c sl bl (C)	20	8
317 A94	1.40b on 75c sl bl (O)	20	8
	Nos. 314-317,C112 (5)	1.10	62

People Attacking Presidential Palace A118

Arms of Bolivia and Argentina A119

1947, Sept.	**Litho.**	***Perf. 13½***	
318 A118	20c bl grn	5	5
a.	Imperf. (pair)		
319 A118	50c lil rose	10	6
320 A118	1.40b grnsh bl	15	8
a.	Imperf. (pair)		
321 A118	3.70b dl org	25	12
322 A118	4b violet	35	20
323 A118	10b olive	75	45
	Nos. 318-323,C113-C117 (11)	2.90	1.91

Issued to commemorate the first anniversary of the Revolution of July 21, 1946.

1947, Oct. 23
324 A119 1.40b dp org 12 8

Issued to commemorate the meeting of Presidents Enrique Hertzog of Bolivia and Juan D. Peron of Argentina at Yacuiba on October 23, 1947. See also No. C118.

Statue of Christ above La Paz — A120

Designs: 2b, Child kneeling before cross of Golgotha. 3b, St. John Bosco. No. 328, Virgin of Copacabana. No. 329, Pope Pius XII blessing University of La Paz.

1948, Sept. 26 Unwmk. *Perf. 11½*
325 A120 1.40b bl & yel 50 18
326 A120 2b yel grn & sal 75 22
327 A120 3b grn & gray 1.25 25
328 A120 5b vio & sal 1.50 30
329 A120 5b red brn & lt grn 2.00 30
Nos. 325-329,C119-C123 (10) 11.10 3.30

Issued to publicize the 3rd Inter-American Congress of Catholic Education.

Map and Emblem of Bolivia Auto Club — A125

Pres. Gregorio Pacheco, Map and Post Horn — A126

1948, Oct. 20
330 A125 5b ind & sal 3.50 25

Issued to publicize the International Automobile Races of South America, September-October 1948. See also No. C124.

1950, Jan. 2 Litho. *Perf. 11½*
331 A126 1.40b vio bl 15 10
332 A126 4.20b red 15 10
Nos. 331-332,C125-C127 (5) 70 60

Issued to commemorate the 75th anniversary of the formation of the Universal Postal Union.

No. 273 Surcharged in Black

Bs.2.-
Habilitada

D.S.6-VII-50

1950 *Perf. 10½*
333 A102 2b on 1.05b dk ultra 25 10

Crucifix and View of Potosi A127

Symbols of United Nations A128

Perf. 11½
1950, Sept. 14 Litho. Unwmk.
334 A127 20c violet 10 6
335 A127 30c dp org 10 6
336 A127 50c lil rose 10 6
337 A127 1b carmine 15 6
338 A127 2b blue 20 6
339 A127 6b chocolate 35 15
Nos. 334-339 (6) 1.00 45

Issued to commemorate the 400th anniversary of the appearance of a crucifix at Potosi.

1950, Oct. 24
340 A128 60c ultra 1.50 20
341 A128 2b green 2.00 35

Issued to commemorate the 5th anniversary of the formation of the United Nations, October 24, 1945. See also Nos. C138-C139.

Gate of the Sun and Llama A129

Church of San Francisco A130

Designs: 40c, Avenue Camacho. 50c, Consistorial Palace. 1b, Legislative Palace. 1.40b, Communications Bldg. 2b, Arms. 3b, La Gasca ordering Mendoza to found La Paz. 5b, Capt. Alonso de Mendoza founding La Paz. 10b, Arms; portrait of Mendoza.

1951, Mar. Engr. *Perf. 12½*
Center in Black.
342 A129 20c green 10 10
343 A130 30c dp org 10 10
344 A129 40c bis brn 10 10
345 A129 50c dk red 10 10
346 A129 1b dp pur 15 15
347 A129 1.40b dk vio bl 20 20
348 A129 2b dp pur 20 20
349 A129 3b red lil 30 20
a. Sheet, Nos. 345, 346, 348, 349 1.75 1.75
b. Sheet, imperf. 1.75 1.75
350 A129 5b dk red 35 25
a. Sheet, Nos. 344, 347, 350 1.75 1.75
b. Sheet, imperf. 1.75 1.75
351 A129 10b sepia 75 35
a. Sheet, Nos. 342, 343, 351 1.75 1.75
b. Sheet, imperf. 1.75 1.75
Nos. 342-351,C140-C149 (20) 6.70 6.10

Issued to commemorate the 400th anniversary of the founding of La Paz.

The souvenir sheets measure 150x100mm., and contain marginal inscriptions in black.

Boxing A131

Designs: 50c, Tennis. 1b, Diving. 1.40b, Soccer. 2b, Skiing. 3b, Handball. 4b, Cycling.

Perf. 12½
1951, July 1 Unwmk. Engr.
Center in Black.
352 A131 20c dp bl 25 10
353 A131 50c red 25 15
354 A131 1b claret 30 15
355 A131 1.40b yellow 30 20
356 A131 2b brt car 75 35
357 A131 3b yel brn 1.25 75
a. Sheet, Nos. 352, 353, 356, 357 3.50 3.50
b. Sheet, imperf. 3.50 3.50
358 A131 4b vio bl 1.50 75
a. Sheet, Nos. 354, 355, 358 3.00 3.00
b. Sheet, imperf. 3.00 3.00
Nos. 352-358,C150-C156 (14) 12.45 5.85

The stamps were intended to commemorate the 5th athletic championship matches held at La Paz, October 1948.

The sheets measure 150x100 mm., and contain marginal inscriptions in black.

Eagle and Flag of Bolivia A132

1951, Nov. 5 Litho. *Perf. 11½*
Flag in Red, Yellow and Green.
359 A132 2b aqua 15 15
360 A132 3.50b ultra 15 15
361 A132 5b purple 25 20
362 A132 7.50b gray 40 20
363 A132 15b dp car 50 40
364 A132 30b sepia 1.00 75
Nos. 359-364 (6) 2.45 1.85

Issued to commemorate the centenary of the adoption of Bolivia's national flag.

Eduardo Abaroa A133

Queen Isabella I A134

1952, Mar. *Perf. 11*
365 A133 80c dk car 15 5
366 A133 1b red org 15 15
367 A133 2b emerald 25 15
368 A133 5b ultra 30 20
369 A133 10b lil rose 50 25
370 A133 20b dk brn 1.00 60
Nos. 365-370,C157-C162 (12) 6.40 4.05

Issued to commemorate the 73rd anniversary of the death of Eduardo Abaroa.

1952, July 16 Unwmk. *Perf. 13½*
371 A134 2b vio bl 15 10
372 A134 6.30b carmine 35 25

Issued to commemorate the 500th anniversary of the birth of Queen Isabella I of Spain. See also Nos. C163-C164.

Columbus Lighthouse A135

1952, July 16 Litho.
373 A135 2b vio bl,*bl* 25 20
374 A135 5b car, *sal* 50 30
375 A135 9b emer, *grn* 75 50
Nos. 373-375,C165-C168 (7) 2.55 1.58

Miner — A136

1953, Apr. 9
376 A136 2.50b vermilion 10 8
377 A136 8b violet 15 12

Issued to publicize the nationalization of the mines.

Gualberto Villarroel, Victor Paz Estenssoro and Hernan Siles Zuazo A137

1953, Apr. 9 *Perf. 11½*
378 A137 50c rose lil 5 5
379 A137 1b brt rose 10 10
380 A137 2b vio bl 10 10
381 A137 3b lt grn 15 15
382 A137 4b yel org 15 1
383 A137 5b dl vio 25 1
Nos. 378-383,C169-C175 (13) 2.80 2.2

Issued to commemorate the first anniversary of the Revolution of Apr. 9, 1952.

Map of Bolivia and Cow's Head — A138

Designs: 17b, Same as 5b. 25b, 85b, Map and ear of wheat.

1954, Aug. 2 *Perf. 12x11½*
384 A138 5b car rose 5
385 A138 17b aqua 15
386 A138 25b chlky bl 25 8
387 A138 85b blk brn 50 25
Nos. 384-387,C176-C181 (10) 4.65 1.45

Nos. 384-385 were issued to commemorate the agrarian reform laws of 1953-54. Nos. 386-387 commemorate the 1st National Congress of Agronomy.

Oil Refinery A139

1955, Oct. 9 Unwmk. *Perf. 12x11½*
388 A139 10b ultra & lt ultra 10 10
389 A139 35b rose car & rose 15 10
390 A139 40b dk & lt yel grn 15 10
391 A139 50b red vio & lil rose 20 10
392 A139 80b brn & bis brn 35 15
Nos. 388-392,C182-C186 (10) 4.90 3.00

Nos. 342-351, Surcharged with New Values and Bars in Ultramarine.

1957, Feb. 14 Engr. *Perf. 12½*
Center in Black.
393 A129 50b on 3b red lil 15 5
394 A129 100b on 2b dp pur 15 5
395 A129 200b on 1b dp pur 20 10
396 A129 300b on 1.40b dk vio bl 25 10
397 A129 350b on 20c grn 35 10
398 A129 400b on 40c bis brn 35 10
399 A130 600b on 30c dp org 50 15
400 A129 800b on 50c dk red 60 15
401 A129 1000b on 10b sep 60 25
402 A129 2000b on 5b dk red 1.00 40
Nos. 393-402 (10) 4.15 1.45

See also Nos. C187-C196.

CEPAL Building, Santiago de Chile, and Meeting Hall in La Paz — A140

1957, May 15 Litho. *Perf. 13*
403 A140 150b gray & ultra 15 5
404 A140 350b bis brn & gray 30 10
405 A140 550b chlky bl & brn 35 15
406 A140 750b dp rose & grn 50 20
407 A140 900b grn & brn blk 75 25
Nos. 403-407,C197-C201 (10) 8.90 4.75

Issued to commemorate the seventh session of the C. E. P. A. L. (Comision Economica para la America Latina de las Naciones Unidas), La Paz.

Presidents Siles Zuazo and Aramburu A141

1957, Dec. 15 Unwmk. *Perf. 11½*
408 A141 50b red org 15 5
409 A141 350b blue 40 10
410 A141 1000b redsh brn 75 15
Nos. 408-410,C202-C204 (6) 2.90 70

Issued to commemorate the opening of the Santa Cruz-Yacuiba Railroad and the meeting of the Presidents of Bolivia and Argentina.

Flags of Bolivia and Mexico and Presidents Hernan Siles Zuazo and Adolfo Lopez Mateos
A142

1960, Jan. 30 Litho. *Perf. 11½*
411 A142 350b olive 25 8
412 A142 600b red brn 35 15
413 A142 1500b blk brn 75 25
Nos. 411-413,C205-C207 (6) 4.60 1.53

Issued for an expected visit of Mexico's President Adolfo Lopez Mateos. On sale Jan. 30-Feb. 1, 1960.

Indians and Mt. Illimani
A143

Refugee Children
A144

1960, Mar. 26 Unwmk.
414 A143 500b ol bis 35 10
415 A143 1000b blue 60 20
416 A143 2000b brown 1.25 50
417 A143 4000b green 2.50 75
Nos. 414-417,C208-C211 (8) 24.70 10.30

1960, Apr. 7 *Perf. 11½*
418 A144 50b brown 15 5
419 A144 350b claret 20 6
420 A144 400b stl bl 25 8
421 A144 1000b gray brn 75 25
422 A144 3000b sl grn 1.50 70
Nos. 418-422,C212-C216 (10) 6.20 4.34

Issued to publicize World Refugee Year, July 1, 1959-June 30, 1960.

Jaime Laredo
A145

Rotary Emblem and Nurse with Children
A146

1960, Aug. 15 Litho. *Perf. 11½*
423 A145 100b olive 40 10
424 A145 350b dp rose 60 10
425 A145 500b Prus grn 75 15
426 A145 1,000b brown 1.00 25
427 A145 1,500b vio bl 1.75 35
428 A145 5,000b gray 6.00 1.25
Nos. 423-428,C217-C222 (12) 25.25 8.10

Issued to honor violinist Jaime Laredo.

1960, Nov. 19 *Perf. 11½*
429 A146 350b grn, yel & dp bl 25 10
430 A146 500b brn, yel & dp bl 35 10
431 A146 600b vio, yel & dp bl 50 15
432 A146 1,000b gray, yel & dp bl 60 25
Nos. 429-432,C223-C226 (8) 8.45 3.65

Issued for the Children's Hospital, sponsored by the Rotary Club of La Paz.

Designs from Gate of the Sun
A147 A148

Designs: Various prehistoric gods and ornaments from Tiahuanacu excavations.

Perf. 13x12, 12x13
1960, Dec. 16 Litho.
Gold Background.
Surcharge in Black or Dark Red (#436)
Sizes: 21x23, 23x21mm.

433 A147 50b on ½c red 75 50
434 A147 100b on 1c red 50 25
435 A147 200b on 2c blk 1.50 15
436 A147 300b on 5c grn 35 20
437 A147 350b on 10c grn 35 1.25
438 A148 400b on 15c ind 50 25
439 A148 500b on 20c red 50 25
440 A148 500b on 50c red 60 25
441 A148 600b on 22½c grn 75 40
442 A148 600b on 60c vio 90 50
443 A148 700b on 25c vio 1.25 30
444 A148 700b on 1b grn 1.75 1.00
445 A148 800b on 30c red 85 30
446 A148 900b on 40c grn 75 40
447 A148 1000b on 2b bl 90 50
448 A148 1800b on 3b gray 9.00 6.00

Perf. 11
Size: 49½x23mm.
449 A148 4000b on 4b gray 65.00 55.00

Perf. 11x13½
Size: 49x53mm.
450 A147 5000b on 5b gray 17.50 12.50
Nos. 433-450 (18) 103.70 80.00

Nos. 433-450 were not regularly issued without surcharge. Price (set), $20.

The decree for Nos. 433-450 stipulated that seven were for air mail (500b on 50c, 600b on 60c, 700b on 1b, 1,000b, 1,800b, 4,000b and 5,000b), but the overprinting failed to include "Aereo."

The 800b surcharge also exists on the 1c red and gold. This was not listed in the decree.

Miguel de Cervantes
A149

Nuflo de Chaves
A150

1961, Nov. Photo. *Perf. 13x12½*
451 A149 600b ocher & dl vio 50 12

Issued to commemorate Cervantes' appointment as Chief Magistrate of La Paz. See also No. C230.

1961, Nov. Unwmk.
452 A150 1500b dk bl, *buff* 75 30

Issued to commemorate the 400th anniversary of the founding of Santa Cruz de la Sierra. See also Nos. 468, C246.

People below Eucharist Symbol
A151

Hibiscus
A152

1962, Mar. 19 Litho. *Perf. 10½*
453 A151 1000b gray grn, red & yel 1.00 50

Issued to commemorate the Fourth National Eucharistic Congress, Santa Cruz, 1961. See also No. C231.

Nos. 418-422 Surcharged Horizontally with New Value and Bars or Greek Key Border Segment

1962, June *Perf. 11½*
454 A144 600b on 50b brn 30 20
455 A144 900b on 350b cl 40 20
456 A144 1,000b on 400b stl bl 60 25
457 A144 2,000b on 1,000b gray brn 75 40
458 A144 3,500b on 3,000b sl grn 1.25 75
Nos. 454-458,C232-C236 (10) 9.20 4.80

Old value obliterated with two short bars on No. 454; four short bars on Nos. 455-456 and Greek key border on Nos. 457-458. The Greek key obliteration comes in two positions: two full "keys" on top, and one full and two half keys on top.

1962, June 28 Litho. *Perf. 10½*
Flowers in Natural Colors

Flowers: 400b, Bicolored vanda. 600b, Lily. 1000b, Orchid.

459 A152 200b sl bl 30 10
460 A152 400b brown 30 15
461 A152 600b dk bl 60 20
462 A152 1000b violet 1.00 35
Nos. 459-462,C237-C240 (8) 9.80 4.65

Infantry
A153

Anti-Malaria Emblem
A154

Designs: 500b, Cavalry. 600b, Artillery. 2000b, Engineers.

1962, Sept. 5 *Perf. 11½*
Insigne in Red, Yellow & Green
463 A153 400b blk, mar & buff 15 10
464 A153 500b blk, lt & dk grn 20 15
465 A153 600b blk & pale bis 25 20
466 A153 2000b blk & brn 75 50
Nos. 463-466,C241-C244 (8) 4.30 2.95

Issued in honor of Bolivia's Armed Forces.

1962, Oct. 4
467 A154 600b dk & lt vio & yel 40 20

Issued for the World Health Organization drive to eradicate malaria. See No. C245.

Portrait Type of 1961.

Design: 600b, Alonso de Mendoza.

1962 Photo. *Perf. 13x12½*
468 A150 600b rose vio, *bluish* 40 20

Soccer and Flags — A155

Design: 1b, Goalkeeper catching ball (vert.).

1963, Mar. 21 Litho. *Perf. 11½*
Flags in National Colors
469 A155 60c gray 60 15
470 A155 1b gray 90 25

Issued to publicize the 21st South American Soccer Championships. See also Nos. C247-C248.

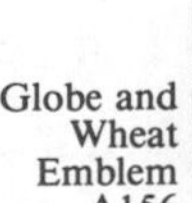

Globe and Wheat Emblem
A156

1963, Aug. 1 Unwmk. *Perf. 11½*
471 A156 60c dk bl, bl & yel 35 15

Issued for the "Freedom from Hunger" campaign of the U.N. Food and Agriculture Organization. See also No. C249.

Oil Derrick and Chart — A157

Designs: 60c, Map of Bolivia. 1b, Students.

1963, Dec. 21 Litho. *Perf. 11½*
472 A157 10c grn & dk brn 15 10
473 A157 60c ocher & dk brn 40 15
474 A157 1b dk bl, grn & yel 50 25
Nos. 472-474,C251-C253 (6) 3.90 1.95

Issued to commemorate the 10th anniversary of the Revolution of Apr. 9, 1952.

Flags of Bolivia and Peru — A158

1966, Aug. 10 Wmk. 90 *Perf. 13½*
Flags in National Colors
475 A158 10c blk & tan 15 10
476 A158 60c blk & lt grn 30 15
477 A158 1b blk & gray 50 20
478 A158 2b blk & rose 75 30
Nos. 475-478,C254-C257 (8) 4.15 1.85

Issued to commemorate the centenary (in 1965) of the death of Marshal Andres Santa Cruz (1792-1865), president of Bolivia and of Peru-Bolivian Confederation.

Children — A159

Perf. 13½
1966, Dec. 16 Unwmk. Litho.
479 A159 30c ocher & sep 25 10

Issued to help poor children. See No. C258.

Map and Flag of Bolivia and Generals Ovando and Barrientos
A160

1966, Dec. 16 Litho. *Perf. 13½*
Flag in Red, Yellow and Green
480 A160 60c vio brn & tan 30 10
481 A160 1b dl grn & tan 45 15

Issued to honor Generals Rene Barrientos Ortuno and Alfredo Ovando C., co-Presidents, 1965-66. See also Nos. C259-C260.

A161

Various Issues 1957-60 and Type A161 Surcharged with New Values and Bars

1966, Dec. 21

On No. 403: "Centenario de la / Cruz Roja / Internacional"

482 A140 20c on 150b gray & ultra 15 5

On Nos. 405-406: "Homenaje a la / Generala / J. Azurduy de / Padilla"

483 A140 30c on 550b chlky bl & brn 15 5
484 A140 2.80b on 750b dp rose & grn 90 50

On No. 424: "CL Aniversario / Heroinas Coronilla"

485 A145 60c on 350b dp rose 25 10

Nos. 429-430 Surcharged

486 A146 1.60b on 350b multi 60 25
487 A146 2.40b on 500b multi 90 40

Revenue Stamps of 1946 surcharged with New Value, "X" and: "XXV Aniversario / Gobierno Busch"

488 A161 20c on 5b red 15 5

Overprinted: "XX Aniversario / Gob. Villaroel"

489 A161 60c on 2b grn 25 10

Overprinted: "Centenario do / Rurrenabaque"

490 A161 1b on 10b brn 40 15

Overprinted: "XXV Aniversario / Dpto. Pando"

491 A161 1.60b on 50c vio 60 25
Nos. 482-491,C261-C272 (22) 14.20 10.20

Sower
A162

"Macheteros"
A163

1967, Sept. 20 Litho. *Perf. 13½x13*

492 A162 70c multi 50 15

Issued to commemorate the 50th anniversary of Lions International. See Nos. C273-C273a.

1968, June 24 *Perf. 13½x13*

Designs (Folklore characters): 60c, Chunchos. 1p, Wiphala. 2p, Diablada.

493 A163 30c gray & multi 15 8
494 A163 60c sky bl & multi 25 15
495 A163 1b gray & multi 40 20
496 A163 2b gray ol & multi 75 30
Nos. 493-496,C274-C277 (8) 4.45 2.43

Issued to publicize the 9th Congress of the Postal Union of the Americas and Spain.

A souvenir sheet exists containing 4 imperf. stamps similar to Nos. 493-496. Bister and gray marginal inscription. Size: 131x81½mm.

Arms of Tarija
A164

Pres. Gualberto Villaroel
A165

1968, Oct. 29 Litho. *Perf. 13½x13*

497 A164 20c pale sal & multi 15 6
498 A164 30c gray & multi 15 8
499 A164 40c dl yel & multi 20 10
500 A164 60c lt yel grn & multi 30 12
Nos. 497-500,C278-C281 (8) 4.40 2.11

Battle of Tablada sesquicentennial.

1968, Nov. 6 Unwmk.

501 A165 20c sep & org 20 6
502 A165 30c sep & dl bl grn 20 6
503 A165 40c sep & dl rose 20 8
504 A165 50c sep & yel grn 25 10
505 A165 1b sep & ol bis 50 15
Nos. 501-505 (5) 1.35 45

Issued to commemorate the 4th centenary of the founding of Cochabamba. See Nos. C282-C286.

ITU Emblem
A166

1968, Dec. 3 Litho. *Perf. 13x13½*

506 A166 10c gray, blk & yel 25 6
507 A166 60c org, blk & ol 50 10

Issued to commemorate the centenary (in 1965) of the International Telecommunication Union. See Nos. C287-C288.

Polychrome Painted Clay Cup, Inca Period — A167

1968, Nov. 14 *Perf. 13½x13*

508 A167 20c dk bl grn & multi 25 6
509 A167 60c vio bl & multi 50 10

Issued to commemorate the 20th anniversary (in 1966) of UNESCO (United Nations Educational, Scientific and Cultural Organization). See Nos. C289-C290.

John F. Kennedy — A168

Tennis Player — A169

1968, Nov. 22 *Perf. 13x13½*

510 A168 10c yel grn & blk 20 10
511 A168 4b vio & blk 2.00 60

Issued in memory of Pres. John F. Kennedy (1917-1963).

A souvenir sheet contains one imperf. stamp similar to No. 511. Green marginal inscription. Size: 131x81½mm.

See Nos. C291-C292.

1968, Dec. 10 *Perf. 13x13½*

512 A169 10c gray, blk & lt brn 20 10
513 A169 20c yel, blk & lt brn 20 10
514 A169 30c ultra, blk & lt brn 20 10

Issued to commemorate the 32nd South American Tennis Championships, La Paz, 1965. See Nos. C293-C294.

A souvenir sheet exists containing 3 imperf. stamps similar to Nos. 512-514. Light brown marginal inscription. Size: 131x81½mm.

Issue of 1863 — A170

1968, Dec. 23 Litho. *Perf. 13x13½*

515 A170 10c yel grn, brn & blk 20 10
516 A170 30c lt bl, brn & blk 20 10
517 A170 2b gray, brn & blk 35 20
Nos. 515-517,C295-C297 (6) 4.50 2.25

Issued to commemorate the centenary of Bolivian postage stamps. See Nos. C295-C297.

A souvenir sheet exists containing 3 imperf. stamps similar to Nos. 515-517. Yellow green marginal inscription. Size: 131x81½mm.

Rifle Shooting
A171

Sports: 50c, Equestrian. 60c, Canoeing.

1969, Oct. 29 Litho. *Perf. 13x13½*

518 A171 40c red brn, org & blk 20 10
519 A171 50c emer, red & blk 20 10
520 A171 60c bl, emer & blk 35 15
Nos. 518-520,C299-C301 (6) 4.60 2.10

Issued to commemorate the 19th Olympic Games, Mexico City, Oct. 12-27, 1968.

A souvenir sheet exists containing 3 imperf. stamps similar to Nos. 518-520. Marginal inscription in red brown, emerald and blue. Size: 130½x81mm.

Temenis Laothoe Violetta
A172

Butterflies: 10c, Papilio crassus. 20c, Catagramma cynosura. 30c, Eunica eurota flora. 80c, Ituna phenarete.

1970, Apr. 24 Litho. *Perf. 13x13½*

521 A172 5c pale lil & multi 15 5
522 A172 10c pink & multi 15 5
523 A172 20c gray & multi 15 5
524 A172 30c yel & multi 15 5
525 A172 80c multi 35 20
Nos. 521-525,C302-C306 (10) 7.20 3.35

A souvenir sheet exists containing 3 imperf. stamps similar to Nos. 521-523. Black marginal inscription. Size: 129½x80mm.

Boy Scout — A173

Design: 10c, Girl Scout planting rose bush.

1970, June 17 *Perf. 13½x13*

526 A173 5c multi 20 5
527 A173 10c multi 20 5

Issued to honor the Bolivian Scout movement. See Nos. C307-C308.

No. 437 Surcharged "EXFILCA 70 / $b. 0.30" and Two Bars in Red

1970, Dec. 6 Litho. *Perf. 13x12*

528 A147 30c on 350b on 10c gold & grn 20 10

EXFILCA 70, 2nd Interamerican Philatelic Exhibition, Caracas, Venezuela, Nov. 27-Dec. 6.

Nos. 455 and 452 Surcharged in Black or Red

1970, Dec. Photo. *Perf. 11½*

529 A144 60c on 900b on 350b cl 35 12
533 A150 1.20b on 1500b dk bl, *buff* (R) 65 20

Amaryllis Yungacensis
A174

Sica Sica Church, EXFILIMA Emblem
A175

Bolivian Flowers: 30c, Amaryllis escobar uriae (horiz.). 40c, Amaryllis evansae (horiz.). 2b, Gymnocalycium chiquitanum.

Perf. 13x13½, 13½x13

1971, Aug. 9 Litho. Unwmk.

534 A174 30c gray & multi 15 10
535 A174 40c multi 15 10
536 A174 50c multi 25 20
537 A174 2b multi 75 50
Nos. 534-537,C310-C313 (8) 5.90 2.50

1971, Nov. 6 *Perf. 14x13½*

538 A175 20c red & multi 25 10

EXFILIMA '71, 3rd Inter-American Philatelic Exhibition, Lima, Peru, Nov. 6-14.

Pres. Hugo Banzer Suarez — A176

1972, Jan. 24 Litho. *Perf. 13½*

539 A176 1.20b blk & multi 75 20

Bolivia's development, Aug. 19, 1971, to Jan. 24, 1972.

Chiriwano de Achocalla Dance — A177

Folk Dances: 40c, Rueda Chapaca. 60c, Kena-kena. 1b, Waca Thokori.

1972, Mar. 23 Litho. *Perf. 13½x13*

540 A177 20c red & multi 10 10
541 A177 40c rose lil & multi 25 20
542 A177 60c cr & multi 35 25
543 A177 1b cit & multi 50 35
Nos. 540-543,C314-C315 (6) 2.95 1.40

Madonna and Child by B. Bitti — A178

Tarija Cathedral, EXFILBRA Emblem — A179

Paintings: 10c, Nativity, by Melchor Perez de Holguin. 50c, Coronation of the Virgin, by G. M. Berrio. 70c, Harquebusier, anonymous. 80c, St. Peter of Alcantara, by Holguin.

1972 Litho. *Perf. 14x13½*

544 A178 10c gray & multi 15 10
545 A178 50c sal & multi 30 10
546 A178 70c lt grn & multi 35 15
547 A178 80c buff & multi 40 20
548 A178 1b multi 50 25
Nos. 544-548,C316-C319 (9) 4.50 1.95

Bolivian paintings. Issue dates: 1b, Aug. 17; others, Dec. 4.

1972, Aug. 26

549 A179 30c multi 25 10

4th Inter-American Philatelic Exhibition, EXFILBRA, Rio de Janeiro, Brazil, Aug. 26-Sept. 2.

Echinocactus Notocactus A180

Designs: Various cacti.

1973, Aug. 6 Litho. *Perf. 13½*

550 A180 20c crim & multi 15 5
551 A180 40c multi 20 8
552 A180 50c multi 25 10
553 A180 70c multi 35 12
Nos. 550-553,C321-C323 (7) 3.20 1.25

Power Station, Santa Isabel A181

Designs: 20c, Tin industry. 90c, Bismuth industry. 1b, Natural gas plant.

1973, Nov. 26 Litho. *Perf. 13½*

554 A181 10c gray & multi 10 5
555 A181 20c tan & multi 10 5
556 A181 90c lt grn & multi 40 12
557 A181 1b yel & multi 40 15
Nos. 554-557,C324-C325 (6) 2.25 87

Bolivia's development.

Cattleya Nobilior — A182

Orchids: 50c, Zygopetalum bolivianum. 1b, Huntleya melagris.

1974, May 15 *Perf. 13½*

558 A182 20c gray & multi 15 5
559 A182 50c lt bl & multi 25 10
560 A182 1b cit & multi 40 15
Nos. 558-560,C327-C330 (7) 7.80 2.45

UPU and Philatelic Exposition Emblems A183

1974, Oct. 9

561 A183 3.50b grn, blk & bl 1.50 60

Centenary of Universal Postal Union: PRENFIL-UPU Philatelic Exhibition, Buenos Aires, Oct. 1-12; EXPO-UPU Philatelic Exhibition, Montevideo, Oct. 20-27.

Gen. Sucre, by I. Wallpher — A184

1974, Dec. 9 Litho. *Perf. 13½*

562 A184 5b multi 1.75 75

Sesquicentennial of the Battle of Ayacucho.

Lions Emblem and Steles A185

1975, Mar. Litho. *Perf. 13½*

563 A185 30c red & multi 50 10

Lions International in Bolivia, 25th anniversary.

España 75 Emblem A186

1975, Mar.

564 A186 4.50b yel, red & blk 1.25 50

Espana 75 International Philatelic Exhibition, Madrid, Apr. 4-13.

Emblem A187

1975 Litho. *Perf. 13½*

565 A187 2.50b lil, blk & sil 1.00 40

First meeting of Postal Ministers, Quito, Ecuador, March 1974, and for the Cartagena Agreement.

Pando Coat of Arms — A188

Designs: Departmental coats of arms.

1975, July 16 Litho. *Perf. 13½*
Gold & Multicolored

566 A188 20c *shown* 10 10
567 A188 2b *Chuquisaca* 75 50
568 A188 3b *Cochabamba* 1.00 75
Nos. 566-568,C336-C341 (9) 4.35 3.50

Sesquicentennial of Republic of Bolivia.

Simón Bolívar — A189

Presidents and Statesmen of Bolivia: 30c, Victor Paz Estenssoro. 60c, Tomas Frias. 1b, Ismael Montes. 2.50b, Aniceto Arce. 7b, Bautista Saavedra. 10b, José Manuel Pando. 15b, José María Linares. 50b, Simon Bolivar.

1975 Litho. *Perf. 13½*
Size: 24x32mm.

569 A189 30c multi 15 5
569A A189 60c multi 20 10
570 A189 1b multi 30 15
571 A189 2.50b multi 75 35
572 A189 7b multi 2.00 1.00
573 A189 10b multi 3.00 1.50
574 A189 15b multi 4.00 2.00

Size: 28x39mm.

575 A189 50b multi 15.00
Nos. 569-575,C346-C353 (16) 53.90

Sesquicentennial of Republic of Bolivia.

"EXFIVIA 75" A190

1975, Dec. 1 Litho. *Perf. 13½*

576 A190 3b multi 1.00 50
a. Souvenir sheet 2.25 1.75

EXFIVIA 75, first Bolivian Philatelic Exposition. No. 576a contains one stamp similar to No. 576 with simulated perforations. Multicolored margin shows emblems of various international philatelic exhibitions. Size: 130x80mm. Sold for 5b.

Chiang Kai-shek, Flags of Bolivia and China — A191

1976, Apr. 4 Litho. *Perf. 13½*

577 A191 2.50b multi, red circle 90 40
578 A191 2.50b multi, bl circle 90 40

Pres. Chiang Kai-shek of China (1887-1975), first death anniversary.

Erroneous red of sun's circle on Chinese flag of No. 577 was corrected on No. 578 with a dark blue overlay.

Naval Insignia — A192

1976, Apr. Litho. *Perf. 13½*

579 A192 50c bl & multi 35 10

Navy anniversary.

Geological Map, Pickax and Lamp A193

1976, May

580 A193 4b multi 1.25 75

Bolivian Geological Institute.

Lufthansa Jet, Bolivian and German Colors A194

1976, May

581 A194 3b multi 1.25 50

Lufthansa, 50th anniversary.

Boy Scout and Scout Emblem — A195

1976, May Litho. *Perf. 13½*

582 A195 1b multi 50 30

Bolivian Boy Scouts, 60th anniversary.

Battle Scene, U.S. Bicentennial Emblem — A196

1976, May 25

583 A196 4.50b bis & multi 2.00 1.00

American Bicentennial.

A souvenir sheet contains one stamp similar to No. 583 with simulated perforations. Multicolored, inscribed margin shows U.S. flags of 1776 and 1976. Size: 130x80mm.

Family, Map of Bolivia A197

Brother Vicente Bernedo A198

1976 *Perf. 13½*
584 A197 2.50b multi 75 50

National Census 1976.

1976, Oct.
585 A198 1.50b multi 50 25

Brother Vicente Bernedo de Potosi (1544-1619), missionary to the Indians.

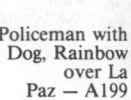

Policeman with Dog, Rainbow over La Paz — A199

1976, Oct.
586 A199 2.50b multi 75 40

Bolivian Police, 150 years of service.

Emblem, Bolivar and Sucre A200

1976, Nov. 18 **Litho.** *Perf. 13½*
587 A200 1.50b multi 75 40

International Congress of Bolivarian Societies.

Pedro Poveda, View of La Paz — A201

1976, Dec.
588 A201 1.50b multi 50 25

Pedro Poveda (1874-1936), educator.

A202

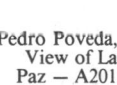

1976, Dec. 17 *Perf. 10½*
594 A202 20c brown 10 5
595 A202 1b ultra 30 10
596 A202 1.50b green 50 10

Boy and Girl — A203

1977, Feb. 4 **Litho.** *Perf. 13½*
599 A203 50c multi 20 5

Christmas 1976, and for 50th anniversary of the Inter-American Children's Institute.

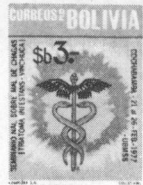

Staff of Aesculapius A204

Supreme Court, La Paz A205

1977, Mar. 18 **Litho.** *Perf. 13½x13*
600 A204 3b multi 90 15

National Seminar on Chagas' disease, Cochabamba, Feb. 21-26.

1977, May 3

Designs: 4b, Manuel Maria Urcullu, first President of Supreme Court. 4.50b, Pantaleon Dalence, President 1883-1889.

601 A205 2.50b multi 45 12
602 A205 4b multi 65 18
603 A205 4.50b multi 75 20

Sesquicentennial of Bolivian Supreme Court.

Newspaper Mastheads A206

Map of Bolivia, Tower and Flag A207

Designs: 2.50b, Alfredo Alexander and Hoy (horiz.). 3b, Jose Carrasco and El Diario (horiz.). 4b, Demetrio Canelas and Los Tiempos. 5.50b, Frontpage of Presencia.

1977, June **Litho.** *Perf. 13½*
604 A206 1.50b multi 35 10
605 A206 2.50b multi 50 15
606 A206 3b multi 65 20
607 A206 4b multi 75 25
608 A206 5.50b multi 1.00 30
Nos. 604-608 (5) 3.25 1.00

Bolivian newspapers and their founders

1977, June
609 A207 3b multi 75 25

90th anniversary of Oruro Club.

Games' Poster A208

Tin Miner and Emblem A209

1977, Oct. 20 **Litho.** *Perf. 13½*
610 A208 5b bl & multi 1.00 30

8th Bolivian Games, La Paz, Oct. 1977.

1977, Oct. 31 **Litho.** *Perf. 13*
611 A209 3b multi 75 25

Bolivian Mining Corporation, 25th anniversary.

Miners, Globe, Tin Symbol A210

Map of Bolivia, Radio Masts A211

1977, Nov. 3
612 A210 6b sil & multi 1.25 40

International Tin Symposium, La Paz, Nov. 14-21.

1977, Nov. 11
613 A211 2.50b bl & multi 50 12

Radio Bolivia, ASBORA, 50th anniversary.

No. 450 Surcharged with New Value, 3 Bars and "EXFIVIA-77"

1977, Nov. 25 **Litho.** *Perf. 11x13½*
614 A147 5b on 5000b on 5b gold & gray 1.10 25

EXFIVIA '77 Philatelic Exhibition, Cochabamba.

Eye, Compass, Book of Law — A212

1978, May 3 **Litho.** *Perf. 13½x13*
615 A212 5b multi 1.00 25

Audit Department, 50th anniversary.

Mt. Illimani A213

Pre-Columbian Monolith A214

Design: 1.50b, Mt. Cerro de Potosi.

Perf. 11x10½, 10½x11
1978, June 1 **Litho.**
616 A213 50c bl & Prus bl 15 5
617 A214 1b brn & lem 25 5
618 A213 1.50b red & bl gray 40 6

Andean Countries, Staff of Aesculapius A215

Map of Americas with Bolivia A216

1978, June 1 *Perf. 10½x11*
626 A215 2b org & blk 50 15

Health Ministers of Andean Countries, 5th meeting.

1978, June 1
627 A216 2.50b dp ultra & red 50 20

World Rheumatism Year.

Central Bank Building — A217

1978, July 26 **Litho.** *Perf. 13½*
628 A217 7b multi 1.50 40

50th anniversary of Bank of Bolivia.

Jesus and Children — A218

1979, Feb. 20 **Litho.** *Perf. 13½*
629 A218 8b multi 1.40 25

International Year of the Child.

Antofagasta Cancel — A219

Eduardo Abaroa, and Chain — A220

Designs: 1b, La Chimba cancel. 1.50b, Mejillones cancel. 5.50b, View of Antofagasta (horiz.). 6.50b, Woman in chains, symbolizing captive province. 8b, Map of Antofagasta Province, 1876. 10b, Arms of province.

1979, Mar. 23 **Litho.** *Perf. 10½*
630 A219 50e buff & blk 10 5
631 A219 1b pink & blk 18 5
632 A219 1.50b pale grn & blk 28 6

Perf. 13½

633 A220 5.50b multi 95 25
634 A220 6.50b multi 1.20 28
635 A220 7b multi 1.25 28
636 A220 8b multi 1.40 35
637 A220 10b multi 1.75 48
Nos. 630-637 (8) 7.11 1.80

Centenary of loss of Antofagasta coastal area to Chile.

Emblem and Map of Bolivia A221

Gymnast A222

1979, Mar. 26 *Perf. 13½x13*
638 A221 3b multi 55 12

Radio Club of Bolivia.

Perf. 13x13½, 13½x13
1979, Mar. 27

Design: 6.50b, Runner and Games emblem (horiz.).

39 A222 6.50b multi 1.20 28
40 A222 10b multi 1.75 48

Southern Cross Sports Games, Bolivia, Nov. 3-12, 1978.

A souvenir sheet contains 1 stamp similar to No. 640 with simulated perforations. Multicolored margin shows various exhibition and sports emblems. Sold for 20b. Size: 0x130mm.

Bulgaria No. 1 — A223

EXFILMAR Emblem — A224

1979, Mar. 30 *Perf. 10½*
41 A223 2.50b multi 45 12

PHILASERDICA '79 International Philatelic Exhibition, Sofia, Bulgaria, May 18-27.

1979, Apr. 2
42 A224 6b multi 1.10 30

Bolivian Maritime Philatelic Exhibition, La Paz, Nov. 18-28.

OAS Emblem, Map of Bolivia — A226

1979, Oct. 22 Litho. *Perf. 14x13½*
644 A226 6b multi 1.10 30

Organization of American States, 9th Congress, La Paz, Oct.-Nov.

Franz Tamayo — A227

Bolivian and Japanese Flags, Hospital — A228

U.N. Emblem and Meeting — A229

Radio Tower and Waves — A230

1979, Dec.
645 A227 2.80b blk & gray 50 15
646 A228 5b multi 90 25
648 A229 5b multi 90 25
649 A230 6b multi 1.10 30

Franz Tamayo, lawyer, birth centenary; Japanese-Bolivian health care cooperation; CEPAL, 18th Congress, La Paz, Sept. 18-26; Bolivian National Radio, 50th anniversary.

Puerto Suarez Iron Ore Deposits A231

1979 Litho. *Perf. 13½x14*
650 A231 9.50b multi 1.70 45

Bolivia No. 19, EXFILMAR Emblem, Bolivian Flag — A232

1980 Litho. *Perf. 13½*
651 A232 4b multi 72 16

EXFILMAR, Bolivian Maritime Philatelic Exhibition, La Paz, Nov. 18-28, 1979.

Juana Azurduy on Horseback — A233

1980 Litho. *Perf. 14x13½*
652 A233 4b multi 72 16

Juana Azurduy de Padilla, independence fighter, birth bicentenary.

La Salle and World Map A234

1980 *Perf. 13½x14*
653 A234 9b multi 1.60 40

St. Jean Baptiste de la Salle (1651-1719), educator.

"Victory" in Chariot, Madrid, Exhibition Emblem, Flags of Bolivia and Spain — A235

1980, Oct. Litho. *Perf. 13½x14*
654 A235 14b multi 2.50 65

ESPAMER '80 Stamp Exhibition, Madrid.

Map of South America, Flags of Argentina, Bolivia and Peru — A236

1980, Oct. *Perf. 14x13½*
655 A236 2b multi 36 8

Ministers of Public Works and Transport of Argentina, Bolivia and Peru meeting.

Santa Cruz-Trinidad Railroad, Inauguration of Third Section — A237

1980, Oct.
656 A237 3b multi 52 12

Flag on Provincial Map — A238

Ara Macao — A239

Perf. 14x13½, 13½x14

1981, May 11 Litho.
657 A238 1b Soldier, flag, map 18 5
658 A238 3b Flag, map 52 12
659 A238 40b shown 7.25 1.60
660 A238 50b Soldier, civilians, horiz. 9.00 2.00

July 17 Revolution memorial.

1981, May 11 *Perf. 14x13½*

Designs: Parrots.

661 A239 4b shown 72 16
662 A239 7b Ara chloroptera 1.25 32
663 A239 8b Ara ararauna 1.50 35
664 A239 9b Ara rubrogenys 1.60 40
665 A239 10b Ara auricollis 1.75 42
666 A239 12b Anodorynchus hyacinthinus 2.25 60
667 A239 15b Ara militaris 2.75 75
668 A239 20b Ara severa 3.50 85
Nos. 661-668 (8) 15.32 3.85

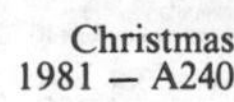

Christmas 1981 — A240

1981, Dec. 7 Litho. *Perf. 10½*
669 A240 1b Virgin and Child, vert. 18 5
670 A240 2b Child, star 36 8

American Airforces Commanders' 22nd Conference, Buenos Aires — A241

1982, Apr. 12 Litho. *Perf. 13½*
671 A241 14b multi 2.50 70

75th Anniv. of Cobija — A242

Simon Bolivar Birth Bicentenary (1983) — A243

1982, July 8 Litho. *Perf. 13½*
672 A242 28b multi 62 24

1982, July 12
673 A243 18b multi 40 16

1983 World Telecommunications Day — A244

1982 World Cup — A245

1982, July 15
674 A244 26b Receiving station 58 20

1982, July 21 *Perf. 11*
675 A245 4b shown 10 5
676 A245 100b Final Act, by Picasso 2.25 90

Girl Playing Piano A246

1982, July 25 *Perf. 13½*
677 A246 16b Boy playing soccer 35 14
678 A246 20b shown 45 18

Prices of premium quality never hinged stamps will be in excess of catalogue price.

Bolivian-Chinese Agricultural Cooperation, 1972-1982 — A247

1982, Aug. 12
679 A247 30b multi 65 26

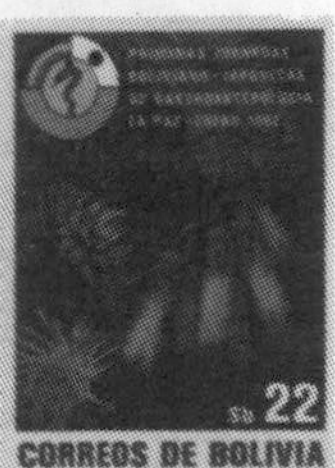

First Bolivian-Japanese Gastroenterology Conference, La Paz, Jan — A248

1982, Aug. 26
680 A248 22b multi 50 20

10th Anniv. of Bolivian Philatelic Federation A249

1982, Aug. 31 Litho. ***Perf. 14x13½***
681 A249 19b Stamps 40 15

Pres. Hernando Siles Birth Centenary A250

1982, Sept. 1
682 A250 20b tan & dk brn 45 18

Scouting Year A251

Cochabamba Philatelic Center, 25th Anniv. A252

1982, Sept. 3 ***Perf. 11***
683 A251 5b Baden-Powell 12 5

1982, Sept. 14
684 A252 3b multi 6 5

Cochabamba Superior Court of Justice Sesquicentennial — A253

1982 Litho. ***Perf. 13½***
685 A253 10b multi 25 10

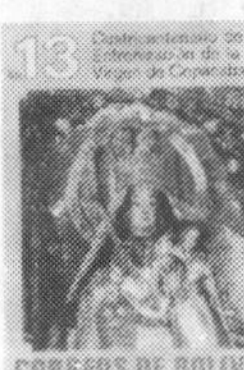

Enthronement of Virgin of Copacabana, 400th Anniv. — A254

Navy Day — A255

1982, Nov. 15 Litho. ***Perf. 13½***
686 A254 13b multi 34 15

1982, Nov. 17
687 A255 14b Port Busch Naval Base 35 15

Christmas 1982 — A256

1982, Nov. 19 ***Perf. 11***
688 A256 10b grn & gray 25 10

10th Youth Soccer Championship, Jan. 22-Feb. 13 — A257

1983, Feb. 13 Litho. ***Perf. 13½***
689 A257 50b multi 1.25 50

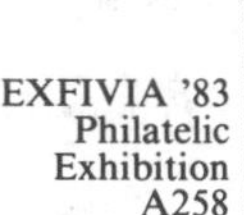

EXFIVIA '83 Philatelic Exhibition A258

1983, Nov. 5 Litho. ***Perf. 13½***
690 A258 150b brn car 1.50 60

Visit of Brazilian Pres. Joao Figueiredo, Feb. — A259

1984, Feb. 7 Litho. ***Perf. 13½x14***
691 A259 150b multi 60 25

Simon Bolivar Entering La Paz, by Carmen Baptista A260

Paintings of Bolivar: 50b, Riding Horse, by Mulato Gil de Quesada (vert.).

Perf. 14x13½, 13½x14

1984, Mar. 30
692 A260 50b multi 20 8
693 A260 200b multi 80 32

Types of 1957-79 Surcharged.

1984, Mar.
694 A223 40b on 2.50b #641 16 5
695 A227 40b on 2.80b #645 16 5
696 A219 60b on 1.50b #632 24 10
697 A216 60b on 2.50b #627 24 10
698 A226 100b on 2b #642 40 16
699 A141 200b on 350b #409 80 32
Nos. 694-699 (6) 2.00 78

Nos. 675, 683-684, 688, C328 Surcharged.

1984, June 27 Litho. ***Perf. 11***
700 A252 500b on 36 #684
701 A245 1000b on 4b #675
702 A256 2000b on 10b #688
703 A251 5000b on 5b #683

Perf. 13½
704 A182 10,000b on 3.80b #C328

Road Safety Education A261

Jose Eustaquio Mendez, 200th Birth Anniv. A262

Cartoons.

1984, Sept. 7 Litho. ***Perf. 11***
705 A261 80b Jaywalker 5 5
706 A261 120b Motorcycle policeman, ambulance 8 5

Perf. 14x13½, 13½x14

1984, Sept. 19

Paintings. 300b, Birthplace, by Jorge Campos. 500b, Mendez Leading the Battle of La Tablada, by M. Villegas, horiz.

707 A262 300b multi 18 8
708 A262 500b multi 22 10

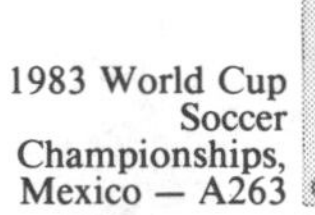

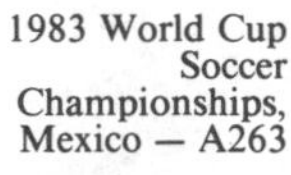

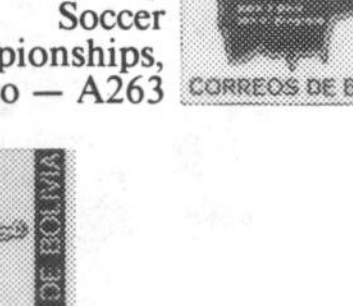

1983 World Cup Soccer Championships, Mexico — A263

Chasqui, Postal Runner — A264

Sponsoring shoe-manufacturers' trademarks and: 100b, 200b, Outline map of Bolivia, national colors. 600b, World map and soccer ball, horiz.

1984, Oct. 26 ***Perf. 11***
709 A263 100b multi 5 5
710 A263 200b multi 8 5
711 A263 600b multi 20 8

1985
712 A264 11000b vio bl 40 16

Intl. Year of Professional Education A265

Intl. Anti-Polio Campaign A266

1985, Apr. 25
713 A265 2000b Natl. Manual Crafts emblem 5 5

1985, May 22
714 A266 20000b lt bl & vio 36 15

Endangered Wildlife — A267

1985, May 22
715 A267 23000b Altiplano boliviano 30 12
716 A267 25000b Sarcorhamphus gryphus 35 14
717 A267 30000b Blastocaros dichotomus 45 18

Nos. 716-717 vert.

Dona Vicenta Juaristi Eguino (b. 1785), Independence Heroine — A268

UN, 40th Anniv. — A269

1985, Oct. Litho. ***Perf. 13½***
718 A268 300000b multi 30 12

1985, Oct. 24 ***Perf. 11***
719 A269 1000000b bl & gold 1.00 40

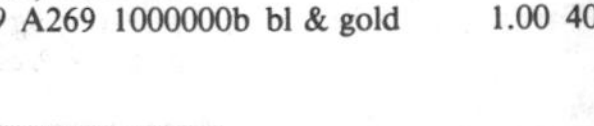

Natl. Soccer Team, 75th Anniv. — A270

1985, Nov.
720 A270 200000b multi 20 8

No. 713 Surcharged.

1986 Litho. ***Perf. 11***
721 A265 200000b on 2000b multi 22 10
722 A265 5000000b on 2000b multi 5.25 2.10

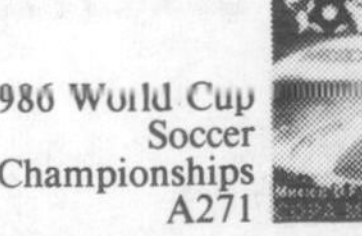

1986 World Cup Soccer Championships A271

Intl. Youth Year
A272 A273

1986
723 A271 300000 Emblems, vert. 32 12
724 A271 550000 Pique trade-mark, vert. 58 24
725 A271 1000000 Azteca Stadium 1.05 42
726 A271 2500000 World cup, vert. 2.65 1.05

1986
727 A272 150000 brt car rose 16 6
728 A272 500000 bl grn 55 35
729 A273 3000000 multi 3.15 1.25

Inscribed 1985.

Alfonso Sobieta Viaduct, Carretera Quillacollo, Confital A274

1986 *Perf. 13½*
730 A274 400000 int bl & gray 42 16

Inter-American Development Bank, 25th anniv.

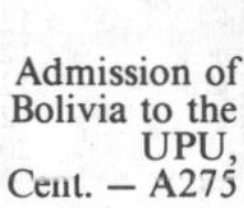

Admission of Bolivia to the UPU, Cent. — A275

1986 *Perf. 11*
731 A275 800000 multi 85 35

Postal Workers Society, 50th Anniv. — A276

1986, Sept. 5
732 A276 2000000 brn & pale brn 2.10 85

Founding of Trinidad, 300th Anniv. A277

1986 *Perf. 13½x14*
733 A277 1400000 Bull and Rider, by Vaca 1.50 60

Bolivian Philatelic Federation, 15th Anniv. A278

1986, Nov. 28
734 A278 600000b No. 19 62 25

Death of a Priest, by Jose Antonio Zampa — A279

Intl. Peace Year — A280

1986, Nov. 21 *Perf. 14x13½*
735 A279 400000 multi 42 16

1986, Sept. 16 *Perf. 11*
736 A280 200000 yel grn & pale grn 22 10

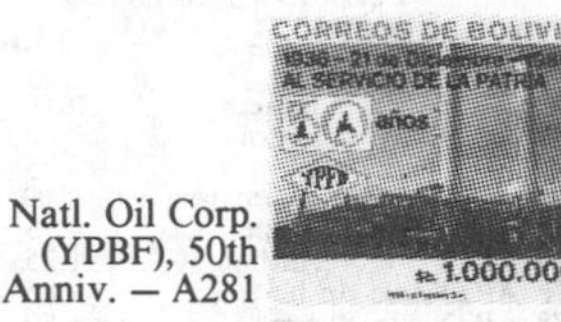

Natl. Oil Corp. (YPBF), 50th Anniv. — A281

1986, Dec. 22 Litho. *Perf. 11*
737 A281,000,000b 1.50 38

Photograph of a Devil-mask Dancer, by Jimencz Cordero — A282

1987, Feb. 13 Litho. *Perf. 14x13½*
738 A28220c multi 30 12

February 10th Society, cent. (in 1985).

State Visit of Richard von Weizsacker, Pres. of Germany, Mar. 20 — A283

1987, Mar. 20 Litho. *Perf. 14x13½*
739 A283 30c Crossed flags 45 18

State Visit of King Juan Carlos of Spain, May 20 — A284

1987, May 20 *Perf. 13½x14*
740 A284 60c Natl. arms 90 35

EXFIVIA '87 — A285

Mount Potosi, 18th cent. engraving.

1987, Oct. Litho. *Perf. 13½*
741 A28550c multi 72 28

Wildlife Conservation A286

1987, Oct.
742 A28620c Condor 30 12
743 A28620c Tapir 30 12
744 A28630c Vicuna 45 18
745 A28630c Armadillo 45 18
746 A28640c Spectacled bears 58 24
747 A28660c Toucans 88 35
Nos. 742-747 (6) 2.96 1.19

Wildlife in danger of extinction.

ESPAMER '87, La Coruna — A287

1987, Oct. Litho. *Perf. 14x13½*
748 A28720c Nina, stern of Santa Maria 30 12
749 A28720c Bow of Santa Maria, Pinta 30 12

Nos. 748-749 printed se-tenant in a continuous design.

AIR POST STAMPS

Aviation School
AP1 AP2

1924, Dec. Unwmk. Engr. *Perf. 14*
C1 AP1 10c ver & blk 35 35
a. Inverted center 1,250.
C2 AP1 15c car & blk 1.50 1.00
C3 AP1 25c dk bl & blk 75 50
C4 AP1 50c org & blk 1.25 1.00
C5 AP2 1b red brn & blk 1.25 1.25
C6 AP2 2b blk brn & blk 2.75 2.75
C7 AP2 5b dk vio & blk 4.50 4.50
Nos. C1-C7 (7) 12.35 11.35

Issued to commemorate the establishing of the National Aviation School.

These stamps were available for ordinary postage. Nos. C1, C3, C5 and C6 exist imperforate. Proofs of the 2b with inverted center exist imperforate and privately perforated.

Emblem of Lloyd Aereo Boliviano — AP3

1928 Litho. *Perf. 11.*
C8 AP3 15c green 1.25 75
a. Imperf. (pair) 35.00
C9 AP3 20c dk bl 25 15
C10 AP3 35c red brn 75 40

Graf Zeppelin Issues.
Nos. C1-C5 Surcharged or Overprinted in Various Colors:

a
CORREO AEREO
R. S. 6-V-1930
5 Cts.

b
CORREO AEREO
R. S.
6-V-1930

1930, May 6 *Perf. 14.*
C11 AP1 (a) 5c on 10c ver & blk (G) 15.00 15.00
C12 AP1 (b) 10c ver & blk (Bl) 15.00 15.00
C13 AP1 (b) 10c ver & blk (Br) 550.00 750.00
C14 AP1 (b) 15c car & blk (V) 15.00 15.00
C15 AP1 (b) 25c dk bl & blk (R) 15.00 15.00
C16 AP1 (b) 50c org & blk (Br) 15.00 15.00
C17 AP1 (b) 50c org & blk (R) 550.00 750.00
C18 AP1 (b) 1b red brn & blk (gold) 175.00 150.00

Experts consider the 50c with silver overprint to be a trial color proof.

Surcharged or Overprinted in Bronze Inks of Various Colors.

C19 AP1 (a) 5c on 10c ver & blk (G) 85.00 85.00
C20 AP1 (b) 10c ver & blk (Bl) 70.00 70.00
C21 AP1 (b) 15c car & blk (V) 85.00 85.00
C22 AP1 (b) 25c dk bl & blk (cop) 85.00 85.00
C23 AP2 (b) 1b red brn & blk (gold) 175.00 175.00

Issued in commemoration of the flight of the airship Graf Zeppelin from Europe to Brazil and return via Lakehurst, N.J.

Nos. C11 to C18 exist with the surcharges inverted, double, or double with one inverted, but the regularity of these varieties is questioned.

Nos. C19 to C23 were intended for use on postal matter forwarded by the Graf Zeppelin. No. C18 was overprinted with light gold or gilt bronze ink. No. C23 was overprinted with deep gold bronze ink. Nos. C13 and C17 were overprinted with trial colors but were sold with the regular printings. The 5c on 10c is known surcharged in black and in blue.

Air Post Stamps of 1928 Issue, Surcharged

Z 1930
Bs. 3.—

1930, May 6 *Perf. 11.*
C24 AP3 1.50b on 15c grn 40.00 40.00
a. Inverted surcharge 80.00 80.00
b. Comma instead of period after "1" 50.00 50.00
C25 AP3 3b on 20c dk bl 40.00 40.00
a. Inverted surcharge 80.00 80.00
b. Comma instead of period after "3" 55.00 55.00
C26 AP3 6b on 35c red brn 60.00 65.00
a. Inverted surcharge 135.00 135.00
b. Comma instead of period after "6" 75.00 75.00

Airplane and Bullock Cart — AP6

Airplane and River Boat — AP7

1930, July 24 Litho. *Perf. 14*
C27 AP6 5c dp vio 60 40
C28 AP7 15c red 60 40
C29 AP7 20c yellow 60 40
C30 AP6 35c yel grn 60 25
C31 AP7 50c dp bl 60 25

C32 AP6 1b lt brn	60	25
C33 AP7 2b dp rose	60	35
C34 AP6 3b slate	3.00	2.00
Nos. C27-C34 (8)	7.20	4.30

Nos. C27 to C34 exist imperforate.

Air Service Emblem AP8

1932, Sept. 16 *Perf. 11.*

C35 AP8 5c ultra	1.00	60
C36 AP8 10c gray	60	30
C37 AP8 15c dk rose	1.00	75
C38 AP8 25c orange	1.00	75
C39 AP8 30c green	80	40
C40 AP8 50c violet	80	40
C41 AP8 1b dk brn	80	40
Nos. C35-C41 (7)	6.00	3.60

Map of Bolivia — AP9

1935, Feb. 1 **Engr.** *Perf. 12.*

C42 AP9 5c brn red	25	20
C43 AP9 10c dk grn	25	20
C44 AP9 20c dk vio	25	20
C45 AP9 30c ultra	25	20
C46 AP9 50c orange	35	20
C47 AP9 1b bis brn	35	30
C48 AP9 1½b yellow	80	20
C49 AP9 2b carmine	80	40
C50 AP9 5b green	1.50	50
C51 AP9 10b dk brn	2.50	1.00
Nos. C42-C51 (10)	7.30	3.40

Air Post Stamps of 1924-30 Surcharged in Red or Green — c

Correo Aéreo
D. S. 25-2-37
0.05

1937, Oct. 6 *Perf. 11, 14.*

C52 AP6 5c on 35c yel grn (R)	50	40
a. "Carreo"	15.00	
C53 AP3 20c on 35c red brn (R)	60	40
C54 AP3 50c on 35c red brn (R)	75	60
a. Inverted surcharge	25.00	
C55 AP3 1b on 35c red brn (R)	1.25	75
C56 AP1 2b on 50c org & blk (R)	1.75	1.00
C57 AP1 12b on 10c ver & blk (G)	7.00	5.00
a. Inverted surcharge	30.00	
C58 AP1 15b on 10c ver & blk (G)	7.00	3.00

Regular Postage Stamps of 1925 Surcharged in Green or Red — d

Correo
Aéreo
D. S.
25-2-37
Bs. 4.—

Perf. 14.

C59 A56 (d) 3b on 50c dp vio (G)	1.75	1.50
C60 A56 (d) 4b on 1b red (G)	2.25	2.00
C61 A57 (c) 5b on 2b org (G)	2.75	2.50
C62 A56 (d) 10b on 5b blk brn (R)	7.00	5.00
a. Double surcharge	50.00	
Nos. C52-C62 (11)	32.60	22.15

Courtyard of Potosi Mint AP10

Miner AP11

Emancipated Woman — AP12

Airplane over Field AP13

Airplanes and Liberty Monument AP14

Pincers, Torch and Good Will Principles — AP15

Airplane over River AP16

Emblem of New Government AP17

Transport Planes over Map of Bolivia AP18

1938, May **Litho.** *Perf. 10½.*

C63 AP10 20c dp rose	35	30
C64 AP11 30c gray	35	30
C65 AP12 40c yellow	35	30
C66 AP13 50c yel grn	50	30
C67 AP14 60c dl bl	50	30
C68 AP15 1b dl red	75	30
C69 AP16 2b bister	1.50	30
C70 AP17 3b lt brn	1.50	30
C71 AP18 5b dk vio	2.00	30
Nos. C63-C71 (9)	7.80	2.70

Chalice — AP19

Virgin of Copacabana AP20

Jesus Christ AP21

Church of San Francisco, La Paz — AP22

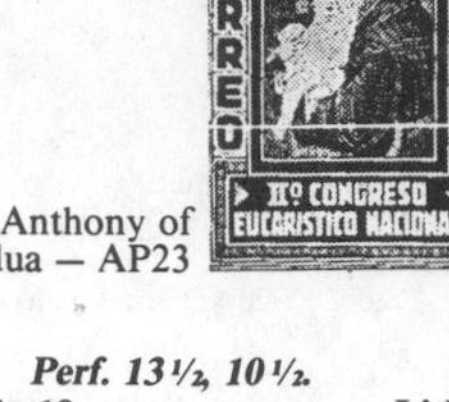

St. Anthony of Padua — AP23

Perf. 13½, 10½.

1939, July 19 **Litho.**

C72 AP19 5c dl vio	75	50
a. Pair, imperf. between	60.00	
C73 AP20 30c lt bl grn	60	30
C74 AP21 45c vio bl	75	30
a. Vertical pair, imperf. between	85.00	
C75 AP22 60c carmine	75	50
C76 AP23 75c vermilion	1.25	1.00
C77 AP23 90c dp bl	85	40
C78 AP22 2b dl brn	1.50	40
C79 AP21 4b dp plum	2.00	60
C80 AP20 5b lt bl	4.00	40
C81 AP19 10b yellow	10.00	40
Nos. C72-C81 (10)	22.45	4.80

Issued to commemorate the second National Eucharistic Congress.

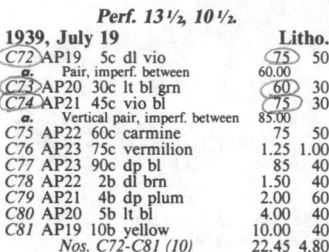

Plane over Lake Titicaca — AP24

Mt. Illimani and Condor — AP25

1941, Aug. 21 *Perf. 13½.*

C82 AP24 10b dl grn	6.00	75
C83 AP24 20b lt ultra	7.00	1.25
C84 AP25 50b rose lil	12.50	1.75
C85 AP25 100b ol bis	30.00	6.00

Counterfeits exist.

Liberty and Clasped Hands — AP26

1942, Nov. 12

C86 AP26 40c rose lake	50	35
C87 AP26 50c ultra	50	35
C88 AP26 1b org brn	60	50
C89 AP26 5b magenta	1.50	35
a. Double impression		
C90 AP26 10b dl brn vio	5.00	2.50
Nos. C86-C90 (5)	8.10	4.05

Issued to commemorate the Conference of Chancellors held January 15, 1942.

General José Ballivián; Old and Modern Transportation — AP27

1943, Nov. 18 **Engr.** *Perf. 12½*

C91 AP27 10c rose vio & brn	15	15
C92 AP27 20c emer & brn	20	15
C93 AP27 30c rose car & brn	30	25
C94 AP27 3b bl & brn	40	30
C95 AP27 5b blk & brn	75	50
Nos. C91-C95 (5)	1.80	1.35

Department of Beni centenary.

Condor and Sun Rising — AP28

Plane — AP29

1944, Sept. 19 **Litho.** *Perf. 13½.*

C96 AP28 40c red vio	15	10
C97 AP28 1b lb vio	20	10
C98 AP29 1.50b yel grn	25	10
C99 AP29 2.50b dk gray bl	50	25

Revolution of Dec. 20, 1943.

Map of National Airways AP30

Map of Bolivian Air Lines AP31

1945, May 31 *Perf. 11*

C100 AP30 10c red	15	10
a. Imperf. (pair)	12.50	
C101 AP30 50c yellow	20	10
a. Imperf. (pair)	20.00	
C102 AP30 90c lt grn	30	10
C103 AP30 5b lt ultra	50	20
C104 AP30 20b dp brn	1.50	60
Nos. C100-C104 (5)	2.65	1.10

10th anniversary of first flight, La Paz to Tacha, Peru, by Panagra Airways.

1945, Sept. 15 *Perf. 13½.*

Centers in Red and Blue.

C105 AP31 20c violet	12	10
C106 AP31 30c org brn	12	10
C107 AP31 50c brt bl grn	12	10
C108 AP31 90c brt vio	12	10
C109 AP31 2b blue	20	15
C110 AP31 3b magenta	30	20
C111 AP31 4b ol bis	50	25
Nos. C105-C111 (7)	1.48	1.00

Issued to commemorate the 20th anniversary of the founding of Lloyd Aereo Boliviano.

No. C76 Surcharged in Blue

1947
Habilitada
Bs. 1.40

1947, Mar. 23

C112 AP23 1.40b on 75c ver	30	30

Mt. Illimani AP32

Arms of Bolivia and Argentina AP33

1947, Sept. 15 **Litho.** *Perf. 11½*

C113 AP32 1b rose car	10	10
C114 AP32 1.40b emerald	15	10
C115 AP32 2.50b blue	25	20
C116 AP32 3b dp org	35	30
C117 AP32 4b rose lil	40	25
Nos. C113-C117 (5)	1.25	95

Issued to commemorate the first anniversary of the Revolution of July 21, 1946.

1947, Oct. 23 *Perf. 13½*

C118 AP33 2.90b ultra	40	40
a. Imperf. (pair)	30.00	
b. Perf. 10½	7.50	6.00

Issued to commemorate the meeting of Presidents Enrique Hertzog of Bolivia and Juan D. Peron of Argentina at Yacuiba, Oct. 23, 1947.

Types of Regular Issue of 1948.

Designs: 2.50b, Statue of Christ above La Paz. 3.70b, Child kneeling before cross. No. C121, St. John Bosco. No. C122, Virgin of Copacabana. 13.60b, Pope Pius XII blessing University of La Paz.

1948, Sept. 26 *Perf. 11½.*

C119	A120	2.50b ver & yel	85	50
C120	A120	3.70b rose & cr	1.00	50
C121	A120	4b rose lil & gray	1.00	40
C122	A120	4b lt ultra & sal	1.00	25
C123	A120	13.60b ultra & lt grn	1.25	40
		Nos. C119-C123 (5)	5.10	2.05

Issued to publicize the 3rd Inter-American Congress of Catholic Education.

Type of Regular Issue of 1948

1948, Oct.

C124	A125	10b emer & sal	2.50	30

Issued to publicize the International Automobile Races of South America, September-October 1948.

Pres. Gregorio Pacheco, Map and Post Horn AP34

L. A. B. Plane AP35

1950, Jan. 2 **Unwmk.**

C125	AP34	1.40b org brn	15	15
C126	AP34	2.50b orange	10	10
C127	AP34	3.30b rose vio	15	15

Issued to commemorate the 75th anniversary of the formation of the Universal Postal Union.

Nos. C100 and C104 Surcharged in Black

XV ANIVERSARIO
PANAGRA
Bs 4.- 1935-1950

1950, May 31 *Perf. 11*

C128	AP30	4b on 10c red	15	15
C129	AP30	10b on 20b dp brn	40	30
a.		Inverted surcharge	25.00	25.00

Issued to commemorate the 15th anniversary of Panagra air services in Bolivia.

1950, Sept. 15 **Litho.** *Perf. 13½*

C130	AP35	20c red org	15	15
C131	AP35	30c purple	15	15
C132	AP35	50c green	15	15
C133	AP35	1b orange	15	15
C134	AP35	3b ultra	15	15
C135	AP35	15b carmine	50	20
C136	AP35	50b chocolate	1.50	50
		Nos. C130-C136 (7)	2.75	1.45

Issued to commemorate the 25th anniversary of the founding of Lloyd Aero Boliviano. No. C132 exists imperforate.

No. C116 Surcharged in Black

Triunfo de la Democracia
24 de Sept.49
Bs. 1.40

1950, Sept. 24 *Perf. 11½*

C137	AP32	1.40b on 3b dp org	25	25

Issued to commemorate the 1st anniversary of the ending of the Civil War of Aug. 24-Sept. 24, 1949.

Symbols of United Nations — AP36

1950, Oct. 24 **Unwmk.**

C138	AP36	3.60b crim rose	75	25
C139	AP36	4.70b blk brn	1.00	25

Issued to commemorate the 5th anniversary of the formation of the United Nations, October 24, 1945.

Gate of the Sun and Llama AP37

Church of San Francisco AP38

Designs: 40c, Avenue Camacho. 50c, Consistorial Palace. 1b, Legislative Palace. 2b, Communications Bldg. 3b, Arms. 4b, La Gasca ordering Mendoza to found La Paz. 5b, Capt. Alonso de Mendoza founding La Paz. 10b, Arms; portrait of Mendoza.

1951, Mar. 1 **Engr.** *Perf. 12½.*

Center in Black.

C140	AP37	20c carmine	20	20
C141	AP38	30c dk vio bl	20	20
C142	AP37	40c dk bl	20	20
C143	AP37	50c bl grn	25	25
C144	AP37	1b red	30	30
C145	AP37	2b red org	50	50
C146	AP37	3b dp bl	50	50
C147	AP37	4b vermilion	60	60
a.		Souv. sheet of 4	1.50	1.50
C148	AP37	5b dk grn	60	60
a.		Souv. sheet of 3	1.50	1.50
C149	AP37	10b red brn	1.00	1.00
a.		Souv. sheet of 3	1.50	1.50
		Nos. C140-C149 (10)	4.35	4.35

400th anniversary of the founding of La Paz.

No. C147a contains C143-C145, C147; No. C148a contains C142, C146, C148; No. C149a contains C140, C141, C149. Black marginal inscriptions. Perf. and imperf., size: 150x100mm.

Horsemanship AP39

Designs: 30c, Basketball. 50c, Fencing. 1b, Hurdling. 2.50b, Javelin throwing. 3b, Relay race. 5b, La Paz stadium.

1951, Aug. 23 **Unwmk.**

Center in Black.

C150	AP39	20c purple	35	10
C151	AP39	30c rose vio	50	15
C152	AP39	50c dp red org	75	15
C153	AP39	1b chocolate	75	15
C154	AP39	2.50b orange	1.00	60
C155	AP39	3b blk brn	1.50	75
a.		Souv. sheet of 3	6.00	5.00
C156	AP39	5b red	3.00	1.50
a.		Souv. sheet of 4	7.00	6.50
		Nos. C150-C156 (7)	7.85	3.40

The stamps were intended to commemorate the 5th South American Games and the 2nd National Sports Congress held at La Paz, October 1948.

No. C155a contains C153-C155; No. C156a contains C150-C152, C156. Black marginal inscriptions. Perf. and imperf., size: 150x100mm.

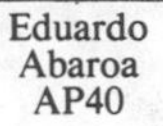

Eduardo Abaroa AP40

Queen Isabella I AP41

1952, Mar. 24 **Litho.** *Perf. 11*

C157	AP40	70c rose red	15	15
C158	AP40	2b org yel	20	25
C159	AP40	3b yel grn	20	25
C160	AP40	5b blue	25	25
C161	AP40	50b rose lil	1.50	75
C162	AP40	100b gray blk	1.75	1.00
		Nos. C157-C162 (6)	4.05	2.65

Issued to commemorate the 73rd anniversary of the death of Eduardo Abaroa.

1952, July 16 *Perf. 13½*

C163	AP41	50b emerald	50	40
C164	AP41	100b brown	1.00	50

Issued to commemorate the 500th anniversary of the birth of Queen Isabella I of Spain. Exist imperforate.

Columbus Lighthouse AP42

1952, July 16

C165	AP42	2b rose lil, *sal*	15	15
C166	AP42	3.70b bl grn, *bl*	15	15
C167	AP42	4.40b org, *sal*	25	10
C168	AP42	20b dk brn, *cr*	50	18

No. C168 exists imperforate.

Soldiers — AP43

Gualberto Villarroel, Victor Paz Estenssoro and Hernan Siles Zuazo AP44

Perf. 13½ (AP43), 11½ (AP44)

1953, Apr. 9 **Litho.**

C169	AP44	3.70b chocolate	20	20
C170	AP43	6b red vio	20	20
C171	AP44	9b brn rose	20	20
C172	AP44	10b aqua	20	20
C173	AP44	16b vermilion	20	20
C174	AP43	22.50b dk brn	40	30
C175	AP44	40b gray	60	20
		Nos. C169-C175 (7)	2.00	1.50

Issued to commemorate the first anniversary of the Revolution of Apr. 9, 1952. Nos. C170 and C174 exist imperf.

Pres. Victor Paz Estenssoro Embracing Indian AP45

Map and Peasant AP46

1954, Aug. 2 *Perf. 12x11½.*

C176	AP45	20b org brn	15	10
C177	AP46	27b brt pink	15	20
C178	AP46	30b red org	25	15
C179	AP46	45b vio brn	40	10
C180	AP45	100b bl grn	75	10
C181	AP46	300b yel grn	2.00	35
		Nos. C176-C181 (6)	3.70	1.00

Nos. C176 and C180 were issued to commemorate the 3rd Inter-American Indian Congress. Nos. C177-C179 and C181 commemorate the agrarian reform laws of 1953-1954.

Oil Derricks AP47

Map of South America and La Paz Arms AP48

1955, Oct. 9 *Perf. 10½*

C182	AP47	55b dk & lt grnsh bl	15	10
C183	AP47	70b dk gray & gray	25	10
C184	AP47	90b dk & lt grn	30	15

Perf. 13.

C185	AP47	500b red lil	1.25	60
C186	AP47	1000b blk brn & fawn	2.00	1.50
		Nos. C182-C186 (5)	3.95	2.45

Nos. C140-C149 Surcharged with New Values and Bars in Black or Carmine.

1957 **Engr.** *Perf. 12½*

Center in Black

C187	AP37	100b on 3b dp bl (C)	15	10
C188	AP37	200b on 2b red org	15	10
C189	AP37	500b on 4b ver	25	15
C190	AP37	600b on 1b red	25	15
C191	AP37	700b on 20c car	40	20
C192	AP37	800b on 40c dk bl (C)	50	30
C193	AP38	900b on 30c dk vio bl (C)	60	15
C194	AP37	1800b on 50c bl grn (C)	1.00	50
C195	AP37	3000b on 5b dk grn (C)	1.50	90
C196	AP37	5000b on 10b red brn (C)	2.50	1.75
		Nos. C187-C196 (10)	7.30	4.30

Unwmk.

1957, May 25 **Litho.** *Perf. 12*

C197	AP48	700b lil & vio	60	40
C198	AP48	1200b pale brn	75	60
C199	AP48	1350b rose car	1.00	75
C200	AP48	2700b bl grn	2.00	1.00
C201	AP48	4000b vio bl	2.50	1.25
		Nos. C197-C201 (5)	6.85	4.00

Issued to commemorate the seventh session of the C. E. P. A. L. (Comision Economica para la America Latina de las Naciones Unidas), La Paz.

Type of Regular Issue, 1957

1957, Dec. 19 *Perf. 11½*

C202	A141	600b magenta	35	10
C203	A141	700b vio bl	50	18
C204	A141	900b pale grn	75	12

Issued to commemorate the opening of the Santa Cruz-Yacuiba Railroad and the meeting of the Presidents of Bolivia and Argentina.

Type of Regular Issue, 1960.

1960, Jan. 30

C205	A142	400b rose cl	75	15
C206	A142	800b sl bl	1.00	30
C207	A142	2000b slate	1.50	60

Issued for an expected visit of Mexico's Pres. Adolfo Lopez Mateos. On sale Jan. 30-Feb. 1, 1960.

Gate of the Sun, Tiahuanacu AP49

Uprooted Oak Emblem AP50

1960, Mar. 26 Litho. *Perf. 11½*
C208 AP49 3,000b gray 2.00 75
C209 AP49 5,000b orange 3.00 1.50
C210 AP49 10,000b rose cl 6.00 2.50
C211 AP49 15,000b bl vio 9.00 4.00

1960, Apr. 7 *Perf. 11½*
C212 AP50 600b ultra 50 50
C213 AP50 700b lt red brn 50 50
C214 AP50 900b dk bl grn 50 50
C215 AP50 1,800b violet 85 85
C216 AP50 2,000b gray 1.00 85
Nos. C212-C216 (5) 3.35 3.20

Issued to publicize World Refugee Year, July 1, 1959-June 30, 1960.

No. C215 exists with "1961" overprint in dark carmine, but was not regularly issued in this form.

Jaime Laredo — AP51

Perf. 11½
1960, Aug. 15 Unwmk. Litho.
C217 AP51 600b rose vio 1.25 40
C218 AP51 700b ol gray 1.50 50
C219 AP51 800b vio brn 1.50 50
C220 AP51 900b dk bl 2.00 50
C221 AP51 1,800b green 2.50 1.50
C222 AP51 4,000b dk gray 6.00 2.50
Nos. C217-C222 (6) 14.75 5.90

Issued to honor the violinist Jaime Laredo.

Type of Regular Issue, 1960.
(Children's Hospital)

1960, Nov. 21 *Perf. 11½*
C223 A146 600b red brn, yel & dp bl 60 35
C224 A146 1,000b ol grn, yel & dp bl 90 35
C225 A146 1,800b plum, yel & dp bl 1.25 60
C226 A146 5,000b blk, yel & dp bl 4.00 1.75

Issued for the Children's Hospital, sponsored by the Rotary Club of La Paz.

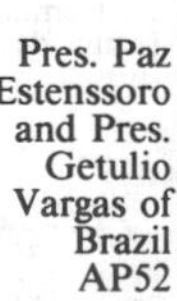

Pres. Paz Estenssoro and Pres. Getulio Vargas of Brazil AP52

1960, Dec. 14 Litho. *Perf. 11½*
C227 AP52 1,200b on 10b org & blk 1.25 1.00

Exists with surcharge inverted.

No. C227 without surcharge was not regularly issued, although a decree authorizing its circulation was published. Counterfeits of surcharge exist.

Pres. Paz Estenssoro and Pres. Frondizi of Argentina AP53

Design: 4,000b, Flags of Bolivia and Argentina.

1961, May 23 *Perf. 10½*
C228 AP53 4,000b brn, red, yel, grn & bl 1.00 90
C229 AP53 6,000b dk grn & blk 1.50 1.25

Issued to commemorate the visit of the President of Argentina, Dr. Arturo Frondizi, to Bolivia.

Miguel de Cervantes — AP54

1961, Oct. Photo. *Perf. 13*
C230 AP54 1400b pale grn & dk ol grn 75 35

Issued to commemorate Cervantes' appointment as Chief Magistrate of La Paz.

Virgin of Cotoca and Symbol of Eucharist AP55

Planes and Parachutes AP56

1962, Mar. 19 Litho. *Perf. 10½*
C231 AP55 1400b brn, pink & yel 1.00 50

Issued to commemorate the 4th National Eucharistic Congress, Santa Cruz, 1961.

Nos. C212-C216 Surcharged Vertically with New Value and Greek Key Border.

1962, June Unwmk. *Perf. 11½*
C232 AP50 1,200b on 600b ultra 1.00 50
C233 AP50 1,300b on 700b lt red brn 90 50
C234 AP50 1,400b on 900b dk bl grn 1.00 50
C235 AP50 2,800b on 1,800b vio 1.50 75
C236 AP50 3,000b on 2,000b gray 1.50 75
Nos. C232-C236 (5) 5.90 3.00

The overprinted segment of Greek key border on Nos. C232-C236 comes in two positions: two full "keys" on top, and one full and two half keys on top.

Flower Type of 1962

Flowers: 100b, 1,800b, Cantua buxifolia. 800b, 10,000b, Cantua bicolor.

1962, June 28 Litho. *Perf. 10½*
Flowers in Natural Colors
C237 A152 100b dk bl 10 10
C238 A152 800b green 50 25
C239 A152 1,800b violet 1.00 50
a. Souv. sheet of 3 5.00 5.00
C240 A152 10,000b dk bl 6.00 3.00

No. C239a contains 3 imperf. stamps similar to Nos. C237-C239, but with the 1,800b background color changed to dark violet blue. Green marginal inscriptions. Size: 130x80mm.

1962, Sept. 5 Litho. *Perf. 11½*

Designs: 1,200b, 5,000b, Plane and oxcart. 2,000b, Aerial photography (plane over South America). Emblem in Red, Yellow & Green

C241 AP56 600b blk & bl 35 20
C242 AP56 1200b multi 50 30
C243 AP56 2000b multi 60 50
C244 AP56 5000b multi 1.50 1.00

Armed Forces of Bolivia.

Malaria Type of 1962

Design: Inscription around mosquito, laurel around globe.

1962, Oct. 4
C245 A154 2000b ind, grn & yel 1.25 75

Issued for the World Health Organization drive to eradicate malaria.

Type of Regular Issue, 1961

Design: 1,200b Pedro de la Gasca (1485-1567).

1962 Unwmk. Photo. *Perf. 13x12½*
C246 A150 1,200b brn, *yel* 50 30

Condor, Soccer Ball and Flags AP57

Alliance for Progress Emblem AP58

Design: 1.80b, Map of Bolivia, soccer ball, goal and flags.

1963, Mar. 21 Litho. *Perf. 11½*
Flags in National Colors
C247 AP57 1.40b blk, ocher & red 1.50 1.00
C248 AP57 1.80b blk, red & ocher 1.50 1.00

Issued to publicize the 21st South American Soccer Championships.

Freedom from Hunger Issue
Type of Regular Issue

Design: 1.20b, Wheat, globe and wheat emblem.

1963, Aug. 1 Unwmk. *Perf. 11½*
C249 A156 1.20b dk grn, bl & yel 1.00 75

Issued for the "Freedom from Hunger" campaign of the U.N. Food and Agriculture Organization.

1963, Nov. 15 *Perf. 11½*
C250 AP58 1.20b dl yel, ultra & grn 1.25 50

Issued to commemorate the second anniversary of the Alliance for Progress, which aims to stimulate economic growth and raise living standards in Latin America.

Type of Regular Issue, 1963

Designs: 1.20b, Ballot box and voters. 1.40b, Map and farmer breaking chain. 2.80b, Miners.

1963, Dec. 21 *Perf. 11½*
C251 A157 1.20b gray, dk brn & rose 60 30
C252 A157 1.40b bis & grn 75 40
C253 A157 2.80b sl & buff 1.50 75

Issued to commemorate the 10th anniversary of the Revolution of Apr. 9, 1952.

Andrés Santa Cruz — AP59

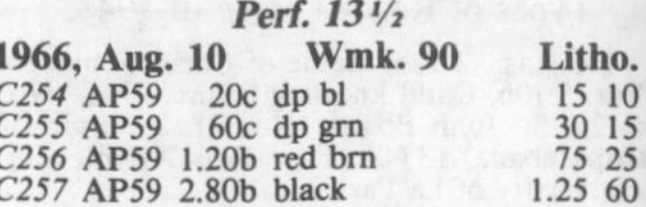

Perf. 13½
1966, Aug. 10 Wmk. 90 Litho.
C254 AP59 20c dp bl 15 10
C255 AP59 60c dp grn 30 15
C256 AP59 1.20b red brn 75 25
C257 AP59 2.80b black 1.25 60

Issued to commemorate the centenary (in 1965) of the death of Marshal Andrés Santa Cruz (1792-1865), president of Bolivia and of Peru-Bolivia Confederation.

Children Type of 1966

Design: 1.40b, Mother and children.

1966, Dec. 16 Unwmk. *Perf. 13½*
C258 A159 1.40b gray bl & blk 1.50 65

Issued to help poor children.

Co-Presidents Type of Regular Issue

1966, Dec. 16 Litho. *Perf. 12½*
Flag in Red, Yellow and Green
C259 A160 2.80b gray & tan 2.00 1.50
C260 A160 10b sep & tan 2.50 1.75
a. Souv. sheet of 4 10.00 10.00

Issued to honor Generals Rene Barrientos Ortuno and Alfredo Ovando C., Co-Presidents, 1965-66.

No. C260a contains 4 imperf. stamps similar to Nos. 480-481 and C259-C260. Dark green marginal inscription. Size: 135x82mm.

Various Issues 1954-62 Surcharged with New Values and Bars

1966, Dec. 21

On No. C177:
"XII Aniversario / Reforma / Agraria"
C261 AP46 10c on 27b brt pink 20 20

On No. C182:
"XXV / Aniversario Paz / del Chaco"
C262 AP47 10c on 55b dk & lt grnsh bl 20 20

On No. C199:
"Centenario de / Tupiza"
C263 AP48 60c on 1350b rose car 30 30

On No. C200:
"XXV / Aniversario / Automovil Club / Boliviano"
C264 AP48 2.80b on 2700b bl grn 3.00 2.50

On No. C201:
"Centenario de la / Cruz Roja / Internacional"
C265 AP48 4b on 4000b vio bl 2.00 1.50

On No. C219:
"CL Aniversario / Heroinas Coronilla"
C266 AP51 1.20b on 800b vio brn 60 50

On No. C222:
"Centenario Himno / Paceño"
C267 AP51 1.40b on 4,000b dk gray 60 50

Nos. C224-C225 Surcharged
C268 A146 1.40b on 1,000b multi 60 60
C269 A146 1.40b on 1,800b multi 60 60

On Nos. C238-C239:
"Aniversario / Centro Filatelico / Cochabamba"
C270 A152 1.20b on 800b multi 50 40
C271 A152 1.20b on 1,800b multi 50 40

Revenue Stamp of 1946 Surcharged with New Value "X" and: "XXV Aniversario / Dpto. Pando / Aéreo"
C272 A161 1.20b on 1b dk bl 75 60
Nos. C261-C272 (12) 9.85 8.30

Lions Emblem and Pre-historic Sculptures AP60

1967, Sept. 20 Litho. *Perf. 13x13½*
C273 AP60 2b red & multi 1.25 1.00
a. Souv. sheet of 2 5.00 5.00

Issued to commemorate the 50th anniversary of Lions International. No. C273a contains 2 imperf. stamps similar to Nos. 492 and C273. Black marginal inscription. Size: 129x80mm.

Folklore Type of Regular Issue

Designs (Folklore characters): 1.20p, Pujllay. 1.40p, Ujusiris. 2p, Morenada. 3p, Aukiaukis.

1968, June 24 *Perf. 13½x13*
C274 A163 1.20b lt yel grn & multi 40 25
C275 A163 1.40b gray & multi 50 30
C276 A163 2b dk ol bis & multi 75 40
C277 A163 3b sky bl & multi 1.25 75

Issued to publicize the 9th Congress of the Postal Union of the Americas and Spain.

A souvenir sheet exists containing 4 imperf. stamps similar to Nos. C274-C277. Bister and gray marginal inscription. Size: 131x81½mm.

Moto Mendez — AP61

1968, Oct. 29 Litho. *Perf. 13½x13*
C278 AP61 1b dp org & multi 50 25
C279 AP61 1.20b lt ultra & multi 60 25
C280 AP61 2b bis brn & multi 1.00 50
C281 AP61 4b bluish lil & multi 1.50 75

Battle of Tablada sesquicentennial.

Pres. Gualberto Villaroel AP62

1968, Nov. 6 *Perf. 13x13½*
C282 AP62 1.40b org & blk 50 40
C283 AP62 3b lt bl & blk 1.00 60
C284 AP62 4b rose & blk 1.25 75
C285 AP62 5b gray grn & blk 1.50 1.00
C286 AP62 10b pale pur & blk 3.00 2.00
Nos. C282-C286 (5) 7.25 4.75

4th centenary of Cochabamba.

ITU Type of Regular Issue

1968, Dec. 3 Litho. *Perf. 13x13½*
C287 A166 1.20b gray, blk & yel 40 20
C288 A166 1.40b bl, blk & gray ol 50 30

Issued to commemorate the centenary (in 1965) of the International Telecommunication Union.

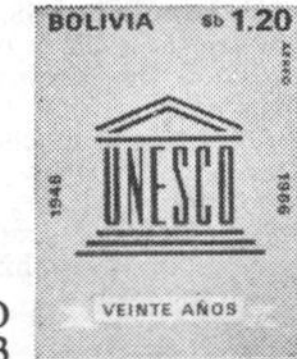

UNESCO Emblem — AP63

1968, Nov. 14 *Perf. 13½x13*
C289 AP63 1.20b pale vio & blk 50 25
C290 AP63 2.80b yel grn & blk 1.00 50

Issued to commemorate the 20th anniversary (in 1966) of UNESCO (United Nations Educational, Scientific and Cultural Organization).

Foreign postal stationery (stamped envelopes, postal cards and air letter sheets) lies beyond the scope of this Catalogue, which is limited to adhesive postage stamps.

Kennedy Type of Regular Issue

1968, Nov. 22 Unwmk.
C291 A168 1b grn & blk 40 30
C292 A168 10b scar & blk 3.00 2.00

Issued in memory of Pres. John F. Kennedy, 1917-1963.

A souvenir sheet contains one imperf. stamp similar to No. C291. Dark violet marginal inscription. Size: 131x81½mm.

Tennis Type of Regular Issue

1968, Dec. 10 *Perf. 13x13½*
C293 A169 1.40b org, blk & lt brn 50 35
C294 A169 2.80b sky bl, blk & lt brn 1.00 75

Issued to commemorate the 32nd South American Tennis Championships, La Paz, 1965.

A souvenir sheet exists containing one imperf. stamp similar to No. C293. Light brown marginal inscription. Size: 131x81½mm.

Stamp Centenary Type of Regular Issue

Design: 1.40b, 2.80b, 3b, Bolivia No. 1.

1968, Dec. 23 Litho. *Perf. 13x13½*
C295 A170 1.40b org, grn & blk 75 35
C296 A170 2.80b pale rose, grn & blk 1.50 75
C297 A170 3b lt vio, grn & blk 1.50 75

Issued to commemorate the centenary of Bolivian postage stamps.

A souvenir sheet exists containing 3 imperf. stamps similar to Nos. C295-C297. Dark brown marginal inscription. Size: 131x81½mm.

Franklin D. Roosevelt — AP64

1969, Oct. 29 Litho. *Perf. 13½x13*
C298 AP64 5b brn, blk & buff 2.00 1.50

Issued to honor Franklin D. Roosevelt (1882-1945), 32nd President of the United States.

Olympic Type of Regular Issue

Sports: 1.20b, Woman runner (vert.). 2.80b, Discus thrower (vert.). 5b, Hurdler.

Perf. 13½x13, 13x13½
1969, Oct. 29 Litho.
C299 A171 1.20b yel grn, bis & blk 60 25
C300 A171 2.80b red, org & blk 1.25 50
C301 A171 5b bl, lt bl, red & blk 2.00 1.00

Issued to commemorate the 19th Olympic Games, Mexico City, Oct. 12-27, 1968.

A souvenir sheet exists containing 3 imperf. stamps similar to Nos. C299-C301. Marginal inscription in blue, yellow green and red brown. Size: 130½x81mm.

Butterfly Type of Regular Issue

Butterflies: 1b, Metamorpha dido wernichei. 1.80b, Heliconius felix. 2.80b, Morpho casica. 3b, Papilio yuracares. 4b, Heliconius melitus.

1970, Apr. 24 Litho. *Perf. 13x13½*
C302 A172 1b sal & multi 50 20
C303 A172 1.80b lt bl & multi 75 40
C304 A172 2.80b multi 1.50 75
C305 A172 3b multi 1.50 75
C306 A172 4b multi 2.00 85
Nos. C302-C306 (5) 6.25 2.95

A souvenir sheet exists containing 3 imperf. stamps similar to Nos. C302-C304. Black marginal inscription. Size: 129½x80mm.

Scout Type of Regular Issue

Designs: 50c, Boy Scout building brick wall. 1.20b, Bolivian Boy Scout emblem.

1970, June 17 Litho. *Perf. 13½x13*
C307 A173 50c yel & multi 20 10
C308 A173 1.20b multi 40 20

Issued to honor the Bolivian Boy Scout movement.

No. C228 Surcharged

1970, Dec. Litho. *Perf. 10½*
C309 AP53 1.20b on 4,000b multi 40 20

Flower Type of Regular Issue

Bolivian Flowers: 1.20b, Amaryllis pseudopardina (horiz.). 1.40b, Rebutia kruegeri. 2.80b, Lobivia pentlandii (horiz.). 4b, Rebutia tunariensis.

Perf. 13x13½, 13½x13
1971, Aug. 9 Litho. Unwmk.
C310 A174 1.20b multi 60 20
C311 A174 1.40b multi 75 25
C312 A174 2.80b multi 1.25 40
C313 A174 4b multi 2.00 75

Two souvenir sheets of 4 exist. One contains imperf. stamps similar to Nos. 534-535 and C310, C312. The other contains imperf. stamps similar to Nos. 536-537, C311, C313. Black marginal inscriptions. Size: 130x80mm.

Dance Type of Regular Issue

Folk Dances: 1.20b, Kusillo. 1.40b, Taquirari.

1972, Mar. 23 Litho. *Perf. 13½x13*
C314 A177 1.20b yel & multi 75 25
C315 A177 1.40b org & multi 1.00 25

Two souvenir sheets of 3 exist. One contains imperf. stamps similar to Nos. 542-543, C314. The other contains imperf. stamps similar to Nos. 540-541, C315. Sheets have Sapporo '72 Olympic Games emblem in multicolor and marginal inscriptions in yellow, green and orange. Size: 80x129mm.

Painting Type of Regular Issue

Bolivian Paintings: 1.40b, Portrait of Chola Pacena, by Cecilio Guzman de Rojas. 1.50b, Adoration of the Kings, by G. Gamarra. 1.60b, Adoration of Pachamama (mountain), by A. Borda. 2b, The Kiss of the Idol, by Guzman de Rojas.

1972 Litho. *Perf. 13½*
C316 A178 1.40b multi 60 25
C317 A178 1.50b multi 60 25
C318 A178 1.60b multi 60 25
C319 A178 2b multi 1.00 40

Two souvenir sheets of 2 exist. One contains imperf. stamps similar to Nos. 548 and C318. The other contains imperf. stamps similar to Nos. C317 and C319. Sheets have "Munich 1972," Olympic and Munich emblems in margins. Size: 129x80mm.

Issue dates: 1.40b, Dec. 4. Others, Aug. 17.

Bolivian Coat of Arms AP65

1972, Dec. 4 *Perf. 13½x14*
C320 AP65 4b lt bl & multi 2.00 1.50

Cactus Type of Regular Issue

Designs: Various cacti.

1973, Aug. 6 Litho. *Perf. 13½*
C321 A180 1.20b tan & multi 50 20
C322 A180 1.90b org & multi 75 30
C323 A180 2b multi 1.00 40

Development Type of Regular Issue

Designs: 1.40b, Highway 1Y4. 2b, Bus crossing bridge.

1973, Nov. 26 Litho. *Perf. 13½*
C324 A181 1.40b sal & multi 50 20
C325 A181 2b multi 75 30

Bolivia's development.

Santos-Dumont and 14-Bis Plane — AP66

1973, July 20
C326 AP66 1.40b yel & blk 1.00 50

Centenary of the birth of Alberto Santos-Dumont (1873-1932), Brazilian aviation pioneer.

Orchid Type of 1974

Orchids: 2.50b, Cattleya luteola (horiz.). 3.80b, Stanhopaea. 4b, Catasetum (horiz.). 5b, Maxillaria.

1974 Litho. *Perf. 13½*
C327 A182 2.50b multi 1.00 35
C328 A182 3.80b rose & multi 1.50 50
C329 A182 4b multi 2.00 60
C330 A182 5b sal & multi 2.50 70

Air Force Emblem, Plane over Map of Bolivia AP67

Designs: 3.80b, Plane over Andes. 4.50b, Triple decker and jet. 8b, Rafael Pabon and double decker. 15b, Jet and "50."

1974 Litho. *Perf. 13x13½*
C331 AP67 3b multi 1.00 75
C332 AP67 3.80b multi 1.50 1.00
C333 AP67 4.50b multi 1.50 1.00
C334 AP67 8b multi 2.50 2.00
C335 AP67 15b multi 5.00 3.00
Nos. C331-C335 (5) 11.50 7.75

Bolivian Air Force, 50th anniversary.

Coat of Arms Type of 1975

Designs: Departmental coats of arms.

1975, July 16 Litho. *Perf. 13½*
Gold & Multicolored
C336 A188 20c *Beni* 10 10
C337 A188 30c *Tarija* 15 10
C338 A188 50c *Potosi* 15 15
C339 A188 1b *Oruro* 35 30
C340 A188 2.50b *Santa Cruz* 75 75
C341 A188 3b *La Paz* 1.00 75
Nos. C336-C341 (6) 2.50 2.15

Sesquicentennial of Republic of Bolivia.

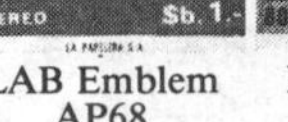

LAB Emblem AP68

Bolivia on Map of Americas AP69

Map of Bolivia, Plane and Kyllmann AP70

1975 Litho. *Perf. 13½*
C342 AP68 1b gold, bl & blk 25 15
C343 AP69 1.50b multi 35 25
C344 AP70 2b multi 50 35

Lloyd Aereo Boliviano, 50th anniversary, founded by Guillermo Kyllmann.

Bolivar, Presidents Perez and Banzer, and Flags
AP71

1975, Aug. 4 Litho. *Perf. 13½*

C345 AP71 3b gold & multi 1.00 75

Visit of Pres. Carlos A. Perez of Venezuela.

Bolivar Type of 1975.

Presidents and Statesmen of Bolivia: 50c, Rene Barrientes O. 2b, Francisco B. O'Connor. 3.80b, Gualberto Villarroel. 4.20b, German Busch. 4.50b, Hugo Banzer Suarez. 20b, José Ballivian. 30b, Andres de Santa Cruz. 40b, Antonio Jose de Sucre.

1975 Litho. *Perf. 13½*

Size: 24x33mm.

C346 A189 50c multi 25 15
C347 A189 2b multi 75 40
C348 A189 3.80b multi 1.00 75
C349 A189 4.20b multi 1.50 1.00

Size: 28x39mm.

C350 A189 4.50b multi 1.50 1.00

Size: 24x33mm.

C351 A189 20b multi 6.00 4.00
C352 A189 30b multi 7.50 5.00
C353 A189 40b multi 10.00 7.00
Nos. C346-C353 (8) 28.50 19.30

UPU Emblem
AP72

1975, Dec. 7 Litho. *Perf. 13½*

C358 AP72 25b bl & multi 6.00 3.50

Centenary of Universal Postal Union (in 1974).

POSTAGE DUE STAMPS

D1

1931 Unwmk. Engr. *Perf. 14, 14½.*

J1 D1 5c ultra 2.25 1.50
J2 D1 10c red 2.25 1.50
J3 D1 15c yellow 2.25 1.50
J4 D1 30c dp grn 2.25 1.50
J5 D1 40c dp vio 2.25 1.50
J6 D1 50c blk brn 2.25 1.50
Nos. J1-J6 (6) 13.50 9.00

Symbol of Youth
D2

Torch of Knowledge
D3

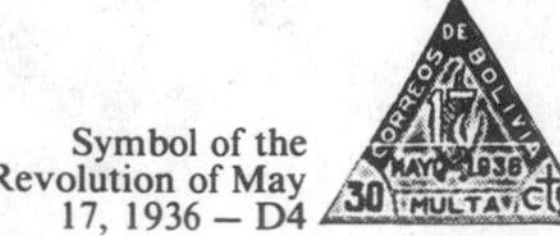

Symbol of the Revolution of May 17, 1936 — D4

1938 Litho. *Perf. 11.*

J7 D2 5c dp rose 1.00 75
a. Pair, imperf. between
J8 D3 10c green 1.00 75
J9 D4 30c gray bl 1.00 75

POSTAL TAX STAMPS

Worker
PT1

Symbols of Communications
PT2

Imprint: "LITO. UNIDAS LA PAZ."

Perf. 13½x10½, 10½, 13½.

1939 Litho. Unwmk.

RA1 PT1 5c dl vio 60 15
a. Double impression

Redrawn

Imprint: "TALL. OFFSET LA PAZ."

1940 *Perf. 12x11, 11.*

RA2 PT1 5c violet 50 15
a. Horizontal pair, imperf. between 2.50
b. Imperf. horiz., pair

Tax of Nos. RA1-RA2 was for the Workers' Home Building Fund.

1944-45 Litho. *Perf. 10½*

RA3 PT2 10c salmon 45 15
RA4 PT2 10c bl ('45) 45 15

A 30c orange inscribed "Centenario de la Creacion del Departmento del Beni" was issued in 1946 and required to be affixed to all air and surface mail to and from the Department of Beni in addition to regular postage. Five higher denominations in the same scenic design were used for local revenue purposes.

Type of 1944 Redrawn.

1947-48 Unwmk. *Perf. 10½.*

RA5 PT2 10c carmine 30 5
RA6 PT2 10c org yel ('48) 25 5
RA7 PT2 10c yel brn ('48) 25 5
RA8 PT2 10c emer ('48) 25 5

Post horn and envelope reduced in size.

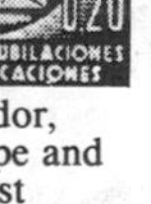

Condor, Envelope and Post Horn — PT3

Communication Symbols — PT4

1951-52

RA9 PT3 20c dp org 40 20
a. Imperf., pair
RA10 PT3 20c grn ('52) 40 20
RA11 PT3 20c bl ('52) 40 20

1952-54 *Perf. 13½, 10½, 10½x12*

RA12 PT4 50c green 50 20
RA13 PT4 50c carmine 50 20
RA14 PT4 3b green 50 20
RA15 PT4 3b ol bis 75 60
RA16 PT4 5b vio ('54) 75 20
Nos. RA12-RA16 (5) 3.00 1.40

No. RA10 and Type of 1951-52. Surcharged with New Value in Black.

1953 *Perf. 10½.*

RA17 PT3 50c on 20c grn 40 20
RA18 PT3 50c on 20c red vio 40 20

Postman Blowing Horn — PT5

1954-55 Unwmk. *Perf. 10½.*

RA19 PT5 1b brown 30 15
RA20 PT5 1b car rose ('55) 30 15

Nos. RA15 and RA14 Surcharged in Black "Bs. 5.-/D. S./21-IV-55"

1955 *Perf. 10½, 10½x12*

RA21 PT4 5b on 3b ol bis 30 10
RA22 PT4 5b on 3b grn 30 10

Tax of Nos. RA3-RA22 was for the Communications Employees Fund.

No. RA21 is known with surcharge in thin type of different font and with comma added after "55".

Plane over Airport — PT6

Planes — PT7

Perf. 10½, 12, 13½,

1955 Unwmk. Litho.

RA23 PT6 5b dp ultra 40 10
a. Vertical pair imperf. between

Perf. 11½

RA24 PT7 10b lt grn 30 10

PT8

PT9

1955 Litho. *Perf. 10½*

RA25 PT8 5b red 40 10

Perf. 12

RA26 PT9 20b dk brn 40 20

Tax of Nos. RA23-RA26 was for the building of new airports.

General Alfredo Ovando and Three Men — PT10

1970, Sept. 26 Litho. *Perf. 13x13½*

RA27 PT10 20c blk & red 25 15

See No. RAC1.

Pres. German Busch — PT11

1971, May 13 Litho. *Perf. 13x13½*

RA28 PT11 20c lil & blk 35 10

AIR POST POSTAL TAX STAMPS

Type of Postal Tax Issue

1970, Sept. 26 Litho. *Perf. 13x13½*

Design: 30c, General Ovando and oil well.

RAC1 PT10 30c bl & grn 30 15

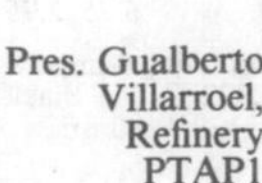

Pres. Gualberto Villarroel, Refinery
PTAP1

1971, May 25 Litho. *Perf. 13x13½*

RAC2 PTAP1 30c lt bl & blk 30 15

Type of 1971 Inscribed: "XXV ANIVERSARIO DE SU GOBIERNO"

1975 Litho. *Perf. 13x13½*

RAC3 PTAP1 30c lt bl & blk 30 15

BOSNIA AND HERZEGOVINA

LOCATION — In what is now Jugoslavia, between Dalmatia and Serbia.
GOVT. — Provinces of Turkey under Austro-Hungarian occupation, 1879-1908; provinces of Austria-Hungary 1908-1918.
AREA — 19,768 sq. mi.
POP. — 2,000,000 (approx. 1918)
CAPITAL — Sarajevo

Following World War I Bosnia and Herzegovina united with the kingdoms of Montenegro and Serbia, and Croatia, Dalmatia and Slovenia, to form the Kingdom of Jugoslavia (See Jugoslavia.)

100 Novcica (Neukreuzer) = 1 Florin (Gulden)

100 Heller = 1 Krone (1900)

Coat of Arms — A1

Type I. The heraldic eaglets on the right side of the escutcheon are entirely blank. The eye of the lion is indicated by a very small dot, which sometimes fails to print. All values except the ½n exist in this type.

Type II. There is a colored line across the lowest eaglet. A similar line sometimes appears on the middle eaglet. The eye of the lion is formed by a large dot which touches the outline of the head above it. All values are found in this type.

Type III. The eaglets and eye of the lion are similar to type I. Each tail feather of the large eagle has two lines of shading and the lowest feather does not touch the curved line below it. In types I and II there are several shading lines in these feathers, and the lowest feather touches the curved line. Only the 5n is found in type III.

Varieties of the Numerals

2 NOVCICA:
A. The "2" has curved tail. All are type I.
B. The "2" has straight tail. All are type II.

15 NOVCICA:
C. The serif of the "1" is short and forms a wide angle with the vertical stroke.
D. The serif of the "1" forms an acute angle with the vertical stroke.

The numerals of the 5n were retouched several times and show minor differences, especially in the flag.

Other Varieties

½ NOVCICA:
All printings of the ½n are type II.

There is a black dot between the curved ends of the ornaments near the lower spandrels.

G. This dot touches the curve at its right. Stamps of this (first) printing are lithographed.

H. This dot stands clear of the curved lines. Stamps of this (second) printing are typographed.

10 NOVCICA:
Ten stamps in each sheet of type II show a small cross in the upper section of the right side of the escutcheon.

Bosnia and Herzegovina stamps can be mounted in Soctt's Austria Album.

Wmk. 91

Wmk. BRIEF-MARKEN or (from 1890) ZEITUNGS-MARKEN in Double-lined Capitals, Across the Sheet (91)

Perf. 9 to 13½ and Compound

1879-94 **Litho.**

Type I

No.	Type	Denom.	Color	Unused	Used
1	A1	½n	blk (type II) ('94)	10.00	*25.00*
2	A1	1n	gray	6.00	2.50
c.			1n gray lil		3.00
4	A1	2n	yellow	7.50	1.50
5	A1	3n	green	10.00	3.00
6	A1	5n	rose red	15.00	60
7	A1	10n	blue	50.00	1.25
8	A1	15n	brown	55.00	7.50
9	A1	20n	gray grn ('93)	225.00	10.00
10	A1	25n	violet	45.00	10.00

No. 2c was never issued. It is usually canceled by blue pencil marks and "mint" copies generally have been cleaned.

Perf. 10½ to 13 and Compound

1894-98 **Typo.**

Type II

No.	Type	Denom.	Color	Unused	Used
1a	A1	½n	black	14.00	*20.00*
2a	A1	1n	gray	5.50	1.50
4a	A1	2n	yellow	4.00	75
5a	A1	3n	green	5.50	1.75
6a	A1	5n	rose red	75.00	50
7a	A1	10n	blue	7.50	1.00
8a	A1	15n	brown	6.50	4.50
9a	A1	20n	gray grn	9.00	5.00
10a	A1	25n	violet	10.00	8.00

Type III

No.	Type	Denom.	Color	Unused	Used
6b	A1	5n	rose red ('98)	2.00	50

All the preceding stamps exist in various shades.

Nos. 1a to 10a were reprinted in 1911 in lighter colors, on very white paper and perf. 12½. Price, set $25.

A2

A3

Perf. 10½, 12½ and Compound

1900 **Typo.**

No.	Type	Denom.	Color	Unused	Used
11	A2	1h	gray blk	38	8
12	A2	2h	gray	38	8
13	A2	3h	yellow	40	12
14	A2	5h	green	38	5
15	A2	6h	brown	75	12
16	A2	10h	red	35	5
17	A2	20h	rose	125.00	5.00
18	A2	25h	blue	1.10	25
19	A2	30h	bis brn	140.00	6.00
20	A2	40h	orange	200.00	10.00
21	A2	50h	red lil	1.25	45
22	A3	1k	dk rose	1.50	65
23	A3	2k	ultra	2.00	1.75
24	A3	5k	dl bl grn	4.50	4.50
			Nos. 11-24 (14)	477.99	29.10

All values of this issue except the 3h exist on ribbed paper.

Nos. 17, 19 and 20 were reprinted in 1911. The reprints are in lighter colors and on whiter paper than the originals. Reprints of Nos. 17 and 19 are perf. 10½ and those of No. 20 are perf. 12½. Price each $3.

Numerals in Black

1901-04 ***Perf. 12½***

No.	Type	Denom.	Color	Unused	Used
25	A2	20h	pink ('02)	75	50
26	A2	30h	bis brn ('03)	75	50
27	A2	35h	blue	1.00	50
a.			35h ultra	*100.00*	6.00
28	A2	40h	org ('03)	1.25	1.00
29	A2	45h	grnsh bl ('04)	85	55
			Nos. 25-29 (5)	4.60	3.05

Nos. 11-16, 18, 21-29 exist imperf. Most of Nos. 11-29 exist perf. 6½; compound with 12½; part perf.; in pairs imperf. between. These were supplied only to some high-ranking officials and never sold at any P.O.

View of Deboj A4

The Carsija at Sarajevo — A17

Designs: 2h, View of Mostar. 3h, Pliva Gate, Jajce. 5h, Narenta Pass and Prenj River. 6h, Rama Valley. 10h, Vrbas Valley. 20h, Old Bridge, Mostar. 25h, Bey's Mosque, Sarajevo. 30h, Donkey post. 35h, Jezero and tourists' pavilion. 40h, Mail wagon. 45h, Bazaar at Sarajevo. 50h, Postal car. 2k, St. Luke's Campanile, Jajce. 5k, Emperor Franz Josef.

Perf. 6½, 9½, 10½ and 12½, also Compounds

1906 **Engr.** **Unwmk.**

No.	Type	Denom.	Color	Unused	Used
30	A4	1h	black	10	12
31	A4	2h	violet	10	12
32	A4	3h	olive	10	12
33	A4	5h	dk grn	10	12
34	A4	6h	brown	20	25
a.			Perf. 13½	20.00	25.00
35	A4	10h	carmine	10	12
36	A4	20h	dk brn	50	30
a.			Perf. 13½	50.00	50.00
37	A4	25h	dp bl	1.50	1.25
38	A4	30h	green	1.65	50
39	A4	35h	myr grn	1.75	50
40	A4	40h	org red	1.75	50
41	A4	45h	brn red	1.75	1.50
42	A4	50h	dl vio	2.00	1.00
43	A17	1k	maroon	4.50	2.00
44	A17	2k	gray grn	6.00	10.00
45	A17	5k	dl bl	5.00	7.50
			Nos. 30-45 (16)	27.10	25.90

Nos. 30-45 exist imperf. Price, set $60 unused, $45 canceled.

Birthday Jubilee Issue

Designs of 1906 Issue, with "1830-1910" in label at bottom.

1910 ***Perf. 12½***

No.	Type	Denom.	Color	Unused	Used
46	A4	1h	black	50	22
47	A4	2h	violet	60	22
48	A4	3h	olive	60	30
49	A4	5h	dk grn	70	12
50	A4	6h	org brn	75	30
51	A4	10h	carmine	70	12
52	A4	20h	dk brn	1.50	1.75
53	A4	25h	dp bl	3.50	3.75
54	A4	30h	green	2.50	3.25
55	A4	35h	myr grn	3.50	3.25
56	A4	40h	org red	3.50	4.00
57	A4	45h	brn red	6.00	7.25
58	A4	50h	dl vio	6.00	7.50
59	A17	1k	maroon	6.00	7.50
60	A17	2k	gray grn	22.50	22.50
61	A17	5k	dl bl	4.00	5.00
			Nos. 46-61 (16)	62.85	67.03

80th birthday of Emperor Franz Josef.

Scenic Type of 1906

Designs (Views): 12h, Jaice. 60h, Konjica. 72h, Vishegrad.

1912

No.	Type	Denom.	Color	Unused	Used
62	A4	12h	ultra	5.00	6.00
63	A4	60h	dl bl	3.00	5.50
64	A4	72h	carmine	15.00	20.00

Price, imperf. set, $75.

Emperor Franz Josef

A23 A24

A25

A26

1912-14

Various Frames

No.	Type	Denom.	Color	Unused	Used
65	A23	1h	ol grn	50	5
66	A23	2h	brt bl	50	5
67	A23	3h	claret	50	5
68	A23	5h	green	50	5
69	A23	6h	dk gray	50	5
70	A23	10h	rose car	50	5
71	A23	12h	dp ol grn	1.50	30
72	A23	20h	org brn	6.00	6
73	A23	25h	ultra	3.00	8
74	A23	30h	org red	3.00	8
75	A24	35h	myr grn	3.00	8
76	A24	40h	dk vio	9.00	8
77	A24	45h	ol brn	4.00	25
78	A24	50h	sl bl	4.00	8
79	A24	60h	brn vio	3.75	8
80	A24	72h	dk bl	4.50	4.00
81	A25	1k	brn vio, *straw*	17.50	50
82	A25	2k	dk gray, *bl*	10.00	35
83	A26	3k	car, *grn*	15.00	12.50
84	A26	5k	dk vio, *gray*	30.00	30.00
85	A25	10k	dk ultra, *gray* ('14)	100.00	110.00
			Nos. 65-85 (21)	217.25	158.74

Price, imperf. set, $450.

A27

A28

1916-17 ***Perf. 12½***

No.	Type	Denom.	Color	Unused	Used
86	A27	3h	dk gray	25	28
87	A27	5h	ol grn	38	50
88	A27	6h	violet	42	50
89	A27	10h	bister	1.90	2.50
90	A27	12h	bl gray	50	70
91	A27	15h	car rose	8	8
92	A27	20h	brown	45	60
93	A27	25h	blue	35	50
94	A27	30h	dk grn	35	50
95	A27	40h	vermilion	35	50
96	A27	50h	green	35	50
97	A27	60h	lake	38	55
98	A27	80h	org brn	1.50	50
a.			Perf. 11½	5.00	4.50
99	A27	90h	dk vio	90	75
a.			Perf. 11½	600.00	*900.00*
101	A28	2k	cl, *straw*	60	75
102	A28	3k	grn, *bl*	1.75	3.25
103	A28	4k	car, *grn*	8.00	11.00
104	A28	10k	dp vio, *gray*	20.00	30.00
			Nos. 86-104 (18)	38.51	53.96

Price, imperf. set, $175.

Emperor Karl I

A29 A30

1917 ***Perf. 12½***

No.	Type	Denom.	Color	Unused	Used
105	A29	3h	ol gray	20	28
a.			Perf. 11½	100.00	110.00
b.			Perf. 12½x11½	20.00	32.50
106	A29	5h	ol grn	12	20
107	A29	6h	violet	50	75
108	A29	10h	org brn	25	6
a.			Perf. 11½x12½	85.00	120.00
b.			Perf. 11½		
109	A29	12h	blue	75	1.00
110	A29	15h	brt rose	12	8
111	A29	20h	red brn	12	12
112	A29	25h	ultra	1.25	65
113	A29	30h	gray grn	35	25
114	A29	40h	ol bis	38	20
115	A29	50h	dp grn	1.25	65
116	A29	60h	car rose	1.25	55
a.			Perf. 11½	22.50	25.00
117	A29	80h	stl bl	35	28
118	A29	90h	dl vio	1.50	2.00
119	A30	2k	car, *straw*	80	50
120	A30	3k	grn, *bl*	20.00	25.00
121	A30	4k	car, *grn*	8.00	10.00
122	A30	10k	dp vio, *gray*	5.00	8.00
			Nos. 105-122 (18)	42.19	50.57

Price, imperf. set, $85.

Nos. 47 and 66 Overprinted in Red **1918**

1918

No.	Type	Denom.	Color	Unused	Used
126	A4	2h	violet	65	65
b.			Inverted overprint	25.00	
d.			Double overprint	20.00	
f.			Double overprint, one inverted		
127	A23	2h	brt bl	75	75
a.			Pair, one without overprint		
b.			Inverted overprint	25.00	
c.			Double overprint	20.00	
d.			Double overprint, one inverted		

Emperor Karl I — A31

1918 **Typo.** ***Perf. 12½, Imperf.***

No.	Type	Denom.	Color	Unused	Used
128	A31	2h	orange	11.50	
129	A31	3h	dk grn	11.50	
130	A31	5h	lt grn	11.50	
131	A31	6h	bl grn	11.50	
132	A31	10h	brown	11.50	
133	A31	20h	brick red	11.50	
134	A31	25h	ultra	11.50	
135	A31	45h	dk sl	11.50	
136	A31	50h	lt bluish grn	11.50	
137	A31	60h	bl vio	11.50	
138	A31	70h	ocher	11.50	
139	A31	80h	rose	11.50	
140	A31	90h	vio brn	11.50	

Engr.

No.	Type	Denom.	Color	Unused	Used
141	A30	1k	ol grn, *grnsh*	*2,250.*	
			Nos. 128-140 (13)	149.50	

Nos. 128-141 were prepared for use in Bosnia and Herzegovina, but were not issued there. They were sold after the Armistice at the Vienna post office for a few days.

SEMI-POSTAL STAMPS

Nos. 33 and 35 Surcharged in Red **1914. 7 Heller**

1914 **Unwmk.** ***Perf. 12½***

No.	Type	Surcharge	Unused	Used
B1	A4	7h on 5h dk grn	50	50
B2	A4	12h on 10h car	50	50

Various minor varieties of the surcharge include "4" with open top, narrow "4" and wide "4".

Nos. B1-B2 exist with double and inverted surcharges. Price about $20 each.

Nos. 33 and 35 Surcharged in Red or Blue **1915. 7 Heller**

1915 ***Perf. 12½***

No.	Type	Surcharge	Unused	Used
B3	A4	7h on 5h dk grn (R)	12.50	12.50
a.		Perf. 9½	200.00	200.00
B4	A4	12h on 10h car (Bl)	40	40

Nos. B3-B4 exist with double and inverted surcharges. Price about $18.50 each.

1915

Nos. 68 and 70 Surcharged in Red or Blue

7 Heller.

1915

No.	Type	Surcharge	Unused	Used
B5	A23	7h on 5h grn (R)	1.00	1.00
a.		"1915" at top and bottom	45.00	55.00
B6	A23	12h on 10h rose car (Bl)	1.75	2.00
a.		Surcharged "7 Heller."	45.00	55.00

Nos. B5-B6 are found in three types differing in length of surcharge lines: I, date

18mm., denomination 14mm. II, date 16mm., denomination 14mm. III, date 18mm., denomination 16mm.

Nos. B5-B6 exist with double and inverted surcharges. Price $15 each.

Nos. B5a and B6a exist double and inverted.

❖ 1916. ❖

Nos. 68 and 70 Surcharged in Red or Blue

7 Heller.

1916

B7 A23 7h on 5h grn (R) 75 1.00
B8 A23 12h on 10h rose car (Bl) 75 1.00

Nos. B7-B8 exist with double and inverted surcharges. Price $12.50 each.

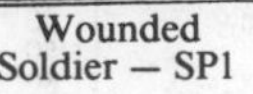

Wounded Soldier — SP1

Blind Soldier — SP2

1916 **Engr.**

B9 SP1 5h (+ 2h) grn 1.00 1.00
B10 SP2 10h (+ 2h) mag 1.50 1.50

Nos. B9-B10 exist imperf. Price, set $27.50.

Nos. 89, 91 Overprinted

WITWEN- UND WAISENWOCHE 1917

1917

B11 A27 10h bister 10 15
B12 A27 15h car rose 10 15

Nos. B11-B12 exist imperf. Price set, $16.

Nos. B11-B12 exist with double and inverted overprint. Price $9 each.

Design for Memorial Church at Sarajevo SP3

Archduke Francis Ferdinand — SP4

Duchess Sophia and Archduke Francis Ferdinand SP5

1917 **Typo.** ***Perf. 11½, 12½***

B13 SP3 10h vio blk 15 38
B14 SP4 15h claret 15 38
B15 SP5 40h dp bl 15 38

Assassination of Archduke Ferdinand and Archduchess Sophia. Sold at a premium of 2h each which helped build a memorial church at Sarajevo.

Exist imperf. Price, set $3.

Blind Soldier — SP6

Emperor Karl I — SP8

Design: 15h, Wounded soldier.

1918 **Engr.** ***Perf. 12½***

B16 SP6 10h (+ 10h) grnsh bl 75 75
B17 SP6 15h (+ 10h) red brn 75 75

Nos. B16-B17 exist imperf. Price, set $18.50.

1918 **Typo.** ***Perf. 12½x13***

Design: 15h, Empress Zita.

B18 SP8 10h gray grn 50 75
B19 SP8 15h brn red 50 75
B20 SP8 40h violet 50 75

Sold at a premium of 10h each which went to the "Karl's Fund."

Nos. B18-B20 exist imperf. Price, set $22.50.

POSTAGE DUE STAMPS

D1

D2

Perf. 9½, 10½, 12½ and Compound

1904 **Unwmk.**

J1 D1 1h blk, red & yel 50 8
J2 D1 2h blk, red & yel 50 25
J3 D1 3h blk, red & yel 50 8
J4 D1 4h blk, red & yel 50 8
J5 D1 5h blk, red & yel 50 8
J6 D1 6h blk, red & yel 25 8
J7 D1 7h blk, red & yel 3.00 3.25
J8 D1 8h blk, red & yel 3.00 70
J9 D1 10h blk, red & yel 75 12
J10 D1 15h blk, red & yel 60 22
J11 D1 20h blk, red & yel 3.50 25
J12 D1 50h blk, red & yel 2.50 20
J13 D1 200h blk, red & grn 10.00 1.00
Nos. J1-J13 (13) 26.10 6.39

Price, imperf. set, $150.

1916-18 ***Perf. 12½***

J14 D2 2h red ('18) 50 50
J15 D2 4h red ('18) 38 38
J16 D2 5h red 50 50
J17 D2 6h red ('18) 38 38
J18 D2 10h red 45 45
J19 D2 15h red 4.00 4.00
J20 D2 20h red 45 45
J21 D2 25h red 1.40 1.40
J22 D2 30h red 1.25 1.25
J23 D2 40h red 10.00 10.00
J24 D2 50h red 32.50 32.50
J25 D2 1k dk bl 4.00 4.00
J26 D2 3k dk bl 17.00 17.00
Nos. J14-J26 (13) 72.81 72.81

Nos. J25 and J26 have colored numerals on a white tablet.

Price, imperf. set, $110.

NEWSPAPER STAMPS

Bosnian Girl — N1

1913 **Unwmk.** ***Imperf.***

P1 N1 2h ultra 50 50
P2 N1 6h violet 2.00 2.00
P3 N1 10h rose 2.00 2.00
P4 N1 20h green 2.50 2.50

After Bosnia and Herzegovina became part of Jugoslavia stamps of type N1 perforated, also imperforate copies snrcharged with new values, were used as regular postage stamps.

un='30000' us='00000' pre='QE' pgs='1'SPECIAL HANDLING STAMPS

"Lightning" — SH1

1916 **Unwmk.** **Engr.** ***Perf. 12½***

P1 SH1 2h vermilion 30 30
a. Perf. 11½x12½ 225.00 225.00
P2 SH1 5h dp grn 50 50
a. Perf. 11½ 17.50 17.50

BRAZIL

Brasil (after 1918)

LOCATION — On the north and east coasts of South America, bordering on the Atlantic Ocean.
GOVT. — Republic
AREA — 3,286,000 sq. mi.
POP. — 132,580,000 (est. 1984)
CAPITAL — Brasilia

Brazil was an independent empire from 1822 to 1889, when a constitution was adopted and the country became officially known as The United States of Brazil.

1000 Reis = 1 Milreis
100 Centavos = 1 Cruzeiro (1942)

Prices of Brazil Nos. 1-13 vary according to condition. Quotations are for fine copies. Very fine to superb specimens sell at much higher prices, and inferior or poor copies sell at reduced prices, depending on the condition of the individual specimen.

Issues of the Empire.

A1

Grayish or Yellowish Paper.

Unwmk.

1843, Aug. 1 **Engr.** ***Imperf.***

1 A1 30r black 2,200. 525.00
a. In pair with No. 2 *90,000.*
2 A1 60r black 750.00 250.00
3 A1 90r black 3,500. 1,450.

Early impressions of Nos. 1 to 3 bring higher prices than quoted which are for copies from worn plates.

A2

A3

Grayish or Yellowish Paper.

1844-46

7 A2 10r black 90.00 30.00
8 A2 30r black 110.00 45.00
9 A2 60r black 90.00 30.00
10 A2 90r black 675.00 200.00
11 A2 180r black 4,500. 1,750.
12 A2 300r black 7,000. 2,400.
13 A2 600r black 6,500. 2,750.

Nos. 8, 9 and 10 exist on thick paper and are considerably scarcer.

Grayish or Yellowish Paper.

1850, Jan. 1

21 A3 10r black 35.00 20.00
22 A3 20r black 90.00 125.00
23 A3 30r black 12.00 4.00
24 A3 60r black 12.00 3.00
25 A3 90r black 110.00 15.00
26 A3 180r black 110.00 70.00
27 A3 300r black 350.00 100.00
28 A3 600r black 450.00 125.00

All values except the 90r were reprinted in 1910 on very thick paper.

1854

37 A3 10r blue 17.50 15.00
38 A3 30r blue 45.00 80.00

A4

1861

39 A4 280r red 200.00 150.00
40 A4 430r yellow 300.00 200.00

Nos. 39 and 40 have been reprinted on thick white paper with white gum. They are printed in aniline inks and the colors are brighter than those of the originals.

1866 ***Perf. 13½.***

42 A3 10r blue 80.00 *125.00*
43 A3 20r black 500.00 350.00
44 A3 30r black 225.00 125.00
45 A3 30r blue *600.00 750.00*
46 A3 60r black 80.00 17.50
47 A3 90r black 400.00 225.00
48 A3 180r black 400.00 225.00
49 A4 280r red 450.00 650.00
50 A3 300r black 750.00 350.00
51 A4 430r yellow 450.00 425.00
52 A3 600r black 450.00 225.00

Fraudulent perforations abound.
A 10r black is questioned.

Emperor Dom Pedro — A5

A6

A7

A8

A8a

A9

A9a

Thick or Thin White Wove Paper.

1866, July 1 — *Perf. 12*

53 A5 10r vermilion 10.00 5.00
a. Bluish paper 550.00 650.00
54 A6 20r red lil 12.00 3.00
a. 20r dl vio 80.00 40.00
b. Bluish paper 175.00 35.00
56 A7 50r blue 25.00 2.00
a. Bluish paper 175.00 17.50
57 A8 80r sl vio 60.00 6.00
a. Bluish paper 225.00 35.00
58 A8a 100r bl grn 22.50 50
a. 100r yel grn 90.00 5.00
b. Bluish paper 1,000. 150.00
59 A9 200r black 90.00 6.00
60 A9a 500r orange 200.00 30.00
Nos. 53-60 (7) 419.50 52.50

The 10r and 20r exist imperf. on both white and bluish paper. Some authorities consider them proofs.

Nos. 58 and 65 are found in two types.

1876-77 — *Rouletted.*

61 A5 10r ver ('77) 45.00 40.00
62 A6 20r red lil ('77) 60.00 30.00
63 A7 50r bl ('77) 60.00 7.00
64 A8 80r vio ('77) 135.00 17.50
65 A8a 100r green 20.00 1.00
66 A9 200r blk ('77) 50.00 6.00
a. Diagonal half used as 100r on cover
67 A9a 500r orange 175.00 35.00
Nos. 61-67 (7) 545.00 136.50

A10 A11

A12 A13

A14 A15

A16 A17

A18 A19

A20

1878-79 — *Rouletted.*

68 A10 10r vermilion 8.00 3.00
69 A11 20r violet 12.00 2.50
70 A12 50r blue 17.50 1.50
71 A13 80r lake 20.00 9.00
72 A14 100r green 20.00 50
73 A15 200r black 125.00 15.00
a. Diagonal half used as 100r on cover
74 A16 260r dk brn 70.00 24.00
75 A18 300r bister 70.00 6.00
76 A19 700r red brn 160.00 110.00
77 A20 1000r gray lil 200.00 45.00
Nos. 68-77 (10) 702.50 216.50

1878, Aug. 21 — *Perf. 12*

78 A17 300r org & grn 75.00 20.00

Nos. 68-78 exist imperforate.

A21 A22

A23

Small Heads

Laid Paper

Perf. 13, 13½ and Compound

1881, July 15

79 A21 50r blue 125.00 20.00
80 A22 100r ol grn 400.00 40.00
81 A23 200r pale red brn 600.00 125.00

On Nos. 79 and 80 the hair above the ear curves forward. On Nos. 83 and 88 it is drawn backward. On the stamps of the 1881 issue the beard is smaller than in the 1882-85 issues and fills less of the space between the neck and the frame at the left.

See also No. 88.

A24 A25

A26 A27

Two types each of the 100 and 200 reis.

100 REIS:

Type I. Groundwork formed of diagonal crossed lines and horizontal lines.

Type II. Groundwork formed of diagonal crossed lines and vertical lines.

200 REIS:

Type I. Groundwork formed of diagonal and horizontal lines.

Type II. Groundwork formed of diagonal crossed lines.

Larger Heads.

Laid Paper

Perf. 12½ to 14 and Compound.

1882-84

82 A24 10r black 7.00 17.50
83 A25 100r ol grn, type 1 30.00 3.50
a. 100r dk grn, type I 30.00 3.50
b. 100r dk grn, type II 175.00 15.00
84 A26 200r pale red brn, type I 80.00 27.50
85 A27 200r pale rose, type II 40.00 5.00
a. Diagonal half used as 100r on cover 20.00

See also No. 86.

A28

A29

A30

Three types of A29.

Type I. Groundwork formed of horizontal lines.

Type II. Groundwork formed of diagonal crossed lines.

Type III. Groundwork solid.

Perf. 13, 13½, 14 and Compound

1884-85

86 A24 10r orange 2.00 2.00
87 A28 20r sl grn 8.00 3.00
a. 20r ol grn 8.00 2.00
88 A21 50r bl, head larger 20.00 3.50
89 A29 100r lil, type II,III 300.00 60.00
90 A29 100r lil, type I 75.00 2.50
91 A30 100r lilac 160.00 4.00

A31

Perf. 13, 13½, 14 and Compound.

1885

92 A31 100r lilac 40.00 1.50

A32

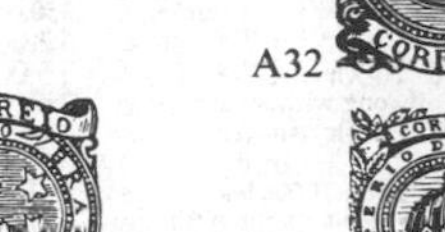

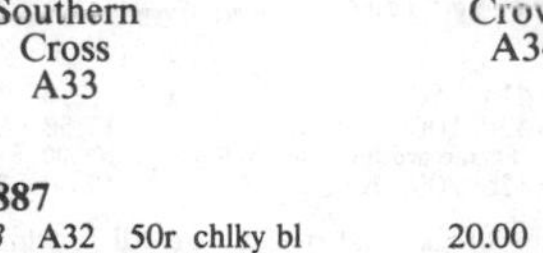

Southern Cross A33 Crown A34

1887

93 A32 50r chlky bl 20.00 4.00
94 A33 300r gray bl 125.00 22.50
95 A34 500r olive 85.00 15.00

A35

A36

Entrance to Bay of Rio de Janeiro — A37

1888

96 A35 100r lilac 30.00 1.00
a. Imperf., pair 90.00 *125.00*
97 A36 700r violet 60.00 *90.00*
98 A37 1000r dl bl 200.00 90.00

Issues of the Republic.

Southern Cross — A38

Wove Paper, Thin to Thick.

Perf. 12½ to 14, 11 to 11½, and 12½ to 14x11 to 11½, Rough or Clean-Cut.

Engraved; Typographed (#102)

1890-91

99 A38 20r gray grn 1.75 1.25
a. 20r bl grn 1.75 1.25
b. 20r emer 13.00 6.00
100 A38 50r gray grn 2.50 1.00
a. 50r ol grn 10.00 1.00
b. 50r yel grn 10.00 5.00
c. 50r dk sl grn 10.00 5.00
d. Horizontal pair, imperf. between
101 A38 100r lil rose 300.00 4.00
102 A38 100r red lil, redrawn 25.00 65
a. Tete beche pair *12,000.* *18,000.*
103 A38 200r purple 8.00 1.00
a. 200r vio 15.00 2.25
b. 200r vio bl 30.00 3.00
104 A38 300r sl vio 50.00 2.50
a. 300r gray 50.00 7.50
b. 300r gray bl 70.00 10.00
c. 300r dk vio 35.00 6.00
105 A38 500r ol bis 16.00 7.50
a. 500r ol gray 16.00 10.00
106 A38 500r slate 16.00 8.00
107 A38 700r chocolate 20.00 20.00
a. 700r fawn 22.50 22.50
108 A38 1000r bister 12.00 2.50
a. 1000r yel buff 25.00 5.00
Nos. 99-108 (10) 451.25 48.40

The redrawn 100r may be distinguished by the absence of the curved lines of shading in the left side of the central oval. The pearls in the oval are not well aligned and there is less shading at right and left of "CORREIO" and "100 REIS."

A 100 reis stamp of type A38 but inscribed "BRAZIL" instead of "E. U. DO BRAZIL" was not placed in issue but postmarked copies are known. A reprint on thick paper was made in 1910.

No. 101 exists imperf., not regularly issued.

Liberty Head A39

Liberty Head A40

Perf. 12½ to 14, 11 to 11½ and 12½ to 14 x 11 to 11 ½

1891, May 1 — **Typo.**

109 A39 100r bl & red 25.00 50
a. Head inverted 110.00 90.00
b. Tete beche pair 575.00 575.00
c. 100r ultra & red 27.50 60

Perf. 11, 11½, 13, 13½, 14 and Compound.

1893, Jan. 18 — **Litho.**

111 A40 100r rose 35.00 50

Sugarloaf Mountain
A41 A41a

A42

Liberty Head — A42a

Hermes — A43

Perf. 11 to 11½, 12½ to 14 and 12½ to 14x11 to 11½.

1894-97 **Unwmk.**
112 A41 10r rose & bl 2.00 50
113 A41a 10r rose & bl 1.50 35
114 A41a 20r org & bl 1.25 30
115 A41a 50r dk bl & bl 5.00 1.50
116 A42 100r car & blk 2.50 25
a. Vertical pair, imperf. between 100.00
118 A42a 200r org & blk 1.50 25
a. Imperf. horiz., pair 75.00
b. Vertical pair, imperf. between 75.00
119 A42a 300r grn & blk 15.00 50
120 A42a 500r bl & blk 25.00 1.25
121 A42a 700r lil & blk 17.50 1.75
122 A43 1000r grn & vio 60.00 1.50
124 A43 2000r blk & gray lil 60.00 15.00
Nos. 112-124 (11) 191.25 23.15

The head of No. 116 exists in five types. See also Nos. 140-150A, 159-161, 166-171d.

Newspaper Stamps Surcharged:

100 **200**
1898 **1898**
100 **200**
a b

100
c **1898**
100

Surcharged on 1889 Issue of type N1.

1898 ***Rouletted***

Green Surcharge.
125 (b) 700r on 500r yel 7.00 10.00
126 (c) 1000r on 700r yel 30.00 30.00
a. Surcharged "700r" 450.00 550.00
127 (c) 2000r on 1000r yel 20.00 12.50
128 (c) 2000r on 1000r brn 17.50 6.00

Violet Surcharge.
129 (a) 100r on 50r brn yel 2.00 *25.00*
130 (c) 100r on 50r brn yel 45.00 50.00
131 (c) 300r on 200r blk 3.50 1.25
a. Double surcharge 150.00 125.00

The surcharge on No. 130 is handstamped. The impression is blurred and lighter in color than on No. 129. The two surcharges differ most in the shapes and serifs of the figures "1."

Counterfeits exist of No. 126a. Black Surcharge.

132 (b) 200r on 100r vio 3.00 1.25
a. Double surcharge 85.00 *150.00*
b. Inverted surcharge 85.00 *150.00*
132C (b) 500r on 300r car 4.50 2.50
133 (b) 700r on 500r grn 7.00 2.25

Blue Surcharge.
134 (b) 500r on 300r car 7.50 5.00

Red Surcharge.
135 (c) 1000r on 700r ultra 20.00 12.50
a. Inverted surcharge 175.00 175.00

Surcharged on 1890-94 Issues:

200 **1898**
1898 **50 RÉIS 50**
d e

Perf. 11 to 14 and Compound.

Black Surcharge.
136 N3 (e) 20r on 10r bl 1.25 2.50
137 N2 (d) 200r on 100r red lil 9.00 6.50
a. Double surcharge 110.00 110.00

Surcharge on No. 137 comes blue to deep black. Blue Surcharge.

138 N3 (e) 50r on 20r grn 3.00 6.00

Red Surcharge.
139 N3 (e) 100r on 50r grn 9.00 10.00
a. Blue surch. 17.50

The surcharge on Nos. 139 and 139a exists double, inverted, one missing, etc.

Types of 1894-97

Perf. 5½ to 7 and 11 to 11½x5½ to 7
140 A41a 10r rose & bl 4.00 8.00
141 A41a 20r org & bl 8.00 8.00
142 A41a 50r dk bl & lt bl 9.00 18.00
143 A42 100r car & blk 15.00 4.00
144 A42a 200r org & blk 9.00 4.00
145 A42a 300r grn & blk 55.00 9.00

Perf. 8½-9½, 8½-9½x11-11½
146 A41a 10r rose & bl 5.00 2.50
147 A41a 20r org & bl 15.00 2.50
147A A41a 50r dk bl & bl 125.00 35.00
148 A42 100r car & blk 25.00 1.50
149 A42a 200r org & blk 10.00 1.25
150 A42a 300r grn & blk 60.00 6.00
150A A43 1000r grn & vio 120.00 12.00

Issue of 1890-93 Surcharged in Violet or Magenta

1899
50 RÉIS

Perf. 11 to 11½, 12½ to 14 and Compound

1899, June 25
151 A38 50r on 20r gray grn 1.00 1.50
a. Double surcharge
152 A38 100r on 50r gray grn 1.50 1.50
b. Double surch. 60.00 60.00
153 A38 300r on 200r pur 6.00 *9.00*
a. Double surcharge 60.00 60.00
154 A38 500r on 300r sl vio 18.00 8.00
a. 500r on 300r gray lil 16.00 6.00
b. Pair, one without surcharge 300.00
155 A38 700r on 500r ol bis 20.00 5.00
a. Pair, one without surcharge 350.00
156 A38 1000r on 700r choc 12.00 5.00
157 A38 1000r on 700r fawn 15.00 5.00
a. Pair, one without surcharge 350.00
158 A38 2000r on 1000r yel buff 45.00 3.50
a. 2000r on 1000r bis 17.50 3.50
b. Pair, one without surcharge 350.00
Nos. 151-158 (8) 118.50 38.50

Types of 1894-97

Perf. 11, 11½, 13 and Compound.

1900
159 A41a 50r green 8.50 50
160 A42 100r rose 17.50 25
a. Frame around inner oval 100.00 5.00
161 A42a 200r blue 12.00 25

Three types exist of No. 161, all of which have the frame around inner oval.

Cabral Arrives at Brazil — A44

Independence Proclaimed A45

"Emancipation of Slaves" — A46

Allegory, Republic of Brazil — A47

1900, Jan. 1 **Litho.** ***Perf. 12½***
162 A44 100r red 6.00 5.50
a. Imperf. (pair) 350.00 350.00
163 A45 200r grn & yel 6.00 5.50
164 A46 500r blue 6.00 5.50
165 A47 700r emerald 6.00 5.50

Discovery of Brazil, 400th anniversary.

Wmk. 97- "CORREIO FEDERAL REPUBLICA DOS ESTADOS UNIDOS DO BRAZIL" in Sheet

Wmk. 98- "IMPOSTO DE CONSUMO REPUBLICA DOS ESTADOS UNIDOS DO BRAZIL" in Sheet

Types of 1894-97.
Wmk. (97? or 98?)

1905 ***Perf. 11, 11½***
166 A41a 10r rose & bl 4.00 2.00
167 A41a 20r org & bl 7.00 75
168 A41a 50r green 12.50 60
169 A42 100r rose 17.50 30
170 A42a 200r dk bl 17.50 20
171 A42a 300r grn & blk 35.00 1.50
Nos. 166-171 (6) 93.50 5.35

Positive identification of Wmk. 97 or 98 places stamp in specific watermark groups below.

Wmk. 97
166b A41a 10r rose & bl 30.00 13.00
167b A41a 20r org & bl 30.00 7.50
168b A41a 50r green 45.00 7.50
169b A42 100r rose 225.00 25.00
170b A42a 200r dk bl 90.00 2.00
171b A42a 300r grn & blk 275.00 17.50
171A A43 1000r grn & vio 225.00 22.50
Nos. 166b-171A (7) 920.00 95.00

Wmk. 98
166c A41a 10r rose & bl 32.50 27.50
167c A41a 20r org & bl 60.00 12.50
168c A41a 50r green 110.00 22.50
169c A42 100r rose 70.00 2.50
170c A42a 200r dk bl 90.00 1.00
171d A42a 300r grn & blk 200.00 22.50
Nos. 166c-171d (7) 562.50 88.50

Allegory, Pan-American Congress — A48

1906, July 23 **Litho.** **Unwmk.**
172 A48 100r car rose 30.00 30.00
173 A48 200r blue 60.00 8.00

Third Pan-American Congress.

Aristides Lobo A48a

Benjamin Constant A49

Pedro Alvares Cabral A50

Eduardo Wandenkolk A51

Manuel Deodoro da Fonseca A52

Floriano Peixoto A53

Prudente de Moraes A54

Manuel Ferraz de Campos Salles A55

Francisco de Paula Rodrigues Alves A56

Liberty Head A57

A58

A59

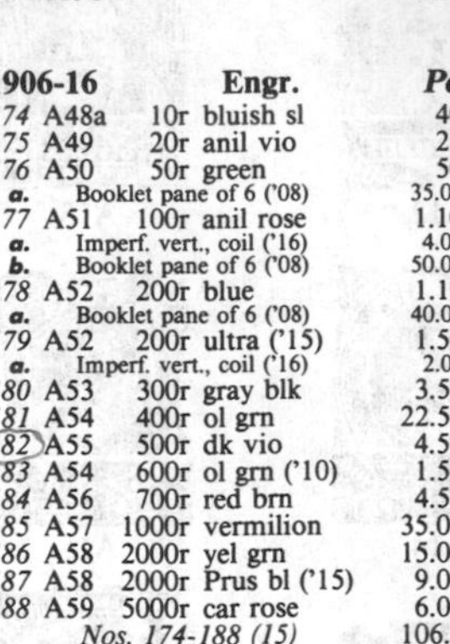

1906-16 **Engr.** ***Perf. 12***
174 A48a 10r bluish sl 40 8
175 A49 20r anil vio 25 8
176 A50 50r green 50 10
a. Booklet pane of 6 ('08) 35.00 *67.50*
177 A51 100r anil rose 1.10 8
a. Imperf. vert., coil ('16) 4.00 50
b. Booklet pane of 6 ('08) 50.00 *67.50*
178 A52 200r blue 1.10 10
a. Booklet pane of 6 ('08) 40.00 *67.50*
179 A52 200r ultra ('15) 1.50 10
a. Imperf. vert., coil ('16) 2.00 50
180 A53 300r gray blk 3.50 15
181 A54 400r ol grn 22.50 1.50
182 A55 500r dk vio 4.50 20
183 A54 600r ol grn ('10) 1.50 50
184 A56 700r red brn 4.50 2.00
185 A57 1000r vermilion 35.00 60
186 A58 2000r yel grn 15.00 40
187 A58 2000r Prus bl ('15) 9.00 50
188 A59 5000r car rose 6.00 1.25
Nos. 174-188 (15) 106.35 7.64

Allegorical Emblems: Liberty, Peace, Industry, etc. — A60

1908, July 14
189 A60 100r carmine 20.00 1.00

National Exhibition, Rio de Janeiro.

Emblems of Peace Between Brazil and Portugal A61

1908, July 14
190 A61 100r red 7.50 75

Issued to commemorate the centenary of the opening of Brazilian ports to foreign commerce. Medallions picture King Carlos I of Portugal and Pres. Affonso Penna of Brazil.

Bonifacio, Bolivar, Hidalgo, O'Higgins, San Martin, Washington — A62

1909

191 A62 200r dp bl 3.50 50

Nilo Peçanha A63

Baron of Rio Branco A64

1910, Nov. 15

192 A63 10,000r brown 6.00 1.00

1913-16

193 A64 1000r dp grn 1.50 20
194 A64 1000r sl ('16) 15.00 30

Cabo Frio — A65

Wmk.99

Wmk. "CORREIO." (99)

1915, Nov. 13 Litho. *Perf. 11½*

195 A65 100r dk grn, *yelsh* 4.00 3.00

Founding of the town of Cabo Frio, 300th anniversary.

Bay of Guajara — A66

1916, Jan. 5

196 A66 100r carmine 8.00 4.50

City of Belem, 300th anniversary.

Revolutionary Flag — A67

1917, Mar. 6

197 A67 100r dp bl 20.00 7.50

Centenary of Revolution of Pernambuco, Mar. 6, 1817.

Rodrigues Alves — A68

Unwmk.

1917, Aug. 31 Engr. *Perf. 12*

198 A68 5000r red brn 50.00 7.50

Liberty Head
A69 A70

Perf. 12½, 13, 13x13½.

1918-20 Typo. Unwmk.

200 A69 10r org brn 30 20
201 A69 20r slate 30 20
202 A69 25r ol gray ('20) 30 20
203 A69 50r green 30.00 2.00
204 A70 100r rose 85 20
a. Imperf. (pair)
205 A70 300r red org 15.00 1.75
206 A70 500r dl vio 15.00 90
Nos. 200-206 (7) 61.75 5.45

Wmk. 100-"CASA DA MOEDA" in Sheet

Because of the spacing of this watermark, a few stamps in each sheet may show no watermark.

207 A69 10r red brn 4.00 1.25
a. Imperf. (pair)
207B A69 20r slate 1.00 80
c. Imperf. (pair)
208 A69 25r ol gray ('20) 50 30
209 A69 50r green 50 20
210 A70 100r rose 37.50 20
a. Imperf. (pair)
211 A70 200r dl bl 5.50 30
212 A70 300r orange 37.50 3.00
213 A70 500r dl vio 37.50 7.00
214 A70 600r orange 1.50 *7.00*
Nos. 207-214 (9) 125.50 20.05

"Education" — A72

1918 Engr. *Perf. 11½.*

215 A72 1000r blue 3.00 20
216 A72 2000r red brn 20.00 5.00
217 A72 5000r dk vio 6.00 6.00

Watermark note below No. 257 also applies to Nos. 215-217.

See also Nos. 233-234, 283-285, 404, 406, 458, 460.

Railroad A73

"Industry" A74

"Aviation" A75

Mercury A76

"Navigation" — A77

Perf. 13½x13, 13x13½

1920-22 Typo. Unwmk.

218 A73 10r red vio 40 20
219 A73 20r ol grn 40 20
220 A74 25r brn vio 30 20
221 A74 50r bl grn 50 20
222 A74 50r org brn ('22) 80 20
223 A75 100r rose red 1.50 20
224 A75 100r org ('22) 3.00 20
225 A75 150r vio ('21) 80 20
226 A75 200r blue 1.50 20
227 A75 200r rose red ('22) 5.00 20
228 A76 300r ol gray 5.00 30
229 A76 400r dl bl ('22) 15.00 1.75
230 A76 500r red brn 10.00 40
Nos. 218-230 (13) 44.20 4.45

See also Nos. 236-257, 265-266, 268-271, 273-274, 276-281, 302-311, 316-322, 326-340, 357-358, 431-434, 436-441, 461-463B, 467-470, 472-474, 488-490, 492-494.

Perf. 11, 11½

Engr. Wmk. 100

231 A77 600r red org 1.25 20
232 A77 1000r claret 3.00 15
a. Perf. 8½ 22.50 4.00
233 A72 2000r dl vio 12.00 40
234 A72 5000r brown 10.00 5.00

Nos. 233 and 234 are inscribed "BRASIL CORREIO". Watermark note below No. 257 also applies to Nos. 231-234.

See also No. 282.

King Albert of Belgium and President Epitacio Pessoa A78

1920, Sept. 19 Engr. *Perf. 11½x11*

235 A78 100r dl red 75 75

This stamp was issued to commemorate the visit of the King and Queen of Belgium to Brazil.

Types of 1920-22 Issue.

Perf. 13x13½, 13x12½.

1922-29 Typo. Wmk. 100

236 A73 10r red vio 20 15
237 A73 20r ol grn 20 15
238 A73 20r gray vio ('29) 20 15
239 A74 25r brn vio 25 10
240 A74 50r bl grn 2.50 *30.00*
241 A74 50r org brn ('23) 35 25
a. Booklet pane of 6
242 A75 100r rose red 18.00 30
243 A75 100r org ('26) 40 10
a. Booklet pane of 6
244 A75 100r turq grn ('28) 25 15
245 A75 150r violet 2.00 15
246 A75 200r blue 300.00 10.00
247 A75 200r rose red 30 15
a. Booklet pane of 6
248 A75 200r ol grn ('28) 2.00 2.50
249 A76 300r ol gray 1.50 20
a. Booklet pane of 6
250 A76 300r rose red ('29) 25 20
251 A76 400r blue 1.50 15
252 A76 400r org ('29) 60 50
253 A76 500r red brn 6.00 40
a. Booklet pane of 6
254 A76 500r ultra ('29) 7.00 15
255 A76 600r brn org ('29) 6.00 2.50
256 A76 700r dl vio ('29) 6.00 1.40
257 A76 1000r turq bl ('29) 8.00 60
Nos. 236-257 (22) 363.50 50.25

Because of the spacing of the watermark, a few stamps in each sheet show no watermark.

"Agriculture" — A79

1922 Unwmk. *Perf. 13x13½.*

258 A79 40r org brn 50 10
259 A79 80r grnsh bl 40 *3.00*

See also Nos. 263, 267, 275.

Declaration of Ypiranga — A80

Dom Pedro I and Jose Bonifacio A81

National Exposition and President Pessoa — A82

Unwmk.

1922, Sept. 7 Engr. *Perf. 14*

260 A80 100r ultra 6.00 40
261 A81 200r red 2.50 30
262 A82 300r green 4.50 30

Issued in commemoration of the centenary of independence and the National Exposition of 1922.

Agriculture Type of 1922

Perf. 13½x12

1923 Wmk. 100 Typo.

263 A79 40r org brn 35 *1.00*

Brazilian Army Entering Bahia — A83

Unwmk.

1923, July 12 Litho. *Perf. 13*

264 A83 200r rose 9.00 4.50

Centenary of the taking of Bahia from the Portuguese.

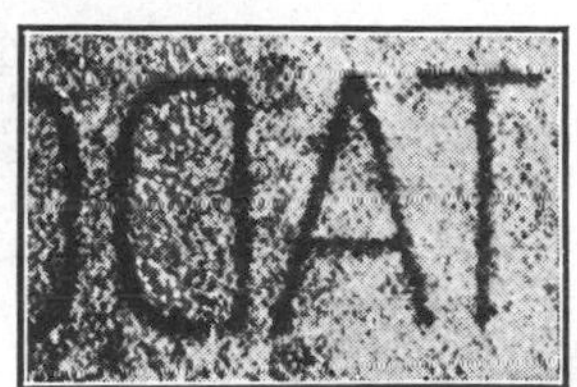

Wmk. 193- ESTADOS UNIDOS DO BRASIL

Types of 1920-22 Issues

Perf. 13x13½

1924 Typo. Wmk. 193

265 A73 10r red vio 4.50 3.00
266 A73 20r ol grn 5.00 3.00
267 A79 40r org brn 3.50 50
268 A74 50r org brn 3.00 *15.00*
269 A75 100r orange 3.50 25
270 A75 200r rose 5.00 20
271 A76 400r blue 3.00 3.00
Nos. 265-271 (7) 27.50 24.95

Arms of Equatorial Confederation, 1824 — A84

Unwmk.

1924, July 2 Litho. *Perf. 11*

272 A84 200r bl, blk, yel, & red 3.50 2.00
a. Red omitted 450.00 450.00

Centenary of the Equatorial Confederation.

Wmk. 101- Stars and CASA DA MOEDA

Types of 1920-22 Issues.

Perf. 9½ to 13½ and Compound.

1924-28 Typo. Wmk. 101

273 A73 10r red vio 15 10
274 A73 20r ol gray 15 10
275 A79 40r org brn 30 12
276 A74 50r org brn 30 10
277 A75 100r red org 60 10
278 A75 200r rose 40 10
279 A76 300r ol gray ('25) 7.00 80
280 A76 400r blue 2.00 25
281 A76 500r red brn 9.00 35

Engr.

282 A77 600r red org ('26) 75 15
283 A72 2000r dl vio ('26) 2.00 15
284 A72 5000r brn ('26) 10.00 60
285 A72 10,000r rose ('28) 12.00 75
Nos. 273-285 (13) 44.65 3.67

Nos. 283 to 285 are inscribed "BRASIL CORREIO".

Ruy Barbosa — A85

1925 Wmk. 100 *Perf. 11½*

286 A85 1000r claret 4.00 2.00

1926 Wmk. 101

287 A85 1000r claret 1.75 25

"Justice" — A86

Scales of Justice and Map of Brazil — A87

Wmk. 206- Star-framed CM, Multiple

Perf. 13½x13

1927, Aug. 11 Typo. Wmk. 206

288 A86 100r dp bl 1.00 50
289 A87 200r rose 1.00 50

Issued in commemoration of the centenary of the founding of the law courses.

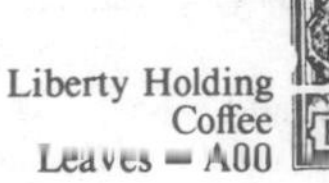

Liberty Holding Coffee Leaves — A88

1928, Mar. 5

290 A88 100r bl grn 1.50 60
291 A88 200r carmine 1.00 50
292 A88 300r ol blk 8.50 40

Issued to commemorate the bicentenary of the introduction of the coffee tree in Brazil.

Official Stamps of 1919 Surcharged in Red or Black **700 Réis**

Perf. 11, 11½

1928 Wmk. 100 Engr.

293 O3 700r on 500r org (R) 3.25 2.25
a. Inverted surcharge 250.00 250.00
294 O3 1000r on 100r rose red (Bk) 2.25 40
295 O3 2000r on 200r dl bl (R) 3.00 60
296 O3 5000r on 50r grn (R) 3.00 75
297 O3 10,000r on 10r ol grn (R) 16.00 1.25
Nos. 293-297 (5) 27.50 5.25

Nos. 293 to 297 were used for ordinary postage.

Stamps in the outer rows of the sheets are often without watermark.

Ruy Barbosa — A89

Perf. 9, 9½x11, 11, and Compound.

1929 Wmk. 101

300 A89 5000r bl vio 12.00 75

See Nos. 405 and 459.

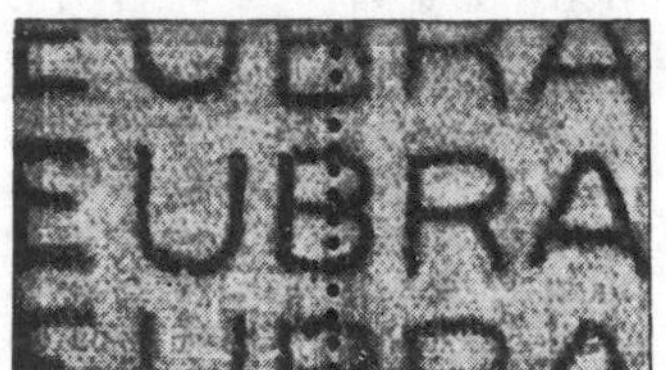

Wmk. 218- E U BRASIL Multiple. (Letters 8 mm. high.)

Wmk. 218 exists both in vertical alignment and in echelon.

Types of 1920-21 Issue.

Perf. 13½x12½.

1929 Typo. Wmk. 218

302 A75 20r gray vio 15 8
a. Wmk. in echelon 20 35
303 A75 50r red brn 15 8
a. Wmk. in echelon 90.00 30.00
304 A75 100r turq grn 25 8
305 A75 200r ol grn 13.00 2.50
306 A76 300r rose red 60 8
a. Wmk. in echelon 75 30
307 A76 400r orange 75 25
308 A76 500r ultra 7.50 50
a. Wmk. in echelon 125.00 17.50
309 A76 600r brn org 9.00 60
310 A76 700r dp vio 2.50 10
311 A76 1000r turq bl 4.00 10
a. Wmk. in echelon 7.50 7.50
Nos. 302-311 (10) 37.90 4.37

Architectural Fantasies
A90 A91

Architectural Fantasy — A92

Perf. 13x13½

1930, June 20 Wmk. 206

312 A90 100r turq bl 1.75 1.00
313 A91 200r ol gray 3.00 75
314 A92 300r rose red 5.00 1.00

Issued in connection with the Fourth Pan-American Congress of Architects and Exposition of Architecture.

Wmk. 221- ESTADOS UNIDOS DO BRASIL, Multiple (Letters 6 mm. high.)

Types of 1920-21 Issues.

1930 Wmk. 221 *Perf. 13x12½.*

316 A75 20r gray vio 10 10
317 A75 50r red brn 15 10
318 A75 100r turq bl 20 10
319 A75 200r ol grn 2.50 20
320 A76 300r rose red 50 20
321 A76 500r ultra 1.25 20
322 A76 1000r turq bl 17.50 60
Nos. 316-322 (7) 22.20 1.50

Imperforates

Since 1930, imperforate or partly perforated sheets of nearly all commemorative and some definitive issues have become obtainable.

Wmk. 222- CORREIO BRASIL and 5 Stars in Squared Circle. (222)

Types of 1920-29 Issue.

Perf. 11, 13½x13, 13x12½

1931-34 Typo. Wmk. 222

326 A75 10r dp brn 10 8
327 A75 20r gray vio 10 8
328 A74 25r brn vio ('34) 10 50
330 A75 50r bl grn 15 10
331 A75 50r red brn 10 10
332 A75 100r orange 25 10
334 A75 200r dp car 35 10
335 A76 300r ol grn 50 10
336 A76 400r ultra 70 10
337 A76 500r red brn 3.00 10
338 A76 600r brn org 3.00 10
339 A76 700r dp vio 3.00 10
340 A76 1000r turq bl 10.00 10
Nos. 326-340 (13) 21.35 1.66

Getulio Vargas and Joao Pessoa A93

Vargas and Pessoa A94

Oswaldo Aranha
A95 A96

Antonio Carlos A97

Pessoa A98

Vargas — A99

Unwmk.

1931, Apr. 29 Litho. *Perf. 14*

342 A93 10r + 10r lt bl 20 *8.00*
343 A93 20r + 20r yel brn 20 *6.00*
344 A95 50r + 50r bl grn, red & yel 20 20
a. Red missing at left 1.25 1.25
345 A93 100r + 50r org 40 40
346 A93 200r + 100r grn 40 40
347 A94 300r + 150r multi 40 40
348 A93 400r + 200r dp rose 1.50 90
349 A93 500r + 250r dk bl 1.00 80
350 A93 600r + 300r brn vio 70 *10.00*
351 A94 700r + 350r multi 1.25 75
352 A96 1000r + 500r brt grn, red & yel 3.00 30
353 A97 2000r + 1000r gray blk & red 6.00 75
354 A98 5000r + 2500r blk & red 25.00 7.00
355 A99 10000r + 5000r brt grn & yel 60.00 15.00
Nos. 342-355 (14) 100.25 50.90

Issued to commemorate the Revolution of Oct. 3, 1930. Prepared as semipostal stamps, Nos. 342-355 were sold as ordinary postage stamps with stated surtax ignored.

Nos. 306, 320 and 250 Surcharged **1931 200 Réis**

Wmk. E U BRASIL Multiple. (218)

1931, July 20 *Perf. 13½x12½*

356 A76 200r on 300r rose red 1.00 1.00
a. Wmk. in echelon 15.00 15.00
b. Inverted surcharge 35.00

Perf. 13x12½

Wmk. 221

357 A76 200r on 300r rose red 30 18
a. Inverted surcharge 40.00 40.00

Perf. 13½x12½

Wmk. 100

358 A76 200r on 300r rose red 50.00 50.00

Map of South America Showing Meridian of Tordesillas A100

Joao Ramalho and Tibiriça
A101

Martim Affonso de Souza
A102

King John III of Portugal
A103

Disembarkation of M. A. de Souza at Sao Vicente — A104

Wmk. 222

1932, June 3 Typo. *Perf. 13*

359	A100	20r dk vio	20	20
360	A101	100r black	50	40
361	A102	200r purple	1.25	20
362	A103	600r red brn	2.50	1.00

Engr.

Wmk. 101

Perf. 9½, 11, 9½x11.

363	A104	700r ultra	3.00	1.50
		Nos. 359-363 (5)	7.45	3.30

Nos. 359 to 363 commemorate the fourth centenary of the first colonization of Brazil at Sao Vicente, in 1532, under the hereditary captaincy of Martim Affonso de Souza.

Revolutionary Issue.

Map of Brazil
A105

Soldier and Flag
A106

Allegory: Freedom, Justice, Equality
A107

Soldier's Head
A108

"LEX" and Sword
A109

Symbolical of Law and Order
A110

Symbolical of Justice
A111

Perf. 11½

1932, Sept. 13 Litho. Unwmk.

364	A105	100r brn org	60	3.00
365	A106	200r dk car	50	1.00
366	A107	300r gray grn	3.00	5.00
367	A108	400r dk bl	10.00	10.00
368	A105	500r blk brn	10.00	10.00
369	A107	600r red	10.00	10.00
370	A106	700r violet	4.50	10.00
371	A108	1000r orange	2.50	10.00
372	A109	2000r dk brn	20.00	27.50
373	A110	5000r yel grn	25.00	47.50
374	A111	10000r plum	27.50	55.00
		Nos. 364-374 (11)	113.60	189.00

Issued by the revolutionary forces in the state of Sao Paulo during the revolt of September, 1932. Subsequenty the stamps were recognized by the Federal Government and placed in general use.

Excellent counterfeits of Nos. 373 and 374 exist.

Counterfeit cancellations abound.

City of Vassouras and Illuminated Memorial — A112

Wmk. 222

1933, Jan. 15 Typo. *Perf. 12*

375	A112	200r rose red	1.50	1.00

Commemorative of the centenary of the founding of the city of Vassouras.

No. 306 Surcharged 200 RÉIS

Perf. 13½x12½

1933, July 28 Wmk. 218

376	A76	200r on 300r rose red	85	75
a.		Wmk.218 in echelon (No. 306a)	15.00	15.00
b.		Wmk. 100 (No. 250)	110.00	110.00

Same Surcharge on No. 320.

Perf. 13x12½.

Wmk. 221

377	A76	200r on 300r rose red	50	40
a.		Inverted surcharge	40.00	
b.		Double surcharge	40.00	

Religious Symbols and Inscriptions — A113

Wmk. 222

1933, Sept. 3 Typo. *Perf. 13*

378	A113	200r dk red	1.00	60

Issued in commemoration of the First National Eucharistic Congress in Brazil.

"Flag of the Race"
A114

1933, Aug. 18

379	A114	200r dp red	1.00	60

Commemorating the raising of the "Flag of the Race" and the 441st anniversary of the sailing of Columbus from Palos, Spain, August 3, 1492.

Republic Figure, Flags of Brazil and Argentina — A115

Wmk. 236- Coat of Arms in Sheet

Watermark (reduced illustration) covers 22 stamps in sheet.

Wmk. 101

1933, Oct. 7 Engr. *Perf. 11½*

380	A115	200r blue	50	35

Thick Laid Paper.

Perf. 11, 11½.

Wmk. 236

381	A115	400r green	90	70
382	A115	600r brt rose	3.50	3.50
383	A115	1000r lt vio	5.50	3.00

Issued in commemoration of the visit of President Justo of the Argentine Republic to Brazil, October 2nd to 7th, 1933.

Allegory: "Faith and Energy"
A116

Allegory of Flight
A117

1933 Typo. Wmk. 222

384	A116	200r dk red	30	15
385	A116	200r dk vio	35	10

See also Nos. 435, 471 and 491.

Wmk. 236

1934, Apr. 15 Engr. *Perf. 12*

386	A117	200r blue	75	75

Issued in commemoration of the first National Aviation Congress at Sao Paulo.

A118

Wmk. 222

1934, May 12 Typo. *Perf. 11*

387	A118	200r dk ol	50	50
388	A118	400r carmine	2.50	2.50
389	A118	700r ultra	2.50	1.50
390	A118	1000r orange	6.00	1.00

Issued in commemoration of the Seventh International Fair at Rio de Janeiro.

Christ of Corcovado — A119

1934, Oct. 20

392	A119	300r dk red	3.00	3.00
a.		Tete beche pair	9.00	11.00
393	A119	700r ultra	12.00	7.50
a.		Tete beche pair	35.00	40.00

Visit of Eugenio Cardinal Pacelli, later Pope Pius XII, to Brazil.

The three printings of Nos. 392-393, distinguishable by shades, sell for different prices.

José de Anchieta
A120

Thick Laid Paper.

1934, Nov. 8 Wmk. 236 *Perf. 11, 12*

394	A120	200r yel brn	1.00	25
395	A120	300r violet	75	40
396	A120	700r blue	3.00	2.50
397	A120	1000r lt grn	6.00	1.00

Issued in commemoration of the 400th anniversary of the birth of Jose de Anchieta, S.J. (1534-1597), Portuguese missionary and "father of Brazilian literature."

"Brazil" and "Uruguay"
A121 A122

Wmk. 222

1935, Jan. 8 Typo. *Perf. 11*

398	A121	200r orange	1.00	60
399	A122	300r yellow	1.25	75
400	A122	700r ultra	5.00	5.00
401	A121	1000r dk vio	12.00	6.00

Visit of President Terra of Uruguay.

View of Town of Igarassu
A123

1935, July 1

402	A123	200r mar & brn	1.50	75
403	A123	300r vio & ol brn	1.50	60

Issued in commemoration of the 400th anniversary of the founding of the captaincy of Pernambuco.

Types of 1918-29.
Thick Laid Paper.

Perf. 9½, 11, 12, 12x11.

1934-36 Engr. Wmk. 236

404	A72	2000r violet	4.50	40
405	A89	5000r bl vio ('36)	12.50	50
406	A72	10000r cl ('36)	10.00	80

No. 404 is inscribed "BRASIL CORREIO".

The lack of a price for a listed item does not necessarily indicate rarity.

Revolutionist A124

Bento Gonçalves da Silva — A125

Duke of Caxias A126

1935, Sept. 20 ***Perf. 11, 12***
407 A124 200r black 1.00 75
408 A124 300r rose lake 1.00 60
409 A125 700r dl bl 4.00 4.00
410 A126 1000r lt vio 4.50 2.50

Centenary of the "Ragged" Revolution.

Federal District Coat of Arms A127

Wmk. 222
1935, Oct. 19 **Typo.** ***Perf. 11***
411 A127 200r blue 4.00 3.00

Issued in commemoration of the Eighth International Sample Fair held at Rio de Janeiro.

Coutinho's Ship — A128

Arms of Fernandes Coutinho — A129

1935, Oct. 25
412 A128 300r maroon 3.50 1.00
413 A129 700r turq bl 4.50 2.50

Issued in commemoration of the 400th anniversary of the establishment of the first Portuguese colony at Espirito Santo by Vasco Fernandes Coutinho.

Gavea, Rock near Rio de Janeiro A130

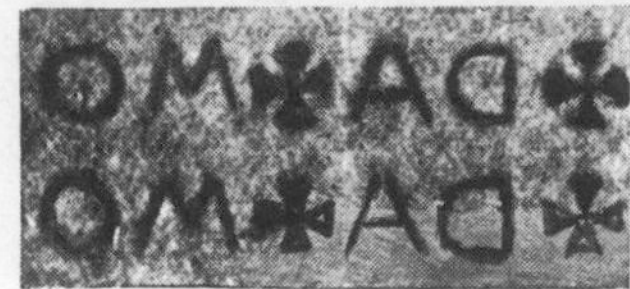
Wmk. 245- Multiple "CASA DA MOEDA DO BRASIL" and Small Formée Cross

1935, Oct. 12 **Wmk. 245** ***Perf. 11***
414 A130 300r brn & vio 2.00 1.50
415 A130 300r blk & turq bl 2.00 1.50
416 A130 300r Prus bl & ultra 2.00 1.50
417 A130 300r crim & blk 2.00 1.50

"Child's Day," Oct. 12.

Viscount of Cairu — A131

Perf. 11, 12x11
1936, Jan. 20 **Engr.** **Wmk. 236**
418 A131 1200r violet 10.00 5.00

Issued in commemoration of the centenary of the death of Jose da Silva Lisboa, Viscount of Cairu (1756-1835).

View of Cameta A132

1936, Feb. 26 ***Perf. 11, 12***
419 A132 200r brn org 1.75 1.25
420 A132 300r green 1.75 75

Issued in commemoration of the 300th anniversary of the founding of the city of Cameta, Dec. 24, 1635.

Coining Press A133

Thick Laid Paper.
1936, Mar. 24 ***Perf. 11***
421 A133 300r pur brn, *cr* 1.25 75

Issued in commemoration of the first Numismatic Congress at Sao Paulo, March, 1936.

Carlos Gomes A134

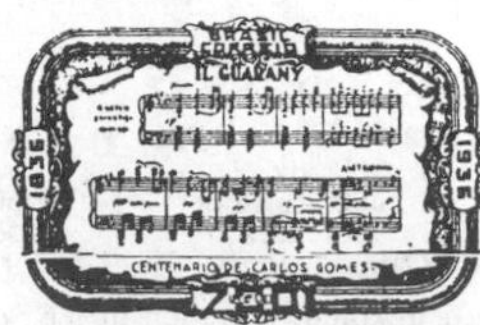

"Il Guarany" — A135

Thick Laid Paper.
1936, July 11 ***Perf. 11, 11x12***
422 A134 300r dl rose 75 50
423 A134 300r blk brn 75 50
424 A135 700r ocher 4.50 1.50
425 A135 700r blue 3.50 1.75

Issued in commemoration of the 100th anniversary of the birth of Antonio Carlos Gomes, who composed the opera "Il Guarany."

Scales of Justice — A136

Wmk. 222
1936, July 4 **Typo.** ***Perf. 11***
426 A136 300r rose 2.00 75

First National Judicial Congress.

Federal District Coat of Arms A137

Wmk. 249- "CORREIO BRASIL" multiple

1936, Nov. 13 **Typo.** **Wmk. 249**
427 A137 200r rose red 1.25 75

Issued in commemoration of the Ninth International Sample Fair held at Rio de Janeiro.

Eucharistic Congress Seal — A138

1936, Dec. 17 **Wmk. 245** ***Perf. 11½***
428 A138 300r grn, yel, bl & blk 1.25 75

Issued in commemoration of the Second National Eucharistic Congress in Brazil.

Botafogo Bay — A139

Thick Laid Paper.
Wmk. 236
1937, Jan. 2 **Engr.** ***Perf. 11***
429 A139 700r blue 1.50 75
430 A139 700r black 1.50 75

Issued to commemorate the birth centenary of Francisco Pereira Passos, engineer who planned the modern city of Rio de Janeiro.

Types of 1920-21, 1933.
Perf. 11, 11½ and Compound.

1936-37		**Typo.**	**Wmk. 249**	
431	A75	10r dp brn	15	10
432	A75	20r dl vio	15	10
433	A75	50r bl grn	15	10
434	A75	100r orange	25	10
435	A116	200r dk vio	50	10
436	A76	300r ol grn	25	10
437	A76	400r ultra	50	10
438	A76	500r lt brn	75	10
439	A76	600r brn org ('37)	1.75	10
440	A76	700r dp vio	3.25	10
441	A76	1000r turq bl	3.50	10
	Nos. 431-441 (11)		11.20	1.10

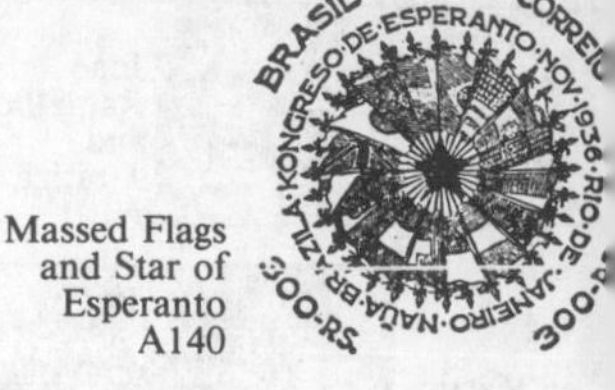

Massed Flags and Star of Esperanto A140

1937, Jan. 19
442 A140 300r green 1.75 75

Ninth Brazilian Esperanto Congress.

Bay of Rio de Janeiro A141

1937, June 9 **Unwmk.** ***Perf. 12½***
443 A141 300r org red & blk 75 75
444 A141 700r bl & dk brn 2.00 75

Issued in commemoration of the Second South American Radio Communication Conference held in Rio de Janeiro, June 7 to 19, 1937.

Globe — A142

1937, Sept. 4 **Wmk. 249** ***Perf. 11, 12***
445 A142 300r green 1.50 75

50th anniversary of Esperanto.

Monroe Palace, Rio de Janeiro A143

Botanical Garden, Rio de Janeiro A144

1937, Sept. 30 **Unwmk.** ***Perf. 12½***
446 A143 200r lt brn & bl 75 50
447 A144 300r org & ol grn 75 50
448 A143 2000r grn & cer 6.50 9.00
449 A144 10000r lake & ind 55.00 45.00

Brig. Gen. Jose da Silva Paes — A145

Eagle and Shield — A146

1937, Oct. 11 **Wmk. 249** ***Perf. 11½***
450 A145 300r blue 1.00 40

Bicentenary of Rio Grande do Sul.

1937, Dec. 2 **Typo.** ***Perf. 11***
451 A146 400r dk bl 1.25 50

Issued in commemoration of the 150th anniversary of the Constitution of the United States of America.

Bags of Brazilian Coffee A147

Frame Engraved, Center Typographed

1938, Jan. 17 Unwmk. *Perf. 12½*

452 A147 1200r multi 6.00 75

Arms of Olinda A148

Perf. 11, 11x11½.

1938, Jan. 24 Engr. Wmk. 249

453 A148 400r violet 75 40

Issued in commemoration of the fourth centenary of the founding of the city of Olinda.

Independence Memorial, Ypiranga — A149

1938, Jan. 24 Typo. *Perf. 11*

454 A149 400r brn ol 1.00 40

Issued to commemorate the proclamation of Brazil's independence by Dom Pedro, Sept. 7, 1822.

Iguaçu Falls — A150

Perf. 12½

1938, Jan. 10 Unwmk. Engr.

455 A150 1000r sep & yel brn 2.50 1.25
456 A150 5000r ol blk & grn 27.50 12.50

Couto de Magalhaes — A151

Perf. 11, 11x11½

1938, Mar. 17 Wmk. 249

457 A151 400r dl grn 75 35

Issued to commemorate the centenary of the birth of General Couto de Magalhaes (1837-1898), statesman, soldier, explorer, writer, developer.

Types of 1918-38

Perf. 11, 12x11, 12x11½, 12.

1938 Engr. Wmk. 249

458 A72 2000r bl vio 8.00 15
459 A89 5000r vio bl 30.00 60
a. 5000r dp bl 25.00 60
460 A72 10000r rose lake 35.00 1.20

No. 458 is inscribed "BRASIL CORREIO".

Types of 1920-22.

1938 Wmk. 245 Typo. *Perf. 11.*

461 A75 50r bl grn 60 1.25
462 A75 100r orange 60 1.25
463 A76 300r ol grn 60 25
463A A76 400r ultra 120.00 60.00
463B A76 500r red brn 60 *17.50*
Nos. 461-463B (5) 122.40 80.25

National Archives Building A152

1938, May 20 Wmk. 249

464 A152 400r brown 75 35

Centenary of National Archives.

Souvenir Sheets.

Sir Rowland Hill A153

1938, Oct. 22 *Imperf.*

465 A153 Sheet of 10 20.00 20.00
a. 400r dl grn, Single stamp 1.25 1.25

Issued in commemoration of the Brazilian International Philatelic Exposition (Brapex).

Issued in sheets measuring 106x118mm. A few perforated sheets exist.

President Vargas A154

1938, Nov. 10 *Perf. 11*

Without Gum

466 A154 Sheet of 10 9.00 15.00
a. 400r sl bl, Single stamp 70 70

Issued in commemoration of the Constitution of Brazil, set up by President Vargas, Nov. 10, 1937. Size: 113x135½mm.

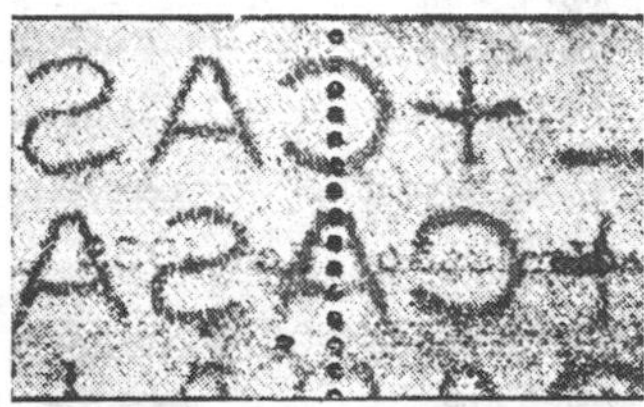
Wmk. 256- "CASA+DA+MOEDA+DO+BRAZIL" in 8mm. Letters

Types of 1920-33.

1939 Typo. Wmk. 256 *Perf. 11.*

467 A75 10r red brn 40 30
468 A75 20r dl vio 40 15
469 A75 50r bl grn 40 10
470 A75 100r yel org 60 10
471 A116 200r dk vio 70 10
472 A76 400r ultra 1.25 10
473 A76 600r dl org 1.25 10
474 A76 1000r turq bl 9.00 10
Nos. 467-474 (8) 14.00 1.05

View of Rio de Janeiro — A155

View of Santos — A156

1939, June 14 Engr. Wmk. 249

475 A155 1200r dl vio 2.50 25

1939, Aug. 23

476 A156 400r dl bl 60 30

Centenary of founding of Santos.

Chalice Vine and Blossoms A157

Eucharistic Congress Seal A158

1939, Aug. 23

477 A157 400r green 2.00 50

Issued in commemoration of the first South American Botanical Congress held in January, 1938.

1939, Sept. 3

478 A158 400r rose red 60 30

Third National Eucharistic Congress.

Duke of Caxias, Army Patron — A159

1939, Sept. 12 Photo. *Rouletted*

479 A159 A400r dp ultra 60 40

Issued for Soldiers' Day.

George Washington — A159a

Emperor Pedro II — A159b

Grover Cleveland — A159c

Statue of Friendship, Given by US — A159d

Unwmk.

1939, Oct. 7 Engr. *Perf. 12*

480 A159a 400r yel org 75 40
481 A159b 800r dk grn 45 25
482 A159c 1200r rose car 1.00 25
483 A159d 1600r dk bl 1.00 40

New York World's Fair.

Benjamin Constant A160

Fonseca on Horseback A161

Manuel Deodoro da Fonseca and President Vargas — A162

Wmk. 249

1939, Nov. 15 Photo. *Rouletted*

484 A160 400r dp grn 60 30
485 A162 1200r chocolate 1.50 40

Engr. *Perf. 11*

486 A161 800r gray blk 90 45

Issued in commemoration of the 50th anniversary of the Proclamation of the Republic.

President Roosevelt, President Vargas and Map of the Americas A163

1940, Apr. 14

487 A163 400r sl bl 1.25 60

Pan American Union, 50th anniversary.

Wmk. 264- "*CORREIO*BRASIL*" Multiple. Letters 7mm. high.

Types of 1920-33.

1940-41 Typo. Wmk. 264 *Perf. 11.*

488 A75 10r red brn 10 25
489 A75 20r dl vio 25 25
489A A75 50r bl grn ('41) 85 *1.50*
490 A75 100r yel org 1.00 8
491 A116 200r violet 75 8
492 A76 400r ultra 5.00 8
493 A76 600r dl org 5.00 8
494 A76 1000r turq bl 12.50 8
Nos. 488-494 (8) 25.45 2.40

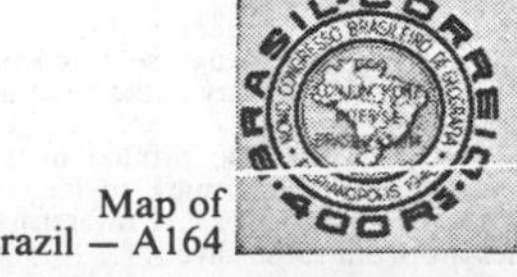
Map of Brazil — A164

1940, Sept. 7 **Engr.**

495 A164 400r carmine 65 35
a. Unwmk. 82.50 50.00

Issued in commemoration of the 9th Brazilian Congress of Geography held at Florianopolis.

Victoria Regia Water Lily — A165

President Vargas — A166

Relief Map of Brazil — A167

1940, Oct. 30 **Wmk. 249** ***Perf. 11***
Without Gum

496 A165 1000r dl vio 1.50 1.50
a. Sheet of ten 15.00 45.00
497 A166 5000r red 12.00 9.00
a. Sheet of ten 130.00 200.00
498 A167 10,000r sl bl 13.50 4.50
a. Sheet of ten 175.00 200.00

New York World's Fair.

All three sheets exist unwatermarked and also with papermaker's watermark of large globe and "AMERICA BANK" in sheet. A few imperforate sheets also exist.

Joaquim Machado de Assis — A168

Pioneers and Buildings of Porto Alegre — A169

1940, Nov. 1

499 A168 400r black 75 30

Birth centenary of Joaquim Maria Machado de Assis, poet and novelist.

1940, Nov. 2 **Wmk. 264**

500 A169 400r green 60 25

Issued to commemorate the bicentenary of the colonization of Porto Alegre.

Proclamation of King John IV of Portugal — A173

1940, Dec. 1 **Wmk. 249**

501 A173 1200r bl blk 2.00 40

Issued in commemoration of the 800th anniversary of Portuguese independence and the 300th anniversary of the restoration of the monarchy.

No. 501 was also printed on paper with papermaker's watermark of large globe and "AMERICA BANK." Unwatermarked copies are from these sheets.

Brazilian Flags and Head of Liberty — A175

Calendar Sheet and Inscription "Day of the Fifth General Census of Brazil" — A176

Wmk. 256

1940, Dec. 18 **Engr.** ***Perf. 11***

502 A175 400r dl vio 75 30
b. Unwmk. 60.00 60.00

Wmk. 245

502A A175 400r dl vio 50.00 50.00

Issued in commemoration of the 10th anniversary of the inauguration of President Vargas.

Wmk. 256

1941, Jan. 14 **Typo.** ***Perf. 11***

503 A176 400r bl & red 45 20

Wmk. 245

504 A176 400r bl & red 3.50 1.00

Fifth general census of Brazil.

King Alfonso Henriques A177

Father Antonio Vieira A178

Salvador Corrêia de Sa e Benevides — A179

President Carmona of Portugal and President Vargas A180

Wmk. 264

1940-41 **Photo.** ***Rouletted***

504A	A177	200r pink	20	15
505	A178	400r ultra	30	20
506	A179	800r brt vio	35	20
506A	A180	5400r sl grn	2.25	1.00

Wmk. 249

507	A177	200r pink	7.50	4.50
507A	A178	400r ultra	35.00	12.00
508	A180	5400r sl grn	3.50	1.75
		Nos. 504A-508 (7)	49.10	19.80

Issued in commemoration of the 800th anniversary of Portuguese Independence.

Jose de Anchieta A181

Amador Bueno A182

Wmk. 264

1941, Aug. 1 **Engr.** ***Perf. 11***

509 A181 1000r gray vio 1.75 80

Society of Jesus, 400th anniversary.

1941, Oct. 20 ***Perf. 11½***

510 A182 400r black 80 50

Issued in commemoration of the 300th anniversary of the acclamation of Amador Bueno (1572-1648) as king of Sao Paulo.

Air Force Emblem A183

1941, Oct. 20 ***Perf. 11***

511 A183 5400r sl grn 6.00 3.50

Issued in connection with Aviation Week, as propaganda for the Brazilian Air Force.

Petroleum A184

Agriculture A185

Steel Industry A186

Commerce A187

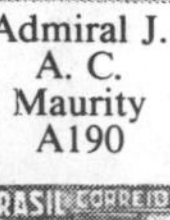

Marshal Peixoto A188

Count of Porto Alegre A189

Admiral J. A. C. Maurity A190

"Armed Forces" A191

Vargas — A192

1941-42 **Wmk. 264** **Typo.** ***Perf. 11***

512	A184	10r yel brn	20	20
513	A184	20r ol grn	10	8
514	A184	50r ol bis	10	8
515	A184	100r bl grn	20	8
516	A185	200r brn org	50	8
517	A185	300r lil rose	25	15
518	A185	400r grnsh bl	75	10
519	A185	500r salmon	35	10
520	A186	600r violet	75	10
521	A186	700r brt rose	35	15
522	A186	1000r gray	2.00	10
523	A186	1200r dl bl	3.50	10
524	A187	2000r gray vio	3.00	10
		Engr.		
525	A188	5000r blue	6.00	15
526	A189	10,000r rose red	7.50	20
527	A190	20,000r dp brn	7.50	40
528	A191	50,000r red ('42)	30.00	22.50
529	A192	100,000r bl ('42)	60	*10.00*
		Nos. 512-529 (18)	63.65	34.67

Nos. 512 to 527 and later issues come on thick or thin paper. The stamps on both papers also exist with three vertical green lines printed on the back, a control mark.

See also Nos. 541-587, 592-593, 656-670.

Bernardino de Campos A193

Prudente de Morais A194

1942, May 25

533 A193 1000r red 2.50 75
534 A194 1200r blue 6.00 50

Issued in commemoration of the 100th anniversary of the birth of Bernardino de Campos and Prudente de Morais, lawyers and statesmen of Brazil.

Head of Indo-Brazilian Bull — A195

1942, May 1 **Wmk. 264** ***Perf. 11½***

535 A195 200r blue 75 40
536 A195 400r org brn 75 40
a. Wmk. 267 75.00 75.00

Issued in commemoration of the second Agriculture and Livestock Show of Central Brazil held at Uberaba. Wmk. 267 is illustrated with Nos. 573-587.

Outline of Brazil and Torch of Knowledge A196

Map of Brazil Showing Goiania A197

Wmk. 264

1942, July 5 **Typo.** ***Perf. 11***

537 A196 400r org brn 60 35

8th Brazilian Congress of Education.

1942, July 5

538 A197 400r lt vio 60 40

Founding of Goiania city.

Seal of Congress A198

1942, Sept. 20 **Wmk. 264**

539	A198	400r ol bis	50	25
a.		Wmk. 267	30.00	15.00

Issued to commemorate the 4th National Eucharistic Congress at Sao Paulo. Wmk. 267 is illustrated with Nos. 573-587.

Types of 1941-42.

1942-47 **Wmk. 245** ***Perf. 11.***

541	A184	20r ol grn	10	40
542	A184	50r ol bis	10	10
543	A184	100r bl grn	40	40
544	A185	200r brn org	65	50
545	A185	400r grnsh bl	40	10
546	A186	600r lt vio	3.00	10
547	A186	700r brt rose	35	80
548	A186	1200r dl bl	1.25	15
549	A187	2000r gray vio ('47)	9.00	9.00
		Engr.		
550	A188	5000r blue	10.00	40
551	A189	10,000r rose red	6.00	1.50
552	A190	20,000r dp brn ('47)	4.50	45
553	A192	100,000r blue	3.50	8.00
		Nos. 541-553 (13)	39.25	21.90

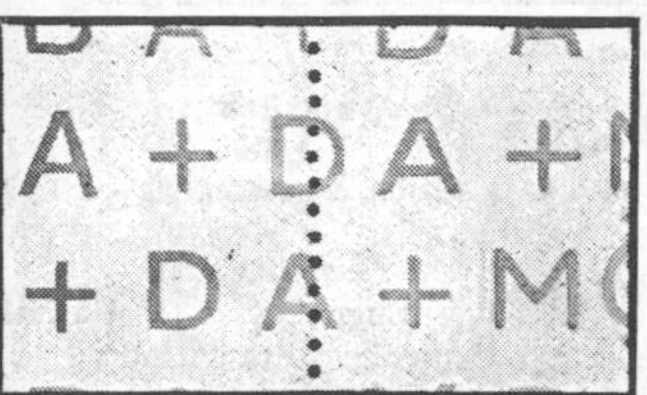

Wmk. 268- "CASA+DA+MOEDA+DO+BRASIL" in 6mm. Letters

Types of 1941-42.

1941-47 **Typo.** **Wmk. 268** ***Perf. 11.***

554	A184	20r ol grn	20	15
555	A184	50r ol bis ('47)	60	60
556	A184	100r bl grn ('43)	20	15
557	A185	200r brn org ('43)	20	10
558	A185	300r lil rose ('43)	15	10
559	A185	400r grnsh bl ('42)	35	15
560	A185	500r sal ('43)	20	10
561	A186	600r violet	70	8
562	A186	700r brt rose ('45)	40	*2.00*
563	A186	1000r gray	75	8
564	A186	1200r dp bl ('44)	1.00	15
565	A187	2000r gray vio ('43)	3.50	10
		Engr.		
566	A188	5000r bl ('43)	5.00	15
567	A189	10,000r rose red ('43)	10.00	45
568	A190	20,000r dp brn ('42)	22.50	50
569	A191	50,000r red ('42)	25.00	3.50
a.		50,000r dk brn red ('47)	17.50	10.00
570	A192	100,000r blue	65	65
		Nos. 554-570 (17)	71.40	9.01

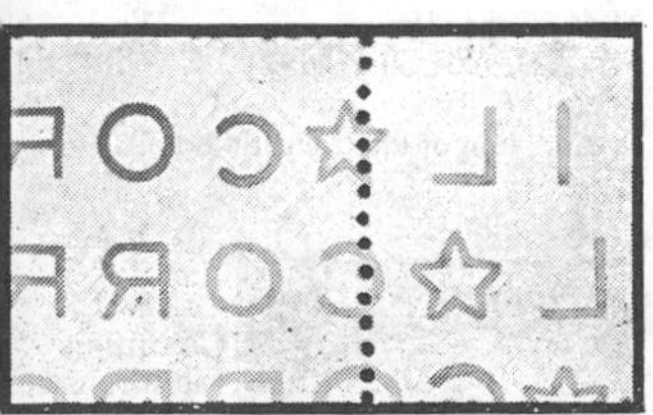

Wmk. 267- "*CORREIO*BRASIL*" Multiple in Small Letters (5 mm. high)

Types of 1941-42.

1942-47 **Typo.** **Wmk. 267**

573	A184	20r ol grn ('43)	20	10
574	A184	50r ol bis ('43)	10	10
575	A184	100r bl grn ('43)	25	10
576	A185	200r brn org ('43)	30	35
577	A185	400r grnsh bl	30	10
578	A185	500r sal ('43)	100.00	15.00
579	A186	600r vio ('43)	60	40
580	A186	700r brt rose ('47)	50	*5.00*
581	A186	1000r gray ('44)	3.00	15
582	A186	1200r dl bl	3.50	10
583	A187	2000r gray vio	3.50	10
		Engr.		
584	A188	5000r blue	6.00	20
585	A189	10,000r rose red ('44)	10.00	85
586	A190	20,000r dp brn ('45)	12.00	60
587	A191	50,000r red ('43)	35.00	7.50
		Nos. 573-587 (15)	175.25	30.65

1942 **Typo.** **Wmk. 249**

592	A184	100r bl grn	5.00	3.50
593	A186	600r violet	5.00	1.00

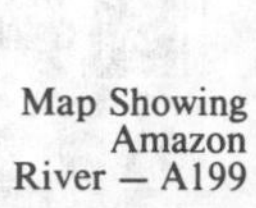

Map Showing Amazon River — A199

1943, Mar. 19 **Wmk. 267** ***Perf. 11***

607	A199	40c org brn	50	50

Issued in commemoration of the 400th anniversary of the discovery of the Amazon River.

Reproduction of Brazil Stamp of 1866 — A200

Adaptation of 1843 "Bull's-eye" A201

1943, Mar. 28 **Wmk. 267**

608	A200	40c violet	75	40
a.		Wmk. 268	*1,000.*	

Centenary of city of Petropolis.

1943, Aug. 1 **Engr.** ***Imperf.***

609	A201	30c black	1.00	50
610	A201	60c black	1.25	50
611	A201	90c black	1.00	50

Centenary of the first postage stamp of Brazil. The 30c and 90c exist unwatermarked; prices $25 and $65.

Souvenir Sheet.

A202

Wmk. 281- Wavy Lines

Wmk. 281 Horizontally or Vertically.

1943 **Engr.** ***Imperf.***

Without Gum.

612	A202	Sheet of three	10.00	9.00
a.		30c blk	2.50	2.50
b.		60c blk	2.50	2.50
c.		90c blk	2.50	2.50

Sheet measures 125 ½x94½mm.

Ubaldino do Amaral A203

"Justice" A204

Perf. 11, 12

1943, Aug. 27 **Typo.** **Wmk. 264**

613	A203	40c dl sl grn	50	25
a.		Wmk. 267	30.00	25.00

Birth centenary of Ubaldino do Amaral, banker and statesman.

1943, Aug. 30 **Wmk. 267**

614	A204	2cr brt rose	1.00	60

Centenary of Institute of Brazilizn Lawyers.

Indo-Brazilian Bull — A205

1943, Aug. 30 **Engr.**

615	A205	40 dk red brn	1.25	75

9th Livestock Show at Bahia.

Jose Barbosa Rodrigues A206

1943, Nov. 13 **Typo.**

616	A206	40c bluish grn	60	25

Birth centenary of Jose Barbosa Rodrigues, botanist.

Charity Hospital, Santos A207

1943, Nov. 7 **Engr.**

617	A207	1cr blue	75	40

400th anniversary of Charity Hospital, Santos.

Pedro Americo — A208

Wmk. 267

1943, Dec. 16 **Typo.** ***Perf. 11***

618	A208	40c brn org	50	25

Issued to commemorate the birth centenary of Pedro Americo de Figueirido e Melo (1843-1905), artist-hero and statesman.

Gen. A. E. Gomes Carneiro A209

1944, Feb. 9 **Engr.**

619	A209	1.20cr rose	1.00	50

50th anniversary of the Lapa siege.

Statue of Baron of Rio Branco — A210

1944, May 13 **Typo.**

620	A210	1cr blue	75	40

Issued to commemorate the unveiling of a statue of the Baron of Rio Branco.

Duke of Caxias A211

1944, May 13 **Unwmk.** ***Perf. 12***

Granite Paper.

621	A211	1.20cr bl grn & pale org	90	50

Centenary of pacification of Sao Paulo and Minas Gerais in an independence movement in 1842.

YMCA Seal — A212

1944, June 7 **Litho.** ***Perf. 11***

Granite Paper.

622	A212	40c dp bl, car & yel	40	25

Centenary of Young Men's Christian Assn.

Chamber of Commerce Rio Grande A213

Wmk. 268

1944, Sept. 25 **Engr.** ***Perf. 12***

623	A213	40c lt yel brn	40	35

Issued to commemorate the centenary of the Chamber of Commerce of Rio Grande.

Martim F. R. de Andrada
A214

1945, Jan. 30 *Perf. 11*
624 A214 40c blue 40 35

Issued to commemorate the centenary of the death of Martim F. R. de Andrada, statesman.

Meeting of Duke of Caxias and David Canabarro
A215

1945, Mar. 19 **Photo.**
625 A215 40c ultra 40 25

Centenary of the pacification of Rio Grande do Sul.

Globe and "Esperanto"
A216

1945, Apr. 16
626 A216 40c lt bl grn 60 30

10th Esperanto Congress, Rio de Janeiro, Apr. 14-22.

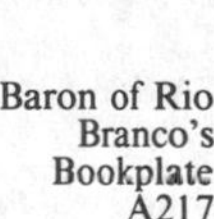

Baron of Rio Branco's Bookplate
A217

1945, Apr. 20 **Wmk. 268** *Perf. 11*
627 A217 40c violet 30 25

Issued to commemorate the centenary of the birth of José Maria da Silva Paranhos, Baron of Rio Branco.

Tranquility
A218

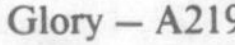

Glory — A219

Victory
A220

Peace
A221

Cooperation
A222

Rouletted 7

1945, May 8 **Engr.** **Wmk. 268**

628	A218	20c dk rose vio	20	20
629	A219	40c dk car	20	20
630	A220	1cr dl org	60	50
631	A221	2cr stl bl	1.50	75
632	A222	5cr green	3.00	1.00
		Nos. 628-632 (5)	5.50	2.65

Victory of the Allied Nations in Europe.
Nos. 628-632 exist on thin card, imperf. and unwatermarked.

Francisco Manoel da Silva — A223

Wmk. 245

1945, May 30 **Typo.** *Perf. 12*
633 A223 40c brt rose 75 40
a. Wmk. 268 11.00 11.00

Issued to commemorate the 150th anniversary of the birth of Francisco Manoel da Silva (1795-1865), composer (in 1831) of the national anthem.

Bahia Institute of Geography and History
A224

1945, May 30 **Wmk. 268** *Perf. 11*
634 A224 40c lt ultra 35 25

Issued to commemorate the 50th anniversary of the founding of the Institute of Geography and History at Bahia.

Emblems of 5th Army and B.E.F.

A225 A226

U.S. Flag and Shoulder Patches
A227

Brazilian Flag and Shoulder Patches
A228

Victory Symbol and Shoulder Patches — A229

1945, July 18 **Litho.**

635	A225	20c multi	25	25
636	A226	40c multi	25	25
637	A227	1cr multi	1.25	75
638	A228	2cr multi	1.75	1.00
639	A229	5cr multi	5.00	1.00
		Nos. 635-639 (5)	8.50	3.25

Issued in honor of the Brazilian Expeditionary Force and the United States Fifth Army Battle against the Axis in Italy.

Radio Tower and Map — A230

1945, Sept. 3 **Engr.**
640 A230 1.20cr gray 60 25

Third Inter-American Conference on Radio Communications.

No. 640 was reproduced on a souvenir card with blue background and inscriptions. Size: 145x161mm.

A 40c lilac stamp, picturing the International Bridge between Argentina and Brazil and portraits of Presidents Justo and Vargas, was prepared late in 1945. It was not issued, but later was sold, without postal value, to collectors. Price, 15 cents.

Adm. Saldanha da Gama — A231

1946, Apr. 7
641 A231 40c gray blk 30 30

Issued to commemorate the centenary of the birth of Admiral Luiz Felipe Saldanha da Gama (1846-1895).

Princess Isabel d'Orleans-Braganca — A232

1946, July 29 **Unwmk.**
642 A232 40c black 35 35

Issued to commemorate the centenary of the birth of Princess Isabel d'Orleans-Braganca.

Post Horn, V and Envelope — A233

Post Office, Rio de Janeiro
A234

Bay of Rio de Janeiro and Plane
A235

Wmk. 268

1946, Sept. 2 **Litho.** *Perf. 11*
643 A233 40c blk & pale org 30 25

Perf. 12½

Engr. **Unwmk.**

Center in Ultramarine.

644	A234	2cr slate	75	25
645	A234	5cr org brn	4.50	1.50
646	A234	10cr dk vio	5.00	75

Center in Brown Orange.

647	A235	1.30cr dk grn	50	50
648	A235	1.70cr car rose	50	50
649	A235	2.20cr dp ultra	75	75
		Nos. 643-649 (7)	12.30	4.50

Nos. 643 to 649 were issued to commemorate the 5th Postal Union Congress of the Americas and Spain.

No. 643 was reproduced on a souvenir card with inscriptions and marginal illustrations of the Palacio da Fazenda, Rio de Janeiro. Size 188x239mm. Sold for 10 cruzeiros.

Liberty — A236

Perf. 11x11½

1946, Sept. 18 **Wmk. 268**
650 A236 40c blk & gray 20 15
a. Unwmk. 150.00

Adoption of the Constitution of 1946.

Columbus Lighthouse, Dominican Republic
A237

1946, Sept. 14 **Litho.** *Perf. 11*
651 A237 5cr Prus grn 6.50 2.50

Orchid
A238

Gen. A. E. Gomes Carneiro
A239

1946, Nov. 8 **Wmk. 268**
652 A238 40c ultra, red & yel 55 30
a. Unwmk. 75.00

Issued to publicize the 4th National Exhibition of Orchids, Rio de Janeiro, November, 1946.

Perf. 10 ½x12

1946, Dec. 6 **Engr.** **Unwmk.**
653 A239 40c dp grn 20 20

Issued to commemorate the centenary of the birth of General Antonio Ernesto Gomes Carneiro.

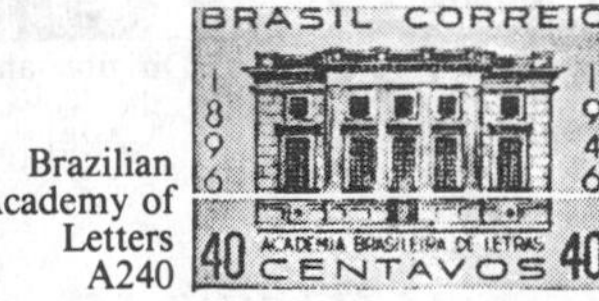

Brazilian Academy of Letters A240

1946, Dec. 14 ***Perf. 11***
654 A240 40c blue 25 20

Issued to commemorate the 50th anniversary of the foundation of the Brazilian Academy of Letters, Rio de Janeiro.

Antonio de Castro Alves — A241

1947, Mar. 14 **Litho.** **Wmk. 267**
655 A241 40c bluish grn 25 25

Issued to commemorate the birth centenary of Antonio de Castro Alves (1847-1871), poet.

Types of 1941-42, Values in Centavos or Cruzeiros.

1947-54	**Wmk. 267**	**Typo.**	***Perf. 11***	
656	A184	2c olive	12	8
657	A184	5c yel brn	12	8
658	A184	10c green	12	8
659	A185	20c brn org	15	8
660	A185	30c dk lil rose	50	8
661	A185	40c blue	25	8
b.		Wmk. 268	800.00	60.00
661A	A185	50c salmon	50	8
662	A186	60c lt vio	90	8
663	A186	70c brt rose ('54)	30	10
664	A186	1cr gray	90	10
665	A186	1.20cr dl bl	2.25	10
a.		Wmk. 268	10.00	9.00
666	A187	2cr gray vio	3.50	8
		Engr.		
667	A188	5cr blue	7.00	10
668	A189	10cr rose red	7.00	10
		Perf. 11, 13.		
669	A190	20cr dp brn	14.00	75
670	A191	50cr red	27.50	50
		Nos. 656-670 (16)	65.11	2.47

The 5cr, 20cr and 50cr also exist with pert. 12 to 13.

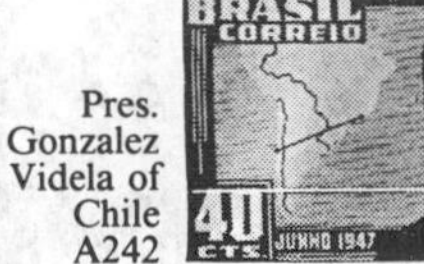

Pres. Gonzalez Videla of Chile A242

1947, June 26 **Unwmk.** ***Perf. 12x11***
671 A242 40c dk brn org 25 20

Issued to commemorate the visit of President Gabriel Gonzalez Videla of Chile, June 1947.

A souvenir folder contains four impressions of No. 671, measures 6 ½x8 ¼inches and has marginal inscriptions, including a coat of arms, in blue.

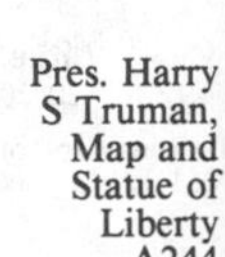

"Peace" and Western Hemisphere — A243

1947, Aug. 15 ***Perf. 11x12***
672 A243 1.20cr blue 35 25

Issued to commemorate the Inter-American Defense Conference at Rio de Janeiro, August-September, 1947.

Pres. Harry S Truman, Map and Statue of Liberty A244

1947, Sept. 1 **Typo.** ***Perf. 12x11***
673 A244 40c ultra 30 25

Visit of U.S. President Harry S Truman to Brazil, Sept. 1947.

Pres. Eurico Gaspar Dutra — A245

Mother and Child — A246

Wmk. 268

1947, Sept. 7 **Engr.** ***Perf. 11***
674 A245 20c green 20 20
675 A245 40c rose car 25 15
676 A245 1.20cr dp bl 50 22

The souvenir sheet containing Nos. 674-676 is listed as No. C73A. See also No. 679.

1947, Oct. 10 **Typo.** **Unwmk.**
677 A246 40c brt ultra 25 20

Issued to mark Child Care Week, 1947.

Arms of Belo Horizonte A247

Globe A248

1947, Dec. 12 **Engr.** **Wmk. 267**
678 A247 1.20cr rose car 60 25

Issued to commemorate the 50th anniversary of the founding of the city of Belo Horizonte.

Dutra Type of 1947.

1948 **Engr.** **Wmk. 267**
679 A245 20c green 3.00 3.00

1948, July 10 **Litho.**
680 A248 40c dl grn & pale lil 50 20

Issued to commemorate the International Exposition of Industry and Commerce, Petropolis, 1948.

Arms of Paranagua A249

Child Reading Book A250

1948, July 29
681 A249 5cr bis brn 3.00 1.00

Issued to commemorate the 300th anniversary of the founding of the city of Paranagua, July 29, 1648.

1948, Aug. 1
682 A250 40c green 30 30

National Education Campaign.

No. 682 was reproduced on a souvenir card with brown orange background and inscriptions. Size: 124x157mm.

Tiradentes A251

Symbolical of Cancer Eradication A252

1948, Nov. 12
683 A251 40c brn org 25 20

Issued to commemorate the 200th anniversary of the birth of Joaquim Jose da Silva Xavier (Tiradentes).

1948, Dec. 14
684 A252 40c claret 25 25

Anti-cancer publicity.

Adult Student A253

1949, Jan. 3 **Wmk. 267** ***Perf. 12x11***
685 A253 60c red vio & pink 25 15

Campaign for adult education.

"Battle of Guararapes," by Vitor Meireles — A254

1949, Feb. 15 ***Perf. 11 ½x12***
686 A254 60c lt bl 1.25 60

Issued to commemorate the 300th anniversary of the Second Battle of Guararapes.

Church of Sao Francisco de Paula A255

Manuel de Nobrega A256

Perf. 11x12

1949, Mar. 8 **Unwmk.** **Engr.**
687 A255 60c dk brn 30 25
a. Souvenir sheet 40.00 40.00

Bicentenary of city of Ouro Fino, state of Minas Gerais.

No. 687a contains one imperf. stamp similar to No. 687, with dates in lower margin. Size: 70x89mm.

1949, Mar. 29 ***Imperf.***
688 A256 60c violet 25 25

Issued to commemorate the 400th anniversary of the founding of the City of Salvador.

Emblem of Brazilian Air Force and Plane A257

1949, June 18
689 A257 60c bl vio 25 25

Issued to honor the Brazilian Air Force.

Star and Angel — A258

1949 **Wmk. 267** **Litho.** ***Perf. 11x12.***
690 A258 60c pink 25 25

Issued to publicize the first Ecclesiastical Congress, Salvador, Bahia.

"U. P. U." Encircling Globe A259

1949, Oct. 22 **Typo.** ***Perf. 12x11***
691 A259 1.50cr blue 40 20

Issued to commemorate the 75th anniversary of the formation of the Universal Postal Union.

Ruy Barbosa A260

Unwmk.

1949, Dec. 14 Engr. *Perf. 12*
692 A260 1.20cr rose car 75 40

Centenary of birth of Ruy Barbosa.

Joaquim Cardinal Arcoverde — A261

Perf. 11x12

1950, Feb. 27 Litho. Wmk. 267
693 A261 60c rose 30 25

Issued to commemorate the birth centenary of Joaquim Cardinal Arcoverde A. Cavalcanti.

Grapes and Factory A262

1950, Mar. 15 *Perf. 12x11*
694 A262 60c rose lake 20 20

Issued to commemorate the 75th anniversary of Italian immigration to the state of Rio Grande do Sul.

Virgin of the Globe A263

Globe and Soccer Players A264

1950, May 31 *Perf. 11x12*
695 A263 60c blk & lt bl 30 20

Issued to commemorate the centenary of the establishment in Brazil of the Daughters of Charity of St. Vincent de Paul.

1950, June 24
696 A264 60c ultra, bl & gray 1.00 50

4th World Soccer Championship.

Symbolical of Brazilian Population Growth A265

1950, July 10 Typo. *Perf. 12x11*
697 A265 60c rose lake 30 20

Issued to publicize the 6th Brazilian census.

Dr. Oswaldo Cruz — A266

1950, Aug. 23 Litho. *Perf. 11x12*
698 A266 60c org brn 30 25

Issued to publicize the 5th International Congress of Microbiology.

View of Blumenau and Itajai River A267

1950, Sept. 9 Wmk. 267 *Perf. 12x11*
699 A267 60c brt pink 25 20

Centenary of the founding of Blumenau.

Amazonas Theater, Manaus A268

1950, Sept. 27
700 A268 60c lt brn red 20 20

Centenary of Amazonas Province.

Arms of Juiz de Fora — A269

1950, Oct. 24 *Perf. 11x12*
701 A269 60c carmine 25 25

Centenary of the founding of Juiz de Fora.

Post Office at Recife A270

1951, Jan. 10 Typo. *Perf. 12x11*
702 A270 60c carmine 20 20
703 A270 1.20cr carmine 30 20

Issued to commemorate the opening of the new building of the Pernambuco Post Office.

Arms of Joinville A271

Jean-Baptiste de La Salle A272

1951, Mar. 9 *Perf. 11x12*
704 A271 60c org brn 20 20

Centenary of the founding of Joinville.

1951, Apr. 30 Litho.
705 A272 60c blue 30 25

Issued to commemorate the 300th anniversary of the birth of Jean-Baptiste de La Salle.

Brazil stamps through 1975 can be mounted in Scott's Brazil Album.

Heart and Flowers A273

Sylvio Romero A274

1951, May 13 Engr.
706 A273 60c dp plum 30 25

Issued to honor Mother's Day, May 14, 1951.

1951, Apr. 21 Litho.
707 A274 60c dl vio brn 20 20

Issued to commemorate the centenary of the birth of Sylvio Romero (1851-1914), poet and author.

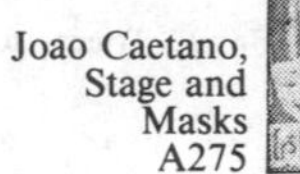

Joao Caetano, Stage and Masks A275

1951, July 9 *Perf. 12x11*
708 A275 60c lt gray bl 25 20

Issued to publicize the first Brazilian Theater Congress, Rio de Janeiro, July 9-13, 1951.

Orville A. Derby — A276

First Mass Celebrated in Brazil — A277

1951, July 23 *Perf. 11x12*
709 A276 2cr slate 40 40

Issued to commemorate the centenary of the birth (in New York State) of Orville A. Derby, geologist.

1951, July 25
710 A277 60c dl brn & buff 30 25

Issued to publicize the 4th Inter-American Congress on Catholic Education, Rio de Janeiro, 1951.

Euclides Pinto Martins A278

1951, Aug. 16 *Perf. 12x11*
711 A278 3.80cr brn & cit 2.25 35

Issued to commemorate the 29th anniversary of the first flight from New York City to Rio de Janeiro.

Monastery of the Rock A279

1951, Sept. 8
712 A279 60c dl brn & cr 25 25

Founding of Vitoria, 4th centenary.

Santos-Dumont and Model Plane Contest A280

Dirigible and Eiffel Tower A281

Perf. 11x12

1951, Oct. 19 Wmk. 267 Litho.
713 A280 60c sal & dk brn 60 40

Unwmk. Engr.
714 A281 3.80cr dk pur 2.25 40

Issued to publicize the Week of the Wing and to commemorate the 50th anniversary of Santos-Dumont's flight around the Eiffel Tower.

In December 1951, Nos. 713 and 714 were privately overprinted: "Exposicao Filatelica Regional Distrito Federal 15-XII-1951 23-XII-1951." These were attached to souvenir sheets bearing engraved facsimiles of Nos. 38, 49 and 51, which were sold by Clube Filatelico do Brasil to mark its 20th anniversary. The overprinted stamps on the sheets were canceled, but 530 "unused" sets were sold by the club.

Farmers and Ear of Wheat — A282

1951, Nov. 10 Litho. Wmk. 267
715 A282 60c dp grn & gray 40 30

Issued to publicize Festival of Grain at Bage, 1951.

Map and Open Bible A283

1951, Dec. 9 *Perf. 12x11*
716 A283 1.20cr brn org 75 40

Issued to publicize the Day of the Bible.

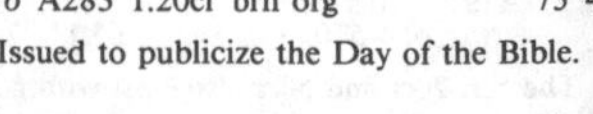

Queen Isabella A284

Henrique Oswald A285

1952, Mar. 10 *Perf. 11x12*
717 A284 3.80cr lt bl 1.00 30

Issued to commemorate the 500th anniversary of the birth of Queen Isabella I of Spain.

1952, Apr. 22
718 A285 60c brown 30 25

Issued to commemorate the centenary of the birth of Henrique Oswald (1852-1931), composer.

Vicente Licinio Cardoso A286

Map and Symbol of Labor A287

1952, May 2
719 A286 60c gray bl 30 25

4th Brazilian Homeopathic Congress.

1952, Apr. 30
720 A287 1.50cr brnsh pink 40 25

Issued to publicize the 5th International Labor Organization Conference for American Countries.

Gen. Polidoro da Fonseca A288

Luiz de Albuquerque M. P. Caceres A289

Portraits: 5cr, Baron de Capanema. 10cr, Minister Eusebio de Queiros.

Unwmk.

1952, May 11 Engr. *Perf. 11*
721 A288 2.40cr lt car 50 35
722 A288 5cr blue 3.50 45
723 A288 10cr dk bl grn 3.50 45

Centenary of telegraph in Brazil.

Perf. 11x12

1952, June 8 Litho. Wmk. 267
724 A289 1.20cr vio bl 30 20

Issued to commemorate the 200th anniversary of the founding of the city of Mato Grosso.

Symbolizing the Glory of Sports A290

1952, July 21 *Perf. 12x11*
725 A290 1.20cr dp bl & bl 85 40

Fluminense Soccer Club, 50th anniversary.

José Antonio Saraiva A291

Emperor Dom Pedro A292

1952, Aug. 16 *Perf. 11x12*
726 A291 60c lil rose 20 20

Issued to commemorate the centenary of the founding of Terezina, capital of Piaui State.

1952, Sept. 3 Wmk. 267
727 A292 60c lt bl & blk 25 20

Issued for Stamp Day and the 2nd Philatelic Exhibition of Sao Paulo.

Flag-encircled Globe — A293

1952, Oct. 24 *Perf. 13½*
728 A293 3.80cr blue 1.50 50

Issued to publicize United Nations Day.

View of Sao Paulo, Sun and Compasses A294

1952, Nov. 8 Litho. *Perf. 12x11*
729 A294 60c dl bl, yel & gray grn 30 25

City Planning Day.

Father Diogo Antonio Feijo — A295

1952, Nov. 9 *Perf. 11x12*
730 A295 60c fawn 20 20

Rodolpho Bernardelli and His "Christ and the Adultress" A297

1952, Dec. 18 *Perf. 12x11*
732 A297 60c gray bl 25 20

Issued to commemorate the centenary of the birth of Rodolpho Bernardelli, sculptor and painter.

Map of Western Hemisphere and View of Rio de Janeiro — A298

1952, Sept. 20
733 A298 3.80cr vio brn & lt grn 90 30

Issued to commemorate the 2nd Congress of American Industrial Medicine, Rio de Janeiro, 1952.

Arms and Head of Pioneer A299

Coffee, Cotton and Sugar Cane — A300

Designs: 2.80cr, Jesuit monk planting tree. 3.80cr and 5.80cr, Spiral, symbolizing progress.

1953, Jan. 25 Litho. *Perf. 11*
734 A299 1.20cr ol brn & blk brn 75 50
735 A300 2cr ol grn & yel 2.50 50
736 A300 2.80cr red brn & dp org 1.75 30
737 A300 3.80cr dk brn & yel grn 1.50 30
738 A300 5.80cr int bl & yel grn 1.00 30
Nos. 734-738 (5) 7.50 1.90

400th anniversary of Sao Paulo.

Ledger and Winged Cap — A301

1953, Feb. 22 *Perf. 12x11*
739 A301 1.20cr dl brn & fawn 40 20

6th Brazilian Accounting Congress.

Joao Ramalho — A302

Wmk. 264

1953, Apr. 8 Engr. *Perf. 11½*
740 A302 60c blue 25 20

Issued to commemorate the fourth centenary of the founding of the city of Santo Andre.

Aarao Reis and Plan of Belo Horizonte A303

1953, May 6 Photo.
741 A303 1.20cr red brn 35 25

Issued to commemorate the centenary of the birth of Aarao Leal de Carvalho Reis (1853-1936), civil engineer.

Training Ship Almirante Saldanha — A304

1953, May 16
742 A304 1.50cr vio bl 50 30

Issued to commemorate the fourth globe-circling voyage of the training ship Almirante Saldanha.

Joaquim Jose Rodrigues Torres, Viscount of Itaborai — A305

1953, July 5 Photo.
743 A305 1.20cr violet 30 20

Centenary of the Bank of Brazil.

Lamp and Rio-Petropolis Highway — A306

1953, July 14
744 A306 1.20cr gray 30 20

Issued to publicize the tenth International Congress of Nursing, Petropolis, 1953.

Bay of Rio de Janeiro A307

1953, July 15
745 A307 3.80cr dk bl grn 60 20

Issued to publicize the fourth World Congress of Baptist Youth, July 1953.

Arms of Jau and Map A308

1953, Aug. 15 Engr.
746 A308 1.20cr purple 30 20

Centenary of the city of Jau.

Ministry of Health and Education Building, Rio A309

Maria Quiteria de Jesus Medeiros A310

1953, Aug. 1
747 A309 1.20cr dp grn 30 20

Issued to publicize the Day of the Stamp and the first Philatelic Exhibition of National Education.

1953, Aug. 21 **Photo.**
748 A310 60c vio bl 25 20

Issued to commemorate the centenary of the death of Maria Quiteria de Jesus Medeiros (1792-1848), independence heroine.

Pres. Odria of Peru — A311

Duke of Caxias Leading his Troops — A312

1953, Aug. 25
749 A311 1.40cr rose brn 30 20

Issued to publicize the visit of Gen. Manuel A. Odria, President of Peru, Aug. 25, 1953.

Engr. (60c, 5.80cr); Photo.
1953, Aug. 25

Designs: 1.20cr, Caxias' tomb. 1.70cr, 5.80cr, Portrait of Caxias. 3.80cr, Arms of Caxias.

750 A312	60c dp grn	50	25
751 A312	1.20cr dp cl	60	25
752 A312	1.70cr sl grn	60	25
753 A312	3.80cr rose brn	1.00	25
754 A312	5.80cr gray vio	1.00	25
	Nos. 750-754 (5)	3.70	1.25

Issued to commemorate the 150th anniversary of the birth of Luis Alves de Lima e Silva, Duke of Caxias.

Quill Pen, Map and Tree — A313

Horacio Hora — A314

1953, Sept. 12 **Photo.**
755 A313 60c ultra 25 20

5th National Congress of Journalism.

1953, Sept. 17 **Litho.** **Wmk. 267**
756 A314 60c org & dp plum 25 20

Issued to commemorate the centenary of the birth of Horacio Pinto de Hora (1853-1890), painter.

Pres. Somoza of Nicaragua A315

Auguste de Saint-Hilaire A316

1953, Sept. 24 **Photo.** **Wmk. 264**
757 A315 1.40cr dk vio brn 30 20

Issued to publicize the visit of Gen. Anastasio Somoza, president of Nicaragua.

1953, Sept. 30
758 A316 1.20cr dk brn car 30 25

Issued to commemorate the centenary of the death of Auguste de Saint-Hilaire, explorer and botanist.

Jose Carlos do Patrocinio A317

Clock Tower, Crato A318

1953, Oct. 9 **Photo.**
759 A317 60c dk sl gray 25 20

Issued to commemorate the centenary of the birth of Jose Carlos do Patrocinio, (1853-1905), journalist and abolitionist.

1953, Oct. 17
760 A318 60c bl grn 25 20

Centenary of the city of Crato.

Joao Capistrano de Abreu A319

Allegory: "Justice" A320

1953, Oct. 23
761 A319 60c dl bl 30 30
762 A319 5cr purple 2.00 30

Issued to commemorate the centenary of the birth of Joao Capistrano de Abreu (1853-1927), historian.

1953, Nov. 17
763 A320 60c indigo 25 20
764 A320 1.20cr dp mag 25 20

Issued to commemorate the 50th anniversary of the Treaty of Petropolis.

Farm Worker in Wheat Field — A321

Teacher and Pupils — A322

1953, Nov. 29 **Photo.** ***Perf. 11½***
766 A321 60c dk grn 30 20

Issued to publicize the Third National Wheat Festival, Erechim, 1953.

1953, Dec. 14
767 A322 60c red 25 25

Issued to publicize the First National Conference of Primary School Teachers, Salvador, 1953.

Zacarias de Gois e Vasconsellos A323

Alexandre de Gusmao A324

Design: 5cr, Porters with Trays of Coffee Beans.

1953-54 **Photo.**
Inscribed: "Centenario do Parana."
768 A323 2cr org brn & blk ('54) 2.50 40
a. Buff paper 90 40
769 A323 5cr dp org & blk 1.75 40

Centenary of the state of Parana.

1954, Jan. 13
770 A324 1.20cr brn vio 30 20

Issued to commemorate the 200th anniversary of the death of Alexandre de Gusmao (1695-1753), statesman, diplomat and writer.

Symbolical of Sao Paulo's Growth — A325

Arms and View of Sao Paulo A326

Designs: 2cr, Priest, settler and Indian. 2.80cr, Jose de Anchieta.

1954, Jan. 25 ***Perf. 11½x11***

771 A325	1.20cr dk vio brn	1.25	50
a.	Buff paper	1.75	1.00
772 A325	2cr lil rose	1.75	60
773 A325	2.80cr pur gray	1.75	1.00

Perf. 11x11½.
Engr.

774 A326	3.80cr dl grn	2.00	50
a.	Buff paper	2.25	2.00
775 A326	5.80cr dl red	2.00	60
a.	Buff paper	5.00	75
	Nos. 771-775 (5)	8.75	3.20

400th anniversary of Sao Paulo.

J. Fernandes Vieira, A. Vidal de Negreiros, A. F. Camarao and H. Dias A327

Perf. 11x11½
1954, Feb. 18 **Photo.** **Unwmk.**
776 A327 1.20cr ultra 40 30

Issued to commemorate the 300th anniversary of the recovery of Pernambuco from the Dutch.

Sao Paulo and Minerva A328

1954, Feb. 24
777 A328 1.50cr dp plum 30 25

Issued to publicize the 10th International Congress of Scientific Organizations, Sao Paulo, 1954.

Stylized Grapes, Jug and Map A329

Monument of the Immigrants A330

1954, Feb. 27 **Photo.** ***Perf. 11½x11***
778 A329 40c dp cl 25 25

Grape Festival, Rio Grande do Sul.

1954, Feb. 28
779 A330 60c dp vio bl 25 25

Issued to commemorate the unveiling of the Monument to the Immigrants of Caxias do Sul.

First Brazilian Locomotive — A331

Perf. 11x11½
1954, Apr. 30 **Unwmk.**
781 A331 40c carmine 50 25

Issued to commemorate the centenary of the first railroad engine built in Brazil.

Pres. Chamoun of Lebanon — A332

1954, May 12 Photo. *Perf. 11½x11*
782 A332 1.50cr maroon 35 30

Issued to commemorate the visit of Pres. Camille Chamoun of Lebanon, 1954.

Sao Jose College, Rio de Janeiro
A333

J. B. Champagnat Marcelin
A334

Apolonia Pinto
A335

1954, June 6 *Perf. 11x11½, 11½x11*
783 A333 60c purple 30 20
784 A334 120cr vio bl 35 25

Issued to commemorate the 50th anniversary of the founding of the Marist Brothers in Brazil.

1954, June 21 Photo.
785 A335 1.20cr brt grn 15 12

Issued to commemorate the centenary of the birth of Apolonia Pinto (1854-1937), actress.

Adm. Margues Tamandare — A336

Portraits: 2c, 5c, 10c, Admiral Margues Tamandare. 20c, 30c, 40c, Oswaldo Cruz. 50c, 60c, 90c, Joaquim Murtinho. 1cr, 1.50cr, 2cr, Duke of Caxias. 5cr, 10cr, Ruy Barbosa. 20cr, 50cr, Jose Bonifacio.

1954-60 Wmk. 267 *Perf. 11x11½*

786	A336	2c vio bl	15	12
787	A336	5c org red	10	5
788	A336	10c brt grn	15	5
789	A336	20c magenta	15	5
790	A336	30c dk gray grn	25	5
791	A336	40c rose red	50	5
792	A336	50c violet	30	5
793	A336	60c gray grn	15	5
794	A336	90c org ('55)	50	15
795	A336	1cr brown	15	5
796	A336	1.50cr blue	10	5
a.		Wmk. 264	20.00	10.00
797	A336	2cr dk bl grn ('56)	60	5
798	A336	5cr rose lil ('56)	50	10
799	A336	10cr lt grn ('60)	1.25	10
800	A336	20cr crim rose ('59)	1.25	10
801	A336	50cr ultra ('59)	7.50	20
		Nos. 786-801 (16)	13.60	1.27

See also Nos. 890, 930-933.

Boy Scout Waving Flag (Statue)
A337

Baltasar Fernandes, Explorer
A338

1954, Aug. 2 Unwmk. *Perf. 11½x11*
802 A337 1.20cr vio bl 60 30

Issued to publicize the International Boy Scout Encampment, Sao Paulo, 1954.

1954, Aug. 15
803 A338 60c dk red 30 25

300th anniversary of city of Sorocaba.

Adeodato Giovanni Cardinal Piazza
A339

Our Lady of Aparecida, Map of Brazil
A340

1954, Sept. 2
804 A339 4.20cr red org 75 35

Issued to commemorate the visit of Adeodato Cardinal Piazza, papal legate to Brazil.

1954

Design: 1.20cr, Virgin standing on globe.

805 A340 60c claret 60 35
806 A340 1.20cr vio bl 80 30

No. 805 was issued to commemorate the 1st Congress of Brazil's Patron Saint (Our Lady of Aparecida); No. 806, the centenary of the proclamation of the dogma of the Immaculate Conception. Both stamps also commemorate the Marian Year.

Issue dates: 60c, Sept. 6; 1.20cr, Sept. 8.

Benjamin Constant and Hand Reading Braille
A341

1954, Sept. 27 Photo. Unwmk.
807 A341 60c dk grn 25 20

Issued to commemorate the centenary of the founding of the Benjamin Constant Institute.

River Battle of Riachuelo
A342

Admiral F. M. Barroso
A343

Dr. Christian F. S. Hahnemann
A344

1954, Oct. 6 *Perf. 11x11½, 11½x11*
808 A342 40c redsh brn 40 25
809 A343 60c purple 30 25

Issued to commemorate the 150th anniversary of the birth of Admiral Francisco Manoel Barroso da Silva (1804-82).

1954, Oct. 8 *Perf. 11½x11*
810 A344 2.70cr dk grn 40 25

Issued to publicize the first World Congress of Homeopathic Medicine.

Nizia Floresta
A345

Ears of Wheat
A346

1954, Oct. 12
811 A345 60c lil rose 25 25

Issued to commemorate the reburial of the remains of Nizia Floresta (Dio Nizia Pinto Lisboa), writer and educator.

1954, Oct. 22
812 A346 60c ol grn 30 25

4th National Wheat Festival, Carazinho.

Basketball Player and Ball-Globe
A347

Allegory of the Spring Games
A348

1954, Oct. 23 Photo.
813 A347 1.40cr org red 50 30

Issued to publicize the second World Basketball Championship Matches, 1954.

Perf. 11½x11
1954, Nov. 6 Wmk. 267
814 A348 60c red brn 40 25

Issued to publicize the 6th Spring Games.

San Francisco Hydroelectric Plant — A349

1955, Jan. 15 *Perf. 11x11½*
815 A349 60c brn org 20 15

Issued to publicize the inauguration of the San Francisco Hydroelectric Plant.

Itutinga Hydroelectric Plant — A350

1955, Feb. 3
816 A350 40c blue 20 15

Issued to publicize the inauguration of the Itutinga Hydroelectric Plant at Lavras.

Rotary Emblem and Bay of Rio de Janeiro — A351

1955, Feb. 23 *Perf. 12x11½*
817 A351 2.70cr sl gray & blk 75 25

Rotary International, 50th anniversary.

Fausto Cardoso Palace
A352

1955, Mar. 17 *Perf. 11x11½*
818 A352 40c hn brn 25 25

Centenary of Aracaju.

Aviation Symbols
A353

1955, Mar. 13 Photo. *Perf. 11½*
819 A353 60c dk gray grn 20 15

Issued to publicize the third National Aviation Congress at Sao Paulo, Mar. 6-13.

Arms of Botucatu
A354

1955, Apr. 14
820 A354 60c org brn 25 20
821 A354 1.20cr brt grn 35 20

Centenary of Botucatu.

Young Racers at Starting Line — A355

Perf. 11½
1955, Apr. 30 Photo. Unwmk.
823 A355 60c org brn 35 20

5th Children's Games.

Marshal Hermes da Fonseca
A356

Congress Altar, Sail and Sugarloaf Mountain
A357

1955, May 12 **Wmk. 267**
824 A356 60c purple 20 20

Issued to commemorate the centenary of the birth of Marshal Hermes da Fonseca.

Engraved; Photogravure (2.70cr)
1955, July 17 Unwmk. *Perf. 11½*

Designs: 2.70cr, St. Pascoal. 4.20cr, Aloisi Benedetto Cardinal Masella.

825 A357 1.40cr green 25 25
826 A357 2.70cr dp cl 50 40
827 A357 4.20cr blue 60 25

Issued to commemorate the 36th World Eucharistic Congress in Rio de Janeiro.

Girl Gymnasts A358

1955, Nov. 12 **Engr.**
Granite Paper
828 A358 60c rose lil 35 20

Issued to publicize the 7th Spring Games.

José B. Monteiro Lobato A359

1955, Dec. 8
Granite Paper
829 A359 40c dk grn 20 15

Issued in honor of Jose B. Monteiro Lobato, author.

Adolfo Lutz — A360

Lt. Col. Vilagran Cabrita — A361

1955, Dec. 18
Granite Paper
830 A360 60c dk grn 20 15

Issued to commemorate the centenary of the birth of Adolfo Lutz, public health pioneer.

1955, Dec. 22 Photo. Wmk. 267
831 A361 60c vio bl 20 15

Issued to commemorate the centenary of the First Battalion of Engineers.

Salto Grande Hydroelectric Dam — A362

1956, Jan. 15 Unwmk. *Perf. 11½*
Granite Paper.
832 A362 60c brick red 20 15

Arms of Mococa A363

"G" and Globe A364

Wmk. 256
1956, Apr. 17 Photo. *Perf. 11½*
833 A363 60c brick red 20 15

Centenary of Mococa, Sao Paulo.

1956, Apr. 14 **Unwmk.**
Granite Paper
834 A364 1.20cr vio bl 30 20

18th International Geographic Congress, Rio de Janeiro, August 1956.

Girls' Foot Race A365

1956, Apr. 28 **Photo.**
Granite Paper.
835 A365 2.50cr brt bl 50 20

6th Children's Games.

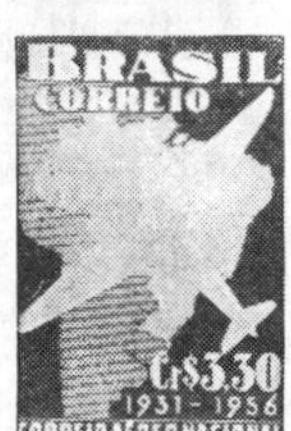
Plane over Map of Brazil — A366

1956, June 12 Wmk. 267 *Perf. 11½*
836 A366 3.30cr brt vio bl 1.00 20

Issued to commemorate the 25th anniversary of the National Airmail Service.

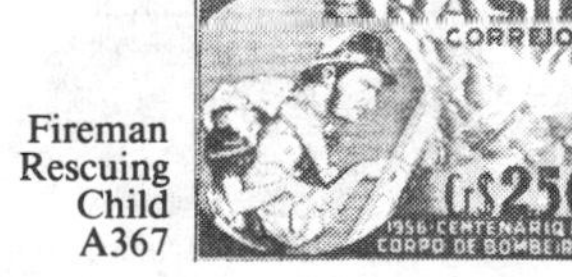
Fireman Rescuing Child A367

1956, July 2 **Wmk. 264**
837 A367 2.50cr crimson 60 25
a. Buff paper 2.25 2.00

Centenary of the Fire Brigade.

Map of Brazil and Open Book A368

1956, Sept. 8 **Wmk. 267**
838 A368 2.50cr brt vio bl 35 20

Issued to commemorate the 50th anniversary of the arrival of the Marist Brothers in Northern Brazil.

Church and Monument, Franca — A369

1956, Sept. 7 **Engr.**
839 A369 2.50cr dk bl 35 20

Centenary of city of Franca, Sao Paulo.

Woman Hurdler A370

1956, Sept. 22 Photo. Unwmk.
Granite Paper.
840 A370 2.50cr dk car 1.00 25

Issued to publicize the 8th Spring Games.

Forest and Map of Brazil — A371

1956, Sept. 30 Wmk. 267 *Perf. 11½*
841 A371 2.50cr dk grn 35 20

Issued to publicize education in forestry.

Baron da Bocaina A372

1956, Oct. 8 Engr. Wmk. 268
842 A372 2.50cr redsh brn 35 20

Issued to commemorate the centenary of the birth of Baron da Bocaina, who introduced the special delivery mail system to Brazil.

Marbleized Paper

Paper with a distinct wavy-line or marbleized watermark (which Brazilians call *marmorizado* paper) has been found on many stamps of Brazil, 1956-68, including Nos. 843-845, 847, 851-854, 858-858A, 864, 878, 880, 882, 884, 886-887, 896, 909, 918, 920-921, 925-928, 936-939, 949, 955-958, 960, 962-964, 978-979, 983, 985-987, 997-998, 1002-1003, 1005, 1009-1012, 1017, 1024, 1026, 1055, 1075, 1078, 1082, C82, C82a, C83-C87, C96, C99, C109.

Quantities are much less than those of stamps on regular paper.

Panama Stamp Showing Pres. Juscelino Kubitschek — A373

1956, Oct. 12 Photo. Wmk. 267
843 A373 3.30cr grn & blk 1.00 25

Issued on America Day, Oct. 12, to commemorate the meeting of the Presidents and the Pan-American Conference at Panama City, July 21-22.

Symbolical of Steel Production A374

Wmk. 267
1957, Jan. 31 Photo. *Perf. 11½*
844 A374 2.50cr chocolate 35 15

Issued to commemorate the second expansion of the National Steel Company at Volta Redonda.

Joaquim E. Gomes da Silva — A375

1957, Mar. 1 Photo. Unwmk.
Granite Paper.
845 A375 2.50cr dk bl grn 35 15

Issued to commemorate the centenary of the birth (in 1856) of Joaquim E. Gomes da Silva.

Allan Kardec A376

Wmk. 268
1957, Apr. 18 Engr. *Perf. 11½*
846 A376 2.50cr dk brn 35 15

Issued in honor of Allan Kardec, pen name of Leon Hippolyto Denizard Rivail, and for the centenary of the publication of his "Codification of Spiritism."

Boy Gymnast A377

1957, Apr. 27 Photo. Unwmk.
Granite Paper.
847 A377 2.50cr lake 75 25

7th Children's Games.

Pres. Craveiro Lopes — A378

Stamp of 1932 — A379

1957, June 7 Engr. Wmk. 267
848 A378 6.50cr blue 75 25

Issued to commemorate the visit of Gen. Francisco Higino Craveiro Lopes, President of Portugal.

1957, July 9 Photo.
849 A379 2.50cr rose 30 15

Issued to commemorate the 25th anniversary of the movement for a constitution.

St. Antonio Monastery, Pernambuco A380

1957, Aug. 24 Engr. Wmk. 267
850 A380 2.50cr dp mag 30 15

Issued to commemorate the 300th anniversary of the emancipation of the Franciscan province of St. Antonio in Pernambuco State.

Volleyball A381

Basketball A382

1957, Sept. 28 Photo. *Perf. 11 ½*
851 A381 2.50cr dl org red 75 25

Issued for the 9th Spring Games.

1957, Oct. 12
852 A382 3.30cr org & brt grn 75 25

Issued to commemorate the second Women's International Basketball Championship, Rio de Janeiro.

Count of Pinhal and Sao Carlos A383

1957, Nov. 4 Wmk. 267 *Perf. 11 ½*
853 A383 2.50cr rose 50 25

Issued to commemorate the centenary of the city of Sao Carlos and to honor the Count of Pinhal, its founder.

Auguste Comte — A384

1957, Nov. 15
854 A384 2.50cr dk red brn 45 25

Issued to commemorate the centenary of the death of Auguste Comte, French mathematician and philosopher.

Radio Station A385

1957, Dec. 10 Wmk. 268
855 A385 2.50cr dk grn 30 15

Opening of Sarapui Central Radio Station.

Admiral Tamandare and Warship A386

Design: 3.30cr, Aircraft carrier.

1957-58 Photo.
856 A386 2.50cr lt bl 45 20

Engr.
857 A386 3.30cr grn ('58) 50 20

Issued to commemorate the 150th anniversary of the birth of Admiral Joaquin Marques de Tamandare, founder of the Brazilian navy.

Coffee Plant and Symbolic "R" — A387

Wmk. 267
1957-58 Photo. *Perf. 11 ½*
858 A387 2.50cr magenta 85 35

Unwmk.
Granite Paper.
858A A387 2.50cr mag ('58) 75 35

Issued to commemorate the centenary (in 1956) of the city of Ribeirao Preto in Sao Paulo state.

Dom John VI — A388

1958, Jan. 28 Engr. Wmk. 268
859 A388 2.50cr magenta 45 25

Issued to commemorate the 150th anniversary of the opening of the ports of Brazil to foreign trade.

Bugler A389

1958, Mar. 18 Wmk. 267
860 A389 2.50cr red 60 25

Issued to commemorate the 150th anniversary of the Brazilian Marine Corps.

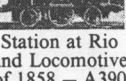

Station at Rio and Locomotive of 1858 — A390

Court House — A391

Wmk. 267
1958, Mar. 29 Photo. *Perf. 11 ½*
861 A390 2.50cr red brn 50 25

Issued to commemorate the centenary of the Central Railroad of Brazil.

1958, Apr. 1 Engr. Wmk. 256
862 A391 2.50cr green 35 15

Issued to commemorate the 150th anniversary of the Military Superior Court.

Emblem and Brazilian Pavilion A392

1958, Apr. 17 Wmk. 267
863 A392 2.50cr dk bl 30 25

World's Fair, Brussels, Apr. 17-Oct. 19.

High Jump — A393

1958, Apr. 20 Photo. Unwmk.
Granite Paper
864 A393 2.50cr crim rose 45 15

8th Children's Games.

Marshal Mariano da Silva Rondon A394

1958, Apr. 19 Engr. Wmk. 267
865 A394 2.50cr magenta 35 15

Issued to honor Marshal Mariano da Silva Rondon and the "Day of the Indian."

Hydroelectric Station A395

1958, Apr. 28 Wmk. 267 *Perf. 11 ½*
866 A395 2.50cr magenta 25 15

Opening of Sao Paulo State power plant.

National Printing Plant A396

1958, May 22 Photo.
867 A396 2.50cr redsh brn 25 15

Issued to commemorate the 150th anniversary of the founding of the National Printing Plant.

Marshal Osorio — A397

1958, May 24
868 A397 2.50cr brt vio 25 15

Issued to commemorate the 150th anniversary of the birth of Marshal Manoel Luiz Osorio.

Pres. Ramon Villeda Morales A398

Fountain A399

1958, June 7 Engr. *Perf. 11 ½*
869 A398 6.50cr dk grn 2.00 75
a. Wmk. 268 6.00 2.00

Issued to commemorate the visit of Pres. Ramon Villeda Morales of Honduras.

1958, June 13
870 A399 2.50cr dk grn 35 15

Issued to commemorate the 150th anniversary of the Botanical Garden, Rio de Janeiro.

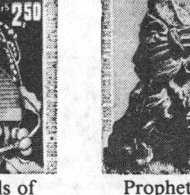

Symbols of Agriculture A400

Prophet Joel A401

1958, June 18 Photo.
871 A400 2.50cr rose car 25 15

Issued to commemorate the 50th anniversary of Japanese immigration to Brazil.

1958, June 21 Engr.
872 A401 2.50cr dk bl 30 15

Issued to commemorate the bicentenary of the Cathedral of Bom Jesus at Matosinhos.

Stylized Globe A402

1958, July 10 Photo.
873 A402 2.50cr dk brn 25 15

Issued to publicize the International Investment Conference, Belo Horizonte.

Brazil stamps through 1975 can be mounted in Scott's Brazil Album.

Julio Bueno Brandao — A403

1958, Aug. 1 Wmk. 268 *Perf. 11½*
874 A403 2.50cr red brn 25 15

Issued to commemorate the centenary of the birth of Julio Bueno Brandao, President of Minas Gerais.

Palacio Tiradentes (House of Congress) A404

1958, July 24 Engr.
875 A404 2.50cr sepia 25 15

Issued to honor the 47th Interparliamentary Conference, Rio de Janeiro, July 24-Aug. 1.

Presidential Palace, Brasilia A405

1958, Aug. 8 Photo. Wmk. 267
876 A405 2.50cr ultra 35 15

Issued to publicize the construction of Brazil's new capital, Brasilia.

Freighters A406

1958, Aug. 22
877 A406 2.50cr blue 45 15

Issued in honor of the Brazilian merchant marine.

Joaquim Caetano da Silva A407

1958, Sept. 2 Unwmk.
Granite Paper
878 A407 2.50cr redsh brn 35 15

Issued in honor of Joaquim Caetano da Silva, scientist and historian.

Giovanni Gronchi A408

Archers A409

1958, Sept. 4 Engr. Wmk. 268
879 A408 7cr dk bl 75 15

Issued to commemorate the visit of Italy's President Giovanni Gronchi to Brazil.

Perf. 11½
1958, Sept. 21 Photo. Unwmk.
Granite Paper
880 A409 2.50cr red org 60 20

Issued to publicize the 10th Spring Games.

Elderly Couple — A410

Machado de Assis — A411

1958, Sept. 27 Wmk. 267
881 A410 2.50cr magenta 35 15

Issued to publicize the Day of the Old People, Sept. 27.

1958, Sept. 28 Unwmk.
882 A411 2.50cr red brn 35 15

Issued to commemorate the 50th anniversary of the death of Joaquim Maria Machado de Assis, writer.

Pres. Vargas and Oil Derrick A412

1958, Oct. 6 Wmk. 268
883 A412 2.50cr blue 25 15

Issued to commemorate the 5th anniversary of Pres. Getulio D. Vargas' oil law.

Globe — A413

Gen. Lauro Sodre — A414

Wmk. 267
1958, Nov. 14 Photo. *Perf. 11½*
884 A413 2.50cr blue 50 15

Issued to commemorate the seventh Inter-American Congress of Municipalities.

1958, Nov. 15 Engr.
885 A414 3.30cr green 15 15

Issued to commemorate the centenary of the birth of Gen. Lauro Sodre.

U. N. Emblem A415

Soccer Player A416

1958, Dec. 26 Photo. *Perf. 11½*
886 A415 2.50cr brt bl 35 15

Issued to commemorate the tenth anniversary of the signing of the Universal Declaration of Human Rights.

1959, Jan. 20
887 A416 3.30cr emer & red brn 50 20

World Soccer Championships of 1958.

Railroad Track and Map A417

Pres. Sukarno of Indonesia A418

1959, Apr. Wmk. 267 *Perf. 11½*
888 A417 2.50cr dp org 30 20

Issued to commemorate the centenary of the linking of Patos and Campina Grande by railroad.

1959, May 20
889 A418 2.50cr blue 25 15

Visit of President Sukarno of Indonesia.

Dom John VI — A419

Boy Polo Players — A420

Perf. 10½x11½
1959, June 12 Wmk. 267
890 A419 2.50cr crimson 30 10

1959, June 13 *Perf. 11½*
891 A420 2.50cr org brn 35 15

9th Children's Games.

Loading Freighter A421

Organ and Emblem A422

1959, July 10
892 A421 2.50cr dk grn 35 15

Issued to honor the merchant marine.

1959, July 16 Photo.
893 A422 3.30cr magenta 20 15

Issued to commemorate the bicentenary of the Carmelite Order in Brazil.

Joachim Silverio de Souza — A423

Symbolic Road — A424

1959, July 20 *Perf. 11½*
894 A423 2.50cr red brn 20 15

Issued to commemorate the birth centenary of Joachim Silverio de Souza, first bishop of Diamantina, Minas Gerais.

1959, Sept. 27 Wmk. 267
895 A424 3.30cr bl grn & ultra 25 15

11th International Roadbuilding Congress.

Girl Athlete — A425

1959, Oct. 4
896 A425 2.50cr lil rose 40 15

11th Spring Games.

Map of Parana A426

1959, Sept. 27
897 A426 2.50cr dk grn 25 15

Issued to commemorate the 25th anniversary of the founding of Londrina, Parana.

Globe and Snipes — A427

Lusignan Cross — A428

1959, Oct. 22 *Perf. 11½*
898 A427 6.50cr dl grn 15 15

Issued to commemorate the World Championship of Snipe Class Sailboats, Porto Alegre, won by Brazilian yachtsmen.

1959, Oct. 24 Engr.
899 A428 6.50cr dl bl 15 15

Issued to commemorate the 4th International Conference on Brazilian-Portuguese Studies, Univeristy of Bahia, Aug. 10-20.

Factory Entrance and Order of Southern Cross — A429

Corcovado Christ, Globe and Southern Cross — A430

1959, Nov. 19 **Photo.**
900 A429 3.30cr org red 15 15

Issued to commemorate the 50th anniversary of the Pres. Vargas Gunpowder Factory.

1959, Nov. 26 ***Perf. 11½***
901 A430 2.50cr blue 40 15

Universal Thanksgiving Day.

Burning Bush A431

1959, Dec. 24 **Wmk. 267**
902 A431 3.30cr lt grn 15 15

Centenary of Presbyterian work in Brazil.

Piraja da Silva and Schistosoma Mansoni A432

1959, Dec. 28
903 A432 2.50cr rose vio 35 15

Issued to commemorate the 25th anniversary of the discovery and identification of schistosoma mansoni, a parasite of the fluke family, by Dr. Piraja da Silva.

Luiz de Matos A433

1960, Jan. 3 **Photo.**
904 A433 3.30cr red brn 15 15

Birth centenary of Luiz de Matos.

L. L. Zamenhof A434

Adel Pinto A435

1960, Mar. 10 **Wmk. 267** ***Perf. 11½***
905 A434 6.50cr emerald 15 15

Issued to commemorate the birth centenary of Lazarus Ludwig Zamenhof (1859-1917), Polish oculist who invented Esperanto in 1887.

1960, Mar. 19 **Engr.** **Wmk. 268**
906 A435 11.50cr rose red 15 15

Issued to commemorate the centenary of the birth of Adel Pinto, civil engineer and railroad expert.

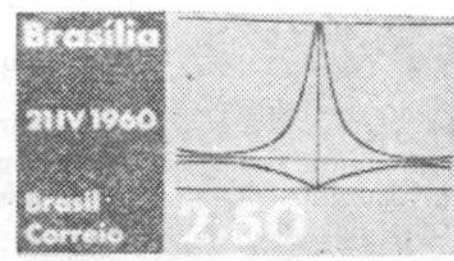

Presidential Palace, Colonnade — A436

Design: 27cr, Plan of Brasilia (like No. C98).

Perf. 11x11½

1960 **Photo.** **Wmk. 267**
907 A436 2.50cr brt grn 40 15
908 A436 27cr salmon 1.00 1.00
Nos. 907-908,C95-C98 (6) 3.20 1.75

No. 907 issued Apr. 21 to commemorate the inauguration of Brazil's new capital, Brasilia, Apr. 21, 1960.

No. 908 issued Sept. 12 to commemorate the birthday of Pres. Juscelino Kubitschek. It measures 105x46½mm., carrying at center a 27cr in design of No. C98, flanked by the chief design features of Nos. 907, C95-C97, with Kubitschek signature below. Issued in sheets of 4 with wide horizontal gutter.

Grain, Coffee, Cotton and Cacao A437

Paulo de Frontin A438

Perf. 11½x11

1960, July 28 **Wmk. 267**
909 A437 2.50cr brown 30 15

Centenary of Ministry of Agriculture.

1960, Oct. 12 **Wmk. 268**
910 A438 2.50cr org red 20 15

Issued to commemorate the centenary of the birth of Paulo de Frontin, engineer.

Girl Athlete Holding Torch — A439

1960, Oct. 18 ***Perf. 11½x11***
911 A439 2.50cr bl grn 30 15

12th Spring Games.

Volleyball and Net A440

Locomotive Wheels A441

Perf. 11½x11

1960, Nov. 12 **Wmk. 268**
912 A440 11cr blue 35 15

International Volleyball Championships.

1960, Oct. 15 ***Perf. 11½x11***
913 A441 2.50cr ultra 25 10

10th Pan-American Railroad Congress.

Symbols of Flight A442

1960, Dec. 16 **Photo.** ***Perf. 11½***
914 A442 2.50cr brn & yel 20 15

Issued to commemorate the International Fair of Industry and Commerce, Rio de Janeiro.

Emperor Haile Selassie I — A443

1961, Jan. 31 ***Perf. 11½x11***
915 A443 2.50cr dk brn 20 15

Issued to commemorate the visit of Emperor Haile Selassie I of Ethiopia to Brazil, Dec. 1960.

Map of Brazil, Open Book and Sacred Heart Emblem A444

Perf. 11x11½

1961, Mar. 13 **Wmk. 268**
916 A444 2.50cr blue 30 15

The 50th anniversary of the operation in Brazil of the Order of the Blessed Heart of Mary.

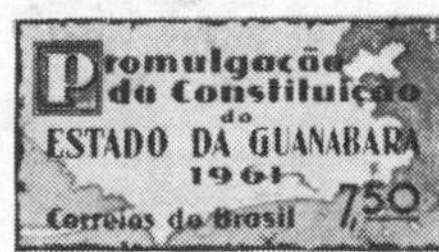

Map of Guanabara A445

1961, March 27 **Wmk. 267**
917 A445 7.50cr org brn 25 15

Issued to commemorate the promulgation of the constitution of the state of Guanabara.

Arms of Agulhas Negras A446

Brazil and Senegal Linked on Map A447

Design: 3.30cr, Dress helmet and sword.

Perf. 11½x11

1961, Apr. 23 **Wmk. 267**
918 A446 2.50cr green 35 15
919 A446 3.30cr rose car 15 15

Issued to commemorate the sesquicentennial of the Agulhas Negras Military Academy.

1961, Apr. 28 **Photo.**
920 A447 27cr ultra 50 20

Issued to commemorate the visit of Afonso Arinos, Brazilian foreign minister, to Senegal to attend its independence ceremonies.

View of Ouro Preto, 1711 A448

1961, June 6 ***Perf. 11x11½***
921 A448 1cr orange 20 20

250th anniversary of Ouro Preto.

War Arsenal A449

1961, June 20 **Wmk. 256**
924 A449 5cr dk red brn 40 15

Issued to commemorate the 150th anniversary of the War Arsenal, Rio de Janeiro.

Coffee Bean and Branch A450

Rabindranath Tagore A451

Perf. 11½x11

1961, June 26 **Wmk. 267**
925 A450 20cr redsh brn 1.50 25

Issued to commemorate the 8th Directorial Committee meeting of the International Coffee Convention, Rio de Janeiro, June 26, 1961.

1961, July 28 **Photo.** **Wmk. 267**
926 A451 10cr rose car 30 15

Issued to commemorate the centenary of the birth of Rabindranath Tagore, Indian poet.

The Catalogue editors cannot undertake to appraise, identify or judge the genuineness or condition of stamps.

Stamp of 1861 and Map of English Channel A452

Design: 20cr, 430r stamp of 1861 and map of Netherlands.

1961, Aug. 1 *Perf. 11x11½*

927 A452 10cr rose 75 20
928 A452 20cr sal pink 2.00 30

Centenary of 1861 stamp issue.

Portrait Type of 1954-60
Designs as Before.

1961 Wmk. 268 *Perf. 11x11½*

930 A336 1cr brown 1.00 50
931 A336 2cr dk bl grn 1.50 50
932 A336 5cr red lil 4.50 30
933 A336 10cr emerald 9.00 30

The 1cr, 5cr and 10cr have patterned background.

Sun, Clouds, Rain and Weather Symbols A453

Dedo de Deus Peak A454

1962, March 23 *Perf. 11½x11*

936 A453 10cr red brn 1.25 30

World Meteorological Day, Mar. 23.

1962, Apr. 14 Photo. Wmk. 267

937 A454 8cr emerald 25 25

Issued to commemorate the 50th anniversary of the climbing of Dedo de Deus (Finger of God) peak.

Dr. Gaspar Vianna and Leishmania Protozoa A455

1962, Apr. 24 *Perf. 11x11½*

938 A455 8cr blue 25 15

Issued to commemorate the 50th anniversary of the discovery by Gaspar Oliveiro Vianna (1885-1914) of a cure for leishmaniasis.

Henrique Dias A456

1962, June 18 Wmk. 267

939 A456 10cr dk vio brn 40 15

Issued to commemorate the 300th anniversary of the death of Henrique Dias, Negro military leader who fought against the Dutch and Spaniards.

The indexes in each volume of the Scott Catalogue contain many listings which help to identify stamps.

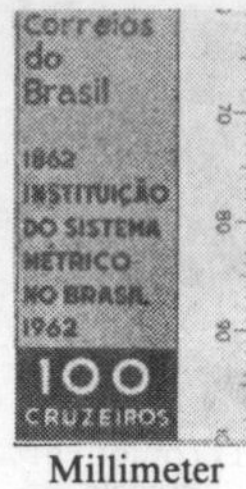

Millimeter Gauge A457

Sailboats, Snipe Class A458

1962, June 26 *Perf. 11½x11*

940 A457 100cr car rose 60 20

Issued to commemorate the centenary of the introduction of the metric system in Brazil.

1962, July 21 Photo. Wmk. 267

941 A458 8cr Prus grn 30 15

Issued to commemorate the 13th Brazilian championships for Snipe Class sailing.

Julio Mesquita A459

1962, Aug. 18 *Perf. 11x11½*

942 A459 8cr dl brn 30 15

Issued to commemorate the centenary of the birth of Julio Mesquita, journalist and founder of Sao Paulo.

Empress Leopoldina — A460

1962, Sept. 7 *Perf. 11½x11*

943 A460 8cr rose cl 25 15

140th anniversary of independence.

Buildings, Brasilia A461

Perf. 11x11½

1962, Oct. 24 Wmk. 267

944 A461 10cr orange 50 15

Issued to commemorate the 51st Interparliamentary Conference, Brasilia.

Pouring Ladle — A462

1962, Oct. 26 *Perf. 11½x11*

945 A462 8cr orange 25 15

Issued to mark the inauguration of the Usiminas State Iron and Steel Foundry at Belo Horizonte, Minas Gerais.

UPAE Emblem A463

1962, Nov. 19 *Perf. 11x11½*

946 A463 8cr brt mag 20 15

Issued to commemorate the 50th anniversary of the founding of the Postal Union of the Americas and Spain, UPAE.

Chimney and Cogwheel Forming "10" — A464

1962, Nov. 26 *Perf. 11½x11*

947 A464 10cr lt bl grn 35 15

Issued to commemorate the 10th anniversary of the National Economic and Development Bank.

Quintino Bocaiuva A465

Soccer Player and Globe A466

Perf. 11½x11

1962, Dec. 27 Photo. Wmk. 267

948 A465 8cr brn org 20 15

Issued to commemorate the 50th anniversary of the death of Quintino Bocaiuva, journalist.

1963, Jan. 14

949 A466 10cr bl grn 20 7

World Soccer Championship of 1962.

Carrier Pigeon A467

1963, Jan. Unwmk. Litho. *Perf. 14*

950 A467 8cr yel, dk bl, red & grn 25 15

Souvenir Sheet

Imperf

951 A467 100cr yel, dk bl, red & grn 1.40 *3.00*

Issued to commemorate 300 years of Brazilian postal service. No. 951 contains one stamp. Black inscription and ultramarine border. Size: 145x57mm.

Issue dates: 8cr, Jan. 25; 100cr, Jan. 31.

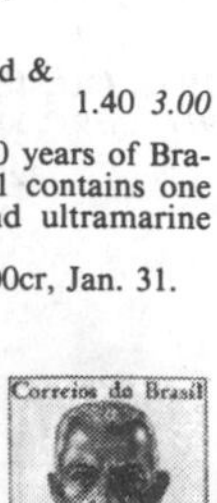

Severino Neiva — A468

Perf. 10½x11½

1963, Jan. 31 Photo. Wmk. 267

952 A468 8cr brt vio 25 10

Radar Tracking Station and Rockets A469

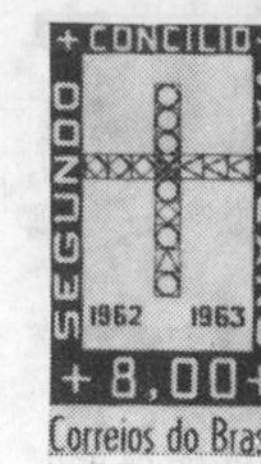

"Cross of Unity" A470

Perf. 11½x11

1963, Mar. 15 Wmk. 268

953 A469 21cr lt ultra 30 15

Issued to publicize the International Aeronautics and Space Exhibition, Sao Paulo.

1963 Wmk. 267 *Perf. 11½x11*

954 A470 8cr red lil 20 15

Issued to commemorate Vatican II, the 21st Ecumenical Council of the Roman Catholic Church.

"ABC" in Geometric Form A471

Basketball Player A472

1963, Apr. 22 Photo. Wmk. 267

955 A471 8cr brt bl & lt bl 20 15

Issued for Education Week, Apr. 22-27, in connection with the 3-year alphabetization program.

1963, May 15

956 A472 8cr dp lil rose 35 15

Issued to commemorate the 4th International Basketball Championships, Rio de Janeiro, May 10-25, 1963.

Games Emblem A473

"OEA" and Map of the Americas A474

1963, May 22 *Perf. 11½x11*

957 A473 10cr car rose 60 15

4th Pan American Games, Sao Paulo.

1963, June 6

958 A474 10cr org & dp org 50 15

Issued to commemorate the 15th anniversary of the charter of the Organization of American States.

José Bonifacio de Andrada — A475

1963, June 13
959 A475 8cr dk brn 20 15

Issued to commemorate the bicentenary of the birth of Jose Bonifacio de Andrada de Silva, statesman.

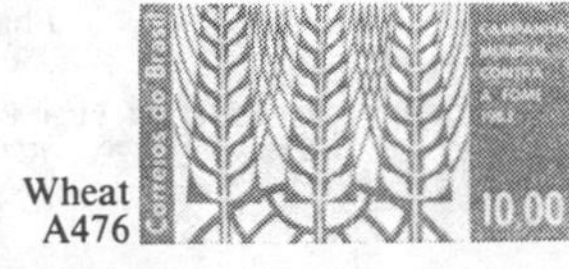

Wheat A476

Perf. 11x11½
1963, June 19 Photo. Wmk. 267
960 A476 10cr blue 50 15

Issued for the "Freedom from Hunger" campaign of the U.N. Food and Agriculture Organization.

Centenary Emblem A477

Joao Caetano A478

1963, Aug. 19 ***Perf. 11½x11***
961 A477 8cr yel org & red 30 15

Centenary of International Red Cross.

1963, Aug. 24 ***Perf. 11½x11***
962 A478 8cr slate 25 15

Death centenary of Joao Caetano, actor.

Symbols of Agriculture, Industry and Atomic Energy A479

Hammer Thrower A480

1963, Aug. 28
963 A479 10cr car rose 40 15

Issued to commemorate the first anniversary of the Atomic Development Law.

1963, Sept. 13
964 A480 10cr gray 75 10

International College Students' Games, Porto Alegre.

A particular stamp may be scarce, but if few collectors want it, its market value may remain relatively low.

Marshal Tito A481

Compass Rose, Map of Brazil and View of Rio de Janeiro A482

1963, Sept. 19
965 A481 80cr sepia 50 30

Visit of Marshal Tito of Jugoslavia.

1963, Sept. 20
966 A482 8cr lt bl grn 20 15

8th International Leprology Congress.

Oil Derrick and Storage Tank A483

1963, Oct. 3 ***Perf. 11x11½***
967 A483 8cr dk sl grn 20 15

Issued to commemorate the 10th anniversary of Petrobras, the national oil company.

"Spring Games" A484

1963, Nov. 5 Photo. Wmk. 267
968 A484 8cr yel & org 25 20

1963 Spring Games.

Borges de Medeiros — A485

1963, Nov. 29 ***Perf. 11½x11***
969 A485 8cr red brn 20 15

Issued to commemorate the centenary of the birth of Dr. Borges de Medeiros (1863-1962), Governor of Rio Grande do Sul.

Sao Joao del Rei A486

1963, Dec. 8 ***Perf. 11x11½***
970 A486 8cr vio bl 20 15

250th anniversary of Sao Joao del Rei.

Dr. Alvaro Alvim A487

1963, Dec. 19
971 A487 8cr dk gray 20 15

Issued to commemorate the centenary of the birth of Dr. Alvaro Alvim (1863-1928), X-ray specialist and martyr of science.

Viscount de Mauá A488

Mandacaru Cactus and Emblem A489

1963, Dec. 28 ***Perf. 11½x11***
972 A488 8cr rose car 20 15

Issued to commemorate the sesquicentennial of the birth of Viscount de Mauá, founder of first Brazilian railroad.

1964, Jan. 23 Photo. Wmk. 267
973 A489 8cr dl grn 25 15

Issued to commemorate the 10th anniversary of the Bank of Northeast Brazil.

Coelho Netto A490

Lauro Müller A491

1964, Feb. 21 ***Perf. 11½x11***
974 A490 8cr brt vio 20 15

Birth centenary of Coelho Netto, writer.

1964, March 8 Wmk. 267
975 A491 8cr dp org 20 15

Issued to commemorate the centenary of the birth of Lauro Siverino Müller, politician and member of the Brazilian Academy of Letters.

Child Holding Spoon A492

1964, March 25 ***Perf. 11x11½***
976 A492 8cr yel brn & yel 25 15

Issued for "School Meals Week."

Chalice Rock A493

Allan Kardec A494

1964, Apr. 9 Engr. ***Perf. 11½x11***
977 A493 80cr red org 40 20

Issued for tourist publicity.

1964, Apr. 18 Photo.
978 A494 30cr sl grn 75 15

Issued to commemorate the centenary of "O Evangelho" (Gospel) of the codification of Spiritism.

Heinrich Lübke A495

Pope John XXIII A496

Perf. 11½x11
1964, May 8 Photo. Wmk. 267
979 A495 100cr red brn 75 18

Issued to commemorate the visit of President Heinrich Lübke of Germany.

1964, June 29 Wmk. 267
980 A496 20cr dk car rose 30 20
a. Unwmk. 30 20

Issued in memory of Pope John XXIII.

Pres. Senghor of Senegal — A497

1964, Sept. 19 Wmk. 267
981 A497 20cr dk brn 35 15

Issued to commemorate the visit of Leopold Sedar Senghor, President of Senegal.

Botafago Bay and Sugarloaf Mountain — A498

Designs: 100cr, Church of Our Lady of the Rock (vert.). 200cr, Copacabana beach.

Perf. 11x11½, 11½x11
1964-65 Photo.
983 A498 15cr org & bl 40 25
984 A498 100cr brt grn & red brn, *yel* 50 18

985 A498 200cr blk & red 2.50 35
a. Souv. sheet of 3 ('65) 6.00 5.00

Issued to commemorate the 4th centenary of Rio de Janeiro. See Nos. 993-995a.

No. 985a contains three imperf. stamps similar to Nos. 986-985, but printed in brown with marginal inscriptions and border in deep orange. Size: 129x79mm. Sold for 320cr. Issued Dec. 30, 1965.

A souvenir card containing one lithographed facsimile of No. 984, imperf., exists, but has no franking value. Marginal inscriptions in green. Size: 100x125mm. Sold by P.O. for 250cr.

Pres. Charles de Gaulle A499

Pres. John F. Kennedy A500

1964, Oct. 13 ***Perf. 11½x11***
986 A499 100cr org brn 30 15

Issued to commemorate the visit of Charles de Gaulle, President of France, Oct. 13-15.

1964, Oct. 24 Photo. Wmk. 267
987 A500 100cr slate 30 15

Issued in memory of President John F. Kennedy (1917-63).

"Prophet" by A. F. Lisbao – A501

1964, Nov. 18 ***Perf. 11½x11***
988 A501 10cr slate 30 6

Issued to commemorate the 150th anniversary of the death of the sculptor Antonio Francisco Lisbao, "O Aleijadinho" (The Cripple).

Antonio Goncalves Dias – A502

Designs: 30cr, Euclides da Cunha. 50cr, Prof. Angelo Moreira da Costa Lima. 200cr, Tiradentes. 500cr, Dom Pedro I. 1000cr, Dom Pedro II.

1965-66 Wmk. 267 ***Perf. 11x11½***
989 A502 30cr brt bluish grn ('66) 2.00 25
989A A502 50cr dl brn ('66) 1.50 10
990 A502 100cr blue 60 10
991 A502 200cr brn org 2.00 10
992 A502 500cr red brn 6.00 50
992A A502 1000cr sl bl ('66) 10.00 50
Nos. 989-992A (6) 22.10 1.55

Statue of St. Sebastian, Guanabara Bay – A503

The Arches A504

Design: 35cr, Estacio de Sá(1520-67), founder of Rio de Janeiro.

1965 Photo. ***Perf. 11½***
Size: 24x37mm.
993 A503 30cr bl & rose red 50 15

Lithographed and Engraved
Perf. 11x11½
994 A504 30cr lt bl & blk 50 15

Photo. ***Perf. 11½***
Size: 21x39mm.
995 A503 35cr blk & org 25 25
a. Souv. sheet of 3 4.00 5.00

Issued to commemorate the 4th centenary of Rio de Janeiro. Issue dates: No. 993, Mar. 5. No. 994, Nov. 30. No. 995, July 28. No. 995a, Dec. 30.

No. 995a contains three imperf. stamps similar to Nos. 993-995, but printed in deep orange with marginal inscriptions and border in brown. Size: 130x79mm. Sold for 100cr.

Sword and Cross – A505

1965, Apr. 15 Wmk. 267 ***Perf. 11½***
996 A505 120cr gray 40 15

Issued to commemorate the first anniversary of the democratic revolution.

Vital Brazil – A506

Shah of Iran – A507

1965, Apr. 28 Wmk. 267 ***Perf. 11½***
997 A506 120cr dp org 50 15

Centenary of birth of Vital Brazil, M.D.

A souvenir card containing one impression similar to No. 997, imperf., exists, printed in dull plum. Sold by P.O. for 250cr. Size: 114x180mm.

1965, May 5 Photo.
998 A507 120cr rose cl 40 15

Issued to commemorate the visit of Shah Mohammed Riza Pahlavi of Iran.

Marshal Mariano da Silva Rondon A508

Lions' Emblem A509

1965, May 7 Engr.
999 A508 30cr claret 45 15

Issued to commemorate the centenary of the birth of Marshal Mariano da Silva Rondon (1865-1958), explorer and expert on Indians.

1965, May 14 Photo.
1000 A509 35cr pale vio & blk 25 15

Issued to commemorate the 12th convention of the Lions Clubs of Brazil, Rio de Janeiro, May 11-16.

ITU Emblem, Old and New Communication Equipment – A510

1965, May 21 ***Perf. 11½***
1001 A510 120cr yel & grn 50 20

Issued to commemorate the centenary of the International Telecommunication Union.

Epitacio Pessoa – A511

Statue of Admiral Barroso – A512

1965, May 23 Photo.
1002 A511 35cr bl gray 20 15

Issued to commemorate the centenary of the birth of Epitacio da Silva Pessoa (1865-1942), jurist, president of Brazil, 1919-22.

1965, June 11
1003 A512 30cr blue 40 15

Centenary of the naval battle of Riachuelo.

A souvenir card containing one lithographed facsimile of No. 1003, imperf., exists. Size: 100x139½mm.

José de Alencar and Indian Princess – A513

1965, June 24 ***Perf. 11½x11***
1004 A513 30cr dp plum 45 15

Issued to commemorate the centenary of the publication of "Iracema" by Jose de Alencar.

A souvenir card containing one lithographed facsimile of No. 1004, printed in rose red and imperf., exists. Size: 100x141½mm.

Winston Churchill A514

1965, June 25 ***Perf. 11x11½***
1005 A514 200cr slate 1.00 25

Issued in memory of Sir Winston Spencer Churchill (1874-1965), statesman and World War II leader.

Scout Jamboree Emblem – A515

1965, July 17 Photo.
1006 A515 30cr dl bl grn 50 15

Issued to commemorate the First Pan-American Boy Scout Jamboree, Fundao Island, Rio de Janeiro, July 15-25.

ICY Emblem A516

1965, Aug. 25 Wmk. 267 ***Perf. 11½***
1007 A516 120cr dl bl & blk 40 15

International Cooperation Year, 1965.

Leoncio Correias A517

Emblem A518

1965, Sept. 1 ***Perf. 11½x11***
1008 A517 35cr sl grn 20 15

Issued to commemorate the centenary of the birth of Leoncio Correias, poet.

1965, Sept. 4
1009 A518 30cr brt rose 30 15

Issued to publicize the Eighth Biennial Fine Arts Exhibition, Sao Paulo, Nov.-Dec., 1965.

Pres. Saragat of Italy – A519

1965, Sept. 11 Photo. Wmk. 267
1010 A519 100cr sl grn, *pink* 25 12

Visit of Pres. Giuseppe Saragat of Italy.

Grand Duke and Duchess of Luxembourg – A520

1965, Sept. 17 *Perf. 11x11½*
1011 A520 100cr brn ol 25 12

Issued to commemorate the visit of Grand Duke Jean and Grand Duchess Josephine Charlotte of Luxembourg.

Biplane — A521

1965, Oct. 8 Photo. *Perf. 11½x11*
1012 A521 35cr ultra 25 15

Issued to publicize the 3rd Aviation Week Philatelic Exhibition, Rio de Janeiro.

A souvenir card carries one impression of this 35cr, imperf. Size: 102x140mm. Sold for 100cr.

Flags of OAS Members A522

1965, Nov. 17 *Perf. 11x11½*
1013 A522 100cr brt bl & blk 40 20

Issued to commemorate the second meeting of Foreign Ministers of the Organization of American States, Rio de Janeiro.

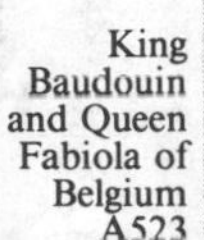

King Baudouin and Queen Fabiola of Belgium A523

1965, Nov. 18
1014 A523 100cr gray 40 20

Visit of King and Queen of Belgium.

"Coffee Beans" — A524

Perf. 11½x11
1965, Dec. 21 Photo. Wmk. 267
1015 A524 30cr brown 60 15

Brazilian coffee publicity.

Conveyor and Loading Crane A525

1966, Apr. 1 *Perf. 11x11½*
1016 A525 110cr tan & dk sl grn 40 25

Issued to commemorate the opening of the new terminal of the Rio Doce Iron Ore Company at Tubarao.

Demand, as well as supply, determines a stamp's market value. One is as important as the other.

Pouring Ladle and Steel Beam A526

Prof. de Rocha Dissecting Cadaver A527

Perf. 11½x11
1966, Apr. 16 Photo. Wmk. 267
1017 A526 30cr *dp org* 35 15

Issued to commemorate the 25th anniversary of the National Steel Company (nationalization of the steel industry).

1966, Apr. 26
1018 A527 30cr brt bluish grn 60 15

Issued to commemorate the 50th anniversary of the discovery and description of Rickettsia prowazeki, the cause of typhus fever, by Prof. Henrique de Rocha Lima.

Battle of Tuiuti A528

Perf. 11x11½
1966, May 24 Photo. Wmk. 267
1019 A528 30cr gray grn 60 15

Centenary of the Battle of Tuiuti.

Symbolic Water Cycle — A529

Pres. Shazar of Israel — A530

1966, July 1 *Perf. 11½x11*
1020 A529 100cr lt brn & bl 45 20

Hydrological Decade (UNESCO), 1965-74.

1966, July 18 Photo. Wmk. 267
1021 A530 100cr ultra 50 20

Visit of Pres. Zalman Shazar of Israel.

Imperial Academy of Fine Arts A531

Perf. 11x11½
1966, Aug. 12 Engr. Wmk. 267
1022 A531 100cr red brn 90 20

150th anniversary of French art mission.

Military Service Emblem A532

1966, Sept. 6 Photo. *Perf. 11x11½*
1023 A532 30cr yel, ultra & grn 40 15
a. With commemorative border 3.00 3.00

Issued to publicize the new Military Service Law. No. 1023a, issued in sheets of four, measures 103½x47mm. It carries at left a single 30cr, type A532, in deeper tones of yellow and ultramarine, Wmk. 264. Top and bottom "frames" in ultramarine are inscribed "Departmento dos Correios e Telegrafos" and "100 Cruzeiros." Inscription at right: "Bloco Comemorativo da Nova Lei do Serviço Militar." Without gum.

Sold for 100cr.

Rubén Dario — A533

Perf. 11½x11
1966, Sept. 20 Photo. Wmk. 267
1024 A533 100cr brt rose lil 40 15

Issued to commemorate the 50th anniversary of the death of Rubén Dario (pen name of Felix Rubén Garcia Sarmiento (1867-1916), Nicaraguan poet, newspaper correspondent and diplomat.

Ceramic Candlestick from Santarem — A534

1966, Oct. 6 *Perf. 11x11½*
1025 A534 30cr dk brn, *sal* 35 15

Centenary of Goeldi Museum at Belem.

Arms of Santa Cruz — A535

Perf. 11½x11
1966, Oct. 15 Photo. Wmk. 267
1026 A535 30cr sl grn 40 15

Issued to publicize the First National Tobacco Exposition, Santa Cruz.

UNESCO Emblem A536

1966, Oct. 24 Engr. *Perf. 11½*
1027 A536 120cr black 90 25
a. With commemorative border 4.75 4.75

Issued to commemorate the 20th anniversary of UNESCO (United Nations Educational, Scientific and Cultural Organization). No. 1027a issued in sheets of 4 with red control number measures 102x48mm. It carries at right a design similar to No. 1027. Inscribed at left: "Bloco comemorativo do 20 degree aniversario da UNESCO," "Cr$150" and "Departmento dos Correios e Telegrafos". Unwatermarked granite paper, without gum. Solf for 150cr.

Captain Antonio Correia Pinto and Map of Lages — A537

Formee Cross and Southern Cross — A538

Perf. 11½x11
1966, Nov. 22 Photo. Wmk. 267
1028 A537 30cr sal pink 35 15

Issued to commemorate the bicentenary of the arrival of Capt. Antonio Correia Pinto.

1966, Dec. 4 *Perf. 11½*
1029 A538 100cr bl grn 45 15

Issued to commemorate LUBRAPEX 1966 philatelic exhibition at the National Museum of Fine Arts, Rio de Janeiro.

Madonna and Child — A539

Madonna and Child — A540

Perf. 11½x11
1966, Dec. Photo. Wmk. 267
1030 A539 30cr bl grn 30 15

Perf. 11½
1031 A540 35cr sal & ultra 25 20
a. 150cr sal & ultra 2.50 3.00

Christmas 1966.

No. 1031a measures 46x103mm. and is printed in sheets of 4. It is inscribed "Pax Hominibus" (but not "Brasil Correio") and carries the Madonna shown on No. 1031. Issued without gum.

Issue dates: 30cr, Dec. 8; 35cr, Dec. 22; 150cr, Dec. 28.

Arms of Laguna A541

1967, Jan. 4 Engr. *Perf. 11x11½*
1032 A541 60cr sepia 25 15

Issued to commemorate the centenary of the Post and Telegraph Agency of Laguna, Santa Catarina.

Railroad Bridge
A542

1967, Feb. 16 Photo. Wmk. 267
1033 A542 50cr dp org 60 20

Centenary of the Santos-Jundiai railroad.

Black Madonna of Czestochowa, Polish Eagle and Cross — A543

1967, Mar. 12 ***Perf. 11x11½***
1034 A543 50cr yel, bl & rose red 60 20

Issued to commemorate the thousandth anniversary of the adoption of Christianity in Poland.

Research Rocket
A544

Anita Garibaldi
A545

1967, March 23 ***Perf. 11½x11***
1035 A544 50cr blk & brt bl 75 30

World Meteorological Day, March 23.

Perf. 11x11½
1967-69 Photo. Wmk. 267

Portraits: 1c, Mother Joana Angelica. 2c, Marilia de Dirceu. 3c, Dr. Rita Lobato. 6c, Ana Neri. 10c, Darcy Vargas.

1036	A545	1c dp ultra	15	5
1037	A545	2c red brn	15	5
1038	A545	3c brt grn	25	8
1039	A545	5c black	50	8
1040	A545	6c brown	50	8
1041	A545	10c dk sl grn ('69)	1.50	30
		Nos. 1036-1041 (6)	3.05	64

Issue dates: 1c, May 3; 2c, Aug. 14; 3c, June 7; 5c, Apr. 14; 6c, May 14, 1967; 10c, June 18, 1969.

VARIG Airlines — A546

Lions Emblem and Globes
A547

The only foreign revenue stamps listed in this Catalogue are those authorized for prepayment of postage.

Madonna and Child, by Robert Feruzzi — A548

1967, May 8 ***Perf. 11½x11***
1046 A546 6c brt bl & blk 30 25

40th anniversary of VARIG Airlines.

1967, May 9 Engr. ***Perf. 11x11½***
1047 A547 6c green 50 25
a. Souv. sheet 2.50 *3.00*

Issued to commemorate the 50th anniversary of Lions International. No. 1047a contains one imperf. stamp similar to No. 1047. Green inscription and Lions emblem in margin. Size: 131x80mm. Sold for 15c.

1967, May 14 Photo. ***Perf. 11½x11***
1048 A548 5c violet 30 25
a. 15c, souv. sheet 2.50 *3.00*

Issued for Mother's Day. No. 1048a contains one 15c imperf. stamp in design of No. 1048. Violet marginal inscription. Size: 129x77mm.

Prince Akihito and Princess Michiko
A549

1967, May 25 ***Perf. 11x11½***
1049 A549 10c blk & pink 40 20

Issued to commemorate the visit to Brazil of Crown Prince Akihito and Princess Michiko of Japan.

Carrier Pigeon and Radar Screen
A550

Brother Vicente do Salvador
A551

Perf. 11½x11
1967, June 20 Photo. Wmk. 267
1050 A550 10c sl & brt pink 35 20

Issued to commemorate the opening of the Communications Ministry in Brasilia.

1967, June 28 Engr.
1051 A551 5c brown 35 25

Issued to commemorate the 400th anniversary of the birth of Brother Vicente do Salvador (1564-1636), founder of Franciscan convent in Rio de Janeiro, and historian.

Boy, Girl and 4-S Emblem
A552

1967, July 12 Photo. ***Perf. 11½***
1052 A552 5c grn & blk 30 20

National 4-S (4-H) Day.

Möbius Strip
A553

1967, July 21 ***Perf. 11x11½***
1053 A553 5c brt bl & blk 30 20

Issued to commemorate the 6th Brazilian Mathematical Congress.

Fish
A554

1967, Aug. 1 ***Perf. 11½***
1054 A554 5c slate 50 20

Bicentenary of city of Piracicaba.

Golden Rose and Papal Arms — A555

1967, Aug. 15
1055 A555 20c mag & yel 1.25 40

Issued to commemorate the offering of a golden rose by Pope Paul VI to the Virgin Mary of Fatima (Our Lady of Peace), Patroness of Brazil.

General Sampaio
A556

King Olaf of Norway
A557

1967, Aug. 25 Engr. ***Perf. 11½x11***
1056 A556 5c blue 30 20

Issued to honor General Antonio de Sampaio, hero of the Battle of Tutui.

1967, Sept. 8 Photo.
1057 A557 10c brn org 30 20

Visit of King Olaf of Norway.

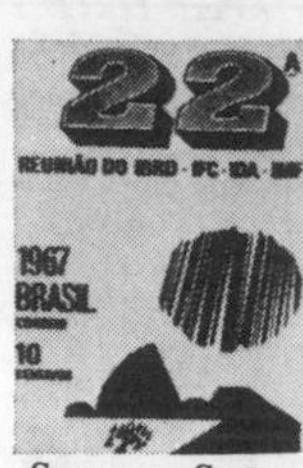

Sun over Sugar Loaf, Botafogo Bay
A558

Nilo Peçanha
A559

Photogravure and Embossed
1967, Sept. 25 Wmk. 267 ***Perf. 11½***
1058 A558 10c blk & dp org 30 20

Issued to commemorate the 22nd meeting of the International Monetary Fund, International Bank for Reconstruction and Development, International Financial Corporation and International Development Association.

Perf. 11½x11
1967, Oct. 1 Photo. Wmk. 267
1059 A559 5c brn vio 30 20

Issued to commemorate the centenary of the birth of Nilo Peçanha (1867-1924), President of Brazil 1909-1910.

Virgin of the Apparition and Basilica of Aparecida
A560

Cockerel, Festival Emblem
A561

1967, Oct. 11 ***Perf. 11½***
1060 A560 5c ultra & dl yel 50 20
a. Souv. sheet of 2 3.50 *4.50*

Issued to commemorate the 250th anniversary of the discovery of the statue of Our Lady of the Apparition, now in the National Basilica of the Apparition at Aparecida do Norte.

No. 1060a contains imperf. 5c and 10c stamps similar to No. 1060. Blue marginal inscriptions with pink and blue design. Issued Dec. 27, 1967, for Christmas. Size: 77½x129mm.

Engraved and Photogravure
1967, Oct. 16 ***Perf. 11½x11***
1061 A561 20c blk & multi 75 40

Second International Folksong Festival.

Balloon, Plane and Rocket
A562

Perf. 11x11½
1967, Oct. 18 Photo. Unwmk.
1062 A562 10c blue 60 30
a. 15c, souv. sheet 3.00 *3.50*

Issued for the Week of the Wing, Oct. 18-23. No. 1062a contains one imperf. 15c stamp similar to No. 1062, blue marginal design and inscription; it was issued Oct. 23. Size: 130x75mm.

Pres. Arthur Bernardes — A563

Portraits of Brazilian Presidents: 20c, Campos Salles. 50c, Wenceslau Pereira Gomes Braz. 1cr, Washington Pereira de Souza Luiz. 2cr, Castello Branco.

Perf. 11x11½

1967-68 Photo. Wmk. 267

1063 A563 10c blue 30 20
1064 A563 20c dk red brn 1.00 20

Engr.

1065 A563 50c blk ('68) 5.00 30
1066 A563 1cr lil rose ('68) 8.00 30
1067 A563 2cr emer ('68) 1.50 30
Nos. 1063-1067 (5) 15.80 1.30

Carnival of Rio — A564

Ships, Anchor and Sailor — A565

1967, Nov. 22 *Perf. 11½x11*

1070 A564 10c lem, ultra & pink 35 20
a. 15c, souv. sheet 3.50 *4.50*

Issued for International Tourist Year, 1967. No. 1070a contains a 15c imperf. stamp in design of No. 1070. Pink marginal design and inscription. Size: 76x130mm. Issued Nov. 24.

1967, Dec. 6

1071 A565 10c ultra 40 25

Issued for Navy Week.

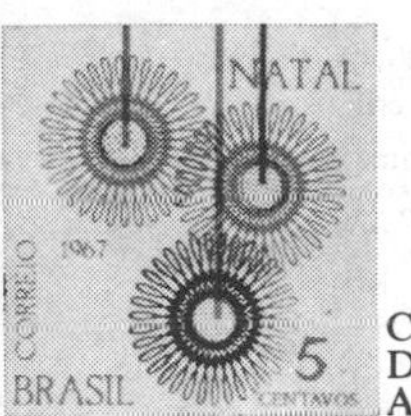

Christmas Decorations A566

1967, Dec. 8 *Perf. 11½*

1072 A566 5c car, yel & bl 40 20

Christmas 1967.

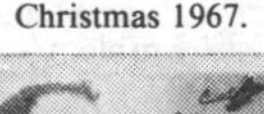

Olavo Bilac, Planes, Tank and Aircraft Carrier A567

Perf. 11x11½

1967, Dec. 16 Photo. Wmk. 267

1073 A567 5c brt bl & yel 40 20

Issued for Reservists' Day and to honor Olavo Bilac, sponsor of compulsory military service.

Rodrigues de Carvalho — A568

1967, Dec. 18 Engr. *Perf. 11½x11*

1074 A568 10c green 30 20

Issued to commemorate the centenary of the birth of Rodrigues de Carvalho, poet and lawyer.

Orlando Rangel A569

1968, Feb. 29 Photo. *Perf. 11x11½*

1075 A569 5c lt grnsh bl & blk 60 30

Issued to commemorate the centenary of the birth of Orlando de Fonseca Rangel, pioneer of pharmaceutical industry in Brazil.

Virgin of Paranagua and Diver A570

Map of Brazil Showing Manaus A571

1968, Mar. 9 *Perf. 11½x11*

1076 A570 10c dk sl grn & brt yel grn 50 25

Issued to commemorate the 250th anniversary of the first underwater explorations at Paranagua.

1968, Mar. 13 Photo. Wmk. 267

1077 A571 10c yel, grn & red 40 25

Issued to publicize the free port of Manaus on the Amazon River.

Human Rights Flame A572

Paul Harris and Rotary Emblem A573

1968, Mar. 21 *Perf. 11½x11*

1078 A572 10c bl & sal 40 25

International Human Rights Year.

1968, Apr. 19 Litho. Unwmk.
Without Gum

1079 A573 20c grn & org brn 1.50 70

Issued to commemorate the centenary of the birth of Paul Percy Harris (1868-1947), founder of Rotary International.

Pedro Alvares Cabral and his Fleet — A574

Design: 20c, First Mass celebrated in Brazil.

1968 Without Gum *Perf. 11½*

1080 A574 10c multi 85 45
1081 A574 20c multi 1.15 60

Issued to commemorate the 500th anniversary of the birth of Pedro Alvares Cabral, navigator, who took possession of Brazil for Portugal.

Issue dates: 10c, Apr. 22; 20c, July 11.

College Arms — A575

1968, Apr. 22 Photo. Wmk. 267

1082 A575 10c vio bl, red & gold 80 35

Centenary of St. Luiz College, Sao Paulo.

Motherhood, by Henrique Bernardeli A576

1968, May 12 Litho. Unwmk.
Without Gum

1083 A576 5c multi 50 30

Issued for Mother's Day.

Harpy Eagle A577

Photogravure and Engraved

1968, May 28 Wmk. 267

1084 A577 20c brt bl & blk 1.75 50

Sesquicentennial of National Museum.

Brazilian and Japanese Women — A578

1968, June 28 Litho. Unwmk.
Without Gum

1085 A578 10c yel & multi 80 40

Issued to commemorate the inauguration of Varig's direct Brazil-Japan airline.

Horse Race A579

Perf. 11x11½

1968, July 16 Litho. Unwmk.
Without Gum

1086 A579 10c multi 50 30

Centenary of the Jockey Club of Brazil.

Musician Wren A580

Designs: 10c, Red-crested cardinal (vert.). 50c, Royal flycatcher (vert.).

Perf. 11½x11, 11x11½

1968-69 Engr. Wmk. in Sheet
Without Gum

1087 A580 10c multi ('69) 75 30
1088 A580 20c multi 1.25 30
1089 A580 50c multi 1.75 60

Some stamps in each sheet of Nos. 1087-1089 show parts of a two-line papermaker's watermark: "WESTERPOST / INDUSTRIA BRASILEIRA" with diamond-shaped emblem between last two words. Entire watermark appears in one sheet margin.

Issue dates: 10c, Aug. 20, 1969. 20c, July 19, 1968. 50c, Aug. 2, 1968.

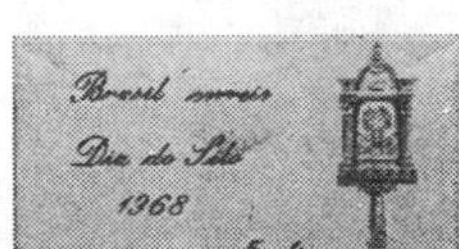

Mailbox and Envelope A581

Photogravure and Engraved

1968, Aug. 1 Wmk. 267 *Perf. 11*

1091 A581 5c cit, blk & grn 25 20

Issued for Stamp Day, 1968 and to commemorate the 125th anniversary of the first Brazilian postage stamps.

Emilio Luiz Mallet A582

Map of South America A583

Perf. 11½x11

1968, Aug. 25 Engr. Wmk. 267

1092 A582 10c pale pur 25 20

Issued to honor Marshal Emilio Luiz Mallet, Baron of Itapevi, patron of the marines.

1968, Sept. 5 Photo.

1093 A583 10c dp org 20 20

Visit of President Eduardo Frei of Chile.

Seal of Portuguese Literary School — A584

Photogravure and Engraved

1968, Sept. 10 *Perf. 11½*

1094 A584 5c pink & grn 25 20

Centenary of Portuguese Literary School.

Map of Brazil and Telex Tape A585

1968, Sept. Photo. *Perf. 11x11½*

1095 A585 20c cit & brt grn 60 25

Linking of 25 Brazilian cities by teletype.

Soldiers' Heads on Medal — A586

Perf. 11½x11

1968, Sept. 24 Litho. Unwmk.

Without Gum

1096 A586 5c bl & gray 30 25

8th American Armed Forces Conference.

Clef, Notes and Sugarloaf Mountain A587

1968, Sept. 30 *Perf. 11½*

Without Gum

1097 A587 6c blk, yel & red 60 30

Third International Folksong Festival.

Catalogue prices for unused stamps up to mid-1953 are for hinged copies matching the condition specified in this volume's introduction.

Catalytic Cracking Plant — A588

1968, Oct. 4

Without Gum

1098 A588 6c bl & multi 60 40

Issued to commemorate the 15th anniversary of Petrobras, the national oil company.

Child Protection A589

Whimsical Girl — A590

Design: 5c, School boy walking toward the sun.

Perf. 11½x11, 11x11½

1968, Oct. 16 Litho. Unwmk.

Without Gum

1099 A590 5c gray & lt bl 50 40
1100 A589 10c brt bl, dk red & blk 60 30
1101 A590 20c multi 75 30

Issued to commemorate the 22nd anniversary of the United Nations Children's Fund.

Children with Books A591

1968, Oct. 23 *Perf. 11x11½*

Without Gum

1102 A591 5c multi 35 25

Issued to publicize Book Week.

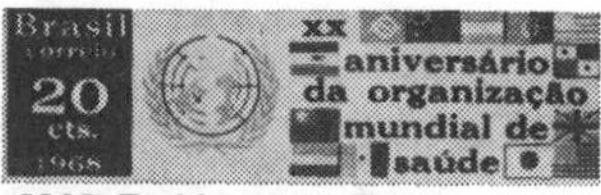

U.N. Emblem and Flags — A592

1968, Oct. 24 *Perf. 11½x11*

Without Gum

1103 A592 20c blk & multi 75 35

Issued to commemorate the 20th anniversary of the World Health Organization.

Jean Baptiste Debret, Self-portrait — A593

Perf. 11x11½

1968, Oct. 30 Litho. Unwmk.

Without Gum

1104 A593 10c dk gray & pale yel 50 25

Issued to commemorate the bi-centenary of the birth of Jean Baptiste Debret, (1768-1848), French painter who worked in Brazil (1816-31). Design includes his "Burden Bearer."

Queen Elizabeth II — A594

1968, Nov. 4 *Perf. 11½*

Without Gum

1105 A594 70c lt bl & multi 1.75 1.00

Issued to commemorate the visit of Queen Elizabeth II of Great Britain.

Francisco Braga — A595

Perf. 11½x11

1968, Nov. 19 Wmk. 267

1106 A595 5c dl red brn 40 25

Issued to commemorate the centenary of the birth of Antonio Francisco Braga, composer of the Hymn of the Flag.

Brazilian Flag — A596

1968, Nov. 19 Unwmk. *Perf. 11½*

Without Gum

1107 A596 10c multi 50 30

Issued for Flag Day.

Clasped Hands and Globe A597

Perf. 11x11½

1968, Nov. 25 Typo. Unwmk.

Without Gum

1108 A597 5c multi 30 25

Issued for Voluntary Blood Donor's Day.

Old Locomotive — A598

1968, Nov. 28 Litho. *Perf. 11½*

Without Gum

1109 A598 5c multi 1.00 50

Centenary of the Sao Paulo Railroad.

Bell — A599

Francisco Caldas, Jr. — A600

Design: 6c, Santa Claus and boy.

1968 Without Gum *Perf. 11½x11*

1110 A599 5c multi 50 25
1111 A599 6c multi 50 25

Christmas 1968.
Issue dates: 5c, Dec. 12; 6c, Dec. 20.

1968, Dec. 13

Without Gum

1112 A600 10c crim & blk 35 20

Issued to commemorate the centenary of the birth of Francisco Caldas, Jr., journalist and founder of Correio de Povo, newspaper.

Map of Brazil, War Memorial and Reservists' Emblem — A601

Perf. 11x11½

1968, Dec. 16 Photo. Wmk. 267

1113 A601 5c bl grn & org brn 50 25

Issued for Reservists' Day.

Radar Antenna A602

Viscount of Rio Branco A603

Perf. 11½x11

1969, Feb. 28 Litho. Unwmk.
Without Gum

1114 A602 30c ultra, lt bl & blk 1.25 60

Issued to publicize the inauguration of EMBRATEL, satellite communications ground station bringing U.S. television to Brazil via Telstar.

1969, Mar. 16
Without Gum

1115 A603 5c blk & buff 35 25

Issued to commemorate the 150th anniversary of the birth of Jose Maria da Silva Paranhos, Viscount of Rio Branco (1819-1880), statesman.

St. Gabriel — A604

1969, Mar. 24
Without Gum

1116 A604 5c multi 50 25

Issued to honor St. Gabriel as patron saint of telecommunications.

Shoemaker's Last and Globe — A605

Perf. 11x11½

1969, Mar. 29 Litho. Unwmk.
Without Gum

1117 A605 5c multi 35 25

Issued to publicize the 4th International Shoe Fair, Novo Hamburgo.

Allan Kardec A606

1969, Mar. 31 Photo. Wmk. 267

1118 A606 5c brt grn & org brn 40 25

Issued to commemorate the centenary of the death of Allan Kardec (pen name of Leon Hippolyto Denizard Rivail, 1803-1869), French physician and spiritist.

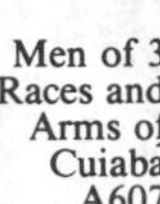

Men of 3 Races and Arms of Cuiaba A607

1969, Apr. 8 Litho. Unwmk.
Without Gum

1119 A607 5c blk & multi 30 25

Issued to commemorate the 250th anniversary of the founding of Cuiaba, capital of Matto Grosso.

State Mint — A608

1969, Apr. 11 *Perf. 11½*
Without Gum

1120 A608 5c ol bis & org 60 40

Issued to commemorate the opening of the state money printing plant.

Brazilian Stamps and Emblem A609

Perf. 11x11½

1969, Apr. 30 Litho. Unwmk.
Without Gum

1121 A609 5c multi 40 25

Issued to commemorate the 50th anniversary of the Sao Paulo Philatelic Society.

St. Anne, Baroque Statue — A610

1969, May 8 *Perf. 11½*
Without Gum

1122 A610 5c lem & multi 60 40

Issued for Mother's Day.

ILO Emblem A611

Perf. 11x11½

1969, May 13 Photo. Wmk. 267

1123 A611 5c dp rose red & gold 35 20

Issued to commemorate the 50th anniversary of the International Labor Organization.

Diving Platform and Swimming Pool A612

Mother and Child at Window A613

Lithographed and Photogravure
Perf. 11½x11

1969, June 13 Unwmk.
Without Gum

1124 A612 20c bis brn, blk & bl grn 1.00 50

40th anniversary of the Cearense Water Sports Club, Fortaleza.

1969 Litho. *Perf. 11½*

Designs: 20c, Modern sculpture by Felicia Leirner. 50c, "The Sun Sets in Brasilia," by Danilo di Prete. 1cr, Angelfish, painting by Aldemir Martins.

Size: 24x36mm.

1125 A613 10c org & multi 85 30

Size: 33x34mm.

1126 A613 20c red & multi 85 60

Size: 33x53mm.

1127 A613 50c yel & multi 3.00 1.50

Without Gum

1128 A613 1cr gray & multi 4.00 1.50

Issued to publicize the 10th Biennial Art Exhibition, Sao Paulo, Sept.-Dec. 1969.

Angelfish A614

Fish — A615

Fish: 10c, Tetra. 15c, Piranha. No. 1130c, Megalamphodus megalopterus. 30c, Black tetra.

Wmk. 267

1969, July 21 Litho. *Perf. 11½*

1129 A614 20c multi 1.00 50

Souvenir Sheet

1969, July 24 Unwmk. ***Imperf.***

1130 A615 Sheet of four 5.50 *7.00*
- ***a.*** 10c yel & multi 1.00 1.00
- ***b.*** 15c brt bl & multi 1.00 1.00
- ***c.*** 20c grn & multi 1.00 1.00
- ***d.*** 30c org & multi 1.00 1.00

Issued to publicize the work of ACAPI, an organization devoted to the preservation and development of fish in Brazil.

No. 1130 contains 4 stamps (size: 38½x21mm.). Greenish margin with commemorative inscription, marine life design and ACAPI emblem. Size: 132½x98½mm.

L. O. Teles de Menezes A616

Mailman A617

Perf. 11½x11

1969, July 26 Photo. Wmk. 267

1131 A616 50c dp org & bl grn 1.75 1.50

Centenary of Spiritism press in Brazil.

1969, Aug. 1

1132 A617 30c blue 1.75 1.00

Issued for Stamp Day.

Map of Brazil A618

Gen. Tasso Fragoso A620

Railroad Bridge A619

Perf. 11½

1969, Aug. 25 Unwmk. Litho.
Without Gum

1133 A618 10c lt ultra, grn & yel 30 25

Perf. 11x11½

1134 A619 20c multi 1.00 40

Perf. 11½x11

Engr. Wmk. 267
With Gum

1135 A620 20c green 1.00 50

No. 1133 honors the Army as guardian of security; No. 1134, as promoter of development. No. 1135 commemorates the birth centenary of Gen. Tasso Fragoso.

Jupia Dam, Parana River — A621

Perf. 11½

1969, Sept. 10 Litho. Unwmk.
Without Gum

1136 A621 20c lt bl & multi 50 50

Issued to commemorate the inauguration of the Jupia Dam, part of the Urubupunga hydroelectric system serving Sao Paulo.

Gandhi and Spinning Wheel A622

1969, Oct. 2 ***Perf. 11x11½***

1137 A622 20c yel & blk 50 30

Issued to commemorate the centenary of the birth of Mohandas K. Gandhi (1869-1948), leader in India's fight for independence.

Santos Dumont, Eiffel Tower and Module Landing on Moon — A623

1969, Oct. 17 *Perf. 11½*
Without Gum
1138 A623 50c dk bl & multi 2.50 1.50

Man's first landing on the moon, July 20, 1969. See note after U.S. No. C76.

Smelting Plant — A624

1969, Oct. 26 Unwmk. *Perf. 11½*
Without Gum
1139 A624 20c multi 50 40

Expansion of Brazil's steel industry.

Steel Furnace A625

1969, Oct. 31 **Litho.**
Without Gum
1140 A625 10c yel & multi 50 40

25th anniversary of Acesita Steel Works.

Water Vendor, by J. B. Debret — A626

Design: 30c, Street Scene, by Debret.

1969-70
Without Gum
1141 A626 20c multi 1.50 50
1141A A626 30c multi 1.50 1.00

Issued to commemorate the 200th anniversary of the birth of Jean Baptiste Debret (1768-1848), painter.

Issue dates: 20c, Nov. 5, 1969; 30c, May 19, 1970.

Exhibition Emblem — A627

1969, Nov. 15 *Perf. 11½x11*
Without Gum
1142 A627 10c multi 50 25

Issued to publicize the ABUEXPO 69 Philatelic Exposition, Sao Paulo, Nov. 15-23.

Plane — A628

1969, Nov. 23
Without Gum
1143 A628 50c multi 3.50 1.50

Issued to publicize the year of the expansion of the national aviation industry.

Pelé Scoring A629

1969-70
Without Gum
1144 A629 10c multi 30 30
Souvenir Sheet
Imperf
1145 A629 75c multi ('70) 3.50 3.50

Issued to commemorate the 1,000th goal scored by Pelé, Brazilian soccer player.

No. 1145 contains one imperf. stamp with simulated perforations, commemorative marginal inscription. Size: 80x119mm.

Issued dates: 10c, Nov. 28, 1969. 75c, Jan. 23, 1970.

Madonna and Child from Villa Velha Monastery A630

Perf. 11½
1969, Dec. Unwmk. Litho.
Without Gum
1146 A630 10c gold & multi 50 25
Souvenir Sheet
Imperf
1147 A630 75c gold & multi 13.00 *15.00*

Christmas 1969.

No. 1147 has simulated perforations; commemorative inscription and Christmas decorations in margin. Size: 136x102mm.

Issue dates: 10c, Dec. 8; 75c, Dec. 18.

Destroyer and Submarine A631

Perf. 11x11½
1969, Dec. 9 Engr. Wmk. 267
1148 A631 5c bluish gray 50 25

Issued for Navy Day.

Dr. Herman Blumenau A632

1969, Dec. 26 *Perf. 11½*
1149 A632 20c gray grn 1.25 40

Issued to commemorate the 150th anniversary of the birth of Dr. Herman Blumenau (1819-1899), founder of Blumenau, Santa Catarina State.

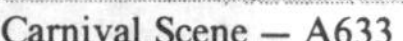

Carnival Scene — A633

Sugarloaf Mountain, Mask, Confetti and Streamers A634

Designs: 5c, Jumping boy and 2 women (vert.). 20c, Clowns. 50c, Drummer.

1969-70 Litho. Unwmk.
Without Gum
1150 A633 5c multi 50 30
1151 A633 10c multi 50 30
1152 A633 20c multi 65 40
1153 A634 30c multi ('70) 3.75 3.00
1154 A634 50c multi ('70) 3.50 2.50
Nos. 1150-1154 (5) 8.90 6.50

Carico Carnival, Rio de Janeiro.

Issue dates: Nos. 1150-1152, Dec. 29, 1969. Nos. 1153-1154, Feb. 5, 1970.

Opening Bars of "Il Guarani" with Antonio Carlos Gomes Conducting A635

1970, Mar. 19 Litho. *Perf. 11½*
Without Gum
1155 A635 20c blk, yel, gray & brn 75 40

Issued to commemorate the centenary of the opera Il Guarani, by Antonio Carlos Gomes.

Church of Penha A636

1970, Apr. 6 Unwmk. *Perf. 11½*
Without Gum
1156 A636 20c blk & multi 40 20

Issued to commemorate the 400th anniversary of the Church of Penha, State of Esperito Santo.

Assembly Building A637

Designs: 50c, Reflecting Pool. 1cr, Presidential Palace.

1970, Apr. 21
Without Gum
1157 A637 20c multi 1.50 75
1158 A637 50c multi 3.75 3.00
1159 A637 1cr multi 3.75 3.00

10th anniversary of Brasilia.

Symbolic Water Design A638

1970, May 5 Unwmk. *Perf. 11½*
Without Gum
1161 A638 50c multi 3.00 3.00

Issued to publicize the Rondon Project for the development of the Amazon River basin.

Marshal Manoel Luiz Osorio and Osorio Arms — A639

1970, May 8
Without Gum
1162 A639 20c multi 2.00 1.00

Issued to commemorate the inauguration of the Marshal Osorio Historical Park.

Madonna, from San Antonio Monastery, Rio de Janeiro A640

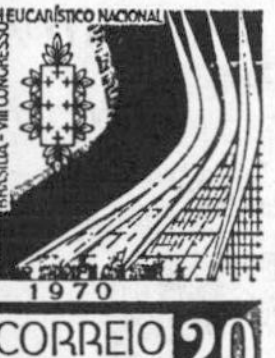
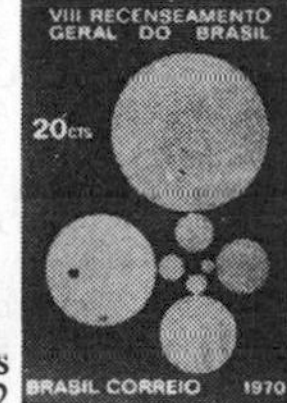
Detail from Brasilia Cathedral — A641

1970, May 10
Without Gum

1163 A640 20c multi 60 50

Issued for Mother's Day.

1970, May 27 Engr. Wmk. 267

1164 A641 20c lt yel grn 40 30

8th National Eucharistic Congress, Brasilia.

Census Symbol — A642

Perf. 11½
1970, June 22 Unwmk. Litho.
Without Gum

1165 A642 20c grn & yel 75 75

Issued to publicize the 8th general census.

Soccer Cup, Maps of Brazil and Mexico A643

Swedish Flag and Player Holding Rimet Cup — A644

Designs: 2cr, Chilean flag and soccer. 3cr, Mexican flag and soccer.

1970
Without Gum

1166 A643 50c blk, lt bl & gold 1.00 1.00
1167 A644 1cr pink & multi 3.00 1.50
1168 A644 2cr gray & multi 6.00 1.50
1169 A644 3cr multi 5.00 1.00

Issued to commemorate the 9th World Soccer Championships for the Jules Rimet Cup, Mexico City, May 30-June 21. No. 1166 commemorates Brazil's victory.

Issue dates: No. 1166, June 24; Nos. 1167-1169, Aug. 4.

Corcovado Christ and Map of South America A645

1970, July 18
Without Gum

1170 A645 50c brn, dk red & bl 3.00 3.00

Issued to publicize the 6th World Congress of Marist Brothers' Alumni.

Pandia Calogeras — A646

Perf. 11½x11
1970, Aug. 25 Photo. Unwmk.

1171 A646 20c bl grn 75 50

Issued to honor Pandia Calogeras, Minister of War.

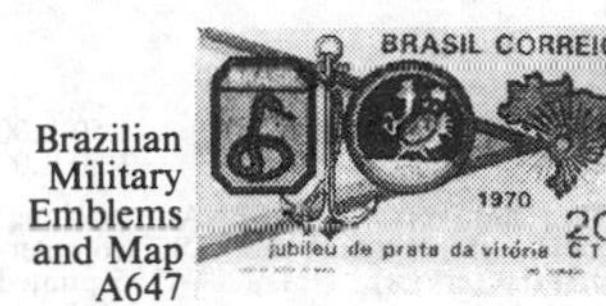
Brazilian Military Emblems and Map A647

Perf. 11x11½
1970, Sept. 8 Litho. Unwmk.
Without Gum

1172 A647 20c gray & multi 60 50

25th anniversary of victory in World War II.

Annunciation (Brazilian Primitive Painting) A648

1970, Sept. 29 Perf. 11½
Without Gum

1173 A648 20c multi 1.75 1.00

Issued for St. Gabriel's (patron saint of communications) Day.

Boy in Library A649

U.N. Emblem A650

1970, Oct. 23
Without Gum

1174 A649 20c multi 1.60 1.00

Issued to publicize Book Week.

1970, Oct. 24
Without Gum

1175 A650 50c dk bl, lt bl & sil 2.00 1.50

25th anniversary of the United Nations.

Rio de Janeiro, 1820 — A651

Designs: 50c, LUBRAPEX 70 emblem. 1cr, Rio de Janeiro with Sugar Loaf Mountain, 1970. No. 1179, like 20c.

1970, Oct.
Without Gum

1176 A651 20c multi 2.00 1.00
1177 A651 50c yel brn & blk 4.00 2.00
1178 A651 1cr multi 4.00 3.75

Souvenir Sheet
Imperf

1179 A651 1cr multi 13.00 *17.00*

Issued to commemorate LUBRAPEX 70, third Portuguese-Brazilian Philatelic Exhibition, Rio de Janeiro, Oct. 24-31. No. 1179 contains one stamp, black marginal inscription. Size: 60x80mm.

Issue dates: Nos. 1176-1178, Oct. 27. No. 1179, Oct. 31.

Holy Family by Candido Portinari A652

1970, Dec. Litho. Perf. 11½
Without Gum

1180 A652 50c multi 1.50 1.50

Souvenir Sheet
Imperf

1181 A652 1cr multi 17.00 *24.00*

Christmas 1970. No. 1181 contains one stamp with simulated perforations. Light yellow green margin with red and black inscription. Size: 106x52mm. Issue dates: 50c, Dec. 1; 1cr, Dec. 8.

Battleship A653

CIH Emblem A654

1970, Dec. 11 Litho. Perf. 11½
Without Gum

1182 A653 20c multi 1.75 75

Navy Day.

1971, Mar. 28 Litho. Perf. 11½
Without Gum

1183 A654 50c blk & red 2.00 1.75

Third Inter-American Housing Congress, Mar. 27-Apr. 3.

Links Around Globe — A655

1971, Mar. 31 Litho. Perf. 12½x11
Without Gum

1184 A655 20c grn, yel, blk & red 85 50

International year against racial discrimination.

Morpho Melacheilus — A656

Design: 1cr, Papilio thoas brasiliensis.

Perf. 11x11½
1971, Apr. 28 Litho. Unwmk.
Without Gum

1185 A656 20c multi 1.50 60
1186 A656 1cr multi 7.50 4.00

Madonna and Child — A657

1971, May 9 Litho. Perf. 11½
Without Gum

1187 A657 20c multi 1.50 40

Mother's Day, 1971.

Basketball A658

1971, May 19
Without Gum

1188 A658 70c multi 2.25 1.50

6th World Women's Basketball Championship.

Certain countries cancel stamps in full sheets and sell them (usually with gum) for less than face value. Dealers generally sell "CTO".

Map of Trans-Amazon Highway
A660 A659

Perf. 11½

1971, July 1 Unwmk. Litho.

Without Gum

1189 A659 40c multi 7.50 3.00
1190 A660 1cr multi 7.50 6.00

Trans-Amazon Highway. Nos. 1189-1190 printed se-tenant in sheets of 28 (4x7). Horizontal rows contain 2 pairs of 1189-1190 with a label between. Each label carries different inscription.

Man's Head, by Victor Mairelles de Lima — A661

Design: 1cr, Arab Violinist, by Pedro Americo.

1971, Aug. 1

Without Gum

1191 A661 40c pink & multi 2.00 1.00
1192 A661 1cr gray & multi 5.00 2.00

Stamp Day.

Duke of Caxias and Map of Brazil — A662

1971, Aug. 23 Photo.

1193 A662 20c yel grn & red brn 75 60

Army Day.

Anita Garibaldi — A663

1971, Aug. 30 Litho.

Without Gum

1194 A663 20c multi 75 50

Anita Garibaldi (1821-1849), heroine in liberation of Brazil.

Xavante Jet and Santos Dumont's Plane, 1910 — A664

1971, Sept. 6

Without Gum

1195 A664 40c yel & multi 2.00 90

First flight of Xavante jet plane.

Flags and Map of Central American Nations A665

"71" in French Flag Colors A666

1971, Sept. 15

Without Gum

1196 A665 40c ocher & multi 1.60 60

Sesquicentennial of the independence of Central American nations.

1971, Sept. 16

Without Gum

1197 A666 1.30cr ultra & multi 2.00 1.50

French Exhibition.

Black Mother, by Lucillo de Albuquerque A667

Archangel Gabriel A668

1971, Sept. 28

Without Gum

1198 A667 40c multi 1.00 60

Centenary of law guaranteeing personal freedom starting at birth.

1971, Sept. 29 *Perf. 11½x11*

Without Gum

1199 A668 40c multi 1.00 75

St. Gabriel's Day.

Bridge over River — A669

Children's Drawings: 35c, People crossing bridge. 60c, Woman with hat.

1971, Oct. 25 *Perf. 11½*

Without Gum

1200 A669 35c pink, bl & blk 75 60
1201 A669 45c blk & multi 2.00 60
1202 A669 60c ol & multi 75 60

Children's Day.

Werkhäuserii Superba — A670

1971, Nov. 16

Without Gum

1203 A670 40c bl & multi 3.00 1.00

In memory of Carlos Werkhauser, botanist.

Greek Key Pattern "25" — A671

Design: 40c, like 20c but inscribed "sesc / servicio social / do comercio."

1971, Dec. 3

Without Gum

1204 A671 20c blk & bl 1.50 1.00
1205 A671 40c blk & org 1.50 1.00

25th anniversary of SENAC (national apprenticeship system) and SESC (commercial social service). Nos. 1204-1205 printed se-tenant.

Gunboat A672

1971, Dec. 8 *Perf. 11*

Without Gum

1206 A672 20c bl & multi 1.00 50

Navy Day.

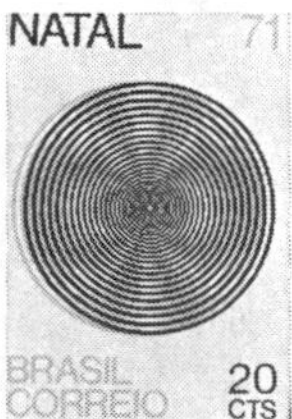

Cross and Circles — A673

Washing of Bonfim Church, Salvador, Bahia — A674

1971, Dec. 11

1207 A673 20c car & bl 50 40
1208 A673 75c sil & gray 1.00 *3.00*
1209 A673 1.30cr blk, yel, grn & bl 6.00 2.50

Christmas 1971.

1972, Feb. 18 Litho. *Perf. 11½x11*

Designs: 40c, Grape Festival, Rio Grande do Sul. 75c, Festival of the Virgin of Nazareth, Belem. 1.30cr, Winter Arts Festival, Ouro Preto. Without Gum

1210 A674 20c sil & multi 1.50 75
1211 A674 40c sil & multi 2.75 75
1212 A674 75c sil & multi 2.75 3.00
1213 A674 1.30cr sil & multi 6.00 3.00

Pres. Lanusse and Flag of Argentina A675

1972, Mar. 13 *Perf. 11x11½*

Without Gum

1214 A675 40c bl & multi 3.00 2.50

Visit of Lt. Gen. Alejandro Agustin Lanusse, president of Argentina.

Presidents Castello Branco, Costa e Silva and Garrastazu Medici A676

1972, Mar. 29

Without Gum

1215 A676 20c emer & multi 1.50 60

Anniversary of 1964 revolution.

Post Office Emblem — A677

Perf. 11½x11

1972, Apr. 10 Photo. Unwmk.

1216 A677 20c red brn 2.00 20

No. 1216 is luminescent.

Pres. Thomas and Portuguese Flag — A678

1972, Apr. 22 Litho. *Perf. 11*

Without Gum

1217 A678 75c ol brn & multi 2.50 2.00

Visit of Pres. Americo Thomas of Portugal to Brazil, Apr. 22-27.

Soil Research (CPRM) A679

1972, May 3 *Perf. 11½*

Without Gum

1218 A679 20c *shown* 1.50 50
1219 A679 40c *Offshore oil rig* 3.50 85
1220 A679 75c *Hydroelectric dam* 1.50 1.75
1221 A679 1.30cr *Iron ore production* 3.50 1.40

Industrial development. Stamps are inscribed with names of industrial firms.

Souvenir Sheet

SEMANA·DE·ARTE·
MODERNA-1922
BRASIL CORREIO 1,00

Poster for Modern Art Week 1922
A680

1972, May 5

1222	A680	1cr blk & car	30.00	30.00

50th anniversary of Modern Art Week. No. 1222 contains one stamp. Silver margin with black inscription. Size: 78x110mm.

Mailman, Map of Brazil and Letters
A681

Designs: 45c, "Telecommunications" (vert.). 60c, Tropospheric scatter system. 70c, Road map of Brazil and worker.

1972, May 26
Without Gum

1223	A681	35c bl & multi	1.50	50
1224	A681	45c sil & multi	1.75	1.75
1225	A681	60c blk & multi	1.75	1.50
1226	A681	70c multi	2.00	1.50

Unification of communications in Brazil.

Development Type and

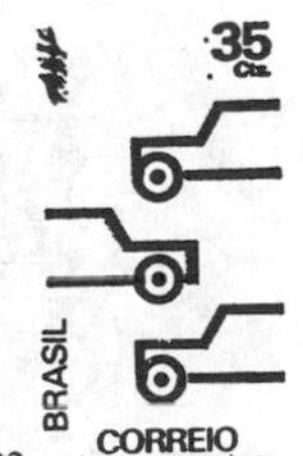

Automobiles — A682

Designs: 45c, Ships. 70c, Ingots.

Perf. 11x11½, 11½x11

1972, June 21 **Photo.**

1227	A682	35c blk, mag & org	1.25	50

Litho.

1228	A679	45c lil & multi	1.25	60
1229	A679	70c vio & multi	1.25	40

Industrial development. The 35c is luminescent.

Soccer — A683

Designs: 75c, Folk music. 1.30cr, Plastic arts.

Perf. 11½x11

1972, July 7 **Photo.** **Unwmk.**

1230	A683	20c blk & yel	1.00	50
1231	A683	75c blk & ver	2.00	3.50
1232	A683	1.30cr blk & ultra	4.00	3.50

150th anniversary of independence. No. 1230 publicizes the 1972 sports tournament, a part of independence celebrations.

Nos. 1230-1232 are luminescent.

Souvenir Sheet

Shout of Independence, by Pedro Américo de Figueiredo e Melo — A684

1972, July 19 **Litho.** ***Perf. 11½***
Without Gum

1233	A684	1cr multi	6.00	*10.00*

4th Interamerican Philatelic Exhibition, EXFILBRA, Rio de Janeiro, Aug 26-Sept. 2. No. 1233 contains one stamp (55x37mm.). Black and multicolored margin with white inscription. Size: 125x87mm.

Figurehead
A685

Designs: 60c, Gauchos dancing fandango. 75c, Acrobats (capoeira). 1.15cr, Karajá (ceramic) doll. 1.30cr, Mock bullfight (bumba meu boi).

1972, Aug. 6
Without Gum

1234	A685	45c multi	1.00	35
1235	A685	60c org & multi	2.00	1.50
1236	A685	75c gray & multi	35	35
1237	A685	1.15cr multi	65	65
1238	A685	1.30cr yel & multi	6.00	2.00
		Nos. 1234-1238 (5)	10.00	4.85

Brazilian folklore.

Map of Brazil, by Diego Homem, 1568 — A686

Designs: 1cr, Map of Americas, by Nicholas Visscher, 1652. 2cr, Map of Americas, by Lopo Homem, 1519.

1972, Aug. 26 **Litho.** ***Perf. 11½***
Without Gum

1239	A686	70c multi	50	50
1240	A686	1cr multi	9.00	1.00
1241	A686	2cr multi	4.50	1.50

4th Inter-American Philatelic Exhibition, EXFILBRA, Rio de Janeiro, Aug. 26-Sept. 2.

Dom Pedro Proclaimed Emperor, by Jean Baptiste Debrçt
A687

Designs: 30c, Founding of Brazil (people with imperial flag; vert.). 1cr, Coronation of Emperor Dom Pedro (vert.). 2cr, Dom Pedro commemorative medal. 3.50cr, Independence Monument, Ipiranga.

1972, Sept. 4 **Litho.** ***Perf. 11½x11***

1242	A687	30c yel & grn	1.50	1.50
1243	A687	70c pink & rose lil	1.50	1.00
1244	A687	1cr buff & red brn	10.00	1.50
1245	A687	2cr pale yel & blk	5.00	1.50
1246	A687	3.50cr gray & blk	9.00	5.00
		Nos. 1242-1246 (5)	27.00	10.50

Sesquicentennial of independence.

Souvenir Sheet

"Automobile Race" — A688

1972, Nov. 14 ***Perf. 11½***

1247	A688	2cr multi	13.50	17.00

Emerson Fittipaldi, Brazilian world racing champion. No. 1247 contains one stamp. Multicolored margin with race car design and black inscription. Size: 120x86½mm.

Numeral and Post Office Emblem — A689

Möbius Strip
A689a

Perf. 11½x11

1972-75 **Unwmk.** **Photo.**

1248	A689	5c orange	35	5
a.		Wmk. 267	20	8
1249	A689	10c brn ('73)	20	5
a.		Wmk. 267	4.00	8
1250	A689	15c brt bl ('75)	14	5
1251	A689	20c ultra	35	5
1252	A689	25c sep ('75)	25	5
1253	A689	30c dp car	40	10
1254	A689	40c dk grn ('73)	20	10
1255	A689	50c olive	30	10
1256	A689	70c red lil ('75)	30	10

Engr. ***Perf. 11½***

1257	A689a	1cr lil ('74)	45	10
1258	A689a	2cr grnsh bl ('74)	65	12
1259	A689a	4cr org & vio ('75)	1.40	20
1260	A689a	5cr brn, car & buff ('74)	2.00	20
1261	A689a	10cr grn, blk & buff ('74)	4.50	30
		Nos. 1248-1261 (14)	11.49	1.57

The 5cr and 10cr have beige lithographed multiple Post Office emblem underprint.

Nos. 1248-1261 are luminescent. Nos. 1248a and 1249a are not.

Hand Writing "Mobral"
A690

Designs: 20c, Multiracial group and population growth curve. 1cr, People and hands holding house. 2cr, People, industrial scene and upward arrow.

1972, Nov. 28 **Litho.** ***Perf. 11½***
Without Gum

1262	A690	10c blk & multi	25	50
1263	A690	20c blk & multi	1.25	75
1264	A690	1cr blk & multi	11.00	30
1265	A690	2cr blk & multi	2.50	75

Publicity for: "Mobral" literacy campaign (10c); Centenary of census (20c); Housing and retirement fund (1cr); Growth of gross national product (2cr).

Congress Building, Brasilia, by Oscar Niemeyer, and "Os Guerreiros," by Bruno Giorgi — A691

1972, Dec. 4
Without Gum

1266	A691	1cr bl, blk & org	11.00	6.00

Meeting of National Congress, Brasilia, Dec. 4 8.

Holy Family (Clay Figurines)
A692

Retirement Plan
A693

1972, Dec. 13 **Photo.** ***Perf. 11½x11***

1267	A692	20c ocher & blk	1.00	50

Christmas 1972. Luminescent.

Perf. 11½x11, 11x11½

1972, Dec. 20 **Litho.**

Designs: No. 1269, School children and traffic lights (horiz.). 70c, Dr. Oswaldo Cruz with Red Cross, caricature. 2cr, Produce, fish and cattle (horiz.).

Without Gum

1268	A693	10c blk, bl & dl org	50	50
1269	A693	10c org & multi	1.00	1.00
1270	A693	70c blk, red & brn	9.00	3.75
1271	A693	2cr grn & multi	15.00	6.50

Publicity for: Agricultural workers' assistance program (No. 1268); highway and transportation development (No. 1269); centenary of the birth of Dr. Oswaldo Cruz (1872-1917), Director of Public Health Institute (70c); agricultural and cattle export (2cr). Nos. 1268-1271 are luminescent.

Sailing Ship, Navy
A694

Designs: 10c, Monument, Brazilian Expeditionary Force. No. 1274, Plumed helmet, Army. No. 1275, Rocket, Air Force.

Lithographed and Engraved

1972, Dec. 28 ***Perf. 11x11½***

Without Gum

1272 A694 10c brn, dk brn & blk 2.00 1.50
1273 A694 30c lt ultra, grn & blk 2.00 1.50
1274 A694 30c yel grn, bl grn & blk 2.00 1.50
1275 A694 30c lil, mar & blk 2.00 1.50

Armed Forces Day. Nos. 1272-1275 are se-tenant in blocks of 4 with greenish blue label showing Navy, Army and Air Force insignia in black.

Rotary Emblem and Cogwheels A695

Perf. 11½

1973, Mar. 21 Litho. Unwmk.

1276 A695 1cr ultra, grnsh bl & yel 2.50 1.50

Rotary International serving Brazil 50 years.

Swimming A696

Designs: No. 1278, Gymnastics. No. 1279, Volleyball (vert.).

1973 Photo. *Perf. 11x11½, 11½x11*

1277 A696 40c brt bl & red brn 50 50
1278 A696 40c grn & org brn 3.75 1.00
1279 A696 40c vio & org brn 1.00 1.00

Issue dates: No. 1277, Apr. 19; No. 1278, May 22; No. 1279, Oct. 15.

Flag of Paraguay A697

Perf. 11½

1973, Apr. 27 Litho. Unwmk.

1280 A697 70c multi 3.00 1.25

Visit of Pres. Alfredo Stroessner of Paraguay, Apr. 25-27.

"Communications" — A698

Design: 1cr, Neptune, map of South America and Africa.

1973, May 5 ***Perf. 11x11½***

1281 A698 70c multi 1.25 1.00
1282 A698 1cr multi 6.00 3.00

Inauguration of the Ministry of Communications Building, Brasilia (70c); and of the first underwater telephone cable between South America and Europe, Bracan 1 (1cr).

Congress Emblem — A699

1973, May 19 ***Perf. 11½x11***

1283 A699 1cr org & pur 4.50 3.00

24th Congress of the International Chamber of Commerce, Rio de Janeiro, May 19-26.

Swallowtailed Manakin — A700

Birds: No. 1285, Orange-backed oriole. No. 1286, Brazilian ruby (hummingbird).

1973 Litho. ***Perf. 11x11½***

1284 A700 20c multi 50 20
1285 A700 20c multi 50 20
1286 A700 20c multi 50 20

Issue dates: No. 1284, May 26; No. 1285, June 6; No. 1286, June 19.

Tourists A701

1973, June 28 Litho. ***Perf. 11x11½***

1287 A701 70c multi 1.50 1.00

National Tourism Year.

Conference at Itu — A702

Satellite and Multi-spectral Image — A703

1973 ***Perf. 11½x11***

1288 A702 20c *shown* 75 50
1289 A702 20c *Decorated wagon* 75 50
1290 A702 20c *Indian* 75 50
1291 A702 20c *Graciosa Road* 75 50

Centenary of the Itu Convention (1288); sesquicentennial of the July 2 episode (1289); 400th anniversary of the founding of Niteroi (1290); centenary of Graciosa Road (1291).

Issue dates: No. 1291, July 29; others July 2.

1973, July 11 ***Perf. 11½***

Designs: 70c, Official opening of Engineering School, 1913. 1cr, Möbius strips and "IMPA."

1292 A703 20c blk & multi 30 50
1293 A703 70c dk bl & multi 2.50 1.25
1294 A703 1cr lil & multi 3.50 1.25

Institute for Space Research (20c); School of Engineering, Itajuba, 60th anniversary (70c); Institute for Pure and Applied Mathematics (1cr).

Santos-Dumont and 14-Bis Plane — A704

Designs (Santos-Dumont and): 70c, No. 6 Balloon and Eiffel Tower. 2cr Demoiselle plane.

Lithographed and Engraved

1973, July 20 ***Perf. 11x11½***

1295 A704 20c lt grn, brt grn & brn 1.25 30
1296 A704 70c yel, rose red & brn 3.00 1.50
1297 A704 2cr bl, vio bl & brn 3.00 1.50

Centenary of the birth of Alberto Santos-Dumont (1873-1932), aviation pioneer.

Mercator Map A705

Design: No. 1299, Same, red border on top and at left.

Photogravure and Engraved

1973, Aug. 1 Wmk. 267

1298 A705 40c red & blk 3.50 1.50
1299 A705 40c red & blk 3.00 3.00
Block of 4 30.00 15.00

Stamp Day. Nos. 1298-1299 are printed se-tenant horizontally and tete beche vertically in sheets of 55. Blocks of 4 have red border all around.

Gonçalves Dias — A706

Perf. 11½x11

1973, Aug. 10 Wmk. 267

1300 A706 40c vio & blk 1.00 50

Sesquicentenary of the birth of Antonio Gon-çalves Dias (1823-1864), poet.

Souvenir Sheet

Copernicus and Sun — A707

Perf. 11x11½

1973, Aug. 15 Litho. Unwmk.

1301 A707 1cr multi 4.50 5.00

500th anniversary of the birth of Nicolaus Copernicus (1473-1543), Polish astronomer. No. 1301 contains one stamp; multicolored margin. Size: 124x86mm.

Folklore Festival Banner — A708

1973, Aug. 22 ***Perf. 11½***

1302 A708 40c ultra & multi 1.25 60

Folklore Day, Aug. 22.

Masonic Emblem A709

1973, Aug. 24 Photo. ***Perf. 11x11½***

1303 A709 1cr Prus bl 3.50 2.00

Free Masons of Brazil, 1822-1973.

Nature Protection A710

Designs: No. 1305, Fire protection. No. 1306, Aviation safety. No. 1307, Safeguarding cultural heritage.

1973, Sept. 20 Litho. ***Perf. 11x11½***

1304 A710 40c brt grn & multi 75 40
1305 A710 40c dk bl & multi 75 40
1306 A710 40c lt bl & multi 75 40
1307 A710 40c pink & multi 75 40

Souvenir Sheet

St. Gabriel and Proclamation of Pope Paul VI — A711

Lithographed and Engraved

1973, Sept. 29 Unwmk. ***Perf. 11½***

1308 A711 1cr bis & blk 9.00 10.00

1st National Exhibition of Religious Philately, Rio de Janeiro, Sept. 29-Oct. 6. No. 1308 contains one stamp; bister margin and black inscription. Size: 123x87½mm.

St. Teresa — A712

Photogravure and Engraved

Perf. 11½x11

1973, Sept. 30 Wmk. 267

1309 A712 2cr dk org & brn 6.00 2.50

Centenary of the birth of St. Teresa of Lisieux, the Little Flower (1873-1897), Carmelite nun.

Monteiro Lobato and Emily A713

Perf. 11½

1973, Oct. 12 Litho. Unwmk.

1310 A713 40c *shown* 1.00 50
1311 A713 40c *Aunt Nastacia* 1.00 50
1312 A713 40c *Snubnose, Peter and Rhino* 1.00 50
1313 A713 40c *Viscount de Sabugosa* 1.00 50
1314 A713 40c *Dona Benta* 1.00 50
Block of 5 + label 5.00 5.00

Monteiro Lobato, author of children's books. Nos. 1310-1314 printed in sheets of 30 stamps and 6 labels.

Soapstone Sculpture of Isaiah (detail) — A714

Baroque Art in Brazil: No. 1316, Arabesque, gilded wood carving (horiz.). 70c, Father José Mauricio Nunes Garcia and music score. 1cr, Church door, Salvador, Bahia. 2cr, Angels, church ceiling painting by Manoel da Costa Athayde (horiz.).

1973, Nov. 5

1315 A714 40c multi 30 30
1316 A714 40c multi 30 30
1317 A714 70c multi 1.50 1.40
1318 A714 1cr multi 9.00 3.00
1319 A714 2cr multi 4.00 3.00
Nos. 1315-1319 (5) 15.10 8.00

Old and New Telephones — A715

1973, Nov. 28 ***Perf. 11x11½***

1320 A715 40c multi 50 40

50th anniversary of Brazilian Telephone Company.

Symbolic Angel — A716

1973, Nov. 30 ***Perf. 11½***

1321 A716 40c ver & multi 50 40

Christmas 1973.

"Gaiola" A717

Designs: River boats.

1973, Nov. 30 Litho. ***Perf. 11x11½***

1322 A717 40c *shown* 50 50
1323 A717 70c *"Regatao"* 1.50 1.50
1324 A717 1cr *"Jangada"* 6.50 3.00
1325 A717 2cr *"Saveiro"* 6.00 3.00

Nos. 1322-1325 are luminescent.

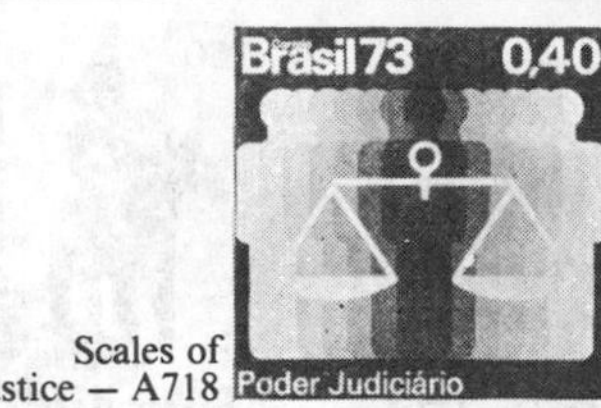

Scales of Justice — A718

1973, Dec. 5 ***Perf. 11½***

1326 A718 40c mag & vio 75 35

To honor the High Federal Court, created in 1891. Luminescent.

José Placido de Castro A719

Scarlet Ibis and Victoria Regia A720

Lithographed and Engraed
Perf. 11½x11

1973, Dec. 12 Wmk. 267

1327 A719 40c lil rose & blk 90 35

Centenary of the birth of Jose Placido de Castro, liberator of the State of Acre.

Perf. 11½x11

1973, Dec. 28 Litho. Unwmk.

Designs: 70c, Jaguar and spathodea campanulata. 1cr, Scarlet macaw and carnauba palm. 2cr, Rhea and coral tree.

1328 A720 40c brn & multi 1.50 50
1329 A720 70c brn & multi 3.75 2.00
1330 A720 1cr bis & multi 6.00 40
1331 A720 2cr bis & multi 11.00 4.50

Nos. 1328-1331 are luminescent.

Saci Perere, Mocking Goblin — A721

Characters from Brazilian Legends: 80c, Zumbi, last chief of rebellious slaves. 1cr, Chico Rei, African king. 1.30cr, Little Black Boy of the Pasture. 2.50cr, Iara, Queen of the Waters.

Perf. 11½x11

1974, Feb. 28 Litho. Unwmk.

Size: 21x39mm.

1332 A721 40c multi 50 25
1333 A721 80c multi 1.00 75
1334 A721 1cr multi 2.00 50

Perf. 11½

Size: 32½x33mm.

1335 A721 1.30cr multi 3.50 1.00
1336 A721 2.50cr multi 13.50 3.00
Nos. 1332-1336 (5) 20.50 5.50

Nos. 1332-1336 are luminescent.

Pres. Costa e Silva Bridge A722

1974, Mar. 11

1337 A722 40c multi 75 35

Inauguration of the Pres. Costa e Silva Bridge, Rio Niteroi, connecting Rio de Janeiro and Guanabara State.

"The Press" A723

1974, Mar. 25 ***Perf. 11½***

1338 A723 40c *shown* 60 40
1339 A723 40c *"Radio"* 30 30
1340 A723 40c *"Television"* 50 40

Communications Commemorations: No. 1338, bicentenary of first Brazilian newspaper, published in London by Hipolito da Costa; No. 1339, founding of the Radio Sociedade do Rio de Janeiro by Roquette Pinto; No. 1340, installation of first Brazilian television station by Assis Chateaubriand. Luminescent.

"Reconstruction" — A724

1974, Mar. 31

1341 A724 40c multi 1.00 45

10 years of progress. Luminescent.

Corcovado Christ, Marconi, Colors of Brazil and Italy — A725

1974, Apr. 25 Litho. ***Perf. 11½***

1342 A725 2.50cr multi 7.50 3.00

Centenary of the birth of Guglielmo Marconi (1874-1937), Italian physicist and inventor. Luminescent.

Stamp Printing Press, Stamp Designing A726

1974, May 6

1343 A726 80c multi 1.00 50

Brazilian mint.

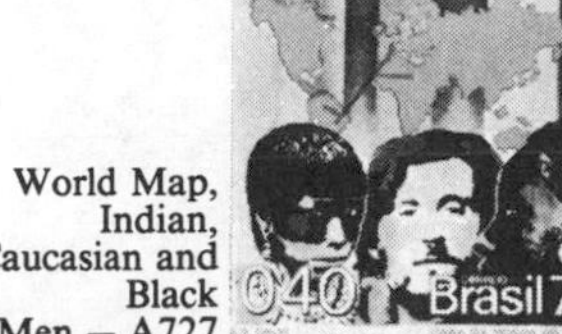

World Map, Indian, Caucasian and Black Men — A727

Designs (World Map and): No. 1345, Brazilians. No. 1346, Cabin and German horseback rider. No. 1347, Italian farm wagon. No. 1348, Japanese woman and torii.

1974, May 3 Unwmk.

1344 A727 40c multi 50 35
1345 A727 40c multi 30 30
1346 A727 2.50cr multi 5.00 1.75
1347 A727 2.50cr multi 7.50 1.75
1348 A727 2.50cr multi 1.75 1.00
Nos. 1344-1348 (5) 15.05 5.15

Ethnic and migration influences in Brazil.

Sandstone Cliffs, Sete Cidades National Park — A728

Design: 80c, Ruins of Cathedral of Sao Miguel das Missões.

Lithographed and Engraved

1974, June 8 ***Perf. 11x11½***

1349 A728 40c multi 1.00 50
1350 A728 80c multi 1.00 50

Tourist publicity.

Souvenir Sheet

Soccer — A729

1974, June 20 Litho. ***Perf. 11½***

1351 A729 2.50cr multi 4.50 6.00

World Cup Soccer Championship, Munich, June 13-July 7. No. 1351 has multicolored margin. Size: 130x95mm.

Church and College, Caraça A730

1974, July 6 Litho. ***Perf. 11x11½***

1352 A730 40c multi 75 35

Bicentenary of the College (Seminary) of Caraça.

Wave on Television Screen A731

1974, July 15 ***Perf. 11½***

1353 A731 40c blk & bl 50 40

TELEBRAS, Third Brazilian Congress of Telecommunications, Brasilia, July 15-20.

Fernao Dias Paes — A732

1974, July 21 ***Perf. 11½***
1354 A732 20c grn & multi 40 30

3rd centenary of the expedition led by Fernao Dias Paes exploring Minas Gerais and the passage from South to North in Brazil.

Mexican Flag — A733

1974, July 24 Litho. ***Perf. 11½***
1355 A733 80c multi 3.50 1.25

Visit of Pres. Luis Echeverria Alvares of Mexico, July 24-29.

Flags of Brazil and Germany A734

1974, Aug. 5 ***Perf. 11x11½***
1356 A734 40c multi 1.00 50

World Cup Soccer Championship, 1974, victory of German Federal Republic.

Souvenir Sheet

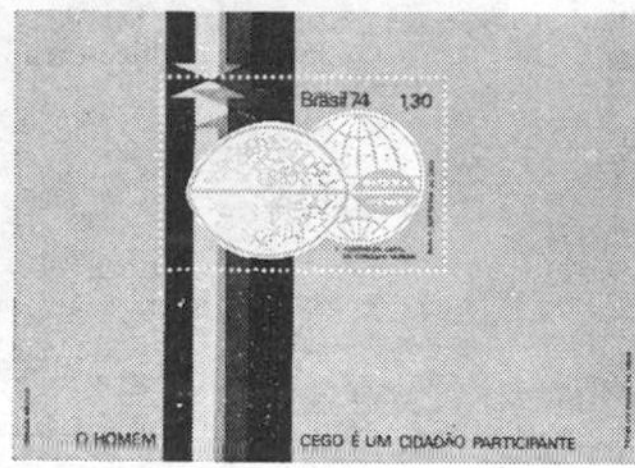

Congress Emblem — A735

1974, Aug. 7 ***Perf. 11½***
1357 A735 1.30cr multi 1.00 *2.00*

5th World Assembly of the World Council for the Welfare of the Blind, Sao Paulo, Aug. 7-16. No. 1357 has ocher margin with black inscription. Stamp and margin inscribed in Braille with name of Assembly. Size: 126x88½mm.

Raul Pederneiras, Caricature by J. Carlos — A736

Lithographed and Engraved

1974, Aug. 15 ***Perf. 11½x11***
1358 A736 40c buff, blk & ocher 50 40

Centenary of the birth of Raul Pederneiras (1874-1953), journalist, professor of law and fine arts.

Society Emblem and Landscape A737

1974, Aug. 19 Litho. ***Perf. 11x11½***
1359 A737 1.30cr multi 1.75 1.00

13th Congress of the International Union of Building and Savings Societies.

Souvenir Sheet

Five Women, by Di Cavalcanti — A738

1974, Aug. 26 Litho. ***Perf. 11½***
1360 A738 2cr multi 3.00 *6.00*

LUBRAPEX 74, 5th Portuguese-Brazilian Philatelic Exhibition, Sao Paulo, Nov. 26-Dec. 4. No. 1360 has gray marginal inscription. Size of stamp: 37x55mm., size of sheet: 87x125mm.

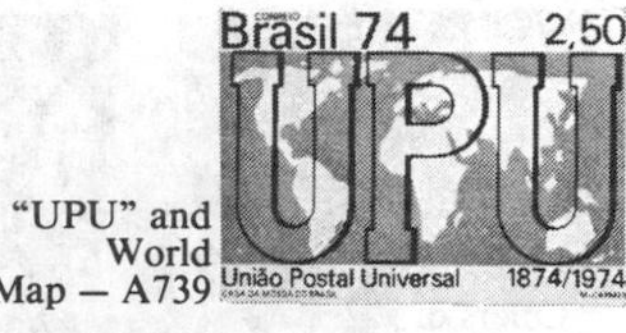

"UPU" and World Map — A739

1974, Oct. 9 Litho. ***Perf. 11½***
1361 A739 2.50cr blk & brt bl 7.50 2.25

Centenary of Universal Postal Union.

Hammock (Antillean Arawak Culture) A740

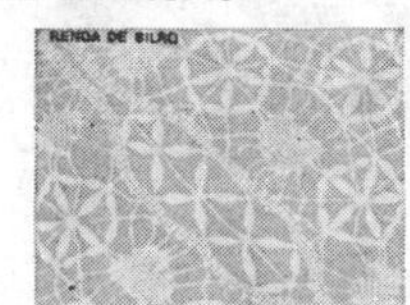

Bilro Lace — A741

Singer of "Cord" Verses — A742

Ceramic Figure by Master Vitalino — A743

1974, Oct. 16 Litho. ***Perf. 11½***
1362 A740 50c dp rose lil 2.00 40
1363 A741 50c lt & dk bl 2.50 40
1364 A742 50c yel & red brn 60 40
1365 A743 50c brt yel & dk brn 75 40

Popular Brazilian crafts.

Branch of Coffee A744

1974, Oct. 27 Unwmk. ***Perf. 11***
1366 A744 50c multi 1.00 60

Centenary of city of Campinas.

Hornless Tabapua A745

Animals of Brazil: 1.30cr, Creole horse. 2.50cr, Brazilian mastiff.

1974, Nov. 10 ***Perf. 11½***
1367 A745 80c multi 1.75 75
1368 A745 1.30cr multi 1.75 75
1369 A745 2.50cr multi 12.00 2.50

Angel — A746

1974, Nov. 18 ***Perf. 11½x11***
1370 A746 50c ultra & multi 75 30

Christmas 1974.

Solteira Island Hydroelectric Dam — A747

1974, Nov. 11 ***Perf. 11½***
1371 A747 50c blk & yel 1.40 50

Inauguration of the Solteira Island Hydroelectric Dam over Parana River.

The Girls, by Carlos Reis — A748

1974, Nov. 26
1372 A748 1.30cr multi 1.00 50

LUBRAPEX 74, 5th Portuguese-Brazilian Philatelic Exhibition, Sao Paulo, Nov. 26-Dec. 4.

Youths, Judge, Scales A749

1974, Dec. 20 Litho. ***Perf. 11½***
1373 A749 90c yel, red & bl 50 35

Juvenile Court of Brazil, 50th anniversary.

Long Distance Runner — A750

1974, Dec. 23
1374 A750 3.30cr multi 1.25 75

Sao Silvestre long distance running, 50th anniversary.

News Vendor, 1875, Masthead, 1975 — A751

1975, Jan. 4
1375 A751 50c multi 1.75 75

Centenary of the newspaper "O Estado de S. Paulo."

Sao Paulo Industrial Park A752

Designs: 1.40cr, Natural rubber industry, Acre. 4.50cr, Manganese mining, Amapa.

1975, Jan. 24 Litho. ***Perf. 11x11½***
1376 A752 50c vio bl & yel 2.25 40
1377 A752 1.40cr yel & brn 1.00 40
1378 A752 4.50cr yel & blk 10.00 40

Economic development.

Condition is the all-important factor of price. Prices quoted are for stamps in fine condition.

Fort of the Holy Cross A753

Designs: No. 1380, Fort of the Three Kings. No. 1381, Fort of Monteserrat. 90c, Fort of Our Lady of Help.

Lithographed, Engraved

1975, Mar. 14 ***Perf. 11½***

1379	A753	50c yel & red brn	30	20
1380	A753	50c yel & red brn	50	20
1381	A753	50c yel & red brn	1.00	20
1382	A753	90c yel & red brn	30	20

Colonial forts.

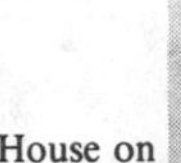

House on Stilts, Amazon Region A754

Designs: 50c, Modern houses and plan of Brasilia. 1.40cr, Indian hut, Rondonia. 3.30cr, German-style cottage (Enxaimel), Santa Catarina.

1975, Apr. 18 **Litho.** ***Perf. 11½***

1383	A754	50c yel & multi	2.25	2.50
1384	A754	50c yel & multi	15.00	7.50
1385	A754	1cr yel & multi	1.50	25
1386	A754	1.40cr yel & multi	3.00	3.00
1387	A754	1.40cr yel & multi	1.00	1.00
1388	A754	3.30cr yel & multi	1.50	1.50
1389	A754	3.30cr yel & multi	6.00	4.50
		Nos. 1383-1389 (7)	30.25	20.25

Brazilian architecture. Nos. 1383-1384, 1386-1387, 1388-1389 printed setenant in sheets of 50. Nos. 1383, 1386, 1388 have yellow strip at right side, others at left; No. 1385 has yellow strip on both sides.

Astronotus Ocellatus A755

Designs: Brazilian fresh-water fish.

1975, May 2 **Litho.** ***Perf. 11½***

Pale Green and Multicolored

1390	A755	50c *shown*	2.25	40
1391	A755	50c *Colomesus psitacus*	40	25
1392	A755	50c *Phallocerus caudimaculatus*	40	40
1393	A755	50c *Symphysodon discus*	75	50

Soldier's Head in Brazil's Colors, Plane, Rifle and Ship — A756

Brazilian Otter — A757

1975, May 8 ***Perf. 11½x11***

1394	A756	50c vio bl & multi	50	35

In honor of the veterans of World War II, on the 30th anniversary of victory.

1975, June 17 **Litho.** ***Perf. 11½***

Designs: 70c, Brazilian pines (horiz.). 3.30cr, Marsh cayman (horiz.).

1395	A757	70c bl, grn & blk	1.50	50
1396	A757	1cr multi	1.50	1.00
1397	A757	3.30cr multi	1.25	75

Nature protection.

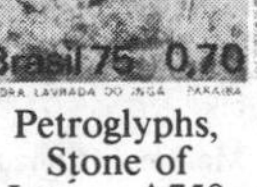

Petroglyphs, Stone of Inga — A758

Marjoara Vase, Para — A759

Vinctifer Comptoni, Petrified Fish A760

1975, July 8 **Litho.** ***Perf. 11½***

1398	A758	70c multi	1.00	40
1399	A759	1cr multi	65	40
1400	A760	1cr multi	65	40

Archaeological discoveries.

Immaculate Conception, Franciscan Monastery, Vitoria A761

Post and Telegraph Ministry A762

1975, July 15

1401	A761	3.30cr bl & multi	1.50	1.25

Holy Year 1975 and 300th anniversary of establishment of the Franciscan Province in Southern Brazil.

1975, Aug. 8 **Engr.** ***Perf. 11½***

1402	A762	70c dk car	1.00	30

Stamp Day 1975.

Sword Dance, Minas Gerais A763

Folk Dances: No. 1404, Umbrella Dance, Pernambuco. No. 1405, Warrior's Dance, Alagoas.

1975, Aug. 22 **Litho.** ***Perf. 11½***

1403	A763	70c gray & multi	50	50
1404	A763	70c pink & multi	50	50
1405	A763	70c yel & multi	50	50

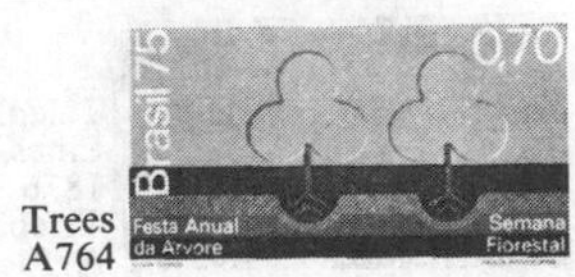

Trees A764

1975, Sept. 15 ***Perf. 11x11½***

1406	A764	70c multi	40	25

Annual Tree Festival.

Globe, Radar and Satellite — A765

1975, Sept. 16 ***Perf. 11½***

1407	A765	3.30cr multi	1.00	75

Inauguration of 2nd antenna of Tangua Earth Station, Rio de Janeiro State.

Woman Holding Flowers and Globe A766

1975, Sept. 23

1408	A766	3.30cr multi	1.50	1.00

International Women's Year 1975.

Tile, Railing and Column, Alcantara A767

Cross and Monastery, Sao Cristovao — A768

Design: No. 1411, Jug and Clock Tower, Goias (vert.).

1975, Sept. 27 **Litho.** ***Perf. 11½***

1409	A767	70c multi	50	50
1410	A768	70c multi	90	50
1411	A768	70c multi	90	50

Historic cities.

"Books teach how to live" A769

1975, Oct. 23 **Litho.** ***Perf. 11½***

1412	A769	70c multi	30	30

Day of the Book.

ASTA Congress Emblem A770

1975, Oct. 27 ***Perf. 11x11½***

1413	A770	70c multi	30	30

American Society of Travel Agents, 45th World Congress, Rio de Janeiro, Oct. 27-Nov. 1.

Angels — A771

1975, Nov. 11

1414	A771	70c red & brn	35	20

Christmas 1975.

Map of Americas, Waves — A772

Dom Pedro II — A773

1975, Nov. 19 ***Perf. 11½x12***

1415	A772	5.20cr gray & multi	6.00	2.25

2nd Interamerican Conference of Telecommunications (CITEL), Rio de Janeiro, Nov. 19-27.

1975, Dec. 2 **Engr.** ***Perf. 12***

1416	A773	70c vio brn	1.25	50

Dom Pedro II (1825-1891), emperor of Brazil, birth sesquicentennial.

People and Cross A774

1975, Nov. 27 **Litho.** ***Perf. 11x11½***

1417	A774	70c lt bl & dp bl	65	65

National Day of Thanksgiving.

Guarapari Beach, Espirito Santo A775

Designs: No. 1419, Salt Stone beach, Piaui. No. 1420, Cliffs, Rio Grande Do Sul.

1975, Dec. 19 **Litho.** ***Perf. 11½***

1418	A775	70c multi	35	35
1419	A775	70c multi	35	35
1420	A775	70c multi	35	35

Tourist publicity.

Triple Jump, Games Emblem A776

1975, Dec. 22 *Perf. 11x11½*
1421 A776 1.60cr bl grn & blk 35 35

Triple jump world record by Joao Carlos de Oliveira in 7th Pan-American Games, Mexico City, Oct. 12-26.

UN Emblem and Headquarters — A777

1975, Dec. 29 *Perf. 11½*
1422 A777 1.30cr dp bl & vio bl 30 30

United Nations, 30th anniversary.

Light Bulbs, House and Sun A778

Design: No. 1424, Gasoline drops, car and sun.

1976, Jan. 16
1423 A778 70c multi 50 20
1424 A778 70c multi 50 15

Energy conservation.

Concorde A779

1976, Jan. 21 Litho. *Perf. 11x11½*
1425 A779 5.20cr bluish blk 35 35

First commercial flight of supersonic jet Concorde from Paris to Rio de Janeiro, Jan. 21.

Souvenir Sheet

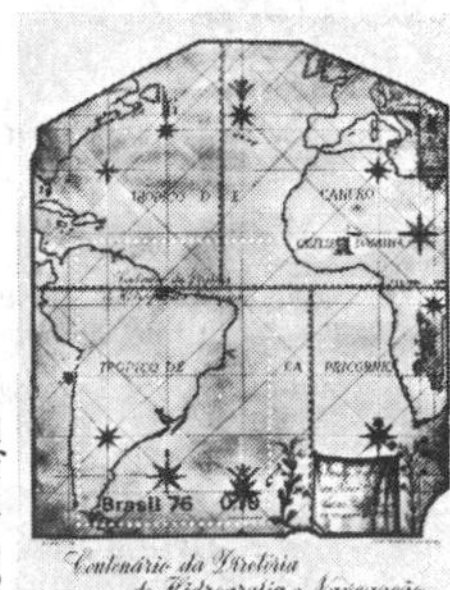
Nautical Map of South Atlantic, 1776 A780

1976, Feb. 2 *Perf. 11½*
1426 A780 70c sal & multi 75 1.50

Centenary of the Naval Hydrographic and Navigation Institute. Size: 88x123mm.

A little time given to the study of the arrangement of the Scott Catalogue can make it easier to use effectively.

Telephone Lines, 1876 Telephone A781

1976, Mar. 10 Litho. *Perf. 11x11½*
1427 A781 5.20cr org & bl 1.00 60

Centenary of first telephone call by Alexander Graham Bell, March 10, 1876.

Eye and Exclamation Point — A782

Kaiapo Body Painting — A783

1976, Apr. 7 Litho. *Perf. 11½x11*
1428 A782 1cr vio red brn & brn 75 75

World Health Day: "Foresight prevents blindness."

1976, Apr. 19 Litho. *Perf. 11½*

Designs: No. 1430, Bakairi ceremonial mask. No. 1431, Karajá feather headdress.

1429 A783 1cr lt vio & multi 20 20
1430 A783 1cr lt vio & multi 20 20
1431 A783 1cr lt vio & multi 20 20

Preservation of indigenous culture.

Itamaraty Palace, Brasilia A784

1976, Apr. 20
1432 A784 1cr multi 90 90

Diplomats' Day. Itamaraty Palace, designed by Oscar Niemeyer, houses the Ministry of Foreign Affairs.

Watering Can over Stones, by Jose Tarcisio A785

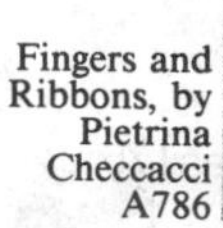
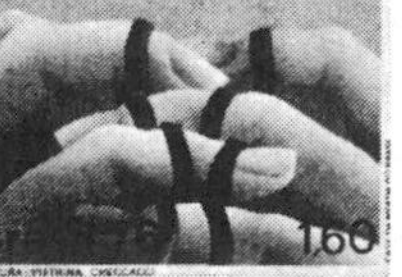
Fingers and Ribbons, by Pietrina Checcacci A786

1976, May 14 Litho. *Perf. 11½*
1433 A785 1cr multi 35 35
1434 A786 1.60cr multi 45 35

Modern Brazilian art.

Basketball A787

Orchid A788

Designs (Olympic Rings and): 1.40cr, Yachting. 5.20cr, Judo.

1976, May 21 Litho. *Perf. 11½*
1435 A787 1cr emer & blk 20 15
1436 A787 1.40cr dk bl & blk 25 15
1437 A787 5.20cr org & blk 75 50

21st Olympic Games, Montreal, Canada, July 17-Aug. 1.

1976, June 4 *Perf. 11½x11*

Design: No. 1439, Golden-faced lion monkey.

1438 A788 1cr multi 35 30
1439 A788 1cr multi 35 30

Nature protection.

Film Camera, Brazilian Colors — A789

1976, June 19
1440 A789 1cr vio bl, brt grn & yel 30 25

Brazilian film industry.

Bahia Woman — A790

Designs: 10c, Oxcart driver (horiz.). 20c, Raft fishermen (horiz.). 30c, Rubber plantation worker. 40c, Cowboy (horiz.). 50c, Gaucho. 80c, Gold panner. 1cr, Banana plantation worker. 1.10cr, Grape harvester. 1.30cr, Coffee picker. 1.80cr, Farmer gathering wax palms. 2cr, Potter. 5cr, Sugar cane cutter. 7cr, Salt mine worker. 10cr, Fisherman. 15cr, Coconut seller. 20cr, Lacemaker.

Perf. 11½x11, 11x11½

1976-78 **Photo.**

1441	A790	10c red brn ('77)	15	5
1442	A790	15c brown	50	50
1443	A790	20c vio bl	15	5
1444	A790	30c lil rose	15	5
1445	A790	40c org ('77)	20	5
1446	A790	50c citron	15	5
1447	A790	80c sl grn	75	5
1448	A790	1cr black	25	5
1449	A790	1.10cr mag ('77)	25	5
1450	A790	1.30cr red ('77)	25	5
1451	A790	1.80cr dk vio bl ('78)	35	5

Engr.

1452	A790	2cr brn ('77)	45	5
1453	A790	5cr dk pur ('77)	1.00	5
1454	A790	7cr violet	3.00	5
1455	A790	10cr yel grn ('77)	1.10	5
1456	A790	15cr gray grn ('78)	2.75	5
1457	A790	20cr blue	2.75	5
		Nos. 1441-1457 (17)	14.20	1.30

See Nos. 1653-1657

Hyphessobrycon Innesi — A791

Designs: Brazilian fresh-water fish.

1976, July 12 Litho. *Perf. 11x11½*
1460 A791 1cr *shown* 60 50
1461 A791 1cr *Copeina arnoldi* 60 50
1462 A791 1cr *Prochilodus insignis* 60 50
1463 A791 1cr *Crenicichla lepidota* 60 50
1464 A791 1cr *Ageneiosus* 60 50
1465 A791 1cr *Corydoras reticulatus* 60 50
Nos. 1460-1465 (6) 3.60 3.00

Nos. 1460-1465 printed se-tenant in sheets of 36.

Santa Marta Lighthouse A792

1976, July 29 Engr. *Perf. 12x11½*
1466 A792 1cr blue 50 30

300th anniversary of the city of Laguna.

Children on Magic Carpet A793

1976, Aug. 1 Litho. *Perf. 11½x12*
1467 A793 1cr multi 25 20

Stamp Day.

Nurse's Lamp and Head A794

1976, Aug. 12 Litho. *Perf. 11½*
1468 A794 1cr multi 25 20

Brazilian Nurses' Association, 50th anniversary.

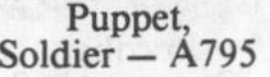
Puppet, Soldier — A795

Winner's Medal — A796

Designs: 1.30cr, Girl's head. 1.60cr, Hand with puppet head on each finger (horiz.).

1976, Aug. 20
1469 A795 1cr multi 25 20
1470 A795 1.30cr multi 25 20
1471 A795 1.60cr multi 25 20

Mamulengo puppet show.

1976, Aug. 21
1472 A796 5.20cr multi 1.00 50

27th International Military Athletic Championships, Rio de Janeiro, Aug. 21-28.

Family Protection — A797

1976, Sept. 12
1473 A797 1cr lt & dk bl 25 20

National organizations SENAC and SESC helping commercial employees to improve their living standard, both commercially and socially.

Dying Tree — A798

1976, Sept. 20 Litho. ***Perf. 11½***
1474 A798 1cr gray & multi 25 20

Protection of the environment.

Atom Symbol, Electron Orbits A799

1976, Sept. 21
1475 A799 5.20cr multi 1.00 50

20th General Conference of the International Atomic Energy Agency, Rio de Janeiro, Sept. 21-29.

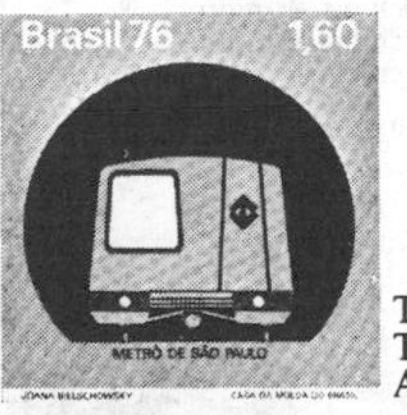

Train in Tunnel A800

1976, Sept. 26
1476 A800 1.60cr multi 35 25

Inauguration of Sao Paulo subway, first in Brazil.

St. Francis and Birds A801

1976, Oct. 4
1477 A801 5.20cr multi 1.10 50

St. Francis of Assisi, 750th death anniversary.

Ouro Preto School of Mining — A802

1976, Oct. 12 Engr. ***Perf. 12x11½***
1478 A802 1cr dk vio 50 50

Ouro Preto School of Mining, centenary.

Three Kings A803

Designs: Children's drawings.

1976, Nov. 4 Litho. ***Perf. 11½***
1479 A803 80c *shown* 50 35
1480 A803 80c *Santa Claus on donkey* 50 35
1481 A803 80c *Virgin and Child and Angels* 30 35
1482 A803 80c *Angels with candle* 50 35
1483 A803 80c *Nativity* 50 35
Nos. 1479-1483 (5) 2.30 1.75

Christmas 1976. Nos. 1479-1483 printed se-tenant in sheets of 35.

Souvenir Sheet

30,000 Reis Banknote — A804

1976, Nov. 5 Litho. ***Perf. 11½***
1484 A804 80c multi 25 *1.50*

Opening of 1000th branch of Bank of Brazil, Barra do Bugres, Mato Grosso. No. 1484 contains one stamp. Size of stamp: 38x56½mm.; size of sheet: 125x87mm.

Virgin of Monte Serrat, by Friar Agostinho A805

St. Joseph, 18th Century Wood Sculpture — A806

Designs: 5.60cr, The Dance, by Rodolfo Bernadelli, 19th century. 6.50cr, The Caravel, by Bruno Giorgi, 20th century abstract sculpture.

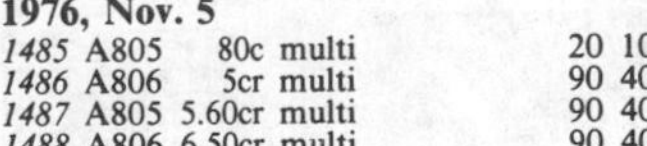
1976, Nov. 5
1485 A805 80c multi 20 10
1486 A806 5cr multi 90 40
1487 A805 5.60cr multi 90 40
1488 A806 6.50cr multi 90 40

Development of Brazilian sculpture.

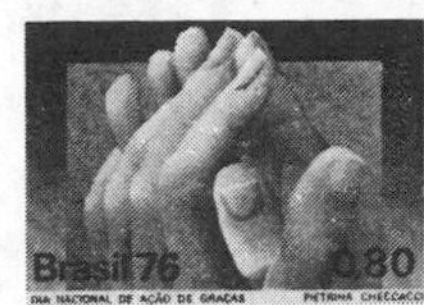

Praying Hands A807

1976, Nov. 25
1489 A807 80c multi 30 25

National Day of Thanksgiving.

Sailor, 1840 — A808

Design: 2cr, Marine's uniform, 1808.

1976, Dec. 13 Litho. ***Perf. 11½x11***
1490 A808 80c multi 30 25
1491 A808 2cr multi 45 25

Brazilian Navy.

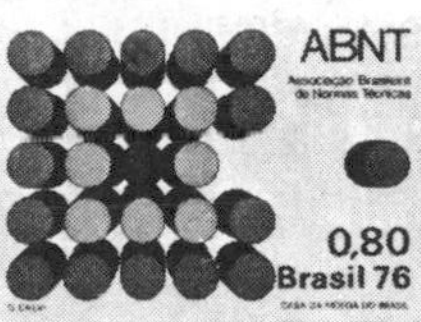

"Natural Resources and Development" — A809

1976, Dec. 17 ***Perf. 11½***
1492 A809 80c multi 25 20

Brazilian Bureau of Standards, founded 1940.

Wheel of Life — A810

Designs: 5.60cr, Beggar, sculpture by Agnaldo dos Santos. 6.50cr, Benin mask.

1977, Jan. 14
1493 A810 5cr multi 1.00 40
1494 A810 5.60cr multi 1.00 40
1495 A810 6.50cr multi 1.75 40

FESTAC '77, 2nd World Black and African Festival, Lagos, Nigeria, Jan. 15-Feb. 12.

A811

1977, Jan. 20 Litho. ***Perf. 11½***
1496 A811 6.50cr bl & yel grn 1.25 65

Rio de Janeiro International Airport.

Seminar Emblem with Map of Americas A812

Salicylate, Microphoto A813

1977, Feb. 6
1497 A812 1.10cr gray, vio bl & bl 50 20

6th Inter-American Budget Seminar.

1977, Apr. 10 Litho. ***Perf. 11½***
1498 A813 1.10cr multi 25 10

International Rheumatism Year.

Lions International Emblem A814

1977, Apr. 16
1499 A814 1.10cr multi 25 20

25th anniversary of Brazilian Lions International.

Heitor Villa Lobos A815

1977, Apr. 26 ***Perf. 11x11½***
1500 A815 1.10cr *shown* 25 20
1501 A815 1.10cr *Chiquinha Gonzaga* 25 20
1502 A815 1.10cr *Noel Rosa* 25 20

Brazilian composers.

Farmer and Worker — A816

Medicine Bottles and Flask — A817

1977, May 8 Litho. ***Perf. 11½***
1503 A816 1.10cr grn & multi 25 20
1504 A817 1.10cr lt & dk grn 25 20

Support and security for rural and urban workers (No. 1503) and establishment in 1971 of Medicine Distribution Center (CEME) for low-cost medicines (No. 1504).

Churchyard Cross, Porto Seguro — A818

Views, Porto Seguro: 5cr, Beach and boats. 5.60cr, Our Lady of Pena Chapel. 6.50cr, Town Hall.

1977, May 25 Litho. *Perf. 11½*

1505 A818 1.10cr multi 25 15
1506 A818 5cr multi 2.50 40
1507 A818 5.60cr multi 1.00 50
1508 A818 6.50cr multi 1.50 60

Centenary of Brazil's membership in Universal Postal Union.

Diario de Porto Alegre A819

1977, June 1

1509 A819 1.10cr multi 25 20

150th anniversary of Diario de Porto Alegre, newspaper.

Blue Whale A820

1977, June 3

1510 A820 1.30cr multi 28 20

Protection of marine life.

"Life and Development" A821

1977, June 20

1511 A821 1.30cr multi 25 20

National Development Bank, 25th anniversary.

Train Leaving Tunnel A822

1977, July 8 Engr. *Perf. 11½*

1512 A822 1.30cr black 25 20

Centenary of Sao Paulo-Rio de Janeiro railroad.

Vasum Cassiforme A823

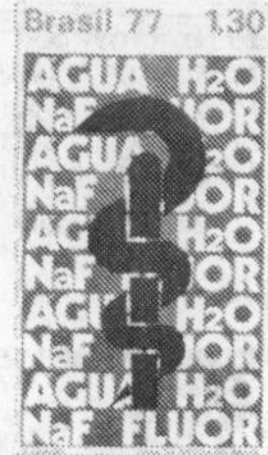
Caduceus, Formulas for Water and Fluoride A824

Sea Shells: No. 1514, Strombus goliath. No. 1515, Murex tenuivaricosus.

1977, July 14 Litho.

1513 A823 1.30cr bl & multi 25 20
1514 A823 1.30cr brn & multi 25 20
1515 A823 1.30cr grn & multi 25 20

1977, July 15 *Perf. 11½x11*

1516 A824 1.30cr multi 25 20

3rd International Odontology Congress, Rio de Janeiro, July 15-21.

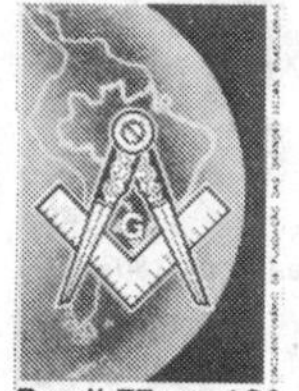
Masonic Emblem, Map of Brazil — A825

"Stamps Don't Sink or Lose their Way" — A826

1977, July 18 *Perf. 11½*

1517 A825 1.30cr bl, lt bl & blk 25 20

50th anniversary of the founding of the Brazilian Grand Masonic Lodge.

1977, Aug. 1

1518 A826 1.30cr multi 25 20

Stamp Day 1977.

Dom Pedro's Proclamation — A827

Horses and Bulls — A828

1977, Aug. 11 Litho. *Perf. 11½*

1519 A827 1.30cr multi 25 20

150th anniversary of Brazilian Law School.

Perf. 11½x11, 11x11½

1977, Aug. 20 Litho.

Designs: No. 1521, King on horseback. No. 1522, Joust (horiz.).

1520 A828 1.30cr ocher & multi 25 20
1521 A828 1.30cr bl & multi 25 20
1522 A828 1.30cr yel & multi 25 20

Brazilian folklore.

2000-reis Doubloon A829

Brazilian Colonial Coins: No. 1524, 640r pataca. No. 1525, 20r copper "vintem."

1977, Aug. 31 *Perf. 11½*

1523 A829 1.30cr vio bl & multi 25 15
1524 A829 1.30cr dk red & multi 25 15
1525 A829 1.30cr yel & multi 25 15

Pinwheel A830

Neoregelia Carolinae A831

1977, Sept. 1

1526 A830 1.30cr multi 25 15

National Week.

1977, Sept. 21 Litho. *Perf. 11½*

1527 A831 1.30cr multi 25 15

Nature preservation.

Pen, Pencil, Letters — A832

1977, Oct. 15 Litho. *Perf. 11½*

1528 A832 1.30cr multi 25 15

Primary education, sesquicentennial.

Dome and Telescope A833

1977, Oct. 15

1529 A833 1.30cr multi 25 15

National Astrophysics Observatory, Brasópolis, sesquicentennial.

"Jahu" Hydroplane (Savoia Marchetti S-55) A834

Design: No. 1531, PAX, dirigible.

1977, Oct. 17

1530 A834 1.30cr multi 50 25
1531 A834 1.30cr multi 50 25

50th anniversary of crossing of South Atlantic by Joao Ribeiro de Barros from Genoa to Sao Paulo (No. 1530) and 75th anniversary of the PAX airship (No. 1531).

O'Guarani — A835

1977, Oct. 24

1532 A835 1.30cr multi 25 15

Book Day and to honor José Martiniano de Alencar, writer, jurist.

Waves — A836

1977, Nov. 5 Litho. *Perf. 11½*

1533 A836 1.30cr multi 25 15

Amateur Radio Operators' Day.

Nativity A837

Designs (Folk Art): 2cr, Annunciation. 5cr, Nativity.

1977, Nov. 10

1534 A837 1.30cr bis & multi 35 15
1535 A837 2cr bis & multi 50 15
1536 A837 5cr bis & multi 1.00 25

Christmas 1977.

Emerald — A838

Designs: No. 1538, Topaz. No. 1539, Aquamarine.

1977, Nov. 19

1537 A838 1.30cr multi 25 20
1538 A838 1.30cr multi 25 20
1539 A838 1.30cr multi 25 20

PORTUCALE 77, 2nd International Topical Exhibition, Porto, Nov. 19-20.

Angel with Cornucopia — A839

1977, Nov. 24 Litho. *Perf. 11½*
1540 A839 1.30cr multi 25 20

National Thanksgiving Day.

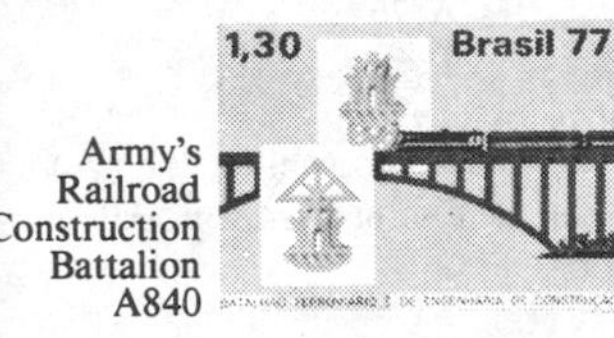

Army's Railroad Construction Battalion A840

Designs: No. 1542, Navy's Amazon flotilla. No. 1543, Air Force's postal service (plane).

1977, Dec. 5
1541 A840 1.30cr multi 25 20
1542 A840 1.30cr multi 25 20
1543 A840 1.30cr multi 25 20

Civilian services of armed forces.

Varig Emblem, Jet A841

1977, Dec. *Perf. 11x11½*
1544 A841 1.30cr bl & blk 25 20

50th anniversary of Varig Airline.

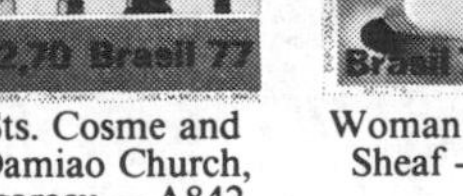

Sts. Cosme and Damiao Church, Igaracu — A842

Woman Holding Sheaf — A843

Brazilian Architecture: 7.50cr, St. Bento Monastery Church, Rio de Janeiro. 8.50cr, Church of St. Francis of Assisi, Ouro Preto. 9.50cr, St. Anthony Convent Church, Joao Pessoa.

1977, Dec. 8
1545 A842 2.70cr multi 50 15
1546 A842 7.50cr multi 1.50 35
1547 A842 8.50cr multi 1.50 40
1548 A842 9.50cr multi 2.00 45

1977, Dec. 19 *Perf. 11½*
1549 A843 1.30cr multi 25 20

Brazilian diplomacy.

Soccer Ball and Foot — A844

Designs: No. 1551, Soccer ball in net. No. 1552, Symbolic soccer player.

1978, Mar. 1 Litho. *Perf. 11½*
1550 A844 1.80cr multi 40 20
1551 A844 1.80cr multi 40 20
1552 A844 1.80cr multi 40 20

11th World Cup Soccer Championship, Argentina, June 1-25.

"La Fosca" on La Scala Stage and Carlos Gomes A845

1978, Feb. 9
1553 A845 1.80cr multi 40 20

Bicentenary of La Scala in Milan, and to honor Carlos Gomes (1836-1893), Brazilian composer.

Symbols of Postal Mechanization — A846

1978, Mar. 15 Litho. *Perf. 11½*
1554 A846 1.80cr multi 25 20

Opening of Postal Staff College.

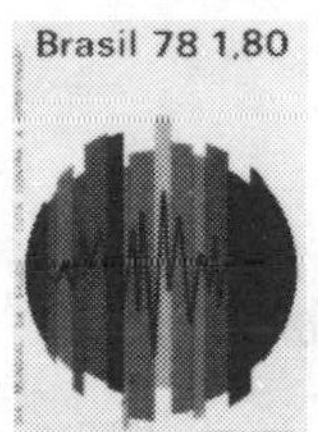

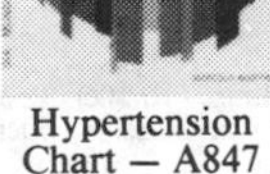

Hypertension Chart — A847

Waves from Antenna Uniting World — A848

1978, Apr. 4
1555 A847 1.80cr multi 30 20

World Health Day, fight against hypertension.

1978, May 17 Litho. *Perf. 12x11½*
1556 A848 1.80cr multi 25 20

10th World Telecommunications Day.

Brazilian Canary A849

Birds: 8.50cr, Cotinga. 9.50cr, Tanager fastuosa.

1978, June 5 *Perf. 11½x12*
1557 A849 7.50cr multi 2.00 75
1558 A849 8.50cr multi 2.00 1.00
1559 A849 9.50cr multi 2.00 1.25

Inocencio Serzedelo Correa and Manuel Francisco Correa, 1893 A850

1978, June 20 Litho. *Perf. 11x11½*
1560 A850 1.80cr multi 25 20

85th anniversary of Union Court of Audit.

Post and Telegraph Building A851

1978, June 22 *Perf. 11½*
1561 A851 1.80cr multi 25 25

Souvenir Sheet

Imperf

1562 A851 7.50cr multi 1.00 1.50

Inauguration of Post and Telegraph Building (ECT), Brasilia, and for BRAPEX, 3rd Brazilian Philatelic Exhibition, Brasilia, June 23-28 (No. 1562). No. 1562 has buff margin with black inscription. Size: 70x90mm.

Ernesto Geisel — A852

1978, June 22 Engr. *Perf. 11½*
1563 A852 1.80cr dl grn 25 15

Ernesto Geisel, President of Brazil.

Savoia-Marchetti S-64, Map of South Atlantic — A853

1978, July 3 Litho.
1564 A853 1.80cr multi 30 20

50th anniversary of first crossing of South Atlantic by Carlos del Prete and Arturo Ferrarin.

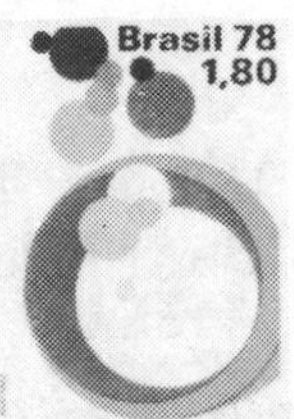

Symbolic of Smallpox Eradication A854

Brazil No. 68 A855

1978, July 25
1565 A854 1.80cr multi 30 20

Eradication of smallpox.

1978, Aug. 1
1566 A855 1.80cr multi 30 25

Stamp Day, centenary of the "Barba Branca" (white beard) issue.

Stormy Sea, by Seelinger A856

1978, Aug. 4
1567 A856 1.80cr multi 30 25

Helios Seelinger, painter, birth centenary.

Guitar Players A857

Musicians and Instruments: No. 1569, Flutes. No. 1570, Percussion instruments.

1978, Aug. 22 Litho. *Perf. 11½*
1568 A857 1.80cr multi 30 15
1569 A857 1.80cr multi 30 15
1570 A857 1.80cr multi 30 20

Children at Play A858

1978, Sept. 1 Litho. *Perf. 11½*
1571 A858 1.80cr multi 30 20

National Week.

Collegiate Church A859

1978, Sept. 6 Engr.
1572 A859 1.80cr red brn 30 20

Restoration of patio of Collegiate Church, Sao Paulo.

Justice by A. Geschiatti A860

1978, Sept. 18 Litho.
1573 A860 1.80cr blk & ol 30 20

Federal Supreme Court, sesquicentennial.

Iguacu Falls — A861

Design: No. 1575, Yellow ipecac.

1978, Sept. 21

1574	A861	1.80cr multi	30	20
1575	A861	1.80cr multi	30	20

Iguacu National Park.

Stages of Intelsat Satellite A862

1978, Oct. 9 Litho. *Perf. 11½*

1576	A862	1.80cr multi	30	20

Flag of Order of Christ A863

Brazilian Flags: No. 1578, Principality of Brazil. No. 1579, United Kingdom. No. 1580, Imperial Brazil. No. 1581, National flag (current).

1978, Oct. 13

1577	A863	1.80cr multi	1.40	65
1578	A863	1.80cr multi	1.40	65
1579	A863	1.80cr multi	1.40	65
1580	A863	8.50cr multi	1.40	65
1581	A863	8.50cr multi	1.40	65
a.		Block of 5 + label	6.75	7.50

7th LUBRAPEX Philatelic Exhibition, Porto Alegre. Nos. 1577-1581 printed se-tenant in blocks of 5 plus label showing Acorianos monument.

Mail Street Car A864

Mail Transportation: No. 1583, Overland mail truck. No. 1584, Mail delivery truck. 7.50cr. Railroad mail car. 8.50cr, Mail coach. 9.50cr, Post riders.

1978, Oct. 21 *Perf. 11x11½*

1582	A864	1.80cr multi	75	40
1583	A864	1.80cr multi	75	40
1584	A864	1.80cr multi	75	40
1585	A864	7.50cr multi	75	40
1586	A864	8.50cr multi	73	40
1587	A864	9.50cr multi	75	50
		Nos. 1582-1587 (6)	4.50	2.50

18th Universal Postal Union Congress, Rio de Janeiro, 1979. Nos. 1582-1587 printed se-tenant.

Gaucho Herding Cattle, and Cactus — A865

1978, Oct. 23 *Perf. 11½x11*

1588	A865	1.80cr multi	30	20

Joao Guimaraes Rosa, poet and diplomat, 70th birthday.

St. Anthony's Hill, by Nicholas A. Taunay A866

Landscape Paintings: No. 1590, Castle Hill, by Victor Meirelles. No. 1591, View of Sabara, by Alberto da Veiga Guignard. No. 1592, View of Pernambuco, by Frans Post.

1978, Nov. 6 Litho. *Perf. 11½*

1589	A866	1.80cr multi	30	20
1590	A866	1.80cr multi	30	20
1591	A866	1.80cr multi	30	20
1592	A866	1.80cr multi	30	20

Angel with Harp — A867

Designs: No. 1594, Angel with lute. No. 1595, Angel with oboe.

1978, Nov. 10

1593	A867	1.80cr multi	30	20
1594	A867	1.80cr multi	30	20
1595	A867	1.80cr multi	30	20

Christmas 1978.

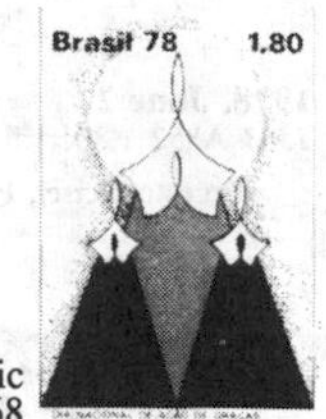

Symbolic Candles — A868

1978, Nov. 23

1596	A868	1.80cr blk, gold & car	30	20

National Thanksgiving Day.

Red Crosses and Activities A869

1978, Dec. 5 Litho. *Perf. 11x11½*

1597	A869	1.80cr blk & red	30	20

70th anniversary of Brazilian Red Cross.

Paz Theater, Belem — A870

Designs: 12cr, José de Alencar Theater, Portaleza. 12.50cr, Municipal Theater, Rio de Janeiro.

1978, Dec. 6 *Perf. 11½*

1598	A870	10.50cr multi	1.10	25
1599	A870	12cr multi	1.10	25
1600	A870	12.50cr multi	1.10	25

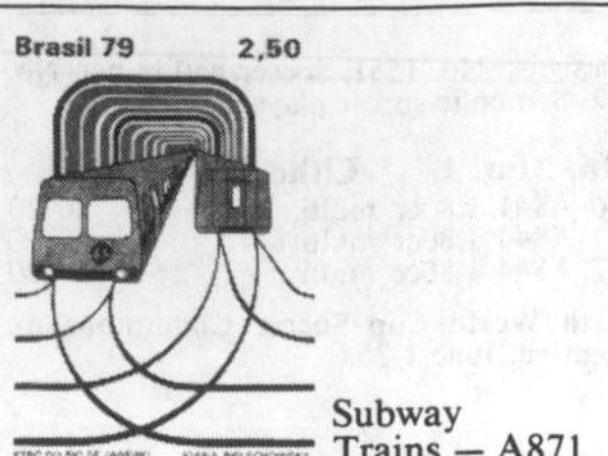

Subway Trains — A871

1979, Mar. 5 Litho. *Perf. 11½*

1601	A871	2.50cr multi	40	20

Inauguration of Rio de Janeiro's subway system.

Old and New Post Offices A872

Designs: No. 1603, Old and new mail boxes. No. 1604, Manual and automatic mail sorting. No. 1605, Old and new planes. No. 1606, Telegraph and telex machine. No. 1607, Mailmen's uniforms.

1979, Mar. 20 Litho. *Perf. 11x11½*

1602	A872	2.50cr multi	40	30
1603	A872	2.50cr multi	40	30
1604	A872	2.50cr multi	40	30
1605	A872	2.50cr multi	40	30
1606	A872	2.50cr multi	40	30
1607	A872	2.50cr multi	40	30
		Nos. 1602-1607 (6)	2.40	1.80

10th anniversary of the new Post and Telegraph Department, and 18th Universal Postal Union Congress, Rio de Janeiro, Sept.-Oct., 1979.

O'Day 23 Class Yacht A873

Yachts and Stamp Outlines: 10.50cr, Penguin Class. 12cr, Hobie Cat Class. 12.50cr, Snipe Class.

1979, Apr. 18 Litho. *Perf. 11x11½*

1608	A873	2.50cr multi	50	30
1609	A873	10.50cr multi	1.00	50
1610	A873	12cr multi	1.00	40
1611	A873	12.50cr multi	1.25	40

Brasiliana '79, 3rd World Thematic Stamp Exhibition, Sao Conrado, Sept. 15-23.

Children, IYC Emblem — A874

1979, May 30 Litho. *Perf. 11½*

1612	A874	2.50cr multi	50	20

International Year of the Child and Children's Book Day.

Giant Water Lily — A875

Designs: 12cr, Amazon manatee. 12.50cr, Arrau (turtle).

1979, June 5 Litho. *Perf. 11½*

1613	A875	10.50cr multi	1.00	50
1614	A875	12cr multi	1.25	60
1615	A875	12.50cr multi	1.25	60

Amazon National Park, nature conservation.

Bank Emblem A876

1979, June 7

1616	A876	2.50cr multi	25	15

Northwest Bank of Brazil, 25th anniversary.

Physician Tending Patient 15th Cent. Woodcut A877

1979, June 30

1617	A877	2.50cr multi	25	15

National Academy of Medicine, 50th anniversary.

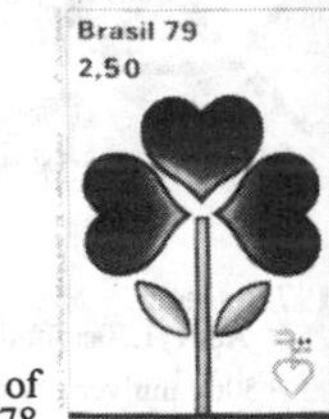

Flower made of Hearts — A878

1979, July 8 Litho. *Perf. 11½*

1618	A878	2.50cr multi	25	15

35th Brazilian Cardiology Congress.

Souvenir Sheet

Hotel Nacional, Rio de Janeiro A879

1979, July 16

1619	A879	12.50cr multi	1.00	1.50

Brasiliana '79 comprising 1st Inter-American Exhibition of Classical Philately and 3rd World Topical Exhibition, Rio de Janeiro, Sept. 15-23. No. 1619 has multicolored margin showing hang glider. Size: 87x125mm.

The first price column gives the catalogue value of an unused stamp, the second that of a used stamp.

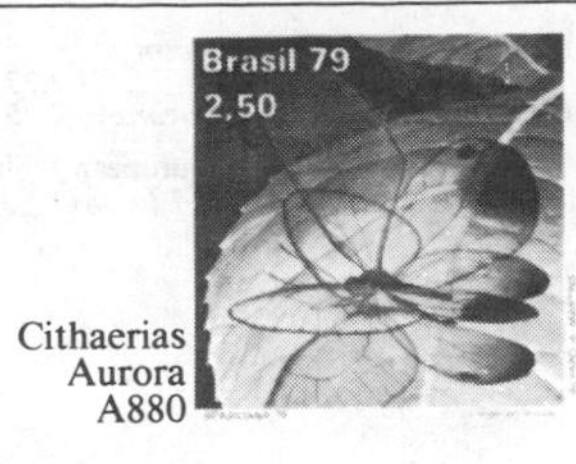

Cithaerias Aurora
A880

Moths: 10.50cr, Evenus regalis. 12cr, Caligo eurilochus. 12.50cr, Diaethria clymena janeira.

1979, Aug. 1

1620 A880 2.50cr multi 30 15
1621 A880 10.50cr multi 1.00 45
1622 A880 12cr multi 1.25 60
1623 A880 12.50cr multi 1.25 60

Stamp Day 1979.

EMB-121 Xingo
A881

1979, Aug. 19 Litho. *Perf. 11½*

1624 A881 2.50cr vio bl 25 20

Embraer, Brazilian aircraft company, 10th anniversary.

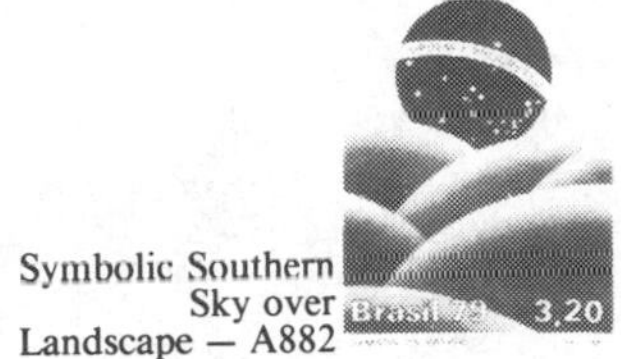

Symbolic Southern Sky over Landscape — A882

1979, Sept. 12

1625 A882 3.20cr multi 25 20

National Week.

Our Lady of the Apparition — A883

1979, Sept. 8 Litho. *Perf. 11½*

1626 A883 2.50cr multi 25 20

Statue of Our Lady of the Apparition, 75th anniversary of coronation.

"UPU," Envelope and Mail Transport — A884

"UPU" and: No. 1628, Post Office emblems. 10.50cr, Globe. 12cr, Flags of Brazil and U.N. 12.50cr, UPU emblem.

1979, Sept. 12 *Perf. 11x11½*

1627 A884 2.50cr multi 30 20
1628 A884 2.50cr multi 30 20
1629 A884 10.50cr multi 1.00 60
1630 A884 12cr multi 1.25 75
1631 A884 12.50cr multi 1.25 75
Nos. 1627-1631 (5) 4.10 2.50

18th Universal Postal Union Congress, Rio de Janeiro, Sept.-Oct. 1979.

Pyramid Fountain, Rio de Janeiro — A885

Fountains: 10.50cr, Facade, Marilia, Ouro Preto (horiz.). 12cr, Boa Vista, Recife.

Perf. 12x11½, 11½x12

1979, Sept. 15

1632 A885 2.50cr multi 30 20
1633 A885 10.50cr multi 1.00 60
1634 A885 12cr multi 1.25 75

Brasiliana '79, 1st Interamerican Exhibition of Classical Philately.

Church of the Glory
A886

Landscapes by Leandro Joaquim: 12cr, Fishing on Guanabara Bay. 12.50cr, Boqueirao Lake and Carioca Arches.

1979, Sept. 15 *Perf. 11½*

1635 A886 2.50cr multi 30 20
1636 A886 12cr multi 1.25 65
1637 A886 12.50cr multi 1.25 65

Brasiliana '79, 3rd World Topical Exhibition, Sao Conrado, Sept. 15-23.

World Map
A887

1979, Sept. 20

1638 A887 2.50cr multi 30 20

3rd World Telecommunications Exhibition, Geneva, Sept. 20-26.

"UPU" and UPU Emblem — A888

1979, Oct. 9 Litho. *Perf. 11½x11*

1639 A888 2.50cr multi 30 20
1640 A888 10.50cr multi 1.00 60
1641 A888 12cr multi 1.25 65
1642 A888 12.50cr multi 1.25 65

Universal Postal Union Day.

IYC Emblem, Feather Toy
A889

IYC Emblem and Toys: No. 1644, Bumble bee, ragdoll. No. 1645, Flower, top. No. 1646, Wooden acrobat.

1979, Oct. 12 *Perf. 11½*

1643 A889 2.50cr multi 40 20
1644 A889 3.20cr multi 40 25
1645 A889 3.20cr multi 40 25
1646 A889 3.20cr multi 40 25

International Year of the Child.

Adoration of the Kings — A890

Christmas 1979: No. 1648, Nativity. No. 1649 Jesus and the Elders in the Temple.

1979, Nov. 12 Litho. *Perf. 11½*

1647 A890 3.20cr multi 30 25
1648 A890 3.20cr multi 30 25
1649 A890 3.20cr multi 30 25

Souvenir Sheet

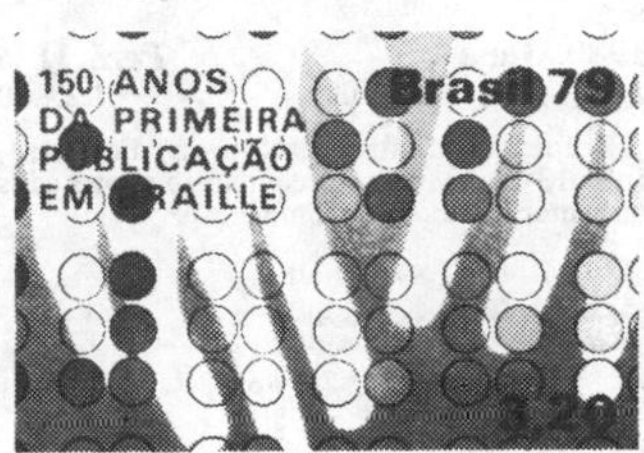

Hands Reading Braille — A891

Lithographed and Embossed

1979, Nov. 20. *Perf. 11½*

1650 A891 3.20cr multi 75 1.25

Publication of Braille script, 150th anniversary. Multicolored margin shows extension of stamp design with Braille printed and embossed. Size: 127x87½mm.

Wheat Harvester
A892

Steel Mill
A893

1979, Nov. 22

1651 A892 3.20cr multi 25 25

Thanksgiving 1979.

1979, Nov. 23

1652 A893 3.20cr multi 30 25

COSIPA Steelworks, Sao Paulo, 25th anniversary.

Type of 1976 and

A894

Designs: 70c, Women grinding coconuts. 2cr, Coconuts. 2.50cr, Basket weaver. 3cr, Mangoes. 3.20cr, River boatman. 4cr, Corn. 5cr, Onions. 7cr, Oranges. 10cr, Maracuja. 12cr, Pineapple. 15cr, Bananas. 17cr, Guarana. 20cr, Sugar cane. 21cr, Harvesting ramie (China grass). 24cr, Beekeeping. 27cr, Man leading pack mule. 30cr, Silkworm. 34cr, Cacao. 38cr, Coffee. 42cr, Soybeans. 45cr, Mandioca. 50cr, Wheat. 57cr, Peanuts. 66cr, Grapes. 100cr, Cashews. 140cr, Tomatoes. 200cr, Mamona. 500cr, Cotton.

Photogravure, Engraved (21cr)

1979 *Perf. 11x11½, 11½x11*

1653 A790 70c gray grn 20 5
1654 A790 2.50cr sepia 15 5
1655 A790 3.20cr bl, horiz. 15 5
1656 A790 21cr purple 50 10
1657 A790 27cr sep, horiz. 60 15
Nos. 1653-1657 (5) 1.60 40

1980-83 Photo. *Perf. 11½x11*

1658 A894 2cr yel brn ('82) 5 5
1659 A894 3cr red ('82) 5 5
1660 A894 4cr orange 15 5
1661 A894 5cr dk pur ('82) 8 5
1662 A894 7cr org ('81) 20 5
1663 A894 10cr bl grn ('82) 20 5
1664 A894 12cr dk grn ('81) 28 5
1665 A894 15cr gldn brn ('83) 10 5
1666 A894 17cr brn org ('82) 30 5
1667 A894 20cr ol ('82) 28 10
1668 A894 24cr bis ('82) 20 5
1669 A894 30cr blk ('82) 20 10
1670 A894 34cr brown 45 10
1671 A894 38cr red ('83) 20 10
1672 A894 42cr green 7.50 50
1673 A894 45cr sep ('83) 75 10
1674 A894 50cr yel org ('82) 22 10
1675 A894 57cr brn ('83) 22 10
1676 A894 66cr pur ('81) 5.00 15
1677 A894 100cr dk red brn ('81) 3.00 5
1678 A894 140cr red ('82) 3.50 15

Engr.

1678A A894 200cr grn ('82) 3.75 10
1679 A894 500cr brn ('82) 7.50 15
Nos. 1658-1679 (23) 34.18 2.30

See Nos. 1928-1941.

Plant Inside Raindrop — A896

Light Bulb Containing: 17cr+7cr, Sun. 20cr+8cr, Windmill. 21cr+9cr, Dam.

1980, Jan. 2 Litho. *Perf. 12*

1680 A896 3.20cr multi 25 15
1681 A896 24cr (17 + 7) 2.50 1.25
1682 A896 28cr (20 + 8) 3.00 1.50
1683 A896 30cr (21 + 9) 4.50 1.75

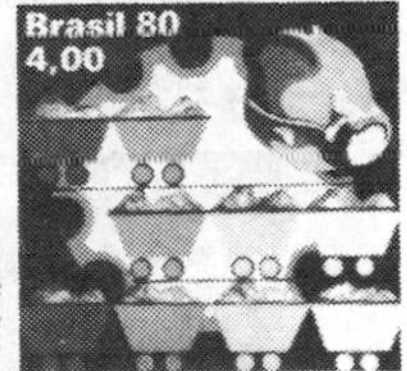

Anthracite Industry
A897

1980, Mar. 19 Litho. *Perf. 11½*

1684 A897 4cr multi 30 15

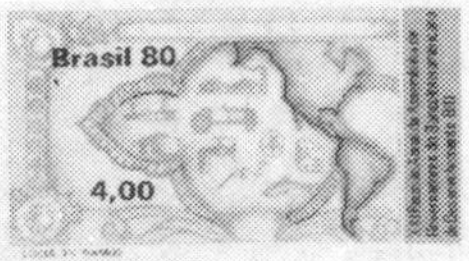

Map of Americas, Symbols of Development — A898

1980, Apr. 14 Litho. *Perf. 11x11½*

1685 A898 4cr multi 30 15

21st Assembly of Inter-American Development Bank Governors, Rio de Janeiro, Apr. 14-16.

Tapirape Mask, Mato Grosso
A899

1980, Apr. 18 *Perf. 11½*

1686 A899 4cr *shown* 30 15
1687 A899 4cr *Tukuna mask, Amazonas,* vert. 30 15
1688 A899 4cr *Kanela mask, Maranhao,* vert. 30 15

Brazilian Television, 30th Anniversary
A900

1980, May 5 **Litho.** *Perf. 11½*

1689 A900 4cr multi 30 15

Duke of Caixas, by Miranda
A901

The Worker, by Candido Partinari
A902

1980, May 7

1690 A901 4cr multi 30 15

Duke of Caixas, death centenary.

1980, May 18

Paintings: 28cr, Mademoiselle Pogany, by Constantin Brancusi. 30cr, The Glass of Water, by Francisco Aurelio de Figueiredo.

1691 A902 24cr multi 2.00 1.00
1692 A902 28cr multi 2.00 1.00
1693 A902 30cr multi 3.00 1.00

Graf Zeppelin, 50th Anniversary of Atlantic Crossing
A903

1980, June **Litho.** *Perf. 11x11½*

1694 A903 4cr multi 35 15

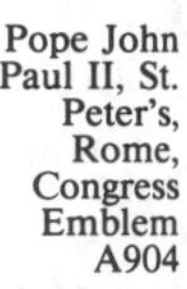

Pope John Paul II, St. Peter's, Rome, Congress Emblem
A904

Pope, Emblem and Brazilian Churches: No. 1696, Fortaleza (vert.) 24cr. Apericida 28cr. Rio de Janeiro, 30cr, Brasilia.

1980, June 24 *Perf. 12*

1695 A904 4cr multi 30 15
1696 A904 4cr multi 30 15
1697 A904 24cr multi 1.50 40
1698 A904 28cr multi 1.50 40
1699 A904 30cr multi 3.00 40
Nos. 1695-1699 (5) 6.60 1.50

Visit of Pope John Paul II to Brazil, June 30-July 12; 10th National Eucharistic Congress, Fortaleza, July 9-16.

First Transatlantic Flight, 50th Anniversary — A905

1980, June **Litho.** *Perf. 11x11½*

1700 A905 4cr multi 35 15

Souvenir Sheet

Yacht Sail, Exhibition Emblem — A906

1980, June *Perf. 11½*

1701 A906 30cr multi 1.25 2.00

Brapex IV Stamp Exhibition, Fortaleza, June 13-21. Multicolored margin shows sails on water. Size: 125x88mm.

Rowing, Moscow '80 Emblem
A907

1980, June 30

1702 A907 4cr *shown* 30 15
1703 A907 4cr *Target shooting* 30 15
1704 A907 4cr *Bicycling* 30 15

22nd Summer Olympic Games, Moscow, July 19-Aug. 3.

Rondon Community Works Project
A908

1980, July 11

1705 A908 4cr multi 30 15

Helen Keller and Anne Sullivan
A909

1980, July 28

1706 A909 4cr multi 30 15

Helen Keller (1880-1968), blind deaf writer and lecturer taught by Anne Sullivan (1867-1936).

Souvenir Sheet

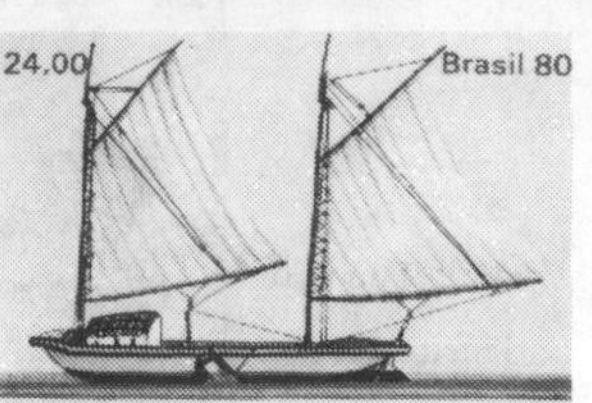
Sao Francisco River Canoe — A910

1980, Aug. 1 **Litho.** *Perf. 11½*

1707 A910 24cr multi 1.00 2.00

Stamp Day. Light blue and black margin shows river canoe, Postal and Telegraph Museum emblem. Size: 125½x86½mm.

Microscope, Red Cross, Insects, Brick and Tile Houses — A911

1980, Aug. 5 *Perf. 11½x11*

1708 A911 4cr multi 30 15

National Health Day.

Brazilian Postal Administration, 15th Anniversary — A912

1980, Sept. 16 **Litho.** *Perf. 12*

1709 A912 5cr multi 40 20

Souvenir Sheet

St. Gabriel World Union, 6th Congress
A913

1980, Sept. 29 *Perf. 11½x12*

1710 A913 30cr multi 1.50 2.00

No. 1710 has red and orange margin. Size: 125x86mm.

Cattleya Amethystoglossa — A914

1980, Oct. 3 *Perf. 11½*

1711 A914 5cr *shown* 35 20
1712 A914 5cr *Laelia cinnabarina* 35 20
1713 A914 24cr *Zygopetalum crinitum* 2.25 1.00
1714 A914 28cr *Laelia tenebrosa* 2.25 1.00

Espamer 80, American-European Philatelic Exhibition, Madrid, Oct. 3-12.

Red-tailed Amazon Parrot
A915

Capitao Rodrigo, Hero of Erico Verissimo's "O Continento"
A916

Parrots: No. 1716, Vinaceous Amazon. No. 1717, Brown-backed. No. 1718, Red-spectacled.

1980, Oct. 18 **Litho.** *Perf. 12*

1715 A915 5cr multi 35 20
1716 A915 5cr multi 35 20
1717 A915 28cr multi 2.25 1.00
1718 A915 28cr multi 2.25 1.00

Lubrapex '80 Stamp Exhibition, Lisbon, Oct. 18-26.

1980, Oct. 23

1719 A916 5cr multi 35 20

Book Day.

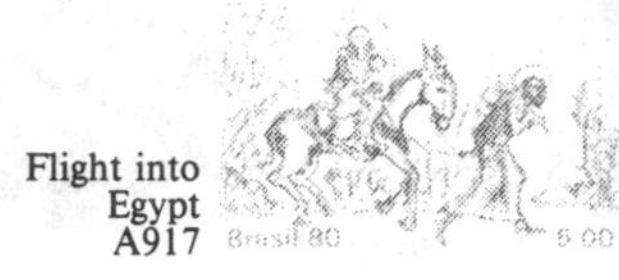
Flight into Egypt
A917

1980, Nov. 5

1720 A917 5cr multi 35 20

Christmas 1980.

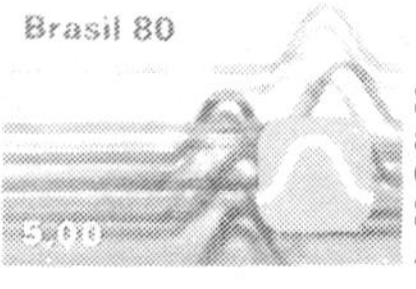
Sound Waves and Oscillator Screen
A918

1980, Nov. 7

1721 A918 5cr multi 35 20

Telebras Research Center inauguration.

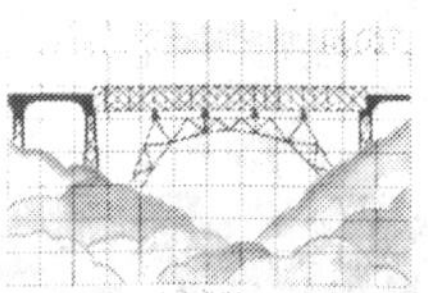
Carvalho Viaduct, Paranagua-Curitiba Railroad — A919

1980, Nov. 10

1722 A919 5cr multi 50 20

Engineering Club centenary.

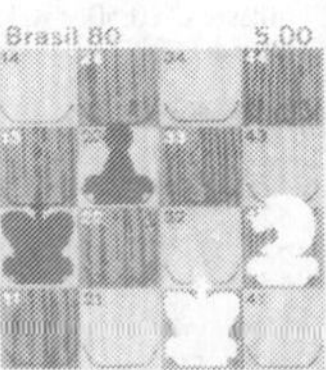
Portable Chess Board — A920

1980, Nov. 18 Litho. *Perf. 11½*
1723 A920 5cr multi 50 50

Postal chess contest.

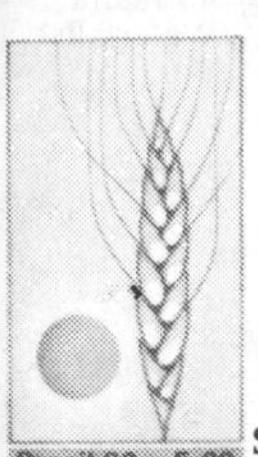

Sun and Wheat — A921

1980, Nov. 27 *Perf. 11½x11*
1724 A921 5cr multi 40 40

Thanksgiving 1980

Father Anchieta Writing "Virgin Mary, Mother of God" on Sand of Iperoig Beach — A922

1980, Dec. 8 *Perf. 12*
1725 A922 5cr multi 35 20

Christ Carrying Cross, By O Aleijadinho A923

Antonio Francisco Lisboa (O Aleijadinho), 250th Birth Anniversary: Paintings of the life of Christ: a. Mount of Olives. b. Arrest in the Garden. c. Flagellation. d. Crown of Thorns. f. Crucifixion.

1980, Dec. 29
1726 Block of 6 3.50 3.00
a.-f. A923 5cr any single 60 35

Agricultural Productivity — A924

1981, Jan. 2 Litho. *Perf. 11x11½*
1727 A924 30cr *shown* 1.65 35
1728 A924 35cr *Domestic markets* 1.50 35
1729 A924 40cr *Exports* 1.50 35

Boy Scout and Campfire A925

1981, Jan. 22 Litho. *Perf. 11x11½*
1730 A925 5cr shown 35 20
1731 A925 5cr Scouts cooking 35 20
1732 A925 5cr Scout, tents 35 20

4th Pan-American Scout Jamboree.

Souvenir Sheet

Mailman, 1930 — A926

1981, Mar. 11 Litho. *Perf. 11*
1733 Sheet of 3 4.50 4.50
a. A926 30cr shown 1.00 1.00
b. A926 35cr Mailman, 1981 1.00 1.00
c. A926 40cr Telegram messenger, 1930 1.00 1.00

Department of Posts and Telegraphs, 50th anniversary. No. 1733 has black marginal inscription. Size: 100x70mm.

Souvenir Sheet

The Hunter and the Jaguar, by Felix Taunay (1795-1881) A927

1981, Apr. 10 Litho. *Perf. 11*
1734 A927 30cr multi 1.65 *3.00*

Size: 70x90mm.

Lima Barreto and Rio de Janeiro, 1900 A928

1981, May 13 Litho. *Perf. 11½*
1735 A928 7cr multi 35 30

Lima Barreto, writer, birth centenary.

Maraca Indian Funerary Urn — A929

1981, May 18
1736 A929 7cr shown 35 30
1737 A929 7cr Marajoara triangular jug 35 30
1738 A929 7cr Tupi-Guarani bowl 35 30

Lophornis Magnifica A930

Designs: Hummingbirds.

1981, May 22 *Perf. 11½*
1739 A930 7cr shown 60 30
1740 A930 7cr Phaethornis pretrei 60 30
1741 A930 7cr Chrysolampis mosquitus 60 30
1742 A930 7cr Heliactin cornuta 60 30

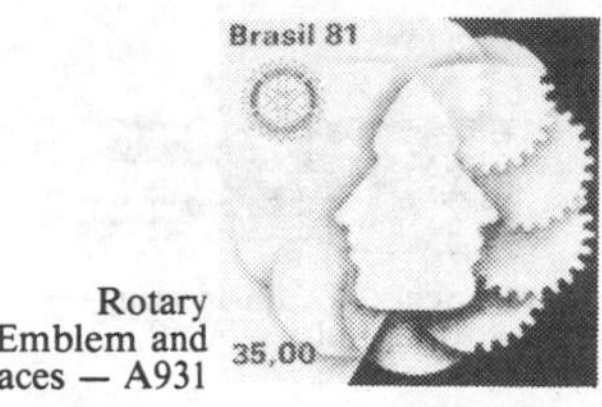

Rotary Emblem and Faces — A931

1981, May 31
1743 A931 7cr Emblem, hands 35 30
1744 A931 35cr shown 2.00 1.50

72nd Convention of Rotary Intl., Sao Paulo.

Environmental Protection — A932

1981, June 5 *Perf. 12*
1745 A932 7cr shown 35 30
1746 A932 7cr Forest 35 30
1747 A932 7cr Clouds (air) 35 30
1748 A932 7cr Village (soil) 35 30

Nos. 1745-1748 se-tenant.

Biplane, 1931 (Airmail Service, 50th Anniv.) A933

1981, June 10 *Perf. 11½*
1749 A933 7cr multi 35 30

Madeira-Mamore Railroad, 50th Anniv. of Nationalization — A934

1981, July 10 Litho. *Perf. 11x11½*
1750 A934 7cr multi 35 30

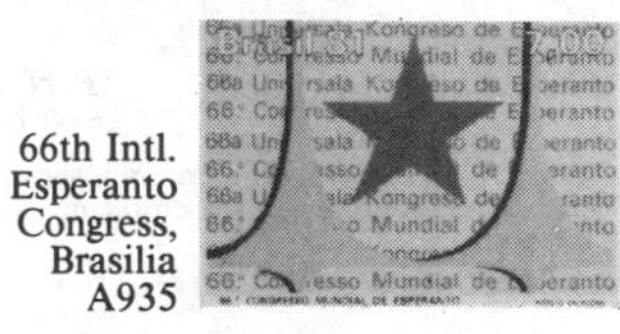
66th Intl. Esperanto Congress, Brasilia A935

1981, July 26 *Perf. 12*
1751 A935 7cr grn & blk 35 30

No. 79 — A936

1981, Aug. 1
1752 A936 50cr shown 2.50 50
1753 A936 55cr No. 80 2.50 50
1754 A936 60cr No. 81 2.50 50

Stamp Day; centenary of "small head" stamps.

Institute of Military Engineering, 50th Anniv. A937

1981, Aug. 11 Litho. *Perf. 11½*
1755 A937 12cr multi 35 30

Reisado Dancers A938

1981, Aug. 22
1756 A938 50cr Dancers, diff. 1.65 35
1757 A938 55cr Sailors 1.65 38
1758 A938 60cr shown 1.65 42

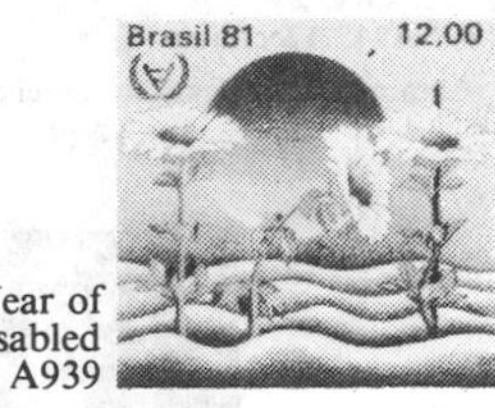

Intl. Year of the Disabled A939

1981, Sept. 17 Litho. *Perf. 11½*
1759 A939 12cr multi 30 20

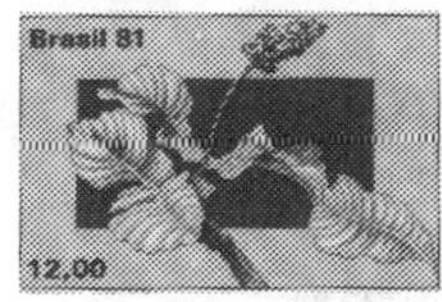

Flowers of the Central Plateau A940

1981, Sept. 21 Litho. *Perf. 12*
1760 A940 12cr Palicourea rigida 40 20
1761 A940 12cr Dalechampia caperonioides 40 20
1762 A940 12cr Cassia clausseni, vert. 40 20
1763 A940 12cr Eremanthus sphaerocephalus, vert. 40 20

Virgin of Nazareth Statue — A941

Christ the Redeemer Statue, Rio de Janeiro, 50th Anniv. — A942

1981, Oct. 10 Litho. *Perf. 12*
1764 A941 12cr multi 35 20

Candle Festival of Nazareth, Belem.

1981, Oct. 12
1765 A942 12cr multi 35 20

World Food Day — A943

1981, Oct. 16
1766 A943 12c multi 35 20

75th Anniv. of Santos-Dumont's First Flight — A944

1981, Oct. 23 Litho. *Perf. 12*
1767 A944 60cr multi 1.65 50

Father José de Santa Rita Durao, Titlepage of his Epic Poem Caramuru, Diego Alvares Correia (Character) A945

1981, Oct. 29
1768 A945 12cr multi 35 20

Caramuru publication centenary; World Book Day.

Christmas 1981 — A946

Designs: Creches and figurines. 55cr, 60cr vert.

1981, Nov. 10 Litho. *Perf. 12*
1769 A946 12cr multi 18 10
1770 A946 50cr multi 1.75 35
1771 A946 55cr multi 1.75 38
1772 A946 60cr multi 1.75 40

State Flags A947

Designs: a. Alagoas. b. Bahia. c. Federal District. d. Pernambuco. e. Sergipe.

1981, Nov. 19
1773 Block of 5 plus label 1.65 1.65
a.-e. A947 12cr, any single 30 30

Label shows arms of Brazil.

Thanksgiving 1981 — A948

1981, Nov. 26 Litho. *Perf. 11½*
1776 A948 12cr multi 30 15

Ministry of Labor, 50th Anniv. A949

1981, Nov. 26
1777 A949 12cr multi 30 15

School of Engineering, Itajuba — A950

1981, Nov. 30 *Perf. 11x11½*
1778 A950 15cr lt grn & pur 45 15

Theodomiro C. Santiago, founder, birth centenary.

Sao Paulo State Police Sesquicentennial A951

1981, Dec. 15 Litho. *Perf. 12*
1779 A951 12cr Policeman with saxophone 40 15
1780 A951 12cr Mounted policemen 40 15

Army Library Centenary A952

1981, Dec. 17
1781 A952 12cr multi 30 15

Souvenir Sheet

Philatelic Club of Brazil, 50th Anniv. A953

1981, Dec. 18 *Perf. 11*
1782 A953 180cr multi 6.00 *6.00*

No. 1782 has multicolored margin showing "Bull's Eye" stamps designs, emblem. Size: 89x69mm.

Brigadier Eduardo Gomes A954

1982, Jan. 20 Litho. *Perf. 11x11½*
1783 A954 12cr bl & blk 45 15

Birth Centenary of Henrique Lage, Industrialist — A956

1982, Mar. 14 Litho. *Perf. 11½*
1785 A956 17cr multi 70 16

1982 World Cup Soccer — A957

TB Bacillus Centenary — A958

Designs: Various soccer players.

1982, Mar. 19
1786 A957 75cr multi 1.75 60
1787 A957 80cr multi 1.75 65
1788 A957 85cr multi 1.75 65

Souvenir Sheet
Imperf
1789 Sheet of 3 5.00 *10.00*
a. A957 100cr like #1786 1.65
b. A957 100cr like #1787 1.65
c. A957 100cr like #1788 1.65

No. 1789 has black marginal inscription. Size: 125x87mm.

1982, Mar. 24 *Perf. 12*
1790 A958 90cr Microscope, lung 1.50 80
1791 A958 100cr Lung, pills 1.50 90

Nos. 1790-1791 se-tenant.

Souvenir Sheet

A959

1982, Apr. 17 Litho. *Perf. 11*
1792 Sheet of 3 4.00 3.75
a. A959 75cr Laelia Purpurata 1.25 70
b. A959 80cr Oncidium flexuosum 1.25 75
c. A959 85cr Cleistes revoluta 1.40 80

BRAPEX V Stamp Exhibition, Blumenau. No. 1792 has black marginal inscription. Size: 100x70mm.

Oil Drilling Centenary A960

1982, Apr. 18 *Perf. 11½*
1793 A960 17cr multi 30 15

400th Birth Anniv. of St. Vincent de Paul A961

1982, Apr. 24 Litho. *Perf. 11½*
1794 A961 17cr multi 30 15

Seven Steps of Guaira (Waterfalls) A962

1982, Apr. 29
1795 A962 17cr Fifth Fall 30 15
1796 A962 21cr Seventh Fall 40 20

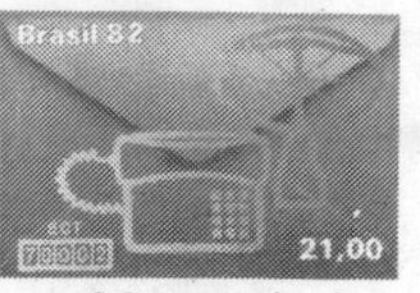

Ministry of Communications, 15th Anniv. — A963

1982, May 15
1797 A963 21cr multi 40 20

Museology Course, Natl. Historical Museum, 50th Anniv. A964

1982, May 18
1798 A964 17cr blk & sal pink 30 15

Vale de Rio Doce Mining Co. — A965

1982, June 1
1799 A965 17cr Gears 30 15

Martin Afonso de Souza Reading Charter to Settlers A966

1982, June 3 Litho. *Perf. 11½*
1800 A966 17cr multi 30 15

Town of Sao Vincente, 450th anniv.

Armadillo A967

1982, June 4
1801 A967 17cr shown 1.00 15
1802 A967 21cr Wolves 1.00 20
1803 A967 30cr Deer 3.00 25

Film Strip and Award A968

1982, June 19
1804 A968 17cr multi 30 15

20th anniv. of Golden Palm award for The Promise Keeper, Cannes Film Festival.

Souvenir Sheet

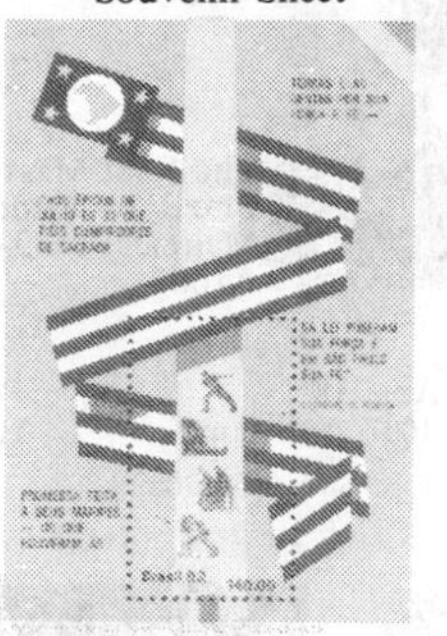

50th Anniv. of Constitutionalist Revolution — A969

1982, July 9 Litho. *Perf. 11*
1805 A969 140cr multi 2.25 2.25

Multicolored margin continues design. Size: 70x100mm.

Church of Our Lady of O'Sabara — A970

St. Francis of Assisi, 800th Birth Anniv. — A971

Baroque Architecture, Minas Gerais State: No. 1807, Church of Our Lady of the Rosary, Diamantina (horiz.). No. 1808, Town Square, Mariana (horiz.).

1982, July 16 *Perf. 11½*
1806 A970 17cr multi 30 15
1807 A970 17cr multi 30 15
1808 A970 17cr multi 30 15

1982, July 24
1809 A971 21cr multi 35 20

Stamp Day and Centenary of Pedro II "Large Head" Stamps A972

1982, Aug. 1
1810 A972 21cr No. 82 35 20

Port of Manaus Free Trade Zone A973

1982, Aug. 15 *Perf. 11x11½*
1811 A973 75cr multi 1.25 70

Canceled-to-order stamps are often from remainders. Most collectors of canceled stamps prefer postally used specimens.

Scouting Year — A974

1982, Aug. 21 Litho. *Perf. 11*
1812 Sheet of 2 4.75 *5.50*
a. A974 85cr Baden-Powell 1.75 *2.00*
b. A974 185cr Scout 2.80 *3.00*

Black marginal inscription, emblem. Size: 100x70mm.

Orixas Folk Costumes of African Origin A975

1982, Aug. 21 *Perf. 11½*
1813 A975 20cr Iemanja 30 16
1814 A975 20cr Xango 30 16
1815 A975 20cr Oxumare 30 16

10th Anniv. of Central Bank of Brazil Currency Museum A976

1982, Aug. 31
1816 A976 25cr 12-florin coin, 1645, obverse and reverse 38 20
1817 A976 25cr Emperor Pedro's 6.40-reis coronation coin, 1822 38 20

National Week A977

1982, Sept. 1
1818 A977 25cr Don Pedro proclaiming independence 38 20

St. Theresa of Avila (1515-1582) A978

1982, Oct. 4
1819 A978 85cr Portrait 1.30 75

Instruments — A979

1982, Oct. 15 Litho. *Perf. 11½x11*
1820 A979 75cr Instruments 1.15 70
1821 A979 80cr Dancers 1.20 72
1822 A979 85cr Musicians 1.30 75
a. Souvenir sheet of 3 3.75 *4.50*

Lubrapex '82, 4th Portuguese-Brazilian Stamp Exhibition. No. 1822a contains Nos. 1820-1822 (perf. 11), without "LUBRAPEX 82."

Aviation Industry Day — A980

1982, Oct. 17 *Perf. 12*
1823 A980 24cr Embraer EMB-312 trainer plane 36 20

Bastos Tigre, Poet, Birth Centenary, and "Saudade" Text A981

1982, Oct. 29
1824 A981 24cr multi 36 20

Book Day.

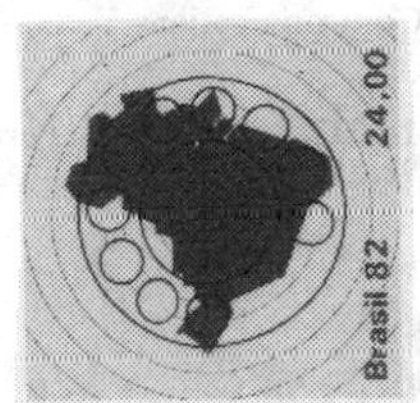

10th Anniv. of Brazilian Telecommunications Co. — A982

1982, Nov. 9 Litho. *Perf. 11½*
1825 A982 24cr multi 36 20

Christmas 1982 — A983

Children's Drawings.

1982, Nov. 10
1826 A983 24cr Nativity 36 20
1827 A983 24cr Angels 36 20
1828 A983 30cr Nativity, diff. 45 45
1829 A983 30cr Flight into Egypt 45 45

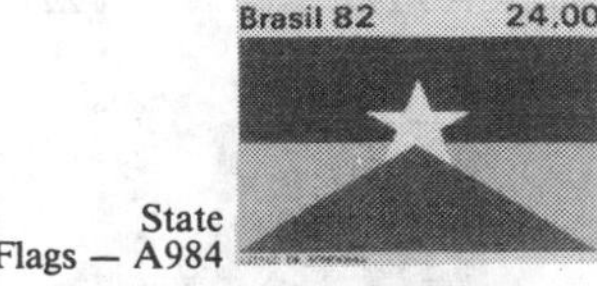

State Flags — A984

Designs: a. Ceara. b. Espirito Santo. c. Paraiba. d. Grande de Norte. e. Rondonia.

1982, Nov. 19
1830 Block of 5 plus label 6.50 6.50
a.-e. A984 24cr any single 1.25 20

Thanksgiving 1982 — A985

1982, Nov. 25
1835 A985 24cr multi 36 20

Homage to the Deaf — A986

1982, Dec. 1
1836 A986 24cr multi 36 20

Naval Academy Bicentenary A987

Training Ships.

1982, Dec. 14
1837 A987 24cr Brazil 40 20
1838 A987 24cr Benjamin Constant 40 20
1839 A987 24cr Almirante Saldanha 40 20

Souvenir Sheet

No. 12 — A988

1982, Dec. 18 Litho. *Perf. 11*
1840 A988 200cr multi 5.00 *6.00*

BRASILIANA '83 Intl. Stamp Exhibition, Rio de Janeiro, July 29-Aug. 7. Multicolored margin shows Regional Administration building. Size: 100x70mm.

Brasiliana '83 Carnival A989

1983, Feb. 9 Litho. *Perf. 11½*
1841 A989 24cr Samba drummers 18 10
1842 A989 130cr Street parade 1.25 50
1843 A989 140cr Dancer 1.25 52
1844 A989 150cr Male dancer 1.25 55

Antarctic Expedition A990

1983, Feb. 20 Litho. *Perf. 11½*
1845 A990 150cr Support ship Barano de Teffe 1.50 55

50th Anniv. of Women's Rights — A991

1983, Mar. 8
1846 A991 130cr multi 1.50 50

Itaipu Hydroelectric Power Station Opening — A992

1983, Mar. Litho. *Perf. 12*
1847 A992 140cr multi 1.50 45

Cancer Prevention A993

Martin Luther (1483-1546) A994

Designs: 30cr, Microscope. 38cr, Antonio Prudente, Paulista Cancer Assoc. founder, Camargo Hospital. Se-tenant.

1983, Apr. 18
1848 A993 30cr multi 20 10
1849 A993 38cr multi 25 12

1983, Apr. 18
1850 A994 150cr pale grn & blk 1.50 50

Agricultural Research A995

1983, Apr. 26 Litho. *Perf. 11½*
1851 A995 30cr Chestnut tree 20 6
1852 A995 30cr Genetic research 20 6
1853 A995 38cr Tropical soy beans 25 8

Prices of premium quality never hinged stamps will be in excess of catalogue price.

Father Rogerio Neuhaus (1863-1934), Centenary of Ordination — A996

1983, May 3 *Perf. 11½x11*
1854 A996 30cr multi 25 6

30th Anniv. of Customs Cooperation Council — A997

1983, May 5 *Perf. 11x11½*
1855 A997 30cr multi 25 6

World Communications Year — A998

1983, May 17 Litho. *Perf. 11½*
1856 A998 250cr multi 1.65 50

Toucans A999

1983, May 21
1857 A999 30cr Tucanucu 15 6
1858 A999 185cr White-breasted 1.65 38
1859 A999 205cr Green-beaked 1.65 40
1860 A999 215cr Black-beaked 1.65 45

Souvenir Sheet

Resurrection, by Raphael (1483-1517) — A1000

1983, May 25 *Perf. 11*
1861 A1000 250cr multi 2.25 *3.00*

Hohenzollern 980 Locomotive, 1875 — A1001

Various locomotives.

1983, June 12 Litho. *Perf. 11½*
1862 A1001 30cr shown 20 6
1863 A1001 30cr Baldwin No. 1, 1881 20 6
1864 A1001 38cr Fowler No. 1, 1872 25 8

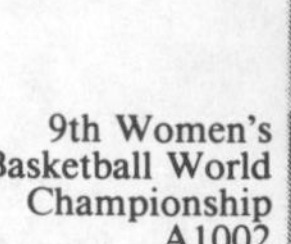
9th Women's Basketball World Championship A1002

1983, July 24 Litho. *Perf. 11½x11*
1865 A1002 30cr Players, front view 20 6
1866 A1002 30cr Players, rear view 20 6

Simon Bolivar (1783-1830) A1003

1983, July 24 *Perf. 12*
1867 A1003 30cr multi 20 6

Children's Polio and Measles Vaccination Campaign A1004

1983, July 25
1868 A1004 30cr Girl, measles 20 6
1869 A1004 30cr Boy, polio 20 6

20th Anniv. of Master's Program in Engineering — A1005

1983, July 28 *Perf. 11½x11*
1870 A1005 30cr Minerva (goddess of wisdom), computer tape 20 6

No. 1, Guanabara Bay — A1006

1983, July 29 Engr.
1871 A1006 185cr shown 1.50 38
1872 A1006 205cr No. 2 1.50 40
1873 A1006 215cr No. 3 1.50 45

Souvenir Sheet
Perf. 11

1874 Sheet of 3 8.75 *10.00*
a. A1006 185cr No. 1 2.25 *3.00*
b. A1006 205cr No. 2 2.25 *3.00*
c. A1006 215cr No. 3 2.25 *3.00*

BRASILIANA '83 Intl. Stamp Show, Rio de Janeiro, July 29-Aug. 7. No. 1874 View of Guanabara Bay in one continuous design. Size: 101x70mm.

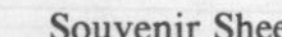
Souvenir Sheet

The First Mass in Brazil, by Vitor Meireles (1833-1903) A1007

1983, Aug. 18 *Perf. 11*
1875 A1007 250cr multi 2.00 1.50

Size: 101x70mm.

EMB-120 Brasilia Passenger Plane A1008

1983, Aug. 19 *Perf. 12*
1876 A1008 30cr multi 20 6

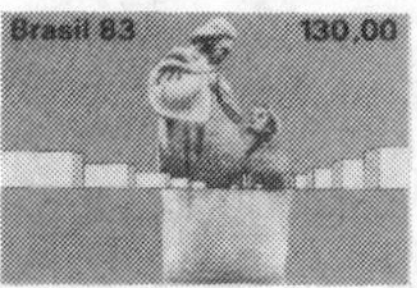
Vision of Don Bosco Centenary A1009

1983, Aug. 30
1877 A1009 130cr multi 75 25

Independence Week — A1010

1983, Sept. 1 Litho. *Perf. 11½*
1878 A1010 50cr multi 25 12

National Steel Corp., 10th Anniv. A1011

1983, Sept. 17 Litho. *Perf. 11½*
1879 A1011 45cr multi 18 10

Cactus A1012

1983, Sept. 12 Litho. *Perf. 11½*
1880 A1012 45cr Pilosocereus gounellei 25 10
1881 A1012 45cr Melocactus bahiensis 25 10
1882 A1012 57cr Cereus jamacaru 30 12

1st National Eucharistic Congress — A1013

1983, Oct. 12 Litho. *Perf. 11½*
1883 A1013 45cr multi 18 10

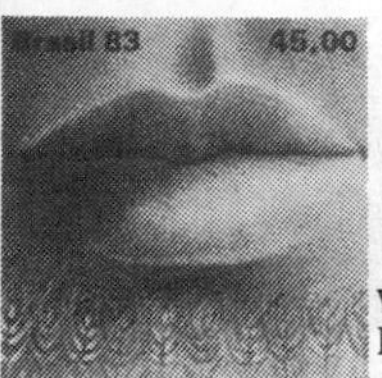

World Food Program A1014

1983, Oct. 14 Litho. *Perf. 11½*
1884 A1014 45cr Mouth, grain 18 10
1885 A1014 57cr Fish, sailboat 24 12

Souvenir Sheet

Louis Breguet, Death Centenary — A1015

1983, Oct. 27 Litho. *Perf. 11*
1886 A1015 376cr Telegraph transmitter 2.00 1.50

Brown and multicolored margin shows portrait and telegraph lines. Size: 70x99mm.

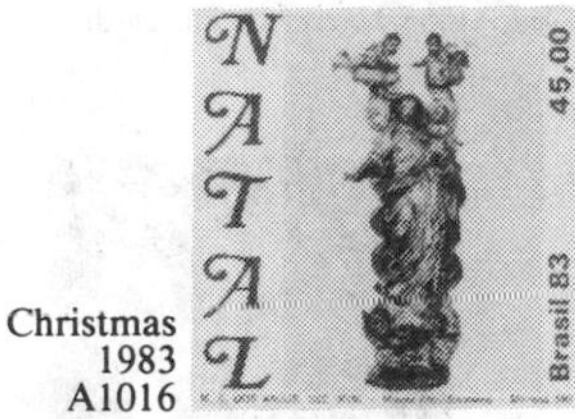

Christmas 1983 A1016

17th-18th Cent. Statues: 45cr, Our Lady of the Angels. 315cr, Our Lady of the Parturition. 335cr, Our Lady of Joy. 345cr, Our Lady of the Presentation.

1983, Nov. 10 Litho. *Perf. 11½*
1887 A1016 45cr multi 25 10
1888 A1016 315cr multi 1.65 60
1889 A1016 335cr multi 1.65 65
1890 A1016 345cr multi 1.65 70

Marshal Mascarenhas Birth Centenary A1017

1983, Nov. 13 Litho. *Perf. 11½*
1891 A1017 45cr Battle sites 18 10

Commander of Brazilian Expeditionary Force in Italy.

State Flags A1018

Designs: a. Amazonas. b. Goias. c. Rio de Janiero. d. Mato Grosso Do Sol. e. Parana.

1983, Nov. 17 Litho. *Perf. 11½*
1892 Block of 5 plus label 3.00 3.00
a.-e. A1018 45cr any single 50 20

Nos. 1892-1896 printed se-tenant with label showing arms of Republic.

Thanksgiving 1983 — A1018a

1983, Nov. 24 Litho. *Perf. 12*
1896 A1018a 45cr Madonna, wheat 30 10

Manned Flight Bicentenary A1019

1983, Dec. 15 Litho. *Perf. 12*
1897 A1019 345cr Montgolfiere balloon, 1783 5.00 50

Ethnic Groups A1020

1984, Jan. 20 Litho. *Perf. 12*
1898 A1020 45cr multi 18 5

50th anniv. of publication of Masters and Slaves, sociological study by Gilberto Freyre.

Centenary of Crystal Palace, Petropolis A1021

1984, Feb. 2
1899 A1021 45cr multi 18 5

Souvenir Sheet

Flags (Sculpture with 40 Figures), by Victor Brecheret (b. 1894) — A1022

1984, Feb. 22 Litho. *Perf. 11*
1900 A1022 805cr multi 1.75 1.00

Size: 100x70mm.

Naval Museum Centenary A1023

1984, Mar. 23 Litho. *Perf. 11½*
1901 A1023 620cr Figurehead, frigate, 1847 1.30 60

Slavery Abolition Centenary A1024

1984, Mar. 25
1902 A1024 585cr Broken chain, raft 1.15 65
1903 A1024 610cr Freed slave 1.25 70

Souvenir Sheet

Visit of King Carl XVI Gustaf of Sweden A1025

1984, Apr. 2 *Perf. 11*
1904 A1025 2105cr multi 4.50 2.50

Multicolored margin shows palaces, arms. Size: 99x69mm.

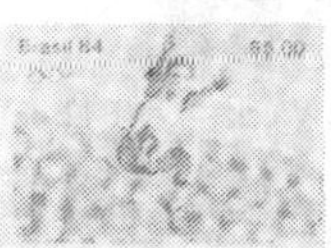

1984 Summer Olympics A1026

1984, Apr. 13 *Perf. 11½*
1905 A1026 65cr Long jump 14 8
1906 A1026 65cr 100-meter race 14 8
1907 A1026 65cr Relay race 14 8
1908 A1026 585cr Pole vault 1.15 65
1909 A1026 610cr High jump 1.25 70
1910 A1026 620cr Hurdles 1.30 80
Nos. 1905-1910 (6) 4.12 2.39

Nos. 1905-1910 se-tenant.

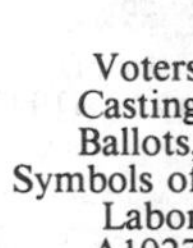

Voters Casting Ballots, Symbols of Labor A1027

Pres. Getulio Vargas Birth Centenary: Symbols of Development.

1984, Apr. 19 Litho. *Perf. 11½*
1911 A1027 65cr shown 20 8
1912 A1027 65cr Oil rig, blast furnace 20 8
1913 A1027 65cr High-tension towers 20 8

Columbus, Espana '84 Emblem — A1028

1984, Apr. 27
1914 A1028 65cr Pedro Cabral 20 8
1915 A1028 610cr shown 1.50 70

Map of Americas, Heads — A1029

Lubrapex '84 — A1030

1984, May 7 Litho. *Perf. 11½*
1916 A1029 65cr multi 14 8

Pan-American Association of Finance and Guarantees, 8th Assembly.

1984, May 8 *Perf. 11½x11*

18th Century Paintings, Mariana Cathedral.

1917 A1030 65cr Hunting scene 20 8
1918 A1030 585cr Pastoral scene 1.40 62
1919 A1030 610cr People under umbrellas 1.50 70
1920 A1030 620cr Elephants 1.65 72

Souvenir Sheet

Intl. Fedn. of Soccer Associations, 80th Anniv. — A1031

1984, May 21 *Perf. 11*
1921 A1031 2115cr Globe 4.50 2.50

Multicolored margin shows various World Cup games emblems. Size: 99x68mm.

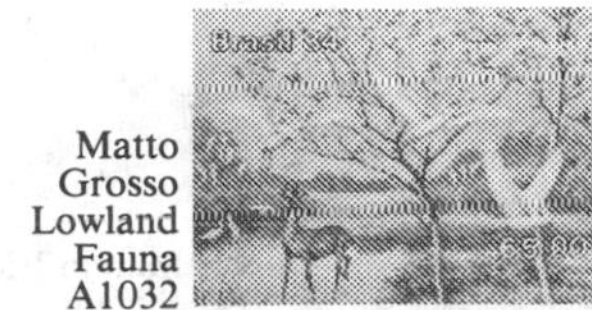

Matto Grosso Lowland Fauna A1032

1984, June 5 Litho. *Perf. 11½*
1922 Strip of 3 75 30
a. A1032 65cr Deer 25 8
b. A1032 65cr Jaguar 25 8
c. A1032 60cr Alligator 25 10

First Letter Mailed in Brazil, by Guido Mondin — A1033

1984, June 8 *Perf. 12x11½*
1923 A1033 65cr multi 20 8

Postal Union of Americas and Spain, first anniv. of new headquarters.

Brazil-Germany Air Service, 50th Anniv.
A1034 A1035

1984, June 19
1924 A1034 610cr Dornier-Wal seaplane 1.25 70
1925 A1035 620cr Steamer Westfalen 1.30 72

Woolly Spider Monkey, World Wildlife Fund Emblem — A1036

1984, July 6 ***Perf. 11½***
1926 A1036 65cr Mother, baby 70 8
1927 A1036 80cr Monkey 50 10

Agriculture Type of 1980

Designs: 65cr, Rubber tree. 80cr, Brazil nuts. 120cr, Rice. 150cr, Eucalyptus. 300cr, Pinha da Parana. 800cr, Carnauba. 1000cr, Babacu. 2000cr, Sunflower.

Photogravure (65, 80, 120, 150cr), Engraved

1984-85 ***Perf. 11x11½***
1934 A894 65cr lilac 14 8
1935 A894 80cr brn red 18 10
1936 A894 120cr dk sl bl 26 8
1937 A894 150cr Eucalyptus 10 5
1938 A894 300cr rose mag 35 15
1939 A894 800cr grnsh bl 1.00 15
1940 A894 1000cr lemon 1.00 15
1941 A894 2000cr yel org ('85) 50 25
Nos. 1934-1941 (8) 3.53 1.01

Marajo Isld. Buffalo
A1037

1984, July 9 **Litho.** ***Perf. 12***
1942 Strip of 3 75 25
a. A1037 65cr Approaching stream 20 8
b. A1037 65cr Standing on bank 20 8
c. A1037 65cr Drinking 20 8

Continuous design.

Banco Economico Sesquicentenary — A1038

1984, July 13 ***Perf. 11½***
1943 A1038 65cr Bank, coins 20 8

Historic Railway Stations
A1039

1984, July 23 **Litho.** ***Perf. 11½***
1944 A1039 65cr Japeri 14 8
1945 A1039 65cr Luz, vert. 14 8
1946 A1039 80cr Sao Joao del Rei 18 10

Souvenir Sheet

Girl Scouts in Brazil, 65th Anniv. — A1040

1984, Aug. 13 ***Perf. 11***
1947 A1040 585cr Girl scout 1.50 1.00

Multicolored margin shows Juliet Lowe, scouts. Size: 100x70mm.

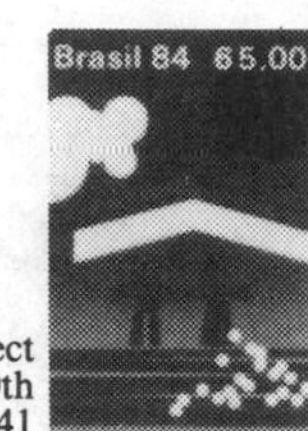

Housing Project Bank, 20th Anniv. — A1041

1984, Aug. 21 **Litho.** ***Perf. 11½***
1948 A1041 65cr Couple sheltered from rain 20 8

Independence Week — A1042

Children's Drawings.

1984, Sept. 3
1949 A1042 100cr Explorer & ship 20 12
1950 A1042 100cr Sailing ships 20 12
1951 A1042 100cr "BRASIL" mural 20 12
1952 A1042 100cr Children under rainbow 20 12

Rio de Janeiro Chamber of Commerce Sesquicentenary — A1043

1984, Sept. 10
1953 A1043 100cr Monument, worker silhouette 20 12

Death Sesquicentenary of Don Pedro I (IV of Portugal) — A1044

1984, Sept. 23 ***Perf. 12x11½***
1954 A1044 1000cr Portrait 2.00 1.25

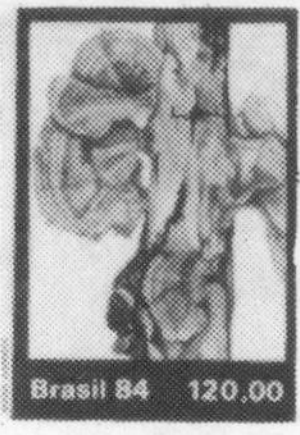

Local Mushrooms
A1045

1984, Oct. 22 ***Perf. 11½***
1955 A1045 120cr Pycnoporus sanguineus 24 15
1956 A1045 1050cr Calvatia sp 2.30 1.25
1957 A1045 1080cr Pleurotus sp, horiz. 2.40 1.30

Book Day — A1046

1984, Oct. 23 ***Perf. 11½***
1958 A1046 120cr Girl in open book 24 15

New State Mint Opening — A1047

1984, Nov. 1
1959 A1047 120cr multi 24 15

Informatics Fair & Congress
A1048

1984, Nov. 5 **Litho.** ***Perf. 12***
1960 A1048 120cr Eye, computer terminal 12 5

Org. of American States, 14th Assembly — A1049

1984, Nov. 14
1961 A1049 120cr Emblem, flags 12 5

State Flags
A1050

Designs: a. Maranhaio. b. Mato Grosso. c. Minas Gerais. d. Piaui. e. Santa Catarina.

1984, Nov. 19 ***Perf. 11½***
1962 Block of 5 plus label 1.50 1.50
a.-e. A1050 120cr, any single 30 10

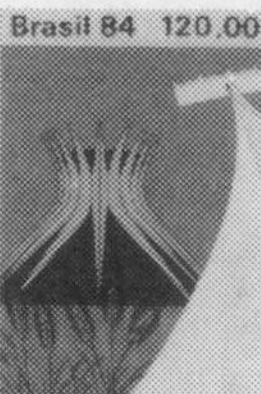

Thanksgiving 1984 — A1051

1984, Nov. 22
1963 A1051 120cr Bell tower, Brasilia 14 6

Christmas 1984
A1052

Paintings: No. 1964, Nativity, by Djanira. No. 1965, Virgin and Child, by Glauco Rodrigues. No. 1966, Flight into Egypt, by Paul Garfunkel. No. 1967, Nativity, by Di Cavalcanti.

1984, Dec. 3 **Litho.** ***Perf. 12***
1964 A1052 120cr multi 12 5
1965 A1052 120cr multi 12 5
1966 A1052 1050cr multi 1.10 40
1967 A1052 1080cr multi 1.10 40

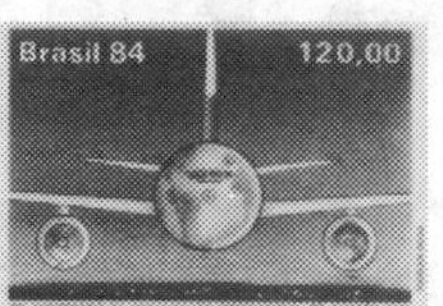

40th Anniv., International Civil Aviation Organization — A1053

1984, Dec. 7 **Litho.** ***Perf. 12***
1968 A1053 120cr Aircraft, Earth globe 12 5

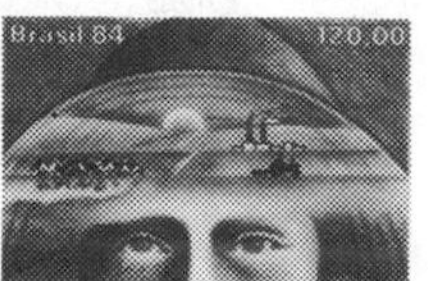

25th Anniv., North-Eastern Development — A1054

1984, Dec. 14 **Litho.** ***Perf. 12***
1969 A1054 120cr Farmer, field 12 5

Emilio Rouede
A1055

Painting: Church of the Virgin of Safe Travels, by Rouede.

1985, Jan. 22 **Litho.** ***Perf. 12***
1970 A1055 120cr multi 12 5

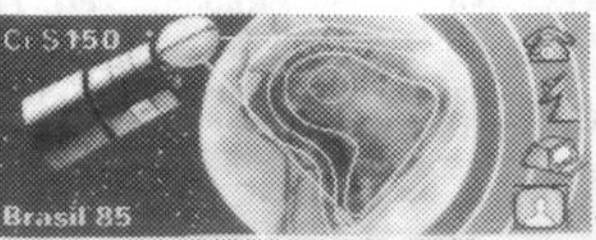

BRASILSAT — A1056

1985, Feb. 8 **Litho.** ***Perf. 11½x12***
1971 A1056 150cr Satellite, Brazil 14 6

Metropolitan Railways — A1057

1985, Mar. 2 Litho. *Perf. 11x11½*
1972 A1057 200cr Passenger trains 14 8

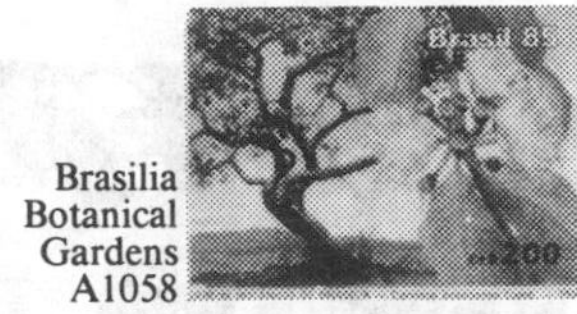
Brasilia Botanical Gardens A1058

1985, Mar. 8 Litho. *Perf. 11½x12*
1973 A1058 200cr Caryocar brasiliense 14 8

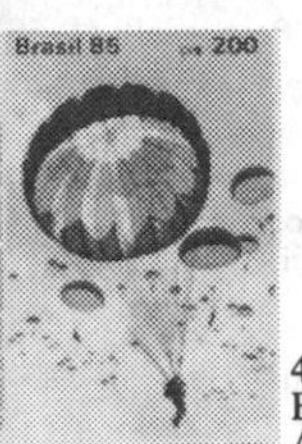
40th Anniv., Brazilian Paratroops A1059

1985, Mar. 8 Litho. *Perf. 11½x12*
1974 A1059 200cr Parachute drop 14 8

Natl. Climate Awareness Program — A1060

1985, Mar. 18 Litho. *Perf. 11½x12*
1975 A1060 500cr multi 30 14

Thoroughbred Horses — A1061

1985, Mar. 19 Litho. *Perf. 12*
1976 A1061 1000cr Campolina 60 28
1977 A1061 1500cr Marajoara 1.10 42
1978 A1061 1500cr Mangalarga marchador 1.10 42

Ouro Preto — A1062

1985, Apr. 18 Litho. *Perf. 11½x12*
1979 A1062 220cr shown 14 6
1980 A1062 220cr St. Miguel des Missoes 14 6
1981 A1062 220cr Olinda 14 6

Polivolume, by Mary Vieira — A1063

Rio Branco Inst. 40th Anniv.

1985, Apr. 20 Litho.
1982 A1063 220cr multi 14 6

Natl. Capital, Brasilia, 25th Anniv. — A1064

1985, Apr. 22 Litho.
1983 A1064 220cr Natl. Theater, acoustic shell 14 6
1984 A1064 220cr Catetinho Palace, JK Memorial 14 6

Numerals — A1065

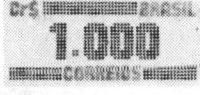

Dot Numeral A1065a

1985-86 Photo. *Perf. 11½*

1985	A1065	50cr	lake	5	5
1986	A1065	100cr	dp vio	6	5
1987	A1065	150cr	violet	5	5
1988	A1065	200cr	ultra	8	5
1989	A1065	220cr	green	10	6
1990	A1065	300cr	ryl bl	18	12
1991	A1065	500cr	ol blk	30	22
1992	A1065a	1000cr	brn ol ('86)	18	10
1993	A1065a	2000cr	brt grn ('86)	35	22
1994	A1065a	3000cr	dl vio	42	32
1995	A1065a	5000cr	brn	58	42
	Nos. 1985-1995 (11)			2.35	1.66

Marshall Rondon, 120th Birth Anniv. A1066

1985, May 5 *Perf. 11x11½*
1996 A1066 220cr multi 14 6

Educator, protector of the Indians, building superintendent of telegraph lines.

Candido Fontoura (1885-1974) A1067

Brapex VI A1068

1985, May 14 *Perf. 12x11½*
1997 A1067 220cr multi 14 6

Pioneer of the Brazilian pharmaceutical industry.

1985, May 18 *Perf. 11½x11*

Cave paintings: No. 1998, Deer, Cerca Grande. No. 1999, Lizards, Lapa do Caboclo. No. 2000, Running deer, Grande Abrigo de Santana do Riacho.

1998 A1068 300cr multi 18 8
1999 A1068 300cr multi 18 8
2000 A1068 2000cr multi 1.10 50
a. Souvenir sheet of 3, perf. 10½x11 1.65 75

No. 2000a contains Nos. 1998-2000; margin inscribed. Size: 100x70mm.

Wildlife Conservation A1069

Birds in Marinho dos Abrolhos National Park.

1985, June 5 *Perf. 11½x12*
2001 A1069 220cr Fregata magnificens 14 5
2002 A1069 220cr Sula dactylatra 14 5
2003 A1069 220cr Anous stolidus 14 5
2004 A1069 2000cr Pluvialis squatarola 1.25 50

U.N. Infant Survival Campaign A1070

1985, June 11 *Perf. 12x11½*
2005 A1070 220cr Mother breastfeeding infant 12 5
2006 A1070 220cr Hand, eyedropper, children 12 5
a. Pair, #2005-2006 25 10

Helicopter Rescue, Search Ship, Diver — A1071

1985, June 22 Litho. *Perf. 11½x11*
2007 A1071 220cr multi 15 10

Sea Search & Rescue.

Souvenir Sheet

World Cup Soccer, Mexico, 1986 A1072

1985, June 23 *Perf. 11*
2008 A1072 2000cr Player dribbling, World Cup 1.25 85

No. 2008 has multicolored margin continuing the design. Size: 70x99mm.

Intl. Youth Year A1073

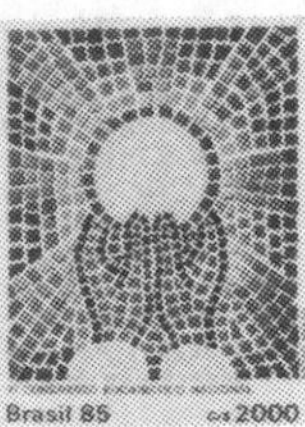
11th Natl. Eucharistic Congress A1074

1985, June 28 *Perf. 12*
2009 A1073 220cr Circle of children 15 10

1985, July 16 *Perf. 12x11½*
2010 A1074 2000cr Mosaic, Priest raising host 1.25 85

Director Humberto Mauro, Scene from Sangue Mineiro, 1929 — A1075

1985, July 27
2011 A1075 300cr multi 18 12

Cataguases Studios, 60th anniv.

Escola e Sacro Museum, Convent St. Anthony, Joao Pessoa, Paraiba A1076

1985, Aug. 5 *Perf. 11½x12*
2012 A1076 330cr multi 20 15

Paraiba State 400th anniv.

Inconfidencia Museum A1077

Cabanagem Insurrection, 150th Anniv. A1078

1985, Aug. 11 *Perf. 12x11½*
2013 A1077 300cr shown 18 12
2014 A1077 300cr Museum of History & Diplomacy 18 12

1985, Aug. 14

Design: Revolutionary, detail from an oil painting by Guido Mondin.

2015 A1078 330cr multi 20 15

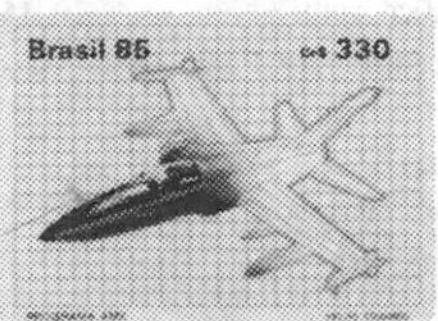
AMX Subsonic Air Force Fighter Plane A1079

1985, Aug. 19 *Perf. 11½x12*
2016 A1079 330cr multi 20 15

AMX Project, joint program with Italy.

16th-17th Century Military Uniforms A1080

1985, Aug. 26 *Perf. 12x11½*
2017 A1080 300cr Captain, cross-bowman 20 12
2018 A1080 300cr Harquebusier, sergeant 20 12
2019 A1080 300cr Musketeer, pike-man 20 12
2020 A1080 300cr Fusilier, pikeman 20 12

Farrouphilha Insurrection, 150th Anniv. — A1081

Design: Bento Goncalves and insurrectionist cavalry on Southern battlefields, detail of an oil painting by Guido Mondin.

1985, Sept. 20 *Perf. 11½x12*
2021 A1081 330cr multi 20 15

Aparados da Serra National Park A1082

1985, Sept. 23
2022 A1082 3100cr Ravine 80 52
2023 A1082 3320cr Mountains 85 55
2024 A1082 3480cr Forest, waterfall 90 60

President-elect Tancredo Neves — A1083

Design: Portrait, Natl. Congress, Alvorada Palace, Federal Supreme Court.

1985, Oct. 10 Litho. *Perf. 11x11½*
2025 A1083 330cr multi 20 12

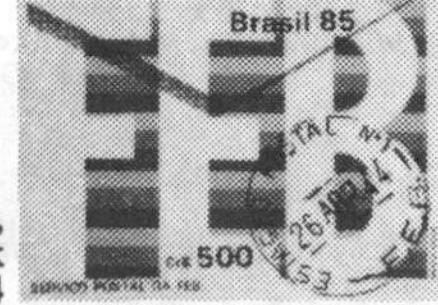

FEB, Postmark A1084

1985, Oct. 10 *Perf. 11½x12*
2026 A1084 500cr multi 20 15

Brazilian Expeditionary Force Postal Service, 41st anniv.

Foreign postal stationery (stamped envelopes, postal cards and air letter sheets) lies beyond the scope of this Catalogue, which is limited to adhesive postage stamps.

Rio de Janeiro-Niteroi Ferry Service, 150th Anniv. — A1085

1985, Oct. 14 *Perf. 11½x12*
2027 A1085 500cr Segunda 20 15
2028 A1085 500cr Terceira 20 15
2029 A1085 500cr Especuladora 20 15
2030 A1085 500cr Urca 20 15

Muniz M-7 Inaugural Flight, 50th Anniv. — A1086

1985, Oct. 22
2031 A1086 500cr multi 20 15

UN 40th Anniv. A1087

Natl. Press System A1088

1985, Oct. 24 *Perf. 11½x11*
2032 A1087 500cr multi 20 15

1985, Nov. 7
2033 A1088 500cr Newspaper mast-head, reader 20 15

Diario de Pernambuco, newspaper, 160th anniv.

Christmas 1985 A1089

1985, Nov. 11 *Perf. 11½x12*
2034 A1089 500cr Christ in Manger 20 15
2035 A1089 500cr Adoration of the Magi 20 15
2036 A1089 500cr Flight to Egypt 20 15

Para A1090

State Flags: No. 2037b, Rio Grande do Sul. No. 2037c, Acre. No. 2037d, Sao Paulo.

1985, Nov. 19 *Perf. 12*
2037 Block of 4 80 60
a.-d. A1090 500cr, any single 20 15

Thanksgiving Day — A1091

1985, Nov. 28 *Perf. 12x11½*
2038 A1091 500cr Child gathering wheat 20 15

Economic Development of Serra dos Carajas Region — A1092

1985, Dec. 11 Litho. *Perf. 11½x12*
2039 A1092 500cr multi 14 6

Fr. Bartholomeu Lourenco de Gusmao (1685-1724), Inventor, the Aerostat — A1093

1985, Dec. 19 Litho. *Perf. 11x11½*
2040 A1093 500cr multi 14 6

The Trees, by Da Costa E Silva (b. 1885), Poet — A1094

1985, Dec. 20 Litho. *Perf. 12x11½*
2041 A1094 500cr multi 14 6

Souvenir Sheet

1986 World Cup Soccer Championships, Mexico — A1095

1986, Mar. 3 Litho. *Perf. 11*
2042 A1095 10000cr multi 2.25 2.00

LUBRAPEX '86, philatelic exhibition. No. 2042 has multicolored margin continuing the design and picturing FIFA emblem and flags. Size: 69x99mm.

Halley's Comet — A1096

1986, Apr. 11 Litho. *Perf. 11½x12*
2043 A1096 .50cz multi 8 5

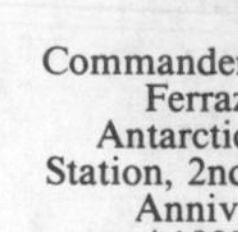

Commander Ferraz Antarctic Station, 2nd Anniv. A1097

1986, Apr. 25
2044 A1097 .50cz multi 8 6

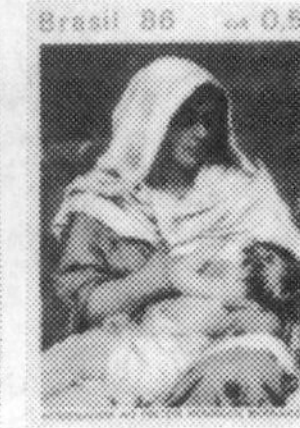

Labor Day A1098

Maternity, by Henrique Bernardelli (1858-1936) A1099

1986, May 1 Litho. *Perf. 12x11½*
2045 A1098 .50cz multi 8 5

1986, May 8
2046 A1099 .50cz multi 8 5

Amnesty Intl., 25th Anniv. A1100

1986, May 28 Litho. *Perf. 11½x12*
2047 A1100 .50cz multi 8 5

Butterflies A1101

1985, June 5 *Perf. 12x11½*
2048 A1101 .50cz Pyrrhopyge rufi-cauda 10 5
2049 A1101 .50cz Prepona eugenes diluta 10 5
2050 A1101 .50cz Pierriballia mande-la molione 10 5

Score from Opera "Il Guarani" and Antonio Carlos Gomes (1836-1896), Composer A1102

1986, July 11 *Perf. 11½x12*
2051 A1102 .50cz multi 8 5

Natl. Accident Prevention Campaign — A1103

1986, July 30 Litho. *Perf. 11½x11*
2052 A1103 .50cz Lineman 5 5

Souvenir Sheet

Stamp Day — A1104

1986, Aug. 1 *Perf. 11*
2053 A1104 5cz No. 53 85 35

Brazilian Philatelic Society, 75th anniv., and Dom Pedro II issue, Nos. 53-60, 120th anniv. No. 2053 has beige and vermilion inscribed margin picturing Emperor Dom Pedro II. Size: 70x99mm.

Architecture A1105

Famous Men A1106

Designs: .10cz, House of Garcia D'Avila, Nazare de Mata, Bahia. .20cz, Church of Our Lady of the Assumption, Anchieta Village. .50cz, Fort Reis Magos, Natal. 1cz, Pilgrim's Column, Alcantara Village, 1648. 2cz, Cloisters, St. Francis Convent, Olinda. 5cz, St. Anthony's Chapel, Sao Roque. 10cz, St. Lawrence of the Indians Church, Niteroi. 20cz, Principe da Beiro Fort, Mato Dentro. 50cz, Jesus of Matozinhos Church.

1986-87 Photo. *Perf. 11½x11*
2055 A1105 .10cz sage grn 5 5
2057 A1105 .20cz brt blue 5 5
2059 A1105 .50cz orange 5 5
2064 A1105 1cz golden brn 12 8
2065 A1105 2cz dull rose 25 18
2068 A1105 5cz lt olive grn 60 45
2073 A1105 10cz slate blue ('87) 50 35
2073B A1105 20cz lt red brn ('87) 75 58
2073C A1105 50cz brn org ('87) 2.25 1.75
Nos. 2055-2073C (9) 4.62 3.54

Issue dates: .10cz, Aug. 11. .20cz, Dec. 8; .50cz, Aug. 19. 1cz, Nov. 19; 2cz, Nov. 9; 5cz, Dec. 30; 10cz, June 2, 1987; 20cz, Oct. 1987; 50cz, Sept. 18, 1987.

1986 *Perf. 12x11½, 11½x12*

Designs: No. 2074, Juscelino Kubitschek de Oliveira, president 1956-61, and Alvorado Palace, Brasilia. No. 2075, Octavio Mangabeira, statesman, and Itamaraty Palace, Rio de Janeiro, horiz.

2074 A1106 .50cz multi 5 5
2075 A1106 .50cz multi 5 5

Issue dates: No. 2074, Aug. 21. No. 2075, Aug. 27.

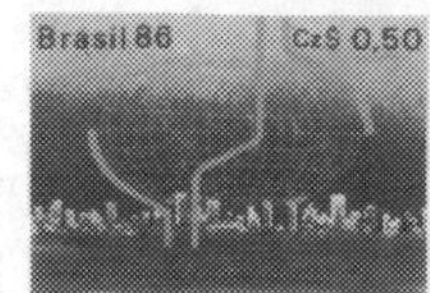
World Gastroenterology Congress, Sao Paulo — A1107

1986, Sept. 7 *Perf. 11½x12*
2076 A1107 .50cz multi 5 5

Federal Broadcasting System, 50th Anniv. — A1108

Intl. Peace Year — A1109

1986, Sept. 15 *Perf. 12x11½*
2077 A1108 .50cz multi 5 5

1986, Sept. 16

Painting (detail): War and Peace, by Candido Portinari.

2078 A1109 .50cz multi 5 5

Ernesto Simoes Filho (b. 1886), Publisher of La Tarde A1110

1986, Oct. 4 Litho. *Perf. 11½x12*
2079 A1110 .50cz multi 8 6

Famous Men — A1111

Federal Savings Bank, 125th Anniv. — A1112

Designs: No. 2080, Title page from manuscript, c. 1683-94, by Gregorio Mattose e Guerra (b. 1636), author. No. 2081, Manuel Bandeira (1886-1968), poet, text from I'll Go Back to Pasargada.

1986, Oct. 29 *Perf. 11½x11*
2080 A1111 .50cz lake & beige 8 6
2081 A1111 .50cz lake & dl grn 8 6

1986, Nov. 4 *Perf. 12x11½*
2082 A1112 .50cz multi 8 6

Flowering Plants A1113

Glauber Rocha, Film Industry Pioneer A1114

Perf. 12x11½, 11½x12
1986, Sept. 23
2083 A1113 .50cz Urera mitis 8 6
2084 A1113 6.50cz Couroupita guyanensis 52 40
2085 A1113 6.90cz Bauhinia variegata, horiz. 55 42

1986, Nov. 20 *Perf. 12x11½*
2086 A1114 .50cz multi 8 6

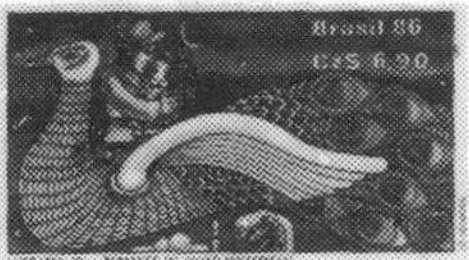
LUBRAPEX '86 — A1115

Cordel Folk Tales: No. 2087, Romance of the Mysterious Peacock. No. 2088, History of the Empress Porcina.

1986, Nov. 21 *Perf. 11x12*
2087 A1115 6.90cz multi 55 42
2088 A1115 6.90cz multi 55 42
a. Souv. sheet of 2, #2087-2088, perf. 11 1.10 85

No. 2088a has inscribed decorative margin picturing folk figures. Size: 70x100mm.

Christmas A1116

Birds: .50cz, And Christ child. 6.50cz, And tree. 7.30cz, Eating fruit.

1986, Nov. 10 *Perf. 11½x12*
2089 A1116 .50cz multi 5 5
2090 A1116 6.50cz multi 65 48
2091 A1116 7.30cz multi 75 58

Military Uniforms, c. 1930 — A1117

Bartolomeu de Gusmao Airport, 50th Anniv. — A1118

Designs: No. 2092, Navy lieutenant commander, dreadnought Minas Gerais. No. 2093, Army flight lieutenant, WACO S.C.O. biplane, Fortaleza Airport.

1986, Dec. 15 *Perf. 12x11½*
2092 A1117 .50cz multi 5 5
2093 A1117 .50cz multi 5 5

Fortaleza Air Base, 50th anniv. (No. 2093).

1986, Dec. 26
2094 A1118 1cz multi 10 5

Heitor Villa-Lobos (1887-1959), Conductor A1119

1987, Mar. 5 Litho. *Perf. 12x11½*
2095 A1119 1.50cz multi 15 12

Natl. Air Force C-130 Transport Plane, Flag, the Antarctic — A1120

1987, Mar. 9 *Perf. 11x11½*
2096 A1120 1cz multi 12 8

Antarctic Project.

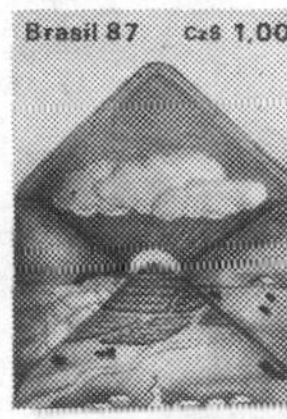
Special Mail Services — A1121

1987, Mar. 20 *Perf. 12x11½*
2097 A1121 1cz Rural delivery 10 8
2098 A1121 1cz Intl. express 10 8

TELECOM '87, Geneva A1122

1987, May 5 *Perf. 11½x12*
2099 A1122 2cz Brazilsat, wave, globe 20 15

10th Pan American Games, Indianapolis, Aug. 7-25 — A1123

1987, May 20 *Perf. 12x11½*
2100 A1123 18cz multi 1.40 1.05

The lack of a price for a listed item does not necessarily indicate rarity.

Natl. Fine Arts Museum, 150th Anniv
A1124

1987, May *Perf. 11½x12*

2101 A1124 1cz multi 15 12

Marine Conservation — A1125

1987, June 5

2102 A1125 2cz Eubalaena australis 14 10
2103 A1125 2cz Eretmochelys imbricata 14 10

Federal Court of Appeal, 40th Anniv.
A1126

1987, June 15

2104 A1126 2cz multi 12 8

Military Club, Cent. — A1127

1987, June 26 *Perf. 12x11½*

2105 A1127 3cz multi 18 12

Agriculture Institute of Campinas, Cent.
A1128

1987, June 27 *Perf. 11½x12*

2106 A1128 2cz multi 12 8

Entomological Society, 50th Anniv. — A1129

1987, July 17

2107 A1129 3cz Zoolea lopiceps 14 10
2108 A1129 3cz Fulgora servillei 14 10

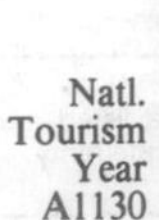
Natl. Tourism Year
A1130

Designs: No. 2109, Monuments and Sugarloaf Mountain, Rio de Janeiro. No. 2110, Colonial church, sailboats, parrot, cashews.

1987, Aug. 4

2109 A1130 3cz multi 15 12
2110 A1130 3cz multi 15 12

Royal Portuguese Cabinet of Literature, 150th Anniv. — A1131

1987, Aug. 27 *Perf. 12x11½*

2111 A1131 30czver & brt grn 1.50 1.15

Sport Club Intl. — A1132

Championship soccer clubs, Brazil's Gold Cup: No. 2112b, Sao Paulo. No. 2112c, Guarani. No. 2112d, Regatas do Flamengo.

1987, Aug. 29 *Perf. 11½x12*

2112 Block of 4 60 40
a.-d. A1132 3cz any single 15 10

St. Francis Convent, 400th Anniv.
A1133

1987, Oct. 4

2113 A1133 4cz multi 20 15

SEMI-POSTAL STAMPS

National Philatelic Exhibition Issue.

SP1

Wmk. Coat of Arms in Sheet. (236)

1934, Sept. 16 **Engr.** *Imperf.*

Thick Paper

B1 SP1 200r + 100r dp cl 75 1.50
B2 SP1 300r + 100r ver 75 1.50
B3 SP1 700r + 100r brt bl 8.00 15.00
B4 SP1 1000r + 100r blk 8.00 15.00

The surtax was to help defray the expenses of the exhibition. Issued in sheets of 60, inscribed "EXPOSICAO FILATELICA NACIONAL".

Red Cross Nurse and Soldier
SP2

Wmk. 222

1935, Sept. 19 **Typo.** *Perf. 11*

B5 SP2 200r + 100r pur & red 1.00 1.00
B6 SP2 300r + 100r ol brn & red 1.00 75
B7 SP2 700r + 100r turq bl & red 12.00 8.00

3rd Pan-American Red Cross Conference. Exist imperf.

Three Wise Men and Star of Bethlehem
SP3

Angel and Child
SP4

Southern Cross and Child — SP5

Mother and Child — SP6

Wmk. 249

1939, Dec. 20 **Litho.** *Perf. 10½*

B8 SP3 100r + 100r chlky bl & bl blk 50 50
a. Horiz. or vert. pair, imperf. between 45.00
B9 SP4 200r + 100r brt grnsh bl 1.00 1.00
a. Horizontal pair, imperf. between 45.00
B10 SP5 400r + 200r ol grn & ol 1.00 25
B11 SP6 1200r + 400r crim & brn red 5.00 1.50
a. Vertical pair, imperf. between 45.00

The surtax was distributed to charitable institutions.

AIR POST STAMPS

Official Stamps of 1913 Surcharged

SERVIÇO AEREO 200 Rs.

1927, Dec. 28 **Unwmk.** *Perf. 12*

Center in Black.

C1 O2 50r on 10r gray 15 15
a. Inverted surcharge 275.00
b. Top ornaments missing 60.00
C2 O2 200r on 1000r blk brn 2.00 4.00
a. Double surch. 275.00
C3 O2 200r on 2000r red brn 2.00 7.00
a. Double surch. 300.00
C4 O2 200r on 5000r brn 1.50 1.50
a. Double surch. 275.00
b. Double surcharge, one inverted 300.00
c. Triple surch. 400.00
C5 O2 300r on 500r org 1.50 1.50
C6 O2 300r on 600r vio 60 50
b. Pair, one without surch.
C6A O2 500r on 10r gray 375.00 525.00
C7 O2 500r on 50r gray 1.50 50
a. Double surch. 275.00 275.00
C8 O2 1000r on 20r ol grn 90 20
a. Double surch. 275.00 *225.00*
C9 O2 2000r on 100r ver 2.50 1.75
a. Pair, one without surcharge 1,000.
C10 O2 2000r on 200r bl 2.50 1.75
C11 O2 2000r on 10,000r blk 2.00 60
C12 O2 5000r on 20,000r bl 4.00 4.00
C13 O2 5000r on 50,000r grn 4.00 4.00
C14 O2 5000r on 100,000r org 20.00 25.00
C15 O2 10,000r on 500,000r brn 25.00 17.50
C16 O2 10,000r on 1,000,000r dk brn 20.00 20.00
Nos. C1-C6,C7-C16 (16) 90.15 89.95

Nos. C1, C1b, C7, C8 and C9 have small diamonds printed over the numerals in the upper corners.

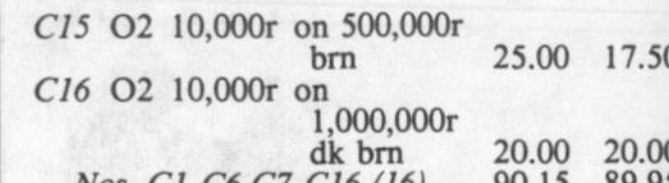

Monument to de Gusmao — AP1

Santos-Dumont's Airship — AP2

Augusto Severo's Airship "Pax" — AP3

Santos-Dumont's Biplane "14 Bis" — AP4

Ribeiro de Barros's Seaplane "Jahu" — AP5

Perf. 11, 12½x13, 13x13½.

1929 **Typo.** **Wmk. 206**

C17 AP1 50r bl grn 25 20
C18 AP2 200r red 1.25 20
C19 AP3 300r brt bl 1.50 20
C20 AP4 500r red vio 2.00 20
C21 AP5 1000r org brn 6.00 40
Nos. C17-C21 (5) 11.00 1.20

See also Nos. C32-C36.

Bartholomeu de Gusmao
AP6

Augusto Severo
AP7

Alberto Santos-Dumont — AP8

Perf. 9, 11 and Compound.

1929-30 **Engr.** **Wmk. 101**

C22 AP6 2000r lt grn ('30) 10.00 25

C23 AP7	5000r carmine	10.00 1.00
C24 AP8	10,000r ol grn	10.00 1.25

See also Nos. C37, C40.

Allegory: Airmail Service between Brazil and the United States — AP9

1929 Typo. Wmk. 206

C25 AP9	3000r violet	10.00 65

See also Nos. C38, C41. Nos. C23-C25 exist imperforate.

Air Post Stamps of 1929 Surcharged in Blue or Red

ZEPPELIN
2$500

1931, Aug. 16 *Perf. 12½x13½.*

C26 AP2	2500r on 200r red (Bl)	20.00 22.50
C27 AP3	5000r on 300r brt bl (R)	22.50 27.50

No. C25 Surcharged 2.500 REIS

1931, Sept. 2 *Perf. 11*

C28 AP9	2500r on 3000r vio	17.50 *20.00*
a.	Inverted surcharge	200.00
b.	Surcharged on front and back	200.00

Regular Issues of 1928-29 Surcharged

ZEPPELIN
3$500

Perf. 11, 11½.

1932, May Wmk. 101

C29 A89	3500r on 5000r gray lil	20.00 22.50
C30 A72	7000r on 10,000r rose	20.00 24.00
b.	Horiz. pair, imperf. between	*1,000.*

Imperforates

Since 1933, imperforate or partly perforated sheets of nearly all of the airmail issues have become available.

Flag and Airplane — AP10

Wmk. 222

1933, June 7 Typo. *Perf. 11*

C31 AP10	3500r grn, yel & dk bl	4.00 85

See also Nos. C39, C42.

1934 Wmk. 222

C32 AP1	50r bl grn	1.00 1.00
C33 AP2	200r red	1.25 60
C34 AP3	300r brt bl	2.50 1.25
C35 AP4	500r red vio	1.25 50
C36 AP5	1000r org brn	3.00 40
	Nos. C32-C36 (5)	9.00 3.75

1934 Wmk. 236 Engr. *Perf. 12x11.*

Thick Laid Paper.

C37 AP6	2000r lt grn	5.00 1.00

Types of 1929, 1933.

Perf. 11, 11½, 12.

1937-40 Typo. Wmk. 249

C38 AP9	3000r violet	20.00 1.50
C39 AP10	3500r grn, yel & dk bl	2.00 1.25

Engr.

C40 AP7	5000r ver ('40)	5.00 60

Watermark note after No. 501 also applies to No. C40.

Types of 1929-33.

Perf. 11, 11½x12

1939-40 Typo. Wmk. 256

C41 AP9	3000r violet	1.00 50
C42 AP10	3500r bl, dl grn & yel ('40)	75 40

Map of the Western Hemisphere Showing Brazil AP11

1941, Jan. 14 Engr. *Perf. 11*

C43 AP11	1200r dk brn	2.50 50

5th general census of Brazil.

No. 506A Overprinted in Carmine

AÉREO
"10 Nov."
937-941

1941, Nov. 10 Wmk. 264 *Rouletted.*

C45 A180	5400r sl grn	2.00 1.00
a.	Overprint inverted	175.00

Issued in commemoration of the fourth anniversary of President Varges' new constitution.

Nos. 506A and 508 Surcharged in Black

AÉREO
"10 Nov."
937-942
Cr.$ 5,40

1942, Nov. 10 Wmk. 264

C47 A180	5.40cr on 5400r sl grn	2.00 1.00
a.	Wmk. 249	50.00 50.00
b.	Surcharge inverted	75.00 75.00

Issued in commemoration of the fifth anniversary of President Vargas' new constitution. The status of No. C47a is questioned.

Southern Cross and Arms of Paraguay AP12

Wmk. 270--Wavy Lines and Seal

Wmk. 270

1943, May 11 Engr. *Perf. 12½*

C48 AP12	1.20cr lt gray bl	1.00 50

Issued in commemoration of the visit of President Higinio Morinigo of Paraguay.

Map of South America — AP13

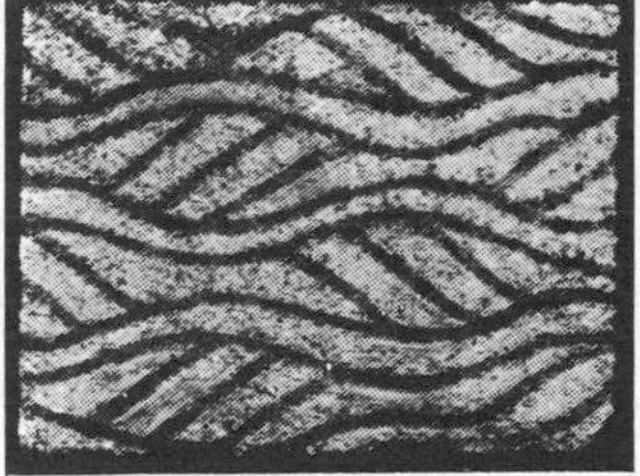
Wmk. 271- Wavy Lines

1943, June 30 Wmk. 271 *Perf. 12½*

C49 AP13	1.20cr multi	1.00 50

Visit of President Penaranda of Bolivia.

Numeral of Value AP14

1943, Aug. 7

C50 AP14	1cr blk & dl yel	3.00 2.00
a.	Double impression	50.00
C51 AP14	2cr blk & pale grn	4.00 2.00
a.	Double impression	60.00
C52 AP14	5cr blk & pink	5.00 2.75

Centenary of Brazil's first postage stamps.

Souvenir Sheet.

AP15

Without Gum *Imperf.*

C53 AP15	Sheet of three	50.00 50.00
a.	1cr blk & dl yel	13.00 13.00
b.	2cr blk & pale grn	13.00 13.00
c.	5cr blk & pink	13.00 13.00

Issued to commemorate the 100th anniversary of the first postage stamps of Brazil and the second Philatelic Exposition (Brapex). Printed in panes of 6 sheets, perforated 12½ between. Each sheet is perforated on two or three sides. Size approximately 155x155mm. Inscriptions are printed in light brown.

Law Book — AP16

1943, Aug. 13 *Perf. 12½*

C54 AP16	1.20cr rose & lil rose	60 25

Issued to commemorate the second Inter-American Conference of Lawyers.

Semi-Postal Stamps of 1939 Surcharged in Red, Carmine or Black

20
Cts.

1944, Jan. 3 Wmk. 249 *Perf. 10½*

C55 SP5	20c on 400r + 200r ol grn & ol (R)	60 50
C56 SP5	40c on 400r + 200r ol grn & ol (Bk)	1.10 35
C57 SP5	60c on 400r + 200r ol grn & ol (C)	1.10 25
C58 SP5	1cr on 400r + 200r ol grn & ol (Bk)	1.40 30
C59 SP5	1.20cr on 400r + 200r ol grn & ol (C)	1.65 30
	Nos. C55-C59 (5)	5.85 1.70

No. C59 is known with surcharge in black but its status is questioned.

Bartholomeu de Gusmao and the "Aerostat" — AP17

Wmk. 268

1944, Oct. 23 Engr. *Perf. 12*

C60 AP17	1.20cr rose car	50 20

Week of the Wing.

L. L. Zamenhof AP18

1945, Apr. 16 Litho. *Perf. 11*

C61 AP18	1.20cr dl brn	60 30

Issued to commemorate the Esperanto Congress held in Rio de Janeiro, April 14-22, 1945.

Map of South America AP19

Baron of Rio Branco AP20

1945, Apr. 20

C62 AP19	1.20cr gray brn	50 25
C63 AP20	5cr rose lil	1.50 40

Issued to commemorate the centenary of the birth of Jose Maria de Silva Paranhos, Baron of Rio Branco.

Dove and Flags of American Republics AP21

Perf. 12x11

1947, Aug. 15 Engr. Unwmk.

C64 AP21	2.20cr dk bl grn	50 25

Issued to commemorate the Inter-American Defense Conference at Rio de Janeiro August-September, 1947.

Santos-Dumont Monument, St. Cloud, France — AP22

Bay of Rio de Janeiro and Rotary Emblem — AP23

1947, Nov. 15 Typo. *Perf. 11x12*
C65 AP22 1.20cr org brn & ol 50 25

Issued to commemorate the Week of the Wing and to honor the Santos-Dumont monument which was destroyed in World War II.

1948, May 16 Engr. *Perf. 11.*
C66 AP23 1.20cr dp cl 60 40
C67 AP23 3.80r dl vio 1.25 40

Issued in honor of the 39th convention of Rotary International, Rio de Janeiro, May 1948.

Hotel Quitandinha, Petropolis AP24

1948, July 10 Litho. Wmk. 267
C68 AP24 1.20cr org brn 35 25
C69 AP24 3.80cr violet 65 30

Issued to commemorate the International Exposition of Industry and Commerce, Petropolis, 1948.

Musician and Singers AP25

1948, Aug. 13 Engr. Unwmk.
C70 AP25 1.20cr blue 50 20

Issued to commemorate the centenary of the establishment of the National School of Music.

Luis Batlle Berres AP26

1948, Sept. 2 Typo.
C71 AP26 1.70cr blue 35 25

Issued to commemorate the visit of President Luis Batlle Berres of Uruguay, September, 1948.

Merino Ram AP27

Perf. 12x11.

1948, Oct. 10 Wmk. 267
C72 AP27 1.20cr dp org 70 30

Issued to publicize the International Livestock Exposition at Bage.

Eucharistic Congress Seal — AP28

Unwmk.

1948, Oct. 23 Engr. *Perf. 11*
C73 AP28 1.20cr dk car rose 40 30

Issued to commemorate the 5th National Eucharistic Congress, Porto Alegre, October 24 to 31.

Souvenir Sheet

AP28a

1948, Dec. 14 Engr. *Imperf.*
Without Gum
C73A AP28a Sheet of three 55.00 67.50

No. C73A contains one each of Nos. 674-676. Issued in honor of President Eurico Gasper Dutra and the armed forces. Exists both with and without number on back. Measures 130x75mm. Marginal inscriptions typographed in black.

Church of Prazeres, Guararapes — AP29

Perf. 11½x12.

1949, Feb. 15 Litho. Wmk. 267
C74 AP29 1.20cr pink 1.50 75

Issued to commemorate the 300th anniversary of the Second Battle of Guararapes.

Thomé de Souza Meeting Indians — AP30

Perf. 11x12.

1949, Mar. 29 Engr. Unwmk.
C75 AP30 1.20cr blue 35 25

Issued to commemorate the 400th anniversary of the founding of the City of Salvador.

A souvenir folder, issued with No. C75, has an engraved 20cr red brown postage stamp portraying John III printed on it, and a copy of No. C75 affixed to it and postmarked. Paper is laid, inscriptions are in red brown and size of folder front is 100x150mm. Price, $5.

Franklin D. Roosevelt AP31

1949, May 20 Unwmk. *Imperf.*
C76 AP31 3.80cr dp bl 1.00 80
a. Souvenir sheet 12.00 15.00

No. C76a measures 85x110mm., with deep blue inscriptions in upper and lower margins. It also exists with papermaker's watermark.

Joaquim Nabuco — AP32

1949, Aug. 30 *Perf. 12*
C77 AP32 3.80cr rose lil 70 40
a. Wmk. 256, imperf. 25.00

Issued to commemorate the centenary of the birth of Joaquim Nabuco (1849-1910), lawyer and writer.

Maracana Stadium AP33

Soccer Player and Flag — AP34

Perf. 11x12, 12x11

1950, June 24 Litho. Wmk. 267
C78 AP33 1.20cr ultra & sal 1.25 40
C79 AP34 5.80cr bl, yel grn & yel 3.50 50

Issued to publicize the 4th World Soccer Championship at Rio de Janeiro.

Symbolical of Brazilian Population Growth — AP35

1950, July 10 *Perf. 12x11*
C80 AP35 1.20cr red brn 40 15

Issued to publicize the 6th Brazilian census.

J. B. Marcelino Champagnat AP36

1956, Sept. 8 Engr. *Perf. 11½*
C81 AP36 3.30cr rose lil 35 15

Issued to commemorate the 50th anniversary of the arrival of the Marist Brothers in Northern Brazil.

Santos-Dumont's 1906 Plane — AP37

1956, Oct. 16 Photo.
C82 AP37 3cr dk bl grn 1.25 30
a. Souvenir sheet of four 9.00 9.00
b. 3cr dk car 2.25 90
C83 AP37 3.30cr brt ultra 30 10
C84 AP37 4cr dp cl 60 10
C85 AP37 6.50cr red brn 20 10
C86 AP37 11.50cr org red 1.25 35
Nos. C82-C86 (5) 3.60 95

Issued to commemorate the 50th anniversary of the first flight by Santos-Dumont.

No. C82a measures 123½x156mm. and contains four copies of No. C82b. Inscribed in dark carmine in four languages: "50TH ANNIVERSARY OF THE FIRST FLIGHT OF THE HEAVIER THAN THE AIR." Issued Oct. 14, 1956.

Lord Baden-Powell AP38

1957, Aug. 1 Unwmk.
Granite Paper
C87 AP38 3.30cr dp red lil 40 15

Issued to commemorate the centenary of the birth of Lord Baden-Powell, founder of the Boy Scouts.

UN Emblem, Soldier and Map of Suez Canal Area AP39

Wmk. 267

1957, Oct. 24 Engr. *Perf. 11½*
C88 AP39 3.30cr dk bl 30 20

Issued to honor the Brazilian contingent of the United Nations Emergency Force.

Basketball Player — AP40

1959, May 30 Photo. *Perf. 11½*
C89 AP40 3.30cr brt red brn & bl 40 15

Brazil's victory in the World Basketball Championships of 1959.

Symbol of Flight AP41

1959, Oct. 21 Wmk. 267
C90 AP41 3.30cr dp ultra 20 10

Issued to publicize Week of the Wing.

Caravelle AP42

1959, Dec. 18 *Perf. 11½*
C91 AP42 6.50cr ultra 15 10

Inauguration of Brazilian jet flights.

Pres. Adolfo Lopez Mateos AP43

World Refugee Year Emblem AP45

1960, Jan. 19 Photo. Wmk. 267
C92 AP43 6.50cr brown 15 10

Issued to commemorate the visit of President Adolfo Lopez Mateos of Mexico.

1960, Feb. 23 *Perf. 11½*
C93 AP44 6.50cr dp org 20 12

Visit of Pres. Dwight D. Eisenhower.

Tower at Brasilia AP46

1960, Apr. 7 Wmk. 268
C94 AP45 6.50cr blue 15 10

Issued to publicize World Refugee Year, July 1, 1959-June 30, 1960.

Type of Regular Issue and AP46.

Designs: 3.30cr, Square of the Three Entities. 4cr, Cathedral. 11.50cr, Plan of Brasilia.

Perf. 11x11½, 11½x11

1960, Apr. 21 Photo. Wmk. 267
C95 A436 3.30cr violet 20 15
C96 A436 4cr blue 1.25 15
C97 AP46 6.50cr rose car 15 15
C98 A436 11.50cr brown 20 15

Issued to commemorate the inauguration of Brazil's new capital, Brasilia, Apr. 21, 1960.

Chrismon and Oil Lamp AP47

1960, May 16 *Perf. 11x11½*
C99 AP47 3.30cr lil rose 15 15

Issued to publicize the Seventh National Eucharistic Congress at Curitiba.

Cross, Sugarloaf Mountain and Emblem AP48

1960, July 1 Wmk. 267
C100 AP48 6.50cr brt bl 15 10

Issued to commemorate the 10th Congress of the World Baptist Alliance, Rio de Janeiro.

Boy Scout AP49

Caravel AP50

Pres. Dwight D. Eisenhower AP44

1960, July 23 *Perf. 11½x11*
C101 AP49 3.30cr org ver 15 10

Boy Scouts of Brazil, 50th anniversary.

1960, Aug. 5 Engr. Wmk. 268
C102 AP50 6.50cr black 15 10

Issued to commemorate the 500th anniversary of the birth of Prince Henry the Navigator.

Maria E. Bueno AP51

1960, Dec. 15 Photo. *Perf. 11x11½*
C103 AP51 60cr pale brn 15 10

Issued to commemorate the victory at Wimbledon of Maria E. Bueno, women's singles tennis champion.

War Memorial, Sugarloaf Mountain and Allied Flags AP52

1960, Dec. 22 Wmk. 268
C104 AP52 3.30cr lil rose 15 10

Issued to commemorate the reburial of Brazilian servicemen of World War II.

Power Line and Map AP53

Malaria Eradication Emblem AP54

1961, Jan. 20 *Perf. 11½x11*
C105 AP53 3.30cr lil rose 10 10

Issued to commemorate the inauguration of Three Marias Dam and hydroelectric station in Minas Gerais.

1962, May 24 Wmk. 267 Engr.
C106 AP54 21cr blue 10 10

Issued for the World Health Organization drive to eradicate malaria.

F. A. de Varnhagen – AP55

1966, Feb. 17 Photo. Wmk. 267
C107 AP55 45cr red brn 30 15

Issued to commemorate the 150th anniversary of the birth of Francisco Adolfo de Varnhagen, Viscount of Porto Seguro (1816-1878), historian and diplomat.

Map of the Americas and Alliance for Progress Emblem AP56

1966, March 14 *Perf. 11x11½*
C108 AP56 120cr grnsh bl & vio bl 40 15

Issued to commemorate the fifth anniversary of the Alliance for Progress.

A souvenir card contains one impression of No. C108, imperf. Black inscriptions. Size: 113x160mm.

Nun and Globe AP57

Face of Jesus from Shroud of Turin AP58

1966, Mar. 25 Photo. *Perf. 11½x11*
C109 AP57 35cr violet 20 10

Issued to commemorate the centenary of the arrival of the teaching Sisters of St. Dorothea.

1966, June 3 Photo. Wmk. 267
C110 AP58 45cr brn org 25 15

Issued to commemorate Vatican II, the 21st Ecumenical Council of the Roman Catholic Church, Oct. 11, 1962-Dec. 8, 1965.

A souvenir card contains one impression of No. C110, imperf. Brown orange inscription and head of Jesus in margin. Size: 100x39mm.

Admiral Mariz e Barros AP59

"Youth" by Eliseu Visconti AP60

1966, June 13 Photo. Wmk. 267
C111 AP59 35cr red brn 20 10

Death centenary of Admiral Antonio Carlos Mariz e Barros, who died in the Battle of Itaperu.

1966, July 31 *Perf. 11½x11*
C112 AP60 120cr red brn 50 20

Birth centenary of Eliseu Visconti, painter.

SPECIAL DELIVERY STAMPS

No. 191 Surcharged

1930 Unwmk. *Perf. 12*
E1 A62 1000r on 200r dp bl 3.00 1.50
a. Inverted surcharge 500.00

POSTAGE DUE STAMPS

D1

D2

1889 Unwmk. Typo. *Rouletted.*

J1	D1	10r carmine	1.50	75
J2	D1	20r carmine	1.75	1.30
J3	D1	50r carmine	3.50	2.00
J4	D1	100r carmine	2.00	1.00
J5	D1	200r carmine	32.50	10.00
J6	D1	300r carmine	4.00	5.00
J7	D1	500r carmine	4.00	5.00
J8	D1	700r carmine	7.50	7.00
J9	D1	1000r carmine	7.50	7.00
		Nos. J1-J9 (9)	64.25	39.05

Counterfeits are common.

1890

J10	D1	10r orange	50	20
J11	D1	20r ultra	75	20
J12	D1	50r olive	1.00	20
J13	D1	200r magenta	3.00	30
J14	D1	300r bl grn	2.00	65
J15	D1	500r slate	2.50	2.25
J16	D1	700r purple	3.50	5.00
J17	D1	1000r dk vio	5.00	4.00
		Nos. J10-J17 (8)	18.25	12.80

Perf. 11 to 11½, 12½ to 14 and Compound.

1895-1901

J18	D2	10r dk bl ('01)	1.00	50
J19	D2	20r yel grn	10.00	3.00
J20	D2	50r yel grn ('01)	7.50	3.50
J21	D2	100r brick red	7.75	40

J22 D2 200r violet 5.00 25
a. 200r gray lil ('98) 14.00 1.50
J23 D2 300r dl bl 3.50 2.00
J24 D2 2000r brown 10.00 10.00
Nos. J18-J24 (7) 44.75 19.65

1906 **Wmk. 97**
J25 D2 100r brick red 6.50 2.50

Wmk. (97? or 98?)
J26 D2 200r violet 6.00 1.00
a. Wmk. 97 275.00 85.00
b. Wmk. 98 10.00 45.00

D3

D4

1906-10 Unwmk. Engr. ***Perf. 12***
J28 D3 10r slate 15 10
J29 D3 20r brt vio 15 10
J30 D3 50r dk grn 20 10
J31 D3 100r carmine 1.50 50
J32 D3 200r dp bl 80 25
J33 D3 300r gray blk 30 50
J34 D3 400r ol grn 80 75
J35 D3 500r dk vio 30.00 30.00
J36 D3 600r vio ('10) 1.00 *2.50*
J37 D3 700r red brn 25.00 25.00
J38 D3 1000r red 1.25 *2.50*
J39 D3 2000r green 4.00 5.00
J40 D3 5000r choc ('10) 1.25 *12.00*
Nos. J28-J40 (13) 66.40 79.30

Perf. 12½, 11, 11x10½.
1919-23 **Typo.**
J41 D4 5r red brn 15 30
J42 D4 10r violet 30 30
J43 D4 20r ol gray 25 20
J44 D4 50r grn ('23) 25 25
J45 D4 100r red 1.50 1.25
J46 D4 200r blue 7.00 2.00
J47 D4 400r brn ('23) 1.75 1.75
Nos. J41-J47 (7) 11.20 6.05

Perf. 12½, 12½x13½.
1924-35 **Wmk. 100**
J48 D4 5r red brn 25 20
J49 D4 100r red 75 30
J50 D4 200r sl bl ('29) 1.00 50
J51 D4 400r dp brn ('29) 1.50 1.00
J52 D4 600r dk vio ('29) 1.75 1.10
J53 D4 600r org ('35) 75 50
Nos. J48-J53 (6) 6.00 3.60

1924 Wmk. 193 ***Perf. 11x10½.***
J54 D4 100r red 40.00 40.00
J55 D4 200r sl bl 5.00 5.00

Perf. 11x10½, 13x13½.
1925-27 **Wmk. 101**
J56 D4 20r ol gray 25 20
J57 D4 100r red 1.50 40
J58 D4 200r sl bl 4.50 50
J59 D4 400r brown 2.50 1.75
J60 D4 600r dk vio 6.00 3.50
Nos. J56-J60 (5) 14.75 6.35

Wmk. E U BRASIL Multiple. (218)
1929-30 ***Perf. 12½x13½.***
J61 D4 100r lt red 25 20
J62 D4 200r bl blk 40 25
J63 D4 400r brown 40 25
J64 D4 1000r myr grn 75 50

Perf. 11, 12½x13, 13.
1931-36 **Wmk. 222**
J65 D4 10r lt vio ('35) 15 10
J66 D4 20r blk ('33) 20 15
J67 D4 50r bl grn ('35) 30 25
J68 D4 100r rose red ('35) 30 25
J69 D4 200r sl bl ('35) 50 35
J70 D4 400r blk brn ('35) 2.50 2.50
J71 D4 600r dk vio 40 25
J72 D4 1000r myr grn 60 40
J73 D4 2000r brn ('36) 1.00 1.00
J74 D4 5000r ind ('36) 1.50 1.25
Nos. J65-J74 (10) 7.45 6.50

1938 Wmk. 249 ***Perf. 11.***
J75 D4 200r sl bl 2.25 75

1940 Typo. Wmk. 256
J76 D4 10r lt vio 60 60
J77 D4 20r black 60 60
J79 D4 100r rose red 60 60
J80 D4 200r myr grn 60 60

1942 **Wmk. 264**
J81 D4 10r lt vio 15 10
J82 D4 20r ol blk 15 10
J83 D4 50r lt bl grn 15 10
J84 D4 100r vermilion 40 30
J85 D4 200r gray bl 40 30
J86 D4 400r claret 40 30
J87 D4 600r rose vio 30 20
J88 D4 1000r dk bl grn 30 20
J89 D4 2000r dp yel brn 75 50
J90 D4 5000r indigo 40 30
Nos. J81-J90 (10) 3.40 2.40

1949 **Wmk. 268**
J91 D4 10c pale rose lil 5.00 4.00
J92 D4 20r black 30.00 30.00

No. J92 exists in shades of gray ranging to gray olive.

OFFICIAL STAMPS

Pres. Affonso Penna O1

Pres. Hermes da Fonseca O2

Unwmk.
1906, Nov. 15 Engr. ***Perf. 12***
O1 O1 10r org & grn 20 15
O2 O1 20r org & grn 35 15
O3 O1 50r org & grn 1.20 15
O4 O1 100r org & grn 35 15
O5 O1 200r org & grn 65 15
O6 O1 300r org & grn 1.75 30
O7 O1 400r org & grn 4.50 65
O8 O1 500r org & grn 2.00 50
O9 O1 700r org & grn 3.50 2.00
O10 O1 1000r org & grn 2.50 75
O11 O1 2000r org & grn 3.00 90
O12 O1 5000r org & grn 6.50 90
O13 O1 10,000r org & grn 8.00 50
Nos. O1-O13 (13) 34.50 7.25

The portrait is the same but the frame differs for each denomination of this issue.

1913, Nov. 15
Center in Black
O14 O2 10r gray 30 20
O15 O2 20r ol grn 30 20
O16 O2 50r gray 35 15
O17 O2 100r vermilion 65 15
O18 O2 200r blue 75 25
O19 O2 500r orange 2.50 60
O20 O2 600r violet 4.00 90
O21 O2 1000r blk brn 5.00 75
O22 O2 2000r red brn 6.50 75
O23 O2 5000r brown 8.00 1.00
O24 O2 10,000r black 12.00 3.75
O25 O2 20,000r blue 30.00 30.00
O26 O2 50,000r green 45.00 35.00
O27 O2 100,000r org red 150.00 150.00
O28 O2 500,000r brown 225.00 245.00
O29 O2 1,000,000r dk brn 250.00 260.00
Nos. O14-O29 (16) 740.35 728.70

The portrait is the same on all denominations of this series but there are eight types of the frame.

Pres. Wenceslau Braz — O3

Perf. 11, 11½
1919, Apr. 11 **Wmk. 100**
O30 O3 10r ol grn 40 1.00
O31 O3 50r green 50 50
O32 O3 100r rose red 75 40
O33 O3 200r dl bl 1.00 40
O34 O3 500r orange 6.50 7.50
Nos. O30-O34 (5) 9.15 9.80

The official decree called for eleven stamps in this series but only five were issued. See Nos. 293-297.

NEWSPAPER STAMPS

N1

Rouletted
1889, Feb. 1 Unwmk. Litho.
P1 N1 10r yellow 2.50 3.00
a. Pair, imperf. between 125.00 175.00
P2 N1 20r yellow 6.00 7.00
P3 N1 50r yellow 10.00 6.00
P4 N1 100r yellow 4.00 3.00
P5 N1 200r yellow 3.00 1.50
P6 N1 300r yellow 3.00 1.50
P7 N1 500r yellow 17.50 8.00
P8 N1 700r yellow 3.00 10.00
P9 N1 1000r yellow 3.00 10.00
Nos. P1-P9 (9) 52.00 50.00

1889, May 1
P10 N1 10r olive 50 20
P11 N1 20r green 50 25
P12 N1 50r brn yel 65 25
P13 N1 100r violet 1.35 1.00
P14 N1 200r black 1.25 1.00
P15 N1 300r carmine 8.00 8.00
P16 N1 500r green 40.00 40.00
P17 N1 700r ultra 20.00 25.00
P18 N1 1000r brown 8.00 15.00
Nos. P10-P18 (9) 80.25 90.70

N2

N3

White Wove Paper Thin to Thick
Perf. 11 to 11½, 12½ to 14 and 12½ to 14x11 to 11½
1890 **Typo.**
P19 N2 10r blue 7.00 5.00
a. 10r ultra 7.00 5.00
P20 N2 20r emerald 20.00 7.50
P21 N2 100r violet 8.00 4.50

1890-93
P22 N3 10r blue 50 25
a. 10r ultra 1.25 50
P23 N3 10r ultra, *buff* 1.00 50
P24 N3 20r green 1.00 60
a. 20r emer 1.25 75
P25 N3 50r yel grn ('93) 6.00 4.00

POSTAL TAX STAMPS

Icarus from the Santos-Dumont Monument at St. Cloud, France — PT1

Perf. 13½x12½, 11.
1933, Oct. 1 Typo. Wmk. 222
RA1 PT1 100r dp brn 50 10

No. RA1 was issued in commemoration of the Brazilian aviator, Santos-Dumont. It did not pay postage but its use was obligatory as a tax on all correspondence sent to countries in South America, the United States and Spain. Its use on correspondence to other countries was optional. The money obtained from its sale was added to funds for the construction of airports throughout Brazil.

Father Joseph Damien and Children PT2

Father Bento Dias Pacheco PT3

Perf. 12x11
1952, Nov. 24 Litho. Wmk. 267
RA2 PT2 10c yel brn 25 15

1953, Nov. 30
RA3 PT2 10c yel grn 25 15

1954, Nov. 22 Photo. ***Perf. 11½***
RA4 PT3 10c vio bl 20 15

1955-66, Nov. 24
RA5 PT3 10c dk car rose 20 15
RA6 PT3 10c org red ('57) 20 10
RA7 PT3 10c dp emer ('58) 15 10
RA8 PT3 10c red lil ('61) 15 10
RA9 PT3 10c choc ('62) 15 10
RA10 PT3 10c sl ('63) 15 10
RA11 PT3 2cr dp mag ('64) 15 10
RA12 PT3 2cr vio ('65) 15 10
RA13 PT3 2cr org ('66) 15 10

1968, Nov. 25
RA14 PT3 50c brt yel grn 1.25 75

1969, Nov. 28
RA15 PT3 5c dp plum 50 25

Eunice Weaver PT4

Father Nicodemo PT5

1971, Nov. 24
RA16 PT4 10c sl grn 1.00 40

1973, Nov. 24
RA17 PT4 10c brt rose lil ('73) 20 10

1975, Nov. 24 Litho. Unwmk.
RA18 PT5 10c sepia 20 10

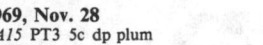

Father Vicente Borgard (1888-1977) PT6

Father Bento Dias Pacheco PT7

1983, Nov. 24 Photo. ***Perf. 11½***
RA19 PT6 10cr brown 60 60

1984, Nov. 24 Photo. ***Perf. 11½***
RA20 PT7 30cr dp bl 5 5

1985, Nov. 24 Litho. ***Perf. 11½***
RA21 PT7 100cr lake 8 6

Use of Nos. RA2-RA21 was required for one week. The tax was for the care and treatment of lepers.

Fr. Pacheco Type of 1984
1986, Nov. 24 Litho. ***Perf. 11½***
RA22 PT7 .10cz gray brn 5 5

Use of No. RA22 was required for one week. The tax was for the care and treatment of lepers.

Fr. Pacheco Type of 1984

1987, Nov. 24 Photo. *Perf. 11½*

RA23 PT7 30c sage grn 5 5

Use of No. RA23 was required for one week. The tax was for the care and treatment of lepers.

POSTAL TAX SEMI-POSTAL STAMP

Icarus — PTSP1

Wmk. 267

1947, Nov. 15 Typo. *Perf. 11*

RAB1 PTSP1 40c + 10c brt red 35 20
a. Pair, imperf. between *350.00*

Aviation Week, November 15-22, 1947, and compulsory on all domestic correspondence during that week.

BULGARIA

LOCATION — Southeastern Europe bordering on the Black Sea on the east and the Danube River on the north.
GOVT. — Republic
AREA — 42,823 sq. mi.
POP. — 8,929,332 (1983)
CAPITAL — Sofia

In 1885 Bulgaria, then a principality under the suzerainty of the Sultan of Turkey, was joined by Eastern Rumelia. Independence from Turkey was obtained in 1908.

100 Centimes = 1 Franc
100 Stotinki = 1 Lev (1881)

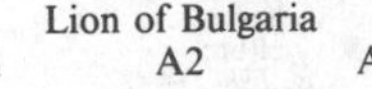

Lion of Bulgaria
A1 A2 A3

Wmk. 168- Wavy Lines and EZGV in Cyrillic

Perf. 14½x15

1879, June 1 Wmk. 168 Typo.

Laid Paper.

1 A1 5c blk & yel 45.00 16.00
2 A1 10c blk & grn 125.00 32.50
3 A1 25c blk & vio 120.00 12.50
a. Imperf.

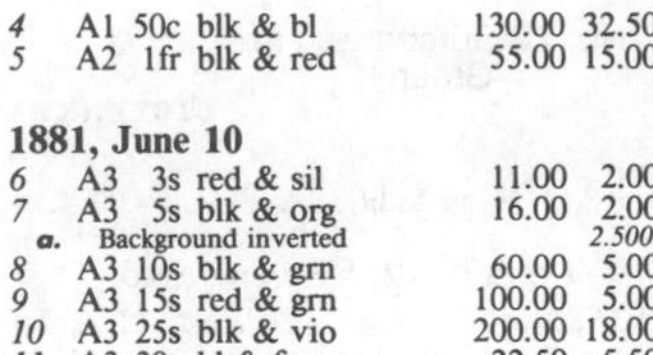

4 A1 50c blk & bl 130.00 32.50
5 A2 1fr blk & red 55.00 15.00

1881, June 10

6 A3 3s red & sil 11.00 2.00
7 A3 5s blk & org 16.00 2.00
a. Background inverted *2,500.*
8 A3 10s blk & grn 60.00 5.00
9 A3 15s red & grn 100.00 5.00
10 A3 25s blk & vio 200.00 18.00
11 A3 30s bl & fawn 22.50 5.50

1882, Dec. 4

12 A3 3s org & yel 1.10 50
a. Background inverted *2,000.*
13 A3 5s grn & pale grn 7.00 50
a. 5s rose & pale rose (error) *1,800. 1,500.*
14 A3 10s rose & pale rose 9.00 50
15 A3 15s red vio & pale lil 7.00 35
16 A3 25s bl & pale bl 7.00 50
17 A3 30s vio & grn 8.00 55
18 A3 50s bl & pink 8.00 80

See also Nos. 207-210, 286.

A4 A5

Surcharged in Black, Carmine or Vermilion

1884, May 1

Typo. Surcharge

19 A4 3s on 10s rose (Bk) 145.00 50.00
20 A4 5s on 30s bl & fawn (C) 75.00 32.50
20A A4 5s on 30s bl & fawn (Bk) *2,500. 2,500.*
21 A5 15s on 25s bl (C) 200.00 32.50

On some values the surcharge may be found inverted or double.

1885, June

Litho. Surcharge

21B A4 3s on 10s rose (Bk) 40.00 32.50
21C A4 5s on 30s bl & fawn (V) 40.00 32.50
21D A5 15s on 25s bl (V) 40.00 32.50
22 A5 50s on 1fr blk & red (Bk) 125.00 100.00

Forgeries of Nos. 19-22 are plentiful.

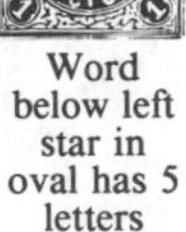

Word below left star in oval has 5 letters
A6

Third letter below left star is "A"
A7

1885, May 25

23 A6 1s gray vio & pale gray 9.00 4.00
24 A7 2s sl grn & pale gray 9.00 3.00

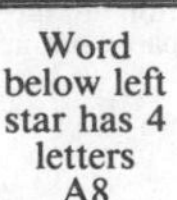

Word below left star has 4 letters
A8

Third letter below left star is "b" with cross-bar in upper half
A9

A10

1886-87

25 A8 1s gray vio & pale gray 85 20
26 A9 2s sl grn & pale gray 85 20
27 A10 1 l blk & red ('87) 25.00 4.00

A11

Perf. 10½, 11, 11½, 13, 13½.

1889 Wove Paper. Unwmk.

28 A11 1s lilac 20 5
29 A11 2s gray 75 10
30 A11 3s bis brn 50 10
31 A11 5s yel grn 25 5
a. Vertical pair, imperf. between
32 A11 10s rose 1.50 12
33 A11 15s orange 80 10
34 A11 25s blue 1.25 12
35 A11 30s dk brn 10.50 8
36 A11 50s green 75 30
37 A11 1 l org red 65 35
Nos. 28-37 (10) 17.15 1.37

The 10s orange is a proof.

Nos. 28-34 are known imperforate. Price, set $225. See Nos. 39, 41-42.

No. 35 Surcharged in Black **15**

1892, Jan. 26

38 A11 15s on 30s brn 8.00 1.00
a. Inverted surcharge *100.00 75.00*

1894 *Perf. 10½, 11, 11½.*

Pelure Paper.

39 A11 10s red 11.00 40
a. Imperf. *80.00*

No. 26 Surcharged in Red **01**

Wmk. Wavy Lines. (168)

1895, Oct. 25 *Perf. 14½x15*

Laid Paper.

40 A9 1s on 2s sl grn & pale gray 60 20
a. Inverted surcharge *9.00 6.00*
b. Double surcharge *90.00 90.00*
c. Pair, one without surcharge *175.00 175.00*

This surcharge on No. 24 is a proof.

Wmk. Coat of Arms in the Sheet.

1896, Apr. 30 *Perf. 11½, 13*

Wove Paper.

41 A11 2 l rose & pale rose 3.50 2.50
42 A11 3 l blk & buff 3.50 2.50

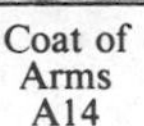

Coat of Arms
A14

Cherry Wood Cannon
A15

1896, Feb. 2 *Perf. 13*

43 A14 1s bl grn 50 15
44 A14 5s dk bl 50 15
45 A14 15s purple 75 30
46 A14 25s red 7.00 1.50

Baptism of Prince Boris.

Examples of Nos. 41-46 from sheet edges show no watermark.

Nos. 43, 45-46 were also printed on rough unwatermarked paper.

1901, Apr. 20 Litho. Unwmk.

53 A15 5s carmine 1.25 1.25
54 A15 15s yel grn 1.25 1.25

Insurrection of Independence in April, 1876, 25th anniversary.

Exist imperf. Forgeries exist.

Nos. 30 and 36 Surcharged in Black **5**

1901, Mar. 24 Typo.

55 A11 5s on 3s bis brn 1.75 1.00
a. Inverted surcharge *60.00 60.00*
b. Pair, one without surcharge *100.00 100.00*
56 A11 10s on 50s grn 2.25 1.00
a. Inverted surcharge *70.00 70.00*
b. Pair, one without surcharge *100.00 100.00*

Tsar Ferdinand
A17

Fighting at Shipka Pass
A18

ONE LEV:

Type I. The numerals in the upper corners have, at the top, a sloping serif on the left side and a short straight serif on the right.

Type II. The numerals in the upper corners are of ordinary shape without the serif at the right.

1901-05 Typo. *Perf. 12½*

57 A17 1s vio & gray blk 15 5
58 A17 2s brnz grn & ind 15 5
a. Imperf.
59 A17 3s org & ind 20 6
60 A17 5s emer & brn 3.50 5
61 A17 10s rose & blk 2.25 5
62 A17 15s cl & gray blk 1.00 5
63 A17 25s bl & blk 1.00 5
64 A17 30s bis & gray blk 22.50 12
65 A17 50s dk bl & brn 1.25 8
66 A17 1 l red org & brnz grn, type I 3.00 20
67 A17 1 l brn red & brnz grn, II('05) 60.00 1.75
68 A17 2 l car & blk 6.00 1.40
69 A17 3 l sl & red brn 7.50 3.25
Nos. 57-69 (13) 108.50 7.16

1902, Aug. 29 Litho. *Perf. 11½*

70 A18 5s lake 1.00 50
71 A18 10s bl grn 1.00 50
72 A18 15s blue 5.00 2.50

Battle of Shipka Pass, 1877.

Imperf. copies are proofs.

Excellent forgeries of Nos. 70 to 72 exist.

No. 62 Surcharged in Black **10**

1903, Oct. 1 *Perf. 12½*

73 A17 10s on 15s 8.50 40
a. Invtd. surch. *80.00 70.00*
b. Double surcharge *80.00 70.00*
c. Pair, one without surcharge *150.00 150.00*
d. 10s on 10s rose & blk *350.00 350.00*

Ferdinand in 1887 and 1907
A19

1907, Aug. 12 Litho. *Perf. 11½*

74 A19 5s dp grn 7.50 1.25
75 A19 10s red brn 13.00 1.25
76 A19 25s dp bl 20.00 2.50

Accession to the throne of Ferdinand I, 20th anniversary.

Nos. 74-76 imperf. are proofs. Nos. 74-76 exist in pairs imperforate between.

Stamps of 1889 Overprinted **1909**

1909

77 A11 1s lilac 1.50 60
a. Inverted overprint *30.00 25.00*
b. Double overprint, one inverted *35.00 35.00*

78 A11 5s yel grn 1.50 60
a. Inverted ovpt. 35.00 35.00
b. Double overprint 35.00 35.00

With Additional Surcharge **5** or **10**

79 A11 5s on 30s brn (Bk) 2.00 35
a. "5" double
b. "1990" for "1909" *1,000. 800.00*
80 A11 10s on 15s org (Bk) 2.00 75
a. Inverted surcharge 25.00 25.00
b. "1909" omitted *40.00 40.00*
81 A11 10s on 50s dk grn (R) 2.00 75
a. "1990" for "1909" 150.00 150.00
b. Black surcharge 75.00 75.00

Stamps of 1901

Surcharged with Value Only.

83 A17 5s on 15s cl & gray blk (Bl) 1.90 60
a. Inverted surcharge 30.00 30.00
84 A1710s on 15s cl & gray blk (Bl) 5.00 40
a. Inverted surcharge 30.00 30.00
85 A1725s on 30s brn bis & gray blk (R) 6.25 85
a. Double surcharge 100.00 100.00
b. "2" of "25" omitted 125.00 125.00
c. Blue surcharge *400.00 250.00*

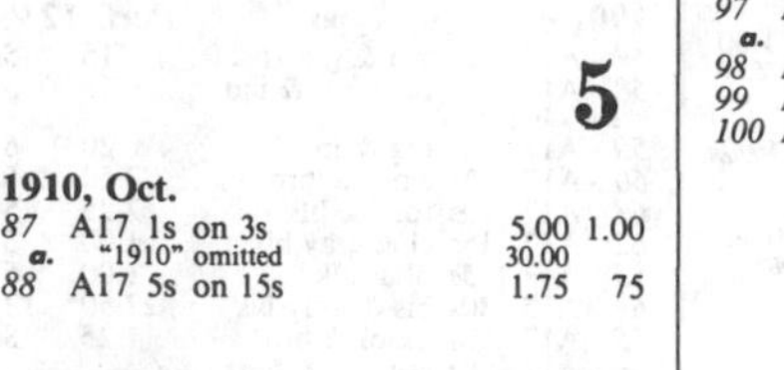

1910

Nos. 59 and 62 Surcharged in Blue

5

1910, Oct.
87 A17 1s on 3s 5.00 1.00
a. "1910" omitted 30.00
88 A17 5s on 15s 1.75 75

Tsar Assen's Tower (Crown over lion) A20

Tsar Ferdinand A21

City of Trnovo A22

Tsar Ferdinand A23

Tsar Ferdinand A24

Isker River A25

Ferdinand A26

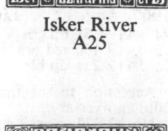

Rila Monastery (Crown at upper right) A27

Tsar and Princes A28

Ferdinand in Robes of Ancient Tsars A29

Monastery of Holy Trinity — A30

View of Varna — A31

1911, Feb. 14 Engr. *Perf. 12*
89 A20 1s myr grn 15 5
90 A21 2s car & blk 15 5
91 A22 3s lake & blk 40 8
92 A23 5s grn & blk 1.00 5
93 A24 10s dp red & blk 1.25 5
94 A25 15s brn bis 2.50 10
95 A26 25s ultra & blk 50 6
96 A27 30s bl & blk 6.50 15
97 A28 50s ocher & blk 15.00 20
a. Center inverted *3,000.*
98 A29 1 l chocolate 5.75 25
99 A30 2 l dl pur & blk 1.50 80
100 A31 3 l bl vio & blk 6.25 2.75
Nos. 89-100 (12) 40.95 4.59

See also Nos. 114-120, 161-162.

Tsar Ferdinand — A32

1912, Aug. 2 Typo. *Perf. 12½*
101 A32 5s ol grn 2.50 1.00
a. 5s pale grn *350.00 150.00*
102 A32 10s claret 4.00 2.25
103 A32 25s slate 5.25 2.50

25th year of reign of Tsar Ferdinand.

ОСВОБ. ВОЙНА

Nos. 89-95 Overprinted in Various Colors

1912-1913

1913, Aug. 6 Engr.
104 A20 1s myr grn (C) 16 10
105 A21 2s car & blk (Bl) 16 10
107 A22 3s lake & blk (Bl Bk) 25 15
108 A23 5s grn & blk (R) 16 8
109 A24 10s dp red & blk (Bk) 38 6
110 A25 15s brn bis (G) 75 35
111 A26 25s ultra & blk (R) 3.50 50
Nos. 104-111 (7) 5.36 1.34

Victory over the Turks in Balkan War of 1912-1913.

10 CT.

No. 95 Surcharged in Red

1915, July 6
112 A26 10s on 25s 50 10

No. 28 Surcharged in Green

3
СТОТИНКИ

113 A11 3s on 1s lil 4.00 4.50

Types of 1911 Re-engraved.

1915, Nov. 7 *Perf. 11½, 14*
114 A20 1s dk bl grn 5 5
115 A23 5s grn & brn vio 1.25 5
116 A24 10s red brn & brnsh blk 20 5
117 A25 15s ol grn 30 5
118 A26 25s ind & blk 20 5
119 A27 30s ol grn & red brn 20 5
120 A29 1 l dk brn 60 45
Nos. 114-120 (7) 2.80 75

No. 114 is 19 ½ m m. wide; No. 89, 18½mm. No. 118 is 19¼mm. wide; No. 95, 18¼mm. No. 120 is 20mm. wide; No. 98, 19mm. The re-engraved stamps also differ from the 1911 issue in many details of design. Nos. 114-120 exist imperforate.

The 5s and 10s exist perf. 14x11½.

For Nos. 114-116 and 118 overprinted with Cyrillic characters and "1916-1917," see Romania Nos. 2N1-2N4.

Coat of Arms — A33

Peasant and Bullock — A34

Soldier and Mt. Sonichka A35

View of Nish A36

Town and Lake Okhrida — A37

Demir-Kapiya (Iron Gate) — A37a

View of Gevgeli — A38

Perf. 11½, 12½x13, 13x12½.
1917-19 Typo.
122 A33 5s green 35 15
123 A34 15s slate 12 6
124 A35 25s blue 12 6
125 A36 30s orange 12 10
126 A37 50s violet 60 30
126A A37a 2 l brn org ('19) 60 35
127 A38 3 l claret 85 75
Nos. 122-127 (7) 2.76 1.77

Commemorative of the liberation of Macedonia. A 11 dark green was prepared but not issued. Price $2.50.

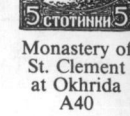

View of Veles A39

Monastery of St. Clement at Okhrida A40

1918 *Perf. 13x14*
128 A39 1s gray 5 5
129 A40 5s green 5 5

Tsar Ferdinand A41

Plowing with Oxen A42

1918, July 1 *Perf. 12½x13*
130 A41 1s dk grn 5 5
131 A41 2s dk brn 5 5
132 A41 3s indigo 35 15
133 A41 10s brn red 35 15

30th anniversary of Tsar Ferdinand's accession to the throne.

1919 *Perf. 13½x13.*
134 A42 1s gray 5 5

Sobranye Palace — A43

Tsar Boris III — A44

1919 *Perf. 11½x12, 12x11½*
135 A43 1s black 5 5
137 A43 2s ol grn 5 5

1919, Oct. 3
138 A44 3s org brn 5 5
139 A44 5s green 5 5
140 A44 10s rose red 5 5
141 A44 15s violet 5 5
142 A44 25s dp bl 5 5
143 A44 30s chocolate 18 5
144 A44 50s yel brn 18 5
Nos. 138-144 (7) 61 35

First anniversary of enthronement of Tsar Boris III.

Nos. 135-144 exist imperforate.

Birthplace of Vazov at Sopot and Cherrywood Cannon A47

"The Bear Fighter"- a Character from "Under the Yoke" — A48

The indexes in each volume of the Scott Catalogue contain many listings which help to identify stamps.

Ivan Vazov in 1870 and 1920 — A49

Vazov — A50

Homes of Vazov at Plovdiv and Sofia — A51

The Monk Paisii — A52

1920, Oct. 20 Photo. *Perf. 11½*

No.	Type	Description		
147	A47	30s brn red	10	5
148	A48	50s dk grn	12	6
149	A49	1 l db	25	20
150	A50	2 l lt brn	70	45
151	A51	3 l blk vio	1.10	50
152	A52	5 l dp bl	1.25	60
		Nos. 147-152 (6)	3.52	1.86

Issued to commemorate the 70th birthday of Ivan Vazov (1850-1921), Bulgarian poet and novelist.

Several values of this series exist imperforate and in pairs imperforate between.

Tsar Ferdinand A53 A54

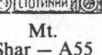

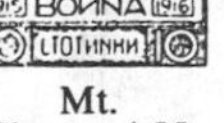
Mt. Shar — A55

Bridge over Vardar River — A56

View of Ohrid — A57

Perf. 13x14, 14x13

1921, June 11 Typo.

No.	Type	Description		
153	A53	10s claret	5	5
154	A54	10s claret	5	5
155	A55	10s claret	5	5
156	A56	10s rose lil	5	5
157	A57	20s blue	30	25
		Nos. 153-157 (5)	50	45

Nos. 153-157 were intended to be issued in 1915 to commemorate the liberation of Macedonia. They were not put in use until 1921. A 50s violet was prepared but never placed in use. Price $2.50.

View of Sofia — A58

"The Liberator," Monument to Alexander II — A59

Monastery at Shipka Pass — A62

Tsar Boris III — A63

Harvesting Grain — A64

Tsar Assen's Tower (No crown over lion) — A65

Rila Monastery (Rosette at upper right) — A66

1921-23 Engr. *Perf. 12*

No.	Type	Description		
158	A58	10s bl gray	8	5
159	A59	20s dp grn	8	5
160	A63	25s bl grn ('22)	8	5
161	A22	50s orange	8	5
162	A22	50s dk bl ('23)	2.50	2.50
163	A62	75s dl vio	16	5
164	A62	75s dp bl ('23)	30	12
165	A63	1 l carmine	30	15
166	A63	1 l dp bl ('22)	30	5
167	A64	2 l brown	35	6
168	A65	3 l brn vio	38	9
169	A66	5 l lt bl	2.50	30
170	A63	10 l vio brn	6.75	1.10
		Nos. 158-170 (13)	13.86	4.62

Bourchier in Bulgarian Costume A67

James David Bourchier A68

View of Rila Monastery A69

1921, Dec. 31

No.	Type	Description		
171	A67	10s red org	5	5
172	A67	20s orange	5	5
173	A68	30s dp gray	6	5
174	A68	50s bluish gray	6	5
175	A68	1 l dl vio	25	6
176	A69	1½ l ol grn	25	15
177	A69	2 l dp grn	25	15
178	A69	3 l Prus bl	65	30
179	A69	5 l red brn	1.25	50
		Nos. 171-179 (9)	2.87	1.36

Issued to commemorate the death of James D. Bourchier, Balkan correspondent of the London Times.

Postage Due Stamps of 1919-22 Surcharged — a

10 СТОТИНКИ

1924

No.	Type	Description		
182	D6	10s on 20s yel	5	5
183	D6	20s on 5s gray grn	5	5
a.		20s on 5s emer	10.00	10.00
184	D6	20s on 10s vio	5	5
185	D6	20s on 30s org	5	5

Nos. 182 to 185 were used for ordinary postage.

Regular Issues of 1919-23 Surcharged in Blue or Red:

1 ЛЕВЪ b **3 ЛЕВА** c

No.	Type	Description		
186	A43 (a)	10s on 1s blk (R)	5	5
187	A44 (b)	1 l on 5s emer (Bl)	15	5
188	A22 (c)	3 l on 50s dk bl (R)	30	15
189	A63 (b)	6 l on 1l car (Bl)	90	30
		Nos. 182-189 (8)	1.60	75

The surcharge of No. 188 comes in three types: normal, thick and thin.

Nos. 182, 184-189 exist with inverted surcharge.

Lion of Bulgaria A70 A71

Tsar Boris III A72

New Sofia Cathedral A73

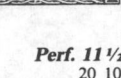

Harvesting A74

1925 Typo. *Perf. 13, 11½*

No.	Type	Description		
191	A70	10s red & bl, *pink*	6	5
192	A70	15s car & org, *bl*	6	5
193	A70	30s blk & buff	6	5
a.		Cliche of 15s in plate of 30s		
194	A71	50s choc, *grn*	10	5
195	A72	1 l dl grn	50	5
196	A73	2 l dk grn & buff	1.10	5
197	A74	4 l lake & yel	1.10	5
		Nos. 191-197 (7)	2.98	35

Several values of this series exist imperforate and in pairs imperforate between.

See also Nos. 199, 201.

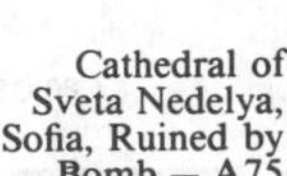

Cathedral of Sveta Nedelya, Sofia, Ruined by Bomb — A75

1926 *Perf. 11½*

No.	Type	Description		
198	A75	50s gray blk	20	10

A76 A77

Type A72 Re-engraved. (Shoulder at left does not touch frame.)

1926

No.	Type	Description		
199	A76	1 l gray	70	5
a.		1l grn	70	5
201	A76	2 l ol brn	80	5

Center Embossed

No.	Type	Description		
202	A77	6 l dp bl & pale lem	1.75	15
203	A77	10 l brn blk & brn org	6.00	1.00

Christo Botev — A78

Tsar Boris III — A79

1926, June 2

No.	Type	Description		
204	A78	1 l ol grn	45	15
205	A78	2 l sl vio	1.25	15
206	A78	4 l red brn	1.25	75

Issued to commemorate the 50th anniversary of the death of Christo Botev (1847-1876), Bulgarian revolutionary and poet.

Lion Type of 1881.

1927-29 *Perf. 13.*

No.	Type	Description		
207	A3	10s dk red & db	10	5
208	A3	15s blk & org ('29)	10	5
209	A3	30s dk bl & bis brn ('28)	10	5
a.		30s ind & buff	10	5
210	A3	50s blk & rose red ('28)	15	5

1928, Oct. 3 *Perf. 11½*

No.	Type	Description		
211	A79	1 l ol grn	1.10	5
212	A79	2 l dp brn	1.25	5

St. Clement A80

Konstantin Miladinov A81

George S. Rakovski A82

Drenovo Monastery A83

Paisii — A84

Tsar Simeon — A85

Lyuben Karavelov
A86

Vassil Levski
A87

Georgi Benkovski — A88

Tsar Alexander II — A89

1929, May 12

No.	Type	Denom.	Color	Unused	Used
213	A80	10s	dk vio	15	10
214	A81	15s	vio brn	15	5
215	A82	30s	red	15	5
216	A83	50s	ol grn	30	5
217	A84	1 l	org brn	75	10
218	A85	2 l	dk bl	85	15
219	A86	3 l	dl grn	2.00	50
220	A87	4 l	ol brn	3.00	25
221	A88	5 l	brown	2.00	40
222	A89	6 l	Prus grn	2.75	1.00
			Nos. 213-222 (10)	12.10	2.65

Issued to commemorate the millenary of Tsar Simeon and the 50th anniversary of the liberation of Bulgaria from the Turks.

Royal Wedding Issue.

Tsar Boris and Fiancée, Princess Giovanna
A90

Queen Ioanna and Tsar Boris — A91

1930, Nov. 12 ***Perf. 11½***

No.	Type	Denom.	Color	Unused	Used
223	A90	1 l	green	25	30
224	A91	2 l	dl vio	35	40
225	A90	4 l	rose red	35	40
226	A91	6 l	dk bl	40	45

Fifty-five copies of a miniature sheet incorporating one each of Nos. 223-226 were printed and given to royal, governmental and diplomatic personages.

Tsar Boris III
A92 A93

Perf. 11½, 12x11½, 13.

1931-37 **Unwmk.**

No.	Type	Denom.	Color	Unused	Used
227	A92	1 l	bl grn	30	5
228	A92	2 l	carmine	50	5
229	A92	4 l	red org ('34)	1.00	5
230	A92	4 l	yel org ('37)	25	5
231	A92	6 l	dp bl	90	5
232	A92	7 l	dp bl ('37)	25	6
233	A92	10 l	sl blk	11.00	60
234	A92	12 l	lt brn	50	15
235	A92	14 l	lt brn ('37)	35	20
236	A93	20 l	cl & org brn	1.25	40
			Nos. 227-236 (10)	16.30	1.66

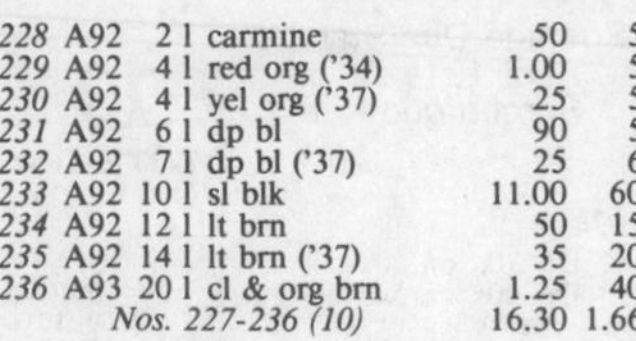

Nos. 230-233 and 235 have outer bars at top and bottom as shown on cut A92; Nos. 227-229 and 234 are without outer bars. See also Nos. 251, 252, 279-280, 287.

Balkan Games Issues.

Gymnast
A95

Soccer — A96

Riding — A97

Swimmer
A100

"Victory"
A101

Designs: 6 l, Fencing. 10 l, Bicycle race.

1931, Sept. 18 ***Perf. 11½***

No.	Type	Denom.	Color	Unused	Used
237	A95	1 l	lt grn	1.00	60
238	A96	2 l	garnet	1.00	60
239	A97	4 l	carmine	2.25	90
240	A95	6 l	Prus bl	4.50	1.50
241	A95	10 l	red org	11.00	4.50
242	A100	12 l	dk bl	37.50	9.00
243	A101	50 l	ol brn	35.00	27.50
			Nos. 237-243 (7)	92.25	44.60

1933, Jan. 5

No.	Type	Denom.	Color	Unused	Used
244	A95	1 l	bl grn	1.40	1.25
245	A96	2 l	blue	2.50	1.25
246	A97	4 l	brn vio	3.50	1.50
247	A95	6 l	brt rose	6.50	2.25
248	A95	10 l	ol brn	35.00	12.50
249	A100	12 l	orange	72.50	25.00
250	A101	50 l	red brn	140.00	110.00
			Nos. 244-250 (7)	261.40	153.75

Nos. 244-250 were sold only at the philatelic agency.

Boris Type of 1931.
Outer Bars at Top and Bottom Removed.

1933 ***Perf. 13.***

No.	Type	Denom.	Color	Unused	Used
251	A92	6 l	dp bl	90	5

Type of 1931 Surcharged in Blue **2**

1934

No.	Type	Denom.	Color	Unused	Used
252	A92	2 (l) on 3 l	ol brn	6.00	35

Soldier Defending Shipka Pass
A102

Shipka Battle Memorial
A103

Color-Bearer
A104

Veteran of the War of Liberation, 1878
A105

Widow and Orphans — A106

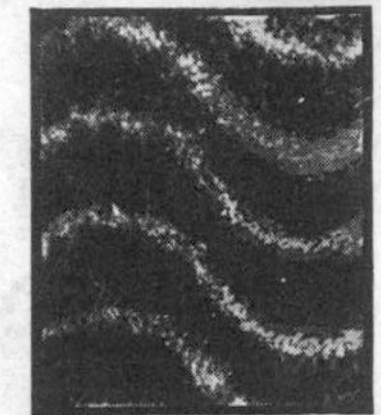

Wmk. 145- Wavy Lines

Perf. 10½, 11½

1934, Aug. 26 **Wmk. 145**

No.	Type	Denom.	Color	Unused	Used
253	A102	1 l	green	55	45
254	A103	2 l	pale red	55	30
255	A104	3 l	bis brn	1.65	1.40
256	A105	4 l	dk car	1.40	70
257	A104	7 l	dk bl	2.50	2.25
258	A106	14 l	plum	6.75	6.75
			Nos. 253-258 (6)	13.40	11.85

Issued to commemorate the unveiling of the Shipka Pass Battle memorial.

An unwatermarked miniature sheet incorporating one each of Nos. 253-258 was put on sale in 1938 in five cities at a price of 8,000 leva. Printing: 100 sheets.

1934, Sept. 21

No.	Type	Denom.	Color	Unused	Used
259	A102	1 l	brt grn	55	45
260	A103	2 l	dl org	55	30
261	A104	3 l	yellow	1.65	1.40
262	A105	4 l	rose	1.40	70
263	A104	7 l	blue	2.50	2.25
264	A106	14 l	ol bis	6.75	6.75
			Nos. 259-264 (6)	13.40	11.85

An unwatermarked miniature sheet incorporating one each of Nos. 259-263 was issued.

Velcho A. Djamjiyata
A108

Capt. G. S. Mamarchev
A109

1935, May 5 ***Perf. 11½***

No.	Type	Denom.	Color	Unused	Used
265	A108	1 l	dp bl	1.00	35
266	A109	2 l	maroon	1.00	40

Issued in commemoration of the centenary of a Bulgarian uprising against the Turks.

Soccer Game
A110

Cathedral of Alexander Nevski
A111

Soccer Team
A112

Symbolical of Victory
A113

Player and Trophy
A114

The Trophy
A115

1935, June 14

No.	Type	Denom.	Color	Unused	Used
267	A110	1 l	green	1.50	1.25
268	A111	2 l	bl gray	3.50	1.90
269	A112	4 l	crimson	5.50	3.00
270	A113	7 l	brt bl	11.00	3.50
271	A114	14 l	orange	11.00	4.75
272	A115	50 l	lil brn	85.00	75.00
			Nos. 267-272 (6)	117.50	89.40

5th Balkan Soccer Tournament.

Gymnast on Parallel Bars
A116

Youth in "Yunak" Costume
A117

Girl in "Yunak" Costume
A118

Pole Vaulting
A119

Stadium, Sofia
A120

Yunak Emblem
A121

1935, July 10

No.	Type	Denom.	Color	Unused	Used
273	A116	1 l	green	2.00	1.40
274	A117	2 l	lt bl	2.50	1.40
275	A118	4 l	carmine	5.25	2.25
276	A119	7 l	dk bl	5.25	3.50
277	A120	14 l	dk brn	5.25	3.50
278	A121	50 l	red	57.50	55.00
			Nos. 273-278 (6)	77.75	67.05

Issued to commemorate the 8th tournament of the Yunak Gymnastic Organization at Sofia, July 12-14.

Boris Type of 1931.

1935 **Wmk. 145** ***Perf. 12½, 13***

No.	Type	Denom.	Color	Unused	Used
279	A92	1 l	green	45	5
280	A92	2 l	carmine	22.50	5

Janos Hunyadi A122

King Ladislas Varnenchik A123

Varna Memorial — A124

King Ladislas III — A125

Battle of Varna, 1444 — A126

1935, Aug. 4 *Perf. 10½, 11½*

281	A122	1 l brn org	90	75
282	A123	2 l maroon	90	75
283	A124	4 l vermilion	4.50	3.50
284	A125	7 l dl bl	2.00	1.25
285	A126	14 l green	2.00	1.25
		Nos. 281-285 (5)	10.30	7.50

Issued to commemorate the Battle of Varna, and the death of the Polish King, Ladislas Varnenchik (1424-1444).

Lion Type of 1881.

1935 **Wmk. 145** *Perf. 13.*

286	A3	10s dk red & db	1.00	15

Boris Type of 1933.

Outer Bars at Top and Bottom Removed.

287	A92	6 l gray bl	75	10

Dimitr Monument A127

Haji Dimitr A128

Haji Dimitr and Stefan Karaja A129

Taking the Oath — A130

Birthplace of Dimitr A131

1935, Oct. 1 **Unwmk.** *Perf. 11½*

288	A127	1 l green	1.50	50
289	A128	2 l brown	2.00	1.00
290	A129	4 l car rose	4.00	3.25
291	A130	7 l blue	5.25	5.00
292	A131	14 l orange	5.25	5.00
		Nos. 288-292 (5)	18.00	14.75

Issued to commemorate the 67th anniversary of the death of the Bulgarian patriots, Haji Dimitr and Stefan Karaja.

Numeral A132

Lion A133

1936-39 *Perf. 13x12½, 13*

293	A132	10s red org ('37)	5	5
294	A132	15s emerald	5	5
295	A133	30s maroon	8	5
296	A133	30s yel brn ('37)	8	5
297	A133	30s Prus bl ('37)	10	5
298	A133	50s ultra	12	5
299	A133	50s dk car ('37)	15	5
300	A133	50s sl grn ('39)	6	5
		Nos. 293-300 (8)	69	40

Meteorological Station, Mt. Moussalla A134

Peasant Girl A135

Town of Nessebr A136

1936, Aug. 16 **Photo.** *Perf. 11½*

301	A134	1 l purple	1.40	1.00
302	A135	2 l ultra	1.40	90
303	A136	7 l dk bl	3.75	2.25

Issued to commemorate the fourth Geographical and Ethnographical Congress, Sofia, August, 1936.

Sts. Cyril and Methodius A137

Displaying the Bible to the People A138

1937, June 2

304	A137	1 l dk grn	22	20
305	A137	2 l dk plum	22	20
306	A138	4 l vermilion	40	30
307	A137	7 l dk bl	1.75	1.50
308	A138	14 l rose red	1.75	1.50
		Nos. 304-308 (5)	4.34	3.70

Millennium of Cyrillic alphabet.

Princess Marie Louise A139

Tsar Boris III A140

1937, Oct. 3

310	A139	1 l yel grn	30	8
311	A139	2 l brn red	30	12
312	A139	4 l scarlet	40	20

Issued in honor of Princess Marie Louise.

1937, Oct. 3

313	A140	2 l brn red	30	20

Issued to commemorate the 19th anniversary of the accession of Tsar Boris III to the throne. See No. B11.

National Products Issue.

Peasants Bundling Wheat A141

Sunflower A142

Wheat — A143

Chickens and Eggs — A144

Cluster of Grapes — A145

Rose and Perfume Flask — A146

Strawberries A147

Girl Carrying Grape Clusters A148

Rose — A149

Tobacco Leaves — A150

1938 *Perf. 13.*

316	A141	10s orange	5	5
317	A141	10s red org	5	5
318	A142	15s brt rose	30	6
319	A142	15s dp plum	30	6
320	A143	30s gldn brn	10	6
321	A143	30s cop brn	10	6
322	A144	50s black	10	6
323	A144	50s indigo	10	8
324	A145	1 l yel grn	70	8
325	A145	1 l green	70	8
326	A146	2 l rose pink	65	8
327	A146	2 l rose brn	65	6
328	A147	3 l dp red lil	1.25	20
329	A147	3 l brn lake	1.25	20
330	A148	4 l plum	85	20
331	A148	4 l gldn brn	85	20
332	A149	7 l vio bl	1.50	85
333	A149	7 l dp bl	1.50	85
334	A150	14 l dk brn	2.25	1.40
335	A150	14 l red brn	2.25	1.40
		Nos. 316-335 (20)	15.50	6.08

Several values of this series exist imperforate.

Crown Prince Simeon

A151 A153

Designs: 2 l, Same portrait as 1 l, value at lower left. 14 l, Similar to 4 l, but no wreath.

1938, June 16

336	A151	1 l brt grn	10	6
337	A151	2 l rose pink	12	6
338	A153	4 l dp org	13	8
339	A151	7 l ultra	65	50
340	A151	14 l dp brn	65	50
		Nos. 336-340 (5)	1.65	1.20

First birthday of Prince Simeon.

Tsar Boris III

A155 A156

Various Portraits of Tsar.

1938, Oct. 3

341	A155	1 l lt grn	10	6
342	A156	2 l rose brn	60	8
343	A156	4 l gldn brn	15	6
344	A156	7 l brt ultra	30	30
345	A156	14 l dp red lil	35	35
		Nos. 341-345 (5)	1.50	85

20th anniversary, reign of Tsar Boris III.

Early Locomotive A160

Designs: 2 l, Modern locomotive. 4 l, Train crossing bridge. 7 l, Tsar Boris in cab.

1939, Apr. 26

346	A160	1 l yel grn	15	8
347	A160	2 l cop brn	15	8
348	A160	4 l red org	1.00	30
349	A160	7 l dk bl	2.25	1.50

Issued in commemoration of the 50th anniversary of Bulgarian State Railways.

Post Horns and Arrows — A164

Central Post Office, Sofia — A165

1939, May 14 **Typo.**

350	A164	1 l yel grn	12	6
351	A165	2 l brt car	18	6

Issued in commemoration of the 60th anniversary of the establishment of the postal system.

Gymnast on Bar A166

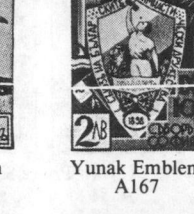

Yunak Emblem A167

Discus Thrower A168

Athletic Dancer A169

Weight Lifter — A170

1939, July 7 **Photo.**

352	A166	1 l yel grn & pale grn	20	15
353	A167	2 l brt rose	20	15
354	A168	4 l brn & gldn brn	30	30
355	A169	7 l dk bl & bl	70	90
356	A170	14 l plum & rose vio	3.00	3.75
		Nos. 352-356 (5)	4.40	5.25

Issued to commemorate the 9th tournament of the Yunak Gymnastic Organization at Sofia, July 4-8.

Tsar Boris III — A171

Bulgaria's First Stamp — A172

1940-41 **Typo.**

356A	A171	1 l dl grn ('41)	75	5
357	A171	2 l brt crim	20	5

1940, May 19 **Photo.** ***Perf. 13***

Design: 20 l, Similar design, scroll dated "1840-1940."

358	A172	10 l ol blk	1.00	1.00
359	A172	20 l indigo	1.00	1.00

Centenary of first postage stamp. Exist imperf.

Peasant Couple and Tsar Boris — A174

Flags over Wheat Field and Tsar Boris — A175

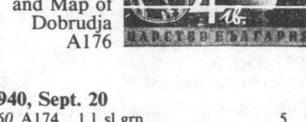

Tsar Boris and Map of Dobrudja A176

1940, Sept. 20

360	A174	1 l sl grn	5	5
361	A175	2 l rose red	10	8
362	A176	4 l dk brn	15	8
363	A176	7 l dk bl	60	40

Issued in commemoration of the return of Dobrudja from Romania.

Fruit A177

Bees and Flowers A178

Plowing A179

Shepherd and Sheep A180

Tsar Boris III — A181

Perf. 10, 10½x11½, 11½, 13.

1940-44 **Typo.** **Unwmk.**

364	A177	10s red org	5	5
365	A178	15s blue	5	5
366	A179	30s ol brn ('41)	5	5
367	A180	50s violet	15	5
368	A181	1 l brt grn	5	5
369	A181	2 l rose car	7	5
370	A181	4 l red org	15	5
371	A181	6 l red vio ('44)	30	5
372	A181	7 l blue	30	5
373	A181	10 l bl grn ('41)	35	15
		Nos. 364-373 (10)	1.52	60

See No. 440.

1940-41 **Wmk. 145** ***Perf. 13.***

373A	A180	50s vio ('41)	10	5
374	A181	1 l brt grn	10	5
375	A181	2 l rose car	15	5
376	A181	7 l dl bl	40	8
377	A181	10 l bl grn	60	20
		Nos. 373A-377 (5)	1.35	43

Watermarked vertically or horizontally.

P. R. Slaveikov A182

Sofronii, Bishop of Vratza A183

Saint Ivan Rilski A184

Martin S. Drinov A185

Monk Khrabr A186

Kolio Ficheto A187

1940, Sept. 23 **Photo.** **Unwmk.**

378	A182	1 l brt bl grn	6	5
379	A183	2 l brt car	8	5
380	A184	3 l dp red brn	15	8
381	A185	4 l red org	12	8
382	A186	7 l dp bl	1.00	75
383	A187	10 l dp red brn	1.50	1.10
		Nos. 378-383 (6)	2.91	2.11

Issued in commemoration of the liberation of Bulgaria from the Turks in 1878.

Johannes Gutenberg A188

N. Karastoyanov, First Bulgarian Printer A189

1940, Dec. 16

384	A188	1 l sl grn	10	8
385	A189	2 l org brn	10	8

Issued in commemoration of the 500th anniversary of the invention of the printing press and the 100th anniversary of the first Bulgarian printing press.

Christo Botev — A190

Botev with his Insurgent Band — A191

Monument to Botev — A192

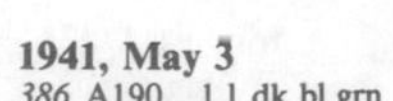

1941, May 3

386	A190	1 l dk bl grn	10	5
387	A191	2 l crim rose	15	5
388	A192	3 l dk brn	50	50

Issued in honor of Christo Botev, patriot and poet.

Palace of Justice, Sofia — A193

Designs: 20l, Workers' hospital. 50l, National Bank.

1941-43 **Engr.** ***Perf. 11½***

389	A193	14 l lt gray brn ('43)	20	15
390	A193	20 l gray grn ('43)	40	25
391	A193	50 l lt bl gray	2.00	2.00

Macedonian Woman — A196

Outline of Macedonia and Tsar Boris III — A197

View of Aegean Sea — A198

Poganovski Monastery A199

City of Okhrida — A200

1941, Oct. 3 **Photo.** ***Perf. 13***

392	A196	1 l sl grn	5	5
393	A197	2 l crimson	6	5
394	A198	2 l red org	10	5
395	A199	4 l org brn	10	8
396	A200	7 l dp gray bl	40	40
		Nos. 392-396 (5)	71	63

Issued to commemorate the acquisition of Macedonian territory from neighboring countries.

Peasant Working in a Field — A201

Designs: 15s, Plowing. 30s, Apiary. 50s, Women harvesting fruit. 3 l, Shepherd and sheep. 5 l, Inspecting cattle.

1941-44

397	A201	10s dk vio	5	5
398	A201	10s dk bl	5	5
399	A201	15s Prus bl	5	5
400	A201	50s dk ol brn	5	5
401	A201	30s red org	5	5

No.	Type	Description	Unused	Used
402	A201	30s dk sl grn	5	5
403	A201	50s bl vio	6	5
404	A201	50s red lil	8	5
405	A201	3 l hn brn	55	40
406	A201	3 l dk brn ('44)	1.65	1.75
407	A201	5 l sepia	70	75
408	A201	5 l vio bl ('44)	1.65	1.75
		Nos. 397-408 (12)	4.99	5.05

Girls Singing A207

Boys in Camp A208

Raising Flag — A209

Camp Scene — A210

Folk Dancers — A211

1942, June 1 **Photo.**

No.	Type	Description	Unused	Used
409	A207	1 l dk bl grn	8	5
410	A208	2 l scarlet	15	6
411	A209	4 l ol gray	15	6
412	A210	7 l dp bl	16	15
413	A211	14 l fawn	30	30
		Nos. 409-413 (5)	84	62

National "Work and Joy" movement.

Wounded Soldier — A212

Soldier's Farewell — A213

Designs: 4 l, Aiding wounded soldier. 7 l, Widow and orphans at grave. 14 l, Tomb of Unknown Soldier. 20 l, Queen Ioanna visiting wounded.

1942, Sept. 7

No.	Type	Description	Unused	Used
414	A212	1 l sl grn	8	6
415	A213	2 l brt rose	8	6
416	A213	4 l yel org	8	5
417	A213	7 l dk bl	10	5
418	A213	14 l brown	12	8
419	A213	20 l ol blk	20	10
		Nos. 414-419 (6)	66	40

Issued to aid war victims. No. 419 was printed in sheets of 50, alternating with 50 labels.

A particular stamp may be scarce, but if few collectors want it, its market value may remain relatively low.

Legend of Kubrat — A218

Cavalry Charge — A219

Designs: 30s, Rider of Madara. 50s, Christening of Boris I. 1 l, School, St. Naum. 2 l, Crowning of Tsar Simeon by Boris I. 3 l, Golden era of Bulgarian literature. 4 l, Sentencing of the Bogomil Basil. 5 l, Proclamation of 2nd Bulgarian Empire. 7 l, Ivan Assen II at Trebizond. 10 l, Deporting the Patriarch Jeftimi. 14 l, Wandering minstrel. 20 l, Monk Paisii. 30 l, Monument, Shipka Pass.

1942, Oct. 12

No.	Type	Description	Unused	Used
420	A218	10s bluish blk	5	5
421	A219	15s Prus grn	5	5
422	A219	30s dk rose vio	5	5
423	A219	50s indigo	5	5
424	A219	1 l sl grn	5	5
425	A219	2 l crimson	5	5
426	A219	3 l brown	5	5
427	A219	4 l orange	6	6
428	A219	5 l grnsh blk	6	6
429	A219	7 l dk bl	8	8
430	A219	10 l brn blk	15	15
431	A219	14 l ol blk	15	15
432	A219	20 l hn brn	50	50
433	A219	30 l black	75	75
		Nos. 420-433 (14)	2.10	2.10

Tsar Boris III — A234

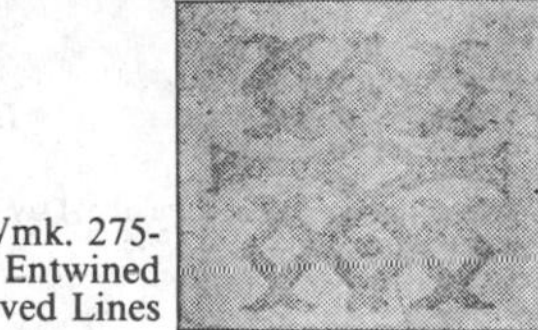

Wmk. 275- Entwined Curved Lines

Designs: Various portraits of Tsar.

Perf. 13, Imperf.

1944, Feb. 28 **Photo.** **Wmk. 275**

Frames in Black.

No.	Type	Description	Unused	Used
434	A234	1 l ol grn	5	5
435	A234	2 l red brn	12	12
436	A234	4 l brown	14	14
437	A234	5 l gray vio	20	25
438	A234	7 l sl bl	20	25
		Nos. 434-438 (5)	71	81

Issued in memory of Tsar Boris III (1894-1943).

Tsar Simeon II — A239

Perf. 11½, 13

1944, June 12 **Typo.** **Unwmk.**

No.	Type	Description	Unused	Used
439	A239	3 l red org	20	5

Shepherd Type of 1940

1944

No.	Type	Description	Unused	Used
440	A180	50s yel grn	20	10

Parcel Post Stamps of 1944 Overprinted in Black or Orange

ВСИЧКО ЗА ФРОНТА

1945, Jan. 25 ***Perf. 11½***

No.	Type	Description	Unused	Used
448	PP5	1 l dk car	5	5
449	PP5	7 l rose lil	5	5
450	PP5	20 l org brn	8	5
451	PP5	30 l dk brn car	15	5
452	PP5	50 l red org	25	12
453	PP5	100 l bl (O)	60	30

The overprint reads: "Everything for the Front".

No. 448 with Additional Surcharge of New Value in Black.

No.	Type	Description	Unused	Used
454	PP5	4 l on 1 l dk car	5	5
		Nos. 448-454 (7)	1.23	67

Nos. 368 to 370 Overprinted in Black

СЬБИРАЙТЕ СТАРО ЖЕЛѢЗО

1945, Mar. 15 ***Perf. 11½, 13***

No.	Type	Description	Unused	Used
455	A181	1 l brt grn	5	5
456	A181	2 l rose car	10	5
457	A181	4 l red org	15	5

The overprint reads: "Collect old iron."

Overprinted in Black

СЬБИРАЙТЕ ХАРТИЕНИ ОТПАДЬЦИ

No.	Type	Description	Unused	Used
458	A181	1 l brt grn	5	5
459	A181	2 l rose car	10	5
460	A181	4 l red org	15	5

The overprint reads: "Collect discarded paper."

Overprinted in Black

СЬБИРАЙТЕ ВСЬКАКВИ ПАРЦАЛИ

No.	Type	Description	Unused	Used
461	A181	1 l brt grn	5	5
462	A181	2 l rose car	10	5
463	A181	4 l red org	15	5
		Nos. 455-463 (9)	90	45

The overprint reads: "Collect all kinds of rags."

Oak Tree — A245

Imperf., Perf. 11½.

1945 **Litho.** **Unwmk.**

No.	Type	Description	Unused	Used
464	A245	4 l vermilion	8	6
465	A245	10 l blue	8	6

Imperf

No.	Type	Description	Unused	Used
466	A245	50 l brn lake	20	20

Slav Congress, Sofia, March, 1945.

A246

A247

Lion Rampant A248

Arms of Bulgaria A249

A251

A252

Arms of Bulgaria A253 A254

Two types of 2 l and 4 l: Type I: Large crown close to coat of arms. Type II: Smaller crown standing high.

1945-46 **Photo.** ***Perf. 13***

No.	Type	Description	Unused	Used
469	A246	30s yel grn	5	5
470	A247	50s pck grn	5	5
471	A248	1 l dk grn	5	5
472	A249	2 l choc (I)	5	5
a.		Type II	5	5
473	A249	4 l dk bl (I)	8	5
a.		Type II	5	5
475	A251	5 l red vio	5	5
476	A251	9 l sl gray	6	5
477	A252	10 l Prus bl	8	5
478	A253	15 l brown	10	5
479	A254	20 l carmine	20	6
480	A254	20 l gray blk	20	6
		Nos. 469-480 (11)	97	57

Breaking Chain — A255

1 Lev Coin — A256

Water Wheel — A257

Coin and Symbols of Agriculture and Industry — A258

Unwmk.

1945, June 4 Litho. *Imperf.*

Laid Paper.

481	A255	50 l brn red, *pink*	10	8
482	A255	50 l org, *pink*	10	8
483	A256	100 l gray bl, *pink*	15	12
484	A256	100 l brn, *pink*	15	12
485	A257	150 l dk ol gray, *pink*	30	25
486	A257	150 l dl car, *pink*	30	25
487	A258	200 l dp bl, *pink*	45	40
488	A258	200 l ol grn, *pink*	45	40
		Nos. 481-488 (8)	2.00	1.70

Souvenir Sheets.

489	Sheet of four	2.50	2.50
a.	50 l vio bl	25	25
b.	100 l vio bl	25	25
c.	150 l vio bl	25	25
d.	200 l vio bl	25	25
490	Sheet of four	2.50	2.50
a.	50 l brn org	25	25
b.	100 l brn org	25	25
c.	150 l brn org	25	25
d.	200 l brn org	25	25

Nos. 481 to 490 were issued to publicize Bulgaria's Liberty Loan.

Nos. 489 and 490 measure 90x122mm. and contain one each of types A255-A258. Margin inscription: "March 9, 1935, Sofia" in Bulgarian characters.

Olive Branch — A260

1945, Sept. 1 Typo. *Perf. 13*

491	A260	10 l org brn & yel grn	6	5
492	A260	50 l dl red & dp grn	25	15

Victory of Allied Nations, World War II.

September 9, 1944 — A261

Numeral and Broken Chain — A262

1945, Sept. 7

493	A261	1 l gray grn	5	5
494	A261	4 l dp bl	5	5
495	A261	5 l rose lil	5	5
496	A262	10 l lt bl	5	5
497	A262	20 l brt car	22	12
498	A261	50 l brt bl grn	50	30
499	A261	100 l org brn	55	50
		Nos. 493-499 (7)	1.47	1.12

Issued to commemorate the 1st anniversary of Bulgaria's liberation.

Old Postal Savings Emblem — A263

First Bulgarian Postal Savings Stamp — A264

Child Putting Coin in Bank — A265

Postal Savings Building, Sofia — A266

1946, Apr. 12

500	A263	4 l brn org	6	5
501	A264	10 l dk ol	12	5
502	A265	20 l ultra	12	6
503	A266	50 l sl gray	65	65

Issued to commemorate the 50th anniversary of Bulgarian Postal Savings.

Refugee Children — A267

Wounded Soldier A268

Nurse Assisting Wounded Soldier — A269

Design: 35 l, 100 l, Red Cross hospital train.

1946, Apr. 4

Cross in Carmine

504	A267	2 l dk ol	5	5
505	A268	4 l violet	10	5
506	A267	10 l plum	10	6
507	A268	20 l ultra	12	6
508	A269	30 l brn org	15	10
509	A268	35 l gray blk	18	18
510	A269	50 l vio brn	25	25
511	A268	100 l gray brn	85	85
		Nos. 504-511 (8)	1.80	1.60

See also Nos. 553 to 560.

Advancing Troops A271

Grenade Thrower A272

Attacking Planes — A274

Designs: 5l, Horse-drawn cannon. 9 l, Engineers building pontoon bridge. 10 l, 30 l, Cavalry charge. 40 l, Horse-drawn supply column. 50 l, Motor transport column. 60 l, Infantry, tanks and planes.

1946, Aug. 9 Typo. Unwmk.

512	A271	2 l dk red vio	5	5
513	A272	4 l dk gray	5	5
514	A271	5 l dk org red	5	5
515	A274	6 l blk brn	5	5
516	A271	9 l rose lil	5	5
517	A271	10 l dp vio	5	5
518	A271	20 l dp bl	25	15
519	A271	30 l red org	25	15
520	A271	40 l dk ol bis	30	20
521	A271	50 l dk grn	30	20
522	A271	60 l red brn	42	35
		Nos. 512-522 (11)	1.82	1.35

Bulgaria's participation in World War II.

Arms of Russia and Bulgaria A279

Lion Rampant A280

1946, May 23

523	A279	4 l red org	8	8
525	A279	20 l turq grn	20	15

Issued to commemorate the Congress of the Bulgarian-Soviet Association, May 1946. The 4 l exists in dk car rose and 20 l in blue, price, set $10.

1946, May 25 *Imperf.*

526	A280	20 l blue	35	25

Issued to commemorate the Day of the Postage Stamp, May 26, 1946.

Alexander Stambolisky A281

Flags of Albania, Romania, Bulgaria and Jugoslavia A282

1946, June 13 *Perf. 12*

527	A281	100 l red org	3.00	3.00

Issued to commemorate the 23rd anniversary of the death of Alexander Stambolisky, agrarian leader.

1946, July 6 *Perf. 11½*

528	A282	100 l blk brn	75	80

Issued to publicize the 1946 Balkan Games.

Sheet of 100 arranged so that all stamps are tete beche vertically and horizontally, except two center rows in left pane which provide 10 vertical pairs that are not tete beche vertically.

St. Ivan Rilski — A283

A284

A285

Rila Monastery A286

Views of Rila Monastery A287

1946, Aug. 26

529	A283	1 l red brn	7	6
530	A284	4 l blk brn	8	6
531	A285	10 l dk grn	12	8
532	A286	20 l dp bl	16	10
533	A287	50 l dk red	75	65
		Nos. 529-533 (5)	1.18	95

Millenary of Rila Monastery.

People's Republic

A288

1946, Sept. 15 Typo.

534	A288	4 l brn lake	5	5
535	A288	20 l dl bl	5	5
536	A288	50 l ol bis	18	18

No. 535 is inscribed "BULGARIA" in Latin characters.

Issued to commemorate the referendum of September 8, 1946, resulting in the establishment of the Bulgarian People's Republic.

Partisan Army A289

Snipers A290

Soldiers: Past and Present — A291

Design: 30 l, Partisans advancing.

1946, Dec. 2

537 A289	1 l	vio brn	5	5
538 A290	4 l	dl grn	5	5
539 A291	5 l	chocolate	5	5
540 A290	10 l	crimson	5	5
541 A289	20 l	ultra	25	15
542 A290	30 l	ol bis	25	15
543 A291	50 l	black	30	30
		Nos. 537-543 (7)	1.00	80

Relief Worker and Children A294

Child with Gift Parcels A295

Waiting for Food Distribution A296

Mother and Child A297

1946, Dec. 30

545 A294	1 l	dk vio brn	5	5
546 A295	4 l	brt red	5	5
547 A295	9 l	ol bis	5	5
548 A294	10 l	sl gray	10	5
549 A296	20 l	ultra	15	6
550 A297	30 l	dp brn org	15	10
551 A296	40 l	maroon	25	20
552 A294	50 l	pck grn	45	40
		Nos. 545-552 (8)	1.25	96

"Bulgaria" is in Latin characters on No. 548.

Red Cross Types of 1946

1947, Jan. 31

Cross in Carmine

553 A267	2 l	ol bis	5	5
554 A268	4 l	ol blk	5	5
555 A267	10 l	bl grn	10	10
556 A268	20 l	brt bl	20	20
557 A269	30 l	yel grn	28	28
558 A268	35 l	grnsh gray	32	32
559 A269	50 l	hn brn	45	45
560 A268	100 l	dk bl	65	65
		Nos. 553-560 (8)	2.10	2.10

Laurel Branch, Allied and Bulgarian Emblems A298

Dove of Peace A299

1947, Feb. 28

561 A298	4 l	olive	5	5
562 A299	10 l	brn red	6	6
563 A299	20 l	dp bl	20	20

Issued to commemorate the return to peace at the close of World War II. "Bulgaria" in Latin characters on No. 563.

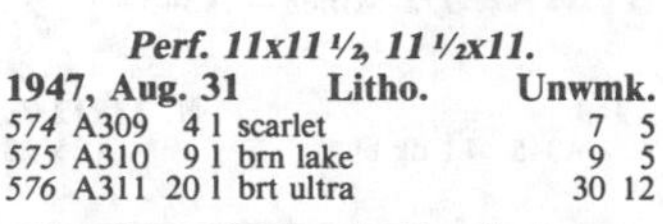

A302

Guerrilla Fighters A303 A304

1947, Jan. 21 *Perf. 11½*

567 A302	10 l	choc & brn org	25	25
568 A303	20 l	dk bl & bl	25	25
569 A304	70 l	dp cl & rose	12.50	12.50

Issued to honor the anti-fascists.

Hydroelectric Station — A305

Miner A306

Symbols of Industry A307

Tractor — A308

1947, Aug. 6

570 A305	4 l	ol grn	8	5
571 A306	9 l	red brn	15	12
572 A307	20 l	dp bl	25	25
573 A308	40 l	ol brn	60	60

Exhibition Building A309

Former Home of Alphonse de Lamartine A310

Symbols of Agriculture and Horticulture — A311

Perf. 11x11½, 11½x11.

1947, Aug. 31 **Litho.** **Unwmk.**

574 A309	4 l	scarlet	7	5
575 A310	9 l	brn lake	9	5
576 A311	20 l	brt ultra	30	12

Issued to publicize the Plovdiv International Fair, 1947. See No. C54.

Basil Evstatiev Aprilov — A312

1947, Oct. 19 **Photo.** *Perf. 11*

577 A312	40 l	brt ultra	35	25

Issued to commemorate the centenary of the death of Basil Evstatiev Aprilov, educator and historian. See also No. 603.

Balkan Games Issue.

Bicycle Race A313

Basketball A314

Chess — A315

Designs: 20 l, Soccer players. 60l, Four flags of participating nations.

1947, Sept. 29 **Typo.** *Perf. 11½*

578 A313	2 l	plum	25	20
579 A314	4 l	dk ol grn	25	20
580 A315	9 l	org brn	55	20
581 A315	20 l	brt ultra	1.10	30
582 A315	60 l	vio brn	2.25	1.50
		Nos. 578-582 (5)	4.40	2.40

People's Theater, Sofia A316

National Assembly A317

Central Post Office, Sofia A318

Presidential Mansion A319

1947-48 **Typo.** *Perf. 12½*

583 A316	50s	yel grn	5	5
584 A317	50s	yel grn	5	5
585 A318	1 l	green	5	5
586 A319	1 l	green	5	5
587 A316	2 l	brn lake	5	5
588 A317	2 l	lt brn	5	5
589 A316	4 l	dp bl	6	5
590 A317	4 l	dp bl	8	5
591 A316	9 l	carmine	40	5
592 A317	20 l	dp bl	85	30
		Nos. 583-592 (10)	1.69	75

On Nos. 583-592 inscription reads "Bulgarian Republic." No. 592 is inscribed in Latin characters.

Redrawn.

НАРОДНА

added to inscription.

593 A318	1 l	green	6	5
594 A318	2 l	brn lake	8	5
595 A318	4 l	dp bl	10	5

Cyrillic inscription beneath design on Nos. 593-595 reads "Bulgarian People's Republic".

Geno Kirov — A320

Actors' Portraits: 1 l, Zlatina Nedeva. 2 l, Ivan Popov. 3 l, Athanas Kirchev. 4 l, Elena Snejina. 5 l, Stoyan Bachvarov.

Perf. 10½

1947, Dec. 8 **Unwmk.** **Litho.**

596 A320	50s	bis brn	5	5
597 A320	1 l	lt bl grn	5	5
598 A320	2 l	sl grn	5	5
599 A320	3 l	dp bl	6	6
600 A320	4 l	scarlet	8	8
601 A320	5 l	red brn	8	8
		Nos. 596-601,B22-B26 (11)	145.07	107.77

National Theater, 50th anniversary.

Merchant Ship "Fatherland" — A321

1947, Dec. 19

602 A321	50 l	Prus bl, *cr*	40	25

B. E. Aprilov A322

Bulgarian Worker A323

1948, Feb. 19 *Perf. 11*

603 A322	4 l	brn car, *cr*	10	10

Issued to commemorate the centenary of the death of Basil Evstatiev Aprilov, educator and historian.

1948, Feb. 29 **Photo.** *Perf. 11½x12*

604 A323	4 l	dp bl, *cr*	20	10

2nd Bulgarian Workers' Congress.

Self-education A324

Accordion Player A325

Factory Recess
A326

Girl Throwing Basketball
A327

1948, Mar. 31 **Photo.**

605	A324	4 l red	6	6
606	A325	20 l dp bl	18	15
607	A326	40 l dl grn	25	15
608	A327	60 l brown	70	50

Nicholas Vaptzarov — A328

Portraits: 9 l, P. K. Iavorov. 15 l, Christo Smirnenski. 20 l, Ivan Vazov. 45 l, P. R. Slaveikov.

1948, May 18 **Litho.** ***Perf. 11***

Cream Paper.

611	A328	4 l brt ver	7	5
612	A328	9 l lt brn	8	5
613	A328	15 l claret	10	6
614	A328	20 l dp bl	12	12
615	A328	45 l green	40	40
		Nos. 611-615 (5)	77	68

Soviet Soldier
A329

Civilians Offering Gifts to Soldiers
A330

Designs: 20 l, Soldiers, 1878 and 1944. 60 l, Stalin and Spasski Tower.

1948, July 5 **Photo.**

Cream Paper.

616	A329	4 l brn org	6	5
617	A330	10 l ol grn	6	5
618	A330	20 l dp bl	15	12
619	A329	60 l ol brn	60	50

Issued to honor the Soviet Army.

Demeter Blagoev
A331

Monument to Bishop Andrey
A332

Designs: 9 l, Gabriel Genov. 60 l, Marching youths.

1948, Sept. 6 **Litho.**

Cream Paper.

620	A331	4 l dk brn	5	5
621	A331	9 l brn org	5	5
622	A332	20 l dp bl	12	9
623	A332	60 l brown	80	65

No. 623 is inscribed in Cyrillic characters.

Issued to commemorate, the 25th anniversary of the National Insurrection of 1923.

Christo Smirnenski
A333

Battle of Grivitza, 1877
A334

1948, Oct. 2 **Photo.** ***Perf. 11½***

Cream Paper

624	A333	4 l blue	7	5
625	A333	16 l red brn	15	6

Issued to commemorate the 25th anniversary of the death of Christo Smirnenski, poet, 1898-1923.

1948, Nov. 1

626	A334	20 l blue	20	12

Issued to publicize Romanian-Bulgarian friendship. See Nos. C56-C57.

Bath, Gorna Banya
A335

Bath, Bankya
A336

Mineral Bath, Sofia
A337

Maliovitza
A338

1948-49 **Typo.** ***Perf. 12½.***

627	A335	2 l red brn	15	5
628	A336	3 l red org	15	5
629	A337	4 l dp bl	20	5
630	A338	5 l vio brn	18	5
631	A336	10 l red vio	25	5
632	A338	15 l ol grn ('49)	35	5
633	A335	20 l dp bl	1.25	20
		Nos. 627-633 (7)	2.53	50

Latin characters on No. 633. See also No. 653.

Emblem of the Republic — A339

1948-50

634	A339	50s red org	5	5
634A	A339	50s org brn ('50)	6	5
635	A339	1 l green	6	5
636	A339	9 l black	15	8

Botev's Birthplace, Kalofer — A340

Christo Botev — A341

Cyrillic Inscription:
"Chr. Botev 1848-1948."

Designs: 9 l, Steamer "Radetzky." 15 l, Kalofer village. 20 l, Botev in uniform. 40 l, Botev's mother. 50 l, Pen, pistol and wreath.

Perf. 11x11½, 11½

1948, Dec. 21 **Photo.**

Cream Paper.

638	A340	1 l dk grn	5	5
639	A341	4 l vio brn	5	5
640	A340	9 l violet	5	5
641	A340	15 l brown	8	6
642	A341	20 l blue	20	10
643	A340	40 l red brn	35	25
644	A341	50 l ol blk	45	35
		Nos. 638-644 (7)	1.23	91

Issued to commemorate the centenary of the birth of Christo Botev, Bulgarian national poet.

Lenin — A342

Lenin Speaking — A343

1949, Jan. 24 **Unwmk.** ***Perf. 11½***

Cream Paper.

645	A342	4 l brown	15	7
646	A343	20 l brn red	40	25

25th anniversary of the death of Lenin.

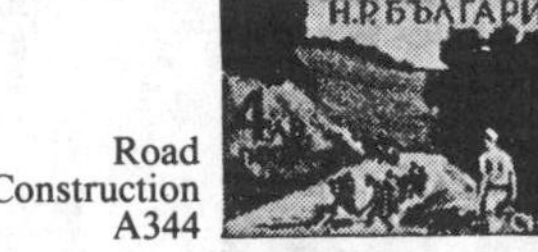

Road Construction
A344

Designs: 5 l, Tunnel construction. 9 l, Locomotive. 10 l, Textile worker. 20 l, Female tractor driver. 40 l, Workers in truck.

1949, Apr. 6 ***Perf. 10½***

Inscribed: "CHM".

Cream Paper.

647	A344	4 l dk red	10	5
648	A344	5 l dk brn	15	8
649	A344	9 l dk sl grn	25	15
650	A344	10 l violet	30	20
651	A344	20 l dl bl	65	55
652	A344	40 l brown	1.10	80
		Nos. 647-652 (6)	2.55	1.83

Issued to honor the Workers' Cultural Brigade.

Type of 1948.
Redrawn.
Country Name and "POSTA" in Latin Characters.

1949 **Typo.** ***Perf. 12½***

653	A337	20 l dp bl	70	15

Miner — A345

1949 ***Perf. 11x11½.***

654	A345	4 l dk bl	25	8

George Dimitrov
A347

A348

1949, July 10 **Photo.**

656	A347	4 l red brn	15	5
657	A348	20 l dk bl	40	25

Issued in tribute to Prime Minister George Dimitrov, 1882-1949.

Power Station
A349

Grain Towers
A350

Farm Machinery
A351

Tractor Parade
A352

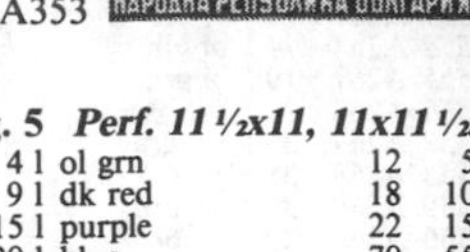

Agriculture and Industry
A353

1949, Aug. 5 ***Perf. 11½x11, 11x11½.***

658	A349	4 l ol grn	12	5
659	A350	9 l dk red	18	10
660	A351	15 l purple	22	15
661	A352	20 l blue	70	55
662	A353	50 l org brn	2.25	1.25
		Nos. 658-662 (5)	3.47	2.10

Issued to publicize Bulgaria's Five Year Plan.

Grenade and Javelin Throwers
A354

Hurdlers
A355

Motorcycle and Tractor
A356

Boy and Girl Athletes
A357

1949, Sept. 5

663	A354	4 l brn org	30	20
664	A355	9 l ol grn	60	35

665 A356 20 l vio bl 1.25 1.00
666 A357 50 l red brn 3.00 2.00

Frontier Guards
A358 A359

1949, Oct. 31
667 A358 4 l chnt brn 15 5
668 A359 20 l gray bl 60 40

See also No. C60.

George Dimitrov A360

Allegory of Labor A361

Laborers of Both Sexes A362

Workers and Flags of Bulgaria and Russia A363

Perf. 11½
1949, Dec. 13 **Photo.** **Unwmk.**
669 A360 4 l org brn 12 5
670 A361 9 l purple 20 8
671 A362 20 l dl bl 35 35
672 A363 50 l red 75 75

Joseph V. Stalin — A364

Stalin and Dove — A365

1949, Dec. 21
673 A364 4 l dp org 20 8
674 A365 40 l rose brn 60 50

Issued to commemorate the 70th anniversary of the birth of Joseph V. Stalin.

Kharalamby Stoyanov A366

Railway Strikers A367

Communications Strikers — A368

1950, Feb. 15
675 A366 4 l yel brn 10 5
676 A367 20 l vio bl 20 10
677 A368 60 l brn ol 60 55

Issued to commemorate the 30th anniversary (in 1949) of the General Railway and Postal Employees' Strike of 1919.

Miner A369

Locomotive A370

Shipbuilding A371

Tractor A372

Farm Machinery — A373

Stalin Central Heating Plant — A374

Textile Worker — A375

1950-51 *Perf. 11½, 13.*
678 A369 1 l ol 12 5
679 A370 2 l gray blk 20 5
680 A371 3 l gray bl 30 5
681 A372 4 l dk bl grn 2.50 75
682 A373 5 l hn brn 60 10
682A A373 9 l gray blk ('51) 30 6
683 A374 10 l dp plum ('51) 40 10
684 A375 15 l dk car ('51) 60 6
685 A375 20 l dk bl ('51) 1.00 60
Nos. 678-685 (9) 6.02 1.82

No. 685 is inscribed in Latin characters. See Nos. 750-751A.

Vassil Kolarov — A377

1950, Mar. 6 *Perf. 11½*
Size: 21½x31½mm.
686 A377 4 l red brn 6 5

Size: 27x39½mm.
687 A377 20 l vio bl 35 30

Issued in memory of Vassil Kolarov (1877-1950).

No. 687 has altered frame and is inscribed in Latin characters.

Stanislav Dospevski, Self-portrait A378

King Kaloyan and Desislava A379

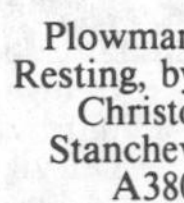

Plowman Resting, by Christo Stanchev A380

Statue of Dimtcho Debelianov, by Ivan Lazarov A381

"Harvest," by V. Dimitrov A382

Design: 9l, Nikolai Pavlovich, self-portrait.

1950, Apr. 15 *Perf. 11½*
688 A378 1 l dk ol grn 35 15
689 A379 4 l dk red 1.00 30
690 A378 9 l chocolate 1.00 30
691 A380 15 l brown 1.75 35
692 A380 20 l dp bl 2.25 1.10
693 A381 40 l red brn 3.25 1.75
694 A382 60 l dp org 4.50 2.25
Nos. 688-694 (7) 14.10 6.20

Latin characters on No. 692.

Ivan Vazov and Birthplace A383

1950, June 26
695 A383 4 l ol grn 12 10

Issued to commemorate the centenary of the birth of Ivan Vazov (1850-1921), poet.

Road Building — A384

Men of Three Races and "Stalin" Flag — A385

Perf. 11½x11, 11x11½
1950, Sept. 19
696 A384 4 l brn red 5 5
697 A385 20 l vio bl 40 25

2nd National Peace Conference.

Molotov, Kolarov, Stalin and Dimitrov — A386

Spasski Tower and Flags — A387

Russian and Bulgarian Women A388

Loading Russian Ship A389

Perf. 11½
1950, Oct. 10 **Unwmk.** **Photo.**
698 A386 4 l brown 10 5
699 A387 9 l rose car 15 6
700 A388 20 l gray bl 20 20
701 A389 50 l dk grnsh bl 1.10 65

Issued to commemorate the 2nd anniversary of the Soviet-Bulgarian treaty of mutual assistance.

St. Constantine Sanatorium A390

Children at Seashore A391

Design: 5 l, Rest home.

1950 **Typo.**
702 A390 1 l dk grn 6 5
703 A391 2 l carmine 18 5
704 A391 5 l dp org 25 15
705 A391 10 l dp bl 65 35

Originally prepared in 1945 as "Sunday Delivery Stamps," this issue was released for ordinary postage in 1950.

Runners — A393

Designs: 9 l, Cycling. 20 l, Putting the Shot. 40 l, Volleyball.

1950, Aug. 21 **Photo.** *Perf. 11*
706 A393 4 l dk grn 25 20
707 A393 9 l red brn 45 40
708 A393 20 l gray bl 90 65
709 A393 40 l plum 2.00 1.50

Marshal Fedor I. Tolbukhin A394

Natives Greeting Tolbukhin A395

Perf. 11½x11, 11x11½.

1950, Dec. 10 Photo. Unwmk.

710	A394	4 l claret	12	10
711	A395	20 l dk bl	50	30

Issued to publicize the return of Dobrich and part of the province of Dobruja from Romania to Bulgaria.

Dimitrov's Birthplace A396

George Dimitrov
A397 A398

Various Portraits, Inscribed:

Г.ДИМИТРОВ

Design: 2 l, Dimitrov Museum, Sofia.

1950, July 2 *Perf. 10½*

712	A396	50s ol grn	12	5
713	A397	50s brown	12	5
714	A397	1 l redsh brn	22	5
715	A396	2 l gray	22	5
716	A397	4 l claret	40	15
717	A397	9 l red brn	55	35
718	A398	10 l brn red	60	50
719	A396	15 l ol gray	60	50
720	A396	20 l dk bl	1.65	75
		Nos. 712-720,C61 (10)	6.73	2.50

Issued to commemorate the first anniversary of the death of George Dimitrov, statesman. No. 720 is inscribed in Latin characters.

A. S. Popov — A400

1951, Feb. 10

722	A400	4 l red brn	25	15
723	A400	20 l dk bl	50	25

No. 723 is inscribed in Latin characters.

Arms of Bulgaria
A401 A402

1950 Unwmk. Typo. *Perf. 13*

724	A401	2 l dk brn	6	5
725	A401	3 l rose	8	5
726	A402	5 l carmine	10	5
727	A402	9 l aqua	25	5

Nos. 724-727 were prepared in 1947 for official use but were issued as regular postage stamps Oct. 1, 1950.

The only foreign revenue stamps listed in this Catalogue are those authorized for prepayment of postage.

Heroes Chankova, Antonov-Malchik, Dimitrov and Dimitrova
A403

Stanke Dimitrov-Marek
A404

George Kirkov
A405

George Dimitrov at Leipzig
A406

Natcho Ivanov and Avr. Stoyanov — A407

Portraits: 9 l, Anton Ivanov. 15 l, Christo Michailov.

1951, Mar. 25 Photo. *Perf. 11½*

728	A403	1 l red vio	15	6
729	A404	2 l dk red brn	15	8
730	A405	4 l car rose	15	10
731	A405	9 l org brn	45	15
732	A405	15 l ol brn	75	30
733	A406	20 l dk bl	1.10	75
734	A407	50 l ol gray	2.25	1.25
		Nos. 728-734 (7)	5.00	2.69

First Bulgarian Tractor
A408

First Steam Roller
A409

First Truck
A410

Bulgarian Embroidery
A411

Designs: 15 l, Carpet. 20 l, Tobacco and roses. 40 l, Fruits.

Perf. 11x10½

1951, Mar. 30 Photo. Unwmk.

735	A408	1 l ol brn	10	5
736	A409	2 l violet	15	5
737	A410	4 l red brn	25	10
738	A411	9 l purple	35	20
739	A409	15 l dp plum	50	45
740	A411	20 l vio bl	80	50
741	A410	40 l dp grn	1.25	1.00

Perf. 13.

Size: 23x18½mm.

742	A408	1 l purple	6	5
743	A409	2 l Prus grn	15	5
744	A410	4 l red brn	15	5
		Nos. 735-744 (10)	3.76	2.50

See also Nos. 894, 973.

Turkish Attack on Mt. Zlee Dol
A412

Designs: 4 l, Georgi Benkovski speaking to rebels. 9 l, Cherrywood cannon of 1876 and Russian cavalry, 1945. 20 l, Rebel, 1876 and partisan, 1944. 40 l, Benkovski and Dimitrov.

1951, May 3 *Perf. 10½*

Cream Paper.

745	A412	1 l redsh brn	15	10
746	A412	4 l dk grn	15	10
747	A412	9 l vio brn	45	40
748	A412	20 l dp bl	60	70
749	A412	40 l dk red	85	1.00
		Nos. 745-749 (5)	2.20	2.30

Issued to commemorate the 75th anniversary of the "April" revolution.

Industrial Types of 1950.

1951 *Perf. 13*

750	A369	1 l violet	15	5
751	A370	2 l dk brn	15	5
751A	A372	4 l dk yel grn	1.00	10

Demeter Blagoev Addressing 1891 Congress at Busludja — A413

1951 Photo. *Perf. 11*

752	A413	1 l purple	25	15
753	A413	4 l dk grn	35	15
754	A413	9 l dp cl	60	50

Issued to commemorate the 60th anniversary of the first Congress of the Bulgarian Social-Democratic Party.
See also Nos. 1174-1176.

Day Nursery
A414

Designs: 4 l, Model building construction. 9 l, Playground. 20 l, Children's town.

1951, Oct. 10 Unwmk.

755	A414	1 l brown	12	6
756	A414	4 l dp plum	22	10
757	A414	9 l bl grn	65	30
758	A414	20 l dp bl	1.10	75

Issued to publicize Children's Day, Sept. 25, 1951.

Order of Labor
A415 A416

1952, Feb. 1 *Perf. 13*

Reverse of Medal

759	A415	1 l red brn	5	5
760	A415	4 l bl grn	10	5
761	A415	9 l dk bl	35	10

Obverse of Medal

762	A416	1 l carmine	5	5
763	A416	4 l green	10	5
764	A416	9 l purple	35	10
		Nos. 759-764 (6)	1.00	40

No. 764 has numeral at lower left and different background.

Workers and Symbols of Industry — A417

Design: 4 l, Flags and Dimitrov, Chervenkov.

1951, Dec. 29 *Perf. 11*

Inscribed: "16 XII 1951."

765	A417	1 l ol blk	6	5
766	A417	4 l chocolate	15	5

Issued to publicize the Third Congress of Bulgarian General Workers' Professional Union.

Dimitrov and Chemical Works — A418

George Dimitrov and V. Chervenkov — A419

Portrait: 80s, Dimitrov.

Unwmk.

1952, June 18 Photo. *Perf. 11*

767	A418	16s brown	32	25
768	A419	44s brn car	45	30
769	A418	80s brt bl	1.00	60

Issued to commemorate the 70th anniversary of the birth of George Dimitrov.

Vassil Kolarov Dam — A420

Republika Power Station — A421

1952, May 16 *Perf. 13*

770	A420	4s dk grn	6	5
771	A420	12s purple	8	5

772 A420 16s red brn 12 5
773 A420 44s rose brn 50 10
774 A420 80s brt bl 1.75 25
Nos. 770-774 (5) 2.51 50

No. 774 is inscribed in Latin characters.

1952, June 30 ***Perf. 13, Pin Perf.***

775 A421 16s dk brn 25 5
776 A421 44s magenta 90 15

Nikolai I. Vapzarov A422

Designs: Various portraits.

1952, July 23 ***Perf. 10½***

777 A422 16s rose brn 15 15
778 A422 44s dk red brn 60 25
779 A422 80s dk ol brn 1.40 80

Issued to commemorate the 10th anniversary of the death of Nikolai I. Vapzarov, poet and revolutionary.

Dimitrov and Youth Conference — A423

Designs: 16s, Resistance movement incident. 44s, Frontier guards and industrial scene. 80s, George Dimitrov and young workers.

1952, Sept. 1 ***Perf. 11x11½***

780 A423 2s brn car 12 5
781 A423 16s purple 16 15
782 A423 44s dk grn 45 40
783 A423 80s dk brn 1.00 85

Issued to commemorate the 40th anniversary of the founding conference of the Union of Social Democratic Youth.

Assault on the Winter Palace — A424

Designs: 8s, Volga-Don Canal. 16s, Symbols of world peace. 44s, Lenin and Stalin. 80s, Himlay hydroelectric station.

Perf. 11½

1952, Nov. 6 Unwmk. Photo.
Dated: "1917-1952"

784 A424 4s red brn 6 5
785 A424 8s dk grn 8 5
786 A424 16s dk bl 10 5
787 A424 44s brown 28 20
788 A424 80s ol brn 65 40
Nos. 784-788 (5) 1.17 75

Issued to commemorate the 35th anniversary of the Russian revolution.

Vassil Levski — A425

Design: 44s, Levski and comrades.

1953, Feb. 19 Cream Paper ***Perf. 11***

789 A425 16s brown 10 6
790 A425 44s brn blk 25 15

Issued to commemorate the 80th anniversary of the death of Vassil Levski, patriot.

Ferrying Artillery and Troops into Battle A426

Soldier A427

Mother and Children A428

Designs: 44s, Victorious soldiers. 80s, Soldier welcomed. 1 l, Monuments.

1953, Mar. 3 ***Perf. 10½***

791 A426 8s Prus grn 12 5
792 A427 16s dp brn 16 6
793 A426 44s dk sl grn 32 16
794 A426 80s dl red brn 65 40
795 A426 1 l black 80 65
Nos. 791-795 (5) 2.05 1.32

Issued to commemorate the 75th anniversary of Bulgaria's independence from Turkey.

1953, Mar. 9

796 A428 16s sl grn 10 5
797 A428 16s brt bl 10 5

Issued to commemorate Women's Day.

Woodcarvings at Rila Monastery
A429 A430

Designs: 12s, 16s, 28s, Woodcarvings, Rila Monastery. 44s, Carved Ceilings, Trnovo. 80s, 1 l, 4 l, Carvings, Pasardjik.

1953 Unwmk. Photo. ***Perf. 13.***

798 A429 2s gray brn 5 5
799 A430 8s dk sl grn 6 5
800 A430 12s brown 10 5
801 A430 16s rose lake 20 5
802 A429 28s dk ol grn 24 10
803 A430 44s dk brn 40 10
804 A430 80s ultra 65 20
805 A430 1 l vio bl 1.40 30
806 A430 4 l rose lake 2.75 1.25
Nos. 798-806 (9) 5.85 2.15

Karl Marx A431

"Das Kapital" A432

1953, Apr. 30 ***Perf. 10½***

807 A431 16s brt bl 15 10
808 A432 44s dp brn 35 25

70th anniversary of the death of Karl Marx.

Labor Day Parade — A433

Joseph V. Stalin — A434

1953, Apr. 30 ***Perf. 13***

809 A433 16s brn red 20 5

Issued to publicize Labor Day, May 1, 1953.

1953, May 23 ***Perf. 13x13½***

810 A434 16s dk gray 20 5
811 A434 16s dk brn 20 5

Death of Joseph V. Stalin, Mar. 5, 1953.

Georgi Delchev A435

Battle Scene A436

Peasants Attacking Turkish Troops A437

1953, Aug. 8 ***Perf. 13***

812 A435 16s dk brn 8 5
813 A436 44s purple 30 20
814 A437 1 l dp cl 45 25

Issued to commemorate the 50th anniversary of the Ilinden Revolt (Nos. 812 and 814) and the Preobrazhene Revolt (No. 813).

Soldier and Rebels — A438

Design: 44s, Soldier guarding industrial construction.

1953, Sept. 18

815 A438 16s dp cl 10 5
816 A438 44s grnsh bl 25 15

Issued to publicize Army Day.

George Dimitrov and Vassil Kolarov A439

Demeter Blagoev A440

Designs: 16s, Citizens in revolt. 44s, Attack.

1953, Sept. 22

817 A439 8s ol gray 10 5
818 A439 16s dk red brn 15 5
819 A439 44s cerise 42 25

September Revolution, 30th anniversary.

1953, Sept. 21

Portraits: 44s, G. Dimitrov and D. Blagoev.

820 A440 16s brown 16 5
821 A440 44s red brn 25 20

Issued to commemorate the 50th anniversary of the formation of the Social Democratic Party.

Railway Viaduct — A441

Pouring Molten Metal — A442

Designs: 16s, Welder and storage tanks. 80s, Harvesting machine.

1953, Oct. 17

826 A441 8s brt bl 6 5
827 A441 16s grnsh blk 12 5
828 A442 44s brn red 25 18
829 A441 80s orange 45 40

Month of Bulgarian-Russian friendship.

Belladonna A443

Kolarov Library, Sofia A444

Medicinal Flowers: 4s, Jimson weed. 8s, Sage. 12s, Dog rose. 16s, Gentian. 20s, Poppy. 28s, Peppermint. 40s, Bear grass. 44s, Coltsfoot. 80s, Cowslip. 1l, Dandelion. 2l, Foxglove.

1953 Unwmk. Photo. ***Perf. 13.***
White or Cream Paper

830 A443 2s dl bl 6 5
831 A443 4s brn org 6 5
832 A443 8s bl grn 10 6
833 A443 12s brn org 12 6
834 A443 12s bl grn 12 6
835 A443 16s vio bl 15 8
836 A443 16s dp red brn 15 8
837 A443 20s car rose 16 10
838 A443 28s dk gray grn 35 10
839 A443 40s dk bl 42 22
840 A443 44s brown 42 22
841 A443 80s yel brn 70 45
842 A443 1 l hn brn 2.50 60
843 A443 2 l purple 4.25 1.65
a. Souvenir sheet 30.00 30.00
Nos. 830-843 (14) 9.56 3.78

No. 843a contains 12 stamps, one of each denomination above, printed in dark green, with floral border and frame of inscriptions. Size: 161x172mm. Sold for 6 leva.

1953, Dec. 16

854 A444 44s brown 25 15

Issued to commemorate the 75th anniversary of the founding of the Kolarov Library, Sofia.

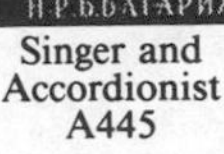

Singer and Accordionist A445

Lenin and Stalin A446

Design: 44s, Dancers.

1953, Dec. 26

855	A445	16s red brn	10	5
856	A445	44s dk grn	25	15

1954, Mar. 13

Designs: 44s, Lenin statue. 80s, Lenin mausoleum, Moscow. 1 l, Lenin. Cream Paper.

857	A446	16s brown	15	5
858	A446	44s rose brn	22	5
859	A446	80s blue	35	20
860	A446	1 l dp ol grn	50	40

30th anniversary of the death of Lenin.

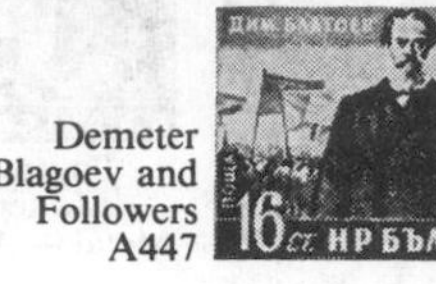

Demeter Blagoev and Followers A447

Design: 44s, Blagoev at desk.

1954, Apr. 28

Cream Paper

861	A447	16s dp red brn	15	5
862	A447	44s blk brn	35	15

Issued to commemorate the 30th anniversary of the death of Demeter Blagoev.

George Dimitrov A448

Dimitrov and Refinery A449

1954, June 11

Cream Paper

863	A448	44s lake	20	8
864	A449	80s brown	40	12

Issued to commemorate the 5th anniversary of the death of George Dimitrov.

Train Leaving Tunnel A450

1954, July 30

Cream Paper

865	A450	44s dk grn	40	15
866	A450	44s blk brn	40	15

Day of the Railroads, Aug. 1, 1954.

Miner at Work — A451

1954, Aug. 19

Cream Paper

867	A451	44s grnsh blk	25	10

Issued to publicize Miners' Day.

Academy of Science — A452

1954, Oct. 27

Cream Paper

868	A452	80s black	50	25

Issued to commemorate the 85th anniversary of the foundation of the Bulgarian Academy of Science.

Gymnastics — A453

Horsemanship A454

Designs: 44s, Wrestling. 2 l, Skiing.

1954, Dec. 21

869	A453	16s dk gray grn	55	25
870	A453	44s brn red	65	30
871	A454	80s cop brn	1.40	85
872	A453	2 l vio bl	3.25	2.50

Welcoming Liberators A455

Soldier's Return A456

Designs: 28s, Refinery. 44s, Dimitrov and Workers. 80s, Girl and boy. 1 l, George Dimitrov.

1954, Oct. 4

Cream Paper

873	A455	12s brn car	5	5
874	A456	16s dp car	5	5
875	A455	28s indigo	15	5
876	A455	44s redsh brn	18	5
877	A456	80s dp bl	80	35
878	A456	1 l dk grn	80	35
		Nos. 873-878 (6)	2.03	90

10th anniversary of Bulgaria's liberation.

Recreation at Workers' Rest Home A457

Metal Worker and Furnace A458

Portraits: 80s, Dimitrov, Blagoev, and Kirkov.

Unwmk.

1954, Dec. 28 Photo. *Perf. 13*

Cream Paper

879	A457	16s dk grn	16	5
880	A458	44s brn org	16	6
881	A457	80s dp vio bl	40	25

Issued to commemorate the 50th anniversary of Bulgaria's trade union movement.

Geese — A459

Designs: 4s, Chickens. 12s, Hogs. 16s, Sheep. 28s, Telephone building. 44s, Communist party headquarters. 80s, Apartment buildings. 1 l, St. Kiradgieff Mills.

1955-56

882	A459	2s dk bl grn	10	5
883	A459	4s ol grn	15	5
884	A459	12s dk red brn	25	5
885	A459	16s brn org	38	8
886	A459	28s vio bl	18	6
887	A459	44s lil red,*cr*	35	6
a.		44s brn red	2.50	20
888	A459	80s dk red brn	45	15
889	A459	1 l dk bl grn	85	25
		Nos. 882-889 (8)	2.71	75

Issue dates: No. 887, Apr. 20, 1956; others, Feb. 19, 1955.

Textile Worker — A460

Mother and Child — A461

Design: 16s, Woman feeding calf.

1955, Mar. 5

890	A460	12s dk brn	6	5
891	A460	16s dk grn	12	5
892	A461	44s dk car rose	40	10
893	A461	44s blue	40	10

Women's Day, Mar. 8, 1955.

No. 744 Surcharged in Blue.

1955, Mar. 8 *Perf. 13*

894	A410	16s on 4 l red brn	40	5

May Day Demonstration of Workers A462

Sts. Cyril and Methodius A463

Design: 44s, Three workers and globe.

1955, Apr. 23 Photo.

895	A462	16s car rose	9	5
896	A462	44s blue	25	10

Labor Day, May 1, 1955.

1955, May 21

Cream Paper

Designs: 8s, Paisii Hilendarski. 16s, Nicolas Karastoyanov's printing press. 28s, Christo Botev. 44s, Ivan Vazov. 80s, Demeter Blagoev and socialist papers. 2 l, Blagoev printing plant, Sofia.

897	A463	4s dp bl	5	5
898	A463	8s olive	5	5
899	A463	16s black	8	5
900	A463	28s hn brn	15	6
901	A463	44s brown	30	8
902	A463	80s rose red	50	25
903	A463	2 l black	1.50	65
		Nos. 897-903 (7)	2.63	1.19

Issued to commemorate the 1100th anniversary of the creation of the Cyrillic alphabet. Latin lettering at bottom on Nos. 901-903.

Sergei Rumyantzev A464

Mother and Children A465

Portraits: 16s, Christo Jassenov. 44s, Geo Milev.

1955, June 30 Unwmk. *Perf. 13*

Cream Paper

904	A464	12s org brn	15	5
905	A464	16s lt brn	15	5
906	A464	44s grnsh blk	35	20

Issued to commemorate the 25th anniversary of the deaths of Sergei Rumyanchev, Christo Jassenov and Geo Milev. Latin lettering at bottom of No. 906.

1955, July 30

Cream Paper

907	A465	44s brn car	25	15

Issued to commemorate the World Congress of Mothers in Lausanne, 1955.

Young People of Three Races — A466

Friedrich Engels and Book — A467

1955, July 30

Cream Paper

908	A466	44s blue	25	8

Issued to commemorate the fifth World Festival of Youth in Warsaw, July 31-Aug. 14, 1955.

1955, July 30

909	A467	44s brown	30	15

Issued to commemorate the 60th anniversary of the death of Friedrich Engels.

Entrance to Fair, 1892 — A468

Statuary Group at Fair, 1955 — A469

Designs: 44s, "Fruit of our Land." 80s, Woman holding Fair emblem.

1955, Aug. 31

Cream Paper

910	A468	4s dp brn	5	5
911	A469	16s dk car rose	5	5
912	A468	44s ol blk	20	12
913	A469	80s dp bl	45	20

Issued to commemorate the 16th International Plovdiv Fair. Latin lettering on Nos. 912-913.

Catalogue prices for unused stamps up to mid-1953 are for hinged copies matching the condition specified in this volume's introduction.

Friedrich von Schiller — A470

Portraits: 44s, Adam Mickiewicz. 60s, Hans Christian Andersen. 80s, Baron de Montesquieu. 1 l, Miguel de Cervantes. 2 l, Walt Whitman.

1955, Oct. 31
Cream Paper

914 A470	16s brown		10	5
915 A470	44s brn red		32	10
916 A470	60s Prus bl		48	10
917 A470	80s black		50	10
918 A470	1 l rose vio		1.10	45
919 A470	2 l ol grn		1.50	70
	Nos. 914-919 (6)		4.00	1.50

Issued in honor of various anniversaries of famous writers. Nos. 918 and 919 are issued in sheets alternating with labels without franking value. The labels show title pages for Leaves of Grass and Don Quixote in English and Spanish, respectively. Latin lettering on Nos. 915-919.

Karl Marx Industrial Plant A471

Friendship Monument A472

I. V. Michurin — A473

Designs: 4s, Alexander Stambolisky Dam. 16s, Bridge over Danube. 1 l, Vladimir V. Mayakovsky.

1955, Dec. 1 **Unwmk.**

920 A471	2s sl blk	5	5
921 A471	4s dp bl	5	5
922 A471	16s dk bl grn	6	5
923 A472	44s red brn	22	8
924 A473	80s dk grn	35	15
925 A473	1 l gray blk	55	20
	Nos. 920-925 (6)	1.28	58

Issued to publicize Russian-Bulgarian friendship.

Library Seal — A474

Krusto Pishurka — A475

Portrait: 44s, Bacho Kiro.

1956, Feb. 10 ***Perf. 11x10½***
Cream Paper

926 A474	12s car lake	5	5
927 A475	16s dp brn	10	5
928 A475	44s sl blk	35	12

Issued to commemorate the 100th anniversary of the National Library. Latin lettering at bottom of No. 928.

Canceled to Order
Beginning about 1956, some issues were sold in sheets canceled to order. Prices in second column when much less than unused are for "CTO" copies. Postally used stamps are valued at slightly less than, or the same as, unused.

Quinces A476

Cherrywood Cannon A477

Designs: 8s, Pears. 16s, Apples. 44s, Grapes.

1956 **Photo.** ***Perf. 13***

929 A476	4s carmine	85	8
930 A476	8s bl grn	38	10
931 A476	16s lil rose	90	5
932 A476	44s dp vio	90	25

Latin lettering on No. 932. See also Nos. 964-967.

1956, Apr. 28 ***Perf. 11x10½***

Design: 44s, Cavalry attack.

933 A477	16s dk cl	15	5
934 A477	44s dk sl grn	25	10

Issued to commemorate the 80th anniversary of the April (1876) Uprising against Turkish rule.

Demeter Blagoev and Birthplace A478

Cherries — A479

1956, May 30 ***Perf. 11***

935 A478	44s Prus bl	30	10

Issued to commemorate the centenary of the birth of Demeter Blagoev (1856-1924), writer.

1956 **Unwmk.** ***Perf. 13***

Designs: 12s, Plums. 28s, Peaches. 80s, Strawberries.

936 A479	2s rose car	6	5
937 A479	12s blue	15	5
938 A479	28s org brn	25	5
939 A479	80s dp car	80	30

Latin lettering on No. 939.

Gymnastics A480

Pole Vaulting A481

Designs: 12s, Discus throw. 44s, Soccer, 80s, Basketball. 1 l, Boxing.

Perf. 11x10½, 10½x11
1956, Aug. 29

940 A480	4s brt ultra	12	5
941 A480	12s brick red	16	6
942 A481	16s yel brn	30	18
943 A481	44s dk grn	45	28
944 A480	80s dk red brn	95	60
945 A481	1 l dp mag	1.50	80
	Nos. 940-945 (6)	3.48	1.97

Latin lettering on Nos. 943-945.

Issued to publicize the forthcoming 16th Olympic Games at Melbourne, Nov. 22-Dec. 8, 1956.

Tobacco, Rose and Distillery A482

People's Theater A483

1956, Sept. 1 ***Perf. 13***

946 A482	44s dp car	40	20
947 A482	44s ol grn	40	20

17th International Plovdiv Fair.

1956, Nov. 16 **Unwmk.**

Design: 44s, Dobri Woinikoff and Sawa Dobroplodni, dramatists.

948 A483	16s dl red brn	15	6
949 A483	44s dk bl grn	25	10

Bulgarian Theater centenary.

Benjamin Franklin A484

Cyclists, Palms and Pyramids A485

Portraits: 20s, Rembrandt. 40s, Mozart. 44s, Heinrich Heine. 60s, G. B. Shaw. 80s, Dostoevski. 1 l, Henrik Ibsen. 2 l, Pierre Curie.

1956, Dec. 29

950 A484	16s dk ol grn	10	5
951 A484	20s brown	18	5
952 A484	40s dk car rose	18	6
953 A484	44s dk vio brn	22	8
954 A484	60s dk sl	30	15
955 A484	80s dk brn	45	15
956 A484	1 l bluish grn	75	45
957 A484	2 l Prus grn	1.65	80
	Nos. 950-957 (8)	3.83	1.79

Issued in honor of great personalities of the world.

1957, Mar. 6 **Photo.** ***Perf. 10½***

958 A485	80s hn brn	70	30
959 A485	80s Prus grn	70	30

Fourth Egyptian bicycle race.

Woman Technician A486

"New Times" Review A487

Designs: 16s, Woman and children. 44s, Woman feeding chickens.

1957, Mar. 8

960 A486	12s dp bl	6	5
961 A486	16s hn brn	8	5
962 A486	44s sl grn	30	12

Women's Day, Mar. 8, 1957. Latin lettering on 44s.

1957, Mar. 8 **Unwmk.**

963 A487	16s dp car	20	6

Issued to commemorate the 60th anniversary of the founding of the "New Times" review.

Fruit Type of 1956.

Designs: 4s, Quinces. 8s, Pears. 16s, Apples. 44s, Grapes.

1957 **Photo.** ***Perf. 13***

964 A476	4s yel grn	5	5
965 A476	8s brn org	12	5
966 A476	16s rose red	15	5
967 A476	44s org yel	55	10

Latin lettering on No. 967.

Sts. Cyril and Methodius A488

Basketball A489

1957, May 22 ***Perf. 11***

968 A488	44s ol grn & buff	40	15

Issued for the centenary of the first public veneration of Sts. Cyril and Methodius, inventors of the Cyrillic alphabet.

1957, June 20 **Photo.** ***Perf. 10½x11***

969 A489	44s dk grn	1.10	30

Issued to commemorate the 10th European Basketball Championship at Sofia.

Dancer and Spasski Tower, Moscow — A490

Certain countries cancel stamps in full sheets and sell them (usually with gum) for less than face value. Dealers generally sell "CTO".

1957, July 18 *Perf. 13*
970 A490 44s blue 35 15

Issued to publicize the Sixth World Youth Festival in Moscow.

George Dimitrov A491

1957, July 18
971 A491 44s dp car 40 15

75th anniversary of the birth of George Dimitrov (1882-1949).

Vassil Levski — A492

1957, July 18 *Perf. 11*
972 A492 44s grnsh blk 40 15

Issued to commemorate the 120th anniversary of the birth of Vassil Levski, patriot and national hero.

No. 742 Surcharged in Carmine.

1957 **Unwmk.** *Perf. 13*
973 A408 16s on 1 l pur 10 5

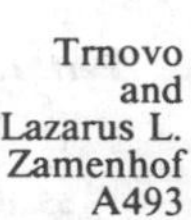
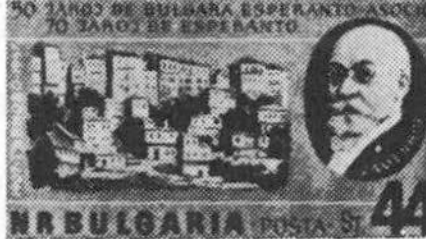

Trnovo and Lazarus L. Zamenhof A493

1957, July 27
974 A493 44s sl grn 55 20

Issued to commemorate the 50th anniversary of the Bulgarian Esperanto Society and the 70th anniversary of Esperanto.

Bulgarian Veteran of 1877 War and Russian Soldier — A494

Design: 44s, Battle of Shipka Pass.

1957, Aug. 13
975 A494 16s dk bl grn 15 5
976 A494 44s brown 35 6

Issued to commemorate the 80th anniversary of Bulgaria's liberation from the Turks. Latin lettering on No. 976.

Woman Planting Tree — A495

Red Deer in Forest — A496

Designs: 16s, Dam, lake and forest. 44s, Plane over forest. 80s, Fields on edge of forest.

1957, Sept. 16 **Photo.** *Perf. 13*
977 A495 2s dp grn 5 5
978 A496 12s dk brn 7 5
979 A496 16s Prus bl 8 5
980 A496 44s Prus grn 18 8
981 A496 80s yel grn 35 20
Nos. 977-981 (5) 73 43

Latin lettering on Nos. 980 and 981.

Lenin — A497

Designs: 16s, Cruiser "Aurora." 44s, Dove over map of communist area. 60s, Revolutionaries and banners. 80s, Oil refinery.

1957, Oct. 29 *Perf. 11*
982 A497 12s chocolate 15 5
983 A497 16s Prus grn 30 5
984 A497 44s dp bl 60 12
985 A497 60s dk car rose 70 25
986 A497 80s dk grn 1.25 35
Nos. 982-986 (5) 3.00 82

Issued to commemorate the 40th anniversary of the Communist Revolution.
Latin lettering on Nos. 984-985.

Globes A498

1957, Oct. 4 *Perf. 13*
987 A498 44s Prus bl 30 18

Issued to commemorate the fourth International Trade Union Congress, Leipzig, Oct. 4-15.

Vassil Kolarov Hotel A499

Health Resorts: 4s, Skis and Pirin Mountains. 8s, Old house at Koprivspitsa. 12s, Rest home at Velingrad. 44s, Momin-Prochod Hotel. 60s, Nesebr Hotel, shoreline and peninsula. 80s, Varna beach scene. 1 l, Hotel at Varna.

1958 **Photo.** *Perf. 13*
988 A499 4s blue 5 5
989 A499 8s org brn 6 5
990 A499 12s dk grn 6 5
991 A499 16s green 10 5
992 A499 44s dk bl grn 18 8
993 A499 60s dp bl 30 12
994 A499 80s fawn 45 20
995 A499 1 l dk red brn 55 30
Nos. 988-995 (8) 1.75 90

Issued to publicize various Bulgarian health resorts. Latin lettering on 44s, 60s, 80s, and 1l.
Issue dates: Nos. 991-994, Jan. 20. Others, July 5.

Mikhail I. Glinka — A500

Portraits: 16s, Jan A. Komensky (Comenius). 40s, Carl von Linne. 44s, William Blake. 60s, Carlo Goldoni. 80s, Auguste Comte.

1957, Dec. 30
996 A500 12s dk brn 16 5
997 A500 16s dk grn 16 5
998 A500 40s Prus bl 16 6
999 A500 44s maroon 16 10
1000 A500 60s org brn 60 20
1001 A500 80s dp plum 2.00 1.25
Nos. 996-1001 (6) 3.24 1.71

Issued to honor famous men of other countries. Latin lettering on Nos. 999-1001.

Young Couple, Flag, Dimitrov A501

People's Front Salute A502

1957, Dec. 28 *Perf. 11*
1002 A501 16s car rose 15 6

Issued to commemorate the 10th anniversary of Dimitrov's Union of the People's Youth.

1957, Dec. 28
1003 A502 16s dk vio brn 15 6

15th anniversary of the People's Front.

Hare A503

Animals: 12s, Red deer (doe) (vert.). 16s, Red deer (stag). 44s, Chamois. 80s, Brown bear. 1 l, Wild boar.

Perf. 10½

1958, Apr. 5 **Unwmk.** **Photo.**
1004 A503 2s lt & dk ol grn 6 5
1005 A503 12s sl grn & red brn 15 5
1006 A503 16s bluish grn & dk red brn 18 5
1007 A503 44s bl & brn 20 10
1008 A503 80s bis & dk brn 65 20
1009 A503 1 l stl bl & dk brn 90 35
Nos. 1004-1009 (6) 2.14 80

Price, imperf. set $4.

Marx and Lenin A504

Designs: 16s, Marchers and flags. 44s, Lenin blast furnaces.

1958, July 2 *Perf. 11*
1010 A504 12s dk brn 12 5
1011 A504 16s dk car 15 5
1012 A504 44s dk bl 60 15

Issued to commemorate the 7th Congress of the Bulgarian Communist Party.

Wrestlers — A505

1958, June 20 *Perf. 10½*
1013 A505 60s dk car rose 65 50
1014 A505 80s dp brn 1.10 75

World Wrestling Championship, Sofia.

Chessmen and Globe A506

Perf. 10½

1958, July 18 **Unwmk.** **Photo.**
1015 A506 80s grn & yel grn 1.40 1.25

5th World Students' Chess Games, Varna.

Conference Emblem A507

1958, Sept. 24
1016 A507 44s blue 30 15

Issued to commemorate the World Trade Union Conference of Working Youth, Prague, July 14-20.

Swimmer A508

Designs: 28s, Dancer (vertical). 44s, Volleyball (vertical).

1958, Sept. 19 *Perf. 11x10½*
1017 A508 16s brt bl 15 6
1018 A508 28s brn org 25 15
1019 A508 44s brt grn 38 15

1958 Students' Games.

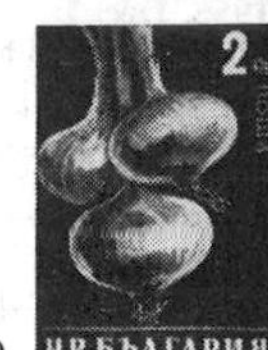

Onions — A509

Vegetables: 12s, Garlic. 16s, Peppers. 44s, Tomatoes. 80s, Cucumbers. 1 l, Eggplant.

1958, Sept. 20 *Perf. 13*
1020 A509 2s org brn 5 5
1021 A509 12s Prus bl 5 5
1022 A509 16s dk grn 6 5
1023 A509 44s dp car 15 5
1024 A509 80s dp grn 35 12
1025 A509 1 l brt pur 55 15
Nos. 1020-1025 (6) 1.21 47

See No. 1072.
Price, imperf. set $3.50.

Plovdiv Fair Building A510

1958, Sept. 14 **Unwmk.** *Perf. 11*
1026 A510 44s dp car 35 12

18th International Plovdiv Fair.

Attack — A511

Design: 44s, Fighter dragging wounded man.

1958, Sept. 23 Photo. *Perf. 11*

1027 A511 16s org ver 12 6
1028 A511 44s lake 30 10

Issued to commemorate the 35th anniversary of the September Revolution.

Emblem, Brussels Fair — A512

1958, Oct. 13 *Perf. 11*

1029 A512 1 l blk & brt bl 2.00 2.00

Brussels World's Fair, Apr. 17-Oct. 19. Price imperf. $8.50

Runner at Finish Line — A513

Woman Throwing Javelin — A514

Sports: 60s, High jumper. 80s, Hurdler. 4 l, Shot putter.

1958, Nov. 30

1030 A513 16s red brn, *pnksh* 30 20
1031 A514 44s ol, *yelsh* 30 20
1032 A514 60s dk bl, *bluish* 55 30
1033 A514 80s dp grn, *grnsh* 70 30
1034 A513 4 l dp rose cl, *pnksh* 4.75 2.00
Nos. 1030-1034 (5) 6.60 3.00

1958 Balkan Games.
Latin lettering on Nos. 1032-1033.

Christo Smirnenski A515

1958, Dec. 22

1035 A515 16s dk car 15 6

Issued to commemorate the 60th anniversary of the birth of Christo Smirnenski, poet, 1898-1923.

Girls Harvesting — A516

Girl Tending Calves A517

Designs: 16s, Boy and girl laborers. 40s, Boy pushing wheelbarrow. 44s, Headquarters building.

1959, Nov. 29 Photo.

1036 A516 8s dk ol grn 5 5
1037 A517 12s redsh brn 6 5
1038 A516 16s vio brn 8 5
1039 A517 40s Prus bl 12 5
1040 A516 44s dp car 60 20
Nos. 1036-1040 (5) 91 40

Issued to commemorate the 4th Congress of Dimitrov's Union of People's Youth.

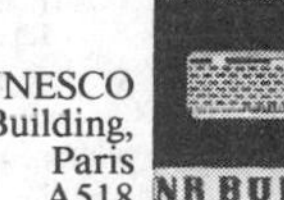

UNESCO Building, Paris A518

1959, Mar. 28 Unwmk. *Perf. 11*

1041 A518 2 l dp red lil, *cr* 1.25 1.25

Opening of UNESCO Headquarters, Paris, Nov. 3, 1958. Price imperf. $3.50.

Skier — A519

Soccer Players — A520

1959, Mar. 28 *Perf. 11*

1042 A519 1 l bl, *cr* 1.10 55

Forty years of skiing in Bulgaria.

1959, Mar. 25

1043 A520 2 l chnt, *cr* 1.40 90

Issued to commemorate the 1959 European Youth Soccer Championship.

Russian Soldiers Installing Telegraph Wires — A521

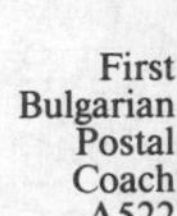

First Bulgarian Postal Coach A522

Designs: 60s, Stamp of 1879. 80s, First Bulgarian automobile. 1 l, Television tower. 2 l, Strike of railroad and postal workers, 1919.

1959, May 4

1044 A521 12s dk grn & cit 8 5
1045 A522 16s dp plum 12 5
1046 A521 60s dk brn & yel 25 10
1047 A522 80s hn brn & sal 35 20
1048 A521 1 l blue 50 25
1049 A522 2 l dk red brn 1.25 1.25
Nos. 1044-1049 (6) 2.55 1.90

Issued to commemorate the 80th anniversary of the Bulgarian post. Latin lettering on Nos. 1046-1049.

Two imperf. souvenir sheets exist with olive borders and inscriptions. One contains one copy of No. 1046 in black & ochre, and measures 92x121mm. The other sheet contains one copy each of Nos. 1044-1045 and 1047-1048 in changed colors: 12s, olive green & ocher; 16s, deep claret & ocher; 80s, dark red & ocher; 1 l, olive & ocher. Each sheet sold for 5 leva.

Price, each $25.

Great Tits A523

Birds: 8s, Hoopoe. 16s, Great spotted woodpecker (vert.). 45s, Gray partridge (vert.) 60s, Rock partridge. 80s, European cuckoo.

1959, June 30 Photo.

1050 A523 2s ol & sl grn 5 5
1051 A523 8s dp org & blk 6 5
1052 A523 16s chnt & dk brn 15 10
1053 A523 45s brn & blk 16 15
1054 A523 60s dp bl & gray 38 20
1055 A523 80s dp bl grn & gray 70 30
Nos. 1050-1055 (6) 1.50 85

Bagpiper — A524

Designs: 12s, Acrobats. 16s, Girls exercising with hoops. 20s, Male dancers. 80s, Ballet dancers. 1 l, Ceramic pitcher. 16s, 20s, 80s are horizontal.

1959, Aug. 29 Unwmk. *Perf. 11*
Surface-colored Paper.

1056 A524 4s dk ol 5 5
1057 A524 12s scarlet 5 5
1058 A524 16s maroon 6 5
1059 A524 20s dk bl 20 10
1060 A524 80s brt grn 40 25
1061 A524 1 l brn org 75 40
Nos. 1056-1061 (6) 1.51 90

Issued to publicize the 7th International Youth Festival, Vienna. Latin inscriptions on Nos. 1060-1061.

Partisans in Truck A525

Designs: 16s, Partisans and soldiers shaking hands. 45s, Refinery. 60s, Tanks. 80s, Harvester. 1.25 l, Children with flag (vert.).

1959, Sept. 8

1062 A525 12s red & Prus grn 5 5
1063 A525 16s red & dk pur 6 5
1064 A525 45s red & int bl 10 5
1065 A525 60s red & ol grn 15 8
1066 A525 80s red & brn 35 15
1067 A525 1.25 l red & dp brn 90 45
Nos. 1062-1067 (6) 1.61 83

15th anniversary of Bulgarian liberation.

Soccer A526

1959, Oct. 10 Unwmk. *Perf. 11*

1068 A526 1.25 l dp grn, *yel* 4.00 3.00

50 years of Bulgarian soccer.

Price, set imperf. in changed colors, $8. unused, $5. canceled.

Batak Defenders A527

1959, Aug. 8

1069 A527 16s dp cl 20 10

Issued to commemorate the 300th anniversary of the settlement of Batak.

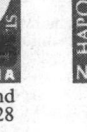

Post Horn and Letter — A528

Bird-shaped Lyre — A529

Design: 1.25 l, Dove and letter.

1959, Nov. 23

1070 A528 45s emer & blk 30 10
1071 A528 1.25 l lt bl, red & blk 60 30

Issued for International Letter Writing Week Oct. 5-11.

Type of 1958 Surcharged "45 CT." in Dark Blue.

Design: Tomatoes.

1959 Photo. *Perf. 13*

1072 A509 45s on 44s scar 55 15

1960, Feb. 23 Unwmk. *Perf. 10½*

Design: 1.25l, Lyre.

1073 A529 80s emer & blk 35 15
1074 A529 1.25 l brt red & blk 60 30

Issued to commemorate the 50th anniversary of Bulgaria's State Opera.

N. I. Vapzarov A530

Parachute and Radio Tower A531

1959, Dec. 14 *Perf. 11*

1075 A530 80s yel grn & red brn 35 12

Issued to commemorate the 50th anniversary of the birth of N. I. Vapzarov, poet and patriot.

1959, Dec. 3 Photo.

1076 A531 1.25 l dp grnsh bl & yel 1.40 65

Issued to publicize the third Congress of Voluntary Participants in Defense.

Cotton Picker A532 — Harvester Combine A533

Designs: 2s, Kindergarten. 4s, Woman doctor and child. 10s, Woman milking cow. 12s, Woman holding tobacco leaves. 15s, Woman working loom. 16s, Stalin textile mill, Dimitrovgrad. 25s, Rural electrification. 28s, Woman picking sunflowers. 40s, "Cold-well" hydroelectric dam. 45s, Miner. 60s, Foundry worker. 80s. Woman harvesting grapes. 1 l, Worker and peasant with cog-wheel. 1.25 l, Industrial worker. 2 l, Party leader.

1959-61 Photo. *Perf. 13*

1077 A533 2s brn org ('60) 5 5
1077A A532 4s gldn brn ('61) 5 5
1078 A532 5s dk grn 5 5
1079 A533 10s red brn ('61) 5 5
1080 A532 12s red brn 5 5
1081 A533 15s red lil ('60) 6 5
1082 A533 16s dp vio ('60) 6 5
1083 A533 20s orange 8 5
1084 A532 25s brt bl ('60) 8 5
1085 A532 28s brt grn 15 5
1086 A533 40s brt grnsh bl 22 5
1087 A532 45s choc ('60) 16 5
1088 A533 60s scarlet 30 10
1089 A532 80s ol ('60) 38 12
1090 A532 1 l maroon 38 12
1090A A533 1.25 l dl bl ('61) 1.25 40
1091 A532 2 l dp car ('60) 85 30
Nos. 1077-1091 (17) 4.22 1.64

Issued to commemorate the early completion of the 5-year plan (in 1959).

L. L. Zamenhof — A534

Path of Lunik 3 — A535

1959, Dec. 5 Unwmk. *Perf. 11*

1092 A534 1.25 l dk grn & yel grn 60 50

Lazarus Ludwig Zamenhof (1859-1917), inventor of Esperanto.

1960, Mar. 28 *Perf. 11*

1093 A535 1.25 l Prus bl & brt yel 3.75 2.75

Flight of Lunik 3 around moon.
Price, imperf. $8.

Skier A536

1960, Apr. 15 Litho.

1094 A536 2 l ultra, blk & brn 1.10 50

8th Winter Olympics, Squaw Valley, CA, Feb. 18-29. Price, imperf. $4 unused, $2 canceled.

Vela Blagoeva — A537

Portraits: 28s, Anna Maimunkova. 45s, Vela Piskova. 60s, Rosa Luxemburg. 80s, Klara Zetkin. 1.25 l, N. K. Krupskaya.

1960, Apr. 27 Photo. *Perf. 11*

1095 A537 16s rose & red brn 5 5
1096 A537 28s cit & ol 8 5
1097 A537 45s ol grn & sl grn 20 5
1098 A537 60s lt bl & Prus bl 20 10
1099 A537 80s red org & dp brn 35 15
1100 A537 1.25 l dl yel & ol 60 25
Nos. 1095-1100 (6) 1.48 65

International Women's Day, Mar. 8, 1960.

Lenin — A538

Design: 45s, Lenin sitting.

1960, May 12

1101 A538 16s red brn 35 20
1102 A538 45s sal pink & blk 75 30

90th anniversary of the birth of Lenin.

Women Playing Basketball — A539

1960, June 3 *Perf. 11*

1103 A539 1.25 l yel & sl grn 1.10 50

Issued to commemorate the seventh European Women's Basketball championships.

Parachutist A541

Design: 1.25l, Parachutes.

1960, June 29 Litho.

1105 A541 16s lil & dk bl 60 30
1106 A541 1.25 l bl & cl 1.50 45

Issued to commemorate the 5th International Parachute Championships.

Yellow Gentian — A542

Flowers: 5s, Tulips. 25s, Turk's-cap lily. 45s, Rhododendron. 60s, Lady's-slipper. 80s, Violets.

1960, July 27 Photo. *Perf. 11*

1107 A542 2s beige, grn & yel 15 5
1108 A542 5s yel grn, grn & car rose 15 5
1109 A542 25s pink, grn & org 20 5
1110 A542 45s pale lil, grn & rose lil 35 15
1111 A542 60s yel, grn & org 75 15
1112 A542 80s gray, grn & vio bl 90 35
Nos. 1107-1112 (6) 2.50 80

Soccer A543

Sports: 12s, Wrestling. 16s, Weight lifting. 45s, Woman gymnast. 80s, Canoeing. 2 l, Runner.

1960, Aug. 29 Unwmk. *Perf. 11*
Athletes' Figures in Pink

1113 A543 8s brown 5 5
1114 A543 12s violet 5 5
1115 A543 16s Prus bl 8 8
1116 A543 45s dp plum 16 10
1117 A543 80s blue 25 20
1118 A543 2 l dp grn 1.00 50
Nos. 1113-1118 (6) 1.59 98

17th Olympic Games, Rome, Aug. 25-Sept. 11.

Price, set imperf. in changed colors, $5.50

Globes A544

Unwmk.
1960, Oct. 12 Photo. *Perf. 11*

1125 A544 1.25 l bl & ultra 55 30

Issued to commemorate the 15th anniversary of the World Federation of Trade Unions.

Alexander Popov — A545

1960, Oct. 12

1126 A545 90s bl & blk 75 20

Issued to commemorate the centenary of the birth of Alexander Popov, radio pioneer.

Bicyclists A546

1960, Sept. 22

1127 A546 1 l yel, red org & blk 1.25 75

The 10th Tour of Bulgaria Bicycle Race.

Jaroslav Vesin — A547

1960, Nov. 22 Unwmk. *Perf. 11*

1128 A547 1 l brt cit & ol grn 2.25 1.00

Birth centenary of Jaroslav Vesin, painter.

U.N. Headquarters A548 — Costume of Kyustendil A549

1961, Jan. 14 Photo. *Perf. 11*

1129 A548 1 l brn & yel 1.25 75
a. Souvenir sheet 4.75 4.75

15th anniv. of the UN. No. 1129 sold for 2 l.

Price, imperf. $4.50.

No. 1129a sold for 2.50 l and contains one copy of No. 1129, imperf. in dark olive and pink with orange marginal inscription. Size: 74x58mm.

1961, Jan. 28

Designs (Regional Costumes): 16s, Pleven. 28s, Sliven. 45s, Sofia. 60s, Rhodope. 80s, Karnobat.

1130 A549 12s sal, sl grn & yel 10 5
1131 A549 16s pale lil, brn vio & buff 10 5
1132 A549 28s pale grn, sl grn & rose 15 6
1133 A549 45s bl & red 30 8
1134 A549 60s grnsh bl, Prus bl & yel 50 18
1135 A549 80s yel, sl grn & pink 65 35
Nos. 1130-1135 (6) 1.80 77

Theodor Tiro (Fresco) A550

Designs: 60s, Boyana Church. 1.25 l, Duchess of Dessislava (fresco).

1961, Jan. 28 Photo.

1136 A550 60s yel grn, blk & grn 50 15
1137 A550 80s yel, sl grn & org 50 15
1138 A550 1.25 l yel grn, hn brn & buff 1.00 35

700th anniversary of murals in Boyana Church.

Clock Tower, Vratsa — A551 — Wooden Jug — A552

Designs: 12s, Clock tower, Bansko. 20s, Anguchev House, Mogilitsa. 28s, Oslekov House, Koprivspitsa (horiz.). 40s, Pasha's house. Melnik (horiz.). 45s, Lion sculpture. 60s, Man on horseback, Madara. 80s, Fresco, Bratchkovo monastery. 1 l, Tsar Assen coin.

1961, Feb. 25 Unwmk. *Perf. 11*
Denomination and Stars in Vermilion.

1139 A551 8s ol grn 5 5
1140 A551 12s lt vio 5 5
1141 A552 16s dk red brn 5 5
1142 A551 20s brt bl 5 5
1143 A551 28s grnsh bl 8 5
1144 A551 40s red brn 12 6

1145 A552 45s ol gray 15 8
1146 A552 60s slate 30 10
1147 A552 80s dk ol gray 50 12
1148 A552 1 l green 65 25
Nos. 1139-1148 (10) 2.00 86

Capercaillie
A553

Birds: 4s, Dalmatian pelican. 16s, Ring-necked pheasant. 80s, Great bustard. 1 l, Lammergeier. 2 l, Hazel hen.

1961, March 31
1149 A553 2s blk, sal & Prus grn 5 5
1150 A553 4s blk, yel grn & org 5 5
1151 A553 16s brn, lt grn & org 7 5
1152 A553 80s brn, bluish grn & yel 30 5
1153 A553 1 l blk, lt bl & yel 45 18
1154 A553 2 l brn, bl & yel 1.10 60
Nos. 1149-1154 (6) 2.02 98

Radio Tower and Winged Anchor
A554

1961, Apr. 1 Unwmk. *Perf. 11*
1155 A554 80s brt grn & blk 40 15

Issued to commemorate the 50th anniversary of the Transport Workers' Union.

T. G. Shevchenko
A555

Water Polo
A556

1961, Apr. 27
1156 A555 1 l ol & blk 2.00 1.00

Issued to commemorate the centenary of the death of Taras G. Shevchenko, Ukrainian poet.

1961, May 15

Designs: 5s, Tennis. 16s, Fencing. 45s, Throwing the discus. 1.25 l, Sports Palace. 2 l, Basketball. 5 l, Sports Palace, different view. 5s, 16s, 45s and 1.25 l, are horizontal.

Black Inscriptions
1157 A556 4s lt ultra 5 5
1158 A556 5s org ver 5 5
1159 A556 16s ol grn 15 5
1160 A556 45s dl bl 20 6
1161 A556 1.25 l yel brn 70 20
1162 A556 2 l lilac 90 45
Nos. 1157-1162 (6) 2.05 86

Souvenir Sheet
Imperf
1163 A556 5 l yel grn, dl bl & yel 10.00 10.00

Nos. 1157-1163 were issued to publicize the 1961 World University Games, Sofia, Aug. 26-Sept. 3.
No. 1163 measures 66x66mm.
Price, #1157-1162 in changed colors, imperf. $5.

Monk Seal
A557

Black Sea Fauna: 12s, Jellyfish. 16s, Dolphin. 45s, Black Sea sea horse (vert.). 1 l, Starred sturgeon. 1.25 l, Thornback ray.

1961, June 19 *Perf. 11*
1164 A557 2s grn & blk 5 5
1165 A557 12s Prus grn & pink 5 5
1166 A557 16s ultra & vio bl 6 5
1167 A557 45s lt bl & brn 18 5
1168 A557 1 l yel grn & Prus grn 45 20
1169 A557 1.25 l lt vio bl & red brn 80 35
Nos. 1164-1169 (6) 1.59 75

Hikers — A558

Designs: 4s, "Sredetz" hostel (horiz.). 16s, Tents. 1.25 l, Mountain climber.

1961, Aug. 25 Litho. *Perf. 11*
1170 A558 4s yel grn, yel & blk 5 5
1171 A558 12s lt bl, cr & blk 5 5
1172 A558 16s grn, cr & blk 6 5
1173 A558 1.25 l bis, cr & blk 60 10

"Know Your Country" campaign.

Demeter Blagoev Addressing 1891 Congress at Busludja — A559

1961, Aug. 5 Photo.
1174 A559 45s dk red & buff 18 15
1175 A559 80s bl & pink 30 20
1176 A559 2 l dk brn & pale cit 70 40

Issued to commemorate the 70th anniversary of the first Congress of the Bulgarian Social-Democratic Party.

The Golden Girl — A560

Fairy Tales: 8s, The Living Water. 12s, The Golden Apple. 16s, Krali-Marko, hero. 45s, Samovila-Vila, Witch. 80s, Tom Thumb.

1961, Oct. 10 Unwmk. *Perf. 11*
1177 A560 2s bl, blk & org 15 5
1178 A560 8s rose lil, blk & gray 18 5
1179 A560 12s bl grn, blk & pink 18 5
1180 A560 16s red, blk, bl & gray 30 20
1181 A560 45s ol grn, blk & pink 60 30
1182 A560 80s ocher, blk & dk car 90 40
Nos. 1177-1182 (6) 2.31 1.05

Caesar's Mushroom
A561

Miladinov Brothers and Title Page
A562

Designs: Various mushrooms.

1961, Dec. 20 Photo. *Perf. 11*
Denominations in Black
1183 A561 2s lem & red 5 5
1184 A561 4s ol grn & red brn 5 5
1185 A561 12s bis & red brn 5 5
1186 A561 16s lil & red brn 5 5
1187 A561 45s car rose & yel 15 6
1188 A561 80s brn org & sep 30 15
1189 A561 1.25 l vio & dk brn 65 20
1190 A561 2 l org brn & brn 1.10 50
Nos. 1183-1190 (8) 2.40 1.11

Price, denomination in dark grn, imperf. set $5 unused, $3 canceled.

1961, Dec. 21 Unwmk. *Perf. 10½*
1191 A562 1.25 l ol & blk 50 15

Issued to commemorate the centenary of the publication of "Collected Folksongs" by the Brothers Miladinov, Dimitri and Konstantin.

Nos. 1079-1085, 1087, 992, 1023, 1090-1091 and 806 Surcharged with New Value in Black, Red or Violet.

1962, Jan. 1
1192 A533 1s on 10s red brn 5 5
1193 A532 1s on 12s red brn 5 5
1194 A532 2s on 15s red lil 8 5
1195 A533 2s on 16s dp vio (R) 8 5
1196 A533 2s on 20s org 8 5
a. "2 CT." on 2 lines 8 5
1197 A532 3s on 25s brt bl (R) 10 5
a. Black surch. 7.50 5.50
1198 A532 3s on 28s brt grn (R) 12 5
1199 A532 5s on 45s choc 15 5
1200 A499 5s on 44s dk bl grn (R) 15 10
1201 A509 5s on 44s dp car (V) 15 10
1202 A532 10s on 1 l mar 28 15
1203 A532 20s on 2 l dp car 75 30
1204 A430 40s on 4 l rose lake (V) 1.65 65
Nos. 1192-1204 (13) 3.69 1.70

Freighter "Varna"
A563

Designs: 5s, Tanker "Komsomoletz." 20s, Liner "G. Dimitrov."

1962, Mar. 1 Photo. *Perf. 10½*
1205 A563 1s lt grn & brt bl 5 5
1206 A563 5s lt bl & grn 20 6
1207 A563 20s gray bl & grnsh bl 75 20

Dimitrov working as Printer
A564

Roses
A565

Design: 13s, Griffin, emblem of state printing works.

1962, March 19 Unwmk.
1208 A564 2s ver, blk & yel 5 5
1209 A564 13s red org, blk & yel 45 15

Issued to commemorate the 80th anniversary (in 1961) of the George Dimitrov state printing works.

1962, March 28
Various Roses in Natural Colors
1210 A565 1s dp vio 5 5
1211 A565 2s sal & dk car 5 5
1212 A565 3s gray & car 8 5
1213 A565 4s dk grn 15 5
1214 A565 5s ultra 20 10
1215 A565 6s bluish grn & dk car 45 20
1216 A565 8s cit & car 1.00 30
1217 A565 13s blue 2.00 1.00
Nos. 1210-1217 (8) 3.98 1.80

Malaria Eradication Emblem and Mosquito
A566

Design: 20s, Malaria eradication emblem.

1962, Apr. 19
1218 A566 5s org brn, yel & blk 45 15
1219 A566 20s emer, yel & blk 90 40

WHO drive to eradicate malaria.
Price, imperf. $4.50 unused, $2.50 canceled.

Lenin and First Issue of Pravda
A567

1962, May 4 Unwmk. *Perf. 10*
1220 A567 5s dp rose & sl 50 20

Issued to commemorate the 50th anniversary of Pravda, Russian newspaper founded by Lenin.

Blackboard and Book — A568

1962, May 21 Photo.
1221 A568 5s Prus bl, blk & yel 20 6

The 1962 Teachers' Congress.

Soccer Player and Globe
A569

1962, May 26 *Perf. 10½*
1222 A569 13s brt grn, blk & lt brn 90 35

World Soccer Championship, Chile, May 30-June 17. Price, imperf. in changed colors, $4 unused, $3 canceled.

George Dimitrov
A570

1962, June 18 Photo.
1223 A570 2s dk grn 15 5
1224 A570 5s turq bl 45 15

Issued to commemorate the 80th anniversary of the birth of George Dimitrov (1882-1949), communist leader and premier of the Bulgarian Peoples' Republic.

Bishop — A571

Chessmen: 2s, Rook. 3s, Queen. 13s, Knight. 20s, Pawn.

1962, July 7 Unwmk. *Perf. 10½*

1225 A571 1s gray, emer & blk 5 5
1226 A571 2s gray, lem & blk 5 5
1227 A571 3s gray, lil & blk 10 5
1228 A571 13s gray, dk org & blk 55 20
1229 A571 20s gray, bl & blk 1.00 40
Nos. 1225-1229 (5) 1.75 75

Issued to commemorate the 15th Chess Olympics, Varna. Nos. 1225-1229 were also issued imperf. in changed colors.

An imperf. souvenir sheet contains one 20s horizontal stamp showing five chessmen. Lilac and gray border of sea horses and waves. Size: 75x66mm.

Rila Mountain A572

Designs: 2s, Pirin mountain. 6s, Nesebr, Black Sea. 8s, Danube. 13s, Vidin Castle. 1 l, Rhodope mountain.

1962-63 *Perf. 13*

1230 A572 1s dk bl grn 5 5
1231 A572 2s blue 6 5
1232 A572 6s grnsh bl 15 5
1233 A572 8c lilac 20 5
1234 A572 13s yel grn 50 15
1234A A572 1 l dp grn ('63) 4.00 50
Nos. 1230-1234A (6) 4.96 85

13 =

No. 974 Surcharged in Red

1962, July 14 *Perf. 13*

1235 A493 13s on 44s sl grn 2.00 1.25

Issued to commemorate the 25th Bulgarian Esperanto Congress, Burgas, July 14-16.

Girl and Festival Emblem A573

Design: 5s, Festival emblem.

1962, Aug. 18 Photo. *Perf. 10½*

1236 A573 5s grn, lt bl & pink 20 6
1237 A573 13s lil, lt bl & gray 45 10

Issued to commemorate the 8th Youth Festival for Peace and Friendship, Helsinki, July 28-Aug. 6, 1962.

Parnassius Apollo — A574

1962, Sept. 13
Various Butterflies in Natural Colors

1238 A574 1s pale cit & dk grn 5 5
1239 A574 2s rose & brn 8 5
1240 A574 3s buff & red brn 10 5
1241 A574 4s gray & brn 12 5
1242 A574 5s lt gray & brn 15 5
1243 A574 6s gray & blk 20 5
1244 A574 10s pale grn & blk 95 30
1245 A574 13s buff & red brn 1.50 50
Nos. 1238-1245 (8) 3.15 1.10

Planting Machine A575

Designs: 2s, Electric locomotive. 3s, Blast furnace. 13s, Blagoev and Dimitrov and Communist flag.

1962, Nov. 1 *Perf. 11½*

1246 A575 1s bl grn & dk ol grn 5 5
1247 A575 2s bl & Prus bl 8 5
1248 A575 3s car & brn 15 5
1249 A575 13s plum, red & blk 45 20

Bulgarian Communist Party, 8th Congress.

Title Page of "Slav-Bulgarian History" — A576

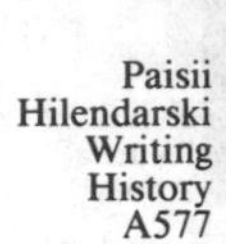

Paisii Hilendarski Writing History A577

1962, Dec. 8 Unwmk. *Perf. 10½*

1250 A576 2s ol grn & blk 8 5
1251 A577 5s brn org & blk 25 5

Issued to commemorate the 200th anniversary of "Slav-Bulgarian History."

Aleco Konstantinov A578

1963, Mar. 5 Photo. *Perf. 11½*

1252 A578 5s red, grn & blk 20 10

Issued to commemorate the centenary of the birth of Aleco Konstantinov (1863-1897), writer. Printed with alternating red brown and black label showing Bai Ganu, hero from Konstantinov's books.

Arms of Bulgaria A579

Sofia University A580

Designs: No. 1255, Levski Stadium, Sofia. No. 1256, Arch, Nissaria. No. 1257, Parachutist.

1963, Feb. 20 Unwmk. *Perf. 10*

1253 A579 1s brn red 5 5
1254 A580 1s red brn 5 5
1255 A580 1s bl grn 5 5
1256 A580 1s dk grn 5 5
1257 A580 1s brt bl 5 5
Nos. 1253-1257 (5) 25 25

Vassil Levski A581

Boy, Girl and Dimitrov A582

1963, Apr. 11 Photo.

1258 A581 13s grnsh bl & buff 75 25

Issued to commemorate the 90th anniversary of the death of Vassil Levski, revolutionary leader in the fight for liberation from the Turks.

1963, Apr. 25 Unwmk. *Perf. 11½*

Design: 13s, Girl with book and boy with hammer.

1259 A582 2s org, ver, red brn & blk 8 5
1260 A582 13s bluish grn, brn & blk 45 10

Issued to commemorate the 10th Congress of Dimitrov's Union of the People's Youth.

Red Squirrel A583

Sun Coast Promenade A584

Animals: 2s, Hedgehog. 3s, European polecat. 5s, Pine marten. 13s, Badger. 20s, Otter. (2s, 3s, 13s, horiz.)

1963, Apr. 30
Red Numerals

1261 A583 1s grn & brn, *grnsh* 5 5
1262 A583 2s grn & blk *yel* 5 5
1263 A583 3s grn & brn, *bis* 6 5
1264 A583 5s vio & red brn, *lil* 15 6
1265 A583 13s red brn & blk, *pink* 65 20
1266 A583 20s blk & brn, *bl* 1.00 25
Nos. 1261-1266 (6) 1.96 66

1963, Mar. 12 Unwmk. *Perf. 13*

Black Sea Resorts: 2s, 3s, 13s, Views of Gold Sand. 5s, 20s, Sun Coast.

1267 A584 1s blue 5 5
1268 A584 2s vermilion 40 5
1269 A584 2s car rose 55 5
1270 A584 3s ocher 28 5
1271 A584 5s lilac 28 5
1272 A584 13s bl grn 80 12
1273 A584 20s green 1.40 30
Nos. 1267-1273 (7) 3.76 67

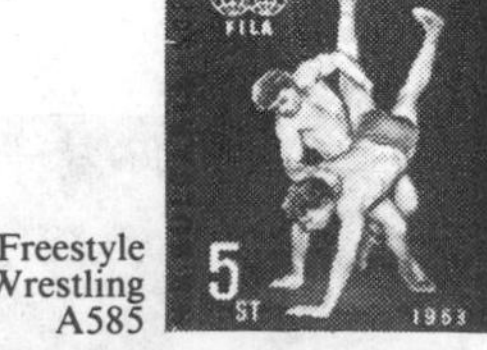

Freestyle Wrestling A585

Design: 20s, Freestyle wrestling (horiz.).

1963, May 31 *Perf. 11½*

1274 A585 5s yel bis & blk 15 10
1275 A585 20s org brn & blk 75 30

Issued to commemorate the 15th International Freestyle Wrestling Competitions, Sofia.

"Women for Peace" A586

1963, June 24 Unwmk. *Perf. 11½*

1276 A586 20s bl & blk 55 20

Issued to commemorate the World Congress of Women, Moscow, June 24-29.

Esperanto Emblem and Arms of Sofia — A587

Moon, Earth and Lunik 4 — A588

1963, June 29 Photo.

1277 A587 13s multi 65 20

Issued to commemorate the 48th World Esperanto Congress, Sofia, Aug. 3-10.

1963, July 22

Designs: 2s, Radar equipment. 3s, Satellites and moon.

1278 A588 1s ultra 5 5
1279 A588 2s red lil 10 5
1280 A588 3s grnsh bl 15 5

Issued to commemorate Russia's rocket to the moon, Apr. 2, 1963.

= MOSTRA EUROPEISTICA·1963 13 RICCIONE

Nos. 1211-1212 and 1215 Overprinted or Surcharged in Green, Ultramarine or Black

1963, Aug. 31 *Perf. 10½*

1281 A565 2s (G) 30 15
1282 A565 5s on 3s (U) 45 15
1283 A565 13s on 6s 85 35

Issued to commemorate the International Stamp Fair, Riccione, Aug. 31.

Women's Relay Race A589

Designs: 2s, Hammer thrower. 3s, Women's long jump. 5s, Men's high jump. 13s, Discus thrower.

Perf. 11½
1963, Sept. 13 Photo. Unwmk.
Flags in National Colors

1284 A589 1s sl grn 10 5
1285 A589 2s purple 15 5
1286 A589 3s Prus bl 20 5
1287 A589 5s maroon 60 30
1288 A589 13s chnt brn 2.00 1.25
Nos. 1284-1288 (5) 3.05 1.70

Issued to publicize the Balkan Games. A multicolored, 50s, imperf. souvenir sheet shows design of women's relay race. Size: 74x70mm.

"Slav-Bulgarian History" — A590

1963, Sept. 19 *Perf. 10½*
1289 A590 5s sal pink, sl & yel 18 5

5th International Slavic Congress.

Revolutionists
A591

Christo
Smirnenski
A592

1963, Sept. 22 *Perf. 11½*
1290 A591 2s brt red & blk 12 5

Issued to commemorate the 40th anniversary of the September Revolution.

1963, Oct. 28 *Perf. 10½*
1291 A592 13s pale lil & ind 35 15

Issued to commemorate the 65th anniversary of the birth of Christo Smirnenski, poet.

Columbine
A593

Horses
A594

1963, Oct. 9 **Photo.** *Perf. 11½*
1292 A593 1s *shown* 5 5
1293 A593 2s *Edelweiss* 5 5
1294 A593 3s *Primrose* 10 5
1295 A593 5s *Water lily* 10 6
1296 A593 6s *Tulips* 15 8
1297 A593 8s *Larkspur* 25 12
1298 A593 10s *Alpine clematis* 60 20
1299 A593 13s *Anemone* 1.10 30
Nos. 1292-1299 (8) 2.40 91

1963, Dec. 28 **Unwmk.** *Perf. 10½*

Designs: 2s, Charioteer and chariot. 3s, Trumpeters. 5s, Woman carrying tray with food. 13s, Man holding bowl. 20s, Woman in armchair. Designs are from a Thracian tomb at Kazanlik.

1300 A594 1s gray, org & dk red 5 5
1301 A594 2s gray, ocher & pur 5 5
1302 A594 3s gray, dl yel & sl grn 8 5
1303 A594 5s pale grn, ocher & brn 15 6
1304 A594 13s pale grn, bis & blk 45 15
1305 A594 20s pale grn, org & dk car 80 30
Nos. 1300-1305 (6) 1.58 66

World Map
and Emblem
A595

Designs: 2s, Blood transfusion. 3s, Nurse bandaging injured wrist. 5s, Red Cross nurse. 13s, Henri Dunant.

1964, Jan. 27 *Perf. 10½*
1306 A595 1s lem, blk & red 5 5
1307 A595 2s ultra, blk & red 5 5
1308 A595 3s gray, sl, blk & red 6 5
1309 A595 5s brt bl, blk & red 15 6
1310 A595 13s org yel, blk & red 45 18
Nos. 1306-1310 (5) 76 39

Centenary of International Red Cross.

Speed
Skating
A596

Sports: 2s, 50s, Women's figure skating. 3s, Cross-country skiing. 5s, Ski jump. 10s, Ice hockey goalkeeper. 13s, Ice hockey players.

1964, Feb. 21 **Unwmk.** *Perf. 10½*
1311 A596 1s grnsh bl, ind & ocher 5 5
1312 A596 2s brt pink, ol grn & dk sl grn 5 5
1313 A596 3s dl grn, dk grn & brn 8 5
1314 A596 5s bl, blk & yel brn 20 5
1315 A596 10s gray, org & blk 45 15
1316 A596 13s lil, blk & lil rose 75 25
Nos. 1311-1316 (6) 1.58 60

Miniature Sheet
Imperf
1317 A596 50s gray, Prus grn & pink 4.50 3.50

Issued to commemorate 9th Winter Olympic Games, Innsbruck, Jan. 29-Feb. 9, 1964.
No. 1317 measures 64x67½mm.

Mask of
Nobleman, 2nd
Century — A597

Designs: 2s, Thracian horseman. 3s, Ceramic jug. 5s, Clasp and belt. 6s, Copper kettle. 8s, Angel. 10s, Lioness. 13s, Scrub woman, contemporary sculpture.

1964, Mar. 14 **Photo.** *Perf. 10½*
Gray Frame
1318 A597 1s dp grn & red 5 5
1319 A597 2s ol gray & red 5 5
1320 A597 3s bis & red 10 6
1321 A597 5s ind & red 20 6
1322 A597 6s org brn & red 25 8
1323 A597 8s brn red & red 45 10
1324 A597 10s ol & red 50 15
1325 A597 13s gray ol & red 75 25
Nos. 1318-1325 (8) 2.35 80

2,500 years of Burgarian art.

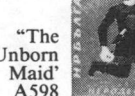

"The
Unborn
Maid'
A598

Fairy Tales: 2s, Grandfather's Glove. 3s, The Big Turnip. 5s, The Wolf and the Seven Kids. 8s, Cunning Peter. 13s, The Wheat Cake.

1964, Apr. 17 **Unwmk.** *Perf. 10½*
1326 A598 1s bl grn, red & org brn 5 5
1327 A598 2s ultra, ocher & blk 5 5
1328 A598 3s cit, red & blk 6 5
1329 A598 5s dp rose, brn & blk 10 5
1330 A598 8s yel grn, red & blk 20 15
1331 A598 13s lt vio bl, grn & blk 70 30
Nos. 1326-1331 (6) 1.16 65

Ascalaphus
Otomanus
A599

Insects: 2s, Nemoptera coa. (vert.). 3s, Saga natalia (grasshopper). 5s, Rosalia alpina (vert.). 13s, Anisoplia austriaca (vert.). 20s, Scolia flavitrons.

1964, May 16 **Photo.** *Perf. 11½*
1332 A599 1s brn org, yel & blk 5 5
1333 A599 2s dl bl grn, bis & blk 6 5
1334 A599 3s gray, grn & blk 10 8
1335 A599 5s lt ol grn, blk & vio 15 10
1336 A599 13s vio, bis & blk 60 18
1337 A599 20s gray bl, yel & blk 90 30
Nos. 1332-1337 (6) 1.86 76

Soccer — A600

Designs: 13s, Women's volleyball. 60s, Map of Europe and European Women's Volleyball Championship Cup (rectangular, size: 60x69mm.).

1964, June 8 **Unwmk.** *Perf. 11½*
1338 A600 2s bl, dk bl, ocher & red 20 10
1339 A600 13s bl, dk bl, ocher & red 75 30

Miniature Sheet
Imperf
1340 A600 60s ultra, ocher, red & gray 3.25 2.50

Issued to commemorate the 50th anniversary of the Levski Physical Culture Association.

Peter
Beron
and
Title
Page
of
Primer
A601

1964, June 22 *Perf. 11½*
1341 A601 20s red brn & dk brn, *grysh* 1.25 1.00

Issued to commemorate the 140th anniversary of the publication of the first Bulgarian primer.

Robert Stephenson's "Rocket"
Locomotive, 1825 — A602

Designs: 2s, Modern steam locomotive. 3s, Diesel locomotive. 5s, Electric locomotive. 8s, Freight train on bridge. 13s, Diesel locomotive and tunnel.

1964, July 1 **Photo.** *Perf. 11½*
1342 A602 1s org brn, blk, bis & gray 5 5
1343 A602 2s org brn, blk, Prus bl & ol 5 5
1344 A602 3s org brn, blk, grn & gray 6 5
1345 A602 5s org brn, blk & bl 15 5
1346 A602 8s org brn, blk, bl & gray 30 10
1347 A602 13s org brn, blk, yel & gray 75 25
Nos. 1342-1347 (6) 1.36 55

German
Shepherd
A603

1964, Aug. 22 **Photo.**
1348 A603 1s *shown* 5 5
1349 A603 2s *Setter* 5 5
1350 A603 3s *Poodle* 6 5
1351 A603 4s *Pomeranian* 15 5
1352 A603 5s *St. Bernard* 18 5
1353 A603 6s *Terrier* 25 10
1354 A603 10s *Pointer* 1.25 35
1355 A603 13s *Dachshund* 2.50 70
Nos. 1348-1355 (8) 4.49 1.40

Partisans — A604

Designs: 2s, People welcoming Soviet army. 3s, Russian aid to Bulgaria. 4s, Blast furnace, Kremikovski. 5s, Combine. 6s, Peace demonstration. 8s, Sentry. 13s, Demeter Blagoev and George Dimitrov.

1964, Sept. 9 **Unwmk.** *Perf. 11½*
Flag in Red
1356 A604 1s lt & dp ultra 5 5
1357 A604 2s ol bis & dp ol 5 5
1358 A604 3s rose lil & mar 6 5
1359 A604 4s lt vio & vio 6 5
1360 A604 5s org & red brn 15 5
1361 A604 6s bl & dp bl 20 5
1362 A604 8s lt grn & grn 30 10
1363 A604 13s fawn & red brn 65 20
Nos. 1356-1363 (8) 1.52 60

Issued to commemorate the 20th anniversary of People's Government of Bulgaria.

М М панаир
ПЛОВДИВ - 1964
No. 967
Surcharged
ST 20

1964, Sept. 13 *Perf. 13*
1364 A476 20s on 44s org yel 1.00 30

International Plovdiv Fair.

Gymnast on Parallel Bars A606

Vratcata Mountain Road A607

Sports: 2s, Long jump. 3s, Woman diver. 5s, Soccer. 13s, Women's volleyball. 20s, Wrestling.

1964, Oct. 10 ***Perf. 11½***

1366 A606 1s pale grn, grn & red 5 5
1367 A606 2s pale vio, vio bl & red 5 5
1368 A606 3s bl grn, brn & red 6 5
1369 A606 5s pink, pur & red 15 8
1370 A606 13s bl, Prus grn & red 50 15
1371 A606 20s yel, grn & red 90 25
Nos. 1366-1371 (6) 1.71 63

Issued for the 18th Olympic Games, Tokyo. Oct. 10-25. See No. B27.

1964, Oct. 26 Photo. ***Perf. 12½x13***

Bulgarian Views: 2s, Ritlite mountain road. 3s, Pines, Malovica peak. 4s, Pobitite rocks. 5s, Erkupria. 6s, Rhodope mountain road.

1372 A607 1s dk sl grn 5 5
1373 A607 2s brown 5 5
1374 A607 3s grnsh bl 8 5
1375 A607 4s dk red brn 15 5
1376 A607 5s dp grn 25 5
1377 A607 6s bl vio 40 5
Nos. 1372-1377 (6) 98 30

Mail Coach, Plane and Rocket A608

1964, Oct. 3 Unwmk. ***Perf. 11½***

1378 A608 20s grnsh bl 1.65 80

Issued to commemorate the first national stamp exhibition, Sofia, Oct. 3-18. Issued in sheets of 12 stamps and 12 labels (woman's head and inscription, 5x5) arranged around one central label showing stylized bird design.

Students Holding Book — A609

1964, Dec. 30 **Photo.**

1379 A609 13s lt bl & blk 50 15

Issued to commemorate the 8th International Students' Congress, Sofia.

500-Year-Old Walnut Tree at Golemo Drenovo — A610

Designs: Various Old Trees.

1964, Dec. 28

1380 A610 1s blk, buff & cl brn 5 5
1381 A610 2s blk, pink & dp cl 5 5
1382 A610 3s blk, yel & dk brn 6 5
1383 A610 4s blk, lt bl & Prus bl 8 5
1384 A610 10s blk, pale grn & grn 35 10
1385 A610 13s blk, pale bis & dk ol grn 65 20
Nos. 1380-1385 (6) 1.24 50

Soldiers' Monument A611

1965, Jan. 1 **Unwmk.**

1386 A611 2s red & blk 20 10

Issued to honor Bulgarian-Soviet friendship.

Olympic Medal Inscribed "Olympic Glory" A612

1965, Jan. 27 Photo. ***Perf. 11½***

1387 A612 20s org brn, gold & blk 90 30

Issued to commemorate Bulgarian victories in the 1964 Olympic Games.

"Victory Over Fascism" A613

Design: 13s, "Fight for Peace" (dove and globe).

1965, Apr. 16 ***Perf. 11½***

1388 A613 5s gray, blk & ol bis 15 5
1389 A613 13s gray, blk & bl 40 20

Issued to commemorate the 20th anniversary of victory over Fascism, May 9, 1945.

Vladimir M. Komarov and Section of Globe — A614

Designs: 2s, Konstantin Feoktistov. 5s, Boris B. Yegorov. 13s, Komarov, Feoktistov and Yegorov. 20s, Spaceship Voskhod.

1965, Feb. 15 **Photo.**

1390 A614 1s pale lil & dk bl 5 5
1391 A614 2s lt bl, ind & dl vio 5 5
1392 A614 5s pale grn, grn & ol grn 15 5
1393 A614 13s pale pink, dp rose & mar 45 15
1394 A614 20s lt bl, vio bl, grnsh bl & yel 80 25
Nos. 1390-1394 (5) 1.50 55

Russian 3-man space flight, Oct. 12-13, 1964.

Imperfs. in changed colors. Four low values se-tenant.
Price, set $3 unused, $1.50 canceled.

Bullfinch — A615

Birds: 2s, European golden oriole. 3s, Common rock thrush. 5s, Barn swallow. 8s, European roller. 10s, European goldfinch. 13s, Rosy pastor starling. 20s, Nightingale.

1965, Apr. 20 Unwmk. ***Perf. 11½***
Birds in Natural Colors

1395 A615 1s bl grn 5 5
1396 A615 2s rose lil 5 5
1397 A615 3s rose 5 5
1398 A615 5s brt bl 10 5
1399 A615 8s citron 35 6
1400 A615 10s gray 1.25 18
1401 A615 13s lt vio bl 1.25 30
1402 A615 20s emerald 2.50 60
Nos. 1395-1402 (8) 5.60 1.34

Sting Ray — A616

Black Sea Fish: 2s, Belted bonito. 3s, Hogfish. 5s, Gurnard. 10s, Scad. 13s, Turbot.

1965, June 10 Photo. ***Perf. 11½***
Gray Frames

1403 A616 1s org, blk & gold 5 5
1404 A616 2s ultra, ind & sil 5 5
1405 A616 3s emer, blk & gold 12 5
1406 A616 5s dp car, blk & gold 20 10
1407 A616 10s grnsh bl, blk & sil 85 25
1408 A616 13s red brn, blk & gold 1.25 40
Nos. 1403-1408 (6) 2.52 90

Plane, Bus, Train, Ship and Whale — A617

ITU Emblem and Communications Symbols — A618

1965, Apr. 30

1409 A617 13s multi 50 15

Issued to publicize the fourth International Conference of Transport, Dock and Fishery Workers, Sofia, May 10-14.

1965, May 17

1410 A618 20s multi 70 25

Issued to commemorate the centenary of the International Telecommunication Union.

Col. Pavel Belyayev and Lt. Col. Alexei Leonov — A619

Design: 20s, Leonov floating in space.

1965, May 20 **Unwmk.**

1411 A619 2s gray, dl bl & dk brn 10 8
1412 A619 20s multi 1.75 60

Space flight of Voskhod 2 and the first man floating in space, Lt. Col. Alexei Leonov.

ICY Emblem — A620

1965, May 15 **Photo.**

1413 A620 20s org, ol & blk 70 20

International Cooperation Year, 1965.

Corn A621

Marx and Lenin A622

Designs: 2s, Wheat. 3s, Sunflowers. 4s, Sugar beet. 5s, Clover. 10s, Cotton. 13s, Tobacco.

1965, Apr. 1 ***Perf. 12½x13***

1414 A621 1s org yel 5 5
1415 A621 2s brt grn 5 5
1416 A621 3s dp org 8 5
1417 A621 4s olive 15 5
1418 A621 5s brt rose 25 5
1419 A621 10s grnsh bl 70 10
1420 A621 13s bister 1.00 20
Nos. 1414-1420 (7) 2.28 55

1965, June ***Perf. 10½***

1421 A622 13s red & dk brn 60 20

Issued to commemorate the 6th Conference of Postal Ministers of Communist Countries, Peking, June 21-July 15.

Film and UNESCO Emblem A623

1965, June 30

1422 A623 13s dp bl, blk & lt gray 50 20

Balkan Film Festival, Varna.

Ballerina — A624

1965, July 10 **Photo.**
1423 A624 5s dp lil rose & blk 60 30

Issued to publicize the Second International Ballet Competition, Varna.

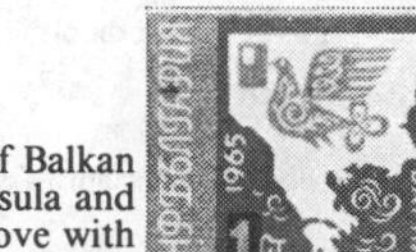

Map of Balkan Peninsula and Dove with Letter — A625

Col. Pavel Belyayev and Lt. Col. Alexei Leonov — A626

Designs: 2s, Sailboat and modern buildings. 3s, Fish and plants. 13s, Symbolic sun and rocket. 40s, Map of Balkan Peninsula and dove with letter (like 1s).

1965, July 23-Aug. 7 ***Perf. 10½***
1424 A625 1s sil, dp ultra & yel 5 5
1425 A625 2s sil, pur & yel 6 5
1426 A625 3s gold, grn & yel 15 8
1427 A625 13s gold, hn brn & yel 75 50
1428 A626 20s sil, bl & brn 90 55
Nos. 1424-1428 (5) 1.91 1.23

Miniature Sheet
Imperf
1429 A625 40s gold & brt bl 2.75 1.50

Balkanphila 1965 Philatelic Exhibition, Varna, Aug. 7-15, and visit of Russian astronauts Belyayev and Leonov. The 20s and 40s were issued Aug. 7.

No. 1429 has gold denomination and inscription in margin. Size: 69x61½mm.

Price, #1428 imperf. in changed colors, 90 cents.

Woman Gymnast — A627

Designs: 2s, Woman gymnast on parallel bars. 3s, Weight lifter. 5s, Automobile and chart. 10s, Women basketball players. 13s, Automobile and map of rally.

1965, Aug. 14 ***Perf. 10½***
1430 A627 1s crim, brn & blk 5 5
1431 A627 2s rose vio, dp cl & blk 5 5
1432 A627 3s dp car, brn & blk 6 5
1433 A627 5s fawn, red brn & blk 20 5
1434 A627 10s dp lil rose, dp cl & blk 75 20
1435 A627 13s lil, cl & blk 90 25
Nos. 1430-1435 (6) 2.01 65

Issued to commemorate various sports events in Bulgaria during May-June, 1965.

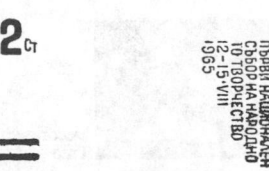

No. 989 Surcharged

1965, Aug. 12 ***Perf. 13***
1436 A499 2s on 8s org brn 75 40

Issued to publicize the First National Folklore Competition, Aug. 12-15.

Escaping Prisoners A628

Apples A629

1965, July 23 ***Perf. 10½***
1437 A628 2s slate 20 10

Issued to commemorate the 40th anniversary of the escape of political prisoners from Bolshevik Island.

1965, July 1 ***Perf. 13***

Fruit: 2s, Grapes. 3s, Pears. 4s, Peaches. 5s, Strawberries. 6s, Walnuts.

1438 A629 1s dp org 5 5
1439 A629 2s lt ol grn 5 5
1440 A629 3s bister 5 5
1441 A629 4s orange 6 5
1442 A629 5s car rose 30 5
1443 A629 6s yel brn 50 15
Nos. 1438-1443 (6) 1.01 40

Dressage — A630

Horsemanship: 2s, Three-day test. 3s, Jumping. 5s, Race. 10s, Steeplechase. 13s, Hurdle race.

1965, Sept. 30 **Unwmk.** ***Perf. 10½***
1444 A630 1s bluish gray, blk & dk vio 5 5
1445 A630 2s buff, blk & hn brn 5 5
1446 A630 3s gray, blk & dk car rose 5 5
1447 A630 5s gray ol, dk grn & red brn 8 5
1448 A630 10s lt gray, blk & dk red brn 65 25
1449 A630 13s sal, dk grn & dk red brn 1.10 35
Nos. 1444-1449 (6) 1.98 80

See also No. B28.

Smiling Children — A631

Designs: 2s, Two girl Pioneers. 3s, Bugler. 5s, Pioneer with model plane. 8s, Two singing girls in national costume. 13s, Running boy.

1965, Oct. 24 **Photo.**
1450 A631 1s dk bl grn & yel grn 5 5
1451 A631 2s vio & dp rose 5 5
1452 A631 3s ol & lem 10 5
1453 A631 5s dp bl & bis 15 6
1454 A631 8s ol bis & org 35 15
1455 A631 13s rose car & vio 85 30
Nos. 1450-1455 (6) 1.55 66

Issued to honor the Dimitrov Pioneer Organization.

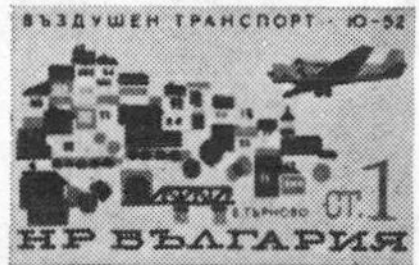

U-52 Plane over Trnovo A632

Designs: 2c, IL-14 over Plovdiv. 3s, Mi-4 Helicopter over Dimitrovgrad. 5s, Tu-104 over Ruse. 13s, IL-18 over Varna. 20s, Tu-114 over Sofia.

1965, Nov. 25 ***Perf. 10½***
1456 A632 1s gray, bl & red 5 5
1457 A632 2s gray, lil & red 5 5
1458 A632 3s gray, grnsh bl & red 6 5
1459 A632 5s gray, org & red 10 8
1460 A632 13s gray, bis & red 65 15
1461 A632 20s gray, lt grn & red 90 40
Nos. 1456-1461 (6) 1.81 78

Issued to publicize the development of Bulgarian Civil Air Transport.

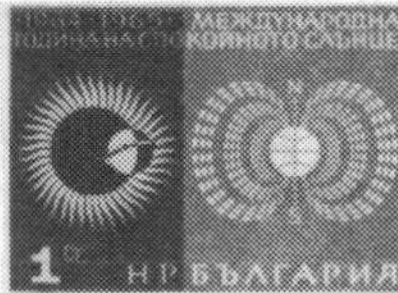

IQSY Emblem, and Earth Radiation Zones A633

Designs (IQSY Emblem and): 2s, Sun with corona. 13s, Solar eclipse.

1965, Dec. 15 **Photo.** ***Perf. 10½***
1462 A633 1s grn, yel & ultra 5 5
1463 A633 2s yel, red lil & red 5 5
1464 A633 13s bl, yel & blk 45 20

International Quiet Sun Year, 1964-65.

"North and South Bulgaria" A634

"Martenitsa" Emblem A635

1965, Dec. 6
1465 A634 13s brt yel grn & blk 55 25

Issued to commemorate the centenary of the Union of North and South Bulgaria.

1966, Jan. 10 **Photo.** ***Perf. 10½***

"Spring" in Folklore: 2s, Drummer. 3s, Bird ornaments. 5s, Dancer "Lazarka." 8s, Vase with flowers. 13s, Bagpiper.

1466 A635 1s rose lil, vio bl & gray 5 5
1467 A635 2s gray, blk & crim 5 5
1468 A635 3s red, vio & gray 5 5
1469 A635 5s lil, blk & crim 10 5
1470 A635 8s rose lil, brn & pur 25 8
1471 A635 13s bl, blk & rose lil 60 25
Nos. 1466-1471 (6) 1.10 53

Church of St. John the Baptist, Nessebr A636

Designs: 1s, Christ, fresco from Bojana Church. 2s, Ikon "Destruction of Idols" (horiz.). 3s, Bratchkovo Monastery. 4s, Zemen Monastery (horiz.). 13s, Nativity, ikon from Arbanassi. 20s, Ikon "Virgin and Child," 1342.

1966, Feb. 25 **Litho.** ***Perf. 11½***
1472 A636 1s gray & multi *2.75* *2.25*
1473 A636 2s gray & multi 20 15
1474 A636 3s multi 20 15
1475 A636 4s multi 20 15
1476 A636 5s multi 25 20
1477 A636 13s gray & multi 40 25
1478 A636 20s multi 75 60
Nos. 1472-1478 (7) 4.75 3.75

2,500 years of art in Bulgaria.

Georgi Benkovski and T. Kableshkov — A637

Designs: 1s, Proclamation of April Uprising, Koprivstitsa. 3s, Dedication of flag, Panaguriste. 5s, V. Petleshkov and Z. Dyustabanov. 10s, Botev landing at Kozlodui. 13s, P. Volov and Ilarion Dragostinov.

1966, March 3 **Photo.** ***Perf. 10½***
Center in Black
1479 A637 1s red brn & gold 5 5
1480 A637 2s brt red & gold 5 5
1481 A637 3s ol grn & gold 6 5
1482 A637 5s stl bl & gold 10 5
1483 A637 10s brt rose lil & gold 25 5
1484 A637 13s lt vio & gold 60 15
Nos. 1479-1484 (6) 1.11 40

Issued to commemorate the 90th anniversary of the April Uprising against the Turks.

Elephant A638

Animals from Sofia Zoo: 2s, Tiger. 3s, Chimpanzee. 4s, Siberian ibex. 5s, Polar bear. 8s, Lion. 13s, Bison. 20s, Kangaroo.

1966, May 23 **Litho.**
1485 A638 1s yel, blk & gray 5 5
1486 A638 2s dl yel, org yel & blk 5 5
1487 A638 3s pale grn, bis & blk 6 5
1488 A638 4s tan, brn & blk 15 5
1489 A638 5s lt bl & blk 20 5
1490 A638 8s pale rose, bis & blk 20 15
1491 A638 13s cit, brn & blk 65 30
1492 A638 20s pale lil, bis & blk 1.25 45
Nos. 1485-1492 (8) 2.61 1.15

WHO Headquarters, Geneva — A639

1966, May 3 **Photo.**
1493 A639 13s dp bl & sil 75 20

Issued to commemorate the inauguration of the World Health Organization Headquarters, Geneva.

Worker A640

1966, May 9 **Photo.** ***Perf. 10½***
1494 A640 20s gray & rose 65 20

Sixth Trade Union Congress.

Yantra River Bridge, Biela — A641

Designs: No. 1496, Maritsa River Bridge, Svilengrad. No. 1497, Fountain, Samokov. No. 1498, Ruins of Fort, Kaskovo. 8s, Old Fort, Ruse. 13s, House, Gabrovo.

1966, Feb. 10 Photo. *Perf. 13*

1495 A641 1s Prus bl 5 5
1496 A641 1s brt grn 5 5
1497 A641 2s ol grn 5 5
1498 A641 2s dk red brn 5 5
1499 A641 8s red brn 30 10
1500 A641 13s dk bl 50 15
Nos. 1495-1500 (6) 1.00 45

Souvenir Sheet

Moon Allegory — A642

1966, Apr. 29 *Imperf.*

1501 A642 60s blk, plum & sil 3.00 2.00

Issued to commemorate the first Russian soft landing on the moon by Luna 9, Feb. 3, 1966. Size: 70x50mm.

Steamer Radetzky and Bugler A643

1966, May 28 *Perf. 10½*

1502 A643 2s multi 20 5

Issued to commemorate the 90th anniversary of the participation of the Danube steamer Radetzky in the uprising against the Turks.

Standard Bearer Nicola Simov-Kuruto A644

1966, May 30

1503 A644 5s bis, grn & ol 25 12

Issued to honor Nicola Simov-Kuruto, hero of the Turkish War.

UNESCO Emblem — A645

1966, June 8

1504 A645 20s gold, blk & ver 70 25

20th anniv. of UNESCO.

Condition is the all-important factor of price. Prices quoted are for stamps in fine condition.

Youth Federation Badge — A646

1966, June 6 Photo. *Perf. 10½*

1505 A646 13s sil, bl & blk 40 15

Issued to publicize the 7th Assembly of the International Youth Federation.

Soccer — A647

Designs: Various soccer scenes. 50s, Jules Rimet Cup.

1966, June 27

1506 A647 1s gray, yel brn & blk 5 5
1507 A647 2s gray, crim & blk 5 5
1508 A647 5s gray, ol bis & blk 15 5
1509 A647 13s gray, ultra & blk 40 15
1510 A647 20s gray, Prus bl & blk 70 30
Nos. 1506-1510 (5) 1.35 60

Miniature Sheet

Imperf

1511 A647 50s gray, dp lil rose & gold 3.00 1.50

Issued to commemorate the World Soccer Cup Championship, Wembley, England, July 11-30. Size of No. 1511: 60x64mm.

Woman Javelin Thrower — A648

Designs: No. 1513, Runner. No. 1514, Young man and woman carrying banners (vert.).

1966 Photo. *Perf. 10½*

1512 A648 2s grn, yel & ver 5 5
1513 A648 13s dp grn, yel & sal pink 45 15
1514 A648 13s bl, lt bl & sal 45 20

Nos. 1512-1513 commemorate the 3rd Spartacist Games; issued Aug. 10. No. 1514 commemorates the 3rd congress of the Bulgarian Youth Federation; issued May 25.

Wrestlers Nicolas Petrov and Dan Kolov — A649

1966, July 29

1515 A649 13s bis brn, dk brn & lt ol grn 55 20

3rd International Wrestling Championships.

Map of Balkan Countries, Globe and UNESCO Emblem — A650

1966, Aug. 26 *Perf. 10½x11½*

1516 A650 13s ultra, lt grn & pink 30 15

First Congress of Balkanologists.

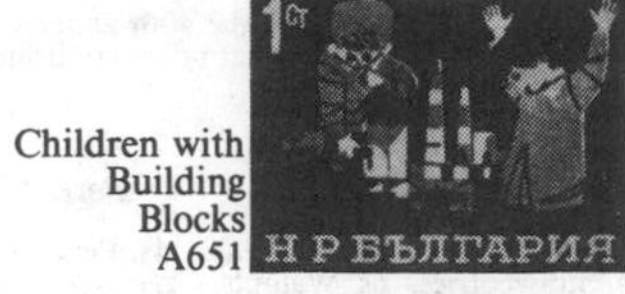

Children with Building Blocks A651

Designs: 2s, Bunny and teddy bear with book. 3s, Children as astronauts. 13s, Children with pails and shovel.

1966, Sept. 1 *Perf. 10½*

1517 A651 1s dk car, org & blk 5 5
1518 A651 2s emer, blk & red brn 5 5
1519 A651 3s ultra, org & blk 10 5
1520 A651 13s bl, rose & blk 75 20

Issued for Children's Day.

Yuri A. Gagarin and Vostok 1 — A652

Designs: 2s, Gherman S. Titov and Vostok 2. 3s, Andrian G. Nikolayev, Pavel R. Popovich, and Vostoks 3 & 4. 5s, Valentina Tereshkova, Valeri Bykovski and Vostoks 5 and 6. 8s, Vladimir M. Komarov, Boris B. Yegorov, Konstantin Feoktistov and Voskhod 1. 13s, Pavel Belyayev, Alexei Leonov and Voskhod 2.

1966, Sept. 29 Photo. *Perf. 11½x11*

1521 A652 1s sl & gray 5 5
1522 A652 2s plum & gray 5 5
1523 A652 3s yel brn & gray 6 5
1524 A652 5s brn red & gray 8 6
1525 A652 8s ultra & gray 10 10
1526 A652 13s Prus bl & gray 45 15
Nos. 1521-1526,B29 (7) 1.54 56

Russian space explorations.

St. Clement, 14th Century Wood Sculpture — A653

1966, Oct. 27 Photo. *Perf. 11½x11*

1527 A653 5s red, buff & brn 25 5

Issued to commemorate the 1050th anniversary of the birth of St. Clement of Ochrida.

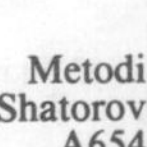

Metodi Shatorov A654

Portraits: 3s, Vladimir Trichkov. 5s, Valcho Ivanov. 10s, Raiko Daskalov. 13s, General Vladimir Zaimov.

1966, Nov. 8 *Perf. 11x11½*

Gold Frame, Black Denomination

1528 A654 2s crim & bl vio 5 5
1529 A654 3s mag & blk 5 5
1530 A654 5s car rose & dk bl 10 5
1531 A654 10s org & ol 35 10
1532 A654 13s red & brn 45 15
Nos. 1528-1532 (5) 1.00 40

Issued to honor fighters against fascism.

George Dimitrov A655

Steel Worker A656

1966, Nov. 14 Photo. *Perf. 11½x11*

1533 A655 2s mag & blk 5 5
1534 A656 20s fawn, gray & blk 50 20

Bulgarian Communist Party, 9th Congress.

Deer's Head Drinking Cup A667

Gold Treasure: 2s, 6s, 10s, Various Amazon's head jugs. 3s, Ram's head cup. 5s, Circular plate. 8s, Deer's head cup. 13s, Amphora. 20s, Ram drinking horn.

1966, Nov. 28 *Perf. 12x11½*

Vessels in Gold and Brown; Black Inscriptions

1535 A667 1s gray & vio 5 5
1536 A667 2s gray & grn 7 5
1537 A667 3s gray & dk bl 10 5
1538 A667 5s gray & red brn 15 5
1539 A667 6s gray & Prus bl 18 5
1540 A667 8s gray & brn ol 1.10 15
1541 A667 10s gray & sep 1.10 20
1542 A667 13s gray & dk vio bl 1.10 30
1543 A667 20s gray & vio brn 1.25 35
Nos. 1535-1543 (9) 5.10 1.25

The gold treasure from the 4th century B.C. was found near Panagyurishte in 1949.

Tourist House, Bansko — A668

Tourist Houses: No. 1545, Belogradchik. No. 1546, Triavna. 20s, Rila.

1966, Nov. 29 Photo. *Perf. 11x11½*

1544 A668 1s dk bl 5 5
1545 A668 2s dk grn 5 5
1546 A668 2s brn red 5 5
1547 A668 20s lilac 50 15

Decorated Tree — A669

Design: 13s, Jug with bird design.

1966, Dec. 12 ***Perf. 11***

1548	A669	2s grn, pink & gold	5	5
1549	A669	13s brn lake, rose, emer & gold	45	15

Issued for New Year, 1967.

Pencho Slavikov, Author — A670

Dahlia — A671

Portraits: 2s, Dimcho Debeljanov, author. 3s, P. H. Todorov, author. 5s, Dimitri Dobrovich, painter. 8s, Ivan Markvichka, painter. 13s, Ilya Bezhkov, painter.

1966, Dec. 15 ***Perf. 10½x11***

1550	A670	1s bl, ol & org	5	5
1551	A670	2s org, brn & gray	5	5
1552	A670	3s ol, bl & org	5	5
1553	A670	5s gray, red brn & org	8	5
1554	A670	8s lil, dk gray & bl	35	8
1555	A670	13s bl, vio & lil	45	15
		Nos. 1550-1555 (6)	1.03	43

1966, Dec. 29

Flowers: No. 1557, Clematis. No. 1558, Foxglove. No. 1559, Narcissus. 3s, Snowdrop. 5s, Petunia. 13s, Tiger lily. 20s, Bellflower. Flowers in Natural Colors

1556	A671	1s gray & lt brn	5	5
1557	A671	1s gray & dl bl	5	5
1558	A671	2s gray & dl lil	5	5
1559	A671	2s gray & brn	5	5
1560	A671	3s gray & dk grn	15	6
1561	A671	5s gray & dp ultra	20	12
1562	A671	13s gray & brn	55	15
1563	A671	20s gray & ultra	90	25
		Nos. 1556-1563 (8)	2.00	78

Ringnecked Pheasant — A672

Game: 2s, Rock partridge. 3s, Gray partridge. 5s, Hare. 8s, Roe deer. 13s, Red deer.

1967, Jan. 28 ***Perf. 11x10½***

1564	A672	1s lt ultra, dk brn & ocher	5	5
1565	A672	2s pale yel grn & dk grn	5	5
1566	A672	3s lt bl, blk & cr	15	5
1567	A672	5s lt grn & blk	15	5
1568	A672	8s pale bl, dk brn & ocher	65	15
1569	A672	13s bl & dk brn	1.25	35
		Nos. 1564-1569 (6)	2.30	70

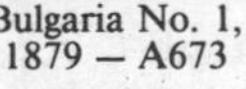

Bulgaria No. 1, 1879 — A673

Thracian Coin, 6th Century, B.C. — A674

1967, Feb. 4 **Photo.** ***Perf. 10½***

1570	A673	10s emer, blk & yel	85	35

Issued to publicize the 10th Congress of the Bulgarian Philatelic Union.

1967, March 30 ***Perf. 11½x11***

Coins: 2s, Macedonian tetradrachma, 2nd century, B.C. 3s, Tetradrachma of Odessus, 2nd century, B.C. 5s, Philip II of Macedonia, 4th century, B.C. 13s, Thracian King Seuthus VII, 4th century, B.C., obverse and reverse. 20s, Apollonian coin, 5th century, B.C., obverse and reverse. Size: 25x25mm.

1571	A674	1s brn, blk & sil	5	5
1572	A674	2s red lil, blk & sil	5	5
1573	A674	3s grn, blk & sil	10	5
1574	A674	5s brn org, blk & sil	20	5

Size: 37½x25mm.

1575	A674	13s brt bl, blk & brnz	85	40
1576	A674	20s vio, blk & sil	1.50	75
		Nos. 1571-1576 (6)	2.75	1.35

Partisans Listening to Radio — A675

Design: 20s, George Dimitrov addressing crowd and Bulgarian flag.

1967, Apr. 20 ***Perf. 11x11½***

1577	A675	1s red, gold, buff & sl grn	5	5
1578	A675	20s red, gold, dl red, grn & blk	60	20

Issued to commemorate the 25th anniversary of the Union of Patriotic Front Organizations.

Nikolas Kofardjiev A676

Portraits: 2s, Petko Napetov. 5s, Petko D. Petkov. 10s, Emil Markov. 13s, Traitcho Kostov.

1967, Apr. 24 ***Perf. 11½x11***

1579	A676	1s brn red, gray & blk	5	5
1580	A676	2s ol grn, gray & blk	5	5
1581	A676	5s brn, gray & blk	8	5
1582	A676	10s dp bl, gray & blk	17	10
1583	A676	13s mag, gray & blk	40	12
		Nos. 1579-1583 (5)	75	37

Issued to honor fighters against fascism.

Symbolic Flower and Flame — A677

1967, May 18 **Photo.** ***Perf. 11x11½***

1584	A677	13s gold, yel & lt grn	50	15

First Cultural Congress, May 18-19.

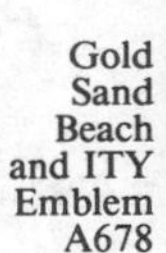

Gold Sand Beach and ITY Emblem A678

Designs: 20s, Hotel, Pamporovo. 40s, Nessebr Church.

1967, June 12 **Photo.** ***Perf. 11x11½***

1585	A678	13s ultra, yel & blk	25	15
1586	A678	20s Prus bl, blk & buff	35	20
1587	A678	40s brt grn, blk & ocher	90	45

Issued for International Tourist Year, 1967.

Angora Cat — A679

Cats: 2s, Siamese (horiz.). 3s, Abyssinian. 5s, Black European. 13s, Persian (horiz.). 20s, Striped domestic.

Perf. 11½x11, 11x11½

1967, June 19

1588	A679	1s dl vio, dk brn & buff	5	5
1589	A679	2s ol, sl & brt bl	10	5
1590	A679	3s dl bl & brn	10	5
1591	A679	5s grn, blk & yel	15	5
1592	A679	13s dl red brn, sl & org	70	20
1593	A679	20s gray grn, brn & buff	1.25	40
		Nos. 1588-1593 (6)	2.35	80

Scene from Opera "The Master of Boyana" by K. Iliev A680

Songbird on Keyboard — A681

1967, June 19

1594	A680	5s gray, vio bl & dp car	15	5
1595	A681	13s gray, dp car & dk bl	45	15

Issued to commemorate the 3rd International Competition for Young Opera Singers.

George Kirkov A682

1967, June 24 ***Perf. 11x11½***

1596	A682	2s rose red & dk brn	15	5

Issued to commemorate the centenary of the birth of George Kirkov (1867-1919), revolutionist.

Symbolic Tree and Stars — A683

1967, July 28 **Photo.** ***Perf. 11½x11***

1597	A683	13s dp bl, car & blk	45	15

Issued to commemorate the 11th Congress of Dimitrov's Union of the People's Youth.

Roses and Distillery A684

Designs: No. 1599, Chick and incubator. No. 1600, Cucumbers and hothouse. No. 1601, Lamb and sheep farm. 3s, Sunflower and oil mill. 4s, Pigs and pig farm. 5s, Hops and hop farm. 6s, Corn and irrigation system. 8s, Grapes and Bolgar tractor. 10s, Apples and cultivated tree. 13s, Bees and honey. 20s, Bee, blossoms and beehives.

1967 ***Perf. 11x11½***

1598	A684	1s multi	5	5
1599	A684	1s dk car, yel & blk	5	5
1600	A684	2s vio, lt grn & blk	5	5
1601	A684	2s brt grn, gray & blk	5	5
1602	A684	3s yel grn, yel & blk	5	5
1603	A684	4s brt pur, yel & blk	6	5
1604	A684	5s ol bis, yel grn & blk	10	8
1605	A684	6s ol, brt grn & blk	15	10
1606	A684	8s grn, bis & blk	15	10
1607	A684	10s multi	30	10
1608	A684	13s grn, bis brn & blk	45	15
1609	A684	20s grnsh bl, brt pink & blk	60	20
		Nos. 1598-1609 (12)	2.06	1.03

Issue dates: Nos. 1598-1601, 1607 and 1609, July 15; Nos. 1602-1606 and 1608, July 24.

Map of Communist Countries, Spasski Tower A685

Designs: 2s, Lenin speaking to soldiers. 3s, Fighting at Wlodaja, 1918. 5s, Marx, Engels and Lenin. 13s, Oil refinery. 20s, Molniya communication satellite.

1967, Aug. 25 ***Perf. 11***

1610	A685	1s multi	5	5
1611	A685	2s mag & ol	5	5
1612	A685	3s mag & dl vio	5	5
1613	A685	5s mag & red	8	5
1614	A685	13s mag & ultra	25	15
1615	A685	20s mag & bl	55	18
		Nos. 1610-1615 (6)	1.03	53

Issued to commemorate the 50th anniversary of the Russian October Revolution.

Rod, "Fish" and Varna — A686

1967, Aug. 29 **Photo.** ***Perf. 11***

1616	A686	10s multi	50	20

7th World Angling Championships, Varna.

Skiers and Winter Olympics' Emblem — A687

Sports and Emblem: 2s, Ski jump. 3s, Biathlon. 5s, Ice hockey. 13s, Figure skating couple.

1967, Sept. 20 **Photo.** ***Perf. 11***

1617	A687	1s dk bl grn, red & blk	5	5
1618	A687	2s ultra, blk & ol	5	5
1619	A687	3s vio brn, bl & blk	5	5
1620	A687	5s grn, yel & blk	10	5
1621	A687	13s vio bl, blk & buff	40	15
		Nos. 1617-1621,B31 (6)	90	40

Issued to publicize the 10th Winter Olympic Games, Grenoble, France, Feb. 6-18, 1968.

Bogdan Mountain A688

Mountain Peaks: 2s, Czerny. 3s, Ruen (vert.). 5s, Persenk. 10s, Botev. 13s, Rila (vert.). 20s, Vihren.

1967, Sept. 25 Engr. *Perf. 11½*

1622	A688	1s sl grn & yel	5	5
1623	A688	2s sep & pale bl	5	5
1624	A688	3s ind & lt bl	5	5
1625	A688	5s sl grn & lt bl	10	5
1626	A688	10s dp cl & lt bl	15	6
1627	A688	13s dk gray & lt bl	30	10
1628	A688	20s ind & rose	60	20
		Nos. 1622-1628 (7)	1.30	56

George Rakovski A689

1967, Oct. 20 Photo. *Perf. 11*

1629	A689	13s yel grn & blk	45	15

Issued to commemorate the centenary of the death of George Rakovski, revolutionary against Turkish rule.

Yuri A. Gagarin, Valentina Tereshkova and Alexei Leonov — A690

Designs: 2s, Lt. Col. John H. Glenn, Jr., and Maj. Edward H. White. 5s, Earth and Molniya 1. 10s, Gemini 6 and 7. 13s, Luna 13 moon probe. 20s, Gemini 10 and Agena rocket.

1967, Nov. 25

1630	A690	1s Prus bl, blk & yel	5	5
1631	A690	2s dl bl, blk & dl yel	5	5
1632	A690	5s vio bl, grnsh bl & blk	8	5
1633	A690	10s dk bl, blk & red	25	10
1634	A690	13s grnsh bl, brt yel & blk	40	12
1635	A690	20s dl bl, blk & red	55	30
		Nos. 1630-1635 (6)	1.38	67

Achievements in space exploration.

View of Trnovo A691

Various Views of Trnovo

1967, Dec. 5 Photo. *Perf. 11*

1636	A691	1s multi	5	5
1637	A691	2s multi	5	5
1638	A691	3s multi	5	5
1639	A691	5s multi	15	5
1640	A691	13s multi	30	20
1641	A691	20s multi	45	25
		Nos. 1636-1641 (6)	1.05	65

Issued to publicize the restoration of the ancient capital Veliko Trnovo.

Ratchenitza Folk Dance, by Ivan Markv'1653ichka — A692

1967, Dec. 9

1642	A692	20s gold & gray grn	1.40	1.10

Issued to commemorate the Belgo-Bulgarian Philatelic Exposition, Brussels, Dec. 9-10. Printed in sheets of 8 stamps and 8 labels.

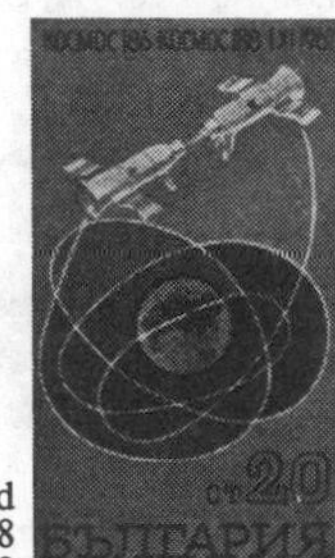

Cosmos 186 and 188 Docking — A693

Design: 40s, Venus 4 and orbits around Venus (horiz.).

1968, Jan.

1643	A693	20s vio, gray & pink	55	20
1644	A693	40s rose car, gray, sil & blk	1.10	40

Issued to commemorate the docking maneuvers of the Russian spaceships Cosmos 186 and Cosmos 188, Nov. 1, 1967, and the flight to Venus of Venus 4, June 12-Nov. 18, 1967.

Crossing the Danube, by Orenburgski — A694

Paintings: 2s, Flag of Samara, by J. Veschin (vert.). 3s, Battle of Pleven by Orenburgski. 13s, Battle of Orlovo Gnezdo, by N. Popov (vert.). 20s, Welcome for Russian Soldiers, by D. Gudienov.

1968, Jan. 25 Photo. *Perf. 11*

1645	A694	1s gold & dk grn	5	5
1646	A694	2s gold & dk bl	5	5
1647	A694	3s gold & cl brn	5	5
1648	A694	13s gold & dk vio	50	20
1649	A694	20s gold & Prus grn	75	30
		Nos. 1645-1649 (5)	1.40	65

Issued to commemorate the 90th anniversary of the liberation from Turkey.

Shepherds, by Zlatyn Boyadjiev — A695

Paintings: 2s, Wedding dance, by V. Dimitrov. (vert.). 3s, Partisans' Song, by Ilya Petrov. 5s, Portrait of Anna Penchovich, by Nikolai Pavlovich (vert.). 13s, Self-portrait, by Zachary Zograf (vert.). 20s, View of Old Plovdiv, by T. Lavrenov. 60s, St. Clement of Ochrida, by A. Mitov.

1967, Dec. Litho. *Perf. 11½*
Size: 45x38mm., 38x45mm.

1650	A695	1s gray & multi	8	5
1651	A695	2s gray & multi	10	5

Size: 55x35mm.

1652	A695	3s gray & multi	20	10

Size: 38x45mm., 45x38mm.

1653	A695	5s gray & multi	40	15
1654	A695	13s gray & multi	90	35
1655	A695	20s gray & multi	1.25	60
		Nos. 1650-1655 (6)	2.93	1.30

Miniature Sheet
Imperf.
Size: 65x84mm.

1656	A695	60s multi	4.00	3.00

Marx Statue, Sofia — A696

Maxim Gorky — A697

1968, Feb. 20 Photo. *Perf. 11*

1657	A696	13s blk & red	35	10

150th anniversary of birth of Karl Marx.

1968, Feb. 20

1658	A697	13s ver & grnsh blk	40	15

Issued to commemorate the centenary of the birth of Maxim Gorky (1868-1936), Russian writer.

Folk Dancers — A698

Designs: 5s, Runners. 13s, Doves. 20s, Festival poster, (head, flowers and birds). 40s, Globe and Bulgaria No. 1 under magnifying glass.

1968, Mar. 20

1659	A698	2s multi	5	5
1660	A698	5s multi	10	5
1661	A698	13s multi	20	10
1662	A698	20s multi	45	25
1663	A698	40s multi	1.00	50
		Nos. 1659-1663 (5)	1.80	95

Issued to publicize the 9th Youth Festival for Peace and Friendship, Sofia, July 28-Aug. 6.

Bellflower — A699

Flowers: 2s, Gentian. 3s, Crocus. 5s, Iris. 10s, Dog-tooth violet. 13s, Sempervivum. 20s, Dictamnus.

1968, Apr. 25 *Perf. 11*
Flowers in Natural Colors

1664	A699	1s dl bl & blk	5	5
1665	A699	2s yel grn & blk	5	5
1666	A699	3s gray grn & blk	5	5
1667	A699	5s brn org & blk	15	5
1668	A699	10s ultra & blk	20	10
1669	A699	13s rose lil & blk	65	15
1670	A699	20s ol & blk	90	30
		Nos. 1664-1670 (7)	2.05	75

"The Unknown Hero," Tale by Ran Bosilek A700

Design: 20s, The Witch and the Young Man (Hans Christian Andersen fairy tale.)

1968, Apr. 25 Photo. *Perf. 10½*

1671	A700	13s blk & multi	40	20
1672	A700	20s blk & multi	50	30

Bulgarian-Danish Philatelic Exhibition.

Memorial Church, Shipka A701

Steeplechase A702

1968, May 3

1673	A701	13s multi	75	30

Bulgarian Stamp Exhibition in West Berlin.

1968, June 24 Photo. *Perf. 10½*

Designs (Olympic Rings and): 1s, Gymnast on bar. 3s, Fencer. 10s, Boxer. 13s, Woman discus thrower.

1674	A702	1s red & blk	5	5
1675	A702	2s gray, blk & rose brn	5	5
1676	A702	3s mag, gray & blk	5	5
1677	A702	10s grnsh bl, blk & lem	20	5
1678	A702	13s vio bl, gray & pink	55	20
		Nos. 1674-1678,B33 (6)	1.70	50

Issued to publicize the 19th Olympic Games, Mexico City, Oct. 12-27.

Battle of Buzluja A703

Design: 13s, Haji Dimitr and Stefan Karaja.

1968, July 1

1679	A703	2s sil & red brn	5	5
1680	A703	13s gold & sl grn	35	15

Issued to commemorate the centenary of the death of the patriots Haji Dimitr and Stefan Karaja.

Lakes of Smolian A704

Sofia Zoo, Cent. A705

Bulgarian Scenes: 2s, Ropotamo Lake. 3s, Erma-Idreloto mountain pass. 8s, Isker River dam. 10s, Slanchev Breg (sailing ship). 13s, Cape Caliacra. 40s, Old houses, Sozopol. 2 l, Chudnite Skali ("Strange Mountains").

1968 Photo. *Perf. 13*

1681	A704	1s Prus grn	5	5
1682	A704	2s dk grn	5	5
1683	A704	3s dk brn	5	5
1684	A704	8s ol grn	15	8
1685	A704	10s redsh brn	20	10
1686	A704	13s dk ol grn	30	10
1687	A704	40s Prus bl	80	35
1688	A704	2 l sepia	5.00	1.25
		Nos. 1681-1688 (8)	6.60	2.03

1968, July 29 *Perf. 10½*

1689	A705	1s Cinereous vulture	5	5
1690	A705	2s Crowned crane	5	5
1691	A705	3s Zebra	15	5
1692	A705	5s Leopard	25	6
1693	A705	13s Indian python	45	15
1694	A705	20s African crocodile	80	30
		Nos. 1689-1694 (6)	1.75	66

Human Rights Flame — A706

1968, July 8

1695 A706 20s dp bl & gold 50 20

International Human Rights Year, 1968.

Congress Hall, Varna, and Emblem A707

1968, Sept. 17 Photo. *Perf. 10½*

1696 A707 20s bis, grn & red 45 15

Issued to publicize the 56th International Dental Congress, Varna.

Flying Swans — A708

Rose A709

Stag Beetle A710

Designs: 2s, Jug. 20s, Five Viking ships.

1968 Photo. *Perf. 10½*

1697	A709	2s grn & ocher	1.00	1.00
1698	A708	5s dp bl & gray	1.00	1.00
1699	A709	13s dp plum & lil rose	1.00	1.00
1700	A708	20s dp vio & gray	1.00	1.00

Issued to publicize cooperation with the Scandinavian countries. Nos. 1697 and 1700 are printed with connecting label showing bridge made of flags of Scandinavian countries.

Issue dates: 5s, 13s, Sept. 12. Others, Nov. 22.

Perf. 12½x13, 13x12½

1968, Aug. 26

Insects: No. 1702, Ground beetle (Procerus scabrosus). No. 1703, Ground beetle (Calosoma sycophania). No. 1704, Scarab beetle (Horiz.). No. 1705, Saturnid moth (horiz.).

1701	A710	1s brn ol	5	5
1702	A710	1s dk bl	5	5
1703	A710	1s dk grn	5	5
1704	A710	1s org brn	5	5
1705	A710	1s magenta	5	5
		Nos. 1701-1705 (5)	25	25

Turks Fighting Insurgents, 1688 — A711

1968, Aug. 22 *Perf. 10½*

1706 A711 13s multi 50 10

Issued to commemorate the 280th anniversary of the Tchiprovtzi insurrection.

Christo Smirnenski — A712

1968, Sept. 28 Litho. *Perf. 10½*

1707 A712 13s gold, red org & blk 40 10

Issued to commemorate the 70th birthday of Christo Smirnenski (1898-1923), poet.

Dalmatian Pelican — A713

Birds: 2s, Little egret. 3s, Crested grebe. 5s, Common tern. 13s, European spoonbill. 20s, Glossy ibis.

1968, Oct. 28 Photo.

1708	A713	1s sil & multi	5	5
1709	A713	2s sil & multi	5	5
1710	A713	3s sil & multi	8	5
1711	A713	5s sil & multi	10	8
1712	A713	13s sil & multi	40	10
1713	A713	20s sil & multi	85	35
		Nos. 1708-1713 (6)	1.53	68

Issued to publicize the Srebirna wild life reservation.

Carrier Pigeon A714

1968, Oct. 19

1714	A714	20s emerald	70	35
a.		Sheet of 4 + labels	4.25	2.25

Issued to publicize the 2nd National Stamp Exhibition in Sofia, Oct. 25-Nov. 15. No. 1714a contains 4 No. 1714 and 5 decorative labels of two types with commemorative inscriptions. Gold frame. Size: 133x161½mm. No. 1714 was issued only as sheet No. 1714a.

A little time given to the study of the arrangement of the Scott Catalogue can make it easier to use effectively.

Man and Woman from Lovetch A715

Regional Costumes: 1s, Silistra. 3s, Jambol. 13s, Chirpan. 20s, Razgrad. 40s, Ihtiman.

1968, Nov. 20 Litho. *Perf. 13½*

1715	A715	1s dp org & multi	5	5
1716	A715	2s Prus bl & multi	6	5
1717	A715	3s multi	15	5
1718	A715	13s multi	25	8
1719	A715	20s multi	50	25
1720	A715	40s grn & multi	1.25	45
		Nos. 1715-1720 (6)	2.26	93

St. Arsenius A716

Designs (10th century Murals and Icons): 2s, Procession with relics of St. Ivan Rilsky (horiz.). 3s, St. Michael Torturing the Soul of the Rich Man. 13s, St. Ivan Rilsky. 20s, St. John. 40s, St. George. 1 l, Procession meeting relics of St. Ivan Rilsky (horiz.).

Perf. 11½x12½, 12½x11½

1968, Nov. 25 Photo.

1721	A716	1s gold & multi	5	5
1722	A716	2s gold & multi	5	5
1723	A716	3s gold & multi	15	5
1724	A716	13s gold & multi	60	18
1725	A716	20s gold & multi	1.25	35
1726	A716	40s gold & multi	1.75	70
		Nos. 1721-1726 (6)	3.85	1.38

Souvenir Sheet

Imperf

1727 A716 1 l gold & multi 5.50 4.50

Issued to commemorate the millenium of Rila Monastery. No. 1727 also publicizes "Sofia 1969," International Philatelic Exhibition, May 31-June 8, 1969. No. 1727 contains one stamp (size: 57x51mm.), gray margin with emblems of Philatelic Exhibition. Size: 100x75mm.

Medlar A717

Herbs: No. 1729, Camomile. 2s, Lily-of-the-valley. 3s, Belladonna. 5s, Mallow. 10s, Buttercup. 13s, Poppies. 20s, Thyme.

1969, Jan. 2 Litho. *Perf. 10½*

1728	A717	1s blk, grn & org red	5	5
1729	A717	1s blk, grn & yel	5	5
1730	A717	2s blk, emer & grn	5	5
1731	A717	3s blk & multi	5	5
1732	A717	5s blk & multi	10	5
1733	A717	10s blk, grn & yel	16	8
1734	A717	13s blk & multi	30	15
1735	A717	20s blk, lil & grn	65	20
		Nos. 1728-1735 (8)	1.41	68

Silkworms and Spindles A718

Designs: 2s, Silkworm, cocoons and pattern. 3s, Cocoons and spinning wheel. 5s, Cocoons, woof-and-warp diagram. 13s, Silk moth, Cocoon and spinning frame. 20s, Silk moth, eggs and shuttle.

1969, Jan. 30 Photo. *Perf. 10½*

1736	A718	1s bl, grn, sl & blk	5	5
1737	A718	2s dp car, sil & blk	5	5
1738	A718	3s Prus bl, sil & blk	5	5
1739	A718	5s pur, ver, sil & blk	8	6
1740	A718	13s red lil, ocher, sil & blk	30	15
1741	A718	20s grn, org, sil & blk	50	20
		Nos. 1736-1741 (6)	1.03	56

Bulgarian silk industry.

Attack and Capture of Emperor Nicephorus A719

Sts. Cyril and Methodius, Mural, Troian Monastery A720

Designs (Manasses Chronicle): No. 1742, Death of Ivan Asen. 3s, Khan Kroum feasting after victory. No. 1748, Invasion of Bulgaria by Prince Sviatoslav of Kiev. No. 1750, Russian invasion and campaigns of Emperor John I Zimisces, c. 972 A.D. 40s, Tsar Ivan Alexander, Jesus and Constantine Manasses.

Horizontal designs: No. 1743, Kings Nebuchadnezzar, Balthazar, Darius and Cyrus. No. 1745, Kings Cambyses, Gyges and Darius. 5s, King David and Tsar Ivan Alexander. No. 1749, Persecution of Byzantine army after battle of July 26, 811. No. 1751, Christening of Bulgarian Tsar Boris, 865. 60s, Arrival of Tsar Simeon in Constantinople and his succeeding surprise attack on that city.

1969 Photo. *Perf. 14x13½, 13½x14*

Gold Frame

1742	A719	1s multi	5	5
1743	A719	1s multi	5	5
1744	A719	2s multi	5	5
1745	A719	2s multi	5	5
1746	A719	3s multi	10	5
1747	A719	5s multi	10	5
1748	A719	13s multi	30	8
1749	A719	13s multi	30	10
1750	A719	20s multi	60	20
1751	A719	20s multi	60	20
1752	A719	40s multi	1.00	50
1753	A719	60s multi	1.75	60
		Nos. 1742-1753 (12)	4.95	1.98

1969, Mar. 23

1754 A720 28s gold & multi 85 40

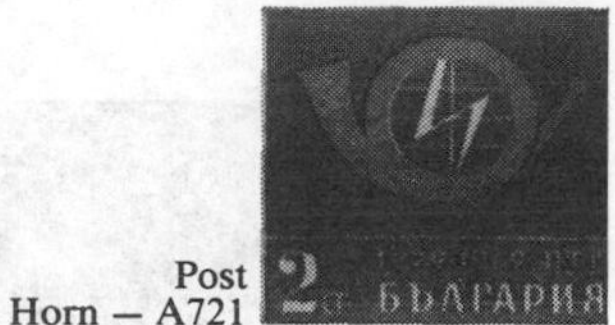

Post Horn — A721

Designs: 13s, Bulgaria Nos. 1 and 534. 20s, Street fighting at Stackata, 1919.

1969, Apr. 15 Photo. *Perf. 10½*

1755 A721 2s grn & yel 5 5

1756	A721	13s multi	40	10
1757	A721	20s dk bl & lt bl	50	20

Issued to commemorate the 90th anniversary of the Bulgarian postal administration.

The Fox and the Rabbit A722

Children's Drawings: 2s, Boy reading to wolf and fox. 13s, Two birds and cat. singing together.

1969, Apr. 21

1758	A722	1s emer, org & blk	5	5
1759	A722	2s org, lt bl & blk	5	5
1760	A722	13s lt bl, ol & blk	50	15

Issued for Children's Week.

ILO Emblem — A723

1969, Apr. 28

1761	A723	13s dl grn & blk	30	15

Issued to commemorate the 50th anniversary of the International Labor Organization.

St. George and SOPHIA 69 Emblem A724

Designs: 2s, Virgin Mary and St. John Bogoslov. 3s, Archangel Michael. 5s, Three Saints. 8s, Jesus Christ. 13s, Sts. George and Dimitrie. 20s, Christ, the Almighty. 40s, St. Dimitrie. 60s, The 40 Martyrs. 80s, The Transfiguration.

1969, Apr. 30 *Perf. 11x12*

1762	A724	1s gold & multi	5	5
1763	A724	2s gold & multi	5	5
1764	A724	3s gold & multi	5	5
1765	A724	5s gold & multi	10	5
1766	A724	8s gold & multi	15	5
1767	A724	13s gold & multi	30	10
1768	A724	20s gold & multi	60	20
1769	A724	40s gold & multi	1.25	40
a.		Sheet of four	5.00	3.50
1770	A724	60s gold & multi	1.75	80
1771	A724	80s gold & multi	2.50	90
		Nos. 1762-1771 (10)	6.80	2.65

Old Bulgarian art from the National Art Gallery. No. 1769a contains 4 of No. 1769 with center gutter showing Alexander Nevski Shrine. See note on SOPHIA 69 after Nos. C112-C120.

St. Cyril Preaching A725

St. Sophia Church — A726

Design: 28s, St. Cyril and followers.

1969, June 20 Litho. *Perf. 10½*

1772	A725	2s sil, grn & red	15	5
1773	A725	28s sil, dk bl & red	65	35

Issued to commemorate the 1100th anniversary of the death of St. Cyril (827-869), apostle to the Slavs, inventor of Cyrillic alphabet. Issued in sheets of 25 with setenant labels; Cyrillic inscription on label of 2s, Glagolitic inscription on label of 28s.

1969, May 25 *Perf. 13x12½*

Sofia Through the Ages: 1s, Roman coin with inscription "Ulpia Serdica." 2s, Roman coin with Aesculapius Temple. 4s, Bojana Church. 5s, Sobranie Parliament. 13s, Vasov National Theater. 20s, Alexander Nevski Shrine. 40s, Clement Ochrida University. 1l, Coat of arms.

1774	A726	1s gold & bl	5	5
1775	A726	2s gold & ol grn	5	5
1776	A726	3s gold & red brn	5	5
1777	A726	4s gold & pur	8	5
1778	A726	5s gold & plum	10	5
1779	A726	13s gold & brt grn	25	10
1780	A726	20s gold & vio bl	45	15
1781	A726	40s gold & dp car	1.10	35
		Nos. 1774-1781 (8)	2.13	85

Souvenir Sheet

Imperf

1782	A726	1 l grn, gold & red	2.50	2.50

Issued to show historic Sofia in connection with the International Philatelic Exphibition. Sofia, May 31-June 8.

No. 1782 contains one stamp (size: 43½x43½mm.). Emblems of 8 preceding philatelic exhibitions in metallic ink in margin; gold inscription. Size: 80x72mm.

No. 1782 was overprinted in green "IBRA 73" and various symbols, and released May 4, 1973, for the Munich Philatelic Exhibition. The overprint also exists in gray.

St. George A727

1969, June 9 Litho. *Perf. 11½*

1783	A727	40s sil, blk & pale rose	1.10	50

Issued to commemorate the 38th FIP (Federation Internationale de Philatelie) Congress, June 9-11.

Hand Planting Sapling A728

1969, Apr. 28 Photo. *Perf. 11*

1784	A728	2s ol grn, blk & lil	10	5

Issued to publicize 25 years of the reforestation campaign.

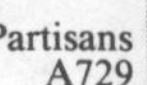

Partisans A729

Dsigns: 2s, Combine harvester. 3s, Dam. 5s, Flutist and singers. 13s, Factory. 20s, Lenin, Dimitrov, Russian and Bulgarian flags.

1969, Sept. 9

1785	A729	1s blk, pur & org	5	5
1786	A729	2s blk, ol bis & org	5	5
1787	A729	3s blk, bl grn & org	5	5
1788	A729	5s blk, brn red & org	10	5
1789	A729	13s blk, bl & org	30	10
1790	A729	20s blk, brn & org	55	20
		Nos. 1785-1790 (6)	1.10	50

25th anniversary of People's Republic.

Women Gymnasts A730

Design: 20s, Wrestlers.

1969, Sept. Photo. *Perf. 11*

1791	A730	2s bl, blk & pale brn	5	5
1792	A730	20s red org & multi	60	25

Third National Spartakiad.

Tchanko Bakalov Tcherkovski A731

1969, Sept.

1793	A731	13s multi	30	10

Birth centenary of Tchanko Bakalov Techerkovski, poet.

Woman Gymnast A732

Designs: 2s, Two women with hoops. 3s, Woman with hoop. 5s, Two women with spheres.

1969, Oct.

Gymnasts in Light Gray

1794	A732	1s grn & dk bl	5	5
1795	A732	2s bl & dk bl	5	5
1796	A732	3s emer & sl grn	8	5
1797	A732	5s org & pur	12	8
		Nos. 1794-1797,B35-B36 (6)	1.70	73

Issued to publicize the World Championships for Artistic Gymnastics, Varna.

The first price column gives the catalogue value of an unused stamp, the second that of a used stamp.

The Priest Rilski, by Zachary Zograf — A733

Paintings from the National Art Gallery. 2s, Woman at Window, by Vasil Stoilov. 3s, Workers at Rest, by Nenko Balkanski (horiz.). 4s, Woman Dressing (Nude), by Ivan Nenov. 5s, Portrait of a Woman, by N. Pavlovich. 13s, Falstaff, by Duzunov Kr. Sarafov. No. 1804, Portrait of a Woman, by N. Mihajlov (horiz.). No. 1805, Workers at Mealtime, by Stojan Sotirov (horiz.). 40s, Self-portrait, by Tcheno Togorov.

Perf. 11½x12, 12x11½

1969, Nov. 10

1798	A733	1s gold & multi	5	5
1799	A733	2s gold & multi	5	5
1800	A733	3s gold & multi	5	5
1801	A733	4s gold & multi	8	5
1802	A733	5s gold & multi	10	5
1803	A733	13s gold & multi	40	10
1804	A733	20s gold & multi	80	30
1805	A733	20s gold & multi	80	30
1806	A733	40s gold & multi	1.50	80
		Nos. 1798-1806 (9)	3.83	1.75

Roman Bronze Wolf — A734

Design: 2s, Roman statue of woman, found at Silistra (vert.).

1969, Oct. Photo. *Perf. 11*

1807	A734	2s sil, ultra & gray	10	5
1808	A734	13s sil, dk grn & gray	45	15

City of Silistra's 1,800th anniversary.

Worker and Factory — A735

1969 *Perf. 13*

1809	A735	6s ultra & blk	15	8

25th anniversary of the factory militia.

European Hake — A736

Designs: No. 1811, Deep-sea fishing trawler. Fish: 2s, Atlantic horse mackerel. 3s, Pilchard. 5s, Dentex macrophthalmus. 10s, Chub mackerel. 13s Otolithes macrognathus. 20s, Lichia vadigo.

1969 *Perf. 11*

1810	A736	1s ol grn & blk	5	5
1811	A736	1s ultra, ind & gray	5	5
1812	A736	2s lil & blk	5	5
1813	A736	3s vio bl & blk	5	5
1814	A736	5s rose cl, pink & blk	18	6
1815	A736	10s gray & blk	35	10
1816	A736	13s ver, sal & blk	50	12
1817	A736	20s ocher & blk	90	25
		Nos. 1810-1817 (8)	2.13	73

Marin Drinov A737

1969, Nov. 10 Litho. *Perf. 11*
1818 A737 20s blk & red org 40 15

Issued to commemorate the centenary of the Bulgarian Academy of Science, founded by Marin Drinov.

Trapeze Artists A738

Pavel Bania Sanatorium A739

Circus Performers: 2s, Jugglers. 3s, Jugglers with loops. 5s, Juggler and bear on bicycle. 13s, Woman and performing horse. 20s, Musical clowns.

1969 Photo. *Perf. 11*
1819 A738 1s dk bl & multi 5 5
1820 A738 2s dk grn & multi 5 5
1821 A738 3s dk vio & multi 8 5
1822 A738 5s multi 8 5
1823 A738 13s multi 40 15
1824 A738 20s multi 75 30
Nos. 1819-1824 (6) 1.41 65

1969, Dec. Photo. *Perf. 10½*

Health Resorts: 5s, Chisar Sanatorium. 6s, Kotel Children's Sanatorium. 20s, Narechen Polyclinic.

1825 A739 2s blue 5 5
1826 A739 5s ultra 10 6
1827 A739 6s green 12 10
1828 A739 20s emerald 35 10

G. S. Shonin, V. N. Kubasov and Spacecraft — A740

Designs: 2s, A. V. Filipchenko, V. N. Volkov, V. V. Gorbatko and spacecraft. 3s, Vladimir A. Shatalov, Alexei S. Yeliseyev and spacecraft. 28s, Three spacecraft in orbit.

1970, Jan. Photo. *Perf. 11*
1829 A740 1s rose car, ol grn & blk 5 5
1830 A740 2s bl, dl cl & blk 5 5
1831 A740 3s grnsh bl, vio & blk 5 5
1832 A740 28s vio bl, lil rose & lt bl 75 25

Issued to commemorate the Russian space flights of Soyuz 6, 7 and 8, Oct. 11-13, 1969.

Khan Krum and Defeat of Emperor Nicephorus, 811 — A741

Bulgarian History: 1s, Khan Asparuch and Bulgars crossing the Danube (679). 3s, Conversion of Prince Boris to Christianity, 865. 5s, Tsar Simeon and battle of Akhelo, 917. 8s, Tsar Samuel defeating the Byzantines, 976. 10s, Tsar Kaloyan defeating Emperor Baldwin, 1205. 13s, Tsar Ivan Assen II defeating Greek King Theodore Komnine, 1230. 20s, Coronation of Tsar Ivailo, 1277.

1970, Feb. *Perf. 10½*
1833 A741 1s gold & multi 5 5
1834 A741 2s gold & multi 5 5
1835 A741 3s gold & multi 5 5
1836 A741 5s gold & multi 5 5
1837 A741 8s gold & multi 14 6
1838 A741 10s gold & multi 25 10
1839 A741 13s gold & multi 35 15
1840 A741 20s gold & multi 60 20
Nos. 1833-1840 (8) 1.54 71

See also Nos. 2126-2133.

Bulgarian Pavilion, EXPO '70 — A742

1970 *Perf. 12½*
1841 A742 20s brn, sil & org 65 45

Issued to publicize EXPO '70 International Exposition, Osaka, Japan, Mar. 15-Sept. 13, 1970.

Soccer A743

Designs: Various views of soccer game.

1970, Mar. 4 Photo. *Perf. 12½*
1842 A743 1s bl & multi 5 5
1843 A743 2s rose car & multi 5 5
1844 A743 3s ultra & multi 8 5
1845 A743 5s grn & multi 12 10
1846 A743 20s emer & multi 50 10
1847 A743 40s red & multi 1.10 30
Nos. 1842-1847 (6) 1.90 65

Issued to publicize the 9th World Soccer Championships for the Jules Rimet Cup, Mexico City, May 30-June 21, 1970. See No. B37.

Lenin A744

Designs: 13s, Lenin portrait. 20s, Lenin writing.

1970, Apr. 22
1848 A744 2s vio bl & multi 5 5
1849 A744 13s brn & multi 35 10
1850 A744 20s multi 75 20

Centenary of birth of Lenin (1870-1924).

Tephrocactus Alexanderi V. Bruchii — A745

Cacti: 2s, Opuntia drummondii. 3s, Hatiora cilindrica. 5s, Gymnocalycium vatteri. 8s, Helianthо cereus grandiflorus. 10s, Neochilenia andreaeana. 13s, Peireskia vargasii v. longispina. 20s, Neobesseya rosiflora.

1970 Photo. *Perf. 12½*
1851 A745 1s multi 5 5
1852 A745 2s dk grn & multi 5 5
1853 A745 3s multi 5 5
1854 A745 5s bl & multi 10 5
1855 A745 8s brn & multi 25 5
1856 A745 10s vio bl & multi 95 20
1857 A745 13s brn red & multi 95 20
1858 A745 20s pur & multi 1.25 40
Nos. 1851-1858 (8) 3.65 1.05

Rose — A746

Designs: Various Roses.

1970, June 8 Litho. *Perf. 13½*
1859 A746 1s gray & multi 5 5
1860 A746 2s gray & multi 5 5
1861 A746 3s gray & multi 5 5
1862 A746 4s gray & multi 6 5
1863 A746 5s gray & multi 10 5
1864 A746 13s gray & multi 30 15
1865 A746 20s gray & multi 90 35
1866 A746 28s gray & multi 1.50 55
Nos. 1859-1866 (8) 3.01 1.30

Gold Bowl — A747

Designs: Various bowls and art objects from Gold Treasure of Thrace.

1970, June 15 Photo. *Perf. 12½*
1867 A747 1s blk, bl & gold 5 5
1868 A747 2s blk, lt vio & gold 5 5
1869 A747 3s blk, ver & gold 6 5
1870 A747 5s blk, yel grn & gold 10 6
1871 A747 13s blk, org & gold 70 15
1872 A747 20s blk, lil & gold 85 25
Nos. 1867-1872 (6) 1.81 61

EXPO Emblem, Rose and Bulgarian Woman — A748

Designs (EXPO Emblem and): 2s, Three women. 3s, Woman and fruit. 28s, Dancers. 40s, Mt. Fuji and pavilions.

1970, June 20
1873 A748 1s gold & multi 10 5
1874 A748 2s gold & multi 10 5
1875 A748 3s gold & multi 12 5
1876 A748 28s gold & multi 80 25

Miniature Sheet
Imperf
1877 A748 40s gold & multi 1.50 90

Issued to publicize EXPO '70 International Exposition, Osaka, Japan, Mar. 15-Sept. 13. No. 1877 contains one stamp with simulated perforations; gray margin with blue border and roses. Size: 75½x90mm.

Ivan Vasov A749

1970, Aug. 1 Photo. *Perf. 12½*
1878 A749 13s vio bl 40 10

Issued to commemorate the 120th anniversary of the birth of Ivan Vasov, author.

U.N. Emblem — A750

1970, Aug. 1
1879 A750 20s Prus bl & gold 45 15

25th anniversary of the United Nations.

George Dimitrov A751

Retriever A752

1970, Aug.
1880 A751 20s blk, gold & org 55 20

Issued to commemorate the 70th anniversary of BZNC (Bulgarian Communist Party).

1970 Photo. *Perf. 12½*

Dogs: 1s, Golden retriever (horiz.). 3s, Great Dane. 4s, Boxer. 5s, Cocker spaniel. 13s, Doberman pinscher. 20s, Scottish terrier. 28s, Russian greyhound (horiz).

1881 A752 1s multi 5 5
1882 A752 2s multi 5 5
1883 A752 3s multi 8 5
1884 A752 4s multi 10 6
1885 A752 5s multi 10 8
1886 A752 13s multi 50 15
1887 A752 20s multi 1.00 35
1888 A752 28s multi 1.50 45
Nos. 1881-1888 (8) 3.38 1.24

Volleyball A753

Designs: No. 1890, Two women players. No. 1891, Woman player. No. 1892, Man player.

1970, Sept. Photo. *Perf. 12½*
1889 A753 2s dk red brn, bl & blk 10 5
1890 A753 2s ultra, org & blk 15 5
1891 A753 20s Prus bl, yel & blk 80 20
1892 A753 20s grn, yel & blk 80 20

World Volleyball Championships.

Enrico Caruso and "I Pagliacci" by Ruggiero Leoncavallo — A754

Opera Singers and Operas: 2s, Christina Morfova and "The Bartered Bride" by Bedrich Smetana. 3s, Peter Reitchev and "Tosca" by Giacomo Puccini. 10s, Svetana Tabakova and "The Flying Dutchman" by Richard Wagner. 13s, Katia Popova and "The Masters" by Paroshkev Hadjev. 20s, Feodor Chaliapin and "Boris Godunov" by Modest Musorgski.

1970, Oct. 15 Photo. *Perf. 14*

1893 A754 1s blk & multi 8 8
1894 A754 2s blk & multi 8 8
1895 A754 3s blk & multi 8 8
1896 A754 10s blk & multi 18 12
1897 A754 13s blk & multi 25 15
1898 A754 20s blk & multi 95 25
Nos. 1893-1898 (6) 1.62 76

Issued to honor opera singers in their best roles.

Ivan Assen II Coin — A755

Coins from 14th Century with Ruler's Portrait: 2s, Theodor Svetoslav. 3s, Mikhail Chichman. 13s, Ivan Alexander and Mikhail Assen. 20s, Ivan Sratsimir. 28s, Ivan Chichman (initials).

1970, Nov. *Perf. 12½*

1899 A755 1s buff & multi 5 5
1900 A755 2s gray & multi 5 5
1901 A755 3s multi 8 5
1902 A755 13s multi 25 12
1903 A755 20s lt bl & multi 70 15
1904 A755 28s multi 90 25
Nos. 1899-1904 (6) 2.03 67

Fireman A756

Design: 3s, Fire engine.

1970 Litho. *Perf. 12½*

1905 A756 1s blk, gray & yel 5 5
1906 A756 3s blk, gray & red 10 5

Fire protection publicity.

Bicyclists A757

Congress Emblem A758

1970 Photo.

1907 A757 20s grn, yel & pink 60 15

For the 20th Bulgarian bicycle race.

1970

1908 A758 13s gold & multi 40 10

For the 7th World Congress of Sociology, Varna, Sept. 14-19.

Beethoven — A759

Friedrich Engels — A760

1970

1909 A759 28s lil rose & dk bl 75 25

Bicentenary of the birth of Ludwig van Beethoven (1770-1827), composer.

1970 Photo. *Perf. 12½*

1910 A760 13s ver, tan & brn 40 15

Sesquicentennial of the birth of Friedrich Engels (1820-1895), German socialist, collaborator of Karl Marx.

Miniature Sheets

Luna 16 A761

Design (Russian moon mission): 80s, Lunokhod 1, unmanned vehicle on moon (horiz.).

1970 Photo. *Imperf.*

1911 A761 80s plum, sil, blk & bl 2.25 2.50
1912 A761 1 l vio bl, sil & red 4.50 3.00

No. 1911 commemorates Lunokhod 1, Nov. 10-17. Size: 60x72mm. No. 1912, Luna 16 mission, Sept. 12-24. Size: 50x68mm.

Issue dates: 80s, Dec. 18; 1 lev, Nov. 10.

Snowflake A762

1970, Dec. 15 Photo. *Perf. 12½x13*

1913 A762 2s ultra & multi 8 5

New Year 1971.

Birds and Flowers A763

Folk Art: 2s, Bird and flowers. 3s, Flying birds. 5s, Birds and flowers. 13s, Sun. 20s, Tulips and pansies.

1971, Jan. 25 *Perf. 12½x13½*

1914 A763 1s multi 5 5
1915 A763 2s multi 5 5
1916 A763 3s multi 5 5
1917 A763 5s multi 5 5
1918 A763 13s multi 20 10
1919 A763 20s multi 70 15
Nos. 1914-1919 (6) 1.10 45

Spring 1971.

Girl, by Zeko Spiridonov A764

Modern Bulgarian Sculpture: 2s, Third Class (people looking through train window), by Ivan Funev. 3s, Bust of Elin Pelin, by Marko Markov. 13s, Bust of Nina, by Andrej Nikolov. 20s, Monument to P. K. Yavorov (kneeling woman), by Ivan Lazarov. 28s, Engineer, by Ivan Funev. 1l, Refugees, by Sekul Krimov (horiz.).

1971, Feb. *Perf. 12½*

1920 A764 1s gold & vio 6 6
1921 A764 2s gold & dk ol grn 6 6
1922 A764 3s gold & rose brn 10 8
1923 A764 13s gold & dk grn 35 15
1924 A764 20s gold & red brn 60 15
1925 A764 28s gold & dk brn 90 25
Nos. 1920-1925 (6) 2.07 75

Souvenir Sheet

Imperf

1926 A764 1 l gold, dk brn & buff 2.50 2.00

No. 1926 has green marginal inscription. Size: 60x72mm.

Runner A765

Design: 20s, Woman putting the shot.

1971, Mar. 13 Photo. *Perf. 12½x13*

1927 A765 2s brn & multi 10 5
1928 A765 20s dp grn, org & blk 1.25 25

2nd European Indoor Track and Field Championships.

Bulgarian Secondary School, Bolgrad — A766

Educators: 20s, Dimiter Mitev, Prince Bogoridi and Sava Radoulov.

1971, March 16 *Perf. 12½*

1929 A766 2s sil, brn & grn 5 5
1930 A766 20s sil, brn & vio 55 20

First Bulgarian secondary school, 1858, in Bolgrad, USSR.

Communards — A767

1971, Mar. 18 Photo. *Perf. 12½x13*

1931 A767 20s rose mag & blk 60 20

Centenary of the Paris Commune.

Dimitrov Facing Goering, Quotation, FIR Emblem — A768

1971, Apr. 11 *Perf. 12½*

1932 A768 2s grn, gold, blk & red 5 5
1933 A768 13s plum, gold, blk & red 70 15

International Federation of Resistance Fighters (FIR), 20th anniversary.

George S. Rakovski — A769

1971, Apr. 14

1934 A769 13s ol & blk brn 30 10

150th anniversary of birth of George S. Rakovski (1821-1867), revolutionary against Turkish rule.

Edelweiss Hotel, Borovets A770

Designs: 2s, Panorama Hotel, Pamporovo. 4s, Boats at Albena, Black Sea. 8s, Boats at Rousalka. 10s, Shtastlivetsa Hotel, Mt. Vitosha.

1971 *Perf. 13*

1935 A770 1s brt grn 5 5
1936 A770 2s ol gray 5 5
1937 A770 4s brt bl 8 5
1938 A770 8s blue 15 5
1939 A770 10s bluish grn 25 6
Nos. 1935-1939 (5) 58 26

Technological Progress — A771

Designs: 1s, Mason with banner (vert.). 13s, Two men and doves (vert.).

1971, Apr. 20 Photo. *Perf. 12½*

1940 A771 1s gold & multi 5 5
1941 A771 2s gray bl & multi 5 5
1942 A771 13s lt grn & multi 40 15

Tenth Congress of Bulgarian Communist Party.

Panayot Pipkov and Anthem A772

1971, May 20
1943 A772 13s sil, blk & brt grn 40 15

Birth centenary of Panayot Pipkov, composer.

Mammoth
A773

Prehistoric Animals: 2s, Bear (vert.). 3s, Hipparion (horse). 13s, Platybelodon. 20s, Dinotherium (vert.). 28s, Saber-tooth tiger.

1971, May 29 *Perf. 12½*
1944 A773 1s dl bl & multi 6 5
1945 A773 2s lil & multi 6 5
1946 A773 3s multi 10 8
1947 A773 13s multi 50 10
1948 A773 20s dp grn & multi 90 20
1949 A773 28s multi 1.50 30
Nos. 1944-1949 (6) 3.12 78

Khan Asparuch Crossing Danube, 679 A.D., by Boris Angelushev — A774

Historical Paintings: 3s, Reception at Trnovo, by Ilya Petrov. 5s, Chevartov's Troops at Benkovsky, by P. Morozov. 8s, Russian Gen. Gurko and People in Sofia, 1878, by D. Gudjenko. 28s, People Greeting Red Army, by S. Venov.

1971, Mar. 6 *Perf. 13½x14*
1950 A774 2s gold & multi 5 5
1951 A774 3s gold & multi 5 5
1952 A774 5s gold & multi 15 6
1953 A774 8s gold & multi 30 10
a. Souv. sheet of 4 1.50 75
1954 A774 28s gold & multi 2.50 85
Nos. 1950-1954 (5) 3.05 1.11

No. 1953a contains one each of Nos. 1950-1953. Gold decoration in gutter between stamps. Size: 137½x130mm.

In 1973, No. 1953a was surcharged 1 lev and overprinted "Visitez la Bulgarie", airline initials and emblems, and, on the 5s stamp, "Par Avion".

Freed Black, White and Yellow Men — A775

1971, May 20 Photo. *Perf. 12½*
1955 A775 13s bl, blk & yel 40 15

International Year against Racial Discrimination.

Map of Europe, Championship Emblem — A776

"XXX" Supporting Barbell — A777

1971, June 19
1956 A776 2s lt bl & multi 5 5
1957 A777 13s yel & multi 70 15

30th European Weight Lifting Championships, Sofia, June 19-27.

Facade, Old House, Koprivnica
A778

Designs: Decorated facades of various old houses in Koprivnica.

1971, July 10 Photo. *Perf. 12½*
1958 A778 1s grn & multi 5 5
1959 A778 2s brn & multi 5 5
1960 A778 6s vio & multi 10 8
1961 A778 13s dk red & multi 55 15

Frontier Guard and German Shepherd
A779

1971, July 31 *Perf. 13*
1962 A779 2s grn & ol grn 10 5

25th anniversary of the Frontier Guards.

Congress of Busludja, Bas-relief — A780

1971, July 31 *Perf. 12½*
1963 A780 2s dk red & ol grn 10 5

80th anniversary of the first Congress of the Bulgarian Social Democratic party.

Young Woman, by Ivan Nenov — A781

Paintings: 2s, Lazarova in Evening Gown, by Stefan Ivanov. 3s, Performer in Dress Suit, by Kyril Zonev. 13s, Portrait of a Woman, by Detchko Uzunov. 20s, Woman from Kalotina, by Vladimir Dimitrov. 40s, Gorjanin (Mountain Man), by Stoyan Venev.

1971, Aug. 2 *Perf. 14x13½*
1964 A781 1s grn & multi 5 5
1965 A781 2s grn & multi 5 5
1966 A781 3s grn & multi 5 5
1967 A781 13s grn & multi 35 10
1968 A781 20s grn & multi 75 35
1969 A781 40s grn & multi 1.50 55
Nos. 1964-1969 (6) 2.75 1.15

National Art Gallery.

Wrestlers
A782

Designs: 13s, Wrestlers.

1971, Aug. 27 *Perf. 12½*
1970 A782 2s grn, blk & bl 5 5
1971 A782 13s red org, blk & bl 55 10

European Wrestling Championships.

Young Workers
A783

Post Horn Emblem
A784

1971 Photo. *Perf. 13*
1972 A783 2s dk bl 10 5

25th anniversary of the Young People's Brigade.

1971, Sept. 15 *Perf. 12½*
1973 A784 20s dp grn & gold 60 20

8th meeting of postal administrations of socialist countries, Varna.

FEBS Waves Emblem — A785

1971, Sept. 20
1974 A785 13s blk, red & mar 60 20

7th Congress of European Biochemical Association (FEBS), Varna.

Statue of Republic — A786

Design: 13s, Bulgarian flag.

1971, Sept. 20 *Perf. 13x12½*
1975 A786 2s gold, yel & dk red 5 5
1976 A786 13s gold, grn & red 45 20

25th anniversary of the Bulgarian People's Republic.

Cross Country Skiing and Winter Olympics Emblem
A787

Sport and Winter Olympics Emblem: 2s, Downhill skiing. 3s, Ski jump and skiing. 4s, Women's figure skating. 13s, Ice hockey. 28s, Slalom skiing. 1l, Torch and stadium.

1971, Sept. 25 *Perf. 12½*
1977 A787 1s dk grn & multi 6 5
1978 A787 2s vio bl & multi 6 5
1979 A787 3s ultra & multi 6 5
1980 A787 4s dp plum & multi 10 5
1981 A787 13s dk bl & multi 60 10
1982 A787 28s multi 1.35 35
Nos. 1977-1982 (6) 2.23 65

Miniature Sheet

Imperf
1983 A787 1l multi 4.50 2.75

11th Winter Olympic Games, Sapporo, Japan, Feb. 3-13, 1972.
Size of No. 1983: 70x80mm.

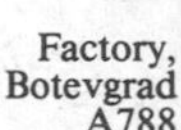

Factory, Botevgrad
A788

Industrial Buildings: 2s, Petro-chemical works, Pleven (vert.). 10s, Chemical works, Vratsa. 13s, Maritsa-Istok Power Station, Dimitrovgrad. 40s, Electronics works, Sofia.

1971 Photo. *Perf. 13*
1984 A788 1s violet 5 5
1985 A788 2s orange 6 5
1986 A788 10s dp pur 20 8
1987 A788 13s lil rose 25 10
1988 A788 40s dp brn 75 15
Nos. 1984-1988 (5) 1.31 43

UNESCO Emblem
A789

1971, Nov. 4 *Perf. 12½*
1989 A789 20s lt bl, blk, gold & red 60 20

25th anniv. of UNESCO.

Soccer Player, by Kyril Zonev (1896-1971)
A790

Paintings by Kyril Zonev: 2s, Landscape (horiz.). 3s, Self-portrait. 13s, Lilies. 20s, Landscape (horiz.). 40s, Portrait of a Young Woman.

1971, Nov. 10 *Perf. 11x12*
1990 A790 1s gold & multi 8 8
1991 A790 2s gold & multi 8 8
1992 A790 3s gold & multi 8 8
1993 A790 13s gold & multi 25 10
1994 A790 20s gold & multi 1.00 30
1995 A790 40s gold & multi 1.40 45
Nos. 1990-1995 (6) 2.89 1.09

Salyut Space Station — A791

Canceled-to-order stamps are often from remainders. Most collectors of canceled stamps prefer postally used specimens.

Astronauts Dobrovolsky, Volkov and Patsayev — A792

Designs: 13s, Soyuz 11 space transport. 40s, Salyut and Soyuz 11 joined.

1971, Dec. 20 *Perf. 12½*

1996 A791 2s dk grn, yel & red 5 5
1997 A791 13s multi 25 15
1998 A791 40s dk bl & multi 1.25 35

Souvenir Sheet

Imperf

1999 A792 80s multi 2.25 1.75

Salyut-Soyuz 11 space mission, and in memory of the Russian astronauts Lt. Col. Georgi T. Dobrovolsky, Vladislav N. Volkov and Victor I. Patsayev, who died during the Soyuz 11 space mission, June 6-30, 1971. Size of No. 1999: 70x73½mm.

Oil Tanker Vihren — A793

1972, Jan. 8 **Photo.** *Perf. 12½*

2000 A793 18s lil rose, vio & blk 70 20

Bulgarian shipbuilding industry.

Goce Delchev A794

Portraits: 5s, Jan Sandanski. 13s, Damjan Gruev.

1972, Jan. 21 **Photo.** *Perf. 12½*

2001 A794 2s brick red & blk 5 5
2002 A794 5s grn & blk 12 6
2003 A794 13s lem & blk 40 15

Centenary of the births of Bulgarian patriots Delchev (1872-1903) and Sandanski, and of Macedonian Gruev (1871-1906).

Gymnast with Ball, Medals — A795

Designs: 18s, Gymnast with hoop, and medals. 70s, Gymnasts with hoops, and medals.

1972, Feb. 10

2004 A795 13s grn, brn, red & gold 65 15
2005 A795 18s brn, grn, red & gold 85 25

Miniature Sheet

Imperf

2006 A795 70s gold, brn, grn & red 3.00 2.00

5th World Women's Gymnastic Championships, Havana, Cuba. Size of No. 2006: 61½x73mm.

View of Melnik, by Petar Mladenov — A796

Paintings from National Art Gallery: 2s, Plower, by Pencho Georgiev. 3s, Funeral, by Alexander Djendov. 13s, Husband and Wife, by Vladimir Dimitrov. 20s, Nursing Mother, by Nenko Balkanski. 40s, Paisii Hilendarski Writing History, by Koio Denchev.

1972, Feb. 20 *Perf. 13½x14*

2007 A796 1s grn & multi 6 5
2008 A796 2s grn & multi 6 5
2009 A796 3s grn & multi 10 8
2010 A796 13s grn & multi 40 12
2011 A796 20s grn & multi 70 20
2012 A796 40s grn & multi 1.25 35
Nos. 2007-2012 (6) 2.57 85

Paintings from National Art Gallery.

Worker — A797

Singing Harvesters A798

1972, Mar. 7 *Perf. 12½*

2013 A797 13s sil & multi 30 10

7th Bulgarian Trade Union Congress.

Perf. 11½x12, 12x11½

1972, Mar. 31

Designs: Paintings by Vladimir Dimitrov.

2014 A798 1s *shown* 8 5
2015 A798 2s *Harvester* 8 5
2016 A798 3s *Women Diggers* 12 10
2017 A798 13s *Fabric Dyers* 35 10
2018 A798 20s *"My Mother"* 75 15
2019 A798 40s *Self-portrait* 1.50 35
Nos. 2014-2019 (6) 2.88 80

90th anniversary of birth of Vladimir Dimitrov, painter.

"Your Heart is your Health" — A799

St. Mark's Basilica and Wave — A800

1972, Apr. 30 *Perf. 12½*

2020 A799 13s red, blk & grn 60 15

World Health Day.

1972, May 6 *Perf. 13x12½*

Design: 13s, Ca' D'Oro and wave.

2021 A800 2s ol grn, bl grn & lt bl 5 5
2022 A800 13s red brn, vio & lt grn 60 15

UNESCO campaign to save Venice.

Dimitrov in Print Shop, 1901 — A801

Designs: Life of George Dimitrov.

1972, May 8 **Photo.** *Perf. 12½*

Gold and Multicolored

2023 A801 1s *shown* 6 5
2024 A801 2s *Dimitrov as leader of 1923 uprising* 6 5
2025 A801 3s *Leipzig trial, 1933* 6 5
2026 A801 5s *as Communist functionary, 1935* 10 6
2027 A801 13s *as leader and teacher, 1948* 15 10
2028 A801 18s *addressing youth rally, 1948* 65 15
2029 A801 28s *with Pioneers, 1948* 1.00 25
2030 A801 40s *Mausoleum* 1.50 50
2031 A801 80s *Portrait* 2.50 70
a. Souvenir sheet 6.00 4.00
Nos. 2023-2031 (9) 6.08 1.91

90th anniversary of the birth of George Dimitrov (1882-1949), communist leader.

No. 2031a contains one imperf. stamp similar to No. 2031, but in different colors. Gold marginal inscription. Size: 86x82mm.

Price, #2031 imperf. in slightly changed colors, $4.

Paisii Hilendarski — A802

Design: 2s, Flame and quotation.

1972, May 12

2032 A802 2s gold, grn & brn 5 5
2033 A802 13s gold, grn & brn 40 15

250th anniversary of the birth of the monk Paisii Hilendarski (1722-1798), writer of Bulgarian-Slavic history.

Foreign postal stationery (stamped envelopes, postal cards and air letter sheets) lies beyond the scope of this Catalogue, which is limited to adhesive postage stamps.

Canoeing, Motion and Olympic Emblems — A803

Designs (Motion and Olympic emblems and): 2s, Gymnastics. 3s, Swimming, women's. 13s, Volleyball. 18s, Jumping. 40s, Wrestling. 80s, Stadium and sports.

1972, June 25

Figures of Athletes in Silver & Black

2034 A803 1s lt bl & multi 5 5
2035 A803 2s org & multi 8 8
2036 A803 3s multi 10 10
2037 A803 13s yel & multi 20 10
2038 A803 18s multi 55 25
2039 A803 40s pink & multi 1.60 40
Nos. 2034-2039 (6) 2.58 98

Miniature Sheet

Imperf

Size: 62x60mm.

2040 A803 80s gold, ver & yel 2.50 1.50

20th Olympic Games, Munich, Aug. 26-Sept. 11.

Angel Kunchev A804

1972, June 30 **Photo.** *Perf. 12½*

2041 A804 2s mag, dk pur & gold 10 5

Centenary of the death of Angel Kunchev, patriot and revolutionist.

Zlatni Pyassatsi — A805

1972, Sept. 16

2042 A805 1s *shown* 5 5
2043 A805 2s *Drouzhba* 5 5
2044 A805 3s *Slunchev Bryag* 8 5
2045 A805 13s *Primorsko* 18 10
2046 A805 28s *Roussalka* 65 30
2047 A805 40s *Albena* 1.00 35
Nos. 2042-2047 (6) 2.01 90

Bulgarian Black Sea resorts.

Bronze Medal, Olympic Emblems, Canoeing A806

Designs (Olympic Emblems and): 2s, Silver medal, broad jump. 3s, Gold medal, boxing. 18s, Gold medal, wrestling. 40s, Gold medal, weight lifting.

1972, Sept. 29

2048 A806 1s Prus bl & multi 5 5
2049 A806 2s dk grn & multi 5 5
2050 A806 3s org brn & multi 5 5
2051 A806 18s ol & multi 50 20
2052 A806 40s multi 1.00 35
Nos. 2048-2052 (5) 1.65 70

Bulgarian victories in 20th Olympic Games.

Stoj Dimitrov — A807

Resistance Fighters: 2s, Cvetko Radoinov. 3s, Bogdan Stivrodski. 5s, Mirko Laiev. 13s, Nedelyo Nikolov.

1972, Oct. 30 Photo. *Perf. 12½x13*

2053 A807 1s ol & multi 5 5
2054 A807 2s multi 5 5
2055 A807 3s multi 6 6
2056 A807 5s multi 10 8
2057 A807 13s multi 25 10
Nos. 2053-2057 (5) 51 34

"50 Years USSR" A808

1972, Nov. 3 Photo. *Perf. 12½x13*

2058 A808 13s gold, red & yel 25 10

50th anniversary of Soviet Union.

Turk's-cap Lily — A809

Protected Plants: 2s, Gentian. 3s, Sea daffodil. 4s, Globe flower. 18s, Primrose. 23s, Pulsatilla vernalis. 40s, Snake's-head.

1972, Nov. 25 *Perf. 12½*

Flowers in Natural Colors

2059 A809 1s ol bis 5 5
2060 A809 2s ol bis 5 5
2061 A809 3s ol bis 8 5
2062 A809 4s ol bis 10 8
2063 A809 18s ol bis 25 10
2064 A809 23s ol bis 70 25
2065 A809 40s ol bis 1.35 45
Nos. 2059-2065 (7) 2.58 1.03

No. 2052 Overprinted in Red СВЕТОВЕН ПЪРВЕНЕЦ

1972, Nov. 27

2066 A806 40s multi 1.10 35

Bulgarian weight lifting Olympic gold medalists.

Dobri Chintulov A810

1972, Nov. 28 Photo. *Perf. 12½*

2067 A810 2s gray, dk & lt grn 20 5

Dobri Chintulov, writer, 150th birth anniversary.

Forehead Band — A811

Designs (14th-19th Century Jewelry): 2s, Belt buckles. 3s, Amulet. 8s, Pendant. 23s, Earrings. 40s, Necklace.

1972, Dec. 27 Engr. *Perf. 14x13½*

2068 A811 1s red brn & blk 5 5
2069 A811 2s emer & blk 5 5
2070 A811 3s Prus bl & blk 6 5
2071 A811 8s dk red & blk 16 12
2072 A811 23s red org & multi 60 25
2073 A811 40s vio & blk 1.35 55
Nos. 2068-2073 (6) 2.27 1.07

Skin Divers A812

Designs: 2s, Shelf-1 underwater house and divers. 18s, Diving bell and diver (vert.). 40s, Elevation balloon and divers (vert.).

1973, Jan. 24 Photo. *Perf. 12½*

2074 A812 1s lt bl, blk & yel 5 5
2075 A812 2s blk, bl & org yel 5 5
2076 A812 18s blk, Prus bl & dl org 60 20
2077 A812 40s blk, ultra & bis 1.35 45

Bulgarian deep-sea research in the Black Sea.

A souvenir sheet of four contains imperf. 20s stamps in designs of Nos. 2074-2077 with colors changed. Gray marginal inscriptions. Size: 118x99mm. Sold for 1 lev. Price $4 unused, $2.50 canceled.

Execution of Levski, by Boris Angelushev A813

Design: 20s, Vassil Levski, by Georgi Danchev.

1973, Feb. 19 *Perf. 13x12½*

2078 A813 2s dl rose & Prus grn 5 5
2079 A813 20s dl grn & brn 1.00 25

Centenary of the death of Vassil Levski (1837-1873), patriot, executed by the Turks.

Kukersky Mask, Elhovo Region A814

Nicolaus Copernicus A815

Kukersky Masks at pre-Spring Festival: 2s, Breznik. 3s, Hissar. 13s, Radomir. 20s, Karnobat. 40s, Pernik.

1973, Feb. 26 *Perf. 12½*

2080 A814 1s dp rose & multi 8 8
2081 A814 2s emer & multi 8 8
2082 A814 3s vio & multi 8 8
2083 A814 13s multi 40 15
2084 A814 20s multi 45 20
2085 A814 40s multi 2.50 1.75
Nos. 2080-2085 (6) 3.59 2.34

1973, Mar. 21 Photo. *Perf. 12½*

2086 A815 28s ocher, blk & cl 1.40 60

500th anniversary of the birth of Nicolaus Copernicus (1473-1543), Polish astronomer.

Vietnamese Worker and Rainbow — A816

1973, Apr. 16

2087 A816 18s lt bl & multi 40 15

Peace in Viet Nam.

Poppy — A817

Designs: Wild flowers.

1973, May Photo. *Perf. 13*

2088 A817 1s *shown* 5 5
2089 A817 2s *Daisy* 6 5
2090 A817 3s *Peony* 7 5
2091 A817 13s *Centaury* 25 10
2092 A817 18s *Corn cockle* 2.50 1.65
2093 A817 28s *Ranunculus* 60 35
Nos. 2088-2093 (6) 3.53 2.25

Christo Botev — A818

1973, June 2

2094 A818 2s pale grn, buff & brn 6 5
2095 A818 18s pale brn, gray & grn 70 45

125th anniversary of the birth of Christo Botev (1848-1876), poet.

"Suffering Worker" — A819

Design: 1s, Asen Halachev and revolutionists.

1973, June 6 Photo. *Perf. 13*

2096 A819 1s gold, red & blk 5 5
2097 A819 2s gold, org & dk brn 5 5

50th anniversary of Pleven uprising.

Muskrat A820

Perf. 12½x13, 13x12½

1973, June 29 Litho.

2098 A820 1s *shown* 5 5
2099 A820 2s *Racoon* 5 5
2100 A820 3s *Mouflon (vert.)* 6 5
2101 A820 12s *Fallow deer (vert.)* 20 15
2102 A820 18s *European bison* 45 20
2103 A820 40s *Elk* 2.25 1.50
Nos. 2098-2103 (6) 3.06 2.00

Aleksandr Stamboliski — A821

1973, June 14 Photo. *Perf. 12½*

2104 A821 18s dp brn & org 50 30
a. 18s org 2.50 1.25

50th anniversary of the death of Aleksandr Stamboliski (1879-1923), leader of Peasants' Party and premier.

Trade Union Emblem — A822

Stylized Sun, Olympic Rings — A823

1973, Aug. 27 Photo. *Perf. 12½*

2105 A822 2s yel & multi 8 5

8th Congress of World Federation of Trade Unions, Varna, Oct. 15-22.

1973, Aug. 29 *Perf. 13*

Designs: 28s, Emblem of Bulgarian Olympic Committee and Olympic rings. 80s, Soccer, emblems of Innsbruck and Montreal 1976 Games (horiz.).

2106 A823 13s multi 65 45
2107 A823 28s multi 1.10 55

Souvenir Sheet

2108 A823 80s multi 4.00 2.50

Olympic Congress, Varna. No. 2108 contains one stamp. Blue and gray green margin shows emblems of various Olympic committees and games. Size: 60x77½ mm. It also exists imperf.; also with violet margin, imperf.

Revolutionists with Communist Flag — A824

Designs: 5s, Revolutionists on flatcar blocking train. 13s, Raising Communist flag (vert.). 18s, George Dimitrov and Vassil Kolarov.

1973, Sept. 22 Photo. *Perf. 12½*

2109 A824 2s mag & multi 5 5
2110 A824 5s mag & multi 8 6
2111 A824 13s mag & multi 35 15
2112 A824 18s mag & multi 90 50

50th anniversary of the September Revolution.

Warrior Saint A825

Murals from Boyana Church: 1s, Tsar Kaloyan and 2s, his wife Dessislava. 5s, "St. Wystratti." 10s, Tsar Constantine Assen. 13s, Deacon Laurentius. 18s, Virgin Mary. 20s, St. Ephraim. 28s, Jesus. 80s, Jesus in the Temple (horiz.).

1973, Sept. 24

2113 A825 1s gold & multi 10 8
2114 A825 2s gold & multi 10 8
2115 A825 3s gold & multi 10 8
2116 A825 5s gold & multi 10 8
2117 A825 10s gold & multi 25 10
2118 A825 13s gold & multi 35 10
2119 A825 18s gold & multi 50 25
2120 A825 20s gold & multi 70 30
2121 A825 28s gold & multi 2.50 60
Nos. 2113-2121 (9) 4.70 1.67

Miniature Sheet

Imperf

2122 A825 80s gold & multi 5.50 3.50

No. 2122 contains one stamp with simulated perforations. Gold margin with view of Boyana Church. Size: 56x76½mm.

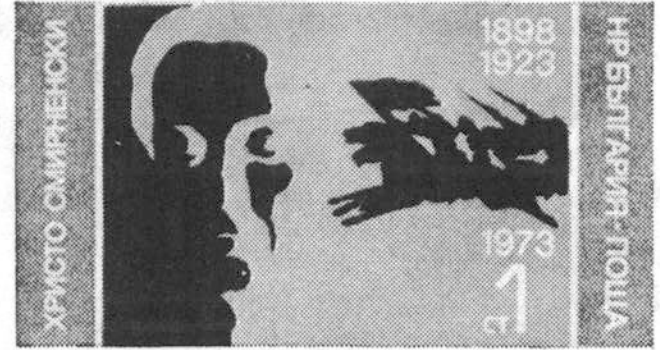

Christo Smirnenski — A826

1973, Sept. 29 Photo. *Perf. 12½*

2123 A826 1s multi 5 5
2124 A826 2s vio bl & multi 20 5

75th anniversary of the birth of Christo Smirnenski (1898-1923), poet.

Human Rights Flame — A827

1973, Oct. 10

2125 A827 13s dk bl, red & gold 30 20

25th anniversary of the Universal Declaration of Human Rights.

Type of 1970

History of Bulgaria: 1s, Tsar Theodor Svetoslav receiving Byzantine envoys. 2s, Tsar Mihail Shishman's army in battle with Byzantines. 3s, Tsar Ivan Alexander's victory at Russocastro. 4s, Patriarch Euthimius at the defense of Turnovo. 5s, Tsar Ivan Shishman leading horsemen against the Turks. 13s, Momchil attacking Turks at Umour. 18s, Tsar Ivan Stratsimir meeting King Sigismund's crusaders. 28s, The Boyars Balik, Theodor and Dobrotitsa, meeting ship bringing envoys from Anne of Savoy.

1973, Oct. 23 *Perf. 13*

Silver and Black Vignettes

2126 A741 1s ol bis 8 8
2127 A741 2s Prus bl 8 8
2128 A741 3s lilac 10 8
2129 A741 4s green 10 8
2130 A741 5s violet 10 8
2131 A741 13s org & brn 20 10
2132 A741 18s ol grn 35 15
2133 A741 28s yel brn & brn 1.00 45
Nos. 2126-2133 (8) 2.01 1.10

Fin Class — A828

1973, Oct. 29 Litho. *Perf. 13*

Sailboats: 2s, Flying Dutchman. 3s, Soling class. 13s, Tempest class. 20s, Class 470. 40s, Tornado class.

2134 A828 1s ultra & multi 8 8
2135 A828 2s grn & multi 8 8
2136 A828 3s dk bl & multi 10 8
2137 A828 13s dl vio & multi 30 10
2138 A828 20s gray bl & multi 65 25
2139 A828 40s multi 2.75 1.50
Nos. 2134-2139 (6) 3.96 2.09

Price, set imperf. in changed colors, $12.50.

Village, by Bencho Obreshkov — A829

Paintings: 2s, Mother and Child, by Stoyan Venev. 3s, Rest (woman), by Tsenko Boyadjiev. 13s, Flowers in Vase, by Sirak Skitnik. 18s, Meri Kuneva (portrait), by Ilya Petrov. 40s, Winter in Plovdiv, by Zlatyu Boyadjiev. 13s, 18s, 40s, vertical.

Perf. 12½x12, 12x12½

1973, Nov. 10

2140 A829 1s gold & multi 8 8
2141 A829 2s gold & multi 8 8
2142 A829 3s gold & multi 8 8
2143 A829 13s gold & multi 20 18
2144 A829 18s gold & multi 40 30
2145 A829 40s gold & multi 2.00 1.10
Nos. 2140-2145 (6) 2.84 1.82

Souvenir Sheet

Paintings by Stanislav Dospevski: No. 2146a, Domnica Lambreva. No. 2146b, Self-portrait. Both vertical.

2146 A829 Sheet of 2 4.00 2.50
a. 50s gold & multi 1.00 75
b. 50s gold & multi 1.00 75

Bulgarian paintings. No. 2146 commemorates the 150th birth anniv. of Stanislav Dospevski; gold margin and brown inscription. Size: 100x96mm.

Souvenir Sheet

Soccer A830

1973, Dec. 10 Photo. *Perf. 13*

2147 A830 28s multi 6.00 3.50

No. 2147 sold for 1l. Size: 65x100mm. Exists overprinted for Argentina 78.

Angel and Ornaments A831

Designs: 1s, Attendant facing right. 2s, Passover table and lamb. 3s, Attendant facing left. 8s, Abraham and ornaments. 13s, Adam and Eve. 28s, Expulsion from Garden of Eden.

1974, Jan. 21 Photo. *Perf. 13*

2148 A831 1s fawn, yel & brn 10 8
2149 A831 2s fawn, yel & brn 10 8
2150 A831 3s fawn, yel & brn 10 8
2151 A831 5s sl grn & yel 10 8
2152 A831 8s sl grn & yel 28 10
2153 A831 13s lt brn, yel & ol 40 20
2154 A831 28s lt brn, yel & ol 75 30
Nos. 2148-2154 (7) 1.83 92

Woodcarvings from Rozhen Monastery, 19th century. Nos. 2148-2150, 2151-2152, 2153-2154 printed se-tenant.

Lenin, by N. Mirtchev — A832

Design: 18s, Lenin visiting Workers, by W. A. Serov.

1974, Jan. 28 Litho. *Perf. 12½x12*

2155 A832 2s ocher & multi 5 5
2156 A832 18s ocher & multi 45 20

50th anniversary of the death of Lenin.

1974, Jan. 28

Design: Demeter Blagoev at Rally, by G. Kowachev.

2157 A832 2s multi 8 5

50th anniversary of the death of Demeter Blagoev, founder of Bulgarian Communist Party.

Catalogue prices for unused stamps up to mid-1953 are for hinged copies matching the condition specified in this volume's introduction.

Sheep A833

Designs: Domestic animals.

1974, Feb. 1 Photo. *Perf. 13*

2158 A833 1s *shown* 8 8
2159 A833 2s *Goat* 8 8
2160 A833 3s *Pig* 8 8
2161 A833 5s *Cow* 12 8
2162 A833 13s *Buffalo cow* 30 10
2163 A833 20s *Horse* 80 25
Nos. 2158-2163 (6) 1.46 67

Comecon Emblem A83

1974, Feb. 11 Photo. *Perf. 13*

2164 A834 13s sil & multi 40 10

25th anniversary of the Council of Mutual Economic Assistance.

Soccer — A835

Designs: Various soccer action scenes.

1974, Mar. Photo. *Perf. 13*

2165 A835 1s dl grn & multi 8 8
2166 A835 2s brt grn & multi 8 8
2167 A835 3s sl grn & multi 8 8
2168 A835 13s ol & multi 10 10
2169 A835 28s bl grn & multi 60 25
2170 A835 40s emer & multi 1.35 40
Nos. 2165-2170 (6) 2.29 99

Souvenir Sheet

2171 A835 1 l grn & multi 4.00 2.50

World Soccer Championship, Munich, June 13-July 7. No. 2171 contains one stamp. Red margin with emblem and inscription in white; soccer cup in yellow and gold. Size: 67x78½mm. No. 2171 exists imperf.

Salt Production A836

Children's Paintings: 1s, Cosmic Research for Peaceful Purposes. 3s, Fire Dancers. 28s, Russian-Bulgarian Friendship (train and children). 60s, Spring (birds).

1974, Apr. 15 Photo. *Perf. 13*

2172 A836 1s lil & multi 8 8
2173 A836 2s lt grn & multi 8 8
2174 A836 3s bl & multi 15 8
2175 A836 28s sl & multi 1.75 1.00

Souvenir Sheet

Imperf

2176 A836 60s bl & multi 2.50 1.75

Third World Youth Philatelic Exhibition, Sofia, May 23-30. No. 2176 contains one stamp with simulated perforations, rose and lilac border. Size: 70x70mm.

Folk Singers — A837

Designs: 2s, Folk dancers (men). 3s, Bagpiper and drummer. 5s, Wrestlers. 13s, Runners (women). 18s, Gymnast.

1974, Apr. 25 *Perf. 13*

2178 A837 1s ver & multi 5 5
2179 A837 2s org brn & multi 5 5
2180 A837 3s brn red & multi 5 5
2181 A837 5s bl & multi 20 5
2182 A837 13s ultra & multi 1.10 35
2183 A837 18s vio bl & multi 65 20
Nos. 2178-2183 (6) 2.10 75

4th Amateur Arts and Sports Festival

Aster A838

Flowers: 2s, Petunia. 3s, Fuchsia. 18s, Tulip. 20s, Carnation. 28s, Pansy. 80s, Sunflower.

1974, May **Photo.** *Perf. 13*

2184 A838 1s grn & multi 5 5
2185 A838 2s vio bl & multi 5 5
2186 A838 3s ol & multi 5 5
2187 A838 18s brn & multi 22 10
2188 A838 20s multi 50 20
2189 A838 28s dl bl & multi 1.25 55
Nos. 2184-2189 (6) 2.12 1.00

Souvenir Sheet

2190 A838 80s multi 2.50 1.25

No. 2190 contains one stamp. Deep ultramarine margin with white inscription and flower design. Size: 78x60mm.

Automobiles and Emblems — A839

1974, May 15 **Photo.** *Perf. 13*

2191 A839 13s multi 35 15

International Automobile Federation (FIA) Spring Congress, Sofia, May 20-24.

Old and New Buildings, UNESCO Emblem A840

1974, June 15

2192 A840 18s multi 35 15

UNESCO Executive Council, 94th Session, Varna.

Certain countries cancel stamps in full sheets and sell them (usually with gum) for less than face value. Dealers generally sell "CTO".

Postrider A841

Designs: 18s, First Bulgarian mail coach. 28s, UPU Monument, Bern.

1974, Aug. 5

2193 A841 2s ocher, blk & vio 5 5
2194 A841 18s ocher, blk & grn 40 20

Souvenir Sheet

2195 A841 28s ocher, blk & bl 2.50 1.25

Centenary of Universal Postal Union.

No. 2195 contains one stamp, multicolored marginal inscription. Size: 79x58mm. Exists imperf.

Pioneer and Komsomol Girl — A842

"Bulgarian Communist Party" — A843

Designs: 2s, Pioneer and birds. 60s, Emblem with portrait of George Dimitrov.

1974, Aug. 12

2196 A842 1s grn & multi 5 5
2197 A842 2s bl & multi 5 5

Souvenir Sheet

2198 A842 60s red & multi 2.50 1.75

30th anniversary of Dimitrov Pioneer Organization, Septemvrilche. No. 2198 contains one stamp, gold margin with black inscription. Size: 60x83mm.

1974, Aug. 20

Symbolic Designs: 2s, Russian liberators. 5s, Industrialization. 13s, Advanced agriculture and husbandry. 18s, Scientific and technical progress.

2199 A843 1s bl gray & multi 5 5
2200 A843 2s bl gray & multi 5 5
2201 A843 5s gray & multi 8 5
2202 A843 13s gray & multi 25 10
2203 A843 18s gray & multi 35 15
Nos. 2199-2203 (5) 78 40

30th anniversary of the People's Republic.

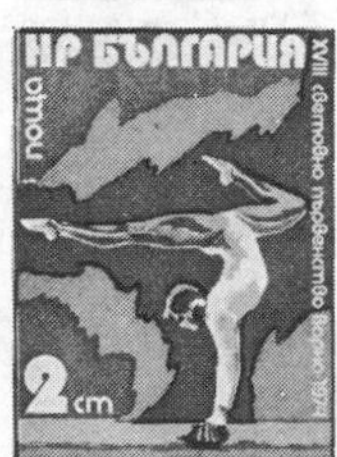
Gymnast on Parallel Bars — A844

Design: 13s, Gymnast on vaulting horse.

1974, Oct. 18 **Photo.** *Perf. 13*

2204 A844 2s multi 8 5
2205 A844 13s multi 35 20

18th Gymnastic Championships, Varna.

Souvenir Sheet

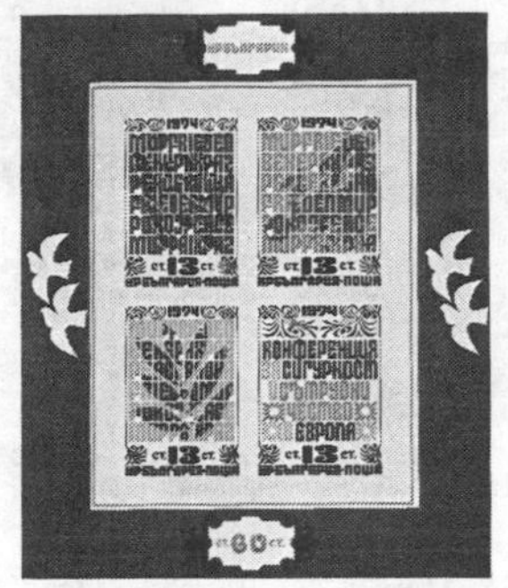
Symbols of Peace — A845

1974, Oct. 29 **Photo.** *Perf. 13*

2206 A845 Sheet of 4 2.75 1.50
a. 13s *Doves* 25 15
b. 13s *Map of Europe* 25 15
c. 13s *Olive Branch* 25 15
d. 13s *Inscription* 25 15

1974 European Peace Conference. "Peace" in various languages written on Nos. 2206a-2206c. No. 2206 has yellow, brown and lilac margin. Size: 97½x117mm. Sold for 60s. Exists imperf.

Nib and Envelope — A846

1974, Nov. 20

2207 A846 2s yel, blk & grn 10 5

Introduction of postal zone numbers.

Flowers A847

1974, Dec. 5

2208 A847 2s emer & multi 8 5

St. Todor, Ceramic Icon A848

Apricot Blossoms A849

Designs: 2s, Medallion, Veliko Turnovo. 3s, Carved capital. 5s, Silver bowl. 8s, Goblet. 13s, Lion's head finial. 18s, Gold plate with Cross. 28s, Breastplate with eagle.

1974, Dec. 18 **Photo.** *Perf. 13*

2209 A848 1s org & multi 5 5
2210 A848 2s pink & multi 5 5
2211 A848 3s bl & multi 5 5
2212 A848 5s lt vio & multi 8 5
2213 A848 8s brn & multi 15 8
2214 A848 13s multi 28 10
2215 A848 18s red & multi 40 15
2216 A848 28s ultra & multi 1.25 55
Nos. 2209-2216 (8) 2.31 1.08

Art works from 9th-12th centuries.

1975, Jan. **Photo.** *Perf. 13*

Fruit Tree Blossoms: 2s, Apple. 3s, Cherry. 19s, Pear. 28s, Peach.

2217 A849 1s org & multi 5 5
2218 A849 2s multi 5 5
2219 A849 3s car & multi 5 5
2220 A849 19s lem & multi 40 15
2221 A849 28s ver & multi 1.00 30
Nos. 2217-2221 (5) 1.55 60

Tree and Book A850

1975, Mar. 25 **Photo.** *Perf. 13*

2222 A850 2s gold & multi 12 5

Forestry High School, 50th anniversary.

Souvenir Sheet

Farmers' Activities (Woodcuts) — A851

1975, Mar. 25

2223 A851 Sheet of 4 1.25 75
a. 2s *Farmer with ax and flag*
b. 5s *Farmers on guard*
c. 13s *Dancing couple*
d. 18s *Woman picking fruit*

Bulgarian Agrarian Peoples Union, 75th anniversary. No. 2223 has orange and green margin. Size: 102x95mm.

Michelangelo, Self-portrait A852

Designs: 13s, Night (horiz.). 18s, Day (horiz.). Both designs after sculptures from Medici Tomb, Florence.

1975

2224 A852 2s plum & dk bl 5 5
2225 A852 13s vio bl & plum 25 10
2226 A852 18s brn & grn 55 18

Souvenir Sheet

2227 A852 2s ol & red 2.00 2.00

500th birth anniversary of Michelangelo Buonarotti (1475-1564), Italian sculptor, painter and architect. No. 2227 issued to publicize ARPHILA 75 International Philatelic Exhibition, Paris, June 6-16. Marginal inscriptions and border in gold, red and green. Sheet sold for 60s. Size: 69x83mm.

Issue dates: Nos. 2224-2226, Mar. 28. No. 2227, Mar. 31.

Souvenir Sheet

Spain No. 1 and Espana 75 Emblem A853

1975, Apr. 4
2228 A853 40s multi 4.50 3.00

Espana 75 International Philatelic Exhibition, Madrid, Apr. 4-13. No. 2228 contains one stamp; bright ultramarine margin with white design and inscription, bister post horn. Size: 70x102mm.

Gabrov Costume — A854

Regional Costumes: 3s, Trnsk. 5s, Vidin. 13s, Gocedelchev. 18s, Risen.

1975, Apr. Photo. *Perf. 13*
2229 A854 2s bl & multi 5 5
2230 A854 3s emer & multi 5 5
2231 A854 5s org & multi 12 8
2232 A854 13s ol & multi 35 12
2233 A854 18s multi 75 30
Nos. 2229-2233 (5) 1.32 60

Red Star and Arrow — A855

Standard Kilogram and Meter — A856

Design: 13s, Dove and broken sword.

1975, May 9
2234 A855 2s red, blk & gold 5 5
2235 A855 13s bl, blk & gold 40 18

Victory over Fascism, 30th anniversary.

1975, May 9 *Perf. 13x13½*
2236 A856 13s sil, lil & blk 30 10

Centenary of International Meter Convention, Paris, 1875.

IWY Emblem, Woman's Head — A857

Ivan Vasov — A858

1975, May 20 Photo. *Perf. 13*
2237 A857 13s multi 30 10

International Women's Year 1975.

1975, May

Design: 13s, Ivan Vasov, seated.

2238 A858 2s buff & multi 5 5
2239 A858 13s gray & multi 30 10

125th birth anniversary of Ivan Vasov.

Nikolov and Sava Kokarechkov — A859

Designs: 2s, Mitko Palaouzov and Ivan Vassilev. 5s, Nicolas Nakev and Stevtcho Kraychev. 13s, Ivanka Pachkoulova and Detelina Mintcheva.

1975, May 30
2240 A859 1s multi 5 5
2241 A859 2s multi 5 5
2242 A859 5s multi 10 5
2243 A859 13s multi 30 15

Teen-age resistance fighters, killed during World War II.

Mother Feeding Child, by John E. Millais A861

Etchings: 2s, The Dead Daughter, by Goya. 3s, Reunion, by Beshkov. 13s, Seated Nude, by Renoir. 20s, Man in a Fur Hat, by Rembrandt. 40s, The Dream, by Daumier (horiz.). 1l, Temptation, by Dürer.

Photogravure and Engraved

1975, Aug. *Perf. 12x11½, 11½x12*
2248 A861 1s yel grn & multi 5 5
2249 A861 2s org & multi 5 5
2250 A861 3s lil & multi 5 5
2251 A861 13s lt bl & multi 30 10
2252 A861 20s ocher & multi 45 25
2253 A861 40s rose & multi 1.40 40
Nos. 2248-2253 (6) 2.30 90

Souvenir Sheet

2254 A861 1l emer & multi 2.50 1.75

World Graphics Exhibition. No. 2254 contains one stamp; gray green marginal inscription and border. Size: 80x95mm.

Letter "Z" from 12th Century Manuscript A862

Whimsical Globe — A863

Initials from Illuminated Manuscripts: 2s, "B" from 17th century prayerbook. 3s, "V" from 16th century Bouhovo Gospel. 8s, "B" from 14th century Turnovo collection. 13s, "V" from Dobreisho's Gospel, 13th century. 18s, "E" from 11th century Enina book of the Apostles.

1975, Aug. Litho. *Perf. 11½*
2255 A862 1s multi 5 5
2256 A862 2s multi 5 5
2257 A862 3s multi 5 5
2258 A862 8s multi 15 5
2259 A862 13s multi 25 10
2260 A862 18s multi 65 18
Nos. 2255-2260 (6) 1.20 48

Bulgarian art.

1975, Aug. Photo. *Perf. 13*
2261 A863 2s multi 12 5

Festival of Humor and Satire.

Lifeboat Dju IV and Gibraltar-Cuba Route — A864

1975, Aug. 5 Photo. *Perf. 13*
2262 A864 13s multi 25 15

Oceanexpo 75, First International Ocean Exhibition, Okinawa, July 20, 1975-Jan. 18, 1976.

Sts. Cyril and Methodius A865

Sts. Constantine and Helena A866

St. Sophia Church, Sofia, Woodcut by V. Zahriev — A867

1975, Aug. 21
2263 A865 2s ver, yel & brn 5 5
2264 A866 13s grn, yel & brn 30 15

Souvenir Sheet

2265 A867 50s org & multi 2.00 1.25

Balkanphila V, philatelic exhibition, Sofia, Sept. 27-Oct. 5. No. 2265 has bluish gray and orange margin. Size: 89x85mm.

Peace Dove and Map of Europe — A868

1975, Nov. Photo. *Perf. 13*
2266 A868 18s ultra, rose & yel 55 30

European Security and Cooperation Conference, Helsinki, Finland, July 30-Aug. 1. No. 2266 printed in sheets of 5 stamps and 4 labels, arranged checkerwise.

Acherontia Atropos A869

Designs: Moths.

1975 Photo. *Perf. 13*
2267 A869 1s *shown* 5 5
2268 A869 2s *Daphnis nerii* 5 5
2269 A869 3s *Smerinthus ocellata* 5 5
2270 A869 10s *Deilephila nicea* 20 8
2271 A869 13s *Choerocampa elpenor* 25 10
2272 A869 18s *Macroglossum fuciformis* 90 30
Nos. 2267-2272 (6) 1.50 63

Soccer Player — A870

1975, Sept. 21
2273 A870 2s multi 12 5

8th Inter-Toto (soccer pool) Soccer Championships, Varna.

Constantine's Rebellion Against the Turks, 1403 — A871

Designs (Woodcuts): 2s, Campaign of Vladislav III, 1443-1444. 3s, Battles of Turnovo, 1598 and 1686. 10s, Battle of Liprovsko, 1688. 13s, Guerrillas, 17th century. 18s, Return of exiled peasants.

1975, Nov. 27 Photo. *Perf. 13*

2274 A871 1s bis, grn & blk 5 5
2275 A871 2s bl, car & blk 5 5
2276 A871 3s yel, lil & blk 8 6
2277 A871 10s org, grn & blk 20 8
2278 A871 13s grn, lil & blk 25 10
2279 A871 18s pink, grn & blk 55 25
Nos. 2274-2279 (6) 1.18 59

Bulgarian history.

Red Cross and First Aid — A872

Design: 13s, Red Cross and dove.

1975, Dec. 1

2280 A872 2s red brn, red & blk 5 5
2281 A872 13s bl grn, red & blk 25 10

90th anniversary of Bulgarian Red Cross.

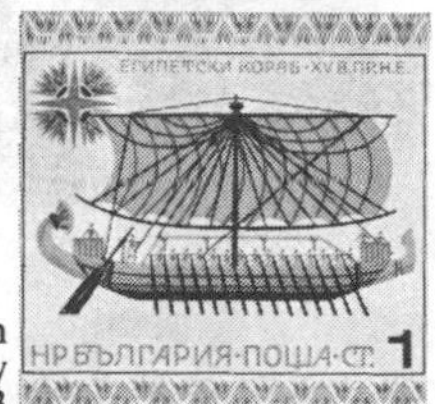

Egyptian Galley A873

Historic Ships: 2s, Phoenician galley. 3s, Greek trireme. 5s, Roman galley. 13s, Viking longship. 18s, Venetian galley.

1975, Dec. 15 Photo. *Perf. 13*

2282 A873 1s multi 5 5
2283 A873 2s multi 5 5
2284 A873 3s multi 5 6
2285 A873 5s multi 12 6
2286 A873 13s multi 35 15
2287 A873 18s multi 65 25
Nos. 2282-2287 (6) 1.27 62

See Nos. 2431-2436, 2700-2705.

Souvenir Sheet

Ethnographical Museum, Plovdiv — A874

1975, Dec. 17

2288 A874 Sheet of 3 4.25 4.00
a. 80s grn, yel & dk brn 1.25 1.00

European Architectural Heritage Year. No. 2288 contains 3 stamps and 3 labels showing stylized bird. Olive margin and inscription. Size: 160x96½mm.

Dobri Hristov — A875

1975, Dec. *Perf. 13*

2289 A875 5s brt grn, yel & brn 12 5

Dobri Hristov, musician, birth centenary.

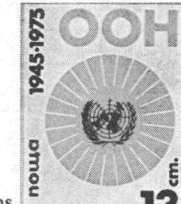

United Nations Emblem — A876

1975, Dec.

2290 A876 13s gold, blk & mag 25 10

United Nations, 30th anniversary.

Glass Ornaments — A877

Design: 13s, Peace dove, decorated ornament.

1975, Dec. 22 Photo. *Perf. 13*

2291 A877 2s brt vio & multi 5 5
2292 A877 13s gray & multi 25 10

New Year 1976.

Downhill Skiing — A878

Designs (Winter Olympic Games Emblem and): 2s, Cross country skier (vert.). 3s, Ski jump. 13s, Biathlon (vert.). 18s, Ice hockey (vert.). 23s, Speed skating (vert.). 80s, Figure skating, pair (vert.).

1976, Jan. 30 *Perf. 13½*

2293 A878 1s sil & multi 5 5
2294 A878 2s sil & multi 5 5
2295 A878 3s sil & multi 5 5
2296 A878 13s sil & multi 25 10
2297 A878 18s sil & multi 35 20
2298 A878 23s sil & multi 85 40
Nos. 2293-2298 (6) 1.60 85

Souvenir Sheet

2299 A878 80s sil & multi 2.25 1.50

12th Winter Olympic Games, Innsbruck, Austria, Feb. 4-15. No. 2299 has light blue margin with white inscription. Size: 71x80mm.

Electric Streetcar, Sofia, 1976 — A879

Design: 13s, Streetcar and trailer, 1901.

1976, Jan. 12 Photo. *Perf. 13½x13*

2300 A879 2s gray & multi 5 5
2301 A879 13s gray & multi 25 10

75th anniversary of Sofia streetcars.

Stylized Bird — A880

Designs: 5s, Dates "1976" and "1956" and star. 13s, Hammer and sickle. 50s, George Dimitrov.

1976, Mar. 1 *Perf. 13*

2302 A880 2s gold & multi 5 5
2303 A880 5s gold & multi 15 5
2304 A880 13s gold & multi 25 10

Souvenir Sheet

2305 A880 50s gold & multi 1.25 70

11th Bulgarian Communist Party Congress. No. 2305 contains one stamp; crimson margin. Size: 56x64mm.

A. G. Bell and Telephone, 1876 A881

1976, Mar. 10

2306 A881 18s dk brn, yel & ocher 40 20

Centenary of first telephone call by Alexander Graham Bell, Mar. 10, 1876.

Mute Swan — A882

Waterfowl: 2s, Ruddy shelduck. 3s, Common shelduck. 5s, Garganey teal. 13s, Mallard. 18s, Red-crested pochard.

1976, Mar. 27 Litho. *Perf. 11½*

2307 A882 1s vio bl & multi 5 5
2308 A882 2s yel grn & multi 5 5
2309 A882 3s bl & multi 5 5
2310 A882 5s multi 20 5
2311 A882 13s pur & multi 55 15
2312 A882 18s grn & multi 80 15
Nos. 2307-2312 (6) 1.70 50

Априлското въстание 1876-1976
НР БЪЛГАРИЯ
поща 1 ст

Guerrillas — A883

Designs (Woodcuts by Stoev): 2s, Peasants with rifle and proclamation. 5s, Raina Knaginia with horse and guerrilla. 13s, Insurgents with cherrywood cannon.

1976, Apr. 5 Photo. *Perf. 13*

2313 A883 1s multi 5 5
2314 A883 2s multi 5 5
2315 A883 5s multi 10 5
2316 A883 13s multi 25 10

Centenary of uprising against Turkey.

Guard and Dog A884

Design: 13s, Men on horseback, observation tower.

1976, May 15

2317 A884 2s multi 5 5
2318 A884 13s multi 25 12

30th anniversary of Border Guards.

Construction Worker — A885

1976, May 20

2319 A885 2s multi 12 5

Young Workers Brigade, 30th anniversary.

Busludja, Bas-relief A886
AES Complex A887

Design: 5s, Memorial building.

1976, May 28 Photo. *Perf. 13*

2320 A886 2s grn & multi 5 5
2321 A886 5s vio bl & multi 12 5

First Congress of Bulgarian Social Democratic Party, 85th anniversary.

1976, Apr. 7

Designs: 8s, Factory. 10s, Apartment houses. 13s, Refinery. 20s, Hydroelectric station.

2322 A887 5s green 10 5
2323 A887 8s maroon 14 5
2324 A887 10s green 18 8
2325 A887 13s violet 30 12
2326 A887 20s brt grn 40 16
Nos. 2322-2326 (5) 1.12 46

Five-year plan accomplishments.

Children Playing Around Table — A888

Designs (Kindergarten Children): 2s, with doll carriage and hobby horse. 5s, playing ball. 23s, in costume.

1976, June 15

2327 A888 1s grn & multi 5 5
2328 A888 2s yel & multi 5 5
2329 A888 5s lil & multi 10 5
2330 A888 23s rose & multi 50 20

Demeter Blagoev — A889

Christo Botev — A890

1976, May 28

2331 A889 13s bluish blk, red & gold 30 15

Demeter Blagoev (1856-1924), writer, political leader, 120th birth anniversary.

1976, May 25

2332 A890 13s ocher & sl grn 30 15

Christo Botev (1848-1876), poet, death centenary. Printed se-tenant with yellow green and ocher label, inscribed with poem.

Boxing, Montreal Olympic Emblem — A891

Belt Buckle — A892

Designs (Montreal Olympic Emblem): 1s, Wrestling (horiz.). 3s, 1l, Weight lifting. 13s, One-man kayak. 18s, Woman gymnast. 28s, Woman diver. 40s, Woman runner.

1976, June 25

2333	A891	1s org & multi	5	5
2334	A891	2s multi	5	5
2335	A891	3s lil & multi	5	5
2336	A891	13s multi	25	8
2337	A891	18s multi	35	15
2338	A891	28s bl & multi	50	25
2339	A891	40s lem & multi	1.00	45
		Nos. 2333-2339 (7)	2.25	1.08

Souvenir Sheet

2340 A891 1 l org & multi 2.25 1.50

21st Olympic Games, Montreal, Canada, July 17-Aug. 1. No. 2340 contains one stamp; multicolored margin. Size: 69x79mm.

1976, July 30 Photo. *Perf. 13*

Thracian Art (8th-4th Centuries): 2s, Brooch. 3s, Mirror handle. 5s, Helmet cheek cover. 13s, Gold ornament. 18s, Lion's head (harness decoration). 20s, Knee guard. 28s, Jeweled pendant.

2341	A892	1s brn & multi	5	5
2342	A892	2s bl & multi	5	5
2343	A892	3s multi	5	5
2344	A892	5s cl & multi	10	5
2345	A892	13s pur & multi	25	12
2346	A892	18s multi	35	15
2347	A892	20s multi	45	16
2348	A892	28s multi	65	25
		Nos. 2341-2348 (8)	1.95	88

Composite of Bulgarian Stamp Designs A893

1976, June 5

2349 A893 50s red & multi 1.50 1.00

International Federation of Philately (F.I.P.), 50th anniversary and 12th Congress. No. 2349 has multicolored margin. Size: 73x102mm.

Partisans at Night, by Ilya Petrov — A894

Paintings: 5s, Old Town, by Tsanko Lavenov. 13s, Seated Woman, by Petrov (vert.). 18s, Seated Boy, by Petrov (vert.). 28s, Old Plovdiv, by Lavenov (vert.). 80s, Ilya Petrov, self-portrait (vert.).

1976, Aug. 11 Photo. *Perf. 14*

2350	A894	2s multi	5	5
2351	A894	5s multi	10	5
2352	A894	13s ultra & multi	30	12
2353	A894	18s multi	40	15
2354	A894	28s multi	60	25
		Nos. 2350-2354 (5)	1.45	62

Souvenir Sheet

2354A A894 80s multi 1.50 1.40

No. 2354A has green border. Size: 60x83mm.

Souvenir Sheet

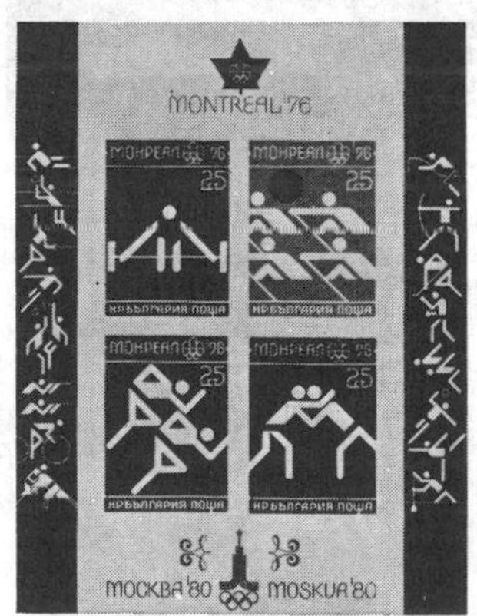
Olympic Sports and Emblems — A895

1976, Sept. 6 Photo. *Perf. 13*

2355	A895	Sheet of 4	1.75	1.40
a.		25s *Weight Lifting*	40	25
b.		25s *Rowing*	40	25
c.		25s *Running*	40	25
d.		25s *Wrestling*	40	25

Medalists, 21st Olympic Games, Montreal. No. 2355 has gold margin, green and red inscription. Size: 98x117mm.

Souvenir Sheet

Fresco and UNESCO Emblem — A896

1976, Dec. 3

2356 A896 50s red & multi 1.50 80

U.N. Educational, Scientific and Cultural Organization, 30th anniversary. No. 2356 has brown and orange margin. Size: 71x80mm.

"The Pianist" by Jendov — A897

Fish and Hook — A898

Designs (Caricatures by Jendov): 5s, Imperialist "Trick or Treat." 13s, The Leader, 1931.

1976, Sept. 30 Photo. *Perf. 13*

2357	A897	2s grn & multi	5	5
2358	A897	5s pur & multi	10	5
2359	A897	13s mag & multi	30	12

Alex Jendov (1901-1953), caricaturist.

1976, Sept. 21 Photo. *Perf. 13*

2360 A898 5s multi 18 5

World Sport Fishing Congress, Varna.

St. Theodore A899

Frescoes: 3s, St. Paul. 5s, St. Joachim. 13s, Melchizedek. 19s, St. Porphyrius. 28s, Queen. 1 l, The Last Supper.

1976, Oct. 4 Litho. *Perf. 12x12½*

2361	A899	2s gold & multi	5	5
2362	A899	3s gold & multi	5	5
2363	A899	5s gold & multi	10	5
2364	A899	13s gold & multi	45	12
2365	A899	19s gold & multi	50	20
2366	A899	28s gold & multi	90	30
		Nos. 2361-2366 (6)	2.05	77

Miniature Sheet

Perf. 12

2367 A899 1l gold & multi 2.25 1.40

Frescoes from Zemen Monastery, 14th century. No. 2367 has gold and vermilion border. Size: 60x75mm.

Document A900

1976, Oct. 5

2368 A900 5s multi 15 5

State Archives, 25th anniversary.

Cinquefoil A901

Designs: 1s, Chestnut. 5s, Holly. 8s, Yew. 13s, Daphne. 23s, Judas tree.

1976, Oct. 14 Photo. *Perf. 13*

2369	A901	1s car & grn	5	5
2370	A901	2s grn & multi	5	5
2371	A901	5s multi	10	5
2372	A901	8s multi	18	5
2373	A901	13s brn & multi	35	12
2374	A901	23s multi	70	25
		Nos. 2369-2374 (6)	1.43	57

Dimitri Polianov — A902

1976, Nov. 19

2375 A902 2s dk pur & ocher 12 5

Dimitri Polianov (1876-1953), poet, birth centenary.

Christo Botev, by Zlatyu Boyadjiev A903

Paintings: 2s, Partisan Carrying Cherrywood Cannon, by Ilya Petrov. 3s, "Necklace of Immortality" (man's portrait), by Detchko Uzunov. 13s, "April 1876," by Georgi Popoff. 18s, Partisans, by Stoyan Venev. 60s, The Oath, by Svetlin Ruseff.

1976, Dec. 8

2376	A903	1s bis & multi	5	5
2377	A903	2s bis & multi	5	5
2378	A903	3s bis & multi	5	5
2379	A903	13s bis & multi	30	10
2380	A903	18s bis & multi	45	15
		Nos. 2376-2380 (5)	90	40

Souvenir Sheet

Imperf

2381 A903 60s gold & multi 1.40 80

Uprising against Turkish rule, centenary. No. 2381 contains one stamp; gold border. Size: 44x82mm.

Canceled-to-order stamps are often from remainders. Most collectors of canceled stamps prefer postally used specimens.

"Pollution" and Tree — A904

Design: 18s, "Pollution" obscuring sun.

1976, Nov. 10 *Perf. 13*

2382 A904 2s ultra & multi 5 5
2383 A904 18s bl & multi 40 15

Protection of the environment.

Congress Emblem — A904a

Flags — A904b

1976, Nov. 28 **Photo.** *Perf. 13*

2384 A904a 2s multi 5 5
2384A A904b 13s multi 25 15

33rd BSIS Congress (Bulgarian Socialist Party).

Tobacco Workers, by Stajkov A905

Paintings by Stajkov: 2s, View of Melnik. 13s, Shipbuilder.

1976, Dec. 16 **Photo.** *Perf. 13*

2385 A905 1s multi 5 5
2386 A905 2s multi 5 5
2387 A905 13s multi 40 15

Veselin Stajkov (1906-1970), painter, 70th birth anniversary.

Snowflake — A906

1976, Dec. 20

2388 A906 2s sil & multi 12 5

New Year 1977.

Prices of premium quality never hinged stamps will be in excess of catalogue price.

Zachary Stoyanov — A907

1976, Dec. 30

2389 A907 2s multi 12 5

Zachary Stoyanov (1851-1889), historian, 125th birth anniversary.

Bronze Coin of Septimus Severus — A908

Roman Coins: 2s, 13s, 18s, Bronze coins of Caracalla (diff.). 23s, Copper coin of Diocletian.

1977, Jan. 28 **Photo.** *Perf. 13½x13*

2390 A908 1s gold & multi 5 5
2391 A908 2s gold & multi 5 5
2392 A908 13s gold & multi 30 12
2393 A908 18s gold & multi 40 20
2394 A908 23s gold & multi 70 30
Nos. 2390-2394 (5) 1.50 72

Coins struck in Serdica (modern Sofia).

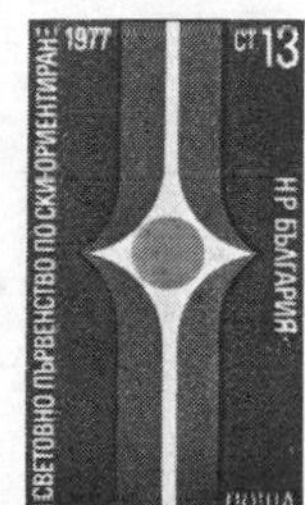

Skis and Compass A909

Tourist Congress Emblem A910

1977, Feb. 14 *Perf. 13*

2395 A909 13s ultra, red & lt bl 30 15

2nd World Ski Orienteering Championships.

1977, Feb. 24 **Photo.** *Perf. 13*

2396 A910 2s multi 12 5

5th Congress of Bulgarian Tourist Organization.

Bellflower — A911

Designs: Various bellflowers.

1977, Mar. 2

2397 A911 1s yel & multi 5 5
2398 A911 2s rose & multi 5 5
2399 A911 3s lt bl & multi 5 5
2400 A911 13s multi 30 12
2401 A911 43s yel & multi 1.00 40
Nos. 2397-2401 (5) 1.45 67

Vasil Kolarov — A912

Union Congress Emblem — A913

1977, Mar. 21 **Photo.** *Perf. 13*

2402 A912 2s bl & blk 12 5

Vasil Kolarov (1877-1950), politician.

1977, Mar. 25

2403 A913 2s multi 12 5

8th Bulgarian Trade Union Congress, Apr. 4-7.

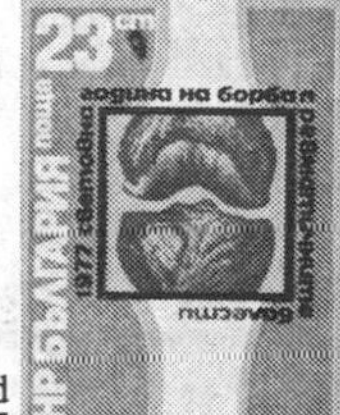

Wolf A914

Wild Animals: 2s, Red fox. 10s, Weasel. 13s, European wildcat. 23s, Jackal.

1977, May 16 **Litho.** *Perf. 12½x12*

2404 A914 1s multi 5 5
2405 A914 2s multi 5 5
2406 A914 10s multi 22 6
2407 A914 13s multi 40 10
2408 A914 23s multi 70 25
Nos. 2404-2408 (5) 1.42 51

Diseased Knee — A915

1977, Mar. 31 **Photo.** *Perf. 13*

2409 A915 23s multi 45 20

World Rheumatism Year.

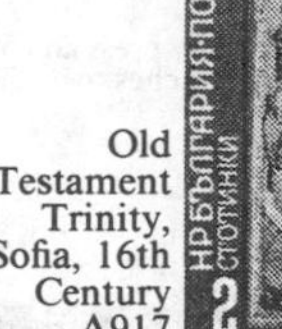

Writers' Congress Emblem A916

1977, June 7

2410 A916 23s lt bl & yel grn 80 30

International Writers Congress: "Peace, the Hope of the Planet." No. 2410 printed in sheets of 8 stamps and 4 labels with signatures of participating writers.

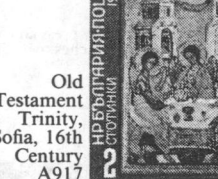

Old Testament Trinity, Sofia, 16th Century A917

Icons: 1s, St. Nicholas, Nessebur, 13th century. 3s, Annunciation, Royal Gates, Veliko Turnovo, 16th century. 5s, Christ Enthroned, Nessebur, 17th century. 13s, St. Nicholas, Elena, 18th century. 23s, Presentation of the Virgin, Rila Monastery, 18th century. 35s, Virgin and Child, Tryavna, 19th century. 40s, St. Demetrius on Horseback, Provadia, 19th century. 1l, The 12 Holidays, Rila Monastery, 18th century.

1977, May 10 **Photo.** *Perf. 13*

2411 A917 1s blk & multi 5 5
2412 A917 2s grn & multi 5 5
2413 A917 3s brn & multi 5 5
2414 A917 5s bl & multi 10 5
2415 A917 13s ol & multi 28 14
2416 A917 23s mar & multi 50 20
2417 A917 35s grn & multi 75 35
2418 A917 40s dp ultra & multi 1.00 55
Nos. 2411-2418 (8) 2.78 1.44

Miniature Sheet

Imperf

2419 A917 1 l gold & multi 2.75 1.75

Bulgarian icons. No. 2419 has decorative orange border. Size: 101x100mm.

Souvenir Sheet

St. Cyril A918

1977, June 7 **Photo.** *Perf. 13*

2420 A918 1 l gold & multi 2.50 1.50

1150th anniversary of the birth of St. Cyril (827-869), reputed inventor of Cyrillic alphabet. No. 2420 has violet blue and gold margin showing ancient Cyrillic writing. Size: 103x87mm.

Congress Emblem — A919

1977, May 9

2421 A919 2s red, gold & grn 12 5

13th Komsomol Congress.

Newspaper Masthead — A920

1977, June 3 Photo. *Perf. 13*
2422 A920 2s multi 12 5

Centenary of Bulgarian daily press and 50th anniversary of Rabotnichesko Delo newspaper.

Patriotic Front Emblem — A921

Weight Lifting — A922

1977, May 26
2423 A921 2s gold & multi 12 5

8th Congress of Patriotic Front.

1977, June 15
2424 A922 13s dp brn & multi 20 12

European Youth Weight Lifting Championships, Sofia, June.

Women Basketball Players — A923

1977, June 15 *Perf. 13*
2425 A923 23s multi 50 25

7th European Women's Basketball Championships.

Wrestling — A924

Designs (Games' Emblem and): 13s, Running. 23s, Basketball. 43s, Women's gymnastics.

1977, Apr. 15
2426 A924 2s multi 5 5
2427 A924 13s multi 30 12
2428 A924 23s multi 55 18
2429 A924 43s multi 1.00 40

UNIVERSIADE '77, University Games, Sofia, Aug. 18-27.

TV Tower, Berlin — A925

1977, Aug. 12 Litho. *Perf. 13*
2430 A925 25s bl & dk bl 60 25

SOZPHILEX 77 Philatelic Exhibition, Berlin, Aug. 19-28.

Ship Type of 1975

Historic Ships: 1s, Hansa cog. 2s, Santa Maria, caravelle. 3s, Golden Hind, frigate. 12s, Santa Catherina, carrack. 13s, La Corone, galleon. 43s, Mediterranean galleass.

1977, Aug. 29 Photo. *Perf. 13*
2431 A873 1s multi 5 5
2432 A873 2s multi 5 5
2433 A873 3s multi 5 5
2434 A873 12s multi 30 6
2435 A873 13s multi 30 10
2436 A873 43s multi 1.25 40
Nos. 2431-2436 (6) 2.00 71

Ivan Vasov National Theater A926

Buildings, Sofia: 13s, Party Headquarters. 23s, House of the People's Army. 30s, Clement Ochrida University. 80s, National Gallery. 1 l, National Assembly.

1977, Aug. 30 Photo. *Perf. 13*
2437 A926 12s red, *gray* 28 8
2438 A926 13s red brn, *gray* 28 10
2439 A926 23s bl, *gray* 50 18
2440 A926 30s ol, *gray* 65 25
2441 A926 80s vio, *gray* 1.75 70
2442 A926 1 l cl, *gray* 2.25 85
Nos. 2437-2442 (6) 5.71 2.16

Map of Europe A927

1977 June 10
2443 A927 23s brn, bl & grn 50 25

21st Congress of the European Organization for Quality Control, Varna.

Union of Earth and Water, by Rubens A928

Rubens Paintings: 23s, Venus and Adonis. 40s, Pastoral Scene (man and woman). 1 l, Portrait of a Lady in Waiting.

1977, Sept. 23 Litho. *Perf. 12*
2444 A928 13s gold & multi 30 10
2445 A928 23s gold & multi 45 18
2446 A928 40s gold & multi 80 35

Souvenir Sheet

2447 A928 1 l gold & multi 2.00 1.50

Peter Paul Rubens (1577-1640), 400th birth anniversary. No. 2447 has gold border. Size: 72x88mm.

George Dimitrov A929

1977, June 17 Photo. *Perf. 13*
2448 A929 13s red & dp cl 30 12

George Dimitrov (1882-1947), first Prime Minister of Bulgaria.

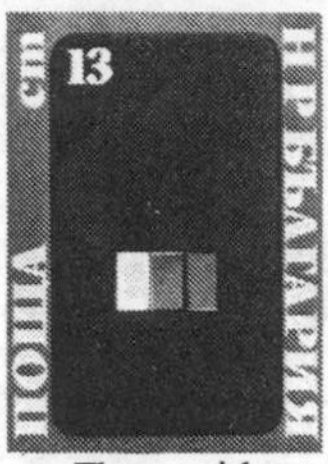

Flame with Star — A930

Smart Pete on Donkey, by Ilya Beshkov — A931

1977, May 17
2449 A930 13s gold & multi 30 12

3rd Bulgarian Culture Congress.

1977, May 19
2450 A931 2s multi 12 5

11th National Festival of Humor and Satire, Gabrovo.

Elin Pelin — A932

13th Canoe World Championships — A933

Albena, Black Sea A933a

Dr. Pirogov — A934

Writers: 2s, Pelin (Dimitur Ivanov Stojanov, (1877-1949), 5s Peju K. Jaworov (1878-1914). Artists: 13s, Boris Angelushev (1902-1966), 23s, Ceno Todorov (Ceno Todorov Dikov, 1877-1953). Each printed with label showing scenes from authors' works or illustrations by the artists.

1977, Aug. 26 Photo. *Perf. 13*
2451 A932 2s gold & brn 5 5
2452 A932 5s gold & gray grn 10 5
2453 A932 13s gold & cl 30 10
2454 A932 23s gold & bl 65 18

1977, Sept. 1 Photo. *Perf. 13*
2455 A933 2s shown 5 5
2456 A933 23s 2-man canoe 45 18

1977, Oct. 5 Photo. *Perf. 13*
2456A A933a 35s shown 85 30
2456B A933a 43s Rila Monastery 1.00 35

Sheet contains 4 each plus label.

1977, Oct. 14 Photo. *Perf. 13*
2457 A934 13s ol, ocher & brn 30 12

Centenary of visit by Russian physician N. J. Pirogov during war of liberation from Turkey.

Peace Decree, 1917 A935

Old Soldier with Grandchild A936

Designs: 13s, Lenin, 1917. 23s, "1917" as a flame.

1977, Oct. 21
2458 A935 2s blk, buff & red 5 5
2459 A935 13s multi 25 10
2460 A935 23s multi 45 18

60th anniversary of Russian October Revolution.

1977, Sept. 30

Designs (Festival Posters): 13s, "The Bugler." 23s, Liberation Monument, Sofia (detail). 25s, Samara flag.

2461 A936 2s multi 5 5
2462 A936 13s multi 30 10
2463 A936 23s multi 50 18
2464 A936 25s multi 60 25

Liberation from Turkish rule, centenary.

Souvenir Sheet

Games' and Sports Emblems — A937

1977, Aug. 10 Photo. *Perf. 13½x13*
2465 A937 1 l multi 2.25 1.25

University Games '77, Sofia. No. 2465 has multicolored margin. Size: 83x75mm.

Conference Building — A938

1977, Sept. 12 *Perf. 13½*
2466 A938 23s multi 50 25

64th Interparliamentary Union Conference, Sofia.

Ornament A940

Design: 13s, Different ornament.

1977, Dec. 1
2468 A940 2s gold & multi 5 5
2469 A940 13s sil & multi 25 12

New Year 1978.

Railroad Bridge — A941

1977, Nov. 9
2470 A941 13s grn, yel & gray 35 15

Transport Organization, 50th anniversary.

Petko Ratchev Slaveikov — A942

1977, Nov. 15
2471 A942 8s gold & vio brn 20 5

Petko Ratchev Slaveikov (1827-95), poet, birth sesquicentennial. No. 2471 printed in sheets of 8 stamps and 8 labels in 4 alternating vertical rows. Pink and black label shows woman rocking cradle.

Soccer Player — A943

Design: 23s, Soccer player and Games' emblem. 50s, Soccer players.

1978, Jan. 30 **Photo.** *Perf. 13*
2472 A943 13s multi 25 10
2473 A943 23s multi 50 18

Souvenir Sheet

2474 A943 50s ultra & multi 1.50 1.00

11th World Cup Soccer Championship, Argentina, June 1-25.

No. 2474 contains one stamp; cup and Argentina '78 emblem in margin. Size: 75x62mm.

Todor Zhivkov and Leonid I. Brezhnev — A944

Ostankino Tower, Moscow, Bulgarian Post Emblem — A945

1977, Sept. 7 **Photo.** *Perf. 13*
2475 A944 18s gold, car & brn 35 18

Bulgarian-Soviet Friendship. No. 2475 issued in sheets of 3 stamps and 3 labels.

1978, Mar. 1
2476 A945 13s multi 25 10

20th anniversary of the Comecon Postal Organization (Council of Mutual Economic Assistance).

Leo Tolstoy — A946

Shipka Pass Monument A947

Portraits: 5s, Fedor Dostoevski. 13s, Ivan Sergeevich Turgenev. 23s, Vasili Vasilievich Vershchagin. 25s, Giuseppe Garibaldi. 35s, Victor Hugo.

1978, Mar. 28 **Photo.** *Perf. 13*
2477 A946 2s yel & dk grn 5 5
2478 A946 5s lem & brn 10 5
2479 A946 13s tan & sl grn 30 10
2480 A946 23s gray & vio brn 55 12
2481 A946 25s yel grn & blk 60 15
2482 A946 35s lt bl & vio bl 1.10 40
Nos. 2477-2482 (6) 2.70 87

Souvenir Sheet

2483 A947 50s multi 1.25 60

Centenary of Bulgaria's liberation from Ottoman rule. No. 2483 has yellow ornaments in margin. Size: 55x73mm.

Burgarian and Russian Colors A948

1978, Mar. 18
2484 A948 2s multi 12 5

30th anniversary of Russo-Bulgarian cooperation.

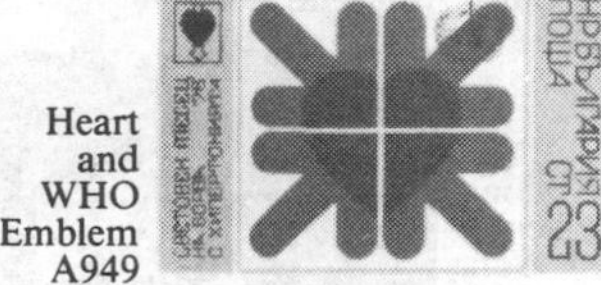
Heart and WHO Emblem A949

1978, May 12
2485 A949 23s gray, red & org 50 18

World Health Day, fight against hypertension.

Goddess A950

Ceramics (2nd-4th Centuries) and Exhibition Emblem: 5s, Mask of bearded man. 13s, Vase. 23s, Vase. 35s, Head of Silenus. 53s, Cock.

1978, Apr. 26
2486 A950 2s grn & multi 5 5
2487 A950 5s multi 10 5
2488 A950 13s multi 28 12
2489 A950 23s multi 50 25
2490 A950 35s multi 75 35
2491 A950 53s car & multi 1.25 50
Nos. 2486-2491 (6) 2.93 1.32

Philaserdica Philatelic Exhibition.

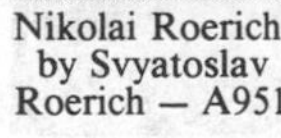

Nikolai Roerich, by Svyatoslav Roerich — A951

"Mind and Matter," by Andrei Nikolov — A952

1978, Apr. 5
2492 A951 8s multi 15 6
2493 A952 13s multi 25 12

Nikolai K. Roerich (1874-1947) and Andrei Nikolov (1878-1959), artists.

Bulgarian Flag and Red Star — A953

1978, Apr. 18
2494 A953 2s vio bl & multi 12 5

Burgarian Communist Party Congress.

Young Man, by Albrecht Dürer A954

Paintings: 23s, Bathsheba at Fountain, by Rubens. 25s, Portrait of a Man, by Hans Holbein the Younger. 35s, Rembrandt and Saskia, by Rembrandt. 43s, Lady in Mourning, by Tintoretto. 60s, Old Man with Beard, by Rembrandt. 80s, Knight in Armor, by Van Dyck.

1978, June 19 **Photo.** *Perf. 13*
2495 A954 13s multi 25 8
2496 A954 23s multi 45 10
2497 A954 25s multi 50 15
2498 A954 35s multi 70 18
2499 A954 43s multi 85 30
2500 A954 60s multi 1.25 40
2501 A954 80s multi 1.60 55
Nos. 2495-2501 (7) 5.60 1.76

Dresden Art Gallery paintings.

Doves and Festival Emblem — A955

1978, May 31
2502 A955 13s multi 25 12

11th World Youth Festival, Havana, July 28-Aug. 5.

Fritillaria Stribrnyi — A956

Rare Flowers: 2s, Fritillaria drenovskyi. 3s, Lilium rhodopaeum. 13s, Tulipa urumoffii. 23s, Lilium jankae. 43s, Tulipa rhodopaea.

1978, June 27
2503 A956 1s multi 5 5
2504 A956 2s multi 5 5
2505 A956 3s multi 10 5
2506 A956 13s multi 30 10
2507 A956 23s multi 50 18
2508 A956 43s multi 1.00 40
Nos. 2503-2508 (6) 2.00 83

Yacht Cor Caroli and Map of Voyage A957

1978, May 19 **Photo.** *Perf. 13*
2509 A957 23s multi 50 25

First Bulgarian around-the-world voyage, Capt. Georgi Georgiev, Dec. 20, 1976-Dec. 20, 1977.

Market, by Naiden Petkov — A958

Views of Sofia: 5s, Street, by Emil Stoichev. 13s, Street, by Boris Ivanov. 23s, Tolbukhin Boulevard, by Nikola Tanev. 35s, National Theater, by Nikola Petrov. 53s, Market, by Anton Mitov.

1978, Aug. 28 Litho. ***Perf. 12½x12***

2510 A958 2s multi	5	5
2511 A958 5s multi	10	5
2512 A958 13s multi	25	10
2513 A958 23s multi	45	15
2514 A958 35s multi	75	25
2515 A958 53s multi	1.25	40
Nos. 2510-2515 (6)	2.85	1.00

Miniature Sheet

Sleeping Venus, by Giorgione — A959

1978, Aug. 7 Photo. ***Imperf.***

2516 A959 1 l multi 2.75 1.00

No. 2516 has light green decorative margin. Size: 71x71mm.

View of Varna — A960

1978, July 13 Photo. ***Perf. 13***

2517 A960 13s multi 30 15

63rd Esperanto Congress, Varna, July 29-Aug. 5.

Black Woodpecker A961

Woodpeckers: 2s, Syrian. 3s, Three-toed. 13s, Middle spotted. 23s, Lesser spotted. 43s, Green

1978, Sept. 1

2518 A961 1s multi	5	5
2519 A961 2s multi	5	5
2520 A961 3s multi	5	5
2521 A961 13s multi	30	10
2522 A961 23s multi	50	18
2523 A961 43s multi	1.25	35
Nos. 2518-2523 (6)	2.20	78

"September 1923" — A962

1978, Sept. 5

2524 A962 2s red & brn 12 5

55th anniversary of September uprising.

Souvenir Sheet

National Theater, Sofia A963

Photogravure and Engraved

1978, Sept. 1 ***Perf. 12x11½***

2525 Sheet of 4	3.75	1.50
a. A963 40s *shown*	90	25
b. A963 40s *Festival Hall, Sofia*	90	25
c. A963 40s *Charles Bridge, Prague*	90	25
d. A963 40s *Belvedere Palace, Prague*	90	25

PRAGA '78 and PHILASERDICA '79 Philatelic Exhibitions. No. 2525 has pink marginal inscriptions and PRAGA and PHILASERDICA emblems. Size: 153x112mm.

Black and White Hands, Human Rights Emblem — A964

1978, Oct. 3 Photo. ***Perf. 13x13½***

2526 A964 13s multi 25 12

Anti-Apartheid Year.

Gotse Deltchev A965

Bulgarian Calculator A966

1978, Aug. 1 Photo. ***Perf. 13***

2527 A965 13s multi 25 10

Gotse Deltchev (1872-1903), patriot.

1978, Sept. 3

2528 A966 2s multi 12 5

International Sample Fair, Plovdiv.

Guerrillas — A967

1978, Aug. 1

2529 A967 5s blk & rose red 12 5

75th anniversary of the Ilinden and Preobrazhene revolts.

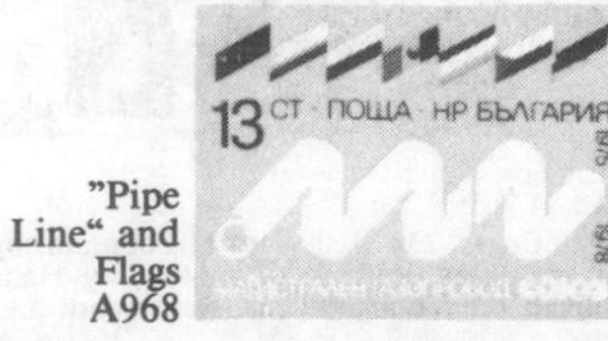

"Pipe Line" and Flags A968

1978, Oct. 3

2530 A968 13s multi 30 12

Construction of gas pipe line from Orenburg to Russian border.

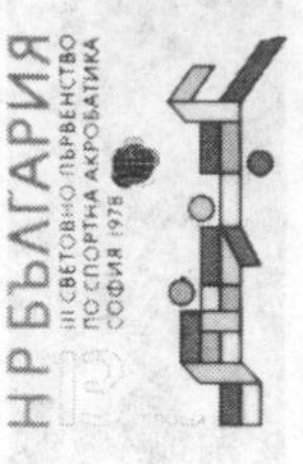

Three Acrobats — A969

1978, Oct. 4 ***Perf. 13x13½***

2531 A969 13s multi 25 12

3rd World Acrobatic Championships, Sofia, Oct. 6-8.

Christo G. Danov — A970

1978, Sept. 18 Photo. ***Perf. 13***

2532 A970 2s dp cl & ocher 12 5

Christo G. Danov (1828-1911), 1st Bulgarian publisher. No. 2532 printed with se-tenant label showing early printing press.

Insurgents, by Todor Panajotov A971

1978, Sept. 20

2533 A971 2s multi 12 5

Vladaja mutiny, 60th anniversary.

Salvador Allende — A972

Human Rights Flame — A973

1978, Oct. 11 Photo. ***Perf. 13***

2534 A972 13s dk brn & org red 25 12

Salvador Allende (1908-1973), president of Chile.

1978, Oct. 18

2535 A973 23s multi 45 15

Universal Declaration of Human Rights, 30th anniversary.

"Strength for my Arm" by Zlatyu Boyadjiev — A974

Burgarian Paintings: 1s, Levski and Matei Mitkaloto, by Kalina Tasseva. 3s, Rumena, woman military leader, by Nikola Mirchev (horiz.). 13s, Kolju Ficeto, by Elza Goeva. 23s, Family, National Revival Period, by Naiden Petkov.

Perf. 12x12½, 12½x12

1978, Oct. 25 **Litho.**

2536 A974 1s multi	5	5
2537 A974 2s multi	5	5
2538 A974 3c multi	5	5
2539 A974 13s multi	25	10
2540 A974 23s multi	45	12
Nos. 2536-2540 (5)	85	37

1300th anniversary of Bulgaria (in 1981).

Souvenir Sheet

Tourism Building, Plovdiv — A975

Design: No. 2541b, Chrelo Tower, Rila Cloister.

1978, Nov. 1 Photo. ***Perf. 13***

2541 Sheet of 5	5.25	3.00
a. A975 43s multi	1.00	40
b. A975 43s multi	1.00	40

Conservation of European architectural heritage. No. 2541 contains 3 No. 2541a, 2 No. 2541b and ornamental label. Lilac marginal inscription. Size: 116x116mm.

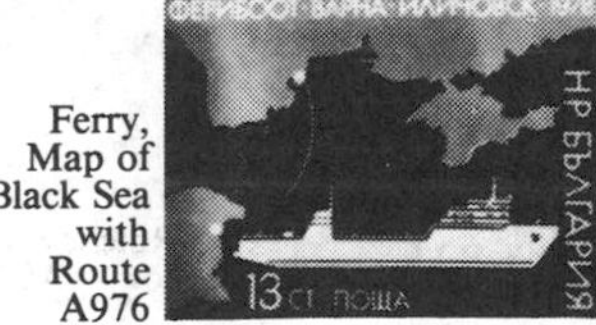

Ferry, Map of Black Sea with Route A976

1978, Nov. 1 Photo. ***Perf. 13***

2542 A976 13s multi 30 15

Opening of Ilychovsk-Varna Ferry.

Bird, from Marble Floor, St. Sofia Church — A977

1978, Nov. 20

2543 A977 5s multi 15 5

3rd Bulgaria '78, National Philatelic Exhibition, Sofia. Printed se-tenant with label showing emblems of Bulgaria '78 and Philaserdica '79.

Initial, 13th Century Gospel — A978

Designs: 13s, St. Cyril, miniature, 1567. 23s, Book cover, 16th century. 80s, St. Methodius, miniature, 13th century.

1978, Dec. 15 Photo. *Perf. 13*

2544	A978	2c multi	5	5
2545	A978	13s multi	25	10
2546	A978	23s multi	45	18

Souvenir Sheet

2547	A978	80s multi	2.00	85

Centenary of the Cyril and Methodius National Library. No. 2547 shows Gospel page. Size: 63x95mm.

Bulgaria No. 53 A979

Bulgarian Stamps: 13s, No. 534. 23s, No. 968. 35s, No. 1176 (vert.). 53s, No. 1223 (vert.). 1 l, No. 1.

1978, Dec. 30

2548	A979	2s ol grn & red	5	5
2549	A979	13s ultra & rose car	28	10
2550	A979	23s rose lil & ol grn	50	15
2551	A979	35s brt bl & blk	75	30
2552	A979	53s ver & sl grn	1.40	50
		Nos. 2548-2552 (5)	2.98	1.10

Souvenir Sheet

2553	A979	1 l multi	2.25	1.25

Philaserdica '79, International Philatelic Exhibition, Sofia, May 18-27, 1979, and centenary of Bulgarian stamps. No. 2553 has green and black marginal inscription and UPU emblem. Size: 62x88mm. See Nos. 2560-2564. No. 2553 exists imperf.

St. Clement of Ochrida — A980

1978, Dec. 8

2554	A980	2s multi	12	5

Clement of Ochrida University, 90th anniversary.

Ballet Dancers A981

1978, Dec. 22

2555	A981	13s multi	30	15

Bulgarian ballet, 50th anniversary.

Nikola Karastojanov A982

1978, Dec. 12

2556	A982	2s multi	12	5

Nikola Karastojanov (1778-1874), printer. No. 2556 printed se-tenant with label showing printing press.

Christmas Tree Made of Birds — A983

Design: 13s, Post horn.

1978, Dec. 22

2557	A983	2s multi	5	5
2558	A983	13s multi	25	12

New Year 1979.

COMECON Building, Moscow, Members' Flags — A984

1979, Jan. 25 Photo. *Perf. 13*

2559	A984	13s multi	30	12

Council for Mutual Economic Aid (COMECON), 30th anniversary.

Philaserdica Type of 1978
Designs as Before

1979, Jan. 30

2560	A979	2s brt bl & red	5	5
2561	A979	13s grn & dk car	25	10
2562	A979	23s org brn & multi	45	15
2563	A979	35s dl red & blk	70	30
2564	A979	53s vio & dk ol	1.25	50
		Nos. 2560-2564 (5)	2.70	1.10

Philaserdica "79.

Bank Building, Commemorative Coin — A985

1979, Feb. 13

2565	A985	2s yel, gray & sil	12	5

Centenary of Bulgarian People's Bank.

Foreign postal stationery (stamped envelopes, postal cards and air letter sheets) lies beyond the scope of this Catalogue, which is limited to adhesive postage stamps.

Aleksander Stamboliski A986

1979, Feb. 28

2566	A986	2s org & dk brn	12	5

Aleksander Stamboliski (1879-1923), leader of peasant's party and premier.

Flower with Child's Face, IYC Emblem — A987

Stylized Heads, World Association Emblem A988

1979, Mar. 8

2568	A987	23s multi	45	18

International Year of the Child.

1979, Mar. 20

2569	A988	13s multi	25	12

8th World Congress for the Deaf, Varna, June 20-27.

"75" and Trade Union Emblem A989

1979, Mar. 20

2570	A989	2s sl grn & org	12	5

75th anniversary of Bulgarian Trade Unions.

Souvenir Sheet

Sculptures in Sofia — A990

Designs: 2s, Soviet Army Monument (detail). 5s, Mother and Child, Central Railroad Station. 13s, 23s, 25s, Bas-relief from Monument of the Liberators.

1979, Apr. 2 Photo. *Perf. 13*

2571	A990	Sheet of 5 + label	2.00	1.00
	a.	2s multi		6
	b.	5s multi		12
	c.	13s multi		35
	d.	23s multi		60
	e.	25s multi		75

Centenary of Sofia as capital. No. 2571 has ultramarine and red border. Size: 106x103mm.

Rocket Launch, Space Flight Emblems A991

Designs (Intercosmos and Bulgarian-USSR Flight Emblems and): 25s, Link-up (horiz.). 35s, Parachute descent. 1 l, Globe, emblems and orbit (horiz.).

1979, Apr. 11

2572	A991	12s multi	25	12
2573	A991	25s multi	50	20
2574	A991	35s multi	70	30

Souvenir Sheet

2575	A991	1l multi	2.25	1.10

First Bulgarian cosmonaut on Russian space flight. No. 2575 has space emblems in margin. Size: 68x85mm.

A slightly larger imperf sheet similar to No. 2575 with control numbers at bottom and rockets at sides exists.

Nicolai Rukavishnikov — A992

Design: 13s, Rukavishnikov and Soviet cosmonaut Georgi Ivanov.

1979, May 14 Photo. *Perf. 13*

2576	A992	2s multi	5	5
2577	A992	13s multi	30	12

Col. Nicolai Rukavishnikov, first Bulgarian astronaut.

Souvenir Sheet

Thracian Gold-leaf Collar — A993

1979, May 16

2578	A993	1 l multi	2.25	1.25

48th International Philatelic Federation Congress, Sofia, May 16-17. No. 2578 has ultramarine and carmine decorative margin. Size: 77x86mm.

Post Horn, Carrier Pigeon, Jet, Globes and UPU Emblem — A994

Designs (Post Horn, Globes and ITU Emblem): 5s, 1st Bulgarian and modern telephones. 13s, Morse key and teleprinter. 23s, Old radio transmitter and radio towers. 35s, Bulgarian TV tower and satellite.

1979, May 8 *Perf. 13½x13*

2579	A994	2s	multi	5	5
2580	A994	5s	multi	10	5
2581	A994	13s	multi	30	10
2582	A994	23s	multi	55	15
2583	A994	35s	multi	85	30
		Nos. 2579-2583 (5)		1.85	65

Souvenir Sheet

Design: 50s, Ground receiving station.

Perf. 13

2584	A994	50s	vio, blk & gray	1.50	90

International Telecommunications Day and centenary of Bulgarian Postal and Telegraph Services. No. 2584 has ocher marginal inscription and emblems. Size of stamp: 39x28mm. Size of sheet: 65x70mm. No. 2584 exists imperf.

Hotel Vitosha-New Otani — A996

1979, May 20

2586	A996	2s	ultra & pink	12	5

Philaserdica '79 Day.

Horseman Receiving Gifts, by Karellia and Boris Kuklievi — A997

1979, May 23

2587	A997	2s	multi	12	5

Bulgarian-Russian Friendship Day.

Man on Donkey, by Boris Angeloushev — A998

Four Women, by Albrecht Dürer — A999

1979, May 23 **Photo.** *Perf. 13½*

2588	A998	2s	multi	12	5

12th National Festival of Humor and Satire, Gabrovo.

Lithographed and Engraved

1979, May 31 *Perf. 14x13½*

Dürer Engravings: 23s, Three Peasants. 25s, The Cook and his Wife. 35s, Portrait of Helius Eobanus Hessus. 80s, Rhinoceros (horiz.).

2589	A999	13s	multi	30	10
2590	A999	23s	multi	50	15
2591	A999	25s	multi	60	20
2592	A999	35s	multi	80	25

Souvenir Sheet

Imperf

2593	A999	80s	multi	1.75	1.25

Albrecht Durer (1471-1528), German engraver and painter. No. 2593 has lilac and brown decorative margin. Size: 81x81mm.

R. Todorov (1879-1916) A1000

Bulgarian Writers: No. 2595, Dimitri Dymov (1909-1966). No. 2596, S. A. Kostov (1879-1939).

1979, June 26 **Photo.** *Perf. 13*

2594	A1000	2s	multi	8	5
2595	A1000	2s	sl grn & yel grn	8	5
2596	A1000	2s	dp cl & yel	8	5

Nos. 2594-2596 each printed se-tenant with label showing title page or character from writer's work.

Moscow '80 Emblem, Runners A1001

Moscow '80 Emblem and: 13s, Pole vault (horiz.). 25s, Discus. 35s, Hurdles (horiz.). 43s, High jump (horiz.). 1 l, Long jump.

1979, May 15 *Perf. 13*

2597	A1001	2s	multi	5	5
2598	A1001	13s	multi	25	15
2599	A1001	25s	multi	50	20
2600	A1001	35s	multi	1.00	40
2601	A1001	43s	multi	1.25	50
2602	A1001	1 l	multi	2.75	1.10
		Nos. 2597-2602 (6)		5.80	2.40

Souvenir Sheet

2602A	A1001	2 l	multi	6.75	5.00

22nd Summer Olympic Games, Moscow, July 19-Aug. 3, 1980.

Rocket A1002

1979, Sept. 4 **Photo.**

Designs: 5c, Flags of U.S.S.R. and Bulgaria. 13s, "35."

2603	A1002	2s	multi	5	5
2604	A1002	5s	multi	10	5
2605	A1002	13s	multi	25	12

35th anniversary of liberation.

Moscow '80 Emblem, Gymnast A1003

Designs: Moscow '80 Emblem and gymnasts. 13s horiz.

1979, July 31 **Photo.** *Perf. 13*

2606	A1003	2s	multi	5	5
2607	A1003	13s	multi	25	15
2608	A1003	25s	multi	60	20
2609	A1003	35s	multi	90	35
2610	A1003	43s	multi	1.25	40
2611	A1003	1 l	multi	2.75	1.25
		Nos. 2606-2611 (6)		5.80	2.40

Souvenir Sheet

2612	A1003	2 l	multi	6.75	5.00

22nd Summer Olympic Games, Moscow, July 19-Aug. 3, 1980. No. 2612 has light and dark blue margin showing Moscow '80 emblem; black control number. Size: 67x89mm.

Theater Institute, 18th Congress A1004

1979, July 8 **Photo.** *Perf. 13*

2613	A1004	13s	ultra & blk	25	10

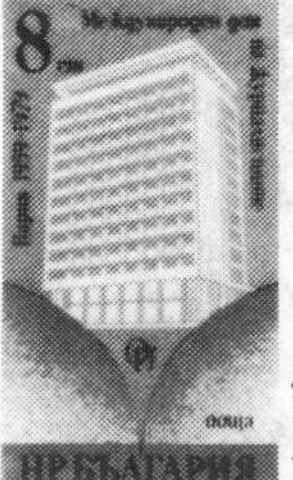

Journalists' Vacation House, Varna, 20th Anniversary A1005

1979, July 17

2614	A1005	8s	multi	16	5

Icon Type of 1977

Virgin and Child by: 13s, 23s, Nesebar, 16th century (diff.). 35s, 43s, Sozopol, 16th century (diff.). 53s, Samokov, 19th century. Inscribed 1979.

1979, Aug. 7 **Litho.** *Perf. 12½*

2615	A917	13s	multi	30	10
2616	A917	23s	multi	50	15
2617	A917	35s	multi	75	18
2618	A917	43s	multi	90	25
2619	A917	53s	multi	1.25	35
		Nos. 2615-2619 (5)		3.70	1.03

Anton Besenschek — A1006

1979, Aug. 9 **Photo.** *Perf. 13x13½*

2620	A1006	2s	dk ol grn & pale yel	12	5

Bulgarian stenography centenary.

Bulgarian Alpine Club, 50th Anniversary A1007

1979, Aug. 28 *Perf. 13*

2621	A1007	2s	multi	12	5

Public Health Ordinance A1008

1979, Aug. 31 *Perf. 13½*

2622	A1008	2s	multi	12	5

Public Health Service centenary. No. 2622 printed with label showing Dimitar Mollov, founder.

Isotope Measuring Device — A1009

1979, Sept. 8 *Perf. 13½x13*

2623	A1009	2s	multi	12	5

International Sample Fair, Plovdiv.

Games' Emblem A1010

1979, Sept. 20 *Perf. 13*
2624 A1010 5s multi 12 5

Universiada '79, World University Games, Mexico City, Sept.

Sofia Locomotive Sports Club, 50th Anniversary — A1011

1979, Oct. 2
2625 A1011 2s bl & org red 12 5

Ljuben Karavelov A1012

1979, Oct. 4 **Photo.** *Perf. 13*
2626 A1012 2s bl & sl grn 12 5

Ljuben Karavelov (1837-1879), poet and freedom fighter.

Biathlon, Lake Placid '80 Emblem — A1013

1979, Oct. 20
2627 A1013 2s *shown* 5 5
2628 A1013 13s *Speed skating* 30 10
2629 A1013 23s *Downhill skiing* 50 15
2630 A1013 43s *Luge* 95 30

Souvenir Sheet
Imperf.
2631 A1013 1 l *Slalom* 2.25 1.75

13th Winter Olympic Games, Lake Placid, N.Y., Feb. 12-24. No. 2631 has gold and bluish green margin showing Lake Placid '80 emblem. Size: 70x78mm.

Woman from Thrace, by Decko Uzunov — A1014

Decko Uzunov, 80th Birthday: 12s, Apparition in Red. 23s, Composition.

1979, Oct. 31 *Perf. 14*
2632 A1014 12s multi 25 8
2633 A1014 13s multi 25 10
2634 A1014 23s multi 45 15

Swimming, Moscow '80 Emblem — A1016

1979, Nov. 30 **Photo.** *Perf. 13*
2636 A1016 2s *Two-man kayak, vert.* 5 5
2637 A1016 13s *Swimming, vert.* 25 15
2638 A1016 25s *shown* 50 20
2639 A1016 35s *One-man kayak* 1.00 30
2640 A1016 43s *Diving, vert* 1.25 60
2641 A1016 1 l *Diving, vert. (diff.)* 2.75 1.10
Nos. 2636-2641 (6) 5.80 2.40

Souvenir Sheet
2642 A1016 2 l *Water polo, vert.* 6.75 5.00

22nd Summer Olympic Games, Moscow, July 19-Aug. 3, 1980. No. 2642 has multicolored margin showing Moscow '80 emblem; black control number. Size: 66x88mm.

Nikola Vapzarov A1017

1979, Dec. 7 **Photo.** *Perf. 13*
2643 A1017 2s cl & rose 12 5

Vapzarov (1909-1942), poet and freedom fighter. No. 2643 printed with label showing smokestacks.

The First Socialists, by Bojan Petrov — A1018

Paintings: 13s, Demeter Blagoev Reading Newspaper, by Demeter Gjudshenov, 1892. 25s, Workers' Party March, by Sotir Sotirov, 1917. 35s, Dawn in Plovdiv, by Johann Leviev (vert.).

Perf. 12½x12, 12x12½
1979, Dec. 10 **Litho.**
2644 A1018 2s multi 5 5
2645 A1018 13s multi 30 10
2646 A1018 25s multi 55 15
2647 A1018 35s multi 80 20

Sharpshooting, Moscow '80 Emblem A1019

1979, Dec. 22 **Photo.** *Perf. 13*
2648 A1019 2s *shown* 5 5
2649 A1019 13s *Judo,* horiz. 25 15
2650 A1019 25s *Wrestling,* horiz. 50 20
2651 A1019 35s *Archery* 1.00 30
2652 A1019 43s *Fencing,* horiz. 1.25 60
2653 A1019 1 l *Fencing* 2.75 1.10
Nos. 2648-2653 (6) 5.80 2.40

Souvenir Sheet
2654 A1019 2 l *Boxing* 6.75 5.00

Procession with Relics, 11th Century Fresco A1020

Frescoes of Sts. Cyril and Methodius, St. Clement's Basilica, Rome: 13s, Reception by Pope Hadrian II. 23s, Burial of Cyril the Philosopher, 18th century. 25s, St. Cyril. 35s, St. Methodius.

1979, Dec. 25
2655 A1020 2s multi 5 5
2656 A1020 13s multi 30 10
2657 A1020 23s multi 50 12
2658 A1020 25s multi 55 15
2659 A1020 35s multi 80 25
Nos. 2655-2659 (5) 2.20 67

Bulgarian Television Emblem A1021

1979, Dec. 29 *Perf. 13½*
2660 A1021 5s vio bl & lt bl 12 5

Bulgarian television, 25th anniversary. No. 2660 printed with label showing Sofia television tower.

Doves in Girl's Hair A1022

Design: 2s, Children's heads, mosaic (vert.).

1979 *Perf. 13*
2661 A1022 2s multi 12 5
2662 A1022 13s multi 25 10

International Year of the Child. Issue dates: 2s, July 17; 13s, Dec. 14.

Puppet on Horseback, IYC Emblem A1023

Thracian Rider, Votive Tablet, 3rd Century A1024

1980, Jan. 22 **Photo.** *Perf. 13*
2663 A1023 2s multi 12 5

UNIMA, International Puppet Theater Organization, 50th anniversary (1979); International Year of the Child (1979).

1980, Jan. 29 **Photo.** *Perf. 13x13½*

National Archaeological Museum Centenary; 13s, Deines stele, 5th century B.C.

2664 A1024 2s brn & gold 5 5
2665 A1024 13s multi 25 10

Dimitrov Meeting Lenin in Moscow, by Alexander Poplilov A1026

1980, Mar. 28 *Perf. 12x12½*
2667 A1026 13s multi 25 10

Lenin, 110th birth anniversary.

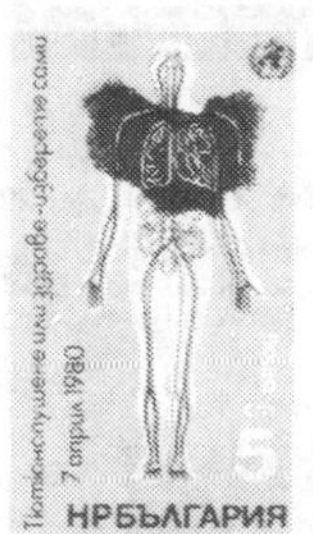

Circulatory System, Lungs Enveloped in Smoke — A1027

1980, Apr. 7 *Perf. 13*
2668 A1027 5s multi 12 5

World Health Day fight against cigarette smoking.

Basketball, Moscow '80 Emblem A1027a

1980, Apr. 10 **Photo.** *Perf. 13*
2669 A1027a 2s shown 5 5
2670 A1027a 13s soccer 25 15
2671 A1027a 25s hockey 50 20
2672 A1027a 35s cycling 1.00 30
2673 A1027a 43s handball 1.25 60
2674 A1027a 1 l volleyball 2.75 1.10
Nos. 2669-2674 (6) 5.80 2.40

Souvenir Sheet
2675 A1027a 2 l weightlifting 6.75 5.00

Souvenir Sheet

Intercosmos Emblem, Cosmonauts — A1028

1980, Apr. 22 *Perf. 12*
2676 A1028 50s multi 1.25 70

Intercosmos cooperative space program. Multicolored margin shows planets, stars and emblems. Size: 111x102mm.

Penio Penev (1930-1959), Poet — A1029

1980, Apr. 22 Photo. *Perf. 13*

2677 A1029 5s multi 12 5

Se-tenant with label showing quote from author's work.

Penny Black — A1030

1980, Apr. 24 *Perf. 13*

2678 A1030 25s dk red & sep 50 20

London 1980 International Stamp Exhibition, May 6-14; printed se-tenant with label showing Rowland Hill between every two stamps.

Demeter H. Tchorbadjiiski, Self-portrait — A1031

1980, Apr. 29

2679 A1031 5s *shown* 10 5
2680 A1031 13s *"Our People"* 25 10

Nikolai Giaurov A1032

Raising Red Flag Reichstag Building, Berlin A1033

1980, Apr. 30

2681 A1032 5s multi 12 5

Nikolai Giaurov (b. 1930), opera singer; printed se-tenant with label showing Boris Godunov.

1980, May 6 *Perf. 13x13½*

Armistice, 35th Anniversary: 13s, Soviet Army memorial, Berlin-Treptow.

2682 A1033 5s multi 10 5
2683 A1033 13s multi 25 10

The lack of a price for a listed item does not necessarily indicate rarity.

Numeral — A1034

1979 *Perf. 14*

2684 A1034 2s ultra 5 5
2685 A1034 5s rose car 12 5

75th Anniv. of Teachers' Union A1034a

1980, May 12 Photo. *Perf. 13*

2685A A1034a 5s multi 10 5

Warsaw Pact, 25th Anniversary A1035

1980, May 14 Photo. *Perf. 13*

2686 A1035 13s multi 25 10

A1036

10th Intl. Ballet Competition, Varna — A1037

1980, June 10

2687 A1036 2s multi 5 5
2688 A1036 13s multi 25 15
2689 A1036 25s multi 50 20
2690 A1036 35s multi 1.00 30
2691 A1036 43s multi 1.25 60
2692 A1036 1 l multi 2.75 1.10
Nos. 2687-2692 (6) 5.80 2.40

Souvenir Sheet

2693 A1036 2l multi 6.75 5.00

22nd Summer Olympic Games, Moscow, July 19-Aug. 3.

1980, Sept. Photo. *Perf. 13*

2694 A1037 13s multi 35 12

Hotel Europa, Sofia A1038

Hotels: No. 2696, Bulgaria, Burgas, vert. No. 2697, Plovdiv, Plovdiv. No. 2698, Riga, Russe, vert. No. 2699, Varna, Djuba.

1980, July 11

2695 A1038 23s lt ultra & multi 45 18
2696 A1038 23s org & multi 45 18
2697 A1038 23s gray & multi 45 18
2698 A1038 23s bl & multi 45 18
2699 A1038 23s yel & multi 45 18
Nos. 2695-2699 (5) 2.25 90

See No. 2766.

Ship Type of 1975

Ships of 16th, 17th Centuries: 5s, Christ of Lubeck, galleon. 8s, Roman galley. 13s, Eagle, Russian galleon. 23s, Mayflower. 35c, Maltese galley. 53, Royal Louis, galleon.

1980, July 14

2700 A873 5s multi 10 5
2701 A873 8s multi 15 5
2702 A873 13s multi 25 10
2703 A873 23s multi 45 18
2704 A873 35s multi 70 20
2705 A873 53s multi 1.10 35
Nos. 2700-2705 (6) 2.75 93

Int'l Year of the Child, 1979 — A1040

Designs: Children's drawings and IYC emblem. 43s, Tower. 5s, 25s, 43s, vert.

1980 Litho. *Perf. 12½x12, 12x12½*

2708 A1040 3s multi 5 5
2709 A1040 5s multi 10 5
2710 A1040 8s multi 15 5
2711 A1040 13s multi 25 10
2712 A1040 25s multi 50 15
2713 A1040 35s multi 70 20
2714 A1040 43s multi 85 25
Nos. 2708-2714 (7) 2.60 85

Helicopter, Missile Transport, Tank — A1041

1980, Sept. 23 Photo. *Perf. 13*

2715 A1041 3s *shown* 5 5
2716 A1041 5s *Jet, radar, rocket* 12 5
2717 A1041 8s *Helicopter, ships* 15 5

Bulgarian People's Army, 35th anniversary.

St. Anne, by Leonardo da Vinci A1042

Da Vinci Paintings: 8s, 13s, Annunciation (diff.). 25s, Adoration of the Kings. 35s, Lady with the Ermine. 50s, Mona Lisa.

1980, Nov.

2718 A1042 5s multi 10 5
2719 A1042 8s multi 18 5
2720 A1042 13s multi 30 10
2721 A1042 25s multi 55 15
2722 A1042 35s multi 80 25
Nos. 2718-2722 (5) 1.93 60

Souvenir Sheet

Imperf

2723 A1042 50s multi 1.25 55

No. 2723 has multicolored margin showing human figure. Size: 57½x81mm.

International Peace Conference, Sofia — A1043

1980, Sept. 4 Photo. *Perf. 13*

2724 A1043 25s multi 50 20

Jordan Jowkov (1880-1937), Writer — A1044

1980, Sept. 19

2725 A1044 5s multi 12 5

Se-tenant with label showing scene from Jowkov's work.

International Samples Fair, Plovdiv — A1045

1980, Sept. 24 *Perf. 13½x13*

2726 A1045 5s multi 12 5

Blooming Cacti — A1045a

1980, Nov. 4 Photo. *Perf. 13*

2726A A1045a 5s multi 10 5
2726B A1045a 13s multi 25 10
2726C A1045a 25s multi 50 20
2726D A1045a 35s multi 70 28
2726E A1045a 53s multi 1.10 35
Nos. 2726A-2726E (5) 2.65 98

Souvenir Sheet

25th Anniv. of Bulgarian UN Membership — A1045b

1980, Nov. 25
2726F A1045a 60s multi 3.25 3.00

World Ski Racing Championship, Velingrad — A1046

1981, Jan. 17 Photo. *Perf. 13*
2727 A1046 43s multi 85 30

Hawthorn A1047 Slalom A1048

Designs: Medicinal herbs.

1981, Jan.

2728	A1047	3s shown	5	5
2729	A1047	5s St. John's wort	10	5
2730	A1047	13s Common elder	28	10
2731	A1047	25s Blackberries	55	20
2732	A1047	35s Lime	75	30
2733	A1047	43s Wild briar	90	35
		Nos. 2728-2733 (6)	2.63	1.05

1981, Feb. 27 Photo. *Perf. 13*
2734 A1048 43s multi 85 35

Evian Alpine World Ski Cup Championship, Borovets.

Nuclear Traces, Research Institute — A1049

1981, Mar. 10 *Perf. 13½x13*
2735 A1049 13s gray & blk 30 10

Nuclear Research Institute, Dubna, USSR, 25th anniversary.

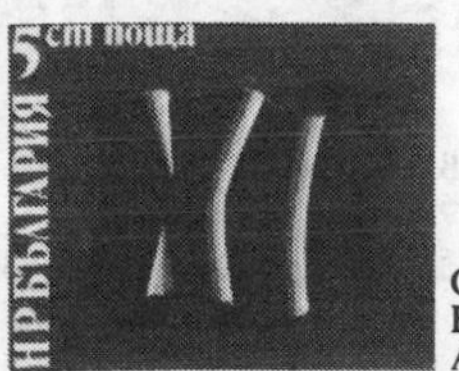

Congress Emblem A1050

1981, Mar. 12 *Perf. 13½*

2736	A1050	5s shown	10	5
2737	A1050	13s Stars	25	10
2738	A1050	23s Teletape	45	18

Souvenir Sheet

2739 A1050 50s Demeter Blagoev, George Dimitrov 1.25 75

12th Bulgarian Communist Party Congress. Nos. 2736-2738 each printed se-tenant with label. No. 2739 has red marginal inscription. Size: 65x87mm.

Paintings by Zachary Zograf — A1050a

1981, Mar. 23 Photo. *Perf. 12x12½*

2739A	A1050a	5s multi	10	5
2739B	A1050a	13s multi	28	10
2739C	A1050a	23s multi	50	18
2739D	A1050a	25s multi	55	20
2739E	A1050a	35s multi	80	28
		Nos. 2739A-2739E (5)	2.23	81

Nos. 2739A-2739C are vert.

EXPO '81, Plovdiv A1050b

1981, Apr. 7

2739F	A1050b	5s multi	10	5
2739G	A1050b	8s multi	18	5
2739H	A1050b	13s multi	30	10
2739J	A1050b	25s multi	55	20
2739K	A1050b	53s multi	1.25	35
		Nos. 2739F-2739K (5)	2.38	75

Centenary of Bulgarian Shipbuilding — A1050c

1981, Apr. 15 Photo. *Perf. 13*

2739L	A1050c	35s Georgi Dimitrov, liner	70	28
2739M	A1050c	43s 5th from RMS, freighter	85	35
2739N	A1050c	53s Khan Asparuch, tanker	1.10	40

Arabian Horse A1051

1980, Nov. 27 Litho. *Perf. 12½x12*

2740	A1051	3s multi	5	5
2741	A1051	5s multi	10	5
2742	A1051	13s multi	30	10
2743	A1051	23s multi	50	18
2744	A1051	35s multi	80	28
		Nos. 2740-2744 (5)	1.75	66

Vassil Stoin, Ethnologist, Birth Centenary — A1052

1980, Dec. 5 Photo. *Perf. 13½x13*
2745 A1052 5s multi 12 5

12th Bulgarian Communist Party Congress — A1052a

1980, Dec. 26 Photo. *Perf. 13x13½*
2745A A1052a 5s Party symbols 12 5

New Year A1053

1980, Dec. 8 *Perf. 13*

2746	A1053	5s shown	10	5
2747	A1053	13s Cup, date	25	12

Culture Palace, Sofia A1053a

1981, Mar. 13 Photo. *Perf. 13*
2747A A1053a 5s multi 10 5

Vienna Hofburg Palace A1054

1981, May 15 Photo. *Perf. 13*
2748 A1054 35s multi 70 28

WIPA 1981 Intl. Philatelic Exhibition, Vienna, May 22-31.

34th Farmers' Union Congress A1055

1981, May 18 *Perf. 13½*

2749	A1055	5s shown	10	5
2750	A1055	8s Flags	15	6
2751	A1055	13s Flags, diff.	25	12

Wild Cat A1056

1981, May 27

2752	A1056	5s shown	10	5
2753	A1056	13s Boar	30	12
2754	A1056	23s Mouflon	55	18
2755	A1056	25s Mountain goat	60	20
2756	A1056	35s Stag	85	28
2757	A1056	53s Roe deer	1.40	40
		Nos. 2752-2757 (6)	3.80	1.23

Souvenir Sheet

Perf. 13½x13

2758 A1056 1 l Stag (diff.) 2.50 1.25

EXPO '81 Intl. Hunting Exhibition, Plovdiv. Nos. 2752-2757 each se-tenant with labels showing various hunting rifles. No. 2758 contains one stamp (48½x39mm.); multicolored margin shows hunter with bird. Size: 79x104mm.

25th Anniv. of UNESCO Membership A1057

1981, June 11 *Perf. 13*
2759 A1057 13s multi 30 12

Hotel Type of 1980

1981, July 13 Photo. *Perf. 13*
2766 A1038 23s Veliko Tirnovo Hotel 45 18

Flying Figure, Sculpture by Velichko Minekov — A1059

Bulgarian Social Democratic Party Buzludja Congress, 90th Anniv. (Minkov Sculpture): 13s, Advancing Female Figure.

1981, July 16 *Perf. 13½*

2767	A1059	5s multi	10	5
2768	A1059	13s multi	25	12

Kukeri, by Georg Tschapkanov A1060

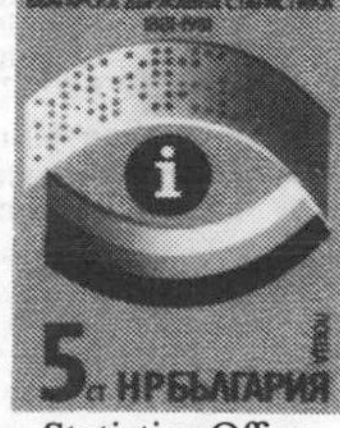

Statistics Office Centenary A1061

1981, May 28 Photo. *Perf. 13*
2769 A1060 5s multi 12 5

13th Natl. Festival of Humor and Satire.

1981, June 9
2770 A1061 5s multi 12 5

Gold Dish A1063

Designs: Goldsmiths' works, 7th-9th cent.

1981, July 21

2772	A1063	5s multi	10	5
2773	A1063	13s multi	30	12
2774	A1063	23s multi	55	18
2775	A1063	25s multi	60	20
2776	A1063	35s multi	85	28
2777	A1063	53s multi	1.40	40
	Nos. 2772-2777 (6)		3.80	1.23

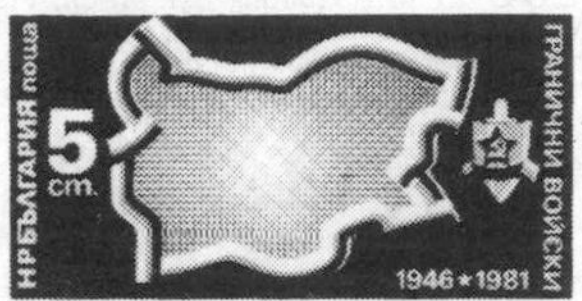

35th Anniv. of Frontier Force — A1064

1981, July 28 *Perf. 13½x13*

2778 A1064 5s multi 12 5

1300th Anniv. of First Bulgarian State — A1065

Designs: No. 2779, Sts. Cyril and Methodius. No. 2780, 9th cent. bas-relief. 8s, Floor plan, Round Church, Preslav, 10th cent. 12s, Four Evangelists of King Ivan Alexander, miniature, 1356. No. 2783, King Ivan Asen II memorial column. No. 2784, Warriors on horseback. 16s, April uprising, 1876. 23s, Russian liberators, Tirnovo. 25s, Social Democratic Party founding, 1891. 35s, September uprising, 1923. 41s, Fatherland Front. 43s, Prime Minister George Dimitrov, 5th Communist Party Congress, 1948. 50s, Lion, 10th cent. bas-relief. 53s, 10th Communist Party Congress. 55s, Kremikovski Metalurgical Plant, 1 l, Brezhnev, Gen. Todor Jovkov.

1981, Aug. 10

2779	A1065	5s multi	10	5
2780	A1065	5s multi	10	5
2781	A1065	8s multi	15	6
2782	A1065	12s multi	25	10
2783	A1065	13s multi	25	12
2784	A1065	13s multi	25	12
2785	A1065	16s multi	32	15
2786	A1065	23s multi	45	18
2787	A1065	25s multi	50	20
2788	A1065	35s multi	70	30
2789	A1065	41s multi	85	35
2790	A1065	43s multi	85	35
2791	A1065	53s multi	1.10	45
2792	A1065	55s multi	1.10	50
	Nos. 2779-2792 (14)		6.97	2.98

Souvenir Sheets

2793	A1065	50s multi	1.10	70
2794	A1065	1 l multi	2.25	1.25

Nos. 2791-2794 have multicolored margins showing flags and arms. Size: 83x75mm.

European Volleyball Championship A1066

1981, Sept. 16 *Perf. 13*

2795 A1066 13s multi 25 12

Pegasus, Bronze Sculpture (Word Day) — A1067

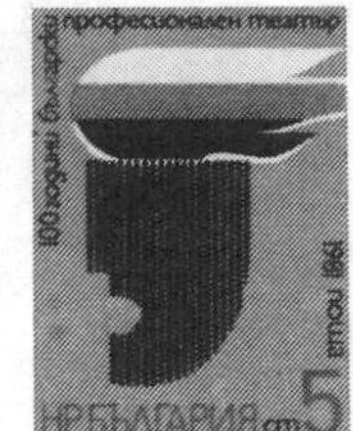

World Food Day — A1068

1981, Oct. 2

2796 A1067 5s ol & cr 12 5

1981, Oct. 16

2797 A1068 13s multi 25 12

Professional Theater Centenary A1069

1981, Oct. 30

2798 A1069 5s multi 12 5

Anti-Apartheid Year — A1070

1981, Dec. 2

2799 A1070 5s multi 12 5

Espana '82 World Cup Soccer — A1071

Designs: Various soccer players.

1981, Dec.

2800	A1071	5s multi	12	12
2801	A1071	13s multi	35	25
2802	A1071	43s multi	1.00	35
2803	A1071	53s multi	1.40	50

Heritage Day A1072

1981, Nov. 21 **Photo.** *Perf. 13*

2804 A1072 13s multi 25 12

Souvenir Sheet

2804A A1072 60s multi 1.75 1.50

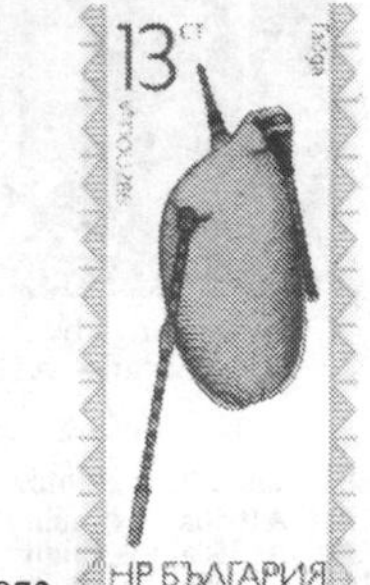

Bagpipe — A1073

Public Libraries and Reading Rooms, 125th Anniv — A1074

1982, Jan. 14

2805	A1073	13s shown	30	12
2806	A1073	25s Flutes	60	25
2807	A1073	30s Rebec	75	30
2808	A1073	35s Flute, recorder	85	35
2809	A1073	44s Mandolin	1.10	45
	Nos. 2805-2809 (5)		3.60	1.47

1982, Jan. 20

2810 A1074 5s dk grn 12 5

Souvenir Sheet

Intl. Decade for Women (1975-1985) — A1075

1982, Mar. 8

2811 A1075 1 l multi 2.50 1.50

Size: 65x78mm.

New Year 1982 A1076

1981, Dec. 22 **Photo.** *Perf. 13*

2812	A1076	5s Ornament	10	5
2813	A1076	13s Ornament, diff.	25	12

The Sofia Plains, by Nicolas Petrov (1881-1916) — A1077

1982, Feb. 10 *Perf. 12½*

2814	A1077	5s shown	10	5
2815	A1077	13s Girl Embroidering	30	12
2816	A1077	30s Fields of Peshtera	70	30

25th Anniv. of UNICEF (1981) — A1078

Mother and Child Paintings.

1982, Feb. 25 *Perf. 14*

2817	A1078	53s Vladimir Dimitrov	1.25	50
2818	A1078	53s Basil Stoilov	1.25	50
2819	A1078	53s Ivan Milev	1.25	50
2820	A1078	53s Liliana Russeva	1.25	50

Figures, by Vladamir Dimitrov (1882-1961) — A1079

1982, Mar. 8 **Litho.**

2821	A1079	5s shown	10	5
2822	A1079	8s Landscape	18	6
2823	A1079	13s View of Istanbul	30	12
2824	A1079	25s Harvesters, vert.	55	25
2825	A1079	30s Woman in a Landscape, vert.	65	30
2826	A1079	35s Peasant Woman, vert.	80	40
	Nos. 2821-2826 (6)		2.58	1.18

Souvenir Sheet

2827 A1079 50s Self-portrait 1.25 75

No. 2827 contains one stamp (54x32mm.); olive green and brown margin. Size: 65x58mm.

Trade Union Congress A1080

1982, Apr. 8 **Photo.** *Perf. 13½*

2828	A1080	5s Dimitrov reading union paper	10	5
2829	A1080	5s Culture Palace	10	5

Nos. 2828-2829 se-tenant with label showing text.

Marsh Snowdrop A1081

Designs: Medicinal plants.

1982, Apr. 10 Photo. *Perf. 13*
2830 A1081 3s shown 6 5
2831 A1081 5s Chicory 10 5
2832 A1081 8s Chamaenerium angustifolium 15 6
2833 A1081 13s Solomon's seal 30 12
2834 A1081 25s Violets 55 25
2835 A1081 35s Centaury 80 35
Nos. 2830-2835 (6) 1.96 88

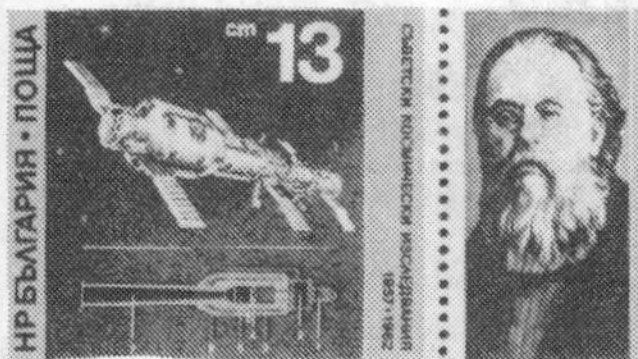
Cosmonauts' Day — A1082

1982, Apr. 12 *Perf. 13½*
2836 A1082 13s Salyut-Soyuz link-up 30 12

Se-tenant with label showing K.E. Tsiolkovsky (space pioneer).

Souvenir Sheet

SOZFILEX Stamp Exhibition — A1083

1982, May 7 *Perf. 13*
2837 A1083 50s Dimitrov, emblems 1.25 70

Size: 62x82mm.

14th Komsomol Congress (Youth Communists) — A1084

1982, May 25
2838 A1084 5s multi 12 5

PHILEXFRANCE '82 Intl. Stamp Exhibition, Paris, June 11-21 — A1085

1982, May 28
2839 A1085 42s France #1, Bulgaria #1 90 35

19th Cent. Fresco A1086

Designs: Various floral pattern frescoes.

1982, June 8 *Perf. 11½*
2840 A1086 5s red & multi 10 5
2841 A1086 13s grn & multi 30 10
2842 A1086 25s vio & multi 55 20
2843 A1086 30s ol grn & multi 65 30
2844 A1086 42s bl & multi 95 35
2845 A1086 60s brn & multi 1.40 55
Nos. 2840-2845 (6) 3.95 1.55

Souvenir Sheet

George Dimitrov (1882-1949), First Prime Minister — A1087

1982, June 15 *Perf. 13*
2846 A1087 50s multi 1.25 70

Multicolored margin shows natl. colors, olive branch. Size: 77x52mm.

9th Congress of the National Front — A1088

1982, June 21 Photo. *Perf. 13*
2847 A1088 5s Dimitrov 12 5

35th Anniv. of Balkan Bulgarian Airline A1089

1982, June 28 *Perf. 13½x13*
2848 A1089 42s multi 85 35

Nuclear Disarmament A1090

1982, July 15 *Perf. 13*
2849 A1090 13s multi 30 12

Ludmila Zhiukova (b. 1942), Artist — A1091

1982, July Photo. *Perf. 13*
2850 A1091 5s multi 10 5
2851 A1091 13s multi 24 10

Souvenir Sheet

2852 A1091 1l multi 2.00 1.00

No. 2852 has multicolored margin showing Jirkova's paintings. Size: 62x67mm.

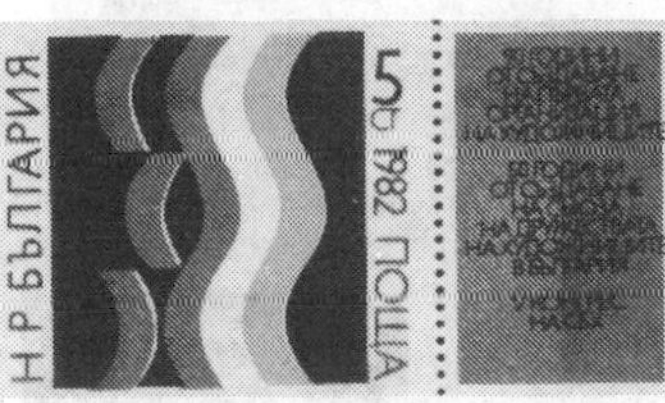
5th Congress of Bulgarian Painters — A1092

1982, July 27 *Perf. 13½*
2853 A1092 5s multi 10 5

Se-tenant with label showing text.

Flag of Peace Youth Assembly — A1092a

Various children's drawings.

1982, Aug. 10 *Perf. 14*
2853A A1092a 3s multi 6 5
2853B A1092a 5s multi 10 5
2853C A1092a 8s multi 18 8
2853D A1092a 13s multi 30 10

Souvenir Sheet
Perf. 14, Imperf.
2853E A1092a 50s In balloon 1.00 50

10th Anniv. of UN Conference on Human Environment, Stockholm — A1093

1982, Nov. 10 *Perf. 13*
2854 A1093 13s dk bl & grn 24 10

Park Hotel Moskva, Sofia — A1094

October Revolution, 65th Anniv. — A1095

Design: No. 2856, Tchernomore, Varna.

1982, Oct. 20 Photo. *Perf. 13*
2855 A1094 32s lt blue & multi 60 25
2856 A1094 32s pink & multi 60 25

1982, Nov. 4
2857 A1095 13s Cruiser Aurora, Sputnik II 24 10

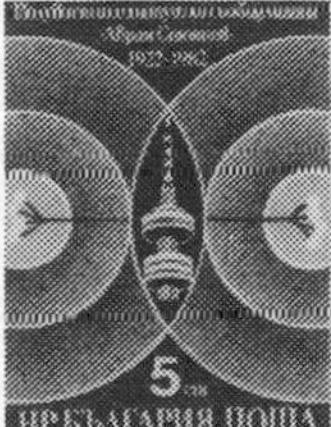
60th Anniv. of Institute of Communications A1096

1982, Dec. 9
2858 A1096 5s ultra 10 5

60th Anniv. of USSR A1097

1982, Dec. 9
2859 A1097 13s multi 24 10

The Piano, by Pablo Picasso (1881-1973) A1098

Perf. 11½x12½
1982, Dec. 24 Litho.
2860 A1098 13s shown 28 10
2861 A1098 30s Portrait of Jacqueline 55 25
2862 A1098 42s Maternity 80 35

Souvenir Sheet
2863 A1098 1 l Self-portrait 2.00 1.00

Size of No. 2863: 62x80mm.

2nd Flag of Peace Youth Assembly — A1099

Various children's drawings. 8s, 13s, 50s vert.

1982, Dec. 28 *Perf. 14*
2864 A1099 3s multi 6 5
2865 A1099 5s multi 10 5
2866 A1099 8s multi 18 8
2867 A1099 13s multi 28 10
2868 A1099 25s multi 50 20
2869 A1099 30s multi 55 25
Nos. 2864-2869 (6) 1.67 73

Souvenir Sheet

Perf. 14, Imperf.
2870 A1099 50s Shaking hands 1.00 50

New Year A1100

1982, Dec. 28 Photo. *Perf. 13*
2872 A1100 5s multi 10 5
2873 A1100 13s multi 24 10

Robert Koch (TB Bacillus Centenary) A1101

1982, Dec. 28
2874 A1101 25s shown 55 20
2875 A1101 30s Simon Bolivar 60 25
2876 A1101 30s Rabindranath Tagore (1861-1941) 60 25

Vassil Levski (1837-1873), Revolutionary A1102

1983, Jan. 10 Photo. *Perf. 13x13½*
2877 A1102 5s ol & brn 10 5

Universiade Games — A1103

1983, Feb. 15 *Perf. 13*
2878 A1103 30s Downhill skiing 50 25

Fresh-water Fish — A1104

1983, Mar. 24 Photo. *Perf. 13½x13*
2879 A1104 3s Pike 6 5
2880 A1104 5s Sturgeon 10 5
2881 A1104 13s Chub 30 12
2882 A1104 25s Perch 55 22
2883 A1104 30s Catfish 60 25
2884 A1104 42s Trout 80 35
Nos. 2879-2884 (6) 2.41 1.04

Karl Marx (1818-1883) A1105

1983, Apr. 5 *Perf. 13x13½*
2885 A1105 13s multi 25 12

Jaroslav Hasek (1883-1923) — A1106

1983, Apr. 20 Photo. *Perf. 13*
2886 A1106 13s multi 25 12

Martin Luther (1483-1546) A1107

1983, May 10
2887 A1107 13s multi 25 12

55th Anniv. of Komsomol Youth Movement — A1108

1983, May 13
2888 A1108 5s "PMC" 10 5

National Costumes A1109

1983, May 17 Litho. *Perf. 14*
2889 A1109 5s Chaskovov 10 3
2890 A1109 8s Pernik 16 8
2891 A1109 13s Burgas 25 12
2892 A1109 25s Tolbukhin 45 22
2893 A1109 30s Blagoevgrad 50 25
2894 A1109 42s Topolovgrad 70 35
Nos. 2889-2894 (6) 2.16 1.07

6th Satire and Humor Biennial, Gabrovo — A1111

Design: Old Man Feeding Chickens.

1983, May 20
2900 A1111 5s multi 10 5

Christo Smirnensky (1898-1983), Poet — A1112

1983, May 25
2901 A1112 5s multi 10 5

17th Intl. Geodesists' Congress — A1113

1983, May 27
2902 A1113 30s Emblem 60 30

Interarch '83 Architecture Exhibition, Sofia — A1114

1983, June 6
2903 A1114 30s multi 60 30

8th European Chess Championships, Plovdiv — A1115

1983, June 20 Photo. *Perf. 13*
2904 A1115 13s Chess pieces, map of Europe 25 12

Souvenir Sheets

BRASILIANA '83 Philatelic Exhibition — A1116

1983, June 24
2905 A1116 1 l Brazilian and Bulgarian stamps 2.25 1.10

Multicolored margin shows symbols and text. Size: 75x104mm.

Social Democratic Party Congress of Russia, 80th Anniv. A1118

Design: Lenin addressing congress.

1983, July 29 Photo. *Perf. 13*
2907 A1118 5s multi 10 5

Ilinden-Preobrazhensky Insurrection, 80th Anniv. — A1119

1983, July 29
2908 A1119 5s Gun, dagger, book 10 5

Institute of Mining and Geology, Sofia, 30th Anniv. — A1120

1983, Aug. 10
2909 A1120 5s multi 10 5

60th Anniv. of September 1923 Uprising — A1121

1983, Aug. 19
2910 A1121 5s multi 10 5
2911 A1121 13s multi 25 12

Angora Cat A1123

1983, Sept. 26 ***Perf. 13***
2917 A1123 5s shown 10 5
2918 A1123 13s Siamese 28 10
2919 A1123 20s Abyssinian, vert. 50 20
2920 A1123 25s Persian 60 25
2921 A1123 30s European, vert. 75 30
2922 A1123 42s Indochinese 1.00 42
Nos. 2917-2922 (6) 3.23 1.32

Animated Film Festival — A1124

1983, Sept. 15 Photo. ***Perf. 14x13½***
2923 A1124 5s Articulation layout 10 5

Trevethick's Engine, 1804 — A1125

Locomotives: 13s, Blenkinsop's Prince Royal, 1810. 42s, Hedley's Puffing Billy, 1812. 60s, Adler (first German locomotive), 1835.

1983, Oct. 20 ***Perf. 13***
2924 A1125 5s multi 10 5
2925 A1125 13s multi 30 10
2926 A1125 42s multi 1.00 42
2927 A1125 60s multi 1.40 60

See Nos. 2983-2987.

Souvenir Sheet

Liberation Monument, Plovdiv — A1126

1983, Nov. 4
2928 A1126 50s multi 1.25 75

Philatelic Federation, 90th anniv. Gold marginal inscription. Size: 66x79mm.

Sofia Opera, 75th Anniv. — A1127

Composers' Assoc., 50th Anniv. — A1128

1983, Dec. 2 ***Perf. 13x13½***
2929 A1127 5s Mask, lyre, laurel 10 5

1983, Dec. 5

Composers: 5s, Ioan Kukuzel (14th cent.) 8s, Atanasov. 13s, Petko Stainov. 20s, Veselin Stodiov. 25s, Liubomir Pipkov. 30s, Pancho Vladigerov. Se-tenant with labels showing compositions.

2930 A1128 5s multi 10 5
2931 A1128 8s multi 16 8
2932 A1128 13s multi 28 10
2933 A1128 20s multi 45 20
2934 A1128 25s multi 55 25
2935 A1128 30s multi 70 30
Nos. 2930-2935 (6) 2.24 98

New Year 1984 A1129

1983, Dec. 10 ***Perf. 13***
2936 A1129 5s multi 10 5

Angelo Donni, by Raphael A1130

1983, Dec. 22 ***Perf. 14***
2937 A1130 5s shown 10 5
2938 A1130 13s Cardinal 28 10
2939 A1130 30s Baldassare Castiglioni 65 30
2940 A1130 42s Donna Belata 95 42

Souvenir Sheet

2941 A1130 1 l Sistine Madonna 2.50 1.25

No. 2941 has silver marginal inscription. Size: 60x98mm.

Bat, World Wildlife Emblem — A1131

Various bats and rodents.

1983, Dec. 30 ***Perf. 13***
2942 A1131 12s multi 24 8
2943 A1131 13s multi 26 10
2944 A1131 20s multi 40 20
2945 A1131 30s multi 65 30
2946 A1131 42s multi 95 42
Nos. 2942-2946 (5) 2.50 1.10

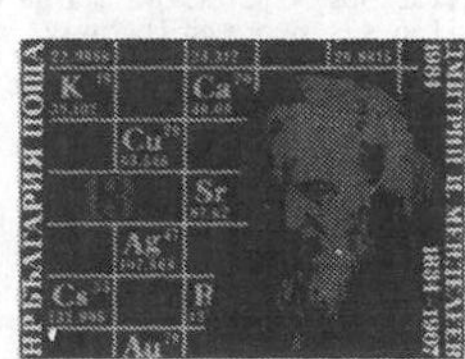

Dmitri Mendeleev (1834-1907), Russian Chemist — A1132

1984, Mar. 14
2947 A1132 13s multi 26 10

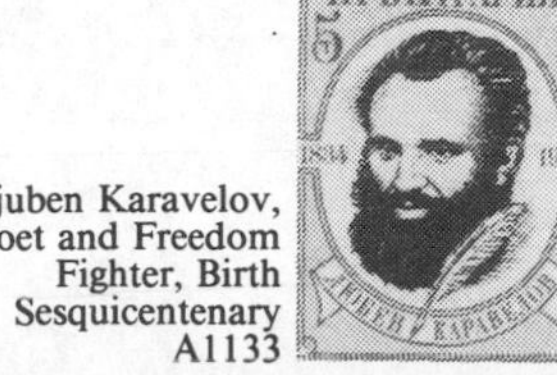

Ljuben Karavelov, Poet and Freedom Fighter, Birth Sesquicentenary A1133

1984, Jan. 31 ***Perf. 13x13½***
2948 A1133 5s multi 10 5

Tanker Gen. V.I. Zaimov A1137

1984, Mar. 22 ***Perf. 13½***
2959 A1137 5s shown 10 5
2960 A1137 13s Mesta 30 10
2961 A1137 25s Veleka 60 25
2962 A1137 32s Ferry 75 32
2963 A1137 42s Cargo ship Rossen 1.00 42
Nos. 2959-2963 (5) 2.75 1.14

Souvenir Sheet

World Cup Soccer Commemorative of 1982, Spain No. 2281 — A1137a

1984, Apr. 18 Photo. ***Perf. 13x13½***
2963A A1137a 2l multi 4.00 2.00

ESPANA '84. No. 2963A has multicolored decorative margin containing exhibition and FIP emblems; black control number. Size: 89x110mm.

Dove with Letter over Globe — A1138

Berries — A1139

1984, Apr. 24 ***Perf. 13***
2964 A1138 5s multi 10 5

World Youth Stamp Exhibition, Pleven, Oct. 5-11.

1984, May 5
2965 A1139 5s Cherries 10 5
2966 A1139 8s Strawberries 16 8
2967 A1139 13s Blackberries 30 10
2968 A1139 20s Raspberries 50 22
2969 A1139 42s Currants 1.00 48
Nos. 2965-2969 (5) 2.06 93

6th Republican Spartikiade Games — A1140

1984, May 23
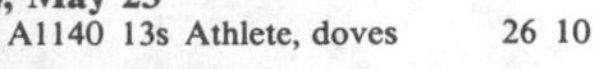
2970 A1140 13s Athlete, doves 26 10

6th Amateur Art Festival — A1142

1984, June 12
2972 A1142 5s Folk singer, drum 10 5

Bulgarian-Soviet Relations, 50th Anniv. — A1143

1984, June 27
2973 A1143 13s Initialed seal 26 10

Doves and Pigeons — A1144

1984, July 6 Litho. ***Perf. 14***
2974 A1144 5s Rock dove 10 5
2975 A1144 13s Stock dove 30 10
2976 A1144 20s Wood pigeon 50 20
2977 A1144 30s Turtle dove 70 30
2978 A1144 42s Domestic pigeon 1.00 42
Nos. 2974-2978 (5) 2.60 1.07

1st Natl. Communist Party Congress, 60th Anniv. — A1145

1984, May 18 Photo. ***Perf. 13½x13***
2979 A1145 5s multi 10 5

Souvenir Sheet

Intl. Stamp Exhibition, Essen, May 26-31 — A1146

Europa Conference stamps: No. 2980a, 1980. No. 2980b, 1981.

1984, May 22 *Perf. 13x13½*
2980 Sheet of 2 15.00 12.50
a.-b. A1146 1.50 l multi 7.50 6.25

No. 2980 has multicolored margin picturing exhibition emblem; black control number. Size: 94x147mm.

Mount Everest — A1147

1984, May 31 *Perf. 13*
2981 A1147 5s multi 10 5

1st Bulgarian Everest climbing expedition, Apr. 20-May 9.

Souvenir Sheet

UPU Congress, Hamburg — A1148

1984, June 11 *Perf. 13½x13*
2982 A1148 3 l Sailing ship 15.00 12.50

No. 2982 has multicolored decorative margin picturing figureheads, congress and association emblems; black control number. Size: 100x107mm.

Locomotives Type of 1983

1984, July 31 *Perf. 13*
2983 A1125 13s Best Friend of Charleston, 1830, USA 28 14
2984 A1125 25s Saxonia, 1836, Dresden 50 25
2985 A1125 30s Lafayette, 1837, USA 60 30
2986 A1125 42s Borsig, 1841, Germany 85 42
2987 A1125 60s Philadelphia, 1843, Austria 1.25 65
Nos. 2983-2987 (5) 3.48 1.76

September 9 Revolution, 40th Anniv. A1149

1984, Aug. 4
2988 A1149 5s K, production quality emblem 10 5
2989 A1149 20s Victory Monument, Sofia 40 20
2990 A1149 30s Star, "9" 60 30

Paintings by Nenko Balkanski (1907-1977) — A1150

1984, Sept. 17 *Perf. 14*
2991 A1150 5s Boy Playing Harmonica, vert. 10 5
2992 A1150 30s A Paris Window, vert. 60 30
2993 A1150 42s Double Portrait 85 42

Souvenir Sheet

2994 A1150 1 l Self-portrait, vert. 2.00 1.00

No. 2994 has multicolored decorative margin. Size: 65x110mm.

MLADPOST '84 International Youth Stamp Exhibition, Pleven — A1151

Buildings in Pleven: 5s, Mausoleum to Russian soldiers, 1877-78 Russo-Turkish War. 13s, Panorama Building.

1984, Sept. 20 *Perf. 13*
2995 A1151 5s multi 10 5
2996 A1151 13 multi 28 14

Septembrist Young Pioneers Org., 40th Anniv. — A1152

1984, Sept. 21 **Photo.** *Perf. 13*
2997 A1152 5s multi 10 5

Nikola Vapzarov A1153

1984, Oct. 2
2998 A1153 5s mar & pale yel 10 5

Natl. Soccer, 75th Anniv. A1154

1984, Oct. 3
2999 A1154 42s multi 85 42

Souvenir Sheet

MLADPOST '84 — A1155

1984, Oct. 5 **Photo.** *Perf. 13*
3000 A1155 50s multi 1.00 50

Bridges and Maps — A1156

1984, Oct. 5 **Photo.** *Perf. 13½x13*
3001 A1156 5s Devil's Bridge, Arda River 10 5
3002 A1156 13s Koljo-Fitscheto, Bjala 28 14
3003 A1156 30s Asparuchow, Warna 65 32
3004 A1156 42s Bebresch Highway Bridge, Botevgrad 90 45

Intl. Olympic Committee, 90th Anniv. — A1158

1984, Oct. 24 **Photo.** *Perf. 13*
3007 A1158 13s multi 28 14

Pelecanus Crispus — A1159

1984, Nov. 2
3008 A1159 5s Adult, young 10 5
3009 A1159 13s Two adults 28 14
3010 A1159 20s Adult in water 40 20
3011 A1159 32s In flight 65 32

World Wildlife Fund.

Anton Ivanov (1884-1942), Labor Leader — A1160

1984, Nov. 2
3012 A1160 5s multi 10 5

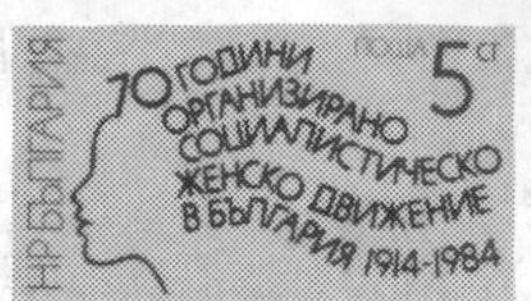

Women's Socialist Movement, 70th Anniv. — A1161

1984, Nov. 9
3013 A1161 5s multi 10 5

Telecommunication Towers — A1162

1984, Nov. 23
3014 A1162 5s Snezhanka 10 5
3015 A1162 1 l Orelek 2.00 1.00

Snowflakes, New Year 1985 — A1163

1984, Dec. 5
3016 A1163 5s Doves, posthorns 10 5
3017 A1163 13s Doves, blossom 28 14

Paintings by Stoyan Venev (b. 1904) — A1164

1984, Dec. 10 **Litho.**

3018	A1164	5s	September Nights	10	5
3019	A1164	30s	Man with Three Medals	60	30
3020	A1164	42s	The Best	85	42

Butterflies A1165

1984, Dec. 14 ***Perf. 11½***

3021	A1165	13s	Inachis io	28	14
3022	A1165	25s	Papilio machaon	50	25
3023	A1165	30s	Brintesia circe	60	30
3024	A1165	42s	Anthocaris cardamines	85	42
3025	A1165	60s	Vanessa atalanta	1.20	60
			Nos. 3021-3025 (5)	3.43	1.71

Souvenir Sheet

3026	A1165	1 l	Limenitis populi	2.00	1.00

No. 3026 has multicolored margin picturing Limenitis populi. Size: 75x60mm.

Cesar Augusto Sandino (1895-1934), Nicaraguan Freedom Fighter — A1166

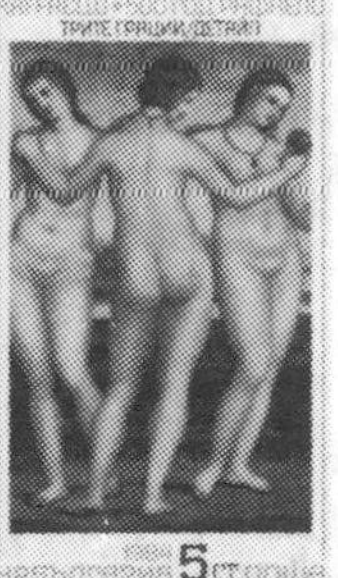

Raphael, 500th Birth Anniv. (1983) — A1167

1984, Dec. 18 **Photo.** ***Perf. 13x13½***

3027	A1166	13s	multi	28	14

1984, Dec. 28 **Litho.** ***Perf. 14***

3028	A1167	5s	The Three Graces	10	5
3029	A1167	13s	Cupid and the Graces	28	14
3030	A1167	30s	Original Sin	60	30
3031	A1167	42s	La Fornarina	85	42

Souvenir Sheet

3032	A1167	1 l	Galatea	2.00	1.00

No. 3032 has multicolored margin continuing design. Size: 106x95mm.

The indexes in each volume of the Scott Catalogue contain many listings which help to identify stamps.

Cruise Ship Sofia, Maiden Voyage — A1168

1984, Dec. 29 **Photo.** ***Perf. 13***

3033	A1168	13s	bl, dk bl & yel	28	14

Predators A1170

1985, Jan. 17

3035	A1170	13s	Conepatus leuconotus	28	14
3036	A1170	25s	Prionodon linsang	50	25
3037	A1170	30s	Ictonix striatus	60	30
3038	A1170	42s	Hemigalus derbyanus	85	42
3039	A1170	60s	Galidictis fasciata	1.20	60
			Nos. 3035-3039 (5)	3.43	1.71

Nikolai Liliev (1885-1960), Poet, UNESCO Emblem — A1171

1985, Jan. 25

3040	A1171	30s	multi	60	30

Zviatko Radojnov (1895-1942), Labor Leader — A1172

1985, Jan. 29

3041	A1172	5s	dk red & dk brn	10	5

Dr. Assen Zlatarov (1885-1936), Chemist A1173

1985, Feb. 14

3042	A1173	5s	multi	10	5

Souvenir Sheet

Akademik, Research Vessel — A1174

1985, Mar. 1

3043	A1174	80s	multi	1.60	80

UNESCO Intl. Oceanographic Commission, 25th anniv. No. 3043 has multicolored inscribed margin picturing UN and commission emblems and marine life. Size: 90x60mm.

Souvenir Sheet

Lenin — A1175

1985, Mar. 12

3044	A1175	50s	multi	1.00	50

No. 3044 has tan, dark red and silver margin continuing the design. Size: 56x88mm.

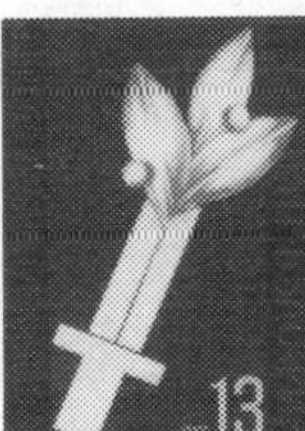

Warsaw Treaty Org., 30th Anniv. — A1176

1985, Mar. 19

3045	A1176	13s	multi	28	14

Composers A1177

1985, Mar. 25

3046	A1177	42s	Bach	85	42
3047	A1177	42s	Mozart	85	42
3048	A1177	42s	Tchaikovsky	85	42
3049	A1177	42s	Mussorgsky	85	42
3050	A1177	42s	Verdi	85	42
3051	A1177	42s	Tenev	85	42
			Nos. 3046-3051 (6)	5.10	2.52

Children's Drawings Type of 1982

Inscribed 1985. Various children's drawings.

1985, Mar. 26 **Litho.** ***Perf. 14***

3052	A1099	5s	multi	10	5
3053	A1099	8s	multi	16	8
3054	A1099	13s	multi	28	14
3055	A1099	20s	multi	40	20
3056	A1099	25s	multi	50	25
3057	A1099	30s	multi	60	30
			Nos. 3052-3057 (6)	2.04	1.02

Souvenir Sheet

3058	A1099	50s	Children dancing, vert.	1.00	50

3rd Banner of Peace Intl. Assembly, Sofia. No. 3058 has multicolored decorative margin. Exists with and without blue control number. Size: 71x111mm.

St. Methodius, 1100th Death Anniv. — A1179

1985, Apr. 6 **Photo.** ***Perf. 13***

3059	A1179	13s	multi	28	14

Victory Parade, Moscow, 1945 A1180

Designs: 13s, 11th Infantry on parade, Sofia. 30s, Soviet soldier, orphan. 50s, Soviet flag-raising, Berlin.

1985, Apr. 30 ***Perf. 13½***

3060	A1180	5s	multi	10	5
3061	A1180	13s	multi	28	14
3062	A1180	30s	multi	60	30

Souvenir Sheet

Perf. 13

3063	A1180	50s	multi	1.00	50

Defeat of Nazi Germany, end of World War II, 40th anniv. Nos. 3060-3062 printed se-tenant with labels picturing Soviet (5s, 30s) and Bulgarian medals of honor. No. 3063 has multicolored decorative margin picturing postwar scenes, Soviet Orders of the Patriotic War and Victory. Size: 90x124mm.

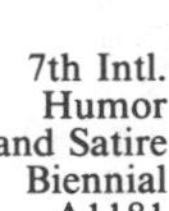

7th Intl. Humor and Satire Biennial A1181

1985, Apr. 30 ***Perf. 13½***

3064	A1181	13s	yel, sage grn & red	28	14

No. 3064 printed se-tenant with label picturing Gabrovo Cat emblem.

Intl. Youth Year — A1182

1985, May 21 ***Perf. 13***

3065	A1182	13s	multi	28	14

Ivan Vasov (1850-1921), Poet — A1183

1985, May 30 *Perf. 13½*

3066 A1183 5s tan & sep 10 5

No. 3066 printed se-tenant with label picturing Vasov's birthplace in Sopot.

Soviet War Memorial, Haskovo City Arms A1184

1985, June 1 *Perf. 13*

3067 A1184 5s multi 10 5

Haskovo millennium.

12th World Youth Festival, Moscow — A1185

1985, June 25

3068 A1185 13s multi 28 14

Indira Gandhi (1917-1984), Prime Minister of India — A1186

1985, June 26

3069 A1186 30s org yel, sep & ver 60 30

Vasil Aprilov, Founder — A1187

1985, June 30

3070 A1187 5s multi 10 5

1st secular school, Gabrovo, 150th anniv.

A particular stamp may be scarce, but if few collectors want it, its market value may remain relatively low.

INTERSTENO '85 — A1188

1985, June 30

3071 A1188 13s multi 28 14

Congress for the Intl. Union of Stenographers and Typists, Sofia.

Alexander Nevski Cathedral A1189

1985, July 9

3072 A1189 42s multi 85 42

World Tourism Org., general assembly, Sofia.

UN, 40th Anniv. A1190

1985, July 16

3073 A1190 13s multi 28 14

Admission of Bulgaria to UN, 30th Anniv. — A1191

1985, July 16

3074 A1191 13s multi 28 14

Roses — A1192

1985, July 20 **Litho.**

3075	A1192	5s	Rosa damascena	10	5
3076	A1192	13s	Rosa trakijka	28	14
3077	A1192	20s	Rosa radiman	40	20
3078	A1192	30s	Rosa marista	60	30
3079	A1192	42s	Rosa valentina	85	42
3080	A1192	60s	Rosa maria	1.20	60
			Nos. 3075-3080 (6)	3.43	1.71

Helsinki Conference, 10th Anniv. — A1193

1985, Aug. 1 **Photo.**

3081 A1193 13s multi 28 14

European Swimming Championships, Sofia — A1194

1985, Aug. 2 **Litho.** *Perf. 12½*

3082	A1194	5s	Butterfly stroke	10	5
3083	A1194	13s	Water polo, vert.	28	14
3084	A1194	42s	Diving, vert.	85	42
3085	A1194	60s	Synchronized swimming	1.20	50

The 60s exists with central design inverted.

Natl. Tourism Assoc., 90th Anniv. A1195

1985, Aug. 15 **Photo.** *Perf. 13*

3086 A1195 5s multi 10 5

1986 World Cup Soccer Championships, Mexico — A1196

Various soccer plays. Nos. 3087-3090 vert.

1985, Aug. 29 *Perf. 13*

3087	A1196	5s	multi	10	5
3088	A1196	13s	multi	28	14
3089	A1196	30s	multi	60	30
3090	A1196	42s	multi	85	42

Souvenir Sheet

3091 A1196 1 l multi 2.00 1.00

No. 3091 has multicolored margin picturing soccer cup, emblem and stadium. Size: 55x77mm.

Union of Eastern Rumelia and Bulgaria, 1885 — A1197

1985, Aug. 29 *Perf. 14x13½*

3092 A1197 5s multi 10 5

Computer Design Portraits — A1198

1985, Sept. 23 *Perf. 13*

3093	A1198	5s	Boy	10	5
3094	A1198	13s	Youth	28	14
3095	A1198	30s	Cosmonaut	60	30

Intl. Exhibition of the Works of Youth Inventors, Plovdiv.

St. John the Baptist Church, Nessebar A1199

Natl. restoration projects: 13s, Tyrant Hreljo Tower, Rila Monastery. 35s, Soldier, fresco, Ivanovo Rock Church. 42s, Archangel Gabriel, fresco, Bojana Church. 60s, Thracian Woman, fresco, Tomb of Kasanlak, 3rd century B.C. 1L, The Horseman of Madara, bas-relief.

1985, Sept. 25 **Litho.** *Perf. 12½*

3096	A1199	5s	multi	10	5
3097	A1199	13s	multi	28	14
3098	A1199	35s	multi	70	35
3099	A1199	42s	multi	85	42
3100	A1199	60s	multi	1.25	65
			Nos. 3096-3100 (5)	3.18	1.61

Souvenir Sheet

Imperf

3101 A1199 1 l multi 2.00 1.00

UNESCO, 40th anniv. No. 3101 has multicolored margin picturing the site and UNESCO emblem. Size: 100x83mm.

Souvenir Sheet

Ludmila Zhishkova Cultural Palace, Sofia — A1200

1985, Oct. 8 *Perf. 13*

3102 A1200 1 l multi 2.00 1.00

UNESCO 23rd General Assembly, Sofia. No. 3102 has multicolored margin showing the assembly site; UNESCO emblem. Size: 62x96mm.

Colosseum, Rome — A1201

1985, Oct. 15 Photo. *Perf. 13½*
3103 A1201 42s multi 85 42

ITALIA '85. No. 3103 printed se-tenant with label picturing the exhibition emblem.

Souvenir Sheet

Cultural Congress, Budapest — A1202

Designs: No. 3104a, St. Cyril, patron saint of Europe. No. 3104b, Map of Europe. No. 3104c, St. Methodius, patron saint of Europe.

Perf. 13, 13 Vert. (#3104b)
1985, Oct. 22 Photo.
3104 Sheet of 3 3.00 1.50
a.-c. A1202 50s, any single 1.00 50

Helsinki Congress, 10th anniv. No. 3104 has blue and green inscribed margin. Size: 105x93mm.

Flowers — A1203

1985, Oct. 22 Photo. *Perf. 13x13½*
3105 A1203 5s Gladiolus hybridy 10 5
3106 A1203 5s Iris germanica 10 5
3107 A1203 5s Convolvulus tricolor 10 5

Historic Sailing Ships A1204

1985, Oct. 28 Photo. *Perf. 13*
3108 A1204 5s Dutch 10 5
3109 A1204 12s Sea Sovereign, Britain 24 12
3110 A1204 20s Mediterranean 40 20
3111 A1204 25s Royal Prince, Britain 50 25
3112 A1204 42s Mediterranean 85 42
3113 A1204 60s British battleship 1.20 60
Nos. 3108-3113 (6) 3.29 1.64

The only foreign revenue stamps listed in this Catalogue are those authorized for prepayment of postage.

Souvenir Sheet

PHILATELIA '85, Cologne — A1205

Designs: No. 3114a, Cologne Cathedral. No. 3114b, Alexander Nevski Cathedral, Sofia.

1985, Nov. 4 *Imperf.*
3114 Sheet of 2 1.25 62
a.-b. A1205 30s, any single 60 30

No. 3114 has pale yellow green margin picturing exhibition emblem. Size: 110x55mm.

Conspiracy to Liberate Bulgaria from Turkish Rule, 150th Anniv. — A1206

Freedom fighters and symbols: No. 3115, Georgi Stojkov Rakowski (1820-1876). No. 3116, Batscho Kiro (1835-1876). No. 3117, Sword, Bible and hands.

1985, Nov. 6 *Perf. 13*
3115 A1206 5s multi 10 5
3116 A1206 5s multi 10 5
3117 A1206 13s multi 25 12

Liberation from Byzantine Rule, 800th Anniv. A1207

Paintings: 5s, The Revolt 1185, by G. Bogdanov. 13s, The Revolt 1185, by Alexander Tersiev. 30s, Battle Near Klokotnitza, by B. Grigorov and M. Ganowski. 42s, Velika Tarnovo Town Wall, by Zanko Lawrenov. 1 l, St. Dimitriev Church, 12th cent.

1985, Nov. 15 Litho.
3118 A1207 5s multi 10 5
3119 A1207 13s multi 25 12
3120 A1207 30s multi 60 30
3121 A1207 42s multi 85 42

Souvenir Sheet

Imperf

3122 A1207 1 l multi 2.00 1.00

No. 3122 has buff, olive bister and dark green margin picturing city arms of Velika Tarnovo. Size: 74x80mm.

Souvenir Sheet

BALKANPHILA '85 — A1208

1985, Nov. 29 Photo. *Perf. 13*
3123 A1208 40s Dove, posthorn 80 40

No. 3123 has blue and violet blue inscribed margin picturing exhibition emblem. Size: 55x80mm.

Intl. Post and Telecommunications Development Program — A1209

1985, Dec. 2
3124 A1209 13s multi 28 14

Anton Popov (1915-1942), Freedom Fighter — A1210

1985, Dec. 11 Photo. *Perf. 13*
3125 A1210 5s lake 10 5

New Year 1986 A1211

1985, Dec. 11 Photo. *Perf. 13*
3126 A1211 5s Doves, snowflake 10 5
3127 A1211 13s Doves 28 14

Hunting Dogs and Prey — A1212

Designs: 5s, Pointer and partridge. 8s, Irish setter and pochard. 13s, English setter and mallard. 20s, Cocker spaniel and woodcock. 25s, German pointer and rabbit. 30s, Balkan hound and boar. 42s, Shorthaired dachshund and fox.

1985, Dec. 27 Litho. *Perf. 13x12½*
3128 A1212 5s multi 10 5
3129 A1212 8s multi 16 8
3130 A1212 13s multi 28 14
3131 A1212 20s multi 40 20
3132 A1212 25s multi 50 25
3133 A1212 30s multi 60 30
3134 A1212 42s multi 85 42
Nos. 3128-3134 (7) 2.89 1.44

Intl. Year of the Handicapped — A1213

1985, Dec. 30 Photo. *Perf. 13*
3135 A1213 5s multi 10 5

George Dimitrov (1882-1949) — A1214

1985, Dec. 30 Photo. *Perf. 13*
3136 A1214 13s brn lake 25 12

7th Intl. Communist Congress, Moscow.

UN Child Survival Campaign — A1215

1986, Jan. 21 Photo. *Perf. 13*
3137 A1215 13s multi 28 14

UNICEF, 40th anniv.

Demeter Blagoev (1856-1924) A1216

1986, Jan. 28 Photo. *Perf. 13*
3138 A1216 5s dk lake, car & dk red 10 5

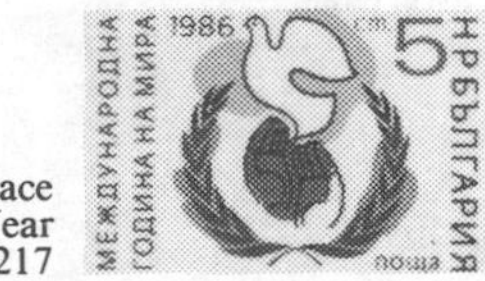

Intl. Peace Year A1217

1986, Jan. 31 *Perf. 13½*
3139 A1217 5s multi 10 5

Orchids — A1218

1986, Feb. 12 Litho. *Perf. 13x12½*

3140 A1218	5s	Dactylorhiza romana	10	5
3141 A1218	13s	Epipactis palustris	25	12
3142 A1218	30s	Ophrys cornuta	60	30
3143 A1218	32s	Limodorum abortivum	65	32
3144 A1218	42s	Cypripedium calceolus	85	42
3145 A1218	60s	Orchis papilionacea	1.20	60
a.		Miniature sheet of 6	3.75	1.75
		Nos. 3140-3145 (6)	3.65	1.81

Size: 177x109mm.

Hares and Rabbits A1219

1986, Feb. 24 *Perf. 12½x12*

3146 A1219	5s	multi	10	5
3147 A1219	25s	multi	50	25
3148 A1219	30s	multi	60	30
3149 A1219	32s	multi	65	32
3150 A1219	42s	multi	85	42
3151 A1219	60s	multi	1.20	60
		Nos. 3146-3151 (6)	3.90	1.94

Bulgarian Eagle, Newspaper, 140th Anniv. — A1220

Design: Front page of first issue and Ivan Bogorov, journalist.

1986, Feb. 2 Photo. *Perf. 13*

3152 A1220	5s	multi	10	5

Souvenir Sheet

Halley's Comet A1221

Comet's orbit in the Solar System: No. 3153a, 1980. No. 3153b, 1910-1986. No. 3153c, 1916-1970. No. 3153d, 1911.

1986, Mar. 7 *Perf. 13½x13*

3153	Sheet of 4	2.00	1.00
a.-d.	A1221 25s, any single	50	25

No. 3153 has violet black and violet gray margin picturing Edmond Halley, Planet-A, Vega, Giotto and Pioneer space probes, and Bulgarian observatory telescope. Size: 121x115mm.

Vladimir Bachev (1935-1967), Poet — A1222

1986, Mar. 12 *Perf. 13x13½*

3154 A1222	5s	dp bl & bl	10	5

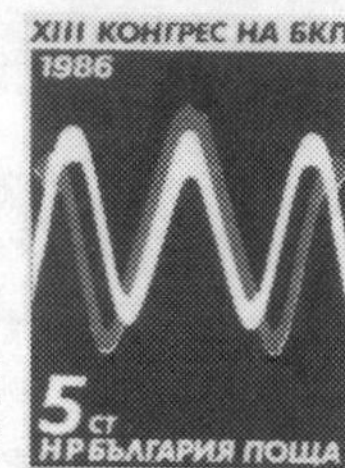

13th Natl. Communist Party Congress A1223

1986, Mar. 17 *Perf. 13*

3155 A1223	5s	Wavy lines	10	5
3156 A1223	8s	Star	16	8
3157 A1223	13s	Worker	28	14

Souvenir Sheet

Imperf

3158 A1223	50s	Scaffold, flags	1.00	50

No. 3158 has dark red inscribed margin. Size: 60x78mm.

Souvenir Sheet

1st Manned Space Flight, 25th Anniv. — A1224

Designs: No. 3159a, Vostok I, 1961. No. 3159b, Yuri Gagarin (1934-1968), Russian cosmonaut.

1986, Mar. 28 *Perf. 13½x13*

3159	Sheet of 2	2.00	1.00
a.-b.	A1224 50s, any single	1.00	50

No. 3159 has greenish black and greenish blue margin picturing star chart, Soyuz-Salyut space lab, Vostok 6, Intercosmos emblem and Apollo 11. Size: 105x101mm.

April Uprising against the Turks, 110th Anniv. — A1225

Monuments: 5s, 1876 Uprising monument, Panagjuriste. 13s, Christo Botev, Vraca.

1986, Mar. 30 *Perf. 13*

3160 A1225	5s	multi	10	5
3161 A1225	13s	multi	28	14

Souvenir Sheet

Levsky-Spartak Sports Club, 75th Anniv. — A1226

1986, May 12 *Imperf.*

3162 A1226	50s	Rhythmic gymnastics	1.00	50

No. 3162 has dull grayish violet and gray margin picturing athletes. Size: 80x65mm.

35th Congress of Bulgarian Farmers, Sofia — A1227

1986, May 19 *Perf. 13*

3163 A1227	5s	Congress emblem	10	5
3164 A1227	8s	Emblem on globe	16	8
3165 A1227	13s	Flags	28	14

Conference of Transport Ministers from Socialist Countries — A1228

1986, May 27 *Perf. 13x13½*

3166 A1228	13s	multi	28	14

17th Intl. Book Fair, Sofia — A1229

1986, May 28

3167 A1229	13s	blk, brt red & grysh blk	28	14

1986 World Cup Soccer Championships, Mexico — A1230

Various soccer plays; attached labels picture Mexican landmarks.

1986, May 30 *Perf. 13½*

3168 A1230	5s	multi, vert.	10	5
3169 A1230	13s	multi	28	14
3170 A1230	20s	multi	40	20
3171 A1230	30s	multi	60	30
3172 A1230	42s	multi	85	42
3173 A1230	60s	multi, vert.	1.20	60
		Nos. 3168-3173 (6)	3.43	1.71

Souvenir Sheet

Perf. 13

3174 A1230	1 l	Azteca Stadium	2.00	1.00

Treasures of Preslav — A1231

Gold artifacts: 5s, Embossed brooch. 13s, Pendant with pearl cross, vert. 20s, Crystal and pearl pendant. 30s, Embossed shield. 42s, Pearl and enamel pendant, vert. 60s, Enamel shield.

1986, June 7 *Perf. 13½x13, 13x13½*

3175 A1231	5s	multi	10	5
3176 A1231	13s	multi	28	14
3177 A1231	20s	multi	40	20
3178 A1231	30s	multi	60	30
3179 A1231	42s	multi	85	42
3180 A1231	60s	multi	1.20	60
		Nos. 3175-3180 (6)	3.43	1.71

World Fencing Championships, Sofia, July 25-Aug. 3 — A1232

1986, July 25 Photo. *Perf. 13*

3181 A1232	5s	Head cut, lunge	10	5
3182 A1232	13s	Touche	28	14
3183 A1232	25s	Lunge, parry	50	25

Flower Type of 1985

1986, July 29 *Perf. 13x13½*

3184 A1203	8s	Ipomoea tricolor	16	8
3185 A1203	8s	Anemone coronaria	16	8
3186 A1203	32s	Lilium auratum	65	32

STOCKHOLMIA '86 — A1233

1986, Aug. 25

3187 A1233	42s	sep, sal brn & lake	85	42

No. 3187 printed in sheets of 3 plus 3 labels picturing folk art.

Miniature Sheet

Environmental Conservation A1234

Designs: No. 3188a, Ciconia ciconia. No. 3188b, Nuphar lutea. No. 3188c, Salamandra salamandra. No. 3188d, Nymphaea alba.

1986, Aug. 25 Litho. *Perf. 14*
3188 Sheet of 4 + label 1.80 90
a.-d. A1234 30s, any single 60 30

No. 3188 contains center label picturing the oldest oak tree in Bulgaria, Granit Village. Size: 139x90mm.

Natl. Arms, Building of the Sobranie — A1235

1986, Sept. 13 Photo. *Perf. 13*
3189 A1235 5s Prus grn, yel grn & red 10 5

People's Republic of Bulgaria, 40th anniv.

15th Postal Union Congress — A1236

1986, Sept. 24
3190 A1236 13s multi 28 14

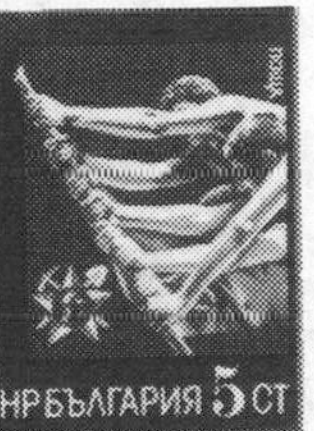
Natl. Youth Brigade Movement, 40th Anniv. A1237

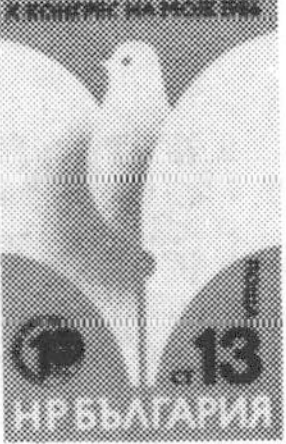
Intl. Organization of Journalists, 10th Congress A1238

1986, Oct. 4
3191 A1237 5s multi 10 5

1986, Oct. 13
3192 A1238 13s bl & dk bl 28 14

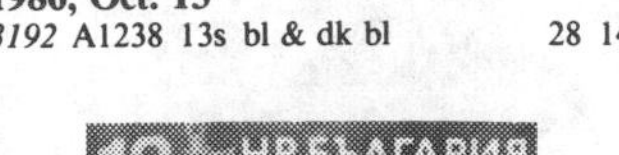

Sts. Cyril and Methodius, Disciples — A1239

1986, Oct. 23 *Perf. 13½*
3193 A1239 13s dk brn & buff 28 14

Sts. Cyril and Methodius in Bulgaria, 1100th anniv. No. 3193 printed se-tenant with inscribed label.

Telephones in Bulgaria, Cent. — A1240

1986, Nov. 5 *Perf. 13*
3194 A1240 5s multi 10 5

World Weight Lifting Championships — A1241

1986, Nov. 6
3195 A1241 13s multi 28 14

Ships A1242

1986, Nov. 20

3196	A1242	5s King of Prussia	10	5
3197	A1242	13s East Indiaman, 18th cent.	28	14
3198	A1242	25s Shebek, 18th cent.	50	25
3199	A1242	30s St Paul	60	30
3200	A1242	32s Topsail schooner, 18th cent.	65	32
3201	A1242	42s Victory	85	42
		Nos. 3196-3201 (6)	2.98	1.48

Souvenir Sheet

European Security and Cooperation Congress, Vienna — A1243

Various buildings and emblems: No. 3202a, Bulgaria. No. 3202b, Austria. No. 3202c, Donau Park, UN.

Perf. 13, Imperf. x13 (#3202b)
1986, Nov. 27
3202 Sheet of 3 3.00 1.50
a.-c. A1243 50s, any single 1.00 50

No. 3202 has blue and yellow-green inscribed margin. Exists imperf. bearing control number. Size: 106x90mm.

Rogozen Thracian Pitchers A1244

1986, Dec. 5 *Perf. 13*
3203 A1244 10s Facing left 20 10
3204 A1244 10s Facing right 20 10

Union of Bulgarian Philatelists, 14th Congress. Nos. 3203-3204 printed se-tenant with labels picturing carved figures on pitchers in blocks of 4.

New Year 1987 A1245

1986, Dec. 9
3205 A1245 5s shown 10 5
3206 A1245 13s Snow flakes 28 14

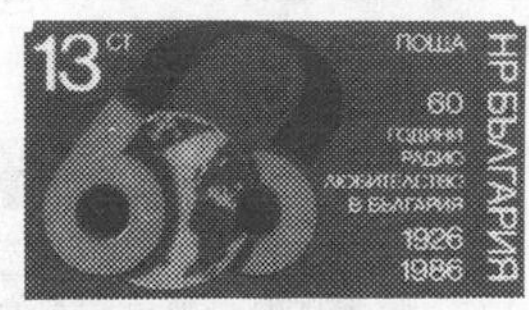
Home Amateur Radio Operators in Bulgaria, 60th Anniv. — A1246

1986, Dec. 10
3207 A1246 13s multi 28 14

Miniature Sheet

Paintings by Bulgarian Artists — A1247

Designs: No. 3208a, Red Tree, by Danail Dechev (1891-1962). No 3208b, Troopers Confront Two Men, by Ilya Beshkov (1901-1958). No. 3208c, View of Melnik, by Veselin Stajkov (1906-1970). No. 3208d, View of Houses through Trees, by Kyril Zonev (1896-1961).

1986, Dec. 10 Litho. *Perf. 14*
3208 Sheet of 4 2.25 1.10
a.-b. A1247 25s, any single 50 25
c.-d. A1247 30s, any single 60 30

Sofia Academy of Art, 90th anniv. Size: 146x102mm.

Augusto Cesar Sandino (1893-1934), Nicaraguan Revolutionary, and Flag — A1248

1986, Dec. 16 Photo. *Perf. 13*
3209 A1248 13s multi 28 14

Sandinista movement in Nicaragua, 25th anniv.

Smoyan Mihylovsky (b. 1856), Writer — A1249

Ran Bossilek (b. 1886) A1250

Title Page from Bulgarian Folk Songs of the Miladinov Brothers A1251

Annivs. and events: No. 3211, Pentcho Slaveyckov (b. 1861), writer. No. 3212, Nickola Atanassov (b. 1886), musician.

1986, Dec. 17

3210	A1249	5s multi	10	5
3211	A1249	5s multi	10	5
3212	A1249	8s multi	16	8
3213	A1250	8s multi	16	8
3214	A1251	10s multi	20	10
		Nos. 3210-3214 (5)	72	36

A1252

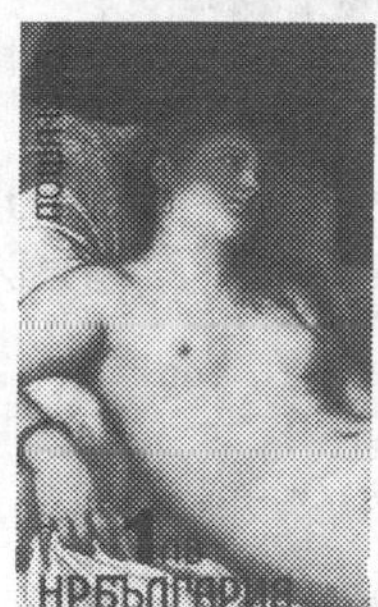
Paintings by Titian — A1253

Various portraits.

1986, Dec. 23 Litho. *Perf. 14*

3215	A1252	5s multi	10	5
3216	A1252	13s multi	28	14
3217	A1252	20s multi	40	20
3218	A1252	30s multi	60	30
3219	A1252	32s multi	65	32
3220	A1252	42s multi	85	42
a.		Min. sheet of 6, #3215-3220	3.00	1.50
		Nos. 3215-3220 (6)	2.88	1.43

Souvenir Sheet

3221 A1253 1 l multi 2.00 1.00

Size of No. 3220a: 150x166mm. No. 3221 has inscribed multicolored margin continuing the design and bearing black control number. Size: 106x76mm.

Rayko Daskalov (b. 1886), Politician A1254

1986, Dec. 23 Photo. *Perf. 13*

3222 A1254 5s deep claret 10 5

Sports Cars — A1255

1986, Dec. 30 Litho. *Perf. 13½*

3223 A1255 5s 1905 Fiat 10 5
3224 A1255 10s 1928 Bugatti 20 10
3225 A1255 25s 1936 Mercedes 50 25
3226 A1255 32s 1952 Ferrari 65 32
3227 A1255 40s 1985 Lotus 80 40
3228 A1255 42s 1986 McLaren 85 42
Nos. 3223-3228 (6) 3.10 1.54

Varna Railway Inauguration, 120th Anniv. — A1257

1987, Jan. 19 Photo.

3229 A1257 5s multi 15 6

Dimcho Debelianov (1887-1916), Poet — A1258

1987, Jan. 20 Photo. *Perf. 13*

3230 A1258 5s blue, dull yel & deep blue 15 6

L.L. Zamenhof, Creator of Esperanto A1259

1987, Feb. 12

3231 A1259 13s multi 15 6

Mushrooms A1260

10th Natl. Trade Unions Congress A1261

1987, Feb. 6 Litho. *Perf. 11½*

3232 A1260 5s Amanita rubescens 15 6
3233 A1260 20s Boletus regius 60 30
3234 A1260 30s Leccinum aurantiacum 90 45
3235 A1260 32s Coprinus comatus 95 48
3236 A1260 40s Russula vesca 1.20 60
3237 A1260 60s Cantharellus cibarius 1.80 90
a. Miniature sheet of 6, Nos. 3232-3237 5.75
Nos. 3232-3237 (6) 5.60 2.79

1987, Mar. 20 Photo. *Perf. 13*

3238 A1261 5s dark red & vio 15 6

Rogozen Thracian Treasure A1262

Embossed and gilded silver artifacts: 5s, Plate, Priestess Auge approaching Heracles. 8s, Pitcher, lioness attacking stag. 20s, Plate, floral pattern. 30s, Pitcher, warriors on horseback dueling. 32s, Urn, decorative pattern. 42s, Pitcher (not gilded), winged horses.

1987, Mar. 31

3239 A1262 5s multi 15 6
3240 A1262 8s multi 24 12
3241 A1262 20s multi 60 30
3242 A1262 30s multi 90 45
3243 A1262 32s multi 95 48
3244 A1262 42s multi 1.25 62
Nos. 3239-3244 (6) 4.09 2.03

Miniature Sheet

Modern Architecture — A1263

Designs: No. 3245a, Ludmila Zhivkova conference center, Varna. No. 3245b, Ministry of Foreign Affairs, Sofia. No. 3245c, Interpred Building, Sofia. No. 3245d, Hotel, Sandanski.

1987, Apr. 7 *Perf. 13½x13*

3245 Sheet of 4 3.75 1.80
a.-d. A1263 30s any single 90 45

No. 3245 has inscribed decorative margin. Exists imperf. with black control number. Size: 108x101mm.

European Freestyle Wrestling Championships A1264

1987, Apr. 22 *Perf. 13*

3246 A1264 5s multi 15 6
3247 A1264 13s multi, diff. 38 18

CAPEX '87, Toronto A1265

1987, Apr. 24

3248 A1265 42s multi 1.25 42

10th Congress of the Natl. Front — A1266

1987, May 11

3249 A1266 5s multi 15 6

15th Communist Youth Congress — A1267

1987, May 13

3250 A1267 5s George Dimitrov 15 6

8th Humor and Satire Biennial, Gabrovo A1268

1987, May 15 *Perf. 13x13½*

3251 A1268 13s multi 38 12

13th World Rhythmic Gymnastics Championships, Varna — A1269

Gymnasts.

1987, Aug. 5 Photo. *Perf. 13*

3252 A1269 5s Maria Gigova 14 6
3252A A1269 8s Iliana Raeva 20 10
3252B A1269 13s Anelia Ralenkova 32 16
3252C A1269 25s Pilyana Georgieva 65 32
3252D A1269 30s Lilia Ignatova 75 38
3252E A1269 42s Bianca Panova 1.05 52
Nos. 3252-3252E (6) 3.11 1.54

Souvenir Sheet

Perf. 13x13½

3252F A1269 1 l Neshka Robeva, trainer 2.50 1.25

No. 3252F has pale violet and ultramarine margin picturing exercises. Exists imperf with black control number. Size: 79x88mm.

Vasil Kolarov — A1270

1987, June 3 *Perf. 13*

3253 A1270 5s dark red, yel & dark blue 15 6

Stela Blagoeva (b.1887) A1271

1987, June 4

3254 A1271 5s pink & sepia 15 6

Rabotnichesko Delo Newspaper, 60th Anniv. — A1272

1987, May 28

3255 A1272 5s black & lake 15 6

Deer A1273

1987, June 23 Litho.

3256 A1273 5s Capreolus capreolus, vert. 15 6
3257 A1273 10s Alces alces 30 15
3258 A1273 32s Dama dama, vert. 95 48
3259 A1273 40s Cervus nippon, vert. 1.20 60
3260 A1273 42s Cervus elaphus 1.25 62
3261 A1273 60s Rangifer tarandus, vert. 1.80 90
a. Miniature sheet of 6, Nos. 3256-3261, imperf. 5.75 2.85
Nos. 3256-3261 (6) 5.65 2.81

Size of No. 3261a: 144x130mm.

Vassil Levski (b. 1837) A1274

Various portraits.

1987, June 19 **Photo.**
3262 A1274 5s red brn & dark grn 15 6
3263 A1274 13s dark grn & red brn 40 20

Namibia Day
A1275

1987, July 8
3264 A1275 13s org, blk & dark red 40 20

Georgi Kirkov (1867-1919), Revolutionary
A1276

1987, July 17 ***Perf. 13x13½***
3265 A1276 5s claret & deep claret 15 6

Bees and Plants — A1277

1987, July 29 **Litho.** ***Perf. 13***
3266 A1277 5s Phacelia tanacetifolia 15 6
3267 A1277 10s Helianthus annuus 30 15
3268 A1277 30s Robinia pseudoacacia 90 45
3269 A1277 32s Lavandula vera 95 48
3270 A1277 42s Tilia parvifolia 1.25 62
3271 A1277 60s Onobrychis sativa 1.80 90
a. Min. sheet of 6, Nos. 3266-3271 5.35 2.75
Nos. 3266-3271 (6) 5.35 2.66

BULGARIA '89 — A1278

1987, Sept. 3 ***Perf. 13½x13***
3272 A1278 13s No. 1 40 20

HAFNIA '87 — A1279

1987, Sept. 8 ***Perf. 13***
3273 A1279 42s multi 1.25 62

No. 3273 issued in sheets of 3 plus 2 labels picturing emblems of the HAFNIA '87 and BULGARIA '89 exhibitions, and 1 label with background similar to Denmark Type A32 with castle instead of denomination.

Portrait of a Girl, by Stefan Ivanov
A1280

Paintings in the Sofia City Art Galler: 8s, Grape-gatherer, by Bencho Obreshkov. 20s, Portrait of a Lady with a Hat, by David Perets. 25s, Listeners of Marimba, by Kiril Tsonev. 32s, Boy with an Harmonica, by Nenko Balkanski. 60s, Rumyana, by Vasil Stoilov.

1987, Sept. 15 **Litho.** ***Perf. 14***
3274 A1280 5s shown 15 6
3275 A1280 8s multi 25 12
3276 A1280 20s multi 60 30
3277 A1280 25s multi 75 38
3278 A1280 32s multi 95 48
3279 A1280 60s multi 1.80 90
Nos. 3274-3279 (6) 4.50 2.24

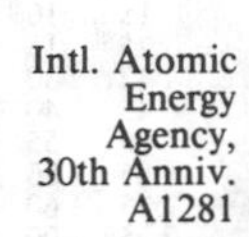

Intl. Atomic Energy Agency, 30th Anniv.
A1281

1987, Sept. 15 **Photo.** ***Perf. 13½x13***
3280 A1281 13s re, lt blue & emer 40 20

Songbirds
A1282

1987, Oct. 12 **Litho.** ***Perf. 12½x12***
3281 A1282 5s Troglodytes troglodytes 15 6
3282 A1282 13s Emberiza citrinella 40 20
3283 A1282 20s Sitta europaea 60 30
3284 A1282 30s Turdus merula 90 45
3285 A1282 42s Coccothraustes coccothraustes 1.25 62
3286 A1282 60s Cinclus cinclus 1.80 90
a. Miniature sheet of 6, Nos. 3281-3286 5.25 2.25
Nos. 3281-3286 (6) 5.10 2.53

Size of No. 3286a: 115x105mm.

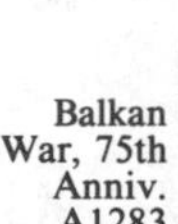

Balkan War, 75th Anniv.
A1283

1987, Sept. 15 **Photo.** ***Perf. 13½***
3287 A1283 5s buff, blk & brt org 14 6

SEMI-POSTAL STAMPS

Regular Issues of 1911-20 Surcharged:

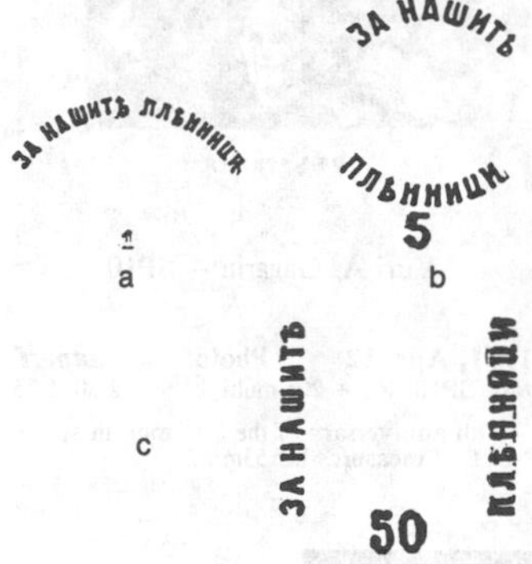

Perf. 11½x12, 12x11½.

1920, June 20 **Unwmk.**
B1 A43 (a) 2s + 1s ol grn 5 5
B2 A44 (b) 5s + 2½s grn 5 5
B3 A44 (b) 10s + 5s rose 5 5
B4 A44 (b) 15s + 7½s vio 5 5
B5 A44 (b) 25s + 12½s dp bl 5 5
B6 A44 (b) 30s + 15s choc 5 5
B7 A44 (b) 50s + 25s yel brn 5 5
B8 A29 (c) 1 l + 50s dk brn 15 15
B9 A37a (a) 2 l + 1 l brn org 25 35
B10 A38 (a) 3 l + 1½ l cl 55 65
Nos. B1-B10 (10) 1.30 1.50

Surtax aided ex-prisoners of war. Price, Nos. B1-B7 imperf., $12.50.

Souvenir Sheet

SP1

1937, Nov. 22 **Photo.** ***Imperf.***
B11 SP1 2 l + 18 l ultra 4.00 4.00

Issued to commemorate the 19th anniversary of the accession of Tsar Boris III to the throne. Size: 80x115mm.

Stamps of 1917-21 Surcharged in Black

Наводненнето
1939
1+1
лсва

1939, Oct. 22 ***Perf. 12½, 12***
B12 A34 1 l + 1 l on 15s sl 10 10
B13 A69 2 l + 1 l on 1½l ol grn 12 12
B14 A69 4 l + 2 l on 2 l dp grn 18 18
B15 A69 7 l + 4 l on 3 l Prus bl 45 45
B16 A69 14 l + 7 l on 5 l red brn 80 80
Nos. B12-B16 (5) 1.65 1.65

The surtax aided victims of the Sevlievo flood.

The surcharge on Nos. B13-B16 omits "leva."

Map of Bulgaria — SP2

1947, June 6 **Typo.** ***Perf. 11½***
B17 SP2 20 l + 10 l dk brn red & grn 40 45

Issued to commemorate the 30th Jubilee Esperanto Congress, Sofia, 1947.

Postman
SP3

Radio Towers
SP6

Designs: 10 l+5 l, Lineman. 20 l+10 l, Telephone operators.

1947, Nov. 5
B18 SP3 4 l + 2l ol brn 6 6
B19 SP3 10 l + 5l brt red 15 15
B20 SP3 20 l + 10l dp ultra 15 15
B21 SP6 40 l + 20l choc 75 75

Christo Ganchev — SP7

Actors' Portraits: 10 l+6 l, Adriana Budevska. 15 l+7 l, Vasil Kirkov. 20 l+15 l, Sava Ognianov. 30 l+20 l, Krostyu Sarafov.

1947, Dec. 8 **Litho.** ***Perf. 10½***
B22 SP7 9 l + 5 l Prus grn 10 10
B23 SP7 10 l + 6 l car lake 18 18
B24 SP7 15 l + 7 l rose vio 18 18
B25 SP7 20 l + 15 l ultra 18 18
B26 SP7 30 l + 20 l vio brn 45 45
Nos. B22-B26 (5) 1.09 1.09

National Theater, 50th anniversary.

Souvenir Sheet

Olympic Emblem — SP8

1964, Oct. 10 **Litho.** ***Imperf.***
B27 SP8 40s + 20s bis, red & bl 3.50 2.25

Issued to commemorate the 18th Olympic Games, Tokyo, Oct. 10-25. No. B27 measures 60x68mm.

Horsemanship Type of 1965

Miniature Sheet

Design: 40s+20s, Hurdle race.

1965, Sept. 30 **Photo.** ***Imperf.***
B28 A630 40s + 20s bluish gray, gold & vio blk 3.00 1.50

No. B28 measures 80x79mm.

Space Exploration Type of 1966

Designs: 20s+10s, Yuri A. Gagarin, Alexei Leonov and Valentina Tereshkova. 30s+10s, Rocket and globe.

1966, Sept. 29 Photo. *Perf. 11½x11*
B29 A652 20s + 10s pur & gray 1.00 50

Miniature Sheet
Imperf.
B30 A652 30s + 10s gray, fawn & blk 2.00 1.25

Issued to publicize Russian space explorations. No. B30 measures 59x51mm.

Winter Olympic Games Type of 1967

Sports and Emblem: 20s+10s, Slalom. 40s+10s, Figure skating couple.

1967, Sept. Photo. *Perf. 11*
B31 A687 20s + 10s multi 1.35 45

Souvenir Sheet
Imperf.
B32 A687 40s + 10s multi 2.50 1.25

Issued to publicize the 10th Winter Olympic Games, Grenoble, France, Feb. 6-8, 1968. No. B32 has silver and bister marginal design. Size: 68x68mm.

Type of Olympic Games Issue, 1968

Designs: 20s+10s, Rowing. 50s+10s, Stadium, Mexico City, and communications satellite.

1968, June 24 Photo. *Perf. 10½*
B33 A702 20s + 10s vio bl, gray & pink 1.00 35

Miniature Sheet
Imperf.
B34 A702 50s + 10s gray, blk & Prus bl 2.50 1.50

Issued to publicize the 19th Olympic Games, Mexico City, Oct. 12-27. No. B34 measures 75x75mm.

Sports Type of Regular Issue, 1969

Designs: 13s+5s, Woman with ball. 20s+10s, Acrobatic jump.

1969, Oct. Photo. *Perf. 11*
Gymnasts in Light Gray
B35 A732 13s + 5s brt rose & vio 50 15
B36 A732 20s + 10s cit & bl grn 90 35

Issued to publicize the Championships for Artistic Gymnastics in Varna.

Miniature Sheet

Soccer Ball SP9

1970, Mar. 4 Photo. *Imperf.*
B37 SP9 80s + 20s org, blk, sil & bl 3.00 2.00

Issued to publicize the 9th World Soccer Championships for the Jules Rimet Cup, Mexico City, May 30-June 21, 1970. No. B37 measures 55x73½mm.

Souvenir Sheet

Yuri A. Gagarin — SP10

1971, Apr. 12 Photo. *Imperf.*
B38 SP10 40s + 20s multi 2.50 1.75

10th anniversary of the first man in space. No. B38 measures 80x53mm.

Bulgarian Lion, Magnifying Glass, Stamp Tongs — SP11

1971, July 10 Photo. *Perf. 12½*
B39 SP11 20s + 10s brn org, blk & gold 1.00 50

11th Congress of Bulgarian Philatelists, Sofia, July, 1971.

AIR POST STAMPS

Regular Issues of 1925-26 Overprinted in Various Colors

1927-28 Unwmk. *Perf. 11½.*
C1 A76 2 l ol (R) ('28) 90 75
C2 A74 4 l lake & yel (Bl) 90 75
C3 A77 10 l brn blk & brn org (G) ('28) 14.00 13.00

Overprinted Vertically and Surcharged with New Value.
C4 A77 1 on 6l dp bl & (l) pale lem (C) 90 75
a. Inverted surcharge *450.00 400.00*
b. Pair, one without surcharge *600.00*

Nos. C2-C4 overprinted in changed colors were not issued, price set $17.50.

Dove Delivering Message AP1

Junkers Plane, Rila Monastery AP2

1931, Oct. 28 Typo.
C5 AP1 1 (l) dk grn 25 10
C6 AP1 2 (l) maroon 25 10
C7 AP1 6 (l) dp bl 35 22
C8 AP1 12 (l) carmine 35 35
C9 AP1 20 (l) dk vio 90 65
C10 AP1 30 (l) dp org 1.40 1.40
C11 AP1 50 (l) org brn 2.75 1.65
Nos. C5-C11 (7) 6.25 4.47

Counterfeits exist.

1932, May 9
C12 AP2 18 l bl grn 15.00 15.00
C13 AP2 24 l dp red 15.00 15.00
C14 AP2 28 l ultra 15.00 15.00

1938, Dec. 27
C15 AP1 1 (l) vio brn 20 10
C16 AP1 2 (l) green 20 15
C17 AP1 6 (l) dp rose 75 30
C18 AP1 12 (l) pck bl 90 35

Counterfeits exist.

Mail Plane — AP3

Plane over Tsar Assen's Tower — AP4

Designs: 4 l, Plane over Bachkovski Monastery. 6 l, Bojurishte Airport, Sofia. 10 l, Plane, train and motorcycle. 12 l, Planes over Sofia Palace. 16 l, Plane over Pirin Valley. 19 l, Plane over Rila Monastery. 30 l, Plane and Swallow. 45 l, Plane over Sofia Cathedral. 70 l, Plane over Shipka Monument. 100 l, Plane and Royal Cipher.

1940, Jan. 15 Photo. *Perf. 13.*
C19 AP3 1 l dk grn 8 6
C20 AP4 2 l crimson 85 6
C21 AP4 4 l red org 10 8
C22 AP3 6 l dp bl 15 10
C23 AP4 10 l dk brn 25 15
C24 AP3 12 l dl brn 42 30
C25 AP3 16 l brt bl vio 45 40
C26 AP3 19 l sapphire 60 55
C27 AP4 30 l rose lake 85 80
C28 AP4 45 l gray vio 2.25 1.60
C29 AP4 70 l rose pink 2.25 2.00
C30 AP4 100 l dp sl bl 7.25 6.50
Nos. C19-C30 (12) 15.50 12.60

Nos. 368 and 370 Overprinted in Black

1945, Jan. 26
C31 A181 1 l brt grn 5 5
C32 A181 4 l red org 5 5

A similar overprint on Nos. O4, O5, O7 and O8 was privately applied.

Type of Parcel Post Stamps of 1944 Surcharged or Overprinted in Various Colors

Imperf.
C37 PP5 10 l on 100 l dl yel (Bl) 12 10
C38 PP5 45 l on 100 l dl yel (C) 18 15
C39 PP5 75 l on 100 l dl yel (G) 25 25
C40 PP5 100 l dl yel (V) 45 35

Plane and Sun — AP16

Pigeon with Letter — AP17

Plane and Letter AP18

Wings and Posthorn AP19

Winged Letter AP20

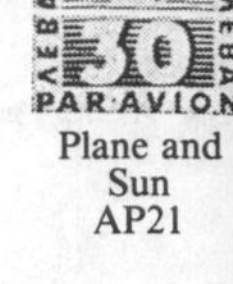

Plane and Sun AP21

Pigeon and Posthorn AP22

Mail Plane AP23

Conventionalized Figure Holding Pigeon — AP24

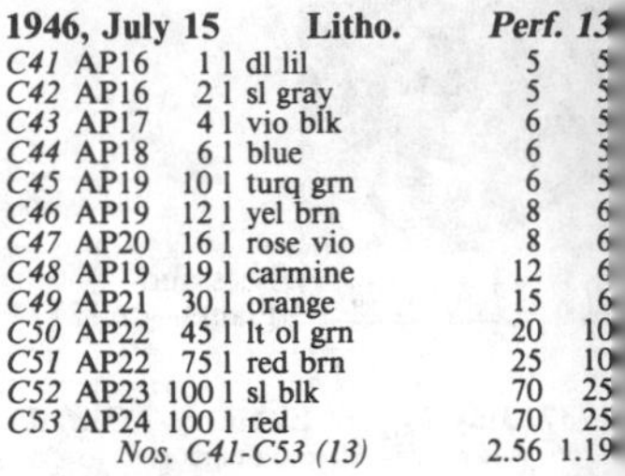

1946, July 15 Litho. *Perf. 13*
C41 AP16 1 l dl lil 5 5
C42 AP16 2 l sl gray 5 5
C43 AP17 4 l vio blk 6 5
C44 AP18 6 l blue 6 5
C45 AP19 10 l turq grn 6 5
C46 AP19 12 l yel brn 8 6
C47 AP20 16 l rose vio 8 6
C48 AP19 19 l carmine 12 6
C49 AP21 30 l orange 15 6
C50 AP22 45 l lt ol grn 20 10
C51 AP22 75 l red brn 25 10
C52 AP23 100 l sl blk 70 25
C53 AP24 100 l red 70 25
Nos. C41-C53 (13) 2.56 1.19

No. C47 exists imperf. Price $90.

People's Republic

Plane over Plovdiv AP25

1947, Aug. 31 Photo. *Imperf.*
C54 AP25 40 l dl ol grn 60 60

Plovdiv International Fair, 1947.

Baldwin's Tower — AP26

1948, May 23 Litho. *Perf. 11½*
C55 AP26 50 l ol brn, *cr* 1.10 90

Issued to commemorate Stamp Day and the 10th Congress of Bulgarian Philatelic Societies, June 1948.

Catalogue prices for unused stamps up to mid-1950 are for hinged copies matching the condition specified in this volume's introduction.

Romanian and Bulgarian Parliament Buildings AP27

Romanian and Bulgarian Flags, Bridge over Danube AP28

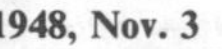

1948, Nov. 3 **Photo.**

Cream Paper

C56 AP27 40 l ol gray 25 15
C57 AP28 100 l red vio 65 50

Issued to publicize Romanian-Bulgarian friendship.

Mausoleum of Pleven — AP29

1949, June 26
C58 AP29 50 l brown 1.75 1.75

Issued to commemorate the 7th Congress of Bulgarian Philatelic Associations, June 26-27, 1949.

Symbols of the U.P.U. AP30

Frontier Guard and Dog AP31

1949, Oct. 10 ***Perf. 11½***
C59 AP30 50 l vio bl 1.25 85

Issued to commemorate the 75th anniversary of the formation of the Universal Postal Union.

1949, Oct. 31
C60 AP31 60 l ol blk 1.25 1.25

Dimitrov Mausoleum AP32

1950, July 3 ***Perf. 10½.***
C61 AP32 40 l ol brn 3.00 1.50

Issued to commemorate the first anniversary of the death of George Dimitrov, statesman.

Belogradchic Rocks — AP33

Air View of Plovdiv Fair — AP34

Designs: 16s, Beach, Varna. 20s, Harvesting grain. 28s, Rila monastery. 44s, Studena dam. 60s, View of Dimitrovgrad. 80s, View of Trnovo. 1 l, University building, Sofia. 4 l, Partisans' Monument.

1954, Apr. 1 **Unwmk.** ***Perf. 13***
C62 AP33 8s ol blk 6 5
C63 AP34 12s rose brn 6 5
C64 AP33 16s brown 10 5
C65 AP33 20s brn red, *cr* 15 5
C66 AP33 28s dp bl, *cr* 20 5
C67 AP33 44s vio brn, *cr* 20 5
C68 AP33 60s red brn, *cr* 28 8
C69 AP34 80s dk grn, *cr* 28 25
C70 AP33 1 l dk bl grn, *cr* 1.40 50
C71 AP34 4 l dp bl 3.00 1.10
Nos. C62-C71 (10) 5.73 2.23

Glider on Mountainside AP35

Designs: 60s, Glider over airport. 80s, Three gliders.

1956, Oct. 15 **Photo.**
C72 AP35 44s brt bl 20 10
C73 AP35 60s purple 35 15
C74 AP35 80s dk bl grn 55 20

Issued to commemorate the 30th anniversary of glider flights in Bulgaria.

Passenger Plane AP36

1957, May 21 **Unwmk.** ***Perf. 13***
C75 AP36 80s dp bl 80 50

Issued to commemorate the tenth anniversary of civil aviation in Bulgaria.

Sputnik 3 over Earth AP37

1958, Nov. 28 ***Perf. 11***
C76 AP37 80s brt grnsh bl 2.25 2.25

International Geophysical Year, 1957-58. Price, imperf. $7.50.

Lunik 1 Leaving Earth for Moon — AP38

1959, Feb. 28 ***Perf. 10½***
C77 AP38 2 l brt bl & ocher 4.50 4.25

Launching of 1st man-made satellite to orbit moon. Price, imperf. in slightly different colors, $6.50 unused, $7.50 canceled.

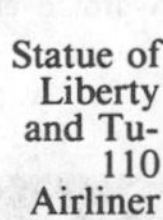

Statue of Liberty and Tu-110 Airliner AP39

Perf. 10½

1959, Nov. 11 **Photo.** **Unwmk.**
C78 AP39 1 l vio bl & pink 2.00 1.50

Visit of Khrushchev to U.S. Price, imperf. $4.50 unused, $5 canceled.

Lunik 2 and Moon — AP40

1960, June 23 **Litho.** ***Perf. 11***
C79 AP40 1.25 l bl, blk & yel 4.00 2.50

Russian rocket to the Moon, Sept. 12, 1959.

Sputnik 5 and Dogs Belka and Strelka — AP41

1961, Jan. 14 **Photo.** ***Perf. 11***
C80 AP41 1.25 l brt grnsh bl & org 4.50 3.25

Russian rocket flight of Aug. 19, 1970.

Maj. Yuri A. Gagarin and Vostok 1 — AP42

1961, Apr. 26 **Unwmk.**
C81 AP42 4 l grnsh bl, blk & red 4.00 2.50

First manned space flight, Apr. 12, 1961.

Soviet Space Dogs AP43

1961, June 28 ***Perf. 11***
C82 AP43 2 l sl & dk car 2.75 1.50

Venus-bound Rocket — AP44

1961, June 28
C83 AP44 2 l brt bl, yel & org 4.50 2.50

Issued to commemorate the Soviet launching of the Venus space probe, Feb. 12, 1961.

Maj. Gherman Titov AP45

Design: 1.25l, Spaceship Vostok 2.

1961, Nov. 20 **Photo.** ***Perf. 11x10½***
C84 AP45 75s dk ol grn & gray grn 2.50 1.50
C85 AP45 1.25 l vio bl, lt bl & pink 3.00 2.25

Issued to commemorate the first manned space flight around the world, Maj. Gherman Titov of Russia, Aug. 6-7, 1961.

Iskar River Narrows AP46

Designs: 2s, Varna and sailboat. 3s, Melnik. 10s, Trnovo. 40s, Pirin mountains.

1962, Feb. 3 **Unwmk.** ***Perf. 13***
C86 AP46 1s bl grn & gray bl 5 5
C87 AP46 2s bl & pink 10 5
C88 AP46 3s brn & ocher 30 5
C89 AP46 10s blk & lem 60 6
C90 AP46 40s dk grn & grn 1.50 40
Nos. C86-C90 (5) 2.55 61

Hyushin Turboprop Airliner AP47

1962, Aug. 18 ***Perf. 11***
C91 AP47 13s bl & blk 60 25

15th anniversary of TABSO airline.

Konstantin E. Tsiolkovsky and Rocket Launching — AP48

Design: 13s, Earth, moon and rocket on future flight to the moon.

1962, Sept. 24 ***Perf. 11***
C92 AP48 5s dp grn & gray 2.00 90
C93 AP48 13s ultra & yel 1.10 35

13th meeting of the International Astronautical Federation.

Maj. Andrian G. Nikolayev — AP49

Designs: 2s, Lt. Col. Pavel R. Popovich. 40s, Vostoks 3 and 4 in orbit.

1962, Dec. 9 **Photo.** **Unwmk.**
C94 AP49 1s bl, sl grn & blk 15 5
C95 AP49 2s bl grn, grn & blk 30 5
C96 AP49 40s dk bl grn, pink & blk 2.00 1.00

First Russian group space flight of Vostoks 3 and 4, Aug. 12-15, 1962.

Spacecraft "Mars 1" Approaching Mars — AP50

Design: 13s, Rocket launching spacecraft, Earth, Moon and Mars.

1963, Feb. 25 Unwmk. *Perf. 11*

C97	AP50	5s multi	70	25
C98	AP50	13s multi	1.40	40

Issued to commemorate the launching of the Russian spacecraft "Mars 1," Nov. 1, 1962.

Lt. Col. Valeri F. Bykovski AP51

Designs: 2s, Lt. Valentina Tereshkova. 5s, Globe and trajectories.

1963, Aug. 26 Unwmk. *Perf. 11½*

C99	AP51	1s pale vio & Prus bl	10	5
C100	AP51	2s cit & red brn	10	5
C101	AP51	5s rose & dk red	20	6

Issued to commemorate the space flights of Valeri Bykovski, June 14-19, and Valentina Tereshkova, first woman cosmonaut, June 16-19, 1963. An imperf. souvenir sheet contains one 50s stamp showing Spasski tower and globe in lilac and red brown. Light blue border with red brown inscription. Size: 77x67mm. Price $1.50. See also No. CB3.

Nos. C99-C100 Surcharged in Magenta or Green

1964, Aug. 22

C102	AP51	10s on 1s pale vio & Prus bl (M)	40	20
C103	AP51	20s on 2s cit & red brn (G)	80	25

Issued to commemorate the International Space Exhibition in Riccione, Italy. Overprint in Italian on No. C103.

St. John's Monastery, Rila — AP52

Design: 13s, Notre Dame, Paris; French inscription.

1964, Dec. 22 Photo. *Perf. 11½*

C104	AP52	5s pale brn & blk	20	10
C105	AP52	13s lt ultra & sl bl	80	30

Issued to commemorate the philatelic exhibition at St. Ouen (Seine) organized by the Franco-Russian Philatelic Circle and philatelic organizations in various People's Democracies.

Paper Mill, Bukijovtz AP53

Designs: 10s, Metal works, Plovdiv. 13s, Metal works, Kremikovtsi. 20s, Oil refinery, Stara-Zagora. 40s, Fertilizer plant, Stara-Zagora. 1 l, Rest home, Meded.

1964-68 Unwmk. *Perf. 13*

C106	AP53	8s grnsh bl	15	5
C107	AP53	10s red lil	20	6
C108	AP53	13s brt vio	30	8
C109	AP53	20s sl bl	1.00	15
C110	AP53	40s dk ol grn	1.50	25
C111	AP53	1 l red ('68)	2.50	45
		Nos. C106-C111 (6)	5.65	1.04

Three-master AP54

Veliko Turnovo — AP55

Means of Communication: 2s, Postal coach. 3s, Old steam locomotive. 5s, Early cars. 10s, Montgolfier balloon. 13s, Early plane. 20s, Jet planes. 40s, Rocket and satellites. 1 l, Postrider.

1969, Mar. 31 Photo. *Perf. 13x12½*

C112	AP54	1s gray & multi	5	5
C113	AP54	2s gray & multi	5	5
C114	AP54	3s gray & multi	5	5
C115	AP54	5s gray & multi	8	5
C116	AP54	10s gray & multi	15	10
C117	AP54	13s gray & multi	28	10
C118	AP54	20s gray & multi	55	25
C119	AP54	40s gray & multi	1.00	45
		Nos. C112-C119 (8)	2.21	1.10

Miniature Sheet

Imperf

C120	AP54	1 l gold & org	2.25	2.00

Issued to publicize SOFIA 1969 Philatelic Exhibition, Sofia, May 31-June 8. No. C120 contains one stamp, silver marginal inscription. Size: 57x54mm.

1973, July 30 Photo. *Perf. 13*

Designs: Historic buildings in various cities.

C121	AP55	2s *shown*	5	5
C122	AP55	13s *Roussalka*	30	15
C123	AP55	20s *Plovdiv*	1.75	1.25
C124	AP55	28s *Sofia*	65	30

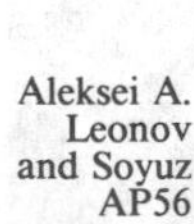

Aleksei A. Leonov and Soyuz AP56

Designs: 18s, Thomas P. Stafford and Apollo. 28s, Apollo and Soyuz over earth. 1 l, Apollo Soyuz link-up.

1975, July 15

C125	AP56	13s bl & multi	25	10
C126	AP56	18s pur & multi	35	15
C127	AP56	28s multi	80	35

Souvenir Sheet

C128	AP56	1 l vio & multi	2.75	1.75

Apollo Soyuz space test project (Russo-American cooperation), launching July 15; link-up July 17.

Balloon Over Plovdiv — AP57

1977, Sept. 3

C129	AP57	25s yel, brn & red	50	25

Alexei Leonov Floating in Space — AP58

Designs: 25s, Mariner 6, US spacecraft. 35s, Venera 4, USSR Venus probe.

1977, Oct. 14 Photo. *Perf. 13½*

C130	AP58	12s multi	25	8
C131	AP58	25s multi	50	20
C132	AP58	35s multi	75	30

Space era, 20 years.

TU-154, Balkanair Emblem — AP59

1977 *Perf. 13*

C133	AP59	35s ultra & multi	1.10	50

30th anniversary of Bulgarian airline, Balkanair, No. C133 issued in sheets of 6 stamps and 3 labels (in lilac) with commemorative inscription and Balkanair emblem.

Baba Vida Fortress AP60

Design: 35s, Peace Bridge, connecting Rousse, Bulgaria, with Giurgiu, Romania.

1978 Photo. *Perf. 13*

C134	AP60	25s multi	60	20
C135	AP60	35s multi	80	28

The Danube, European Intercontinental Waterway. Issued in sheets containing 5 each of Nos. C134-C135 and 2 labels, one showing course of Danube, the other hydrofoil and fish.

Red Cross AP61

1978, Mar. Photo. *Perf. 13*

C136	AP61	25s multi	50	20

Centenary of Bulgarian Red Cross.

Clock Tower, Byalla Cherkva — AP62

Clock Towers: 23s, Botevgrad. 25s, Pazardgick. 35s, Grabovo. 53s, Tryavna.

1979, June 5 Litho. *Perf. 12x12½*

C137	AP62	13s multi	25	10
C138	AP62	23s multi	45	18
C139	AP62	25s multi	50	20
C140	AP62	35s multi	65	28
C141	AP62	53s multi	1.10	45
		Nos. C137-C141 (5)	2.95	1.21

1980, Oct. 22 Photo. *Perf. 12x12½*

C142	AP62	12s Bjala	28	12
C143	AP62	23s Rasgrad	50	22
C144	AP62	25s Karnabat	55	25
C145	AP62	35s Serlievo	75	35
C146	AP62	53s Berkovitza	1.10	50
		Nos. C142-C146 (5)	3.18	1.44

15th World Parachute Championships, Kazanluk — AP63

1980

C147	AP63	13s *shown*	25	10
C148	AP63	25s *Parachutist*	50	20

DWVY-1 Aircraft — AP64

1981, June 27 Litho. *Perf. 12½*

C149	AP64	5s shown	10	5
C150	AP64	12s LAS-7	28	10
C151	AP64	25s LAS-8	55	20
C152	AP64	35s DAR-1	75	28
C153	AP64	45s DAR-3	1.00	38
C154	AP64	55s DAR-9	1.25	45
		Nos. C149-C154 (6)	3.93	1.46

Women in Space, 20th Anniv. — AP65

1983, June 28

C155	Sheet of 2	2.00	1.00
a.	AP65 50s Valentina Tereshkova	1.00	50
b.	AP65 50s Svetlana Savitskava	1.00	50

Multicolored margin shows Vostok 6, Soyuz T-7 and stars. Size: 122x76mm.

Certain countries cancel stamps in full sheets and sell them (usually with gum) for less than face value. Dealers generally sell "CTO".

World Communications Year — AP66

1983, July 20 **Photo.** ***Perf. 13***

C156 AP66 5s TV tower, Tolbukhin 10 5
C157 AP66 13s Postwoman 25 12
C158 AP66 30s TV tower, Mt. Botev 60 30
a. Strip of 3 (# C156-C158) 95 50

Emblems of World Communications Year, Bulgarian Post, UPU and ITU on attached margins.

Souvenir Sheet

Geophysical Map of the Moon, Russia's Luna I, II and III Satellites — AP67

1984, Oct. 24 **Photo.** ***Perf. 13***

C159 AP67 1 l multi 2.00 1.00

Conquest of Space. No. C159 has multicolored margin picturing moon walker, cosmonaut and lunar surface. Size: 79x57mm.

Intl. Civil Aviation Org., 40th Anniv. — AP68

1984, Dec. 21 **Photo.** ***Perf. 13***

C160 AP68 42s Balkan Airlines jet 85 42

Balkan Airlines — AP69

Design: Helicopter MU-8, passenger jet TU-154 and AN-21 transport plane.

1987, Aug. 25 **Photo.** ***Perf.***

C161 AP69 25s multi 75 38

AIR POST SEMI-POSTAL STAMPS

Statue of Liberty, Plane and Bridge SPAP1

Perf. 11½.

1947, May 24 **Unwmk.** **Litho.**

CB1 SPAP1 70l + 30l red brn 1.25 1.10

Issued to honor the 5th Philatelic Congress, Trnovo, and the Centenary International Philatelic Exhibition, New York, May, 1947.

Bulgarian Worker SPAP2

1948, Feb. 28 **Photo.** ***Perf. 12x11½.***

CB2 SPAP2 60 l hn brn, *cr* 55 35

Issued to commemorate the 2nd Bulgarian Workers' Congress, and sold by subscription only, at a premium of 16 levas over face value.

Type of Air Post Stamps, 1963

Design: Valeri Bykovski and Valentina Tereshkova.

1963, Aug. 26 **Unwmk.** ***Perf. 11½***

CB3 AP51 20s + 10s pale bluish grn & dk grn 1.35 60

See note after No. C101.

SPECIAL DELIVERY STAMPS

Postman on Bicycle — SD1

Mail Car — SD2

Postman on Motorcycle — SD3

1939 **Unwmk.** **Photo.** ***Perf. 13***

E1 SD1 5l dp bl 60 20
E2 SD2 6l cop brn 25 20
E3 SD3 7l gldn brn 35 25
E4 SD2 8l red org 60 25
E5 SD1 20l brt rose 1.25 60
Nos. E1-E5 (5) 3.05 1.50

POSTAGE DUE STAMPS

D1

D2

Large Lozenge Perf. 5½ to 6½.

1884 **Typo.** **Unwmk.**

J1 D1 5s orange 200.00 22.50
J2 D1 25s lake 100.00 16.00
J3 D1 50s blue 8.00 7.50

1886 ***Imperf.***

J4 D1 5s orange 100.00 4.00
J5 D1 25s lake 160.00 4.00
J6 D1 50s blue 5.50 4.25

1887 ***Perf. 11½.***

J7 D1 5s orange 12.50 1.75
J8 D1 25s lake 12.50 1.75
J9 D1 50s blue 5.00 1.75

Same, Redrawn. 24 horizontal lines of shading in upper part instead of 30 lines.

1892 ***Perf. 10½, 11½***

J10 D1 5s orange 12.50 2.00
J11 D1 25s lake 12.50 2.00

1893

Pelure Paper.

J12 D2 5s orange 15.00 5.50

D3

D4

1895 ***Imperf.***

J13 D3 30s on 50s bl 9.00 3.00

Perf. 10½, 11½

J14 D3 30s on 50s bl 9.00 3.50

Wmk. Coat of Arms in the Sheet.

1896 ***Perf. 13***

J15 D4 5s orange 4.25 1.10
J16 D4 10s purple 2.75 1.10
J17 D4 30s green 2.00 65

Nos. J15-J17 are also known on unwatermarked paper from the edges of sheets.

In 1901 a cancellation, "T" in circle, was applied to Nos. 60-65 and used provisionally as postage dues.

D5

D6

1901-04 **Unwmk.** ***Perf. 11½***

J19 D5 5s dl rose 30 15
J20 D5 10s yel grn 65 15
J21 D5 20s dl bl ('04) 5.00 22
J22 D5 30s vio brn 55 22
J23 D5 50s org ('02) 8.50 5.50
Nos. J19-J23 (5) 15.00 6.24

Nos. J19-J23 exist imperf. and in pairs imperf. between. Price, imperf., $250.

1915 **Unwmk.** ***Perf. 11½***

Thin Semi-Transparent Paper.

J24 D6 5s green 15 5
J25 D6 10s purple 25 5
J26 D6 20s dl rose 25 8
J27 D6 30s dp org 1.40 30
J28 D6 50s dp bl 45 25
Nos. J24-J28 (5) 2.50 73

1919-21 ***Perf. 11½, 12x11½***

J29 D6 5s emerald 10 6
a. 5s gray grn ('21) 30 15
J30 D6 10s violet 10 6
J31 D6 20s salmon 10 6
a. 20s yel 10 6
J32 D6 30s orange 10 8
a. 30s red org ('21) 65 65
J33 D6 50s blue 10 5
J34 D6 1 l emer ('21) 18 5
J35 D6 2 l rose ('21) 18 5
J36 D6 3 l brn org ('21) 30 5
Nos. J29-J36 (8) 1.16 47

Stotinki values of the above series surcharged 10s or 20s were used as ordinary postage stamps. See Nos. 182-185.

The 1919 printings are on thicker white paper with clean-cut perforations, the 1921 printings on thicker grayish paper with rough perforations.

Most of this series exist imperforate and in pairs imperforate between.

Heraldic Lion D7

Lion of Trnovo D8

National Arms — D9

1982, Aug. 15

Thin Paper

J37 D7 1 l ol bis 40 30
J38 D7 2 l rose brn 40 30
J39 D7 6 l brn vio 1.25 50

1933, Apr. 10

J40 D8 20s dk brn 5 5
J41 D8 40s dp bl 5 5
J42 D8 80s car rose 5 5
J43 D9 1 l org brn 30 25
J44 D9 2 l olive 40 35
J45 D9 6 l dl vio 15 10
J46 D9 14 l ultra 30 18
Nos. J40-J46 (7) 1.30 1.03

National Arms D10

Arms of the People's Republic D11

1947, June **Typo.** ***Perf. 10½***

J47 D10 1 l chocolate 5 5
J48 D10 2 l dp cl 5 5
J49 D10 8 l dp org 12 6
J50 D10 20 l blue 25 12

1951 ***Perf. 11½x10½***

J51 D11 1 l chocolate 5 5
J52 D11 2 l claret 5 5
J53 D11 8 l red org 25 15
J54 D11 20 l dp bl 70 50

OFFICIAL STAMPS

Bulgarian Coat of Arms O1 O2

1942 **Unwmk.** **Typo.** ***Perf. 13***

O1 O1 10s yel grn 5 5
O2 O1 30s red 5 5
O3 O1 50s bister 5 5
O4 O2 1 l vio bl 5 5
O5 O2 2 l dk grn 5 5
O6 O2 3 l lilac 6 5
O7 O2 4 l rose 8 5
O8 O2 5 l carmine 12 5
Nos. O1-O8 (8) 51 40

1944 ***Perf. 10½x11½***

O9 O2 1 l blue 25 15
O10 O2 2 l brt red 25 15

Lion Rampant O3 O4

O5

1945 *Imperf.*

O11	O5	1 l pink	5	5

Perf. 10½x11½, Imperf.

O12	O3	2 l bl grn	5	5
O13	O4	3 l bis brn	5	5
O14	O4	4 l lt ultra	5	5
O15	O5	5 l brn lake	5	5
		Nos. O11-O15 (5)	25	25

In 1950, four stamps prepared for official use were issued as regular postage stamps. See Nos. 724-727.

PARCEL POST STAMPS

Weighing Packages — PP1

Parcel Post — PP2

Designs: 3 l, 8 l, 20 l, Parcel post truck. 4 l, 6 l, 10 l, Motorcycle.

Perf. 12½x13½, 13½x12½.

1941-42 **Photo.** **Unwmk.**

Q1	PP1	1 l sl grn	5	5
Q2	PP2	2 l crimson	5	5
Q3	PP2	3 l dl brn	5	5
Q4	PP2	4 l red org	5	5
Q5	PP1	5 l dp bl	5	5
Q6	PP1	5 l sl grn ('42)	5	5
Q7	PP2	6 l red vio	5	5
Q8	PP2	6 l hn brn ('42)	5	5
Q9	PP1	7 l dk bl	5	5
Q10	PP1	7 l dk brn ('42)	6	5
Q11	PP2	8 l brt bl grn	6	5
Q12	PP2	8 l grn ('42)	6	5
Q13	PP2	9 l ol gray	10	5
Q14	PP2	9 l dp ol ('42)	10	5
Q15	PP2	10 l orange	10	5
Q16	PP2	20 l gray vio	40	6
Q17	PP2	30 l dl blk	55	10
Q18	PP2	30 l sep ('42)	50	10
		Nos. Q1-Q18 (18)	2.38	1.01

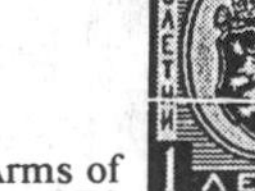
Arms of Bulgaria — PP5

1944 **Litho.** *Imperf.*

Q21	PP5	1 l dk car	5	5
Q22	PP5	3 l bl grn	5	5
Q23	PP5	5 l dl bl grn	5	5
Q24	PP5	7 l rose lil	6	5
Q25	PP5	10 l dp bl	6	5
Q26	PP5	20 l org brn	12	5
Q27	PP5	30 l dk brn car	15	5
Q28	PP5	50 l red org	35	12
Q29	PP5	100 l blue	60	25
		Nos. Q21-Q29 (9)	1.49	72

POSTAL TAX STAMPS

The use of stamps Nos. RA1 to RA18 was compulsory on letters, etc., to be delivered on Sundays and holidays. The money received from their sale was used toward maintaining a sanatorium for employees of the post, telegraph and telephone services.

View of Sanatorium PT1

Sanatorium, Peshtera PT2

1925-29 **Unwmk.** **Typo.** *Perf. 11½*

RA1	PT1	1 l *grnsh bl*	3.25	15
RA2	PT1	1 l choc ('26)	3.25	10
RA3	PT1	1 l org ('27)	3.75	15
RA4	PT1	1 l pink ('28)	5.50	15
RA5	PT1	1 l vio, *pnksh* ('29)	5.00	15
RA6	PT2	2 l bl grn	40	15
RA7	PT2	2 l vio ('27)	40	20
RA8	PT2	5 l dp bl	3.50	1.00
RA9	PT2	5 l rose ('27)	4.50	50
		Nos. RA1-RA9 (9)	29.55	2.55

St. Constantine Sanatorium PT3

1930-33

RA10	PT3	1 l red brn & ol grn	6.00	15
RA11	PT3	1 l ol grn & yel ('31)	75	15
RA12	PT3	1 l red vio & ol brn ('33)	75	15

Trojan Rest Home — PT4

Sanatorium PT5

Wmk. Wavy Lines. (145)

1935 *Perf. 11, 11½.*

RA13	PT4	1 l choc & red org	45	10
RA14	PT4	1 l emer & ind	45	10
RA15	PT5	5 l red brn & ind	2.00	45

St. Constantine Sanatorium PT6

Children at Seashore PT7

Rest Home — PT8

1941 **Unwmk.** **Photo.** *Perf. 13*

RA16	PT6	1 l dk ol grn	5	5
RA17	PT7	2 l red org	15	5
RA18	PT8	5 l dp bl	30	15

BURUNDI

LOCATION — Central Africa, adjoining the ex-Belgian Congo Republic, Rwanda and Tanzania.
GOVT. — Republic.
AREA — 10,759 sq. mi.
POP. — 4,920,000 (est. 1983).
CAPITAL — Bujumbura.

Burundi was established as an independent country on July 1, 1962. With Rwanda, it had been a U.N. trusteeship territory (Ruanda-Urundi) administered by Belgium. A military coup overthrew the monarchy November 28, 1966.

100 Centimes = 1 Franc

Flower Issue of Ruanda-Urundi, 1953 Overprinted:

Royaume du

Burundi

Perf. 11½

1962, July 1 **Unwmk.** **Photo.**

Flowers in Natural Colors

1	A27	25c dk grn & dl org	20	15
2	A27	40c grn & sal	20	15
3	A27	60c bl grn & pink	40	30
4	A27	1.25fr dk grn & bl	14.00	13.00
5	A27	1.50fr vio & ap grn	60	50
6	A27	5fr dp plum & lt bl grn	85	60
7	A27	7fr dk grn & fawn	1.65	1.10
8	A27	10fr dp plum & pale ol	2.25	1.65
		Nos. 1-8 (8)	20.15	17.45

Animal Issue of Ruanda-Urundi, 1959-61 with Similar Overprint or Surcharge in Black or Violet Blue

Size: 23x33mm., 33x23mm.

9	A29	10c brn, crim & blk brn	5	5
10	A30	20c gray, ap grn & blk	5	5
11	A29	40c mag, blk & gray grn	5	5
12	A30	50c grn, org yel & brn	6	5
a.		Larger ovpt. and bar	10	10
13	A29	1fr brn, ultra & blk	15	15
14	A30	1.50fr blk, gray & org (VB)	15	15
15	A29	2fr grnsh bl, ind & brn	15	15
16	A30	3fr brn, dp car & blk	15	15
17	A30	3.50fr on 3fr brn, dp car & blk	20	20
18	A30	4fr on 10fr multi ("XX" 6 mm wide)	30	30
a.		"XX" 4 mm wide	90	90
19	A30	5fr multi	30	30
20	A30	6.50fr red, org yel & brn	50	35
21	A30	8fr bl, mag & blk	60	45
a.		vio bl ovpt.	1.25	1.25
22	A30	10fr multi	60	60

Size: 45x26½mm.

23	A30	20fr multi	1.25	1.25
24	A30	50fr red, org, dp bl & brn (ovpt. bars 2mm wide)	2.50	2.25
a.		Ovpt. bars 4mm wide	3.75	2.25
		Nos. 9-24 (16)	7.06	6.50

On No. 12a, "Burundi" is 13mm. long; bar is continuous line across sheet. On No. 12, "Burundi" is 10mm.; bar is 29mm. No. 12a was issued in 1963.

Two types of overprint exist on 10c, 40c, 1fr and 2fr: I, "du" is below "me"; bar 22½mm. II, "du" below "oy"; bar 20mm.

The 50c and 3fr exist in two types, besides the larger 50c overprint listed as No. 12: I, "du" is closer to "Royaume" than to "Burundi"; bar is less than 29mm; wording is centered above bar. II, "du" is closer to "Burundi"; bar is more than 30mm.; wording is off-center leftward.

King Mwami Mwambutsa IV and Royal Drummers — A1

Flag and Arms of Burundi — A2

Design: 2fr, 8fr, 50fr, Map of Burundi and King.

Unwmk.

1962, Sept. 27 **Photo.** *Perf. 14*

25	A1	50c dl rose car & dk brn	10	5
26	A2	1fr dk grn, red & emer	15	5
27	A1	2fr brn ol & dk brn	20	5
28	A1	3fr ver & dk brn	45	20
29	A2	4fr Prus bl, red & emer	35	5
30	A1	8fr vio & dk brn	65	12
31	A1	10fr brt grn & dk brn	1.00	18
32	A2	20fr brn, red & emer	2.50	38
33	A1	50fr brt pink & dk brn	4.25	75
		Nos. 25-33 (9)	9.65	1.83

Issued to commemorate Burundi's independence, July 1, 1962.

Ruanda-Urundi Nos. 151-152 Surcharged:

Photogravure, Surcharge Engraved

1962, Oct. 31 *Perf. 11½*

Inscription in French

34	A31	3.50fr on 3fr ultra & red	22	15
35	A31	6.50fr on 3fr ultra & red	40	30
36	A31	10fr on 3fr ultra & red	60	50

Inscription in Flemish

37	A31	3.50fr on 3fr ultra & red	22	15
38	A31	6.50fr on 3fr ultra & red	40	30
39	A31	10fr on 3fr ultra & red	60	50
		Nos. 34-39 (6)	2.44	1.90

Issued in memory of Dag Hammarskjold, Secretary General of the United Nations, 1953-61.

King Mwami Mwambutsa IV, Map of Burundi and Emblem — A3

1962, Dec. 10 **Photo.** *Perf. 14*

40	A3	8fr yel, bl grn & blk brn	1.25	30
41	A3	50fr gray grn, bl grn & blk brn	3.25	70

Issued for the World Health Organization drive to eradicate malaria.

Stamps of type A3 without anti-malaria emblem are listed as Nos. 27, 30 and 33.

Sowing Seed over Africa — A4

1963, Mar. 21 *Perf. 14x13*

42	A4	4fr ol & dl pur	12	10
43	A4	8fr dp org & dl pur	30	20
44	A4	15fr emer & dl pur	40	30

Issued for the "Freedom from Hunger" campaign of the U.N. Food and Agriculture Organization.

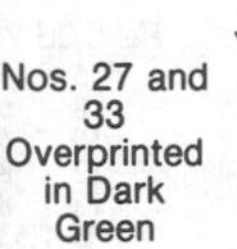
Nos. 27 and 33 Overprinted in Dark Green

1963, June 19 **Unwmk.** *Perf. 14*

45	A1	2fr brn ol & dk brn	3.25	2.50
46	A1	50fr brt pink & dk brn	3.75	2.50

Conquest and peaceful use of outer space.

Types of 1962 Inscribed: "Premier Anniversaire" in Red or Magenta

1963, July 1 **Photo.**

47	A2	4fr ol, red & emer (R)	15	8
48	A1	8fr org & dk brn (M)	25	15
49	A1	10fr lil & dk brn (M)	40	25
50	A2	20fr gray, red & emer (R)	80	50

First anniversary of independence.

Nos. 26 and 32 Surcharged in Brown

1963, Sept. 24 **Unwmk.** *Perf. 14*

51	A2	6.50fr on 1fr dk grn, red & emer	75	20
52	A2	15fr on 20fr brn, red & emer	1.50	50

Red Cross Flag over Globe with Map of Africa — A5

1963, Sept. 26 *Perf. 14x13*

53	A5	4fr emer, car & gray	25	12
54	A5	8fr brn ol, car & gray	50	25
55	A5	10fr bl, car & gray	75	35
56	A5	20fr lil, car & gray	1.50	60

Centenary of International Red Cross. See No. B7.

"1962", Arms of Burundi, U.N. and UNESCO Emblems — A6

U.N. Agency Emblems: 8fr, International Telecommunications Union. 10fr, World Meteorological Organization. 20fr, Universal Postal Union. 50fr, Food and Agriculture Organization.

1963, Nov. 4 **Unwmk.** *Perf. 14*

57	A6	4fr yel, ol grn & blk	15	10
58	A6	8fr pale lil, Prus bl & blk	30	12
59	A6	10fr bl, lil & blk	40	18
60	A6	20fr yel grn, grn & blk	70	30
61	A6	50fr yel, red brn & blk	1.75	60
a.		Souv. sheet of 2	5.25	5.25
		Nos. 57-61 (5)	3.30	1.30

Issued to commemorate the first anniversary of Burundi's admission to the United Nations. No. 61a contains two imperf. stamps with simulated perforations similar to Nos. 60-61. The 20fr stamp shows the FAO and the 50fr the WMO emblems. Gray margin with black inscription. Size: 111x73½mm.

UNESCO Emblem, Scales and Map — A7

Designs: 3.50fr, 6.50fr, Scroll, scales and "UNESCO". 10fr, 20fr, Abraham Lincoln, broken chain and scales.

1963, Dec. 10 **Litho.** *Perf. 14x13½*

62	A7	50c pink, lt bl & blk	5	5
63	A7	1.50fr org, lt bl & blk	7	5
64	A7	3.50fr fawn, lt grn & blk	18	15
65	A7	6.50fr lt vio, lt grn & blk	35	18
66	A7	10fr bl, bis & blk	60	20
67	A7	20fr pale brn, ocher, bl & blk	1.20	35
		Nos. 62-67 (6)	2.45	98

Issued to commemorate the 15th anniversary of the Universal Declaration of Human Rights and the centenary of the American Emancipation Proclamation (Nos. 66-67).

Ice Hockey — A8

Impala — A9

Designs: 3.50fr, Women's figure skating. 6.50fr, Torch. 10fr, Men's speed skating. 20fr, Slalom.

Unwmk.

1964, Jan. 25 **Photo.** *Perf. 14*

68	A8	50c ol, blk & gold	10	5
69	A8	3.50fr lt brn, blk & gold	30	10
70	A8	6.50fr pale gray, blk & gold	75	20
71	A8	10fr gray, blk & gold	1.00	27
72	A8	20fr tan, blk & gold	2.00	65
		Nos. 68-72 (5)	4.15	1.27

Issued to publicize the 9th Winter Olympic Games, Innsbruck, Jan. 29-Feb. 9, 1964.

A souvenir sheet contains two stamps (10fr+5fr and 20fr+5fr) in tan, black and gold. Size: 121x65mm.

Canceled to Order

Starting about 1964, prices in the used column are for "canceled to order" stamps. Postally used copies sell for much more.

1964 **Litho.** *Perf. 14x13, 13x14*

Size: 21½x35mm., 35x21½mm.

Animals: 1fr, 5fr, Hippopotamus (horiz.). 1.50fr, 10fr, Giraffe. 2fr, 8fr, Cape buffalo (horiz.). 3fr, 6.50fr, Zebra (horiz.). 3.50fr, 15fr, Defassa waterbuck. 20fr, Cheetah. 50fr, Elephant. 100fr, Lion.

73	A9	50c multi	10	5
74	A9	1fr multi	15	5
75	A9	1.50fr multi	20	5
76	A9	2fr multi	28	5
77	A9	3fr multi	35	6
78	A9	3.50fr multi	38	7

Size: 26x42mm., 42x26mm.

79	A9	4fr multi	45	8
80	A9	5fr multi	55	10
81	A9	6.50fr multi	65	10
82	A9	8fr multi	80	20
83	A9	10fr multi	1.00	20
84	A9	15fr multi	1.25	33

Perf. 14

Size: 53x33mm.

85	A9	20fr multi	1.65	40
86	A9	50fr multi	4.50	65
87	A9	100fr multi	7.75	1.35
		Nos. 73-87 (15)	20.06	3.74

See Nos. C1-C7.

Burundi Dancer — A10

Designs: Various Dancers and Drummers.

Unwmk.

1964, Aug. 21 **Litho.** *Perf. 14*

Dancers Multicolored

88	A10	50c gold & emer	8	5
89	A10	1fr gold & vio bl	10	5
90	A10	4fr gold & brt bl	25	10
91	A10	6.50fr gold & red	40	18
92	A10	10fr gold & brt bl	60	25
93	A10	15fr gold & emer	90	30
94	A10	20fr gold & red	1.25	45
a.		Souv. sheet of 3	3.00	3.00
		Nos. 88-94 (7)	3.58	1.38

1965, Sept. 10

Dancers Multicolored

88a	A10	50c sil & emer	8	5
89a	A10	1fr sil & vio bl	8	5
90a	A10	4fr sil & brt bl	15	10
91a	A10	6.50fr sil & red	20	15
92a	A10	10fr sil & brt bl	35	20
93a	A10	15fr sil & emer	40	35
94b	A10	20fr sil & red	60	60
c.		Souv. sheet of 3	3.00	3.00
		Nos. 88a-94b (7)	1.86	1.50

Issued to commemorate the New York World's Fair, 1964-65. No. 94a contains one each of Nos. 92-94, gold background and bright blue border. No. 94c, dated "1965" in yellow, contains one each of Nos. 92a-94b, silver background and bright blue border. Size of souvenir sheets: 120x100mm.

Pope Paul VI and King Mwami Mwambutsa IV — A11

22 Sainted Martyrs — A12

Designs: 4fr, 14fr, Pope John XXIII and King Mwami.

1964, Nov. 12 **Photo.** *Perf. 12*

95	A11	50c brt bl, gold & red brn	10	5
96	A12	1fr mag, gold & sl	10	5
97	A11	4fr pale rose lil, gold & brn	35	8
98	A12	8fr red, gold & brn	35	15
99	A11	14fr lt grn, gold & brn	85	30
100	A11	20fr red brn, gold & grn	1.25	60
		Nos. 95-100 (6)	3.00	1.23

Issued to commemorate the canonization of 22 African martyrs, Oct. 18, 1964.

Shot Put A13

African Purple Gallinule A14

Sports: 1fr, Discus. 3fr, Swimming (horiz.). 4fr, Running. 6.50fr, Javelin, woman. 8fr, Hurdling (horiz.). 10fr, Broad jump (horiz.). 14fr, Diving, woman. 18fr, High jump (horiz.). 20fr, Vaulting (horiz.).

1964, Nov. 18 **Litho.** *Perf. 14*

101	A13	50c ol & multi	5	5
102	A13	1fr brt pink & multi	6	5
103	A13	3fr multi	15	10
104	A13	4fr multi	18	12
105	A13	6.50fr multi	25	18
106	A13	8fr lt bl & multi	35	20
107	A13	10fr multi	42	25
108	A13	14fr multi	60	30
109	A13	18fr bis & multi	75	40
110	A13	20fr gray & multi	85	50
		Nos. 101-110 (10)	3.66	2.15

Issued to commemorate the 18th Olympic Games, Tokyo, Oct. 10-25, 1964. See also No. B8.

1965 **Unwmk.** *Perf. 14*

Birds in Natural Colors

Size: 21x35mm.

Birds: 1fr, 5fr, Little bee eater. 1.50fr, 6.50fr, Secretary bird. 2fr, 8fr, Yellow-billed stork. 3fr, 10fr, Congo peacock. 3.50fr, 15fr, African anhinga. 20fr, Saddle-billed stork. 50fr, Abyssinian ground hornbill. 100fr, Crowned crane.

111	A14	50c tan, grn & blk	5	5
112	A14	1fr pink, mag & blk	5	5
113	A14	1.50fr bl & blk	6	5
114	A14	2fr yel grn, dk grn & blk	8	5
115	A14	3fr yel, brn & blk	10	5
116	A14	3.50fr yel grn, dk grn & blk	10	6

Size: 26x43mm.

117	A14	4fr tan, grn & blk	12	8
118	A14	5fr pink, mag & blk	15	8
119	A14	6.50fr bl & blk	25	10
120	A14	8fr yel grn, dk grn & blk	30	10
121	A14	10fr yel, brn & blk	40	12
122	A14	15fr yel grn, dk grn & blk	75	15

Size: 33x53mm.

123	A14	20fr rose lil & blk	95	60

124	A14	50fr yel, brn & blk	2.50	40
125	A14	100fr grn, yel & blk	5.25	80
		Nos. 111-125 (15)	11.11	2.74

Issue dates: Nos. 111-116, Mar. 31. Nos. 117-122, Apr. 16. Nos. 123-125, Apr. 30. See Nos. C8-C16.

Relay Satellite and Morse Key — A15

Designs: 3fr, Telstar and old telephone handpiece. 4fr, Relay satellite and old wall telephone. 6.50fr, Orbiting Geophysical Observatory and radar screen. 8fr, Telstar II and headphones. 10fr, Sputnik II and radar aerial. 14fr, Syncom and transmission aerial. 20fr, Interplanetary Explorer and tracking aerial.

1965, July 3 Litho. *Perf. 13*

126	A15	1fr multi	5	5
127	A15	3fr multi	10	5
128	A15	4fr multi	10	10
129	A15	6.50fr multi	20	15
130	A15	8fr multi	30	18
131	A15	10fr multi	35	20
132	A15	14fr multi	50	28
133	A15	20fr multi	60	35
		Nos. 126-133 (8)	2.20	1.36

Issued to commemorate the centenary of the International Telecommunication Union. Perf. and imperf. souvenir sheets of two contain one each of Nos. 131 and 133. Bluish black margin and gold inscription. Size: 120x86mm. Price, both sheets, $7.50.

Globe and ICY Emblem — A16

Designs: 4fr, Map of Africa and U.N. development emblem. 8fr, Map of Asia and Colombo Plan emblem. 10fr, Globe and U.N. emblem. 18fr, Map of the Americas and Alliance for Progress emblem. 25fr, Map of Europe and EUROPA emblems. 40fr, Map of Outer Space and satellite with U.N. wreath.

1965, Oct. 1 Litho. *Perf. 13*

134	A16	1fr ol grn & multi	5	5
135	A16	4fr dl bl & multi	15	5
136	A16	8fr pale yel & multi	20	12
137	A16	10fr lil & multi	25	12
138	A16	18fr sal & multi	40	20
139	A16	25fr gray & multi	75	20
140	A16	40fr bl & multi	1.10	25
a.		Souv. sheet of 3	3.25	3.25
		Nos. 134-140 (7)	2.90	99

Issued for the International Cooperation Year. No. 140a contains one each of Nos. 138-140. Gray margin with multicolored inscription. Size: 101½x100mm.

Protea A17

Flowers: 1fr, 5fr, Crossandra. 1.50fr, 6.50fr, Ansellia. 2fr, 8fr, Thunbergia. 3fr, 10fr, Schizoglossum. 3.50fr, 15fr, Dissotis. 4fr, 20fr, Protea. 50fr, Gazania. 100fr, Hibiscus. 150fr, Markhamia.

1966 Unwmk. *Perf. 13½*

Size: 26x26mm.

141	A17	50c multi	5	5
142	A17	1fr multi	5	5
143	A17	1.50fr multi	5	5
144	A17	2fr multi	7	5
145	A17	3fr multi	10	5
146	A17	3.50fr multi	10	5

Size: 31x31mm.

147	A17	4fr multi	12	5
148	A17	5fr multi	15	8
149	A17	6.50fr multi	20	10
150	A17	8fr multi	25	12
151	A17	10fr multi	30	15
152	A17	15fr multi	60	20

Size: 39x39mm.

153	A17	20fr multi	75	20
154	A17	50fr multi	2.00	50
155	A17	100fr multi	3.75	75
156	A17	150fr multi	5.50	1.10
		Nos. 141-156 (16)	14.04	3.55

Issue dates: Nos. 141-147, Feb. 28; Nos. 148-153, May 18; Nos. 154-156, June 15. See Nos. C17-C25.

Souvenir Sheets

Allegory of Prosperity and Equality Tapestry by Peter Colfs — A18

1966, Nov. 4 Litho. *Perf. 13½*

157	A18	Sheet of 7 (1.50fr)	1.25	50
158	A18	Sheet of 7 (4fr)	3.25	1.25

Issued to commemorate the 20th anniversary of UNESCO (United Nations Educational, Scientific and Cultural Organization). Each sheet contains 6 stamps showing a reproduction of the Colfs tapestry from the lobby of the General Assembly Building, New York, and one stamp with the UNESCO emblem plus a label. The labels on Nos. 157-158 and C26 are inscribed in French or English. The 3 sheets with French inscription have light blue marginal border. The 3 sheets with English inscription have pink border. Size: 203x124mm. See No. C26.

Republic

Nos. 141-152, 154-156 Overprinted

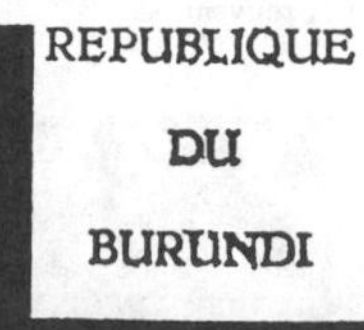

1967 Litho. *Perf. 13½*

Size: 26x26mm.

159	A17	50c multi	5	5
160	A17	1fr multi	5	5
161	A17	1.50fr multi	6	5
162	A17	2fr multi	8	5
163	A17	3fr multi	12	5
164	A17	3.50fr multi	15	5

Size: 31x31mm.

165	A17	4fr multi	1.65	60
166	A17	5fr multi	32	5
167	A17	6.50fr multi	40	5
168	A17	8fr multi	50	5
169	A17	10fr multi	62	7
170	A17	15fr multi	75	10

Size: 39x39mm.

171	A17	50fr multi	7.50	2.50
172	A17	100fr multi	12.50	5.00
173	A17	150fr multi	10.00	4.25
		Nos. 159-173 (15)	34.75	12.97

Nos. 111, 113, 116, 118-125 Overprinted "REPUBLIQUE DU BURUNDI" and Horizontal Bar

1967 Litho. *Perf. 14*

Birds in Natural Colors

Size: 21x35mm.

174	A14	50c multi	2.50	1.25
175	A14	1.50fr bl & blk	5	5
176	A14	3.50fr multi	12	5

Size: 26x43mm.

177	A14	5fr multi	15	5
178	A14	6.50fr bl & blk	18	5
179	A14	8fr multi	35	5
180	A14	10fr yel, brn & blk	65	7
181	A14	15fr multi	1.25	10

Size: 33x53mm.

182	A14	20fr multi	4.00	75
183	A14	50fr multi	8.00	2.75
184	A14	100fr multi	12.00	5.50
		Nos. 174-184 (11)	29.25	10.67

Haplochromis Multicolor — A19

Various Tropical Fish.

1967 Photo. *Perf. 13½*

Size: 42x19mm.

186	A19	50c multi	6	5
187	A19	1fr multi	6	5
188	A19	1.50fr multi	8	5
189	A19	2fr multi	10	5
190	A19	3fr multi	15	5
191	A19	3.50fr multi	18	5

Size: 50x25mm.

192	A19	4fr multi	32	5
193	A19	5fr multi	40	5
194	A19	6.50fr multi	48	5
195	A19	8fr multi	55	5
196	A19	10fr multi	65	7
197	A19	15fr multi	95	10

Size: 59x30mm.

198	A19	20fr multi	1.25	20
199	A19	50fr multi	2.75	35
200	A19	100fr multi	5.75	60
201	A19	150fr multi	8.25	85
		Nos. 186-201 (16)	21.98	2.67

Issue Dates: Nos. 186-191, Apr. 4; Nos. 192-197, Apr. 28; Nos. 198-201, May 18. See Nos. C46-C54.

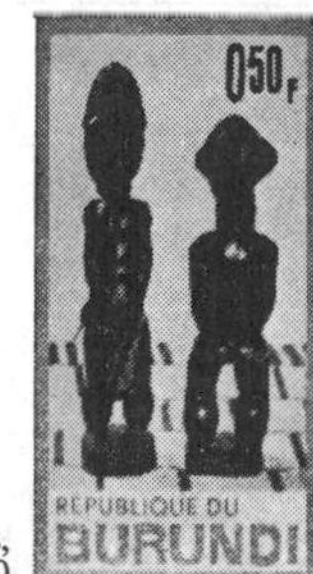

Ancestor Figures, Ivory Coast — A20

African Art: 1fr, Seat of Honor, Southeast Congo. 1.50fr, Antelope head, Aribinda Region. 2fr, Buffalo mask, Upper Volta. 4fr, Funeral figures, Southwest Ethiopia.

1967, June 5 Photo. *Perf. 13½*

202	A20	50c sil & multi	5	5
203	A20	1fr sil & multi	5	5
204	A20	1.50fr sil & multi	10	5
205	A20	2fr sil & multi	12	5
206	A20	4fr sil & multi	18	5
		Nos. 202-206,C36-C40 (10)	2.52	1.36

Scouts on Hiking Trip — A21

Designs: 1fr, Cooking at campfire. 1.50fr, Lord Baden-Powell. 2fr, Boy Scout and Cub Scout giving Scout sign. 4fr, First aid.

1967, Aug. 9 Photo. *Perf. 13½*

207	A21	50c sil & multi	5	5
208	A21	1fr sil & multi	8	6
209	A21	1.50fr sil & multi	10	6
210	A21	2fr sil & multi	12	8
211	A21	4fr sil & multi	18	8
		Nos. 207-211,C41-C45 (10)	4.08	1.63

Issued to commemorate the 60th anniversary of the Boy Scouts and the 12th Boy Scout World Jamboree, Farragut State Park, Idaho, Aug. 1-9.

The Gleaners, by Francois Millet A22

Paintings Exhibited at EXPO '67: 8fr, The Water Carrier of Seville, by Velazquez. 14fr, The Triumph of Neptune and Amphitrite, by Nicolas Poussin. 18fr, Acrobat Standing on a Ball, by Picasso. 25fr, Marguerite van Eyck, by Jan van Eyck. 40fr, St. Peter Denying Christ, by Rembrandt.

1967, Oct. 12 Photo. *Perf. 13½*

212	A22	4fr multi	25	8
213	A22	8fr multi	35	10
214	A22	14fr multi	50	12
215	A22	18fr multi	65	20
216	A22	25fr multi	1.00	35
217	A22	40fr multi	1.50	50
a.		Souv. sheet of 2	2.50	2.00
		Nos. 212-217 (6)	4.25	1.35

Issued to commemorate EXPO '67 International Exhibition, Montreal, Apr. 28-Oct. 27. Printed in sheets of 10 stamps and 2 labels inscribed in French or English. No. 217a contains one each of Nos. 216-217. Blue margin with black and red inscription. Size: 105x105mm. Exists imperf.

Place de la Revolution and Pres. Michel Micombero — A23

Designs: 5fr, President Michel Micombero and flag. 14fr, Formal garden and coat of arms. 20fr, Modern building and coat of arms.

1967, Nov. 23 *Perf. 13½*

218	A23	5fr multi	15	10
219	A23	14fr multi	40	20

220 A23	20fr multi	60	20
221 A23	30fr multi	90	45

First anniversary of the Republic.

Madonna by Carlo Crivelli — A24

Designs: 1fr, Adoration of the Shepherds by Juan Bautista Mayno. 4fr, Holy Family by Anthony Van Dyck. 14fr, Nativity by Maitre de Moulins.

1967, Dec. 7 Photo. *Perf. 13½*

222 A24	1fr multi	6	5
223 A24	4fr multi	15	10
224 A24	14fr multi	50	30
225 A24	26fr multi	1.20	50

Christmas 1967.

Printed in sheets of 25 and one corner label inscribed "Noel 1967" and giving name of painting and painter.

Slalom — A25

Designs: 10fr, Ice hockey. 14fr, Women's skating. 17fr, Bobsled. 26fr, Ski jump. 40fr, Speed skating. 60fr, Hand holding torch, and Winter Olympics emblem.

1968, Feb. 16 Photo. *Perf. 13½*

226 A25	5fr sil & multi	25	5
227 A25	10fr sil & multi	38	5
228 A25	14fr sil & multi	50	10
229 A25	17fr sil & multi	60	10
230 A25	26fr sil & multi	95	15
231 A25	40fr sil & multi	1.50	25
232 A25	60fr sil & multi	2.50	40
	Nos. 226-232 (7)	6.68	1.10

Issued to publicize the 10th Winter Olympic Games, Grenoble, France, Feb. 6-18. Issued in sheets of 10 stamps and label.

The Lacemaker, by Vermeer A26

Paintings: 1.50fr, Portrait of a Young Man, by Botticelli. 2fr, Maja Vestida, by Goya (horiz.).

1968, Mar. 29 Photo. *Perf. 13½*

233 A26	1.50fr gold & multi	8	5
234 A26	2fr gold & multi	12	8
235 A26	4fr gold & multi	25	12
	Nos. 233-235,C59-C61 (6)	3.15	1.30

Issued in sheets of 6.

Moon Probe — A27

Designs: 6fr, Russian astronaut walking in space. 8fr, Weather satellite. 10fr, American astronaut walking in space.

1968, May 15 Photo. *Perf. 13½*

Size: 35x35mm.

236 A27	4fr sil & multi	20	10
237 A27	6fr sil & multi	30	10
238 A27	8fr sil & multi	40	10
239 A27	10fr sil & multi	45	15
	Nos. 236-239,C62-C65 (8)	4.75	1.28

Issued to publicize peaceful space explorations.

A souvenir sheet contains one 25fr stamp in Moon Probe design and one 40fr in Weather Satellite design. Margin in silver and deep red lilac; black inscription. Stamp size: 41x41mm. Sheet size: 109x83mm. Price $2. Sheet exists imperf. Price $3.

Salamis Aethiops — A28

Butterflies: 1fr, 5fr, Graphium ridleyanus. 1.50fr, 6.50fr, Cymothoe. 2fr, 8fr, Charaxes cupale. 3fr, 10fr, Papilio bromius. 3.50fr, 15fr, Teracolus annae. 20fr, Salamis aethiops. 50fr, Papilio zonobia. 100fr, Danais chrysippus. 150fr, Salamis temora.

1968

Size: 30x33½mm.

240 A28	50c gold & multi	5	5
241 A28	1fr gold & multi	5	5
242 A28	1.50fr gold & multi	6	5
243 A28	2fr gold & multi	8	5
244 A28	3fr gold & multi	10	6
245 A28	3.50fr gold & multi	12	6

Size: 33½x37½mm.

246 A28	4fr gold & multi	20	8
247 A28	5fr gold & multi	25	8
248 A28	6.50fr gold & multi	55	8
249 A28	8fr gold & multi	65	8
250 A28	10fr gold & multi	75	10
251 A28	15fr gold & multi	85	15

Size: 41x46mm.

252 A28	20fr gold & multi	1.50	20
253 A28	50fr gold & multi	3.00	25
254 A28	100fr gold & multi	5.00	55
255 A28	150fr gold & multi	7.50	80
	Nos. 240-255 (16)	20.71	2.69

Issue dates: Nos. 240-245, June 7; Nos. 246-251, June 28. Nos. 252-255, July 19. See Nos. C66-C74.

Women, Along the Manzanares, by Goya — A29

Paintings: 7fr, The Letter, by Pieter de Hooch. 11fr, Woman Reading a Letter, by Gerard Terborch. 14fr, Man Writing a Letter, by Gabriel Metsu.

1968, Sept. 30 Photo. *Perf. 13½*

256 A29	4fr multi	15	8
257 A29	7fr multi	25	12
258 A29	11fr multi	40	18
259 A29	14fr multi	60	25
	Nos. 256-259,C84-C87 (8)	5.25	1.58

International Letter Writing Week.

Soccer — A30

Designs: 7fr, Basketball. 13fr, High jump. 24fr, Relay race. 40fr, Javelin.

1968, Oct. 24

260 A30	4fr gold & multi	10	5
261 A30	7fr gold & multi	18	6
262 A30	13fr gold & multi	35	10
263 A30	24fr gold & multi	70	20
264 A30	40fr gold & multi	1.15	30
	Nos. 260-264,C88-C92 (10)	7.43	2.11

Issued to commemorate the 19th Olympic Games, Mexico City, Oct. 12-27. Printed in sheets of 8.

Virgin and Child, by Fra Filippo Lippi — A31

Paintings: 5fr, The Magnificat, by Sandro Botticelli. 6fr, Virgin and Child, by Albrecht Durer. 11fr, Madonna del Gran Duca, by Raphael.

1968, Nov. 26 Photo. *Perf. 13½*

265 A31	3fr multi	15	8
266 A31	5fr multi	20	10
267 A31	6fr multi	24	15
268 A31	11fr multi	45	25
a.	Souv. sheet of 4	2.00	2.00
	Nos. 265-268,C93-C96 (8)	3.14	1.48

Christmas 1968.

No. 268a contains one each of Nos. 265-268, decorative border and inscription. Size: 120x120mm. See Nos. C93-C96.

WHO Emblem and Map of Africa — A32

1969, Jan. 22

269 A32	5fr gold, dk grn & yel	18	8
270 A32	6fr gold, vio & ver	28	12
271 A32	11fr gold, pur & red lil	45	20

Issued to commemorate the 20th anniversary of the World Health Organization in Africa.

Nos. 265-268 Overprinted in Silver

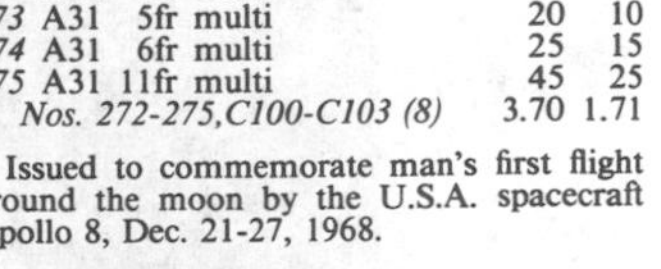

1969, Feb. 17 Photo. *Perf. 13½*

272 A31	3fr multi	15	8
273 A31	5fr multi	20	10
274 A31	6fr multi	25	15
275 A31	11fr multi	45	25
	Nos. 272-275,C100-C103 (8)	3.70	1.71

Issued to commemorate man's first flight around the moon by the U.S.A. spacecraft Apollo 8, Dec. 21-27, 1968.

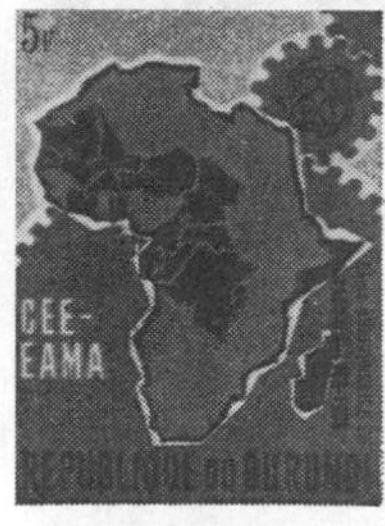

Map of Africa, and CEPT Emblem A33

Designs: 14fr, Plowing with tractor. 17fr, Teacher and pupil. 26fr, Maps of Europe and Africa and CEPT (Conference of European Postal and Telecommunications Administrations) emblem (horiz.).

1969, Mar. 12 Photo. *Perf. 13*

276 A33	5fr multi	12	8
277 A33	14fr multi	40	15
278 A33	17fr multi	50	20
279 A33	26fr multi	65	25

Issued to commemorate the 5th anniversary of the Yaoundé (Cameroun) Agreement, creating the European and African-Malgache Economic Community.

Resurrection, by Gaspard Isenmann A34

Paintings: 14fr, Resurrection by Antoine Caron. 17fr, Noli me Tangere, by Martin Schongauer. 26fr, Resurrection, by El Greco.

1969, Mar. 24

280 A34	11fr gold & multi	30	10
281 A34	14fr gold & multi	40	15
282 A34	17fr gold & multi	50	18
283 A34	26fr gold & multi	75	25
a.	Souv. sheet of 4	3.00	3.00

Easter 1969.

No. 283a contains one each of Nos. 280-283; gold and blue border and inscription. Size: 100½x125mm.

Potter — A35

Designs (ITU Emblem and): 5fr, Farm workers. 7fr, Foundry worker. 10fr, Woman testing corn crop.

1969, May 17 Photo. *Perf. 13½*

284 A35	3fr multi	12	6
285 A35	5fr multi	20	6
286 A35	7fr multi	30	12
287 A35	10fr multi	40	18

Issued to commemorate the 50th anniversary of the International Labor Organization.

Industry and Bank's Emblem A36

Designs (African Development Bank Emblem and): 17fr, Communications. 30fr, Education. 50fr, Agriculture.

1969, July 29 Photo. *Perf. 13½*

288	A36	10fr gold & multi	35	10
289	A36	17fr gold & multi	60	20
290	A36	30fr gold & multi	1.00	30
291	A36	50fr gold & multi	1.60	50
a.		Souv. sheet of 4	3.75	3.75

Issued to publicize the 5th anniversary of the African Development Bank. No. 291a contains one each of Nos. 288-291, gold decorative border. Size: 103x124mm.

Girl Reading Letter, by Vermeer A37

Paintings: 7fr, Graziella (young woman), by Auguste Renoir. 14fr, Woman writing a letter, by Gerard Terborch. 26fr, Galileo Galilei, painter unknown. 40fr, Ludwig van Beethoven, painter unknown.

1969, Oct. 24 Photo. *Perf. 13½*

292	A37	4fr multi	18	5
293	A37	7fr multi	30	10
294	A37	14fr multi	65	18
295	A37	26fr multi	1.10	28
296	A37	40fr multi	1.50	40
a.		Souv. sheet of 2	3.50	3.50
		Nos. 292-296 (5)	3.73	1.01

Issued for International Letter Writing Week, Oct. 7-13.

No. 296a contains one each of Nos. 295-296. Buff decorative margin with commemorative inscription. Size: 133x75mm.

Moon Landing Issue

Rocket Launching A38

Designs: 6.50fr, Rocket in space. 7fr, Separation of landing module from capsule. 14fr, 26fr, Landing module landing on moon. 17fr, Capsule in space. 40fr, Neil A. Armstrong leaving landing module. 50fr, Astronaut on moon.

1969, Nov. 6 Photo. *Perf. 13½*

297	A38	4fr bl & multi	30	10
298	A38	6.50fr vio bl & multi	42	25
299	A38	7fr vio bl & multi	42	25
300	A38	14fr blk & multi	70	38
301	A38	17fr vio bl & multi	1.10	50
		Nos. 297-301,C104-C106 (8)	7.24	3.58

Souvenir Sheet

302	A38	Souv. sheet of 3	6.00	6.00
a.		26fr multi	1.00	1.00
b.		40fr multi	1.50	1.50
c.		50fr multi	2.00	2.00

See note after Algeria No. 427.

On No. 302 stamp designs extend into inscribed margin. Size: 140x88mm.

Madonna and Child, by Rubens — A39

Paintings: 6fr, Madonna and Child with St. John, by Giulio Romano. 10fr, Magnificat Madonna, by Botticelli.

1969, Dec. 2 Photo.

303	A39	5fr gold & multi	15	8
304	A39	6fr gold & multi	25	10
305	A39	10fr gold & multi	50	15
a.		Souvenir sheet of 3	1.50	1.50
		Nos. 303-305,C107-C109 (6)	4.45	1.28

Christmas 1969.

No. 305a contains one each of Nos. 303-305. Gold frame with inscription. Size: 110x87mm.

Sternotomis Bohemani — A40

Designs: Various Beetles and Weevils.

1970 *Perf. 13½*

Size: 39x28mm.

306	A40	50c multi	5	5
307	A40	1fr multi	5	5
308	A40	1.50fr multi	5	5
309	A40	2fr multi	5	5
310	A40	3fr multi	8	5
311	A40	3.50fr multi	9	5

Size: 46x32mm.

312	A40	4fr multi	18	5
313	A40	5fr multi	22	5
314	A40	6.50fr multi	30	5
315	A40	8fr multi	40	5
316	A40	10fr multi	50	5
317	A40	15fr multi	75	5

Size: 52x36mm.

318	A40	20fr multi	1.00	6
319	A40	50fr multi	2.00	35
320	A40	100fr multi	3.75	70
321	A40	150fr multi	5.50	1.00
		Nos. 306-321,C110-C118 (25)	36.37	4.82

Issue dates: Nos. 306-313, Jan. 20; Nos. 314-318, Feb. 17; Nos. 319-321, Apr. 3.

Jesus Condemned to Death — A41

Stations of the Cross, by Juan de Aranoa y Carredano: 1.50fr, Jesus carries His Cross. 2fr, Jesus falls the first time. 3fr, Jesus meets His mother. 3.50fr, Simon of Cyrene helps carry the cross. 4fr, Veronica wipes the face of Jesus. 5fr, Jesus falls the second time.

1970, Mar. 16 Photo. *Perf. 13½*

322	A41	1fr gold & multi	5	5
323	A41	1.50fr gold & multi	6	6
324	A41	2fr gold & multi	8	6
325	A41	3fr gold & multi	15	6
326	A41	3.50fr gold & multi	18	8
327	A41	4fr gold & multi	22	10
328	A41	5fr gold & multi	30	10
a.		Souv. sheet of 7 + label	1.10	1.10
		Nos. 322-328,C119-C125 (14)	5.09	2.18

Easter 1970.

No. 328a contains one each of Nos. 322-328 and label showing three crosses. Gold decorative border. Size: 154x123mm.

Parade and EXPO '70 Emblem — A42

Designs (EXPO '70 Emblem and): 6.50fr, Aerial view. 7fr, African pavilions. 14fr, Pagoda (vert.). 26fr, Recording pavilion and pool. 40fr, Tower of the Sun (vert.). 50fr, Flags of participating nations.

1970, May 5 Photo. *Perf. 13½*

329	A42	4fr gold & multi	15	5
330	A42	6.50fr gold & multi	25	5
331	A42	7fr gold & multi	30	6
332	A42	14fr gold & multi	45	12
333	A42	26fr gold & multi	75	18
334	A42	40fr gold & multi	1.10	30
335	A42	50fr gold & multi	1.65	40
		Nos. 329-335 (7)	4.65	1.16

Issued to publicize EXPO '70 International Exhibition, Osaka, Japan, March 15-Sept. 13, 1970. See No. C126.

White Rhinoceros — A43

Designs, FAUNA: Camel, dromedary, okapi, addax, Burundi cow (2 stamps of each animal in 2 different poses). MAP OF THE NILE: Delta and pyramids, dhow, cataract, Blue Nile and crowned crane, Victoria Nile and secretary bird, Lake Victoria and source of Nile on Mt. Gikizi.

1970, July 8 Photo. *Perf. 13½*

336	A43	7fr multi	75	10
a.		Sheet of 18	14.00	2.75

Issued in sheets of 18 (3x6) stamps of different designs, to publicize the southernmost source of the Nile on Mt. Gikizi in Burundi. See No. C127.

Winter Wren, Firecrest, Skylark and Crested Lark — A44

Birds: 2fr, 3.50fr and 5fr, vertical; others horizontal.

1970, Sept. 30 Photo. *Perf. 13½*

Stamp Size: 44x33mm.

337	A44	2fr Block of four	75	20
a.		*Northern shrike*	18	
b.		*European starling*	18	
c.		*Yellow wagtail*	18	
d.		*Bank swallow*	18	
338	A44	3fr Block of four	1.10	20
a.		*Winter wren*	25	
b.		*Firecrest*	25	
c.		*Skylark*	25	
d.		*Crested lark*	25	
339	A44	3.50fr Block of four	1.40	20
a.		*Woodchat shrike*	35	
b.		*Common rock thrush*	35	
c.		*Black redstart*	35	
d.		*Ring ouzel*	35	
340	A44	4fr Block of four	1.65	20
a.		*European Redstart*	40	
b.		*Hedge sparrow*	40	
c.		*Gray wagtail*	40	
d.		*Meadow pipit*	40	
341	A44	5fr Block of four	2.00	20
a.		*Eurasian hoopoe*	50	
b.		*Pied flycatcher*	50	
c.		*Great reed warbler*	50	
d.		*Eurasian kingfisher*	50	
342	A44	6.50fr Block of four	2.50	25
a.		*House martin*	60	
b.		*Sedge warbler*	60	
c.		*Fieldfare*	60	
d.		*European Golden oriole*	60	
		Nos. 337-342,C132-C137 (12)	47.15	5.80

Nos. 337-342 are printed in sheets of 16 containing 4 blocks of 4.

Library, U.N. Emblem — A45

Designs: 5fr, Students taking test, and emblem of University of Bujumbura. 7fr, Students in laboratory and emblem of Ecole Normale Supérieure of Burundi. 10fr, Students with electron-microscope and Education Year emblem.

1970, Oct. 23

343	A45	3fr gold & multi	12	5
344	A45	5fr gold & multi	16	5
345	A45	7fr gold & multi	24	8
346	A45	10fr gold & multi	32	10

Issued for International Education Year.

Pres. and Mrs. Michel Micombero — A46

Designs: 7fr, Pres. Michel Micombero and Burundi flag. 11fr, Pres. Micombero and Revolution Memorial.

1970, Nov. 28 Photo. *Perf. 13½*

347	A46	4fr gold & multi	15	6
348	A46	7fr gold & multi	25	12
349	A46	11fr gold & multi	40	17
a.		Souvenir sheet of 3	1.00	1.00

Issued to commemorate the 4th anniversary of independence. No. 349a contains 3 stamps similar to Nos. 347-349, but inscribed "Poste Aerienne." Dark gray and gold margin with commemorative inscription. Size: 125x143mm. Exists imperf.

See Nos. C140-C142.

Lenin with Delegates A47

Designs (Lenin, Paintings): 5fr, addressing crowd. 6.50fr, with soldier and sailor. 15fr, speaking from balcony. 50fr, Portrait.

1970, Dec. 31 Photo. *Perf. 13½*
Gold Frame

350 A47 3.50fr dk red brn 14 6
351 A47 5fr dk red brn 20 8
352 A47 6.50fr dk red brn 28 12
353 A47 15fr dk red brn 65 25
354 A47 50fr dk red brn 2.25 35
Nos. 350-354 (5) 3.52 86

Lenin's birth centenary (1870-1924).

Lion — A48

1971, March 19 Photo. *Perf. 13½*
Size: 38x38mm.

355 A48 1fr Strip of four 32 20
a. *Lion* 8
b. *Cape buffalo* 8
c. *Hippopotamus* 8
d. *Giraffe* 8
356 A48 2fr Strip of four 48 20
a. *Hartebeest* 12
b. *Black rhinoceros* 12
c. *Zebra* 12
d. *Leopard* 12
357 48 3fr Strip of four 60 25
a. *Grant's gazelles* 15
b. *Cheetah* 15
c. *African white-backed vultures* 15
d. *Johnston's okapi* 15
358 A48 5fr Strip of four 1.00 40
a. *Chimpanzee* 25
b. *Elephant* 25
c. *Spotted hyenas* 25
d. *Beisa* 25
359 A48 6fr Strip of four 1.25 45
a. *Gorilla* 30
b. *Gnu* 30
c. *Wart hog* 30
d. *Cape hunting dog* 30
360 A48 11fr Strip of four 2.75 90
a. *Sable antelope* 65
b. *Caracal lynx* 65
c. *Ostriches* 65
d. *Bongo* 65
Nos. 355-360,C146-C151 (12) 30.15 5.95

The Resurrection, by Il Sodoma — A49

Paintings: 6fr, Resurrection, by Andrea del Castagno. 11fr, Noli me Tangere, by Correggio.

1971, Apr. 2

361 A49 3fr gold & multi 15 5
362 A49 6fr gold & multi 30 10
363 A49 11fr gold & multi 55 15
a. Souvenir sheet of 3 1.10 1.10
Nos. 361-363,C143-C145 (6) 2.45 88

Easter 1971. No. 363a contains one each of Nos. 361-363. Red and gold margin. Size: 120x85mm. Sheet exists imperf.

Young Venetian Woman, by Dürer — A50

Dürer Paintings: 11fr, Hieronymus Holzschuher. 14fr, Emperor Maximilian I. 17fr, Holy Family, from Paumgartner Altar. 26fr, Haller Madonna. 31fr, Self-portrait, 1498.

1971, Sept. 20

364 A50 6fr multi 25 12
365 A50 11fr multi 45 22
366 A50 14fr multi 55 28
367 A50 17fr multi 70 35
368 A50 26fr multi 1.00 50
369 A50 31fr multi 1.25 60
a. Souvenir sheet of 2 2.50 2.50
Nos. 364-369 (6) 4.20 2.07

International Letter Writing Week. Paintings by Dürer. 500th anniversary of the birth of Albrecht Dürer (1471-1528), German painter and engraver. No. 369a contains one each of Nos. 368-369. Tan margin with portrait of Erasmus. Size: 137x80mm. Exists imperf.

Nos. 364-369, 369a Overprinted in Black and Gold: "VIème CONGRES / DE L'INSTITUT INTERNATIONAL / DE DROIT D'EXPRESSION FRANCAISE"

1971, Oct. 8

370 A50 6fr multi 25 6
371 A50 11fr multi 45 12
372 A50 14fr multi 55 15
373 A50 17fr multi 70 20
374 A50 26fr multi 1.00 30
375 A50 31fr multi 1.25 35
a. Souvenir sheet of 2 2.50 2.50
Nos. 370-375 (6) 4.20 1.18

6th Congress of the International Legal Institute of the French-speaking Area, Usumbura, Aug. 10-19.

Madonna and Child, by Il Perugino — A51

Paintings of the Madonna and Child by: 5fr, Andrea del Sarto. 6fr, Luis de Morales.

1971, Nov. 2 Photo. *Perf. 13½*

376 A51 3fr dk grn & multi 12 5
377 A51 5fr dk grn & multi 20 6
378 A51 6fr dk grn & multi 27 8
a. Souvenir sheet of 3 75 75
Nos. 376-378,C153-C155 (6) 2.79 1.14

Christmas 1971. No. 378a contains one each of Nos. 376-378. Multicolored border. Size: 125x81mm. Sheet exists imperf.

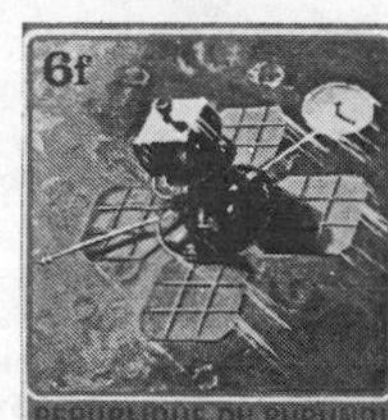

Lunar Orbiter A52

Designs: 11fr, Vostok. 14fr, Luna 1. 17fr, Apollo 11 astronaut on moon. 26fr, Soyuz 11. 40fr, Lunar Rover (Apollo 15).

1972, Jan. 15

379 A52 6fr gold & multi 35 18
380 A52 11fr gold & multi 45 22
381 A52 14fr gold & multi 55 28
382 A52 17fr gold & multi 80 40
383 A52 26fr gold & multi 80 65
384 A52 40fr gold & multi 1.25 65
a. Souvenir sheet of 6 4.25 4.25
Nos. 379-384 (6) 4.20 2.38

Conquest of space. See No. C156.

No. 384a contains one each of Nos. 379-384 inscribed "APOLLO 16." Multicolored margin inscribed "La Conquête de l'Espace." Size: 134x135mm.

Slalom and Sapporo '72 Emblem — A53

Designs (Sapporo '72 Emblem and): 6fr, Figure skating, pairs. 11fr, Figure skating, women's. 14fr, Ski jump. 17fr, Ice hockey. 24fr, Speed skating, men's. 26fr, Snow scooter. 31fr, Downhill skiing. 50fr, Bobsledding.

1972, Feb. 3

385 A53 5fr sil & multi 15 5
386 A53 6fr sil & multi 20 7
387 A53 11fr sil & multi 35 10
388 A53 14fr sil & multi 45 15
389 A53 17fr sil & multi 55 15
390 A53 24fr sil & multi 75 18
391 A53 26fr sil & multi 80 20
392 A53 31fr sil & multi 1.00 25
393 A53 50fr sil & multi 1.60 40
Nos. 385-393 (9) 5.85 1.55

11th Winter Olympic Games, Sapporo, Japan, Feb. 3-13. Printed in sheets of 12. See No. C157.

Issue dates: Nos. 385-390, Feb. 1; Nos. 391-393, Feb. 21.

Ecce Homo, by Quentin Massys — A54

Paintings: 6.50fr, Crucifixion, by Rubens. 10fr, Descent from the Cross, by Jacopo da Pontormo. 18fr, Pietà, by Ferdinand Gallegos. 27fr, Trinity, by El Greco.

1972, Mar. 20 Photo. *Perf. 13½*

394 A54 3.50fr gold & multi 8 5
395 A54 6.50fr gold & multi 20 8
396 A54 10fr gold & multi 30 12
397 A54 18fr gold & multi 50 20
398 A54 27fr gold & multi 1.25 30
a. Souvenir sheet of 5 + label 3.00 2.50
Nos. 394-398 (5) 2.33 75

Easter 1972. Printed in sheets of 8 with label. No. 398a contains one each of Nos. 394-398 and decorative label. Dark brown and gold margin. Size: 120x157mm. Exists imperf.

Gymnastics, Olympic Rings and "Motion" A55

1972, May 19

399 A55 5fr *shown* 18 6
400 A55 6fr *Javelin* 20 7
401 A55 11fr *Fencing* 42 13
402 A55 14fr *Bicycling* 52 17
403 A55 17fr *Pole vault* 65 20
Nos. 399-403,C158-C161 (9) 5.62 1.81

Souvenir Sheet

404 A55 Souv. sheet of 2 3.50 2.50
a. 31fr *Discus* 90 90
b. 40fr *Soccer* 1.20 1.20

20th Olympic Games, Munich, Aug. 26-Sept. 11. No. 404 has multicolored margin with Olympic flag, "Motion" and commemorative inscription. Size: 126x80mm.

Prince Rwagasore, Pres. Micombero, Burundi Flag, Drummers A56

Designs: 7fr, Rwagasore, Micombero, flag, map of Africa, globe. 13fr, Micombero, flag, globe.

1972, Aug. 24 Photo. *Perf. 13½*

405 A56 5fr sil & multi 15 5
406 A56 7fr sil & multi 25 8
407 A56 13fr sil & multi 45 15
a. Souvenir sheet of 3 1.00
Nos. 405-407,C162-C164 (6) 2.85 95

10th anniversary of independence.

No. 407a contains one each of Nos. 405-407. Silver and light blue margin with black inscription. Size: 146x80mm.

Madonna and Child, by Andrea Solario — A57

Paintings of the Madonna and Child by: 10fr, Raphael. 15fr, Botticelli.

1972, Nov. 2

408 A57 5fr lt bl & multi 15 5
409 A57 10fr lt bl & multi 30 10
410 A57 15fr lt bl & multi 45 15
a. Souvenir sheet of 3 1.00
Nos. 408-410,C165-C167 (6) 3.45 1.07

Christmas 1972. Sheets of 20 stamps and one label. No. 410a contains one each of Nos. 408-410. Deep carmine and gold border. Size: 128x81mm.

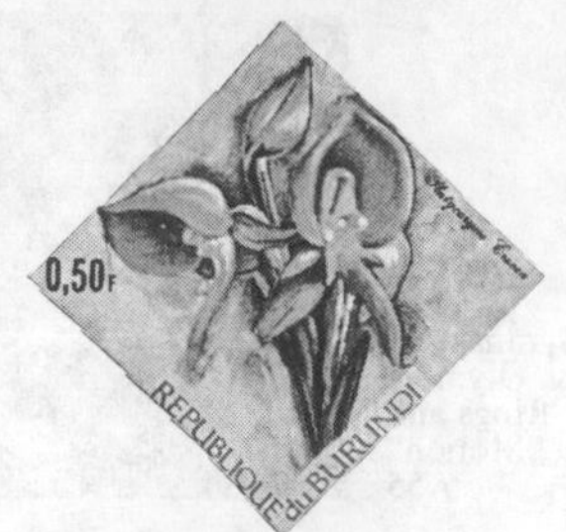

Platycoryne Crocea — A58

1972

Size: 33x33mm.

411	A58	50c shown	5	5
412	A58	1fr *Cattleya trianaei*	5	5
413	A58	2fr *Eulophia cucullata*	7	5
414	A58	3fr *Cymbidium hamsey*	10	5
415	A58	4fr *Thelymitra pauciflora*	13	6
416	A58	5fr *Miltassia*	17	8
417	A58	6fr *Miltonia*	20	10

Size: 38x38mm.

418	A58	7fr Like 50c	23	12
419	A58	8fr Like 1fr	27	13
420	A58	9fr Like 2fr	30	15
421	A58	10fr Like 3fr	35	17
		Nos. 411-421,C168-C174 (18)	6.39	2.15

Orchids. Issue dates: Nos. 411-417, Nov. 6; Nos. 418-421, Nov. 29.

Henry Morton Stanley — A59

Designs: 7fr, Porters, Stanley's expedition. 13fr, Stanley entering Ujiji.

1973, Mar. 19 Photo. *Perf. 13½*

422	A59	5fr gold & multi	15	5
423	A59	7fr gold & multi	20	7
424	A59	13fr gold & multi	40	13
		Nos. 422-424,C175-C177 (6)	2.55	85

Exploration of Africa by David Livingstone (1813-1873) and Henry Morton Stanley (John Rowlands; 1841-1904).

Crucifixion, by Roger van der Weyden — A60

Paintings: 5fr, Flagellation of Christ, by Caravaggio. 13fr, The Burial of Christ, by Raphael.

1973, Apr. 10

425	A60	5fr gold & multi	15	5
426	A60	7fr gold & multi	20	7
427	A60	13fr gold & multi	40	13
a.		Souvenir sheet of 3	1.00	1.00
		Nos. 425-427,C178-C180 (6)	3.00	85

Easter 1973. No. 427a contains one each of Nos. 425-427. Multicolored margin. Size: 121x73mm.

INTERPOL Emblem, Flag — A61

Design: 10fr, INTERPOL flag and emblem. 18fr, INTERPOL Headquarters and emblem.

1973, May 19 Photo. *Perf. 13½*

428	A61	5fr sil & multi	15	5
429	A61	10fr sil & multi	30	12
430	A61	18fr sil & multi	55	22
		Nos. 428-430,C181-C182 (5)	2.75	1.09

50th anniversary of International Criminal Police Organization (INTERPOL).

Signs of the Zodiac, Babylon — A62

Designs: 5fr, Greek and Roman gods representing planets. 7fr, Ptolemy (No. 433a) and Ptolemaic solar system. 13fr, Copernicus (No. 434a) and heliocentric system.

1973, July 27 Photo. *Perf. 13½*

431	A62	3fr Block of four	40	20
a.		3fr in UL	10	5
b.		3fr in UR	10	5
c.		3fr in LL	10	5
d.		3fr in LR	10	5
432	A62	5fr Block of four	50	20
a.		5fr in UL	12	5
b.		5fr in UR	12	5
c.		5fr in LL	12	5
d.		5fr in LR	12	5
433	A62	7fr Block of four	65	20
a.		7fr in UL	16	5
b.		7fr in UR	16	5
c.		7fr in LL	16	5
d.		7fr in LR	16	5
434	A62	13fr Block of four	1.50	40
a.		13fr in UL	35	10
b.		13fr in UR	35	10
c.		13fr in LL	35	10
d.		13fr in LR	35	10
e.		Souvenir sheet of 4	5.25	2.75
		Nos. 431-434,C183-C186 (8)	18.05	4.70

500th anniversary of the birth of Nicolaus Copernicus (1473-1543), Polish astronomer.

Nos. 431-434 are printed in sheets of 32 containing 8 blocks of 4. No. 434e contains one each of Nos. 431-434. Gold and multicolored margin. Size: 136x136mm.

Flowers and Butterflies — A63

Designs: Each block of 4 contains 2 flower and 2 butterfly designs. The 1fr, 2fr, 5fr and 11fr have flower designs listed as "a" and "d" numbers, butterflies as "b" and "c" numbers; the arrangement is reversed for the 3fr and 6fr.

1973, Sept. 3 Photo. *Perf. 13*

Stamp Size: 34x41½mm.

435	A63	1fr Block of 4	32	20
a.		*Protea cynaroides*	8	5
b.		*Precis octavia*	8	5
c.		*Epiphora bauhiniae*	8	5
d.		*Gazania longiscapa*	8	5
436	A63	2fr Block of 4	32	20
a.		*Kniphofia*	8	5
b.		*Cymothoe coccinata*	8	5
c.		*Nudaurelia zambesina*	8	5
d.		*Freesia refracta*	8	5
437	A63	3fr Block of 4	48	20
a.		*Calotis eupompe*	12	5
b.		*Narcissus*	12	5
c.		*Cineraria hybrida*	12	5
d.		*Cyrestis camillus*	12	5
438	A63	5fr Block of 4	80	20
a.		*Iris tingitana*	20	5
b.		*Pappilio demodocus*	20	5
c.		*Catopsilia avelaneda*	20	5
d.		*Nerine sarniensis*	20	5
439	A63	6fr Block of 4	1.00	25
a.		*Hypolimnas dexithea*	25	6
b.		*Zantedeschia tropicalis*	25	6
c.		*Sandersonia aurantiaca*	25	6
d.		*Drurya antimachus*	25	6
440	A63	11fr Block of 4	2.00	45
a.		*Nymphaea capensis*	50	10
b.		*Pandoriana pandora*	50	10
c.		*Precis orythia*	50	10
d.		*Pelargonium domestica*	50	10
		Nos. 435-440,C187-C192 (12)	43.92	6.45

Virgin and Child, by Giovanni Bellini — A64

Virgin and Child by: 10fr, Jan van Eyck. 15fr, Giovanni Boltraffio.

1973, Nov. 13 Photo. *Perf. 13*

441	A64	5fr gold & multi	15	5
442	A64	10fr gold & multi	30	8
443	A64	15fr gold & multi	45	12
a.		Souvenir sheet of 3	1.00	1.00
		Nos. 441-443,C193-C195 (6)	3.45	95

Christmas 1973. No. 443a contains one each of Nos. 441-443 with multicolored margin. Size: 143x79mm.

Pietà, by Paolo Veronese — A65

Paintings: 10fr, Virgin and St. John, by van der Weyden. 18fr, Crucifixion, by van der Weyden. 27fr, Burial of Christ, by Titian. 40fr, Pietà, by El Greco.

1974, Apr. 19 Photo. *Perf. 14x13½*

444	A65	5fr gold & multi	15	5
445	A65	10fr gold & multi	30	10
446	A65	18fr gold & multi	55	18
447	A65	27fr gold & multi	85	25
448	A65	40fr gold & multi	1.35	30
a.		Souvenir sheet of 5	3.25	3.25
		Nos. 444-448 (5)	3.20	88

Easter 1974. No. 448a contains one each of Nos. 444-448, rose brown and gold margin. Size: 145x120mm.

Fish — A66

Designs: Fish.

1974, May 30 Photo. *Perf. 13*

Stamp Size: 35x35mm.

449	A66	1fr Block of 4	20	20
a.		*Haplochromis multicolor*	5	5
b.		*Pantodon buchholzi*	5	5
c.		*Tropheus duboisi*	5	5
d.		*Distichodus sexfasciatus*	5	5
450	A66	2fr Block of 4	24	20
a.		*Pelmatochromis kribensis*	6	5
b.		*Nannaethiops tritaeniatus*	6	5
c.		*Polycentropsis abbreviata*	6	5
d.		*Hemichromis bimaculatus*	6	5
451	A66	3fr Block of 4	36	20
a.		*Ctenopoma acutirostre*	9	5
b.		*Synodontis angelicus*	9	5
c.		*Tilapia melanopleura*	9	5
d.		*Aphyosemion bivittatum*	9	5
452	A66	5fr Block of 4	60	20
a.		*Monodactylus argenteus*	15	5
b.		*Zanclus canescens*	15	5
c.		*Pygoplites diacanthus*	15	5
d.		*Cephalopholis argus*	15	5
453	A66	6fr Block of 4	72	20
a.		*Priacanthus arenatus*	18	5
b.		*Pomacanthus arcuatus*	18	5
c.		*Scarus guacamaia*	18	5
d.		*Zeus faber*	18	5
454	A66	11fr Block of 4	1.32	32
a.		*Lactophrys quadricornis*	33	8
b.		*Balistes vetula*	33	8
c.		*Acanthurus bahianus*	33	8
d.		*Holocanthus ciliaris*	33	8
		Nos. 449-454,C207-C212 (12)	23.69	4.42

Soccer and Cup A67

Designs: Various soccer scenes and cup.

1974, July 4 Photo. *Perf. 13*

455	A67	5fr gold & multi	15	
456	A67	6fr gold & multi	18	
457	A67	11fr gold & multi	33	
458	A67	14fr gold & multi	42	
459	A67	17fr gold & multi	50	
a.		Souvenir sheet of 3	2.75	2.75
		Nos. 455-459,C196-C198 (8)	4.16	

World Soccer Championship, Munich, June 13-July 7. No. 459a contains 3 stamps similar to Nos. C196-C198 without "Poste Aerienne." Gold and multicolored margin with picture of Munich City Hall. Size: 88x142mm.

Nos. 455-459 and 459a exist imperf.

Flags over UPU Headquarters, Bern — A68

Designs: No. 461, G.P.O., Usumbura. No. 462, Mailmen ("11F" in UR). No. 463, Mailmen ("11F" in UL). No. 464, UPU emblem. No. 465, Means of transportation. No. 466, Pigeon over globe showing Burundi. No. 467, Swiss flag, pigeon over map showing Bern.

1974, July 23

460	A68	6fr gold & multi	35	
461	A68	6fr gold & multi	35	
462	A68	11fr gold & multi	60	
463	A68	11fr gold & multi	60	
464	A68	14fr gold & multi	75	
465	A68	14fr gold & multi	75	
466	A68	17fr gold & multi	95	
467	A68	17fr gold & multi	95	
a.		Souvenir sheet of 8	5.50	4.25
		Nos. 460-467,C199-C206 (16)	19.80	
		Set, used		2.00

Centenary of Universal Postal Union. Stamps of same denomination printed se-tenant (continuous design) in sheets of 40.

No. 467a contains one each of Nos. 460-467. Violet, gold and light blue margin. Size: 96x162mm.

St. Ildefonso Writing Letter, by El Greco
A69

Paintings: 11fr, Lady Sealing Letter, by Chardin. 14fr, Titus at Desk, by Rembrandt. 17fr, The Love Letter, by Vermeer. 26fr, The Merchant G. Gisze, by Holbein. 31fr, Portrait of Alexandre Lenoir, by David.

1974, Oct. 1 Photo. *Perf. 13*

468 A69 6fr gold & multi 18
469 A69 11fr gold & multi 33
470 A69 14fr gold & multi 42
471 A69 17fr gold & multi 50
472 A69 26fr gold & multi 78
473 A69 31fr gold & multi 93
a. Souvenir sheet of 2 2.25 2.25
Nos. 468-473 (6) 3.14

International Letter Writing Week, Oct. 6-12. No. 473a contains one each of Nos. 472-473. Multicolored margin. Size: 95x105mm. Sheet exists imperf.

Virgin and Child, by Bernaert van Orley — A70

Paintings of the Virgin and Child: 10fr, by Hans Memling. 15fr, by Botticelli.

1974, Nov. 7 Photo. *Perf. 13*

474 A70 5fr gold & multi 15
475 A70 10fr gold & multi 30
476 A70 15fr gold & multi 45
a. Souvenir sheet of 3 1.00 1.00
Nos. 474-476,C213-C215 (6) 3.45

Christmas 1974. Sheets of 20 stamps and one label. No. 476a contains one each of Nos. 474-476, gold and multicolored margin. Size: 137x90mm. Sheet exists imperf.

Apollo-Soyuz Space Mission and Emblem — A71

1975, July 10 Photo. *Perf. 13*

477 A71 26fr Block of 4 1.60
a. *A.A. Leonov, V.N. Kubasov, Soviet flag* 40
b. *Soyuz and Soviet flag* 40
c. *Apollo and American flag* 40
d. *D.K. Slayton, V.D. Brand, T.P. Stafford, American flag* 40
478 A71 31fr Block of 4 2.20
a. *Apollo-Soyuz link-up* 55
b. *Apollo, blast-off* 55
c. *Soyuz, blast-off* 55
d. *Kubasov, Leonov, Slayton, Brand, Stafford* 55
Nos. 477-478,C216-C217 (4) 8.20

Apollo Soyuz space test project (Russo-American cooperation), launching July 15; link-up, July 17. Nos. 477-478 are printed in sheets of 32 containing 8 blocks of 4.

Addax
A72

1975, July 31 Photo. *Perf. 13½*

479 A72 1fr Strip of four 20
a. *shown* 5
b. *Roan antelope* 5
c. *Nyala* 5
d. *White rhinoceros* 5
480 A72 2fr Strip of four 24
a. *Mandrill* 6
b. *Eland* 6
c. *Salt's dik-dik* 6
d. *Thomson's gazelles* 6
481 A72 3fr Strip of four 36
a. *African small-clawed otter* 9
b. *Reed buck* 9
c. *Indian civet* 9
d. *Cape buffalo* 9
482 A72 5fr Strip of four 60
a. *White-tailed gnu* 15
b. *African wild asses* 15
c. *Black-and-white colobus monkey* 15
d. *Gerenuk* 15
483 A72 6fr Strip of four 72
a. *Dama gazelle* 18
b. *Black-backed jackal* 18
c. *Sitatungas* 18
d. *Zebra antelope* 18
484 A72 11fr Strip of four 1.32
a. *Fennec* 33
b. *Lesser kudus* 33
c. *Blesbok* 33
d. *Serval* 33
Nos. 479-484,C218-C223 (12) 24.44

Jonah, by Michelangelo — A73

Designs: Paintings from Sistine Chapel.

1975, Dec. 3 Photo. *Perf. 13*

485 A73 5fr *shown* 15
486 A73 5fr *Libyan Sybil* 15
487 A73 13fr *Prophet Isaiah* 40
488 A73 13fr *Delphic Sybil* 40
489 A73 27fr *Daniel* 80
490 A73 27fr *Cumaean Sybil* 80
a. Souvenir sheet of 6 4.00 4.00
Nos. 485-490,C228-C233 (12) 9.90

Michelangelo Buonarotti (1475-1564), Italian sculptor, painter and architect. Stamps of same denominations printed se-tenant in sheets of 18 stamps and 2 labels. No. 490a contains one each of Nos. 485-490; brown & gold margin, black inscription. Size: 137x111mm.

Speed Skating
A74

Basketball
A75

Designs (Innsbruck Games Emblem and): 24fr, Figure skating, women's. 26fr, Two-man bobsled. 31fr, Cross-country skiing.

1976, Jan. 23 Photo. *Perf. 14x13½*

491 A74 17fr dp bl & multi 60
492 A74 24fr multi 90
493 A74 26fr multi 95
494 A74 31fr plum & multi 1.10
a. Souvenir sheet of 3 4.25 4.25
Nos. 491-494,C234-C236 (7) 7.50

12th Winter Olympic Games, Innsbruck, Austria, Feb. 4-15.

No. 494a contains 3 stamps similar to Nos. C234-C236, perf. 13½, without "POSTE AERIENNE." Multicolored margin with snowflakes and Games' emblem. Size: 130x62½mm.

1976, May 3 Litho. *Perf. 13½*

Designs (Montreal Games Emblem and): Nos. 496, 499, 503b, Pole vault. Nos. 497, 500, 503d, Running. Nos. 498, 501, 503a, Soccer. No. 502, 503c, Basketball.

495 A75 14fr bl & multi 50
496 A75 14fr ol & multi 50
497 A75 17fr mag & multi 60
498 A75 17fr ver & multi 60
499 A75 28fr ol & multi 95
500 A75 28fr mag & multi 95
501 A75 40fr ver & multi 1.40
502 A75 40fr bl & multi 1.40
Nos. 495-502,C237-C242 (14) 14.30

Souvenir Sheet

503 A75 Sheet of 4 3.20 60
a. 14fr red & multi 42
b. 17fr ol & multi 50
c. 28fr bl & multi 80
d. 40fr mag & multi 1.20

21st Olympic Games, Montreal, Canada, July 17-Aug. 1. Stamps of same denomination printed se-tenant in sheets of 20.

No. 503 has gold inscription, black Montreal Olympic emblem and multicolored band in margin. Size: 115x120mm.

Virgin and Child, by Dirk Bouts — A76

Virgin and Child by: 13fr, Giovanni Bellini. 27fr, Carlo Crivelli.

1976, Oct. 18 Photo. *Perf. 13½*

504 A76 5fr gold & multi 15
505 A76 13fr gold & multi 40
506 A76 27fr gold & multi 80
a. Souvenir sheet of 3 1.50
Nos. 504-506,C250-C252 (6) 4.03

Christmas 1976. Sheets of 20 stamps and descriptive label. No. 506a contains one each of Nos. 504-506; multicolored margin. Size: 123x80mm.

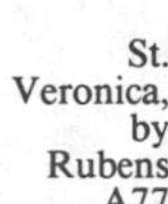

St. Veronica, by Rubens
A77

Paintings by Rubens: 21fr, Christ on the Cross. 27fr, Descent from the Cross. 35fr, The Deposition.

1977, Apr. 5 Photo. *Perf. 13*

507 A77 10fr gold & multi 30
508 A77 21fr gold & multi 62
509 A77 27fr gold & multi 80
510 A77 35fr gold & multi 1.05
a. Souvenir sheet of 4 3.00

Easter 1977. Sheets of 30 stamps and descriptive label. No. 510a contains 4 stamps similar to Nos. 507-510 inscribed "POSTE AERIENNE." Multicolored margin. Size: 111x85mm.

Alexander Graham Bell
A78

Intelsat Satellite, Modern and Old Telephones
A79

Designs: No. 513, Switchboard operator, c. 1910, and wall telephone. No. 514, Intelsat and radar. No. 515, A.G. Bell and first telephone. No. 516, Satellites around globe and videophone.

1977, May 17 Photo. *Perf. 13*

511 A78 10fr multi 16
512 A79 10fr multi 16
513 A78 17fr multi 28
514 A79 17fr multi 28
515 A78 26fr multi 45
516 A79 26fr multi 45
Nos. 511-516,C253-C256 (10) 3.44

Centenary of first telephone call by Alexander Graham Bell, Mar. 10, 1876. Stamps of same denomination printed se-tenant in sheets of 32.

Buffon's Kob — A80

1977, Aug. 22 Photo. *Perf. 14x14½*

517 A80 2fr Strip of four 24
a. *shown* 6
b. *Marabous* 6
c. *Brindled gnu* 6
d. *River hog* 6
518 A80 5fr Strip of four 60
a. *Zebras* 15
b. *Shoebill* 15
c. *Striped hyenas* 15
d. *Chimpanzee* 15
519 A80 8fr Strip of four 96
a. *Flamingos* 24
b. *Nile crocodiles* 24
c. *Green mamba* 24
d. *Greater kudus* 24
520 A80 11fr Strip of four 1.36
a. *Hyrax* 34
b. *Cobra* 34
c. *Jackals* 34
d. *Verreaux's eagles* 34
521 A80 21fr Strip of four 2.56
a. *Honey badger* 64
b. *Harnessed antelopes* 64
c. *Secretary bird* 64
d. *Klipspringer* 64
522 A80 27fr Strip of four 2.80
a. *African big-eared fox* 70
b. *Elephants* 70
c. *Vulturine guineafowl* 70
d. *Impalas* 70
Nos. 517-522,C258-C263 (12) 40.67

The Goose Girl, by Grimm — A81

Fairy Tales: 5fr, by Grimm Brothers. 11fr, by Aesop. 14fr, by Hans Christian Andersen. 17fr, by Jean de La Fontaine. 26fr, English fairy tales.

1977, Sept. 14 *Perf. 14*

523 A81 5fr Block of four 75
a. *shown* 18
b. *The Two Wanderers* 18
c. *The Man of Iron* 18
d. *Snow White and Rose Red* 18
524 A81 11fr Block of four 1.65
a. *The Quarreling Cats* 40
b. *The Blind and the Lame* 40
c. *The Hermit and the Bear* 40
d. *The Fox and the Stork* 40

525 A81 14fr Block of four 2.00
a. *The Princess and the Pea* 50
b. *The Old Tree Mother* 50
c. *The Ice Maiden* 50
d. *The Old House* 50
526 A81 17fr Block of four 2.50
a. *The Oyster and the Suitors* 60
b. *The Wolf and the Lamb* 60
c. *Hen with the Golden Egg* 60
d. *The Wolf as Shepherd* 60
527 A81 26fr Block of four 4.00
a. *Three Heads in the Well* 1.00
b. *Mother Goose* 1.00
c. *Jack and the Beanstalk* 1.00
d. *Alice in Wonderland* 1.00
Nos. 523-527 (5) 10.90

Security Council Chamber, UN Nos. 28, 46, 37, C7 — A82

Designs (UN Stamps and): 8fr, UN General Assembly, interior. 21fr, UN Meeting Hall.

1977, Oct. 10 Photo. *Perf. 13½*
528 A82 8fr Block of four 1.25
a. No. 25 30
b. No. C5 30
c. No. 23 30
d. No. 2 30
529 A82 10fr Block of four 1.50
a. No. 28 35
b. No. 46 35
c. No. 37 35
d. No. C7 35
530 A82 21fr Block of four 3.00
a. No. 45 75
b. No. 42 75
c. No. 17 75
d. No. 13 75
e. Souvenir sheet of 3 1.30
Nos. 528-530,C264-C266 (6) 19.75

25th anniversary (in 1976) of the United Nations Postal Administration. No. 530e contains 8fr in design of No. 529d, 10fr in design of No. 530b, 21fr in design of No. 528c; silver margin. Size: 128x76mm.

Virgin and Child — A83

Designs: Paintings of the Virgin and Child.

1977, Oct. 31 Photo. *Perf. 14x13*
531 A83 5fr By Meliore Toscano 15
532 A83 13fr By J. Lombardos 40
533 A83 27fr By Emmanuel Tzanes, 1610-1680 80
a. Souvenir sheet of 3 1.50
Nos. 531-533,C267-C269 (6) 4.05

Christmas 1977. Sheets of 24 stamps with descriptive label. No. 533a contains one each of Nos. 531-533; gold and multicolored margin. Size: 130x72mm.

Cruiser Aurora, Russia Nos. 211, 303, 1252, 187 — A84

Designs (Russian Stamps and): 8fr, Kremlin, Moscow. 11fr, Pokrovski Cathedral, Moscow. 13fr, Labor Day parade, 1977 and 1980 Olympic Games emblem.

1977, Nov. 14 Photo. *Perf. 13*
534 A84 5fr Block of four 75
a. No. 211 18
b. No. 303 18
c. No. 1252 18
d. No. 187 18
535 A84 8fr Block of four 1.25
a. No. 856 25
b. No. 1986 25
c. No. 908 25
d. No. 2551 25
536 A84 11fr Block of four 1.75
a. No. 3844b 40
b. No. 3452 40
c. No. 3382 40
d. No. 3837 40
537 A84 13fr Block of four 2.00
a. No. 4446 50
b. No. 3497 50
c. No. 2926 50
d. No. 2365 50
Nos. 534-537 (4) 5.75

60th anniversary of Russian October Revolution.

Ship at Dock, Arms and Flag — A85

Burundi Arms and Flag and: 5fr, Men at lathes. 11fr, Male leopard dance. 14fr, Coffee harvest. 17fr, Government Palace.

1977, Nov. 25 Photo. *Perf. 13½*
538 A85 1fr sil & multi 5
539 A85 5fr sil & multi 15
540 A85 11fr sil & multi 35
541 A85 14fr sil & multi 42
542 A85 17fr sil & multi 50
Nos. 538-542 (5) 1.47

15th anniversary of independence.

Virgin and Child, by Rubens — A86

Paintings of the Virgin and Child by: 13fr, Rubens. 17fr, Solario. 27fr, Tiepolo. 31fr, Gerard David. 40fr, Bellini.

1979, Feb. Photo. *Perf. 14x13*
543 A86 13fr multi 40
544 A86 17fr multi 50
545 A86 27fr multi 80
546 A86 31fr multi 95
547 A86 40fr multi 1.20
Nos. 543-547 (5) 3.85

Christmas 1978. See No. C270.

Abyssinian Hornbill — A87

1979 Photo. *Perf. 13½x13*
548 A87 1fr *shown* 5
549 A87 2fr *Snakebird* 6
550 A87 3fr *Melittophagus pusillus* 10
551 A87 5fr *Flamingo* 15
552 A87 8fr *Afropavo congenis* 28
553 A87 10fr *Gallinule* 35
554 A87 20fr *Martial eagle* 65
555 A87 27fr *Ibis* 85
556 A87 50fr *Saddle-billed stork* 1.65
Nos. 548-556 (9) 4.14

See Nos. C273-C281.

Mother and Infant, IYC Emblem A88

IYC Emblem and: 20fr, Infant. 27fr, Girl with doll. 50fr, Children in Children's Village.

1979, July 19 Photo. *Perf. 14*
557 A88 10fr multi 30
558 A88 20fr multi 50
559 A88 27fr multi 65
560 A88 50fr multi 1.10

International Year of the Child. See No. B82.

Virgin and Child, by del Garbo — A89

Virgin and Child by: 27fr, Giovanni Penni. 31fr, G. Romano. 50fr, Jacopo Bassano.

1979, Oct. 12
561 A89 20fr multi 60
562 A89 27fr multi 80
563 A89 31fr multi 95
564 A89 50fr multi 1.50
Nos. 561-564,B83-B86 (8) 7.85

Christmas 1979. See Nos. C271, CB48.

Rowland Hill, Penny Black — A90

Stamps of Burundi: 27fr, German East Africa Nos. 17, N17. 31fr, Nos. 4, 24. 40fr, Nos. 29, 294. 60fr, Heinrich von Stephan, Nos. 464-465.

1979, Nov. 6
565 A90 20fr multi 60
566 A90 27fr multi 80
567 A90 31fr multi 95
568 A90 40fr multi 1.20
569 A90 60fr multi 1.80
Nos. 565-569 (5) 5.35

Sir Rowland Hill (1795-1879), originator of penny postage. See No. C272.

A91

1980, Oct. 24 Photo. *Perf. 13x13½*
570 A91 20fr 110-meter hurdles 75
571 A91 20fr Hurdles, Thomas Munkelt 75
572 A91 20fr Hurdles, R.D.A. 75
573 A91 30fr Discus 1.10
574 A91 30fr Discus, V. Rassh-chupkin 1.10
575 A91 30fr Discus, U.R.S.S. 1.10
576 A91 40fr Soccer, Tchecoslovaquie 1.50
577 A91 40fr "Football" 1.50
578 A91 40fr shown 1.50
Nos. 570-578 (9) 10.05

22nd Summer Olympic Games, Moscow, July 19-Aug. 3. Stamps of same denomination se-tenant.

Virgin and Child, by Mainardi — A92

Christmas 1980 (Paintings): 30fr, Holy Family, by Michelangelo. 40fr, Virgin and Child, by di Cosimo. 45fr, Holy Family, by Fra Bartolomeo.

1980, Dec. 12 Photo. *Perf. 13½x13*
579 A92 10fr multi 20
580 A92 30fr multi 60
581 A92 40fr multi 85
582 A92 45fr multi 90
Nos. 579-582,B87-B90 (8) 5.27

UPRONA Party National Congress, 1979 — A93

1980, Dec. 29 *Perf. 14x13½*
583 A93 10fr multi 30
584 A93 40fr multi 1.20
585 A93 45fr multi 1.35

Johannes Kepler, Dish Antenna A94

1981, Feb. 12 *Perf. 14*
586 A94 10fr shown 30
587 A94 40fr Satellite 1.20
588 A94 45fr Satellite, diff. 1.35
a. Souvenir sheet of 3 3.00

350th death anniversary of Johannes Kepler and first earth satellite station in Burundi. No. 588a contains Nos. 586-588;

gold and red margin shows trajectory. Size: 78x109mm.

Lion A95

1983, Apr. 22 Photo. *Perf. 13*

589 A95 2fr shown 6
590 A95 3fr Giraffes 10
591 A95 5fr Rhinoceros 15
592 A95 10fr Water buffalo 30
593 A95 20fr Elephant 60
594 A95 25fr Hippopotamus 75
595 A95 30fr Zebra 90
596 A95 50fr Warthog 1.50
597 A95 60fr Oryx 1.80
598 A95 65fr Wild dog 2.00
599 A95 70fr Leopard 2.10
600 A95 75fr Wildebeest 2.50
601 A95 85fr Hyena 3.50
Nos. 589-601 (13) 16.26

Nos. 589-601 Overprinted in Silver with World Wildlife Fund Emblem

1983 Photo. *Perf. 13*

589a A95 2fr multi 6
590a A95 3fr multi 10
591a A95 5fr multi 15
592a A95 10fr multi 30
593a A95 20fr multi 60
594a A95 25fr multi 75
595a A95 30fr multi 90
596a A95 50fr multi 1.50
597a A95 60fr multi 1.80
598a A95 65fr multi 2.00
599a A95 70fr multi 2.10
600a A95 75fr multi 2.25
601a A95 85fr multi 2.50
Nos. 589a-601a (13) 15.01

20th Anniv. of Independence, July 1, 1982 — A96

Flags, various arms, map or portrait.

1983 *Perf. 14*

602 A96 10fr multi 30
603 A96 25fr multi 75
604 A96 30fr multi 90
605 A96 50fr multi 1.50
606 A96 65fr multi 2.00
Nos. 602-606 (5) 5.45

Christmas 1983 — A97

Virgin and Child paintings: 10fr, by Luca Signorelli (1450-1523). 25fr, by Esteban Murillo (1617-1682). 30fr, by Carlo Crivelli (1430-1495). 50fr, by Nicolas Poussin (1594-1665).

1983, Oct. 3 Litho. *Perf. 14½x13½*

607 A97 10fr multi 30
608 A97 25fr multi 75
609 A97 30fr multi 90
610 A97 50fr multi 1.50
Nos. 607-610,B91-B94 (8) 7.00

See Nos. C285, CB50.

Condition is the all-important factor of price. Prices quoted are for stamps in fine condition.

Butterflies — A98

1984, June 29 Photo. *Perf. 13*

611 A98 5fr Cymothoe coccinata 25
612 A98 5fr Papilio zalmoxis 25
613 A98 10fr Asterope pechueli 50
614 A98 10fr Papilio antimachus 50
615 A98 30fr Papilio hesperus 1.40
616 A98 30fr Bebearia mardania 1.40
617 A98 35fr Euphaedra neophron 1.65
618 A98 35fr Euphaedra perseis 1.65
619 A98 65fr Euphaedra imperialis 3.00
620 A98 65fr Pseudocraea striata 3.00
Nos. 611-620 (10) 13.60

Stamps of the same denomination printed horizontally se-tenant.

19th UPU Congress, Hamburg A99

UPU emblem and: 10fr, German East Africa, Nos. 17, N17. 30fr, Nos. 4, 24. 35fr, Nos. 294, 595. 65fr, Dr. Heinrich von Stephan, Nos. 464-465.

1984, July 14 Litho. *Perf. 13x13½*

621 A99 10fr multi 30
622 A99 30fr multi 90
623 A99 35fr multi 1.00
624 A99 65fr multi 2.00

See No. C286.

1984 Summer Olympics — A100

Gold medalists: 10fr, Jesse Owens (USA), track and field, Berlin, 1936. 30fr, Rafer Johnson (USA), decathlon, 1960. 35fr, Bob Beamon (USA), long jump, 1968. 65fr, Kipchoge Keino (Kenya), 3000-meter steeplechase, 1972.

1984, Aug. 6 *Perf. 13½x13*

625 A100 10fr multi 50
626 A100 30fr multi 1.40
627 A100 35fr multi 1.65
628 A100 65fr multi 3.00

See No. C287.

Christmas 1984 — A101

Paintings: 10fr, Rest During the Flight into Egypt, by Murillo (1617-1682). 25fr, Virgin and Child, by R. del Garbo. 30fr, Virgin and Child, by Botticelli (1445-1510). 50fr, The Adoration of the Shepherds, by Giacomo da Bassano (1517-1592).

1984, Dec. 15 *Perf. 13½*

629 A101 10fr multi 30
630 A101 25fr multi 75
631 A101 30fr multi 90
632 A101 50fr multi 1.50
Nos. 629-632,B95-B98 (8) 7.00

See Nos. C288, CB51.

Flowers A102

1986, July 31 Photo. *Perf. 13x13½*

633 A102 2fr Thunbergia 5
634 A102 3fr Saintpaulia 5
635 A102 5fr Clivia 8
636 A102 10fr Cassia 16
637 A102 20fr Strelitzia 32
638 A102 35fr Gloriosa 55
Nos. 633-638,C289-C294 (12) 10.21

Intl. Peace Year — A103

1986, May 1 Litho. *Perf. 14*

639 A103 10fr Rockets as housing 18
640 A103 20fr Atom as flower 35
641 A103 30fr Handshake 55
642 A103 40fr Globe, chicks 72
a. Souv. sheet of 4, Nos. 639-642 1.80

No. 642a has light blue decorative margin. Exists imperf. Size: 85x120mm.

Great Lake Nations Economic Community (CEPGI), 10th Anniv. — A104

Outline maps of Lake Tanganyika, CEPGI emblem and: 5fr, Aviation. 10fr, Agriculture. 15fr, Industry. 25fr, Electrification. 35fr, Flags of Burundi, Rwanda and Zaire.

Perf. 13½x14½

1986, May 1 Photo.

643 A104 5fr multi 14
644 A104 10fr multi 28
645 A104 15fr multi 38
646 A104 25fr multi 65
647 A104 35fr multi 90
a. Souv. sheet of 5 + label 2.35
Nos. 643-647 (5) 2.35

No. 647a has gold and dark brown violet decorative margin. Size: 118x114mm.

SEMI-POSTAL STAMPS

Prince Louis Rwagasore — SP1

Prince and Stadium SP2

Design: 1.50fr+75c, 6.50fr+3fr, Prince and memorial monument.

Perf. 14x13, 13x14

1963, Feb. 15 Photo. Unwmk.

B1 SP1 50c + 25c brt vio 5 5
B2 SP2 1fr + 50c red org & dk bl 6 6
B3 SP2 1.50fr + 75c lem & dk vio 10 8
B4 SP1 3.50fr + 1.50fr lil rose 15 12
B5 SP2 5fr + 2fr rose pink & dk bl 25 15
B6 SP2 6.50fr + 3fr gray ol & dk vio 30 20
Nos. B1-B6 (6) 91 66

Issued in memory of Prince Louis Rwagasore (1932-61), son of King Mwami Mwambutsa IV and Prime Minister. The surtax was for the stadium and monument in his honor.

Red Cross Type of Regular Issue
Souvenir Sheet

1963, Sept. 26 Litho. *Imperf.*

B7 A5 Sheet of four 4.00 4.00
a. 4fr + 2fr fawn, red & blk 65 65
b. 8fr + 2fr grn, red & blk 75 75
c. 10fr + 2fr gray, red & blk 85 85
d. 20fr + 2fr ultra, red & blk 1.25 1.25

Issued to commemorate the centenary of the International Red Cross. The surtax was for Red Cross work in Burundi. Pale yellow margin with black and red inscription. Size: 90x140mm.

Olympic Type of Regular Issue
Souvenir Sheet

Designs: 18fr+2fr, Hurdling (horiz.). 20fr+5fr, Vaulting (horiz.).

1964, Nov. 18 *Perf. 13½*

B8 A13 Sheet of two 6.00 5.50
a. 18fr + 2fr yel grn & multi 2.50 2.00
b. 20fr + 5fr brt pink & multi 2.50 2.00

Issued to commemorate the 18th Olympic Games, Tokyo, Oct. 10-25, 1964. No. B8 has ornamental red brown border and black and blue marginal inscriptions. Size: 115x71mm.

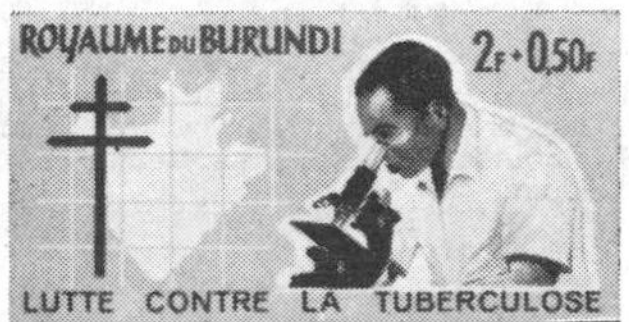

Scientist with Microscope and Map of Burundi — SP3

Lithographed and Photogravure

1965, Jan. 28 Unwmk. *Perf. 14½*

B9 SP3 2fr + 50c tan, red & dk brn 12 8
B10 SP3 4fr + 1.50fr pink, red & grn 28 12
B11 SP3 5fr + 2.50fr ocher, red & vio 40 16
B12 SP3 8fr + 3fr gray, red & dk bl 50 25
B13 SP3 10fr + 5fr grnsh gray, red & red brn 75 32
Nos. B9-B13 (5) 2.05 93

Souvenir Sheet

Perf. 13x13½

B14 SP3 10fr + 10fr pale ol, red & dk brn 1.75 1.75

Issued for the fight against tuberculosis. No. B14 contains one stamp. Tan, red & dark brown margin. Size: 100x71mm.

Coat of Arms, 10fr Coin, Reverse SP4

Designs (Coins of Various Denominations): 4fr+50c, 8fr+50c, 15fr+50c, 40fr+50c, King Mwambutsa IV, obverse.

Lithographed; Embossed on Gilt Foil

1965, Aug. 9 ***Imperf.***

Diameter: 39mm.

B15 SP4 2fr + 50c crim & org 10 10
B16 SP4 4fr + 50c ultra & ver 15 15

Diameter: 45mm.

B17 SP4 6fr + 50c org & gray 20 20
B18 SP4 8fr + 50c bl & mag 30 30

Diameter: 56mm.

B19 SP4 12fr + 50c lt grn & red lil 50 50
B20 SP4 15fr + 50c yel grn & lt lil 60 60

Diameter: 67mm.

B21 SP4 25fr + 50c vio bl & buff 1.00 1.00
B22 SP4 40fr + 50c brt pink & red brn 1.50 1.50
Nos. B15-B22 (8) 4.35 4.35

Stamps are backed with patterned paper in blue, orange and pink engine-turned design.

Prince Louis Rwagasore and Pres. John F. Kennedy SP5

Designs: 4fr+1fr, 20fr+5fr, Prince Louis and memorial. 20fr+2fr, 40fr+5fr, Pres. John F. Kennedy and library shelves. 40fr+2fr, King Mwambutsa IV at Kennedy grave, Arlington (vert.).

1966, Jan. 21 Photo. ***Perf. 13½***

B23 SP5 4fr + 1fr gray bl & dk brn 20 5
B24 SP5 10fr + 1fr pale grn, ind & brn 35 10
B25 SP5 20fr + 2fr lil & dp grn 75 15
B26 SP5 40fr + 2fr gray grn & dk brn 1.25 20

Souvenir Sheet

B27 SP5 Sheet of two 3.00 2.00
a. 20fr + 5fr gray bl & dk brn 1.00 90
b. 40fr + 5fr lil & dp grn 1.50 1.00

Issued in memory of Prince Louis Rwagasore and President John F. Kennedy. No. B27 has brown margin with picture of King Mwambutsa IV and inscription. Size: 75x90mm.

Republic

Winston Churchill and St. Paul's, London SP6

Designs: 15fr+2fr, Tower of London and Churchill. 20fr+3fr, Big Ben and Churchill.

1967, March 23 Photo. ***Perf. 13½***

B28 SP6 4fr + 1fr multi 20 6
B29 SP6 15fr + 2fr multi 70 20
B30 SP6 20fr + 3fr multi 90 35

Issued in memory of Sir Winston Churchill (1874-1965), statesman and World War II leader.

A souvenir sheet contains one airmail stamp, 50fr+5fr, with Churchill portrait centered, marginal decorations and inscriptions. Size: 80x80mm. Exists perf. and imperf. Price, each sheet, $3.50.

Nos. B28-B30 Overprinted

1967, July 14 Photo. ***Perf. 13½***

B31 SP6 4fr + 1fr multi 30 12
B32 SP6 15fr + 2fr multi 85 40
B33 SP6 20fr + 3fr multi 1.25 60

50th anniversary of Lions International. Exist with dates transposed.

The souvenir sheets described below No. B30 also received this Lions overprint. Price, each $3.50.

Blood Transfusion and Red Cross — SP7

Designs: 7fr+1fr, Stretcher bearers and wounded man. 11fr+1fr, Surgical team. 17fr+1fr, Nurses tending blood bank.

1969, June 26 Photo. ***Perf. 13½***

B34 SP7 4fr + 1fr multi 20 5
B35 SP7 7fr + 1fr multi 30 8
B36 SP7 11fr + 1fr multi 60 8
B37 SP7 17fr + 1fr multi 65 15
Nos. B34-B37,CB9-CB11 (7) 4.95 1.26

Issued to commemorate the 50th anniversary of the League of Red Cross Societies.

Pope Paul VI and Map of Africa — SP8

Designs: 3fr+2fr, 17fr+2fr, Pope Paul VI (vert.). 10fr+2fr, Flag made of flags of African Nations. 14fr+2fr, View of St. Peter's, Rome. 40fr+2fr, 40fr+5fr, Martyrs of Uganda. 50fr+2fr, 50fr+5fr, Pope on Throne. All designs include portrait of Pope Paul VI.

1969, Sept. 12 Photo. ***Perf. 13½***

B38 SP8 3fr + 2fr multi 15 5
B39 SP8 5fr + 2fr multi 30 5
B40 SP8 10fr + 2fr multi 60 10
B41 SP8 14fr + 2fr multi 85 12
B42 SP8 17fr + 2fr multi 1.00 15
B43 SP8 40fr + 2fr multi 2.00 35
B44 SP8 50fr + 2fr multi 2.25 40
Nos. B38-B44 (7) 7.15 1.22

Souvenir Sheet

B45 SP8 Sheet of 2 4.00 3.50
a. 40fr + 5fr multi 1.75 1.50
b. 50fr + 5fr multi 2.00 1.75

Issued to commemorate the visit of Pope Paul VI to Uganda, July 31-Aug. 2. No. B45 contains 2 stamps, yellow margin with black inscription and church window design. Size: 80x102mm.

Virgin and Child, by Albrecht Dürer — SP9

Paintings: 11fr+1fr, Madonna of the Eucharist, by Sandro Botticelli. 20fr+1fr, Holy Family, by El Greco.

1970, Dec. 14 Photo. ***Perf. 13½***

Gold Frame

B46 SP9 6.50fr + 1fr multi 30 10
B47 SP9 11fr + 1fr multi 45 15
B48 SP9 20fr + 1fr multi 85 28
a. Souvenir sheet of 3 1.75 1.75
Nos. B46-B48,CB12-CB14 (6) 4.30 1.42

Christmas 1970. No. B48a contains one each of Nos. B46-B48 with ornamental border and inscription. Size: 135x75mm.

Nos. 376-378 Surcharged in Gold and Black

1971, Nov. 27

B49 A51 3fr + 1fr multi 22 10
B50 A51 5fr + 1fr multi 30 15
B51 A51 6fr + 1fr multi 38 18
a. Souvenir sheet of 3 1.10 1.10
Nos. B49-B51,CB19-CB21 (6) 3.55 1.11

25th anniversary of the United Nations International Children's Fund (UNICEF). No. B51a contains 3 stamps similar to Nos. B49-B51 with 2fr surtax each. Size: 125x81mm.

"La Polenta," by Pietro Longhi SP10

Designs: 3fr+1fr, Archangel Michael, Byzantine icon from St. Mark's 6fr+1fr, "Gossip," by Pietro Longhi. 11fr+1fr, "Diana's Bath," by Giovanni Batista Pittoni. All stamps inscribed UNESCO.

1971, Dec. 27

B52 SP10 3fr + 1fr gold & multi 15 6
B53 SP10 5fr + 1fr gold & multi 24 10
B54 SP10 6fr + 1fr gold & multi 35 12
B55 SP10 11fr + 1fr gold & multi 60 20
a. Souvenir sheet of 4 1.20 1.00
Nos. B52-B55,CB22-CB25 (8) 4.32 1.50

The surtax was for the UNESCO campaign to save the treasures of Venice. No. B55a contains 4 stamps similar to Nos. B52-B55, but with 2fr surtax instead 1f. Gold and black ornamental margin. Size: 113x131½mm. Sheet exists imperf.

Nos. 408-410 Surcharged "+1F" in Silver

1972, Dec. 12 Photo. ***Perf. 13½***

B56 A57 5fr + 1fr multi 25 7
B57 A57 10fr + 1fr multi 45 13
B58 A57 15fr + 1fr multi 65 20
a. Souvenir sheet of 3 1.50 1.40
Nos. B56-B58,CB26-CB28 (6) 4.10 1.17

Christmas 1972. No. B58a contains 3 stamps similar to Nos. B56-B58, but with 2fr surtax. Deep carmine and gold border. Size: 128x81mm.

Nos. 441-443 Surcharged "+1F" in Silver

1973, Dec. 14 Photo. ***Perf. 13***

B59 A64 5fr + 1fr multi 20 6
B60 A64 10fr + 1fr multi 40 12
B61 A64 15fr + 1fr multi 60 18
a. Souvenir sheet of 3 1.25 1.25
Nos. B59-B61,CB29-CB31 (6) 3.80 1.18

Christmas 1973. No. B61a contains 3 stamps similar to Nos. B59-B61 with 2fr surtax each. Size: 143x79mm.

Christmas Type of 1974

1974, Dec. 2 Photo. ***Perf. 13***

B62 A70 5fr + 1fr multi 25 15
B63 A70 10fr + 1fr multi 40 25
B64 A70 15fr + 1fr multi 60 38
a. Souvenir sheet of 3 1.50 1.50
Nos. B62-B64,CB32-CB34 (6) 4.30 2.63

No. B64a contains 3 stamps similar to Nos. B62-B64 with 2fr surtax each. Size: 137x90mm.

Nos. 485-490 Surcharged "+ 1F" in Silver and Black

1975, Dec. 22 Photo. ***Perf. 13***

B65 A73 5fr + 1fr #485 25
B66 A73 5fr + 1fr #486 25
B67 A73 13fr + 1fr #487 55
B68 A73 13fr + 1fr #488 55
B69 A73 27fr + 1fr #489 1.00
B70 A73 27fr + 1fr #490 1.00
a. Souvenir sheet of 6 5.00 5.00
Nos. B65-B70,CB35-CB40 (12) 10.20

Michelangelo Buonarroti (1475-1564), 500th birth anniversary. No. B70a contains 6 stamps similar to Nos. B65-B70 with 2fr surcharge each. Size: 132x106mm.

Nos. 504-506 Surcharged "+1f" in Silver and Black

1976, Nov. 25 Photo. ***Perf. 13½***

B71 A76 5fr + 1fr multi 18
B72 A76 13fr + 1fr multi 45
B73 A76 27fr + 1fr multi 85
a. Souvenir sheet of 3 1.75 1.75
Nos. B71-B73,CB41-CB43 (6) 4.33

Christmas 1976. No. B73a contains 3 stamps similar to Nos. B71-B73 with 2fr surtax each. Size: 123x80mm.

Nos. 531-533 Surcharged "+1fr" in Silver and Black

1977 Photo. ***Perf. 14x13***

B74 A83 5fr + 1fr multi 18
B75 A83 13fr + 1fr multi 45
B76 A83 27fr + 1fr multi 85
a. Souvenir sheet of 3 1.75 1.75
Nos. B74-B76,CB44-CB46 (6) 4.31

Christmas 1977. No. B76a contains 3 stamps similar to Nos. B74-B76 with 2fr surtax each. Size: 130x71mm.

Christmas Type of 1979

1979, Feb. Photo. ***Perf. 14x13***

B77 A86 13fr + 1fr multi 45
B78 A86 17fr + 1fr multi 55
B79 A86 27fr + 1fr multi 85
B80 A86 31fr + 1fr multi 1.00
B81 A86 40fr + 1fr multi 1.25
Nos. B77-B81 (5) 4.10

Christmas 1978.

IYC Type of 1979

1979, July 19 Photo. ***Perf. 14***

B82 Sheet of 4, multi 2.50 2.00
a. A88 10fr + 2fr like #557 22 15
b. A88 20fr + 2fr like #558 48 30
c. A88 27fr + 2fr like #559 55 40
d. A88 50fr + 2fr like #560 1.10 65

International Year of the Child. No. B82 has multicolored margin showing detail from Virgin and Child by Rubens, IYC emblem. Size: 131x85mm.

Christmas Type of 1979

1979, Dec. 10 Photo. ***Perf. 13½***

B83 A89 20fr + 1fr like #561 65
B84 A89 27fr + 1fr like #562 85
B85 A89 31fr + 1fr like #563 95
B86 A89 50fr + 2fr like #564 1.55

Christmas Type of 1980

1981, Jan. 16 Photo. *Perf. 13½x13*
B87 A92 10fr + 1fr like #579 22
B88 A92 30fr + 1fr like #580 65
B89 A92 40fr + 1fr like #581 85
B90 A92 50fr + 1fr like #582 1.00

Christmas Type of 1983

1983, Nov. 2 Litho. *Perf. 14½x13½*
B91 A97 10fr + 1fr like #607 32
B92 A97 25fr + 1fr like #608 78
B93 A97 30fr + 1fr like #609 95
B94 A97 50fr + 1fr like #610 1.50

Christmas Type of 1984

1984, Dec. 15 *Perf. 13½*
B95 A101 10fr + 1fr like #629 32
B96 A101 25fr + 1fr like #630 78
B97 A101 30fr + 1fr like #631 95
B98 A101 50fr + 1fr like #632 1.50

AIR POST STAMPS

Animal Type of Regular Issue

Animals: 6fr, Zebra. 8fr, Cape buffalo (bubalis). 10fr, Impala (vert.). 14fr, Hippopotamus. 15fr, Defassa waterbuck (vert.). 20fr, Cheetah. 50fr, Elephant.

Unwmk.

1964, July 2 Litho. *Perf. 14*

Size: 42x21mm., 21x42mm.

C1 A9 6fr multi 25 5
C2 A9 8fr multi 32 8
C3 A9 10fr multi 42 10
C4 A9 14fr multi 60 15
C5 A9 15fr multi 65 18

Size: 53x32½mm.

C6 A9 20fr multi 85 30
C7 A9 50fr multi 2.25 75
Nos. C1-C7 (7) 5.34 1.61

Bird Type of Regular Issue

Birds: 6fr, Secretary bird. 8fr, African anhinga. 10fr, African peacock. 14fr, Bee eater. 15fr, Yellow-billed stork. 20fr, Saddle-billed stork. 50fr, Abyssinian ground hornbill. 75fr, Martial eagle. 130fr, Lesser flamingo.

1965, June 10 Litho. *Perf. 14*

Size: 26x43mm.

C8 A14 6fr multi 25 5
C9 A14 8fr multi 30 8
C10 A14 10fr multi 40 10
C11 A14 14fr multi 50 12
C12 A14 15fr multi 60 15

Size: 33x53mm.

C13 A14 20fr multi 70 13
C14 A14 50fr multi 1.75 40
C15 A14 75fr multi 2.50 50
C16 A14 130fr multi 4.50 75
Nos. C8-C16 (9) 11.50 2.28

Flower Type of Regular Issue

Flowers: 6fr, Dissotis. 8fr, Crossandra. 10fr, Ansellia. 14fr, Thunbergia. 15fr, Schizoglossum. 20fr, Gazania. 50fr, Protea. 75fr, Hibiscus. 130fr, Markhamia.

1966, Oct. 10 Unwmk. *Perf. 13½*

Size: 31x31mm.

C17 A17 6fr multi 22 5
C18 A17 8fr multi 30 8
C19 A17 10fr multi 40 10
C20 A17 14fr multi 50 12
C21 A17 15fr multi 50 15

Size: 39x39mm.

C22 A17 20fr multi 50 18
C23 A17 50fr multi 1.25 40
C24 A17 75fr multi 1.85 50
C25 A17 130fr multi 3.35 75
Nos. C17-C25 (9) 8.87 2.33

Tapestry Type of Regular Issue

Souvenir Sheet

1966, Nov. 4 Unwmk. *Perf. 13½*
C26 A18 Sheet of 7 (14fr) 2.50 1.25

See note after No. 158.

Republic

Nos. C17-C25, Overprinted

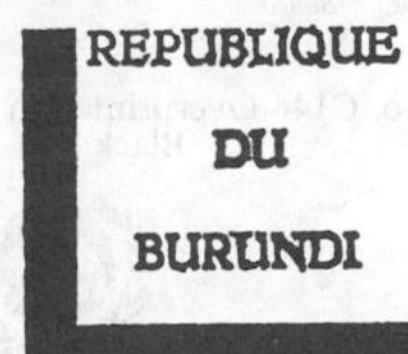

1967 Litho. *Perf. 13½*

Size: 31x31mm.

C27 A17 6fr multi 38 13
C28 A17 8fr multi 45 15
C29 A17 10fr multi 50 17
C30 A17 14fr multi 95 25
C31 A17 15fr multi 95 25

Size: 39x39mm.

C32 A17 20fr multi 1.40 35
C33 A17 50fr multi 3.75 1.00
C34 A17 75fr multi 6.00 1.00
C35 A17 130fr multi 8.00 2.10
Nos. C27-C35 (9) 22.38 5.40

Nos. C8-C16 Overprinted "REPUBLIQUE / DU / BURUNDI" and Horizontal Bar

1967 Litho. *Perf. 14*

Size: 26x43mm.

C35A A14 6fr multi *30*
C35B A14 8fr multi *35*
C35C A14 10fr multi *40*
C35D A14 14fr multi *60*
C35E A14 15fr multi *95*

Size: 33x53mm

C35F A14 20fr multi *1.50*
C35G A14 50fr multi *3.75*
C35H A14 75fr multi *6.00*
C35I A14 130fr multi *6.75*
Nos. C35A-C35I (9) 20.60

African Art Type of Regular Issue

African Art: 10fr, Spirit of Bakutu figurine, Equatorial Africa. 14fr, Pearl throne of Sultan of the Bamum, Cameroun. 17fr, Bronze head of Mother Queen of Benin, Nigeria. 24fr, Statue of 109th Bakouba king, Kata-Mbula, Central Congo. 26fr, Baskets and lances, Burundi.

1967, June 5 Photo. *Perf. 13½*
C36 A20 10fr gold & multi 20 12
C37 A20 14fr gold & multi 25 12
C38 A20 17fr gold & multi 30 12
C39 A20 24fr gold & multi 42 25
C40 A20 26fr gold & multi 85 50
Nos. C36-C40 (5) 2.02 1.11

Boy Scout Type of Regular Issue

Designs: 10fr, Scouts on hiking trip. 14fr, Cooking at campfire. 17fr, Lord Baden-Powell. 24fr, Boy Scout and Cub Scout giving Scout sign. 26fr, First aid.

1967, Aug. 9 *Perf. 13½*
C41 A21 10fr gold & multi 30 20
C42 A21 14fr gold & multi 45 20
C43 A21 17fr gold & multi 55 20
C44 A21 24fr gold & multi 85 35
C45 A21 26fr gold & multi 1.40 35
Nos. C41-C45 (5) 3.55 1.30

Issued to commemorate the 60th anniversary of the Boy Scouts and the 12th Boy Scout World Jamboree, Farragut State Park, Idaho, Aug. 1-9.

A souvenir sheet of 2 contains one each of Nos. C44-C45 and 2 labels in the designs of Nos. 208-209 with commemorative inscriptions was issued Jan. 8, 1968. Size: 100x100mm.

Fish Type of Regular Issue

Designs: Various Tropical Fish

1967, Sept. 8 Photo. *Perf. 13½*

Size: 50x23mm.

C46 A19 6fr multi 25 5
C47 A19 8fr multi 35 6
C48 A19 10fr multi 40 8
C49 A19 14fr multi 55 10
C50 A19 15fr multi 55 12

Size: 58x27mm.

C51 A19 20fr multi 75 14
C52 A19 50fr multi 1.75 25
C53 A19 75fr multi 2.75 35
C54 A19 130fr multi 4.50 60
Nos. C46-C54 (9) 11.85 1.75

Boeing 707 of Air Congo and ITY Emblem — AP1

Designs: 14fr, Boeing 727 of Sabena over lake. 17fr, Vickers VC10 of East African Airways over lake. 26fr, Boeing 727 of Sabena over airport.

1967, Nov. 3 Photo. *Perf. 13*
C55 AP1 10fr blk, yel brn & sil 25 10
C56 AP1 14fr blk, org & sil 40 15
C57 AP1 17fr blk, brt bl & sil 50 20
C58 AP1 26fr blk, brt rose lil & sil 85 30

Issued to commemorate the opening of the jet airport at Bujumbura and for International Tourist Year, 1967.

Paintings Type of Regular Issue

Paintings: 17fr, Woman with Cat, by Renoir. 24fr, The Jewish Bride, by Rembrandt (horiz.). 26fr, Pope Innocent X, by Velazquez.

1968, Mar. 29 Photo. *Perf. 13½*
C59 A26 17fr multi 70 30
C60 A26 24fr multi 90 35
C61 A26 26fr multi 1.10 40

Issued in sheets of 6.

Space Type of Regular Issue

Designs: 14fr, Moon Probe. 18fr, Russian astronaut walking in space. 25fr, Weather satellite. 40fr, American astronaut walking in space.

1968, May 15 Photo. *Perf. 13½*

Size: 41x41mm.

C62 A27 14fr sil & multi 50 10
C63 A27 18fr sil & multi 60 18
C64 A27 25fr sil & multi 90 20
C65 A27 40fr sil & multi 1.40 35

Issued to publicize peaceful space explorations.

Butterfly Type of Regular Issue

Butterflies: 6fr, Teracolus annae. 8fr, Graphium ridleyanus. 10fr, Cymothoc. 14fr, Charaxes eupale. 15fr, Papilio bromius. 20fr, Papilio zenobia. 50fr, Salamis aethiops. 75fr, Danais chrysippus. 130fr, Salamis temora.

1968, Sept. 9 Photo. *Perf. 13½*

Size: 38x42mm.

C66 A28 6fr gold & multi 25 5
C67 A28 8fr gold & multi 30 5
C68 A28 10fr gold & multi 35 5
C69 A28 14fr gold & multi 40 5
C70 A28 15fr gold & multi 40 8

Size: 44x49mm.

C71 A28 20fr gold & multi 60 12
C72 A28 50fr gold & multi 1.40 18
C73 A28 75fr gold & multi 2.50 25
C74 A28 130fr gold & multi 4.00 40
Nos. C66-C74 (9) 10.20 1.23

Painting Type of Regular Issue

Paintings: 17fr, The Letter, by Jean H. Fragonard. 26fr, Young Woman Reading Letter, by Jan Vermeer. 40fr, Lady Folding Letter, by Elisabeth Vigee-Lebrun. 50fr, Mademoiselle Lavergne, by Jean Etienne Liotard.

1968, Sept. 30 Photo. *Perf. 13½*
C84 A29 17fr multi 45 12
C85 A29 26fr multi 85 20
C86 A29 40fr multi 1.15 28
C87 A29 50fr multi 1.40 35

Issued for International Letter Writing Week, Oct. 7-13.

Olympic Games Type of 1968

Designs: 10fr, Shot put. 17fr, Running. 26fr, Hammer throw. 50fr, Hurdling. 75fr, Broad jump.

1968, Oct. 24
C88 A30 10fr gold & multi 25 8
C89 A30 17fr gold & multi 45 12
C90 A30 26fr gold & multi 75 20
C91 A30 50fr gold & multi 1.40 40
C92 A30 75fr gold & multi 2.10 60
Nos. C88-C92 (5) 4.95 1.40

Issued to commemorate the 19th Olympic Games, Mexico City, Oct. 12-27.

Christmas Type of 1968

Paintings: 10fr, Virgin and Child, by Correggio. 14fr, Nativity, by Federigo Baroccio. 17fr, Holy Family, by El Greco. 26fr, Adoration of the Magi, by Maino.

1968, Nov. 26 Photo. *Perf. 13½*
C93 A31 10fr multi 30 15
C94 A31 14fr multi 45 20
C95 A31 17fr multi 55 25
C96 A31 26fr multi 80 30
a. Souv. sheet of 4 2.25

No. C96a contains one each of Nos. C93-C96, decorative border and inscriptions. Size: 120x120mm.

Human Rights Flame, Hand and Globe — AP2

1969, Jan. 22
C97 AP2 10fr multi 30 10
C98 AP2 14fr multi 42 10
C99 AP2 26fr lil & multi 80 25

International Human Rights Year, 1968.

Nos. C93-C96 Overprinted in Silver

1969, Feb. 17 Photo. *Perf. 13½*
C100 A31 10fr multi 40 15
C101 A31 14fr multi 55 25
C102 A31 17fr multi 70 28
C103 A31 26fr multi 1.00 45

Issued to commemorate man's first flight around the moon by the U.S. spacecraft Apollo 8, Dec. 21-27, 1968.

Moon Landing Type of 1969

Designs: 26fr, Neil A. Armstrong leaving landing module. 40fr, Astronaut on moon. 50fr, Splashdown in the Pacific.

1969, Nov. 6 Photo. *Perf. 13½*
C104 A38 26fr gold & multi 1.00 50
C105 A38 40fr gold & multi 1.50 75
C106 A38 50fr gold & multi 1.80 85

See note after Algeria No. 427.

Christmas Type of 1969

Paintings: 17fr, Madonna and Child, by Benvenuto da Garofalo. 26fr, Madonna and Child, by Jacopo Negretti. 50fr, Madonna and Child, by Il Giorgione. All horizontal.

1969, Dec. 2 Photo.
C107 A39 17fr gold & multi 75 15
C108 A39 26fr gold & multi 1.00 25
C109 A39 50fr gold & multi 1.80 55
a. Souvenir sheet of 3 3.00 3.00

No. C109a contains one each of Nos. C107-C109. Gold frame with black and red inscription. Size: 87x110mm.

Insect Type of Regular Issue

Designs: Various Beetles and Weevils.

1970 *Perf. 13½*

Size: 46x32mm.

C110 A40 6fr gold & multi 20 5
C111 A40 8fr gold & multi 25 5
C112 A40 10fr gold & multi 35 5
C113 A40 14fr gold & multi 50 5
C114 A40 15fr gold & multi 60 5

Size: 52x36mm.

C115 A40 20fr gold & multi 2.00 6
C116 A40 50fr gold & multi 4.00 50

C117 A40 75fr gold & multi 6.00 50
C118 A40 130fr gold & multi 7.50 80
Nos. C110-C118 (9) 21.40 2.11

Issue dates: Nos. C110-C115, Jan. 20. Nos. C116-C118, Feb. 27.

Easter Type of 1970

Stations of the Cross, by Juan de Aranoa y Carredano: 8fr, Jesus meets the women of Jerusalem. 10fr, Jesus falls a third time. 14fr, Jesus stripped. 15fr, Jesus nailed to the cross. 18fr, Jesus dies on the cross. 20fr, Descent from the cross. 50fr, Jesus laid in the tomb.

1970, Mar. 16 Photo. *Perf. 13½*
C119 A41 8fr gold & multi 25 10
C120 A41 10fr gold & multi 30 12
C121 A41 14fr gold & multi 45 18
C122 A41 15fr gold & multi 50 20
C123 A41 18fr gold & multi 55 22
C124 A41 20fr gold & multi 60 25
C125 A41 50fr gold & multi 1.40 60
a. Souv. sheet of 7 + label 3.50 3.50
Nos. C119-C125 (7) 4.05 1.67

No. C125a contains one each of Nos. C119-C125 and label showing Ascension. Gold decorative border. Size: 154x123mm.

EXPO '70 Type of Regular Issue

Souvenir Sheet

Designs: 40fr, Tower of the Sun (vert.). 50fr, Flags of participating nations (vert.).

1970, May 5 Photo. *Perf. 13½*
C126 A42 Souv. sheet of 2 2.75 2.75
a. 40fr multi 95 95
b. 50f multi 1.20 1.20

Issued to publicize EXPO '70 International Exhibition, Osaka, Japan, March 15-Sept. 13, 1970. No. C126 has gold and black decorative border. Size: 104½x80mm.

Rhinoceros Type of Regular Issue

Designs, FAUNA: Camel, dromedary, okapi, rhinoceros, addax, Burundi cow (2 stamps of each animal in 2 different poses). MAP OF THE NILE: Delta and pyramids, dhow, cataract, Blue Nile and crowned crane, Victoria Nile and secretary bird, Lake Victoria and source of Nile on Mt. Gikizi.

1970, July 8 Photo. *Perf. 13½*
C127 A43 14fr multi 56 20
a. Sheet of 18 10.50

Issued in sheets of 18 (3x6) stamps of different designs, to publicize the southernmost source of the Nile on Mt. Gikizi in Burundi.

U.N. Emblem and Headquarters, N.Y. — AP3

Designs (U.N. Emblem and): 11fr, Security Council and mural by Per Krohg. 26fr, Pope Paul VI and U Thant. 40fr, Flags in front of U.N. Headquarters, N.Y.

1970, Oct. 23 Photo. *Perf. 13½*
C128 AP3 7fr gold & multi 20 5
C129 AP3 11fr gold & multi 35 8
C130 AP3 26fr gold & multi 75 15
C131 AP3 40fr gold & multi 1.20 25
a. Souvenir sheet of 2 2.00 1.75

Issued to commemorate the 25th anniversary of the United Nations. No. C131a contains 2 stamps similar to Nos. C130-C131 but without "Poste Aerienne"; blue margin with gold ornament, black inscription and U.N. emblem. Size: 123x80mm. Exists imperf.

Bird Type of Regular Issue

Birds: 8fr, 14fr, 30fr, vertical; 10fr, 20fr, 50fr, horizontal.

1970 Photo. *Perf. 13½*
Stamp size: 52x44mm.
C132 A44 8fr Block of four 2.50 25
a. *Northern shrike* 60 6
b. *European starling* 60 6
c. *Yellow wagtail* 60 6
d. *Bank swallow* 60 6
C133 A44 10fr Block of four 3.00 35
a. *Winter wren* 70 8
b. *Firecrest* 70 8
c. *Skylark* 70 8
d. *Crested lark* 70 8
C134 A44 14fr Block of four 3.75 50
a. *Woodchat shrike* 90 12
b. *Common rock thrush* 90 12
c. *Black redstart* 90 12
d. *Ring ouzel* 90 12
C135 A44 20fr Block of four 6.00 65
a. *European redstart* 1.40 15
b. *Hedge sparrow* 1.40 15
c. *Gray wagtail* 1.40 15
d. *Meadow pipit* 1.40 15
C136 A44 30fr Block of four 8.50 1.05
a. *Eurasian hoopoe* 2.00 25
b. *Pied flycatcher* 2.00 25
c. *Great reed warbler* 2.00 25
d. *Eurasian kingfisher* 2.00 25
C137 A44 50fr Block of four 14.00 1.75
a. *House martin* 3.50 40
b. *Sedge warbler* 3.50 40
c. *Fieldfare* 3.50 40
d. *European Golden oriole* 3.50 40
Nos. C132-C137 (6) 37.75 4.55

Nos. C132-C137 are printed in sheets of 16 containing 4 blocks of 4.

Queen Fabiola and King Baudouin of Belgium AP4

Designs: 20fr, Pres. Michel Micombero and King Baudouin. 40fr, Pres. Micombero and coats of arms of Burundi and Belgium.

1970, Nov. 28 Photo. *Perf. 13½*
C140 AP4 6fr gold, dp brn & dp plum 30 10
C141 AP4 20fr gold, dp brn & dp plum 90 30
C142 AP4 40fr gold, dp brn & dp plum 1.85 60
a. Souvenir sheet of 3 3.00 3.00

Issued to commemorate the visit of the King and Queen of Belgium. No. C142a contains 3 stamps similar to Nos. C140-C142, but without "Poste Aerienne." Deep plum and gold margin with commemorative inscription. Size: 143½x108mm.

Easter Type of Regular Issue

Paintings of the Resurrection: 14fr, by Louis Borrassa. 17fr, Piero della Francesca. 26fr, Michel Wohlgemuth.

1971, Apr. 2 Photo. *Perf. 13½*
C143 A49 14fr gold & multi 40 15
C144 A49 17fr gold & multi 45 18
C145 A49 26fr gold & multi 60 25
a. Souvenir sheet of 3 1.90 1.50

Easter 1971. No. C145a contains one each of Nos. C143-C145. Red and gold margin. Size: 120x85mm. Sheet exists imperf.

Animal Type of Regular Issue

1971 Photo. *Perf. 13½*
Size: 44x44mm.
C146 A48 10fr Strip of four 2.00 25
a. *Lion* 45 6
b. *Cape buffalo* 45 6
c. *Hippopotamus* 45 6
d. *Giraffe* 45 6
C147 A48 14fr Strip of four 3.00 45
a. *Hartebeest* 70 10
b. *Black rhinoceros* 70 10
c. *Zebra* 70 10
d. *Leopard* 70 10
C148 A48 17fr Strip of four 3.50 50
a. *Grant's gazelles* 80 12
b. *Cheetah* 80 12
c. *African white-backed vultures* 80 12
d. *Johnston's okapi* 80 12
C149 A48 24fr Strip of four 4.50 65
a. *Chimpanzee* 1.00 15
b. *Elephant* 1.00 15
c. *Spotted Hyenas* 1.00 15
d. *Beisa* 1.00 15
C150 A48 26fr Strip of four 5.00 80
a. *Gorilla* 1.10 20
b. *Gnu* 1.10 20
c. *Warthog* 1.10 20
d. *Cape hunting dog* 1.10 20
C151 A48 31fr Strip of four 5.75 90
a. *Sable antelope* 1.40 22
b. *Caracal lynx* 1.40 22
c. *Ostriches* 1.40 22
d. *Bongo* 1.40 22
Nos. C146-C151 (6) 23.75 3.55

No. C146 Overprinted in Gold and Black

LUTTE CONTRE LE RACISME ET LA DISCRIMINATION RACIALE

1971, July 20 Photo. *Perf. 13½*
C152 A48 10fr Strip of four 1.20 24
a. *Lion* 30 5
b. *Cape buffalo* 30 5
c. *Hippopotamus* 30 5
d. *Giraffe* 30 5

International Year Against Racial Discrimination.

Christmas Type of Regular Issue

Paintings of the Madonna and Child by: 14fr, Cima de Conegliano. 17fr, Fra Filippo Lippi. 31fr, Leonardo da Vinci.

1971, Nov. 2 Photo. *Perf. 13½*
C153 A51 14fr red & multi 55 25
C154 A51 17fr red & multi 65 30
C155 A51 31fr red & multi 1.00 40
a. Souvenir sheet of 3 2.25 2.25

Christmas 1971. No. C155a contains one each of Nos. C153-C155. Multicolored margin. Size: 125x81mm. Sheet exists imperf.

Spacecraft Type of Regular Issue

Souvenir Sheet

1972, Jan. 15 Photo. *Perf. 13½*
C156 A52 Sheet of 6, multi 3.00 2.00
a. 6fr *Lunar Orbiter* 15 8
b. 11fr *Vostok* 30 15
c. 14fr *Luna 1* 35 18
d. 17fr *Apollo 11 astronaut on moon* 42 20
e. 26fr *Soyuz 11* 70 35
f. 40fr *Lunar rover (Apollo 15)* 95 50

Conquest of space. No. C156 has dark blue and multicolored margin. Size: 134x135mm.

Sapporo '72 Type of Regular Issue

Souvenir Sheet

Designs (Sapporo '72 Emblem and): 26fr, Snow scooter. 31fr, Downhill skiing. 50fr, Bobsledding.

1972, Feb. 3
C157 A53 Sheet of 3 3.00 2.50
a. 26fr sil & multi 70 50
b. 31fr sil & multi 80 60
c. 50fr sil & multi 1.25 80

11th Winter Olympic Games, Sapporo, Japan, Feb. 3-13. No. C157 contains 3 stamps, arranged vertically. Silver decorative margin with blue and black inscription. Size: 106x125mm.

Olympic Games Type of 1972

1972, July 24 Photo. *Perf. 13½*
C158 A55 24fr *Weight lifting* 72 23
C159 A55 26fr *Hurdles* 78 25
C160 A55 31fr *Discus* 95 30
C161 A55 40fr *Soccer* 1.20 40

20th Olympic Games, Munich, Aug. 26-Sept. 11.

Independence Type of 1972

Designs: 15fr, Prince Rwagasore, Pres. Micombero, Burundi flag, drummers. 18fr, Rwagasore, Micombero, flag, map of Africa, globe. 27fr, Micombero, flag, globe.

1972, Aug. 24 Photo. *Perf. 13½*
C162 A56 15fr gold & multi 50 17
C163 A56 18fr gold & multi 60 20
C164 A56 27fr gold & multi 90 30
a. Souvenir sheet of 3 2.25 2.25

10th anniversary of independence.
No. C164a contains one each of Nos. C162-C164. Gold and light blue margin with black inscription. Size: 146x80mm.

Christmas Type of 1972

Paintings of the Madonna and Child by: 18fr, Sebastiano Mainardi. 27fr, Hans Memling. 40fr, Lorenzo Lotto.

1972, Nov. 2 Photo. *Perf. 13½*
C165 A57 18fr dk car & multi 55 17
C166 A57 27fr dk car & multi 80 25
C167 A57 40fr dk car & multi 1.20 35
a. Souvenir sheet of 3 2.75 2.75

Christmas 1972. No. C167a contains one each of Nos. C165-C167, slate green and gold border. Size: 128x81mm.

Orchid Type of Regular Issue

1973, Jan. 18 Photo. *Perf. 13½*
Size: 38x38mm.
C168 A58 13fr *Thelymitra pauciflora* 42 10
C169 A58 14fr *Miltassia* 45 12
C170 A58 15fr *Miltonia* 50 13
C171 A58 18fr *Platycoryne crocea* 55 15
C172 A58 20fr *Cattleya trinaei* 60 17
C173 A58 27fr *Eulophia cucullata* 85 20
C174 A58 36fr *Cymbidium hamsey* 1.10 27
Nos. C168-C174 (7) 4.47 1.14

African Exploration Type of 1973

Designs: 15fr, Livingstone writing his diary. 18fr, "Dr. Livingstone, I presume." 27fr, Livingstone and Stanley discussing expedition.

1973, Mar. 19 Photo. *Perf. 13½*
C175 A59 15fr gold & multi 45 15
C176 A59 18fr gold & multi 55 18
C177 A59 27fr gold & multi 80 27
a. Souvenir sheet of 3 2.10 2.10

Exploration of Africa by David Livingstone and Henry Morton Stanley. No. C177a contains 3 stamps similar to Nos. C175-C177, but without "Poste Aerienne." Gold and violet decorative margin. Size: 100x140mm.

Easter Type of 1973

Paintings: 15fr, Christ at the Pillar, by Guido Reni. 18fr, Crucifixion, by Mathias Grunewald. 27fr, Descent from the Cross, by Caravaggio.

1973, Apr. 10
C178 A60 15fr gold & multi 55 15
C179 A60 18fr gold & multi 70 18
C180 A60 27fr gold & multi 1.00 27
a. Souvenir sheet of 3 2.10 2.10

Easter 1973. No. C180a contains one each of Nos. C178-C180. Multicolored margin. Size: 121x73mm.

INTERPOL Type of Regular Issue

Designs: 27fr, INTERPOL emblem and flag. 40fr, INTERPOL flag and emblem.

1973, May 19 Photo. *Perf. 13½*
C181 A61 27fr gold & multi 80 32
C182 A61 40fr gold & multi 95 38

50th anniversary of International Criminal Police Organization (INTERPOL).

Copernicus Type of Regular Issue

Designs: 15fr, Copernicus (C183a), Earth, Pluto, and Jupiter. 18fr, Copernicus (No. C184a), Venus, Saturn, Mars. 27fr, Copernicus (No. C185a), Uranus, Neptune, Mercury. 36fr, Earth and various spacecrafts.

1973, July 27 Photo. *Perf. 13½*
C183 A62 15fr Block of four 2.75 60
a. 15fr in UL 65 15
b. 15fr in UR 65 15
c. 15fr in LL 65 15
d. 15fr in LR 65 15
C184 A62 18fr Block of four 3.00 70
a. 18fr in UL 75 16
b. 18fr in UR 75 16
c. 18fr in LL 75 16
d. 18fr in LR 75 16
C185 A62 27fr Block of four 4.00 1.00
a. 27fr in UL 1.00 25
b. 27fr in UR 1.00 25
c. 27fr in LL 1.00 25
d. 27fr in LR 1.00 25
C186 A62 36fr Block of four 5.25 1.40
a. 36fr in UL 1.25 35
b. 36fr in UR 1.25 35
c. 36fr in LL 1.25 35
d. 36fr in LR 1.25 35
e. Souvenir sheet of 4 14.00 14.00

500th anniversary of the birth of Nicolaus Copernicus (1473-1543), Polish astronomer. Nos. C183-C186 are printed in sheets of 32 containing 8 blocks of 4. No. C186e contains one each of Nos. C183-C186. Gold and multicolored margin. Size: 136x136mm.

Flower-Butterfly Type of 1973

Designs: Each block of 4 contains 2 flower and 2 butterfly designs. The 10fr, 14fr, 24fr and 31fr have flower designs listed as "a" and "d" numbers, butterflies as "b" and "c" numbers; the arrangement is reversed for the 17fr and 26fr.

1973, Sept. 28 Photo. *Perf. 13*
Stamp Size: 35x45mm.

C187 A63 10fr Block of 4 4.00 40
a. *Protea cynaroides* 90 10
b. *Precis octavia* 90 10
c. *Epiphora bauhiniae* 90 10
d. *Gazania longiscapa* 90 10
C188 A63 14fr Block of 4 5.00 55
a. *Kniphofia* 1.25 13
b. *Cymothoe coccinata* 1.25 13
c. *Nudaurelia zambesina* 1.25 13
d. Freesia refracta 1.25 13
C189 A63 17fr Block of 4 6.00 65
a. *Calotis eupompe* 1.40 15
b. *Narcissus* 1.40 15
c. *Cineraria hybrida* 1.40 15
d. *Cyrestis camillus* 1.40 15
C190 A63 24fr Block of 4 7.00 95
a. *Iris tingitana* 1.65 23
b. *Papilio demodocus* 1.65 23
c. *Catopsilia avelaneda* 1.65 23
d. *Nerine sarniensis* 1.65 23
C191 A63 26fr Block of 4 8.00 1.10
a. *Hypolimnas dexithea* 2.00 25
b. *Zantedeschia tropicalis* 2.00 25
c. *Sandersonia aurantiaca* 2.00 25
d. *Drurya antimachus* 2.00 25
C192 A63 31fr Block of 4 9.00 1.30
a. *Nymphaea capensis* 2.25 30
b. *Pandoriana pandora* 2.25 30
c. *Precis orythia* 2.25 30
d. *Pelargonium domestica* 2.25 30
Nos. C187-C192 (6) 39.00 4.95

Christmas Type of 1973

Virgin and Child by: 18fr, Raphael. 27fr, Pietro Perugino. 40fr, Titian.

1973, Nov. 19

C193 A64 18fr gold & multi 55 15
C194 A64 27fr gold & multi 80 22
C195 A64 40fr gold & multi 1.20 33
a. Souvenir sheet of 3 2.75 2.75

Christmas 1973. No. C195a contains one each of Nos. C193-C195 with multicolored margin. Size: 143x79mm.

Soccer Type of Regular Issue

Designs: Various soccer scenes and cup.

1974, July 4 Photo. *Perf. 13*

C196 A67 20fr gold & multi 60
C197 A67 26fr gold & multi 78
C198 A67 40fr gold & multi 1.20

World Cup Soccer Championships, Munich, June 13-July 7. For souvenir sheet see No. 459a.

UPU Type of 1974

Designs: No. C199, Flags over UPU Headquarters, Bern. No. C200, G.P.O., Usumbura. No. C201, Mailmen ("26F" in UR). No. C202, Mailmen ("26F" in UL). No. C203, UPU emblem. No. C204, Means of transportation. No. C205, Pigeon over globe showing Burundi. No. C206, Swiss flag, pigeon over map showing Bern.

1974, July 23

C199 A68 24fr gold & multi 1.25
C200 A68 24fr gold & multi 1.25
C201 A68 26fr gold & multi 1.50
C202 A68 26fr gold & multi 1.50
C203 A68 31fr gold & multi 2.00
C204 A68 31fr gold & multi 2.00
C205 A68 40fr gold & multi 2.50
C206 A68 40fr gold & multi 2.50
a. Souvenir sheet of 8 12.00 12.00
Nos. C199-C206 (8) 14.50

Centenary of Universal Postal Union. Stamps of same denomination printed setenant (continuous design) in sheets of 40. No. C206a contains one each of Nos. C199-C206. Violet, gold and light blue margin. Size: 96x162mm.

Fish Type of 1974

1974, Sept. 9 Photo. *Perf. 13*
Size: 35x35mm.

C207 A66 10fr Block of 4 2.00 25
a. *Haplochromis multicolor* 50 6
b. *Pantodon buchholzi* 50 6
c. *Tropheus duboisi* 50 6
d. *Distichodus sexfasciatus* 50 6
C208 A66 14fr Block of 4 2.50 35
a. *Pelmatochromis kribensis* 60 8
b. *Nannaethiops tritaeniatus* 60 8
c. *Polycentropsis abbreviata* 60 8
d. *Hemichromis bimaculatus* 60 8
C209 A66 17fr Block of 4 3.00 40
a. *Ctenopoma acutirostre* 75 10
b. *Synodontis angelicus* 75 10
c. *Tilapia melanopleura* 75 10
d. *Aphyosemion bivittatum* 75 10
C210 A66 24fr Block of four 3.75 60
a. *Monodactylus argenteus* 90 15
b. *Zanclus canescens* 90 15
c. *Pygoplites diacanthus* 90 15
d. *Cephalopholis argus* 90 15
C211 A66 26fr Block of 4 4.00 70
a. *Priacanthus arenatus* 1.00 17
b. *Pomacanthus arcutus* 1.00 17
c. *Scarus guacamaia* 1.00 17
d. *Zeus faber* 1.00 17
C212 A66 31fr Block of 4 5.00 80
a. *Lactophrys quadricornis* 1.25 20
b. *Balistes vetula* 1.25 20
c. *Acanthurus bahianus* 1.25 20
d. *Holocanthus ciliaris* 1.25 20
Nos. C207-C212 (6) 20.25 3.10

Christmas Type of 1974

Paintings of the Virgin and Child: 18fr, by Hans Memling. 27fr, by Filippino Lippi. 40fr, by Lorenzo di Gredi.

1974, Nov. 7 Photo. *Perf. 13*

C213 A70 18fr gold & multi 55 45
C214 A70 27fr gold & multi 80 65
C215 A70 40fr gold & multi 1.20 95
a. Souvenir sheet of 3 3.00 3.00

Christmas 1974. Sheets of 20 stamps and one label. No. C215a contains one each of Nos. C213-C215, gold and multicolored border. Size: 137x90mm. Sheet exists imperf.

Apollo-Soyuz Type of 1975

1975, July 10 Photo. *Perf. 13*

C216 A71 27fr Block of 4 1.80
a. *A.A. Leonov, V.N. Kubasov, Soviet flag* 45
b. *Soyuz and Soviet flag* 45
c. *Apollo and American flag* 45
d. *Slayton, Brand, Stafford, American flag* 45
C217 A71 40fr Block of 4 2.60
a. *Apollo-Soyuz link-up* 65
b. *Apollo, blast-off* 65
c. *Soyuz, blast-off* 65
d. *Kubasov, Leonov, Slayton, Brand, Stafford* 65

Apollo Soyuz space test project (Russo-American cooperation), launching July 15; link-up, July 17. Nos. C216-C217 are printed in sheets of 32 containing 8 blocks of 4.

Animal Type of 1975

1975, Sept. 17 Photo. *Perf. 13½*

C218 A72 10fr Strip of four 1.75
a. *Addax* 42
b. *Roan antelope* 42
c. *Nyala* 42
d. *White rhinoceros* 42
C219 A72 14fr Strip of four 2.50
a. *Mandrill* 60
b. *Eland* 60
c. *Salt's dik-dik* 60
d. *Thomson's gazelles* 60
C220 A72 17fr Strip of four 3.00
a. *African small-clawed otter* 75
b. *Reed buck* 75
c. *Indian civet* 75
d. *Cape buffalo* 75
C221 A72 24fr Strip of four 4.00
a. *White-tailed gnu* 1.00
b. *African wild asses* 1.00
c. *Black-and-white colobus monkey* 1.00
d. *Gerenuk* 1.00
C222 A72 26fr Strip of four 4.50
a. *Dama gazelle* 1.10
b. *Black-backed jackal* 1.10
c. *Sitatungas* 1.10
d. *Zebra antelope* 1.10
C223 A72 31fr Strip of four 5.25
a. *Fennec* 1.30
b. *Lesser kudus* 1.30
c. *Blesbok* 1.30
d. *Serval* 1.30
Nos. C218-C223 (6) 21.00

Nos. C218-C219 Overprinted in Black and Silver with IWY Emblem and: "ANNEE INTERNATIONALE / DE LA FEMME"

1975, Nov. 19 Photo. *Perf. 13½*

C224 A72 10fr Strip of four 1.20 24
a. *Addax* 30 5
b. *Roan antelope* 30 5
c. *Nyala* 30 5
d. *White rhinoceros* 30 5
C225 A72 14fr Strip of four 1.68 35
a. *Mandrill* 42 8
b. *Oryx* 42 8
c. *Dik-dik* 42 8
d. *Thomson's gazelles* 42 8

International Women's Year 1975.

Nos. C222-C223 Overprinted in Black and Silver with U.N. Emblem and: "30eme ANNIVERSAIRE DES/ NATIONS UNIES"

1975, Nov. 19

C226 A72 26fr Strip of four 3.15 60
a. *Dama gazelle* 76 15
b. *Wild dog* 76 15
c. *Sitatungas* 76 15
d. *Striped duiker* 76 15
C227 A72 31fr Strip of four 3.75 65
a. *Fennec* 93 15
b. *Lesser kudus* 93 15
c. *Blesbok* 93 15
d. *Serval* 93 15

United Nations, 30th anniversary.

Michelangelo Type of 1975

Designs: Paintings from Sistine Chapel.

1975, Dec. 3 Photo. *Perf. 13*

C228 A73 18fr *Zachariah* 70
C229 A73 18fr *Joel* 70
C230 A73 31fr *Erythrean Sybil* 1.25
C231 A73 31fr *Prophet Ezekiel* 1.25
C232 A73 40fr *Persian Sybil* 1.65
C233 A73 40fr *Prophet Jeremiah* 1.65
a. Souvenir sheet of 6 7.25
Nos. C228-C233 (6) 7.20

Michelangelo Buonarotti (1475-1564), Italian sculptor, painter and architect. Stamps of same denominations printed se-tenant in sheets of 18 stamps and 2 labels. No. C233a contains one each of Nos. C228-C233, green & gold margin, black inscription. Size: 137x111mm.

Olympic Games Type, 1976

Designs (Olympic Games Emblem and): 18fr, Ski jump. 36fr, Slalom. 50fr, Ice hockey.

1976, Jan. 23 Photo. *Perf. 14x13½*

C234 A74 18fr ol brn & multi 65
C235 A74 36fr grn & multi 1.40
C236 A74 50fr pur & multi 1.90
a. Souvenir sheet of 4 4.00 2.75

12th Winter Olympic Games, Innsbruck, Austria, Feb. 4-15.

No. C236a contains 4 stamps similar to Nos. 491-494, perf. 13½, inscribed "POSTE AERIENNE." Multicolored margin with snowflakes and Games' emblem. Size: 100x103mm.

Hurdles — AP5

Designs (Montreal Games Emblem and): Nos. C238, C241, C243b, High jump. Nos. C239, C242, C243a, Athlete on rings. No. C240, C243c, Hurdles.

1976, May 3 Litho. *Perf. 13½*

C237 AP5 27fr grn & multi 85
C238 AP5 27fr dk bl & multi 85
C239 AP5 31fr ocher & multi 1.10
C240 AP5 31fr grn & multi 1.10
C241 AP5 50fr dk bl & multi 1.75
C242 AP5 50fr ocher & multi 1.75
Nos. C237-C242 (6) 7.40

Souvenir Sheet

C243 AP5 Sheet of 3 3.40 60
a. 27fr ocher & multi 78
b. 31fr dk bl & multi 95
c. 50fr grn & multi 1.50

21st Olympic Games, Montreal, Canada, July 17-Aug. 1. Stamps of same denomination printed se-tenant in sheets of 20.

No. C243 has gold inscription, Montreal Olympic emblem and multicolored band in margin. Size: 100x120mm.

Battle of Bunker Hill, by John Trumbull

AP6 AP7

Paintings: 26fr, Franklin, Jefferson and John Adams. 36fr, Declaration of Independence, by John Trumbull.

1976, July 16 Photo. *Perf. 13*

C244 AP6 18fr gold & multi 70
C245 AP7 18fr gold & multi 70
C246 AP6 26fr gold & multi 90
C247 AP7 26fr gold & multi 90
C248 AP6 36fr gold & multi 1.50
C249 AP7 36fr gold & multi 1.50
a. Souvenir sheet of 6 5.00 3.00
Nos. C244-C249 (6) 6.20

American Bicentennial. Stamps of same denomination printed se-tenant in sheets of 50. No. C249a contains one each of Nos. C244-C249 with Bicentennial emblem in margin. Size: 102x148mm.

Christmas Type of 1976

Paintings: 18fr, Virgin and Child with St. Anne, by Leonardo da Vinci. 31fr, Holy Family with Lamb, by Raphael. 40fr, Madonna of the Basket, by Correggio.

1976, Oct. 18 Photo. *Perf. 13½*

C250 A76 18fr gold & multi 54
C251 A76 31fr gold & multi 94
C252 A76 40fr gold & multi 1.20
a. Souvenir sheet of 3 2.80 1.75

Christmas 1976. Sheets of 20 stamps and descriptive label. No. C252a contains one each of Nos. C250-C252; multicolored margin. Size: 123x80mm.

A.G. Bell Type of 1977

Designs: 10fr, A.G. Bell and first telephone. Nos. C253, 17fr, A.G. Bell speaking into microphone. Nos. C254, C257e, Satellites around globe and videophone. No. C255, Switchboard operator, c.1910, and wall telephone. Nos. C256, 26fr, Intelsat satellite, modern and old telephones. No. C257c, Intelsat and radar.

1977, May 17 Photo. *Perf. 13*

C253 A78 18fr multi 28
C254 A79 18fr multi 28
C255 A78 36fr multi 55
C256 A79 36fr multi 55

Souvenir Sheet

C257 Sheet of 5 3.50 2.00
a. A78 10fr multi 30 14
b. A78 17fr multi 50 22
c. A79 18fr multi 54 25
d. A79 26fr multi 80 45
e. A79 36fr multi 1.05 50

Centenary of first telephone call by Alexander Graham Bell, Mar. 10, 1876. No. C257 contains 3 postage (10fr, 17fr, 26fr) and 2 air post stamps (18fr, 36fr). Multicolored margin with ITU emblem and old telephone. Size: 120x135mm.

Animal Type of 1977

1977, Aug. 22 Photo. *Perf. 14x14½*

C258 A80 9fr Strip of four 1.65
a. *Buffon's kob* 40
b. *Marabous* 40
c. *Brindled gnu* 40
d. *River hog* 40
C259 A80 13fr Strip of four 2.25
a. *Zebras* 55
b. *Shoebill* 55
c. *Striped hyenas* 55
d. *Chimpanzee* 55
C260 A80 30fr Strip of four 4.50
a. *Flamingos* 1.10
b. *Nile Crocodiles* 1.10
c. *Green mamba* 1.10
d. *Greater kudus* 1.10
C261 A80 35fr Strip of four 5.50
a. *Hyrax* 1.25
b. *Cobra* 1.25
c. *Jackals* 1.25
d. *Verreaux's eagles* 1.25
C262 A80 54fr Strip of four 8.25
a. *Honey badger* 2.00
b. *Harnessed antelopes* 2.00
c. *Secretary bird* 2.00
d. *Klipspringer* 2.00
C263 A80 70fr Strip of four 10.00
a. *African big-eared fox* 2.50
b. *Elephants* 2.50
c. *Vulturine guineafowl* 2.50
d. *Impalas* 2.50
Nos. C258-C263 (6) 32.15

UN Type of 1977

Designs (UN Stamps and): 24fr, UN buildings by night. 27fr, UN buildings and view of Manhattan. 35fr, UN buildings by day.

1977, Oct. 10 Photo. *Perf. 13½*

C264 A82 24fr Block of four 3.75
a. No. 77 95
b. No. 78 95
c. No. 40 95
d. No. 32 95
C265 A82 27fr Block of four 4.00
a. No. 50 1.00
b. No. 21 1.00
c. No. 30 1.00
d. No. 44 1.00
C266 A82 35fr Block of four 6.25
a. No. C6 1.50
b. No. 105 1.50
c. No. 4 1.50
d. No. 1 1.50
e. Souvenir sheet of 3 2.75

25th anniversary (in 1976) of the United Nations Postal Administration. No. C266e contains 24fr in design of No. C265b, 27fr in design of No. C266a, 35fr in design of No. C264c; silver margin. Size: 128x76mm.

Christmas Type of 1977

Designs: Paintings of the Virgin and Child.

1977, Oct. 31 Photo. *Perf. 14x13*

C267 A83 18fr Master of Moulins 55
C268 A83 31fr Workshop of Lorenzo de Credi 95
C269 A83 40fr Palma Vecchio 1.20
a. Souvenir sheet of 3 (# C267-C269) 3.00 2.00

Sheets of 24 stamps and descriptive label.

Christmas 1978 Type of 1979
Souvenir Sheet

1979, Feb. Photo. *Perf. 14x13½*

C270 Sheet of 5, multi 4.00
a. A86 13fr like #543 40
b. A86 17fr like #544 50
c. A86 27fr like #545 80
d. A86 31fr like #546 95
e. A86 40fr like #547 1.20

No. C270 has green, gold and black margin. Size: 114x120mm.

Christmas Type of 1979
Souvenir Sheet

1979, Oct. 12 *Perf. 13½*

C271 Sheet of 4, multi 4.00 2.50
a. A89 20fr like #561 60 32
b. A89 27fr like #562 80 45
c. A89 31fr like #563 95 55
d. A89 50fr like #564 1.50 85

Hill Type of 1979
Souvenir Sheet

1979, Nov. 6

C272 Sheet of 5, multi 7.00 3.50
a. A90 20fr like #565 80 32
b. A90 27fr like #566 1.10 45
c. A90 31fr like #567 1.25 55
d. A90 40fr like #568 1.65 70
e. A90 50fr like #569 2.00 1.00

Sir Rowland Hill (1795-1879), originator of penny postage.

Bird Type of 1979

1979 Photo. *Perf. 13½x3*

C273 A87 6fr like #548 18
C274 A87 13fr like #549 40
C275 A87 18fr like #550 55
C276 A87 26fr like #551 78
C277 A87 31fr like #552 95
C278 A87 36fr like #553 1.10
C279 A87 40fr like #554 1.20
C280 A87 54fr like #555 1.65
C281 A87 70fr like #556 2.10
Nos. C273-C281 (9) 8.91

Olympic Type of 1980
Souvenir Sheet

1980, Oct. 24 Photo. *Perf. 13½*

C282 Sheet of 9 8.50
a. A91 20fr like #570 60
b. A91 20fr like #571 60
c. A91 20fr like #572 60
d. A91 30fr like #573 90
e. A91 30fr like #574 90
f. A91 30fr like #575 90
g. A91 40fr like #576 1.20
h. A91 40fr like #577 1.20
i. A91 40fr like #578 1.20

22nd Summer Olympic Games, Moscow, July 19-Aug. 3. No. C282 has multicolored margin showing Moscow '80 emblem. Size: 144½x112mm.

Christmas Type of 1980
Souvenir Sheet

1980, Dec. 12 Photo. *Perf. 13½x13*

C283 Sheet of 4 3.75 2.75
a. A92 10fr like #579 30 20
b. A92 30fr like #580 90 60
c. A92 40fr like #581 1.20 80
d. A92 45fr like #582 1.35 90

Multicolored decorative margin. Size: 133½x104mm.

UPRONA Type of 1980
Souvenir Sheet

1980, Dec. 29 *Perf. 14½x13½*

C284 Sheet of 3 3.00
a. A93 10fr like #583 30
b. A93 40fr like #584 1.20
c. A93 45fr like #585 1.35

No. C284 has light blue and gold decorative margin. Size: 109x68mm.

Christmas Type of 1983
Souvenir Sheet

1983, Oct. 3 Litho. *Perf. 14½x13½*

C285 Souvenir sheet of 4 3.50
a. A97 10fr like #607 30
b. A97 25fr like #608 75
c. A97 30fr like #609 90
d. A97 50fr like #610 1.50

No. C285 has gold and deep lilac-rose decorative margin. Size: 106x152mm.

UPU Congress Type of 1984

1984, July 14 *Perf. 13x13½*

C286 Souvenir sheet of 4 4.25
a. A99 10fr like #621 30
b. A99 30fr like #622 90
c. A99 35fr like #623 1.00
d. A99 65fr like #624 2.00

No. C286 has multicolored margin picturing the Conference Center, Hamburg. Size: 148x84mm.

Summer Olympics Type of 1984

1984, Aug. 6 *Perf. 13½x13*

C287 Souvenir sheet of 4 4.25
a. A100 10fr like #625 30
b. A100 30fr like #626 90
c. A100 35fr like #627 1.00
d. A100 65fr like #628 2.00

No. C287 has multicolored decorative margin. Size: 119x99mm.

Christmas Type of 1984

1984, Dec. 15 *Perf. 13½*

C288 Souvenir sheet of 4 3.50
a. A101 10fr like #629 30
b. A101 25fr like #630 75
c. A101 30fr like #631 90
d. A101 50fr like #632 1.50

Size: 126x92mm.

Flower Type of 1986 with Dull Lilac Border.

1986, July 31 Photo. *Perf. 13x13½*

C289 A102 70fr like #633 1.10
C290 A102 75fr like #634 1.20
C291 A102 80fr like #635 1.30
C292 A102 85fr like #636 1.40
C293 A102 100fr like #637 1.60
C294 A102 150fr like #638 2.40
Nos. C289-C294 (6) 9.00

AIR POST SEMI-POSTAL STAMPS

Coin Type of Semi-Postal Issue

Designs (Coins of Various Denominations): 3fr+1fr, 11fr+1fr, 20fr+1fr, 50fr+1fr, Coat of Arms, reverse. 5fr+1fr, 14fr+1fr, 30fr+1fr, 100fr+1fr, King Mwambutsa IV, obverse.

Lithographed; Embossed on Gilt Foil
1965, Nov. 15 *Imperf.*

Diameter: 39mm.

CB1 SP4 3fr + 1fr lt & dk vio 10 10
CB2 SP4 5fr + 1fr pale grn & red 15 15

Diameter: 45mm.

CB3 SP4 11fr + 1fr org & lil 25 25
CB4 SP4 14fr + 1fr red & emer 30 30

Diameter: 56mm.

CB5 SP4 20fr + 1fr ultra & blk 40 40
CB6 SP4 30fr + 1fr dp org & mar 60 60

Diameter: 67mm.

CB7 SP4 50fr + 1fr bl & vio bl 1.00 1.00
CB8 SP4 100fr + 1fr rose & dp cl 2.25 2.25
Nos. CB1-CB8 (8) 5.05 5.05

Stamps are backed with patterned paper in blue, orange, and pink engine-turned design.

Red Cross Type of Semi-Postal Issue

Designs: 26fr+3fr, Laboratory. 40fr+3fr, Ambulance and thatched huts. 50fr+3fr, Red Cross nurse with patient.

1969, June 26 Photo. *Perf. 13½*

CB9 SP7 26fr + 3fr multi 75 20
CB10 SP7 40fr + 3fr multi 1.10 30
CB11 SP7 50fr + 3fr multi 1.35 40

Issued to commemorate the 50th anniversary of the League of Red Cross Societies. perf. and imperf. souvenir sheets exist containing 3 stamps similar to Nos. CB9-CB11, but without "Poste Aerienne." Gold frame with green commemorative inscription. Size: 90½x97mm.

Christmas Type of Semi-Postal Issue

Paintings: 14fr+3fr, Virgin and Child, by Velazquez. 26fr+3fr, Holy Family, by Joos van Cleve. 40fr+3fr, Virgin and Child, by Rogier van der Weyden.

1970, Dec. 14 Photo. *Perf. 13½*

CB12 SP9 14fr + 3fr multi 50 17
CB13 SP9 26fr + 3fr multi 90 30
CB14 SP9 40fr + 3fr multi 1.30 42
a. Souvenir sheet of 3 3.00 3.00

No. CB14a contains one each of Nos. CB12-CB14 with ornamental border and inscription. Size: 135x75mm.

No. C147 Surcharged in Gold and Black

LUTTE CONTRE
L'ANALPHABETISME

1971, Aug. 9 Photo. *Perf. 13½*

CB15 A48 14fr + 2fr Strip of four 1.60 32
a. *Hartebeest* 40 8
b. *Black rhinoceros* 40 8
c. *Zebra* 40 8
d. *Leopard* 40 8

UNESCO campaign against illiteracy.

No. C148 Surcharged in Gold and Black

AIDE INTERNATIONALE
AUX REFUGIES

1971, Aug. 9

CB16 A48 17fr + 1fr Strip of four 1.85 35
a. *Grant's gazelles* 45 8
b. *Cheetah* 45 8
c. *African white-backed vultures* 45 8
d. *Johnston's okapi* 45 8

International help for refugees.

Nos. C150-C151 Surcharged in Black and Gold

+1F

75eme ANNIVERSAIRE DES
JEUX OLYMPIQUES MODERNES
(1896-1971)

a

+1F

JEUX PRE-OLYMPIQUES
MUNICH 1972

b

1971, Aug. 16

CB17 A48(a) 26fr + 1fr Strip of four 4.50 90
a. *Gorilla* 1.10 22
b. *Gnu* 1.10 22
c. *Warthog* 1.10 22
d. *Cape hunting dog* 1.10 22
CB18 A48(b) 31fr + 1fr Strip of four 6.00 1.20
a. *Sable antelope* 1.50 30
b. *Caracal lynx* 1.50 30
c. *Ostriches* 1.50 30
d. *Bongo* 1.50 30

75th anniversary of modern Olympic Games (No. CB17); Olympic Games, Munich, 1972 (No. CB18).

Nos. C153-C155 Surcharged

1971, Nov. 27 Photo. *Perf. 13½*

CB19 A51 14fr + 1fr multi 65 15
CB20 A51 17fr + 1fr multi 75 20
CB21 A51 31fr + 1fr multi 1.25 33

25th anniversary of the United Nations International Children's Fund (UNICEF).

Casa D'Oro, Venice
SPAP1

Views in Venice: 17fr+1fr, Doge's Palace. 24fr+1fr, Church of Sts. John and Paul. 31fr+1fr, Doge's Palace and Piazzetta at Feast of Ascension, by Canaletto.

1971, Dec. 27

CB22 SPAP1 10fr + 1fr gold & multi 33 15
CB23 SPAP1 17fr + 1fr gold & multi 65 22
CB24 SPAP1 24fr + 1fr gold & multi 90 30
CB25 SPAP1 31fr + 1fr gold & multi 1.10 35
a. Souvenir sheet of 4 3.00 3.00

The surtax was for the UNESCO campaign to save the treasures of Venice. No. CB25a contains 4 stamps similar to Nos. CB22-CB25, but with 2fr surtax instead 1fr. Gold and black ornamental margin. Size: 113x131½mm. Sheet exists imperf.

Nos. C165-C167 Surcharged "+1F" in Silver

1972, Dec. 12 Photo. *Perf. 13½*

CB26 A57 18fr + 1fr multi 55 17
CB27 A57 27fr + 1fr multi 95 25
CB28 A57 40fr + 1fr multi 1.25 35
a. Souvenir sheet of 3 2.75 2.75

Christmas 1972. No. CB28a contains 3 stamps similar to Nos. CB26-CB28 but with 2fr surtax. Slate green and gold border. Size: 128x81mm.

Nos. C193-C195 Surcharged "+1F" in Silver

1973, Dec. 14 Photo. *Perf. 13*

CB29 A64 18fr + 1fr multi 55 17
CB30 A64 27fr + 1fr multi 80 25
CB31 A64 40fr + 1fr multi 1.25 40
a. Souvenir sheet of 3 3.00 3.00

Christmas 1973. No. CB31 contains 3 stamps similar to Nos. CB29-CB31 with 2fr surtax each. Size: 143x79mm.

Christmas Type of 1974

1974, Dec. 2 Photo. *Perf. 13*

CB32 A70 18fr + 1fr multi 65 40
CB33 A70 27fr + 1fr multi 1.00 60
CB34 A70 40fr + 1fr multi 1.40 85
a. Souvenir sheet of 3 3.50 3.50

Christmas 1974. No. CB34a contains 3 stamps similar to Nos. CB32-CB34 with 2fr surtax. Size: 137x90mm.

Nos. C228-C233 Surcharged "+ 1F" in Silver and Black

1975, Dec. 22 Photo. *Perf. 13*

CB35 A73 18fr + 1fr # C228 70
CB36 A73 18fr + 1fr # C229 70
CB37 A73 31fr + 1fr # C230 1.10
CB38 A73 31fr + 1fr # C231 1.10

CB39	A73	40fr + 1fr # C232	1.50	
CB40	A73	40fr + 1fr # C233	1.50	
a.		Souvenir sheet of 6	8.50	8.50
		Nos. CB35-CB40 (6)	6.60	

Michelangelo Buonarroti (1475-1564), 500th birth anniversary. No. CB40a contains 6 stamps similar to Nos. CB35-CB40 with 2fr surtax each. Size: 132x106mm.

Nos. C250-C252 Surcharged "+1f" in Silver and Black

1976, Nov. 25 Photo. *Perf. 13½*

CB41	A76	18fr + 1fr multi	60	
CB42	A76	31fr + 1fr multi	1.00	
CB43	A76	40fr + 1fr multi	1.25	
a.		Souvenir sheet of 3	3.00	3.00

Christmas 1976. No. CB43a contains 3 stamps similar to Nos. CB41-CB43 with 2fr surtax each. Size: 123x80mm.

Nos. C267-C269 Surcharged "+1fr" in Silver and Black

1977 Photo. *Perf. 14x13*

CB44	A83	18fr + 1fr multi	58	
CB45	A83	31fr + 1fr multi	1.00	
CB46	A83	40fr + 1fr multi	1.25	
a.		Souvenir sheet of 3	3.00	3.00

Christmas 1977. No. CB46a contains 3 stamps similar to Nos. CB44-CB46 with 2fr surtax each. Size: 130x71mm.

Christmas 1978 Type of 1979

Souvenir Sheet

1979, Feb. Photo. *Perf. 14x13*

CB47	Sheet of 5	6.00
a.	A86 13fr + 2fr multi	60
b.	A86 17fr + 2fr multi	75
c.	A86 27fr + 2fr multi	1.10
d.	A86 31fr + 2fr multi	1.40
e.	A86 40fr + 2fr multi	1.75

No. CB47 has gold, black and blue border. Size: 115x121mm.

Christmas Type of 1979

Souvenir Sheet

1979, Dec. 10 Photo. *Perf. 13½*

CB48	Sheet of 4	5.50
a.	A89 20fr + 2fr like #561	90
b.	A89 27fr + 2fr like #562	1.10
c.	A89 31fr + 2fr like #563	1.40
d.	A89 50fr + 2fr like #564	2.00

No. CB48 has multicolored decorative margin.
Size: 86x110mm.

Christmas Type of 1980

Souvenir Sheet

1981, Jan. 16 Photo. *Perf. 13½x13*

CB49	Sheet of 4	5.00
a.	A92 10fr + 2fr like #579	42
b.	A92 30fr + 2fr like #580	1.10
c.	A92 40fr + 2fr like #581	1.50
d.	A92 50fr + 2fr like #582	1.90

Christmas 1980. Multicolored decorative margin. Size: 133x104mm.

Christmas Type of 1983

1983, Nov. 2 Litho. *Perf. 14½x13½*

CB50	Souvenir sheet of 4	3.60
a.	A97 10fr + 1fr like #607	32
b.	A97 25fr + 1fr like #608	78
c.	A97 30fr + 1fr like #609	1.00
d.	A97 50fr + 1fr like #610	1.50

No. CB50 has gold and bright blue decorative margin. Size: 106x152mm.

Christmas Type of 1984

1984, Dec. 15 *Perf. 13½*

CB51	Souvenir sheet of 4	3.60
a.	A101 10fr + 1fr like #629	32
b.	A101 25fr + 1fr like #630	78
c.	A101 30fr + 1fr like #631	1.00
d.	A101 50fr + 1fr like #632	1.50

Size: 126x92mm.

CAMBODIA

Khmer Republic

LOCATION — Southern Indo-China.
GOVT. — Republic
AREA — 69,866 sq. mi.
POP. — 7,640,000 (est. 1974).
CAPITAL — Phnom Penh.

Before 1951, Cambodia used stamps of Indo-China. In October, 1970, the Kingdom of Cambodia became the Khmer Republic.

100 Cents = 1 Piaster
100 Cents = 1 Riel (1955)

Imperforates
Most Cambodia stamps exist imperforate in issued and trial colors, and also in small presentation sheets in issued colors.

Apsaras — A1

King Norodom Sihanouk — A3

Enthronement Hall — A2

1951-52 Unwmk. Engr. *Perf. 13*

1	A1	10c dk bl grn	55	55
2	A1	20c cl & org brn	35	20
3	A1	30c pur & ind	35	20
4	A1	40c ultra & brt bl grn	35	20
5	A2	50c dk grn & dk ol grn	35	20
6	A3	80c bl blk & dk bl grn	70	70
7	A2	1pi ind & pur	80	80
8	A3	1.10pi dp car & brt red	80	80
9	A3	1.50pi blk brn & red brn ('51)	1.10	80
10	A1	1.50pi dp car & cer	1.10	80
11	A2	1.50pi ind & dp ultra	1.10	90
12	A3	1.90pi ind & dp ultra	1.50	1.40
13	A2	2pi dp car & org brn	1.40	90
14	A3	3pi dp car & org brn	1.90	1.40
15	A1	5pi ind & pur	7.75	3.50
a.		Souvenir sheet of 1	27.50	
16	A2	10pi pur & ind	14.00	7.25
a.		Souvenir sheet of 1	27.50	
17	A3	15pi dk pur & pur	19.00	10.00
a.		Souvenir sheet of 1	32.50	
		Nos. 1-17 (17)	53.10	30.60

Nos. 15a, 16a, 17a sold in a booklet for 30pi.

Phnom Daun Penh — A4

East Gate, Angkor Thom A5

Arms of Cambodia A6

Methods of Mail Transport A7

1954-55 Unwmk. *Perf. 13*

18	A4	10c rose car	6	6
a.		Souvenir sheet of 5 ('55)	22.50	
19	A4	20c dk grn	6	6
20	A4	30c indigo	6	6
21	A4	40c dk pur	6	6
22	A4	50c dk vio brn	6	6
23	A5	70c chocolate	20	20
a.		Souvenir sheet of 5 ('55)	22.50	
24	A5	1pi red vio	20	20
25	A5	1.50pi red	20	20
26	A6	2pi rose red	40	40
a.		Souvenir sheet of 5 ('55)	22.50	
27	A6	2.50pi green	60	60
28	A7	2.50pi bl grn	80	60
a.		Souvenir sheet of 5 ('55)	22.50	
29	A6	3pi ultra	90	75
30	A7	4pi blk brn	1.00	1.00
31	A6	4.50pi purple	1.20	1.00
32	A7	5pi rose red	1.25	1.00
33	A6	6pi chocolate	1.50	1.00
34	A7	10pi purple	1.50	1.50
35	A7	15pi dp bl	2.00	1.85
36	A5	20pi ultra	4.00	2.50
37	A5	30pi bl grn	6.00	5.00
		Nos. 18-37 (20)	22.05	18.10

The four souvenir sheets each contain five different stamps: No. 18a (10c, 20c, 30c, 40c, 50c); No. 23a (70c, 1pi, 1.50pi, 20pi, 30pi); No. 26a (2pi, 2.50pi green, 3pi, 4.50pi, 6pi); No. 28a (2.50pi blue green, 4pi, 5pi. 10pi, 15pi). Size of Nos. 18a, 26a and 28a: 120x120mm. Size of No. 23a: 160x92mm.

King Norodom Suramarit A8

King Norodom Suramarit and Queen Kossamak Nearirat Serey Vathana A9

Portraits: 50c (No. 39), 2.50r, 4r, 6r, 15r, Queen Kossamak Nearirat Serey Vathana.

Perf. 14x13(A8), 13(A9)

1955, Nov. 24 Engr. Unwmk.

38	A8	50c violet	10	10
39	A8	50c indigo	10	10
40	A8	1r car lake	15	15
41	A9	1.50r dk brn	40	40
42	A9	2r blk & ind	40	30
43	A8	2r dp ultra	25	40
44	A8	2.50r dk vio brn	40	40
45	A9	3r brn org & car	40	40
46	A8	4r dk grn	60	60
47	A9	5r blk & dk grn	60	60
48	A8	6r dp plum	90	75
49	A8	7r dk brn	1.10	75
50	A9	10r brn car & vio	90	90
51	A8	15r purple	1.65	1.10
52	A8	20r dp grn	2.00	1.75
		Nos. 38-52 (15)	9.95	8.70

Issued to commemorate the coronation of King Norodom Suramarit and Queen Kossamak Nearirat Serey Vathana.
See also Nos. 74-75.

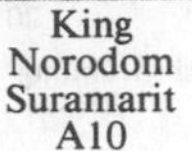

King Norodom Suramarit A10

Prince Sihanouk, Globe and Flags A11

Portrait: 3r, 5r, 50r, Queen Kossamak Nearirat Serey Vathana.

1956, Mar. 8 *Perf. 13*

53	A10	2r dk red	1.00	1.00
54	A10	3r dk bl	1.40	1.40
55	A10	5r yel grn	2.00	2.00
56	A10	10r dk grn	5.00	5.00
57	A10	30r dk vio	10.50	10.50
58	A10	50r rose lil	20.00	20.00
		Nos. 53-58 (6)	39.90	39.90

Issued to commemorate the coronation of King Norodom Suramarit and Queen Kossamak Nearirat Serey Vathana.

1957, Mar. 1

59	A11	2r grn, ultra & car	50	40
60	A11	4.50r ultra	50	40
61	A11	8.50r carmine	50	40

Issued to commemorate the first anniversary of Cambodia's admission to the United Nations (in 1956).

Type of Semi-Postal Stamps, 1957.

1957, May 12 Unwmk. *Perf. 13*

62	SP1	1.50r vermilion	45	45
63	SP1	6.50r bluish vio	60	60
64	SP1	8r dk grn	60	60

Issued to commemorate the 2500th anniversary of the birth of Buddha.

King Ang Duong A12

1958, Mar. 4

65	A12	1.50r pur & brn	15	15
66	A12	5r ol gray & ol	40	30
67	A12	10r cl & dl brn	80	50
a.		Souvenir sheet of 3	3.00	3.00

Issued to honor King Ang Duong (1795-1860).
No. 67a contains one each of Nos. 65-67. Sold for 25r. Size: 155x93mm.

King Norodom I — A13

1958-59 Engr. *Perf. 12½x13*

68	A13	2r ultra & ol	30	30
69	A13	6r org & sl grn	70	70
70	A13	15r grn & ol gray	1.00	1.00
a.		Souvenir sheet of 3 ('59)	3.00	3.00

Issued in honor of King Norodom I (1835-1904).
No. 70a contains one each of Nos. 68-70. Sold for 32r. Size: 155x93mm.
Issue dates: Nos. 68-70, Nov. 3, 1958. No. 70a, Jan. 31, 1959.

A little time given to the study of the arrangement of the Scott Catalogue can make it easier to use effectively.

Children of the World — A14

1959, Dec. 9 Unwmk. *Perf. 13*

71	A14	20c rose vio	6	6
72	A14	50c blue	12	12
73	A14	80c rose car	20	20

Issued to promote friendship among the children of the world.

Nos. 49 and 52 with Black Border.

1960 *Perf. 14x13*

74	A8	7r dk brn & blk	1.00	1.00
75	A8	20r dp grn & blk	1.00	1.00

Issued to commemorate the death of King Norodom Suramarit.

Port of Sihanoukville, Prince Sihanouk and Serpent Naga — A15

(double size) 20r 

1960, Apr. *Perf. 13x12½*

76	A15	2r car & sep	35	35
a.		Cambodian 20r	1.10	1.10
77	A15	5r ultra & dp brn	35	35
a.		Cambodian 20r	1.50	1.50
78	A15	20r lil & dk bl	1.25	90

Issued to commemorate the opening of the port of Sihanoukville. By error the denomination in Cambodian on the 2r and 5r was engraved as 20r; it was corrected later.

Ceremonial Plow — A16

1960 *Perf. 12*

79	A16	1r magenta	35	35
80	A16	2r brown	35	35
81	A16	3r bluish grn	35	35

Feast of the Sacred Furrow.

Works of Sangkum Issue

Fight Against Illiteracy A17

Water Conservation, Dam at Chhouksar — A18

The first price column gives the catalogue value of an unused stamp, the second that of a used stamp.

Dove, Factory and Books A19

Buddhist Ceremony A20

Designs: 6r, Workman and house. 10r, Woman in rice field.

1960, Sept. 1 Engr. *Perf. 13*

82	A17	2r dk grn, brn & dk bl	22	18
a.		Souvenir sheet of 3	3.00	3.00
83	A18	3r brn & grn	32	27
a.		Souvenir sheet of 3	3.00	3.00
84	A19	4r rose car, vio & grn	35	32
85	A17	6r brn, org & grn	45	40
86	A17	10r ultra, grn & bis	90	80
87	A20	25r dk car, red & mag	2.00	1.50
		Nos. 82-87 (6)	4.24	3.47

No. 82a contains one each of Nos. 82, 85 and 87, and sold for 42r. No. 83a contains one each of Nos. 83, 84 and 86, and sold for 23r. Marginal inscriptions in bister. Size: 149x100mm. Nos. 82a-83a were issued Dec. 5, 1960.

Cambodian Flag and Dove A21

Frangipani A22

1960, Dec. 24 Engr. *Perf. 13*
Flag in Ultramarine and Red.

88	A21	1.50r brn & grn	25	25
89	A21	5r org red	35	35
90	A21	7r grn & ultra	85	85
a.		Souvenir sheet of 3	3.00	3.00
b.		Souvenir sheet of 3 (colors changed)	5.75	5.75

Issued as peace propaganda. No. 90a contains one each of Nos. 88-90 and sold for 16r. No. 90b contains one of each denomination with colors changed to: 1.50r orange red, 5r green & ultramarine, 7r brown & green. No. 90b sold for 20r. Marginal inscriptions in bistre. Size: 146½x93mm.

1961, July 1 Unwmk. *Perf. 13*

Flowers: 5r, Oleander. 10r, Amaryllis.

91	A22	2r lil rose, yel & grn	30	30
92	A22	5r ultra, lil rose & grn	50	50
93	A22	10r vio, car & grn	1.25	1.25
a.		Souv. sheet of 3	3.50	3.50

No. 93a contains one each of Nos. 91-93. Gold marginal inscription. Size: 130x100mm. Sold for 20r.

Krishna in Chariot, Khmer Frieze A23

Independence Monument A24

1961-63 Typo. *Perf. 14x13½*

94	A23	1r lilac	10	10
94A	A23	2r bl ('63)	1.25	75
95	A23	3r emerald	25	25
96	A23	6r orange	45	25
a.		Souv. sheet of 3	7.00	7.00

Issued to honor Cambodian armed forces.

No. 94A issued in coils. No. 96a contains one each of Nos. 94, 95, 96. Orange marginal inscriptions. Size: 149x85mm. Sold for 12r.

1961, Nov. 9 Engr. *Perf. 13x12½*

97	A24	2r green	30	30
98	A24	4r gray brn	30	30
a.		Souvenir sheet of 2	1.20	1.20
		Nos. 97-98,C15-C17 (5)	41.35	21.35

Issued to commemorate the tenth anniversary of Independence. No. 98a contains one each of Nos. 97-98 with gold marginal inscription. Size: 150x85mm.

Nos. 27 and 31 Overprinted in Red: "VIe CONFERENCE MONDIALE BOUDDIQUE 12-11-1961"

1961, Nov. 11 *Perf. 13*

99	A6	2.50pi (r) grn	35	35
100	A6	4.50pi (r) pur	50	50

Sixth World Conference of Buddhism.

Highway (American Aid) — A25

Foreign Aid: 2r, Power station (Czech aid). 4r, Textile factory (Chinese aid). 5r, Hospital (Russian aid). 6r, Airport (French aid).

1961, Dec. Engr. *Perf. 13*

101	A25	2r org & rose car	20	12
102	A25	3r bl, grn & org brn	30	20
103	A25	4r dl bl, org brn & mag	35	22
104	A25	5r dl grn & lil rose	40	35
105	A25	6r dk bl & org brn	55	40
a.		Souvenir sheet of 5	3.25	3.25
		Nos. 101-105 (5)	1.80	1.29

Issued to publicize foreign aid to Cambodia. No. 105a contains one each of Nos. 101-105 with bister marginal inscription. Size: 148x84mm.

Malaria Eradication Emblem — A26

1962, Apr. 7 Unwmk. *Perf. 13*

106	A26	2r mag & brn	25	18
107	A26	4r grn & dk brn	38	32
108	A26	6r vio & ol bis	45	38

Issued for the World Health Organization drive to eradicate malaria.

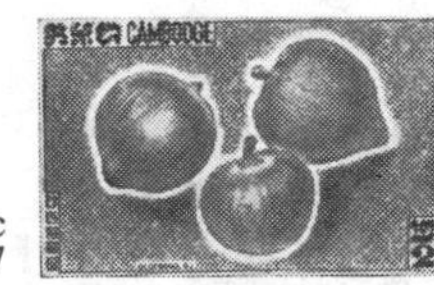

Turmeric A27

Fruits: 4r, Cinnamon. 6r, Mangosteens.

1962, June 4 Engr.

109	A27	2r gray & bis	38	35
110	A27	4r dk bl grn & ol gray	38	35
111	A27	6r dk bl, grn & mag	60	50
a.		Souv. sheet of 3	2.00	2.00

Nos. 111a contains one each of Nos. 109-111 with marginal inscription in gray. Size: 149x84mm. Sold for 15r.

Pineapples — A28

Designs: 5r, Sugar cane. 9r, Sugar palms.

1962 Unwmk. *Perf. 13*

112	A28	2r bluish grn & brn	40	35
113	A28	5r brn & grn	50	40
114	A28	9r Prus grn & brn	75	50

No. 73 Surcharged

1962, Nov. 9 *Perf. 13*

115	A14	50c on 80c rose car	30	30

No. 97 Surcharged with New Value in Red and Overprinted in Black with Two Bars and: "INAUGURATION / DU / MONUMENT"

1962

116	A24	3r on 2r grn	25	18

Dedication of Independence Monument.

Corn, Rice and FAO Emblem A29

1963, Mar. 21 Engr. *Perf. 13*

117	A29	3r multi	55	45
118	A29	6r org red, vio bl & ocher	55	45

Issued for the "Freedom from Hunger" campaign of the U.N. Food and Agriculture Organization.

Preah Vihear, Ancient Temple — A30

Tonsay Lake — A31

1963, June 15 *Perf. 12½x13*

119	A30	3r cl, brn & sl grn	25	25
120	A30	6r org, sl grn & grnsh blk	50	38
121	A30	15r bl, choc & grn	1.00	85

Return by Thailand of Preah Vihear on the Mekong River.

No. 44 Surcharged with New Value and Bars

1963 Engr. *Perf. 14x13*

122	A8	3r on 2½r dk vio brn	35	35

Perf. 12x12½, 12½x12

1963, Aug. 1 Photo.

Designs: 7r, Popokvil Falls. 20r, Beach (horiz.).

123	A31	3r multi	20	20
124	A31	7r multi	45	30
125	A31	20r multi	1.20	70

UNESCO Emblem, Scales and Globe A32

1963, Dec. 10 **Engr.** ***Perf. 13***
126 A32 1r vio bl, rose cl & grn 20 20
127 A32 3r yel grn, vio bl & rose cl 35 35
128 A32 12r rose cl, yel grn & vio bl 75 75

Issued to commemorate the 15th anniversary of the Universal Declaration of Human Rights.

Kouprey A33

1964, March 3 **Unwmk.** ***Perf. 13***
129 A33 50c grn, dk brn & org brn 15 15
130 A33 3r org, brn, dk brn & grn 25 25
131 A33 6r bl, dk brn & grn 40 30

Black-billed Magpie — A34

Birds: 6r, Kingfisher. 12r, Gray heron.

1964, May 2 **Engr.** ***Perf. 13***
132 A34 3r dk bl, ind & grn 20 20
133 A34 6r ind, org & brn 60 40
134 A34 12r Prus grn, ind & red brn 1.00 85

Emblem of Royal Cambodian Airline A35

1964 **Unwmk.** ***Perf. 13x12½***
135 A35 1.50r rose car & pur 20 20
136 A35 3r ver & dk bl 25 20
137 A35 7.50r ultra & car 60 50

Issued to commemorate the 8th anniversary of the Royal Cambodian Airline.

Prince Norodom Sihanouk — A36

1964 **Engr.** ***Perf. 12½x13***
138 A36 2r purple 18 18
139 A36 3r red brn 25 25
140 A36 10r dk bl 70 60

Issued to commemorate the 10th anniversary of the Sangkum (political party).

Woman Weaver A37

Khmer Handicrafts: 3r, Metal worker. 5r, Basket maker.

1965, Feb. 1 ***Perf. 13x12½***
141 A37 1r multi 15 15
142 A37 3r red lil, red brn & gray ol 35 25
143 A37 5r grn, dk brn & car 40 30

Nos. 139-140 Overprinted in Black or Red: "CONFERENCE / DES PEUPLES / INDOCHINOIS"

1965, Mar. 1 ***Perf. 12½x13***
144 A36 3r red brn 40 40
145 A36 10r dk bl (R) 60 40

Conference of the people of Indo-China.

ITU Emblem, Old and New Communication Equipment — A38

1965, May 17 **Engr.** ***Perf. 13***
146 A38 3r grn & ol bis 30 30
147 A38 4r red & bl 40 30
148 A38 10r vio & rose lil 70 60

Issued to commemorate the centenary of the International Telecommunication Union.

Cotton Plant — A39

Designs: 3r, Peanut plant. 7.50r, Coconut palm.

1965, Aug. 2 ***Perf. 12½x13***
149 A39 1.50r org, sl grn & pur 25 25
150 A39 3r bl, yel, grn & brn 38 38
151 A39 7.50r org brn & sl grn 70 70

Preah Ko Temple, Rolouoh — A40

Temples at Angkor: 5r, Baksei Chamkrong, Rolouoh. 7r, Banteay Srei (Citadel of Women). 9r, Angkor Wat. 12r, Bayon, Angkor Thom.

1966, Feb. 1 **Engr.** ***Perf. 13***
152 A40 3r gray ol, sal & dl grn 45 28
153 A40 5r lil, dk grn & redsh brn 50 40
154 A40 7r dk grn, redsh brn & bis 60 45
155 A40 9r vio bl, pur & dk grn 80 55
156 A40 12r dk grn, rose car & ver 1.00 75
Nos. 152-156 (5) 3.35 2.43

WHO Headquarters, Geneva — A41

1966, July 1 **Photo.** ***Perf. 12½x13***
WHO Emblem in Blue and Yellow
157 A41 2r blk & pale rose 20 15
158 A41 3r blk & yel grn 25 20
159 A41 5r blk & lt bl 35 25

Issued to commemorate the inauguration of World Health Headquarters, Geneva.

Tree Planting — A42 UNESCO Emblem — A43

1966, July 22 **Engr.** ***Perf. 12½x13***
160 A42 1r brn, dl brn & brt grn 15 10
161 A42 3r org, dl brn & brt grn 25 20
162 A42 7r gray, dl brn & brt grn 50 30

Issued for Arbor Day.

1966 **Photo.** ***Perf. 13***
163 A43 3r multi 30 30
164 A43 7r multi 50 30

Issued to commemorate the 20th anniversary of UNESCO (United Nations Educational, Scientific and Cultural Organization).

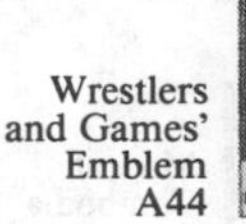

Wrestlers and Games' Emblem A44

Designs (Games Emblem and): 3r, Stadium, Phnom Penh. 7r, Swordsmen. 10r, Indian club swingers. Bas-reliefs from Angkor Wat.

1966, Nov. 25 **Engr.** ***Perf. 13***
165 A44 3r vio bl 22 18
166 A44 4r green 25 18
167 A44 7r dk car rose 38 22
168 A44 10r dk brn 50 35

Issued to commemorate the GANEFO Games.

Indian Wild Boar — A45

Designs: 5r, Muntjac (vert.). 7r, Elephant.

Perf. 13x12½, 12½x13
1967, Feb. 20 **Engr.**
169 A45 3r brt bl, grn & blk 25 20
170 A45 5r multi 35 20
171 A45 7r multi 50 30

Nos. 152-153, 155-156 and 121 Overprinted in Red: "ANNEE INTERNATIONALE DU TOURISME 1967"

1967, Apr. 27 **Engr.** ***Perf. 13***
172 A40 3r multi 25 25
173 A40 5r multi 35 25
174 A40 9r multi 50 45
175 A40 12r multi 60 60
176 A40 15r multi 70 70
Nos. 172-176 (5) 2.40 2.25

International Tourist Year, 1967.

No. 154 Overprinted in Red: "MILLENAIRE / DE BANTEAY SREI / 967-1967"

1967, Apr. 27
177 A40 7r multi 65 35

Issued to commemorate the millennium of the Banteay Srei Temple at Angkor.

Royal Ballet Dancer — A46

Various Dancers

1967, June **Engr.** ***Perf. 13***
178 A46 1r orange 15 15
179 A46 3r Prus bl 30 25
180 A46 5r ultra 45 35
181 A46 7r car rose 60 55
182 A46 10r multi 90 70
Nos. 178-182 (5) 2.40 2.00

Issued to publicize the Cambodian Royal Ballet.

Nos. 128 and 70 Surcharged in Red

Journée Internationale
de l'Alphabétisation
8-9-67
6ʳ

1967, Sept. 8 **Engr.**
183 A32 6r on 12r multi 50 40
184 A13 7r on 15r grn & ol gray 60 45

Issued for International Literacy Day, Sept. 8. The surcharge on No. 184 is adapted to fit the shape of the stamp.

Symbolic Water Cycle — A47

1967, Nov. 1 **Typo.** ***Perf. 13x14***
185 A47 1r blk, bl & org 15 15
186 A47 6r lil, lt bl & org 40 25
187 A47 10r dk bl, emer & org 65 40

Hydrological Decade (UNESCO), 1965-74.

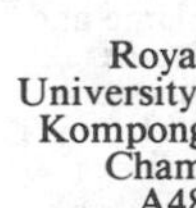

Royal University, Kompong Cham A48

Designs: 6r, Engineering School, Phnom Penh. 9r, University Center, Sangkum Reastr Niyum.

1968, Mar. 1 **Engr.** ***Perf. 13***
188 A48 4r vio bl & multi 30 30
189 A48 6r sl & multi 45 45
190 A48 9r Prus bl & multi 65 45

Vaccination and WHO Emblem A49

Design: 7r, Malaria control and WHO emblem (man spraying DDT).

1968, July 8 **Engr.** ***Perf. 13***

191 A49 3r ultra	20	18
192 A49 7r dp bl	45	30

Issued for the 20th anniversary of the zexit World Health Organization.

Stadium, Mexico City — A50

Designs: 2r, Wrestling. 3r, Bicycling. 5r, Boxing (vert.). 7.50r, Torch bearer (vert.).

1968, Oct. 12 **Engr.** ***Perf. 13***

193 A50 1r brn ol, grn & brn red	17	15
194 A50 2r brn, dk bl & rose cl	20	17
195 A50 3r plum, Prus bl & sep	30	25
196 A50 5r dk pur	38	30
197 A50 7.50r multi	42	38
Nos. 193-197 (5)	1.47	1.25

Issued to commemorate the 19th Olympic Games, Mexico City, Oct. 12-27.

Red Cross Team A51

1968, Nov. 1 **Engr.** ***Perf. 13***

198 A51 3r Prus bl, grn & red	30	15

Issued to honor the Cambodian Red Cross.

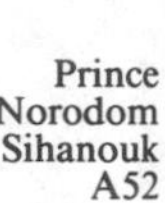

Prince Norodom Sihanouk A52

Design: 8r, Soldiers wading through swamp.

1968, Nov. 9

199 A52 7r emer, ultra & pur	50	30
200 A52 8r bl, grn & dp brn	60	30

15th anniversary of independence.

Human Rights Flame and Prince Sihanouk A53

1968, Dec. 10 **Engr.** ***Perf. 13***

201 A53 3r blue	25	18
202 A53 5r brt plum	40	25
203 A53 7r multi	50	30

International Human Rights Year.

ILO Emblem A54

1969, May 1 **Engr.** ***Perf. 13***

204 A54 3r ultra	22	18
205 A54 6r dp car	35	25
206 A54 9r bl grn	30	30

Issued to commemorate the 50th anniversary of the International Labor Organization.

Globe, Red Cross, Crescent, Lion and Sun Emblems A55

1969, May 8

207 A55 1r bl, red & yel	15	15
208 A55 3r sl grn, red & vio brn	22	20
209 A55 10r brt lil, red & brn	60	30

Issued to commemorate the 50th anniversary of the League of Red Cross Societies.

Papilio Oeacus A56

Butterflies: 4r, Papilio agamenon. 8r, Danaus plexippus.

1969, Oct. 10 **Engr.** ***Perf. 13***

210 A56 3r lil, blk & yel	60	25
211 A56 4r ver, blk & grn	80	35
212 A56 8r yel grn, dk brn & org	1.25	45

Map of Cambodia and Diesel Engine A57

Designs: Various railroad stations and trains.

1969, Nov. 27 **Engr.** ***Perf. 13***

213 A57 3r multi	55	20
214 A57 6r sl grn & lt brn	75	28
215 A57 8r black	1.00	38
216 A57 9r dk grn & bl	1.25	38

Issued to publicize the new rail link between Phnom Penh and Sihanoukville.

Tripletail A58

Fish: 7r, Sleeper goby. 9r, Snakehead.

1970, Jan. 29 **Photo.** ***Perf. 13***

217 A58 3r multi	40	12
218 A58 7r multi	65	27
219 A58 9r multi	90	35

Wat Maniratanaram — A59

Monasteries: 2r, Wat Tepthidaram (vert.). 6r, Wat Patumavati. 8r, Wat Unnalom.

1970, Apr. 29 **Photo.** ***Perf. 13***

220 A59 2r multi	12	10
221 A59 3r multi	25	15
222 A59 6r multi	38	25
223 A59 8r multi	50	38

U.P.U. Headquarters and Monument, Bern — A60

1970, May 20

224 A60 1r grn & multi	5	5
225 A60 3r scar & multi	6	6
226 A60 4r dp bl & multi	10	8
227 A60 10r brn & multi	18	15

Issued to commemorate the inauguration of the new Universal Postal Union Headquarters in Bern.

Open Book and Satellite Earth Receiving Station — A61

1970, May 17 **Photo.** ***Perf. 13***

228 A61 3r dk vio bl & multi	10	5
229 A61 4r sl grn & multi	12	8
230 A61 9r brn ol & multi	18	15

World Telecommunications Day.

Nelumbium Speciosum A62

Flowers: 4r, Eichhornia crassipes. 13r, Nymphea lotus.

1970, Aug. 17 **Photo.** ***Perf. 13***

231 A62 3r multi	8	8
a. Cambodian and Arabic 3's transposed	1.00	
232 A62 4r multi	12	12
233 A62 13r multi	20	20

Elephant God, Basrelief at Banteay Srei — A63

1970, Sept. 21 **Engr.** ***Perf. 13***

234 A63 3r lil rose & dp grn	10	6
235 A63 4r bl grn, grn & lil rose	12	7
236 A63 7r bl grn, dk brn & grn	18	10

Issued for World Meteorological Day.

Khmer Republic

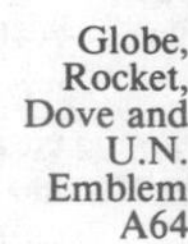

Globe, Rocket, Dove and U.N. Emblem A64

1970, Nov. 9 **Photo.** ***Perf. 12½x12***

237 A64 3r blk & multi	10	7
238 A64 5r brn red & multi	12	10
239 A64 10r dp vio & multi	18	10

25th anniversary of the United Nations.

Education Year Emblem A65

1970, Nov. 9 **Engr.** ***Perf. 13x12½***

240 A65 1r blue	5	5
241 A65 3r brt rose lil	10	6
242 A65 8r bl grn	20	10

Issued for International Education Year.

Chuon-Nath — A66

1971, Jan. 27 **Photo.** ***Perf. 13***

243 A66 3r ol grn & multi	7	5
244 A66 8r pur & multi	12	8
245 A66 9r vio & multi	18	10

In memory of Chuon-Nath (1883-1969), Cambodian language expert.

Soldiers in Battle A67

1971, March 18 **Photo.** ***Perf. 13***

246 A67 1r gray & multi	5	5
247 A67 3r bis & multi	15	10
248 A67 10r bl & multi	50	25

National territorial defense.

U.N. Emblem, Men of Four Races A68

1971, March 21

249 A68 3r bl & multi	6	5
250 A68 7r grn & multi	12	10
251 A68 8r brt rose & multi	18	12

International year against racial discrimination.

General Post Office, Phnom Penh — A69

1971, Apr. 19

252 A69 3r bl & multi	18	10
253 A69 9r lil rose & multi	50	20
254 A69 10r blk & multi	55	25

Canceled-to-order stamps are often from remainders. Most collectors of canceled stamps prefer postally used specimens.

Symbolic Globe and Waves A70

Design: 7r, 8r, ITU emblem and waves.

1971, May 17 Photo. *Perf. 13*

255 A70 3r grn, blk & bl 5 5
256 A70 4r yel & multi 13 5
257 A70 7r lil, blk & red 8 8
258 A70 8r sal pink, blk & red 15 10

3rd World Telecommunications Day.

Erythrina Indica A71

Wild Flowers: 3r, Bauhinia variegata. 6r, Butea frondosa. 10r, Lagerstroemia floribunda (vert.).

1971, July 5 *Perf. 13x12 1/2, 12 1/2x13*

259 A71 2r lt ultra & multi 8 5
260 A71 3r yel grn & multi 10 8
261 A71 6r bl & multi 18 12
262 A71 10r brn & multi 30 25

Khmer Coat of Arms A72

Flag and Square of the Republic A73

1971, Oct. 9 Engr. *Perf. 13*

263 A72 3r brt grn & bis 8 5
264 A73 3r pur & multi 8 5
265 A73 4r dp cl & multi 8 5
266 A72 8r org & bis 10 7
267 A72 10r lt brn & bis 15 8
a. Souvenir sheet of 3 1.25 1.25
268 A73 10r sl grn & multi 15 8
a. Souvenir sheet of 3 1.00 1.00
Nos. 263-268 (6) 64 38

First anniversary of the Republic. No. 267a contains one each of Nos. 263, 266-267 with olive marginal inscriptions. Sold for 25fr. No. 268a contains one each of Nos. 264-265 and 268 with purple marginal inscription. Sold for 20r. Size of sheets: 129x100mm.

UNICEF Emblem — A74

1971, Dec. 11

269 A74 3r blk brn 6 5
270 A74 5r ultra 10 6
271 A74 9r dk pur & brn red 18 10

25th anniversary of the United Nations International Children's Fund (UNICEF).

Book Year Emblem A75

1972, Feb. 7

272 A75 3r bl, grn & vio 8 5
273 A75 8r vio, grn & bl 15 8
274 A75 9r emer & multi 18 10
a. Souvenir sheet of 3 90 90

International Book Year 1972. No. 274a contains one each of Nos. 272-274 with emerald marginal inscription. Size: 159x99mm. Sold for 23r.

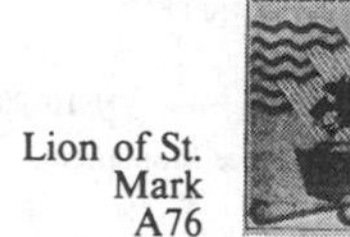

Lion of St. Mark A76

Designs: 5r, Waves engulfing St. Mark's Basilica. 10r, Bridge of Sighs (vert.).

1972, Feb. 7 Engr. *Perf. 13*

275 A76 3r lil rose & org brn 8 5
276 A76 5r yel grn & org brn 15 7
277 A76 10r org brn, bl & yel grn 25 18
a. Souvenir sheet of 3 85 85

UNESCO campaign to save Venice. No. 277a contains one each of Nos. 275-277. Yellow green marginal inscription. Size: 140x99mm. Sold for 23r.

U.N. Emblem A77

1972, Mar. 28

278 A77 3r dp car 8 5
279 A77 6r dp bl 18 12
280 A77 9r dp org 20 17
a. Souvenir sheet of 3 90 90

25th anniversary. United Nations Economic Commission for Asia and the Far East (ECAFE), No. 280a contains one each of Nos. 278-280. Deep blue marginal inscription. Size: 138x100mm. Sold for 23r.

Dancing Apsarases A78

"UIT" A79

1972, May 5 Engr. *Perf. 13*

281 A78 1r gldn brn 5 5
282 A78 3r violet 8 6
283 A78 7r rose cl 18 15
284 A78 8r ol brn 20 15
285 A78 9r bl grn 22 18
286 A78 10r ultra 25 20
287 A78 12r purple 30 25
288 A78 14r Prus bl 40 28
Nos. 281-288 (8) 1.68 1.32

1972, May 17 Litho.

289 A79 3r blk, yel & grnsh bl 10 5
290 A79 9r blk, dp lil rose & bl grn 25 13
291 A79 14r blk, brn & bl grn 35 25

4th World Telecommunications Day.

"Human Environment" — A80

1972, June 5 Engr.

292 A80 3r org, plum & grn 10 7
293 A80 12r brt grn & plum 40 25
294 A80 15r plum & brt grn 48 32
a. Souv. sheet of 3 1.40 1.40

U.N. Conference on Human Environment, Stockholm, June 5-16. No. 294a contains one each of Nos. 292-294. Green marginal inscription. Size: 129x100mm. Sold for 35r.

Javan Rhinoceros A81

1972, Aug. 1 Engr. *Perf. 13*

295 A81 3r *shown* 6 5
296 A81 4r *Serow* 6 5
297 A81 6r *Malayan sambar* 10 7
298 A81 7r *Banteng* 12 8
299 A81 8r *Water buffalo* 12 8
300 A81 10r *Gaur* 15 10
Nos. 295-300 (6) 61 43

Nos. 263, 267, 134, 293, 294 Overprinted in Red

XXE JEUX OLYMPIQUES MUNICH 1972

1972, Sept. 9 Engr. *Perf. 13*

301 A72 3r brt grn & bis 30 10
302 A72 10r org & bis 60 30
303 A34 12r multi 90 35
304 A80 12r brt grn & plum 90 35
305 A80 15r plum & brt grn 1.10 50
Nos. 301-305 (5) 3.80 1.60

20th Olympic Games, Munich, Aug. 26-Sept. 11.

Raising Khmer Flag — A82

1972, Oct. 9 Photo. *Perf. 12 1/2x13*

306 A82 3r multi 8 5
307 A82 5r brt rose & multi 10 6
308 A82 9r yel grn & multi 16 10

2nd anniversary of the establishment of the Khmer Republic.

Stupa and Crest A83

Apsaras A84

1973, May 12 Engr. *Perf. 13*

309 A83 3r ocher & multi 8 5
310 A83 12r yel grn & multi 20 18
311 A83 14r bl & multi 30 23
a. Souvenir sheet of 3 1.25 1.25

New Constitution. No. 311a contains one each of Nos. 309-311 with brown marginal inscription. Size: 128 1/2x99mm. Sold for 34r.

1973, July 23 Engr. *Perf. 13*

Sculptures from Angkor Wat: 8r, 10r, Devata (different).

312 A84 3r brn blk 7 5
313 A84 8r Prus grn 13 13
314 A84 10r ol bis 17 17
a. Souvenir sheet of 3 90 90

No. 314a contains one each of Nos. 312-314 with black marginal inscription. Size: 130x100mm. Sold for 25r.

INTERPOL Emblem A85

Marshal Lon Nol A86

1973, Oct. 2 Engr. *Perf. 13*

315 A85 3r grn & multi 8 5
316 A85 7r red brn & multi 15 13
317 A85 10r ol & multi 20 20
a. Souvenir sheet of 3 1.00 1.00

50th anniversary of the International Criminal Police Organization. No. 317a contains one each of Nos. 315-317; black marginal inscription. Size: 123x100mm. Sold for 30r.

1973, Oct. 9

318 A86 3r lt grn, blk & brn 12 7
319 A86 8r brn, ol & blk 25 15
320 A86 14r blk & brn 42 25
a. Souvenir sheet of 3 1.50 1.50

Marshal Lon Nol, first president of the Republic. No. 320a contains stamps similar to Nos. 318-320 in changed colors; greenish black marginal inscription. Size: 129x99mm. Sold for 50r.

Nos. 248, 243 and 307 Surcharged with New Value, 2 Bars and Overprinted in Red or Silver: "4th ANNIVERSAIRE/DE LA REPUBLIQUE"

1974 Photo. *Perf. 13, 12 1/2x13*

321 A67 10r multi (R) 5 5
322 A66 50r on 3r multi 20 15
323 A82 100r on 5r multi 45 30

4th anniversary of independence.

Copernicus and "Nerva" — A87

Designs: Copernicus, various spacecraft and events.

1974, Sept. 10 Litho. *Perf. 13*

324 A87 1r *shown*
325 A87 5r *Mariner II*
326 A87 10r *Apollo*
327 A87 25r *Telstar*
328 A87 50r *Space walk*
329 A87 100r *Moon landing*
330 A87 150r *Separation of spaceship and module*
Nos. 324-330,C32-C33(9) 19.00 19.00

500th anniversary of the birth of Nicolaus Copernicus (1473-1543), Polish astronomer.

Carrier Pigeon and UPU Emblem — A88

Design: 60r, Sailing ship and UPU emblem.

1974, Nov. 2

331 A88 10r multi 5 5
332 A88 60r multi 25 15

Centenary of Universal Postal Union. A souvenir sheet containing one No. 332 exists. See No. C34.

Importation Prohibited
The U.S. Treasury Department prohibited the importation of stamps of Cambodia (Khmer Republic) as of Apr. 17, 1975.

SEMI-POSTAL STAMPS.

Nos. 8, 12, 14 and 15 Surcharged in Black

+60c
AIDE A L'ETUDIANT

1952, Oct. 20 Unwmk. *Perf. 13*

B1 A3 1.10pi + 40c dp car & brt red 3.00 3.00
B2 A3 1.90pi + 60c ind & dp ultra 3.00 3.00
B3 A3 3pi + 1pi dp car & org brn 3.00 3.00
B4 A1 5pi + 2pi ind & pur 3.00 3.00

Preah Stupa — SP1

1957, Mar. 15 Engr. *Perf. 13*

B5 SP1 1.50r + 50c ind, ol & red 60 60
B6 SP1 6.50r + 1.50r red lil, ol & red 1.00 1.00
B7 SP1 8r + 2r bl, ol & red 1.50 1.50

Issued to commemorate the 2500th anniversary of the birth of Buddha. See Nos. 62-64.

Type of Regular Issue, 1959, with Red Typographed Surcharge

\+ 0,30

1959, Dec. 9

B8 A14 20c + 20c rose vio 6 6
B9 A14 50c + 30c bl 12 12
B10 A14 80c + 50c rose car 18 18

The surtax was for the Red Cross.

Nos. 107-108 Surcharged and Overprinted in Red: "1863-1963 CENTENAIRE DE LA CROIX ROUGE"

1963, Oct. 1 Unwmk. *Perf. 13*

B11 A26 4r + 40c grn & dk brn 60 60
B12 A26 6r + 60c vio & ol bis 75 75

Centenary of International Red Cross.

Nos. 263, 267, 293-294, 134 Surcharged in Red

SECOURS AUX
VICTIMES DE GUERRE

1972, Nov. 15 Engr. *Perf. 13*

B13 A72 3r + 2r multi 20 20
B14 A72 10r + 6r multi 40 30
B15 A80 12r + 7r multi 50 35
B16 A34 12r + 7r multi 50 35
B17 A80 15r + 8r multi 80 65
Nos. B13-B17 (5) 2.40 1.85

Surtax was for war victims. Surcharge arranged differently on Nos. B15-B17.

AIR POST STAMPS.

Kinnari — AP1

Unwmk.

1953, Apr. 16 Engr. *Perf. 13*

C1 AP1 50c dp grn 45 45
a. Souvenir sheet of 4 50.00 50.00
C2 AP1 3pi red brn 55 45
a. Souvenir sheet of 3 50.00 50.00
C3 AP1 3.30pi rose vio 75 50
C4 AP1 4pi dk brn & dp bl 90 50
C5 AP1 5.10pi brn, red & org 1.10 80
C6 AP1 6.50pi dk brn & lil rose 1.10 1.10
a. Souvenir sheet of 2 50.00 50.00
C7 AP1 9pi lil rose & dp grn 1.65 1.65
C8 AP1 11.50pi multi 3.25 2.50
C9 AP1 30pi dk brn, bl grn & org 4.75 2.75
Nos. C1-C9 (9) 14.50 10.70

No. C1a contains one each of the 50c, 3.30pi, 5.10pi and 30pi, and sold for 50pi. No. C2a contains one each of the 3pi, 4pi and 11.50pi, and sold for 25pi. No C6a contains one each of the 6.50pi and 9pi, and sold for 20pi. Marginal inscriptions in brown. Size: 129x100mm.

AP2

1957, Dec. 11

C10 AP2 50c maroon 12 8
C11 AP2 1r emerald 20 15
C12 AP2 4r ultra 90 55
C13 AP2 50r car rose 4.25 3.75
C14 AP2 100r grn, bl & car 6.75 5.00
a. Souvenir sheet of 5 20.00 20.00
Nos. C10-C14 (5) 12.22 9.53

No. C14a contains one each of Nos. C10-C14, and sold for 160r. Size: 159x93mm.

Independence Type of 1961

1961, Nov. 9 *Perf. 13x12½*

C15 A24 7r multi 70 40
C16 A24 30r grn, car & ultra 1.75 1.40
C17 A24 50r ind, grn & ol 3.25 2.50
a. Souvenir sheet of 3 7.25 7.25

Issued to commemorate the tenth anniversary of Independence. No. C17a contains one each of Nos. C15-C17 with gold marginal inscription. Size: 150x85mm.

No. C15 Surcharged with New Value in Red and Overprinted in Black with Two Bars and: "INAUGURATION DU MONUMENT"

1962, Nov. 9

C18 A24 12r on 7r multi 1.10 90

Dedication of Independence Monument.

Hanuman, Monkey God — AP3

1964, Sept. 1 Engr. *Perf. 13*

C19 AP3 5r multi 50 27
C20 AP3 10r ol bis, lil rose & grn 70 35
C21 AP3 20r vio, bl & ol bis 95 55
C22 AP3 40r bl, ol bis & dk bl 2.00 1.10
C23 AP3 80r multi 3.50 3.00
Nos. C19-C23 (5) 7.65 5.27

Nos. C19-C22 Surcharged in Red

1964, Oct.

C24 AP3 3r on 5r multi 35 30
C25 AP3 6r on 10r multi 50 45
C26 AP3 9r on 20r multi 70 60
C27 AP3 12r on 40r multi 1.10 90

18th Olympic Games, Tokyo, Oct. 10-25.

Certain unlisted issues of Cambodia, starting in 1972, are mentioned and briefly described in "For the Record" at the back of this volume.

Garuda, 12th Century, Angkor Thom — AP4

1973, Jan. 18 Engr. *Perf. 13*

C28 AP4 3r carmine 8 6
C29 AP4 30r vio bl 75 50
C30 AP4 50r dl pur 1.25 80
C31 AP4 100r dl grn 2.50 1.50

Copernicus Type of 1974

Designs: 200r, Copernicus and Skylab II; 250r, Copernicus, Concorde and solar eclipse

1974, Sept. 10 Litho. *Perf. 1*

C32 A87 200r multi
C33 A87 250r multi

500th anniversary of the birth of Nicolau Copernicus (1473-1543), Polish astronomer. A souvenir sheet containing No. C32 i perf., size 110x82mm. A souvenir sheet con taining No. C33 is imperf., size 83x111mm.

UPU Type of 1974

Design: 700r, Rocket, globe and UPU emblem.

1974, Nov. 2

C34 A88 700r gold & multi 2.80 2.0

Centenary of Universal Postal Union. A souvenir sheet containing one No. C34 exists

POSTAGE DUE STAMPS

D1

Frieze, Angkor Wat — D2

1957 Unwmk. Typo. *Perf. 13½*
Denomination in Black.

J1 D1 10c ver & pale bl 12 1
J2 D1 50c ver & pale bl 18 1
J3 D1 1r ver & pale bl 22 2
J4 D1 3r ver & pale bl 33 3
J5 D1 5r ver & pale bl 60 6
Nos. J1-J5 (5) 1.45 1.4

1974, Feb. 18 Engr. *Perf. 12½x1*

J6 D2 2r ocher 8
J7 D2 6r green 13 1
J8 D2 8r dp car 20 1
J9 D2 10r vio bl 27 2

CAMEROUN

(Kamerun)

LOCATION — On the west coast of Africa, north of the equator.
GOVT. — Republic.
AREA — 456,054 sq. mi.
POP. — 9,060,000 (est. 1983).
CAPITAL — Yaounde.

Before World War I, Cameroun (Kamerun) was a German Protectorate. It was occupied during the war by Great Britain and France and in 192 was mandated to these countries by the League of Nations. The French-mandated part became the independent State of Cameroun on January 1, 1960. The Southern Cameroons, a United Kingdom Trust Territory, joined this state to form the Federal Republic of Cameroun on October 1, 1961. The name was changed to United Republic of Cameroon on May 20, 1972.

Stamps of Southern Cameroons are listed under Cameroons in Volume 1.

100 Pfennig = 1 Mark
12 Pence = 1 Shilling
100 Centimes = 1 Franc

Issued under German Dominion.

A1 A2

Stamps of Germany, 1889-1900, Overprinted in Black.

1897 Unwmk. *Perf. 13½x14½*

1 A1 3pf yel brn 10.50 13.00
a. 3pf red brn 27.50 50.00
b. 3pf dk brn 15.00 *37.50*
2 A1 5pf green 5.75 3.50
3 A2 10pf carmine 4.00 4.00
4 A2 20pf ultra 4.50 6.50
5 A2 25pf orange 21.00 35.00
6 A2 50pf red brn 17.50 27.50
Nos. 1-6 (6) 63.25 89.50

Kaiser's Yacht "Hohenzollern"
A3 A4

1900 Unwmk. Typo. *Perf. 14*

7 A3 3pf brown 1.50 1.50
8 A3 5pf green 21.00 90
9 A3 10pf carmine 55.00 1.40
10 A3 20pf ultra 30.00 2.25
11 A3 25pf org & blk, *yel* 1.50 *6.00*
12 A3 30pf org & blk, *sal* 2.00 *5.00*
13 A3 40pf lake & blk 2.00 *5.00*
14 A3 50pf pur & blk, *sal* 2.25 *6.25*
15 A3 80pf lake & blk, *rose* 3.00 *12.50*

Engr. *Perf. 14½x14*

16 A4 1m carmine 72.50 65.00
17 A4 2m blue 6.75 *65.00*
18 A4 3m blk vio 6.00 *110.00*
19 A4 5m sl & car 150.00 *400.00*
Nos. 7-19 (13) 353.50 680.80

Wmk. 125- Lozenges

1905-18 Wmk. 125 Typo.

20 A3 3pf brn ('18) 75
21 A3 5pf grn ('06) 80 1.75
b. Booklet pane of 6,(2 No. 21 + 4 No. 22) 77.50
c. Booklet pane of 5 + label 375.00
22 A3 10pf carmine 80 80
b. Booklet pane of 5 + label 550.00
23 A3 20pf ultra ('14) 2.25 *200.00*
24 A4 1m car ('15) 2.25
25 A4 5m sl & car ('13) 18.00 *5,000.*

The 3pf and 1m were not placed in use.

Issued under British Occupation.

Stamps of German Cameroun Surcharged

C. E. F.
½ d.

Wmk. Lozenges (125) (#54-56, 65); Unwmk. (Other Values.)

1915 *Perf. 14, 14½*

Blue Surcharge.

53 A3 ½p on 3pf brn 11.50 17.50
54 A3 ½p on 5pf grn 4.50 7.50
a. Double surcharge 600.00 300.00
b. blk surcharge 8.00 10.00
55 A3 1p on 10pf car 4.50 7.50
a. "1" with thin serifs 16.00 20.00
b. Double surcharge 300.00 300.00
c. Black surcharge 35.00 50.00
d. "C.E.F." omitted *2,750.*
e. "1d" double *2,500.*

Black Surcharge.

56 A3 2p on 20pf ultra 5.00 *15.00*
57 A3 2½p on 25pf org & blk, *yel* 22.50 32.50
a. Double surcharge *3,500.*
58 A3 3p on 30pf org & blk, *sal* 17.50 *32.50*
59 A3 4p on 40pf lake & blk 17.50 *32.50*
60 A3 6p on 50pf pur & blk, *sal* 17.50 *32.50*
61 A3 8p on 80pf lake & blk, *rose* 17.50 32.50

Surcharged

C. E. F.
1s.

62 A4 1sh on 1m car 250.00 *400.00*
a. "S" inverted 1,000. *1,500.*
63 A4 2sh on 2m bl 250.00 *400.00*
a. "S" inverted 1,000. *1,500.*
64 A4 3sh on 3m blk vio 250.00 *400.00*
a. "S" inverted 1,000. *1,500.*
b. Double surcharge *5,000.*
65 A4 5sh on 5m sl & car 250.00 *400.00*
a. "S" inverted 1,000. *1,500.*
Nos. 53-65 (13) 1,118. 1,810.

The letters "C. E. F." are the initials of "Cameroons Expeditionary Force."

Issued under French Occupation.

Stamps of Gabon, 1910, Overprinted

Corps Expéditionnaire
Franco-Anglais
CAMEROUN

1915 Unwmk. *Perf. 13½x14.*

101 A10 10c red & car 25.00 9.00
102 A13 1c choc & org 75.00 22.50
103 A13 2c blk & choc 110.00 62.50
104 A13 4c vio & dp bl 110.00 65.00
105 A13 5c ol gray & grn 25.00 9.00
105A A13 10c red & car *16,000.* *17,500.*
106 A13 20c ol brn & dk vio 125.00 120.00
107 A14 25c dp bl & choc 47.50 15.00
108 A14 30c gray blk & red 125.00 110.00
109 A14 35c dk vio & grn 37.50 15.00
a. Double ovpt. 1,400. 1,400.
110 A14 40c choc & ultra 125.00 110.00
111 A14 45c car & vio 130.00 110.00
112 A14 50c bl grn & gray 130.00 120.00
113 A14 75c org & choc 190.00 120.00
114 A15 1fr dk brn & bis 175.00 130.00
115 A15 2fr car & brn 200.00 160.00
Nos. 101-105,106-115 (15) 1,630. 1,178.

The overprint is vertical, reading up, on Nos. 101-106, 114-115, and horizontal on Nos. 107-113.

Stamps of Middle Congo, Issue of 1907, Overprinted

Occupation
Francaise
du Cameroun

1916 Unwmk.

116 A1 1c ol gray & brn 52.50 52.50
117 A1 2c vio & brn 70.00 60.00
118 A1 4c bl & brn 70.00 60.00
119 A1 5c dk grn & bl 16.00 15.00
120 A2 35c vio brn & bl 70.00 52.50
121 A2 45c vio & red 47.50 42.50

The overprint is horizontal on Nos. 116-119, and vertical, reading down, on Nos. 120-121.

Same Overprint On Stamps of French Congo, 1900.

Wmk. Branch of Thistle. (122)

122 A4 15c dl vio & ol grn 70.00 67.50
a. Inverted overprint 100.00 100.00

Wmk. Branch of Rose Tree. (123)

123 A5 20c yel grn & org 90.00 65.00
124 A5 30c car rose & org 60.00 40.00
125 A5 40c org brn & brt grn 40.00 37.50
126 A5 50c gray vio & lil 60.00 40.00
127 A5 75c red vio & org 60.00 40.00

Wmk. Branch of Olive. (124)

128 A6 1fr gray lil & ol 75.00 47.50
129 A6 2fr car & brn 75.00 47.50
Nos. 116-129 (14) 856.00 667.50

The overprint is horizontal on No. 122; vertical, reading down or up, on Nos. 123-129.

Counterfeits exist of Nos. 101-129.

Stamps of Middle Congo, Issue of 1907 Overprinted

CAMEROUN
Occupation
Française

1916-17 Unwmk.

130 A1 1c ol gray & brn 6 6
131 A1 2c vio & brn 8 6
132 A1 4c bl & brn 14 8
133 A1 5c dk grn & bl 22 10
134 A1 10c car & bl 75 42
135 A1 15c brn vio & rose ('17) 75 35
136 A1 20c brn & bl 42 25
137 A2 25c bl & grn 52 35
a. Triple ovpt. 425.00
138 A2 30c scar & grn 30 30
a. Double ovpt. 300.00
139 A2 35c vio brn & bl 52 40
140 A2 40c dl grn & brn 1.00 42
141 A2 45c vio & red 1.00 48
142 A2 50c bl grn & red 1.00 60
143 A2 75c brn & bl 1.10 60
144 A3 1fr dp grn & vio 95 60
145 A3 2fr vio & gray grn 5.75 3.50
146 A3 5fr bl & rose 7.00 4.25
Nos. 130-146 (17) 21.56 12.82

Nos. 130 to 146 exist on ordinary paper and, with the exception of No. 132, on chalk surfaced paper. Nos. 137 to 146 are known with inverted "S" in "Francaise."

On Nos. 137 to 146 there is a space of 7mm. between "Cameroun" and "Occupation."

Provisional French Mandate.

Types of Middle Congo, 1907, Overprinted

CAMEROUN

1921

147 A1 1c ol grn & org 5 5
148 A1 2c brn & rose 5 5
149 A1 4c gray & lt grn 15 15
150 A1 5c dl red & org 15 15
a. Double overprint 600.00
151 A1 10c bl grn & lt grn 25 22
152 A1 15c bl & org 25 22
153 A1 20c red brn & ol 30 22
154 A2 25c sl & org 30 22
155 A2 30c rose & ver 35 22
156 A2 35c gray & ultra 42 40
157 A2 40c ol grn & org 35 30
158 A2 45c brn & rose 35 22
159 A2 50c bl & ultra 35 30
160 A2 75c red brn & lt grn 42 30
161 A3 1fr sl & org 1.00 80
162 A3 2fr ol grn & rose 3.50 2.75
163 A3 5fr dl red & gray 4.25 4.00
Nos. 147-163 (17) 12.49 10.57

The 2c, 4c, 15c, 25c and 50c exist with overprint omitted.

Nos. 152, 162, 163, 158, 160 Surcharged with New Value and Bars.

1924-25

164 A1 25c on 15c bl & org ('25) 40 40
165 A3 25c on 2fr ol grn & rose 40 40
166 A3 25c on 5fr red & gray 50 50
a. Pair, one without new value and bars
167 A2 65c on 45c brn & rose ('25) 1.00 1.00
168 A2 85c on 75c red brn & lt grn ('25) 1.00 1.00
Nos. 164-168 (5) 3.30 3.30

French Mandate

Herder and Cattle Crossing Sanaga River — A5

Tapping Rubber Tree — A6

Rope Suspension Bridge — A7

1925-38 Typo. *Perf. 14x13½*

170 A5 1c ol grn & brn vio, *lav* 5 5
171 A5 2c rose & grn,*grnsh* 5 5
172 A5 4c bl & blk 6 6
173 A5 5c org & red vio, *lav* 6 5
174 A5 10c red brn & org, *yel* 8 8
175 A5 15c sl grn & grn 10 10
176 A5 15c lil & red ('27) 52 40

Perf. 13½x14.

177 A6 20c ol brn & red brn 25 22
178 A6 20c grn ('26) 25 22
179 A6 20c brn red & ol brn ('27) 30 18
180 A6 25c lt grn & blk 52 22
181 A6 30c bluish grn & ver 25 22
182 A6 30c dk grn & grn ('27) 30 18
183 A6 35c brn & blk 25 22
184 A6 35c dl grn & grn ('38) 85 48
185 A6 40c org & vio 1.00 60
186 A6 45c dp rose & cer 25 22
187 A6 45c vio & org brn ('27) 1.50 1.10
188 A6 50c lt grn & cer 25 5
189 A6 55c ultra & car ('38) 1.00 80
190 A6 60c red vio & blk 25 22
191 A6 60c brn red ('26) 15 15
192 A6 65c ind & brn 15 15
193 A6 75c ind & dp bl 42 30

No.	Type	Description	Unused	Used
194	A6	75c org brn & red vio ('27)	42	25
195	A6	80c car & brn ('38)	85	60
196	A6	85c dp rose & bl	52	25
197	A6	90c brn red & cer ('27)	1.50	80

Perf. 14x13½.

No.	Type	Description	Unused	Used
198	A7	1fr ind & brn	65	42
199	A7	1fr dl bl ('26)	35	30
200	A7	1fr ol brn & red vio ('27)	60	35
201	A7	1fr grn & dk brn ('29)	1.00	70
202	A7	1.10fr rose red & dk brn ('28)	2.50	1.90
203	A7	1.25fr gray & dp bl ('33)	3.75	2.00
204	A7	1.50fr dl bl ('27)	55	30
205	A7	1.75fr brn & org ('33)	75	55
206	A7	1.75fr dk bl & lt bl ('38)	75	48
207	A7	2fr dl grn & brn org	1.25	52
208	A7	3fr ol brn & red vio ('27)	4.00	95
209	A7	5fr brn & blk, *bluish*	1.90	95
a.		Cliché of 2fr in plate of 5fr	*1,300.*	
210	A7	10fr org & vio ('27)	7.25	3.75
211	A7	20fr rose & ol grn ('27)	12.00	6.75
		Nos. 170-211 (42)	49.45	28.14

Common Design Types pictured in section at front of book.

No. 199 Surcharged with New Value and Bars in Red.

1926

No.	Type	Description	Unused	Used
212	A7	1.25fr on 1fr dl bl	35	35

Colonial Exposition Issue.

Common Design Types

Name of Country in Black.

1931 Engr. *Perf. 12½.*

No.	Type	Description	Unused	Used
213	CD70	40c dp grn	2.00	1.90
214	CD71	50c violet	3.00	2.75
215	CD72	90c red org	3.00	2.75
216	CD73	1.50fr dl bl	3.75	3.25

Paris International Exposition Issue.

Common Design Types

1937 *Perf. 13.*

No.	Type	Description	Unused	Used
217	CD74	20c dp vio	1.00	1.00
218	CD75	30c dk grn	90	90
219	CD76	40c car rose	90	90
220	CD77	50c dk brn	90	90
221	CD78	90c red	1.00	1.00
222	CD79	1.50fr ultra	1.00	1.00
		Nos. 217-222 (6)	5.70	5.70

French Colonial Art Exhibition.

Common Design Type

Souvenir Sheet.

1937 *Imperf.*

No.	Type	Description	Unused	Used
222A	CD77	3fr org red & blk	3.50	3.50

Size: 118x99mm.

New York World's Fair Issue.

Common Design Type

1939 *Perf. 12½x12.*

No.	Type	Description	Unused	Used
223	CD82	1.25fr car lake	90	90
224	CD82	2.25fr ultra	90	90

Mandara Woman — A19

Falls on M'bam River near Banyo — A20

Elephants A21

Man in Yare — A22

1939-40 Engr. *Perf. 13*

No.	Type	Description	Unused	Used
225	A19	2c blk brn	5	5
226	A19	3c magenta	5	5
227	A19	4c dp ultra	6	6
228	A19	5c red brn	6	6
229	A19	10c dp bl grn	5	5
230	A19	15c rose red	18	6
231	A19	20c plum	18	6
232	A20	25c blk brn	30	30
233	A20	30c dk red	30	25
234	A20	40c ultra	42	40
235	A20	45c sl grn	1.25	1.00
236	A20	50c brn car	42	30
237	A20	60c pck bl	48	35
238	A20	70c plum	1.65	1.50
239	A21	80c Prus bl	1.25	1.10
240	A21	90c Prus bl	65	40
241	A21	1fr car rose	90	48
242	A21	1fr choc ('40)	90	42
243	A21	1.25fr car rose	2.50	1.65
244	A21	1.40fr org red	90	70
245	A21	1.50fr chocolate	70	52
246	A21	1.60fr blk brn	1.25	1.25
247	A21	1.75fr dk bl	65	48
248	A21	2fr dk grn	75	65
249	A21	2.25fr dk bl	65	42
250	A21	2.50fr brt red vio	90	65
251	A21	3fr dk vio	52	35
252	A22	5fr blk brn	65	42
253	A22	10fr brt red vio	1.25	1.00
254	A22	20fr dk grn	2.00	1.50
		Nos. 225-254 (30)	21.87	16.48

Stamps of 1925-40 Overprinted in Black or Orange "CAMEROUN FRANCAIS 27.8.40."

1940 *Perf. 14x13½, 13½x14, 13.*

No.	Type	Description	Unused	Used
255	A19	2c blk brn (O)	42	42
256	A19	3c magenta	42	42
257	A19	4c dp ultra (O)	52	52
258	A19	5c red brn	1.75	1.75
259	A19	10c dp bl grn (O)	42	42
260	A19	15c rose red	65	65
260A	A19	20c plum (O)	4.75	3.75
261	A20	25c blk brn	52	42
b.		Inverted ovpt.	175.00	175.00
261A	A20	30c dk red	4.50	3.50
262	A20	40c ultra	2.25	1.50
263	A20	45c sl grn	1.75	1.25
264	A6	50c lt grn & cer	90	42
a.		Inverted ovpt.	160.00	
265	A20	60c pck bl	2.25	1.50
266	A20	70c plum	80	80
267	A21	80c Prus bl (O)	2.25	1.90
268	A21	90c Prus bl (O)	52	52
269	A21	1.25fr car rose	80	52
270	A21	1.40fr org red	1.25	90
271	A21	1.50fr chocolate	52	52
272	A21	1.60fr blk brn (O)	90	52
273	A21	1.75fr dk bl (O)	1.25	1.25
274	A21	2.25fr dk bl (O)	65	65
275	A21	2.50fr brt red vio	65	65
276	A7	5fr brn & blk, *bluish*	8.50	6.25
277	A22	5fr blk brn	9.50	8.50
278	A7	10fr org & vio	12.00	8.50
278A	A22	10fr brt red vio	24.00	18.00
279	A7	20fr rose & ol grn	26.00	20.00
279A	A22	20fr dk grn	150.00	140.00

Same Overprint on Stamps of 1939.

Perf. 12½x12.

No.	Type	Description	Unused	Used
280	CD82	1.25fr car lake	2.25	2.25
281	CD82	2.25fr ultra	2.25	2.25
		Nos. 255-281 (31)	265.19	230.50

Issued to note Cameroun's affiliation with General de Gaulle's "Free France" movement.

Foreign postal stationery (stamped envelopes, postal cards and air letter sheets) lies beyond the scope of this Catalogue, which is limited to adhesive postage stamps.

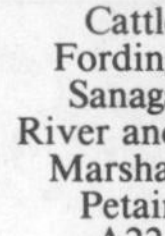

Cattle Fording Sanaga River and Marshal Petain A22a

1941 Engr. *Perf. 12½x12*

No.	Type	Description	Unused	Used
281A	A22a	1fr green	65	
281B	A22a	2.50fr dk bl	65	

Nos. 281A-281B were issued by the Vichy government, and were not placed on sale in Cameroun.

Lorraine Cross and Joan of Arc Shield — A23

1941 Photo. *Perf. 14x14½*

No.	Type	Description	Unused	Used
282	A23	5c brown	5	5
283	A23	10c dk bl	5	5
284	A23	25c emerald	6	6
285	A23	30c dp org	6	6
286	A23	40c dk sl grn	5	5
287	A23	80c red brn	12	5
288	A23	1fr dp red lil	5	5
289	A23	1.50fr brt red	10	5
290	A23	2fr gray blk	30	12
291	A23	2.50fr brt ultra	35	18
292	A23	4fr dl vio	65	52
293	A23	5fr bister	70	65
294	A23	10fr dp brn	75	65
295	A23	20fr dp grn	1.50	1.00
		Nos. 282-295 (14)	4.79	3.54

Eboue Issue

Common Design Type

1945 Unwmk. Engr. *Perf. 13.*

No.	Type	Description	Unused	Used
296	CD91	2fr black	30	30
297	CD91	25fr Prus grn	1.00	1.00

Surcharged with New Values and Bars in Red, Carmine or Black.

1946 *Perf. 14x14½.*

No.	Type	Description	Unused	Used
297A	A23	50c on 5c brn (R)	25	25
298	A23	60c on 5c brn (R)	40	40
a.		Inverted surcharge	87.50	
299	A23	70c on 5c brn (R)	40	40
300	A23	1.20fr on 5c brn (C)	40	40
301	A23	2.40fr on 25c emer	30	30
302	A23	3fr on 25c emer	60	60
302A	A23	4.50fr on 25c emer	1.00	1.00
303	A23	15fr on 2.50fr brt ultra (C)	1.00	1.00
		Nos. 297A-303 (8)	4.35	4.35

Zebu and Herder A25

Tikar Women — A26

Porters Carrying Bananas — A27

Bowman A28

Lamido Horsemen A29

Farmer — A30

1946 Engr. *Perf. 12½x12, 12x12½.*

No.	Type	Description	Unused	Used
304	A25	10c bl grn	5	5
305	A25	30c brn org	5	5
306	A25	40c brt ultra	5	5
307	A26	50c ol brn	5	5
308	A26	60c dp plum	6	6
309	A26	80c chnt brn	30	8
310	A27	1fr org red	6	6
311	A27	1.20fr dp grn	40	25
312	A27	1.50fr dk car	1.25	95
313	A28	2fr black	6	6
314	A28	3fr dk car	12	5
314A	A28	3.60fr red brn	65	48
315	A28	4fr dp bl	30	22
316	A29	5fr brn car	65	22
317	A29	6fr ultra	65	10
318	A29	10fr sl grn	70	12
319	A30	15fr grnsh bl	1.10	48
320	A30	20fr dk grn	1.25	35
321	A30	25fr black	1.75	70
		Nos. 304-321 (19)	9.50	4.38

Imperforates

Most Cameroun stamps from 1952 onward exist imperforate in issued and trial colors, and also in small presentation sheets in issued colors.

Military Medal Issue.

Common Design Type

Engraved and Typographed

1952 Unwmk. *Perf. 13.*

No.	Type	Description	Unused	Used
322	CD101	15fr multi	3.75	2.50

Issued to commemorate the centenary of the creation of the French Military Medal.

Porters Carrying Bananas A32

Picking Coffee Beans A33

1954 Engr.

No.	Type	Description	Unused	Used
323	A32	8fr red vio, org brn & vio bl	52	25
324	A32	15fr brn red, yel & blk brn	90	42
325	A33	40fr blk brn, org brn & lil rose	90	42

FIDES Issue

Common Design Type

Designs: 5fr, Plowmen. 15fr, Wouri bridge. 20fr, Technical instruction. 25fr, Mobile medical station.

1956 Unwmk. *Perf. 13*

No.	Type	Description	Unused	Used
326	CD103	5fr org brn & bl grn	52	40

327 CD103 15fr aqua, sl & bit 85 60
328 CD103 20fr grnsh bl & dp ultra 85 60
329 CD103 25fr dp ultra 1.25 95

Coffee Issue

Coffee A35

1956 Engr. *Perf. 13*
330 A35 15fr car & brt red 75 40

Autonomous Government

Flag and Woman Holding Child A36

1958
331 A36 20fr multi 45 10

Issued to commemorate the anniversary of the installation of the first autonomous government of Cameroun.

Men Looking to the Sun — A37

1958
332 A37 20fr sep & brn red 50 40

Issued to commemorate the tenth anniversary of the signing of the Universal Declaration of Human Rights.

Flower Issue
Common Design Type

Design: 20fr, Randia malleifera.

1959 Photo. *Perf. 12½x12*
333 CD104 20fr dp grn, yel & rose 40 20

Loading Bananas A38

Harvesting Bananas — A39

1959 Engr. *Perf. 13*
334 A38 20fr dk grn & org 30 8
335 A39 25fr mar & sl grn 40 10

Independent State

Map and Flag of Cameroun — A40

Prime Minister Ahmadou Ahidjo — A41

1960 Unwmk. Engr. *Perf. 13*
336 A40 20fr multi 40 10
337 A41 25fr blk, grn & pale lem 45 15

Declaration of independence, Jan. 1, 1960.

Uprooted Oak Emblem A42

1960
338 A42 30fr red brn, ultra & yel grn 60 55

Issued to publicize World Refugee Year, July 1, 1959-June 30, 1960.

C.C.T.A. Issue
Common Design Type

1960
339 CD106 50fr dl cl & sl 1.00 60

U.N. Headquarters, New York, and Flag — A43

1961, May 20 *Perf. 13*
Flag in Green, Red and Yellow
340 A43 15fr grn, dk bl & brn 40 35
341 A43 25fr dk bl & grn 45 35
342 A43 85fr red, dk bl & vio brn 1.35 1.20

Issued to commemorate Cameroun's admission to the United States, Sept. 20, 1960.

Federal Republic

Stamps of 1946-60 Surcharged in Red or Black: REPUBLIQUE FEDERALE 2d

Two types of 2sh6p:
I. Large figures. "2/6" measures 8x3¾mm.
II. Small figures. "2/6" measures 6x2½mm.

Perf. 12x12½, 13
1961, Oct. 1 Engr.
343 A27 ½p on 1fr org red (#310) 25 25
344 A28 1p on 2fr blk (#313) 35 25
345 CD103 1½p on 5fr org brn & dk brn (#326) 35 25
346 A29 2p on 10fr sl grn (#318) 40 30
347 CD103 3p on 15fr aqua, sl & blk (#327) 45 35
348 A35 4p on 15fr car & brt red (Bk) (#330) 60 45
349 A38 6p on 20fr dk grn & org (#334) 75 50
350 A41 1sh on 25fr blk, grn & pale lem (#337) 1.50 1.25
351 A42 2sh6p on 30fr red brn, ultra & yel grn (#338) (I) 2.50 2.50
a. Type II 6.50 6.50
Nos. 343-351 (9) 7.15 6.10

Issued for use in the former United Kingdom Trust Territory of Southern Cameroons.

The "Republique Federale" overprint is in one line on Nos. 345, 347-349, in two vertical lines on No. 350. See Nos. C38-C40.

President Ahidjo and Prime Minister Foncha A45

Unwmk.
1962, Jan. 1 Engr. *Perf. 13*
352 A45 20fr vio & choc 7.50 6.50
353 A45 25fr dk grn & brn 12.50 10.00
354 A45 60fr car & dl grn 35.00 32.50

Same Surcharged for Use in Southern Cameroons 3 d

355 A45 3p on 20fr vio & choc 140.00 140.00
356 A45 6p on 25fr dk grn & brn 140.00 140.00
357 A45 2sh6p on 60fr car & dl grn 140.00 140.00

Issued to commemorate the reunification of the former French and British Sections of Cameroun. It is reported that Nos. 352-357 were withdrawn after a few days and destroyed.

Mustache Monkey A46

Designs: 1fr, 4fr, Elephant, Ntem Falls. 1.50fr, 3fr, Buffon's kob, Dschang. 2fr, 5fr, Hippopotamus. 6fr, 15fr, Mustache monkey. 8fr, 30fr, Manatee, Lake Ossa. 10fr, 25fr, Buffalo, Batouri. 20fr, 40fr, Giraffes, Waza Reservation (vert.).

1962 Unwmk. Engr. *Perf. 12*
358 A46 50c brn, brt grn & bl 10 5
359 A46 1fr gray brn, bl grn & org 10 5
360 A46 1.50fr brn, lt grn & sl grn 10 5
361 A46 2fr dk gray, grnsh bl & grn 10 5
362 A46 3fr brn, org & lil rose 10 6
363 A46 4fr brn, yel grn & bl grn 12 6
364 A46 5fr gray brn, grn & sal 15 8
365 A46 6fr brn, yel & bl 18 10
366 A46 8fr dk bl, red & grn 25 15
367 A46 10fr ol blk, org & brt bl 25 8
368 A46 15fr brn, Prus bl & bl 30 8
369 A46 20fr brn & gray 40 12
370 A46 25fr red brn, grn & yel 60 30
371 A46 30fr blk, org & bl 85 40
372 A46 40fr dp cl, yel grn & blk 1.20 60
Nos. 358-372 (15) 4.80 2.23

See also Nos. 396-397.

African and Malgasy Union Issue
Common Design Type

1962, Sept. 8 Photo. *Perf. 12½x12*
373 CD110 30fr multi 1.00 70

Issued to commemorate the first anniversary of the African and Malgasy Union.

Village and Map of Cameroun A48

Designs: 20fr, 25fr, Sun rising over city. 50fr, Hands holding scroll.

1962, Oct. 1 Engr. *Perf. 13*
374 A48 9fr pur, ol & dk brn 20 20
375 A48 18fr grn, org brn & dk bl 35 25
376 A48 20fr lil rose, ol bis & ind 35 25
377 A48 25fr bl, red org & sep 50 30
378 A48 50fr dk red, sep & bl 1.00 75
Nos. 374-378 (5) 2.40 1.75

Issued to commemorate the first anniversary of the reunification of Cameroun.

"School under the Trees" — A49

1962, Nov. 5 Photo. *Perf. 12x12½*
379 A49 20fr ver, emer & yel 40 20

Literacy and popular education campaign.

Telstar and Globe A50

1963, Feb. 9 Engr. *Perf. 13*
Size: 36x22mm.
380 A50 1fr dk bl, ol & pur 5 5
381 A50 2fr dk bl, cl & grn 8 8
382 A50 3fr dk grn, ol & dp cl 12 12
383 A50 25fr grn, dp cl & brt bl 70 60

Issued to commemorate the first television connection of the United States and Europe through the Telstar satellite, July 11-12, 1962. See No. C45.

High Frequency Transmission Station, Mt. Bankolo — A51

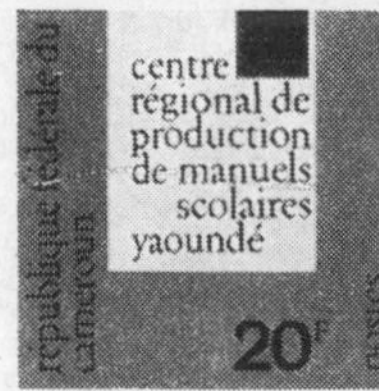

"Yaounde-Regional Center of Textbook Production" – A52

Design: 20fr, Station and wiring plan.

1963, May 18 Photo. *Perf. 12x12½*

384	A51	15fr multi	25	20
385	A51	20fr multi	35	25

Issued to publicize the high frequency telegraph connection Douala-Yaounde. See No. C46.

1963, Aug. 10 Unwmk. *Perf. 12½*

386	A52	20fr emer, blk & red	35	20
387	A52	25fr org, blk & red	45	25
388	A52	100fr gold, blk & red	1.75	1.00

Issued to publicize the UNESCO regional center for the production of school books at Yaounde.

Pres. Ahmadou Ahidjo and Flag – A53

Design: 18fr, Flag and map of Cameroun.

1963, Oct. 1 *Perf. 12x12½*

Flag in Green, Red and Yellow

389	A53	9fr grn, bl & dk brn	15	15
390	A53	18fr grn, bl & lil	30	25
391	A53	20fr grn, blk & yel grn	35	30

Second anniversary of reunification.

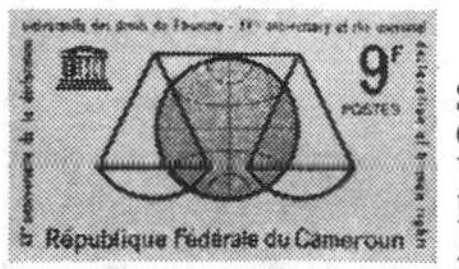

Scales, Globe, UNESCO Emblem A54

1963, Dec. 10 Photo. *Perf. 12½x12*

392	A54	9fr ultra, blk & sal	15	12
393	A54	18fr brt yel grn, blk & rose red	30	20
394	A54	25fr rose red, blk & brt yel grn	40	30
395	A54	75fr yel, blk & ultra	1.35	75

Issued to commemorate the 15th anniversary of the Universal Declaration of Human Rights.

Animal Type of 1962

Design: 10fr, 25fr, Lion, Waza National Park, North Cameroun.

1964, June 20 Engr. *Perf. 13*

396	A46	10fr red brn, bis & grn	25	10
397	A46	25fr grn & bis	50	25

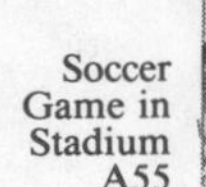

Soccer Game in Stadium A55

Designs: 18fr, Pile of sports equipment. 30fr, Stadium (outside), flags and map of Africa.

1964, July 11 Engr. *Perf. 13*

398	A55	10fr grn, bl & red brn	20	10
399	A55	18fr car, grn & vio	30	20
400	A55	30fr blk, dk bl & org brn	50	30

Tropics Cup Games, Yaounde, July 11-19.

Europafrica Issue, 1964

Common Design Type and

Palace of Justice, Yaounde – A56

Design: 40fr, Emblems of Science, Agriculture, Industry and Education and two sunbursts.

1964, July 20 Photo. *Perf. 12x13*

401	A56	15fr multi	50	40
402	CD116	40fr multi	1.00	85

Issued to commemorate the first anniversary of the economic agreement between the European Economic Community and the African and Malgache Union.

Hurdling and Olympic Flame – A57

Design: 10fr, Runners (vert.).

1964, Oct. 10 Engr. *Perf. 13*

403	A57	9fr red, yel grn & blk	85	60
404	A57	10fr red, vio & ol gray	85	60

18th Olympic Games, Tokyo, Oct. 10-25. See Nos. C49, C49a.

Bamileke Dance Dress – A58

Ntem Falls, Ebolowa Region – A59

Designs: 18fr, Dance mask, Bamenda region. 25fr, Fulani horseman, North Cameroun (horiz.).

1964 Unwmk. *Perf. 13*

405	A58	9fr red, yel grn & bl	15	10
406	A58	18fr bl, red & brn	30	20
407	A59	20fr dk car, grn & ol	35	20
408	A58	25fr dk brn, org & car	45	30

See also No. C50.

Cooperation Issue

Common Design Type

1964, Nov. 7 Engr.

409	CD119	18fr dk bl, yel grn & dk brn	35	20
410	CD119	30fr red brn, bl grn & dk brn	60	25

Memorial Stone – A60

Diesel Train A61

1965, Jan. 1 Engr. *Perf. 13*

411	A60	12fr bl, ind & grn	25	15

Typo. *Perf. 14x13*

412	A61	20fr rose car, yel & grn	40	20

Issued to commemorate the laying of the first rail of the Mbanga-Kumba Railroad, March 28, 1964.

Red Cross Station and Ambulance A62

Design: 50fr, Red Cross nurse and infant (vert.).

1965, May 8 Engr. *Perf. 13*

413	A62	25fr car, sl grn & ocher	45	25
414	A62	50fr gray, red & red brn	90	45

Issued for the Cameroun Red Cross.

Coins Inserted in Map of Cameroun, and Bankbook – A63

Savings Bank Building – A64

Design: 20fr, Bankbook and coins inserted in cacao pod-shaped bank (horiz.).

1965, June 10

Size: 22x37mm.

415	A63	9fr grn, red & org	20	20

Size: 48x27mm., 27x48mm

416	A64	15fr choc, ultra & grn	30	25
417	A63	20fr ocher, brt grn & brn	35	30

Federal Postal Savings Banks.

Soccer Players and Africa Cup – A65

Unwmk.

1965, June 26 Engr. *Perf. 13*

418	A65	9fr car, brn & yel	20	15
419	A65	20fr car, sl bl & yel	35	25

Issued to honor the Cameroun Oryx Club, winner of the club champions' Africa Cup, February 1965.

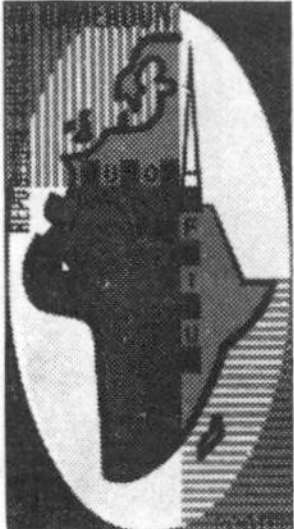

Symbolic Map of Europe and Africa – A66

Designs: 40fr, Delegates around conference table.

1965, July 20 Photo. *Perf. 12x12½*

420	A66	5fr car, blk & lil	10	10
421	A66	40fr brn, buff, grn & ultra	70	50

Issued to commemorate the second anniversary of the economic agreement between the European Economic Community and the African and Malgache Union.

UPU Monument, Bern – A67

1965, July 26 Engr. *Perf. 13*

422	A67	30fr blk & red	55	40

Issued to commemorate the fifth anniversary of Cameroun's admission to the UPU.

ICY Emblem – A68

1965, Sept. 11 Unwmk. *Perf. 13*

423	A68	10fr dk bl & car rose	25	25

Issued for the International Cooperation Year, 1964-65. See also No. C57.

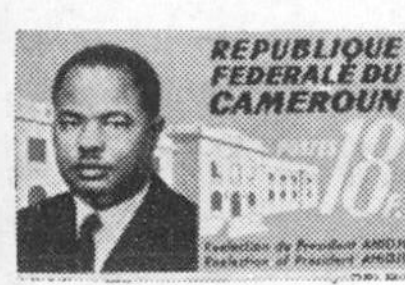

Pres. Ahidjo and Government House A69

Design: 9fr, 20fr, Pres. Ahidjo and Government House (vert.).

Perf. 12x12½, 12½x12

1965, Oct. 1 Photo. Unwmk.

Portrait in Dark Brown; Building in Gray

424	A69	9fr dp red, brt pink, & brt bl	15	12
425	A69	18fr brt yel & blk	30	18
426	A69	20fr vio bl, brt bl & org	35	20
427	A69	25fr yel grn & blk	45	25

Reelection of Pres. Ahmadou Ahidjo.

National Tourist Office, Yaounde A70

Designs: 9fr, Pouss Musgum houses. 18fr, Great Calao's dance (North Cameroun). 20fr, Gate of Sultan's Palace, Foumban (vert.).

1965 Engr. *Perf. 13*

428	A70	9fr brn, rose red & grn	15	10
429	A70	18fr brt bl, brn & grn	30	25
430	A70	20fr bl, brn & choc	35	20
431	A70	25fr mar, emer & gray	35	20

See also No. C58.

Mountain Hotel, Buea — A71

Designs: 20fr, Hotel of the Deputies, Yaounde. 35fr, Dschang Health Center.

1966

432	A71	9fr sl grn, rose cl & brn	20	15
433	A71	20fr brt bl, sl grn & blk	35	20
434	A71	35fr brn, sl grn & car	60	45
		Nos. 432-434,C63-C69 (10)	8.55	4.75

Issue dates: Nos. 432-433, Apr. 6; No. 434, June 4.

Bas-relief, Foumban A72

Designs: 18fr, Ekoi mask (vert.). 20fr,Mother and child, carving, Bamileke (vert.). 25fr, Ceremonial stool, Bamoun.

1966, Apr. 15 Unwmk.

435	A72	9fr red & blk	25	15
436	A72	18fr brt grn, org brn & choc	35	25
437	A72	20fr brt bl, red brn & pur	45	25
438	A72	25fr pur & dk brn	50	30

Issued to commemorate the International Negro Arts Festival, Dakar, Senegal, Apr. 1-24.

WHO Headquarters, Geneva — A73

1966, May 3 Photo. *Perf. 12½x13*

439	A73	50fr ultra, red brn & yel	85	50

Issued to commemorate the inauguration of the World Health Organization Headquarters, Geneva.

ITU Headquarters, Geneva — A74

1966, May 3 Photo. *Perf. 12½x13*

440	A74	50fr ultra & yel	85	50

Issued to publicize the International Telecommunication Union Headquarters, Geneva.

Phaeomeria Magnifica A75

"6" and Men Dancing around U.N. Emblem A76

Flowers: 18fr, Hibiscus (rose of China). 20fr, Mountain rose.

1966, May 20 *Perf. 12x12½*

Flowers in Natural Colors

Size: 22x36mm.

441	A75	9fr red brn	15	10
442	A75	18fr green	30	15
443	A75	20fr dk grn	35	15
		Nos. 441-443,C70-C72 (6)	3.60	1.15

See also No. 469.

1966, Sept. 20 Engr. *Perf. 13*

Design: 50fr, U.N. General Assembly (horiz.).

444	A76	50fr ultra, grn & vio brn	85	20
445	A76	100fr red brn, grn & ultra	1.75	75

Issued to commemorate the 6th anniversary of Cameroun's admission to the United Nations.

Prime Minister's Residence, Buea — A77

Designs (Prime Minister's Residences): 18fr, at Yaounde, front view. 20fr, at Yaounde, side view. 25fr, at Buea, front view.

1966, Oct. 1 Photo.

446	A77	9fr multi	15	12
447	A77	18fr multi	30	18
448	A77	20fr multi	35	15
449	A77	25fr multi	40	25

5th anniversary of re-unification.

Learning to Write and UNESCO Emblem A78

Design: No. 451, Children's heads and UNICEF emblem.

1966, Nov. 24 Engr. *Perf. 13*

450	A78	50fr red lil, bl & brn	85	45
451	A78	50fr red lil, blk & brt bl	85	45

No. 450 commemorates the 20th anniversary of UNESCO (United Nations Educational, Scientific and Cultural Organization), No. 451 commemorates the 20th anniversary of UNICEF (United Nations International Children's Emergency Fund).

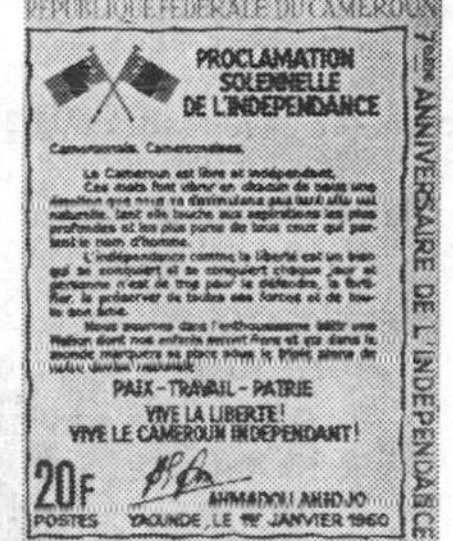

Independence Proclamation — A79

1967, Jan. 1 Engr. *Perf. 13*

452	A79	20fr grn, red & yel	45	35

7th anniversary of independence.

Map of Africa and Madagascar, Railroad Tracks and Symbols — A80

Design: 25fr, Map of Africa and Madagascar and train.

1967, Feb. 21 Photo. *Perf. 13*

453	A80	20fr multi	35	25
454	A80	25fr multi	45	25

Issued to commemorate the 5th Conference of African and Madagascan Railroad Technicians.

Lions Emblem and Forest — A81

Design: 100fr, Lions emblem and palms.

1967, Mar. 3

455	A81	50fr multi	85	50
456	A81	100fr multi	1.75	1.00

Lions International, 50th anniversary.

Jet and I.C.A.O. Emblem — A82

Dove and I.A.E.A. Emblem A83

Perf. 13x12½, 12½x13

1967, March 15 Photo.

457	A82	50fr ultra, lt bl, brn & gold	85	50
458	A83	50fr ultra & emer	85	50

Issued to honor United Nations agencies: No. 457, the International Civil Aviation Organization; No. 458, the International Atomic Energy Agency.

Rotary International Emblem A84

1967, Apr. 17 Photo. *Perf. 12½*

459	A84	25fr crim, vio bl & gold	45	25

Issued to commemorate the 10th anniversary of the Douala, Cameroun, branch of Rotary International.

Pomelo — A85

Bird-of-Paradise Flower — A86

Fruit: 2fr, Papaya. 3fr, Custard apple. 4fr, Breadfruit. 5fr, Coconut. 6fr, Mango. 8fr, Avocado. 10fr, Pineapple. 30fr, Bananas.

1967, May 10 Photo. *Perf. 12x12½*

460	A85	1fr multi	7	5
461	A85	2fr multi	7	5

462	A85	3fr multi	12	5
463	A85	4fr multi	12	5
464	A85	5fr multi	15	6
465	A85	6fr multi	20	6
466	A85	8fr multi	25	10
467	A85	10fr multi	30	12
468	A85	30fr multi	70	30
		Nos. 460-468 (9)	1.98	84

1967, June 22 Photo. *Perf. 12x12½*
Size: 22x36mm.

469	A86	15fr lt bl & multi	25	10

Sanaga Falls and ITY Emblem — A87

1967, Aug. 14 Photo. *Perf. 13x12½*

470	A87	30fr multi	50	30

Issued for International Tourist Year 1967.

Art of Cameroun: Coconut Harvest A88

Designs (Carved Bas-relief): 20fr, Lion hunt. 30fr, Women carrying baskets. 100fr, Carved chest.

1967, Sept. 22 *Perf. 12½x13*

471	A88	10fr brn, bl & car	15	10
472	A88	20fr brn, yel & grn	35	20
473	A88	30fr emer, brn & car	50	20
474	A88	100fr red org, brn & emer	1.75	70

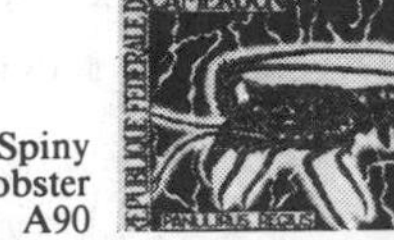

Coat of Arms A89

1968, Jan. 1 Litho. *Perf. 12½x13*

475	A89	30fr gold & multi	60	30

Spiny Lobster A90

Designs (Fish and Crustaceans): 10fr, River crayfish. 15fr, Nile mouth-breeder. 20fr, Sole. 25fr, Common pike. 30fr, Crab. 40fr, Spadefish (vert.). 50fr, Shrimp (vert.). 55fr, African snakehead. 60fr, Threadfin.

1968, July 25 Engr. *Perf. 13*

476	A90	5fr brn, vio bl & dl grn	10	5
477	A90	10fr ultra, brn ol & sl	15	6
478	A90	15fr sal, red lil & sep	20	10
479	A90	20fr red brn, dp bl & sep	25	12
480	A90	25fr lt brn, emer & sl	40	15
481	A90	30fr mag, dk bl & dk brn	50	15
482	A90	40fr sl bl & org	60	20
483	A90	50fr emer, gray & rose car	75	30
484	A90	55fr lt brn, Prus bl & dk brn	85	40
485	A90	60fr brn, bl grn & ind	1.00	50
		Nos. 476-485 (10)	4.80	2.03

Tanker, Refinery and Map of Area Served — A91

1968, July 30 Photo. *Perf. 12½*

486	A91	30fr multi	45	20

Issued to commemorate the opening of the Port Gentil (Gabon) Refinery, June 12, 1968.

Human Rights Flame A92

1968, Sept. 14 Photo. *Perf. 12½x13*

487	A92	15fr bl & sal	25	12

Issued for International Human Rights Year. See also No. C110.

Pres. Ahmadou Ahidjo A93

1969, Apr. 10 Photo. *Perf. 12½x12*

488	A93	30fr car & multi	45	20

Chocolate Vat — A94

Designs: 30fr, Chocolate factory. 50fr, Candy making (vert.).

1969, Apr. 24 Engr. *Perf. 13*

489	A94	15fr red brn, ind & choc	25	10
490	A94	30fr grn, blk & red brn	45	20
491	A94	50fr brn & multi	75	30

Cameroun chocolate industry.

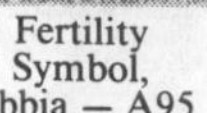

Fertility Symbol, Abbia — A95

Diesel Train on Bridge — A96

Art and Folklore from Abbia: 10fr, Two toucans (horiz.). 15fr, Forest symbol. 30fr, Vulture attacking monkey (horiz.). 70fr, Oliphant player.

1969, May 30 Engr. *Perf. 13*

492	A95	5fr ultra, Prus bl & brt rose lil	10	6
493	A95	10fr bl, ol gray & org	18	8
494	A95	15fr ultra, dk red & blk	20	15
495	A95	30fr brt bl, lem & grn	45	18
496	A95	70fr brt bl, dk grn & ver	1.10	50
		Nos. 492-496 (5)	2.03	97

Perf. 12½x13, 13x12½
1969, July 11 Photo.

Design: 30fr, Kumba Railroad station (horiz.).

497	A96	30fr bl & multi	45	20
498	A96	50fr blk & multi	85	40

Opening of Mbanga-Kumba Railroad.

Development Bank Issue
Common Design Type

1969, Sept. 10 Engr. *Perf. 13*

499	CD130	30fr vio bl, grn & ocher	50	20

Issued to commemorate the 5th anniversary of the African Development Bank.

ASECNA Issue
Common Design Type

1969, Dec. 12 Engr. *Perf. 13*

500	CD132	100fr sl grn	1.50	90

Red Sage — A99

Design: 30fr, Passionflower.

1970, Mar. 24 Photo. *Perf. 12x12½*
Size: 22x36½mm.

501	A99	15fr yel grn & multi	25	15
502	A99	30fr multi	40	15

See Nos. C140-C141.

U.P.U. Headquarters Issue
Common Design Type

1970, May 20 Engr. *Perf. 13*

503	CD133	30fr bl, pur & grn	45	18
504	CD133	50fr gray, red & bl	75	25

Brewery A100

> The Catalogue editors cannot undertake to appraise, identify or judge the genuineness or condition of stamps.

Design: 30fr, Cellar with barrels.

1970, July 9 Engr. *Perf. 13*

505	A100	15fr brn, gray & dk grn	20	15
506	A100	30fr bl grn, dk brn & brn red	40	15

Cameroun brewing industry.

Ozila Dancers — A101

Cameroun Doll — A102

Design: 50fr, Ozila dancer and drummer.

1970, Oct. 19 Engr. *Perf. 13*

507	A101	30fr multi	40	15
508	A101	50fr red & multi	75	30

1970, Nov. 2

Designs: 15fr, Doll in short skirt. 30fr, Doll with basket on back.

509	A102	10fr car & multi	20	12
510	A102	15fr dk grn & multi	28	15
511	A102	30fr brn red & multi	50	20

Cogwheels and Grain A103

1970, Feb. 9 Photo. *Perf. 13*

512	A103	30fr multi	40	20

Europafrica Economic Conference.

Federal University, Yaounde A104

1971, Jan. 19 Engr.

513	A104	50fr multi	60	20

Inauguration of Federal University at Yaounde.

Presidents Ahidjo and Pompidou, Flags of Cameroun and France — A105

1971, Feb. 9 Photo. *Perf. 13*
514 A105 30fr multi 60 50

Visit of Georges Pompidou, President of France.

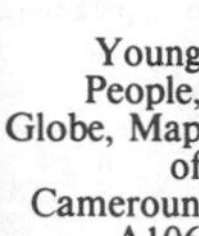

Young People, Globe, Map of Cameroun A106

1971, Feb. 11
515 A106 30fr bl & multi 35 13

Fifth National Youth Festival, Feb. 11.

Gerbera Hybrida — A107

Men of Four Races — A108

Designs: 40fr, Opuntia polyantha (cactus). 50fr, Hemerocallis hybrida (lily).

1971, Mar. 14 Photo.
516 A107 20fr multi 27 10
517 A107 40fr grn & multi 45 22
518 A107 50fr bl & multi 60 20

1971, March 21 *Perf. 13x12½*

Design: 30fr, Hands and globe.

519 A108 20fr grn & multi 25 7
520 A108 30fr ultra & multi 40 13

International year against racial discrimination.

Crowned Cranes at Waza Camp A109

Designs: 20fr, Canoe on Sanaga River. 30fr, Sanaga River.

1971, Apr. 9. Engr. *Perf. 13*
521 A109 10fr red, grn & blk 12 8
522 A109 20fr dk grn, brn & red 27 8
523 A109 30fr red, dk grn & brt bl 35 12

International Court, The Hague — A110

1971, June 14 Engr. *Perf. 13*
524 A110 50fr ultra, org brn & sl grn 60 25

25th anniversary of the International Court in The Hague, Netherlands.

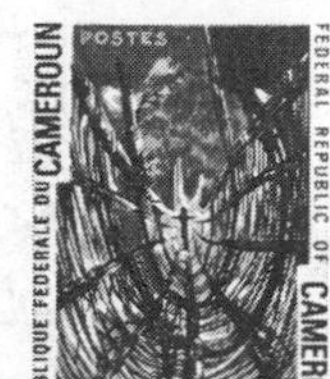

Liana Bridge — A111

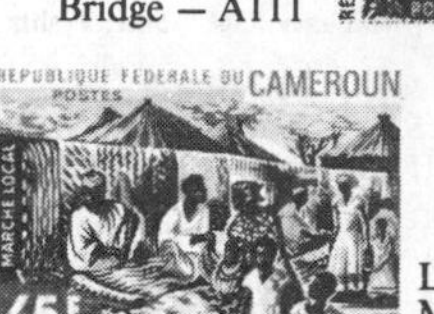

Local Market A112

Bamoun Horseman — A113

1971, Aug. 16 Photo. *Perf. 13*
525 A111 40fr multi 50 20
526 A112 45fr multi 55 20

1971, Sept. 18

African Art: 15fr, Animal fetish statuette.

527 A113 10fr brn & yel 12 5
528 A113 15fr dp brn & org yel 18 8

Communications Satellite and Globe — A114

1971, Oct. 14 *Perf. 13x12½*
529 A114 40fr Prus bl, sl grn & org 45 18

Pan-African telecommunications system.

UNICEF Emblem A115

Design: 50fr, UNICEF emblem and grain (vert.).

1971, Dec. 11 Engr. *Perf. 13*
530 A115 40fr sl grn, bl grn & plum 60 30
531 A115 50fr dp bl, dk red & lt grn 85 40

25th anniversary of the United Nations International Children's Fund (UNICEF).

Houses from South-Central Region — A116

Design: 15fr, Adamaua round houses.

1972, Jan. 15 Photo. *Perf. 13*
532 A116 10fr dk bl & multi 10 8
533 A116 15fr blk & multi 20 12

Giraffe — A117

Designs: 5fr, Home industries. 10fr, Smith (horiz.). 15fr, Women carrying burdens.

Perf. 13x13½, 13½x13
1972, Feb. 18 Litho.
534 A117 2fr multi 8 5
535 A117 5fr blk, org & red 12 5
536 A117 10fr multi 20 5
537 A117 15fr multi 25 10

Youth Day 1972.

Soccer Players and Field — A118

1972, Feb. 22 *Perf. 13½*

Designs: 20fr, African Soccer Cup (vert.). 45fr, Team captains shaking hands (vert.).

538 A118 20fr gray & multi 25 15
539 A118 40fr gray & multi 50 30
540 A118 45fr yel & multi 60 35

African Soccer Cup, Yaoundé, Feb. 23-Mar. 5.

Government Building, Yaoundé, and Laurel — A119

1972, Apr. 6 Photo. *Perf. 12½x12*
541 A119 40fr multi 35 20

110th session of Inter-Parliamentary Council, Yaoundé, Apr. 1972.

"Fantasia," North Cameroun A120

Bororo Woman — A121

Design: 40fr, Boat on Wouri River and Mt. Cameroun.

Perf. 13x12½, 12½x13
1972, Apr. 24
542 A120 15fr dk vio & multi 25 10
543 A121 20fr multi 25 10
544 A120 40fr multi 40 20

Chemical Apparatus A122

1972, May 15 Engr. *Perf. 13*
545 A122 40fr lil, red & grn 35 18

President Ahmadou Ahidjo Prize.

United Republic

Solanum Macranthum A123

Design: 45fr, Wax plant.

1972, July 20 Photo. *Perf. 13*
546 A123 40fr multi 40 18
547 A123 45fr yel & multi 42 20

Charaxes Ameliae A124

Design: 45fr, Papilio tynderaeus.

1972, Aug. 20 Photo. *Perf. 13*
548 A124 40fr bl, dk bl & gold 50 25
549 A124 45fr lt grn, blk & gold 55 30

No. 468 Surcharged

40 F

1972, Aug. 30 Photo. *Perf. 12x12½*
550 A85 40fr on 30fr multi 40 20

Resurrection Lily — A125

Great Blue Touraco — A126

Flowers: 45fr, Candlestick cassia. 50fr, Amaryllis.

1972, Sept. 16 *Perf. 13*

551 A125 40fr lt grn & multi 40 20
552 A125 45fr multi 45 25
553 A125 50fr lt bl & multi 55 30

Perf. 12½x13, 13x12½

1972, Nov. 20 **Litho.**

Design: 45fr, Red-faced lovebirds (horiz.).

554 A126 10fr yel & multi 10 7
555 A126 45fr yel & multi 45 20

Cotton (North) — A127

Designs: 10fr, Cacao (south central). 15fr, Logging (southeast and southern coast). 20fr, Coffee (west). 45fr, Tea (northwest and southwest).

1973, Mar. 26 Photo. ***Perf. 12½x13***

556 A127 5fr blk & multi 6 6
557 A127 10fr blk & multi 8 8
558 A127 15fr blk & multi 13 10
559 A127 20fr blk & multi 18 15
560 A127 45fr blk & multi 45 20
Nos. 556-560 (5) 90 59

Third 5-Year Plan.

Flag and Map of Cameroun, Pres. Ahidjo and No. 331 — A128

Design: 20fr, Proclamation of independence, Pres. Ahidjo and No. 336.

1973, May 20 **Engr.** ***Perf. 13***

561 A128 10fr ultra & multi 10 10
562 A128 20fr multi 20 12

First anniversary of the United Republic of Cameroun. See Nos. C200-C201.

Bamoun Mask — A129 Dr. Hansen — A130

Designs: Various Bamoun masks.

1973, July 10 **Engr.** ***Perf. 13***

563 A129 5fr grn, brn & blk 5 5
564 A129 10fr lil, brn & blk 10 6
565 A129 45fr red, brn & blk 35 20
566 A129 100fr ultra, brn & blk 80 50

1973, July 25 **Engr.** ***Perf. 13***

567 A130 45fr multi 40 20

Centenary of the discovery by Dr. Armauer G. Hansen of the Hansen bacillus, the cause of leprosy.

No. 556 Surcharged with New Value, 2 Bars, and Overprinted in Ultramarine: "SECHERESSE/SOLIDARITE AFRICAINE"

1973, Aug. 16 Photo. ***Perf. 12½x13***

568 A127 100fr on 5fr multi 80 60

African solidarity in drought emergency.

Dancers, South West Africa — A131

WMO Emblem — A132

Designs: Southwest African dances.

1973, Aug. 17 ***Perf. 13***

569 A131 10fr multi 8 6
570 A131 25fr multi 20 15
571 A131 45fr multi 45 20

1973, Sept. 1 **Engr.** ***Perf. 13***

572 A132 45fr grn & ultra 40 25

Centenary of international meteorological cooperation.

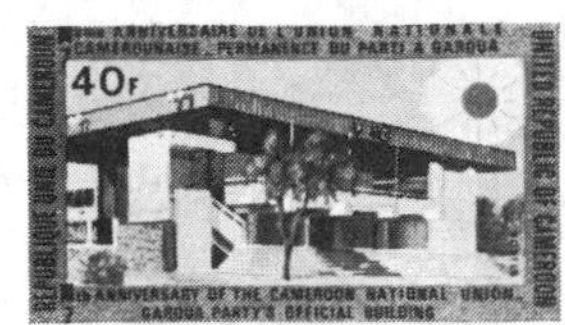

Garoua Party Headquarters — A133

1973, Sept. 1 **Photo.**

573 A133 40fr multi 40 25

7th anniversary of Cameroun National Union.

African Postal Union Issue, 1973

Common Design Type

1973, Sept. 12 **Engr.**

574 CD137 100fr brt bl, bl & sl grn 90 60

11th anniversary of African and Malagasy Posts and Telecommunications Union (UAMPT).

Avocados — A135

1973, Sept. 20

575 A135 10fr *shown* 15 6
576 A135 20fr *Mangos* 25 13
577 A135 45fr *Plums* 45 20
578 A135 50fr *Custard apple* 65 25

Kirdi Village A136.

Views: 45fr, Mabas village. 50fr, Fishing village.

1973, Oct. 25 **Engr.** ***Perf. 13***

579 A136 15fr blk, bis & grn 20 10
580 A136 45fr mag, brn & org 45 25
581 A136 50fr grn, blk & org 50 30

Handshake on Map of Africa — A137

1974, May 15 **Engr.** ***Perf. 12½x13***

582 A137 40fr car & multi 35 18
583 A137 45fr ind & multi 40 20

10th anniversary of the Organization for African Unity.

Spinning Mill A138

1974, May 25 **Engr.** ***Perf. 13x12½***

584 A138 45fr multi 40 25

CICAM Industrial Complex.

Carved Panel from Bilinga A139

Cameroun Art (Carvings): 40fr, Detail from Bubinga chair. 45fr, Detail Acajou Ngollon panel.

1974, May 30

585 A139 10fr brt grn & ocher 10 6
586 A139 40fr red & brn 35 20
587 A139 45fr bl & rose brn 40 25

Zebu — A140

1974, June 1 ***Perf. 13½***

588 A140 40fr multi 35 23

North Cameroun cattle raising. See No. C210.

Laying Rail Section A141

Designs: 5fr, Map showing line Yaoundéto Ngaoundéré (vert.). 40fr, Welding rail joint (vert.). 100fr, Train on Djerem River Bridge.

Perf. 12½x13, 13x12½

1974, June 10 **Engr.**

589 A141 5fr multi 8 5
590 A141 20fr multi 18 10
591 A141 40fr multi 35 20
592 A141 100fr multi 85 65

Opening of Yaoundé-Ngaoundéré railroad line.

No. 466 Surcharged

1974, June 1 Photo. ***Perf. 12x12½***

593 A85 40fr on 8fr multi 40 20

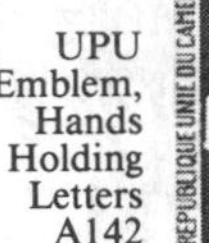

UPU Emblem, Hands Holding Letters A142

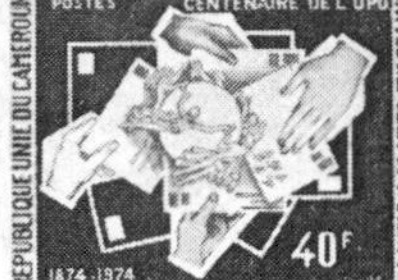

1974, Oct. 8 **Engr.** ***Perf. 13***

594 A142 40fr multi 28 18

Centenary of Universal Postal Union. See Nos. C218-C219.

Presidents and Flags of Cameroun, CAR, Congo, Gabon and Meeting Center — A143

1974, Dec. 8 **Photo.** ***Perf. 13***

595 A143 40fr gold & multi 35 20

10th anniversary of Central African Customs and Economic Union (Union Douanière et Economique de l'Afrique Centrale, UDEAC). See also No. C223.

=100F

No. 589 Surcharged in Violet Blue

10 DECEMBRE 1974

1974, Dec. 10 **Engr.** ***Perf. 12½x13***

596 A141 100fr on 5fr multi 80 70

Catalogue prices for unused stamps up to mid-1953 are for hinged copies matching the condition specified in this volume's introduction.

Virgin of Autun, 15th Century Sculpture A144

Design: 45fr, Virgin and Child, by Luis de Morales (c. 1509-1586).

1974, Dec. 20 **Photo.** ***Perf. 13***
597 A144 40fr gold & multi 35 25
598 A144 45fr gold & multi 40 30

Christmas 1974.

Cockscomb A145

1975, Mar. 10 **Photo.** ***Perf. 13***
599 A145 5fr *shown* 8 5
600 A145 40fr *Costus spectabilis* 35 20
601 A145 45fr *Mussaenda erythrophylla* 38 25

Tropical plants.

Fishing by Night — A146

Design: 45fr, Fishing by day.

1975, Apr. 1 **Engr.** ***Perf. 13***
602 A146 40fr bl & multi 35 20
603 A146 45fr bl & multi 40 25

Afo Akom Statue and Chief's Stool — A147

1975, Apr. 1 **Photo.**
604 A147 40fr multi 30 20
605 A147 45fr multi 35 20
606 A147 200fr multi 1.60 1.10

Tree Fungus — A148

Design: 40fr, Chrysalis.

1975, Apr. 14
607 A148 15fr brn & multi 15 10
608 A148 40fr blk & multi 40 23

Ministry of Posts and Telecommunications — A149

1975, July 21 **Engr.** ***Perf. 13***
609 A149 40fr brn, grn & Prus bl 35 25
610 A149 45fr Prus bl, brn & grn 40 30

Presbyterian Church, Elat — A150

Designs: No. 612, Foumban Mosque. 45fr, Catholic Church, Ngaoundere.

1975, Aug. 20 **Engr.** ***Perf. 13***
611 A150 40fr multi 32 20
612 A150 40fr multi 32 20
613 A150 45fr multi 38 25

Plowing A151

Design: No. 615, Corn harvest (vert.).

Perf. 13x12½, 12½x13
1975, Dec. 15 **Photo.**
614 A151 40fr dp grn & multi 32 20
615 A151 40fr dp grn & multi 32 20

Green revolution.

Zamengoe Satellite Monitoring Station — A152

Design: 100fr, Radar (vert.).

1976, May 20 **Litho.** ***Perf. 13***
616 A152 40fr multi 30 25
617 A152 100fr multi 85 60

Porcelain Rose — A153

Design: 50fr, Flower of North Cameroun.

1976, July 20 **Litho.** ***Perf. 12½***
618 A153 40fr multi 30 20
619 A153 50fr multi 40 25

Leopard Dance — A154

Telephone Exchange — A155

1976, Sept. 15 **Litho.** ***Perf. 12***
620 A154 40fr gray & multi 32 25

See Nos. C233-C234.

1976, Oct. 5 ***Perf. 13***
621 A155 50fr multi 45 30

Centenary of first telephone call by Alexander Graham Bell, Mar. 10, 1876.

Young Men Building House — A156

Design: 45fr, Young women working in field.

1976, Oct. 10 **Litho.** ***Perf. 12***
622 A156 40fr multi 32 25
623 A156 45fr multi 40 30

10th National Youth Day.

Konrad Adenauer, Cologne Cathedral — A157

1976, Oct. 20
624 A157 100fr multi 85 60

Konrad Adenauer (1876-1967), German chancellor, birth centenary.

Party Headquarters, Douala — A158

Design: No. 626, Party Headquarters, Yaounde.

1976, Dec. 28 **Litho.** ***Perf. 12***
625 A158 50fr org & multi 40 30
626 A158 50fr bl & multi 40 30

10th anniversary of the Cameroun National Union.

Bamoun Copper Pipe — A159

Ostrich — A160

1977, Feb. 4 **Litho.** ***Perf. 12½***
627 A159 50fr multi 40 30

2nd World Black and African Festival, Lagos, Nigeria, Jan. 15-Feb. 12. See No. C239.

1977, Mar. 20 **Litho.** ***Perf. 12***

Design: 50fr, Crowned cranes.

628 A160 30fr multi 25 15
629 A160 50fr multi 40 25

Cameroun No. 609 and Switzerland No. 3L1 — A161

1977, June 5 **Litho.** ***Perf. 12***
630 A161 50fr multi 40 30

Jufilex Philatelic Exhibition, Bern, Switzerland. See Nos. C252-C253.

No. 617 Overprinted in French and English in Red: "To the Welfare of the / families of martyrs and / freedom fighters of Palestine."

1977, Aug. 22 **Litho.** ***Perf. 13***
635 A152 100fr multi 85 60

Palestinian fighters and their families.

Certain countries cancel stamps in full sheets and sell them (usually with gum) for less than face value. Dealers generally sell "CTO".

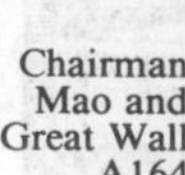

Chairman Mao and Great Wall
A164

1977, Sept. 9 **Engr.** ***Perf. 13***
636 A164 100fr ol & brn 85 60

Mao Tse-tung (1893-1976), Chinese communist leader, first death anniversary.

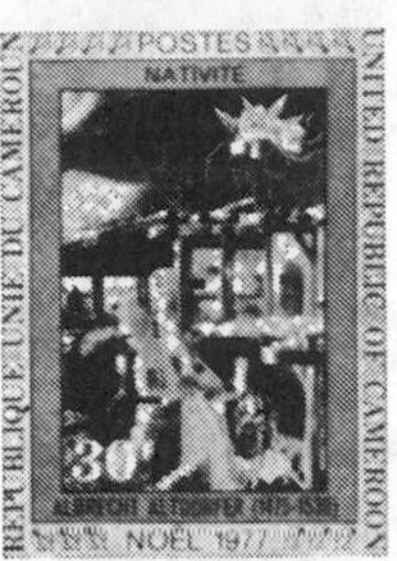

Nativity, by Albrecht Altdorfer
A165

Design: 50fr, Madonna of the Grand Duke, by Raphael.

1977, Dec. 15 **Litho.** ***Perf. 12½x12***
637 A165 30fr multi 25 20
638 A165 50fr multi 40 30

Christmas 1977. See Nos. C264-C265.

Gazelle and Rotary Emblem
A166

Pres. Ahidjo, Flag and Map of Cameroun
A167

1978, Feb. 11 **Litho.** ***Perf. 12***
639 A166 50fr org & multi 40 30

Rotary Club of Yaounde, 20th anniversary.

1978, Apr. 3 **Litho.** ***Perf. 12½***
640 A167 50fr multi 40 20

New flag of Cameroun. See No. C266.

Cardioglossa Escalerae — A168

Design: 60fr, Cardioglossa elegans.

1978, Apr. 5
641 A168 50fr multi 40 25
642 A168 60fr multi 50 35

See No. C267.

> Canceled-to-order stamps are often from remainders. Most collectors of canceled stamps prefer postally used specimens.

Jules Verne and "From Earth to Moon" — A169

1978, Oct. 10 **Litho.** ***Perf. 12***
643 A169 250fr multi 2.50 2.00

Jules Verne (1828-1905), science fiction writer, birth sesquicentennial. See No. C276.

Hypolimnas Salmacis Drury — A170

Butterflies: 25fr, Euxanthe trajanus ward. 30fr, Euphaedra cyparissa cramer.

1978, Oct. 15
644 A170 20fr multi 20 15
645 A170 25fr multi 25 20
646 A170 30fr multi 30 20

Men Planting Seedlings — A171

1978, Oct. 30 ***Perf. 12½***
647 A171 10fr multi 10 8
648 A171 15fr multi 15 10

Green barrier against the desert.

Carved Bamun Drum — A172

Designs: 60fr, String instrument (Gueguerou; horiz.).

1978, Nov. 20 **Litho.** ***Perf. 12½***
649 A172 50fr multi 50 30
650 A172 60fr multi 60 40

See No. C277.

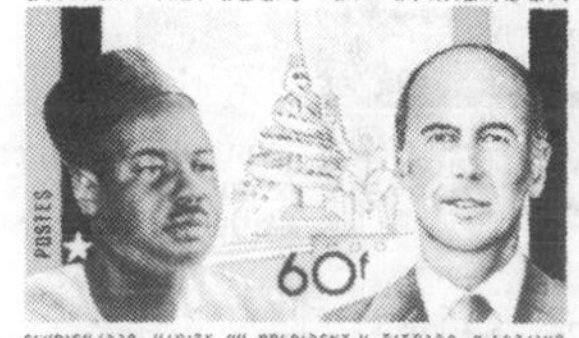

Pres. Ahidjo, Giscard D'Estaing, Flags of Cameroun and France — A173

1979, Feb. 8 **Photo.** ***Perf. 13***
651 A173 60fr multi 60 40

Visit of Pres. Valery Giscard D'Estaing of France to Cameroun.

Human Rights Emblem, Globe, Scroll and African — A174

1979, Feb. 11 **Litho.** ***Perf. 12x12½***
652 A174 5fr multi 5 5

Universal Declaration of Human Rights, 30th anniversary (in 1978). See No. C278. See No. 803.

Boy and Girl Greeting Sun — A175

1979, Aug. 15 **Litho.** ***Perf. 12***
653 A175 50fr multi 50 30

International Year of the Child.

Protected Animals
A176

Nos. 655, 658 vert.

1979, Sept. 20 ***Perf. 12½***
654 A176 50fr Rhinoceros 50 30
655 A176 60fr Giraffe 60 40
656 A176 60fr Gorilla 60 40
657 A176 100fr Leopard 1.00 60
658 A176 100fr Elephant 1.00 60
Nos. 654-658 (5) 3.70 2.30

Eugene Jamot, Map of Cameroun, Tsetse Fly — A177

1979, Nov. 5 **Engr.** ***Perf. 13***
659 A177 50fr multi 50 30

Eugene Jamot (1879-1937), discoverer of sleeping sickness cure.

Annunciation, by Fra Filippo Lippi — A178

Paintings; 50fr, Rest During the Flight to Egypt, C. 1620. No. 622, Flight into Egypt, by Jan Joest, No. 663, Nativity, by Joest. 100fr, Nativity, by Botticelli.

1979, Dec. 6 **Litho.** ***Perf. 12½x12***
660 A178 10fr multi 10 6
661 A178 50fr multi 55 35
662 A178 60fr multi 65 45
663 A178 60fr multi 65 45
664 A178 100fr multi 1.10 65
Nos. 660-664 (5) 3.05 1.96

Christmas 1979. Nos. 662-663 printed se-tenant.

Piper Capense
A179

Medicinal Plants: 60fr, Bracken fern.

1979, Dec. 15 **Litho.** ***Perf. 12½***
665 A179 50fr multi 50 30
666 A179 60fr multi 60 40

Pres. Ahidjo, Cameroun Map, Arms and No. 331 — A180

1980, Feb. 12 **Litho.** ***Perf. 12½***
667 A180 50fr multi 50 30

Independence, 20th anniversary.

Congress Building, Bafoussam
A181

1980, Feb. 12
668 A181 50fr multi 50 30

Cameroun National Union, 3rd Ordinary Congress, Bafoussam, Feb. 12-17.

Rotary Emblem, Map of Cameroun — A182

Rotary International, 75th Anniversary: No. 670, Anniversary emblem.

1980, Mar. 15 Litho. *Perf. 12½*

669	A182	200fr multi	2.00	1.20
670	A182	200fr multi	2.00	1.20
a.		Souvenir sheet of 2	4.00	2.50

No. 670a contains Nos. 669-670; multicolored margin shows emblems of various Rotary clubs. Size: 175x140mm.

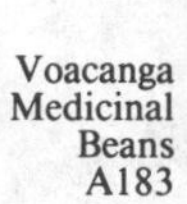

Voacanga Medicinal Beans A183

1980, Dec. 3 Litho. *Perf. 12½*

671	A183	50fr *shown*	50	30
672	A183	60fr *Voacanga tree,* vert.	60	40
673	A183	100fr *Voacanga flower,* vert.	1.00	60

Violet Mellowstone A184

1980, Dec. 5

674	A184	50fr *shown*	60	30
675	A184	60fr *Patula*	70	40
676	A184	100fr *Cashmere bouquet*	1.25	60

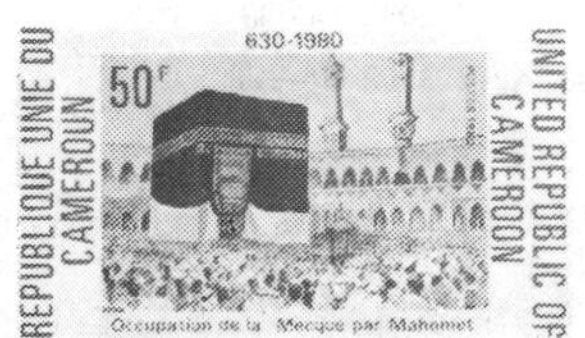
Occupation of Mecca by Mohammed, 1350th Anniversary — A185

1980, Dec. 9

677	A185	50fr multi	50	30

African Slender-snouted Crocodile (Endangered Species) — A186

1980, Dec. 24

678	A186	200fr *shown*	2.50	1.20
679	A186	300fr *Buffon's antelope,* vert.	3.25	1.80

Bororo Girls and Roumsiki Peaks — A187

1980, Dec. 29

680	A187	50fr *shown*	50	30
681	A187	60fr *Dschang tourist center*	60	40

Banana Tree A188

1981, Feb. 5

682	A188	50fr *shown*	50	30
683	A188	60fr *Cattle,* vert.	60	40

Girl on Crutches — A189

1981, Feb. 20 Litho. *Perf. 12½*

684	A189	60fr shown	60	40
685	A189	150fr Boy in motorized wheelchair	1.50	1.00

International Year of the Disabled.

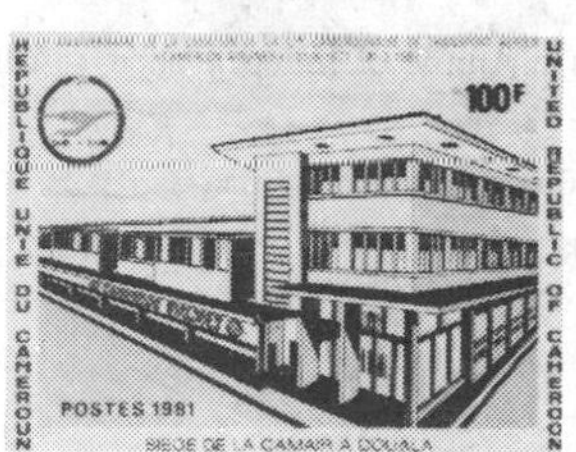
Air Terminal, Douala Airport — A190

1981, Apr. 4 Litho. *Perf. 12½*

686	A190	100fr shown	1.00	65
687	A190	200fr Boeing 747	2.00	1.40
688	A190	300fr Douala Intl. Airport	3.00	2.00

Cameroun Airlines, 10th anniv.

Pres. Ahidjo Presenting Trophy to Canon Soccer Team — A191

Prices of premium quality never hinged stamps will be in excess of catalogue price.

1981, Apr. 20

689	A191	60fr shown	60	40
690	A191	60fr Union team captain	60	40

1979 African Soccer Cup champions.

Scaly Anteater A192

Designs: Endangered species.

1981, July 20 Litho. *Perf. 12½*

691	A192	50fr Moutourou	50	32
692	A192	50fr Tortoise	50	32
693	A192	100fr shown	1.00	65

Prince Charles and Lady Diana, St. Paul's Cathedral — A193

1981, July 29 Litho. *Perf. 12½*

694	A193	500fr shown	4.50	3.00
695	A193	500fr Couple, royal coach	4.50	3.00
a.		Souvenir sheet of 2	9.00	6.00

Royal wedding. No. 695a contains Nos. 694-695; multicolored margin shows flowers. Size: 145x94mm.

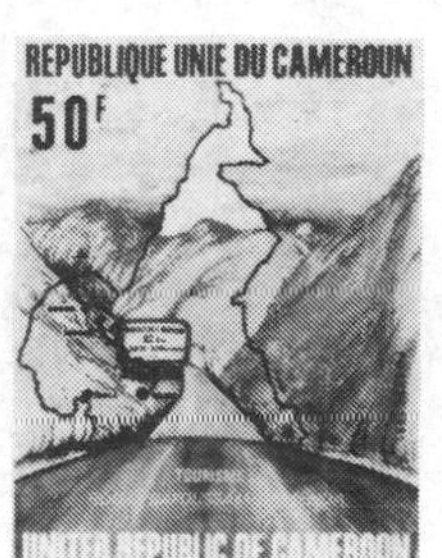
Bafoussam-Bamenda Highway — A194

1981, Sept. 10 Litho. *Perf. 12½*

696	A194	50fr multi	50	32

Freighter Cam Iroko (Cameroun Shipping Line) A195

1981, Sept. 25

697	A195	60fr multi	60	40

20th Anniv. of Reunification — A196

1981, Oct. 10 *Perf. 12½x13*

698	A196	50fr multi	50	32

Medicinal Plants — A197

1981, Dec. 31 Litho. *Perf. 12½*

699	A197	60fr Voacanga thouarsii	60	40
700	A197	70fr Cassia alata	70	45

Easter 1982 — A198

Paintings: 100fr, Christ in the Garden of Olives, by Delacroix. 200fr, Descent from the Cross, by Giotto. 250fr, Pieta in the Countryside, by Bellini.

1982, Apr. 10 Litho. *Perf. 13*

701	A198	100fr multi	80	50
702	A198	200fr multi	1.50	1.00
703	A198	250fr multi	2.00	1.40

PHILEXFRANCE '82 Stamp Exhibition, Paris, June 11-21 — A199

1982, Apr. 25 *Perf. 12*

704	A199	90fr multi	90	60

Snakeskin Handbag — A200

1982, Apr. 30 *Perf. 12½*

705	A200	60fr shown	60	40
706	A200	70fr Clay water jug	70	50

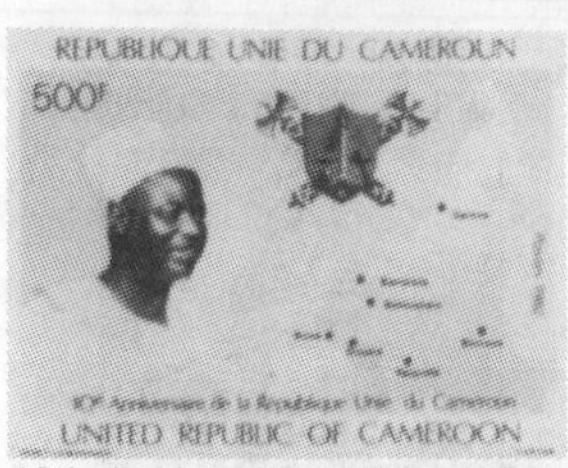

10th Anniv. of Republic — A201

1982, May 20 *Perf. 13*
707 A201 500fr multi 5.00 3.00

Town Hall, Douala — A202

1982, June 15 Litho. *Perf. 12½*
708 A202 40fr shown 40 30
709 A202 60fr Yaounde 60 40

See Nos. 730-731, 757-758, 790-791.

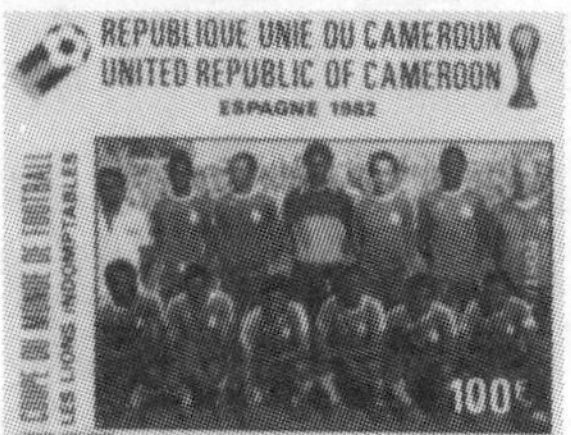

1982 World Cup — A203

1982, July 10 *Perf. 13*
710 A203 100fr Natl. team 1.00 65
711 A203 200fr Semi-finalists 2.00 1.20
712 A203 300fr Players, vert. 3.00 1.90
713 A203 400fr Natl. team 2nd line-up 4.00 2.50
a. Souvenir sheet of 2 9.00 5.00

No. 713a contains 2 Nos. 713; multicolored margin. Size: 217x95mm.

Partridge — A204

1982 *Perf. 12½x13*
714 A204 10fr shown 10 6
715 A204 15fr Turtle dove 15 10
716 A204 20fr Swallow 20 12
717 A204 200fr Bongo antelope 2.00 1.20
718 A204 300fr Black colobus 3.00 1.90
Nos. 714-718 (5) 5.45 3.38

Issue dates: 200fr, 300fr, July 20; others Aug. 10.
See No. 804.

Scouting Year A205

1982, Sept. 30 Litho. *Perf. 13x12½*
719 A205 200fr Campfire 1.75 1.20
720 A205 400fr Baden-Powell 3.50 2.50

25th Anniv. of the Presbyterian Church in Cameroun — A206

Perf. 13x12½, 12½x13
1982, Oct. 30
721 A206 45fr Buea Chapel 35 20
722 A206 60fr Nyasoso Chapel, vert. 45 30

ITU Plenipotentiaries Conference, Nairobi, Sept. — A207

1982, Oct. 5 Litho. *Perf. 12½x13*
723 A207 70fr multi 50 35

Italy's Victory in 1982 World Cup — A208

1982, Nov. *Perf. 13*
724 A208 500fr multi 5.75 3.00
725 A208 1000fr multi 11.00 6.00

30th Anniv. of Customs Cooperation Council — A209

1983, Jan. 10 *Perf. 12½x13*
726 A209 250fr Emblem 2.00 1.25
727 A209 250fr Headquarters, Brussels 2.00 1.25

2nd Yaounde Medical Conference — A210

1983, Jan. 23 Litho. *Perf. 13*
728 A210 60fr grn & multi 70 30
729 A210 70fr brn & multi 80 35

City Hall Type of 1982

1983, Feb. 25 Litho. *Perf. 12½*
730 A202 60fr Bafoussam 60 40
731 A202 70fr Garoua 70 45

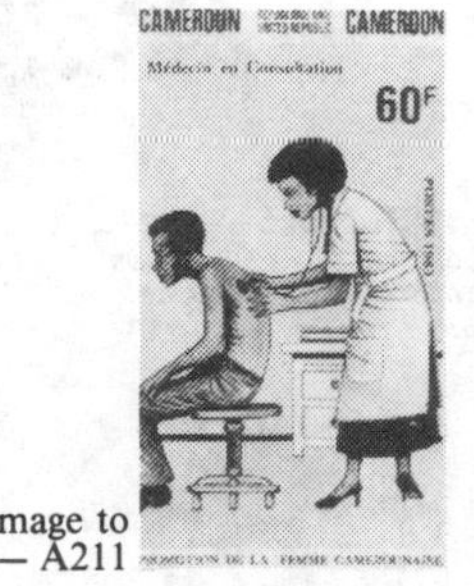

Homage to Women — A211

1983, Apr. 25 Litho. *Perf. 12½*
733 A211 60fr Nurse 60 30
734 A211 70fr Lawyer 70 35

11th Anniv. of Independence — A212

Flag and Pres. Paul Biya.

1983, May 18 Litho. *Perf. 13*
735 A212 60fr dk grn & multi 60 40
736 A212 70fr dk bl & multi 70 45

25th Anniv. of Intl. Maritime Org. A213

1983, May 23 *Perf. 13x12½*
737 A213 500fr multi 3.75 2.25

Eagle — A214

1983, June 15 Litho. *Perf. 12½x13*
738 A214 25fr shown 25 15
739 A214 30fr Sparrowhawk 30 20
740 A214 50fr Purple heron 50 30

Pearl Mask, by Wery-Nwen-Nto, 1899 — A215

1983, July 25 Litho. *Perf. 12*
741 A215 60fr shown 60 40
742 A215 70fr Basket with lid 70 45

World Communications Year — A216

1983, Aug. 20 Litho. *Perf. 12*
743 A216 90fr Mobile Post Office (horiz.) 45 30
744 A216 150fr Telegraph Operator 75 50
745 A216 250fr Tom-Tom 1.25 80

Endangered Species — A217

1983, Sept. 22 *Perf. 12*
746 A217 200fr Civet Cat 1.25 65
747 A217 200fr Gorilla (vert.) 1.25 65
748 A217 350fr Cobaya (vert.) 2.00 1.25

Lake Tizon A218

1983, Nov. 25 Litho. *Perf. 13*
749 A218 60fr shown 30 22
750 A218 70fr Mt. Cameroon 35 25

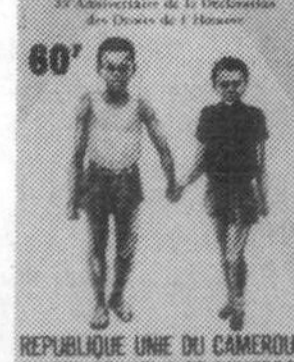

Human Rights Declaration, 35th Anniv — A219

1983, Dec. 20 Litho. *Perf. 12½x13*

751 A219 60fr multi 30 22
752 A219 70fr multi 35 25

Christmas 1983 — A220

Designs: 60fr, Christmas tree. 200fr, Stainedglass window, Yaounde Cathedral. No. 755, Rest during Flight into Egypt, by Philipp Otto Runge. No. 756, Angel of the Annunciation. 60fr, 200fr, No. 756 vert.

1983, Dec. 20 Litho. *Perf. 12½*

753 A220 60fr multi 30 22
754 A220 200fr multi 1.00 65
755 A220 500fr multi 2.50 1.60
756 A220 500fr multi 2.50 1.60
a. Souvenir sheet of 3 6.00 4.00

No. 756a contains Nos. 754-756. Size: 140x90mm.

City Hall Type of 1982

1984, Apr. 20 Litho. *Perf. 12½*

757 A202 60fr Bamenda 30 20
758 A202 70fr Mbalmayo 35 22

Catholic Church, Zoetele — A221

1984, July 25 Litho. *Perf. 13*

759 A221 60fr shown 30 22
760 A221 70fr Protestant Church, Yaounde 35 25

Endangered Species — A222

1984, Aug. 15

761 A222 250fr Wild pig 1.25 80
762 A222 250fr Deer 1.25 80

1984, Oct. 10 Litho. *Perf. 13½*

763 A222 60fr Nightingale 28 20
764 A222 60fr Vultures 28 20

Bamenda Farming Fair — A223

1984, Dec. 10 Litho. *Perf. 13*

765 A223 60fr Corn 28 20
766 A223 70fr Cattle 32 22
767 A223 300fr Potatoes 1.35 90

Foreign postal stationery (stamped envelopes, postal cards and air letter sheets) lies beyond the scope of this Catalogue, which is limited to adhesive postage stamps.

International Civil Aviation Organization, 40th Anniv. — A224

1984, Dec. 20 Litho. *Perf. 12½*

768 A224 200fr Icarus 90 60
769 A224 200fr ICAO emblem, vert. 90 60
770 A224 300fr Boeing 747 1.35 90
771 A224 300fr Solar Princess painting 1.35 90

Olymphilex '85, Lausanne — A225

1985, Apr. 5 Photo. *Perf. 13*

772 A225 150fr Wrestlers, exhibition emblem 65 65

Domestic Musical Instruments A226

1985, Apr. 23 *Perf. 13½*

773 A226 60fr Balafons (xylophone) 25 25
774 A226 70fr Guitar 28 28
775 A226 100fr Flute 42 42

INTELSAT Org., 20th Anniv. — A227

1985, May 8 *Perf. 13*

776 A227 125fr Intelsat V 52 52
777 A227 200fr Intelcam, Yaounde 85 85

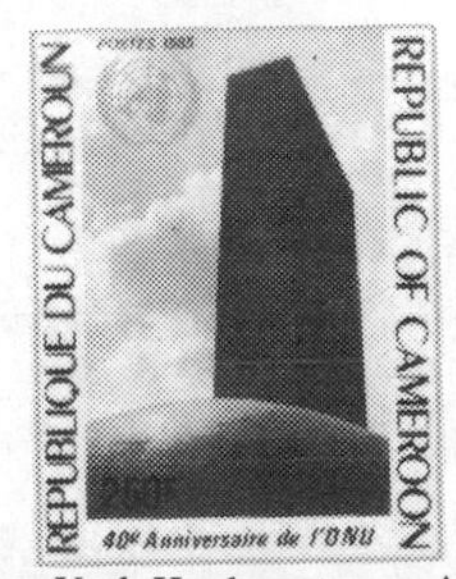

New York Headquarters — A228

UN, 40th Anniv.

1985, May 30

778 A228 250fr multi 1.10 1.10
779 A228 500fr multi 2.25 2.25

Pres. Mitterand, Biya — A229

1985, June 20

780 A229 60fr multi 28 28
781 A229 70fr multi 32 32

Visit of Pres. Mitterand of France.

UNICEF A230

UN Infant Survival Campaign A231

1985, July 15

782 A230 60fr multi 28 28
783 A231 300fr multi 1.40 1.40

Visit of Pope John Paul II, Aug. 10-14 — A232

1985, Aug. 9 *Perf. 13x12½*

784 A232 60fr Pope, papal arms 28 28
785 A232 70fr Pope, crosier 32 32

Size: 60x40mm.

786 A232 300fr Pres. Biya, John Paul II 1.40 1.40
a. Souvenir sheet of 3 2.00 2.00

No. 786a contains Nos. 784-786; margin contains inscriptions. Size: 138x100mm.

Landscapes — A233

1985, July 25 Litho. *Perf. 12½*

787 A233 60fr Lake Barumbi, Kumba 25 25
788 A233 70fr Bonando Pygmy Village, Doume 28 28
789 A233 150fr Cameroun River 62 62

City Hall Type of 1982

1985, July 30

790 A202 60fr Ngaoundere 25 25
791 A202 60fr D'Ebolowa 25 25

Wildlife A234

Wood Sculptures A235

1985, Aug. 20 *Perf. 13½*

792 A234 125fr Porcupine 55 55
793 A234 200fr Squirrel 90 90
794 A234 350fr Hedgehog 1.65 1.65

1985, Sept. 15

795 A235 60fr Mask 28 28
796 A235 70fr Mask, diff. 32 32
797 A235 100fr Wood bas-relief, horiz. 45 45

Birds — A236

1985, Nov. 10

798 A236 140fr Toucans 75 75
799 A236 150fr Rooster 80 80
800 A236 200fr Red-throated bee-eater 1.10 1.10

American Peace Corps in Cameroun, 25th Anniv. — A237

1986, Jan. 1 Litho. *Perf. 12½*

801 A237 70fr multi 38 38
802 A237 100fr multi 55 55

Stamps of 1979-1982 Redrawn.

1986, Mar. *Perf. 13, 13½*

803 A174 5fr multi 5 5
804 A204 10fr multi 6 6

Nos. 803-804 inscribed "Republic of Cameroon" instead of "United Republic of Cameroon."

Easter — A238

Insects — A239

Paintings: 210fr, Head of the Virgin, by Pierre-Paul Prud'Hon (1758-1823). 350fr, The Stoning of St. Steven, by Van Scorel (1495-1562).

1986, Apr. 15 *Perf. 13½*

805	A238	210fr	multi	1.15	1.15
806	A238	350fr	multi	1.90	1.90

1986, Apr. 20

807	A239	70fr	Honeybee	38	38
808	A239	70fr	Dragonfly	38	38
809	A239	100fr	Grasshopper	55	55

Nos. 808-809 horiz.

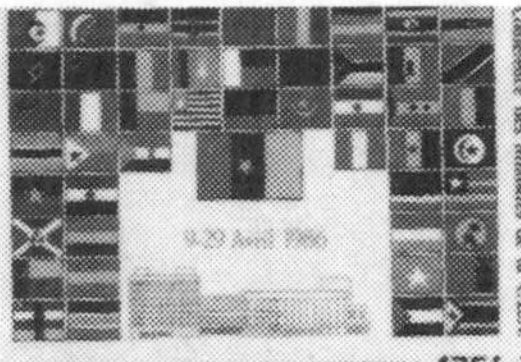

Flags, Conference Center — A240

1986, Apr. 25 **Litho.** *Perf. 13*

810	A240	100fr	Map, vert.	55	55
811	A240	175fr	shown	95	95

Conference of Ministers of the Economic Commission for Africa, Apr. 9-29.

Statues — A241

1986, July 5 **Litho.** *Perf. 13½*

812	A241	70fr	Bronze earth mother	40	40
813	A241	100fr	Wood funerary figure	60	60
814	A241	130fr	Wood equestrian figure	80	80

Queen Elizabeth II, 60th Birthday — A242

1986, July 15 **Litho.** *Perf. 13*

815	A242	100fr	Elizabeth	60	60
816	A242	175fr	Elizabeth, Pres. Biya	1.10	1.10
817	A242	210fr	Elizabeth, diff.	1.25	1.25

Natl. Democratic Party, 1st Anniv. — A243

1986, July 25 *Perf. 12½*

818	A243	70fr	Party headquarters, Bamenda	40	40
819	A243	70fr	Pres. Biya, vert.	40	40
820	A243	100fr	Presidential address, vert.	60	60

Kwem Mask Dancers of the Northeast — A244

1986, Aug. 1 *Perf. 13½*

821	A244	100fr	multi	60	60
822	A244	130fr	multi	80	80

Endangered Species A245

1986, Aug. 20

823	A245	300fr	Varanus niloticus	1.75	1.75
824	A245	300fr	Panthera pardus	1.75	1.75

Intl. Peace Year — A246

Designs: 175fr, 200fr, Desmond Tutu, South Africa, Nobel Peace Prize winner. 250fr, UN and IPY emblems.

1986, Sept. 7 **Litho.** *Perf. 13½*

825	A246	175fr	multi	1.10	1.10
826	A246	200fr	multi	1.25	1.25
827	A246	250fr	multi	1.50	1.50

Natl. Federation of Associations for the Handicapped A247

African Vaccination Year A248

1986, Oct. 30 **Litho.** *Perf. 13½*

828	A247	70fr	multi	40	40

1986, Nov. 9

829	A248	70fr	Family under umbrella	40	40
830	A248	100fr	Child immunization	55	55

Arbor Day — A249

1986, Dec. 20 **Litho.** *Perf. 13½*

831	A249	70fr	Afforestation map	40	40
832	A249	100fr	Hands, seedling	55	55

Agricultural Development — A250

1986, Dec. 24

833	A250	70fr	ONCPB seminar	40	40
834	A250	70fr	Coconut farming, Dibombari	40	40
835	A250	200fr	Pineapple farm	1.10	1.10

Insects Destructive to Agriculture A251

1987, Sept. 25 **Litho.** *Perf. 13½*

836	A251	70fr	Antestiopsis lineaticollis intricata	50	50
837	A251	100fr	Distantiella theobroma	72	72

4th African Games, Nairobi — A252

1987, Oct. 1 *Perf. 12½*

838	A252	100fr	Shot put	72	72
839	A252	140fr	Pole vault	1.00	1.00

Maroua Agricultural Show — A253

1988, Jan. 6

840	A253	70fr	Millet field	50	50
841	A253	100fr	Cotton	72	72
842	A253	150fr	Cattle	1.10	1.10

SEMI-POSTAL STAMPS.

Curie Issue
Common Design Type

1938 **Unwmk.** *Perf. 13*

B1	CD80	1.75fr + 50c brt ultra	4.50	4.00

French Revolution Issue
Common Design Type
Photogravure; Name and Value Typographed in Black.

1939

B2	CD83	45(c) + 25(c) grn	5.00	5.00
B3	CD83	70(c) + 30(c) brn	5.00	5.00
B4	CD83	90(c) + 35(c) red org	5.00	5.00
B5	CD83	1.25fr + 1fr rose pink	5.25	5.25
B6	CD83	2.25fr + 2fr bl	6.25	6.25
		Nos. B2-B6 (5)	26.50	26.50

Stamps of 1925-33 Surcharged in Black

OEUVRES DE GUERRE

+ 2 frs.

1940 *Perf. 14x13½.*

B7	A7	1.25fr + 2fr gray & dp bl	7.50	7.50
B8	A7	1.75fr + 3fr brn & org	7.50	7.50
B9	A7	2fr + 5fr dl grn & brn org	7.50	7.50

The surtax was used for war relief work.

Regular Stamps of 1939 Surcharged in Black

+ 5 Frs.
SPITFIRE

1940 *Perf. 13.*

B10	A20	25c + 5fr blk brn	75.00	70.00
B11	A20	45c + 5fr sl grn	75.00	70.00
B12	A20	60c + 5fr pck bl	90.00	82.50
B13	A20	70c + 5fr plum	90.00	82.50

The surtax was used to purchase Spitfire planes for the Free French army.

The lack of a price for a listed item does not necessarily indicate rarity.

Common Design Type and

Military Doctor SP2

Cameroun Militiaman — SP4

1941 **Photo.** ***Perf. 13½***

B13A	SP2	1fr + 1fr red	75	
B13B	CD86	1.50fr + 3fr mar	75	
B13C	SP4	2.50fr + 1fr dk bl	75	

Nos. B13A-B13C were issued by the Vichy government, and were not placed on sale in Cameroun.

Nos. 281A-281B were surcharged "OEUVRES COLONIALES" and surtax (including change of denomination of the 2.50fr to 50c). These were issued in 1944 by the Vichy government, and not placed on sale in Cameroun.

New York World's Fair Stamps, 1939 Surcharged in Black

+
SPITFIRE 10fr.
Général de GAULLE

1941 ***Perf. 12½x12.***

B14	CD82	1.25fr + 10fr car lake	62.50	55.00
B15	CD82	2.25fr + 10fr ultra	62.50	55.00

New York World's Fair Stamps, 1939, Surcharged in Black or Blue

+ 10 Frs.
AMBULANCE
LAQUINTINIE

1941

B16	CD82	1.25fr + 10fr car lake (Bl)	11.00	8.75
B17	CD82	2.25fr + 10fr ultra (Bk)	11.00	8.75

The surtax was used to purchase ambulances for the Free French army.

Regular Stamps of 1933-39 Surcharged in Black

Valmy
+ 100 frs.

1943 ***Perf. 14x13½, 13, 12½x12.***

B21	A7	1.25fr + 100 gray & dp bl	5.50	5.50
B22	A21	1.25fr + 100fr car rose	5.50	5.50
B23	CD82	1.25fr + 100fr car lake	5.50	5.50
B24	A21	1.50fr + 100fr choc	5.50	5.50
B25	CD82	2.25fr + 100fr ultra	5.50	5.50
		Nos. B21-B25 (5)	27.50	27.50

Red Cross Issue
Common Design Type

1944 **Photo.** ***Perf. 14½x14.***

B28	CD90	5fr + 20fr rose	1.25	1.10

The surtax was for the French Red Cross and national relief.

Tropical Medicine Issue
Common Design Type

1950 **Engr.** ***Perf. 13***

B29	CD100	10fr + 2fr dk bl grn & dk grn	2.50	2.50

The surtax was for charitable work.

Independent State

Map and Flag — SP7

Unwmk.

1961, Mar. 25 **Engr.** ***Perf. 13***

B30	SP7	20fr + 5fr grn, car & yel	65	65
B31	SP7	25fr + 10fr multi	75	75
B32	SP7	30fr + 15fr car, yel & grn	1.10	1.10

The surtax was for the Red Cross.

Federal Republic

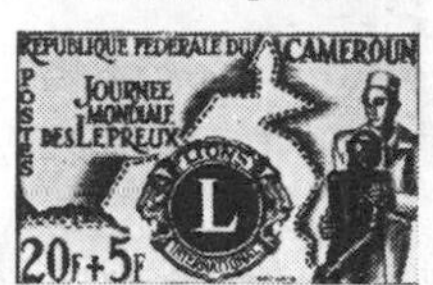

Map of Cameroun, Lions Emblem and Physician Helping Leper — SP8

1962, Jan. 28

B33	SP8	20fr + 5fr blk, mar & red brn	60	60
B34	SP8	25fr + 10fr ultra, mar & red brn	70	70
B35	SP8	50fr + 15fr grn, mar & red brn	1.25	1.25

Issued for leprosy relief work.

Anti-Malaria Issue
Common Design Type

1962, Apr. 7 ***Perf. 12½x12***

B36	CD108	25fr + 5fr rose lil	75	70

Issued for the World Health Organization drive to eradicate malaria.

Freedom from Hunger Issue
Common Design Type

1963, Mar. 21 **Engr.** ***Perf. 13***

B37	CD112	18fr + 5fr grn, dk ultra & brn	65	50
B38	CD112	25fr + 5fr red brn & grn	80	60

AIR POST STAMPS.

Common Design Type
Perf. 14½x14.

1942 **Unwmk.** **Photo.**

C1	CD87	1fr dk org	18	18
C2	CD87	1.50fr brt red	18	18
C3	CD87	5fr brn red	18	18
C4	CD87	10fr black	38	38
C5	CD87	25fr ultra	45	45
C6	CD87	50fr dk grn	65	65
C7	CD87	100fr plum	90	90
		Nos. C1-C7 (7)	2.92	2.92

Victory Issue
Common Design Type

1946, May 8 **Engr.** ***Perf. 12½***

C8	CD92	8fr dk vio brn	38	38

Issued to commemorate the European victory of the Allied Nations in World War II.

Chad to Rhine Issue
Common Design Types

1946, June 6

C9	CD93	5fr dk bl grn	50	50
C10	CD94	10fr dk rose vio	50	50
C11	CD95	15fr red	60	60
C12	CD96	20fr brt bl	60	60
C13	CD97	25fr org red	75	75
C14	CD98	50fr gray	95	95
		Nos. C9-C14 (6)	3.90	3.90

Plane and Map AP9

Seaplane Alighting AP10

Plane and Freighters AP11

1946 **Photo.** ***Perf. 13, 13½***

C15	AP9	25c brn red	5	5
C16	AP9	50c green	5	5
C17	AP9	1fr brt vio	5	5
C18	AP10	2fr ol grn	18	18
C19	AP10	3fr chocolate	18	18
C20	AP10	4fr dp ultra	15	15
C21	AP10	6fr bl grn	18	18
C22	AP10	7fr brt vio	22	22
C23	AP10	12fr orange	2.75	2.75
C24	AP10	20fr crimson	65	65
C25	AP11	50fr dk ultra	70	70
		Nos. C15-C25 (11)	5.16	5.16

Nos. C15 to C25 were "issued" in 1941 in France by the Vichy Government, but were not sold in Cameroun until 1946.

V8

This 100fr stamp and eight denominations of types AP9, AP10 and AP11 without "RF" monogram were issued by the Vichy Government in 1943-44, but were not on sale in Cameroun.

Birds over Mountains — AP12

Cavalry and Plane — AP13

Warrior, Dance Mask and Nose of Plane — AP14

Perf. 12½.

1947, Feb. 10 **Unwmk.** **Engr.**

C26	AP12	50fr dk grn	90	50
C27	AP13	100fr brn red	1.90	30
C28	AP14	200fr black	3.75	90

U.P.U. Issue
Common Design Type

1949, July ***Perf. 13.***

C29	CD99	25fr multi	2.75	2.25

Issued to commemorate the 75th anniversary of the Universal Postal Union.

Humsiki Peak — AP16

1953, Feb. 16

C30	AP16	500fr grnsh blk, dk vio & vio bl	10.00	2.00

Edéa Dam and Sacred Ibis — AP17

1953, Nov. 18

C31	AP17	15fr choc, brn lake & ultra	1.20	50

Issued to publicize the official dedication of Edea Dam on the Sanaga River.

Liberation Issue
Common Design Type

1954, June 6

C32	CD102	15fr dk grnsh bl & bl grn	2.25	1.75

10th anniversary of the liberation of France.

Dr. Eugene Jamot, Research Laboratory and Tsetse Flies — AP19

1954, Nov. 29

C33	AP19	15fr dk grn, ind & dk brn	1.40	1.25

Issued to commemorate the 75th anniversary of the birth of Dr. Eugene Jamot.

Logging — AP20

Designs: 100fr, Giraffes. 200fr, Port of Douala.

1955, Jan. 24

C34	AP20	50fr ol grn, brn & vio brn	70	15
C35	AP20	100fr grnsh bl, brn & dk brn	2.00	30
C36	AP20	200fr dk grn, choc & dp ultra	2.75	50

Federal Republic

Air Afrique Issue
Common Design Type

Unwmk.

1962, Feb. 17 Engr. *Perf. 13*

C37	CD107	25fr mar, pur & lt grn	60	55

Founding of Air Afrique (African Airlines).

Nos. C35-C36 and C30 Surcharged in Red with New Value, Bars and: "REPUBLIQUE FEDERALE"

Two types of 5sh:
I. "5/-" measures 6½x4mm.
II. "5/" measures 3¾x3mm. No dash after diagonal line.

Three types of 10sh:
I. "10/-" measures 9x3¾mm.
II. "10/-" measures 7x2½-3mm.
III. "1" of "10/" vertically in line with last "E" of "FEDERALE".

Two types of £1:
I. "REPUBLIQUE / FEDERALE" 17¼mm. wide.
II. "REPUBLIQUE / FEDERALE" 22mm. wide.

1961, Oct. 1 Engr. *Perf. 13*

C38	AP20	5sh on 100fr (I)	4.00	4.00
a.		Type II	10.00	10.00
C39	AP20	10sh on 200fr (I)	8.00	8.00
a.		Type II	35.00	35.0
b.		Type III	8.00	8.00
C40	AP16	£1 on 500fr (I)	15.00	15.00
a.		Type II	22.50	22.50

Issued for use in the former United Kingdom Trust Territory of Southern Cameroons.

Kapsikis Mokolo — AP21

Designs: 50fr, Cocotieres Hotel, Douala. 100fr, Cymothoe sangaris butterflies. 200fr, Ostriches, Waza Reservation.

1962, June 15

C41	AP21	50fr sl grn, bl & dl red	75	45
C42	AP21	100fr multi	1.65	60
C43	AP21	200fr dk grn, blk & bis	3.50	1.00
C44	AP21	500fr vio brn, bl & ocher	7.50	2.50

Telstar Type of Regular Issue

1963, Feb. 9

Size: 48x27mm.

C45	A50	100fr dk grn & red brn	1.75	1.00

See note after No. 383.

Edea Relay Station — A22

1963, May 18 Photo. *Perf. 12x12½*

C46	AP22	100fr multi	1.75	1.00

Issued to publicize the high frequency telegraph connection Douala-Yaounde.

African Postal Union Issue

Common Design Type

1963, Sept. 8 Unwmk. *Perf. 12½*

C47	CD114	85fr ultra, ocher & red	1.75	1.50

Air Afrique Issue, 1963

Common Design Type

1963, Nov. 19 *Perf. 13x12*

C48	CD115	50fr pink, gray, blk & grn	85	60

Olympic Games Type of 1964

Design: 300fr, Greco-Roman wrestlers (ancient).

1964, Oct. 10 Engr. *Perf. 13*

C49	A57	300fr red, dk brn & dl grn	5.00	3.00
a.		Sheet of 3	6.50	6.50

Issued to commemorate the 18th Olympic Games, Tokyo, Oct. 10-25. No. C49a contains one each of Nos. 403-404 and C49. Size: 168x99mm.

Kribi Port — AP25

1964, Oct. 26 Unwmk. *Perf. 13*

C50	AP25	50fr red brn, ultra & grn	85	50

Black Rhinoceros — AP26

1965, Dec. 15 Engr. *Perf. 13*

C51	AP26	250fr brn red, grn & dk brn	4.50	1.75

Pres. John F. Kennedy — AP27

1964, Dec. 8 Photo. *Perf. 12½*

C52	AP27	100fr grn, yel grn & brn	1.75	1.75
a.		Souv. sheet of 4	7.00	7.00

Issued in memory of Pres. John F. Kennedy (1917-63). No. C52a contains 4 No. C52; green marginal inscription. Size: 128x90mm.

Abraham Lincoln — AP28

1965, Apr. 20 Unwmk. *Perf. 13*

C53	AP28	100fr multi	1.65	1.25

Abraham Lincoln, death centenary.

Syncom Satellite and ITU Emblem — AP29

1965, May 17 Engr.

C54	AP29	70fr red, dk bl, & blk	1.25	90

Centenary of International Telecommunication Union.

Winston Churchill — AP30

Design: 18fr, Churchill, battleship and oak leaves with acorns.

Perf. 13x12½

1965, May 28 Photo. Unwmk.

C55	AP30	12fr org, dk brn & ultra	1.00	75
C56	AP30	18fr org, dk brn, & ultra	1.00	75
a.		Strip of 2 + label	2.50	2.00

Issued in memory of Sir Winston Spencer Churchill, statesman and World War II leader. No. C56a contains Nos. C55-C56 and label between inscribed "Sir Winston Churchill 1874 1965.'

ICY Type of Regular Issue

1965, Sept. 11 Engr. *Perf. 13*

C57	A68	100fr dk red & dk bl	1.65	1.10

International Cooperation Year, 1964-65.

Racing Boat, Sanaga River, Edea — AP31

1965, Oct. 27 Unwmk. *Perf. 13*

C58	AP31	50fr brn, dk grn & sl	90	50

Edward H. White Floating in Space and Gemini IV — AP32

Designs: 50fr, Vostok 6. 200fr, Gemini V and REP (rendezvous evaluation pod). 500fr, Gemini VI & VII rendezvous.

1966, March 30 Engr. *Perf. 13*

C59	AP32	50fr car rose & dk sl grn	85	50
C60	AP32	100fr red lil & vio bl	1.65	1.00
C61	AP32	200fr ultra & dk pur	3.00	2.00
C62	AP32	500fr brt bl & ind	8.00	4.50

Man's conquest of space.

Hotel Type of Regular Issue

1966

Designs: 18fr, Mountain Hotel, Buea. 25fr, Hotel Akwa Palace, Douala. 50fr, Terminus Hotel, Yaounde. 60fr, Imperial Hotel, Yaounde. 85fr, Independence Hotel, Yaounde. 100fr, Hunting Lodge, Mora (vert.). 150fr, Boukarous (round huts), Waza Camp.

C63	A71	18fr sl grn, brt bl & blk	25	20
C64	A71	25fr car, ultra & sl	40	25
C65	A71	50fr choc, grn & ocher	85	50
C66	A71	60fr choc, grn & brt bl	90	50
C67	A71	85fr dk car rose, dl bl & grn	1.25	75
C68	A71	100fr brn, grn & sl	1.65	75
C69	A71	150fr brn, dl bl & ocher	2.10	1.00
		Nos. C63-C69 (7)	7.40	3.95

Issue dates: Nos. C63-C64, Apr. 6; Nos. C65-C69, June 4.

Flower Type of Regular Issue

Flowers: 25fr, Hibiscus mutabilis. 50fr, Delonix regia. 100fr, Bougainvillea.

1966, May 20 Photo. *Perf. 12½*

Flowers in Natural Colors

Size: 26x45mm.

C70	A75	25fr sl grn	40	15
C71	A75	50fr brt grnsh bl	75	20
C72	A75	100fr gold	1.65	40

Military Police — AP33

Design: 25fr, "Army," soldier, tanks and parachutes. 60fr, "Navy," and "Vigilante." 100fr, "Air Force," plane.

1966, June 21 Engr. *Perf. 13*

C73	AP33	20fr vio bl, org brn & dl pur	30	20
C74	AP33	25fr dk grn, dl pur & brn	40	25
C75	AP33	60fr bl grn, bl & ind	1.00	45
C76	AP33	100fr brn, Prus bl & car rose	1.65	1.00

Issued to honor Cameroun's armed forces.

Wembley Stadium, London — AP34

Design: 200fr, Soccer.

1966, July 20

C77	AP34	50fr grn, cop red & sl	85	40
C78	AP34	200fr red, bl & grn	3.00	1.75

Issued to commemorate the 8th World Cup Soccer Championship, Wembley, England, July 11-30.

Air Afrique Issue, 1966
Common Design Type

1966, Aug. 31 Photo. *Perf. 13*
C79 CD123 25fr red lil, blk & gray 40 20

Issued to commemorate the introduction of DC-8F planes by Air Afrique.

Yaoundé Cathedral — AP35

Designs: 18fr, Buea Cathedral. 30fr, Orthodox Church, Yaoundé. 60fr, Mosque, Garoua.

1966, Dec. 19 Engr. *Perf. 13*
C80 AP35 18fr choc, bl & grn 30 25
C81 AP35 25fr brn, grn & brt vio 40 25
C82 AP35 30fr lil, grn & dl red 45 30
C83 AP35 60fr mar, brt grn & grn 1.00 50

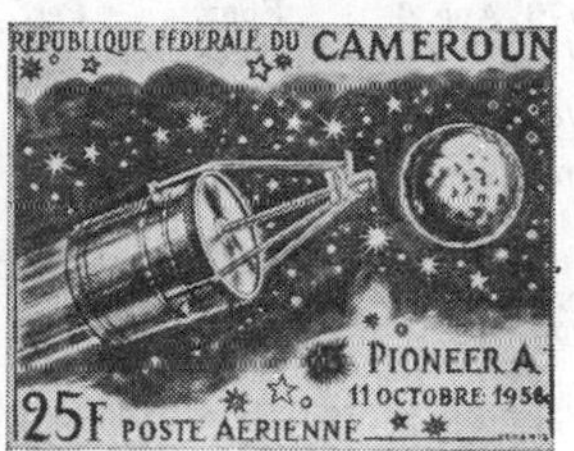

Pioneer A and Moon — AP36

Designs: 50fr, Ranger 6. 100fr, Luna 9. 250fr, Luna 10.

1967, Apr. 30 Engr. *Perf. 13*
C84 AP36 25fr grn, bl & bis 40 25
C85 AP36 50fr grn, dk pur & brn 85 50
C86 AP36 100fr red brn, brt bl & lil 1.75 1.00
C87 AP36 250fr red brn, sl & brn 4.00 3.00

"Conquest of the Moon."

Flower Type of Regular Issue

Flowers: 200fr, Thevetia Peruviana. 250fr, Amaryllis.

1967, June 22 Photo. *Perf. 12½*
Size: 26x46mm.
C88 A86 200fr multi 3.00 1.35
C89 A86 250fr multi 4.00 1.75

African Postal Union Issue, 1967
Common Design Type

1967, Sept. 9 Engr. *Perf. 13*
C90 CD124 100fr red brn, Prus bl & brt lil 1.60 1.00

Skis, Ice Skates, Olympic Flame and Emblem — AP38

1967, Oct. 11 Engr. *Perf. 13*
C91 AP38 30fr ultra & sep 55 30

Issued to publicize the 10th Winter Olympic Games, Grenoble, Feb. 6-8, 1968.

Cameroun Exhibit, EXPO '67 — AP39

Designs: 100fr, Bangwa house poles carved with ancestor figures. 200fr, Canadian Pavilions.

1967, Oct. 18
C92 AP39 50fr mag, ol & mar 75 35
C93 AP39 100fr dk grn, mar & dk brn 1.75 80
C94 AP39 200fr brn, lil rose & sl grn 3.50 1.75

Issued to commemorate EXPO '70, International Exhibition, Montreal, Apr. 28-Oct. 27, 1967.

See note after No. C116 regarding 1969 moon overprint.

Konrad Adenauer and Cologne Cathedral — AP40

Design: 70fr, Adenauer and Chancellery, Bonn.

1967, Dec. 1 Photo. *Perf. 12½*
C95 AP40 30fr multi 50 30
C96 AP40 70fr multi 1.25 60
a. Strip of 2 + label 1.80 1.00

Issued in memory of Konrad Adenauer (1876-1967), chancellor of West Germany (1949-63). No. C96a contains Nos. C95-C96 and label between showing the CEPT design of the 1967 Europa issues.

Pres. Ahidjo, King Faisal and View of Mecca — AP41

Design: 60fr, Pres. Ahidjo, Pope Paul VI and view of Rome.

1968, Feb. 18 Photo. *Perf. 12½*
C97 AP41 30fr multi 45 25
C98 AP41 60fr multi 90 45

Issued to commemorate President Ahidjo's Pilgrimage to Mecca and visit to Rome.

Earth on Television Transmitted by Explorer VI — AP42

Designs: 30fr, Molniya spacecraft. 40fr, Earth on television screen transmitted by Molniya.

1968, Apr. 20 Engr. *Perf. 13*
C99 AP42 20fr multi 30 15
C100 AP42 30fr multi 45 25
C101 AP42 40fr multi 60 30

Telecommunication by satellite.

Forge — AP43

Boxing — AP44

Designs: No. C103, Tea harvest. No. C104, Trans-Cameroun railroad (diesel train emerging from tunnel). 40fr, Rubber harvest. 60fr, Douala Harbor (horiz.).

1968, June 5 Engr. *Perf. 13*
C102 AP43 20fr red brn, dk grn & ind 30 15
C103 AP43 30fr dk brn, grn & ultra 45 25
C104 AP43 30fr ind, sl grn & bis brn 45 25
C105 AP43 40fr ol bis, dk grn & bl grn 50 30
C106 AP43 60fr ultra, dk brn & sl 90 60
Nos. C102-C106 (5) 2.60 1.55

Issued to publicize the Second Economic Development Five-Year Plan.

1968, Aug. 19 Engr. *Perf. 13*

Design: 50fr, Broad jump. 60fr, Athlete on rings.

C107 AP44 30fr brt grn, dk grn & choc 45 25
C108 AP44 50fr brt grn, brn red & choc 75 45
C109 AP44 60fr brt grn, ultra & choc 90 50
a. Min. sheet of 3 2.25 2.25

Issued to commemorate the 19th Olympic Games, Mexico City, Oct. 12-27. No. C109a contains one each of Nos. C107-C109. Size: 128x99mm.

Human Rights Type of Regular Issue

1968, Sept. 14 Photo. *Perf. 12½x13*
C110 A92 30fr grn & brt pink 40 22

International Human Rights Year, 1968.

Martin Luther King, Jr. — AP45

Portraits: No. C112, Mahatma Gandhi and map of India. 40fr, John F. Kennedy. 60fr, Robert F. Kennedy. No. C115, Rev. Martin Luther King, Jr. No. C116, Mahatma Gandhi.

1968, Dec. 5 Photo. *Perf. 12½*
C111 AP45 30fr bl & blk 50 30
C112 AP45 30fr multi 50 30
C113 AP45 40fr pink & blk 60 40
C114 AP45 60fr bluish lil & blk 90 60
C115 AP45 70fr yel grn & blk 1.00 70
a. Souv. sheet of 4 3.00 3.00
C116 AP45 70fr multi 1.00 70
Nos. C111-C116 (6) 4.50 3.00

Issued to honor exponents of non-violence. The 2 King stamps (Nos. C111 and C115), the 2 Gandhi stamps (Nos. C112 and C116) and the 2 Kennedy stamps (Nos. C113-C114) are each printed as triptychs with a descriptive label between. No. C115a contains one each of Nos. C112-C115; black marginal inscription. Size: 122x160mm.

In 1969 Nos. C111-C116 and C94 were overprinted in carmine capitals: "Premier Homme / sur la Lune / 20 Juillet 1969" and "First Man / Landing on Moon / 20 July 1969".

PHILEXAFRIQUE Issue

The Letter, by Armand Cambon AP46

1968, Dec. 10
C117 AP46 100fr multi 1.65 1.25

Issued to publicize PHILEXAFRIQUE, Philatelic Exhibition in Abidjan, Feb. 14-23, 1969. Printed with alternating light green label.

2nd PHILEXAFRIQUE Issue
Common Design Type

Design: 50fr, Cameroun No. 199 and Wouri Bridge.

1969, Feb. 14 Engr. *Perf. 13*
C118 CD128 50fr sl grn, ol & dl bl 85 85

Issued to commemorate the opening of PHILEXAFRIQUE, Abidjan, Feb. 14.

Caladium Bicolor — AP47

Flowers: 50fr, Aristolochia elegans. 100fr, Gloriosa simplex.

1969, May 14 Photo. *Perf. 12½*

C119	AP47	30fr lil & multi	45	30
C120	AP47	50fr grn & multi	85	50
C121	AP47	100fr brn & multi	1.50	80

Issued to publicize the 3rd International Flower Show, Paris, Apr. 23-Oct. 5.

Douala Post Office — AP48

Designs: 50fr, Buea Post Office. 100fr, Bafoussam Post Office.

1969, June 19 Engr. *Perf. 13*

C122	AP48	30fr grn, vio bl & brn	35	20
C123	AP48	50fr sl, emer & red brn	70	40
C124	AP48	100fr dk brn, brt grn & brn	1.40	75

Coronation of Napoleon I, by Jacques Louis David — AP49

Napoleon Crossing Saint Bernard, after J. L. David — AP50

1969, July 4 Photo. *Perf. 12x12½*

C125	AP49	30fr vio bl & multi	75	30

Die-cut Perf. 10

Embossed on Gold Foil

C126	AP50	1000fr gold	25.00	25.00

Bicentenary of birth of Napoleon I.

William E. B. Dubois (1868-1963), American Writer — AP51

Portraits: 15fr, Dr. Price Mars, Haiti (1876-1969). No. C128, Aimé Cesaire, Martinique (1913-). No. C130, Langston Hughes, U.S. (1902-1967). No. C131, Marcus Garvey, Jamaica (1887-1940). 100fr, Rene Maran, Martinique (1887-1960).

1969, Sept. 25 Photo. *Perf. 12½*

C127	AP51	15fr lt bl & blk	20	10
C128	AP51	30fr lem & blk	40	20
C129	AP51	30fr rose brn & blk	40	20
C130	AP51	50fr gray & blk	65	35
C131	AP51	50fr emer & blk	65	35
C132	AP51	100fr yel & blk	1.35	85
a.		Min. sheet of 6	4.00	4.00
		Nos. C127-C132 (6)	3.65	2.05

Issued to honor Negro writers.

No. C132a contains one each of Nos. C127-C132. Size: 114x125mm.

ILO Emblem — AP52

1969, Oct. 29 Photo. *Perf. 13*

C133	AP52	30fr blk, bl grn & gray	50	20
C134	AP52	50fr blk, dp lil rose & gray	85	40

Issued to commemorate the 50th anniversary of the International Labor Organization.

Armstrong, Collins and Aldrin Splashdown in the Pacific — AP53

Design: 500fr, Landing module and Nell A. Armstrong's first step on moon.

1969, Nov. 29 Photo. *Perf. 12½*

C135	AP53	200fr multi	3.00	1.50
C136	AP53	500fr multi	6.50	3.75

See note after Algeria No. 427.

Pres. Ahidjo, Arms and Map of Cameroun — AP54

Embossed on Gold Foil

1970, Jan. 1 *Die-cut Perf. 10*

C137	AP54	1000fr gold & multi	12.50	12.50

10th anniversary of independence.

Hotel Mont Fébé, Yaoundé — AP55

1970, Jan. 15 Engr. *Perf. 13*

C138	AP55	30fr lt brn, sl grn & gray	50	20

Lenin — AP56

1970, Jan. 25 Photo. *Perf. 12½*

C139	AP56	50fr org & blk	70	40

Issued to commemorate the centenary of the birth of Nikolai Lenin (1870-1924), Russian Communist leader.

Plant Type of Regular Issue

Designs. 50fr, Cleome speciosa (caper). 100fr, Mussaenda erythrophylla (madder).

1970, Mar. 24 Photo. *Perf. 12½*

Size: 26x46mm.

C140	A99	50fr blk & multi	60	40
C141	A99	100fr multi	1.20	60

Map of Africa and Lions Emblem Pinpointing Yaoundé — AP57

1970, May 2 Photo. *Perf. 12½*

C142	AP57	100fr multi	1.35	75

Issued to commemorate the 13th Lions International Congress of District 13, Yaounde, May 2, 1970.

U.N. Emblem and Doves — AP58

Design: 50fr, U.N. emblem and dove (vert.).

1970, June 26 Engr. *Perf. 13*

C143	AP58	30fr brn & org	40	25
C144	AP58	50fr Prus bl & sl bl	65	35

25th anniversary of the United Nations.

Japanese Pavilion and EXPO Emblem — AP59

Designs (EXPO Emblem and): 100fr, Map of Japan (vert.). 150fr, Australian pavilion.

1970, Aug. 1 Engr. *Perf. 13*

C145	AP59	50fr ind, lt grn & ver	65	35
C146	AP59	100fr bl, lt grn & red	1.35	65
C147	AP59	150fr choc, bl & gray	2.00	1.00

Issued to commemorate EXPO '70 International Exhibition, Osaka, Japan, Mar. 15-Sept. 13.

Charles de Gaulle — AP60

Pelé and Team — AP61

Design: 200fr, de Gaulle in unifrom.

1970, Aug. 27

C148	AP60	100fr grn, vio bl & ol brn	1.50	75
C149	AP60	200fr ol brn, vio bl & grn	3.00	1.40
a.		Strip of 2 + label	5.00	2.50

Issued to commemorate the 30th anniversary of the rallying of the Free French.

Nos. C148-C149 were printed in same sheet flanking a label showing maps of Cameroun and France, and Cross of Lorraine.

1970, Oct. 14 Photo. *Perf. 12½*

Designs: 50fr, Aztec Stadium, Mexico City (horiz.). 100fr, Mexican soccer team (horiz.).

C150 AP61 50fr multi 75 35
C151 AP61 100fr multi 1.50 75
C152 AP61 200fr multi 3.00 1.50

Issued to publicize the 9th World Soccer Championships for the Jules Rimet Cup, Mexico City, May 30-June 21, and the final victory of Brazil over Italy.

Ludwig van Beethoven AP62

1970, Nov. 23 Engr. *Perf. 13*
C153 AP62 250fr multi 2.75 1.50

Issued to commemorate the bicentenary of the birth of Ludwig van Beethoven (1770-1827), composer.

Christ at Emmaus, by Rembrandt — AP63

Design: 150fr, The Anatomy Lesson, by Rembrandt.

1970, Dec. 5 Photo. *Perf. 12x12½*
C154 AP63 70fr grn & multi 80 40
C155 AP63 150fr multi 1.80 90

Charles Dickens — AP64

Designs: 50fr, Scenes from David Copperfield. 100fr, Dickens holding quill.

1970, Dec. 22 *Perf. 13*
C156 AP64 40fr blk & rose 50 25
C157 AP64 50fr bis & multi 60 30
C158 AP64 100fr rose & multi 1.20 60

Death centenary of Charles Dickens (1812-1870), English novelist. Nos. C156-C158 printed se-tenant.

De Gaulle Type of 1970 Overprinted with Black Border and: "IN MEMORIAM / 1890-1970"

1971, Jan. 15 Engr. *Perf. 13*
C159 AP60 100fr vio bl, emer & brn red 1.20 60
C160 AP60 200fr brn red, emer & vio bl 2.40 1.20
a. Strip of 2 + label 4.25 2.00

In memory of Gen. Charles de Gaulle (1890-1970), President of France.

Timber Storage, Douala — AP65

Designs (Industrialization): 70fr, ALUCAM aluminum plant, Edea (vert.). 100fr, Mbakaou Dam.

1971, Feb. 14 Engr. *Perf. 13*
C161 AP65 40fr dk red, bl grn & ol brn 50 20
C162 AP65 70fr ol brn, sl grn & brt bl 80 40
C163 AP65 100fr Prus bl, yel grn & red brn 1.20 60

Relay Race — AP66

Designs: 50fr, Torch bearer (vert.). 100fr, Discus.

1971, Apr. 24 Engr. *Perf. 13*
C164 AP66 30fr dk brn, ver & ind 40 20
C165 AP66 50fr blk, bl & choc 70 35
C166 AP66 100fr multi 1.25 50

75th anniversary of revival of Olympic Games.

Fishing Trawler — AP67

Designs: 40fr, Local fishermen, Northern Cameroun. 70fr, Fishing harbor, Douala. 150fr, Shrimp boats, Douala.

1971, May 14 Engr. *Perf. 13*
C167 AP67 30fr lt brn, bl & grn 35 20
C168 AP67 40fr sl grn, bl & dk brn 45 25
C169 AP67 70fr dk brn, bl & red org 85 40
C170 AP67 150fr multi 1.80 90

Cameroun fishing industry.

Cameroun No. 123 and War Memorial, Yaounde — AP68

Designs (Cameroun Stamps): 25fr, No. C33 and Jamot memorial. 40fr, No. 431 and government buildings, Yaounde. 50fr, No. 19 and Imperial German postal emblem. 100fr, No. 101 and World War II memorial.

1971, Aug. 1 Engr. *Perf. 13*
C171 AP68 20fr grn, ocher & dk brn 25 10
C172 AP68 25fr dk brn, vio bl & sl grn 30 15
C173 AP68 40fr grn, mar & sl 45 25
C174 AP68 50fr dk brn, blk & ver 60 30
C175 AP68 100fr mar, sl grn & org 1.20 60
Nos. C171-C175 (5) 2.80 1.40

PHILATECAM 1971 Philatelic Exhibition.

Cameroun Flag, Pres. Ahidjo and Reunification Highway — AP69

Typographed, Silk Screen, Embossed
1971, Oct. 1 *Perf. 12½*
C176 AP69 250fr gold & multi 3.75 3.00

PHILATECAM Philatelic Exhibition, Yaounde-Douala.

African Postal Union Issue, 1971
Common Design Type

1971, Nov. 13 Photo. *Perf. 13x13½*
C177 CD135 100fr bl & multi 1.35 65

Annunciation, by Fra Angelico — AP71

Paintings: 45fr, Virgin and Child, by Andrea del Sarto. 150fr, Christ Child with Lamb, detail from Holy Family, by Raphael (vert.).

Perf. 13x13½, 13½x13
1971, Dec. 19
C178 AP71 40fr multi 40 20
C179 AP71 45fr multi 60 30
C180 AP71 150fr multi 2.00 90

Christmas 1971.

Cameroun Airlines Emblem AP72

1972, Feb. 2 Photo. *Perf. 12½x12*
C181 AP72 50fr lt bl & multi 60 30

Inauguration of Cameroun Airlines.

Doge's Palace, by Ippolito Caffi AP73

Paintings: 100fr, 200fr, Details from "Regatta on the Grand Canal," by School of Canaletto.

1972 Photo. *Perf. 13*
C182 AP73 40fr gold & multi 50 25
C183 AP73 100fr gold & multi 1.20 60
C184 AP73 200fr gold & multi 2.50 1.20

UNESCO campaign to save Venice.

Astronauts Patsayev, Dobrovolsky and Volkov — AP74

1972, May 1 Photo. *Perf. 13x13½*
C185 AP74 50fr multi 60 25

Salute-Soyuz 11 space mission, and in memory of the Russian astronauts Victor I. Patsayev, Georgi T. Dobrovolsky and Vladislav N. Volkov, who died during Soyuz 11 space mission, June 6-30, 1971.

U.N. Headquarters, Chinese Flag and Gate of Heavenly Peace — AP75

1972, May 19 *Perf. 13*
C186 AP75 50fr blk, scar & gold 50 25

Admission of People's Republic of China to United Nations.

United Republic

REPUBLIQUE UNIE DU CAMEROUN
50F
UNITED REPUBLIC OF CAMEROON

Olympic Rings, Swimming AP76

Designs (Olympic Rings and): No. C188, Boxing (vert.). 200fr, Equestrian.

1972, Aug. 1 Engr. *Perf. 13*
C187 AP76 50fr lake & sl grn 60 30
C188 AP76 50fr choc & sl 60 30
C189 AP76 200fr cl, gray & dk brn 2.25 1.10
a. Min. sheet of 3 3.25 3.25

20th Olympic Games, Munich, Aug. 26-Sept. 11. No. C189a contains stamps similar to Nos. C187-C189, but in changed colors. The 50fr (swimming) is Prussian blue, violet & brown; the 50c (boxing) lilac, Prussian blue & brown; the 200fr, Prussian blue & brown. Size: 139x99mm.

The indexes in each volume of the Scott Catalogue contain many listings which help to identify stamps.

Nos. C187-C189 Overprinted in Red or Black

NATATION MARK SPITZ
MEDAILLES D'OR
a

SUPER WELTER
KOTTYSCH
MEDAILLE D'OR
b

CONCOURS COMPLET
MEADE
MEDAILLE D'OR
c

1972, Oct. 23 **Engr.** ***Perf. 13***

C190	AP76 (a)	50fr lake & sl grn (R)	60	30
C191	AP76 (b)	50fr choc & sl	60	30
C192	AP76	200fr cl, gray & dk brn	2.50	1.20

Gold Medal Winners in 20th Olympic Games: Mark Spitz, USA, swimming (C190); Dieter Kottysch, West Germany, light middleweight boxing (C191); Richard Meade, Great Britain, 3-day equestrian (C192).

Madonna with Angels, by Cimabue AP77

Design: 140fr, Madonna of the Rose Arbor, by Stefan Lochner.

1972, Dec. 21 **Photo.** ***Perf. 13***

C193	AP77	45fr gold & multi	60	30
C194	AP77	140fr gold & multi	1.40	70

Christmas 1972.

St. Teresa, the Little Flower — AP78

Design: 100fr, Lisieux Cathedral and St. Teresa.

1973, Jan. 2 **Engr.**

C195	AP78	45fr vio bl, pur & mar	50	25
C196	AP78	100fr mag, ultra & brn	1.00	55

Centenary of the birth of St. Teresa of Lisieux (1873-1897), Carmelite nun.

African Unity Hall, Addis Ababa and Emperor Haile Selassie — AP79

1973, Mar. 14 **Photo.** ***Perf. 13***

C197	AP79	45fr yel & multi	40	25

80th birthday of Emperor Haile Selassie of Ethiopia.

Corn, Grain, Healthy and Starving People — AP80

1973, Apr. 10 **Typo.** ***Perf. 13***

C198	AP80	45fr multi	40	20

World Food Program, 10th anniversary.

Hearts and Blood Vessels — AP81

1973, May 5 **Engr.**

C199	AP81	50fr dk car rose & dk vio bl	40	25

"Your Heart is Your Health" and for the 25th anniversary of the World Health Organization.

Type of Regular Issue

Designs: 45fr, Map of Cameroun, Pres. Ahidjo and No. C176. 70fr, National colors and commemorative inscriptions.

1973, May 20 **Engr.** ***Perf. 13***

C200	A128	45fr grn & multi	40	25
C201	A128	70fr red & multi	60	40

First anniversary of the United Republic of Cameroun.

Scout Emblem and Flags — AP82

1973, July 31 **Typo.** ***Perf. 13***

C202	AP82	40fr multi	40	25
C203	AP82	45fr multi	45	30
C204	AP82	100fr multi	85	65

Cameroun's admission to the World Scout Conference, Mar. 26, 1971.

African Weeks Issue

Head and City Hall, Brussels — AP83

1973, Sept. 17 **Engr.** ***Perf. 13***

C205	AP83	40fr dp brn & rose cl	40	25

African Weeks, Brussels, Sept. 15-30.

Map of Africa with Cameroun — AP84

1973, Sept. 29 **Engr.** ***Perf. 13***

C206	AP84	40fr blk, red & grn	50	25

Help for handicapped children.

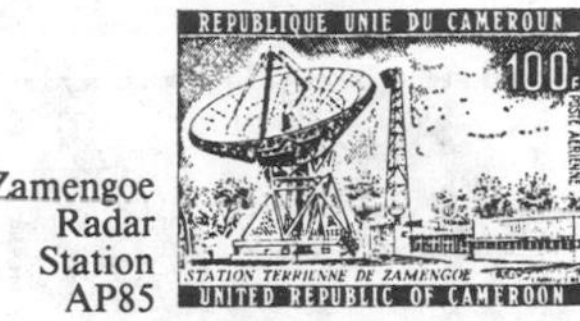

Zamengoe Radar Station AP85

1973, Dec. 8 **Engr.** ***Perf. 13***

C207	AP85	100fr bl, lt brn & grn	85	60

Chancellor Rolin Madonna, by Van Eyck AP86

Design: 140fr, Nativity, by Federigo Barocei.

1973, Dec. 11 **Photo.** ***Perf. 13***

C208	AP86	45fr gold & multi	45	30
C209	AP86	140fr gold & multi	1.50	1.10

Christmas 1973.

Zebu Type of 1974

Design: Zebu herd.

1974, June 1 **Litho.** ***Perf. 13***

C210	A140	45fr multi	40	20

North Cameroun cattle raising.

Churchill and Union Jack AP87

1974, July 10 **Engr.** ***Perf. 13***

C211	AP87	100fr blk, bl & red	90	60

Birth centenary of Winston Churchill (1874-1965).

A particular stamp may be scarce, but if few collectors want it, its market value may remain relatively low.

Soccer, Arms of Frankfurt, Dortmund, Gelsenkirchen and Stuttgart — AP88

Designs: 100fr, Soccer and arms of Berlin, Hamburg, Hanover and Düsseldorf. 200fr, Soccer cup and game.

1974, Aug. 5 **Photo.** ***Perf. 13***

C212	AP88	45fr gray, sl & org	40	20
C213	AP88	100fr gray, sl & org	85	60
C214	AP88	200fr org, sl & bl	1.65	1.00
		Strip of 3, Nos. C212-C214	3.25	2.00

World Cup Soccer Championship, Munich, June 13-July 7. Nos. C212-C214 printed se-tenant in sheets containing 5 triptychs.

Nos. C212-C214 Overprinted in Dark Blue: "7th JULY 1974 / R.F.A. 2 HOLLANDE 1 / 7 JUILLET 1974"

1974, Sept. 16 **Photo.** ***Perf. 13***

C215	AP88	45fr multi	40	25
C216	AP88	100fr multi	85	65
C217	AP88	200fr multi	1.65	1.20
		Strip of 3, Nos. C215-C217	3.25	2.25

World Cup Soccer Championship, 1974, victory of German Federal Republic.

UPU Type of 1974

Designs: 100fr, Cameroun No. 503. 200fr, Cameroun No. C29.

1974, Oct. 8 **Engr.** ***Perf. 13***

C218	A142	100fr bl & multi	65	48
C219	A142	200fr red & multi	1.25	95

Centenary of Universal Postal Union.

Copernicus and Planets Circling Sun — AP89

1974, Oct. 15 **Engr.** ***Perf. 13***

C220	AP89	250fr multi	2.00	1.50

500th anniversary of the birth of Nicolaus Copernicus (1473-1543), Polish astronomer.

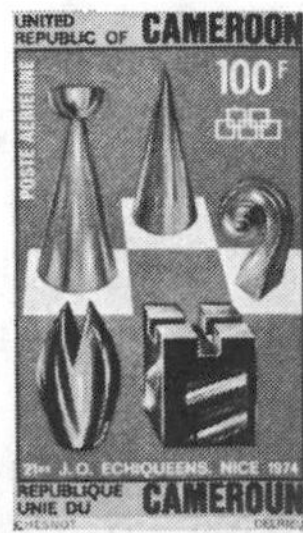

Chess Pieces — AP90

1974, Nov. 3 **Photo.** ***Perf. 13x12½***

C221	AP90	100fr multi	75	65

21st Chess Olympiad, Nice, France, June 6-30.

Mask and ARPHILA Emblem — AP91

1974, Nov. 30 **Engr.** ***Perf. 13***

C222	AP91	50fr choc & mag	40	25

ARPHILA 75, Paris, June 6-16, 1975.

Presidents and Flags of Cameroun, CAR, Gabon and Congo — AP92

1974, Dec. 8 **Photo.**

C223	AP92	100fr gold & multi	80	60

See note after No. 595.

Man Landing on Moon — AP93

1974, Dec. 15 **Engr.**

C224	AP93	200fr brn, bl & car	1.60	1.20

5th anniversary of man's first landing on the moon.

Charles de Gaulle and Félix Eboué — AP94

1975, Feb. 24 **Typo.** ***Perf. 13***

C225	AP94	45fr multi	50	25
C226	AP94	200fr multi	2.10	1.20

Felix A. Eboué (1884-1944), Governor of Chad, first colonial governor to join Free French in WWII, 30th death anniversary.

Marquis de Lafayette AP95

Designs: 140fr, George Washington and soldiers. 500fr, Benjamin Franklin and Independence Hall.

1975, Oct. 20 **Engr.** ***Perf. 13***

C227	AP95	100fr vio bl & multi	80	60
C228	AP95	140fr brn & multi	1.10	90
C229	AP95	500fr grn & multi	4.00	2.50

American Bicentennial.

The Burning Bush, by Nicolas Froment AP96

Painting: 500fr, Adoration of the Kings, by Gentile da Fabriano (horiz.).

1975, Dec. 25 **Photo.** ***Perf. 13***

C230	AP96	50fr gold & multi	50	25
C231	AP96	500fr gold & multi	4.75	2.50

Christmas 1975.

Concorde and Route: Paris-Dakar-Rio de Janeiro — AP97

1976, July 20 **Litho.** ***Perf. 13***

C232	AP97	500fr lt bl & multi	4.50	2.50
a.		Souvenir sheet	5.50	5.50

First commercial flight of supersonic jet Concorde from Paris to Rio de Janeiro, Jan. 21. No. C232a contains one stamp; black marginal inscription giving specifications of Concorde. Size: 130x93mm. Sold for 600fr.

Dance Type of 1976

Designs: 50fr, Dancers and drummer. 100fr, Woman dancer.

1976, Sept. 15 **Litho.** ***Perf. 12***

C233	A154	50fr gray & multi	40	30
C234	A154	100fr gray & multi	80	50

Virgin and Child, by Giovanni Bellini — AP98

Paintings: 30fr, Adoration of the Shepherds, by Le Brun. 60fr, Adoration of the Kings, by Rubens. 500fr, The Newborn, by Georges de la Tour.

1976, Dec. 15 **Litho.** ***Perf. 12½***

C235	AP98	30fr gold & multi	25	15
C236	AP98	60fr gold & multi	50	35
C237	AP98	70fr gold & multi	55	40
C238	AP98	500fr gold & multi	4.00	2.50
a.		Souvenir sheet of 4	5.50	5.50

Christmas 1976. No. C238a contains one each of Nos. C235-C238; black and gold marginal inscription. Size: 150x120mm.

Festival Type of 1977

Design: 60fr, Traditional Chief on his throne, sculpture.

1977, Feb. 4 **Litho.** ***Perf. 12½***

C239	A159	60fr multi	50	35

2nd World Black and African Festival, Lagos, Nigeria, Jan. 15-Feb. 12.

Crucifixion, by Matthias Grunewald — AP99

Paintings: 125fr, Christ on the Cross, by Velazquez (vert.). 150fr, The Deposition, by Titian.

1977, Apr. 2 **Litho.** ***Perf. 12½***

C240	AP99	50fr gold & multi	40	30
C241	AP99	125fr gold & multi	1.00	60
C242	AP99	150fr gold & multi	1.25	80
a.		Souvenir sheet of 3	2.75	2.75

Easter 1977. No. C242a contains one each of Nos. C240-C242, perf. 12; black and gold marginal inscription and black control number. Size: 210x115mm. Sold for 350fr.

Lions Emblem, Map of Africa — AP100

Rotary Emblem AP101

1977, Apr. 29 **Litho.** ***Perf. 12½***

C243	AP100	250fr multi	2.00	1.50

Lions Club of Douala, 19th Congress, Apr. 29-30.

1977, May 18

C244	AP101	60fr multi	50	35

Rotary Club of Douala, 20th anniversary.

Antoine de Saint-Exupery AP102

Charles Lindbergh and Spirit of St. Louis — AP103

Designs: 50fr, Jean Mermoz and his plane. 80fr, Maryse Bastié and her plane. 100fr, Sikorsky S-43. 300fr, Concorde.

1977, May 20 **Engr.** ***Perf. 13***

C245	AP103	50fr org & bl	40	30
C246	AP102	60fr mag & org	50	35
C247	AP103	80fr mag & bl	60	45
a.		Souvenir sheet of 3	1.75	1.75
C248	AP103	100fr grn & yel	80	60
C249	AP103	300fr multi	2.50	1.85
C250	AP103	500fr multi	4.00	2.75
a.		Souvenir sheet of 3	8.50	8.50
		Nos. C245-C250 (6)	8.80	6.30

Aviation pioneers and events. No. C247a contains one each of Nos. C245-C247; blue marginal inscription. Size: 170x100mm. Sold for 200fr. No. C250a contains one each of Nos. C248-C250; blue marginal inscription. Size: 190x100mm. Sold for 1000fr.

Sassenage Castle, Grenoble — AP104

1977, May 21 **Litho.** ***Perf. 12½***

C251	AP104	70fr multi	55	40

10th anniversary of International French Language Council.

Jufilex Type of 1977

Designs: 70fr, Switzerland (Zurich) No. 1L1 and Cameroun No. 16. 100fr, Switzerland (Geneva) No. 2L1 and Cameroun No. 254.

1977, June 5 **Litho.** ***Perf. 12***

C252	A161	70fr multi	55	40
C253	A161	100fr multi	80	60

Jufilex Philatelic Exhibition, Bern, Switzerland.

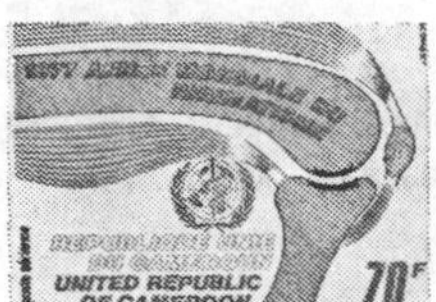

Diseased Knee, WHO Emblem AP105

1977, Oct. 15 **Engr.** ***Perf. 13***

C260	AP105	70fr multi	55	40

World Rheumatism Year.

Demand, as well as supply, determines a stamp's market value. One is as important as the other.

Nos. C249 and C232 Overprinted in Red: "PREMIER VOL PARIS-NEW YORK / FIRST FLIGHT PARIS-NEW YORK / 22 Nov. 1977-22nd Nov. 1977"

Engraved, Lithographed

1977, Nov. 22 ***Perf. 13***

C262 AP103	300fr multi		2.50	1.85
C263 AP97	500fr multi		4.00	3.00

Concorde, first commercial flight Paris to New York.

Christmas Type of 1977

Paintings: 60fr, Virgin and Child with 4 Saints, by Bellini (horiz.). 400fr, Adoration of the Shepherds, by George de la Tour (horiz.).

1977, Dec. 15 Litho. ***Perf. 12x12½***

C264 A165	60fr multi	50	35
C265 A165	400fr multi	3.50	2.50

Christmas 1977.

Flag Type of 1978

Design: 60fr, New flag, Pres. Ahidjo and spear.

1978, Apr. 3 Litho. ***Perf. 12½***

C266 A167	60fr multi	50	25

New flag of Cameroun.

Frog Type of 1978

Design: 100fr, Cardioglossa trifasciata.

1978, Apr. 5

C267 A168	100fr multi	85	60

L'Arlesienne, by Van Gogh — AP106

Painting: No. C269, Burial of Christ, by Albrecht Dürer.

1978, May 15 Litho. ***Perf. 12½***

C268 AP106	200fr multi	2.00	1.60
C269 AP106	200fr multi	2.00	1.60

Vincent Van Gogh (1853-1890), 125th birth anniversary and Albrecht Dürer (1471-1528), 450th death anniversary.

Leprosy Distribution on World Map, Raoul Follereau — AP107

1978, June 6 Litho. ***Perf. 12***

C270 AP107	100fr multi	1.00	80

25th World Leprosy Day.

Capt. Cook and Siege of Quebec — AP108

Design: 250fr, Capt. Cook, Adventure and Resolution, map of voyages.

1978, July 26 Engr. ***Perf. 13***

C271 AP108	100fr multi	1.00	80
C272 AP108	250fr multi	2.50	2.00

Capt. James Cook (1728-1779), explorer.

Argentine Soccer Team, Coat of Arms and Rimet Cup — AP109

Designs: 200fr, Two soccer players (vert.). 1000fr, Soccer ball illuminating world map (vert.).

1978, Sept. 1 Litho. ***Perf. 13***

C273 AP109	100fr multi	1.00	80
C274 AP109	200fr multi	2.00	1.60
C275 AP109	1000fr multi	10.00	8.00

11th World Cup Soccer Championship, Argentina, June 1-25.

Jules Verne Type of 1978

Design: 400fr, Jules Verne and "20,000 Leagues Under the Sea" (horiz.).

1978, Oct. 10 Litho. ***Perf. 12***

C276 A169	400fr multi	4.00	3.20

Jules Verne (1828-1905), science fiction writer, birth sesquicentennial.

Musical Instrument Type of 1978

Design: 100fr, Man playing Mvet zither.

1978, Nov. 20 Litho. ***Perf. 12½***

C277 A172	100fr multi	1.00	60

Human Rights Type of 1979

1979, Feb. 11 Litho. ***Perf. 12x12½***

C278 A174	500fr multi	5.00	4.00

Universal Declaration of Human Rights, 30th anniversary (in 1978).

Lions Emblem, Map of District 403 — AP110

1979, Apr. 26 Litho. ***Perf. 12½***

C279 AP110	60fr multi	60	40

21st Congress of Lions Club of Yaounde.

Penny Black, Hill, Cameroun No. 9 — AP111

1979, Aug. 30 Engr. ***Perf. 13***

C280 AP111	100fr multi	1.00	60

Sir Rowland Hill (1795-1879), originator of penny postage.

"TELECOM 79" — AP112

1979, Sept. 26 Litho. ***Perf. 13x12½***

C281 AP112	100fr multi	1.00	60

3rd World Telecommunications Exhibition, Geneva, Sept. 20-26.

Pope Paul VI — AP113

1979, Oct. 23 Engr. ***Perf. 12½x13***

C282 AP113	100fr *shown*	1.00	65
C283 AP113	100fr *John Paul I*	1.00	65
C284 AP113	100fr *John Paul II*	1.00	65

"Double Eagle" over French Coastline AP114

Design: No. C286, Balloonists and balloon.

1979, Dec. 15 Litho. ***Perf. 12½***

C285 AP114	500fr multi	6.00	3.50
C286 AP114	500fr multi	6.00	3.50

First Transatlantic balloon crossing.

100-Meter Race — AP115

Designs: 150fr, Figure skating pairs. 200fr, Javelin. 300fr, Wrestling.

1980, Dec. 18 Litho. ***Perf. 12½***

C287 AP115	100fr yel brn & brn	1.00	60
C288 AP115	150fr bl & brn	1.50	90
C289 AP115	200fr grn & brn	2.00	1.20
C290 AP115	300fr red & brn	3.00	1.80

22nd Summer Olympic Games, Moscow, July 19-Aug. 3; 13th Winter Olympic Games, Lake Placid, Feb. 12-24 (150fr).

Alan Shepard and Freedom 7 — AP116

1981, Sept. 15 Litho. ***Perf. 12½***

C291 AP116	500fr shown	5.00	3.00
C292 AP116	500fr Yuri Gagarin, Vostok I	5.00	3.00

Manned space flight, 20th anniv.

4th African Scouting Conference, Abidjan, June — AP117

1981, Oct. 5

C293 AP117	100fr Emblem, salute, badge	1.00	65
C294 AP117	500fr Scout saluting	5.00	3.00

Guernica (detail), by Pablo Picasso (1881-1973) — AP118

Design: No. C296, Landscape, by Paul Cezanne (1839-1906).

1981, Nov. 10 Litho. ***Perf. 12½***

C295 AP118	500fr multi	5.00	3.00
C296 AP118	500fr multi	5.00	3.00

Christmas 1981 — AP119

Designs: 50fr, Virgin and Child, by Froment (vert.). 60f, San Zeno Altarpiece, by Mantegna (vert.). 400fr, Flight into Egypt, by Giotto.

1981, Dec. 1 Litho. ***Perf. 12½***

C297 AP119	50fr multi	50	30
C298 AP119	60fr multi	60	40
C299 AP119	400fr multi	4.00	2.40
a.	Souvenir sheet of 3	5.25	3.25

No. C299a contains Nos. C297-C299 (perf. 13x13½); green and gold marginal inscription. Size: 190x112mm.

The only foreign revenue stamps listed in this Catalogue are those authorized for prepayment of postage.

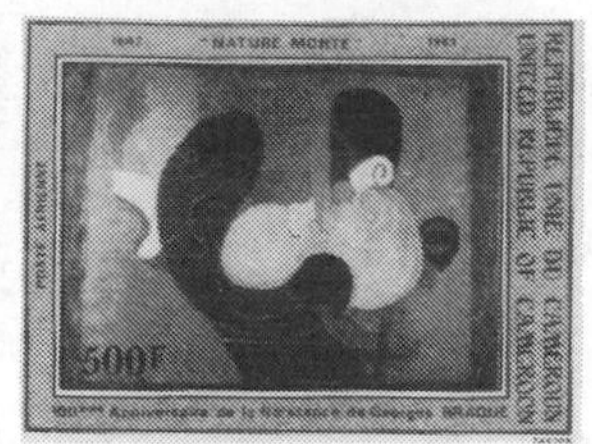

Still Life, by Georges Braque (1882-1963) — AP120

Paintings: No. C301, Olympia, by Edouard Manet (1832-1883).

1982, Dec. 5	**Litho.**	***Perf. 13***		
C300 AP120	500fr multi		4.50	3.00
C301 AP120	500fr multi		4.50	3.00

Pres. John F. Kennedy (1917-1963) AP121

1983, Mar. 15	**Litho.**	***Perf. 13***		
C302 AP121	500fr multi		5.00	3.00

Lions District 403 (Douala), 2nd Convention, May — AP122

1983, May 5	**Litho.**	***Perf. 12½***		
C303 AP122	70fr multi		60	45
C304 AP122	150fr multi		1.40	1.00

Jeanne of Aragon by Raphael AP123

Design: No. C306, Massacre of Scio by Delacroix.

1983, Oct. 15	**Litho.**	***Perf. 13***		
C305 AP123	500fr multi		2.75	1.50
C306 AP123	500fr multi		2.75	1.50

Easter 1984 — AP124

Designs: 200fr, Pieta, by G. Hernandez. 500fr, Martyrdom of St. John the Evangelist, by C. Le Brun.

1984, Mar. 30	**Litho.**	***Perf. 13***		
C307 AP124	200fr multi		1.00	65
C308 AP124	500fr multi		2.50	1.60
a.	Souvenir sheet of 2		3.50	2.25

No. C308a contains Nos. C307-C308. Size: 160x106mm.

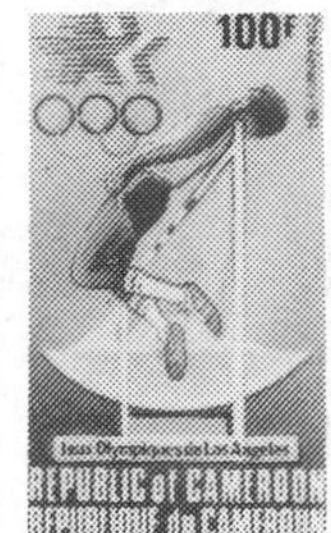

1984 Summer Olympics AP125

1984, Apr. 30		***Perf. 12½***		
C309 AP125	100fr	High jump	50	32
C310 AP125	150fr	Volleyball	75	48
C311 AP125	250fr	Handball	1.25	80
C312 AP125	500fr	Bicycling	2.50	1.60

European Soccer Championship, June 12-27 — AP126

1984, June 5	**Litho.**	***Perf. 12½***		
C313 AP126	250fr	Player in red shorts	1.25	80
C314 AP126	250fr	Yellow shorts	1.25	80
C315 AP126	500fr	Players	2.50	1.65
a.		Souvenir sheet of 3	5.00	2.50

No. C315a contains Nos. C313-C315 in changed panel colors. Size: 131x85mm.

Presidential Oath — AP127

1984	**Litho.**	***Perf. 13***		
C316 AP127	60fr	French inscription	28	20
a.		English inscription	28	20
C317 AP127	70fr	French inscription	32	22
a.		English inscription	32	22
C318 AP127	200fr	French inscription	95	60
a.		English inscription	95	60

Issue dates: French, Sept. 15; English, Nov.

Catalogue prices for unused stamps up to mid-1953 are for hinged copies matching the condition specified in this volume's introduction.

Famous Men — AP128

Paintings: C316, Diana in the Bath, by Watteau (1684-1721). C317, Portrait of Diderot (1713-1784).

1984, Sept. 20	**Litho.**	***Perf. 13***		
C319 AP128	500fr	Witteau	2.25	1.50
C320 AP128	500fr	Diderot, vert.	2.25	1.50

Nos. C309-C312 in Changed Colors with Added Inscriptions as Noted

1984, Sept. 25	**Litho.**	***Perf. 12½***		
C321 AP125	100fr	MOEGENBURG (R.F.A.) 11-08-84	45	30
C322 AP125	150fr	U.S.A. 11-08-84	68	45
C323 AP125	250fr	YOUGOSLAVIE 9-08-84	1.15	80
C324 AP125	500fr	GORSKI (U.S.A.) 3-08-84	2.25	1.50

Moon Landing, 15th Anniv. — AP129

1984, Nov. 15	**Litho.**	***Perf. 12½***		
C325 AP129	500fr	Neil Armstrong	2.25	1.50
C326 AP129	500fr	Apollo 12 launching	2.25	1.50

Louis Pasteur (1822-1895), Chemist, Microbiologist — AP130

Designs: No. 328, Mourning Woman (detail), Mausoleum of Henri Claude d'Harcourt, by sculptor Jean Baptiste Pigalle (1714-1785).

1985, Oct. 10	**Litho.**	***Perf. 13***		
C327 AP130	500fr multi		2.75	2.75
C328 AP130	500fr multi		2.75	2.75

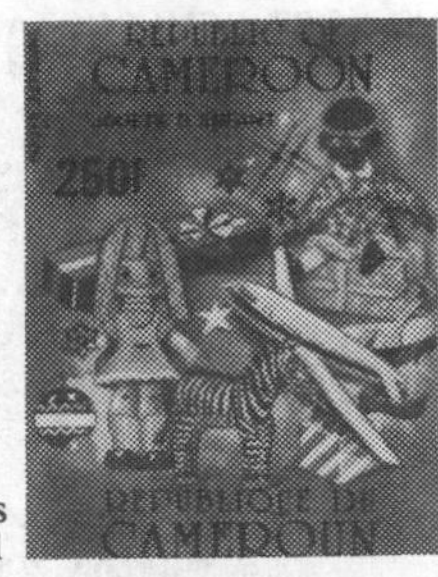

Christmas AP131

Designs: 250fr, Children's gifts. 300fr, Akono Church. 400fr, Holy Family and drummer boy. 500fr, The Virgin with the Blue Diadem, by Raphael.

1985, Dec. 20	**Litho.**	***Perf. 13***		
C329 AP131	250fr multi		1.40	1.40
C330 AP131	300fr multi		1.65	1.65
C331 AP131	400fr multi		2.25	2.25
C332 AP131	500fr multi		2.75	2.75

1986 World Cup Soccer Championships, Mexico — AP132

1986		***Perf. 13½***		
C333 AP132	250fr	Argentina, winner	1.40	1.40
C334 AP132	300fr	Stadium	1.65	1.65
C335 AP132	400fr	Mexican team	2.25	2.25

Famous Men — AP133

Designs: No. C336, Pierre Curie (1859-1906), chemist, atom, and elements. No. C337, Jean Mermoz (1901-1936), aviator, and aircraft.

1986, Sept. 10	**Litho.**	***Perf. 12½***		
C336 AP133	500fr multi		2.75	2.75
C337 AP133	500fr multi		2.75	2.75

AIR POST SEMI-POSTAL STAMPS.

V9

V10

Stamps of the designs shown above were issued in 1942 by the Vichy Government, but were not placed on sale in Cameroun.

POSTAGE DUE STAMPS.

Man Felling Tree — D1

Perf. 14x13½

1925-27		Unwmk.		Typo.
J1	D1	2c lt bl & blk	15	15
J2	D1	4c ol bis & red vio	15	15
J3	D1	5c vio & blk	28	28
J4	D1	10c red & blk	28	28
J5	D1	15c gray & blk	38	38
J6	D1	20c ol grn & blk	45	45
J7	D1	25c yel & blk	50	50
J8	D1	30c bl & org	60	60
J9	D1	50c brn & blk	75	75
J10	D1	60c bl grn & rose red	90	90
J11	D1	1fr dl red & grn, grnsh	1.25	1.25
J12	D1	2fr red & vio ('27)	2.25	2.25
J13	D1	3fr org brn & ultra ('27)	3.25	3.25
		Nos. J1-J13 (13)	11.19	11.19

Carved Figures — D2

D3

1939		Engr.	Perf. 14x13	
J14	D2	5c brt red vio	6	6
J15	D2	10c Prus bl	50	50
J16	D2	15c car rose	6	6
J17	D2	20c blk brn	6	6
J18	D2	30c ultra	6	6
J19	D2	50c dk grn	22	22
J20	D2	60c brn vio	22	22
J21	D2	1fr dk vio	45	45
J22	D2	2fr org red	80	80
J23	D2	3fr dk bl	1.25	1.25
		Nos. J14-J23 (10)	3.68	3.68

A 10c stamp, type D2, without "RF" was issued in 1944 by the Vichy Government, but was not placed on sale in Cameroun.

1947		Unwmk.	Perf. 13.	
J24	D3	10c dk red	5	5
J25	D3	30c dp org	5	5
J26	D3	50c grnsh blk	6	6
J27	D3	1fr dk car	15	15
J28	D3	2fr dp yel grn	30	30
J29	D3	3fr dp red lil	32	32
J30	D3	4fr dp ultra	32	32
J31	D3	5fr red brn	38	38
J32	D3	10fr pck bl	60	60
J33	D3	20fr sepia	1.00	1.00
		Nos. J24-J33 (10)	3.23	3.23

Federal Republic

Hibiscus — D4

Flowers: No. J35, Erythrine. No. J36, Plumeria lutea. No. J37, Ipomoea. No. J38, Hoodia gordonii. No. J39, Grinum. No. J40, Ochna. No. J41, Gloriosa. No. J42, Costus spectabilis. No. J43, Bougainvillea spectabilis. No. J44, Delonix regia. No. J45, Haemanthus. No. J46, Ophthalmophyllum. No. J47, Titanopsis. No. J48, Amorphophallus. No. J49, Zingiberacee.

Unwmk.

1963, Apr. 10		Engr.	Perf. 11	
J34	D4	50c car, bl, grn & yel	5	5
J35	D4	50c car, bl, grn & yel	5	5
J36	D4	1fr mag, grn & yel	6	6
J37	D4	1fr mag, grn & yel	6	6
J38	D4	1.50fr dk grn, lil & yel	5	5
J39	D4	1.50fr dk grn, lil & yel	5	5
J40	D4	2fr org ver, yel & grn	12	12
J41	D4	2fr org ver, yel & grn	12	12
J42	D4	5fr mag, grn & yel	15	15
J43	D4	5fr mag, grn & yel	15	15
J44	D4	10fr crim, grn & yel	32	32
J45	D4	10fr crim, grn & yel	32	32
J46	D4	20fr grn, yel & lil	70	70
J47	D4	20fr grn, yel & lil	70	70
J48	D4	40fr lil & yel	1.25	1.25
J49	D4	40fr lil & yel	1.25	1.25
		Nos. J34-J49 (16)	5.40	5.40

The two types of each value in Nos. J34-J49 were printed tete beche, se-tenant at the base.

MILITARY STAMP

M1

1963, July 1		Unwmk.	Perf. 13	
M1	M1	rose cl	2.25	2.25

CAPE JUBY

LOCATION — Northwest coast of Africa in Spanish Sahara.
GOVT. — Spanish administration.
AREA — 12,700 sq. mi.
POP. — 9,836.
CAPITAL — Villa Bens (Cape Juby).

By agreement with France, Spain's Sahara possessions were extended to include Cape Juby and in 1916 Spanish troops occupied the territory. It is attached for administrative purposes to Spanish Sahara.

100 Centimos = 1 Peseta

Stamps of Rio de Oro, 1914 Surcharged in Violet, Red or Green

CABO JUBI
5
CÉNTIMOS

1916		Unwmk.	Perf. 13.	
1	A6	5c on 4p rose (V)	115.00	20.00
2	A6	10c on 10p dl vio (R)	42.50	20.00
3	A6	15c on 50c dk brn (G)	57.50	37.50
4	A6	15c on 50c dk brn (R)	42.50	20.00
5	A6	40c on 1p red vio (G)	90.00	45.00
6	A6	40c on 1p red vio (R)	75.00	25.00
		Nos. 1-6 (6)	422.50	167.50

Nos. 1-6 exist with inverted surcharge. Prices about twice those quoted.

Stamps of Spain, 1876-1917, Overprinted in Red or Black

1919			Imperf.	
7	A21	1/4c bl grn (R)	25	6
		Perf. 13x12½, 14.		
8	A46	2c dk brn (Bk)	25	6
a.		Double overprint	20.00	9.00
b.		Double overprint (Bk + R)	55.00	37.50
9	A46	5c grn (R)	55	6
a.		Double overprint	20.00	9.00
b.		Inverted overprint	28.50	18.50
10	A46	10c car (Bk)	65	10
a.		Double overprint (Bk + R)	55.00	37.50
11	A46	15c ocher (Bk)	3.00	20
b.		Double overprint	20.00	9.00
c.		Red control #	4.50	4.50
d.		As "c," inverted ovpt.	15.00	
12	A46	20c ol grn (R)	16.50	3.00
13	A46	25c dp bl (R)	2.75	30
a.		Double overprint	20.00	9.00
14	A46	30c bl grn (R)	2.75	40
15	A46	40c rose (Bk)	2.75	40
16	A46	50c sl bl (R)	3.25	40
17	A46	1p lake (Bk)	9.00	3.00
18	A46	4p dp vio (R)	35.00	14.00
19	A46	10p org (Bk)	47.50	15.00
		Nos. 7-19 (13)	124.20	36.98

Nos. 8-19 have blue control number or back.
Nos. 8-13, 15, 17-19 exist imperf.

Same Overprint on Stamps of Spain, 1920-21.

1922			Imperf.	
20	A47	1c bl grn (R)	25.00	13.00

Engr. **Perf. 13x12½.**

Blue Control Number on Back.

23	A46	20c violet	125.00	42.50

A 2c litho. exists, price $300.

Same Overprint on Stamps of Spain, 1922-23.

1925			Perf. 13½x13.	
25	A49	5c red vio	5.50	2.50
26	A49	10c bl grn	16.00	2.50
28	A49	20c violet	35.00	8.00

Spain #331, 2c ol grn, exists. Price $300 unused, $80 canceled

Seville-Barcelona Exposition Issue.
Stamps of Spain, 1929, Overprinted in Red or Blue.

CABO JUBY

1929			Perf. 11.	
29	A52	5c rose lake (Bl)	25	20
30	A53	10c grn (R)	25	20
31	A50	15c Prus bl (R)	25	20
32	A51	20c pur (R)	25	20
33	A50	25c brt rose (Bl)	25	20
34	A52	30c blk brn (Bl)	30	40
35	A53	40c dk bl (R)	30	40
36	A51	50c dp org (Bl)	50	60
37	A52	1p bl blk (R)	14.00	8.50
38	A53	4p dp rose (Bl)	17.50	17.50
39	A53	10p brn (Bl)	17.50	12.50
		Nos. 29-39 (11)	51.35	40.90

Stamps of Spanish Morocco, 1928-33, Overprinted in Black or Red

Cabo Juby

1934			Perf. 14.	
40	A7	1c brt rose (Bk)	35	40
41	A2	2c dk vio (R)	3.25	45
42	A2	5c dp bl (R)	3.25	65
43	A2	10c dk grn (Bk)	7.00	1.25
43A	A10	10c dk grn (R)	2.25	1.90
44	A2	15c org brn (Bk)	16.00	6.00
45	A7	20c sl grn (R)	6.50	3.75
46	A3	25c cop red (Bk)	3.25	3.25
47	A10	30c red brn (Bk)	6.50	3.75
48	A13	40c dp bl (R)	22.50	14.00
49	A13	50c red org (Bk)	42.50	22.50
50	A4	1p yel grn (Bk)	26.00	12.50
51	A5	2.50p red vio (Bk)	57.50	27.50
52	A6	4p ultra (R)	75.00	35.00

No. 43A and 1c, 20c, 30c, 40c, 50c, with control numbers.

Same Overprint in Black on Stamp of Spanish Morocco, 1932.

53	A2	1c car rose ("Ct")	1.40	65
		Nos. 40-53 (15)	273.25	133.55

Stamps of Spanish Morocco, 1933-35, Overprinted in Black, Blue or Red

CABO JUBY

1935-36				
54	A8	2c grn (R)	55	15
55	A9	5c mag (Bk)	2.25	20
55A	A10	10c dk grn (R) ('36)	12.50	2.25
56	A11	15c yel (Bl)	5.00	1.50
57	A12	25c crim (Bk)	42.50	2.50
58	A8	1p sl blk (R)	7.50	3.75
59	A9	2.50p brn (Bl)	30.00	14.00
60	A11	4p yel grn (R)	40.00	17.00
61	A12	5p blk (R)	40.00	22.50
		Nos. 54-61 (9)	180.30	63.85

Same Overprint in Black or Red on Stamps of Spanish Morocco, 1935.

1935			Perf. 13½.	
62	A14	25c vio (R)	3.50	1.50
63	A15	30c crim (Bk)	3.50	1.25
64	A14	40c org (Bk)	4.75	1.50
65	A15	50c brt bl (R)	9.25	1.50
66	A14	60c dk bl grn (R)	11.00	3.50
67	A15	2p brn lake (Bk)	60.00	22.50

Same Overprint on Stamps of Spanish Morocco, 1933.

Perf. 13½, 14.

68	A7	1c brt rose (Bk)	20	10
		Perf. 14		
69	A7	20c sl grn (R)	4.75	2.25
		Nos. 62-69 (8)	96.95	34.10

Same Overprint on Stamps of Spanish Morocco, 1937.

1937			Perf. 13½.	
70	A21	1c dk bl (Bk)	25	10
71	A21	2c org brn (Bk)	25	10
72	A21	5c cer (Bk)	25	10
73	A21	10c emer (Bk)	25	10
74	A21	15c brt bl (Bk)	30	15
75	A21	20c red brn (Bk)	30	15
76	A21	25c mag (Bk)	30	15
77	A21	30c red org (Bk)	30	15
78	A21	40c org (Bk)	1.00	60
79	A21	50c ultra (R)	1.00	60
80	A21	60c yel grn (Bk)	1.00	60
81	A21	1p bl vio (Bk)	1.00	60
82	A21	2p Prus bl (Bk)	55.00	50.00
83	A21	2.50p gray blk (R)	55.00	50.00
84	A21	4p dk brn (Bk)	55.00	50.00
85	A22	10p vio blk (R)	55.00	50.00
		Nos. 70-85 (16)	226.20	203.40

Issued in commemoration of the First Year of the Revolution.

Same Overprint in Black on Types of Spanish Morocco, 1939.

Designs: 5c, Spanish quarter. 10c, Moroccan quarter. 15c, Street scene, Larache. 20c, Tetuan.

1939		Photo.	Perf. 13½.	
86	A25	5c vermillion	60	45
87	A25	10c dp grn	60	45
88	A25	15c brn lake	60	55
89	A25	20c brt bl	60	55

Same Overprint in Black or Red on Stamps of Spanish Morocco, 1940.

1940 *Perf. 11½x11.*
90 A26 1c dk brn (Bk) 15 6
91 A27 2c ol grn (R) 15 6
92 A28 5c dk bl (R) 15 6
93 A29 10c dk red lil (Bk) 20 6
94 A30 15c dk grn (R) 20 6
95 A31 20c pur (R) 20 6
96 A32 25c blk brn (R) 20 15
97 A33 30c brt grn (Bk) 20 15
98 A34 40c sl grn (R) 60 25
99 A35 45c org ver (Bk) 60 25
100 A36 50c brn org (Bk) 60 25
101 A37 70c saph (R) 1.50 60
102 A38 1p ind & brn (Bk) 3.50 60
103 A39 2.50p choc & dk grn (Bk) 8.25 4.25
104 A40 5p dk cer & sep (Bk) 8.25 4.25
105 A41 10p dk ol grn & brn org (Bk) 25.00 16.00
Nos. 90-105 (16) 49.75 27.11

Stamps of Spanish Morocco, 1944. Overprinted in Black or Red

CABO JUBY

1944 **Unwmk.** *Perf. 12½.*
106 A47 1c choc & lt bl 10 10
107 A48 2c sl grn & lt grn 10 10
108 A49 5c choc & grnsh blk (R) 10 10
109 A50 10c brt ultra & red org 10 10
110 A51 15c sl grn & lt grn 10 10
111 A52 20c dp cl & blk (R) 10 10
112 A53 25c lt bl & choc 10 10
113 A47 30c yel grn & brt ultra (R) 10 10
114 A48 40c choc & red vio 10 10
115 A49 50c brt ultra, & red brn 10 10
116 A50 75c yel grn & brt ultra (R) 90 40
117 A51 1p brt ultra & choc 90 40
118 A52 2.50p blk & brt ultra (R) 2.50 2.00
119 A53 10p sal & gray blk (R) 17.50 14.00
Nos. 106-119 (14) 22.80 17.80

Same Overprint on Stamps of Spanish Morocco, 1946.

1946 *Perf. 10½x10.*
120 A54 1c pur & brn 10 10
121 A55 2c dk Prus grn & vio blk (R) 10 10
122 A54 10c dp org vio bl 10 10
123 A55 15c dk bl & bl grn 10 10
124 A54 25c yel grn & ultra 10 10
125 A56 40c dk bl & brn (R) 10 10
126 A55 45c blk & rose 20 20
127 A57 1p dk Prus grn & dp bl 1.00 45
128 A58 2.50p dp org & grnsh gray (R) 3.00 2.25
129 A59 10p dk bl & gray (R) 10.00 6.75
Nos. 120-129 (10) 14.80 10.25

Same Overprint in Carmine, Black or Brown on Stamps of Spanish Morocco, 1948.

1948 *Perf. 10, 10x10½*
130 A64 2c pur & brn 8 8
131 A65 5c dp cl & vio 8 8
132 A66 15c brt ultra & bl grn (Bk) 8 8
133 A67 25c blk & Prus grn 8 8
134 A65 35c brt ultra & gray blk 10 10
135 A68 50c red & vio (Br) 10 10
136 A66 70c dk gray grn & ultra (Bk) 10 10
137 A67 90c cer & dk gray grn (Bk) 10 10
138 A68 1p brt ultra & vio (Br) 25 25
139 A64 2.50p vio brn & sl grn 1.00 60
140 A69 10p blk & dp ultra 3.25 2.50
Nos. 130-140 (11) 5.22 4.07

SEMI-POSTAL STAMPS.

Types of Semi-Postal Stamps of Spain, 1926, Overprinted

CABO–JUBY

1926 **Unwmk.** *Perf. 12½, 13*
B1 SP1 1c orange 9.00 5.00
B2 SP2 2c rose 9.00 5.00
B3 SP3 5c blk brn 2.50 2.00
B4 SP4 10c dk grn 1.40 1.10
B5 SP1 15c dk vio 75 75
B6 SP4 20c vio brn 75 75
B7 SP5 25c dp car 75 75
B8 SP1 30c ol grn 75 75
B9 SP3 40c ultra 8 8
B10 SP2 50c red brn 8 8
B11 SP4 1p vermilion 8 8
B12 SP3 4p bister 90 65
B13 SP5 10p lt vio 1.65 1.40
Nos. B1-B13 (13) 27.69 18.39

AIR POST STAMPS.

Spanish Morocco, Nos. C1 to C10 Overprinted in Black

CABO JUBY

1938, June 1 **Unwmk.** *Perf. 13½.*
C1 AP1 5c brown 20 8
C2 AP1 10c brt grn 20 8
C3 AP1 25c crimson 15 8
C4 AP1 40c lt bl 2.25 1.25
C5 AP2 50c brt mag 20 8
C6 AP2 75c dk bl 20 30
C7 AP1 1p sepia 20 30
C8 AP1 1.50p dp vio 1.25 65
C9 AP1 2p dp red brn 3.00 1.65
C10 AP1 3p brn blk 8.00 5.50
Nos. C1-C10 (10) 15.65 9.97

Strait of Gibraltar — AP3

Designs: 5c, Ketama landscape. 10c, Mosque, Tangier. 15c, Velez. 90c, Sanjurjo.

1942, Apr. 1 **Photo.** *Perf. 12½*
C11 AP3 5c dp bl 10 10
C12 AP3 10c org brn 10 10
C13 AP3 15c grnsh blk 10 10
C14 AP3 90c dk rose 60 45
C15 AP3 5p black 2.25 1.65
Nos. C11-C15 (5) 3.15 2.40

SPECIAL DELIVERY STAMPS.

Special Delivery Stamp of Spain Overprinted "CABO JUBY" as on Nos. 7-28.

1919 **Unwmk.** *Perf. 14*
E1 SD1 20c red (Bk) 1.60 1.00
b. Double overprint 28.50 16.50

Spanish Morocco No. E4 Overprinted in Red

Cabo Juby

1934
E2 SD2 20c black 7.00 6.75

Spanish Morocco No. E5 Overprinted in Black

CABO JUBY

1935
E3 SD3 20c vermilion 3.50 1.00

Same Overprint on Spanish Morocco, No. E6.

1937 *Perf. 13½.*
E4 SD4 20c brt car 1.00 60

Issued in commemoration of the First Year of the Revolution.

Same Overprint on Spanish Morocco, No. E8.

1940 *Perf. 11½x11.*
E5 SD5 25c scarlet 45 30

SEMI-POSTAL SPECIAL DELIVERY STAMP.

Type of Semi-Postal Special Delivery Stamp of Spain, 1926, Overprinted

CABO–JUBY

1926 **Unwmk.** *Perf. 12½, 13.*
EB1 SPSD1 20c ultra & blk 2.50 1.75

CAPE VERDE

LOCATION — A group of 10 islands and five islets in the Atlantic Ocean, about 500 miles due west of Senegal.
GOVT. — Republic.
AREA — 1,557 sq. mi.
POP. — 296,093 (1980).
CAPITAL — Praia.

The Portuguese territory of Cape Verde became independent on July 5, 1975.

1000 Reis = 1 Milreis
100 Centavos = 1 Escudo (1913)

Crown of Portugal
A1

King Luiz
A2

Perf. 12½, 13½.

1877 **Unwmk.** **Typo.**
1 A1 5r black 1.75 1.25
2 A1 10r yellow 17.50 8.00
3 A1 20r bister 1.25 1.00
4 A1 25r rose 1.65 1.00
a. Perf. 13½ 7.00 5.00
5 A1 40r blue 65.00 30.00
a. Cliche of Mozambique in Cape Verde plate, in pair with #5 1,250. 1,000.
b. As "a," perf. 13½ 1,900. 1,900.
6 A1 50r green 65.00 42.50
7 A1 100r lilac 7.00 2.75
8 A1 200r orange 3.00 2.50
a. Perf. 13½ 7.00 5.00
9 A1 300r brown 2.75 2.25

1881-85
10 A1 10r green 1.75 1.50
11 A1 20r car ('85) 3.75 2.50
a. Perf. 13½ 40.00 30.00
12 A1 25r vio ('85) 2.75 2.00
13 A1 40r yel buff 1.75 1.50
a. Imperf. 90
b. Cliche of Mozambique in Cape Verde plate, in pair with #13 90.00 90.00
c. As "b," imperf. 30.00
14 A1 50r blue 5.50 3.75

Reprints of the 1877-85 issues are on smooth white chalky paper, ungummed, and on thin white paper with shiny white gum. They are perf. 13½. Price, $2.75 each.

1886 **Embossed** *Perf. 12½, 13½*
Chalk-Surfaced Paper.
15 A2 5r black 2.75 2.00
16 A2 10r green 3.00 2.25
17 A2 20r carmine 4.25 3.00
a. Perf. 13½ 5.50 4.50
18 A2 25r violet 4.50 2.00
19 A2 40r chocolate 5.00 2.50
a. Perf. 13½ 7.50 5.00
20 A2 50r blue 5.00 2.25
21 A2 100r yel brn 5.25 2.75
22 A2 200r gray lil 12.00 8.00
23 A2 300r orange 14.00 10.00

The 25, 50 and 100r have been reprinted in aniline colors with clean-cut Perf. 13½. Price $3.50 each.

Cape Verde stamps can be mounted in Scott's annual Portugal Supplement.

King Carlos
A3 A4

Perf. 11½, 12½, 13½.

1894-95 **Typo.**
24 A3 5r orange 1.20 90
25 A3 10r redsh vio 1.25 1.00
26 A3 15r chocolate 2.25 1.50
a. Perf. 12½ 125.00 85.00
27 A3 20r lavender 2.75 1.75
28 A3 25r dp grn 2.75 2.00
a. Perf. 12½ 3.00 2.00
29 A3 50r lt bl 2.25 2.00
a. Perf. 13½ 7.00 2.50
30 A3 75r car ('95) 9.00 5.50
a. Perf. 13½ 25.00 15.00
31 A3 80r yel grn ('95) 11.00 7.00
a. Perf. 13½ 16.50 11.00
32 A3 100r brn, *buff* ('95) 7.50 2.25
a. Perf. 12½ 37.50 15.00
33 A3 150r car, *rose* ('95) 15.00 11.00
a. Perf. 12½ 110.00 90.00
b. Perf. 11½ 37.50 25.00
34 A3 200r dk bl, *lt bl* ('95) 12.50 8.00
a. Perf. 12½ 100.00 80.00
35 A3 300r dk bl, *sal* ('95) 22.50 13.50

1898-1903 *Perf. 11½.*
Name and Value in Black except 500r
36 A4 2½r gray 25 20
37 A4 5r orange 25 20
38 A4 10r lt grn 30 20
39 A4 15r brown 3.75 1.50
40 A4 15r gray grn ('03) 1.25 1.00
41 A4 20r gray vio 1.10 50
42 A4 25r sea grn 2.50 1.00
a. Perf. 12½ 60.00 25.00
43 A4 25r car ('03) 80 25
44 A4 50r dk bl 2.50 90
45 A4 50r brn ('03) 2.50 2.00
46 A4 65r sl bl ('03) 12.50 *12.50*
47 A4 75r rose 6.00 3.00
48 A4 75r lil ('03) 2.25 1.75
49 A4 80r violet 5.25 3.50
50 A4 100r dk bl, *bl* 1.75 1.10
51 A4 115r org brn, *pink* ('03) 10.00 *10.00*
52 A4 130r brn, *straw* ('03) 10.00 *10.00*
53 A4 150r brn, *straw* 6.00 4.00
54 A4 200r red vio, *pnksh* 2.50 2.00
55 A4 300r dk bl, *rose* 7.50 3.75
56 A4 400r dl bl, *straw* ('03) 7.50 6.00
57 A4 500r blk & red, *bl* ('01) 7.50 3.75
58 A4 700r vio, *yelsh* ('01) 20.00 12.50
Nos. 36-58 (23) 113.95 81.60

Regular Issues Surcharged in Red or Black

Two spacing types of surcharge. See note above Angola No. 61.

On Issue of 1886.

1902, Dec. 1 *Perf. 12½, 13½*
59 A2 65r on 5r blk (R) 4.00 3.00
60 A2 65r on 200r gray lil 4.00 3.00
61 A2 65r on 300r org 4.00 3.00
62 A2 115r on 10r grn 4.00 3.00
63 A2 115r on 20r rose 4.00 3.00
a. Perf. 13½ 30.00 20.00
64 A2 130r on 50r bl 4.00 3.00
65 A2 130r on 100r brn 4.00 3.00
66 A2 400r on 25r vio 2.00 1.75
67 A2 400r on 40r choc 3.00 2.75
a. Perf. 13½ 30.00 22.50

On Issue of 1894.

Perf. 11½, 12½, 13½.
68 A3 65r on 10r red vio 6.50 4.00
69 A3 65r on 20r lav 6.00 3.00
70 A3 65r on 100r brn, *buff* 6.00 4.00
a. Perf 12½ 15.00 10.00
71 A3 115r on 5r org 3.25 2.50
a. Inverted surcharge 15.00 15.00
72 A3 115r on 25r bl grn 3.00 2.40
a. Perf. 11½ 17.50 8.00
73 A3 115r on 150r car, *rose* 6.00 5.00
a. Perf. 13½ 25.00 15.00
74 A3 130r on 75r car 3.25 2.75
a. Perf. 13½ 37.50 25.00
75 A3 130r on 80r yel grn 3.00 2.75
76 A3 130r on 200r dk bl, *bl* 4.00 2.50
77 A3 400r on 50r lt bl 4.00 3.00
a. Inverted surcharge 40.00 40.00
b. Perf. 13½ 50.00 40.00
78 A3 400r on 300r dk bl, *sal* 2.00 1.50

On Newspaper Stamp of 1893.

79 N1 400r on 2½r brn 1.65 1.50
a. Inverted surcharge 12.50
b. Perf. 12½ 37.50 25.00
Nos. 59-79 (21) 81.65 60.40

Reprints of Nos. 59, 66, 67, and 77 have shiny white gum and clean-cut perforation 13½. Price $1 each.

Overprinted in Black On Nos. 39, 42, 44, 47 — PROVISORIO

1902-03 *Perf. 11½*

80 A4 15r brown 1.50 1.10
81 A4 25r sea grn 1.50 1.10
82 A4 50r bl ('03) 1.75 1.40
83 A4 75r rose ('03) 2.50 2.00
a. Invtd. ovpt. 20.00 20.00

No. 46 Surcharged in Black — 50 RÉIS

1905, July 1

84 A4 50r on 65r sl bl 2.50 2.25

Stamps of 1898-1903 Overprinted in Carmine or Green

1911, Aug. 20

85 A4 2½r gray 30 25
86 A4 5r orange 30 25
87 A4 10r lt grn 90 80
88 A4 15r gray grn 55 30
89 A4 20r gray vio 1.00 1.00
90 A4 25r car (G) 1.00 50
91 A4 50r brown 6.50 4.25
92 A4 75r red lil 1.25 75
93 A4 100r dk bl, *bl* 1.25 90
94 A4 115r org brn, *pink* 70 2.00
95 A4 130r brn, *straw* 70 2.00
96 A4 200r red vio, *pnksh* 5.00 5.00
97 A4 400r dl bl, *straw* 2.00 2.00
98 A4 500r blk & red, *bl* 2.25 1.75
99 A4 700r vio, *straw* 2.25 1.75
Nos. 85-99 (15) 25.95 23.50

King Manuel II — A5

Overprinted in Carmine or Green.

1912 *Perf. 11½x12*

100 A5 2½r violet 15 2.00
101 A5 5r black 15 12
102 A5 10r gray grn 25 25
103 A5 20r car (G) 2.00 1.10
104 A5 25r vio brn 40 25
105 A5 50r dk bl 3.25 2.50
106 A5 75r bis brn 70 50
107 A5 100r brn, *lt grn* 70 50
108 A5 200r dk grn, *sal* 1.10 90
109 A5 300r *azure* 1.10 90

Perf. 14½x15.

110 A5 400r blk & bl 3.00 2.50
111 A5 500r ol grn & vio brn 3.00 2.50
Nos. 100-111 (12) 15.80 14.02

Vasco da Gama Issue of Various Portuguese Colonies.

Common Design Types CD20-CD27 Surcharged — REPUBLICA CABO VERDE ¼ C.

On Stamps of Macao.

1913, Feb. 13 *Perf. 12½ to 16*

112 ¼c on ½a bl grn 1.25 1.25
113 ½c on 1a red 1.25 1.25
114 1c on 2a red vio 1.25 1.25
115 2½c on 4a yel grn 1.25 1.25
116 5c on 8a dk bl 6.00 6.00
117 7½c on 12a vio brn 5.50 5.50
118 10c on 16a bis brn 2.50 2.50
119 15c on 24a bis 4.50 4.50
Nos. 112-119 (8) 23.50 23.50

On Stamps of Portuguese Africa.

Perf. 14 to 15.

120 ¼c on 2½r bl grn 90 90
121 ½c on 5r red 90 90
122 1c on 10r red vio 90 90
123 2½c on 25r yel grn 90 90
124 5c on 50r dk bl 2.00 2.00
125 7½c on 75r vio brn 2.75 2.75
126 10c on 100r bis brn 2.25 2.25
127 15c on 150r bis 3.00 3.00
Nos. 120-127 (8) 13.60 13.60

On Stamps of Timor.

128 ¼c on ½a bl grn 1.25 1.25
129 ½c on 1a red 1.25 1.25
130 1c on 2a red vio 1.25 1.25
131 2½c on 4a yel grn 1.25 1.25
132 5c on 8a dk bl 5.50 5.50
133 7½c On 12a vio brn 5.50 5.50
134 10c on 16a bis brn 2.75 2.75
135 15c on 24a bis 3.00 3.00
Nos. 128-135 (8) 21.75 21.75

No. 75 Overprinted in Red

1913 *Perf. 11½, 12½, 13½.*

137 A3 130r on 80r yel grn 3.50 2.75

Nos. 73 and 76 overprinted but not issued. Prices, $10, $12.

Same Overprint on No. 83 in Green

1914 *Perf. 12*

139 A4 75r rose 3.50 2.75
a. "PROVISORIO" double (G and R) 30.00 27.50

Ceres — A6

Perf. 11½, 12 x 11½, 15 x 14.

1914-26 **Typo.**

Name and Value in Black.

144 A6 ¼c ol brn 10 10
a. Imperf.
145 A6 ½c black 10 10
146 A6 1c bl grn 1.15 1.00
147 A6 1c yel grn ('22) 10 10
148 A6 1½c lil brn 10 10
149 A6 2c carmine 15 12
150 A6 2c gray ('26) 25 3.00
151 A6 2½c lt vio 10 5
152 A6 3c org ('22) 30 25
153 A6 4c rose ('22) 12 2.00
154 A6 4½c gray ('22) 15 3.00
155 A6 5c dp bl 1.10 60
156 A6 5c brt bl ('22) 15 15
157 A6 6c lil ('22) 15 2.75
158 A6 7c ultra ('22) 15 2.75
159 A6 7½c yel brn 15 2.75
160 A6 8c slate 55 40
161 A6 10c org brn 15 12
162 A6 12c bl grn ('22) 35 25
163 A6 15c plum 7.50 5.50
164 A6 15c brn rose ('22) 25 15
165 A6 20c yel grn 20 15
166 A6 24c ultra ('26) 1.50 1.50
167 A6 25c choc ('26) 1.50 1.50
168 A6 30c brn, *grn* 4.50 4.50
169 A6 30c gray grn ('22) 35 25
170 A6 40c brn, *pink* 5.00 5.00
171 A6 40c turq bl ('22) 75 22
172 A6 50c org, *sal* 5.00 5.00
173 A6 50c vio ('26) 1.00 40
174 A6 60c dk bl ('22) 90 60
175 A6 60c rose ('26) 1.00 60
176 A6 80c brt rose ('22) 3.50 1.40
177 A6 1e grn *bl* 5.00 5.00
178 A6 1e rose ('22) 5.00 3.00
179 A6 1e dp bl ('26) 4.00 2.00
180 A6 2e dk vio ('22) 5.00 2.75
181 A6 5e buff ('26) 9.00 6.50
182 A6 10e pink ('26) 17.50 12.00
183 A6 20e pale turq ('26) 50.00 25.00
Nos. 144-183 (40) 133.82 102.61

Provisional Issue of 1902 Overprinted in Carmine

1915 *Perf. 11½, 12½, 13½*

184 A2 115r on 10r grn 1.75 1.75
a. Perf. 13½ 20.00 20.00
185 A2 115r on 20r rose 2.00 2.00
a. Perf. 13½ 20.00 20.00
186 A2 130r on 50r bl 1.75 1.75
187 A2 130r on 100r brn 1.10 1.10
188 A3 115r on 5r org 75 50
a. Invtd. ovpt. 22.50
189 A3 115r on 25r bl grn 1.10 1.00
a. Perf. 11½ 20.00 20.00
190 A3 115r on 150r car, *rose* 75 50
191 A3 130r on 75r car 1.25 1.25
192 A3 130r on 80r yel grn 1.10 1.10
a. Inverted overprint 22.50
193 A3 130r on 200r bl, *bl* 1.25 1.25
a. Perf. 12½ 55.00 45.00
Nos. 184-193 (10) 12.80 12.20

CABO VERDE CORREIOS ½ C.

War Tax Stamps of Portuguese Africa Surcharged

1921, Feb. 3 *Perf. 15x14, 11½*

194 WT1 ¼c on 1c grn 25 25
195 WT1 ½c on 1c grn 45 30
a. "½" instead of "½" 8.50 8.50
196 WT1 1c green 45 35

Nos. 127 and 126 Surcharged — 2 C.

Perf. 14 to 15.

197 CD27 2c on 15c on 150r bis 1.40 1.40
198 CD26 4c on 10c on 100r bis brn 1.75 1.50
a. On No. 118 (error) 110.00 110.00

No. 50 Surcharged — 6 C. REPUBLICA

Perf. 12.

200 A4 6c on 100r dk bl, *bl* 1.75 1.00
a. Accent on "U" of surch. 7.50 7.50

Stamps of 1913-15 Surcharged — $04

1922, Apr. *Perf. 11½, 12½, 13½*

On No. 137

201 A3 4c on 130r on 80r yel grn 2.00 2.00

On Nos. 191-193

202 A3 4c on 130r on 75r car 2.50 2.50
203 A3 4c on 130r on 80r yel grn 2.00 2.00
204 A3 4c on 130r on 200r bl, *bl* 1.25 90
a. Perf. 12½ 20.00 20.00

Surcharge of Nos. 201-204 with smaller $ occurs once in sheet of 28. Price eight times normal.

Nos. 78-79 Surcharged — República 40 C.

1925 *Perf. 13½, 11½*

205 A3 40c on 400r on 300r bl, *sal* 90 60
206 N1 40c on 400r on 2½r brn 55 50

No. 176 Surcharged — 70 C.

1931, Nov. *Perf. 12x11½*

214 A6 70c on 80c brt rose 3.00 2.25

Ceres — A7

Wmk. Maltese Cross. (232)

1934, May 1 *Perf. 12x11½*

215 A7 1c bister 10 1.00
216 A7 5c ol brn 10 10
217 A7 10c violet 10 10
218 A7 15c black 10 10
219 A7 20c gray 10 10
220 A7 30c dk grn 13 10
221 A7 40c red org 40 25
222 A7 45c brt bl 75 50
223 A7 50c brown 60 40
224 A7 60c ol grn 60 40
225 A7 70c brn org 60 40
226 A7 80c emerald 60 40
227 A7 85c dp rose 2.50 2.00
228 A7 1e maroon 2.00 40
229 A7 1.40e dk bl 2.75 2.00
230 A7 2e dk vio 3.50 1.40
231 A7 5e ap grn 15.00 4.50
232 A7 10e ol bis 25.00 13.00
233 A7 20e orange 55.00 25.00
Nos. 215-233 (19) 109.93 52.15

Vasco da Gama Issue

Common Design Types

1938 **Unwmk.** *Perf. 13½x13.*

Name and Value in Black.

234 CD34 1c gray grn 5 1.00
235 CD34 5c org brn 10 1.00
236 CD34 10c dk car 10 10
237 CD34 15c dk vio brn 75 45
238 CD34 20c slate 30 25
239 CD35 30c rose vio 30 25
240 CD35 35c brt grn 40 30
241 CD35 40c brown 30 25
242 CD35 50c brt red vio 30 25
243 CD36 60c gray blk 45 40
244 CD36 70c brn vio 45 30
245 CD36 80c orange 45 30
246 CD36 1e red 60 25
247 CD37 1.75e blue 1.50 60
248 CD37 2e dk bl grn 2.25 1.00
249 CD37 5e ol grn 6.50 2.00
250 CD38 10e bl vio 9.00 2.00
251 CD38 20e red brn 25.00 5.00
Nos. 234-251 (18) 48.80 15.70

Outline Map of Africa — A8

1939, June 23 **Litho.** *Perf. 11½x12*

252 A8 80c vio, *pale rose* 4.00 2.00
253 A8 1.75e bl, *pale bl* 20.00 17.50
254 A8 20e brn, *buff* 60.00 20.00

Issued to commemorate the visit of the President of Portugal to this colony in 1939.

Nos. 239 and 221 Surcharged with New Value and Bars in Black.

1948 **Unwmk.** *Perf. 13½x13*

255 CD35 10c on 30c rose vio 1.40 2.00

Perf. 12x11½

Wmk. 232

256 A7 25c on 40c red org 1.50 2.00

Machado Pt., Sao Vicente — A9

Brava Creek, Sao Nicolao — A10

Designs: 10c, Ribeira Grande. 1e, Harbor, Sao Vicente. 1.75e, Mindelo, distant view. 2e, Joao de Evora Beach. 5e, Mindelo. 10e, Volcano, Fire Island. 20e, Mt. Paul.

Perf. 14½

1948, Oct. 1 Litho. Unwmk.

257 A9 5c vio brn & bis 30 30
258 A9 10c ol grn & pale grn 30 20
259 A10 50c mag & lil rose 60 25
260 A10 1e brn vio & rose lil 2.00 1.00
261 A10 1.75e ultra & grnsh bl 2.50 1.50
262 A10 2e dk brn & buff 12.00 1.50
263 A10 5e ol grn & yel 17.50 7.00
264 A10 10e red & cr 22.50 12.00
265 A10 20e dk vio & bis 55.00 20.00
Nos. 257-265 (9) 112.70 43.75

Common Design Types pictured in section at front of book

Lady of Fatima Issue.
Common Design Type

1948, Dec.
266 CD40 50c dk bl 10.00 6.00

U.P.U. Symbols — A10a

1949, Oct. Perf. 14
267 A10a 1e red vio & pink 4.00 4.00

U.P.U., 75th anniversary

Holy Year Issue
Common Design Types

1950, May Perf. 13x13½
268 CD41 1e org brn 60 50
269 CD42 2e slate 3.00 1.75

Holy Year Conclusion Issue
Common Design Type

1951, Oct. Unwmk. Perf. 14
270 CD43 2e pur & lil 1.25 1.00

Stamps of 1938 Surcharged with New Value and Bars in Black.

Perf. 13½x13

1951, May 21 Unwmk.
271 CD35 10c on 35c brt grn 40 *1.50*
272 CD36 20c on 70c brn vio 60 *1.50*
273 CD36 40c on 70c brn vio 1.50 *2.00*
274 CD36 50c on 80c org 2.50 *3.00*
275 CD37 1e on 1.75e bl 3.00 *4.00*
276 CD38 2e on 10e bl vio 5.00 *7.50*
a. 1e on 10e bl vio 100.00 100.00
Nos. 271-276 (6) 13.00 19.50

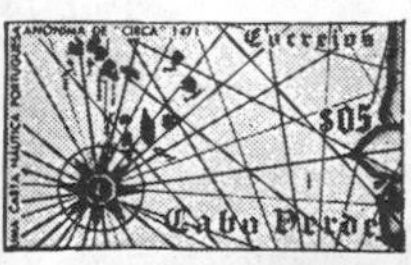

Map of Cape Verde Islands, 1502 — A11

Vicente Dias and Gonçalo de Cintra — A12

Portraits: 30c, Diogo Alfonso and Alvaro Fernandes. 50c, Lançarote and Soeiro da Costa. 1e, Diogo Gomes and Antonio da Nola. 2e, Prince Fernando and Prince Henry the Navigator. 3e, Antao Gonçalves and Dinis Dias. 5e, Alfonso Goncalves Baldaia and Joao Fernandes. 10e, Dinis Eanes da Gra and Alvaro de Freitas. 20e, Map of Cape Verde Islands, 1502.

1952, Feb. 24 Perf. 14
277 A11 5c multi 10 10
278 A12 10c multi 10 10
279 A12 30c multi 10 10
280 A12 50c multi 13 10
281 A12 1e multi 20 13
282 A12 2e multi 1.00 15
283 A12 3e multi 6.00 90
284 A12 5e multi 3.00 50
285 A12 10e multi 4.50 1.10
286 A11 20e multi 10.00 1.40
Nos. 277-286 (10) 25.13 4.58

Medical Congress Issue.
Common Design Type

Design: Hypodermic Injection.

1952, June Perf. 13½
287 CD44 20c ol grn & dk brn 40 30

No. 247 Surcharged with New Values and "X" in Black.

1952, Jan. 25 Perf. 13½x13
288 CD37 10c on 1.75e bl 1.75 1.75
289 CD37 20c on 1.75e bl 1.75 1.75
290 CD37 50c on 1.75e bl 6.00 6.00
291 CD37 1e on 1.75e bl 75 75
292 CD37 1.50e on 1.75e bl 75 75
Nos. 288-292 (5) 11.00 11.00

Facade of Jeronymos Convent — A13

Perf. 13½

1953, Jan. Unwmk. Litho.
293 A13 10c brn & pale ol 10 10
294 A13 50c pur & fawn 40 25
295 A13 1e dk grn & fawn 1.00 65

Issued to commemorate the Exhibition of Sacred Missionary Art held at Lisbon in 1951.

Stamp of Portugal and Arms of Colonies — A13a

1953 Photo.
Stamp and Arms Multicolored.
296 A13a 50c lil rose & gray 85 50

Centenary of Portuguese stamps.

Sao Paulo Issue
Common Design Type

1954 Litho. Perf. 13½
297 CD46 1e grn, cr & gray 35 15

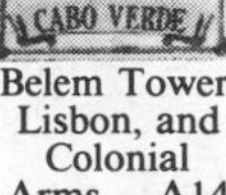

Belem Tower, Lisbon, and Colonial Arms — A14

Arms of Praia — A15

1955, May 15 Litho. Perf. 13½
298 A14 1e multi 30 20
299 A14 1.60e buff & multi 50 30

Issued to publicize the visit of Pres. Francisco H. C. Lopes.

1958, June 14 Perf. 12x11½
300 A15 1e multi 30 20
301 A15 2.50e pink & multi 60 25

Centenary of city of Praia.

Fair Emblem, Globe and Arms — A15a

1958 Perf. 12x11½
302 A15a 2e multi 45 40

World's Fair, Brussels, Apr. 17-Oct. 19.

Tropical Medicine Congress Issue
Common Design Type

Design: Aloe vera.

1958, Sept. 5 Perf. 13½
303 CD47 3e multi 3.00 2.00

Prince Henry — A16

Antonio da Nola — A17

1960, June 25 Litho. Perf. 13½
304 A16 2e multi 30 15

Issued to commemorate the 500th anniversary of the death of Prince Henry the Navigator.

1960, Oct. Unwmk. Perf. 14½

Design: 2.50e, Diogo Gomes.

305 A17 1e multi 45 30
306 A17 2.50e multi 1.00 65

Discovery of Cape Verde, 500th anniversary.

School Children A18

1960
307 A18 2.50e multi 75 50

Issued to commemorate the 10th anniversary of the Commission for Technical Cooperation in Africa South of the Sahara (C.C.T.A.).

Arms of Praia — A19

Designs: Arms of various cities and towns of Cape Verde.

1961, July Litho. Perf. 13½
308 A19 5c *shown* 5 5
309 A19 15c *Nova Sintra* 5 5
310 A19 20c *Ribeira Brava* 5 5
311 A19 30c *Assomada* 10 10
312 A19 1e *Maio* 60 10
313 A19 2e *Mindelo* 50 10
314 A19 2.50e *Santa Maria* 90 18
315 A19 3e *Pombas* 1.75 30
316 A19 5e *Sal-Rei* 1.75 30
317 A19 7.50e *Tarrafal* 1.00 40
318 A19 15e *Maria Pia* 1.75 60
319 A19 30e *San Felipe* 3.50 1.35
Nos. 308-319 (12) 12.00 3.58

Sports Issue
Common Design Type

Sports: 50c, Throwing javelin. 1e, Discus throwing. 1.50e, Cricket. 2.50e, Boxing. 4.50e, Hurding. 12.50e, Golf.

1962, Jan. 18 Perf. 13½
320 CD48 50c lt brn 10 10
321 CD48 1e lt grn 70 25
322 CD48 1.50e lt bl grn 40 20
323 CD48 2.50e pale vio bl 60 30
324 CD48 4.50e orange 1.00 60
325 CD48 12.50e beige 2.25 1.50
Nos. 320-325 (6) 5.05 2.95

Anti-Malaria Issue
Common Design Type

Design: Anopheles pretoriensis.

1962 Litho. Perf. 13½
326 CD49 2.50e multi 1.00 70

Issued for the World Health Organization drive to eradicate malaria.

Airline Anniversary Issue
Common Design Type

1963, Oct. Unwmk. Perf. 14½
327 CD50 2.50e gray & multi 60 40

Issued to commemorate the 10th anniversary of Transportes Aereos Portugueses.

National Overseas Bank Issue
Common Design Type

Design: 1.50e, Jose da Silva Mendes Leal.

1964, May 16 Perf. 13½
328 CD51 1.50e multi 60 50

Issued to commemorate the centenary of the National Overseas Bank of Portugal.

ITU Issue
Common Design Type

1965, May 17 Litho. Perf. 14½
329 CD52 2.50e buff & multi 1.50 1.00

Issued to commemorate the centenary of the International Telecommunication Union.

Militia Drummer, 1806 — A20

Designs: 1e, Soldier, Militia, 1806. 1.50e, Grenadier officer, 1833. 2.50e, Grenadier, 1833. 3e, Cavalry officer, 1834. 4e, Grenadier, 1835. 5e, Artillery officer, 1848. 10e, Drum major, infantry, 1856.

1965, Dec. 1 Litho. Perf. 14½
330 A20 50c multi 12 12
331 A20 1e multi 30 18
332 A20 1.50e multi 45 18
333 A20 2.50e multi 1.00 25
334 A20 3e multi 1.50 40
335 A20 4e multi 1.00 40
336 A20 5e multi 1.00 45
337 A20 10e multi 2.00 1.50
Nos. 330-337 (8) 7.37 3.48

National Revolution Issue
Common Design Type

Design: 1e, Dr. Adriano Moreira School and Health Center.

1966, May 28 Litho. Perf. 12
338 CD53 1e multi 30 30

National Revolution, 40th anniversary.

Navy Club Issue
Common Design Type

Designs: 1e, Capt. Fontoura da Costa and gunboat Mandovy. 1.50e, Capt. Carvalho Araujo and minesweeper Augusto Castilho.

1967, Jan. 31 Litho. *Perf. 13*
339 CD54 1e multi 60 30
340 CD54 1.50e multi 1.00 40

Centenary of Portugal's Navy Club.

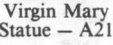

Virgin Mary Statue — A21

Pres. Rodrigues Thomaz — A22

1967, May 13 Litho. *Perf. 12½x13*
341 A21 1e multi 20 15

Issued to commemorate the 50th anniversary of the apparition of the Virgin Mary to 3 shepherd children at Fatima.

1968, Feb. 9 Litho. *Perf. 13½*
342 A22 1e multi 20 20

Issued to commemorate the 1968 visit of Pres. Americo de Deus Rodrigues Thomaz.

Cabral Issue

Pedro Alvares Cabral — A23

Design: 1e, Cantino's world map, 1502 (horiz.).

1968, Apr. 22 Litho. *Perf. 14*
343 A23 1e multi 70 30
344 A23 1.50e multi 80 30

See note after Angola No. 545.

Sao Vicente Harbor — A24

Physic Nut — A25

Designs: 1.50e, Peanut plant. 2.50e, Castor-oil plant. 3.50e, Yams. 4e, Date palm. 4.50e, Guavas. 5e, Tamarind. 10e, Bitter cassava. 30e, Woman carrying fruit baskets.

1968, Oct. 15 Litho. *Perf. 14*
345 A24 50c multi 6 5
346 A25 1e multi 10 5
347 A25 1.50e multi 15 15
348 A25 2.50e multi 25 10
349 A25 3.50e multi 30 15
350 A25 4e multi 30 15
351 A25 4.50e multi 40 15
352 A25 5e multi 40 15
353 A25 10e multi 80 35
354 A25 30e multi 3.00 1.35
Nos. 345-354 (10) 5.76 2.65

Admiral Coutinho Issue
Common Design Type

Design: 30c, Adm. Coutinho and map showing route of first flight from Lisbon to Rio de Janeiro (vert.).

1969, Feb. 17 Litho. *Perf. 14*
355 CD55 30c multi 20 10

Issued to commemorate the centenary of the birth of Admiral Carlos Viegas Gago Coutinho (1869-1959), explorer and aviation pioneer.

Vasco da Gama — A26

King Manuel I — A27

Vasco da Gama Issue

1969, Aug. 29 Litho. *Perf. 14*
356 A26 1.50e multi 20 10

Issued to commemorate the 500th anniversary of the birth of Vasco da Gama (1469-1524), navigator.

Administration Reform Issue
Common Design Type

1969, Sept. 25 Litho. *Perf. 14*
357 CD56 2e multi 20 20

King Manuel I Issue

1969, Dec. 1 Litho. *Perf. 14*
358 A27 3e multi 40 20

Issued to commemorate the 500th anniversary of the birth of King Manuel I.

Marshal Carmona Issue
Common Design Type

Design: 2.50e, Antonio Oscar Carmona in marshal's uniform.

1970, Nov. 15 Litho. *Perf. 14*
359 CD57 2.50e multi 40 20

Galleons on Sanaga River — A28

1972, May 25 Litho. *Perf. 13*
360 A28 5e lil rose & multi 40 20

4th centenary of the publication of The Lusiads by Luiz Camoens.

Olympic Games Issue
Common Design Type

Design: 4e, Basketball and boxing, Olympic emblem.

1972, June 20 *Perf. 14x13½*
361 CD59 4e multi 40 20

20th Olympic Games, Munich, Aug. 26-Sept. 11.

Lisbon-Rio de Janeiro Flight Issue
Common Design Type

Design: 3.50e, "Lusitania" landing at San Vicente.

1972, Sept. 20 Litho. *Perf. 13½*
362 CD60 3.50e multi 50 20

WMO Centenary Issue
Common Design Type

1973, Dec. 15 Litho. *Perf. 13*
363 CD61 2.50e ultra & multi 50 20

Centenary of international meteorological cooperation.

Mindelo Desalination Plant — A29

1974 Litho. *Perf. 13½*
364 A29 4e multi 75 40

Opening of the Mindelo desalination plant.

Republic
No. 343 Overprinted:
"INDEPENDENCIA / 5-Julho-75"

1975, Dec. 19 Litho. *Perf. 14*
365 A23 1e multi 25 15

Proclamation of Independence.

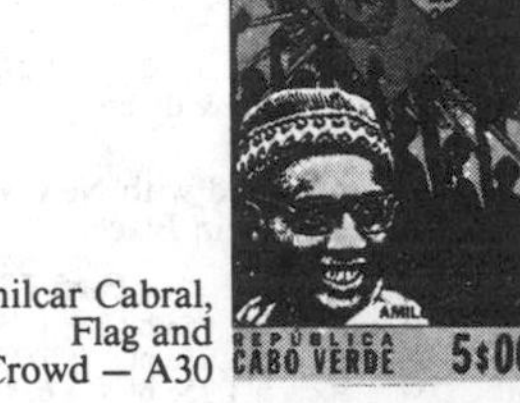

Amilcar Cabral, Flag and Crowd — A30

1976, Jan. 20
366 A30 5e multi 50 20

3rd anniversary of the assassination of Amilcar Cabral (1924-1973), revolutionary leader.

Rising Sun, Coat of Arms, Liberated People — A31

1976, July 5 Litho. *Perf. 14*
367 A31 50c multi 10 10
368 A31 3e multi 45 20
369 A31 15e multi 1.25 60
370 A31 50e multi 4.00 2.00
a. Miniature sheet of 4 *20.00 20.00*

First anniversary of independence. No. 370a contains one each of Nos. 367-370. Size: 154x110mm.

No. 351 Overprinted with Row of Stars and: "REPUBLICA / DE"

1976 Litho. *Perf. 14*
372 A25 4.50e multi 3.00 2.25

Amilcar Cabral, Map and Flag of Cape Verde A32

1976, Sept. 19 *Perf. 14*
373 A32 1e multi 20 20

Party of International Action (PAICC), 20th anniversary.

Electronic Tree and ITU Emblem — A33

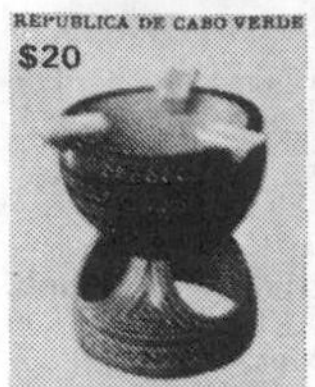

Ashtray — A34

1977, May 17 Litho. *Perf. 13½x13*
374 A33 5.50e multi 40 20

World Telecommunications Day.

1977, July 5 Litho. *Perf. 14*

Carved Coconut Shells: 30c, Bell on stand. 50c, Lamp with Adam and Eve. 1e, Hollow shell with Nativity. 1.50e, Desk lamp. 5e, Jar. 10e, Jar with hinged cover. 20e, Tobacco jar with palms. 30e, Stringed instrument.

375 A34 20c lil & multi 12 5
376 A34 30c rose & multi 20 5
377 A34 50c sal & multi 12 8
378 A34 1e lt grn & multi 20 12
379 A34 1.50e org yel & multi 25 20
380 A34 5e gray & multi 40 12
381 A34 10e lt bl & multi 80 20
382 A34 20e yel & multi 1.50 80
383 A34 30e rose lil & multi 2.50 1.25
Nos. 375-383 (9) 6.09 2.87

Cape Verde No. 1 and Coat of Arms — A35

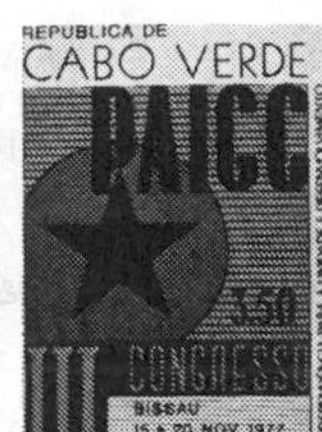

Congress Emblem — A36

1977, Sept. 12 Litho. *Perf. 13½*
384 A35 4e bl & multi 30 12
385 A35 8e lil & multi 70 28

Centenary of Cape Verde stamps.

1977, Nov. 15 *Perf. 14*
386 A36 3.50e multi 30 10

African Party of Independence of Guinea-Bissau and Cape Verde (PAIGC), 3rd congress, Nov. 15-20.

No. 363 Overprinted with Row of Stars and: "REPUBLICA / DE"

1978, May 1 *Perf. 12*
387 CD61 2.50e ultra & multi 30 10

No. 355 Surcharged with New Value and Bars

1978, May 1 *Perf. 14*
388 CD55 3e on 30c multi 30 12

Antenna and ITU Emblem — A37

1978, May 17 Litho. Perf. 14
389 A37 3.50e sil & multi 30 15

10th World Telecommunications Day.

Freighter Cabo Verde — A38

1978, June 25 Litho. Perf. 14
391 A38 1e multi 20 10

First ship of Cape Verde merchant marine.

Map of Africa and Equality Emblem — A39

1978, June 21
392 A39 4.50e multi 40 20

Anti-Apartheid Year.

Human Rights Emblem — A40

1978, Dec. 10 Litho. Perf. 14
393 A40 1.50e multi 20 5
394 A40 2e multi 30 15

Universal Declaration of Human Rights, 30th anniversary.

Children and Balloons, IYC Emblem — A41

IYC Emblem and Child's Drawing: 3.50e, Children and flowers.

1979, June 1 Litho. Perf. 14
395 A41 1.50e multi 20 5
396 A41 3.50e multi 30 15

International Year of the Child.

Pindjiguiti Massacre Monument A42

Natl. Youth Week A42a

1979, Aug. 3 Perf. 13
397 A42 4.50e multi 40 15

Massacre of Pindjiguiti, 20th anniversary.

1979, Sept. 1 Litho. Perf. 14
397A A42a 3.50e Poster 70 15

Centenary of Mindelo — A43

1980, Apr. 23 Litho. Perf. 12½
398 A43 4e multi 30 15

Flag of Cape Verde — A44

Stylized Bird, "V" — A45

1980, July 5 Litho. Perf. 12½
399 A44 4e multi 30 15
400 A45 4e multi 30 15
401 A45 7e multi 60 20
402 A45 11e multi 90 30

5th anniversary of independence No. 399 issued June 1, others July 5.

1980 Natl. Census — A45a

1980, May 13
402A A45a 3.50e multi 70
402B A45a 4.50e multi 90

Running — A46

1980, June 6
403 A46 1e *shown* 20 15
404 A46 2.50e *Boxing* 20 10
405 A46 3e *Basketball* 20 15
406 A46 4e *Volleyball* 30 15
407 A46 20e *Swimming* 1.75 40
408 A46 50e *Tennis* 4.00 1.00
Nos. 403-408 (6) 6.65 1.95

Souvenir Sheet

Perf. 13

409 A46 30e *Soccer*, horiz. 10.00

22nd Summer Olympic Games, Moscow, July 19-Aug. 3. No. 409 has multicolored margin showing Misha, the bear, and Olympic flame. Size: 99x67mm.

Thunnus Alalunga A47

1980, Nov. 11 Litho. Perf. 13
410 A47 50c shown 10 10
411 A47 4.50e Trachurus trachurus 30 15
412 A47 8e Muraena helena 60 20
413 A47 10e Corvina nigra 80 20
414 A47 12e Katsuwonus pelamis 1.00 30
415 A47 50e Prionace glauca 4.00 1.00
Nos. 410-415 (6) 6.80 1.95

Lochnera Rosea — A48

1980, Dec. 29
416 A48 50c shown 10 10
417 A48 4.50e Poinciana regia-bojer 30 15
418 A48 8e Mirabilis jalapa 60 20
419 A48 10e Nerium oleander 80 20
420 A48 12e Bougainvillia litoralis 1.00 30
421 A48 30e Hibiscus 2.50 60
Nos. 416-421 (6) 5.30 1.55

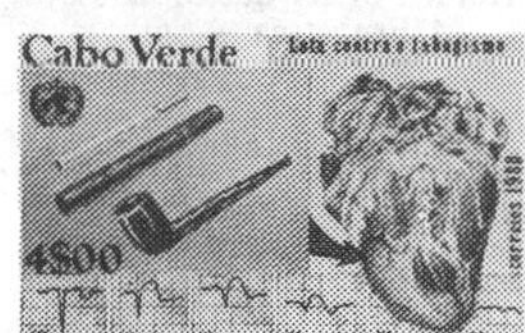

WHO Anti-smoking Campaign — A48a

1980, Sept. 19 Perf. 12½
421A A48a 4e multi 80
421B A48a 7e multi 1.40

Arca Verde A49

1980, Nov. 30 Litho. Perf. 12½x12
422 A49 3e shown 20 10
423 A49 5.50e Ilha do Maio 40 20
424 A49 7.50e Ilha de Komo 60 20
425 A49 9e Boa Vista 70 20
426 A49 12e Santo Antao 1.00 30
427 A49 30e Santiago 2.50 60
Nos. 422-427 (6) 5.40 1.60

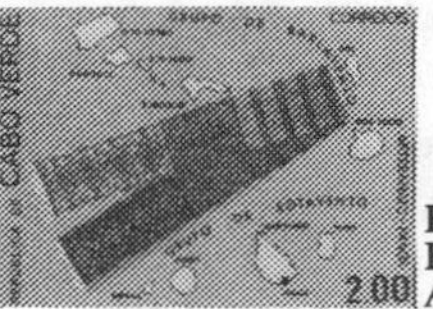

Hand-woven Bag, Map A49a

Various hand-woven articles. 10e vert.

1978, May 21 Litho. Perf. 14
427A A49a 50c multi 10
427B A49a 1.50e multi 30
427C A49a 2e multi 40
427D A49a 3e multi 60
427E A49a 10e multi 2.00
Nos. 427A-427E (5) 3.40

Desert Erosion Prevention Campaign — A50

1981, Mar. 30 Litho. Perf. 13
428 A50 4.50e multi 40 20
429 A50 10.50e multi 80 30

6th Anniv. of Constitution A51

1981, Apr. 15
430 A51 4.50e multi 40 20

Souvenir Sheet

Austria No. B336 A52

1981, May 18
431 A52 50e multi 4.00

WIPA '81 Philatelic Exhibition, Vienna, Austria, May 22-31. No. 431 has multicolored margin showing Prince Eugene statue, exhibition emblem. Size: 108x63mm.

Antenna — A53

1981, Aug. 25 Litho. Perf. 12½
432 A53 4.50e shown 40 20
433 A53 8e Dish antenna 60 20
434 A53 20e Dish antenna, diff. 1.75 50

Cape Verde stamps can be mounted in Scott's annual Portugal Supplement.

Intl. Year of the Disabled A54

1981, Dec. 25 Litho. *Perf. 12½*

435 A54 4.50e multi		30	15

Purple Gallinule — A55

1981, Dec. 30

436 A55 1e	Egret, vert.	10	10
437 A55 4.50e	Barn owl, vert.	30	15
438 A55 8e	Passerine, vert.	55	15
439 A55 10e	shown	60	15
440 A55 12e	Guinea fowl	75	20
Nos. 436-440 (5)		2.30	75

Souvenir Sheet

Perf. 13

441 A55 50e	Razo. Isld. lark	3.00	2.00

No. 441 contains one stamp (31x39mm.); multicolored margin continues design. Size: 80x56mm.

CILSS Congress, Praia, Jan. 17 — A56

1982, Jan. 17 *Perf. 13x12½*

442 A56 11.50e multi		65	30

Amilcar Cabral Soccer Championship — A57

Designs: Soccer players and flags.

1982, Feb. 10 Litho. *Perf. 12½*

443 A57 4.50e multi		30	15
444 A57 7.50e multi		45	15
445 A57 11.50e multi		75	20

1982 World Cup — A58

Designs: Soccer players and ball.

1982, Apr. 25

446 A58 1.50e multi		10	10
447 A58 4.50e multi		30	15
448 A58 8e multi		55	15
449 A58 10.50e multi		60	20
450 A58 12e multi		75	20
451 A58 20e multi		1.25	30
Nos. 446-451 (6)		3.55	1.10

Souvenir Sheet

452 A58 50e multi		3.00	2.00

No. 452 has multicolored margin continuing design. Size: 83x91mm.

First Anniv of Women's Organization — A59

1982, Apr. 15 Litho. *Perf. 12½x12*

453 A59 4.50e	Marching	30	15
454 A59 8e	Farming	55	15
455 A59 12e	Child care	75	20

Estaleiros Navais Port, St. Vincent — A59a

1982, July 5 Litho. *Perf. 13x12½*

455A A59a 10.50e multi		60	

Natl. independence, 7th anniv.

Return of Barque Morrissey-Ernestina — A60

1982, July 5 Litho. *Perf. 13*

456 A60 12e multi		75	

Butterflies — A61

1982, July 27 Litho.

457 A61 2e	Hypolimnas misippus	8	
458 A61 4.50e	Melanitis lede	18	
459 A61 8e	Catopsilia florella	30	
460 A61 10.50e	Colias electo	42	
461 A61 11.50e	Danaus chrysippus	48	
462 A61 12e	Papilio demodecus	50	
Nos. 457-462 (6)		1.96	

Francisco Xavier da Cruz (1905-1958), Composer — A62

Design: 14e, Eugenio Tavares (1867-1930), poet.

1983, Feb. 20 Litho. *Perf. 13*

463 A62 7e multi		28	
464 A62 14e multi		55	

World Communications Year — A63

1983, Oct. 10 Litho.

465 A63 13e multi		52	

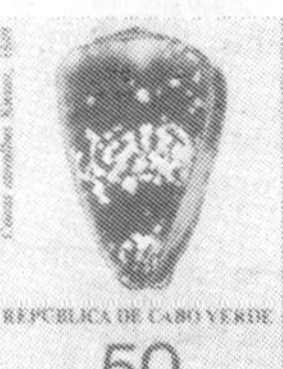

Local Seashells — A64

1983, Nov. 30 *Perf. 13½*

466 A64 50c	Conus ateralbus	5	
467 A64 1e	Conus decoratus	5	
468 A64 3e	Conus salreiensis	12	
469 A64 10e	Conus verdensis	40	
470 A64 50e	Conus cuneolus	2.00	
Nos. 466-470 (5)		2.62	

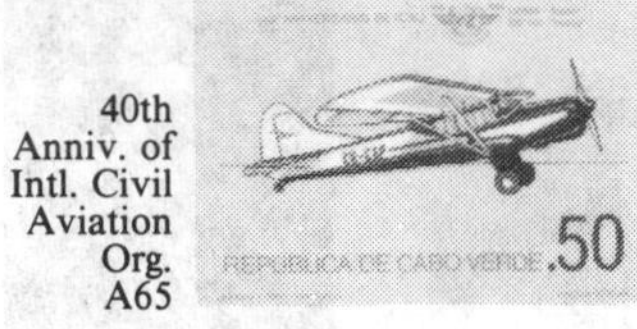

40th Anniv. of Intl. Civil Aviation Org. A65

Airplanes: 50c, Ogma-Auster D5/160, 1966. 2e, De Havilland DH-104 Dove, 1945. 10e, Hawker Siddeley 748-200, 1972. 13e, De Havilland Dragon Rapide, 1945. 20e, De Havilland Twin Otter, 1977. 50e, Britten-Norman Islander, 1971.

1984, Feb. 15 Litho.

471 A65 50c multi		5	
472 A65 2e multi		8	
473 A65 10e multi		40	
474 A65 13e multi		52	
475 A65 20e multi		80	
476 A65 50e multi		2.00	
Nos. 471-476 (6)		3.85	

Amilcar Cabral — A66

1983, Jan. 17 Litho. *Perf. 14½*

477 A66 7e multi		25	
478 A66 10.50e multi		36	
a. Souvenir sheet of 2, #477-478		1.05	

Amilcar Cabral Symposium, Jan. 17-20. No. 478a has pale green and bluish green inscribed margin picturing Cabral quote. Sold for 30e. Size: 130x70mm.

Christianity in Cape Verde, 450th Anniv. — A67

1983, Dec. 10 Photo. *Perf. 14½*

479 A67 7e	Cross overshadowing islands	18	

Natl. Solidarity Campaign A68

1984, Sept. 12 *Perf. 13½*

480 A68 6.50e multi		35	
481 A68 13.50e multi		75	

2nd Conference of Natl. Women's Orgs., Mar. 23-27 — A69

1985, Mar. 27 Litho. *Perf. 13½*

482 A69 8e multi		20	

Miniature Sheet

483 A69 30e multi		75	

Size: 99x80mm.

Natl. Independence, 10th Anniv. — A70

1985, July 5 Litho. *Perf. 14*

484 A70 8c multi		28	
485 A70 12e multi		42	

Intl. Year of the Child — A71

1985, Sept. 12 Litho. *Perf. 14*

486 A71 12e multi		75	

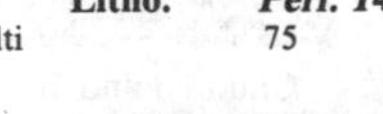

Vapor, by Hundertwasser A72

Photogravure and Engraved

1986, Apr. 25 *Perf. 14*

Black Surcharge

487 A72 30e on 10e multi		1.05	

Souvenir Sheets

Background Color

488	Sheet of 4	7.00	
a. A72 50e yel & multi		1.75	
489	Sheet of 4	7.00	
a. A72 50e red & multi		1.75	

490 Sheet of 4 7.00
a. A72 50e grn & multi 1.75

Nos. 488-490 have gray decorative margins; dark gray control numbers. Sizes: 190x259mm.

World Wildlife Fund — A73

Perf. 13½x14½

1986, June 15 Litho.
491 A73 8e Mabuya vaillanti 28
492 A73 10e Tarentola gigas brancoensis 35
493 A73 15e Tarentola gigas gigas 52
494 A73 30e Hemidactylus bouvieri 1.05

Souvenir Sheet

495 Sheet of 2 3.50
a. A73 50e Mabuya vaillanti 1.75
b. A73 50e Hemidactylus bouvieri 1.75

No. 495 printed with center label picturing progress union emblem. Nos. 495a-495b have bister margin; printed without WWF emblem. Size: 130x60mm.

World Food Day — A74

1986, June 20 ***Perf. 14***
496 A74 8e Caldron 28
497 A74 12e Mortar & pestle 42
498 A74 15e Quern stone 52

Intl. Peace Year — A75

1986, Dec. 24 Litho. ***Perf. 14***
499 A75 12e multi 42
500 A75 30e multi 1.05

Natl. Child Survival Campaign — A76

1987, Mar. 27 Litho. ***Perf. 14***
501 A76 8e multi 28
502 A76 10e multi 35
503 A76 12e multi 42
504 A76 16e multi 55
505 A76 100e multi 3.50

Tourism A77

1987, May 17
506 A77 1e Bay, Mindelo 5
507 A77 2.50e Hill country 8
508 A77 5e Mountain peak 15
509 A77 8e Monument 25
510 A77 10e Mountain peaks 30
511 A77 12e Beached boats 38
512 A77 100e Harbor 3.00
Nos. 506-512 (7) 4.21

Ships — A78

1987, Aug. 3 ***Perf. 13½x14½***
513 A78 12e Carvalho, 1937 38
514 A78 16e Nauta, 1943 50
515 A78 50e Maria Sony, 1911 1.60

Souvenir Sheet

516 Sheet of 2 4.00
a. A78 60e Madalan, 1928 2.00

No. 516 has inscribed multicolored margin picturing map. Size: 106x105mm.

AIR POST STAMPS.

Common Design Type
Name and Value in Black
Perf. 13½x13.

1938, July 26 Unwmk.
C1 CD39 10c scarlet 50 45
C2 CD39 20c purple 50 45
C3 CD39 50c orange 50 45
C4 CD39 1e ultra 50 45
C5 CD39 2e lil brn 1.10 70
C6 CD39 3e dk grn 2.00 1.50
C7 CD39 5e red brn 6.00 1.50
C8 CD39 9e rose car 10.00 3.00
C9 CD39 10e magenta 14.00 4.50
Nos. C1-C9 (9) 35.10 13.00

No. C7 exists with overprint "Exposicao Internacional de Nova York, 1939-1940" and Trylon and Perisphere.

POSTAGE DUE STAMPS.

D1

D2

1904 Unwmk. Typo. ***Perf. 12.***
J1 D1 5r yel grn 28 50
J2 D1 10r slate 28 50
J3 D1 20r yel brn 50 60
J4 D1 30r red org 90 1.00
J5 D1 50r gray brn 50 1.00
J6 D1 60r red brn 6.50 6.50
J7 D1 100r lilac 1.40 1.75
J8 D1 130r dl bl 1.40 1.75
J9 D1 200r carmine 1.75 2.00
J10 D1 500r dl vio 4.50 5.00
Nos. J1-J10 (10) 18.01 20.60

Overprinted in Carmine or Green

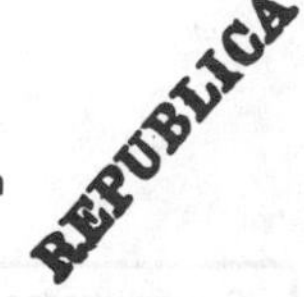

1911
J11 D1 5r yel grn 15 15
J12 D1 10r slate 15 15
J13 D1 20r yel brn 25 20
J14 D1 30r orange 25 20
J15 D1 50r gray brn 25 20
J16 D1 60r red brn 50 40
J17 D1 100r lilac 50 40
J18 D1 130r dl bl 70 50
J19 D1 200r car (G) 1.25 75
J20 D1 500r dl vio 1.75 1.75
Nos. J11-J20 (10) 5.75 4.70

1921 ***Perf. 11½.***
J21 D2 ½c yel grn 10 25
J22 D2 1c slate 10 25
J23 D2 2c red brn 10 25
J24 D2 3c orange 10 25
J25 D2 5c gray brn 10 25
J26 D2 6c lt brn 10 10
J27 D2 10c red vio 10 10
J28 D2 13c dl bl 40 75
J29 D2 20c carmine 40 75
J30 D2 50c gray 1.25 1.50
Nos. J21-J30 (10) 2.75 4.45

Common Design Type
Photogravure and Typographed

1952 Unwmk. ***Perf. 14.***
Numeral in Red, Frame Multicolored.
J31 CD45 10c chocolate 8 8
J32 CD45 30c blk brn 10 10
J33 CD45 50c dk bl 15 15
J34 CD45 1e dk bl 20 20
J35 CD45 2e red brn 20 20
J36 CD45 5e ol grn 40 40
Nos. J31-J36 (6) 1.13 1.13

NEWSPAPER STAMP.

N1

1893 Typo. Unwmk. ***Perf. 11½***
P1 N1 2½r brown 75 50
a. Perf. 12½ 2.00 2.25
b. Perf. 13½ 5.75 2.50

POSTAL TAX STAMPS.

Pombal Issue
Common Design Types

1925 Unwmk. Engr. ***Perf. 12½.***
RA1 CD28 15c dl vio & blk 40 40
RA2 CD29 15c dl vio & blk 40 40
RA3 CD30 15c dl vio & blk 40 40

St. Isabel — PT1

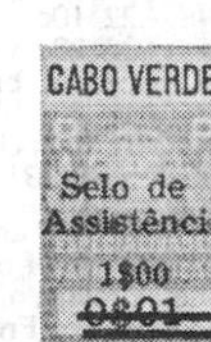

PT2

1948 Litho. ***Perf. 11***
RA4 PT1 50c dk grn 2.50 2.00
RA5 PT1 1e hn brn 5.50 3.00

No. RA5 Surcharged with New Value and Bars

1959
RA6 PT1 50c on 1e hn brn 1.00 75

Perf. 14
RA7 PT1 50c car rose 1.50 80
RA8 PT1 1e blue 1.50 80

St. Isabel Type Redrawn

1967-72 Litho. ***Perf. 14***
RA9 PT1 30c (bl panel) 15 15
RA10 PT1 50c (lil rose panel) 50 50
RA11 PT1 50c (red panel) ('72) *2.25 2.25*
RA12 PT1 1e (brn panel) 60 60
RA13 PT1 1e (red lil panel) ('72) *2.25 2.25*
Nos. RA9-RA13 (5) 5.75 5.75

Nos. RA9-RA13 are inscribed "ASSISTENCIA" in large letters in bottom panel and "PORTUGAL" and "CABO VERDE" in small letters in upper left corner.

Revenue Stamps Surcharged in Green, Blue or Black

1967-72 Typo. ***Perf. 12***
Black "CABO VERDE" & Value
Pale Green Burelage
RA14 PT2 50c on 1c org (Bl) ('71) 1.50 60
a. Black surcharge ('68?) *10.00 8.75*
RA15 PT2 50c on 2c org (G) ('69) *1.75 1.00*
a. Blue surcharge 1.50 60
b. Black surcharge ('68?) *10.00 8.00*
c. Inverted surcharge (Bk)
RA16 PT2 50c on 3c org (G) ('72) 1.50 60
RA17 PT2 50c on 5c org (G) ('72) 70 60
RA18 PT2 50c on 10c org (G) ('71) 85 85
RA19 PT2 1e on 1c org (Bk) 4.50 4.00
RA20 PT2 1e on 2c org (G) ('71) 1.65 1.65
a. Blue surcharge ('71) 1.50 60
b. Black surcharge 4.50 4.00
Nos. RA14-RA20 (7) 12.45 9.30

POSTAL TAX DUE STAMPS.

Pombal Issue.
Common Design Types

1925 Unwmk. ***Perf. 12½.***
RAJ1 CD31 30c dl vio & blk 50 50
RAJ2 CD32 30c dl vio & blk 50 50
RAJ3 CD33 30c dl vio & blk 50 50

CAROLINE ISLANDS

LOCATION — A group of about 549 small islands in the West Pacific Ocean, north of the Equator.
GOVT. — Former German colony.
AREA — 550 sq. mi.
POP. — 40,000 (approx. 1915.)

100 Pfennig = 1 Mark

Stamps of Germany 1889-90 Overprinted in Black

Overprinted at 56 degree Angle

1900 Unwmk. ***Perf. 13½x14½***
1 A9 3pf dk brn 13.00 15.00
2 A9 5pf green 16.00 15.00
3 A10 10pf carmine 18.00 18.00
4 A10 20pf ultra 22.50 25.00
5 A10 25pf orange 57.50 60.00
6 A10 50pf red brn 57.50 60.00
Nos. 1-6 (6) 184.50 193.00

1899
Overprinted at 48 degree Angle
1a A9 3pf lt brn 700.00 850.00
2a A9 5pf green 850.00 750.00
3a A10 10pf carmine 82.50 200.00
4a A10 20pf ultra 82.50 200.00
5a A10 25pf orange *2,000. 4,000.*
6a A10 50pf red brn *1,250. 2,400.*

Kaiser's Yacht "Hohenzollern"
A3 A4

1900-10 Typo. ***Perf. 14***
7 A3 3pf brown 75 *1.50*
8 A3 5pf green 75 *2.25*
9 A3 10pf carmine 75 *6.00*
a. Half used as 5pf on cover, back-stamped in Jaluit ('05) *150.00*
10 A3 20pf ultra 1.25 *10.00*
a. Half used as 10pf on cover ('10) *8,500.*
11 A3 25pf org & blk, *yel* 1.65 *17.50*
12 A3 30pf org & blk, *sal* 1.65 *17.50*
13 A3 40pf lake & blk 1.65 *20.00*
14 A3 50pf pur & blk, *sal* 2.00 *21.00*
15 A3 80pf lake & blk, *rose* 3.00 *25.00*

Engr. *Perf. 14½x14*

16 A4 1m carmine 4.00 *75.00*
17 A4 2m blue 7.00 *100.00*
18 A4 3m blk vio 10.50 *200.00*
19 A4 5m sl & car 175.00 700.00
Nos. 7-19 (13) 209.95

No. 9a is known as the "typhoon provisional" the stock of 5pf stamps having been destroyed during a typhoon. Covers (cards) without backstamp, price about $90.

Forged cancellations are found on Nos. 7-19.

No. 7 Handstamp Surcharged **5 Pf**

1910, July 12

20 A3 5pf on 3pf brn *6,500.*

Price is for stamp tied to cover. Stamps on piece sell for about one-third less.

Wmk. 125

Wmk. Lozenges (125)

1915-19 **Typo.**

21 A3 3pf brn ('19) 1.00
22 A3 5pf green 15.00

Engr.

23 A4 5m sl & car 20.00

Nos. 21-23 were never placed in use.

CASTELLORIZO

(Castelrosso)

LOCATION — A Mediterranean island in the Dodecanese group lying close to the coast of Asia Minor and about 60 miles east of Rhodes.
GOVT. — Former Italian Colony.
AREA — 4 sq. mi.
POP. — 2,238 (1936).

Formerly a Turkish possession, Castellorizo was occupied by the French in 1915 and ceded to Italy after World War I.

25 Centimes = 1 Piastre
100 Centimes = 1 Franc

Issued under French Occupation

Stamps of French Offices in Turkey Overprinted **B. N. F. CASTELLORIZO**

1920 **Unwmk.** *Perf. 14x13½*

1 A2 1c gray 30.00 30.00
a. Inverted ovpt. 60.00 60.00
b. Double ovpt. 77.50 77.50
2 A2 2c vio brn 30.00 30.00
3 A2 3c red org 30.00 30.00
a. Inverted overprint 60.00 60.00
4 A2 5c green 30.00 30.00
a. Inverted overprint 60.00 60.00
5 A3 10c rose 35.00 35.00
6 A3 15c pale red 50.00 50.00
a. Inverted overprint 85.00 85.00
7 A3 20c brn vio 55.00 55.00
8 A5 1pi on 25c bl 55.00 55.00
9 A3 30c lilac 55.00 55.00
10 A4 40c red & pale bl 85.00 85.00
a. Inverted ovpt. 325.00 325.00
11 A6 2pi on 50c bis brn & lav 85.00 85.00
a. Inverted ovpt. 325.00 325.00
12 A6 4pi on 1fr cl & ol grn 110.00 110.00
a. Double ovpt. 350.00 350.00
b. Inverted ovpt. 350.00 350.00
13 A6 20pi on 5fr dk bl & buff 350.00 350.00
a. Double overprint 825.00 825.00
Nos. 1-13 (13) 1,000. 1,000.

On Nos. 10-13 the overprint is placed vertically.

No. 1-9 were overprinted in blocks of 25. Position 4 had "CASTELLORIZO" inverted and Positions 8 and 18 had "CASTELLORISO". The later variety also occurred in the setting of the form for Nos. 10-13.

"B. N. F." are the initials of "Base Navale Francaise".

Overprinted in Black or Red **O. N. F. Castellorizo**

1920

On Stamps of French Offices in Turkey

14 A2 1c gray 14.00 14.00
15 A2 2c vio brn 14.00 14.00
16 A2 3c red org 16.00 16.00
17 A2 5c grn (R) 16.00 16.00
19 A3 10c rose 16.00 16.00
20 A3 15c pale red 22.50 22.50
21 A3 20c brn vio 45.00 45.00
22 A5 1pi on 25c bl (R) 40.00 40.00
23 A3 30c lil (R) 40.00 40.00
24 A4 40c red & pale bl 40.00 40.00
25 A6 2pi on 50c bis brn & lav 40.00 40.00
26 A6 4pi on 1fr cl & ol grn 45.00 45.00
28 A6 20pi on 5fr dk bl & buff 225.00 225.00
Nos. 14-28 (13) 573.50 573.50

On Nos. 25, 26 and 28 the two lines of the overprint are set wider apart than on the lower values.

"O.N.F." are the initials of "Occupation Navale Francaise."

Overprint on 8pi on 2fr (#37), price $700.

On Stamps of France

30 A22 10c red 17.50 13.00
a. Inverted ovpt. 87.50
31 A22 25c bl (R) 17.50 13.00
a. Inverted ovpt. 87.50

This overprint exists on 8 other 1900-1907 denominations of France (5c, 15c, 20c, 30c, 40c, 50c, 1fr, 5fr). These are believed not to have been issued or postally used.

Stamps of France, 1900-1907, Handstamped in Black or Violet **O F CASTELLORISO**

1920

33 A22 5c green 110.00 110.00
34 A22 10c red 110.00 110.00
35 A22 20c vio brn 110.00 110.00
36 A22 5c blue 110.00 110.00
37 A18 50c bis brn & lav 775.00 775.00
38 A18 1fr cl & ol grn (V) 775.00 775.00
Nos. 33-38 (6) 1,990. 1,990.

Nos. 1-38 are considered speculative.

Forgeries of overprints on Nos. 1-38 exist. They abound of Nos. 33-38.

Stamps of French Offices in Turkey handstamped "Occupation Francaise Castellorizo" were made privately.

Issued under Italian Dominion.

100 Centesimi = 1 Lira

Italian Stamps of 1906-20 Overprinted **CASTELROSSO**

1922 **Wmk. Crown (140)** *Perf. 14*

51 A48 5c green 90 *4.50*
52 A48 10c claret 38 *4.50*
53 A48 15c slate 38 *4.50*
54 A50 20c brn org 38 *4.50*
a. Double ovpt. 90.00
55 A49 25c blue 38 *4.50*
56 A49 40c brown 7.50 4.50
57 A49 50c violet 7.50 4.50
58 A49 60c carmine 7.50 4.50
59 A49 85c chocolate 90 *4.50*
Nos. 51-59 (9) 25.82

Map of Castellorizo; Flag of Italy — A1

1923

60 A1 5c gray grn 32 *3.75*
61 A1 10c dl rose 32 *3.75*
62 A1 25c dl bl 32 *3.75*
63 A1 50c gray lil 32 *3.75*
64 A1 1 l brown 32 *3.75*
Nos. 60-64 (5) 1.60

Italian Stamps of 1901-20 Overprinted **CASTELROSSO**

1924

65 A48 5c green 45 *15.00*
66 A48 10c claret 45 *15.00*
67 A48 15c slate 45 *15.00*
68 A50 20c brn org 45 *15.00*
69 A49 25c blue 45 *15.00*
70 A49 40c brown 45 *15.00*
71 A49 50c violet 45 *15.00*
72 A49 60c carmine 45 *15.00*
a. Double ovpt. 90.00
73 A49 85c red brn 45 *15.00*
74 A46 1 l brn & grn 45 *15.00*
Nos. 65-74 (10) 4.50

Ferrucci Issue

Types of Italian Stamps of 1930, Overprinted in Red or Blue **CASTELROSSO**

1930 **Wmk. Crowns (140)**

75 A102 20c violet 1.10 *2.00*
76 A103 25c dk grn 1.10 *2.00*
77 A103 50c black 1.10 *2.00*
78 A103 1.25 l dp bl 1.10 *2.00*
79 A104 5 l + 2 l dp car (Bl) 4.75 *10.50*
Nos. 75-79 (5) 9.15

Garibaldi Issue

Types of Italian Stamps of 1932, Overprinted in Red or Blue **CASTELROSSO**

1932

80 A138 10c brown 5.50 *11.00*
81 A138 20c red brn (Bl) 5.50 *11.00*
82 A138 25c dp grn 5.50 *11.00*
83 A138 30c bluish sl 5.50 *11.00*
84 A138 50c red vio (Bl) 5.50 *11.00*
85 A141 75c cop red (Bl) 5.50 *11.00*
86 A141 1.25 l dl bl 5.50 *11.00*
87 A141 1.75 l + 25c brn 5.50 *11.00*
88 A144 2.55 l + 50c org (Bl) 5.50 *11.00*
89 A145 5 l + 1 l dl vio 5.50 *11.00*
Nos. 80-89 (10) 55.00

Caroline Islands stamps can be mounted in Scott's Germany Part II Album.

CENTRAL AFRICA

LOCATION — Western Africa, north of equator.
GOVT. — Empire
AREA — 241,313 sq. mi.
POP. — 2,610,000 (est. 1974)
CAPITAL — Bangui

The former French colony of Ubangi-Shari, a unit in French Equatorial Africa, proclaimed itself the Central African Republic Dec. 1, 1958. It became the Central African Empire Dec. 4, 1976. It became the Central African Republic again in 1979.

100 Centimes = 1 Franc

Central African Republic

Premier Barthelemy Boganda and Flag — A1

Design: 25fr, Barthelemy Boganda and flag (horiz.).

1959 Unwmk. Engr. *Perf. 13*
1 A1 15fr multi 25 20
2 A1 25fr multi 40 20

Issued to commemorate the first anniversary of the establishment of the Republic and to honor Premier Barthelemy Boganda (1910-1959).

Imperforates
Most stamps of Central African Republic exist imperforate in issued and trial colors, and also in small presentation sheets in issued colors.

C.C.T.A. Issue
Common Design Type

1960 Unwmk. *Perf. 13*
3 CD106 50fr lt grn & dk bl 1.15 85

Dactyloceras Widenmanni — A2

Designs: Various butterflies.

1960-61
4 A2 50c bl grn & dk red ('61) 5 5
5 A2 1fr multi 5 5
6 A2 2fr dk grn & brn ('61) 6 5
7 A2 3fr vel grn & dk red ('61) 6 6
8 A2 5fr dk sl grn, pale grn & ol grn 8 8
9 A2 10fr multi 20 10
10 A2 20fr multi 35 18
11 A2 85fr multi 1.35 80
Nos. 4-11 (8) 2.20 1.37

No. 2 Overprinted: "FETE NATIONALE 1-12-1960"

1960
12 A1 25fr multi 1.10 1.10

National Holiday, Dec. 1, 1960.

Louis Pasteur and Pasteur Institute, Bangui — A3

1961, Feb. 25 Unwmk. *Perf. 13*
13 A3 20fr multi 65 65

Opening of Pasteur Institute at Bangui.

Common Design Types pictured in section at front of book.

Flag, Map, and U.N. Emblem A4

1961, Mar. 4 Engr.
14 A4 15fr multi 30 20
15 A4 25fr multi 40 30
16 A4 85fr multi 1.35 1.10

Issued to commemorate the admission of Central African Republic to the United Nations.

No. 15 Overprinted in Green: "FETE NATIONALE 1-12-61" and Star

1961, Dec. 1
17 A4 25fr multi 1.40 1.40

National Holiday, Dec. 1.

No. 16 Surcharged in Red Brown: "U.A.M. CONFERENCE DE BANGUI 25-27 Mars 1962"

1962, March 25
18 A4 50fr on 85fr multi 1.20 1.20

Issued to commemorate the conference of the African and Malgache Union at Bangui, March 25-27.

Abidjan Games Issue
Common Design Type

Designs. 20fr, Hurdling. 50fr, Bicycling.

1962, July 21 Photo. *Perf. 12½x12*
19 CD109 20fr multi 30 25
20 CD109 50fr multi 80 55

See No. C6.

African-Malgache Union Issue
Common Design Type

1962, Sept. 8 Unwmk.
21 CD110 30fr multi 55 45

Issued to commemorate the first anniversary of the African and Malgache Union.

President David Dacko — A5

Soldiers with Flag — A6

1962 *Perf. 12*
22 A5 20fr multi 30 12
23 A5 25fr multi 35 15

1963, Aug. 13 Photo.
24 A6 20fr blk & multi 30 20

National Army, third anniversary.

Waves Around Globe — A6a

Design: 100fr, Orbit patterns around globe.

1963, Sept. 19 Unwmk. *Perf. 12½*
25 A6a 25fr plum & grn 45 40
26 A6a 100fr org, bl & grn 1.75 1.65

Issued to publicize space communications.

Young Pioneers A7

1963, Oct. 14 Engr. *Perf. 12½*
27 A7 50fr grnsh bl, vio bl & brn 70 50

Issued to honor Young Pioneers.

Boali Falls — A8

1963, Oct. 28 *Perf. 13*
28 A8 30fr bl, grn & red brn 45 30

Colotis Evippe — A9

Designs: Various butterflies.

1963, Nov. 18 Photo. *Perf. 12½x13*
29 A9 1fr multi 15 15
30 A9 3fr multi 20 20
31 A9 4fr multi 25 25
32 A9 60fr multi 1.00 1.00

UNESCO Emblem, Scales and Tree — A9a

1963, Dec. 10 *Perf. 13*
33 A9a 25fr grn, ol & red brn 45 35

Issued to commemorate the 15th anniversary of the Universal Declaration of Human Rights.

Leaves and IQSY Emblem A10

1964, Apr. 20 Engr. *Perf. 13*
34 A10 25fr org, Prus grn & bis 1.10 1.00

International Quiet Sun Year, 1964-65.

Child — A11

"All Men Are Men" — A12

Designs: Heads of Children.

1964, Aug. 13 Unwmk. *Perf. 13*
35 A11 20fr rose lil, red brn & lt ol grn 35 25
36 A11 25fr brick red, red brn & bl 40 30
37 A11 40fr lt ol grn, red brn & rose lil 60 45
38 A11 50fr dl cl, red brn & lt grn 80 50
a. Min. sheet of 4 2.25 2.25

No. 38a contains one each of Nos. 35-38. Size: 144x99mm.

Cooperation Issue
Common Design Type

1964, Nov. 7 Engr.
39 CD119 25fr grn, mag & dk brn 45 30

1964, Dec. 1 Litho. *Perf. 13x12½*
40 A12 25fr multi 42 20

Issued to publicize National Unity.

Putting Yoke on Oxen — A13

Designs: 50fr, Ox pulling harrow. 85fr, Team of oxen in field. 100fr, Hay wagon.

1965, Apr. 28 Engr. *Perf. 13*
41 A13 25fr sl grn, sep & rose 40 30
42 A13 50fr sl grn, lt bl & brn 75 45
43 A13 85fr bl, grn & red brn 1.25 75
44 A13 100fr multi 1.50 1.00

Telegraph Receiver by Pouget-Maisonneuve — A14

Designs: 30fr, Chappe telegraph (vert.). 50fr, Doignon regulator (vert.). 85fr, Pouillet telegraph transcriber.

1965, May 17 Unwmk.
45 A14 25fr red, grn & ultra 40 30
46 A14 30fr lake & grn 50 35
47 A14 50fr car & vio 85 50
48 A14 85fr red lil & sl 1.25 80

Issued to commemorate the centenary of the International Telecommunication Union.

"Health" A15

Designs: 25fr, "Clothes;" shuttle, cloth and women. 60fr, "Teaching;" student and school. 85fr, "Food;" mother feeding child, tractor in wheat field.

1965, June 10 Engr. *Perf. 13*
49 A15 25fr ultra, brt grn & brn 40 30
50 A15 50fr ultra, brn & grn 75 50
51 A15 60fr grn, ultra & brn 90 65
52 A15 85fr multi 1.35 75

Issued to publicize the slogans and aims of "M.E.S.A.N." (Mouvement d'Evolution Sociale de l'Afrique Noire). See No. C30.

Caterpillars and Moth on Coffee Branch — A16

Designs: 3fr, Hawk moth and caterpillar on coffee leaves (horiz.). 30fr, Platyedra moth and larvae on cotton plant.

1965, Aug. 25 Engr. *Perf. 13*

53	A16	2fr dk pur, dp org & sl grn	5	5
54	A16	3fr blk, sl grn & red	8	8
55	A16	30fr red lil, red & sl grn	1.00	40

Issued to publicize plant protection.

Boy Scout, Tents and Animals A17

Design: 25fr, Campfire and Scout emblem.

1965, Sept. 27 Unwmk. *Perf. 13*

56	A17	25fr red org, bl & red lil	40	22
57	A17	50fr brn & Prus bl	80	55

Issued to honor the Boy Scouts.

Nos. 30, 1 and 22 Surcharged in Black or Brown

5 F

Engraved; Photogravure
Perf. 13, 12, 12½x13

1965, Aug. 26 Unwmk.

58	A9	2fr on 3fr multi	1.75	1.75
59	A1	5fr on 15fr multi	1.75	1.75
60	A5	10fr on 20fr multi (Br)	2.00	2.00

The surcharges are adjusted to shape of stamps.

U.N. Emblem and Wheat A18

1965, Oct. 16 Engr. *Perf. 13*

61	A18	50fr ocher, sl grn & brt bl	90	60

Issued for the "Freedom from Hunger Campaign" of the United Nations Food and Agriculture Organization.

Diamond Cutter A19

1966, March 14 Engr. *Perf. 13*

62	A19	25fr car rose, dk pur & brn	40	25

5 F

Nos. 43-44 Surcharged

1966, Feb.

63	A13	5fr on 85fr multi	25	25
64	A13	10fr on 100fr multi	45	45

Issue dates: No. 63, Feb. 17. No. 64, Feb. 15.

Prices of premium quality never hinged stamps will be in excess of catalogue price.

Statue of Mbaka Woman Porter A20

WHO Headquarters, Geneva A21

1966, Apr. 9 Photo. *Perf. 13x12½*

65	A20	25fr multi	40	25

Issued to commemorate the International Negro Arts Festival. Dakar, Senegal, Apr. 1-24.

1966, May 3 Photo. Unwmk.

66	A21	25fr pur, bl & yel	40	25

Issued to commemorate the inauguration of the World Health Organization Headquarters, Geneva.

Eulophia Cucullata — A22

Orchids: 5fr, Lissochilus horsfalii. 10fr, Tridactyle bicaudata. 15fr, Polystachya. 20fr, Eulophia alta. 25fr, Microcelia macrorrhynchium.

1966, May 16 Photo. *Perf. 12x12½*
Orchids in Natural Colors

67	A22	2fr dk red	8	5
68	A22	5fr brn org & vio	10	8
69	A22	10fr bl grn & blk	15	10
70	A22	15fr lt grn & dk brn	25	15
71	A22	20fr dk grn	35	20
72	A22	25fr lt ultra & brn	45	20
		Nos. 67-72 (6)	1.38	78

Congo Forest Mouse A23

Rodents: 10fr, One-stripe mouse. 20fr, Dollman's tree mouse (vert.).

1966, Sept. 15 Photo. *Perf. 12½x12*

73	A23	5fr yel & multi	12	10
74	A23	10fr tan & multi	18	10
75	A23	20fr lt grn & multi	35	25

UNESCO Emblem — A24

Pres. Jean Bedel Bokassa — A25

1966, Dec. 5 Photo. *Perf. 13*

76	A24	30fr multi	45	25

Issued to commemorate the 20th anniversary of UNESCO (United Nations Educational, Scientific and Cultural Organization).

1967, Jan. 1 *Perf. 12x12½*

77	A25	30fr yel grn, blk & bis brn	50	25

No. 72 Surcharged with New Value and "XX"

1967, May 8 Photo. *Perf. 12x12½*

78	A22	10fr on 25fr multi	20	10

See also No. C43.

Central Market, Bangui A26

1967, Aug. 8 Photo. *Perf. 12½x13*

79	A26	30fr multi	50	30

Safari Hotel, Bangui A27

1967, Sept. 26 Photo. *Perf. 12½x13*

80	A27	30fr multi	50	30

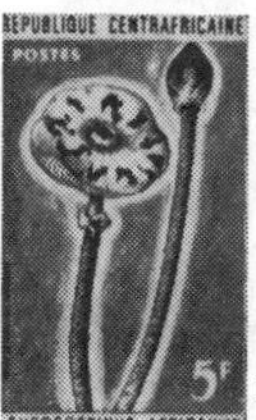

Leucocoprinus Africanus — A28

Various Mushrooms

1967, Oct. 3 Engr. *Perf. 13*

81	A28	5fr dk brn, ol & ocher	12	10
82	A28	10fr dk brn, ultra & yel	18	13
83	A28	15fr dk brn, sl grn & yel	25	17
84	A28	30fr multi	60	25
85	A28	50fr multi	85	50
		Nos. 81-85 (5)	2.00	1.15

Map, Radio Tower, Projector and People A29

1967, Oct. 31

86	A29	30fr emer, ocher & ind	50	30

Radiovision service.

African Hair Style — A30

Various African Hair Styles.

1967, Nov. 7 Engr. *Perf. 13*

87	A30	5fr ultra, dk brn & bis brn	10	8
88	A30	10fr car, dk brn & bis brn	20	12
89	A30	15fr dp grn, dk brn & bis brn	25	15
90	A30	20fr org, dk brn & bis brn	35	15
91	A30	30fr red lil, dk brn & bis brn	50	25
		Nos. 87-91 (5)	1.40	75

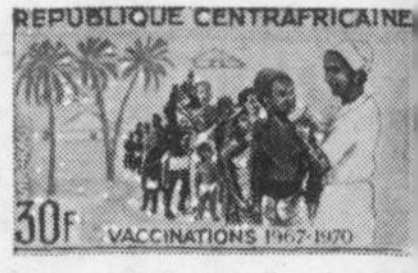

Nurse Vaccinating Children A31

1967, Nov. 14

92	A31	30fr dk red brn & brt grn	50	2

Vaccination campaign, 1967-70.

Douglas DC-3 — A32

Designs: 2fr, Beechcraft Baron. 5fr, Douglas DC-4.

1967, Nov. 24

93	A32	1fr brn red, ind & grn	6	6
94	A32	2fr brt bl, blk & brt pink	6	6
95	A32	5fr grnsh bl, blk & emer	13	12
		Nos. 93-95,C47-C49 (6)	11.85	6.1

Pierced Stone, Kwe Tribe — A33

Designs: 30fr, Primitive dwelling at Toulou (horiz.). 100fr, Megaliths, Bouar. 130fr, Rock painting (people), Toulou (horiz.).

1967, Dec. 26 Engr. *Perf. 13*

96	A33	30fr crim, ind & mar	50	30
97	A33	50fr ol brn, ocher & dk grn	80	40
98	A33	100fr dk brn, brt bl & brn	1.60	70
99	A33	130fr dk red, brn & dk grn	2.00	90

Issued to publicize the 6th Pan-African Prehistoric Congress, Dakar.

Tanker, Refinery and Map of Area Served — A33a

1968, July 30 Photo. *Perf. 12½*

100	A33a	30fr multi	40	20

Issued to commemorate the opening of the Port Gentil (Gabon) Refinery, June 12, 1968.

Bulldozer Clearing Land — A34

Designs: 10fr, Baoule cattle. 20fr, 15,000-spindle spinning machine. No. 104, Automatic Diederichs looms. No. 105, Bulldozer.

1968, Oct. 1 Engr. *Perf. 13*

101	A34	5fr blk, grn & dk brn	7	5
102	A34	10fr blk, pale grn & bis brn	18	15
103	A34	20fr grn, red brn & yel	30	18
104	A34	30fr brn, ol & ultra	50	20
105	A34	30fr ind, red brn & sl grn	50	20
		Nos. 101-105 (5)	1.55	78

Issued to publicize "Operation Bokassa."

Bangui Mosque A35

1968, Oct. 14
106 A35 30fr grn, bl & ocher 45 20

Hunting Knife of Baya and Boufi Tribes A36

Designs: 20fr, Hunting knife of Nzakara tribe. 30fr, Crossbow of Babinga and Babenzele (pygmy) tribes.

1968, Nov. 19 Engr. *Perf. 13*
107 A36 10fr lem, Prus bl & ultra 15 12
108 A36 20fr ultra, dk ol & sl grn 30 17
109 A36 30fr sl grn, ultra & brn org 45 17

"Ville de Bangui," 1958 — A37

River Boats: 30fr, "J. B. Gouandjia," 1968. 50fr, "Lamblin," 1944.

1968, Dec. 10 Engr. *Perf. 13*
Size: 36x22mm.
110 A37 10fr mag, brt grn & vio bl 15 10
111 A37 30fr bl, grn & brn 50 20
112 A37 50fr brn, sl & ol grn 85 40
Nos. 110-112,C62-C63 (5) 5.00 2.40

Woman Javelin Thrower — A38

Sport Designs: 10fr, Women runners. 15fr, Soccer.

1969, Mar. 18 Photo. *Perf. 13x12½*
113 A38 5fr multi 10 6
114 A38 10fr multi 17 10
115 A38 15fr multi 25 12
Nos. 113-115,C71-C72 (5) 2.77 1.23

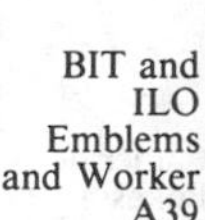

BIT and ILO Emblems and Worker A39

1969, May 20 Photo. *Perf. 12½x13*
116 A39 30fr dp bl, grn & ol brn 40 15
117 A39 50fr dp car, grn & ol brn 75 35

Issued to commemorate the 50th anniversary of the International Labor Organization.

Pres. Jean Bedel Bokassa A40

Garayah A41

1969, Dec. 1 Litho. *Perf. 13x13½*
118 A40 30fr ver & multi 40 20

ASECNA Issue
Common Design Type

1969, Dec. 12 Engr. *Perf. 13*
119 CD132 100fr dp bl 1.50 70

1970, Jan. 6 Engr. *Perf. 13*

Musical Instuments: 15fr, Ngombi (harp; horiz.). 30fr, Xylophone (horia.). 50fr, Ndala (lute; horiz.). 130fr, Gatta and babyon (drums).

120 A41 10fr yel grn, dk grn & ocher 15 12
121 A41 15fr bl grn, ocher & dk brn 25 15
122 A41 30fr mar, ocher & dk brn 45 20
123 A41 50fr rose car & ind 75 45
124 A41 130fr brt bl, brn & ol 2.00 70
Nos. 120-124 (5) 3.60 1.62

U.P.U. Headquarters Issue
Common Design Type

1970, May 20 Engr. *Perf. 13*
125 CD133 100fr ultra, ver & red brn 1.00 50

Loading Platform and Flour Storage Bins A42

Designs: 50fr, Flour milling machinery. 100fr, View of mill.

1970, Feb. 24 Litho. *Perf. 14*
126 A42 25fr sl & multi 35 18
127 A42 50fr lil & multi 70 32
128 A42 100fr red & multi 1.40 75

Inauguration of SICPAD (Societe Industrielle Centrafricaine des Produits Alimentaires et Derives), a part of Operation Bokassa, Feb. 22, 1968.

Pres. Bokassa — A43

1970, Aug. 13 Litho. *Perf. 14*
129 A43 30fr multi 3.25 2.75
130 A43 40fr multi 4.75 3.50

Cheese Factory, Sarki — A44

Silk Worm — A45

Designs: 10fr, M'Bali Ranch. 20fr, Zebu (vert.).

Perf. 13x13½, 13½x13
1970, Sept. 15
131 A44 5fr red & multi 20 10
132 A44 10fr red & multi 4.00 3.50
133 A44 20fr red & multi 65 45
134 A45 40fr red & multi 1.10 75
Nos. 131-134,C83 (5) 7.95 5.90

Issued to publicize Operation Bokassa, a national development plan.

Gnathonemus Monteiri — A46

River Fish: 20fr, Mormyrus proboscirostris. 30fr, Marcusenius wilverthi. 40fr, Gnathonemus elephas. 50fr, Gnathonemus curvirostris.

1971, Apr. 6 Photo. *Perf. 12½*
135 A46 10fr multi 15 10
136 A46 20fr multi 30 20
137 A46 30fr multi 50 25
138 A46 40fr multi 65 25
139 A46 50fr multi 80 40
Nos. 135-139 (5) 2.40 1.20

Berberati Cathedral A47

1971, July 20 Litho. *Perf. 13½*
140 A47 5fr grn & multi 10 8

New Roman Catholic Cathedral at Berberati.

Charles de Gaulle — A48

Gray Galago — A49

1971, Aug. 20 *Perf. 13½x13*
141 A48 100fr brt bl & multi 1.50 1.10

In memory of Gen. Charles de Gaulle (1890-1970), president of France.

1971, Oct. 25 Photo. *Perf. 13*

Designs: 40fr, Elegant galago. 100fr, Calabar potto (horiz.). 150fr, Bosman's potto (horiz.). 200fr, Oustalet's colobo (horiz.).

142 A49 30fr pink & multi 50 40
143 A49 40fr lt bl & multi 70 50
144 A49 100fr multi 1.40 1.00
145 A49 150fr multi 2.25 1.25
146 A49 200fr multi 3.25 1.50
Nos. 142-146 (5) 8.10 4.65

Alan B. Shepard — A50

Designs: No. 148, Yuri Gagarin. No. 149, Edwin E. Aldrin, Jr. No. 150, Alexel Leonov. No. 151, Neil A. Armstrong on moon. No. 152, Lunokhod I on moon.

1971, Nov. 19 Litho. *Perf. 14*
147 A50 40fr vio & multi 50 25
148 A50 40fr vio & multi 50 25
149 A50 100fr multi 1.35 60
150 A50 100fr multi 1.35 60
151 A50 200fr red & multi 2.50 1.00
152 A50 200fr red & multi 2.50 1.00
Nos. 147-152 (6) 8.70 3.70

Space achievements of United States and Russia.

"Operation Bokassa" and Pres. Bokassa A51

1971, Dec. 1 Photo. *Perf. 13*
153 A51 40fr red & multi 60 22

12th anniversary of independence.

Racial Equality Emblem A52

1971, Dec. 6 Litho.
154 A52 50fr multi 60 25

International Year Against Racial Discrimination.

Bokassa School Emblem and Cadets — A53

Book Year Emblem — A54

1972, Jan. 1 Photo.
155 A53 30fr gold & multi 45 20

J. B. Bokassa Military School.

1972, Mar. 11 Photo. ***Perf. 12½x13***
156 A54 100fr red brn, gold & org 1.10 65

International Book Year 1972.

"Your Heart is your Health" A55

1972, Apr. 7 Photo. ***Perf. 13x12½***
157 A55 100fr yel, blk & car 1.10 65

World Health Day.

Red Cross Workers in Village — A56

1972, May 8 ***Perf. 13***
158 A56 150fr multi 2.00 90

25th World Red Cross Day.

Globe A57

1972, May 17 **Litho.**
159 A57 50fr yel, blk & dp org 60 30

4th World Telecommunications Day.

Pres. and Mrs. Bokassa and Family — A58

1972, May 28 ***Perf. 14***
160 A58 30fr yel & multi 40 15

Mother's Day. Mothers' gold medal awarded to Catherine Bokassa.

Pres. Bokassa Planting Cotton, Map of Africa — A59

1972, June 5 Photo. ***Perf. 13***
161 A59 40fr yel & multi 50 25

Operation Bokassa, a national development plan.

Foreign postal stationery (stamped envelopes, postal cards and air letter sheets) lies beyond the scope of this Catalogue, which is limited to adhesive postage stamps.

Postal Checking and Savings Center A60

1972, June 21
162 A60 30fr yel org & multi 40 18

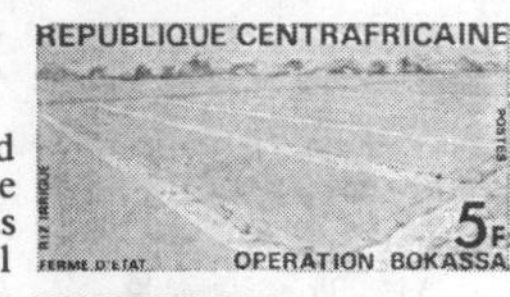

Irrigated Rice Fields A61

"Le Pacifique" Apartment House A62

Designs: 25fr, Plowing rice field. No. 166, Swimming pool, Hotel St. Sylvestre. No. 167, Entrance, Hotel St. Sylvestre. No. 168, J. B. Bokassa University.

1972 Litho. ***Perf. 13x13½***
163 A61 5fr multi 7 6
164 A61 25fr multi 32 15

Engr. ***Perf. 13***
165 A62 30fr multi 35 15
166 A62 30fr multi 35 15
167 A62 40fr multi 45 25
168 A62 40fr multi 45 20
Nos. 163-168 (6) 1.99 96

Operation Bokassa. Issue dates: 5fr, 25fr, Nov. 10; No. 165, June 27; Nos. 166-167, Dec. 9; No. 168, Aug. 26.

Bull Chasing Woman on Clock Face — A63

Designs (Scenes Painted on Clock Faces): 10fr, Men and open cooking fire. 20fr, Fishermen. 30fr, Palms, monkeys and giraffe. 40fr, Warriors.

1972, July 31 Photo. ***Perf. 12½***
169 A63 5fr dk red & multi 8 5
170 A63 10fr brt bl & multi 10 6
171 A63 20fr grn & multi 25 10
172 A63 30fr yel & multi 45 20
173 A63 40fr vio & multi 50 30
Nos. 169-173 (5) 1.38 71

HORCEN Central African clock and watch factory.

Protestant Youth Center — A64

Design: 10fr, Postal runner carrying mail in cleft stick (vert.).

1972, Aug. 12 ***Perf. 13***
174 A64 10fr multi 15 8
175 A64 20fr multi 25 10
Nos. 174-175,C95-C98 (6) 5.50 2.48

Centraphilex 1972, Central African Philatelic Exhibition, Bangui.

Mail Truck — A65

1972, Oct. 23 Photo. ***Perf. 13***
176 A65 100fr ocher & multi 1.35 50

Universal Postal Union Day.

Mother Teaching Child to Write — A66

Central African Mothers: 10fr, Caring for infant. 15fr, Combing child's hair. 20fr, Teaching to read. 180fr, Nursing. 190fr, Teaching to walk.

1972, Dec. 27 ***Perf. 13½x13***
177 A66 5fr multi 8 5
178 A66 10fr lil & multi 12 7
179 A66 15fr dl org & multi 20 8
180 A66 20fr yel grn & multi 25 12
181 A66 180fr multi 2.25 75
182 A66 190fr pink & multi 2.25 1.10
Nos. 177-182 (6) 5.15 2.17

Farmer Carrying Sheaf — A67

1973, May 30 Photo. ***Perf. 13***
183 A67 50fr vio bl & multi 55 35

10th anniversary of the World Food Program.

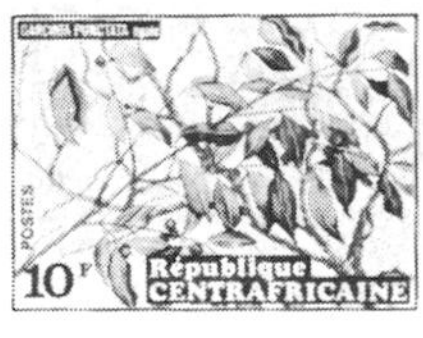

Garcinia Punctata A68

African Flora: 20fr, Bertiera racemosa. 30fr, Corynanthe pachyceras. 40fr, Combretodendron africanum. 50fr, Xylopia Villosa (vert.).

1973, June 8
184 A68 10fr pale bl & multi 10 7
185 A68 20fr multi 20 10
186 A68 30fr lt gray & multi 40 15
187 A68 40fr multi 40 30
188 A68 50fr multi 50 35
Nos. 184-188 (5) 1.60 97

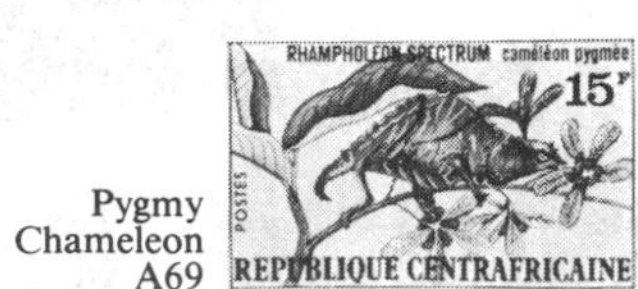

Pygmy Chameleon A69

1973, June 26 Photo. ***Perf. 13***
189 A69 15fr multi 20 10

Caterpillar — A70

Designs: Various caterpillars.

1973, Aug. 6 Photo. ***Perf. 13***
190 A70 3fr multi 5 5
191 A70 5fr multi 8 5
192 A70 25fr multi 30 15

No. 184 Surcharged with New Value, 2 Bars, and Overprinted in Red: "SECHERESSE SOLIDARITE AFRICAINE"

1973, Aug. 16
193 A68 100fr on 10fr multi 90 75

African solidarity in drought emergency.

African Postal Union Issue
Common Design Type

1973, Sept. 12 Engr. ***Perf. 13***
194 CD137 100fr dk brn, red org & ol 90 65

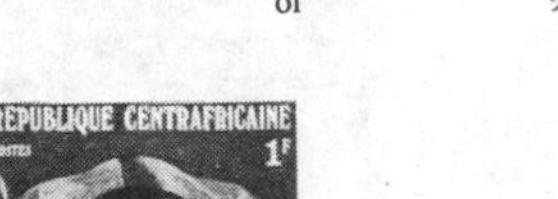

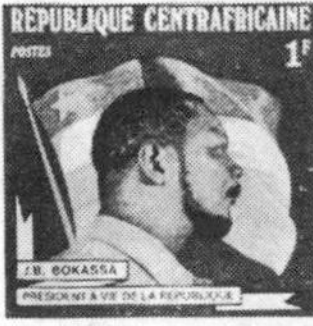

Pres. Bokassa and CAR Flag — A71

1973, Nov. 30 Photo. ***Perf. 12½***
195 A71 1fr brn & multi 5 5
196 A71 2fr pur & multi 5 5
197 A71 3fr vio bl & multi 5 5
198 A71 5fr ocher & multi 5 5
199 A71 10fr multi 10 7
200 A71 15fr org & multi 15 10
201 A71 20fr multi 20 15
202 A71 30fr dk grn & multi 30 20
203 A71 40fr dk brn & multi 40 30
Nos. 195-203,C117-C118 (11) 2.85 2.07

INTERPOL Emblem A72

1973, Dec. 20 ***Perf. 13x12½***
204 A72 50fr yel & multi 50 40

50th anniversary of the International Criminal Police Organization.

Catherine Bokassa Center A73

Design: 40fr, Ambulance in front of Catherine Bokassa Center.

1974, Jan. 24 Engr. ***Perf. 13***
205 A73 30fr multi 25 18
206 A73 40fr multi 32 25

Catherine Bokassa Center for Mothers and Children.

Cigarette-making Machine — A74

Designs: 10fr, Cigarette in ashtray, and factory. 30fr, Hand lighting cigarette, and Administration Building.

1974, Jan. 29

207	A74 5fr sl grn & multi	7	5
208	A74 10fr sl grn & multi	10	10
209	A74 30fr sl grn & multi	25	15

Publicity for Centra cigarettes.

"Communications" A75

1974, June 8 Photo. *Perf. 12½x13*

210	A75 100fr multi	1.00	70

World Telecommunications Day.

People and WPY Emblem A76

1974, June 20 Engr. *Perf. 13*

211	A76 100fr red, sl grn & brn	1.00	70

World Population Year.

Mother, Child, WHO Emblem — A77

1974, July 10

212	A77 100fr multi	1.00	45

26th anniversary of World Health Organization.

Hoeing A78

Designs: 10fr, Battle scene ("yesterday"). 15fr, Pastoral scene ("today"). 20fr, Rice planting. 25fr, Storehouse. 40fr, Veterans Headquarters. Borders show tanks and tractors.

1974, Nov. 15 Litho. *Perf. 13*

213	A78 10fr multi	10	7
214	A78 15fr multi	12	8
215	A78 20fr multi	18	10
216	A78 25fr multi	22	15
217	A78 30fr multi	25	15
218	A78 40fr multi	35	15
	Nos. 213-218 (6)	1.22	70

Veterans' activities.

Presidents and Flags of Cameroun, CAR, Congo, Gabon and Meeting Center — A79

1974, Dec. 8 Photo. *Perf. 13*

219	A79 40fr gold & multi	40	22

See No. C126 and note after Cameroun No. 595.

House in OCAM City — A80

Designs: Scenes in housing development, OCAM City.

1975, Feb. 1 Photo. *Perf. 13*

220	A80 30fr multi	30	17
221	A80 40fr multi	40	22
222	A80 50fr multi	45	30
223	A80 100fr multi	90	65

1975, Feb. 22

Designs: Cottage scenes in J. B. Bokassa "pilot village."

224	A80 25fr multi	20	12
225	A80 30fr multi	25	15
226	A80 40fr multi	40	20

Foreign Ministry A81

Television Station A82

1975, Feb. 28 *Perf. 13x12½*

227	A81 40fr multi	40	18

Perf. 13

228	A82 40fr multi	40	18

Public buildings, Bangui.

Bokassa's Saber — A83

Design: 40fr, Bokassa's baton.

1975, Feb. 22 Photo. *Perf. 13*

229	A83 30fr dp bl & multi	25	17
230	A83 40fr vio bl & multi	35	20

Jean Bedel Bokassa, President for Life and Marshal of the Republic. See Nos. C127-C128.

Do Not Enter — A84

Traffic Signs: 10fr, Stop. 20fr, No parking. 30fr, School. 40fr, Intersection.

1975, Mar. 20

231	A84 5fr ultra & red	5	5
232	A84 10fr ultra & red	10	8
233	A84 20fr ultra & red	15	10
234	A84 30fr ultra & multi	20	17
235	A84 40fr ultra & multi	40	20
	Nos. 231-235 (5)	90	60

Buffon's Kob — A85

Designs: 15fr, Wart hog. 20fr, Waterbuck. 30fr, Lion.

1975, June 24 Photo. *Perf. 13*

236	A85 10fr dl grn & multi	10	7
237	A85 15fr lem & multi	15	8
238	A85 20fr yel grn & multi	20	13
239	A85 30fr lt bl & multi	30	17

Crane Lifting Log onto Truck — A86

Designs: 10fr, Forest (vert.). 15fr, Tree felling (vert.). 100fr, Log pile. 150fr, Logs transported by raft. 200fr, Lumberyard.

1975, Nov. 28 Engr. *Perf. 13*

240	A86 10fr multi	8	5
241	A86 15fr multi	12	8
242	A86 50fr multi	40	25
243	A86 100fr multi	75	55
244	A86 150fr multi	1.10	90
245	A86 200fr multi	1.50	1.10
	Nos. 240-245 (6)	3.95	2.93

Promotion of Central African wood.

Women's Heads and Various Occupations — A87

1975, Dec. 10 Photo.

246	A87 40fr multi	35	20
247	A87 100fr multi	75	55

International Women's Year 1975.

Alexander Graham Bell — A88

1976, Mar. 25 Litho. *Perf. 12½x13*

248	A88 100fr yel & blk	75	50

Centenary of first telephone call by Alexander Graham Bell, Mar. 10, 1876.

Satellite and ITU Emblem — A89

Design: No. 250, UPU emblem, various forms of mail transport.

1976 Engr. *Perf. 13*

249	A89 100fr vio bl, cl & grn	75	50
250	A89 100fr car, grn & ocher	90	70

World Telecommunications Day (No. 249); Universal Postal Union Day (No. 250).

Soyuz on Launching Pad — A90

Design: 50fr, Apollo rocket.

1976, June 14 Litho. *Perf. 14x13½*

251	A90 40fr multi	42	18
252	A90 50fr multi	55	25
	Nos. 251-252,C135-C137 (5)	6.91	2.91

Apollo Soyuz space test project, Russo-American cooperation, launched July 15, link-up July 17, 1975.

Drurya Antimachus — A91

Butterfly: 40fr, Argema mittrei (vert.).

1976, Sept. 20 Litho. *Perf. 12½*

253	A91 30fr ocher & multi	25	15
254	A91 40fr ultra & multi	35	20

See Nos. C145-C146.

Slalom, Piero Gros — A92

Design: 60fr, Karl Schnabel and Toni Innauer.

1976, Sept. 23 *Perf. 13½*

255	A92 40fr multi	42	20
256	A92 60fr multi	65	32
	Nos. 255-256,C147-C149 (5)	6.92	3.17

12th Winter Olympic Games winners, Innsbruck.

The lack of a price for a listed item does not necessarily indicate rarity.

Viking Components A93

Design: 60fr, Viking take-off.

1976, Dec.

No.	Type	Description	Unused	Used
257	A93	40fr multi	42	18
258	A93	60fr multi	65	30
		Nos. 257-258,C151-C153 (5)	6.92	2.88

Viking Mars project.

Empire

Stamps of 1973-76 Overprinted with Bars and "EMPIRE CENTRAFRICAIN" in Black, Green, Violet Blue, Silver, Carmine, Brown or Red

Printing and Perforations as Before

1977, March

No.	Type	Description	Unused	Used
259	A70	3fr (#190; B)	5	5
260	A78	10fr (#213;B)	12	10
261	A84	10fr (#232;VB)	12	10
262	A85	10fr (#236;C)	15	12
263	A85	15fr (#237;C)	20	15
264	A86	15fr (#241;B)	17	12
265	A78	20fr (#215;B)	20	18
266	A85	20fr (#238;C)	20	18
267	A78	25fr (#216;B)	25	20
268	A80	25fr (#224;B)	25	20
269	A80	30fr (#220;VB)	30	25
270	A80	30fr (#225;B)	30	25
271	A85	30fr (#239;C)	30	25
272	A79	40fr (#219;B)	35	30
273	A80	40fr (#221;VB)	40	30
274	A80	40fr (#226;B)	35	30
275	A81	40fr (#227;B & S)	35	30
276	A82	40fr (#228;B)	35	30
277	A84	40fr (#235;VB)	30	25
278	A91	40fr (#254;B)	30	25
279	A86	50fr (#242;Br)	45	35
280	A75	100fr (#210;B)	90	70
281	A76	100fr (#211;B)	90	70
282	A77	100fr (#212;G)	1.00	80
283	A88	100fr (#248;R)	1.00	80
284	A89	100fr (#249;B)	1.00	80
285	A89	100fr (#250;B)	1.00	80
		Nos. 259-285 (27)	11.26	9.10

Stamps of 1975-76 Overprinted "EMPIRE CENTRAFRICAIN" in Black on Silver Panel

1977, Apr. 1

No.	Type	Description	Unused	Used
286	A83	40fr multi (#230)	30	25
287	A90	40fr multi (#251)	40	30
288	A92	40fr multi (#255)	30	25
289	A93	40fr multi (#257)	30	25
290	A90	50fr multi (#252)	50	35
291	A92	60fr multi (#256)	50	35
292	A93	60fr multi (#258)	50	35
		Nos. 286-292 (7)	2.80	2.10

Pierre and Marie Curie A94

Design: 60fr, Wilhelm C. Roentgen.

1977, Apr. 1 Litho. *Perf. 13½*

No.	Type	Description	Unused	Used
293	A94	40fr multi	35	18
294	A94	60fr multi	60	30
		Nos. 293-294,C180-C182 (5)	6.80	2.88

Nobel Prize winners.

Italy No. C42 and Faustine Temple, Rome — A95

Design: 60fr, Russia No. C12 and St. Basil's Cathedral, Moscow.

1977, Apr. 11 Litho. *Perf. 11*

No.	Type	Description	Unused	Used
295	A95	40fr multi	35	18
296	A95	60fr multi	60	30
		Nos. 295-296,C184-C186 (5)	6.80	2.88

75th anniversary of the Zeppelin.

Lindbergh over Paris — A96

Designs: 60fr, Santos Dumont and "14 bis." 100fr, Bleriot and monoplane. 200fr, Roald Amundsen and "N24." 300fr, Concorde. 500fr, Lindbergh and Spirit of St. Louis.

1977, Sept. 30 Litho. *Perf. 13½*

No.	Type	Description	Unused	Used
297	A96	50fr multi	50	25
298	A96	60fr multi	60	30
299	A96	100fr multi	95	38
300	A96	200fr multi	1.90	80
301	A96	300fr multi	3.00	1.20
		Nos. 297-301 (5)	6.95	2.93

Souvenir Sheet

No.	Type	Description	Unused	Used
302	A96	500fr multi	4.75	2.25

History of aviation, famous fliers. No. 302 has multicolored margin showing Spirit of St. Louis and Concorde. Size: 117x91½mm.

Emperor Bokassa I, Central African Flag — A98

Shot on Goal A97

Designs: 60fr, Heading ball in net. 100fr, Backfield defense. 200fr, Argentina '78 poster. 300fr, Mario Zagalo and stadium. 500fr, Ferenc Puskas.

1977, Nov. 18 Litho. *Perf. 13½*

No.	Type	Description	Unused	Used
303	A97	50fr multi	50	25
304	A97	60fr multi	60	30
305	A97	100fr multi	95	35
306	A97	200fr multi	1.90	80
307	A97	300fr multi	3.00	1.20
		Nos. 303-307 (5)	6.95	2.90

Souvenir Sheet

No.	Type	Description	Unused	Used
308	A97	500fr multi	4.75	2.25

World Soccer Championships, Argentina, June 1-25, 1978. No. 308 has multicolored margin showing Argentina '78 emblem, World Cup and Stadium. Size: 120x81mm.

1977, Dec. 4 Litho. *Perf. 13½*

No.	Type	Description	Unused	Used
309	A98	40fr multi	30	25
310	A98	60fr multi	50	35
311	A98	100fr multi	80	60
312	A98	150fr multi	1.20	90
		Nos. 309-312,C188-C189 (6)	6.90	4.60

Coronation of Emperor Bokassa I, Dec. 4.

Lilium — A99

Electronic Tree, ITU Emblem — A100

Design: 10fr, Hibiscus.

1977 Litho. *Perf. 13½x14*

No.	Type	Description	Unused	Used
313	A99	5fr multi	5	5
314	A99	10fr multi	10	5

1977

No.	Type	Description	Unused	Used
315	A100	100fr blk, org & brn	1.20	90

World Telecommunications Day.

Bible and People A101

1977 Litho. *Perf. 14x13½*

No.	Type	Description	Unused	Used
316	A101	40fr multi	40	20

Bible Week.

People and Rotary Emblem A102

1977

No.	Type	Description	Unused	Used
317	A102	60fr multi	60	30

Rotary Club of Bangui, 20th anniversary.

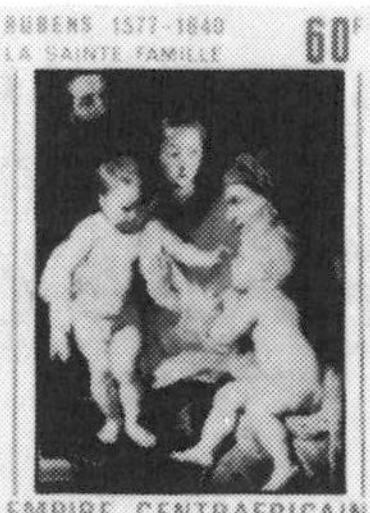

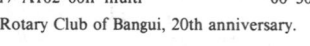

Holy Family, by Rubens A103

Rubens Paintings: 150fr, Marie de Medicis. 200fr, Son of artist. 300fr, Neptune. 500fr, Marie de Medicis (different).

1978, Jan. 26

No.	Type	Description	Unused	Used
318	A103	60fr multi	60	30
319	A103	150fr multi	1.40	60
320	A103	200fr multi	1.90	80
321	A103	300fr multi	3.00	1.20

Souvenir Sheet

No.	Type	Description	Unused	Used
322	A103	500fr gold & multi	4.75	2.25

Peter Paul Rubens (1577-1640), 400th birth anniversary. No. 322 contains one stamp; multicolored margin shows entire painting. Size: 89x116mm.

Rhinoceros — A104

Endangered Animals and Wildlife Fund Emblem: 50fr, Slender-nosed crocodile. 60fr, Leopard (vert.). 100fr, Giraffe (vert.). 200fr, Elephant. 300fr, Gorilla (vert.).

1978, Feb. 21 Litho. *Perf. 13½*

No.	Type	Description	Unused	Used
323	A104	40fr multi	35	18
324	A104	50fr multi	50	25
325	A104	60fr multi	60	30
326	A104	100fr multi	95	42
327	A104	200fr multi	1.90	80
328	A104	300fr multi	3.00	1.25
		Nos. 323-328 (6)	7.30	3.20

Bokassa Sports Palace A105

Design: 60fr, Sports Palace, side view.

1978 *Perf. 14*

No.	Type	Description	Unused	Used
329	A105	40fr multi	32	25
330	A105	60fr multi	50	35

Automatic Telephone Exchange, Bangui A106

1978

No.	Type	Description	Unused	Used
331	A106	40fr multi	40	20
332	A106	60fr multi	60	30

Diligence and Satellite — A107

Designs (UPU Emblem and): 50fr, Steam locomotive and communications via satellite. 60fr, Paddle-wheel steamer and ship-to-shore communication via satellite. 80fr, Old mail truck and satellite.

1978, May 17 *Perf. 13½*

No.	Type	Description	Unused	Used
333	A107	40fr multi	40	20
334	A107	50fr multi	50	25
335	A107	60fr multi	60	30
336	A107	80fr multi	80	40
		Nos. 333-336,C191-C192 (6)	5.30	2.65

Century of progress of posts and telecommunications.

Mask
A108

Capt. Cook on "Endeavour"
A109

Designs: 30fr, Mask. 60fr, Women dancers (horiz.). 100fr, Men dancers (horiz.).

Perf. 13½x14, 14x13½

1978, July 11 **Litho.**

337 A108 20fr blk & yel 20 10
338 A108 30fr blk & brt bl 30 15
339 A108 60fr blk & multi 60 30
340 A108 100fr blk & multi 1.00 50

Black-African World Arts Festival, Lagos.

1978, Aug. 30 *Perf. 14½*

Designs: 60fr, Resolution off Hawaii (horiz.). 200fr, Hawaiians welcoming Capt. Cook (horiz.). 350fr, Masked rowers in Hawaiian boat (horiz.).

341 A109 60fr multi 60 30
342 A109 80fr multi 80 40
343 A109 200fr multi 2.00 1.00
344 A109 350fr multi 3.50 1.75

Capt. James Cook (1728-1779), explorer.

Dürer, Self-portrait
A110

Dürer Paintings: 80fr, The Four Apostles. 200fr, Virgin and Child. 350fr, Emperor Maximilian I.

1978, Oct. 24 **Litho.** *Perf. 13½*

345 A110 60fr multi 60 30
346 A110 80fr multi 80 40
347 A110 200fr multi 2.00 1.00
348 A110 350fr multi 3.50 1.75

Albrecht Dürer (1471-1528), German painter.

Tutankhamen's Gold Mask — A111

Treasures of Tutankhamen: 60fr, King and Queen, gold back panel of throne. 80fr, Gilt folding chair. 100fr, King wearing crowns of Upper and Lower Egypt, painted wood sculpture. 120fr, Lion's head. 150fr, Tutankhamen, wood stature. 180fr, Gold throne. 250fr, Gold miniature coffin.

1978, Nov. 22

349 A111 40fr multi 40 20
350 A111 60fr multi 60 30
351 A111 80fr multi 80 40
352 A111 100fr multi 1.00 50
353 A111 120fr multi 1.20 60
354 A111 150fr multi 1.50 75
355 A111 180fr multi 1.80 90
356 A111 250fr multi 2.50 1.25
Nos. 349-356 (8) 9.80 4.90

Tutankhamen, c. 1358 B.C., King of Egypt.

Lenin at Smolny Institute — A112

Designs: 60fr, 200fr, 300fr, Various Lenin portraits. 100fr, Ulyanov family (horiz.). 150fr, Lenin, Cruiser "Aurora" and flag (horiz.). 500fr, "Aurora" and star.

1978, Nov. *Perf. 14*

357 A112 40fr multi 40 20
358 A112 60fr multi 60 30
359 A112 100fr blk & gold 1.00 50
360 A112 150fr blk, gold & red 1.50 75
361 A112 200fr multi 2.00 1.00
362 A112 300fr multi 3.00 1.50
Nos. 357-362 (6) 8.50 4.25

Souvenir Sheet

363 A112 500fr multi 5.25

60th anniversary of the Soviet Union. No. 363 has red marginal inscription and hammer and sickle emblem. Size: 78x110mm.

Catherine Bokassa
A113

Design: 60fr, Emperor Bokassa.

1978, Dec. 4 **Litho.** *Perf. 13*

364 A113 40fr multi 40 20
365 A113 60fr multi 60 30

First anniversary of coronation. See No. C202.

Rowland Hill, Letter Scale and G.B. No. 1 — A114

Designs (Rowland Hill and): 50fr, U.S. No. 1, mailman on bicycle. 60fr, Austria No. P4 and 19th century mailman. 80fr, Switzerland No. 2L1, postilion and mailcoach.

1978, Dec. 9 **Litho.** *Perf. 13½*

366 A114 40fr multi 40 20
367 A114 50fr multi 50 25
368 A114 60fr multi 60 30
369 A114 80fr multi 80 40
Nos. 366-369,C203-C204 (6) 5.30 2.65

Sir Rowland Hill (1795-1879), originator of penny postage.

Nos. 303-307 Overprinted in Silver: "VAINQUEUR: ARGENTINE"

1978, Dec. 27

370 A97 50fr multi 50 25
371 A97 60fr multi 60 30
372 A97 100fr multi 1.00 50
373 A97 200fr multi 2.00 1.00
374 A97 300fr multi 3.00 1.50
Nos. 370-374 (5) 7.10 3.55

Souvenir Sheet

No. 308 Overprinted in Silver: "ARGENTINE-PAYS BAS 3-1 / 25 juin 1978"

375 A97 500fr multi 5.00 2.50

Argentina's victory in World Cup Soccer Championship 1978.

Children Painting and Dutch Portrait — A115

Designs (UNICEF, Eagle Emblems and): 50fr, Eskimo children skiing, and ski jump. 60fr, Children with toy racing car, and Carl Benz with early car model. 80fr, Children launching rocket, and Intelsat.

1979, Mar. 6 **Litho.** *Perf. 13½*

376 A115 40fr multi 40 20
377 A115 50fr multi 50 25
378 A115 60fr multi 60 30
379 A115 80fr multi 80 40
Nos. 376-379,C206-C207 (6) 5.30 2.65

International Year of the Child.

High Jump, Moscow '80 Emblem and "M" — A116

Designs (Moscow '80 Emblem, Various Sports and): 50fr, Bicycling and "O". 60fr, Weight lifting and "C". 80fr, Judo and "K".

1979, Mar. 16 **Litho.** *Perf. 13*

380 A116 40fr multi 32 15
381 A116 50fr multi 40 20
382 A116 60fr multi 48 25
383 A116 80fr multi 65 30
Nos. 380-383,C209-C210 (6) 4.85 2.40

22nd Olympic Games, Moscow, July 19-Aug. 3, 1980. Background letters on Nos. 380-383, C209-C210 spell "Mockba." A 1500fr gold embossed stamp showing emblems and Discobolus exists.

Memorial, Bangui, Butterfly, Hibiscus — A117

Design: 150fr, Canoe, truck and letters.

1979, June 8 **Litho.** *Perf. 12x12½*

384 A117 60fr multi 48 25
385 A117 150fr multi 1.20 60

Philexafrique II, Libreville, Gabon, June 8-17. No. 384, 385 each printed in sheets of 10 with 5 labels showing exhibition emblem.

Schoolgirl
A118

1979, July 25 **Litho.** *Perf. 12½x12*

386 A118 70fr multi 55 22

International Bureau of Education, Geneva, 50th anniversary.

Chicken
A119

Designs: 20fr, Bull. 40fr, Sheep.

1979, Aug. *Perf. 13*

387 A119 10fr multi 8 5
388 A119 20fr multi 16 8
389 A119 40fr multi 32 15

National Husbandry Association. See No. C211.

Souvenir Sheet

Virgin and Child, by Dürer
A120

1979, Aug. *Perf. 13½*

390 A120 500fr lt grn & dl red 4.00 1.85

Albrecht Dürer (1471-1528), German engraver and printer. No. 390 has dull red and light green margin showing entire etching. Size: 90x115mm.

Nos. 257-258 Overprinted "ALUNISSAGE/APOLLO XI/ juillet/ 1969" and Emblem

1979, Nov. 11 **Litho.** *Perf. 13½*

391 A93 40fr multi 32 15
392 A93 60fr multi 48 25
Nos. 391-392,C212-C214 (5) 5.60 2.80

Apollo 11 moon landing, 10th anniversary.

Girl and Rose
A121

1979, Dec. 15

393 A121 30fr *Butterfly and girl,* vert. 24 12
394 A121 40fr *shown* 32 16
395 A121 60fr *Hansel and Gretel,* vert. 48 24

396 A121 200fr *Cinderella* 1.60 80
397 A121 250fr *Mermaid*, vert. 2.00 1.00
Nos. 393-397 (5) 4.64 2.32

International Year of the Child.

Locomotive, U.S. Type A27, Hill — A122

Locomotives, Hill and Stamps: 100fr, France No. 1. 150fr, Germany type All. 250fr, Great Britain No. 32. 500fr, CAR No. 2.

1979, Dec. 20
398 A122 60fr multi 48 24
399 A122 100fr multi 80 40
400 A122 150fr multi 1.20 60
401 A122 250fr multi 2.00 1.00

Souvenir Sheet

402 A122 500fr multi 4.25 2.25

Sir Rowland Hill (1795-1879), originator of penny postage. No. 402 has multicolored margin showing Hill and Penny Black. Size: 116x78½mm.

Basketball, Moscow '80 Emblem — A123

Pre-Olympic Year: Men's or women's basketball.

1979, Dec. 28 Litho. *Perf. 14½*
403 A123 50fr multi 40 20
404 A123 125fr multi 1.00 50
405 A123 200fr multi 1.60 80
406 A123 300fr multi 2.40 1.20
407 A123 500fr multi 4.00 2.00
Nos. 403-407 (5) 9.40 4.70

Nos. 313-314, 337-338 Overprinted "REPUBLIQUE CENTRAFRICAINE" in Black on Silver Panel and

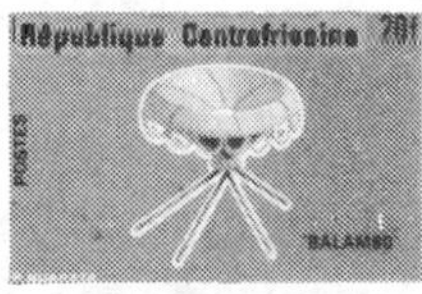

Balambo Chair A124

Perf. 13½x14, 14x13½

1980, Mar. 20 Litho.
408 A99 5fr multi 5 5
409 A99 10fr multi 8 5
410 A124 20fr multi 16 8
411 A108 20fr multi 16 8
412 A108 30fr multi 24 12
Nos. 408-412 (5) 69 38

Viking Satellite A125

1980, Apr. 8 *Perf. 13½*
413 A125 40fr *shown* 32 16
414 A125 50fr *Apollo-Soyuz* 40 20
415 A125 60fr *Voyager* 48 24
416 A125 100fr *European Space Agency emblem, flags* 80 40
Nos. 413-416,C221-C222 (6) 4.80 2.40

Walking, Olympic Medal, Moscow '80 Emblem — A126

1980, July 25 Litho. *Perf. 13½*
417 A126 30fr *shown* 24 12
418 A126 40fr *Relay race* 32 16
419 A126 70fr *Running* 55 25
420 A126 80fr *High jump* 65 32
Nos. 417-420,C231-C232 (6) 3.76 1.85

Agricultural Development A127

1980, Nov. 4 Litho. *Perf. 13½*
421 A127 30fr *shown* 24 12
422 A127 40fr *Telecommunications* 32 16
423 A127 70fr *Engineering* 55 25
424 A127 100fr *Civil engineering* 80 40
Nos. 421-424,C234-C235 (6) 4.71 2.33

Europe-Africa cooperation.

Nos. 403-407 Overprinted with Medal and Country

1980, Nov. 12 *Perf. 14½*
425 A123 50fr multi 40 20
426 A123 125fr multi 1.00 50
427 A123 200fr multi 1.60 80
428 A123 300fr multi 2.40 1.20
429 A123 500fr multi 4.00 2.00
Nos. 425-429 (5) 9.40 4.70

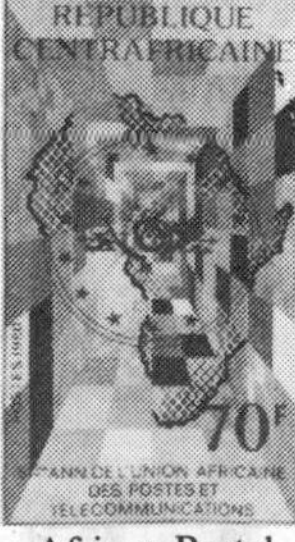

Virgin and Child, by Raphael A128

African Postal Union, 5th Anniversary A129

Christmas 1980: Virgin and Child paintings by Raphael.

1980, Dec. 20 *Perf. 12½*
430 A128 60fr multi 50 25
431 A128 150fr multi 1.20 60
432 A128 250fr multi 2.00 1.00

1980, Dec. 24 Photo. *Perf. 13½*
433 A129 70fr multi 55 25

Peruvian Soccer Team, Soccer Cup — A130

1981, Jan. 13 Litho. *Perf. 13½*
434 A130 10fr shown 8 5
435 A130 15fr Scotland 12 6
436 A130 20fr Mexico 16 8
437 A130 25fr Sweden 20 10
438 A130 30fr Austria 25 12
439 A130 40fr Poland 32 16
440 A130 50fr France 40 20
441 A130 60fr Italy 50 25
442 A130 70fr Germany 60 30
443 A130 80fr Brazil 65 32
Nos. 434-443,C237-C238 (12) 5.68 2.84

ESPANA '82 World Cup Soccer Championship.

13th World Telecommunications Day — A131

1981, May 17 Litho. *Perf. 12½*
144 A131 150fr multi 1.20 60

Apollo 15 Crew on Moon — A132

Space Exploration: Columbia space shuttle.

1981, June 10 Litho. *Perf. 14*
445 A132 100fr multi 80 40
446 A132 150fr multi 1.20 60
447 A132 200fr multi 1.60 80
448 A132 300fr multi 2.40 1.20

Souvenir Sheet

449 A132 500fr multi 4.00 2.00

No. 449 has multicolored margin continuing design of stamp. Size: 103x78mm.

Family of Acrobats with Monkey, by Picasso A133

Picasso Birth Centenary: 50fr, The Balcony. 80fr, The Artist's Son as Pierrot. 100fr, The Three Dancers.

1981, June 30 *Perf. 13½*
450 A133 40fr multi 32 16
451 A133 50fr multi 40 20
452 A133 80fr multi 65 32
453 A133 100fr multi 80 40
Nos. 450-453,C245-C246 (6) 4.97 2.48

First Anniv. of Zimbabwe's Independence — A134

1981, July 9 Litho. *Perf. 12½*
454 A134 100fr multi 80 80
455 A134 150fr multi 1.20 60
456 A134 200fr multi 1.60 80

Prince Charles and Lady Diana — A135

1981, July, 24 *Perf. 14*
457 A135 75fr Charles 60 30
458 A135 100fr Diana 80 40
459 A135 150fr St. Paul's Cathedral 1.20 60
460 A135 175fr shown 1.40 70

Souvenir Sheet

461 A135 500fr Couple 4.00 2.00

Royal Wedding. No. 461 has multicolored margin showing flowers. Size: 70x91mm.

Nos. 417-420 Overprinted with Event, Winner and Country in Gold.

1981 Litho. *Perf. 13½*
462 A126 30fr multi 24 12
463 A126 40fr multi 32 16
464 A126 70fr multi 55 25
465 A126 80fr multi 65 32
Nos. 462-465,C248-C249 (6) 3.76 1.85

Prince Charles and Lady Diana — A136

1981, Aug. 20 Litho. *Perf. 13½*
466 A136 40fr shown 32 16
467 A136 50fr Crowned Prince of Wales 40 20
468 A136 80fr Diana 65 32
469 A136 100fr Naval training 80 40
Nos. 466-469,C251-C252 (6) 4.97 2.48

Royal wedding.

1906 Renault — A137

1981, Sept. 22 Litho. *Perf. 12½*
470 A137 20fr shown 16 8
471 A137 40fr Mercedes-Benz, 1937 32 16
472 A137 50fr Matra-Ford, 1969 40 20

473 A137 110fr Tazio Nuvolari, 1927 90 45
474 A137 150fr Jackie Stewart, 1965 1.20 60
Nos. 470-474 (5) 2.98 1.49

Souvenir Sheet

Perf. 10

475 A137 450fr Finish line, 1914 3.75 2.00

Grand Prix of France, 75th anniv. No. 475 has multicolored margin continuing design. Size: 104x80mm.

World Food Day — A138

1981, Oct. 16

476 A138 90fr multi 72 36
477 A138 110fr multi 90 45

Navigators and their Ships — A139

1981, Sept. 4 Litho. *Perf. 13½*

478 A139 40fr C.V. Rietschoten 32 16
479 A139 50fr M. Pajot 40 20
480 A139 60fr K. Jaworski 50 25
481 A139 80fr M. Birch 65 32
Nos. 478-481,C254-C255 (6) 4.27 2.13

Downfall of Empire A140

1981, Oct. 6

482 A140 5fr Sword through crown 5 5
483 A140 10fr like #482 8 5
484 A140 25fr Victory holding map 20 10
485 A140 60fr like #484 50 25
486 A140 90fr Toppled Bokassa statue 72 36
487 A140 500fr like #486 4.00 2.00
Nos. 482-487 (6) 5.55 2.81

Komba — A141

1981, Nov. 17

488 A141 50fr shown 40 20
489 A141 90fr Dodoro, horiz. 72 36
490 A141 140fr Kaya, horiz. 1.15 60

Central African States Bank A142

1981, Dec. 12 Litho. *Perf. 12½x13*

491 A142 90fr multi 72 36
492 A142 110fr multi 90 45

Christmas 1981 — A143

Virgin and Child Paintings.

1981, Dec. 24

493 A143 50fr Fra Angelico, 1430 40 20
494 A143 60fr Cosimo Tura, 1484 50 25
495 A143 90fr Bramantino 72 36
496 A143 110fr Memling 90 45
Nos. 493-496,C260-C261 (6) 5.27 2.66

Scouting Year — A144

1982, Jan. 13 *Perf. 12½*

497 A144 100fr Hiking 80 40
498 A144 150fr Scouts, horiz. 1.20 60
499 A144 200fr Hiking 1.60 80
500 A144 300fr Salute, flag, vert. 2.40 1.20

Souvenir Sheet

501 A144 500fr Scout, Baden-Powell, vert. 4.00 2.00

No. 501 contains one stamp (perf. 13); multicolored margin shows hike, emblem. Size: 84x113mm.

Elephant A145

1982, Jan. 22 *Perf. 13½*

502 A145 60fr shown 50 25
503 A145 90fr Giraffes 72 36
504 A145 100fr Addaxes 80 40
505 A145 110fr Okapi 90 45
Nos. 502-505,C263-C264 (6) 9.32 4.66

Norman Rockwell Illustrations A146

1982, Feb. 17 *Perf. 13½x14*

506 A146 30fr Grandfather snowman 25 12
507 A146 60fr Croquet players 50 25
508 A146 110fr Women talking 90 45
509 A146 150fr Searching 1.20 60

AT 16 Dirigible A147

1982, Feb. 27 Litho. *Perf. 13½*

510 A147 5fr shown 5 5
511 A147 10fr Beyer-Garrat locomotive 8 5
512 A147 20fr Bugatti 24 "Royale," 1924 16 8
513 A147 110fr Vickers "Valentia," 1928 90 45
Nos. 510-513,C266-C267 (6) 7.59 3.88

Bellvue Garden, by Edouard Manet (1832-1883) — A148

Anniversaries: 400fr, Goethe (1749-1832) (vert.). Nos. 519-520, Princess Diana, 21st birthday, July 1 (vert.). 300fr, George Washington (1732-1799) (vert.).

1982, Apr. 6 Litho. *Perf. 13*

517 A148 200fr multi 1.60 80
517A A148 300fr multi 2.40 1.25
518 A148 400fr multi 3.25 1.60
519 A148 500fr multi 4.00 2.00

Souvenir Sheet

520 A148 500fr multi 4.00 2.00

No. 520 has multicolored margin showing flowers. Size: 80x104mm.

23rd Olympic Games, Los Angeles, 1984 — A149

1982, July 24 Litho. *Perf. 13½*

521 A149 5fr Soccer 5 5
522 A149 10fr Boxing 8 5
523 A149 20fr Running 16 8
524 A149 110fr Long jump 90 45
Nos. 521-524,C269-C270 (6) 7.69 3.88

21st Birthday of Princess Diana — A150

Portraits.

1982, July 20 Litho. *Perf. 13½*

525 A150 5fr multi 5 5
526 A150 10fr multi 8 5
527 A150 20fr multi 16 8
528 A150 110fr multi 90 45
Nos. 525-528,C272-C273 (6) 7.69 3.88

Nos. 457-461 Overprinted in Blue: "NAISSANCE ROYALE 1982"

1982, Aug. 20 *Perf. 14*

529 A135 75fr multi 60 30
530 A135 110fr multi 90 45
531 A135 150fr multi 1.25 60
532 A135 175fr multi 1.40 70

Souvenir Sheet

533 A135 500fr multi 4.00 2.00

Birth of Prince William of Wales, June 21.

2nd UN Conference on Peaceful Uses of Outer Space, Vienna, Aug. 9-21 — A151

Various satellites and space scenes.

1982, Aug. 15 Litho. *Perf. 13½*

534 A151 5fr multi 5 5
535 A151 10fr multi 8 5
536 A151 20fr multi 16 8
537 A151 110fr multi 90 45
Nos. 534-537,C277-C278 (6) 7.69 3.88

Sakpa Basket A152

Baskets and bowls.

1982, Sept. 2 *Perf. 13*

538 A152 5fr shown 5 5
539 A152 10fr like 5fr 8 5
540 A152 25fr Ngbenda gourd, vert. 20 10
541 A152 60fr like 25fr 48 24
542 A152 120fr Ta ti ngou jugs 1.00 50
543 A152 175fr Kangu bowls 1.60 80
544 A152 300fr Kolongo bowls, vert. 2.50 1.25
Nos. 538-544 (7) 5.91 2.99

1982 World Cup Soccer Championships, Spain — A152a

Various soccer plays.

1982, Sept. Litho. *Perf. 13½x13*
Overprinted in Silver or Gold.

545 A152a 60fr Italy, 1st, 2nd 25 12
546 A152a 150fr Poland, 3rd 62 30
547 A152a 300fr France, 4th 1.25 62

Souvenir Sheet

548 A152a 500fr Italy, 1st (G) 2.00 1.00

Not issued without overprint. No. 548 has multicolored margin inscribed with final score. Size: 104x81mm.

13th World UPU Day — A153

1982, Oct. 9

549 A153 60fr multi 48 24
550 A153 120fr multi 1.00 50

Comb and Hairpins A154

1982, Oct. 20 *Perf. 13x12½*

551 A154 20fr multi 16 8
552 A154 30fr multi 24 12
553 A154 60fr multi 48 24
554 A154 80fr multi 65 32
555 A154 120fr multi 1.00 50
Nos. 551-555 (5) 2.53 1.26

Artist Pierre Ndarata and No. 69 — A155

1982, Oct. *Perf. 13*

556 A155 40fr Jean Tubind at easel, vert. 32 16
557 A155 70fr shown 56 28
558 A155 90fr like 70fr 72 36
559 A155 140fr like 40fr 1.35 68

TB Bacillus Centenary A156

1982, Nov. 30 *Perf. 13½x13*

560 A156 100fr vio & blk 80 40
561 A156 120fr red org & blk 1.00 50
562 A156 175fr bl & blk 1.60 80

10th Anniv. of UN Conference on Human Environment A157

1982, Dec. 8

563 A157 120fr multi 1.00 50
564 A157 150fr multi 1.20 60
565 A157 300fr multi 2.50 1.25

Granary A158

1982, Dec. 15 *Perf. 13*

566 A158 60fr multi 48 24
567 A158 80fr multi 65 32
568 A158 120fr multi 1.00 50
569 A158 200fr multi 1.60 80

ITU Plenipotentiaries Conference, Nairobi, Sept. — A159

1982, Dec.

570 A159 100fr multi 80 40
571 A159 120fr multi 1.00 50

UN Decade for African Transportation and Communication, 1978-88 — A160

1983, Jan. 31 Litho. *Perf. 13½x13*

572 A160 5fr Modes of communication 5 5
573 A160 60fr like 5fr 50 25
574 A160 120fr Map, jet 1.00 50
575 A160 175fr like 120fr 1.60 80

Chess Champions — A161

Men and Chess Pieces: 5fr, Steinitz, first world champion, 1886. 10fr, Aaron Niemzovitch, castle. 20fr, Alexander Alekhine, knights. 110fr, Botvinnik. 300fr, Boris Spassky, glass pieces. 500fr, Bobby Fischer, king, knight. 600fr, Korchnoi, Karpov, pawn.

1983, Jan. 15

576 A161 5fr multi 5 5
577 A161 10fr multi 8 5
578 A161 20fr multi 16 8
579 A161 110fr multi 90 45
580 A161 300fr multi 2.50 1.25
581 A161 500fr multi 4.00 2.00
Nos. 576-581 (6) 7.69 3.88

Souvenir Sheet

582 A161 600fr multi 5.00 2.50

No. 582 contains one stamp (56x33mm.); multicolored margin shows 18th cent. chess set. 300fr, 500fr, 600fr air mail.

Marshal Tito (1892-1980) A162

1983, Jan. 22

583 A162 20fr George Washington 16 8
a. Souvenir sheet 25 15
584 A162 110fr shown 90 45
a. Souvenir sheet 1.00 50

Size of Nos. 583a-584a: 62x98mm.

Easter 1983 A163

Rembrandt Paintings.

1983, Apr. 16

585 A163 100fr Entombment 80 40
586 A163 300fr Crucifixion 2.50 1.25
587 A163 400fr Descent from the Cross 3.25 1.75

Vintage Cars and their Makers A164

Designs: 10fr, Emile Levassor, Rene Panhard, 1895 car. 20fr, Henry Ford, 1896 car. 30fr, Louis Renault, 1899 car. 80fr, Ettore Bugatti, type 37, 1925. 400fr, Enzo Ferrari, 815 sport, 1940. 500fr, Ferdinand Porsche, 356 coupe, 1951. 600fr, Karl Benz, velociped, 1886. 400fr, 500fr, 600fr airmail.

1983, June 3 Litho. *Perf. 13½*

588 A164 10fr multi 8 5
589 A164 20fr multi 16 8
590 A164 30fr multi 24 12
591 A164 80fr multi 65 32
592 A164 400fr multi 3.25 1.75
593 A164 500fr multi 4.00 2.00
Nos. 588-593 (6) 8.38 4.32

Souvenir Sheet

594 A164 600fr multi 5.00 2.50

No. 594 has multicolored margin showing cars. Size: 77x87mm.

25th Anniv. of Intl. Maritime Org. — A165

1983, July 8 Litho. *Perf. 12½x13*

595 A165 40fr multi 32 16
596 A165 100fr multi 80 40

World Communications Year — A166

1983, July 22

597 A166 50fr multi 40 20
598 A166 130fr multi 1.05 52

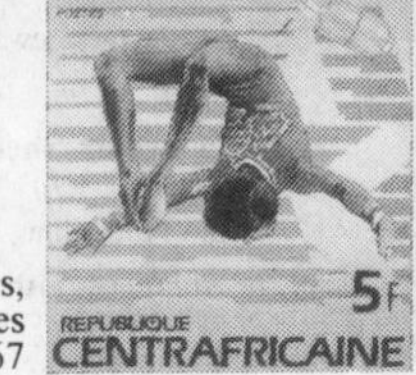

Pre-Olympics, Los Angeles A167

1983, Aug. 3 Litho. *Perf. 13*

599 A167 5fr Gymnast 5 5
600 A167 40fr Javelin throwing 32 16
601 A167 60fr Pole vault 48 24
602 A167 120fr Fencing 96 48
603 A167 200fr Cycling 1.60 80
604 A167 300fr Sailing 2.40 1.25
Nos. 599-604 (6) 5.81 2.98

Souvenir Sheet

605 A167 600fr Handball 5.00 2.50

Multicolored margin shows various players. Size: 109x81mm.

Namibia Day — A168

1983, Sept. 16 Litho. *Perf. 13*

606 A168 100fr multi 80 40
607 A168 200fr multi 1.60 80

Manned Flight Bicentenary — A169

Designs: 50fr, J. Montgolfier and his balloon, 1783. 100fr, J.P. Blanchard, English Channel crossing, 1785. 200fr, L.-J. Gay-Lussac, 4000-meter balloon ascent, 1804. 300fr, Giffard and his dirigible, 1852. 400fr, Santos Dumont, dirigible, Eiffel Tower. 500fr, A. Laquot, captive observation balloon, 1914. 600fr, J.A. Charles, first gas balloon; G. Tissandier, dirigible, 1883.

1983, Sept. 30 Litho. *Perf. 13½*

608 A169 50fr multi 25 12
609 A169 100fr multi 50 25
610 A169 200fr multi 1.00 50
611 A169 300fr multi 1.50 75
612 A169 400fr multi 2.00 1.00
613 A169 500fr multi 2.50 1.25
Nos. 608-613 (6) 7.75 3.87

Souvenir Sheet

614 A169 600fr multi 3.00 1.50

No. 614 has multicolored margin continuing design. Size: 79x85mm. 400fr, 500fr, 600fr airmail.

Black Rhinoceros and World Wildlife Emblem — A170

Various black rhinoceroses.

1983, Nov. 14

615 A170 10fr multi 5 5
616 A170 40fr multi 20 10
617 A170 70fr multi 35 18
618 A170 180fr multi 90 45

UPU Day, World Communications Year — A171

1983, Nov. 2 Litho. Perf. 13
619 A171 205fr multi 1.65 85

2nd Anniv. of the Natl. Military Committee A172

Gen. Andre Kolingba, head of state.

1983, Sept. 1 Perf. 12½
620 A172 65fr sil & multi 32 16
621 A172 130fr gold & multi 65 32

Earth Satellite Receiving Station, Bangui M'Poko — A173

1983 Perf. 13
622 A173 130fr multi 65 32

Natl. Day of the Handicapped and the Elderly — A174

1983, Dec. 20 Engr. Perf. 13x12½
623 A174 65fr vio & org 32 16
624 A174 130fr ultra & org 65 32
625 A174 205fr dk grn & org 1.05 52

Fishing Resources A175

1983, Dec. 31 Litho. Perf. 12½
626 A175 25fr Breeding tank 12 6
627 A175 65fr Net fishing 32 16
628 A175 100fr Dam fishing 50 25
629 A175 130fr Still life with fish 65 32
630 A175 205fr Basket trap 1.05 52
Nos. 626-630 (5) 2.64 1.31

The indexes in each volume of the Scott Catalogue contain many listings which help to identify stamps.

Wildlife Protection — A176

1984, Jan. 25 Perf. 13
631 A176 30fr Forest fire 15 8
632 A176 130fr Hunters 65 32

Packet Ship Pericles — A177

1984, June Litho. Perf. 12½
633 A177 65fr shown 32 16
634 A177 110fr CC-1500 locomotive 55 28
635 A177 120fr Three-master Pereire 60 30
636 A177 240fr PLM series 210, 1868 1.20 60
637 A177 250fr Admella 1.25 62
638 A177 350fr 231-726 locomotive, 1937 1.75 90
639 A177 400fr Royal William 2.00 1.00
640 A177 440fr Pacific S3/6, 1908 2.20 1.10
641 A177 500fr Great Britain 2.50 1.25
642 A177 500fr Henschel 151 series 45, 1937 2.50 1.25
Nos. 633-642 (10) 14.87 7.46

J. W. Goethe, Scene from Faust A178

Designs: 100fr, Henri Dunant, Red Cross Founder, Battle of Solferino, 125th anniv. 200fr, Alfred Nobel, Nobel Foundation headquarters. 300fr, Lord Baden-Powell, World Scouting Jamboree, Alberta, 1983. 400fr, John F. Kennedy, first man on the Moon, 1969. 500fr, 600fr, wedding of Prince and Princess of Wales.

1984, Feb. 25 Litho. Perf. 13½
643 A178 50fr multi 24 12
644 A178 100fr multi 48 24
645 A178 200fr multi 1.00 50
646 A178 300fr multi 1.50 1.50
647 A178 400fr multi 1.90 95
648 A178 500fr multi 2.25 1.10
Nos. 643-648 (6) 7.37 4.41

Souvenir Sheet

649 A178 600fr multi 2.50 1.25

No. 649 has multicolored decorative margin. Size: 400fr, 500fr, airmail.

Old Masters A179

Paintings: 50fr, Madonna and Child, by Raphael. 100fr, Madonna with Pear, by Durer. 200fr, Aldobrandini Madonna, by Raphael. 300fr, Madonna with Carnation, by Durer. 400fr, Virgin and Child, by Correggio. 500fr, La Bohemienne, by Modigliani. 600fr, Madonna and Child on the Throne, by Raphael.

1984, Mar. 30 Litho. Perf. 13½
650 A179 50fr multi 24 12
651 A179 100fr multi 48 24
652 A179 200fr multi 95 48
653 A179 300fr multi 1.50 75
654 A179 400fr multi 2.00 1.00
655 A179 500fr multi 2.50 1.25
Nos. 650-655 (6) 7.67 3.84

Miniature Sheet

656 A179 600fr multi 3.00 1.50

No. 656 contains 1 stamp, size 30 x 59mm, with design continuing into margin. Size: 80x111mm. 400fr, 500fr and 600fr are airmail.

Space — A180

1984, Aug. 6 Litho. Perf. 13½
657 A180 20fr Galileo, Ariane rocket 10 5
658 A180 70fr Piccard, X-15, balloon 35 18
659 A180 150fr Oberth, satellite 75 38
660 A180 205fr Einstein, satellites 1.05 55
661 A180 300fr Curie, Viking vehicle 1.50 75
662 A180 500fr Merbold, Spacelab 2.50 1.25
Nos. 657-662 (6) 6.25 3.16

Miniature Sheet

663 A180 600fr Armstrong, Apollo 11, horiz. 3.00 1.50

No. 663 contains 1 stamp, size 42x36mm, with design continuing into margin. Size: 75x60mm. 300fr, 500fr and 600fr are airmail.

Forestry Resources A181

UNICEF A182

1984, Oct. 9 Litho. Perf. 13x12½
664 A181 70fr Forest 35 18
665 A181 130fr Logging 65 32

1984, Oct. 27 Litho. Perf. 13x12½
666 A182 10fr Weighing child 5 5
667 A182 30fr Vaccinating child 15 8
668 A182 65fr Giving liquids 35 18
669 A182 100fr Balancing diet 50 25

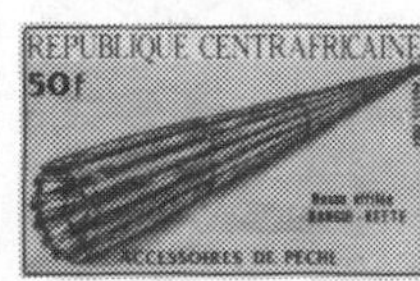
Fishing Traps A183

1984, Nov. 6 Litho. Perf. 13
670 A183 50fr Bangui-Kette 25 12
671 A183 80fr Mbres 40 20
672 A183 150fr Bangui-Kette 75 38

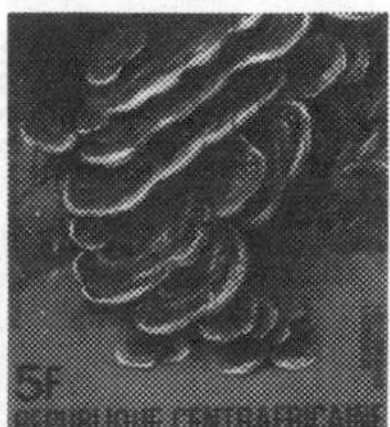
Mushrooms A184

1984, Nov. 15 Litho. Perf. 13½
673 A184 5fr Leptoporus lignosus 5 5
674 A184 10fr Phlebopus sudanicus 5 5
675 A184 40fr Termitomyces letestui 16 8
676 A184 130fr Lepiota esculenta 52 25
677 A184 300fr Termitomyces aurantiacus 1.25 62
678 A184 500fr Termitomyces robustus 2.00 1.00
Nos. 673-678 (6) 4.03 2.05

Souvenir Sheet

679 A184 600fr Tricholoma-lobayensis 2.50 1.25

Nos. 677-679 are airmail. No. 679 has multicolored margin continuing the design. Size: 68x90mm.

1984 Winter Olympics, Sarajevo A184a

Gold medalists, communications satellite and events: 30fr, Gaetan Boucher, Canada, 1000 and 1500-meter speed skating. 90fr, W. Hoppe, R. Wetzig, D. Schauerhammer and A. Kirchner, German Democratic Republic, 4-man bobsled. 140fr, Paoletta Magoni, Italy, women's slalom. 200fr, Jayne Torvill and Christopher Dean, Great Britain, ice dancing. 400fr, Matti Nykaenen, Finland, 90-meter ski jumping. 500fr, USSR, ice hockey. 600fr, Bill Johnson, US, men's downhill.

1984, Nov. 30 Litho. Perf. 13½
679A A184a 30fr multi 15 8
679B A184a 90fr multi 45 22
679C A184a 140fr multi 65 32
679D A184a 200fr multi 1.00 50
679E A184a 400fr multi 2.00 1.00
679F A184a 500fr multi 2.50 1.25
Nos. 679A-679F (6) 6.75 3.37

Souvenir Sheet

679G A184a 600fr multi 3.00 1.50

Nos. 679E-679G are airmail. No. 679G has multicolored margin continuing the design. Size: 79x58mm.

Flowers — A185

1984, Nov. 22 Litho. Perf. 13½
680 A185 65fr Hibiscus 35 18
681 A185 130fr Canna Indica 65 32
682 A185 205fr Eichlornia Crassipes 1.05 52

Economic Campaign — A186

1984, Dec. 3 Litho. *Perf. 13½*

683 A186 25fr Cotton planting 12 6
684 A186 40fr Selling cotton crop 18 10
685 A186 130fr Cotton market 65 32

World Food Day A187

1984, Dec. 10 Litho. *Perf. 13½*

686 A187 205fr Picking corn 1.10 52

OLYMPHILEX '85 — A188

Publicity posters from previous Games and host city landmarks.

1985, Mar 18 Litho. *Perf. 13½*

687 A188 5fr Stockholm, 1912 5 5
688 A188 10fr Paris, 1924 8 4
689 A188 20fr London, 1948 14 8
690 A188 100fr Tokyo, 1964 70 35
691 A188 400fr Mexico 2.75 1.40
692 A188 500fr Munich, 1972 3.50 1.75
Nos. 687-692 (6) 7.22 3.67

Souvenir Sheet

693 A188 600fr Athens, 1896, Baron Pierre de Coubertin 4.25 2.25

Nos. 691-693 are airmail. No. 693 contains one stamp (size: 60x30mm); multicolored margin pictures montage of places and events. Size: 107x68mm.

Anniversaries and Events — A189

Famous men: 50fr, Abraham Lincoln, American Civil War soldiers. 90fr, Auguste Piccard (1884-1962), inventor, bathyscaphe Trieste. 120fr, Gottlieb Daimler (1834-1900), 1938 Mercedes Type 540. 200fr, Louis Bleriot (1872-1936), inventor, plane. 350fr, Anatoly Karpov, world chess champion. 400fr, Jean Henri Dunant (1828-1910), Red Cross founder, worker caring for wounded soldier.

1984, Dec. 22 Litho. *Perf. 13½*

694 A189 50fr multi 20 10
695 A189 90fr multi 38 20
696 A189 120fr multi 50 25
697 A189 200fr multi 82 40
698 A189 350fr multi 1.40 70
698A A189 400fr multi 1.75 90
Nos. 694-698A (6) 5.05 2.55

Nos. 698-698A are airmail.

Souvenir Sheet

Queen Mother, 85th Birthday A189a

1984 Litho. *Perf. 13½*

698B A189a 600fr multi 4.00 2.00

No. 698B has multicolored margin continuing the portrait. Size: 79x114mm.

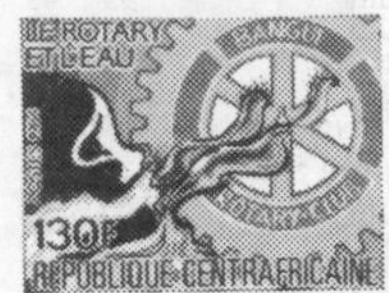

Bangui Rotary Club and Water — A190

1984, Dec. 29

699 A190 130fr multi 52 25
700 A190 205fr multi 85 42

Nos. 637-640, C302A Overprinted with Exhibitions in Red.

1985, Mar. 13 Litho. *Perf. 12½*

701 A177 250fr Argentina '85, Buenos Aires 1.00 50
702 A177 350fr Tsukuba Expo '85 1.40 70
703 A177 400fr Italia '85, Rome 1.60 80
704 A177 440fr Mophila '85, Hamburg 1.75 90

Souvenir Sheet

Perf. 13½x13

705 AP89 500fr Olymphilex '85, Lausanne 2.00 1.00

500fr airmail.

Beetles — A191

1985, Mar. Litho. *Perf. 13½*

706 A191 15fr Chelorrhina polyphemus 6 5
707 A191 20fr Fornasinius russus 8 5
708 A191 25fr Goliathus giganteus 10 5
709 A191 65fr Goliathus meleagris 25 12

Audubon Birth Bicentenary — A192

Illustrations of North American bird species by John Audubon.

1985, Mar. 25 Litho. *Perf. 13½*

710 A192 40fr Cyanocitta cristata 18 10
711 A192 80fr Caprimulgus carolinensis 32 16
712 A192 130fr Campephilus principales 52 25
713 A192 250fr Calocitta formosa 1.00 50
714 A192 300fr Coccizus minor, horiz. 1.25 62
715 A192 500fr Hirundo rustica, horiz. 2.00 1.00
Nos. 710-715 (6) 5.27 2.63

Souvenir Sheet

716 A192 600fr Dryocopus pileatus, horiz. 2.50 1.25

Nos. 714-716 are airmail. No. 716 has multicolored margin continuing the design. Size: 69x104mm.

Intl. Youth Year A193

Famous children's book authors and scenes from their best-known novels: 100fr, The Jungle Book, 1894, by Rudyard Kipling (1865-1936), vert. 200fr, Les Cavaliers, 1967, by Joseph Kessel (1898-1979). 300fr, Twenty-Thousand Leagues Under the Sea, 1873, by Jules Verne (1828-1905). 400fr, The Adventures of Tom Sawyer, 1876, by Mark Twain (1835-1910).

1985, Apr. Litho. *Perf. 13*

718 A193 100fr multi 40 20
719 A193 200fr multi 80 40
720 A193 300fr multi 1.20 60
721 A193 400fr multi 1.60 80

Philexafrica '85, Lome — A194

Designs: No. 722, UPU emblem, Postmen unloading parcel post van. No. 723, Exhibition emblem, scout troop.

1985, May 15 *Perf. 13x12½*

722 A194 200fr multi 80 40
723 A194 200fr multi 80 40

Nos. 722-723 se-tenant with center label picturing a map of Africa or the UAPT emblem.

Battle of Solferino, Founding of the Red Cross, 125th Anniv., Founder Jean-Henri Dunant (1828-1910) A195

Anniversaries and events: 150fr, Rabies vaccine centenary, Louis Pasteur (1822-1895), chemist, microbiologist, vert. 300fr, Girl Guides, 75th anniv., vert. 450fr, Elizabeth, the Queen Mother, 85th birthday, vert. 500fr, Statue of Liberty, cent., vert.

1985, June *Perf. 13*

724 A195 150fr multi 60 30
725 A195 200fr multi 80 40
726 A195 300fr multi 1.20 60
727 A195 450fr multi 1.80 90
728 A195 500fr multi 2.00 1.00
Nos. 724-728 (5) 6.40 3.20

1986 World Cup Soccer Championships, Mexico — A196

Famous soccer players and match scenes.

1985, July 24 Litho. *Perf. 13½*

730 A196 5fr Pele 5 5
731 A196 10fr Tony Schumacher 5 5
732 A196 20fr Paolo Rossi 10 5
733 A196 350fr Kevin Keegan 1.65 85
734 A196 400fr Michel Platini 1.90 95
735 A196 500fr Karl Heinz Rummenigge 2.25 1.10
Nos. 730-735 (6) 6.00 3.05

Souvenir Sheet

736 A196 600fr Diego Armando Maradona 2.75 1.40

Nos. 734-736 are airmail. No. 736 has multicolored margin picturing bullfight scenes. Size: 95x64mm.

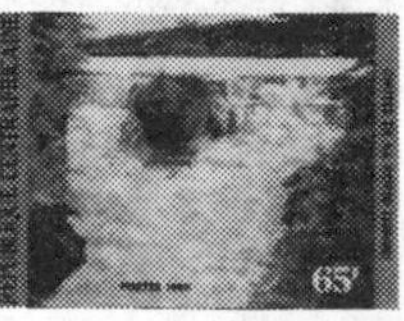

Kotto Waterfalls A197

1985, July 27 Litho. *Perf. 13½*

737 A197 65fr multi 30 15
738 A197 90fr multi 40 20
739 A197 130fr multi 60 30

State Visit of Pope John Paul II — A198

Portraits.

1985, Aug. 14

740 A198 65fr multi 30 15
741 A198 130fr multi 60 30

Natl. Economic Development Campaign — A199

Designs: 5fr, Troops plowing. 60fr, Soldier preparing field for planting, vert. 130fr, Planting cotton seeds, vert.

1985, Sept. 1 *Perf. 13*

742 A199 5fr multi 5 5
743 A199 60fr multi 28 14
744 A199 130fr multi 60 30

A particular stamp may be scarce, but if few collectors want it, its market value may remain relatively low.

Queen Mother, 85th Birthday — A200

1985, Sept. 16 Litho. *Perf. 13½*

745 A200 100fr Age 4, with brother 42 20
746 A200 200fr Duchess of York, 1923 82 40
747 A200 300fr Reviewing Irish Guards, 1928 1.25 62
748 A200 350fr Family portrait, 1936 1.40 70
749 A200 400fr George VI coronation, 1937 1.75 90
750 A200 500fr Wedding anniv., 1948 2.00 1.00
Nos. 745-750 (6) 7.64 3.82

Souvenir Sheet

751 A200 600fr Christening Prince Charles, 1948 2.50 1.25

Nos. 749-751 are airmail. No. 751 has multicolored margin picturing baptism of Prince Henry, Dec. 21, 1984. Size: 75x87mm.

Dr. Rene Labusquiere (1919-1977), Promoter of Preventive Medicine A201

1985, Sept. 22 Litho. *Perf. 13½*

752 A201 10fr multi 5 5
753 A201 45fr multi 18 10
754 A201 110fr multi 45 22

Natl. Postal Service — A202

1985, Oct. 9 *Perf. 12½*

755 A202 15fr Loading mail van 6 5
756 A202 60fr Bangui P.O., van 30 15
757 A202 150fr Hdqtrs, Bangui, and vans 80 40

Space Research — A203

Designs: 40fr, Yuri Gagarin and Sergei Korolev, Soviet cosmonauts. 110fr, Nicolaus Copernicus, Cassini probe. 240fr, Galileo, Viking orbiter. 300fr, Theodor von Karman (1881-1963), American aeronautical engineer, and space shuttle recovering Palapa B satellite. 450fr, Percival Lowell (1855-1916), American astronomer, and Viking probe. 500fr, Dr. U. Merbold and orbiting space station project Colombo. 600fr, Apollo 11 Project, first step on Moon by Neil Armstrong.

1985, Oct. 31 Litho. *Perf. 13½*

758 A203 40fr multi 18 10
759 A203 110fr multi 60 32
760 A203 240fr multi 1.25 65
761 A203 300fr multi 1.65 85
762 A203 450fr multi 2.50 1.25
763 A203 500fr multi 2.75 1.40
Nos. 758-763 (6) 8.93 4.57

Souvenir Sheet

Imperf

764 A203 600fr multi 3.25 1.75

Nos. 762-764 are airmail. No. 764 has multicolored margin continuing the design. Size: 96x68mm.

Solar Energy Apparatus, Damara A204

1985, Nov. 4 Litho. *Perf. 13½*

765 A204 65fr multi 32 16
766 A204 130fr multi 70 35

Girl Guides Nature Study — A205

1985, Nov. 16 *Perf. 13*

767 A205 250fr shown 1.40 70
768 A205 250fr Quaka Sugar Refinery 1.40 70

PHILEXAFRICA '85, Lome, Togo, Nov. 16-24. Nos. 767-768 se-tenant with center labels picturing map of Africa or UAPT emblem.

State Visit of Pres. Mitterand of France, Dec. 12-13 — A206

1985-86 Litho. *Perf. 13x12½*

769 A206 65fr multi 32 16
770 A206 130fr multi 70 35
770A A206 160fr multi ('86) 85 42

Nos. 769-770 issued Dec. 12.

UN 40th Anniv., Central Africa Admission, 25th Anniv. — A207

1985, Dec. 18 *Perf. 13½*

771 A207 140fr multi 75 38

Intl. Youth Year A208

Designs: 40fr, Madonna with the Carnation, 1470, by Leonardo da Vinci. 80fr, Johann Sebastian Bach. 100fr, St. John at Patmos, 1619, by Velazquez. 250fr, The Erl King score, by Franz Schubert. 400fr, Portrait of Vicente Osorio de Moscoso, by Goya. 500fr, The Young Mozart Playing in Paris, 1764. 600fr, Woman in a Plumed Hat, 1901, by Picasso.

1985, Dec. 28

772 A208 40fr multi 18 10
773 A208 80fr multi 40 20
774 A208 100fr multi 52 28
775 A208 250fr multi 1.40 70
776 A208 400fr multi 2.00 1.00
777 A208 500fr multi 2.75 1.40
Nos. 772-777 (6) 7.25 3.68

Souvenir Sheet

778 A208 600fr multi 3.25 1.65

Nos. 776-778 are airmail. No. 778 has multicolored margin picturing Picasso, his studio and Paris residence. Size: 79x79mm.

Halley's Comet A209

Designs: 100fr, Edmond Halley, British astronomer. 200fr, Sir Isaac Newton's telescope and comet sighting. 300fr, Halley and Newton observing comet. 350fr, US probe. 400fr, Soviet probe plotting comet's perihelion. 500fr, Isodensity photograph of comet. 600fr, Comet, Earth, Sun and probe.

1985, Dec. 31

779 A209 100fr multi 52 28
780 A209 200fr multi 1.10 55
781 A209 300fr multi 1.65 85
782 A209 350fr multi 1.90 95
783 A209 400fr multi 2.00 1.00
784 A209 500fr multi 2.75 1.40
Nos. 779-784 (6) 9.92 5.03

Souvenir Sheet

785 A209 600fr multi 3.25 1.65

Nos. 783-785 are airmail. No. 785 has multicolored margin continuing the design. Size: 70x101mm.

Christopher Columbus (1451-1506) — A210

Various events leading to the discovery of America and beyond.

1986

786 A210 90fr Plotting course 48 24
787 A210 110fr Receiving blessing 60 30
788 A210 240fr Fleet in port 1.25 65
789 A210 300fr Trade with natives 1.65 85
790 A210 400fr Storm at sea 2.00 1.00
791 A210 500fr Fleet at sea 2.75 1.40
Nos. 779-784 (6) 9.92 5.03

Souvenir Sheet

792 A210 600fr Portrait 3.25 1.65

Nos. 790-792 are airmail. No. 792 has multicolored margin picturing exotic birds and flagship. Size: 71x101mm.

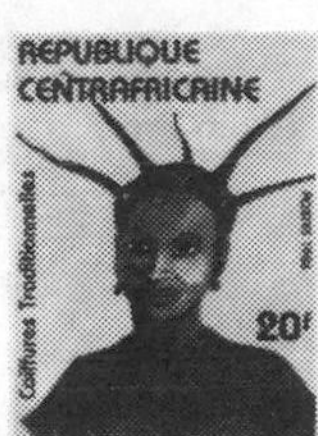

Hairstyles — A211

France-Central Africa Week — A212

1986, May 21 Litho. *Perf. 12½*

793 A211 20fr multi 10 5
794 A211 30fr multi 14 6
795 A211 65fr multi 25 12
796 A211 160fr multi 90 45

1986, May 26

797 A212 40fr Communications, horiz. 22 12
798 A212 60fr Youth, horiz. 35 18
799 A212 100fr Basket maker 55 28
800 A212 130fr Bicycling 70 35

Centrapalm Palm Oil — A213

Designs: 25fr, 65fr, Refinery, Bossongo, and palm tree. 120fr, 160fr, Refinery and palm tree, vert.

1986, Aug. 12 Litho. *Perf. 13½*

801 A213 25fr multi 14 8
802 A213 65fr multi 35 18
803 A213 120fr multi 75 38
804 A213 160fr multi 1.00 50

Dogs and Cats A214

1986, Sept. 9

805 A214 10fr Pointer 6 5
806 A214 20fr Egyptian mau 12 6
807 A214 200fr Newfoundland 1.25 65
808 A214 300fr Borzoi 1.90 95
809 A214 400fr Persian red 2.50 1.25
Nos. 805-809 (5) 5.83 2.96

Souvenir Sheet

810 A214 500fr Spaniel, Burmese-Malayan 3.00 1.50

Nos. 808-810 are airmail. No. 810 has dark olive bister margin picturing King Charles spaniel, Burmese zibeline and kitten. Size: 95x60mm.

African Coffee Producers Organization, 25th Anniv. A215

1986, Sept. 25 Litho. *Perf. 13*

811 A215 160fr multi 90 45

1986 World Cup Soccer Championships, Mexico — A216

Satellites, final scores, World Cup and athletes: 30fr, Muller, Socrates. 110fr, Scifo, Ceulemans. 160fr, Stopyra, Platini. 350fr, Brehme, Schumacher. 450fr, Maradona. 500fr, Schumacher, Burruchaga.

1986, Nov. 12 ***Perf. 13½***

812 A216 30fr multi 18 10
813 A216 110fr multi 60 30
814 A216 160fr multi 90 45
815 A216 350fr multi 2.00 1.00
816 A216 450fr multi 2.50 1.25
Nos. 812-816 (5) 6.18 3.10

Souvenir Sheet

817 A216 500fr multi 2.75 1.40

Nos. 816-817 are airmail. No. 817 has multicolored margin continuing the design, picturing Maradona, Burruchaga, Briegel, stadium and final scores. Size: 110x68mm.

US Anniversaries and Events — A217

Designs: 15fr, Judith Resnik. 25fr, Frederic Auguste Bartholdi. 70fr, Elvis Presley. 300fr, Ronald McNair. 450fr, Christa McAuliffe. 500fr, McAuliffe, Scobee, Smith, Resnik, Onizuka, McNair, Jarvis.

1986, Nov. 19

818 A217 15fr multi 10 5
819 A217 25fr multi 14 8
820 A217 70fr multi 40 20
821 A217 300fr multi 1.65 80
822 A217 450fr multi 2.50 1.25
Nos. 818-822 (5) 4.79 2.38

Souvenir Sheet

823 A217 500fr multi 2.75 1.50

US space shuttle Challenger explosion; Statue of Liberty, cent. Nos. 822-823 are air mail. No. 823 has multicolored decorative margin. Size: 86x86mm.

Flora and Fauna A218

1986, May 30 **Litho.** ***Perf. 13½***

824 A218 25fr Allamanda neri-ifolia 14 6
825 A218 65fr Taurotragus eurycerus 38 18
826 A218 160fr Plumieria acuminata 88 45
827 A218 300fr Acinonyx jubatus 1.65 58
828 A218 400fr Eulophia erthoplata 2.20 1.10
829 A218 500fr Leopard 2.75 1.40
Nos. 824-829 (6) 8.00 3.77

Souvenir Sheet

830 A218 600fr Derby's eland, eulophia cucul-lata 3.25 1.65

Nos. 824, 826, 828 vert. Nos. 828-830 are airmail. No. 830 contains one stamp (size: 51x30mm); multicolored margin continues the design, picturing eland and orchids in habitat. Size: 100x69mm.

Intl. Peace Year — A219

Air Africa, 25th Anniv. — A220

1986, Nov. 29

831 A219 160fr multi 88 45

1986, Dec. 15

832 A220 200fr multi 1.10 55

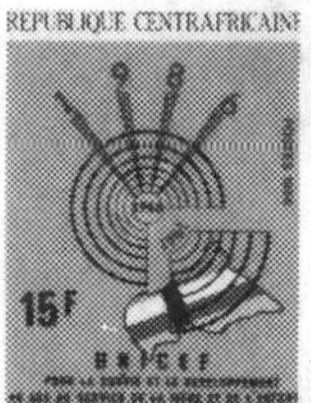

UNICEF, 40th Anniv. — A221

1986, Dec. 24

833 A221 15fr shown 8 5
834 A221 130fr Child immunization 70 35
835 A221 160fr Youth, food, map 88 45

German Railways Sesquicentenary — A222

Inventors and locomotives: 40fr, Alfred de Glehn, Prussian Railways DH2 Green Elephant. 70fr, Rudolf Diesel, S3/6 No. 1829 Rheingold. 160fr, Carl Golsdorf, Trans-Europe Express train Type 103. 300fr, Wilhelm Schmidt, Beyer Garratt locomotive. 400fr, Monsieur de Bousquet, Series 3500 compound locomotive. 500fr, Werner von Siemens, 1980s electric locomotive.

1986, Dec. 31

836 A222 40fr multi 22 10
837 A222 70fr multi 38 18
838 A222 160fr multi 88 45
839 A222 300fr multi 1.65 58
840 A222 400fr multi 2.20 1.10
Nos. 836-840 (5) 5.33 2.41

Souvenir Sheet

841 A222 500fr multi 2.75 1.40

Nos. 840-841 are airmail. No. 841 contains one stamp (size: 42x36mm); multicolored decorative margin pictures 19th century Locomotive 220. Size: 83x67mm.

Agriculture Radio Project A223

1986, Dec. 27 **Litho.** ***Perf. 13½***

842 A223 170fr shown 1.00 50
843 A223 265fr Satellite communication 1.55 78

Pan-African Telecommunications Union congress, Dec. 7, 1986.

Space A224

Scientists and inventions: 25fr, Sir William Herschel (1738-1822), British astronomer, and Miranda satellite. 65fr, Wernher von Braun (1912-1977), American engineer, and Mars rover. 160fr, Rudolf Hanel, Mariner Mark II and Titan. 300fr, Patrick Baudry, Hermes shuttle and Eureka platform. 400fr, U. Keller, Halley's Comet and Giotto probe. 500fr, Wubbo Ockels, Ulf Merbold and Columbus European Space Station. 600fr, Wilhelm Obers (1758-1840) and Mariner Mark II surveying asteroids. Nos. 844-849 vert.

1987, Jan. 27

844 A224 25fr multi 15 8
845 A224 65fr multi 38 20
846 A224 160fr multi 95 48
847 A224 300fr multi 1.75 90
848 A224 400fr multi 2.50 1.25
849 A224 500fr multi 3.00 1.50
Nos. 844-849 (6) 8.73 4.41

Souvenir Sheet

850 A224 600fr multi 3.50 1.75

Nos. 848-850 are airmail. No. 850 has multicolored margin picturing man-made and natural satellites and La Genese. Size: 106x66mm.

No. 820 Surcharged.

1987, Feb. 20 **Litho.** ***Perf. 13½***

851 A217 485fr on 70fr Elvis Presley 2.75 1.40

1992 Barcelona Olympics A225

Athletes and landmarks or sights: 30fr, Soccer player, Lady with Umbrella fountain. 150fr, Judo, Barcelona Cathedral. 265fr, Cyclist, Church of the Holy Family, by Gaudi. 350fr, Gymnast, Tomb of Columbus. 495fr, Runner, human tower. 500fr, Swimmer, Statue of Columbus.

1987, June 4

852 A225 30fr multi 18 10
853 A225 150fr multi 82 40
854 A225 265fr multi 1.45 72
855 A225 350fr multi 1.90 95
856 A225 495fr multi 2.70 1.35
Nos. 852-856 (5) 7.05 3.52

Souvenir Sheet

857 225 500fr multi 2.75 1.40

Nos. 855-857 are airmail. No. 857 has multicolored margin picturing Columbus monument, Barcelona Port. Size: 87x63mm.

A266

1988 Winter Olympics, Calgary A227

1987, June 26

858 A266 20fr Two-man luge 12 6
859 A226 140fr Cross-country skiing 78 40
860 A226 250fr Women's figure skating 1.40 80
861 A226 300fr Hockey 1.65 82
862 A226 400fr Men's slalom 2.20 1.10
Nos. 858-862 (5) 6.15 3.18

Souvenir Sheet

863 A227 500fr Downhill skiing 2.75 1.35

Nos. 861-863 are airmail. No. 863 has multicolored margin continuing the design and picturing Intelsat 5. Size: 103x77mm.

Intl. Peace Year — A228

1987, July 20

864 A228 50fr dull ultra, sepia & blk 28 14
865 A228 160fr lt olive green, sepia & blk 90 45

Pygmy Soccer Team from Nola — A230

1987, Nov. 30 **Litho.** ***Perf. 13***

870 A230 90fr multi 65 32
871 A230 160fr multi 1.15 58

Integration of the pygmy people into Central African society.

Demand, as well as supply, determines a stamp's market value. One is as important as the other.

SEMI-POSTAL STAMPS

Central African Republic
Anti-Malaria Issue
Common Design Type

Perf. 12½x12

1962, Apr. 7 Engr. Unwmk.
B1 CD108 25fr + 5fr sl 70 70

Issued for the World Health Organization drive to eradicate malaria.

Freedom from Hunger Issue
Common Design Type

1963, Mar. 21 ***Perf. 13***
B2 CD112 25fr + 5fr bis, Prus grn & brn 65 65

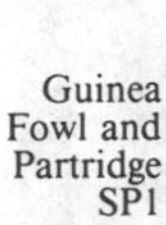

Guinea Fowl and Partridge SP1

Designs: 10fr+5fr, Yellow-backed duiker and snail. 20fr+5fr, Elephant, tortoise and hippopotamus playing tug-of-war. 30fr+10fr, Cuckoo and tortoise. 50fr+20fr, Patas monkey and leopard.

1971, Feb. 9 Photo. ***Perf. 12½x12***
B3 SP1 5fr + 5fr multi 1.20 60
B4 SP1 10fr + 5fr multi 1.75 1.25
B5 SP1 20fr + 5fr multi 2.50 1.75
B6 SP1 30fr + 10fr multi 3.50 2.50
B7 SP1 50fr + 20fr multi 7.00 5.00
Nos. B3-B7 (5) 15.95 11.10

Lengue Dancer — SP2

Dancers: 40fr+10fr, Le Lengue. 100fr+40fr, Teke. 140fr+40fr, Englabolo.

1971 Litho. ***Perf. 13***
B8 SP2 20fr + 5fr multi 35 20
B9 SP2 40fr + 10fr multi 65 40
B10 SP2 100fr + 40fr multi 1.75 90
B11 SP2 140fr + 40fr multi 2.25 1.20

AIR POST STAMPS

Central African Republic

Abyssinian Roller — AP1

Birds: 200fr, Gold Coast touraco. 500fr, African fish eagle.

Unwmk.

1960, Sept. 3 Engr. ***Perf. 13***
C1 AP1 100fr vio bl, org brn & emer 1.50 65
C2 AP1 200fr multi 3.00 1.25
C3 AP1 500fr Prus bl, emer & red brn 7.50 3.00

Olympic Games Issue
French Equatorial Africa No. C37 Surcharged in Red Like Chad No. C1.

1960, Dec. 15 ***Perf. 13***
C4 AP8 250fr on 500fr grnsh blk, blk & sl 6.50 6.50

Issued to commemorate the 17th Olympic Games, Rome, Aug. 25-Sept. 11.

Air Afrique Issue
Common Design Type

1962, Feb. 17 Unwmk. ***Perf. 13***
C5 CD107 50fr vio, lt grn & red brn 75 70

Founding of Air Afrique airline.

Pole Vault — AP1a

1962, July 21 Photo. ***Perf. 12x12½***
C6 AP1a 100fr grn, yel, brn & blk 1.50 1.00

Abidjan games.

Red-faced Lovebirds — AP2

Bird: 50fr, Great blue touraco.

1962-63 Engr. ***Perf. 13***
C7 AP2 50fr sl grn, bl grn & org 75 35
C8 AP2 250fr multi ('63) 3.75 2.10

Issue dates: 50fr, Nov. 15, 1962; 250fr, Mar. 11, 1963.

Runner with Torch and Palm Branch — AP3

1962, Dec. 24
C9 AP3 100fr gray grn, brn & car 1.50 1.00

Tropics Cup Games, Bangui, Dec. 24-31.

African Postal Union Issue
Common Design Type

1963, Sept. 8 Photo. ***Perf. 12½***
C10 CD114 85fr emer, ocher & red 1.25 85

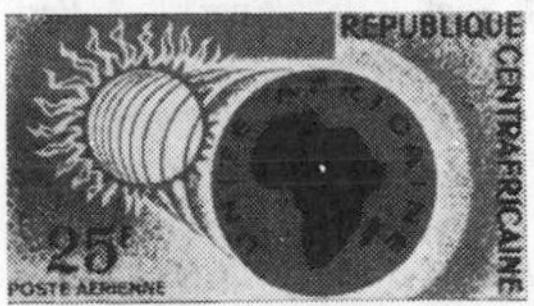

Sun Shining on Africa — AP4

1963, Nov. 9 ***Perf. 13x12***
C11 AP4 25fr bl, yel & vio bl 40 30

Issued for African unity.

Europafrica Issue
Common Design Type

1963, Nov. 30 ***Perf. 12x13***
C12 CD116 50fr ultra, yel & dk brn 1.35 1.10

Diesel Engine — AP5

Designs: Various Locomotives; 25fr, 50fr, vertical.

1963, Dec. 1 Engr. ***Perf. 13***
C13 AP5 20fr brn, cl & dk grn 30 30
C14 AP5 25fr brn, bl & choc 40 30
C15 AP5 50r brn, red lil & vio 80 60
C16 AP5 100fr brn, grn & dl red brn 1.65 1.20
a. Min. sheet of 4 3.25 3.25

Bangui-Douala railroad project.
No. C16a contains one each of Nos. C13-C16. Size: 189x99mm.

Bangui Cathedral — AP6

1964, Jan. 21 Unwmk. ***Perf. 13***
C17 AP6 100fr yel grn, org brn & bl 1.50 90

Radar Tracking Station and WMO Emblem — AP7

1964, Mar. 23 Engr. ***Perf. 13***
C18 AP7 50fr org brn, bl & pur 75 65

World Meteorological Day.

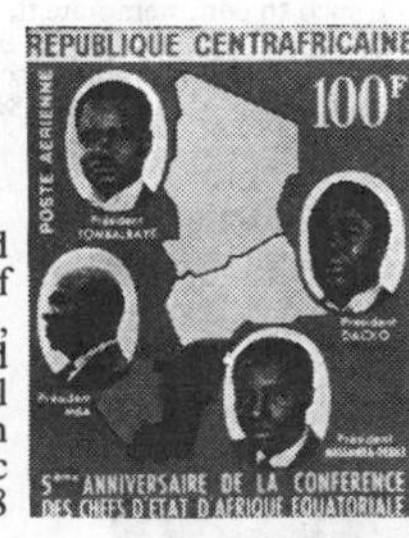

Map and Presidents of Chad, Congo, Gabon and Central African Republic AP8

1964, June 23 Photo. ***Perf. 12½***
C19 AP8 100fr multi 1.50 1.00

Issued to commemorate the 5th anniversary of the Conference of Chiefs of State of Equatorial Africa.

Javelin Throwers — AP9

Designs: 50fr, Basketball game. 100fr, Four runners. 250fr, Swimmers, one in water.

1964, June 23 Engr. ***Perf. 13***
C20 AP9 25fr grn, dk brn & lt vio bl 40 20
C21 AP9 50fr blk, car & grn 75 40
C22 AP9 100fr grn, vio bl & dk brn 1.50 80
C23 AP9 250fr grn, blk & car 3.75 2.25
a. Min. sheet 6.50 6.50

Issued for the 18th Olympic Games, Tokyo, Oct. 10-25, 1964.
No. C23a contains one each of Nos. C20-C23. Size: 128½x99mm.

John F. Kennedy — AP10

1964, July 4 Photo. ***Perf. 12½***
C24 AP10 100fr lil, brn & blk 1.65 1.35
a. Min. sheet of 4 7.50 7.50

Issued in memory of President John F. Kennedy.

Industrial Symbols, Maps of Africa and Europe — AP11

1964, Dec. 19 Unwmk. ***Perf. 13x12***
C25 AP11 50fr yel, org & grn 75 70

See note after Cameroun No. 402.

International Cooperation Year Emblem — AP12

1965, Jan. 2 ***Perf. 13***
C26 AP12 100fr red brn, yel & bl 1.50 90

International Cooperation Year.

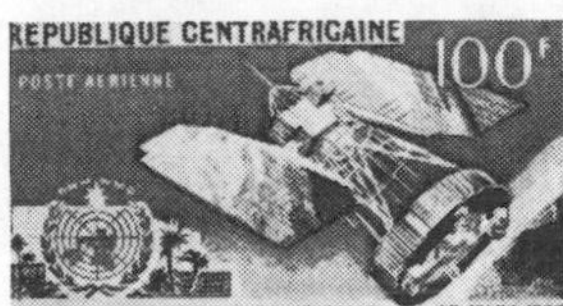

Nimbus Weather Satellite — AP13

1965, Mar. 23 **Engr.** ***Perf. 13***
C27 AP13 100fr org brn, ultra & blk 1.60 1.00

Fifth World Meteorological Day.

Lincoln and Statue of Liberty — AP14

1965, Apr. 15 **Photo.** ***Perf. 13***
C28 AP14 100fr bluish grn, ind & bis 1.60 90

Centenary of death of Abraham Lincoln.

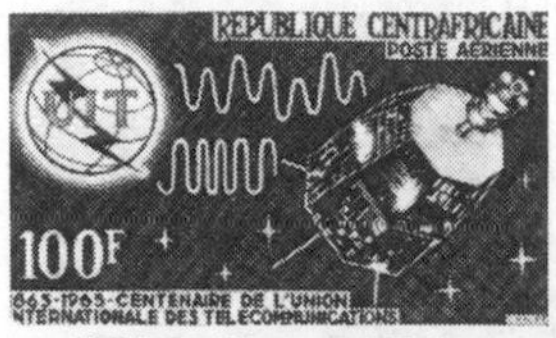

ITU Emblem and Relay Satellite — AP15

1965, May 17 **Engr.** ***Perf. 13***
C29 AP15 100fr dk grn vio bl & brn 1.60 90

Issued to commemorate the centenary of the International Telecommunication Union.

"Housing," New Home in Village — AP16

1965, June 10 **Unwmk.**
C30 AP16 100fr ultra, brn & sl grn 1.50 90

See note after No. 52.

Europafrica Issue

Tractor, Cotton Picker, Cotton, Sun and Emblem — AP17

1965, Nov. 7 **Photo.** ***Perf. 12x13***
C31 AP17 50fr multi 70 50

See note after Chad No. C11.

Mercury by Antoine Coysevox AP18

Father Holding Sick Child AP19

1965, Dec. 5 **Engr.** ***Perf. 13***
C32 AP18 100fr red brn, bl & blk 1.60 1.00

Issued to commemorate the fifth anniversary of Central African Republic's admission to the Universal Postal Union.

1965, Dec. 12

Design: 100fr, Mother and child.

C33 AP19 50fr dk bl, car & blk 75 50
C34 AP19 100fr red brn, red & brt grn 1.50 1.00

Issued to honor the Red Cross.

Air Afrique Issue
Common Design Type

1966, Aug. 31 **Photo.** ***Perf. 13***
C35 CD123 25fr bl, blk & lem 40 15

Issued to commemorate the introduction of DC-8F planes by Air Afrique.

Surveyor Spacecraft on Moon — AP20

Designs: No. C37, Luna 9 on Moon and Earth. 200fr, Rocket take-off, Jules Verne's "From the Earth to the Moon."

1966, Oct. 24 **Photo.** ***Perf. 12x12½***
C36 AP20 130fr multi 2.00 1.20
C37 AP20 130fr multi 2.00 1.20
C38 AP20 200fr multi 3.00 1.80
a. Souv. sheet of 3 8.00 8.00

Issued to commemorate the conquest of the Moon. No. C38a contains one each of Nos. C36-C38, black marginal inscription and control number. Size: 132x158mm.

Eugene A. Cernan, Gemini 9 and Agena Rocket — AP21

Design: No. C40, Pavel R. Popovich and rocket.

1966, Nov. 14 **Photo.** ***Perf. 13***
C39 AP21 50fr multi 75 35
C40 AP21 50fr multi 75 35

Issued to honor American and Russian astronauts.

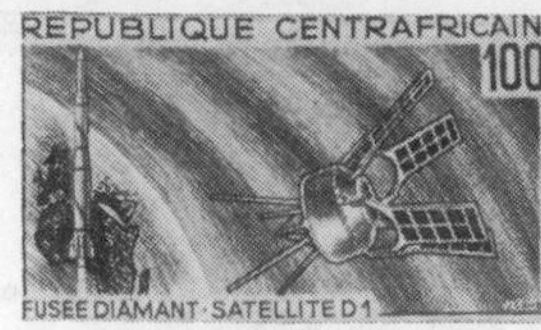

Diamant Rocket, D-1 Satellite and Globe with Map of Africa — AP22

1966, Nov. 14 **Engr.**
C41 AP22 100fr brt rose lil & brn 1.60 70

Issued to commemorate the launching of France's first satellite, Nov. 26, 1965, and the launching of the D-1 satellite, Feb. 17, 1966.

Exchange of Agricultural and Industrial Products between Africa and Europe — AP23

1966, Dec. 5 **Photo.** ***Perf. 12x13***
C42 AP23 50fr multi 75 45

See note after Gabon No. C46.

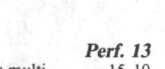

No. C35 Surcharged

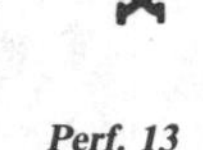

1967, May 8 ***Perf. 13***
C43 CD123 5fr on 25fr multi 15 10

The surcharge obliterates the "2" of the original 25fr denomination.

DC-8F Over M'Poko Airport, Bangui — AP24

1967, July 3 **Engr.** ***Perf. 13***
C44 AP24 100fr sl, dk grn & brn 1.60 75

View of EXPO '67, Montreal — AP25

1967, July 17
C45 AP25 100fr vio bl, dk red brn & dk grn 1.50 70

Issued to commemorate the International Exposition. EXPO '67, Montreal, Apr. 28-Oct. 27.

African Postal Union Issue, 1967
Common Design Type

1967, Sept. 9 **Engr.** ***Perf. 13***
C46 CD124 100fr brt grn, dk car rose & plum 1.50 70

Potez 25 TOE — AP26

Designs: 200fr, Junkers 52. 500fr, Caravelle 11R.

1967, Nov. 24 **Engr.** ***Perf. 13***
C47 AP26 100fr brt bl, brn & gray grn 1.60 65
C48 AP26 200fr dk brn, grn & ind 2.75 1.25
C49 AP26 500fr bl, ind & org brn 7.25 4.00

Presidents Boganda and Bokassa — AP27

1967, Dec. 1 **Photo.** ***Perf. 12½***
C50 AP27 130fr org, red, lt bl & blk 2.00 1.35

9th anniversary of the republic.

Pres. Jean Bedel Bokassa AP28

1968, Jan. 1 ***Perf. 12½x12***
C51 AP28 30fr multi 50 30

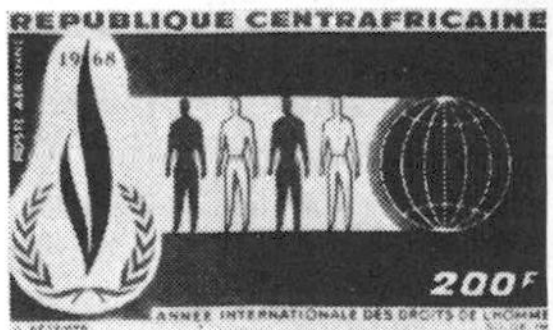

Human Rights Flame, Men and Globe — AP29

1968, Mar. 26 **Photo.** ***Perf. 13***
C52 AP29 200fr brt grn, vio & ver 3.00 1.50

International Human Rights Year.

Man, WHO Emblem and Tsetse Fly — AP30

1968, Apr. 8 **Engr.**
C53 AP30 200fr multi 3.00 1.50

Issued to commemorate the 20th anniversary of the World Health Organization.

Javelin Thrower — AP31

Space Probe Landing on Venus — AP32

Design: No. C55, Downhill skier.

1968, Apr. 16 Engr. *Perf. 13*

C54 AP31 200fr choc, dk red & Prus bl	3.00	1.60
C55 AP31 200fr dk red, choc & Prus bl	3.00	1.60

The 1968 Olympic Games.

1968, Apr. 23

C56 AP32 100fr ultra, dk & brt grn	1.50	70

Issued to commemorate the Venus exploration by Venus IV, Oct. 18, 1967.

Marie Curie and "Cancer Destroyed" — AP33

1968, Apr. 30

C57 AP33 100fr vio, brt bl & brn	1.50	70

Issued to commemorate the centenary of the birth of Marie Curie (1867-1934), scientist.

Nos. C36-C37 and C47-C48 Surcharged with New Value

Photogravure; Engraved

1968, Sept. 16 *Perf. 12x12½, 13*

C58 AP20 5fr on 130fr multi	10	8
C59 AP26 10fr on 100fr multi	15	10
C60 AP26 20fr on 200fr multi	30	12
C61 AP20 50fr on 130fr multi	80	55

On No. C58 the old denomination has been obliterated with "XIX", on No. C61 the obliteration is a rectangular bar. On Nos. C59-C60 the last zero of the old denomination has been obliterated with a black square.

River Boat Type of Regular Issue

Craft: 100fr, "Pie X," Bangui, 1894. 130fr, "Ballay," Bangui, 1891.

1968, Dec. 10 Engr. *Perf. 13*

Size: 48x27mm.

C62 A37 100fr bl, dk brn & ol	1.50	70
C63 A37 130fr brt pink, sl grn & sl	2.00	1.00

PHILEXAFRIQUE Issue

Mme. de Sévigné, French School, 17th Century AP34

1968, Dec. 17 Photo. *Perf. 12½*

C64 AP34 100fr brn & multi	1.60	1.40

Issued to publicize PHILEXAFRIQUE, Philatelic Exhibition in Abidjan, Feb. 14-23. Printed with alternating brown label.

2nd PHILEXAFRIQUE Issue

Common Design Type

Design: 50fr, Ubangi No. J16, cotton field and Pres. Bokassa.

1969, Feb. 14 Engr. *Perf. 13*

C65 CD128 50fr bis brn, blk & dk grn	90	90

Issued to commemorate the opening of PHILEXAFRIQUE, Abidjan, Feb. 14.

Holocerina Angulata Aur. — AP35

Butterflies and Moths: 20fr, Nudaurelia dione fabr. 30fr, Eustera troglophylla hamp. (vert.). 50fr, Aurivillius aratus west. 100fr, Epiphora albida druce.

1969, Feb. 25 Photo.

C66 AP35 10fr yel & multi	15	6
C67 AP35 20fr vio & multi	30	15
C68 AP35 30fr multi	45	20
C69 AP35 50fr multi	85	40
C70 AP35 100fr multi	1.65	80
Nos. C66-C70 (5)	3.40	1.61

Boxing — AP36

Sport Design: 100fr, Basketball.

1969, Mar. 18 Photo. *Perf. 13*

C71 AP36 50fr multi	75	35
C72 AP36 100fr yel & multi	1.50	60

Apollo 8 over Moonscape — AP37

1969, May 27 Photo. *Perf. 13*

C73 AP37 200fr dp bl, gray & yel	3.00	1.35

Issued to commemorate the U.S. Apollo 8 mission, the first men in orbit around the moon, Dec. 21-27, 1968.

Market Cross, Nuremberg, and Toys — AP38

1969, June 3

C74 AP38 100fr blk, brt rose lil & emer	1.50	1.00

Issued to publicize the International Toy Fair in Nuremberg, Germany.

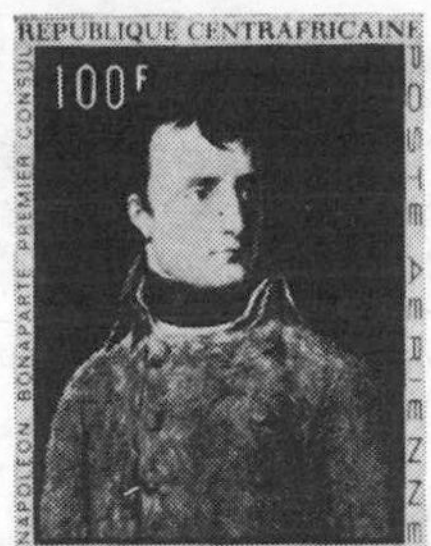

Napoleon as First Consul, by Anne-Louis Girodet-Trioson — AP39

Designs: 130fr, Napoleon meeting Emperor Francis II, by Antoine Jean Gros (horiz.). 200fr, The Wedding of Napoleon and Marie-Louise, by Georges Rouget (horiz.).

1969, Nov. 4 Photo. *Perf. 12½*

C75 AP39 100fr multi	1.75	1.25
C76 AP39 130fr brn & multi	2.50	1.50
C77 AP39 200fr multi	4.00	3.00

Issued to commemorate the bicentenary of the birth of Napoleon Bonaparte (1769-1821).

Pres. Bokassa, Map of Africa and Flag AP40

Franklin Delano Roosevelt AP41

1970, Jan. 1 *Die-cut; Perf. 10½*

Embossed on Gold Foil

C78 AP40 2000fr gold	25.00	25.00

1970 Litho. *Perf. 13½x14*

Design: No. C80, Lenin.

C79 AP41 100fr gold, yel, blk & bl	1.35	80
C80 AP41 100fr gold, yel, blk & red	1.25	70

No. C79 issued to commemorate the 25th anniversary of the death of Pres. Franklin Delano Roosevelt (1882-1945); Nos. C80 commemorates the centenary of the birth of Lenin (1870-1924).

Issue dates: No. C79, Apr. 29; No. C80. Apr. 22.

No. C73 Overprinted in Red:

ATTERRISSAGE
d'APOLLO 12
19 novembre 1969

1970, June 1 Photo. *Perf. 13*

C81 AP37 200fr multi	8.50	6.50

Issued to commemorate the moon landing mission of Apollo 12, Nov. 14-24, 1969.

AP42

1970, Sept. 15 Litho. *Perf. 10*

C82 AP42 Triptych	2.50	1.25
a. 100fr *Dancer*	1.25	50
b. 100fr *Still life*	1.25	50

Issued to publicize Knokphila 70, 6th International Philatelic Exhibition at Knokke, Belgium, July 4-10. The two stamps and violet blue label are printed se-tenant and imperf. between stamps and label.

Sericulture Type of Regular Issue

1970, Sept. 15 *Perf. 10*

C83 A45 140fr multi	2.00	1.10

Issued to publicize Operation Bokassa, a plan for the development of the country.

C.A.R. Flag, EXPO Emblem and Pavilion AP43

1970, Dec. 18 Litho. *Perf. 13½x13*

C84 AP43 200fr red & multi	2.75	1.35

International Exposition EXPO '70, Osaka, Japan.

Soccer AP44

1970, Dec. 8 *Perf. 13x13½*

C85 AP44 200fr multi	2.75	1.35

World Soccer Championships, Mexico, May 30-June 21, 1970.

Dove — AP45

1970, Dec. 31

C86 AP45 200fr bl, yel & blk	2.75	1.35

25th anniversary of the United Nations.

Presidents Mobutu, Bokassa, and Tombalbaye — AP46

1971, Jan. 10

C87 AP46 140fr multi	2.00	90

Return of Central African Republic to the United States of Central Africa which also includes Congo Democratic Republic and Chad.

Satellite over Globe — AP47

1971, May 17 Photo. *Perf. 12½*
C88 AP47 100fr multi 1.35 65

3rd World Telecommunications Day.

African Postal Union Issue, 1971

Common Design Type

Design: 100fr, Carved head and UAMPT building, Brazzaville, Congo.

1971, Nov. 13 Photo. *Perf. 13x13½*
C89 CD135 100fr bl & multi 1.35 65

Child and Education Year Emblem — AP48

1971, Nov. 11 Litho. *Perf. 13x13½*
C90 AP48 140fr multi 1.75 75

25th anniversary of the United Nations Educational, Scientific and Cultural Organization (UNESCO).

Fight Against Cancer — AP49 Gamal Abdel Nasser — AP50

1971, Nov. 20 Photo. *Perf. 12½*
C91 AP49 100fr grn & multi 1.35 60

1972, Jan. 15
C92 AP50 100fr dk red, blk & bis 1.25 60

In memory of Gamal Abdel Nasser (1918-1970), president of Egypt.

Olympic Rings and Boxing — AP51

Design: No. C94, Track and Olympic rings (vert.).

1972, May 26 Engr. *Perf. 13*
C93 AP51 100fr brn org & sep 1.50 60
C94 AP51 100fr grn & vio 1.50 60
a. Miniature sheet of 2 3.00 3.00

20th Olympic Games, Munich, Aug. 20-Sept. 10. No. C94a contains 2 stamps similar to Nos. C93-C94, but in changed colors. The boxing stamp is red lilac and green, the track stamp ocher and red lilac. Size: 129x98mm.

Tiling's Mail Rocket, 1931, and Mailman — AP52

Designs: 50fr, DC-3 and mailman riding camel (vert.). 150fr, Sirio satellite and rocket (vert.). 200fr, Intelsat 4 and rocket.

1972, Aug. 12
C95 AP52 40fr bl, org & ind 50 25
C96 AP52 50fr bl, brn & org 60 25
C97 AP52 150fr brn, org & gray 1.75 80
C98 AP52 200fr brn, bl & org 2.25 1.00
a. Souv. sheet of 4 5.25 5.25

Centraphilex 1972, Central African Philatelic Exhibition, Bangui. No. C98a contains one each of Nos. C95-C98. Brown marginal inscription. Size: 200x99½mm.

Europafrica Issue

Arrows with Symbols of Agriculture and Industry — AP53

1972, Nov. 17 Litho. *Perf. 13*
C99 AP53 100fr multi 1.10 60

Nos. C93-C94, C94a Overprinted

a. POIDS-MOYEN / LEMECHEV MEDAILLE D'OR

b. LONGUER / WILLIAMS MEDAILLE D'OR

1972, Nov. 24 Engr.
C100 AP51 (a) 100fr brn org & sep 1.35 60
C101 AP51 (b) 100fr grn & vio 1.35 60
a. Miniature sheet of 2 3.00 3.00

Gold Medal Winners in 20th Olympic Games: Viatschesiav Lemechev, USSR, middleweight boxing (C100); Randy Williams, USA, broad jump (C101).

Lunar Rover and Module — AP54

1972, Dec. 18 Engr. *Perf. 13*
C102 AP54 100fr sl grn, bl & gray 1.20 65

Apollo 16 U.S. moon mission, Apr. 15-27, 1972.

Virgin and Child, by Francesco Pesellino AP55

Design: 150fr, Adoration of the Child with St. John the Baptist and St. Romuald, by Fra Filippo Lippi.

1972, Dec. 25 Photo.
C103 AP55 100fr gold & multi 1.25 65
C104 AP55 150fr gold & multi 1.85 1.00

Christmas 1972.

Parthenon, Athens, Spyridon Louis, Marathon, 1896 — AP56

Designs (Olympic Rings and): 40fr, Arc de Triomphe, Paris, H. Barrelet, single scull, 1900. 50fr, Old Courthouse and Western Arch, St. Louis, Myer Prinstein, triple jump, 1904. 100fr, Tower, London, Henry Taylor, swimming, 1908. 150fr, City Hall, Stockholm, Greco-Roman wrestling, 1912.

1972, Dec. 28 Engr.
C105 AP56 30fr brt grn, mag & brn 40 12
C106 AP56 40fr vio bl, emer & brn 50 18
C107 AP56 50fr car rose, vio bl & Prus bl 60 25
C108 AP56 100fr sl, red lil & brn 1.25 55
C109 AP56 150fr red lil, blk & Prus bl 1.85 90
Nos. C105-C109 (5) 4.60 2.00

Olympic Games 1896-1912.

WHO Emblem, Surgeon and Nurse — AP57

1973, Apr. 7 Photo. *Perf. 13*
C110 AP57 100fr multi 1.25 70

World Health Organization, 25th anniversary.

World Map, Arrows, Waves — AP58

1973, May 17 Litho. *Perf. 12½*
C111 AP58 200fr lt bl, dp org & blk 2.00 1.20

5th International Telecommunications Day.

Head and City Hall, Brussels — AP58a

1973, Sept. 17 Engr. *Perf. 13*
C112 AP58a 100fr pur, ocher & brn 1.25 70

African Weeks, Brussels, Sept. 15-30, 1973.

Europafrica Issue

Map of Central African Republic with Industry and Agriculture, Young Man — AP59

1973, Sept. 28 Engr. *Perf. 13*
C113 AP59 100fr sep, grn & org 1.10 70

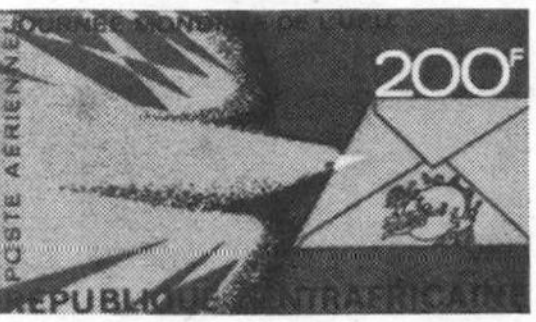

Carrier Pigeon with Letter and UPU Emblem — AP60

1973, Oct. 9 Photo.
C114 AP60 200fr multi 2.25 1.40

Universal Postal Union Day.

WMO Emblem, Weather Map — AP61

1973, Oct. 20 Engr. *Perf. 13*
C115 AP61 150fr brt ultra & sl grn 1.50 75

Centenary of international meteorological cooperation.

Copernicus, Heliocentric System — AP62

1973, Nov. 2 Photo.
C116 AP62 100fr gold & multi 1.15 70

500th anniversary of the birth of Nicolaus Copernicus (1473-1543), Polish astronomer.

Pres. Bokassa AP63

Pres. Bokassa — AP64

Rocket Launch and Apollo 17 Badge — AP65

1973, Nov. 30 Photo. *Perf. 12½*

C117 AP63 50fr multi 50 35
C118 AP64 100fr multi 1.00 70

1973, Dec. 15 Engr. *Perf. 13*

Designs: 65fr, Capsule over moonscape (horiz.). 100fr, Moon landing (horiz.). 150fr, Astronauts on moon. 200fr, Splashdown with parachutes and badge.

C119 AP65 50fr ver, gray grn & brn 50 40
C120 AP65 65fr dk brn, brn red & sl grn 60 50
C121 AP65 100fr ver, sl & choc 1.00 70
C122 AP65 150fr brn, ol & sl grn 1.40 1.00
C123 AP65 200fr red, bl & sl grn 2.00 1.40
Nos. C119-C123 (5) 5.50 4.00

Apollo 17 U.S. moon mission, Dec. 7-19, 1972.

St. Teresa — AP66

UPU Emblem, Letter — AP67

1973, Dec. 25

C124 AP66 500fr vio bl & grnsh bl 5.00 3.00

Centenary of the birth of St. Teresa of the Infant Jesus, the Little Flower (1873-1897), Carmelite nun.

1974, Oct. 9 Engr. *Perf. 13*

C125 AP67 500fr multi 5.00 3.50

Centenary of Universal Postal Union.

Presidents and Flags of Cameroun, CAR, Gabon and Congo — AP68

1974, Dec. 8 Photo. *Perf. 13*

C126 AP68 100fr gold & multi 90 65

See note after Cameroun No. 595.

The only foreign revenue stamps listed in this Catalogue are those authorized for prepayment of postage.

Marshal Bokassa AP69

Design: 100fr, Bokassa in Marshal's uniform with cape.

1975, Feb. 22 Photo. *Perf. 13*

C127 AP69 50fr tan & multi 40 30
C128 AP69 100fr tan & multi 80 60

Jean Bedel Bokassa, President for Life and Marshal of the Republic.

Mask, Map of Africa, Arphila Emblem AP70

Albert Schweitzer and Dugout, Lambarene AP71

1975, Aug. 25 Engr. *Perf. 13*

C129 AP70 100fr brt bl, red brn & red 1.00 50

ARPHILA 75 International Philatelic Exhibition, Paris, June 6-16.

1975, Sept. 30 Engr. *Perf. 13*

C130 AP71 200fr blk, ultra & ol 2.00 1.00

Dr. Albert Schweitzer (1875-1965), medical missionary and musician.

Pres. Bokassa's Houseboat, Bow — AP72

Design: 40fr, Pres. Bokassa's houseboat, stern.

1976, Feb. 22 Litho. *Perf. 13*

C131 AP72 30fr multi 25 15
C132 AP72 40fr multi 35 20

Monument to Franco-CAR Cooperation AP73

Presidents and Flags of France and CAR AP74

1976, Mar. 5

C133 AP73 100fr multi 80 50
C134 AP74 200fr multi 1.60 1.00

Official visit of Pres. Valery Giscard d'Estaing to Central African Republic, Mar. 5-8.

Apollo Soyuz Type, 1976

Designs: 100fr, Soyuz space ship. 200fr, Apollo space ship. 300fr, Astronauts and cosmonauts in cabin. 500fr, Apollo and Soyuz after link-up.

1976, June 14 Litho. *Perf. 14x13½*

C135 A90 100fr multi 1.00 38
C136 A90 200fr multi 2.00 85
C137 A90 300fr multi 3.00 1.25

Souvenir Sheet

C138 A90 500fr multi 4.75 2.25

Apollo Soyuz space test project, Russo-American cooperation, launched July 15, link-up July 17. No. C138 has multicolored margin showing Apollo Soyuz insignia. Size: 103½x78mm.

French Hussar AP75

Uniforms: 125fr, Scottish "Black Watch." 150fr, German dragoon. 200fr, British grenadier. 250fr, American ranger. 450fr, American dragoon.

1976, July 4 *Perf. 13½*

C139 AP75 100fr multi 95 30
C140 AP75 125fr multi 1.20 50
C141 AP75 150fr multi 1.50 60
C142 AP75 200fr multi 1.90 70
C143 AP75 250fr multi 2.25 90
Nos. C139-C143 (5) 7.80 3.00

Souvenir Sheet

C144 AP75 450fr multi 4.25 1.90

American Bicentennial. No. C144 has U.S. Bicentennial emblem in tri-color in margin, black inscription. Size: 118x80mm.

Acherontia Atropos — AP76

Design: 100fr, Papilio nireus and heniocha marnois.

1976, Sept. 20 Litho. *Perf. 12½*

C145 AP76 50fr multi 40 25
C146 AP76 100fr multi 80 50

Olympic Winners Type, 1976

Designs: 100fr, Women's figure skating, Dorothy Hamill (vert.). 200fr, Ice skating, Alexander Gorshkov and Ludmilla Pakhomova. 300fr, Men's figure skating, John Curry (vert.). 500fr, Down-hill skiing, Rosi Mittermaier (vert.).

1976, Sept. 23 Litho. *Perf. 13½*

C147 A92 100fr multi 95 40
C148 A92 200fr multi 1.90 90
C149 A92 300fr multi 3.00 1.35

Souvenir Sheet

C150 A92 500fr multi 4.75 2.25

12th Winter Olympic Games winners, Innsbruck. No. C150 has multicolored margin showing Olympic flags and eternal flame, black inscriptions. Size: 103x78mm.

Viking Mars Type, 1976

Designs: 100fr, Phases of Mars landing. 200fr, Viking descending on Mars (horiz.). 300fr, Viking probe. 500fr, Viking flight to Mars (horiz.).

1976, Dec.

C151 A93 100fr multi 95 35
C152 A93 200fr multi 1.90 85
C153 A93 300fr multi 3.00 1.20

Souvenir Sheet

C154 A93 500fr multi 4.75 2.25

Viking Mars project. No. C154 has multicolored margin showing flight control room. Size: 102x77mm.

Empire

Stamps of 1973-76 Overprinted with Bars and "EMPIRE CENTRAFRICAIN" in Black, Violet Blue or Gold

Printing and Perforations as Before

1977, March

C155 AP68 100fr (#C126;B) 90 70
C156 AP70 100fr (#C129;VB) 90 70
C157 AP73 100fr (#C133;G) 90 70
C158 AP71 200fr (#C130;B) 2.00 1.50
C159 AP67 500fr (#C125;B) 5.50 4.00
Nos. C155-C159 (5) 10.20 7.60

No bar on No. C159.

Stamps of 1976 Overprinted "EMPIRE CENTRAFRICAIN" in Black on Silver Panel

1977, Apr. 1

C160 AP76 50fr (#C145) 50 30
C161 A90 100fr (#C135) 90 70
C162 AP75 100fr (#C139) 80 60
C163 AP76 100fr (#C146) 80 60
C164 A92 100fr (#C147) 80 60
C165 A93 100fr (#C151) 80 60
C166 AP75 125fr (#C140) 1.00 80
C167 AP75 150fr (#C141) 1.20 90
C168 A90 200fr (#C136) 2.00 1.50
C169 AP75 200fr (#C142) 1.60 1.20
C170 A92 200fr (#C148) 1.60 1.20
C171 A93 200fr (#C152) 1.60 1.20
C172 AP75 250fr (#C143) 2.00 1.50
C173 A90 300fr (#C137) 3.00 2.25
C174 A92 300fr (#C149) 2.50 1.85
C175 A93 300fr (#C153) 2.50 1.85
Nos. C160-C175 (16) 23.60 17.65

Souvenir Sheets

C176 AP75 450fr (#C144) 3.75 3.75
C177 A90 500fr (#C138) 4.00 4.00
C178 A92 500fr (#C150) 4.00 4.00
C179 A93 500fr (#C154) 4.00 4.00

Overprint on type AP75 is in upper and lower case letters.

Nobel Prize Type, 1977

Designs: 100fr, Rudyard Kipling. 200fr, Ernest Hemingway. 300fr, Luigi Pirandello. 500fr, Rabindranath Tagore.

1977, Apr. 1 Litho. *Perf. 13½*

C180 A94 100fr multi 95 35
C181 A94 200fr multi 1.90 85
C182 A94 300fr multi 3.00 1.20

Souvenir Sheet

C183 A94 500fr multi 4.75 2.25

Nobel Prize winners. No. C183 has multicolored margin with black inscription. Size: 118x80mm.

Zeppelin Type of 1977

Designs: 100fr, Germany No. C42 and North Pole. 200fr, Germany No. C44 and Science and Industry Building, Chicago. 300fr, Germany No. C35 and Brandenburg Gate, Berlin. 500fr, U.S. No. C14 and U.S. Capitol, Washington, D.C.

1977, Apr. 11 Litho. *Perf. 11*

C184 A95 100fr multi 95 35
C185 A95 200fr multi 1.90 85
C186 A95 300fr multi 3.00 1.20

Souvenir Sheet

C187 A95 500fr multi 4.75 2.25

75th anniversary of Zeppelin. No. C187 has multicolored margin showing early Zeppelin and 15 Zeppelin stamps from various countries. Size: 129x90mm.

Bokassa Type of 1977

1977, Dec. 4 Litho. *Perf. 13½*

C188 A98 200fr multi 1.60 1.00
C189 A98 300fr multi 2.50 1.50
a. Souvenir sheet, 500fr 4.00 3.00

Coronation of Emperor Bokassa I, Dec. 4. No. C189a contains a horizontal stamp in similar design; multicolored margin with eagle and government buildings. Size: 112x80mm. A 2500fr gold embossed horizontal stamp in similar design exists.

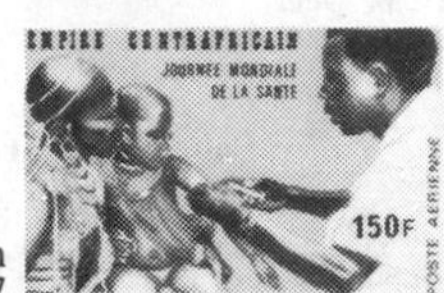

Vaccination AP77

1977 Litho. *Perf. 14x13½*

C190 AP77 150fr multi 1.50 75

World Health Day.

Communications Type of 1978

Designs: 100fr, Balloon and spaceships docking in space. 200fr, Hydrofoil and Concorde. 500fr, Tom-tom and Zeppelin.

1978, May 17 Litho. *Perf. 13½*

C191 A107 100fr multi 1.00 50
C192 A107 200fr multi 2.00 1.00

Souvenir Sheet

C193 A107 500fr multi 5.50 3.50

Century of progress of posts and telecommunications. No. C193 contains one stamp (53x35mm.); multicolored margin shows allegory of posts. Size: 104x70mm.

Clement Ader and his Plane — AP78

Designs: 50fr, Wilbur and Orville Wright and plane. 60fr, John W. Alcock, Arthur W. Brown and plane. 100fr, Alan Cobham and plane 150fr, Claude Dornier and hydroplane. 500fr, Wilbur and Orville Wright and plane.

1978, Sept. 19 *Perf. 14*

C194 AP78 40fr multi 45 20
C195 AP78 50fr multi 55 25
C196 AP78 60fr multi 65 30
C197 AP78 100fr multi 1.10 50
C198 AP78 150fr multi 1.60 75
Nos. C194-C198 (5) 4.35 2.00

Souvenir Sheet

C199 AP78 500fr multi 5.50 2.75

History of aviation. No. C199 has multicolored margin showing Concorde. Size: 116x80mm.

Philexafrique II-Essen Issue

Common Design Types

Designs: No. C200, Crocodile and Central African Rep. No. C3. No. C201, Birds and Mecklenburg-Schwerin No. 1.

1978, Nov. 1 Litho. *Perf. 12½*

C200 CD138 100fr multi 1.00 50
C201 CD139 100fr multi 1.00 50

Nos. C200-C201 printed se-tenant.

Bokassa Type 1978

Design: 150fr, Catherine and Jean Bedel Bokassa (horiz.).

1978, Dec. 4 Litho. *Perf. 13*

C202 A113 150fr multi 1.50 75

First anniversary of coronation. A 1000fr gold embossed souvenir sheet showing Emperor Bokassa exists.

Rowland Hill Type of 1978

Designs (Rowland Hill and): 100fr, Mailman and Tuscany No. 23. 200fr, Balloon and France No. 1. 500fr, Central Africa Nos. 1-2.

1978, Dec. 27

C203 A114 100fr multi 1.00 50
C204 A114 200fr multi 2.00 1.00

Souvenir Sheet

C205 A114 500fr multi 5.00 2.50

Sir Rowland Hill (1795-1879), originator of penny postage. No. C205 contains one stamp (37½x39mm.); multicolored margin shows Penny Black. Size: 83x85mm. 1500fr gold embossed stamp and souvenir sheet exist.

IYC Type of 1979

Designs (UNICEF, Eagle Emblems and): 100fr, Chinese girl flying kites and German Do-X flying boat, 1929. 200fr, Boys playing leapfrog, hurdler and Olympic emblem. 500fr, Child with abacus and Albert Einstein with his equation.

1979, Mar. 6 *Perf. 13½*

C206 A115 100fr multi 1.00 50
C207 A115 200fr multi 2.00 1.00

Souvenir Sheet

C208 A115 500fr multi 5.00 2.50

International Year of the Child. No. C208 contains one stamp (56x33mm.); multicolored margin shows various spacecraft. Size: 110x79mm. 1500fr gold embossed stamp and souvenir sheet exist.

Olympic Type of 1979

Designs (Moscow '80 Emblem, various Sports and): 100fr, Hurdles and "B". 200fr, Broad jump and "A".

1979, Mar. 16 Litho. *Perf. 13*

C209 A116 100fr multi 1.00 50
C210 A116 200fr multi 2.00 1.00

22nd Olympic Games, Moscow, July 19-Aug. 3, 1980. A 1500fr gold embossed souvenir sheet exists showing diver, runner and javelin.

Type of 1979

Design: 60fr, Horse.

1979, Aug. Litho. *Perf. 13*

C211 A119 60fr multi 48 25

National Husbandry Association.

Nos. C151-C154 Overprinted "ALUNISSAGE/APOLLO XI/ JUILLET 1969" and Emblem in Black or Silver

1979, Oct. Litho. *Perf. 14x13½*

C212 A93 100fr multi 80 40
C213 A93 200fr multi 1.60 80
C214 A93 300fr multi 2.40 1.20

Souvenir Sheet

C215 A93 500fr multi (S) 4.25 2.25

Apollo 11 moon landing, 10th anniversary.

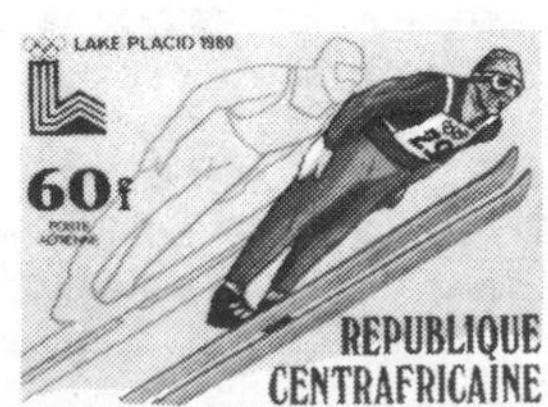

Ski Jump, Lake Placid '80 Emblem — AP79

Lake Placid Emblem and: 100fr, Downhill skiing. 200fr, Hockey. 300fr, Slalom. 500fr, Bobsledding.

1979, Nov. 11 Litho. *Perf. 13½*

C216 AP79 60fr multi 48 25
C217 AP79 100fr multi 80 40
C218 AP79 200fr multi 1.60 80
C219 AP79 300fr multi 2.40 1.20

Souvenir Sheet

C220 AP79 500fr multi 4.25 2.25

13th Winter Olympics Games, Lake Placid, N.Y., Feb. 12-24, 1980. No. C220 has multicolored margin showing skiers. Size 113x78mm.

Space Type of 1980

1980, Apr. 8 Litho. *Perf. 13½*

C221 A125 150fr *Early satellites* 1.20 60
C222 A125 200fr *Space shuttle* 1.60 80

Souvenir Sheet

C223 A125 500fr *Apollo 11, Armstrong* 4.00 2.00

Space explorations No. C223 has multicolored margin showing Neil Armstrong on moon. Size: 85x58½mm.

Nos. C216-C220 Overprinted:
a. VAINQUEUR / INNAVER / AUTRICHE
b. VAINQUEUR / MOSER-PROELL / AUTRICHE
c. VAINQUEUR / ETATS-UNIS
d. VAINQUEUR / STENMARK / SUEDE
e. VAINQUEURS / SCHAERER-BENZ / SUISSE

1980, May 12 Litho. *Perf. 13½*

C224 AP79 (a) 60fr multi 48 25
C225 AP79 (b) 100fr multi 80 40
C226 AP79 (c) 200fr multi 1.60 80
C227 AP79 (d) 300fr multi 2.40 1.20

Souvenir Sheet

C228 AP79 (e) 500fr multi 4.00 2.00

World Telecommunications Day — AP80

1980, June 26 Litho. *Perf. 12½*

C229 AP80 100fr multi 80 40
C230 AP80 150fr multi, vert. 1.20 60

Olympic Type of 1980

1980, July 25 Litho. *Perf. 13½*

C231 A126 100fr *Boxing* 80 40
C232 A126 150fr *Hurdles* 1.20 60

Souvenir Sheet

C233 A126 250fr *Long jump* 2.00 1.00

22nd Summer Olympic Games, Moscow, July 19-Aug. 3. No. C233 contains one stamp (39x36mm); multicolored margin shows satellite, Olympic rings, Moscow '80 emblem, Kremlin. Size: 87x84mm.

Europe-Africa Type of 1980

1980, Nov. 4 Litho. *Perf. 13½*

C234 A127 150fr *Meteorology* 1.20 60
C235 A127 200fr *Aviation* 1.60 80

Souvenir Sheet

C236 A127 500fr *Concorde jet* 4.00 2.00

No. C236 contains one stamp (41½x29mm.); multicolored margin showing jet, flags and maps. Size: 89x64½mm.

Soccer Type of 1981

1981, Jan. 13 Litho. *Perf. 13½*

C237 A130 100fr Netherlands 80 40
C238 A130 200fr Spain 1.60 80

Souvenir Sheet

C239 A130 500fr Argentina 4.00 2.00

ESPANA '82 World Cup Soccer Championship. No. C239 has multicolored margin showing soccer scenes and teams. Size: 119x87mm.

Jacob Wrestling with the Angel, by Rembrandt AP81

Rembrandt Paintings: 90fr, Christ during the Storm. 150fr, Jeremiah Mourning the Destruction of Jerusalem. 250fr, Tobit Accusing Anne of Theft of a Goat. 500fr, Belshazzar's Feast (horiz.).

1981, Feb. 20 *Perf. 12½*

C240 AP81 60fr multi 50 25
C241 AP81 90fr multi 70 35
C242 AP81 150fr multi 1.20 60
C243 AP81 250fr multi 2.00 1.00

Souvenir Sheet

C244 AP81 500fr multi 4.00 2.00

No. C244 has gray and light brown margin showing figures by Rembrandt. Size: 105x80mm.

Picasso Type of 1981

Paintings: 150fr, Woman in Mirror with Self-portrait. 200fr, Woman Sleeping, The Dream. 500fr, Portrait of Maia (the Artist's Daughter).

1981, June 30 Litho. *Perf. 13½*

C245 A133 150fr multi 1.20 60
C246 A133 200fr multi 1.60 80

Souvenir Sheet

C247 A133 500fr multi 4.00 2.00

No. C247 contains one stamp (42x46mm.); multicolored margin shows entire painting. Size: 78½x113½mm.

Nos. C231-C233 Overprinted with Event, Winner and Country in Gold.

1981 Litho. *Perf. 13½*

C248 A126 100fr multi 80 40
C249 A126 150fr multi 1.20 60

Souvenir Sheet

C250 A126 250fr multi 2.00 1.00

Royal Wedding Type of 1981

1981, Aug. 20 Litho. *Perf. 13½*

C251 A136 150fr Prince of Wales arms 1.20 60
C252 A136 200fr Palace 1.60 80

Souvenir Sheet

C253 A136 500fr St. Paul's Cathedral 4.00 2.00

No. C253 contains one stamp (60x32mm.); multicolored margin shows arms. Size: 120x70mm.

Navigator Type of 1981

1981, Sept. 4 Litho. *Perf. 13½*

C254 A139 100fr O. Kersauson 80 40
C255 A139 200fr Chichester 1.60 80

Souvenir Sheet

C256 A139 500fr A. Colas 4.00 2.00

No. C256 has multicolored margin showing ships. Size: 100x80mm.

Lizard AP82

1981, Oct. 30 *Perf. 12½x13*

C257 AP82 30fr shown 25 12
C258 AP82 60fr Snake 50 25
C259 AP82 110fr Crocodile 90 45

Christmas Type of 1981

1981, Dec. 24 *Perf. 13½*

C260 A143 140fr Correggio 1.15 60
C261 A143 200fr Gentileschi, 1610 1.60 80

Souvenir Sheet

C262 A143 500fr Holy Family, by Cranach 4.00 2.00

No. C262 contains one stamp (41x50mm.); multicolored margin shows entire painting. Size: 81x98mm.

Animal Type of 1982

1982, Jan. 22 Litho. *Perf. 13½*

C263 A145 300fr Mandrill 2.40 1.20
C264 A145 500fr Lion 4.00 2.00

Souvenir Sheet

C265 A145 600fr Nile crocodiles 5.00 2.50

No. C265 contains one stamp (47x38mm.); multicolored margin shows crocodiles. Size: 100x80mm.

Transportation Type of 1982

1982, Feb. 27 Litho. *Perf. 13½*

C266 A147 300fr Savannah cargo ship 2.40 1.25
C267 A147 500fr Columbia space shuttle 4.00 2.00

Souvenir Sheet

C268 A147 600fr Spirit of Locomotion emblem 5.00 2.50

No. C268 contains one stamp (39x43mm.); multicolored margin shows modes of transportation. Size: 101x81mm.

Olympic Type of 1982

1982, July 24 Litho. *Perf. 13½*

C269 A149 300fr Diving 2.50 1.25
C270 A149 500fr Equestrian 4.00 2.00

Souvenir Sheet

C271 A149 600fr Basketball 5.00 2.50

No. C271 contains one stamp (38x56mm.); multicolored margin shows city views. Size: 80x108mm.

Diana Type of 1982

1982, July 20 Litho. *Perf. 13½*

C272 A150 300fr multi 2.50 1.25
C273 A150 500fr multi 4.00 2.00

Souvenir Sheet

C274 A150 600fr multi 5.00 2.50

No. C274 contains one stamp (56x32mm.). Size: 120x75mm.

Christmas 1982 AP83

Raphael Paintings.

1982, Dec. *Perf. 13*

C275 AP83 150fr Beautiful Gardener 1.20 60
C276 AP83 500fr Holy Family 4.00 2.00

Space Type of 1982

Various satellites and space scenes.

1982, Aug. 15 Litho. *Perf. 13½*

C277 A151 300fr multi 2.50 1.25
C278 A151 500fr multi 4.00 2.00

Souvenir Sheet

C279 A151 600fr multi 5.00 2.50

No. C279 has multicolored margin showing planets, satellite. Size: 105x67mm.

Birth of Prince William of Wales, June 21, 1982 — AP84

1983, Jan. 22

C280 AP84 500fr Diana, William 4.00 2.00

Souvenir Sheet

C281 AP84 600fr Family 5.00 2.50

Size of No. C281: 120x70mm.

Manned Flight Bicentenary AP85

1983, Apr.

C282 AP85 65fr Robert's & Hullin's balloon 52 25
C283 AP85 130fr John Wise's, 1859 1.05 52
C284 AP85 350fr Mail balloon, 1870 2.75 1.35
C285 AP85 400fr Dirigible Underberg 3.25 1.65

Souvenir Sheet

C286 AP85 500fr Montgolfiere, 1783 4.00 2.00

No. C286 has multicolored margin continuing design. Size: 117x91mm.

Pre-Olympics — AP86

Various equestrian events.

1983, July Litho. *Perf. 13*

C287 AP86 100fr multi 80 40
C288 AP86 200fr multi 1.60 80
C289 AP86 300fr multi 2.50 1.25
C290 AP86 400fr multi 3.25 1.65

Souvenir Sheet

C291 AP86 500fr multi 4.00 2.00

Multicolored margin continues design. Size: 104x81mm.

Endangered Animals, Rotary Emblem — AP87

1983, Nov. 14 Litho. *Perf. 13½*

C292 AP87 500fr Lions, gray parrot, deer, elephant 2.50 1.25

Souvenir Sheet

C293 AP87 600fr Leopard 3.00 1.50

No. C293 contains one stamp (47x32mm.); multicolored margin shows Rotary emblem, rhinoceros, map, bird. Size: 112x75mm.

Christmas 1983 AP88

Paintings: 130fr, Annunciation, by da Vinci. 205fr, Virgin of the Rocks, by da Vinci. 350fr, Adoration of the Shepherds, by Rubens. 500fr, Virgin and Child with Donor, by Rubens.

1984, Jan. 3 Litho. *Perf. 13*

C294 AP88 130fr multi 65 32
C295 AP88 205fr multi 1.05 52
C296 AP88 350fr multi 1.75 85
C297 AP88 500fr multi 2.50 1.25

1984 Summer Olympics — AP89

Various gymnastic and rhythmic gymnastic events. 65fr, 100fr, 205fr, 350fr vert.

1984, Mar. 13 Litho. *Perf. 13*

C298 AP89 65fr multi 32 16
C299 AP89 100fr multi 50 25
C300 AP89 130fr multi 65 32
C301 AP89 205fr multi 1.05 52
C302 AP89 350fr multi 1.75 85
Nos. C298-C302 (5) 4.27 2.10

Souvenir Sheet

Perf. 13½x13

C302A AP89 500fr Rhythmic formation 2.50 1.25

No. C302A has multicolored margin showing the Los Angeles skyline. Size: 103x78mm.

Summer Olympics Winners AP90

1985, Jan. 7 Litho. *Perf. 14*

C303 AP90 60fr 400 meter relay 25 14
C304 AP90 140fr 400 meter hurdles 58 30
C305 AP90 300fr 5000 meter race 1.40 70
C306 AP90 440fr Decathlon 1.80 90

Souvenir Sheet

C307 AP90 500fr 800 meter race, horiz. 2.00 1.00

Size: 102x76mm.

Christmas 1984 — AP91

Paintings by Titian: 130fr, Virgin and Infant Jesus. 350fr, Virgin with Rabbit. 400fr, Virgin and Child.

1985, Jan. 17 Litho. *Perf. 13*

C308 AP91 130fr multi 55 28
C309 AP91 350fr multi 1.45 75
C310 AP91 400fr multi 1.65 85

Audubon Bicentenary — AP92

1985, Jan. 25 Litho. *Perf. 13*

C311 AP92 60fr Otus asio 25 14
C312 AP92 110fr Coccizus minor, vert. 48 24
C313 AP92 200fr Zenaidura macroura, vert. 85 42
C314 AP92 500fr Aix sponsa 2.10 1.05

Christmas 1985 AP93

Religious paintings: 100fr, Virgin with Angels, by the Master of Burgo de Osma. 200fr, Nativity, by Louis Le Nain (1593-1648). 400fr, Virgin and Child with Dove, by Piero de Cosimo (1462-1521).

1985, Dec. 24 Litho. *Perf. 13*

C315 AP93 100fr multi 52 28
C316 AP93 200fr multi 1.10 55
C317 AP93 400fr multi 2.25 1.10

Halley's Comet — AP94

1986, Mar. 8

C318 AP94 110fr Edmond Halley 60 30
C319 AP94 130fr Giotto probe 70 35
C320 AP94 200fr Comet, planet 1.10 55
C321 AP94 300fr Vega probe 1.65 80
C322 AP94 400fr Space shuttle 2.25 1.10
Nos. C318-C322 (5) 6.30 3.10

Catalogue prices for unused stamps up to mid-1953 are for hinged copies matching the condition specified in this volume's introduction.

Christmas AP95

Painting details: 250fr, Nativity, by Giotto. 440fr, Adoration of the Magi, by Botticelli, vert. 500fr, Nativity, by Giotto, diff.

1986, Dec. 24	**Litho.**	***Perf. 13 1/2***	
C323 AP95 250fr multi		1.40	70
C324 AP95 440fr multi		2.40	1.20
C325 AP95 500fr multi		2.75	1.40

Tennis at the 1988 Olympics — AP96

Various plays.

1986, Dec. 31	***Perf. 12 1/2***		
C326 AP96 150fr multi		82	40
C327 AP96 250fr multi, vert.		1.40	70
C328 AP96 440fr multi, vert.		2.40	1.20
C329 AP96 600fr multi		3.25	1.65

1988 Summer Olympics, Seoul — AP97

1987, June 15	**Litho.**	***Perf. 13***	
C330 AP97 100fr Triple jump, vert.		55	28
C331 AP97 200fr High jump		1.10	55
C332 AP97 300fr Long jump		1.65	82
C333 AP97 400fr Pole vault, vert.		2.25	1.10

Souvenir Sheet

C334 AP97 500fr High jump, diff.	2.75	1.40

No. C334 has multicolored decorative margin picturing Olympic Village, Seoul. Size: 105x87mm.

AIR POST SEMI-POSTAL STAMPS

Central African Republic

Isis of Kalabsha SPAP1

Unwmk.

1964, March 7	**Engr.**	***Perf. 13***	
CB1 SPAP1 25fr + 10fr ol, ultra & brt pink		1.00	1.00
CB2 SPAP1 50fr + 10fr dk bl grn, ol & red brn		1.50	1.50
CB3 SPAP1 100fr + 10fr ol gray, lil & mar		2.50	2.50

Issued to publicize the UNESCO world campaign to save historic monuments in Nubia.

African Infants and Globe — SPAP2

1971, Dec. 11	**Litho.**	***Perf. 13x13 1/2***	
CB4 SPAP2 140fr + 50fr multi		2.50	1.50

25th anniversary of the United Nations International Children's Fund (UNICEF), and Children's Day.

POSTAGE DUE STAMPS

Central African Republic

Sternotomis Virescens — D1

Beetles: No. J2, Sternotomis gama. No. J3, Augosoma centaurus. No. J4, Phosphorus virescens and ceroplesis carabarica. No. J5, Cetoine scaraboidae. No. J6, Ceroplesis S.P. No. J7, Macrorhina S.P. No. J8, Cetoine scaraboidae. No. J9, Phryneta leprosa. No. J10, Taurina longiceps. J11, Monohamus griseoplagiatus. J12, Jambonus trifasciatus.

Unwmk.

1962, Oct. 15	**Engr.**	***Perf. 11***	
J1 D1 50c grn & dp org		5	5
J2 D1 50c grn & dp org		5	5
J3 D1 1fr blk, brn & lt grn		10	10
J4 D1 1fr blk, brn & lt grn		10	10
J5 D1 2fr blk, org & yel grn		10	10
J6 D1 2fr blk & red org		10	10
J7 D1 5fr brn, org & grn		18	18
J8 D1 5fr brn, org, grn & red		18	18
J9 D1 10fr blk, grn & brn		45	45
J10 D1 10fr blk, brn & grn		45	45
J11 D1 25fr blk, bl grn & brn		70	70
J12 D1 25fr blk, brn & bl grn		70	70
Nos. J1-J12 (12)		3.16	3.16

Each two stamps of the same denomination are printed together in the sheet, se-tenant at the base.

Giant Anteater — D2

1985, Jan. 25	**Litho.**	***Perf. 12 1/2***	
J13 D2 5fr multi		5	5
J14 D2 20fr multi		10	5
J15 D2 30fr multi		14	8

MILITARY STAMPS

Central African Republic

No. 1 Overprinted

Unwmk.

1962, Jan. 1	**Engr.**	***Perf. 13***	
M1 A1 bl, car, grn & yel		12.50	12.50

=

No. 1 Overprinted

FM

1963			
M2 A1 bl, car, grn & yel		13.50	13.50

OFFICIAL STAMPS

Central African Republic

Coat of Arms — O1

Imprint: "d'apres G. RICHER SO.GE.IM."

Perf. 13x12 1/2

1965-69	**Litho.**	**Unwmk.**	
Arms in Original Colors			
O1 O1 1fr blk & brn org		6	6
O2 O1 2fr blk & vio		7	6
O3 O1 5fr blk & gray		10	6
O4 O1 10fr blk & grn		28	12
O5 O1 20fr blk & red brn		45	32
O6 O1 30fr blk & emer ('69)		80	60
O7 O1 50fr blk & dk bl		1.00	80
O8 O1 100fr blk & bis		2.10	1.25
O9 O1 130fr blk & ver ('69)		3.25	2.50
O10 O1 200fr blk & cl		4.50	3.00
Nos. O1-O10 (10)		12.61	8.77

Redrawn

Imprint: "d'apres G. RICHER DELRIEU"

1971	**Photo.**	***Perf. 12x12 1/2***	
Arms in Original Colors			
O11 O1 5fr blk & gray		18	18
O12 O1 30fr blk & emer		45	28
O13 O1 40fr blk & dp cl		60	35
O14 O1 100fr blk & bis		1.40	70
O15 O1 140fr blk & lt bl		2.50	1.00
O16 O1 200fr blk & cl		3.25	1.60
Nos. O11-O16 (6)		8.38	4.11

Empire

Nos. O11, O13-O16 Overprinted with Bar and "EMPIRE CENTRAFRICAIN"

1977	**Litho.**	***Perf. 12x12 1/2***	
O17 O1 5fr multi		18	15
O18 O1 40fr multi		35	28
O19 O1 100fr multi		80	55
O20 O1 140fr multi		1.20	85
O21 O1 200fr multi		1.85	1.35
Nos. O17-O21 (5)		4.38	3.18

Type of 1965 Inscribed: "EMPIRE CENTRAFRICAIN"

1978, July	**Litho.**	***Perf. 12 1/2***	
O22 O1 1fr multi		5	5
O23 O1 2fr multi		5	5
O24 O1 5fr multi		5	5
O25 O1 10fr multi		12	12
O26 O1 15fr multi		15	15
O27 O1 20fr multi		20	20
O28 O1 30fr multi		30	30
O29 O1 40fr multi		40	40
O30 O1 50fr multi		50	50
O31 O1 60fr multi		60	60
O32 O1 100fr multi		1.00	1.00
O33 O1 130fr multi		1.30	1.30
O34 O1 140fr multi		1.40	1.40
O35 O1 200fr multi		2.00	2.00
Nos. O22-O35 (14)		8.12	8.12

CENTRAL LITHUANIA

LOCATION — North of Poland and east of Lithuania
CAPITAL — Vilnius

At one time Central Lithuania was a grand duchy of Lithuania but at the end of the 18th Century it fell under Russian rule. After World War I, Lithuania regained her sovereignty but certain areas were occupied by Poland. During the Russo-Polish war this territory was seized by Lithuania whose claim was promptly recognized by the Soviet Government. Under the leadership of the Polish General Zeligowski the territory was recaptured and it was during this occupation the stamps of Central Lithuania came into being. Subsequently the territory became a part of Poland.

100 Fennigi = 1 Markka

Coat of Arms — A1

Perf. 11 1/2, Imperf.

1920-21	**Typo.**	**Unwmk.**	
1 A1 25f red		40	75
2 A1 25f dk grn ('21)		40	75
3 A1 1m blue		40	75
4 A1 1m dk brn ('21)		40	75
5 A1 2m violet		50	75
6 A1 2m org ('21)		50	75
Nos. 1-6 (6)		2.60	4.50

ŚRODKOWA LITWA 4 MAR. 4 POCZTA

Lithuanian Stamps of 1919 Surcharged in Blue or Black

Perf. 11 1/2x12, 12 1/2x11 1/2, 14

Wmk. Wavy Lines. (145)

1920, Nov. 23			
13 A5 2m on 15sk lil		10.00	10.00
a. Invtd. surch.		250.00	
14 A5 4m on 10sk red		10.00	10.00
a. Invtd. surch.		250.00	
15 A5 4m on 20sk dl bl (Bk)		10.00	10.00
a. Invtd. surch.		250.00	
16 A5 4m on 30sk buff		10.00	10.00
a. Invtd. surch.		250.00	
17 A6 6m on 50sk lt grn		10.00	10.00
a. 4m on 50sk lt grn (error)		250.00	
b. 10m on 50sk lt grn (error)		250.00	
18 A6 6m on 60sk vio & red		10.00	10.00
a. 4m on 60sk vio & red (error)		250.00	
b. 10m on 60sk vio & red (error)		250.00	
19 A6 6m on 75sk bis & red		10.00	10.00
a. 4m on 75sk bis & red (error)		250.00	
b. 10m on 75sk bis & red (error)		250.00	
20 A8 10m on 1auk gray & red		15.00	15.00
a. Invtd. surch.		375.00	
21 A8 10m on 3auk lt brn & red		500.00	550.00
22 A8 10m on 5auk bl grn & red		500.00	550.00
Nos. 13-22 (10)		1,085.	1,185.

Reprints of Nos. 17a, 17b, 18a, 18b, 19a, 19b. Price, each $75.
Counterfeits of Nos. 21-22 exist.

Lithuanian Girl — A2

Warrior
A3

Holy Gate of Vilnius
A4

Tower and Cathedral, Vilnius
A5

Rector's Insignia
A6

Gen. Lucien Zeligowski — A7

Perf. 11½, Imperf.

1920 **Litho.** **Unwmk.**

No.	Type	Description	Unused	Used
23	A2	25f gray	25	50
24	A3	1m orange	25	50
25	A4	2m claret	50	1.00
26	A5	4m gray grn & buff	75	1.00
27	A6	6m rose & gray	1.50	1.25
28	A7	10m brn & yel	2.50	3.00
		Nos. 23-28 (6)	5.75	7.25

St. Anne's Church, Vilnius
A8

St. Stanislas Cathedral, Vilnius
A9

White Eagle and White Knight Vytis — A10

Queen Hedwig and King Ladislas II Jagello — A11

Coat of Arms of Vilnius
A12

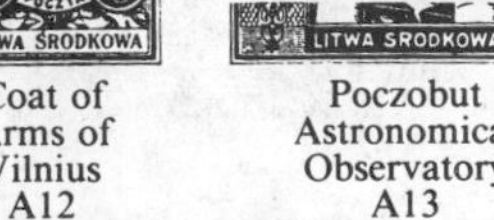
Poczobut Astronomical Observatory
A13

Union of Lithuania and Poland — A14

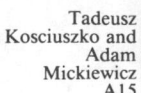

Tadeusz Kosciuszko and Adam Mickiewicz
A15

1921 *Perf. 11½, 13½, 14, Imperf.*

No.	Type	Description	Unused	Used
35	A8	1(m) dk gray & yel	50	75
36	A9	2(m) rose & grn	50	75
37	A10	3(m) dk grn	50	75
38	A11	4(m) brn & buff	50	75
39	A12	5(m) red brn	50	75
40	A13	6(m) sl & buff	50	1.00
41	A14	10(m) red vio & buff	1.25	1.75
42	A15	20(m) blk brn & buff	1.50	1.75
		Nos. 35-42 (8)	5.75	8.25

Peasant Girl Sowing
A16

White Eagle and Vytis
A17

Great Theater at Vilnius
A18

Allegory: Peace and Industry
A19

Gen. Zeligowski Entering Vilnius
A20

Gen. Zeligowski
A21

1921-22 *Perf. 11½, Imperf.*

No.	Type	Description	Unused	Used
53	A16	10m brn ('22)	3.50	4.00
54	A17	25m red & yel ('22)	3.50	3.50
55	A18	50m dk bl ('22)	4.00	4.00
56	A19	75m vio ('22)	5.50	5.50
57	A20	100m bl & bis	4.25	5.50
58	A21	150m ol grn & brn	4.50	5.50
		Nos. 53-58 (6)	25.25	28.00

Nos. 53-56 commemorate the opening of the National Parliament; Nos. 57-58, the anniversary of the entry of General Zeligowski into Vilnius.

SEMI-POSTAL STAMPS.

Nos. 1-6 Surcharged in Black or Red

NA
ŚLĄSK
2 M.

1921 **Unwmk.** *Perf. 11½, Imperf.*

No.	Type	Description	Unused	Used
B1	A1	25f + 2m red (Bk)	90	1.50
B2	A1	25f + 2m dk grn	90	1.50
B3	A1	1m + 2m bl	1.25	2.00
B4	A1	1m + 2m dk brn	1.25	2.00
B5	A1	2m + 2m vio	1.50	2.00
B6	A1	2m + 2m org	1.25	2.00
		Nos. B1-B6 (6)	7.05	11.00

The surcharge means "For Silesia 2 marks." The stamps were intended to provide a fund to assist the plebiscite in Upper Silesia.

Nos. 25, 26 Surcharged:

+1
a

+1 M
b

Perf. 11½, Imperf.

No.	Type	Description	Unused	Used
B13	A4 (a)	2m + 1(m) cl	2.50	3.00
B14	A5 (b)	4m + 1m gray grn & buff	2.50	3.00

Nos. 25-26, 28 with inset 1 M

Perf. 11½, Imperf.

No.	Type	Description	Unused	Used
B17	A4	2m + 1m cl	1.50	1.50
B18	A5	4m + 1m gray grn & buff	1.50	1.50
B19	A7	10m + 2m brn & yel	1.50	1.50
		Nos. B13-B19 (5)	9.50	10.50

POSTAGE DUE STAMPS.

University, Vilnius
D1

Castle Hill, Vilnius
D2

Castle Ruins, Troki
D3

Holy Gate, Vilnius
D4

St. Stanislas Cathedral
D5

St. Anne's Church, Vilnius
D6

1920-21 **Unwmk.** *Perf. 11½, Imperf.*

No.	Type	Description	Unused	Used
J1	D1	50f red vio	40	75
J2	D2	1m green	40	75
J2	D3	2m red vio	40	75
J4	D4	3m red vio	60	1.00
J5	D5	5m red vio	1.00	1.50
J6	D6	20m scarlet	3.00	3.50
		Nos. J1-J6 (6)	5.80	8.25

CHAD

(Tchad)

LOCATION — Central Africa, south of Libya.
GOVT. — Republic
AREA — 495,572 sq. mi.
POP. — 5,122,000 (est. 1984)
CAPITAL — N'djamena

A former dependency of Ubangi-Shari, Chad became a separate French colony in 1920. In 1934, the colonies of Chad, Gabon, Middle Congo and Ubangi-Shari were grouped in a single administrative unit known as French Equatorial Africa, with the capital at Brazzaville. The Republic of Chad was proclaimed November 28, 1958.

100 Centimes = 1 Franc

Types of Middle Congo, 1907-17, Overprinted

TCHAD

Perf. 14x13½, 13½x14.

1922 **Unwmk.**

No.	Type	Description	Unused	Used
1	A1	1c red & vio	15	15
a.		Overprint omitted	100.00	
2	A1	2c ol brn & sal	25	25
a.		Ovpt. omitted	160.00	
3	A1	4c ind & vio	35	35
4	A1	5c choc & grn	45	45
5	A1	10c dp grn & gray grn	75	75
6	A1	15c vio & red	95	95
7	A1	20c grn & vio	2.50	2.50
8	A2	25c ol brn & brn	4.75	4.75
9	A2	30c rose & pale rose	60	60
10	A2	35c dl bl & dl rose	1.10	1.10
11	A2	40c choc & grn	1.10	1.10
12	A2	45c vio & grn	1.10	1.10
13	A2	50c dk bl & pale bl	1.25	1.25
14	A2	60c on 75c vio,*pnksh*	2.00	2.00
a.		"TCHAD" omitted	150.00	
b.		"60" omitted	150.00	
15	A1	75c red & vio	1.10	1.10
16	A3	1fr ind & sal	5.25	5.25
17	A3	2fr ind & vio	8.25	8.25
18	A3	5fr ind & ol brn	7.00	7.00
		Nos. 1-18 (18)	38.90	38.90

Stamps of 1922 Overprinted in Various Colors:

AFRIQUE EQUATORIALE FRANÇAISE
a

AFRIQUE EQUATORIALE FRANÇAISE
b

1924-33

No.	Type	Description	Unused	Used
19	A1 (a)	1c red & vio	5	5
a.		"TCHAD" omitted	95.00	
b.		Dbl. ovpt.	87.50	
20	A1 (a)	2c ol brn & sal	5	5
a.		"TCHAD" omitted	95.00	
b.		Dbl. ovpt.	100.00	
21	A1 (a)	4c ind & vio	5	5
a.		"TCHAD" omitted	525.00	
22	A1 (a)	5c choc & grn (B1)	55	32
a.		"TCHAD" omitted	95.00	
23	A1 (a)	5c choc & grn	32	30
a.		"TCHAD" omitted	125.00	
24	A1 (a)	10c dp grn & gray grn (B1)	32	30
25	A1 (a)	10c dp grn & gray grn	32	30
26	A1 (a)	10c red org & blk ('25)	25	25
27	A1 (a)	15c vio & red	32	30
28	A1 (a)	20c grn & vio	32	30
29	A2 (b)	25c ol brn & brn	32	30
30	A2 (b)	30c rose & pale rose	18	18
31	A2 (b)	30c gray & bl (R) ('25)	18	18
32	A2 (b)	30c dk grn & grn ('27)	55	55
a.		"Afrique Equatoriale Francaise" omitted	150.00	
33	A2 (b)	35c ind & dl rose	20	20
34	A2 (b)	40c choc & grn	55	55
a.		Dbl. overprint (R + Bk)	150.00	
35	A2 (b)	45c vio & grn	42	42
a.		Dbl. overprint (R + Bk)	150.00	
36	A2 (b)	50c dk bl & pale bl	42	42
a.		Inverted overprint	87.50	
37	A2 (b)	50c grn & vio ('25)	55	55
38	A2 (b)	65c org brn & bl ('28)	1.25	1.25
39	A2 (b)	75c red & vio	32	32
40	A2 (b)	75c dp bl & lt bl (R) ('25)	25	25
a.		"TCHAD" omitted	100.00	
41	A2 (b)	75c rose & dk brn ('28)	1.25	1.25
42	A2 (b)	90c brn red & pink ('30)	3.50	3.50
43	A3 (b)	1fr ind & sal	80	80
44	A3 (b)	1.10fr dl grn & bl ('28)	1.25	1.25
45	A3 (b)	1.25fr org brn & lt bl ('33)	3.50	3.50
46	A3 (b)	1.50fr ultra & bl ('30)	3.50	3.50
47	A3 (b)	1.75fr ol brn & vio ('33)	27.50	27.50
48	A3 (b)	2fr ind & vio	1.40	1.25
49	A3 (b)	3fr red vio ('30)	5.50	5.50
50	A3 (b)	5fr ind & ol brn	1.40	1.25
		Nos. 19-50 (32)	57.34	56.69

Types of 1922 Overprinted Type "b" and Surcharged with New Values.

1924-27

No.	Type	Description	Unused	Used
51	A2	60c on 75c dk vio, *pnksh*	35	35
a.		"60" omitted	85.00	
52	A3	65c on 1fr brn & ol grn ('25)	85	85
53	A3	85c on 1fr brn & ol grn ('25)	85	85
54	A2	90c on 75c brn red & rose red ('27)	85	85

55 A3 1.25fr on 1fr dk bl & ultra (R) ('26) 25 25
a. "Afrique Equatoriale Francaise" omitted 100.00
56 A3 1.50fr on 1fr ultra & bl ('27) 85 85
57 A3 3fr on 5fr org brn & dl red ('27) 2.50 2.50
58 A3 10fr on 5fr ol grn & cer ('27) 6.00 6.00
59 A3 20fr on 5fr vio & ver ('27) 9.25 9.25
Nos. 51-59 (9) 21.75 21.75

Colonial Exposition Issue.
Common Design Types
Name of Country in Black.

1931 **Engr.** ***Perf. 12½***
60 CD70 40c dp grn 2.50 2.50
61 CD71 50c violet 2.50 2.50
62 CD72 90c red org 2.50 2.50
63 CD73 1.50fr dl bl 2.50 2.50

Republic

"Birth of the Republic" A1

"Solidarity of the Community" A2

1959 **Unwmk.** **Engr.** ***Perf. 13***
64 A1 15fr ultra, grn & mar 20 10
65 A2 25fr dk grn & dp cl 32 10

Issued to commemorate the first anniversary of the proclamation of the Republic.

Imperforates
Most Chad stamps from 1959 onward exist imperforate in issued and trial colors, and also in small presentation sheets in issued colors.

Common Design Types pictured in section at front of book.

C.C.T.A. Issue
Common Design Type

1960
66 CD106 50fr rose lil & dk pur 70 65

Flag and Map of Chad and U.N. Emblem — A3

Unwmk.
1961, Jan. 11 **Engr.** ***Perf. 13***
Flag in blue, yellow and carmine.
67 A3 15fr brn & dk bl 30 20
68 A3 25fr org brn & dk bl 38 20
69 A3 85fr sl grn & dk bl 1.25 70

Admission of Chad to United Nations.

Chari Bridge and Hippopotamus — A4

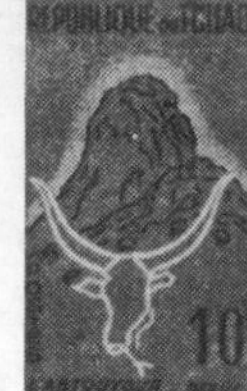

Abtouyoua Mountain and Ox — A5

Designs: 50c, Biltine and dorcas gazelle. 1fr, Logone and elephant. 2fr, Batha and lion. 3fr, Salamat and buffalo. 4fr, Ouaddai and Kudu. 15fr, Bessada and giant eland. 20fr, Tibesti mountains and mouflon. 25fr, Rocherg and antelope. 30fr, Kanem and cheetah. 60fr, Borkou and oryx. 85fr, Gorge of Archet and addax.

Perf. 13½x14, 14x13½
1961-62 **Typo.**
70 A5 50c yel grn & dk grn ('62) 5 5
71 A5 1fr bl grn & dk bl grn ('62) 5 5
72 A5 2fr dk red brn & blk ('62) 5 5
73 A5 3fr ocher & dl grn ('62) 6 6
74 A5 4fr dk crim & blk ('62) 8 8
75 A4 5fr yel & blk 10 10
76 A5 10fr pink & blk 15 10
77 A5 15fr lil & blk ('62) 25 8
78 A5 20fr red & blk 30 15
79 A5 25fr bl & blk ('62) 40 15
80 A5 30fr ultra & blk ('62) 50 20
81 A5 60fr yel & ol grn ('62) 90 30
82 A5 85fr org & blk 1.20 50
Nos. 70-82 (13) 4.09 1.87

First anniversary of Independence.

Abidjan Games Issue
Common Design Type

Designs: 20fr, Relay race. 50fr, High jump.

1962, July 21 **Photo.** ***Perf. 12½x12***
83 CD109 20fr brn, lt grn & blk 30 15
84 CD109 50fr brn, lt grn & blk 60 45

See No. C8.

African-Malgache Union Issue
Common Design Type

1962, Sept. 8 **Unwmk.**
85 CD110 30fr dk bl, bluish grn, red & gold 50 45

Issued to commemorate the first anniversary of the African and Malgache Union.

Pres. Ngarta Tombalbaye — A7

1963, Apr. 22 ***Perf. 12x12½***
86 A7 20fr multi 30 15
87 A7 85fr multi 1.20 45

Space Communciations Issue

Waves Around Globe — A8

Design: 100fr, Orbit patterns around globe.

Perf. 12½
1963, Sept. 19 **Unwmk.** **Photo.**
88 A8 25fr grn & pur 40 35
89 A8 100fr pink & ultra 1.50 1.10

Ancestral Mask — A9

Excavated Sao Art: 5fr, Clay weight. 25fr, Ancestral clay statuette. 60fr, Gazelle, bronze. 80fr, Bronze pectoral.

1963, Dec. 2 **Engr.** ***Perf. 13***
90 A9 5fr brt grn & red brn 10 5
91 A9 15fr gray, dl cl & red 25 15
92 A9 25fr dk bl & org brn 40 25
93 A9 60fr org brn & sl grn 90 40
94 A9 80fr org red & ol 1.20 40
Nos. 90-94 (5) 2.85 1.25

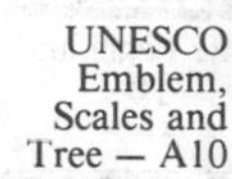

UNESCO Emblem, Scales and Tree — A10

1963, Dec. 10
95 A10 25fr grn & mar 40 30

Issued to commemorate the 15th anniversary of the Universal Declaration of Human Rights.

Potter A11

Designs: 30fr, Boatmaker. 50fr, Weaver. 85fr, Smiths.

Perf. 12½
1964, Feb. 5 **Unwmk.** **Engr.**
96 A11 10fr bl, blk & org 15 10
97 A11 30fr yel, blk & car 45 20
98 A11 50fr grn, blk & car 75 30
99 A11 85fr pur, blk & yel 85 50

Barograph and WMO Emblem A12

1964, March 23 ***Perf. 13***
100 A12 50fr red lil, pur & ultra 85 45

Fourth World Meteorological Day.

Cotton A13

Design: 25fr, Royal poinciana.

1964, Apr. 6 **Photo.** ***Perf. 12½x13***
101 A13 20fr multi 40 20
102 A13 25fr multi 40 20

Co-operation Issue
Common Design Type

1964, Nov. 7 **Engr.** ***Perf. 13***
103 CD119 25fr ver, dk bl & dk brn 40 30

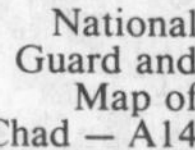

National Guard and Map of Chad — A14

Design: 25fr, Infantry, flag and map (vert.).

Perf. 12½x13, 13x12½
1964, Dec. 11 **Photo.**
104 A14 20fr multi 35 20
105 A14 25fr lt bl & multi 40 20

Issued to honor the army of Chad.

Aoudad or Barbary Sheep — A15

Animals: 10fr, Addax. 20fr, Oryx. 25fr, Derby's eland (vert.). 30fr, Giraffe, buffalo and lion, Zakouma Park (vert.). 85fr, Great kudu at water hole. (vert.).

Perf. 12½x12, 12x12½
1965, Jan. 11 **Unwmk.**
106 A15 5fr dk brn, ultra & yel 7 5
107 A15 10fr ultra, org & blk 18 12
108 A15 20fr multi 30 15
109 A15 25fr multi 40 20
110 A15 30fr multi 45 25
111 A15 85fr multi 1.25 65
Nos. 106-111 (6) 2.65 1.42

Olsen Perforator A16

Designs: 60fr, Milde telephone (vert.). 100fr, Distributor of Baudot telegraph.

1965, May 17 **Engr.** ***Perf. 13***
112 A16 30fr choc, red, grn & ver 45 30
113 A16 60fr red brn, sl grn & ver 90 60
114 A16 100fr sl grn, red brn & ver 1.40 1.00

Issued to commemorate the centenary of the International Telecommunication Union.

Motorized Police — A17

Perf. 12½x12
1965, June 22 **Photo.** **Unwmk.**
115 A17 25fr ol, dk grn, gold & brn 40 25

Issued to honor the national police.

Guitar A18

Musical Instruments from National Museum: 1fr, Drum and stool (vert.). 3fr, Shoulder drums (vert.). 15fr, Viol. 60fr, Harp (vert.).

1965, Oct. 26 **Engr.** ***Perf. 13***
Size: 22x36, 36x22mm.
116 A18 1fr car, emer & brn 6 5
117 A18 2fr red, brt lil & brn 6 5
118 A18 3fr red & sep 6 6
119 A18 15fr red, ocher & sl grn 25 15
120 A18 60fr mar & sl grn 90 40
Nos. 116-120,C23 (6) 2.68 1.16

Head and Bowl
A19

WHO Headquarters, Geneva
A20

Sao Art: 20fr, Head. 60fr, Head with crown. 80fr, Circlet with human head. From excavations at Bouta Kebira and Gawi.

1966, Apr. 1 Engr. *Perf. 13*

121 A19 15fr ol, choc & ultra 20 15
122 A19 20fr dk red, brn & bl grn 30 20
123 A19 60fr brt bl, choc & ver 90 50
124 A19 80fr brn org, grn & pur 1.20 60

Issued to publicize the International Negro Arts Festival, Dakar, Senegal, Apr. 1-24.

No. 86 Surcharged with New Value and Two Bars in Orange

1966, Apr. 15 Photo. *Perf. 12x12½*

125 A7 25fr on 20fr multi 40 20

1966, May 3

126 A20 25fr car, lt ultra & yel 40 30
127 A20 32fr emer, ultra & yel 45 35

Issued to commemorate the inauguration of the World Health Organization Headquarters, Geneva.

Staff of Mercury and Map of Africa
A21

1966, May 24 *Perf. 12½x12*

128 A21 30fr multi 45 20

Central African Customs and Economic Union (Union Douaniere et Economique de l'Afrique Centrale, UDEAC).

Soccer Player — A22

Design: 60fr, Soccer player facing left.

1966, July 12 Engr. *Perf. 13*

129 A22 30fr grn, bl grn & mar 45 25
130 A22 60fr dk bl, gray & car 90 50

Issued to commemorate the 8th World Cup Soccer Championship, Wembley, England, July 11-30.

Young Men, Flag and Emblem
A23

1966, Aug. 11 Photo. *Perf. 12½x13*

131 A23 25fr dk bl & multi 40 25

Chad Youth Movement.

Greek Columns and UNESCO Emblem — A24

1966, Aug. 23 Engr. *Perf. 13*

132 A24 32fr sl bl, vio & car rose 50 30

Issued to commemorate the 20th anniversary of UNESCO (United Nations Educational, Scientific and Cultural Organization).

Reconstructed Skull of Chadanthropus — A25

1966, Sept. 20 Engr. *Perf. 13*

133 A25 30fr gray, red & ocher 45 20

Issued to commemorate Yves Coppens' discovery of Lake Chad man.

Stone Axe — A26

Prehistoric Tools: 30fr, Flint arrow head. 85fr, Bone harpoon. 100fr, Sandstone millstone with grinder.

1966, Dec. 11 Engr. *Perf. 13*

134 A26 25fr dp bl, red & dk brn 32 18
135 A26 30fr brn, dp bl & blk 45 22
136 A26 85fr dk red, brt bl & brn 1.20 55
137 A26 100fr Prus grn, dk brn & bis brn 1.40 70
a. Min. sheet of 4 3.75 3.75

No. 137a contains one each of Nos. 134-137. Size: 128x99mm.

Map of Chad and Various Sports — A27

1967, Apr. 10 Photo. *Perf. 12x12½*

138 A27 25fr multi 40 25

Issued for Sports Day, Apr. 10, 1967.

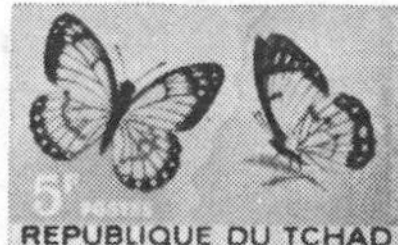

Colotis Protomedia
A28

Various Butterflies.

1967, May 23 Photo. *Perf. 12½x12*

139 A28 5fr bl & multi 10 8
140 A28 10fr emer & multi 20 12
141 A28 20fr org & multi 30 20
142 A28 130fr red & multi 1.75 90

WHO Headquarters, Brazzaville — A29

1967, Sept. 23 Photo. *Perf. 12½x13*

143 A29 30fr vio bl & multi 45 25

Issued to commemorate the opening of the Regional Office of the United Nations World Health Organization, Brazzaville.

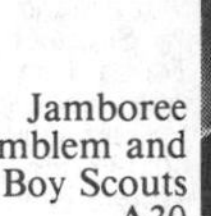

Jamboree Emblem and Boy Scouts
A30

Design: 32fr, Jamboree emblem and Boy Scout.

1967, Oct. 17 Photo. *Perf. 12½x13*

144 A30 25fr multi 35 15
145 A30 32fr multi 50 25

Issued to publicize the 12th Boy Scout World Jamboree, Farragut State Park, Idaho, Aug. 1-9.

Great Mills of Chad — A31

Design: 30fr, Lake reclamation project, grain fields.

1967, Nov. 14 Engr. *Perf. 13*

146 A31 25fr brt bl, ind & sep 35 15
147 A31 30fr ultra, emer & ol brn 40 25

Economic development of Chad.

Woman and Harp Player
A32

Rock Paintings: 30fr, Giraffes. 50fr, Camel rider hunting ostrich.

1967, Dec. 19 Engr. *Perf. 13*
Size: 36x22mm.

148 A32 15fr bl, sal & mar 20 12
149 A32 30fr grnsh bl, sal & mar 45 25
150 A32 50fr emer, sal & mar 75 32
Nos. 148-150,C38-C39 (5) 4.75 2.24

Issued to commemorate the Balloud expedition in the Ennedi Mountains. See also Nos. 163-166.

Rotary Emblem
A33

Map of Chad, WHO Emblem, Well, Physicians, Mother and Child
A34

1968, Jan. 9 Photo. *Perf. 13x12½*

151 A33 50fr multi 75 35

Rotary Club of Chad, 10th anniversary.

1968, Apr. 6 *Perf. 13x12½*

152 A34 25fr multi 35 20
153 A34 32fr multi 50 30

Issued to commemorate the 20th anniversary of the World Health Organization.

"Water" Aiding Agriculture and Industry
A35

1968, Apr. 23 Engr. *Perf. 13*

154 A35 50fr grnsh bl, brn & brt grn 70 30

Hydrological Decade (UNESCO), 1965-74.

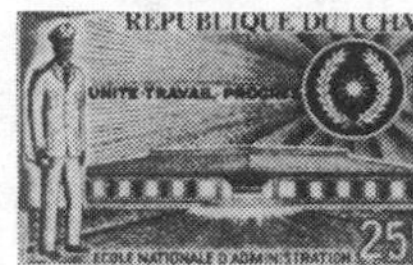

National Administration School — A36

1968, Aug. 20 Engr. *Perf. 13*

155 A36 25fr sl, brn red & rose vio 35 20

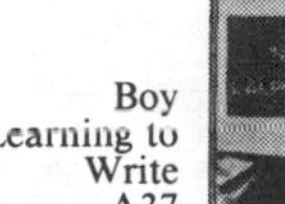

Boy Learning to Write
A37

1968, Sept. 10

156 A37 60fr dk bl, dk brn & blk 75 35

Issued for National Literacy Day.

Cotton Harvest
A38

Loom, Fort Archambault Factory — A39

Tiger Moth — A40

1968, Sept. 24 Engr. *Perf. 13*

157 A38 25fr Prus bl, choc & dk grn 35 13
158 A39 30fr brt grn, ol & ultra 45 20

Issued to publicize the cotton industry.

1968, Oct. 1 Photo.

Designs (Moths): 30fr, Owlet. 50fr, Saturnid (Gynanisa maja). 100fr, Saturnid (Epiphora bauhiniae).

159 A40 25fr multi 30 15
160 A40 30fr multi 40 20
161 A40 50fr multi 70 35
162 A40 100fr multi 1.25 50

Rock Paintings Type of 1967

Rock Paintings: 2fr, Archers. 10fr, Costumes (4 women, 1 man). 20fr, Funeral vigil. 25fr, Dispute.

1968, Nov. 19 Engr. *Perf. 13*
Size: 36x22mm.

163	A32	2fr scar, sal & brn	6	5
164	A32	10fr pur, sal & dk red	15	6
165	A32	20fr grn, sal & mar	30	15
166	A32	25fr bl, sal & mar	40	20

Man and Human Rights Flame — A41

St. Paul — A42

1968, Dec. 10 Engr. *Perf. 13*
167 A41 32fr grn, brt bl & red 50 30

International Human Rights Year.

1969, May 6 Litho. *Perf. 12½x13*

Apostles: 1fr, St. Peter. 2fr, St. Thomas. 5fr, St. John the Evangelist. 10fr, St. Bartholomew. 20fr, St. Matthew. 25fr, St. James the Less. 30fr, St. Andrew. 40fr, St. Jude. 50fr, St. James the Greater. 85fr, St. Philip. 100fr, St. Simon.

168	A42	50c multi	5	5
169	A42	1fr multi	5	5
170	A42	2fr multi	5	5
171	A42	5fr multi	8	5
172	A42	10fr multi	15	8
173	A42	20fr multi	28	15
174	A42	25fr multi	35	17
175	A42	30fr multi	42	20
176	A42	40fr multi	55	25
177	A42	50fr multi	65	30
178	A42	85fr multi	1.00	55
179	A42	100fr multi	1.20	60
		Nos. 168-179 (12)	4.83	2.50

Issued to commemorate the Jubilee Year of the Catholic Church in Chad. Nos. 168-179 printed se-tenant in sheets of 12 (4x3).

Tractors and Trucks — A43

1969, June 19 Engr. *Perf. 13*
180 A43 32fr grn, red brn & ind 40 25

Issued to commemorate the 50th anniversary of the International Labor Organization.

Deborah Meyer, U.S., 200 Meter Freestyle — A44

Woman with Flowers, by Veneto — A45

Winners of 1968 Olympic Games: No. 182, Roland Matthes, East Germany, 100 meter backstroke. No. 183, Klaus DiBiasi, Italy, springboard diving. No. 184, Bruno Cipolla, Primo Baran and Renzo Sambo, Italy, pair with coxswain. No. 185, Annemarie Zimmermann and Rosewitha Esser, West Germany, women's kayak tandem. No. 186, Sailing, Great Britain. No. 187, Pierre Trentin, France, 1000 meter bicycling. No. 188, Pier Franco Vianelli, Italy, 196 kilometer bicycle road race. No. 189, Daniel Morelon and Pierre Trentin, France, tandem. No. 190, Daniel R. Rebillard, France, 4000 meter pursuit (bicycle). No. 191, Ingrid Becker, West Germany, pentathlon. No. 192, Jean J. Guyon, France, equestrian. No. 193, Olympic dressage team, West Germany. No. 194, Bernd Klinger, West Germany, small bore rifle. No. 195, Manfred Wolke, East Germany, welterweight. No. 196, Randy Matson, U.S., shot put. No. 197, Colette Besson, France, 400 meter run. No. 198, Mohammed Gammoudi, Tunisia, 5,000 meter run. No. 199, Tommie Smith, U.S., 200 meter run. No. 200, David Hemery, Great Britain, 200 meter hurdles. No. 201, Willie Davenport, U.S., 110 meter hurdles. No. 202, Bob Beamon, U.S., broad jump. No. 203, Sawao Kato, Japan, all around gymnastics. No. 204, Dick Fosbury, U.S., high jump.

Paintings: No. 206, Holy Family, by Murillo (horiz.). No. 207, Adoration of the Kings, by Rubens. No. 208, Portrait of an African Woman, by Bezombes. No. 209, Three Negroes, by Rubens. No. 210, Mother and Child, by Gauguin.

1969, June 30 Litho. *Perf. 12½x13*

181	A44	1fr *Meyer*	35	35
182	A44	1fr *Matthes*	35	35
183	A44	1fr *DiBiasi*	35	35
184	A44	1fr *Cipolla, Baran & Sambo*	35	35
185	A44	1fr *Zimmermann & Esser*	35	35
186	A44	1fr *Sailing, Great Britain*	35	35
187	A44	1fr *Trentin*	35	35
188	A44	1fr *Vianelli*	35	35
189	A44	1fr *Morelon & Trentin*	35	35
190	A44	1fr *Rebillard*	35	35
191	A44	1fr *Becker*	35	35
192	A44	1fr *Guyon*	35	35
193	A44	1fr *Dressage, Germ.*	35	35
194	A44	1fr *Klinger*	35	35
195	A44	1fr *Wolke*	35	35
196	A44	1fr *Matson*	35	35
197	A44	1fr *Besson*	35	35
198	A44	1fr *Gammoudi*	35	35
199	A44	1fr *Smith*	35	35
200	A44	1fr *Hemery*	35	35
201	A44	1fr *Davenport*	35	35
202	A44	1fr *Beamon*	35	35
203	A44	1fr *Kato*	35	35
204	A44	1fr *Fosbury*	35	35

Perf. 12½x13, 13x12½

205	A45	1fr *Veneto*	35	35
206	A45	1fr *Murillo*	35	35
207	A45	1fr *Rubens*	35	35
208	A45	1fr *Bezombes*	35	35
209	A45	1fr *Rubens*	35	35
210	A45	1fr *Gauguin*	35	35
		Nos. 181-210 (30)	10.50	10.50

Issued to stress the brotherhood of mankind.

Cochlospermum Tinctorium — A46

Flowers: 4fr, Parkia biglobosa. 10fr, Pancratium trianthum. 15fr, Morning glory.

1969, July 8 Photo. *Perf. 12½x13*

211	A46	1fr pink, yel & blk	5	5
212	A46	4fr dk grn, yel & red	5	5
213	A46	10fr dk grn, yel & gray	15	8
214	A46	15fr vio bl & multi	20	10

Meat Freezer, Farcha — A47

Design: 30fr, Cattle at Farcha slaughterhouse.

1969, Aug. 19 Engr. *Perf. 13*

215	A47	25fr sl grn, ocher & red brn	32	18
216	A47	30fr red brn, sl grn & gray	38	25

Economic development in Chad.

Development Bank Issue
Common Design Type

1969, Sept. 10
217 CD130 30fr dl red, grn & ocher 40 20

Issued to commemorate the 5th anniversary of the African Development Bank.

Tilapia Nilotica — A48

Fish: 3fr, Citharinus latus. 5fr, Tetraodon fahaka strigosus. 20fr, Hydrocyon forskali.

1969, Nov. 25 Engr. *Perf. 13*

218	A48	2fr choc, grn & gray	5	5
219	A48	3fr gray, red & bl	8	5
220	A48	5fr ocher, blk & yel	10	8
221	A48	20fr blk, red & grn	32	18

ASECNA Issue
Common Design Type

1969, Dec. 12 Engr. *Perf. 13*
222 CD132 30fr orange 30 15

Pres. François Tombalbaye A49

Lenin A50

1970, Jan. 11 Litho. *Perf. 14*
223 A49 25fr multi 38 20

1970, Apr. 22 Photo. *Perf. 11½*
224 A50 150fr gold, blk & buff 1.85 1.00

Issued to commemorate the centenary of the birth of Lenin (1870-1924), Russian communist leader.

U.P.U. Headquarters Issue
Common Design Type

1970, May 20 Engr. *Perf. 13*
225 CD133 30fr dk red, pur & brn 40 12

Adult Education Class and U.N. Emblem — A52

1970, June 16 Litho. *Perf. 14*
226 A52 100fr bl & multi 1.20 30

Issued for International Education Year.

Bull's Head, Symbols of Weather and Agriculture A53

Ahmed Mangue A54

1970, July 22 Engr. *Perf. 13*
227 A53 50fr org, gray & grn 55 15

Issued for World Meteorological Day.

Lithographed an Engraved

1970, Sept. 15 *Perf. 13*
228 A54 100fr gold, car & blk 1.10 25

Issued in memory of Ahmed Mangue, Minister of Education.

Tanner A55

Designs: 2fr, Cloth dyer (vert.). 3fr, Camel turning oil press (horiz.). 4fr, Water carrier. 5fr, Copper worker (horiz.).

1970, Oct. 10 Engr. *Perf. 13*

229	A55	1fr ol brn, bl & brn	5	5
230	A55	2fr dk brn, ol & ind	5	5
231	A55	3fr pur, ol brn & rose car	5	5
232	A55	4fr choc, lem & bl grn	6	6
233	A55	5fr red, choc & sl grn	5	5
		Nos. 229-233 (5)	26	26

U.N. Emblem, Grain and Dove — A56

1970, Oct. 24 Photo. *Perf. 12x12½*
234 A56 32fr dk bl & multi 40 25

25th anniversary of United Nations.

OCAM Headquarters, Map of Africa, Stars — A57

1971, Jan. 23 Photo. *Perf. 12½x12*
235 A57 30fr dk grn & multi 40 25

OCAM (Organisation Commune Africaine, Malgache et Mauricienne) Summit Conference, N'djamena, Jan. 22-30.

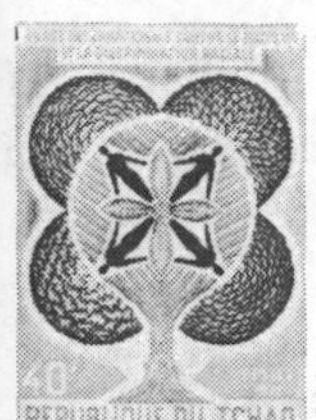

Symbolic Tree — A58

1971, March 21 Engr. *Perf. 13*

236 A58 40fr bl grn, dk red & grn 50 25

International year against racial discrimination.

Map of Africa, Radar Antenna A59

Designs (Map of Africa and): 40fr, Communications tower. 50fr, Communications satellite.

1971, May 17 Engr. *Perf. 13*

237 A59 5fr ultra, org & dk red 10 8
238 A59 40fr pur, emer & brn 40 20
239 A59 50fr dk red, blk & brn 60 30

3rd World Telecommunications Day.

UNICEF Emblem and Children — A60

1971, Dec. 11

240 A60 50fr Prus bl, emer & brt pink 60 30

25th anniversary of the United Nations International Children's Fund (UNICEF).

Gorane Nangara Dancers A61

Dancers: 15fr, Girls' initiation dance, Yondo. 30fr, Women of M'Boum (vert.). 40fr, Men of Sara Kaba (vert.).

1971, Dec. 18 Litho. *Perf. 13*

241 A61 10fr blk & multi 15 5
242 A61 15fr brn org & multi 25 8
243 A61 30fr bl & multi 50 15
244 A61 40fr yel grn & multi 65 18

Presidents Pompidou and Tombalbaye, Map with Paris and Fort Lamy — A62

1972, Jan. 25 Photo. *Perf. 13*

245 A62 40fr bl & multi 50 30

Visit of Pres. Georges Pompidou of France, Jan. 1972.

President Tombalbaye — A63

1972, Apr. 13 Litho. *Perf. 13*

246 A63 30fr multi 30 15
247 A63 40fr multi 40 20

See Nos. C112-C113.

Downhill Skiing — A64

Designs: 75fr, Women's figure skating. 150fr, Luge.

1972, Apr. 13 *Perf. 13½*

248 A64 25fr multi 25 13
249 A64 75fr multi 75 38
250 A64 150fr multi 1.50 75
Nos. 248-250,C114-C115 (5) 5.80 2.91

11th Winter Olympic Games, Sapporo, Japan.

Heart A65

Gorrizia Dubiosa A66

1972, Apr. 25 Engr. *Perf. 13*

251 A65 100fr pur, bl & car 1.20 25

"Your heart is your health," World Health Month.

1972, May 6 Photo.

Insects: 2fr, Spider (argiope sector). 3fr, Silk spider (nephila senegalense). 4fr, Beetle (oryctes boas). 5fr, Dragonfly (hemistigma albipunctata).

252 A66 1fr grn & multi 8 6
253 A66 2fr bl & multi 8 6
254 A66 3fr car rose & multi 8 6
255 A66 4fr yel grn & multi 8 6
256 A66 5fr dp grn & multi 8 6
Nos. 252-256 (5) 40 30

Scout Greeting — A67

Designs: 70fr, Mountain climbing. 80fr, Canoeing.

1972, May 15

257 A67 30fr multi 30 15
258 A67 70fr multi 70 35
259 A67 80fr multi 80 40
Nos. 257-259,C118-C119 (5) 4.00 2.25

Scout Jamboree.

Hurdles, Motion and Olympic Emblems A68

Designs (Motion and Olympic Emblems and): 130fr, Gymnast on rings. 150fr, Swimming. 300fr, Bicycling.

1972, June 9 Litho. *Perf. 13½*

260 A68 30fr blk & multi 60 18
261 A68 130fr blk & multi 1.40 38
262 A68 150fr blk & multi 1.80 45

Souvenir Sheet

263 A68 300fr blk & multi 3.50 3.00

20th Olympic Games, Munich, Aug. 26-Sept. 10. No. 263 contains one stamp. Black marginal inscription and multicolored torch. Size: 101x86mm.

Ski Jump, Kasaya, Japan — A69

Designs: 75fr, Cross-country skiing, P. Tyldum, Sweden. 100fr, Figure-skating, pairs, L. Rodnina and A. Ulanov, USSR. 130fr, Men's speed skating, A. Schenk, Netherlands.

1972, June 15 *Perf. 14½*

264 A69 25fr gold & multi 25 13
265 A69 75fr gold & multi 75 38
266 A69 100fr gold & multi 1.00 50
267 A69 130fr gold & multi 1.30 65
Nos. 264-267,C130-C131 (6) 6.80 3.41

11th Winter Olympic Games, gold-medal winners. Nos. 264-267 exist se-tenant with label showing earth satellite.

TV Tower and Weight-lifting — A70

Designs (TV Tower, Munich and): 40fr, Woman sprinter. 60fr, Soccer goalkeeper.

1972, Aug. 15 Litho. *Perf. 14½*

268 A70 20fr gold & multi 20 10
269 A70 40fr gold & multi 40 20
270 A70 60fr gold & multi 60 30
Nos. 268-270,C135-C137 (6) 4.90 2.45

20th Summer Olympic Games, Munich. Nos. 268-270 exist se-tenant with label showing arms of Munich.

Dromedary A71

Domestic Animals: 30fr, Horse. 40fr, Dog. 45fr, Goat.

1972, Aug. 29 Engr. *Perf. 13*

271 A71 25fr pur & bis 35 12
272 A71 30fr red lil & ind 40 15
273 A71 40fr emer & lt brn 50 15
274 A71 45fr dk bl & brn 55 20

Tobacco Cultivation A72

Design: 50fr, Plowing.

1972, Oct. 24 Engr. *Perf. 13*

275 A72 40fr dk brn, dk car & sl grn 40 20
276 A72 50fr ultra, brn & sl grn 50 25

Massa Warrior — A73

Design: 20fr, Moundang warrior.

1972, Nov. 15 Photo. *Perf. 14x13*

277 A73 15fr org & multi 25 25
278 A73 20fr yel & multi 30 25

King Faisal and Pres. Tombalbaye — A74

1972, Nov. 17 Litho. *Perf. 13*

279 A74 100fr gold & multi 1.00 60

Visit of King Faisal of Saudi Arabia. See No. C143.

Gen. Gowon and Pres. Tombalbaye — A75

1972, Dec. 7

280 A75 70fr multi 75 40

Visit of Gen. Yakubu Gowon of Nigeria.

Olympic Emblem and 100-meter Sprint, Valeri Borzov, USSR — A76

Designs (Olympic Emblem and): 20fr, Shotput, Komar, Poland. 40fr, Hammer throw, Bondartchuk, USSR. 60fr, Discus, Danek, Czechoslovakia.

1972, Dec. 22 *Perf. 11*

281 A76 10fr multi 10 5
282 A76 20fr multi 20 10
283 A76 40fr multi 40 20
284 A76 60fr multi 60 30
Nos. 281-284,C148-C149 (6) 5.30 2.65

20th Summer Olympic Games, winners.

Olympic Emblem and Fencing, Woyda, Poland — A77

Designs (Olympic Emblem and): 30fr, 3-day equestrian event, Richard Meade, Gt. Britain. 50fr, Two-man sculls, Brietzke-Mager, East Germany.

1972, Dec. 22

285 A77 20fr gold & multi 20 10
286 A77 30fr gold & multi 30 15
287 A77 50fr gold & multi 50 25
Nos. 285-287,C151-C152 (5) 5.00 2.50

20th Summer Olympic Games, winners.

Soviet Flag and Shield — A78

1972, Dec. 30 **Litho.** *Perf. 12*

288 A78 150fr red & multi 1.35 65

50th anniversary of the Soviet Union.

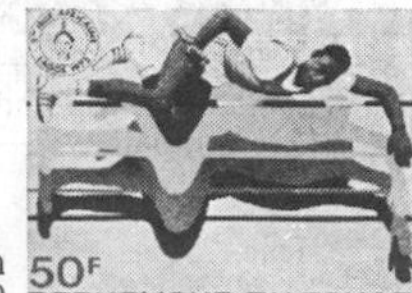

High Jump — A79

Designs (Games Emblem and): 125fr, Running. 200fr, Shot put. 250fr, Discus.

1973, Jan. 17 **Litho.** *Perf. 13½x13*

289 A79 50fr vio bl & multi 50 22
290 A79 125fr ol & multi 1.20 60
291 A79 200fr lil & multi 2.00 1.00

Souvenir Sheet

292 A79 20fr brn & multi 3.00 3.00

2nd African Games, Lagos, Nigeria, Jan. 7-18. No. 292 contains one stamp. Ultramarine margin with inscription and black Games emblems. Size: 101½x85mm.

No. 271 Surcharged with New Value, 2 Bars, and Overprinted in Red: "SECHERESSE SOLIDARITE AFRICAINE"

1973, Aug. 16 **Engr.** *Perf. 13*

293 A71 100fr on 25fr multi 1.00 65

African solidarity in drought emergency.

African Postal Union Issue

Common Design Type

1973, Sept. 17 **Engr.** *Perf. 13*

294 CD137 100fr cl, sl grn & brn ol 1.00 60

Dinothrombium Tinctorium A80

Rotary Emblem A81

1974, Sept. 3 **Photo.** *Perf. 13*

295 A80 25fr *shown* 22 12
296 A80 30fr *Bupreste sternocera* 25 15
297 A80 40fr *Diptere hyperechia* 35 20
298 A80 50fr *Chrysis* 45 27
299 A80 100fr *Longicorn beetle* 85 40
300 A80 130fr *Spider* 1.10 50
Nos. 295-300 (6) 3.22 1.64

1975, Apr. 11 **Typo.** *Perf. 13*

301 A81 50fr multi 45 25

Rotary International, 70th anniversary.

Craterostigma Plantagineum — A82

Flowers: 10fr, Tapinanthus globiferus. 15fr, Commelina forskalaei (vert.). 20fr, Adenium obesum. 25fr, Yellow hibiscus. 30fr, Red hibiscus. 40fr, Kigelia africana.

1975, Sept. 25 **Photo.** *Perf. 13*

302 A82 5fr org & multi 5 5
303 A82 10fr gray bl & multi 8 5
304 A82 15fr yel grn & multi 13 8
305 A82 20fr lt brn & multi 17 10
306 A82 25fr lil & multi 20 12
307 A82 30fr bis & multi 25 13
308 A82 40fr ultra & multi 32 18
Nos. 302-308 (7) 1.20 71

A. G. Bell, Satellite and Waves — A83

1976, June 10 **Litho.** *Perf. 12½*

309 A83 100fr bl, brn & ocher 80 50
310 A83 125fr lt grn, brn & ocher 1.00 60

Centenary of first telephone call by Alexander Graham Bell, Mar. 10, 1876.

Ice Hockey, USSR — A84

Design: 90fr, Ski jump, Karl Schnabl, Austria.

1976, June 21 *Perf. 14*

311 A84 60fr multi 60 30
312 A84 90fr multi 85 35

12th Winter Olympic Games, winners. See Nos. C178-C180.

High Hurdles A85

1976, July 12 **Litho.** *Perf. 13½*

313 A85 45fr multi 45 25

21st Summer Olympic Games, Montreal, Canada.

See Nos. C187-C190.

Mars Landing and Viking Rocket A86

Design (Mars Landing and): 90fr, Viking trajectory, Earth to Mars.

1976, July 23 *Perf. 14*

314 A86 45fr multi 42 25
315 A86 90fr multi 85 42
Nos. 314-315,C191-C193 (5) 6.52 2.97

Viking Mars project.

Robert Koch, Medicine — A87

Design: 90fr, Anatole France, literature.

1976, Dec. 15

316 A87 45fr multi 50 25
317 A87 90fr multi 85 42
Nos. 316-317,C196-C198 (5) 7.05 3.12

Nobel Prize winners.

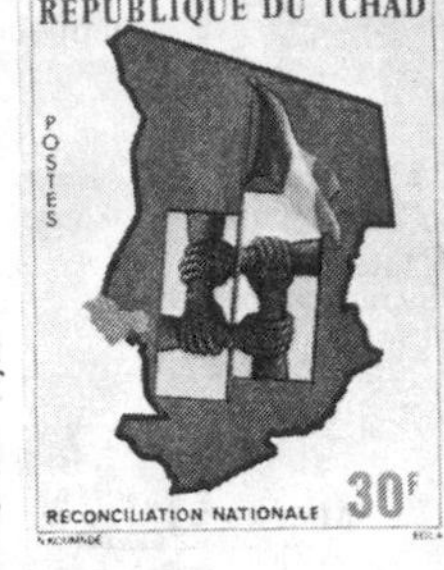

Map and Flag of Chad, Clasped Hands A88

Designs: 60fr, like 30fr. 120fr, Map of Chad, people and various occupations.

1976, Sept. 15 **Litho.** *Perf. 12½x13*

318 A88 30fr multi 25 18
319 A88 60fr org & multi 50 30
320 A88 120fr brn & multi 1.00 65

National reconciliation.

Freed Political Prisoners — A89

Designs: 60fr, Parade of cadets. 120fr, like 30fr.

1976, Sept. 25 **Litho.** *Perf. 12½*

321 A89 30fr bl & multi 25 18
322 A89 60fr blk & multi 50 30
323 A89 120fr red & multi 1.00 65

Revolution of Apr. 13, 1975, first anniversary.

Decorated Calabashes — A90

Designs: Various pyrographed calabashes.

1976, Nov. **Litho.** *Perf. 12½x13*

324 A90 30fr multi 25 18
325 A90 60fr multi 50 30
326 A90 120fr multi 1.00 65

Germany No. C57 and Friedrichshafen, Germany — A91

1977, Mar. 30 *Perf. 14*

327 A91 100fr multi 95 42
Nos. 327,C206-C209 (5) 2.35 1.82

75th anniversary of the Zeppelin.

Elizabeth II in Coronation Regalia and Clergy — A92

Design: 450fr, Elizabeth II and Prince Philip.

1977, June 15 Litho. *Perf. 14x13½*

328 A92 250fr multi 2.75 70

Souvenir Sheet

329 A92 450fr multi 4.75 2.00

25th anniversary of the reign of Elizabeth II. No. 329 has multicolored margin showing Buckingham Palace and heraldic supporters. Size: 110x91mm.

Simon Bolivar — A93

Famous Personalities: 175fr, Joseph J. Roberts. No. 332, Queen Wihelmina of Netherlands. No. 333, Charles de Gaulle. 325fr, King Baudouin and Queen Fabiola of Belgium.

1977, June 15 *Perf. 13½x14*

330 A93 150fr multi 1.40 50
331 A93 175fr multi 1.65 60
332 A93 200fr multi 1.85 65
333 A93 200fr multi 1.85 65
334 A93 325fr multi 3.25 1.00
Nos. 330-334 (5) 10.00 3.40

Post and Telecommunications Emblem — A94

Map of Chad and Waves — A95

REPUBLIQUE DU TCHAD

120F

Society Emblem — A96

Perf. 13 (A94); 12½ (A95); 13½x13 (A96)

1977, Aug. 15 Litho.

335 A94 30fr yel & blk 25 18
336 A95 60fr multi 50 30
337 A96 120fr multi 1.00 65

Telecommunications (30fr); National Telecommunications School, 10th anniversary (60fr); International Telecommunication Society of Chad (120fr).

WHO Emblem and Man (Back Pain) — A97

Designs (WHO Emblem and): 60fr, Woman's head (neck pain; horiz.). 120fr, Leg (knee pain).

Perf. 12½x13, 13x12½

1977, Nov. 10 Engr.

338 A97 30fr multi 25 18
339 A97 60fr multi 50 30
340 A97 120fr multi 1.00 65

World Rheumatism Year.

World Cup Emblems and Saving a Goal — A98

Designs (Argentina '78, World Cup Emblems and): 60fr, Heading the ball. 100fr, Referee whistling a goal. 200fr, World Cup poster. 300fr, Pele. 500fr, Helmut Schoen and Munich stadium.

1977, Nov. 25 Litho. *Perf. 13½*

341 A98 40fr multi 35 15
342 A98 60fr multi 60 27
343 A98 100fr multi 95 42
344 A98 200fr multi 1.90 75
345 A98 300fr multi 3.00 1.15
Nos. 341-345 (5) 6.80 2.74

Souvenir Sheet

346 A98 500fr multi 4.75 1.85

World Cup Soccer Championship, Argentina '78. No. 346 has multicolored margin showing Argentina '78 emblem and stadium. Size: 119x80½mm.

Nos. 328-329 Overprinted in Silver: "ANNIVERSAIRE DU COURONNEMENT 1953-1978"

1978, Sept. 13 *Perf. 14x13½*

347 A92 250fr multi 2.00 1.00

Souvenir Sheet

348 A92 450fr multi 4.00 2.00

25th anniversary of coronation of Queen Elizabeth II. Size of No. 348: 111x92mm.

Abraham and Melchisedek, by Rubens — A99

Rubens Paintings: 120fr, Helene Fourment (vert.). 200fr, David and the Elders of Israel. 300fr, Anne of Austria (vert.). 500fr, Marie de Medicis (vert.).

1978, Nov. 23 Litho. *Perf. 13½*

349 A99 60fr multi 60 30
350 A99 120fr multi 1.20 60
351 A99 200fr multi 2.00 1.00
352 A99 300fr multi 3.00 1.50

Souvenir Sheet

353 A99 500fr multi 5.50 2.75

Peter Paul Rubens (1577-1640). No. 353 has multicolored margin showing entire painting. Size: 78x103mm.

Dürer Portrait A100

Dürer Paintings: 150fr, Jacob Muffel. 250fr, Young Woman. 350fr, Oswolt Krel.

1978, Nov. 23

354 A100 60fr multi 60 30
355 A100 150fr multi 1.50 75
356 A100 250fr multi 2.50 1.25
357 A100 350fr multi 3.50 1.75

Albrecht Dürer (1471-1528), German painter.

Head, Village and Fly — A101

1978, Nov. 28 *Perf. 13*

358 A101 60f multi 60 30

National Health Day.

Nos. 341-346 Overprinted in Silver:
a. 1962 BRESIL-TCHECOSLOVAQUIE / 3-1
b. 1966 / GRANDE BRETAGNE / - ALLEMAGNE (RFA) / 4-2
c. 1970 BRESIL-ITALIE 4-1
d. 1974 ALLEMAGNE (RFA)- / PAY BAS 2-1
e. 1978 / ARGENTINE -/ PAY BAS / 3-1
f. ARGENTINE -PAYS BAS / 3-1

1978, Dec. 30 Litho. *Perf. 13½*

359 A98(a) 40fr multi 40 20
360 A98(b) 60fr multi 60 30
361 A98(c) 100fr multi 1.00 50
362 A98(d) 200fr multi 2.00 1.00
363 A98(e) 300fr multi 3.00 1.50
Nos. 359-363 (5) 7.00 3.50

Souvenir Sheet

364 A98(f) 500fr multi 5.00 2.50

World Soccer Championship winners. Size of No. 364: 119x80½mm.

UPU Emblems, Camel Caravan, Satellites — A102

Design: 150fr, Obus woman and houses, Massa Territory, hibiscus.

1979, June 8 Litho. *Perf. 12x12½*

365 A102 60fr multi 60 30
366 A102 150fr multi 1.50 75

Philexafrique II, Libreville, Gabon, June 8-17. Nos. 365, 366 each printed in sheets of 10 with 5 labels showing exhibition emblem.

Wildlife Fund Emblem and Gazelle A103

Protected Animals: 50fr, Addax. 60fr, Oryx antelope. 100fr, Cheetah. 150fr, Zebra. 300fr, Rhinoceros.

1979, Sept. 15 Litho. *Perf. 14½*

367 A103 40fr multi 40 20
368 A103 50fr multi 50 25
369 A103 60fr multi 60 30
370 A103 100fr multi 1.00 50
371 A103 150fr multi 1.50 75
372 A103 300fr multi 3.00 1.50
Nos. 367-372 (6) 7.00 3.50

Souvenir Sheet

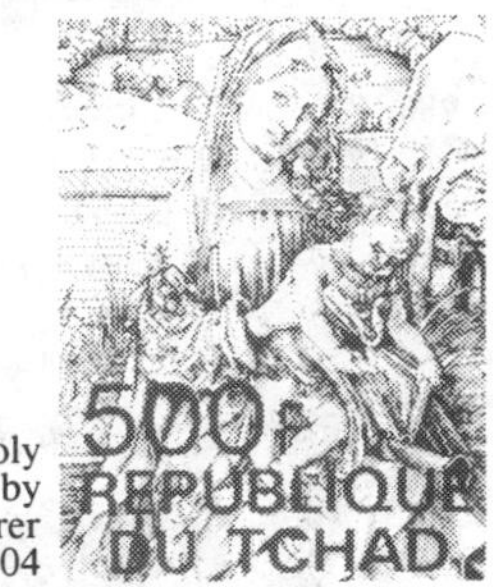

Holy Family, by Dürer A104

1979, Sept. 1 *Perf. 13½*

373 A104 500fr brn & dl red 5.50 2.75

Albrecht Dürer (1471-1528), German engraver and painter. No. 373 has brown and dull red margin showing entire etching. Size: 90x115mm.

Boy and Handpainted Doors — A105

IYC Emblem and: 75fr, Oriental girl. 100fr, Caucasian girl, doves. 150fr, African boys. 250fr, Pencil and outlines of child's hands.

1979, Sept. 19 Litho. *Perf. 13½*

374 A105 65fr multi 65 32
375 A105 75fr multi 75 38
376 A105 100fr multi 1.00 50
377 A105 150fr multi 1.50 75

Souvenir Sheet

378 A105 20fr multi 2.75 1.40

International Year of the Child. No. 378 has multicolored margin showing IYC emblem, children and trains. Size: 103x78mm.

Nos. 314-315 Overprinted "ALUNISSAGE/APOLLO XI/JUILLET 1969" and Emblem

1979, Nov. 26 Litho. *Perf. 13½x14*

379 A86 45fr multi 45 22
380 A86 90fr multi 90 45
Nos. 379-380,C240-C242 (5) 6.85 3.42

Apollo 11 moon landing, 10th anniversary.

Ski Jump, Lake Placid '80 Emblem A106

Lake Placid '80 Emblem and: 20fr, Slalom (vert.). 40fr, Biathlon (vert.). 150fr, Women's slalom (vert.). 350fr, Cross-country skiing. 500fr, Downhill skiing.

1979, Dec. 18 *Perf. 14½*
381 A106 20fr multi 22 10
382 A106 40fr multi 45 20
383 A106 60fr multi 65 30
384 A106 150fr multi 1.65 75
385 A106 350fr multi 3.75 1.75
386 A106 500fr multi 5.50 2.50
Nos. 381-386 (6) 12.22 5.60

13th Winter Olympic Games, Lake Placid, N.Y., Feb. 12-24, 1980.

Jet over Map of Africa A107

1980, Feb. 20 Litho. *Perf. 12½*
387 A107 15fr yel & multi 15 8
388 A107 30fr bl & multi 30 15
389 A107 60fr red & multi 60 30

ASECNA (Air Safety Board), 20th anniversary.

1982 World Cup Soccer Championships, Spain — A108

1982 Litho. *Perf. 13½*
390 A108 30fr Hungary 12 6
391 A108 40fr Italy 16 8
392 A108 50fr Algeria 20 10
393 A108 60fr Argentina 25 12
Nos. 390-393,C258-C259 (6) 2.30 1.14

21st Birthday of Princess Diana A109

1982, July 2 Litho. *Perf. 13½*
395 A109 30fr 1961 30 15
396 A109 40fr 1965 40 20
397 A109 50fr 1967 50 25
398 A109 60fr 1975 60 30
Nos. 395-398,C260-C261 (6) 5.60 2.80

1984 Olympic Games, Los Angeles — A110

1982, Aug. 2 Litho. *Perf. 13½*
399 A110 30fr Gymnast 30 15
400 A110 40fr Equestrian 40 20
401 A110 50fr Judo 50 25
402 A110 60fr High jump 60 30
403 A110 80fr Hurdles 80 40
404 A110 300fr Woman gymnast 3.00 1.50
Nos. 399-404 (6) 5.60 2.80

Souvenir Sheet

405 A110 500fr Relay race 5.00 2.50

No. 405 contains one stamp (56x39mm.); multicolored margin continues design. Size: 110x82mm. Nos. 403-405 airmail.

Scouting Year — A111

Scouts from various countries.

1982, July 15
406 A111 30fr West Germany 30 15
407 A111 40fr Upper Volta 40 20
408 A111 50fr Mali 50 25
409 A111 60fr Scotland 60 30
410 A111 80fr Kuwait 80 40
411 A111 300fr Chad 3.00 1.50
Nos. 401-411 (11) 15.50 7.75

Souvenir Sheet

412 A111 500fr Chad, diff. 5.00 2.50

No. 412 contains one stamp (53x35mm.); multicolored margin shows banner around globe. Size: 110x75mm. Nos. 410-412 airmail.

Nos. 395-398, C260-C262 Overprinted: "21 JUIN 1982 / WILLIAM ARTHUR PHILIP LOUIS/ PRINCE DE GALLES"

1982, Oct. 4 Litho. *Perf. 13½*
413 A109 30fr multi 30 15
414 A109 40fr multi 40 20
415 A109 50fr multi 50 25
416 A109 60fr multi 60 30
417 A109 80fr multi 80 40
418 A109 300fr multi 3.00 1.50
Nos. 413-418 (6) 5.60 2.80

Souvenir Sheet

419 A109 500fr multi 5.00 2.50

Birth of Prince William of Wales, June 21. Nos. 417-419 airmail.

1982 World Cup — A112

Various players and flags.

1982, Nov. 30
420 A112 30fr multi 30 15
421 A112 40fr multi 40 20
422 A112 50fr multi 50 25
423 A112 60fr multi 60 30
424 A112 80fr multi 80 40
425 A112 300fr multi 3.00 1.50
Nos. 420-425 (6) 5.60 2.80

Souvenir Sheet

426 A112 500fr multi 5.00 2.50

No. 426 contains one stamp (56x32mm.). Size: 110x80mm. Nos. 424-426 airmail.

Chess Champions — A113

1982, Dec. 24
427 A113 30fr Philidor 30 15
428 A113 40fr Paul Morphy 40 20
429 A113 50fr Howard Staunton 50 25
430 A113 60fr Jean-Paul Capablanca 60 30
431 A113 80fr Boris Spassky 80 40
432 A113 300fr Anatole Karpov 3.00 1.50
Nos. 427-432 (6) 5.60 2.80

Souvenir Sheet

433 A113 500fr Victor Korchnoi 5.00 2.50

No. 433 contains one stamp (53x35mm.). Size: 98x80mm. Nos. 431-433 airmail.

2nd UN Conference on Peaceful Uses of Outer Space, Vienna, Aug. 9-21 A114

Inventors and Satellites 30fr, K.E. Tsiolkovsky, Soyuz. 40fr, RH Goddard, space telescope design. 50fr, Korolev, ultraviolet telescope. 60fr, von Braun, Columbia space shuttle. 80fr, Esnault Pelterie, Ariana rocket. 300fr, H. Oberth, orbital space station. 500fr, Pres. Kennedy, Apollo 11 badge, lunar rover.

1983, Jan. 31 Litho. *Perf. 13½*
434 A114 30fr multi 30 15
435 A114 40fr multi 40 20
436 A114 50fr multi 50 25
437 A114 60fr multi 60 30
438 A114 80fr multi 80 40
439 A114 300fr multi 3.00 1.50
Nos. 434-439 (6) 5.60 2.80

Souvenir Sheet

440 A114 500fr multi 5.00 2.50

No. 440 contains one stamp (42x50mm.); multicolored margin continues design. Size: 85x85mm. Nos. 438-440 airmail.

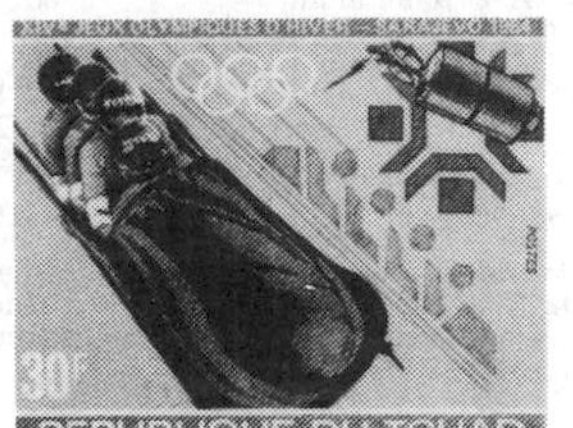

Bobsledding — A115

1983, Apr. 25 Litho. *Perf. 13½*
441 A115 30fr shown 25 15
442 A115 40fr Speed skating 30 20
443 A115 50fr Cross-country skiing 40 25
444 A115 60fr Hockey 50 30
445 A115 80fr Ski jumping 65 40
446 A115 300fr Downhill skiing 2.50 1.50
Nos. 441-446 (6) 4.60 2.80

Souvenir Sheet

447 A115 500fr Figure skating 4.00 2.50

14th Winter Olympic Games, Sarajevo, Jugoslavia, Feb. 8-19, 1984. Nos. 445-447 airmail No. 447 has multicolored margin showing figure skating scenes. Size: 100x80mm.

First Manned Balloon Flight, 200th Anniv. A116

Designs: 25fr, Hot air balloon, Montgolfier Brothers. 45fr, Captive balloon, Pilatre De Rozier. 50fr, First parachute descent, Jacques Garnerin. 60fr, Chelsea balloon, J.P. Blanchard.

1983, May 30 Litho. *Perf. 13½*
448 A116 25fr multi 25 12
449 A116 45fr multi 45 22
450 A116 50fr multi 50 2
451 A116 60fr multi 60 3
Nos. 448-451,C268-C269 (6) 3.85 1.8

1984 Olympics. Los Angeles A117

1983, Nov. 15 Litho. *Perf. 13½*
452 A117 25fr Kayak 12
453 A117 45fr Long jump 12 1
454 A117 50fr Boxing 24 1
455 A117 60fr Discus 28 1
456 A117 80fr Running 38 2
457 A117 350fr Equestrian 1.75 9
Nos. 452-457 (6) 2.89 1.5

Souvenir Sheet

458 A117 500fr Gymnastics 2.50 1.2

No. 458 has multicolored margin showing various gymnastics. Size: 90x93mm. 80fr 350fr, 500fr airmail.

Nos. 427-433 Overprinted: "60e ANNIVERSAIRE FEDERATION / MONDIALE D'ECHECS 1924-1984"

1983, Dec. 27 Litho. *Perf. 13½*
459 A113 30fr multi 14
460 A113 40fr multi 20 1
461 A113 50fr multi 24 1
462 A113 60fr multi 28 1
463 A113 80fr multi 38 2
464 A113 300fr multi 1.50 7
Nos. 459-464 (6) 2.74 1.3

Souvenir Sheet

465 A113 500fr multi 2.50 1.2

World Chess Fedn., 60th anniv.

Nos. 406-412 Ovptd. with Emblem for the 15th World Scout Jamboree, Alberta, Canada, 1983.

1983, Dec. 27 Litho. *Perf. 13½*
466 A111 30fr multi 14
467 A111 40fr multi 20 1
468 A111 50fr multi 24 1
469 A111 60fr multi 28 1
470 A111 80fr multi 38 2
471 A111 300fr multi 1.50 7
Nos. 466-471 (6) 2.74 1.3

Souvenir Sheet

472 A111 500fr multi 2.50 1.2

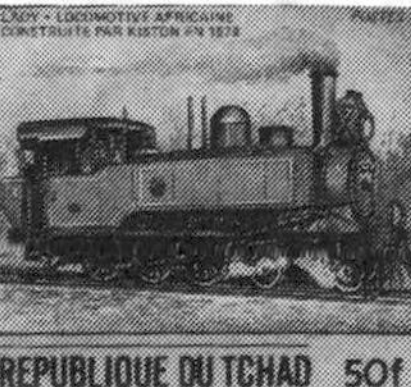

Locomotive "Lady," 1879 A118

1984, Mar. 15
473 A118 50fr shown 20 10
474 A118 200fr Sailboat, Lake Chad 95 48
475 A118 300fr Graf Zeppelin 1.40 70
476 A118 350fr Renault desert transport, 1930 1.65 85
477 A118 400fr Bloch 120 monoplane 1.90 95
478 A118 500fr Air Africa DC-8 2.25 1.10
Nos. 473-478 (6) 8.35 4.18

Souvenir Sheet

479 A118 600fr Intelsat V satellite 2.75 1.40

Nos. 477-479 airmail. No. 479 has multicolored margin continuing design. Size: 85x110mm.

Liberation, 2nd Anniv. — A119

Pres. Hissein Habre — A120

1984, June 6 *Perf. 12½*
480 A119 50fr multi 24 12

1984, June 18 *Perf. 12½x13*
481 A120 125fr multi 60 30

Anniversaries and Events — A121

Designs: 50fr, Pres. Habre, civil war martyrs. 200fr, Paul Harris, Rotary Intl. headquarters, Illinois. 300fr, Alfred Nobel, will establishing fund for Prizes. 350fr, Raphael, detail from Virgin with Child and St. John the Baptist. 400fr, Rembrandt, detail from The Holy Family. 500fr, J.W. Goethe, scene from Faust. 600fr, Rubens, detail from Helene Forement and Her Two Children.

1984, Jan. 16 **Litho.** *Perf. 13½*
482 A121 50fr multi 20 10
483 A121 200fr multi 95 48
484 A121 300fr multi 1.40 70
485 A121 350fr multi 1.65 85
486 A121 400fr multi 1.90 95
487 A121 500fr multi 2.25 1.10
Nos. 482-487 (6) 8.35 4.18

Souvenir Sheet

488 A121 600fr multi 2.75 1.40

Nos. 486-488 are airmail. No. 488 has multicolored margin picturing Rubens painting crucifixion. Size: 79x87mm.

Homage to Our Martyred Dead — A122

1984, Feb. 22 **Litho.** *Perf. 13½*
500 A122 50fr multi 20 10
501 A122 80fr multi 38 20
502 A122 120fr multi 55 28
503 A122 200fr multi 95 45
504 A122 250fr multi 1.25 65
Nos. 500-504 (5) 3.33 1.68

Nos. 503-504 airmail.

World Communications Year — A123

1984, Feb. 29 **Litho.** *Perf. 13½*
505 A123 50fr sil & multi 20 10
506 A123 60fr sil & multi 28 14
507 A123 70fr sil & multi 32 16
508 A123 125fr sil & multi 60 30
509 A123 250fr sil & multi 1.25 65
Nos. 505-509 (5) 2.65 1.35

Nos. 508-509 airmail.

Anniversaries and Events — A123a

Designs: 50fr, Durer, detail from Madonna of the Rosary. 200fr, Henri Dunant, Red Cross founder, Battle of Solferino. 300fr, Early telephone, Goonhilly Downs Satellite Station, Britain. 350fr, J.F. Kennedy, Neil Armstrong's first step on Moon, 1969. 400fr, Europe-Africa Satellite infrared photograph. 500fr, Prince Charles and Lady Diana.

1984
510 A123a 50fr multi 20 10
511 A123a 200fr multi 90 45
512 A123a 300fr multi 1.40 70
513 A123a 350fr multi 1.65 85
514 A123a 400fr multi 1.90 75
515 A123a 500fr multi 2.50 1.25
a. Souvenir sheet of one 3.50 1.75
Nos. 510-515 (6) 8.55 4.10

Nos. 514-515 are airmail. No. 515a has multicolored decorative margin picturing cherubs. Size: 110x60mm. A 600fr souvenir sheet picturing a wedding photograph of Prince Charles and Lady Diana exists.

Development of Communications — A123b

Ships and locomotives.

1984, Aug. 1 **Litho.** *Perf. 12½*
517 A123b 90fr Indiaman, East India Co. 40 20
518 A123b 100fr Nord 701, 1885 45 22
519 A123b 125fr Vera Cruz 60 30
520 A123b 150fr Columbia, 1888 70 35
521 A123b 200fr Carlisle Castle 90 45
522 A123b 250fr Rete Mediterranea, 1900 1.25 65
523 A123b 300fr Britannia 1.40 70
524 A123b 350fr Mav 114 1.65 85
Nos. 517-524 (8) 7.35 3.72

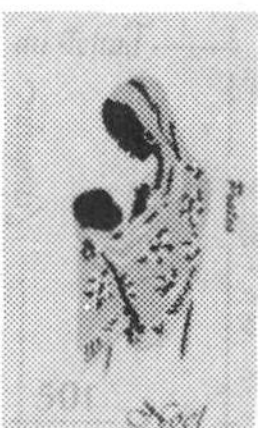

Christmas — A124

1984, Dec. 28 **Litho.** *Perf. 13*
525 A124 50fr lt bl & org brn 22 12
526 A124 60fr ver & org brn 25 14
527 A124 80fr emer & org brn 34 18
528 A124 85fr rose lil & org brn 35 18
529 A124 100fr org yel & org brn 42 22
530 A124 135fr dp bl vio & org brn 58 30
Nos. 525-530 (6) 2.16 1.14

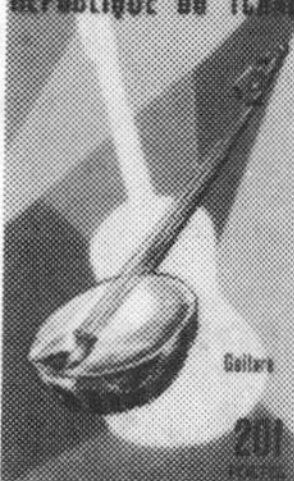

European Music Year A125

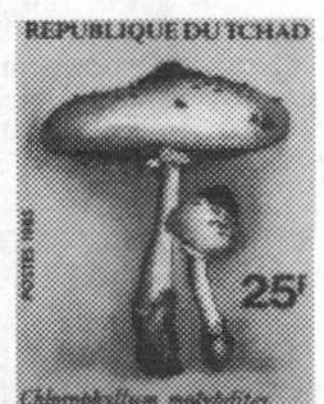

Mushrooms A126

Instruments.

1985, Apr. 30 **Litho.** *Perf. 12x12½*
531 A125 20fr Guitar 6 5
532 A125 25fr Harp 8 5
533 A125 30fr Xylophone 10 5
534 A125 50fr Shoulder drum 20 10
535 A125 70fr like #534 28 14
536 A125 80fr like #532 32 16
537 A125 100fr like #531 40 20
538 A125 250fr like #533 1.00 50
Nos. 531-538 (8) 2.44 1.25

1985, May 15 **Litho.** *Perf. 12½*
539 A126 25fr Chlorophyllum molybdites 8 5
540 A126 30fr Tulostoma volvulatum 10 5
541 A126 50fr Lentinus tuberregium 20 10
542 A126 70fr like #541 28 14
543 A126 80fr Podaxis pistillaris 32 16
544 A126 100fr like #539 40 20
Nos. 539-544 (6) 1.38 70

Anniversaries and Events — A127

Designs: 25fr, Abraham Lincoln. 45fr, Henri Dunant, Geneva birthplace and red cross. 50fr, Gottlieb Daimler, 1887 Motor Carriage. 60fr, Louis Bleriot, Bleriot XI monoplane, 1909. 80fr, Paul Harris, Chicago site of Rotary Intl. founding. 350fr, Auguste Piccard, bathyscaphe Trieste, 1953. 600fr, Anatoly Karpov, 1981 world chess champion.

1985, May 25 **Litho.** *Perf. 13½*
545 A127 25fr multi 10 5
546 A127 45fr multi 18 8
547 A127 50fr multi 20 10
548 A127 60fr multi 25 12
549 A127 80fr multi 35 18
550 A127 350fr multi 1.40 70
551 A127 600fr multi 2.75 1.40
Nos. 545-551 (7) 5.23 2.63

Nos. 548-551 are airmail.

Souvenir sheets of one exist for Nos. 545-551. A 1500fr stamp picturing the Paul Harris Commemorative Medal exists.

Intl. Youth Year — A128

1985, May 30 **Litho.** *Perf. 13*
552 A128 70fr Development levels, vert. 28 14
553 A128 200fr Globe 80 40

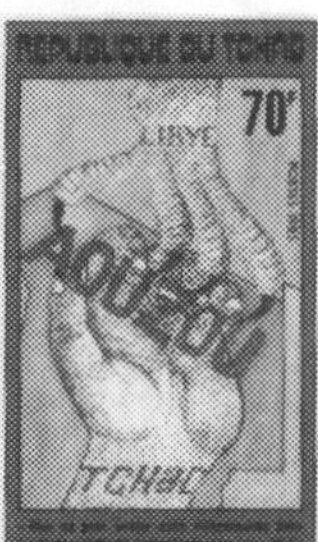

A129

3rd Anniv. of the Republic A130

Perf. 13, 12½x13
1985, June 7 **Litho.**
554 A129 70fr Hand, claw 28 14
555 A129 70fr Hands, map 28 14
556 A130 70fr Pres. Hissein Habre 28 14
557 A129 110fr like #554 45 22
558 A129 110fr like #555 45 22
559 A130 110fr like #556 45 22
Nos. 554-559 (6) 2.19 1.08

Audubon Birth Bicent. A131

Mammals A132

1985, July 20 **Engr.** *Perf. 13*
560 A131 70fr Stork 30 15
561 A131 110fr Ostrich 50 25
562 A131 150fr Marabou 70 35
563 A131 200fr Snake eagle 90 45

Souvenir Sheet

564 A131 500fr like 200fr 2.25 1.10

No. 564 has sepia and olive green margin picturing various species. Size: 130x100mm.

1985, Oct. 1
565 A132 50fr Waterbuck 25 12
566 A132 70fr Kudus, horiz. 58 28
567 A132 250fr Shaggy mouflon 1.25 65

Souvenir Sheet

568 A132 500fr White rhinoceros 2.75 1.40

No. 568 has Prussian blue, henna brown and sepia margin continuing the design. Size: 130x100mm.

UN, 40th Anniv. — A133

1985, Oct. 24
569 A133 200fr brt bl, red & brn 90 45

Chad Admission to UN, 25th Anniv. — A134

1985, Oct. 24
570 A134 300fr red, brt bl & yel 1.65 80

President's Visit to the Nation's Interior A135

1986, June 7 Litho. *Perf. 12½x13*
571 A135 100fr multi 55 28
572 A135 170fr multi 95 48
573 A135 200fr multi 1.10 55

SEMI-POSTAL STAMPS

Anti-Malaria Issue
Common Design Type
Perf. 12½x12

1962, Apr. 7 Engr. Unwmk.
B1 CD108 25fr + 5fr org 65 65

Issued for the World Health Organization drive to eradicate malaria.

Freedom from Hunger Issue
Common Design Type

1963, Mar. 21 *Perf. 13*
B2 CD112 25fr + 5fr dk grn, dk bl & brn 65 65

Red Cross, Mother and Children — SP1

1974, Oct. 2 Photo. *Perf. 12½x13*
B3 SP1 30fr + 10fr multi 35 30

Red Cross of Chad, first anniversary.

AIR POST STAMPS

Olympic Games Issue
French Equatorial Africa No. C37 Surcharged in Red

Unwmk.
1960, Dec. 15 Engr. *Perf. 13*
C1 AP8 250fr on 500fr grnsh blk, blk & sl 9.00 9.00

Issued to commemorate the 17th Olympic Games, Rome, Aug. 25-Sept. 11. Surcharge 46mm. wide; illustration reduced.

Red Bishops — AP1

Discus Thrower — AP2

Designs (birds in pairs): 100fr, Scarlet-chested sunbird. 200fr, African paradise flycatcher. 250fr, Malachite kingfisher. 500fr, Nubian carmine bee-eater.

1961-63 Unwmk. Engr. *Perf. 13*
C2 AP1 50fr dk grn, mag & blk 60 25
C3 AP1 100fr multi 1.50 70
C4 AP1 200fr multi 3.00 1.25
C5 AP1 250fr dk bl, grn & dp org ('63) 4.00 2.00
C6 AP1 500fr multi 8.50 4.00
Nos. C2-C6 (5) 17.60 8.20

Air Afrique Issue
Common Design Type

1962, Feb. 17 Unwmk. *Perf. 13*
C7 CD107 25fr lt bl, org brn & blk 40 18

Issued to commemorate the founding of Air Afrique (African Airlines).

Abidjan Games Issue

1962, July 21 Photo. *Perf. 12x12½*
C8 AP2 100fr brn, lt grn & blk 1.50 85

African Postal Union Issue
Common Design Type

1963, Sept. 8 Unwmk. *Perf. 12½*
C9 CD114 85fr dk bl, ocher & red 1.00 45

Air Afrique Issue, 1963
Common Design Type

1963, Nov. 19 *Perf. 13x12*
C10 CD115 50fr multi 90 60

Europafrica Issue
Common Design Type

1963, Nov. 30 Photo. *Perf. 12x13*
C11 CD116 50fr dp grn, yel & dk brn 75 55

Mail Truck and Broussard Plane — AP4

Unwmk.
1963, Dec. 16 Engr. *Perf. 13*
C12 AP4 100fr sl grn, ultra & red brn 1.50 50

Chiefs of State Issue

Map and Presidents of Chad, Congo, Gabon and Central African Republic AP4a

1964, June 23 Photo. *Perf. 12½*
C13 AP4a 100fr multi 1.35 65

See note after Central African Republic No. C19.

Europafrica Issue, 1964

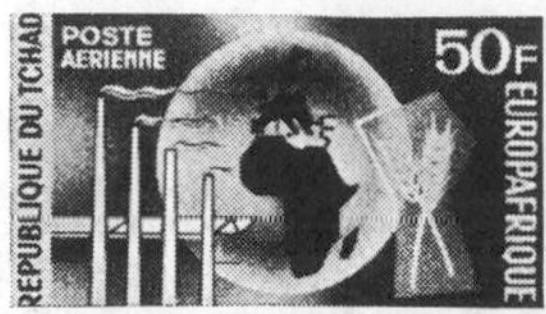

Globe and Emblems of Industry and Agriculture — AP5

1964, July 20 *Perf. 13x12*
C14 AP5 50fr brn, pur & dp org 65 45

See note after Cameroun No. 402.

Soccer — AP6

Designs: 50fr, Javelin throw (vert.). 100fr, High jump (vert.). 200fr, Runners.

1964, Aug. 12 Engr. *Perf. 13*
C15 AP6 25fr yel grn, sl grn & org brn 35 25
C16 AP6 50fr org brn, ind & brt bl 75 50
C17 AP6 100fr blk, red & brt grn 1.50 1.00
C18 AP6 200fr bis, blk & car 3.00 1.65
a. Min. sheet of 4 6.00 6.00

Issued for the 18th Olympic Games, Tokyo, Oct. 10-25, 1964. No. C18a contains one each of Nos. C15-C18. Size: 191x99mm.

Communications Symbols — AP7

1964, Nov. 2 Litho. *Perf. 12½x13*
C19 AP7 25fr lil, dk brn & lt red brn 40 20

Issued to commemorate the Pan-African and Malagasy Posts and Telecommunications Congress, Cairo, Oct. 24-Nov. 6.

President John F. Kennedy — AP8

1964, Nov. 3 Photo. *Perf. 12½*
C20 AP8 100fr multi 1.75 1.25
a. Souv. sheet of 4 7.00 7.00

Issued in memory of Pres. John F. Kennedy (1917-1963). No. C20a contains 4 No. C20; black marginal inscription. Size: 90x129mm.

ICY Emblem — AP9

1965, July 5 Photo. *Perf. 13*
C21 AP9 100fr multi 1.50 85

International Cooperation Year, 1965.

Abraham Lincoln — AP10

1965, Sept. 7 Unwmk. *Perf. 13*
C22 AP10 100fr multi 1.50 85

Centenary of death of Abraham Lincoln.

Musical Instrument Type of Regular Issue

Design: 100fr, Xylophone (marimba).

1965, Oct. 26 Engr. *Perf. 13*
Size: 48x27mm.
C23 A18 100fr ocher, brt bl & vio bl 1.35 45

Winston Churchill — AP11

1965, Nov. 23 Engr. *Perf. 13*
C24 AP11 50fr dk grn & blk 75 35

Issued in memory of Sir Winston Spencer Churchill (1874-1965), statesman and World War II leader.

Condition is the all-important factor of price. Prices quoted are for stamps in fine condition.

Dr. Albert Schweitzer and Outstretched Hands — AP12

1966, Feb. 15 Photo. *Perf. 12½*
C25 AP12 100fr multi 1.50 75

Issued in memory of Dr. Albert Schweitzer (1875-1965), medical missionary, theologian and musician.

Air Afrique Issue, 1966
Common Design Type

1966, Aug. 31 Photo. *Perf. 13*
C26 CD123 30fr yel grn, blk & gray 45 25

Issued to commemorate the introduction of DC-8F planes by Air Afrique.

White-throated Bee-eater — AP13

Birds: 50fr, Blue-eared glossy starling. 200fr, African pygmy kingfisher. 250fr, Red-throated bee-eater. 500fr, Little green bee-eater.

1966-67 Photo. *Perf. 13x12½*
C27 AP13 50fr gold & multi 50 25
C28 AP13 100fr bluish gray & multi 1.00 45
C29 AP13 200fr grnsh gray & multi 2.00 1.00
C30 AP13 250fr pale bl & multi 2.50 1.20
C31 AP13 500fr pale sal & multi 5.00 2.50
Nos. C27-C31 (5) 11.00 5.40

Issue dates: 100fr, 200fr, 500fr, Oct. 18, 1966. Others, Mar. 21, 1967.

Congress Hall — AP14

1967, Jan. 5 Photo. *Perf. 12½*
C32 AP14 25fr multi 40 20

Opening of the new Congress Hall.

Breguet 19 Biplane — AP15

Planes: 30fr, Latecoère 631 hydroplane. 50fr, Douglas DC-3. 100fr, Piper Cherokee 6.

1967, Aug. 1 Engr. *Perf. 13*
C33 AP15 25fr sky bl, sl grn & lt brn 40 20
C34 AP15 30fr sky bl, ind & grn 45 25
C35 AP15 50fr sky bl, ol bis & sl grn 75 40
C36 AP15 100fr dk bl, sl grn & dk red 1.50 75

First anniversary of Air Chad.

African Postal Union Issue, 1967
Common Design Type

1967, Sept. 9 Engr. *Perf. 13*
C37 CD124 100fr ol, brt pink & red brn 1.35 70

Rock Painting Type of Regular Issue

Rock Paintings: 100fr, Masked dancers. 125fr, Rabbit hunt.

1967, Dec. 19 Engr. *Perf. 13*
Size: 48x27mm.
C38 AP32 100fr brt grn, sal & mar 1.50 65
C39 AP32 125fr ultra, sal & mar 1.85 90

Issued to commemorate the Balloud expedition in the Ennedi Mountains.

Downhill Skiing — AP16

Design: 100fr, Ski jump (vert.).

1968, Feb. 5 Engr. *Perf. 13*
C40 AP16 30fr red lil, brt grn & dk ol 45 25
C41 AP16 100fr vio bl, brt bl & sl grn 1.50 85

Issued to commemorate the 10th Winter Olympic Games, Grenoble, France, Feb. 6-18.

Konrad Adenauer — AP17

1968, Mar. 19 Photo. *Perf. 12½*
C42 AP17 52fr grn, dk brn & lt lil 80 45
a. Souv. sheet of 4 3.25 3.25

Issued in memory of Konrad Adenauer (1876-1967), chancellor of West Germany (1949-63). No. C42a contains four No. C42. Margin with black inscription and 1967 CEPT (Europa) emblem. Size: 120½x169mm.

The Snake Charmer, by Henri Rousseau — AP18

Design: 130fr, "War" by Henri Rousseau.

1968, May 14 Photo. *Perf. 13½*
Size: 41x41mm.
C43 AP18 100fr ultra & multi 1.50 60
Size: 48x35mm.
Perf. 12½
C44 AP18 130fr brn & multi 1.80 80

Hurdlers — AP19

Design: 80fr, Relay race.

1968, Oct. 16 Engr. *Perf. 13*
C45 AP19 32fr cop red, grn & choc 50 20
C46 AP19 80fr ultra, choc & car 1.00 30

Issued to commemorate the 19th Olympic Games, Mexico City, Oct. 12-27.

PHILEXAFRIQUE Issue

The Actor Wolf (Bernard), by Jacques L. David AP20

1969, Jan. 15 Photo. *Perf. 12½*
C47 AP20 100fr multi 1.50 90

Issued to publicize PHILEXAFRIQUE, Philatelic Exhibition in Abidjan, Feb. 14-23. Printed with alternating lilac rose label.

2nd PHILEXAFRIQUE Issue
Common Design Type

Design: 50fr, Chad No. J12 and Moundang Dancers.

1969, Feb. 14 Engr. *Perf. 13*
C48 CD128 50fr red, brt bl, brn & grn 75 50

Issued to commemorate the opening of PHILEXAFRIQUE, Abidjan, Feb. 14.

Gustav Nachtigal and Tibesti Gorge, 1869 — AP21

Design: No. C50, Heinrich Barth and Lake Chad, 1851.

1969, Feb. 17
C49 AP21 100fr vio bl, dk brn & brn 1.25 35
C50 AP21 100fr grn, pur & bl 1.25 35

Issued to honor the German explorers Gustav Nachtigal (1834-1885) and Heinrich Barth (1821-1865), and to commemorate the state visit of the President of West Germany Heinrich Lubke.

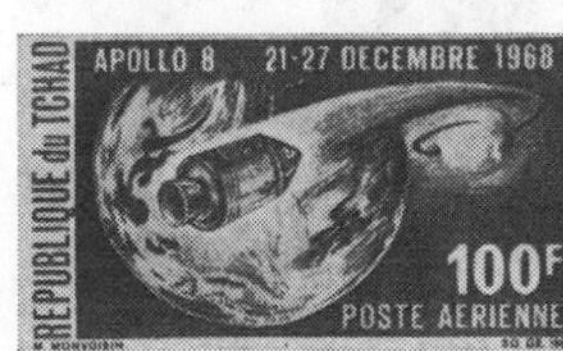

Apollo 8, Earth and Moon — AP22

1969, Apr. 10 Photo. *Perf. 13*
C51 AP22 100fr multi 1.25 65

Issued to commemorate the U.S. Apollo 8 mission, the first men in orbit around the moon, Dec. 21-27, 1968.

Mahatma Gandhi — AP23

Portraits: No. C53, John F. Kennedy. No. C54, Rev. Dr. Martin Luther King, Jr. No. C55, Robert F. Kennedy.

1969, May 20 Photo. *Perf. 12½*
C52 AP23 50fr blk & lt grn 65 35
C53 AP23 50fr blk & tan 65 35
C54 AP23 50fr blk & pink 65 35
C55 AP23 50fr blk & lt vio bl 65 35
a. Souv. sheet of 4 3.00 3.00

Issued to honor exponents of non-violence. No. C55a contains one each of Nos. C52-C55. Black marginal inscription. Size: 120x159mm.

Presidents Tombalbaye and Mobutu, Map and Flags of Chad and Congo — AP24

Embossed on Gold Foil

1969 *Die-cut; Perf. 13½*
C56 AP24 1000fr gold, dk bl & red 16.00 16.00

Issued to commemorate the first anniversary of the establishment of the Union of Central African States, comprising Chad, Congo Democratic Republic and Central African Republic.

Napoleon Visiting Hospital, by Alexandre Veron-Bellecourt — AP25

Paintings: 85fr, Battle of Wagram, by Horace Vernet. 130fr, Battle of Austerlitz, by Francois Pascal Gerard.

1969, July 23 Photo. *Perf. 12x12½*
C57 AP25 30fr multi 60 45
C58 AP25 85fr multi 1.50 1.10
C59 AP25 130fr multi 2.50 1.75

Bicentenary of birth of Napoleon I.

A little time given to the study of the arrangement of the Scott Catalogue can make it easier to use effectively.

Apollo 11 Issue

Astronaut on Moon — AP26

Embossed on Gold Foil

1969, Oct. 17 ***Die-cut; Perf. 13½***

C60 AP26 1000fr gold	16.00	16.00

See note after Algeria No. 427.

Village Life, by Goto Narcisse — AP27

Designs: No. C62, Women at the Market, by Iba N'Diaye. No. C63, Woman with Flowers, by Iba N'Diaye (vert.).

1970 Photo. ***Perf. 12x12½, 12½x12***

C61 AP27 100fr multi	1.10	30
C62 AP27 250fr grn & multi	3.00	70
C63 AP27 250fr brn & multi	3.00	70

Issue dates: Mar. 17, 100fr. Aug. 28, Nos. C62-C63.

EXPO Emblem and Osaka Print — AP28

Designs (EXPO Emblem and): 100fr, Tower of the Sun. 125fr, Osaka print (diff. design).

1970, June 30 Engr. ***Perf. 13***

C64 AP28 50fr bl, red brn & sl grn	70	18
C65 AP28 100fr red, yel grn & Prus bl	1.35	28
C66 AP28 125fr blk, dk red & bis	1.60	40

Issued to publicize EXPO '70 International Exhibition, Osaka, Japan, Mar. 15-Sept. 13.

Nos. C28-C30 Surcharged in Carmine with New Value and Bars and Overprinted:
a. "APOLLO XI / 1er debarquement sur la lune / 20 juillet 1969"
b. "APOLLO XII / Exploration de la lune / 19 novembre 1969"
c. "APOLLO XIII / Exploit spatial / 11-17 avril 1970"

1970, July 9 Photo. ***Perf. 13x12½***

C67 AP13 (a) 50fr on 100fr multi	65	40
C68 AP13 (b) 100fr on 200fr multi	1.30	60
C69 AP13 (c) 125fr on 250fr multi	1.60	80

Space missions of Apollo 11, 12 and 13.

DC-8 "Fort Lamy" over Airport — AP29

1970, Aug. 5 ***Perf. 12½***

C70 AP29 30fr dk sl grn & multi	40	15

The Visitation, Venetian School, 15th Century AP30

Paintings, Venetian School: 25fr, Nativity, 15th century. 30fr, Virgin and Child, c. 1350.

1970, Dec. 15 Photo. ***Perf. 12½x12***

C71 AP30 20fr gold & multi	30	15
C72 AP30 25fr gold & multi	32	20
C73 AP30 30fr gold & multi	40	25

Christmas 1970. See Nos. C105-C108.

Post Office Mauritius and Emblem AP31

Designs (PHILEXOCAM Emblem and): 20fr, Tuscany No. 23. 30fr, France No. 8. 60fr, United States No. 2. 80fr, Japan No. 8. 100fr, Saxony No. 1.

1971, Jan. 23 Engr. ***Perf. 13***

C74 AP31 10fr lt bl grn, bis & dk bl	15	5
C75 AP31 20fr brt grn, blk & bis	25	8
C76 AP31 30fr mar, blk & org brn	40	15
C77 AP31 60fr car lake, org brn & blk	70	25
C78 AP31 80fr bl, bis brn & dl bl	90	38
C79 AP31 100fr bl, dl bl & bis brn	1.35	45
a. Souvenir sheet of 6	4.00	4.00
Nos. C74-C79 (6)	3.75	1.36

Publicity for PHILEXOCAM, philatelic exhibition, Fort Lamy, Jan. 23-30. No. C79a contains one each of Nos. C74-C79 with orange brown marginal inscription. Size: 158x130mm.

Gamal Abdel Nasser — AP32

1971, Feb. 16 Photo. ***Perf. 12½***

C80 AP32 75fr multi	75	20

In memory of Gamal Abdel Nasser (1918-1970), President of Egypt.

Presidents Mobutu, Bokassa and Tombalbaye — AP33

1971, Apr. 28 Photo. ***Perf. 13***

C81 AP33 100fr multi	1.00	50

Return of Central African Republic to the United States of Central Africa which also includes Congo Democratic Republic and Chad.

Map of Africa, Communications Network and Symbols — AP34

1971, May 17 Engr. ***Perf. 13***

C82 AP34 125fr ultra, sl grn & brn red	1.40	30

Pan-African telecommunications system.

Boys Around Campfire, Torii — AP35

1971, Aug. 24 Photo. ***Perf. 12½***

C83 AP35 250fr multi	2.75	85

13th Boy Scout World Jamboree, Asagiri Plain, Japan, Aug. 2-10.

White Egret — AP36

1971, Sept. 28 Photo. ***Perf. 13x12½***

C84 AP36 1000fr blk, dk bl & ocher	10.00	7.00

Greek Marathon Runners — AP37

Designs: 45fr, Ancient Olympic Stadium. 75fr, Greek wrestlers. 130fr, Olympic Stadium, Athens, 1896.

1971, Oct. 5 ***Perf. 12½***

C85 AP37 40fr multi	50	25
C86 AP37 45fr multi	55	35
C87 AP37 75fr multi	85	40
C88 AP37 130fr multi	1.40	75

75th anniversary of modern Olympic Games.

Duke Ellington — AP38

Portraits: 50fr, Sidney Bechet. 100fr, Louis Armstrong.

1971, Oct. 20 Litho. ***Perf. 13***

C89 AP38 50fr multi	65	18
C90 AP38 75fr lt bl & multi	90	23
C91 AP38 100fr multi	1.25	35

Famous American jazz musicians.

Charles de Gaulle — AP39

Design: No. C93, Félix Eboué.

Lithographed and Embossed

1971, Nov. 9 ***Perf. 12½***

C92 AP39 200fr grn, yel grn & gold	3.50	3.50
C93 AP39 200fr bl, lt bl & gold	3.50	3.50
a. Souvenir sheet of 2	7.50	7.50

First anniversary of the death of Charles de Gaulle (1890-1970), president of France. No. C93a contains one each of Nos. C92-C93 with brown and ocher label carrying commemorative inscription and de Gaulle's signature. Size: 110x70mm.

African Postal Union Issue, 1971

Common Design Type

Design: 100fr, Sao antelope head and UAMPT building, Brazzaville, Congo.

1971, Nov. 13 Photo. ***Perf. 13x13½***

C94 CD135 100fr bl & multi	1.10	35

Apollo 15 Rocket AP40

Designs: 80fr, Apollo 15 capsule (horiz.). 150fr, Lunar module on Moon (horiz.). 250fr, Astronaut making tests. 300fr, Moon-buggy. No. C100, Successful splashdown (horiz.). No. C101, Apollo 15 insignia.

1972, Jan. 5 Litho. ***Perf. 13½***

C95 AP40 40fr multi	32	15
C96 AP40 80fr multi	65	33
C97 AP40 150fr multi	1.20	60
C98 AP40 250fr multi	2.00	1.00
C99 AP40 300fr multi	2.40	1.20
C100 AP40 500fr multi	4.00	2.00
Nos. C95-C100 (6)	10.57	5.28

Souvenir Sheet

C101 AP40 500fr multi	4.00	1.85

Apollo 15 moon landing. No. C101 has multicolored margin with American flag, and portraits of the families of astronauts Scott, Worden and Irwin. Size: 103x84mm.

Soyuz 2 Link-up — AP41

Designs: 30fr, Soyuz 2 on launching pad (vert.). 50fr, No. C108, Cosmonauts in uniform. 200fr, V. I. Patzaev. No. C106, V. N. Volkov, 400fr, G. L. Dobrovolsky. No. C109, Three cosmonauts.

1972, Jan. 5 *Perf. 13½x13*

C102 AP41 30fr multi 25 13
C103 AP41 50fr multi 40 20
C104 AP41 100fr multi 80 40
C105 AP41 200fr multi 1.60 80
C106 AP41 300fr multi 2.40 1.20
C107 AP41 400fr multi 3.25 1.60
Nos. C102-C107 (6) 8.70 4.33

Souvenir Sheets

C108 AP41 300fr multi 3.00 1.50
C109 AP41 400fr multi 4.00 2.00

Soyuz 2 link-up project. No. C108 has multicolored margin depicting launching pad, No. C109, Moscow sky-line. Size: 100x79mm.

Bobsledding — AP42

Design: 100fr, Slalom.

1972, Feb. 24 Engr. *Perf. 13*

C110 AP42 50fr Prus bl & rose red 60 20
C111 AP42 100fr red lil & sl grn 1.20 35

11th Winter Olympic Games, Sapporo, Japan, Feb. 3-13.

Pres. Tombalbaye Type, 1972

1972, Apr. 13 Litho. *Perf. 13*

C112 A63 70fr multi 70 35
C113 A63 80fr multi 80 40

11th Winter Olympic Type, 1972

Designs: 130fr, Speed skating. No. C115, Ice hockey. No. C116, Ski jumping. 250fr, 4-man bobsled.

1972, Apr. 13 *Perf. 13½*

C114 A64 130fr multi 1.30 65
C115 A64 200fr multi 2.00 1.00

Souvenir Sheets

C116 A64 200fr multi 2.00 1.00
C117 A64 250fr multi 2.50 1.25

11th Winter Olympic Games, Sapporo, Japan. Nos. C116 and C117 have multicolored margins showing Japanese religious figures. Size: 99x79mm.

Scout Jamboree Type, 1972

Designs: 100fr, Cooking preparation. 120fr, Lord Baden Powell. 250fr, Hiking.

1972, May 15

C118 A67 100fr multi 1.00 60
C119 A67 120fr multi 1.20 75

Souvenir Sheet

C120 A67 250fr multi 2.50 1.50

Scout Jamboree. No. C120 has multicolored margin showing African veldt and ostrich. Size: 102x81mm.

The first price column gives the catalogue value of an unused stamp, the second that of a used stamp.

Zebras — AP43

Designs: 30fr, Mandrills. 100fr, African elephants. 130fr, Gazelles. 150fr, Hippopotamuses. 200fr, Lion cub.

1972, May 15 Litho. *Perf. 13*

C121 AP43 20fr multi 20 10
C122 AP43 30fr multi 30 15
C123 AP43 100fr multi 1.00 50
C124 AP43 130fr multi 1.30 65
C125 AP43 150fr multi 1.50 75
Nos. C121-C125 (5) 4.30 2.15

Souvenir Sheet

C126 AP43 200fr multi 2.00 1.00

African wild animals. No. C126 has multicolored margin showing map of Africa, sun and various animals. Size: 102½x79mm.

View of Venice, by Caffi — AP44

Paintings by Ippolito Caffi: 40fr, Sailing ship and Doge's Palace (vert.). 140fr, Grand Canal (vert.).

1972, May 23 Photo.

C127 AP44 40fr gold & multi 50 15
C128 AP44 45fr gold & multi 60 20
C129 AP44 140fr gold & multi 1.50 1.00

UNESCO campaign to save Venice.

11th Winter Olympic Winners Type, 1972

Designs: 150fr, Slalom, B. Cochran, U.S. 200fr, Women's figure skating, B. Schuba, Austria. 250fr, Ice hockey, USSR. 300fr, 2-man bobsled. W. Zimmerer and P. Utzschneider, West Germany.

1972, June 15 *Perf. 14½*

C130 A69 150fr gold & multi 1.50 75
C131 A69 200fr gold & multi 2.00 1.00

Souvenir Sheets

C132 A69 250fr gold & multi 2.00 1.25
C133 A69 300fr gold & multi 3.00 1.75

11th Winter Olympic gold medal winners. Nos. C130-C131 exist se-tenant with label showing earth satellite. Nos. C132-C133 have multicolored margins showing satellite orbiting earth. Size: 127x89mm.

Daudet, "Tartarin de Tarascon," Book Year Emblem — AP45

1972, July 22 Engr. *Perf. 13*

C134 AP45 100fr dk red, lil & dk brn 1.20 30

International Book Year, 1972, and to honor Alphonse Daudet (1840-1897), French writer.

20th Summer Olympics Type, 1972

Designs (TV Tower, Munich and): 100fr, Gymnast. 120fr, Pole vault. 150fr, Fencing. 250fr, Hammer throw. 300fr, Boxing.

1972, Aug. 15

C135 A70 100fr gold & multi 1.00 50
C136 A70 120fr gold & multi 1.20 60
C137 A70 150fr gold & multi 1.50 75

Souvenir Sheets

C138 A70 250fr gold & multi 2.50 1.25
C139 A70 300fr gold & multi 3.00 1.50

20th Summer Olympic Games, Munich, Nos. C135-C137 exist se-tenant with label showing arms of Munich. Nos. C138-C139 have multicolored margin with Munich views. Size: 127x89mm.

Lunokhod on Moon — AP46

Design: 100fr, Luna 16 on moon and rocket in flight (vert.).

1972, Sept. 19

C140 AP46 100fr dk bl, pur & bis 1.20 50
C141 AP46 150fr sl, brn & lil 1.80 75

Russian moon missions.

Farcha Laboratory, Cattle, Scientist — AP47

1972, Nov. 11 Photo. *Perf. 13*

C142 AP47 75fr yel & multi 70 35

20th anniversary of the Farcha Laboratory for veterinary research.

King Faisal and Holy Kaaba, Mecca — AP48

1972, Nov. 17

C143 AP48 75fr multi 75 40

Visit of King Faisal of Saudi Arabia.

Christmas Type of 1970

Designs: 40fr, Virgin and Child, by Giovanni Bellini. 75fr, Virgin and Child, by Dall"Occhio. 80fr, Nativity, by Fra Angelico (horiz.). 95fr, Adoration of the Kings, by Il Perugino.

1972, Dec. 15 Photo. *Perf. 13*

C144 AP30 40fr gold & multi 50 15
C145 AP30 75fr gold & multi 85 25
C146 AP30 80fr gold & multi 1.00 28
C147 AP30 95fr gold & multi 1.10 38

Christmas 1972.

20th Summer Olympic Winners Type, 1972

Designs (Olympic Emblems and): 150fr, Pole vault, Nordwig, East Germany. 250fr, Hurdles, Milburn, U.S. 300fr, Javelin, Wolfermann, West Germany.

1972, Dec. 22

C148 A76 150fr multi 1.50 75
C149 A76 250fr multi 2.50 1.25

Souvenir Sheet

C150 A76 300fr multi 3.00 1.50

20th Summer Olympic Games winners. No. C150 has multicolored margin showing Olympic emblems. Size: 111½x82mm.

Summer Olympic Winners Type, 1972

Designs (Olympic Emblem and): 150fr, Dressage, Mancinelli, Italy. No. C152; Finn class sailing, Serge Maury, France. No. C153, Swimming, Mark Spitz.

1972, Dec. 22 Litho. *Perf. 11*

C151 A77 150fr gold & multi 1.50 75
C152 A77 250fr gold & multi 2.50 1.25

Souvenir Sheet

C153 A77 250fr multi 2.50 1.25

20th Summer Olympic Games, winners. No. C153 has gold and multicolored margin showing Olympic emblem and flame. Size: 111x82½mm.

Copernicus and Solar System — AP49

1973, Mar. 31 Engr. *Perf. 13*

C154 AP49 250fr gray, mag & brn 2.75 1.50

500th anniversary of the birth of Nicolaus Copernicus (1473-1543), Polish astronomer.

Skylab over Africa — AP50

Design: 150fr, Skylab.

1974, Aug. 6 Engr. *Perf. 13*

C155 AP50 100fr mar, bl & ol 1.00 55
C156 AP50 150fr brn, bl & sl grn 1.40 75

Exploits of Skylab, U.S. manned space station.

Soccer — AP51

Designs: 125fr, 150fr, Soccer players; 125fr, vertical.

1974, Oct. 22 Engr. *Perf. 13*

C157 AP51 50fr dl red & choc 45 25
C158 AP51 125fr red & dp grn 1.10 65
C159 AP51 150fr grn & rose red 1.35 75

World Cup Soccer Championship, Munich, June 13-July 7.

Family and WPY Emblem — AP52

1974, Nov. 11
C160 AP52 250fr multi 2.25 1.40

World Population Year.

Mail Delivery by Canoe — AP53

Designs (UPU Emblem and): 40fr, Diesel train. 100fr, Jet. 150fr, Spacecraft.

1974, Dec. 20 Engr. *Perf. 13*
C161 AP53 30fr car & multi 28 18
C162 AP53 40fr ultra & blk 35 20
C163 AP53 100fr brn, ultra & blk 90 55
C164 AP53 150fr grn, lil & ol 1.40 85

Centenary of Universal Postal Union.

Women of Different Races, IWY Emblem — AP54

1975, June 25 Photo. *Perf. 13*
C165 AP54 250fr bl & multi 2.10 1.25

International Women's Year 1975.

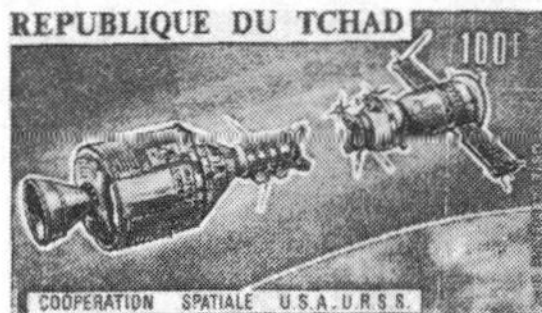

Apollo and Soyuz Before Link-up — AP55

Design: 130fr, Apollo and Soyuz after link-up.

1975, July 15 Engr. *Perf. 13*
C166 AP55 100fr ultra, choc & grn 1.00 50
C167 AP55 130fr vio bl, brn & grn 1.20 75

Apollo Soyuz space test project (Russo-American space cooperation), launching July 15; link-up July 17.

Soccer Player, View of Montreal — AP56

Designs (Olympic Rings, Montreal Skyline): 100fr, Discus thrower. 125fr, Runner.

1975, Oct. 14 Engr. *Perf. 13*
C168 AP56 75fr car & sl grn 70 38
C169 AP56 100fr car, choc & bl grn 1.00 50
C170 AP56 125fr brn, bl & car 1.25 75

Pre-Olympic Year 1975.

Nos. C166-C167 Overprinted: "JONCTION / 17 JUILLET 1975"

1975, Nov. 4 Engr. *Perf. 13*
C171 AP55 100fr multi 1.00 50
C172 AP55 130fr multi 1.20 70

Apollo-Soyuz link-up in space, July 17.

Stylized British and American Flags, "200" — AP57

1975, Dec. 5 Engr. *Perf. 13*
C173 AP57 150fr vio bl, car & ol bis 1.35 75

American Bicentennial.

Adoration of the Shepherds, by Murillo — AP58

Paintings: 75fr, Adoration of the Shepherds, by Georges de La Tour. 80fr, Virgin and Child with Bible, by Rogier van der Weyden (vert.). 100fr, Holy Family, by Raphael (vert.).

1975, Dec. 15 Litho. *Perf. 13x12½*
C174 AP58 40fr yel & multi 40 20
C175 AP58 75fr yel & multi 70 38
C176 AP58 80fr yel & multi 80 40
C177 AP58 100fr yel & multi 1.00 45

Christmas 1975.

12th Winter Olympic Winners Type, 1976

Designs: 250fr, 4-man bobsled, West Germany. 300fr, Speed skating, J. E. Storholt, Norway. 500fr, Downhill skiing, F. Klammer, Austria.

1976, June 21 *Perf. 14*
C178 A84 250fr multi 2.40 1.10
C179 A84 300fr multi 2.85 1.35

Souvenir Sheet

C180 A84 500fr multi 5.00 2.00

12th Winter Olympic Games winners, Innsbruck. No. C180 has multicolored margin showing snowflakes. Size: 114x78mm.

Paul Revere's Ride and Portrait by Copley — AP59

Designs: 125fr, George Washington crossing Delaware. 150fr, Lafayette offering his services to America. 200fr, Rochambeau at Yorktown with Washington. 250fr, Benjamin Franklin presenting Declaration of Independence. 400fr, Count de Grasse's victory at Cape Charles.

1976, July 4 Litho. *Perf. 14*
C181 AP59 100fr multi 95 45
C182 AP59 125fr multi 1.20 60
C183 AP59 150fr multi 1.40 70
C184 AP59 200fr multi 1.90 85
C185 AP59 250fr multi 2.50 95
Nos. C181-C185 (5) 7.95 3.55

Souvenir Sheet

C186 AP59 400fr multi 4.00 1.85

American Bicentennial. No. C186 has multicolored margin showing George Washington and his staff. Size: 113x78mm.

Summer Olympics Type, 1976

Designs: 100fr, Boxing. 200fr, Pole vault. 300fr, Shot put. 500fr, Sprint.

1976, July 12
C187 A85 100fr multi 90 50
C188 A85 200fr multi 1.85 85
C189 A85 300fr multi 2.75 1.10

Souvenir Sheet

C190 A85 500fr multi 4.00 2.00

21st Summer Olympic Games, Montreal. No. C190 has multicolored margin showing Olympic stadium. Size: 103x77mm.

Viking Mars Project Type, 1976

Designs (Mars Lander and): 100fr, Viking landing on Mars. 200fr, Capsule over Mars. 250fr, Lander over Mars. 450fr, Lander and probe.

1976, July 23 Litho. *Perf. 14*
C191 A86 100fr multi 95 50
C192 A86 200fr multi 1.90 85
C193 A86 250fr multi 2.40 95

Souvenir Sheet

C194 A86 450fr multi 4.25 2.00

Viking Mars project, No. C194 has multicolored margin showing Viking probe. Size: 114x89mm.

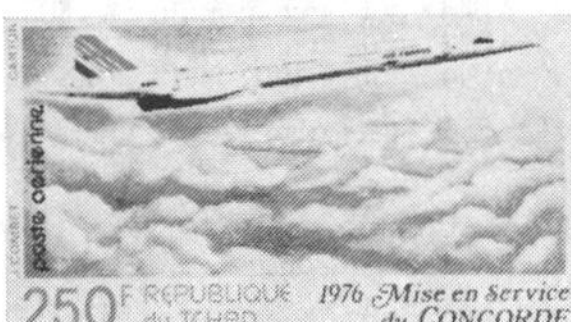

Concorde — AP60

1976, Oct. 15 Litho. *Perf. 12½*
C195 AP60 250fr bl, blk & ver 2.00 75

First commercial flight of supersonic jet Concorde, Jan. 21.

Nobel Prize Type, 1976

Designs: 100fr, Albert Einstein, physics. 200fr, Dag Hammarskjold, peace. 300fr, Shinichiro Tomanaga, physics. 500fr, Alexander Fleming, medicine.

1976, Dec. 15
C196 A87 100fr multi 95 50
C197 A87 200fr multi 1.90 85
C198 A87 300fr multi 2.85 1.10

Souvenir Sheet

C199 A87 500fr multi 4.75 2.00

Nobel Prize winners. No. C199 has multicolored margin showing reverse and obverse of Nobel medal. Size: 116x79mm.

Adoration of the Shepherds, by Gerard van Honthorst — AP61

Paintings: 30fr, Nativity, by Albrecht Altdorfer (vert.). 60fr, Nativity, by Hans Holbein (vert.). 150fr, Adoration of the Kings, by Gerard David.

1976, Dec. 22 Litho. *Perf. 12½*
C200 AP61 30fr gold & multi 25 15
C201 AP61 60fr gold & multi 50 30
C202 AP61 120fr gold & blk 1.00 60
C203 AP61 150fr gold & blk 1.20 70

Christmas 1976.

Lesdiguieres Bridge, by Jongkind — AP62

Design: 120fr, Sailing Ship and Boats, by Johan Barthold Jongkind (1819-1891).

1976, Dec. 27 Photo. *Perf. 13*
C204 AP62 100fr multi 80 45
C205 AP62 120fr multi 1.00 60

Centenary of impressionism.

Zeppelin Type of 1977

Designs: 125fr, Germany No. C40 and North Pole. 150fr, Germany No. C45 and Chicago department store. 175fr, Germany No. C38 and scenes of New York and London. 200fr, 500fr, U.S. No. C15 and New York.

1977, Mar. 30 *Perf. 11*
C206 A91 125fr multi 1.20 50
C207 A91 150fr multi 1.40 60
C208 A91 175fr multi 1.65 70
C209 A91 200fr multi 2.00 85

Souvenir Sheet

C210 A91 500fr multi 5.00 2.00

75th anniversary of the Zeppelin. No. 2210 has multicolored margin showing world map with cancellations of Zeppelin flights. Size: 130x91mm.

Sassenage Castle, Grenoble — AP63

1977, May 21 Litho. *Perf. 12½*
C211 AP63 100fr multi 80 45

10th anniversary of the International French Language Council.

Lafayette and Ships — AP64

Designs: 120fr, Abraham Lincoln, eagle and flags (vert.). 150fr, James Madison and family.

1977, July 30 Engr. *Perf. 13*
C212 AP64 100fr multi 80 60
C213 AP64 120fr multi 1.00 70
C214 AP64 150fr multi 1.20 90

American Bicentennial.

Lindbergh and Spirit of St. Louis — AP65

Designs: 100fr, Concorde. 150fr, 200fr, 300fr, Various Lindbergh portraits and Spirit of St. Louis.

1977, Sept. 27

C215	AP65	100fr multi	80	60
C216	AP65	120fr multi	1.00	70
C217	AP65	150fr multi	1.20	90
C218	AP65	200fr multi	1.60	1.10
C219	AP65	300fr multi	2.40	1.65
		Nos. C215-C219 (5)	7.00	4.95

Charles A. Lindbergh's solo transatlantic flight from New York to Paris, 50th anniversary, and first supersonic transatlantic flight of Concorde.

Mariner 10 — AP66

Spacecraft: 200fr, Lunokhod on moon, Luna 21. 300fr, Viking on Mars.

1977, Oct. 10 Engr. *Perf. 13*

C220	AP66	100fr multi	80	60
C221	AP66	200fr multi	1.60	1.20
C222	AP66	300fr multi	2.40	1.60

Running — AP67

Designs: 60fr, Volleyball. 120fr, Soccer. 125fr, Basketball.

1977, Oct. 24 Engr. *Perf. 13*

C223	AP67	30fr multi	25	20
C224	AP67	60fr multi	50	35
C225	AP67	120fr multi	1.00	70
C226	AP67	125fr multi	1.00	75

No. C215 Overprinted: "PARIS NEW-YORK / 22.11.77"

1977, Nov. 22

C227	AP65	100fr multi	80	60

Concorde, first commercial flight Paris to New York.

Virgin and Child, by Rubens AP68

Rubens Paintings: 60fr, Virgin and Child and Two Donors. 100fr, Adoration of the Shepherds. 125fr, Adoration of the Kings.

1977, Dec. 20 Litho. *Perf. 12½x12*

C228	AP68	30fr multi	25	20
C229	AP68	60fr multi	50	35
C230	AP68	100fr multi	80	60
C231	AP68	125fr multi	1.00	75

Christmas 1977.

Antoine de Saint-Exupéry — AP69

Designs: 50fr, Wilbur and Orville Wright and Flyer. 80fr, Hugo Junkers and his plane. 100fr, Gen. Italo Balbo and his plane. 120fr, Concorde. 500fr, Wilbur and Orville Wright and Flyer.

1978, Oct. 25 Litho. *Perf. 13½*

C232	AP69	40fr multi	40	20
C233	AP69	50fr multi	50	25
C234	AP69	80fr multi	80	40
C235	AP69	100fr multi	1.00	50
C236	AP69	120fr multi	1.20	60
		Nos. C232-C236 (5)	3.90	1.95

Souvenir Sheet

C237	AP69	500fr multi	5.50	2.75

History of aviation and 75th anniversary of 1st powered flight. No. C237 has multicolored margin showing Concorde in flight. Size: 104x99mm.

Philexafrique II-Essen Issue

Common Design Types

Designs: No. C238, Rhinoceros and Chad No. C6. No. C239, Kingfisher and Mecklenburg-Strelitz No. 1.

1978, Nov. 1 *Perf. 12½*

C238	CD138	100fr multi	1.00	50
C239	CD139	100fr multi	1.00	50

Nos. C238-C239 printed se-tenant.

Nos. C191-C194 Overprinted "ALUNISSAGE/APOLLO XI/ JUILLET 1969"

1979, Nov. 26 Litho. *Perf. 13½x14*

C240	A86	100fr multi	1.00	50
C241	A86	200fr multi	2.00	1.00
C242	A86	250fr multi	2.50	1.25

Souvenir Sheet

C243	A86	450fr multi	4.75	2.50

Apollo 11 moon landing, 10th anniversary.

Hurdles, Moscow '80 Emblem — AP70

Moscow '80 Emblem and: 30fr, Field hockey. 250fr, Swimming. 350fr, Running. 500fr, Yachting.

1979, Nov. 30 *Perf. 13½*

C244	AP70	15fr multi	20	8
C245	AP70	30fr multi	40	15
C246	AP70	250fr multi	2.75	1.25
C247	AP70	350fr multi	3.75	1.75

Souvenir Sheet

C248	AP70	500fr multi	5.75	2.75

Pre-Olympic Year. No. C248 has multicolored margin showing Moscow '80 emblem. Size: 118x80mm.

Austria Jubilee Issue of 1910, Canoe, Hill — AP71

Hill, Stamps and Vessels: 100fr, U.S. type A97, dhow. 200fr, France No. 21, Sidewheeler. 300fr, Holstein No. 16, ocean liner. 500fr, Chad No. J13, ocean liner.

1979, Dec. 3 *Perf. 14x13½*

C249	AP71	65fr multi	75	35
C250	AP71	100fr multi	1.10	50
C251	AP71	200fr multi	2.25	1.00
C252	AP71	300fr multi	3.25	1.50

Souvenir Sheet

C253	AP71	500fr multi	5.75	2.75

Sir Rowland Hill (1795-1879), originator of penny postage. No. C253 has multicolored margin showing early stamps. Size: 114x91mm.

Nos. C244-C245, C249-C250 Overprinted: "POSTES 1981" in Red or Overprinted and Surcharged Silver on Red.

Perf. 13½, 14x13½

1981, Nov. 15 Litho.

C254	AP70	30fr on 15fr multi	30	15
C255	AP70	30fr multi	30	15
C256	AP71	60fr on 65fr multi	60	30
C257	AP71	60fr on 100fr multi	60	30

Soccer Type of 1982

1982 Litho. *Perf. 13½*

C258	A108	80fr Brazil	32	16
C259	A108	300fr Spain	1.25	62

Souvenir Sheet

C259A	A108	500fr like 300fr	2.25	1.10

No. C259A contains one stamp (size: 42x51mm); multicolored margin pictures Spanish cultural attractions. Size: 77x100mm.

Diana Type of 1982

1982, July 2 Litho. *Perf. 13½*

C260	A109	80fr 1977	80	40
C261	A109	300fr 1980	3.00	1.50

Souvenir Sheet

C262	A109	500fr 1981	5.00	2.50

No. C262 has multicolored margin showing family tree. Size: 78x75mm.

Manned Flight Bicentenary AP72

Balloons: 100fr, Charles' and Roberts', 1783 (vert.). 200fr, J.P. Blanchard, Berlin, 1788 (vert.). 300fr, Charles Green, London, 1837. 400fr, Modern blimp. 500fr, Montgolfiere, 1783 (vert.).

1983, Apr. Litho. *Perf. 13*

C263	AP72	100fr multi	75	40
C264	AP72	200fr multi	1.50	75
C265	AP72	300fr multi	2.25	1.10
C266	AP72	400fr multi	3.00	1.50

Souvenir Sheet

C267	AP72	500fr multi	5.00	2.50

No. C267 has multicolored margin continuing design. Size: 80x98mm.

Balloon Type

Designs: 80fr, Steam Powered Airship, H. Giffard. 250fr, Graf Zeppelin; Airship L-1, first flight. 300fr, 1st Balloon Flight, Montgolfier and Rozier.

1983, May 30 Litho. *Perf. 13*

C268	A116	80fr multi	80	40
C269	A116	250fr multi	1.25	60

Souvenir Sheet

C270	A116	300fr multi	3.00	1.50

Multicolored margin depicts crowd watching balloon ascent. Size: 57x95mm.

1984 Summer Olympics — AP73

Various kayak scenes.

1984, Mar. 1 Litho. *Perf. 13*

C271	AP73	100fr multi	45	22
C272	AP73	200fr multi	90	45
C273	AP73	300fr multi	1.40	70
C274	AP73	400fr multi	1.90	95

Souvenir Sheet

C275	AP73	500fr multi	2.25	1.10

No. C275 has multicolored margin continuing design. Size: 105x81mm.

IYY, PHILEXAFRICA '85 — AP74

1985, May 2 Litho. *Perf. 13*

C280	AP74	200fr Boy scout, tree	80	40
C281	AP74	200fr Air Chad Fokker 27	80	40

Printed se-tenant with center label.

IYY, PHILEXAFRICA Type of 1985

1985, Nov. 1 Litho. *Perf. 13x12½*

C283	AP74	250fr Girl, Scout ceremony	1.40	70
C284	AP74	250fr Communications and transportation	1.40	70

Nos. C283-C284 printed se-tenant with center labels picturing map of Africa or UAPT emblem.

ASCENA Airlines, 25th Anniv. — AP75

1985, Aug. 15 *Perf. 12½*

C285	AP75	70fr bl & multi	30	15
C286	AP75	110fr org & multi	45	22
C287	AP75	250fr yel & multi	1.10	55

Victor Hugo (1802-1885), French Novelist — AP76

Scene from Les. Miserables.

1985, Nov. 24 Engr. *Perf. 13*

C288 AP76 70fr org brn, chlky bl & dp brn 30 15
C289 AP76 110fr lake, dk brn & dk grn 60 30
C290 AP76 250fr brt org, blk & dk red 1.40 70
C291 AP76 300fr dk red, cl & sl bl 1.65 85

Christmas 1985 — AP77

1985, Dec. 22 Litho. *Perf. 13½*

C292 AP77 250fr Adoration of the Magi 1.40 70

AIR POST SEMI-POSTAL STAMPS

Ramses II Battling the Hittites (from Abu Simbel) — SPAP1

Unwmk.

1964, March 9 Engr. *Perf. 13*

CB1 SPAP1 10fr + 5fr red, grn & vio 35 30
CB2 SPAP1 25fr + 5fr red, grn & vio brn 50 40
CB3 SPAP1 50fr + 5fr red, grn & sl grn 1.00 90

Issued to publicize the UNESCO world campaign to save historic monuments in Nubia.

Lions Emblem SPAP2

1967, July 5 Photo. *Perf. 13*

CB4 SPAP2 50fr + 10fr multi 90 35

Issued to commemorate the 50th anniversary of Lions International and to publicize the Lions work for the blind.

POSTAGE DUE STAMPS

TCHAD

Postage Due Stamps of France Overprinted

A. E. F.

1928 Unwmk. *Perf. 14x13½*

J1 D2 5c lt bl 18 18
J2 D2 10c gray brn 18 18
J3 D2 20c ol grn 22 22
J4 D2 25c brt rose 40 40
J5 D2 30c lt red 50 50
J6 D2 45c bl grn 70 70
J7 D2 50c brn vio 75 75
J8 D2 60c yel brn 90 90
J9 D2 1fr red brn 90 90
J10 D2 2fr org red 3.00 3.00
J11 D2 3fr brt vio 1.50 1.50
Nos. J1-J11 (11) 9.23 9.23

Huts — D3

Canoe — D4

1930 Typo. *Perf. 14x13½, 13½x14.*

J12 D3 5c dp bl & ol 25 25
J13 D3 10c dk red & brn 32 32
J14 D3 20c grn & brn 55 55
J15 D3 25c lt bl & brn 65 65
J16 D3 30c bis brn & Prus bl 65 65
J17 D3 45c Prus bl & ol 80 80
J18 D3 50c red vio & brn 1.10 1.10
J19 D3 60c gray lil & bl blk 1.50 1.50
J20 D4 1fr bis brn & bl blk 1.50 1.50
J21 D4 2fr vio & brn 3.00 3.00
J22 D4 3fr dp red & brn 24.00 24.00
Nos. J12-J22 (11) 34.32 34.32

In 1934 stamps of Chad were superseded by those of French Equatorial Africa.

Republic

Rhinoceros — D5

Tibesti Pictographs: No. J24, Kudu. No. J25, Two antelopes. No. J26, Three antelopes. No. J27, Ostrich. No. J28, Horned bull. No. J29, Bull. No. J30, Wild swine. No. J31, Elephant. No. J32, Rhinoceros. No. J33, Warrior with spear and shield. No. J34, Masked archer.

Unwmk.

1962, Apr. 20 Engr. *Perf. 13*

J23 D5 50c ol bis 6 6
J24 D5 50c brn red 6 6
J25 D5 1fr blue 8 8
J26 D5 1fr green 8 8
J27 D5 2fr vermilion 12 12
J28 D5 2fr maroon 12 12
J29 D5 5fr sl grn 22 22
J30 D5 5fr vio bl 22 22
J31 D5 10fr brown 50 50
J32 D5 10fr org brn 50 50
J33 D5 25fr car rose 1.25 1.25
J34 D5 25fr violet 1.25 1.25
Nos. J23-J34 (12) 4.46 4.46

The two designs of the same denomination are printed se-tenant.

Kanem Doll — D6

Dolls: 2fr, Kotoko. 5fr, Leather doll. 10fr, Kotoko. 25fr, Guera.

1969, Sept. 19 Engr. *Perf. 14x13*

J35 D6 1fr grn, ver & brn 5 5
J36 D6 2fr ver, yel grn & brn 5 5
J37 D6 5fr grn, brn & sl grn 10 5
J38 D6 10fr grn, lil & brn 18 18
J39 D6 25fr rose, bl & brn 38 22
Nos. J35-J39 (5) 76 55

MILITARY STAMPS

Flag Bearer and Map of Chad — M1

1st Regiment Emblem — M2

No. 78 Overprinted "F.M."

1965 Typo. *Perf. 14x13½*

M1 A5 20fr red & blk 135.00 135.00

1968 Unwmk. Litho. *Perf. 13x12½*

M2 M1 tan & multi 1.40 90

1972, Jan. 21 Photo. *Perf. 13*

M3 M2 bl & multi 65 40

OFFICIAL STAMPS

Flag and Map of Chad — O1

Perf. 13½x14

1966-71 Typo. Unwmk.

Flag in blue, yellow and carmine.

O1 O1 1fr lt bl 6 5
O2 O1 2fr gray 6 5
O3 O1 5fr black 7 6
O4 O1 10fr vio bl 10 8
O5 O1 25fr orange 25 12
O6 O1 30fr brt grn 38 18
O7 O1 40fr car ('71) 45 18
O8 O1 50fr red lil 60 25
O9 O1 85fr green 90 45
O10 O1 100fr brown 1.40 50
O11 O1 200fr red 2.50 90
Nos. O1-O11 (11) 6.77 2.82

CHILE

LOCATION — Southwest corner of South America
GOVT. — Republic
AREA — 292,135 sq. mi.
POP. — 11,682,260 (est. 1982)
CAPITAL — Santiago

100 Centavos = 1 Peso
1000 Milesimos = 100 Centesimos = 1 Escudo (1960)
100 Centavos = 1 Peso (1975)

Prices of early Chile stamps vary according to condition. Quotations for Nos. 1-14 are for fine copies. Very fine to superb specimens sell at much higher prices, and inferior or poor copies sell at reduced prices, depending on the condition of the individual specimen.

Pen cancellations are common on the 1862-67 issues. Such stamps sell for much less than the quoted prices which are for those with handstamped postal cancellations.

Christopher Columbus — A1

Wmkd.

1 5 5 5
a b c d

10 10 20
e f g

London Prints.

1853 Wmk. b. Engr. *Imperf.*

Blued Paper.

1 A1 5c brn red *500.00* 55.00
  a. White paper 90.00

Wmk. e.

White Paper.

2 A1 10c dp brt bl *800.00* 125.00
  a. Blued paper *650.00*
  b. Diagonal half used as 5c on cover *425.00*

Santiago Prints.

Impressions Fine and Clear.

1854 Wmk. b and e

White Paper.

3 A1 5c pale red brn 450.00 45.00
  a. 5c dp red brn *500.00* 50.00
  b. 5c chnt *800.00* 150.00
4 A1 5c brnt sien *1,500.* 225.00
  a. 5c dl choc *2,750.* 1,200.
5 A1 10c dp bl *1,250.* 125.00
  a. 10c sl bl 125.00
  b. 10c grnsh bl 1,200.
  c. Half used as 5c on cover 550.00
6 A1 10c lt dl bl *1,250.* 125.00
  a. 10c pale bl 125.00
  b. Diagonal half used as 5c on cover 400.00

Litho.

7 A1 5c red brn *2,250.* 300.00
  a. 5c pale brn *1,600.* 250.00

London Print.

1855 Blued Paper Wmk. c. Engr.

8 A1 5c brn red 175.00 12.50

Santiago Prints.

Impressions Worn and Blurred.

1856-62 Wmk. b and e

White Paper.

9 A1 5c rose red ('58) 40.00 6.00
  a. 5c car red ('62) 100.00 20.00
  b. 5c org red ('61) 250.00 150.00
  c. 5c dl redsh brn ('57) 250.00 25.00
  d. Printed on both sides *650.00*
  e. Double impression
10 A1 10c dp bl 200.00 25.00
  a. 10c sky bl ('57) 200.00 25.00
  b. 10c lt bl 200.00 25.00
  c. 10c ind bl 250.00 75.00
  d. Half used as 5c on cover *175.00*

London Prints.

1862 Wmk. a, f and g

11 A1 1c lem yel 30.00 37.50
  a. Double impression *950.00*
12 A1 10c brt bl 50.00 10.00
  a. 10c dp bl 50.00 10.00
  b. Blued paper 125.00 25.00
  c. Wmkd. "20" (error) *4,000.* *3,000.*
  d. Half used as 5c on cover 150.00
13 A1 20c green 75.00 45.00
  a. 20c emer

Santiago Print.

1865 Wmk. d.

14 A1 5c rose red 30.00 12.50
  a. 5c car red 35.00 12.50
  b. Printed on both sides *300.00*
  c. Laid paper *225.00*
  d. Double impression *225.00*

The 5c rose red (shades) on unwatermaked paper, either wove or ribbed, and on paper watermarked Chilean arms in the sheet are reprints made about 1870.

No. 13 has been reprinted in the color of issue and in fancy colors, both from the original engraved plate and from lithographic transfers. The reprints are on paper without watermark or with watermark CHILE and Star.

A2

A3

1867 Unwmk. *Perf. 12*

15 A2 1c orange 17.50 2.50
Pen cancellation 25
16 A2 2c black 25.00 3.75
Pen cancellation 40
17 A2 5c red 17.50 1.25
Pen cancellation 10
18 A2 10c blue 17.50 2.50
Pen cancellation 25
19 A2 20c green 25.00 3.75
Pen cancellation 35

Unused prices for Nos. 15-19 are for stamps with original gum.

1877 *Rouletted*

20 A3 1c gray 2.50 1.25
21 A3 2c orange 15.00 3.75
22 A3 5c dl lake 17.50 1.00
23 A3 10c blue 15.00 2.50
a. Diagnoal half used as 5c on cover
24 A3 20c green 16.00 3.75

The panel inscribed "CENTAVO" is straight on No. 22.

A4

A5

Columbus — A6

1878-99 *Rouletted*

25 A4 1c grn ('81) 1.00 20
26 A4 2c rose ('81) 1.25 20
27 A5 5c dl lake ('78) 5.00 50
28 A5 5c ultra ('83) 1.25 10
29 A5 10c org ('85) 2.00 40
a. 10c yel 8.00 1.00
30 A5 15c dk grn ('92) 1.50 50
31 A5 20c gray ('86) 1.25 50
32 A5 25c org brn ('92) 2.00 50
33 A5 30c rose car ('99) 5.00 2.00
34 A5 50c lil ('78) 50.00 10.00
35 A5 50c vio ('85) 2.50 1.00
36 A6 1p dk brn & blk ('92) 25.00 2.00
a. Imperf. horiz. or vert. pair 125.00
Nos. 25-36 (12) 97.75 17.90

Columbus
A7 A8

1894 Re-engraved.

37 A7 1c bl grn 1.00 20
38 A7 2c car lake 1.00 20

In type A4 there is a small colorless ornament at each side of the base of the numeral, above the "E" and "V" of "CENTAVO". In type A7 these ornaments are missing, the figure "1" is broader than in type A4 and the head of the figure "2" is formed by a curved line instead of a ball.

1900-01

Type I. There is a heavy shading of short horizontal lines below "Chile" and the adjacent ornaments.

Type II. There is practically no shading below "Chile" and the ornaments.

Type I.

39 A8 1c yel grn 1.00 20
40 A8 2c brn rose 2.00 20
41 A8 5c dp bl 12.50 20
42 A8 10c violet 7.50 40
a. Horizontal pair, imperf. between
43 A8 20c gray 5.00 1.00
44 A8 30c dp org ('01) 6.00 1.00
45 A8 50c red brn 7.50 1.75
a. Horiz. pair, imperf. btwn. 75.00
Nos. 39-45 (7) 41.50 4.75

Type II.

46 A8 1c yel grn ('01) 1.00 20
47 A8 2c rose ('01) 1.00 20
48 A8 5c dl bl ('01) 5.00 20
a. Printed on both sides
49 A8 10c vio ('01) 6.00 50

Columbus
A9 A10

1900

Black Surcharge

50 A9 5c on 30c rose car 1.00 20
a. Inverted surcharge 37.50 20.00
b. Double surcharge 125.00 80.00
c. Double surcharge, both inverted 125.00 80.00
d. Double surcharge, one inverted 125.00 80.00
e. Surcharged on front and back 125.00 80.00

1901-02 *Perf. 12*

51 A10 1c green 35 20
52 A10 2c carmine 50 20
53 A10 5c ultra 1.00 10
54 A10 10c red & blk 2.50 40
55 A10 30c vio & blk 7.50 40
56 A10 50c red org & blk 9.00 3.00
Nos. 51-56 (6) 20.85 4.30

Diez

No. 44 Surcharged in Dark Blue

1903 *Rouletted.*

57 A8 10c on 30c org 2.50 50
a. Inverted surcharge 25.00 15.00
b. Double surcharge 30.00 15.00
c. Double surch., one inverted 30.00 15.00
d. Double surch., both inverted 30.00 15.00
e. Stamp design printed on both sides

Pedro de Valdivia
A11

Coat of Arms
A12

A13

Telegraph Stamps Surcharged or Overprinted in Black

Type I. Animal at left has neither mane nor tail.

Type II. Animal at left has mane and tail.

1904 *Perf. 12.*

58 A11 1c on 20c ultra 35 20
a. Imperf. horiz. pair 50.00 50.00
b. Inverted surcharge 60.00 60.00
59 A13 2c yel brn, I 35 20
a. Inverted overprint 25.00 25.00
b. Pair, one without overprint 60.00 60.00
60 A13 5c red, I 60 20
a. Inverted overprint 25.00 25.00
c. Pair, one without overprint 60.00 60.00
61 A13 10c ol grn, I 2.00 60
a. Inverted overprint 60.00 60.00

Perf. 12½ to 16.

62 A13 2c yel, brn, II 6.00 4.00
63 A11 3c on 5c brn red 60.00 55.00
a. Inverted surcharge
64 A12 3c on 1p brn, II 50 30
a. Double surcharge 60.00 60.00
65 A13 5c red, II 10.00 7.50
a. Inverted overprint
66 A13 10c ol grn, II 22.50 13.00
67 A11 12c on 5c brn red 1.25 50
a. No star at left of "Centavos" 2.50 1.50
b. Inverted surcharge 50.00 50.00
c. Double surcharge 60.00 60.00
Nos. 62-67 (6) 100.25 80.30

Counterfeits exist of the overprint and surcharge varieties of Nos. 57-67.

Columbus
A14 A15

Columbus — A16

1905-09 *Perf. 12.*

68 A14 1c green 30 20
69 A14 2c carmine 30 20
70 A14 3c yel brn 75 30
71 A14 5c ultra 75 10
72 A15 10c gray & blk 1.50 20
73 A15 12c lake & blk 7.50 2.50
74 A15 15c vio & blk 1.50 20
75 A15 20c org brn & blk 3.50 20
76 A15 30c bl grn & blk 4.50 30
77 A15 50c ultra & blk 5.00 30
78 A16 1p gold, grn & gray 17.50 9.00
Nos. 68-78 (11) 43.10 13.50

A 20c dull red and black, type A15, was prepared but not issued. Price $125. "Specimen" copies of Nos. 74, 76-78 exist, punched to prevent postal use.

Nos. 73, 78 Surcharged in Blue or Red

ISLAS DE
JUAN FERNANDEZ

ISLAS DE
JUAN FERNANDEZ

5 10 Cts.
a *b*

1910

79 A15 (a) 5c on 12c lake & blk (Bl) 60 20
80 A16 (b) 10c on 1p gold, grn & gray (R) 1.50 40
81 A16 (b) 20c on 1p gold, grn & gray (R) 2.00 80
82 A16 (b) 1p gold, grn & gray (R) 4.00 1.50

The 1p is overprinted "ISLAS DE JUAN FERNANDEZ" only. The use of these stamps throughout Chile was authorized.

Independence Centenary Issue.

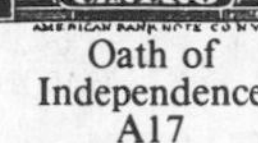
Oath of Independence
A17

Monument to O'Higgins
A26

Gen. Manuel Blanco Encalada — A29

Designs: 2c, Battle of Chacabuco. 3c, Battle of Roble. 5c, Battle of Maipu. 10c, Naval Engagement of "Lautaro" and "Esmeralda." 12c, Capturing the "Maria Isabel." 15c, First Sortie of Liberating Forces. 20c, Abdication of O'Higgins. 25c, Chile's First Congress. 50c, Monument to Jose M. Carrera. 1p, Monument to San Martin. 5p, Gen. Jose Ignacio Zenteno. 10p, Adm. Lord Thomas Cochrane.

1910

Center in Black.

83 A17 1c dk grn 40 20
a. Center inverted *7,000.*
84 A17 2c lake 40 20
85 A17 3c red brn 1.25 60
86 A17 5c dp bl 75 10
87 A17 10c gray brn 1.25 40
88 A17 12c vermilion 3.00 1.20
89 A17 15c slate 3.00 60
90 A17 20c red org 4.00 1.00
91 A17 25c ultra 5.00 2.00
92 A26 30c violet 4.00 1.00
93 A26 50c ol grn 9.00 3.00
94 A26 1p yel org 20.00 7.50
95 A29 2p red 20.00 7.50
96 A29 5p yel grn 55.00 25.00
97 A29 10p dk vio 50.00 22.50
Nos. 83-97 (15) 177.05 72.80

Columbus
A32

De Valdivia
A33

Mateo de Toro Zambrano
A34

Bernardo O'Higgins
A35

Ramon Freire
A36

F. A. Pinto
A37

Joaquin Prieto
A38

Manuel Bulnes
A39

Manuel Montt
A40

José Joaquin Perez
A41

Federico Errazuriz Zanartu
A42

Anibal Pinto
A43

Designs: 2p, Domingo Santa Maria. 5p, Jose de Balmaceda. 10p, Federico Errazuriz Echaurren.

Outer backgrounds consist of horizontal and diagonal lines.

1911 Engr. *Perf. 12.*

98 A32 1c dp grn 30 10
99 A33 2c scarlet 30 10
100 A34 3c sepia 1.00 40
101 A35 5c dk bl 30 5
102 A36 10c gray & blk 1.00 20
a. Center inverted 1,100. 800.00
103 A37 12c car & blk 1.50 20
104 A38 15c vio & blk 1.20 20
a. Center inverted *1,100.*
105 A39 20c org red & blk 2.50 20
a. Center inverted 90.00 85.00
106 A40 25c lt bl & blk 3.00 75
107 A41 30c bis brn & blk 4.50 30
108 A42 50c myr grn & blk 5.50 30
109 A43 1p grn & blk 10.00 40
110 A43 2p ver & blk 17.50 1.50
111 A43 5p ol grn & blk 65.00 10.00
112 A43 10p org yel & blk 55.00 8.00
Nos. 98-112 (15) 168.60 22.70

See also Nos. 117, 121, 123, 127-128, 133-141, 143, 155A, 157-161, 165-169, 171-172.

Columbus
A47

Toro Z.
A48

Freire
A49

O'Higgins
A50

1912-13 Engr. *Perf. 12.*

113 A47 2c scarlet 25 10
114 A48 4c blk brn 35 10
115 A49 8c gray 1.40 20
116 A50 10c bl & blk 1.40 10
a. Center inverted 700.00 600.00
b. Imperf. horizontally or vertically, pair 70.00
117 A37 14c car & blk 1.50 20
121 A38 40c vio & blk 6.50 60
123 A40 60c lt bl & blk 14.00 1.75
Nos. 112-123 (8) 80.40 11.05

See also Nos. 125-126, 131, 164, 170, 173.

Cochrane
A52

Columbus
A53

1915 Engr. *Perf. 13½x14.*

124 A52 5c sl bl 75 10
a. Imperf., pair 16.00

See also Nos. 155, 162-163.

1918

125 A49 8c slate 14.00 60

No. 125 is from a plate made in Chile to resemble No. 115. The top of the head is further from the oval, the spots of color enclosed in the figures "8" are oval instead of round, and there are many small differences in the design.

1921

Worn Plate.

126 A49 8c gray 37.50 9.00

No. 126 differs from No. 125 in not having diagonal lines in the frame and only a few diagonal lines above the shoulders (due to wear), while No. 125 has diagonal lines in the oval up to the level of the forehead.

1915-25 Typo. *Perf. 13½x14½*

127 A32 1c gray grn 30 10
128 A33 2c red 30 10
129 A53 4c brn ('18) 40 10

Frame Litho.; Head Engr.

131 A50 10c bl & blk 2.00 5
a. 10c dk bl & blk 2.00 5
b. Imperf., pair 150.00
c. Center inverted 450.00
133 A38 15c vio & blk 1.50 10
134 A39 20c org red & blk 2.75 10
a. 20c brn org & blk 2.75 10
135 A40 25c dl bl & blk 1.00 20
136 A41 30c bis brn & blk 3.00 20
137 A42 50c dp grn & blk 3.00 20

Perf. 14

138 A43 1p grn & blk 15.00 30
139 A43 2p red & blk 17.50 20
a. 2p ver & blk 55.00 1.00
140 A43 5p ol grn & blk ('20) 45.00 1.00
141 A43 10p org & blk ('25) 50.00 2.50
Nos. 127-141 (13) 141.75 5.15

The frames have crosshatching on the 15c, 20c, 30c, 2p, 5p and 10p. They have no crosshatching on the 10c, 25c, 50c and 1p.

Nos. 131a and 134a are printed from new head plates which give blacker and heavier impressions. No. 131a exists with; (a) frame lithographed and head engraved; (b) frame typographed and head engraved; (c) frame typographed and head lithographed. No. 134a is with frame typographed and head engraved.

A 4c stamp with portrait of Balmaceda and a 14c with portrait of Manuel de Salas were prepared but not placed in use. Both stamps were sent to the paper mill at Puente Alto for destruction. They were not all destroyed as some were privately preserved and sold.

Columbus
A54

Manuel Rengifo
A55

Types of 1915-20 Re-drawn.

1918-20 *Perf. 13½x14½*

143 A32 1c gray grn ('20) 40 20
144 A54 4c brown 75 20

No. 143 has all the lines much finer and clearer than No. 127. The white shirt front is also much less shaded.

1921

145 A55 40c dk vio & blk 3.00 20

Pan-American Congress Building
A56

Admiral Juan José Latorre
A57

1923, Apr. 25 Typo. *Perf. 14½x14*

146 A56 2c red 25 15
147 A56 4c brown 25 15

Typo.; Center Engr.

148 A56 10c bl & blk 25 15
149 A56 20c org & blk 60 20
150 A56 40c dl vio & blk 1.00 30
151 A56 1p grn & blk 1.25 50
152 A56 2p red & blk 5.00 60
153 A56 5p dk grn & blk 17.50 4.00
Nos. 146-153 (8) 26.10 6.05

Fifth Pan-American Congress.

Typographed; Head Engraved

1927 *Perf. 13½x14½*

154 A57 80c dk brn & blk 3.50 80

Wmk. 215-Small Star in Shield, Multiple

Types of 1915-25 Issues.
Inscribed: "Chile Correos".

Perf. 13½x14½

1928-31 Engr. Wmk. 215

155 A52 5c sl bl 1.40 30

Frame Typo.; Center Engr.

155A A38 15c vio & blk *500.00*
156 A55 40c dk vio & blk 85 10
157 A42 50c dp grn & blk 3.00 10

Perf. 14

158 A43 1p grn & blk 1.40 10
159 A43 2p red & blk 5.00 20
160 A43 5p ol grn & blk 11.00 40
161 A43 10p org & blk 11.00 1.50
Nos. 155,156-161 (7) 33.65 2.70

Paper of Nos. 155-161 varies from thin to thick.

Types of 1915-25 Issues.
Inscribed: "Correos de Chile"

1928 Engr. *Perf. 13½x14½*

162 A52 5c dp bl 60 10

1929 Litho.

163 A52 5c lt grn 60 10

Frame Litho.; Center Engr.

164 A50 10c bl & blk 2.50 10
165 A38 15c vio & blk 2.75 10
166 A39 20c org red & blk 6.50 12
167 A40 25c bl & blk 1.25 10
168 A41 30c brn & blk 90 30
169 A42 50c dp grn & blk 75 10
Nos. 163-169 (7) 15.25 92

Redrawn.

Frame Typographed; Center Lithographed

1929

170 A50 10c bl & blk 3.00 6
171 A38 15c vio & blk 2.50 20
172 A39 20c org red & blk 4.00 25

1931 Unwmk.

173 A50 10c bl & blk 1.00 30

In the redrawn stamps the lines behind the portraits are heavier and completely fill the ovals. There are strong diagonal lines above the shoulders. On No. 170 the head is larger than on Nos. 164 and 173.

A58

Prosperity of Saltpeter Trade
A59 A60

Perf. 13½x14

1930, July 21 Litho. Wmk. 215

Size: 20x25 mm.

175 A58 5c yel grn 50 20
176 A58 10c red brn 50 20
177 A58 15c violet 50 20
178 A59 25c dp gray 2.00 60
179 A60 70c dk bl 5.00 1.50

Perf. 14

Size: 24½x30 mm.

180 A60 1p dk gray grn 3.75 75
Nos. 175-180 (6) 12.25 3.45

Issued to commemorate the centenary of the first shipment of saltpeter from Chile, July 21, 1830.

Manuel Bulnes
A61

Bernardo O'Higgins
A62

1931 *Perf. 13½, 14*

181 A61 20c dk brn 1.25 10

1932

182 A62 10c dp bl 1.50 10

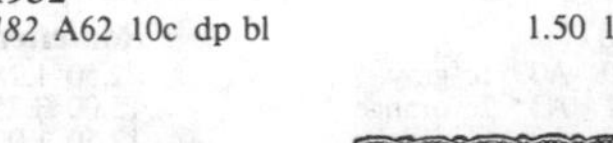

Mariano Egana — A63

Joaquin Tocornal — A64

1934 *Perf. 13½x14*

183 A63 30c magenta 75 20

Perf. 14

184 A64 1.20p brt bl 1.25 30

Centenary of the constitution.

José Joaquin Perez — A65

1934 *Perf. 13½x14*

185 A65 30c brt pink 2.00 10

Atacama Desert — A66

Fishing Boats — A67

Coquito Palms — A68

Sheep — A69

Mining — A70

Lonquimay Forest — A71

Colliery at Port Lota — A72

Shipping at Valparaiso — A73

Puntiagudo Volcano — A74

Diego de Almagro — A75

Cattle — A76

Mining Saltpeter — A77

Wmk. 215

1936, Mar. 1	Litho.	Perf. 14	
186 A66	5c vermilion	35	20
187 A67	10c violet	25	15
188 A68	20c magenta	25	15
189 A69	25c grnsh bl	2.50	80
190 A70	30c lt grn	25	15
191 A71	40c blk, *cr*	2.50	75
192 A72	50c bl, *bluish*	1.25	30
	Engr.		
193 A73	1p dk grn	1.25	50
194 A74	1.20p dp bl	1.50	70
195 A75	2p dk brn	1.50	85
196 A76	5p cop red	4.00	2.00
197 A77	10p dk vio	10.00	7.00
	Nos. 186-197 (12)	25.60	13.55

Issued in commemoration of the 400th anniversary of the discovery of Chile by Diego de Almagro.

Laja Waterfall A78

Agriculture A79

Boldo Tree A79a

Nitrate Industry A80

Mineral Spas A81

Copper Mine A82

Mining A83

Fishing in Chiloé A84

Osorno Volcano — A85

Mercantile Marine — A86

Lake Villarrica — A87

State Railways — A88

Perf. 13½x14

1938-40	Litho.	Wmk. 215	
198 A78	5c brn car ('39)	25	10
199 A79	10c sal pink ('39)	25	10
200 A79a	15c brn org ('40)	25	10
201 A80	20c lt bl	25	10
202 A81	30c brt pink	25	10
203 A82	40c lt grn ('39)	25	6
204 A83	50c violet	25	10
	Engr.	*Perf. 14*	
205 A84	1p org brn	25	10
206 A85	1.80p dp bl	65	30
207 A86	2p car lake	25	10
208 A87	5p dk sl grn	50	10
209 A88	10p rose vio ('40)	1.25	10
	Nos. 198-209 (12)	4.65	1.36

See also Nos. 217-227.

Map of the Americas — A89

Unwmk.

1940, Sept. 11	Litho.	Perf. 14	
210 A89	40c dl grn & yel grn	25	10

Pan American Union, 50th anniversary.

Camilo Henriquez — A90

Founding of Santiago A93

Designs: 40c, Pedro de Valdivia. 1.10p, Benjamin Vicuna Mackenna. 3.60p, Diego Barros Arana.

Perf. 14½x14, 14½.

1941, Jan. 23	Engr.	Wmk. 215	
211 A90	10c car lake	25	15
212 A90	40c green	40	12
213 A90	1.10p red	1.25	75
214 A93	1.80p blue	1.25	75
215 A90	3.60p indigo	3.75	2.50
	Nos. 211-215 (5)	6.90	4.27

400th anniversary of Santiago.

Types of 1938.

Perf. 13½x14.

1942-46	Unwmk.	Litho.	
217 A79	10c sal pink ('43)	25	10
218 A79a	15c brn org ('43)	25	10
219 A80	20c lt bl ('43)	25	10
220 A81	30c brt pink ('43)	30	10
221 A82	40c yel grn	1.00	10
222 A83	50c vio ('43)	25	10
	Engr.	*Perf. 14.*	
223 A84	1p brn org	2.00	10
225 A86	2p car lake ('43)	25	10
226 A87	5p dk sl grn ('43)	65	10
227 A88	10p rose vio ('46)	1.00	10
	Nos. 217-227 (10)	6.20	1.00

Valentin Letelier A95

University of Chile A98

Designs: 40c, Andrés Bello. 90c, Manuel Bulnes. 1.80p, Manuel Montt.

1942, Nov. 1	Perf. 14x14½, 14 (1p)		
228 A95	30c rose red	25	10
229 A95	40c dp grn	25	10
230 A95	90c rose vio	1.50	1.00
231 A98	1p dp brn	1.00	60
232 A95	1.80p dk bl	3.00	2.00
	Nos. 228-232 (5)	6.00	3.80

University of Chile centenary. See also No. C89.

Manuel Bulnes A100

Map Showing Strait of Magellan A104

Designs: 30c, Juan Williams Wilson. 40c, Diego Duble Almeida. 1p, JoséMardones.

1944, Mar. 2	Litho.	Perf. 14	
233 A100	15c black	25	15
234 A100	30c dp rose	25	15
235 A100	40c yel grn	25	15
236 A100	1p brn car	1.25	40
237 A104	1.80p ultra	1.75	1.00
	Nos. 233-237 (5)	3.75	1.85

Issued to commemorate the 100th anniversary of the occupation of the Strait of Magellan.

Red Cross and Lamp of Life — A105

Serpent and Cup — A106

1944, Oct. 18		Unwmk.	
238 A105	40c grn, red & blk	35	15
239 A106	1.80p ultra & red	90	50

Issued to commemorate the 80th anniversary of the International Red Cross Society.

Bernardo O'Higgins — A107

"Embrace of Maipú" (O'Higgins Joining San Martin) — A108

Designs: 40c, Abdication of O'Higgins. 1.80p, Battle of Rancagua.

1945	Engr.	Perf. 14 (15c), 14½	
	Center in Black.		
240 A107	15c carmine	25	15
241 A108	30c brown	35	15
242 A108	40c dp grn	35	15
243 A108	1.80p dk bl	1.75	1.20

Issued to commemorate the centenary of the death of Bernardo O'Higgins in 1842.

Proposed Columbus Lighthouse A111

Canceled-to-order stamps are often from remainders. Most collectors of canceled stamps prefer postally used specimens.

Wmk. 215

1945, Sept. 10 Litho. Perf. 14
244 A111 40c lt grn 30 20

Issued in honor of the discovery of America by Columbus and the Memorial Lighthouse to be erected in his memory.

Andrés Bello — A112

1946 Engr.
245 A112 40c dk grn 20 10
246 A112 1.80p dk bl 20 15

Issued to commemorate the 80th anniversary of the death of Andres Bello, poet and educator.

Map Showing Chile's Claims of Antarctic Territory A113

1947, May 12 Litho. Perf. 14½
247 A113 40c carmine 50 15
248 A113 2.50p dp bl 1.00 40

Eusebio Lillo and Ramon Carnicer A114

1947, Sept. 18 Engr.
249 A114 40c dk grn 20 12

Centenary of national anthem.

Miguel de Cervantes Saavedra A115

1947, Oct. 11 Wmk. 215
250 A115 40c dk car 30 20

Issued to commemorate the 400th anniversary of the birth of Miguel de Cervantes Saavedra, novelist, playwright and poet.

Arturo Prat Chacon and Iquique Naval Battle A116

1948, Dec. 24 Perf. 14½
251 A116 40c dp bl 20 8

Issued to commemorate the centenary of the birth of Arturo Prat Chacon, Chilean naval hero.

Bernardo O'Higgins — A117

Perf. 13½x14.
1948 Wmk. 215 Litho.
252 A117 60c black 10 10

See also No. 262.

No. 203 Surcharged in Black

VEINTE
CTS.

1948
253 A82 20c on 40c lt grn 10 10

Chilean Pigeons — A118

American Skunk — A119

Designs not illustrated, FAUNA: Chilean Otter. Southern sea lions. Sugar-cane borer moth. Emperor penguins. Bat. Chinchilla. Grant's stag beetle. Trevally (fish). Chilean slender lizard. Crested caracara. Red-gartered coot. Chilean guemal (deer). Spiny rock lobster. Tilefish. Praying mantis. Torrent duck. Red conger. FLORA: Araucarian pine (monkey puzzle tree). Evening primrose. Chilean red bell flower. Loxodon (flower). Boldo tree. Coquito palm trees.

Wmk. 215

1948, Dec. 6 Litho. Perf. 14
254 A118 60c ultra 35 20
a. Block of 25 10.00
255 A119 2.60p green 50 35
a. Block of 25 15.00

Issued in panes of 100 stamps, divisible into four blocks of 25 different designs.

The stamps commemorate the centenary (in 1944) of the publication of the first volume of Claudio Gay's Natural History of Chile. See also No. C124.

Benjamin Vicuna Mackenna — A121

1949, Mar. 22 Engr. Perf. 13½x14
257 A121 60c dp bl 10 10

See also No. C126.

Symbols of Arts and Crafts Education A122

Heinrich von Stephan A123

Design: 2.60p, Badge and book.

Unwmk.

1949, Nov. 11 Litho. Perf. 14
258 A122 60c lil rose 20 10
259 A122 2.60p vio bl 50 30

Issued to commemorate the centenary of the foundation of Chile's School of Arts and Crafts. See also Nos. C127-C128.

1950, Jan. 6 Engr.
260 A123 60c dp car 20 10
261 A123 2.50p dp bl 50 30

Issued to commemorate the 75th anniversary of the formation of the Universal Postal Union. See also Nos. C129-C130.

O'Higgins Type of 1948.

1950 Litho. Perf. 13x14
262 A117 60c black 10 8

Gen. Jose de San Martin — A124

Queen Isabella I — A125

Wmk. 215

1951, Mar. 16 Engr. Perf. 14
263 A124 60c dp bl 10 8

Issued to commemorate the centenary of the death of Gen. Jose de San Martin. See also No. C165.

1952, Mar. 20
264 A125 60c brt bl 10 8

Issued to commemorate the 500th anniversary of the birth of Queen Isabella I of Spain. See also No. C166.

Bernardo O'Higgins A126

Mateo de Toro Zambrano A127

1952 Unwmk. Litho. Perf. 13½x14
265 A126 1p dk bl grn 10 8

See also No. 275.

Nos. 252 and 262 Surcharged "40 Ctvs." in Red.

1952, Sept.
266 A117 40c on 60c blk 10 8

Wmk. 215

267 A117 40c on 60c blk 10 8

1953, Mar. 13 Wmk. 215
268 A127 80c green 10 8

See also No. 285.

Valdivia Arms — A128

Old Fort — A129

Designs: 3p, Modern Valdivia. 5p, Street in ancient Valdivia.

1953, May Perf. 14
269 A128 1p brt ultra 20 10
270 A129 2p dl rose vio 20 10
271 A129 3p bl grn 30 20
272 A129 5p dp brn 30 20
Nos. 269-272,C167 (5) 2.00 85

Issued to commemorate the 4th centenary of the founding of Valdivia, capital of Valdivia province.

José Toribio Medina — A130

1953, June Engr. Perf. 14½
273 A130 1p brown 15 15
274 A130 2.50p dp bl 30 20

Issued to commemorate the centenary of the birth of Jose Toribio Medina (1852-1930), historian and bibliographer.

O'Higgins Type of 1952.

Perf. 13½x14
1953, Oct. Wmk. 215 Litho.
275 A126 1p dk bl grn 10 8

Stamp of 1853 — A131

1953, Oct. 15 Engr. Perf. 14½
276 A131 1p chocolate 20 15

Centenary of Chile's first postage stamps.

Souvenir sheet including No. 276 is noted below No. C168.

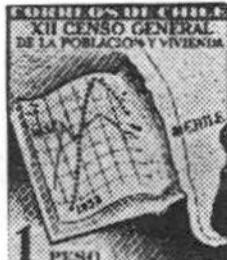
Census Chart and Map — A132

1953, Nov. 5 Litho. Perf. 13½x14
277 A132 1p bl grn 10 10
278 A132 2.50p vio bl 20 10
279 A132 3p chocolate 30 20
280 A132 4p carmine 40 20

Issued to publicize the 12th general census of population and housing.

Arms of Angol A133

Ignacio Domeyko A134

1954, May 28 Unwmk. Perf. 14
281 A133 2p dp car 15 8

Issued to commemorate the 400th anniversary of the founding of Angol, capital of Malleco province.

1954, Aug. 16 Engr. Perf. 13½x14
282 A134 1p grnsh bl 10 5

Issued to commemorate the 150th anniversary of the birth of Ignacio Domeyko (1802-

1889), mineralogist and educator. See also No. C171.

Early Steam Locomotive — A135

1954, Sept. 10 Wmk. 215 ***Perf. 14½***
283 A135 1p red 15 10

Issued to commemorate the centenary (in 1951) of the first South American railroad. See also No. C172.

Adm. Arturo Prat Chacon — A136

Arms of Vina del Mar — A137

1954 Unwmk. Litho. ***Perf. 14***
284 A136 2p dk vio bl 10 8

Issued to commemorate the 75th anniversary of the naval Battle of Iquique.

Toro Zambrano Type of 1953

1954, Nov. 6 ***Perf. 13½x14***
285 A127 80c green 10 5

1955, Mar. 5 Wmk. 215 ***Perf. 14***

Design: 2p, Arms of Valparaiso.

286 A137 1p vio bl 10 8
287 A137 2p carmine 10 8

Issued to publicize the first International Philatelic Exhibition, Valparaiso, March 1955.

Dr. Alejandro del Rio — A138

1955, May 24 ***Perf. 13½x14***
288 A138 2p vio bl 10 8

14th Pan-American Sanitary Conference.

Christ of the Andes, Emblems of Chile, Argentina A139

1955, Aug. 31 Unwmk. ***Perf. 14½***
289 A139 1p vio bl 15 10

Issued to publicize the reciprocal visits of Presidents Juan D. Peron and Carlos Ibanez del Campo. See also No. C173.

Prices of premium quality never hinged stamps will be in excess of catalogue price.

Manuel Rengifo — A140

Portraits: 5p, Mariano Egana. 50p, Diego Portales.

1955-56 Unwmk. ***Perf. 14x14½***
290 A140 3p vio bl 10 8
291 A140 5p dk car rose 15 8
292 A140 50p rose lil ('56) 1.75 40

Issued to commemorate the centenary of the death of Joaquin Prieto (1786-1854), soldier and political leader; president, 1831-41. See No. QRA1.

Jose M. Carrera A141

Ramon Freire A142

Portraits: 5p, Manuel Bulnes. 10p, Pres. Francisco A. Pinto. 50p, Manuel Montt.

Perf. 14x14½

1956-58 Unwmk. Litho.
293 A141 2p purple 10 5
293A A142 3p lt vio bl 10 5
294 A141 5p redsh brn (19½x23mm) 10 5
a. Size 19x22mm 10 8
295 A142 10p vio (19x22¼mm) 15 5
a. Perf. 13½x14 (19¼x22½mm) ('58) 50 8
296 A141 50p rose red 35 10
Nos. 293-296 (5) 80 30

No. 294 has yellow gum; No. 294a, white gum.

Wmk. 215

297 A141 2p dl pur 10 8
298 A142 3p vio bl 10 8

Federico Santa Maria — A143

Gabriela Mistral — A144

Unwmk.

1957, Jan. 31 Engr. ***Perf. 14***
299 A143 5p dk red brn 15 8

Issued to commemorate the 25th anniversary of the Federico Santa Maria Technical University. See Nos. C190-C191.

Souvenir sheet including No. 299 is noted below No. C191.

1958, Jan. 10
300 A144 10p red brn 15 5

Issued in honor of Gabriela Mistral, poet and educator. See also No. C192.

Arms of Osorno A145

Arms of Santiago A146

Design: 50p, Garcia Hdo. de Mendoza.

1958, Mar. 23 Litho. ***Perf. 14***
301 A145 10p carmine 15 10

Engr.
302 A145 50p green 40 15

Issued to commemorate the 400th anniversary of the founding of the city of Osorno, capital of Osorno province.

Souvenir sheet including No. 302 in red brown is noted below No. C193.

1958, Oct. 18 Unwmk. ***Perf. 14***
303 A146 10p dk vio 15 5

Issued to publicize the National Philatelic Exposition, Santiago, Oct. 18-26.

Souvenir sheet including No. 303 in deep red is noted below No. C194.

Symbolical Savings Bank A147

Modern Map of Antarctica A148

1958, Dec. 18
304 A147 10p dk bl 15 5

Issued to commemorate the centenary of the Savings Bank for Public Employees.

Souvenir sheet including No. 304 in violet is noted below No. C195.

1958, Aug. 28 Unwmk. ***Perf. 14***
305 A148 40p rose car 20 10

Issued to commemorate the International Geophysical Year, 1957-1958. See No. C214.

Antarctic Map and "La Araucana" A149

Map of Strait of Magellan, 1588 A150

1958 Litho. ***Perf. 14***
310 A149 10p vio bl 15 10

Engr.
311 A150 200p dl pur 2.25 75

See also Nos. C199-C200.

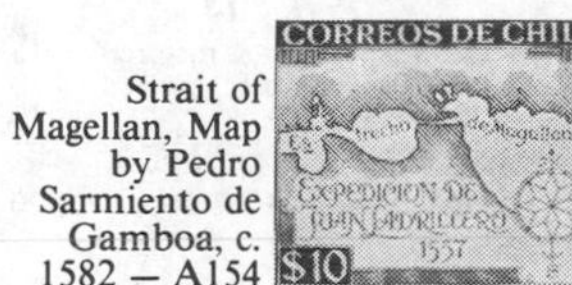

Valdivia River Bridge — A153

1959, Feb. 9 Engr. ***Perf. 14***
319 A153 40p green 20 10

Issued to commemorate the centenary of the German School in Valdivia and to publicize the Valdivia Philatelic Exhibition, Feb. 9-18.

Souvenir sheet including No. 319 is noted below No. C213.

Strait of Magellan, Map by Pedro Sarmiento de Gamboa, c. 1582 — A154

1959, Aug. 27 Lighographed
320 A154 10p dl pur 20 10

Issued to commemorate the 400th anniversary of the Juan Ladrillero expedition to explore the Strait of Magellan, 1557-1558. See also No. C215.

Diego Barros Arana — A155

Henri Dunant — A156

1959, Aug. 27
321 A155 40p ultra 20 10

Issued to commemorate the 50th anniversary of the death of Diego Barros Arana (1830-1907), historian. See No. C216.

1959, Oct. 6 Unwmk. ***Perf. 14***
322 A156 20p red & red brn 15 5

Issued to commemorate the centenary of the Red Cross idea. See No. C217.

Manuel Bulnes A157

Francisco A. Pinto A158

Choshuenco Volcano — A159

Designs: No. 326, Choshuenco volcano, redrawn. 5c, Manuel Montt. 10c, Maule River Valley. 20c, 1e, Inca Lake.

1960-67 Litho. ***Perf. 13x14***
323 A157 5m bluish grn 5 5
324 A158 1c carmine 5 5

Perf. 14

Size: 29x25mm.

325 A159 2c ultra ('61) 10 5

Perf. 14x13

Size: 23½x18mm.

326 A159 2c ultra ('62) 5 5

Perf. 13x14

327 A157 5c blue 10 5

Perf. 14

Size: 29x25mm.

328 A159 10c grn ('62) 25 10
329 A159 20c Prus bl ('62) 40 15
329A A159 1e bluish grn ('67) 50 25
Nos. 323-329A (8) 1.50 75

On No. 325 "Volcan Choshuenco" is at upper left, below "Correos." On No. 326, it is at bottom, above "Centesimos."

Refugee Family — A160

1960, Apr. 7 ***Perf. 14½***
330 A160 1c green 15 10

Issued to publicize World Refugee Year, July 1, 1959-June 30, 1960. A souvenir sheet is noted below No. C218.

Type of Air Post Issue, 1962, and

Arms of Chile A161

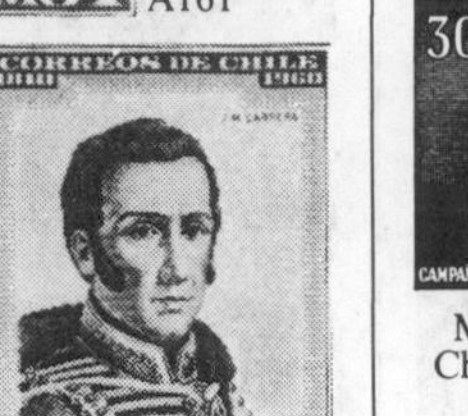

José M. Carrera — A162

Designs: No. 332, Palace of Justice. 5c, National Memorial. 10c, Manuel de Toro y Zambrano and Martinez de Rozas. 20c, Manuel de Salas and Juan Egana. 50c, Manuel Rodriguez and Juan Mackenna.

Wmk. 215 (#331, 1e); Unwmk.

1960-65 Engr. *Perf. 14½*

331 A161 1c mar & sep 20 10
332 A161 1c brn & cl ('62) 15 5
333 A162 5c grn & Prus grn ('61) 15 5
334 AP54 10c brn & vio brn ('64) 20 5
334A AP54 20c ind & bl grn ('65) 20 5
335 AP54 50c red brn & mar ('65) 35 15
336 A162 1e gray ol & brn 1.25 50
Nos. 331-336,C218A-C220D (14) 5.00 2.05

Issued to commemorate the 150th anniversary of the formation of the first National Government. A souvenir sheet is noted below No. C220B. See also No. C285.

Family — A163

Design: 10c, Various buildings.

Unwmk.

1960, Jan. 18 Litho. *Perf. 14*

337 A163 5c green 20 8
338 A163 10c brt vio 20 8

Issued to publicize the 13th population census (No. 337) and the second housing census (No. 338).

Chamber of Deputies A164

1961, Aug. 14 Unwmk. *Perf. 14½*

339 A164 2c red brn 60 10

Issued to commemorate the 150th anniversary of the first National Congress. See also No. C245.

Soccer Players and Globe A165

Design: 5c, Goalkeeper and stadium (vert.).

1962, May 30 Engr. *Perf. 14½*

340 A165 2c blue 20 10
341 A165 5c green 30 10

Issued to commemorate the World Soccer Championship, Chile, May 30-June 17. Note on souvenir sheet follows No. C247.

Mother and Child — A166

Centenary Emblem — A167

1963, Mar. 21 Litho. *Perf. 14*

342 A166 3c maroon 10 5

Issued for the "Freedom from Hunger" campaign of the U.N. Food and Agriculture Organization. See also No. C248.

1963, Aug. 23 Unwmk. *Perf. 14*

343 A167 3c red & gray 15 8

Issued to commemorate the centenary of the International Red Cross. See No. C249.

Fireman Carrying Woman — A168

Enrique Molina — A169

1963, Dec. 20 Unwmk. *Perf. 14*

344 A168 3c violet 10 8

Issued to commemorate the centenary of the Santiago Fire Brigade. See No. C250.

1964, Nov. 14 Litho. *Perf. 14*

Design: No. 346, Magr. Carlos Casanueva.

345 A169 4c bis brn 15 5
346 A169 4c rose cl 10 5

Issued to honor Enrique Molina, founder of the University of Concepcion, and Msgr. Carlos Casanueva, rector of the Catholic University, 1920-53. See Nos. C257-C258.

Easter Island Statue A170

Copihue, National Flower A171

Design: 30c, Robinson Crusoe.

1965-69 Litho. *Perf. 14x14½*

347 A170 60c rose lil 10 6
347A A170 10c rose pink ('68) 10 6

Perf. 14

348 A171 15c yel grn & rose red 15 8
348A A171 20c yel grn & rose red ('69) 10 6

Perf. 14x14½

349 A170 30c rose cl 20 15

Skier — A172

Lorenzo Sazie — A173

1965, Aug. 30 *Perf. 14*

350 A172 4c bl grn 10 5

World Skiing Championships, Chile, 1966.

1966, Feb. 9 Litho. *Perf. 14x14½*

351 A173 1e green 60 10

Issued to commemorate the centenary of the death of Dr. Lorenzo Sazie, dean of the Faculty of Medicine, University of Santiago.

German Riesco, President in 1901-1906 — A174

Portrait: 30c, Jorge Montt (1847-1922), president in 1891-1896.

1966 Unwmk. *Perf. 13x14*

354 A174 30c violet 10 5
355 A174 50c dl brn 10 5

William Wheelwright and S.S. Chile — A175

1966, Aug. 2 *Perf. 14½*

358 A175 10c ultra & lt bl 10 8

Issued to commemorate the 125th anniversary (in 1965) of the arrival of the paddle steamers "Chile" and "Peru." See also No. C268.

Learning to Read — A176

1966, Aug. 13 Litho. *Perf. 14*

359 A176 10c red brn 10 8

Literacy campaign.

U.N. and ICY Emblems A177

1966, Oct. 28 Unwmk. *Perf. 14½*

360 A177 1e grn & brn 1.00 20

International Cooperation Year, 1965. See No. C269.

Capt. Luis Pardo and Ship in Antarctica A178

1967, Jan. Litho. *Perf. 14½*

361 A178 20c turq bl 10 10

Issued to commemorate the 50th anniversary of the rescue of the Shackleton South Pole expedition by Capt. Luis Pardo of Chile. See also No. C271.

Family A179

Trees and Mountains A180

1967, Apr. 13 Unwmk. *Perf. 14*

362 A179 10c mag & blk 5 5

Issued to publicize the 8th International Conference for Family Planning, Santiago, April 1967. See also No. C272.

1967, June 9 Litho. *Perf. 14½*

363 A180 10c bl grn & lt bl 5 5

Reforestation Campaign. See No. C274.

Lions Emblem — A181

1967, July 12 Litho. *Perf. 14*

364 A181 20c Prus bl & yel 15 10

Issued to commemorate the 50th anniversary of Lions International. See also Nos. C275-C276.

Chilean Flag A182

1967, Oct. 20 Unwmk. *Perf. 14½*

365 A182 80c crim & ultra 15 10

Issued to commemorate the sesquicentennial of the national flag. See No. C277.

José Maria Cardinal Caro — A183

1967, Dec. 4 Engr. *Perf. 14½*
366 A183 20c dp car 60 20

Issued to commemorate the centenary of the birth of Jose Maria Cardinal Caro, the first Chilean cardinal. See No. C279.

San Martin and O'Higgins A184

1968, Apr. 23 Litho. Unwmk.
367 A184 3e blue 10 6

Issued to commemorate the sesquicentennial of the Battles of Chacabuco and Maipu. See No. C280.

Farm Couple — A185

1968, June 18 *Perf. 14½*
368 A185 20c blk, org & grn 20 10

Agrarian reforms. See No. C281.

Juan I. Molina A186

1968, Aug. 27 Litho. *Perf. 14½*
369 A186 2e red lil 10 6

Issued to honor Juan I. Molina, educator and scientist. See also No. C282.

Hand Holding Cogwheel — A187

1968, Sept. *Perf. 14x14½*
370 A187 30c dp car 10 6

Fourth census of manufacturers.

Map of Chiloé Province, Sailing Ship and Coastal Vessel A188

1968, Oct. 7 *Perf. 14½*
371 A188 30c ultra 10 6

Issued to commemorate the anniversaries of the founding of five towns in Chiloé Province. See also No. C283.

Automobile Club Emblem — A189

1968, Nov. 10 Engr. *Perf. 14½x14*
372 A189 1e car rose 10 6

Issued to commemorate the 40th anniversary of the Automobile Club of Chile. See No. C284.

Francisco Garcia Huidobro A190

Design: 5e, King Philip V of Spain.

1968, Dec. 31 Litho. *Perf. 14½*
373 A190 2e pale rose & ultra 10 6
374 A190 5e brn & yel grn 15 8

Issued to commemorate the 225th anniversary of the founding of the State Mint (Casa de Moneda de Chile). See Nos. C288-C289.

Satellite and Radar Station A191

1969, May 20 Litho. *Perf. 14½*
375 A191 30c blue 10 5

Issued to publicize the inauguration of ENTEL-Chile, the first commercial satellite communications ground station, Longovilo. See No. C290.

Red Cross, Crescent and Lion and Sun Emblems A192

1969, Sept. Litho. *Perf. 14½*
376 A192 2e vio bl & red 10 6

Issued to commemorate the 50th anniversary of the League of Red Cross Societies. See No. C291.

Rapel Hydroelectric Plant — A193

1969, Nov. 18 Litho. *Perf. 14½*
377 A193 40c green 10 8

See No. C292.

Col. Rodriguez Monument A194

1969, Nov. 24
378 A194 2e rose cl 10 6

Issued to commemorate the 150th anniversary of the death of Col. Manuel Rodriguez. See No. C293.

EXPO '70 Emblem — A195

1069, Dec. 2 Litho. *Perf. 14*
379 A195 3e blue 8 5

Issued to publicize EXPO '70 International Exhibition, Osaka, Japan, March 15-Sept. 13, 1970. See No. C294.

Open Book A196

1969, Dec. 3 *Perf. 14½*
380 A196 40c red brn 5 5

Issued to commemorate the 400th anniversary of the translation of the Bible into Spanish by Casiodoro de Reina. See No. C295.

Globes and ILO Emblem A197

1969, Dec. 17 *Perf. 14½*
381 A197 1e grn & blk 8 5

Issued to commemorate the 50th anniversary of the International Labor Organization. See No. C296.

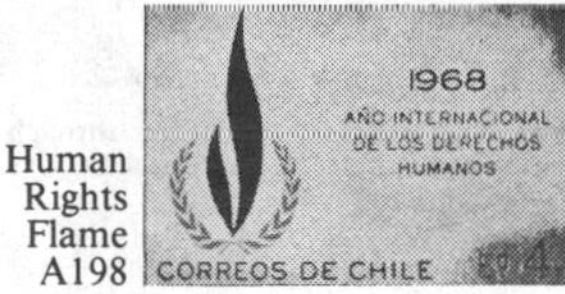

Human Rights Flame A198

1969, Dec. 18
382 A198 4e bl & red 8 5

Human Rights Year, 1968. See No. C297.

Policarpo Toro and Easter Island A199

1970, Jan. 26 *Perf. 14½*
383 A199 5e lilac 8 5

Issued to commemorate the 80th anniversary of the acquisition of Easter Island. See No. C298.

Sailing Ship and Arms of Valdivia A200

1970, Feb. 4 Litho. *Perf. 14½*
384 A200 40c dk car 10 5

Issued to commemorate the 150th anniversary of the capture of Valdivia during Chile's war of independence by Thomas Cochrane (1775-1860), naval commander. See No. C299.

Paul Harris and Rotary Emblem — A201

1970, Mar. 18 Litho. *Perf. 14*
385 A201 10e vio bl 10 5

Issued to commemorate the centenary of the birth of Paul Harris (1868-1947), founder of Rotary International. See No. C300.

Mahatma Gandhi — A202

Santo Domingo Church, Santiago, Chile — A203

1970, Apr. 1 Litho. *Perf. 14½*
386 A202 40c bl grn 10 5

Issued to commemorate the centenary of the birth of Mohandas L. Gandhi (1869-1948), leader in India's fight for independence. See No. C301.

1970, Apr. 30 Engr.

Designs: 2e, Casa de Moneda de Chile (horiz.). 3e, Pedro de Valdivia. 5e, Bridge (horiz.). 10e, Ambrosio O'Higgins.

387	A203	2e vio brn	10	5
388	A203	3e dk red	8	5
389	A203	4e dk bl	8	5
390	A203	5e brown	10	5
391	A203	10e green	10	8
		Nos. 387 391 (5)	46	28

Issued to commemorate the exploration and development of Chile by Spanish explorers.

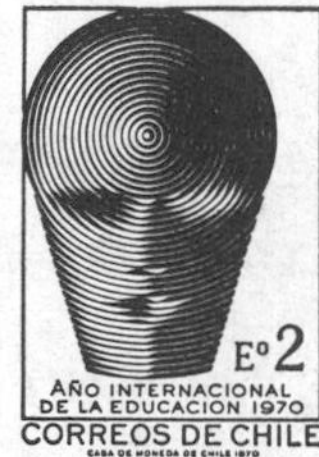

Education Year Emblem — A204

Virgin and Child — A205

1970, July 17 Litho. *Perf. 14½*
392 A204 2e claret 8 5

Issued for International Education Year. See No. C302.

1970, July 28
393 A205 40c green 8 5

Issued to publicize the O'Higgins National Shrine at Maipu. See No. C303.

Scott's editorial staff cannot undertake to identify, authenticate or appraise stamps and postal markings.

Torch and Snake — A206

Copper Symbol, Chile Arms — A207

1970, Aug. 11
394 A206 40c cl & lt bl 5 5

Issued to commemorate the International Cancer Congress, Houston, Texas, May 22-29. See No. C304.

1970, Oct. 21 Litho. *Perf. 14½*
395 A207 40c car & lt red brn 5 5

Issued to commemorate the nationalization of the copper industry. See No. C305.

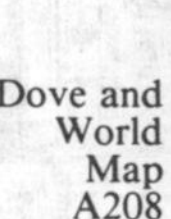

Dove and World Map A208

1970, Oct. 22
396 A208 3e rose mag & pur 8 5

Issued to commemorate the 25th anniversary of the United Nations. See No. C306.

No. 375 Surcharged in Red

1970, Dec. 24 Litho. *Perf. 14½*
397 A191 52c on 30c bl 10 8

Freighter and Ship's Wheel — A209

1971, Jan. 18 Litho. *Perf. 14*
398 A209 52c dp car 8 5

National Maritime Commission. See No. C307.

Bernardo O'Higgins and Ship A210

1971, Feb. 3 *Perf. 14½*
399 A210 5e grnsh bl & grn 8 5

The 150th anniversary of the expedition to liberate Peru from Spanish rule. See No. C309.

Youth, Girl and U.N. Emblem A211

1971, Feb. 11 Litho. *Perf. 14½*
400 A211 52c dk bl & brn 8 5

First meeting in Latin America of the Executive Council of UNICEF (U.N. Children's Fund), Santiago, May 20-31, 1969. See No. C310.

Chilean Boy Scout Emblem — A212

1971, Feb. 10 *Perf. 14*
401 A212 1e grn & brn 8 5

Founding of Chilean Boy Scouts, 60th anniversary. See No. C311.

Satellite and Radar Station A213

1971, May 25 Litho. *Perf. 14½*
402 A213 40c dl grn 10 5

First commercial Chilean satellite communications ground station, Longovilo. See No. C312.

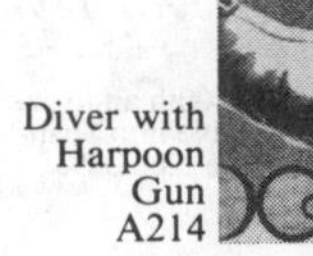

Diver with Harpoon Gun A214

1971, Sept. 1
403 A214 1.15e lt & dk grn 10 5
404 A214 2.35e vio bl & dp vio bl 8 5

10th World Championship of Underwater Fishing.

Ferdinand Magellan and Sailing Ship A215

1971, Nov. 3
405 A215 35c lt vio & brn vio 8 5

450th anniversary of first trip through and discovery of the Strait of Magellan, Oct. 21-Nov. 28, 1520.

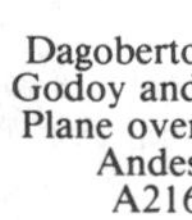

Dagoberto Godoy and Plane over Andes A216

1971, Nov. 4
406 A216 1.15e bl & grn 8 5

First trans-Andean flight, Dec. 12, 1918.

Virgin of San Cristobal — A217

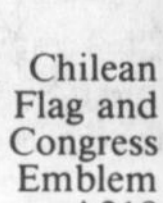

Chilean Flag and Congress Emblem A218

Designs (Congress Emblem and): 4.35e, Church of San Francisco. 9.35e, Central post office (horiz.). 18.35e, La Posada (Inn) del Corregidor (horiz.).

1971

407	A217	1.15e dk bl	15	8
408	A218	2.35e ultra & car	10	5
409	A217	4.35e brn red	10	5
410	A217	9.35e violet	10	5
411	A217	18.35e lil rose	15	8
		Nos. 407-411 (5)	60	31

10th Congress of the Postal Union of the Americas and Spain, Santiago. Issue dates: 2.35e, 4.35e, Nov. 5; 1.15e, Nov. 11; 9.35e, Nov. 18; 18.35e, Nov. 19.

Observation Dome, Cerro el Tololo Observatory A219

1971, Dec. 18
412 A219 1.95e lt & dk bl 8 5

Boeing 707 over Easter Island A220

1971, Dec. 18
413 A220 2.35e dk brn & yel 8 5

Inauguration of flights to Easter Island.

Alonso de Ercilla y Zuniga — A221

1972, Mar. 20 Engr. *Perf. 14*
414 A221 1e dk red 8 5

4th centenary (in 1969) of "La Araucana," by Alonso de Ercilla y Zuniga (1533-1596), Spanish author. See No. C313.

Map of Antarctica and Dog Sled A222

1972, Mar. 20 Litho. *Perf. 14½x15*
415 A222 1.15e vio bl & blk 10 5
416 A222 3.50e bl grn & grn 8 5

10th anniversary (in 1971) of the Antarctic Treaty pledging peaceful uses of and scientific cooperation in Antarctica.

"Your Heart is your Health" — A223

1972, Apr. 2 Litho. *Perf. 14½*
417 A223 1.15e blk & car 8 5

World Health Day.

People and Statement by Pres. Allende A224

Conference Hall and U.N. Emblem — A225

1972, Apr. 13 Litho. *Perf. 14½*

418	A224	35c dl grn & buff	10	8
419	A225	1.15e ultra & pur	8	5
420	A224	4e dk pur & pale rose	10	8
421	A225	6e org & vio bl	10	5

3rd United Nations Conference on Trade and Development (UNCTAD III), Santiago, Apr.-May 1972. Design A224 is perforated horizontally in the middle.

Soldier, 1822, Andes, Military College Emblem A226

1972, June 9
422 A226 1.15e bl & yel 8 5

Sesquicentennial of Bernardo O'Higgins Military College.

Miner Holding Copper Ingot, Chilean Flag — A227

Sailing Ship — A228

1972, July 11 Litho. *Perf. 15x14½*
423 A227 1.15e bl & rose red 8 5
424 A227 5e bl, blk & rose red 10 5

Nationalization of copper industry.

1972, Aug. 4
425 A228 1.15e vio brn 8 5

Sesquicentennial of the Arturo Pratt Naval Training School.

Mt. Calan Observatory — A229

1972, Aug. 31 Litho. *Perf. 14½*
426 A229 50c ultra 10 5

University of Chile Mt. Calan Observatory.

Carrier Pigeon — A230

1972, Oct. 9 Litho. *Perf. 14½*
427 A230 1.15e red lil & vio 8 5

International Letter Writing Week, Oct. 9-15.

René Schneider and Army Flag — A231

1972, Oct. 25 *Perf. 14*
428 A231 2.30e multi 8 5

2nd anniversary of the death of Gen. René Schneider. No. 428 is perforated vertically in the middle.

Book and Young People A232

1972, Oct. 31 *Perf. 14½*
429 A232 50c blk & dp org 8 5

International Book Year 1972.

Guitar and Earthen Jar — A233

Designs: 2.65e, Fish and produce. 3.50e, Stove, pots and rug (vert.).

1972, Nov. 20 Litho. *Perf. 14½*
430 A233 1.15e red & blk 8 5
431 A233 2.65e ultra & rose lake 8 5
432 A233 3.50e red & red brn 8 5

Tourism Year of the Americas.

José M. Carrera Before Execution A234

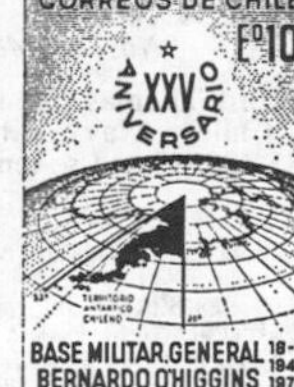

Map of Antarctica, Flag at O'Higgins Base A235

1973, Feb. 1 Litho. *Perf. 14½*
433 A234 2.30e lt ultra 8 5

Sesquicentennial of the death of José Miguel Carrera (1785-1821), Chilean revolutionist and dictator.

1973, Feb. 8
434 A235 10e ultra & red 8 5

25th anniversary of the Bernardo O'Higgins Antarctic Base.

Naval Air Service Emblem, Destroyer A236

La Silla Observatory A237

1973, Mar. 16 Litho. *Perf. 14½*
435 A236 20e brt bl & ocher 8 5

Chilean Naval Aviation, 50th anniversary.

1973, Apr. 25 Litho. *Perf. 14½*
436 A237 2.30e ultra & blk 8 5

INTERPOL Emblem A238

Designs: 50e, Fingerprint over globe.

1973, Sept. 23 Litho. *Perf. 14½*
437 A238 30e bis & ultra 10 8
438 A238 50e blk & red 25 8

50th anniversary of International Criminal Police Organization.

Grapes — A239

Design: 100e, Globe inscribed "Chile Exporta Vino."

1973, Dec. 10 Litho. *Perf. 14½*
439 A239 20e buff & lil 10 8
440 A239 100e bl & cl 10 8

Chilean wine export.

UPU Headquarters, Bern — A240

1974, Apr. 4
441 A240 500e on 45c grn 8 5

Centenary of Universal Postal Union. No. 441 was not issued without dark green surcharge and overprint.

Bernardo O'Higgins, Armed Forces Emblems A241

1974, Apr. 11 Litho. *Perf. 14½*
442 A241 30e *shown* 8 5
443 A241 30e *Soldiers with mortar* 8 5
444 A241 30e *Navy anti-aircraft gunners* 8 5
445 A241 30e *Pilot in cockpit* 8 5
446 A241 30e *Mounted policeman* 8 5
Nos. 442-446 (5) 40 25

Honoring the Armed Forces.

Soccer Ball and Globe — A242

Traffic Police — A243

Design: 1000e, Soccer ball and stadium (horiz.).

1974 Litho. *Perf. 14*
447 A242 500e dk red & org 10 5
448 A242 1000e bl & ind 20 10

World Cup Soccer Championship, Munich, June 13-July 7.

A souvenir sheet contains 2 imperf. stamps similar to Nos. 447-448, with blue marginal inscription. Printed on thin card. Size: 90x119mm.

Nos. 386, 355 Surcharged

1974, June Litho. *Perf. 14½*
449 A202 100e on 40c bl grn 10 5

Perf. 13x14
450 A174 300e on 50c dl brn 10 5

1974, June 20 *Perf. 14½*
451 A243 30e red brn & grn 10 5

Traffic safety.

Santiago-Fiji Air Service — A244

1974, Sept. 5 Litho. *Perf. 14½x14*
Brown & Green
452 A244 Block of 4 1.00 50
a. 200e *Easter Island turtle* 20 10
b. 200e *Polynesian dancer* 20 10
c. 200e *Map of Fiji Islands* 20 10
d. 200e *Kangaroo* 20 10

Inauguration of air service by LAN (Chile's national airline) from Santiago to Easter Island, Tahiti, Fiji, Australia.

Globe Cut to Show Mantle and Core — A245

1974, Sept. 9 *Perf. 14x14½*
453 A245 500e red brn & org 10 5

International Volcanology Congress, Santiago, Sept. 9-14.

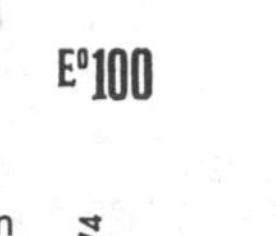

No. 393 Surcharged in Brown

1974, Oct. 24 Litho. *Perf. 14½*
454 A205 100e on 40c grn 10 8

Inauguration of the O'Higgins National Shrine at Maipu, Oct. 24, 1974.

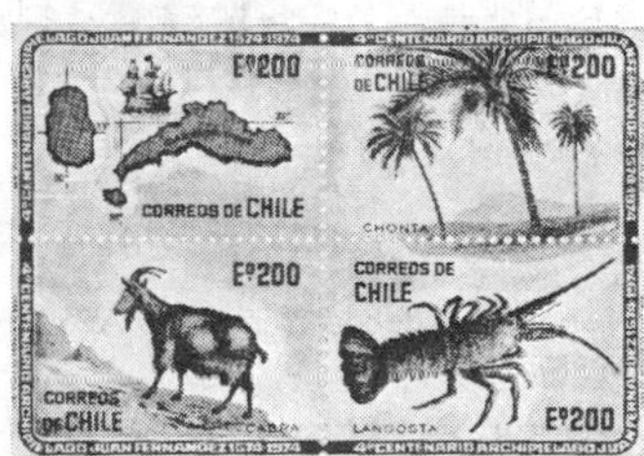

Juan Fernandez Archipelago — A246

1974, Nov. 22 Litho. *Perf. 14½x14*
Blue & Brick Red
455 A246 Block of 4 75 50
a. 200e *Robinson Crusoe Island* 15 10
b. 200e *Chonta palms* 15 10
c. 200e *Mountain goat* 15 10
d. 200e *Crayfish* 15 10

400th anniversary of discovery of Juan Fernandez Archipelago.

O'Higgins and Bolivar A247

1974, Dec. 9 *Perf. 14½*
456 A247 100e red brn & buff 8 5

Sequicentennial of the Battles of Junin and Ayacucho.

Foreign postal stationery (stamped envelopes, postal cards and air letter sheets) lies beyond the scope of this Catalogue, which is limited to adhesive postage stamps.

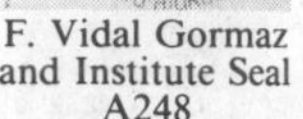

F. Vidal Gormaz and Institute Seal A248

Albert Schweitzer A249

1975, Jan. 22 Litho. ***Perf. 14½***

457	A248	100e	rose cl & bl	10	6

Centenary of the Naval Hydrographic Institute; F. Vidal Gormaz was first commandant.

1975, Apr. 7 Litho. ***Perf. 14x14½***

458	A249	500e	yel & red brn	12	6

Dr. Albert Schweitzer (1875-1965), medical missionary, birth centenary.

E° 70.-

No. 395 Surcharged in Red

Revalorizada
1975

1975, Apr. 7 ***Perf. 14½***

459	A207	70e	on 40c car & lt red brn	10	6

Volunteer Lifeboat Service — A250

1975, Apr. 15 Litho. ***Perf. 14½x14***

Dark Blue & Gray Olive

460	A250		Block of 4	75	50
a.		150e	*Lighthouse*	15	10
b.		150e	*Shipwreck*	15	10
c.		150e	*Lifeboat*	15	10
d.		150e	*Sailor reaching for life preserver*	15	10

Valparaiso Volunteer Lifeboat service, 50th anniversary.

Frigate Lautaro A251

Photogravure & Engraved

1975, May 21

Emerald & Black

461	A251	500e	*shown*	20	10
462	A251	500e	*Corvette Baquedano*	20	10
463	A251	500e	*Cruiser Chacabuco*	20	10
464	A251	500e	*Brigantine Goleta Esmeralda*	20	10

Orange & Black

465	A251	800e	*Frigate Lautaro*	25	10
466	A251	800e	*Corvette Baquedano*	25	10
467	A251	800e	*Cruiser Chacabuco*	25	10
468	A251	800e	*Brigantine Goleta Esmeralda*	25	10

Ultramarine & Black

469	A251	1000e	*Frigate Lautaro*	35	12
470	A251	1000e	*Corvette Baquedano*	35	12
471	A251	1000e	*Cruiser Chacabuco*	35	12
472	A251	1000e	*Brigantine Goleta Esmeralda*	35	12
			Nos. 461-472 (12)	3.20	1.28

Shipwreck of training frigate Lautaro, 30th anniversary. Stamps of some denomination printed se-tenant in sheets of 25 (5x5) with 7 Lautaro stamps and 6 each of the others.

A souvenir card contains impressions of Nos. 469-472 with ultramarine and orange marginal inscription and decoration. Size: 118x150mm.

Happy Mother, by Alfredo Valenzuela P. — A252

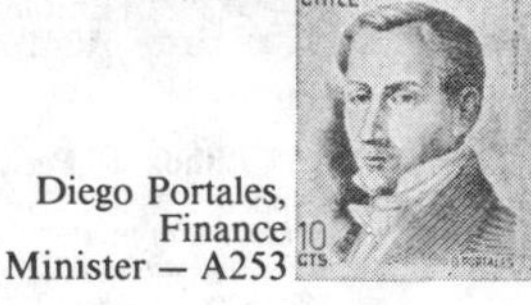

Diego Portales, Finance Minister — A253

Paintings: No. 474, Young Girl, by Francisco Javier Mandiola. No. 475, Lucia Guzman, by Pedro Lira Rencoret. No. 476, Woman, by Magdalena Mira Mena.

1975, Oct. 13 Litho. ***Perf. 14½***

473	A252	50c	multi	12	8
474	A252	50c	multi	12	8
475	A252	50c	multi	12	8
476	A252	50c	multi	12	8

International Women's Year 1975. Gray inscription on back, printed beneath gum, gives details about painting shown.

A souvenir card contains impressions of Nos. 473-476 with black and blue marginal inscription and decoration. Size: 149x120mm.

Inscribed D. Portales

1975-78 Litho. ***Perf. 13x14***

477	A253	10c	gray grn	8	5
478	A253	20c	vio ('76)	8	5
479	A253	30c	org ('76)	8	5
480	A253	50c	lt brn	8	5
481	A253	1p	blue	8	5
482	A253	1.50p	ocher ('76)	10	5
483	A253	2p	gray ('77)	10	5
483A	A253	2.50p	cit ('78)	10	5
483B	A253	3.50p	pnksh rose ('78)	20	5
484	A253	5p	rose cl	20	5
			Nos. 477-484 (10)	1.10	50

See Nos. 635-639.

Cochrane and Liberating Squadron, 1820 — A254

Designs: No. 486, Capture of Valdivia, 1820. No. 487, Capture of Three-master Esmeralda, 1820. No. 488, Cruiser Cochrane, 1874. No. 489, Destroyer Cochrane, 1962.

1976, Jan. 6 ***Perf. 14½***

485	A254	1p	multi	12	8
486	A254	1p	multi	12	8
487	A254	1p	multi	12	8
488	A254	1p	multi	12	8
489	A254	1p	multi	12	8
			Nos. 485-489 (5)	60	40

Lord Thomas Cochrane, first commander of Chilean Navy, birth bicentenary. Nos. 485-489 printed se-tenant.

Flags of Chile and Bolivia A255

1976, May 25 Litho. ***Perf. 14½***

490	A255	1.50p	multi	15	8

Sesquicentennial of Bolivia's independence.

Lake of the Inca, OAS Emblem A256

1976, June 11

491	A256	1.50p	multi	12	8

6th General Assembly of the Organization of American States.

George Washington A257

1976, July

492	A257	5p	multi	35	15

American Bicentennial.

Minerva and Academy Emblem A258

1976, July

493	A258	2.50p	multi	12	8

Polytechnic Military Academy, 50th anniversary.

Araucan Indian — A259

Designs: 2p, Condor with broken chain. 3p, Winged woman, symbolizing rebirth.

1976, Sept. 20 Litho. ***Perf. 14½***

494	A259	1p	bl & multi	12	8
495	A259	2p	bl & multi	15	8
496	A259	3p	yel & multi	25	12

3rd anniversary of the Military Junta. Nos. 494-496 printed se-tenant.

View, Antarctica A260

1977, Feb. 10 Litho. ***Perf. 14½***

497	A260	2p	multi	12	6

Visit of President Augusto Pinochet to Antarctica.

School Emblem, Planted Field — A261

Justice — A262

1977, Mar. 10 ***Perf. 14½***

498	A261	2p	multi	12	6

Centenary of advanced agricultural education.

1977, Mar. 30 Litho. ***Perf. 14½***

499	A262	2p	brn & sl	12	6

Supreme Court of Justice, sesquicentennial.

Eye with Globe, Caduceus A263

1977, Mar. 30 Litho. ***Perf. 14½***

500	A263	2p	multi	12	6

11th Pan-American Ophthalmological Congress.

Mounted Policeman — A264

Designs: No. 502, Policewoman with children. No. 503, Paine Peaks and Osorno Volcano, crossed rifle emblem. No. 504, Crossed rifle emblem, mounted and motorcycle policemen, helicopter and automobile. (horiz.).

1977, Apr. 27

501	A264	2p	multi	12	6
502	A264	2p	multi	12	6
503	A264	2p	multi	12	6
504	A264	2p	multi	12	6

Chilean police organization, 50th anniversary.

The lack of a price for a listed item does not necessarily indicate rarity.

Intelsat Satellite over Globe — A265

1977, May 17 Litho. *Perf. 14½*
505 A265 2p multi 12 6

World Telecommunications Day.

El Mercurio's First Front Page, Press and Ship A266

1977, July 5 Litho. *Perf. 14½*
506 A266 2p multi 12 6

El Mercurio de Valparaiso, first Chilean newspaper, 150th anniversary.

St. Francis, Birds and Cross A267 — Science and Technology A268

1977, July 26 Litho. *Perf. 14½*
507 A267 5p multi 25 12

St. Francis of Assisi, 750th death anniversary.

1977, Aug. 26 Litho. *Perf. 14½*
508 A268 4p multi 20 10

Young Mother Weaving — A269

Designs: No. 510, Handicapped boy in wheelchair and nurse. No. 511, Children dancing in circle (horiz.). No. 512, Old man and home (horiz.).

1977, Sept. 13 Litho. *Perf. 14½*
509 A269 5p multi 25 8
510 A269 5p multi 25 8
511 A269 10p multi 50 12
512 A269 10p multi 50 12

4th anniversary of Government Junta and social services of armed forces.

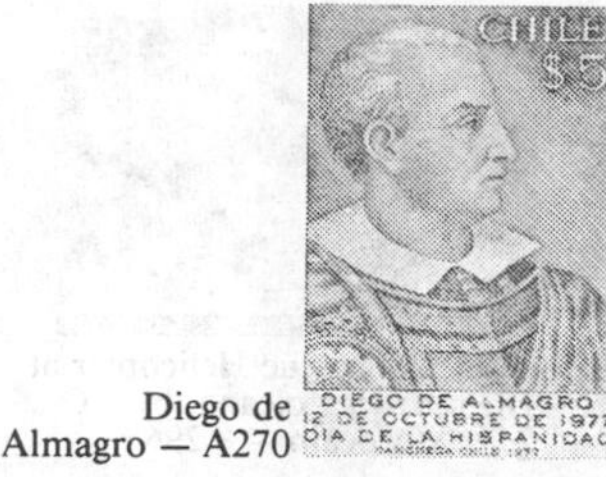
Diego de Almagro — A270

1977, Oct. 31 Engr. *Perf. 14½*
513 A270 5p rose & car 25 6

Diego de Almagro (1475-1538), leader of Spanish expedition to Chile.

Bell, Letters, Dove and Child A271

1977, Dec. 12 Litho. *Perf. 14½*
514 A271 2.50p multi 12 6

Christmas 1977.

Loading Timber A272

1978 Litho. *Perf. 15*
515 A272 10p multi 50 12
516 A272 20p multi 1.00 12

No. 516 inscribed "CORREOS," ship is flying Chilean flag.

Papal Arms and Globe A273

University A274

1978 Litho. *Perf. 14½*
521 A273 10p multi 50 12
522 A274 25p multi 1.25 20

World Peace Day (10p); Catholic University of Valparaiso, 50th anniversary (25p). Issue dates: 10p, July 28; 25p, July 31.

O'Higgins, by Gil de Castro — A275

1978, Aug. 20 Litho. *Perf. 15*
523 A275 10p multi 50 12

Bernardo O'Higgins (1778-1842), soldier and statesman.

Chacabuco Victory Monument A276

1978, Sept. 11
524 A276 10p multi 50 12

160th anniversary of O'Higgins victory at Chacabuco, and 5th anniversary of military government.

Teacher Writing on Blackboard — A277

1978, Sept. 21
525 A277 15p multi 75 12

10th anniversary and 9th Reunion of Inter-american Council for Education, Science and Culture (C.I.E.C.C.), Sept. 21-29.

First National Fleet, by Thomas Somerscales — A278

Design: 30p, Last Moments of Rancagua Battle, by Pedro Subercaseaux.

1978 Litho. *Perf. 15*
526 A278 20p multi 1.00 12
527 A278 30p multi 1.50 20

Bernardo O'Higgins (1778-1842), soldier and statesman.
Issue dates: 20p, Oct. 9; 30p, Oct. 2.

San Martin-O'Higgins Medal, by Rene Thenot, 1942 — A279

1978, Oct. 20
528 A279 7p multi 35 8

José de San Martin and Bernardo O'Higgins, 200th birth anniversaries.

Council Emblem — A280

1978, Nov. 27 Litho. *Perf. 14½*
529 A280 50p multi 3.00 50

International Council of Military Sports, 30th anniversary.

Three Kings — A281 — Virgin and Child — A282

1978, Dec. 14 Litho. *Perf. 14½*
530 A281 3p multi 15 8
531 A282 11p multi 60 25

Christmas 1978.

Philippi Brothers A283

1978, Dec. 29 Litho. *Perf. 14½x15*
532 A283 3.50p multi 20 8

Bernardo E. Philippi (1811-1852) and Rodulfo A. Philippi (1808-1904), scientists and travelers.

No. 477 Surcharged in Bright Green

1979 Litho. *Perf. 13x14*
533 A253 3.50p on 10c gray grn 25 15

Flags of Chile and Salvation Army — A284

1979, Mar. 17 Litho. *Perf. 14½*
534 A284 10p multi 75 50

Salvation Army in Chile, 70th anniversary.

Pope Paul VI — A285

1979, Mar. 30
535 A285 11p multi 80 50

In memory of Pope Paul VI (1897-1978).

Battle of Maipu Monument — A286

1979, Apr. 17 Litho. *Perf. 14½*
536 A286 8.50p multi 65 40

Bernardo O'Higgins (1778-1842), Liberator of Chile.

Battle of Angamos A287

Naval Battles: No. 538, Iquique. No. 539, Punta Gruesa.

1979, May 21 Litho. *Perf. 14½*

537 A287 3.50p multi 25 15
538 A287 3.50p multi 25 15
539 A287 3.50p multi 25 15

Centenary of victorious naval battles against Peru.

1903 Ambulance and Red Cross A288

1979, June 29 Litho. *Perf. 14½*

540 A288 25p multi 1.50 90

75th anniversary of Chilean Red Cross.

Diego Portales — A289

1979-86 Litho. *Perf. 13½*

542 A289 1.50p ocher 10 5
543 A289 2p gray ('81) 12 10
545 A289 3.50p red 20 10
546 A289 4.50p bl grn ('81) 25 15
547 A289 5p rose cl 30 15
548 A289 6p emerald 35 20
549 A289 7p yel ('82) 30 20
550 A289 10p bl ('82) 45 20
550A A289 12p org ('86) 14 8
Nos. 542-550A (9) 2.21 1.23

1.50p, 3.50p, 5p and 6p inscribed "D. Portales."

People and Flag — A290

1979, Aug. 28 Litho. *Perf. 14½*

551 A290 10p multi 60 35

Jugoslavian immigration, centenary.

Coat of Arms and Mt. Castillo A290a

1979, Oct. 12 Litho. *Perf. 14½*

552 A290a 20p multi 1.20 75

Coyhaique 50th anniv.

IYC Emblem, Playground — A291

IYC Emblem, Children's Drawings: 11p, Girl and shadow (vert.). 12p, Dancing.

1979, Oct. 9 *Perf. 14½*

553 A291 9.50p multi 60 35
554 A291 11p multi 65 40
555 A291 12p multi 70 40

International Year of the Child.

Telecom 79 — A292

1979, Oct. 26 Litho. *Perf. 14½*

556 A292 15p multi 90 50

3rd World Telecommunications Exhibition, Geneva, Sept. 20-26.

Puerto Williams, 25th Anniversary — A293

1979, Nov. 21

557 A293 3.50p multi 20 10

Adoration of the Kings A294

1979, Dec. 4 Litho. *Perf. 15*

558 A294 3.50p multi 20 10

Christmas 1979.

Rafael Sotomayor, Minister of War — A295

Military Heroes: No. 560, Erasmo Escala. No. 561, Emilio Sotomayor. No. 562, Eleuterio Ramirez

1979, Dec. 29 *Perf. 13½*

559 A295 3.50p ocher & brn 20 10
560 A295 3.50p ocher & brn 20 10
561 A295 3.50p ocher & brn 20 10
562 A295 3.50p ocher & brn 20 10

Nos. 559-562 printed se-tenant in blocks of four.

Bell UH-1 Rescue Helicopter at Tinguiririca Volcano, by S.O. Mococain — A296

Air Force, 50th Anniversary: No. 564, Flying boat Catalina Skua over Antarctic, by E.F. Alvarez. No. 565, F5-E Tiger II over Andes, by M.M. Barria.

1980, Mar. 21 Litho. *Perf. 13½*

563 A296 3.50p *shown* 20 10
564 A296 3.50p *Jet* 20 10
565 A296 3.50p *Sea plane* 20 10

The Death of Bueras, by Pedro Leon Carmona — A297

1980, Apr. 14 Litho. *Perf. 13½*

566 A297 12p multi 70 40

Charge of Bueras, Battle of Maipo, 1818.

Rotary International, 75th Anniversary — A298

1980, Apr. 15

567 A298 10p multi 60 30

Gen. Manuel Baquedano, by Pedro Subercaseaux A299

Gen. Pedro Lagos, Battle Scene, by Subercaseaux — A300

Battle of Morro de Arica Centenary (Subercaseaux Paintings): No. 570, Commander Juan J. San Martin, battle scene.

1980, June 7 Litho. *Perf. 13½*

568 A299 3.50p multi 20 10
569 A300 3.50p multi 20 10
570 A300 3.50p multi 20 10

Score and Perez's Silhouette — A301

1980, June 27 Litho. *Perf. 13½*

571 A301 6p multi 35 20

Osman Perez Freire (1880-1930), composer, and fragment from his song "Ay, Ay, Ay."

Mt. Gasherbrum II, Chilean Flag, Ice Pick — A302

1980, July 9

572 A302 15p multi 90 50

Chilean Himalayan expedition, June 1979.

"Charity," Stained-glass Window A303

1980, July 18

573 A303 10p multi 60 30

Daughters of Charity, 125th anniversary in Chile.

Condor, Colors of Chile A304

1980, Sept. 11 Litho. *Perf. 13½*

574 A304 3.50p multi 20 10

17th anniversary of constitution.

Inca Child Mummy A305

Pablo Burchard, by Pedro Lira A306

1980, Sept. 14

575 A305 5p *shown* 30 15
576 A305 5p *Claudio Gay* 30 15

National Museum of Natural History (founded by Claudio Gay, 1800-1873) sesquicentennial. Nos. 575-576 se-tenant with gutter between giving history of museums and mummy.

1980, Sept. 27 Litho. *Perf. 13½*
577 A306 3.50p multi 20 10

Museum of Fine Art centenary (directed by Burchard, 1932).

Santiago International Fair — A307

1980, Oct. 30
578 A307 3.50p multi 20 10

Nativity — A308

Christmas 1980: 3.50p, Family (vert.).

1980, Nov. 25 Litho. *Perf. 13½*
579 A308 3.50p multi 20 10
580 A308 10.50p multi 65 35

Infantryman 1879 — A309

Congress Emblem — A310

Designs: Pacific War period uniforms, 1879. Nos. 581-584 se-tenant.

1980, Nov. 27
581 A309 3.50p *shown* 20 10
582 A309 3.50p *Cavalry officer* 20 10
583 A309 3.50p *Artillery officer* 20 10
584 A309 3.50p *Engineer colonel* 20 10

1980, Dec. 1
585 A310 11.50p multi 70 40

23rd International Congress of Military Medicine and Pharmacy.

Successful Eradication of Hoof and Mouth Disease A311

1981, Jan. 16 Litho. *Perf. 13½*
586 A311 9.50p multi 45 15

The Catalogue editors cannot undertake to appraise, identify or judge the genuineness or condition of stamps.

Maoi Statues, Easter Island A312

1981, Jan. 28 Litho. *Perf. 13½*
587 A312 3.50p shown 16 10
588 A312 3.50p Robinson Crusoe Island 16 10
589 A312 10.50p Penguins, Antarctic Territory 65 50

National Heroine Javiera Carrera, by O.M. Pizarro, Birth Bicentenary — A313

1981, Mar. 20
590 A313 3.50p multi 16 10

UPU Membership Centenary A314

1981, Apr. 1
591 A314 3.50p multi 16 10

C130 Hercules Air Force Transport Plane Unloading Cargo — A315

1981, Apr. 21
592 A315 3.50p multi 16 10

Lieutenant Marsh Air Force Base, first anniversary.

13th World Telecommunications Day — A316

1981, May 17 Litho. *Perf. 13½*
593 A316 3.50p multi 16 10

Arturo Prat Naval Base A317

1981, June 23 Litho. *Perf. 13½*
594 A317 3.50p multi 16 10

Capt. Jose Luis Araneda A318

1981, June 26
595 A318 3.50p multi 16 10

Battle of Sangrar centenary.

Philatelic Society of Chile, 90th Anniv. — A319

1981, July 29 Litho. *Perf. 13½*
596 A319 4.50p multi 20 10

Minister Recabarren and Chief Conuepan Giving Speeches, by Hector Robles Acuna — A320

1981, Aug. 7
597 A320 4.50p multi 20 10

Temuco city centenary.

Exports A321

1981, Aug. 31 Litho. *Perf. 13½*
598 A321 14p multi 65 35

Palacio de Moneda (Govt. Mint) — A322

1981, Sept. 11
599 A322 4.50p multi 20 15

Natl. liberation, 8th anniv.

St. Vincent de Paul, 400th Birth Anniv. A323

1981, Sept. 27 Litho. *Perf. 13½*
600 A323 4.50p multi 25 10

Andres Bello, Statesman, Birth Bicentenary A324

1981, Sept. 29
601 A324 4.50p Coin 25 10
602 A324 9.50p Bust, books 50 15
603 A324 11.50p Statue, arms 60 25

2nd Congress of South American Uniformed Police — A325

1981, Oct. 15
604 A325 4.50p multi 25 10

World Food Day A326

1981, Oct. 16
605 A326 5.50p multi 30 10

Uniform Type of 1980

1879 Parade Uniforms. Nos. 544-547 se-tenant.

1981, Nov. 6 *Perf. 13½*
606 A309 5.50p Infantry private 30 10
607 A309 5.50p Cadet 30 10
608 A309 5.50p Cavalryman 30 10
609 A309 5.50p Artilleryman 30 10

Intl. Year of the Disabled A327

1981, Nov. 11
610 A327 5.50p multi 30 10

Christmas 1981 — A328

1981, Nov. 25
611 A328 5.50p Nativity 30 10
612 A328 11.50p Three Kings 60 25

50th Anniv. of Federico Santa Maria Technical University — A329

1981, Dec 1 Litho. *Perf. 13½*
613 A329 5.50p multi 30 10

Dario Sales (1881-1941), Educator — A330

1981, Dec. 4
614 A330 5.50p multi 30 10

FIDA '82, 2nd Natl. Air Force Fair A331

1982, Mar. 6 Litho. *Perf. 13½*
615 A331 4.50p multi 25

1982 Constitution — A332

1982, Mar. 11
616 A332 4.50p Cardinal Caro, family 25
617 A332 11p Diego Portales 65
618 A332 30p Bernardo O'Higgins 1.80

Panamerican Institute of Geography and History, 12th General Assembly A333

1982, Mar. 22 Litho. *Perf. 13½*
619 A333 4.50p multi 25

American Air Forces Cooperation System — A334

1982, Apr. 12
620 A334 4.50p multi 25

Pedro Montt A335 — Fish Exports A336

1982
621 A335 4.50p lt vio 25

1982, May 3 Litho. *Perf. 13½*
622 A336 20p multi 1.20

Scouting Year — A337

1982, May 21 Litho. *Perf. 13*
623 Pair 50
a.-b. A337 4.50p multi 25

Battle of Concepcion Centenary — A338

Designs: Chacabuco Regiment officers killed in battle.

1982, June 18 Litho. *Perf. 13½*
624 Block of 4 1.00
a. A338 4.50p I. Carrera Pinto 25
b. A338 4.50p A. Perez Canto 25
c. A338 4.50p J. Montt Salamanca 25
d. A338 4.50p L. Cruz Martinez 25

UN World Assembly on Aging, July 26-Aug 6 — A339

1982, Aug. 5
625 A339 4.50p multi 25

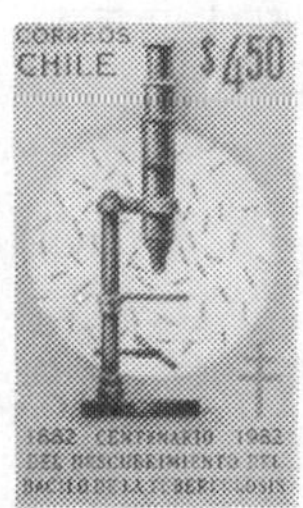

TB Bacillus Centenary — A340

1982, Aug. 31
626 A340 4.50p multi 20

9th Anniv. of National Liberation — A341

1982, Sept. 11 Litho. *Perf. 13½*
627 A341 4.50p multi 20

Christmas 1982 — A342

Children's drawings.

1982, Nov. 2
628 A342 10p multi 45
629 A342 25p multi, vert. 1.00

Nos. 416-417 Surcharged in Green or Black.

1982, Nov. *Perf. 14½x15, 14½*
630 A222 1p on 3.50p bl grn & grn (G) 5
631 A223 2p on 1.15p blk & car 8

Marist Alumni, 9th World Congress — A342a

Design: 7p, Virgin Mary and Marcellus Champagnat (founder of Marist Brotherhood), stained glass window, Church of the Sacred Heart of Jesus, Barcelona.

1982, Nov. 11 Litho. *Perf. 13½*
631A A342a 7p multi 30

El Sur Newspaper Centenary A342b

1982, Nov. 15
631B A342b 7p Wooden handpress, masthead 30

110th Anniv. of South American Steamship Co. — A342c

1982, Dec. 20
631C A342c 7p Steamer Copiapo 30

60th Anniv. of Radio Club of Chile — A342d

1982, Dec. 29
631D A342d 7p multi 30

First Anniv. of Postal Agreement with Order of Malta — A343

1983, Mar. 30 Litho. *Perf. 13½*
632 A343 25p Arms of Order of Malta 1.00
633 A343 50p Chile 2.00

Se-tenant.

D. Portales Type of 1975 Inscribed Diego Portales and:

Ramon Barros Luco A344

Juan Luis Sanfuentes A344a

1983-84 Litho. *Perf. 13½*
634 A344 1p grnsh bl 5 5
635 A253 1p chlky bl 5 5
636 A253 1.50p ocher 6 5

636A	A344	2p	dl vio ('84)	5	5
637	A253	2p	ol gray	8	5
638	A253	2.50p	lemon	10	5
640	A253	3.50p	pink ('84)	8	5
641	A344	5p	crim rose	12	5
642	A344a	5p	red ('84)	10	5
643	A344	7p	ultra	28	8
645	A344a	9p	brn ('84)	22	8
646	A344a	9p	grn ('84)	22	8
647	A344a	10p	black	25	8
			Nos. 634-647 (13)	1.66	77

50th Anniv. of Bureau of Investigation A345

1983, June 19 Litho. *Perf. 13½*
649 A345 20p multi 80

Antonio Cardinal Samore (1905-1983) — A346

1983, June 26
650 A346 30p multi 1.20

Centenary of Cliff Elevators in Valparaiso A347

1983, Aug. 19 Litho. *Perf. 13½*
651 A347 40p multi 1.00

Pucara de Quitor Settlement Ruins, San Pedro de Atacama — A348

Designs: No. 653, Llamas, rock painting, Rio Ibanez, Aisen. No. 654, Duck-shaped jug with human head, Diaguita cultures. No. 655, Puoko Tangata carved stone head, Easter Isld. (vert.).

1983, Aug. 26
652 A348 7p multi 18
653 A348 7p multi 18
654 A348 7p multi 18
655 A348 7p multi 18

10th Anniv. of National Liberation — A349

1983, Sept. 11 Litho. *Perf. 13½*
656 A349 7p Angel with broken chains 18
657 A349 7p Couple, flag 18
658 A349 10p Family, torch 25
659 A349 40p Coat of arms, "10" 1.00

Nos. 656-659 se-tenant.

Famous Hondurans — A350

Designs: No. 660, Francisco Morazan (1792-1842), Advocate of United Central America. No. 661, Jose Cecilio Del Valle (1777-1834), Scholar and Leader of Pan Americanism.

1983, Oct. 3 Litho. *Perf. 13½*
660 A350 7p multi 18
661 A350 7p multi 18

World Communications Year A351 A352

1983, Oct. 13 Litho. *Perf. 13½*
662 A351 7p Central P.O. 18
663 A352 7p Challenger spaceship 18

Nos. 662-663 printed se-tenant.

Christmas 1983 — A353

Childrens' Drawings: 10p Chilean Peasant, Hanny Chacon. 30p, Holy Family. Lucrecia Cardenas, vert.

1983, Nov. 14 Litho. *Perf. 13*
664 A353 10p multi 25
665 A353 30p multi 75

Design descriptions printed on back on top of gum.

State Railways Centenary — A354

Train Cars: a. Presidential coach, 1911. b. Service coach, 1910; tender, 1929. c. Locomotive Type 80, 1929.

1984, Jan. 4 Litho. *Perf. 13½*
666 Strip of 3 70
a.-c. A354 9p, any single 22

3rd Intl. Air Fair, Santiago, Mar. 3-11 — A355

1984, Jan. 31 Litho. *Perf. 13½*
667 A355 9p Flags, plane 22

20th Anniv. of Nuclear Energy Commission — A356

1984, Apr. 16 Litho. *Perf. 13*
668 A356 9p multi 22

Nos. 656-657 Surcharged in Purple.

1984, June 11 Litho. *Perf. 13½*
669 A349 9p on 7p #656 18
670 A349 9p on 7p #657 18

Antarctic Colonization — A357

1984, June 18
671 A357 15p Women's expedition 30
672 A357 15p Villa las Estrellas Station 30
673 A357 15p Scouts, flag, Air Force base 30

Nos. 671-673 se-tenant.

10th Anniv. of Regionalization — A358

Designs: a. Parinacota Church, Tarapaca. b. El Tatio geyser, Antofagasta. c. Copper mining, Atacama. d. Tololo Observatory, Coquimbo. e. Valparaiso Harbor, Valparaiso. f. Ahu Akivi head sculptures, Easter Isld. g. St. Francis Church, Santiago. h. El Hunique House, O'Higgins. i. Colburn Machicura Dam and Hydroelectric Power Station, Maule. j. Sta. Juana de Guadalcazar Fort, Bio-Bio. k. Indian woman, Araucania. l. Guar Isld. Church, Los Lagos. m. Main road, Gen. del Campo. n. Shepherds' Monument, Magellanes and Antarctic. o. Family, Villa las Estrellas Station, Antarctic.

1984, July 11
6740. Sheet of 15 2.75
a.-o. A358 9p multi, any single 18

Capt. Pedro Sarmiento de Gamboa, Map, 1584 — A359

1984, July 31 Litho. *Perf. 13*
675 A359 100p multi 2.00

400th anniv. of Spanish presence in Straits of Magellan.

State Bank of Chile Centenary — A360

1984, Sept. 6 Litho. *Perf. 13½*
676 A360 35p Founder Antonio Varas de la Barra, coin 70

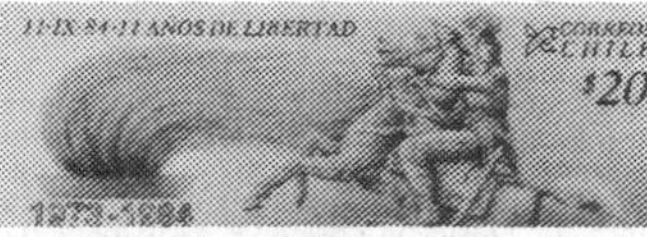

11th Anniv. of Liberation — A361

1984, Sept. 11
677 A361 20p Monument to O'Higgins 40

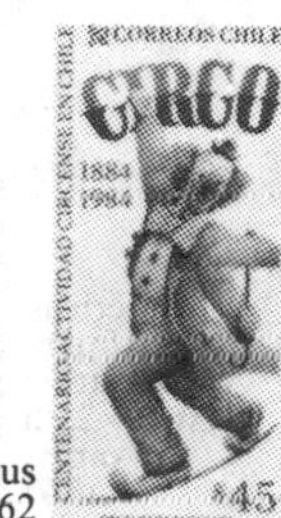

Circus Centenary — A362

1984, Sept. 28 Litho. *Perf. 13½*
678 A362 45p Clown 90

Endangered Species, World Wildlife Emblem — A363

1985, July Litho. *Perf. 13½*
679 A363 9p Chinchilla 18
680 A363 9p Blue whale 18
681 A363 9p Sea lions 18
682 A363 9p Chilean huemuls 18

Nos. 679-682 se-tenant.

Christmas 1984 — A364

Children's drawings.

1984, Nov. 20 Litho. *Perf. 13½*
683 A364 9p Shepherds 18
684 A364 40p Bethlehem 80

The indexes in each volume of the Scott Catalogue contain many listings which help to identify stamps.

Santiago University Planetarium Opening — A365

1984, Dec. 29
685 A365 10p multi 20

Flora and Fauna — A366

Wildlife: a. Conepatus chinga. b. Leucocoryne purpurea. c. Himantopus himantopus. d. Lutra felina. e. Balbisia peduncularis. f. Psittacus cyanalysias. g. Pudu Pudu. h. Fuschia magellanica. i. Diuca diuca. j. Dusicyon griseus. k. Alstroemeria sierrae. l. Glaucidium nanum.

1985, Feb.
686 Block of 12 2.40
a.-l. A366 10p, Any single 20

American Airforces Cooperation System, 25th Anniv. A367

1985, Mar. 26
687 A367 45p Emblem, flags 90

Chile-Argentina Peace Treaty — A368

1985, May 2 Litho. *Perf. 13½*
688 A368 20p Papal arms, flags 25

Fr. Joseph Kentenich (1885-1968), Founder, Intl. Schonstatt Movement of Catholic Laymen A369

1985, May 19 Litho. *Perf. 13½*
689 A369 40p Portrait, La Florida Sanctuary, Santiago 48

Antarctic Treaty, 25th Anniv. — A370

Resources, research: 15p, Krill, pack ice, map. 20p, Seismological Station, O'Higgins' Base. 35p, Georeception Station, dish receiver.

1985, June 21
690 A370 15p multi 18
691 A370 20p multi 24
692 A370 35p multi 42

Canis Fulvipes — A371

Endangered wildlife: No. 693b, Phoenicoparrus jamesi. No. 693c, Fulica gigantea. No. 693d, Lutra provocax.

1985, Aug. 9 Litho. *Perf. 13½*
693 Block of 4 1.00
a.-d. A371 20p, any single 25

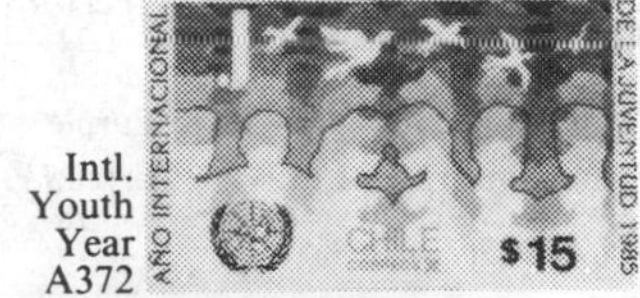

Intl. Youth Year A372

UN, 40th Anniv. A373

1985, Aug. 31
694 A372 15p multi 18
695 A373 15p multi 18

Nos. 694-695 printed se-tenant.

Gen. Jose Miguel Carrera Verdugo (1785-1821) — A374

1985, Oct. 8 Litho. *Perf. 13½*
696 A374 40p multi 45

Farmer and Ox-drawn Hay Cart — A375

Folklore: No. 697b, Street photographer, wet plate camera. No. 697c, One-man band. No. 697d, Basket maker.

1985, Oct.
697 Block of 4 40
a.-d. A375 10p, any single 10

Christmas 1985 — A376

Winning children's drawings, 7th natl. design contest.

1985, Nov. 4
698 A376 15p Nativity 16
699 A376 100p Father Christmas, vert. 1.10

Nos. 698-699 inscribed in black on gummed side with child's name, age, school and region.

16th Armed Forces Conference — A377

Designs: 20p, Cavalryman, Directorial Escort, 1818. 35p, Officer, Grand Guard, 1813.

1985, Nov. 15 Litho. *Perf. 13½*
700 A377 20p multi 22
701 A377 35p multi 38

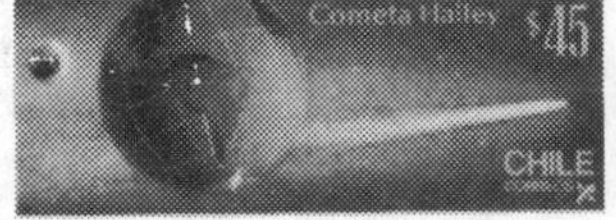

Halley's Comet — A378

1985, Nov. 29 Litho. *Perf. 13½*
702 A378 45p multi 48
a. Souvenir sheet

No. 702a has multicolored margin picturing US space shuttle during take-off; black control number. Exists imperf. Size: 90x105mm.

Natl. Solidarity Campaign — A379

1985
703 A379 5p red & bl 5

Campaign for Prevention of Forest Fires — A380

1985, Dec. 27
704 A380 40p Forest 45
705 A380 40p Fire destruction 45

Nos. 704-705 printed se-tenant in continuous design.

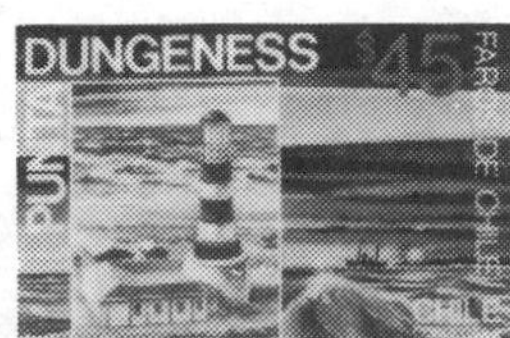

Dungeness Point Lighthouse, Straits of Magellan — A381

1986, Jan. 26
706 A381 45p shown 50
707 A381 45p Evangelistas Lighthouse 50

Nos. 706-707 printed se-tenant in a continuous design.

View of Santiago, Mackenna — A382

1986, Jan. 28
708 A382 30p multi 35

Benjamin Vicuna Mackenna (d. 1886), municipal superintendent of Santiago, 1872-1875.

Diego Portales, Natl. Crest, Text — A382a

1986, Feb. Litho. *Perf. 13½*
708A A382a 12p on 3.50p multi 14

No. 708A not issued without surcharge.

1986 World Cup Soccer Championships, Mexico — A383

Host stadiums: 15p, Natl. Stadium, Chile, 1962. 20p, Aztec Stadium, Mexico, 1970. 35p, Maracana Stadium, Brazil, 1950. 50p, Wembley Stadium, Great Britain, 1966.

1986, Feb. 18
709 A383 15p multi 18
710 A383 20p multi 22
711 A383 35p multi 40
712 A383 50p multi 55

Environmental Conservation — A384

1986, Feb. 28
713 A384 20p Water 24
714 A384 20p Air 24
715 A384 20p Soil 24

Sailing Ship Santiaguillo, Flags — A385

1986, Mar. 20
716 A385 40p multi 48

Discovery of Valparaiso Bay, 450th anniv.

Interamerican Development Bank, 25th Anniv. — A386

1986, Apr. 9
717 A386 45p multi 55

St. Rosa de Lima (1586-1617), Sanctuary at Pelequen — A387

1986, Apr. 30 Litho. *Perf. 13½*
718 A387 15p multi 18

Maoi Statues, Easter Is. — A388

1986, May 15
719 A388 60p Raraku Volcano 65
a. Souv. sheet 1.15
720 A388 100p Tongariki Ruins 1.10
a. Souv. sheet 1.90

Nos. 719a-720a have multicolored margins continuing the designs and bearing black control numbers. Sizes: 90x105mm, 104x90mm (100p).

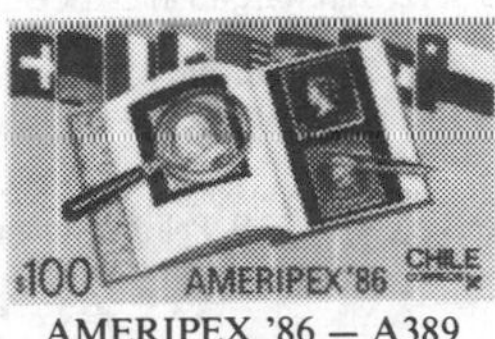

AMERIPEX '86 — A389

1986, May 23
721 A389 100p multi 1.10

Historic Naval Ships — A390

1986, May 30
722 A390 35p Schooner Ancud, 1843 38
723 A390 35p Armed merchantman Aguilar, 1830 38
724 A390 35p Corvette Esmeralda, 1856 38
725 A390 35p Frigate O'Higgins, 1834 38

Printed se-tenant. See Nos. 752-753.

Paintings by Juan Francisco Gonzalez (1853-1933) A391

1986, June 24
726 A391 30p Rush and Chrysanthemums 32
727 A391 30p Gate of La Serena 32

Exports — A392

Designs: No. 728a, Saltpeter. No. 728b, Iron. No. 728c, Copper. No. 728d, Molybdenum.

1986 Litho. *Perf. 13½*
728 Block of 4 56
a.-d. A392 12p, any single 14

Antarctic Fauna — A393

Designs: No. 729a, Sterna vittata. No. 729b, Phalacrocorax atriceps. No. 729c, Aptenodytes forsteri. No. 729d, Catharacta lonnberg.

1986, July 16 Litho. *Perf. 13½*
729 Block of 4 1.80
a.-d. A393 40p, any single 45

Writers — A394

Designs: No. 730, Pedro de Ona (1570-1643). No. 731, Vicente Huidobro (1893-1948).

1986, Aug. 19
730 A394 20p multi 22
731 A394 20p multi 22

Printed se-tenant in a continuous design.

Military Academy, Cent. — A395

1986, Sept. 8 Litho. *Perf. 13½*
732 A395 45p Major-General, 1878 48
733 A395 45p Major, 1950 48

Nos. 732-733 printed se-tenant.

Art A396

1986, Oct. 17 *Perf. 13½*
734 A396 30p Diaguita urn, duck jug 30
735 A396 30p Mapuche silver ornament, embroidery 30

Nos. 734-735 printed se-tenant.

Christmas — A397

8th Natl. design contest-winning children's drawings.

1986, Nov. 19 Litho. *Perf. 13½*
736 A397 15p multi 16
737 A397 105p multi 1.10

Nos. 736-737 inscribed in black on gummed side with child's name, age, school and region.

Intl. Peace Year — A398

1986, Nov. 26
738 A398 85p multi 88

Natl. Women Volunteers — A399

1986, Dec. 15 Litho. *Perf. 13½*
739 A399 15p multi 16

Crowning of Our Lady of Mt. Carmel, Patron of Chile, by Pius XI, 60th Anniv. — A400

1986, Dec. 19
740 A400 25p multi 28

Andean Railways Kitson-Meyer No. 59, 1907, designed by Robert Sterling — A401

1987, Jan. 27 Litho. *Perf. 13½*
741 A401 95p multi 1.05

Arturo Prat Naval Base, Greenwich Island, the Antarctic, 40th Anniv. — A402

1987, Feb. 6
742 A402 100p Storage and power supplies 1.15
743 A402 100p Working and living quarters 1.15

Nos. 742-743 printed se-tenant in continuous design.

State Visit of Pope John Paul II, Apr. 1-6, 1987 A403

Pope John Paul II and: 20p, Christ the Redeemer statue. 25p, Votive Church, Maipu. 90p, Cross of the Seas, Straits of Magellan. 115p, Virgin of the Hill.

1987, Apr. 6 Litho. *Perf. 13½*
744 A403 20p multi 20
745 A403 25p multi 25
746 A403 90p multi 90
747 A403 115p multi 1.25
a. Souv. sheet of one 2.50

No. 747a has multicolored margin picturing enlargement of the statue, papal arms and black control number. Sold for 250p. Size: 104x89mm.

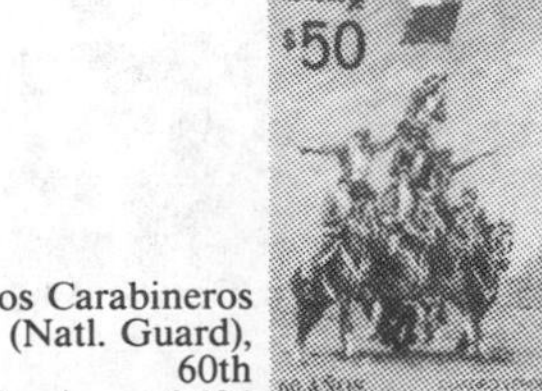

Los Carabineros (Natl. Guard), 60th Anniv. — A404

A particular stamp may be scarce, but if few collectors want it, its market value may remain relatively low.

World Youth Soccer Championships A405

1987, Apr. 21

748 A404 50p Cavalry showman-ship 50
749 A404 50p Air-sea rescue 50

Printed se-tenant.

1987, May 28

Designs: No. 750a, Two players. No. 750b, Concepcion Stadium, kick play. No. 750c, Antofagasta Stadium, dribbling the ball. No. 750d, Valparaiso Stadium, heading the ball.

750 Block of 4 1.80
a.-d. A405 45p any single 45

Souvenir Sheet

751 A405 45p Four players 1.50

No. 751 contains one No. 750a and has decorative multicolored margin inscribed with black control number; publicizes the 1988 Summer Olympics, Seoul. Sold for 150p. Size: 89x105mm.

Naval Ships Type of 1986

1987, May 29

752 A390 60p Battleship Almirante Latorre, 1913 60
753 A390 60p Cruiser O'Higgins, 1936 60

Diego Portales (1793-1837), Finance Minister — A406

1987, June 16

754 A406 30p multi 30

Public Works Ministry, Cent. — A407

1987, June 26

755 A407 25p multi 25

Infantry School, Cent. — A408

1987, July 9

756 A408 50p Entrance 50
757 A408 100p Soldiers, natl. flag 1.00

Miniature Sheet

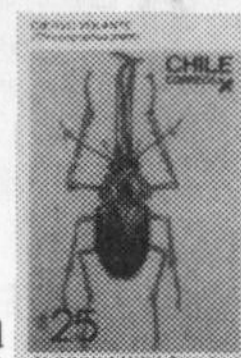

Flora and Fauna — A409

Designs: a. Chiasognathus granti. b. Calidris alba. c. Hippocamelus antisensis. d. Jubaea chilensis. e. Colias vauthieri. f. Pandion haliaetus. g. Cephalorhynchus commersonii. h. Austrocedrus chilensis. i. Jasus frontalis. j. Stephanoides fernandensis. k. Vicugna vicugna. l. Thyrsopteris elegans. m. Lithodes antarctica. n. Pterocnemia pennata. o. Lagidium viscacia. p, Cereus atacamensis.

1987, July 30

758 Sheet of 16 4.00
a.-p. A409 25p any single 25

Size: 165x116mm.

Intl. Year of Shelter for the Homeless — A410

1987, Aug. 6

759 A410 40p multi 40

FISA '87, Santiago — A412

1987, Oct. 16 Litho. *Perf. 13½*

761 A412 20p multi 18

25th Intl. agriculture and exports exhibition.

Rear Admiral Carlos Condell de la Haza (1843-1887), Naval Hero at the Battle of the Pacific — A413

1987, Nov. 7

762 A413 50p multi 45

Christmas 1987 — A414

COBRE '87, Intl. Conference on Copper — A415

Children's drawings: 30p, Holy Family, by Ximena Soledad Rosales Opazo. 100p, Star Over Bethlehem, by Marcelo Bordones Meneses, horiz.

1987, Nov. 13

763 A414 30p multi 28
764 A414 100p multi 90

1987, Nov. 23

765 A415 40p Foundry 35
a. Souv. sheet of one 1.35

No. 765 has multicolored decorative margin picturing molecular structure of copper. Sold for 150p. Size:88x104mm.

Ramon Freire (1787-1851), Chief of State — A416

1987, Dec. 29 *Perf.*

766 A416 20p 18

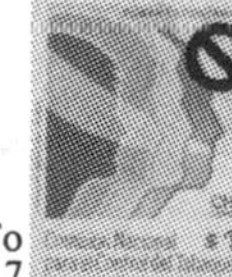

To Smoke Is To Contaminate — A417

1987 Litho. *Perf. 13½*

767 A417 15p blue & ver 14

Natl. Comission for the Control of Smoking.

SEMI-POSTAL STAMPS

S. S. Abtao and Captain Policarpo Toro SP1

S. S. Abtao and Brother Eugenio Eyraud SP2

Perf. 14½x15

1940, Mar. 1 Engr. Unwmk.

B1 SP1 80c + 2.20p dk grn & lake 2.00 1.75
B2 SP2 3.60p + 6.40p lake & dk grn 2.00 1.75

Issued in commemoration of the 50th anniversary of Chilean ownership of Easter Island. The surtax was used for charitable institutions.

These stamps were printed together in a sheet containing fifteen of each value, of which nine pairs are se-tenant.

Pedro de Valdivia — SP3

Portraits: 10c+10c, Jose Toribio Medina.

1961, Apr. 29 Photo. *Perf. 13x12½*

B3 SP3 5c + 5c pale brn & sl grn 1.00 25
B4 SP3 10c + 10c buff & vio blk 75 25

Printed without charge by the Spanish Mint as a gift to Chile. The surtax was to aid the 1960 earthquake victims and to increase teachers' salaries. See also Nos. CB1-CB2.

E° 27 + 3

"Centenario de la Organización Meteorológica Mundial IMO-W-MO 1973"

No. 402 Surcharged in Dark Green

1974, Mar. 25 Litho. *Perf. 14½*

B5 A213 27e + 3e on 40c dl grn 8 5

Centenary of international meteorological cooperation.

The 3e surtax of Nos. B5-B10 was for modernization of the postal system.

E° 27 + 3

"V Centenario del Nacimiento de Copérnico 1473 - 1973"

No. 412 Surcharged in Dark Blue

1974, Apr. 25 Litho. *Perf. 14½*

B6 A219 27e + 3e on 1.95e lt & dk bl 8 5

500th anniversary of the birth of Nicolaus Copernicus (1473-1534), Polish astronomer.

E° 27 + 3

" Centenario de la ciudad de Viña del Mar 1874 - 1974 "

No. 329A Surcharged

1974, May 2 Litho. *Perf. 14*

B7 A159 27e + 3e on 1e bluish grn 8 5

Centenary of the city of Vina del Mar.

No. 377 Surcharged

1974, June 7 Litho. *Perf. 14½*

B8 A193 47e + 3e on 40c grn 8 5

Nos. 395 and 380 Surcharged in Red

1974

B9 A207 67e + 3e on 40c multi 8 5
B10 A196 97e + 3e on 40c red brn 8 5

Issue dates: No. B9, July 9; No. B10, June 20.

AIR POST STAMPS

Bernardo O'Higgins — AP1

Black Surcharge.

Lithographed; Center Engraved

1927 Unwmk. *Perf. 13½x14.*

No.	Type	Description	Unused	Used
C1	AP1	40c on 10c blk brn & bl	325.00	35.00
C2	AP1	80c on 10c blk brn & bl	325.00	60.00
C3	AP1	1.20p on 10c blk brn & bl	325.00	60.00
C4	AP1	1.60p on 10c blk brn & bl	325.00	60.00
C5	AP1	2p on 10c blk brn & bl	325.00	60.00
		Nos. C1-C5 (5)	1,625.	275.00

Nos. C1 to C5 were issued for air post service between Santiago and Valparaiso, and are not known without surcharge.

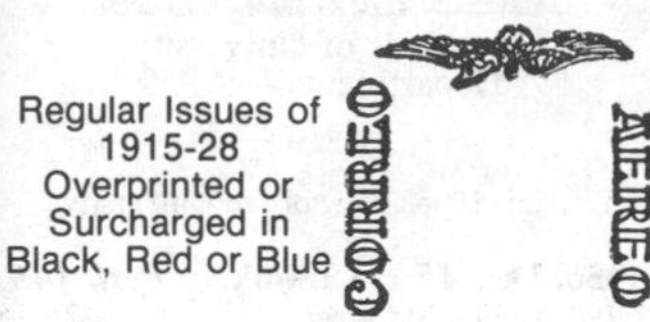

Regular Issues of 1915-28 Overprinted or Surcharged in Black, Red or Blue

Inscribed: "Chile Correos".

1928-29 *Perf. 13½x14, 14*

No.	Type	Description	Unused	Used
C6	A39	20c brn org & blk (Bk)	50	20
C6A	A55	40c dk vio & blk (R)	50	20
C6B	A43	1p grn & blk (Bl)	1.50	60
C6C	A43	2p red & blk (Bl)	2.50	40
f.		2p ver & blk (Bl)	110.00	27.50
C6D	A43	5p ol grn & blk (Bl)	3.75	1.00
C6E	A50	6p on 10c dp bl & blk (R)	60.00	32.50
C7	A43	10p org & blk (Bk) ('29)	12.50	4.00
C8	A43	10p org & blk (Bl)	55.00	32.50
		Nos. C6-C8 (8)	136.25	71.40

On Nos. C6B to C6D, C7 and C8 the overprint is larger than on the other stamps of the issue.

Same Overprint or Surcharge on Nos. 155, 156, 158-161.

Inscribed: "Chile Correos".

1928-32 Wmk. 215

No.	Type	Description	Unused	Used
C9	A55	40c vio & blk (R)	60	30
C10	A43	1p grn & blk (Bl)	1.75	50
C11	A43	2p red & blk (Bl)	10.00	2.00
C12	A52	3p on 5c sl bl (R)	40.00	27.50
C13	A43	5p ol grn & blk (Bl)	7.50	2.00
C14	A43	10p org & blk (Dk)	40.00	10.00
		Nos. C9-C14 (6)	99.85	42.30

Same Overprint on Nos. 166-169, 172 and 158 in Black, Red or Blue.

Inscribed: "Correos de Chile"

1928-30

No.	Type	Description	Unused	Used
C15	A39	20c org red & blk (#166) (Bk) ('29)	1.25	60
C16	A39	20c org red & blk (#172) (Bk) ('30)	40	20
C17	A40	25c bl & blk (R)	60	20
C18	A41	30c brn & blk (Bk)	35	20
a.		Double ovpt., one inverted	*350.00*	*350.00*
C19	A42	50c dp grn & blk (R)	50	20
		Nos. C15-C19 (5)	3.10	1.40

Inscribed: "Chile Correos".

1932 *Perf. 13½x14, 14.*

No.	Type	Description	Unused	Used
C21	A43	1p yel grn & blk (Bk)	3.75	2.00

Condor on Andes AP1a

Los Cerrillos Airport AP2

Airplane Crossing Andes — AP3

1931 Litho. *Perf. 13½x14, 14½x14*

No.	Type	Description	Unused	Used
C22	AP1a	5c yel grn	35	20
C23	AP1a	10c yel brn	35	20
C24	AP1a	20c rose	35	20
C25	AP2	50c dk bl	1.75	50
C26	AP3	50c blk brn	85	40
C27	AP3	1p purple	75	30
C28	AP3	2p bl blk	1.50	40
a.		2p bluish sl	1.50	40
C29	AP2	5p lt red	3.75	35
		Nos. C22-C29 (8)	9.65	2.55

Airplane over City — AP4

Wings over Chile — AP5

Condor AP6

Airplane and Star of Chile AP7

Condor and Statue of Canpolican AP8

Two Airplanes over Globe AP9

Seaplane AP10

Airplane AP11

Airplane and Southern Cross — AP12

Airplane and Symbols of Space — AP13

Perf. 13½x14

1934-39 Engr. Wmk. 215

Size: 21x25 mm.

No.	Type	Description	Unused	Used
C30	AP4	10c yel grn ('35)	25	10
C31	AP4	15c dk grn ('35)	35	20
C32	AP4	20c dp bl ('36)	20	12
C33	AP5	30c blk brn ('35)	20	12
C34	AP5	40c ind ('38)	20	12
C35	AP5	50c dk brn ('36)	20	12
C36	AP6	60c vio blk ('35)	20	12
C37	AP7	70c bl ('35)	35	20
C38	AP8	80c ol blk ('35)	20	12

Perf. 14

Size: 24½x29 mm.

No.	Type	Description	Unused	Used
C39	AP9	1p sl blk	20	12
C40	AP9	2p grnsh bl	20	12
C41	AP10	3p org brn ('35)	25	15
C42	AP10	4p brn ('35)	25	15
C43	AP10	5p org red	25	15
C44	AP11	6p yel brn ('35)	35	20
a.		6p brn ('39)	3.75	2.00
C45	AP11	8p grn ('35)	30	15
C46	AP11	10p brn lake	35	20
C47	AP12	20p olive	35	20
C48	AP12	30p gray blk	35	20
C49	AP13	40p gray vio	1.00	60
C50	AP13	50p brn vio	1.00	60
		Nos. C30-C50 (21)	7.00	4.06

Nos. C30-C50 have been re-issued in slightly different colors, with white gum. The first printings are considerably scarcer.

See also Nos. C90-C107B, C148-C154.

Types of 1931 Surcharged in Black or Red

LAN Cts.80

Perf. 13½x14, 14½x14.

1940 Wmk. 215

No.	Type	Description	Unused	Used
C51	AP1a	80c on 20c lt rose	60	20
C52	AP2	1.60p on 5p lt red	3.75	1.25
C53	AP3	5.10p on 2p sl bl (R)	3.00	1.50

The surcharge on No. C52 measures 21½mm.

Plane and Weather Vane — AP14

Plane and Caravel — AP23

Designs (Plane and): 20c, Globe. 30c, Chilean flag. 40c, Star of Chile and Southern Cross. 50c, Mountains. 60c, Tree. 70c, Lakes. 80c, Shore. 90c, Sunrise. 2p, Compass. 3p, Telegraph lines. 4p, Rainbow. 5p, Factory. 10p, Snow-capped mountain.

1941-42 Wmk. 215 Litho. *Perf. 14.*

No.	Type	Description	Unused	Used
C54	AP14	10c ol gray	25	15
C55	AP14	20c dp rose	25	15
C56	AP14	30c bl vio	25	15
C57	AP14	40c dl red brn	25	15
C58	AP14	50c red org ('42)	65	20
C59	AP14	60c dp grn	25	15
C60	AP14	70c rose	50	30
C61	AP14	80c ultra ('42)	3.00	50
C62	AP14	90c dk brn	75	30
C63	AP23	1p brt bl	50	30
C64	AP23	2p rose lake	75	40
C65	AP23	3p dk bl grn & yel grn	1.10	65
C66	AP23	4p bl vio & buff	1.65	85
C67	AP23	5p dk org red ('42)	15.00	6.00
C68	AP23	10p gray grn & bl grn	8.50	5.00
		Nos. C54-C68 (15)	33.65	15.25

The 1p, dated "1541-1941", commemorates the 400th anniversary of Santiago.

1942-46 Unwmk.

No.	Type	Description	Unused	Used
C69	AP14	10c ultra ('43)	25	15
C70	AP14	10c rose lil ('45)	25	15
C71	AP14	20c dl grn ('43)	25	15
C72	AP14	20c cop brn ('45)	25	15
C73	AP14	30c dl vio ('44)	25	15
C74	AP14	30c ol blk ('45)	25	15
C75	AP14	40c red brn ('44)	50	20
C76	AP14	40c ultra ('45)	25	15
C77	AP14	50c rose ('43)	25	15
C78	AP14	50c org red ('45)	25	15
C79	AP14	60c orange	25	15
C79B	AP14	60c dp grn ('46)	25	15
C80	AP14	70c rose ('45)	75	40
C81	AP14	80c sl grn	25	15
C82	AP14	90c brn ('45)	75	40
C83	AP23	1p gray grn & lt bl ('43)	35	20
C84	AP23	2p org red ('43)	75	20
C85	AP23	3p dk pur & pale org ('43)	75	20
C86	AP23	4p bl grn & yel grn	75	40
C87	AP23	5p dk rose car ('43)	65	30
a.		5p dk car rose ('44)	30	20
C88	AP23	10p saph ('43)	75	40
		Nos. C69-C88 (21)	9.00	4.50

No. C83 is without dates "1541-1941."

See Nos. C109-C123, C145-C147.

Coat of Arms and Plane AP29

1942, Nov. 5 Engr. *Perf. 14½*

No.	Type	Description	Unused	Used
C89	AP29	100p car lake	35.00	25.00

University of Chile centenary.

Types of 1934-39.

Perf. 13½x14.

1944-55 Unwmk. Engr.

No.	Type	Description	Unused	Used
C90	AP4	10c yel grn ('55)	35	25
C92	AP4	20c dp bl	20	12
C93	AP5	30c blk brn	20	12
C94	AP5	40c indigo	20	12
C95	AP5	50c dk brn ('47)	20	12
C96	AP6	60c sl vio	20	12
C97	AP7	70c bl ('48)	20	12
C98	AP8	80c ol blk	20	12

Perf. 14

No.	Type	Description	Unused	Used
C99	AP9	1p sl blk	20	12
C100	AP9	2p grnsh bl	35	15
C101	AP10	3p org brn ('45)	20	12
C102	AP10	4p brown	20	12
C103	AP10	5p org red	50	20
C104	AP11	6p yel brn ('46)	50	20
C105	AP11	8p green	50	20
C106	AP11	10p brn lake	1.25	20
C107	AP12	20p ol gray ('45)	1.00	20
a.		Imperf., pair	100.00	
C107B	AP13	50p rose vio ('50)	25.00	4.00
		Nos. C90-C107B (18)	31.45	6.60

Plane and Radio Tower — AP30

1945 Unwmk. Litho. *Perf. 14*

No.	Type	Description	Unused	Used
C108	AP30	1.60p brt vio	75	30

Types of 1941-42.

1946-48 Wmk. 215

No.	Type	Description	Unused	Used
C109	AP14	10c rose lil ('47)	20	12
C110	AP14	20c dk red brn ('48)	20	12
C111	AP14	20c dl grn ('48)	2.50	40
C112	AP14	30c blk ('48)	20	12
C113	AP14	40c ultra ('48)	20	12
C114	AP14	60c ol grn ('48)	20	12
C115	AP14	80c ol brk ('48)	20	12
C116	AP14	90c choc ('48)	25	15
C117	AP23	1p gray grn & lt bl ('48)	25	12
C118	AP30	1.60p brt vio	25	12
C119	AP30	1.80p brt vio ('48)	25	12
C119A	AP23	2p org red	50	15
C120	AP23	3p dk pur & pale org ('47)	2.00	40
C121	AP23	4p bl grn & yel grn ('48)	1.50	60
C122	AP23	5p rose car ('47)	1.00	30
C123	AP23	10p saph ('47)	1.25	30
		Nos. C109-C123 (16)	10.95	3.38

No. C117 is without dates "1541-1941."

Araucarian Pine — AP31

1948

C124 AP31 3p carmine 60 60
a. Block of 25 20.00

Issued in panes of 100 stamps, divisible into four blocks of 25 different designs, the same animals, insects, birds, fish, flowers and trees of Chile as illustrated and described for Nos. 254-255.

The stamps commemorate the centenary (in 1944) of the publication of the first volume of Claudio Gay's Natural History of Chile.

Air Line Emblem and Planes — AP32

1949 Wmk. 215 Litho. *Perf. 14.*

C125 AP32 2p ultra 40 25

Issued to commemorate the 20th anniversary of the establishment of Chile's National Air Line.

Benjamin Vicuna Mackenna AP33

Factory, Badge and Book AP34

1949, Mar. 22 Engr. *Perf. 13½x14*

C126 AP33 3p dk car rose 20 12

Unwmk.

1949, Nov. 11 Litho. *Perf. 14*

Design: 10p, Column and cogwheel.

C127 AP34 5p green 60 40
C128 AP34 10p red brn 1.00 60

Issued to commemorate the centenary of the founding of Chile's School of Arts and Crafts.

Plane and Globe — AP35

1950, Jan. Engr.

C129 AP35 5p green 25 20
C130 AP35 10p red brn 60 40

Issued to commemorate the 75th anniversary of the formation of the Universal Postal Union.

Plane over Snow-capped Mountain AP36

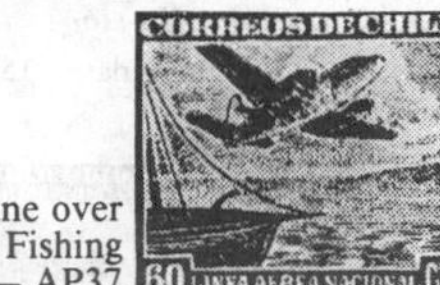

Plane over Fishing Boat — AP37

Araucarian Pine and Plane — AP38

Plane Above River — AP39

Plane and: 40c, Coast and Sunrise. 2p, Chilean flag. 3p, Dock crane. 5p, Blast furnace. 10p, Mountain lake. 20p, Cable cars.

Imprint: "Especies Valoradas-Chile"

1950-54 Wmk. 215 Litho. *Perf. 14*

C135 AP36 20c yel brn ('54) 20 10
C136 AP36 40c pur ('52) 20 10
C137 AP37 60c lt bl ('53) 1.50 60
C138 AP38 1p dl grn 20 10
C139 AP38 2p brn red 20 10
C140 AP38 3p vio bl 20 10
C141 AP39 4p red org ('54) 20 10
C142 AP38 5p violet 20 10
C143 AP39 10p yel grn ('53) 20 10
C144 AP39 20p red brn ('54) 40 10
Nos. C135-C144 (10) 3.50 1.50

See also Nos. C155-C164, C207-C212.

Nos. C115, C81 and C116 Surcharged with New Value in Carmine or Black.

1951-52 Wmk. 215

C145 AP14 40c on 80c ol blk (C) ('52) 20 10

Unwmk.

C146 AP14 40c on 80c sl grn (C) ('52) 5.00 3.00

Wmk. 215

C147 AP14 1p on 90c choc 20 10

Types of 1934-39.

1951-53 Unwmk. Engr. *Perf. 14*

C148 AP9 1p dp bl 20 12
C149 AP9 2p blue 35 15
C150 AP11 6p bis brn ('52) 50 20
C151 AP12 30p dk gray ('53) 5.00 75
C152 AP13 40p dk pur brn 15.00 2.00
C153 AP13 50p dk pur 25.00 8.00
Nos. C148-C153 (6) 46.05 11.22

Wmk. 215

C154 AP13 50p dk pur ('52) 1.00 50

Types of 1950-54.
Designs as Before.
Imprint: "Especies Valoradas-Chile"

1951-55 Unwmk. Litho. *Perf. 14*

C155 AP36 20c yel brn ('54) 20 10
C156 AP36 40c purple 20 10
C157 AP37 60c lt bl ('53) 25 15
C158 AP38 1p dk bl grn ('55) 20 10
C159 AP38 2p brn red 20 10
C160 AP38 3p vio bl 20 10
C161 AP39 4p red org ('52) 35 20
C162 AP38 5p violet 35 20
C163 AP39 10p emerald 35 10
C164 AP39 20p brown 50 15
Nos. C155-C164 (10) 2.80 1.30

San Martin Crossing Andes AP40

Perf. 14½.

1951, Mar. 16 Wmk. 215 Engr.

C165 AP40 5p red vio 40 25

Issued to commemorate the centenary of the death of Gen. Jose de San Martin.

Isabella Type of Regular Issue, 1952.

1952, Mar. 21 *Perf. 14*

C166 A125 10p carmine 50 30

Issued for the 500th anniversary of the birth of Queen Isabella I of Spain.

A souvenir card without franking value was issued for the Hispano-Chilean Philatelic Exhibition at Santiago, Oct. 12, 1969. It contains 2 imperf. stamps similar to Nos. 264 and C166-60c green and 10p rose red. Size: 115x137½mm.

Ancient Fortress — AP42

1953, Apr. 28

C167 AP42 10p brn car 1.00 25

4th centenary of the founding of Valdivia.

Stamp Centenary Type of 1953.

1953, Oct. 15 Engr. *Perf. 14½*

C168 A131 100p dp grnsh bl 1.50 1.00

Issued to commemorate the centenary of Chile's first postage stamps.

An imperf. souvenir sheet contains one each of Nos. 276 and C168, with inscriptions in black at top and bottom center. Sheet measures 178x229mm. It is stated that this sheet was not valid for postage.

Early Plane and Stylized Modern Version — AP44

Unwmk.

1954, May 26 Engr. *Perf. 14*

C170 AP44 3p dp bl 15 10

Issued to commemorate the 25th anniversary of the founding of Chile's National Air Line.

Domeyko Type of Regular Issue, 1954.

1954, Aug. 16 *Perf. 13½x14*

C171 A134 5p org brn 20 10

Issued to commemorate the 150th anniversary (in 1952) of the birth of Ignacio Domeyko.

Railroad Type of Regular Issue, 1954.

1954, Sept. 10 Wmk. 215 *Perf. 14½*

C172 A135 10p dk pur 40 20

Issued to commemorate the centenary (in 1951) of the first South American railroad.

An imperforate souvenir sheet contains one each of Nos. 283 and C172. Size: 174x232mm. Price, $200.

Presidential Visits Type of 1955

1955, May 24

C173 A139 100p red 1.25 1.00

Issued to publicize the reciprocal visits of Presidents Juan D. Peron and Carlos Ibanez del Campo.

Jet Plane in Clouds — AP48

Comet Air Liner — AP49

Designs: 2p, Helicopter over bridge. 10p, Oil derricks and plane. 50p, Control tower and plane. 200p, Beechcraft monoplane. 500p, Douglas DC-6.

Perf. 14½x14, 14x13½ (AP49)

1955-56 Engr. Wmk. 215

C174 AP48 1p dp red lil ('56) 20 10
C175 AP48 2p pale brn ('56) 10 5
C176 AP48 10p bluish grn ('56) 10 5
C177 AP48 50p rose ('56) 60 25
C178 AP49 100p green 75 15
C179 AP49 200p dp ultra 5.00 75
C180 AP49 500p dk car 6.00 75
Nos. C174-C180 (7) 12.75 2.10

Stamps similar to type AP49, but inscribed in escudo currency, are listed as type AP58.

1956-58 Unwmk.

Designs: 5p, Train and plane. 20p, Jet plane and Easter Island statue.

C183 AP48 5p violet 10 5
C184 AP48 10p grn ('57) 10 5
C185 AP48 20p ultra 10 5
C186 AP48 50p rose ('57) 10 5
C187 AP49 100p bl grn ('57) 40 15
a. Lithographed ('60) 40 20
C188 AP49 200p dp ultra ('57) 40 15
C189 AP49 500p car ('58) 60 20
Nos. C183-C189 (7) 1.80 70

Symbols of University Departments — AP50

Design: 100p, View of the University.

1956, Dec. 15 Unwmk. *Perf. 14½*

C190 AP50 20p green 25 15
C191 AP50 100p dk vio bl 1.00 60

Issued to commemorate the 25th anniversary of the Federico Santa Maria Technical University, Valparaiso.

A souvenir sheet contains one each of Nos. 299, C190-C191, imperf. It was not issued for postal use, though some served postally. Size: 127x160mm. Price, $25.

Mistral Type of Regular Issue, 1958

1958, Jan. 10 Engr. *Perf. 14*

C192 A144 100p green 20 10

Issued in honor of Gabriela Mistral, poet and educator.

Ambrosio O'Higgins — AP51

1958, March 23

C193 AP51 100p lt bl 25 15

Issued to commemorate the 400th anniversary of the founding of the city of Osorno.

A souvenir sheet contains one each of Nos. 302 and C193, imperf. and printed in red brown. It was not issued for postal use, though some served postally. Size: 155x138mm. Price, $15.

Exhibition Type of Regular Issue

1958, Oct. 18 Unwmk.

C194 A146 50p dl grn 15 10

Issued to publicize the National Philatelic Exhibition, Santiago, Oct. 18-26.

A souvenir sheet contains one each of Nos. 303 and C194, imperf. and printed in deep red. It was not issued for postal use, though some served postally. Size: 188x220mm. Price, $15.

Bank Type of Regular Issue, 1958.

1958, Dec. 18 Engr. *Perf. 14*

C195 A147 50p redsh brn 15 10

Issued to commemorate the centenary of the Savings Bank for Public Employees.

A souvenir sheet contains one each of Nos. 304 and C195, printed in dull violet, imperf. It was not issued for postal use, though some served postally. Price, $150.

Antarctic Types of Regular Issue

1958 **Litho.** ***Perf. 14***
C199 A149 20p violet 20 10

Engr.
C200 A150 500p dk bl 2.50 1.25

Symbols of Various Religions AP52

Perf. 14½

1959, Jan. 23 **Unwmk.** **Engr.**
C206 AP52 50p dk car rose 15 10

Issued to commemorate the 10th anniversary of the Universal Declaration of Human Rights.

Types of 1950-54.
Imprint: "Casa de Moneda de Chile."

Designs: 1p, Araucarian pine and plane. 10p, Plane over mountain lake. 20p, Plane and cable cars. 50p, Plane silhouette over shore. 100p, Plane over map of Antarctica. 200p, Plane over natural arch rock.

1959 **Litho.** ***Perf. 14***
C207 AP38 1p dk bl grn 60 30
a. Wmk. 215 30.00
C208 AP39 10p emerald 40 10
C209 AP39 20p red brn 25 10
C210 AP39 50p yel grn 25 10
C211 AP39 100p car rose 25 10
C212 AP39 200p brt bl 40 10
Nos. C207-C212 (6) 2.15 80

Carlos Anwandter — AP53

1959, June 18 **Engr.** ***Perf. 14***
C213 AP53 20p rose car 20 10

Issued to commemorate the centenary of the German School in Valdivia, founded by Carlos Anwandter.

A souvenir sheet contains one each of Nos. 319 and C213, imperf. It was not issued for postal use, though some served postally. Price, $20.

IGY Type of Regular Issue, 1958.

1959, Aug. 28 **Unwmk.** ***Perf. 14***
C214 A148 50p green 20 10

Issued to commemorate the International Geophysical Year, 1957-58.

Ladrillero Type of Regular Issue.

1959, Aug. 28 **Litho.**
C215 A154 50p green 20 10

Issued to commemorate the 400th anniversary (in 1957) of the Juan Ladrillero expedition.

Barros Arana Type of Regular Issue.

1959, Aug. 28
C216 A155 100p purple 40 20

Issued to commemorate the 50th anniversary of the death of Diego Barros Arana (1830-1907), historian.

Red Cross Type of Regular Issue.

1959, Oct. 6
C217 A156 50p red & blk 25 15

Centenary of Red Cross idea.

Demand, as well as supply, determines a stamp's market value. One is as important as the other.

WRY Type of Regular Issue, 1960.

1960, Apr. 7 **Unwmk.** ***Perf. 14½***
C218 A160 10c violet 25 15

Issued to publicize World Refugee Year, July 1, 1959-June 30, 1960.

A souvenir sheet contains two stamps similar to Nos. 330 and C218, the 1c printed in blue, the 10c airmail in maroon. The sheet is imperf., printed on thin cardboard and has border, inscriptions and WRY emblems in dark green with drab background. Size: 160x204mm. Price, $90.

Type of Regular Issue, 1960-62, and

José Agustin Eyzaguirre and José Miguel Infante AP54

Designs: 2c, Palace of Justice. 5c, National memorial. No. C220, Arms of Chile. No. C220A, José Gaspar Marin and J. Gregorio Argomedo. 50c, Archbishop J. I. Cienfuegos and Brother Camilo Henriquez. 1e, Bernardo O'Higgins.

1960-65 **Unwmk.** **Engr.** ***Perf. 14½***
C218A AP54 2c mar & gray vio ('62) 15 10
C219 A162 5c vio bl & dl pur ('61) 20 10

Wmk. 215
C220 A161 10c dk brn & red brn 20 10

Unwmk.
C220A AP54 10c vio brn & brn ('64) 20 10
C220B AP54 20c dk bl & dl pur ('64) 25 10
C220C AP54 50c bl grn & ind ('65) 50 20
C220D A162 1e dk red & red brn ('63) 1.00 40
Nos. C218A-C220D (7) 2.50 1.10

Issued to commemorate the 150th anniversary of the formation of the first National Government.

A souvenir sheet contains two airmail stamps: a 5c brown similar to No. C219 (National Memorial) and a 10c green, type A161. The sheet is imperf., printed on heavy paper with papermaker's watermark, and has green inscriptions. Size: 120x168mm. Price, $30.

Map and Rotary Emblem — AP55

Unwmk.

1960, Dec. 1 **Litho.** ***Perf. 14***
C221 AP55 10c blue 25 15

Issued to commemorate the South American Rotary Regional Conference, Santiago, 1960.

A souvenir sheet contains one 10c maroon, type AP55, with brown marginal inscription. Size: 118x158mm. Price, $14.

The souvenir sheet was overprinted in green "El Mundo Unida Contra la Malaria" and the outline of a mosquito, and released in October, 1962. Price, $27.50.

Plane over Mountain Lake — AP56

Designs: 1m, Araucarian pine and plane. 2m, Chilean flag and plane. 3m, Plane and dock crane. 4m, Plane above river (vignette like AP39). 5m, Blast furnace. 2c, Plane over cable cars. 5c, Plane silhouette over shore. 10c, Plane over map of Antarctica. 20c, Plane over natural arch rock.

Imprint: "Casa de Moneda de Chile."

1960-62 **Litho.** ***Perf. 14***
C222 AP56 1m orange 10 10
C223 AP56 2m yel grn 10 5
C224 AP56 3m violet 10 5
C225 AP56 4m gray ol 10 5
C226 AP56 5m brt bl grn 10 5
C227 AP56 1c ultra 10 5
C228 AP56 2c red brn ('61) 20 5
C229 AP56 5c yel grn ('61) 1.25 10
C230 AP56 10c car rose ('62) 30 10
C231 AP56 20c brt bl ('62) 30 10
Nos. C222-C231 (10) 2.65 70

Oil Derricks and Douglas DC-6 AP57

Beechcraft Monoplane AP58

Designs: 5m, Train and plane. 2c, Jet plane and Easter Island statue. 5c, Control tower and plane. 10c, Comet airliner. 50c, Douglas DC-6.

Perf. 14x13½

1960-67 **Unwmk.** **Litho.**
C234 AP57 5m red brn 5 5
C235 AP57 1c dl bl 5 5
C236 AP57 2c ultra ('62) 5 5
C237 AP57 5c rose red ('64) 5 5
C238 AP58 10c ultra ('67) 5 6
C239 AP58 20c car ('62) 5 5
C240 AP58 50c grn ('63) 5 5
Nos. C234-C240 (7) 35 36

Stamps similar to type AP58, but inscribed in peso ($) currency, are listed as type AP49.

Congress Type of Regular Issue.

1961, Oct. 5 ***Perf. 14½***
C245 A164 10c gray grn 75 25

Issued to commemorate the 150th anniversary of the first National Congress.

Soccer Type of Regular Issue, 1962.

Designs: 5c, Goalkeeper and stadium (vert.). 10c, Soccer players and globe.

Perf. 14½

1962, May 30 **Unwmk.** **Engr.**
C246 A165 5c rose lil 15 10
C247 A165 10c dk car 25 15

Issued to commemorate the World Soccer Championship, Chile, May 30-June 17.

A souvenir sheet of four contains one each of Nos. 340-341, C246-C247, imperf., with light brown marginal inscriptions. Size: 123x194mm. Sold for 7.50 escudos (face value, 22 centavos). Price, $5.

Hunger Type of Regular Issue.

Design: 20c, Mother with empty bowl (horiz.).

1963, Mar. 21 **Litho.** ***Perf. 14***
C248 A166 20c green 10 5

Issued for the "Freedom from Hunger" campaign of the U.N. Food and Agriculture Organization.

Red Cross Type of Regular Issue.

Design: 20c, Centenary emblem and plane silhouette (horiz.).

1963, Sept. 6 **Unwmk.** ***Perf. 14***
C249 A167 20c gray & red 15 10

Centenary of International Red Cross.

Fire Engine of 1860's AP59

1963, Dec. 20 **Litho.** ***Perf. 14½***
C250 AP59 30c red 15 10

Centenary of the Santiago Fire Brigade.

Western Hemisphere AP60

1964, Apr. 9 **Unwmk.** ***Perf. 14½***
C254 AP60 4c ultra 10 5

Issued in memory of President John F. Kennedy and to honor the Alliance for Progress.

Battle of Rancagua AP61

1965, May 7 **Engr.** ***Perf. 14½***
C255 AP61 5c dl grn p sep 10 5

Issued to commemorate the sesquicentennial of the Battle of Rancagua, Oct. 7, 1814.

ITU Emblem, Old and New Communication Equipment AP62

1965, May 7 **Litho.** ***Perf. 14½x14***
C256 AP62 40c red & mar 10 5

Issued to commemorate the centenary of the International Telecommunication Union.

Portrait Type of 1964

Portraits: No. C257, Enrique Molina. No. C258, Msgr. Carlos Casanueva.

1965, June **Litho.** ***Perf. 14***
C257 A169 60c brt vio 10 5
C258 A169 60c green 10 5

See note after No. 346.

Skier Type of Regular Issue 1965

Design: 20c, Skier (horiz.).

1965, Aug. 30 **Unwmk.** ***Perf. 14***
C259 A172 20c ultra 10 5

World Skiing Championships, Chile, 1966.

Fishing Boats, Angelmo Harbor AP63

Aviators' Monument AP64

1965
C260 AP63 40c brown 10 5

Perf. 14x14½
C262 AP64 1e car rose 15 5

Andrés Bello — AP65

1965, Nov. 29 **Engr.** **Unwmk.**
C263 AP65 10 dk car rose 15 10

Issued to commemorate the centenary of the death of Andres Bello (1780?-1865), Venezuela-born writer and educator.

Skiers AP66 Basketball AP67

1966, Apr. 6 **Litho.** ***Perf. 14***
C264 AP66 4e dk bl & red brn 60 15

World Skiing Championships, Partillo, Aug. 1966.

1966, Apr. 28
C265 AP67 13c rose car 10 5

International Basketball Championships.

Slalom AP68

Perf. 14½x15
1966, July 20 **Litho.** **Unwmk.**
C266 AP68 75c rose car & lil 10 5
C267 AP68 3e ultra & lt bl 20 10

International Skiing Championships, Partillo, August 1966. A souvenir sheet of 2 contains imperf. stamps similar to Nos. C266-C267. Marginal inscription in ultramarine and rose carmine. No gum. Size: 109x140mm. Price $2.50.

Ship Type of Regular Issue

1966 **Litho.** ***Perf. 14½***
C268 A175 70c Prus grn & yel grn 10 10

See note below No. 358.

ICY Type of Regular Issue

1966, Oct. 28 **Unwmk.** ***Perf. 14½***
C269 A177 3e bl & car 50 20

International Cooperation Year, 1965.
A souvenir sheet of 2 contains imperf. stamps similar to Nos. 360 and C269. Brown marginal inscription. No gum. Size: 111x140mm. Price $2.25.

Chilean Flag and Ships — AP69

1966, Nov. 21 **Litho.** ***Perf. 14***
C270 AP69 13c dl red brn 10 5

Centenary of the city of Antofagasta.

Pardo Type of Regular Issue

Design: 40c, Pardo and map of Chile's claim to Antarctica.

1967, Jan. 6 **Unwmk.** ***Perf. 14½***
C271 A178 40c ultra 10 5

See note below No. 361.

Family Type of Regular Issue

1967, Apr. 13 **Litho.** ***Perf. 14***
C272 A179 80c brt bl & blk 10 5

Issued to publicize the 8th International Conference for Family Planning, Santiago, April 1967.

Ruben Dario and Title Page of "Azul" AP70

1967, May 15 **Engr.** ***Perf. 14½***
C273 AP70 10c dk bl 10 5

Issued to commemorate the centenary of the birth of Ruben Dario (pen name of Felix Ruben Garcia Sarmiento, 1867-1916), Nicaraguan poet, newspaper correspondent and diplomat.

Tree Type of Regular Issue

1967, June 9 **Litho.**
C274 A180 75c grn & pale rose 10 5

Reforestation Campaign.

Lions Type of Regular Issue

1967 **Litho.** ***Perf. 14***
C275 A181 1e pur & yel 10 5
C276 A181 5e bl & yel 1.00 15

Issued to commemorate the 50th anniversary of Lions International. A souvenir sheet without franking value contains 3 imperf. stamps, 20c, 1e and 5e, in violet blue and yellow. Marginal inscription and design in violet blue and yellow. Size: 110x140mm. Price, $7.50.
Issue dates: 1e, July 12; 5e, Aug. 11.

Flag Type of Regular Issue

1967, Oct. 20 **Unwmk.** ***Perf. 14½***
C277 A182 50c ultra & crim 10 10

Sesquicentennial of the national flag.

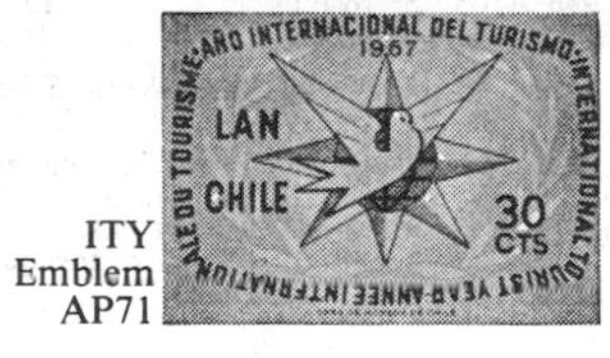

ITY Emblem AP71

1967, Nov. 22 **Litho.** ***Perf. 14½***
C278 AP71 30c lt vio bl & blk 10 5

Issued for International Tourist Year, 1967.

Caro Type of Regular Issue, 1967.

1967, Dec. 4 **Engr.** ***Perf. 14½***
C279 A183 40c violet 60 25

Issued to commemorate the centenary of the birth of José Maria Cardinal Caro.

Type of Regular Issue, 1968

1968, Apr. 23 **Litho.** ***Perf. 14½***
C280 A184 2e brt vio 10 5

Issued to commemorate the sesquicentennial of the Battles of Chacabuco and Maipu. A souvenir sheet of 2 contains imperf. stamps similar to Nos. 367 and C280. Gold marginal inscription commemorates the battles and the First Trans-Andes Philatelic Week, Apr. 4-10. Price, $4. A second sheet exists with the 2e in green and the 3e in brown. Size: 139½x100mm. Price, $4.

Farm Type of Regular Issue

1968, June 18 **Unwmk.**
C281 A185 50c blk, org & grn 10 5

Issued to publicize the agrarian reforms.

Juan I. Molina AP72

1968, Aug. 27 **Litho.** ***Perf. 14½***
C282 AP72 1e brt grn 10 5

Issued to honor Juan I. Molina, educator and scientist.

Map of Chiloé Province — AP73 British Crown and Map of Chile — AP74

Perf. 14½
1968, Oct. 7 **Unwmk.** **Litho.**
C283 AP73 1e rose cl 10 5

Issued to commemorate the anniversaries of the founding of five towns in Chiloe Province.

Auto Club Type of Regular Issue

1968, Nov. 10 **Engr.** ***Perf. 14½x14***
C284 A189 5e ultra 20 10

Issued to commemorate the 40th anniversary of the Automobile Club of Chile.

1968, Nov. 12 **Litho.** ***Perf. 14½***

Designs: 50c, Chilean coat of arms (horiz.; similar to type A161). 3e, British coat of arms (horiz.).

C285 AP74 50c grn & brn 20 10
C286 AP74 3e bl & org brn 10 5
Engr.
C287 AP74 5e pur & mag 20 10

Visit of Queen Elizabeth II of Great Britain, Nov. 11-18. A souvenir sheet of 3 contains imperf., lithographed stamps similar to Nos. C285-C287. Dark blue marginal inscription. Size: 124½x190mm. The souvenir sheet also publicizes the British-Chilean Philatelic Exhibition. Price, $8.

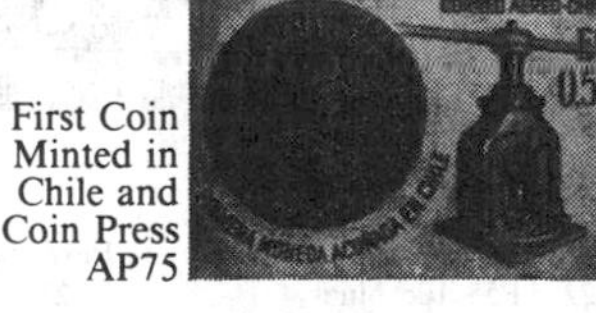

First Coin Minted in Chile and Coin Press AP75

Design: 1e, Chile No. 128.

1968, Dec. 31 **Litho.** ***Perf. 14½***
C288 AP75 50c ocher & vio brn 10 5
C289 AP75 1e lt bl & dp org 10 5

Issued to commemorate the 225th anniversary of the founding of the State Mint (Casa de Moneda de Chile).
A souvenir sheet of 4 contains imperf. stamps similar to Nos. 373-374, C288-C289. Brown marginal inscription. Size: 150x119mm. Price, $2.

Satellite Type of Regular Issue

1969, May 20 **Litho.** ***Perf. 14½***
C290 A191 2e rose lil 10 5

Issued to publicize the inauguration of ENTEL-Chile, the first commercial satellite communications ground station, Longovilo.

Red Cross Type of Regular Issue

1969, Sept. **Litho.** ***Perf. 14½***
C291 A192 5e blk & red 10 5

Issued for the 50th anniversary of the League of Red Cross Societies.
A souvenir card contains 2 imperf. stamps similar to Nos. 376 and C291, with red marginal inscription. Size: 109x140mm. Price $3.

Dam Type of Regular Issue

1969, Nov. 18 **Litho.** ***Perf. 14½***
C292 A193 3e blue 10 5

Rodriguez Type of Regular Issue

1969, Nov. 24
C293 A194 30c brown 10 5

Issued to commemorate the 150th anniversary of the death of Col. Manuel Rodriguez.

EXPO '70 Type of Regular Issue

1969, Dec. 1 **Litho.** ***Perf. 14***
C294 A195 5e red 15 10

Issued to publicize EXPO '70 International Exposition, Osaka, Japan, March 15-Sept. 13, 1970.

Bible Type of 1969

1969, Dec. 2 ***Perf. 14½***
C295 A196 1e green 10 5

Issued to commemorate the 400th anniversary of the translation of the Bible into Spanish by Casiodoro de Reina.

ILO Type of Regular Issue

1969, Dec. 17 ***Perf. 14½***
C296 A197 2e rose lil & blk 10 5

Issued to commemorate the 50th anniversary of the International Labor Organization.

Human Rights Year Type of 1969

1969, Dec. 18
C297 A198 4e brn & red 10 5

Human Rights Year, 1968.
A souvenir sheet of 2 contains imperf. stamps similar to Nos. 382 and C297. Blue commemorative marginal inscription. Size: 110x140mm. Price, $3.50.

Easter Island Type of 1970

1970, Jan. 26
C298 A199 50c dl grnsh bl 10 5

Issued to commemorate the 80th anniversary of the acquisition of Easter Island.

Ship Type of Regular Issue

1970, Feb. 4 **Litho.** ***Perf. 14½***
C299 A200 2e dp ultra 20 5

Issued to commemorate the 150th anniversary of the capture of Valdivia during Chile's war of independence by Thomas Cochrane (1775-1860), naval commander.

Rotary Type of Regular Issue

1970, Mar. 18 **Litho.** ***Perf. 14***
C300 A201 1e rose cl 10 5

Issued to commemorate the centenary of the birth of Paul Harris (1868-1947), founder of Rotary International.

Gandhi Type of Regular Issue

1970, Apr. 1 **Litho.** ***Perf. 14½***
C301 A202 1e red brn 10 5

Issued to commemorate the centenary of the birth of Mohandas K. Gandhi (1869-1948), leader in India's fight for independence.

Education Year Type of 1970

1970, July 17 **Litho.** ***Perf. 14½***
C302 A204 4e red brn 10 5

Issued for International Education Year.

National Shrine Type of 1970

1970, July 28 **Litho.** ***Perf. 14½***
C303 A205 1e ultra 10 5

Issued to publicize the O'Higgins National Shrine at Maipu.

Cancer Type of Regular Issue

1970, Aug. 11

C304	A206	2e brn & lt ol	10	10

Issued to commemorate the International Cancer Congress, Houston, Texas, May 22-29.

Copper Type of Regular Issue

1970, Oct. 21 Litho. *Perf. 14½*

C305	A207	3e grn & lt red brn	10	5

Nationalization of the copper industry.

United Nations Type of 1970

1970, Oct. 22

C306	A208	5e dk car & grn	40	5

United Nations, 25th anniversary.

Freighter Type of Regular Issue

1971, Jan. 18 Litho. *Perf. 14*

C307	A209	5e lt red brn	10	5

National Maritime Commission.

No. C290 Surcharged in Red

1971, Jan. 21 Litho. *Perf. 14½*

C308	A191	52c on 2e rose lil	20	5

Liberation Type of Regular Issue

1971, Feb. 3 *Perf. 14½*

C309	A210	1e gray bl & brn	5	5

The 150th anniversary of the expedition to liberate Peru.

UNICEF Type of Regular Issue

1971, Feb. 11 Litho. *Perf. 14½*

C310	A211	2e bl & grn	5	5

First meeting in Latin America of the Executive Council of UNICEF, Santiago, May 20-31, 1969.

Boy Scout Type of Regular Issue

1971, Feb. 10 *Perf. 14*

C311	A212	5c dk car & ol	10	5

Founding of Chilean Boy Scouts, 60th anniversary.

Satellite Type of Regular Issue

1971, May 25 Litho. *Perf. 14½*

C312	A213	2e brown	10	5

First commercial Chilean satellite communications ground station, Longovilo.

De Ercilla Type of Regular Issue

1972, Mar. 20 Engr. *Perf. 14*

C313	A221	2e Prus bl	10	5

4th centenary (in 1969) of "La Araucana," by Alonso de Ercilla y Zuniga (1533-1596).

A souvenir card contains impressions of Nos. 414 and C313 with black marginal inscription commemorating Espana 75 Philatelic Exhibition. Size: 165x220mm.

AIR POST SEMI-POSTAL STAMPS

Type of Semi-Postal Stamps, 1961.

Portraits: 10c+10c, Alonso de Ercilla. 20c+20c, Gabriela Mistral.

Perf. 13x12½

1961, Apr. 29 Photo. Unwmk.

CB1	SP3	10c + 10c sal & choc	75	25
CB2	SP3	20c + 20c gray & dp cl	75	25

Printed without charge by the Spanish Mint as a gift to Chile. The surtax was to aid the 1960 earthquake victims and to increase teachers' salaries.

ACKNOWLEDGMENT OF RECEIPT STAMPS

AR1

1894 Unwmk. *Perf. 11½.*

H1	AR1	5c brown	50	50
a.		Imperf., pair	3.00	

The black stamp of design similar to AR1 inscribed "Avis de Paiement" was prepared for use on notices of payment of funds but was not regularly issued.

POSTAGE DUE STAMPS

D1

D2

Handstamped

1894 Unwmk. *Perf. 13*

J1	D1	2c blk, *straw*	15.00	7.00
J2	D1	4c blk, *straw*	15.00	7.00
J3	D1	6c blk, *straw*	15.00	7.00
J4	D1	8c blk, *straw*	15.00	7.00
J5	D2	10c blk, *straw*	15.00	7.00
J6	D1	16c blk, *straw*	15.00	7.00
J7	D1	20c blk, *straw*	15.00	7.00
J8	D1	30c blk, *straw*	15.00	7.00
J9	D1	40c blk, *straw*	15.00	7.00
		Nos. J1-J9 (9)	135.00	63.00

J1a	D1	2c blk, *yel*	62.50	60.00
J2a	D1	4c blk, *yel*	50.00	40.00
J3a	D1	6c blk, *yel*	37.50	35.00
J4a	D1	8c blk, *yel*	15.00	12.50
J5a	D2	10c blk, *yel*	15.00	12.50
J6a	D1	16c blk, *yel*	15.00	12.50
J7a	D1	20c blk, *yel*	15.00	12.50
J8a	D1	30c blk, *yel*	15.00	12.50
J9a	D1	40c blk, *yel*	15.00	12.50
		Nos. J1a-J9a (9)	240.00	210.00

Counterfeits exist.

D3

1895 Litho. *Perf. 11.*

J19	D3	1c red, *yel*	5.00	2.00
J20	D3	2c red, *yel*	5.00	2.00
J21	D3	4c red, *yel*	4.00	2.00
J22	D3	6c red, *yel*	5.00	2.00
J23	D3	8c red, *yel*	3.00	2.00
J24	D3	10c red, *yel*	3.00	2.00
J25	D3	20c red, *yel*	2.00	1.25
J26	D3	40c red, *yel*	3.00	2.00
J27	D3	50c red, *yel*	3.00	2.00
J28	D3	60c red, *yel*	6.00	3.00
J29	D3	80c red, *yel*	6.00	3.50
J30	D3	1p red, *yel*	6.00	3.50
		Nos. J19-J30 (12)	51.00	27.25

Nos. J19-J30 were printed in sheets of 100 (10x10) containing all 12 denominations.

Counterfeits of Nos. J19-J42 exist.

1896 *Perf. 13½*

J31	D3	1c red, *straw*	85	50
J32	D3	2c red, *straw*	85	50
J33	D3	4c red, *straw*	85	50
J34	D3	6c red, *straw*	2.00	75
J35	D3	8c red, *straw*	85	50
J36	D3	10c red, *straw*	85	50
J37	D3	20c red, *straw*	85	50
J38	D3	40c red, *straw*	12.50	10.00
J39	D3	50c red, *straw*	12.50	10.00
J40	D3	60c red, *straw*	12.50	10.00
J41	D3	80c red, *straw*	12.50	10.00
J42	D3	100c red, *straw*	25.00	20.00
		Nos. J31-J42 (12)	82.10	63.75

D4

D5

1898 *Perf. 13.*

J43	D4	1c scarlet	50	30
J44	D4	2c scarlet	1.25	60
J45	D4	4c scarlet	50	30
J46	D4	10c scarlet	50	30
J47	D4	20c scarlet	50	30
		Nos. J43-J47 (5)	3.25	1.80

1924 *Perf. 11½, 12½.*

J48	D5	2c bl & red	75	50
J49	D5	4c bl & red	75	50
J50	D5	8c bl & red	75	50
J51	D5	10c bl & red	75	50
J52	D5	20c bl & red	75	30
J53	D5	40c bl & red	75	50
J54	D5	60c bl & red	75	50
J55	D5	80c bl & red	75	50
J56	D5	1p bl & red	1.00	60
J57	D5	2p bl & red	2.00	1.25
J58	D5	5p bl & red	2.00	1.25
		Nos. J48-J58 (11)	11.00	6.90

Nos. J48-J58 were printed in sheets of 150 containing all 11 denominations, and in sheets of 50 containing the five lower denominations, providing various se-tenants.

All values of this issue exist imperforate, also with center inverted, but are not believed to have been regularly issued. Those with inverted centers sell for about 10 times normal stamps.

OFFICIAL STAMPS

For Domestic Postage.

O1

Single-lined frame.
Control number in violet.

1907 Unwmk. *Imperf.*

O1	O1	dl bl, "CARTA" in org	30.00	22.50
O2	O1	red, "OFICIO" in bl	30.00	22.50
O3	O1	vio, "PAQUETE" in red	30.00	22.50
O4	O1	org, *bl,* "EP" in vio	30.00	22.50

The diagonal inscription in differing color indicates type of usage: CARTA for letters of ordinary weight; OFICIO, heavy letters to 100 grams; PAQUETE, parcels to 100 grams; E P (Encomienda Postal), heavier parcels; C (Certificado), as on No. O8, registration including postage.

Varieties include CARTA, PAQUETE and E P inverted, OFICIO omitted, etc.

Double-lined frame.

Large control number in black.

Perf. 11.

O5	O1	bl, "CARTA" in yel	7.50	6.25
O6	O1	red, "OFICIO" in bl	7.50	5.00
O7	O1	brn, "PAQUETE" in grn	7.50	5.00
O8	O1	grn, "C" in red	150.00	110.00

Nos. O5-O8 exist in tete beche pairs; with CARTA, OFICIO or PAQUETE double or inverted, and other varieties.

Counterfeits of Nos. O1-O8 exist.

For Foreign Postage.

Regular Issues of 1892-1909 Overprinted in Red — a

On Stamps of 1904-09.

1907 ***Perf. 12.***

O9 A14 1c green 7.50 7.50
a. Inverted ovpt. 25.00
O10 A12 3c on lp brn 20.00 20.00
a. Inverted ovpt. 75.00
O11 A14 5c ultra 15.00 15.00
a. Inverted ovpt. 50.00
O12 A15 10c gray & blk 15.00 15.00
O13 A15 15c vio & blk 20.00 20.00
O14 A15 20c org brn & blk 20.00 20.00
O15 A15 50c ultra & blk 62.50 62.50

On Stamp of 1892.

Rouletted.

O16 A6 1p dk brn & blk 150.00 125.00

Counterfeits of Nos. O9-O16 exist.

Regular Issues of 1915-25 Overprinted in Red or Blue — b

1926 ***Perf. 13½x14, 14.***

O17 A52 5c sl bl (R) 1.75 40
O18 A50 10c bl & blk (R) 2.75 60
O19 A39 20c org red & blk (Bl) 1.25 30
O20 A42 50c dp grn & blk (Bl) 1.25 30
O21 A43 1p grn & blk (R) 4.00 50
O22 A43 2p ver & blk (Bl) 2.75 80
Nos. O17-O22 (6) 13.75 2.90

Nos. O21 and O22 are overprinted vertically at each side.

Nos. O17 to O22 were for the use of the Biblioteca Nacional.

Servicio del

Regular Issue of 1915-25 Overprinted in Red — c

ESTADO

1928 ***Perf. 13½x14, 14.***

O23 A50 10c bl & blk 6.00 1.50
O24 A39 20c brn org & blk 2.75 75
O25 A40 25c dl bl & blk 7.00 75
O26 A42 50c dp grn & blk 4.00 75
O27 A43 1p grn & blk 4.50 1.00
Nos. O23-O27 (5) 24.25 4.75

The overprint on Nos. O23 to O26 is 16½mm. high; on No. O27 it is 20mm.

Servicio del

Regular Issues of 1928-30 Overprinted in Red — d

ESTADO

On Stamp Inscribed: "Correos de Chile".

1930-31

O28 A50 10c bl & blk 2.75 1.00

Wmk. Small Star in Shield, Multiple. (215)

On Stamps Inscribed: "Correos de Chile".

O29 A50 10c bl & blk 6.00 2.00
O30 A39 20c org red & blk 75 35
O31 A40 25c bl & blk 75 35
O32 A42 50c dp grn & blk 1.50 50

On Stamps Inscribed: "Chile Correos".

O33 A42 50c dp grn & blk 1.50 50
O34 A43 1p grn & blk 1.50 75
Nos. O28-O34 (7) 14.75 5.45

Same Overprint on No. 181.

1933 ***Perf. 13½x14.***

O35 A61 20c dk brn 75 35

Same Overprint in Red on No. 182.

1935 **Wmk. 215**

O36 A62 10c dp bl 75 50

No. 163 Overprinted Type "b" in Red.

Inscribed: "Correos de Chile".

1934

O37 A52 5c lt grn 65 50

Overprint "b" on No. 182.

1935

O38 A62 10c dp bl 65 50

Same Overprint in Black on No. 181.

1936 **Wmk. 215** ***Perf. 13½x14.***

O39 A61 20c dk brn 10.00 50

Overprint "b" in Red on No. 158.

1938 ***Perf. 14.***

O40 A43 1p grn & blk 2.50 1.00

Nos. 204 and 205 Overprinted Type "d" in Black.

1939 ***Perf. 13½x14, 14.***

O41 A83 50c violet 3.75 1.25
O42 A84 1p org brn 5.00 3.50

Stamps of 1938-40 Overprinted Type "b" in Black, Red or Blue.

1940-46 ***Perf. 13½x14, 14.***

O43 A79 10c sal pink ('45) 2.00 1.50
O44 A79a 15c brn org 1.00 35
O45 A80 20c lt bl (R) ('42) 1.25 50
O46 A81 30c brn pink (Bl) 65 35
O47 A82 40c lt grn 65 35
O48 A83 50c vio ('45) 3.75 75
O49 A84 1p org brn ('42) 2.50 75
O50 A85 1.80p dp bl (R) ('45) 10.00 6.25
O51 A86 2p car lake ('42) 2.00 1.25
Nos. O43-O51 (9) 23.80 12.05

Overprint "b" in Black on Nos. 223, 225.

Unwmk.

O58 A84 1p brn org 2.50 1.25
O59 A86 2p car lake ('46) 4.50 1.50

Regular Issues of 1938-43 Overprinted Diagonally in Carmine, Black or Blue — e

Perf. 13½x14, 14.

1948-54 **Unwmk.** **Wmk. 215**

O60 A80 20c lt bl, #219 (C) 65 35
O61 A81 30c brt pink, #202 (Bl) ('54) 1.25 50
O62 A82 40c brt grn, #203 ('54) 2.50 1.25
O63 A83 50c vio #222 ('49) 75 35
O64 A84 1p org brn, #205 2.50 1.00
O65 A86 2p car lake, #207 ('54) 1.00 50
O66 A87 5p dk sl grn, #208 (C) ('51) 2.50 1.00
Nos. O60-O66 (7) 11.15 4.95

Overprint "e" Diagonally on Nos. 265 and 275 in Red or Black.

Perf. 13½x14, 13x14

1953-55 **Unwmk.** **Wmk. 215**

O67 A126 1p dk bl grn, #265 (R) 1.00 50
O68 A126 1p dk bl grn, #265 (Bk) ('55) 75 50
O69 A126 1p dk bl grn, #275 (R) ('55) 75 50

Overprint "e" Horizontally on Nos. 207, 209 in Black or Blue

1955-56 **Wmk. 215** ***Perf. 14.***

O70 A86 2p car lake ('56) 2.50 75
O71 A88 10p rose vio (Bl) 3.00 1.75

Overprint "e" Horizontally on Nos. 293-295 and Types of 1956 Regular Issue in Black or Red.

1956 **Unwmk.** ***Perf. 14x14½.***

O72 A141 2p purple 1.00 60
O73 A142 3p lt vio bl (R) 3.00 2.00
O74 A141 5p redsh brn 75 30
O75 A142 10p vio (19x22¼mm) (R) 3.00 1.75
a. Perf. 13½x14 (19½x22½mm) ('58) 50 30
O76 A141 50p rose red 2.50 1.00

No. 310 Overprinted in Red Vertically, Reading Down, Similar to Type "e."

Size of Overprint: 21x2½mm.

1958 **Litho.** ***Perf. 14***

O77 A149 10p vio bl *275.00 30.00*

Overprint "e" Horizontally on No. 327 in Red.

1960 **Unwmk.** ***Perf. 13x14***

O79 A157 5c blue 2.50 1.00

POSTAL TAX STAMPS

Talca Issue.

A 10c blue postal tax stamp, inscribed "Bicentenario de Talca" and picturing a coat of arms, was issued in 1942. It was sold only in Talca and was required for a time on all domestic letters sent from that city. The tax helped pay for Talca's bicentenary celebration. Price 10 cents.

Nos. 326 and 347 Surcharged — E° 0,10 Art. 77 LEY 17272

1970 Unwmk. Litho. ***Perf. 14x13***
RA1 A159 10c on 2c ultra 10 8
Perf. 14x14½
RA2 A170 10c on 6c rose lil 10 8

Chilean Arms — PT1

Perf. 14½x14
1970, Apr. 23 Litho. Unwmk.
RA3 PT1 10c blue 15 8

No. RA3 Surcharged in Red

E°0,15 E°0,15

a b

1971-72
RA4 PT1 (a) 15c on 10c bl 5 5
RA5 PT1 (b) 15c on 10c bl ('72) 10 8

Type of 1970

1972, July Litho. ***Perf. 14½x14***
RA6 PT1 15c rose red 15 8

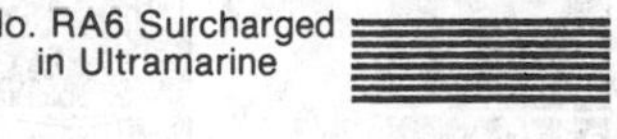

No. RA6 Surcharged in Ultramarine — E°0,20

1972-73
RA7 PT1 20c on 15c rose red 12 6
RA8 PT1 50c on 15c rose red ('73) 15 8

No. RA8 has 9 bars instead of 8.

The surtax on Nos. RA1-RA8 was for modernization of postal system. Compulsory on all inland mail.

PARCEL POST

POSTAL TAX STAMP

Pres. J. J. Prieto V. — PPT1

Unwmk.
1957, Apr. 8 Litho. ***Perf. 14***
QRA1 PPT1 15p green 25 15

The surtax aided the Prieto Foundation. No. QRA1 was required on parcel post entering or leaving Chile.

CHINA

LOCATION — Eastern Asia
GOVT. — Republic
AREA — 2,903,475 sq. mi.
POP. — 462,798,093 (1948)

10 Candareen = 1 Mace
10 Mace = 1 Tael
100 Cents = 1 Dollar (Yuan) (1897)

Issues of the Imperial Maritime Customs Post

Imperial Dragon — A1

1878 Unwmk. Typo. ***Perf. 12½***
Thin Paper
Stamps printed 2½ mm. apart
1 A1 1c green 125.00 37.50
a. Imperf. (pair) 1,500.
2 A1 3c brn red 60.00 27.50
a. Imperf. (pair) 1,500.
3 A1 5c orange 100.00 30.00
a. Imperf. (pair) 1,800.

Imperforate proofs of Nos. 1-3 have an extra circle near the dragon's lower left foot.

1882
Thin or Pelure Paper
Stamps printed 4½ mm apart
4 A1 1c green 200.00 85.00
5 A1 3c brn red 400.00 35.00
6 A1 5c org yel 3,500. 500.00

1883 ***Rough to smooth Perf. 12½***
Medium to Thick Opaque Paper
Stamps printed 2 to 3¼ mm. apart
7 A1 1c green 110.00 35.00
a. Vertical pair, imperf. between 1,900.
8 A1 3c brn red 150.00 18.00
a. Vertical pair, imperf. between *1,700.*
9 A1 5c yellow 225.00 30.00

Nos. 1 to 9 were printed from plates of 25, 20 or 15 individual copper dies, but only No. 5 exists in the 15-die setting. Many different printings and plate settings exist. All values occur in a wide variety of shades and papers. The effect of climate on certain papers has produced the varieties on so-called toned papers in Nos. 1 to 15.

Counterfeits, frequently with forged cancellations, occur in all early Chinese issues.

Imperial Dragon — A2

Wmk. 103

Wmk. Yin-Yang Symbol (103)
1885 ***Perf. 12½***
10 A2 1c green 15.00 6.00
a. Vertical pair, imperf. between 1,300.
b. Horiz. pair, imperf. between
11 A2 3c lilac 20.00 7.00
a. Horizontal pair, imperf. between 300.00
b. Vertical pair, imperf. between 400.00
12 A2 5c grnsh yel 40.00 11.00
a. 5c bis brn 45.00 12.00
b. Vertical pair, imperf. between 1,000.
c. Horizontal pair, imperf. between 900.00

1888 ***Perf. 11½-12***
13 A2 1c green 8.00 3.50
14 A2 3c lilac 14.00 2.50
b. Double impression
15 A2 5c grnsh yel 12.00 4.00
b. Horiz. pair, imperf. vert. 600.00
c. Double impression 300.00 200.00

Nos. 10 to 15 were printed from plates made of 40 individual copper dies, arranged in two panes of 20 each. Several different settings exist of all values.

Imperforates of Nos. 13-15 are considered proofs by most authorities.

Stamps overprinted "Formosa" in English or Chinese are proofs.

"Shou" and "Wu Fu" — A3

Dragon and Hydrangea Leaves — A4

"Pa Kua" Signs in Corners A5

Dragon and Peony A6

Carp, the Messenger Fish A7

Dragon, "Pa Kua" and Immortelle A8

Dragons and "Shou" — A9

Dragons and Giant Peony — A10

Junk on the Yangtse — A11

1894 Lithographed in Shanghai
16 A3 1c org red 6.75 3.50
a. Vertical pair, imperf. between 300.00 250.00
b. Horizontal pair, imperf. between 300.00 300.00
c. Imperf. horizontally (pair) 200.00 200.00
17 A4 2c green 6.00 2.25
a. Horizontal pair, imperf. between 275.00
18 A5 3c org yel 5.50 2.25
a. Vertical pair, imperf. between 250.00 250.00
b. Horizontal pair, imperf. between 250.00 250.00
19 A6 4c rose pink 24.00 11.00
a. Horizontal pair, imperf. between 300.00
20 A7 5c dl org 40.00 17.50
a. Horizontal pair, imperf. between 300.00
21 A8 6c brown 10.50 4.00
a. Vertical pair, imperf. between 250.00
b. Horizontal pair, imperf. between 250.00
22 A9 9c dl grn 27.50 7.50
a. Imperf., pair 250.00
b. Imperf. vert., pair 300.00
c. Imperf horiz., pair 250.00
d. Vertical pair, imperf. between 300.00
e. Tete beche pair 350.00 350.00

f. Tete bêche pair, imperf. horizontally 1,600.
g. Tete beche pair, imperf. vertically 1,600.
h. Vert. strip of 3, imperf. between 375.00
23 A10 12c orange 40.00 15.00
24 A11 24c carmine 100.00 27.50
a. Vertical pair, imperf. between 900.00

Nos. 16 to 24 were issued to commemorate the 60th birthday of Tsz'e Hsi, the Empress Dowager. All values exist in several distinct shades.

On March 20, 1896, the Customs Post was changed, by Imperial Edict, to a National Post and the dollar was adopted as the unit of currency. The effective date of the Imperial Edict was January 1, 1897 and until that date the Customs Post continued operating.

Time was required to work out details of the Imperial Post and design new stamps. As a provisional measure, stocks of Nos. 16 to 24 were ordered surcharged with new values in dollars and cents. It is believed that only the Shanghai office stock of Nos. 16 to 24 (plus any reserve stock at the printers) was surcharged with small figures of value. Other post offices throughout China were instructed to return all unoverprinted stocks on receipt of the new surcharges.

Early in the year it was apparent that all stamps would be exhausted before the new issues were ready (Nos. 86 to 97), and since the stones from which Nos. 16 to 24 had been printed no longer existed, new stones were made from the original transfers. A printing from the new stones was made early in 1897 and surcharged with large figures of value spaced 2½mm. below the Chinese characters. During the surcharging, sheets from the 1894 (original) printing were received from outlying post offices and surcharged as they arrived. A small quantity of the 1897 printing reached the public without surcharge (Nos. 16n to 24n).

Additional stamps were still required and another printing was made from the new stones and surcharged with large figures, but in a new setting with 1½mm. between the Chinese characters and the value. Additional sheets of the 1894 printing were received from the most distant post offices and were also surcharged with the 1½mm. setting. Thus there are four different sets of the large-figure surcharges. All these stamps were regularly issued but no attempt was made by the post office to separate printings. Some values are difficult to distinguish as to printing, particularly in used condition.

1897 Lithographed in Shanghai

16n A3 1c red org 175.00
17n A4 2c yel grn 200.00
18n A5 3c chr yel 125.00
p. 3c yel buff 400.00
19n A6 4c pale rose 175.00
20n A7 5c yellow 125.00
21n A8 6c red brn 250.00
22n A9 9c yelsh grn 300.00
23n A10 12c pale org yel 400.00
24n A11 24c rose red 350.00

Nos. 16n to 24n were new printings from new stones. These stamps were prepared solely for surcharging and were not regularly issued without surcharge. The colors of the 1897 printings are pale or dull; the gum is thin and white. The 1894 printing has a thicker, yellowish gum.

The set of nine values on thick unwatermarked paper is a special printing ordered by P. G. von Mollendorf, a Customs official, for presentation purposes. Price, set, $100.

Issues of the Chinese Government Post

Preceding Issues Surcharged in Black

貳洋暫
分銀作
2
cents.

Small Numerals

Surcharged on Nos. 13-15

1897, Jan. 2 *Perf. 11½-12*

25 A2 1c on 1c grn 12.00 3.50
26 A2 2c on 3c lil 32.50 7.50
27 A2 5c on 5c grnsh yel 30.00 6.00

Surcharged on Nos. 16-24

28 A5 ½c on 3c org yel 6.00 2.50
a. "1" instead of "½" 140.00 140.00
b. Horizontal pair, imperf. between 300.00
c. Imperf. horizontally (pair) 250.00 250.00
d. Double surcharge 400.00
e. Vert. pair, imperf. between 400.00
29 A3 1c on 1c org red 2.75 1.75
a. Inverted surcharge 700.00 500.00
30 A4 2c on 2c grn 3.75 1.75
a. Imperf. vertically (pair) 250.00
b. Vertical pair, imperf. between 300.00
c. Double surcharge 350.00
d. Inverted surcharge 600.00
e. Horizontal pair, imperf. between 275.00
31 A6 4c on 4c rose pink 3.50 2.25
a. Double surch. 400.00 400.00
b. Vertical pair, imperf. between 275.00 275.00
c. Horizontal pair, imperf. between 275.00 275.00
32 A7 5c on 5c dl org 4.50 2.25
a. Vertical pair, imperf. between 400.00
33 A8 8c on 6c brn 6.00 5.00
a. Vertical pair, imperf. between 225.00 225.00
b. Vertical strip of three, imperf. between 300.00 300.00
c. Horizontal pair, imperf. between 275.00 275.00
34 A8 10c on 6c brn 18.00 11.00
a. 10c on 6c choc 18.00 11.00
b. Vertical pair, imperf. between 225.00 225.00
c. Imperf. vertically (pair) 300.00
35 A9 10c on 9c dl grn 19.00 11.00
a. Double surcharge 600.00 600.00
b. Invtd. surch. 1,500. 1,500.
36 A10 10c on 12c org 40.00 20.00
a. Imperf. horizontally (pair) 300.00
37 A11 30c on 24c car 57.50 40.00
a. Vert. pair, imperf. between 1,250.

Preceding Issues Surcharged in Black

貳洋暫
分銀作
2
cents.

Large Numerals

Numerals 2½mm. below Chinese characters

1897, March

Surcharged on Nos. 16 to 24

38 A5 ½c on 3c org yel 400.00 100.00
b. Inverted surch. 600.00
39 A3 1c on 1c org red 55.00 40.00
40 A4 2c on 2c grn 125.00 70.00
41 A6 4c on 4c rose pink 125.00 50.00
b. Horiz. pair, imperf. between 2,500.
42 A7 5c on 5c dl org 32.50 32.50
43 A8 8c on 6c brn 375.00 375.00
44 A9 10c on 9c dl grn 175.00 100.00
45 A10 10c on 12c org 1,600. 225.00
46 A11 30c on 24c car 350.00 300.00
b. 2mm spacing between "30" and "cents." 2,000.

Same Surcharge on Nos. 16n to 24n

47 A5 ½c on 3c chr yel 2.00 1.25
a. "cen" for "cent" 175.00 150.00
b. Vertical pair, imperf. between 150.00 150.00
c. Imperf. horizontally (pair) 100.00 100.00
d. As "a," imperf. horiz. (pair) 1,200. 1,200.
48 A3 1c on 1c red org 3.25 2.50
a. Horiz. pair, imperf. between 300.00
49 A4 2c on 2c yel grn 2.75 1.40
50 A6 4c on 4c pale rose 3.25 2.00
a. Horizontal pair, imperf. between 150.00 150.00
51 A7 5c on 5c yel 4.50 2.75
52 A8 8c on 6c red brn 30.00 18.00
53 A9 10c on 9c yelsh grn 25.00 13.00
a. 10c on 9c emer 25.00 12.50
54 A10 10c on 12c pale org yel 25.00 18.00
55 A11 30c on 24c rose red 85.00 30.00
a. 2mm spacing between "30" and "cents" 250.00 200.00
b. Vertical pair, imperf. between 2,500.

Numerals 1½mm. below Chinese characters

1897, May

Surcharged on Nos. 16 to 24

56 A5 ½c on 3c org yel *300.00 90.00*
57 A3 1c on 1c org red 60.00 650.00
58 A4 2c on 2c grn 100.00
59 A6 4c on 4c rose pink 40.00 35.00
60 A7 5c on 5c dl org 30.00 27.50
61 A8 8c on 6c brn 350.00 200.00
62 A9 10c on 9c dl grn 50.00 25.00
63 A10 10c on 12c org 300.00 175.00
64 A11 30c on 24c car *2,250.*

Same Surcharge on Nos. 16n to 24n

65 A5 ½c on 3c yel 1.10 90
a. Invtd. surch. 400.00 200.00
b. ½mm spacing 1,200. 700.00
66 A3 1c on 1c red org 2.25 1.50
67 A4 2c on 2c yel grn 3.50 2.25
a. Inverted surcharge 1,000.
68 A6 4c on 4c pale rose 47.50 27.50
a. Inverted surcharge 300.00 200.00
69 A7 5c on 5c yel 45.00 27.50
70 A9 10c on 9c gray grn 35.00 17.50
a. Inverted surcharge 250.00 175.00
71 A10 10c on 12c brn org 75.00 27.50
72 A11 30c on 24c pale rose 1,500. 600.00

Same Surcharge (1½mm. Spacing) on Type A12, and

A12

A12a

Redrawn Designs

Printed from New Stones

1897

73 A12 ½c on 3c yel 110.00 42.50
a. ½mm spacing 400.00 300.00
74 A12a 2c on 2c yel grn 20.00 3.00
a. Horizontal pair, imperf. between 400.00

Nos. 73 and 74 were surcharged on stamps printed from new stones, which differ slightly from the originals. On No. 73 the numeral "3" and symbols in the four corner panels have been enlarged and strengthened. On No. 74, the numeral "2" has a thick, flat base.

Surcharged on 1888 Issue

75 A2 1c on 1c grn 82.50
76 A2 2c on 3c lil 200.00
77 A2 5c on 5c grnsh yel 60.00

Nos. 75-77 were not regularly issued.

Type A13 Surcharged in Black:

A13

政郵清大
分壹當
one cent
a

政郵清大
貳洋暫
分銀作
2 cents
b

政郵清大
貳洋暫
分銀作
2
cents
c

政郵清大
肆洋暫
分銀作
4
cents.
d

政郵清大
肆洋暫
分銀作
4
cents.
e

政郵清大
當
壹
圓
1 dollar.
f

政郵清大
當
壹
圓
1 dollar
g

1897 Unwmk. *Perf. 12 to 15*

78 A13 (a) 1c on 3c red 15.00 3.50
a. No period after "cent" 50.00 25.00
b. Central character with large "box" 32.50 20.00
79 A13 (b) 2c on 3c red 50.00 20.00
a. Invtd. surch. 500.00 300.00
b. Inverted "S" in "CENTS" 70.00 70.00
c. No period after "CENTS" 70.00 70.00
d. Comma after "CENTS" 70.00 70.00
e. Double surch. 1,000.
f. Double surcharge, both inverted
g. Double surch. (blk. & grn.) *10,000.*
80 A13 (c) 2c on 3c red 20.00 10.00
81 A13 (d) 4c on 3c red 1,500. 1,750.
a. Double surch. (blk. & vio.) 3,500. 2,500.
82 A13 (e) 4c on 3c red 75.00 27.50
83 A13 (f) $1 on 3c red
a. No period after "r"
84 A13 (g) $1 on 3c red 250.00 85.00
85 A13 (g) $5 on 3c red 3,500. 2,500.
a. Inverted surcharge *5,000. 3,750.*

A few copies of the 3c red exist without surcharge; one cancelled. No. 79 with green surcharge is a trial printing.

Dragon
A14

Carp
A15

Wild Goose — A16

"Imperial Chinese Post"

Lithographed in Japan

Perf. 11, 11½, 12

1897, Aug. 16 Wmk. 103

86 A14 ½c pur brn 2.00 1.00
a. Horizontal pair, imperf. between 225.00
87 A14 1c yellow 2.25 1.00
88 A14 2c orange 2.00 1.00
a. Imperf. horizontally (pair) 250.00
89 A14 4c brown 2.75 1.00
a. Horizontal pair, imperf. between 350.00
90 A14 5c rose red 4.00 1.00
91 A14 10c dk grn 8.00 1.00
92 A15 20c maroon 15.00 5.25
93 A15 30c red 18.00 8.00
94 A15 50c yel grn 22.00 10.00
a. 50c blk grn 275.00
b. 50c bl grn 400.00
95 A16 $1 car & rose 90.00 50.00
a. Imperf. vertically (pair) 1,500.
96 A16 $2 org & yel 450.00 500.00
a. Imperf vertically (pair) 1,600.
97 A16 $5 yel grn & pink 250.00 225.00

The inner circular frames and outer frames of Nos. 86 to 91 differ for each denomination.

No. 97 imperforate was not regularly issued. Copies have been privately perforated and offered as No. 97. Shades occur in most values of this issue.

Dragon
A17

Carp
A18

Wild Goose — A19

"Chinese Imperial Post"

Engraved in London

1898 Wmk. 103 *Perf. 12 to 16*

98 A17 ½c chocolate 45 10
a. Vertical pair, imperf. between 200.00
99 A17 1c ocher 45 10
a. Vertical pair, imperf. between 90.00 90.00
b. Horizontal pair, imperf. between 125.00 125.00
100 A17 2c scarlet 60 10
a. Vertical pair, imperf. between 60.00 60.00
b. Imperf. vertically (pair)
101 A17 4c org brn 1.50 10
a. Vertical pair, imperf. between 100.00
b. Imperf. vertically (pair) 75.00 75.00
c. Horiz. pair, imperf. between 150.00 150.00
d. Horiz. strip of 3, imperf. between 200.00 200.00
102 A17 5c salmon 2.00 50
a. Vertical pair, imperf. between 90.00 90.00
b. Horizontal pair, imperf. between 100.00 100.00
103 A17 10c dk bl grn 2.25 20
a. Vert. or horiz. pair, imperf. between 100.00 100.00

104 A18 20c claret 7.00 75
a. Horizontal pair, imperf. between 200.00
b. Imperf. horiz. (pair) 125.00 125.00
105 A18 30c dl rose 9.00 65
a. Horizontal pair, imperf. between 200.00
b. Imperf. horizontally (pair) 250.00
106 A18 50c lt grn 18.00 2.00
a. Vertical pair, imperf. between 275.00
107 A19 $1 red & pale rose 70.00 6.00
108 A19 $2 brn, red & yel 125.00 25.00
109 A19 $5 dp grn & sal 190.00 50.00
a. Horizontal pair, imperf. between 1,500.
b. Vert. pair, imperf. between 1,750.

No. 98 surcharged "B. R. A.-5-Five Cents" in three lines in black or green, was surcharged by British military authorities shortly after the Boxer riots for use from military posts in an occupied area along the Peking-Mukden railway. Usually canceled in violet.

1902-03 Unwmk. *Perf. 12 to 16*
110 A17 ½c brown 40 8
a. Horiz. or vert. pair, imperf. between 90.00 90.00
111 A17 1c ocher 40 8
a. Horizontal pair, imperf. between 50.00 50.00
b. Vertical pair, imperf. between 60.00 60.00
c. Vert. pair, imperf. horiz. 40.00 40.00
112 A17 2c scarlet 75 8
a. Horiz. or vert. pair, imperf. between 45.00 45.00
c. Vert. pair, imperf. horiz. 40.00 40.00
d. Horiz. pair, imperf. vert. 40.00 40.00
e. Vert. strip of 3 imperf. between 75.00 75.00
113 A17 4c org brn 1.25 20
a. Horiz. or vert. pair, imperf. between 75.00 75.00
114 A17 5c rose red 9.00 1.25
a. Vertical pair, imperf. between 110.00
b. Vert. pair, imperf. horiz. 90.00
115 A17 5c orange 7.50 1.25
a. 5c yel 60.00 10.00
b. Vertical pair, imperf. between 90.00
c. Horizontal pair, imperf. between 125.00
116 A17 10c green 8.25 15
a. Vertical pair, imperf. between 50.00
b. Horizontal pair, imperf. between 55.00
c. Vert. pair, imperf. horiz. 50.00
d. Vert. strip of 3, imperf. between 95.00
117 A18 20c red brn 5.00 25
a. Horizontal pair, imperf. between 125.00
b. Vertical pair, imperf. between 100.00
118 A18 30c dl red 8.50 35
a. Vertical pair, imperf. between 200.00
119 A18 50c yel grn 12.00 50
120 A19 $1 red & pale rose 42.50 1.50
121 A19 $2 brn red & yel 100.00 8.50
122 A19 $5 dp grn & sal 165.00 45.00
Nos. 110-122 (13) 360.55 59.19

Postage
1 Cent
Paid

Diagonal Half of No. 112 Surcharged on Stamp and Envelope

1903
123 A17 1c on half of 2c scar, on cover 400.00

Excellent forgeries of No. 123 are plentiful, particularly on pieces of cover.

1905-10
124 A17 2c grn ('08) 60 5
a. Horizontal pair, imperf. between 45.00 45.00
b. Vertical pair, imperf. between 52.50 52.50
c. Imperf. vertically (pair) 55.00
d. Horiz. strip of 4, imperf. between 135.00
125 A17 3c sl grn ('10) 1.00 6
a. Horiz. or vert. pair, imperf. between 90.00
126 A17 4c ver ('09) 1.50 12
127 A17 5c violet 1.75 12
a. 5c lil 2.50 12
b. Horiz. or vert. pair, imperf. between 60.00
d. Vert. pair, imperf. horiz. 35.00
128 A17 7c mar ('10) 5.00 70
129 A17 10c ultra ('08) 3.00 10
a. Horiz. or vert. pair, imperf. between 125.00
c. Vert. pair, imperf. horiz. 85.00 60.00
130 A18 16c ol grn ('07) 15.00 1.75
Nos. 124-130 (7) 27.85 2.90

Temple of Heaven, Peking — A20

1909 *Perf. 14*
131 A20 2c org & grn 1.25 35
132 A20 3c org & bl 1.50 50
133 A20 7c org & brn vio 1.75 50

Issued to commemorate the first year of the reign of Hsuan T'ung, who later became Henry Pu-yi and then Emperor Kang Teh of Manchukuo.

Stamps of 1902-10 Overprinted with Chinese Characters

Foochow Issue

Overprinted in Red or Black 立中時臨

1912 *Perf. 12 to 16*
134 A17 3c sl grn (R) 65.00 35.00
135 A19 $1 red & pale rose (Bk) 900.00 750.00
136 A19 $2 brn red & yel (Bk) 1,200. 800.00
137 A19 $5 dp grn & sal (Bk) 1,300. 825.00

The overprint "Ling Shih Chung Li" or "Provisional Neutrality," signified that the Post Office was conducted neutrally by agreement between the Manchu and opposing forces.

Nanking Issue

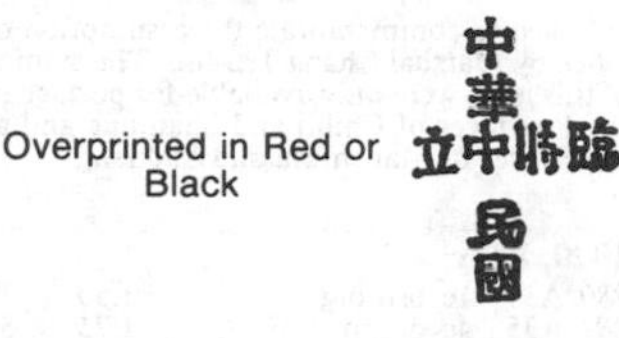
Overprinted in Red or Black

138 A17 1c ocher (R) 50.00 30.00
139 A17 3c sl grn (R) 47.50 30.00
140 A17 7c mar (Bk) 200.00 150.00
141 A18 16c ol grn (R) 800.00 600.00
142 A18 50c yel grn (R) 1,300. 900.00
143 A19 $1 red & pale rose (Bk) 1,200. 825.00
144 A19 $2 brn red & yel (Bk) 2,250. 2,250.
145 A19 $5 dp grn & sal (Bk) 4,000. 4,000.

Vertical overprint reads: "Chung Hwa Min Kuo" (Republic of China).

Stamps of this issue were also used in Shanghai and Hankow.

Additional values were overprinted but not issued. Excellent forgeries of the overprints of Nos. 134-145 exist.

Issues of the Republic

Overprinted in Black or Red

a 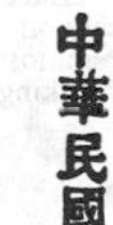

Overprinted by the Maritime Customs Statistical Department, Shanghai.

146 A17 ½c brn (Bk) 40 6
a. Inverted overprint 6.00 6.00
b. Double overprint 50.00
147 A17 1c ocher (R) 45 6
a. Vert. pair, imperf. horiz. 60.00 60.00
b. Invtd. ovpt. 52.50 42.50
c. Double overprint 60.00 60.00
d. Horizontal pair, imperf. between 60.00 60.00
e. Horiz. pair, imperf. vert. 42.50
f. Pair, one without overprint 42.50
148 A17 2c grn (R) 1.00 5
a. Vertical pair, imperf. between 60.00 60.00
149 A17 3c sl grn (R) 1.00 5
a. Inverted overprint 45.00 25.00
b. Horiz. or vert. pair, imperf. between 60.00 60.00
d. Horiz. pair, imperf. vert. 45.00
150 A17 4c ver (Bk) 1.00 10
a. Vertical pair, imperf. between 400.00
151 A17 5c vio (R) 2.25 12
a. Horizontal pair, imperf. between
152 A17 7c mar (Bk) 2.50 45
153 A17 10c ultra (R) 2.25 10
a. Double overprint 80.00
b. Pair, one without overprint 350.00
c. Brnsh red overprint 7.50 5.00
d. Inverted overprint 125.00 125.00
154 A18 16c ol grn (R) 4.25 1.00
155 A18 20c red brn (Bk) 4.50 30
156 A18 30c rose red (Bk) 6.00 60
157 A18 50c yel grn (R) 8.00 40
158 A19 $1 red & pale rose (Bk) 35.00 1.25
a. Inverted overprint 2,000.
159 A19 $2 brn red & yel (Bk) 60.00 8.00
a. Inverted overprint 150.00 150.00
160 A19 $5 dp grn & sal (Bk) 150.00 125.00
Nos. 146-160 (15) 278.60 137.54

Stamps with blue overprint similar to the preceding were not an official issue but were privately made by a printer in Tientsin.

Overprinted in Red

b 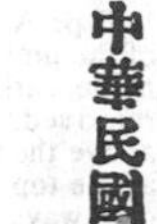

Overprinted by the Commercial Press, Shanghai

Type "b" differs from "a" in that the top character is shifted slightly to right and the bottom character is larger and has small "legs".

161 A17 1c ocher (R) 1.75 12
a. Inverted overprint 40.00 40.00
b. Vertical pair, imperf. between 60.00
c. Double ovpt. 60.00
162 A17 2c grn (R) 14.00 12
a. Inverted overprint 650.00 300.00
b. Vertical pair, imperf. between 85.00
c. Horizontal pair, imperf. between 110.00
d. Horiz. strip of 3, imperf. btwn. 250.00

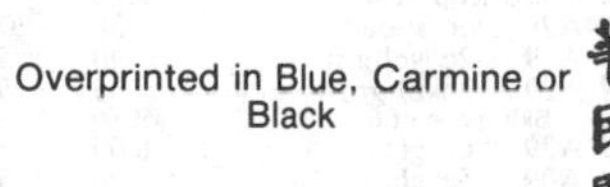
Overprinted in Blue, Carmine or Black

Overprinted by Waterlow & Sons, London

163 A17 ½c brn (Bl) 20 5
a. Vertical pair, imperf. between 325.00 325.00
164 A17 1c ocher (C) 20 5
a. Horizontal pair, imperf. between 55.00
165 A17 2c grn (C) 45 5
166 A17 3c sl grn (C) 60 5
a. Inverted overprint 500.00
167 A17 4c ver (Bk) 1.00 15
168 A17 5c vio (C) 1.25 20
169 A17 7c mar (Bk) 5.00 1.50
170 A17 10c ultra (C) 1.50 12
a. Vertical pair, imperf. between 175.00 150.00
171 A18 16c ol grn (R) 5.00 1.00
172 A18 20c red brn (Bk) 4.50 50
173 A18 30c dl red (Bk) 5.50 50
174 A18 50c yel grn (R) 10.50 1.25
175 A19 $1 red & pale rose (Bk) 30.00 2.00
176 A19 $2 brn red & yel (Bk) 77.50 45.00
177 A19 $5 dp grn & sal (C) 150.00 110.00
Nos. 163-177 (15) 293.20 162.42

Due to instructions issued to postmasters throughout China at the time of the Revolution, a number of them prepared unauthorized overprints using the same characters as the overprints prepared by the government. While many were made in good faith, some, like the blue overprints from Tientsin, were bogus, and the status of certain others is extremely dubious.

Dr. Sun Yat-sen — A21

1912, Dec. 14 *Perf. 14½*
178 A21 1c orange 1.10 90
179 A21 2c yel grn 1.10 90
180 A21 3c sl grn 1.10 90
181 A21 5c rose lil 1.75 1.00
182 A21 8c dp brn 2.50 1.75
183 A21 10c dl bl 2.00 1.75
184 A21 16c ol grn 6.00 2.00
185 A21 20c maroon 7.50 2.25
186 A21 50c dk grn 20.00 11.00
187 A21 $1 brn red 57.50 25.00
188 A21 $2 yel brn 200.00 165.00
189 A21 $5 gray 125.00 65.00
Nos. 178-189 (12) 425.55 277.45

Issued in honor of the leader of the Revolution.

President Yuan Shih-kai — A22

1912, Dec. 14
190 A22 1c orange 70 50
191 A22 2c yel grn 70 50
192 A22 3c sl grn 70 50
193 A22 5c rose lil 1.00 60
194 A22 8c dp brn 3.00 1.50
195 A22 10c dl bl 1.75 1.25
196 A22 16c ol grn 3.75 2.75
197 A22 20c maroon 4.50 2.75
198 A22 50c dk grn 24.00 13.00
199 A22 $1 brn red 32.50 20.00
200 A22 $2 yel brn 55.00 22.50
201 A22 $5 gray 95.00 65.00
Nos. 190-201 (12) 222.60 130.85

Issued in honor of the first president of the Republic.

Junk — A24

Reaping Rice — A25

Gateway, Hall of Classics, Peking — A26

DESIGN A24
London Printing: Vertical shading lines under top panel fine, junk with clear diagonal shading lines on sails, right pennant of junk usually long, lines in water weak except directly under junk.

Peking Printing: Vertical shading lines under top panel and inner vertical frame line much heavier, water and sails of junk more evenly and strongly colored, white wave over "H" of "CHINA" pointed upward, touching the junk.

DESIGN A25
London: Front hat brim thick and nearly straight, left foot touches shadow.

Peking: Front hat brim thin and strongly upturned, left foot and sickle clearly outlined in white, shadow of middle tree lighter than those of the right and left trees.

DESIGN A26
London: Light colored walk clearly defined almost to the doorway, figure in right doorway "T" shaped with strong horizontal crossbar, white panel in base of central tower rectangular, vertical stroke in top left character uniformly thick at its base, tree to right of doorway ends in minute dots.

Peking: Walk more heavily shaded near doorway, especially at right; figure in right doorway more like a "Y", white panel at base of central tower is a long oval, right vertical stroke in top left character incurved near its base, tree at right has five prominent dots at top.

London Printing: By Waterlow & Sons, London, perforated 14 to 15.

Peking Printing: By the Chinese Bureau of Engraving and Printing, Peking, perforated 14.

London Printing

1913, May 5 *Perf. 14-15*
202 A24 ½c blk brn 30 5
a. Horiz. or vert. pair, imperf. btwn. 100.00

203 A24 1c orange 30 5
a. Horizontal pair, imperf. between 150.00
b. Vertical pair, imperf. between 80.00
c. Horiz. strip of 5, imperf. between 225.00
204 A24 2c yel grn 65 5
a. Horizontal pair, imperf. between 125.00
205 A24 3c bl grn 1.10 5
a. Horizontal pair, imperf. between 100.00
b. Vertical pair, imperf. between 250.00
206 A24 4c scarlet 1.75 5
207 A24 5c rose lil 3.00 6
208 A24 6c gray 1.75 10
209 A24 7c violet 2.75 75
210 A24 8c brn org 3.25 20
211 A24 10c dk bl 3.25 6
a. Horizontal pair, imperf. between 200.00 200.00
b. Vertical pair, imperf. between 225.00 150.00
212 A25 15c brown 10.00 50
213 A25 16c ol grn 3.50 50
214 A25 20c brn red 5.75 15
215 A25 30c brn vio 7.50 20
a. Horiz. pair, imperf. between 225.00 175.00
216 A25 50c green 11.00 20
217 A26 $1 ocher & blk 40.00 35
218 A26 $2 bl & blk 50.00 2.50
219 A26 $5 scar & blk 82.50 22.50
220 A26 $10 yel grn & blk 450.00 375.00
Nos. 202-220 (19) 678.35 403.32

First Peking Printing

1915 ***Perf. 14***
221 A24 ½c blk brn 25 5
222 A24 1c orange 25 5
223 A24 2c yel grn 35 5
224 A24 3c bl grn 50 5
225 A24 4c scarlet 1.40 5
226 A24 5c rose lil 1.40 5
a. Bklt. pane of 4 100.00
227 A24 6c gray 1.75 12
228 A24 7c violet 2.25 60
229 A24 8c brn org 1.75 6
230 A24 10c dk bl 1.75 5
a. Bklt. pane of 4 100.00
231 A25 15c brown 10.00 75
232 A25 16c ol grn 4.00 20
233 A25 20c brn red 3.25 5
234 A25 30c brn vio 3.25 8
235 A25 50c green 5.50 6
236 A26 $1 ocher & blk 15.00 20
237 A26 $2 bl & blk 22.50 60
a. Center invtd. *6,000. 5,000.*
238 A26 $5 scar & blk 50.00 6.00
239 A26 $10 yel grn & blk 225.00 75.00
Nos. 221-239 (19) 350.15 84.07

1919
240 A24 1½c violet 45 8
241 A25 13c brown 60 6
242 A26 $20 yel & blk 1,500. 1,300.

Nos. 226 and 230 overprinted in red with five characters in vertical column were for postal savings use.

The higher values of the 1913-19 issues are often overprinted with Chinese characters, which are the names of various postal districts. Stamps were frequently stolen while in transit to post offices. The overprints served to protect them, since the stamps could only be used in the districts for which they were overprinted.

Yeh Kung-cho, Hsu Shi-chang and Chin Yun-peng — A27

1921, Oct. 10
243 A27 1c orange 4.75 75
244 A27 3c bl grn 4.75 75
245 A27 6c gray 4.75 75
246 A27 10c blue 4.75 75

National Post Office, 25th anniversary.

A28

1923 **Red Surcharge**
247 A28 2c on 3c bl grn 1.25 10
a. Inverted surcharge 1,500. 1,350.

Second Peking Printing

A29

A30

A31

Types of 1913-19 Issues Re-engraved

Type A29: Most of the whitecaps in front of the junk have been removed and the water made darker. The shading lines have been removed from the arabesques and pearls above the top inscription. The inner shadings at the top and sides of the picture have been cut away.

Type A30: The heads of rice in the side panels have a background of crossed lines instead of horizontal lines. The Temple of Heaven is strongly shaded and has a door. There are rows of pearls below the Chinese characters in the upper corners. The arabesques above the top inscription have been altered and are without shading lines.

Type A31: The curved line under the inscription at top is single instead of double. There are four vertical lines, instead of eight, at each side of the picture. The trees at the sides of the temple had foliage in the 1913-19 issues, but now the branches are bare. There are numerous other alterations in the design.

1923 ***Perf. 14***
248 A29 ½c blk brn 30 5
a. Horizontal pair, imperf. between 75.00 75.00
b. Horiz. pair, imperf. vert. 60.00 60.00
249 A29 1c orange 30 5
a. Imperf., pair 45.00
b. Horiz. pair, imperf. vert. 60.00
c. Booklet pane of 6 60.00
d. Booklet pane of 4 30.00
250 A29 1½c violet 30 20
251 A29 2c yel grn 40 5
252 A29 3c bl grn 45 5
a. Bklt. pane of 6 50.00
253 A29 4c gray 6.00 5
254 A29 5c claret 90 5
a. Bklt. pane of 4 60.00
255 A29 6c scarlet 1.10 5
256 A29 7c violet 1.65 15
257 A29 8c orange 1.50 5
258 A29 10c blue 1.50 5
a. Bklt. pane of 6 75.00
b. Bklt. pane of 2 90.00
259 A30 13c brown 6.00 8
260 A30 15c dp bl 2.25 5
261 A30 16c ol grn 3.25 10
262 A30 20c brn red 3.00 5
263 A30 30c purple 4.00 6
264 A30 50c dp grn 14.00 6
265 A31 $1 org brn & sep 15.00 10
266 A31 $2 bl & red brn 22.50 15
267 A31 $5 red & sl 42.50 35
268 A31 $10 grn & cl 110.00 12.50
269 A31 $20 plum & bl 250.00 30.00
Nos. 248-269 (22) 486.90 44.30

Nos. 249 and 275 exist with webbing watermark from experimental printing.

To prevent speculation and theft, the dollar denominations were overprinted with single characters in red for use in Kwangsi ($1-$20) and Kweichow ($1-$5).

See Nos. 275, 324.

Temple of Heaven, Peking — A32

1923, Oct. 17 ***Perf. 14***
270 A32 1c orange 1.75 30
271 A32 3c bl grn 2.00 50
272 A32 4c red 3.00 50
273 A32 10c blue 7.50 1.25

Adoption of Constitution, October, 1923.

No. 253 Surcharged in Red

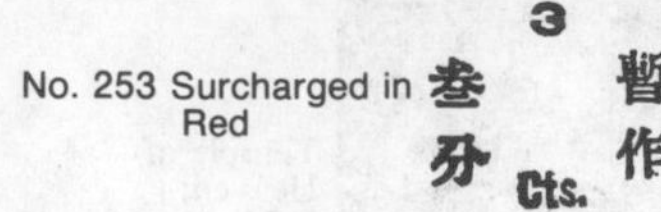

1925
274 A29 3c on 4c gray 2.00 10
a. Invtd. surch. 1,500. 1,500.
b. Vertical pair, imperf. between

Junk Type of 1923

1926
275 A29 4c ol grn 1.00 10
a. Imperf. vertically (pair) 75.00
b. Horiz. pair, imperf. between 90.00
c. Horiz. strip of 3, imperf. between 100.00

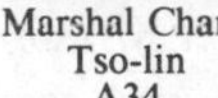

Marshal Chang Tso-lin A34

President Chiang Kai-shek A35

1928, Mar. 1 ***Perf. 14***
276 A34 1c brn org 1.00 25
277 A34 4c ol grn 1.75 35
278 A34 10c dl bl 8.75 1.25
279 A34 $1 red 45.00 25.00

Issued to commemorate the assumption of office by Marshal Chang Tso-lin. The stamps of this issue were only available for postage in the Provinces of Chihli and Shantung and at the Offices in Manchuria and Sinkiang.

1929, May
280 A35 1c brn org 1.50 35
281 A35 4c ol grn 1.75 50
282 A35 10c dk bl 21.00 1.50
283 A35 $1 dk red 100.00 37.50

Issued to commemorate the unification of China.

Sun Yat-sen Mausoleum, Nanking — A36

1929, May 30 ***Perf. 14***
284 A36 1c brn org 60 35
285 A36 4c ol grn 95 35
286 A36 10c dk bl 7.50 1.25
287 A36 $1 dk red 60.00 37.50

Issued in commemoration of Dr. Sun Yat-sen on the occasion of the transfer of his remains from Peiping to the mausoleum at Nanking.

Nos. 224 and 252 Surcharged in Red

壹 1 暫
分 Ct. 作

1930
288 A24 1c on 3c bl grn 2.00 2.00
289 A29 1c on 3c bl grn 50 5
a. No period after "Ct" 12.50 8.00

See Nos. 311, 325, 330.

Dr. Sun Yat-sen — A37

Type I. Double-lined circle in the sun.

Type II. Heavy, single-lined circle in the sun.

Printed by De la Rue & Co., Ltd., London

Perf. 11½x12½, 12½x13, 12½, 13½
1931 **Engr.**

Type I

290 A37 1c orange 15 5
291 A37 2c ol grn 15 5
292 A37 4c green 45 5
293 A37 20c ultra 45 5
294 A37 $1 org brn & dk brn 3.75 8
295 A37 $2 bl & org brn 7.50 20
296 A37 $5 dl red & blk 12.50 75
Nos. 290-296 (7) 24.95 1.23

Stamps issued prior to 1933 were printed by a wet-paper process, and owing to shrinkage such stamps are 1-1½ mm. narrower than the later dry-printed stamps. Early printings are perf. 12½x13. Nos. 304, 305 and 306 were later perf. 11½x12½.

1931-37

Type II

297 A37 2c ol grn 15 5
298 A37 4c green 15 5
299 A37 5c grn ('33) 15 5
300 A37 15c dk grn 3.00 40
301 A37 15c scar ('34) 20 5
302 A37 20c ultra ('37) 50 5
303 A37 25c ultra 50 5
304 A37 $1 org brn & dk brn 4.00 5
305 A37 $2 bl & org brn 7.50 25
306 A37 $5 dl red & blk 15.00 50
Nos. 297-306 (10) 31.15 1.50

See Nos. 631 to 635 for other stamps of type A37.

"Nomads in the Desert" — A38

1932 **Unwmk.** ***Perf. 14***
307 A38 1c dp org 20.00 15.00
308 A38 4c ol grn 20.00 15.00
309 A38 5c claret 20.00 15.00
310 A38 10c dp bl 20.00 15.00

Issued to commemorate the Northwest Scientific Expedition of Sven Hedin. A small quantity of this issue was sold at face at Peking and several other cities. The bulk of the issue was given to Hedin and sold at $5 (Chinese) a set for funds to finance the expedition. Letters franked with these stamps were carried without additional charge.

No. 252 Surcharged in Black Like No. 288

1932
311 A29 1c on 3c bl grn 1.00 10

Martyrs Issue

Teng Keng A39

Ch'en Ying-shih A40

Chu Chih-hsin A45

Sung Chiao-jen A46

The only foreign revenue stamps listed in this Catalogue are those authorized for prepayment of postage.

Huang Hsing A47

Liao Chung-kai A48

1932-34 *Perf. 14*
312 A39 ½c blk brn 5 8
313 A40 1c org ('34) 5 8
314 A39 2½c rose lil ('33) 5 8
315 A48 3c dp brn ('33) 5 8
316 A45 8c brn org 22 8
317 A46 10c dl vio 30 8
318 A45 13c bl grn 22 8
319 A46 17c brn ol 22 8
320 A47 20c brn red 22 8
321 A48 30c brn vio 22 8
322 A47 40c orange 22 8
323 A40 50c grn ('34) 30 8
Nos. 312-323 (12) 2.12 96

Perfs. 12 to 13 and compound and with secret marks are listed as Nos. 402-439. No. 316 re-drawn is No. 485.

Junk Type of 1923 Issue

1933 *Perf. 14*
324 A29 6c brown 16.00 25

No. 275 Surcharged in Red Like No. 288

325 A29 1c on 4c ol grn 1.10 10
a. No period after Ct

Tan Yuan-chang — A49

1933, Jan. 9
326 A49 2c ol grn 1.10 30
327 A49 5c green 1.40 35
328 A49 25c ultra 6.75 1.00
329 A49 $1 red 45.00 20.00

Issued in commemoration of Tan Yuan-chang more commonly known as Tan Yen-kai, a prominent statesman in China since the revolution of 1912 and President of the Executive Department of the National Government. The stamps were placed on sale January 9, 1933, the date of the ceremony in celebration of the completion of the Tan Yuan-chang Memorial Hall and Tomb at Mukden.

No. 251 Surcharged in Red Like No. 288

1935 *Perf. 14*
330 A29 1c on 2c yel grn 1.10 6

Emblem of New Life Movement A50

Four Virtues of New Life A51

Lighthouse — A52

1936, Jan. 1
331 A50 2c ol grn 75 25
332 A50 5c green 1.25 25
333 A51 20c dk bl 6.00 1.00
334 A52 $1 rose red 20.00 4.00

"New Life" movement.

Methods of Mail Transportation A53

Maritime Scene — A54

Shanghai General Post Office — A55

Ministry of Communications, Nanking — A56

1936, Oct. 10
335 A53 2c orange 60 25
336 A54 5c green 75 20
337 A55 25c blue 5.00 60
338 A56 $1 dk car 20.00 2.50

Issued in commemoration of the 40th anniversary of the founding of the Chinese Post Office.

Nos. 260 and 261 Surcharged in Red

339 A30 5c on 15c dp bl 1.25 5
340 A30 5c on 16c ol grn 1.40 5

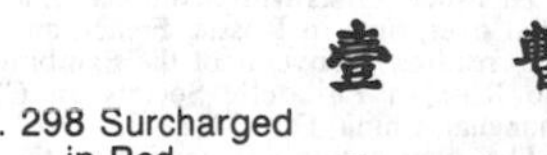

No. 298 Surcharged in Red

1937

Type II
341 A37 1c on 4c grn 55 5
a. Upper left character missing

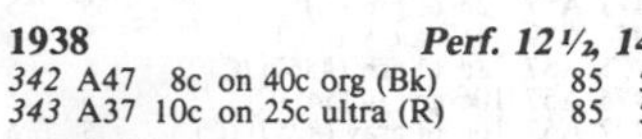
Nos. 322 and 303 Surcharged in Black or Red

1938 *Perf. 12½, 14*
342 A47 8c on 40c org (Bk) 85 5
343 A37 10c on 25c ultra (R) 85 5

Dr. Sun Yat-sen — A57

Type I. Coat button half circle. Six lines of shading above head. Top frame partially shaded with vertical lines.

Type II. Coat button complete circle. Nine lines of shading above head. Top frame partially shaded with vertical lines.

Type III. Coat button complete circle. Nine lines of shading above head. Top frame line fully shaded with vertical lines.

Printed by the Chung Hwa Book Co.

1938 Unwmk. Engr. *Perf. 12½*

Type I
344 A57 $1 hn & dk brn 30.00 2.50
345 A57 $2 dp bl & org brn 12.00 80
346 A57 $5 red & grnsh blk 52.50 9.00

1939

Type II
347 A57 $1 hn & dk brn 6.50 50
348 A57 $2 dp bl & org brn 8.50 1.00

1939-41

Type III
349 A57 2c ol grn 10 10
350 A57 3c dl cl 10 5
351 A57 5c green 10 5
352 A57 5c ol grn 10 5
353 A57 8c ol grn 15 5
354 A57 10c green 10 5
355 A57 15c scarlet 15 15
356 A57 15c dk vio brn ('41) 2.25 2.50
357 A57 16c ol gray 30 8
358 A57 25c dk bl 22 15
359 A57 $1 hn & dk brn 2.25 15
360 A57 $2 dp bl & org brn 2.50 15
a. Imperf., pair 250.00
361 A57 $5 red & grnsh blk 1.50 15
362 A57 $10 dk grn & dl pur 6.25 60
363 A57 $20 rose lake & dk bl 14.00 5.50
Nos. 349-363 (15) 30.07 9.78

Several values exist imperforate, but these were not regularly issued. No. 361 imperforate was sold as waste paper.

See Nos. 368-401, 506-524.

Chinese and American Flags and Map of China — A58

Printed by American Bank Note Co.

Frame Engraved, Center Lithographed
1939, July 4 Unwmk. *Perf. 12*
Flag in Deep Rose and Ultramarine
364 A58 5c dk grn 75 22
365 A58 25c dp bl 1.50 45
366 A58 50c brown 1.75 90
367 A58 $1 rose car 3.50 1.40

Issued in commemoration of the 150th anniversary of the Constitution of the United States of America.

Type of 1939-41 Issue
Re-engraved

2c, 1939-41

Re-engraved

8c, 1939-41

Re-engraved

1940 *Perf. 12½*
368 A57 2c ol grn 15 10
369 A57 8c ol grn 15 10

Type of 1938-41 Issue

1940 Unwmk. *Perf. 14*

Type III
370 A57 2c ol grn 50 50
371 A57 5c green 1.50 40
372 A57 $1 hn & dk brn 45.00 9.00
373 A57 $2 dp bl & org brn 12.00 3.00
374 A57 $5 red & grnsh blk 12.00 3.00
375 A57 $10 dk grn & dl pur 12.00 3.00
Nos. 370-375 (6) 83.00 18.90

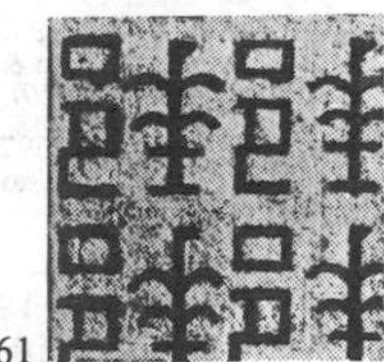
Wmk. 261

Type of 1939-41

Wmk. Character Yu (Post) Multiple (261)

1940 *Perf. 12½*

Type III
376 A57 $1 hn & dk brn 4.50 3.00
377 A57 $2 dp bl & org brn 6.00 1.50
378 A57 $5 red & grnsh blk 6.00 4.50
379 A57 $10 dk grn & dl pur 10.00 4.50
380 A57 $20 rose lake & dp bl 12.00 4.50
Nos. 376-380 (5) 38.50 18.00

Printed by the Dah Tung Book Co.
Type III with secret marks

Five Cent

Type III. Characters joined.
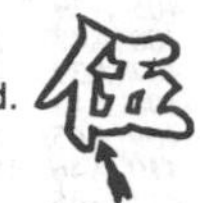

Secret Mark. Characters not joined.

Eight Cent

Type III. Characters not joined.

Secret Mark. Characters joined.

Ten Cent

Type III. Characters sharp and well-proportioned.

Secret Mark. Characters coarse and varying in thickness.

Dollar Values

Type III.

Secret Mark.

1940 Unwmk. *Perf. 14*
381 A57 5c green 5 5
382 A57 5c ol grn 5 5
383 A57 8c ol grn 45 5
a. Without "star" in uniform button 65 65
384 A57 10c green 8 5
385 A57 30c scarlet 8 5
386 A57 50c dk bl 8 5
387 A57 $1 org brn & sep 85 5
388 A57 $2 dp bl & yel brn 85 5
389 A57 $5 red & sl grn 85 12
390 A57 $10 dk grn & dl pur 1.50 25
391 A57 $20 rose lake & dk bl 3.00 50
Nos. 381-391 (11) 7.84 1.27

Type III with secret marks

1940 Wmk. 261 *Perf. 14*
392 A57 5c green 8 5
393 A57 5c ol grn 8 5
394 A57 10c green 12 5
395 A57 30c scarlet 12 5
396 A57 50c dk bl 12 5
397 A57 $1 org brn & sep 1.50 25
398 A57 $2 dp bl & yel brn 3.00 1.50
399 A57 $5 red & sl grn 3.00 1.75

400 A57 $10 dk grn & dl pur 9.00 3.75
401 A57 $20 rose lake & dk bl 10.00 4.50
Nos. 392-401 (10) 27.02 12.00

Nos. 383, 384, 385, 397, 400 and 401 exist perf. 12½, but were not issued with this perforation.

Types of 1932-34
Martyrs Issue with secret mark

1932-34 Issue. In the left Chinese character in bottom row, the two parts are not joined.

Secret Mark, 1940-41 Issue. The two parts are joined.

Perf. 12½, 13 and Compound.

1940-41 **Wmk. 261**

402 A39 ½c ol blk 8 5
403 A40 1c orange 8 5
404 A46 2c dp bl ('41) 8 12
405 A39 2½c rose lil 8 5
406 A48 3c dp yel brn 8 8
407 A39 4c pale vio ('41) 8 8
408 A48 5c dl red org ('41) 8 8
409 A45 8c dp org 8 8
410 A46 10c dl vio 8 8
411 A45 13c dp yel grn 8 8
412 A48 15c brn car 8 8
413 A46 17c brn ol 8 8
414 A47 20c lt bl 8 8
415 A45 21c ol brn ('41) 8 8
416 A40 25c red vio ('41) 8 8
417 A46 28c ol ('41) 8 12
418 A48 30c brn car 8 8
a. Vert. pair, imperf. btwn. 125.00
419 A47 40c orange 8 8
420 A40 50c green 8 8

Unwmk.

421 A39 ½c ol blk 8 5
422 A40 1c orange 8 5
a. Without secret mark 75
b. Horiz. pair, imperf. vert. 25.00
423 A46 2c dp bl 8 5
a. Vert. pair, imperf. horiz. 9.00
b. Horiz. pair, imperf. between 150.00
424 A39 2½c rose lil 8 5
425 A48 3c dp yel brn 8 5
426 A39 4c pale vio 8 5
427 A48 5c dl red org 8 5
428 A45 8c dp org 8 5
429 A46 10c dl vio 8 5
430 A45 13c dp yel grn 8 5
431 A48 15c brn car 8 5
432 A46 17c brn ol 8 5
433 A47 20c lt bl 8 5
a. Vert. pair, imperf. horiz. 110.00
b. Horiz. pair, imperf. vert. 110.00
434 A45 21c ol brn 8 5
435 A40 25c rose vio 8 5
436 A46 28c olive 8 5
437 A48 30c brn car 1.75 25
438 A47 40c orange 8 5
439 A40 50c green 8 5
Nos. 402-439 (38) 4.71 2.66

Several values exist imperforate, but they were not regularly issued.

Regional Surcharges.

The regional surcharges, Nos. 440 to 448, 482 to 484, 486 to 491 and 525 to 549, have been listed according to the basic stamps, with black or red surcharges. The surcharges of the individual provinces, plus Hong Kong and Shanghai, are noted in small type. These surcharges are identified by the following letters:

a- Hong Kong	i- Kwangsi
b- Shanghai	j- Kwantung
bx- Anhwei	k- Western Szechwan
c- Hunan	l- Yunnan
d- Kansu	m- Honan
e- Kiangsi	n- Shensi
f- Eastern Szechwan	o- Kweichow
g- Chekiang	p- Hupeh
h- Fukien	

The numeral following each letter is the surcharge denomination.

Regional Surcharges on Stamps of 1939-40:

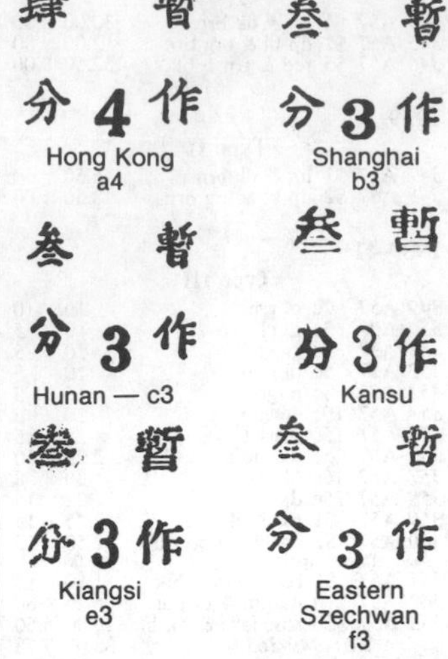

Hong Kong a4 · Shanghai b3 · Hunan — c3 · Kansu · Kiangsi e3 · Eastern Szechwan f3

Chekiang — g3

1940-41 Unwmk. *Perf. 12½, 14*
Parenthetical number indicates basic stamp

Carmine Surcharge

440 A57(a4) 4c on 5c ol grn (#382) 30 15
a. Lower right character duplicated at left 22.50 25.00

Black Surcharge

441 A57(b3) 3c on 5c grn (#351) 30 22
442 A57(c3) 3c on 5c ol grn (#352) 52 38
(d3) Kansu 50 50
443 A57(b3) 3c on 5c grn (#381) 22 22
444 A57 3c on 5c ol grn (#382) (b3, e3, f3) 22 22
r. Lower left character duplicated at right (Kiangsi) 45.00 40.00

The Kansu surcharges of No. 442 are of six types. Differences include formation of top part of fen character (at left of "3"), fen with low right hook, height of "3" (5mm. to 4mm.), space between upper and lower characters (6 to 9mm.), etc.

1940-41 Wmk. 261 *Perf. 14*

445 A57 3c on 5c grn (#392) (b3, e3) 22 22
(c3) Hunan 35 45
r. Lower left character duplicated at right (Kiangsi) 30.00 30.00
446 A57(b3) 3c on 5c ol grn (#393) 40 40
(f3) Eastern Szechwan 60 70
r. Lower left character duplicated at right (Eastern Szechwan) 45.00 50.00

Red Surcharge

447 A57 (g3) 3c on 5c grn (#392) 1.25 50
448 A57 (g3) 3c on 5c ol grn (#393) 3.00 2.00

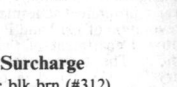

Dr. Sun Yat-sen — A59

Printed by American Bank Note Co.

1941 Unwmk. Engr. *Perf. 12*

449 A59 ½c sepia 5 5
450 A59 1c orange 5 5
451 A59 2c brt ultra 5 5
452 A59 5c green 5 5
453 A59 8c red org 5 5
454 A59 8c turq grn 5 5
455 A59 10c brt grn 5 5
456 A59 17c olive 1.50 1.50
457 A59 25c rose vio 5 5
458 A59 30c scarlet 5 5
459 A59 50c dk bl 6 5
460 A59 $1 brn & blk 10 5
461 A59 $2 bl & blk 10 7
a. Center invert. 5,000.
462 A59 $5 scar & blk 20 10
463 A59 $10 grn & blk 2.50 75
464 A59 $20 rose vio & blk 2.50 75
Nos. 449-464 (16) 7.41 3.72

Industry and Agriculture — A60

Printed by Chung Hwa Book Co.

1941, June 21 *Perf. 12½*

465 A60 8c green 5 5
466 A60 21c red brn 10 10
467 A60 28c dk ol grn 18 18
468 A60 33c vermilion 28 22
469 A60 50c dp ultra 30 28
470 A60 $1 dk vio 75 60
Nos. 465-470 (6) 1.66 1.43

Issued to promote the Thrift Movement and its aim to "Save for Reconstruction."

Souvenir Sheet

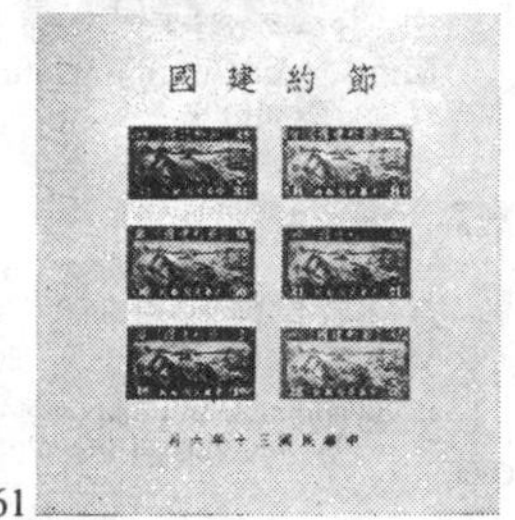

A61

Typo. *Imperf.*

471 A61 Sheet of six 15.00 15.00
a. 8c dl grn 1.50 1.50
b. 21c dk org brn 1.50 1.50
c. 28c dl yel grn 1.50 1.50
d. 33c red 1.50 1.50
e. 50c dl bl 1.50 1.50
f. $1 dk vio 1.50 1.50

Issued in sheets measuring 155x171mm. without gum.

This sheet exists with additional blue marginal overprints in Russia, French and Chinese reading "Souvenir of the Exhibition of the Russian Philatelic Society in China, Shanghai, China, Feb. 28, 1943."

The overprinting was applied by the society, and when so overprinted this sheet had no franking power.

Stamps of 1939-41 Overprinted in Carmine or Blue

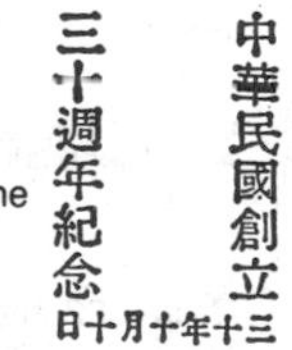

1941, Oct. 10 *Perf. 12½, 14, 13*

472 A40 1c dl org (Bl) 5 5
473 A57 2c ol grn (C) 5 5
474 A39 4c pale vio (C) 5 5
475 A57 8c ol grn (#369) (C) 5 5
476 A57 10c grn (#354) (C) 5 5
477 A57 16c ol gray (#257) (C) 5 5
478 A45 21c ol brn (C) 7 7
479 A46 28c ol (C) 40 30
480 A57 30c scar (Bl) 60 50
481 A57 $1 hn & dk brn (#359) (Bl) 1.00 80
Nos. 472-481 (10) 2.37 1.97

Chinese Republic, 30th anniversary.

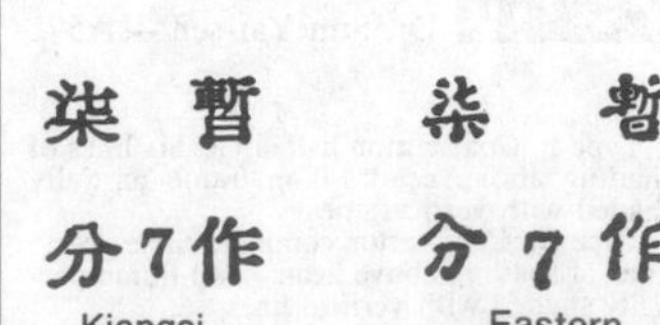

Kiangsi e7 · Eastern Szechwan f7

Chekiang g7 · Fukien h7

1941 Unwmk. *Perf. 12½, 14*

482 A57 7c on 8c ol grn (#353) (g7, h7) 30 30
483 A57 7c on 8c ol grn (#369) (f7) 28 28
484 A57 7c on 8c ol grn (#383) (e7, g7, h7) 35 35
a. Without "star" in uniform button 50.00

Type of 1932-34 Re-engraved

1941 Unwmk. *Perf. 14*

485 A45 8c dp org 7.50 9.00

The original stamps are 19½mm. wide, the re-engraved 21mm.

Eleven other values of the Martyrs Issue and types A37 and A57 exist re-engraved, but were not issued.

Hunan c1 · Kiangsi e1

Fukien — h1 · Kwangsi — i1

Kwangtung — j1

1942

Red Surcharge

486 A39 1c on ½c blk brn (#312) (cl, il) 40 45
487 A39 1c on ½c ol blk (#421) (c1,e1,h1,i1) 40 40
488 A59 1c on ½c sep (#449) (c1,j1) 25 30

Hunan c40 · Eastern Szechwan f40

Western Szechwan k40 · Yunnan l40

Red Surcharge

489 A57 (f40) 40c on 50c dk bl (#386) 40 40
(k40) Western Szechwan 1.75 1.75
(l40) Yunnan 1.25 1.25
a. Inverted surcharge (Yunnan) 85.00

Wmk. 261

490 A40 (c40) 40c on 50c grn (#420) 40 40

Unwmk.

491 A59 (c40) 40c on 50c dk bl (#459) 25 15

Dr. Sun Yat-sen — A62

Central Trust Printing

Perf. 10½-11, 11½-12½, 13 and Compounds

1942-43 **Typo.**

Without Gum

No.	Type	Description	Unused	Used
492	A62	10c dp grn ('43)	6	6
493	A62	16c dl ol brn	5.00	5.75
a.		Perf 10½	175.00	85.00
494	A62	20c dk ol grn ('43)	12	10
a.		Perf. 11	4.00	4.00
495	A62	25c brn vio	8	25
496	A62	30c dl ver	8	8
a.		Perf. 11	2.00	2.00
497	A62	40c dk red brn ('43)	25	25
a.		Perf. 11x13	35.00	
b.		Perf. 11	13.00	13.00
498	A62	50c sage grn	6	5
a.		Perf. 11	1.50	1.50
499	A62	$1 rose lake	6	6
a.		Perf. 11	25.00	25.00
500	A62	$1 dl grn ('43)	6	6
501	A62	$1.50 dp bl ('43)	6	6
a.		Perf. 11	200.00	
502	A62	$2 dk bl grn	6	6
503	A62	$3 dk yel ('43)	6	6
504	A62	$4 red brn	6	6
505	A62	$5 cer ('43)	6	6
		Nos. 492-505 (14)	6.07	6.96

Many shades and part-perforate varieties exist. See Nos. 550 to 563 for other stamps of type A62 with secret mark and new values and colors.

Type of 1938

Thin Paper Without Gum

1942-44 **Unwmk.** **Engr.** ***Imperf.***

No.	Type	Description	Unused	Used
506	A57	$10 red brn	10	8
507	A57	$20 bl grn	30	10
508	A57	$20 rose red ('44)	4.50	60
509	A57	$30 dl vio ('43)	45	30
510	A57	$40 rose red ('43)	10	5
511	A57	$50 blue	1.10	1.10
512	A57	$100 org brn ('43)	1.50	1.10

Rouletted

No.	Type	Description	Unused	Used
513	A57	$5 lil gray ('44)	2.25	90
a.		Rouletted x perf. 12½	25.00	
514	A57	$10 red brn	1.75	40
515	A57	$50 blue	2.25	90
a.		Rouletted x imperf.		
		Nos. 506-515 (10)	14.30	5.53

1942-45 ***Perf. 12½ to 15***

No.	Type	Description	Unused	Used
516	A57	$4 dp bl ('43)	10	6
517	A57	$5 lil gray ('43)	10	7
518	A57	$10 red brn	10	7
519	A57	$20 bl grn ('43)	10	10
520	A57	$20 rose red ('45)	30.00	30.00
521	A57	$30 dl vio ('43)	10	10
522	A57	$40 rose ('43)	50	25
523	A57	$50 blue	50	25
524	A57	$100 org brn ('45)	30.00	30.00
		Nos. 516-524 (9)	61.50	60.90

附加已付 國内平信

No. 493 Overprinted in Black or Red

1942

No.	Type	Description	Unused	Used
525	A62 (i)	16c dl ol brn (Bk)	25.00	25.00
		(c) Hunan	250.00	
		(k) Western Szechwan	50.00	50.00
		(m) Honan	350.00	350.00
r.		Perf. 10½ (Kwangsi)	275.00	
		(n) Shensi	75.00	75.00
s.		Inverted ovpt. (Shensi)	100.00	
526	A62 (d)	16c dl ol brn (R)	4.50	6.00
		(bx) Anhwei	175.00	175.00
		(e) Kiangsi	12.50	12.50
		(f) Eastern Szechwan	15.00	15.00
r.		Perf. 10½ (E. Szechwan)	375.00	
		(h) Fukien	52.50	52.50
		(j) Kwangtung	275.00	300.00
		(l) Yunnan	13.00	13.00
		(o) Kweichow	45.00	45.00
		(p) Hupeh, perf. 10½	325.00	325.00
s.		Horiz. pair, imperf. between (Yunnan)	200.00	
f.		Perf. 13 (Hupeh)	650.00	450.00

This overprint means "Domestic Ordinary Letter Surcharge Paid." It was applied in various sizes and types by 14 districts, 9 using red ink, 5 using black. (The Anhwei overprint comes in two types.) These overprinted stamps were briefly sold for $1.16 before the government ordered their sale suspended. The vertical bars and 50c surcharge of Nos. 527-528 were then applied.

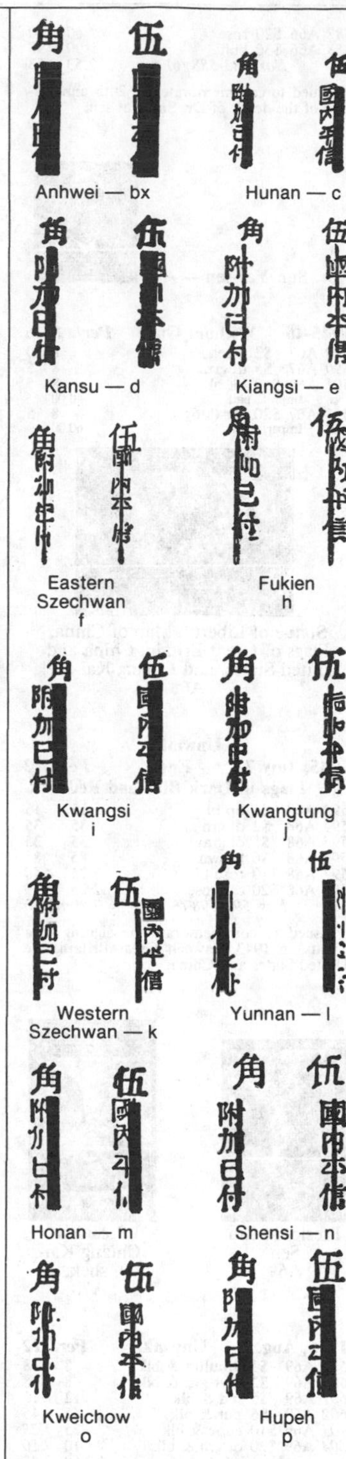

Anhwei — bx | Hunan — c | Kansu — d | Kiangsi — e | Eastern Szechwan f | Fukien h | Kwangsi i | Kwangtung j | Western Szechwan — k | Yunnan — l | Honan — m | Shensi — n | Kweichow o | Hupeh p

Nos. 525-526 Surcharged "50 cents" and 2 Vertical Bars in Black or Red

1942 **Unwmk.**

No.	Type	Description	Unused	Used
527	A62	50c on 16c dl ol brn (Bk) (c,f)	1.50	1.50
		(i) Kwangsi	1.75	1.75
		(k) Western Szechwan	3.75	3.75
r.		Inverted surch. (W. Szech.)	75.00	
s.		"k" surch. on #493	60.00	
		(m) Honan	4.50	4.50
		(n) Shensi	1.75	1.75
528	A62 (d)	50c on 16c dl ol brn (R)	1.00	1.00
		(bx) Anhwei	13.00	13.00
		(e) Kiangsi	4.00	3.25
		(h) Fukien	4.00	
		(j) Kwangtung	2.25	2.25
		(l) Yunnan	4.50	
		(o) Kweichow	2.00	2.00
		(p) Hupeh	1.50	1.50
r.		Inverted surch. (Kweichow)	25.00	
s.		"p" surch. on #526f	35.00	35.00

Many varieties of Nos. 527-528 exist, including narrow or wide spacing between the two top characters, or between the vertical bars, or both.

Surcharges on stamps perf. 10½ (basic No. 493a) usually sell at much higher prices.

伍 改 角50作

General Issue

伍 改 角50作 — Hunan c50

伍 改 角50作 — Eastern Szechwan f50

伍 改 角50作 — Chekiang g50

伍 改 角50作 — Kwangsi i50

伍 改 角50作 — Kwangtung j50

伍 改 角50作 — Western Szechwan k50

伍 改 角50作 — Honan — m50

伍 改 角50作 — Shensi — n50

伍 改 角50作 — Kweichow — o50

No. 493 Surcharged in Black, Red or Carmine

1943 **Unwmk.**

No.	Type	Description	Unused	Used
529	A62	50c on 16c dl ol brn (Bk) (m50, n50)	2.50	2.50
r.		Perf. 11x13 (Shensi)	65.00	
530	A62	50c on 16c dl ol brn (R,C)	40	40
a.		General Issue (C)	40	40
		General Issue (C) (c50) Hunan	1.50	1.50
r.		Inverted surch. (Hunan)	35.00	
		(f50) Eastern Szechwan	1.10	1.10
		(g50) Chekiang	13.00	
		(i50) Kwangsi	2.25	2.25
		(j50) Kwangtung	1.75	1.75
		(k50) Western Szechwan	3.00	3.00
		(m50) Honan	3.75	3.75
		(o50) Kweichow	1.75	1.75
s.		"05" instead of "50" (Kweichow)	250.00	

Many varieties of Nos. 529-530 exist, such as narrow or wide spacing horizontally or vertically between the overprinted Chinese characters.

Surcharges on No. 493a (perf. 10½) usually sell at much higher prices.

The General Issue type, No. 530a, was distributed to all head offices, which in turn supplied the post offices under their direction. It is surcharged in carmine; the other stamps listed under No. 530 are surcharged in red or carmine.

貳 改 角20作 — Hunan c20

貳 改 角(20)作 — Kansu d20

貳 改 角20作 — Kiangsi e20

貳 改 角20作 — Eastern Szechwan f20

貳 改 角20作 — Fukien h20

貳 改 角20作 — Kwangsi i20

貳 改 角20作 — Kwangtung j20

貳 改 角20作 — Western Szechwan k20

貳 改 角20作 — Yunnan l20

貳 改 角20作 — Honan m20

貳 改 角20作 — Shensi n20

貳 改 角20作 — Kweichow o20

貳 改 角20作 — Hupeh — p20

1943 **Unwmk.**

No.	Type	Description	Unused	Used
531	A45 (n20)	20c on 13c bl grn (#318) (Bk)	8	10
		(d20) Kansu	40	45
		(k20) Western Szechwan	22	25
532	A45 (i20)	20c on 13c bl grn (#318) (R)	22	22
		(c20) Hunan	475.00	
		(e20) Kiangsi	52.50	
		(j20) Kwangtung	15.00	15.00
		(p20) Hupeh	30	45

Wmk. 261

No.	Type	Description	Unused	Used
533	A45 (n20)	20c on 13c dp yel grn (#411) (Bk)	22	25
		(d20) Kansu	35	35
		(k20) Western Szechwan	30	30
		(l20) Yunnan	1.25	1.25
		(m20) Honan	535.00	
534	A45	20c on 13c dp yel grn (#411) (R) (f20, p20)	15	15
		(c20) Hunan	20	20
		(e20) Kiangsi	18	18
		(h20) Fukien	40	40
		(i20) Kwangsi	30	30
		(j20) Kwangtung	7.00	7.00
		(o20) Kweichow	50	40

Unwmk.

No.	Type	Description	Unused	Used
535	A45 (n20)	20c on 13c dp yel grn (#430) (Bk)	15	18
		(d20) Kansu	20	30
		(k20) Western Szechwan	10.50	10.50
		(l20) Yunnan	28	30
		(m20) Honan	50	50

536 A45 20c on 13c dp yel grn (#430) (R) (f20, i20, j20, p20) 15 18
(c20) Hunan 1.75 1.75
(e20) Kiangsi 22 30
(o20) Kweichow 30 30
537 A57 20c on 16c ol gray (#357) (Bk) (d20) 15 18
(c20) Hunan 22 25
(k20) Western Szechwan 22 25
(m20) Honan 80 80
(n20) Shensi 22 25
538 A57 20c on 16c ol gray (#357) (R) (e20, i20, o20) 22 30
(c20) Hunan 1.00 1.10
(j20) Kwangtung 19.50 21.00

Wmk. 261

539 A46 (i20) 20c on 17c brn ol (#413) (R) 15 18
(c20) Hunan 40 45
(j20) Kwangtung 15.00 15.00

Unwmk.

540 A46 (k20) 20c on 17c brn ol (#432) (Bk) 22 22
(d20) Kansu 1.25 1.50
(m20) Honan 12.00 12.00
541 A46 20c on 17c brn ol (#432) (R) (e20, j20, o20) 22 30
542 A59 (m20) 20c on 17c ol (#456) (Bk) 75.00 80.00
543 A59 (c20) 20c on 17c ol (#456) (R) 1.75 1.75

Wmk. 261

544 A45 (e20) 20c on 21c ol brn (#415) (R) 40 45

Unwmk.

545 A45 (c20) 20c on 21c ol brn (#434) (Bk) 8 8
(d20) Kansu 25 30
(k20) Western Szechwan 22 18
(l20) Yunnan 22 18
(m20) Honan 38 45
546 A45 (f20) 20c on 21c ol brn (#434) (R) 8 8
(e20) Kiangsi 22 25
(h20) Fukien 22 25
(i20) Kwangsi 15 15
(j20) Kwangtung 15 15
(o20) Kweichow 25 25
(p20) Hupeh 22 25

Wmk. 261

547 A46 (e20) 20c on 28c ol (#417) (R) 300.00 350.00

Unwmk.

548 A46 (l20) 20c on 28c (#436) (Bk) 15 18
(d20) Kansu 9.00 9.00
(k20) Western Szechwan 12.00 12.00
(m20) Honan 12.00 12.00
549 A46 20c on 28c ol (#436) (R) (c20,h20) 8 8
(e20) Kiangsi 15 18
(i20) Kwangsi 15 18
(j20) Kwangtung 15 18
(o20) Kweichow 40 40

Many varieties of Nos. 531-549 exist, such as narrow or wide spacing between the overprinted Chinese characters, and "20" higher or lower than illustrated.

Catalogue prices for unused stamps up to mid-1953 are for hinged copies matching the condition specified in this volume's introduction.

Type of 1942-43
Pacheng Printing

1944-46 Unwmk. *Perf. 12*
Without Gum

550 A62 30c chocolate 40 *3.00*
551 A62 $1 green 2.75 2.20
552 A62 $2 dk vio brn 8 8
a. Imperf., pair 2.50 2.50
553 A62 $2 dk bl grn 15 15
a. Perf. 10½ 50.00 55.00
554 A62 $2 dp bl 10 10
555 A62 $3 lt yel 12 8
556 A62 $4 vio brn 8 8
a. Imperf., pair 50.00
557 A62 $5 car ('46) 8 6
a. Perf. 10½ 75.00 70.00
558 A62 $6 gray vio ('45) 8 6
559 A62 $10 red brn ('45) 8 6
a. Imperf., pair 50.00
560 A62 $20 dp ultra ('46) 8 6
561 A62 $50 dk grn ('46) 12 6
562 A62 $70 lil ('46) 15 8
563 A62 $100 lt brn ('46) 8 6
Nos. 550-563 (14) 4.35 6.13

In the Pacheng printing of the Central Trust type stamps, the secret mark "C" has been added below the lower left foliate ornament beneath the sun emblem. On the $3, it is below the right ornament. New values also include a "P" at right of sun emblem on the $6 and $10, and at right of necktie on the $20. Some values of Pacheng printing exist on paper with elephant watermark in sheet.

Dr. Sun Yat-sen
A63

Allegory of Savings
A64

1944-46 Unwmk. Typo. *Perf. 12½*
Without Gum

565 A63 40c brn red 8 5
566 A63 $2 gray brn 8 5
567 A63 $3 red 8 5
a. $3 org red 1.50 1.25
568 A63 $3 lt red brn ('45) 35 25
569 A63 $6 pale lil gray ('45) 8 5
570 A63 $10 dl lake ('45) 8 5
571 A63 $20 rose ('45) 8 5
a. Perf. 15½ 30.00
572 A63 $50 lt brn ('46) 15 5
573 A63 $70 rose vio ('46) 10 5
Nos. 565-573 (9) 1.08 65

1944-45 Engr. *Perf. 13*
Without Gum

574 A64 $40 ind ('45) 8 5
575 A64 $50 yel grn ('45) 8 5
576 A64 $100 yel brn 8 5
577 A64 $200 dk grn ('45) 15 15

All four values were printed on thick paper; the first three were also printed on thin paper.

Dr. Sun Yat-sen
A65 A66

1944, Dec. 25 Litho.
Without Gum

578 A65 $2 dp grn 12 12
579 A65 $5 fawn 18 18
580 A65 $6 dl rose vio 30 35
581 A65 $10 vio bl 50 60
582 A65 $20 carmine 75 85
Nos. 578-582 (5) 1.85 2.10

50th anniversary of the Kuomintang.

1945, Mar. 12
Without Gum

583 A66 $2 gray grn 8 8
584 A66 $5 red brn 22 22
585 A66 $6 dk vio bl 28 28
586 A66 $10 lt bl 45 45
587 A66 $20 rose 60 60
588 A66 $30 buff 90 90
Nos. 583-588 (6) 2.53 2.53

Issued to commemorate the 20th anniversary of the death of Dr. Sun Yat-sen.

Dr. Sun Yat-sen — A67

1945-46 Without Gum *Perf. 12½*

589 A67 $2 green 8 10
590 A67 $5 dl grn 8 5
591 A67 $10 dk bl 8 5
a. Impref., pair 40.00
592 A67 $20 car ('46) 8 5
a. Imperf., pair 60.00

Statue of Liberty, Map of China, Flags of Great Britain, China and United States, and Chiang Kai-shek
A68

Unwmk.
1945, July 7 Engr. *Perf. 12*
Flags in Dark Blue and Red

593 A68 $1 dp bl 15 15
594 A68 $2 dl grn 35 35
595 A68 $5 ol gray 35 35
596 A68 $6 brown 85 85
597 A68 $10 rose lil 3.25 *4.50*
598 A68 $20 car rose 2.25 *5.50*
Nos. 593-598 (6) 7.20 11.70

Issued to commemorate the signing of a Treaty in 1943 between Great Britain, the United States and China.

President Lin Sen
A69

President Chiang Kai-shek
A70

1945, Aug. Unwmk. *Perf. 12*

599 A69 $1 dp ultra & blk 8 8
600 A69 $2 myr grn & blk 8 8
601 A69 $5 red & blk 12 12
602 A69 $6 pur & blk 45 45
603 A69 $10 choc & blk 75 *1.25*
604 A69 $20 ol grn & blk 1.10 *1.50*
Nos. 599-604 (6) 2.58 3.48

Issued in memory of President Lin Sen (1864-1943).

1945, Oct. 10
Flag in Rose Red and Violet Blue

605 A70 $2 green 38 38
606 A70 $4 dk bl 38 38
607 A70 $5 ol gray 38 38
608 A70 $6 bis brn 90 90
609 A70 $10 gray 1.25 1.25
610 A70 $20 red vio 2.00 2.00
Nos. 605-610 (6) 5.29 5.29

Issued to commemorate the inauguration of Chiang Kai-shek as president, October 10, 1943.

President Chiang Kai-shek — A71

1945, Oct. 10 Typo. *Perf. 13*
Without Gum
Flag in Carmine and Blue

611 A71 $20 grn & bl 10 8
612 A71 $50 bis brn & bl 20 12
613 A71 $100 blue 18 15
614 A71 $300 rose red & bl 18 15

Issued to commemorate the Victory of the Allied Nations over Japan.

C. N. C. Surcharges

The green surcharges on Nos. 615 to 621, and the surcharges on Nos. 647 to 721, and 768 to 774 represent Chinese National Currency and were applied at Shanghai.

Stamps of 1938-41 Surcharged in Black with Chinese Characters and New Value in Checkered Rectangle at Bottom, Resurcharged in Green

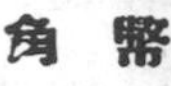

1945 *Perf. 12, 12½*

615 A57 10c on $20 on 3c dl cl (#350) 6 5
616 A46 15c on $30 on 2c dp bl (#423) 6 10
a. Horiz. pair, imperf. between 90.00
b. Vert. pair, imperf. between 85.00
617 A59 25c on $50 on 1c org (#450) 6 10
618 A57 50c on $100 on 3c dl cl (#350) 6 10
619 A40 $1 on $200 on 1c org (#422) 6 10
a. Horiz. pair, imperf. between 90.00
620 A57 $2 on $400 on 3c dl cl (#350) 6 10
621 A59 $5 on $1000 on 1c org (#450) 6 10

The black (first) surcharges on Nos. 615 to 621 represent Nanking puppet government currency.

In the green surcharge, the characters at the left express the new value and are either two or four in number.

Types of 1932-34, Re-engraved, Overprinted in Black and Surcharged in Green with Horizontal Bar and Four or Five Chinese Characters

Perf. 14

622 A47 $10 on 20c brn red 3.00 4.50
623 A47 $20 on 40c org 12.00 15.00
a. Green surcharge inverted 40.00
624 A48 $50 on 30c vio brn 7.50 10.50

These provisional surcharges were applied in Honan in National currency to stamps of the Hwa Pei (North China) government. The black overprint reads: "Hwa Pei."

The two-character "Hwa Pei" overprint was applied to various stamps in 1941-43 by the North China puppet government. See Nos. 8N1-8N53, 8N60-8N84.

Dr. Sun Yat-sen
A72 A73

1945, Dec. Typo. *Perf. 12*
Without Gum

625 A72 $20 dp car 6 6
626 A72 $30 dp bl 6 6
627 A72 $40 orange 8 6
628 A72 $50 green 12 6
629 A72 $100 dk brn 12 8
630 A72 $200 brn vio 12 10
Nos. 625-630 (6) 56 42

Type of 1931-37
Perf. 12½, 13x12½, 13½

1946 Unwmk.

631 A37 $1 dk vio 10 10
632 A37 $2 ol grn 10 10
633 A37 $20 brt yel grn 12 10

634 A37 $30 chocolate 12 10
635 A37 $50 red org 15 8
Nos. 631-635 (5) 59 48

1946-47 Engr. *Perf. 14*
Without Gum

636 A73 $20 carmine 15 5
637 A73 $30 dk bl ('47) 6 5
638 A73 $50 purple 12 5
639 A73 $70 red org ('47) 7.00 1.10
640 A73 $100 dk car 6 5
641 A73 $200 ol grn ('47) 8 5
642 A73 $500 brt bl grn ('47) 15 5
643 A73 $700 red brn ('47) 15 15
644 A73 $1000 rose lake 15 5
645 A73 $3000 blue 50 5
646 A73 $5000 dp grn & ver 75 8
Nos. 636-646 (11) 9.17 1.73

念 20.00 國
圓 幣

Stamps of 1932-41 Surcharged in Black

Perf. 12½, 13, 13x12, 14
Wmk. 261

647 A45 $20 on 8c dp org (#409) 8 15
648 A39 $30 on ½c ol blk (#402) 1,000.
649 A45 $50 on 21c ol brn (#415) 8 15
650 A45 $70 on 13c dp yel grn (#411) 8 10
651 A46 $100 on 28c ol (#417) 8 15

Unwmk.

652 A39 $3 on 2½c rose lil (#424) 50 75
653 A48 $10 on 15c brn car (#431) 8 10
654 A45 $20 on 8c dp org (#428) 8 10
655 A47 $20 on 20c lt bl (#433) 8 10
656 A39 $30 on ½c ol blk (#421) 8 10
657 A45 $50 on 21c ol brn (#434) 8 10
657A A45 $70 on 13c bl grn (#318) 75.00 85.00
658 A45 $70 on 13c dp yel grn (#430) 8 25
659 A46 $100 on 28c ol (#436) 8 10

伍 國
拾
圓 50.00 幣

Stamps of 1931-1946 Surcharged in Black or Carmine

Perf. 12½, 13, 14
1946-47 Wmk. 261

660 A57 $50 on 5c grn (#392) 8 10
661 A57 $50 on 5c ol grn (#393) 20.00 19.00
662 A48 $50 on 5c dl red org (#408) 5 30
663 A40 $100 on 1c org (#403) 5 25

Perf. 12, 12½, 12½x13, 13, 14
1946-47 Unwmk.

664 A57 $20 on 3c dl cl (#350) 8 15
665 A45 $20 on 8c dp org (#428) 8 10
666 A57 $50 on 3c dl cl (#350) 15 10
667 A57 $50 on 5c ol grn (#352) 8 10
668 A57 $50 on 5c ol grn (#382) 8 20
669 A48 $50 on 5c dl red org (#427) 8 10
670 A59 $50 on 5c grn (#452) 10 10
671 A62 $50 on $1 dl grn (#500) 8 10
672 A40 $100 on 1c org (#422) 8 10
a. Without secret mark (No. 422a) 60.00
673 A57 $100 on 3c dl cl (#350) 8 10
674 A57 $100 on 8c ol grn (#353) 12.00 10.00
675 A57 $100 on 8c ol grn (#369) 10 10
676 A57 $100 on 8c ol grn (#383) 10 10
a. Without "star" in uniform button (No. 383a) 25.00 25.00
677 A59 $100 on 8c turq grn (#454) 15 10
678 A37 $100 on $1 dk vio (#631) 20 10
679 A73 $100 on $20 car (#636) 1.40 15
680 A57 $200 on 10c grn (#354) 25 10
681 A57 $200 on 10c grn (#384) 25 10
682 A37 $200 on $4 dl bl 10 10
a. Double surch. 15.00
683 A62 $250 on $1.50 dp bl (#501) 8 20
a. Perf. 11 125.00 150.00
684 A37 $250 on $2 ol grn (#632) 20 10
685 A37 $250 on $5 car 10 10
686 A57 $300 on 10c grn (#354) 8 10
687 A59 $300 on 10c brt grn (#455) 8 15
688 A57 $500 on 3c dl cl (#350) 15 10
689 A37 $500 on $20 brt yel grn (#633) 8 10
690 A37 $800 on $30 choc (#634) 8 10
691 A37 $1000 on 2c ol grn (#297) 50 20
692 A62 $1000 on $2 dk vio brn (#552) 12 12
a. Imperf., pair 20.00 20.00
693 A62 $1000 on $2 dk bl grn (#553) 8 8
694 A62 $1000 on $2 dp bl (#554) 8 12
695 A67 $1000 on $2 grn (#589) 10 12
696 A62 $2000 on $5 car (#557) 10 12
697 A67 $2000 on $5 dl grn (C) (#590) 15 20
Nos. 664-697 (34) 17.42 13.91

Nos. 682 and 685 were not issued without surcharge. No. 682 is perf. 13x13½; No. 685, perf. 12x12½.

The characters at the left express the new value and vary in number.

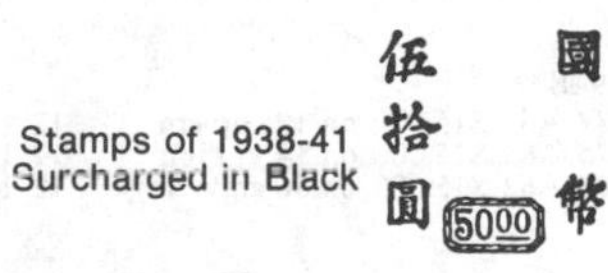

Stamps of 1938-41 Surcharged in Black

Perf. 12, 12½, 13, 14
1946 Wmk. 261

698 A45 $20 on 8c dp org (#409) 80.00 90.00
699 A57 $50 on 5c grn (#392) 8 25
700 A57 $50 on 5c ol grn (#393) 8 25

1946-48 Unwmk.

700A A57 $20 on 5c grn (#381) 500.00
701 A57 $20 on 8c ol grn (#353) 6 10
702 A57 $20 on 8c ol grn (#369) 25 30
703 A57 $20 on 8c ol grn (#383) 6 10
a. Without "star" in uniform button (No. 383a) 3.25 3.25
b. Inverted surch. 22.50
c. Double surcharge, one on back 40.00 30.00
d. Double surch. 40.00
704 A45 $20 on 8c dp org (#428) 6 15
a. Double surch. 20.00
705 A59 $20 on 8c red org (#453) 10 15
706 A59 $20 on 8c turq grn (#454) 6 10
a. Inverted surch. 17.50
b. Double surcharge 17.50
707 A57 $50 on 5c grn (#351) 3.00 3.00
708 A57 $50 on 5c ol grn (#352) 6 10
a. Inverted surch. 30.00
709 A57 $50 on 5c grn (#381) 6 15
710 A57 $50 on 5c ol grn (#382) 10 10
711 A48 $50 on 5c dl red org (#427) 10 10
a. Inverted surch. 25.00
712 A59 $50 on 5c grn (#452) 10 10
a. Double surch. 15.00

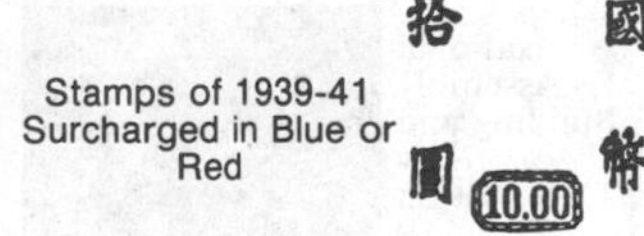

Stamps of 1939-41 Surcharged in Blue or Red

1946 Wmk. 261 *Perf. 12½*

713 A40 $10 on 1c org (Bl) (#403) 5 10
a. Inverted surch. 35.00
714 A48 $20 on 3c dp yel brn (#406) (Bl) 300.00 175.00

1946 Unwmk. *Perf. 12, 12½, 13*

715 A40 $10 on 1c org (Bl) (#422) 5 10
a. Without secret mark (No. 422a) 6.50 6.50
b. Inverted surcharge 9.00 12.00
716 A59 $10 on 1c org (Bl) (#450) 5 10
a. Double surch. 25.00
717 A57 $20 on 2c ol grn (R) (#368) 5 10
718 A59 $20 on 2c brt ultra (R) (#451) 5 10
a. Inverted surch. 17.50
b. Double surch. 15.00
719 A57 $20 on 3c dl cl (Bl) (#350) 5 10
a. Double surch. 20.00
720 A48 $20 on 3c dp yel brn (Bl) (#425) 5 15
721 A39 $30 on 4c pale vio (R) (#426) 5 15
a. Inverted surch. 8.00

President Chiang Kai-shek — A74

Perf. 14, 10½-11½
1946, Oct. 31 Engr. Unwmk.

722 A74 $20 carmine 22 15
723 A74 $30 green 22 15
724 A74 $50 vermilion 22 15
725 A74 $100 yel grn 22 15
726 A74 $200 yel org 22 15
727 A74 $300 magenta 22 15
Nos. 722-727 (6) 1.32 90

60th birthday of Chiang Kai-shek.

Perf. 14 stamps were printed by Dah Tung Book Co. and have no gum. Perf. 10½-11½ stamps were printed by Dah Yeh Printing Co.; the earlier ones are gumless, the later ones gummed.

Assembly House, Nanking — A75

1946, Nov. 15 Litho. *Perf. 14*
Without Gum

728 A75 $20 green 6 10
729 A75 $30 blue 6 10
730 A75 $50 dk brn 6 10
a. Horiz. pair, imperf. between 50.00 60.00
731 A75 $100 carmine 6 10

Convening of National Assembly.

Entrance to Dr. Sun Yat-sen Mausoleum A76

Dr. Sun Yat-sen A77

1947, May 1 Engr.

732 A76 $100 dp grn 10 12
733 A76 $200 dp bl 10 12
734 A76 $250 carmine 10 12
735 A76 $350 lt brn 10 12
736 A76 $400 dp cl 10 12
Nos. 732-736 (5) 50 60

First anniversary of return of Chinese National Government to Nanking.

1947 *Perf. 12½, 11½x12½*

737 A77 $500 ol grn 10 5
738 A77 $1000 grn & car 15 5
739 A77 $2000 dp bl & red brn 15 6
740 A77 $5000 org red & blk 15 6

Confucius A78

Confucius' Lecturing School A79

Tomb of Confucius A80

Temple of Confucius — A81

1947, Aug. 27 Litho. *Perf. 14*
Without Gum

741 A78 $500 car rose 8 10

Engr.

742 A79 $800 yel brn 8 15
743 A80 $1250 bl grn 8 15
744 A81 $1800 blue 8 15

Sun Yat-sen and Plum Blossoms A82

Chinese Flag and Map of Taiwan A83

1947-48 Engr. *Perf. 14*
Without Gum

745 A82 $150 dk bl 8 15
746 A82 $250 dp lil 20 10
747 A82 $500 bl grn 6 10
748 A82 $1000 red 6 6
749 A82 $2000 vermilion 15 6
750 A82 $3000 blue 5 6
751 A82 $4000 gray ('48) 15 6
752 A82 $5000 dk brn 6 6
753 A82 $6000 rose lil ('48) 15 6
754 A82 $7000 lt red brn ('48) 15 6
755 A82 $10,000 dp bl & car 65 6
756 A82 $20,000 car & yel grn 45 6
757 A82 $50,000 grn & dk bl 65 6
758 A82 $100,000 dl yel & ol grn ('48) 1.00 6
759 A82 $200,000 vio brn & dp bl ('48) 1.25 25
760 A82 $300,000 sep & org brn ('48) 1.25 25
761 A82 $500,000 dk Prus grn & sep ('48) 1.40 25
Nos. 745-761 (17) 7.76 1.76

See Nos. 788-799.

1947, Oct. 25
With Gum

762 A83 $500 carmine 10 20
763 A83 $1250 dp grn 10 20

Second anniversary, restoration of Taiwan to China.

Mobile Post Office — A84

Street-Corner Branch Post Office — A85

1947, Nov. 5

764 A84 $500 carmine 8 *15*
765 A85 $1000 lilac 8 *15*
766 A85 $1250 green 8 *15*
767 A84 $1800 dp bl 8 *15*

伍 國 佰 圓 500 幣

Stamps and Type of 1943-47 Surcharged in Black or Green

1947-48 Unwmk. *Perf. 12½, 13, 14*

768 A37 $500 on $20 brt yel grn (#633) 8 6
769 A73 $1250 on $70 red org (#639) 8 *15*
770 A82 $1800 on $350 yel org 8 *12*
771 A62 $2000 on $3 dk yel ('48) (#503) 8 10
772 A63 $2000 on $3 red (#567) 8 10
  a. On #567a 3.00 1.25
773 A62 $3000 on $3 lt yel ('48) (#555) 8 10
774 A63 $3000 on $3 lt red brn (G) ('48) (#568) 8 10
  Nos. 768-774 (7) 56 73

The characters at the left express the new value and vary in number.

伍 國 千 圓 5000 幣

No. 640 Surcharged

1948, Aug. *Perf. 14*

775 A73 $5000 on $100 dk car 3.50 5.50

No. 775 received its surcharge in Kwangsi for use in that province.

Map of China and Mail-carrying Vehicles A86

Rural Mail Delivery A87

Early and Modern Mail Transportation A88

1947, Dec. 16 Engr. *Perf. 12*

776 A86 $100 violet 8 10
777 A87 $200 brt grn 8 10
778 A87 $300 red brn 8 10
779 A88 $400 scarlet 8 10
780 A88 $500 brt vio bl 8 10
  Nos. 776-780 (5) 40 50

Issued to commemorate the 50th anniversary of the Chinese Postal Administration.

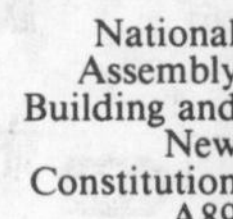

National Assembly Building and New Constitution A89

1947, Dec. 25 *Perf. 14*

Without Gum

781 A89 $2000 brt red 8 10
782 A89 $3000 blue 8 10
783 A89 $5000 dp grn 8 10

Issued to commemorate the first anniversary of the adoption of China's new constitution, Dec. 25, 1946.

Chinese Stamps of 1947 and 1912 — A90

Perf. 14, Imperf.

1948, Mar. 20 Litho.

Without Gum

784 A90 $5000 dk car rose 20 30
  a. Vert. pair, imperf. between 30.00
785 A90 $5000 dk grn 20 30
  a. Vert. pair, imperf. between 20.00

Issued to commemorate stamp exhibitions at Nanking, Mar. 20 (No. 784), and at Shanghai, May 19 (No. 785).

Sun Yat-sen Memorial Hall, Taipei — A91

1948, Apr. 28 Engr. *Perf. 14*

786 A91 $5000 violet 12 20
787 A91 $10000 red 12 20

Issued to commemorate the third anniversary of the restoration of Formosa to China.

Sun Yat-sen Type of 1947-48

1948

Without Gum

788 A82 $20000 rose pink 15 15
789 A82 $30000 chocolate 10 15
790 A82 $40000 green 8 5
791 A82 $50000 dp bl 10 5
792 A82 $100000 dl grn 10 5
793 A82 $200000 brn vio 15 5
794 A82 $300000 yel grn 45 5
795 A82 $500000 lil rose 45 8
796 A82 $1000000 claret 38 8
797 A82 $2000000 vermilion 90 15
798 A82 $3000000 ol bis 1.50 25
799 A82 $5000000 ultra 2.75 50
  Nos. 788-799 (12) 7.11 1.61

Zeros for "cents" omitted.

Early Ship and Modern Hai Tien — A92

Passenger Ship Kiang Ya — A93

1948, Aug. 16

Without Gum

800 A92 $20000 blue 6 10
801 A92 $30000 rose lil 6 10
802 A93 $40000 yel brn 6 15
803 A93 $60000 vermilion 6 15

Issued to commemorate the 75th anniversary of the China Merchants' Steam Navigation Company.

圓仟伍作改☆☆ 500000 ☆☆

Type of 1947-48 Surcharged in Black

1948 Unwmk. *Perf. 14*

804 A82 $4000 on $100 car 10 2.00
805 A82 $5000 on $100 car 6 8
806 A82 $8000 on $700 red brn 10 8

圓仟伍作改 5000.00

Stamps of 1942-46 Surcharged in Black or Red

1948 *Perf. 12½, 13*

807 A62 $5000 on $1 dl grn (#500) 8 8
808 A62 $5000 on $1 grn (#551) 2.75 3.50
809 A62 $5000 on $2 dk bl grn (#502) 8 10
810 A72 $10000 on $20 dp car (#625) 8 10
811 A62 $20000 on 10c dp grn (#492) 8 10
812 A62 $20000 on 50c sage grn (R) (#498) 8 10
813 A62 $30000 on 30c dl ver (#496) 8 10
  a. Perf. 10½ 15.00 15.00
  Nos. 807-813 (7) 3.23 4.08

圓仟伍萬壹作改 15000

Nos. 492, 556 and 558 Surcharged in Black or Carmine

1948

814 A62 $15,000 on 10c dp grn 12 15
815 A62 $15,000 on $4 vio brn 12 15
816 A62 $15,000 on $6 gray vio (C) 12 15

圓萬肆作改 40000

No. 498, 494 and 504 Surcharged in Black

1948 Unwmk. *Perf. 11½, 13*

817 A62 $15,000 on 50c sage grn 12 15
818 A62 $40,000 on 20c dk ol grn 12 15
  a. Perf. 11 6.50 6.50
819 A62 $60,000 on $4 red brn 12 15

Gold Yuan Surcharges

(Nos. 820-885E)

金圓 ½分

Stamps of 1942-47 Surcharged in Black, Carmine or Red

1948 *Perf. 14, 13, 11*

820 A62 ½c on 30c dl ver (#496) 8 *20*
821 A82 ½c on $500 bl grn (Bk) (#747) 8 10
822 A82 ½c on $500 bl grn (C) (#747) 8 10
823 A73 1c on $20 car (#636) 8 *50*
824 A62 2c on $1.50 dp bl (R) (#501) 8 *25*
825 A62 3c on $5 cer (#505) 8 *25*
826 A62 4c on $1 rose lake (#499) 8 *20*
827 A62 5c on 50c sage grn (#498) 8 10
  a. Perf. 11 3.50 3.50
  Nos. 820-827 (8) 64 1.70

On No. 820-827, the position of the surcharged denomination and "Gold Yuan" characters varies, the aim being to obliterate the original denomination.

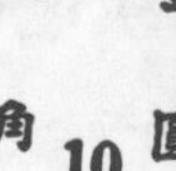

Stamps of 1940-48 Surcharged in Black, Violet, Carmine, Blue or Green

Perf. 12, 12½, 13, 14, 12½x13

1948-49

828 A63 5c on $20 rose (#571) 8 *15*
829 A72 5c on $30 dp bl (C) (#626) 8 50
  a. Double surch. 15.00
830 A57 10c on 2c ol grn (#368) 8 10
831 A39 10c on 2½c rose lil (#424) 8 12
832 A62 10c on 25c brn vio (V) (#495) 8 10
833 A63 10c on 40c brn red (#565) 6 *15*
834 A62 10c on $1 dl grn (#500) 6 10
834A A62 10c on $1 grn (#551) 40.00 40.00
835 A63 10c on $2 gray brn (#566) 8 10
836 A62 10c on $20 ultra (C) (#560) 8 12
836A A63 10c on $20 rose (#571) 40.00 40.00
837 A67 10c on $20 car (#592) 12 12
837A A73 10c on $20 car (#636) 50 75
838 A72 10c on $30 dp bl (C) (#626) 8 *25*
839 A63 10c on $70 rose vio (#573) 8 10
  a. Double surch. 12.00
840 A82 10c on $7000 lt red brn (#754) 20 20
841 A82 10c on $20,000 rose pink (#788) 8 *50*
842 A63 20c on $6 pale lil gray (#569) 8 10
843 A37 20c on $30 choc (#634) 8 *30*
844 A73 20c on $30 dk bl (C) (#637) 8 *50*
845 A73 20c on $100 dk car (#640) 8 *40*
  a. Inverted surch. 17.00
  b. Double surch. 12.50
846 A39 50c on ½c blk brn (#312) 17.50 18.00
847 A39 50c on ½c ol blk (#421) 8 10
  a. Inverted surch. 25.00
848 A62 50c on 20c dk ol grn (#494) 8 10
849 A62 50c on 30c dl ver (Bl) (#496) 8 *30*
850 A62 50c on 40c dk red brn (V) (#497) 8 *30*
  a. Perf. 11 4.50 5.25
851 A63 50c on 40c brn red (V) (#565) 8 10
852 A62 50c on $4 vio brn (#556) 8 *15*

853 A62 50c on $4 vio brn (Bl) (#556) 8 *30*
854 A62 50c on $20 dp ultra (C) (#560) 8 10
855 A67 50c on $20 car (V) (#592) 8 *20*
856 A73 50c on $20 car (#636) 8 10
857 A62 50c on $70 lil (C) (#562) 8 10
858 A82 50c on $6000 rose lil (#753) 20 25
859 A82 50c on $6000 rose lil (Bl) (#753) 12 15
860 A62 $1 on 30c choc (#550) 10 12
a. Perf. 11 40.00
861 A62 $1 on 40c dk red brn (#497) 8 12
a. Perf. 11 3.25 3.75
862 A62 $1 on $1 rose lake (#499) 8 10
863 A62 $1 on $5 car (#557) 8 10
864 A63 $2 on $2 gray brn (R) (#566) 8 10
865 A72 $2 on $20 dp car (#625) 8 10
866 A73 $2 on $100 dk car (#640) 8 10
867 A46 $5 on 17c brn ol (#432) 8 10
868 A63 $5 on $2 gray brn (#566) 10 12
869 A82 $5 on $3000 bl (C) (#750) 8 10
870 A47 $8 on 20c lt bl (#433) 8 *15*
871 A82 $8 on $30,000 choc (C) (#789) 10 12
872 A47 $10 on 40c org (#438) 20 10
873 A63 $10 on $2 gray brn (G) (#566) 8 10
874 A63 $10 on $2 gray brn (C) (#566) 10 12
875 A63 $20 on $2 gray brn (C) (#566) 10 12
875A A73 $20 on $20 car (#636) 1.25 80
876 A62 $50 on 30c dl ver (#496) 8 10
877 A63 $50 on $2 gray brn (Bl) (#566) 12 15
878 A73 $80 on $20 car (#636) 15 20
879 A62 $100 on $1 grn (#551) 15 20
a. Perf. 11 30.00
880 A63 $100 on $2 gray brn (C) (#566) 15 20
880A A82 $50,000 on $20,000 rose pink (#788) 45 40
880B A82 $100,000 on $30,000 choc (V) (#789) 50 40

Wmk. 261

881 A39 10c on 2½c rose lil (#405) 8 *50*
882 A39 50c on ½c ol blk (#402) 8 *50*
Nos. 828-882 (61) 105.27 110.13

Characters at left express the new value. Style of characters and numerals varies.

改作郵票
金圓伍佰圓
500⁰⁰

Nos. Q7 to Q9 Surcharged in Black or Carmine

1948 Unwmk. *Perf. 12½*

883 PP2 $200 on $3000 red org 10 10
884 PP2 $500 on $5000 dk bl (C) 10 12
885 PP2 $1000 on $10,000 vio 20 20

金圓
念萬圓
200000

Nos. 788-791 Surcharged in Gold Yuan in Red or Black at Foochow

1949, Apr. 30 Unwmk. *Perf. 14*

885A A82 $20,000 on $40,000 grn 3.50 3.50
885B A82 $50,000 on $30,000 choc (B) 3.50 4.25
885C A82 $100,000 on $20,000 rose pink (B) 3.50 3.50
885D A82 $200,000 on $40,000 grn 3.50 3.50
885E A82 $200,000 on $50,000 dp bl 3.50 4.25
Nos. 885A-885E (5) 17.50 19.00

Nos. 885A-885E were issued in Fukien Postal District.

Dr. Sun Yat-sen — A94

1949 Unwmk. Engr. *Perf. 14*
Without Gum

886 A94 $1 orange 5 5
887 A94 $10 green 5 5
888 A94 $20 vio brn 5 *10*
889 A94 $50 dk Prus grn 8 *10*
890 A94 $100 org brn 5 5
891 A94 $200 red org 6 6
892 A94 $500 rose lil 5 5
893 A94 $800 car rose 20 *30*
894 A94 $1000 blue 5 5

Redrawn
Engr.
Perf. 12½

894A A94 $10 green 20 *1.50*
b. Perf. 14 2.25 *2.75*
894C A94 $20 vio brn 10 10
d. Perf. 14 45 *1.25*
Nos. 886-894C (11) 94 2.41

Small "T" at left of necktie on Nos. 894A-894d.

Redrawn

1949 Litho. *Perf. 12½*
Without Gum

895 A94 $50 grnsh gray 10 *1.00*
896 A94 $100 dk org brn 5 *15*
897 A94 $200 org red 10 *1.00*
898 A94 $1000 dp bl 6 *20*
899 A94 $5000 lt bl 6 10
900 A94 $10,000 sepia 6 10
Nos. 895-900 (6) 43 2.55

Diagonal lines have been added to the background of the redrawn design.
See Nos. 945-958, 973-981.

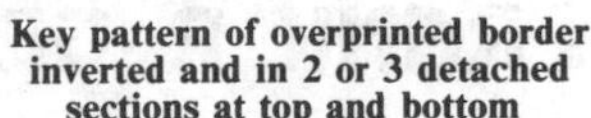

Plane, Train and Ship — A95

Two types, 50c on $20:
I. Thick numerals in "20." Vertical stroke in lower right corner of vignette. (Dah Tung Book Co.)
II. Thin "20." No vertical stroke in corner. (Central Trust.)

Two types, $2 on $50, $10 on $30, $100 on $50 and $300 on $50:
III. "Y" in lower right corner of vignette. (Dah Yeh Printing Co.)
IV. No "Y" in corner. (Dah Tung, Central Trust or Chung Ming.)

Two types, $50 on $300 and $1000 on $100:
V. Projection on left frame column below foliate ornament. (Dah Yeh Printing Co.)
VI. No projection. (Dah Tung Book Co.)

Gold Yuan Surcharge in Various Colors on Revenue Stamps

Lithographed; Nos. 923, 933, 935-936 Engraved

1949 *Perf. 12½, 13, 14*
Without Gum

915 A95 50c on $20 red brn, I (Bk) 8 5
a. 50c on $20 brn, II (Bk) 8 5
916 A95 $1 on $15 red org (Bk) 10 *30*
917 A95 $2 on $50 dk bl, IV (C) 8 *10*
d. Type III 25 *50*
917A A95 $3 on $50 dk bl (Bl) 8 6
917C A95 $3 on $50 dk bl (Bk) 8 5
918 A95 $5 on $500 brn (Dk Br) 8 5
919 A95 $10 on $30 dk vio, III (Bl) 8 5
a. Type IV 45 15
b. Dbl. surch., IV
920 A95 $15 on $20 org brn (Bl) 8 5
921 A95 $25 on $20 org brn (G) 8 5
922 A95 $50 on $50 dk bl (R O) 8 5
923 A95 $50 on $300 grn, VI (C) 8 5
a. $50 on $300 yel grn, V (C) 10 10
924 A95 $80 on $50 dk bl (Dk Br) 8 *20*
925 A95 $100 on $50 dk bl, IV (Bk) 8 5
a. Type III 1.25 *2.50*
926 A95 $200 on $50 dk bl (Bk) 8 5
927 A95 $200 on $500 brn (Bl) 20 15
928 A95 $300 on $50 dk bl, III (C) 15 *20*
a. Type IV 45 45
929 A95 $300 on $50 dk bl (Br) 50 45
930 A95 $500 on $15 red org (Bl) 20 20
931 A95 $500 on $30 dk vio (Bk) 20 20
932 A95 $1000 on $50 dk bl (C) 25 30
933 A95 $1000 on $100 ol grn, V (Bk) 25 *50*
a. Type VI 3.00 3.00
934 A95 $1500 on $50 dk bl (Bl) 1.25 1.25
935 A95 $2000 on $300 grn (Bl) 25 10
936 A95 $5000 on $100 ol grn (C) 150.00
Nos. 915-935 (23) 4.39 4.51

No. 936 was officially authorized, but never issued.

Key pattern of overprinted border inverted and in 2 or 3 detached sections at top and bottom

Litho.
Hankow Prints
Without Gum

937 A95 $50 on $10 sl grn (Bk) 3.00 3.00
938 A95 $100 on $10 sl grn (Bl) 4.50 4.50
939 A95 $500 on $10 sl grn (Bk) 4.50 3.75
940 A95 $1000 on $10 sl grn (Bl) 1.75 1.75
941 A95 $5000 on $20 red brn (Bl) 4.50 4.50
942 A95 $10,000 on $20 red brn (Bk) 4.50 4.50
943 A95 $50,000 on $20 red brn (Bl) 5.25 5.25
944 A95 $100,000 on $20 red brn (Bk) 6.00 6.00
944A A95 $500,000 on $20 red brn (Bl) 150.00 75.00
944B A95 $2,000,000 on $20 red brn (G) 250.00 125.00
944C A95 $5,000,000 on $20 red brn (Bl) 600.00 150.00
Nos. 937-944C (11) 1,034. 383.25

The basic revenue stamps of Nos. 915-944C were the work of several printers. There are three main types, differing in the bottom label. Nos. 922 and 925 are in a second type: Nos. 923 and 930 in a third. Varieties of paper, color and overprint exist.
Counterfeits exist of Nos. 944A-944C.

Type of 1949 Redrawn

1949 Without Gum *Perf. 12½*

945 A94 $500 rose lil 7 12
946 A94 $2000 violet 8 15
947 A94 $20,000 ap grn 8 15
948 A94 $50,000 rose pink 15 25
949 A94 $80,000 brn red 90 1.00
950 A94 $100,000 bl grn 50 40
Nos. 945-950 (6) 1.78 2.07

Zeros for "cents" omitted on No. 950.

Redrawn Coarse Impression

1949 Litho.
Without Gum
Size: 18¼x20¾mm.

951 A94 $50 green 60 1.25
952 A94 $1000 dp bl 50 60
953 A94 $5000 carmine 60 60
954 A94 $10,000 brown 75 1.25
955 A94 $20,000 orange 60 90
956 A94 $50,000 blue 60 50
957 A94 $200,000 violet 75 1.25
958 A94 $500,000 vio brn 75 50
Nos. 951-958 (8) 5.15 6.85

Zeros for "cents" omitted on Nos. 957-958.

Locomotive and Ship — A96

1949, May 1 Litho. *Perf. 12½*
Without Gum

959 A96 orange 85 40
a. Rouletted 2.75 1.75

Nos. 959, C62, E12 and F2 were printed without denomination and sold at the daily rate of the yuan. This was necessitated by the gold yuan inflation.

Revenue Stamps Overprinted in Black

1949, May *Perf. 12½, 13, 14*

Without Gum

960 A95	$30 dk vio		85.00	50.00

Engr.

961 A95	$200 vio brn		10.00	7.50
962 A95	$500 dk grn		10.00	7.50

A similar overprint appears on Nos. C63, E13 and F3, differing in second and third characters of bottom row.

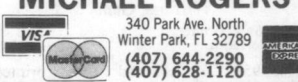

Silver Yuan Surcharge in Various Colors

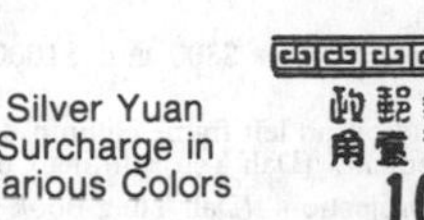

1949 **Litho.**

963	A95	1c on $5000 brn (G)	90	1.10
964	A95	4c on $100 ol grn (Bl)	38	45
965	A95	4c on $3000 org (Bk)	38	45
966	A95	10c on $50 dk bl (RV)	60	75
967	A95	10c on $1000 car (Bk)	60	38
a.		Inverted surch.	55.00	
968	A95	20c on $1000 red (V)	60	90
b.		Inverted surch.	24.00	
968A	A95	50c on $30 dk vio (C)	75	90
969	A95	50c on $50 dk bl (C)	1.40	90
970	A95	$1 on $50 dk bl (Bk)	1.00	75
		Nos. 963-970 (9)	6.61	6.58

Nos. 963-965 and 967 are engraved.

Sun Type of 1949 Redrawn
Coarse Impression

1949 *Perf. 12½, 13 or Compound*

973 A94	1c ap grn		1.75	60
974 A94	2c orange		1.10	60
975 A94	4c bl grn		10	10
976 A94	10c dp lil		10	30
977 A94	16c org red		60	*1.75*
978 A94	20c blue		38	38
979 A94	50c dk brn		1.75	*3.75*
980 A94	100c dp bl		150.00	140.00
981 A94	500c scarlet		175.00	165.00
	Nos. 973-981 (9)		330.78	312.48

Flying Geese Over Globe
A97

Pigeons, Globe and Wreath
A98

1949, May **Litho.** *Perf. 12½*

Without Gum

984 A97	$1 brn org	3.75	2.50
985 A97	$2 blue	7.50	3.00
986 A97	$5 car rose	11.00	6.25
987 A97	$10 bl grn	22.50	8.00

Five other denominations - 10c, 16c, 50c, $20 and $50 - were also printed at Shanghai, but were not issued.

Engraved and Typographed

1949, Aug. 1 Without Gum *Imperf.*

988 A98	$1 org red & blk	3.50	4.25

Issued to commemorate the 75th anniversary of the formation of the Universal Postal Union.

Exists with black denomination omitted.

Summer Palace, Peiping — A99

Bronze Bull and Kunming Lake — A100

Engraved and Typographed

1949, Aug. *Rouletted*

Without Gum

989 A99	15c org brn & grn	25	*1.00*
990 A100	40c dl grn & car	35	*1.00*
a.	2nd and 3rd characters at top transposed	60.00	75.00

Silver Yuan Surcharge in Black on 1949 Sun Yat-sen Issues

1949 *Perf. 12½, 14*

991 A94	1c on $100 org brn (890)	3.25	3.25
992 A94	1c on $100 dk org brn (896)	3.25	3.25
993 A94	2½c on $500 rose lil (892)	3.75	3.75
a.	Inverted surch.	24.00	
994 A94	2½c on $500 rose lil (945)	3.75	3.75
995 A94	15c on $10 grn (887)	7.50	5.00
a.	Inverted surch.	27.50	
996 A94	15c on $20 vio brn (894C)	12.00	7.50
	Nos. 991-996 (6)	33.50	26.50

Silver Yuan Surcharge in Black or Carmine

5 伍分

997 A94	2½c on $50 grn (951)	90	60
998 A94	2½c on $50,000 bl (956)	90	60
999 A94	5c on $1000 dp bl (952) (C)	1.25	90
1000 A94	5c on $20,000 org (955)	1.25	90
1001 A94	5c on $200,000 vio (957) (C)	1.25	1.25
1002 A94	5c on $500,000 vio brn (958)	1.25	1.25
1003 A94	10c on $5000 car (953)	1.75	2.00
1004 A94	10c on $10,000 brn (954)	1.75	1.75
1005 A94	15c on $200 red org (891)	3.00	3.00
1006 A94	25c on $100 dk org brn (896)	6.75	5.00
	Nos. 997-1006 (10)	20.05	17.25

REPUBLIC OF CHINA

(Taiwan)

LOCATION — Taiwan (since 1949) (Formosa)
GOVT. — Republic
AREA — 13,892 sq. mi.
POP. — 16,700,000 (est. 1978)
CAPITAL — Taipei

Stamps issued and used in Taiwan after Chinese Communist forces occupied the Chinese mainland include Taiwan Nos. 91-96, 101-103, J10-J17.

Type of 1949 with Value Omitted Surcharged in Various Colors

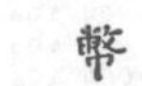

1950, Jan. 1 Unwmk. *Perf. 12½*

1007 A97	$1 grn (Bk)	15.00	2.50
1008 A97	$2 grn (C)	30.00	6.50
1009 A97	$5 grn (V)	450.00	25.00
1010 A97	$10 grn (Br)	400.00	80.00
1011 A97	$20 grn (Dk Bl)	900.00	400.00
	Nos. 1007-1011 (5)	1,795.	514.00

Two printings of the $1 and $2 show minor differences.

Cheng Ch'eng-kung (Koxinga) — A101

1950, June 26 Typo. *Rouletted*

Without Gum

1012 A101	3c dk gray grn	50	20
1013 A101	10c org brn	50	10
1014 A101	15c org yel	7.50	1.50
1015 A101	20c emerald	1.25	15
1016 A101	30c claret	16.00	8.00
1017 A101	40c red org	1.75	15
1018 A101	50c chocolate	4.00	30
1019 A101	80c carmine	4.00	1.50
1020 A101	$1 ultra	4.50	15
1021 A101	$1.50 green	12.50	1.25
1022 A101	$1.60 blue	16.00	75
1023 A101	$2 red vio	21.00	75
1024 A101	$5 aqua	62.50	5.25
	Nos. 1012-1024 (13)	152.00	20.05

Part perforate pairs exist of the 10c, 20c, and 80c.

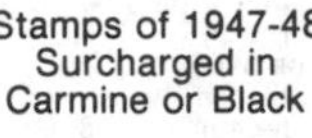

Stamps of 1947-48 Surcharged in Carmine or Black

1950, Mar. 25 *Perf. 14*

1025 A82	3c on $30,000 choc	2.00	2.00
1026 A82	3c on $40,000 grn (C)	2.00	2.00
1027 A82	3c on $50,000 dp bl (C)	2.50	2.50
1028 A82	5c on $200,000 brn vio	2.50	2.00
1029 A82	10c on $4000 gray	5.00	4.00
a.	Inverted surch.	60.00	
1030 A82	10c on $6000 rose lil	8.00	4.00
a.	Inverted surch.	140.00	
1031 A82	10c on $20,000 rose pink	8.00	4.00
1032 A82	10c on $2,000,000 ver	8.00	4.00
a.	Inverted surch	85.00	
1033 A82	20c on $500,000 lil rose	8.00	4.00
a.	Inverted surch.	110.00	
1034 A82	20c on $1,000,000 cl	10.00	7.00
a.	Inverted surch.	110.00	
1035 A82	30c on $3,000,000 ol bis	12.00	9.00
1036 A82	50c on $5,000,000 ultra (C)	20.00	9.50
	Nos. 1025-1036 (12)	88.00	54.00

Allegory of Election — A102

Perf. 12x12½, Imperf.

1951, Mar. 20 Engr. Unwmk.

Without Gum

1037 A102	40c carmine	3.00	45
a.	Horiz. pair, imperf. btwn.	60.00	
1038 A102	$1 dp bl	6.00	1.25
1039 A102	$1.60 purple	9.00	2.00
1040 A102	$2 brown	14.00	3.50

Adoption of local self-government in Taiwan.

Souvenir Sheet
Imperf

1041 A102 $2 dp bl grn 55.00 55.00

Marginal inscriptions publicize Postal Commemorative Day, Mar. 20, 1951. Size: 100x71 mm.

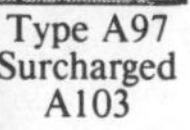

Type A97 Surcharged
A103

Farmer and Scroll Announcing Tax Reduction
A104

Surcharge in Various Colors

1951, July 19 ***Perf. 12½***
Without Gum

1042 A103 $5 grn (R Br) 17.50 4.50
1043 A103 $10 grn (Bk) 45.00 5.00
1044 A103 $20 grn (R) 200.00 20.00
1045 A103 $50 grn (P) 350.00 40.00

1952, Jan. 1 ***Imperf., Perf 14***
Without Gum

1046 A104 20c red org 3.50 1.75
1047 A104 40c dk grn 7.00 2.50
1048 A104 $1 brown 9.50 6.00
1049 A104 $1.40 dp bl 15.00 5.00
1050 A104 $2 dk gray 27.50 17.50
1051 A104 $5 brn car 35.00 10.00
Nos. 1046-1051 (6) 97.50 42.75

Land tax reduction of 37.5% in Taiwan.

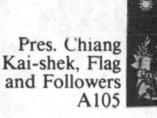

Pres. Chiang Kai-shek, Flag and Followers
A105

Imperf., Perf. 14

1952, Mar. 1 **Unwmk.**
Without Gum
Flag in Violet Blue and Carmine

1052 A105 40c rose car 4.00 60
a. Vert. pair, imperf. btwn. 60.00
1053 A105 $1 dp grn 8.00 2.00
1054 A105 $1.60 brn org 15.00 1.50
a. Horiz. pair, imperf. btwn. 125.00
1055 A105 $2 brt bl 25.00 6.00
1056 A105 $5 vio brn 30.00 3.00
Nos. 1052-1056 (5) 82.00 13.10

Issued to commemorate the 2nd anniversary of Chiang Kai-shek's return to the presidency.
See Nos. 1064-1069.

Nos. 975, 976, 978 and 979 Surcharged in Black

叁 臺
分 幣
3

1952 ***Perf. 12½***

1057 A94 3c on 4c bl grn 1.75 1.00
1058 A94 3c on 10c dp lil 1.75 1.00
a. Inverted surch.
1059 A94 3c on 20c bl 1.75 1.00
1060 A94 3c on 50c dk brn 1.75 1.00

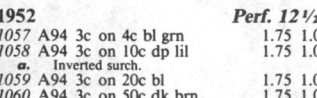

Geese Type of 1949 with Value Omitted Surcharged

圓拾壹幣

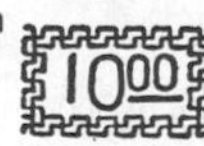

1952, Dec. 8

1061 A97 $10 grn (P) 40.00 7.50
1062 A97 $20 grn (R) 150.00 15.00
1063 A97 $50 grn (Bk) 850.00 650.00

Chiang Type of 1952
Redrawn
Perf. 12½

1953, Mar. 1 **Engr.** **Unwmk.**
Without Gum
Flag in Dark Blue & Carmine

1064 A105 10c red org 5.50 50
1065 A105 20c green 5.50 50
1066 A105 40c rose pink 10.00 75
1067 A105 $1.40 blue 18.00 1.00
1068 A105 $2 brown 25.00 2.00
1069 A105 $5 rose vio 50.00 3.00
Nos. 1064-1069 (6) 114.00 7.75

Third anniversary of Chiang Kai-shek's return to presidency.
Many differences in redrawn design. Price, imperf. set, $114.

Nos. 1020, 1014, 1016 and 1022 Surcharged in Various Colors

3 叁
cts. 分

1953-54 ***Rouletted***

1070 A101 3c on $1 ultra (C) 1.50 25
1070A A101 10c on 15c org yel (G) ('54) 13.00 60
1071 A101 10c on 30c cl (Bl) 1.50 30
1072 A101 20c on $1.60 bl (Bk) 1.50 30

Chinese characters and ornamental device at bottom differ on each value.

Nurse and Patients — A106

1953, July 1 **Litho.** ***Perf. 12½***
Without Gum
Cross in Red, Burelage Color in Italics

1073 A106 40c brn, *buff* 6.00 1.00
1074 A106 $1.60 bl, *bl* 9.00 80
1075 A106 $2 grn, *yel* 22.50 1.25
1076 A106 $5 red org, *org* 30.00 4.50

Issued to honor the Chinese Anti-Tuberculosis Association.

Pres. Chiang Kai-shek — A107

1953, Oct. 31 **Engr.**
Without Gum

1077 A107 10c dk brn 75 25
1078 A107 20c lilac 2.25 25
1079 A107 40c dp grn 2.25 15
1080 A107 50c dp pink 2.25 40
1081 A107 80c brn bis 12.50 5.50
1082 A107 $1 dp ol grn 5.75 35
1083 A107 $1.40 dp bl 10.00 70
1084 A107 $1.60 dp car 12.50 55
1085 A107 $1.70 ap grn 7.50 5.00
1086 A107 $2 brown 8.00 35
1087 A107 $3 dk bl 45.00 12.50
1088 A107 $4 aqua 18.00 1.10
1089 A107 $5 red org 9.00 1.40
1090 A107 $10 dk grn 16.00 2.25
1091 A107 $20 dk brn lake 45.00 5.50
a. Souvenir folder 50.00
Nos. 1077-1091 (15) 196.75 36.25

67th birthday of Pres. Chiang Kai-shek.
No. 1091a contains Nos. 1077-1091 imperf., arranged in 3 sheets of 5 stamps each.

Silo Highway Bridge
A108

Forest of Evergreens
A109

Design: $1.60 and $5, Silo bridge, side view.

1954, Jan. 28 **Unwmk.** ***Perf. 12½***
Without Gum
Various Frames

1092 A108 40c vermilion 2.00 50
1093 A108 $1.60 bl vio 27.50 1.00
1094 A108 $3.60 sepia 11.00 2.00
1095 A108 $5 magenta 35.00 3.00
a. Souv. sheet 60.00

Opening of Silo bridge, 1st anniversary.
No. 1095a contains one each of Nos. 1092-1095 imperforate.

1954, Mar. 12 ***Perf. 12x12½***

Design: $10, Nursery.

Without Gum

1096 A109 40c bl grn 12.00 75
1097 A109 $10 red vio 35.00 4.50

Issued to publicize forest conservation.

Runner
A110

Globe, Bridge and Ship
A111

1954, Mar. 29
Without Gum

1098 A110 40c dp ultra 12.00 1.25
1099 A110 $5 carmine 35.00 6.00

Issued to publicize 11th Youth Day, March 29, 1954.

1954, Oct. 21 ***Perf. 12***
Without Gum

1100 A111 40c red org 12.00 30
1101 A111 $5 dp bl 8.00 1.50

Issued to publicize the second Overseas Chinese Day, October 21, 1954.

Ex-Prisoner with Broken Chains — A112

Designs: $1, Ex-prisoner with torch and flag, UN emblem. $1.60, Torch and date.

1955, Jan. 23

1102 A112 40c bl grn 2.00 40
a. Vert. pair, imperf. btwn. 150.00
1103 A112 $1 sepia 15.00 2.50
1104 A112 $1.60 lake 20.00 2.25

Issued to honor anti-Communist Chinese prisoners who fought with the North Korean army, released January 23, 1955.

Certain countries cancel stamps in full sheets and sell them (usually with gum) for less than face value. Dealers generally sell "CTO".

Nos. 1019-1021, 1017 Surcharged in Brown, Blue or Green:

分 叁   角 壹
0.10
a   b

角 貳
0.20
c

1955 ***Rouletted***

1105 A101(a) 3c on $1 ultra (Br) 2.00 60
1106 A101(b) 10c on 80c car (Bl) 2.00 60
1107 A101(b) 10c on $1.50 grn (Bl) 2.00 60
1108 A101(c) 20c on 40c red org (G) 2.00 60

Hand Planting Evergreen Tree — A113

Chiang Kai-shek, Flags, Building
A114

Design: $50, Seedling and map of Taiwan.

1955, Apr. 1 ***Perf. 12***
Without Gum

1109 A113 $20 dp car 14.00 1.50
1110 A113 $50 blue 30.00 6.00

Issued to publicize forest conservation.

1955, May 20 **Engr.** ***Perf. 12***
Without Gum

1111 A114 20c olive 1.50 10
1112 A114 40c bl grn 2.00 10
1113 A114 $2 car rose 5.00 60
1114 A114 $7 dp ultra 8.50 1.25
a. Souvenir sheet of 4 22.50 22.50

No. 1114a contains one each of Nos. 1111-1114, imperforate, with ornamental border typographed in red.
First anniversary of Pres. Chiang Kai-shek's re-election.

Armed Forces Emblem — A115

1955, Sept. 3
Without Gum

1115 A115 40c dk bl 1.75 20
1116 A115 $2 org ver 12.50 60
1117 A115 $7 bl grn 11.50 1.25
a. Sheet of three 35.00 35.00

Armed Forces Day, Sept. 3.
No. 1117a measures 147x104mm. and contains one each of Nos. 1115-1117.

Nos. 1017, 1018 and C64 Surcharged in Magenta

角 貳

0.20

1955 **Typo.** ***Rouletted***

1118 A101 20c on 40c red org 2.25 60

1119 A101 20c on 50c choc 2.25 60
1120 AP6 20c on 60c dp bl 2.25 60

Flags of U.N. and China A116

1955, Oct. 24 Engr. *Perf. 11½*
Without Gum

1121 A116 40c dk bl 1.75 20
1122 A116 $2 dk car rose 6.00 60
1123 A116 $7 sl grn 7.25 1.25

Issued to commemorate the tenth anniversary of the United Nations, Oct. 24, 1955.

Pres. Chiang Kai-shek A117 | Birthplace of Sun Yat-sen A118

1955, Oct. 31 Photo. *Perf. 13½*

1124 A117 40c dk bl, red & brn 1.75 20
1125 A117 $2 grn, red & dk bl 5.00 60
1126 A117 $7 brn, red & grn 6.75 1.25
a. Souvenir sheet of 3 17.50 17.50

69th birthday of Pres. Chiang Kai-shek.
No. 1126a measures 147x105 mm. and contains one each of Nos. 1124-1126, imperf.

1955, Nov. 12 Engr. *Perf. 12*
Without Gum

1127 A118 40c blue 1.75 20
1128 A118 $2 red brn 4.00 75
1129 A118 $7 rose lake 7.00 1.25

90th anniversary, birth of Sun Yat-sen.

角貳

No. 959a Surcharged in Bright Green

0.20

1956 Litho. *Rouletted*

1130 A96 20c on org 45 15

See No. 1213.

China Map and Transportation Methods — A119

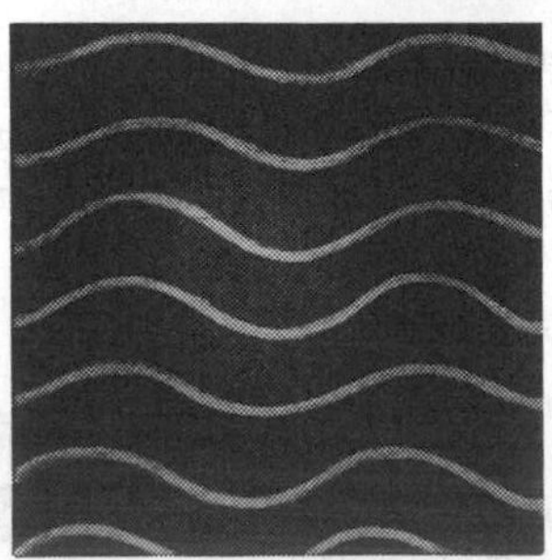

Wmk. 281

Wmk. Wavy Lines (281)
1956, Mar. 20 Engr. *Perf. 12*
Without Gum

1131 A119 40c dk car 60 15
1132 A119 $1 int blk 1.10 45
1133 A119 $1.60 chocolate 2.25 20
1134 A119 $2 dk grn 3.00 45

Issued to commemorate the 60th anniversary of the founding of the modern Chinese postal system.

Souvenir Sheets
Imperf

1135 A119 $2 magenta 6.25 6.25
1136 A119 $2 red 6.25 6.25

Issued for the exhibition for the 60th anniversary of the modern Chinese postal system, March 20, 1956.
Nos. 1135-36 measure 148x103mm. Marginal floral design and inscription in red and silver (No. 1135), and red and gold (No. 1136).

Children at Play — A120

Early and Modern Locomotives A121

1956, Apr. 4 Unwmk. *Perf. 12*
Without Gum

1137 A120 40c emerald 60 10
1138 A120 $1.60 dk bl 1.50 20
1139 A120 $2 dk car 2.00 70

Children's Day, Apr. 4, 1956.

1956, June 9 Wmk. 281 (vert.)
Without Gum

1140 A121 40c rose car 1.25 10
1141 A121 $2 blue 1.75 15
1142 A121 $8 green 5.00 80

75th anniversary of Chinese Railroads.

Pres. Chiang Kai-shek
A122 A123

A124

Various Portraits of Chiang
Perf. 14½x13½, 14½ (A123), 13½x14½

1956, Oct. 31 Photo. Unwmk.

1143 A122 20c red org 75 10
1144 A122 40c car rose 1.20 10
1145 A123 $1 brt ultra 1.50 20
1146 A123 $1.60 red lil 2.00 20
1147 A124 $2 red brn 4.00 25
1148 A124 $8 brt grnsh bl 9.00 1.00
Nos. 1143-1148 (6) 18.45 1.85

Issued in honor of the 70th birthday of Pres. Chiang Kai-shek.

Types of Special Delivery, Air Post and Registration Stamps of 1949 Surcharged in Black or Maroon

分叁 分叁

a b

c

0.10

1956 Unwmk. Litho. *Rouletted*
Without Gum

1150 SD2(a) 3c red vio 85 20
a. Perf. 12½ 1.50 60
1151 AP5(b) 3c bl grn (M) 85 20
1152 R2(c) 10c brt red 85 20

Telecommunications Emblem and Radio Tower — A125

Wmk. 281
1956, Dec. 28 Engr. *Perf. 12*
Without Gum

1153 A125 40c dp ultra 20 10
1154 A125 $1.40 carmine 40 10
1155 A125 $1.60 dk grn 50 10
1156 A125 $2 chocolate 2.75 30

Issued to commemorate the 75th anniversary of the founding of the Chinese telegraph service.

Map of China A126 | Mother Instructing Mencius A127

Pin Perf., Perf. 12x12½
1957 Litho. Wmk. 281
Without Gum

1157 A126 3c brt bl 45 6
1158 A126 10c violet 45 10
1159 A126 20c red org 45 10
1160 A126 40c rose red 45 10

Unwmk.

1161 A126 $1 org brn 80 10
1162 A126 $1.60 green 1.25 20
Nos. 1157-1162 (6) 3.85 66

Map inscription reads: "Recovery of Mainland."
See Nos. 1177-1182.

Unwmk.
1957, May 12 Engr. *Perf. 12*

Design: $3, Mother tattooing Yueh Fei.

Without Gum

1163 A127 40c green 50 20
1164 A127 $3 redsh brn 1.25 35

Issued to honor Mother's Day, 1957.

Badge of Chinese Boy Scouts A128

1957, Aug. 11
Without Gum

1165 A128 40c lilac 25 10
1166 A128 $1 green 45 15
1167 A128 $1.60 dk bl 65 20

Issued to commemorate the centenary of the birth of Lord Baden-Powell and to publicize the World Scout Jubilee Jamboree, England, Aug. 1-12.

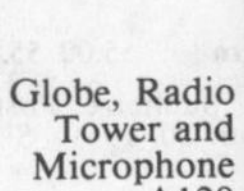

Globe, Radio Tower and Microphone A129

1957, Sept. 16
Without Gum

1168 A129 40c vermilion 25 10
1169 A129 50c brt rose lil 45 20
1170 A129 $3.50 dk bl 1.10 35

Issued to commemorate the 30th anniversary of Chinese broadcasting.

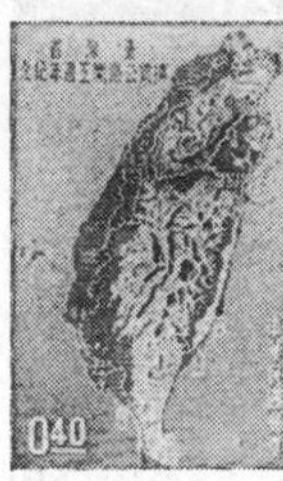

Map of Taiwan — A130

1957, Oct. 26
Without Gum

1171 A130 40c bl grn 45 10
1172 A130 $1.40 lt ultra 1.15 35
1173 A130 $2 gray 1.50 40

Issued to commemorate the start of construction on the Cross Island Highway, Taiwan.

Freighter "Hai Min" and River Boat "Kiang Foo" A131

1957, Dec. 16 Engr. *Perf. 12*
Without Gum

1174 A131 40c dp ultra 25 10
1175 A131 80c rose lake 60 15
1176 A131 $2.80 vermilion 1.50 50

Issued to commemorate the 85th anniversary of the establishment of the China Merchants Steam Navigation Co.

Type of 1957
Pin Perf., Perf. 12x12½
1957, Dec. 25 Typo. Unwmk.
Without Gum
Dark Blue Frames

1177 A126 3c brt bl 30 10
1178 A126 10c violet 30 15
1179 A126 20c brick red 30 15
1180 A126 40c rose red 70 25
1181 A126 $1 dp org brn 70 15
1182 A126 $1.60 dp grn 1.00 15
Nos. 1177-1182 (6) 3.30 95

Butterfly A132 | Mme. Chiang Kai-shek Orchid A133

Perf. 13½
1958, Mar. 20 Unwmk. Photo.
Various Insects in Natural Colors

1183 A132 10c pale grn, grn & blk 40 10
1184 A132 40c lem, pink, grn & blk 40 15
1185 A132 $1 yel grn & mar 55 15
1186 A132 $1.40 yel, org & blk 75 20

1187 A132 $1.60 pale brn & dk pur 80 20
1188 A132 $2 brt yel, org & blk 1.00 30
Nos. 1183-1188 (6) 3.90 1.10

1958, Mar. 20

Orchids: 20c, Formosan Wilson (horiz.). $1.40, Klotzsch. $3, Fitzgerald (horiz.).

Orchids in Natural Colors

1189 A133 20c chocolate 30 15
1190 A133 40c purple 45 15
1191 A133 $1.40 dk vio brn 60 25
1192 A133 $3 dk bl 90 50

World Health Organization Emblem — A134

1958, May 28 Engr. *Perf. 12*
Without Gum

1193 A134 40c dk bl 15 10
1194 A134 $1.60 brick red 40 10
1195 A134 $2 dp red lil 75 30

Issued to commemorate the 10th anniversary of the World Health Organization.

President's Mansion, Taipei — A135

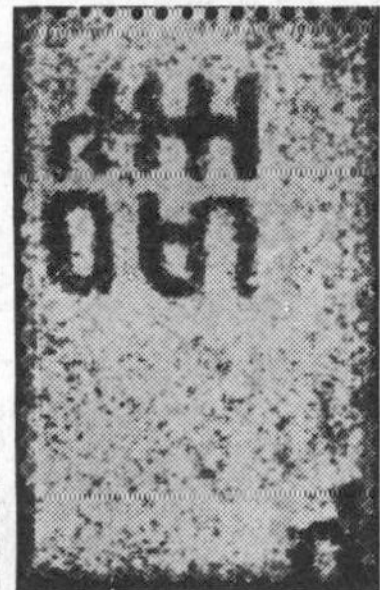

Wmk. 323 - (found with "Yu" in various arrangements)

Wmk. Seal Character "Yu" (323)
1958, Sept. 20 Engr. *Perf. 12*
Without Gum

1196 A135 $10 bl grn 4.25 10
a. Granite paper ('63) 3.75 10
1197 A135 $20 car rose 6.00 30
a. Granite paper ('63) 5.75 10
1198 A135 $50 red brn 25.00 1.75
1199 A135 $100 dk bl 42.50 3.50

See Nos. 1349-1351.

Taiwan Farm Scene A136

1958, Oct. 1 Unwmk.
Without Gum

1200 A136 20c emerald 18 8
1201 A136 40c black 18 8
1202 A136 $1.40 brt mag 70 10
1203 A136 $3 ultra 1.75 40

Issued to commemorate the tenth anniversary of the Joint Commission on Rural Reconstruction.

Pres. Chiang Kai-shek A137

1958, Oct. 31 Photo. *Perf. 13½*
Without Gum

1204 A137 40c multi 55 15

Issued to honor Pres. Chiang Kai-shek on his 72nd birthday.

UNESCO Building, Paris A138

1958, Nov. 3 Engr. *Perf. 12*
Without Gum

1205 A138 20c dk bl 12 8
1206 A138 40c green 18 8
1207 A138 $1.40 org ver 70 10
1208 A138 $3 red lil 1.00 40

Issued to commemorate the opening of UNESCO (U. N. Educational, Scientific and Cultural Organization) Headquarters in Paris, Nov. 3.

Flame from Liberty Torch Encircling Globe — A139

1958, Dec. 10 Unwmk.
Without Gum

1209 A139 40c green 12 8
1210 A139 60c gray brn 18 8
1211 A139 $1 carmine 50 15
1212 A139 $3 ultra 1.00 40

Issued to commemorate the tenth anniversary of the signing of the Universal Declaration of Human Rights.

0.20
角貳

No. 959a Surcharged in Bright Green

Rouletted
1958, Dec. 11 Litho. Unwmk.
Without Gum

1213 A196 20c on org 30 10

Ballot Box, Scales and Constitution A140

1958, Dec. 25 Engr. *Perf. 12*
Without Gum

1214 A140 40c green 18 8
1215 A140 50c dl pur 25 8
1216 A140 $1.40 car rose 75 15
1217 A140 $3.50 dk bl 1.25 50

Issued to commemorate the 10th anniversary of the adoption of the constitution.

Chu Kwang Tower, Quemoy — A141

1959-60 Wmk. 323 Litho. *Perf. 12*
Without Gum

1218 A141 3c orange 12 5
1218A A141 5c lt yel grn ('60) 12 8
1219 A141 10c lilac 12 5
1220 A141 20c ultra 12 5
1221 A141 40c brown 20 5
1222 A141 50c bluish grn 35 5
1223 A141 $1 rose red 55 5
1224 A141 $1.40 yel grn 75 5
1225 A141 $2 gray grn 75 8
1226 A141 $2.80 rose pink 1.50 8
1227 A141 $3 sl bl 1.50 9
Nos. 1218-1227 (11) 6.08 68

See Nos. 1270-1283.

ILO Emblem and Headquarters, Geneva A142

1959, June 15 Engr. *Perf. 12*
Without Gum

1228 A142 40c blue 12 6
1229 A142 $1.60 dk brn 30 6
1230 A142 $3 brt bl grn 60 15
1231 A142 $5 org ver 1.50 40

Issued to commemorate the 40th anniversary of the International Labor Organization.

Bugler and Tents A143

1959, July 8 Unwmk.
Without Gum

1232 A143 40c carmine 20 10
1233 A143 50c dk bl 60 15
1234 A143 $5 green 1.50 50

Issued to publicize the 10th World Boy Scout Jamboree, at Makiling National Park, Philippines, July 17-26.

Inscribed Stone, Mt. Tai-wu, Quemoy — A144

Map of Taiwan Straits A145

1959, Sept. 3 Engr. *Perf. 12*
Without Gum

1235 A144 40c brown 20 10
1236 A145 $1.40 ultra 50 15
1237 A145 $2 green 1.10 30
1238 A144 $3 dk bl 1.40 40

Defense of Quemoy and Matsu islands.

Pigeons Circling Globe A146

1959, Oct. 4
Without Gum

1239 A146 40c blue 15 10
1240 A146 $1 rose car 30 15
1241 A146 $2 gray brn 50 10
1242 A146 $3.50 red org 1.10 40

Issued for International Letter Writing Week, Oct. 4-10.

National Taiwan Science Hall, Taipei — A147

Design: $3, Front view.

1959, Nov. 12 Photo. *Perf. 13x13½*

1243 A147 40c multi 85 15
1244 A147 $3 multi 1.75 45

Emblem A148

1959, Dec. 7 Engr. *Perf. 12*
Without Gum

1245 A148 40c bl grn 25 10
1246 A148 $1.60 red lil 60 15
1247 A148 $3 orange 1.00 30

Issued to commemorate the 10th anniversary of the International Confederation of Free Trade Unions.

Sun Yat-sen, Lincoln and Flags A149

Perf. 13½, 12
1959, Dec. 25 Photo. Unwmk.

1248 A149 40c multi 30 15
1249 A149 $3 multi 40 25

Issued to honor Sun Yat-sen and Abraham Lincoln as "Leaders of Democracy."

Mailman on Motorcycle Delivering Night Mail A150

Postal Launch A151

1960, Mar. 20 Engr. *Perf. 11½*
Without Gum

1250 A150 $1.40 dk vio brn 80 15
1251 A151 $1.60 ultra 1.10 20

Issued to publicize the Prompt Delivery Service.

WRY Uprooted Oak Emblem — A152

1960, Apr. 7 Photo. *Perf. 13*

1252 A152 40c blk, red brn & emer 35 10
1253 A152 $3 blk, red org & grn 75 30

Issued to publicize World Refugee Year, July 1, 1959-June 30, 1960.

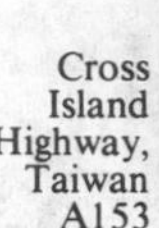

Cross Island Highway, Taiwan A153

Design: $1, $2, Road through tunnel (vert.).

Perf. 11½

1960, May 9 Engr. Unwmk.
Without Gum

1254 A153 40c green 40 10
1255 A153 $1 dk bl 1.25 40
1256 A153 $2 brn vio 50 20
1257 A153 $3 brown 1.75 25
a. Souv. sheet of 2, wmk. 323 30.00 30.00

Issued to commemorate the opening of the Cross Island Highway, Taiwan.

No. 1257a contains imperf. copies of Nos. 1255 and 1257, with multicolored pictorial background and marginal inscriptions in red. Size: 144x103mm.

Red Overprint on Nos. 1237-1238 Chinese and English: "Welcome U.S. President Dwight D. Eisenhower 1960"

1960, June 18 Unwmk. *Perf. 12*

1258 A145 $2 green 50 15
a. Invtd. ovpt. 205.00 200.00
1259 A144 $3 dk bl 1.00 40

Issued to commemorate President Eisenhower's visit to China, June 18, 1960.

Phonopost — A154

1960, June 27
Without Gum

1260 A154 $2 red org 80 20

Issued to publicize the Phonopost Service of the Chinese armed forces.

Two Horses and Groom, by Han Kan — A155

Paintings from Palace Museum, Taichung: $1, Two Riders, by Wei Yen. $1.60, Flowers and Birds by Hsiao Yung (vert.). $2, Pair of Mandarin Ducks by Monk Hui Ch'ung.

1960, Aug. 4 Photo. *Perf. 13*

1261 A155 $1 ol gray, blk & brn 1.10 30
1262 A155 $1.40 bis brn, blk & fawn 1.25 30
1263 A155 $1.60 multi 1.75 40
1264 A155 $2 beige, blk & gray grn 3.25 75

Chinese paintings, 7th-11th centuries.

Youth Corps Flag and Summer Activities A156

Reforestation A157

Design: $3, similar to 50c (horiz.).

1960, Aug. 20 Engr. *Perf. 12*
Without Gum

1265 A156 50c sl grn 40 10
1266 A156 $3 cop brn 1.40 40

Summer activities of China Youth Corps.

1960, Aug. 29 Photo. *Perf. 13½x13*

Designs: $2, Protection of forest. $3, Timber industry.

1267 A157 $1 multi 60 10
1268 A157 $2 multi 1.50 40
1269 A157 $3 multi 1.50 40
a. Souvenir sheet of 3 2.25 2.25

Issued to commemorate the Fifth World Forestry Congress, Seattle, Washington, Aug. 29-Sept. 10.

No. 1269a contains Nos. 1267-1269 assembled as a triptych, 65½x40mm. and imperf., but with simulated black perforations. Marginal inscriptions in carmine. Size of sheet: 99x144½mm.

Chu Kwang Tower, Quemoy A158

Diver A159

1960-61 Wmk. 323 Litho. *Perf. 12*
Without Gum

1270 A158 3c lt red brn 15 5
1271 A158 40c pale vio 15 5
1272 A158 50c org ('61) 15 5
1273 A158 60c rose lil 15 5
1274 A158 80c pale grn 20 5
1275 A158 $1 gray grn ('61) 1.50 5
1276 A158 $1.20 gray ol 75 5
1277 A158 $1.50 ultra 75 6
1278 A158 $2 car rose ('61) 1.65 8
1279 A158 $2.50 pale bl 1.65 8
1280 A158 $3 bluish grn 1.50 8
1281 A158 $3.20 lt red brn 2.75 8
1282 A158 $3.60 vio bl ('61) 2.50 18
1283 A158 $4.50 vermilion 4.50 25
Nos. 1270-1283 (14) 18.35 1.16

1962-64

Granite Paper
Without Gum

1270a A158 3c lt red brn 30 5
1270B A158 10c emer ('63) 75 5
1271a A158 40c pale vio 30 5
1274a A158 80c pale grn 50 5
1275a A158 $1 gray grn ('63) 2.00 5
1278a A158 $2 car rose 2.25 7
1281a A158 $3.20 red brn ('64) 2.25 6
1282A A158 $4 brt bl grn 4.50 15
1283a A158 $4.50 vermilion 2.25 20
Nos. 1270a-1283a (9) 15.10 73

Two types of No. 1271a: I. Seven lines in "0" of "40." II. Eight lines in "0."

Perf. 12½

1960, Oct. 25 Photo. Unwmk.

Sports: 80c, Discus thrower. $2, Basketball. $2.50, Soccer. $3, Hurdling. $3.20, Runner.

1284 A159 50c ultra, yel & org 45 10
1285 A159 80c rose cl, pur & yel 45 15
1286 A159 $2 blk, red org & yel 80 25
1287 A159 $2.50 org & blk 1.25 30
1288 A159 $3 multi 1.40 50
1289 A159 $3.20 multi 2.25 60
Nos. 1284-1289 (6) 6.60 1.90

Bronze Wine Container, 1751-1111 B.C. — A160

Flat Bowl, 1111-771 B.C. — A161

Designs: $1, Cauldron, 1111-771 B.C. $1.20, Porcelain vase, 960-1126 A.D. $1.50, Perforated tube, 1111-771 B.C. $2, Jug in shape of monk's cap, 1368-1661 A.D. $2.50, Jade flower vase, 1368-1661, A.D.

Art Series I

1961-62 Photo. *Perf. 13*

1290 A160 80c lt ol, blk & dk vio 80 12
1291 A160 $1 sal, bl & blk 85 15
1292 A160 $1.20 yel, brn & ultra 1.10 30
1293 A160 $1.50 lil, bl & sep 1.10 40
1294 A160 $2 pale grn, dk grn & red brn 1.65 30
1295 A160 $2.50 grnsh bl & dk vio 2.00 35
Nos. 1290-1295 (6) 7.50 1.62

Art Series II

Designs: 80c, Palace perfumer, 1662-1911. $1, Corn vase, 770-221 B.C. $2, Jade tankard, 960-1126 A.D. $4, Glazed washer, 1127-1279 A.D. $4.50, Jade chimera, 8 B.C.-206 A.D.

1296 A160 80c pink, brn, bl & yel 50 10
1297 A160 $1 cit, blk & brn 1.65 20
1298 A161 $1.50 sal & ind 1.65 50
1299 A160 $2 bl, blk & rose 1.65 40
1300 A161 $4 red, blk & bluish gray 5.25 40
1301 A161 $4.50 grnsh bl, blk & brn 4.75 1.00
Nos. 1296-1301 (6) 15.45 2.60

Art Series III (1962)

Designs: 80c, Topaz twin wine vessels, 1662-1911 A.D. $1, Squat pouring vase, 1751-1111 B.C. $2.40, Vase, 1368-1661 A.D. $3, Wine vase, 1751-1111 B.C. $3.20, Covered porcelain jar, 1662-1911 A.D. $3.60, Perforated disc, 206 B.C.-8 A.D.

1302 A160 80c crim, blk & ocher 40 10
1303 A160 $1 bl & vio blk 50 10
1304 A160 $2.40 hn brn, blk & bl 1.75 40
1305 A160 $3 bl, blk & pink 4.00 1.25
1306 A160 $3.20 ultra, lt grn & red 5.25 25
1307 A160 $3.60 yel, blk & brn 4.00 75
Nos. 1302-1307 (6) 15.90 2.85

Issued to publicize ancient Chinese art treasures.

Farmer with Mechanized Plow — A162

Madame Chiang Kai-shek and League Emblem — A163

1961, Feb. 4 Engr. *Perf. 12*
Without Gum

1308 A162 80c rose vio 38 10
1309 A162 $2 green 1.25 40
1310 A162 $3.20 vermilion 1.25 20

Issued to publicize the 1961 agricultural census.

Unwmk.

1961, March 8 Photo. *Perf. 13*
Portrait in Black

1311 A163 80c lt grn & car rose 75 10
1312 A163 $1 yel grn & car rose 1.75 25
1313 A163 $2 org brn & car rose 1.75 25
1314 A163 $3.20 lil & car rose 4.00 50

Issued to commemorate the 10th anniversary of the Chinese Women's Anti-Aggression League.

Spiny Lobster and Mail Order Service Emblem A164

Jeme Tien-yow and Pataling Tunnel A165

1961, Mar. 20 Engr. *Perf. 11½*
Without Gum

1315 A164 $3 sl grn 1.50 25

Issued to publicize the mail order service for consumer goods.

1961, Apr. 26 *Perf. 11½*
Without Gum

Design: $2, Jeme Tien-yow and 1909 locomotive (horiz.).

1316 A165 80c lilac 35 10
1317 A165 $2 black 1.50 40

Issued to commemorate the centenary of the birth of Jeme Tien-yow, builder of the Peking-Kalgan railroad.

Map of China inscribed: "Recovery of the Mainland" — A166

Pres. Chiang Kai-shek — A167

1961, May 20 Photo. *Perf. 13½*

1318 A166 80c multi	1.10	15
1319 A167 $2 multi	3.75	75
a. Souvenir sheet of 2	2.25	2.25

Issued to commemorate the first anniversary of Pres. Chiang Kai-shek's 3rd term inauguration.

No. 1319a contains one each of Nos. 1318-1319, imperf. with simulated perforations and red marginal inscription. Without gum. Size: 135x100mm.

Convair 880-M, Biplane of 1921 and Flag — A168

1961, July 1 *Perf. 13x12½*

1320 A168 $10 multi	4.00	50

40th anniversary of civil air service.

Sun Yat-sen and Chiang Kai-shek — A169

Flag and Map of China — A170

Perf. 13½

1961, Oct. 10 Unwmk. Photo.

1321 A169 80c gray, lt brn & sl	1.25	10
1322 A170 $5 gray, ultra, red & beige	4.75	90
a. Souvenir sheet of 2	3.00	3.00

Issued to commemorate the 50th anniversary of the Republic of China. No. 1322a contains one each of Nos. 1321-1322, imperf. with simulated perforations and red marginal inscription. No gum. Size of sheet: 135x99mm.

Green Lake — A171

Lotus Pond A172

Oil Refinery — A173

Taiwan Scenery: $2, Sun-Moon Lake. $3.20, Wulai waterfalls.

Perf. 13½x14, 14x13½

1961, Oct. 31 Unwmk.

1323 A171 80c multi	70	15
1324 A172 $1 multi	2.00	50
1325 A172 $2 multi	2.00	50
1326 A171 $3.20 multi	4.25	75

1961, Nov. 14 *Perf. 11½*

Designs: $1.50, Steel works. $2.50, Aluminum plant. $3.20, Fertilizer plant (horiz.).

1327 A173 80c multi	60	10
1328 A173 $1.50 multi	1.75	80
1329 A173 $2.50 multi	1.75	80
1330 A173 $3.20 multi	3.50	70

Issued to publicize Chinese industrial development and in connection with the Golden Jubilee Convention of the Chinese Institute of Engineers, Nov. 13-16.

Atomic Reactor, Tsing-Hwa University A174

Atomic Reactor in Operation A175

Design: $3.20, Atomic symbol and laboratory, Tsing-Hwa (horiz.).

1961-62 Photo. *Perf. 12½*

1331 A174 80c multi	1.25	10
1332 A175 $2 multi ('62)	2.75	1.40
1333 A175 $3.20 multi ('62)	4.00	90

Issued to commemorate the inauguration on Apr. 13, 1961, of the first Chinese atomic reactor at the National Tsing-Hwa University Institute of Nuclear Science.

Microwave Reflector and Telegraph Wires — A176

Design: $3.20, Microwave parabolic antenna and mountains (horiz.).

1961, Dec. 28 *Perf. 12½*

1334 A176 80c multi	60	12
1335 A176 $3.20 multi	3.00	90

Issued to commemorate the 80th anniversary of Chinese telecommunications.

Mechanical Postal Equipment and Twine Tying Machine A176a

Wmk. 323

1962, Mar. 20 Engr. *Perf. 11½*

Without Gum

1336 A176a 80c chocolate	1.10	15

Yu Shan Observatory A177

Observation Balloon, Earth and Cumulus Clouds A178

Design: $1, Map showing route of typhoon Pamela, Sept. 1961 (horiz.).

1962

Without Gum

1337 A177 80c brown	50	10
1338 A178 $1 bluish blk	2.25	40
1339 A178 $2 green	2.25	80

Issue dates: 80c, $2, Mar. 23; $1, May 7. World Meteorological Day, Mar. 23.

Child Receiving Milk, U.N. Emblem A179

1962, Apr. 4

Without Gum

1340 A179 80c rose red	25	10
1341 A179 $3.20 green	1.75	75
a. Souvenir sheet of 2	2.00	2.00

Issued to commemorate the 15th anniversary of UNICEF (United Nations Children's Emergency Fund.) No. 1341a contains one each of Nos. 1340-1341 imperf. with simulated perforations and red marginal inscription. Size: 135x100mm.

Malaria Eradication Emblem — A180

Perf. 12½

1962, Apr. 7 Unwmk. Photo.

1342 A180 80c dk bl, red & lt grn	75	10
1343 A180 $3.60 brn, pink & grn	1.50	75

Issued for the World Health Organization drive to eradicate malaria.

Yu Yu-jen A181

Cheng Ch'eng-kung (Koxinga) A182

1962, Apr. 24 *Perf. 13*

1344 A181 80c gray, blk & pink	1.10	10

Issued to honor Yu Yu-jen, newspaper reporter, revolutionary leader and co-worker of Sun Yat-sen, on his 84th birthday.

1962, Apr. 29

1345 A182 80c dp cl	75	10
1346 A182 $2 dk grn	1.75	25

Issued to commemorate the 300th anniversary (in 1961) of the recovery of Taiwan from the Dutch by Koxinga.

Emblem of International Cooperative Alliance A183

Clasped Hands Across Globe A184

Wmk. 323

1962, July 7 Engr. *Perf. 12*

Without Gum

1347 A183 80c brown	60	10
1348 A184 $2 violet	1.75	50

Issued to publicize the International Cooperative Movement and to commemorate the 40th International Cooperative Day, July 7, 1962.

Mansion Type of 1958

1962, July 20

Without Gum

1349 A135 $5 gray grn	2.25	6
a. Granite paper ('63)	2.75	10
1350 A135 $5.60 violet	2.75	8
a. Granite paper ('63)	4.25	10
1351 A135 $6 orange	3.00	10
a. Granite paper ('63)	4.75	10

"Art and Science" — A185

Designs: $2, "Education," book and UNESCO emblem (horiz.). $3.20, "Communications," globes (horiz.).

1962, Aug. 28 Wmk. 323 *Perf. 12*

Without Gum

1352 A185 80c lil rose	28	15
1353 A185 $2 rose cl	1.50	60
1354 A185 $3.20 yel grn	1.40	40

Issued to publicize the activities of UNESCO in China.

Emperor T'ai Tsung, T'ang Dynasty, 627-649 A186

Emperors: $2, T'ai Tsu, Sung dynasty, 960-975. $3.20, T'ai Tsu, Yuan dynasty (Genghis Khan), 1206-27. $4, T'ai Tsu, Ming dynasty, 1368-98.

1962, Sept. 20 Photo. Unwmk.

1355 A186 80c multi	1.25	20
1356 A186 $2 multi	6.00	1.35
1357 A186 $3.20 multi	7.00	1.10
1358 A186 $4 multi	6.00	1.65

Lions International Emblem A187

1962, Oct. 8 *Perf. 13*

1359 A187 80c multi	75	10
1360 A187 $3.60 multi	2.25	85
a. Souvenir sheet of 2	3.00	3.00

Issued to commemorate the 45th anniversary of Lions International. No. 1360a contains one each of Nos. 1359-1360, imperf. with simulated perforations and gold marginal inscription. Size: 100x75mm.

Pole Vaulting — A188

Shooting A189

1962, Oct. 25 Unwmk. *Perf. 13*
1361 A188 80c multi 1.00 15
1362 A189 $3.20 multi 2.00 40

Sports meet.

Young Farmers and 4-H Emblem A190

Flag and Liner of China Merchants' Steam Navigation Co. A191

Design: $3.20, 4-H emblem and rice.

Wmk. 323
1962, Dec. 7 Engr. *Perf. 12*
Without Gum
1363 A190 80c carmine 50 10
1364 A190 $3.20 green 1.40 50
a. Souvenir sheet of 2 2.50 2.50

Issued to commemorate the 10th anniversary of the 4-H Club in China. No. 1364a contains one each of Nos. 1363-1364, imperf. with simulated perforations and red lithographed marginal inscription. Size: 135x100mm.

Perf. 13½
1962, Dec. 16 Unwmk. Photo.

Design: $3.60, Company's Pacific navigation chart and freighter (horiz.).

1365 A191 80c multi 95 10
1366 A191 $3.60 multi 2.75 85

Issued to commemorate the 90th anniversary of the China Merchants' Steam Navigation Co., Ltd.

Farm Woman, Tractor and Plane Dropping Food over Mainland — A192

Perf. 12½
1963, Mar. 21 Unwmk. Photo.
1367 A192 $10 multi 4.50 90

Issued for the "Freedom from Hunger" campaign of the U.N. Food and Agriculture Organization.

Condition is the all-important factor of price. Prices quoted are for stamps in fine condition.

Torch, Young Couple and Martyrs' Monument, Canton A193

Wmk. 323
1963, Mar. 29 Engr. *Perf. 11½*
Without Gum
1368 A193 80c purple 35 8
1369 A193 $3.20 green 1.75 40

Issued for the 20th Youth Day.

Swallows, Pagoda and AOPU Emblem — A194

Designs: $2, Northern gannet (horiz.). $6, Japanese crane and pine.

Unwmk.
1963, Apr. 1 Photo. *Perf. 13*
1370 A194 80c multi 2.00 15
1371 A194 $2 multi 2.00 15
1372 A194 $6 multi 7.00 1.75

Issued to commemorate the first anniversary of the formation of the Asian-Oceanic Postal Union, AOPU.

Refugee Girl (Li Ying) and Map of China — A195

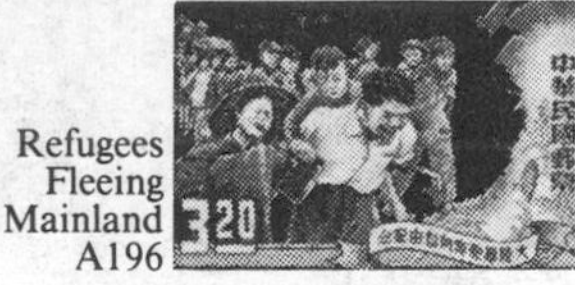

Refugees Fleeing Mainland A196

Wmk. 323
1963, June 27 Engr. *Perf. 11½*
Without Gum
1373 A195 80c bluish blk 85 15
1374 A196 $3.20 dp cl 1.95 25

Issued to commemorate the first anniversary of the evacuation of Chinese mainland refugees from Hong Kong to Taiwan. Designs from photographs of refugees.

Nurse and Red Cross A197

Basketball Player, Stadium and Asian Cup — A198

Design: $10, Globe and Red Cross.

Perf. 12½
1963, Sept. 1 Unwmk. Photo.
1375 A197 80c blk & car 2.00 20
1376 A197 $10 sl, gray & car 7.00 2.00

Centenary of International Red Cross.

Wmk. 323
1963, Nov. 20 Engr. *Perf. 12*
Without Gum

Design: $2, Hands reaching for ball and Asian cup.

1377 A198 80c lil rose 40 10
1378 A198 $2 violet 2.25 75

Issued to commemorate the 2nd Asian Basketball Championship, Taipei, Nov. 20.

U.N. Emblem, Torch and Men — A199

Scales and Men of Various Races — A200

1963, Dec. 10 Wmk. 323 *Perf. 11½*
Without Gum
1379 A199 80c brt grn 40 8
1380 A200 $3.20 maroon 1.10 20

Universal Declaration of Human Rights, 15th anniversary.

Village and Orchids A201

"Kindle the Fire of Conscience" A202

Perf. 13½x13
1963, Dec. 17 Photo. Unwmk.
1381 A201 40c multi 1.10 10
1382 A202 $4.50 multi 4.00 75

Issued to commemorate the contribution of the Good-People-Good-Deeds campaign to improve ethical standards.

Sun Yat-sen and Book, "Three Principles of the People" A203

1963, Dec. 25 *Perf. 13*
1383 A203 $5 bl & multi 3.75 30

"Land-to-the-Tillers" program, 10th anniversary.

Torch A204

Hands Unchained A205

Wmk. 323
1964, Jan. 23 Engr. *Perf. 11½*
Without Gum
1384 A204 80c red org 25 8
1385 A205 $3.20 indigo 1.25 15

Liberty Day, 10th anniversary.

Broadleaf Cactus A206

Wu Chih-hwei A207

Designs: $1, Crab cactus. $3.20, Nopalxochia. $5, Grizzly bear cactus.

Perf. 12½
1964, Feb. 27 Unwmk. Photo.
Plants in Original Colors
1386 A206 80c dp plum & fawn 55 10
1387 A206 $1 dk bl & car 1.40 40
1388 A206 $3.20 green 2.00 10
1389 A206 $5 lil & yel 2.75 40

Wmk. 323
1964, Mar. 25 Engr. *Perf. 11½*
Without Gum
1390 A207 80c blk brn 1.00 12

Issued to commemorate the centenary of the birth of Wu Chih-hwei (1865-1953), politician and leader of the Kuomintang.

Chu Kwang Tower, Quemoy — A208

Perf. 13x12½
1964-66 Wmk. 323 Litho.
Granite Paper; Without Gum

No.	Type	Value	Color	Unused	Used
1391	A208	3c	sepia	10	5
1392	A208	5c	brt yel grn ('65)	10	5
1393	A208	10c	yel grn	10	5
1394	A208	20c	sl grn ('65)	10	5
1395	A208	40c	rose red	10	5
1396	A208	50c	brown	10	5
1397	A208	80c	org ('65)	22	5
1398	A208	$1	vio ('65)	28	5
1399	A208	$1.50	brt lil ('66)	38	15
1400	A208	$2	lil rose	38	6
1401	A208	$2.50	ultra ('65)	38	6
1402	A208	$3	slate	65	10
1403	A208	$3.20	brt bl	80	6
1404	A208	$4	brt grn	1.00	8
			Nos. 1391-1404 (14)	4.69	91

Nurses Holding Candles A209

Florence Nightingale and Student Nurse A210

1964, May 12 Engr. *Perf. 11½*
Without Gum

1406 A209 80c vio bl	75	8
1407 A210 $4 red	2.25	25

Issued for Nurses Day.

Shihmen Reservoir A211

Designs: $1, Irrigation system. $3.20, Main dam and power plant. $5, Spillway.

Perf. 12½
1964, June 14 Unwmk. Photo.

1408 A211 80c multi	1.10	10
1409 A211 $1 multi	1.10	10
1410 A211 $3.20 multi	2.00	15
1411 A211 $5 multi	5.50	75

Completion of Shihmen Reservoir.

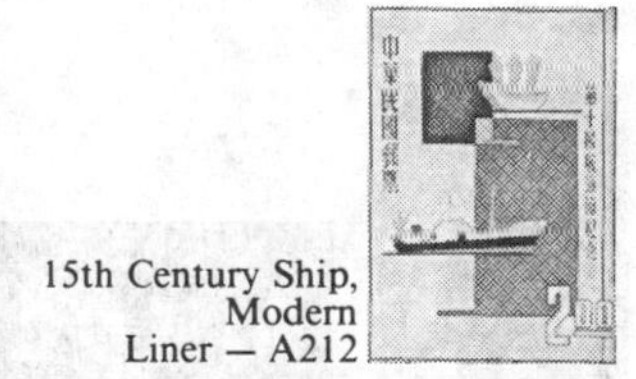
15th Century Ship, Modern Liner — A212

Wmk. 323
1964, July 11 Engr. *Perf. 11½*
Without Gum

1412 A212 $2 orange	55	8
1413 A212 $3.60 brt grn	1.10	20

China's 10th Navigation Day.

Bananas A213

Unwmk.
1964, July 25 Photo. *Perf. 14*

1414 A213 80c *shown*	1.10	8
1415 A213 $1 *Oranges*	2.25	40
1416 A213 $3.20 *Pineapple*	2.75	25
1417 A213 $4 *Watermelon*	4.75	65

Artillery, Warships, Jet Fighters — A214

Wmk. 323
1964, Sept. 3 Engr. *Perf. 11½*
Without Gum

1418 A214 80c dk bl	35	8
1419 A214 $6 vio brn	1.90	40

Issued for the 10th Armed Forces Day.

Unisphere, Flags of China and U.S. — A215

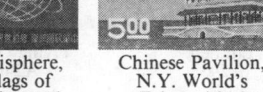

Chinese Pavilion, N.Y. World's Fair — A216

1964, Sept. 10 Photo. Unwmk.

1420 A215 80c vio & multi	75	8
1421 A216 $5 bl & multi	3.50	45

New York World's Fair, 1964-65. See Nos. 1450-1451.

Cowboy Carrying Calf, and Ranch A217

Bicycling A218

Wmk. 323
1964, Sept. 24 Engr. *Perf. 11½*
Without Gum

1422 A217 $2 brn lake	95	10
1423 A217 $4 dk vio bl	2.25	40

Animal Protection Week, Sept. 24-30.

1964, Oct. 10 Without Gum

Sports: $1, Runner. $3.20, Gymnast on rings. $10, High jump.

1424 A218 80c vio bl	45	6
1425 A218 $1 rose red	85	10
1426 A218 $3.20 dl bl grn	1.65	10
1427 A218 $10 lilac	4.50	1.50

18th Olympic Games, Tokyo, Oct. 10-25.

Hsü Kuang-chi A219

Pharmaceutical Industry A220

Textile Industry A221

1964, Nov. 8 Engr. *Perf. 11½*
Without Gum

1428 A219 80c indigo	1.10	10

Issued to honor Hsü Kuang-chi (1562-1633), scholar and statesman.

1964, Nov. 11 Photo. Unwmk.

Designs: $2, Chemical industry. $3.60, Cement industry.

1429 A220 40c multi	65	8
1430 A221 $1.50 multi	1.75	40
1431 A220 $2 multi	2.00	15
1432 A221 $3.60 multi	3.50	30

Dr. Sun Yat-sen A222

Eleanor Roosevelt and Scales of Justice A223

1964, Nov. 24 Engr. Wmk. 323
Without Gum

1433 A222 80c green	95	8
1434 A222 $3.60 purple	1.75	25

Founding of the Kuomintang by Sun Yat-sen, 70th anniversary.

Unwmk.
1964, Dec. 10 Photo. *Perf. 13*

1435 A223 $10 vio & brn	2.00	40

Issued to honor Eleanor Roosevelt (1884-1962) on the 16th anniversary of the Universal Declaration of Human Rights.

Scales, Code Book and Plum Blossom A224

Rotary Emblem and Mainspring A225

Wmk. 323
1965, Jan. 11 Engr. *Perf. 11½*
Without Gum

1436 A224 80c car rose	40	8
1437 A224 $3.20 dl sl grn	1.10	20

The 20th Judicial Day.

1965, Feb. 23 Wmk. 323 *Perf. 11½*
Without Gum

1438 A225 $1.50 vermilion	40	8
1439 A225 $2 emerald	1.10	15
1440 A225 $2.50 bluc	1.40	25

Rotary International, 60th anniversary.

Double Carp Design A226

Madame Chiang Kai-shek A227

Wmk. 323
1965, Mar. 29 Engr. *Perf. 11½*
Granite Paper; Without Gum

1441 A226 $5 purple	5.50	25
1442 A226 $5.60 dp bl	3.25	2.00
1443 A226 $6 brown	2.75	50
1444 A226 $10 lil rose	5.50	20
1445 A226 $20 rose car	6.75	40
1446 A226 $50 green	13.00	1.25
1447 A226 $100 crim rose	30.00	2.25
Nos. 1441-1447 (7)	66.75	6.85

1965, Apr. 17 Photo. Unwmk.

1448 A227 $2 multi	3.50	10
1449 A227 $6 sal & multi	9.00	1.00

Chinese Women's Anti-Aggression League, 15th anniversary.

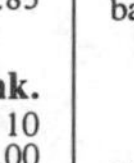

Unisphere and Chinese Pavilion — A228

"100 Birds Paying Homage to Queen Phoenix" and Unisphere — A229

1965, May 8

1450 A228 $2 bl & multi	2.25	10
1451 A229 $10 red, ocher & bis	9.00	75

New York World's Fair, 1964-65.

ITU Emblem, Old and New Communication Equipment A230

Design: $5, similar to 80c (vert.).

Perf. 13½x13, 13x13½
1965, May 17 Photo. Unwmk.

1452 A230 80c multi	40	8
1453 A230 $5 multi	2.50	50

Issued to commemorate the centenary of the International Telecommunication Union.

Red Sea Bream A231

Fish: 80c, White pomfret. $2, Skipjack (vert.). $4, Moonfish.

1965, July 1 *Perf. 13*

1454 A231 40c multi	38	6
1455 A231 80c multi	75	6
1456 A231 $2 multi	1.10	8
1457 A231 $4 multi	2.25	30

Issued for Fishermen's Day.

Confucius A232

ICY Emblem A233

Portraits: $2.50, Yueh Fei. $3.50, Wen Tien-hsiang. $3.60, Mencius.

Wmk. 323
1965-66 Engr. *Perf. 11½*
Without Gum

1458 A232 $1 dp car	65	6
1459 A232 $2.50 blk brn	65	8
1460 A232 $3.50 dk red	1.40	15
1461 A232 $3.60 dk bl	2.00	20

Issue dates: Nos. 1458, 1461, Sept. 28, 1965. Nos. 1459-1460, Sept. 3, 1966.
The $2.50 and $3.50 have colored background.
See Nos. 1507-1508.

Unwmk.
1965, Oct. 24 Photo. *Perf. 13*

Design: $6, ICY emblem (horiz.).

1462	A233	$2	brn, blk & gold	75	8
1463	A233	$6	brt grn, red & gold	3.50	1.00

International Cooperation Year, 1965.

Street Crossing and Traffic Light
A234

Sun Yat-sen
A235

Wmk. 323

1965, Nov. 1 Engr. *Perf. 11½*

Without Gum

1464	A234	$1	brn vio	1.00	8
1465	A234	$4	crime rose	1.75	20

Issued to publicize traffic safety.

Perf. 13½

1965, Nov. 12 Unwmk. Photo.

Designs: $4, Dr. Sun Yat-sen, portrait at right. $5, Sun Yat-sen and flags (horiz.).

1466	A235	$1	multi	85	8
1467	A235	$4	multi	1.75	25
1468	A235	$5	multi	4.50	1.00

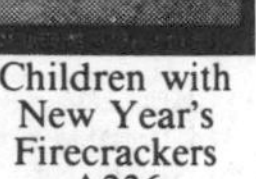

Children with New Year's Firecrackers
A236

Dragon Dance, "Dragon Playing Ball"
A237

1965, Dec. 1 Photo. *Perf. 13*

1469	A236	$1	multi	1.75	10
1470	A237	$4.50	multi	2.00	75

Lien Po from "Marshal and Prime Minister Reconciled" – A238

Facial Paintings for Chinese Operas: $3, Kuan Yü from "Reunion at Ku City." $4, Gen. Chang Fei from "The Battle of Chang Pan Hill." $6, Buddha from "The Flower-Scattering Angel."

1966, Feb. 15 Unwmk. *Perf. 11½*

1471	A238	$1	ol & multi	3.50	30
1472	A238	$3	multi	3.00	25
1473	A238	$4	multi	3.50	30
1474	A238	$6	ver & multi	5.25	2.00

Postal Service Emblem Held by Carrier Pigeon – A239

Stone, Mt. Tai-wu, Quemoy, and Mailman
A240

Designs (postal service emblem and): $3, Postal Museum. $4, Mailman climbing symbolic slope.

1966, Mar. 20 Photo. *Perf. 12½*

1475	A239	$1	grn & multi	70	8
1476	A240	$2	multi	70	8
1477	A240	$3	multi	1.10	15
1478	A239	$4	multi	2.00	50

China postal service, 70th anniversary.

Fishing on a Snowy Day, "Five Dynasties" (907-960)
A241

Paintings from Palace Museum: $3.50, Calves on the Plain, Sung artist (960-1126). $4.50, Winter landscape, Sung artist (960-1126). $5, Magpies, by Lin Ch'un, Southern Sung dynasty (1127-1279).

1966, May 20 Photo. *Perf. 13*

1479	A241	$2.50	blk, brn & red	1.40	8
1480	A241	$3.50	bis brn, blk & gray	1.10	10
1481	A241	$4.50	blk, buff & sl	1.10	40
1482	A241	$5	multi	3.00	50

Issued to commemorate the inauguration of Pres. Chiang Kai-shek for a fourth term.

Dragon Boat Race – A242

Lion Dance – A243

Design: $4, Lady Chang O flying to the Moon.

1966 Unwmk.

1483	A242	$2.50	multi	2.75	8
1484	A242	$4	multi	1.75	8
1485	A243	$6	multi	1.50	25

Issued for the Dragon Boat, Mid-Autumn and Lunar New Year Festivals. Issue dates: $2.50, June 23; $4, Sept. 29; $6, Nov. 26.

Flags of China and Argentina
A244

1966, July 9 Photo. *Perf. 13*

1486	A244	$10	multi	2.50	25

Issued to commemorate the 150th anniversary of Argentina's Independence.

Lin Sen
A245

Flying Geese
A246

Wmk. 323

1966, Aug. 1 Engr. *Perf. 11½*

Without Gum

1487	A245	$1	dk brn	90	8

Issued to commemorate the centenary of the birth of Lin Sen (1867-1943), Chairman of the Nationalist Government of China (1931-43).

1966-67 *Perf. 11½ Rough*

Granite Paper; Without Gum

1496	A246	$3.50	brown	38	5
1497	A246	$4	vermilion	50	5
1498	A246	$4.50	brt grn	65	15
1499	A246	$5	rose lil	65	5
1500	A246	$5.50	yel grn ('67)	65	15
1501	A246	$6	brt bl	1.90	40
1502	A246	$6.50	violet	1.25	25
1503	A246	$7	black	1.10	5
1504	A246	$8	car rose ('67)	1.25	15
			Nos. 1496-1504 (9)	8.33	1.30

The $4.50, $5, $6, $7 and $8 were reissued with gum in 1970-71.

Pres. Chiang Kai-shek in Chung San Robe – A247

Design: $5, Chiang Kai-shek in marshal's uniform.

Unwmk.

1966, Oct. 31 Photo. *Perf. 13*

1505	A247	$1	multi	90	10
1506	A247	$5	multi	3.75	50

Issued to commemorate Chiang Kai-shek's inauguration for a fourth term as president, May 20, 1966.

Famous Men Type of 1965-66 with Frame Line

Portraits: No. 1507, Tsai Yuan-pei (1868-1940), educator. No. 1508, Chiu Ching (1875-1907), woman educator and revolutionist.

1967 Wmk. 323 Engr. *Perf. 11½*

Without Gum

1507	A232	$1	vio bl	75	15
1508	A232	$1	black	75	15

Issue dates: No. 1507, Jan. 11. No. 1508, July 15.

No. 1507 is on granite paper.

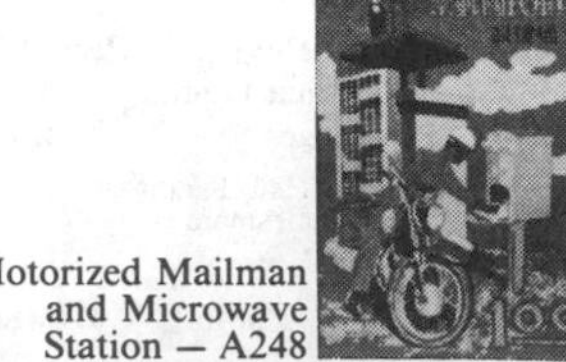

Motorized Mailman and Microwave Station – A248

"Transportation" and Radar Weather Station – A249

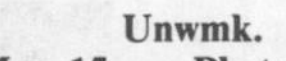

Unwmk.

1967, Mar. 15 Photo. *Perf. 13*

1511	A248	$1	multi	1.00	5
1512	A249	$5	multi	2.00	20

Issued to publicize the progress in communication and transportation services.

Pres. Chiang Kai-shek and Chinese Flag – A250

Chu Yuan, 332-295 B.C. – A251

Design: $4, Different frame.

1967, May 20 Litho. *Perf. 13*

1513	A250	$1	multi	1.50	10
1514	A250	$4	multi	3.00	20

First anniversary of President Chiang Kai-shek's 4th-term inauguration.

Wmk. 323

1967, June 12 Engr. *Perf. 11½*

Portraits: $2, Li Po (705-760). $2.50, Tu Fu (712-770). $3, Po Chu-i (772-846).

Granite Paper; Without Gum

1515	A251	$1	black	65	5
1516	A251	$2	brown	1.00	8
1517	A251	$2.50	brn blk	1.25	20
1518	A251	$3	grnsh blk	1.25	15

Issued for Poets' Day.

Hotei, Wood Carving
A252

World Map
A253

Handicrafts: $2.50, Vase and plate. $3, Dolls. $5, Palace lanterns.

Perf. 11½

1967, Aug. 12 Unwmk. Photo.

1519	A252	$1	gray & multi	40	8
1520	A252	$2.50	multi	80	8
1521	A252	$3	multi	1.10	15
1522	A252	$5	multi	1.75	40

Taiwan handicraft industry.

Wmk. 323

1967, Sept. 25 Engr. *Perf. 11½*

Granite Paper; Without Gum

1523	A253	$1	vermilion	18	6
1524	A253	$5	blue	90	25

Issued to commemorate the first Conference of the World Anti-Communist League, WACL, Taipei, Sept. 25-29.

Players on Stilts: "The Fisherman and the Woodcutter"
A254

Unwmk.

1967, Oct. 10 Photo. *Perf. 13*

1525	A254	$4.50	multi	75	25

Issued for the 56th National Day.

Maroon Oriole — A255

Formosan Birds: $1, Formosan barbet (vert.). $2.50, Formosan green pigeon. $3, Formosan blue magpie. $5, Crested serpent eagle (vert.). $8, Mikado pheasants.

1967, Nov. 25 Photo. *Perf. 11*

Granite Paper

1526	A255	$1	multi	25	15
1527	A255	$2	multi	50	15
1528	A255	$2.50	multi	50	20
1529	A255	$3	multi	65	20
1530	A255	$5	multi	1.40	30
1531	A255	$8	multi	2.00	75
	Nos. 1526-1531 (6)			5.30	1.75

Chung Hsing Pagoda — A256

Buddha, Changhua A257

Designs: $2.50, Seashore, Yeh Liu Park. $5, National Palace Museum, Taipei.

Unwmk.

1967, Dec. 10 Photo. *Perf. 13*

1532	A256	$1	multi	30	8
1533	A257	$2.50	multi	90	30
1534	A257	$4	multi	1.25	20
1535	A257	$5	multi	2.00	50

Issued for International Tourist Year 1967.

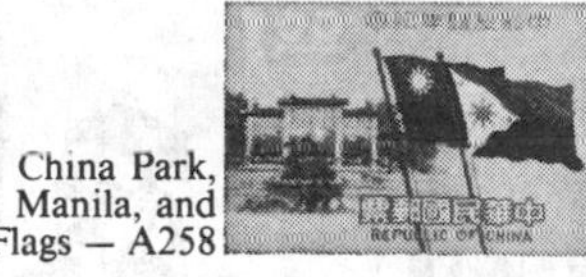

China Park, Manila, and Flags — A258

1967, Dec. 30 *Perf. 13½*

1536	A258	$1	multi	50	6
1537	A258	$5	multi	1.50	25

Sino-Philippine Friendship Year 1966-67.

Sun Yat-sen Building, Yangmingshan

A259 A259a

Perf. 13x12½

1968-75 Litho. Wmk. 323

Granite Paper

1538	A259	5c	lt brn	10	5
1539	A259	10c	grnsh blk	10	5
1540	A259	50c	brt rose lil	10	5
1541	A259	$1	vermilion	20	5
1542	A259	$1.50	emerald	40	10
1543	A259	$2	plum	40	5
1544	A259	$2.50	blue	40	5
1545	A259	$3	grnsh bl	80	10
	Nos. 1538-1545 (8)			2.50	50

Coil Stamps

Perf. 13 Horiz.

Photo. Unwmk.

1546	A259a	$1	car rose ('70)	40	15
1547	A259a	$1	ver ('75)	35	10

Issued dates: 50c, $1, $2.50, Jan. 23, 1968; No. 1546, Mar. 20, 1970; No. 1547, Jan. 28, 1975; others July 11, 1968.

Inscription on No. 1546 is in color with white background. On No. 1547 it is white with colored background.

Harvesting Sugar Cane A260

Jade Cabbage, 1662-1911 A261

Unwmk.

1968, Mar. 1 Photo. *Perf. 13*

1548	A260	$1	ol & multi	50	10
1549	A260	$4	multi	75	30

1968, Mar. 29 Unwmk. *Perf. 13*

Ancient Art Treasures: $1.50, Jade battle axe. $2, Porcelain flower bowl, 960-1126 A.D. (horiz.). $2.50, Cloisonne enamel vase, 1723-1736 A.D. $4, Agate flower holder in shape of finger citrus, 1662-1911 A.D. (horiz.). $5, Sacrificial kettle, 1111-771 B.C.

1550	A261	$1	rose & multi	30	8
1551	A261	$1.50	bl & multi	60	25
1552	A261	$2	bl & multi	75	10
1553	A261	$2.50	dl rose & multi	75	25
1554	A261	$4	pink & multi	80	30
1555	A261	$5	bl & multi	1.25	40
	Nos. 1550-1555 (6)			4.45	1.38

View of City in Cathay (1) — A262

Views: No. 1557, City and wall of Forbidden City (2). No. 1558, Wall at right, bridge at left (3). No. 1559, Queen's ship landing at left (4). No. 1560, Palace (5). $5, City wall and gate. $8, Suburb around Great Bridge. Design from scroll "A City in Cathay," painted 1736.

1968, June 18 Photo. *Perf. 13½*

Size: 50x29mm.

1556	A262	$1	multi	30	10
1557	A262	$1	multi	30	10
1558	A262	$1	multi	30	10
1559	A262	$1	multi	30	10
1560	A262	$1	multi	30	10

Size: 60x31mm.

Perf. 13x13½

1561	A262	$5	multi	2.00	80
1562	A262	$8	multi	3.00	90
	Nos. 1556-1562 (7)			6.50	2.20

Nos. 1556-1560 printed se-tenant in sheet of 50 with horizontal strips of five containing one of each.

See Nos. 1610-1614.

Entrance Gate, Taroko Gorge A263

Design: $8, Sun Yat-sen Building, Yangmingshan.

1968, Feb. 12 Photo. *Perf. 13*

1563	A263	$5	multi	1.10	25
1564	A263	$8	multi	1.10	25

The 17th Annual Conference of the Pacific Area Travel Association.

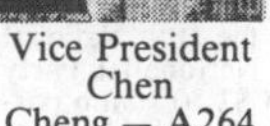

Vice President Chen Cheng — A264

Flying Geese — A265

1968, Mar. 5

1565	A264	$1	brn & multi	80	10

Issued in memory of Vice President Chen Cheng (1898-1965).

Wmk. 323

1968, Mar. 20 Litho. *Perf. 12*

Granite Paper

1566	A265	$1	vermilion	45	12

Souvenir Sheet

Imperf

1567	A265	$3	green	90	90

Issued to commemorate the 90th anniversary of Chinese postage stamps. No. 1567 contains one stamp with simulated perforations, yellow decorative margin with red inscription. Size: 75x100mm.

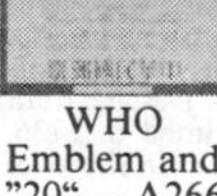

WHO Emblem and "20" — A266

Symbolic Water Cycle — A267

1968, Apr. 7 Engr. *Perf. 12*

Granite Paper

1568	A266	$1	green	35	5
1569	A266	$5	scarlet	90	30

Issued to commemorate the 20th anniversary of the World Health Organization.

Wmk. 323

1968, June 6 Litho. *Perf. 11½*

Granite Paper

1570	A267	$1	grn & org	35	8
1571	A267	$4	brt bl & org	90	8

Hydrological Decade (UNESCO) 1965-74.

Broadcasting to Mainland China A268

Dual Carriers for F.M. Broadcasting A269

Wmk. 323

1968, Aug. 1 Litho. *Perf. 12*

Granite Paper

1572	A268	$1	bl, vio bl & gray	35	8
1573	A269	$4	lt ultra & ver	90	15

Issued to commemorate the 40th anniversary of the Broadcasting Corporation of China, and the inauguration of frequency modulation broadcasting.

Human Rights Flame A270

Crop Improvement and Extension Work A271

1968, Sept. 3

Granite Paper

1574	A270	$1	multi	35	15
1575	A270	$5	multi	90	15

International Human Rights Year 1968.

Wmk. 323

1968, Sept. 30 Litho. *Perf. 12*

Granite Paper

1576	A271	$1	yel, bis & dk brn	30	5
1577	A271	$5	yel, emer & dk grn	90	50

Joint Commission on Rural Reconstruction, 20th anniversary.

Javelin — A272

Designs: $2.50, Weight lifting. $5, Pole vault (horiz.). $8, Woman hurdling (horiz.).

Unwmk.

1968, Oct. 12 Photo. *Perf. 13*

1578	A272	$1	multi	30	5
1579	A272	$2.50	multi	40	15
1580	A272	$5	multi	70	10
1581	A272	$8	pink & multi	1.00	30

Issued to commemorate the 19th Olympic Games, Mexico City, Oct. 12-27.

Pres. Chiang Kai-shek and Whampoa Military Academy A273

Designs: $2, Pres. Chiang Kai-shek reviewing forces of the Northern Expedition. $2.50, Suppression of bandits, reconstruction work and New Life Movement emblem. $3.50, Marco Polo Bridge near Peking and victory parade, Nanking. $4, Original copy of Constitution of Republic of China. $5, Nationalist Chinese flag flying over mainland China.

1968, Oct. 31 *Perf. 11½x12*

1582	A273	$1	multi	50	8
1583	A273	$2	multi	70	20
1584	A273	$2.50	multi	70	20
1585	A273	$3.50	multi	85	20
1586	A273	$4	multi	1.00	40
1587	A273	$5	multi	1.40	40
	Nos. 1582-1587 (6)			5.15	1.48

Chiang Kai-shek's achievements for China.

Cock — A274

1968, Nov. 12 Litho. *Perf. 12*
Granite Paper

1588 A274 $1 pink & multi 9.00 15
1589 A274 $4.50 lil & multi 9.00 2.25

Issued for use on New Year's greetings.

Flag — A275

1968, Dec. 25 Wmk. 323 *Perf. 12½*
Granite Paper

1590 A275 $1 multi 50 6
1591 A275 $5 lt bl & multi 1.10 20

Constitution of the Republic of China, 20th anniversary.

Jade Belt Buckle, 1662-1911 A276

Ancient Art Treasures: $1.50, Yellow jade vase, 960-1126 A.D. (vert.). $2, Cloisonne enamel square teapot, 1662-1911 A.D. $2.50, Kuei, sacrificial bronze vessel, 722-481 B.C. $4, Heavenly ball vase, 1368-1661 A.D. (vert.). $5, Gourd-shaped vase, 1662-1911 A.D. (vert.).

Unwmk.
1969, Jan. 15 Photo. *Perf. 13*

1592 A276 $1 dl rose & multi 28 5
1593 A276 $1.50 rose & multi 35 15
1594 A276 $2 brt rose & multi 35 10
1595 A276 $2.50 lt bl & multi 55 20
1596 A276 $4 tan & multi 75 20
1597 A276 $5 pale bl & multi 1.00 40
Nos. 1592-1597 (6) 3.28 1.10

Servicemen and Savings Emblem — A277

Wmk. 323
1969, Feb. 1 Engr. *Perf. 12*
Granite Paper

1598 A277 $1 dl red brn 40 8
1599 A277 $4 dp bl 1.10 15

Issued to commemorate the 10th anniversary of the Military Savings Program.

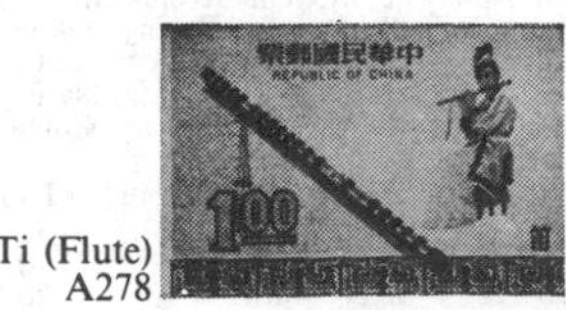
Ti (Flute) A278

Musical Instruments: $2.50, Sheng (13 bamboo pipes connected at the base). $4, P'i p'a (lute). $5, Cheng (zither).

Unwmk.
1969, Mar. 16 Photo. *Perf. 13*

1600 A278 $1 buff & multi 28 5
1601 A278 $2.50 lt ap grn & multi 45 10
1602 A278 $4 pink & multi 1.00 40
1603 A278 $5 lt grnsh bl & multi 1.00 25

Sun Yat-sen Building and Kuomintang Emblem A279

Double Carp Design A280

1969, Mar. 29 Litho. *Perf. 13½*

1604 A279 $1 multi 40 5

Issued to commemorate the 10th National Congress of the Chinese Nationalist Party (Kuomintang), Mar. 29. A $2.50 stamp portraying Sun Yat-sen and Chiang Kai-shek was prepared but not issued.

Perf. 13½x12½
1969-74 Engr. Wmk. 323
Granite Paper

1606 A280 $10 dk bl ('74) 1.10 20
a. Perf. 11½ 1.75 15
1607 A280 $20 dk brn ('74) 2.25 20
a. Perf. 11½ 2.50 20
1608 A280 $50 grn ('74) 5.50 75
a. Perf. 11½ 6.50 75
1609 A280 $100 brt red ('74) 8.75 2.00
a. Perf. 11½ 10.00 2.50

The 1969 issue is 27mm. high; 1974, 28mm. See No. 1980.

Bridal Procession — A281

Designs: No. 1610, Musicians and standard bearer from bridal procession. $2.50, Emigrant farm family in oxcart. $5, Art gallery. $8, Roadside food stands. Designs from scroll "A City in Cathay," painted in 1736. Nos. 1610-1611 printed se-tenant in sheets of 30 (6x5).

Perf. 13½
1969, May 20 Unwmk. Photo.

1610 A281 $1 multi 30 10
1611 A281 $1 multi 30 10
1612 A281 $2.50 multi 80 40
1613 A281 $5 multi 90 50
1614 A281 $8 multi 1.50 80
Nos. 1610-1614 (5) 3.80 1.90

ILO Emblem — A282

Wmk. 323
1969, June 15 Engr. *Perf. 11½*
Granite Paper

1615 A282 $1 dk bl 28 5
1616 A282 $8 dk car 90 30

International Labor Organization, 50th anniversary.

Family at Dinner Table and Dressing — A283

Pupils in Laboratory and Playing — A284

Designs: $2.50, Housecleaning and obeying traffic rules. $4, Recreation (music, fishing, basketball) and education.

Wmk. 323
1969, July 15 Engr. *Perf. 11½*

1617 A283 $1 brick red 22 5
1618 A283 $2.50 blue 85 25
1619 A283 $4 green 85 20

Model Citizen's Life Movement.

1969, Sept. 1 Wmk. 323 *Perf. 11½*

Design: $1, $5, Pupils with book and various school activities (horiz.).

Granite Paper

1620 A284 $1 brt red 25 8
1621 A284 $2.50 brt grn 45 10
1622 A284 $4 dk bl 55 15
1623 A284 $5 brown 75 25

Issued to commemorate the first anniversary of the free 9-year education system.

Wild Flowers and Pheasants, by Lu Chih (Ming) — A285

Paintings: $2.50, Bamboo and birds, Sung dynasty. $5, Flowers and Birds, Sung dynasty. $8, Cranes and Flowers, by G. Castiglione, S.J. (1688-1766).

1969, Oct. 9 Photo. *Perf. 13½*

1624 A285 $1 multi 22 8
1625 A285 $2.50 multi 45 15
1626 A285 $5 multi 90 25
1627 A285 $8 multi 1.50 40

Golden Scepter Rose A286

Rocket and Radar Station A287

Roses: $1, "Charles Mollerin," called black rose. $5, Peace. $8, Josephine Bruce.

1969, Oct. 31 Litho. *Perf. 14*

1628 A286 $1 lt vio & multi 42 10
1629 A286 $2.50 lt bl & multi 70 20
1630 A286 $5 dl org & multi 1.25 50
1631 A286 $8 ap grn & multi 1.40 40

Wmk. 323
1969, Nov. 21 Engr. *Perf. 11½*

1632 A287 $1 rose cl 30 10

The 30th Air Defense Day.

Symbol of International Cooperation A288

Pekingese A289

1969, Nov. 25

1633 A288 $1 rose cl 40 8
1634 A288 $5 green 1.10 20

Issued to commemorate the 5th General Assembly of the Asian Parliamentary Union, Taipei, Nov. 24-28.

1969, Dec. 1 Litho. *Perf. 12*
Granite Paper

1635 A289 50c red & multi 65 8
1636 A289 $4.50 grn & multi 4.00 60

Issued for use on New Year's greetings.

Satellite, Earth Station and Map of Taiwan A290

Unwmk.
1969, Dec. 28 Photo. *Perf. 13*

1637 A290 $1 brn & multi 30 10
1638 A290 $5 vio bl & multi 85 30
1639 A290 $8 pur & multi 1.00 50

Issued to commemorate the inauguration of the Communication Satellite Earth Station at Chin-Shan-Li, Dec. 28.

Agate Grinding Stone, 1662-1911 A291

Ancient Art Treasures: $1, Carved lacquer ware vase, 1662-1911 (vert.). $2, White jade Chin-li-chih melons, 1662-1911. $2.50, Black jade shepherd and ram, 206 B.C.-220 A.D. $4, Chien-lung twin porcelain vase, 1736-1796 (vert.). $5, Ju porcelain vase with 3 bulls, 960-1126 (vert.).

1970, Jan. 23

1640 A291 $1 lt grnsh bl & multi 20 8
1641 A291 $1.50 pale bl & multi 35 15
1642 A291 $2 grn & multi 35 15
1643 A291 $2.50 pink & multi 50 15
1644 A291 $4 ol bis & multi 85 15
1645 A291 $5 ultra & multi 1.10 30
Nos. 1640-1645 (6) 3.35 98

Hsuan Chuang A292

Chu Hsi A293

Design: $2.50, Hua To.

Wmk. 323
1970, Feb. 20 Engr. *Perf. 11½*
Granite Paper

1646 A292 $1 car rose 52 10
1647 A293 $2.50 bl grn 85 15
1648 A293 $4 blue 1.10 20

Issued in memory of Hsuan Chuang (602-664), who propagated Buddhism in China; Chu Hsi (1130-1200), who developed Neo-Confucianism, and Hua To (3rd century A.D.) physician and surgeon.

EXPO '70 Pavilion, Emblem and Flags of Participants A294

Design: $5, Chinese pavilion, EXPO '70 emblem, exhibition and Chinese flags.

Unwmk.

1970, Mar. 13 Photo. *Perf. 13*

1649 A294 $5 org red & multi 65 25
1650 A294 $8 lt bl & multi 95 40

EXPO '70 International Exhibition, Osaka, Japan, Mar. 15-Sept. 13.

Nimbus III and WMO Emblem A295

Design: $1, Agricultural meteorological station and tropical landscape (vert.).

Perf. 14x13½, 13½x14

1970, Mar. 23 Litho. Wmk. 323

Granite Paper

1651 A295 $1 grn & multi 35 8
1652 A295 $8 bl & multi 1.10 40

10th Annual World Meteorological Day.

Martyrs' Shrine, Taipei A296

Shrine's Gate — A297

Unwmk.

1970, Mar. 29 Photo. *Perf. 13*

1653 A296 $1 multi 35 8
1654 A297 $8 multi 1.00 40

Issued to commemorate the completion of the Martyrs' Shrine in Northern Taipei, dedicated to the memory of 72 young revolutionaries who died March 29, 1911.

Yueh Fei Fighting for Lost Territories A298

Characters from Chinese Operas: $2.50, Emperor Shun and stepmother. $5, The Lady Warrior Chin Liang-yu. $8, Kuan Yu and groom.

1970, May 4 Unwmk. *Perf. 13½*

1655 A298 $1 multi 30 10
1656 A298 $2.50 multi 50 25
1657 A298 $5 multi 75 30
1658 A298 $8 multi 1.50 50

"One Hundred Horses" (Detail) by Lang Shih-ning — A299

Three Horses Playing — A300

Designs (Horses): No. 1660, Trees in left background. No. 1661, Tree trunk in lower left corner. No. 1662, Group of trees at right. No. 1663, Barren tree at right. $8, Groom roping horses. Designs from scroll "One Hundred Horses" by Lang Shih-ning (Giuseppe Castiglione, 1688-1766). Nos. 1659-1663 printed se-tenant in sheets of 50 (5x10).

Perf. 13½

1970, June 18 Unwmk. Photo.

1659 A299 $1 multi 30 8
1660 A299 $1 multi 30 8
1661 A299 $1 multi 30 8
1662 A299 $1 multi 30 8
1663 A299 $1 multi 30 8
1664 A300 $5 bis & multi 1.25 60
1665 A300 $8 dl yel & multi 1.75 75
Nos. 1659-1665 (7) 4.50 1.75

Lai-tsu Amusing his Old Parents — A301

Chinese Fairy Tales: No. 1667, Man disguised as deer, and hunters. No. 1668, Boy cooling his father's bed. No. 1669, Boy fishing through ice. No. 1670, Son reunited with old mother. No. 1671, Emperor tasting mother's medicine. No. 1672, Boy saving oranges for mother. No. 1673, Boy saving father from tiger.

Wmk. 323

1970, July 10 Litho. *Perf. 13½*

Granite Paper

1666 A301 10c red & multi 5 5
1667 A301 10c car rose & multi 5 5
1668 A301 10c lt vio & multi 5 5
1669 A301 10c gray & multi 5 5
1670 A301 10c emer & multi 5 5
1671 A301 50c bis & multi 10 5
1672 A301 $1 sky bl & multi 30 5
1673 A301 $1 dp bl & multi 30 5
Nos. 1666-1673 (8) 95 40

See Nos. 1726-1733.

Man's First Step onto Moon — A302

Designs: $1, Pres. Chiang Kai-shek's message brought to the moon. $5, Neil A. Armstrong, Michael Collins, Edwin E. Aldrin, Jr., and moon (horiz.).

Perf. 13½x13, 13x13½

1970, July 21 Photo. Unwmk.

1674 A302 $1 yel & multi 40 10
1675 A302 $5 lt yel grn & multi 75 25
1676 A302 $8 bl & multi 1.10 50

Issued to commemorate the first anniversary of man's first landing on the moon.

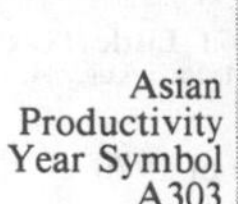

Asian Productivity Year Symbol A303

Wmk. 323

1970, Aug. 18 Litho. *Perf. 13½*

Granite Paper

1677 A303 $1 emer & multi 30 5
1678 A303 $5 bl & multi 65 20

Issued to publicize Asian Productivity Year.

Flags of China and U.N. — A304

1970, Sept. 19 Wmk. 323 *Perf. 12*

Granite Paper

1679 A304 $5 bl, car & blk 90 25

Issued to commemorate the 25th anniversary of the United Nations.

Postal Zone Map of Taiwan A305

Postal Code Emblem A306

1970, Oct. 8 Litho.

1680 A305 $1 lt bl & multi 30 8
1681 A306 $2.50 grn & multi 75 25

Issued to publicize the postal code system.

Eleventh Month Scroll — A307

Designs: A scroll series, "Activities of the 12 Months," painted on silk by a group of painters of the Ch'ien Lung court (1736-1796). Chinese number in parenthesis at right of denomination tells month.

Jan., Feb., Mar. Scrolls

(一) (二) (三)

Perf. 13½x13

1970-71 Photo. Unwmk.

1682 A307 $1 multi 1.25 20
1683 A307 $2.50 multi 1.75 30
1684 A307 $5 multi 3.00 50

A little time given to the study of the arrangement of the Scott Catalogue can make it easier to use effectively.

Apr., May, June Scrolls

(四) (五) (六)

1685 A307 $1 multi 24 8
1686 A307 $2.50 multi 55 20
1687 A307 $5 multi 80 40

July, Aug., Sept. Scrolls

(七) (八) (九)

1688 A307 $1 multi 24 8
1689 A307 $2.50 multi 55 20
1690 A307 $5 multi 80 30

Oct., Nov., Dec. Scrolls

(十) (一十) (二十)

1691 A307 $1 multi 24 8
1692 A307 $2.50 multi 55 20
1693 A307 $5 multi 80 30
Nos. 1682-1693 (12) 10.77 2.84

Issue dates: Nos. 1691-1693, Oct. 21, 1970. Nos. 1682-1684, Jan. 14, 1971. Nos. 1685-1687, Apr. 26, 1971. Nos. 1688-1690, Aug. 27, 1971.

Family at Home — A308

Piggy Bank — A309

Design: $4, Family of 5 going on an excursion (vert.).

Perf. 13½x14, 14x13½

1970, Nov. 11 Litho. Wmk. 323

Granite Paper

1694 A308 $1 multi 28 8
1695 A308 $4 yel grn & multi 80 20

Issued to publicize family planning.

1970, Dec. 1 *Perf. 12½x12*

Granite Paper

1696 A309 50c multi 50 8
1697 A309 $4.50 bl & multi 2.25 40

Issued for use on New Year's greetings.

Tibia Fusus Shells A310

Rare Taiwan Shells: $2.50, Harpeola kurodai. $5, Conus stupa kuroda. $8, Entemnotrochus rumphii.

1971, Feb. 25 *Perf. 13x13½*

1698 A310 $1 vio & multi 24 8
1699 A310 $2.50 multi 32 20
1700 A310 $5 org & multi 80 40
1701 A310 $8 grn & multi 1.40 25

Sun Yat-sen Building, Yangmingshan A311

Passbook and Postal Savings Certificate A312

Perf. 13½x12½

1971 Litho. Wmk. 323

Granite Paper

1702 A311 5c brown 8 5
1703 A311 10c dk gray 8 5
1704 A311 50c brt rose lil 10 5
1705 A311 $1 vermilion 10 5
1706 A311 $1.50 ultra 35 5
1707 A311 $2 plum 35 5
1708 A311 $2.50 emerald 75 5
1709 A311 $3 aqua 75 5
Nos. 1702-1709 (8) 2.56 40

Perf. 13½x14

1971, Mar. 20 Litho. Wmk. 323

Design: $4, People and hand dropping coin into bank.

1712 A312 $1 yel grn & multi 18 8
1713 A312 $4 ver & multi 75 20

Publicizing Chinese Postal Savings Service.

Cooperation Emblem, Farmers A313

Rock Monkey A314

Design: $8, Chinese teaching rice farming to Africans (horiz.).

Unwmk.

1971, May 20 Photo. *Perf. 13*

1714 A313 $1 multi 25 8
1715 A313 $8 multi 1.10 40

Sino-African Technical Cooperation Committee, 10th anniversary.

1971, June 25 *Perf. 11½*

Taiwan Animals: $2, White-face flying squirrel. $3, Chinese pangolin. $5, Formosan sika deer. ($2, $3, $5 are horiz.).

1716 A314 $1 gold & multi 30 15
1717 A314 $2 gold & multi 30 20
1718 A314 $3 gold & multi 65 20
1719 A314 $5 gold & multi 65 40

Pitcher — A315

Designs: $2.50, Players at base (horiz.). $4, Hitter and catcher.

1971, July 29 Photo. *Perf. 13*

1720 A315 $1 multi 28 8
1721 A315 $2.50 multi 40 20
1722 A315 $4 multi 65 20

Pacific Regional competition for the 1971 Little League World Series.

中華少年棒球世界冠軍紀念

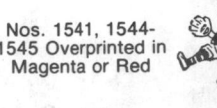

Nos. 1541, 1544-1545 Overprinted in Magenta or Red

Perf. 13x12½

1971, Sept. 9 Litho. Wmk. 323

Granite Paper

1723 A259 $1 ver (M) 25 8
1724 A259 $2.50 bl (R) 65 25
1725 A259 $3 grnsh bl (R) 50 30

Chinese victory in 1971 Little League World Series, Williamsport, Pa., Aug. 24.

Fairy Tale Type of 1970

Chinese Fairy Tales (Filial Piety): No. 1726, Birds and elephant helping in rice field. No. 1727, Son gathering mulberries for mother. No. 1728, Son gathering firewood. No. 1729, Son, mother and bandits. No. 1730, Son carrying heavy burden. 50c, Son digging for bamboo shoots in winter. No. 1732, Man and wife working as slaves. No. 1733, Father, son and carriage.

1971, Sept. 22 *Perf. 13½*

Granite Paper

1726 A301 10c dp org & multi 8 5
1727 A301 10c lil & multi 8 5
1728 A301 10c ocher & multi 8 5
1729 A301 10c dp car & multi 8 5
1730 A301 10c lt ultra & multi 8 5
1731 A301 50c multi 10 5
1732 A301 $1 emer & multi 30 5
1733 A301 $1 lt red brn & multi 30 5
Nos. 1726-1733 (8) 1.10 40

Flag of China, "Double Ten" and Anniversary Emblems A316

Designs (Flag of China and): $2.50, National anthem. $5, Gen. Chiang Kai-shek. $8, Sun Yat-sen.

1971, Oct. 10 Photo. *Perf. 13*

1734 A316 $1 org & multi 28 8
1735 A316 $2.50 multi 40 15
1736 A316 $5 grn & multi 80 40
1737 A316 $8 ol & multi 1.00 40

60th National Day.

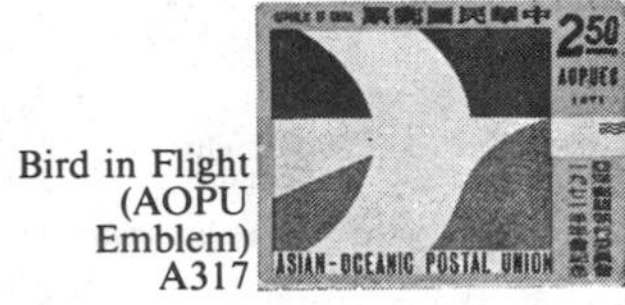

Bird in Flight (AOPU Emblem) A317

Perf. 13½x14

1971, Nov. 8 Litho. Wmk. 323

1738 A317 $2.50 yel & multi 75 20
1739 A317 $5 org & multi 75 20

Asian-Oceanic Postal Union Executive Committee Session, Taipei, Nov. 8-15.

"White Frost Hawk," by Lang Shih-ning A318

Dog Series I

Designs: $2, "Star-Glancing Wolf." $2.50, "Golden-Winged Face." $5, "Young Black Dragon." $8, "Young Gray Dragon."

Designs from painting series "Ten Prized Dogs," by Lang Shih-ning (Giuseppe Castiglione, 1688-1766).

Perf. 13½x13

1971, Nov. 16 Litho. Unwmk.

1740 A318 $1 *Facing left* 35 8
1741 A318 $2 *Lying down* 42 10
1742 A318 $2.50 *Scratching* 50 20
1743 A318 $5 *Facing right* 90 30
1744 A318 $8 *Looking back* 1.65 60
Nos. 1740-1744 (5) 3.82 1.28

Dog Series II

Designs: $1, "Black with Snow-white Paws." $2, "Yellow Leopard." $2.50, "Flying Magpie." $5, "Heavenly Lion." $8, "Mottled Tiger."

1972, Jan. 12

1745 A318 $1 *Facing right* 35 10
1746 A318 $2 *Walking* 42 10
1747 A318 $2.50 *Sleeping* 50 20
1748 A318 $5 *Facing left* 90 30
1749 A318 $8 *Sitting* 2.00 50
Nos. 1745-1749 (5) 4.17 1.20

Squirrels — A319

Perf. 13½x12½

1971, Dec. 1 Wmk. 323

1750 A319 Block of 4, multi 90 45
a. 50c in UL corner 15 6
b. 50c in UR corner 15 6
c. 50c in LL corner 15 6
d. 50c in LR corner 15 6
1751 A319 Block of 4, multi 4.75 3.25
a. $4.50 in UL corner 1.10 55
b. $4.50 in UR corner 1.10 55
c. $4.50 in LL corner 1.10 55
d. $4.50 in LR corner 1.10 55

New Year 1972.

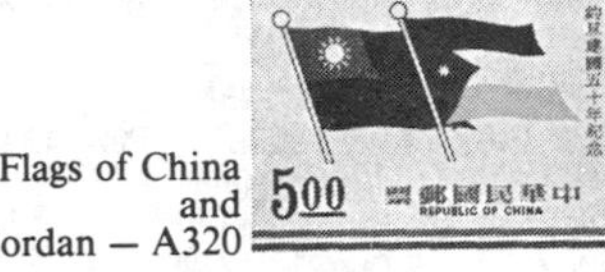

Flags of China and Jordan — A320

1971, Dec. 16 *Perf. 13½*

Granite Paper

1752 A320 $5 multi 85 20

50th anniversary of the founding of the Hashemite Kingdom of Jordan.

Cargo Ship "Hai King" — A321

Design: $7, Ocean liner and map of Pacific Ocean (vert.).

1971, Dec. 16 *Perf. 12½*

1753 A321 $4 grn, dk bl & red 50 20
1754 A321 $7 ocher & multi 80 20

Centenary of China Merchants Steam Navigation Co.

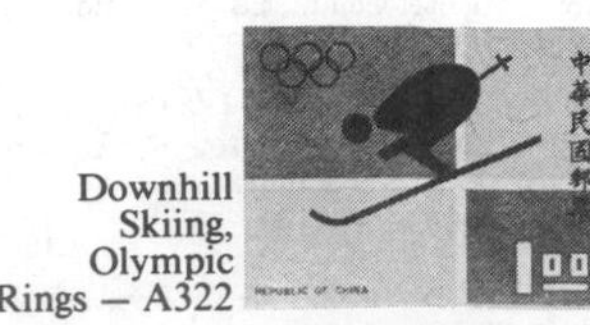

Downhill Skiing, Olympic Rings — A322

Designs: $5, Cross-country skiing. $8, Giant slalom.

1972, Feb. 3 *Perf. 13½*

1755 A322 $1 org, blk & bl 25 8
1756 A322 $5 yel grn, dp org & blk 75 20
1757 A322 $8 red, gray & blk 90 20

11th Winter Olympic Games, Sapporo, Japan, Feb. 3-13.

Vase, 18th Century — A323

Porcelain Series I

Porcelain Masterworks of Ching Dynasty: $2, Covered jar. $2.50, Pitcher. $5, Vase with 5 openings and dragon design. $8, Covered jar with children design.

Perf. 11½

1972, Mar. 20 Photo. Unwmk.

1758 A323 $1 vio & multi 35 8
1759 A323 $2 plum & bl 35 15
1760 A323 $2.50 org ver & bl 35 15
1761 A323 $5 bis brn & bl 65 25
1762 A323 $8 sl grn & multi 1.00 40
Nos. 1758-1762 (5) 2.70 1.03

See Nos. 1812-1821, 1864-1868.

Nine Flying Doves — A324

Perf. 13½x14

1972, Apr. 1 Litho. Wmk. 323

1763 A324 $1 lt bl & blk 28 8
1764 A324 $5 lt vio & blk 85 20

Asian-Oceanic Postal Union, 10th anniversary.

"Dignity with Self-reliance" — A325

Perf. 13½x12½

1972-75 Litho. Wmk. 323

1765 A325 5c brn & yel 5 5
1766 A325 10c bl & org 5 5
1767 A325 20c cl & yel grn ('75) 5 5
1768 A325 50c lil & lil rose 5 5
1769 A325 $1 red & brt bl 10 5
1770 A325 $1.50 yel & dk bl 25 5
1771 A325 $2 mar & org 25 6
1772 A325 $2.50 emer & ver 25 7
1773 A325 $3 red & lt grn 32 8
Nos. 1765-1773 (9) 1.37 51

Souvenir Sheet

Imperf

1775 A325 Sheet of 2 1.50 1.50

No. 1775 commemorates ROCPEX '72 Philatelic Exhibition, Taipei, Oct. 24-Nov. 2. It contains 2 stamps similar to Nos. 1771 and 1773 with simulated perforations. Orange brown margin with white inscriptions. Size: 69x100mm.

Issue dates: $1, $1.50, $2, $3, May 20, 1972; 5c, 10c, 50c, $2.50, No. 1775, Oct. 24, 1972; 20c, 1975.

Emperor Shih-tsung's Procession — A326

Messengers on Horseback — A327

Designs from scrolls depicting Emperor Shih-tsung's (reigned 1522-1566) journey to and from tombs at Cheng-tien. No. 1776 shows land journey and is designed from right to left. No. 1779 shows return trip by boat and is designed from left to right. The five stamps of Nos. 1776 and 1780 are numbered 1 to 5 in Chinese (see illustrations with Nos. 1682-1686 for numerals).

1972 Photo. Unwmk. Perf. 13½

1776 A326 Strip of 5, *Departure* 1.25 35
- *a.* $1 *shown* (1) 20 5
- *b.* $1 *Seven carriages* (2) 20 5
- *c.* $1 *Carriage drawn by 23 horses* (3) 20 5
- *d.* $1 *Procession* (4) 20 5
- *e.* $1 *Emperor under 2 canopies* (5) 20 5

1777 A327 $2.50 *shown* 70 8
1778 A327 $5 *Guards with flags, fans & spears* 1.00 20
1779 A327 $8 *Sedan chair carried by 28 men* 1.75 40
1780 A326 Strip of 5, *Return trip* 1.25 35
- *a.* $1 *Three barges* (1) 20 5
- *b.* $1 *Procession, sedan chairs* (2) 20 5
- *c.* $1 *Two barges with trunks* (3) 20 5
- *d.* $1 *Procession on land* (4) 20 5
- *e.* $1 *Procession, 2 sedan chairs* (5) 20 5

1781 A327 $2.50 *Courtiers at city welcoming Emperor* 70 8
1782 A327 $5 *Orchestra on horseback* 1.00 20
1783 A327 $8 *Barges* 1.00 40
Nos. 1776-1783 (8) 8.65 2.06

Issue dates: No. 1776-1779, June 14; Nos. 1780-1783, July 12.

First Day Covers A328

Magnifying Glass, Tongs, Gauge A329

Design: $2.50, Sun Yat-sen stamp of 1971 (type A311) under magnifying glass.

Wmk. 323

1972, Aug. 9 Engr. Perf. 12

1784 A328 $1 dk vio bl 25 5
1785 A328 $2.50 brt brn 30 8
1786 A329 $8 scarlet 90 20

Promotion of philately. Printed in sheets of 40. Each sheet contains 4 blocks of 10 stamps surrounded by margins with inscriptions.

Nos. 1768-1770, 1772 Overprinted in Dark Blue or Red

Perf. 13½x12½

1972, Sept. 9 Litho. Wmk. 323

1787 A325 $1 red & brt bl (DB) 20 8
1788 A325 $1.50 yel & dk bl (R) 40 20
1789 A325 $2 mar & org (R) 40 8
1790 A325 $3 red & lt grn (DB) 40 15

China's championship victories in the Little League World Series, Gary, Ind., and in the Senior League World Series, Williamsport, Pa., Aug. 1972.

Emperor Yao (2357-2258 B.C.) A330

Mountain Climbing A331

Rulers: $4, Emperor Shun (ruled 2255-2208 B.C.). $4.50, Yu, the Great (ruled 2205-2198 B.C.). $5, King T'ang (ruled 1783-1754 B.C.). $5.50, King Wen (ruled 1171-1122 B.C.). $6, King Wu (ruled 1121-1114 B.C.). $7, Chou Kung (died 1105 B.C.). $8, Confucius (551-479 B.C.).

1972-73 Engr. Perf. 12

Granite Paper

1791 A330 $3.50 dk bl 32 20
1792 A330 $4 rose red 32 20
1793 A330 $4.50 bluish lil 40 20
1794 A330 $5 brt grn 45 20
1795 A330 $5.50 dp org ('73) 65 20
1796 A330 $6 dp cl ('73) 65 25
- *a.* Perf. 13½x12½ ('76) 65 25

1797 A330 $7 sep ('73) 65 25
- *a.* Perf. 13½x12½ ('76) 65 25

1798 A330 $8 ind ('73) 1.00 30
- *a.* gray, perf. 13½x12½ ('76) 1.00 30

Nos. 1791-1798 (8) 4.44 1.80

In the first printing, Nos. 1791-1794, 1796-1798 measure 32mm. high. In a 1974 reissue they are 33mm.

Unwmk.

1972, Oct. 31 Photo. Perf. 12

Designs (China Youth Corps emblem and): $2.50, Skiing (skiers forming circle). $4, Diving. $8, Parachute jumping.

1800 A331 $1 grn & multi 15 8
1801 A331 $2.50 bl & multi 35 8
1802 A331 $4 org & multi 45 20
1803 A331 $8 multi 1.00 40

China Youth Corps, 20th anniversary.

JCI Emblem — A332

1972, Nov. 12 Litho. Wmk. 323

1804 A332 $1 multi 20 8
1805 A332 $5 org & multi 50 15
1806 A332 $8 multi 75 40

27th Junior Chamber International (JCI) World Congress, Taipei, Nov. 12-19.

Electronic Mail Sorter A333

Plane, Ship and Pier A334

Design: $5, Highway overpass over railroad.

Wmk. 323

1972, Nov. 12 Engr. Perf. 11½

1807 A333 $1 red 20 8
1808 A334 $2.50 blue 35 15
1809 A334 $5 dk vio & brn 75 30

Progress of communications system on Taiwan.

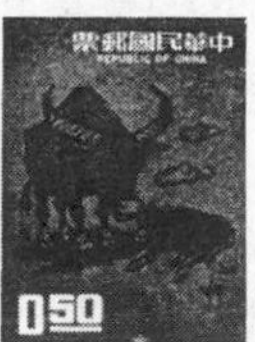

Cow and Calf (Parental Love) — A335

1972, Dec. 1 Litho. Perf. 12

1810 A335 50c red & blk 38 8
1811 A335 $4.50 yel, red & brn 1.00 30

New Year 1973. Printed in sheets of 80, divided into 4 panes of 20, separated by vertical and horizontal gutters 2 rows wide. 20 red chops meaning "Happy New Year" are printed in the gutters.

Porcelain Type of 1972 and

Stem Bowl with Dragons A336

Porcelain Series II

1973 Photo. Perf. 11½

Porcelain Masterworks of Ming Dynasty: $1, Covered vase with fruits and flowers. $2, Vase with ornamental and floral design. $2.50, Vase imitating ancient bronze. $5, Flask with flowers of 4 seasons. $8, Garlic head vase.

1812 A323 $1 gray & multi 15 5
1813 A323 $2 lt brn & multi 25 8
1814 A323 $2.50 brt grn & multi 35 10
1815 A323 $5 ultra & multi 60 25
1816 A323 $8 ol & multi 90 40
Nos. 1812-1816 (5) 2.25 88

Porcelain Series III

Ming Porcelain: $2, Refuse container with dragons. $2.50, Covered jar with lotus. $5, Covered jar with horses. $8, Bowl with figures of immortals.

1817 A336 $1 gray & multi 15 5
1818 A336 $2 lt vio & multi 25 8
1819 A336 $2.50 dk red & multi 45 10
1820 A336 $5 bl & multi 45 20
1821 A336 $8 dp org & multi 90 30
Nos. 1817-1821 (5) 2.20 73

Issue dates: Nos. 1812-1816, Jan. 10; Nos. 1817-1821, Mar. 24.
See Nos. 1865-1868.

Oyster Fairy and Fisherman's Dance — A337

1973, Feb. 7 Photo. Perf. 11½

Granite Paper

1822 A337 $1 *Kicking shuttlecock* (vert.) 40 5
1823 A337 $4 *shown* 65 20
1824 A337 $5 *Rowing boat over land* 65 20
1825 A337 $8 *Old man carrying young lady* (vert.) 1.00 30

Chinese folklore popular entertainment.

Bamboo Boat A338

Taiwanese Handicrafts: $2.50, Painted marble vase (vert.). $5, Painted glass plate. $8, Doll, bridegroom carrying bride on back (vert.).

Perf. 13½x14½, 14½x13½

1973, Mar. 9 Photo.

1826 A338 $1 multi 20 5
1827 A338 $2.50 multi 40 10
1828 A338 $5 multi 65 20
1829 A338 $8 multi 1.00 30

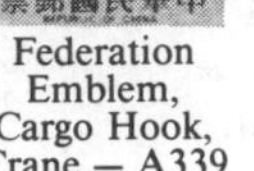

Federation Emblem, Cargo Hook, Crane — A339

Emblem, Tractor, New Buildings — A340

Wmk. 323

1973, Apr. 2 Litho. Perf. 12½

1830 A339 $1 sal & multi 10 5
1831 A340 $5 bl & blk 55 20

12th convention of International Federation of Asian and Western Pacific Contractors Association, Taipei, Apr. 2-10.

Pres. Chiang Kai-shek, Flag of China A341

Lin Tse-hsü A342

Design: $4, like $1 with different border.

Unwmk.

1973, May 20 Photo. Perf. 12

1832 A341 $1 yel & multi 30 5
1833 A341 $4 dk grn & multi 75 20

First anniversary of Pres. Chiang Kai-shek's inauguration for a fifth term.

Wmk. 323

1973, June 3 Engr. Perf. 12

1834 A342 $1 sepia 15 6

Lin Tse-hsü (1785-1850), Governor of Hunan and Kwantung, who destroyed large quantity of opium at Humen, Kwantung, June 3, 1839.

Willows and Palace Gate in the Morning — A343

Lady Watering Peonies, Stone Ornament A344

Design from scroll "Spring Morning in the Han Palace," by Chiu Ying. The five stamps of No. 1835 are numbered 1 to 5 and the five stamps of No. 1838 are numbered 6-10 in Chinese (see illustrations with Nos. 1682-1691 for numerals). The stamps are numbered and listed from right to left.

1973 Photo. Unwmk. Perf. 11½
Granite Paper

1835 A343 Strip of 5 90 25
- a. $1 *shown* (1) 12 5
- b. $1 *Ladies feeding peacocks* (2) 12 5
- c. $1 *Lady watering peonies* (3) 12 5
- d. $1 *Pear tree in bloom* (4) 12 5
- e. $1 *Lady musicians* (5) 12 5

1836 A344 $5 *shown* 75 20
1837 A344 $8 *Lady musicians* 1.10 30
1838 A343 Strip of 5 90 25
- a. $1 *Ladies playing go* (6) 12 5
- b. $1 *Various games* (7) 12 5
- c. $1 *Talking and playing music* (8) 12 5
- d. $1 *Artist painting portrait* (9) 12 5
- e. $1 *Sentries guarding wall* (10) 12 5

1839 A344 $5 *Ladies playing go* 75 20
1840 A344 $8 *Girl chasing butterfly* 1.10 30
Nos. 1835-1840 (6) 5.50 1.50

Issue dates: Nos. 1835-1837, June 20; Nos. 1838-1840, July 18.

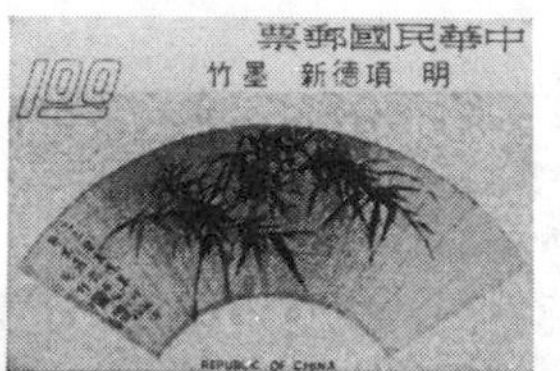
Fan, Bamboo Design, by Hsiang Tehsin — A345

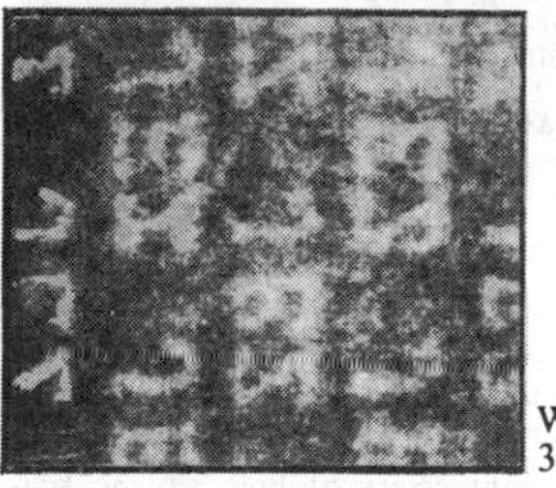
Wmk. 368

Designs: Painted fans, Ming dynasty.

Wmk. JEZ Multiple (368)
1973, Aug. 15 Photo. Perf. 12½x13

1841 A345 $1 bis & multi 15 6
1842 A345 $2.50 bis & multi 35 8
1843 A345 $5 bis & multi 55 20
1844 A345 $8 bis & multi 90 30

See Nos. 1934-1937.

Little League Emblem A346

INTERPOL Emblem A347

Wmk. 370

Wmk. Geometrical Design (370)
1973, Sept. 9 Litho. Perf. 13½

1845 A346 $1 yel, car & dk bl 25 6
1846 A346 $4 yel, grn & dk bl 50 20

Chinese victory in Little League Twin Championships, Gary, Ind., and Williamsport, Pa.

Wmk. 370
1973, Sept. 11 Litho. Perf. 12

1847 A347 $1 bl & org 10 5
1848 A347 $5 grn & org 45 20
1849 A347 $8 mag & org 70 30

50th anniversary of International Criminal Police Organization.

Ch'iu Feng-chia — A348

Wmk. 323
1973, Oct. 5 Engr. Perf. 11½

1850 A348 $1 vio blk 30 8

2nd meeting of overseas Hakkas, Taipei, Oct. 5-7, and to honor Ch'iu Feng-chia (1864-1912), Hakka scholar, poet and revolutionist.

Tsengwen Reservoir A349

Tsengwen Dam — A350

Perf. 13½
1973, Oct. 31 Photo. Unwmk.

1851 A349 Strip of 3 45 15
- a. $1 *Upper shore* 10 5
- b. $1 *shown* 10 5
- c. $1 *Lower shore* 10 5

Perf. 12x11½

1852 A350 $5 *shown* 55 20
1853 A350 $8 *Spillway* 80 30

Inauguration of Tsengwen Reservoir. No. 1851 printed se-tenant in sheets of 15.

Tiger — A351

Wmk. 370
1973, Dec. 1 Litho. Perf. 12½

1854 A351 50c multi 25 6
1855 A351 $4.50 multi 80 20

New Year 1974.

"Snow-dotted Eagle," by Lang Shih-ning — A352

Designs: No. 1857, "Comfortable Ride." No. 1858, "Red Flower Eagle." No. 1859, "Cloud-running Steed." No. 1860, "Sky-running steed." $2.50, "Red Jade Seat." $5, "Thunderclap Steed." $8, "Arabian Champion." Designs from painting series "Ten Prized Horses," by Lang Shih-ning (Giuseppe Castiglione, 1688-1766).

1973 Litho. Unwmk. Perf. 13
Without Gum

1856 A352 50c *shown* 8 5
1857 A352 $1 *Pinto, blk tail* 22 5
1858 A352 $1 *Facing left* 22 5
1859 A352 $1 *Facing right* 22 5
1860 A352 $1 *Pinto, white tail* 22 5
1861 A352 $2.50 *Palomino* 50 8
1862 A352 $5 *Grazing* 75 20
- a. Souvenir sheet of 4 1.40

1863 A352 $8 *Brown stallion* 1.25 25
Nos. 1856-1863 (8) 3.46 78

Nos. 1857-1860 printed se-tenant in sheets of 50. No. 1862a contains 4 stamps with simulated perforations similar to Nos. 1856-1857, 1861-1862. Bluish green ornamental margin, black inscription. Size: 150x120mm.

Issue dates: 50c, $2.50, $5, Nov. 21; others Dec. 21.

Porcelain Types of 1972-73
Porcelain Series IV

Porcelain Masterworks of Sung Dynasty: $1, Vase. $2, Three-tiered vase. $2.50, Lotus-shaped bowl. $5, Incense burner. $8, Incense burner on stand.

1974, Jan. 16 Photo. Perf. 11½

1864 A323 $1 ultra & multi 12 5
1865 A336 $2 multi 28 8
1866 A336 $2.50 red & multi 35 8
1867 A336 $5 lil & multi 55 20
1868 A336 $8 grn & multi 75 30
Nos. 1864-1868 (5) 2.05 71

Juggler — A353

Taroko Gorge, Hualien — A354

Design: $8, Magician producing dishes from his robe (horiz.).

1974, Feb. 6 Photo. Perf. 11½

1869 A353 $1 yel & multi 15 5
1870 A353 $8 yel & multi 60 30

1974, Mar. 22 Photo. Perf. 12

Designs: $2.50, Luce Chapel, Tunghai University. $5, Tzu En Pagoda, Sun Moon Lake. $8, Goddess of Mercy, Keelung.

1871 A354 $1 multi 12 5
1872 A354 $2.50 multi 40 8
1873 A354 $5 multi 60 15
1874 A354 $8 multi 1.00 25

Taiwan landmarks.

Fighting Cocks (Brass) A355

Designs: $2.50, Grapes and bowl with fruit (imitation jade). $5, Fisherman (wood carving; vert.). $8, Basket with plastic roses (vert.).

Perf. 13½x14½, 14½x13½
1974, Apr. 10

1875 A355 $1 bl grn & multi 12 5
1876 A355 $2.50 brn & multi 38 8
1877 A355 $5 crim & multi 50 15
1878 A355 $8 multi 1.00 25

Taiwanese handicraft products.

Sun Yat-sen Memorial Hall — A356

Designs: $2.50, Reaching-moon Tower, Cheng Ching Lake. $5, Orchid Island (boats). $8, Penghu Interisland Bridge.

1974, May 15 Photo. Perf. 11½
Granite Paper

1879 A356 $1 bl & multi 12 5
1880 A356 $2.50 bl & multi 35 8
1881 A356 $5 bl & multi 50 15
1882 A356 $8 bl & multi 1.00 25

Taiwan landmarks.

Pres. Chiang and Gate of Whampoa Military Academy — A357

Marching Cadets and Entrance Gate — A358

Wmk. 323
1974, June 16 Engr. Perf. 11½

1883 A357 $1 car rose 35 5
1884 A358 $14 vio bl 1.40 50

50th anniversary of the founding of the Whampoa Military Academy.

Long-distance Runner and Olympic Rings — A359

The Boy Wang Ch'i Fighting Invaders — A360

Design: $8, Women's relay race and Olympic rings.

1974, June 23 Litho. Perf. 12½

1885 A359 $1 bl, blk & red 12 5
1886 A359 $8 pink, blk & red 80 25

80th anniversary of International Olympic Committee.

1974, July 15 Wmk. 370 Perf. 13½

Folk Tales: No. 1888, T'i Ying pleading for her father before the Emperor. No. 1889, Wen Yen-po flushing out ball caught in tree. No. 1890, Boy Wang Hua returning gold piece he found. No. 1891, Pu Shih, a rich sheep raiser and benefactor. No. 1892, K'ung Yung as a child choosing smallest pear. No. 1893, Tung Yu studying. No. 1894, Szu Ma-kuang saving playmate from drowning in water jar.

1887 A360 50c ol & multi 5 5
1888 A360 50c ultra & multi 5 5
1889 A360 50c ocher & multi 5 5
1890 A360 50c red brn & multi 5 5
1891 A360 $1 grn & multi 12 5

1892 A360	$1	lil & multi	12	5
1893 A360	$1	bl & multi	12	5
1894 A360	$1	car & multi	12	5
		Nos. 1887-1894 (8)	68	40

Same denominations printed in blocks of four in sheets of 100.

Myrtle, by Wei Sheng — A361

Silk Fan Paintings, Sung Dynasty (960-1279 A.D.): $2.50, Cabbage and Insects, by Hsu Ti. $5, Hibiscus, Cat and Dog, by Li Ti. $8, Pomegranate and Birds, by Wu Ping. Fans from National Palace Museum.

Perf. 13x12½

1974, Aug. 14 Photo. Wmk. 368

1895 A361	$1	multi	15	5
1896 A361	$2.50	multi	40	8
1897 A361	$5	multi	70	15
1898 A361	$8	multi	1.00	25

See Nos. 1950-1953.

Battle at Marco Polo Bridge, July 7, 1937 A362

Wmk. 370

1974, Sept. 3 Litho. *Perf. 13½*

1899 A362 $1 multi 10 5

Souvenir Sheet

Wmk. 323

Without Gum; Granite Paper

1900	Sheet of 8	1.00
a.	A362 $1, Single stamp	12

20th Armed Forces Day. No. 1900 commemorates Armed Forces Stamp Exhibition, Sun Yat-sen Memorial Hall, Sept. 3-9. Sheet has yellow ornamental margin with black inscription. Size: 106x146mm.

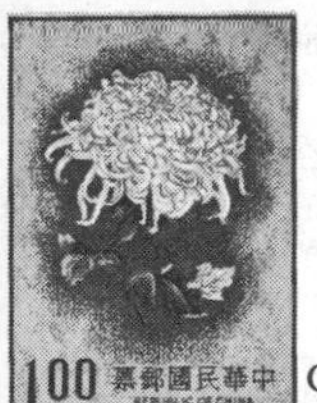

Chrysanthemum A363

Designs: Various chrysanthemums.

Unwmk.

1974, Sept. 30 Photo. *Perf. 12*

Granite Paper

1901 A363	$1	lil & multi	12	5
1902 A363	$2.50	multi	35	8
1903 A363	$5	org & multi	50	15
1904 A363	$8	multi	85	25

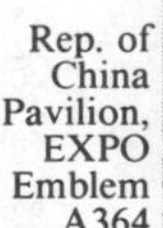

Rep. of China Pavilion, EXPO Emblem A364

The first price column gives the catalogue value of an unused stamp, the second that of a used stamp.

Map of Fair Grounds, Chinese Flag A364a

Wmk. 370

1974, Oct. 10 Litho. *Perf. 13*

1905 A364	$1	multi	20	5
1906 A364a	$8	multi	75	25

EXPO '74, Spokane, Wash., May 4-Nov. 4. Theme, "Preserve the Environment."

Steel Mill, Kaohsiung A365

Taichung Harbor A366

Designs: $1, Taiwan North Link Railroad and map. $2, Oil refinery. $2.50, Electric train. $3.50, Taoyuan International Airport. $4, Taiwan North-South Highway and map. $4.50, Kaohsiung shipyard. $5, Su-ao Port.

Perf. 13x12½, 12½x13

1974, Oct. 31 Wmk. 323

1907 A365	50c	lil, yel & brn	5	5
1908 A365	$1	grn & org	10	5
1909 A365	$2	bl & yel	15	5
1910 A365	$2.50	emer & org	15	8
1911 A366	$3	ocher & ultra	28	10
1912 A366	$3.50	sl grn & yel	32	12
1913 A366	$4	brn & yel	40	14
1914 A366	$4.50	ver & bl	40	15
1915 A366	$5	sep & dk bl	55	16
		Nos. 1907-1915 (9)	2.40	90

Major construction projects.

See Nos. 2009-2017, 2068-2076.

Agaricus Bisporus A367

Edible Mushrooms: $2.50, Pleurotus ostreatus. $5, Dictyophora indusiata. $8, Flammulina velutipes.

Perf. 11½

1974, Nov. 15 Unwmk. Photo.

1916 A367	$1	multi	10	5
1917 A367	$2.50	multi	38	8
1918 A367	$5	multi	65	16
1919 A367	$8	multi	80	25

9th International Scientific Congress on the Cultivation of Edible Fungi, Taipei, Nov. 1974.

Batters and World Map — A368

Pitcher and Championship Banners A369

Wmk. 323

1974, Nov. 24 Litho. *Perf. 13½*

1920 A368	$1	multi	15	5
1921 A369	$8	multi	75	25

China's victory in 1974 Little League Baseball World Series Triple Championships.

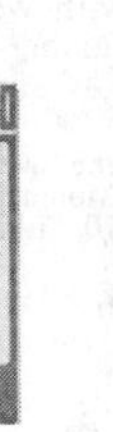

Rabbit A370

Acrobat with Iron Rod A371

Wmk. 323

1974, Dec. 10 Photo. *Perf. 12½*

1922 A370	50c	org & multi	10	5
1923 A370	$4.50	brn & multi	50	15

New Year 1975.

1975, Jan. 15 Unwmk. *Perf. 11½*

Design: $5, Two acrobats spinning tops (horiz.).

Granite Paper

1924 A371	$4	yel & multi	30	15
1925 A371	$5	yel & multi	50	20

Children Watching Puppet Show — A372

Ceremonial New Year Greetings — A373

Designs from scroll "Festivals for the New Year," by Ting Kuan-p'eng. Nos. 1926a-1926e are numbered 1-5 in Chinese.

1975, Feb. 25 Photo. *Perf. 11½*

Granite Paper

1926 A372		Strip of 5	55	20
a.	$1	*Ceremonial New Year Greetings (1)*	8	5
b.	$1	*Man with trained monkey (2)*	8	5
c.	$1	*Crowd and musicians (3)*	8	5
d.	$1	*Picnic under a tree (4)*	8	5
e.	$1	*shown (5)*	8	5
1927 A373	$2.50	*shown*	40	8
1928 A373	$5	*Children buying firecrackers*	55	20
1929 A373	$8	*Children and man with trained monkey*	1.40	60

Sun Yat-sen Memorial Hall, Taipei A374

Sun Yat-sen's Handwriting — A375

Sun Yat-sen, Bronze Statue in Memorial Hall — A376

Sun Yat-sen Memorial Hall, St. John's University, N.Y. A377

Perf. 13½x14, 14x13½

1975, Mar. 12 Litho.

1930 A374	$1	grn & multi	12	5
1931 A375	$4	yel grn & multi	38	15
1932 A376	$5	yel & multi	50	20
1933 A377	$8	gray & multi	80	30

Dr. Sun Yat-sen (1866-1925), statesman and revolutionary leader, 50th death anniversary.

Fan Type of 1973 Inscribed "Landscape" (1st Character, 2nd Row)

水山

Designs: Painted fans, Ming Dynasty. Second row of inscription gives design description.

Perf. 12½x13

1975, Apr. 16 Photo. Wmk. 368

1934 A345	$1	bis & multi	12	5
1935 A345	$2.50	bis & multi	35	8
1936 A345	$5	bis & multi	50	20
1937 A345	$8	bis & multi	80	30

Yuan-chin coin, 1122-221 B.C. — A378

Ancient Chinese Coins: $4, Pan-liang, 221-207 B.C. $5, Five chu, 206 B.C.-220 A.D. $8, Five chu, 502-557 A.D.

Wmk. 323

1975, May 20 Litho. *Perf. 13*

1938 A378	$1	sal & multi	12	5
1939 A378	$4	yel & multi	35	15
1940 A378	$5	dl yel & multi	50	20
1941 A378	$8	lt vio & multi	80	30

The Cloth-bag Monk, by Chang Hung (1577-1668) A379

Chinese Paintings: $4, Lao-tzu Riding Buffalo, by Chao Pu-chih (1053-1110). $5, Portrait of Shih-te, by Wang Wen (1497-1576). $8, Splashed-ink Immortal, by Liang K'ai (early 13th century).

Perf. 11 1/2

1975, June 18 Photo. Unwmk.

Granite Paper

1942 A379 $2 blk, buff & ver 15 8
1943 A379 $4 blk, gray & red 35 15
1944 A379 $5 blk, yel & ver 45 20
1945 A379 $8 tan, red & blk 80 30

Chu Yin Reading by the Light of Fireflies — A380

Folk Tales: No. 1947, Hua Mu-lan going to war for her father. No. 1948, King Kou Chien tasting gall. $5, Chou Ch'u killing tiger.

Perf. 14x13 1/2

1975, July 16 Litho. Wmk. 368

1946 A380 $1 ol & multi 12 5
1947 A380 $2 bis brn & multi 20 8
1948 A380 $2 lt grn & multi 20 8
1949 A380 $5 bl & multi 60 16

See Nos. 2108-2111.

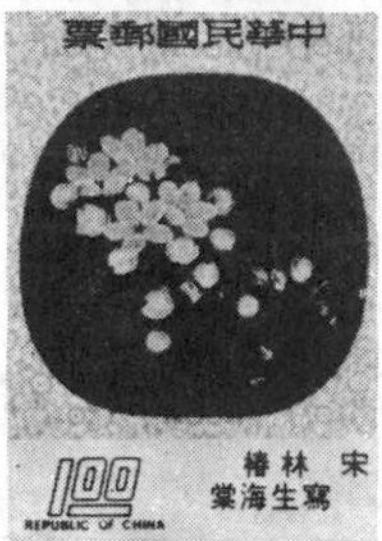

Cherry-Apple Blossoms, by Lin Ch'un — A381

Silk Fan Paintings, Sung Dynasty: $2, Spring Blossoms and Butterfly, by Ma K'uei. $5, Monkeys and Deer, by I Yüan-chih. $8, Tame Sparrow among Bamboo.

Perf. 13x12 1/2

1975, Aug. 15 Litho. Wmk. 323

1950 A381 $1 multi 12 5
1951 A381 $2 multi 30 8
1952 A381 $5 multi 60 16
1953 A381 $8 multi 85 30

See Nos. 2001-2004.

Gen. Chang Tzu-chung (1891-1940) A382

Portraits: No. 1955, Maj. Gen. Kao Chih-hong (1908-1937). No. 1956, Capt. Sha Shih-chiun (1896-1938). No. 1957, Maj. Gen. Hsieh Chin-yuan (1905-1941). No. 1958, Lt. Yen Hai-wen (1916-1937). No. 1959, Lt. Gen. Tai An-lan (1905-1942).

Wmk. 323

1975, Sept. 3 Engr. Perf. 12

1954 A382 $2 carmine 28 8
1955 A382 $2 sepia 28 8
1956 A382 $2 dl grn 28 8
1957 A382 $5 vio blk 65 20
1958 A382 $5 vio bl 65 20
1959 A382 $5 dk bl 65 20
Nos. 1954-1959 (6) 2.79 84

Martyrs of the resistance fight against Japan.

Lotus Pond with Willows, by Madame Chiang — A383

Paintings by Madame Chiang Kai-shek: $5, Sun Breaks through Mountain Clouds. $8, A Pair of Pine Trees. $10, Fishing and Farming.

Perf. 13 1/2

1975, Oct. 31 Litho. Unwmk.

1960 A383 $2 multi 25 10
1961 A383 $5 multi 50 25
1962 A383 $8 multi 75 40
1963 A383 $10 multi 95 50

Cauldron with Phoenix Handles, 481-221 B.C. — A384

Ancient Bronzes: $2, Rectangular cauldron, 1122-722 B.C. (vert.). $8, Flat jar, 481-221 B.C. $10, 3-legged wine vessel, 1766-1122 B.C. (vert.).

1975, Nov. 12 Photo. Perf. 12

1964 A384 $2 pink & multi 18 10
1965 A384 $5 lt bl & multi 50 25
1966 A384 $8 yel & multi 75 40
1967 A384 $10 lil & multi 95 50

Dragon, Nine-Dragon Wall, Peihai A385

Techi Dam A386

Wmk. 323

1975, Dec. 1 Litho. Perf. 12 1/2

1968 A385 $1 org & multi 10 5
1969 A385 $5 grn & multi 50 20

New Year 1976.

1975, Dec. 17 Unwmk. Perf. 13 1/2

Design: $10, Panoramic view of Techi Dam.

1970 A386 $2 grn & multi 20 8
1971 A386 $10 bl & multi 90 40

Completion of Techi Dam, Tachia River.

Biathlon and Olympic Rings — A387

Designs (Olympic Rings and): $5, Luge. $8, Skiing.

1976, Jan. 15 Litho. Perf. 13 1/2

1972 A387 $2 bl & multi 20 8
1973 A387 $5 bl & multi 45 16
1974 A387 $8 bl & multi 65 25

12th Winter Olympic Games, Innsbruck, Austria, Feb. 4-15.

Chin, Oldest Chinese Instrument A388

Musical Instruments: $5, Se, c. 2900 B.C. $8, Standing kong-ho (harp). $10, Sleeping kong-ho.

1976, Feb. 11 Unwmk. Perf. 14

1975 A388 $2 yel & multi 22 8
1976 A388 $5 org & multi 45 16
1977 A388 $8 grnsh bl & multi 70 25
1978 A388 $10 multi 85 32

Double Carp Type of 1969

Perf. 13 1/2x12 1/2

1976, Dec. 15 Engr. Unwmk.

1980 A280 $14 car rose 1.10 25

Mail Collecting A389

Mail Sorting — A390

Designs: $8, Mail transport. $10, Mail delivery.

Wmk. 323

1976, Mar. 20 Litho. Perf. 13 1/2

1984 A389 $2 yel & multi 22 8
1985 A390 $5 grn & multi 45 16
1986 A390 $8 bl & multi 65 25
1987 A389 $10 org & multi 85 32
a. Souvenir sheet of 4 2.50 2.50

80th anniversary of postal service. No. 1987a contains one each of Nos. 1984-1987; buff margin with red inscription. Size: 130x100mm.

Pres. Chiang Kai-shek A391

People Paying Homage — A392

Designs: No. 1990, Pres. Chiang lying in state. No. 1991, Hearse leaving funeral chapel. $5, People along funeral route. $8, Spirit tablet in Tzuhu Guest House. $10, Tzuhu Guest House, Pres. Chiang's burial place.

1976, Apr. 4

1988 A391 $2 gray & multi 25 8
1989 A392 $2 gray & multi 25 8
1990 A392 $2 gray & multi 25 8
1991 A392 $2 gray & multi 25 8
1992 A392 $5 gray & multi 45 20
1993 A392 $8 gray & multi 75 30
1994 A392 $10 gray & multi 80 40
Nos. 1988-1994 (7) 3.00 1.22

Pres. Chiang Kai-shek (1887-1975), first death anniversary.

Flags of China and USA — A393

Wmk. 323

1976, May 29 Litho. Perf. 13 1/2

1995 A393 $2 multi 25 8
1996 A393 $10 yel & multi 90 40

American Bicentennial.

Coin, 12th Century B.C. — A394

Cauldron, Shang Dynasty — A395

Bronze Shovel Coins (pu): $5, Pointed-feet coin, 481-221 B.C. $8, Round-feet coin, 722-481 B.C. $10, Square-feet coin, 3rd-2nd centuries B.C.

1976, June 16

1997 A394 $2 sal & multi 18 8
1998 A394 $5 lt bl & multi 50 16
1999 A394 $8 gray & multi 75 25
2000 A394 $10 multi 95 32

Fan Painting Type of 1975

Silk Fan Paintings, Sung Dynasty: $2, Hibiscus, by Li Tung. $5, Lilies, by Lin Ch'un. $8, Deer and Pine, by Mou Chung-fu. $10, Quail and Wild Flowers, by Li An-chung.

Perf. 13x12 1/2

1976, July 14 Litho. Wmk. 323

2001 A381 $2 multi 22 8
2002 A381 $5 multi 45 20
2003 A381 $8 multi 65 30
2004 A381 $10 multi 85 35

1976, Aug. 25 Photo. Perf. 11 1/2

Granite Paper

Ancient Bronzes: $5, 3-legged cauldron, Chou Dynasty (1122-722 B.C.). $8, Wine container, Chou Dynasty. $10, Wine vessel with spout, Shang Dynasty (1766-1122 B.C.).

2005 A395 $2 rose & multi 22 8
2006 A395 $5 lt bl & multi 45 16
2007 A395 $8 yel & multi 75 25
2008 A395 $10 lil & multi 95 32

Construction Types of 1974

Designs: $1, Taiwan North Link railroad and map. $2, Railroad electrification. $3, Taichung Harbor. $4, Taiwan North-South Highway and map. $5, Steel Mill, Kaohsiung. $6, Taoyuan International Airport. $7, Kaohsiung shipyard. $8, Oil refinery. $9, Su-ao Port.

Perf. 13 1/2x12 1/2, 12 1/2x13 1/2

1976 Litho. Wmk. 323

2009 A365 $1 car & grn 10 5
2010 A365 $2 org & multi 20 5
2011 A366 $3 vio & multi 25 10
2012 A366 $4 car & multi 32 15
2013 A365 $5 grn & brn 40 20
2014 A366 $6 brn & multi 45 20
2015 A366 $7 brn & multi 50 25
2016 A365 $8 car & grn 65 30
2017 A366 $9 ol & bl 65 30
Nos. 2009-2017 (9) 3.52 1.60

Canceled-to-order stamps are often from remainders. Most collectors of canceled stamps prefer postally used specimens.

Chiang Kai-shek and Mother — A396

Sun Yat-sen and Chiang Kai-shek at Canton Station — A397

Design: $5, Chiang Kai-shek, portrait.

1976, Oct. 31 Litho. *Perf. 13½*

2023	A396	$2 multi	25	8
2024	A396	$5 multi	50	20
2025	A397	$10 multi	95	40

Pres. Chiang Kai-shek, 90th anniversary of birth.

Flags of Kuomintang and China — A398

Sun Yat-sen and Chiang Kai-shek A399

1976, Nov. 12 *Perf. 13½x14*

2026	A398	$2 multi	25	8
2027	A399	$10 multi	95	40
a.		Souvenir sheet of 2	1.50	1.50

11th National Kuomintang Congress, Taipei.

No. 2027a contains one each of Nos. 2026-2027; yellow margin with red inscription. Size: 110x87mm.

Brazen Serpent — A400

1976, Dec. 15 Wmk. 323 *Perf. 12½*

2028	A400	$1 red, lil & gold	10	5
2029	A400	$5 plum, yel & gold	50	16

New Year 1977.

Bird and Plum Blossoms, by Ch'en Hung-shou A401

Chinese Paintings: $8, "Wintry Days" (pine), by Yang Wei-chen. $10, Rock and Bamboo, by Hsia Ch'ang.

Perf. 11½

1977, Jan. 12 Photo. Unwmk.

Granite Paper

2030	A401	$2 multi	25	8
2031	A401	$8 multi	60	30
2032	A401	$10 multi	90	35

Black-naped Orioles — A402

Birds of Taiwan: $8, Common Kingfisher. $10, Chinese pheasant-tailed jacana.

1977, Feb. 16 Litho.

2033	A402	$2 multi	25	8
2034	A402	$8 multi	60	30
2035	A402	$10 multi	90	35

See Nos. 2163-2165.

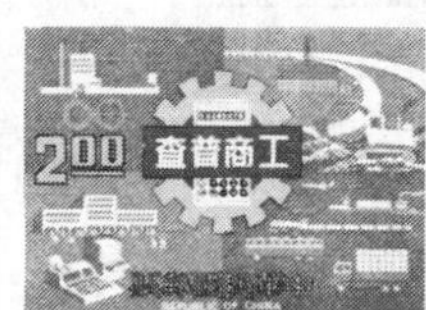

Census Emblem, Industry and Commerce A403

Perf. 13½

1977, Mar. 16 Litho. Unwmk.

2036	A403	$2 red & multi	25	8
2037	A403	$10 pur & multi	90	35

Industry and Commerce Census.

Green Mountains Rising into Clouds, by Madame Chiang — A404

Landscapes, by Madame Chiang Kai-shek: $5, Boat in the Beauty of Spring. $8, Scholar beside Waterfall. $10, Water Rises to Meet the Bridge.

Perf. 11½

1977, Mar. 31 Unwmk. Photo.

Granite Paper

2038	A404	$2 multi	24	5
2039	A404	$5 multi	50	12
2040	A404	$8 multi	75	20
2041	A404	$10 multi	90	25

League Emblem A405

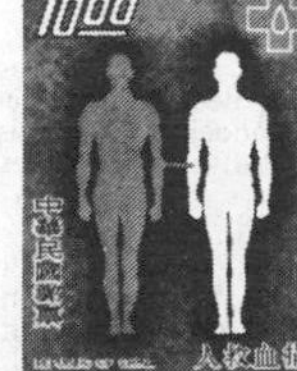

Blood Donation A406

1977, Apr. 18 Litho. *Perf. 12½*

2042	A405	$2 car & multi	28	5
2043	A405	$10 grn & multi	90	25

10th World Anti-Communist League Conference.

1977, May 5 Wmk. 323 *Perf. 13½*

Design: $2, Donating blood (horiz).

2044	A406	$2 red & blk	25	5
2045	A406	$10 red & blk	95	25

Blood donation movement.

San-hsien A407

Musical Instruments: $5, Tung-hsiao (bamboo flute). $8, Yang-chin (butterfly harpsichord). $10, Pai-hsiao (pipes). Background shows musician playing instrument.

Unwmk.

1977, June 21 Photo. *Perf. 14*

2046	A407	$2 multi	24	5
2047	A407	$5 multi	50	12
2048	A407	$8 multi	75	20
2049	A407	$10 multi	90	25

Idea Leuconoe — A408

Protected Butterflies: $4, Hebomoia glaucippe formosana. $6, Stichophthalma howqua formosana. $10, Atrophaneura horishana.

1977, July 20 Litho. *Perf. 13½*

2050	A408	$2 ver & multi	24	5
2051	A408	$4 lt grn & multi	50	10
2052	A408	$6 lt bl & multi	75	15
2053	A408	$10 yel & multi	90	25

National Palace Museum A409

Temple — A410

Children's Drawings: $2, Sea Goddess Festival. $4, Boats on Shore of Lan-yu.

Wmk. 323

1977, Aug. 27 Litho. *Perf. 13½*

2054	A409	$1 multi	10	5
2055	A409	$2 multi	22	5
2056	A409	$4 multi	35	10
2057	A410	$5 multi	45	12

8th Exhibition of World School Children's Art.

Carved Lacquer Plate, Wan-li Ware — A411

Ancient Carved Lacquer Ware: $5, Bowl, Ching dynasty. $8, Round box, Ming dynasty. $10, Four-tiered box, Ching dynasty.

Perf. 13x14

1977, Sept. 28 Photo. Wmk. 368

2058	A411	$2 multi	22	5
2059	A411	$5 multi	50	12
2060	A411	$8 multi	75	20
2061	A411	$10 multi	90	25

Lions International, Emblem and Activities — A412

Unwmk.

1977, Oct. 8 Litho. *Perf. 13*

2062	A412	$2 multi	20	5
2063	A412	$10 multi	70	25

International Association of Lions Clubs, 60th anniversary.

Nos. 2069 and 2075 Overprinted in Claret

1977
中華民國青少年、青少年棒球隊再獲世界三冠軍紀念

Perf. 13½x12½

1977, Sept. 9 Litho. Unwmk.

2064	A365	$2 org & multi	25	5
2065	A365	$8 car & grn	65	20

Little League baseball championship.

Chinese Quality Mark — A413

Perf. 13x12½

1977, Oct. 14 Litho. Unwmk.

2066	A413	$2 red & multi	20	5
2067	A413	$10 bl & multi	70	25

International Standardization Day.

Construction Types of 1974 Redrawn: Numerals Outlined

Designs as 1976 Issue.

Perf. 13½x12½, 12½x13½

1977 Litho. Unwmk.

Granite Paper

2068	A365	$1 car & dp grn	10	5
2069	A365	$2 ver & multi	20	5
2070	A366	$3 vio & multi	25	7
2071	A366	$4 car & multi	32	10
2072	A365	$5 grn & multi	40	12
2073	A366	$6 sep & multi	45	15
2074	A366	$7 sep & multi	50	18
2075	A365	$8 red lil & multi	65	20
2076	A366	$9 ol & multi	65	22
		Nos. 2068-2076 (9)	3.52	1.14

Numerals are in solid color on Nos. 1907-1915, 2009-2017; in outline on Nos. 2068-2076.

Man and Heart — A414

Perf. 13½x12½

1977, Nov. 12 Litho. Wmk. 323

2077	A414	$2 multi	25	5
2078	A414	$10 multi	90	25

Physical health, cardiac care.

White Stallion — A415

Design: $5, Two horses (horiz.). Designs from painting "100 Horses," by Lang Shih-ning.

Perf. 12½

1977, Dec. 1 Unwmk. Litho.

2079 A415 $1 red & multi 10 5
2080 A415 $5 emer & multi 50 15

New Year 1978.

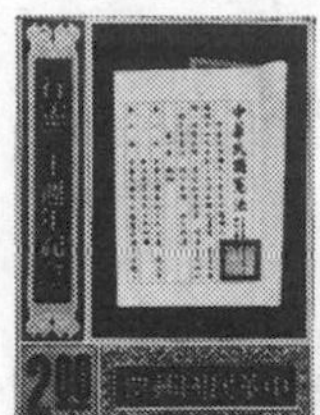
First Page of Constitution A416

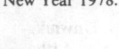

Pres. Chiang Accepting Constitution, 1946 — A417

1977, Dec. 25 Litho. *Perf. 13½*

2081 A416 $2 multi 25 6
2082 A417 $10 multi 90 30

30th anniversary of the Constitution.

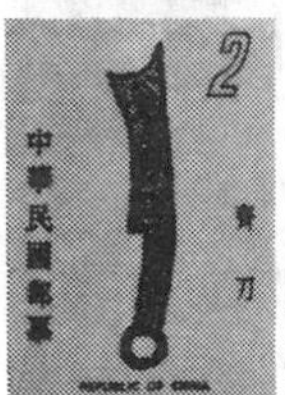
Knife Coin with 3 Characters, 403-221 B.C. — A418

Designs: Ancient knife coins.

1978, Jan. 18 Wmk. 323 *Perf. 13½*

2083 A418 $2 sal & multi 20 5
2084 A418 $5 lt bl & blk 45 16
2085 A418 $8 lt gray & multi 65 25
2086 A418 $10 tan & multi 85 32

China No. 1 and Flag of China — A419

Designs: $5, No. 464 (Sun Yat-sen). $10, No. 1204 (Chiang Kai-shek).

1978, Feb. 21 Litho. *Perf. 13½*

2087 A419 $2 brn & multi 25 8
2088 A419 $5 bl & multi 50 16
2089 A419 $10 org & multi 90 32
a. Souvenir sheet of 3 1.75

Centenary of Chinese postage stamps. No. 2089a contains one each of Nos. 2087-2089; orange and dark carmine margin. Size: 143x101mm.

Sun Yat-Sen Memorial Hall — A420

China Nos. 2079 and 2 — A421

Perf. 14x12½, 12½x14

1978, Mar. 20 Wmk. 323

2090 A420 $2 multi 30 8
2091 A421 $10 multi 80 32

ROCPEX '78 Philatelic Exhibition, Taipei, Mar. 20-29.

Chiang Kai-shek with Revolutionary Army — A422

Designs (Chiang Kai-shek); $2, as young man, 1912 (vert.). $8, Making speech at Mt. Lu, July 17, 1937. $10, Reviewing Armed Forces on National Day, 1956, and Chinese flags (vert.).

1978, Apr. 5 Wmk. 323 *Perf. 13½*

2092 A422 $2 vio & multi 20 8
2093 A422 $5 grn & multi 45 16
2094 A422 $8 bl & multi 65 25
2095 A422 $10 vio bl & multi 80 32

Pres. Chiang Kai-shek (1887-1975).

Nuclear Reactor and Plant — A423

Poem by Wen Cheng-ming (1470-1559) — A424

Perf. 13½x12½

1978, Apr. 28 Unwmk.

2096 A423 $10 multi 75 32

First nuclear power plant on Taiwan.

Wmk. 323

1978, May 20 Litho. *Perf. 13½*

Chinese Calligraphy: $2, Letter by Wang Hsi-chih (307-365). $4, Eulogy by Chu Sui-liang (596-658). $8, From Autobiography of Huai-su, Tang Dynasty. $10, Poem by Ch'ang Piao, Sung Dynasty.

2097 A424 $2 multi 15 8
2098 A424 $4 multi 28 16
2099 A424 $6 multi 40 24
2100 A424 $8 multi 55 32
2101 A424 $10 multi 70 40
Nos. 2097-2101 (5) 2.08 1.20

Head and Dao Cancer Fund Emblem A425

Carved Lacquer Vase, Ming Dynasty A426

1978, June 15 Litho. *Perf. 13½*

2102 A425 $2 red, org & ol 18 8
2103 A425 $10 dk & lt bl & grn 72 40

Cancer prevention.

1978, July 12

Ancient Carved Lacquer Ware: $2, Box with dragon and cloud design, Ch'ing dynasty (horiz.). $5, Double box on legs, Ch'ing dynasty (horiz.). $8, Round box with peonies, Ming dynasty (horiz.).

2104 A426 $2 gray ol & multi 20 8
2105 A426 $5 gray ol & multi 35 16
2106 A426 $8 gray ol & multi 60 25
2107 A426 $10 gray ol & multi 75 32

Tsu Ti Practicing with his Sword — A427

Folk Tales: No. 2109, Pan Ch'ao, diplomat and governor. No. 2110, Tien Tan's "Fire Bull Battle." $5, Liang Hung-yu, a general's wife, who served as drummer in battle.

Wmk. 323

1978, Aug. 16 Litho. *Perf. 13½*

2108 A427 $1 multi 10 5
2109 A427 $2 bis & multi 18 8
2110 A427 $2 gray & multi 18 8
2111 A427 $5 multi 35 16

Nos. 2012 and 2014 Overprinted in Red

1978

中華民國青年青少年及少年棒球隊三獲世界三冠軍紀念

1978, Sept. 9 *Perf. 12½x13*

2112 A366 $4 multi 28 16
2113 A366 $6 multi 45 25

Triple championships won by Chinese teams in Little League World Series. "1978" overprint on $4 at left, on $6 at right.

Ixias Pyrene — A428

Protected Butterflies: $4, Euploea sylvestor swinhoei. $6, Cyrestis thyodamas formosana. $10, Byasa polyeuctes termessus.

1978, Sept. 20

2114 A428 $2 multi 20 8
2115 A428 $4 multi 32 16
2116 A428 $6 multi 45 25
2117 A428 $10 multi 80 40

Scout Symbols A429

Tropical Tomatoes A430

1978, Oct. 5 Litho. *Perf. 13½*

2118 A429 $2 multi 35 8
2119 A429 $10 multi 55 40

5th Chinese Boy Scout Jamboree, Cheng Ching Lake, Oct. 5-12.

1978, Oct. 23 Wmk. 323

Design: $10, Tropical tomatoes (horiz.).

2120 A430 $2 multi 10 8
2121 A430 $10 multi 65 40

International Symposium on Tropical Tomatoes, Taiwan, Oct. 23-28.

Sino-Saudi Bridge A431

Design: $6, Buttresses of bridge, flags of Taiwan and Saudi Arabia (horiz.).

1978, Oct. 31

2122 A431 $2 multi 10 8
2123 A431 $6 multi 60 25

Completion of Sino-Saudi Bridge over Cho-Shui River.

National Flag — A432

1978-80 *Perf. 13½*

2124 A432 $1 red & dk bl 8 5
a. Bklt. pane of 16 ($5, $6, $8, $10, 3 $1, 9 $2) 4.50
2125 A432 $2 red & dk bl 15 8
a. Bklt. pane of 15 + label 2.50
2126 A432 $3 lt grn & multi ('80) 50 12
2127 A432 $4 bis & multi ('80) 60 15
2128 A432 $5 lt grn & multi 42 20
2129 A432 $6 brn org & multi 50 24
2130 A432 $7 dk brn & multi ('80) 60 28
2131 A432 $8 dk grn & multi 75 32
2132 A432 $10 brt bl & multi ('79) 1.00 40
2133 A432 $12 brt rose lil & multi ('80) 1.00 45
Nos. 2124-2133 (10) 5.60 2.29

Two types exist: 1. Second line (red) below flag is same width as blue line. 2. Second line is a hairline, notably thinner. The $3, $4, $7 and $12 were issued only in type 2; Nos. 2129, 2132, 2134, 2124a, only in type 1; others in both types.

Nos. 2129-2133 have colorless inscriptions and denomination in a panel of solid color.

Coil Stamp

1980, Jan. 15 *Perf. 12 Horiz.*

2134 A432 $2 multi 15 6

See Nos. 2288-2300.

Prices of premium quality never hinged stamps will be in excess of catalogue price.

Three Rams, by Emperor Hsuan-tsung
A433

Taoyuan International Airport
A434

Wmk. 323

1978, Dec. 1 Litho. *Perf. 12½*

2135 A433 $1 multi	5	5
2136 A433 $5 multi	45	20

New Year 1979.

1978, Dec. 31 *Perf. 13½*

Design: $10, Passenger terminal and control tower (horiz.).

2137 A434 $2 multi	15	8
2138 A434 $10 multi	60	40

Completion of Taoyuan International Airport.

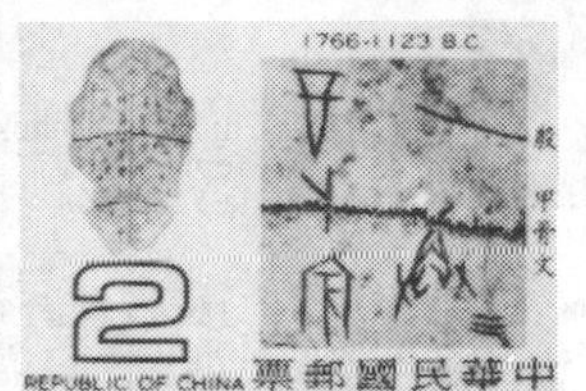

Oracle Bones and Inscription, 1766-1123 B.C. — A435

Antiquities and Inscriptions: $5, Lehchi cauldron, 722-481 B.C. $8, Small seal (turtle), 206 B.C.-8 A.D. $10, Inscribed stone tablet, 175-183 A.D.

1979, Jan. 17

2139 A435 $2 multi	10	8
2140 A435 $5 multi	28	20
2141 A435 $8 multi	55	32
2142 A435 $10 multi	70	40

Origin and development of Chinese characters.

Chihkan Tower, 1653 — A436

Taiwan Scenery: $5, Shrine of Confucius, 1665. $8, Shrine of Koxinga, 1661. $10, Eternal Castle and moat.

1979, Feb. 11 Litho. *Perf. 13½*

2143 A436 $2 multi	10	8
2144 A436 $5 multi	28	20
2145 A436 $8 multi	55	32
2146 A436 $10 multi	70	40

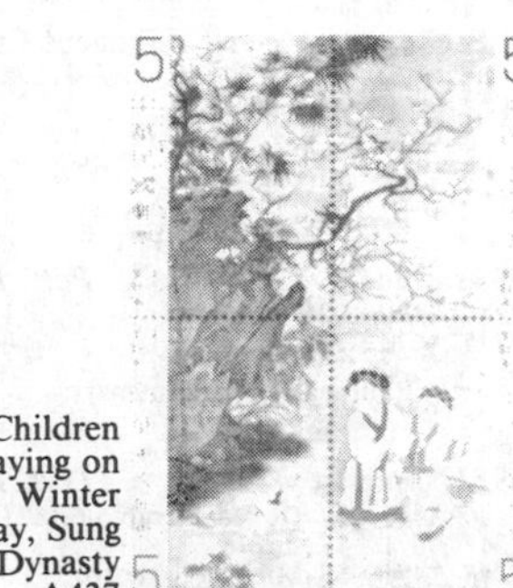

Children Playing on Winter Day, Sung Dynasty
A437

1979, Mar. 8

2147 A437 Block of four	1.40	60
a. $5 in UL corner	35	15
b. $5 in UR corner	35	15
c. $5 in LL corner	35	15
d. $5 in LR corner	35	15
e. Souvenir sheet of 4	2.00	1.00

No. 2147e contains No. 2147; pink and black margin. Size: 101x145mm.

Lu Hao-tung
A438

Yellow Jade Brush Holder
A439

Perf. 13x12½

1979, Mar. 29 Engr. Wmk. 323

2148 A438 $2 blue	10	8

Lu Hao-tung (1868-1895), revolutionist.

Unwmk.

1979, Apr. 12 Photo. *Perf. 12*

Ancient Brush Washers: $5, White jade, Ming Dynasty. $8, Dark green jade, Ch'ing Dynasty. $10, Bluish jade, Ch'ing Dynasty. All horiz.

Granite Paper

2149 A439 $2 multi	10	8
2150 A439 $5 multi	35	20
2151 A439 $8 multi	55	32
2152 A439 $10 multi	70	40

Plum Blossoms, National Flower
A440

Plum Blossoms
A440a

City Houses and Garden — A441

Perf. 13x12½

1979-87 Engr. Wmk. 323

Granite Paper

2153 A440 $10 dk bl	70	40
2154 A440 $20 brown	1.10	80
b. Plain paper ('87)	1.00	80
2154A A440 $40 brt car ('85)	2.25	1.25
2155 A440 $50 dl grn	2.75	2.00
a. Plain paper ('87)	2.50	2.00
2156 A440 $100 vermilion	5.75	4.00

Perf. 14x13½

2156A A440a $300 pur & red org ('83)	21.00	10.00
2156B A440a $500 ver & brn ('82)	32.50	15.00

See No. 2510

Perf. 13x12½, 12½x13

1979, June 5 Litho.

Design: $10, Rural landscape (horiz.).

2157 A441 $2 multi	10	8
2158 A441 $10 multi	50	40

Protection of the Environment.

Bankbook and Computer Department
A442

Designs: $2, Children at counter (vert.). $5, People standing in line (vert.). $10, Hand putting coin in savings bank, symbolic tree.

1979, July 1 Wmk. 323 *Perf. 13½*

2159 A442 $2 multi	18	8
2160 A442 $5 multi	40	20
2161 A442 $8 multi	60	32
2162 A442 $10 multi	70	40

Postal savings, 60th anniversary.

Bird Type of 1977

Birds of Taiwan: $2, Swinoe's pheasant. $8, Steere's babbler. $10, Formosan yuhina.

1979, Aug. 8 *Perf. 11½*

2163 A402 $2 multi	10	8
2164 A402 $8 multi	55	32
2165 A402 $10 multi	65	40

Rowland Hill, Penny Black
A443

Perf. 13½x13

1979, Aug. 27 Litho. Wmk. 323

2166 A443 $10 multi	60	40

Sir Rowland Hill (1795-1879), originator of penny postage.

Jar with Rope Design, Shang Dynasty — A444

Ancient Chinese Pottery: $5, Two-handled jar, Shang dynasty. $8, Red jar with "ears," Han dynasty. $10, Green glazed jar, Han dynasty.

1979, Sept. 12 *Perf. 13½*

2167 A444 $2 multi	12	8
2168 A444 $5 multi	42	20
2169 A444 $8 multi	65	32
2170 A444 $10 multi	85	40

Children and IYC Emblem — A445

1979, Sept. 28 Litho. *Perf. 13½*

2171 A445 $2 multi	10	8
2172 A445 $10 multi	60	40

International Year of the Child.

Trade Symbols, Competition Emblem
A446

1979, Nov. 11 Litho. *Perf. 13½*

2173 A446 $2 bl & multi	10	8
2174 A446 $10 grn & multi	60	40

10th National Vocational Training Competition, Taichung, Nov. 11.

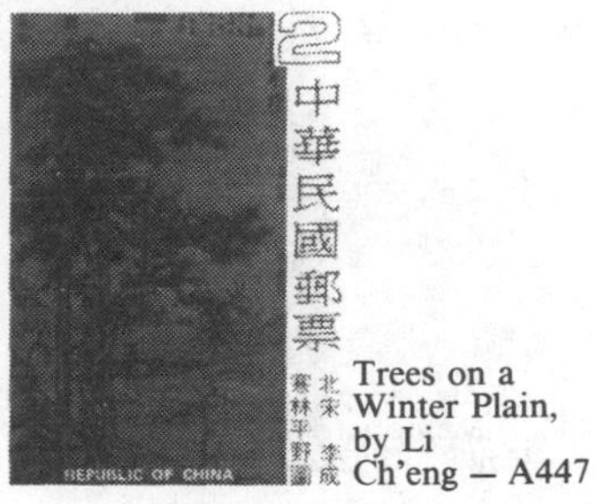

Trees on a Winter Plain, by Li Ch'eng — A447

Paintings: $5, Bamboo, Wen T'ung. $8, Old tree, bamboo and rock, by Chao Meng-fu. $10, Twin Pines, by Li K'an.

1979, Nov. 21

2175 A447 $2 multi	10	8
2176 A447 $5 multi	38	20
2177 A447 $8 multi	60	32
2178 A447 $10 multi	75	40

Monkey — A448

1979, Dec. 1 *Perf. 12½*

2179 A448 $1 yel & multi	5	5
2180 A448 $6 tan & multi	45	25

New Year 1980.

Rotary Emblem and "75" — A449

Rotary International, 75th Anniversary. $12, Anniversary emblem (vert.).

Wmk. 323

1980, Feb. 23 Litho. *Perf. 13½*

2181 A449 $2 multi	10	6
2182 A449 $12 multi	80	50

Mt. Hohuan
A450

Taiwan Landscapes (East-West Cross-Island Highway): $2, Tunnel of Nine Turns (vert.). $12, Bridge, Tien Hsiang (vert.).

1980, Mar. 1

2183 A450 $2 multi	10	6
2184 A450 $8 multi	60	24
2185 A450 $12 multi	90	50

Shih Chien-Ju — A451

Perf. 13½x12½

1980, Mar. 29 **Engr.**

Granite Paper

2186 A451 $2 red brn 10 6

Shih Chien-Ju (1879-1900), revolutionist.

Chung-cheng Memorial Hall — A452

1980, Apr. 4 **Litho.** ***Perf. 13½***

2187 A452	$2	*shown*	15	6
2188 A452	$8	*Quotation*	60	24
2189 A452	$12	*Bronze statue*	90	50

Chiang Kai-shek (1887-1975), 5th anniversary of death.

Melon-shaped Jade Brush Washer, Ming Dynasty — A453

Jade Pottery: $2, Jar with dragons, Sung dynasty (vert.). $8, Monk's alms bowl, Ch'ing dynasty. $10, Yellow jade brush washer, Ch'ing dynasty.

1980, May 20 **Photo.** ***Perf. 12***

Granite Paper

2190 A453	$2	multi	10	6
2191 A453	$5	multi	32	20
2192 A453	$8	multi	55	32
2193 A453	$10	multi	70	40

Energy Conservation — A454

1980, July 15 **Litho.** ***Perf. 13½***

2194 A454	$2	multi	10	6
2195 A454	$12	multi	80	50

Soldier, T'ang Dynasty Pottery — A455

1980, Aug. 18 **Litho.** ***Perf. 13½***

2196 A455	$2	*shown*	10	6
2197 A455	$5	*Roosters*	35	20
2198 A455	$8	*Horse*	55	32
2199 A455	$10	*Camel*	70	40

Confucius Returning Lost Article — A456

Folk Tales: $1, Grinding mortar into a needle. No. 2202, Wen Tien-hsiang in jail. $5, Sending coal in snow.

Perf. 14x13½

1980, Sept. 23 **Litho.** **Wmk. 323**

2200 A456	$1	multi	5	5
2201 A456	$2	multi	10	6
2202 A456	$2	multi	10	6
2203 A456	$5	multi	35	20

Railroad Electrification — A457

1980, Oct. 10 ***Perf. 13½x14***

2204 A457	$2	*shown*	10	6
2205 A457	$2	*Taichung Harbor*	10	6
2206 A457	$2	*Chiang Kai-shek Airport*	10	6
2207 A457	$2	*Steel Mill*	10	6
2208 A457	$2	*Sun Yat-sen Freeway*	10	6
2209 A457	$2	*Nuclear power plant*	10	6
2210 A457	$2	*Petrochemical plants*	10	6
2211 A457	$2	*Su-ao Harbor*	10	6
2212 A457	$2	*Kaohsiung shipyard*	10	6
2213 A457	$2	*North link railroad*	10	6
a.		Souvenir sheet of 10	1.50	
		Nos. 2204-2213 (10)	1.00	60

Completion of major construction projects. Nos. 2204-2213 se-tenant. No. 2213a contains one each of Nos. 2204-2213. Size: 218x100mm.

10th National Savings Day — A458

Wmk. 323

1980, Oct. 25 **Litho.** ***Perf. 13½***

2214 A458	$2	*Ancient coin and coin banks*	10	6
2215 A458	$12	*shown*	80	35

Landscape, by Ch'iu Ying, Ming Dynasty — A459

1980, Nov. 12 **Litho.** ***Perf. 13½***

2216 A459	Block of 4	1.50	80
a.	$5 in UL corner	35	20
b.	$5 in UR corner	35	20
c.	$5 in LL corner	35	20
d.	$5 in LR corner	35	20
e.	Souvenir sheet	1.75	1.00

No. 2216e contains No. 2216a-2216d; yellow and brown decorative margin. Size: 102x145½mm.

Cock — A460

Faces, Flag, Census Form — A461

1980, Dec. 1 ***Perf. 12½***

2217 A460	$1	multi	5	5
2218 A460	$6	multi	40	24
a.		Souvenir sheet of 4	1.10	

New Year 1980. No. 2218a contains 2 each Nos. 2217-2218; black marginal inscription. Size: 77x102mm.

1980, Dec. 13 ***Perf. 13½***

2219 A461	$2	*shown*	10	6
2220 A461	$12	*Buildings*, horiz.	80	50

1980 population and housing census.

TIROS-N Satellite — A462

Design: $10, Central weather bureau (horiz.).

1981, Jan. 28 **Litho.** ***Perf. 13½***

2221 A462	$2	multi	10	6
2222 A462	$10	multi	70	50

Completion of meteorological satellite ground station, Taipei.

"Happiness" — A463

1981, Feb. 3 ***Perf. 13½x12½***

New Year 1981 (Calligraphy): No. 2224, Wealth. No. 2225, Longevity. No. 2226, Joy. Nos. 2223-2226 se-tenant.

2223 A463	$5	multi, 5 at B	35	15
2224 A463	$5	multi, 5 at R	35	15
2225 A463	$5	multi, 5 at L	35	15
2226 A463	$5	multi, 5 at T	35	15

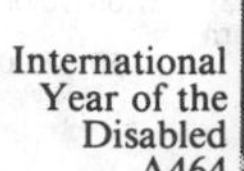

International Year of the Disabled — A464

1981, Feb. 19 **Litho.** ***Perf. 13½***

2227 A464	$2	multi	10	6
2228 A464	$12	multi	80	55

Mt. Ali — A465

1981 Mar. 1

2229 A465	$2	shown	10	
2230 A465	$7	Oluanpi Beach	48	2
2231 A465	$12	Sun Moon Lake	80	3

A $2 multicolored stamp for the 12th National Kuomintang Congress at Taipei was prepared for release Mar. 29, 1981, but not issued. It showed Sun Yat-sen, Chiang Kai-shek, flags of China and the Koumintang and a map of China.

Children in Forest A467

Children's Day: Drawings.

1981, Apr. 4

2233 A467	$1	multi	5	
2234 A467	$2	multi	10	
2235 A467	$5	multi	38	2
2236 A467	$7	multi	52	2

Chiang Kai-shek Memorial Hall — A468

1981, Apr. 5 ***Perf. 12½x13½***

2237 A468	20c bluish lil	5	5
a.	Photo. ('87)	5	5
2238 A468	40c crim rose	5	5
a.	Photo. ('87)	5	5
2239 A468	50c dl red brn	5	5

Chiang Kai-shek (1887-1975), 6th anniversary of death.

Cloisonne Enamel Brush Washer, 15th Cent. A469

Cloisonne Enamel: $5, Ritual vessel, 15th cent. (vert.). $8, Plate, 17th cent. $10, Vase, Ming Dynasty (vert.).

1981, May 20 **Photo.** ***Perf. 12***

Granite Paper

2240 A469	$2	multi	10	6
2241 A469	$5	multi	25	20
2242 A469	$8	multi	40	32
2243 A469	$10	multi	50	40

Early and Modern Locomotives A470

Linnaeus Crab A471

Wmk. 323

1981, June 9 **Litho.** ***Perf. 12½***

2244 A470	$2	shown	10	6
2245 A470	$14	Trains, horiz.	80	52

Railroad service centenary.

1981, June 14 ***Perf. 13½***

2246 A471	$2	De Haan crab, horiz.	10	6
2247 A471	$5	shown	30	20
2248 A471	$8	Miers crab, horiz.	50	32
2249 A471	$14	Rathbun crab	85	52

Central Weather Bureau, 40th Anniv. — A472

1981, July 1 Litho. *Perf. 13½*
2250 A472 $2 multi 10 6
2251 A472 $14 multi 80 50

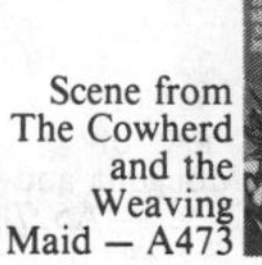

Scene from The Cowherd and the Weaving Maid — A473

Designs: Scenes from the Cowherd and the Weaving Maid.

1981, Aug. 6 Litho. *Perf. 13½x14*
2252 A473 $2 multi 10 6
2253 A473 $4 multi 25 12
2254 A473 $8 multi 60 24
2255 A473 $14 multi 1.10 42

First Lasography Exhibition — A474

Lasography Designs.

1981, Aug. 15 *Perf. 13½*
2256 A474 $2 multi 10 6
2257 A474 $5 multi 30 15
2258 A474 $8 multi 50 24
2259 A474 $14 multi 90 42

Soccer Players
A475 A476

1981, Sept. 9 Litho. *Perf. 13½*
2260 A475 $5 multi 30 15
2261 A476 $5 multi 30 15

Sports Day. Se-tenant.

A477

70th Anniv. of Republic: No. 2263, Eastward Expedition (soldiers on Hill). No. 2264, Northward Expedition (Chiang on horse). No. 2265, Resistance War with Japan (Chiang, fist raised). No. 2266, Suppression of Communist Rebels (Battle scene). No. 2267, Counter-offensive and unification. $8, Chiang Kai-shek. $14, Sun Yat-sen.

1981 Litho. Wmk. 323 *Perf. 13½*
2262 A477 $2 multi 10 6
2263 A477 $2 multi 10 6
2264 A477 $2 multi 10 6
2265 A477 $2 multi 10 6
2266 A477 $3 multi 20 10
2267 A477 $3 multi 20 10
2268 A477 $8 multi 55 25
2269 A477 $14 multi 1.00 40
a. Souvenir sheet of 8 2.50 1.25
Nos. 2262-2269 (8) 2.35 1.09

No. 2269a contains Nos. 2262-2269; multicolored decorative margin. Size: 117x168mm. Nos. 2262-2269 issued Oct. 10; No. 2269a, Oct. 25.

ROCPEX TAIPEI '81 Intl. Philatelic Exhibition, Taipei, Oct. 25-Nov. 2 — A478

1981, Oct. 25
2270 A478 $2 multi 10 6
2271 A478 $14 multi 95 40

Boys Playing Games (#2272a) A479

Design: "One Hundred Boys," Sung Dynasty scroll. Two strips of 5 each in continuous design.

1981, Nov. 12
2272 Block of 10 1.50 60
a.-e. A479 $2 single (top) 15 6
f.-j. A479 $2 single (bottom) 15 6

New Year 1982 (Year of the Dog) — A480

Information Week, Dec. 6-12 — A481

Wmk. 323

1981, Dec. 1 Litho. *Perf. 12½*
2273 A480 $1 multi 5 5
2274 A480 $10 multi 70 30
a. Souvenir sheet of 4 1.40 75

No. 2274a contains 2 each Nos. 2273-2274; black marginal inscription. Size: 78x103mm.

1981, Dec. 7 *Perf. 14x13½*
2275 A481 $2 multi 10 6

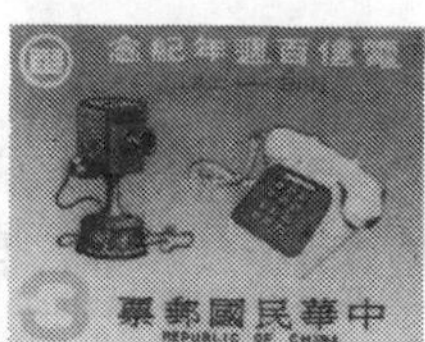

Telecommunications Centenary — A482

Perf. 14x13½, 13½x14

1981, Dec. 28
2276 A482 $2 Telephone, vert. 10 6
2277 A482 $3 Old, new phones 15 10
2278 A482 $8 Submarine cable 55 25
2279 A482 $18 Computers, vert. 1.25 65

Floral Arrangement A483

Designs: Various floral arrangements in Ming vases.

Wmk. 323

1982, Jan. 23 Litho. *Perf. 13½*
2280 A483 $2 multi 10 6
2281 A483 $3 multi 15 10
2282 A483 $8 multi 55 25
2283 A483 $18 multi 1.25 65

The Ku Cheng Reunion — A484

Designs: Opera scenes.

Wmk. 323

1982, Feb. 15 Litho. *Perf. 13½*
2284 A484 $2 multi 10 6
2285 A484 $3 multi 15 10
2286 A484 $4 multi 30 12
2287 A484 $18 multi 1.25 65

Flag Type of 1978
Value Colorless in Colored Panel

1981 Litho. *Perf. 13½*

Panel Color

2288 A432 $1 dk bl 5 5
2289 A432 $1.50 lt ol 8 5
2290 A432 $2 dk ol bis 10 6
2291 A432 $3 red 15 10
2292 A432 $4 blue 30 12
2293 A432 $5 sepia 35 15
2294 A432 $6 orange 40 20
2295 A432 $7 green 45 22
2296 A432 $8 magenta 55 25
2297 A432 $9 ol grn 60 28
2298 A432 $10 dk pur 65 30
2299 A432 $12 lilac 80 40
2300 A432 $14 dk grn 95 45
Nos. 2288-2300 (13) 5.43 2.63

Second line (red) below flag is a hairline, notably thinner.

Tubercle Bacillus Centenary A485

Cheng Shih-liang, Revolutionary A486

Wmk. 323

1982, Mar. 24 Litho. *Perf. 13½*
2309 A485 $2 multi 10 6

Perf. 13½x12½

1982, Mar. 29 Engr.

Granite Paper

2310 A486 $2 car rose 10 6

Children's Day — A487

Designs: Various children's drawings. $2 vert.

1982, Apr. 4 Litho.
2311 A487 $2 multi 10 6
2312 A487 $3 multi 15 10
2313 A487 $5 multi 32 15
2314 A487 $8 multi 55 25

Dentists' Day — A488

1982, May 4 Litho. *Perf. 13½*
2315 A488 $2 Tooth, boy 10 6
2316 A488 $3 Flossing, brushing 15 10
2317 A488 $10 Examination 70 30

Champleve Enamel Cup and Saucer, 18th Cent. A489

Painted Enamelware: $5, Cloisonne gold-plated duck Ch'ien-lung period (1736-1795) (vert.). $8, Incense burner, K'ang-hsi period (1662-1722). $12, Cloisonne pitcher, Ch'ien-lung period (vert.).

1982, May 20 Photo. *Perf. 12*

Granite Paper

2318 A489 $2 multi 10 6
2319 A489 $5 multi 30 16
2320 A489 $8 multi 50 26
2321 A489 $12 multi 80 40

See Nos. 2348-2351.

Poets' Day — A490

Tang Dynasty Poetry Illustrations (618-906): $2, Spring Dawn, by Meng Hao-Jan. $3, On Looking for a Hermit and Not Finding Him, by Chia Tao. $5, Summer Dying, by Liu Yu-Hsi. $18, Looking at the Snow Drifts on South Mountain, by Tsu Yung.

Wmk. 323

1982, June 25 Litho. *Perf. 13½*
2322 A490 $2 multi 10 6
2323 A490 $3 multi 15 10
2324 A490 $5 multi 35 16
2325 A490 $18 multi 1.25 60

See Nos. 2352-2355.

5th World Women's Softball Championship, Taipei, July 1-12 — A491

1982, July 2
2326 A491 $2 lt grn & multi 10 6
2327 A491 $18 tan & multi 1.25 60

Scouting Year A492

1982, July 18

2328 A492 $2 Crossing bridge, Baden-Powell 10 6

2329 A492 $18 Emblem, camp 1.25 60

Stamp in Tongs A493

1982, Aug. 9

2330 A493 $2 shown 10 6

2331 A493 $18 Album stamps magnified 1.25 60

Carved Lion, Tsu Shih Temple — A494

Hsun Kuan Saving Hsiang-cheng City — A495

Tsu Shih Temple of Sanhsia Architecture: $3, Lion brackets (horiz.). $5, Sub-lintels. $18, Tiled roof (horiz.).

1982, Sept. 1 Litho. *Perf. 13½*

2332 A494 $2 multi 10 6

2333 A494 $3 multi 15 10

2334 A494 $5 multi 35 15

2335 A494 $18 multi 1.25 60

1982, Oct. 15 *Perf. 14x13½*

Designs: Scenes from The Thirty-Six Examples of Filial Piety, Folk Tale collection by Wu Yen-huan.

2336 A495 $1 multi 5 5

2337 A495 $2 multi 10 6

2338 A495 $3 multi 15 10

2339 A495 $5 multi 40 15

30th Anniv. of China Youth Corps A496

1982, Oct. 31

2340 A496 $2 Riding 10 6

2341 A496 $3 Raising flag, vert. 15 10

2342 A496 $18 Mountain climbing 1.25 60

Seated Lohan (Buddhist Saint) — A497

New Year 1983 (Year of the Boar) — A498

Paintings of Lohan, Hanging Scrolls by Liu Sung-nien, 13th cent.

Perf. 13x12½

1982, Nov. 12 Litho. Wmk. 323

2343 A497 $2 multi 10 6

2344 A497 $3 multi 15 10

2345 A497 $18 multi 1.25 60

a. Souvenir sheet of 3 1.75 75

No. 2345a contains Nos. 2343-2345; marginal inscription. Size: 140x102mm. No. 2345a comes overprinted in red in the sheet margins.

1982, Dec. 1 *Perf. 12½*

2346 A498 $1 multi 5 5

2347 A498 $10 multi 70 30

a. Souvenir sheet of 4 1.75 75

No. 2347a contains 2 each Nos. 2346-2347; marginal inscription. Size: 78x102mm.

Enamelware Type of 1982

Designs: $2, Square basin, Ch'ing Dynasty (1644-1911). $3, Vase, Ch'ien-lung period (1736-1795) (vert.). $4, Tea pot, Ch'ien-lung period. $18, Elephant vase, Ch'ing Dynasty (vert.).

1983, Jan. 5 Photo. *Perf. 12*

Granite Paper

2348 A489 $2 multi 10 6

2349 A489 $3 multi 15 10

2350 A489 $4 multi 25 12

2351 A489 $18 multi 1.25 60

Poetry Illustration Type of 1982

Sung Dynasty Poetry: $2, Seeing the Flowers Fade Away. $3, River. $5, Freckled with Clouds is the Azure Sky. $11, Yielding Fine Fragrance in the Snow. Nos. 2352-2355 vert.

Wmk. 323

1983, Feb. 10 Litho. *Perf. 13½*

2352 A490 $2 multi 10 6

2353 A490 $3 multi 15 8

2354 A490 $5 multi 35 16

2355 A490 $11 multi 80 30

Mt. Jade, Taiwan — A499

1983, Mar. 1

2356 A499 $2 Wawa Valley, vert. 10 6

2357 A499 $3 University Pond, vert. 15 8

2358 A499 $18 shown 1.10 60

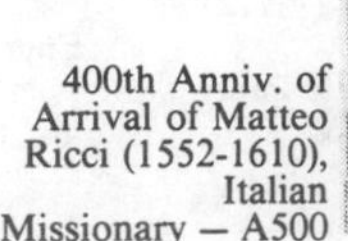

400th Anniv. of Arrival of Matteo Ricci (1552-1610), Italian Missionary — A500

Perf. 14x13½

1983, Apr. 3 Litho. Wmk. 323

2359 A500 $2 Globe 10 6

2360 A500 $18 Great Wall 1.40 60

Mandarin Phonetic Symbols, 70th Anniv. A501

Scenes from Lady White Snake Fairytale A502

Wmk. 323

1983, May 22 Litho. *Perf. 13½*

2361 A501 $2 Wu Ching-heng, inventor 10 6

2362 A501 $18 Children writing 1.40 60

1983, June 15 *Perf. 14x13½*

2363 A502 $2 multi 10 6

2364 A502 $3 lt bl & multi 15 10

2365 A502 $3 org & multi 15 10

2366 A502 $18 multi 1.25 60

Bamboo Jug — A503

Various bamboo carved objects. Nos. 2367-2369 Ch'ing dynasty.

Wmk. 323

1983, July 14 Litho. *Perf. 13½*

2367 A503 $2 shown 10 6

2368 A503 $3 Tao-t'ieh motif vase 15 10

2369 A503 $4 Landscape sculpture 25 12

2370 A503 $18 Brush holder, Ming dynasty 1.25 60

World Communications Year — A504

Wmk. 323

1983, Aug. 5 Litho. *Perf. 13½*

2371 A504 $2 Globe 10 6

2372 A504 $18 Emblem 1.40 60

Fishing Industry (Local Fish) A505

1983, Aug. 20

2373 A505 $2 Epinephelus tauvina 10 6

2374 A505 $18 Saurida undosquamis 1.40 60

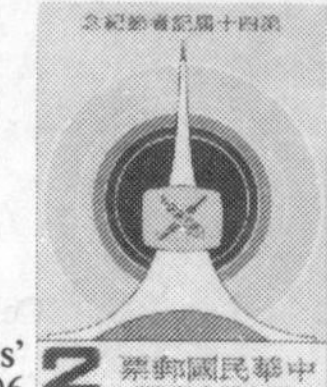

40th Journalists' Day — A506

1983, Sept. 1

2375 A506 $2 multi 10 6

Views of Mongolia and Tibet — A507

1983, Sept. 15

2376 A507 $2 Village 10 6

2377 A507 $3 Potala Palace 15 10

2378 A507 $5 Sheep grazing 35 15

2379 A507 $11 Camel caravan 80 32

2nd East Asian Bird Protection Conference, Oct. — A508

1983, Oct. 8 Litho. *Perf. 13½*

2380 A508 $2 Lanius cristatus, vert. 10 6

2381 A508 $18 Butastur indicus 1.40 60

Plum Blossoms, photography by Hu Ch'ung-hsien — A509

1983, Oct. 31 Litho. *Perf. 14x13½*

2382 A509 $2 multi 10 6

2383 A509 $3 multi 15 10

2384 A509 $5 multi 35 15

2385 A509 $11 multi 80 32

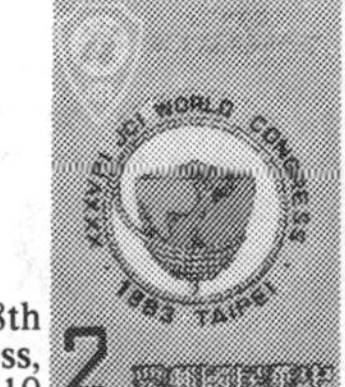

Jaycees Intl., 38th World Congress, Taipei — A510

1983, Nov. 6 *Perf. 13x13½, 13½x13*

2386 A510 $2 JCI and Congress emblems 10 6

2387 A510 $18 Globe and emblems (horiz.) 1.40 60

8th Asian-Pacific Cardiology Congress — A511

1983, Nov. 27 Litho. *Perf. 13½*

2388 A511 $2 shown 10 6

2389 A511 $18 Electrocardiogram 1.40 60

New Year 1984 (Year of the Rat) — A512

1983, Dec. 1 Litho. *Perf. 12½*
2390 A512 $1 multi 5 5
2391 A512 $10 multi 70 30
a. Souvenir sheet of 4 1.50 65

No. 2391a contains 2 each Nos. 2390-2391; marginal inscription. Size: 78x102mm.

Literacy Week A513

1983, Dec. 17 Litho. *Perf. 13½*
2392 A513 $2 shown 10 6
2393 A513 $18 Modern family, vert. 1.40 60

World Freedom Day — A514

1984, Jan. 23 Litho. *Perf. 13½*
2394 A514 $2 Korean War Patriots 10 6
2395 A514 $18 Intl. support 1.40 60

Drama Day — A515

Yuan Dynasty Poetry Illustrations by Tien-shih Lin (Poems by): $2, Kuan Yun-shih. $3, Po Pu. $5, Chang Ko-chiu. $18, Shang Cheng-shu.

1984, Feb. 15 Litho. *Perf. 13½*
2396 A515 $2 multi 10 6
2397 A515 $3 multi 15 10
2398 A515 $5 multi 32 16
2399 A515 $18 multi 1.25 60

A516

A517

A518

Arbor Day — A519

1984, Mar. 12 Litho. *Perf. 13½x14*
2400 A516 $2 multi 10 6
2401 A517 $2 multi 10 6
2402 A518 $2 multi 10 6
2403 A519 $2 multi 10 6

Nos. 2400-2403 se-tenant.

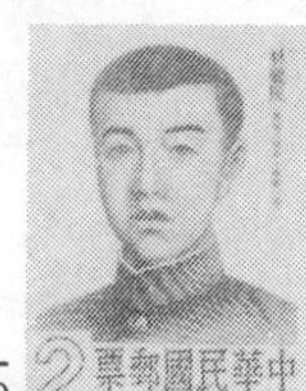
Lin Chueh-min — A520

1984, Mar. 29 Engr. *Perf. 13x12½*
Granite Paper
2404 A520 $2 dk grn 10 6

Central News Agency, 60th Anniv. — A521

Perf. 14x13½
1984, Apr. 1 Litho. Wmk.
2405 A521 $2 Emblem 10 6
2406 A521 $10 Emblem, satellite, dish antenna 70 30

God of Longevity A522

Ch'ing Dynasty Enamelware A523

Paintings by Chang Ta-chien (1899-1983): $2, Five Auspicious Tokens. $18, Lotus Blossoms in Ink Splash.

Wmk. 323
1984, Apr. 20 Litho. *Perf. 11½*
2407 A522 $2 multi 10 6
2408 A522 $5 multi 32 15
2409 A522 $18 multi 1.10 60

1984, May 20 Photo. *Perf. 12*
Granite Paper
2410 A523 $2 Cup, pot, plate, horiz. 10 6
2411 A523 $3 Wine jug 15 10
2412 A523 $4 Teapot 32 12
2413 A523 $18 Candle holder 1.25 60

China Airlines World-wide Service Inauguration A524

1984, May 31 Litho. *Perf. 13½x14*
2414 A524 $2 Jet circling globe 10 6
2415 A524 $7 Globe, jet 50 28
2416 A524 $11 New York City 80 45
2417 A524 $18 Amsterdam 1.25 60

30th Navigation Day A525

Perf. 13½x13
1984, July 11 Litho. Wmk. 323
2418 A525 $2 Container ship 10 6
2419 A525 $18 Oil tanker 1.40 60

1984 Summer Olympics A526

Alpine Plants A527

Perf. 13½x14, 14x13½
1984, July 28
2420 A526 $2 Judo, horiz. 10 6
2421 A526 $5 Archery 32 15
2422 A526 $18 Swimming, horiz. 1.25 60

1984, Aug. 8 *Perf. 13*
2423 A527 $2 Gentiana arisanensis 10 6
2424 A527 $3 Epilobium nankotaizanense 15 10
2425 A527 $5 Adenophora uehatae 32 15
2426 A527 $18 Aconitum fukutomei 1.25 60

The Eighteen Scholars, Sung Dynasty Hanging Scroll — A528

Details.

Wmk. 323
1984, Aug. 20 Litho. *Perf. 13*
2427 A528 $2 Playing instruments 10 6
2428 A528 $3 Playing chess 15 10
2429 A528 $5 Practicing calligraphy 32 15
2430 A528 $18 Painting 1.25 60

Athletics Day
A529 A530

1984, Sept. 9
2431 A529 $5 Two players 30 15
2432 A530 $5 One player 30 15

Asian-Pacific Parliamentarians' Union, 20th Anniv. — A531

1984, Sept. 9
2433 A531 $10 "20," map of Asia 60 30

Postal Museum Opening — A532

1984, Oct. 10 Litho. *Perf. 12½*
2434 A532 $2 No. 1458 10 6
2435 A532 $5 No. 296 32 15
2436 A532 $18 Museum 1.25 60
a. Souvenir sheet of 3 1.75 1.00

No. 2436a contains Nos. 2434-2436. Size: 129x91mm.

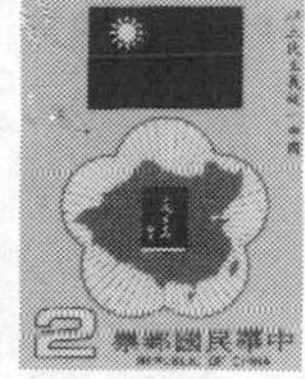
Flag, Alliance Emblem — A533

1984, Oct. 16 *Perf. 13½*
2437 A533 $2 multi 10 6

Grand Alliance for China's Reunification Under the Three Principles of the People Convention, Taipei, Oct. 16-17.

Veteran's Assistance A534

Pine Tree A535

1984, Nov. 1 Litho. *Perf. 13½*
2438 A534 $2 Vignettes 10 6

1984-88
2439 A535 $2 shown 10 6
2440 A535 $8 Bamboo 60 25
2441 A535 $10 Plum, grayish tan background 75 30
a. pale yel bis background 50 30

Issue dates: Nos. 2439-2441, Nov. 12. No. 2441a, Jan. 12, 1988. See Nos. 2495-2497.

New Year 1985 (Year of the Ox) — A536

1984, Dec. 1 *Perf. 12x12½*
2442 A536 $1 multi 5 5

2443 A536 $10 multi 55 30
a. Miniature sheet of 4 (2 each #2442-2443) 1.50 75

Size of No. 2443a: 78x102mm.

Judicial Day 1985 — A537

1985, Jan. 11 **Litho.** ***Perf. 13½***
2444 A537 $5 Scales, legal codes 30 15

Quemoy and Matsu Scenes — A538

1985, Jan. 23 **Litho.** ***Perf. 13½x14***
2445 A538 $2 Ku-kang Lake, Quemoy 10 6
2446 A538 $5 Kuang-hai Stone, Quemoy 40 15
2447 A538 $8 Sheng-li Reservoir, Matsu 70 25
2448 A538 $10 Tung-chu Lighthouse, Matsu 85 30

Sir Robert Hart (1835-1911) A539

1985, Feb. 15 **Litho.** ***Perf. 14x13½***
2449 A539 $2 No. 1 10 6

Inspector General of Chinese Customs, 1863-1908, and founder of the Chinese Postal Service.

Lo Fu-hsing (1886-1914) A540

1985, Feb. 24 ***Perf. 13x13½***
2450 A540 $2 multi 10 6

Tsou Jung (1882-1905) — A541

Perf. 13½x12½
1985, Mar. 29 **Engr.**
Granite Paper
2451 A541 $3 green 15 10

Chung-cheng Memorial Hall Main Gate — A542

1985, Apr. 5 **Litho.** ***Perf. 13***
2452 A542 $2 shown 10 6
2453 A542 $8 Tzuhu Memorial 60 24
2454 A542 $10 Chiang Kai-shek, vert. 80 30

Tenth death anniv. of Chiang Kai-shek (1887-1975).

Mother's Day — A543

1985, May 8 **Litho.** ***Perf. 13½***
2455 A543 $2 Carnation 10 6
2456 A543 $2 Day lily 10 6
a. Se-tenant pair 20 12

Kaohsiung Cross-Harbor Tunnel, 1st Anniv. — A544

1985, May 18
2457 A544 $5 Tunnel to Chi-chin Island 25 15

Girl Scouts, 75th Anniv. — A545

Wmk. 323
1985, June 1 **Litho.** ***Perf. 13½***
2458 A545 $2 multi 10 6
2459 A545 $18 multi 1.40 36

Poetry Illustration Type of 1982

Designs from The Book of Odes, Confucius.

1985, June 22 **Litho.** **Wmk. 323**
2460 A490 $2 Spring 10 6
2461 A490 $5 Summer 30 15
2462 A490 $8 Fall 50 24
2463 A490 $10 Winter 60 30

Fruit — A546

Perf. 13½x14
1985, July 5 **Litho.** **Wmk. 323**
2464 A546 $2 Wax Jambo 12 8
2465 A546 $3 Guava 15 10
2466 A546 $5 Carambola 35 15
2467 A546 $8 Litchi nut 65 25

Ch'ing Dynasty (1644-1911) Ivory Carvings — A547

1985, July 18 **Wmk. 323** ***Perf. 13½***
2468 A547 $2 Dragon Boat 12 8
2469 A547 $3 Landscape 15 10
2470 A547 $5 Melon, water container 35 15
2471 A547 $18 Brush holder, vert. 1.40 58

T'ang Dynasty (618-907) Aristocrat — A548

Designs: $5, Sung Dynasty (960-1280) palace woman. $8, Yuan Dynasty (1280-1368) aristocrat. $11, Ming-Dynasty (1368-1644) aristocrat.

1985, Aug. 1 **Wmk. 323** ***Perf. 13½***
2472 A548 $2 multi 12 8
2473 A548 $5 multi 35 15
2474 A548 $8 multi 60 25
2475 A548 $11 multi 80 32

4th Asian Conference on Costume, Aug. 3. See Nos. 2549-2552, 2605-2608.

Social Welfare Program A549

Perf. 13½x14
1985, Aug. 1 **Wmk. 323**
2476 A549 $2 Heart, bird feeding young 12 8

Historic Sites A550

Wmk. 323
1985, Sept. 3 **Litho.** ***Perf. 13½***
2477 A550 $2 Taipei North Gate 12 8
2478 A550 $5 San Domingo Fort, Tamsui 35 15
2479 A550 $8 Lung Shun Temple, Lukang 60 25
2480 A550 $10 Confucius Temple, Changhua 80 30

Bonsai A551

Trade Shows A552

Perf. 13½x14
1985, Sept. 22 **Wmk. 323**
2481 A551 $2 Oak 10 6
2482 A551 $5 Five-leaf pine 35 15
2483 A551 $8 Lohan pine 60 24
2484 A551 $18 Banyan 1.40 55

1985, Oct. 5 ***Perf. 13½***

Taipei World Trade Center and show emblems: No. 2485a, Sporting goods. No. 2485b, Toys and gifts. No. 2485c, Electronics. No. 2485d, Machinery. Se-tenant in continuous design.

2485 Strip of 4 60 24
a.-d. A552 $2, Any single 15 6

Scenes of Modern Taiwan, Map, Flag A553

1985, Oct. 25
2486 A553 $2 shown 10 6
2487 A553 $18 Chiang Kai-shek, Triumphal Arch 1.40 55

Defeat of Japanese army, end of World War II, and return of Taiwan to control of the Republic, 40th anniv.

7th Asian Conference on Mental Retardation A554

Sun Yat-sen and Birthplace A555

1985, Nov. 8 ***Perf. 14x13½***
2488 A554 $2 multi 10 6
2489 A554 $11 multi 1.00 32

1985, Nov. 12 ***Perf. 13½***
2490 A555 $2 multi 10 6
2491 A555 $18 multi 1.40 55

Postal Life Insurance, 50th Anniv. — A556

New Year 1986 (Year of the Tiger) — A557

1985, Dec. 1
2492 A556 $2 multi 10 6

1985, Dec. 1 ***Perf. 12½***
2493 A557 $1 multi 5 5
2494 A557 $10 multi 50 30
a. Miniature sheet of 4 (2 each #2493-2494) 1.10 1.10

Flora Type of 1984

1986, Jan. 10 **Litho.** ***Perf. 13½***
2495 A535 $1 Pine 5 5
2496 A535 $11 Bamboo 55 32
2497 A535 $18 Plum, lt bl background 90 55

Flora Type of 1984

Wmk. 323
1988, Feb. 12 **Litho.** ***Perf. 13½***
2498 A535 $1.50 Pine 12 10

2499 A535 $7.50 Bamboo 58 45
2500 A535 $18 Plum, lt grnsh bl background 1.35 1.00

No. 2500 has value expressed in dollars and cents.

Cultural Renaissance Movement — A558

Painting: Hermit Anglers on a Mountain Stream, Ming Dynasty, 1386-1644. Se-tenant in a continuous design.

1986, Jan. 28 Litho. *Perf. 13½*
2507 Strip of 5 50 30
a.-e. A558 $2, any single 10 6

See No. 2604.

Plum Blossom Type of 1979

Perf. 13½x12½

1986, Jan. 10 Engr. Wmk. 323
2510 A440 $40 car rose 2.50 1.75

Floral Arrangements A559

Wmk. 323

1986, Feb. 20 Litho. *Perf. 13½*
2517 A559 $2 multi 12 8
2518 A559 $5 multi 30 20
2519 A559 $8 multi 50 35
2520 A559 $10 multi 62 42

Natl. Postal Service, 90th Anniv. A560

Designs: $2, Unloading express mail at airport. $5, Motorcycle delivery, vert. $8, Technological innovations, vert. $10, Electronic sorting machine.

1986, Mar. 20
2521 A560 $2 multi 12 8
2522 A560 $5 multi 30 20
2523 A560 $8 multi 50 35
2524 A560 $10 multi 62 42
a. Souvenir sheet of 4, #2521-2524 1.55 1.05

No. 2524a has pale salmon and red decorative margin. Size: 130x100mm.

Chen Tien-hua (1875-1905), Revolutionary A561

Perf. 13½x12½

1986, Mar. 29 Engr.

Granite Paper

2525 A561 $2 violet 12 8

Yushan Natl. Park A562

Various views.

1986, Apr. 10 Litho. *Perf. 13½*
2526 A562 $2 multi 12 8
2527 A562 $5 multi 30 20
2528 A562 $8 multi 50 35
2529 A562 $10 multi 62 42

Power Plants A563

1986, Apr. 29
2530 A563 $2 Hydro-electric 12 8
2531 A563 $8 Thermo-electric 50 35
2532 A563 $10 Nuclear 62 42

Economic prosperity through energy development.

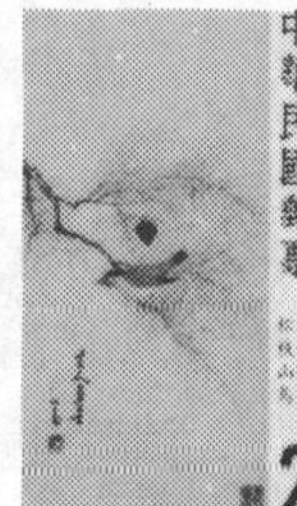

Paintings by P'u Hsin-yu (1896-1963) A564

1986, May 22 *Perf. 11½*
2533 A564 $2 Bird 12 8
2534 A564 $8 Landscape 50 35
2535 A564 $10 Woman in forest 62 42

Asian Productivity Org., 25th Anniv. A565

1986, June 3 *Perf. 13x13½*
2536 A565 $2 multi 12 8
2537 A565 $11 multi 68 45

Natl. Productivity Center, 30th anniv.

Coral-reef Fish A566

Designs: No. 2538a, Chrysiptera starcki. No. 2538b, Chelmon rostratus. No. 2538c, Chaetodon xanthurus. No. 2538d, Chaetodon quadrimaculatus. No. 2538e, Chaetodon meyeri. No. 2538f, Genicanthus semifasciatus. No. 2538g, Genicanthus semifasciatus. No. 2538h, Pomacanthus annularis. No. 2538i, Lienardella fasciata. No. 2538j, Balistapus undulatus.

1986, June 3 *Perf. 13½*
2538 Block of 10 1.25 80
a.-j. A566 $2, any single 12 8

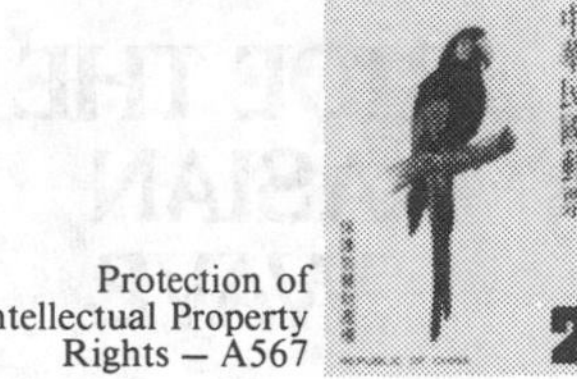

Protection of Intellectual Property Rights — A567

1986, June 12
2539 A567 $2 Macaw 12 8

Nos. 2294 and 2297 Ovptd. "60th ANNIVERSARY OF NORTHWARD EXPEDITION BY THE NATIONAL REVOLUTIONARY ARMY" in Chinese and Surcharged with Fleur-de-lis and New Value.

1986, July 9 Litho. *Perf. 13½*
2540 A432 $2 on $6 multi 12 8
2541 A432 $8 on $9 multi 48 32

Bridges A568

1986, July 30
2542 A568 $2 Tzu Mu, 1965 12 8
2543 A568 $5 Chang Hung, 1968 30 20
2544 A568 $8 Kuan Fu, 1977 48 32
2545 A568 $10 Kuan Tu, 1983 60 40

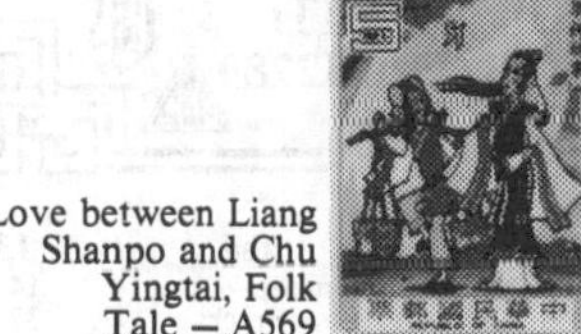

Love between Liang Shanpo and Chu Yingtai, Folk Tale — A569

Cartoons by Huang Mu-ts'un: No. 2546a, Yingtai disguised to go to school. No. 2546b, Yingtai and Shanpo meet in class. No. 2546c, The friends at pond. No. 2546d, Yingtai summoned home for arranged marriage. No. 2546e, Yingtai and Shanpo ascend to heaven as butterflies.

1986, Aug. 12 *Perf. 12½*
2546 Strip of 5 1.50 1.00
a.-e. A569 $5, any single 30 20

Social Awareness Campaign A570

1986, Sept. 12 Litho. *Perf. 13½*
2547 A570 $2 Rainbow, children 12 8
2548 A570 $8 Children, adults 48 32

Folk Costumes — A571

Designs: $2, Shang Dynasty (1766-1122 B.C.) aristocrat. $5, Warring States (403-221 B.C.) aristocrat. $8, Later Han Dynasty (A.D. 25-221) empress. $10, Flying ribbons gown, Wei and Tsin Dynasties (A.D. 221-420) aristocrat.

1986, Sept. 23 Litho. *Perf. 13½*
2549 A571 $2 multi 12 8
2550 A571 $5 multi 30 20
2551 A571 $8 multi 50 35
2552 A571 $10 multi 62 42

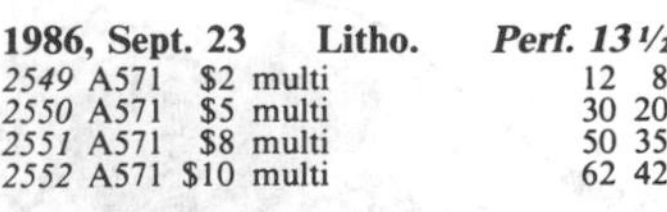

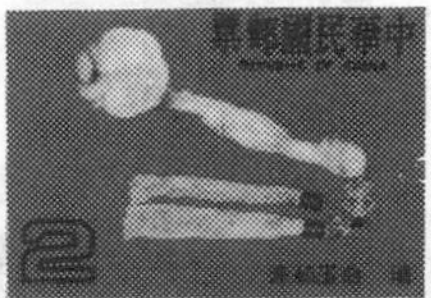

Ch'ing Dynasty Ju-i Scepters A572

1986, Oct. 10 Photo. *Perf. 14½x15*
2553 A572 $2 White jade 12 8
2554 A572 $3 Red coral 18 12
2555 A572 $4 Redwood and gems 24 16
2556 A572 $18 Gilded wood 1.10 75

See Nos. 2582-2585.

Chiang Kai-Shek A573

Portrait and: $5, Map and flag. $8, Emblem. $10, Flags on globe.

1986, Oct. 31 Litho. *Perf. 13½*
2557 A573 $2 multi 12 8
2558 A573 $5 multi 30 20
2559 A573 $8 multi 48 32
2560 A573 $10 multi 60 40
a. Souv. sheet of 4, #2557-2560 1.50 1.00

No. 2560a has pale orange inscribed margin. Size: 120x90mm.

Cultural Heritage A574

Architecture: $2, Chin-Kuang Fu land development and defense fund building, 1826. $5, Erh-sha-wan Gun Emplacement, Keelung, 1841, restored 1979. $8, Fort Hsi T'ai, 1886. $10, Matsu Temple, Peng-hu, renovated 1563-1624.

1986, Nov. 14 Litho. *Perf. 13½*
2561 A574 $2 multi 12 8
2562 A574 $5 multi 30 20
2563 A574 $8 multi 48 32
2564 A574 $10 multi 60 40

New Year 1987 (Year of the Hare) — A575

1986, Dec. 1 *Perf. 12½*
2565 A575 $1 dl pink & multi 6 5
2566 A575 $10 pale grn & multi 60 40
a. Souv. sheet of 4, 2 each #2565-2566 1.35 1.35

No. 2566a has inscribed margin. Size: 78x102mm.

Kenting, 1st Natl. Park — A576

1987, Jan. 8 Litho. *Perf. 13½*

2567	A576	$2	Garden	14	6
2568	A576	$5	Shore rocks	32	14
2569	A576	$8	Shore and hill	52	22
2570	A576	$10	Shore and rocks, diff.	65	28

Folk Art — A577

Puppets: $2, Hand puppet. $5, Marionette. $18, Shadow puppet.

1987, Feb. 12 Litho. *Perf. 14x13½*

2571	A577	$2	multi	14	6
2572	A577	$5	multi	32	14
2573	A577	$18	multi	1.20	80

Speedpost
A578

Wu Yueh (1878-1905), Revolutionary
A579

1987, Mar. 20 Litho. *Perf. 14x13½*

2574	A578	$2	multi	14	6
2575	A578	$18	multi	1.20	80

Stamp Day.

Perf. 13½x12½

1987, Mar. 29 Engr.

2576	A579	$2	orange	14	6

Landscapes Painted by Madame Chiang Kai-shek — A580

Designs: $2, Singing Creek with Bamboo Orchestra. $5, Mountains Draped in Clouds. $8, Vista of Tranquility. $10, Mountains after a Snowfall.

1987, Apr. 10 Litho. *Perf. 13½*

2577	A580	$2	blk, buff & ver	14	10
2578	A580	$5	blk, buff & ver	35	25
2579	A580	$8	blk, buff & ver	55	38
2580	A580	$10	blk, buff & ver	70	48

Stone Sculptures — A581

Designs: a. Head of a Bodhisattva, sandstone, Norther Wei Dynasty (386-534). b. Standing Buddha, limestone, Northern Ch'i Dynasty (550-577). c. Head of a Bodhisattva, sandstone, T'ang Dynasty (618-907). d. Seated Buddha, alabaster, T'ang Dynasty.

1987, Apr. 23

2581		Strip of 4	1.40	1.00
a.-d.	A581 $5	any single	35	25

No. 2581a shows seven Chinese characters at left; No. 2581c shows five.

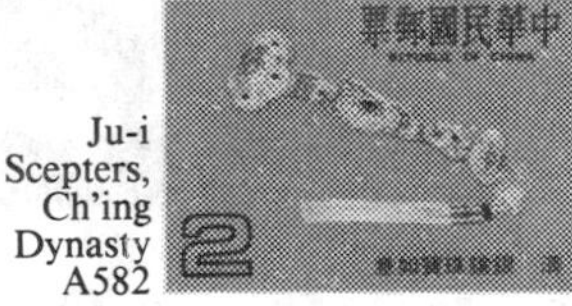

Ju-i Scepters, Ch'ing Dynasty
A582

1987, May 7 Photo. *Perf. 14½x15*

2582	A582	$2	Silver and gems	14	10
2583	A582	$3	Gold and gems	20	15
2584	A582	$4	Gilded, jade and inlaid gems	28	20
2585	A582	$18	Gilded, inlaid malachite	1.25	95

Feitsui Reservoir Inauguration
A583

1987, June 6 Litho. *Perf. 13½x14*

2586	A583	$2	Reservoir	14	10
2587	A583	$18	Hsintien Stream, reservoir	1.25	95

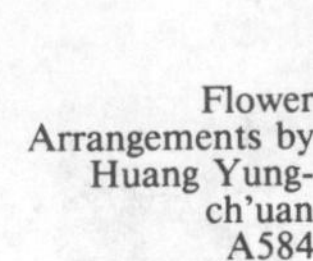

Flower Arrangements by Huang Yung-ch'uan
A584

Lions Club Intl. 70th Annual Convention, Taipei — A585

1987, June 19 *Perf. 13½*

2588	A584	$2	multi	14	10
2589	A584	$5	multi	35	28
2590	A584	$8	multi	55	42
2591	A584	$10	multi	70	52

1987, July 1

2592	A585	$2	multi	14	10
2593	A585	$18	multi	1.25	95

Sino-Japanese War, 50th Anniv.
A586

Wang Yun-Wu (1888-1979), Lexicographer
A587

1987, July 7 *Perf. 14x13½*

2594	A586	$1	Battle front	8	6
2595	A586	$2	Chiang Kai-shek giving speech	14	10
2596	A586	$5	Public donating funds	35	28
2597	A586	$6	Troops marching	42	32
2598	A586	$8	Signing of peace treaty	58	45
2599	A586	$18	Parade	1.25	95
			Nos. 2594-2599 (6)	2.82	2.16

1987, Aug. 14 *Perf. 13½*

2600	A587	$2	gray blk	14	10

Memorial Hall Type of 1981

Perf. 12½x13½

1987, Sept. 24 Photo.

2601	A468	10c	lake	5	5
2602	A468	30c	brt grn	5	5
2603	A468	60c	brt blue	5	5

A588

Cultural Renaissance Movement — A589

Scroll, 1543, by Weng Chen-ming (1470-1559), a copy of Chao Po-su's *Red Cliff*. Nos. 2604a-2604e and 2604f-2604j are printed in continuous designs.

1987, Sept. 22 Engr. *Perf. 13½*

2604	Block of 10	2.50	1.90
a.-e.	A588 $3 any single	24	18
f.-j.	A589 $3 any single	24	18

Folk Costumes — A590

Designs: $1.50, Han woman, early Ch'ing Dynasty (1644-1911). $3, Wife of a Ch'ing Dynasty Manchu Bannerman. $7.50, Urban woman wearing Manchu ch'i-p'ao dress, c. 1912. $18, Short jacket over long skirt, c. 1920.

1987, Oct. 2 Litho.

2605	A590	$1.50 multi	12	10
2606	A590	$3 multi	24	16
2607	A590	$7.50 multi	58	45
2608	A590	$18 multi	1.40	1.05

Intl. Symposium on Confucianism, Taipei, Nov. 12-17 — A591

New Year 1988 (Year of the Dragon) — A592

1987, Nov. 12 *Perf. 13½x14*

2609	A591	$3 Ta Chen Tian temple, Taichung	24	16
2610	A591	$18 Confucius	1.40	1.05

1987, Dec. 1 *Perf. 12½*

2611	A592	$1.50 multi	12	8
2612	A592	$12 multi	95	65
a.		Souv. sheet of 4, 2 each Nos. 2611-2612	2.25	2.25

No. 2612a has inscribed margin. Size: 78x102mm.

Constitution, 40th Anniv. — A593

1987, Dec. 25 Litho. *Perf. 13½*

2613	A593	$3 multi	22	16
2614	A593	$16 multi, diff.	1.20	90

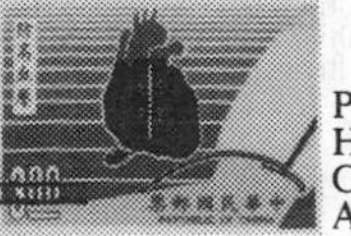

Prevent Hypertension Campaign A594

1988, Jan. 8 *Perf. 12½x13½*

2615	A594	$3 multi	22	16

Fruit Tree Blossoms — A595

Wmk. 323

1988, Feb. 4 Litho. *Perf. 13½*

2616	A595	$3 Prunus mume	22	16
2617	A595	$7.50 Prunus armeniaca	58	45
2618	A595	$12 Prunus persica	90	68
a.		Min. sheet of 3, Nos. 2616-2618	1.70	1.70

No. 2618a has bright pink inscribed margin. Size: 121x80mm.

SEMI-POSTAL STAMPS

SP1

Red or Blue Surcharge

1920, Dec. 1 Unwmk. *Perf. 14, 15*

B1	SP1	1c on 2c grn	5.25	1.25
B2	SP1	3c on 4c scar (B)	6.75	1.90
B3	SP1	5c on 6c gray	10.50	2.75

The surcharge represents the actual franking value. The extra cent helped victims of the 1919 Yellow River flood.

War Refugees SP2

Black Surcharge

1944, Oct. 10 Engr. *Perf. 12*

B4	SP2	$2 +$2 on 50c + 50c brt ultra	25	25
B5	SP2	$4 +$4 on 8c + 8c brt grn	25	25
B6	SP2	$5 +$5 on 21c + 21c red brn	75	75
B7	SP2	$6 +$6 on 28c + 28c ol grn	1.10	1.10
B8	SP2	$10 +$10 on 33c + 33c red	1.65	1.65
B9	SP2	$20 +$20 on $1 + $1 vio	3.25	3.25
a.		Sheet of six	12.50	12.50
		Nos. B4-B9 (6)	7.25	7.25

The borders of each stamp differ slightly in design.

The surtax was for war refugees.

No. B9a measures 191x112mm. and contains one each of Nos. B4 to B9 with marginal inscriptions in olive green, red brown and bright green.

Nos. B4-B8 exist without surcharge, but were not regularly issued.

Great Wall of China SP4

Chinese Refugee Family SP5

1948, July 5 Litho. *Perf. 14, Imperf.*

Without Gum

Cross in Carmine

B11	SP4	$5000 + $2000 vio	12	12
B12	SP4	$10,000 + $2000 brn	12	12
B13	SP4	$15,000 + $2000 gray	12	12
a.		Cross omitted		

The surtax was for anti-tuberculosis work.

Republic of China (Taiwan)

1954, Oct. 1 Engr. *Perf. 12*

Without Gum

B14	SP5	40c + 10c dp bl	9.25	1.50
B15	SP5	$1.60 + 40c lil rose	18.00	3.50
B16	SP5	$5 + $1 red	42.50	25.00

The surtax was used to aid in the evacuation of Chinese from North Viet Nam.

AIR POST STAMPS

Curtiss "Jenny" over Great Wall (Bars of Republic flag on tail.) — AP1

Unwmk.

1921, July 1 Engr. *Perf. 14*

C1	AP1	15c bl grn & blk	17.50	8.50
C2	AP1	30c scar & blk	12.50	7.50
C3	AP1	45c dl vio & blk	12.50	7.50
C4	AP1	60c dk bl & blk	17.50	8.50
C5	AP1	90c ol grn & blk	20.00	10.00
		Nos. C1-C5 (5)	80.00	42.00

(Nationalist sun emblem on tail.) — AP2

1929, July 5

C6	AP2	15c bl grn & blk	2.50	50
C7	AP2	30c dk red & blk	4.00	1.00
C8	AP2	45c dk vio & blk	7.50	3.00
C9	AP2	60c dk bl & blk	7.50	3.00
C10	AP2	90c ol grn & blk	10.00	5.00
		Nos. C6-C10 (5)	31.50	12.50

Junkers F-13 over Great Wall AP3

1932-37

C11	AP3	15c gray grn	10	6
C12	AP3	25c org ('33)	10	5
C13	AP3	30c red	30	10
C14	AP3	45c brn vio	10	8
C15	AP3	50c dk brn ('33)	10	8
C16	AP3	60c dk bl	10	8
C17	AP3	90c ol grn	30	10
C18	AP3	$1 yel grn ('33)	30	10
C19	AP3	$2 brn ('37)	30	10
C20	AP3	$5 brn car ('37)	1.00	75
		Nos. C11-C20 (10)	2.70	1.50

Type of 1932-37, with secret mark

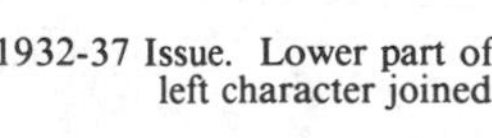

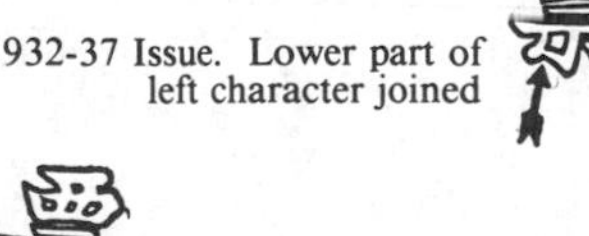

1932-37 Issue. Lower part of left character joined

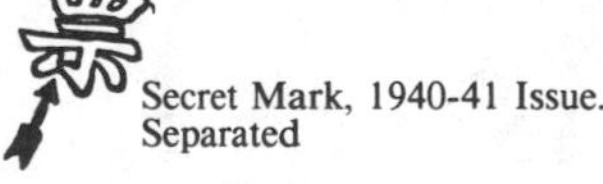

Secret Mark, 1940-41 Issue. Separated

Wmk. Character Yu (Post) Multiple (261)

1940-41 *Perf. 12, 12½, 12½x13, 13*

C21	AP3	15c gray grn	10	20
C22	AP3	25c yel org	15	25
C23	AP3	30c red	10	10
a.		Vert. pair, imperf. between	175.00	
C24	AP3	45c dl rose vio ('41)	8	25
C25	AP3	50c brown	8	25
C26	AP3	60c dp bl ('41)	10	30
C27	AP3	90c ol ('41)	10	30
C28	AP3	$1 ap grn ('41)	12	30
C29	AP3	$2 lt brn ('41)	12	30
C30	AP3	$5 lake	12	25
		Nos. C21-C30 (10)	1.07	2.50

Unwmk.

Perf. 12½, 13, 13½

C31	AP3	15c gray grn ('41)	6	6
C32	AP3	25c lt org ('41)	6	6
C33	AP3	30c lt red ('41)	6	6
C34	AP3	45c dl rose vio ('41)	8	8
C35	AP3	50c brown	6	6
C36	AP3	60c bl ('41)	6	6
C37	AP3	90c lt ol ('41)	6	6
C38	AP3	$1 ap grn ('41)	10	10
C39	AP3	$2 lt brn ('41)	15	15
C40	AP3	$5 lake ('41)	12	12
		Nos. C31-C40 (10)	81	81

圓叁拾伍幣國

Nos. C11 and C12 Surcharged in Black

1946, May 2 Unwmk. *Perf. 14*

C41	AP3	$53 on 15c gray grn	20	*35*
C42	AP3	$73 on 25c org	775.00	825.00

Forgeries of No. C42 exist.

On Nos. C23, C21, C22, C29 and C30

Perf. 13, 13x12, 12½

Wmk. 261

C43	AP3	$23 on 30c red	10	*40*
C44	AP3	$53 on 15c gray grn	7.00	*9.00*
C45	AP3	$73 on 25c yel org	30	*50*
C46	AP3	$100 on $2 lt brn	10	*40*
C47	AP3	$200 on $5 lake	15	*45*

On Nos. C33, C31, C32, C39 and C40

Perf. 13, 13x12, 13x12½, 12½

Unwmk.

C48	AP3	$23 on 30c lt red	(5)	5
a.		Inverted surcharge	110.00	
b.		"2300" omitted	55.00	
c.		Last character (kuo) of surch. omitted	75.00	
C49	AP3	$53 on 15c gray grn	(5)	5
a.		Horiz. pair, imperf. between		750.00
C50	AP3	$73 on 25c lt org	(5)	5
a.		Inverted surcharge	600.00	
C51	AP3	$100 on $2 lt brn	(5)	5
C52	AP3	$200 on $5 lake	(5)	5
a.		Inverted surcharge	90.00	

The surcharges on Nos. C41-C52 represent Chinese national currency and were applied at Shanghai.

Douglas DC-4 over Sun Yat-sen Mausoleum, Nanking AP4

1946, Sept. 10 Litho. *Perf. 14*

Without Gum

C53	AP4	$27 blue	15	10

圓萬壹作改

No. C23 Surcharged in Black

Perf. 13x12

1948, May 18 Wmk. 261

C54	AP3	$10,000 on 30c red	10	*50*

Same, in Black or Carmine, on Nos. C33, C32, C37, C36, C18 and C38

Perf. 12½, 13x12½, 14

Unwmk.

C55	AP3	$10,000 on 30c lt red	(8)	*10*
C56	AP3	$20,000 on 25c lt org	(8)	*12*
C57	AP3	$30,000 on 90c lt ol (C)	(8)	*15*
C58	AP3	$50,000 on 60c bl (C)	10	*20*
C59	AP3	$50,000 on $1 yel grn (C)	45.00	45.00
C60	AP3	$50,000 on $1 ap grn (C)	10	*20*

改作壹萬圓

No. C53 Surcharged in Black

Perf. 14

C61	AP4	$10,000 on $27 bl	(8)	*15*
		Nos. C54-C61 (8)	45.62	46.42

Douglas DC-4 and Arrow — AP5

Perf. 12½

1949, May 2 Unwmk. Litho.

Without Gum

C62	AP5	bl grn	2.25	2.25
a.		Rouletted	3.50	3.50

See note after No. 959.

政郵國民華中
費空航內國

Revenue Stamp Overprinted in Blue

1949, May Engr. *Perf. 14*

C63	A95	$100 ol grn	20.00	21.00

See note after No. 962.

Republic of China (Taiwan)

Cheng Ch'eng-kung (Koxinga) — AP6

Rouletted

1950, Sept. 26 Unwmk. Typo.

Without Gum

C64	AP6	60c dp bl	12.50	2.00

Plane over City Gate, Taipei — AP7

Jet Planes above Chung Shan Bridge — AP8

Two Doves Near Koxinga Shrine — AP9

1954 Engr. *Perf. 11½*

Without Gum

C65	AP7	$1 dk brn	7.00	50
a.		Vert. pair, imperf. btwn.		300.00
C66	AP8	$1.60 ol blk	4.50	40
a.		Vert. pair, imperf. btwn.	200.00	
b.		Horiz. pair, imperf. between	150.00	175.00
C67	AP9	$5 grnsh bl	5.50	50

No. C67 Surcharged in Red

1958, Dec. 11

C68	AP9	$3.50 on $5 grnsh bl	1.50	25

Sea Gull AP10

Sabre Jets in Bomb Burst Formation AP11

1959, Mar. 20 Photo. *Perf. 13*

C69	AP10	$8 bl, gray & blk	1.40	25

1960, Feb. 29 Unwmk. *Perf. 13*

Plane Formations: $2, Loop (horiz.). $5, Diamond formation passing over grounded plane (horiz.).

C70	AP11	$1 multi	1.75	40
C71	AP11	$2 multi	1.75	25
C72	AP11	$5 multi	3.75	50

Issued to honor the Chinese Air Force and the "Thunder Tiger" aerobatic team.

Jet Airliner over Pitan Bridge — AP12

Designs: $6, Jet over Tropic of Cancer monument, Kiai (vert.). $10, Jet over Lion Head mountain, Sinchu (vert.).

1963, Aug. 14 Photo. *Perf. 13*

C73	AP12	$2.50 multi	1.25	8
C74	AP12	$6 multi	2.25	12
C75	AP12	$10 multi	4.50	1.00

Boeing 727 over Chilin Pavilion, Grand Hotel — AP13

Design: $8, Boeing 727 over National Palace Museum, Taipei.

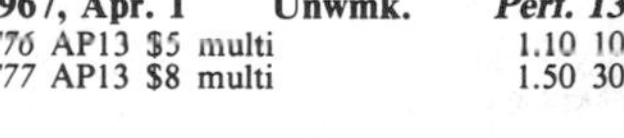

1967, Apr. 1 Unwmk. *Perf. 13*

C76	AP13	$5 multi	1.10	10
C77	AP13	$8 multi	1.50	30

Wild Geese Flying over Mountains — AP14

Designs (Wild Geese flying over): $5, The sea. $8, The land (horiz.).

1969, Aug. 14 Photo. *Perf. 13*

C78	AP14	$2.50 multi	55	10
C79	AP14	$5 multi	85	20
C80	AP14	$8 multi	1.10	30

Presidental Palace and Tzu-Ch'iang Squadron AP15

1980, June 18 Litho. *Perf. 13½*

C81 AP15 $5 *shown* 25 20
C82 AP15 $7 *China Airlines jet* 35 32
C83 AP15 $12 *China flag, jet* 60 50

Civil Aeronautics Administration, 37th Anniv. — AP16

Jet Airliners over: $7, Chiang Kai-shek Intl. Airport, vert. $11, Chung Cheng Memorial Hall. $18, Sun Yat-sen Memorial Hall.

Perf. 14x13½, 13½x14

1984, Jan. 20 Litho.

C84 AP16 $7 multi 70 22
C85 AP16 $11 multi 1.10 32
C86 AP16 $18 multi 1.75 60

Airplane AP17

1987, Aug. 4 Litho. *Perf. 13½*

C87 AP17 $9 multi 68 52
C88 AP17 $14 multi 1.05 80
C89 AP17 $18 multi 1.35 1.00

SPECIAL DELIVERY STAMPS

Design: Dragon in irregular oval.

Stamp 8x2½ inches, divided into four parts by perforation or serrate rouletting.

Prices of Nos. E1-E8 are for used parts. Complete unused strips of four are exceptionally scarce.

"Chinese Imperial Post Office" in lines, repeated to form the background which is usually lighter in color than the rest of the design.

Dragon's head facing downward
Background with period after "POSTOFFICE".
No Date

1905 Unwmk. *Perf. 11*

E1 10c grass grn 175.00

Serrate Roulette in Black

E2 10c dp grn 125.00

1907-10

Dragon's head facing forward
Background with no period after "POSTOFFICE"
No Date

E3 10c lt bluish grn 75.00

1909-11

Background with date at bottom

E4 10c grn (Feb. 1909) 35.00
E5 10c bl grn (Jan. 1911) 22.50

1912

"Imperial Post Office" in serifed letters repeated to form the background.
No Date, No Border
Background of 30 or 28 lines

E6 10c grn (30 lines) 35.00
a. 28 lines 40.00

Background of 35 lines of sans-serif letters
Colored Border

E8 10c green 40.00

On No. E8 the medallion in the third section has Chinese characters in the background instead of the usual English inscriptions. E6 and E8 occur with many types of four-character overprints reading "Republic of China," applied locally but unofficially at various post offices.

1913

Design: Wild Goose. Stamp 7½x2¾inches, divided into five parts.
"Chinese Post Office" in sans-serif letters, repeated to form the background of 28 lines. With border.
Serrate Roulette in Black

E9 10c green 200.00 19.00

Unused prices for Nos. E9-E10 are for complete strips of five parts. Used prices are for single parts.

1914

"Chinese Post Office" in antique letters, forming a background of 29 or 30 lines. No border.
Serrate Roulette in Green

E10 10c green 57.50 1.25

On No. E9 the background is in sans-serif capitals, the Chinese and English inscriptions are on white tablets and the serial numbers are in black.

On No. E10 the background is in antique capitals and extends under the inscriptions. The serial numbers are in green.

NOTE:

In February, 1916, the Special Delivery Stamps were demonetized and became merely receipts without franking value. To mark this, four of the five sections of the stamp had the letters A, B, C, D either handstamped or printed on them.

SD1

1941 Unwmk. Typo. *Rouletted*
Without Gum

E11 SD1 ($2) car & yel 17.50 4.00

Motorcycle Messenger — SD2

1949, July Litho. *Perf. 12½*
Without Gum

E12 SD2 red vio 1.25 1.50
a. Rouletted 3.50 *4.75*

See note after No. 959.

Revenue Stamp Overprinted in Purple Brown

1949

Without Gum

E13 A95 $10 grnsh gray 11.00 11.00

See note after No. 962.

REGISTRATION STAMPS

R1

1941 Unwmk. Typo. *Rouletted*
Without Gum

F1 R1 ($1.50) grn & buff 13.00 3.50

Mountain Scene — R2

1949, July Litho. *Perf. 12½*
Without Gum

F2 R2 carmine 1.40 1.40
a. Rouletted 2.50 *3.50*

See note after No. 959.

Revenue Stamp Overprinted in Carmine

1949

F3 A95 $50 dk bl 10.50 10.50

See note after No. 962.

POSTAGE DUE STAMPS

Regular Issue of 1902-03 Overprinted in Black — POSTAGE DUE 欠資

1904 Unwmk. *Perf. 14 to 15*

J1 A17 ½c chocolate 6.00 1.40
J2 A17 2c ocher 6.00 1.10
J3 A17 2c scarlet 6.00 1.90
J4 A17 4c red brn 6.00 1.90
J5 A17 5c salmon 10.00 1.90
J6 A17 10c dk bl grn 12.00 2.25
a. Vertical pair, imperf. between 300.00
Nos. J1-J6 (6) 46.00 10.45

D1

D2

D3

1904 Engr.

J7 D1 ½c blue 2.25 15
a. Horizontal pair, imperf. between 150.00 150.00
J8 D1 1c blue 3.25 15
J9 D1 2c blue 2.25 15
a. Horizontal pair, imperf. between 135.00 135.00
J10 D1 4c blue 4.50 35
J11 D1 5c blue 5.00 40
J12 D1 10c blue 5.00 75
J13 D1 20c blue 13.00 4.00
J14 D1 30c blue 17.50 4.50
Nos. J7-J14 (8) 52.75 10.45

Arabic numeral of value at left on Nos. J12 to J14.

1911

J15 D1 1c brown 4.50 1.00
J16 D1 2c brown 6.25 1.50

The ½c, 4c, 5c and 20c in brown exist but were not issued as they arrived in China after the downfall of the Ching dynasty.

Issue of 1904 Overprinted in Red — 臨時中立

1912

J19 D1 ½c blue 350.00 275.00
J20 D1 4c blue 400.00 325.00
J21 D1 5c blue 450.00 425.00
J22 D1 10c blue 600.00 550.00
J23 D1 20c blue 1,500. 1,300.
J24 D1 30c blue 1,500. 1,300.

Nos. J15-J16 exist with this overprint, but were not regularly issued.

1912

Overprinted in Red

J25 D2 ½c blue 25 15
J26 D2 1c brown 30 20
a. Horizontal pair, imperf. between 125.00
b. Inverted overprint 165.00
J27 D2 2c brown 50 30
J28 D2 4c blue 1.50 40
J29 D2 5c blue 85.00 60.00
J30 D2 5c brown 1.50 50
a. Inverted overprint 100.00 80.00
J31 D2 10c blue 4.00 65
J32 D2 20c blue 6.00 1.50
J33 D2 30c blue 11.00 4.00
Nos. J25-J33 (9) 110.05 67.70

1912

Overprinted in Black

J34 D3 ½c blue 6.00 2.00
J35 D3 ½c brown 1.00 35
J36 D3 1c brown 60 35
a. Inverted overprint 135.00
J37 D3 2c brown 2.00 65
J38 D3 4c blue 4.00 1.00
J39 D3 5c brown 4.00 1.25
a. Horizontal pair, imperf. between 225.00
J40 D3 10c blue 11.00 2.00
J41 D3 20c brown 20.00 7.00
J42 D3 30c blue 25.00 8.00
Nos. J34-J42 (9) 73.60 22.60

D4

Printed by Waterlow & Sons

1913, May *Perf. 14, 15*

J43 D4 ½c blue 50 15
a. Horizontal pair, imperf. between 200.00
J44 D4 1c blue 1.00 10
J45 D4 2c blue 1.00 15
J46 D4 4c blue 2.50 20
J47 D4 5c blue 3.00 20
J48 D4 10c blue 5.00 50
J49 D4 20c blue 7.50 80
J50 D4 30c blue 10.00 2.00
Nos. J43-J50 (8) 30.50 4.10

Printed by the Chinese Bureau of Engraving & Printing

1915 Re-engraved *Perf. 14*

J51 D4 ½c blue 60 10
J52 D4 1c blue 1.25 10
J53 D4 2c blue 1.25 10
J54 D4 4c blue 1.25 10
J55 D4 5c blue 1.75 25
J56 D4 10c blue 2.50 35
J57 D4 20c blue 7.00 40
J58 D4 30c blue 20.00 1.50
Nos. J51-J58 (8) 35.60 2.90

In the upper part of the stamps of type D4 there is an ornament of five marks like the letter "V". Below this is a curved label with an inscription in Chinese characters. On the 1913 stamps there are two complete background lines between the ornament and the label. The 1915 stamps show only one unbroken line at this place. There are other minute differences in the engraving of the stamps of the two issues.

D5

1932 *Perf. 14*

J59 D5 ½c orange 12 8
J60 D5 1c orange 12 8
J61 D5 2c orange 12 8
J62 D5 4c orange 25 25
J63 D5 5c orange 25 25
J64 D5 10c orange 60 35
J65 D5 20c orange 60 35
J66 D5 30c orange 60 35
Nos. J59-J66 (8) 2.66 1.79

欠 暫
資 作

Regular Stamps of 1939 Overprinted in Black or Red

1940
J67 A57 $1 hn & dk brn (Bk) 1.10 1.10
J68 A57 $2 dl bl & org brn (R) 1.50 1.50

Type of 1932
Printed by The Commercial Press, Ltd.

Perf. 12½, 12½x13, 13

1940-41 **Engr.**
J69 D5 ½c yel org 6 8
J70 D5 1c yel org 15 20
J71 D5 2c yel org ('41) 6 8
J72 D5 4c yel org 6 8
J73 D5 5c yel org ('41) 10 12
J74 D5 10c yel org ('41) 10 12
J75 D5 20c yel org ('41) 10 12
J76 D5 30c yel org 10 12
J77 D5 50c yel org 10 12
J78 D5 $1 yel org 10 15
J79 D5 $2 yel org 20 25
Nos. J69-J79 (11) 1.13 1.41

D6

Thin Paper Without Gum

1944 **Typo.** ***Perf. 13***
J80 D6 10c bluish grn 5 5
J81 D6 20c lt chlky bl 5 5
J82 D6 40c dl rose 5 5
J83 D6 50c bluish grn 5 5
J84 D6 60c dl bl 5 5
J85 D6 $1 dl rose 10 10
J86 D6 $2 lil brn 12 15
Nos. J80-J86 (7) 47 50

D7

1945 **Without Gum** **Unwmk.**
J87 D7 $2 rose car 5 6
J88 D7 $6 rose car 5 6
J89 D7 $8 rose car 5 6
J90 D7 $10 rose car 6 8
J91 D7 $20 rose car 6 8
J92 D7 $30 rose car 6 8
Nos. J87-J92 (6) 33 42

D8

Thin Paper Without Gum

1947 **Litho.** ***Perf. 14***
J93 D8 $50 plum 8 8
J94 D8 $80 plum 8 8
J95 D8 $100 plum 8 8
J96 D8 $160 plum 8 8
J97 D8 $200 plum 8 8
J98 D8 $400 vio brn 8 8
J99 D8 $500 vio brn 8 8
a. Vert. pair, imperf. between 20.00
J100 D8 $800 vio brn 8 8
J101 D8 $2000 vio brn 8 8
Nos. J93-J101 (9) 72 72

Type of 1945, Redrawn
Surcharged with New Value in Black

1948 **Engr.** ***Perf. 13½x14***
Without Gum
J102 D7 $1000 on $20 dp cl 10 12
J103 D7 $2000 on $30 dp cl 10 12
J104 D7 $3000 on $50 dp cl 10 12
J105 D7 $4000 on $100 dp cl 10 12
J106 D7 $5000 on $200 dp cl 10 12
J107 D7 $10,000 on $300 dp cl 12 15
J108 D7 $20,000 on $500 dp cl 12 15
J109 D7 $30,000 on $1000 dp cl 15 20
Nos. J102-J109 (8) 89 1.10

There are many differences in the redrawn design.

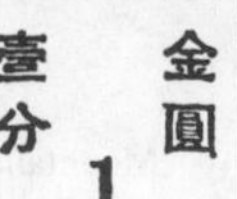
資欠作改
壹 金
分 圓
1

No. 627 Surcharged in Black

1949 ***Perf. 12***
J110 A72 1 (c) on $40 org 10 12
J111 A72 2 (c) on $40 org 10 12
J112 A72 5 (c) on $40 org 10 12
J113 A72 10 (c) on $40 org 10 12
J114 A72 20 (c) on $40 org 10 12
J115 A72 50 (c) on $40 org 12 15
J116 A72 $1 on $40 org 12 15
J117 A72 $2 on $40 org 12 15
J118 A72 $5 on $40 org 12 15
J119 A72 $10 on $40 org 20 25
Nos. J110-J119 (10) 1.18 1.45

Republic of China (Taiwan)

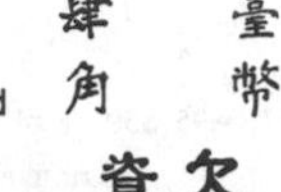
肆 臺
角 幣
資欠
40 40

No. 438 Surcharged in Green or Black

1951 **Unwmk.** ***Perf. 12½***
J120 A47 40c on 40c org (G) 7.50 6.00
J121 A47 80c on 40c org (G) 7.50 6.00

政郵國民華中
角壹幣台資欠
10

Revenue Stamps Surcharged in Various Colors

1953 **Unwmk.** ***Perf. 12½, 14***
Without Gum
J122 A95 10c on $50 dk bl (O) 6.75 2.50
J123 A95 20c on $100 ol grn (Dk Br) 6.75 2.50
J124 A95 40c on $20 org brn 8.25 75
J125 A95 80c on $500 sl grn (Dk Bl) 14.00 1.50
J126 A95 $1 on $30 dk vio (G) 14.00 5.00
Nos. J122-J126 (5) 49.75 12.25

D9

1956 **Unwmk.** **Litho.** ***Perf. 12½***
Without Gum
J127 D9 20c rose car, & lt bl 25 10
J128 D9 40c grn & buff 25 10
J129 D9 80c brn & gray 50 10
J130 D9 $1 ultra & pink 50 15

500
資欠
伍
圓

No. 1197 Surcharged in Dark Violet

Wmk. 323
1961, Dec. 28 **Engr.** ***Perf. 12***
Without Gum
J131 A135 $5 on $20 car rose 1.50 1.00

010
資欠
壹
角

Nos. 1274, 1282-1283 Surcharged in Black, Carmine Rose or Blue

1964-65 **Litho.**
J132 A158 10c on 80c pale grn 15 10
J133 A158 20c on $3.60 vio bl (CR) ('65) 15 10
J134 A158 40c on $4.50 ver (B) ('65) 25 10

D10

1966-76 **Wmk. 323** ***Perf. 12½***
Granite Paper; Without Gum
J135 D10 10c dk brn & lil 10 8
J136 D10 20c bl & yel 10 8
J137 D10 50c vio bl & lt bl ('70) 25 8
J138 D10 $1 pur & sal 20 8
J139 D10 $2 grn & lt bl 25 8
J140 D10 $5 red & sal 50 30
a. org red & pale yel 50 30
J141 D10 $10 lil rose & pink ('76) 1.00 60
Nos. J135-J141 (7) 2.40 1.30

The 50c, $10 and No. J140a are gummed. The $1 and $2 were reissued with gum in 1968 and 1973 respectively. No. J140a and the $10 are on ordinary paper.

D11

1984, Mar. 15 **Litho.** ***Perf. 12½***
J142 D11 $1 rose & vio 5 5
J143 D11 $2 yel & bl 10 8
J144 D11 $5 bl & yel 25 16
J145 D11 $10 yel & lil rose 50 32

PARCEL POST STAMPS

PP1

PP2

PP3

1945-48 **Unwmk.** **Engr.** ***Perf. 13***
Without Gum
Q1 PP1 $500 green 45 8
Q2 PP1 $1000 blue 45 8
Q3 PP1 $3000 rose red 1.50 13
Q4 PP1 $5000 brown 25.00 2.00
Q5 PP1 $10,000 lil gray 40.00 2.50
Q6 PP1 $20,000 red org 1000.00
Nos. Q1-Q5 (5) 67.40 4.79

No. Q6 was prepared but not issued.

Perf. 12½
Q7 PP2 $3000 red org 60 10
Q8 PP2 $5000 dk bl 70 12
Q9 PP2 $10,000 violet 70 20
Q10 PP2 $20,000 dk red 70 20

Perf. 13½
Q11 PP3 $1000 org yel 70 25
Q12 PP3 $3000 bl grn 90 25
Q13 PP3 $5000 org red 90 25
Q14 PP3 $7000 dl bl 90 25
Q15 PP3 $10,000 car rose 1.00 25
Q16 PP3 $30,000 olive 1.00 25
Q17 PP3 $50,000 indigo 1.00 25
Q18 PP3 $70,000 org brn 1.25 25
Q19 PP3 $100,000 dp plum 1.25 25

Denomination Tablet Without Inner Frame
Q20 PP3 $200,000 dk grn 1.75 40
Q21 PP3 $300,000 pink 1.75 40
Q22 PP3 $500,000 vio brn 1.75 50
Q23 PP3 $3,000,000 sl bl 2.00 75
Q24 PP3 $5,000,000 lilac 2.00 75
Q25 PP3 $6,000,000 ol gray 2.25 85
Q26 PP3 $8,000,000 scarlet 2.25 1.00
Q27 PP3 $10,000,000 sage grn 3.50 1.25
Nos. Q11-Q27 (17) 26.15 8.15

Zeros for "cents" omitted on Nos. Q23-Q27.

圓拾圓金
10
圓拾圓金

Parcel Post Stamps of 1945-48 Surcharged in Black or Carmine

1949 **Unwmk.** ***Perf. 13½***
Q32 PP3 $10 on $3000 bl grn 40 10
Q33 PP3 $20 on $5000 org red 40 10
Q34 PP3 $50 on $10,000 car rose 40 10
Q35 PP3 $100 on $3,000,000 sl bl (C) 60 15
Q36 PP3 $200 on $5,000,000 lil 1.00 15
Q37 PP3 $500 on $1000 org yel 2.00 25
Q38 PP3 $1000 on $7500 dl bl 2.00 40
Nos. Q32-Q38 (7) 6.80 1.25

Five characters in each line on Nos. Q33 to Q38.

MILITARY STAMPS

No. 454 Overprinted in Dull Red 郵 軍

1943-44 **Unwmk.** ***Perf. 12***
M1 A59 8c turq grn 1.50 1.50

Nos. 383, 453-454 Overprinted in Red 郵 軍

6mm. between characters

Perf. 14, 12½
M2 A57 8c ol grn 1.10 1.10
a. 8mm between characters 1.75 1.75
M3 A59 8c red org 175.00
M4 A59 8c turq grn 3.00 3.00

郵 軍

No. 493 Overprinted in Red

Perf. 13
M5 A62 16c dl ol brn 1.50 1.50
a. Perf. 10½-11 85.00

No. M5 overprinted in black is a proof.

Stamps of 1942-44 Overprinted in Carmine or Black 郵 軍

M6 A62 50c sage grn (C) 1.25 1.25
M7 A62 $1 rose lake (Bk) 1.50 1.50
M8 A62 $1 dl grn (Bk) 1.75 1.75
M9 A62 $2 dk bl grn (C) 3.00 3.00
M10 A62 $2 dk vio brn ('44) (Bk) 15.00 20.00

Nos. 383 and 357 Overprinted in Red 郵 軍

1944 ***Perf. 12, 14***
M11 A57 8c ol grn 1.75 1.75
a. Right character inverted 125.00
M12 A57 16c ol gray 9.00 9.00

Anti-Aircraft Guns — M1

1945, Jan. 1 Typo. *Perf. 12 1/2*
Thin Paper Without Gum
M13 M1 rose 70 1.75

TAIWAN

(Formosa)
100 Sen = 1 Yen
100 Cents = 1 Dollar

Stamps and Types of Japan (Taiwan) Overprinted in Black

中華民國
臺灣省

Values in Sen and Yen
Black Overprint

1945 Unwmk. Litho. *Imperf.*
Stamps Divided by Lines of Colored Dashes.

1 A1 3s carmine 60 40
2 A1 5s bl grn 75 30
3 A1 10s pale bl 85 30
a. Inverted ovpt. 35.00
b. Double ovpt. 40.00
4 A1 30s dk bl 1.00 1.00
5 A1 40s violet 1.25 80
6 A1 50s gray brn 1.10 1.25
7 A1 1y ol grn 1.25 1.40

Same Overprint on Types of Japan A99 and A100

8 A99 5y gray grn 4.00 2.50
9 A100 10y brn vio 6.00 3.50
a. Invtd. ovpt. 135.00
Nos. 1-9 (9) 16.80 11.45

The basic stamps of this issue were prepared by Japanese authorities for Taiwan use before the end of World War II when the island reverted to Chinese control. They are printed on crude buff or white wove paper. The overprint translates: "For Use in Taiwan, Chinese Republic."

A second overprinting of Nos. 2-3 was made with a different font.

China, Nos. 728-731, Surcharged in Black

限臺灣省貼用
70 錢拾柒

1946 *Perf. 14*
10 A75 70s on $20 grn 10 7
a. Inverted surcharge 135.00
11 A75 1y on $30 bl 20 15
12 A75 2y on $50 dk brn 30 25
13 A75 3y on $100 car 30 25

Issued to commemorate the convening of the Chinese National Assembly.

China Issues and Types of 1940-1946 Surcharged in Black

用貼灣臺限

a

錢 拾

Perf. 12 1/2, 12 1/2x13, 13, 13x12 1/2, 14
1946-47
14 A46 2s on 2c dp bl ('47) 5 5
15 A48 5s on 5c dl red org 5 5
16 A39 10s on 4c pale vio 5 5
17 A48 30s on 15c brn car 5 5
18 A73 50s on $20 car ('47) 5 5
19 A37 65s on $20 brt yel grn ('47) 5 5
20 A47 1y on 20c lt bl 5 5
a. Inverted surch. 65.00
21 A37 1y on $30 choc ('47) 5 5
22 A37 2y on $50 red org ('47) 5 5
23 A73 3y on $100 dk car ('47) 10 10
24 A73 5y on $200 ol grn ('47) 10 10
25 A73 10y on $500 brt bl grn ('47) 10 10
26 A73 20y on $700 red brn ('47) 30 30
27 A73 50y on $1000 rose lake ('47) 60 60
28 A73 100y on $3000 bl ('47) 95 95
Nos. 14-28 (15) 2.60 2.60

The bottom line of the surcharge expresses the new value and consists of 2, 3 or 4 characters.

Same Surcharge on China No. 412

1947 Wmk. 261 *Perf. 13*
28A A48 30s on 15c brn car 30.00 35.00

Type of China, 1946, Inscribed:

貼 臺
用 湾

1947 Unwmk. Engr. *Perf. 11, 11 1/2*
29 A74 70c carmine 15 15
30 A74 $1 green 15 15
31 A74 $2 vermilion 15 15
32 A74 $3 yel grn 15 15
33 A74 $7 yel org 25 25
34 A74 $10 magenta 25 25
Nos. 29-34 (6) 1.10 1.10

60th birthday of Chiang Kai-shek.

Type of China, 1947, Inscribed:

用貼灣臺

1947 *Perf. 14*
35 A76 50c dp grn 15 15
36 A76 $3 dp bl 15 15
37 A76 $7.50 carmine 15 15
38 A76 $10 lt brn 15 15
39 A76 $20 dp cl 15 15
Nos. 35-39 (5) 75 75

First anniversary of return of Chinese National Government to Nanking.

Dr. Sun Yat-sen — A1

1947, July 10
Without Gum
40 A1 $1 dk brn 5 5
41 A1 $2 org brn 5 5
42 A1 $3 bl grn 5 5
43 A1 $5 vermilion 5 5
44 A1 $9 dp bl 5 5
45 A1 $10 brt rose car 5 5
46 A1 $20 dp grn 5 5
47 A1 $50 rose lil 10 10
48 A1 $100 blue 18 18
49 A1 $200 dk red 15 15
Nos. 40-49 (10) 78 78

The 30c gray and $7.50 orange were not regularly issued without surcharge.

Type of 1947 Surcharged in Black

改作伍佰圓

b

500.00

1948 Unwmk. *Perf. 14*
51 A1 $25 on $100 bl 75 25
52 A1 $500 on $7.50 org 75 50
53 A1 $1000 on 30c gray 3.00 1.40

Stamps of China, 1943-48, Surcharged Type "a" in Black or Carmine

1948-49 *Perf. 12 1/2, 14*
54 A73 $5 on $70 red org 15 15
55 A62 $10 on $3 dk yel 20 20
56 A82 $10 on $150 dk bl (C) 15 15
57 A82 $20 on $250 dp lil (C) 15 15
58 A67 $100 on $20 car 125.00 125.00
59 A82 $1000 on $20,000 rose pink ('49) 1.50 60
Nos. 54-59 (6) 127.15 126.25

The bottom line of the surcharge expresses the new value and consists of 2 or 3 characters.

Type of 1947

1949 Engr. *Perf. 14*
63 A1 $25 ol grn 15 12
64 A1 $5000 ocher 30 15
65 A1 $10,000 ap grn 30 15
66 A1 $20,000 ol bis 30 15
67 A1 $30,000 indigo 30 15
68 A1 $40,000 vio brn 30 15
Nos. 63-68 (6) 1.65 87

No. 42 and Type of 1947 Surcharged Type "b" in Black, Carmine Violet or Red Violet

1949
69 A1 $300 on $3 bl grn 25 20
70 A1 $1000 on $3 bl grn (C) 75 20
71 A1 $2000 on $3 bl grn (V) 50 45
72 A1 $3000 on $3 bl grn (RV) 2.25 38
73 A1 $3000 on $7.50 org 16.50 1.75
Nos. 69-73 (5) 20.25 2.98

Stamps of China, 1940-47, Surcharged Type "a" in Black or Carmine

Perf. 12 1/2, 13x13 1/2, 14
74 A39 $2 on 2 1/2c rose lil (#424) 10 10
75 A72 $5 on $40 org (#627) 10 10
76 A73 $5 on $50 pur (C) (#638) 10 10
77 A73 $5 on $100 dk car (#640) 10 10
78 A57 $20 on 2c ol grn (#368) 15 15
81 A63 $100 on $20 rose (#571) 15 10
82 A67 $200 on $10 dk bl (C) (#591) 25 25
84 A57 $500 on $30 dl vio (#521) 20 20
86 A62 $800 on $4 red brn (#504) 50 50
87 A67 $5000 on $10 dk bl (#591) 95 95
88 A67 $10,000 on $20 car (#592) 2.25 1.75
89 A82 $200,000 on $3000 bl (C) (#750) 50.00 24.00
Nos. 74-89 (12) 54.85 28.30

貳分 臺幣

Northeastern Provinces No. 47, Surcharged in Green, Red Violet, Black or Blue

2 ★★★ 2

1949-50
91 A2 2c on $44 dk car rose (G) 2.25 1.00
92 A2 5c on $44 dk car rose (RV) ('50) 2.50 1.50
a. vio surcharge 2.50 2.00
93 A2 10c on $44 dk car rose (RV) ('50) 8.00 90
94 A2 20c on $44 dk car rose (Bk) ('50) 8.00 2.50
a. Double surcharge 30.00
95 A2 30c on $44 dk car rose (Bl) ('50) 9.00 2.65
96 A2 50c on $44 dk car rose (Bl) ('50) 14.00 5.25
Nos. 91-96 (6) 43.75 13.80

China 959a, Overprinted in Black

用貼湾臺限

Ovpt. 15mm. Wide

1949 Unwmk. *Rouletted 9 1/2*
97 A96 orange 60 20

China Nos. 567, 498 and 640 Surcharged Type "a" in Black

1948-49 Unwmk. *Perf. 12 1/2, 13, 14*
98 A63 $20 on $3 red 1.00 30
99 A62 $50 on 50c sage grn 30 10
a. Perf. 11 12.00 12.00
100 A73 $600 on $100 dk car 1.50 60

Botton line of surcharge consists of 3 characters.

No. 99 has two settings of surcharge: I. Spacing 10mm. between rows of characters. II. Spacing 12mm.

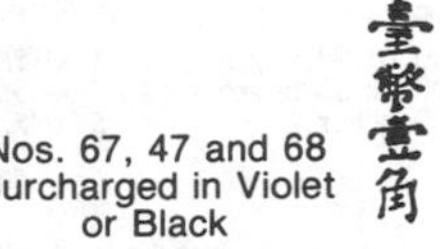
Nos. 67, 47 and 68 Surcharged in Violet or Black

10

1949 *Perf. 14*
101 A1 2c on $30,000 ind (V) 2.00 2.00
102 A1 10c on $50 rose lil 3.00 1.50
103 A1 10c on $40,000 vio brn 2.50 2.50

Numerals slightly larger on Nos. 101 and 103.

For similar surcharges on C

AIR POST STAMP

China No. C62a, Overprinted in Black

用貼湾臺限

Ovpt. 15mm. Wide

1949 Unwmk. *Rouletted 9 1/2*
C1 AP5 bl grn 60 50

SPECIAL DELIVERY STAMP

China No. E12a, Overprinted in Black

用貼灣臺限

Ovpt. 12 1/2mm. Wide

1950 Unwmk. *Rouletted 9 1/2*
E1 SD2 red vio 60 *1.00*

REGISTRATION STAMP

China No. F2a Overprinted in Black

用貼灣臺限

Ovpt. 12mm. Wide

1950 Unwmk. *Rouletted 9 1/2*
F1 R2 carmine 60 50

TAIWAN POSTAGE DUE STAMPS

D1

Unwmk.
1948, Feb. 10 Litho. *Perf. 14*
Without Gum
J1 D1 $1 blue 10 *40*
J2 D1 $3 blue 10 *40*
J3 D1 $5 blue 10 *40*
J4 D1 $10 blue 10 *40*
J5 D1 $20 blue 10 *40*
Nos. J1-J5 (5) 50 2.00

作改
伍拾圓

Nos. J1-J4 Surcharged in Carmine

50.00

1948, Dec. 4
J6 D1 $50 on $1 bl 2.00 2.50
J7 D1 $100 on $3 bl 2.00 2.50
J8 D1 $300 on $5 bl 2.00 2.50
J9 D1 $500 on $10 bl 2.00 2.50

Nos. 70, 72 and 64 Handstamped in Violet 欠 資

1949, Aug. 5
J10 A1 $1000 on $3 bl grn 5.00 5.50
J11 A1 $3000 on $3 bl grn 5.00 5.50
J12 A1 $5000 ocher 5.00 5.50

No. 48 Surcharged in Various Colors

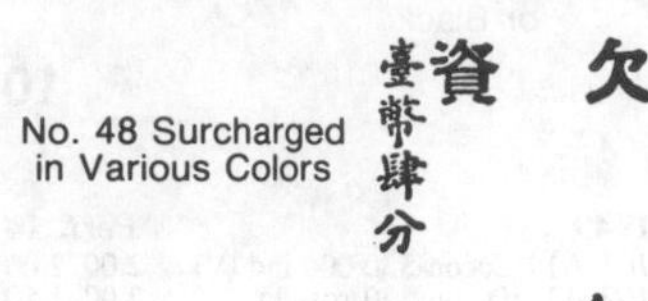

1950
J13 A1 4c on $100 bl (Br) 2.00 2.50
J14 A1 10c on $100 bl (RV) 2.25 2.25
J15 A1 20c on $100 bl (Bk) 2.25 2.25
J16 A1 40c on $100 bl (C) 6.00 6.00
J17 A1 $1 on $100 bl (Bl) 11.00 8.00
Nos. J13-J17 (5) 23.50 21.00

PARCEL POST STAMPS

Type of China, Parcel Post Stamps of 1945-48 With Added Inscription:

1949 Unwmk. Engr. *Perf. 14*
Q1 PP3 $100 bluish grn 60.00 20
Q2 PP3 $300 rose car 60.00 20
Q3 PP3 $500 ol grn 60.00 20
Q4 PP3 $1000 slate 60.00 20
Q5 PP3 $3000 dp plum 60.00 20

Numerals slightly larger on Nos. 101 and 103. Chinese characters in lower corners have colorless background; denomination tablet in color.

OCCUPATION STAMPS

Issued Under Japanese Occupation

Kwangtung

China No. 297 Overprinted in Black

1942 Unwmk. *Perf. 12½*
1N1 A37 2c ol grn 1.00 1.00
a. Inverted ovpt. 35.00

Same Overprint in Red or Black on Stamps of China, 1939-41
Perf. 12½, 14
1N2 A57 3c dl cl (#350) 60 60
1N3 A57 8c ol grn (#383) 60 60
1N4 A57 10c grn (#354) (R) 60 60
1N5 A57 10c grn (#384) (R) 60 60
1N6 A57 16c ol gray (#357) 1.00 1.00
1N7 A57 30c scar (#385) 60 60
1N8 A57 50c dk bl (#386) (R) 60 60
1N9 A57 $1 org brn & sep (#387) 2.00 2.00
1N10 A57 $2 dp bl & yel brn (#388) 1.00 1.00
1N11 A57 $5 red & sl grn (#389) 1.75 1.75
1N12 A57 $10 dk grn & dl pur (#390) 4.00 4.00
1N13 A57 $20 rose lake & dk bl (#391) 1.75 1.75

Same Overprint on China Nos. 422 and 433
Perf. 12½
1N14 A40 1c orange 50 50
a. Inverted ovpt. 37.50 37.50
1N15 A47 20c lt bl 1.00 1.00

Same Overprint on Stamps of China, 1941
Perf. 12
1N16 A59 1c orange 50 50
1N17 A59 5c green 50 50
1N18 A59 8c turq grn 50 50
1N19 A59 10c brt grn 50 50
1N20 A59 17c olive 1.00 1.00
1N21 A59 30c scarlet 1.00 1.00
1N22 A59 50c dk bl 1.00 1.00
Nos. 1N1-1N22 (22) 22.60 22.60

Stamps of China, 1939-41 Overprinted in Black 貼 粵 用 省

1942 *Perf. 12½, 14*
1N23 A57 2c ol grn (#368) 50 50
1N24 A57 3c dl cl (#350) 50 50
1N25 A57 5c ol grn (#352) 50 50
1N26 A57 8c ol grn (#353) 140.00
1N27 A57 8c ol grn (#369) 60 60
1N28 A57 10c grn (#354) 90 90
1N29 A57 16c ol gray (#357) 90 90
1N30 A57 25c dk bl (#358) 90 90
1N31 A57 30c scar (#385) 50 50
1N32 A57 50c dk bl (#386) 50 50
1N33 A57 $1 org brn & sep (#387) 1.50 1.50
1N34 A57 $2 dp bl & yel brn (#388) 1.50 1.50
1N35 A57 $5 red & sl grn (#389) 2.50 2.50
1N36 A57 $10 dk grn & dl pur (#390) 3.50 3.50
1N37 A57 $20 rose lake & dk bl (#391) 5.00 5.00
Nos. 1N23-1N25,1N27-1N37 (14) 19.80 19.80

Same Overprint on China Nos. 397-401

1942 Wmk. 261 *Perf. 14*
1N38 A57 $1 org brn & sep 4.00 4.00
1N39 A57 $2 dp bl & yel brn 4.00 4.00
1N40 A57 $5 red & sl grn 5.00 4.00
1N41 A57 $10 dk grn & dl pur 5.00 4.00
1N42 A57 $20 rose lake & dk bl 8.00 7.00
Nos. 1N38-1N42 (5) 26.00 23.00

Same Overprint on Stamps of China, 1941

1942 Unwmk. *Perf. 12*
1N43 A59 2c brt ultra 25 25
1N44 A59 5c green 25 25
1N45 A59 8c red org 25 25
1N46 A59 8c turq grn 25 25
1N47 A59 10c brt grn 60 60
1N48 A59 17c olive 60 60
1N49 A59 25c rose vio 60 60
1N50 A59 30c scarlet 60 60
1N51 A59 50c dk bl 50 50
1N52 A59 $1 brn & blk 1.00 1.00
1N53 A59 $2 bl & blk 1.00 1.00
1N54 A59 $5 scar & blk 1.00 1.00
1N55 A59 $10 grn & blk 2.25 2.25
1N56 A59 $20 rose vio & blk 3.00 3.00
Nos. 1N43-1N56 (14) 12.15 12.15

China Nos. 354 and 369 Surcharged in Black

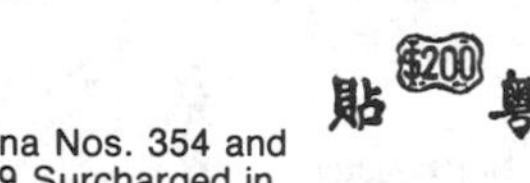

1945 Unwmk. *Perf. 12½*
1N57 A57 $200 on 10c grn 60.00 35.00
1N58 A57 $400 on 8c ol grn 60.00 35.00

China No. 422 Surcharged in Black 肆佰圓 暫售

1945
1N59 A40 $400 on 1c org 400.00 400.00

OCCUPATION POSTAGE DUE STAMPS

China, No. J79 Surcharged Diagonally with New Value Between Parallel Lines in Black

1945 Unwmk. *Perf. 12½*
1NJ1 D5 $100 on $2 yel org 400.00 400.00
a. Inverted surch. 550.00

MENG CHIANG (Inner Mongolia)

Nos. 297-298, 301-303 Overprinted

疆 蒙 疆 蒙

Characters 4mm. High — I
Characters 5mm. High — II

1941 Engr. Unwmk.
2N1 A37 2c #297, I 50 50
a. Type II 60 60
2N2 A37 4c #298, II 9.00 9.00
a. Type I 15.00 15.00
2N3 A37 15c #301, I 50 50
a. Type II 1.00 1.00
2N4 A37 20c #302, II 1.50 1.00
a. Type I 1.50 1.50
2N5 A37 25c #303, II 1.50 1.00
a. Type I 14.00 14.00

On Nos. 312, 314, 318, 321

1941 *Perf. 14*
2N6 A39 ½c #312, I 90 90
a. Type II 6.00 6.00
2N7 A39 2½c #314, II 35 30
a. Type I 40 40
2N8 A45 13c #318, II 1.25 1.00
a. Type I 32.50 32.50
2N9 A48 30c #321, II 27.50 27.50

On Stamps of 1939-41

1941 *Perf. 12½*
2N10 A57 2c #368, II 35 35
2N11 A57 3c #350, I 25 25
a. Type II 35 35
2N12 A57 5c #352, I 25 25
a. Type II 35 35
2N13 A57 8c #353, I 25 25
a. Type II 35 35
2N14 A57 8c #369, II 2.25 1.75
2N15 A57 10c #354, II 60 40
2N16 A57 16c #357, II 85 75
2N17 A57 $1 #359, II 3.50 3.50
a. Type I 250.00 250.00
b. #347, I 37.50 37.50
2N18 A57 $5 #361, II 20.00 20.00

On Stamps of 1940 with Secret Marks

1941 Unwmk. *Perf. 14*
2N19 A57 5c #382, II 30 30
2N20 A57 8c #383, I 35 30
a. Type II 16.50 16.50
2N21 A57 10c #384, I 35 30
a. Type II 50 40
2N22 A57 30c #385, I 90 35
a. Type II 1.25 90
2N23 A57 50c #386, I 1.25 75
a. Type II 1.25 90
2N24 A57 $1 #387, I 3.50 3.50
a. Type II 6.00 6.00
2N25 A57 $2 #388, I 4.00 4.00
a. Type II 12.00 8.00
2N26 A57 $5 #389, I 14.00 14.00
a. Type II 22.50 22.50
2N27 A57 $10 #390, II 22.50 22.50
a. Type I 27.50 27.50
2N28 A57 $20 #391, II 32.50 32.50
a. Type I 37.50 37.50

On Stamps of 1940 with Secret Marks

1941 Wmk. 261 *Perf. 14*
2N29 A57 10c #394, II 1.25 90
2N30 A57 30c #395, II 1.75 1.75
a. Type I 32.50 32.50
2N31 A57 50c #396, II 1.75 1.75

On Stamps of 1940-41 (Martyrs) with Secret Marks

Perf. 12½, 13 & Compound

1941 Wmk. 261
2N32 A39 ½c #402, II 5.00 3.00
2N33 A40 1c #403, I 30 25
a. Type II 30 30
2N34 A39 2½c #405, II 20.00 20.00
a. Type I 22.50 22.50
2N35 A48 3c #406, II 30 30
2N36 A46 10c #410, II 2.00 1.75
a. Type I 2.25 1.75
2N37 A46 17c #413, II 13.50 13.50
a. Type I 22.50 22.50
2N38 A40 25c #416, II 1.75 60
2N39 A48 30c #418, II 16.50 14.00
a. Type I 22.50 22.50
2N40 A47 40c #419, II 60 35
a. Type I 1.75 1.75
2N41 A40 50c #420, I 3.50 1.75
a. Type II 13.50 13.50

Unwmk.
2N42 A39 ½c #421, I 30 30
a. Type II 30 30
2N43 A40 1c #422, I 30 30
a. Type II 90 30
2N44 A46 2c #423, I 30 30
2N45 A48 3c #425, I 40 40
a. Type II 50 30
2N46 A39 4c #426, II 60 30
2N47 A45 8c #428, II 4.00 4.00
a. Type I 37.50 37.50
2N48 A46 10c #429, I 6.00 4.00
a. Type II 16.50 16.50
2N49 A45 13c #430, I 1.75 90
a. Type II 3.00 2.25
2N50 A48 15c #431, II 1.00 1.00
2N51 A46 17c #432, I 90 75
a. Type II 1.00 75
2N52 A47 20c #433, II 1.00 50
a. Type I 1.25 1.25
2N53 A45 21c #434, II 1.00 1.00
2N54 A40 25c #435, I 1.25 1.25
2N55 A46 28c #436, II 1.00 1.00
2N56 A40 50c #439, II 2.00 2.00
a. Type I 3.50 1.75

China Nos. 297-298, 302 Surcharged in Black 蒙 疆

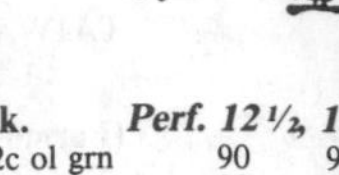

1942 Unwmk. *Perf. 12½, 13*
2N57 A37 1c on 2c ol grn 90 90
2N58 A37 2c on 4c grn 90 75
2N59 A37 10c on 20c ultra 12.00 12.00

Same, on China No. 313
Perf. 14
2N60 A40 ½c on 1c org 2.00

Same, on Stamps of China, 1938-41
Perf. 12½
2N61 A57 1c on 2c ol grn (#368) 50 30
2N62 A57 4c on 8c ol grn (#353) 2.50 2.00
a. Inverted surch 50.00 50.00
2N63 A57 4c on 8c ol grn (#369) 75 75
2N64 A57 5c on 10c grn (#354) 50 35
2N65 A57 8c on 16c ol gray (#357) 1.00 60
2N66 A57 50c on $1 hn & dk brn (#359) 2.50 2.50
a. 50c on $1 hn & dk brn (#347) 20.00 20.00
b. 50c on $1 hn & dk brn (#344) 200.00 200.00
2N67 A57 $1 on $2 dp bl & org brn (#360) 12.50 12.50

No. 2N66b was issued without gum.

Same, on Stamps of China, 1940
Perf. 14
2N68 A57 4c on 8c ol grn (#383) 25 25
2N69 A57 15c on 30c scar (#385) 60 60
a. Inverted surch. 50.00 50.00
2N70 A57 25c on 50c dk bl (#386) 1.00 1.00
2N71 A57 50c on $1 org brn & sep (#387) 1.50 1.00
2N72 A57 $1 on $2 dp bl & yel brn (#388) 3.00 2.50
2N73 A57 $5 on $10 dk grn & dl pur (#390) 10.00 10.00
2N74 A57 $10 on $20 rose lake & dk bl (#391) 37.50 37.50

Same, on China No. 395

1942 Wmk. 261 *Perf. 14*
2N75 A57 15c on 30c scar 25.00 25.00

Same, on China Nos. 418 and 419
Perf. 12½, 13
2N76 A48 15c on 30c brn car 12.00 12.00
2N77 A47 20c on 40c org 2.50 2.50

Same, on Stamps of China, 1940-41

1942 Unwmk.
2N78 A40 ½c on 1c org 20 20
2N79 A39 2c on 4c pale vio 40 35
2N80 A47 10c on 20c lt bl 75 60
2N81 A47 20c on 40c org 3.00 2.50
2N82 A40 25c on 50c grn 7.00 7.00

Same Surcharge on "New Peking" Prints
Perf. 14
2N83 A37 1c on 2c ol grn 15 15
2N84 A37 2c on 4c dl grn 15 15
2N85 A46 5c on 10c dl vio 30 30
2N86 A57 8c on 16c ol gray 30 30
2N87 A47 10c on 20c red brn 50 50
2N88 A48 15c on 30c brn car 75 75
2N89 A47 20c on 40c org 75 75
2N90 A40 25c on 50c grn 1.00 1.00
2N91 A57 50c on $1 org brn & sep 2.00 2.00
2N92 A57 $1 on $2 dp bl & org brn 14.00 14.00
2N93 A57 $5 on $10 dk grn & dl pur 17.50 17.50

The "New Peking" printings were made by the Chinese Bureau of Engraving and Printing for use in Japanese controlled areas of North China. They are on thin, poor quality paper, with dull gum or without gum and there are slight alterations in the designs.

Dragon-Carved Pillar and Doves — A1

Mining Coal — A2

Wmk. Characters in Circle in Sheet

1943 Engr. *Perf. 12 x Pin-perf 12*

2N94 A1 4f dp org 15 *30*
2N95 A1 8f dk bl 25 *50*

Issued to commemorate the 5th anniversary of the Inner Mongolia post and telegraph service.

The watermark, which is 40mm. in diameter and covers four stamps, occurs three times in the sheet.

1943 Unwmk. Photo. *Perf. 12*

2N96 A2 8f Prus grn 12 *30*
2N97 A2 4f brn red 25 *50*

Issued to commemorate the 2nd anniversary of the "Greater East Asia War".

Flying Horse — A3

Yun Wang — A4

1944 *Perf. 12½x12, 12x12½*

2N98 A3 4f rose 15 *30*
2N99 A4 8f dl bl 25 *50*

Issued to commemorate the 5th anniversary of the founding of the Federal Autonomous Government of Mongolia, September 1, 1939.

Industrial Plant — A5

1944, Dec. 8 Photo. *Perf. 12x12½*

2N100 A5 8f red brn 10 *50*

Issued to commemorate the 3rd anniversary of the "Greater East Asia War" and to encourage production increase.

New Peking Printings of 1942 Overprinted in Black

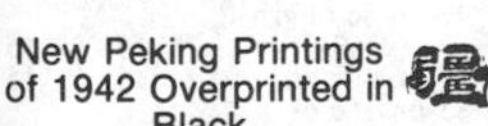

1945 Unwmk. Engr. *Perf. 14*

Without Gum

2N101 A37 2c ol grn 10 10
2N102 A37 4c dl grn 1.25 1.25
2N103 A37 5c green 10 10
2N104 A57 $1 org brn & sep 75 75
2N105 A57 $2 dp bl & org brn 3.00 3.00
2N106 A57 $5 red & grnsh blk 10.00 10.00

Same Overprint on New Peking Printings of Martyrs Issue

2N107 A40 1c orange 10 10
2N108 A45 8c dp org 10 10
2N109 A46 10c dl vio 15 15
2N110 A47 20c red brn 15 15
2N111 A48 30c brn car 10 10
2N112 A47 40c orange 10 10
2N113 A40 50c green 35 35
Nos. 2N101-2N113 (13) 16.25 16.25

Stamps of Meng Chiang, 1941, With Additional Surcharge in Red or Black

1945

2N114 A39 10c on ½c ol blk (#2N42) (R) 25 25
a. 10c on ½c ol bk (#2N42a) 75
2N115 A40 10c on 1c org (#2N43a) (R) 25 25
a. Without secret mark (China #313) 20.00 20.00
2N116 A37 50c on 2c ol grn (#2N1a) (Bk) 40 40
2N117 A57 50c on 2c ol grn (#2N10) (Bk) 10 10
2N118 A39 50c on 4c pale vio (#2N46) (R) 25 25
2N119 A57 50c on 5c ol grn (#2N12a) (R) 15 15
a. On #2N12
2N120 A57 50c on 5c ol grn (#2N19) (R) 25 25
Nos. 2N114-2N120 (7) 1.65 1.65

Same Surcharge on Nos. 2N32, 2N33a

1945 Wmk. 261

2N121 A39 10c on ½c ol blk (R) 7.50 7.50
2N122 A40 10c on 1c org (R) 50 50

Same Surcharge on Nos. 2N107 2N101-2N103 and 2N108

1945 Unwmk.

2N123 A40 10c on 1c org (R) 20 20
2N124 A37 50c on 2c ol grn (Bk) 15 15
2N125 A37 50c on 4c dl grn (R) 2.50 2.50
2N126 A37 50c on 5c grn 20 20
2N127 A45 $1 on 8c dp org (R) 35 35
Nos. 2N123-2N127 (5) 3.40 3.40

NORTH CHINA HONAN

Nos. 297-298, 301-303 Overprinted

南 河 南 河
I II

1941 Engr. Unwmk.

3N1 A37 2c #297, II 60 60
a. Type I 1.50 1.50
3N2 A37 4c #298, I 2.25 1.75
a. Type II 7.00 7.00
3N3 A37 15c #301, II 50 50
a. Type I 60 50
3N4 A37 20c #302, I 2.50 50
3N5 A37 25c #303, II 7.00 7.00

1941 *Perf. 14*

3N6 A39 ½c #312, I 30 30
a. Type II 4.00 4.00
3N7 A39 2½c #314, II 25 25
a. Type I 30 30
3N8 A45 13c #318, II 50 30
a. Type I 37.50 37.50
3N9 A48 30c #321, II 4.00 2.00
3N10 A47 40c #322, II 37.50 37.50

On Stamps of 1939-41

1941 *Perf. 12½*

3N11 A57 2c #368, II 25 25
3N12 A57 3c #350, II 25 25
a. Type I 30 30
3N13 A57 5c #352, II 25 25
a. Type I 30 30
3N14 A57 8c #353, II 25 25
a. Type I 60 60
3N15 A57 10c #354, II 25 25
3N16 A57 16c #357, II 25 25
3N17 A57 $1 #359, II 4.00 3.25
a. Type I 165.00 165.00
b. On #347, I 30.00 30.00
3N18 A57 $5 #361, II 32.50 32.50

On Stamps of 1940 with Secret Marks

1941 Unwmk. *Perf. 14*

3N20 A57 5c #382, II 90 25
3N21 A57 8c #383, II 25 25
3N22 A57 10c #384, II 25 25
3N23 A57 30c #385, II 1.25 40
a. Type I 1.50 1.00
3N24 A57 50c #386, I 1.50 1.25
a. Type II 3.50 2.25
3N25 A57 $1 #387, I 3.50 1.75
a. Type II 27.50 25.00
3N26 A57 $2 #388, I 5.00 4.00
a. Type II 6.00 3.50
3N27 A57 $5 #389, I 7.00 7.00
a. Type II 22.50 22.50
3N28 A57 $10 #390, II 20.00 20.00
a. Type I 65.00 65.00
3N29 A57 $20 #391, II 32.50 32.50
a. Type I 35.00 35.00

On Stamps of 1940 with Secret Marks

1941 Wmk. 261 *Perf. 14*

3N30 A57 5c #392, II 7.00 1.25
3N31 A57 5c #393, II 3.50 50
3N32 A57 30c #395, II 4.00 1.75
a. Type I 7.00 3.50
3N33 A57 50c #396, II 7.00 7.00

On Stamps of 1940-41 (Martyrs) with Secret Marks

Perf. 12½, 13 & Compound

1941 Wmk. 261

3N34 A39 ½c #402, II 25 25
3N35 A40 1c #403, II 25 25
a. Type I 25 25
3N36 A39 2½c #405, II 6.00 3.50
3N37 A46 10c #410, I 90 30
a. Type II 2.25 1.75
3N38 A45 13c #411, II 25 25
3N39 A46 17c #413, II 50 25
a. Type I 4.00 1.75
3N40 A40 25c #416, II 50 25
3N41 A47 40c #419, II 75 25
a. Type I 6.00 1.50

Unwmk.

3N42 A39 ½c #421, II 25 25
a. Type I 25 25
3N43 A40 1c #422, I 25 25
a. Type II 50 25
3N44 A46 2c #423, I 3.00 60
3N45 A48 3c #425, I 50 50
3N46 A39 4c #426, II 25 25
3N47 A46 10c #429, I 13.50 7.00
3N48 A45 13c #430, II 75 25
a. Type I 5.00 1.75
3N49 A48 15c #431, II 25 25
3N50 A46 17c #432, II 25 25
a. Type I 5.00 1.50
3N51 A47 20c #433, II 25 25
a. Type I 30.00 4.00
3N52 A45 21c #434, II 25 25
3N53 A40 25c #435, I 1.25 90
3N54 A46 28c #436, II 25 25

Overprinted in Red

坡 嘉 新
念紀落陷

1942

3N55 A39 4c #3N46 90 90
3N56 A57 8c #3N14 8.00 8.00
3N57 A57 8c #369, II 3.00 3.00

The fall of Singapore.

Overprinted in Red

國建國洲滿
念紀年週十

1942

3N58 A57 2c #3N11 2.50 2.50
3N59 A39 4c #3N46 3.50 3.50
3N60 A57 8c #369, II 15.00 15.00
3N61 A57 8c #3N14 15.00 15.00

Tenth anniv. of the formation of Manchukuo.

Hopei

Nos. 297-298, 301-303 Overprinted

北 河 北 河
I II

1941 Engr. Unwmk.

4N1 A37 2c #297, II 40 40
a. Type I 60 60
4N2 A37 4c #298, I 75 60
a. Type II 27.50 27.50
4N3 A37 15c #301, II 40 40
a. Type I 1.50 90
4N4 A37 20c #302, II 60 60
4N5 A37 25c #303, II 2.25 1.75
a. Type I 37.50 37.50

On Nos. 312, 314, 318, 321

1941 *Perf. 14*

4N6 A39 ½c #312, II 25 25
a. Type I 50 50
4N7 A39 2½c #314, II 25 25
a. Type I 35 25
4N8 A45 13c #318, II 75 50
a. Type I 1.25 1.25
4N9 A48 30c #321, II 1.75 1.25

On Stamps of 1939-41

1941 *Perf. 12½*

4N10 A57 2c #368, II 25 25
4N11 A57 2c #349, II 25 25
4N12 A57 3c #350, II 25 25
a. Type I 90 60
4N13 A57 5c #352, II 25 25
a. Type I 50 50
4N14 A57 8c #353, II 25 25
a. Type I 60 60
4N15 A57 8c #369, II 75 30
4N16 A57 10c #354, II 25 25
4N17 A57 16c #357, II 25 25
4N18 A57 $1 #359, II 2.25 2.25
a. On #347, I 135.00 135.00
4N19 A57 $2 #360, II 2.25 2.25
a. Type I 25.00 25.00
4N20 A57 $5 #361, II 16.50 16.50
a. Type I 20.00 20.00
4N21 A57 $10 #362, II 55.00 55.00
4N22 A57 $20 #363, II 160.00 160.00

On Stamps of 1940 with Secret Marks

1941 Unwmk. *Perf. 14*

4N24 A57 5c #382, II 25 25
a. Type I 25 25
4N25 A57 8c #383, II 25 25
a. Type I 27.50 27.50
4N26 A57 10c #384, II 25 25
a. Type I 60 50
4N27 A57 30c #385, II 25 25
4N28 A57 50c #386, II 75 25
a. Type I 90 75
4N29 A57 $1 #387, II 1.75 90
a. Type I 2.25 1.75
4N30 A57 $2 #388, II 6.00 1.75
a. Type I 11.00 7.00
4N31 A57 $5 #389, II 12.00 12.00
a. Type I 17.50 17.50
4N32 A57 $10 #390, II 16.50 16.50
a. Type I 22.50 22.50
4N33 A57 $20 #391, II 27.50 27.50
a. Type I 32.50 32.50

On Stamps of 1940 with Secret Marks

1941 Wmk. 261 *Perf. 14*

4N34 A57 5c #392, II 25 25
4N35 A57 5c #393, II 25 25
4N36 A57 10c #394, II 25 25
4N37 A57 30c #395, II 50 50
a. Type I 1.50 1.25
4N38 A57 50c #396, II 75 60

On Stamps of 1940-41 (Martyrs) with Secret Marks

Perf. 12½, 13 & Compound

1941 Wmk. 261

4N39 A39 ½c #402, II 25 25
4N40 A40 1c #403, II 25 25
a. Type I 25 25
4N41 A46 2c #404, II 25 25
4N42 A39 2½c #405, II 25 25
4N43 A48 3c #406, II 25 25
4N44 A46 10c #410, II 50 50
a. Type I 50 30
4N45 A45 13c #411, II 50 50
4N46 A46 17c #413, II 50 50
a. Type I 90 75
4N47 A40 25c #416, II 60 50
4N48 A48 30c #418, II 60 50
a. Type I 9.00 9.00
4N49 A47 40c #419, II 60 50
a. Type I 1.75 1.50
Nos. 4N39-4N49 (11) 4.55 4.25

Unwmk.

4N50 A39 ½c #421, II 25 25
a. Type I 25 25
4N51 A40 1c #422, II 25 25
a. Type I 25 25
4N52 A46 2c #423, I 50 50
4N53 A48 3c #425, II 25 25
a. Type I 50 50
4N54 A39 4c #426, II 50 50
4N55 A45 8c #428, II 50 50
a. Type I 75 60
4N56 A46 10c #429, II 50 50
4N57 A45 13c #430, II 75 75
a. Type I 75 60
4N58 A48 15c #431, II 50 50
4N59 A46 17c #432, II 60 50
a. Type I 1.50 1.00
4N60 A47 20c #433, II 50 50
a. Type I 1.50 1.00
4N61 A45 21c #434, II 50 50
4N62 A40 25c #435, II 75 50
a. Type I 1.50 1.00
4N63 A46 28c #436, II 50 50

Honan Singapore Overprint in Red

1942

4N64 A39 4c #4N54 50 50
4N65 A57 8c #4N25 1.50 1.50
4N66 A57 8c #4N14 1.75 1.75
4N67 A57 8c #4N15 2.00 2.00

Honan Anniv. of Manchukuo Overprint in Red

1942

4N68 A57 2c #4N10 3.00 3.00
4N69 A39 4c #4N54 1.25 1.25
4N70 A57 8c #4N14 25.00 25.00
4N71 A57 8c #4N25 3.00 3.00

Shansi

Nos. 297-298, 301, 303 Overprinted

西 山 西 山
I II

1941 Engr. Unwmk.

5N1 A37 2c #297, II 90 50
a. Type I 1.50 75
5N2 A37 4c #298, I 5.00 1.25
a. Type II 55.00 32.50
5N3 A37 15c #301, I 75 50
a. Type II 75 50
5N4 A37 25c #303, II 1.50 60
a. Type I 22.50 22.50

On Nos. 312, 314, 318, 321

1941 ***Perf. 14***
5N5 A39 ½c #312, II 25 25
a. Type I 60 30
5N6 A39 2½c #314, II 25 25
a. Type I 50 50
5N7 A45 13c #318, II 60 60
a. Type I 55.00 55.00
5N8 A48 30c #321, II 3.50 3.50

On Stamps of 1939-41

1941 ***Perf. 12½***
5N9 A57 2c #368, II 50 50
5N10 A57 3c #350, II 50 50
a. Type I 3.50 1.00
5N11 A57 5c #352, II 50 50
a. Type I 90 40
5N12 A57 8c #353, II 50 50
a. Type I 90 50
5N13 A57 8c #369, II 16.50 11.00
5N14 A57 10c #354, II 50 30
5N15 A57 16c #357, II 90 90
5N16 A57 $1 #359, II 4.00 2.25
5N17 A57 $2 #360, II 14.00 14.00
5N18 A57 $5 #361, II 25.00 25.00
Nos. 5N9-5N18 (10) 62.90 55.45

On Stamps of 1940 with Secret Marks

1941 **Unwmk.** ***Perf. 14***
5N19 A57 5c #382, II 25 25
5N20 A57 8c #383, II 50 50
5N21 A57 10c #384, II 50 50
a. Type I 60 30
5N22 A57 30c #385, I 75 50
a. Type II 75 75
5N23 A57 50c #386, I 90 75
a. Type II 90 90
5N24 A57 $1 #387, I 5.00 2.50
a. Type II 14.00 5.00
5N25 A57 $2 #388, I 7.00 2.50
a. Type II 7.00 5.00
5N26 A57 $5 #389, II 9.00 9.00
a. Type I 27.50 27.50
5N27 A57 $10 #390, II 14.00 14.00
a. Type I 16.50 16.50
5N28 A57 $20 #391, II 25.00 25.00
a. Type I 27.50 27.50

On Stamps of 1940 with Secret Marks

1941 **Wmk. 261** ***Perf. 14***
5N29 A57 5c #392, II 40 40
5N30 A57 5c #393, II 40 40
5N31 A57 10c #394, II 75 75
5N32 A57 30c #395, I 30.00 30.00
5N33 A57 50c #396, I 2.50 1.50
Nos. 5N29-5N33 (5) 34.05 33.05

On Stamps of 1940-41 (Martyrs) with Secret Marks

Perf. 12½, 13 & Compound

1941 **Wmk. 261**
5N34 A39 ½c #402, II 25 25
5N35 A40 1c #403, II 25 25
a. Type I 25 25
5N36 A46 2c #404, II 50 50
5N37 A39 2½c #405, I 1.50 1.50
5N38 A46 10c #410, I 1.75 1.25
5N39 A45 13c #411, II 35 35
5N40 A46 17c #413, I 11.00 8.00
5N41 A40 25c #416, II 60 60
5N42 A48 30c #418, II 27.50 27.50
a. Type I 27.50 27.50
5N43 A47 40c #419, II 60 60
a. Type I 12.00 7.00
5N44 A40 50c #420, II 90 75
a. Type I 15.00 9.00

Unwmk.
5N45 A39 ½c #421, II 25 25
a. Type I 25 25
5N46 A40 1c #422, II 25 25
a. Type I 25 25
5N47 A46 2c #423, II 25 25
5N48 A48 3c #425, I 2.00 1.25
5N49 A39 4c #426, II 25 25
5N50 A45 8c #428, I 5.00 1.75
a. Type II 5.00 2.25
5N51 A46 10c #429, I 11.00 10.00
a. Type II 20.00 20.00
5N52 A45 13c #430, I 6.50 1.25
a. Type II 6.00 4.00
5N53 A48 15c #431, II 75 60
5N54 A46 17c #432, II 75 60
a. Type I 90 90
5N55 A47 20c #433, II 75 60
a. Type I 90 90
5N56 A45 21c #434, II 75 60
5N57 A40 25c #435, I 1.25 75
5N58 A46 28c #436, II 90 75
5N59 A40 50c #439, II 3.00 1.75

Honan Singapore Overprint in Red

1942
5N60 A39 4c #5N49 90 90
5N61 A57 8c #5N20 3.00 3.00
5N62 A57 8c #5N12 3.00 3.00
5N63 A57 8c #5N13 10.00 10.00

Honan Anniv. of Manchukuo Overprint in Red

1942
5N64 A57 2c #5N9 1.50 1.50
5N65 A39 4c #5N49 1.50 1.50
5N66 A57 8c #5N12 15.00 15.00
5N67 A57 8c #5N13 18.00 18.00
5N68 A57 8c #5N20 15.00 15.00
Nos. 5N64-5N68 (5) 51.00 51.00

Shantung

Nos. 297-298, 301-303 Overprinted

東 山 (I) 東 山 (II)

1941 **Engr.** **Unwmk.**
6N1 A37 2c #297, II 25 25
a. Type I 50 40
6N2 A37 4c #298, I 1.75 90
a. Type II 1.75 1.25
6N3 A37 15c #301, II 25 25
a. Type I 90 50
6N4 A37 20c #302, II 50 25
6N5 A37 25c #303, II 1.50 1.25
a. Type I 80.00 80.00

On Nos. 312, 314, 318

1941 ***Perf. 14***
6N6 A39 ½c #312, II 25 25
a. Type I 40 25
6N7 A39 2½c #314, II 25 25
a. Type I 25 25
6N8 A45 13c #318, II 25 25
a. Type I 9.00 7.00

On Stamps of 1939-41

1941 ***Perf. 12½***
6N9 A57 2c #349, II 25 25
6N10 A57 2c #368, II 25 25
6N11 A57 3c #350, II 25 25
a. Type I 50 25
6N12 A57 5c #352, II 25 25
a. Type I 25 25
6N13 A57 8c #353, II 25 25
a. Type I 25 25
6N14 A57 8c #369, II 25 25
6N15 A57 10c #354, II 25 25
6N16 A57 16c #357, II 60 60
6N17 A57 $1 #359, II 4.00 4.00
a. Type I 135.00 135.00
b. On No. 347, I 25.00 25.00
6N18 A57 $5 #361, II 20.00 20.00
Nos. 6N9-6N18 (10) 26.35 26.35

On Stamps of 1940 with Secret Marks

1941 **Unwmk.** ***Perf. 14***
6N20 A57 5c #382, II 25 25
6N21 A57 8c #383, I 20 20
a. Type II 25 25
6N22 A57 10c #384, II 25 25
6N23 A57 30c #385, II 50 25
a. Type I 1.25 1.25
6N24 A57 50c #386, II 90 75
a. Type I 1.25 90
6N25 A57 $1 #387, II 90 75
a. Type I 3.00 3.00
6N26 A57 $2 #388, II 2.50 2.00
a. Type I 6.00 5.00
6N27 A57 $5 #389, II 7.00 6.00
a. Type I 14.00 14.00
6N28 A57 $10 #390, II 16.50 16.50
a. Type I 22.50 22.50
6N29 A57 $20 #391, II 25.00 25.00
a. Type I 32.50 32.50

On Stamps of 1940 with Secret Marks

1941 **Wmk. 261** ***Perf. 14***
6N30 A57 5c #392, II 25 25
6N31 A57 5c #393, II 25 25
6N32 A57 10c #394, II 2.00 1.75
6N33 A57 30c #395, II 2.00 1.00
a. Type I 7.00 6.00
6N34 A57 50c #396, II 1.50 75
a. Type I 2.25 1.75
Nos. 6N30-6N34 (5) 6.00 4.00

On Stamps of 1940-41 (Martyrs) with Secret Marks

Perf. 12½, 13 & Compound

1941 **Wmk. 261**
6N35 A39 ½c #402, II 25 25
6N36 A40 1c #403, II 25 25
a. Type I 25 25
6N37 A39 2½c #405, II 1.75 1.50
6N38 A46 10c #410, I 90 40
6N39 A45 13c #411, II 50 25
6N40 A46 17c #413, II 1.50 50
a. Type I 3.00 1.25
6N41 A40 25c #416, II 50 50
6N42 A48 30c #418, I 9.00 9.00
6N43 A47 40c #419, II 50 50
a. Type I 9.00 9.00
6N44 A40 50c #420, II 1.00 60
Nos. 6N35-6N44 (10) 16.15 13.75

Unwmk.
6N45 A39 ½c #421, II 25 25
a. Type I 25 25
6N46 A40 1c #422, II 25 25
a. Type I 25 25
b. On No. 422a, II 32.50 32.50
6N48 A46 2c #423, II 25 25
6N49 A48 3c #425, I 50 50
a. Type II 75 50
6N50 A39 4c #426, II 25 25
6N51 A45 8c #428, II 25 25
a. Type I 6.00 6.00
6N52 A46 10c #429, I 2.50 1.75
6N53 A45 13c #430, II 25 25
a. Type I 60 60
6N54 A48 15c #431, II 25 25
6N55 A46 17c #432, II 25 25
a. Type I 60 60
6N56 A47 20c #433, II 25 25
a. Type I 60 60
6N57 A45 21c #434, II 25 25
6N58 A40 25c #435, I 90 75
6N59 A46 28c #436, II 50 30
6N60 A40 50c #439, II 3.00 3.00

Honan Singapore Overprint in Red

1942
6N61 A39 4c #6N50 50 50
6N62 A57 8c #6N13 3.00 3.00
6N63 A57 8c #6N21a 1.75 1.75
6N64 A57 8c #6N14 7.00 7.00

Honan Anniv. of Manchukuo Overprint in Red

1942
6N65 A57 2c #6N10 1.50 1.50
6N66 A39 4c #6N50 1.25 1.25
6N67 A57 8c #6N13 10.00 10.00
6N68 A57 8c #6N14 16.50 16.50
6N69 A57 8c #6N21a 1.50 1.50
Nos. 6N65-6N69 (5) 30.75 30.75

Supeh

Nos. 297-298, 301-302 Overprinted

北 蘇 (I) 北 蘇 (II)

1941 **Engr.** **Unwmk.**
7N1 A37 2c #297, I 2.25 2.25
a. Type II 5.00 5.00
7N2 A37 4c #298, I 15.00 15.00
7N3 A37 15c #301, I 60 50
a. Type II 75 60
7N4 A37 20c #302, II 75 60

On Nos. 312, 314, 318

1941 ***Perf. 14***
7N5 A39 ½c #312, I 60 60
7N6 A39 2½c #314, II 50 50
a. Type I 50 50
7N7 A45 13c #318, II 50 50
a. Type I 55.00 55.00

On Stamps of 1939-41

1941 ***Perf. 12½***
7N8 A57 2c #368, II 50 50
7N9 A57 3c #350, II 50 50
a. Type I 7.00 6.00
7N10 A57 5c #352, II 50 50
a. Type I 50 50
7N11 A57 8c #353, I 50 50
a. Type II 1.75 1.75
7N12 A57 8c #369, II 16.50 16.50
7N13 A57 10c #354, II 50 50
7N14 A57 16c #357, II 50 50
7N15 A57 $1 #359, II 6.00 6.00
a. On No. 347, I 100.00 100.00
Nos. 7N8-7N15 (8) 25.50 25.50

On Stamps of 1940 with Secret Marks

1941 **Unwmk.** ***Perf. 14***
7N17 A57 5c #382, II 20 20
7N18 A57 8c #383, II 20 20
7N19 A57 10c #384, I 50 40
a. Type II 60 40
7N20 A57 30c #385, II 75 40
a. Type I 75 60
7N21 A57 50c #386, II 75 40
a. Type I 1.25 75
7N22 A57 $1 #387, I 7.00 4.00
a. Type II 14.00 14.00
7N23 A57 $2 #388, I 8.00 7.00
a. Type II 8.00 8.00
7N24 A57 $5 #389, I 14.00 14.00
a. Type II 37.50 37.50
7N25 A57 $10 #390, II 22.50 22.50
a. Type I 27.50 27.50
7N26 A57 $20 #391, II 32.50 32.50
a. Type I 32.50 32.50

On Stamps of 1940 with Secret Marks

1941 **Wmk. 261** ***Perf. 14***
7N27 A57 10c #394, II 50 30
7N28 A57 30c #395, I 3.00 2.25
7N29 A57 50c #396, I 3.00 2.25

On Stamps of 1940-41 (Martyrs) with Secret Marks

Perf. 12½, 13 & Compound

1941 **Wmk. 261**
7N30 A39 ½c #402, II 25 25
7N31 A40 1c #403, II 25 25
a. Type I 25 25
7N32 A46 2c #404, II 25 25
7N33 A39 2½c #405, I 10.00 10.00
7N34 A46 10c #405, I 3.50 3.00
7N35 A45 13c #411, II 1.50 1.00
7N36 A46 17c #413, II 75 30
a. Type I 27.50 27.50
7N37 A40 25c #416, II 75 50
7N38 A48 30c #418, I 3.50 3.00
7N39 A47 40c #419, II 60 40
a. Type I 2.25 2.25
7N40 A40 50c #420, I 32.50 32.50
Nos. 7N30-7N40 (11) 53.85 51.45

Unwmk.
7N41 A39 ½c #421, II 20 20
a. Type I 25 25
7N42 A40 1c #422, II 20 20
7N43 A46 2c #423, I 2.25 1.75
7N44 A48 3c #425, I 50 50
7N45 A39 4c #426, II 25 25
7N46 A46 10c #429, I 16.50 16.50
7N47 A45 13c #430, I 60 60
7N48 A48 15c #431, II 60 30
7N49 A46 17c #432, II 75 50
a. Type I 75 75
7N50 A47 20c #433, II 50 30
a. Type I 1.50 1.25
7N51 A45 21c #434, II 50 30
7N52 A40 25c #435, I 1.50 1.25
a. Type II 1.75 1.50
7N53 A46 28c #436, II 40 40
Nos. 7N41-7N53 (13) 24.75 23.05

Honan Singapore Overprint in Red

1942
7N54 A37 4c #298, II 32.50 32.50
7N55 A39 4c #7N45 1.50 1.50
7N56 A57 8c #7N11a 3.00 3.00
7N57 A57 8c #7N12 7.00 7.00

Honan Anniv. of Manchukuo Overprint in Red

1942
7N58 A57 2c #7N8 1.75 1.75
7N59 A39 4c #7N45 1.25 1.25
7N60 A57 8c #7N11a 37.50 37.50
7N61 A57 8c #7N12 20.00 20.00

North China

For use in Honan, Hopei, Shansi, Shantung and Supeh (Northern Kiangsu)

Stamps of China, 1931-37 Surcharged North China (Hwa Pei) and Half of Original Value

北 華
分 壹

1942 **Unwmk.** ***Perf. 14, 12½***
8N1 A40 ½c on 1c org (#313) 15 15
8N2 A37 1c on 2c ol grn (#297) 25 20
8N3 A37 2c on 4c grn (#298) 50 20
8N4 A45 4c on 8c brn org (#316) 90.00

Same Surcharge on Stamps of 1938-41

Perf. 12½
8N5 A57 1c on 2c ol grn (#349) 1.25 1.25
8N6 A57 1c on 2c ol grn (#368) 30 15
8N7 A57 4c on 8c ol grn (#353) 75 40
8N8 A57 4c on 8c ol grn (#369) 15 15
8N9 A57 5c on 10c grn 15 15
8N10 A57 8c on 16c ol gray 50 20
8N11 A57 50c on $1 hn & dk brn (#359) 1.25 1.25
8N12 A57 50c on $1 hn & dk brn (#344) 200.00 200.00
8N13 A57 50c on $1 hn & dk brn (#347) 22.50 22.50
8N14 A57 $1 on $2 dp bl & org brn (#360) 3.00 3.00
8N15 A57 $1 on $2 dp bl & org brn (#345) 9.00 9.00
8N16 A57 $1 on $2 dp bl & org brn (#348) 50.00 50.00

No. 8N12 was issued without gum.

Same Surcharge on China Nos. 383-388, 390-391

Perf. 14
8N17 A57 4c on 8c ol grn 10 10
8N18 A57 5c on 10c grn 10 10
8N19 A57 15c on 30c scar 10 10
a. Invtd. surch. 60.00 60.00
8N20 A57 25c on 50c dk bl 15 10
8N21 A57 50c on $1 org brn & sep 65 50

8N22 A57 $1 on $2 dp bl & yel brn 1.50 1.00
8N23 A57 $5 on $10 dk grn & dl pur 20.00 20.00
8N24 A57 $10 on $20 rose lake & dk bl 12.50 12.50

Same Surcharge on China Nos. 394-396

Wmk. 261

8N25 A57 5c on 10c grn 20 20
8N26 A57 15c on 30c scar 50 40
8N27 A57 25c on 50c dk bl 30 20

Same Surcharge on Stamps of 1940-41

1942 Wmk. 261 *Perf. 12½, 13*

8N28 A40 ½c on 1c org 10 10
8N29 A46 1c on 2c dp bl 10 10
8N30 A45 4c on 8c dp org 7.00 7.00
8N31 A46 5c on 10c dl vio 10 10
8N32 A48 15c on 30c brn car 35 20
8N33 A47 20c on 40c org 20 10
8N34 A40 25c on 50c grn 50 30

Unwmk.

8N35 A40 ½c on 1c org (#422) 10 10
a. ½c on 1c org (#422a) 2.00 2.00
8N36 A46 1c on 2c dp bl 10 10
8N37 A39 2c on 4c pale vio 10 10
8N38 A45 4c on 8c dp org 10 10
8N39 A46 5c on 10c dl vio 10 10
8N40 A47 10c on 20c lt bl 10 10
8N41 A47 20c on 40c org 20 15
8N42 A40 25c on 50c grn 1.25 1.00

Same Surcharge on "New Peking" Prints

Perf. 14

8N43 A37 1c on 2c ol grn 10 10
8N44 A37 2c on 4c dl grn 10 10
a. Inverted surch. 30.00
8N45 A45 4c on 8c dp org 10 10
8N46 A57 8c on 16c ol gray 10 10
8N47 A47 10c on 20c red brn 15 10
8N48 A48 15c on 30c brn car 25 10
8N49 A47 20c on 40c org 20 10
a. Inverted surch. 35.00
8N50 A40 25c on 50c grn 30 15
8N51 A57 50c on $1 org brn & sep 20 10
8N52 A57 $1 on $2 dp bl & org brn 1.50 1.00
8N53 A57 $5 on $10 dk grn & dl pur 6.00 6.00

See note after No. 2N93.

Nos. 8N44, 8N17 and 8N46 with Additional Overprint in Red

邦友
界租 還交
念紀

1943 Unwmk. *Perf. 14*

8N54 A37 2c on 4c dl grn 10 10
8N55 A57 4c on 8c ol grn 10 10
8N56 A57 8c on 16c ol gray 20 20

Issued to commemorate the return of the Foreign Concessions to China.

Nos. 8N44, 8N7 and 8N46 with Additional Overprint in Red

局總 政郵
立成
念紀年週五

1943, Aug. 15 *Perf. 14, 12½*

8N57 A37 2c on 4c dl grn 10 10
8N58 A57 4c on 8c ol grn 15 15
8N59 A57 8c on 16c ol gray 30 30

Issued to commemorate the fifth anniversary of the North China Postal Service.

Stamps of China, 1934-41, Overprinted in Black

北 華

1943, Nov. 1

8N60 A40 1c org (#313) 10 10
8N61 A40 1c org (#422) 10 10
8N62 A57 10c grn (#354) 10 10
8N63 A57 $2 dp bl & yel brn (#388) 12.00 10.00
8N64 A57 $5 red & grnsh blk (#361) 3.50 3.00
8N65 A57 $5 red & sl grn (#389) 3.00 2.50
8N66 A57 $10 dk grn & dl pur (#390) 10.00 9.00
8N67 A57 $20 rose lake & dk bl (#391) 70.00 60.00
Nos. 8N60-8N67 (8) 98.80 84.80

Same Overprint on "New Peking" Prints

8N68 A40 1c orange 10 10
8N69 A37 2c ol grn 10 10
8N70 A37 4c dl grn 10 10
8N71 A37 5c green 10 10
8N72 A57 9c ol grn 10 10
8N73 A46 10c dl vio 10 10
8N74 A57 16c ol gray 10 10
8N75 A57 18c ol gray 10 10
8N76 A47 20c henna 15 10
8N77 A48 30c brn car 15 10
8N78 A47 40c brt org 20 10
a. Inverted ovpt. 30.00 30.00
8N79 A40 50c green 20 10
8N80 A57 $1 org brn & sep 50 25
8N81 A57 $2 bl & org brn 60 30
8N82 A57 $5 red & sl grn 1.25 1.00
8N83 A57 $10 dk grn & dl pur 2.50 2.50
8N84 A57 $20 rose lake & dk bl 5.00 5.00
Nos. 8N68-8N84 (17) 11.35 10.25

See note after No. 2N93.

Nos. 8N70 and 8N62 with Additional Overprint in Red

戰 参
念紀年週一

1944, Jan. 9

8N85 A37 4c dl grn 15 15
8N86 A57 10c green 15 15

Issued to commemorate the first anniversary of the declaration of war against the Allies by North China.

Nos. 8N72, 8N75, 8N79 and 8N80 with Additional Overprint in Red

會員委務政
念紀年週四

1944, Mar. 30

8N87 A57 9c ol grn 15 15
8N88 A57 18c ol gray 20 20
8N89 A40 50c green 40 40
8N90 A57 $1 org brn & sep 75 75
a. red ovpt. inverted 25.00 25.00

Issued to commemorate the fourth anniversary of the North China Political Council.

Shanghai-Nanking Nos. 9N101-9N104 Surcharged North China (Hwa Pei) and New Value in Red or Black

華北玖分 (a)
華北壹角捌分 (b)
華北叁角陸分 (c)
華北玖角 (d)

1944 *Perf. 12½x12, 12x12½*

8N91 OS1 (a) 9c on 50c org 10 10
8N92 OS1 (b) 18c on $1 grn (R) 15 15
a. Dble. surch. 25.00 25.00
8N93 OS2 (c) 36c on $2 dp bl (R) 15 15
8N94 OS2 (d) 90c on $5 car rose 25 25

Nos. 8N72, 8N75, 8N79 and 8N80 Overprinted in Red or Blue

立成局總政郵
念紀年週六

1944, Aug. 15

8N95 A57 9c ol grn 10 10
8N96 A57 18c ol gray 10 10
8N97 A40 50c green 20 20
8N98 A57 $1 org brn & sep (Bl) 35 35

Issued to commemorate the sixth anniversary of the General Post Office Department of North China.

North China Nos. 8N76, 8N79-8N81 Overprinted in Blue or Black

席主汪
念紀典葬

1944, Dec. 5

8N99 A47 20c hn (Bl) 12 12
8N100 A40 50c grn (Bl) 12 12
8N101 A57 $1 org brn & sep (Bl) 18 18
8N102 A57 $2 bl & org brn 18 18

Issued to commemorate the death of Wang Ching-wei, puppet ruler of China.

North China Nos. 8N76, 8N79-8N81 Overprinted in Red or Black

年週二戰参
念紀

1945

8N103 A47 20c henna 12 12
8N104 A40 50c grn (R) 20 20
8N105 A57 $1 org brn & sep 20 20
8N106 A57 $2 bl & org brn 35 35

Issued to commemorate the second anniversary of the declaration of war.

Shanghai-Nanking Nos. 9N105-9N106 Surcharged in Red

華北伍角

1945 *Perf. 12x12½*

8N107 OS3 50c on $3 lt org 10 10
8N108 OS3 $1 on $6 bl 15 15

Issued to commemorate the return of the foreign concessions in Shanghai.

Dragon Pillar
OS1

Dr. Sun Yat-sen
OS2

Designs: $2, Long Bridge and White Pagoda. $5, Tower in Imperial City. $10, Marble Boat, Summer Palace.

1945 Unwmk. Litho. *Perf. 14*
Various Papers

8N109 OS1 $1 dl yel 8 8
8N110 OS1 $2 dp bl 6 6
8N111 OS1 $5 carmine 15 15
8N112 OS1 $10 dl grn 15 15

Issued to commemorate the fifth anniversary of the North China Political Council.

1945
Without Gum; Various Papers

8N113 OS2 $1 bister 15 10
8N114 OS2 $2 dk bl 18 10
8N115 OS2 $5 fawn 25 15
8N116 OS2 $10 sage grn 40 25
8N117 OS2 $20 dl vio 50 30
8N118 OS2 $50 brown 12.50 6.00
Nos. 8N113-8N118 (6) 13.98 6.90

Nos. 8N113-8N118 without "Hwa Pei" overprint are proofs.

Wutai Mountain, Shansi — OS3

Designs: $10, Kaifeng Iron Pagoda. $20, International Bridge, Tientsin. $30, Taishan Mountain, Shantung. $50, General Post Office, Peking.

1945, Aug. 15
Without Gum; Various Papers

8N119 OS3 $5 gray grn 5 5
8N120 OS3 $10 dl brn 5 5
8N121 OS3 $20 dl pur 7 7
8N122 OS3 $30 sl bl 8 8
8N123 OS3 $50 carmine 15 15
Nos. 8N119-8N123 (5) 40 40

Issued to commemorate the seventh anniversary of the North China Postal Directorate.

Shanghai and Nanking

China Nos. 299-303 Surcharged

貳角伍分 25 (a)
暫 陸 暫 售 圓 6.00 售 (b)

1942-45 Unwmk. *Perf. 12½, 13½*

9N1 A37(b) $6 on 5c grn 10 10
9N2 A37(b) $20 on 15c scar 10 10
9N3 A37(b) $500 on 15c dk grn 15 15
9N4 A37(b) $1000 on 20c ultra 15 15
9N5 A37(b) $1000 on 25c ultra 15 15

A $1000 on 20c ultramarine, No. 293, exists. Price $200.

Same Surcharge on Stamps of 1939-41

Perf. 12½

9N6 A57(a) 25c on 5c ol grn (#352) 10 10
9N7 A57(a) 30c on 2c ol grn (#368) 10 10
9N8 A57(a) 50c on 3c dl cl (#350) 10 10
9N9 A57(a) 50c on 5c ol grn (#352) 10 10
9N10 A57(a) 50c on 8c ol grn (#353) 10 10
9N11 A57(b) $1 on 8c ol grn (#353) 10 10
9N12 A57(b) $1 on 8c ol grn (#369) 5.00 5.00
9N13 A57(b) $1 on 15c dk vio brn (#356) 10 10
9N14 A57(b) $1.30 on 16c ol gray (#357) 10 10
9N15 A57(b) $1.50 on 3c dl cl (#350) 10 10
9N16 A57(b) $2 on 5c ol grn (#352) 10 10
9N17 A57(b) $2 on 10c grn (#354) 10 10
9N18 A57(b) $3 on 15c dk vio brn (#356) 10 10
9N19 A57(b) $4 on 16c ol gray (#357) 10 10
9N20 A57(b) $5 on 15c dk vio brn (#356) 10 10
9N21 A57(b) $6 on 5c grn (#351) 10 10
a. Perf. 14 (#371) 15.00 15.00
9N22 A57(b) $6 on 5c ol grn (#352) 10 10
9N23 A57(b) $6 on 8c ol grn (#353) 10 10
9N24 A57(b) $6 on 8c ol grn (#369) 450.00 450.00
9N25 A57(b) $6 on 10c grn (#354) 10 10
9N26 A57(b) $10 on 10c grn (#354) 10 10

9N27 A57(b) $10 on 16c ol gray (#357) 10 10
9N28 A57(b) $20 on 3c dl cl (#350) 10 10
9N29 A57(b) $20 on 15c scar (#355) 10 10
9N30 A57(b) $20 on 15c dk vio brn (#356) 10 10
9N31 A57(b) $20 on $2 dp bl & org brn (#360) 50 50
9N32 A57(b) $100 on 3c dl cl (#350) 10 10
9N33 A57(b) $500 on 8c ol grn (#353) 40 40
9N34 A57(b) $500 on 8c ol grn (#369) 12.50 12.50
9N35 A57(b) $500 on 10c grn (#354) 10 10
9N36 A57(b) $500 on 15c scar (#355) 10 10
9N37 A57(b) $500 on 15c dk vio brn (#356) 10 10
9N38 A57(b) $500 on 16c ol gray (#357) 10 10
9N39 A57(b) $1000 on 25c dk bl (#358) 10 10
9N40 A57(b) $2000 on $5 red & grnsh blk (#361) 25 25
Nos. 9N1-9N23,9N25-9N40 (39) 22.20 22.20

Nos. 381-391 Surcharged with Type "b"

Perf. 14

9N41 A57 $1 on 8c ol grn 10 10
9N42 A57 $1.70 on 30c scar 10 10
a. Perf. 12½ 15 15
9N43 A57 $2 on 5c ol grn 10 10
9N44 A57 $2 on $1 org brn & sep 35 35
9N45 A57 $3 on 8c ol grn 10 10
a. $3 on 8c ol grn (#383a) 10 10
b. "3" with flat top 10 10
9N46 A57 $6 on 5c grn 10 10
9N47 A57 $6 on 5c ol grn 10 10
9N48 A57 $6 on 8c ol grn 10 10
9N49 A57 $10 on 10c grn 10 10
a. Perf. 12½ 25 25
9N50 A57 $20 on $2 dp bl & yel brn 15 15
9N51 A57 $50 on 30c scar 10 10
9N52 A57 $50 on 50c dk bl 10 10
9N53 A57 $50 on $5 red & sl grn 15 15
9N54 A57 $50 on $20 rose lake & dk bl 60 60
9N55 A57 $100 on $10 dk grn & dl pur 30 30
9N56 A57 $200 on $20 rose lake & dk bl 10 10
9N57 A57 $500 on 8c ol grn 3.00 3.00
a. $500 on 8c ol grn (#383a) 12.50 12.50
9N58 A57 $500 on 10c grn 15 15
9N59 A57 $1000 on 30c scar 15 15
9N60 A57 $1000 on 50c dk bl 15 15
9N61 A57 $1000 on $2 dp bl & yel brn 75 75
9N62 A57 $2000 on $5 red & sl grn 30 30

China Nos. 392-395 and 399-401 Surcharged with Type "b"

1942-45 **Wmk. 261** ***Perf. 14***

9N63 A57 $2 on $1 org brn & sep, perf. 12½ 30 30
9N64 A57 $6 on 5c grn 10 10
9N65 A57 $6 on 5c ol grn 10 10
9N66 A57 $50 on $5 red & sl grn 10 10
a. Numeral tablet vio 10 10
9N67 A57 $100 on $10 dk grn & dl pur 15 15
9N68 A57 $200 on $20 rose lake & dk bl 15 15
9N69 A57 $500 on 10c grn 25 25
9N70 A57 $1000 on 30c scar 50 50
9N71 A57 $5000 on $10 dk grn & dl pur, perf. 12½ 3.50 3.50
a. Perf. 14 30.00 30.00
Nos. 9N41-9N71 (31) 12.30 12.30

Nos. 9N63 and 9N71 were not issued without surcharge. A $50 on 30c scarlet exists.

Same Surcharge on Stamps of 1940-41

Perf. 12½, 13
Wmk. 261

9N72 A46 $30 on 2c dp bl 35.00 35.00

A $7.50 on ½c and a $15 on 1c are known.

Unwmk.

9N73 A39 $7.50 on ½c ol blk 10 10
9N74 A40 $15 on 1c org 10 10
a. Without secret mark 30.00 30.00
9N75 A46 $30 on 2c dp bl 10 10
9N76 A40 $200 on 1c org 10 10
9N77 A45 $200 on 8c dp org 10 10
Nos. 9N73-9N77 (5) 50 50

Same Surcharge on Stamps of 1941

Perf. 12

9N78 A59(a) 5c on ½c sep 10 10
9N79 A59(a) 10c on 1c org 10 10
9N80 A59(a) 20c on 1c org 10 10
9N81 A59(a) 40c on 5c grn 10 10
9N82 A59(b) $5 on 5c grn 10 10
9N83 A59(b) $10 on 10c brt grn 10 10
9N84 A59(b) $50 on ½c sep 10 10
9N85 A59(b) $50 on 1c org 10 10
9N86 A59(b) $50 on 17c ol 10 10
9N87 A59(b) $200 on 5c grn 10 10
9N88 A59(b) $200 on 8c turq grn 10 10
9N89 A59(b) $200 on 8c red org 10 10
9N90 A59(b) $500 on $5 scar & blk 15 15
9N91 A59(b) $1000 on 1c org 15 15
9N92 A59(b) $1000 on 25c rose vio 25 25
9N93 A59(b) $1000 on 30c scar 25 25
9N94 A59(b) $1000 on $2 bl & blk 40 40
9N95 A59(b) $1000 on $10 grn & blk 25 25
9N96 A59(b) $2000 on $5 scar & blk 50 50
Nos. 9N78-9N96 (19) 3.15 3.15

Stamps of China 1939-41 Surcharged in Red or Blue

念紀界租回收
八月一日 三十二年
分伍角貳

1943 **Unwmk.** ***Perf. 12, 12½***

9N97 A57 25c on 5c grn 5 5
9N98 A59 50c on 8c red org (Bl) 5 5
9N99 A57 $1 on 16c ol gray 10 10
9N100 A59 $2 on 50c dk bl 10 10

Issued to commemorate the return of the foreign concessions in Shanghai.

Wheat and Cotton — OS1

Purple Mountain, Nanking OS2

Perf. 12½x12, 12x12½

1944 **Engr.** **Unwmk.**

9N101 OS1 50c orange 5 5
9N102 OS1 $1 green 5 5
9N103 OS2 $2 dp bl 5 5
9N104 OS2 $5 car rose 10 5

Issued to commemorate the fourth anniversary of the establishment of the puppet government at Nanking.

Map of Foreign Concessions in Shanghai — OS3

1944 ***Perf. 12x12½***

9N105 OS3 $3 lt org 5 10
9N106 OS3 $6 blue 5 10

Issued to commemorate the first anniversary of the return of the foreign concessions in Shanghai.

Nos. 9N101-9N104 Surcharged in Black with Type "b"

1945, Mar. 30

9N107 OS1 $15 on 50c org 5 5
9N108 OS1 $30 on $1 grn 5 5
9N109 OS2 $60 on $2 dp bl 5 5
9N110 OS2 $200 on $5 car rose 10 10

China Nos. C31, C32, C36 and C38 Surcharged in Red, Green, Orange or Carmine

防空
1000

暫售
壹仟圓

1945 ***Perf. 12½, 13***

9N111 AP3 $150 on 15c gray grn (R) 5 5
9N112 AP3 $250 on 25c yel org (G) 5 5
9N113 AP3 $600 on 60c dp bl (O) 10 10
9N114 AP3 $1,000 on $1 ap grn (C) 15 15

Issue as air raid precaution propaganda.

SHANGHAI AND NANKING AIR POST STAMPS

China Nos. C35 and C38 Surcharged in Black

10

付已費空航之片明內國

The surcharges on Nos. 9NC1-9NC7 were in Japanese currency because all air mail then was carried by Japanese planes.

1941 **Unwmk.** ***Perf. 12½***

The surcharges translate: (10c) "Airmail fee for postcard within the nation has been paid." (20c) "Airmail fee for letter within the nation has been paid."

9NC1 AP3 10(s) on 50c brn 10 10
9NC2 AP3 20(s) on $1 ap grn 10 10

Two types of surcharge exist on No. 9NC1.

Similar Surcharge on No. C28

1941 **Wmk. 261** ***Perf. 13***

9NC3 AP3 20(s) on $1 ap grn 7.50 7.50

Nos. C37 and C39 Surcharged

35

付已費空航函信本日寄

1941 **Unwmk.** ***Perf. 12½, 13***

The surcharges translate: (18c and 25c) "Airmail fee for postcard to Japan has been paid." (35c) "Airmail fee for letter to Japan has been paid."

9NC4 AP3 18(s) on 90c lt ol 10 10
9NC5 AP3 25(s) on 90c lt ol 10 10
9NC6 AP3 35(s) on $2 lt brn 10 10

No. 9NC6 with Additional Surcharge in Red

Perf. 12½

9NC7 AP3 60(s) on 35(s) on $2 lt brn 10 10

SHANGHAI AND NANKING POSTAGE DUE STAMPS

Postage Due Stamps of China 1932 Surcharged in Black

壹 改
圓 作
100

1945 **Unwmk.** ***Perf. 14***

9NJ1 D5 $1 on 2c org 10 10
9NJ2 D5 $2 on 5c org 10 10
9NJ3 D5 $5 on 10c org 10 10
9NJ4 D5 $10 on 20c org 10 10

Northeastern Provinces

民 中
國 華

With the end of World War II and the collapse of Manchukuo, the Northeastern Provinces reverted to China. In many Manchurian towns and cities, the Manchukuo stamps were locally handstamped in ideograms: "Republic of China," "China Postal Service" or "Temporary Use for China." A typical example is shown above.

Dr. Sun Yat-sen
A1 A2

Black Surcharge

1946, Feb. **Unwmk.** **Typo.** ***Perf. 14***

1 A1 50c on $5 red 8 5
2 A1 50c on $10 grn 8 5
3 A1 $1 on $10 grn 8 5
4 A1 $2 on $20 brn vio 8 5
5 A1 $4 on $50 brn 15 10
Nos. 1-5 (5) 47 30

The two characters at left express the new value.

Stamps of China, 1938-41 Overprinted

用貼北東限

1946, Apr. ***Perf. 12½, 13, 13½, 14***

6 A40 1c org (#422) 8 5
7 A48 3c dp yel brn (#425) 8 5
8 A48 5c dl red org (#427) 8 5
9 A57 10c grn (#354) 8 5
10 A57 10c grn (#384) 8 5

11 A47 20c lt bl (#433) 8 5
a. Horiz. pair, imperf. between 45.00
Nos. 6-11 (6) 48 30

1946, July Engr. *Perf. 14*
Without Gum

12	A2	5c lake	12	8
13	A2	10c orange	12	8
14	A2	20c yel grn	12	8
15	A2	25c blk brn	12	8
16	A2	50c red org	12	8
17	A2	$1 blue	12	8
18	A2	$2 dk vio	12	8
19	A2	$2.50 indigo	12	8
20	A2	$3 brown	12	8
21	A2	$4 org brn	12	8
22	A2	$5 dk grn	12	8
23	A2	$10 crimson	12	8
24	A2	$20 olive	12	8
25	A2	$50 bl vio	12	8
		Nos. 12-25 (14)	1.68	1.12

Two types of $4, $10, $20 and $50: I. Character *kuo* directly left of sun emblem is open at upper and lower left corners of "box." Diagonal stroke from top center to lower right has no hook at bottom. II. Character is closed at left corners. Diagonal stroke has hook at bottom.

See Nos. 47-52, 61-63.

China Nos. 728-731 Surcharged in Black

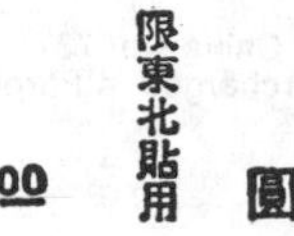

1946

26	A75	$2 on $20 grn	12	12
27	A75	$3 on $30 bl	12	12
28	A75	$5 on $50 dk brr	12	12
29	A75	$10 on $100 car	12	12

Convening of Chinese National Assembly.

Type of China, 1946, Inscribed:

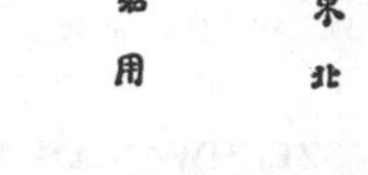

1947 Engr. *Perf. 11, 11½*

30	A74	$2 carmine	10	10
31	A74	$3 green	10	10
32	A74	$5 vermilion	10	10
33	A74	$10 yel grn	12	12
34	A74	$20 yel org	12	12
35	A74	$30 magenta	12	12
		Nos. 30-35 (6)	66	66

60th birthday of Chiang Kai-shek.

Type of China, 1947, Inscribed:

1947 Unwmk. Engr. *Perf. 14*

36	A76	$2 dp grn	10	10
37	A76	$4 dp bl	10	10
38	A76	$6 carmine	10	10
39	A76	$10 lt brn	10	10
40	A76	$20 dp cl	10	10
		Nos. 36-40 (5)	50	50

First anniversary of return of Chinese National Government to Nanking.

China Nos. 644 to 646 and 634 Surcharged in Black

用貼北東限 叁佰圓 改作 300

1947 *Perf. 12½, 14*

41	A73	$100 on $1000 rose lake	10	7
42	A73	$300 on $3000 bl	12	8
43	A73	$500 on $5000 dp grn & ver	15	8
44	A37	$500 on $30 choc	15	12

Type of 1946

1947 Engr. *Perf. 14*
Without Gum

47	A2	$44 dk car rose	12.50	12.50
48	A2	$100 dp grn	5	5
49	A2	$200 rose brn	5	5
50	A2	$300 bluish grn	6	6
51	A2	$500 rose car	6	6
52	A2	$1000 dp org	8	8
		Nos. 47-52 (6)	12.80	12.80

Stamps and Types of 1946-47 Surcharged in Black or Red

壹仟伍佰圓 改作 1500

1948 Unwmk. *Perf. 14*

53	A2	$1500 on 20c yel grn	25	25
54	A2	$3000 on $1 bl	10	10
55	A2	$4000 on 25c blk brn (R)	10	10
56	A2	$8000 on 50c red org	10	10
57	A2	$10,000 on 10c org	15	15
58	A2	$50,000 on $109 dk grn (R)	30	33
59	A2	$100,000 on $65 dl grn	30	40
60	A2	$500,000 on $22 gray (R)	30	40
		Nos. 53-60 (8)	1.60	1.83

Type of 1946

1949
Without Gum

61	A2	$22 gray	15.00
62	A2	$65 dl grn	20.00
63	A2	$109 dk grn	30.00

POSTAGE DUE STAMPS

D1

1947 Unwmk. Engr. *Perf. 14*
Without Gum

J1	D1	10c dk bl	5	*15*
J2	D1	20c dk bl	5	*15*
J3	D1	50c dk bl	5	*15*
J4	D1	$1 dk bl	5	*15*
J5	D1	$2 dk bl	5	*15*
J6	D1	$5 dk bl	5	*15*
		Nos. J1-J6 (6)	30	*90*

Nos. J1 to J3 Surcharged in Red

拾圓 改作

1948

J7	D1	$10 on 10c dk bl	5	*15*
J8	D1	$20 on 20c dk bl	5	*15*
J9	D1	$50 on 50c dk bl	5	*15*

The surcharge reads "Changed to . . . dollars." Characters at the left express the new value and vary on each denomination.

MILITARY STAMPS

No. 16 Surcharged in Black

郵軍 作暫 圓肆拾肆

1947 Unwmk. *Perf. 14*

M1 A2 $44 on 50c red org 1.75 1.75

The surcharge reads: "Army Post. Temporarily for 44 dollars."

China No. M13 Overprinted in Black

用貼北東限

Perf. 12½
Thin Paper Without Gum

M2 M1 rose 25 25

China No. M13 Overprinted in Black

用貼北東限

M3 M1 rose 3.50 3.00

PARCEL POST STAMP

China No. Q25 Surcharged in Black

用貼北東限 伍拾萬圓 改作

1948 Unwmk. Engr. *Perf. 13½*
Without Gum

Q1 PP3 $500,000 on $5,000,000 lil 47.50

Anhwei Province

China Type A95 Handstamp Surcharged

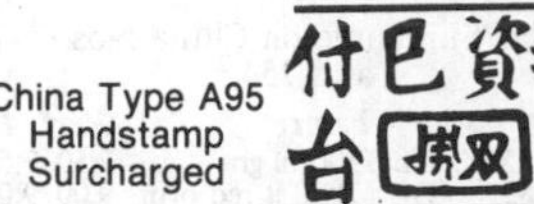

1949, Mar. 16 Litho.

1 A95 On $1000 car 45.00

SPECIAL DELIVERY STAMP

China Type A95 with Similar Surcharge

1949, Mar 16 Litho.

E1 A95 On $500 brn 45.00

REGISTRATION STAMP

China Type A95 with Similar Surcharge

1949, Mar. 16 Litho.

F1 A95 On $3000 org 45.00

ACKNOWLEDGMENT OF RECEIPT STAMP

China Type A95 with Similar Surcharge

1949, Mar. 16 Litho.

H1 A95 On $20 red brn 45.00

Fukien Province

Stamps of China, 1945-49, Surcharged

郵資 壹分 1

1949 Engr. *Perf. 14*
Without Gum

1	A82	1c on $500 bl grn	6.00	6.00
2	A82	1c on $7000 lt red brn	11.00	11.00
3	A82	2c on $2,000,000 ver	2.75	2.75
4	A82	2½c on $50,000 dp bl	3.75	3.75
5	A73	4c on $100 dk car	2.75	2.75
6	A73	10c on $200 ol grn	2.75	2.75
7	A82	10c on $3000 bl	1.75	1.75
8	A82	10c on $4000 gray	2.25	2.25
9	A82	10c on $6000 rose lil	1.75	1.75
10	A82	10c on $100,000 dl grn	1.75	1.75
11	A82	10c on $1,000,000 cl	1.75	1.75
12	A82	40c on $200,000 brn vio	4.50	4.50

The surcharge on No. 2 is handstamped and in slightly larger characters.

Issue dates: No. 2, May 10; others, June.

China Nos. 973, 975-978 Overprinted

州福

1949, June Litho. *Perf. 12½, 13*

13	A94	1c ap grn	5.25	3.75
14	A94	4c bl grn	1.75	75
15	A94	10c dp lil	22.50	9.00
16	A94	16c org red	4.50	4.50
17	A94	20c blue	11.00	7.50

Same Overprint on China Nos. 959, 959a

Perf. 12½, Rouletted

1949, July Litho.

18 A96 orange 7.50 7.50

Same Overprint on Fukien Nos. 1, 3-4, 11 in Black or Red

1949, June Engr. *Perf. 14*

19	A82	1c on $500 bl grn	45.00	32.50
20	A82	2c on $2,000,000 ver	7.50	6.00
21	A82	2½c on $50,000 dp bl	7.50	6.00
22	A82	10c on $4000 gray	15.00	12.00
23	A82	10c on $1,000,000 cl	45.00	32.50

AIR POST STAMP

China Nos. C62, C62a Overprinted as Nos. 13-17

Perf. 12½, Rouletted

1949, July Litho.

C1 AP5 bl grn 7.50 7.50

SPECIAL DELIVERY STAMP

China No. E12, E12a Overprinted as Nos. 13-17

Perf. 12½, Rouletted

1949, July Litho.

E1 SD2 red vio 7.50 7.50

FUKIEN PROVINCE REGISTRATION STAMPS

China Nos. F2, F2a Overprinted as Nos. 13-17

Perf. 12½, Rouletted

1949, July Litho.

F1 R2 carmine 7.50 7.50

Hunan Province

China No. 640 Surcharged

郵資已付 湘 國內平信

1949, May Engr. *Perf. 14*

1 A73 On $100 dk car 3.50 3.50

The first printing of surcharge on No. 1 is in smaller characters.

China Nos. 797, 788, 750, 747 Surcharged

伍分 湘

1949, May Engr. *Perf. 14*

2	A82	1c on $2,000,000 ver	6.00	6.00
3	A82	2c on $20,000 rose pink	6.00	6.00
4	A82	5c on $3000 bl	6.00	6.00
5	A82	10c on $500 bl grn	6.00	6.00

AIR POST STAMP

China No. 790 Surcharged

國內航空 湘 郵資已付

1949, May **Engr.** ***Perf. 14***

C1 A82 On $40,000 grn 3.50 3.50

SPECIAL DELIVERY STAMP

China No. 637 Surcharged as No. F1 in Red

1949, May **Engr.** ***Perf. 14***

E1 A73 On $30 dk bl 2.00 2.00

HUNAN REGISTRATION STAMP

China No. 754 Surcharged

國內掛號 湘 郵資已付

1949, May **Engr.** ***Perf. 14***

F1 A73 On $7000 lt red brn 3.00 3.00

Hupeh Province

China Type A95 Surcharged

1

1949, May **Litho.**

1 A95 1c on $20 red brn 10.00 10.00
2 A95 10c on $20 red brn 10.00 10.00

Kansu Province

China No. 959 Handstamped in Purple

限甘寧青區 貼用

1949, Aug. **Litho.** ***Perf. 12½***

1 A96 orange 125.00

AIR POST STAMP

Same Handstamp Overprinted on China No. C62 in Red

1949, Aug. **Litho.** ***Perf. 12½***

C1 AP5 bl grn 125.00

Counterfeits exist.

Kiangsi Province

China Nos. 789-791 Surcharged

國內平信 郵資已付 贛

1949 **Engr.** ***Perf. 14***

1 A82 On $30,000 choc 4.50 4.50
2 A82 On $40,000 grn 7.50 7.50
3 A82 On $50,000 dp bl 7.50 7.50

KIANGSI AIR POST STAMP

Similar Surcharge on China No. 754

1949 **Engr.** ***Perf. 14***

C1 A82 On $7000 lt red brn 15.00 15.00

Third and fourth characters in right column of surcharge read "Air Mail" in Chinese on No. C1, "Registered" on Nos. F1-F2.

SPECIAL DELIVERY STAMP

Similar Surcharge on China No. 750

1949 **Engr.** ***Perf. 14***

E1 A82 On $3000 bl 6.00 6.00

See note below No. C1.

KIANGSI REGISTRATION STAMPS

Similar Surcharge on China Nos. 747 and 754

1949 **Engr.** ***Perf. 14***

F1 A82 On $500 bl grn 7.50 7.50
F2 A82 On $7000 lt red brn 9.00 9.00

Kwangsi Province

China Nos. 811 and 818 Also Surcharged in Red

桂區 銀圓 伍分

1949, May 21 **Typo.**

6 A62 5c on $20,000 on 10c dp grn 6.00 6.00
7 A62 5c on $40,000 on 20c dk ol grn 11.00 11.00

China Stamps of 1946-48 Surcharged in Black or Red

桂區 銀圓2分 a

桂區 銀圓壹角貳分 b

1949 **Engr.** ***Perf. 14***

Type "a" Surcharge

8 A82 ½c on $500,000 lil rose 11.00 11.00
9 A82 1c on $200,000 brn vio 3.25 3.25
10 A82 2c on $300,000 yel grn 22.50 22.50
11 A73 5c on $3000 bl 3.25 3.25
12 A82 5c on $3000 bl 3.25 3.25
13 A82 5c on $40,000 grn 4.50 4.50

Type "b" Surcharge

14 A82 13c on $50,000 dp bl (R) 4.50 4.50
15 A82 13c on $50,000 dp bl 10.50 10.50
16 A82 17c on $7000 lt red brn 4.50 4.50
17 A82 21c on $100,000 dl grn 4.50 4.50

Shensi Province

China Nos. 747, 750 Surcharged

國內平信 郵資已付 (陝)

1949, May **Engr.** ***Perf. 14***

1 A82 On $500 bl grn 3.50 3.50
2 A82 On $3000 bl 3.50 3.50

AIR POST STAMP

Similar Surcharge on China No. 754

1949, May **Engr.** ***Perf. 14***

C1 A82 On $7000 lt red brn 4.50 4.50

SPECIAL DELIVERY STAMP

Similar Surcharge on China No. 746 in Red

1949, May **Engr.** ***Perf. 14***

E1 A82 On $250 dp lil 3.50 3.50

SHENSI REGISTRATION STAMPS

Similar Surcharge on China Nos. 626, 637 in Red

1949, May **Typo.** ***Perf. 12***

F1 A72 On $30 dp bl 7.00 7.00
F2 A73 On $30 dk bl 3.50 3.50

Szechwan Province

Re-engraved Issue of China, 1923, Overprinted

限四川貼用

1933 **Unwmk.** ***Perf. 14***

1 A29 1c orange 1.00 15
2 A29 5c claret 1.00 15
3 A30 50c dp grn 3.75 1.40

The overprint reads "For use in Szechwan Province exclusively".

Same Overprint on Sun Yat-sen Issue of 1931-37 Type II

1933-34 ***Perf. 12½***

4 A37 2c ol grn 15 20
5 A37 5c green 15 15
6 A37 15c dk grn 90 45
7 A37 15c scar ('34) 75 1.50
8 A37 25c ultra 75 20
9 A37 $1 org brn & dk brn 5.00 1.50
10 A37 $2 bl & org brn 10.00 3.00
11 A37 $5 dl red & blk 30.00 12.00
Nos. 4-11 (8) 47.70 19.00

Same Overprint on Martyrs Issue of 1932-34

1933 ***Perf. 14***

12 A39 ½c blk brn 30 15
13 A40 1c orange 15 15
14 A39 2½c rose lil 1.50 50
15 A48 3c dp brn 90 15
16 A45 8c brn org 1.10 15
17 A46 10c dl vio 2.25 15
18 A45 13c bl grn 2.25 15
19 A46 17c brn ol 3.00 75
20 A47 20c brn red 3.00 15
21 A48 30c brn vio 3.00 15
22 A47 40c orange 6.75 40
23 A40 50c green 13.00 50
Nos. 12-23 (12) 37.20 3.35

Stamps of China, 1947-48, Surcharged

國內平信郵資 每重貳拾公分 蓉

1949 **Engr.** ***Perf. 14***

24 A82 On $150 dk bl 15.00 15.00
25 A82 On $250 dp lil 15.00 15.00
26 A82 On $500 bl grn 3.00 3.00
27 A82 On $1000 red 9.00 9.00
28 A82 On $2000 ver 3.00 3.00
29 A82 On $3000 bl 3.00 3.00
30 A82 On $4000 gray 3.00 3.00
31 A82 On $5000 dk brn 15.00 15.00
32 A82 On $6000 rose lil 3.00 3.00
33 A82 On $7000 lt red brn 15.00 15.00
34 A82 On $10,000 dk bl & car 3.00 3.00
35 A82 On $20,000 rose pink 6.00 6.0
36 A82 On $30,000 choc 3.00 3.0
37 A82 On $50,000 grn & dk bl 3.00 3.0
38 A82 On $50,000 dp bl 4.50 4.5
39 A82 On $100,000 dl yel & ol 5.25 5.2
40 A82 On $100,000 dl grn 6.00 6.0
41 A82 On $200,000 vio brn & dp bl 6.00 6.0
42 A82 On $200,000 brn vio 6.00 6.0
43 A82 On $300,000 sep & org brn
44 A82 On $300,000 yel grn 11.00 11.0
45 A82 On $500,000 dk Prus grn & sep 3.00 3.0
46 A82 On $1,000,000 cl 9.75 9.7
47 A82 On $2,000,000 ver 6.00 6.0
48 A82 On $3,000,000 ol bis 6.00 6.0
49 A82 On $5,000,000 ultra 22.50 22.5

Several of Nos. 24-49 exist with inverted surcharge and a few with bottom character of left row repeated in right row, same position.

Counterfeits exist.

China No. 737 Surcharged in Purple

2

1949 ***Perf. 12½***

50 A77 2c on $500 ol grn 10.50 10.50

China No. 975 Handstamp Surcharged in Purple

蓉 2½ 貳分半

1949 **Litho.**

51 A94 2½c on 4c bl grn 9.00 9.00

SZECHWAN AIR POST STAMPS

China Nos. C55-C59, C61 Surcharged

國內航空資 每重貳拾公分 蓉

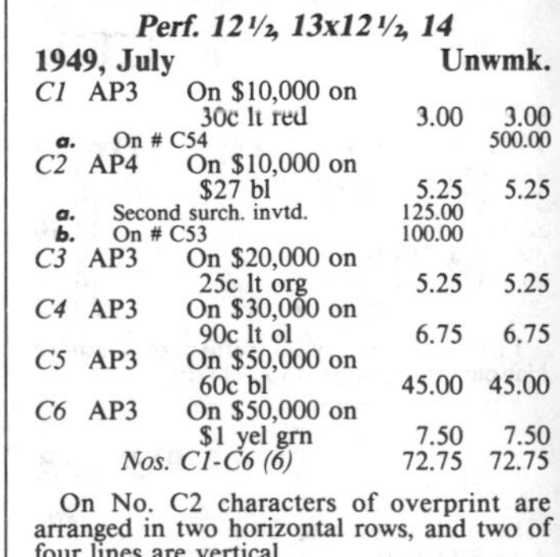

Perf. 12½, 13x12½, 14

1949, July **Unwmk.**

C1 AP3 On $10,000 on 30c lt red 3.00 3.00
a. On # C54 500.00
C2 AP4 On $10,000 on $27 bl 5.25 5.25
a. Second surch. invtd. 125.00
b. On # C53 100.00
C3 AP3 On $20,000 on 25c lt org 5.25 5.25
C4 AP3 On $30,000 on 90c lt ol 6.75 6.75
C5 AP3 On $50,000 on 60c bl 45.00 45.00
C6 AP3 On $50,000 on $1 yel grn 7.50 7.50
Nos. C1-C6 (6) 72.75 72.75

On No. C2 characters of overprint are arranged in two horizontal rows, and two of four lines are vertical.

SZECHWAN REGISTRATION STAMPS

Stamps of China, 1944-47, Surcharged

國內信函 掛號郵資 蓉

Engraved; Typographed (A72)

1949 ***Perf. 12, 13, 14***

F1 A64 On $100 yel brn 30.00

F2 A72 On $100 dk brn 45.00
F3 A64 On $200 dk grn 15.00
F4 A72 On $200 brn vio 15.00
F5 A73 On $200 ol grn 75.00
F6 A73 On $500 brt bl grn 75.00
F7 A73 On $700 red brn 100.00
F8 A73 On $5000 dp grn & ver 65.00
Nos. F1-F8 (8) 420.00

PARCEL POST STAMP

China No. Q10 Surcharged 分 蓉 壹

1949 Engr. *Perf. 12½*
Q1 PP2 1c on $20,000 dk red 75.00

No. Q1 is also found with surcharged value repeated in 5 characters at top of stamp.

Tsingtau

China Nos. 890, 899, 945, 894 Handstamp Surcharged in Purple Blue or Red 壹 銀 分 圓 (島青)

Engraved; Lithographed
1949, May *Perf. 14, 12½*
1 A94 1c on $100 org brn (P) 20.00 20.00
2 A94 4c on $5000 lt bl (P) 16.00 14.00
3 A94 6c on $500 rose lil (B) 14.00 12.00
4 A94 10c on $1000 bl (R) 14.00 12.00

Yunnan Province

Stamps of China, 1923-26, Overprinted 用貼省滇限

The overprint reads "For exclusive use in the Province of Yunnan". It was applied to prevent stamps being purchased in the depreciated currency of Yunnan and used elsewhere.

1926 Unwmk. *Perf. 14*
1 A29 ½c blk brn 15 10
2 A29 1c orange 20 10
3 A29 1½c violet 25 20
4 A29 2c yel grn 40 20
5 A29 3c bl grn 30 15
6 A29 4c ol grn 30 15
7 A29 5c claret 50 15
8 A29 6c red 40 25
9 A29 7c violet 40 30
10 A29 8c brn org 50 40
11 A29 10c dk bl 50 15
12 A30 13c brown 85 60
13 A30 15c dk bl 75 60
14 A30 16c ol grn 85 60
15 A30 20c brn red 1.25 25
16 A30 30c brn vio 2.00 60
17 A30 50c dp grn 1.75 75
18 A31 $1 org brn & sep 7.00 2.00
19 A31 $2 bl & red brn 14.00 6.00
20 A31 $5 red & sl 90.00 75.00
Nos. 1-20 (20) 122.35 88.55

Unification Issue of China, 1929, Overprinted in Red 貼 滇 用 省

1929 *Perf. 14*
21 A35 1c brn org 1.00 40
22 A35 4c ol grn 1.40 65
23 A35 10c dk bl 3.00 1.65
24 A35 $1 dk red 55.00 42.50

Similar Overprint in Black on Sun Yat-sen Mausoleum Issue
Characters 15½-16mm. apart

25 A36 1c brn org 75 30
26 A36 4c ol grn 1.10 60
27 A36 10c dk bl 3.00 1.50
28 A36 $1 dk red 32.50 18.00

London Print Issue of China, 1931-37, Overprinted 用貼省滇限

1932-34 Unwmk. *Perf. 12½*
Type I (double circle)
29 A37 1c orange 50 50
30 A37 2c ol grn 75 75
31 A37 4c green 85 85
32 A37 20c ultra 1.25 1.25
33 A37 $1 org brn & dk brn 17.50 12.50
34 A37 $2 bl & org brn 35.00 22.50
35 A37 $5 dl red & blk 100.00 75.00
Nos. 29-35 (7) 155.85 113.35

Type II (single circle)
36 A37 2c ol grn 40 20
37 A37 4c green 75 75
38 A37 5c green 50 50
39 A37 15c dk grn 2.50 1.75
40 A37 15c scar ('34) 1.50 1.50
41 A37 25c ultra 1.75 1.75
42 A37 $1 org brn & dk brn 20.00 12.50
43 A37 $2 bl & org brn 40.00 20.00
44 A37 $5 dl red & blk 90.00 75.00
Nos. 36-44 (9) 157.40 113.95

Nos. 36-39, 41-44 were overprinted in London as well as in Peiping. The overprints differ in minor details. Price of London overprints (8), $350.

Tan Yuan-chang Issue of China, 1933, Overprinted 貼 滇 用 省

1933 *Perf. 14*
45 A49 2c ol grn 75 40
46 A49 5c green 90 60
47 A49 25c ultra 2.00 1.25
48 A49 $1 red 25.00 18.00

Martyrs Issue of China, 1932-34, Overprinted 用貼省滇限

1933
49 A39 ½c blk brn 32 25
50 A40 1c orange 40 25
51 A39 2½c rose lil 65 40
52 A48 3c dp brn 80 52
53 A45 8c brn org 1.65 1.00
54 A46 10c dl vio 1.10 52
55 A45 13c bl grn 1.25 52
56 A46 17c brn ol 2.75 1.00
57 A47 20c brn red 1.25 80
58 A48 30c brn vio 2.75 1.00
59 A47 40c orange 20.00 16.00
60 A40 50c green 20.00 16.00
Nos. 49-60 (12) 52.92 38.26

China No. 324 was overprinted with characters arranged vertically, like Sinkiang No. 114, but was not issued.

China Stamps of 1945-49 Surcharged in Black or Blue 壹 滇 省 貼 角10 用

Engraved; Lithographed; Typographed
1949 *Perf. 12, 12½, 14*
61 A82 1c on $200,000 brn vio 1.75 1.75
62 A82 1.2c on $40,000 grn 2.50 2.50
63 A94 6c on $200 red org 1.50 1.50
64 A94 10c on $20,000 org 1.50 1.50
65 A94 12c on $50 dk Prus grn (Bl) 1.75 1.75
66 A72 12c on $50 grnsh gray (Bl) 2.25 2.25
67 A72 12c on $200 brn vio (Bl) 1.10 1.10
68 A94 30c on $20 vio brn 1.50 1.50
69 A82 $1.20 on $100,000 dl grn 4.50 4.50

China No. 888 and 630 Surcharged 4 肆 郵 分 資 滇

1949 Engr. *Perf. 14*
70 A94 4c on $20 vio brn 75.00

Typo. *Perf. 12*
71 A72 12c on $200 brn vio 100.00

Manchuria

Kirin and Heilungkiang Issue

Stamps of China, 1923-26, Overprinted 用貼黑吉限

The overprint reads: "For use in Ki-Hei District" the two names being abbreviated.

The intention of the overprint was to prevent the purchase of stamps in Manchuria, where the currency was depreciated, and their resale elsewhere.

1927 Unwmk. *Perf. 14*
1 A29 ½c blk brn 10 10
2 A29 1c orange 10 10
3 A29 1½c violet 20 20
4 A29 2c yel grn 25 15
5 A29 3c bl grn 20 20
6 A29 4c ol grn 25 10
7 A29 5c claret 25 15
8 A29 6c red 35 20
9 A29 7c violet 35 25
10 A29 8c brn org 35 20
11 A29 10c dk bl 35 10
12 A30 13c brown 1.25 30
13 A30 15c dk bl 75 30
14 A30 16c ol grn 75 30
15 A30 20c brn red 1.25 50
16 A30 30c brn vio 1.25 50
17 A30 50c dp grn 4.00 50
18 A31 $1 org brn & sep 12.00 2.00
19 A31 $2 bl & red brn 17.50 10.00
20 A31 $5 red & sl 90.00 75.00
Nos. 1-20 (20) 131.50 91.35

Several values of this issue exist with inverted overprint, double overprint and in pairs with one overprint omitted. These "errors" were not regularly issued. Forgeries also exist.

Chang Tso-lin Stamps of 1928 Overprinted in Red or Blue 貼 吉 用 黑

1928 *Perf. 14*
21 A34 1c brn org (R) 40 30
22 A34 4c ol grn (R) 75 50
23 A34 10c dl bl (R) 2.00 1.25
24 A34 $1 red (Bl) 22.50 15.00

Unification Issue of China, 1929, Overprinted in Red as in 1928

1929
25 A35 1c brn org 75 40
26 A35 4c ol grn 1.00 60
27 A35 10c dk bl 3.00 1.75
28 A35 $1 dk red 40.00 25.00

Similar Overprint in Black on Sun Yat-sen Mausoleum Issue of China
Characters 15-16mm. apart

1929 *Perf. 14*
29 A36 1c brn org 75 75
30 A36 4c ol grn 75 75
31 A36 10c dk bl 2.00 1.50
32 A36 $1 dk red 25.00 15.00

Sinkiang

Stamps of China, 1913-19, Overprinted in Black or Red

限新省貼用
a

The first character of overprint "a" is ½mm. out of alignment, to the left, and the overprint measures 16mm.

1915 Unwmk. *Perf. 14, 15*
1 A24 ½c blk brn 35 25
2 A24 1c orange 35 15
3 A24 2c yel grn 40 25
4 A24 3c sl grn 40 25
5 A24 4c scarlet 50 30
6 A24 5c rose lil 60 50
7 A24 6c gray 75 50
8 A24 7c violet 1.00 90
9 A24 8c brn org 75 60
10 A24 10c dk bl 1.40 1.25
11 A25 15c brown 1.25 1.25
12 A25 16c ol grn 3.00 2.00
13 A25 20c brn red 3.00 2.00
14 A25 30c brn vio 4.00 2.00
15 A25 50c dp grn 10.00 7.50
16 A26 $1 ocher & blk (R) 60.00 25.00
a. Second & third characters of ovpt. transposed *1,000.*
Nos. 1-16 (16) 87.75 44.70

Stamps of China, 1913-19, Overprinted in Black or Red

b 

The five characters of overprint "b" are correctly aligned and measure 15½mm.

1916-19
17 A24 ½c blk brn 40 15
18 A24 1c orange 40 15
19 A24 1½c violet 40 30
20 A24 2c yel grn 40 15
21 A24 3c sl grn 40 15
22 A24 4c scarlet 40 30
23 A24 5c rose lil 50 30
24 A24 6c gray 60 25
25 A24 7c violet 1.00 75
26 A24 8c brn org 35 15
27 A24 10c dk bl 25 15
28 A25 13c brown 1.00 40
29 A25 15c brown 1.00 50
30 A25 16c ol grn 60 30
31 A25 20c brn red 40 30
32 A25 30c brn vio 75 50
33 A25 50c dp grn 1.00 50
34 A26 $1 ocher & blk (R) 6.00 1.50
35 A26 $2 dk bl & blk (R) 12.50 4.00
36 A26 $5 scar & blk (R) 35.00 15.00
37 A26 $10 yel grn & blk (R) 110.00 82.50
38 A26 $20 yel & blk (R) 350.00 300.00
Nos. 17-38 (22) 523.35 408.30

China Nos. 243-246 Overprinted 用貼省新限

1921 *Perf. 14*
39 A27 1c orange 1.10 90
40 A27 3c bl grn 1.50 1.50
41 A27 6c gray 4.50 3.00
42 A27 10c blue 37.50 30.00

Constitution Issue of China, 1923, Overprinted 貼 新 疆 用 省

1923
43 A32 1c orange 1.75 35
44 A32 3c bl grn 1.75 50
45 A32 4c red 5.00 75
46 A32 10c blue 12.50 5.00

Stamps of China, 1923-26, Overprinted Type "b" as in 1916-19, in Black or Red,

1924
Re-engraved
47 A29 ½c blk brn 20 8
48 A29 1c orange 20 8
49 A29 1½c violet 20 8
50 A29 2c yel grn 20 8
51 A29 3c bl grn 25 8
52 A29 4c gray 2.00 1.25
53 A29 5c claret 35 8
54 A29 6c red 40 15
55 A29 7c violet 35 15
56 A29 8c org brn *5.00* *2.00*
57 A29 10c dk bl 35 15
58 A30 13c red brn 50 25
59 A30 15c dp bl 50 30
60 A30 16c ol grn 60 30
61 A30 20c brn red 60 20
62 A30 30c brn vio 1.00 25
63 A30 50c dp grn 1.25 40
64 A31 $1 org brn & sep (R) 5.00 75
65 A31 $2 bl & red brn (R) 10.00 2.00
66 A31 $5 red & sl (R) 35.00 5.00

67 A31 $10 grn & cl (R) 100.00 60.00
68 A31 $20 plum & bl (R) 125.00 100.00
Nos. 47-68 (22) 288.95 173.63

See Nos. 69, 114.

Same Overprint on China No. 275.

1926
69 A29 4c ol grn 40 12

Chang Tso-lin Stamps of China, 1928, Overprinted in Red or Blue

1928 ***Perf. 14***
70 A34 1c brn org (R) 60 35
71 A34 4c ol grn (R) 1.25 70
72 A34 10c dl bl (R) 2.75 1.75
73 A34 $1 red (Bl) 25.00 17.50

Unification Issue of China, 1929, Overprinted in Red as in 1928

1929
74 A35 1c brn org 75 50
75 A35 4c ol grn 1.25 1.00
76 A35 10c dk bl 3.00 2.00
77 A35 $1 dk red 42.50 25.00

Similar Overprint in Black on Sun Yat-sen Mausoleum Issue of China Characters 15mm. apart

1929 ***Perf. 14***
78 A36 1c brn org 1.65 60
79 A36 4c ol grn 2.00 90
80 A36 10c dk bl 6.25 1.75
81 A36 $1 dk red 40.00 18.00

Stamps of Sun Yat-sen Issue of 1931-37 Overprinted

用貼省新限

1932 **Type I** ***Perf. 12½***
82 A37 1c orange 50 60
83 A37 2c ol grn 1.00 1.25
84 A37 4c green 75 75
85 A37 20c ultra 1.00 1.25
86 A37 $1 org brn & dk brn 4.00 4.00
87 A37 $2 bl & org brn 6.00 5.00
88 A37 $5 dl red & blk 14.00 12.50
Nos. 82-88 (7) 27.25 25.35

No. 83 was overprinted in Shanghai in 1938. The overprint differs in minor details.

1932-38

Type II
89 A37 2c ol grn 15 15
90 A37 4c green 15 15
91 A37 5c green 15 15
92 A37 15c dk grn 40 35
93 A37 15c scar ('34) 35 30
93A A37 20c ultra ('38) 30 50
94 A37 25c ultra 35 30
95 A37 $1 org brn & dk brn 2.00 1.75
96 A37 $2 bl & org brn 3.00 3.00
97 A37 $5 dl red & blk 12.00 10.00
Nos. 89-97 (10) 18.85 16.65

Nos. 89, 90 and 94 were overprinted in London, Peiping and Shanghai. Nos. 92, 95-97 exist with London and Peiping overprints. Nos. 91 and 93 exist with Peiping and Shanghai overprints. No. 93A is a Shanghai overprint. The overprints differ in minor details.

Tan Yuan-chang Issue of China, 1933, Overprinted as in 1928

1933 ***Perf. 14***
98 A49 2c ol grn 40 30
99 A49 5c green 1.00 75
100 A49 25c ultra 2.00 1.50
101 A49 $1 red 25.00 20.00

Stamps of China Martyrs Issue of 1932-34 Overprinted

用貼省新限

1933-34
102 A39 ½c blk brn 10 10
103 A40 1c orange 10 10
104 A39 2½c rose lil 10 10
105 A48 3c dp brn 10 10
106 A45 8c brn org 10 10
107 A46 10c dl vio 10 10
108 A45 13c bl grn 20 20
109 A46 17c brn ol 20 20
110 A47 20c brn red 35 35
111 A48 30c brn vio 35 35
112 A47 40c orange 48 48
113 A40 50c green 55 55
Nos. 102-113 (12) 2.73 2.73

Nos. 102-113 were originally overprinted in Peiping. In 1938, Nos. 103-105, 108-112 were overprinted in Shanghai. The two overprints differ in minor details. No. 105, Shanghai overprint, is scarce. Price $35.

China No. 324 Overprinted Type "b" as in 1924

1936 ***Perf. 14***
114 A29 6c brown 9.00 8.00

Stamps of China, 1939-40 Overprinted in Black

1940-45 **Unwmk.** ***Perf. 12½***

Type III
115 A57 2c ol grn 8 5
116 A57 3c dl cl ('41) 8 5
117 A57 5c green 8 5
118 A57 5c ol grn 8 5
119 A57 8c ol grn ('41) 8 5
120 A57 10c grn ('41) 8 5
121 A57 15c scarlet 8 5
122 A57 16c ol gray ('41) 15 5
123 A57 25c dk bl 8 5
124 A57 $1 hn & dk brn (type II) 2.50 2.50
125 A57 $2 dp bl & org brn (type I) 3.00 2.50
126 A57 $5 red & grnsh blk 10.00 10.00
Nos. 115-126 (12) 16.29 15.45

Perf. 14

With Secret Marks
127 A57 8c ol grn (#383a) 8 5
a. On #383 4.00 4.00
128 A57 10c grn ('41) 90 75
129 A57 30c scar ('45) 8 5
130 A57 50c dk bl ('45) 8 5
131 A57 $1 org brn & sep 15 10
132 A57 $2 dp bl & org brn 30 25
133 A57 $5 red & sl grn 45 40
134 A57 $10 dk grn & dl pur 1.00 1.00
135 A57 $20 rose lake & dk bl 1.75 1.50
Nos. 127-135 (9) 4.79 4.15

Wmk. Character Yu (Post) (261)

Perf. 14
136 A57 5c ol grn 8 8
137 A57 10c green 15 10
138 A57 30c scarlet 15 15
139 A57 50c dk bl 18 18

Martyrs Issue, 1940-41, Overprinted in Black

用貼省新限

Perf. 12, 12½, 13, 13x12, 13½x13

1941-45 **Wmk. 261**
140 A40 1c orange 15 10
141 A39 2½c rose lil 15 10
142 A45 8c dp org ('45) 90 75
143 A46 10c dl vio 15 10
144 A45 13c dp yel grn 40 30
145 A46 17c brn ol 50 40
146 A40 25c red vio ('45) 60 50
147 A47 40c org ('45) 90 75
Nos. 140-147 (8) 3.75 3.00

Unwmk.
148 A39 ½c ol blk 8 5
149 A40 1c org ('45) 8 5
150 A46 2c dp bl ('45) 8 5
151 A48 3c dp yel brn 8 5
152 A39 4c pale vio ('45) 8 5
153 A45 8c dp org 8 5
154 A45 13c dp yel grn ('45) 12 10
155 A48 15c brn car ('45) 12 10
156 A46 17c brn ol ('45) 30 25
157 A47 20c lt bl ('45) 15 10
158 A45 21c ol brn ('45) 25 20
159 A46 28c ol ('45) 25 20
160 A47 40c org ('45) 1.50 1.25
161 A40 50c grn ('45) 25 20
Nos. 148-161 (14) 3.42 2.70

Stamps of China, 1942-43 Overprinted in Carmine, Black or Red

用貼省新限

1944 ***Perf. 12½, 13***

Without Gum
162 A62 10c dp grn (C) 6 5
163 A62 20c dk ol grn (C) 6 5
164 A62 25c vio brn 6 5
165 A62 30c dk org 6 5
166 A62 40c red brn 6 5
167 A62 50c sage grn 6 5
a. Perf. 11 1.00 1.00
168 A62 $1 rose lake 6 5
169 A62 $1 dl grn 6 5
170 A62 $1.50 dp bl (C) 6 5
171 A62 $2 dk bl grn (R) 6 5
172 A62 $3 yellow 6 5
173 A62 $5 cerise 6 5
Nos. 162-173 (12) 72 60

Same Overprint on Stamps of China, 1942-43, in Black

1944-46 ***Imperf.***
174 A57 $10 red brn 20.00 20.00
175 A57 $20 rose red 25 25
176 A57 $30 dl vio 40 35
177 A57 $40 rose red 45 40
178 A57 $50 bl ('46) 350.00 400.00
179 A57 $100 org brn 90 75

Perf. 13½
180 A57 $4 dp bl 8 5
181 A57 $5 lil gray 8 5
182 A57 $10 red brn 8 5
183 A57 $20 bl grn 50 50
184 A57 $20 rose red 25.00 25.00
185 A57 $30 dl vio 65 60
186 A57 $40 rose 75 75
187 A57 $50 blue 1.00 1.00
188 A57 $100 org brn 25.00 25.00
Nos. 174-177,179-188 (14) 75.14 74.75

Nos. 162 and 164 Surcharged in Black

改作壹 / 角貳分

1944, Aug. 1
194 A62 12c on 10c dp grn 15 8
195 A62 24c on 25c brn vio 20 10

Stamps of China, 1940-41, Overprinted in Black at Chengtu, Szechwan

用貼省新限

1943
196 A57 10c grn (#354) 1.50 1.50
197 A47 20c lt bl (#433) 1.50 1.50

Wmk. 261 ***Perf. 14***
198 A57 50c dk bl (#396) 1.50 1.50

China Nos. 565 and 567 Overprinted in Black

用貼省新限

1945 **Unwmk.** ***Perf. 12½***
200 A63 40c brn red 8 8
201 A63 $3 red 8 8

China Nos. 640-642, 788, 750, 753 Surcharged in Black or Red

改作 / 伍分 / 用貼省新限

1949 **Engr.** ***Perf. 14***
202 A73 1c on $100 dk car 2.00 2.00
203 A73 3c on $200 ol grn (R) 2.00 2.00
204 A73 5c on $500 brt bl grn (R) 2.00 2.00
205 A82 10c on $20,000 rose pink 3.50 3.50
206 A82 50c on $4000 gray (R) 4.00 4.00
207 A82 $1 on $6000 rose lil 10.00 10.00
Nos. 202-207 (6) 23.50 23.50

AIR POST STAMPS

Sinkiang Nos. 53, 57, 59, 32 Overprinted in Red

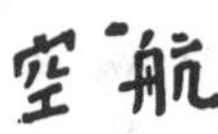

1932-33 **Unwmk.** ***Perf. 14***
C1 A29 5c cl ('33) 125.00 75.00
C2 A29 10c dk bl ('33) 125.00 60.00
C3 A30 15c dp bl 1,000. 250.00
C4 A25 30c brn vio 375.00 275.00

Counterfeits exist of Nos. C1-C19.

Air Post Stamps of China, 1932-37 Handstamped in Dull Red

用貼省新限

1942
C5 AP3 15c gray grn 1.00 75
C6 AP3 25c orange 200.00 200.00
C7 AP3 30c red 60 60
C8 AP3 45c brn vio 1.00 75
C9 AP3 50c dk brn 8.00 8.00
C10 AP3 60c dk bl 1.00 75
C11 AP3 90c ol grn 12.50 12.50
C12 AP3 $1 yel grn 1.00 75
Nos. C5-C12 (8) 225.10 224.10

Same Handstamped Overprint on Air Post Stamps of China, 1940-41

1942 **Wmk. 261** ***Perf. 12½, 13, 13½***
C13 AP3 15c gray grn 65 50
C14 AP3 25c yel org 65 50

1942 **Unwmk.**
C15 AP3 25c lt org 75 60
C16 AP3 30c lt red 75 75
C17 AP3 50c brown 1.00 75
C18 AP3 $2 lt brn 8.00 8.00
C19 AP3 $5 lake 8.00 8.00
Nos. C15-C19 (5) 18.50 18.10

Twelve values exist with this overprint in black. Their status has not been determined. Inverted overprints exist in both red and black.

Official Perforated Characters

For use on official mail, various Sinkiang stamps were perforated with an arrangement of four Chinese characters ("For Official Business Only"). These include Nos. 1-38, 47-69, 114.

OFFICES IN TIBET

12 Pies = 1 Anna
16 Annas = 1 Rupee

Stamps of China, Issues of 1902-10, Surcharged

分半 / Three Pies

1911 **Unwmk.** ***Perf. 12 to 16***
1 A17 3p on 1c ocher 3.00 3.50
a. Inverted surcharge 375.00
2 A17 ½a on 2c grn 3.00 3.50
3 A17 1a on 4c ver 3.00 3.50
4 A17 2a on 7c mar 4.00 5.00
5 A17 2½a on 10c ultra 7.00 8.00
6 A18 3a on 16c ol grn 12.00 14.00
a. Large "S" in "Annas" 375.00
7 A18 4a on 20c red brn 12.00 14.00
8 A18 6a on 30c rose red 20.00 22.50
9 A18 12a on 50c yel grn 45.00 50.00
10 A19 1r on $1 red & pale rose 160.00 185.00
11 A19 2r on $2 red & yel 400.00 450.00
Nos. 1-11 (11) 669.00 759.00

CHINA, PEOPLE'S REPUBLIC OF

LOCATION — Eastern Asia
GOVT. — Communist Republic
POP. — 1,015,400,000 (est. 1983)
CAPITAL — Beijing (Peking)

The communists completed their conquest of all mainland China in 1949. They established the Central Government and General Postal Administration in Peking. They ordered all but two regions to stop selling regional issues by June 30, 1950, extending validity one year from that date. The Northeast and Port Arthur-Dairen regions were exempted because their currency had a different value. These two regions stopped using separate issues at the end of 1950. Thereafter unified issues were used throughout mainland China.

After currency revaluation Mar. 1, 1955, reprints were prepared and put on sale by the Philatelic Agency in order to supply stocks of exhausted issues for collectors. Minor differences in design or paper distinguish the reprints. They are of commemorative and special issues up to the gymnastics set of 1952. Many exist canceled to order. Reprints are plentiful and inexpensive. Prices are for original issues. Reprint distinctions are footnoted.

Commemorative issues, beginning in 1949, and special issues, beginning in 1951, bear 4 numbers in lower margin: 1. Issue number. 2. Total of stamps in set. 3. Position of stamp in set. 4. Cumulative number of stamp (usually in parenthesis). A fifth number, the year of issue, was added in 1952.

The numbering system varies at times, with all numbers omitted on Nos. 938-1046.

In certain sets listings include parenthetically the position-in-set number. During some periods these parentheses in listings hold the stamp's cumulative number.

All stamps to the beginning of 1960 were issued without gum, except as noted. After that date, most stamps have gum, which is translucent and almost invisible. All issues are unwatermarked, unless otherwise noted.

100 fen = 1 yuan ($)

Prices fluctuate for most P.R.C. issues, and for Communist Regional issues. Information is inadequate or lacking about quantities printed and issued, existence of large stocks, and possible release of remainders.

Prices quoted represent averages and indicate relative values.

Lantern and Gate of Heavenly Peace — A1

Globe and Hand Holding Hammer — A2

1949, Oct. 8 Litho. *Perf. 12½*

1	A1	$30 blue	1.25	1.50
2	A1	$50 rose red	1.25	1.50
3	A1	$100 green	1.25	1.50
4	A1	$200 maroon	1.25	1.50

First session of Chinese People's Political Conference. See also Nos. 1L121-1L124.

Original

Reprint

Reprints have altered ornament on lantern base. On originals, it is a full oval; in reprints, only a partial circle. Price, set, 50 cents.

1949, Nov. 16

5	A2	$100 carmine	4.00	2.50
6	A2	$300 sl grn	4.00	1.50
7	A2	$500 dk bl	4.00	4.00

Asiatic and Australasian Congress of the World Federation of Trade Unions, Peking.

The $100, imperf., is of dubious status.

See also Nos. 1L133-1L135.

Original

Reprint

Reprints show heavier shading on index finger and thumb. Price, set 75 cents.

Conference Hall, Peking — A3

Mao Tse-tung on Rostrum — A4

1950, Feb. 1 Engr. *Perf. 14*

8	A3	$50 red	3.00	3.00
9	A3	$100 blue	3.00	3.00
10	A4	$300 red brn	3.00	2.00
11	A4	$500 green	3.00	2.00

Chinese People's Political Conference. See also Nos. 1L136-1L139.

Original

Reprint

Nos. 8-9: First character in top inscription shows a square, reprints an oblong.

Nos. 10-11: Originals have heavy cross-hatching and lines which touch back of head and top of rostrum. Reprints have lighter lines which do not touch head or top of rostrum. Reprints, price set $1.25.

Gate of Heavenly Peace (same size) — A5

First Issue: Top line of shading broken at right.

1950, Feb. 10 Litho. *Perf. 12½*

12	A5	$200 green	1.00	1.00
13	A5	$300 brn red	10	30
14	A5	$500 red	15	12
15	A5	$800 orange	11.00	12
16	A5	$1000 dl vio	15	10
17	A5	$2000 olive	1.00	50
18	A5	$5000 brt pink	15	1.00
19	A5	$8000 blue	15	3.00
20	A5	$10,000 brown	15	1.50
		Nos. 12-20 (9)	13.85	7.64

1950, June 9 Typo.

Second Issue: Top line of shading extends to frame line at right.

21	A5	$1000 dl vio	15	10
22	A5	$3000 red brn	15	10
23	A5	$10,000 brown	15	10

中國人民郵政 貳佰圓

1949 Unit Issue of China Surcharged in Blue, Black, Green or Red

1950, Mar. Litho. *Perf. 12½*

24	SD2	$100 on red vio (Bl)	3.00	3.00
a.		Rouletted	20	40
25	R2	$200 on red (Bk)	13.00	2.00
a.		Rouletted	1.75	50
26	AP5	$300 on bl grn (Bk)	20	85
a.		Rouletted	10	75
27	A96	$500 on org (G)	10	30
a.		Perf. 14	90.00	60.00
28	A96	$800 on org (R)	8.00	75
a.		Rouletted	1.75	20
b.		Perf. 14	100.00	60.00
29	A96	$1000 on org (Bk)	5	25
a.		Perf. 14	10	20

Harvesters with Ox — A6

1950, May

30	A6	$20,000 on $10,000 red	200.00	15.00

No. 30 is surcharged on an unissued stamp of East China.

Flag, Mao Tse-tung, Gate of Heavenly Peace — A7

1950, July 1 *Perf. 14*

Yellow Stars

31	A7	$800 grn & red	14.00	2.50
32	A7	$1000 brn & red	14.00	5.00
33	A7	$2000 dk brn & red	14.00	6.00
34	A7	$3000 dk bl & red	14.00	7.00

Inauguration of the People's Republic, Oct. 1, 1949. See also Nos. 1L150-1L153.

Original

Reprint

Originals have a single curved line in jacket button, reprints have an extra dot in button. Price, set $1.50.

中國人民郵政 伍拾圓 ☆ 50

Sun Yat-sen Stamps of Northeastern Provinces Surcharged in Red, Black or Blue

1950, July 1 Engr.

35	A2	$50 on 20c yel grn (R)	50	4.00
36	A2	$50 on 25c blk brn (R)	1.50	1.75
37	A2	$50 on 50c red org (Bk)	15	50
38	A2	$100 on $2.50 ind (R)	35	50
39	A2	$100 on $3 brn (Bk)	6.00	50
40	A2	$100 on $4 org brn, Type II (Bl)	4.00	2.75
a.		Type I	50.00	50.00
41	A2	$100 on $5 dk grn (Bk)	6.00	50
42	A2	$100 on $10 crim, Type II (Bl)	6.00	4.00
a.		Type I	100.00	
43	A2	$400 on $20 ol, Type II (Bl)	6.00	4.00
a.		Type I	125.00	100.00
44	A2	$400 on $44 dk car rose (Bl)	20	2.50
45	A2	$400 on $65 dl grn (R)	25.00	8.00
46	A2	$400 on $100 dp grn (R)	6.00	2.50
47	A2	$400 on $200 rose brn (Bk)	30.00	3.50
48	A2	$400 on $300 bluish grn (R)	30.00	3.50
		Nos. 35-48 (14)	121.70	38.50

中國人民郵政 貳佰圓 ★★ 200

Flying Geese Type of China Surcharged in Red, Blue, Green, Brown or Black

1950, Aug. 1 ***Perf. 12½, Imperf.***

No.	Type	Description	Unused	Used
49	A97	$50 on 10c dk bl (R)	5	25
50	A97	$100 on 16c ol, imperf. (Bl)	5	25
51	A97	$100 on 50c dl grn, imperf. (Bl)	5	12
52	A97	$200 on $1 org (G)	10	12
53	A97	$200 on $2 bl (Br)	2.00	20
54	A97	$400 on $5 car rose (Bk)	15	25
55	A97	$400 on $10 bl grn (Bk)	15	80
56	A97	$400 on $20 pur (Bk)	20	1.00
		Nos. 49-58 (10)	12.75	8.99

Dove of Peace, by Picasso — A8

Chinese Flag and "1" — A9

1950, Aug. 1 **Engr.** ***Perf. 14***

No.	Type	Description	Unused	Used
57	A8	$400 brown	5.00	3.00
58	A8	$800 green	5.00	3.00
59	A8	$2000 blue	5.00	3.00

World Peace Campaign. See also Nos. 1L154-1L156.

Paper of originals appears bright under ultraviolet lamp. That of reprints looks dull. Price, set 75 cents.

1950 **Engr. & Litho.**

Flag in Red & Yellow

No.	Type	Description	Unused	Used
60	A9	$100 purple	8.00	3.50
61	A9	$400 red brn	8.00	6.00
62	A9	$800 green	8.00	3.50
63	A9	$1000 lt ol	8.00	4.00
64	A9	$2000 blue	8.00	6.00
		Nos. 60-64 (5)	40.00	23.00

First anniversary of the Chinese People's Republic. Size of $800: 38x46 mm.; others 26x32 mm.

Issue dates: No. 62, Oct. 1; others Oct. 31. See also Nos. 1L157-1L161.

$800

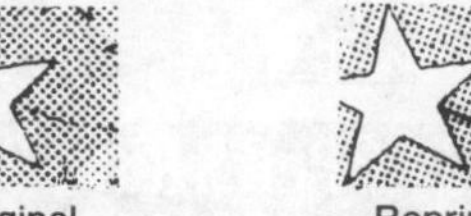

Original Reprint

Reprints are a brighter red, leaves beside "1" are gray brown instead of reddish brown. On the $800 the arrangement of dots in background differs in relationship to large star. Price, set $1.00.

Gate of Heavenly Peace (same size) — A10

"Communication" and Map of China — A11

Third Issue: Cloud almost touches character at upper left. Cloud breaks inner frame line at top.

1950 **Litho.**

No.	Type	Description	Unused	Used
65	A10	$100 lt grnsh bl	40.00	6.75
66	A10	$200 green	140.00	8.50
67	A10	$300 dk car	1.00	*4.25*
68	A10	$400 grnsh gray	40	*4.25*
69	A10	$500 carmine	25	*5.00*
70	A10	$800 orange	2.00	35
71	A10	$2000 gray ol	50	60
		Nos. 65-71 (7)	184.15	29.70

Issue dates: $800, Oct. 8; $500, $2000, Dec. 1; others, Oct. 6.

1950, Nov. 1 **Litho.**

No.	Type	Description	Unused	Used
72	A11	$400 grn & brn	4.00	4.00
73	A11	$800 car & grn	4.00	3.00

First All-China Postal Conference, Peking.

Original Reprint

Originals have 3 lines below horizontal bar between 1st & 2nd character; reprints have four. Price, set 50 cents.

Stalin and Mao Tse-tung — A12

1950, Dec. 1 **Engr.** ***Perf. 14***

No.	Type	Description	Unused	Used
74	A12	$400 red	6.00	4.00
75	A12	$800 dp grn	6.00	3.00
76	A12	$2000 dk bl	6.00	4.00

Signing of Sino-Soviet Treaty of Friendship, Alliance and Mutual Assistance. See also Nos. 1L176-1L178.

Paper of originals appears bright under ultraviolet lamp. That of reprints looks dull. Price, set $1.50.

East China Issue of 1949 Surcharged in Red, Black, Brown or Blue

Train and Postal Runner — A12a

1950, Dec. **Litho.** ***Perf. 12½***

No.	Type	Description	Unused	Used
77	A12a	$50 on $10 dp ultra (R)	5	10
78	A12a	$100 on $15 org ver (Bk)	6	10
a.		$100 on $15 red (Bk), perf. 14	10	10
79	A12a	$300 on $50 car (Bk)	5	20
80	A12a	$400 on $1600 vio bl (Br)	50	15
81	A12a	$400 on $2000 brn vio (Bl)	20	15
		Nos. 77-81 (5)	86	70

East China Issue of 1949 Surcharged in Red or Black

Chairman Mao — A12b

1950, Dec.

No.	Type	Description	Unused	Used
82	A12b	$50 on $10 ultra (R)	15	10
83	A12b	$400 on $15 ver (Bk)	15	10
84	A12b	$400 on $2000 grn (Bk)	75	10

(same size) — A13

(same size) — A14

Fourth Issue: Similar to 3rd issue, but large cloud does not break inner frame line at top.

1950-51 **Litho.**

No.	Type	Description	Unused	Used
85	A13	$100 lt bl	1.00	1.00
86	A13	$200 dl grn	1.20	1.20
87	A13	$300 dl lil	25	*7.00*
88	A13	$400 gray grn	25	1.00
89	A13	$500 carmine	5	*1.50*
90	A13	$800 orange	40.00	1.25
a.		Imperf., pair	*1,200.*	
91	A13	$1000 violet	35	1.00
92	A13	$2000 olive	120.00	4.00
93	A13	$3000 brown	5	*8.00*
94	A13	$5000 pink	5	*8.00*
		Nos. 85-94 (10)	163.20	33.95

Issue dates: $200, $300, $500, $800, $2000, $5000, Dec. 22, 1950; others June 8, 1951.

1951, Jan. 18 **Engr.** ***Perf. 14***

Fifth Issue: Colored network on surface in salmon.

No.	Type	Description	Unused	Used
95	A14	$10,000 brown	50	*10.00*
96	A14	$20,000 olive	50	*7.50*
97	A14	$30,000 green	12.00	*15.00*
98	A14	$50,000 violet	45.00	12.50
99	A14	$100,000 scarlet	950.00	75.00
100	A14	$200,000 blue	950.00	75.00
		Nos. 95-100 (6)	1,958.	195.00

Unit Issue of China Surcharged

中國人民郵政
伍
圓

5

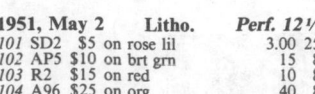

1951, May 2 **Litho.** ***Perf. 12½***

No.	Type	Description	Unused	Used
101	SD2	$5 on rose lil	3.00	25
102	AP5	$10 on brt grn	15	8
103	R2	$15 on red	10	8
104	A96	$25 on org	40	8

Issued for use in Northeast China, but available for use throughout China. Nos. 101-104 rouletted were sold for philatelic purposes only. Price, set $1.25

Chairman Mao Tse-tung — A15

1951, July 1 **Engr.** ***Perf. 14***

No.	Type	Description	Unused	Used
105	A15	$400 chestnut	2.50	1.50
106	A15	$500 dp grn	2.50	1.50
107	A15	$800 crimson	2.50	1.50

30th anniversary of the Chinese Communist Party.

Reprints are on whiter, thinner and harder paper. Price, set 60 cents.

Picasso Dove — A16

1951, Aug. 15 ***Perf. 12½***

No.	Type	Description	Unused	Used
108	A16	$400 org brn	4.50	2.50
109	A16	$800 bl grn	4.50	1.50
110	A16	$1000 dl vio	4.50	2.50

Reprints are perf. 14. Price, set $1.50.

Remittance Stamp of China Surcharged in Carmine or Black

(same size) — A17

Engraved, Commercial Press

1951, Sept. ***Perf. 12½***

No.	Type	Description	Unused	Used
111	A17	$50 on $2 bl grn (C)	20	75

Typographed Kang Hwa Printing Co.

Roul. 9½

No.	Type	Description	Unused	Used
112	A17	$50 on $2 gray bl (C)	50	75
113	A17	$50 on $5 red org (Bk)	5	75
114	A17	$50 on $50 gray (C)	4.75	75

Lithographed, Central Trust Co.

Perf. 13

No.	Type	Description	Unused	Used
115	A17	$50 on $50 gray blk (C)	5	75

Lithographed, Chung Hwa Book Co.

Perf. 11½

No.	Type	Description	Unused	Used
116	A17	$50 on $50 gray (C)	1.75	75
a.		Perf. 11½x10	50	50
		Nos. 111-116 (6)	7.30	4.50

National Emblem — A18

Engraved; Background Network Lithographed in Yellow.

1951, Oct. 1 ***Perf. 14***

No.	Type	Description	Unused	Used
117	A18	$100 Prus bl	4.50	2.00
118	A18	$200 brown	4.50	1.50

119 A18 $400 orange 4.50 2.00
120 A18 $500 green 4.50 1.50
121 A18 $800 carmine 4.50 1.50
Nos. 117-121 (5) 22.50 8.50

Reprints exist but difficult to distinguish; paper whiter, and colors slightly brighter. Price, set $1.

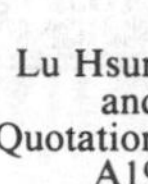

Lu Hsun and Quotation A19

1951, Oct. 19 Litho. *Perf. 12½*
122 A19 $400 lilac 4.00 3.00
123 A19 $800 green 4.00 3.00

15th anniversary of the death of Lu Hsun (1881-1936), writer.

Original

Reprint

Reprints have dot in triangle at lower right; no dot in original. Price, set, 30 cents.

Peasant Uprising, Chintien — A20

Design: Nos. 126-127, Coin of Taiping Regime and decrees of peasant government.

1951, Dec. 15 Engr. *Perf. 14*
124 A20 $400 green 5.00 2.00
125 A20 $800 scarlet 5.00 2.00
126 A20 $800 orange 5.00 2.00
127 A20 $1000 dp bl 5.00 3.00

Centenary of Taiping Peasant Rebellion.

Original

Reprint

Reprints of Nos. 124-125 have additional short stroke at upper left.

Original

Reprint

Reprints of Nos. 126-127 have two short strokes on scale near tail of right dragon on coin. Price, Nos. 124-127, 50 cents.

Old and New Methods of Agriculture — A21

1952, Jan. 1
128 A21 $100 scarlet 3.00 3.00
129 A21 $200 brt bl 3.00 3.00
130 A21 $400 dp brn 3.00 2.00
131 A21 $800 green 3.00 2.00

Agrarian reform.

Original

Reprint

One short horizontal line between legs of plower; 2 lines in reprints. Price, set 50 cents.

Potala Monastery, Lhasa A22

Designs: Nos. 134-135, Farmer plowing with yaks.

1952, Mar. 15 *Perf. 12½*
132 A22 $400 vermilion 4.00 3.00
133 A22 $800 claret 4.00 3.00
134 A22 $800 bl grn 4.00 2.00
135 A22 $1000 dl vio 4.00 2.00

Liberation of Tibet.

Reprints, perf. 14, have a small Chinese character at lower left of the vignette which is missing in the original.
Price, set 50 cents.

Children of Four Races — A23

Hammer and Sickle on Numeral 1 — A24

1952, Apr. 12 Litho.
136 A23 $400 dl grn 15 5
137 A23 $800 vio bl 15 5

International Child Protection Conference, Vienna.

1952, May 1

Designs: No. 139, Dove rising from worker's hand. No. 140, Dove, hammer, wheat and chimneys.

138 A24 $800 scarlet 5 5
139 A24 $800 bl grn 5 5
140 A24 $800 org brn 20 5

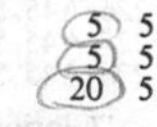

Labor Day.

Physical Exercises A25

Stamps printed in blocks of four for each color, each block representing a specific setting-up exercise; exercises coincided with a national radio program. Where exercise positions are identical within the block, the serial number (in parenthesis) is the only means of differentiation.

1952, June 20
141 A25 $400 ver, blk. of 4 15.00 15.00
  a. Right arm forward (1) 2.00 1.00
  b. Left arm forward (2) 2.00 1.00
  c. as "a" (3) 2.00 1.00
  d. as "b" (4) 2.00 1.00
142 A25 $400 bl, blk. of 4 15.00 15.00
  a. Arms outstretched (5) 2.00 1.00
  b. Knee-bend (6) 2.00 1.00
  c. as "a" (7) 2.00 1.00
  d. Rest (8) 2.00 1.00
143 A25 $400 brn red, blk. of 4 15.00 15.00
  a. Arms forward (9) 2.00 1.00
  b. Arms outstretched (10) 2.00 1.00
  c. as "b" (11) 2.00 1.00
  d. Rest (12) 2.00 1.00
144 A25 $400 yel grn, blk. of 4 15.00 15.00
  a. Arms outstretched (13) 2.00 1.00
  b. Sideways bend (14) 2.00 1.00
  c. as "a" (15) 2.00 1.00
  d. Hands on hips (16) 2.00 1.00
145 A25 $400 red org, blk. of 4 15.00 15.00
  a. as 144a (17) 2.00 1.00
  b. Alternate toe touch (18) 2.00 1.00
  c. as "a" (19) 2.00 1.00
  d. Rest (20) 2.00 1.00
146 A25 $400 dl bl, blk. of 4 15.00 15.00
  a. Stretch (21) 2.00 1.00
  b. Toe touch (22) 2.00 1.00
  c. Hands on floor (23) 2.00 1.00
  d. Rest (24) 2.00 1.00
147 A25 $400 org, block of 4 15.00 15.00
  a. Leg forward (25) 2.00 1.00
  b. Leg extended back (26) 2.00 1.00
  c. as "a" (27) 2.00 1.00
  d. Rest (28) 2.00 1.00
148 A25 $400 dl pur, block of 4 15.00 15.00
  a. Jumping jack (29) 2.00 1.00
  b. Rest (30) 2.00 1.00
  c. as "a" (31) 2.00 1.00
  d. as "b" (32) 2.00 1.00
149 A25 $400 yel bis, blk. of 4 15.00 15.00
  a. Left leg raised (33) 2.00 1.00
  b. Hands on hips (34) 2.00 1.00
  c. Right leg raised (35) 2.00 1.00
  d. as "b" (36) 2.00 1.00
150 A25 $400 sky bl, blk. of 4 15.00 15.00
  a. Arms raised forward (37) 2.00 1.00
  b. Arms above head (38) 2.00 1.00
  c. Arms outstretched (39) 2.00 1.00
  d. Rest (40) 2.00 1.00
Nos. 141-150 (10) 150.00 150.00

Originals are on thin gray paper, colors darker. Reprints on thicker white paper, colors brighter. Price, set $7.

Hunting, Wei Dynasty, A.D. 386-580 A26

Designs from Murals in Cave Temples at Tunhuang, Kansu Province: No. 152, Lady attendants, Sui Dynasty, 581-617 A.D. No. 153, Gandharvas (mythology), Tang Dynasty, 618-906. No. 154, Dragon, Tang Dynasty.

1952, July 1 Engr.
151 A26 $800 sl grn (1) 12 6
152 A26 $800 choc (2) 12 6
153 A26 $800 ind (3) 12 6
154 A26 $800 blk (4) 12 6

"Glorious Mother Country," 1st series.

Marco Polo Bridge, near Peking A27

Designs: No. 156, Cavalry passing through Great Wall. No. 157, Departure of New Fourth Army. No. 158, Mao Tse-tung and Gen. Chu Teh planning counter-attack.

1952, July 7 Litho. *Perf. 14*
155 A27 $800 brt bl 10 6
156 A27 $800 bl grn 20 6
157 A27 $800 plum 10 6
158 A27 $800 scarlet 5 6

15th anniversary of war against Japan.

Soldier and Tanks A28

Designs: No. 159, Soldier, sailor and airman (vert.). No. 161, Sailor and warships. No. 162, Airman and planes.

1952, Aug. 1 Engr. *Perf. 12½*
159 A28 $800 carmine 10 6
160 A28 $800 dp grn 20 6
161 A28 $800 purple 10 6
162 A28 $800 org brn 10 6

25th anniversary of People's Liberation Army.

Huai River Sluice Dam A29

Designs: No. 164, Train on the Chengtu-Chungking Railway. No. 165, Oil refinery and derricks in the Northwest. No. 166, Mechanized state farm.

1952, Oct. 1 *Perf. 14*
163 A29 $800 dk vio 10 6
164 A29 $800 red 10 6
165 A29 $800 dk vio brn 10 6
166 A29 $800 dp grn 10 6

"Glorious Mother Country," 2nd series.

Doves and Globe A30

Designs: Nos. 167-168, Picasso dove over Pacific (vert.). $2500, as No. 169.

1952, Oct. 2 *Perf. 14*
167 A30 $400 maroon 10 5
168 A30 $800 red 10 5
169 A30 $800 brn org 10 6
170 A30 $2500 dp grn 20 15

Peace Conference of the Asian and Pacific Regions.

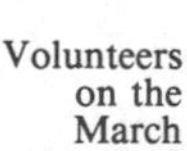

Volunteers on the March A31

Designs: No. 172, Chinese peasants loading supplies. No. 173, Volunteers attacking across river. No. 174, Meeting of Chinese and Korean troops.

1952, Oct. 25
171 A31 $800 bl grn (1) 10 6
172 A31 $800 ver (2) 10 6
173 A31 $800 vio (3) 15 6
174 A31 $800 lake brn (4) 20 6

2nd anniversary of Chinese Volunteers in Korea.

Woman Textile Worker A32

Design: No. 176, Farm woman with sickle.

1953, Mar. 10

175 A32 $800 carmine 12 10
176 A32 $800 emerald 15 10

International Women's Day.

Textile Worker A33

Karl Marx A34

Designs: $200, Shepherdess. $250, Stone lion. $800, Lathe operator. $1600, Coal miners. $2000, Corner tower of Forbidden City, Peking.

1953 Litho. *Perf. 14; 12½ ($250)*

177 A33 $50 magenta 10 8
178 A33 $200 emerald 8 10
179 A33 $250 ultra 60 10
180 A33 $800 bl grn 5 6
181 A33 $1600 gray 10 25
182 A33 $2000 red org 5 15
Nos. 177-182 (6) 98 74

Issue dates: Nos. 177-181, Mar. 25; No. 182, May 23.

1953, May 20 Engr. *Perf. 14*

183 A34 $400 dk brn 10 8
184 A34 $800 sl grn 20 8

135th anniversary of the birth of Karl Marx (1818-1883).

Workers and Banners — A35

1953, June 25

185 A35 $400 Prus bl 15 5
186 A35 $800 carmine 10 5

7th All-China Trade Union Congress.

Picasso Dove — A36

1953, July 25

187 A36 $250 bl grn 20 8
188 A36 $400 org brn 10 10
189 A36 $800 purple 15 12

World Peace.

Groom, Wei Dynasty, 386-580 A37

Scenes from Tunhuang Murals: No. 191, Court Players, Wei Dynasty. No. 192, Battle Scene, Sui Dynasty, 581-617. No. 193, Oxdrawn palanquin, Tang Dynasty, 618-906.

1953, Sept. 1

190 A37 $800 dp grn (1) 25 6
191 A37 $800 red org (2) 5 6
192 A37 $800 Prus bl (3) 12 6
193 A37 $800 car (4) 5 6

"Glorious Mother Country," 3rd series.

Stalin and Mao on Kremlin Terrace A38

Statue of Stalin at Volga-Don Canal — A39

Designs: No. 195, Lenin proclaiming Soviet power. No. 197, Stalin as orator.

1953, Oct. 5

194 A38 $800 grn (1) 30 8
195 A38 $800 car (2) 15 8
196 A39 $800 brt bl (3) 12 8
197 A39 $800 org brn (4) 10 8

35th anniversary of the Russian October Revolution.

Stamps in same designs with two additional characters meaning "Soviet" in the single-line Chinese inscription, and in different colors, were unofficially released at several small post offices in Hunan, Fukien and Canton areas in February, 1953, but were withdrawn after only a small number had been sold. Price, set $3500 unused, $2000 canceled.

Compass, 3rd Century B.C. — A40

Designs: No. 199, Seismoscope, later Han Dynasty. No. 200, Drum cart to measure distance, Chin Dynasty. No. 201, Armillary sphere, Ming Dynasty.

1953, Dec. 1

198 A40 $800 ind (1) 18 6
199 A40 $800 dk grn (2) 5 6
200 A40 $800 dk sl grn (3) 10 6
201 A40 $800 choc (4) 10 6

Major inventions by ancient and medieval Chinese scientists.

"Glorious Mother Country," 4th series.

Francois Rabelais A41

(same size) Gate of Heavenly Peace A42

Designs: $400, José Marti, Cuban revolutionary. $800, Chu Yuan (350-275 B.C.), philosopher. $2200, Nicolaus Copernicus, astronomer.

1953, Dec. 30

202 A41 $250 sl grn (3) 10 5
203 A41 $400 brn blk (4) 10 5
204 A41 $800 ind (1) 10 5
205 A41 $2200 choc (2) 10 10

1954, April 16 Litho.

Sixth Issue: Inscription at upper right.

206 A42 $50 carmine 5 5
207 A42 $100 lt bl 5 6
208 A42 $200 green 5 6
209 A42 $250 ultra 75 8
210 A42 $400 gray grn 5 8
211 A42 $800 orange 5 6
212 A42 $1600 gray 5 40
213 A42 $2000 olive 5 20
Nos. 206-213 (8) 1.10 99

Textile Plant, Harbin — A43

Lenin — A44

1954, May 1 Engr.

Designs: $200, Tangku Harbor. $250, Tienshui-Lanchow railroad bridge, Kansu Province. $400, Heavy machine-building plant, Taiyuan, Shansi. No. 218, Automatic blast, furnace, Anshan, Manchuria. No. 219, Fushun open-cut coal mine. $2000, Automatic power plant, Northeast. $3200, Prospecting in Tayeh district, Hupeh.

214 A43 $100 brn ol 10 5
215 A43 $200 bl grn 10 5
216 A43 $250 violet 5 5
217 A43 $400 black 10 5
218 A43 $800 claret 5 5
219 A43 $800 indigo 5 5
220 A43 $2000 red 5 15
221 A43 $3200 dk brn 15 25
Nos. 214-221 (8) 65 70

Economic progress.

1954, June 30 Engr.

Designs: $400, Lenin and Stalin Monument, Gorki (horiz.). $2000, Lenin proclaiming Soviet power.

222 A44 $400 dp grn 10 8
223 A44 $800 dk brn 5 12
224 A44 $2000 dp car 40 12

30th anniversary of the death of Lenin.

Pottery Vessels, Neolithic Period, 2000 B. C. — A45

Archeological Treasures: No. 226, Stone clime, Shang Dynasty, c. 1200 B.C. No. 227, Kuo Chi Tsu-pai bronze basin, Middle Chou Dynasty, 816 B.C. No. 228, Lacquered box and wine cup, Warring States Period, 403-221 B.C.

1954, Aug. 25

225 A45 $800 brown 10 6
226 A45 $800 indigo 10 6
227 A45 $800 Prus bl 10 6
228 A45 $800 dk car 10 6

"Glorious Mother Country," 5th series.

Pipe Production, Anshan Steel Mill — A46

Stalin Statue, by Tomsky — A47

Design: $800, Rolling mill, Anshan.

1954, Oct. 1

229 A46 $400 Prus grn 30 15
230 A46 $800 vio brn 30 15

1954, Oct. 15

Designs: $800, Stalin portrait. $2000, Stalin viewing hydroelectric plant.

Size: 21x45mm.

231 A47 $400 black 40 12

Size: 26x37mm.

232 A47 $800 blk brn 10 12

Size: 42x26mm.

233 A47 $2000 dp red 10 12

First anniversary of the death of Stalin.

Exhibition Building, Peking — A48

1954, Nov. 7

234 A48 $800 brn, *cr* 6.50 3.00

Russian Economic and Cultural Exhibition, Peking. No. 234 measures 52½x24½mm. It also exists 53½x24mm.

Apprentices and Lathe A49

Design: $800, Heavy machinery and workers.

1954, Dec. 15

235 A49 $400 dk ol grn 15 10
236 A49 $800 brt red 10 10

Progress in technology.

Woman Worker Voting — A50

People Celebrating Opening of Congress — A51

1954, Dec. 30
237 A50 $400 dp cl 5 12
238 A51 $800 brt red 15 10

First National Congress.

Flags, Worker and Woman Holding Constitution — A52

1954, Dec. 30
239 A52 $400 brn, *buff* 15 7
240 A52 $800 brt red, *yel* 15 10

Adoption of Constitution.

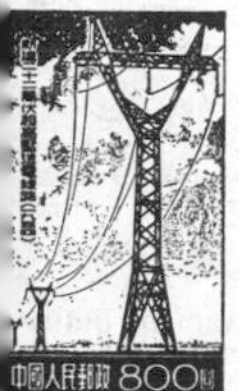
High-tension Pylon — A53

1955, Feb. 25
241 A53 $800 dk Prus bl 25 15

Development of electric power.

Factory Health Workers and Red Cross A54

Engraved; Cross Typographed

1955, June 25
242 A54 8f dp grn & red 9.50 30

50th anniversary of Chinese Red Cross.

Stalin and Mao in Kremlin A55

Soviet Specialist and Chinese Worker — A56

1955, July 25 **Engr.**
243 A55 8f brn red 6.00 15
244 A56 20f ol blk 6.00 40

5th anniversary of Sino-Soviet Friendship Treaty.

Demand, as well as supply, determines a stamp's market value. One is as important as the other.

Chang Heng (78-139), Astronomer — A57

Portraits of Scientists: No. 246, Tsu Chung-chih (429-500), mathematician. No. 247, Chang Sui (683-727), astronomer. No. 248, Li Shih-chen (1518-1593), physician and pharmacologist.

1955, Aug. 25 ***Perf. 14***
245 A57 8f sep, *buff* 40 5
a. Min. sheet, sep, *white* 2.50 1.00
246 A57 8f dp grn, *buff* 40 5
a. Min. sheet, dp grn, *white* 2.50 1.00
247 A57 8f blk, *buff* 40 5
a. Min. sheet, blk, *white* 2.50 1.00
248 A57 8f cl, *buff* 40 5
a. Min. sheet, cl, *white* 2.50 1.00

Miniature sheets contain one imperf. stamp each. Size: 63x90mm.

Steel Pouring Ladle A58

1955-56 **Litho.**

Bluish Black Frames, Multicolored Centers.

Position-in-set number in ( ).

249 A58 8f *shown* (1) 25 5
250 A58 8f *High tension line* (2) 25 5
251 A58 8f *Mechanized coal mining* (3) 25 5
252 A58 8f *Tank cars and derricks* (4) 25 5
253 A58 8f *Heavy machine shop* (5) 25 5
254 A58 8f *Soldier on guard* (6) 25 5
255 A58 8f *Spinning machine* (7) 25 5
256 A58 8f *Workers discussing 5-year plan* (8) 25 5
257 A58 8f *Combine harvester* (9) 25 5
258 A58 8f *Milk production* (10) 25 5
259 A58 8f *Dam* (11) 25 5
260 A58 8f *Pottery industry* (12) ('56) 25 5
261 A58 8f *Truck* (13) 25 5
262 A58 8f *Ship at dock* (14) 25 5
263 A58 8f *Geological survey* (15) 25 5
264 A58 8f *Higher education* (16) 25 5
265 A58 8f *Family* (17) 25 5
266 A58 8f *Workers' rest home* (18) ('56) 25 5
Nos. 249-266 (18) 4.50 90

First Five Year Plan. Issue dates: Nos. 249-257, Oct. 1, 1955; Nos. 258-259, 261-265, Dec. 15, 1955; Nos. 260, 266, Feb. 24, 1956.

Lenin — A59

Engels — A60

1955, Dec. 15 **Engr.** ***Perf. 14***
267 A59 8f dk bl grn 4.50 10
268 A59 20f dk rose car 4.50 1.25

85th anniversary of the birth of Lenin.

1955, Dec. 15
269 A60 8f dp org 4.50 10
270 A60 20f brown 4.50 1.25

135th anniversary of the birth of Friedrich Engels (1820-1895), German socialist.

Storming Lu Ting Bridge A61

Crossing Great Snow Mountains — A62

1955, Dec. 30
271 A61 8f dk red 4.00 25
272 A62 8f dk bl 4.00 75

Long March of Chinese Communist army, 20th anniversary.

Miner A63

Gate of Heavenly Peace A64

Designs: 1f, Machinist. 2f, Airman. 2½f, Nurse. 4f, Soldier. 8f, Steel worker. 10f, Scientist. 20f, Farm woman. 50f, Sailor.

1955-56 **Litho.** ***Perf. 14***
273 A63 ½f org brn 3.00 5
274 A63 1f purple 3.00 10
275 A63 2f green 3.00 5
276 A63 2½f bl ('56) 3.00 5
277 A63 4f gray ol 3.00 10
278 A63 8f red org (Peking printing) 3.00 35
a. Perf. 12½ (Shanghai printing) 90.00 20.00
279 A63 10f cl ('56) 22.50 5
280 A63 20f dp bl 4.50 5
281 A63 50f gray 4.50 5
Nos. 273-281 (9) 49.50 85

Engr.

282 A64 $1 cl ('56) 1.25 25
283 A64 $2 sep ('55) 2.25 25
284 A64 $5 ind ('56) 5.75 40
285 A64 $10 dp org ('56) 12.00 4.00
286 A64 $20 gray vio ('56) 22.50 16.00
Nos. 282-286 (5) 43.75 20.90

Nos. 282-286 are the 7th Gate Issue.

Trucks, Mountains, Highway Map — A65

Suspension Bridge over Tatu River — A66

Design: No. 289, First truck arriving in Lhasa, and the Potala.

1956, Mar. 10 **Engr.**
287 A65 4f dp bl 40 10
288 A66 8f dk brn 40 10
289 A65 8f carmine 40 10

Completion of Sikang-Tibet and Chinghai-Tibet Highways.

Summer Palace and Marble Boat — A67

Famous Views of Imperial Peking: No. 291, Peihai Park with Jade Belt Marble Bridge. No. 292, Gate of Heavenly Peace. No. 293, Temple of Heaven. No. 294, Great Throne Hall, Forbidden City.

1956-57
290 A67 4f car rose (1) 50 10
291 A67 4f bl grn (2) 50 10
292 A67 8f red org (3) ('57) 50 10
293 A67 8f Prus bl (4) 50 10
294 A67 8f yel brn (5) 50 10
Nos. 290-294 (5) 2.50 50

Issue dates: No. 292, Feb. 20, 1957; others, June 15, 1956.
No. 292 exists with sun rays in background.

Salt Making A68

Designs: No. 296, Dwelling of the Eastern Han period. No. 297, Duck hunting and harvesting. No. 298, Carriage crossing bridge.

1956, Oct. 1
295 A68 4f gray ol 15 5
296 A68 4f sl bl 15 5
297 A68 8f gray brn 15 5
298 A68 8f sepia 15 5

Murals, Tung Han Dynasty, 250 B.C.-220 A.D., found near Chengtu.

Ancient Coins and "Save" A69

1956, Oct. 1
299 A69 4f yel brn 3.00 12
300 A69 8f rose red 3.00 12

Promotion of saving.

Gate of Heavenly Peace — A70

Sun Yat-sen — A71

1956, Nov. 10
301 A70 4f dk grn 3.25 10
302 A70 8f brt red 3.25 10
303 A70 16f dk car 3.25 20

8th National Congress of the Communist Party of China.

1956, Nov. 12
304 A71 4f brn, *cr* 4.50 5
305 A71 8f dp bl, *cr* 4.50 80

90th anniversary of birth of Sun Yat-sen.

Weight Lifting — A72

Designs: No. 306, Shot put. No. 308, Track. No. 309, Soccer. No. 310, Bicycling.

1957, Mar. 20 Litho. *Perf. 12½*

Hibiscus red and green; inscription in brown.

306	A72	4f dp car (2)	30	5
307	A72	4f red lil (5)	30	5
308	A72	8f dk bl grn (1)	30	5
309	A72	8f dp bl (3)	30	5
310	A72	8f dp yel brn (4)	30	5
		Nos. 306-310 (5)	1.50	25

First National Workers' Sports Meeting.

Truck Factory No. 1, Changchun — A73

Designs: 8f, Trucks rolling off assembly line.

1957, May 1 Engr. *Perf. 14*

311	A73	4f lt brn	20	5
312	A73	8f sl grn	20	5

China's truck industry.

Nanchang Uprising — A74

Designs: No. 314, Mao and Chu Teh at Chingkanshan. No. 315, Crossing Yellow River. No. 316, Liberation of Nanking, Apr. 23, 1949.

1957

313	A74	4f blk vio (1)	3.50	15
314	A74	4f sl grn (2)	3.50	25
315	A74	8f red brn (3)	3.50	10
316	A74	8f dp bl (4)	3.50	10

30th anniversary of People's Liberation Army. Issue dates: Nos. 313, 315, Aug. 10; No. 314, Aug. 30; No. 316, Dec. 30.

Congress Emblem — A75

1957, Sept. 30

317	A75	8f chocolate	3.75	12
318	A75	22f indigo	3.75	20

4th International Trade Union Congress, Leipzig, Oct. 4-15.

Yangtze River Bridge A76

Design: 20f, Road leading to and over bridge.

1957, Oct. 1

319	A76	8f scarlet	30	10
320	A76	20f sl bl	30	5

Completion of Yangtze River Bridge at Wuhan.

Fireworks over Kremlin — A77

Designs: 8f, Hammer and sickle over globe and broken chain. 20f, Stylized dove and olive branch. 22f, Hands of three races holding book with Marx and Lenin. 32f, Star and pylon.

1957, Nov. 7

321	A77	4f brt red	4.00	10
322	A77	8f chocolate	4.00	10
323	A77	20f dp grn	4.00	10
324	A77	22f red brn	4.00	10
325	A77	32f dp bl	4.00	75
		Nos. 321-325 (5)	20.00	1.15

40th anniversary of Russian October Revolution.

Map of Yellow River Basin A78

Designs: No. 327, Sanmen Gorge dam and powerhouse. No. 328, Ocean liner on Yellow River. No. 329, Dam, irrigation canals and tree-bordered fields.

1957, Dec. 30

326	A78	4f dp org (1)	3.50	20
327	A78	4f dp bl (2)	3.50	25
328	A78	8f dp lake (3)	3.50	10
329	A78	8f bl grn (4)	3.50	10

Yellow River control plan.

Old Man and Young Drummer A79

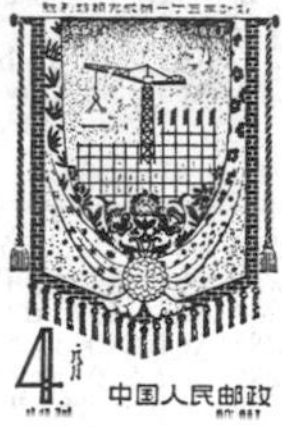

Crane, Dove and Flowers A80

1957, Dec. 30 Litho.

330	A79	8f *shown* (1)	20	10
331	A79	8f *Plowman* (2)	20	5
332	A79	8f *Woman planting tree* (3)	20	5
333	A79	8f *Harvest* (4)	20	5

Agricultural cooperation.

1958, Jan. 30 Engr.

Designs (Congratulatory Banner and): 8f, Crane with hot ingots, cotton bolls and wheat. 16f, Train on bridge, ship and plane.

334	A80	4f emer, *cr*	25	5
335	A80	8f red, *cr*	25	10
336	A80	16f ultra, *cr*	25	5

Fulfillment of First Five-Year Plan.

Sungyu Pagoda, Honan — A81

Trilobite, Kaoli — A82

Ancient Pagodas: No. 338, Chienhsun Pagoda, Yunnan. No. 339, Sakyamuni Pagoda, Shansi. No. 340, Flying Rainbow Pagoda, Shansi.

1958, Mar. 15 Engr.

337	A81	8f sep (1)	30	5
338	A81	8f Prus bl (2)	30	5
339	A81	8f mar (3)	30	5
340	A81	8f dp grn (4)	30	10

1958, Apr. 15

Designs: 8f, Lufeng dinosaur. 16f, Choukoutien sino-megaceros.

341	A82	4f black	25	8
342	A82	8f sepia	25	12
343	A82	16f sl grn	25	8

Prehistoric animals of China.

Heroes Monument A83

1958, May 1

344	A83	8f scarlet	7.50	80
	a.	Souvenir sheet	16.00	9.00

Unveiling of People's Heroes Monument, Peking. No. 344a contains one imperf. stamp, scarlet marginal inscription. Size: 87x137mm. Issued May 30.

Karl Marx — A84

Cogwheels and Factories — A85

Design: 22f, Marx Speaking to German Workers' Educational Association, London, painting by Zhukow.

1958, May 5

345	A84	8f chocolate	6.00	30
346	A84	22f dk grn	6.00	60

140th anniversary of the birth of Karl Marx (1818-1883).

1958, May 25

347	A85	4f brt grnsh bl	6.00	*3.00*
348	A85	8f red lil	6.00	75

8th All-China Trade Union Congress, Peking.

Dove over Globe — A86

Mother and Child — A87

1958, June 1

349	A86	8f vio bl	6.00	10
350	A86	20f bl grn	6.00	1.50

4th Congress of the International Democratic Women's Federation, Vienna, Austria June 1958.

1958, June 1 Litho.

Designs (Children): No. 352, Watering sunflowers. No. 353, Playing hide-and-seek. No. 354, Sailing toy boat.

351	A87	8f grn & multi (1)	3.75	25
352	A87	8f grn & multi (2)	3.75	25
353	A87	8f grn & multi (3)	3.75	25
354	A87	8f grn & multi (4)	3.75	25

Children's Day.

Kuan Han-ching — A88

Designs (Operas): 4f, "Dream of Butterflies." 20f, "The Riverside Pavilion."

1958, June 20 Engr.

355	A88	4f ind, *cr*	6.00	*1.00*
356	A88	8f brn, *cr*	6.00	25
357	A88	20f blk, *cr*	6.00	35
	a.	Souvenir sheet of 3, *white*	125.00	35.00

700th anniversary of publication of works of Kuan Han-ching (1210-1280), dramatist. No. 357a contains 3 imperf. stamps similar to Nos. 355-357. Dark brown marginal inscription. Size: 130x100mm. Issued June 28.

Planetarium A89

Design: 20f, Telescope and stars over Peking.

1958, June 25

358	A89	8f dk grn	5.25	15
359	A89	20fr indigo	5.25	35

First Chinese planetarium, Peking.

Marx and Engels — A90

Wild Goose and Broadcasting Tower — A91

Design: 8f, Cover of first edition of the Communist Manifesto.

1958, July 1

360	A90	4f dk red vio	4.75	1.75
361	A90	8f Prus bl	4.75	15

110th anniversary of publication of the Communist Manifesto.

1958, July 10

362	A91	4f ultra	4.75	15
363	A91	8f dp grn	4.75	60

1st Conference of the Ministers of Posts and Telecommunications of Socialist Countries, Moscow, Dec. 3-17, 1957.

Peony and Doves — A92

Bronze Weather Vane — A93

Designs: 8f, Olive branch with ribbon and clouds. 22f, Atomic energy symbol over factories.

1958, July 20

364	A92	4f red	8.25	1.00
365	A92	8f green	8.25	9.00
366	A92	22f red brn	8.25	3.00

Congress for Disarmament and International Cooperation, Stockholm, July 17-22.

1958, Aug. 25

Designs: No. 368, Weather balloon. No. 369, Typhoon tower and weather map of Asia.

367	A93	8f yel bis & blk (1)	30	10
368	A93	8f bl & blk (2)	30	10
369	A93	8f brt grn & blk (3)	30	10

Meteorological services in ancient and modern China.

"5" Encircling IUS Emblem — A94

1958, Sept. 4

370	A94	8f rose lil	6.00	15
371	A94	22f dp bl grn	6.00	35

5th Congress of the International Union of Students, Peking, Sept. 4-13.

Telegraph Building, Peking — A95

1958, Sept. 29

372	A95	4f grnsh blk	50	8
373	A95	8f rose red	50	8

Opening of Telegraph Building, Peking.

Exhibition Emblem and Exhortation A96

Designs: No. 375, Dragon over clouds signifying "aiming high." No. 376, Flying horses, signifying "great leap forward" in production.

1958, Oct. 1

374	A96	8f sl grn (1)	5.00	15
375	A96	8f rose car (2)	5.00	15
376	A96	8f red brn (3)	5.00	60

National Exhibition of Industry and Communications, Peking.

The only foreign revenue stamps listed in this Catalogue are those authorized for prepayment of postage.

Worker and Excavator A97

Design: 8f, Completed dam and pylon.

1958, Oct. 25

377	A97	4f dk brn	15	10
378	A97	8f dp Prus bl	25	5

Completion of the 13 Ming Tombs Reservoir.

Sputnik over Armillary Sphere — A98

Designs: 8f, Sputnik 3 in orbit. 10f, Trajectories of 3 Sputniks over earth.

1958, Oct. 30

379	A98	4f scarlet	2.00	10
380	A98	8f dp vio bl	2.00	10
381	A98	10f dp grn	2.00	60

Anniversary of first earth satellite launched by the USSR.

Chinese and North Korean Soldiers A99

Designs: No. 383, Chinese soldier embracing Korean woman. No. 384, Chinese girl presenting flowers to returning soldier.

1958, Nov. 20

382	A99	8f brt pur (1)	40	20
383	A99	8f chnt (2)	40	10
384	A99	8f rose car (3)	40	10

Return of the Chinese Volunteers from Korea.

Forest and Mountains A100

Peony A101

Designs: No. 386, Mounted forest patrol No. 387, Mechanized lumbering (horiz.). No. 388, Tree-planting: "Turning the Country Green" (horiz.).

1958, Dec. 15

385	A100	8f dp bl grn (1)	85	30
386	A100	8f sl grn (2)	85	10
387	A100	8f dk pur (3)	85	10
388	A100	8f ind (4)	85	20

Afforestation.

1958, Sept. 25 **Litho.**

Designs: 3f, Lotus. 5f, Chrysanthemums.

389	A101	1½f lil rose	5.00	15
390	A101	3f bl grn	5.00	50
391	A101	5f dp org	5.00	5

Atomic Reactor A102

Design: 20f, Cyclotron.

1958, Dec. 30 **Engr.**

392	A102	8f dp bl	5.25	*1.00*
393	A102	20f dp brn	5.25	15

Inauguration of China's first atomic reactor and cyclotron, Peking.

Children Launching Model Planes A103

Camel Carrying Load A104

Designs: 8f, Gliders over trees. 10f, Parachutists descending. 20f, Small monoplanes in mid-air.

1958, Dec. 30

394	A103	4f carmine	35	10
395	A103	8f dp sl grn	35	5
396	A103	10f dk brn	35	5
397	A103	20f Prus bl	35	5

Sports-aviation publicity.

1959, Jan. 1

Designs: No. 399, Pomegranates. No. 400, Rooster. No. 401, Theatrical figure.

398	A104	8f vio & blk (1)	3.25	5
399	A104	8f dp bl grn & blk (2)	3.25	15
400	A104	8f red & blk (3)	3.25	15
401	A104	8f dp bl & blk (4)	3.25	40

Paper cut-outs (folk art).

Red Flag, Mao and Workers — A105

Women Workers and Atomic Model — A106

Designs: 8f, Traditional and modern blast furnaces. 10f, Steel works and workers.

1959

402	A105	4f brt red	6.00	30
403	A105	8f lake	6.00	30
404	A105	10f dp red	6.00	30

"Great Leap Forward" in steel production. Issue dates: 4f, 8f, Feb. 19; 10f, May 25.

1959, Mar. 8

Design: 22f, Chinese and Soviet women holding banners dated "3.8".

405	A106	8f emer, *cr*	40	15
406	A106	22f mag, *cr*	40	5

International Women's Day.

Natural History Museum — A107

1959, Apr. 1

407	A107	4f grnsh bl	25	10
408	A107	8f ol brn	25	10

Opening of Museum of Natural History, Peking.

Wheat — A108

Designs on Chinese Flag: No. 410, Rice. No. 411, Cotton bolls. No. 412, Soybeans, rapeseed and peanuts.

1959, Apr. 25

409	A108	8f red (1)	40	10
410	A108	8f red (2)	40	10
411	A108	8f red (3)	40	10
412	A108	8f red (4)	40	10
		Block of 4 (Nos. 409-412)	3.00	50

Successful harvest, 1958. Printed setenant in blocks of four.

Marx, Lenin and Workers — A109

Designs: 8f, Black, yellow and white fists holding banner. 22f, Steel workers parading with banners dated "5.1."

1959, May 1

413	A109	4f ultra	5.00	30
414	A109	8f red	5.00	30
415	A109	22f emerald	5.00	30

International Labor Day.

Peking Airport — A110

Design: 10f, Plane loading on runway.

1959, June 20

416	A110	8f lil & blk	5.00	20
417	A110	10f ol gray & blk	5.00	20

Opening of new Peking Airport.

Students with Marx-Lenin Banners A111

Design: 8f, Workers with banners of Mao.

1959, July 1 **Photo.** ***Perf. 11x11½***

418	A111	4f gray, red & dk brn	7.50	2.25
419	A111	8f bis, red & dk brn	7.50	2.25

40th anniversary of the May 4th students' uprising.

Frederick Joliot-Curie — A112

Design: 22f, Three races, dove and olive branch.

1959, July 25 Engr. *Perf. 11½*

420 A112 8f vio brn 6.00 *1.25*
421 A112 22f dk vio 6.00 5

10th anniversary of the World Peace Movement.

Stamp Printing Plant, Peking A113

1959, Aug. 15 *Perf. 11x11½*

422 A113 8f dp bl grn 6.75 90

Sino-Czechoslovak cooperation in stamp production.

Table Tennis — A114

1959, Aug. 30 Litho. *Perf. 14*

423 A114 4f blk & bl 60 15
424 A114 8f blk & red 60 10

25th World Table Tennis Championships, Dortmund, German Democratic Republic.

Soviet Space Rocket — A115

1959, Sept. 10 Photo. *Perf. 11½*

425 A115 8f Prus bl, red & blk 10.50 1.00

Launching of first Russian space rocket, Jan. 2, 1959.

Backyard Steel Production A116

Mao and Gate of Heavenly Peace A117

Designs: No. 426, Sun rising over "industry and agriculture." No. 428, Farming. No. 429, Trade. No. 430, Education. No. 431, Militia. No. 432, Communal dining. No. 433, Nursery. No. 434, Care for the aged. No. 435, Health services. No. 436, Flutist; culture and sports. No. 437, Flower symbolizing unity of industry, agriculture, trade, education and armed forces.

Position-in-set number in ( ).

1959, Sept. 25 Engr.

426 A116 8f rose (1) 30 8
427 A116 8f vio brn (2) 30 8
428 A116 8f dp org (3) 30 8
429 A116 8f sl grn (4) 30 8
430 A116 8f dp bl (5) 30 8
431 A116 8f ind (6) 30 8
432 A116 8f ind (7) 30 8
433 A116 8f lil rose (8) 30 8
434 A116 8f gray blk (9) 30 8
435 A116 8f emer (10) 30 8
436 A116 8f dk vio (11) 30 8
437 A116 8f red (12) 30 8
Nos. 426-437 (12) 3.60 96

First anniversary of Peoples' Communes.

1959, Sept. 28 Photo. *Perf. 11½x11*

Designs: 8f, Marx, Lenin and Kremlin. 22f, Dove over globe. With Gum

438 A117 8f lt brn & red 6.75 3.00
439 A117 8f dl bl & red 6.75 1.00
440 A117 22f bl grn & red 6.75 50

See note after No. 456.

National Emblem — A118 Blast Furnaces — A119

1959, Oct. 1 Litho. *Perf. 14*

441 A118 4f pale grn, red & gold 4.00 5.00
442 A118 8f gray, red & gold 4.00 50
443 A118 10f lt bl, red & gold 4.00 50
444 A118 20f pale brn, red & gold 4.00 2.00

Engraved and Photogravure

1959, Oct. 1 *Perf. 11½x11*

Designs: No. 446, Large coal mine. No. 447, Planer, Wuhan heavy machinery plant. No. 448, Wuhan Yangtze River Bridge. No. 449, Combine harvester. No. 450, Hsinankiang hydroelectric station. No. 451, Spinning machine. No. 452, Kirin chemical fertilizer plant. With Gum

445 A119 8f brn & rose red (1) 30 10
446 A119 8f brn & gray (2) 30 10
447 A119 8f brn & yel brn (3) 30 10
448 A119 8f brn & stl bl (4) 30 10
449 A119 8f brn & org (5) 30 10
450 A119 8f brn & ol (6) 30 10
451 A119 8f brn & bl grn (7) 30 15
452 A119 8f brn & vio (8) 30 15
Nos. 445-452 (8) 2.40 90

Celebration at Gate of Heavenly Peace — A120

Mao Proclaiming Republic — A121

Designs: 10f, Workers and factory (vert.). No. 455, People rejoicing (vert.).

1959, Oct. 1 Litho. *Perf. 14*

Inscribed: 1949-1959.

453 A120 8f cr & multi 3.00 35
454 A120 10f cr & multi 3.00 35
455 A120 20f cr & multi 3.00 35

Engr.

456 A121 20f dp car 15.00 8.50

Nos. 438-456 commemorate 10th anniversary of the Proclamation of the People's Republic of China.

Pioneer Bugler — A122

Exhibition Emblem, Communications Symbols — A123

Designs: No. 457, Pioneers' emblem. No. 459, Schoolgirl. No. 460, Girl using rain gauge. No. 461, Boy planting tree. No. 462, Girl figure skater.

1959, Nov. 10 Photo. *Perf. 11½*

457 A122 4f red yel & blk (1) 1.25 15
458 A122 4f Prus bl & red (2) 1.25 15
459 A122 8f brn & red (3) 1.25 15
460 A122 8f dk bl & red (4) 1.25 15
461 A122 8f red & grn (5) 1.25 15
462 A122 8f mag & red (6) 1.25 15
Nos. 457-462 (6) 7.50 90

10th anniversary of the Young Pioneers. Black inscription on No. 457 engraved.

1959, Dec. 1 Engr.

Design: 8f, Exhibition emblem and chimneys.

463 A123 4f dk bl 35 12
464 A123 8f red 35 8

Exhibition of Industry and Communications, Peking.

Palace of Nationalities A124

Engraved, Frame Lithographed

1959, Dec. 10 *Perf. 14*

465 A124 4f red & blk 1.85 10
466 A124 8f brt grn & blk 1.85 15

Inauguration of the Cultural Palace of Nationalities, Peking.

Athletes' Monument and Track — A125

Designs: No. 468, Parachuting. No. 469, Marksmanship. No. 470, Diving. No. 471, Table tennis. No. 472, Weight lifting. No. 473, High jump. No. 474, Rowing. No. 475, Track. No. 476, Basketball. No. 477, Traditional Chinese fencing. No. 478, Motorcycling. No. 479, Gymnastics. No. 480, Bicycling. No. 481, Horsemanship. No. 482, Soccer.

1959, Dec. 28 Litho.

467 A125 8f bis, blk & gray (1) 60 15
468 A125 8f dl bl, blk & gray (2) 60 15
469 A125 8f red brn & blk (3) 60 15
470 A125 8f grn, blk & brn (4) 60 15
471 A125 8f brt grn, blk, brn & gray (5) 60 15
472 A125 8f gray, blk & brn (6) 60 15
473 A125 8f dl bl, blk & brn (7) 60 15
474 A125 8f Prus grn, blk & brn (8) 60 15
475 A125 8f org, blk & brn (9) 60 15
476 A125 8f dl vio, blk & brn (10) 60 15
477 A125 8f lt ol, blk & brn (11) 60 15
478 A125 8f bl, blk & gray (12) 60 15
479 A125 8f gray bl, blk, grn, & bl (13) 60 15
480 A125 8f gray, blk, brn, & vio (14) 60 15
481 A125 8f red org, blk, brn, & gray (15) 60 15
482 A125 8f lt gray, blk, brn, & red (16) 60 15
Nos. 467-482 (16) 9.60 2.40

First National Sports Meeting, Peking.

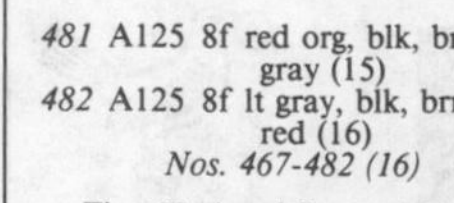

Wheat and Main Pavilion A126

Designs (Pavilion and): 8f, Meteorological symbols. 10f, Domestic animals. 20f, Fish.

Engraved and Lithographed

1960, Jan. 20

Cream Background

483 A126 4f blk & org 45 10
484 A126 8f blk & dl bl 45 10
485 A126 10f blk & org brn 45 10
486 A126 20f blk & grnsh bl 45 20

Opening of the National Agricultural Exhibition Halls, Peking.

With Gum

From No. 487 onward all stamps were issued with gum except as noted.

Conference Hall, Tsunyi A127

Designs: 8f, Mao addressing conference. 10f, Crossing Chinsha River.

Engraved (4f, 10f); Photogravure (8f)

1960, Jan. 25 *Perf. 11x11½*

487 A127 4f vio & bl 9.00 1.00
488 A127 8f red & multi 9.00 *5.00*
489 A127 10f sl grn 9.00 2.00

25th anniversary of the Communist Party Conference at Tsunyl.

Clara Zetkin (1857-1933) A128

Chinese and Russian Workers A129

Designs: 8f, Mother, child and dove. 10f, Woman tractor driver. 22f, Women of three races.

1960, Mar. 8 Photo. *Perf. 11½x11*

490 A128 4f blk & multi 85 15
491 A128 8f blk & multi 85 15
492 A128 10f blk & multi 85 15
493 A128 22f blk & multi 85 15

50th anniversary of International Women's Day.

1960, Mar. 10

Designs: 8f, Chinese and Russian flags. 10f, Chinese and Russian soldiers.

494 A129 4f dk brn 9.00 1.50
495 A129 8f red, yel & blk 9.00 1.50
496 A129 10f dp bl 9.00 5.00

10th anniversary of Sino-Soviet Treaty of Friendship. Black inscription engraved on No. 495.

Flags of Hungary and China A130

Design: 8f, Parliament Building, Budapest.

1960, Apr. 4 *Perf. 11x11½*

497 A130 8f yel, blk, red & grn 7.50 1.00
498 A130 8f bl, red & blk 7.50 4.00

15th anniversary of the liberation of Hungary.

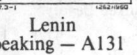

Lenin Speaking — A131

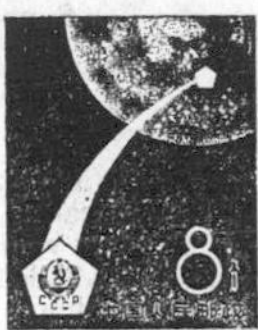

Lunik 2, Earth and Russian Arms — A132

Designs: 8f, Portrait of Lenin. 20f, Lenin talking with Smolny Palace guard.

Engraved (4f, 20f); Engraved and Photogravure (8f).

1960, Apr. 22 *Perf. 11½x11*

499 A131 4f vio brn 8.25 2.00
500 A131 8f org red & blk 8.25 6.00
501 A131 20f dk brn 8.25 2.00

90th anniversary of the birth of Lenin.

1960, Apr. 30 **Engr.** *Perf. 11½*

Design: 10f, Lunik 3 over earth.

502 A132 8f red 3.00 35
503 A132 10f green 3.00 35

Russian space flights.

Pioneers and Flags of Czechoslovakia and China — A133

View of Prague with Charles Bridge A134

Perf. 11½x11; 11x11½

1960, May 9 **Photo.**

504 A133 8f yel & multi 7.50 2.50
505 A133 8f dp grn 7.50 2.50

15th anniversary of the liberation of Czechoslovakia.

Nostril Bouquet A135

Designs: Various goldfish.
Position-in-set number in ( ).

1960, June 1 *Perf. 11x11½*

506 A135 4f *shown* (1) 7.25 50
507 A135 4f *Black-back dragon eye* (2) 7.25 50
508 A135 4f *Bubble eye* (3) 7.25 50
509 A135 4f *Red tiger head* (4) 7.25 50
510 A135 8f *Pearl scale* (5) 7.25 50
511 A135 8f *Blue dragon eye* (6) 7.25 50
512 A135 8f *Skyward eye* (7) 7.25 50
513 A135 8f *Red cap* (8) 7.25 50
514 A135 8f *Purple cap* (9) 7.25 4.00
515 A135 8f *Red head* (10) 7.25 4.00
516 A135 8f *Red and white dragon eye* (11) 7.25 4.00
517 A135 8f *Red dragon eye* (12) 7.25 4.00
Nos. 506-517 (12) 87.00 20.00

Sow with Litter A136

Designs: No. 519, Pig being inoculated. No. 520, Pigs. No. 521, Pig and mechanized feeding. No. 522, Pig and bales.

1960, June 15

518 A136 8f red & blk (1) 5.50 50
519 A136 8f dp grn & blk (2) 5.50 50
520 A136 8f lil rose & blk (3) 5.50 50
521 A136 8f lt yel grn & blk (4) 5.50 50
522 A136 8f org & blk (5) 5.50 1.75
Nos. 518-522 (5) 27.50 3.75

Flag Inscribed "Serving the Workers" A137

Flowers, Flags of North Korea and China A138

Design: 8f, Inscribed stone seal.

1960, July 30 **Photo.** *Perf. 11½x11*

523 A137 4f lt grn, red, pink & brn 6.75 2.50

Photogravure & Engraved

524 A137 8f pale bl, red & bis 6.75 2.50

3rd National Congress for Literature and Arts, Peking.

1960, Aug. 15 **Photo.**

Design: 8f, Flying horse of Korea.

525 A138 8f red & multi 7.50 3.00
526 A138 8f ultra, red & ind 7.50 3.00

15th anniversary of the liberation of Korea.

Railroad Station, Peking — A139

Design: 10f, Train arriving at station.

1960, Aug. 30 *Perf. 11½*

527 A139 8f bl, cr & brn 4.00 2.50
528 A139 10f bluish grn, cr & ind 4.00 2.50

Opening of new Peking Railroad Station.

Catalogue prices for unused stamps up to mid-1953 are for hinged copies matching the condition specified in this volume's introduction.

Girls and Flags of North Viet Nam and China A140

Lake of the Returning Sword, Hanoi A141

Worker and Fresh-air Installation A142

1960, Sept. 2 *Perf. 11x11½, 11½x11*

529 A140 8f red & multi 2.25 60
530 A141 8f red, gray grn & gray 2.25 40

15th anniversary of the Democratic Republic of North Viet Nam.

1960, Sept. 10 *Perf. 11½*

Designs: No. 532, Exterminator. No. 533, Window cleaning. No. 534, Medical examination of child. No. 535, Physical exercise.

531 A142 8f blk & org (1) 1.00 10
532 A142 8f ind & sl (2) 1.00 15
533 A142 8f brn & bl (3) 1.00 20
534 A142 8f mar & ocher (4) 1.00 30
535 A142 8f ind & brt grn (5) 1.00 25
Nos. 531-535 (5) 5.00 1.00

National health campaign.

Great Hall of the People — A143

Design: 10fr, Inside view.

1960, Oct. 1

536 A143 8f yel & multi 4.50 2.50
537 A143 10f brn & multi 4.50 2.50

Completion of the Great Hall of the People, Peking.

Dr. Norman Bethune A144

Engels Addressing Congress at The Hague A145

Design: No. 539, Dr. Bethune operating on a soldier.

Photogravure (No. 538); Engraved (No. 539)

1960, Nov. 20 *Perf. 11½x11*

538 A144 8f red & multi 1.50 20
539 A144 8f sepia 1.50 20

Dr. Norman Bethune (1890-1939), Canadian surgeon with 8th Army.

Engraved (No. 540); Photogravure (No. 541).

1960, Nov. 28

Designs: 10f, Portrait of Engels.

540 A145 8f brown 7.00 4.75
541 A145 10f bl & multi 7.00 4.75

140th anniversary of the birth of Friedrich Engels (1820-1895), German Socialist.

"Hwang Shi Ba" A146

Freighter A147

1960-61 **Photo.**

Various Chrysanthemums in Natural Colors.

542 A146 4f bl gray (1) 4.50 60
543 A146 4f pink (2) 4.50 60
544 A146 8f dk gray (3) 4.50 60
545 A146 8f dp bl (4) 4.50 60
546 A146 8f grn (5) 4.50 60
547 A146 8f mag (6) 4.50 60
548 A146 8f ol (7) 4.50 60
549 A146 8f grnsh bl (8) 4.50 60
550 A146 10f gray (9) 4.50 60
551 A146 10f choc (10) 4.50 60
552 A146 20f dp bl (11) 4.50 60
553 A146 20f brt red (12) 4.50 60
554 A146 22f ol bis (13) 4.50 60
555 A146 22f car (14) 4.50 60
556 A146 30f grnsh gray (15) 4.50 60
557 A146 30f brt pink (16) 4.50 60
558 A146 35f dp grn (17) 4.50 60
559 A146 52f brt lil rose (18) 4.50 60
Nos. 542-559 (18) 81.00 10.80

Issue dates: Nos. 548-550, 557-559, Dec. 10, 1960; Nos. 545-547, 554-556, Jan. 18, 1961; Nos. 542-544, Feb. 24, 1961.

1960, Dec. 15 *Perf. 11½*

Without Gum

560 A147 8f dp bl 8.00 1.50

Launching of first 10,000-ton Chinese-built freighter.

Pantheon, Paris — A148

Design: 8f, Proclamation of the Commune.

Engraved and Photogravure

1961, Mar. 18 *Perf. 11½x11*

561 A148 8f gray blk & red 4.00 1.00
562 A148 8f brn & red 4.00 1.00

90th anniversary of the Paris Commune.

Championship Symbol and Jasmine — A149

Designs: 10f, Table tennis racket and ball; Temple of Heaven. 20f, Table tennis match. 22f, Peking workers' gymnasium.

1961, Apr. 5 **Photo.** *Perf. 11*

563 A149 8f multi 60 15
564 A149 10f multi 60 10
565 A149 20f multi 60 10

566 A149 22f multi 60 25
a. Souv. sheet of 4 100.00 80.00

26th World Table Tennis Championships, Peking. No. 566a contains one each of Nos. 563-566. Red and bister marginal inscription and decoration. Size: 150x100mm.

Jeme Tien-yow — A150

Design: 10f, Train and tunnel, Peking-Changchow Railroad.

1961, June 20 ***Perf. 11½x11***
567 A150 8f ol grn & blk 1.25 15
568 A150 10f org brn & brn 1.25 15

Centenary of the birth of Jeme Tien-yow, railroad construction engineer.

Congress Building, Shanghai — A151

Designs: 8f, August 1st Building, Nanchang. 10f, Provisional Central Government Office, Juikin. 20f, Pagoda Hill, Yenan. 30f, Gate of Heavenly Peace, Peking.

1961, July 1 ***Perf. 11½***
569 A151 4f gold, red & cl 6.25 50
570 A151 8f gold, red & bl grn 6.25 50
571 A151 10f gold, red & yel brn 6.25 1.00
572 A151 20f gold, red & ultra 6.25 50
573 A151 30f gold, red & org red 6.25 60
Nos. 569-573 (5) 31.25 3.10

40th anniversary of the Chinese Communist Party.

August 1 Building, Nanchang — A152

Designs: 1½f, 2f, as 1f. 3f, 4f, 5f, Trees and Sha Cho Pa Building, Juikin. 8f, 10f, 20f, Pagoda Hill, Yenan. 22f, 30f, 50f, Gate of Heavenly Peace, Peking.

1961-62 **Engr.** ***Perf. 11***
Without Gum
Size: 24x16mm
574 A152 1f vio bl 2.75 50
575 A152 1½f maroon 2.75 10
576 A152 2f indigo 2.75 50
577 A152 3f dl vio 2.75 10
578 A152 4f green 2.75 10
579 A152 5f gray 2.75 50
580 A152 8f sepia 2.75 5
581 A152 10f brt lil rose 2.75 5
582 A152 20f grnsh bl 2.75 5
583 A152 22f brown 2.75 5
584 A152 30f blue 2.75 5
585 A152 50f vermilion 2.75 5
Nos. 574-585 (12) 33.00 2.10

Issue dates: 1f, 1½f, 5f, July 20, 1962; others July 20, 1961. See Nos. 647-654, 1059-1064.

Flowers, Flags of Mongolia and China A153

Design: 10f, Parliament, Ulan Bator, and statue of Sukhe Bator.

1961, July 11 **Photo.** ***Perf. 11x11½***
586 A153 8f crim, ultra & yel 8.00 1.00
587 A153 10f org, blk & yel 8.00 6.25

40th anniversary of the Mongolian People's Republic.

Military Museum — A154

1961, Aug. 1 ***Perf. 11½***
Photogravure & Engraved
588 A154 8f gray bl, brn & grn 7.50 60
589 A154 10f gray, blk & grn 7.50 15

Opening of the People's Revolutionary Military Museum.

Uprising at Wuchang A155

Sun Yat-sen — A156

Perf. 11x11½, 11½x11
1961, Oct. 10 **Photo.**
590 A155 8f gray & blk 8.50 *1.75*
591 A156 10f tan & blk 8.50 25

50th anniversary of the 1911 Revolution.

Donkey — A157

Rejoicing Tibetans — A158

Designs: 8f, 10f, 20f, 22f, Horses; 30f, 50f, Camels. Ceramic statuettes from Tang Dynasty (618-906) graves.

1961, Nov. 10 ***Perf. 11½x11***
Statuettes in Original Colors
592 A157 4f dl bl 1.25 25
593 A157 8f gray grn 1.25 25
594 A157 8f dp pur 1.25 25
595 A157 10f dp bl 1.25 20
596 A157 20f olive 1.25 25
597 A157 22f bl grn 1.25 10
598 A157 30f red brn 1.25 25
599 A157 50f slate 1.25 25
Nos. 592-599 (8) 10.00 1.80

1961, Nov. 25

Designs: 8f, Woman sower. 10f, Celebration of bumper crop. 20f, People's representatives. 30f, Tibetan children.

600 A158 4f brn & ocher 9.00 5
601 A158 8f brn & lt bl grn 9.00 20
602 A158 10f brn & yel 9.00 5
603 A158 20f brn & rose 9.00 1.50
604 A158 30f brn & bluish gray 9.00 1.50
Nos. 600-604 (5) 45.00 3.30

Rebirth of the Tibetan people.

Lu Hsun — A159

1962, Feb. 26
605 A159 8f red brn & blk 50 15

80th anniversary of the birth of Lu Hsun, writer.

An Chi Bridge, Chao Hsien — A160

Bridges of Ancient China: 8f, Pao Tai, Soochow. 10f, Chu Pu, Kwan Hsien. 20f, Chen Yang, San Kiang.

1962, May 15 ***Perf. 11***
606 A160 4f dk gray bl 1.00 10
607 A160 8f dp grn 1.00 10
608 A160 10f brown 1.00 5
609 A160 20f grnsh bl 1.00 45

Tu Fu — A161

Cranes and Bamboo — A162

Design: 4f, Tu Fu memorial pavilion, Chengtu.

1962, May 25 ***Perf. 11½x11***
610 A161 4f ol bis & blk 7.50 25
611 A161 8f grnsh bl & blk 7.50 50

Poet Tu Fu, 1,250th anniversary of birth.

1962, June 10

Designs: 10f, Two cranes in flight. 20f, Crane on rock.

612 A162 8f tan & multi 4.00 1.25
613 A162 10f bl & multi 4.00 70
614 A162 20f bis & multi 4.00 70

"The Sacred Crane," from paintings by Chen Chi-fo.

Cuban Soldier and Flag — A163

Designs: 10f, Sugar cane worker. 22f, Militiaman and woman.

1962, July 10 ***Perf. 11x11½***
615 A163 8f car, rose & blk 12.00 1.50
616 A163 10f grn & blk 12.00 50
617 A163 22f ultra & blk 12.00 9.00

Support of Cuba.

Torch and Map of Algeria — A164

Mei Lan-fang — A165

Design: 22f, Algerian soldiers and flag.

1962, July 10 ***Perf. 11½x11***
618 A164 8f dp brn & red org 45 20
619 A164 22f ocher & dp brn 45 30

Support of Algeria.

1962 ***Perf. 11½x11, 11x11½***

Designs (Mei Lan-fang in Women's Roles): No. 621, Beating drum. No. 622, With fan. 10f, Lady Yu with swords. 20f, With bag. 22f, Heavenly Maiden (horiz.). 30f, With spinning wheel (horiz.). 50f, Kneeling (horiz.). $3, Scene from opera "Drunken Beauty."

620 A165 4f tan & multi 9.00 1.00
621 A165 8f tan & multi 9.00 1.00
622 A165 8f gray & multi 9.00 10
623 A165 10f gray & multi 9.00 1.00
624 A165 20f lt grn & multi 9.00 50
625 A165 22f cr & multi 9.00 4.00
626 A165 30f lt bl & multi 9.00 5.00
627 A165 50f buff & multi 9.00 6.00
Nos. 620-627 (8) 72.00 18.60

Souvenir Sheet
Perf. 11
628 A165 $3 brn & multi 500.00 350.00

Stage art of Mei Lan-fang, actor.

Issue dates: 4f, 8f, 10f, Aug. 8; $3, Sept. 15; others Sept. 1. Imperfs. exist. Price, set $300.

No. 628 contains one stamp (48x58mm); Prussian blue margin with white ornamental design. Size: 108x147mm.

Flower Drum Dance, Han — A166

Folk Dances: 8f, Ordos, Mongolia. 10f, Catching shrimp, Chuang. 20f, Friend, Yi. 30f, Fiddle dance, Tibet. 50f, Tambourine dance, Uighur.

Cumulative numbers 246-251 at lower right.

1962, Oct. 15 **Litho.** ***Perf. 12½***
Without Gum
629 A166 4f cr & multi 40 5
630 A166 8f cr & multi 40 5
631 A166 10f cr & multi 40 10
632 A166 20f cr & multi 40 40
633 A166 30f cr & multi 40 30
634 A166 50f cr & multi 40 40
Nos. 629-634 (6) 2.40 1.30

See Nos. 696-707.

Soldiers Storming Winter Palace — A167

Design: 8f, Lenin leading soldiers (vert.).

1962, Nov. 7 **Photo.** ***Perf. 11½***
635 A167 8f blk & red 13.00 20
636 A167 20f sl grn & red 13.00 75

45th anniversary of the Russian Revolution.

Monument and Map of Albania
A168

Tsai Lun, Inventor of Papermaking
A169

Design: 10f, Albanian flag and Girl Pioneer.

1962, Nov. 28 ***Perf. 11½x11***

637	A168	8f Prus bl & sep	1.00	30
638	A168	10f red, yel, & blk	1.00	30

50th anniversary of Albanian independence.

1962, Dec. 1 ***Perf. 11½x11***

Designs: No. 640, Paper making. No. 641, Sun Szu-miao, physician. No. 642, Writing medical treatise. No. 643, Shen Ko, geologist. No. 644, Making field notes. No. 645, Kuo Shou-chin, astronomer. No. 646, Astronomical instrument.

Cumulative numbers 297-304 at lower right.

639	A169	4f multi	40	20
640	A169	4f multi	40	10
641	A169	8f multi	40	15
642	A169	8f multi	40	20
643	A169	10f multi	40	10
644	A169	10f multi	40	25
645	A169	20f multi	40	25
646	A169	20f multi	40	25
		Nos. 639-646 (8)	3.20	1.50

Scientists of ancient China.

Building Type of 1961

Designs: 1f, 2f, Building, Nanchang. 3f, 4f, Trees and Sha Cho Pa Building. 8f, 10f, 20f, Pagoda Hill, Yenan. 30f, Gate of Heavenly Peace, Peking.

1962, Jan. Litho. ***Rough Perf. 12½***
Size: 21x16mm.

647	A152	1f ultra	45	10
648	A152	2f grnsh gray	45	10
649	A152	3f vio gray	45	10
650	A152	4f green	45	10
651	A152	8f dk ol, perf. 14	45	10
a.		Perf. 12½		50
652	A152	10f brt rose lil	45	10
653	A152	20f sl bl	45	10
654	A152	30f dl bl	45	10
		Nos. 647-654 (8)	3.60	80

Tank Monument, Havana
A170

Crowd in Havana — A171

Designs: No. 656, Cuban revolutionaries. No. 658, Crowd in Peking. No. 659, Cuban soldier. No. 660, Castro and Cuban flag.

Perf. 11½, 11x11½

1963, Jan. 1 **Photo.**

655	A170	4f red & blk brn	9.00	15
656	A170	4f grn & blk	9.00	15
657	A171	8f dl red & brn	9.00	1.00
658	A171	8f dl red & brn	9.00	20
659	A170	10f ocher & blk	9.00	3.00
660	A170	10f red, bl & blk	9.00	*10.00*
		Nos. 655-660 (6)	54.00	14.50

4th anniversary of the Cuban revolution.

Green Dragontail
A172

Karl Marx
A173

Position-in-set number in ( ).

1963 **Without Gum** ***Perf. 11***
Butterflies in Natural Colors.

661	A172	4f *Tibetan clouded yellow* (1)	1.50	15
662	A172	4f *Tritailed glory* (2)	1.50	15
663	A172	4f *Neumogeni jungle queen* (3)	1.50	15
664	A172	4f *Washan swordtail* (4)	1.50	40
665	A172	4f *Striped ringlet* (5)	1.50	15
666	A172	8f *shown* (6)	1.50	10
667	A172	8f *Dilunulated peacock* (7)	1.50	15
668	A172	8f *Yamfly* (8)	1.50	5
669	A172	8f *Golden kaiser-i-hind* (9)	1.50	5
670	A172	8f *Mushaell hairstreak* (10)	1.50	5
671	A172	10f *Yellow orange-tip* (11)	1.50	5
672	A172	10f *Great jay* (12)	1.50	10
673	A172	10f *Striped punch* (13)	1.50	5
674	A172	10f *Hainan violet-beak* (14)	1.50	5
675	A172	10f *Omeiskipper* (15)	1.50	5
676	A172	20f *Philippines birdwing* (16)	1.50	15
677	A172	20f *Richtofenis red apollo* (17)	1.50	15
678	A172	22f *Blue-banded king crow* (18)	1.50	20
679	A172	30f *Solskyi copper* (19)	1.50	50
680	A172	50f *Yunnan clipper* (20)	1.50	1.25
		Nos. 661-680 (20)	30.00	3.95

Issue dates: Nos. 666-675, July 15; others Apr. 5.

1963, May 5 ***Perf. 11½***

Designs: No. 682, "Workers of the World, Unite" on cover of first edition of Communist Manifesto. No. 683, Marx and Engels.

Without Gum

681	A173	8f blk, gold & sal (1)	7.50	2.50
682	A173	8f gold & red (2)	7.50	2.50
683	A173	8f gold & choc (3)	7.50	2.50

145th anniversary of birth of Karl Marx (1818-1883), German political philosopher.

Child with Top — A174

Designs (Child): No. 685, eating berries. No. 686, as traffic policeman. No. 687, with windmill. No. 688, listening to caged cricket. No. 689, with sword. No. 690, embroidering. No. 691, with umbrella. No. 692, playing with sand. No. 693, playing table tennis. No. 694, learning to add. No. 695, with kite.

1963, June 1 **Litho.** ***Perf. 12½***
Without Gum
Multicolored Designs

684	A174	4f grnsh gray (1)	40	5
685	A174	4f tan (2)	40	5
686	A174	8f gray (3)	40	5
687	A174	8f bl (4)	40	5
688	A174	8f tan (5)	40	5
689	A174	8f dp gray (6)	40	5
690	A174	8f cit (7)	40	5
691	A174	8f gray (8)	40	5
692	A174	10f grn (9)	40	15
693	A174	10f vio (10)	40	15
694	A174	20f bis (11)	40	40
695	A174	20f grn (12)	40	40
		Nos. 684-695 (12)	4.80	1.50

Children's Day. Price, imperf set $15.

Dance Type of 1962

Folk Dances: 4f, Weavers' dance, Puyi. 8f, Kazakh. 10f, Olunchun. 20f, Labor dance, Kaochan. 30f, Reed pipe dance, Miao. 50f, Fan dance, Korea.

Cumulative numbers 261-266 at lower right.

1963, June 15 ***Perf. 12½***
Without Gum

696	A166	4f cr & multi	40	5
697	A166	8f cr & multi	40	5
698	A166	10f cr & multi	40	10
699	A166	20f cr & multi	40	25
700	A166	30f cr & multi	40	30
701	A166	50f cr & multi	40	50
		Nos. 696-701 (6)	2.40	1.25

1963, June 30 **Without Gum**

Folk Dances: 4f, "Wedding Ceremony," Yu. 8f, "Encircling Mountain Forest," Pai. 10f, Long drum dance, Yao. 20f, Third day of the third month dance, Li. 30f, Knife dance, Kawa. 50f, Peacock dance, Thai.

Cumulative numbers 279-284 at lower right.

702	A166	4f cr & multi	40	5
703	A166	8f cr & multi	40	5
704	A166	10f cr & multi	40	10
705	A166	20f cr & multi	40	30
706	A166	30f cr & multi	40	30
707	A166	50f cr & multi	40	40
		Nos. 702-707 (6)	2.40	1.20

Giant Panda Eating Apples — A175

Table Tennis Player — A176

Designs: No. 709, Giant panda eating bamboo shoots. 10f, Two pandas (horiz.).

1963, Aug. 5 **Photo.** ***Perf. 11½x11***
Size: 28x38mm.

708	A175	8f pale bl & blk	6.00	15
709	A175	8f pale bl & blk	6.00	2.00

Perf. 11½
Size: 50x29mm.

710	A175	10f ol & blk	6.00	10

Price, imperf set $18.

1963, Sept. 10 **Engr.** ***Perf. 11½***

Design: No. 712, Trophies won by Chinese team.

711	A176	8f dk ol grn	9.00	70
712	A176	8f brown	9.00	5

27th World Table Tennis Championships.

Snub-nosed Langur — A177

Jade-green Screen Mountain — A178

Designs: 10f, Two monkeys playing. 22f, Two monkeys grooming.

1963, Sept. 23 **Photo.** ***Perf. 11½x11***

713	A177	8f gray & multi	1.50	10
714	A177	10f gray & multi	1.50	10
715	A177	22f gray & multi	1.50	2.00

Price, imperf set $14.

Engraved and Photogravure

1963, Oct. 15 ***Perf. 11½***

Hwang Shan Landscapes (Yellow Mountains), Anhwei Province. Nos. 724-731 horizontal.

716	A178	4f *shown* (1)	2.00	20
717	A178	4f *"Guests Welcoming Pines"* (2)	2.00	35
718	A178	4f *Pines and Rock Behind the Sea* (3)	2.00	25
719	A178	4f *Terrace of Keeping Cool* (4)	2.00	10
720	A178	8f *Mount of Heavenly Capital* (5)	2.00	20
721	A178	8f *Mount of Scissors* (6)	2.00	20
722	A178	8f *Forest of Ten Thousand Pines* (7)	2.00	20
723	A178	8f *"Brush Blooming in Dream"* (8)	2.00	20
724	A178	10f *Mount of Lotus Flower* (9)	2.00	20
725	A178	10f *Cumulus Cloud over West Sea* (10)	2.00	20
726	A178	10f *Old Pines of Hwang Shan* (11)	2.00	20
727	A178	10f *"Watching the Clouds over West Sea"*	2.00	10
728	A178	20f *Mount of Stalagmites* (13)	2.00	30
729	A178	22f *"Stone Monkey Watching the Sea"* (14)	2.00	25
730	A178	30f *Forest of Lions* (15)	2.00	*6.00*
731	A178	50f *Three Fairy Tales of Pen Lai* (16)	2.00	20
		Nos. 716-731 (16)	32.00	9.15

Soccer Player — A179

Athletes and Banners — A180

Designs: No. 733, Discus, women's. No. 734, Diving, men's. No. 735, Gymnastics, women's.

Engraved and Photogravure

1963, Nov. 17 ***Perf. 11***

732	A179	8f gray, red & blk (1)	7.50	20
733	A179	8f gray, ultra & blk (2)	7.50	20
734	A179	8f lt grn, brn & blk (3)	7.50	20
735	A179	8f gray, lil rose & blk (4)	7.50	20

Photo. ***Perf. 11½***
736 A180 10f red & multi (5) 7.50 40
Nos. 732-736 (5) 37.50 1.20

Games of the Newly Emerging Forces, Djakarta.

Clay Rooster and Goat — A181

Chinese Folk Toys: No. 738, Cloth camel. No. 739, Cloth tigers. No. 740, Clay ox and rider. No. 741, Cloth rabbit, wooden doll, clay roosters. No. 742, Straw rooster. No. 743, Cloth donkey and bird. No. 744, Clay lion. No. 745, Cloth tiger and tumbler doll.

1963, Dec. 10 Litho. ***Perf. 11½***
Toys Multicolored; Without Gum
737 A181 4f bis (1) 25 8
738 A181 4f gray (4) 25 8
739 A181 4f lt bl (7) 25 8
740 A181 8f bis (2) 25 8
741 A181 8f gray (5) 25 8
742 A181 8f lt bl (8) 25 8
743 A181 10f bis (3) 25 8
744 A181 10f gray (6) 25 8
745 A181 10f lt bl (9) 25 8
Nos. 737-745 (9) 2.25 72

Armed Vietnamese Family — A182

Flags of Cuba and China — A183

Design: No. 747, Militia with Vietnamese flag.

1963, Dec. 20 Photo. ***Perf. 11½x11***
746 A182 8f tan, blk & red 2.00 15
747 A182 8f red & multi 2.00 25

Liberation of South Viet Nam.

1964, Jan. 1

Design: No. 749, Boy waving Cuban flag.

748 A183 8f red, yel, bl & ind 9.25 50
749 A183 8f multi 9.25 2.50

5th anniversary of the liberation of Cuba.

Woman Driving Tractor — A184

Woman of the People's Commune: No. 751, harvesting. No. 752, picking cotton. No. 753, picking fruit. No. 754, reading book. No. 755, on guard duty.

1964, Mar. 8
750 A184 8f ol, pink & brn (1) 60 10
751 A184 8f brn yel & org (2) 60 10
752 A184 8f gray & multi (3) 60 10
753 A184 8f blk, org & bl (4) 60 10
754 A184 8f grn & multi (5) 60 10
755 A184 8f lil & multi (6) 60 10
Nos. 750-755 (6) 3.60 60

Certain countries cancel stamps in full sheets and sell them (usually with gum) for less than face value. Dealers generally sell "CTO".

Chinese and African Men A185

Design: No. 757, African drummer.

1964, Apr. 12 Photo. ***Perf. 11***
756 A185 8f red & multi 1.25 10
757 A185 8f blk & dk brn 1.25 10

African Freedom Day.

Marx, Engels, Lenin and Stalin — A186

Design: No. 759, Banners and workers.

1964, May 1 ***Perf. 11½***
758 A186 8f gold, red & blk 12.00 *5.00*
759 A186 8f gold, red & blk 12.00 *4.00*

Labor Day.

Orchard, Yenan A187

Yenan, Shrine of the Chinese Revolution: No. 761, Central Auditorium, Yang Chia Ling. No. 762, Mao's office and residence. No. 763, Auditorium, Wang Chia Ping. No. 764, Border Region Assembly Hall. No. 765, Pagoda Hill and Bridge.

1964, July 1 Photo. ***Perf. 11x11½***
760 A187 8f multi (1) 2.00 20
761 A187 8f multi (2) 2.00 20
762 A187 8f multi (3) 2.00 20
763 A187 8f multi (4) 2.00 20
764 A187 8f multi (5) 2.00 20
765 A187 52f multi (6) 2.00 85
Nos. 760-765 (6) 12.00 1.85

Map and Flag of Viet Nam — A188

Alchemist's Glowing Crucible — A189

1964, July 20 ***Perf. 11½***
766 A188 8f multi 18.00 1.25

Victory in South Viet Nam.

1964, Aug. 5 ***Perf. 11½x11***
Position-in-set number in ( ).
767 A189 4f *shown* (1) 1.75 10
768 A189 4f *Night-shining jade* (2) 1.75 10
769 A189 8f *Pur. Kuo's cap* (3) 1.75 5
770 A189 8f *Chao pink* (4) 1.75 5
771 A189 8f *Yao yellow* (5) 1.75 10
772 A189 8f *Twin beauty* (6) 1.75 5
773 A189 8f *Ice-veiled ruby* (7) 1.75 5
774 A189 10f *Gold-sprinkled Chinese ink* (8) 1.75 8
775 A189 10f *Cinnabar jar* (9) 1.75 8
776 A189 10f *Lan Tien jade* (10) 1.75 5
777 A189 10f *Imperial robe yellow* (11) 1.75 8
778 A189 10f *Hu red* (12) 1.75 8
779 A189 20f *Pea green* (13) 1.75 2.00
780 A189 43f *Wei purple* (14) 1.75 2.00
781 A189 50f *Intoxicated celestial peach* (15) 1.75 2.00
Nos. 767-781 (15) 26.25 6.87

Souvenir Sheet
Perf. 11½
Without Gum
782 A189 $2 *Glorious crimson & great gold pink* 125.00 75.00

No. 782 contains one stamp (48x59mm.). Bluish gray and silver border. Size: 77x136mm.

Wine Cup — A190

Grain Harvest — A191

Designs: Sacrificial bronze vessels of Yin dynasty, prior to 1050 B.C.

Engraved and Photogravure
1964, Aug. 25 ***Perf. 11½x11***
783 A190 4f *shown* (1) 1.65 60
784 A190 4f *Ku beaker* (2) 1.65 60
785 A190 8f *Kuang wine urn* (3) 1.65 8
786 A190 8f *Chia wine cup* (4) 1.65 8
787 A190 10f *Tsun wine vessel* (5) 1.65 10
788 A190 10f *Yu wine urn* (6) 1.65 10
789 A190 20f *Tsun wine vessel* (7) 1.65 20
790 A190 20f *Ceremonial cauldron* (8) 1.65 20
Nos. 783-790 (8) 13.20 1.96

1964, Sept. 26 Photo.

Designs: No. 792, Students planting trees. No. 793, Study period. No. 794, Scientific experimentation.

791 A191 8f multi (1) 55 10
792 A191 8f multi (2) 55 10
793 A191 8f multi (3) 55 10
794 A191 8f multi (4) 55 10

Youth helping in agriculture.

Marx, Engels, Trafalgar Square, London — A192

People with Banners — A193

1964, Sept. 28 ***Perf. 11½***
795 A192 8f red, gold & red brn 27.50 12.00

Centenary of the First International.

1964, Oct. 1

Designs: No. 797, Gate of Heavenly Peace and Chinese flag. No. 798, People with banners, facing left.

796 A193 8f cr & multi (1) 10.00 25
797 A193 8f cr & multi (2) 10.00 25
798 A193 8f cr & multi (3) 10.00 25
a. Souv. sheet of three 175.00 75.00
Strip of three, Nos. 796-798 35.00 3.00

15th anniversary of the People's Republic. Nos. 796-798 printed se-tenant. No. 798a contains Nos. 796-798 as continuous design without separating perfs. Red and gold marginal inscription. Size: 153x114mm.

Oil Derricks — A194

Designs: 4f, Geological surveyors and truck (horiz.). 8f, "Christmas tree" and extraction accessories. 10f, Oil refinery. 20f, Tank cars (horiz.).

1964, Oct. 1
799 A194 4f lt bl & multi 9.00 10
800 A194 8f lt bl & multi 9.00 5
801 A194 8f lil & multi 9.00 15
802 A194 10f sl & multi 9.00 5
803 A194 20f brn & multi 9.00 *8.00*
Nos. 799-803 (5) 45.00 8.35

Oil industry.

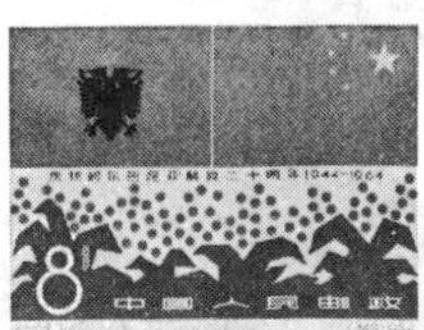
Albanian and Chinese Flags A195

Design: 10f, Enver Hoxha and Albanian coat of arms.

1964, Nov. 29 ***Perf. 11x11½***
804 A195 8f red & multi 15.00 75
805 A195 10f red, yel & blk 15.00 7.50

20th anniversary of the liberation of Albania.

Power Dam Construction A196

Designs: No. 807, Installation of turbogenerator rotor. No. 808, Main dam. 20f, Pylon.

1964, Dec. 15 *Perf. 11½*

806 A196 4f multi 10.00 10
807 A196 8f multi 10.00 10
808 A196 8f multi 10.00 5
809 A196 20f multi 10.00 7.50

Hsin An Kiang Dam and hydroelectric power station.

Fertilizer Industry — A197

Designs (Chemical Industry): No. 811, Plastics. No. 812, Medicines. No. 813, Rubber. No. 814, Insecticides. No. 815, Industrial acids. No. 816, Industrial alkalies. No. 817, Synthetic fibers.

Photogravure & Engraved

1964, Dec. 30

810 A197 8f red & blk (1) 60 15
811 A197 8f yel grn & blk (2) 60 10
812 A197 8f brn & blk (3) 60 10
813 A197 8f lil rose & blk (4) 60 10
814 A197 8f bl & blk (5) 60 10
815 A197 8f org & blk (6) 60 20
816 A197 8f vio & blk (7) 60 20
817 A197 8f brt grn & blk (8) 60 20
Nos. 810-817 (8) 4.80 1.15

Mao Studying Map — A198

Mao Tse-tung — A199

Design: No. 819, Victory at Lushan Pass.

1965, Jan. 31 **Photo.** *Perf. 11*

818 A198 8f red & multi 12.00 4.50
819 A198 8f red & multi 12.00 4.50

Perf. 11½x11

820 A199 8f gold & multi 12.00 4.50

Tsunyi Conference, 30th anniversary.

Conference Hall, Bandung — A200

Lenin — A201

1965, Apr. 18 *Perf. 11½x11*

Design: No. 822, Asians and Africans applauding.

821 A200 8f cr & multi 25 8
822 A200 8f cr & multi 25 8

10th anniversary of the Bandung, Indonesia, Conference, Apr. 1955.

1965, Apr. 25 *Perf. 11½*

823 A201 8f red, choc & sal 16.00 5.25

95th anniversary of the birth of Lenin.

Chinese Player — A202

1965, Apr. 25 *Perf. 11½*

Emerald, Gold, Red & Black

824 A202 8f *shown* (1) 15 8
825 A202 8f *European woman* (2) 15 8
826 A202 8f *Chinese woman* (3) 15 8
827 A202 8f *European man* (4) 15 8
Block of 4, Nos. 824-827 75 50

28th World Table Tennis Championships, Ljubljana, Jugoslavia, Apr. 15-25. Nos. 824-827 printed se-tenant.

Climbers on Mt. Minya Konka — A203

Marx and Lenin — A204

Mountain Climbers: No. 829, on Muztagh Ata. No. 830, on Mt. Jolmo Lungma (Mt. Everest). No. 831, Women camping on Kongur Tiubie Tagh. No. 832, on Shisha Pangma.

Photogravure & Engraved

1965, May 25

828 A203 8f bl, blk & ol (1) 1.00 20
829 A203 8f bl, blk & ol (2) 1.00 20
830 A203 8f ultra, blk & gray (3) 1.00 20
831 A203 8f lt bl, blk & yel gray (4) 1.00 20
832 A203 8f ultra, blk & gray (5) 1.00 20
Nos. 828-832 (5) 5.00 1.00

Chinese mountaineering achievements, 1957-64.

1965, June 21 **Photo.** *Perf. 11½x11*

833 A204 8f red, yel & blk 16.00 5.25

Postal Ministers' Congress, Peking.

Tseping Valley A205

Chingkang Mountains, Cradle of the Chinese Revolution.

1965, July 1 *Perf. 11x11½*

834 A205 4f *shown* (1) 3.00 10
835 A205 8f *San Wan Tsun* (2) 3.00 10
836 A205 8f *Octagon Bldg., Mao Ping* (3) 3.00 15
837 A205 8f *River and Bridge at Lung Shih* (4) 3.00 85
838 A205 8f *Ta Ching Tsun* (5) 3.00 8
839 A205 10f *Bridge across the Lung Yuan* (6) 3.00 8
840 A205 10f *Hwang Yang Mountain* (7) 3.00 2.00
841 A205 52f *Chingkang peaks* (8) 3.00 2.00
Nos. 834-841 (8) 24.00 5.36

Soldiers with Books — A206

1965, Aug. 1 *Perf. 11½*

Without Gum

842 A206 8f *shown* (1) 4.00 2.25
843 A206 8f *Soldiers reading Little Red Books* (2) 4.00 2.25
844 A206 8f *With shell and artillery* (3) 4.00 30
845 A206 8f *Rifle instruction* (4) 4.00 30
846 A206 8f *Sewing jacket* (5) 4.00 30
847 A206 8f *Bayonet charge* (6) 4.00 3.25
848 A206 8f *With Banner* (7) 4.00 3.25
849 A206 8f *Military band* (8) 4.00 3.25
Nos. 842-849 (8) 32.00 15.15

People's Liberation Army. Nos. 846-849 vertical.

"Welcome to Peking" — A207

Designs: No. 851, Chinese and Japanese young men. No. 852, Chinese and Japanese girls. No. 853, Musical entertainment. No. 854, Emblem of meeting.

1965, Aug. 25 *Perf. 11½x11*

850 A207 4f yel & multi 60 10
851 A207 8f pink & multi 60 12
852 A207 8f multi 60 12
853 A207 10f multi 60 12
854 A207 22f lt bl & multi 60 25
Nos. 850-854 (5) 3.00 71

Chinese-Japanese Youth Meeting, Peking.

North Vietnamese Soldier — A208

Peoples of the World — A209

Designs: No. 856, Soldier with guns. No. 857, Soldier giving victory salute.

1965, Sept. 2 *Perf. 11½x11*

855 A208 8f red & red brn (1) 60 15
856 A208 8f red & blk (2) 60 15
857 A208 8f red & vio brn (3) 60 15

Perf. 11½

858 A209 8f blk & red (4) 60 15

Struggle of the people of Viet Nam.

Mao Tse-tung at His Desk — A210

Crossing Yellow River A211

Victory Monument — A212

Design: No. 862, Recruits in cart.

1965, Sept. 3 *Perf. 11*

859 A210 8f red & multi (1) 5.75 2.00

Perf. 11x11½, 11½x11

860 A211 8f red & dk grn (2) 5.75 6.00
861 A212 8f red & dk brn (3) 5.75 50
862 A211 8f red & dk grn (4) 5.75 50

20th anniversary of victory over Japan.

Soccer — A213

National Games Opening Ceremonies — A214

Designs: No. 864, Archery. No. 865, Javelin. No. 866, Gymnastics. No. 867, Volleyball. No. 869, Bicycling. 20f, Diving. 22f, Hurdles. 30f, Weight lifting. 43f, Basketball. Position-in-set number in ( ).

Perf. 11½x11, 11 (A214)

1965, Sept. 28

863 A213 4f red & multi (1) 4.00 25
864 A213 4f gray & multi (2) 4.00 25
865 A213 8f dk grn & multi (3) 4.00 25
866 A213 8f lil rose & multi (4) 4.00 25
867 A213 8f dp grn & multi (5) 4.00 25
868 A214 10f red, gold & multi (6) 4.00 25
869 A213 10f ol & multi (7) 4.00 25
870 A213 20f ultra & multi (8) 4.00 60
871 A213 22f org & multi (9) 4.00 75
872 A213 30f dp bl & multi (10) 4.00 1.25
873 A213 43f red lil & multi (11) 4.00 2.50
Nos. 863-873 (11) 44.00 6.85

2nd National Games.

Government Building A215

Textile Workers A216

Designs: 4f, 20f, as 1f. 1½f, 5f, 22f, Gate of Heavenly Peace. 2f, 8f, 30f, People's Hall. 3f, 10f, 50f, Military Museum.

1965-66 ***Perf. 11½x11***

Without Gum

874 A215 1f brown 10 5
875 A215 1½f red lil 10 30
876 A215 2f green 10 5
877 A215 3f bl grn 10 5
878 A215 4f brt bl 10 5
879 A215 5f vio brn ('66) 20 5
880 A215 8f rose red 20 5
881 A215 10f gray ol 20 5
882 A215 20f violet 20 6
883 A215 22f orange 1.00 6
884 A215 30f yel grn 1.00 5
885 A215 50f dp bl ('66) 1.00 75
Nos. 874-885 (12) 4.30 1.57

1965, Nov. 30

886 A216 8f *shown* (1) 7.75 5
887 A216 8f *Machine shop* (2) 7.75 10
888 A216 8f *Welder* (3) 7.75 5
889 A216 8f *Students* (4) 7.75 1.50
890 A216 8f *Militia* (5) 7.75 1.50
Nos. 886-890 (5) 38.75 3.20

Women workers.

Soccer — A217

Children's Sports: No. 892, Racing. No. 893, Tobogganing and skating. No. 894, Gymnastics. No. 895, Swimming. No. 896, Rifle practice. No. 897, Jumping rope. No. 898, Table tennis.

1966, Feb. 25 ***Perf. 11***

891 A217 4f emer & multi (1) 8 5
892 A217 4f yel brn & multi (2) 8 5
893 A217 8f bl & multi (3) 18 10
894 A217 8f yel & multi (4) 18 10
895 A217 8f grnsh bl & multi (5) 18 10
896 A217 8f grn & multi (6) 18 10
897 A217 10f org & multi (7) 25 12
898 A217 52f grnsh gray & multi (8) 1.40 60
Nos. 891-898 (8) 2.53 1.22

Mobile Transformer A218

New Industrial Machinery: No. 900, Electron microscope (vert.). No. 901, Lathe. No. 902, Vertical boring and turning machine (vert.). No. 903, Gear-grinding machine. No. 904, Hydraulic press. No. 905, Milling machine. No. 906, Electron accelerator (vert.).

Photogravure & Engraved

Perf. 11x11½, 11½x11

1966, Mar. 30

899 A218 4f yel & blk (1) 4.50 15
900 A218 8f blk & lt ultra (2) 4.50 15
901 A218 8f sal pink & blk (3) 4.50 15
902 A218 8f ol & blk (4) 4.50 15
903 A218 8f rose lil & blk (5) 4.50 15
904 A218 10f gray & blk (6) 4.50 1.00
905 A218 10f bl grn & blk (7) 4.50 1.00
906 A218 22f lil & blk (8) 4.50 1.00
Nos. 899-906 (8) 36.00 3.75

Military and Civilian Workers A219

Women in Various Occupations: No. 908, Train conductor. No. 909, Red Cross worker. No. 910, Kindergarten teacher. No. 911, Road sweeper. No. 912, Hairdresser. No. 913, Bus conductor. No. 914, Traveling saleswoman. No. 915, Canteen worker. No. 916, Rural mail carrier.

1966, May 10 ***Perf. 11x11½***

907 A219 8f red & multi (1) 25 12
908 A219 8f pale grn & multi (2) 25 12
909 A219 8f yel & multi (3) 25 12
910 A219 8f grn & multi (4) 25 12
911 A219 8f sal & multi (5) 25 12
912 A219 8f pale bl & bl (6) 25 12
913 A219 8f yel & multi (7) 25 12
914 A219 8f tan & multi (8) 25 12
915 A219 8f yel grn & multi (9) 25 12
916 A219 8f grn & multi (10) 25 12
Nos. 907-916 (10) 2.50 1.20

Statue "Thunderstorm" — A220

Design: 22f, Open book and association emblem.

1966, June 27 With Gum ***Perf. 11***

917 A220 8f red & blk 1.00 10
918 A220 22f red, gold & yel 1.50 20

Afro-Asian Writers' Association Conference, Peking.

Sun Yat-sen — A221

1966, Nov. 12 ***Perf. 11½x11***

919 A221 8f sep & lt buff 12.50 5.00

Birth centenary of Sun Yat-sen.

Athletes Holding Portrait of Mao — A222

Two Women Athletes with Little Red Book A223

Designs: No. 921, Athletes holding Little Red Books. No. 923, Athletes reading Mao texts.

1966, Dec. 31 ***Perf. 11***

920 A222 8f red & multi (1) 8.25 2.00
921 A222 8f red & multi (2) 8.25 2.00

Perf. 11x11½

922 A223 8f bl & multi (3) 8.25 2.00
923 A223 8f bl & multi (4) 8.25 2.00

1st Athletic Games of the New Emerging Nations.

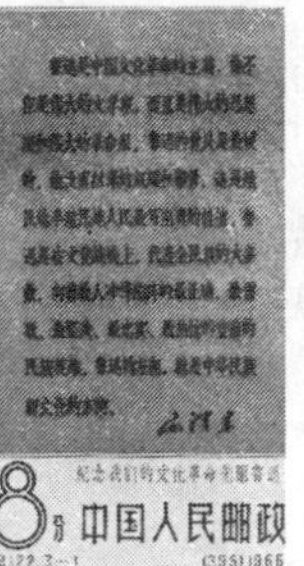

Appreciation of Lu Hsun by Mao — A224

"Be Resolute ...," by Mao Tse-tung — A225

Designs: No. 925, Portrait of Lu Hsun. No. 926, Lu Hsun's handwriting (3 vert. rows).

Engraved and Photogravure; Photogravure (No. 925)

1966, Dec. 31 ***Perf. 11½***

924 A224 8f red & blk (1) 8.00 3.00
925 A224 8f red & multi (2) 8.00 3.00
926 A224 8f red & blk (3) 8.00 3.00

Lu Hsun, Revolutionary writer (1881-1936).

Perf. 11½x11, 11½ (No. 928)

1967, Mar. 10 **Photo.**

Designs: No. 928, Drilling crew fighting natural gas fire (horiz.). No. 929, Attempt to close fire-engulfed valve. Sizes: Nos. 927, 929, 26x38mm.; No. 928, 49x29mm.

927 A225 8f red, gold & blk 7.00 3.00
928 A225 8f brick red & blk 7.00 3.00
929 A225 8f brick red & blk 7.00 3.00

Heroic oil well firefighters.

Liu Ying-chun — A226

1967, Mar. 25 ***Perf. 11½x11***

930 A226 8f *shown* (1) 5.00 2.00
931 A226 8f *With book by Mao* (2) 5.00 2.00
932 A226 8f *Holding bridle of horse* (3) 5.00 2.00
933 A226 8f *With film slide* (4) 5.00 2.00
934 A226 8f *Lecturing* (5) 5.00 2.00
935 A226 8f *Fatal attempt to stop runaway horse* (6) 5.00 2.00
Nos. 930-935 (6) 30.00 12.00

In memory of soldier Liu Ying-chun, hero.

Industrial Growth — A227

Design: No. 937, Banners and people facing left: agricultural growth.

1967, Apr. 15 ***Perf. 11***

936 A227 8f red & multi 6.75 2.00
937 A227 8f red & multi 6.75 2.00

Third Five-Year Plan.

Mao Tse-tung — A228

Thoughts of Mao — A229

1967, Apr. 20 ***Perf. 11½***

938 A228 8f red & multi 12.00 2.00

Red & Gold

939 A229 8f *39 characters* 12.00 3.50
940 A229 8f *50 characters* 12.00 3.50
941 A229 8f *39 characters in 6 lines* 12.00 3.50
942 A229 8f *53 characters* 12.00 3.50
943 A229 8f *46 characters* 12.00 3.50
Strip of five 75.00 30.00

Gold & Red

944 A229 8f *41 characters* 12.00 3.50
945 A229 8f *49 characters* 12.00 3.50
946 A229 8f *35 characters* 12.00 3.50
947 A229 8f *22 characters* 12.00 3.50
948 A229 8f *29 characters* 12.00 3.50
Strip of five 75.00 30.00
Nos. 938-948 (11) 132.00 37.00

Thoughts of Mao Tse-tung. Nos. 939-943, Nos. 944-948 printed se-tenant in strips of 5 each.

No numbers appear below design on Nos. 938-1046.

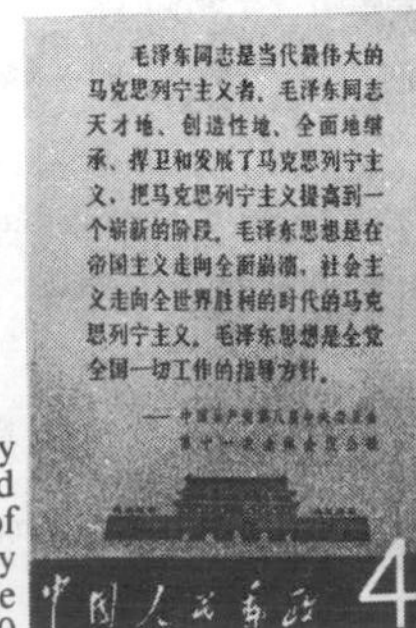

Text by Mao and Gate of Heavenly Peace A230

Mao and Lin Piao — A231

Designs: No. 950, Mao and poem. No. 951, Mao among people of various races. No. 952, Mao facing left and Red Guards with books. No. 953, Mao with upraised right hand. No. 954, Mao leaning on rail (horiz.). 10f, Mao and Lin Piao in discussion (horiz.).

Engraved and Photogravure

1967 ***Perf. 11x11½***

Size: 36x56mm.

949 A230 4f yel, red & mar 9.50 2.00

Photo.

950 A230 8f yel, brn, & red 9.50 2.00
951 A230 8f yel, red & multi 9.50 2.00
952 A230 8f yel, red & multi 9.50 2.00

Perf. 11

Size: 36x50, 50x36mm.

953 A231 8f blk & multi 9.50 2.00
954 A231 8f blk & multi 50.00 20.00
955 A231 8f lt bl & multi 18.00 20.00
956 A231 10f blk & multi 37.50 20.00
Nos. 949-956 (8) 153.00 70.00

"Mao Tse-tung Our Great Teacher." Issue dates: Nos. 949-953, May 1; Nos. 954-956, Sept. 20.

Mao Text (4 lines) — A232

Parade of Supporters — A233

Design: No. 958, Mao text (5 lines).

Engraved and Photogravure

1967, May 23 ***Perf. 11½***

957 A232 8f blk, red & yel 14.00 5.50
958 A232 8f blk, red & yel 14.00 5.50

Photo. ***Perf. 11***

959 A233 8f multi 14.00 5.50

25th anniversary of Mao Tse-tung's "Talks on Literature and Art" in Yenan.

Mao Tse-tung — A234

1967 **Engr.** ***Perf. 11***

960 A234 4f brown 16.00 5.00
961 A234 8f carmine 16.00 5.00
962 A234 35f dk brn 16.00 5.00
963 A234 43f vermilion 16.00 5.00
964 A234 52f carmine 16.00 5.00
Nos. 960-964 (5) 80.00 25.00

46th anniversary of Chinese Communist Party. Issue dates: 8f, July 1, others September.

Mao, "Sun of the Revolution" — A235

Design: No. 966, Mao and people of various races.

1967, Oct. 1 ***Perf. 11½x11***

965 A235 8f multi 15.00 7.50
966 A235 8f multi 15.00 7.50

18th anniversary of the People's Republic of China.

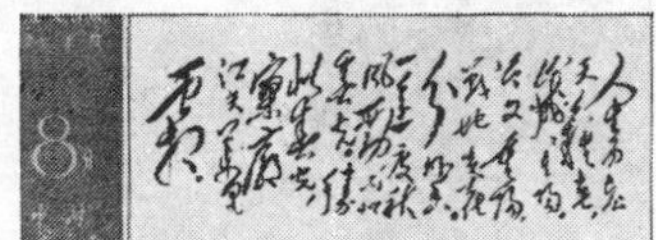
"September 9" — A236

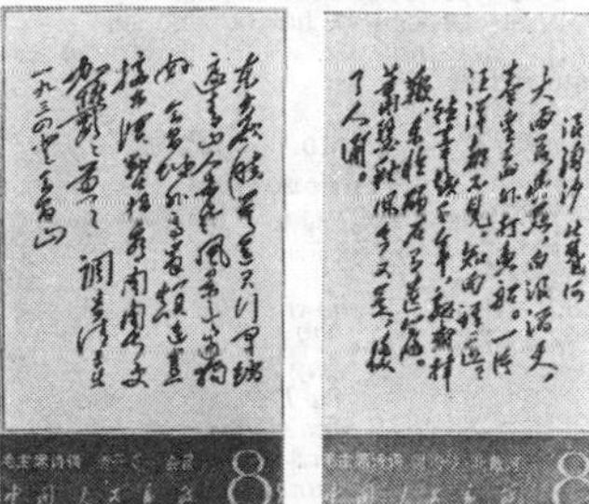
"Huichang" A237 "Peitaiho" A238

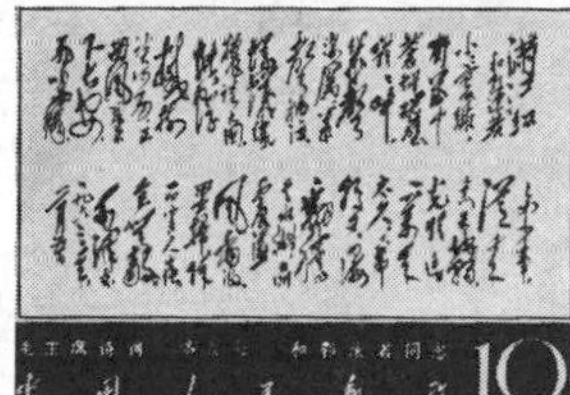
Reply to Comrade Kuo Mo-jo — A239

Mao Tse-tung Writing Poems — A240

Designs (Poems by Mao): No. 967, "The Long March." No. 968, "Liupanshan." No. 969, shown. No. 970, "The Cave of the Fairies." No. 971, "Snow." No. 972, "Lushan Pass." Nos. 973-974, shown. No. 975, "Conquest of Nanking." No. 976, "The Yellow Crane Pavilion." No. 977, "Swimming." No. 978, shown. No. 979, "Changsha."

1967-68 **Photo.** ***Perf. 11***

Red and Yellow Frame; Poem Written in Black

Size: 79x18½mm.

967 A236 4f *9 characters, UL panel ('68)* 14.00 4.75
968 A236 4f *11 characters, UL panel ('68)* 14.00 4.75

Perf. 11½

Size: 60x24mm.

969 A236 8f *shown, 10 characters in UL panel* 8.50 1.75
970 A236 8f *21 characters in UL panel* 8.50 1.75
971 A236 8f *11 characters in UL panel* 14.00 4.75
972 A236 8f *9 characters in UL panel* 14.00 4.75

Size: 29x50mm.

973 A237 8f *shown* 8.50 1.75
974 A238 8f *shown* 14.00 4.75
975 A238 8f *3 rows in bottom panel* 8.50 1.75
976 A238 8f *2 rows in bottom panel* 14.00 4.75

Perf. 11

Size: 52x38mm.

977 A239 8f *3 short vert. rows, at left of poem* 14.00 4.75
978 A239 10f *shown* 14.00 4.75
979 A239 10f *undivided text* 8.50 1.75
980 A240 10f red, yel & multi 11.00 4.75
Nos. 967-980 (14) 165.50 51.50

Poems by Mao Tse-tung. Issue dates: Nos. 969-970, 980, Oct. 1, 1967; Nos. 973-974, 977, May 20, 1968; others July 20, 1968.

Lin Piao's Epigram on Mao Tse-tung A241

1967, Dec. 26 **Photo.** ***Perf. 11x11½***

981 A241 8f red & gold 17.50 8.00

Mao and Parade of Artists — A242

"Raid on White Tiger Regiment" — A243

"Red Detachment of Women" — A244

1968 ***Perf. 11½x11; 11 (983, 990)***

982 A242 8f *shown* (56x36mm) 7.50 2.00
983 A242 8f *"The Red Lantern"* (vert.) 7.50 2.00
984 A243 8f *shown* 7.50 2.00
985 A243 8f *"Shachiapang" (women & soldier)* 7.50 2.00
986 A243 8f *"On the Dock"* 7.50 2.00
987 A243 8f *"Taking Bandits' Fort"* 7.50 2.00
988 A244 8f *shown* 15.00 7.00
989 A244 8f *"The White-haired Girl"* 15.00 7.00
990 A242 8f *Mao with Orchestra & Chorus* (50x36mm) 12.00 5.00
Nos. 982-990 (9) 87.00 31.00

Mao's direction for revolutionary literature and art. Issue dates: Nos. 982-987, Jan. 30; Nos. 988-990, May 1.

"Unite still more closely . . ." — A245

1968, May 31 **Photo.** ***Perf. 11***

991 A245 8f red, gold & red brn 22.50 8.00

Mao Tse-tung's statement of support of Afro-Americans.

Statement about Cultural Revolution A246

Directives of Chairman Mao: No. 993, Experiences of Revolutionary Committee. No. 994, Leadership role of Revolutionary Committee. No. 995, Basic principle of reform. No. 996, Purpose of Cultural Revolution.

1968, July 20 **Photo.** ***Perf. 11½***

Red, Yellow & Brown

992 A246 8f *shown* 15.00 4.00
993 A246 8f *5 lines over signature* 15.00 4.00
994 A246 8f *4½ lines over signature* 15.00 4.00
995 A246 8f *4 lines over signature* 15.00 4.00
996 A246 8f *8 lines over signature* 15.00 4.00
Strip of five 140.00 90.00

Printed se-tenant in horizontal strips of 5 within sheet.

Lin Piao's Statement, July 26, 1965 — A247

Engraved & Photogravure

1968, Aug. 1

997 A247 8f red, gold & blk 7.50 5.00

41st anniversary of the Chinese People's Liberation Army.

A little time given to the study of the arrangement of the Scott Catalogue can make it easier to use effectively.

Mao Tse-tung Going to An Yuan, 1921
A248

1968, Aug. 1 ***Perf. 11x11½***
998 A248 8f multi 12.00 6.00

Shade varieties include varying amount of red in clouds.

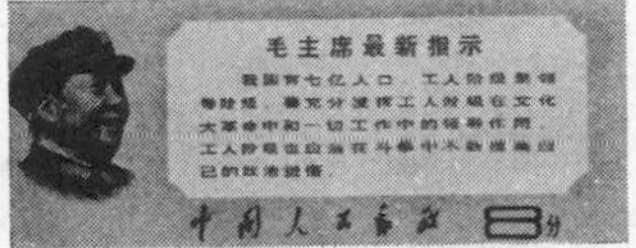

Directive of Chairman Mao — A249

1968, Nov. 30 ***Perf. 11½***
999 A249 8f red & blk brn 25.00 8.00

China Map, Worker, Farmer and Soldier — A249a

1968, Nov. Photo. ***Perf. 11½x11***
999A A249a 8f red, bl & bis *4,500. 2,500.*

Map inscribed: "The entire nation is red." Issued in Canton and quickly withdrawn because Taiwan appears white instead of red.

Woman, Miner and Soldier Holding Little Red Book
A250

1968, Dec. 26 ***Perf. 11x11½***
1000 A250 8f multi 9.00 1.50

Yangtze Bridge, Nanking
A251

Road across Bridge — A252

Designs: No. 1003, Side view. 10f, Aerial view.

Lithographed, Perf. 11½x11 (A251); Photogravure, Perf. 11½ (A252)
1969

Without Gum
1001 A251 4f multi 4.00 2.00
1002 A252 8f multi 4.00 4.00
1003 A252 8f multi 4.00 2.00
1004 A251 10f multi 4.00 2.00

Inauguration of Yangtze Bridge at Nanking on Dec. 29, 1968.

Singer and Pianist
A253

Designs (Piano Music from the Opera, "The Red Lantern"): No. 1006, Woman singer and pianist.

1969, Aug. Photo. ***Perf. 11x11½***
Without Gum
1005 A253 8f multi 4.50 2.00
1006 A253 8f multi 4.50 2.00

Harvest
A254

1969, Oct.
1007 A254 4f *shown* 3.00 2.00
a. Brown omitted 20.00 10.00
1008 A254 8f *Two harvesters* 3.00 2.00
1009 A254 8f *Harvesters with Little Red Books* 5.50 3.00
1010 A254 10f *Red Cross worker examining baby* 3.00 1.00

Agriculture students.

Armed Forces and Slogan — A255

Guarding the Coast — A256

Designs: No. 1013, 43f, Snow patrol (vert.).

1969, Oct. ***Perf. 11½***
1011 A255 8f red & multi 3.00 *2.00*
a. Bayonets omitted 90.00 40.00
1012 A256 8f bl & multi 3.00 *2.00*
1013 A256 8f bl & multi 3.00 *2.00*
1014 A256 35f blk & multi 3.00 *3.00*
1015 A256 43f blk & multi 3.00 *3.00*
Nos. 1011-1015 (5) 15.00 12.00

Defense of Chen Pao-tao (Damansky Islands) in Ussuri River.

Farm Woman — A257

Designs: 8f, Foundry worker. 10f, Soldier.

1969, Dec. ***Perf. 10; 11½ (#1017)***
Without Gum
1016 A257 4f ver & dk pur 50 1.25
1017 A257 8f ver & dk brn 50 1.25
1018 A257 10f ver & blk 50 1.25

Perforation
Nos. 1016-1018 and some succeeding issues bear two kinds of perforation: clean (Peking) and rough (Shanghai).

Building
A258

Communist Party Building, Shanghai
A259

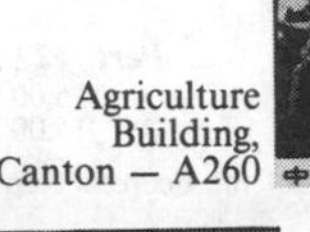

Agriculture Building, Canton — A260

Foundry Worker — A261

Two types of 8f Gate of Heavenly Peace:
I. Strong, definite halo around sun.
II. Halo missing, white shades gradually into red.

1969-72 Photo. ***Perf. 10, 11½***
Without Gum
1019 A258 1f *shown* 6 *25*
1020 A259 1½f *shown* 1.50 1.00
a. Perf. 11½ 6.00 5.00
1021 A260 2f *shown* 6 *15*
1022 A260 3f *1929 Party Day House, Pu Tien* 10 5
1023 A260 4f *Mao's Home and Office, Yunnan* 15 *20*
1024 A261 5f *Woman Tractor Driver* 2.25 75
1025 A260 8f *Gate of Heavenly Peace, type II* 2.25 50
a. Type I 2.25 60
1026 A259 8f *Heroes Monument* 2.25 1.00
a. Perf. 11½ 5.00 4.00
1027 A260 8f *Pagoda Hill, Yenan* 2.25 5.00
1028 A260 8f *Gate of Heavenly Peace (no sun)* 22 10
1029 A260 10f *Monument, Tsu Ping* 30 30
1030 A259 20f *Conference Hall, Tsunyi* 2.25 2.00
a. Perf. 11½ 6.00 4.00
1031 A260 20f *Highway ('72)* 45 30
1032 A260 22f *Shao Shan Village, Birthplace of Mao* 52 50
1033 A260 35f *Conference Hall* 75 50
1034 A260 43f *Chingkang Peaks* 90 50
1035 A259 50f *as 4f, different view* 4.50 2.00
1036 A260 52f *People's Hall, Peking* 1.25 50
1037 A261 $1 *shown ('70)* 4.50 4.00
a. Perf. 11
b. Perf. 11½
Nos. 1019-1037 (19) 26.51 19.60

Kin Hsün-hua
A262

Mounted Patrol — A263

1970, Jan. Without Gum ***Perf. 11½***
1045 A262 8f red & gray brn 5.00 5.00
a. 8f red & blk 5.00 *8.00*

Death of Kin Hsün-hua in Kirin border flood.

1970, Aug. 1
Without Gum
1046 A263 8f yel grn & multi 4.00 4.00

43rd anniversary of the People's Liberation Army.

Beginning with No. 1047 commemorative stamps carry a cumulative number in parenthesis at lower left and the year at lower right. Where such numbers help to identify, they are quoted in parenthesis.

Cpl. Yang Tse-jung — A264

Ensemble — A265

1970, Aug. 1 ***Perf. 11½x11, 11x11½***
1047 A264 8f *shown* (1) 70 70
1048 A264 8f *Armed guards* (2) 70 70
1049 A264 8f *Yang leaping through forest* (3) 70 70
1050 A265 8f *shown* (4) 70 70
1051 A265 8f *Yang in folk costume* (5) 70 70
1052 A265 8f *Four actors* (6) 50 50
Nos. 1047-1052 (6) 4.00 4.00

Scenes from opera "Taking Tiger Mountain by Strategy." Nos. 1048, 1052, horizontal.

Frontier Guard
A266

1971, Jan. Litho. *Perf. 11 ½*
Without Gum

1053 A266 4f multi 2.00 75
a. Perf. 10 60 1.00
b. Perf. 11½x10 5.00
c. Perf. 10x11½ 5.00

Banner of the Commune — A267

Street Battle, Paris, 1871 A268

Designs: 10f, Proclamation of the Commune. 22f, Rally.

Lithographed and Engraved
Perf. 11½x11, 11x11½
1971, Mar. 18

1054 A267 4f sal & multi 1.50 1.50
1055 A268 8f ver, pink & brn 1.50 1.50
1056 A267 10f ver, pink & dk brn 1.50 1.50
1057 A268 22f ver, pink & dk brn 1.50 1.50

Centenary of the Paris Commune.

Redrawn Building Type of 1961

Designs: 2f, 3f, August 1 building, Nanchang. 4f, 52f, Gate of Heavenly Peace, Peking. 10f, 20f, Pagoda Hill, Yenan.

1971 Litho. *Perf. 11x11½*
Size: 21x16mm.

1059 A152 2f sl grn 2.25 3.00
1060 A152 3f sepia 2.25 3.00
1061 A152 4f brt pink 2.25 3.00
1062 A152 10f brt rose lil 2.25 3.00
1063 A152 20f dk bl grn 2.25 3.00
1064 A152 52f orange 2.25 3.00
Nos. 1059-1064 (6) 13.50 18.00

Paper of Nos. 1059-1064 is white. That of Nos. 647-654 is toned.

Communist Party Building, Shanghai — A269

People and Factories — A270

Designs: No. 1068, Peasant Movement Training Institute. No. 1069, Ching Kang Peaks. No. 1070, Conference Building, Tsunyi. No. 1071, Pagoda Hall, Yenan. No. 1073, People and People's Hall, Peking. No. 1074, People and Pagoda Hill, Yenan. 22f, Gate of Heavenly Peace, Peking.

1971, July 1 Photo. *Perf. 11½*
Red and Gold Frame

1067 A269 4f ver (12) 55 55
1068 A269 4f brt grn (13) 55 55

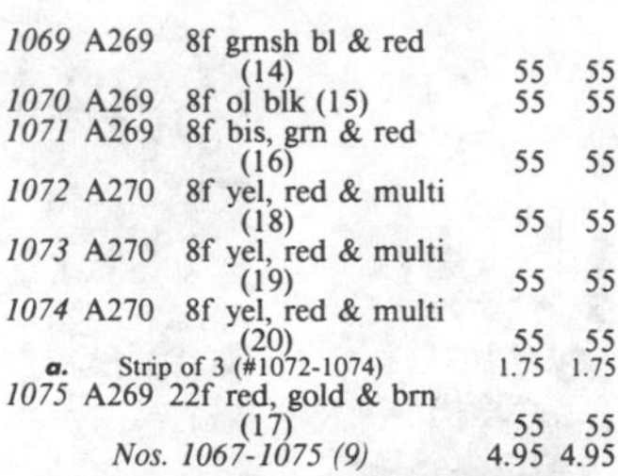

1069 A269 8f grnsh bl & red (14) 55 55
1070 A269 8f ol blk (15) 55 55
1071 A269 8f bis, grn & red (16) 55 55
1072 A270 8f yel, red & multi (18) 55 55
1073 A270 8f yel, red & multi (19) 55 55
1074 A270 8f yel, red & multi (20) 55 55
a. Strip of 3 (#1072-1074) 1.75 1.75
1075 A269 22f red, gold & brn (17) 55 55
Nos. 1067-1075 (9) 4.95 4.95

50th anniversary of the Chinese Communist Party. Nos. 1072-1074 printed se-tenant with continuous design.

Chinese Welcome — A271

Enver Hoxha — A272

Designs: No. 1077, Chinese and African players. No. 1078, Chinese and African girl players. 43f, Games' emblem.

1971, Nov. 3 Litho. *Perf. 11½*

1076 A271 8f lil rose & multi 25 25
1077 A271 8f lt yel & multi 25 25
1078 A271 8f dk grn & multi 25 25
1079 A271 43f grn, gold & org 1.25 1.25

Afro-Asian Table Tennis Games, Peking.

1971, Nov. 3 Photo. *Perf. 11*

Designs: No. 1081, Party's birthplace. No. 1082, Albanian flag. 52f, Albanian partisans (horiz.).

1080 A272 8f Prus bl & multi 3.00 3.00
1081 A272 8f buff & multi 3.00 3.00
1082 A272 8f red, yel & multi 3.00 3.00
1083 A272 52f lt bl & multi 3.00 3.00

30th anniversary of the founding of Albanian Communist Party.

Yenan Pagoda and 1942 Meeting House A273

1972, May 23 Photo. *Perf. 11*
Cumulative numbers in parenthesis.

1084 A273 8f *shown* (33) 1.00 1.00
1085 A273 8f *Uniformed choir* (34) 1.00 1.00
1086 A273 8f *"Brother & Sister"* (35) 1.00 1.00
1087 A273 8f *Outdoor performance* (36) 1.00 1.00
1088 A273 8f *"The Red Signal Lantern"* (37) 1.00 1.00
1089 A273 8f *Dancer from "The Red Company of Women"* (38) 1.00 1.00
Nos. 1084-1089 (6) 6.00 6.00

30th anniversary of the publication of the Discussions on Literature and Art at the Yenan Forum.

Various Ball Games — A274

Workers' Gymnastics A275

1972, June 10

1090 A274 8f *shown* (39) 25 25
1091 A275 8f *shown* (40) 25 25
1092 A275 8f *Tug of war* (41) 25 25
1093 A275 8f *Mountain climbers and tents* (42) 25 25
1094 A275 8f *Children diving & swimming* (43) 25 25
Nos. 1090-1094 (5) 1.25 1.25

10th anniversary of Mao Tse-tung's edict on physical culture.

Ocean Freighter Fenglei — A276

1972, July 10 Photo. *Perf. 11½*

1095 A276 8f *shown* (29) 50 50
1096 A276 8f *Tanker Taching No. 30* (30) 50 50
1097 A276 8f *Cargo-passenger ship Changzeng* (31) 50 50
1098 A276 8f *Dredger Xienfeng* (32) 50 50

Table Tennis Players' Welcome A277

1972, Sept. 2 *Perf. 11½x11, 11x11½*

1099 A277 8f *Championship emblem* (vert.) (45) 25 14
1100 A277 8f *shown* (46) 25 14
1101 A277 8f *Table tennis* (47) 25 14
1102 A277 22f *Women from different countries* (vert.) (48) 1.00 65

First Asian table tennis championships.

Wang Chin-hsi — A278

Workers on Cliffs along Canal — A279

Engraved and Photogravure
1972, Dec. 25 *Perf. 11½x11*

1103 A278 8f multi (44) 75 75

Wang Chin-hsi, the Iron Man, fighter for the working class.

1972, Dec. 30

Designs: No. 1105, Canal flowing through tunnel. No. 1106, Bridge. No. 1107, Canal along cliffs.

1104 A279 8f multi (49) 35 35
1105 A279 8f multi (50) 35 35
1106 A279 8f multi (51) 35 35
1107 A279 8f multi (52) 35 35

Construction of Red Flag Canal, Linhsien county, Honan.

Giant Panda — A280

Woman Coal Miner — A281

Designs: Pandas in various positions. The 8f stamps are horizontal.

Perf. 11½x11, 11x11½
1973, Jan. 15 Photo.
Designs in Black and Red

1108 A280 4f lt yel grn (61) 2.00 2.00
1109 A280 8f buff (59) 2.00 2.00
1110 A280 8f lt tan (60) 2.00 2.00
1111 A280 10f pale grn (58) 2.00 2.00
1112 A280 20f pale bl gray (57) 2.00 2.00
1113 A280 43f pale lil (62) 2.00 2.00
Nos. 1108-1113 (6) 12.00 12.00

1973, Mar. 8 Photo. *Perf. 11½x11*

1114 A281 8f *shown* (63) 40 40
1115 A281 8f *Committee member* (64) 40 40
1116 A281 8f *Telephone line worker* (65) 40 40

International Working Women's Day. Designs are after paintings from an exhibition for 30th anniversary of the Yenan Forum on Literature and Art.

Dancing Girl — A282

Tournament Emblem — A283

1973, June 1 Photo. *Perf. 11*

1117 A282 8f *shown* (86) 25 25
1118 A282 8f *Musician, boy* (87) 25 25
1119 A282 8f *Girl with scarf* (88) 25 25
1120 A282 8f *Boy with tambourine* (89) 25 25
1121 A282 8f *Girl with drum* (90) 25 25
Nos. 1117-1121 (5) 1.25 1.25

Nos. 1117-1121 printed se-tenant.

1973, Aug. 25 Photo. *Perf. 11½*

Designs: No. 1123, Visitors from Asia, Africa and Latin America arriving by plane. No. 1124, Woman player. 22f, African, Asian and Latin American women.

1122 A283 8f multi (91) 40 40
1123 A283 8f multi (92) 40 40
1124 A283 8f multi (93) 40 40
1125 A283 22f multi (94) 40 40

Asian, African and Latin American Table Tennis Friendship Invitational Tournament.

The White-haired Girl — A284

Designs: Scenes from the ballet "The White-haired Girl." Nos. 1126 and 1129 vertical.

1973, Sept. 25 Photo. *Perf. 11½*

1126 A284 8f multi (53) 50 50
1127 A284 8f multi (54) 50 50
1128 A284 8f multi (55) 50 50
1129 A284 8f multi (56) 50 50

Fair Building, Canton — A285

1973, Oct. 15 Photo. *Perf. 11*

1130 A285 8f multi (95)	75	75

Export Commodities Fall Fair, Canton.

Teapot with Blue Phoenix Design — A286

Designs: No. 1132, Silver pot with horse design. No. 1133, Black pottery horse. No. 1134, Woman, clay figurine. No. 1135, Carved stone pillar base. No. 1136, Galloping bronze horse. No. 1137, Bronze inkwell (toad). No. 1138, Bronze lamp, Chang Hsin Palace. No. 1139, Bronze tripod. No. 1140, Square bronze pot. 20f, Bronze wine vessel. 52f, Painted red clay tripod.

1973, Nov. 20 *Perf. 11½*

1131 A286 4f ol bis & multi (66)	25	25
1132 A286 4f ver & multi (67)	25	25
1133 A286 8f yel grn & multi (68)	25	25
1134 A286 8f brt rose & multi (69)	25	25
1135 A286 8f lt vio & multi (70)	25	25
1136 A286 8f yel bis & multi (71)	25	25
1137 A286 8f lt bl & multi (72)	25	25
1138 A286 8f gray & multi (73)	25	25
1139 A286 10f yel bis & multi (74)	25	25
1140 A286 10f dp org & multi (75)	25	25
1141 A286 20f lil & multi (76)	60	60
1142 A286 52f grn & multi (77)	1.50	1.50
Nos. 1131-1142 (12)	4.60	4.60

Excavated works of art.

Marginal Markings

Marginal inscriptions on stamps of 1974 start at lower left with "J" for commemoratives and "T" for "special issues," followed by three numbers indicating (a) set sequence for the year, (b) total of stamps in set, and (c) number of stamp within set. At right appears the year date. Listings include the "c" number parenthetically.

Woman Gymnast — A287

Designs: No. 1144, Gymnast on rings. No. 1145, Aerial split over balance beam, woman. No. 1146, Gymnast on parallel bars. No. 1147, Uneven bars, woman. No. 1148, Gymnast on horse.

1974, Jan. 1 Photo. *Perf. 11½x11*

1143 A287 8f lt grn & multi (1)	35	35
1144 A287 8f lt vio & multi (2)	35	35
1145 A287 8f lt bl & multi (3)	35	35
1146 A287 8f sal & multi (4)	35	35
1147 A287 8f yel & multi (5)	35	35
1148 A287 8f lil rose & multi (6)	35	35
Nos. 1143-1148 (6)	2.10	2.10

Girls Twirling Bamboo Diabolos — A288

Designs: No. 1149, Lion Dance (vert.). No. 1150, Handstand on chairs (vert.). No. 1152, Men balancing jar. No. 1153, Plate spinning (vert.). No. 1154, Twirling umbrella (vert.).

1974, Jan. 21 *Perf. 11*

1149 A288 8f brn & multi (1)	30	30
1150 A288 8f Prus bl & multi (2)	30	30
1151 A288 8f lil & multi (3)	30	30
1152 A288 8f dl bl & multi (4)	30	30
1153 A288 8f ol grn & multi (5)	30	30
1154 A288 8f gray & multi (6)	30	30
Nos. 1149-1154 (6)	1.80	1.80

Traditional acrobatics.

Shao Shan — A289

Transportation by Railroad — A290

Designs: 1½f, Site of 1st National Communist Party Congress. 2f, Peasant Movement Institute, Kwangchow. 3f, Headquarters of Nanchang Uprising. 4f, Great Hall of the People, Peking. 5f, View of Wen Chia Shih. 8f, Tien An Men. 10f, Tzeping in Chingkang Mountains. 20f Site of Kutien Meeting. 22f, Tsunyi Conference site. 35f, Yenan (bridge). 43f, Hsi Pai Ho, Communist Party meeting site. 50f, Fairy Cave, Lushan. 52f, Monument to People's Heroes. $2, Trucks on mountain road.

1974 Litho. *Perf. 11*

Without Gum

1163 A289 1f sl grn & pale grn	5	5
1164 A289 1½f car & buff	5	50
1165 A289 2f dk bl & pale grn	5	5
1166 A289 3f dk ol & yel	5	5
1167 A289 4f red & yel	8	8
1168 A289 5f brn & lt yel	10	10
1169 A289 8f dl mag & buff	15	15
1170 A289 10f bl & pink	20	20
1171 A289 20f dk red & buff	50	50
1172 A289 22f vio & lt yel	55	55
1173 A289 35f mar & lt yel	75	75
1174 A289 43f red brn & buff	1.10	*2.00*
1175 A289 50f dk bl & pink	*6.50*	*1.25*
1176 A289 52f sep & buff	1.25	1.25

Photogravure & Engraved

1177 A290 $1 multi	2.50	1.00
1178 A290 $2 multi	5.00	1.65
Nos. 1163-1178 (16)	18.88	10.13

Capital Stadium — A290a

Design: 8f, Hotel Peking.

1974, Dec. 1 Photo. *Perf. 11*

Without Gum

1179 A290a 4f blk & yel grn	15	*20*
1180 A290a 8f blk & ultra	25	25

"Veteran Secretary" A291

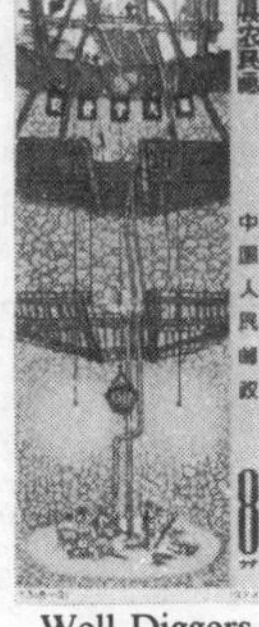
Well Diggers A292

Designs: Nos. 1183-1186 horizontal.

1974, Apr. 20 Photo. *Perf. 11*

1181 A291 8f *shown* (1)	35	35
1182 A292 8f *shown* (2)	35	35
1183 A291 8f *Spring hoeing* (3)	35	35
1184 A291 8f *Farmers* (4)	35	35
1185 A292 8f *Farm* (5)	35	35
1186 A291 8f *Bumper crops* (6)	35	35
Nos. 1181-1186 (6)	2.10	2.10

Paintings by farmers of Huhsien County, shown at exhibition in Peking.

Mailman on Motorcycle — A293

1974, May 15 Photo. *Perf. 11*

1187 A293 8f *shown* (1)	45	45
1188 A293 8f *People of the world* (2)	45	45
1189 A293 8f *Great Wall* (3)	45	45

Centenary of the Universal Postal Union.

Barefoot Doctor Inoculating Children A294

Designs (Barefoot Doctors): No. 1191, Crossing stream at night to reach patient (vert.). No. 1192, Gathering herbs (vert.). No. 1193, Acupuncture treatment for farmer in the field.

Perf. 11x11½, 11½x11

1974, June 26 Photo.

1190 A294 8f multi (82)	35	35
1191 A294 8f multi (83)	35	35
1192 A294 8f multi (84)	35	35
1193 A294 8f multi (85)	35	35

Steel Worker Wang Chin-hsi — A295

1974, Sept. 30 Photo. *Perf. 11*

Designs: No. 1195, Workers studying Mao's writings around campfire. No. 1196, Drilling for oil in winter. No. 1197, Scientific industrial management. No. 1198, Oil derricks and farms. Numbered T.4.

1194 A295 8f multi (5-1)	30	30
1195 A295 8f multi (5-2)	30	30
1196 A295 8f multi (5-3)	30	30
1197 A295 8f multi (5-4)	30	30
1198 A295 8f multi (5-5)	30	30
Nos. 1194-1198 (5)	1.50	1.50

The workers of Taching as examples of achievement.

Members of Tachai Commune — A296

Designs: No. 1200, Farmers leveling mountains and fields in winter. No. 1201, Scientific farming. No. 1202, Trucks carrying surplus harvest. No. 1203, Young workers with banner. Numbered T.5.

1974, Sept. 30

1199 A296 8f multi (5-1)	40	40
1200 A296 8f multi (5-2)	40	40
1201 A296 8f multi (5-3)	40	40
1202 A296 8f multi (5-4)	40	40
1203 A296 8f multi (5-5)	40	40
Nos. 1199-1203 (5)	2.00	2.00

The farmers of Tachai as examples of achievement.

Arms of Republic and Members of Ethnic Groups — A297

Taching Steel Worker — A298

Designs: No. 1206, Tachai farm woman. No. 1207, Soldier, planes and ships. Numbered J.3.

1974, Oct. 1

1204 A297 8f multi (1-1)	1.25	1.25
1205 A298 8f multi (3-1)	35	35
1206 A298 8f multi (3-2)	35	35
1207 A298 8f multi (3-3)	35	35

People's Republic of China, 25th anniversary. Nos. 1205-1207 printed se-tenant.

Export Commodities Fair Building, Canton — A299

1974, Oct. 15

1208 A299 8f multi	50	50

Chinese Export Commodities Fair, Canton.

Guerrillas' Monument, Permet, Albania — A300

Albanian Patriots and Coat of Arms — A301

1974, Nov. 29 Photo. ***Perf. 11½x11***
1209 A300 8f multi 1.75 1.75
1210 A301 8f multi 1.75 1.75

Albania's liberation, 30th anniversary.

Water-cooled Generator — A302

Designs: No. 1212, Motorized rice sprouts transplanter. No. 1213, Universal cylindrical grinding machine. No. 1214, Open-air rock drill (vert.). All dated 1973.

Photogravure and Engraved

1974, Dec. 23 ***Perf. 11***
1211 A302 8f vio & multi (78) 50 50
1212 A302 8f yel grn & multi (79) 50 50
1213 A302 8f ver & multi (80) 50 50
1214 A302 8f bl & multi (81) 50 50

Industrial products.

Congress Delegates — A303

Designs: No. 1216, Red flags, constitution and flowers. No. 1217, Worker, farmer and soldier, agriculture and industry. Numbered J.5.

1975, Jan. 25 Photo. ***Perf. 11½***
1215 A303 8f gold & multi (3-1) 50 50
1216 A303 8f gold & multi (3-2) 50 50
1217 A303 8f gold & multi (3-3) 50 50

Fourth National People's Congress, Peking.

Teacher Studying Revolutionary Works — A304

Designs: No. 1219, Teacher, children and horse. No. 1220, Outdoors class. No. 1221, Class held in boat. Numbered T.9.

1975, Mar. 8 Photo. ***Perf. 11***
1218 A304 8f multi (4-1) 35 35
1219 A304 8f multi (4-2) 35 35
1220 A304 8f multi (4-3) 35 35
1221 A304 8f multi (4-4) 35 35

Rural women teachers and for International Working Women's Day.

"Broadsword," Encounter Position — A305

Designs: No. 1223, Exercise with 2 swords (woman). No. 1224, Graceful boxing (woman). No. 1225, Man leaping with spear. No. 1226, Woman holding cudgel. 43f, Two women with spears against man with cudgel.

1975, June 10 Photo. ***Perf. 11x11½***
Size: 39x29mm.
1222 A305 8f red & multi (6-1) 60 60
1223 A305 8f red & multi (6-2) 60 60
1224 A305 8f red & multi (6-3) 60 60
1225 A305 8f red & multi (6-4) 60 60
1226 A305 8f red & multi (6-5) 60 60

Size: 59x29mm.
1227 A305 43f red & multi (6-6) 1.25 1.25
Nos. 1222-1227 (6) 4.25 4.25

Wushu ("Kung Fu"), self-defense exercises. Tete beche in sheets of 50 (5x10).

Mass Judgment and Criticisms — A306

Designs: No. 1229, Brigade leader writing wall newspaper. No. 1230, Study and criticism on battlefield (horiz.). No. 1231, Former "slave" led into battle by criticism of Lin Piao and Confucius (horiz.). Numbered T. 8.

Perf. 11½x11, 11x11½
1975, Aug. 20 Photo.
1228 A306 8f red & multi (4-1) 60 60
1229 A306 8f red & multi (4-2) 60 60
1230 A306 8f red & multi (4-3) 60 60
1231 A306 8f red & multi (4-4) 60 60

Campaign to encourage criticism of Lin Piao and Confucius.

Athletes Studying Theory of Dictatorship of Proletariat — A307

Designs: No. 1232, Women athletes leading parade (vert.). No. 1234, Women volleyball players. No. 1235, Runner, soldier, farmer and worker (vert.). No. 1236, Young athlete and various sports. No. 1237, Athletes of various races and horse race. 35f, Children and diving tower (vert.). Numbered J. 6.

1975, Sept. 12 Photo. ***Perf. 11½***
1232 A307 8f multi (7-1) 20 20
1233 A307 8f multi (7-2) 20 20
1234 A307 8f multi (7-3) 20 20
1235 A307 8f multi (7-4) 20 20
1236 A307 8f multi (7-5) 20 20
1237 A307 8f multi (7-6) 20 20
1238 A307 35f multi (7-7) 90 90
Nos. 1232-1238 (7) 2.10 2.10

3rd National Sports Meet.

Mountaineers A308

Mt. Everest A309

Design: No. 1240, Mountaineers raising Chinese flag on summit (horiz.). Numbered T.15.

1975 Photo. ***Perf. 11½x11, 11x11½***
1239 A308 8f multi (3-2) 35 35
1240 A308 8f multi (3-3) 35 35
1241 A309 43f multi (3-1) 1.25 1.25

Chinese Mt. Everest expedition.

Agricultural Workers with Book — A310

Designs: No. 1243, Workers carrying load. No. 1244, Woman driving harvester combine. Numbered J.7.

1975, Oct. 1 ***Perf. 11½***
1242 A310 8f multi (3-1) 50 50
1243 A310 8f multi (3-2) 50 50
1244 A310 8f multi (3-3) 50 50

National Conference to promote learning from Tachai's achievements in agriculture.

Girl Giving Boy Red Scarf — A311

Designs (Children): No. 1246, Putting up wall posters criticizing Lin Piao and Confucius. No. 1247, Studying. No. 1248, Harvesting. 52f, Physical training. Numbered T.14.

1975, Dec. 1 Photo. ***Perf. 11½***
1245 A311 8f multi (5-1) 25 25
1246 A311 8f multi (5-2) 25 25
1247 A311 8f multi (5-3) 25 25
1248 A311 8f multi (5-4) 25 25
1249 A311 52f multi (5-5) 1.50 1.50
Nos. 1245-1249 (5) 2.50 2.50

Moral, intellectual and physical progress of Chinese children.

Woman Plowing Rice Field A312

Designs: No. 1251, Mechanized rice planting. No. 1252, Drainage and irrigation. No. 1253, Woman spraying insecticide over cotton field. No. 1254, Combine. Numbered T.13.

1975, Dec. 15 ***Perf. 11***
1250 A312 8f multi (5-1) 35 35
1251 A312 8f multi (5-2) 35 35
1252 A312 8f multi (5-3) 35 35
1253 A312 8f multi (5-4) 35 35
1254 A312 8f multi (5-5) 35 35
Nos. 1250-1254 (5) 1.75 1.75

Priority program of farm mechanization.

Farmland and Irrigation Canal — A313

Designs of Nos. 1255-1270 numbered J.8.

1976, Feb. 20 Photo. ***Perf. 11½***
1255 A313 8f *shown* (16-1) 35 35
1256 A313 8f *Irrigation canal* (16-2) 35 35
1257 A313 8f *Fertilizer plant* (16-3) 35 35
1258 A313 8f *Textile plant* (16-4) 35 35
1259 A313 8f *Anshan Iron and Steel Co.* (16-5) 35 35

Nos. 1255-1270 commemorate fulfillment of 4th Five-year Plan.

1976, Apr. 9
1260 A313 8f *Coal freight trains* (16-6) 35 35
1261 A313 8f *Hydroelectric station* (16-7) 35 35
1262 A313 8f *Ship building* (16-8) 35 35
1263 A313 8f *Oil industry* (16-9) 35 35
1264 A313 8f *Pipe line and port* (16-10) 35 35

1976, June 12
1265 A313 8f *Train on viaduct* (16-11) 35 35
1266 A313 8f *Scientific research* (16-12) 35 35
1267 A313 8f *Classroom* (16-13) 35 35
1268 A313 8f *Health Center* (16-14) 35 35
1269 A313 8f *Apartment houses* (16-15) 35 35
1270 A313 8f *Department store* (16-16) 35 35
Nos. 1255-1270 (16) 5.60 5.60

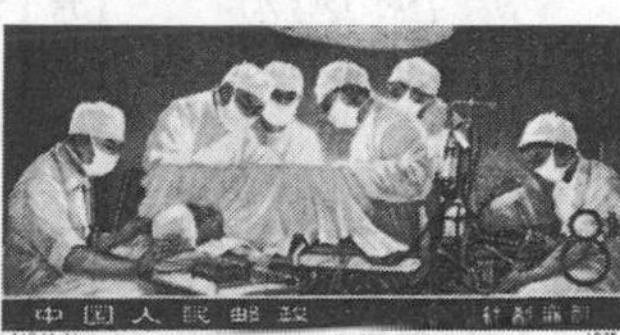

Heart Surgery with Acupuncture Anesthesia — A314

Designs (Operating Room and): No. 1272, Man driving tractor with severed arm restored. No. 1273, Man exercising broken arm in cast. No. 1274, Patient threading needle after cataract operation. Numbered T.12.

1976, Apr. 9 Photo. ***Perf. 11½***
1271 A314 8f brn & multi (4-1) 35 35
1272 A314 8f yel grn & multi (4-2) 35 35
1273 A314 8f bl grn & multi (4-3) 35 35
1274 A314 8f vio bl & multi (4-4) 35 35

Achievements in medical and health services.

Students in May 7 School — A315

Designs: No. 1276, Students as farm workers. No. 1277, Production brigade. Numbered J.9.

1976, May 7 Photo. ***Perf. 11½***
1275 A315 8f multi (3-1) 50 50
1276 A315 8f multi (3-2) 50 50
1277 A315 8f multi (3-3) 50 50

10th anniversary of Chairman Mao's May 7 Directive.

Mass Training in Swimming — A316

Designs: No. 1279, Swimmers crossing Yangtze River. No. 1280, Swimmers walking into the surf. Numbered J.10.

1976, July 16 Photo. ***Perf. 11½***
Size: 47x27mm.
1278 A316 8f multi (3-1) 50 50

Size: 35x27mm.

1279 A316 8f multi (3-2) 50 50
1280 A316 8f multi (3-3) 50 50

Chairman Mao's swim in Yangtze River, 10th anniversary.

Workers, Peasants and Soldiers Going to College — A317

Designs: No. 1282, Classroom. No. 1283, Instruction on construction site. No. 1284, Computer room. No. 1285, Graduates returning home. Numbered T.18.

1976, Sept. 6 Photo. *Perf. 11½*

1281 A317 8f multi (5-1) 35 35
1282 A317 8f multi (5-2) 35 35
1283 A317 8f multi (5-3) 35 35
1284 A317 8f multi (5-4) 35 35
1285 A317 8f multi (5-5) 35 35
Nos. 1281-1285 (5) 1.75 1.75

Success of proletarian education system.

Power Line Repair by Woman — A318

Designs: No. 1287, Insulator repair. No. 1288, Cherry picker. No. 1289, Transformer repair. Numbered T.16.

1976, Sept. 15

1286 A318 8f multi (4-1) 40 40
1287 A318 8f multi (4-2) 40 40
1288 A318 8f multi (4-3) 40 40
1289 A318 8f multi (4-4) 40 40

Maintenance of high power lines.

Lu Hsun — A319

Designs: No. 1291, Lu Hsun sick, writing in bed. No. 1292, Lu Hsun with worker, soldier and peasant. Numbered J.11.

Photogravure and Engraved

1976, Oct. 19 *Perf. 11x11½*

1290 A319 8f multi (3-1) 70 70
1291 A319 8f multi (3-2) 70 70
1292 A319 8f multi (3-3) 70 70

Lu Hsun (1881-1936), writer and revolutionary leader.

Old Farmer Tying Towel on Student's Head — A320

Designs: No. 1294, Student teaching farm woman (horiz.). No. 1295, Students climbing mountain for new water resources. No. 1296, Student testing wheat (horiz.). 10f, Student feeding lamb. 20f, Frontier guards (horiz.). Numbered T.17.

1976, Dec. 22 Photo. *Perf. 11½*

1293 A320 4f multi (6-1) 30 30
1294 A320 8f multi (6-2) 30 30
1295 A320 8f multi (6-3) 30 30
1296 A320 8f multi (6-4) 30 30
1297 A320 10f multi (6-5) 30 30
1298 A320 20f multi (6-6) 1.25 1.25
Nos. 1293-1298 (6) 2.75 2.75

Students' efforts to help poor country people.

Mao's Home, Shaoshan — A321

Designs: No. 1300, School building. No. 1301, Farmers' Association building. 10f, Railroad station. All in Shaoshan. Numbered T.11.

1976, Dec. 26 *Perf. 11*

1299 A321 4f multi (4-1) 40 40
1300 A321 8f multi (4-2) 40 40
1301 A321 8f multi (4-3) 40 40
1302 A321 10f multi (4-4) 40 40

Shaoshan, Mao's birthplace.

Chou En-lai — A322

Designs: No. 1304, Chou giving report at 10th Party Congress. No. 1305, Chou with Wang Chin-hsi, famous oil worker (horiz.). No. 1306, Chou with people of Tachai, 1973 (horiz.). Numbered J.13.

1977, Jan. 8 Photo. *Perf. 11½*

1303 A322 8f multi (4-1) 30 30
1304 A322 8f multi (4-2) 30 30
1305 A322 8f multi (4-3) 30 30
1306 A322 8f multi (4-4) 30 30

Premier Chou En-lai (1898-1976), a founder of Chinese Communist Party, 1st death anniversary.

Liu Hu-lan, an Inspiration A323

Designs: No. 1307, Liu Hu-lan monument. No. 1308, Mao Tse-tung quotation: "A great life-a glorious death." Numbered J.12.

1977, Jan. 31

1307 A323 8f multi (3-1) 32 32
1308 A323 8f multi (3-2) 32 32
1309 A323 8f multi (3-3) 32 32

Liu Hu-lan, Chinese heroine.

Uprising in Taiwan A324

Design: 10f, Gate of Heavenly Peace, Peking; Sun Moon Lake, Taiwan, Taiwanese people holding PRC flag. Numbered J.14.

1977, Feb. 28 Photo. *Perf. 11*

1310 A324 8f multi (2-1) 45 45
1311 A324 10f multi (2-2) 45 45

Uprising of the people of Taiwan, Feb. 28, 1947.

Sharpshooters — A325

Designs: No. 1313, Women horseback riders. No. 1314, Underground defense tunnel. Numbered T.10.

1977, Mar. 8 *Perf. 11½*

1312 A325 8f multi (3-1) 25 25
1313 A325 8f multi (3-2) 25 25
1314 A325 8f multi (3-3) 25 25

Militia women.

Forestry — A326

Designs: 1f, Coal mining. 1½f, Sheepherding. 2f, Export (loading railroad car onto ship). 4f, Hydroelectric station. 5f, Fishery. 8f, Combine in field. 10f, Radio tower and mail truck. 20f, Steel production. 30f, Trucks on mountain road. 40f, Textiles. 50f, Tractor assembly line. 60f, Offshore oil rigs and birds, setting sun. 70f, Railroad bridge, Yangtze Gorge. No numbers.

1977 Photo. *Perf. 11½*

1315 A326 1f yel grn, red & blk 15 5
1316 A326 1½f bl grn, yel grn & brn 15 *50*
1317 A326 2f org, bl & blk 15 7
1318 A326 3f ol & dk grn 15 9
1319 A326 4f lil, org & blk 15 10
1320 A326 5f lt ol & ultra 25 10
1321 A326 8f red & yel 25 10
1322 A326 10f lt grn, org & bl 25 5
1323 A326 20f org, yel & brn 60 5
1324 A326 30f bl, lt grn & blk 70 10
1325 A326 40f multi 80 40
1326 A326 50f cit, red & blk 90 20
1327 A326 60f pur, yel & org 1.25 30
1328 A326 70f bl & multi 1.50 50
Nos. 1315-1328 (14) 7.25 2.61

Address by Party Committee A327

Designs: No. 1330, Planting new rice fields. No. 1331, Farmers reading wall newspaper. No. 1332, Land reclamation. Numbered T.22.

1977, Apr. 9 *Perf. 11x11½*

1329 A327 8f multi (4-1) 30 30
1330 A327 8f multi (4-2) 30 30
1331 A327 8f multi (4-3) 30 30
1332 A327 8f multi (4-4) 30 30

Building Tachai-type communities throughout China.

Worker at Microphone — A328

Designs: No. 1334, Drilling for oil during snowstorm. No. 1335, Crowd advancing under Red banner. No. 1336, Workers, industrial complex, rocket blast-off. Numbered J.15.

1977, Apr. 25 *Perf. 11*

1333 A328 8f multi (4-1) 30 30
1334 A328 8f multi (4-2) 30 30
1335 A328 8f multi (4-3) 30 30
1336 A328 8f multi (4-4) 30 30

Conference on learning from Taching workers in industry.

Mongolians Hailing Anniversary A329

Designs: 10f, Iron and steel complex, iron ore train. 20f, Cattle grazing in improved pasture. Numbered J.16.

1977, May 1 *Perf. 11x11½*

1337 A329 8f multi (3-1) 30 30
1338 A329 10f multi (3-2) 30 30
1339 A329 20f multi (3-3) 60 60

30th anniversary of Inner Mongolian Autonomous Region.

1877 Flag of Romania and Oak Leaves A330

Mihai Viteazu Memorial (16th Century Hero) A331

Design: 10f, Battle of Smirdan, by N. Grigorescu. Numbered J.17.

1977, May 9 Photo. *Perf. 11*

1340 A330 8f multi (3-1) 30 30
1341 A331 10f multi (3-2) 30 30
1342 A331 20f multi (3-3) 60 60

Centenary of Romanian independence.

Yenan "Let 100 Flowers Bloom" A332

Design: No. 1344, Hammer, sickle, gun and flowers; "Proletarian revolutionary literature will prosper." Numbered J.18.

1977, May, 23

1343 A332 8f grn, red & gold 35 35
1344 A332 8f lt brn, red & gold 35 35

Yenan Forum on Literature and Art, 35th anniversary.

The first price column gives the catalogue value of an unused stamp, the second that of a used stamp.

Chu Teh — A333

Designs: No. 1346, Chu Teh, last address to Congress. No. 1347, Chu Teh at his desk (horiz.). No. 1348, Chu Teh on horseback as commander of Red Army. Numbered J.19.

1977, July 6 Photo. *Perf. 11½*

1345 A333 8f multi (4-1)	30	30
1346 A333 8f multi (4-2)	30	30
1347 A333 8f multi (4-3)	30	30
1348 A333 8f multi (4-4)	30	30

Chu Teh (1886-1976), Commander of Red Army, Chairman of National People's Congress.

Military under Mao's Banner — A334

Designs: No. 1350, Red Flag, Soldiers, Chingkang Mountains. No. 1351, Guerrilla fighters returning to base. No. 1352, Guerrillas crossing Yangtze. No. 1353, National defense. Numbered J.20.

1977, Aug. 1

1349 A334 8f multi (5-1)	25	25
1350 A334 8f multi (5-2)	25	25
1351 A334 8f multi (5-3)	25	25
1352 A334 8f multi (5-4)	25	25
1353 A334 8f multi (5-5)	25	25
Nos. 1349-1353 (5)	1.25	1.25

Liberation Army Day, 50th anniversary of People's Army.

Gate of Heavenly Peace, People and Red Flags — A335

Designs: No. 1355, People marching under Red Flag with Mao's portrait. No. 1356, People marching under Red Flag with hammer and sickle. Numbered J.23.

1977, Aug. 22 Photo. *Perf. 11½x11*

1354 A335 8f multi (3-1)	50	50
1355 A335 8f multi (3-2)	50	50
1356 A335 8f multi (3-3)	50	50

11th National Congress of the Communist Party of China.

Chairman Mao — A336

Designs (Mao Portraits): No. 1358, as young man in Shansi. No. 1359, addressing Communist Party in Plenary Session. No. 1360, Proclaiming People's Republic at Gate of Heavenly Peace. No. 1361, at airport with Chou En-lai and Chu Teh (horiz.). No. 1362, Reviewing Army as old man. Numbered J.21.

1977, Sept. 9 Photo. *Perf. 11½*

1357 A336 8f multi (6-1)	25	25
1358 A336 8f multi (6-2)	25	25
1359 A336 8f multi (6-3)	25	25
1360 A336 8f multi (6-4)	25	25
1361 A336 8f multi (6-5)	25	25
1362 A336 8f multi (6-6)	25	25
Nos. 1357-1362 (6)	1.50	1.50

Mao-Tse-tung (1893-1976), first death anniversary.

Mao Memorial Hall — A337

Design: No. 1364, Chairman Hua's inscription. Numbered J.22.

1977, Sept. 9

1363 A337 8f lt ultra & multi	85	85
1364 A337 8f lt grn, tan & gold	85	85

Completion of Mao Memorial Hall.

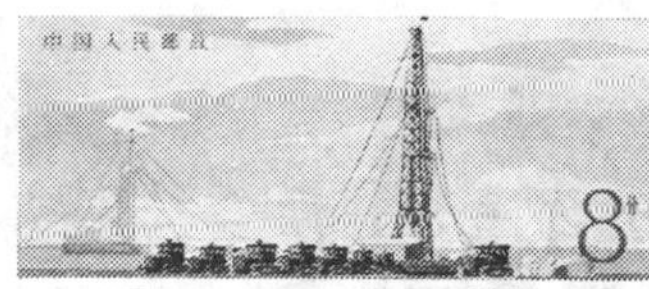
Tractors Moving Drilling Tower — A338

Designs: No. 1366, Shui Pow Tsi oil well and women workers. No. 1367, Construction of oil pipe line, Taching, and silos. No. 1368, Tung Fang Hung oil refinery, Peking. No. 1369, Taching oil loaded into tanker in harbor. 20f, Off-shore drilling platform "Pohai No. 1." Numbered T.19.

1978, Jan. 31 Photo. *Perf. 11*

1365 A338 8f multi (6-1)	25	25
1366 A338 8f multi (6-2)	25	25
1367 A338 8f multi (6-3)	25	25
1368 A338 8f multi (6-4)	25	25
1369 A338 8f multi (6-5)	25	25
1370 A338 8f multi (6-6)	50	50
Nos. 1365-1370 (6)	1.75	1.75

Development of Chinese oil industry.

"Army Teaching Militia" — A339

Design: No. 1372, "Army helping with rice planting." Numbered T.23.

1978, Feb. 5 Photo. *Perf. 11*

1371 A339 8f multi (2-1)	28	28
1372 A339 8f multi (2-2)	28	28

Army and people working as a family.

Red Flags, Mao Tse-tung A340

Constitution and Red Flags A341

Design: No. 1375, Atom symbol over symbols of agriculture and industry. All designs include Great Hall of the People, Peking, and flowers. Numbered J.24.

1978, Feb. 26

1373 A340 8f multi (3-1)	30	30
1374 A341 8f multi (3-2)	30	30
1374 A340 8f multi (3-3)	30	30

5th National People's Congress.

Mao's Eulogy for Lei Feng — A342

Lei Feng, Studying Mao's Works — A343

Design: No. 1377, Chairman Hua's thoughts (5 lines). Numbered J.26.

1978, Mar. 5

1376 A342 8f gold & red (3-1)	50	50
1377 A342 8f gold & red (3-2)	50	50
1378 A343 8f multi (3-3)	50	50

Lei Feng (1940-1962), communist fighter; 15th anniversary of Chairman Mao's eulogy "Learn from Comrade Feng."

Hsiang Ching-yu — A344

Yang Kai-hui — A345

Numbered J.27.

1978, Mar. 8

1379 A344 8f multi (2-1)	25	25
1380 A345 8f multi (2-2)	25	25

Hsiang Ching-yu, pioneer of Women's Movement, executed 1928; Yang Kai-hui, communist fighter, executed 1930.

Conference Emblem — A346

Designs: No. 1382, Banners symbolizing industry, agriculture, defense and science. No. 1383, Red flag, atom symbol and globe. Numbered J.25.

1978, Mar. 18 Litho. *Perf. 11½x11*

1381 A346 8f gold & red (3-1)	30	30
1382 A346 8f multi (3-2)	30	30
1383 A346 8f multi (3-3)	30	30
a. Souvenir sheet of 3	45.00	

National Science Conference. No. 1383a contains one each of Nos. 1381-1383 with simulated perforations; olive margin with atom symbols and inscription. Size: 140x105mm. Sold for 50fen.

Release of Weather Balloon A347

Weather Observations: No. 1385, Radar station, typhoon watch. No. 1386, Computer, weather maps. No. 1387, Local weather observers. No. 1388, Rockets intercepting hail clouds. Numbered T.24.

1978, Apr. 25 Photo. *Perf. 11x11½*

1384 A347 8f multi (5-1)	30	30
1385 A347 8f multi (5-2)	30	30
1386 A347 8f multi (5-3)	30	30
1387 A347 8f multi (5-4)	20	20
1388 A347 8f multi (5-5)	20	20
Nos. 1384-1388 (5)	1.30	1.30

Galloping Horse — A348

Children Playing Soccer — A349

Designs: Galloping Horses, by Hsu Peihung (1895-1953). 40f, 50f, 60f, 70f, $5, horiz. Numbered T.28.

1978, May 5 *Perf. 11½x11, 11x11½*

1389 A348 4f multi (10-1)	20	20
1390 A348 8f multi (10-2)	20	20
1391 A348 8f multi (10-3)	20	20
1392 A348 10f multi (10-4)	20	20
1393 A348 20f multi (10-5)	55	55
1394 A348 30f multi (10-6)	65	65
1395 A348 40f multi (10-7)	90	90
1396 A348 50f multi (10-8)	1.10	1.10
1397 A348 60f multi (10-9)	1.40	1.40
1398 A348 70f multi (10-10)	1.75	1.75
Nos. 1389-1398 (10)	7.15	7.15

Souvenir Sheet

1399 A348 $5 multi	27.50	

No. 1399 contains one stamp showing 4 horses (89x39mm.); black and silver margin shows floral damask pattern. Size: 147x98mm.

1978, June 1 *Perf. 11½*

Designs: No. 1401, Children on the beach. No. 1402, Little girls dancing. No. 1403, Children taking long walks. 20f, Children exercising for good health. Numbered T.21.

Size: 22x27mm.

1400 A349 8f multi (5-2)	25	25
1401 A349 8f multi (5-3)	25	25
1402 A349 8f multi (5-4)	25	25
1403 A349 8f multi (5-5)	25	25

Size: 48x28mm.

1404 A349 20f multi (5-1)	25	25
Nos. 1400-1404 (5)	1.25	1.25

Build up your health while young.

Canceled-to-order stamps are often from remainders. Most collectors of canceled stamps prefer postally used specimens.

Synthetic Fiber Feeder A350

Designs: No. 1406, Drawing out threads. No. 1407, Weaving. No. 1408, Dyeing and printing. No. 1409, Finished products. Numbered T.25.

1978, June 15 Photo. *Perf. 11½*

1405 A350 8f multi (5-1) 25 25
1406 A350 8f multi (5-2) 25 25
1407 A350 8f multi (5-3) 25 25
1408 A350 8f multi (5-4) 25 25
1409 A350 8f multi (5-5) 25 25
Nos. 1405-1409 (5) 1.25 1.25

Chemical fiber industry. Nos. 1405-1409 printed se-tenant in continuous design.

Conference Emblem A351

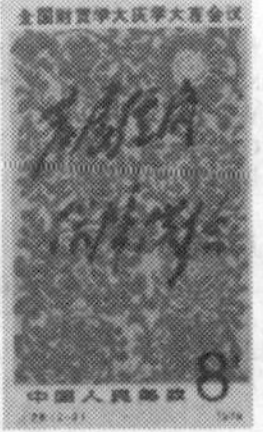

"Develop Economy and Ensure Supplies" A352

Numbered J.28.

1978, June 20 *Perf. 13*

1410 A351 8f multi (2-1) 25 25
1411 A352 8f multi (2-2) 25 25

National Conference on Learning from Taching and Tachai in Finance and Trade.

New Pastures, Mongolia — A353

Designs: No. 1413, Kazakh shepherds selecting sheep for breeding. No. 1414, Mechanized shearing of sheep, Tibet, Numbered T.27.

1978, June 30 Photo. *Perf. 11½*

1412 A353 8f multi (3-1) 30 30
1413 A353 8f multi (3-2) 30 30
1414 A353 8f multi (3-3) 30 30

Learning from Tachai in developing animal husbandry and new pastoral areas.

Coke Oven — A354

Designs: No. 1416, Iron furnace. No. 1417, Pouring steel. No. 1418, Steel rolling. No. 1419, Finished iron and steel products. Numbered T.26.

1978, July 22

1415 A354 8f multi (5-1) 25 25
1416 A354 8f multi (5-2) 25 25
1417 A354 8f multi (5-3) 25 25
1418 A354 8f multi (5-4) 25 25
1419 A354 8f multi (5-5) 25 25
Nos. 1415-1419 (5) 1.25 1.25

Iron and steel industry.

Iron Fist to Prevent Revisionism A355

Jug in Shape of Sheep A356

Designs: No. 1421, "Carrying forward revolutionary tradition." No. 1422, "Strenuous training in military skills to wipe out enemy." Numbered T.32.

1978, Aug. 1 Photo. *Perf. 11½*

1420 A355 8f multi (3-1) 25 25
1421 A355 8f multi (3-2) 25 25
1422 A355 8f multi (3-3) 25 25

"Learn from Hard-boned 6th Company." (A military unit since 1939).

1978, Aug. 26

Arts and Crafts: 4f, Giant lion (toy; horiz.). No. 1425, Rhinoceros (lacquer ware; horiz). 10f, Cat (embroidery). 20f, Bag (weaving; horiz.). 30f, Teapot in shape of peacock (cloisonne). 40f, Plate with lotus, and swan-shaped box (lacquer ware; horiz.). 50f, Dragon flying in sky (ivory). 60f, Sun rising (jade; horiz.). 70f, Flight to human world (ivory). $3, Flying fairies (arts and crafts; horiz.). Numbered T.29.

1423 A356 4f multi (10-1) 20 20
1424 A356 8f multi (10-2) 20 20
1425 A356 8f multi (10-3) 20 20
1426 A356 10f multi (10-4) 20 20
1427 A356 20f multi (10-5) 55 55
1428 A356 30f multi (10-6) 65 65
1429 A356 40f multi (10-7) 90 90
1430 A356 50f multi (10-8) 1.10 1.10
1431 A356 60f multi (10-9) 1.40 1.40
1432 A356 70f multi (10-10) 1.75 1.75
Nos. 1423-1432 (10) 7.15 7.15

Souvenir Sheet

1433 A356 $3 multi 27.50

No. 1433 contains one stamp (85x36mm.). Gold decorative margin. Size: 139x90mm.

Women, Atom Symbol, Rocket and Wheat A357

1978, Sept. 8 Photo. *Perf. 11*

1434 A357 8f multi 60 30

4th National Women's Congress.

Ginseng — A358

Flag, Wheat, Cogwheel, Plane, Atom Symbols — A359

Medicinal Plants: No. 1436, Horn of plenty. No. 1437, Blackberry lily. No. 1438, Balloonflower. 55f, Rhododendron dauricum. Numbered T.30.

1978, Sept. 15

1435 A358 8f multi (5-1) 20 20
1436 A358 8f multi (5-2) 20 20
1437 A358 8f multi (5-3) 20 20
1438 A358 8f multi (5-4) 20 20
1439 A358 55f multi (5-5) 1.40 1.40
Nos. 1435-1439 (5) 2.20 2.20

1978, Oct. 11 Photo. *Perf. 11*

1440 A359 8f multi 60 60

9th National Trade Union Congress.

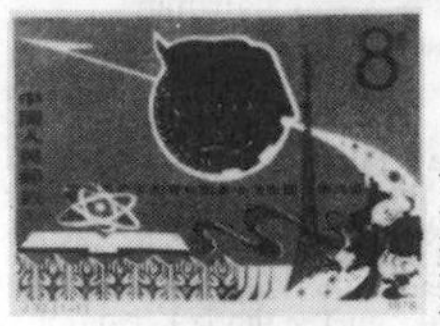

Youth League Emblem A360

1978, Oct. 16

1441 A360 8f multi 60 60

10th National Communist Youth League Congress.

Chinese and Japanese Girls Exchanging Gifts A361

Great Wall and Mt. Fuji — A362

1978, Oct. 22

1442 A361 8f multi 25 25
1443 A362 55f multi 1.25 1.25

Signing of Sino-Japanese Peace and Friendship Treaty.

Moslem, Chinese and Mongolian People — A363

Chinsha River Bridge, West Szechuan — A364

Designs: No. 1445, Loading coal at Holan Mountain. 10f, Irrigated rice fields and boxthorn. Numbered J.29.

1978, Oct. 25

1444 A363 8f multi (3-1) 30 30
1445 A363 8f multi (3-2) 30 30
1446 A363 10f multi (3-3) 30 30

20th anniversary of founding of Ningsia Moslem Autonomous Region.

1978, Nov. 1 Photo. *Perf. 11½x11*

Highway Bridges: No. 1448, Hsinhong bridge, Wuhsi. No. 1449, Chiuhsikou bridge, Fengdu. No. 1450, Chinsha River bridge, West Szechuan. 60f, Shangyeh bridge, Sanmen. $2, Hsiang-kiang River bridge. Numbered T.31.

1447 A364 8f multi (5-1) 20 20
1448 A364 8f multi (5-2) 20 20
1449 A364 8f multi (5-3) 20 20
1450 A364 8f multi (5-4) 20 20
1451 A364 60f multi (5-5) 1.75 1.75
Nos. 1447-1451 (5) 2.55 2.55

Souvenir Sheet

1452 A364 $2 multi 25.00

No. 1452 contains one stamp (86x37mm.). Ultramarine, white and gold margin shows tiny boats. Size: 145x69mm.

Mechanical Transplanting of Rice Seedlings A365

Paintings: No. 1454, Spraying fields. No. 1455, Seed selection. No. 1456, Trade. No. 1457, Delivery of public grain in city. Numbered T.34.

1978, Nov. 30 *Perf. 11½*

1453 A365 8f multi (5-1) 30 30
1454 A365 8f multi (5-2) 30 30
1455 A365 8f multi (5-3) 30 30
1456 A365 8f multi (5-4) 30 30
1457 A365 8f multi (5-5) 30 30
Strip of 5 (#1453-1457) 1.75 1.75

Agricultural progress. Nos. 1453-1457 printed se-tenant in continuous design.

Dancers and Fireworks — A366

Designs: No. 1459, Industry (vert.). 10f, Agriculture (vert.). Numbered J.33.

1978, Dec. 11 Photo. *Perf. 11*

1458 A366 8f multi (3-1) 30 30
1459 A366 8f multi (3-2) 30 30
1460 A366 10f multi (3-3) 30 30

20th anniversary of Kwangsi Chuang Autonomous Region.

Miners with Pneumatic Drill A367

Mine Development: 4f, Old Tibetan peasant reporting to surveyor. 10f, Open-cut mining with power shovel. 20f, Loaded electric train in pit. Numbered T.20.

Photogravure & Engraved

1978, Dec. 29

1461 A367 4f multi (4-1) 8 8
1462 A367 8f multi (4-2) 20 20
1463 A367 10f multi (4-3) 25 25
1464 A367 20f multi (4-4) 45 45

Golden Pheasants Roosting on Rock — A368

Golden Pheasants: 8f, In flight. 45f, Seeking food. Numbered T.35.

1979, Jan. 25 Photo. Perf. 11½

1465	A368	4f multi (3-1)	25	25
1466	A368	8f multi (3-2)	25	25
1467	A368	45f multi (3-3)	95	95

Albert Einstein and his Equation — A369

1979, Mar. 14 Photo. Perf. 11½x11

1468	A369	8f brn gold & blk	50	50

Albert Einstein (1879-1955), theoretical physicist.

Phoenix Battling Monster, Praying Woman A370

Design: 60f, Man riding dragon to heaven. Designs from silk paintings found in Changsha tomb, Warring States Period (475-221 B.C.). Numbered T.33.

1979, Mar. 29 Perf. 11

1469	A370	8f multi (2-1)	25	25
1470	A370	60f multi (2-2)	1.40	1.40

Summer Palace — A371

Photogravure, Photogravure and Envraved ($5)

1979-80 Perf. 13

1471	A371	$1 *Pagoda* ('80)	1.50	75
1472	A371	$2 *Shown*	3.00	1.50
1473	A371	$5 *Temple, Beihai Park* ('80)	10.00	3.75

Hammer and Sickle "51" and Bars from "International" — A372

1979, May 1 Photo. Perf. 11

1474	A372	8f multi	45	30

International Labor Day, 90th anniv.

"Tradition of May 4th Movement" — A373

Young Woman, Rocket, Antenna, Nuclear Reactor A374

1979, May 4

1475	A373	8f multi	30	30
1476	A374	8f multi	30	30

60th anniversary of May 4th Movement.

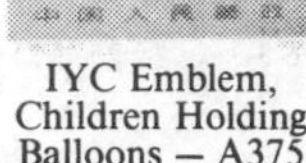

IYC Emblem, Children Holding Balloons — A375

Children of Three Races, IYC Emblem — A376

1979, May 25 Perf. 11½

1477	A375	8f multi	28	28
1478	A376	60f multi	1.65	1.65

International Year of the Child.

Great Wall in Spring A377

Designs (The Great Wall): No. 1480, in summer. No. 1481, in autumn. 60f, in winter. $2, Guard tower. Numbered T.38.

1979, June 25 Photo. Perf. 11

1479	A377	8f multi (4-1)	20	20
1480	A377	8f multi (4-2)	20	20
1481	A377	8f multi (4-3)	20	20
1482	A377	60f multi (4-4)	1.25	1.25

Souvenir Sheet

1483	A377	$2 multi	16.00

No. 1483 has blue gray and gold margin showing Great Wall and towers. Size: 140x78mm.

Roaring Tiger — A379

Manchurian Tiger: 8f, Two young tigers. 60f, Tiger at rest. Numbered T.40.

1979, July 20 Perf. 11½x11

1484	A379	4f multi (3-1)	25	25
1485	A379	8f multi (3-2)	25	25
1486	A379	60f multi (3-3)	1.40	1.40

Mechanical Harvesting — A380

Work of the Communes: No. 1488, Forestry. No. 1489, Raising ducks. No. 1490, Women weaving baskets. 10f, Fishing. Numbered T.39.

1979, Aug. 10 Perf. 11½

1487	A380	4f multi (5-1)	20	20
1488	A380	8f multi (5-2)	20	20
1489	A380	8f multi (5-3)	20	20
1490	A380	8f multi (5-4)	20	20
1491	A380	10f multi (5-5)	20	20
		Nos. 1487-1491 (5)	1.00	1.00

No. 1483 Overprinted with Gold Inscription and "1979"

Souvenir Sheet

1979, Aug. 25 Photo. Perf. 11

1492	A377	$2 multi	75.00

31st International Stamp Exhibition, Riccione, Italy. Size: 140x78mm. Numbered J41 (1-1).

Games Emblem, Sports — A381

Emblem and: No. 1494, Soccer, badminton, high jump, speed skating. No. 1495, Fencing, skiing, gymnastics, diving. No. 1496, Motorcycling, table tennis, basketball, archery. No. 1497, Emblem only (vert.). Numbered J.43.

1979, Sept. 15 Perf. 11½x11

1493	A381	8f multi (4-1)	28	28
1494	A381	8f multi (4-2)	28	28
1495	A381	8f multi (4-3)	28	28
1496	A381	8f multi (4-4)	28	28

Souvenir Sheet

Perf. 11½

1497	A381	$2 multi	10.00

4th National Games. Nos. 1493-1496 printed se-tenant. No. 1497 has gray olive margin showing symbols of various sports. Size of stamp: 22x26mm., size of sheet: 57x62mm.

Flag and Rainbow — A382

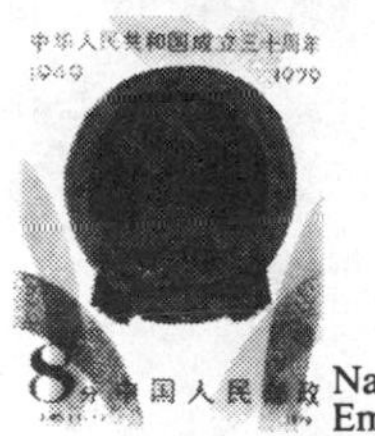

National Emblem — A383

National Anthem A384

Dancers A385

Tractor, Aerial Crop Spraying, Irrigation A386

Designs: No. 1499, Flag and mountains. Nos. 1503-1505, various dances (numbered J.47). No. 1507, Atom symbol. No. 1509, Rocket, submarine, jets (Nos. 1506-1509 numbered J.48). No. 1510, National Emblem.

1979, Oct. 1 Photo. Perf. 11½

1498	A382	8f multi	30	30
1499	A382	8f multi	30	30
1500	A383	8f multi	35	35

Engr. Perf. 11

1501	A384	8f multi	35	35

Photo. Perf. 11½

1502	A385	8f multi (4-1)	30	30
1503	A385	8f multi (4-2)	30	30
1504	A385	8f multi (4-3)	30	30
1505	A385	8f multi (4-4)	30	30
		Block of 4 (#1502-1505)	1.40	
1506	A386	8f multi (4-1)	30	30
1507	A386	8f multi (4-2)	30	30
1508	A386	8f multi (4-3)	30	30
1509	A386	8f multi (4-4)	30	30

Souvenir Sheet

1510	A383	$1 multi	6.50

People's Republic of China, 30th anniversary. Nos. 1502-1505 printed in blocks of 4. No. 1510 has multicolored decorative margin. Size: 67x75mm.

Exhibition Emblem A387

Children Flying Model Planes A388

1979, Oct. 3

1511	A387	8f multi	45	45

Junior National Scientific and Technological Exhibition.

1979, Oct. 3

Designs: No. 1513, Girls and microscope. No. 1514, Children and telescope. No. 1515, Boy catching butterflies. No. 1516, Girl taking meteorological readings. No. 1517, Boys sailing model boat. No. 1518, Girl with book. Numbered T.41.

1512	A388	8f multi (6-1)	20	20
1513	A388	8f multi (6-2)	20	20
1514	A388	8f multi (6-3)	20	20
1515	A388	8f multi (6-4)	20	20
1516	A388	8f multi (6-5)	20	20
1517	A388	60f multi (6-6)	80	80
		Nos. 1512-1517 (6)	1.80	1.80

Souvenir Sheet

Perf. 11

1518	A388	$2 multi	60.00

Study Science from Childhood. No. 1518 contains one stamp (90x40mm.). Light blue margin shows fish. Size: 148x90mm.

Yu Shan Mountain
A389

Taiwan Landscapes: No. 1520, Sun and Moon Lake. No. 1521, Chihkan Tower. No. 1522, Suao-Hualien Highway. 55f, Tian Xiang Falls. 60f, Banping Mountain. Numbered T.42.

1979, Oct. 20 Photo. *Perf. 11x11½*

1519	A389	8f multi (6-1)	30	30
1520	A389	8f multi (6-2)	30	30
1521	A389	8f multi (6-3)	30	30
1522	A389	8f multi (6-4)	30	30
1523	A389	55f multi (6-5)	1.25	1.25
1524	A389	60f multi (6-6)	1.25	1.25
		Nos. 1519-1524 (6)	3.70	3.70

Arts Symbols
A390

Design: 8f, Seals and modernization symbols. Numbered J.39.

1979, Oct. 30

1525	A390	4f multi	20	20
1526	A390	8f multi	35	35

4th National Congress of Literary and Art Workers.

Train in Tunnel
A391

Railroads: No. 1520, Mountain bridge. No. 1521, Freight train. Numbered T.36.

Photogravure and Engraved

1979, Oct. 30

1527	A391	8f multi (3-1)	20	20
1528	A391	8f multi (3-2)	20	20
1529	A391	8f multi (3-3)	20	20

Chrysanthemum Petal — A392

Camellias: No. 1531, Lion head. No. 1532, Camellia chryantha. 10f, Small osmanthus leaf. 20f, Baby face. 30f, Cornelian. 40f, Peony camellia. 50f, Purple gown. 60f, Dwarf rose. 70f, Willow leaf spinel pink. $2, Red jewelry. Numbered T.37.

1979, Nov. 10 Photo. *Perf. 11x11½*

1530	A392	4f multi (10-1)	25	25
1531	A392	8f multi (10-2)	25	25
1532	A392	8f multi (10-3)	25	25
1533	A392	10f multi (10-4)	25	25
1534	A392	20f multi (10-5)	50	50
1535	A392	30f multi (10-6)	65	65
1536	A392	40f multi (10-7)	85	85
1537	A392	50f multi (10-8)	1.00	1.00
1538	A392	60f multi (10-9)	1.25	1.25
1539	A392	70f multi (10-10)	1.40	1.40
		Nos. 1530-1539 (10)	6.65	6.65

Souvenir Sheet

Perf. 11½x11

1540 A392 $2 multi 14.00

No. 1540 contains one stamp (86x36mm.), gold margin with white inscription. Size: 135x90mm.

No. 1540 Overprinted and Numbered in Gold in Margin.

Souvenir Sheet

1979, Nov. 10

1541 A392 $2 multi 47.50

People's Republic of China Philatelic Exhibition, Hong Kong, 1979. Numbered J.42 (1-1).

Norman Bethune Treating Soldier — A393

Design: 70f, Bethune statue.

1979, Nov. 12

1542	A393	8f multi (2-2)	25	25
1543	A393	70f multi (2-1)	1.65	1.65

Dr. Norman Bethune, 40th death anniversary. Numbered J.50.

Central Archives Hall — A394

International Archives Weeks: No. 1545, Gold archive cabinet (vert.). 60f, Pavilion. Numbered J.51.

Perf. 11x11½, 11½x11

1979, Nov. 26 Photo.

1544	A394	8f multi (3-1)	30	30
1545	A394	8f multi (3-2)	30	30
1546	A394	60f multi (3-3)	1.25	1.25

Monkey King in Waterfall Cave — A395

Monkey King, Scenes from Pilgrimage to the West (Novel): No. 1548, Fighting Necha, son of Prince Li. No. 1549, In Mother Queen's peach orchard. No. 1550, In the alchemy furnace. 10f, Subduing the white bone demon. 20f, With palm leaf fan. 60f, In cobweb cave. 70f, Walking on scripture-seeking route. Numbered T.43.

1979, Dec. 1 *Perf. 11½x11*

1547	A395	8f multi (8-1)	25	25
1548	A395	8f multi (8-2)	25	25
1549	A395	8f multi (8-3)	25	25
1550	A395	8f multi (8-4)	25	25
1551	A395	10f multi (8-5)	25	25
1552	A395	20f multi (8-6)	40	40
1553	A395	60f multi (8-7)	1.40	1.40
1554	A395	70f multi (8-8)	1.50	1.50
		Nos. 1547-1554 (8)	4.55	4.55

Stalin Delivering Speech
A396

Design: No. 1555, Portrait of Stalin (vert.). Numbered J. 49.

Perf. 11x11½, 11½x11

1979, Dec. 21 Engr.

1555	A396	8f brn (2-1)	38	38
1556	A396	8f blk (2-2)	38	38

Joseph Stalin (1879-1953).

Peony, by Qi Baishi — A397

1980 Photo. *Perf. 11½*

1557	A397	4f *shown* (16-1)	25	25
1558	A397	4f *Squirrels and grapes* (16-2)	25	25
1559	A397	8f *Crabs candle and wine* (16-3)	25	25
1560	A397	8f *Tadpoles in mountain spring* (16-4)	25	25
1561	A397	8f *Chicks* (16-5)	25	25
1562	A397	8f *Lotus* (16-6)	25	25
1563	A397	8f *Red plum* (16-7)	25	25
1564	A397	8f *Kingfisher* (16-8)	25	25
1565	A397	10f *Bottle gourd* (16-9)	25	25
1566	A397	20f *Voice of autumn* (16-10)	35	35
1567	A397	30f *Wisteria* (16-11)	50	50
1568	A397	40f *Chrysanthemums* (16-12)	65	65
1569	A397	50f *Shrimp* (16-13)	80	80
1570	A397	55f *Litchi* (16-14)	90	90
1571	A397	60f *Cabbages, mushrooms* (16-15)	1.00	1.00
1572	A397	70f *Peaches* (16-16)	1.25	1.25
		Nos. 1557-1572 (16)	7.70	7.70

Souvenir Sheet

1980, May 20 Photo. *Perf. 11½*

1573 A397 $2 Evergreen 11.00

Qi Baishi paintings. Issue dates: Nos. 1557-1560, 1569-1572, Jan. 15; others, May 20. Numbered T. 44. No. 1573 contains one stamp (37½x61mm); brown and tan margin shows portrait of Qi Baishi and inscription. Size: 120x86mm.

Meng Liang Mask from Hongyang Cave Opera — A398

Opera Masks. No. 1575, Li Kui, from Black Whirlwind. No. 1576, Huang Gai, from Meeting of Heroes. No. 1577, 10f, Lu Zhishen, from Wild Boar Forest. 20f, Lian Po, from Reconciliation between the General and Minister. 60f, Zhang Fei, from Reed Marsh. 70f, Dou Erdun, from Stealing the Emperor's Horse, Numbered T. 45.

1980, Jan. 25 *Perf. 11½x11*

1574	A398	4f multi (8-1)	20	20
1575	A398	4f multi (8-2)	20	20
1576	A398	8f multi (8-3)	20	20
1577	A398	8f multi (8-4)	20	20
1578	A398	10f multi (8-5)	20	20
1579	A398	20f multi (8-6)	40	40
1580	A398	60f multi (8-7)	1.25	1.25
1581	A398	70f multi (8-8)	1.40	1.40
		Nos. 1574-1581 (8)	4.05	4.05

Speed Skating, Olympic Rings — A399

Monkey, New Year — A400

Olympic Rings and: No. 1582, Chinese flag. No. 1584, Figure skating. 60f, Downhill skiing. Numbered J. 54.

1980, Feb. 13

1582	A399	8f multi (4-1)	20	20
1583	A399	8f multi (4-2)	20	20
1584	A399	8f multi (4-3)	20	20
1585	A399	60f multi (4-4)	1.10	1.10

13th Winter Olympic Games, Lake Placid, N.Y., Feb. 12-24.

Engraved and Photogravure

1980, Feb. 15 *Perf. 11½*

1586 A400 8f multi 10.00 5.00

Clara Zetkin — A401

Photogravure & Engraved

1980, Mar. 8 *Perf. 11½x11*

1587 A401 8f blk & yel 45 45

International Working Women's Day, 70th anniversary, founded by Clara Zetkin (1857-1933).

Orchard
A402

Afforestation: 8f, Trees lining highway. 10f, Aerial seeding. 20f, Trees surrounding factory. Numbered T.48.

1980, Mar. 12 *Perf. 11x11½*

1588	A402	4f multi (4-1)	10	10
1589	A402	8f multi (4-2)	15	15
1590	A402	10f multi (4-3)	20	20
1591	A402	20f multi (4-4)	40	40

Apsaras, Symbols of Modernization — A403

1980, Mar. 15 Photo. *Perf. 11½*

1592 A403 8f multi 50 50

2nd National Conference of the Scientific and Technical Association of China.

Mail Transport by Ship — A404

1980, Mar. 20 ***Perf. 11x11½***

1593	A404	2f *shown* (4-1)	5	5
1594	A404	4f *Bus* (4-2)	6	6
1595	A404	8f *Train* (4-3)	20	20
1596	A404	10f *Jet* (4-4)	20	20

Numbered T.49.

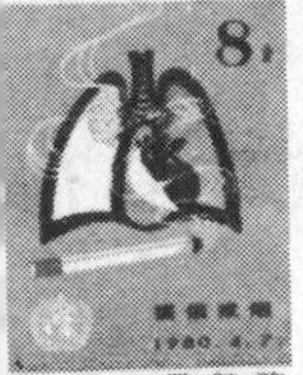
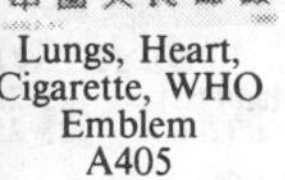

Lungs, Heart, Cigarette, WHO Emblem A405

Statue of Chien Chen (688-763) A406

1980, Apr. 7 ***Perf. 11½x11***

1597	A405	8f *shown* (2-1)	20	20
1598	A405	60f *Faces* (2-2)	1.25	1.25

Fight against cigarette smoking. Numbered J.56.

Perf. 11x11½, 11½x11

1980, Apr. 13

Loan to China by Japan of statue of Chien Chen (Jian Zhen), Buddhist missionary to Japan (754-763): No. 1600, Chien Chen Memorial Hall, Yangchou (horiz.). 60f, Chien Chen's ship (horiz.). His name in Japan is Ganjin. Numbered J.55.

1599	A406	8f multi (3-1)	20	20
1600	A406	8f multi (3-2)	20	20
1601	A406	60f multi (3-3)	1.25	1.25

Lenin's 110th Birthday — A407

Swallow Chick Kite — A408

Photogravure and Engraved

1980, Apr. 22 ***Perf. 11½x11***

1602	A407	8f multi	45	45

1980, May 10 **Photo.** ***Perf. 11½***

Designs: Kites. Numbered T.50.

1603	A408	8f *Shown* (4-1)	20	20
1604	A408	8f *Slender-swallow* (4-2)	20	20
1605	A408	8f *Semi-slender swallow* (4-3)	20	20
1606	A408	70f *Dual swallows* (4-4)	1.25	1.25

Hare Running from Fallen Papaya A409

1980, June 1 **Photo.** ***Perf. 11x11½***

1607		Strip of 4	75	75
a.		A409 8f *Shown* (4-1)	15	15
b.		A409 8f *Hare fox, monkey running away* (4-2)	15	15
c.		A409 8f *Lion instructing animals* (4-3)	15	15
d.		A409 8f *Discovery of fallen papaya* (4-4)	15	15

Gu Dong fairy tale. Nos. 1607a-1607d se-tenant with label telling story. Numbered T.51.

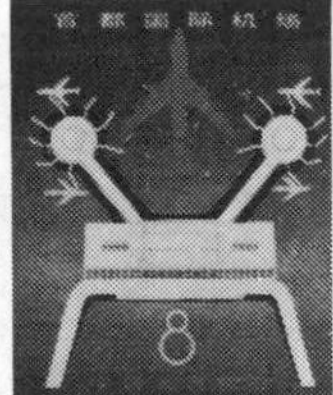

Terminal Building, Jets — A410

1980, June 20 ***Perf. 11½***

1608	A410	8f *Shown* (2-1)	20	20
1609	A410	10f *Runways, jets* (2-2)	25	25

Peking International Airport opening. Numbered T.47.

Sika Stag — A411

White Lotus — A412

1980, July 18 **Photo.** ***Perf. 11½***

1610	A411	4f *Shown* (3-1)	12	12
1611	A411	8f *Doe and fawn* (3-2)	20	20
1612	A411	60f *Herd* (3-3)	1.25	1.25

Numbered T.52.

1980, Aug. 4

1613	A412	8f *Shown* (4-1)	20	20
1614	A412	8f *Rose-tipped snow* (4-2)	20	20
1615	A412	8f *Buddha's seat* (4-3)	20	20
1616	A413	70f *Variable charming face* (4-4)	1.65	1.65

Souvenir Sheet

1617	A412	$1 *Fresh lotus on rippling water*	13.00	

Numbered T.54. No. 1617 contains one stamp (48x88mm); light gray decorative margin. Size: 70x145½mm.

Pearl Cave, Sword-cut Stone Sculptures — A413

Guilin Landscapes: No. 1619, Three mountains, distant views. No. 1620, Nine-horse fresco hill. No. 1621, Egrets around aged banyan. No. 1622, Western hills at sunset (vert.). No. 1623, Moonlight on Lijiang River (vert.). 60f, Springhead,ancient ferry (vert.). 70f, Scenic path, Yangshue (vert.). Numbered T.53.

1980, Aug. 30 **Photo.** ***Perf. 11½***

1618	A413	8f multi (8-1)	15	15
1619	A413	8f multi (8-2)	15	15
1620	A413	8f multi (8-3)	15	15
1621	A413	8f multi (8-4)	15	15
1622	A413	8f multi (8-5)	15	15
1623	A413	8f multi (8-6)	15	15
1624	A413	70f multi (8-7)	1.10	1.10
1625	A413	70f multi (8-8)	1.25	1.25
		Nos. 1618-1625 (8)	3.25	3.25

Entrance Gate and Good Fairies A414

Great Wall, Symbols of Chicago, San Francisco and New York A415

1980, Sept. 13 **Photo.** ***Perf. 11x11½***

1626	A414	8f multi	15	15
1627	A415	70f multi	1.40	1.40

Exhibitions of the People's Republic of China in San Francisco, Chicago and New York, Sept.-Dec. Sheets of 12 were sold only at U.S. exhibitions.

Romanian Flag, Warrior and Scroll — A416

1980, Sept. 20 **Photo.** ***Perf. 11½x11***

1628	A416	8f multi	45	45

2050th anniversary of Dacia, first independent Romanian state.

UNESCO Exhibition of Drawings and Paintings — A417

Numbered J.60.

1980, Oct. 8 ***Perf. 11½***

1629	A417	8f *Sea of Clouds, by Liu Haisu,* (3-1)	20	20
1630	A417	8f *Oriole and Magnolia, by Yu Feian,* vert., (3-2)	20	20
1631	A417	8f *Camels, by Wu Zuoren,* (3-3)	20	20

Quxi Tower, Tarrying Garden — A418

Designs: Scenes from Tarrying Garden. Numbered T.56.

1980, Oct. 25 **Photo.** ***Perf. 11½***

1632	A418	8f *shown* (4-1)	15	15
1633	A418	8f *Yuancui Pavilion* (4-2)	15	15
1634	A418	10f *Hanbi Shanfang* (4-3)	20	20
1635	A418	60f *Guanyun Peak* (4-4)	1.40	1.40

Xu Guangpi (1562-1633), Agronomist A419

Shooting, Olympic Rings A420

Scientists of Ancient China: No. 1637, Li Bing, hydraulic engineer, 3rd century B.C. No. 1638, Jia Sixie, agronomist, 5th century. 60f, Huang Daopo, textile expert, 13th century. Numbered J.58.

Photogravure and Engraved

1980, Nov. 20 ***Perf. 11½x11***

1636	A419	8f multi (4-1)	20	20
1637	A419	8f multi (4-2)	20	20
1638	A419	8f multi (4-3)	20	20
1639	A419	60f multi (4-4)	1.40	1.40

1980, Nov. 26 **Photo.**

1640	A420	4f *shown* (5-1)	6	6
1641	A420	8f *Gymnastics* (5-2)	15	15
1642	A420	8f *Diving* (5-3)	15	15
1643	A420	10f *Volleyball* (5-4)	20	20
1644	A420	60f *Archery* (5-5)	1.40	1.40
		Nos. 1640-1644 (5)	1.96	1.96

Return to International Olympic Committee, 1st anniversary. Numbered J.62.

Chinese River Dolphin A421

Photogravure & Engraved

1980, Dec. 25 ***Perf. 11x11½***

1645	A421	8f *shown* (2-1)	25	25
a.		Booklet pane of 6	1.25	
1646	A421	60f *Dolphins* (2-2)	1.25	1.25
a.		Booklet pane of 1	2.50	

Cock — A422

Photogravure & Engraved

1981, Jan. 5 ***Perf. 11½***

1647	A422	8f multi	1.50	1.50
a.		Bklt. pane of 12	4.75	

New Year 1981. Numbered T.58.

Early Morning in Xishuang Bana A423

Perf. 11x11½, 11½x11

1981, Jan. 20 **Photo.**

1648	A423	4f *shown* (6-1)	6	6
1649	A423	4f *Dai mountain village* (6-2)	6	6
1650	A423	8f *Rainbow over Lanchang River* (6-3)	15	15
1651	A423	8f *Ancient temple* vert. (6-4)	15	15
1652	A423	8f *Moonlit night,* vert. (6-5)	15	15
1653	A423	60f *Phoenix tree,* vert. (6-6)	1.40	1.40
		Nos. 1648-1653 (6)	1.97	1.97

Flower Basket Palace Lantern — A424

Designs: Palace lanterns. Numbered T.60.

1981, Feb. 19 Photo. *Perf. 11½*

1654 A424 4f multi (6-1)	6	6
1655 A424 8f multi (6-2)	15	15
1656 A424 8f multi (6-3)	15	15
1657 A424 8f multi (6-4)	15	15
1658 A424 20f multi (6-5)	40	40
1659 A424 60f multi (6-6)	1.25	1.25
Nos. 1654-1659 (6)	2.16	2.16

Crossing River, Scene from Marking the Gunwale A425

Designs: Scenes from Marking the Gunwale fable.

1981, Mar. 10 Photo. *Perf. 11x11½*

1660 A425 8f Text (5-1)	15	15
1661 A425 8f shown (5-2)	15	15
1662 A425 8f Dropping sword in water (5-3)	15	15
1663 A425 8f Marking gunwale (5-4)	15	15
1664 A425 8f Searching for sword (5-5)	15	15
a. Bklt. pane of 10 (2 each #1660-1664)	2.00	
Nos. 1660-1664 (5)	75	75

Nos. 1660-1664 se-tenant. Numbered T.59.

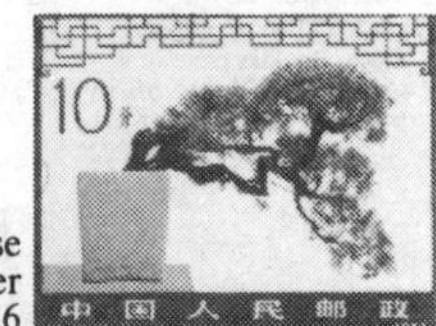

Chinese Juniper A426

Designs: Miniature landscapes. Numbered T.61.

1981, Mar. 31 *Perf. 11½*

1665 A426 4f Chinese elm, vert. (6-1)	6	6
1666 A426 8f Juniper, vert. (6-2)	15	15
1667 A426 8f Maidenhair tree, vert. (6-3)	15	15
1668 A426 10f shown (6-4)	18	18
1669 A426 20f Persimmon (6-5)	40	40
1670 A426 60f Juniper (6-6)	1.10	1.10
Nos. 1665-1670 (6)	2.04	2.04

Vase with Tiger-shaped Handles — A427

Cizhou Kiln Ceramic Pottery: 4f, Vase with two tigers, Song Dynasty (vert.). No. 1672, Black glazed jar, Jin Dynasty. No. 1673, Amphora (vert.). No. 1674, Jar with two phoenixes (Yuan Dynasty). 10f, Flat flask, Yuan Dynasty. Numbered T.62.

1981, Apr. 15 Photo. *Perf. 11½x11*

1671 A427 4f multi (6-1)	6	6
1672 A427 8f multi (6-2)	15	15
1673 A427 8f multi (6-3)	15	15
1674 A427 8f multi (6-4)	15	15
1675 A427 10f multi (6-5)	20	20
1676 A427 60f multi (6-6)	1.25	1.25
Nos. 1671-1676 (6)	1.96	1.96

Panda Bear and Colored Stamps — A428

1981, Apr. 29 Photo. *Perf. 11½x11*

1677 A428 8f shown (2-1)	15	15
1678 A428 60f Boat, bird (2-2)	1.10	1.10
a. Booklet (8 #1677, 1677-1678 se-tenant)	2.50	2.50

Qinchuan Steer A429

Cattle Breeds: No. 1680, Binhu buffalo. No. 1681, Yak. No. 1682, Black and white dairy cows. 10f, Pasture red cow. 55f, Simmental cross-breed. Numbered T.63.

1981, May 5 *Perf. 11x11½*

1679 A429 4f multi (6-1)	6	6
1680 A429 8f multi (6-2)	12	12
1681 A429 8f multi (6-3)	12	12
1682 A429 8f multi (6-4)	12	12
1683 A429 10f multi (6-5)	20	20
1684 A429 55f multi (6-6)	1.00	1.00
Nos. 1679-1684 (6)	1.62	1.62

Mail Delivery Slogan — A430

13th World Telecommunications Day — A431

1981, May 9 *Perf. 11*

1685 A430 8f multi 30 30

Numbered J.70.

1981, May 17 *Perf. 11½x11*

1686 A431 8f multi 30 30

Numbered J.69.

Construction Worker — A432

Telephone Building, Peking — A433

1981, May 20 *Perf. 11½*

1687 A432 8f shown (4-1)	15	15
1688 A432 8f Miner (4-2)	15	15
1689 A432 8f Children crossing street (4-3)	15	15
1690 A432 8f Farm worker (4-4)	15	15

National Safety Month. Numbered J.65.

1981, June 5 Engr. *Perf. 11½x11*

1691 A433 8f vio brn 25 25

Swaythling Cup, Men's Team Table Tennis — A434

36th World Table Tennis Championships Victory: No. 1692a, St. Bride Vase, men's singles (7-3). No. 1692b, Iran Cup, men's doubles (7-4). No. 1692c, G. Geist Prize, women's singles (7-5). No. 1692d, W.J. Pope Trophy, women's doubles (7-6). No. 1692e, Heydusek Prize, mixed doubles (7-7). No. 1694, Marcel Corbillon Cup, women's team. Nos. 1693-1694 printed in sheets of 16 (8 each) with 2 labels. Numbered J.71.

1981, June 30 Photo. *Perf. 11½x11*

1692 Strip of 5	80	80
a.-e. A434 3f multi	15	15
1693 A434 20f multi (7-1)	40	40
1694 A434 20f multi (7-2)	40	40

Chinese Communist Party, 60th Anniv. A435

1981, July 1 Photo. *Perf. 11x11½*

1695 A435 8f multi 35 35

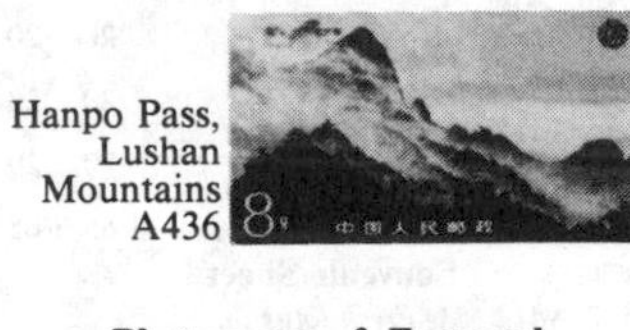

Hanpo Pass, Lushan Mountains A436

Photogravure & Engraved

1981, July 20 *Perf. 12½x12*

1696 A436 8f Five-veteran Peak, vert. (7-1)	12	12
1697 A436 8f shown (7-2)	12	12
1698 A436 8f Yellow Dragon Pool, vert. (7-3)	12	12
1699 A436 8f Sunlit Peak (7-4)	12	12
1700 A436 8f Three-layer Spring, vert. (7-5)	12	12
1701 A436 8f Stone and pines (7-6)	12	12
1702 A436 60f Dragon-head Cliff, vert. (7-7)	1.40	1.40
Nos. 1696-1702 (7)	2.12	2.12

Numbered T.67.

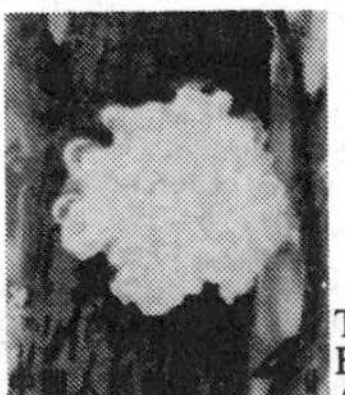

Tremella Fuciformis A437

Designs: Edible mushrooms. Numbered T.66.

1981, Aug. 6 Photo. *Perf. 11½*

1703 A437 4f shown (6-1)	6	6
1704 A437 8f Dictyophora indusiata (6-2)	12	12
1705 A437 8f Hericium erinaceus (6-3)	12	12
1706 A437 8f Russula rubra (6-4)	12	12
1707 A437 10f Lentinus edodes (6-5)	15	15
1708 A437 70f Agaricus bisporus (6-6)	1.10	1.10
Nos. 1703-1708 (6)	1.67	1.67

Quality Month — A438

Lunan Stone Forest, Yunn — A439

1981, Sept. 1 Photo. *Perf. 11½x11*

1709 A438 8f Silver medal (2-1)	25	25
1710 A438 8f Gold medal (2-2)	25	25

Numbered J.66.

1981, Sept. 18 *Perf. 11½*

Designs: Views of limestone formations, Lunan Stone Forest. Nos. 1711-1713 horiz. Numbered T.64.

1711 A439 8f multi (5-1)	12	12
1712 A439 8f multi (5-2)	12	12
1713 A439 8f multi (5-3)	12	12
1714 A439 10f multi (5-4)	15	15
1715 A439 70f multi (5-5)	1.50	1.50
Nos. 1711-1715 (5)	2.01	2.01

Lu Xun, Writer, Birth Centenary A440

1981, Sept. 25

1716 A440 8f shown (2-1)	15	15
1717 A440 20f Portrait (diff.) (2-2)	35	35

Numbered J.67.

Sun Yat-sen and Text A441

70th Anniv. of 1911 Revolution: No. 1719, 72 Martyrs Grave, Huang Hua Gang. No. 1720, Hubei Provincial Government Headquarters, 1911. Numbered J.68.

1981, Oct. 10 Photo. *Perf. 11x11½*

1718 A441 8f multi (3-1)	18	18
1719 A441 8f multi (3-2)	18	18
1720 A441 8f multi (3-3)	18	18

Asian Conference of Parliamentarians on Population and Development, Peking, Oct. 27 — A442

Perf. 11½x11, 11x11½

1981, Oct. 27

1721 A442 8f Tree, vert. (2-1)	12	12
1722 A442 70f shown (2-2)	1.40	1.40

Numbered J.73.

Huang Guo Shu Falls — A443

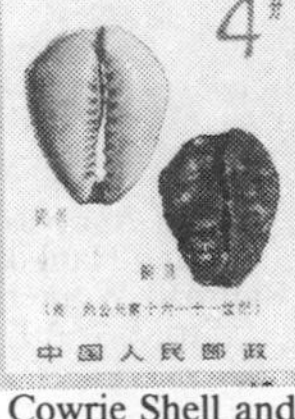
Cowrie Shell and Shell-shaped Coin — A444

Perf. 13x13½, 11½(Photo.)

1981-83 Engr., Photo.

1723 A443 1f Xishuang Banna 5 5
1724 A443 1½f Mt. Hua 5 5
1725 A443 2f Mt. Tai 5 5
1726 A443 3f shown 5 5
a. Photogravure 5 5
1727 A443 4f Hainan Isld. 6 6
a. Photogravure 6 6
1728 A443 5f Tiger Hill, Suzhou 8 8
1729 A443 8f Great Wall 12 12
a. Photogravure 12 12
1730 A443 10f Immense Forest 15 15
a. Photogravure 15 15
1731 A443 20f Mt. Tian 30 30
a. Photogravure 30 30
1732 A443 30f Grassland, Inner Mongolia 45 45
1733 A443 40f Stone Forest 60 60
1734 A443 50f Banping Mountain 75 75
1735 A443 70f Mt. Qomolangma 1.10 1.10
1736 A443 80f Seven-Star Crag 1.25 1.25
1737 A443 $1 Three Gorges, Changjiang River 1.50 1.50
1738 A443 $2 Guilin landscape 3.00 3.00
1739 A443 $5 Mt. Huangshan 7.50 7.50
Nos. 1723-1739 (17) 17.06 17.06
Nos. 1726a-1731a (5) 68 68

Issue dates: Nos. 1737-1739, Oct. 9, 1982; Nos. 1732, 1734-1736 Apr. 1, 1983.

Photogravure and Engraved

1981, Oct. 29 ***Perf. 11½x11***

Ancient Coins. Numbered T.65.

1740 A444 4f shown (8-1) 6 6
1741 A444 4f Shovel (8-2) 6 6
1742 A444 8f Shovel, diff. (8-3) 12 12
1743 A444 8f Shovel, diff. (8-4) 12 12
1744 A444 8f Knife (8-5) 12 12
1745 A444 8f Knife (8-6) 12 12
1746 A444 60f Knife, diff. (8-7) 1.25 1.25
1747 A444 70f Gong (8-8) 1.40 1.40
Nos. 1740-1747 (8) 3.25 3.25

See Nos. 1765-1772.

Intl. Year of the Disabled — A445

1981, Nov. 10 Photo. ***Perf. 11½x11***

1748 A445 8f multi 30 30

Numbered J.72.

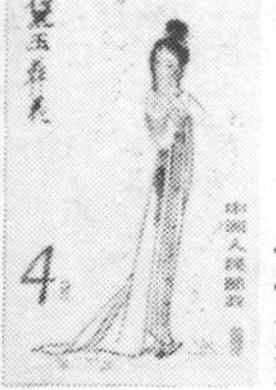
Twelve Beauties, from The Dream of Red Mansions, by Cao Xueqin — A446

1981-82 Photo. ***Perf. 11***

1749 A446 4f Daiyu (12-1) 6 6
1750 A446 4f Baochai (12-2) 6 6
1751 A446 8f Yuanchun (12-3) 12 12
1752 A446 8f Yingchun (12-4) 12 12
1753 A446 8f Tanchun (12-5) 12 12
1754 A446 8f Xichun (12-6) 12 12
1755 A446 8f Xiangyuh (12-7) 12 12
1756 A446 10f Liwan (12-8) 20 20
1757 A446 20f Xifeng (12-9) 40 40
1758 A446 30f Sister Qiao (12-10) 60 60
1759 A446 40f Keqing (12-11) 80 80
1760 A446 80f Miaoyu (12-12) 1.65 1.65
Nos. 1749-1760 (12) 4.37 4.37

Souvenir Sheet

1761 A446 $2 Baoyu, Daiyu 6.75

No. 1761 contains one stamp (59x39mm.); multicolored margin continues design. Size: 140x78mm. Issue dates: Nos. 1749, 1751, 1753, 1755, 1757, 1759, 1761, Nov. 20, 1981; others, Apr. 24, 1982. Numbered T.69.

Women's Team Victory in 3rd World Cup Volleyball Championship A447

1981, Dec. 21 Photo.

1762 A447 8f Girl playing volleyball (2-1) 30 30
1763 A447 20f Girl holding trophy (2-2) 60 60

Numbered J.76.

New Year 1982 (Year of the Dog) — A448

Photogravure & Engraved

1982, Jan. 5 ***Perf. 11½***

1764 A448 8f multi 75 75
a. Bklt. pane of 10 plus label 3.00

Numbered T.70.

Coin Type of 1981

Photogravure & Engraved

1982, Feb. 12

1765 A444 4f Guilian mask (8-1) 6 6
1766 A444 4f Shu shovel (8-2) 6 6
1767 A444 8f Xia zhuan shovel (8-3) 12 12
1768 A444 8f Han Dan shovel (8-4) 12 12
1769 A444 8f Knife (8-5) 12 12
1770 A444 8f Ming knife (8-6) 12 12
1771 A444 70f Jin hua knife (8-7) 1.25 1.25
1772 A444 80f Yi Liu Hua coin (8-8) 1.40 1.40
Nos. 1765-1772 (8) 3.25 3.25

Numbered T.71.

Nie Er (1912-1935), Natl. Anthem Composer A449

1982, Feb. 15 ***Perf. 11x11½***

1773 A449 8f multi 30 30

Numbered J.75.

Intl. Drinking Water and Sanitation Decade, 1981-1990 A450

1982, Mar. 1 ***Perf. 11½x11***

1774 A450 8f multi 20 20

Numbered J.77.

TB Bacillus Centenary A451

1982, Mar. 24 ***Perf. 11x11½***

1775 A451 8f multi 30 30

Numbered J.74.

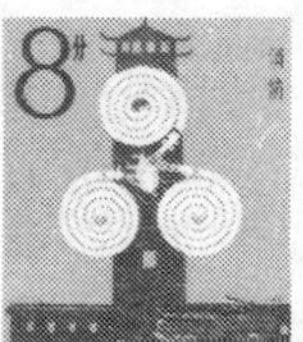
Fire Control — A452

1982, May 8 Photo. ***Perf. 11½x11***

1776 A452 8f Water hoses (2-1) 15 15
1777 A452 8f Chemical extinguisher (2-2) 15 15

Numbered T.76.

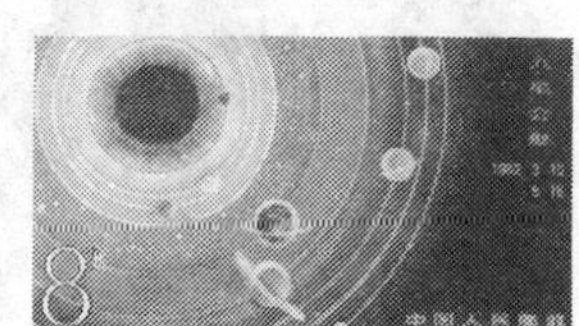
Syzygy of the Nine Planets, Mar. 10 and May 16 — A453

1982, May 16 ***Perf. 11½***

1778 A453 8f multi 30 30

Numbered T.78.

Medicinal Herbs — A454

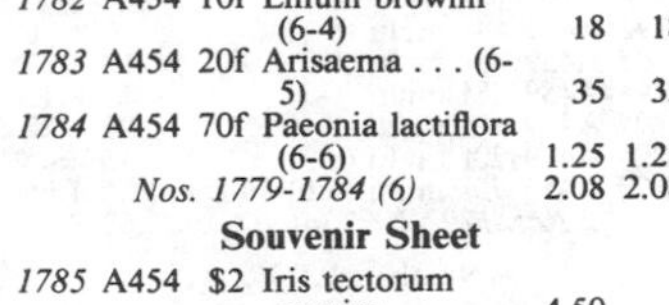
Soong Ching Ling (1893-1981), Sun Yat-sens' Widow — A455

1982, May 20 ***Perf. 11½x11***

1779 A454 4f Hemerocallis flava (6-1) 6 6
1780 A454 8f Fritillaria unibracteata (6-2) 12 12
1781 A454 8f Aconitum carmichaeli (6-3) 12 12
1782 A454 10f Lilium brownii (6-4) 18 18
1783 A454 20f Arisaema . . . (6-5) 35 35
1784 A454 70f Paeonia lactiflora (6-6) 1.25 1.25
Nos. 1779-1784 (6) 2.08 2.08

Souvenir Sheet

1785 A454 $2 Iris tectorum maxim 4.50

No. 1785 contains one stamp (89x39mm.); gold and gray decorative margin. Size: 138x70mm. Nos. 1779-1784 numbered T.72.

1982, May 29 ***Perf. 11½***

1786 A455 8f Addressing Consultative Conference (2-1) 15 15
1787 A455 20f Portrait (2-2) 45 45

Numbered J.82.

Sable A456

1982, June 20 Photo. ***Perf. 11½***

1788 A456 8f shown (2-1) 35 35
1789 A456 80f Sable, diff. (2-2) 1.90 1.90
a. Bklt. pane of 8: 6x8f plus sheetlet of 2 (8f, 80f) 2.00

Numbered T.68.

Natl. Census, July 1 — A457

1982, June 30 ***Perf. 11½x11***

1790 A457 8f multi 15 15

Numbered J.78.

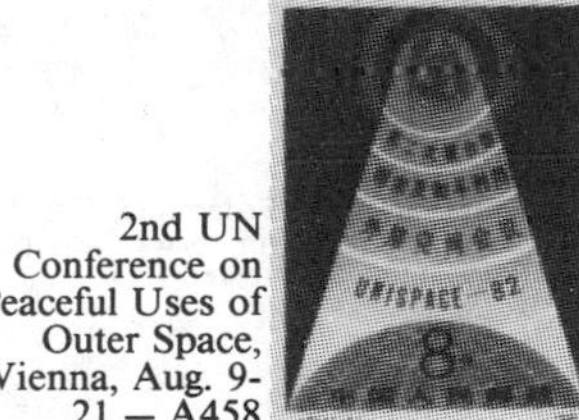
2nd UN Conference on Peaceful Uses of Outer Space, Vienna, Aug. 9-21 — A458

1982, July 25 Photo. ***Perf. 11½x11***

1791 A458 8f multi 15 15

Numbered J.81.

Strolling in Autumn Woods, by Shen Zhou, Ming Dynasty — A459

Fan Paintings (Ming or Qing Dynasty): No. 1793, Jackdaw on Withered Tree, by Tang Yin. No. 1794 Bamboo and Sparrows, by Zhou Zhimian. 10f, Writing Poem under Pine, by Chen Hongshou and Bai Han. 20f, Chrysanthemums, by Yun Shouping, Qing. 70f, Birds, Crape Myrtle and Chinese Parasol, by Wang Wu, Qing.

1982, July 31 *Perf. 11½*

1792 A459 4f multi (6-1) 6 6
1793 A459 8f multi (6-2) 12 12
1794 A459 8f multi (6-3) 12 12
1795 A459 10f multi (6-4) 22 22
1796 A459 20f multi (6-5) 45 45
1797 A459 70f multi (6-6) 1.65 1.65
Nos. 1792-1797 (6) 2.62 2.62

Numbered T.77.

60th Anniv. of Chinese Geological Society — A460

1982, Aug. 25 *Perf. 11½x11*

1798 A460 8f J.79 15 15

Orpiment — A461

1982, Aug. 25 Photo. *Perf. 11½x11*

1799 A461 4f shown (4-1) 6 6
1800 A461 8f Stibnite (4-2) 12 12
1801 A461 10f Cinnabar (4-3) 20 20
1802 A461 20f Wolframite (4-4) 40 40

Numbered T.73.

Souvenir Sheet

Messenger, Tomb Mural, Jiayu Pass, Wei-Jin Period — A462

1982, Aug. 25

1803 A462 $1 multi 5.50

All-China Philatelic Federation, First Congress. Pale green margin, black inscription. Size: 136x80mm. Numbered J.85.

12th Natl. Communist Party Congress — A463

Hoopoe — A464

1982, Sept. 1 *Perf. 11½*

1804 A463 8f multi 30 30

Numbered J.86.

1982, Sept. 10 *Perf. 11½x11*

1805 A464 8f shown (5-1) 12 12
1806 A464 8f Swallows (5-2) 12 12
1807 A464 8f Oriole (5-3) 12 12
1808 A464 20f Swifts (5-4) 35 35
1809 A464 70f Woodpecker (5-5) 1.40 1.40
Nos. 1805-1809 (5) 2.11 2.11

Souvenir Sheet

1810 A464 $2 Cuckoos 5.50

No. 1810 contains one stamp (56x36mm.); gray blue margin shows tree; black inscription. Size: 136x80mm. Numbered T.79.

Japan-China Relations Normalization, 10th Anniv. — A465

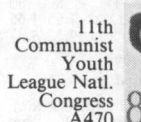

World Food Day — A466

Flower Paintings: 8f, Plum blossoms, by Guan Shanyue. 70f, Hibiscus, by Xiao Shufang.

1982, Sept. 29 *Perf. 11*

1811 A465 8f J.84 (2-1) 12 12
1812 A465 70f J.84 (2-2) 1.40 1.40

1982, Oct. 16 *Perf. 11½*

1813 A466 8f J.80 15 15

Guo Morou (1892-1978), Acad. of Sciences Pres. A467

Bodhisattva, 11th Cent. Sculpture A468

Designs: Portraits. Numbered J.87.

1982, Nov. 16 Photo. *Perf. 11½x11*

1814 A467 8f multi (2-1) 20 20
1815 A467 20f multi (2-2) 40 40

1982, Nov. 19 *Perf. 11*

Liao Dynasty Buddha Sculptures, Lower Huayan Monastery. Numbered T.74.

1816 A468 8f multi (4-1) 12 12
1817 A468 8f multi (4-2) 12 12
1818 A468 8f multi (4-3) 12 12
1819 A468 70f multi (4-4) 1.10 1.10

Souvenir Sheet

Perf. 11x11½

1820 A468 $2 multi 5.50

No. 1820 contains one stamp (36x55mm.); marginal inscription. Size: 130x80mm.

Dr. D.S. Kotnis, Indian Physician in 8th Army A469

Perf. 11½x11, 11x11½

1982, Dec. 9 **Photo.**

1821 A469 8f Portrait, vert. (2-1) 12 12
1822 A469 70f Riding horse (2-2) 1.40 1.40

Numbered J.83.

11th Communist Youth League Natl. Congress A470

1982, Dec. 20 *Perf. 11x11½*

1823 A470 8f J.88 15 15

Bronze Wine Container — A471

Western Zhou Dynasty Bronze (1200-771 B.C.): No. 1825, Three-legged cooking pot. No. 1826, Food bowl. No. 1827, Three-legged cooking pot (diff.). No. 1828, Animal-shaped wine container. 10f, Wine container with lid. 20f, Round food bowl. 70f, Square wine container. Numbered T.75.

Photogravure & Engraved

1982, Dec. 25 *Perf. 11*

1824 A471 4f multi (8-1) 6 6
1825 A471 4f multi (8-2) 6 6
1826 A471 8f multi (8-3) 12 12
1827 A471 8f multi (8-4) 12 12
1828 A471 8f multi (8-5) 12 12
1829 A471 10f multi (8-6) 18 18
1830 A471 20f multi (8-7) 35 35
1831 A471 70f multi (8-8) 1.25 1.25
Nos. 1824-1831 (8) 2.26 2.26

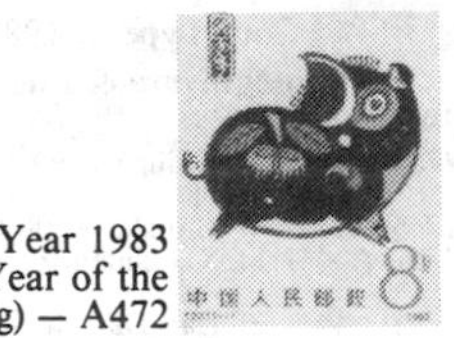

New Year 1983 (Year of the Pig) — A472

1983, Jan. 5 *Perf. 11½*

1832 A472 8f T.80 1.10 1.10
a. Bklt. pane of 12 3.75

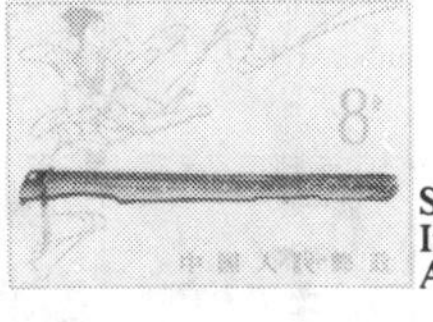

Stringed Instruments A473

Perf. 11½x11, 11x11½

1983, Jan. 20

1833 A473 4f Konghou (5-1) 6 6
1834 A473 8f Ruan (5-2) 18 18
1835 A473 8f Qin, horiz. (5-3) 18 18
1836 A473 10f Piba (5-4) 24 24
1837 A473 70f Sanxian (5-5) 1.65 1.65
Nos. 1833-1837 (5) 2.31 2.31

Numbered T.81.

60th Anniv. of Peking-Hankow Railroad Workers' Strike — A474

1983, Feb. 7 Photo. *Perf. 11½x11*

1838 A474 8f Memorial Tower, Zhengzhou (2-1) 20 20
1839 A474 8f Monument, Jiangan (2-2) 20 20

Numbered J.89.

The Western Chamber, Traditional Opera, by Wang Shifu (1271-1368) A475

Scenes from the opera.

1983, Feb. 21 Photo. *Perf. 11x11½*

1840 A475 8f multi (4-1) 12 12
1841 A475 8f multi (4-2) 12 12
1842 A475 10f multi (4-3) 20 20
1843 A475 80f multi (4-4) 1.75 1.75

Souvenir Sheet

Photogravure and Engraved

Perf. 12

1844 A475 $2 multi 4.50

No. 1844 contains one stamp (27x48mm.). Size:130x80mm. Numbered T.82.

Karl Marx (1818-1883) A476

Photogravure & Engraved

1983, Mar. 14 *Perf. 11½x11*

1845 A476 8f Portrait (2-1) 20 20
1846 A476 20f Making speech (2-2) 40 40

Numbered J.90.

Tomb of the Yellow Emperor A477

Photogravure & Engraved

1983, Apr. 5 *Perf. 11½*

1847 A477 8f Tomb, vert. (3-1) 12 12
1848 A477 10f Hall of Founder of Chinese Culture (3-2) 15 15
1849 A477 20f Cypress tree, vert. (3-3) 30 30

Numbered T.84.

Prices of premium quality never hinged stamps will be in excess of catalogue price.

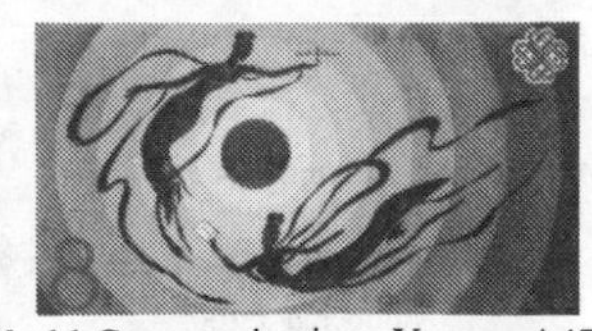

World Communications Year — A478

1983, Apr. 28 Photo. *Perf. 11½*

1850 A478 8f J.91	30	30

Male Chinese Alligator — A479

Photogravure & Engraved

1983, May 24 *Perf. 11*

1851 A479 8f shown (2-1)	12	12
1852 A479 20f Female, hatching eggs (2-2)	30	30

Numbered T.85.

Kitten, by Tan Arxi — A480

Various children's drawings. Numbered T.86.

1983, June 1 *Perf. 11½x11*

1853 A480 8f multi (4-1)	12	12
1854 A480 8f multi (4-2)	12	12
1855 A480 8f multi (4-3)	12	12
1856 A480 8f multi (4-4)	12	12

6th Natl. People's Congress — A481

Photogravure & Engraved

1983, June 6 *Perf. 11x11½*

1857 A481 8f Hall (2-1)	12	12
1858 A481 20f Natl. anthem score (2-2)	30	30

Numbered J.94.

Terra Cotta Figures, Qin Dynasty (221-207 BC) — A482

1983, June 30

1859 A482 8f Soldiers (4-1)	12	12
1860 A482 8f Heads (4-2)	12	12
1861 A482 10f Soldiers, horses (4-3)	15	15
1862 A482 70f Excavation site (4-4)	1.10	1.10
a. Bklt. pane of 8 (#1859, 3 #1860, 3 #1861, #1862)	2.50	

Souvenir Sheet

1863 A482 $2 Soldier leading horse	3.75	
a. Bklt. pane	3.75	

No. 1863 contains one stamp (59x39mm., perf. 11½x11); multicolored margin continues design. Size: 100x86mm. Numbered T.88.

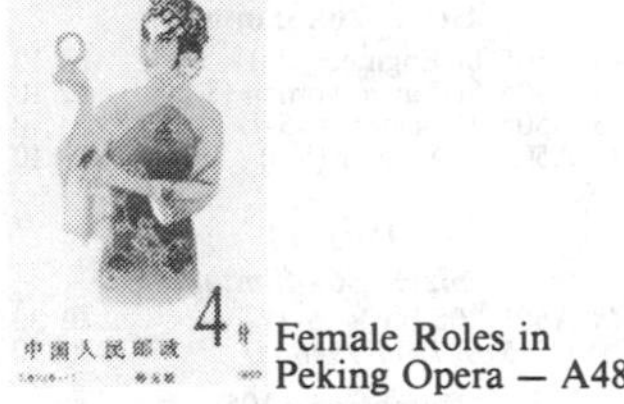

Female Roles in Peking Opera — A483

1983, July 20 Photo. *Perf. 11*

1864 A483 4f Sun Yujiao (8-1)	6	6
1865 A483 8f Chen Miaochang (8-2)	12	12
1866 A483 8f Bai Suzhen (8-3)	12	12
1867 A483 8f Sister Thirteen (8-4)	12	12
1868 A483 10f Qin Xianglian (8-5)	15	15
1869 A483 20f Yang Yuhuan (8-6)	30	30
1870 A483 50f Cui Yingying (8-7)	75	75
1871 A483 80f Mu Guiying (8-8)	1.25	1.25
Nos. 1864-1871 (8)	2.87	2.87

Numbered T.87.

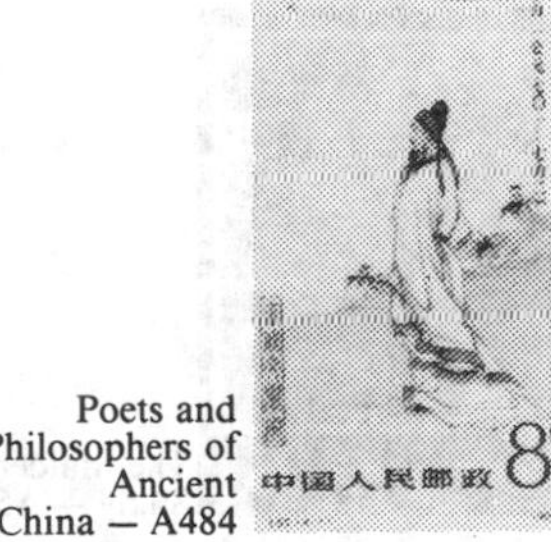

Poets and Philosophers of Ancient China — A484

Paintings by Liu Lingcang.

1983, Aug. 10 Photo. *Perf. 11½*

1872 A484 8f Li Bai (4-1)	12	12
1873 A484 8f Du Fu (4-2)	12	12
1874 A484 8f Han Yu (4-3)	12	12
1875 A484 70f Liu Zongyuan (4-4)	1.50	1.50

Numbered J.92.

5th Natl. Women's Congress — A485

1983, Sept. 1 Photo. *Perf. 11½*

1876 A485 8f J.95 (1-1)	20	20

5th National Games — A486

1983, Sept. 16 Photo. *Perf. 11½*

1877 A486 4f Emblem (6-1)	6	6
1878 A486 8f Gymnast (6-2)	12	12
1879 A486 8f Badminton (6-3)	12	12
1880 A486 8f Diving (6-4)	12	12
1881 A486 20f High jump (6-5)	38	38
1882 A486 70f Wind surfing (6-6)	1.40	1.40
Nos. 1877-1882 (6)	2.20	2.20

Numbered J.93.

Family Planning A487

1983, Sept. 19 *Perf. 11x11½*

1883 A487 8f One child (2-1)	15	15
1884 A487 8f Cultivated land (2-2)	15	15

Numbered T.91.

10th Intl. Trade Union Congress — A488

1983, Oct. 18 Litho. *Perf. 11½*

1885 A488 8f J.98 (1-1)	20	20

Swans A489

Perf. 11x11½ on 3 sides

1983, Nov. 18 Photo.

1886 A489 8f (4-1)	15	15
1887 A489 8f (4-2)	15	15
1888 A489 10f (4-3)	20	20
1889 A489 80f (4-4)	1.25	1.25
a. Booklet pane, 7 #1886, 1 each #1887-1889	2.75	

Numbered T.83.

85th Birth Anniv. of Liu Shaoqi, Political Leader — A490

Various photos. Numbered J.96.

1983, Nov. 24 Photo. *Perf. 11½*

1890 A490 8f multi (4-1)	12	12
1891 A490 8f multi (4-2)	12	12
1892 A490 8f multi (4-3)	12	12
1893 A490 8f multi (4-4)	12	12

CHINAPEX '83 Natl. Philatelic Exhibition — A491

1983, Nov. 29 Photo. *Perf. 11½*

1894 A491 8f No. 117 (2-1)	12	12
1895 A491 20f No. 4L1 (2-2)	30	30

Numbered J.99.

90th Birth Anniv. of Mao Tse-tung — A492

Various portraits. Numbered J.97.

1983, Dec. 26 Photo. *Perf. 11½*

1896 A492 8f 1925 (4-1)	12	12
1897 A492 8f 1945 (4-2)	12	12
1898 A492 10f 1952 (4-3)	15	15
1899 A492 20f 1961 (4-4)	40	40

New Year 1984 (Year of the Rat) — A493

Photogravure and Engraved

1984, Jan. 5 *Perf. 11½*

1900 A493 8f T.90	45	45
a. Bklt. pane of 12	2.00	

Beauties Wearing Flowers — A494

Portions of painting by Zhou Fang (Tang Dynasty). Numbered T.89.

1984, Mar. 24 Photo. *Perf. 11*

1901 A494 8f multi (3-1)	12	12
1902 A494 10f multi (3-2)	20	20
1903 A494 70f multi (3-3)	1.25	1.25

Souvenir Sheet

1904 A494 $2 Entire painting	6.00	

No. 1904 contains one stamp (162x40mm.). Size: 176x66mm.

Chinese Roses — A495

1984, Apr. 20 Photo. *Perf. 11½*

1905 A495 4f Spring of Shanghai (6-1)	6	6
1906 A495 8f Rosy Dawn of Pujiang River (6-2)	12	12
1907 A495 8f Pearl (6-3)	12	12
1908 A495 10f Black whirlwind (6-4)	20	20
1909 A495 20f Yellow flower in battlefield (6-5)	35	35
1910 A495 70f Blue Phoenix (6-6)	1.25	1.25
Nos. 1905-1910 (6)	2.10	2.10

Numbered T.93.

Ren Bishi (1904-50), Statesman — A496

1984, Apr. 30 *Perf. 11½x11*

1911 A496 8f J.100 15 15

Crested Ibis — A497

1984, May 15 Photo. *Perf. 11x11½*

1912 A497 8f Flying (3-1) 12 12
1913 A497 8f Wading (3-2) 12 12
1914 A497 80f Perching (3-3) 1.25 1.25

Numbered T.94.

Chinese Red Cross Society, 80th Anniv. — A498

1984, May 29 *Perf. 11½*

1915 A498 8f J.102 15 15

Gezhou Dam, Yangtze River — A499

1984, June 15 **Photo.**

1916 A499 8f Dam (3-1) 12 12
1917 A499 10f Bridge, vert. (3-2) 15 15
1918 A499 20f Lock Gate No. 2 (3-3) 30 30

Numbered T.95.

Zhuo Zheng Garden, Suzhou — A500

Photogravure & Engraved

1984, June 30 *Perf. 11½x11*

1919 A500 8f Inverted Image Tower (4-1) 12 12
1920 A500 8f Loquat Garden (4-2) 12 12
1921 A500 10f Water Court, Xiao Cang Lang (4-3) 15 15
1922 A500 70f Yuanxiang Hall, Yiyu Study (4-4) 1.10 1.10

Numbered T.96.

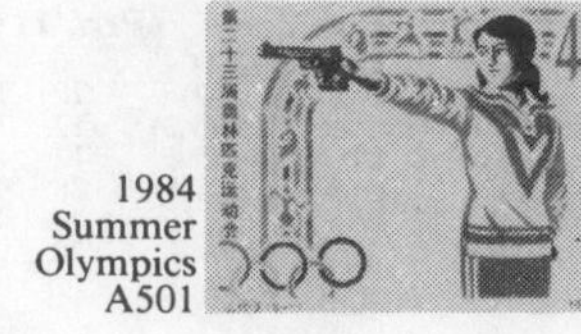

1984 Summer Olympics A501

1984, July 28 Photo. *Perf. 11½*

1923 A501 4f Shooting (6-1) 6 6
1924 A501 8f High jump (6-2) 12 12
1925 A501 8f Weight lifting (6-3) 12 12
1926 A501 10f Gymnastics (6-4) 15 15
1927 A501 20f Volleyball (6-5) 30 30
1928 A501 80f Diving (6-6) 1.25 1.25
Nos. 1923-1928 (6) 2.00 2.00

Souvenir Sheet

1929 A501 $2 Athletes, rings 3.00

No. 1929 contains one stamp (61x38mm.); multicolored decorative margin. Size: 96x70mm. Numbered J.103.

Calligraphy A502

Luanhe River Water Diversion Project A503

Artworks by Wu Changshuo. Numbered T.98.

1984, Aug. 27 Photo. *Perf. 11½*

1930 A502 4f shown (8-1) 5 5
1931 A502 4f A Pair of Peaches (8-2) 5 5
1932 A502 8f Lotus (8-3) 10 10
1933 A502 8f Wistaria (8-4) 10 10
1934 A502 8f Peony (8-5) 10 10
1935 A502 10f Chrysanthemum (8-6) 12 12
1936 A502 20f Plum Blossom (8-7) 25 25
1937 A502 70f Seal Cutting (8-8) 88 88
Nos. 1930-1937 (8) 1.65 1.65

Perf. 11½x11, 11 (#1939)

1984, Sept. 11 **Photo.**

1938 A503 8f multi (3-1) 10 10
1939 A503 10f multi, horiz. (3-2) 15 15
1940 A503 20f multi (3-3) 35 35

Numbered T.97.

Chinese-Japanese Youth — A504

1984, Sept. 24 Photo. *Perf. 11½*

1941 A504 8f Neighbors (3-1) 10 10
1942 A504 20f Planting tree (3-2) 30 30
1943 A504 80f Dancing (3-3) 1.25 1.25

Numbered J.104.

People's Republic, 35th Anniv. — A505

1984, Oct. 1 Photo. *Perf. 11½x11*

Size: 26x35mm.

1944 A505 8f Engineer (5-1) 10 10
1945 A505 8f Farm woman (5-2) 10 10
1946 A505 8f Scientist (5-4) 10 10
1947 A505 8f Soldier (5-5) 10 10

Perf. 11

Size: 36x48mm.

1948 A505 20f Birds (5-3) 30 30
Nos. 1944-1948 (5) 70 70

Numbered J.105.

110th Birth Anniv. of Chen Jiageng A506

1984, Oct. 21 Photo. *Perf. 12½x12*

1949 A506 8f Chen Jiageng (2-1) 10 10
1950 A506 80f Jimei School (2-2) 1.00 1.00

Numbered J.106.

The Maiden's Study — A507

Scenes from The Peony Pavilion, by Tang Xianzu. Numbered T.99.

Photogravure & Engraved

1984, Oct. 30 *Perf. 11*

1951 A507 8f shown (4-1) 10 10
1952 A507 8f In the dreamland (4-2) 10 10
1953 A507 20f Du Liniang drawing self-portrait (4-3) 25 25
1954 A507 70f Married to Liu Mengmai (4-4) 1.00 1.00

Souvenir Sheet

1955 A507 $2 Playing in the garden 3.25

No. 1955 contains one stamp (90x60mm, perf. 11½); multicolored decorative margin continues design. Size: 136x80mm.

Emei Shan Mountain Scenery — A508

1984, Nov. 16

1956 A508 4f Baoguo Temple (6-1) 5 5
1957 A508 8f Leiyin Temple (6-2) 10 10
1958 A508 8f Hongchun Lawn (6-3) 10 10
1959 A508 10f Elephant bath (6-4) 12 12
1960 A508 20f Woyun Temple (6-5) 30 30
1961 A508 80f Shining Cloud Sea at Jinding (6-6) 1.25 1.25
Nos. 1956-1961 (6) 1.92 1.92

Numbered T.100.

Former Party Secretary Ren Bishi (1904-1950) A509

Portraits.

1984, Dec. 15 Photo. *Perf. 11½x11*

1962 A509 8f During the Long March (3-1) 10 10
1963 A509 10f At 7th Natl. Party Congress (3-2) 15 15
1964 A509 20f In motorcade (3-3) 35 35

Chinese Insurance Industry — A510

1984, Dec. 25 *Perf. 11*

1965 A510 8f Flower arrangement 15 15

Numbered T.101.

New Year 1985 (Year of the Ox) — A511

Photogravure & Engraved

1985, Jan. 5 *Perf. 11½*

1966 A511 8f T.102 15 15
a. Bklt. pane of 4 + 8 plus label 2.00

Zunyi Meeting, 50th Anniv. — A512

Paintings: 8f, The Zunyi Meeting, by Liu Xiangping. 20f, The Red Army Successfully Arrived in Northern Shaanxi, by Zhao Yu. Numbered J.107.

1985, Jan. 15 Photo. *Perf. 11x11½*

1967 A512 8f multi (2-1) 10 10
1968 A512 20f multi (2-2) 35 35

Lotus of Good Luck — A513

Lantern Folk Festival: No. 1970, Auspicious dragon and phoenix. No. 1971, A hundred flowers blossoming. 70f, Prosperity and affluence. Numbered T.104.

1985, Feb. 28 *Perf. 11½*
1969 A513 8f multi (4-1) 10 10
1970 A513 8f multi (4-2) 10 10
1971 A513 8f multi (4-3) 10 10
1972 A513 70f multi (4-4) 1.00 1.00

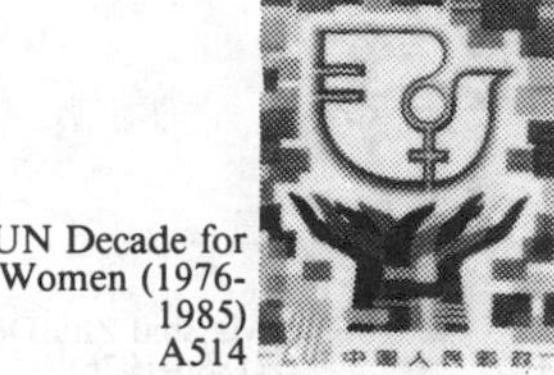
UN Decade for Women (1976-1985) A514

1985, Mar. 8
1973 A514 20f J.108 30 30

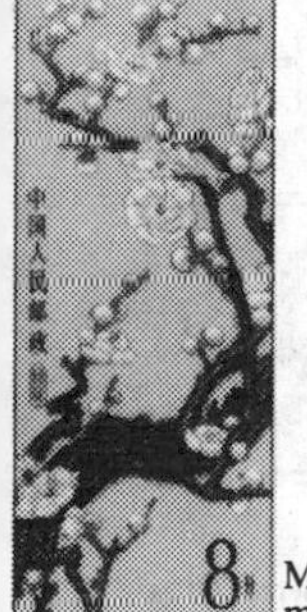
Mei (Prunus mume) — A515

1985, Apr. 5 *Perf. 11*
1974 A515 8f Green calyx (6-1) 10 10
1975 A515 8f Pendant mei (6-2) 10 10
1976 A515 8f Contorted dragon (6-3) 10 10
1977 A515 10f Cinnabar (6-4) 12 12
1978 A515 20f Versicolor mei (6-5) 25 25
1979 A515 80f Apricot mei (6-6) 1.00 1.00
Nos. 1974-1979 (6) 1.67 1.67

Souvenir Sheet

1980 A515 $2 Duplicate and condensed fragrance mei 3.00

No. 1980 contains one stamp (93x52mm, perf. 11½); multicolored margin pictures floral design. Size: 130x70mm. Numbered T.103.

All-China Fed. of Trade Unions — A516

1985, May 1 **Photo.** *Perf. 11*
1981 A516 8f Huizo Guild Hall, Guangzhou 10 10

Numbered J.109.

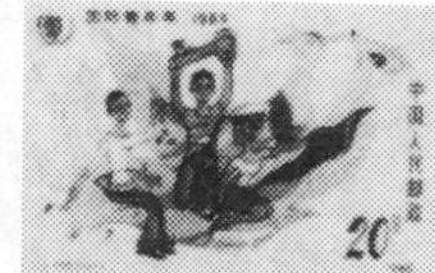
Intl. Youth Year A517

1985, May 4 **Photo.**
1982 A517 20f J.110 30 30

Giant Pandas — A518

Paintings of pandas: 8f, 20f, 50f, 80f, by Han Meilin; $3, by Wu Zuoren.

1985, May 24 *Perf. 11½*
1983 A518 8f multi (4-1), vert. 10 10
1984 A518 20f multi (4-2) 25 25
1985 A518 50f multi (4-3), vert. 65 65
1986 A518 80f multi (4-4) 1.00 1.00

Souvenir Sheet

1987 A518 $3 multi, vert. 4.50

No. 1987 contains one stamp (39x59mm, perf. 11x11½); multicolored margin contains inscriptions. Size: 74x80mm. Numbered T.106.

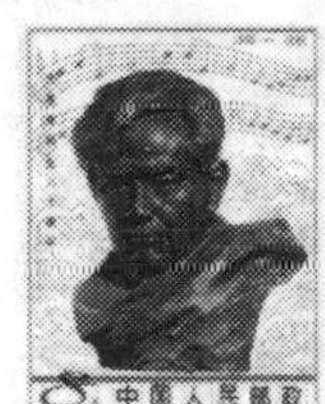

Xian Xinghai (1905-1945), Composer A519

Agnes Smedley, 1892-1950 (3-1) A520

Design: Bust, by Cao Chongen and music from The Yellow River Cantata. Numbered J.111.

1985, June 13 **Photo.** *Perf. 11½x11*
1988 A519 8f multi 10 10

1985, June 25

American journalists: 20f, Anna Louise Strong, 1885-1970 (3-2). 80f, Edgar Snow, 1905-1972 (3-3). Numbered J.112.

1989 A520 8f multi 10 10
1990 A520 20f multi 25 25
1991 A520 80f multi 1.00 1.00

Zheng He's West Seas Expedition, 580th Anniv. — A521

Designs: No. 1992, Portrait of the navigator (4-1). No. 1993, Peace envoy (4-2). 20f, Trade, cultural exchange (4-3). 80f, Honored for navigational feats (4-4). Numbered J.113.

1985, July 11 *Perf. 11½*
1992 A521 8f multi 10 10
1993 A521 8f multi 10 10
1994 A521 20f multi 25 25
1995 A521 80f multi 1.00 1.00

Xu Beihong, 1895-1953, Painter (2-2) A522

Perf. 11½x11, 11x11½

1985, July 19
1996 A522 8f Self-portrait (2-1), vert. 10 10
1997 A522 20f shown 35 35

Numbered J.114.

Lin Zexu, 1785-1850, Statesman, Patriot (2-1) — A523

Design: 80f, Burning opium at Humen, bas-relief (2-2).

1985, Aug. 30 *Perf. 11*
1998 A523 8f multi 10 10

Size: 51x22mm.

1999 A523 80f multi 1.00 1.00

Lin Zexu's ban of the opium trade catalyzed the Anglo-Chinese Opium Wars. Numbered J.115.

Tibet Autonomous Region, 20th Anniv. — A524

1985, Sept. 1 *Perf. 11½x11*
2000 A524 8f Prosperity (3-1) 10 10
2001 A524 10f Celebration (3-2) 15 15
2002 A524 20f Abundant Harvest (3-3) 35 35

Numbered J.116.

End of World War II, 40th Anniv. A525

Woodcuts by Wu Biduan: 8f, The Chinese Army Rose Against the Japanese Agressors at Logouqiao (2-1). 80f, The Eighth Route Army and Militia Fought Around the Great Wall (2-2). Numbered J.117.

1985, Sept. 3 *Perf. 11*
2003 A525 8f multi 10 10
2004 A525 80f multi 1.00 1.00

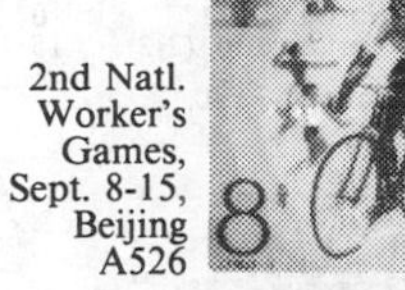
2nd Natl. Worker's Games, Sept. 8-15, Beijing A526

Competitors from various events and: 8f, Men's bicycling (2-1). 20f, Women hurdlers (2-2). Numbered J.118.

1985, Sept. 8 *Perf. 11x11½*
2005 A526 8f multi 10 10
2006 A526 20f multi 35 35

Xinjiang Uygur Autonomous Region, 30th Anniv. A527

1985, Oct. 1 **Photo.** *Perf. 11½*
2007 A527 8f Oasis in the Gobi, woman (3-1) 10 10
2008 A527 10f Oil field, Lake Tianchi (3-2) 18 18
2009 A527 20f Tianshan pasture, woman (3-3) 35 35

Numbered J.119. Size of No. 2008, 60x30mm.

1st Natl. Youth Games, Oct. 6-15, Zhengzhou A528

1985, Oct. 6 *Perf. 11½x11*
2010 A528 8f Girls' track & field (2-1) 10 10
2011 A528 20f Boys' basketball (2-2) 35 35

Numbered J.121

Forbidden City Main Buildings — A529

1985, Oct. 10 *Perf. 11½*
2012 A529 8f multi (4-1) 10 10
2013 A529 8f multi (4-2) 10 10
2014 A529 20f multi (4-3) 25 25
2015 A529 80f multi (4-4) 1.10 1.10

Palace Museum, 60th anniv. Numbered J.120.

Zou Taofen (1895-1935), Journalist A530

1985, Nov. 5 *Perf. 11½x11*
2016 A530 8f Portrait (2-1) 10 10
2017 A530 20f Epitaph by Zhou Enlai (2-2) 35 35

Se-tenant. Numbered J.122.

December 9th Revolution, 50th Anniv. — A531

1985, Dec. 9 *Perf. 11½*
2018 A531 8f Memorial Pavilion 10 10

Numbered J.125

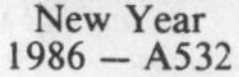

New Year 1986 — A532

Natl. Space Industry — A533

Photogravure & Engraved

1986, Jan. 5 ***Perf. 11½***

2019	A532	8f T.107	6	6
a.		Bklt. pane of 4 + 8 with label between	75	

1986, Feb. 1 **Photo.**

Designs: 4f, 1st experimental satellite. No. 2021, Recoverable satellite. No. 2022, Underwater rocket launch. 10f, Rocket launch. 20f, Earth satellite receiver. 70f, Satellite trajectory diagram. Numbered T.108.

2020	A533	4f multi (6-1)	5	5
2021	A533	8f multi (6-2)	6	6
2022	A533	8f multi (6-3)	6	6
2023	A533	10f multi (6-4)	8	8
2024	A533	20f multi (6-5)	15	15
2025	A533	70f multi (6-6)	52	52
		Nos. 2020-2025 (6)	92	92

Dong Biwu (1886-1975), Party Founder — A534

Lin Boqu (1886-1960), Party Leader — A535

Photogravure and Engraved

1986, Mar. 5 ***Perf. 11½x11***

2026	A534	8f Portrait, 1975 (2-1)	6	6
2027	A534	20f Portrait, 1945 (2-2)	15	15

Numbered J.123.

1986, Mar. 20

2028	A535	8f shown (2-1)	6	6
2029	A535	20f Boqu standing (2-2)	15	15

Numbered J.124.

He Long (1896-1969), Revolution Leader — A536

1986, Mar. 22 ***Perf. 11x11½***

2030	A536	8f shown (2-1)	6	6
2031	A536	20f Long on horseback (2-2)	15	15

Numbered J.126.

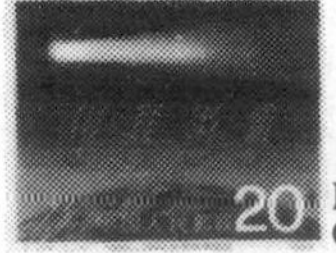

Halley's Comet — A537

1986, Apr. 11 **Photo.** ***Perf. 11½***

2032	A537	20f dk bl & gray	15	15

Numbered T.109.

White Crane A538

Perf. 11x11½, 11½x11

1986, May 22

2033	A538	8f Two cranes (3-1)	6	6
2034	A538	10f One flying (3-2), vert.	8	8
2035	A538	70f Four cranes (3-3), vert.	65	65

Souvenir Sheet

2036	A538	$2 Flock	1.50

Numbered T.110. No. 2036 contains one stamp (size: 116x25mm); beige inscribed margin. Size: 160x52mm.

Li Weihan (1896-1984), Party Leader — A539

1986, June 2 ***Perf. 11x11½***

2037	A539	8f Portrait (2-1)	6	6
2038	A539	20f Writing (2-2)	15	15

Numbered J.127.

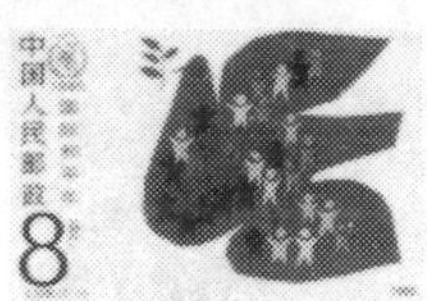

Intl. Peace Year A540

1986, June 16 ***Perf. 11***

2039	A540	8f multi	6	6

Numbered J.128.

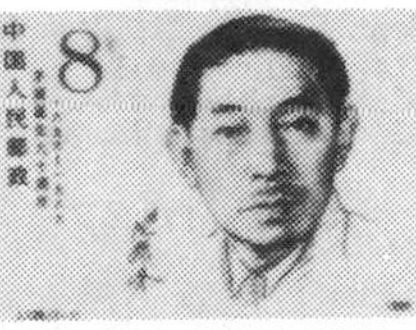

Mao Dun (1896-1981), Writer — A541

1986, July 4 ***Perf. 11x11½***

2040	A541	8f Portrait (2-1)	6	6
2041	A541	20f Portrait, diff. (2-2)	15	15

Numbered J.129.

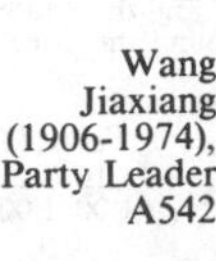

Wang Jiaxiang (1906-1974), Party Leader A542

1986, Aug. 15

2042	A542	8f Portrait (2-1)	6	6
2043	A542	20f Portrait, diff. (2-2)	15	15

Numbered J.130.

Teacher's Day A543

1986, Sept. 10 ***Perf. 11***

2044	A543	8f multi	6	6

Numbered J.131.

Magnolia Liliflora A544

1986, Sept. 23 ***Perf. 11x11½***

2045	A544	8f Blossom (3-1)	6	6
2046	A544	8f Two blossoms (3-2)	6	6
2047	A544	70f Blossom, diff. (3-3)	52	52

Souvenir Sheet

2048	A544	$2 Three blossoms	1.50

Numbered T.111. No. 2048 contains one stamp (size: 132x70mm).

Folk Houses — A545

Perf. 13x13½, 11x11½, (1½f, 3f, #2057-2062)

1986, Apr. 1 **Photo.**

2049	A545	1f Inner Mongolia	5	5
2050	A545	1½f Tibet	5	5
2051	A545	2f Northeastern China	5	5
2052	A545	3f Hunan	5	5
2053	A545	4f So. Yangtse River	5	5
2054	A545	8f Yunnan	6	6
2055	A545	10f Shanghai	8	8
2056	A545	20f Shanghai	15	15
2057	A545	30f Anhui	22	22
2058	A545	40f No. Shaanxi	30	30
2059	A545	50f Sichuan	38	38
2060	A545	90f Taiwan	68	68
2061	A545	$1 Fujian	75	75
2062	A545	$1.10 Zhejiang	80	80
		Nos. 2049-2062 (14)	3.67	3.67

Issue dates: 3f, Dec. 25. 4f, $1, Oct. 15. 20f, 50f, Sept. 10. 40f, Nov. 15. Others, Apr. 1.

Souvenir Sheet

All-China Philatelic Federation, 2nd Congress — A546

1986, Oct. 17 **Litho.** ***Perf. 11½***

2063	A546	$2 Jade lion	1.50

Numbered J.135. No. 2063 has yellow bister, red and black decorative margin.

Leaders of the 1911 Revolution A547

1986, Oct. 10 **Photo.** ***Perf. 11x11½***

2064	A547	8f Sun Yat-sen (3-1)	6
2065	A547	10f Huang Xing (3-2)	8
2066	A547	40f Zhang Taiyan (3-3)	30

Numbered J.132

Souvenir Sheet

Sun Yat-sen (1866-1925) — A548

1986, Nov. 12 ***Perf. 11½***

2067	A548	$2 multi	1.50

No. 2067 has black and gold decorative margin. Size: 82x137mm. Numbered J.133

Marshal Zhu De (1886-1976) A549

Designs: 20f, Orating.

1986, Dec. 1 **Engr.** ***Perf. 11½x11***

2068	A549	8f sep (2-1)	6
2069	A549	20f myr grn (2-2)	15

Numbered J.134.

Sports of Ancient China A550

Stone carvings. Numbered T.113.

Perf. 11½x11, 11x11½

1986, Dec. 20 **Photo.**

2070	A550	8f Archery (4-1), vert.	6
2071	A550	8f Weiqi (4-2)	6
2072	A550	10f Golf (4-3)	8
2073	A550	50f Soccer (4-4), vert.	38

New Year 1987 (Year of the Hare) — A551

Photogravure & Engraved

1987, Jan. 5 ***Perf. 11½***

2074	A551	8f blk, dk pink & yel grn	6
a.		Bklt. pane of 4 + 8 + label	75

Numbered T.112.

Xu Xiake (1587-1621), Ming Dynasty Geographer A552

1987, Feb. 20 Photo. *Perf. 11½*

2075	A552	8f Traveling (3-1)	6
2076	A552	20f Writing in cave (3-2)	15
2077	A552	40f Mountain climbing (3-3)	30

Numbered J.136.

Birds of Prey — A553

1987, Mar. 20

2078	A553	8f Kite (4-1)	6
2079	A553	8f Sea eagle (4-2), vert.	6
2080	A553	10f Vulture (4-3), vert.	8
2081	A553	90f Buzzard (4-4)	65

Numbered T.114.

Liao Zhongkai (1877-1925), Party Leader A554

1987, Apr. 23 *Perf. 11½x11*

2082	A554	8f shown (2-1)	6
2083	A554	20f Liao, He Xiangning (2-2)	15

Numbered J.137.

Kites — A555

1987, Apr. 1

2084	A555	8f Hawk (4-1)	6
2085	A555	8f Dragon (4-2)	6
2086	A555	30f Symbolic octagon (4-3)	22
2087	A555	30f Phoenix (4-4)	22

Numbered T.115. Stamps of the same denomination printed se-tenant in continuous design.

Portraits of Ye Jianying (1897-1986), Central Committee Vice Chairman — A556

1987, Apr. 28

2088	A556	8f multi (3-3)	6
2089	A556	10f multi (3-2)	8
2090	A556	30f multi (3-3)	22

Numbered J.138.

Caves of the Thousand Buddhas, Dunhuang, Gansu Province — A557

Petroglyphs: 8f, Worshipping Bodhisattvas, Northern Liang Dynasty. 10f, Deer King Jatka, Northern Wei Dynasty. 20f, Heavenly Musicians, Northern Wei Dynasty. 40f, Flying Devata, Northern Wei Dynasty. $2, Mahasattva Jataka.

1987, May 20 *Perf. 11½*

2091	A557	8f multi (4-1)	6
2092	A557	10f multi (4-2)	8
2093	A557	20f multi (4-3)	15
2094	A557	40f multi (4-4)	30

Souvenir Sheet

2095	A557	$2 multi	1.50

Numbered T.116. No. 2095 contains one stamp (size: 92x73mm); has multicolored decorative margin. Size: 142x93mm.

Children's Day Festival — A558

Children's drawings: No. 2096, Happy Holiday, by Yan Qinghui, age 7. No. 2097, Peace and Happiness, by Liu Yuan, age 7.

1987, June 1 *Perf. 12½x12*

2096	A558	8f shown (2-1)	6
2097	A558	8f multi, vert. (2-2)	6

Numbered T.117.

Rural Development A559

Postal Savings Bank Inauguration A560

1987, June 25 *Perf. 11½*

2098	A559	8f Village, southeast China (4-1)	6
2099	A559	8f Market (4-2)	6
2100	A559	10f Dairy industry (4-3)	8
2101	A559	20f Theater (4-4)	15

Numbered T.118. Nos. 2099-2100 horiz.

1987, July 1

2102	A560	8f multi	6

Numbered T.119.

Esperanto Language Movement, Cent. — A561

1987, July 26

2103	A561	8f lt olive grn, blk & brt blue	6

Numbered J.139.

People's Liberation Army, 60th Anniv. A562

1987, Aug. 1 *Perf. 11*

2104	A562	8f Flag, Great Wall (4-1)	6
2105	A562	8f Rocket launch, soldier, village (4-2)	6
2106	A562	10f Submarine, sailor (4-3)	8
2107	A562	30f Aircraft, pilot (4-4)	22

Numbered J.140.

Intl. Year of Shelter for the Homeless — A563

1987, Aug. 20 *Perf. 11*

2108	A563	8f	6

Numbered J.141.

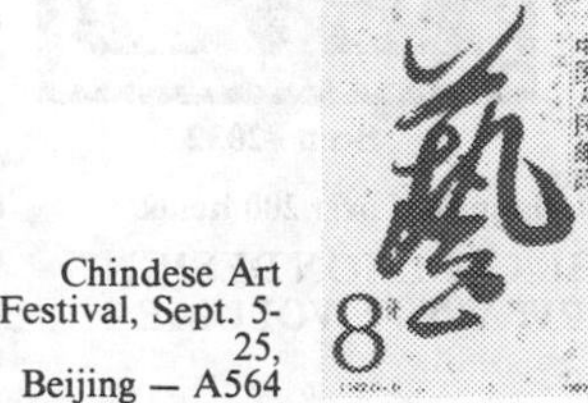

Chindese Art Festival, Sept. 5-25, Beijing — A564

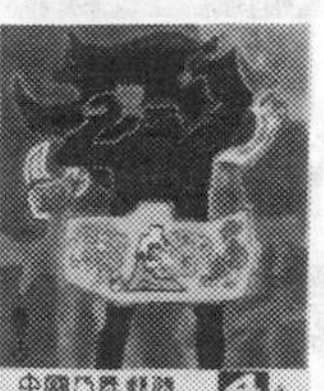

Fairy Tales — A565

1987, Sept. 5 *Perf. 11*

2109	A564	8f	6

Numbered J.142.

1987, Sept. 25 *Perf. 11½*

Designs: 4f, Pan Gu inventing the universe. No. 2111, Nu Wa creating man. No. 2112, Yi shooting nine suns. 10f, Chang'e flying to the moon. 20f, Kua Fu pursuing the sun. 90f, Jing Wei filling the sea. Numbered T.120.

2110	A565	4f multi (6-1)	5
2111	A565	8f multi (6-2)	6
2112	A565	8f multi (6-3)	6
2113	A565	10f multi (6-4)	8
2114	A565	20f multi (6-5)	16
2115	A565	90f multi (6-6)	68
		Nos. 2110-2115 (6)	1.09

Communist Party of China, 13th Natl. Congress — A566

1987, Oct. 25 *Perf. 11*

2116	A566	8f multi	6

Numbered J.143.

Yellow Crane Tower A567

1987, Oct. 30

2117	A567	8f shown (4-1)	5
2118	A567	8f Yue Yang Tower (4-2)	5
2119	A567	10f Teng Wang Pavilion (4-3)	6
2120	A567	90f Peng Lai Pavilion (4-4)	50
a.		Min. sheet of 4, Nos. 2117-2120	85

Numbered T.121. No. 2120a has black on dark beige inscribed margin. Sold for $1.50. Size: 130x93mm.

6th Natl. Games — A568

1987, Nov. 20 *Perf. 11½x11*

2121	A568	8f Pole vault (4-1)	5
2122	A568	8f Softball (4-2)	5
2123	A568	30f Weight lifting (4-3)	18
2124	A568	50f Diving (4-4)	28

Numbered J.144.

Souvenir Sheet

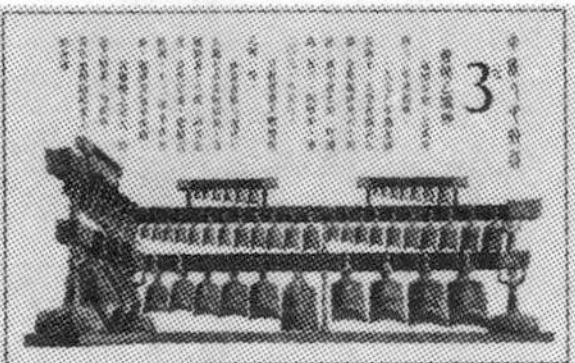

Bronze Bells from the Tomb of Marquis Yi of the Zeng State (c. 433 B.C.), Hubei Province — A569

1987, Dec. 10 Litho. *Imperf.*
2125 A569 $3 multi 2.25

Numbered T.122. No. 2125 has decorative inscribed margin. Size: 92x166mm.

Classic Literature — A570

Outlaws of the Marsh: 8f, Shi Jin practicing martial arts. 10f, Sagacious Lu, the "Tattooed Monk," uprooting a willow tree. 30f, Lin Chong seeking shelter from snow storm at the Mountain Spirit Temple. 50f, Song Jiang helps Ward Chief Chao Gai flee. $2, Outlaws of the Marsh capture treasures. Numbered T.123.

1987, Dec. 20 Photo. *Perf. 11*
2126 A570 8f multi (4-1) 6
2127 A570 10f multi (4-2) 8
2128 A570 30f multi (4-3) 22
2129 A570 50f multi (4-4) 38

Souvenir Sheet

Perf. 11½x11

2130 A570 $2 multi 1.50

No. 2130 contains one stamp (size: 90x60mm); has dull brown, beige and black inscribed margin. Size: 140x87mm.

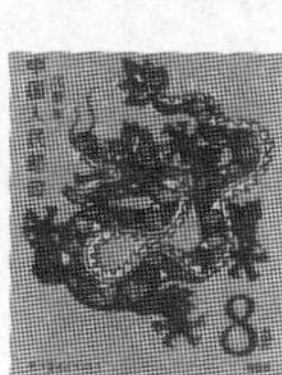

New Year 1987 (Year of the Dragon) A571

Cai Yuanpei (1868-1940), Education Reformer A572

Photo. & Engr.

1988, Jan. 5 *Perf. 11½*
2131 A571 8f multi 6

Numbered T.124.

1988, Jan. 11 Photo. *Perf. 11½x11*
2132 A572 8f shown (2-1) 6
2133 A572 20f Seated (2-2) 15

Numbered J.145.

Tao Zhu (1908-1969), Party Leader A573

1988, Jan. 16 *Perf. 11x11½*
2134 A573 8f shown (2-1) 6
2135 A573 20f Zhu, diff. (2-2) 15

Numbered J.146.

Folklore A574

1988, Feb. 10
2136 A574 8f shown (4-1) 6
2137 A574 10f multi, diff. (4-2) 8
2138 A574 20f multi, diff. (4-3) 15
2139 A574 30f multi, diff. (4-4) 24

Numbered T.125.

SEMI-POSTAL STAMPS

Girl Holding Ball — SP1

1984, Feb. 16 Photo. *Perf. 11½*
B1 SP1 8 + 2f shown (2-1) 15 15
B2 SP1 8 + 2f Boy, panda (2-2) 15 15

Numbered T.92. Surtax was for China Children's Fund.

Hands Reading Braille — SP2

1985, Mar. 15 Photo. *Perf. 11½*
B3 SP2 8f + 2f shown (4-1) 15 15
B4 SP2 8f + 2f Sign language, lip reading (4-2) 15 15
B5 SP2 8f + 2f Artificial limb (4-3) 15 15
B6 SP2 8f + 2f Handicapped person in wheelchair (4-4) 15 15

Surtax for China Welfare Fund. Numbered T.105.

AIR POST STAMPS

Mail Plane and Temple of Heaven — AP1

1951, May 1 Engr. *Perf. 12½*
C1 AP1 $1000 carmine 5 10
C2 AP1 $3000 green 10 10
C3 AP1 $5000 orange 5 15
C4 AP1 $10,000 vio brn & grn 8 25
C5 AP1 $30,000 dk bl & brn 1.50 75
Nos. C1-C5 (5) 1.78 1.35

Planes at Airport — AP2

Designs: 28f, Plane over winding mountain highway. 35f, Plane over railroad yard. 52f, Plane over ship.

1957-58 *Perf. 14*
C6 AP2 16f indigo 16.00 5
C7 AP2 28f ol blk 16.00 10
C8 AP2 35f slate 16.00 4.00
C9 AP2 52f Prus bl ('58) 16.00 50

POSTAGE DUE STAMPS

Grain and Cogwheel D1

Numeral D2

1950, Sept. 1 Typo. *Perf. 12½*
J1 D1 $100 stl bl 5 10
J2 D1 $200 stl bl 5 10
J3 D1 $500 stl bl 5 10
J4 D1 $800 stl bl 10.00 10
J5 D1 $1000 stl bl 15 40
J6 D1 $2000 stl bl 15 40
J7 D1 $5000 stl bl 10 60
J8 D1 $8000 stl bl 10 1.00
J9 D1 $10,000 stl bl 20 2.00
Nos. J1-J9 (9) 10.85 4.80

1954, Aug. 18 Litho. *Perf. 14*
J10 D2 $100 red 50 8
J11 D2 $200 red 15 8
J12 D2 $500 red 50 8
J13 D2 $800 red 5 8
J14 D2 $1600 red 5 15
Nos. J10-J14 (5) 1.25 47

MILITARY STAMPS

Red Star, 8-1 in Center — M1

1953, Aug. 1 Litho. *Perf. 14*
M1 M1 $800 yel, org & red (Army) 9.00 15.00
M2 M1 $800 dp pur, org & red (Air Force) 70.00
M3 M1 $800 bl, org & red (Navy) *6,500.*

NORTHEAST CHINA

The Northeast Liberation Area included the provinces of Liaoning, Kirin, Jehol and Heilungkiang, the area generally known as Manchuria under the Japanese. The first post war issues were local overprints on stamps of Manchukuo. In early 1946, a Ministry of Posts and Telegraphs served the areas already liberated, and in August, 1946, a Communications Committee of the Political Council was established. In June, 1947, these postal services were subordinated to the Harbin General Post Office, and this was extended to Changchun on Oct. 22, 1948, and to

Mukden on Nov. 4, 1948. It was rapidly extended to cover all Manchuria.

All Stamps Issued without Gum

Mao Tse-tung
A1 A2

1946, Feb. Unwmk. Litho. Perf. 11

1L1 A1 $1 violet 9.00 9.00
1L2 A2 $2 vermilion 60 1.00
1L3 A2 $5 orange 60 1.00
a. Booklet pane of 6 150.00
1L4 A2 $10 blue 60 1.00
a. Booklet pane of 6 150.00

Price, imperf set $35.

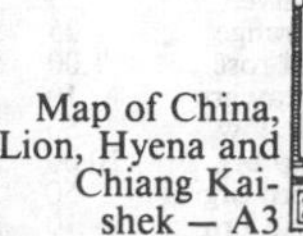

Map of China, Lion, Hyena and Chiang Kai-shek — A3

1946, Dec. 12 Perf. 10½

1L5 A3 $1 violet 1.50 1.50
1L6 A3 $2 orange 1.50 1.50
1L7 A3 $5 org brn 7.00 7.00
1L8 A3 $10 lt grn 11.00 11.00
a. Imperf. pair 30.00

10th anniversary of the capture of Chiang Kai-shek at Sian.

Railroad Workers, Chengchow — A4

1947, Feb. 7 Perf. 10½

1L9 A4 $1 pink 25 *1.00*
1L10 A4 $2 dl grn 50 *1.00*
1L11 A4 $5 pink 1.00 1.00
1L12 A4 $10 dl grn 2.50 2.50

24th anniversary of the Chengchow railroad workers' strike and massacre.

Women (Worker, Soldier and Farmer) — A5

Wmk. Chinese Characters in Sheet

1947, Mar. 8 Perf. 10½x11

1L13 A5 $5 brick red 65 65
1L14 A5 $10 brown 65 65

International Women's Day, March 8.

Same Overprinted in Green ("Northeast Postal Service")

1947, Mar. 18

1L15 A5 $5 brick red 2.50 3.25
1L16 A5 $10 brown 2.50 3.25

Children Carrying Banner — A6

1947, Apr. 4 Perf. 11x10½

Granite Paper

1L17 A6 $5 rose red 3.00 3.00
1L18 A6 $10 lt grn 3.00 4.00
1L19 A6 $30 orange 3.00 5.00

Children's Day.

Nos. 1L1-1L2 Surcharged in Red, Brown, Black, Blue or Green

伍 政
拾
圓 作
5000

1947, Apr. Unwmk. Perf. 11

1L20 A1 $50 on $1 vio (R) 19.00 19.00
a. Brown surcharge 19.00 19.00
1L21 A2 $50 on $2 ver 19.00 19.00
a. Brown surcharge 19.00 19.00
1L22 A1 $100 on $1 vio 19.00 19.00
a. Green surcharge 19.00 19.00
1L23 A2 $100 on $2 ver (Bl) 19.00 19.00
a. Green surcharge 19.00 19.00

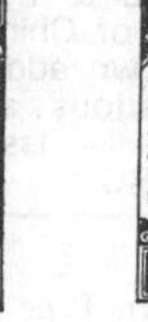

Farmer and Worker — A7 Ax Severing Chain — A8

Wmk. Chinese Characters in Sheet

1947, May 1 Perf. 10½x11

Granite Paper

1L24 A7 $10 org red 1.00 1.00
1L25 A7 $30 ultra 1.50 1.50
1L26 A7 $50 gray grn 2.50 2.50

Labor Day. Price, imperf pairs, set $200.

1947, May 4 Perf. 11

1L27 A8 $10 brt grn 2.50 2.50
1L28 A8 $30 brown 2.50 2.50
1L29 A8 $50 violet 3.00 3.00

28th anniversary of the students' revolt at Peking University against the 1918 peace treaty. Price, imperf pairs, set $200.

Workers with Banner: "Oppose Imperialist Aggression" — A9

1947, May 30 Perf. 10½x11

Banner in Red

1L30 A9 $2 brt lil 2.50 2.50
1L31 A9 $5 brt grn 2.50 2.50
1L32 A9 $10 yellow 2.50 2.50
1L33 A9 $20 violet 2.50 2.50
1L34 A9 $30 red brn 2.50 2.50
1L35 A9 $50 dk bl 2.50 2.50
1L36 A9 $100 brown 2.50 2.50
a. Souvenir sheet of 7 60.00
Nos. 1L30-1L36 (7) 17.50 17.50

22nd anniversary of the Shanghai-Nanking Road incident. No. 1L36a is on granite paper and contains 7 imperf. stamps similar to Nos. 1L30-1L36. Multicolored marginal inscription. Size: 215x158mm. Price, imperf pairs, ordinary paper, set $500.

Mao and Communist Flag — A10

1947, July 1 Perf. 10½x11

1L37 A10 $10 red 4.00 4.00
1L38 A10 $30 brt lil 4.00 4.00
1L39 A10 $50 rose brn 11.00 11.00
1L40 A10 $100 vermilion 13.00 13.00

26th anniversary of the founding of the Chinese Communist Party.

Hand Holding Rifle — A11

1947, July 7 Perf. 10½

1L41 A11 $10 orange 4.00 4.00
1L42 A11 $30 green 4.00 4.00
1L43 A11 $50 dl bl 3.75 3.75
1L44 A11 $100 brown 3.75 3.75
a. Souvenir sheet of 4 45.00 50.00

10th anniversary of the start of Sino-Japanese War. No. 1L44a contains 4 imperf. stamps similar to Nos. 1L41-1L44. Brown marginal inscription. Size: 149x107mm. Exist imperf. Price set of pairs $600.

White Mountain and Black Water, Northeast China — A12

Wmk. Zigzag Lines (141)

1947, Aug. 15 Perf. 10½

1L45 A12 $10 brn org 13.00 10.00
1L46 A12 $30 lt ol grn 1.50 10.00
1L47 A12 $50 bl grn 1.50 10.00
1L48 A12 $100 sepia 13.00 10.00

2nd anniversary of the reoccupation of Northeast China and the surrender of Japan.

Nos. 1L1-1L2 Surcharged in Black, Red, Green or Blue

拾 政
圓 作
1000

1947, Aug. 29 Unwmk. Perf. 11

1L49 A1 $5 on $1 vio 20.00 20.00
a. Red surcharge 20.00 20.00
b. Green surcharge 20.00 20.00
1L50 A2 $10 on $2 ver 20.00 20.00
a. Blue surcharge 20.00 20.00
b. Green surcharge 20.00 20.00

Map of Manchuria — A13

1947, Sept. 18 Unwmk.

White Paper

1L51 A13 $10 gray grn 8.00 8.00
1L52 A13 $20 rose lil 8.00 8.00
1L53 A13 $30 blk brn 8.00 8.00
1L54 A13 $50 carmine 8.00 8.00

16th anniversary of Japanese attack on Mukden, Sept. 18, 1931.

Northeast Political Council Offices A14 — Mao Tse-tung (Value figures repeated) A15

1947, Oct. 10 Perf. 10½

1L55 A14 $10 yel org 25.00 25.00
1L56 A14 $20 rose red 25.00 25.00
1L57 A14 $100 brown 70.00 70.00

35th anniversary of the founding of the Chinese Republic.

1947, Oct. 10 White Paper Perf. 11

1L58 A15 $1 brown 20 1.50
1L59 A15 $5 gray grn 4.00 1.50
1L60 A15 $10 brt grn 12.00 8.00
1L61 A15 $15 bluish lil 12.00 8.00
1L62 A16 $20 brt rose 10 1.50
1L63 A15 $30 green 15 2.00
1L64 A15 $50 blk brn 15.00 10.00
1L65 A15 $90 blue 4.00 4.00

Newsprint

1L66 A15 $100 red 15
1L67 A15 $500 red org 16.00 16.00

Type A22 resembles A15, but has "YUAN" at upper right.

See footnotes following No. 1L72.

1947, Nov. Redrawn

White Paper

1L68 A15 $50 lt grn 75 1.50
1L69 A15 $150 red org 1.00 1.50
a. Wmkd. Chinese characters 2.50
1L70 A15 $250 bluish lil 25 1.50
a. Wmkd. Chinese characters 1.00 1.50

1947, Dec. **Unwmk.**

Newsprint

1L71	A15	$300 green	40.00	25.00
1L72	A15	$1,000 yellow	1.00	1.00
		Nos. 1L68-1L72 (5)	43.00	30.50

Panel below portrait 8½x3mm. on Nos. 1L68-1L70; 7x3mm. on No. 1L58-1L67. Nos. 1L68-1L70 have different ornamental border. Nos. 1L71-1L72 without zeros for cents.

The $1, $90 were also printed on newsprint; the $100, $500, $1,000 also on white paper.

Hand Holding Torch — A16

1947, Dec. 12 **Unwmk.** ***Perf. 11***

White Paper

1L73	A16	$30 rose red	7.00	7.00
1L74	A16	$90 dk bl	7.00	7.00
1L75	A16	$150 green	7.00	7.00

11th anniversary of the capture of Chiang Kai-shek at Sian.

Tomb of Gen. Li Chao-lin A17

Globe and Banner A18

Perf. 10½x11

1948, Mar. 9 **Unwmk.**

1L76	A17	$30 green	10.00	10.00
a.		Granite paper, wmkd.	9.00	9.00
1L77	A17	$150 vio gray	10.00	10.00
a.		Granite paper, wmkd.	9.00	9.00

2nd anniversary of the assassination of Gen. Li Chao-lin, Commander of 3rd Army.

Wmk. Chinese Characters in Sheet

1948, May 1 ***Perf. 11x10½***

1L78	A18	$50 red	8.00	10.00
1L79	A18	$150 green	1.00	15.00
1L80	A18	$250 lilac	1.00	30.00

Labor Day.

Student, Torch and Banner — A19

1948, May 4 **Unwmk.** ***Perf. 10½x11***

Granite paper

1L81	A19	$50 green	10.00	10.00
1L82	A19	$150 brown	10.00	10.00
1L83	A19	$250 red	10.00	10.00

Youth Day, May 4.

Nos. 1L58, 1L61, 1L59, 1L63, 1L65, 1L2-1L4, 1L68-1L69, 1L71 Surcharged in Black, Blue, Red or Green

壹佰圓 10000 改作

1948-49 ***Perf. 11***

1L84	A15	$100 on $1 brn pur	60.00	45.00
a.		Blue surcharge	50.00	50.00
1L85	A15	$100 on $15 bluish lil	17.50	17.50
a.		Blue surcharge	50.00	50.00
1L86	A15	$300 on $5 gray grn (R)	55.00	25.00
1L87	A15	$300 on $30 grn (R)	8.50	10.00
1L88	A15	$300 on $90 bl (R)	8.50	10.00
1L89	A2	$500 on $2 ver	5.00	5.00
1L90	A15	$500 on $50 lt grn (R, '49)	27.50	20.00
1L91	A2	$1500 on $5 org (bl)	5.00	5.00
1L92	A15	$1500 on $150 red org (Gr, '49)	6.00	6.00
1L93	A2	$2500 on $10 bl (R)	5.00	5.00
1L94	A15	$2500 on $300 grn ('49)	5.00	5.00
		Nos. 1L84-1L94 (11)	203.00	153.50

Crane Operator — A20

Wmk. Chinese Characters in Sheet

1948, May ***Perf. 11***

1L95	A20	$100 red & pink	50	50
1L96	A20	$300 vio brn & yel	1.50	1.50
1L97	A20	$500 bl & grn	1.50	1.50

6th All-China Labor Conference, Harbin.

Farmer, Worker and Soldier Saluting A21

Mao Tse-tung ("YUAN" at upper right) A22

1948, Dec. 3 **Unwmk.** ***Perf. 11x10½***

White paper

1L98	A21	$500 vermilion	3.50	3.50
1L99	A21	$1500 brt grn	7.00	7.00
1L100	A21	$2500 brown	11.00	11.00

Liberation of Northeast China.

1949, Feb. ***Perf. 11***

1L101	A22	$300 olive	40	60
1L102	A22	$500 orange	1.00	1.00
1L103	A22	$1500 bl grn	40	60
1L104	A22	$4500 brown	40	60
1L105	A22	$6500 dk bl	40	70
		Nos. 1L101-1L105 (5)	2.60	3.50

See also type A15.

Workers, Globe and Flag A23

Fields and Factories A24

1949, May 1 ***Perf. 11½***

1L106	A23	$1000 red & dl bl	15	30
1L107	A23	$1500 red & pale bl	10	30
1L108	A23	$4500 rose & ol brn	15	40
1L109	A23	$6500 dl org & grn	60	50
1L110	A23	$10,000 mar & ultra	60	60
		Nos. 1L106-1L110 (5)	1.60	2.10

Labor Day.

1949 ***Perf. 10, 11***

1L111	A24	$5000 Prus bl	4.00	1.00
1L112	A24	$10,000 org brn	50	50
1L113	A24	$50,000 green	10	2.00
1L114	A24	$100,000 violet	15	8.00

Production in agriculture and industry.

Workers with Flags — A25

Heroes' Monument, Harbin — A26

1949, July 1 ***Perf. 11***

1L115	A25	$1500 vio, lt bl & red	5	25
1L116	A25	$4500 dk brn, lt bl & ver	1.00	30
1L117	A25	$6500 gray, lt bl & rose red	10	50

28th anniversary of the founding of the Chinese Communist Party.

1949, Aug. 15 ***Perf. 11½x11***

1L118	A26	$1500 brick red	10	50
1L119	A26	$4500 yel grn	25	50
1L120	A26	$6500 lt bl	1.25	50

4th anniversary of the Reoccupation, and the surrender of Japan.

(Enlarged)

"Northeast Postal Service"

The following commemorative issues are similar to those of the People's Republic of China, with the 4 characters shown added in different sizes and various arrangements. Reprints were also issued similar to those of the PRC.

Chinese Lantern Type of PRC, 1949

1949, Sept. 12 **Litho.** ***Perf. 12½***

1L121	A1	$1000 dp bl	4.00	5.00
1L122	A1	$1500 scarlet	4.00	5.00
1L123	A1	$3000 green	4.00	5.00
1L124	A1	$4500 maroon	4.00	5.00

First session of Chinese People's Political Conference.

Reprints exist. Price, set 60 cents.

Factory — A27

1949, Oct. ***Perf. 11x10½***

1L125	A27	$1500 orange	25	40

Nos. 1L101, 1L103-1L105, 1L125 Surcharged in Black or Green

貳仟圓 2000 改作

1949, Nov. 20

1L126	A22	$2000 on $300 ol	35.00	2.50
1L127	A22	$2000 on $4500 pur brn (G)	20.00	15.00
1L128	A22	$2500 on $1500 bl grn	75	3.00
1L129	A22	$2500 on $6500 bl	20.00	10.00
1L130	A27	$5000 on $1500 org	50	70
1L131	A22	$20,000 on $4500 pur brn	30	3.00
1L132	A22	$35,000 on $300 ol	45	4.00
		Nos. 1L126-1L132 (7)	77.00	38.20

Globe and Hammer Type of PRC

1949, Nov. 15 ***Perf. 12½***

1L133	A2	$5000 crimson	40.00	40.00
1L134	A2	$20,000 dp grn	40.00	40.00
1L135	A2	$35,000 vio bl	40.00	40.00

Asiatic and Australasian Congress of the World Federation of Trade Unions, Peking.

Reprints, price, set $25.

Mao and Conference Hall Types of PRC

1950, Feb. 1 ***Perf. 14***

1L136	A3	$1000 vermilion	11.00	11.00
1L137	A3	$1500 dp bl	11.00	11.00
1L138	A4	$5000 dk vio brn	11.00	11.00
1L139	A4	$20,000 green	11.00	11.00

First session of Chinese People's Political Conference.

Reprints exist. Price, set $1.75.

Gate of Heavenly Peace (same size) — A28

1950 ***Perf. 10½***

Narrow horizontal shading

1L140	A28	$500 olive	25	50
1L141	A28	$1000 orange	25	50
1L142	A28	$1000 lil rose	1.00	50
1L143	A28	$2000 gray grn	10	15
1L144	A28	$2500 yellow	50	15
1L145	A28	$5000 dp org	10.00	20
1L146	A28	$10,000 brn org	50	50
1L147	A28	$20,000 vio brn	10	20
1L148	A28	$35,000 dp bl	10	35
1L149	A28	$50,000 brt grn	25	70
		Nos. 1L140-1L149 (10)	13.05	3.75

Flag and Mao Type of PRC

1950, July 1 ***Perf. 14***

Yellow Stars

1L150	A7	$5000 grn & red	11.00	11.00
1L151	A7	$10,000 brn & red	11.00	11.00
1L152	A7	$20,000 dk brn & red	11.00	11.00
1L153	A7	$30,000 dk vio bl & red	12.50	12.50

Inauguration of the People's Republic, Oct 1, 1949.

Reprints exist. Price, set $2.

Picasso Dove Type of PRC

1950, Aug. 1 **Engr.** ***Perf. 14***

1L154	A8	$2500 brown	9.00	9.00
1L155	A8	$5000 green	9.00	9.00
1L156	A8	$20,000 blue	9.00	9.00

World Peace Campaign.

Reprints exist. Price, set $1.25.

Flag Type of PRC

Engraved and Lithographed

1950, Oct. 1

Flag in Red & Yellow

1L157	A9	$1000 purple	10.00	10.00
1L158	A9	$2500 org brn	10.00	10.00
1L159	A9	$5000 dp grn	10.00	10.00
1L160	A9	$10,000 olive	10.00	10.00
1L161	A9	$20,000 blue	10.00	10.00
		Nos. 1L157-1L161 (5)	50.00	50.00

First anniversary of the Chinese People's Republic. Size of No. 1L159: 38x47mm., others 26x33mm.

Reprints exist. Price, set $1.25

Postal Conference Type of PRC

1950, Nov. 1 **Litho.**

1L162	A11	$2500 grn & dp org	4.00	4.00
1L163	A11	$5000 car & grn	4.00	4.00

All-China Postal Conference, Peking.

Reprints exist. Price, set, 60 cents.

Gate of Heavenly Peace (same size) — A29

1950 ***Perf. 10½***

Wide horizontal shading

1L164 A29 $5000 orange 40 1.25
1L165 A29 $30,000 scarlet 25 *3.00*
1L166 A29 $100,000 violet 2.50 3.25

Wmk. Zigzag Lines (141)

1L167 A29 $250 brown 20 30
1L168 A29 $500 olive 20 30
1L169 A29 $1000 lil rose 25 50
1L170 A29 $2000 dl grn ('51) 10 50
1L171 A29 $2500 yellow 15 50
1L172 A29 $5000 orange 20 50
1L173 A29 $10,000 brn org ('51) 30 50
1L174 A29 $12,500 maroon 10 50
1L175 A29 $20,000 dp brn ('51) 30 1.00
Nos. 1L164-1L175 (12) 4.95 12.10

A $50,000 grn was prepared, but not issued, Price $7.50.

Stalin and Mao Tse-tung Type of PRC

Unwmk.

1950, Dec. 1 **Engr.** ***Perf. 14***

1L176 A12 $2500 red 2.00 2.00
1L177 A12 $5000 dp grn 2.00 2.00
1L178 A12 $20,000 dk bl 2.00 2.00

Signing of the Sino-Soviet Treaty of Friendship, Alliance and Mutual Assistance.
Reprints exist. Price, set $1.50.

NORTHEAST CHINA PARCEL POST STAMPS

Locomotive — PP1

1951 **Litho.** ***Imperf., perf. 10½***

1LQ1 PP1 $100,000 pur (P) 40.00
1LQ2 PP1 $300,000 brn (P, I) 150.00
1LQ3 PP1 $500,000 grnsh bl (P, I) 250.00
1LQ4 PP1 $1,000,000 ver (P, I) 400.00

PORT ARTHUR AND DAIREN

The Liaoning Postal Administration was established on April 1, 1946, in accordance with the Sino-Soviet Treaty, but was renamed one week later the Port Arthur and Dairen Postal Administration. On Apr. 3, 1947, it was combined with telecommunications and renamed the Kwantung Post and Telegraph General Administration. On May 1, 1949, the name was again changed to Port Arthur and Dairen Post and Telegraph Administration. Postal tariffs were based on local currency and both Manchukuo and Japanese stamps were overprinted for use.

政郵寧遼
五暫
圓作

Manchukuo Nos. 162 and 94 Handstamp Surcharged in Violet ("Liaoning Post")

1946, Mar. 15

With Gum

2L1 A19 20f on 30f buff 70.00 70.00
2L2 A18 1y on 12f org 40.00 40.00

Same Surcharge on Japan Nos. 260, 337, 195, 244, 263, 342 in Violet, Red or Black

1946, Apr. 1

2L3 A85 20f on 3s grn (V) 15.00 15.00
2L4 A151 1y on 17s gray vio (R) 12.00 12.00
2L5 A57 5y on 6s car 30.00 30.00
2L6 A57 5y on 6s crim 30.00 30.00
2L7 A88 5y on 6s org 20.00 20.00
2L8 A154 15y on 40s dk vio 90.00 90.00
Nos. 2L1-2L8 (8) 307.00 307.00

Surcharge sideways on Nos. 2L5-2L6.

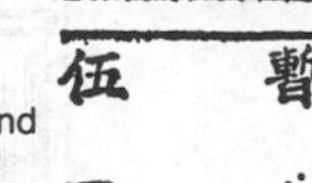

Japan Nos. 260 and 263 Surcharged

1946, Apr.

2L9 A85 1y on 3s grn *350.00*
2L10 A88 5y on 6s org *230.00*

Sha Ho Kow (suburb of Dairen) issue.

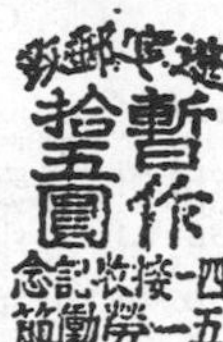

Manchukuo Nos. 84, 88 and 98 Hand-stamp Surcharged in Green, Red or Black

1946, May 1

2L11 A16 1y on 1f red brn (G) 18.00 18.00
2L12 A18 5y on 4f lt ol grn (R) 25.00 25.00
2L13 A19 15y on 30f chnt brn 50.00 50.00

Transfer of postal administration and Labor Day.

七·七
念紀戰抗
拾 暫
伍
圓 作

Manchukuo Nos. 159, 86 and 94 Surcharged in Green, Red or Black

1946, July 7

2L14 A17 1y on 6f crim rose (G) 15.00 15.00
2L15 A17 5y on 2f lt grn (R) 65.00 65.00
2L16 A18 15y on 12f dp org 90.00 90.00

9th anniversary of the outbreak of war with Japan.

復光國民華中
念紀年週一
壹 暫
圓 作
五一·八

Manchukuo Nos. 94, 84 and 158 Surcharged in Black, Green or Red

1946, Aug. 15

2L17 A18 1y on 12f dp org (B) 27.50 27.50
2L18 A16 5y on 1f red brn (G) 50.00 50.00
2L19 A10 15y on 5f gray blk (R) 100.00 100.00

Surrender of Japan, first anniversary.

國民華中
念紀節十雙
五 暫
圓 作

Manchukuo Nos. 159, 94 and 86 Surcharged in Green, Black or Red

1946, Oct. 10

2L20 A17 1y on 6f crim rose (G) 27.50 27.50
2L21 A18 5y on 12f dp org (B) 50.00 50.00
2L22 A17 15y on 2f lt grn (R) 100.00 100.00

35th anniversary of Chinese revolution.

國民華中
世逝迅魯
念紀年週十
拾 暫
五
圓 作

Manchukuo Nos. 84, 159 and 94 Surcharged in Black, Green or Blue

1946, Oct. 19

2L23 A16 1y on 1f red brn (B) 45.00 45.00
2L24 A17 5y on 6f crim rose (G) 70.00 70.00
2L25 A18 15y on 12f dp org (Bl) 110.00 110.00

10th anniversary of the death of Lu Hsun (1881-1936), writer.

建聯蘇祝慶
十二第節軍
念紀年週九
五 暫
圓 作.

Manchukuo Nos. 86, 159 and 95 Surcharged in Red, Green or Black

1947, Feb. 20

2L26 A16 1y on 2f lt grn (R) 45.00 45.00
2L27 A17 5y on 6f crim rose (G) 85.00 85.00
2L28 A10 15y on 13f dk red brn 140.00 140.00

29th anniversary of the Red (USSR) Army.

國 中
政郵東關
拾暫
念五. 紀
圓作
節勵勞一五

Manchukuo Nos. 86, 159 and 162 Surcharged in Red, Green or Black

1947, May 1

2L29 A17 1y on 2f lt grn (R) 22.50 22.50
2L30 A17 5y on 6f crim rose (G) 65.00 65.00
2L31 A19 15y on 30f buff 100.00 100.00

Labor Day.

政郵東關國中
五 暫
圓 作

Manchukuo Nos. 86, 88, 98 and 162 Surcharged ("Kwantung Postal Service, China")

1947, Sept. 15

2L32 A17 5y on 2f lt grn 30.00 25.00
2L33 A18 15y on 4f lt ol grn 50.00 40.00
2L34 A19 20y on 30f red brn 75.00 60.00
2L35 A19 20y on 30f buff 80.00 75.00

軍建聯蘇祝慶
念紀年週卅節
貳 暫
拾
圓 作
政郵東關

Manchukuo Nos. 86 and 159 Surcharged in Red and Green

Sacred Golden Kite (same size) — A1

1948, Feb. 20

2L36 A17 10y on 2f lt grn (R) 100.00 100.00
2L37 A17 20y on 6f crim rose (G) 120.00 120.00
2L38 A1 100y on bl & red brn 500.00 500.00

30th anniversary of the Red (USSR) Army. No. 2L38 is on an ungummed label commemorating the 2600th anniversary of the Japanese Empire.

政郵華中
五 暫
圓 作
電郵東關

Japan No. 260 and Manchukuo Nos. 84, 86 and 88 Surcharged in Red, Blue or Black

1948, July

2L39 A85 5y on 3s grn (R) 80.00 80.00
2L40 A16 10y on 1f red brn (Bl) 145.00 145.00
2L41 A17 50y on 2f lt grn 250.00 250.00
2L42 A18 100y on 4f lt ol grn (R) 600.00 400.00

Smaller Characters on Bottom Line

2L43 A17 10y on 2f lt grn (R) 200.00 145.00
2L44 A16 50y on 1f red brn 250.00 180.00

政 郵 東 關
年週一卅念紀
壹 暫
佰
圓 作
節命革月十

Stamps of Manchukuo Nos. 84, 86 and 88 Surcharged in Blue, Red or Black

1948, Nov. 1

2L45 A16 10y on 1f red brn (Bl) 500.00 500.00
2L46 A17 50y on 2f lt grn (R) 500.00 500.00
2L47 A18 100y on 4f lt ol grn 450.00 450.00

31st anniversary of the Russian Revolution.

年八四祝慶
換勞業農東關
念紀會大覽展
拾 暫
圓 作
電郵東關

Manchukuo Nos. 86 and 161 Surcharged in Red or Green

1948, Nov. 15

2L48 A17 10y on 2f lt grn (R) 700.00 400.00
2L49 A17 50y on 20f brn (G) 700.00 700.00

Kwantung Agricultural and Industrial Exhibition.

政郵東關
貳 暫
拾
圓 作

Manchukuo Nos. 86, 88 and 161 Surcharged in Red, Black or Green

1949, Jan.

2L50 A17 20y on 2f lt grn (R) 500.00
2L51 A18 50y on 4f lt ol grn 700.00
2L52 A17 100y on 20f brn (G) 700.00

Without Gum

From No. 2L56 onward all stamps were issued without gum except as noted.

Farmer and Worker — A2

Train and Ship — A3

Ship at Dock *(No. 2L55)* — A4

(No. 2L56)

1949 Litho. *Perf. 11, 11½*

2L53 A2 5y pale grn 1.50 2.50
2L54 A3 10y orange 10.00 7.00
2L55 A4 50y vermilion 15.00 10.00
2L56 A4 50y red (redrawn) 20.00 15.00

Issue dates: Nos. 2L56, July 7; others Apr. 1.

Worker, Flag and Means of Transport A5

1949, May 1 *Perf. 11*

2L57 A5 10y rose pink 8.00 8.00
a. 10y ver 75.00 75.00

Labor Day. No. 2L57a is from a worn plate.

Mao Tse-tung and Red Flag — A6

Heroes Monument, Dairen — A7

1949, July 1

2L59 A6 50y red 24.00 24.00

28th anniversary of the founding of the Chinese Communist Party.

1949, Sept.

2L60 A7 10y red, bl & ol 15.00 15.00
a. 10y red, bl & pale bl 100.00 100.00

4th anniversary of victory over Japan and opening of the Dairen Industrial Fair.

Nos. 2L53-2L54 Surcharged in Red or Black

暫作 柒圓
a

暫作 伍拾圓
b

c

1949, Sept. With Gum

2L62 A2(a) 7y on 5y lt grn (R) 30.00 25.00
2L63 A2(a) 7y on 5y lt grn 30.00 25.00
2L64 A2(b) 50y on 5y lt grn (R) 85.00 70.00
2L65 A3(b) 100y on 10y org 450.00 350.00
2L66 A3(c) 500y on 10y org (R) 600.00 400.00
Nos. 2L62-2L66 (5) 1,195. 870.00

Size of surcharge on No. 2L63: 16x19mm.
A 500y on 5y light green with red surcharge "c", and a 500y on 10y orange with surcharge "b" were prepared but not issued.

Stalin and Lenin — A8

1949, Nov. 7 *Perf. 11x11½*

2L68 A8 10y dl bl grn (shades) 8.00 8.00

32nd anniversary of the Russian Revolution.

Workers Saluting Mao, Star and Flag — A9

1949, Nov. 16 *Perf. 11*

2L69 A9 35y dk bl, red, & yel 9.00 *10.00*

Founding of the People's Republic of China.

Stalin — A10

(same size) Gate of Heavenly Peace — A11

1949, Dec. 20 *Perf. 11½*

2L70 A10 20y dl mag 21.00 21.00
2L71 A10 35y rose red 21.00 21.00

70th birthday of Stalin.

1950, Mar. 10 Typo. *Perf. 10½*

2L72 A11 10y Prus bl 50 *3.00*
2L73 A11 20y dl grn 14.00 10.00
2L74 A11 35y red 50 *3.00*
2L75 A11 50y dp pur 30 *4.00*
2L76 A11 100y lil rose 50 *7.00*
Nos. 2L72-2L76 (5) 15.80 27.00

NORTH CHINA

The North China Liberation Area included the provinces of Hopeh, Chahar, Shansi and Suiyuan. The original postal service, begun in the Shansi-Hopeh-Chahar Border Area in December, 1937, became the North China Postal and Telegraph Administration in May, 1949.

All Stamps Issued without Gum

Large Victory Issue

Cavalry Man Holding Nationalist Flag — A1

Wmk. Wavy Lines

1946, Mar. *Perf. 10½*

Granite Paper

Size: 34½x42mm.

3L1 A1 $1 red brn 1.00 1.00
a. Newsprint 12.00 12.00
3L2 A1 $2 gray grn 1.00 1.00
3L3 A1 $4 vermilion 1.25 1.00
3L4 A1 $5 vio brn 1.25 1.00
3L5 A1 $8 vio bl 1.25 1.00
3L6 A1 $10 dp car 1.25 1.00
3L7 A1 $12 yellow 3.00 3.00
3L8 A1 $20 lt grn 7.00 7.00
Nos. 3L1-3L8 (8) 17.00 16.00

Defeat of Japan.

Small Victory Issue

Perf. 10½x10, 9½ rough

1946, May Unwmk.

Granite paper

Size: 20x21mm.

3L9 A1 $1 red org 1.00 1.00
3L10 A1 $2 green 1.50 1.00
3L11 A1 $3 lt lil 3.00 *4.00*
3L12 A1 $5 dl pur 4.00 10
3L13 A1 $8 dk bl 6.00 *8.00*
3L14 A1 $10 rose red 1.50 *2.00*
3L15 A1 $15 purple *30.00 20.00*
3L16 A1 $20 green 3.00 3.00
3L17 A1 $30 brt grnsh bl 2.50 *3.50*
3L18 A1 $40 brt rose lil 3.00 *3.00*
3L19 A1 $50 brown *20.00* 25
3L20 A1 $60 myr grn *30.00* 75

Wmk. Wavy Lines

3L21 A1 $100 orange 1.00 *2.00*
3L22 A1 $200 dl bl 1.00 *2.00*
3L23 A1 $500 rose *10.00 25.00*
Nos. 3L9-3L23 (15) 117.50 75.60

North China Postal and Telegraph Administration

Charging Infantrymen A2

Agriculture and Industry A3

1949, Jan. Unwmk. *Imperf.*

White Paper

3L24 A2 50c brn lake 1.25 30
3L25 A2 $1 prus bl 1.25 30

Newsprint

3L26 A2 $2 ap grn 1.25 30
3L27 A2 $3 dl vio 1.25 30
3L28 A2 $5 brown 1.25 30
3L29 A3 $6 dp rose 1.25 80
a. White paper 1.25 80
3L30 A2 $10 bl grn 20 80
3L31 A2 $12 dp car 1.25 30
Nos. 3L24-3L31 (8) 8.95 3.40

No. 3L29 issued in Peking, others in Tientsin.

Remittance Stamps of China Surcharged

A4

壹 $1

叁 $3

1949, Jan. Engr. *Perf. 13*

Small Central Characters

3L32 A4 50c on $50 brn blk 4.00 1.00
3L33 A4 $1 on $50 gray blk 3.00 1.00
3L34 A4 $3 on $50 gray 3.00 1.50

Large Central Characters

3L35 A4 50c on $50 blk 2.00 1.50
3L36 A4 $6 on $20 dk vio brn 2.00 1.50

Issued in Tientsin.

Sun Yat-sen Type A2 of Northeastern Provinces and China No. 640 Surcharged in Black, Red, Green or Blue

改作 人民郵政 三元 華北
a

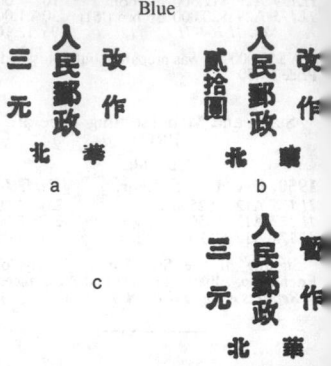

改作 人民郵政 貳拾圓 華北
b

暫作 人民郵政 三元 華北
c

Type "b," bottom character of left vertical row (yuan) differs. Type "c," top character of right vertical row differs.

1949, March 7 *Perf. 14*

3L37 A2 (a) 50c on 5c lake 25 3.00
3L38 A2 (a) $1 on 10c org 25 1.00
3L39 A2 (a) $2 on 20c yel grn 40.00 1.25
a. Surch. inverted 140.00
3L40 A2 (a) $3 on 50c red org 25 3.00
3L41 A2 (a) $4 on $5 dk grn 4.00 1.50
3L42 A2 (a) $6 on $10 crim 1.00 1.00
3L43 A2 (a) $10 on $300 bluish grn 1.25 *2.00*
3L44 A2 (a) $12 on $1 bl 1.25 *1.50*
3L45 A2 (a) $18 on $3 brn 1.25 75
3L46 A2 (b) $20 on 50c red org (Bl) 1.25 25
3L47 A2 (a) $20 on $20 ol, II 1.25 50
a. Type I 10.00 10.00
3L48 A2 (a) $30 on $2.50 ind (R) 1.25 *2.00*
3L49 A2 (a) $40 on 25c blk brn (R) 4.00 1.00
3L50 A2 (a) $50 on $109 dk grn (R) 9.00 2.00
3L51 A2 (b) $80 on $1 bl (R) 15.00 1.00
3L52 A2 (a) $100 on $65 dl grn (R) 18.00 1.50
3L53 A73 (b) $100 on $100 dk car, surch. 16mm. wide (Bl) 25.00 1.30
a. Surch. 14mm. wide 24.00 18.00

1949, Apr.

3L55 A2 (c) $2 on 20c yel grn 1.25 1.50
3L56 A2 (c) $3 on 50c red org 20 *1.00*
3L57 A2 (c) $4 on $5 dk grn 8.00 *2.00*
3L58 A2 (c) $6 on $10 crim, II 4.00 1.00
a. Type I 9.00 1.00
3L59 A2 (c) $12 on $1 bl 75 75

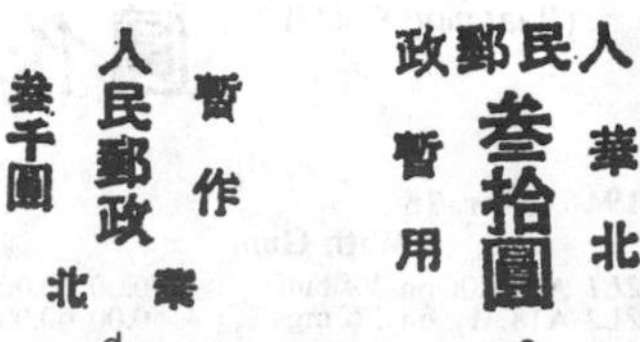

d e

1949, Apr.

3L60 A2 (d) $1 on 25c blk grn (G) 15 *2.50*
3L61 A2 (d) $10 on $300 bluish grn (R) 9.00 2.75
3L62 A2 (d) $20 on 50c red org (G) 12.00 2.00

No.	Type	Description	Unused	Used
3L63	A2 (d)	$20 on $20 ol (R)	6.00	40
3L64	A2 (d)	$40 on 25c blk brn (R)	6.00	1.25
3L65	A2 (d)	$50 on $109 dk grn, surch. 15mm. wide (R)	9.00	1.25
a.		Surch. 13mm. wide	30.00	8.00
3L66	A2 (d)	$80 on $1 bl (R)	6.00	1.25

On Stamps on China

No.	Type	Description	Unused	Used
3L67	A73 (d)	$100 on $100 dk car (G)	50.00	4.00
3L68	A73 (d)	$300 on $700 red brn (Bl)	10.00	1.15
3L69	A82 (d)	$500 on $500 bl grn (R)	7.50	1.00
3L70	A82 (d)	$3000 on $3000 bl (R)	10.00	1.25

On Stamps of Northeastern Provinces

1949, Aug.

No.	Type	Description	Unused	Used
3L71	A2 (e)	$10 on $10 crim (Bl), II	6.00	1.15
a.		Type I	12.00	12.00
3L72	A2 (e)	$30 on 20c yel grn (R)	6.00	1.00
3L73	A2 (e)	$50 on $44 dk car rose (Bl)	6.00	50
3L74	A2 (e)	$100 on $3 brn (Bl)	10.00	1.25
3L75	A2 (e)	$200 on $4 org brn (Bl), II	18.00	4.00
a.		Type I	300.00	150.00

On China No. 754

No.	Type	Description	Unused	Used
3L76	A82	$10 on $7000 lt red brn (Bl)	10.00	4.00
		Nos. 3L37-3L76 (39)	320.10	61.50

Overprints on Nos. 3L71 and 3L76 have 2 characters in center row.

Farmer and Worker on Globe — A5

1949, May 1 **Engr.** ***Perf. 14***

No.	Type	Description	Unused	Used
3L77	A5	$20 crimson	1.75	65
3L78	A5	$40 dk bl	1.75	80
3L79	A5	$60 brn org	1.75	65
3L80	A5	$80 dk grn	1.75	1.25
3L81	A5	$100 purple	1.75	1.00
		Nos. 3L77-3L81 (5)	8.75	4.35

Labor day. Exists imperf. Price, set $12.50. Also issued in blocks of 4, imperf between.

Mao Tse-tung (Chinese Numeral) — A6

Mao Tse-tung (Arabic Numeral) — A7

1949, July 1 ***Perf. 14***

No.	Type	Description	Unused	Used
3L82	A6	$10 red	25	*60*
3L83	A7	$20 dk bl	25	*60*
3L84	A6	$50 orange	2.00	60
3L85	A7	$80 dk grn	30	*1.00*
3L86	A6	$100 purple	2.00	1.00
3L87	A7	$120 olive	20	*1.00*
3L88	A6	$140 vio brn	2.00	1.00
		Nos. 3L82-3L88 (7)	7.00	5.80

28th anniversary of the founding of the Chinese Communist Party. Price, imperf set $35.

(same size) Gate of Heavenly Peace — A8

Farmers and Factory — A9

1949, Nov. 26 **Litho.** ***Perf. 12½***

No.	Type	Description	Unused	Used
3L89	A8	$50 orange	20	3.00
3L90	A8	$100 crimson	5	40
3L91	A8	$200 green	50	50
3L92	A8	$300 rose brn	9.00	1.00
3L93	A8	$400 blue	9.00	1.00
3L94	A8	$500 brown	9.00	60
3L95	A8	$700 violet	3.00	3.00
		Nos. 3L89-3L95 (7)	30.75	9.50

1949, Dec. **Engr.** ***Perf. 14***

No.	Type	Description	Unused	Used
3L96	A9	$1000 orange	2.50	50
3L97	A9	$3000 dk bl	5	40
3L98	A9	$5000 crimson	10	75
3L99	A9	$10,000 red brn	10	1.50

NORTH CHINA PARCEL POST STAMPS

Parcel Post Stamps of China Nos. Q23-Q27 Surcharged in Red, Black or Blue

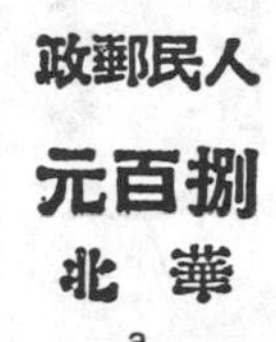

a

b

1949, June

No.	Type	Description	Unused	Used
3LQ1	PP3 (a)	$300 on $6,000,000 ol gray (R)	15.00	
3LQ2	PP3 (a)	$400 on $8,000,000 scar (Bl)	15.00	
3LQ3	PP3 (a)	$500 on $10,000,000 sage grn (R)	18.00	
3LQ4	PP3 (a)	$800 on $5,000,000 lil (R)	25.00	
3LQ5	PP3 (a)	$1000 on $3,000,000 sl bl (R)	35.00	

Surcharged Type "b"

No.	Type	Description	Unused	Used
3LQ6	PP3	$500 on $3,000,000 dk bl	25.00	
3LQ7	PP3	$1000 on $5,000,000 vio gray	40.00	
3LQ8	PP3	$3000 on $8,000,000 ver	75.00	
3LQ9	PP3	$5000 on $10,000,000 dl grn	140.00	
		Nos. 3LQ1-3LQ9 (9)	388.00	

Nos. 3LQ8-3LQ9 have large numerals unboxed.

Remittance Stamps of China (like North China Type A4) Surcharged in Black or Red

政郵民人
紙印裹包
元 六
北 華

a

北 華
圓拾貳
紙印裹包
圓拾貳
北 華

b

Peking Surcharge (a)

1949, June **Litho.** ***Perf. 13***

No.	Description	Unused	Used
3LQ10	$6 on $5 ver	5.00	
3LQ11	$20 on $50 gray	5.00	
3LQ12	$50 on $20 dk vio brn	5.00	
3LQ13	$100 on $10 ol grn	10.00	

Tientsin Surcharge (b)

Engr.

Perf. 14

No.	Description	Unused	Used
3LQ14	$20 on $1 brn org	12.00	6.00
a.	Perf. 12½	20.00	7.00
3LQ15	$30 on $2 dk grn	12.00	4.00
a.	Red surcharge	20.00	7.00
3LQ16	$30 on $10 ol grn	*90.00*	*45.00*
3LQ17	$100 on $10 gray grn (R)	12.00	6.00

Litho.

Perf. 13

No.	Description	Unused	Used
3LQ18	$50 on $5 red	12.00	6.00

Engr.

Perf. 12½

No.	Description	Unused	Used
3LQ19	$20 on $1 org brn	35.00	18.00
3LQ20	$100 on $10 yel grn (R)	60.00	30.00

Typo.

Roulette 9½

No.	Description	Unused	Used
3LQ21	$30 on $2 bl grn (R)	45.00	22.50

The surcharge on No. 3LQ19 is without first and last lines.

Locomotive — PP1

1949, Nov. **Engr.** ***Perf. 14***

No.	Type	Description	Unused	Used
3LQ22	PP1	$500 crimson	5.00	6.00
3LQ23	PP1	$1000 dp bl		10.00
3LQ24	PP1	$2000 green		15.00
3LQ25	PP1	$5000 dp ol		30.00
3LQ26	PP1	$10,000 orange		60.00
3LQ27	PP1	$20,000 red brn		150.00
3LQ28	PP1	$50,000 brn pur		300.00
		Nos. 3LQ22-3LQ28 (7)		571.00

NORTHWEST CHINA

The Northwest China Liberation Area consisted of the provinces of Sinkiang, Tsinghai, Ningsia and the western part of Shensi. The area was first established as the Shensi-Kansu-Ningsia Border Area in October, 1936, after the Long March to Yenan. Remote Sinkiang was not included until late 1949.

All Stamps Issued without Gum

Pagoda on Yenan Hill — A1

1945, Mar. **Litho.** ***Imperf.***

No.	Type	Description	Unused	Used
4L1	A1	$1 green	15.00	
a.		Rouletted 9	80.00	
4L2	A1	$5 dk bl	100.00	
a.		Rouletted 9	115.00	
4L3	A1	$10 rose red	14.00	
a.		Rouletted 9	80.00	
4L4	A1	$50 dl pur	10.00	
4L5	A1	$100 yel org	14.00	
		Nos. 4L1-4L5 (5)	153.00	

First issue; denomination in Chinese and Arabic. Heavy shading at top of vignette. Columns at sides.

Nos. 4L1-4L2 Surcharged in Red:

暫作
三十元

a

暫作
三十圓

b

暫作
三十元

c

暫作
九十元

d

1946, Nov.

No.	Type	Description	Unused	Used
4L6	A1 (a)	$30 on $1 grn	20.00	
4L7	A1 (b)	$30 on $1 grn	*125.00*	
a.		Rectangular lower left character	*675.00*	
4L8	A1 (c)	$30 on $1 grn	15.00	
4L9	A1 (b)	$60 on $1 grn		
4L10	A1 (d)	$90 on $5 dk bl	20.00	

Surcharges on Nos. 4L7a and 4L9 are type "b" as illustrated. Surcharge on No. 4L7 differs from "b," having lower left character as in type "a."

Pagoda on Yenan Hill (same size)
A2 A3

1948, June

No.	Type	Description	Unused	Used
4L11	A2	$100 buff	140.00	
4L12	A2	$300 rose pink	1.00	
4L13	A2	$500 red	3.50	
4L14	A2	$1000 blue	3.50	
4L15	A2	$2000 yel grn	24.00	
4L16	A2	$5000 dl pur	10.00	
		Nos. 4L11-4L16 (6)	182.00	

Second issue; denominations in Chinese only. Many shades and proofs exist.

1948, Dec.

No.	Type	Description	Unused	Used
4L17	A3	10c yel org	1.50	
4L18	A3	20c lemon	1.50	
4L19	A3	$1 dk bl	1.50	
4L20	A3	$2 vermilion	1.50	
4L21	A3	$5 pale bl grn	9.00	
4L22	A3	$10 violet	13.50	
		Nos. 4L17-4L22 (6)	28.50	

Third issue; ornamental border at sides. Many shades exist.

Nos. 4L2 and 4L13 Surcharged in Red or Black

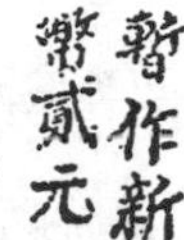

1949, Jan.

No.	Type	Description	Unused	Used
4L23	A1	$1 on $5 dk bl	45.00	
4L24	A2	$2 on $500 red	20.00	

Pagoda on Yenan Hill — A4

1949, May 1

No.	Type	Description	Unused	Used
4L25	A4	50c yel to ol	10	20
4L26	A4	$1 dl bl to ind	15	20
4L27	A4	$3 ol yel to org yel	10	20
4L28	A4	$5 bl grn	50	20
4L29	A4	$10 vio to dp vio	6.00	5.00
4L30	A4	$20 pink to rose red	1.50	2.00
		Nos. 4L25-4L30 (6)	8.35	7.80

Fourth issue; light shading at top of vignette, columns without ornaments at sides. Many shades exist.

China Nos. 959, F2 and E12 Overprinted ("People's Post, Shensi")

1949, June 13 **Engr.** ***Perf. 12½***

No.	Type	Description	Unused	Used
4L31	A96	orange	18.00	18.00
4L32	R2	carmine	25.00	25.00
4L33	SD2	red vio	25.00	25.00

Stamps of China, Sun Yat-sen Type of 1949, Overprinted in Black or Red ("People's Post, Shensi")

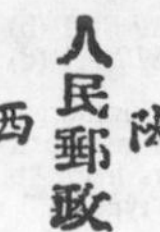

Lithographed; Engraved

1949, July 1 *Perf. 14, 12½*

4L34	A94	$10 grn (887)	1.00	1.00
4L35	A94	$20 vio brn (888)	2.00	2.00
4L36	A94	$20 vio brn (894C)	1.00	1.00
4L37	A94	$50 dk Prus grn (889; R)	5.00	5.00
4L38	A94	$50 grn (951)	5.00	5.00
4L39	A94	$100 org brn (890)	12.00	6.00
4L40	A94	$500 ros lil (892)	18.00	6.00
4L41	A94	$1000 dp bl (952; R)	25.00	8.00
4L42	A94	$2000 vio (946;R)	25.00	8.00
4L43	A94	$5000 car (953)	34.00	15.00
4L44	A94	$10,000 brn (954)	65.00	32.00
		Nos. 4L34-4L44 (11)	193.00	89.00

Kansu-Ningsia-Tsinghai Area, Lanchow Overprints

China Nos. 959a, F2 and E12 Overprinted ("People's Post, Kansu")

1949, Oct. **Engr.** ***Rouletted***

4L45	A96	orange	18.00	18.00

Perf. 12½

4L46	R2	carmine	25.00	25.00
4L47	SD2	red vio	25.00	25.00

Stamps of China, Sun Yat-sen Type of 1949, Overprinted ("People's Post, Kansu")

郵政 人民 (甘)

Engraved; Lithographed

1949, Oct. *Perf. 14, 12½*

4L48	A94	$10 grn (887)	3.25	1.50
4L49	A94	$20 vio brn (888)	3.25	3.00
4L50	A94	$50 dk Prus grn (889)	9.00	8.00
4L51	A94	$100 org brn (890)	3.25	3.00
4L52	A94	$100 dk org brn (896)	5.00	4.00
4L53	A94	$200 red org (891)	6.50	5.00
4L54	A94	$500 rose lil (892)	6.50	5.00
4L55	A94	$1000 bl (894)	3.25	3.00
4L56	A94	$1000 dp bl (898)	6.50	5.00
4L57	A94	$2000 vio (946)	11.00	9.00
4L58	A94	$5000 lt bl (899)	22.00	18.00
4L59	A94	$10,000 sep (900)	30.00	25.00
4L60	A94	$20,000 ap grn (947)	60.00	50.00
		Nos. 4L48-4L60 (13)	169.50	139.50

China Nos. 959, F2 and 791-792 Surcharged in Black or Red ("People's Post, Sinkiang")

政郵民人 (新) 圓壹

1949, Oct.

4L61	A96	$1 on org	25.00	25.00
4L62	R2	$3 on car	25.00	25.00
4L63	A82	10c on $50,000 dp bl (R)	25.00	25.00
4L64	A82	$1.50 on $100,000 dl grn (R)	25.00	30.00

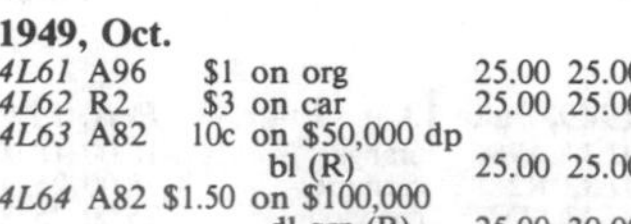

Northwest People's Post

Mao Tse-tung A5

Great Wall A6

1949, Oct. 15 **Litho.** ***Imperf.***

4L65	A5	$50 rose	2.50	2.00
a.		$200 cliche in $50 plate	120.00	
4L66	A6	$100 dk bl	15	15
4L67	A5	$200 orange	15	75
4L68	A6	$400 sepia	2.50	1.25

EAST CHINA

The East China Liberation Area included the provinces of Shantung, Kiangsu, Chekiang, Anhwei and Fukien. The original postal service established in Shantung in 1941, became the East China Posts and Telegraph General Office in July, 1948.

All Stamps Issued without Gum

Mao Tse-tung — A1

Transportation and Tower — A2

1948, Mar. **Litho.** ***Perf. 10½***

5L1	A1	$50 yel org	1.50	1.00
5L2	A1	$100 dp rose	5.00	3.50
5L3	A1	$200 dk vio bl	5.00	3.50
5L4	A1	$300 brt grn	5.00	3.50
5L5	A1	$500 dp bl	2.00	1.50
5L6	A1	$800 vermilion	5.00	4.00
5L7	A1	$1000 dk bl	10.00	8.00
5L8	A1	$5000 rose	20.00	15.00
5L9	A1	$10,000 dp car	35.00	25.00
		Nos. 5L1-5L9 (9)	88.50	65.00

Many varieties, including unissued imperforates exist.

Perf. 9 to 11 and comp.

1949, Apr. **Litho.**

5L10	A2	$1 yel grn	10	10
5L11	A2	$2 bl grn	10	10
5L12	A2	$3 dl red	10	10
5L13	A2	$5 pale brn (ovpt. 4x4 mm)	10	10
a.		Without overprint	60.00	60.00
b.		Overprint 3x3 mm	1.00	1.00
5L14	A2	$10 ultra	15	15
5L15	A2	$13 brt vio	15	15
5L16	A2	$18 brt bl	15	15
5L17	A2	$21 vermilion	20	20
5L18	A2	$30 gray	20	20
5L19	A2	$50 crimson	25	35
5L20	A2	$100 olive	12.00	9.00
		Nos. 5L10-5L20 (11)	13.50	10.60

Seventh anniv. of Shantung Communist Postal Administration. The overprint on the $5, character "yu" meaning "Posts," obliterates Japanese flag on tower, erroneously included in design. Price, imperfs of Nos. 5L10-5L12, 5L13a, 5L14-5L20 on different paper, set $75.

Train and Postal Runner (1949.2.7) A3

Mao, Soldiers, Map A4

1949, Apr. **Litho.** ***Perf. 8 to 11***

5L21	A3	$1 brt emer	10	10
5L22	A3	$2 bl grn	10	10
5L23	A3	$3 dk red	5	10
5L24	A3	$5 brown	5	10
5L25	A3	$10 ultra	40	10
5L26	A3	$13 brt vio	5	10
5L27	A3	$18 brt bl	5	10
5L28	A3	$21 vermilion	5	10
5L29	A3	$30 slate	15	25
5L30	A3	$50 crimson	25	25
5L31	A3	$100 olive	50	50
		Nos. 5L21-5L31 (11)	1.75	1.80

Seventh anniversary of Shantung Post Office, Feb. 7. Imperf. sets were sold by the Philatelic Dept., Tientsin P.O. Price $25. See Nos. 5L69-5L76.

1949, Apr. ***Perf. 9½ to 11 comp.***

5L32	A4	$1 brt emer	5	5
5L33	A4	$2 bl grn	5	5
5L34	A4	$3 dl red	5	5
5L35	A4	$5 brown	5	5
5L36	A4	$10 ultra	5	5
5L37	A4	$13 brt vio	5	5
5L38	A4	$18 brt bl	10	10
5L39	A4	$21 vermilion	10	10
5L40	A4	$30 gray	10	10
5L41	A4	$50 crimson	10	10
5L42	A4	$100 olive	1.50	1.50
		Nos. 5L32-5L42 (11)	2.20	2.20

Victory of Hwai-Hai (Hwaiying and Haichow). Imperf. sets were sold by the Philatelic Dept., Tientsin P.O. Price, set $60.

Stamps of China, Sun Yat-sen Type of 1949, Surcharged in Red or Black

政郵東華 京 圓壹作暫

(Nanking) a

人民券 伍拾圓 東華

(Wuhu) b

1949, May 4 **Engr.** ***Perf. 12½***

5L43	A94 (a)	$1 on $10 grn (894A, R)	50	50
a.		Perf. 13	3.00	3.00
5L44	A94 (a)	$3 on $20 vio brn (894C)	50	50
a.		Perf. 13	75	2.00
b.		Perf. 14	6.00	6.00
c.		Surch. inverted	200.00	

Lithographed, Engraved

1949, May ***Perf. 12½, 14***

5L45	A94 (b)	$30 on $1000 dp bl (898)	7.50	5.00
5L46	A94 (b)	$30 on $1000 bl (894)	7.50	5.00
5L47	A94 (b)	$50 on $200 org red (897)	7.50	5.00
5L48	A94 (b)	$100 on $5000 lt bl (899, R)	16.00	13.00
5L49	A94 (b)	$300 on $10,000 sep (900, R)	50.00	40.00
5L50	A94 (b)	$500 on $200 org red (897)	75.00	60.00
		Nos. 5L45-5L50 (6)	163.50	128.00

Many varieties exist.

China Nos. 915a and 915 Surcharged in Blue, Green, Black or Red

(East China)

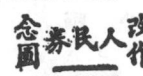

1949, May **Litho.** ***Perf. 12½***

5L51	A95	$5 on 50c on $20 brn, II (B)	14.00	16.00
a.		grn surcharge	65.00	35.00
5L52	A95	$10 on 50c on $20 brn, II	14.00	16.00
5L53	A95	$20 on 50c on $20 red brn, II (R)	14.00	16.00
a.		Type I (R)	18.00	18.00

Stamps of China, Sun Yat-sen Type of 1949, Surcharged in Black or Red

政郵東華 杭 圓叁拾作暫

(Hangchow)

Engraved, No. 5L57 Lithographed

1949, June 25 ***Perf. 14, 12½***

5L54	A94	$1 on $1 org (886)	1.50	1.50
5L55	A94	$3 on $20 vio brn (894C, R)	85	85
5L56	A94	$5 on $100 org brn (890)	4.00	2.00
5L57	A94	$5 on $100 dk org brn (896)	2.00	60
5L58	A94	$10 on $50 dk Prus grn (889, R)	14.00	12.00
5L59	A94	$13 on $10 grn (894A)	30	70
		Nos. 5L54-5L59 (6)	22.65	17.65

East China Liberation Area

Maps of Shanghai and Nanking — A5

1949, May 30 **Litho.** ***Perf. 8½ to 11***

5L60	A5	$1 org ver	10	20
5L61	A5	$2 bl grn	10	20
5L62	A5	$3 brt vio	5	10
5L63	A5	$5 vio brn	6	10
5L64	A5	$10 ultra	10	10
5L65	A5	$30 slate	6	20
5L66	A5	$50 carmine	15	40
5L67	A5	$100 olive	15	20
5L68	A5	$500 orange	1.50	1.50
		Nos. 5L60-5L68 (9)	2.27	3.00

Liberation of Shanghai and Nanking. Many shades, paper and perforation varieties and imperfs. exist.

Train and Postal Runner Type Dated "1949"

1949, July-1950, Feb. ***Perf. 12½, 14***

5L69	A3	$10 dp ultra	5	10
5L70	A3	$15 org ver	5	40
a.		$15 red, perf. 14	40	10
5L71	A3	$30 sl grn	5	10
a.		Perf. 12½	5	10
5L72	A3	$50 carmine	10	40
5L73	A3	$60 bl grn, perf. 14	5	1.00
5L74	A3	$100 ol, perf. 14	3.00	40
5L75	A3	$1600 vio bl ('50)	75	3.00
5L76	A3	$2000 brn vio ('50)	1.00	3.00
		Nos. 5L69-5L76 (8)	5.05	8.40

Chu Teh, Mao, Troops with Flags A7

Mao Tse-tung A8

1949, Aug. 17 ***Perf. 12½***

5L77	A7	$70 orange	5	10
5L78	A7	$270 crimson	5	10
5L79	A7	$370 emerald	40	30
5L80	A7	$470 vio brn	65	40
5L81	A7	$570 blue	10	30
		Nos. 5L77-5L81 (5)	1.25	1.20

22nd anniversary of the People's Liberation Army.

1949, Oct.

5L82	A8	$10 dk bl	2.00	5.00
5L83	A8	$15 vermilion	2.50	2.50
5L84	A8	$70 brown	5	5
5L85	A8	$100 vio brn	10	5
5L86	A8	$150 orange	5	5
5L87	A8	$200 grnsh gray	10	5
5L88	A8	$500 gray bl	10	5
5L89	A8	$1000 rose	5	5
5L90	A8	$2000 emerald	5	10
		Nos. 5L82-5L90 (9)	5.00	7.90

Foreign postal stationery (stamped envelopes, postal cards and air letter sheets) lies beyond the scope of this Catalogue, which is limited to adhesive postage stamps.

中華人民郵政
華東區
肆佰圓
★★★★★

Stamps of China, Sun Yat-sen Type of 1949 Surcharged in Black or Red

1949, Nov. **Litho.** *Perf. 12½*

5L91 A94 $400 on $200 org red (897) 24.00 80
5L92 A94 $1000 on $50 grnsh gray (895, R) 2.00 80
5L93 A94 $1200 on $100 dk org brn (896) 5 *2.00*
5L94 A94 $1600 on $20,000 ap grn (947) 5 *80*
5L95 A94 $2000 on $1000 dp bl (952,R) 5 *80*
a. Perf. 14 90.00 25.00
Nos. 5L91-5L95 (5) 26.15 5.20

EAST CHINA PARCEL POST STAMPS

Parcel Post Stamps of China 1945-48 Surcharged

(Shantung)

20000
山東郵政
貳百圓

1949, Aug. 1 **Engr.** *Perf. 13*

5LQ1 PP1 $200 on $500 grn 8.00 8.00
5LQ2 PP1 $500 on $1000 Bl 8.00 8.00

Perf. 13½

5LQ3 PP3 $200 on $200,000 dk grn 40.00 30.00
5LQ4 PP3 $200 on $10,000,000 sage grn 8.00 8.00
5LQ5 PP3 $500 on $7000 dl bl 90.00 60.00
5LQ6 PP3 $500 on $50,000 ind 8.00 8.00
5LQ7 PP3 $1000 on $10,000 car rose 8.00 8.00
5LQ8 PP3 $1000 on $100,000 dk rose brn 8.00 8.00
5LQ9 PP3 $1000 on $300,000 pink 6.00 6.00
5LQ10 PP3 $1000 on $500,000 vio brn 50.00 45.00
5LQ11 PP3 $1000 on $8,000,000 org ver 8.00 8.00
5LQ12 PP3 $2000 on $5,000,000 dl vio 12.00 12.00
5LQ13 PP3 $2000 on $6,000,000 brn blk 12.00 12.00
5LQ14 PP3 $3000 on $30,000 ol 20.00 17.50
5LQ15 PP3 $3000 on $70,000 org brn 20.00 17.50
5LQ16 PP3 $5000 on $3,000,000 dl bl 25.00 22.50
Nos. 5LQ1-5LQ16 (16) 331.00 278.50

China No. 987 Surcharged

華東郵政
$200 $500
$1000 $2000
$5000 $10,000

1949, Sept. 7 **Litho.** *Perf. 12½*

5LQ17 A97 $200 on $10 bl grn 30.00 15.00
5LQ18 A97 $500 on $10 bl grn 30.00 15.00
5LQ19 A97 $1000 on $10 bl grn 30.00 15.00
5LQ20 A97 $2000 on $10 bl grn 30.00 15.00
5LQ21 A97 $5000 on $10 bl grn 30.00 15.00
5LQ22 A97 $10,000 on $10 bl grn 30.00 15.00
Nos. 5LQ17-5LQ22 (6) 180.00 90.00

Flying Geese Type of China, 1949, and China Nos. 984-986 Surcharged in Red or Black

1950, Jan. 28

5LQ23 A97 $5000 on 10c bl vio (R) 90.00 50.00
5LQ24 A97 $10,000 on $1 brn org 90.00 50.00
5LQ25 A97 $20,000 on $2 bl 90.00 50.00
5LQ26 A97 $50,000 on $5 car rose 90.00 50.00

Parcel Post Stamps of China Nos. Q1-Q4 Surcharged in Red or Black

華東郵政

1950, Jan. 28 **Engr.** *Perf. 13*

5LQ27 PP1 $5000 on $500 grn (R) 20 *40.00*
5LQ28 PP1 $10,000 on $1000 bl (R) 120.00 40.00
5LQ29 PP1 $20,000 on $3000 bl grn 120.00 80.00
5LQ30 PP1 $50,000 on $5000 org red 20.00 40.00

CENTRAL CHINA

The Central Chinese Liberation Area included the provinces of Honan, Hupeh, Hunan and Kiangsi. The area was established between August and September, 1949, following the liberation of Hankow.

All Stamps Issued without Gum

Hupeh Postal and Telegraph Administration

Stamps of China, Sun Yat-sen Type of 1949, Surcharged ("Chinese P.O., Temporary Use")

華中郵政
暫用
100 壹圓

Engraved; Lithographed

1949, June 4 *Perf. 14, 12½*

Thin parallel lines.

6L1 A94 $1 on $200 red org (891) 75 75
6L2 A94 $6 on 10,000 sep (900) 75 75
6L3 A94 $15 on $1 org (886) 75 75
6L4 A94 $30 on $100 org brn (890) 3.50 3.50
6L5 A94 $30 on $100 dk org brn (896) 75 75
6L6 A94 $50 on $20 vio brn (894C) 12.00 12.00
6L7 A94 $80 on $1000 dp bl (898) 2.25 2.25

Thick parallel lines.

6L8 A94 $1 on $200 red org (891) 3.50 3.50
6L9 A94 $3 on $5000 lt bl (899) 50 50
6L10 A94 $10 on $500 rose lil (892) 50 50
6L11 A94 $10 on $500 rose lil (945) 3.50 3.50
6L12 A94 $50 on $20 vio brn (888) 3.50 3.50
6L13 A94 $50 on $20 vio brn (894C) 1.00 1.00
6L14 A94 $80 on $1000 bl (894) 3.50 3.50
6L15 A94 $80 on $1000 dp bl (898) 12.00 12.00
6L16 A94 $100 on $50 dk Prus grn (899) 1.50 1.50
Nos. 6L1-6L16 (16) 50.25 50.25

Kiangsi Postal and Telegraph Administration.

Central Trust Revenue Stamps of China Surcharged ("People's Post, Kiangsi")

(same size) — A1

改作 人民郵政 叁拾圓 江西
$30

改作 人民郵政 陸拾圓 江西
$60

1949, June 20 **Engr.** *Perf. 12½*

6L17 A1 $3 on $30 pur 1.00 1.00
6L18 A1 $15 on $15 red org 1.00 1.00
6L19 A1 $30 on $50 dk bl 1.00 1.00
6L20 A1 $60 on $50 dk bl 1.00 1.00
6L21 A1 $130 on $15 red org 1.00 1.00

The $15 surcharge has 3 characters in left vertical row, the $130 surcharge has 5.

Same Surcharge on Sun Yat-sen Issues of China, 1945-49

Engraved, Lithographed

Perf. 14, 12½

6L22 A82 $1 on $250 dp lil (746) 3.00 3.00
6L23 A94 $5 on $1000 dp bl (898) 3.00 3.00
6L24 A94 $5 on $2000 vio (946) 3.00 3.00
6L25 A94 $5 on $5000 lt bl (899) 1.00 1.00
6L26 A94 $10 on $1000 bl (894) 3.00 3.00
6L27 A82 $20 on $4000 gray 1.00 1.00
6L28 A73 $30 on $100 dk car 3.00 3.00
6L29 A82 $30 on $20,000 rose pink 1.00 1.00
6L30 A94 $80 on $500 rose lil (945) 1.00 1.00
6L31 A94 $100 on $1000 dp bl (898) 1.00 1.00
6L32 A82 $200 on $250 dp lil 2.00 2.00
Nos. 6L17-6L32 (16) 27.00 27.00

Central China Posts and Telegraph Administration

Farmer, Soldier and Worker

A2 A3

I. Top white line of square character (yuan) at upper left does not touch left vertical stroke. No gap in shading between soldier's feet.

II. Top line connects with left vertical stroke. Gap in shading between feet.

Perf. 10 to 11½ & Comp.

1949 **Litho.**

6L33 A2 $1 orange 9.00 9.00
6L34 A2 $3 brn org 3.00 3.00
6L35 A2 $6 emerald 3.00 3.00
6L36 A3 $7 yel brn 50 50
6L37 A2 $10 bl grn 15 30
6L38 A3 $14 org brn 18.00 9.00
6L39 A2 $15 ultra 40 15
6L40 A2 $30 grn, I 10 15
a. Type II 10 15
6L41 A3 $35 gray bl 12.00 9.00
6L42 A2 $50 rose vio 10.00 6.00
6L43 A3 $70 dp grn 15 15
6L44 A2 $80 pink 50 50
6L45 A3 $100 bl grn 30 30
6L46 A3 $220 rose red 4.00 4.00
Nos. 6L33-6L46 (14) 61.10 45.05

Star Enclosing Map of Hankow Area — A4

Two types of $500:
I. Thick numerals of "500". No period after "500".
II. Thin numerals and period.

Two types of $1000:
I. No. period after "1000".
II. Period after "1000".

1949, July

6L48 A4 $110 org brn 25 25
6L49 A4 $130 violet 5.00 25
6L50 A4 $200 dp org 10 25
6L51 A4 $290 brown 2.00 75
6L52 A4 $370 dk bl 2.00 50
6L53 A4 $500 lt bl, I 5.00 1.00
a. $500 bl, II 25.00 6.00
6L54 A4 $1000 dk red, I 35.00 2.50
a. $1000 dl red, II 25.00 4.50
6L55 A4 $5000 brown 1.00 2.00
6L56 A4 $10,000 brt pink 2.00 3.00
Nos. 6L48-6L56 (9) 52.35 10.50

Hankow River Customs Building A5

River Wall, Wuchang — A6

Design: $290, $370, River scene, Hanyang.

1949, Aug. 16 *Perf. 11, Imperf.*

6L57 A5 $70 green 60 80
6L58 A5 $220 crimson 60 80
6L59 A5 $290 brown 60 80
6L60 A5 $370 brt bl 60 80
6L61 A6 $500 purple 60 *1.00*
6L62 A6 $1000 vermilion 60 *1.50*
Nos. 6L57-6L62 (6) 3.60 5.70

Liberation of Hankow, Wuchang and Hanyang.

Nos. 6L35, 6L39 and 6L40 Surcharged in Red ("Honan People's Post")

人民幣 柒拾圓 河南省

1949, July

6L63 A2 $7 on $6 emer 8.50 8.50
6L64 A2 $14 on $15 ultra 10.00 10.00
6L65 A2 $70 on $30 grn 15.00 15.00

Surcharge shown is for $70. The $7 has 5 characters in left column and no bottom line.

Issues of 1949 Overprinted ("Honan People's Post")

河南省 人民幣

1949, Aug.

6L66 A2 $3 brn org 1.00 1.00
6L67 A3 $7 yel brn 1.00 1.00
6L68 A2 $10 bl grn 2.00 2.00
6L69 A3 $14 org brn 2.00 2.00
6L70 A2 $30 yel grn (6L40a) 2.00 2.00
6L71 A3 $35 gray bl 1.00 1.00
6L72 A2 $50 rose vio 7.50 7.50
6L73 A3 $70 dp grn 2.00 2.00

6L74	A4	$110 org brn	14.00	14.00
6L75	A3	$220 rose red	4.00	4.00
6L76	A4	$290 brown	14.00	14.00
6L77	A4	$370 blue	16.00	16.00
6L78	A4	$500 bl, II	24.00	24.00
6L79	A4	$1000 dk red, I	32.00	32.00
6L80	A4	$5000 brown	90.00	90.00
6L81	A4	$10,000 brt pink	200.00	200.00
		Nos. 6L66-6L81 (16)	412.50	412.50

Width of the overprint varies slightly.

Nos. 6L57-6L62 Overprinted ("Honan People's Post") 河南省 人民郵

1949, Aug. *Perf. 11, Imperf.*

6L82	A5	$70 green	4.50	4.50
6L83	A5	$220 crimson	4.50	4.50
6L84	A5	$290 brown	4.50	4.50
6L85	A5	$370 brt bl	4.50	4.50
6L86	A6	$500 purple	4.50	4.50
6L87	A6	$1000 vermilion	4.50	4.50
		Nos. 6L82-6L87 (6)	27.00	27.00

Width of overprint on Nos. 6L82-6L85, 7mm.; on Nos. 6L86-6L87, 12mm.

Changchow Issue Surcharged in Red ("Honan Post")

(same size) Mao Tse-tung — A7

1949, Sept. *Perf. 10*

6L88	A7	$290 on $30 yel grn	50.00	30.00
6L89	A7	$370 on $30 yel grn	70.00	40.00

Issues of 1949 Surcharged 改作 貳佰圓 200⁰⁰

1950, Jan.

6L90	A2	$200 on $1 org	50	2.00
6L91	A2	$200 on $3 brn org	3.00	2.00
6L92	A2	$200 on $6 emer	50	2.00
6L93	A3	$200 on $7 yel brn	3.00	2.00
6L94	A3	$200 on $14 org brn	3.00	2.00
6L95	A3	$200 on $35 gray bl	3.00	2.00
6L96	A3	$200 on $70 dp grn	3.00	2.00
6L97	A2	$200 on $80 pink	3.00	2.00
6L98	A3	$200 on $220 rose red	3.00	2.00
6L99	A4	$200 on $370 bl	50	2.00
6L100	A3	$300 on $70 dp grn	50	2.00
6L101	A2	$300 on $80 pink	50	2.00
6L102	A3	$300 on $220 rose red	10	2.00
6L103	A2	$1200 on $3 brn org	30.00	15.00
6L104	A3	$1200 on $7 yel brn	6.00	3.00
6L105	A3	$1500 on $14 org brn	9.00	2.00
6L106	A2	$2100 on $1 org	40.00	15.00
6L107	A2	$2100 on $6 emer	40.00	15.00
6L108	A3	$2100 on $35 gray bl	13.00	2.50
6L109	A4	$5000 on $370 bl	5.00	3.00
		Nos. 6L90-6L109 (20)	166.60	81.50

Two types of surcharge exist, differing in spacing of characters in top row.

CENTRAL CHINA PARCEL POST STAMPS

Star and Map of Hankow — PP1

1949, Nov. **Litho.** *Perf. 11, 11½*

6LQ1	PP1	$5000 brown	1.00	2.00
6LQ2	PP1	$10,000 scarlet	7.00	4.00
6LQ3	PP1	$20,000 dk sl grn	2.50	6.00
6LQ4	PP1	$50,000 vermilion	1.00	20.00

SOUTH CHINA

The South China Liberation Area included the provinces of Kwantung and Kwangsi and Hainan Island. The South China Postal and Telegraph Administration was organized on or about Nov. 4, 1949.

All Stamps Issued without Gum

Pearl River Bridge, Canton — A1

1949, Nov. 4 **Litho.** *Imperf.*

7L1	A1	$10 green	5	5
7L2	A1	$20 sepia	15	5
7L3	A1	$30 violet	5	5
7L4	A1	$50 carmine	5	5
7L5	A1	$100 ultra	25	15
		Nos. 7L1-7L5 (5)	55	35

China Nos. 993-995 With Additional Overprint in Red ("Liberation of Swatow") 解放 暫用

1949, Nov. 9

7L6	A94	2½c on $500 rose lil (993)	12.50	12.50
a.		Handstamped	30.00	30.00
7L7	A94	2½c on $500 rose lil (994)	20.00	20.00
a.		Handstamped	30.00	30.00
7L8	A94	15c on $10 grn (995)	15.00	15.00
a.		Handstamped	40.00	40.00

On Unit Issues of China, 1949

7L9	A96	org (959)	15.00	12.00
7L10	AP5	bl grn (C62)	15.00	12.00
7L11	SD2	red vio (E12)	15.00	12.00
7L12	R2	car (F2)	15.00	12.00

On Sun Yat-sen and Flying Geese Issues of China

7L13	A94	2c org (974)	30.00	30.00
7L14	A94	4c bl grn (975)	350.00	250.00
7L15	A94	10c dp lil (976)	18.00	14.00
7L16	A94	20c bl (978)	18.00	14.00
7L17	A97	$1 brn org (984)	18.00	14.00
7L18	A97	$10 bl grn (987)	230.00	190.00
		Nos. 7L6-7L18 (13)	771.50	607.50

300

Nos. 7L1-7L3 Surcharged in Red or Green

1950, Jan.

7L19	A1	$300 on $30 vio (R)	3.50	1.00
7L20	A1	$500 on $20 brn (R)	3.50	1.00
7L21	A1	$800 on $30 vio (G)	3.50	1.25
7L22	A1	$1000 on $10 gray grn (R)	3.50	1.00
7L23	A1	$1000 on $20 brn (R)	3.50	1.00
		Nos. 7L19-7L23 (5)	17.50	5.25

SOUTHWEST CHINA

The Southwest China Liberation Area included the provinces of Kweichow, Szechwan, Yunnan, Sikang and Tibet. The Southwest Postal and Telegraph Administration was organized on or about Nov. 15, 1949 after the liberation of Kweiyang, capital of Kweichow Province.

All Stamps Issued without Gum

Chu Teh, Mao and Troops — A1

1949, Dec. **Litho.** *Perf. 12½*

8L1	A1	$10 dp bl	2.00	1.50
8L2	A1	$20 rose cl	15	1.00
8L3	A1	$30 dp org	10	50
8L4	A1	$50 gray grn	35	50
8L5	A1	$100 carmine	10	50
8L6	A1	$200 blue	50	60
8L7	A1	$300 bl vio	1.00	1.50
8L8	A1	$500 dk gray	2.50	2.50
8L9	A1	$1000 pale pur	5.00	5.00
8L10	A1	$2000 green	15.00	15.00
8L11	A1	$5000 orange	40.00	40.00
		Nos. 8L1-8L11 (11)	66.70	68.60

China Nos. 974-975, 984, 986-987 Surcharged ("Kweichow People's Post") 改作 人民郵政 貳拾圓 黔 20⁰⁰ 區

1949, Dec. 1 *Perf. 12½*

8L12	A94	$20 on 2c org	5.00	5.00
8L13	A94	$50 on 4c bl grn	5.00	5.00
8L14	A97	$100 on $1 brn org	8.00	8.00
8L15	A97	$400 on $5 car rose	25.00	25.00
8L16	A97	$2000 on $10 bl grn	60.00	60.00
		Nos. 8L12-8L16 (5)	103.00	103.00

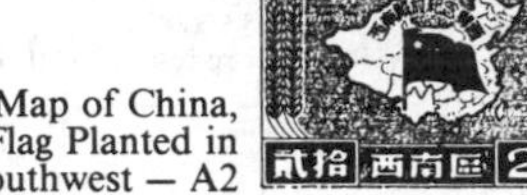

Map of China, Flag Planted in Southwest — A2

1950, Jan. **Litho.** *Perf. 9 to 11½*

8L17	A2	$20 dk bl	10	40
8L18	A2	$30 green	50	40
8L19	A2	$50 red	20	60
8L20	A2	$100 brown	20	60

Liberation of the Southwest.

Nos. 8L5-8L6 Surcharged 圓仟貳作改

Perf. 12½

8L21	A1	$300 on $100 car	15.00	5.00
8L22	A1	$500 on $100 car	15	1.50
8L23	A1	$1200 on $100 car	1.00	3.00
8L24	A1	$1500 on $200 bl	1.00	3.00
8L25	A1	$2000 on $200 bl	25.00	15.00
		Nos. 8L21-8L25 (5)	42.15	27.50

Nos. 8L5-8L6 Overprinted ("East Szechwan") (川東)

1950, Jan.

8L26	A1	$100 carmine	5.00	5.00
8L27	A1	$200 blue	5.00	5.00

Nos. 8L5-8L6 Handstamp Surcharged

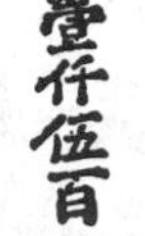

改作

1950, Jan.

8L28	A1	$1200 on $100 car	30.00	20.00
8L29	A1	$1500 on $200 bl	45.00	20.00

Many varieties, including wide and narrow settings, exist.

Nos. 8L17-8L20 Surcharged in Black or Red

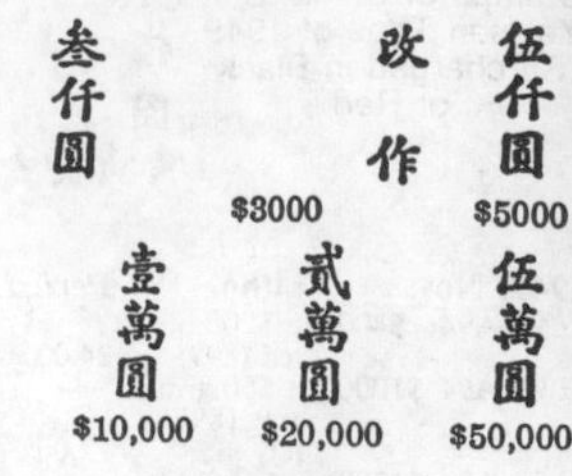

1950 *Perf. 9 to 11½*

8L30	A2	$60 on $30 grn	20.00	6.00
8L31	A2	$150 on $30 grn	20.00	6.00
8L32	A2	$300 on $20 dk bl (R)	2.00	2.50
8L33	A2	$300 on $100 brn	20.00	6.00
8L34	A2	$1500 on $100 brn	24.00	15.00
8L35	A2	$3000 on $50 red	6.00	10.00
8L36	A2	$5000 on $50 red	5.00	12.00
8L37	A2	$10,000 on $50 red	50.00	25.00
8L38	A2	$20,000 on $50 red	3.00	20.00
8L39	A2	$50,000 on $50 red	5.00	30.00
		Nos. 8L30-8L39 (10)	155.00	132.50

Nos. 8L5-8L7 Overprinted ("West Szechwan") 川 西

1950, Jan. *Perf. 12½*

8L40	A1	$100 carmine	20.00	20.00
8L41	A1	$200 pale bl	20.00	20.00
8L42	A1	$300 bl vio	20.00	20.00

Nos. 8L4-8L7 Surcharged 蓉 圓仟貳作改 $2000

1950, Jan.

8L43	A1	$500 on $100 car	8.00	6.00
a.		Narrow spacing	70.00	60.00
8L44	A1	$800 on $100 car	8.00	6.00
8L45	A1	$1000 on $50 gray grn	10.00	8.00
8L46	A1	$2000 on $200 pale bl	17.50	15.00
8L47	A1	$3000 on $300 gray vio	32.50	27.50
		Nos. 8L43-8L47 (5)	76.00	62.50

Two lines of surcharge 7mm. apart on No. 8L43, 4mm. on No. 8L43a.

China Nos. 975 and 977 Surcharged

Perf. 12½, 13 or Compound

1950, Jan.

8L48	A94	$100 on 4c bl grn	12.00	12.00
8L49	A94	$200 on 4c bl grn	25.00	25.00
8L50	A94	$800 on 16c org red	80.00	80.00
8L51	A94	$1000 on 16c org red	225.00	225.00

Unit Issue of China Overprinted ("Southwest People's Post")

西南

1950, Jan. **Engr.** *Perf. 12½*

8L52	A96	orange	125.00	100.00
a.		Rouletted	125.00	120.00
8L53	SD2	red vio	125.00	120.00
8L54	R2	carmine	125.00	120.00

On No. 8L54, space between overprint columns is 3mm. and right column is raised to height of left.

Nos. 8L3, 8L17-8L20 Surcharged in Black or Red

改作 ══ 捌百元 ══

1950, Mar. *Perf. 12½, 9 to 11½*

No.	Type	Description	Unused	Used
8L55	A1	$800 on $30 dp org	42.00	35.00
8L56	A2	$1000 on $50 red	9.00	7.50
8L57	A2	$2000 on $100 brn	12.00	9.00
8L58	A2	$4000 on $20 dk bl (R)	35.00	25.00
8L59	A2	$5000 on $30 gray grn	55.00	45.00
		Nos. 8L55-8L59 (5)	153.00	121.50

CILICIA

LOCATION — A territory of Turkey, in Southeastern Asia Minor.
GOVT. — Former French occupation
AREA — 6,238 sq. mi.
POP. — 383,645.
CAPITAL — Seyhan

British and French forces occupied Cilicia in 1918 and in 1919 its control was transferred to the French. Eventually part of Cilicia was assigned to the French Mandated Territory of Syria but by the Lausanne Treaty of 1923 which fixed the boundary between Syria and Turkey, Cilicia reverted to Turkey.

40 Paras = 1 Piaster

Issued under French Occupation.

The overprint on Nos. 2-93 is often found inverted, double, etc.
Numbers in parentheses are those of basic Turkish stamps.

Turkish Stamps of 1913-19 Handstamped — CILICIE

Perf. 11½, 12, 12½, 13½.

1919 **Unwmk.**

On Pictorial Issue of 1913.

2 A24 2pa red lil (254) 60 60
3 A25 4pa dk brn (255) 60 60
4 A27 6pa dk bl (257) 4.50 3.00
5 A32 1¾pi sl & red brn (262) 1.75 1.10

On Issue of 1915.

6 A17 1pi bl (300) 55 55
7 A21 20pa car rose (318) 60 60
9 A22 20pa car rose (330) 75 75

On Commemorative Issue of 1916.

10 A41 20pa ultra (347) 60 60
11 A41 1pi vio & blk (348) 1.00 1.00
12 A41 5pi yel brn & blk (349) 60 60

On Issue of 1916-18.

13 A44 10pa grn (424) 55 55
14 A47 50pa ultra (428) 8.25 3.00
15 A51 25pi car, *straw* (434) 90 90
16 A52 50pi car (437) 1.10 1.10
17 A52 50pi ind (438) 9.00 9.00

On Issue of 1917.

18 A53 5pi on 2pa Prus bl (547) 2.75 2.50

On Issue of 1919.

19 A47 50pa ultra (555) 7.50 1.75
20 A48 2pi org brn & ind (556) 7.50 1.00
21 A49 5pi pale bl & blk (557) 7.50 1.85

On Newspaper Stamp of 1916.

22 N3 5pa on 10pa gray grn (P137) 90 90

On Semi-Postal Stamps of 1916.

23 A17 1pi bl (B19) 60 60
24 A21 20pa car rose (B28) 45 45
25 A21 1pi ultra (B29) 1.25 1.25

Turkish Stamps of 1913-18 Handstamped — CILICIE

1919

On Pictorial Issue of 1913.

31 A24 2pa red lil (254) 60 60
32 A25 4pa dk brn (255) 60 60

On Issue of 1915.

33 A17 1pi bl (300) 75 75
34 A22 20pa car rose (330) 55 55

On Commemorative Issue of 1916.

35 A41 20pa ultra (347) 1.50 1.50
36 A41 1pi vio & blk (348) 40 40

On Issue of 1917.

40 A53 5pi on 2pa Prus bl (547) 1.50 1.50

On Newspaper Stamp of 1916.

41 N3 5pa on 10pa gray grn (P137) 1.50 1.50

On Semi-Postal Stamps of 1916.

42 A17 1pi bl (B19) 75 75
43 A21 20pa car rose (B28) 55 55

Turkish Stamps of 1913-19 Handstamped — *Cilicie*

1919

On Pictorial Issue of 1913.

51 A24 2pa red lil (254) 60 60
52 A25 4pa dk brn (255) 55 55

On Issue of 1915.

53 A17 1pi bl (300) 38 38
55 A22 5pa ocher (328) 4.00 2.00
56 A22 20pa car rose (330) 40 40

On Commemorative Issue of 1916.

57 A41 20pa ultra (347) 55 55
58 A41 1pi vio & blk (348) 60 60
59 A41 5pi yel brn & blk (349) 75 75

On Issue of 1916

59A A17 1pi bl (372) 35.00 35.00

On Issue of 1916-18.

60 A43 5pa org (421) 5.00 5.00
61 A46 1pi dl vio (426) 3.00 2.00
63 A52 50pi grn, *straw* (439) 12.00 5.50

On Issue of 1917

64 A53 5pi on 2pa Prus bl (547) 7.50 2.75

On Newspaper Stamp of 1916.

65 N3 5pa on 10pa gray grn (P137) 55 55

On Semi-Postal Stamps of 1916.

66 A17 1pi bl (B19) 3.75 1.50
67 A19 20pa car (B26) 11.00 4.50
68 A21 20pa car rose (B28) 85.00 35.00
69 A21 20pa car rose (B31) 2.25 2.25

Turkey No. 424 Handstamped — *T.E.O. Cilicie*

1919

71 A44 10pa green 55 55

"T.E.O." stands for "Territoires Ennemis Occupes."

Turkish Stamps of 1913-19 Overprinted in Black, Red or Blue — T. E. O. Cilicie

1919

In this setting there are various broken and wrong font letters and the letter "i" is sometimes replaced by a "t."

1919 **On Pictorial Issue of 1913.**

75 A30 1pi bl (R) (260) 30 20

On Issue of 1915.

76 A21 20pa car rose (318) 1.65 1.65

On Commemorative Issue of 1916.

77 A41 20pa ultra (347) 30 30
78 A41 1pi vio & blk (348) 60 38

On Issue of 1916-18.

79 A43 5pa org (Bl) (421) 15 15
80 A44 10pa grn (424) 30 30
81 A45 20pa dp rose (Bk) (425) 3.00 3.00
82 A45 20pa dp rose (Bl) (425) 15 15
83 A48 2pi org brn & ind (429) 40 38
83C A49 5pi pale bl & blk (R) (430) 45 38
84 A51 25pi car, *straw* (434) 7.50 5.00
85 A52 50pi grn, *straw* (439) 40.00 32.50

On Issue of 1917.

85A A53 5pi on 2pa Prus bl (547)
86 A53 5pi on 2pa Prus bl (548) 2.00 2.00

On Newspaper Stamps of 1916-19

87 N3 5pa on 10p gray grn (P137) 1.50 1.50
88 N4 5pa on 2pa ol grn (P173) 15 15

On Semi-Postal Stamps of 1915-17

90 A21 20pa car rose (B28) 1.10 1.10
91 A41 10pa car (B42) 15 15
92 A11 10pa on 20pa vio brn (B38) 15 15
93 SP1 10pa red vio (B46) 40 40

It is understood that the Newspaper and Semi-Postal stamps overprinted "Cilicie" were used as ordinary postage stamps.

A1

1920 **Blue Surcharge.** *Perf. 11½.*

98 A1 70pa on 5pa red 45 45
99 A1 3½pi on 5pa red 45 45

Nos. 98-99 exist with surcharge double, inverted, double with one inverted, "OCCUPTTION," etc. Price, $1 to $2 each.

French Offices in Turkey No. 26 Surcharged — T. E. O 20 PARAS

1920 *Perf. 14x13½*

100 A3 20pa on 10c rose red 45 45
a. "PARAS" omitted 13.00 13.00
b. Surcharged on back 2.50 2.50

Three types of "20" exist on No. 100.

Stamps of France, 1900-17, Surcharged — O. M. F. Cilicie 5 PARAS

1920

101 A16 5pa on 2c vio brn 38 38
102 A22 10pa on 5c grn 38 38
103 A22 20pa on 10c red 55 55
104 A22 1pi on 25c bl 45 45
105 A20 2pi on 15c gray grn 5.50 5.50
106 A18 5pi on 40c red & gray bl 9.00 9.00
107 A18 10pi on 50c bis brn & lav 7.50 7.50
108 A18 50pi on 1fr cl & ol grn 50.00 50.00
109 A18 100pi on 5fr dk bl & buff 650.00 650.00
Nos. 101-109 (9) 723.76 723.76

Nos. 106 to 109 surcharged in four lines.
"O.M.F." stands for "Occupation Militaire Francaise."

Stamps of France, 1917, Surcharged — O. M. F. Cilicie SAND. EST 20 PARAS

1920

110 A16 5pa on 2c vio brn 3.00
111 A22 10pa on 5c grn 3.00
112 A22 20pa on 10c red 1.50
113 A22 1pi on 25c bl 1.50
114 A20 2pi on 15c gray grn 7.50
115 A18 5pi on 40c red & gray bl 30.00
116 A18 20pi on 1fr cl & ol grn 60.00
Nos. 110-116 (7) 106.50

On Nos. 115 and 116 "SAND. EST" is placed vertically. "Sand. Est" is an abbreviation of Sandjak de l'Est (Eastern County).
Nos. 110-116 were prepared for use, but never issued.

Stamps of France, 1900-17, Surcharged — O. M. F. Cilicie 10 PARAS

1920

117 A16 5pa on 2c vio brn 15 15
a. Inverted surch. 7.50 6.75
b. Double surcharge 9.00
c. "Cililie" 7.25 7.25
d. Surch. 5 pi (error) 15.00 15.00
119 A22 10pa on 5c grn 15 15
a. Inverted surcharge 7.50 6.75
b. Surch. 5pa (error) 15.00 15.00
121 A22 20pa on 10c red 15 15
a. Inverted surcharge 7.50 6.75
b. Surch. 10pa (error) 16.50 16.50
122 A22 1pi on 25c bl 15 15
a. Double surcharge 12.00
b. Inverted surcharge 7.50 6.75
123 A20 2pi on 15c gray grn 40 40
a. Double surcharge 12.00
b. Inverted surcharge 7.50 6.75
124 A18 5pi on 40c red & gray bl 75 75
a. Double surcharge 17.50
b. Inverted surcharge 11.50 10.00
c. "PIASRTES" 15.00 15.00
125 A18 10pi on 50c bis brn & lav 2.00 2.00
a. "PIASRTES" 15.00 15.00
126 A18 50pi on 1fr cl & ol grn 2.50 2.50
a. "PIASRTES" 18.50 18.50
b. Inverted surch. 20.00 18.00
127 A18 100pi on 5fr dk bl & buff 8.00 8.00
a. "PIASRTES" 40.00 40.00
Nos. 117-127 (9) 14.25 14.25

This surcharge has "O.M.F." in thicker letters than the preceding issues.
There were two printings of this surcharge which may be distinguished by the space of 1 or 2mm. between "Cilicie" and the numeral.
The surcharge on Nos. 119b and 121b is always inverted.

AIR POST STAMPS.

Nos. 123 and 124 Handstamped

Perf. 14x13½

1920, July 15 **Unwmk.**

C1 A20 2pi on 15c gray grn *5,250.*
C2 A18 5pi on 40c red & gray bl *5,250.*
a. "PIASRTES"

A very limited number of Nos. C1 and C2 were used on two air mail flights between Adana and Aleppo. At a later date impressions from a new handstamp were struck "to oblige" on stamps of the regular issue of 1920 (Nos. 123, 124, 125 and 126) that were in stock at the Adana Post Office.
Counterfeits exist.

POSTAGE DUE STAMPS.

Turkish Postage Due Stamps of 1914 Handstamped.

Handstamped — CILICIE

1919 **Unwmk.** *Perf. 12.*

J1 D1 5pa claret 2.00 2.00
J2 D2 20pa red 2.00 2.00

J3	D3	1pi dk bl	4.00	4.00
J4	D4	2pi slate	4.00	4.00

Handstamped CILICIE

J5	D1	5pa claret	2.00	2.00
J6	D2	20pa red	2.00	2.00
J7	D3	1pi dk bl	5.25	5.25
J8	D4	2pi slate	4.50	4.50

Handstamped *Cilicie*

J9	D1	5pa claret	2.25	2.25
J10	D2	20pa red	2.25	2.25
J11	D3	1pi dk bl	4.50	4.50
J12	D4	2pi slate	5.25	5.25

Postage Due Stamps of France Surcharged

O. M. F.
Cilicie
2
PIASTRES

1921

J13	D2	1pi on 10c choc	3.75	3.75
J14	D2	2pi on 20c ol grn	3.75	3.75
J15	D2	3pi on 30c red	4.50	4.50
J16	D2	4pi on 50c vio brn	3.75	3.75

COCHIN CHINA

LOCATION — The southernmost state of French Indo-China in the Cambodian Peninsula.
GOVT. — French Colony
AREA — 26,476 sq. mi.
POP. — 4,615,968
CAPITAL — Saigon

100 Centimes = 1 Franc

Surcharged in Black on Stamps of French Colonies:

5 a

5 C. CH. b

5 c

1886-87 Unwmk. *Perf. 14x13½*

1	A9 (a) 5c on 25c yel, *straw*	125.00	90.00
2	A9 (b) 5c on 2c brn, *buff*	8.00	8.00
3	A9 (b) 5c on 25c yel, *straw*	9.00	9.00
4	A9 (c) 5c on 25c *rose* ('87)	27.50	25.00
a.	Double surcharge, one of type b	*2,500.*	*1,200.*
b.	Triple surcharge, two of type b		
c.	Inverted surcharge		

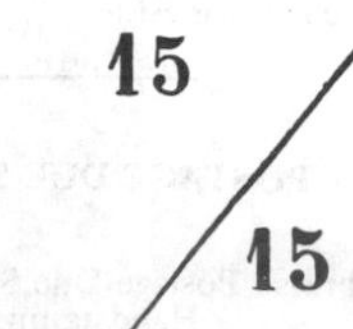

d

1888

5	A9 (d) 15c on half of 30c brn, *bis*		25.00

No. 5 was prepared but not issued.
The so-called Postage Due stamps were never issued.

Stamps of Cochin China were superseded by those of Indo-China in 1892.

COLOMBIA

LOCATION — On the northwest coast of South America, bordering on the Caribbean Sea and the Pacific Ocean.
GOVT. — Republic.
AREA — 456,535 sq. mi.
POP. — 28,240,000 (est. 1984).
CAPITAL — Bogota.

In 1810 the Spanish Viceroyalty of New Granada gained its independence and with Venezuela and Ecuador formed the State of Greater Colombia. In 1832 this state split into three independent units as Venezuela, Ecuador and the Republic of New Granada. The name of the country has been, successively, Granadine Confederation (1858-61), United States of New Granada (1861), United States of Colombia (1861-65), and the Republic of Colombia (1885 to date).

100 Centavos = 1 Peso

> Prices of early Colombia stamps vary according to condition. Quotations for Nos. 1-34 are for fine copies. Very fine to superb specimens sell at much higher prices, and inferior or poor copies sell at reduced prices, depending on the condition of the individual specimen.
>
> In the earlier days many towns did not have handstamps for canceling and stamps were canceled with pen and ink. Pen cancellations, therefore, do not indicate fiscal use. (Postage stamps were not used for revenue purposes.) Prices of Nos. 1-128 are for pen-canceled specimens. Those with handstamped cancellations sell for considerably more.
>
> Fractions of many Colombian stamps of both early and late issues are found canceled, their use to pay postage having been tolerated even though forbidden by the postal laws and regulations. Many are known to have been made for philatelic purposes.

Granadine Confederation

Coat of Arms
A1 A2

Type A1: Asterisks in frame. Wavy lines in background.
Type A2: Diamond-shaped ornaments in frame. Straight lines in background. Numerals larger.

1859 Unwmk. Litho. *Imperf.*
Wove Paper.

1	A1	2½c green	100.00	110.00
a.		2½c yel grn	100.00	110.00
2	A1	5c blue	140.00	90.00
a.		Tete beche pair	*3,000.*	*6,500.*
3	A1	5c violet	250.00	110.00
b.		"50" instead of "5"		
4	A1	10c red brn	110.00	80.00
a.		10c buff	110.00	80.00
6	A1	20c blue	110.00	70.00
a.		20c gray bl	110.00	70.00
b.		Se-tenant with 5c		
c.		Tete beche pair	*25,000.*	*25,000.*
7	A1	1p carmine	70.00	125.00
a.		1p rose	70.00	125.00
8	A1	1p rose, *bluish*	350.00	

The 10c green is an essay.

Reprints of No. 7 are in brown rose or brown red. Wavy lines of background are much broken; no dividing lines between stamps.

1860
Laid Paper.

9	A2	5c lilac	300.00	225.00

Wove Paper.

10	A2	5c gray lil	80.00	65.00
a.		5c lil	80.00	65.00
11	A2	10c yel buff	70.00	60.00
a.		Tete beche pair	*6,000.*	
12	A2	20c blue	175.00	140.00

United States of New Granada

Arms of New Granada — A3

1861

13	A3	2½c black	1,100.	350.00
14	A3	5c yellow	240.00	125.00
a.		5c buff	240.00	125.00
16	A3	10c blue	725.00	175.00
17	A3	20c red	425.00	225.00
18	A3	1p pink	950.00	425.00

There are 54 varieties of the 5c, 20c, and 1 peso.
Forgeries exist of Nos. 13-18.

United States of Colombia

Coat of Arms
A4 A5 A6

1862

19	A4	10c blue	225.00	125.00
20	A4	20c red	*3,000.*	725.00
21	A4	50c green	225.00	160.00
22	A4	1p red lil	550.00	275.00
23	A4	1p red lil, *bluish*	*3,500.*	*1,500.*

No. 23 is on a thinner, coarser wove paper than Nos. 19-22.

1863

24	A5	5c orange	85.00	65.00
a.		Star after "Cent"	100.00	75.00
25	A5	10c blue	200.00	25.00
a.		Period after "10"	225.00	30.00
26	A5	20c red	200.00	80.00
a.		Star after "Cent"	225.00	90.00
b.		Transfer of 50c in stone of 20c	*16,500.*	*5,000.*

Bluish Paper.

28	A5	10c blue	150.00	35.00
a.		Period after "10"	165.00	37.50
29	A5	50c green	175.00	80.00
a.		Star after "Cent"	185.00	90.00

Ten varieties of each.

1864

Wove Paper.

30	A6	5c orange	65.00	40.00
a.		Tete beche	475.00	400.00
31	A6	10c blue	50.00	16.00
a.		Period after 10	50.00	16.00
32	A6	20c scarlet	90.00	55.00
33	A6	50c green	75.00	55.00
34	A6	1p red vio	325.00	175.00

Two varieties of each.

Arms of Colombia
A7 A9

A8

1865

35	A7	1c rose	12.50	12.50
a.		bluish pelure paper	17.50	15.00
36	A8	2½c *lilac*	21.00	13.00
37	A9	5c yellow	40.00	20.00
a.		5c org	40.00	20.00
38	A9	10c violet	60.00	6.50
39	A9	20c blue	60.00	21.00
40	A9	50c green	100.00	55.00
41	A9	50c grn (small figures)	100.00	55.00
42	A9	1p vermilion	110.00	17.50
a.		1p rose red	110.00	17.50
b.		Period after "PESO"	120.00	20.00

Ten varieties of each of the 5c, 10c, 20c, and 50c, and six varieties of the 1 peso. No. 36 was used as a carrier stamp.

A10

A11

A12

A13

A14

A15

A16

1866

White Wove Paper.

45	A10	5c orange	62.50	30.00
46	A11	10c lilac	13.00	7.50
a.		Pelure paper	20.00	13.00
47	A12	20c lt bl	37.50	22.50
a.		Pelure paper	57.50	47.50
48	A13	50c green	16.00	13.50
49	A14	1p rose red, *bluish*	85.00	32.50
a.		1p ver	85.00	32.50
51	A15	5p *green*	425.00	225.00
52	A16	10p *vermilion*	325.00	200.00

There are several varieties of the 1 peso having the letters "U", "N", "S" and "O" smaller.

A17

A18

A19

A20

A21

TEN CENTAVOS:
Type I: "B" of "COLOMBIA" over "V" of "CENTAVOS".

Type II: "B" of "COLOMBIA" over "VO" of "CENTAVOS".

ONE PESO:

Type I: Long thin spear heads Diagonal lines in lower part of shield.

Type II: Short thick spear heads. Horizontal and a few diagonal lines in lower part of shield.

Type III: Short thick spear heads. Crossed lines in lower part of shield. Ornaments at each side of circle are broken. (See No. 97.)

1868

53	A17	5c orange	62.50	55.00
54	A18	10c lil (I)	2.50	1.10
a.		10c red vio (I)	2.50	1.10
b.		10c lil (II)	2.50	1.10
c.		10c red vio (II)	2.50	1.10
d.		Printed on both sides	5.00	2.50
55	A19	20c blue	2.50	1.25
56	A20	50c yel grn	3.00	2.10
57	A21	1p ver (II)	3.00	2.25
a.		Tete beche pair	150.00	125.00
b.		1p rose red (I)	52.50	35.00
c.		1p rose red (II)	3.00	2.25

See also Nos. 83-84, 96-97.

Counterfeits or reprints.

10c. There is a large white dot at the upper left between the circle enclosing the "X" and the ornament below.

50c. There is a shading of dots instead of dashes below the ribbon with motto. There are crossed lines in the lowest section of the shield instead of diagonal or horizontal ones.

1p. The ornaments in the lettered circle are broken. There are crossed lines in the lowest section of the shield. These counterfeits, or reprints, are on white paper, wove and laid, on colored wove paper and in fancy colors.

A22

Two varieties.

1869-70

Wove Paper

59	A22	2½c *violet*	4.00	2.50
a.		Laid paper ('70)	275.00	275.00
b.		Laid batonne paper ('70)	25.00	25.00

Nos. 59, 59a and 59b were used as carrier stamps.

Counterfeits, or reprints, are on magenta paper wove or ribbed.

A23

A24

1870

Wove Paper.

62	A23	5c orange	1.50	1.50
a.		5c yel	1.50	1.50
63	A24	25c *blue*	14.00	14.00

See also No. 89.

In the counterfeits, or reprints, of No. 63, the top of the "2" of "25" does not touch the down stroke. The counterfeits are on paper of various colors.

A25

A26

5 pesos. The ornament at the left of the "C" of "Cinco" cuts into the "C", and the shading of the flag is formed of diagonal lines.

10 pesos. The stars have extra rays between the points, and the central part of the shield has some horizontal lines of shading at each end.

1870

Surface Colored, Chalky Paper

64	A25	5p *green*	90.00	70.00
65	A26	10p *vermilion*	100.00	70.00

See Nos. 77-79.

A27

A28

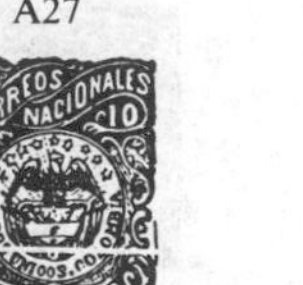
A29

TEN CENTAVOS:

Type I: "S" of "CORREOS" 2½ mm. high. First "N" of "NACIONALES" small.

Type II: "S" of "CORREOS" 2 mm. high. First "N" of "NACIONALES" wide.

1871-74

Thin Porous Paper

66	A27	1c grn ('72)	3.25	3.25
67	A27	1c rose ('73)	3.25	3.25
a.		1c car ('73)	3.25	3.25
68	A28	2c brown	1.50	1.50
a.		2c red brn	1.50	1.50
69	A29	10c vio (I) ('74)	1.60	1.75
a.		10c lil (I) ('74)	1.60	1.75
b.		10c vio (II) ('74)	1.60	1.75
c.		10c lil (II) ('74)	1.60	1.75
d.		Laid paper, as #69 ('72)	125.00	125.00
e.		Laid paper, as "b" ('72)	125.00	125.00

Counterfeits or reprints.

1c. The outer frame of the shield is broken near the upper left corner and the "A" of "Colombia" has no cross-bar.

2c. There are scratches across "DOS" and many white marks around the letters on the large "2". The counterfeits, or reprints, are on white wove and bluish white laid paper.

Condor — A30

Liberty Head
A31 A32

5 pesos, re-drawn: The ornament at the left of the "C" only touches the "C", and the shading of the flag is formed of vertical and diagonal lines.

10 pesos, re-drawn: The stars are distinctly five pointed, and there is no shading in the central part of the shield.

1877

Wove Paper.

73	A30	5c purple	6.25	2.50
a.		5c lil	6.25	2.50
74	A31	10c bis brn	2.25	1.00
a.		10c red brn	2.25	1.00
b.		10c vio brn	2.25	1.00
75	A32	20c blue	3.00	1.35
a.		20c vio bl	7.50	3.75
77	A26	10p *rose*	100.00	70.00
78	A25	5p *lt grn,* redrawn	35.00	35.00
79	A26	10p *rose,* redrawn	12.00	3.00

Stamps of the issues of 1871-77 are known with private perforations of various gauges, also with sewing machine perforation.

In the counterfeits, or reprints, of the 5 pesos the ornament at the left of the "C" of "Cinco" is separated from the "C" by a black line.

In the counterfeits, or reprints, of the 10 pesos the outer line of the double circle containing "10" is broken at the top, below "OS" of "Unidos", and the vertical lines of shading contained in the double circle are very indistinct. There is a colorless dash below the loop of the "P" of "Pesos".

1876-79

Laid Paper.

80	A30	5c lilac	72.50	72.50
81	A31	10c brown	40.00	30.00
82	A32	20c blue	85.00	72.50
83	A20	50c grn ('79)	90.00	70.00
84	A21	1p pale red (II) ('79)	60.00	16.50

1879

Wove Paper.

89	A24	25c green	35.00	37.50

1881

Blue Wove Paper.

93	A30	5c violet	17.50	12.00
a.		5c lil	17.50	12.00
94	A31	10c brown	10.00	2.75
95	A32	20c blue	10.00	4.00
96	A20	50c yel grn	11.00	8.00
97	A21	1p ver (III)	15.00	8.00

For types of 1p, see note over No. 53.

Reprints of the 10c and 20c are much worn. On the 10c the letters "TAVOS" of "CENTAVOS" often touch. On the 20c the letters "NT" of "VEINTE" touch and the left arm of the "T" is too long. Reprints of the 25c, 50c and 1p have the characteristics previously described. The reprints are on white wove or laid paper, on colored papers, and in fancy colors. Stamps on green paper exist only as reprints.

A34

A35

A36

1 centavo: The period before "UNION" is round and there are rays between the stars and the condors.

2 centavos: The "2" s and "C" s in the corners are placed upright.

5 centavos: The last star at the right almost touches the frame.

10 centavos: The letters of the inscription are thin; there are rays between the stars and the condor.

1881 ***Imperf.***

White Wove Paper.

103	A34	1c green	4.50	4.50
104	A35	2c vermilion	1.75	1.75
a.		2c rose	1.75	1.75
106	A34	5c blue	4.00	1.50
a.		Printed on both sides		
107	A36	10c violet	3.50	1.25
108	A34	20c black	4.00	2.00
		Nos. 103-108 (5)	17.75	11.00

The stamps of this issue are found with perforations of various gauges, also sewing machine perforation, all of which are unofficial.

Liberty Head — A37

A37a

1881 ***Imperf.***

109	A37	1c *green*	3.00	5.00
110	A37	2c *lil rose*	3.00	5.00
111	A37	5c *lilac*	5.00	2.50

Nos. 109 to 111 are found with regular or sewing machine perforation, unofficial.

Reprints:

1c. The top line of the stamp and the top frame extend to the left. 2c. There is a curved line over the scroll below the "AV" of "CENTAVOS".

5c. There are scratches across the "5" in the upper left corner. All three values were reprinted on the three colors of paper of the originals.

Redrawn

1 centavo: The period before "UNION" is square and the rays between the stars and the condor have been wholly or partly erased.

2 centavos: The "2's" and "C's" in the corners are placed diagonally.

5 centavos: The last star at the right touches the wing of the condor.

10 centavos: The letters of the inscription are thick; there are no rays under the stars; the last star at the right touches the wing of the condor and this wing touches the frame.

1883 ***Imperf.***

112	A34	1c green	6.50	6.50
113	A37a	2c rose	1.75	1.75
114	A34	5c blue	3.50	1.25
a.		5c ultra	3.50	1.25
b.		Printed on both sides, reverse ultra	30.00	25.00
115	A36	10c violet	3.50	1.90

The stamps of this issue are found with regular or sewing machine perforation, privately applied.

A38

A39

1883 ***Perf. 10½, 12, 13½***

116	A38	1c gray grn,*grn*	1.00	1.00
a.		Imperf., pair	5.00	5.00
117	A39	2c red, *rose*	1.00	1.50
a.		2c org red, rose	1.00	1.50
b.		2c red, *buff*	7.50	7.50
c.		Imperf., pair (#117 or 117a)	5.00	5.00
d.		"DE LOS" in very small caps	10.00	10.00
118	A38	5c bl, *bluish*	2.00	1.75
a.		5c dk bl, *bluish*	2.00	1.25
b.		5c bl	2.50	2.50
c.		Imperf., pair (#118 or 118a)	8.50	8.50
d.		As "b," imperf., pair	12.00	12.00
119	A39	10c org, *yel*	1.25	1.65
a.		"DE LOS" in large caps	62.50	27.50
b.		Imperf., pair	7.50	7.50
120	A39	20c vio, *lil*	1.25	1.60
a.		Imperf., pair	5.00	5.00
122	A38	50c brn, *buff*	3.00	3.50
a.		Perf. 12	3.00	3.50
123	A38	1p cl, *bluish*	5.25	2.25
a.		Imperf., pair	17.50	17.50
		Nos. 116-123 (7)	14.75	13.25

1886 ***Perf. 10½, 11½, 12.***

127	A38	5p brn, *straw*	8.00	8.00
a.		Imperf., pair	35.00	35.00
128	A38	10p *rose*	9.50	9.50
a.		Imperf., pair	35.00	35.00

Republic of Colombia

A40

Simon Bolivar
A41

President Rafael Nunez
A42

1886 ***Perf. 10½ and 13½***

129	A40	1c grn, *grn*	1.75	90
a.		Imperf., pair	7.50	7.50
130	A41	5c bl, *bl*	1.75	50
a.		5c ultra, *bl*	1.75	50
b.		Imperf., pair (#130)	7.50	7.50
131	A42	10c orange	4.00	90
a.		Imperf., pair	10.00	10.00
b.		Pelure paper	5.00	1.25

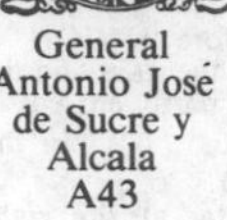

General Antonio José de Sucre y Alcala
A43

General Antonio Narino
A44

1887

133	A43	2c org red,*rose*	2.50	1.25
a.		2c org red, *yel*	6.25	6.25
b.		2c org red	7.25	7.25
c.		Imperf., pair (#133)	11.00	11.00
134	A44	20c pur, *grysh*	3.25	1.25
a.		Imperf., pair	9.00	9.00
b.		Pelure paper	4.00	2.50

Impressions of No. 134 on white, blue or greenish blue paper were not regularly issued.

Arms
A45

Narino
A46

1888

135	A45	50c brn, *buff*	2.00	2.00
a.		Imperf., pair	6.50	6.50
136	A45	1p cl, *bluish*	7.50	2.50
137	A45	1p claret	3.50	1.75
138	A45	5p org brn	9.00	6.00
139	A45	5p black	16.00	10.00
140	A45	10p *rose*	18.50	7.50
		Nos. 135-140 (6)	56.50	29.75

1889

141	A46	20c pur, *grysh*	2.00	1.50
a.		Imperf., pair	10.00	10.00

Impressions on white, blue or greenish blue paper were not regularly issued.

A47

A48

A49

A50

A51

1890-91 ***Perf. 10½, 13½, 11***

142	A47	1c grn, *grn*	2.00	1.65
143	A48	2c org red, *rose*	90	1.00
144	A49	5c bl, *grnsh bl*	1.50	50
a.		5c dp bl, *bl*	1.25	50
b.		Imperf., pair	6.00	6.00
146	A50	10c brn, *yel*	90	50
147	A51	20c vio, pelure paper	4.00	5.00
		Nos. 142-147 (5)	9.30	8.65

A52

A53

A54

Perf. 10½, 12, 13½, 14 to 15½.

1892

Ordinary Paper.

148	A47	1c red, *yel*	80	40
149	A52	2c red, *rose*	40.00	40.00
150	A52	2c green	50	30
a.		2c yel grn	50	30
151	A49	5c blk, *buff*	6.25	40
152	A50	10c bis brn, *rose*	75	40
153	A53	20c brn, *bl*	75	45
154	A45	50c vio, *vio*	1.25	75
155	A54	1p bl, *grnsh*	2.00	50
156	A45	5p red, *pale rose*	8.00	3.25
157	A45	10p blue	15.00	3.50
a.		Thin, pale rose paper	30.00	8.00
		Nos. 148-157 (10)	75.30	49.95

Nos. 148, 150-155 and 157 exist imperf. Price per pair, $5-$7.50.

A55

A55a

1895-99

158	A55	5c org brn, *pale buff*	85	30
a.		Imperf., pair	6.00	6.00
159	A55	5c red brn, *sal* ('97)	85	30
a.		Imperf., pair	6.00	6.00
160	A53	20c yel brn, *grnsh bl* ('97)	5.00	13.00
160A	A53	20c brn, *buff* ('97)	17.50	13.00
161	A55a	50c red vio, *vio* ('99)	1.50	1.40

Type A55a is a redrawing of type A45. The letters of the inscriptions are slightly larger and the numerals "50" slightly smaller than in type A45.

The 20c brown on white paper is believed to be a chemical changeling.

A56

1899

162	A56	1c red, *yel*	75	45
163	A56	5c red brn, *sal*	75	45
164	A56	10c brn, *lil rose*	2.50	2.25
165	A56	50c bl, *lil*	1.40	1.40

Cartagena Issues.

A57

1899 Blue Overprint. ***Imperf.***

167	A57	5c red, *buff*	30.00	30.00
a.		Sewing machine perf.	30.00	30.00
168	A57	10c ultra, *buff*	30.00	30.00
a.		Sewing machine perf.	30.00	30.00

Nos. 168 and 168a differ slightly from the illustration.

A58

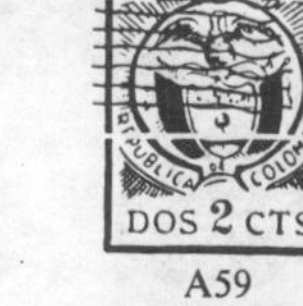

A59

A60

A61

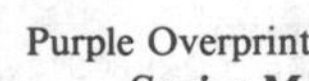

Purple Overprint.

1899 ***Sewing Machine Perf.***

170	A58	1c brn, *buff*	25.00	25.00
a.		Altered from 10c	30.00	30.00
171	A59	2c blk, *buff*	25.00	25.00
a.		Altered from 10c	30.00	30.00
172	A60	5c mar, *grnsh bl*	20.00	20.00
a.		Perf. 12	20.00	20.00
b.		Without ovpt.	12.50	12.50
173	A61	10c red, *sal*	20.00	20.00
a.		Perf. 12	20.00	20.00

Types A58 and A59 illustrate Nos. 170a and 171a, which were made from altered plates of the 10c (No. 168). Nos. 170 and 171 were made from altered plate of the 5c denomination (No. 167), show part of the top flag of the "5" and differ slightly from the illustrations.

Nos. 170-173 exist imperf. Prices about same as perf.

A62

1900 ***Imperf.***

Purple Overprint

174	A62	5c red	30.00	30.00
a.		Perf. 12	40.00	40.00

A63

A64

1901 ***Sewing Machine Perf.***

Purple Overprint.

175	A63	1c black	1.25	1.25
a.		Without overprint	2.75	2.75
b.		Double overprint	3.00	3.00
c.		Imperf., pair	3.00	3.00
d.		Inverted overprint	1.50	1.50
176	A64	2c *rose*	1.25	1.25
a.		Imperf., pair	3.00	3.00
b.		Without overprint	2.75	2.75
c.		Double overprint	3.00	3.00

A65

A66

1901

Rose Overprint

177	A65	1c blue	1.25	1.25
a.		Imperf., pair	3.50	3.50
178	A66	2c brown	1.25	1.25
a.		Imperf., pair	3.50	3.50
b.		Without overprint	1.25	1.25

A67

A68

Sewing Machine or Regular Perf. 12, 12½

1902

Magenta Overprint.

179	A67	5c violet	2.50	2.50
a.		Without overprint	2.50	2.50
b.		Double overprint	2.50	2.50
c.		Imperf., pair	5.50	5.50
180	A68	10c yel brn	2.50	2.50
a.		Double overprint	2.50	2.50
b.		Imperf., pair	5.50	5.50
c.		Without overprint	2.50	2.50
d.		Printed on both sides	3.50	3.50

A69

A70

1902

Magenta Overprint

181	A69	5c yel brn	2.50	2.50
a.		Without overprint	2.25	2.25
b.		Imperf., pair	5.50	5.50
182	A69	10c black	1.75	1.75
a.		Without overprint	1.50	1.50
b.		Imperf., pair	8.50	8.50
183	A70	20c maroon	6.00	3.50
b.		Imperf., pair	15.00	15.00

Nos. 181-183 exist tête bêche. Price of 10c and 20c, each $17.50.

Washed copies of Nos. 167-183 are offered as "without overprint."

Barranquilla Issues.

Magdalena River — A75

Iron Quay at Sabanilla — A76

La Popa Hill — A77

1902-03 ***Imperf.***

184	A75	2c green	3.00	2.75
185	A75	2c dk bl	2.00	2.00
186	A75	2c rose	22.50	22.50
187	A76	10c scarlet	1.25	1.00
188	A76	10c orange	10.00	9.00
189	A76	10c rose	1.25	1.00
190	A76	10c maroon	2.00	2.00
191	A76	10c claret	2.00	2.00
192	A77	20c violet	4.00	4.00
a.		Laid paper		
193	A77	20c dl bl	5.00	5.00
194	A77	20c dl bl, *pink*	*150.00*	*150.00*
195	A77	20c car rose	22.50	22.50
		Nos. 184-195 (12)	225.50	223.75

Sewing Machine Perf. and Perf. 12.

184a	A75	2c green	7.50	7.50
185a	A75	2c dk bl	6.00	6.00
186a	A75	2c carmine	*40.00*	*40.00*
187a	A76	10c scarlet	4.00	4.00
188a	A76	10c orange	*30.00*	*30.00*
189a	A76	10c rose	6.00	6.00
190a	A76	10c maroon	6.00	6.00
191a	A76	10c claret	6.00	6.00
192b	A77	20c purple	60	60
c.		20c lil	60	60
193a	A77	20c dl bl	5.00	5.00
194a	A77	20c dl bl, *rose*	*150.00*	*150.00*
195b	A77	20c car rose	*60.00*	*60.00*
		Nos. 184a-195b (12)	321.10	321.10

See Nos. 240-245.

Cruiser "Cartagena" A78

Bolivar A79

General Prospero Pinzon — A80

A81

A82

1903-04 ***Imperf.***

209 A78 5c blue 3.00 3.00
210 A78 5c bister 4.00 4.00
211 A79 50c yellow 4.50 4.50
212 A79 50c green 5.00 5.00
213 A79 50c scarlet 5.00 5.00
214 A79 50c carmine 5.00 5.00
a. 50c rose 5.00 5.00
215 A79 50c pale brn 5.00 5.00
216 A80 1p yel brn 1.90 1.90
217 A80 1p rose 3.00 3.00
218 A80 1p blue 3.00 3.00
219 A80 1p violet 30.00 30.00
220 A81 5p claret 6.00 6.00
221 A81 5p pale brn 8.00 8.00
222 A81 5p bl grn 7.00 7.00
223 A82 10p pale grn 9.00 9.00
224 A82 10p claret 30.00 30.00
Nos. 209-224 (16) 129.40 129.40

Nos. 216 and 217 measure 20½x26½mm. and No. 218, 18x24 mm. Stamps of this issue exist with forged perforations.

Perf. 12.

209a A78 5c blue 7.00 6.00
210a A78 5c bister 7.50 7.50
211a A79 50c yellow 11.50 10.00
b. 50c org 11.50 10.00
212a A79 50c green 20.00 20.00
213a A79 50c scarlet 9.00 9.00
214b A79 50c rose 9.00 9.00
215a A79 50c pale brn 9.00 9.00
216a A80 1p yel brn 4.00 4.00
217a A80 1p rose 5.50 5.50
218a A80 1p blue 5.50 5.50
219a A80 1p violet 50.00 50.00
220a A81 5p claret 16.00 16.00
221a A81 5p pale brn 17.50 17.50
222a A81 5p bl grn 15.00 15.00
223a A82 10p pale grn 25.00 25.00
224a A82 10p claret 60.00 60.00
Nos. 209a-224a (16) 271.50 269.00

Imperf.
Laid Paper.

240 A76 10c dk bl, *lil* 4.50 4.50
241 A76 10c dk bl, *bluish* 4.50 4.50
242 A76 10c dk bl, *brn* 4.50 4.50
243 A76 10c dk bl, *sal* 9.00 9.00
244 A76 10c dk bl, *grnsh bl* 8.00 8.00
245 A76 10c dk bl, *dp rose* 4.50 4.50
Nos. 240-245 (6) 35.00 35.00

Perf. 12.

240a A76 10c dk bl, *lil* 13.00 13.00
241a A76 10c dk bl, *bluish* 8.00 8.00
242a A76 10c dk bl, *brn* 8.00 8.00
243a A76 10c dk bl, *sal* 70.00 70.00
244a A76 10c dk bl, *grnsh bl* 20.00 20.00
245a A76 10c dk bl, *dp rose* 8.00 8.00
Nos. 240a-245a (6) 127.00 127.00

Medellin Issue.

A83

1902

257 A83 1c grn, *straw* 30 60
a. Imperf., pair 12.00 12.00
258 A83 2c sal, *rose* 30 60
a. Imperf., pair 12.00 12.00
259 A83 5c dp bl, *grnsh* 30 60
a. Imperf., pair 12.00 12.00
260 A83 10c pale brn, *straw* 30 60
a. Imperf., pair 12.00 12.00
261 A83 20c pur, *rose* 50 60
a. Imperf., pair 12.00 12.00
262 A83 50c dl rose, *grnsh* 2.50 3.75
a. Imperf., pair 12.00 12.00
263 A83 1p *yellow* 5.00 7.50
a. Imperf., pair 32.50 32.50
264 A83 5p sl, *bl* 40.00 40.00
a. Imperf., pair 90.00 90.00
265 A83 10p dk brn, *rose* 25.00 25.00
a. Imperf., pair 70.00 70.00
Nos. 257-265 (9) 74.20 79.25

Regular Issue.

A84

A85

A86

A87

A88

A89

A90

A91

A92

1902 ***Imperf.***

266 A84 2c *rose* 25 25
267 A85 4c red, *grn* 30 30
268 A86 5c grn, *bl* 30 30
269 A87 10c *pink* 30 30
270 A88 20c brn, *buff* 30 30
271 A89 50c dk grn, *rose* 1.50 1.50
272 A90 1p pur, *buff* 60 60
273 A91 5p grn, *bl* 4.50 4.50
274 A92 10p grn, *pale grn* 12.00 7.00
Nos. 266-274 (9) 20.05 15.05

Sewing Machine Perf.

266a A84 2c *rose* 1.75 1.75
267a A85 4c red, *grn* 1.75 1.75
268a A86 5c grn, *bl* 2.00 2.00
269a A87 10c *pink* 2.00 2.00
270a A88 20c brn, *buff* 2.00 2.00
271a A89 50c dk grn, *rose* 4.00 3.00
272a A90 1p pur, *buff* 4.00 4.00
273a A91 5p grn, *bl* 30.00 30.00
274a A92 10p grn, *pale grn* 60.00 50.00
Nos. 266a-274a (9) 107.50 96.50

1903 ***Perf. 12***

266b A84 2c *rose* 1.75 1.75
269b A87 10c *pink* 2.00 2.00
270b A88 20c brn, *buff* 2.00 2.00
272b A90 1p pur, *buff* 4.00 4.00
273b A91 5p grn, *bl* 30.00 30.00
274b A92 10p grn, *pale grn* 60.00 50.00
Nos. 266b-274b (6) 99.75 89.75

1903 ***Imperf.***

284 A85 4c bl, *grn* 30 30
285 A86 5c bl, *bl* 30 30
286 A88 20c bl, *buff* 30 30
288 A89 50c bl, *rose* 2.00 2.00

Sewing Machine Perf.

284a A85 4c bl, *grn* 2.00 2.00
285a A86 5c bl, *bl* 2.00 2.00
286a A88 20c bl, *buff* 2.00 2.00
288a A89 50c bl, *rose* 6.00 5.00

Perf. 12

284b A85 4c bl, *grn* 2.00 2.00
285b A86 5c bl, *bl* 2.00 2.00
286b A88 20c bl, *buff* 2.00 2.00
288b A89 50c bl, *rose* 6.00 5.00

A93

1904 **Pelure Paper** ***Imperf.***

303 A93 ½c yel brn 1.40 1.40
304 A90 1c bl grn 1.50 1.50
a. 1c yel grn 1.50 1.50
306 A84 2c blue 1.25 90
307 A86 5c carmine 1.40 1.40
308 A87 10c violet 1.50 1.25
Nos. 303-308 (5) 7.05 6.45

1904 ***Perf. 13***

303a A93 ½c yel brn 3.00 3.00
304b A90 1c bl grn 4.00 4.00
c. 1c yel grn 5.00 5.00
306a A84 2c blue 3.00 3.00

Perf. 12

307a A86 5c carmine 3.50 3.00
308a A87 10c violet 3.50 3.00
Nos. 303a-308a (5) 17.00 16.00

A94

A95

Pres. José Manuel Marroquin — A96

Imprint: "Lit. J. L. Arango Medellin. Col."

1904 **Wove Paper** ***Perf. 12***

314 A94 ½c yellow 90 15
a. Redrawn 90 15
b. Imperf., pair 3.75 3.75
315 A94 1c green 90 6
a. Redrawn 90 6
b. Imperf. pair 3.00 3.00
316 A94 2c rose 90 5
a. Redrawn 90 5
b. Imperf., pair 3.75 3.75
317 A94 5c blue 1.50 15
a. Redrawn 1.50 15
b. Imperf., pair 3.75 3.75
318 A94 10c violet 1.90 22
a. Imperf., pair 4.75 4.75
319 A94 20c black 2.00 30
a. Redrawn 2.00 30
b. Imperf., pair 8.50 8.50
320 A95 1p brown 20.00 3.50
a. Imperf., pair 47.50 47.50
321 A96 5p red & blk, *yel* 65.00 65.00
322 A96 10p bl & blk, *grnsh* 65.00 65.00
Nos. 314-322 (9) 158.10 134.43

On the redrawn types, the imprint is close to the base of the design instead of being spaced from it. On the redrawn 2c and 5c, the lower end of the vertical white line below "OR" of "CORREOS" forms a hook which turns to the right instead of to the left as in the originals. See also Nos. 325-330.

A97

A98

1905 ***Imperf.***

323 A97 50p org yel, *pale pink* 100.00 100.00
324 A98 100p dk bl, *dk rose* 90.00 90.00

Imprint: "Lit. Nacional".

Perf. 10, 13, 13½ and Compound.

1908

325 A94 ½c orange 90 15
a. ½c yel 90 15
b. Imperf., pair 2.25 2.25
c. Without imprint 6.00 6.00
326 A94 1c yel grn 90 6
a. Without imprint 90 6
d. Imperf., pair 3.75 3.75
327 A94 2c red 90 6
a. 2c car 90 6
b. Imperf., pair 3.75 3.75
328 A94 5c blue 80 15
a. Imperf., pair 6.00 6.00
329 A94 10c violet 55.00 1.00
330 A94 20c gray blk 55.00 70
Nos. 325-330 (6) 113.50 2.12

The above stamps may be easily distinguished from those of 1904 by the perforation, by the height of the design, 24mm. instead of 23mm., and by the "Lit. Nacional" imprint.

Camilo Torres A99

Policarpa Salavarrieta A100

Nariño — A101

Bolivar — A102

Francisco José de Caldas A103

Francisco de Paula Santander A104

Bolivar Demanding Liberation of Slaves A105

Bolivar Resigning A106

1910, Aug. **Engr.** ***Perf. 12***

331 A99 ½c vio & blk 1.10 70
a. Center inverted 425.00 425.00
332 A100 1c dp grn 90 70
333 A101 2c scarlet 75 45
334 A102 5c dp bl 1.90 65
335 A103 10c plum 15.00 7.25
336 A104 20c blk brn 22.50 8.00

337 A105 1p dk vio 75.00 27.50
338 A106 10p claret 300.00 210.00
Nos. 331-338 (8) 417.15 255.25

Colombian independence centenary.

Caldas
A107

Torres
A108

Nariño
A109

Santander
A110

Bolivar
A111

José María Cordoba
A112

Monument to Battle of Boyaca
A113

View of Cartagena
A114

Sucre
A115

Rufino Cuervo
A116

Antonio Ricaurte y Lozano
A117

Coat of Arms
A118

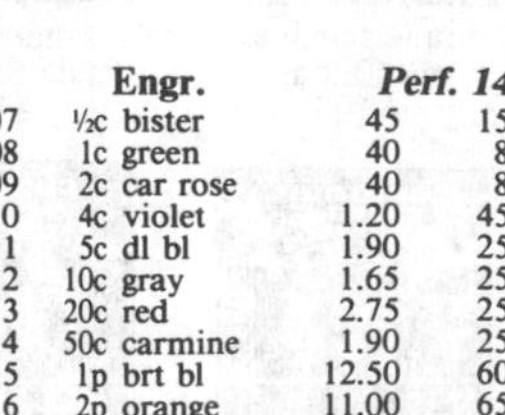

1917 Engr. *Perf. 14*

339	A107	½c bister	45	15
340	A108	1c green	40	8
341	A109	2c car rose	40	8
342	A110	4c violet	1.20	45
343	A111	5c dl bl	1.90	25
344	A112	10c gray	1.65	25
345	A113	20c red	2.75	25
346	A114	50c carmine	1.90	25
347	A115	1p brt bl	12.50	60
348	A116	2p orange	11.00	65
349	A117	5p gray	22.50	7.50
350	A118	10p dk brn	47.50	15.00
		Nos. 339-350 (12)	104.15	25.51

The 1c, 5c, 10c, 50c, 2p, 5p and 10p also exist perf. 11½ and 11½ compounded with 14.

fLithographed varieties of Nos. 343, 345 and 346 are counterfeits made to defraud the government.

Imperforate copies of Nos. 339-350 are not known to have been regularly issued.

See Nos. 373-374, 400-405.

Nos. 318-319, 329-330 Surcharged in Red

1918

On Issue of 1904.

351 A94 ½c on 20c blk 1.50 35
352 A94 3c on 10c vio 3.00 1.00

On Issue of 1908.

353 A94 ½c on 20c gray blk 10.00 7.00
354 A94 3c on 10c vio 15.00 6.25

Nos. 351 to 354 inclusive exist with surcharge reading upward or downward. On one stamp in each sheet the letter "S" in "Especie" is omitted. All denominations exist with a small zero before the decimal in the surcharge.

A119

A120

1918 Litho. *Perf. 13½.*

358 A119 3c red 75 15
a. Imperf., pair 6.00 6.00

1920 Engr. *Perf. 14.*

359 A120 3c red, *org* 45 10
a. Imperf., pair 4.50 4.50

See also Nos. 371-372.

A121

A122

A123

Perf. 10, 13½ and Compound

1920-21 Litho.

360	A121	½c yellow	80	35
361	A121	1c green	1.25	20
362	A121	2c red	90	22
363	A122	3c green	80	22
a.		3c yel grn	80	22
364	A121	5c blue	1.40	30
365	A121	10c violet	4.50	2.25
366	A121	20c dp grn	12.00	5.25
367	A123	50c dk red	12.00	5.50
		Nos. 360-367 (8)	33.65	14.29

The tablet with "PROVISIONAL" was added separately to each design on the various lithographic stones and its position varies slightly on different stamps in the sheet. For some values there were two or more stones, on which the tablet was placed at various angles.

Nos. 360-366 exist imperf.

See No. 375.

No. 342 Surcharged in Red

PROVICIONAL
$003
a

PROVISIONAL
$0.03
(15mm. wide) — b

1921

369 A110(a) 3c on 4c vio 1.10 32
a. Dbl. surcharge 17.50
370 A110(b) 3c on 4c vio 5.00 3.00

See also No. 377.

Types of 1917-21.

1923-24 Engr. *Perf. 13½.*

371 A120 1½c chocolate 1.25 75
372 A120 3c blue 70 18
373 A111 5c cl ('24) 3.00 25
374 A112 10c blue 8.50 60

Litho.

375 A121 10c dk bl 12.00 7.50
Nos. 371-375 (5) 25.45 9.28

No. 342 Surcharged in Red

(18mm. wide)

PROVISIONAL
$003

1924

377 A110 3c on 4c vio 3.75 1.90
a. Double surcharge 17.50
b. Double surcharge, one inverted 17.50
c. With added surch. "3cs." in red

A124

1924-25 Litho. *Perf. 10, 10x13½*

379 A124 1c red 1.00 25
380 A124 3c dp bl ('25) 1.00 25

Exist imperf. Price, each pair $5.

A125

A126

Black, Red or Green Surcharge and Overprint.

Imprint of Waterlow & Sons.

1925 *Perf. 14, 14½.*

382 A125 1c on 3c bis brn (Bk) 45 15
383 A126 4c vio (R) 55 30
a. Inverted surch. 10.00 10.00

Imprint of American Bank Note Co.

Perf. 12.

384 A125 1c on 3c bis brn (Bk) 6.00 5.00
a. Inverted surcharge 13.00 15.00
385 A126 4c vio (G) 60 45
a. Inverted overprint 8.00 8.00

Correos

Provisional

Revenue stamps of basic types A125 and A126 were handstamped as above in violet or blue by the Cali post office in 1925, but were not authorized by the government. Denominations so overprinted are 1c, 2c, 3c, 4c and 5c.

A127

A128

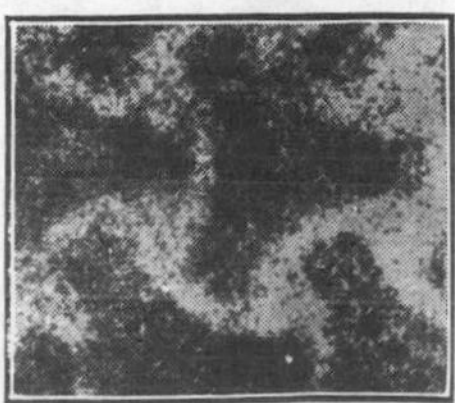

Wmk. 194

Wmk. Multiple Curvilinear Triangles (194)

1926 Litho. *Perf. 10, 13½x1*

395 A127 1c gray grn 50 2
396 A128 4c dp bl 50 2

Exist imperf. Price, each pair $4.

Types of 1917 and

Sabana Station — A129

1926-29 Unwmk. Engr. *Perf. 1*

400	A110	4c dp bl	60	
401	A120	8c dk bl	75	1
402	A107	30c ol bis	7.00	9
403	A129	40c brn & yel brn	11.00	1.5
404	A117	5p violet	9.00	1.0
a.		Perf. 11 ('29)	9.00	1.5
405	A118	10p green	18.50	3.0
a.		Perf. 11 ('29)	37.50	6.0
		Nos. 400-405 (6)	46.85	6.5

Death of Bolivar
A130

1930, Dec. 17 *Perf. 12½*

408 A130 4c dk bl & blk 40 35

Issued to commemorate the centenary of the death of Gen. Simón Bolivar. See also Nos. C80-C82.

Nos. 400 and 402 Surcharged in Red or Dark Blue

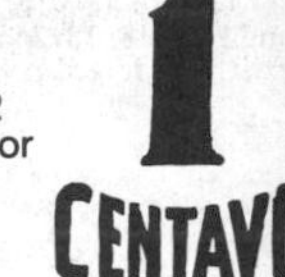

1932, Jan. 20 *Perf. 14*

409 A110 1c on 4c dp bl (R) 45 12
a. Inverted surcharge 8.00 8.00
410 A107 20c on 30c ol bis (Bl) 12.00 1.00
a. Inv. surcharge 25.00
b. Dbl. surcharge 25.00

Emerald Mine — A131

Oil Wells — A132

Coffee Cultivation
A133

Platinum Mine
A134

Gold Mining
A135

Christopher Columbus
A136

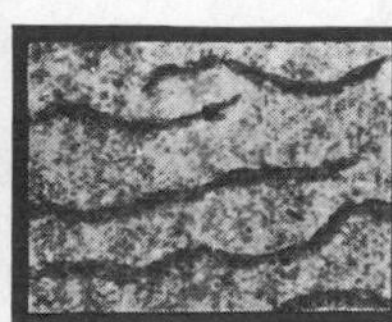
Wmk. 229

Imprint: "Waterlow & Sons Ltd. Londres"

Wmk. Wavy Lines. (229)

1932 Engr. *Perf. 12½*

No.	Type	Description	Unused	Used
411	A131	1c green	90	5
412	A132	2c red	90	5
413	A133	5c brown	1.00	5
414	A134	8c bl blk	5.50	70
415	A135	10c yellow	5.00	12
416	A136	20c dk bl	12.00	50
		Nos. 411-416 (6)	25.30	1.47

See Nos. 441-442, 464-466a, 517.

Pedro de Heredia A137

Coffee Picking A138

Perf. 11½

1934, Jan. 10 Unwmk. Litho.

No.	Type	Description	Unused	Used
417	A137	1c dk grn	3.00	90
418	A137	5c chocolate	4.00	75
419	A137	8c dk bl	3.00	90

400th anniversary of Cartagena. See also Nos. C111-C114.

1934, Dec. Engr. *Perf. 12*

No.	Type	Description	Unused	Used
420	A138	5c brown	3.25	5

Discus Thrower — A139

Allegory of Olympic Games at Barranquilla — A140

Foot Race A141

Tennis A142

Pier at Puerto Colombia A143

The lack of a price for a listed item does not necessarily indicate rarity.

View of the Bay — A144

Post and Telegraph Building — A145

Designs: 2c, Soccer. 10c, Hurdling. 15c, Athlete in stadium. 18c, Baseball. 24c, Swimming. 50c, View of Barranquilla. 2p, Monument to Flag. 5p, Coat of Arms. 10p, Condor.

1935, Jan. 26 Litho. *Perf. 11½*

No.	Type	Description	Unused	Used
421	A139	2c bluish grn & buff	1.75	75
422	A139	4c dp grn	1.75	75
423	A140	5c dk brn & yel	1.75	75
a.		Horizontal pair, imperf. btwn.	300.00	
424	A141	7c dk car	2.50	2.25
425	A142	8c blk & pink	2.75	2.75
426	A141	10c brn & bl	4.25	2.25
427	A143	12c indigo	4.75	3.75
428	A141	15c bl & red brn	8.50	6.25
429	A141	18c dk vio & buff	10.00	10.00
430	A144	20c pur & grn	10.00	7.50
431	A144	24c bluish grn & ultra	10.00	10.00
432	A144	50c ultra & buff	15.00	12.50
433	A145	1p db & bl	135.00	75.00
434	A145	2p dl grn & gray	185.00	135.00
435	A145	5p pur blk & bl	600.00	450.00
436	A145	10p blk & gray	725.00	600.00
		Nos. 421-436 (16)	1,718.	1,319.

3rd National Olympic Games, Barranquilla. Counterfeits of 10p exist.

Oil Wells A155

Gold Mining A157

Imprint: "American Bank Note Co."

1935, Mar. Unwmk. Engr. *Perf. 12*

No.	Type	Description	Unused	Used
437	A155	2c car rose	45	5
439	A157	10c dp org	27.50	15

See also Nos. 468, 470, 498, 516.

No. 347 Surcharged in Black

12 CENTAVOS

1935, Aug. *Perf. 14*

No.	Type	Description	Unused	Used
440	A115	12c on 1p brt bl	4.75	2.25

Types of 1932
Imprint: "Lit. Nacional Bogota"

1935-36 Litho. *Perf. 11, 11½, 12½*

No.	Type	Description	Unused	Used
441	A131	1c lt grn	15	5
a.		Imperf. (pair)	5.00	
442	A133	5c brn ('36)	80	12
a.		Imperf. (pair)	6.00	6.00

Simon Bolivar A159

Tequendama Falls A160

Wmk. Wavy Lines. (229)

1937 Engr. *Perf. 12½*

No.	Type	Description	Unused	Used
443	A159	1c dp grn	25	5
a.		Perf. 14		
444	A160	12c dp bl	3.75	1.40

See also No. 570.

Soccer Player A161

Discus Thrower A162

Runner — A163

1937, Jan. 4 Photo. Unwmk.

No.	Type	Description	Unused	Used
445	A161	3c lt grn	2.25	1.40
446	A162	10c car rose	4.00	2.50
447	A163	1p black	50.00	45.00

National Olympic Games, Manizales.

Exposition Palace A164

Stadium at Barranquilla A165

Monument to the Colors — A166

1937, Jan. 4

No.	Type	Description	Unused	Used
448	A164	5c vio brn	75	45
449	A165	15c blue	6.25	5.00
450	A166	50c org brn	16.00	8.50

Barranquilla National Exposition.

Stamps of 1926-37 Surcharged in Black

1 CENTAVO

1937-38 Unwmk. *Perf. 12½.*

No.	Type	Description	Unused	Used
452	A161	1c on 3c lt grn	1.10	1.10
a.		Invtd. surcharge	2.50	2.50
453	A120	5c on 8c dk bl	55	50
a.		Invtd. surcharge	2.50	2.50

Wmk. Wavy Lines. (229)

No.	Type	Description	Unused	Used
454	A160	2c on 12c dp bl	55	50
455	A134	5c on 8c bl blk	60	60
a.		Invtd. surcharge	2.25	2.25
456	A160	10c on 12c dp bl ('38)	6.25	1.25
a.		Dbl. surcharge	12.00	12.00
		Nos. 452-456 (5)	9.05	3.95

Calle del Arco A168

Entrance to Church of the Rosary A169

Arms of Bogota A170

Gonzalo Jimenez de Quesada A171

Bochica A172

Santo Domingo Convent A173

Mass of the Conquistadors — A174

1938, July 27 Unwmk. *Perf. 12½*

No.	Type	Description	Unused	Used
457	A168	1c yel grn	18	18
458	A169	2c scarlet	20	18
459	A170	5c brn blk	25	18
460	A171	10c brown	70	35
461	A172	15c brt bl	3.25	1.85
462	A173	20c brt red vio	3.25	1.85
463	A174	1p red brn	42.50	32.50
		Nos. 457-463 (7)	50.33	37.09

Bogotá, 400th anniversary.

Types of 1932.
Imprint: "Litografia Nacional Bogota".

1938, Dec. 5 Litho. *Perf. 10½, 11*

No.	Type	Description	Unused	Used
464	A132	2c rose	1.10	40
465	A135	10c yellow	3.00	45
466	A136	20c dl bl	6.25	1.50
a.		20c dk bl, perf. 12½ ('44)	60.00	7.50

Simon Bolivar A175

Coffee Picking A176

Arms of Colombia A177

Christopher Columbus A178

Caldas
A179

Sabana Station
A180

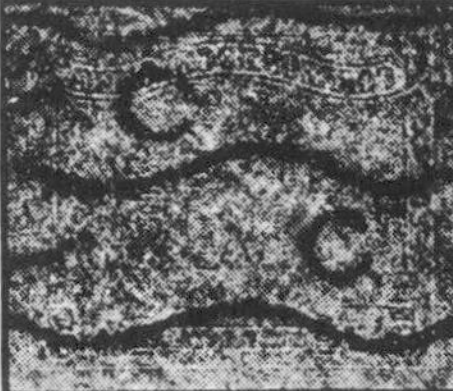
Wmk. 255- Wavy Lines and C Multiple

Imprint:
"American Bank Note Co."
Wmk. 255

1939, Mar. 3 Engr. *Perf. 12*

467 A175 1c green 18 5
468 A155 2c car rose 25 5
469 A176 5c dl brn 25 (5)
470 A157 10c dp org 1.25 5
471 A177 15c dl bl 3.00 22
472 A178 20c vio blk 5.25 30
473 A179 30c ol bis 5.25 45
474 A180 40c bis brn 15.00 4.25
Nos. 467-474 (8) 30.43 5.42

See also Nos. 497-499, 515, 518, 574.

General Santander
A181

Allegory
A182

General Santander
A183

Statue at Cucuta
A184

Birthplace of Santander
A185

Church at Rosario
A186

Paya — A187

Bridge at Boyaca — A188

Death of General Santander — A189

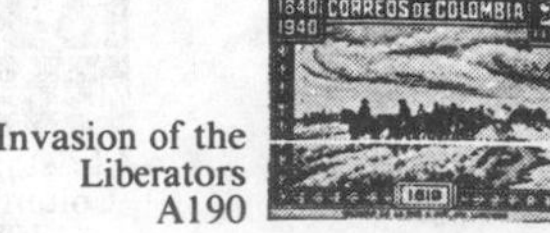
Invasion of the Liberators
A190

Perf. 13x13½, 13½x13
1940, May 6 Engr. Wmk. 229

475 A181 1c ol grn 30 25
476 A182 2c dk car 60 45
477 A183 5c sepia 30 22
478 A184 8c carmine 2.25 1.50
479 A185 10c org yel 1.00 75
480 A186 15c dk bl 2.75 1.65
481 A187 20c green 3.50 2.00
482 A188 50c violet 8.00 6.00
483 A189 1p dp rose 25.00 25.00
484 A190 2p orange 80.00 80.00
Nos. 475-484 (10) 123.70 117.82

Issued in commemoration of the centenary of the death of General Francisco Santander.

Tobacco Plant
A194

General Santander
A195

Garcia Rovira
A196

R. Galan
A197

Antonio Sucre
A198

Arms of Palmira
A199

Wmk. Wavy Lines and C Multiple. (255)

1940-43 Engr. *Perf. 12.*

488 A194 8c rose car & grn 1.50 85
489 A195 15c dp bl ('43) 1.60 35
490 A196 20c gray blk ('41) 4.00 55
491 A197 40c brn bis ('41) 2.75 55
492 A198 1p black 9.50 80
Nos. 488-492 (5) 19.35 3.10

See also Nos. 500, 554.

Unwmk.

1942, July 4 Litho. *Perf. 11*

493 A199 30c claret 2.50 90

Issued to commemorate the 8th National Agricultural Exposition, held at Palmira.

Paradise of Isaacs, Palmira
A200

Signing Treaty of the Wisconsin
A201

1942, July 4

494 A200 50c lt bl grn 3.25 1.25

Issued in honor of the writer, Jorge Isaacs.

1942, Nov. 21 *Perf. 10½*

495 A201 10c dl org 1.60 75
a. "2. XI.1902" instead of "21. XI. 1902" 21.00 22.50
b. Perf. 12 4.50 4.50

Issued in commemoration of the 40th anniversary of the signing of the Treaty of the Wisconsin, November 21, 1902.

No. 470 Surcharged in Black

5
Centavos

1944 Wmk. 255 *Perf. 12.*

496 A157 5c on 10c dp org 20 15

Counterfeits exist of No. 496 with inverted or double surcharge.

Types of 1935-41 and

National Shrine
A202

San Pedro Alejandrino
A203

Imprint:
"Columbian Bank Note Co."

1944-45 Unwmk. Engr. *Perf. 11*

497 A175 1c green 20 10
498 A155 2c rose 20 10
499 A176 5c dl brn 20 5
500 A196 20c gray blk 3.75 1.10
501 A202 30c dl ol grn ('45) 2.00 1.40
502 A203 50c rose 2.50 1.40
Nos. 497-502 (6) 8.85 4.15

No. 499 Surcharged in Black

1
CENTAVO

1944, Oct.

506 A176 1c on 5c dl brn 12 12
507 A176 2c on 5c dl brn 12 12

Nos. 506 and 507 exist with inverted or double surcharge, created by favor.

Flag
A204

Arms
A205

Murillo Toro
A206

Hospital of St. John of God
A207

Virrey Solis — A208

A209

1944, Oct. 10 Litho.

508 A204 2c ultra & bis 40 40
a. Sheet of 18 12.00
b. Imperf., pair 12.50
509 A205 5c ultra & bis 40 40
a. Sheet of 22 15.00
b. Imperf., pair 12.50
510 A206 20c blk & bluish grn 1.10 1.10
a. Sheet of 8 12.00
b. Imperf., pair 18.50
511 A207 40c blk & red 5.00 4.50
a. Sheet of 4 20.00
512 A208 1p blk & red 13.00 13.00
a. Sheet of 2 27.50
Nos. 508-512 (5) 19.90 19.40

Souvenir Sheet.
Perf. 11x11½ All Around, Stamps Imperf.

513 A209 Sheet of five 20.00 20.00

75th anniversary of General Benevolent Association of Cundinamarca. Size of No. 513: 100x87mm.

Nos. 508-513 were printed in composite sheets containing one each of Nos. 508a, 509a, 510a, 511a and 512a, and two of 513. Fifty of these were presented to government officials.

Murillo Toro
A210

San Pedro Alejandrino
A211

1944, Nov. 10 *Perf. 11*

514 A210 5c lt brn 40 22

Types of 1932-39 and A211.
Imprint: "Litografia Nacional Bogota".

1944 Litho. *Perf. 12½.*

515 A175 1c dp grn 45 20
a. 1c ol grn 45 20
b. Imperf., pair 3.00 3.00
516 A155 2c dk car 45 20
a. Imperf., pair 3.00 3.00
517 A135 10c yel org 2.50 75
518 A179 30c gray ol 12.00 5.25
a. Imperf., pair 40.00
519 A211 50c rose 13.00 6.00
Nos. 515-519 (5) 28.40 12.40

No. 469 Overprinted in Green, Blue or Red

Wmk. 255

1945, July 19 Engr. *Perf. 12*

520 A176 5c dl brn (G) 25 12
521 A176 5c dl brn (R) 25 12
522 A176 5c dl brn (Bl) 25 12

Portraits are Joseph Stalin, Franklin D. Roosevelt and Winston Churchill.

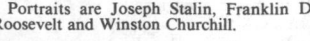

Clock Tower, Cartagena — A212

1945, Nov. 15

523 A212 50c ol blk 5.75 1.75

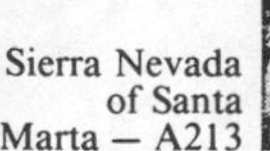
Sierra Nevada of Santa Marta — A213

Designs: 30c, Seaplane Tolima. 50c, San Sebastian Fort, Cartagena.

Unwmk.

1945, Dec. 14 Litho. *Perf. 11*

524	A213	20c lt grn	2.25	1.50
525	A213	30c pale bl	2.25	1.50
526	A213	50c sal pink	2.25	1.50

Issued to commemorate the 25th anniversary of the first airmail service in America, according to the inscription, but earlier services are known to have existed.

No. 442 Surcharged in Black

1
UN CENTAVO

1946, Mar. 8 *Perf. 11x11½, 12½*

527	A133	1c on 5c brn	10	10
a.		Inverted surcharge	1.25	

Gen. Antonio José de Sucre — A216

Wmk. 255

1946, Apr. 16 Engr. *Perf. 12*

Size: 19x26½mm.

528	A216	1c brn & turq grn	22	12
529	A216	2c vio & rose car	22	12

Size: 23x31mm.

530	A216	5c sep & bl	22	12
531	A216	9c dk grn & red	90	90
532	A216	10c ultra & org	80	70
533	A216	20c blk & dp org	80	45
534	A216	30c brn red & grn	1.40	45
535	A216	40c ol blk & red vio	1.40	60
536	A216	50c dp brn & vio	1.40	60
		Nos. 528-536 (9)	7.36	4.06

Map of South America A217

National Observatory A218

Unwmk.

1946, June 7 Litho. *Perf. 11*

537	A217	15c ultra	75	45
a.		Imperf. (pair)	6.00	

1946, Aug.

538	A218	5c fawn	35	12
a.		Imperf. (pair)	6.00	

See No. 565.

Andrés Bello — A219

Joaquin de Cayzedo y Cuero — A220

Wmk. 255

1946, Sept. 3 Engr. *Perf. 12*

539	A219	3c sepia	22	15
540	A219	10c orange	75	45
541	A219	15c sl blk	85	45

Issued to commemorate the 80th anniversary of the death of Andrés Bello (1781-1865), poet and educator. See also No. C145.

1946, Sept. 20 Wmk. 229 *Perf. 12½*

542	A220	2p bluish grn	6.75	1.75

See No. 568.

Type of 1945, Overprinted in Black or Green

V JUEGOS C.
A. Y DEL C.
1946

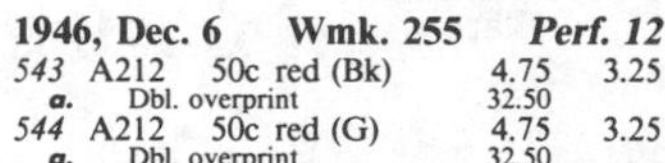

1946, Dec. 6 Wmk. 255 *Perf. 12*

543	A212	50c red (Bk)	4.75	3.25
a.		Dbl. overprint	32.50	
544	A212	50c red (G)	4.75	3.25
a.		Dbl. overprint	32.50	

Issued to commemorate the fifth Central American and Caribbean Championship Games.

Coffee — A221

Engraved and Lithographed

1947, Jan. 10 Wmk. 229 *Perf. 12½*

545	A221	5c multi	60	12

Colombian Orchid: Masdevallia Nycterina — A222

Designs (Orchids): 2c, Miltonia vexillaria. No. 548, Cattleya chocoensis. No. 549, Odontoglossum crispum. No. 550, Cattleya dowiana aurea. 10c, Cattleya labiata trianae.

Engraved and Lithographed

1947, Feb. 7 Wmk. 255 *Perf. 12*

546	A222	1c multi	45	18
547	A222	2c multi	45	18
548	A222	5c multi	1.40	18
549	A222	5c multi	1.40	18
550	A222	5c multi	1.40	18
551	A222	10c multi	2.25	60
		Nos. 546-551 (6)	7.35	1.50

Antonio Nariño A228

Alberto Urdaneta y Urdaneta A229

Perf. 12½

1947, May 9 Litho. Unwmk.

552	A228	5c bl, *grnsh*	40	22
553	A229	10c red brn, *grnsh*	50	22

Issued to commemorate the 4th Pan-American Press Congress, 1946. See also Nos. C146-C147.

Sucre Type of 1940.

1947 Wmk. 255 Engr. *Perf. 12.*

554	A198	1p violet	3.25	1.50

José Celestino Mutis and José Jeronimo Triana A230

Miguel A. Caro and Rufino J. Cuervo — A231

1947 Wmk. 229 *Perf. 12½*

555	A230	25c ol grn	85	40
556	A231	3p dk pur	5.75	4.00

See also Nos. 567, 569.

Metropolitan Cathedral, Plaza Bolivar, Bogota — A232

National Capitol A233

Ministry of Foreign Affairs A234

A235

1948, Apr. 2

557	A232	5c blk brn	15	5
558	A233	10c orange	85	75
559	A234	15c dk bl	85	75
		Nos. 557-559,C148-C149 (5)	3.40	2.85

Miniature Sheet

Imperf

560	A235	50c slate	2.25	2.25

Nos. 557-560 commemorate the 9th Pan-American Conference, Bogota. No. 560 measures 90½x90½mm.

No. RA5A Overprinted in Black

1948 Unwmk. *Perf. 12½*

Without Gum.

561	PT3	1c yel org	10	5

The letter "C" is the initial of "CORREOS".

Nos. RA33, RA24 and RA25 Overprinted in Black

CORREOS

1948 Wmk. 255 *Perf. 12.*

562	PT6	1c olive	6	5
563	PT6	2c green	6	5
564	PT6	20c brown	25	5

Nos. 561-564 exist with inverted and double overprints.

Observatory Type of 1946.

Unwmk.

1948, June 30 Litho. *Perf. 11*

565	A218	5c blue	30	6

Simón Bolivar A236

Carlos Martinez Silva A237

Wmk. 255

1948, May 29 Engr. *Perf. 12*

566	A236	15c green	60	25

Types of 1946-47.

1948 Unwmk. *Perf. 12½*

567	A230	25c green	30	12
568	A220	2p dp grn	80	18
569	A231	3p dp red vio	1.00	22

Falls Type of 1937.

1948 Wmk. 229

570	A160	10c red	15	5

Perf. 13½

1948, Dec. 21 Unwmk. Litho.

571	A237	40c carmine	60	35

Juan de Dios Carrasquilla A238

1949, May 20 Wmk. 229 *Perf. 12½*

572	A238	5c bister	22	12

Issued to commemorate the 75th anniversary of the foundation of the Colombian Society of Agriculture.

The Catalogue editors cannot undertake to appraise, identify or judge the genuineness or condition of stamps.

Julio Garavito Armero A239

Arms of Colombia A240

Wmk. 229

1949, Apr. 24 Engr. *Perf. 12*

573	A239	4c green	45	22

Issued to honor Julio Garavito Armero (1865-1920), mathematician.

Coffee Type of 1939.
Imprint: "American Bank Note Co."

1949, Aug. 4 Wmk. 255

574	A176	5c blue	15	5

1949, Oct. 7 Unwmk. *Perf. 13*

575	A240	15c blue	25	6

Issued to honor the new Constitution. See also Nos. C164-C165.

Shield and Tree A241

Francisco Javier Cisneros A242

1949, Oct. 13 Wmk. 229 *Perf. 12½*

576	A241	5c olive	15	5

Issued to commemorate the 4th anniversary of Colombia's first Forestry Congress and as propaganda for the government's reforestation program.

1949, Dec. 15 Photo. Unwmk.

577	A242	50c red vio & yel	1.50	85
578	A242	50c grn & vio	1.50	85
579	A242	50c brn & lt bl	1.50	85

Issued to commemorate the 50th anniversary (in 1948) of the death of Francisco Javier Cisneros.

Masdevallia Chimaera — A243

Odontoglossum Crispum A244

Eastern Hemisphere — A245

Designs: 3c, Cattleya labiata trianae. 4c, Masdevallia nycterina. 5c, Cattleya dowiana aurea. 11c, Miltonia vexillaria. 18c, Santo Domingo post office.

1950, Aug. 22 Photo. *Perf. 13*

580	A243	1c brown	22	15
581	A244	2c violet	22	15
582	A243	3c rose lil	28	15
583	A243	4c emerald	40	15
584	A243	5c red org	1.10	15
585	A244	11c red	2.50	2.10
586	A244	18c ultra	2.00	90
		Nos. 580-586 (7)	6.72	3.75

Miniature Sheet

Imperf

587	A245	50c org yel	1.85	1.85

Nos. 580-587 commemorate the 75th anniversary (in 1949) of the formation of the Universal Postal Union. No. 587 measures 91x90mm. See No. C199.

Antonio Baraya — A246

Perf. 12½

1950, Nov. 27 Unwmk. Engr.

588	A246	2c red	10	5

Colombian Farm A247

1950, Dec. 28 Photo. *Perf. 11½*

589	A247	5c dp car & buff	30	10
590	A247	5c bl grn & gray	30	10
591	A247	5c vio bl & gray	30	10

Issued to publicize rural life.

Arms of Bogota A248

Arms of Colombia A249

Perf. 12x12½

1950, Dec. 28 Engr. Wmk. 255

592	A248	5p dp grn	3.75	55
593	A249	10p red org	11.00	65

Map and Badge A250

Guillermo Valencia A251

Perf. 12½x13

1951, Jan. 30 Photo. Unwmk.

594	A250	20c red, yel & bl	60	22

Issued to commemorate the 60th anniversary (in 1947) of the formation of the Colombian Society of Engineers.

1951, Oct. 20 Engr. *Perf. 13x13½*

595	A251	25c black	1.40	30

Issued to honor Guillermo Valencia (1873-1943), newspaper founder, governor of Cauca, presidential candidate, author.

No. 468 Overprinted in Black

REVERSION
CONCESION MARES
25 Agosto 1951

1951, Dec. 11 Wmk. 255 *Perf. 12*

596	A155	2c car rose	10	6

Issued to publicize the reversion of the Mares oil concession to Columbia.

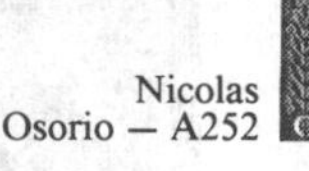

Nicolas Osorio — A252

Portraits: No. 598, Pompilio Martinez. No. 599, Ezequiel Uriocoechea. No. 600, Jose M. Lombana.

Perf. 11½

1952, Aug. 6 Unwmk. Engr.

Various Frames.

597	A252	1c dp bl	10	6
598	A252	1c dp bl	10	6
599	A252	1c dp bl	10	6
600	A252	1c dp bl	10	6

Nos. 597-600 were printed in a single sheet containing four panes of twenty-five each, separated by double rows of ornamental tabs. Although inscribed "sobretasa," the stamps were for ordinary postage.

Types of Postal Tax Stamps of 1945-50 and

Communications Building
A253 A253a

1952 *Perf. 12*

601	A253	5c ultra	22	6

Wmk. 255.

602	PT10	20c brown	6.75	22
603	PT6	25c dk gray	7.50	2.25
604	PT10	25c bl grn	60	10
605	A253a	50c org yel	26.00	12.00
606	A253a	1p rose car	2.00	45
607	A253a	2p lil rose	25.00	6.50
608	A253a	2p violet	1.50	70
		Nos. 601-608 (8)	69.57	22.28

Although inscribed "sobretasa," Nos. 601-608 were issued for ordinary postage.

Cathedral of Manizales — A254

Perf. 11½

1952, Oct. 10 Photo. Unwmk.

609	A254	23c bl & gray blk	40	30

Centenary of city of Manizales.

No. 555 Surcharged in Blue

1a CONFERENCIA 1952 SIDERURGICA
LATINO-AMERICANA.
15

1952, Oct. 30 Wmk. 229 *Perf. 12½*

610	A230	15c on 25c ol grn	45	30

Issued to publicize the Latin American Siderurgical Conference, 1952. See also No. C226.

Queen Isabella I and Monument — A255

Perf. 12½

1953, Mar. 10 Unwmk. Engr.

611	A255	23c bl & blk	90	75

Issued to commemorate the fifth centenary of the birth of Queen Isabella I of Spain.

Nos. 606 and 568 Surcharged with New Values in Dark Blue

1953, Oct. 19 Wmk. 255

612	A253a	40c on 1p rose car	1.40	22
613	A220	50c on 2p dp grn	1.40	22

Manuel Ancizar — A256

Portraits: 23c, José Jeronimo Triana. 30c, Manuel Ponce de Leon. 1p, Agustin Codazzi.

Perf. 12½x13

1953, Nov. Engr. Unwmk.

Frames in Black.

614	A256	14c rose red	50	50
615	A256	23c ultra	50	30
616	A256	30c chocolate	45	20
617	A256	1p emerald	45	15

Issued to commemorate the centenary (in 1950) of the establishment of the Chorographic Commission. See also Nos. 687, 690, 692.

Murillo Toro and Map — A257

Engraved and Lithographed

1953, Dec. 12 Wmk. 255 *Perf. 12*

Black Surcharge.

618	A257	5c on 5p multi	38	22

Issued to publicize the 2nd National Philatelic Exhibition, Bogota, December 1953. See also No. C237.

Nos. 609 and 614 Surcharged with New Value or New Value and Ornaments.

1953 Unwmk. *Perf. 11½, 12½x13.*

619	A254	5c on 23c bl & gray blk (C)	45	30
620	A256	5c on 14c blk & rose red (Bk)	45	40

No. 614 surcharged "CINCO" in blue is listed as No. 687.

Symbolical of St. Francis Receiving Christ's Wounds — A258

1954, Apr. 23 Photo. *Perf. 11½*

621	A258	5c sep & grn	25	10

Issued to commemorate the 400th anniversary of the establishment of Colombia's first Franciscan community.

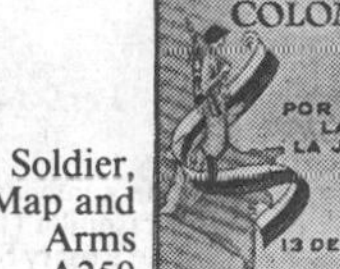

Soldier, Map and Arms A259

1954, June 13 Engr. *Perf. 13*

622	A259	5c dl bl	25	10

Issued to commemorate the first anniversary of the assumption of the presidency by Gen. Gustavo Rojas Pinilla. See also Nos. C255, 637a.

Sports Emblem — A260

Design: 10c, Stadium and athlete holding arms of Colombia.

1954, July 18 Unwmk.

623	A260	5c dp bl	50	22
624	A260	10c red	85	22

Issued to publicize the 7th National Athletic Games, Cali, July 1954. See also Nos. C256-C257.

History Academy Seal — A261

1954, July 24

625	A261	5c ultra & grn	22	10

Issued to commemorate the 50th anniversary (in 1952) of the Colombian Academy of History.

Convent and Cell of St. Peter Claver A262

1954, Sept. 9

627	A262	5c dk grn	20	10
a.		Souvenir sheet	3.25	3.25

Issued to commemorate the 300th anniversary of the death of St. Peter Claver.

No. 627a contains one stamp similar to No. 627, but printed in greenish black. Marginal inscriptions in black. Sheet size: 121x129½mm. See also Nos. C258-C258a.

Mercury — A263

1954, Oct. 29

628	A263	5c orange	40	10

Issued to publicize the first International Fair and Exhibition, Bogota, 1954. See Nos. C259-C260.

Tapestry Madonna A264

College Cloister A265

Designs: 10c, Brother Cristobal de Torres. 20c, College chapel and arms.

Perf. 12½x11½, 11½x12½

1954, Dec. 6

629	A264	5c org & blk	40	18
630	A264	10c blue	40	18
631	A265	15c vio brn	45	18
632	A265	20c blk & brn	90	35
a.		Souvenir sheet	6.25	6.25
Nos. 629-632,C263-C266 (8)			5.85	2.51

Issued to commemorate the 300th anniversary (in 1953) of the founding of the Senior College of Our Lady of the Rosary, Bogota.

No. 632a contains four stamps similar to Nos. 629-632, but printed in different colors: 5c yellow and black, 10c green, 15c dull violet, 20c black and light-blue. Marginal inscriptions in black. Sheet size: 124½x130½mm.

Steel Mill — A266

Jose Marti — A267

1954, Dec. 12 *Perf. 12½x13*

633	A266	5c ultra & blk	30	10

Issued to mark the opening of the Paz del Rio steel mill, October 1954. See No. C267.

1955, Jan. 28 *Perf. 13½x13*

634	A267	5c dp car	20	10

Issued to commemorate the centenary of the birth of José Marti (1853-1895), Cuban patriot. See No. C268.

Arms, Flags and Soldiers Building Bridge A268

1955, Mar. 23 *Perf. 12½*

635	A268	10c claret	25	10

Issued to honor Colombian soldiers who served in Korea, 1951-53. See Nos. 637a, C269.

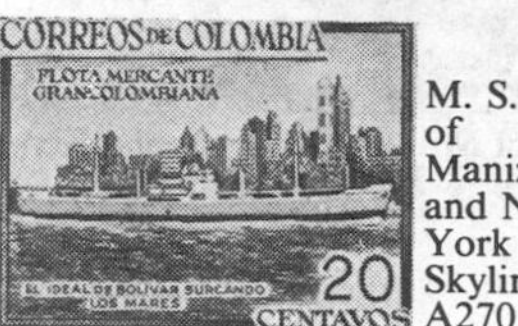

Fleet Emblem — A269

M. S. City of Manizales and New York Skyline A270

1955, Apr. 12 Unwmk.

636	A269	15c dp grn	25	10
637	A270	20c violet	25	10
a.		Souvenir sheet	6.25	6.25

Issued to honor the Grand-Colombian Merchant Fleet. See Nos. C270-271a.

No. 637a contains four stamps similar to Nos. 622, 635-637, but printed in different colors: 5c blue, 10c dark carmine, 15c green, 20c purple. Marginal inscriptions in black. Sheet size: 125x131mm.

Hotel Tequendama and Church of San Diego A271

1955, May 16 Photo. *Perf. 11½x12*

638	A271	5c blue	15	5

See also No. C273.

Bolivar's Country Estate, Bogota A272

1955, Sept. 28 Engr. *Perf. 12½*

639	A272	5c dp ultra	15	5

Issued to commemorate the 50th anniversary of Rotary International. See No. C274.

Belalcazar, Jimenez de Quesada and Balboa A273

Caravels and Columbus A274

Design: 5c, San Martin, Bolivar and Washington.

Engraved and Photogravure

1955, Oct. 29 *Perf. 13x12½*

640	A273	2c yel grn & brn	10	6
641	A273	5c brt bl & brn	22	6
642	A274	23c lt ultra & blk	25	22
a.		Souvenir sheet	7.25	7.25
Nos. 640-642,C275-C280 (9)			16.62	10.59

Issued to publicize the seventh Congress of the Postal Union of the Americas and Spain, Bogota, Oct. 12.-Nov. 9, 1955.

No. 642a contains one each of Nos. 640-642, printed in slightly different shades. It measures 120x132 mm. and is inscribed in black: "Ministerio de Comunicaciones. III Exposicion Filatelica Nacional Bogota 1955."

José Eusebio Caro — A275

1955, Nov. 29 Engr. *Perf. 13½x13*

643	A275	5c brown	12	6

Issued to commemorate the centenary of the death of José Eusebio Caro (1817-1853), poet. See also No. C281.

Departmental Issue

Map — A276

View of San Andres Harbor — A277

Cattle at Waterhole A278

Designs: 2c, Docks, Atlantico. 3c, "Industry," Antioquia. 4c, Cartagena Harbor, Bolivar. No. 647, Steel Mill, Boyaca. No. 648, Cattle, Cordoba. No. 649, Map. No. 650, San Andres Harbor. No. 651, Cacao picker, Cauca. 10c, Coffee picker, Caldas. 15c, Salt Mine Chapel, Zipaquira, Cundinamarca. 20c, Tropical plants and map, Choco. 23c, Harvester, Huila. 25c, Banana Plantation, Magdalena. 30c, Gold mining, Nariño. 40c, Tobacco plantation, Santander. 50c, Oil wells, North Santander. 60c, Cotton plantation, Tolima. 1p, Sugar industry, Cauca. 3p, Amazon river at Leticia, Amazonas. 5p, Windmills and panoramic view, La Guajira. 10p, Rubber plantation, Vaupes.

Engraved; Engraved and Lithographed
Perf. 13½x13, 13x13½, 13

1956 **Unwmk.**

Various Frames.

644	A277	2c car & grn	10	5
645	A276	3c brn vio & blk	10	5
646	A277	4c grn & blk	10	5
647	A276	5c dk brn & bl	20	6
648	A277	5c ol & dk vio brn	35	5
649	A276	5c bl & blk	30	5
650	A277	5c car & grnsh bl	25	5
651	A277	5c ol grn & red brn	25	5
652	A276	10c org & blk	25	6
653	A276	15c ultra & blk	30	10
654	A276	20c dk brn & bl	25	10
655	A277	23c ultra & ver	30	25
656	A277	25c ol grn & blk	30	25
657	A277	30c ultra & brn	25	5
658	A277	40c dl pur & red brn	25	5
659	A277	50c dk grn & blk	25	5
660	A277	60c pale brn & grn	25	5
661	A278	1p mag & grnsh bl	2.00	25
662	A278	2p grn & red brn	2.50	30
663	A278	3p car & blk	3.25	50
664	A278	5p brn & lt ultra	5.00	1.25
665	A276	10p red brn & grn	14.00	6.25
		Nos. 644-665 (22)	30.80	9.92

Nos. 645, 647, 649, 652-654 measure 27x32mm. No. 665 measures 27x37mm. See also Nos. 681-684, 685, 688-689.

Columbus and Proposed Lighthouse A279

1956, Oct. 12 **Photo.** ***Perf. 12***
666 A279 3c gray blk 15 10

Issued in honor of Christopher Columbus. See also Nos. C285, C306.

Altar of St. Elizabeth and Tomb of Jimenez de Quesada A280

1956, Nov. 19 **Unwmk.**
667 A280 5c red lil 15 10

Issued to commemorate the 7th centenary of St. Elizabeth of Hungary, patron saint of Sante Fe de Bogota. See No. C286.

St. Ignatius of Loyola — A281

Javier Pereira — A282

1956, Nov. 26 **Engr.** ***Perf. 12½x13***
668 A281 5c blue 25 8

Issued to commemorate the 400th anniversary of the death of St. Ignatius of Loyola. See No. C287.

1956, Dec. 28 **Unwmk.** ***Perf. 12***
669 A282 5c blue 15 5

Issued to honor 167-year-old Javier Pereira. See No. C288.

Emblem and Dairy Farm A283

Designs: 2c, Emblem and tractor. 5c, Emblem, coffee and corn.

1957, Mar. 5 **Photo.** ***Perf. 14x13½***

670	A283	1c lt ol grn	6	5
671	A283	2c lt brn	6	5
672	A283	5c lt bl	15	7
		Nos. 670-672,C292-C296 (8)	1.97	1.15

25th anniversary of the Agrarian Savings Bank of Colombia.

Arms of Military Academy and Gen. Rafael Reyes A284

Design: 10c, Arms and Academy.

1957, July 20 **Engr.** ***Perf. 12½***

673	A284	5c blue	15	5
674	A284	10c orange	15	5
a.		Souv. sheet of 2	15.00	15.00

Issued to commemorate the 50th anniversary of the Colombian Military Academy. See Nos. C299-C300.

No. 674a contains one each of Nos. 673-674 in slightly different shades. It measures 120x131½mm. with marginal inscriptions in black.

Statue of José Matias Delgado — A285

1957, Sept. 16 **Photo.** ***Perf. 12***
675 A285 2c rose brn 6 5

Issued in honor of Jose Matias Delgado, liberator of El Salvador. See No. C301.

Santo Michelena, Marcos V. Crespo, P. Alcantara Herran and UPU Monument A286

1957, Oct. 10 **Unwmk.**

676	A286	5c green	15	10
677	A286	10c gray	15	5

Issued for International Letter Writing Week and the 14th UPU Congress. See Nos. C302-C303.

St. Vincent de Paul and Children — A287

1957, Oct. 18
678 A287 1c dk ol grn 5 5

Issued to commemorate the centenary of the Colombian Society of St. Vincent de Paul. See No. C304.

Fencer A288

1957, Nov. 22 **Photo.** ***Perf. 12***
679 A288 4c lilac 15 10

Issued to commemorate the third South American Fencing Championship. See No. C305.

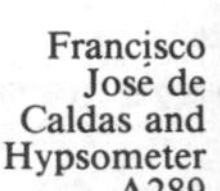

Francisco José de Caldas and Hypsometer A289

1958, May 12 **Unwmk.** ***Perf. 12***
680 A289 10c black 35 10

Issued for the International Geophysical Year, 1957-58. See Nos. C309-C310.

Departmental Issue.
Type of 1956

Designs as Before.

1958 **Engr.** ***Perf. 13***

681	A276	3c ultra & brn	10	5
682	A276	3c ol grn & pur	10	5
683	A276	10c grn & brn	20	5
684	A276	10c dk bl & brn	20	5

Nos. 646, C291, 614, 653, 655, 616, C308, 615 and 611 Surcharged with New Value, and Old Value Obliterated, or Overprinted in Dark Blue or Green.

Perf. 12½, 12½x13, 13.

1958-59 **Unwmk.**

685	A277	2c on 4c grn & blk	15	5
686	AP48	5c dp plum & multi ('59)	15	10
687	A256	5c on 14c blk & rose red ("CINCO") ('59)	45	38
688	A276	5c on 15c ultra & blk	15	5
689	A277	5c on 23c ultra & ver (G)	35	25
690	A256	5c on 30c blk & choc	15	10
691	AP40	10c on 25c rose vio	15	5
692	A256	20c on 23c blk & ultra (G) ('59)	35	30
693	A255	20c on 23c bl & blk ('59)	35	30
		Nos. 685-693 (9)	2.25	1.58

On No. 686 the words "Correo Extra Rapido" are obliterated in dark blue.

Father Rafael Almanza and Church of San Diego, Bogota A290

1958, Oct. 23 **Photo.** ***Perf. 14x13***
695 A290 10c purple 15 5

See also Nos. C313-C314.

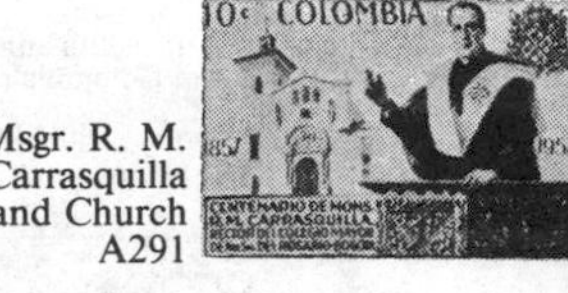

Msgr. R. M. Carrasquilla and Church A291

1959, Jan. 22 ***Perf. 14x13***
696 A291 10c dk red brn 20 5

Issued to commemorate the centenary of the birth of Msgr. R. M. Carrasquilla (1857-1930), rector of Our Lady of the Rosary Seminary, Bogota. See Nos. C315-C316.

Miss Universe 1959 A292

Jorge Eliecer Gaitan A293

1959, June 26 **Photo.** ***Perf. 11½***
697 A292 10c multi 10 5

Issued to honor Luz Marina Zuluaga, Miss Universe, 1959. See Nos. C317-C318.

1959, July 28 **Engr.** ***Perf. 12x13½***

698	A293	10c on 3c gray bl (Bl)	20	5
699	A293	30c rose vio	50	20

Issued in honor of Jorge Eliecer Gaitan (1898-1948), lawyer and politician.

No. 698 exists without blue surcharge.

See also Nos. C319-C320.

Gen. Francisco de Paula Santander — A294

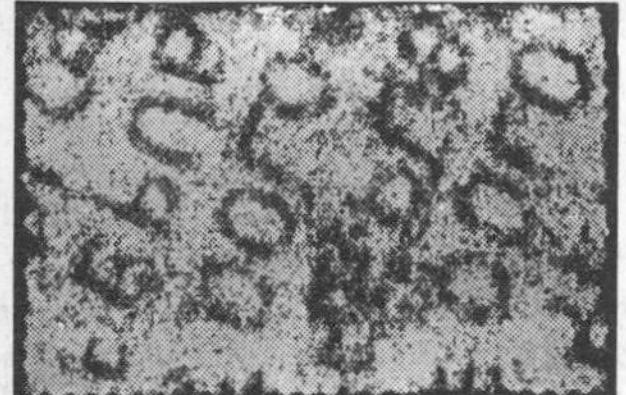
Wmk. 331

Designs: Nos. 701, 703, Simon Bolivar.

Wmk. "REPUBLICA DE COLOMBIA". (331)

1959 Litho. *Perf. 12½*
700 A294 5c brn & yel 15 10
701 A294 5c ultra & bl 15 10
702 A294 10c gray & grn 20 10
703 A294 10c gray & red 20 10

See also No. C389.

Capitol, Bogota A295

1959
704 A295 2c dk bl & red brn 12 10
705 A295 3c blk brn & lil 12 10

Stamp of 1859 and Mail Transport by Mule — A296

Two-Toed Sloth — A297

Designs (various stamps of 1859 and): 10c, Mail boat on the Magdalena river. 25c, Train.

Unwmk.

1959, Dec. 1 Photo. *Perf. 12*
709 A296 5c org & grn 20 15
710 A296 10c rose cl & bl 20 15
711 A296 15c car rose & grn 45 45
712 A296 25c bl & red brn 60 55
Nos. 709-712,C351-C354 (8) 6.10 4.10

Centenary of Colombian postage stamps.

1960, Feb. 12 *Perf. 12*

Designs: 10c, Alexander von Humboldt. 20c, Spider monkey.

713 A297 5c grnsh bl & brn 20 10
714 A297 10c blk & dp car 25 5
715 A297 20c cit & gray brn 20 5
Nos. 713-715,C357-C359 (6) 6.40 4.50

Issued to commemorate the centenary of the death of Alexander von Humboldt (1769-1859), German naturalist and geographer.

Anthurium Andreanum A298

Lincoln Statue, Washington A299

Flower: 20c, Espeletia grandiflora.

1960, May 10
716 A298 5c multi 15 15
717 A298 20c brn, yel & gray ol 10 10
Nos. 716-717,C360-C370 (13) 16.20 15.19

See also Nos. C420-C425.

Wmk. 331

1960, June 10 Litho. *Perf. 10½*
718 A299 20c rose lil & blk 30 20

Issued to commemorate the sesquicentennial of the birth of Abraham Lincoln (1809-1865). See also Nos. C375-C376.

Floredo House, Cradle of the Republic A300

Arms of Santa Cruz de Mompox — A301

Design: 5c, First coins of Republic.

Unwmk.

1960, July 19 Photo. *Perf. 12*
719 A301 5c grn & ocher 10 10
720 A300 20c ol bis & mar 10 10
721 A301 20c multi 20 30
Nos. 719-721,C377-C385 (12) 8.20 6.15

Issued to commemorate the 150th anniversary of Colombia's independence.

St. Isidro and Farm Animals — A302

Design: 20c, Nativity by Gregorio de Arce Vasquez y Ceballos.

1960, Sept. 26 *Perf. 12*
722 A302 10c multi 15 10
723 A302 20c multi 22 10

Issued to honor St. Isidro the Farmer, patron saint of the rural people.
See also Nos. 747, C387-C388, C439-C440.

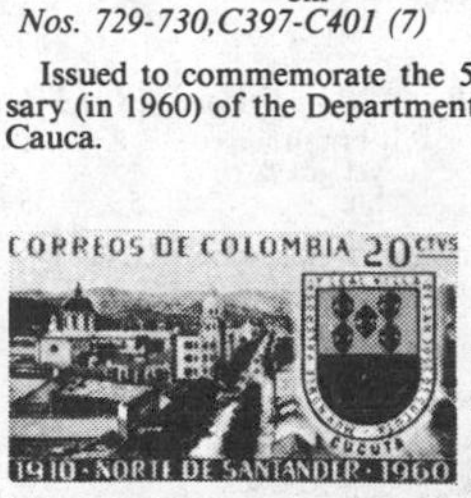

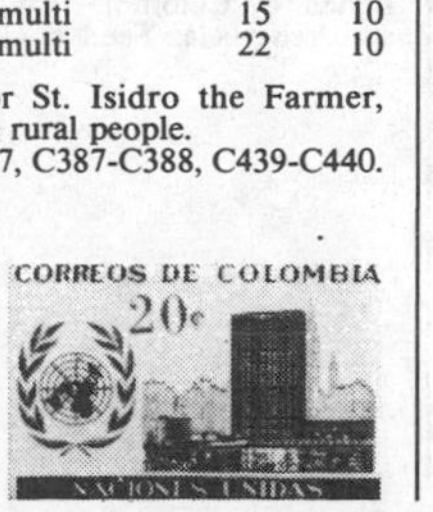

View of Cucuta and Arms A308

Wmk. 331

1960, Oct. 24 Litho. *Perf. 11*
724 A303 20c blk & pink 22 15

Souvenir Sheet

Imperf

725 A303 50c dk brn, brt grn & blk 3.50 3.50

15th anniversary of the United Nations. No. 725 contains one stamp and has dark brown marginal inscription and black number. Size: 55x48½mm.

Pan-American Highway through Colombia A304

Alfonso Lopez A305

Perf. 10½x11

1961, Mar. 7 Unwmk.
726 A304 20c brn & grnsh bl 90 80
Nos. 726,C390-C393 (5) 4.30 3.80

Issued to commemorate the 8th Pan-American Highway Congress, Bogota, May 20-29, 1960.

1961, Mar. 22 Photo. *Perf. 12½*
727 A305 10c brt rose & brn 25 15
728 A305 20c vio & brn 25 15

Issued to honor Alfonso Lopez (1886-1959), President of Colombia. See Nos. C394-C396.

Cauca River Bridge, Cali A306

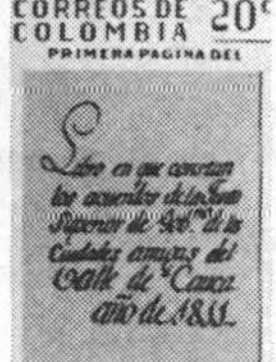

Page from Resolutions of Confederated Cities — A307

1961-62 *Perf. 12½x13, 13½x13*
729 A306 10c red brn, bl, grn & red ('62) 15 6
730 A307 20c pale brn & blk 20 7
Nos. 729-730,C397-C401 (7) 4.00 1.67

Issued to commemorate the 50th anniversary (in 1960) of the Department of Valle del Cauca.

Design: No. 732, Arms of Ocana and Pamplona.

1961, Aug. 29 *Perf. 13x13½*
731 A308 20c bl, blk, yel & red 15 6
732 A308 20c ocher, ultra & red 15 6

Issued to commemorate the 50th anniversary (in 1960) of the Department of North Santander. See Nos. C402-C403.

Arms of Popayan A309

Basketball A310

Designs: No. 734, Arms of Barranquilla. No. 735, Arms of Bucaramanga.

Perf. 12½x13

1961, Oct. 10 Unwmk.

Arms in Multicolor
733 A309 10c bl & sil 15 7
734 A309 20c bl & yel 15 7
735 A309 20c bl & gold 15 7
Nos. 733-735,C404-C408 (8) 3.40 88

Issued to honor Atlantico Department.

1961, Dec. 16 Litho. *Perf. 13½x14*
736 A310 20c *shown* 10 5
737 A310 20c *Runners* 10 5
738 A310 20c *Boxers* 35 15
739 A310 25c *Soccer* 20 7
Nos. 736-739,C414-C418 (9) 4.00 1.32

4th Bolivarian Games, Barranquilla, 1961.

Colombian Anti-Malaria Emblem — A311

Engineers Society Emblem — A312

Design: 50c, Malaria eradication emblem and mosquito in swamp.

1962, Apr. 12 Unwmk. *Perf. 12*
740 A311 20c lt bis & red 22 20
741 A311 50c bis & ultra 25 15
Nos. 740-741,C426-C428 (5) 6.72 6.45

Issued for the World Health Organization drive to eradicate malaria.

1962, June 12 Photo. *Perf. 11½x12*
742 A312 10c multi 30 30
Nos. 742,C429-C432 (5) 3.50 3.30

Issued to commemorate the 75th anniversary of the Colombian Society of Engineers.

Flags of American Nations A313

Woman Casting Ballot and Statue of Policarpa Salavarrieta A314

1962, June 28 ***Perf. 13***

Flags in National Colors

743 A313 25c blk & org ver 15 5

Souvenir Sheet

744 A313 2.50p blk & yel 4.50 4.50

Issued to commemorate the 70th anniversary of the founding of the Organization of American States.

No. 744 contains one stamp, black marginal inscription. Size: 45x55mm.

See also No. C433.

Perf. 12x12½

1962, July 20 Litho. Wmk. 229

745 A314 10c lt bl, gray & blk 10 5

Issued to publicize women's political rights. See also Nos. 752, C434, C448-C450.

Scouts at Campfire and Tents A315

Railroad Map of Colombia A316

Perf. 11½x12

1962, July 28 Photo. Unwmk.

746 A315 10c brt grnsh bl & brn 45 38

Nos. 746,C435-C438 (5) 8.00 6.93

Issued to commemorate the 30th anniversary of the Colombian Boy Scouts.

St. Isidro Type of 1960 Redrawn

1962, Aug. 28 ***Perf. 12***

747 A302 10c pink & multi 15 8

The frame on No. 747 is solid color with white inscription similar to type AP82. See also Nos. C439-C440.

1962, Sept. 28 ***Perf. 12½***

748 A316 10c blk, gray, grn & red 15 5

Nos. 748,C441-C444 (5) 7.75 2.85

Issued to publicize the progress of Colombian railroads and to commemorate the completion of the Atlantic Line from Santa Marta to Bogota.

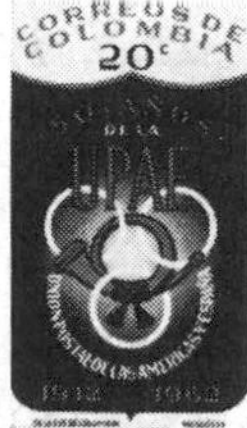

Post Horn — A317

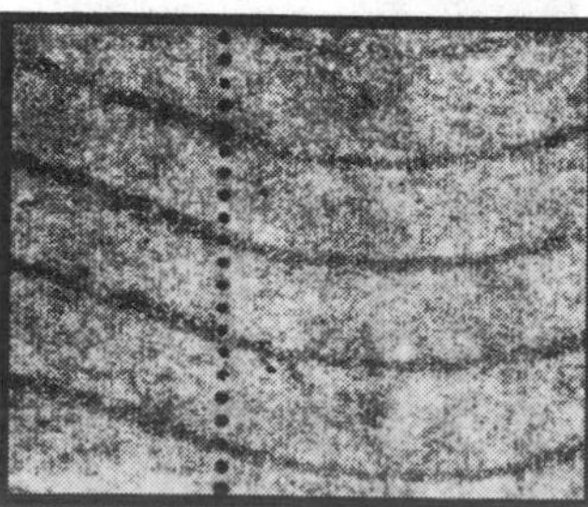

Wmk. 346

The indexes in each volume of the Scott Catalogue contain many listings which help to identify stamps.

Wmk. Parallel Curved Lines. (346)

1962, Oct. 18 Litho. ***Perf. 13½x14***

749 A317 20c gold, dl gray vio & blk 22 5

Issued to commemorate the 50th anniversary of the founding of the Postal Union of the Americas and Spain, UPAE.

See also Nos. C445-C446.

"Virgin of the Rock" A318

Red Cross Centenary Emblem A319

1963, Mar. 11 Wmk. 346

750 A318 60c multi 25 5

Issued to commemorate Vatican II, the 21st Ecumenical Council of the Roman Catholic Church. See also No. C447.

1963, May 1 ***Perf. 12x12½***

751 A319 5c ol bis & red 10 5

Centenary of International Red Cross.

Women's Rights Type of 1962

1963, July 11 Wmk. 346

752 A314 5c org, gray & blk 6 5

See also Nos. C448-C450.

Manuel Mejia J. and Flag of National Coffee Growers Assn. A320

Perf. 12½x13

1965, Feb. 10 Engr. Unwmk.

753 A320 25c rose & blk 25 5

Issued to honor Manuel Mejia J. (1887-1958), banker and manager of the National Coffee Growers Association. See Nos. C464-C466.

Julio Arboleda A321

1966, Mar. 9 Litho. ***Perf. 14x13½***

754 A321 5c lt brn, lt yel grn & blk 5 5

Issued to honor Julio Arboleda (1817-1862), writer, soldier and statesman.

Spanish Galleon, 16th Century A322

History of Maritime Mail: 15c, Rio Hacha brigantine, 1850. 20c, Uraba canoe. 40c, Magdalena River steamship and barge, 1900. 50c, Modern motor ship and sea gull.

1966, June 16 Photo. Unwmk.

755 A322 5c org & multi 10 6

756 A322 15c car rose, blk & brn 15 6

757 A322 20c brt grn, org & blk 15 6

758 A322 40c dp bl & multi 25 10

759 A322 50c pale bl & multi 65 35

Nos. 755-759 (5) 1.30 63

Plumed Hogfish A323

Design: 10p, Bat ray and brittle starfish.

1966, Aug. 25 Photo. ***Perf. 12½x13***

760 A323 80c multi 25 10

761 A323 10p multi 7.25 6.75

Nos. 760-761,C481-C483 (5) 22.00 21.05

Arms of Venezuela, Colombia and Chile A324

1966, Oct. 11 Litho. ***Perf. 14x13½***

762 A324 40c yel & multi 15 7

Issued to commemorate the visits of Eduardo Frei and Raul Leoni, presidents of Chile and Venezuela. See Nos. C484-C485.

Camilo Torres, 1766-1816, Lawyer — A325

Portraits: 60c, Jorge Tadeo Lozano (1771-1816), naturalist. 1p, Francisco Antonio Zea (1776-1822), naturalist and politician.

Perf. 13½x14

1967, Jan. 18 Litho. Unwmk.

763 A325 25c vio & bis 5 5

764 A325 60c dk red brn & bis 10 5

765 A325 1p grn & bis 50 25

Nos. 763-765,C486-C487 (5) 1.15 55

Issued to honor famous men of Colombia.

Map of South America and Arms — A326

1967, Feb. 2 Litho. ***Perf. 14x13½***

766 A326 40c multi 20 10

767 A326 60c multi 20 5

Issued to publicize the Declaration of Bogota for cooperation and world peace, signed by Colombia, Chile, Ecuador, Peru and Venezuela. See No. C488.

Monochaetum Orchid and Bee — A327

Orchid: 2p, Passiflora vitifolia and butterfly.

1967, May 23 Litho. ***Perf. 14***

768 A327 25c multi 10 6

769 A327 2p multi 1.25 1.25

Nos. 768-769,C489-C491 (5) 4.53 2.11

Issued to commemorate the First National Orchid Exhibition and the Topical Philatelic Flora and Fauna Exhibition, Medellin, Apr. 1967.

Lions Emblem — A328

SENA Emblem — A329

1967, July 12 Litho. ***Perf. 13½x14***

770 A328 10p multi 4.00 85

Issued to commemorate the 50th anniversary of Lions International. See No. C492.

Lithograph and Embossed

1967, Sept. 20 Unwmk.

771 A329 5p gold, brt grn & blk 1.50 22

Issued to commemorate the 10th anniversary of National Apprenticeship Service, SENA. See No. C494.

Gold Diadem in Calima Style A330

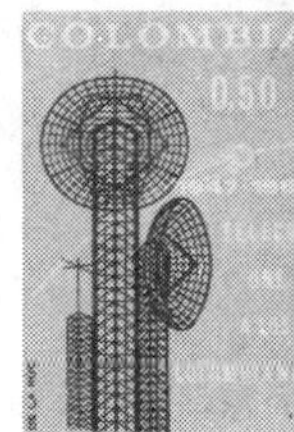

Radar Installation A331

Pre-Columbian Art: 3p, Gold statuette, ornamental globe and bird (horiz.).

Perf. 13½x14, 14x13½

1967, Oct. 13 Photo.

772 A330 1.60p brt rose lil, gold & brn 70 20

773 A330 3p dk bl, gold & brn 1.00 40

Nos. 772-773,C495-C497 (5) 17.40 12.15

Issued to commemorate the meeting of the Universal Postal Union Committee on Postal Studies, Bogota, October, 1967.

1968, May 14 Litho. ***Perf. 13½x14***

Design: 1p, Map of communications network.

774 A331 50c brt yel grn, blk & org brn 15 5

775 A331 1p multi 30 5

Issued to commemorate the 20th anniversary of the National Telecommunications Service (TELECOM). See Nos. C498-C499.

The Eucharist
A332

St. Augustin, by Gregorio Vasquez
A333

1968, June 6 Litho. *Perf. 13½x14*

776 A332 60c multi 15 5

Issued to publicize the 39th Eucharistic Congress, Bogota, Aug. 18-25. See Nos. C500-C501.

1968, Aug. 13 Photo. *Perf. 13*

Designs: 60c, The Gathering of Manna, by Gregorio Vasquez. 1p, The Marriage of the Virgin, by Baltazar de Figueroa. 5p, Jeweled monstrance, c. 1700. 10p, Pope Paul VI, painting by Roman Franciscan nuns.

777	A333	25c multi	5	5
778	A333	60c multi	5	5
779	A333	1p multi	15	6
780	A333	5p multi	80	10
781	A333	10p multi	1.65	50
a.		Souv. sheet of 2	2.75	1.40
Nos. 777-781,C502-C506 (10)			10.45	4.06

Issued to commemorate the 39th Eucharistic Congress. Bogota, Aug. 18-25. No. 781a contains two imperf. stamps similar to Nos. 780-781. Black inscription, Congress emblem in crimson and red control number in margin. Size: 90x89½mm.

Pope Paul VI
A334

Stamp of Antioquia, 1868 — A336

Arms of National University
A335

1968, Aug. 22 Litho. *Perf. 13½x14*

782 A334 25c multi 10 5

Issued to commemorate the visit of Pope Paul VI to Colombia, Aug. 22-24. See Nos. C507-C509.

1968, Oct. 29 Litho. *Perf. 13½x14*

783 A335 80c multi 15 5

Issued to commemorate the centenary of the founding of the National University. See No. C510.

Institute Emblem — A337

1968, Nov. 20 Litho. *Perf. 12x12½*

784 A336 30c emer & bl 20 5

Souvenir Sheet

785 A336 5p lt ol & bl 3.75 3.00

Issued to commemorate the centenary of the first postage stamps of Antioquia and to publicize the 7th National Philatelic Exhibition, Medellin, Nov. 20-29. No. 785 contains one stamp; vermilion margin with white inscription and blue coat of arms and control number. Size: 59x79mm.

1969, Mar. 5 Litho. *Perf. 13½x14*

786 A337 20c multi 15 5

Issued to commemorate the 25th anniversary (in 1967) of the Inter-American Agricultural Sciences Institute. See No. C511.

Battle of Boyaca (Detail), by José Maria Espinosa — A338

Design: 30c, Army of liberation crossing Pisba Pass, by Francisco Antonio Caro.

1969, July 24 Litho. *Perf. 13½x14*

787 A338 20c gold & multi 15 5

788 A338 30c gold & multi 20 5

Issued to commemorate the sesquicentennial of the fight for independence. See No. C517.

"Poverty"
A339

1970, Mar. 1 Litho. *Perf. 14*

789 A339 30c bl & multi 15 5

Issued to publicize the Colombian Institute for Family Welfare and to commemorate the 10th anniversary of the Children's Rights Law.

Greek Mask and Pre-Columbian Symbol of Literary Contest — A340

1970, Sept. 12 Litho. *Perf. 14x13½*

790 A340 30c dk brn, red org & ocher 10 5

Issued to publicize the 3rd Latin American Theatrical Festival of the Universities, Manizales, Sept. 12-20.

Colómbian Stamps, Envelope and Emblem
A341

1970, Sept. 24 Litho. *Perf. 14x13½*

791 A341 2p brt bl & multi 40 5

Issued to publicize Philatelic Week.

Arms of Ibague and Discobolus — A342

1970, Oct. 13

792 A342 80c buff, emer & sep 30 5

9th National Games in Ibague.

St. Theresa, by Baltazar de Figueroa — A343

1970, Oct. 28 Litho. *Perf. 13½x14*

793 A343 2p multi 50 5

Elevation of St. Theresa (1515-1582), to Doctor of the Church. See No. C568.

Casa Cural
A344

1971, May 20 Litho. *Perf. 14x13½*

794 A344 1.10p multi 40 10

Fourth centenary (in 1970) of the founding of Guacari, Valle. See also No. 809.

Dancers and Music, Currulao — A345

Design: 1p, Chicha Maya dancers and music.

1971 Litho. *Perf. 13½x14*

795 A345 1p pink & multi 30 8

796 A345 1.10p lt bl & multi 40 8

Souvenir Sheets

Imperf.

797	A345	Sheet of 3	4.75	4.25
a.		2.50p Napanga	50	50
b.		2.50p Joropo	50	50
c.		5p Guabina	1.00	1.00
798	A345	Sheet of 3	4.75	4.25
a.		4p Bambuco	80	80
b.		4p Cumbia	80	80
c.		4p Currulao	80	80

Size of Nos. 797-798: 78x110mm. Issue dates: No. 795, Dec. 20; No. 796, Aug. 5; Nos. 797-798, Aug. 10.

Constitutional Assembly, by Delgado — A346

1971, Oct. 2 *Perf. 14*

801 A346 80c multi 22 5

Sequicentennial of Gran Colombian Constitutional Assembly in Rosario del Cucuta. See No. C589.

Arrows Emblem — A347

1972, Feb. 24 *Perf. 13½x14*

802 A347 60c blk & gray 40 5

Inter-Governmental Committee on European Migration, 20th anniversary.

Student and World Map
A348

1972, Mar. 15 *Perf. 14x13½*

803 A348 1.10p lt grn & brn 25 5

20th anniversary of ICETEX, an organization which furnishes financial help for educational purposes and for technical studies abroad.

U.N. Emblem, Soldier and Frigate
A349

1972, Apr. 7

804 A349 1.20p lt bl & multi 25 6

20th anniversary of the Colombian Battalion in Korea.

Mother Francisca Josefa del Castillo
A350

Handicraft
A351

1972, Apr. 6 ***Perf. 13½x14***
805 A350 1.20p brn & multi 25 6

Tercentenary (in 1971) of the birth of Mother Francisca Josefa del Castillo, Poor Clare abbess and writer.

1972, Apr. 11
806 A351 1.10p multi 40 15

Colombian artisans. See Nos. C569-C571.

Maxillaria Triloris A352

Emeralds A353

1972, Apr. 20
807 A352 20p grn & multi 5.25 65

10th National Philatelic Exhibition, Medellin.

1972, June 16 Litho. ***Perf. 13½x14***
808 A353 1.10p multi 70 15

Type of 1971

Design: Antonio Nariño House.

1972, June 17 ***Perf. 14x13½***
809 A344 1.10p multi 60 10

4th centenary, town of Leyva.

San Andres and Providencia Islands — A354

1972, June 24 ***Perf. 13½x14***
810 A354 60c bl & multi 20 5

Sesquicentennial of annexation by Colombia of San Andres and Providencia Islands.

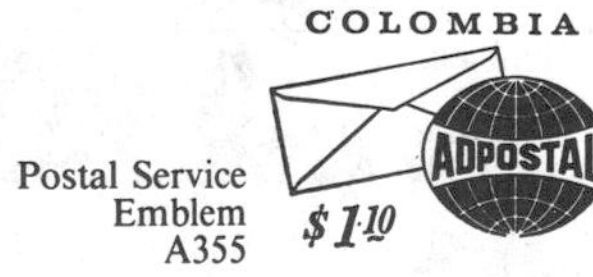

Postal Service Emblem A355

1972, Nov. 15 Litho. ***Perf. 12½x12***
811 A355 1.10p emerald 15 6

Family — A356

1972, Nov. 23
812 A356 60c orange 15 6

Social progress.

Radio League Emblem A357

Human Figure, Tamalameque A358

1973, Apr. 6 Litho. ***Perf. 12x12½***
813 A357 60c lt bl, ultra & red 25 6

40th anniversary of the Colombian Radio Amateurs' League.

1973, June 15 Litho. ***Perf. 13½x14***

Excavated Ceramic Artifacts: 1p, Winged urn, Tairona. 1.10p, Jug, Muisca.

814 A358 60c lt bl & multi 35 10
815 A358 1p org & multi 65 10
816 A358 1.10p vio bl & multi 45 5
Nos. 814-816,C583-C586 (7) 6.00 2.30

Antonio Nariño, by José M. Espinosa — A359

Child — A360

1973, Dec. 13 Litho. ***Perf. 13½x14***
817 A359 60c multi 15 6

Sesquicentennial of the death of General Antonio Nariño (1765-1823).

1973, Dec. 17
818 A360 1.10p multi 22 5

National Campaign for Children's Welfare.

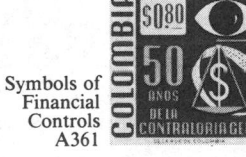

Symbols of Financial Controls A361

1973, Dec. 20 Litho. ***Perf. 14x13½***
819 A361 80c ultra, ocher & blk 15 5

50th anniversary of Comptroller-general's Office.

Mother Laura Montoya — A362

1974, June 18 Litho. ***Perf. 13½x14***
820 A362 1p multi 20 5

Centenary of the birth of Mother Laura Montoya (1874-1949), founder and Mother Superior of the Missionaries of Mary Immaculata and St. Catherine of Siena.

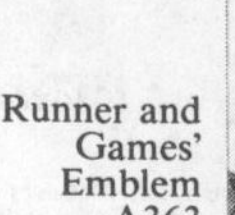

Runner and Games' Emblem A363

1974, July 18 Litho. ***Perf. 14x13½***
821 A363 2p ver, yel & brn 25 10

10th National Games, Pereira.

José Rivera A364

1974, Aug. 3 Litho. ***Perf. 14x13½***
822 A364 10p grn & multi 1.65 15

50th anniversary of the publication of "La Voragine" (The Whirlpool) by José Eustasio Rivera.

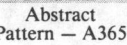

Abstract Pattern — A365

Train Emerging from Tunnel — A366

1974, Oct. 24 Litho. ***Perf. 13½x14***
823 A365 1.10p multi 30 5

Centenary of National Insurance Co. See No. C610.

1974, Nov. 27 Litho. ***Perf. 13½x14***
824 A366 1.10p multi 25 5

Centenary of the Antioquia railroad.

Boy, Puppy and Soccer Ball — A367

Design: 1p, Girl with racket and kitten.

1974, Dec. 9
825 A367 80c multi 20 5
826 A367 1p multi 25 10

Christmas 1974.

Gold Animal A368

Design: 1.10p, Gold necklace.

1975, Apr. 11 Litho. ***Perf. 14x13½***
827 A368 80c ultra, gold & brn 30 6
828 A368 1.10p red, gold & brn 30 6

Pre-Columbian Sinu culture artifacts. See Nos. C621-C622.

Guglielmo Marconi A369

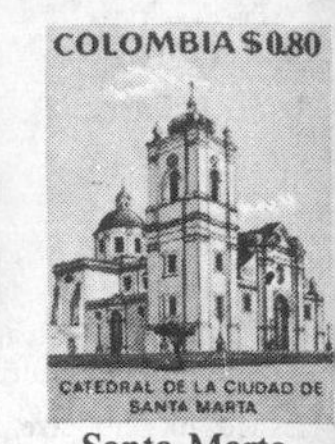

Santa Marta Cathedral A370

1975, June 2 Litho. ***Perf. 13½x14***
829 A369 3p multi 25 10

Birth centenary of Guglielmo Marconi (1874-1937), Italian electrical engineer and inventor.

1975, July 26
830 A370 80c multi 15 5

400th anniversary of Santa Marta City. See No. C623.

Rafael Nuñez — A371

Arms of Medellin — A372

1975, Sept. 28 Litho. ***Perf. 13½x14***
831 A371 1.10p multi 22 6

Rafael Nuñez (1825-1894), philosopher, poet, political leader, birth sesquicentenary.

1975-79 ***Perf. 13½x14, 12 (1.20p)***

832	A372	1p	*Shown*	45	10
833	A372	1.20p	*Ibague* ('76)	22	6
834	A372	1.20p	*Tunja* ('76)	22	5
835	A372	1.50p	*Cucuta*	45	10
836	A372	1.50p	*Cartagena* ('76)	22	5
836A	A372	4p	*Sogamoso* ('79)	70	20
837	A372	5p	*Popayan* ('77)	45	10
838	A372	5p	*Barranquilla* ('77)	40	10
839	A372	10p	*SanGil* ('79)	70	15
839A	A372	10p	*Socorro* ('79)	70	15
			Nos. 832-839A (10)	4.51	1.06

The 1p commemorates the tercentenary of Medellin; No. 835, the centenary of Cucuta's reconstruction.

No. 827 Surcharged **$ 1.20**

1975 ***Perf. 14x13½***
840 A368 1.20p on 80c multi 15 6

A particular stamp may be scarce, but if few collectors want it, its market value may remain relatively low.

Purace Indians, Cauca — A373

1976, Nov. 10 Litho. *Perf. 13½x14*

841 A373 1.50p multi 15 5

Callicore A374

Designs: 5p, Morpho (butterfly). 20p, Anthurium.

1976, Nov. 17 *Perf. 12*

842 A374 3p multi 50 10
843 A374 5p multi 70 15
844 A374 20p multi 2.25 50

Rotary Emblem — A375

1976, Dec. 3 Litho. *Perf. 12*

845 A375 1p multi 15 6

Rotary Club of Colombia, 50th anniversary.

Declaration of Independence, by John Trumbull — A376

1976, Dec. 21 Litho. *Perf. 12*

846 A376 Strip of 3 13.00 15.00
a. 30p, single stamp 4.00 2.00

American Bicentennial. No. 846 printed in sheets of 4 triptychs; black control number in margin showing Bicentennial emblems and personalities of the American Revolution.

Policeman with Dog — A377

1976, Dec. 29 *Perf. 13½x14*

847 A377 1.50p multi 25 5

Honoring the National Police.

Nos. 831, 834, 847 Surcharged in Light Brown

1977, June Litho. *Perf. 13½x14, 12*

848 A371 2p on 1.10p multi 30 5
849 A372 2p on 1.20p multi 22 5
850 A377 2p on 1.50p multi 22 5

Souvenir Sheet

Postal Museum, Bogota — A378

1977, July 27 Litho. *Perf. 14*

855 A378 25p multi 3.25 3.25

Postal Museum, Bogota. No. 855 contains one stamp (50x40mm.); multicolored margin shows Colombian stamps; black control number. Size: 130x105mm.

Mother and Child — A379

1977-78 Litho. *Perf. 12*

856 A379 2p multi 20 5
857 A379 2.50p multi ('78) 1.25 10

National good nutrition plan. Issue dates: 2p, Aug. 30. 2.50p, Jan. 26.

Jacana and Eichhornia A380

Fidel Cano, by Francisco Cano A381

Design: 20p, Mayan cotinga and pyrostegia venusta.

1977, Sept. 6 Litho. *Perf. 14*

858 A380 10p multi 1.00 25
859 A380 20p multi 1.65 38
Nos. 858-859,C644-C647 (6) 5.35 1.37

1977, Sept. 16 *Perf. 14*

860 A381 4p multi 30 5

90th anniversary of El Espectador, newspaper founded by Fidel Cano.

Abacus and Alphabet A382

Cattleya Triannae A383

1977, Sept. 16 *Perf. 13½x14*

861 A382 3p multi 22 6

Popular education.

1978, Apr. 18 Litho. *Perf. 12*

862 A383 2.50p multi 22 5

1979, May 10 Litho. *Perf. 12*

863 A383 3p multi 25 5

Sprinting and Games Emblem A384

Sports: a. sprinting. b. basketball. c. baseball. d. boxing. e. bicycling. f. fencing. g. soccer. h. gymnastics. i. judo. j. weight lifting. k. wrestling. l. swimming. m. tennis. n. target shooting. o. volleyball. p. water polo.

1978, June 27 Litho. *Perf. 14*

868 Sheet of 16 21.00 3.50
a.-p. A384 10p, any single 1.25 20

13th Central American and Caribbean Games, Medellin. No. 863 has black marginal inscription and control number. Size: 200x160mm.

"Sigma 2" by Alvaro Herran A385

1978, June 30

869 A385 8p multi 50 25

Chamber of Commerce, Bogota, centenary.

Gen. Tomás Cipriano de Mosquera A386

1978, Oct. 6 Litho. *Perf. 12*

870 A386 6p multi 60 22

Gen. Tomas Cipriano de Mosquera (1778-1878), statesman.

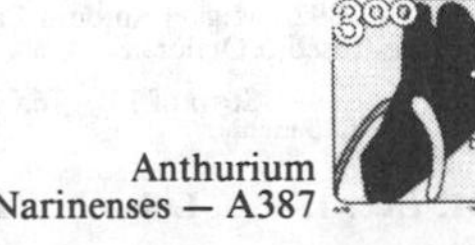
Anthurium Narinenses — A387

1979, July 23 *Perf. 12*

871 A387 3p red & multi 25 6
872 A387 3p pur & multi 25 6
873 A387 3p rose & pur 25 6
874 A387 3p white & multi 25 6

Nos. 871-874 printed in blocks of four, sheets of 100.

Gen. Rafael Uribe, by Acevedo Bernal — A388

1979, Oct. 31 Litho. *Perf. 12*

875 A388 8p multi 50 20

Gen. Rafael Uribe, statesman, 60th death anniversary.

Village, by Leonor Alarcon — A389

1979, Nov. 22 *Perf. 14*

876 A389 15p multi 1.50 50

Community Work Boards, 20th anniversary.

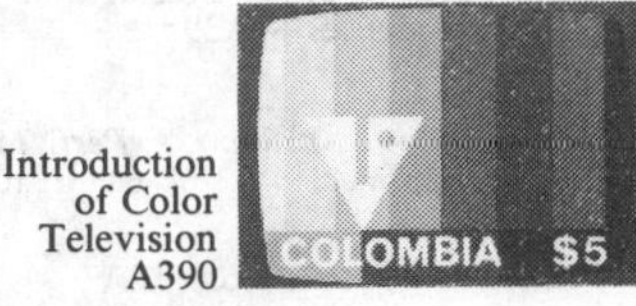
Introduction of Color Television A390

1980, Mar. 4 Litho. *Perf. 14*

877 A390 5p multi 40 10

Bullfight, Arms of Cali — A391

1980, Mar. 25

878 A391 5p multi 60 15

Cali Tourist Festival, Dec. 25, 1979-Jan. 2, 1980.

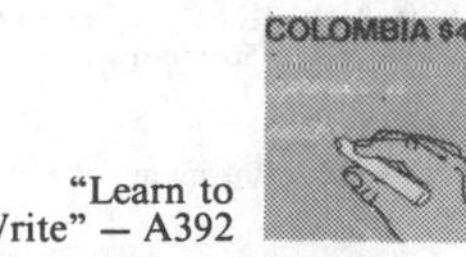
"Learn to Write" — A392

1980, Apr. 25 Litho. *Perf. 12½*

879 Block of 30 9.00 9.00
a. A392 4p, any single 30 8

Each stamp shows letter of alphabet and corresponding animal. Issued in sheets of 90 (30x3).

Villavicencio Festival — A393

Design: 9p, Vallenato festival.

1980 Litho. *Perf. 14*

880 A393 5p multi 45 20
881 A393 9p multi 45 20

Issue dates: 5p, July 15; 9p, June 17.

Gustavo Uribe Ramirez and Tree A394

1980, Aug. 5 Litho. *Perf. 12*
882 A394 10p multi 45 20

Gustavo Uribe Ramirez (1893-1968), ecologist.

Narino Palace (Former Presidential Residence) — A395

1980, Sept. 19 Litho. *Perf. 14*
883 A396 5p multi 60 10

Monument to First Pioneers of 1819, Armenia A396

1980, Oct. 14
884 A396 5p multi 50 10

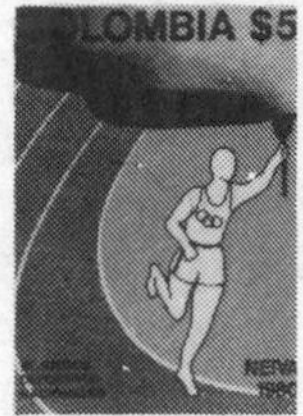
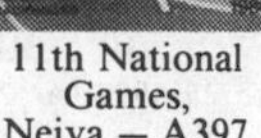
11th National Games, Neiva — A397

Fight against Cancer — A398

1980, Nov. 28 *Perf. 13½x14*
885 A397 5p multi 65 6

1980, Dec. 9
886 A398 10p multi 45 15

Xavier University Law Faculty, 50th Anniversary A399

1980, Dec. 16 Litho. *Perf. 14½*
887 A399 20p multi 80 20

Death of Bolivar — A400

1980, Dec. 17 *Perf. 12*
888 A400 25p multi 1.40 45

Simon Bolivar, death sesquicentennial. See No. C696.

José Maria Obando, President of Colombia A401

115th Anniv. of Constitution (Former Presidents): No. 889b, Jose Hilario Lopez. No. 889c, Manuel Murillo Toro. No. 889d, Santiago Perez. No. 889e, Rafael Reyes. No. 889f, Carlos E. Restrepo. No. 889g, Jose Vicente Concha. No. 889h, Miguel Abadia Mendez. No. 889i, Eduardo Santos. No. 889j, Mariano Ospina Perez.

1981, June 9 Litho. *Perf. 12*
889 Strip of 10 2.25 90
a.-j. A401 5p multi 22 6

1981, Sept. 23 Litho. *Perf. 12*

Designs: No. 890a, Rafael Nunez (1825-1894). No. 890b, Marco Fidel Suarez (1855-1927). No. 890c, Pedro Nel Ospina (1858-1927). No. 890d, Enrique Olaya Herrera (1880-1937). No. 890e, Alfonso Lopez Pumarejo (1886-1959). No. 890f, Aquileo Parra (1825-1900). No. 890g, Santos Gutierrez (1820-1872). No. 890h, Tomas Cipriano de Mosquera (1789-1878). No. 890i, Mariano Ospina Rodriguez. No. 890j, Pedro Alcantara Herran (1800-1872).

890 Strip of 10 25.00
a.-j. A401 7p multi 2.50 40

Designs like No. 889.

1981, Aug. 11 Litho. *Perf. 12*
891 Strip of 10 37.50
a.-j. A401 7p multi 3.75 1.25

1981, Nov. 11 Litho. *Perf. 12*

Designs: No. 892a, Manuel Maria Mallarino. No. 892b, Santos Acosta. No. 892c, Eustorgio Salgar. No. 892d, Julian Trujillo. No. 892e, Francisco Javier Zaldua. No. 892f, Guillermo Leon Valencia. No. 892g, Laureano Gomez. No. 892h, Manuel A. Sanclemente. No. 892i, Miguel Antonio Caro. No. 892j, Jose Eusebio Otalora.e

892 Strip of 10 16.00
a.-j. A401 7p multi 1.50 30

1981, Dec. 15 Litho. *Perf. 12*

Designs: No. 893a, Ruben Piedrahita Arango. No. 893b, Jorge Holguin. No. 893c, Ramon Gonzalez Valencia. No. 893d, Jose Manuel Marroquin. No. 893e, Carlos Holguin. No. 893f, Bartolome Calvo. No. 893g, Sergio Camargo. No. 893h, Jose Maria Rojas Garrido. No. 893i, J.M. Campo Serrano. No. 893j, Eliseo Payan.

893 Strip of 10 12.00
a.-j. A401 7p multi 1.10 20

1982, May 3 *Perf. 12*

Designs: a. Simon Bolivar. b. Francisco de Paula Santander. c. Joaquin Mosquera. d. Domingo Caicedo. e. Jose Ignacio de Marquez. f. Roberto Urdaneta Arbelaez. g. Carlos Lozano y Lozano. h. Guillermo Quintero Calderon. i. Jose de Obaldia. j. Juan de Dios Aranzazu.

894 Strip of 10 11.00
a.-j. A401 7p multi 1.10 20

Jose Maria Villa and West Bridge over Cauca River A404

1981, Nov. 25 Litho. *Perf. 14x13½*
895 A404 60p multi 1.50 30

Agrarian, Mineral and Industrial Credit Bank, 50th Anniv. — A405

Los Nevados Park — A406

1981, Dec. 9 Litho. *Perf. 14*
896 A405 15p multi 50 10

1981, Dec. 10 Litho. *Perf. 13½x14*
897 A406 20p multi 90 15

Girl Sitting on Fence — A407

1982, Feb. 22 Litho. *Perf. 12½x12*
898 Strip of 3 3.00 1.65
a. A407 30p shown 90 30
b. A407 30p Girl, basket 90 30
c. A407 30p Boy, wheelbarrow 90 30

Floral Bouquet — A408

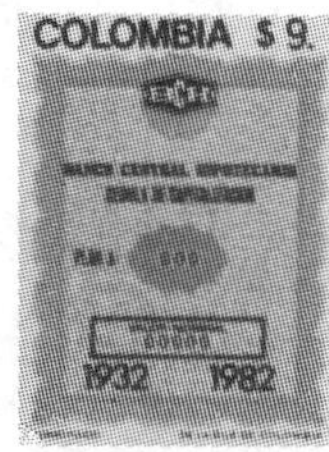

Hipotecario Bank, 50th Anniv. — A409

Designs: Various floral arrangements.

1982, July 28
900 Strip of 10 4.00 2.50
a. A408 7p, any single 35 10

1982, July 29 *Perf. 14*
901 A409 9p blk & grn 30 10

St. Thomas Aquinas (1225-1274) A410

Paintings by Zurbaran.

1982, Aug. 6 Litho. *Perf. 12*
902 A410 5p multi 20 6
903 A410 5p St. Teresa of Avila (1515-1582) 20 6
904 A410 5p St. Francis of Assisi (1182-1226) 20 6

Issue dates: No. 903, Sept. 28; No. 904, Oct. 4.

Arms of Buga City — A411

Gabriel Marquez, 1982 Nobel Prize, Literature — A412

1982-86 Litho. *Perf. 14*
905 A411 10p shown 35 10
905A A411 10p San Juan de Pasto 35 10
906 A411 16p Rionegro 60 20
907 A411 20p Santa Fe de Bogota 60 20
907A A411 20p Santiago de Cali ('86) 24 8
908 A411 23p Honda 80 30
913 A411 55p Antioquia ('86) 60 20
Nos. 905-913 (7) 3.54 1.18

1982, Dec. 10 *Perf. 13½x14*
917 A412 7p gray & grn 30 10

See No. C731-C732.

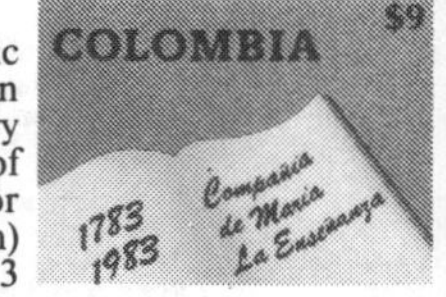

Public Education Bicentenary (Society of Mary for Education) A413

1983, May 6
918 A413 9p gold & blk 50 25

José Maria Espinosa Prieto, Painter — A414

1983, June 3 *Perf. 12*
919 A414 9p Self-portrait, 1860 25 10

250th Anniv. of City of Cucuta — A415

1983, June 23 **Litho.** ***Perf. 12***

920	A415	9p multi	25	6

Porfirio Barba-Jacob (1883-1942), Poet — A416

1983, July 29 **Litho.** ***Perf. 13½x14***

921	A416	9p Portrait	25	6

Simon Bolivar, 200th Birth Anniv. A417

1983, July 24 ***Perf. 12***

922	A417	9p multi	30	10

See Nos. C736-C737.

Royal Spanish Botanical Exhibition, 200th Anniv. — A418

1983, Aug. 18 ***Perf. 14***

923	A418	9p Cinchona Lancefolia	25	10
924	A418	9p Passiflora Laurifolia L.	25	10
925	A418	60p Cinchona Cordiflora	1.65	70
Nos. 923-925,C738-C740 (6)			4.10	1.55

Dawn in the Andes, by Alejandro Obregon A420

1983, Oct. 5 **Litho.** ***Perf. 12***

928	A420	20p multi	50	15

See No. C741.

Francisco de Paula Santander (1792-1840), General — A421

1984, Mar. 6 **Litho.** ***Perf. 14½x14***

929	A421	12p lt ol grn	28	10
930	A421	12p pale car	28	10
931	A421	12p lt ultra	28	10

Admiral Jose Prudencio Padilla (1784-1831) A423

1984, May 17 **Litho.** ***Perf. 12***

933	A423	10p multi	25	8

Luis Antonio Calvo (1882-1945) Composer A424

1984, July 26

934	A424	18p multi	45	15

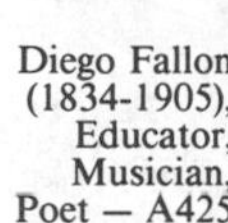

Diego Fallon (1834-1905), Educator, Musician, Poet — A425

1984, Aug. 31 ***Perf. 12***

935	A425	20p multi	45	15

Candelario Obeso (1849-1884), Writer A426

1984, Sept. 4 ***Perf. 14x13½***

936	A426	20p multi	45	15

Site of Marandua, Future City — A427

1984, Sept. 28 ***Perf. 12***

937	A427	15p multi	32	10

See No. C744.

Christmas 1984 A428

Nativity and Children Playing, by Jose Uriel Sierra, Age 7.

1984, Dec. 14

938	A428	12p multi	28	10

See No. C746.

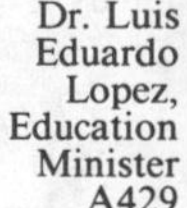

Dr. Luis Eduardo Lopez, Education Minister A429

1984, Dec. 21

939	A429	22p multi	50	16

Independence War Heroine — A430

Maria Concepcion Loperena de Fernandez de Castro.

1985, Jan. 6

940	A430	12p multi	22	8

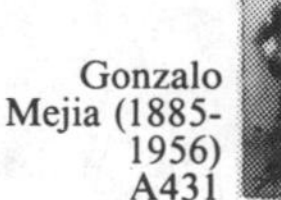
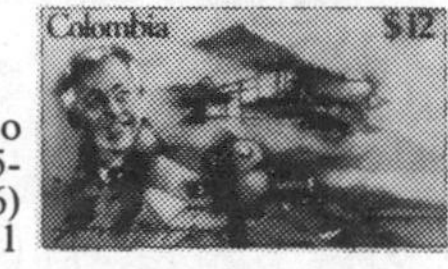

Gonzalo Mejia (1885-1956) A431

1985, Feb. 25

941	A431	12p Portrait, biplane, camera	20	8

Aviation, motion picture and meat exporting industrialist.

Self-portrait with Wife — A432

1985, Feb. 25

942	A432	37p multi	62	20

Pedro Nel Gomez (1899-1984), painter. See No. C748.

Fauna A433

1985 ***Perf. 14 (12p), 13***

943	A433	12p Hydrochaeris hydrochaeris	16	6
944	A433	15p Felis pardalis	20	8
945	A433	15p Tremarctos ornatus, vert.	20	8
946	A433	20p Tapirus pinchaque	28	10

Issued dates: 12p, Apr. 12. No. 944, 20p, Aug. 6. No. 945, Aug. 29.

Carlos Gardel (1890-1935), Entertainer A434

Camina Literacy Program A435

1985, June 23 ***Perf. 14***

947	A434	15p Portrait, Fokker F-31 Trimotor	20	8

1985, Nov. 25 ***Perf. 13½x14***

948	A435	15p Tree, alphabet	20	8

Christmas 1985 — A436

1985, Dec. 4 **Litho.** ***Perf. 13***

949	A436	15p multi	20	8

Rafael Pombo Children's Foundation. See No. C755.

Eduardo Carranza (b. 1913), Poet — A437

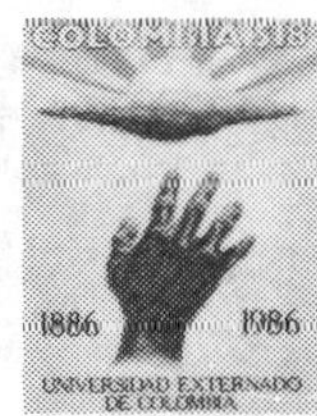

Colombian Free University, Cent. — A438

1986, Feb. 13

950	A437	18p multi	24	8

1986, Feb. 14

951	A438	18p multi	24	8

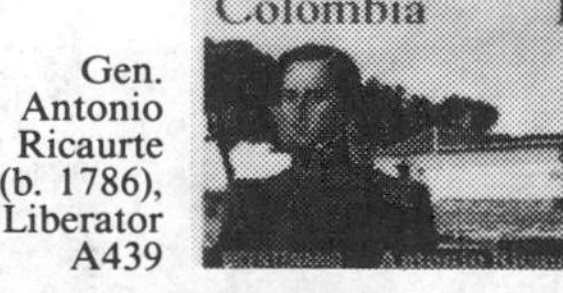

Gen. Antonio Ricaurte (b. 1786), Liberator A439

1986, May 7 **Litho.** ***Perf. 13***

952	A439	18p Leiva birthplace	24	8

Jose Asuncion Silva (1865-1896), Poet, and Scene from Nocturno A440

1986, May 30 **Litho.** ***Perf. 12***

953	A440	18p multi	22	8

> Demand, as well as supply, determines a stamp's market value. One is as important as the other.

Fernando Gomez Martinez (1897-1985), Journalist — A441

1986, June 19

954 A441 24p multi 30 10

Santiago de Cali, 450th Anniv. A442

1986, July 25 Litho. *Perf. 13*

955 A442 25p La Merced 30 10

Monsignor Jose Vicente Castro Silva (1885-1968), Rector of the Mayor del Rosario School — A443

Portrait by Ricardo Gomez.

1986, Aug. 4 Litho. *Perf. 12*

956 A443 20p multi 22 8

Natl. University — A444

1986, Oct. 14 Litho. *Perf. 12*

957 A444 40p multi 45 15

Faculties: Fine Arts, cent., and Architecture, 50th anniv.

Rafael Maya (1897-1980), Poet, and Salamanca University Entrance A445

1986, Oct. 15

958 A445 25p multi 28 10

See No. C772.

Condor in Flight — A446

1986, Nov. 6

963 A446 20p ultra 22 8

Condor Type of 1986 and

Deroptius Accipritrinus — A446a

1987 Litho. *Perf. 12, 14½x14 (30p)*

964 A446 25p ultra ('87) 30 10
965 A446a 30p grn ('87) 35 12

See No. C778. Issue dates: 25p, May 25. 30p, June 8.

Fauna Type of 1987

Design: No. 966, Inia goefrenis, horiz.

1987, Dec. 24 Litho. *Perf. 14x14½*

966 A446a 30p dull vio ('87) 35 12

See No. C779.

Pedro Uribe Mejia (1886-1972), Pioneer of Colombian Coffee Industry — A447

Mompox, 450th Anniv. — A448

1987, Jan. 29 Litho. *Perf. 12*

969 A447 25p multi 45 15

1987, May 3 *Perf. 13½x13*

970 A448 500p Santa Barbara Church 4.75 1.60

Writers A449

Portraits and scenes from works: 70p, Jorge Isaacs (1837-1895), novelist, and scene from *Maria.* 90p, Aurelio Martinez Mutis (1884-1954), poet, and scene from *La Epopeya del Condor.*

1987, Sept. 2 *Perf. 12*

971 A449 70p multi 75 25
972 A449 90p multi 1.00 32

Issue dates: 70p, July 28. 90p, Sept. 2.

Social Security & Communications A450

1987 Litho. *Perf. 13½x13*

973 A450 35p multi 38 14

SEMI-POSTAL STAMP

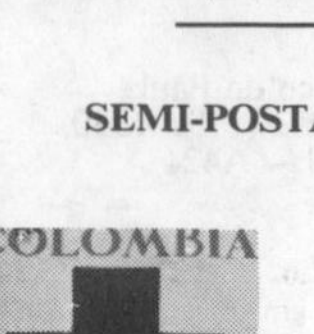

Girl Giving First Aid — SP1

Perf. 13½x14

1966, Apr. 26 Litho. Unwmk.

B1 SP1 5c + 5c multi 10 6

Issued for the Red Cross.

AIR POST STAMPS

No. 341 Overprinted

1er.
Servicio
Postal
Aereo
6-18-19

1919 Unwmk. *Perf. 14.*

C1 A109 2c car rose 3,000. 1,850.
a. Numerals "1" with serifs *7,000. 4,000.*

Used for the first experimental flight from Barranquilla to Puerto Colombia, June 18, 1919.

Issued by Compania Colombiana de Navegacion Aerea.

From 1920 to 1932 the internal airmail service of Colombia was handled by the Compania Colombiana de Navegacion Aerea (1920) and the Sociedad Colombo-Alemana de Transportes Aereos, known familiarly as "SCADTA" (1920-1932). These organizations under government contracts operated and maintained their own post offices, and issued stamps which were the only legal franking for airmail service during this period, both in the internal and international mails. All letters had to bear government stamps as well.

Woman and Boy Watching Plane — AP1

Designs: No. C3, Clouds and small biplane at top. No. C4, Tilted plane viewed close-up from above. No. C5, Flier in plane watching biplane. No. C6, Lighthouse. No. C7, Fuselage and tail of biplane. No. C8, Condor on cliff. No. C9, Plane at rest; pilot foreground. No. C10, Ocean liner.

1920, Feb. Unwmk. Litho. *Imperf.* Without Gum.

C2 AP1 10c grn, red, bl, yel & blk 2,750. 2,250.
C3 AP1 10c bl, red & blk 3,250. 2,250.
C4 AP1 10c yel, red, bl & blk 3,250. 2,250.
C5 AP1 10c bl, red, yel & blk 2,750. 2,250.
C6 AP1 10c bl, grn, red, yel, & blk 2,750. 2,250.
C7 AP1 10c grn, red, bl, red brn & blk 11,000. 4,750.
C8 AP1 10c brn, grn, bl, red & blk 4,750. 3,750.
a. Without overprint
C9 AP1 10c grn, bl, red, yel, red brn & blk 3,250. 2,250.
C10 AP1 10c bl, yel, grn, red & blk 5,250. 3,250.

Flier in Plane Watching Biplane — AP2

1920, March

C11 AP2 10c green 62.50 *100.00*

Four other 10c stamps, similar to No. C11, have two designs showing plane, mountains and water. They are printed in deep green or light brown red. Some authorities state that these four were not used regularly.

Issued by Sociedad Colombo-Alemana de Transportes Aereos (SCADTA)

Seaplane over Magdalena River — AP3

1920-21 Litho. *Perf. 12*

C12 AP3 10c yel ('21) 47.50 37.50
C13 AP3 15c bl ('21) 47.50 40.00
C14 AP3 30c blk, *rose* 21.00 15.00
C15 AP3 30c rose ('21) 42.50 35.00
C16 AP3 50c pale grn 47.50 42.50
Nos. C12-C16 (5) 206.00 170.00

No. C16 Handstamp Surcharged in Violet or Black:

(Illustrations of types "a" to "e" are reduced in size.)

VALOR 10 CENTAVOS
a

VALOR 10 CENTAVOS
b

Valor 10 Céntavos
c

VALOR 30 Ctvos
S.C.A.T.A
d

30¢ 30¢
e

$030
f

$030¢
g

1921

C17 AP3 (a) 10c on 50c 650.00 650.00
C18 AP3 (b) 10c on 50c 575.00 575.00
C19 AP3 (c) 10c on 50c *1,250. 1,000.*
C20 AP3 (b) 30c on 50c 650.00 650.00
C21 AP3 (d) 30c on 50c 850.00 800.00
C22 AP3 (e) 30c on 50c 1,350. 1,000.
C23 AP3 (f) 30c on 50c 1,100. 950.00
C24 AP3 (g) 30c on 50c 1,100. 950.00

The only foreign revenue stamps listed in this Catalogue are those authorized for prepayment of postage.

Plane over Magdalena River — AP4 Plane over Bogota Cathedral — AP5

1921 *Perf. 11½*

C25	AP4	5c org yel	5.25	5.25
C26	AP4	10c sl grn	1.90	1.50
C27	AP4	15c org brn	1.90	1.60
C28	AP4	20c red brn	3.00	2.25
a.		Imperf. vert., pair	200.00	
C29	AP4	30c green	2.25	75
C30	AP4	50c blue	3.00	1.20
C31	AP4	60c vermilion	15.00	12.50
C32	AP5	1p gray blk	17.00	12.50
C33	AP5	2p rose	32.50	25.00
C34	AP5	3p violet	72.50	70.00
C35	AP5	5p ol grn	500.00	475.00
		Nos. C25-C35 (11)	654.30	607.55

Exist imperf.

Nos. C16 and C12 Handstamp Surcharged

(Illustration of type "h" is reduced in size.)

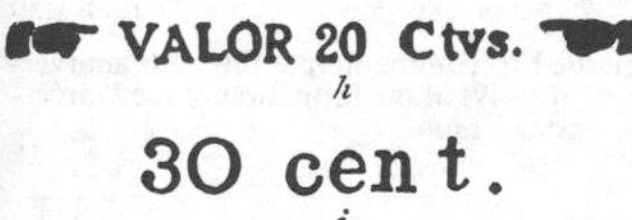

1921-22 *Perf. 12*

C36	AP3 (h)	20c on 50c	1,650.	1,400.
C37	AP3 (i)	30c on 10c	700.00	475.00

Seaplane over Magdalena River — AP6 Plane over Bogota Cathedral — AP7

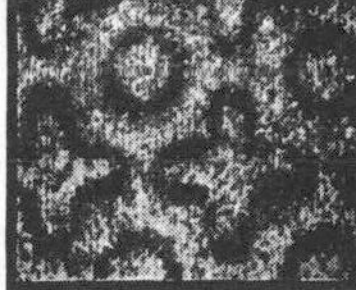

Wmk. 116

Wmk. Crosses and Circles (116)

1923-28 *Perf. 14x14½*

C38	AP6	5c org yel	1.10	30
C39	AP6	10c green	1.10	25
C40	AP6	15c carmine	1.10	25
C41	AP6	20c gray	1.10	15
C42	AP6	30c blue	1.10	15
C43	AP6	40c pur ('28)	9.25	6.00
C44	AP6	50c green	1.65	30
C45	AP6	60c brown	2.50	30
C46	AP6	80c ol grn ('28)	27.50	27.50
C47	AP7	1p black	11.00	3.00
C48	AP7	2p red org	17.50	7.50
C49	AP7	3p violet	37.50	25.00
C50	AP7	5p ol grn	60.00	35.00
		Nos. C38-C50 (13)	172.40	105.70

Nos. C41 and C31 Surcharged in Carmine and Dark Blue:

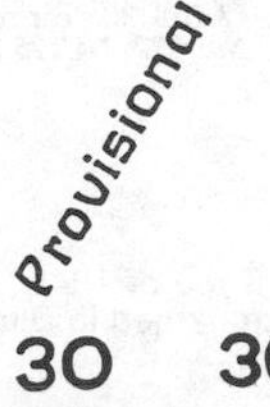

1923

C51	AP6 (j)	30c on 20c gray (C)	85.00	50.00
C52	AP4 (k)	30c on 60c ver (Bl)	72.50	40.00

Nos. C41-C42 Overprinted in Black

1928 **Wmk. 116** *Perf. 14x14½*

C53	AP6	20c gray	75.00	75.00
C54	AP6	30c blue	75.00	75.00

Issued to commemorate the goodwill flight of Lt. Benjamin Mendez from New York to Bogota.

Magdalena River and Tolima Volcano AP8 Columbus' Ship and Plane AP9

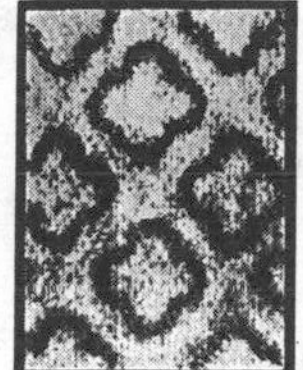

Wmk. 127

Wmk. Quatrefoils. (127)

1929, June 1 *Perf. 14*

C55	AP8	5c yel org	1.00	50
C56	AP8	10c red brn	1.00	40
C57	AP8	15c dp grn	1.00	50
C58	AP8	20c carmine	1.00	20
C59	AP8	30c gray bl	1.00	40
C60	AP8	40c dl vio	1.25	40
C61	AP8	50c dk ol grn	2.50	60
C62	AP8	60c org brn	2.50	60
C63	AP8	80c green	8.00	6.00
C64	AP9	1p blue	9.50	3.50
C65	AP9	2p brn org	15.00	6.00
C66	AP9	3p pale rose vio	30.00	30.00
C67	AP9	5p ol grn	72.50	60.00
		Nos. C55-C67 (13)	146.25	109.10

For International Airmail.

AP10 AP11

1929, June 1 **Wmk. 127** *Perf. 14*

C68	AP10	5c yel org	7.25	7.25
C69	AP10	10c red brn	1.25	3.50
C70	AP10	15c dp grn	1.25	3.50
C71	AP10	20c carmine	1.25	4.00
C72	AP10	25c vio bl	1.25	1.10
C73	AP10	30c gray bl	1.25	1.10
C74	AP10	50c dk ol grn	1.25	2.00
C75	AP10	60c brown	3.25	3.50
C76	AP11	1p blue	6.00	9.00
C77	AP11	2p red org	9.00	12.00
C78	AP11	3p violet	110.00	100.00
C79	AP11	5p ol grn	140.00	150.00
		Nos. C68-79 (12)	283.00	296.95

This issue was sold abroad for use on correspondence to be flown from coastal to interior points of Colombia. Cancellations are those of the country of origin rather than Colombia.

Nos. C63, C66 and C64 Surcharged in Black:

1830 1930
SIMON BOLIVAR
30 cts. 30 cts.
n

1930, Dec. 15

C80	AP8(m)	10c on 80c grn	6.25	6.75
C81	AP9(n)	20c on 3p pale rose vio	12.00	13.00
C82	AP9(n)	30c on 1p bl	13.00	13.00

Issued to commemorate the centenary of the death of Simon Bolivar (1783-1830).

Colombian Government Issues.

Nos. C55-C67 Overprinted in Black:

CORREO AEREO
o

CORREO AEREO
p

Wmk. 127

1932, Jan. 1 **Typo.** *Perf. 14*

C83	AP8(o)	5c yel org	12.00	12.00
C84	AP8(o)	10c red brn	2.50	70
C85	AP8(o)	15c dp grn	4.25	4.25
C86	AP8(o)	20c carmine	2.00	45
C87	AP8(o)	30c gray bl	2.00	75
C88	AP8(o)	40c dl vio	3.00	1.40
C89	AP8(o)	50c dk ol grn	4.75	4.25
C90	AP8(o)	60c org brn	3.75	4.25
C91	AP8(o)	80c green	20.00	20.00
C92	AP9(p)	1p blue	16.00	13.00
C93	AP9(p)	2p brn org	45.00	40.00
C94	AP9(p)	3p pale rose vio	85.00	75.00
C95	AP9(p)	5p ol grn	150.00	160.00
		Nos. C83-C95 (13)	350.25	336.05

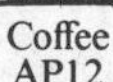

Coffee AP12 Cattle AP13

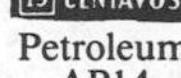

Petroleum AP14 Bananas AP15

Gold — AP16

Emerald AP17

1932-39 **Wmk. 127** **Photo.** *Perf. 14*

C96	AP12	5c org & blk brn	1.40	40
C97	AP13	10c lake & blk	1.50	35
C98	AP14	15c bl grn & vio blk	70	25
C99	AP14	15c ver & vio blk ('39)	4.00	20
C100	AP15	20c car & ol blk	1.10	5
C101	AP15	20c turq grn & ol blk ('39)	5.50	50
C102	AP12	30c dk bl & blk brn	2.25	25
C103	AP15	40c dk vio & ol bis	1.25	22
C104	AP13	50c dk grn & brnsh blk	5.50	2.00
C105	AP14	60c dk brn & blk vio	1.75	40
C106	AP12	80c grn & blk brn	8.50	3.25
C107	AP16	1p dk bl & ol bis	14.00	2.00
C108	AP16	2p org brn & ol bis	15.00	3.50
C109	AP17	3p dk vio & emer	26.00	9.50
C110	AP17	5p gray blk & emer	72.50	30.00
		Nos. C96-C110 (15)	160.95	52.87

Nos. C104, C106-C108 Surcharged:

1533 CARTAGENA 1933
10 10
a

1533 1933
CARTAGENA
20 centavos 20
b

1934, Jan. 5

C111	AP13(a)	10(c)on 50c	6.00	6.00
C112	AP12(a)	15(c)on 80c	8.00	8.00
C113	AP16(b)	20c on 1p	9.00	9.00
C114	AP16(b)	30c on 2p	10.00	10.00

400th anniversary of Cartagena.

Nos. C100 and C103 Surcharged in Black or Carmine:

5 cts 15

1939, Jan. 15

C115	AP15	5c on 20c car & ol blk (Bk)	50	35
C116	AP15	5c on 40c dk vio & ol bis (C)	50	35
C117	AP15	15c on 20c car & ol blk (Bk)	2.25	75
a.		Double surcharge	17.50	
b.		Pair, one double surcharge	17.50	
c.		Invtd. surch.	17.50	17.50

No. CF5 Surcharged in Black.

C118	AP15	5c on 20c car & ol blk	1.00	1.00

Nos. C102-C103 Surcharged in Black or Red

15 cts

1940, Oct. 20

C119	AP12	15c on 30c dk bl & blk brn	1.75	70
a.		Invtd. surch.	17.50	
C120	AP15	15c on 40c dk vio & ol bis (R)	3.75	1.25
a.		Double surcharge	17.50	

Catalogue prices for unused stamps up to mid-1953 are for hinged copies matching the condition specified in this volume's introduction.

Pre-Columbian Monument AP18

Symbol of Legend of El Dorado AP19

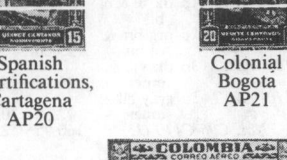

Spanish Fortifications, Cartagena AP20

Colonial Bogota AP21

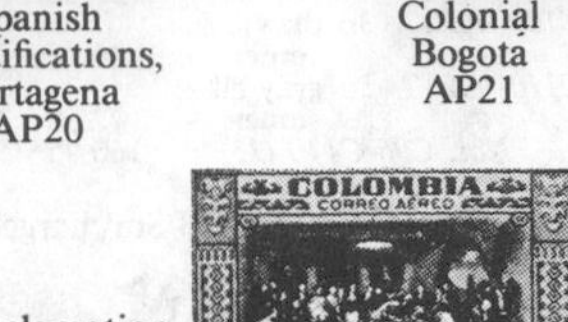

Proclamation of Independence AP22

National Library, Bogota AP23

Unwmk.

1941, Jan. 28 Engr. *Perf. 12*

C121	AP18	5c gray blk	20	10
C122	AP19	10c yel org	20	6
C123	AP20	15c car rose	25	5
C124	AP21	20c yel grn	50	10
a.		Imperf. vert., pair	125.00	
C125	AP18	30c dp bl	50	10
C126	AP19	40c rose lake	1.00	10
C127	AP20	50c turq grn	1.00	10
C128	AP21	60c sepia	1.00	10
C129	AP18	80c ol blk	2.75	70
C130	AP22	1p bl & blk	4.50	70
C131	AP23	2p red org & blk	7.50	3.00
C132	AP22	3p vio & blk	20.00	9.00
C133	AP23	5p lt grn & blk	40.00	30.00
		Nos. C121-C133 (13)	79.40	44.11

See also Nos. C151-C163, C217-C225.

San Sebastian Fort, Cartagena AP24

Bay of Santa Marta AP25

Tequendama Waterfall AP26

National Capitol, Bogota AP27

Unwmk.

1945, Nov. 3 Litho. *Perf. 11*

C134	AP24	5c bl gray	20	10
a.		Imperf., pair	12.00	
C135	AP26	10c yel org	20	10
a.		Imperf., pair	12.00	
C136	AP25	15c rose	20	5
a.		Imperf., pair	12.00	
C137	AP24	20c lt yel grn	45	10
a.		Imperf., pair	12.00	
C138	AP26	30c ultra	45	10
a.		Imperf., pair	12.00	
C139	AP25	40c claret	75	22
a.		Imperf., pair	12.00	
C140	AP24	50c bluish grn	80	25
a.		Imperf., pair	12.00	
C141	AP26	60c lt vio brn	3.25	1.25
a.		Imperf., pair	12.00	
C142	AP25	80c dk sl grn	5.00	1.20
a.		Imperf., pair	15.00	
C143	AP27	1p dk bl	7.00	1.25
a.		Imperf., pair	25.00	
C144	AP27	2p red org	10.00	4.75
a.		Imperf., pair	85.00	
		Nos. C134-C144 (11)	28.30	9.37

Part-perforate varieties exist for all denominations except 80c.

Bello Type of Regular Issue, 1946.

Wmk. 255

1946, Sept. 3 Engr. *Perf. 12*

C145	A219	5c dp bl	25	20

Issued to commemorate the 80th anniversary of the death of Andrés Bello, poet and educator.

Francisco José de Caldas AP29

Manuel del Socorro Rodriguez AP30

Perf. 12½

1947, May 9 Litho. Unwmk.

C146	AP29	5c dp bl, *grnsh*	50	30
C147	AP30	10c red org, *grnsh*	75	65

4th Pan-American Press Congress (1946).

Chancellery Patio AP31

Capitol, Patio Rafael Nunez AP32

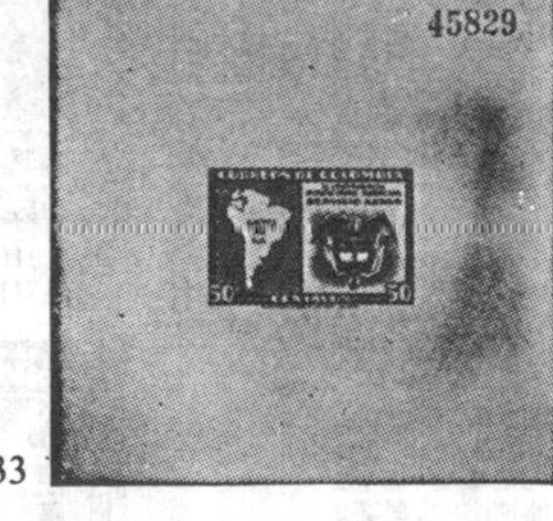
AP33

1948, Apr. 2 Engr. Wmk. 229

C148	AP31	5c dk brn	15	5
C149	AP32	15c dp bl	1.40	1.25

Miniature Sheet

Imperf

C150	AP33	50c brown	2.25	2.25

Nos. C148-C150 commemorate the 9th Pan-American Conference, Bogota. No. C150 measures 90½x90½mm.

Types of 1941.

1948, July 21 Unwmk. *Perf. 12*

C151	AP18	5c org yel	25	5
C152	AP19	10c scarlet	25	5
C153	AP20	15c dp bl	25	5
C154	AP21	20c violet	25	5
C155	AP18	30c yel grn	60	22
C156	AP19	40c gray	70	20
C157	AP20	50c rose lake	75	20
C158	AP21	60c ol gray	1.25	20
C159	AP18	80c red brn	1.50	25
C160	AP22	1p ol grn & vio brn	2.50	50
C161	AP23	2p dp grn & brt bl	4.50	1.00
C162	AP22	3p rose car & blk	9.50	5.50
C163	AP23	5p lt brn & turq grn	25.00	12.00
		Nos. C151-C163 (13)	47.30	20.27

"Air Week" 5c Blue

The War and Air Department issued a 5c blue stamp in May, 1949, to publicize Air Week (Semana de Aviacion). The design shows a coat-of-arms, inscribed "FAC," superimposed upon an outline map of Colombia. This stamp had no franking value and its use was optional during May 16-23.

Justice and Liberty AP34

Wing AP35

Design: 10c, Liberty holding tablet of laws.

1949, Oct. 7 Unwmk. *Perf. 13*

C164	AP34	5c bl grn	15	5
C165	AP34	10c orange	15	5

Issued to honor the new Constitution.

For Domestic Postage.

1950, June 22 Litho. *Perf. 12*

C166	AP35	5c org yel	40	35
C167	AP35	10c brn red	50	40
C168	AP35	15c lt bl	60	40
C169	AP35	20c lt grn	1.10	75
C170	AP35	30c lil gray	2.50	2.50
C171	AP35	60c chocolate	3.25	3.50

With Network as in Parenthesis.

C172	AP35	1p gray (buff)	25.00	25.00
C173	AP35	2p bl (pale grn)	25.00	25.00
C174	AP35	5p red brn (red brn)	70.00	70.00
		Nos. C166-C174 (9)	128.35	127.90

No. C172 was issued both with and without network.

Nos. C151-C157 and C160-C163 Overprinted in Black

1950, July 18

C175	AP18	5c org yel	25	15
C176	AP19	10c scarlet	25	15
C177	AP20	15c dp bl	25	15
C178	AP21	20c violet	35	20
C179	AP18	30c yel grn	60	30
C180	AP19	40c gray	1.25	50
C181	AP20	50c rose lake	75	40
C182	AP22	1p ol grn & vio brn	4.50	3.50
C183	AP23	2p dp grn & brt bl	7.00	5.00
C184	AP22	3p rose car & blk	20.00	20.00
C185	AP23	5p lt brn & turq grn	42.50	42.50
		Nos. C175-C185 (11)	77.70	72.85

Nos. C151-C163 Overprinted in Black

1950, July 12

C186	AP18	5c org yel	25	7
C187	AP19	10c scarlet	25	7
C188	AP20	15c dp bl	25	5
C189	AP21	20c violet	35	5
C190	AP18	30c yel grn	35	5
C191	AP19	40c gray	75	15
C192	AP20	50c rose lake	75	15
C193	AP21	60c ol gray	1.25	25
C194	AP18	80c red brn	1.90	65
C195	AP22	1p ol grn & vio brn	2.00	80
C196	AP23	2p dp grn & brt bl	5.50	2.25
C197	AP22	3p rose car & blk	13.00	12.00
C198	AP23	5p lt brn & turq grn	30.00	25.00
		Nos. C186-C198 (13)	56.60	41.54

On Nos. C175-C198, "L" stands for LANSA, "A" for AVIANCA.

Miniature Sheet

Western Hemisphere — AP36

Unwmk.

1950, Aug. 22 Photo. *Imperf.*

C199	AP36	50c gray	1.50	1.50

Issued to commemorate the 75th anniversary (in 1949) of the formation of the Universal Postal Union.

Types of 1941 Overprinted at Lower Right in Black

Unwmk.

1951, Sept. 15 Engr. *Perf. 12*

C200	AP19	40c org yel	2.50	2.00
C201	AP20	50c ultra	2.50	2.00
C202	AP21	60c gray	2.50	2.00
C203	AP18	80c car rose	1.75	1.50
C204	AP22	1p red org & red brn	6.00	5.00
C205	AP23	2p rose car & bl	6.50	5.00
C206	AP22	3p choc & emer	16.00	13.00
C207	AP23	5p org & gray	47.50	47.50
		Nos. C200-C207 (8)	85.25	78.00

Types of 1941 Overprinted at Lower Right in Black

1951-54

C208	AP19	40c org yel	5.00	80
C209	AP20	50c ultra	6.00	90
C210	AP21	60c gray	4.50	65
a.		Overprint centered	2.50	75
C211	AP18	80c car rose	1.25	45
C212	AP22	1p red org & red brn	5.00	70
C213	AP22	1p ol grn & vio brn ('54)	6.00	1.10
C214	AP23	2p rose car & bl	5.00	75
C215	AP22	3p choc & emer	7.50	2.00
C216	AP23	5p org & gray	15.00	2.75
		Nos. C208-C216 (9)	55.25	10.10

All values except the 2p and 3p exist without overprint.

Types of 1941.

1952, May 10 Engr.

C217	AP18	5c ultra	45	20
C218	AP19	10c ultra	45	25
C219	AP20	15c ultra	45	25
C220	AP21	20c ultra	1.00	40
C221	AP18	30c ultra	2.50	90
C222	AP18	5c car rose	45	20
C223	AP19	10c car rose	45	25
C224	AP21	20c car rose	1.00	30
C225	AP18	30c car rose	2.00	45
		Nos. C217-C225 (9)	8.75	3.20

Type of 1941 Surcharged in Blue

1ª CONFERENCIA 1952 LATINO AMERICANA SIDERURGICA 70 Ctvos.

1952, Oct. 30
C226 AP18 70c on 80c car rose 2.25 1.00

Issued to publicize the Latin American Siderurgical Conference, 1952.

Type of Postal Tax Stamps, 1948-50, Nos. 602 and 604 Surcharged or Overprinted in Black

CORREO 5 AEREO

1953	**Wmk. 255**	**Perf. 12.**		
C227	PT10	5c on 8c bl	15	5
C228	PT10	15c on 20c brn	35	5
C229	PT10	15c on 25c bl grn	1.50	10
C230	PT10	25c bl grn	50	10

Many varieties of overprint or surcharge exist on Nos. C227-C231.

No. 570 Overprinted "AEREO" in Blue.

1953, Aug. **Wmk. 229** ***Perf. 12½***
C231 A160 10c red 22 5

"Extra Rapido"

Stamps inscribed "Extra Rapido" are for use on domestic airmail carried by airlines other than AVIANCA.

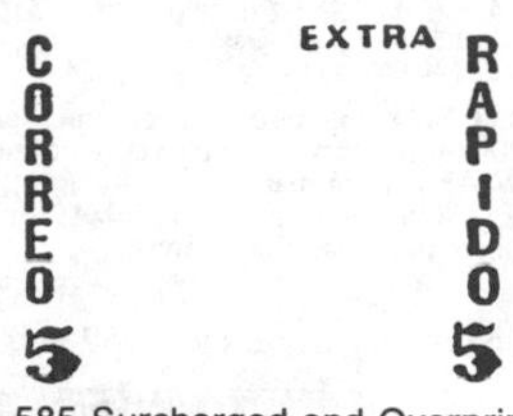

No. 585 Surcharged and Overprinted "Extra Rapido" in Dark Blue

1953 **Unwmk.** ***Perf. 13***
C232 A244 5c on 11c red 50 45

Capitol and Arms — AP37

Revenue Stamps Overprinted "Correo Extra-Rapido"
Gray Security Paper.

1953	**Wmk. 255**	**Engr.**	***Perf. 12***	
C233	AP37	1c on 2c grn	15	6
C234	AP37	50c red org	25	10

AP38

Real Estate Tax Stamps Overprinted "Correo Extra-Rapido" in Black or Carmine

1953				
C235	AP38	5c red org	20	6
C236	AP38	20c brn (C)	30	10

On 20c, overprint is at bottom of stamp and two lines of ornaments cover real estate tax inscription at top.

Castillo y Rada and Map — AP39

Real Estate Tax Stamp Surcharged "Correo Aereo, II Exposicion Filatelica Nacional, Bogota Dicbre 1953, 15 Centavos"

Engraved and Lithographed

1953, Dec. 12
C237 AP39 15c on 10p multi 50 25

Issued to publicize the second National Philatelic Exhibition, Bogota, Dec. 1953.

No. RA45 Overprinted in Black

CORREO
EXTRA-RAPIDO

1953
C238 PT10 10c purple 15 6

Galeras Volcano — AP40

Retreat of San Diego — AP41

Designs: 15c (C241), Las Lajas Shrine, Narino. 15c (C242), 50c, Bolivar monument. 20c, 80c, Ruiz mountain, Manizales. 40c, George Isaacs monument, Cali. 60c, Monkey Fountain, Tunja. 1p, Stadium, Medellin. 2p, Pastelillo Fort, Cartagena. 3p, Santo Domingo University gate. 5p, Las Lajas Shrine. 10p, Map of Colombia.

Perf. 13½x13, 13.

1954, Jan. 15		**Engr.**	**Unwmk.**	
C239	AP40	5c dp red vio	20	10
C240	AP41	10c black	20	10
C241	AP40	15c red org	25	5
C242	AP40	15c car rose	25	5
C243	AP40	20c brown	25	5
C244	AP40	30c brn org	25	5
C245	AP40	40c blue	25	10
C246	AP40	50c dk vio brn	30	10
C247	AP40	60c dk brn	40	10
C248	AP40	80c red brn	90	20

Size: 37x27mm.
Center in Black.

C249	AP41	1p dp bl	3.00	30
C250	AP41	2p dk grn	4.75	45
C251	AP41	3p car rose	11.00	1.50

Size: 38x32mm., 32x38mm.

C252	AP41	5p dk grn & red brn	12.00	3.75
C253	AP40	10p gray grn & red org	15.00	8.50
		Nos. C239-C253 (15)	49.00	15.40

See also Nos. C307-C308.

Condor Carrying Shield AP42

Inscribed: "Correo Extra-Rapido"

1954, Apr. 23 **Litho.** ***Perf. 12½.***
C254 AP42 5c lil rose 90 40

Soldier-Map-Arms Type of Regular Issue, 1954.

1954, June 13 **Engr.** ***Perf. 13***
C255 A259 15c carmine 40 10

Issued to commemorate the first anniversary of the assumption of the presidency by General Rojas Pinilla.

See also No. C271a.

Games Type of Regular Issue, 1954.

Design: 20c, Stadium and Athlete holding arms of Colombia.

1954, July 18				
C256	A260	15c chocolate	80	20
C257	A260	20c dp bl grn	1.50	50

7th National Games, Cali, July 1954.

Church of St. Peter Claver, Cartagena AP45

1954, Sept. 9
C258 AP45 15c brown 35 10
a. Souvenir sheet 3.25 3.25

Issued to commemorate the 300th anniversary of the death of St. Peter Claver.

No. C258a contains one stamp similar to No. C258, but printed in red brown. Marginal inscriptions in black. Sheet size: 120½x127mm.

Mercury Type of Regular Issue, 1954.

1954, Oct. 29
C259 A263 15c dp bl 45 10

Inscribed "Extra Rapido"

C260 A263 50c scarlet 40 10

Issued to publicize the first International Fair and Exhibition, Bogota, 1954.

Archbishop Manuel Jose Mosquera — AP47

Inscribed: "Correo Extra Rapido"

1954, Nov. 17
C261 AP47 2c yel grn 10 8

Issued to commemorate the centenary of the death of Archbishop Manuel Jose Mosquera.

Virgin of Chiquinquira — AP48

Inscribed: "Correo Extra Rapido"

Engraved and Lithographed

1954, Dec. 4
C262 AP48 5c org brn & multi 10 5

See also No. C291.

College Types of Regular Issue, 1954.

Designs: 20c, Brother Cristobal de Torres. 50c, College chapel and arms.

Perf. 12½x11½, 11½x12½

1954, Dec. 6		**Engr.**	**Unwmk.**	
C263	A264	15c org & blk	40	20
C264	A264	20c ultra	60	20
C265	A265	25c dk brn	80	22
C266	A265	50c blk & car	1.90	1.00
a.		Souvenir sheet	6.00	6.00

Issued to commemorate the 300th anniversary (in 1953) of the founding of the Senior College of Our Lady of the Rosary, Bogota.

No. C266a contains four stamps similar to Nos. C263-C266, but printed in different colors: 15c red and black, 20c pale purple, 25c brown, 50c black and olive green. Marginal inscriptions in black. Sheet size: 124½x130½mm.

Steel Mill Type of Regular Issue.

1954, Dec. 12 ***Perf. 12½x13***
C267 A266 20c grn & blk 1.50 90

Issued to mark the opening of the Paz del Rio steel mill, October 1954.

Marti Type of Regular Issue, 1955

1955, Jan. 28 ***Perf. 13½x13***
C268 A267 15c dp grn 40 15

Issued to commemorate the centenary (in 1953) of the birth of José Marti.

Korean Veterans Type of Regular Issue, 1955.

1955, Mar. 23 ***Perf. 12½***
C269 A268 20c dk grn 75 25

Issued to honor Colombian soldiers who served in Korea.

Merchant Fleet Types of Regular Issue, 1955.

1955, Apr. 12			***Perf. 12½***	
C270	A269	25c black	40	10
C271	A270	50c dk grn	80	45
a.		Souvenir sheet	6.00	6.00

Issued to honor the Grand-Colombian Merchant Fleet.

No. C271a contains four stamps similar to Nos. C255, C269-C271, but printed in different colors; 15c lilac red, 20c olive, 25c bluish black, 50c bluish green. Marginal inscriptions in black. Sheet size: 125x131mm.

Pres. Marco Fidel Suarez — AP56

Inscribed: "Correo Extra Rapido"

1955, April 23 ***Perf. 13***
C272 AP56 10c dp bl 15 5

Issued to commemorate the centenary of the birth of Marco Fidel Suarez (1855-1927), president in 1918-1921.

Hotel-Church Type of Regular Issue, 1955.

1955, May 16 **Photo.** ***Perf. 11½x12***
C273 A271 15c rose brn 40 10

Rotary Type of Regular Issue, 1955.

Unwmk.

1955, Oct. 17 **Engr.** ***Perf. 13***
C274 A272 15c dk car rose 40 10

Rotary International, 50th anniversary.

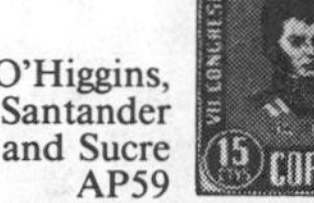

O'Higgins, Santander and Sucre AP59

Ferdinand the Catholic and Queen Isabella I — AP60

Designs: 2c, Atahualpa, Tisquesuza and Montezuma. 20c, Marti, Hidalgo and Petion. 1p, Artigas, Solano Lopez and Murillo. 2p, Abdon Calderon, Baron de Rio Branco and José de La Mar.

Engraved & Photogravure

1955, Oct. 12

Inscribed: "Extra Rapido"

C275	AP59	2c dl brn & blk	10	5
C276	AP60	5c dk brn & yel	20	15

Regular Air Post

C277 AP59 15c rose car & blk 30 15
C278 AP59 20c pale brn & blk 45 15
a. Souvenir sheet of 2 9.50 9.50

Inscribed: "Extra Rapido"

C279 AP60 1p ol gray & brn 9.00 5.25
C280 AP60 2p vio & blk 6.00 4.50
Nos. C275-C280 (6) 16.05 10.25

Issued to publicize the 7th Congress of the Postal Union of the Americas and Spain, Bogota, Oct. 12-Nov. 9, 1955.

No. C278a contains one each of Nos. C277-C278 printed in different shades. It measures 120x132mm. with marginal inscription in black: "Ministerio de Communicaciones. III Exposicion Filatelica Nacional Bogota 1955."

Caro Type of Regular Issue, 1955.

1955, Nov. 29 Engr. *Perf. 13½x13*

C281 A275 15c gray grn 35 5

Issued to commemorate the centenary of the death of Jose Eusebio Caro, poet.

University of Salamanca AP62

Inscribed: "Extra Rapido"

1955, Nov. 29 Unwmk. *Perf. 13*

C282 AP62 20c dk brn 15 5

University of Salamanca, 7th centenary.

Type of Postal Tax Stamp of 1948-50 Surcharged in Black

CORREO
EXTRA-RAPIDO

1956 Wmk. 255 Engr. *Perf. 12*

C283 PT10 2c on 8c bl 6 5

No. 617 Overprinted in Black

EXTRA-RAPIDO

1956 Unwmk. *Perf. 12½x13*

C284 A256 1p blk & emer 25 5

Columbus Type of Regular Issue.

1956, Oct. 11 Photo. *Perf. 12*

C285 A279 15c int bl 50 15

Issued in honor of Christopher Columbus. See also No. C306.

St. Elizabeth Type of Regular Issue

1956, Nov. 19

C286 A280 15c red brn 40 20

Issued to commemorate the 7th centenary of St. Elizabeth of Hungary, patron saint of Santa Fe de Bogota.

St. Ignatius Type of Regular Issue

1956, Nov. 26 Engr. *Perf. 12½x13*

C287 A281 5c brown 25 5

Issued to commemorate the 400th anniversary of the death of St. Ignatius of Loyola.

Javier Pereira — AP63

1956, Dec. 28 Unwmk. *Perf. 12*

C288 AP63 20c rose car 15 10

Issued to honor 167-year-old Javier Pereira.

No. 649 and Type of 1941 Overprinted in Red "EXTRA RAPIDO."

1957 *Perf. 13½x13*

C289 A276 5c bl & blk 9.50 5.50

Perf. 12

C290 AP23 5p org & gray 8.50 6.00

The overprint measures 14mm.

Virgin Type of 1954.

Engraved and Lithographed

1957, May 23 Unwmk. *Perf. 13*

C291 AP48 5c dp plum & multi 8 6

Bank Type of Regular Issue, 1957.

Designs: C292, 20c, Emblem and dairy farm. 10c, Emblem and tractor. 15c, Emblem, coffee and corn. C293, Emblem, cow, horse and herd.

1957 Photo. *Perf. 14x13½*

C292 A283 5c chocolate 20 5
C293 A283 5c orange 15 5
C294 A283 10c green 70 55
C295 A283 15c black 40 8
C296 A283 20c dl red 25 25
Nos. C292-C296 (5) 1.70 98

Nos. C292-C296 issued to commemorate the 25th anniversary of the founding of the Agrarian Savings Bank of Colombia.

No. C292 is inscribed "Extra Rapido."

No. C292 issued Mar. 5, others May 23.

Cyclist AP64

1957, July 6 Unwmk. *Perf. 12*

C297 AP64 2c brown 15 15
C298 AP64 5c ultra 25 25

Seventh Bicycle Tour of Colombia.

Academy Type of Regular Issue.

Designs: 15c, Coat of arms and Gen. Rafael Reyes. 20c, Coat of arms and Academy.

1957, July 20 Engr. *Perf. 12½*

C299 A284 15c rose car 22 5
C300 A284 20c brown 40 8

Issued to commemorate the 50th anniversary of the Colombian Military Academy.

Delgado Type of Regular Issue, 1957.

1957, Sept. 15 Photo. *Perf. 12*

C301 A285 10c sl bl 25 10

Issued in honor of José Matias Delgado, liberator of El Salvador.

UPU Type of Regular Issue, 1957.

1957, Oct. 10

C302 A286 15c dk red brn 25 15
C303 A286 25c dk bl 25 5

Issued for International Letter Writing Week and the 14th UPU Congress.

St. Vincent de Paul Type of Regular Issue, 1957.

1957, Oct. 18

C304 A287 5c rose brn 25 15

Issued to commemorate the centenary of the Colombian Society of St. Vincent de Paul.

Fencing Type of Regular Issue, 1957.

1957, Nov. 23 *Perf. 12*

C305 A288 20c dk red brn 40 35

Issued to commemorate the third South American Fencing Championship.

Columbus Type of Regular Issue, 1956, Inscribed "Extra Rapido."

1958, Jan. 8 Unwmk. *Perf. 12*

C306 A279 3c dk grn 10 7

Scenic Type of 1954.

Design: 25c, Las Lajas Shrine.

1958, June 20 Engr. *Perf. 13*

C307 AP40 25c dk bl 40 7
C308 AP40 25c rose vio 40 7

IGY Type of Regular Issue, 1958.

1958, May 12 Photo. *Perf. 12*

C309 A289 25c green 70 10

Inscribed "Extra Rapido."

C310 A289 1p purple 50 10

Nos. C309-C310 issued for the International Geophysical Year, 1957-58.

No. 659 Overprinted "AEREO" in Carmine.

1958, Oct. 16 Engr. *Perf. 13*

C312 A277 50c dk grn & blk 60 15

Almanza Type of Regular Issue, 1958.

1958, Oct. 23 Photo. *Perf. 14x13*

C313 A290 25c dk gray 40 10

Inscribed "Extra Rapido"

C314 A290 10c ol grn 15 5

Carrasquilla Type of Regular Issue, 1959.

1959, Jan. 22 Photo. *Perf. 14x13*

C315 A291 25c car rose 30 5
C316 A291 1p dk bl 90 25

Issued to commemorate the centenary of the birth (in 1857) of Msgr. R. M. Carrasquilla, rector of Our Lady of the Rosary Seminary, Bogota.

Miss Universe Type of Regular Issue, 1959.

1959, June 26 Unwmk. *Perf. 11½*

C317 A292 1.20p multi 2.00 1.65
C318 A292 5p multi 47.50 47.50

Issued to honor Luz Marina Zuluaga, Miss Universe, 1959.

Gaitan Type of Regular Issue, 1959, Inscribed "Extra Rapido" and Surcharged in Black or Blue.

1959, July 28 Engr. *Perf. 12x13½*

C319 A293 2p on 1p blk 1.50 1.40
C320 A293 2p on 1p blk (Bl) 1.75 1.65

Issued in honor of Jorge Eliecer Gaitan, (1898-1948), lawyer and politician.

The 1p black, type A293, exists without surcharge.

No. C247 Surcharged with New Value in Dark Blue; Old Value Obliterated.

1959, Aug. 24 Unwmk. *Perf. 13*

C321 AP40 50c on 60c dk brn 1.75 55

Regular and Air Post Issues of 1948-1959 Overprinted in Black or Red

1959-60

C322 A283 5c orange 45 40
C323 A287 5c rose brn ('60) 60 60
C324 A281 5c brn (R) 55 45
C325 AP41 10c black 22 8
a. Double ovpt. 3.50 3.50
C326 A160 10c red 50 10
a. Double ovpt. 2.00 2.00
C328 A284 15c rose car 35 5
a. Inverted ovpt. 4.50 4.50
C330 AP40 20c brown 20 5
a. Double ovpt. 2.00 2.00
C331 A284 20c brown 30 30
C332 A288 20c dk red brn ('60) 25 20
C333 AP40 25c rose vio ('60) 25 5
C334 AP40 25c dk bl 25 5
C335 A291 25c car rose 30 10
C336 A290 25c dk gray 25 7
C338 AP40 30c brn org 20 5
C340 AP40 50c on 60c dk brn 50 18
C341 A291 1p dk bl 90 20
a. Double ovpt. 3.50 3.50
C342 A292 1.20p brn, ultra, car & ol 1.50 1.25
C343 AP41 2p dk grn & blk 2.00 30
C344 AP41 3p car rose & blk 5.50 75
a. Double ovpt. 12.00 12.00
C345 AP41 5p dk grn & red brn 7.50 1.65
a. Double ovpt. 12.00 12.00
b. Invert. ovpt. 12.00 12.00
C346 AP40 10p gray grn & red org 9.50 3.50
Nos. C322-C346 (21) 32.07 10.38

Issued following agreement between the Colombian government and AVIANCA to unify the air postage used on all mail carried by AVIANCA.

Vertical overprint on Nos. C342 and C346.

Airmail Stamp of 1919 and Planes AP66

Designs: 60c, No. C349a, C350a, Planes of 1919 and 1959. C349b, C350b, Stamp of 1919 and Planes.

Unwmk.

1959, Dec. 5 Photo. *Perf. 12*

C347 AP66 35c lt bl, blk & red 75 10
C348 AP66 60c yel grn & gray 40 10

Souvenir Sheets.

C349 AP66 Sheet of two 6.75 6.75
a. 1p org & gray 1.00 1.00
b. 1p lil, gray & red 1.00 1.00

Inscribed "Extra Rapido"

1960, May 17

C350 AP66 Sheet of two 6.75 6.75
a. 1.50p red org & gray 1.25 1.25
b. 1.50p ol, gray & rose 1.25 1.25

Nos. C347-C350 issued to commemorate the 40th anniversary of air post service and of the AVIANCA company.

Nos. C349-C350 measure 90x49½mm. with black marginal inscriptions.

Type of Regular Issue, 1959 and

1859 Stamp and Seaplane AP67

Designs (various stamps of 1859 and): 10c, Map of Colombia. 25c, Pres. Mariano Ospina. 1.20p, Plane over mountains.

1959, Dec. 1 Photo. *Perf. 12*

C351 A296 25c choc & red 50 35
C352 AP67 50c ver & ultra 1.25 75
C353 AP67 1.20p yel grn & car 2.75 1.65

Inscribed "Extra Rapido"

C354 A296 10c lem & vio 15 5

Souvenir Sheet

Tete Beche 5c Stamps of 1859 — AP68

Wmk. "REPUBLICA DE COLOMBIA". (331)

1959, Dec. 23 Litho. *Imperf.*

C355 AP68 5p bl, *pink* 16.50 16.50

Nos. C351-C355 issued to commemorate the centenary of Colombian postage stamps.

No. C355 contains a tete beche pair simulating the 5c blue of 1859, No. 2. Sheet sold for 5p. Size: 74½x70mm.

No. C355 exists with inscription "VALOR $5.10" instead of "VALOR $5."

Eldorado Airport, Bogota AP69

1960, Jan. 5 Wmk. 331 Perf. 12½

C356	AP69	35c blk & ocher	75	35
C356A	AP69	60c ver & gray	90	60

Inscribed "Extra Rapido"

C356B	AP69	1p Prus bl & gray	1.25	60

Ant Bear — AP70

Designs: 1.30p, Armadillo. 1.45p, Parrot fish.

Unwmk.

1960, Feb. 12 Photo. Perf. 12

C357	AP70	35c sepia	1.25	15
C358	AP70	1.30p rose car & dk brn	2.50	2.25
C359	AP70	1.45p lt bl, bl & yel	2.00	1.90

Issued to commemorate the centenary of the death of Alexander von Humboldt, German naturalist and geographer (1769-1859).

Flower Type of Regular Issue, 1960

Flowers: Nos. C360, C362, C366, Passiflora mollissima. Nos. C361, C364, C367, Odontoglossum luteo purpureum. Nos. C363, C369, Anthurium andreanum. Nos. C365, C370, Stanhopea tigrina. No. C368, Espeletia grandiflora.

1960, May 10 Photo. Perf. 12

Flowers in Natural Colors.

C360	A298	5c dk bl	15	12
C361	A298	35c maroon	60	7
C362	A298	60c dk bl	1.25	80
C363	A298	1.45p dk brn	1.25	1.25

Inscribed "Extra Rapido"

C364	A298	5c maroon	10	10
C365	A298	10c brown	10	10
C366	A298	1p dk bl	2.50	2.50
C367	A298	1p maroon	2.50	2.50
C368	A298	1p brown	2.50	2.50
C369	A298	1p brown	2.50	2.50
C370	A298	1p brown	2.50	2.50
		Nos. C360-C370 (11)	15.95	14.94

See also Nos. C420-C425.

Fleeing Family and Uprooted Oak Emblem AP71

Perf. 10, 11

1960, May 24 Litho. Wmk. 331

C371	AP71	60c bl grn & gray	45	30

Issued to publicize World Refugee Year, July 1, 1959-June 30, 1960.

Souvenir Sheet

Pan-American Highway Through Colombia — AP72

1960, May 28 Litho. Imperf.

C372	AP72	2.50p brn & aqua	7.50	7.50

Issued to commemorate the 8th Pan-American Highway Congress, Bogota, May 20-29.

No. C372 measures 44x54mm. with brown marginal inscription and black control number.

Lincoln Type of Regular Issue.

1960, June 6 Perf. 10½

C375	A299	40c dl red brn & blk	1.25	90
C376	A299	60c rose red & blk	35	10

Issued to commemorate the sesquicentennial (in 1959) of the birth of Abraham Lincoln.

Type of Regular Issue and

Joaquin Camacho, Jorge Tadeo Lozano and Jose Miguel Pey — AP73

Designs: No. C378, Arms of Cartagena. 35c, 1.45p, Colombian flag. 60c, Andres Rosillo, Antonio Villavicencio and Joaquin Caicedo. 1p, Manuel de Bernardo Alvarez and Joaquin Gutierrez. 1.20p, Jose Antonio Galan statue. 1.30p, Front page of newspaper La Bagatela, 1811. 1.65p, Antonia Santos, Jose Acevedo y Gomez and Liborio Mejia.

Unwmk.

1960, July 20 Photo. Perf. 12

C377	AP73	5c lil & brn	15	10
C378	A301	5c dp bl grn & multi	15	10
C379	AP73	35c multi	25	5
C380	AP73	60c red brn & grn	60	20
C381	AP73	1p ver & sl grn	1.25	90
C382	A301	1.20p ultra & ind	1.25	90
C383	AP73	1.30p org & blk	1.25	90
C384	AP73	1.45p multi	1.65	1.25
C385	AP73	1.65p grn & brn	1.25	1.25
		Nos. C377-C385 (9)	7.80	5.65

Souvenir Sheet

Stamps Inscribed "Extra Rapido"

Flag, Coins and Arms of Mompox and Cartagena — AP74

C386	AP74	Sheet of four	5.50	5.50
a.		50c dp cl & multi	85	85
b.		50c grn & multi	85	85
c.		1p brn ol, yel, bl & car	85	85
d.		1p lil & gray	85	85

Nos. C377-C386 issued to commemorate the 150th anniversary of Colombia's independence.

No. C386 measures 90x75mm.

St. Isidro Type of Regular Issue, 1960.

Designs: 35c, No. C388a, St. Isidro and farm animals. No. C388b, Nativity.

Unwmk.

1960, Sept. 26 Photo. Perf. 12

C387	A302	35c multi	25	10

Souvenir Sheet

Stamps Inscribed "Extra Rapido"

C388	A302	Sheet of two	9.00	9.00
a.		1.50p multi	3.00	3.00
b.		1.50p multi	3.00	3.00

Issued to honor St. Isidro the Farmer, patron saint of the rural people. Black marginal inscription on No. C388. Size: 89½x60mm.

See also Nos. C439-C440.

Type of Regular Issue, 1959

Portrait: 35c, Simon Bolivar.

Wmk. 331

1960, Nov. 23 Litho. Perf. 12½

C389	A294	35c gray	4.50	60

Type of Regular Issue, 1961 (Pan-American Highway)

Perf. 10½x11

1961, Mar. 7 Unwmk.

C390	A304	10c rose lil & emer	85	75
C391	A304	20c ver & lt bl	85	75
C392	A304	30c blk & emer	85	75

Inscribed "Extra Rapido"

C393	A304	10c dk bl & emer	85	75

Issued to commemorate the 8th Pan-American Highway Congress, Bogota, May 20-29, 1960.

Lopez Type of Regular Issue, 1961

1961, Mar. 22 Photo. Perf. 12½

C394	A305	35c bl & brn	75	10

Inscribed "Extra Rapido"

C395	A305	10c emer & brn	25	15

Souvenir Sheet

C396	A305	1p lil & brn	5.00	5.00

Issued to honor Alfonso Lopez (1886-1959), President of Colombia.

No. C396 contains one stamp with margin solidly printed in brown and lilac; colorless inscriptions, and black control number. Size: 60x75mm.

Brother Damian and San Francisco Church, Cali AP75

Designs: No. 398, Emblem of University del Valle (vert.). 1.30p, Fine Arts School, Cali. 1.45p, Agricultural College, Palmira.

Perf. 13x13½, 13½x13

1961, Aug. 17 Photo. Unwmk.

C397	AP75	35c vio brn & ol	45	7
C398	AP75	35c ol & grn	45	7
C399	AP75	1.30p sep & pink	1.25	65
C400	AP75	1.45p multi	1.25	65

Inscribed: "Extra Rapido"

Design: 10c, View of Cali (vert.).

C401	AP75	10c brn & yel grn	25	10
		Nos. C397-C401 (5)	3.65	1.54

Issued to commemorate the 50th anniversary (in 1960) of the department of Valle del Cauca.

View of Cucuta AP76

1961, Aug. 29

C402	AP76	35c brn ol & grn	90	10

Inscribed: "Extra Rapido"

Design: 10c, Church of the Rosary, Cucuta (vert.).

C403	AP76	10c dk brn & gray grn	15	6

Issued to commemorate the 50th anniversary (in 1960) of the department of North Santander.

Old and New Ships of Barranquilla AP77

Arms and View of San Gil AP78

Hotel, Popayan AP79

Statue of Christ in Procession — AP80

Design: 1.45p, View of Velez.

Perf. 12½x13, 13x12½

1961, Oct. 10 Photo. Unwmk.

C404	AP77	35c gold & bl	70	10
C405	AP78	35c bl grn, yel & red	70	10
C406	AP79	35c car & brn	70	10
C407	AP78	1.45p brn & grn	70	30

Inscribed: "Extra Rapido."

C408	AP80	10c brn & yel	15	7
		Nos. C404-C408 (5)	2.95	67

Souvenir Sheets

Types of Regular and Air Post Issues

Designs, No. C409: 35c, Barranquilla arms. 40c, Popayan arms. c, Arms and view of San Gil. d, Holy Week in Popayan. No. C410: a, Old and new ships at Barranquilla. b, Hotel, Popayan. c, Bucaramanga arms. d, Holy Week in Popayan.

C409	Sheet of four	7.50	7.50
a.	A309 35c gold & multi	50	50
b.	A309 40c gold & multi	50	50
c.	AP78 1p bl, yel & red	1.10	1.10
d.	AP80 1p car rose & yel	1.10	1.10

Stamps Inscribed: "Extra Rapido."

C410	Sheet of four	7.50	7.50
a.	AP77 50c gold & car rose	85	85
b.	AP79 50c gold & bl	85	85
c.	A309 50c pink & multi	85	85
d.	AP80 50c bl & yel	85	85

Nos. C404-C408 are in honor of the Atlantico Department. Nos. C409-C410 are in honor of the Departments of Atlantico, Cauca and Santander. The sheets have blue marginal inscriptions, black control numbers. Size: 90x75mm.

Nos. 713, 716 and 715 Overprinted and Surcharged

1961, Sept. Perf. 12

C411	A297	5c grnsh bl & brn	15	10
C412	A298	5c multi	15	8
C413	A297	10c on 20c cit & gray brn	15	8

"Aereo" in script on No. C412.

See also Nos. C420-425.

Sports Type of Regular Issue, 1961

Designs: No. C414, Women divers. No. C415, Tennis, mixed doubles. 1.45p, C419b, Baseball. No. C417, Torch bearer. No. C418, C419a, Bolivar statue and flags of six participating nations. No. C419c, Soccer. No. C419d, Basketball.

1961, Dec. 16 Litho. Perf. 13½x14

C414	A310	35c ultra, yel & brn	85	5
C415	A310	35c car, yel & brn	85	5
C416	A310	1.45p Prus grn, yel & brn	1.25	80

Inscribed: "Extra Rapido"

C417	A310	10c car lake, yel & brn	15	5
C418	A310	10c ol, yel, bl & red	15	5
		Nos. C414-C418 (5)	3.25	1.00

Souvenir Sheet

Stamps Inscribed: "Extra Rapido."

Imperf

C419	Sheet of four	7.25	7.25
a.	A310 50c multi	60	60
b.	A310 50c multi	60	60
c.	A310 1p multi	1.20	1.20
d.	A310 1p multi	1.20	1.20

Issued to publicize the 4th Bolivarian Games, Barranquilla, 1961. No. C419 has black marginal inscription and control number. Size: 74x106mm.

Flower Type of 1960

Flowers: 5c, Passiflora mollissima. 10c, Espeletia grandiflora. 20c, 2p, Odontoglossum luteo purpureum. 25c, Stanhopea tigrina. 60c, Anthurium Andreanum.

Unwmk.

1962, Jan. 30 Photo. *Perf. 12*

Flowers in Natural Colors

C420	A298	5c gray	15	10
C421	A298	10c gray bl	15	10
C422	A298	20c rose lil	15	10
C423	A298	25c citron	40	10
C424	A298	60c lt brn	40	40

Inscribed "Extra Rapido"

C425	A298	2p sal pink	2.75	2.00
		Nos. C420-C425 (6)	4.00	2.80

Anti-Malaria Type of Regular Issue.

Designs: 40c, Colombian anti-malaria emblem. 1p, 1.45p, Malaria eradication emblem and mosquito in swamp.

1962, Apr. 12 Litho. *Perf. 12*

C426	A311	40c yel & red	25	20
C427	A311	1.45p gray & ultra	75	65

Inscribed "Extra Rapido"

C428	A311	1p yel grn & ultra	5.25	5.25

Issued for the World Health Organization drive to eradicate malaria.

Type of Regular Issue, 1962 and

Abelardo Ramos and Engineering School, Cauca — AP81

Designs: 10c, Miguel Triana, Andres A. Arroyo and Monserrate shrine with cable cars. 15c, Diodoro Sanchez and first meeting place of Engineers Society. 2p, Engineers Society emblem.

1962, June 12 Photo. *Perf. 11½x12*

C429	AP81	5c bl & dp rose	10	10
C430	AP81	10c grn & sep	20	15
C431	AP81	15c lil & sep	40	25

Inscribed: "Extra Rapido"

C432	A312	2p blk, yel, red & bl	2.50	2.50

Issued to commemorate the 75th anniversary of the founding of the Colombian Society of Engineers and to publicize the Sixth National Congress of Engineers.

American States Type of 1962.

1962, June 28 Photo. *Perf. 13*

Flags in National Colors

C433	A313	35c blk & bl	50	5

Women's Rights Type of 1962

Perf. 12x12½

1962, July 20 Litho. Wmk. 229

C434	A314	35c ocher, gray & blk	30	5

Issued to publicize women's political rights. See also Nos. C448-C450.

Scout Type of 1962.

Designs: 15c, No. C438, Scouts at campfire and tents. 40c and No. C437, Girl Scouts.

Perf. 11½x12

1962, July 26 Photo. Unwmk.

C435	A315	15c brn & rose	30	25
C436	A315	40c dp cl & pink	35	30
C437	A315	1p bl & buff	1.40	50

Inscribed "Extra Rapido"

C438	A315	1p pur & yel	5.50	5.50

Nos. C435 and C438 issued to commemorate the 30th anniversary of the Colombian Boy Scouts. Nos. C436 and C437 commemorate the 25th anniversary of the Girl Scouts.

Nativity by Gregorio Vasquez — AP82

Design: 2p, St. Isidro, similar to type A302.

Inscribed "Extra Rapido"

Unwmk.

1962, Aug. 28 Photo. *Perf. 12*

C439	AP82	10c gray & multi	15	5
C440	AP82	2p gray & multi	4.75	4.75

See also Nos. C387-C388.

Type of Regular Issue, 1962 and

Pres. Aquileo Parra and Magdalena River Bridge AP83

Design: 5c, Locomotives of 1854 and 1961. 10c, Railroad map of Colombia.

1962, Sept. 28 Photo. *Perf. 12½*

C441	AP83	5c sep & sl grn	20	5
C442	A316	10c multi	15	5

Engr.

C443	AP83	1p dl pur & brn	2.00	20

Inscribed: "Extra Rapido."

C444	AP83	5p bl, brn & dl grn	5.25	2.50

Issued to publicize the progress of Colombian railroads and to commemorate the completion of the Atlantic Line from Santa Maria to Bogota.

UPAE Type of Regular Issue

Designs: 50c, Map of Americas and carrier pigeon. 60c, Post horn.

Perf. 13½x14

1962, Oct. 18 Litho. Wmk. 346

C445	A317	50c sl grn & gold	40	10
C446	A317	60c gold & plum	30	5

Issued to commemorate the 50th anniversary of the founding of the Postal Union of the Americas and Spain, UPAE.

Pope John XXIII — AP84

1963, Mar. 11

C447	AP84	60c gold, red brn, buff & red	30	5

Issued to commemorate Vatican II, the 21st Ecumenical Council of the Roman Catholic Church.

Women's Rights Type of 1962

1963-64 *Perf. 12x12½*

C448	A314	5c sal, gray & blk ('64)	6	5
C449	A314	45c pale grn, gray & blk	50	5
C450	A314	45c brt pink, gray & blk	50	5

Games Emblem — AP85

Perf. 13x14

1963, Aug. 12 Wmk. 346

C451	AP85	20c gray & multi	20	7
C452	AP85	80c buff & multi	20	5

Issued to commemorate the South American Athletic Championships (22nd for men, 12th for women), Cali, June 30-July 7.

Bolivar Statue by Arenas-Betancourt — AP86

Perf. 14x13½

1963, Aug. 30 Unwmk.

C453	AP86	1.90p ol bis & bl	30	5

Centenary of the city of Pereira.

Tennis Player — AP87

1963, Oct. 11 *Perf. 13½x14*

C454	AP87	55c multi	15	5

Issued to commemorate the 30th South American Tennis Championships, Medellin, Oct. 3-13.

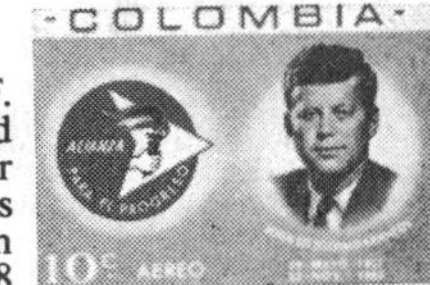

Pres. John F. Kennedy and Alliance for Progress Emblem AP88

1963, Dec. 17 Litho. *Perf. 14x13½*

C455	AP88	10c multi	5	5

Issued to honor President John F. Kennedy (1917-1963).

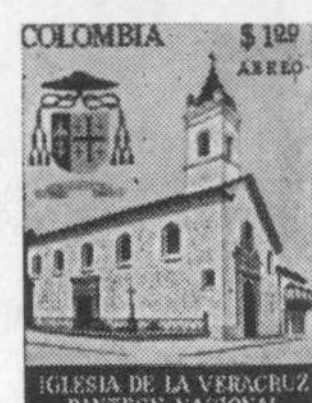

Church of the True Cross, National Pantheon, Bogota — AP89

Design: 2p, Christ of the Martyrs, bell and tomb.

Perf. 13½x14

1964, Mar. 10 Photo. Unwmk.

C459	AP89	1p multi	40	10
C460	AP89	2p multi	50	25

View of Cartagena AP90

1964, Mar. 18 Litho. *Perf. 14x13½*

C461	AP90	3p vio, bl, ocher & brn	2.00	85

Issued to commemorate Cartagena's independence in 1811, Simon Bolivar's visit in 1812 and the siege of 1815.

Eleanor Roosevelt AP91

1964, Nov. 10 Photo. *Perf. 12*

C462	AP91	20c ol & dl red brn	10	5

Issued to honor Eleanor Roosevelt (1884-1962).

Alberto Castilla and Score of "El Bunde" — AP92

1964, Nov. 10 Unwmk.

C463	AP92	30c ol bis & Prus grn	10	5

Issued to honor the Department of Tolima and Maestro Alberto Castilla (1878-1937) who in 1906 founded the Tolima Conservatory of Music in Ibague.

Mejia Type of Regular Issue

Designs (Mejia portrait and): 45c, Women picking coffee. 5p, Mules carrying coffee bags. 10p, Loading coffee on freighter "Manuel Mejia."

1965, Feb. 10 Engr. *Perf. 12½x13*

C464	A320	45c brn & blk	25	5
C465	A320	5p gray grn & blk	3.00	45
C466	A320	10p ultra & blk	4.00	40

Issued to honor Manuel Mejia J. (1887-1958), banker and manager of the National Coffee Growers Association.

ITU Emblem AP93

1965, Oct. 25 Photo. *Perf. 12*
C467 AP93 80c Prus bl, lt bl & red 20 8

Issued to commemorate the centenary of the International Telecommunication Union.

Cattleya Truanae — AP94

Pres. Manuel Murillo Toro Statue, Telegraph and Orbits — AP95

1965, Oct. 3 Litho. *Perf. 13½x14*
C468 AP94 20c yel & multi 10 6

Fifth Philatelic Exhibition.

1965, Nov. 1 *Perf. 13½x14, 14x13½*

Design: No. C470, Telegraph and satellites over South America (horiz.).

C469 AP95 60c multi 20 5
C470 AP95 60c multi 20 5

Centenary of the telegraph in Colombia.

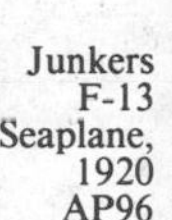

Junkers F-13 Seaplane, 1920 AP96

History of Colombian Aviation: 10c, Dornier Wal, 1924. 20c, Dornier Mercur, 1926. 50c, Trimotor Ford, 1932. 60c, De Havilland biplane, 1930. 1p, Douglas DC-4, 1947. 1.40p, Douglas DC-3, 1944. 2.80p, Superconstellation 1049, 1951. 3p, Boeing 720B jet, 1961.

Perf. 14x13½
1965-66 Photo. Unwmk.

C471	AP96	5c multi	10	5
C472	AP96	10c multi	10	5
C473	AP96	20c multi	15	5
C474	AP96	50c multi	15	5
C475	AP96	60c multi	30	5
C476	AP96	1p multi	50	15
C477	AP96	1.40p multi	60	20
C478	AP96	2.80p multi	1.25	90
C479	AP96	3p multi	1.90	1.25
		Nos. C471-C479 (9)	5.05	2.75

Issue dates: 5c, 60c, 3p, Dec. 13, 1965; 10c, 1p, 1.40p, July 15, 1966; 20c, 50c, 2.80p, Dec. 14, 1966.

Automobile Club Emblem and Car on Road AP97

1966, Feb. 16 Litho. *Perf. 14x13½*
C480 AP97 20c multi 10 6

Issued to commemorate the 25th anniversary (in 1965) of the Automobile Club of Colombia.

Fish Type of Regular Issue, 1966.

Fish: 2p, Flying fish. 2.80p, Queen angelfish. 20p, King mackerel.

1966, Aug. 25 Photo. *Perf. 12½x13*
C481 A323 2p multi 50 20
C482 A323 2.80p multi 1.50 1.50
C483 A323 20p multi 12.50 12.50

Coat of Arms Type of Regular Issue, 1966

1966, Oct. 11 Litho. *Perf. 14x13½*
C484 A324 1p ultra & multi 35 10
C485 A324 1.40p red & multi 30 10

Issued to commemorate the visits of Eduardo Frei and Raul Leoni, presidents of Chile and Venezuela.

Portrait Type of Regular Issue

Portraits: 80c, Father Felix Restrepo Mejia, S.J. (1887-1965), theologian and scholar. 1.70p, Jose Joaquin Casas (1866-1951), educator and diplomat.

Perf. 13½x14
1967, Jan. 18 Litho. Unwmk.
C486 A325 80c dk bl & bis 15 5
C487 A325 1.70p blk & bis 35 15

Famous men of Colombia.

Declaration of Bogota Type of Regular Issue

1967, Feb. 2 Litho. *Perf. 14x13½*
C488 A326 3p multi 50 25

See note after No. 767.

Orchid Type of Regular Issue

Orchids: 1p, Cattleya dowiana aurea (vert.). 1.20p, Masdevallia coccinea (vert.). 5p, Catasetum macrocarpum and bee.

1967, May 23 Litho. *Perf. 14*
C489 A327 1p multi 55 20
C490 A327 1.20p multi 38 10
C491 A327 5p multi 2.25 50
a. Souv. sheet of 3 3.50 3.50

Issued to commemorate the First National Orchid Exhibition and the Topical Philatelic Flora and Fauna Exhibition, Medellin, Apr. 1967. No. C491a contains one each of Nos. C489-C491. Gray margin with black inscription and red control number. Size: 99x149mm.

Lions Type of Regular Issue

1967, July 12 Litho. *Perf. 13½x14*
C492 A328 25c multi 20 5

Lions International, 50th anniversary.

"First Caesarean Section" by Grau AP98

Perf. 14x13½
1967, Sept. 7 Litho. Unwmk.
C493 AP98 80c multi 10 5

Issued to publicize the 6th Congress of Colombian Surgeons, Bogota, Sept. 25.

SENA Type of Regular Issue
Lithographed and Embossed

1967, Sept. 20 *Perf. 13½x14*
C494 A329 2p gold, ver & blk 70 15

Issued to commemorate the 10th anniversary of National Apprenticeship Service, SENA.

Pre-Columbian Art Type of Regular Issue

Designs: 30c, Bird pectoral. 5p Ornamental pectoral. 20p, Pitcher.

1967, Oct. 13 Photo. *Perf. 13½x14*
C495 A330 30c ver, gold & brn 20 5
C496 A330 5p red, gold & brn 2.50 50
a. Souvenir sheet of 2 3.00 2.50
C497 A330 20p vio, gold & brn 13.00 11.00

Issued to commemorate the meeting of the Universal Postal Union Committee on Postal Studies, Bogota, October, 1967; No. C496a also commemorates the 6th National Philatelic Exhibition. No. C496a contains 2 imperf. stamps in changed colors similar to Nos. C495-C496 (30c has green background and 5 p maroon background). Gray margin with red control number. Size: 92x91mm.

Telecommunications Type of Regular Issue

Designs: 50c, Signal lights. 1p, Early Bird satellite, Southern Cross and radar.

Perf. 13½x14
1968, May 14 Litho. Unwmk.
C498 A331 50c blk, ver & emer 15 5
C499 A331 1p ultra, yel & gray 25 5

Issued to commemorate the 20th anniversary of the National Telecommunications Service (TELECOM).

Eucharist Type of Regular Issue

1968, June 6 Litho. *Perf. 13½x14*
C500 A332 80c rose lil, red, yel & blk 15 5
C501 A332 3p bl, red, yel & blk 45 15

Issued to publicize the 39th Eucharistic Congress, Bogota, Aug. 18-25.

Eucharistic Congress Type of Regular Issue

Designs: 80c, The Last Supper, by Gregorio Vasquez (horiz.). 1p, St. Francis Xavier Preaching, by Gregorio Vasquez. 2p, The Dream of the Prophet Elias, by Gregorio Vasquez. 3p, Monstrance, c. 1700. 20p, Pope Paul VI, painting by Roman Franciscan nuns.

1968, Aug. 13 Photo. *Perf. 13*

C502	A333	80c multi	25	5
C503	A333	1p multi	35	5
C504	A333	2p multi	50	10
C505	A333	3p lil & multi	90	10
C506	A333	20p gold & multi	5.75	3.00
		Nos. C502-C506 (5)	7.75	3.30

Issued to commemorate the 39th Eucharistic Congress, Bogota, Aug. 18-25.

Shrine of the Eucharist, Bogota AP99

Designs: 1.20p, Pope Paul VI giving blessing and Papal arms (vert.). 1.80p, Cathedral of Bogota (vert.).

Perf. 14x13½, 13½x14
1968, Aug. 22 Litho.
C507 AP99 80c multi 15 5
C508 AP99 1.20p multi 30 10
C509 AP99 1.80p multi 45 20

Visit of Pope Paul VI to Colombia.

Computer Symbols — AP100

1968, Oct. 29 Litho. *Perf. 13½x14*
C510 AP100 20c buff, car & grn 10 5

Issued to commemorate the centenary of the National University and the First Data Processing Congress in 1967 at the University.

Agriculture Institute Type of Regular Issue

1968, Mar. 5 Litho. *Perf. 13½x14*
C511 A337 1p gray & multi 25 5

Issued to commemorate the 25th anniversary (in 1967) of the Inter-American Agricultural Sciences Institute.

Microscope and Pen — AP101

1969, Mar. 24 Litho. *Perf. 14*
C512 AP101 5p blk, yel, ver & pur 1.65 15

Issued to commemorate the 20th anniversary (in 1968) of the University of the Andes.

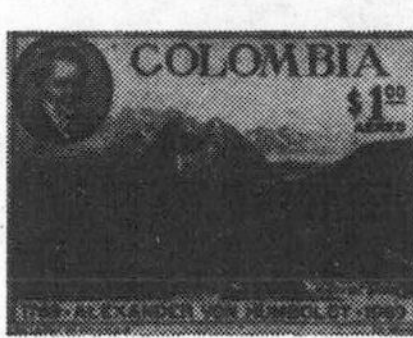

Alexander von Humboldt and Andes AP102

1969, May 3 Litho. *Perf. 14x13½*
C513 AP102 1p grn & brn 20 5

Issued to commemorate the bicentenary of the birth of Alexander von Humboldt (1769-1859), German naturalist and traveler.

Map of Colombia, Amphibian Plane and Letter AP103

Design: 1.50p, No. C516b, Globe, letter, and jet of Avianca airlines.

1969, June 18 Litho. *Perf. 14x13½*
C514 AP103 1p multi 25 6
C515 AP103 1.50p multi 35 15

Souvenir Sheet
Imperf

C516 AP103 Sheet of 2 5.25 5.25
a. 5p grn & multi 1.00 1.00
b. 5p vio & multi 1.00 1.00

Issued to commemorate the 50th anniversary of the first air post flight in Colombia. No. C516 also publicizes the 8th National Philatelic Exhibition, EXFILBA 69, Barranquilla, June 18-22. No. C516 contains 2 stamps in the designs of the 1p and 1.50p; gray margin with commemorative inscription, coats of arms and red control number. Size: 92x92mm.

Independence Type of Regular Issue

1969, July 24 Litho. *Perf. 13½x14*

Design: 2.30p, Simon Bolivar, José Antonio Anzoategui, Francisco de Paula Santander and victorious army entering Bogota, Sept. 18, 1819; painting by Ignacio Castillo Cervantes.

C517 A338 2.30p gold & multi 70 25

Issued to commemorate the sesquicentennial of the fight for independence.

Social Security Emblem AP104

Neurosurgeons' Congress Emblem AP105

1969, Oct. 29 Litho. *Perf. 13½x14*
C518 AP104 20c emer & blk 10 5

Issued to commemorate the 20th anniversary of the Colombian Institute of Social Security.

1969, Oct. 29
C519 AP105 70c vio, red & yel 30 10

Issued to publicize the 13th Congress of Latin-American Neurosurgeons, Bogota.

Junkers F-13 AP106

Designs: No. C521, C522b, Globe with airlines from Bogota and Boeing jet. No. C522a, like No. C520.

1969, Nov. 28 Litho. *Perf. 14x13½*
C520 AP106 2p grn & multi 50 15
C521 AP106 3.50p ultra & multi 70 40

Souvenir Sheet
Imperf

C522 AP106 Sheet of 2 5.25 5.25
a. 3.50p lt grn & multi 75 75
b. 5p ultra & multi 1.10 1.10

Issued to commemorate the 50th anniversary of AVIANCA; No. C522 also publicizes the First Interamerican Philatelic Exhibition, Bogota, Nov. 28-Dec. 7.

No. C522 contains 2 imperf. stamps. Multicolored inscriptions, coat of arms, medals and red control number on light olive margin. Size: 92x90mm.

Child Mailing Letter — AP107

Design: 1.50p, Praying child and gifts.

1969, Dec. 16 Litho. *Perf. 13½x14*
C523 AP107 60c ocher & multi 60 25
C524 AP107 1p multi 60 10
C525 AP107 1.50p multi 70 25

Christmas 1969.

Radar Station and Pre-Columbian Head — AP108

1970, Mar. 25 Litho. *Perf. 14x13½*
C526 AP108 1p dl grn, blk & brick red 40 5

Issued to publicize the opening of the communications satellite earth station at Choconta in Cundinamarca Province.

Certain countries cancel stamps in full sheets and sell them (usually with gum) for less than face value. Dealers generally sell "CTO".

Emblem of Colombian Youth Sports Institute AP109

Art Exhibition Emblem AP110

Design: 2.30p, Games' emblem (dove and 3 rings).

1970, Apr. 6 Litho. *Perf. 13½x14*
C527 AP109 1.50p dk ol grn, yel & blk 40 25
C528 AP109 2.30p red & multi 60 25

Issued to publicize the 9th National Youth Games, Ibague, July 10-20.

1970, Apr. 30 Litho. *Perf. 13½x14*
C529 AP110 30c multi 10 5

Issued to publicize the 2nd Biennial Art Exhibition, Medellin, May 1-June 14.

Eduardo Santos, Rural and Urban Buildings AP111

1970, June 18 Litho. *Perf. 14x13½*
C530 AP111 1p grn, yel & blk 25 5

Issued to commemorate the founding (in 1939) of the Territorial Credit Institute.

U.N. Emblem, Scales and Dove AP112

EXFILCA Emblem AP113

1970, June 26 *Perf. 13½x14*
C531 AP112 1.50p dk bl, lt bl & yel 25 5

25th anniversary of United Nations.

1970, Nov. Litho. *Perf. 13½x14*
C532 AP113 10p bl, gold & blk 5.00 38

Issued to publicize EXFILCA 70, 2nd Interamerican Philatelic Exhibition. Caracas, Venezuela, Nov. 27-Dec. 6.

Mother Juana Ruperta in Napanga Costume and Music by Efrain Orozco AP114

Athlete and Games Emblem AP115

Designs: 1p, Dancers from Eastern Plains and music by Alejandro Wills. No. C535, Guabina man, woman and folk song. No. C536, Bambuco man and woman, and music. No. C537, Man and woman dancing the Cumbia, and music.

1970-71 Litho. *Perf. 13½x14*
C533 AP114 60c dp lil rose & multi 70 20
C534 AP114 1p ultra & multi 50 8
C535 AP114 1.30p bl & multi 65 10
C536 AP114 1.30p emer & multi ('71) 65 10
C537 AP114 1.30p lil & multi ('71) 50 10
Nos. C533-C537 (5) 3.00 58

1971, Mar. 11

Design: 2p, Games emblem.

C542 AP115 1.50p multi 1.30 90
C543 AP115 2p blk, org & grn 1.20 80

6th Pan-American Games, Cali, July 30-Aug. 13.

Gilberto Alzate Avendaño AP116

1971, Apr. 29 Litho. *Perf. 14x13½*
C544 AP116 1p bl & multi 60 38

Gilberto Alzate Avendaño (1910-1960), journalist and popular leader, 10th anniversary of death.

Commemorative Medal — AP117

Lithographed and Embossed

1971, June 21 *Perf. 14x13½*
C545 AP117 1p sl grn & gold 70 40

Centenary (in 1970) of the Bank of Bogota.

Olympic Center — AP118

Soccer — AP119

Designs (Games Emblem and): Nos. C546-C546c, Olympic Center. No. 547, Soccer. No. C548, Wrestling. No. C549, Bicycling. No. C550, Volleyball. No. C551, Diving (women). No. C552, Fencing. No. C553, Sailing. No. C554, Equestrian. No. C555, Jumping. No. C556, Rowing. No. C557, Cali emblem. No. C558, Basketball (women). No. C559, Stadium. No. C560, Baseball. No. C561, Hockey. No. C562, Weight lifting. No. C563, Medals. No. C564, Boxing. No. C565, Gymnastics (women). No. C566, Sharpshooting.

1971, July 16 Litho. *Perf. 13½x14*
C546 AP118 1.30p yel & multi 1.75 30
a. 1.30p grn & multi 1.75 30
b. 1.30p bl & multi 1.75 30
c. 1.30p car & multi 1.75 30
C547 AP119 1.30p emer & multi 1.75 30
C548 AP119 1.30p lil & multi 1.75 30
C549 AP119 1.30p bl & multi 1.75 30
C550 AP119 1.30p car & multi 1.75 30
C551 AP119 1.30p bl & multi 1.75 30
C552 AP119 1.30p car & multi 1.75 30
C553 AP119 1.30p bl & multi 1.75 30
C554 AP119 1.30p gray & multi 1.75 30
C555 AP119 1.30p grn & multi 1.75 30
C556 AP119 1.30p bl & multi 1.75 30
C557 AP118 1.30p org & multi 1.75 30
C558 AP119 1.30p car & multi 1.75 30
C559 AP118 1.30p lt bl & multi 1.75 30
C560 AP119 1.30p plum & multi 1.75 30
C561 AP119 1.30p yel grn & multi 1.75 30
C562 AP119 1.30p pink & multi 1.75 30
C563 AP118 1.30p dp org & multi 1.75 30
C564 AP119 1.30p plum & multi 1.75 30
C565 AP119 1.30p lil rose & multi 1.75 30
C566 AP119 1.30p grn & multi 1.75 30
a. Sheet of 25 (Nos. C546-C566) 45.00 7.25

6th Pan American Athletic Games, Cali. First color in listings is color of emblem. No. C546b appears twice in sheet. No. C566a has marginal multicolored inscription commemorating EXFILCALI 71 Philatelic Exhibition.

Battle of Carabobo, by Martin Tovar y Tovar — AP120

1971, Nov. 25 Litho. *Perf. 13½x14*
C567 AP120 1.50p multi 1.50 25

Sesquicentennial of the Battle of Carabobo.

St. Theresa Type of Regular Issue Overprinted "AEREO"

1972 Litho. *Perf. 13½x14*
C568 A343 2p multi 45 5

See note after No. 793.

Vendor — AP121

Designs: 50c, Woman wearing shawl, and woven shawl. 3p, Fruit vendor (puppet).

1971, Apr. 11 Litho. *Perf. 13½x14*

C569	AP121	50c multi	38	25
C570	AP121	1p multi	40	15
C571	AP121	3p multi	50	35

Colombian artisans.

Mormodes Rolfeanum AP122

1972, Apr. 20 *Perf. 14x13½*

C572	AP122	1.30p multi	40	5

7th World Orchidology Congress, Medellin.

Congo Grande Dancer AP123

Pres. Laureano Gomez, by Ridriguez Cubillos AP124

1972, June 21 Litho. *Perf. 13½x14*

C573	AP123	1.30p multi	60	7

International Carnival of Barranquilla.

No. C453 Surcharged in Brown — **$ 1.30**

1972, Oct. 5 Litho. *Perf. 14x13½*

C574	AP86	1.30p on 1.90p ol bis & bl	80	25

1972, Oct. 17 *Perf. 13½x14*

C575	AP124	1.30p multi	20	5

Laureano Gomez (1898-1966), President of Colombia.

1972, Nov. 28

Design: 1.30p, Guillermo León Valencia Muñoz.

C576	AP124	1.30p multi	25	5

Guillermo León Valencia Muñoz (1909-1971), President of Colombia.

Benito Juarez AP125

Rebecca Fountain AP126

1972, Dec. 12 *Perf. 13½x14*

C577	AP125	1.50p multi	30	10

Centenary of the death of Benito Juarez (1806 1872), revolutionary leader and president of Mexico.

1972, Dec. 19 Litho.

C578	AP126	80c multi	70	40
C579	AP126	1p multi	60	15

"Bucaramanga" — AP127

1972, Dec. 22 *Perf. 14x13½*

C580	AP127	5p multi	1.25	10

350th anniversary of the founding of Bucaramanga.

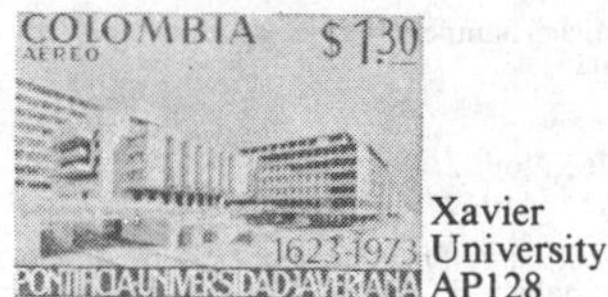

Xavier University AP128

1973, May 8 Litho. *Perf. 14x13½*

C581	AP128	1.30p lt grn & sep	35	8
C582	AP128	1.50p lt bl & sep	35	8

350th anniversary of the founding of Xavier University in Bogota.

Ceramic Type of Regular Issue

Excavated Ceramic Artifacts: 1p, Winged urn, Tairona. 1.30p, Woman and child, Sinu. 1.70p, Two-headed figure, Quimbaya. 3.50p, Man, Tumaco.

1973 Litho. *Perf. 13½x14*

C583	A358	1p multi	1.40	1.25
C584	A358	1.30p multi	70	5
C585	A358	1.70p multi	80	35
C586	A358	3.50p multi	1.65	40

Issue dates: 1p, Oct. 11; others, June 15.

Battle of Maracaibo, by Manuel F. Rincon AP129

1973, July 24 Litho. *Perf. 14x13½*

C587	AP129	10p bl & multi	3.00	25

Battle of Maracaibo, sesquicentennial.

Bank Emblem AP130

1973, Oct. 1 Litho. *Perf. 14x13½*

C588	AP130	2p multi	30	5

50th anniversary of the Bank of the Republic.

No. 801 Overprinted "AEREO"

1973, Oct. 11 *Perf. 14*

C589	A346	80c multi	40	10

Pres. Pedro Nel Ospina, by Coroleano Leudo — AP131

Arms of Toro — AP132

1973, Nov. 9 *Perf. 13½x14*

C590	AP131	1.50p multi	30	8

50th anniversary of the Ministry of Communications founded under Pres. Ospina.

1973, Dec. 1

C591	AP132	1p multi	20	5

4th centenary of the founding of Toro, Valle del Cauca.

Bolivar, Battle of Bombona AP133

1973, Dec. 7 Litho. *Perf. 14x13½*

C592	AP133	1.30p multi	20	6

Sesquicentennial (in 1972) of the Battle of Bombona.

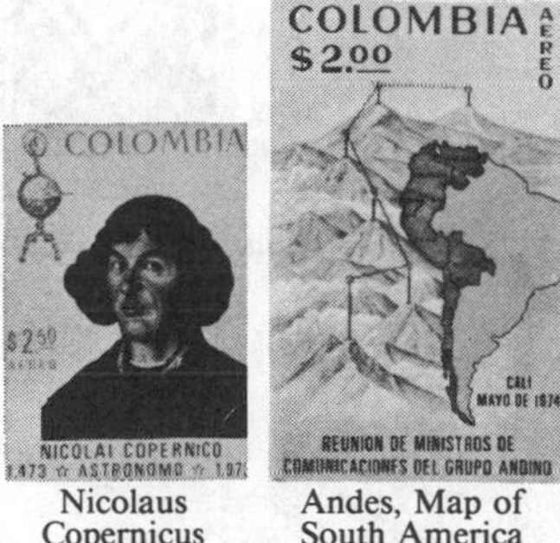

Nicolaus Copernicus AP134

Andes, Map of South America AP135

1974, Feb. 19 Litho. *Perf. 13½x14*

C593	AP134	2.50p multi	70	25

500th anniversary of the birth of Nicolaus Copernicus (1473-1543), Polish astronomer.

1974, May 11 Litho. *Perf. 14*

C594	AP135	2p multi	40	10

Meeting of Communications Ministers of Members of the Andean Group, Cali, May 7-11, 1974.

Television Set AP136

1974, July 16 Litho. *Perf. 14x13½*

C595	AP136	1.30p org, blk & brn	25	5

20th anniversary of Colombian television and 10th anniversary of INRAVISION, the National Institute of Radio and Television.

Championship Emblem — AP137

1974, Aug. 5 Litho. *Perf. 14x13½*

C596	AP137	4.50p multi	45	20

2nd World Swimming Championships, Cali.

Condor — AP138

1974, Aug. 28 *Perf. 14*

C597	AP138	1.50p multi	25	10

Bank of Colombia centenary.

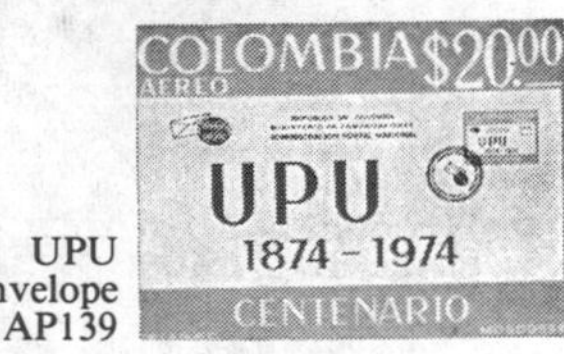

UPU Envelope AP139

1974, Sept. 9 Litho. *Perf. 14*

C598	AP139	20p multi	3.50	40

Centenary of Universal Postal Union.

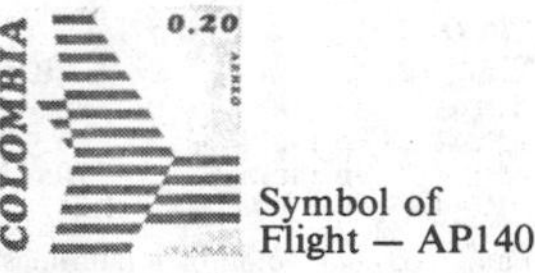

Symbol of Flight — AP140

1974, Sept. *Perf. 12x12½*

C599	AP140	20c olive	8	5

Gen. Jose Maria Cordoba AP141

White-tailed Trogon, Letter AP142

1974, Oct. 14 Litho. *Perf. 13½x14*

C609	AP141	1.30p multi	25	5

Sesquicentennial of the Battles of Junin and Ayacucho.

Insurance Type of 1974

Design: 3p, Abstract pattern.

1974, Oct. 24 Litho. *Perf. 13½x14*

C610	A365	3p multi	40	10

Centenary of National Insurance Company.

Perf. 13½x14, 14x13½

1974, Nov. 14

Designs (UPU Letter and): 1.30p, Keelbilled Toucan (horiz.). 2p, Peruvian cock-of-the-rock (horiz.). 2.50p, Scarlet macaw.

C611	AP142	1p multi	25	8
C612	AP142	1.30p multi	30	5
C613	AP142	2p multi	40	10
C614	AP142	2.50p multi	45	15

Centenary of Universal Postal Union.

Forest No. 1, by Roman Roncancio — AP143

Boy with Thorn in Finger, by Gregorio Vazquez AP144

Paintings: 3p, Women Fruit Vendors, by Miguel Diaz Vargas (1886-1956). 5p, Annunciation, Santaferena School, 17th-18th centuries.

Perf. 13½x14, 14x13½

1975, Mar. 12 **Litho.**

C615	AP143	2p multi	80	10
C616	AP144	3p multi	55	10
C617	AP144	4p multi	70	25
C618	AP144	5p multi	1.25	40

Modern and Colonial Colombian paintings.

Trees and Lake AP145

Design: 6p, Victoria regia, Amazon River.

1975, Mar. 12 *Perf. 14x13½*

C619	AP145	1p yel & multi	22	5
C620	AP145	6p yel & multi	65	10

Nature conservation of trees and Amazon Region.

Gold Treasure Type of 1975

Designs: 2p, Nose pendant. 10p, Alligator-shaped staff ornament.

1975, Apr. 11 **Litho.** *Perf. 14x13½*

C621	A368	2p grn, gold & brn	60	6
C622	A368	10p multi	3.25	85

Pre-Columbian Sinu Culture artifacts.

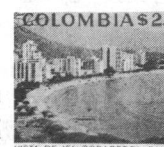

El Rodadero, Santa Maria AP146

1975, July 26 **Litho.** *Perf. 14x13½*

C623	AP146	2p multi	20	5

400th anniversary of Santa Maria City.

Maria de J. Paramo — AP147

1975, Aug. 31 **Litho.** *Perf. 13½x14*

C624	AP147	4p multi	30	5

International Women's Year 1975. Maria de Jesus Paramo de Collazos founded first normal school for women in Bucaramanga in 1875.

"Sugar Cane" — AP148

1976, Mar. 12 **Litho.** *Perf. 13½x14*

C625	AP148	5p blk & emer	1.25	15

4th Congress of Latin-American and Caribbean sugar-exporting countries, Cali, Mar. 8-12.

View of Bogota — AP149

1976, July 2 **Litho.** *Perf. 12*

C626	AP149	10p *shown*	1.75	80
C627	AP149	10p *Barranquilla*	1.75	80
C628	AP149	10p *Cali*	1.75	80
C629	AP149	10p *Medellin*	1.75	80

Habitat, U.N. Conference on Human Settlements, Vancouver, Canada, May 31-June 11. Nos. C626-C629 printed se-tenant in blocks of 4, sheets of 60.

University Emblem and "90" — AP150

1976, Aug. 6 **Litho.** *Perf. 13½x14*

C630	AP150	5p lt bl & multi	75	15

University of Colombia, 90th anniversary.

Miguel Samper AP151

Telephone, 1895 AP152

1976, Oct. 29 **Litho.** *Perf. 13½x14*

C631	AP151	2p multi	30	5

Miguel Samper (1825-1899), economist and writer.

1976, Nov. 2

C632	AP152	3p multi	25	5

Centenary of first telephone call by Alexander Graham Bell, Mar. 10, 1876.

747 Jumbo Jet — AP153

1976, Dec. 3 **Litho.** *Perf. 12*

C633	AP153	2p multi	20	5

Inauguration of 747 jumbo jet service by Avianca.

Convent, Church and Plaza de San Francisco — AP154

1976, Dec. 29 **Litho.** *Perf. 14*

C634	AP154	6p multi	75	20

150th anniversary of the Congress of Panama.

Souvenir Sheet

Bank of the Republic Emblem — AP155

1977, June 6 **Litho.** *Perf. 14*

C635	AP155	25p multi	8.00	8.00

Opening of Philatelic Museum of Medellin under auspices of Banco de la Republica. No. C635 contains one stamp (50x40mm.); multicolored margin shows various orchids; black control number. Size: 130x105mm.

No. C633 Surcharged in Light Brown

1977, June **Litho.** *Perf. 12*

C636	AP153	3p on 2p multi	20	5

Coffee AP156

Coffee Grower, Pack Mule AP157

1977-78 **Litho.** *Perf. 12½*

C640	AP156	3p multi	20	5
C641	AP156	3.50p multi ('78)	25	5

Colombian coffee.

1977, Aug. 9 **Litho.** *Perf. 13½x14*

C642	AP157	10p multi	75	7

National Federation of Coffee Growers, 50th anniversary.

Beethoven and 9th Symphony AP158

Games' Emblem AP159

1977, Aug. 17

C643	AP158	8p multi	75	10

Sesquicentennial of the death of Ludwig van Beethoven (1770-1827).

Bird Type of 1977

Tropical Birds and Plants: No. C644, Woodpecker and meriania. C645, Purple gallinule and water lilies. No. C646, Xipholaena punicea and cochlospermum orinocense. No. C647, Crowned flycatcher and jacaranda copaia.

1977, Sept. 6 **Litho.** *Perf. 14*

C644	A380	5p multi	60	15
C645	A380	5p multi	60	15
C646	A380	10p multi	75	22
C647	A380	10p multi	75	22

1977, Sept. 9 *Perf. 12x12½*

C648	AP159	6p multi	35	10

13th Central American and Caribbean Games, Medellin, 1978.

La Cayetana, by Enrique Grau AP160

Design: No. C650, Water Nymphs, by Beatriz Gonzalez.

1977, Sept. 13 *Perf. 14x13½*

C649	AP160	8p multi	65	22
C650	AP160	8p multi	65	22

Women's suffrage, 20th anniversary.

Judge Francisco Antonio Moreno, by Joaquin Gutierrez AP161

Design: 25p, Viceroy Manuel de Guirior.

1977, Sept. 13 *Perf. 12*

C651	AP161	20p multi	1.75	80
C652	AP161	25p multi	2.50	1.25

Bicentenary of National Library.

Federico Lleras Acosta — AP162

Cauca University Arms — AP163

1977, Sept. 27 **Litho.** *Perf. 14*

C653	AP162	5p multi	38	10

Dr. Federico Lleras Acosta, veterinarian and bacteriologist; birth centenary.

1977, Oct. 14

C654	AP163	5p multi	40	15

Sesquicentennial of the University of Cauca.

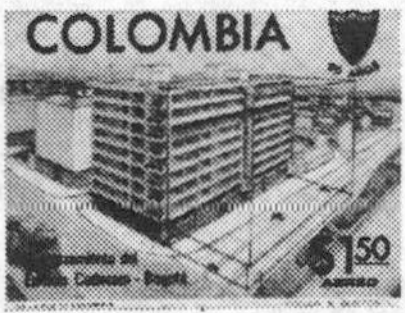

CUDECOM Building, Bogota AP164

1977, Oct. 14

C655	AP164	1.50p multi	15	6

Colombian Society of Engineers, 90th anniversary.

No. C612 Surcharged with New Value and Bars in Brown

1977, Dec. 3 **Litho.** *Perf. 14x13½*

C656	AP142	2p on 1.30p multi	40	15

Lost City, Tayrona Culture AP165

Creator of Energy, by Arenas Betancourt AP166

1978, Apr. 18 **Litho.** *Perf. 12½*

C657	AP165	3.50p multi	30	5

1978, Apr. 25 *Perf. 12*

C658	AP166	4p bl & multi	35	15

Sesquicentennial of Antioquia University Law School.

Column of the Slaves AP167

Statue of Catalina, Cartagena AP168

1978, May 9

C659	AP167	2.50p multi	35	15

Sesquicentennial of Ocaña Convention (meeting of various political groups).

1978, May 30 **Litho.** *Perf. 12*

C660	AP168	4p blk & lt bl	35	15

Sesquicentennial of University of Cartagena.

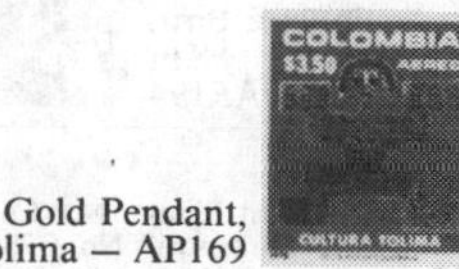

Gold Pendant, Tolima — AP169

1978, July 11 **Litho.** *Perf. 12x12½*

C661	AP169	3.50p multi	30	5

Apotheosis of Spanish Language, by Luis Alberto Acuña — AP170

1978, Aug. 9 *Perf. 14*

C662	AP170	Strip of 3	6.75	6.75
a.		11p, single stamp	1.65	1.65

Millennium of Spanish language. No. C662 printed in sheets of 15 (3x5). Black control number.

Presidential Guard AP171

Figure, Muisca Culture AP172

1978, Aug. 16 *Perf. 13½x14*

C663	AP171	9p multi	60	60

Presidential Guard Battalion, 50th anniversary.

1978, Sept. 12 **Litho.** *Perf. 12½*

C664	AP172	3.50p multi	30	5

Apse of Carmelite Church — AP173

1978, Oct. 12 *Perf. 13*

C665	AP173	30p multi	3.50	60

Souvenir Sheet

Perf. 13½x14

C666	AP173	50p multi	4.50	4.50

ESPAMER '78 Philatelic Exhibition, Bogota, Oct. 12-21. No. C666 contains one stamp; multicolored margin shows enlarged stamp design, ESPAMER emblem and black control number. Size: 125x95mm.

Owl, Gold Ornament, Calima AP174

Virgin and Child, by Gregorio Vasquez AP175

Designs: No. C669, Gold frog, Quimbaya culture. No. C670, Gold nose pendant, Tairona, horiz.

1978-80 **Litho.** *Perf. 12½*

C667	AP174	3.50p multi	30	5
C668	AP174	4p multi ('79)	30	5
C669	AP174	4p multi ('79)	30	5
C670	AP174	5p multi ('80)	30	8

1978, Nov. 28 *Perf. 13½x14*

C671	AP175	2.50p multi	20	5

Christmas 1978.

Bull Ring, Cathedral, Manizales AP176

1979, Jan. 6 **Litho.** *Perf. 14*

C672	AP176	7p multi	90	20

Manizales Fair.

Children Playing Hopscotch, and IYC Emblem — AP177

Designs: No. C674, Child at blackboard and UNESCO emblem (horiz.). No. C675, The Paper Collector, by Omar Gordillo, and U.N. emblem.

Perf. 13½x14, 14x13½

1979, July 19

C673	AP177	8p multi	45	25
C674	AP177	12p multi	65	30
C675	AP177	12p multi	65	30

International Year of the Child.

Rio Prado Hydroelectric Station — AP178

1979, Aug. 24 *Perf. 13½x14*

C676	AP178	5p multi	70	15

Tomb, 6th Century — AP179

1979, Sept. 25 **Litho.** *Perf. 14*

C677	AP179	8p multi	75	25

San Augustin Archaeological Park.

Gonzalo Jimenez de Quesada, by C. Leudo AP180

1979, Oct. 11 *Perf. 12*

C678	AP180	20p multi	2.25	70

Gonzalo Jimenez de Quesada (1500-1579), Spanish conquistador.

Hill, Penny Black, Colombia No. 1 — AP181

1979, Oct. 23 *Perf. 13½x14*

C679	AP181	15p multi	90	30

Sir Rowland Hill (1795-1879), originator of penny postage.

Amazon Region — AP182

Tourism: 14p, San Fernando Fortress.

1979 Litho. *Perf. 13½x14*

C680	AP182	7p multi	50	20
C681	AP182	14p multi	1.25	50

Issue dates: 7p, Nov. 16; 14p, Nov. 9.

Nativity — AP183

Creche Sculptures: No. C682, Three Kings and soldiers. No. C684, Shepherds.

1979, Nov. 30 *Perf. 12*

C682	AP183	3p multi	50	45
C683	AP183	3p multi	50	45
C684	AP183	3p multi	50	45

Christmas 1979. Nos. C682-C684 se-tenant in continuous design.

Magdalena Bridge, Avianca Emblem — AP184

1979, Dec. 5 *Perf. 14*

C685	AP184	15p multi	90	25

Barranquilla, 350th anniversary; Avianca National Airline, 60th anniversary.

Boy Playing Flute, by Judith Leyster — AP185

1980, Feb. 15 *Perf. 13½x14*

C686	AP185	6p multi	38	15

2nd International Music Competition, Ibague, Dec. 1979.

Gen. Antonio Jose de Sucre, 150th Death Anniversary AP186

1980, Feb. 15 Litho. *Perf. 12½x12*

C687	AP186	12p multi	65	25

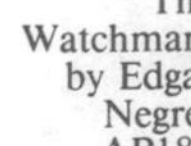
The Watchman, by Edgar Negret AP187

1980, Feb. 26 *Perf. 12x12½*

C688	AP187	25p multi	2.00	90

Virgin Mary, by Real del Sarte, 1929 — AP188

1980, May 23 Litho. *Perf. 14x13½*

C689	AP188	12p multi	45	18

Apparition of the Virgin Mary to Sister Catalina Labouri Gontard, 150th anniversary.

San Gil Produce Market, by Luis Roncancio — AP189

1980, May 27 *Perf. 13½x14*

C690	AP189	12p multi	45	20

Pres. Enrique Olaya Herrera, by Miguel Diaz Vargas — AP190

1980, Oct. 28 Litho. *Perf. 12*

C691	AP190	20p multi	1.40	35

Enrique Olaya Herrera (1880-1936), president, 1930-1934.

The Boy Fishing in a Bucket AP191

Christmas 1980 (Christmas Stories by Rafael Pombo): No. C693, The Frog and the Mouse. No. C694, The Seven Lives of the Cat.

1980, Nov. 21 Litho. *Perf. 14½*

C692	AP191	4p multi	30	25
C693	AP191	4p multi	30	25
C694	AP191	4p multi	30	25

28th World Golf Cup, Cajica — AP192

1980, Dec. 9 Litho. *Perf. 13½x14*

C695	AP192	30p multi	2.00	60

Bolivar Type of 1980

Simon Bolivar Death Sesquicentennial: 6p, Portrait, last words to Colombia (vert.).

1980, Dec. 17 *Perf. 12*

C696	A400	6p multi	90	35

St. Peter Claver Holding Cross — AP193

1981, Jan. 13 *Perf. 14½*

C697	AP193	15p multi	70	25

St. Peter Claver (1580-1654), helped American Indians.

Sculptured Bird, San Augustin — AP194

Archaeological Finds: No. C699, Funeral chamber, Tierradentro. No. C700, Chamber hallway, Tierradentro. No. C701, Statue of man, San Augustin. Nos. C698-C701 se-tenant.

1981, May 12 Litho. *Perf. 14*

C698	AP194	7p multi	40	15
C699	AP194	7p multi	40	15
C700	AP194	7p multi	40	15
C701	AP194	7p multi	40	15

See Nos. C707-C710.

Child with Hobby Horse, by Fernando Botero — AP195

4th Biennial Arts show, Medellin: 20p, Square Abstract, by Omar Rayo. 25p, Flowers, by Alejandro Obregon.

1981, May 15 *Perf. 12*

C702	AP195	20p multi	1.25	25
C703	AP195	25p multi	1.40	40
C704	AP195	50p multi	2.50	75

8th South American Swimming Championships, Medellin — AP196

1981, June 5

C705	AP196	15p multi	75	22

Santamaria Bull Ring, 50th Anniv. — AP197

1981, June 9 Litho. *Perf. 12*

C706	AP197	30p multi	3.00	1.00

Archaeological Type of 1981

Quimbaya Culture: Nos. C707-C710 se-tenant.

1981, Sept. 23 Litho. *Perf. 14*

C707	AP194	9p Man	55	15
C708	AP194	9p Seated man	55	15
C709	AP194	9p Seal, print	55	15
C710	AP194	9p Jug	55	15

1981, Dec. 17 Litho. *Perf. 14*

Calima Culture: Nos. C710A-C710D se-tenant.

C710A	AP194	9p Anthropomorphic container	55	15
C710B	AP194	9p Jar	55	15
C710C	AP194	9p Anthropomorphic jar	55	15
C710D	AP194	9p Urn	55	15

Fruit AP198

1981, Nov. 3 Litho. *Perf. 14*

C711		Block of 6	12.00	9.00
a.-f.	AP198	25p, any single	1.75	70

Revolt of the Comuneros, 200th Anniv. — AP199

1981, Nov. 21 Litho. *Perf. 12*

C712	AP199	20p multi	80	40

Jose Manuel Restrepo, Historian, 1775?-1860? AP200

Andres Bello, 1780?-1865 AP201

1981, Dec. 1 Litho. *Perf. 12*

C713	AP200	35p multi	1.25	30

1981, Dec. 11 Litho. *Perf. 12*

C714	AP201	18p multi	70	20

Colombia's Admission to UPU, 100th Anniv. AP202

Designs: 30p, No. 103. 50p, Hemispheres, Nos. 104-108.

1981 Litho. ***Perf. 12 (30p), Imperf.***

C715 AP202 30p multi 1.00 25
C716 AP202 50p multi 2.00 1.00

No. C716 has red control number. Size: 100x70mm. Dates of issue: No. C715, Dec. 18. No. C716, Dec. 28.

Tourism Type of 1979

1982 Litho. ***Perf. 12***

C717 AP182 20p Solano Bay 70 18
C718 AP182 20p Tota Lake, Boyaca 70 18
C719 AP182 20p Corrales, Boyaca 70 18

Issue dates: No. C717, June 2; others, June 16.

1982 World Cup — AP202a

Designs: Players and team emblems.

1982, June 21 ***Perf. 14***

C720 Sheet of 15 6.00 3.00
a. AP202a 9p any single 40 15

No. C720 has black control number. Size: 181x150mm.

Bogota Gun Club Centenary AP202b

1982, July 16 ***Perf. 12***

C721 AP202b 20p multi 60 20

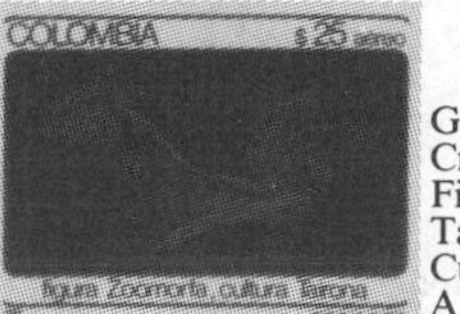

Gold Crocodile Figure, Tairona Culture AP202c

Tairona Culture Exhibit, Gold Museum: Various figures. Nos. C723-C727 vert.

1982, July 28

C722 AP202c 25p lt brn, gold & blk 1.00 40
C723 AP202c 25p brt pink, gold & blk 1.00 40
C724 AP202c 25p grn, gold & blk 1.00 40
C725 AP202c 25p dk bl, gold, & blk 1.00 40
C726 AP202c 25p vio. gold & blk 1.00 40
C727 AP202c 25p red, gold & blk 1.00 40
Nos. C722-C727 (6) 6.00 2.40

Government Buildings, Pereira — AP203

1982, Aug. 4 Litho. ***Perf. 12***

C728 AP203 35p multi 1.25 35

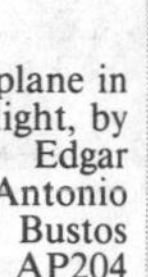

Bi-plane in Flight, by Edgar Antonio Bustos AP204

1982, Aug. 5 ***Perf. 14***

C729 AP204 18p multi 60 20

American Air Forces Cooperation System.

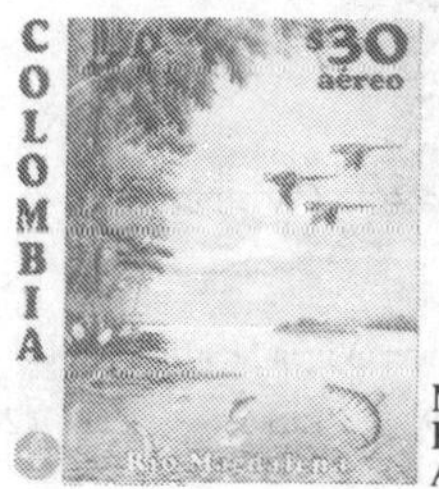

Magdalena River AP205

1982, Oct. 21 Litho. ***Perf. 12***

C730 AP205 30p multi 1.00 30

Marquez Type of 1982

1982, Dec. 10 ***Perf. 13½x14***

C731 A412 25p gray & bl 90 25
C732 A412 30p gray & brn 1.25 30

San Andres Archipelago — AP206

1983, Apr. 9 Litho. ***Perf. 12***

C733 AP206 25p Liberty Fort 70 15

Opening of Las Gaviotas (The Seagulls) Ecological Center, Bogota — AP207

1983, June 1 Litho.

C734 AP207 12p multi 40 15

50th Anniv. of Radio Amateurs League AP208

1983, June 11 ***Perf. 14x13½***

C735 AP208 12p multi 45 15

Bolivar Type of 1983

1983, July 24 ***Perf. 12***

C736 A417 30p multi 90 30
C737 A417 100p multi 3.00 1.25

Botanical Exhibition Type of 1983

1983, Aug. 18 ***Perf. 14***

C738 A418 12p Begonia Guaduensis H.B.K. 35 15
C739 A418 12p Chinchona Ovaliflora 35 15
C740 A418 40p Begonia Urticae L.F. 1.25 35

Cartagena, 450th Anniv. — AP208a

1983, Sept. 9 Litho. ***Perf. 12***

C740A AP208a 12p Customs Square 35 15
C740B AP208a 35p Historic sites, Cartagena 1.00 45

Painting Type of 1983

1983, Oct. 5 Litho. ***Perf. 12***

C741 A420 30p multi 75 18

Scouting Year — AP209

1983, Oct. 24

C742 AP209 12p multi 30 8

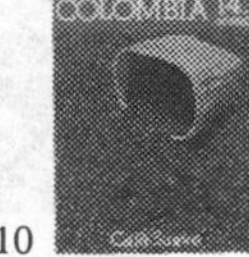

Coffee beans — AP210

1984, Mar. 28 Litho. ***Perf. 14½x14***

C743 AP210 14p multi 30 10

Marandua City Type of 1984

1984, Sept. 28 ***Perf. 12***

C744 A427 30p multi 68 22

45th Congress of Americanists, Bogota, 1985 — AP211

1984, Nov. 2

C745 AP211 45p multi 1.00 32

Christmas Type of 1984

1984, Dec. 14

C746 A428 14p multi 32 10

Contadora Group of Latin American Countries — AP212

Design: Dove, map and flags of Colombia, Mexico, Costa Rica and Venezuela.

1985, Feb. 15

C747 AP212 40p multi 68 32

Gomez Type of 1985

1985, Feb. 25

C748 A432 40p multi 68 32

Birds — AP213

1985

C749 AP213 14p Dryocopus lineatus nuperus 20 6
C750 AP213 20p Xiphorhynchus picus 28 10
C751 AP213 50p Eriocnemis cupreoventris 70 22
C752 AP213 55p Momotus momota 78 25

Issue dates: 14p, Apr. 12. 20p, 50p, Aug. 6. 55p, Aug. 29.

Almirante Padilla Naval School, 50th Anniv. — AP214

1985, July 15

C753 AP214 20p multi 28 10

1985 Census AP215

1985, Oct. 15 ***Perf. 12***

C754 AP215 20p multi 28 10

Christmas Type of 1985

1985, Dec. 4 Litho. ***Perf. 13***

C755 A436 20p Girl, Christmas tree 28 10

Alfonso Lopez Pumarejo (1886-1959), President, 1934-38, 1942-45 — AP216

1986, Jan. 31
C756 AP216 24p multi 30 10

Coffee Berries, Natl. Cycling Team AP217

1986, Feb. 4
C757 AP217 60p multi 75 25

Natl. Coffee Producers Assoc. sponsorship of natl. cycling team, 25th anniv.

Fauna Type of 1985

1986, Feb. 18
C758 A433 50p Pudu mephis-tophiles 65 22

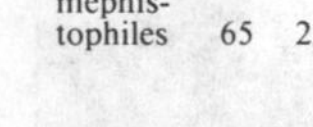

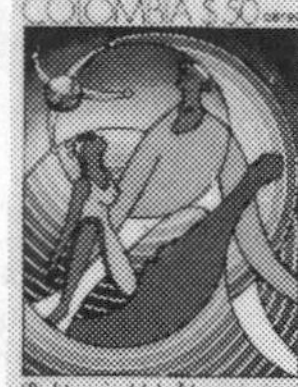

World Communications Day — AP218

1986, May 17 **Litho.** ***Perf. 13***
C759 AP218 50p multi 65 22

Intl. Peace Year — AP219

1986, June 13 **Litho.** ***Perf. 13***
C760 AP219 55p multi 65 22

Visit of Pope John Paul II — AP220

1986, July 1 **Litho.** ***Perf. 13***
C761 AP220 24p Portrait, papal arms 32 10
C762 AP220 55p Portrait, Medellin cathe-dral, horiz. 65 22
C763 AP220 60p Blessing crowd, horiz. 70 24

Souvenir Sheet

C764 AP220 200p Praying, Madon-na of Bogota 1.40 1.40

Nos. C762-C763 each printed in sheets of 20 with se-tenant labels picturing religious symbols.

Enrique Santos Montejo (1886-1971), Journalist AP221

1986, July 15 ***Perf. 12***
C765 AP221 25p multi 30 10

Bach, Handel and Schutz, Composers AP222

1986, July 17 ***Perf. 13***
C766 AP222 70p Bach 82 28
C767 AP222 100p Text, music 1.15 38

Salesian Order Education in Colombia, Cent. AP223

1986, July 23 ***Perf. 12***
C768 AP223 25p De La Salle, founder 30 10

Completion of Coal Mining Complex, El Cerrejon AP224

1986, July 29 **Litho.** ***Perf. 12***
C769 AP224 55p multi 62 20

AP225

Natl. Constitution, Cent. — AP226

Designs: 25p, The Five Signators, by R. Vasquez, detail, and Bogota Cathedral. 200p, Pres. Nunez and Miguel Antonio Caro, Natl. Council of Delegates chairman, and Presidential Palace, constitution.

1986, Aug. 5 **Litho.** ***Perf. 14***
C770 AP225 25p multi 28 10

Souvenir Sheet

Perf. 12

C771 AP226 200p multi 2.25 75

No. C771 has multicolored margin continuing the design and showing black control number. Size: 120x80mm.

Poet Type of 1986

Design: Federico Garcia Lorca (1898-1936), poet, and birthplace, Fuentevaqueros, Granada, Spain.

1986, Sept. 26 **Litho.** ***Perf. 12***
C772 A445 60p multi 68 24

Gratitude for Intl. Aid after the Armero Mudslide Disaster AP227

1986, Nov. 13
C773 AP227 50p multi 55 18

Christmas AP228

Wood sculpture: Virgin Mestiza, Nerina.

1986, Dec. 19 **Litho.** ***Perf. 12***
C774 AP228 25p multi 28 10

AP229

The Apotheosis of Papayan, by Ephrain Martinez Zambrano (1898-1956) — AP229

1987, Jan. 13
C775 AP229 100p Papayan riding horse 1.10 35
C776 AP229 100p Onlook-ers 1.10 35

Nos. C775-C776 printed se-tenant in continuous design.

The Conversion of St. Augustine of Hippo, 1600th Anniv. — AP230

1987, Mar. 16 **Litho.** ***Perf. 12***
C777 AP230 30p multi 32 10

Bird Type of 1987

Design: 30p, Phoenicopterus ruber.

1987, June 8 ***Perf. 14½x14***
C778 A446a 30p lake 35 12

Fauna Type of 1987

Design: 35p, Pseydemys scripta, horiz.

1987, Dec. 24 **Litho.** ***Perf. 14x14½***
C779 A446a 35p dark red brn 40 14

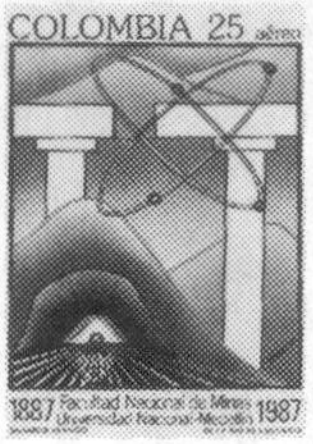

Natl. University School of mining, Medellin, Cent. — AP231

1987, Apr. 10 ***Perf. 13½x13***
C783 AP231 25p multi 30 10

Purebred Horses AP232

1987, June 17 ***Perf. 12***
C784 AP232 60p White horse 70 22
C785 AP232 70p Black horse 85 28

El Espectador Newspaper, Cent. AP233

Design: Frontispieces from 1887, 1915, 1948, 1974 and portraits of founder Don Fidel Cano, editors Don Luis Cano, Luis Gabriel Cano Isaza and Alfonso Cano Isaza.

1987, July 24 ***Perf. 12½x12***
C786 AP233 60p multi 70 22

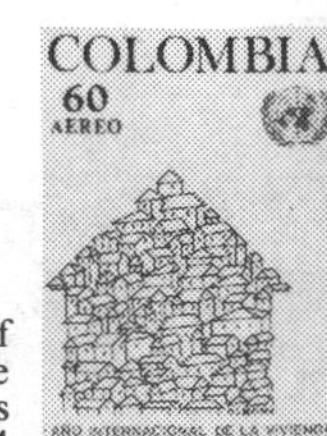

Intl. Year of Shelter for the Homeless AP234

1987, Sept. 21 ***Perf. 14***
C787 AP234 60p 65 22

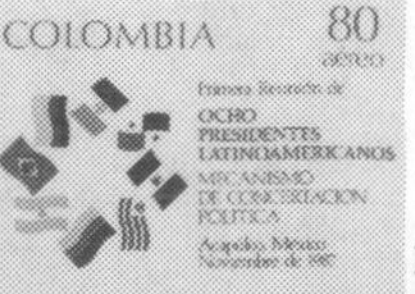

Flags AP235

1987, Nov. 27 Litho. *Perf. 13x13½*
C788 AP235 80p multi 82 28

1st Meeting of the eight Latin-American Presidents, Acapulco, Nov.

Christmas 1987 — AP236

1987, Dec. 8 Litho. *Perf. 14*
C789 AP236 30p multi 30 10

AIR POST SPECIAL DELIVERY STAMPS

Post Horn and Wings APSD1

Unwmk.
1958, May 19 Litho. *Perf. 12*
CE1 APSD1 25c dk bl & red 60 20

Same Overprinted Vertically Red

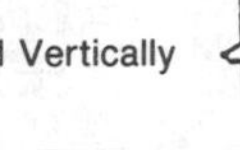

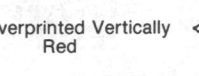

1959
CE2 APSD1 25c dk bl & red 50 20

Jet Plane and Envelope — APSD2

1963, Oct. 4 *Perf. 14*
CE3 APSD2 50c red & blk 30 10

Aviation Type of Air Post Issue

History of Colombian Aviation: 80c, Boeing 727 jet, 1966.

Perf. 14x13½
1966, Dec. 14 Photo. Unwmk.
CE4 AP96 80c crim & multi 45 20

AIR POST REGISTRATION STAMPS

Issued by Sociedad Colombo-Alemana de Transportes Aereos (SCADTA)

No. C41 Overprinted in Red

1923 Wmk. 116 *Perf. 14x14½*
CF1 AP6 20c gray 3.50 1.75

No. C58 Overprinted in Black

1929 Wmk. 127 *Perf. 14*
CF2 AP8 20c carmine 4.50 1.75

Same Overprint on No. C71.
CF3 AP10 20c carmine 9.00 9.00

Colombian Government Issues.
Same Overprint on No. C86.

1932
CF4 AP8 20c carmine 10.00 8.00

No. C100 Overprinted

CF5 AP15 20c car & ol blk 6.25 2.00

SPECIAL DELIVERY STAMP

Special Delivery Messenger — SD1

1917 Unwmk. Engr. *Perf. 14.*
E1 SD1 5c gray grn 3.25 4.50

SD2

1987, July 31 Litho. *Perf. 14*
E2 SD2 25p emer & ver 30 30
E3 SD2 30p emer & ver 35 35

REGISTRATION STAMPS

R1 R2

1865 Unwmk. Litho. *Imperf.*
F1 R1 5c black 100.00 57.50
F2 R2 5c black 85.00 55.00

R3 R4

1870

White Paper.
Vertical Lines in Background.
F3 R3 5c black 2.50 2.50
F4 R4 5c black 2.50 2.50

Horizontal Lines in Background.
F5 R3 5c black 5.00 5.00
F6 R4 5c black 2.50 2.50

Reprints of Nos. F3 to F6 show either crossed lines or traces of lines in background.

R5

1881 *Imperf.*
F7 R5 10c violet 55.00 60.00
a. Sewing machine perf. 62.50 67.50
b. Perf. 11 67.50 70.00

R6

1883 *Perf. 12, 13½*
F8 R6 10c red, *org* 2.00 2.50

R7

1889-95 *Perf. 12, 13½*
F9 R7 10c red, *grysh* 7.50 3.50
F10 R7 10c red, *yelsh* 7.50 3.50
F11 R7 10c dp brn, *rose buff* ('95) 2.00 1.65
F12 R7 10c yel brn, *lt buff* ('92) 2.00 1.65

Nos. F9-F12 exist imperf. Prices same as for perf.

R9

1902 *Imperf.*
F13 R9 20c red brn, *bl* 2.00 2.00
a. Sewing machine perf. 5.25 5.25
b. Perf. 12 5.25 5.25

Medellin Issue.

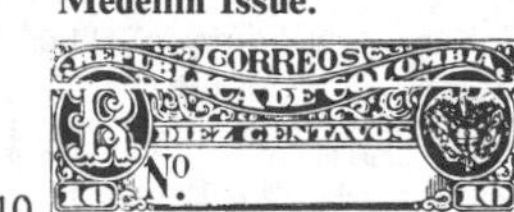
R10

1902 *Perf. 12.*

Wove Paper.
F16 R10 10c blk vio 21.00 21.00
a. Laid paper 17.50 17.50

Regular Issue.

1903 *Imperf.*
F17 R9 20c bl, *bl* 1.90 1.90
a. Sewing machine perf. 5.50 5.50
b. Perf. 12 5.50 5.50

R11

1904 Pelure Paper. *Imperf.*
F19 R11 10c purple 4.25 4.25
a. Sewing machine perf. 4.25 4.25
b. Perf. 12 5.75 5.75

R12

Imprint: "J. L. Arango".

1904 *Perf. 12*

Wove Paper.
F20 R12 10c purple 3.00 75
a. Imperf., pair 9.00 9.00

1909 *Perf. 10, 14, 10x14, 14x10*
Imprint: "Lit. Nacional".
F21 R12 10c purple 3.25 1.00
a. Imperf., pair 7.50 7.50

Execution at Cartagena in 1816 R13

1910, July 20 Engr. *Perf. 12*
F22 R13 10c red & blk 25.00 *90.00*

Centenary of National Independence.

Pier at Puerto Colombia — R14

Tequendama Falls — R15

Perf. 11, 11½, 14, 11½x14
1917, Aug. 25
F23 R14 4c grn & ultra 75 3.50
a. Center inverted 750.00 750.00
F24 R15 10c dp bl 2.75 90

R16

1925 Litho. *Perf. 10x13½*
F25 R16 (10c) blue 3.50 2.25
a. Imperf., pair 10.00 10.00
b. Perf. 13½x10 5.50 5.50

ACKNOWLEDGMENT OF RECEIPT STAMPS

AR1 AR2

1893 Unwmk. Litho. *Perf. 13½.*
H1 AR1 5c ver, *bl* 6.00 6.00

1894 *Perf. 12.*
H2 AR1 5c vermilion 5.00 5.00

1902-03 *Imperf.*
H3 AR2 10c bl, *bl* 4.00 4.00
a. 10c, bl, *grnsh bl* 4.00 4.00
b. Sewing machine perf. 4.00 4.00
c. Perf. 12 4.00 4.00

The handstamp "AR" in circle is believed to be a postmark.

AR3

AR4

1904 Pelure Paper *Imperf.*

H12	AR3	5c pale bl	15.00	15.00
a.		Perf. 12	15.00	15.00

No. 307 Overprinted in Black, Green or Violet **A R**

H13	A86	5c carmine	25.00	25.00

1904 *Perf. 12.*

H16	AR4	5c blue	4.75	4.00
a.		Imperf., pair	12.50	12.50

General José Acevedo y Gómez — AR5

1910, July 20 Engr.

H17	AR5	5c org & grn	8.50	*22.50*

Centenary of National Independence.

Sabana Station AR6

Map of Colombia AR7

1917 *Perf. 14.*

H18	AR6	4c bis brn	2.50	3.00
H19	AR7	5c org brn	2.10	2.50
a.		Imperf., pair	13.50	

LATE FEE STAMPS

LF1

LF2

1886 Unwmk. Litho. *Perf. 10½.*

I1	LF1	2½c *lilac*	4.50	3.50
a.		Imperf., pair	15.00	15.00

1892 *Perf. 12, 13½.*

I2	LF2	2½c dk bl, *rose*	4.00	3.00
a.		Imperf., pair	15.00	
I3	LF2	2½c ultra,*pink*	4.00	3.00

LF3

LF4

1902 *Imperf.*

I4	LF3	5c pur, *rose*	1.25	1.25
a.		Perf. 12	2.50	2.50

1914 *Perf. 10, 13½.*

I6	LF4	2c vio brn	6.00	4.25
I7	LF4	5c bl grn	6.00	4.25

Retardo Retardo 1921

Overprints illustrated above are unauthorized and of private origin.

POSTAGE DUE STAMPS

These are not, strictly speaking, postage due stamps but were issued to cover an additional fee, "Sobreporte", charged on mail to foreign countries with which Colombia had no postal conventions.

D1

D2

D3

1866 Unwmk. Litho. *Imperf.*

J1	D1	25c *blue*	50.00	50.00
J2	D2	50c *yellow*	50.00	50.00
J3	D3	1p *rose*	135.00	110.00

DEPARTMENT STAMPS

These stamps are said to be for interior postage, to supersede the separate issues for the various departments.

Regular Issues Handstamped in Black, Violet, Blue or Green — a

Correos Departa-mentales

On Stamps of 1904.

1909 Unwmk. *Perf. 12.*

L1	A94	½c yellow	3.00	3.00
a.		Imperf., pair	8.50	8.50
L2	A94	1c yel grn	3.00	3.00
L3	A94	2c red	3.75	3.75
a.		Imperf., pair	14.00	14.00
L4	A94	5c blue	4.75	4.75
L5	A94	10c violet	8.00	8.00
L6	A94	20c black	14.00	14.00
L7	A95	1p brown	24.00	24.00

On Stamp of 1902.

L8	A83	10p dk brn, *rose*	22.50	22.50
		Nos. L1-L8 (8)	83.00	83.00

On Stamps of 1908.

Perf. 10, 13, 13½ and Compound.

L9	A94	½c orange	3.00	3.00
a.		Imperf., pair	6.50	6.50
L10	A94	1c green	4.75	4.75
a.		Without imprint	5.50	5.50
L11	A94	2c red	4.75	4.75
a.		Imperf., pair		
L12	A94	5c blue	4.75	4.75
a.		Imperf., pair	10.00	10.00
L13	A94	10c violet	7.50	7.50

On Tolima Stamp of 1888.

Perf. 10½.

L14	A23	1p red brn	12.00	12.00
		Nos. L9-L14 (6)	36.75	36.75

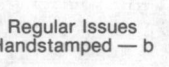

Regular Issues Handstamped — b

On Stamps of 1904.

Perf. 12.

L15	A94	½c yellow	3.00	3.00
L16	A94	1c yel grn	3.00	3.00
L17	A94	2c red	4.75	4.75
L18	A94	5c blue	4.75	4.75
L19	A94	10c violet	7.50	7.50
L20	A94	20c black	13.00	13.00
L21	A94	1p brown	24.00	24.00
		Nos. L15-L21 (7)	60.00	60.00

On Stamps of 1908.

Perf. 10, 13, 13½.

L22	A94	½c orange	3.00	3.00
L23	A94	1c yel grn	9.00	9.00
L24	A94	2c red	4.50	4.50
a.		Imperf., pair	10.00	10.00
L25	A94	5c lt bl	4.50	4.50

The handstamps on Nos. L1 to L25 are, as usual, found inverted and double.

DEPARTMENT REGISTRATION STAMPS

Registration Stamps Handstamped like Nos. L1 to L25.

On Registration Stamp of 1904.

1909 Unwmk. *Perf. 12.*

LF1	R12(a)	10c purple	30.00	30.00
LF2	R12(b)	10c purple	30.00	30.00

On Registration Stamp of 1909.

Perf. 10, 13.

LF3	R12(a)	10c purple	30.00	30.00
LF4	R12(b)	10c purple	30.00	30.00

Nos. LF1-LF4 exist imperf. Price per pair, $20.

DEPARTMENT ACKNOWLEDGMENT OF RECEIPT STAMPS

Acknowledgment of Receipt Stamp of 1904 Handstamped like Nos. L1 to L25.

1909 Unwmk. *Perf. 12.*

LH1	AR4(a)	5c blue	30.00	30.00
a.		Imperf., pair	45.00	
LH2	AR4(b)	5c blue	30.00	30.00
a.		Imperf., pair	45.00	

LOCAL STAMPS FOR THE CITY OF BOGOTA

A1

Pelure Paper.

1889 Unwmk. Litho. *Perf. 12*

LX1	A1	½c black	1.25	1.25
a.		Imperf., pair	6.00	6.00

Impressions on bright blue and blue-gray paper were not regularly issued

A2

A3

White Wove Paper.

1896 *Perf. 12, 13½*

LX2	A2	½c black	1.25	1.25

1903 *Imperf.*

LX3	A3	10c *pink*	1.75	1.75
a.		Perf. 12	6.00	6.00

OFFICIAL STAMPS

Stamps of 1917-1937 Overprinted in Black or Red:

OFICIAL a OFICIAL b

1937 Unwmk. *Perf. 11, 12, 13½.*

O1	A131(a)	1c grn (Bk)	10	5
O2	A157(a)	10c dp org (Bk)	15	15
O3	A107(b)	30c ol bis (Bk)	2.50	1.40
O4	A129(b)	40c brn & yel brn (Bk)	1.50	1.10
O5	A114(b)	50c car (Bk)	1.40	70
O6	A115(b)	1p lt bl (Bk)	6.50	4.00
O7	A116(b)	2p org (Bk)	13.00	6.50
O8	A117(b)	5p gray (Bk)	55.00	35.00
O9	A118(b)	10p dk brn (Bk)	160.00	125.00

Wmk. 229

Perf. 12½.

O10	A132(a)	2c red (Bk)	15	15
O11	A133(a)	5c brn (Bk)	10	10
O12	A160(a)	12c dp bl (R)	1.40	60
O13	A136(b)	20c dk bl (R)	2.25	85
		Nos. O1-O13 (13)	244.05	175.60

Tall, wrong font "I's" in OFICIAL exist on all stamps with "a" overprint.

POSTAL TAX STAMPS

"Greatest Mother" PT1

Perf. 11½

1935, May 27 Unwmk. Litho.

RA1	PT1	5c ol blk & scar	3.00	1.10

This stamp was required on all mail during Red Cross Week in 1935 (May 27-June 3) and in 1936.

Mother and Child — PT2

Perf. 10½, 10½x11.

1937, May 24 Unwmk.

RA2	PT2	5c red	1.00	40

This stamp was required on all mail during Red Cross Week. The tax was for the Red Cross.

Ministry of Posts and Telegraphs Building

PT3 PT4

1939-45 Litho. *Perf. 10½, 12½*

RA3	PT3	¼c dp bl	5	5
RA3A	PT3	¼c dk vio brn ('45)	8	5
RA4	PT3	½c pink	10	5
RA5	PT3	1c violet	55	15
RA5A	PT3	1c yel org ('45)	2.50	90
RA6	PT3	2c pck grn	50	20
RA7	PT3	20c lt brn	3.50	1.00
		Nos. RA3-RA7 (7)	7.28	2.40

These stamps were obligatory on all mail. The tax was for the construction of the new Communications Building.

The 25c of type PT3 and PT4 were not usable on postal matter.

See also No. 561.

Wmk. Wavy Lines (229)

1940, Jan. 20 Engr. *Perf. 12½x13*

RA8	PT4	¼c ultra	6	5
RA9	PT4	½c carmine	6	5
RA10	PT4	1c violet	5	5
RA11	PT4	2c bl grn	35	5
RA12	PT4	20c brown	1.40	35
	Nos. RA8-RA12 (5)		1.92	55

See note after No. RA7.

"Protection" — PT5

1940, Apr. 25 Wmk. 255 *Perf. 12*

RA13	PT5	5c rose car	30	15

See also No. RA17.

Postal Tax Stamps of 1939 Surcharged in Black

$ 0,0½
MEDIO CENTAVO

1943 Unwmk. *Perf. 10½.*

RA14	PT3	½c on 1c vio	5	5
a.		Inverted surcharge	2.25	
RA15	PT3	½c on 2c pck grn	5	5
RA16	PT3	½c on 20c lt brn	15	15

Types of 1940.
Imprint: "Litografia Colombia Bogota S.A."

1944 Litho. *Perf. 11.*

RA17	PT5	5c dk rose	45	22

Imprint: "Lito-Colombia Bogota-Colombia"

RA18	PT4	¼c ultra	8	6

Ministry of Posts and Telegraphs Building — PT6

1945-48 Wmk. 255 Engr. *Perf. 12.*

RA19	PT6	¼c ultra	5	5
RA20	PT6	¼c sep ('46)	5	5
RA21	PT6	½c car rose	5	5
RA22	PT6	½c dp mag ('46)	5	5
RA23	PT6	1c vio ('46)	5	5
RA23A	PT6	1c red org ('46)	5	5
RA24	PT6	2c grn ('46)	8	6
RA25	PT6	20c brn ('46)	1.25	30
a.		20c red brn ('48)	90	15
	Nos. RA19-RA25 (8)		1.63	66

These stamps were obligatory on all mail. The surtax was for the construction of the new Communications Building. See also Nos. 603, RA33.

No. 469 Overprinted in Carmine

1946, May 25

RA26	A176	5c dl brn	50	22

The surtax was for the Red Cross.

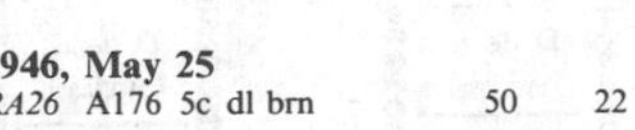

Ministry of Posts and Telegraphs Building — PT7

1946 Unwmk. Litho. *Perf. 11*

RA27	PT7	3c blue	15	8

No. 490 Overprinted in Carmine SOBRETASA

1947 Wmk. 255 *Perf. 12*

RA28	A196	20c gray blk	2.00	1.40

Arms of Colombia and Red Cross — PT8

PT9

Perf. 12½

1947, Sept. Unwmk. Engr.

RA29	PT8	5c car lake	22	15

The surtax of Nos. RA29 and RA40 was for the Red Cross. See also No. RA40.

No. 466 Overprinted Like No. RA28 in Carmine.

RA30	A136	20c dk bl	6.00	4.50

Type of 1945.

1947 Wmk. 255 Engr. *Perf. 12*

RA33	PT6	1c ol bis	6	5

Black Surcharge.

1948 Unwmk. Litho. *Perf. 11.*

RA36	PT9	1c on 5c lt brn	8	5
RA37	PT9	1c on 10c lt vio	8	5
RA38	PT9	1c on 25c red	8	5
RA39	PT9	1c on 50c ultra	8	5

Type of 1947.

1948 *Perf. 10½*

RA40	PT8	5c vermilion	22	15

Ministry of Posts and Telegraphs Building PT10

Mother and Child PT11

1948-50 Wmk. 255 Engr. *Perf. 12*

RA41	PT10	1c rose car ('49)	5	5
RA42	PT10	2c grn ('50)	8	5
RA43	PT10	3c blue	10	5
RA44	PT10	5c gray	10	6
RA45	PT10	10c purple	30	7
	Nos. RA41-RA45 (5)		63	28

A 25c stamp of type PT10 was for use on telegrams, later for regular postage. See Nos. 602, 604.

Unwmk.

1950, May 25 Litho. *Perf. 11*

Dark Blue Surcharge.

RA46	PT11	5c on 2c gray, red, blk & yel	1.10	45
a.		"195" instead of "1950"	2.00	2.00
b.		Top bar and "19" of "1950" omitted	2.00	2.00

Marginal perforations omitted, creating 26 straight-edged copies in each sheet of 44. Surtax for Red Cross.

No. 574 Overprinted in Black SOBRETASA

1950, May 26 Wmk. 255 *Perf. 12*

RA47	A176	5c blue	22	8
a.		Inverted ovpt.	1.25	

Telegraph Stamp Surcharged in Black.

RA48	A253a	8c on 50c org yel	15	8

Fiscal stamps of type A253a were available for postal use after May 9, 1952. See Nos. 605-608.

Arms and Cross — PT12

Bartolome de Las Casas Aiding Youth — PT13

Perf. 12½

1951, May Unwmk. Engr.

RA49	PT12	5c red	30	10
RA50	PT13	5c carmine	30	10

The surtax was for the Red Cross.

No. RA43 Surcharged with New Value in Black.

1951 Wmk. 255 *Perf. 12.*

RA51	PT10	1c on 3c bl	8	5

Type of 1951.

Engraved; Cross Lithographed

1953 Unwmk. *Perf. 12½.*

RA52	PT13	5c grn & car	30	10

The surtax of Nos. RA52-RA60 was for the Red Cross.

No. C254 Overprinted with Cross and Bar in Carmine.

1954

RA53	AP42	5c lil rose	90	55

St. Peter Claver Offering Gifts to Slaves — PT14

Engraved; Cross Typographed

1955, May 2 Unwmk. *Perf. 13*

RA54	PT14	5c dp plum & red	30	10

Issued to commemorate the 300th anniversary of the death of St. Peter Claver.

Jean Henri Dunant and Santiago Samper Brush PT15

Photogravure; Red Cross and "Cruz Roja" Engraved

1956, June 1 Unwmk. *Perf. 13*

RA55	PT15	5c brn & red	30	10

Nurses and Ambulances PT16

1958, June 2 Photo. *Perf. 12*

RA56	PT16	5c gray & red	15	8

St. Louisa de Marillac and Church PT17

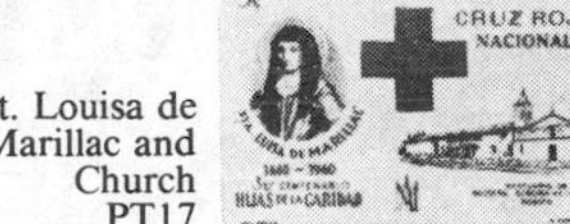

Design: No. RA58, Henri Dunant and battle scene.

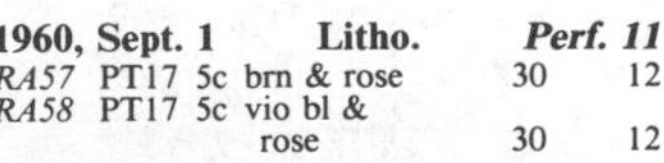

1960, Sept. 1 Litho. *Perf. 11*

RA57	PT17	5c brn & rose	30	12
RA58	PT17	5c vio bl & rose	30	12

No. RA57 issued to commemorate the 3rd centenary of the Sisters of Charity. No. RA58 issued to commemorate the centenary (in 1959) of the Red Cross idea.

Manuelita de la Cruz PT18

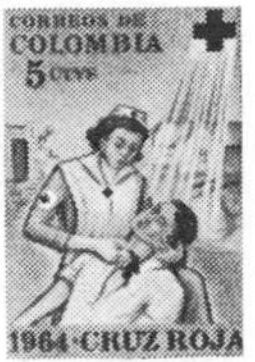

Red Cross Worker and Patient PT19

1961, Nov. 2 Engr. *Perf. 13*

RA59	PT18	5c dl pur & red	22	8
RA60	PT18	5c brn & red	22	8

Issued in memory of Red Cross Nurse Manuelita de la Cruz, who died in the line of duty during the floods of 1955. Obligatory on domestic mail for a month.

1965, Apr. 30 Photo. *Perf. 12*

RA61	PT19	5c bl gray & red	8	6

Obligatory on domestic mail during May.

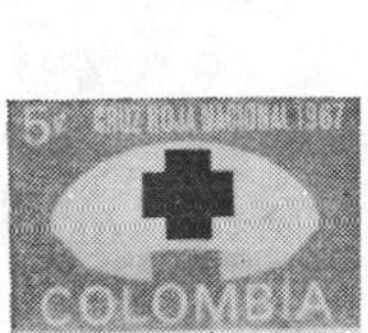

Nurse's Cap PT20

Red Cross — PT21

1967, June 1 Litho. *Perf. 12*

RA62	PT20	5c brt bl & red	8	6

1969, July 1 Litho. *Perf. 12x12½*

RA63	PT21	5c vio bl & red	8	6

Child Care — PT22

1970, July 1 Litho. *Perf. 12½x12*

RA64	PT22	5c lt bl & red	5	5

ANTIOQUIA

Originally a State, now a Department of the Republic of Colombia. Until the revolution of 1885, the separate states making up the United States of Colombia were sovereign governments in their own right. On August 4, 1886, the National Council of Bogota, composed of two delegates from each state, adopted a new constitution which abolished the sovereign rights of states, which then became departments with governors appointed by the President of the Republic. The nine original states represented at the Bogota Convention retained some of their previous rights, as management of their own finances, and all issued postage stamps until as late as 1904. For Panama's issues, see Panama Nos. 1-30.

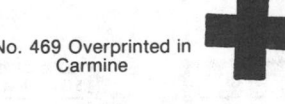

Coat of Arms
A1 A2

A3 A4

Wove Paper.

1868	Unwmk.	Litho.		*Imperf.*
1	A1	2½c blue	*600.00*	*400.00*
2	A2	5c green	*450.00*	*300.00*
3	A3	10c lilac	*1,350.*	*600.00*
4	A4	1p red	*350.00*	*275.00*

Reprints of Nos. 1, 3 and 4 are on a bluish white paper and all but No. 3 have scratches across the design.

A5 A6

A7 A8

A9 A10

1869				
5	A5	2½c blue	3.00	3.00
6	A6	5c green	3.75	3.75
7	A7	5c green	3.75	3.75
8	A8	10c lilac	5.25	2.00
9	A9	20c brown	5.25	3.75
10	A10	1p rose red	10.00	10.00
a.		1p ver	22.50	22.50

Reprints of Nos. 7, 8 and 10 are on a bluish white paper; reprints of Nos. 5 and 10a on white paper. The 10c blue is believed to be a reprint.

A11 A12

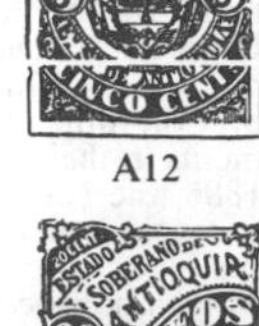

A13 A14

A15 A16

A17 A18

1873				
12	A11	1c yel grn	4.50	4.00
a.		1c grn	4.50	4.00
13	A12	5c green	5.25	4.00
14	A13	10c lilac	20.00	20.00
15	A14	20c yel brn	5.25	5.25
a.		20c dk brn	5.25	5.25
16	A15	50c blue	1.75	1.75
17	A16	1p vermilion	3.00	3.00
18	A17	2p *yellow*	7.50	7.50
19	A18	5p *rose*	67.50	60.00

A19 A20

Liberty Head
A21 A22

Pedro Justo Berrio — A23

1875-85				
20	A19	1c *grn*, unglazed ('76)	1.50	1.50
a.		Glazed paper	2.25	2.25
b.		1c *lt grn*, laid paper ('85)	3.50	3.00
21	A19	1c *blk* ('76)	1.10	70
a.		Laid paper	125.00	100.00
22	A19	1c *bl grn* ('85)	2.25	2.25
23	A19	1c red lil, laid paper ('85)	2.25	2.25
24	A20	2½c blue	2.25	2.25
a.		Pelure paper ('78)	*20,000.*	*1,650.*
25	A21	5c green	15.00	14.00
a.		Laid paper	120.00	80.00
26	A22	5c green	15.00	14.00
a.		Laid paper	120.00	80.00
27	A23	10c lilac	22.50	21.00
a.		Laid paper	120.00	110.00
28	A20	10c vio, pelure paper ('78)	*525.00*	450.00

Arms
A24

Liberty
A25

A26 A27

1878-85				
29	A24	2½c bl, pelure paper	2.25	2.25
30	A24	2½c grn ('83)	2.25	2.25
a.		Laid paper ('83)	60.00	45.00
31	A24	2½c *buff* ('85)	4.50	4.50
32	A25	5c grn ('83)	2.25	2.25
a.		Pelure paper	24.00	21.00
b.		Laid paper ('82)	30.00	9.00
33	A25	5c vio ('83)	5.25	5.25
a.		5c bl vio ('83)	5.25	5.00
34	A26	10c vio, laid paper ('82)	110.00	45.00
35	A26	10c scar ('83)	2.25	2.25
a.		Tete beche pair	50.00	50.00
36	A27	20c brn ('83)	2.25	2.25
a.		Laid paper ('82)	4.50	4.50

A28 A29

Liberty — A30

1883-85				
37	A28	5c brown	4.50	3.25
a.		Laid paper	135.00	75.00
38	A28	5c grn ('85)	90.00	45.00
a.		Laid paper ('85)	100.00	67.50
39	A28	5c yel, laid paper ('85)	4.50	4.50
40	A29	10c bl grn, laid paper	4.50	4.50
41	A29	10c bl, *bl* ('85)	4.50	4.50
42	A29	10c lil, laid paper ('85)	6.00	6.00
a.		Wove paper ('85)	90.00	45.00
43	A30	20c bl, laid paper ('85)	4.50	4.50

Coat of Arms — A31

1886

Wove Paper.

55	A31	1c grn, *pink*	65	65
56	A31	2½c *orange*	65	65
57	A31	5c ultra, *buff*	1.75	1.75
a.		5c bl, *buff*	3.00	3.00
58	A31	10c rose, *buff*	85	75
a.		Transfer of 50c in stone of 10c	72.50	72.50
59	A31	20c dk vio, *buff*	1.50	1.50
61	A31	50c yel brn, *buff*	2.75	2.75
62	A31	1p yel, *grn*	4.50	4.50
63	A31	2p grn, *vio*	4.50	4.50

1887-88				
64	A31	1c red, *vio*	45	45
65	A31	2½c lil, *pale lil*	65	65
66	A31	5c car, *buff*	75	75
67	A31	5c red, *grn*	2.25	2.25
68	A31	10c brn, *grn*	65	65

Medellin Issue.

A32

A33

A34

1888 Type-set.

69	A32	2½c *yellow*	14.00	14.00
70	A33	5c *yellow*	4.50	4.50
71	A34	5c red, *yel*	4.50	4.50

Two varieties of No. 69, six of No. 70 and ten of No. 71.

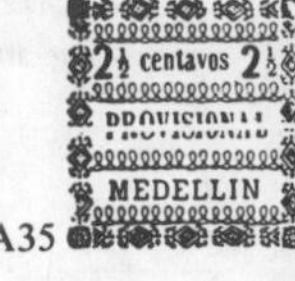

A35

1889				
72	A35	2½c red	4.50	4.50

Ten varieties including "eentavos".

Regular Issue.

Coat of Arms
A36 A37

A38 A39

A40 A41

1889-90	Litho.			*Perf. 13½*
73	A36	1c *rose*	30	30
74	A36	2½c *blue*	30	30
75	A36	5c *yellow*	38	38
76	A36	10c *green*	38	38
78	A37	20c bl ('90)	1.50	1.50
79	A38	50c vio brn ('90)	3.00	3.00
a.		Transfer of 20c in stone of 50c	90.00	90.00
80	A38	50c grn ('90)	2.50	2.50
81	A39	1p red ('90)	2.25	2.25
82	A40	2p *mag* ('90)	13.00	13.00
83	A41	5p *org red* ('90)	18.50	18.50

Nos. 73-76, 82-83 exist imperf.

The so-called "errors" of Nos. 73 to 76, printed on paper of wrong colors, are essays or, possibly, reprints. They exist perforated and imperforate.

See also No. 96.

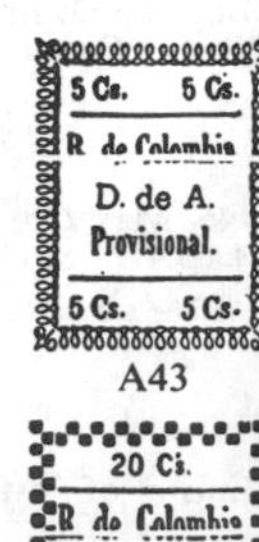

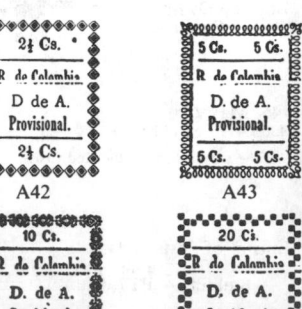

A42 A43

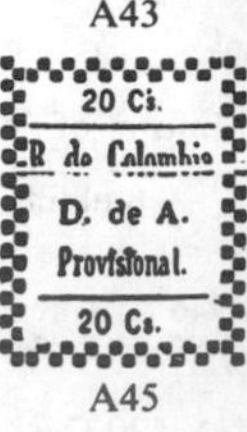

A44 A45

1890	Type-set.			*Perf. 14.*
84	A42	2½c *buff*	1.75	1.75
85	A43	5c *orange*	1.75	1.75
86	A44	10c *buff*	6.00	6.00

No.	Type	Denomination	Unused	Used
87	A44	10c *rose*	6.75	6.75
88	A45	20c *orange*	6.75	6.75

Twenty varieties of the 5c, ten of each of the other values.

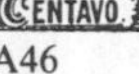
A46

A47

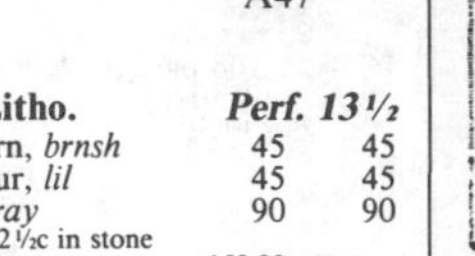

1892 Litho. *Perf. 13½*

No.	Type	Denomination	Unused	Used
89	A46	1c brn, *brnsh*	45	45
90	A46	2½c pur, *lil*	45	45
92	A46	5c *gray*	90	90
a.		Transfer of 2½c in stone of 5c	150.00	

1893

No.	Type	Denomination	Unused	Used
93	A46	1c blue	30	30
94	A46	2½c green	45	45
95	A46	5c vermilion	30	30
96	A36	10c pale brn	30	30

1896 *Perf. 14*

No.	Type	Denomination	Unused	Used
97	A47	2c gray	30	30
98	A47	2c lil rose	30	30
99	A47	2½c brown	30	30
100	A47	2½c stl bl	30	30
101	A47	3c orange	30	30
102	A47	3c ol grn	30	30
103	A47	5c green	30	30
104	A47	5c yel buff	30	30
105	A47	10c brn vio	60	60
106	A47	10c violet	60	60
107	A47	20c brn org	60	60
108	A47	20c blue	1.00	1.00
109	A47	50c gray brn	1.00	1.00
110	A47	50c rose	1.40	1.40
111	A47	1p bl & blk	18.50	18.50
112	A47	1p rose red & blk	18.50	18.50
113	A47	2p org & blk	60.00	60.00
114	A47	2p dk grn & blk	60.00	60.00
115	A47	5p red vio & blk	90.00	90.00
116	A47	5p pur & blk	90.00	90.00

Nos. 115-116 with centers omitted are proofs.

General José María Córdoba — A48

1899 *Perf. 11.*

No.	Type	Denomination	Unused	Used
117	A48	½c grnsh bl	7	12
118	A48	1c sl bl	7	12
119	A48	2c sl brn	7	12
120	A48	3c red	7	12
121	A48	4c bis brn	7	12
122	A48	5c green	7	12
123	A48	10c scarlet	7	12
124	A48	20c gray vio	7	12
125	A48	50c ol bis	7	12
126	A48	1p grnsh blk	7	12
127	A48	2p ol gray	7	12
		Nos. 117-127 (11)	77	1.32

Numerous part-perf. and imperf. varieties of Nos. 117-127 exist.

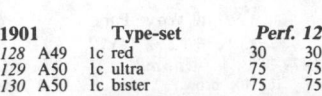

A49

A50

A50a

1901 Type-set *Perf. 12*

No.	Type	Denomination	Unused	Used
128	A49	1c red	30	30
129	A50	1c ultra	75	75
130	A50	1c bister	75	75
130A	A50a	1c dl red	75	75
130B	A50a	1c ultra	6.00	6.00

Eight varieties of No. 128, four varieties of Nos. 129-130B.

A51

A52

Atanasio Girardot A53

Dr. José Félix Restrepo A54

1902 Litho. Wove Paper

No.	Type	Denomination	Unused	Used
131	A51	1c brt rose	22	15
a.		Laid paper	75	75
b.		Imperf., pair	3.00	
132	A51	2c blue	15	15
a.		Transfer of 3c in stone of 2c	6.25	6.25
133	A51	3c green	15	15
a.		Imperf., pair	3.50	
134	A51	4c dl vio	15	15
135	A52	5c rose red	22	22
136	A53	10c rose lil	15	15
a.		Small head	6.25	6.25
b.		10c rose	15	15
137	A53	20c gray grn	22	22
138	A53	30c brt rose	22	22
139	A53	40c blue	22	22
140	A53	50c brn, *yel*	22	22

Laid Paper.

No.	Type	Denomination	Unused	Used
141	A54	1p pur & blk	90	90
142	A54	2p rose & blk	90	90
143	A54	5p sl bl & blk	1.50	1.50
		Nos. 131-143 (13)	5.22	5.15

1903

Wove Paper.

No.	Type	Denomination	Unused	Used
143A	A51	1c blue	15	15
144	A51	2c violet	15	15
a.		Imperf.	3.00	

A55

A56

Francisco Antonio Zea A57

Custodio Garcia Rovira A58

La Pola (Policarpa Salavarrieta) A59

J. M. Restrepo A60

José Fernandez Madrid A61

Juan del Corral A62

1903-04

No.	Type	Denomination	Unused	Used
145	A55	4c yel brn	22	22
146	A55	5c blue	22	22
147	A56	10c yellow	22	22
148	A56	20c purple	22	22
149	A56	30c brown	75	75
150	A56	40c green	75	75
151	A56	50c rose	22	22
152	A57	1p ol gray	75	75
153	A58	2p purple	75	75
154	A59	3p dk bl	75	75
155	A60	4p dl red	1.10	1.10
156	A61	5p red brn	1.10	1.10
157	A62	10p scarlet	4.50	4.50
		Nos. 145-157 (13)	11.55	11.55

Nos. 145-146, 151, 153-157 exist imperf. Price by pair, $3 to $4.

Stamps of these designs are local private post issues.

OFFICIAL STAMPS. Stamps of 1903-04 with overprint "OFICIAL" were never issued.

REGISTRATION STAMPS.

R1

1896 Unwmk. Litho. *Perf. 14*

No.	Type	Denomination	Unused	Used
F1	R1	2½c rose	1.40	1.40
F2	R1	2½c dl bl	1.40	1.40

Cordoba R2

R3

1899 *Perf. 11*

No.	Type	Denomination	Unused	Used
F3	R2	2½c dl bl	30	30
F4	R3	10c red lil	30	30

R4

1902 *Perf. 12*

No.	Type	Denomination	Unused	Used
F5	R4	10c pur, *bl*	38	38
a.		Imperf.		

ACKNOWLEDGMENT OF RECEIPT STAMPS.

AR1

1902-03 Unwmk. Litho. *Perf. 12*

No.	Type	Denomination	Unused	Used
H1	AR1	5c *rose*	1.10	1.10
H2	AR1	5c sl ('03)	38	38

AR2

Purple Handstamp.

1903 *Imperf.*

No.	Type	Denomination	Unused	Used
H3	AR2	10c *pink*	21.00	21.00

LATE FEE STAMPS.

Córdoba — LF1

1899 Unwmk. Litho. *Perf. 11*

No.	Type	Denomination	Unused	Used
I1	LF1	2½c dk grn	30	30
a.		Imperf., pair	3.50	

LF2

LF3

1901 Type-set. *Perf. 12.*

No.	Type	Denomination	Unused	Used
I2	LF2	2½c red vio	65	65
a.		2½c pur	65	65

1902 Litho.

No.	Type	Denomination	Unused	Used
I3	LF3	2½c violet	22	22

City of Medellin

Stamps of the designs shown were not issued by any governmental agency but by the Sociedad de Mejoras Publicas.

BOLIVAR

Originally a State, now a Department of the Republic of Colombia. (See Antioquia.)

A1

1863-66 Unwmk. Litho. *Imperf.*

1 A1 10c green 850.00 500.00
a. Five stars below shield *1,850.* *2,000.*
2 A1 10c red ('66) 30.00 30.00
a. Diagonal half used as 5c on cover 55.00
b. Five stars below shield 75.00 75.00
3 A1 1p red 10.00 10.00

Fourteen varieties of each. Counterfeits of Nos. 1 and 1a exist.

Coat of Arms
A2 A3

A4

A5

1873

4 A2 5c blue 6.75 6.75
5 A3 10c violet 6.75 6.75
6 A4 20c yel grn 27.50 27.50
7 A5 80c vermilion 60.00 60.00

A6

A7

A8

1874-78

8 A6 5c blue 25.00 25.00
9 A7 5c bl ('78) 7.50 7.50
10 A8 10c vio ('77) 3.75 3.75

Simon Bolivar — A9

Dated "1879".

1879 White Wove Paper. *Perf. 12½*

11 A9 5c blue 30 30
a. Imperf., pair 1.00
12 A9 10c violet 22 22
13 A9 20c red 30 30
a. 20c grn (error) 12.50 12.50

Bluish Laid Paper.

15 A9 5c blue 30 30
a. Imperf., pair 2.50
16 A9 10c violet 2.00 2.00
a. Imperf., pair 5.00
17 A9 20c red 40 40
a. Imperf., pair 2.25

Stamps of 80c and 1p on white wove paper and 1p on bluish laid paper were prepared but not placed in use.

Dated "1880".

1880 White Wove Paper *Perf. 12½*

19 A9 5c blue 30 30
a. , pair 2.00
20 A9 10c violet 40 40
a. Imperf., pair 2.00
21 A9 20c red 40 40
a. 20c grn (error) 16.00 16.00
23 A9 80c green 2.75 2.75
24 A9 1p orange 2.75 2.75
a. Imperf., pair 7.00

Bluish Laid Paper.

25 A9 5c blue 30 30
a. Imperf., pair 1.50
26 A9 10c violet 2.75 2.75
27 A9 20c red 40 40
a. Imperf., pair 3.50
28 A9 1p orange 500.00
a. Imperf. *450.00*

A11

A12

A13

A15

A16

Dated "1882".
White Wove Paper.

1882 *Perf. 12, 16x12*

29 A11 5c blue 40 40
30 A12 10c lilac 30 30
31 A13 20c red 40 40
33 A15 80c green 80 80
34 A16 1p orange 80 80

Nos. 29, 30 and 34 are known imperforate. They are printer's waste and were not issued through post offices.

Bolivar
A17

Bolivar
A18

1882 Engr. *Perf. 12*

35 A17 5p bl & rose red 75 75
a. Imperf., pair 6.00
b. Perf. 16 7.50 7.50
c. Perf. 14 7.50 7.50
36 A17 10p brn & bl 2.00 2.00
a. Imperf., pair 10.00
b. Perf. 16 6.75 6.75
c. Rouletted 10.00 10.00

Dated "1883".

1883 Litho. *Perf. 12, 16x12*

37 A11 5c blue 22 22
a. Imperf., pair 1.00
b. Perf. 12 2.75 1.25
38 A12 10c lilac 30 30
39 A13 20c red 30 30
41 A15 80c green 40 40
42 A16 1p orange 75 75
a. Perf. 16x12 2.50 2.50

Dated "1884"

1884

43 A11 5c blue 40 40
a. Perf. 12 11.50 11.50
44 A12 10c lilac 22 22
45 A13 20c red 22 22
a. Perf. 12 5.25 5.25
47 A15 80c green 30 30
a. Perf. 12 2.50 2.50
48 A16 1p orange 40 40

Dated "1885"

1885

49 A11 5c blue 18 18
50 A12 10c lilac 18 18
51 A13 20c red 18 18
53 A15 80c green 30 30
54 A16 1p orange 40 40

The note after No. 34 will also apply to imperforate stamps of the 1884-85 issues.

1891 *Perf. 14.*

55 A18 1c black 40 40
56 A18 5c orange 40 40
a. Imperf., pair 1.00
57 A18 10c carmine 40 40
58 A18 20c blue 75 75
59 A18 50c green 1.10 1.10
60 A18 1p purple 1.10 1.10
Nos. 55-60 (6) 4.15 4.15

Overprinted with 7 Parallel Wavy Lines in Purple

1899

61 A18 1c black 55.00 55.00

The overprint is a control mark.

Bolivar
A19

José Fernandez Madrid
A20

Manuel Rodriguez Torices
A21

José Maria Garcia de Toledo
A22

1903 Laid Paper *Imperf.*

62 A19 50c dk bl, *pink* 75 75
a. bluish paper 75 75
63 A19 50c sl grn, *pink* 75 75
a. rose paper 1.10 1.10
b. grnsh bl paper 2.25 2.25
c. yel paper 2.75 2.75
d. brn paper 2.75 2.75
e. sal paper 6.00 6.00
64 A19 50c pur, *pink* 1.10 1.10
a. white paper 2.50 2.50
b. brn paper 2.50 2.50
c. grnsh bl paper 2.50 2.50
d. lil paper 2.50 2.50
e. rose paper 2.25 2.25
f. yel paper 2.50 2.50
g. sal paper 4.50 4.50
h. As "a," wove paper 8.50 8.50
65 A20 1p org, *sal* 75 75
a. yel paper 4.50 4.50
b. grnsh bl paper 15.00 15.00
66 A20 1p gray grn, *lil* 1.75 1.75
a. yel paper 6.75 6.75
b. sal paper 7.50 7.50
c. grn paper 7.50 7.50
d. white wove paper 10.00
67 A21 5p car rose, *lil* 75 75
a. brn paper 75 75
b. yel paper 1.40 1.40
c. grnsh bl paper 4.50 4.50
d. bluish paper 6.00 6.00
e. sal paper 7.50 7.50
f. rose paper 9.00 9.00
68 A22 10p dk bl, *bluish* 1.50 1.50
a. grnsh bl paper 1.50 1.50
b. rose paper 7.50 7.50
c. sal paper 7.50 7.50
d. yel paper 7.50 7.50
e. brn paper 9.00 9.00
f. lil paper 10.00 10.00
g. white paper 9.00 9.00
69 A22 10p pur, *grnsh bl* 4.50 4.50
a. bluish paper 7.50 7.50
b. rose paper 6.75 6.75
c. yel paper 7.50 7.50
d. brn paper 7.50 7.50

Sewing Machine Perf.
Laid Paper

70 A19 50c dk bl, *pink* 75 75
a. bluish paper 75 75
71 A19 50c sl grn, *pink* 1.75 1.75
72 A19 50c pur, *grnsh bl* 2.50 2.50
a. white paper 2.50 2.50
b. white wove paper 7.50
73 A20 1p org, *sal* 1.75 1.75
74 A20 1p gray grn, *lil* 9.00 9.00
a. yel paper 9.00 9.00
75 A21 5p car rose, *lil* 2.50 2.50
a. yel paper 1.75 1.75
b. brn paper 2.50 2.50
c. bluish paper 5.25 5.25
d. white wove paper 9.00
76 A22 10p dk bl, *bluish* 6.75 6.75
a. grnsh bl paper 4.50 4.50
b. yel paper 9.00 9.00
c. As "b," wove paper 10.00
77 A22 10p pur, *grnsh bl* 6.75 6.75
a. bluish paper 11.00 11.00
b. rose paper 8.25 8.25
c. yel paper 11.00 11.00

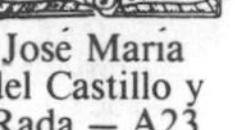
José Maria del Castillo y Rada — A23

Manuel Anguiano — A24

Pantaleon C. Ribon — A25

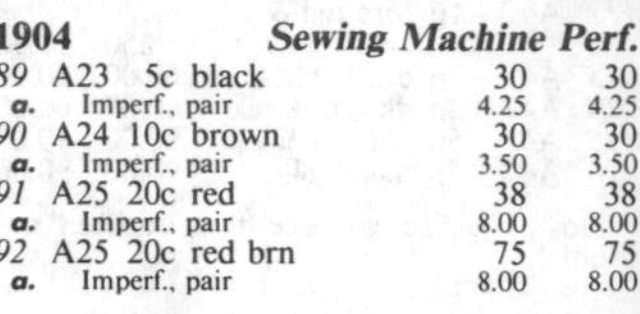

1904 *Sewing Machine Perf.*

89 A23 5c black 30 30
a. Imperf., pair 4.25 4.25
90 A24 10c brown 30 30
a. Imperf., pair 3.50 3.50
91 A25 20c red 38 38
a. Imperf., pair 8.00 8.00
92 A25 20c red brn 75 75
a. Imperf., pair 8.00 8.00

A26

A27

A28

1904 *Imperf.*

93 A26 ½c black 75 75
a. Tete beche pair 4.50 4.50
94 A27 1c blue 1.40 1.40
95 A28 2c purple 1.50 1.50

REGISTRATION STAMPS.

Simon Bolivar
R1 R2

White Wove Paper.
Perf. 12½, 16x12.

1879 Unwmk. Litho.

F1 R1 40c brown 90 90

Bluish Laid Paper.

F2 R1 40c brown 90 90
a. Imperf., pair 4.00

Dated "1880".

1880

White Wove Paper.

F3 R1 40c brown 40 40

Bluish Laid Paper.

F4 R1 40c brown 80 80
a. Imperf., pair 4.50

Dated "1882" to "1885".
White Wove Paper.

1882-85 ***Perf. 16x12***

F5 R2 40c brn (1882) 40 40
a. Perf. 12 22.50
F6 R2 40c brn (1883) 30 30
a. Perf. 12 11.50
F7 R2 40c brn (1884) 30 30
a. Perf. 12 12.00
F8 R2 40c brn (1885) 40 40
a. Perf. 12 3.00

R3

Laid Paper.

1903 ***Imperf.***

F9 R3 20c org, *rose* 75 75
a. sal paper 1.40 1.40
b. grnsh bl paper 4.50 4.50

Sewing Machine perf.

F10 R3 20c org, *rose* 1.50 1.50
a. sal paper 1.50 1.50
b. grnsh bl paper 4.50 4.50

R4

1904

Wove Paper

F11 R4 5c black 4.00 4.00

ACKNOWLEDGMENT OF RECEIPT STAMPS.

AR1

1903 Unwmk. Litho. ***Imperf.***

Laid Paper

H1 AR1 20c org, *rose* 1.50 1.50
a. yel paper 1.50 1.50
b. grnsh bl paper 3.75 3.75
H2 AR1 20c dk bl, *yel* 1.75 1.75
a. brn paper 1.75 1.75
b. rose paper 2.00 2.00
c. sal paper 4.75 4.75
d. grnsh bl paper 4.50 4.50

Sewing Machine Perf.

H3 AR1 20c org, *grnsh bl* 7.50 7.50
a. yel paper 9.00 9.00
H4 AR1 20c dk bl, *yel* 9.00 9.00
a. lil paper 9.00

AR2

1904

Wove Paper.

H5 AR2 2c red 1.40 1.40

LATE FEE STAMPS.

LF1

1903 Unwmk. Litho. ***Imperf.***

Laid Paper.

I1 LF1 20c car rose, *bluish* 75 75
I2 LF1 20c pur, *bluish* 70 70
a. rose paper 1.50 1.50
b. brn paper 1.50 1.50
c. lil paper 1.75 1.75
d. yel paper 7.50 7.50

Sewing Machine Perf.

I13 LF1 20c car rose, *bluish* 75 75
I14 LF1 20c pur, *bluish* 75 75
a. rose paper 1.50 1.50
b. lil paper 1.75 1.75
c. yel paper 7.50 7.50

BOYACA

Originally a State, now a Department of the Republic of Colombia. (See Antioquia.)

Diego Mendoza Perez — A1

1902 Unwmk. Litho. ***Perf. 13½***

Wove Paper.

1 A1 5c bl grn 90 90
a. bluish paper 90.00 90.00
b. Imperf., pair 13.50

Laid Paper.

Perf. 12

2 A1 5c green 100.00 100.00

Coat of Arms
A2 A3

General Prospero Pinzon
A4

Numeral of Value
A5

Monument of Battle of Boyaca — A6

President José Manuel Marroquin — A7

1903 Litho. ***Imperf.***

4 A2 10c dk gray 30 30
5 A3 20c red brn 40 40
6 A5 1p red 3.75 3.75
a. 1p cl 4.50 4.50
8 A6 5p *rose* 1.40 1.40
a. 5p *buff* 12.00 12.00
9 A7 10p *buff* 1.40 1.40
a. 10p *rose* 12.00 12.00
b. Tete beche pair 18.50
Nos. 4-9 (5) 7.25 7.25

Perf. 12.

10 A2 10c dk gray 30 30
11 A3 20c red brn 45 45
12 A4 50c green 40 40
13 A4 50c dl bl 2.00 2.00
14 A5 1p red 40 40
a. 1p cl 3.75 3.75
16 A6 5p *rose* 1.40 1.40
a. 5p *buff* 12.00 12.00
17 A7 10p *buff* 1.40 1.40
a. 10p *rose* 12.00 12.00
b. Tete beche pair 15.00 15.00
Nos. 10-17 (7) 6.35 6.35

Statue of Bolivar — A8

1904

18 A8 10c orange 30 30
a. Imperf., pair 4.50 4.50

CAUCA

Originally a State, now a Department of the Republic of Colombia. (see Antioquia.)

A1

A2

Handstamped.

1879 (?) Unwmk. ***Imperf.***

1 A1 (5c) black *4,000. 3,500.*

1882

2 A2 5c violet 80.00 80.00
a. Figure in lower left corner omitted

A3

A4

1883

3 A3 (5) violet 25.00 25.00
4 A4 (5) violet 60.00 60.00

A5

A7

1890

5 A5 5c red 75.00 75.00

Nos. 1 to 5 were sanctioned, though not authorized, by the national government.

Imperf., Sewing Machine Perf.

1902 **Typeset**

8 A7 10c *rose* 2.25 2.25
9 A7 20c *orange* 1.50 1.50

Stamps of this design are believed to be of private origin and without official sanction.
Items inscribed "No hay estampillas" (No stamps available) and others inscribed "Manuel E. Jimenez" are considered by specialists to be receipt labels, not postage stamps.

CUNDINAMARCA

Originally a State, now a Department of the Republic of Colombia. (See Antioquia.)

Coat of Arms
A1 A2

1870 Unwmk. Litho. ***Imperf.***

1 A1 5c blue 4.75 4.75
2 A2 10c red 15.00 15.00

The counterfeits, or reprints, show traces of the cuts made to deface the dies.

A3

A4

A5

A6

1877-82

3 A3 10c red ('82) 3.00 3.00
a. Laid paper ('77) 4.50 4.50
4 A4 20c grn ('82) 6.75 6.75
a. Laid paper ('77) 7.50 7.50
7 A5 50c pur ('82) 7.50 7.50
8 A6 1p brn ('82) 11.00 11.00

A7

1884

10 A7 5c blue 75 75
11 A7 5c bl (redrawn) 1.50 1.50
a. Tete beche pair 75.00 75.00

The redrawn stamp has no period after "COLOMBIA."

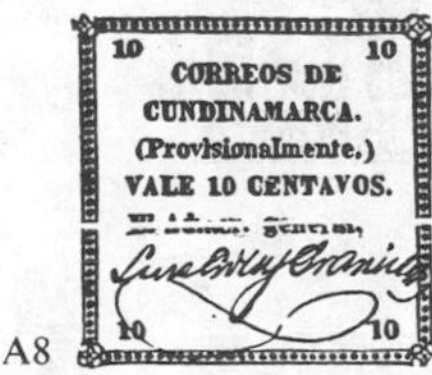

A8

CUNDINAMARCA.
CINCUENTA CVOS.
A9

A10

A11

1883 **Typeset**

13	A8	10c *yellow*	11.00	11.00
14	A9	50c *rose*	11.00	11.00
15	A10	1p *brown*	30.00	30.00
16	A11	2r *green*	*1,600*	

Typeset varieties exist: 4 of the 10c, 2 each of 50c and 1p.

Some experts doubt that No. 16 was issued. The variety without signature and watermarked "flowers" is believed to be a proof. Forgeries exist.

A12

1886 **Litho.**

17	A12	5c blue	75	75
18	A12	10c red	4.50	4.50
19	A12	10c red, *lil*	2.40	2.40
20	A12	20c green	3.75	3.75
a.		20c yel grn	4.50	4.50
21	A12	50c purple	4.50	4.50
22	A12	1p org brn	5.25	5.25

Nos. 17 to 22 have been reprinted. The colors are aniline and differ from those of the original stamps. The impression is coarse and blurred.

A13

A14

Arms
A15 A16

A17

A18

Scott's International Album provides spaces for an extensive representative collection of the world's postage stamps.

A19

A20

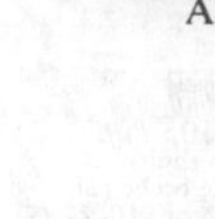
A21

1904 ***Perf. 10½, 12***

23	A13	1c orange	30	30
24	A14	2c gray bl	30	30
25	A15	3c rose	45	45
26	A15	5c ol grn	45	45
27	A16	10c pale brn	45	45
28	A17	15c pink	45	45
29	A18	20c bl, *grn*	45	45
30	A18	20c blue	75	75
31	A19	40c blue	75	75
32	A19	40c bl, *buff*	17.50	17.50
33	A20	50c red vio	75	75
34	A21	1p gray grn	60	60
		Nos. 23-34 (12)	23.20	23.20

Imperf

23a	A13	1c orange	90	90
24a	A14	2c blue	90	90
b.		2c sl	6.00	6.00
25a	A15	3c rose	90	90
26a	A15	5c ol grn	1.50	1.50
27a	A16	10c pale brn	2.50	2.50
28a	A17	15c pink	45	45
29a	A18	20c bl, *grn*	2.25	2.25
30a	A18	20c blue	2.25	2.25
31a	A19	40c blue	75	75
32a	A19	40c bl, *buff*	17.50	17.50
33a	A20	50c red vio	75	75
34a	A21	1p gray grn	75	75
		Nos. 23a-34a (12)	31.40	31.40

REGISTRATION STAMPS.

R1

1883 **Unwmk.** ***Imperf.***

F1	R1	*orange*	15.00	16.50

R2

1904 ***Perf. 12.***

F2	R2	10c bister	1.00	1.00
a.		Imperf.	4.25	4.25

Magdalena

Items inscribed "No hay estampillas" (No stamps available) are considered by specialists to be not postage stamps but receipt labels.

Panama.

Issues of Panama as a state and later Department of Colombia are listed with the Republic of Panama issues (Nos. 1-30).

SANTANDER

Originally a State, now a Department of the Republic of Colombia. (See Antioquia.)

Coat of Arms
A1 A2

1884 **Unwmk.** **Litho.** ***Imperf.***

1	A1	1c blue	30	30
a.		1c gray bl	50	50
2	A2	5c red	50	50
3	A2	10c bluish pur	1.75	1.75
a.		Tete beche pair		

No. 2 exists unofficially perforated 14.

A3

A4

1886 ***Imperf.***

4	A3	1c blue	90	90
5	A3	5c red	30	30
6	A3	10c red vio	50	50
a.		10c dp vio	50	50
b.		Inscribed "CINCO CENTAVOS"	25.00	25.00

The numerals in the upper corners are omitted on No. 5, while on No. 6 there are no numerals in the side panels. No. 6 exists unofficially perforated 12.

1887

7	A4	1c blue	22	22
a.		1c ultra	1.50	1.50
8	A4	5c red	1.50	1.50
9	A4	10c violet	3.75	3.75

A5

A6

A7

1889 ***Perf. 11½ and 13½.***

10	A5	1c blue	30	30
11	A6	5c red	1.50	1.50
12	A7	10c purple	50	50
a.		Imperf., pair	20.00	

A8

A9

1892 ***Perf. 13½***

13	A8	5c red, *rose buff*	75	75

1895-96

14	A9	5c brown	90	90
15	A9	5c yel grn ('96)	90	90

A10

A11

A12

1899 ***Perf. 10***

16	A10	1c *green*	40	40
17	A11	5c *pink*	40	40

Perf. 13½.

18	A12	10c blue	90	90
a.		Perf. 12	1.25	1.25

A13

1903 ***Imperf.***

19	A13	50c red	65	65
a.		50c rose	65	65
b.		"SANTENDER"	3.00	3.00
c.		"Corrcos"	3.00	3.00
d.		"Corceos"	3.00	3.00
e.		Tete beche pair	6.00	6.00
f.		Pair, one without overprint	3.50	3.50

The overprint "Correos de Departmento Bucaramanga" on the 50c red revenue stamp has been proved to be a cancellation.

A14

A15

Arms
A16

Locomotive
A17

A18

A19

A20

1904 ***Imperf.***

22	A14	5c dk grn	30	30
a.		5c yel grn	50	50
24	A15	10c rose	15	15
25	A16	20c brn vio	15	15
26	A17	50c yellow	20	20
27	A18	1p black	20	20
28	A19	5p dk bl	40	40
29	A20	10p carmine	50	50
		Nos. 22-29 (7)	1.90	1.90

1905

30	A14	5c pale bl	50	50
31	A15	10c red brn	50	50
32	A16	20c yel grn	50	50
33	A17	50c red vio	50	50
34	A18	1p dk bl	50	50
35	A19	5p pink	50	50
36	A20	10p red	2.00	2.00
		Nos. 30-36 (7)	5.00	5.00

A21

1907 *Imperf.*
37 A21 ½c on 50c rose 65 65

CITY OF CUCUTA

A71

A72

"Gobierno Provisorio" at Top

1900 Litho. ***Perf. 12 Vertically.***
101 A71 1c (ctvo) *bl grn* 4.50 4.50
a. "cvo." 11.50 11.50
b. "cvos." 4.50 4.50
c. "centavo" 5.25 5.25
103 A71 2c black 3.00 3.00
104 A71 5c *pink* 3.00 3.00
a. Name at side (V) 6.50 6.50
105 A71 10c *pink* 3.00 3.00
a. Name at side (V) 6.50 6.50
106 A71 20c *yellow* 4.50 4.50
a. Name at side (G) 9.00 9.00
Nos. 101-106 (5) 18.00 18.00

"Gobierno Provisional" at Top

Name at Side in Black or Green
108 A72 1c (ctvo.)*bl grn* (Bk) 4.50 4.50
a. "centavo" 17.50 17.50
109 A72 2c *bl grn* (Bk) 2.50 2.50
110 A72 5c blk (G) 2.50 2.50
a. "ctvos." smaller 5.00 5.00
112 A72 10c *pink* (Bk) 2.50 2.50
113 A72 20c *yel* (G) 4.50 4.50
Nos. 108-113 (5) 16.50 16.50

Stamps of these and similar designs on white and yellow paper, with and without surcharges of ½c, 1c or 2c, are believed to have been produced without government authorization.

TOLIMA

Originally a State, now & Department of the Republic of Colombia. (See Antioquia.)

A1

1870 Unwmk. Typeset. ***Imperf.***
White Wove Paper.
1 A1 5c black 60.00 32.50
2 A1 10c black 60.00 32.50

Printed from two settings. Setting I, ten types of 5c. Setting II, six types of 5c and four types of 10c. Blue Laid Batonne Paper.

3 A1 5c black *750.00*

Buff Laid Batonné Paper.
4 A1 5c black 120.00 80.00

Blue Wove Paper
5 A1 5c black 67.50 45.00

Blue Vertically Laid Paper.
6 A1 5c black 100.00 70.00
a. Paper with ruled blue vertical lines

Blue Horizontally Laid Paper
7 A1 5c black 100.00 70.00

Blue Quadrille Paper.
8 A1 5c black 100.00 90.00

Ten varieties each of Nos. 3-5 and 7; 20 varieties each of Nos. 6 and 8.

Official imitations were made in 1886 from new settings of the type. There are only two varieties of each value. They are printed on blue and white paper, wove, batonne, laid, etc.

A2

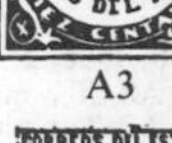
A3

A4

A5

Yellowish White Wove Paper.

1871 Litho. ***Imperf.***
9 A2 5c dp brn 2.25 2.25
a. 5c red brn 2.25 2.25
b. Value reads "CINGO" 37.50 37.50
10 A3 10c blue 6.00 6.00
11 A4 50c green 7.50 7.50
12 A5 1p carmine 12.00 12.00

The 5p stamps, type A2, are bogus varieties made from an altered die of the 5c.

The 10c, 50c and 1 peso stamps have been reprinted on bluish white wove paper. They are from new plates and most copies show traces of fine lines with which the dies had been defaced. Reprints of the 5c have a large cross at the top. The 10c on laid batonnepaper is known only as a reprint.

A6

A7

A8

A9

1879
Grayish or White Wove Paper
14 A6 5c yel brn 45 45
a. 5c pur brn 45 45
15 A7 10c blue 50 50
16 A8 50c grn, *bluish* 50 50
a. White paper 1.50 1.50
17 A9 1p vermilion 2.25 2.25
a. 1p car rose 9.00 9.00

A10

1883 ***Imperf.***
18 A6 5c orange 45 45
19 A7 10c vermilion 90 90
20 A10 20c violet 1.40 1.40

Coat of Arms — A12

1884 ***Imperf.***
23 A12 1c gray 15 15
24 A12 2c rose lil 15 15
a. 2c sl 15 15
25 A12 2½cdl org 15 15
26 A12 5c brown 15 15
27 A12 10c blue 38 38
a. 10c sl 22 22
28 A12 20c lemon 38 38
a. Laid paper 5.00 5.00
29 A12 25c black 30 30
30 A12 50c green 30 30
31 A12 1p vermilion 40 40
32 A12 2p violet 60 60
a. Value omitted 27.50 27.50
33 A12 5p yellow 40 40
34 A12 10p lil rose 1.10 1.10
a. Laid paper 27.50 27.50
b. 10p gray *135.00*
Nos. 23-34 (12) 4.46 4.46

A13

A14

Condor with Long Wings Touching Flagstaffs
A15 A16

1886 Litho. ***Perf. 10½, 11***
White Paper
36 A13 5c brown 1.50 1.50
a. 5c yel brn 1.50 1.50
b. Imperf., pair 20.00
37 A14 10c blue 4.50 4.50
a. Imperf., pair 20.00
38 A15 50c green 1.75 1.75
a. Imperf., pair 20.00
39 A16 1p vermilion 3.00 3.00
a. Imperf., pair 30.00

No. 38 has been reprinted in pale gray green, perforated 10½, and No. 39 in bright vermilion, perforated 11½. The impressions show many signs of wear.

Lilac Tinted Paper.
36c A13 5c org brn 13.00 13.00
37b A14 10c blue 13.00 13.00
38b A15 50c green 9.00 9.00
39b A16 1p vermilion 7.50 7.50

A17

A18

Condor with Short Wings
A19 A20

1886 White Paper ***Perf. 12***
44 A19 1c gray 7.50 7.50
a. Imperf., pair 20.00
45 A17 2c rose lil 8.25 8.25
46 A18 2½cdl org 24.00 24.00
47 A19 5c brown 10.00 10.00
a. Imperf., pair 32.50
48 A20 10c blue 10.00 10.00
a. Imperf., pair 32.50
49 A20 20c lemon 8.25 8.25
a. Tete beche pair 225.00 225.00
50 A20 25c black 7.50 7.50
51 A20 50c green 3.00 3.00
52 A20 1p vermilion 4.50 4.50
a. Imperf., pair 20.00
53 A20 2p violet 9.00 9.00
a. Imperf., pair 25.00
b. Tete beche pair 175.00 175.00
54 A20 5p orange 16.50 16.50
a. Imperf., pair 40.00
55 A20 10p lil rose 8.25 8.25
a. Imperf., pair 20.00

Condor with Long Wings, Upper Flagstaffs Omitted
A21 A22

1886 ***Perf. 12, 12½, 12x11***
56 A15 2½cdl org 75.00 75.00
a. Imperf., pair
b. Transfer of 5c in stone of 2½c
c. Transfer of 10c in stone of 2½c
57 A21 5c brown 7.50 7.50
a. Imperf., pair 20.00
b. Transfer of 10c in stone of 5c
c. As "b," imperf.
58 A14 10c ultra 13.00 13.00
a. Imperf., pair 32.50
b. Transfer of 5c in stone of 10c
59 A22 2p red vio 15.00 15.00
a. Imperf., pair 37.50
b. Without numerals in corners, colored background, imperf. 27.50
c. As "b," white background 27.50 27.50
60 A22 5p pale org 22.50 22.50
a. Imperf., pair 55.00
b. Bottom label inverted *650.00*
c. Tete beche pair
d. Transfer of 2p in stone of 5p

Imperf
61 A13 1c black *150.00*

No. 56 is similar to type A15, and No. 58 similar to type A14, but both have upper flagstaffs omitted.

A23

1888 ***Perf. 10½.***
62 A23 5c red 15 15
a. Imperf., pair 3.50
63 A23 10c green 38 38
a. Imperf., pair 4.00
64 A23 50c blue 1.00 1.00
a. Imperf., pair 6.00 6.00
65 A23 1p red brn 1.75 1.75
a. Imperf., pair 9.00

1895 ***Perf. 12, 13½***
66 A23 1c bl, *rose* 30 30
a. Imperf., pair 9.00
67 A23 2c grn, *lt grn* 30 30
a. Imperf., pair 9.00
68 A23 5c red 15 15
69 A23 10c green 30 30
70 A23 20c bl, *yel* 38 38
a. Imperf., pair 10.00
71 A23 1p brown 2.25 2.25
Nos. 66-71 (6) 3.68 3.68

"No Hay Estampillas"

Items inscribed "No hay estampillas' (No stamps available) are considered by specialists to be not postage stamps but receipt labels.

Honda Issue.

A23a

Black Surcharge.

1896 ***Perf. 12***
78 A23a 1c on 2c grn 45.00 45.00

Excellent counterfeits exist.

Condition is the all-important factor of price. Prices quoted are for stamps in fine condition.

Regular Issue.

A24

A25

A26

A27

A28

A29

A30

A31

Sewing Machine or Regular Perf. 12

1903-04 **Litho.**

79 A24 4c *green* 30 30
80 A25 10c dl bl 30 30
81 A26 20c orange 60 60
82 A27 50c *rose* 22 22
a. 50c *buff* 22 22
84 A28 1p brown 22 22
85 A29 2p gray 22 22
86 A30 5p red 22 22
a. Tete beche pair 6.25 6.25
87 A31 10p *blue* 22 22
a. 10p *lt grn* 22 22
b. 10p *grn glazed* 4.50 4.50
Nos. 79-87 (8) 2.30 2.30

Imperf

79a A24 4c *green* 30 30
80a A25 10c dl bl 22 22
81a A26 20c orange 1.40 1.40
82b A27 50c *rose* 1.75 1.75
c. 50c *buff* 1.75 1.75
84a A28 1p brown 22 22
85a A29 2p gray 22 22
86b A30 5p red 22 22
c. Tete beche pair 6.25 6.25
87c A31 10p *blue* 2.75 2.75
d. Tete beche pair
e. 10p *lt grn* 4.50 4.50
f. 10p *grn glazed* 22.50 22.50
Nos. 79a-87c (8) 7.08 7.08

COMORO ISLANDS

LOCATION — In Mozambique Channel between Madagascar and Mozambique.
GOVT. — Republic.
AREA — 838 sq. mi.
POP. — 385,000 (est. 1983).
CAPITAL — Moroni.

The Comoro Archipelago consists of the islands of Mayotte, Anjouan, Grand Comoro (Grande Comore) and Moheli, which issued their own stamps as French protectorates or colonies from 1887-1914. The archipelago was attached to Madagascar from 1914 to 1946, when it became a separate French territory. In July 1975, Anjouan, Grand Comoro and Moheli united to declare independence as the State of Comoro. Mayotte remained French.

100 Centimes = 1 Franc

A little time given to the study of the arrangement of the Scott Catalogue can make it easier to use effectively.

Anjouan Bay — A2

Comoro Woman Grinding Grain — A3

Moroni Mosque on Grand Comoro A4

1950 **Unwmk.** **Engr.** ***Perf. 13***

30 A2 10c blue 12 12
31 A2 50c green 15 15
32 A2 1fr dk ol brn 15 15
33 A3 2fr brt grn 30 30
34 A3 5fr purple 30 30
35 A3 6fr vio brn 42 42
36 A4 7fr red 42 42
37 A4 10fr dk grn 50 50
38 A4 11fr dp ultra 65 65
Nos. 30-38 (9) 3.01 3.01

Imperforates
Most Comoro Islands stamps exist imperforate in issued and trial colors, and also in small presentation sheets in issued colors.

Military Medal Issue.
Common Design Type

1952 **Engraved and Typographed**
39 CD101 15fr multi 27.50 27.50

Mosque of Ouani, Anjouan — A5

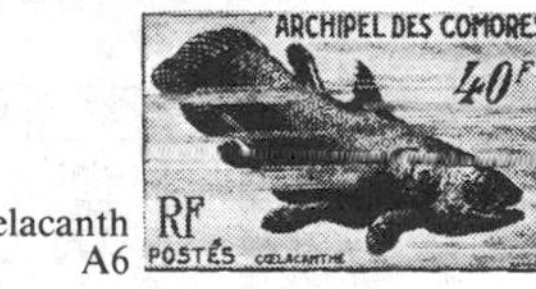

Coelacanth A6

1952-54 **Engr.**
40 A5 15fr dk brn 60 60
41 A5 20fr red brn 75 75
42 A6 40fr aqua & ind ('54) 11.00 8.50

FIDES Issue
Common Design Type

1956 **Unwmk.** ***Perf. 13x12½***
43 CD103 9fr dp vio 75 60

Human Rights Issue
Common Design Type

1958 **Engr.** ***Perf. 13***
44 CD105 20fr ol grn & dk bl 4.00 4.00

Flower Issue
Common Design Type

Design: Colvillea.

1959 **Photo.** ***Perf. 12½x12***
45 CD104 10fr multi 2.50 1.65

View of Dzaoudzi and Radio Symbol A8

Design: 25fr, Radio tower and radio waves over Islands.

1960, Dec. 23 **Engr.** ***Perf. 13***
46 A8 20fr mar, vio bl & grn 70 60
47 A8 25fr ultra, brn & grn 85 85

Comoro radio station.

Harpa Conoidalis — A9

Sea Shells: 50c, Cypraecassis rufa. 2fr, Murex ramosus. 5fr, Turbo marmoratus. 20fr, Pterocera scorpio. 25fr, Charonia tritonis.

1962, Jan. 13 **Photo.**
Shells in Natural Colors
48 A9 50c lil & brn 30 30
49 A9 1fr yel & red 30 30
50 A9 2fr pale grn & pink 40 40
51 A9 5fr yel & grn 80 80
52 A9 20fr sal & brn 1.85 1.85
53 A9 25fr bis & pink 2.50 2.50
Nos. 48-53,C5-C6 (8) 21.65 20.15

Wheat Emblem and Globe — A10

1963, Mar. 21 **Engr.** ***Perf. 13***
54 A10 20fr choc & dk grn 2.25 2.00

Issued for the "Freedom from Hunger" campaign of the U.N. Food and Agriculture Organization.

Red Cross Centenary Issue
Common Design Type

1963, Sept. 2 **Unwmk.** ***Perf. 13***
55 CD113 50fr emer, gray & car 4.00 3.50

Centenary of the International Red Cross.

Human Rights Issue
Common Design Type

1963, Dec. 10 **Engr.**
56 CD117 15fr dk red & yel grn 4.00 3.50

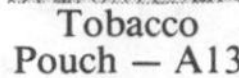

Tobacco Pouch — A13

Grand Comoro Canoe — A14

Designs: 4fr, Censer. 10fr, Carved lamp.

1963, Dec. 27 ***Perf. 13***
Size: 22x36mm.
57 A13 3fr multi 15 15
58 A13 4fr org, dp cl & sl grn 25 25
59 A13 10fr org brn, dk red brn & grn 50 50
Nos. 57-59,C8-C9 (5) 6.90 4.60

Common Design Types pictured in section at front of book.

Philatec Issue
Common Design Type

1964, March 31
60 CD118 50fr dk bl, red & grn 1.65 1.65

1964, Aug. 7 **Photo.** ***Perf. 13x12½***

Design: 30fr, Boutre felucca.

Size: 22x37mm.

61 A14 15fr multi 60 60
62 A14 30fr lt grn & multi 1.00 1.00

See Nos. C10-C11.

Spiny Lobster — A15

Designs: 12fr, Hammerhead shark (horiz.). 20fr, Turtle (horiz.). 25fr, Merou fish.

1965, Dec. 20 **Engr.** ***Perf. 13***
63 A15 1fr grn, lil & ocher 20 20
64 A15 12fr org red, sl & gray 50 40
65 A15 20fr org, red & bl grn 60 50
66 A15 25fr bl grn, dk brn & red 70 60

Hotel Itsandra, Moroni A16

Design: 15fr, Lake Salé, Grand Comoro.

1966, Dec. 19 **Photo.** ***Perf. 12½x13***
67 A16 15fr multi 40 30
68 A16 25fr multi 50 30

See Nos. C18-C19.

Comoro Sunbird A17

Birds: 10fr, Malachite kingfisher. 15fr, Rothschild's fody. 30fr, Cuckoo-roller.

1967, June 20 **Photo.** ***Perf. 12½x13***
Size: 36x23mm.
69 A17 2fr ocher & multi 60 60
70 A17 10fr lil & multi 80 80
71 A17 15fr yel grn & multi 1.00 1.00
72 A17 30fr pink & multi 1.60 1.60
Nos. 69-72,C20-C21 (6) 7.85 5.50

WHO Anniversary Issue
Common Design Type

1968, May 4 **Engr.** ***Perf. 13***
73 CD126 40fr grn, vio & dp car 80 70

Issued for the 20th anniversary of the World Health Organization.

Surgeonfish A19

Design: 25fr, Imperial angelfish.

1968, Aug. 1 Engr. *Perf. 13*
Size: 36x22mm.

74 A19 20fr vio bl, yel & red brn 40 40
75 A19 25fr Prus bl, dk bl & org 50 50

See Nos. C23-C24.

Human Rights Year Issue
Common Design Type

1968, Aug. 10 Engr. *Perf. 13*
76 CD127 60fr brn, grn & org 90 90

Msoila Prayer Rug and Praying Man — A20

Designs: Each stamp shows a different prayer position.

1969, Feb. 27 Engr. *Perf. 13*
77 A20 20fr bl grn, rose red & pur 30 25
78 A20 30fr pur, rose red & bl grn 40 35
79 A20 45fr rose red, pur & bl grn 60 50

Vanilla Flower A21

Design: 15fr, Flower of ylang-ylang tree. 25fr, Poinsettia (country name in upper right corner).

1969-70 Photo. *Perf. 12½x13*
Size: 36x23mm.

80 A21 10fr multi 25 20
81 A21 15fr multi 32 28
82 A21 25fr multi ('70) 50 35
Nos. 80-82,C26-C28 (6) 6.32 4.68

Issue dates: Nos. 80-81, Mar. 20, 1969. No. 82, Mar. 5, 1970.

ILO Issue
Common Design Type

1969, Nov. 24 Engr. *Perf. 13*
83 CD131 5fr org, emer & gray 25 20

Issued for 50th anniversary of the International Labor Organization.

U.P.U. Headquarters Issue
Common Design Type

1970, May 20 Engr. *Perf. 13*
84 CD133 65fr pur, bl grn & red brn 1.25 80

Chiromani Costume, Anjouan — A22

Friday Mosque — A23

Design: 25fr, Bouiboui costume, Grand Comoro.

1970, Oct. 30 Photo. *Perf. 12½x13*
85 A22 20fr grn, yel & red 40 32
86 A22 25fr brn, yel & dk bl 50 40

1970, Dec. 18 Engr. *Perf. 13*
87 A23 5fr rose car, grn & grnsh bl 25 15
88 A23 10fr dp lil, grn & vio 32 25
89 A23 40fr cop red, grn & dp brn 55 45

The first price column gives the catalogue value of an unused stamp, the second that of a used stamp.

Great White Egret A24

Pyrostegia Venusta A25

Birds: 10fr, Comoro pigeon. 15fr, Green-backed heron. 25fr, Comoro blue pigeon. 35fr, Humblot's flycatcher. 40fr, Allen's gallinule.

Perf. 12½x13

1971, March 12 Photo.
90 A24 5fr multi 20 15
91 A24 10fr yel & multi 28 20
92 A24 15fr bl & multi 30 22
93 A24 25fr org & multi 45 35
94 A24 35fr yel grn & multi 85 60
95 A24 40fr gray & multi 1.00 80
Nos. 90-95 (6) 3.08 2.32

1971, July 19 Photo. *Perf. 13*

Flowers: 3fr, Dogbane (horiz.). 20fr, Frangipani.

Size: 22x36, 36x22mm.

96 A25 1fr ver & grn 15 15
97 A25 3fr yel, grn & red 25 20
98 A25 20fr ver & grn 70 45
Nos. 96-98,C37-C38 (5) 3.80 2.30

Lithograph Cone — A26

Sea Shells: 10fr, Pacific lettered cone. 20fr, Aulicus cone. 35fr, Polita nerita. 60fr, Snake-head cowrie.

1971, Oct. 4
99 A26 5fr lt ultra & multi 20 15
100 A26 10fr multi 25 20
101 A26 20fr vio & multi 35 30
102 A26 35fr lt bl & multi 60 45
103 A26 60fr lt vio & multi 80 80
Nos. 99-103 (5) 2.20 1.90

De Gaulle Issue
Common Design Type

Designs: 20fr, Gen. de Gaulle, 1940. 35fr, Pres. de Gaulle, 1970.

1971, Nov. 9 Engr. *Perf. 13*
104 CD134 20fr dk car & blk 50 25
105 CD134 35fr dk car & blk 70 55

First anniversary of the death of Charles de Gaulle (1890-1970), president of France.

Louis Pasteur, Slides, Microscope A27

1972, Aug. 2
106 A27 65fr ind, org, & ol brn 1.00 75

Sesquicentennial of the birth of Louis Pasteur (1822-1895), chemist.

Type of Air Post Issue 1971

Designs: 10fr, View of Goulaivoini. 20fr, Bay, Mitsamiouli. 35fr, Gate and fountain, Foumbouni. 50fr, View of Moroni.

1973, June 28 Photo. *Perf. 13*
107 AP10 10fr bl & multi 25 20
108 AP10 20fr grn & multi 40 35
109 AP10 35fr bl & multi 70 65
110 AP10 50fr bl & multi 85 75
Nos. 107-110,C53 (5) 4.45 3.55

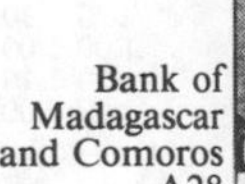

Bank of Madagascar and Comoros A28

Buildings in Moroni: 15fr, Post and Telecommunications Administration. 20fr, Prefecture.

1973, July 10 Photo. *Perf. 13x12½*
111 A28 5fr multi 12 10
112 A28 15fr multi 22 20
113 A28 20fr multi 40 35

Salimata Hamissi Mosque A29

Design: 20fr, Zaouiyat Chaduli Mosque (vert.).

Perf. 12½x13, 13x12½

1973, Oct. 20 Photo.
114 A29 20fr multi 35 30
115 A29 35fr multi 65 60

Cheikh Mausoleum A30

Design: 50fr, Mausoleum of President Said Mohamed Cheikh (different view).

1974, Mar. 16 Engr. *Perf. 13*
116 A30 35fr grn, ol brn & blk 55 45
117 A30 50fr grn, ol brn & blk 75 65

Koran Stand, Anjouan A31

Designs: 15fr, Carved combs (vert.). 20fr, 3-legged table (vert.). 75fr, Sugar press.

1974, May 10 Photo. *Perf. 12½x13*
118 A31 15fr emer & multi 25 20
119 A31 20fr grn & multi 35 25
120 A31 35fr multi 50 40
121 A31 75fr multi 90 75

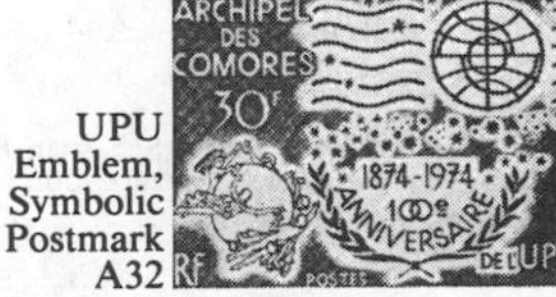

UPU Emblem, Symbolic Postmark A32

1974, Oct. 9 Engr. *Perf. 13x12½*
122 A32 30fr multi 40 35

Centenary of Universal Postal Union.

Bracelet A33

Designs: 35fr, Diadem. 120fr, Saber. 135fr, Dagger.

1975, Feb. 28 Engr. *Perf. 13*
123 A33 20fr multi 35 30
124 A33 35fr grn & multi 55 50
125 A33 120fr bl & multi 1.75 1.50
126 A33 135fr multi 1.85 1.65

Mohani Village, Moheli — A34

Designs: 50fr, Djoezi Village, Moheli. 55fr, Chirazi tombs.

1975, May 26 Photo. *Perf. 13*
127 A34 30fr vio bl & multi 30 20
128 A34 50fr Prus bl & multi 55 40
129 A34 55fr grn & multi 60 65

Skin Diver Photographing Coelacanth — A35

1975, June 27 Engr. *Perf. 13*
130 A35 50fr multi 80 60

1975 coelacanth expedition.

STATE OF COMORO

In 1978 the islands' name became the Federal and Islamic Republic of the Comoros.

Issues of 1971-75 Surcharged and Overprinted with Bars and: "ETAT COMORIEN" in Black, Silver or Red.

Tambourine Player — A36

Design: No. 153, Women dancers and tambourine players.

Printing & Perforations as Before.
A36: Photogravure

1975 *Perf. 13*
131 A25 5fr on 1fr 6 6
132 A25 5fr on 3fr 6 6
133 A17 10fr on 2fr 45 45
134 A28 15fr on 20fr (R) 20 15
135 A29 15fr on 20fr (S) 20 15
136 A33 15fr on 20fr 20 15
137 A31 20fr 28 20
138 A29 25fr on 35fr 35 30
139 A34 30fr 40 35
140 A30 30fr on 35fr 40 35
141 A31 30fr on 35fr 40 35
142 A33 30fr on 35fr 40 35
143 AP10 35fr 45 40
144 SP2 35fr on 35fr + 10fr 45 40
145 A24 40fr 55 45
146 A34 50fr 70 60
147 A35 50fr 70 60
148 A34 50fr on 55fr (S) 70 60
149 A31 75fr 1.10 90
150 A26 75fr on 60fr (S) 1.10 90
151 A33 100fr on 120fr 1.40 1.20
152 A36 100fr bl & multi 1.40 1.20
153 A36 100fr on 150fr (S) 1.40 1.20
154 A33 200fr on 135fr 2.80 2.25
155 A32 500fr on 30fr 7.00 6.00
Nos. 131-155 (25) 23.15 19.62

Nos. 152-155 exist without overprint or surcharge. No. 155 exists with red surcharge.

Comoro Flag, Map and Government Buildings — A37

1976, Nov. 18 Litho. *Perf. 13½*

156 A37 30fr multi	25	15
157 A37 50fr multi	40	25

1st anniversary of independence.

Comoro Flag, UN Headquarters and Emblem — A38

1976, Nov. 25

158 A38 40fr multi	30	20
159 A38 50fr multi	40	25

1st anniversary of United Nations membership.

Islamic Republic

Nos. 156-157 Surcharged and Overprinted with 3 Lines and: "République / Fédérale / et Islamique / des Comores"

1978, July 24 Litho. *Perf. 13½*

160 A37 30fr multi	
161 A37 40fr on 30fr multi	
162 A37 50fr multi	
163 A37 100fr on 50fr multi	

Nos. 160 and 162 were also overprinted to commemorate Queen Elizabeth II coronation anniversary; Capt. James Cook; World Cup Soccer winner; Albrecht Dürer; First powered flight; Railroad anniversary; Voyager I and II; Int. Year of the Child; 1980 Olympic Games; World Cup Soccer, Espana '82.

Italian Ball Game, 18th Century, Modern Soccer — A40

Soccer Cup, Argentina '78 Emblem, Soccer Scene and: 2fr, Ball game, London, 14th century. 3fr, Man and boy with ball, Greece, 5th century B.C. 50fr, Ball game, France, 19th century.

1979 Litho. *Perf. 13*

Black Surcharge and Overprint

169 A40 1fr on 100fr multi	5	5
170 A40 2fr on 75fr multi	5	5
171 A40 3fr on 30fr multi	5	5
172 A40 50fr multi	60	60
Nos. 169-172,C96 (5)	2.75	2.75

Otto Lilienthal and Glider — A41

History of Aviation: No. 174, Wright brothers and Flyer A. No. 175, Louis Bleriot and Bleriot XI. 100fr, Claude Dornier and Dornier-Wall hydrofoil.

1979

Black Overprint and Surcharge

173 A41 30fr multi	30	30
174 A41 50fr multi	1.00	1.00
175 A41 50fr on 75fr multi	1.10	1.10
176 A41 100fr multi	2.00	2.00

Papilio Dardanus Cenea A42

Butterflies: 15fr, Papilio dardanus. 30fr, Chrysiridia croesus. 50fr, Precis octavia. 75fr, Bunaea alcinoe.

1979

Black Overprint and Surcharge

177 A42 5fr on 20fr multi	5	5
178 A42 15fr multi	20	20
179 A42 30fr multi	40	40
180 A42 50fr multi	75	75
181 A42 75fr multi	1.25	1.25
Nos. 177-181 (5)	2.65	2.65

Gallinule A43

Birds: 30fr, Kingfisher. No. 184, Bee-eater. No. 185, Flycatcher. 200fr, Sunbird.

1979 Litho. *Perf. 13*

Black Overprint and Surcharge

182 A43 15fr multi	20	20
183 A43 30fr on 35fr multi	40	40
184 A43 50fr on 20fr multi	80	80
185 A43 50fr on 40fr multi	80	80
186 A43 200fr on 75fr multi	2.00	2.00

Giuseppe Verdi — A44

Composers: 30fr, Johann Sebastian Bach. 40fr, Wolfgang Amadeus Mozart. 50fr, Hector Berlioz.

1979

Black Overprint and Surcharge

187 A44 5fr on 100fr multi	8	8
188 A44 30fr multi	30	30
189 A44 40fr multi	32	32
190 A44 50fr multi	55	55
Nos. 187-190,C98 (5)	1.85	1.85

For Nos. 169-190, C98 without overprint see "For the Record."

Galileo and Voyager I — A46

Exploration of Solar System: 30fr, Kepler and Voyager II. 40fr, Copernicus and Voyager I, 100fr, Huygens and Voyager II.

1979, Feb. 19

196 A46 20fr multi	10	10
197 A46 30fr multi	22	10
198 A46 40fr multi	32	12
199 A46 100fr multi	70	32
Nos. 196-199,C99-C100 (6)	5.74	2.44

Philidor, Anderssen, Steinitz and King — A47

Design: 100fr, Chess pieces and board, Venetian chess player.

1979, Feb. 19

200 A47 40fr multi	28	8
201 A47 100fr multi	70	25

Chess Grand Masters. See No. C102.

Satellite and Radar — A48

Design: 100fr, Satellites, earth and radar.

1979, Sept. 15 Litho. *Perf. 13*

Black Overprint

202 A48 75fr multi	75
203 A48 100fr multi	70

See No. C103.

U.N. No. 42, Satellite over Earth A49

1979, Sept. 15

Black Overprint

204 A49 75fr multi	75

Innsbruck, Olympic Emblems, Skater — A50

1979, Sept. 15

Black Overprint

205 A50 35fr multi	35

Philipp Reis, Telephone Operators — A51

1979, Sept. 15

Black Overprint

206 A51 75fr multi	75

For Nos. 202-206 without overprint see "For the Record."

Charaxes Defulvata — A52

Birds: 50fr, Leptosomus discolor. 75fr, Bee eater.

1979, Apr. 10 Litho. *Perf. 12½*

207 A52 30fr multi	30	12
208 A52 50fr multi	50	22
209 A52 75fr multi	80	35

Litchi Nuts — A53

1979, June 15 Litho. *Perf. 12½*

Fruit: 70fr, Papayas. 100fr, Avocados. 125fr, Bananas.

210 A53 60fr multi	60	30
211 A53 70fr multi	70	35
212 A53 100fr multi	1.00	45
213 A53 125fr multi	1.25	75

Basketball Players — A54

1979, Aug. 28 Litho. *Perf. 13*

214 A54 200fr multi	1.75	1.25

Indian Ocean Olympics.

Dugout on Beach — A61

Anjouan Puppet — A62

1980, Jan. 4 Litho. *Perf. 13*

232 A61 60fr multi	38	15
233 A62 100fr multi	60	30

Sultan Said Ali — A63

1980, Feb. 20 *Perf. 12½x13*
234 A63 40fr *shown* 28 18
235 A63 60fr *Sultan Ahmed* 38 22

Sherlock Holmes, Doyle — A64

1980, Feb. 25 *Perf. 12½*
236 A64 200fr multi 2.00 1.10

Sir Arthur Conan Doyle (1859-1930), writer.

Grand Mosque, Holy Ka'aba, Mecca — A64a

1980, Mar. 12 *Perf. 13x12½*
237 A64a 75fr multi 45 30

Hegira, 1500th anniv.

Year of the Holy City of Jerusalem A65

1980, Mar. 12 *Perf. 13x13½*
238 A65 60fr multi 38 22

Kepler, Copernicus and Pluto — A66

1980, Apr. 30 **Litho.** *Perf. 12½*
239 A66 400fr multi 3.00 2.25

Discovery of Pluto, 50th anniversary.

Muscle System, Avicenna — A67

1980, Apr. 30 **Engr.** *Perf. 13*
240 A67 60fr multi 38 30

Avicenna, Arab physician, birth millennium.

Soccer Players — A69

Designs; Various soccer scenes. 60fr, 150fr, 500fr, vert.

1981, Feb. 20 **Litho.** *Perf. 12½*
241 A69 60fr multi 45 18
242 A69 75fr multi 50 22
243 A69 90fr multi 65 28
244 A69 100fr multi 80 38
245 A69 150fr multi 1.25 42
Nos. 241-245 (5) 3.65 1.48

Souvenir Sheet

246 A69 500fr multi 4.00 1.40

World Cup Soccer 1982. No. 246 has multicolored margin showing emblems. Size: 104x80mm.

Nos. 236-237, 213, and:

Merops Superciliosus A70

Perf. 12½, 13x12½ (No. 248)
1981, Feb. **Litho.**
Red, Black or Blue Surcharge
247 A64 15fr on 200fr multi 15 15
248 A64a 20fr on 75fr multi 18 18
249 A53 40fr on 125fr multi (Bk) 40 40
250 A70 60fr on 75fr multi (Bl) 60 60

A71

Space Exploration: 50fr, Apollo program (vert.). 75fr, 100fr, 500fr, Columbia space shuttle.

1981, July 13 **Litho.** *Perf. 14*
251 A71 50fr multi 32 15
252 A71 75fr multi 45 22
253 A71 100fr multi 65 38
254 A71 450fr multi 3.00 1.50

Souvenir Sheet

255 A71 500fr multi 4.00 1.50

No. 255 has multicolored margin showing Eugene Sanger (1905-1964), and rockets. Size: 104x79mm.

Prince Charles and Lady Diana, Buckingham Palace — A72

1981, Sept. 1 **Litho.** *Perf. 14½*
256 A72 125fr shown 75 30
257 A72 200fr Highwood House 1.50 60
258 A72 450fr Carnarvon Castle 3.00 1.40
a. Souvenir sheet of 3 5.25 2.25

Royal wedding. No. 258a contains Nos. 256-258 in changed colors. Multicolored margin shows flowers, label shows arms of Prince of Wales. Size: 133x98mm.

Flag Type of 1979

1981, Oct. **Litho.** *Perf. 13*
259 O1 5fr multi 5 5
260 O1 15fr multi 8 5
261 O1 25fr multi 15 5
262 O1 35fr multi 22 12
263 O1 75fr multi 45 28
Nos. 259-263 (5) 95 55

Nos. 239, 243, 212, 233 Surcharged.

1981, Nov. **Litho.** *Perf. 12½*
264 A66 5fr on 400fr multi 5 5
265 A69 20fr on 90fr multi 8 5
266 A53 45fr on 100fr multi 28 12
267 A62 45fr on 100fr multi 28 12

75th Anniv. of Grand Prix — A73

Designs: Winners and their Cars.

1981, Dec. 28 **Litho.** *Perf. 12½*
268 A73 20fr Mercedes, 1914 15 5
269 A73 50fr Delage, 1925 35 15
270 A73 75fr Rudi Caracciola, 1926 55 22
271 A73 90fr Stirling Moss, 1955 60 30
272 A73 150fr Maserati, 1957 1.00 45
Nos. 268-272 (5) 2.65 1.17

Souvenir Sheet
Perf. 13

273 A73 500fr Changing wheels, vert. 3.50 1.50

No. 273 has multicolored margin continuing design. Size: 107x86mm.

Scouting Year — A74

1982, Jan. 5
274 A74 50fr Climbing rocks 35 15
275 A74 75fr Boating 50 22
276 A74 250fr Sailing 1.65 75
277 A74 350fr Sailing, diff. 2.50 1.10

Souvenir Sheet
Perf. 13

278 A74 500fr Baden-Powell 3.75 1.75

No. 278 has multicolored margin continuing design. Size: 78x102mm.

21st Birthday of Princess of Wales — A75

Designs: Various portraits of Princess Diana.

1982, July 1 **Litho.** *Perf. 14*
279 A75 200fr multi 1.25 60
280 A75 300fr multi 1.75 90

Souvenir Sheet

281 A75 500fr multi 3.00 1.50

No. 281 has multicolored margin showing portrait. Size: 112x81mm.

Johannes von Goethe (1749-1832) A76

1982, July
282 A76 75fr multi 45 22
283 A76 350fr multi 2.00 1.00

Nos. 256-258a Overprinted in Blue: "NAISSANCE ROYALE 1982"

1982, July 31 *Perf. 14½*
284 A72 125fr multi 75 60
285 A72 200fr multi 1.10 90
286 A72 450fr multi 2.75 2.25
a. Souvenir sheet of 3 5.00 5.00

Birth of Prince William of Wales, June 21.

Nos. 241-246 Overprinted with Finalists and Score in Red.

1982, Sept. 20 **Litho.** *Perf. 12½*
287 A69 60fr multi 38 28
288 A69 75fr multi 45 32
289 A69 90fr multi 50 38
290 A69 100fr multi 60 45
291 A69 1.50fr multi 80 60
Nos. 287-291 (5) 2.73 2.03

Souvenir Sheet

292 A69 500fr multi 3.00 3.00

Italy's victory in 1982 World Cup.

Paintings by Norman Rockwell A77

1982, Oct. 11 **Litho.** *Perf. 14*
293 A77 60fr 1931 45 22
294 A77 75fr 1925 55 22
295 A77 100fr 1922 70 30
296 A77 150fr 1919 1.10 45

297 A77 200fr 1924 1.40 50
298 A77 300fr 1918 2.25 90
Nos. 293-298 (6) 6.45 2.59

Sultans of Anjouan — A78

1982, Dec. *Perf. 12½x13, 13x12½*
299 A78 30fr Said Mohamed Sidi, vert. 22 15
300 A78 60fr Ahmed Abdallah, vert. 38 22
301 A78 75fr Salim 45 30
302 A78 300fr Sidi, Abdallah 1.75 1.25

Landscapes — A79

1983, Sept. 30 **Litho.** *Perf. 13*
303 A79 60fr D'Ziani Lake 38 22
304 A79 100fr Sunset 60 38
305 A79 175fr Anjouan, vert. 1.10 60
306 A79 360fr Itsandra 2.00 1.25
307 A79 400fr Anjouan, diff. 2.50 1.65
Nos. 303-307 (5) 6.58 4.10

Woman from Moheli A80

1983, Oct. 17 **Litho.** *Perf. 12½x13*
308 A80 30fr shown 20 15
309 A80 45fr Woman, diff. 30 18
310 A80 50fr Man from Mayotte 35 18

Thoroughbred Horses — A81

1983, Nov. 30 **Litho.** *Perf. 13*
311 A81 75fr Arabian 45 18
312 A81 100fr Anglo-Arabian 60 28
313 A81 125fr Lippizaner 75 30
314 A81 150fr Tennessee 90 38
315 A81 200fr Appaloosa 1.25 50
316 A81 300fr Pure English 1.75 80
317 A81 400fr Clydesdale 2.50 1.00
318 A81 500fr Andalusian 3.00 1.40
Nos. 311-318 (8) 11.20 4.84

Double Portrait, by Raphael A82

1983, Dec. 30 **Litho.** *Perf. 13*
319 A82 100fr shown 60 30
320 A82 200fr Girl, fresco detail 1.25 45
321 A82 300fr St. George Killing Dragon 1.75 90
322 A82 400fr Balthazar Castiglione 2.50 1.10

Ships and Automobiles — A83

1984, Oct. 9 **Litho.** *Perf. 12½*
323 A83 100fr William Fawcett 42
324 A83 100fr De Dion, 1885 42
325 A83 150fr Lightning 62
326 A83 150fr Benz Victoria, 1893 62
327 A83 200fr Rapido 85
328 A83 200fr Columbia Electric, 1901 85
329 A83 350fr Sindia 1.25
330 A83 350fr Fiat, 1902 1.25
Nos. 323-330 (8) 6.28

Souvenir Sheets

Nos. 255, 273, 278 Ovptd. with Exhibition in Black, Blue or Red.

1985, Mar. 11 *Perf. 14, 13*
335 A71 500fr '85/HAMBOURG (BK) 2.25
336 A73 500fr TSUKUBA EXPO '85 (Bl) 2.25
337 A74 500fr ARGENTINA '85/BUENOS AIRES (R) 2.25

See Nos. C143-C144

Victor Hugo (1802-1885), Author, Pantheon, Paris — A85

Anniversaries and events: 200fr, IYY, Jules Verne (1828-1905), author. 300fr, IYY, Mark Twain (1835-1910), author. 450fr, Queen Mother, 85th birthday, vert. 500fr, Statue of Liberty, cent., vert.

1985, May 27 **Litho.** *Perf. 13*
338 A85 100fr multi 40
339 A85 200fr multi 80
340 A85 300fr multi 1.15
341 A85 450fr multi 1.75
342 A85 500fr multi 2.00
Nos. 338-342 (5) 6.10

Sea Shells — A86

1985, Oct. 23 *Perf. 14*
343 A86 75fr Lambis chiragra 30
344 A86 125fr Strombe lentifinosum 50
345 A86 200fr Tonna gala 80
346 A86 300fr Cymbium glans 1.15
347 A86 450fr Lambis crocata 1.75
Nos. 343-347 (5) 4.50

Comoros Admission to UN, 10th Anniv. — A87

1985, Nov. 12 **Litho.** *Perf. 13x12½*
348 A87 5fr multi 5 5
349 A87 30fr multi 12 6
350 A87 75fr multi 40 20
351 A87 125fr multi 65 32
352 A87 400fr multi 2.00 1.00
Nos. 348-352 (5) 3.22 1.63

Moroni Rotary Club, 20th Anniv. — A88

1985, Nov. 30 *Perf. 13*
353 A88 25fr multi 10 5
354 A88 75fr multi 40 20
355 A88 125fr multi 65 32
356 A88 500fr multi 2.75 1.40

Mushrooms — A89

1985, Dec. 24 *Perf. 13½*
357 A89 75fr Boletus edulis 40 20
358 A89 125fr Sarcoscypha coccinea 65 32
359 A89 200fr Hypholoma fasciculare 1.10 55
360 A89 350fr Astraeus hygrometricus 1.90 95
361 A89 500fr Armillariella mellea 2.75 1.40
Nos. 357-361 (5) 6.80 3.42

Health Year — A90

1986, Oct. 2 **Litho.** *Perf. 15x14½*
362 A90 25fr Pediatric examination 14 8
363 A90 100fr Weighing child 65 32
364 A90 200fr Immunization 1.40 70

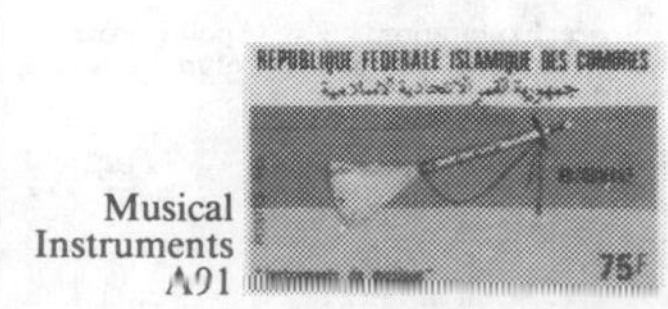

Musical Instruments A91

1986, Dec. 24 **Litho.** *Perf. 13*
365 A91 75fr Ndzoumara 40 20
366 A91 125fr Ndzedze 70 35
367 A91 210fr Gaboussi 1.15 58
368 A91 500fr Ngoma 2.75 1.40

Role of Women in National Development — A92

1987, Mar. 7 **Litho.** *Perf. 13*
369 A92 75fr Working fields 40 20
370 A92 125fr Harvesting crops, vert. 68 35
371 A92 1000fr Basket-weaving 5.25 2.65

SEMI-POSTAL STAMPS

Anti-Malaria Issue

Common Design Type

Perf. 12½x12

1962, Apr. 7 **Engr.** **Unwmk.**
B1 CD108 25fr + 5fr brt pink 1.75 1.75

Issued for the World Health Organization drive to eradicate malaria.

Nurse Feeding Infant — SP1

Mother and Child — SP2

1967, July 3 **Engr.** *Perf. 13*
B2 SP1 25fr + 5fr red, brt grn & choc 1.10 1.10

For the Red Cross.

1974, Aug. 10 **Engr.** *Perf. 13*
B3 SP2 35fr + 10fr red & dk brn 80 80

For the Red Cross.

AIR POST STAMPS

Comoro Village — AP1

Comoro Men and Moroni Mosque — AP2

Design: 200fr, Mosque of Ouani, Anjouan.

1950-54 **Unwmk.** **Engr.** *Perf. 13*
C1 AP1 50fr grn & red brn 2.00 1.00
C2 AP2 100fr dk brn & red 3.00 1.00
C3 AP1 200fr dk grn, rose brn & pur ('54) 12.00 6.00

Liberation Issue
Common Design Type

1954, June 6
C4 CD102 15fr sep & red 14.00 10.50

10th anniversary of the liberation of France.

Madrepora Fructicosa — AP3

Design: 100fr, Coral, shells and sea anemones.

1962, Jan. 13 Photo. *Perf. 12½x13*
C5 AP3 100fr multi 3.00 3.00
C6 AP3 500fr multi 12.50 11.00

Telstar Issue
Common Design Type

1962, Dec. 5 Engr. *Perf. 13*
C7 CD111 25fr dp vio, dl pur & red lil 2.25 1.25

Type of Regular Issue, 1963.

Designs: 65fr, Baskets. 200fr, Pendant.

Unwmk.
1963, Dec. 27 Engr. *Perf. 13*
Size: 26½x48mm.
C8 A13 65fr car, grn & ocher 2.00 1.20
C9 A13 200fr grnsh bl, rose lake & red 4.00 2.50

Boat Type of Regular Issue

Designs: 50fr, Mayotte pirogue. 85fr, Schooner.

1964, Aug. 7 Photo. *Perf. 13*
Size: 27x48mm.
C10 A14 50fr multi 1.50 60
C11 A14 85fr multi 2.25 1.35

Olympic Torch and Boxers — AP4

Order of Star of Grand Comoro — AP5

1964, Oct. 10 Engr. *Perf. 13*
C12 AP4 100fr led brn, dk brn & gray grn 2.50 2.50

18th Olympic Games, Tokyo, Oct. 10-25.

1964, Dec. 10 Photo. *Perf. 13*
C13 AP5 500fr crim, blk, emer & gold 11.00 6.50

ITU Issue
Common Design Type

1965, May 17 Engr. *Perf. 13*
C14 CD120 50fr gray, grnsh bl & ol 8.50 6.50

International Telecommunication Union centenary.

French Satellite A-1 Issue
Common Design Type

Designs: 25fr, Diamant rocket and launching installations. 30fr, A-1 satellite.

1966, Jan. 17 Engr. *Perf. 13*
C15 CD121 25fr dk pur & ultra 2.00 2.00
C16 CD121 30fr dk pur & ultra 2.50 2.50
a. Strip of 2 + label 5.00 5.00

Issued to commemorate the launching of France's first satellite, Nov. 26, 1965. No. C16a contains one each of Nos. C15-C16 and dark purple label with commemorative inscription. Each sheet contains 16 triptychs (2x8).

French Satellite D-1 Issue
Common Design Type

1966, May 16 Engr. *Perf. 13*
C17 CD122 30fr dk grn, org & brn 1.75 1.20

Old Gun Battery, Dzaoudzi — AP6

Design: 200fr, Ksar Castle, Mutsamudu (vert.).

1966, Dec. 19 Photo. *Perf. 13*
C18 AP6 50fr multi 1.00 85
C19 AP6 200fr multi 3.50 2.00

Bird Type of Regular Issue

Birds: 75fr, Madagascar paradise flycatchers. 100fr, Blue-cheeked bee eaters.

1967, June 20 Photo. *Perf. 13*
Size: 27x48mm.
C20 A17 70fr yel grn & multi 1.75 65
C21 A17 100fr lt bl & multi 2.10 85

Woman Skier — AP7

1968, Apr. 29 Engr. *Perf. 13*
C22 AP7 70fr brt grn, lt bl & choc 1.20 75

Issued to commemorate the 10th Winter Olympic Games, Grenoble, France, Feb. 6-18, 1968.

Fish Type of Regular Issue

Designs: 50fr, Moorish idol. 90fr, Diagramma lineatus.

1968, Aug. 1 Engr. *Perf. 13*
Size: 47½x27mm.
C23 A19 50fr plum blk & yel 1.00 90
C24 A19 90fr brt grn, yel & gray grn 1.75 1.35

Swimmer, Butterfly Stroke — AP8

1969, Jan. 27 Photo. *Perf. 12½*
C25 AP8 65fr ver, grnsh bl & blk 1.35 1.00

Issued to commemorate the 19th Olympic Games, Mexico City, Oct. 12-27.

Flower Type of Regular Issue, 1969.

Designs: 50fr, Heliconia sp. (vert.). 85fr, Tuberose (vert.). 200fr, Orchid (angraecum eburneum; vert.).

1969, Mar. 20 Photo. *Perf. 13*
Size: 27x48mm.
C26 A21 50fr gray & multi 1.00 75
C27 A21 85fr multi 1.50 1.00
C28 A21 200fr dk red & multi 2.75 2.10

Concorde Issue
Common Design Type

1969, Apr. 17 Engr.
C29 CD129 100fr pur & brn org 7.50 6.00

View of EXPO, Globe and Moon — AP9

Design: 90fr, Geisha, map of Japan and EXPO emblem.

1970, Sept. 13 Photo. *Perf. 13*
C30 AP9 60fr sl & multi 1.20 75
C31 AP9 90fr multi 1.20 75

EXPO '70 International Exposition, Osaka, Japan, Mar. 15-Sept. 13.

Sunset over Mutsamudu — AP10

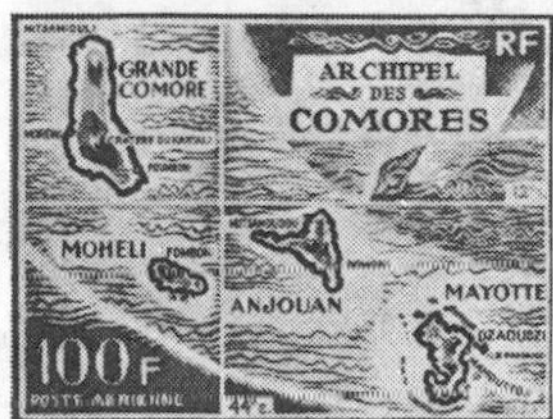

Map of Archipelago — AP11

Designs: 20fr, Sada Village, Mayotte. 65fr, Old Iconi Palace, Grand Comoro. 85fr, Nioumatchoua Island, Moheli.

1971, May 3 Photo. *Perf. 13*
C32 AP10 15fr dk bl & multi 25 10
C33 AP10 20fr multi 45 25
C34 AP10 65fr grn & multi 90 45
C35 AP10 85fr bl & multi 1.10 60

Engr.
C36 AP11 100fr brn red, grn & vio bl 2.00 1.00
Nos. C32-C36 (5) 4.70 2.40

See Nos. 107-110, C45-C49, C53, C62-C64.

Flower Type of Regular Issue

Flowers: 60fr, Hibiscus schizopetalus. 85fr, Acalypha sanderii.

1971, July 19 Photo. *Perf. 13*
Size: 27x48mm.
C37 A25 60fr grn, ver & yel 1.20 60
C38 A25 85fr grn, red & yel 1.50 90

Mural, Moroni Airport — AP12

Designs: 85fr, Mural in Arrival Hall, Moroni Airport. 100fr, View of Moroni Airport.

1972, Mar. 30 Photo. *Perf. 13*
C39 AP12 65fr gray & multi 60 50
C40 AP12 85fr gray & multi 90 50

Engr.
C41 AP12 100fr brn, bl & sl grn 1.50 75

New airport in Moroni.

Eiffel Tower and Moroni Telephone Exchange — AP13

Design: 75fr, Frenchman and Comoro Islander talking on telephone, radio tower and beacons.

1972, Apr. 24
C42 AP13 35fr dl red & gray 35 20
C43 AP13 75fr dk car, vio & bl 70 35

First radio-telephone connection between France and Comoro Islands.

Underwater Spear-fishing — AP14

1972, July 5 Engr. *Perf. 13*
C44 AP14 70fr vio bl, brt grn & mar 1.10 80

Types of 1971

1972, Nov. 15 Photo.

Designs: 20fr, Cape Sima. 35fr, Bambao Palace. 40fr, Domoni Palace. 60fr, Gomajou Peninsula. 100fr, Map of Anjouan Island.

C45 AP10 20fr brn & multi 25 20
C46 AP10 35fr dk grn & multi 45 35
C47 AP10 40fr bl & multi 55 40
C48 AP10 60fr grnsh blk & multi 75 60

Engr.
C49 AP11 100fr mar, bl & sl grn 1.50 1.00
Nos. C45-C49 (5) 3.50 2.55

Pres. Said Mohamed Cheikh — AP15

1973, Mar. 16 Photo. *Perf. 13*
C50 AP15 20fr multi 30 25
C51 AP15 35fr multi 50 25

President Said Mohamed Cheikh (1904-1970).

Mission Internationale pour l'étude du Cœlacanthe

No. C24 Surcharged

1973, Apr. 30 Engr. ***Perf. 13***

C52 A19 120fr on 90fr multi 1.65 1.25

International Commission for Coelacanth Studies.

Map of Grand Comoro AP16

1973, June 28 Engr. ***Perf. 13***

C53 AP16 135fr vio, bl & dk brn 2.25 1.60

See Nos. C65, C68.

Karthala Volcano AP17

1973, July 16 Photo. ***Perf. 13x12½***

C54 AP17 120fr multi 1.65 1.25

Eruption of Karthala, Sept. 1972.

Armauer G. Hansen — AP18

Design: 150fr, Nicolaus Copernicus.

1973, Sept. 5 Engr. ***Perf. 13***

C55 AP18 100fr brn, dk bl & sl grn 1.65 1.25

C56 AP18 150fr grnsh bl, vio bl & choc 2.25 1.50

Centenary of the discovery of the Hansen bacillus, the cause of leprosy (100fr).

500th anniversary of the birth of Nicolaus Copernicus (1473-1543), Polish astronomer (150fr).

Pablo Picasso AP19

1983, Sept. 30 Photo.

C57 AP19 200fr blk & multi 2.75 2.00

Souvenir Sheet

C58 AP19 100fr blk & multi 1.75 1.75

Pablo Picasso (1881-1973), painter. No. C58 contains one stamp; reddish brown marginal inscription. Size: 100x130mm.

Order of the Star of Anjouan — AP20

Said Omar ben Soumeth — AP21

1974, Jan. 7 Photo. ***Perf. 13***

C59 AP20 500fr brn, bl & gold 6.00 5.00

Perf. 13x13½, 13½x13

1974, Jan. 31

Design: 135fr, Grand Mufti Said Omar (horiz.).

C60 AP21 135fr blk & multi 1.60 1.35

C61 AP21 200fr blk & multi 2.75 1.90

Types of 1971-73

1974, Aug. 31 Photo. ***Perf. 13***

Designs (Views on Mayotte): 20fr, Moya Beach. 35fr, Chiconi. 90fr, Port Mamutzu. 120fr, Map of Mayotte.

C62 AP10 20fr bl & multi 30 20

C63 AP10 35fr grn & multi 50 40

C64 AP10 90fr multi 1.20 1.00

Engr.

C65 AP16 120fr ultra & grn 1.50 1.20

Jet Take-off — AP22

1975, Jan. 10 Engr. ***Perf. 13***

C66 AP22 135fr multi 1.75 1.35

First direct route Moroni-Hahaya-Paris.

Rotary Emblem, Meeting House, Map — AP23

1975, Feb. 23 Photo. ***Perf. 13***

C67 AP23 250fr multi 3.25 2.50

Rotary International, 70th anniversary, and Moroni Rotary Club, 10th anniversary.

Map Type of 1973

Design: 230fr, Map of Moheli (horiz.).

1975, May 26 Engr. ***Perf. 13***

C68 AP16 230fr ocher, ol grn & bl 3.25 2.50

STATE OF COMORO

Issues of 1968-75 Surcharged and Overprinted with Bars and: "ETAT COMORIEN" in Black, Silver, Red or Orange.

Printing and Perforations as Before.

1975

C69 AP10 10fr on 20fr #C62 12 8

C70 AP15 20fr (S) 28 18

C71 AP10 30fr on 35fr (R) #C63 40 30

C72 AP15 35fr (S) 45 35

C73 AP10 40fr (O) 55 38

C74 A19 50fr 70 45

C75 A25 75fr on 60fr 1.10 70

C76 AP10 75fr on 60fr 1.10 70

C77 AP10 75fr on 65fr (O) 1.10 70

C78 AP14 75fr on 70fr 1.10 70

C79 AP11 100fr #C36 1.40 90

C80 AP11 100fr #C49 1.40 90

C81 AP18 100fr 1.40 90

C82 AP10 100fr on 85fr (O) 1.40 90

C83 A25 100fr on 85fr 1.40 90

C84 AP10 100fr on 90fr 1.40 90

C85 AP21 100fr on 135fr (S) 1.40 90

C86 AP22 100fr on 135fr 1.40 90

C87 AP19 200fr (S) 2.80 1.85

C88 AP21 200fr (S) 2.80 1.85

C89 AP17 200fr on 120fr 2.80 1.85

C90 AP16 200fr on 120fr 2.80 1.85

C91 AP16 200fr on 135fr 2.80 1.85

C92 AP16 200fr on 230fr 2.80 1.85

C93 AP18 400fr on 150fr 5.60 3.75

C94 AP23 400fr on 250fr 5.60 3.75

C95 AP20 500fr 7.00 4.75

Nos. C69-C95 (27) 53.10 35.09

Surcharged Soccer Type of 1979

Design: 200fr, English soccer game, 19th century, Soccer Cup, Argentina '78 emblem.

1979 Litho. ***Perf. 13***

Black Overprint

C96 A40 200fr multi 2.00 2.00

Aviation Type of 1979

Design: 200fr, Charles Lindbergh and Spirit of St. Louis.

1979

Black Overprint

C97 A41 200fr multi 1.75 1.75

For Nos. C96-C97 without overprint see "For the Record."

Composer Type of 1979

Design: 50fr, Peter I. Tchaikovsky.

1979 Litho. ***Perf. 13***

Black Surcharge

C98 A44 50fr on 200fr multi 60 60

Space Type of 1979

Exploration of Solar System: 200fr, William Herschel and Voyager II. 400fr, Urbain Leverrier and Voyager II. 500fr, Voyagers I and II, symbolic solar system.

1979, Feb. 19

C99 A46 200fr multi 1.40 55

C100 A46 400fr multi 3.00 1.25

Souvenir Sheet

C101 A46 500fr multi 4.00 1.75

No. C101 has multicolored margin showing symbolic design. Size: 130x80mm.

Chess Masters Type of 1979

Chess Grand Masters Alekhine, Spassky, Fischer, and bishop.

1979, Feb. 19

C102 A47 500fr multi 3.50 1.40

Satellite Type of 1979

Design: 200fr, Satellite (diff.), operator and radar.

1979, Sept. 15 Litho. ***Perf. 13***

Black Overprint

C103 A48 200fr multi 2.00

Gymnasts, Olympic Emblems, Fair Poster — AP24

1979, Sept. 15 Litho. ***Perf. 13***

Black Overprint

C104 AP25 250fr multi 2.50

Leonid Brezhnev, Pres. Ford, Astronauts — AP25

Design: 200 fr emblem & earth

1979, Sept. 15.

Black Overprint

C105 AP25 100fr multi 1.00

C106 AP25 200fr multi 2.00

For Nos. C103-C106 without overprint see "For the Record."

Rotary Emblem, Landscape AP26

1979, July 31 ***Perf. 13x12½***

C107 AP26 400fr multi 4.50 2.50

Rotary International.

IYC Emblem, Mother and Child — AP27

1979, July 31 Litho. ***Perf. 13x13½***

C108 AP27 250fr multi 2.50 1.90

International Year of the Child. See No. CB1.

Dimadjou Dispensary, Map of Southern Africa, Emblem AP28

1980, Feb. 23 Litho. ***Perf. 12½***

C109 AP28 100fr *shown* 75 45

C110 AP28 260fr *Globe, Concorde, emblem* 2.00 1.00

Rotary International, 75th anniversary and Moroni Rotary Club, 15th anniversary (100fr).

First Transatlantic Flight, 50th Anniversary — AP29

1980, May 30 Litho. *Perf. 13*
C111 AP29 200fr multi 1.50 1.10

No. C111 Surcharged in Blue

1981, Feb. Litho. *Perf. 13*
C112 AP29 30fr on 200fr multi 30 30

The Dove and the Rainbow, by Picasso — AP30

Picasso Birth Centenary: 70fr, Still Life on a Sideboard. 150fr, Studio with Plaster Head. 250fr, Bowl and Pot (vert.). 500fr, The Red Tablecloth.

1981, June 30 Litho. *Perf. 12½*
C113 AP30 40fr multi 25 12
C114 AP30 70fr multi 40 20
C115 AP30 150fr multi 1.00 50
C116 AP30 250fr multi 1.65 85
C117 AP30 500fr multi 3.25 1.65
Nos. C113-C117 (5) 6.55 3.32

Nos. C114, C109-C110, CB1 Surcharged.

1981, Nov. Litho. *Perf. 12½, 13*
C118 AP30 10fr on 70fr multi 10 6
C119 AP28 10fr on 100fr multi 10 6
C120 AP28 50fr on 260fr multi 30 15
C121 AP27 50fr on 200 + 30fr multi 30 15

Manned Flight Bicentenary — AP31

Balloons. 100fr, 200fr, 300fr, 500fr vert.

1983, Apr. 20 Litho. *Perf. 13*
C122 AP31 100fr Montgolfiere, 1783 60 30
C123 AP31 200fr Lunardi, 1784 1.25 60
C124 AP31 300fr Blanchard and Jeffries, 1785 1.75 90
C125 AP31 400fr Giffard, 1852 2.50 1.25

Souvenir Sheet

C126 AP31 500fr Paris Siege. 1870 3.00 1.50

No. C126 has multicolored margin showing aerial view of Paris and ballon monte cover. Size: 80x104mm.

Pre-Olympic Year Sailing — AP32

1983, June 30 Litho. *Perf. 13*
C127 AP32 150fr Type 470 90 45
C128 AP32 200fr Flying Dutchman 1.25 60
C129 AP32 300fr Type 470, diff. 1.75 80
C130 AP32 400fr Finn 2.50 1.10

Souvenir Sheet

C131 AP32 500fr Solding 3.50 1.75

Multicolored margin continues design. Size: 104x80mm.

1984 Summer Olympics — AP33

1984, July 10 Litho. *Perf. 13*
C132 AP33 60fr Basketball 38 18
C133 AP33 100fr Basketball, diff. 60 30
C134 AP33 165fr Basketball, diff. 1.00 50
C135 AP33 175fr Baseball, horiz. 1.10 50
C136 AP33 200fr Baseball, horiz. 1.25 60
Nos. C132-C136 (5) 4.33 2.08

Souvenir Sheet

C137 AP33 500fr Basketball, diff. 3.00 1.50

Nos. C132-C134 vert. Size of No. C137: 104x80mm.

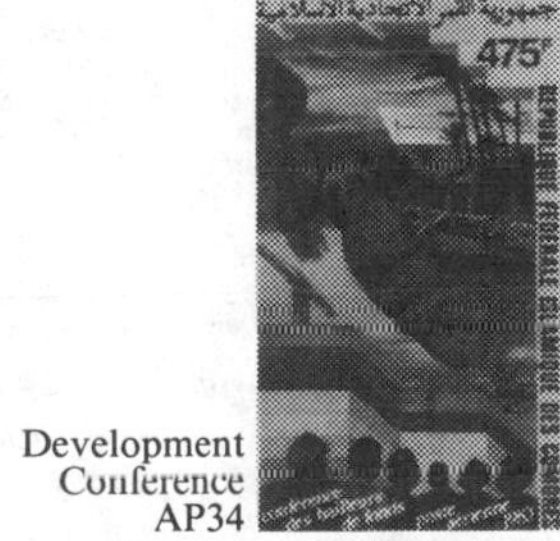

Development Conference AP34

1984, July 2 Litho. *Perf. 13*
C138 AP34 475fr Tools for development 2.50

Audubon Bicentenary — AP35

1985, Jan. 15 Litho. *Perf. 13*
C139 AP35 100fr Hirundo rustica, vert. 42
C140 AP35 125fr Icterus galbula, vert. 52
C141 AP35 150fr Buteo lineatus 62
C142 AP35 500fr Sphyropicus varius 2.10

Nos. C126, C131 Ovptd. with Exhibitions in Red or Gold.

1985, Mar. 11 *Perf. 13*
C143 AP31 500fr Rome, ITALIA '85 emblem (R) 2.25
C144 AP32 500fr OLYMPHILEX / '85 / LAUSANNE (G) 2.25

Moroni Port Missile Defense — AP36

Designs: No. C146, Ngome Ntsoudjini Scout troop.

1985, May 20 Litho. *Perf. 13x12½*
C145 AP36 200fr multi 80
C146 AP36 200fr multi 80

PHILEXAFRICA '85, Lome. Nos. C145-C146 printed se-tenant with center labels picturing map of Africa or UAPT emblem.

Natl. Flag, Sun, Outline Map of Islands — AP37

1985, July 6
C147 AP37 10fr multi 5
C148 AP37 15fr multi 6
C149 AP37 125fr multi 50
C150 AP37 300fr multi 1.15

Natl. independence, 10th anniv.

Runners — AP38

1985, Nov. 12
C151 AP38 250fr shown 1.00
C152 AP38 250fr Mining 1.00

PHILEXAFRICA '85, Lome, Togo, Nov. 16-24. Nos. C151-C152 printed se-tenant with center label picturing map of Africa or UAPT emblem.

Air Transport Union, UTA, 50th Anniv. — AP39

1985, Dec. 30 Litho. *Perf. 13*
C153 AP39 25fr F-AOUL seaplane 10 5
C154 AP39 75fr Camel driver, DC-9 30 15
C155 AP39 100fr Noratlas and Heron DC-4s 52 25
a. Souvenir sheet of 3, #C153-C155, perf. 12½ 80 80
C156 AP39 125fr UTA cargo plane 65 32

Size: 40x52mm.

Perf. 12½x13

C157 AP39 1000fr Aircraft, 1935-1985 5.25 2.75
a. Souvenir sheet of 2, #C156-C157, perf. 12½ 4.55 4.55
Nos. C153-C157 (5) 6.82 3.52

No. C155a has multicolored margin picturing world map. No. C157a has multicolored margin picturing airport and UTA jets. Sizes: 132x111mm.

Halley's Comet — AP40

Comets, astronomers and probes.

1986, Mar. 7 *Perf. 13*
C158 AP40 125fr Edmond Halley, Giotto probe 65 32
C159 AP40 150fr Giacobini-Zinner, 1959 80 40
C160 AP40 225fr Encke, 1961 1.25 60
C161 AP40 300fr Bradfield, 1980 1.65 80
C162 AP40 400fr Planet A probe 2.00 1.00
Nos. C158-C162 (5) 6.35 3.12

1986 World Cup Soccer Championships, Mexico — AP41

Various soccer plays.

1986, June 11 Litho. *Perf. 13*
C163 AP41 125fr multi 70 35
C164 AP41 210fr multi 1.25 60
C165 AP41 500fr multi 2.75 1.40
C166 AP41 600fr multi 3.50 1.75

Tennis at the 1988 Summer Olympics — AP42

Various players.

1987, Jan. 28 Litho. *Perf. 13½*
C167 AP42 150fr multi 82 40
C168 AP42 250fr multi 1.40 70
C169 AP42 500fr multi 2.75 1.40
C170 AP42 600fr multi 3.25 1.65

World Wildlife Fund — AP43

Various pictures of the mongoose lemur.

1987, Feb. 18 *Perf. 13*
C171 AP43 75fr multi, vert. 40 20
C172 AP43 100fr multi 55 28
C173 AP43 125fr multi 70 35
C174 AP43 150fr multi 82 40

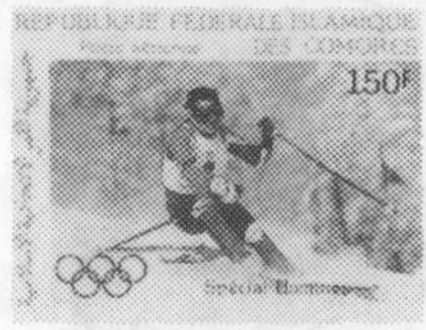

1988 Winter Olympics, Calgary
AP44

1987, Apr. 10 Litho. *Perf. 13½*

C175	AP44	150fr Slalom	82	40
C176	AP44	225fr Ski jumping	1.25	62
C177	AP44	500fr Women's giant slalom	2.75	1.40
C178	AP44	600fr Luge	3.25	1.65

AIR POST SEMI-POSTAL STAMP

Type of Air Post 1979

Design: IYC emblem, mother and son.

1979, July 31 Litho. *Perf. 13½x13*

CB1	AP27	200fr + 30fr multi	1.75	1.75

International Year of the Child.

POSTAGE DUE STAMPS

Anjouan Mosque
D1

Coelacanth
D2

1950 Unwmk. Engr. *Perf. 14x13.*

J1	D1	50c dp grn	30	30
J2	D1	1fr blk brn	30	30

1954

J3	D2	5fr dk brn & grn	42	42
J4	D2	10fr gray & red brn	55	55
J5	D2	20fr ind & bl	85	85

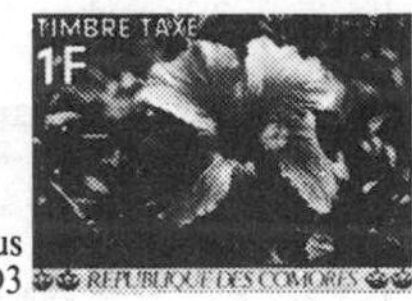

Hibiscus
D3

Designs: 2fr, 15fr, 40fr, 50fr, vertical.

1977, Nov. 19 Litho. *Perf. 13½*

J6	D3	1fr *shown*	5	5
J7	D3	2fr *Pineapple*	5	5
J8	D3	5fr *White butterfly*	6	6
J9	D3	10fr *Chameleon*	6	6
J10	D3	15fr *Blooming banana*	8	6
J11	D3	20fr *Orchids*	10	6
J12	D3	30fr *Allamanda cathartica*	15	10
J13	D3	40fr *Cashews*	22	12
J14	D3	50fr *Custard apple*	25	15
J15	D3	100fr *Breadfruit*	50	25
J16	D3	200fr *Vanilla*	1.00	50
J17	D3	500fr *Ylang ylang*	2.50	1.25
		Nos. J6-J17 (12)	5.02	2.71

OFFICIAL STAMPS

Comoro Flag — O1

Perf. 13x12½

1979-85 Litho. Unwmk.

O1	O1	5fr multi	5	5
O2	O1	10fr multi	6	6
O3	O1	20fr multi	15	6
O4	O1	30fr multi	28	12
O5	O1	40fr multi	38	25
O6	O1	60fr multi ('80)	32	25
O6A	O1	75fr multi ('85)	30	20
O7	O1	100fr multi	75	50
		Nos. O1-O7 (8)	2.29	1.49

Pres. Said Mohamed Cheikh (1904-1970) — O2

1980-85

O8	O2	100fr multi	50	38
O8A	O2	125fr multi ('85)	50	35
O9	O2	400fr multi	2.00	1.40

CONGO DEMOCRATIC REPUBLIC

LOCATION — Central Africa
GOVT. — Republic
AREA — 895,348 sq. mi. (estimated)
POP. — 22,480,000 (est. 1971)
CAPITAL — Kinshasa (Leopoldville)

Congo was an independent state, founded by Leopold II of Belgium, until 1908 when it was annexed to Belgium as a colony. Congo became an independent republic in 1960. The name was changed to Republic of Zaire, Oct. 28, 1971. See Zaire in Vol. IV for later issues.

100 Centimes = 1 Franc
100 Sengi = 1 Li-Kuta,
100 Ma-Kuta = 1 Zaire (1967)

Belgian Congo Flower Issue of 1952-53 Overprinted or Surcharged **CONGO**

1960, June 6 Photo. *Perf. 11½*
Flowers in Natural Colors
Size: 21x25½mm.
Granite Paper

323	A86	10c dp plum & ocher	6	6
324	A86	10c on 15c red & yel grn	10	10
325	A86	20c grn & gray	6	6
326	A86	40c grn & sal	6	5
327	A86	50c on 60c bl grn & pink	10	10
328	A86	50c on 75c dp plum & gray	10	10
329	A86	1fr car & yel	6	5
330	A86	1.50fr vio & ap grn	8	5
331	A86	2fr ol grn & buff	12	6
332	A86	3fr ol grn & pink	20	8
333	A86	4fr choc & lil	25	20
334	A86	5fr dp plum & lt bl grn	25	10
335	A86	6.50fr dk car & lil	35	10
336	A86	8fr grn & lt yel	50	20
337	A86	10fr dp plum & pale ol	70	20
338	A86	20fr vio bl & dl sal	1.40	55

Overprinted **CONGO**

Size: 22x32mm.

339	A86	50fr dp plum & gray bl	7.25	3.50
340	A86	100fr grn & buff	12.50	6.00
		Nos. 323-340 (18)	24.14	11.56

Nos. 324, 327-328 exist without "CONGO" overprint but with surcharge.

Belgian Congo Animal Issue, Nos. 306-317, Overprinted or Surcharged in Red, Blue, Black or Brown **CONGO**

341	A92	10c bl & brn (R)	6	6
342	A93	20c red org & sl (Bl)	6	6
343	A92	40c brn & bl (Bk)	6	6
344	A93	50c brt ultra, red & sep (R)	5	5
345	A92	1fr brn, grn & blk (Br)	6	5
346	A93	1.50fr blk & org yel (R)	8	6
347	A92	2fr crim, blk & brn (Bl)	10	5
348	A93	3.50fr on 3fr blk, gray & lil rose (Bk)	18	7
349	A92	5fr brn, dk brn & brt grn (Br)	25	10
350	A93	6.50fr bl, brn & org yel (R)	28	10
a.		Black overprint	50	25
351	A92	8fr org brn, ol bis & lil (Br)	32	25
352	A93	10fr multi (R)	45	20
		Nos. 341-352 (12)	1.95	1.11

Same Overprint on Belgian Congo No. 318.

1960

353	A94	50c gldn brn, ocher & red brn	60	60

Same Overprint and Surcharge of New Value on Belgian Congo Nos. 321-322.

Inscription in French

354	A95	3.50fr on 3fr gray & red	60	50

Inscription in Flemish

355	A95	3.50fr on 3fr gray & red	60	50

Map of Congo
A93a

1960 Photo. *Perf. 11½*

356	A93a	20c brown	8	5
357	A93a	50c rose red	8	5
358	A93a	1fr green	8	6
359	A93a	1.50fr red brn	12	5
360	A93a	2fr rose car	15	5
361	A93a	3.50fr lilac	17	8
362	A93a	5fr brt bl	23	10
363	A93a	6.50fr gray	30	12
364	A93a	10fr orange	50	25
365	A93a	20fr ultra	75	38
		Nos. 356-365 (10)	2.46	1.19

Issued to commemorate Congo's Independence.

Flag, People and Broken Chain — A94

1961 Unwmk. *Perf. 11½*
Flag in Blue and Yellow

366	A94	2fr rose vio	10	6
367	A94	3.50fr vermilion	12	10
368	A94	6.50fr yel brn	25	12
369	A94	10fr brt grn	38	20
370	A94	20fr car rose	65	45
		Nos. 366-370 (5)	1.50	93

Issued to commemorate the signing of the Independence Agreement by Belgium, Jan. 4, 1959.

Nos. 356-365 Overprinted in Blue, Black or Red: "Conference Coquilhatville Avril Mai 1961"

1961

371	A93a	20c brn (Bl)	60	60
372	A93a	50c rose red (Bk)	60	60
373	A93a	1fr grn (R)	60	60
374	A93a	1.50fr red brn (Bk)	60	60
375	A93a	2fr rose car (Bk)	60	60
376	A93a	3.50fr lil (Bl)	60	60
377	A93a	5fr brt bl (R)	60	60
378	A93a	6.50fr gray (R)	60	60
379	A93a	10fr org (Bk)	60	60
380	A93a	20fr ultra (R)	60	60
		Nos. 371-380 (10)	6.00	6.00

Issued to commemorate the Coquilhatville Conference April-May, 1961.

Pres. Joseph Kasavubu
A95

Kasavubu and Map of Congo
A96

Design: 10fr, 20fr, 50fr, 100fr, Kasavubu i[n] uniform and map.

Perf. 11½

1961, June 30 Unwmk. Photo[.]
Portrait and Inscription in Dark Brown

381	A95	10c yellow	8	[illegible]
382	A95	20c dp rose	8	[illegible]
383	A95	40c bl grn	8	[illegible]
384	A95	50c salmon	8	[illegible]
385	A95	1fr lilac	12	[illegible]
386	A95	1.50fr lt brn	15	[illegible]
387	A95	2fr brt grn	15	[illegible]
388	A96	3.50fr rose pink	20	[illegible]
389	A96	5fr gray	1.75	1[illegible]
390	A96	6.50fr ultra	45	[illegible]
391	A96	8fr olive	50	1[illegible]
392	A95	10fr lt vio	1.10	1[illegible]
393	A95	20fr orange	1.10	1[illegible]
394	A95	50fr lt bl	1.75	4[illegible]
395	A95	100fr ap grn	2.50	7[illegible]
		Nos. 381-395 (15)	10.09	2.5[illegible]

First anniversary of independence.

Nos. 381-387, 389 and 392 Overprinted: "REOUVERTURE du PARLEMENT JUILLET 1961"

1961

Portrait and Inscription in Dark Brown

396	A95	10c yellow	10	8
397	A95	20c dp rose	10	8
398	A95	40c bl grn	10	8
399	A95	50c salmon	42	3[illegible]
400	A95	1fr lilac	42	30
401	A95	1.50fr lt brn	1.10	90
402	A95	2fr brt grn	1.10	90
403	A96	5fr gray	1.10	90
404	A95	10fr lt vio	1.25	1.10
		Nos. 396-404 (9)	5.69	4.64

Issued to commemorate the re-opening of the Congolese parliament, July, 1961.

Dag Hammarskjold and Map of Africa with Congo — A97

Malaria Eradication Emblem and Mosquito — A98

1962, Jan. 20 Photo. *Perf. 11½*
Gray Background

405	A97	10c dk brn	5	5
406	A97	20c Prus bl	5	5
407	A97	30c brown	7	7
408	A97	40c dk bl	7	7
409	A97	50c brn red	10	10
410	A97	3fr ol grn	2.50	1.65
411	A97	6.50fr dk vio	85	55
412	A97	8fr red brn	95	70
		Nos. 405-412 (8)	4.64	3.24

Souvenir Sheets

Imperf

413	A97	25fr blk brn	4.00	4.00
a.		Ovpt. in grn	1.50	1.50

Nos. 405-413 issued in memory of Dag Hammarskjold, Secretary General of the United Nations, 1953-61.

No. 413 contains one stamp and has gold marginal inscription. Size: 65x90mm.

No 413a is overprinted "30 Juin 1962" on stamp and "2eme Anniversaire de l'Independance" on sheet margin. Issued June 30, 1962.

1962, June 15
Granite Paper

414 A98 1.50fr yel, blk & dk red 8 8
415 A98 2fr yel grn, brn & bl grn 42 20
416 A98 6.50fr ultra, blk & mar 20 15

Issued for the World Health Organization drive to eradicate malaria.

Nos. 405-412 Overprinted in Blue, Purple, Black or Carmine

"Paix,
Travail,
Austerite .,,
C. ADOULA
11 juillet 1962

1962, Oct. 15
Gray Background

417 A97 10c dk brn (Bl) 7 5
418 A97 20c Prus bl (P) 7 5
419 A97 30c brn (Bk) 7 5
420 A97 40c dk bl (C) 7 5
421 A97 50c brn red (Bl) 1.75 75
422 A97 3fr ol grn (P) 22 7
423 A97 6.50fr dk vio (Bk) 30 12
424 A97 8fr red brn (C) 42 20
Nos. 417-424 (8) 2.97 1.34

Reorganization of Adoula administration.

Canceled to Order
Starting in 1963, prices in the used column are for "canceled to order" stamps. Postally used copies sell for much more.

A99

1963, Jan. 28 Engr. *Perf. 10½x13*

425 A99 2fr dl pur 1.40 1.50
426 A99 4fr red 10 8
427 A99 7fr dk bl 15 10
428 A99 20fr sl grn 30 20

Issued to commemorate Congo's first participation at the U.P.U. Congress, New Delhi, March, 1963.

Shoebill — A100

Birds: 10c, Pelicans. 20c, Crested guinea fowl (horiz.). 30c, Openbill. 40c, White-bellied storks (horiz.). 2fr, Marabou. 3fr, Greater flamingos (horiz.). 4fr, Congolese peacock. 5fr, Hartlaub ducks (horiz.). 6fr, Secretary bird. 7fr, Black-casqued hornbill (horiz.). 8fr, Sacred ibis and nest. 10fr, Crowned crane (horiz.). 20fr, Saddle-bill stork (horiz.).

1963 Unwmk. Photo. *Perf. 11½*

429 A100 10c pink, ultra & ocher 5 5
430 A100 20c rose red, bl & blk 5 5
431 A100 30c grn, ocher & blk 5 5
432 A100 40c gray, org & blk 5 5
433 A100 1fr brn, emer & gray 5 5
434 A100 2fr gray, red & ind 1.75 50
435 A100 3fr ol grn, blk & rose 8 5
436 A100 4fr car rose, vio bl & grn 8 5
437 A100 5fr lake, lt bl & blk 10 5
438 A100 6fr pur, yel & blk 1.75 50
439 A100 7fr bl grn, blk & ind 15 5
440 A100 8fr yel, org & blk 18 5
441 A100 10fr bl, blk & rose 22 8
442 A100 20fr cit, red & blk 45 10
Nos. 429-442 (14) 5.01 1.68

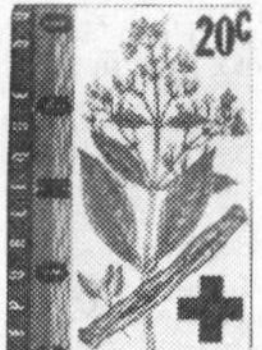

Cinchona Ledgeriana
A101

Red Cross Nurse
A102

Designs: 10c, 30c, 5fr, Strophanthus sarmentosus.

Perf. 12½x13½, 13½x12½
1963, May 25 Engr. Unwmk.
Cross in Red

443 A101 10c vio & dl grn 5 5
444 A101 20c mag & bl 5 5
445 A101 30c grn & org 5 5
446 A101 40c bl & vio 6 6
447 A101 5fr ol & rose cl 12 5
448 A101 7fr org & blk 12 5
449 A102 9fr gray ol & red 18 8
450 A102 20fr pur & red 1.75 1.00
Nos. 443-450 (8) 2.38 1.39

International Red Cross centenary.
A souvenir sheet of three contains imperf. 58fr, 7fr, and 20fr stamps similar to Nos. 447, 448 and 450, but in changed colors. Marginal inscriptions in violet. Size: 109x75mm. Price $15.

Men Joining Hands and Map of Congo — A103

1963, June 29 Photo. *Perf. 11½*

451 A103 4fr multi 1.25 45
452 A103 5fr multi 10 5
453 A103 9fr multi 20 8
454 A103 12fr multi 28 12

Issued to celebrate national reconciliation.

Bulldozer and Kabambare Sewer, Leopoldville — A104

Designs: 30c, 5fr, 12fr, Excavator and blueprint. 50c, 9fr, Building Ituri road.

1963, July 1 Engr. Unwmk.

455 A104 20c multi 5 5
456 A104 30c multi 5 5
457 A104 50c multi 5 5
458 A104 3fr multi 1.25 50
459 A104 5fr multi 10 5
460 A104 9fr multi 18 10
461 A104 12fr multi 22 15
Nos. 455-461 (7) 1.90 95

Issued to publicize aid to Congo by the European Economic Community.

Leopoldville Airport N'Djili — A105

Design: 5fr, 7fr, 50fr, Tail assembly and airport.

1963, Nov. 30 Photo. *Perf. 11½*

462 A105 2fr gray, yel & red brn 5 5
463 A105 5fr mag, vio & yel 8 8
464 A105 6fr bl, yel & dk brn 1.25 55
465 A105 7fr multi 35 22
466 A105 30fr lil, yel & ol 55 38
467 A105 50fr multi 60 40
Nos. 462-467 (6) 2.88 1.68

Issued to publicize Air Congo.

Nos. 425-428 Overprinted with Silver Frame on Three Sides and Black Inscription: "15e anniversaire/10 DECEMBRE 1948/DROITS DE L'HOMME/ 10 DECEMBRE 1963"

Engraved and Typographed
1963, Dec. 10 *Perf. 10½x13*

468 A99 2fr dl pur 6 6
469 A99 4fr red 8 8
470 A99 7fr dk bl 28 28
471 A99 20fr sl grn 30 30

15th anniversary of Universal Declaration of Human Rights.
Nos. 468-471 exist with side date panels transposed ("1963" at left, "1948" at right). Price, each $5.

Laboratory Technician and Atomic Emblem
A106

Designs: 1.50fr, 60fr, University. 8fr, 75fr, First African nuclear reactor. 25fr, 100fr, University and crest.

1964, Feb. 1 Photo. *Perf. 14x12½*

472 A106 50c multi 8 8
473 A106 1.50fr multi 8 8
474 A106 8fr multi 2.50 2.25
475 A106 25fr multi 25 20
476 A106 30fr multi 30 25
477 A106 60fr multi 55 45
478 A106 75fr multi 75 70
479 A106 100fr multi 1.00 85
a. Souv. sheet of 3 3.50 3.50
Nos. 472-479 (8) 5.51 4.86

10th anniversary of Lovanium University, Leopoldville.
No. 479a contains 3 imperf. multicolored stamps: 20fr, design as 50c; 30fr, as 8fr; 100fr. Size: 141x70mm.

Belgian Congo Issues of 1952-59 Overprinted "REPUBLIQUE DU CONGO" and Surcharged in Black on Overprinted Metallic Panels.

1964 *Perf. 11½*

480 A93 1fr on 20c red org & sl (#307) 8 8
481 A86 2fr on 1.50fr multi (#273) 2.10 1.50
482 A93 5fr on 6.50fr multi (#315) 32 20
483 A86 8fr on 6.50fr multi (#278) 40 25

Republic Issues of 1960-61 Surcharged in Black of Overprinted Metallic Rectangles or Ovals.

484 A86 1fr on 6.50fr multi (#335) 8 8
485 A93 1fr on 20c red org & sl (#342) 8 8
486 A86 2fr on 1.50fr multi (#330) 8 8
487 A95 3fr on 20c dp rose & dk brn (#382) 25 20
488 A95 4fr on 40c bl grn & dk brn (#383) 25 20
489 A93 5fr on 6.50fr multi ("Congo" red) (#350) 33 20
a. "Congo" black 33 20
490 A93a 6fr on 6.50fr gray (#363) 33 22
491 A93a 7fr on 20c brn (#356) 50 28
Nos. 480-491 (12) 4.80 3.37

Pole Vault
A107

Sports: 7fr, 20fr, Javelin (vert.). 8fr, 100fr, Hurdling.

Perf. 11½
1964, July 13 Unwmk. Photo.
Granite Paper

492 A107 5fr gray, dk brn & car 6 5
493 A107 7fr rose, vio & emer 1.20 55
494 A107 8fr org, yel, red brn & vio bl 10 5
495 A107 10fr bl, vio brn & mag 10 5
496 A107 20fr gray grn, red brn & ver 25 10
497 A107 100fr lil, dk brn & grn 1.20 30
a. Souv. sheet of 3 5.25 5.25
Nos. 492-497 (6) 2.91 1.10

Issued to commemorate the 18th Olympic Games, Tokyo, Oct. 10-25. No. 497a contains 3 imperf. stamps (20fr orange & dark brown, pole vault; 30fr citron and dark brown, hurdling; 100fr dull green and dark brown, javelin). Dark brown marginal inscription and dull green Olympic rings. Size: 134x85mm. Sheet issued Sept. 10.

National Palace, Leopoldville — A108

1964, Sept. 15
Granite Paper

498 A108 50c lil rose & bl 5 5
499 A108 1fr bl & lil rose 5 5
500 A108 2fr brn red & vio 5 5
501 A108 3fr emer & red 5 5
502 A108 4fr org & vio bl 5 5
503 A108 5fr gray vio & emer 5 5
504 A108 6fr sep & org 8 5
505 A108 7fr gray ol & red brn 8 5
506 A108 8fr rose red & vio bl 2.50 50
507 A108 9fr vio bl & rose red 7 5
508 A108 10fr brn ol & grn 10 5
509 A108 20fr bl & brn org 15 5
510 A108 30fr dk car rose & grn 22 7
511 A108 40fr ultra & dk car rose 33 7
512 A108 50fr brn org & grn 45 7
513 A108 100fr sl & ver 85 15
Nos. 498-513 (16) 5.13 1.41

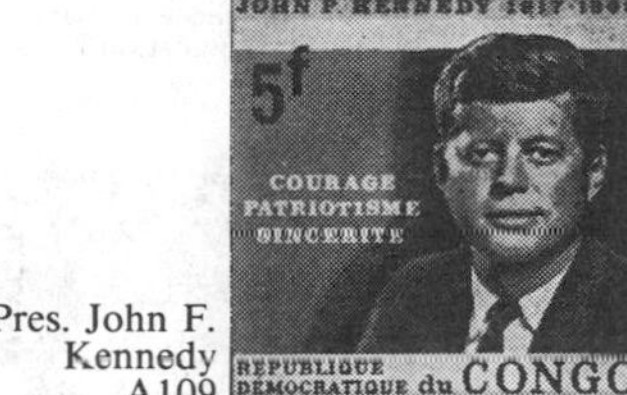

Pres. John F. Kennedy
A109

1964, Dec. 8 Photo. *Perf. 13½*

514 A109 5fr dk bl & blk 8 5
515 A109 6fr rose cl & blk 8 5
516 A109 9fr brn & blk 10 5
517 A109 30fr pur & blk 42 7
518 A109 40fr dl grn & blk 2.50 75
519 A109 60fr red brn & blk 70 30
Nos. 514-519 (6) 3.88 1.27

Souvenir Sheet

520 A109 150fr blk & mar 3.00 3.00

Issued in memory of Pres. John F. Kennedy (1917-63). No. 520 contains one stamp, black marginal inscription. Size: 64x76mm.

Rocket and Unisphere
A110

Basketball
A111

Engraved and Typographed

1965, March 1 Unwmk. *Perf. 12*

521 A110 50c lil & blk 5 5
522 A110 1.50fr bl & lil 5 5
523 A110 2fr red brn & brt grn 5 5
524 A110 10fr brt grn & dk red 1.00 60
525 A110 18fr vio bl & brn 15 8
526 A110 27fr rose red & grn 33 12
527 A110 40fr gray & org 50 18
Nos. 521-527 (7) 2.13 1.13

New York World's Fair, 1964-65.

1965, Apr. Photo. *Perf. 13½*

Designs: 6fr, 40fr, Soccer (horiz.). 15fr, 60fr, Volleyball.

528 A111 5fr blk, grnsh bl & ocher 5 5
529 A111 6fr blk, bl gray & crim 8 5
530 A111 15fr blk, org & yel grn 12 10
531 A111 24fr blk, rose lil & brt grn 30 10
532 A111 40fr blk, brt grn & ultra 1.75 60
533 A111 60fr blk, bl & red lil 55 20
Nos. 528-533 (6) 2.85 1.10

First African Games, Leopoldville, Mar. 31-Apr. 7, 1965.

Earth and Satellites A112

Designs: 9fr, 15fr, 20fr, 40fr, Satellites at left, globe at right.

Perf. 14x14½

1965, June 28 Photo. Unwmk.

534 A112 6fr blk, sal & vio 8 5
535 A112 9fr blk, lt grn & gray 8 5
536 A112 12fr org, gray & blk 10 7
537 A112 15fr grn, ultra & blk 13 7
538 A112 18fr blk, lt grn & gray 1.50 42
539 A112 20fr blk, sal & vio 22 8
540 A112 30fr grn, ultra & blk 33 10
541 A112 40fr org, gray & blk 45 15
Nos. 534-541 (8) 2.89 99

Issued to commemorate the centenary of the International Telecommunication Union.

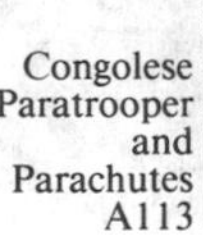

Congolese Paratrooper and Parachutes A113

1965, July 5 *Perf. 13x14*

542 A113 5fr brt bl & brn 5 5
543 A113 6fr org & brn 5 5
544 A113 7fr br grn & brn 60 28
545 A113 9fr brt pink & brn 10 8
546 A113 18fr lem & brn 18 10
Nos. 542-546 (5) 98 56

Fifth anniversary of independence.

Matadi Harbor and ICY Emblem — A114

Designs (ICY Emblem and): 8fr, 25fr, Katanga mines. 9fr, 60fr, Tshopo Dam, Stanleyville.

1965, Oct. 25 Photo. *Perf. 13x14*

547 A114 6fr ultra, blk & yel 8 5
548 A114 8fr org red, blk & bl 10 5
549 A114 9fr bl grn, blk & brn org 10 5
550 A114 12fr car rose, blk & gray 1.15 45
551 A114 25fr ol, blk & rose red 27 12
552 A114 60fr gray, blk & org 55 15
Nos. 547-552 (6) 2.25 87

International Cooperation Year, 1965.

Soldiers Giving First Aid — A115

The Army Serving the Country: 7fr, Bridge building. 9fr, Feeding child. 19fr, Maintenance of telegraph lines. 20fr, House building. 30fr, Soldier and flag. (19fr, 20fr, 30fr, vertical.)

Perf. 12½x13, 13x12½

1965, Nov. 17

553 A115 5fr sal, brn & red 8 5
554 A115 7fr yel & grn 8 5
555 A115 9fr ol & brn 10 5
556 A115 19fr brt grn & brn 90 55
557 A115 20fr lt bl & brn 25 8
558 A115 30fr multi 35 10
Nos. 553-558 (6) 1.76 88

See also Nos. 582-586.

Nos. 551-552 Overprinted with U.N. Emblem and "6e Journee Meteorologique Mondiale / 23.3.66." on Metallic Strip

1966, Mar. 23 Photo. *Perf. 13x14*

559 A114 25fr ol & blk 1.10 55
560 A114 60fr gray & blk 1.10 80

6th World Meteorological Day.

Woman's Head and Goat — A116

Designs: 10fr, Sculptured heads. 12fr, Sitting figure and two heads (vert.). 53fr, Figure with earrings and kneeling woman with bowl (vert.).

Perf. 11½x13, 13x11½

1966, Apr. 23 Litho. Unwmk.

561 A116 10fr red, blk & gray 12 12
562 A116 12fr grn, blk & bl 15 15
563 A116 15fr dp bl, blk & lil 18 18
564 A116 53fr dp rose, blk & vio bl 1.50 1.25

Issued to commemorate the International Negro Arts Festival, Dakar, Senegal, Apr. 1-24.

Pres. Joseph Desiré Mobutu and Fishing Industry A117

Pres. Mobutu and: 4fr, Pyrethrum harvest. 6fr, Building industry. 8fr, Winnowing rice. 10fr, Cotton harvest. 12fr, Banana harvest. 15fr, Cacao harvest. 24fr, Pineapple harvest.

1966, May 1 Photo. *Perf. 11½*

565 A117 2fr dk brn & dk bl 6 6
566 A117 4fr dk brn & org 6 6
567 A117 6fr dk brn & ol 95 85
568 A117 8fr dk brn & brt grnsh bl 7 7
569 A117 10fr dk brn & brn red 10 10
570 A117 12fr dk brn & vio 12 10
571 A117 15fr dk brn & lt ol grn 12 10
572 A117 24fr dk brn & lil rose 30 20
Nos. 565-572 (8) 1.78 1.54

Souvenir Sheet

Design: Pres. Mobutu without cap, and men rolling up sleeves.

Perf. 11x11½

573 A117 Sheet of 4 1.10 1.10
a. 15fr red, blk & ultra 25 25

Issued to honor Lt. Gen. Joseph Desiré Mobutu, President of Congo, and to publicize the "Back to Work" campaign. No. 573 contains four stamps and flag of Congo in margin. Size: 127x94½mm.

Nos. 510-513 Overprinted

1966, June 13 *Perf. 11½*

574 A108 30fr dk car rose & grn 1.00 1.00
575 A108 40fr ultra & dk car rose 1.00 1.00
576 A108 50fr brn org & grn 1.10 1.10
577 A108 100fr sl & ver 1.10 1.10

Issued to commemorate the inauguration of World Health Organization Headquarters, Geneva.

Soccer Player — A118

Designs: 30fr, Two soccer players. 50fr, Three soccer players. 60fr, Jules Rimet Cup, soccer ball and globe.

1966, July 25 Photo. *Perf. 14*

578 A118 10fr ocher, vio & brt grn 10 10
579 A118 30fr brt rose lil, vio & ap grn 35 25
580 A118 50fr ap grn, Prus bl & tan 1.25 1.20
581 A118 60fr brt grn, dk brn & gold 65 55

Issued to commemorate the World Cup Soccer Championship, Wembley, England, July 11-30.

Army Type of 1965

The Army Serving the Country: 2fr, Soldiers giving first aid. 6fr, Feeding child. 10fr, House building (vert.). 18fr, Bridge building. 24fr, Soldier and flag (vert.).

1966, Aug. 8 *Perf. 12½x13, 13x12½*

582 A115 2fr ver, ind & red 5 5
583 A115 6fr ultra red brn 8 8
584 A115 10fr yel grn & red brn 60 55
585 A115 18fr car rose & vio 15 10
586 A115 24fr multi 25 20
Nos. 582-586 (5) 1.13 98

Nos. 578-581 Overprinted in Black, Carmine or Green: "FINALE / ANGLETERRE-ALLEMAGNE / 4-2"

1966, Nov. 14 Photo. *Perf. 14*

587 A118 10fr multi (B or C) 22 22
588 A118 30fr multi (B or G) 70 60
589 A118 50fr multi (B or C) 1.10 90
590 A118 60fr multi (B or C) 1.25 1.00

Issued to commemorate England's victory in the World Soccer Cup Championship. The two colors of the overprint alternate in the sheets.

Souvenir Sheets

Pres. John F. Kennedy — A119

1966, Dec. 28 Engr. *Perf. 13*

591 A119 150fr brown 4.00 4.00
592 A119 150fr slate 4.00 4.00

Issued in memory of Pres. John F. Kennedy. No. 591 has slate green, No. 592 deep orange marginal design. Two imperf. sheets exist: 150fr brown with violet blue margin and 150fr slate with lilac margin. Size: 65x76mm. Price $4.25 each.

5 K

4e Sommet OUA
KINSHASA
du 11 au 14 - 9 - 67

Nos. 498-503 Surcharged in Black, Red or Maroon

1967, Sept. 11 Photo. *Perf. 11½*

593 A108 1k on 2fr brn red & vio 8 5
a. Inverted overprint 9.00
594 A108 3k on 5fr gray vio & emer 15 10
595 A108 5k on 4fr org & vio bl 25 18
596 A108 6.60k on 1fr bl & lil rose (R) 33 25
a. Inverted overprint 6.50
597 A108 9.60k on 50c lil rose & bl 55 40
a. Inverted overprint 6.50
598 A108 9.80k on 3fr emer & red (M) 75 55
Nos. 593-598 (6) 2.11 1.53

Souvenir Sheet

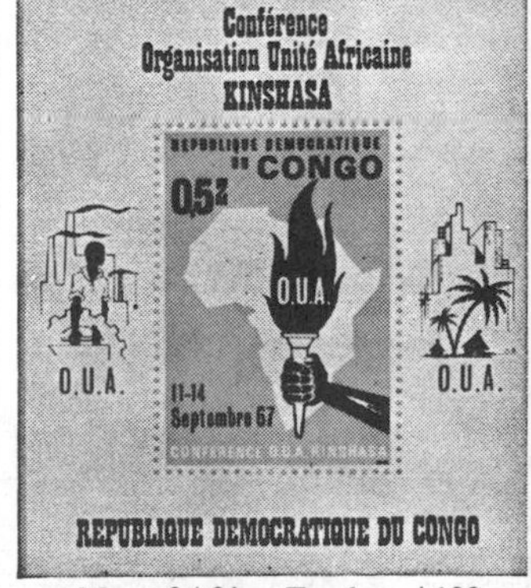

Map of Africa, Torch — A120

599 A120 50k grnsh bl, blk & red 2.25 2.25

Issued to commemorate the 4th meeting of the Organization for African Unity, Kinshasa (Leopoldville), Sept. 9-11. No. 599 has black marginal inscription and design in black and red. Size: 76x90mm.

Souvenir Sheet

Horn Blower and EXPO Emblem — A121

1967, Sept. 28 Engr. *Perf. 11½*
600 A121 50k dk brn 2.50 2.50

Issued to commemorate EXPO '67, International Exhibition, Montreal, Apr. 28-Oct. 27, 1967. No. 600 has ultramarine and orange marginal inscription. Size: 90x75mm.

Nos. 565-566 and 582 Overprinted: "NOUVELLE CONSTITUTION 1967" and Surcharged with New Value on Metallic Panel in Magenta or Brown.

Perf. 11½, 12½x13

1967, Oct. 9 Photo.
601 A117 4k on 2fr dk brn & dk bl (M) 25 20
602 A115 5k on 2fr ver, ind & red (B) 30 25
603 A117 21k on 4fr dk brn & org (M) 1.35 1.00

Issued to commemorate the promulgation of the Constitution, June 4, 1967.

Nos. 528 and 530 Surcharged with New Value and Overprinted: "lere Jeux Congolais / 25/6 au 2/7/1967 / Kinshasa"

1967, Oct. 16 Photo. *Perf. 13½*
604 A111 1k on 5fr multi 12 12
605 A111 9.60k on 15fr multi 75 75

Issued to commemorate the First Congolese Games, Kinshasa, June 25-July 2, 1967.

No. 465 Surcharged with New Value and Overprinted: "ler VOL BAC / ONE ELEVEN / 14/5/67"

1967, Oct. 16 *Perf. 11½*
606 A105 9.60k on 7fr multi 1.00 25

Issued to commemorate the first flight of the BAC 111 in the service of Air Congo, May 14, 1967.

Nos. 547 and 549 Surcharged in Red or Black: "JOURNEE MONDIALE / DE L'ENFANCE / 8-10-67"

1968, Feb. 10 Photo. *Perf. 13x14*
607 A114 1k on 6fr ultra, blk & yel (R) 12 12
608 A114 9k on 9fr bl grn, blk & brn org (B) 75 75

Issued for International Children's Day. The surcharge is on a rectangle printed in metallic ink.

Nos. 498, 504 and 501 Surcharged in Blue or Red: "Annee Internationale / du Tourisme 24-10-1967"

1968, Feb. 10 *Perf. 11½*
609 A108 5k on 50c lil rose & bl (Bl) 27 27
610 A108 10k on 6fr sep & org (R) 60 60
611 A108 15k on 3fr emer & red (R) 85 85

Issued for International Tourist Year. The surcharge is on a rectangle printed in metallic ink.

Nos. 500, 498 and 502 Surcharged in Black, Violet Blue or Gold

1968, July Photo. *Perf. 11½*
612 A108 1k on 2fr brn red & vio 7 7
613 A108 2k on 50c lil rose & bl (VBl) 15 15
614 A108 2k on 50c lil rose & bl (G) 15 15
615 A108 9.60k on 4fr org & vio bl 60 60

The surcharge on No. 612 consists of a black rectangle and new denomination in upper right corner; the surcharge on No. 613 has a violet blue rectangle with denomination printed in white on it; on No. 614 the rectangle is gold and the denomination black; on No. 615 the rectangle is black and the denomination white.

No. 565 Surcharged in White on Black Rectangle.

1968, Oct. Photo. *Perf. 11½*
616 A117 10k on 2fr dk brn & dk bl 60 12

Leopard A122

1968, Nov. 5 Litho. *Perf. 10½*
617 A122 2k brt grnsh bl & blk 12 5
618 A122 9.60k red & blk 60 15

Mobutu Type of 1966 Surcharged

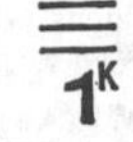

1968, Dec. 20 Photo. *Perf. 11½*
619 A117 15s on 2fr sep & brt bl 5 5
620 A117 1k on 6fr sep & brn 5 5
621 A117 3k on 10fr sep & emer 15 12
622 A117 5k on 12fr sep & org 25 18
623 A117 20k on 15fr scp & brt grn 90 65
624 A117 50k on 24fr sep & brt lil 2.50 1.75
Nos. 619-624 (6) 3.90 2.80

Human Rights Flame — A123

1968, Dec. 30 *Perf. 12½x13*
625 A123 2k lt ultra & brt grn 12 5
626 A123 9.60k grn & dp car 55 35
627 A123 10k brt lil & brn 55 35
628 A123 40k org brn & pur 2.10 1.50

International Human Rights Year.

Type of 1968 Overprinted in Gold

1969, Jan. 27 Photo. *Perf. 12½x13*
629 A123 2k ap grn & red brn 12 6
630 A123 9.60k rose & emer 55 35
631 A123 10k gray & ultra 55 35
632 A123 40k grnsh bl & pur 2.10 1.50

Issued to publicize the 4th summit meeting of OCAM (Organisation Communitee Afrique et Malgache), Kinshasa, Jan. 27.

Kinshasa Fair Emblem and Cotton Boll — A124

Designs (Fair Emblem and): 6k, Copper. 9.60k, Coffee. 9.80k, Diamond. 11.60k, Oil palm fruits.

1969, May 2 Photo. *Perf. 12½x13*
633 A124 2k brt pur, gold & red lil 12 5
634 A124 6k grn, gold & bl grn 35 35
635 A124 9.60k brn, gold & lt brn 55 25
636 A124 9.80k ultra & gold 55 50
637 A124 11.60k hn brn, gold & brn 70 70
Nos. 633-637 (5) 2.27 1.85

Kinshasa Fair, Limete, June 30-July 21.

Fair Entrance, Emblem — A125

Designs (Fair Emblem and): 3k, Gecomin Mining Co. Pavilion. 10k, Administration Building. 25k, Pavilion of the Organization for African Unity.

1969, June 30 Photo. *Perf. 11½*

Granite Paper

638 A125 2k brt rose lil & gold 10 10
639 A125 3k bl & gold 15 15
640 A125 10k lt ol grn & gold 50 40
641 A125 25k cop red & gold 1.15 1.00

Kinshasa Fair, Limete, June 30-July 21.

Congo Arms A126

Pres. Mobutu A127

1969, July-Sept. Litho. *Perf. 14*
642 A126 10s org & blk 5 5
643 A126 15s ultra & blk 5 5
644 A126 30s brt grn & blk 5 5
645 A126 60s brt rose lil & blk 5 5
646 A126 90s dp bis & blk 5 5

Perf. 13

647 A127 1k sky bl & multi 5 5
648 A127 2k org & multi 6 5
649 A127 3k multi 9 6
650 A127 5k brt rose & multi 15 13
651 A127 6k ultra & multi 20 15
652 A127 9.60k multi 35 20
653 A127 10k lt lil & multi 50 25
654 A127 20k yel & multi 1.00 50
655 A127 50k multi 2.50 1.10
656 A127 100k fawn & multi 4.50 2.00
Nos. 642-656 (15) 9.65 4.74

Well Driller, by Oscar Bonnevalle — A128

Paintings: 4k, Preparation of cocoa, by Jean Van Noten. 8k, Dock workers, by Constantin Meunier. 10k, Poultry shop, by Henri Evenepoel. 15k, Steel industry, by Constantin Meunier.

Perf. 13x14, 14x13 (8k)

1969, Dec. 15 Litho.

Size: 41x41mm.

657 A128 3k multi 20 17
658 A128 4k multi 25 20

Size: 28x41mm.

659 A128 8k multi 40 35

Size: 41x41mm.

660 A128 10k multi 65 50
661 A128 15k multi 1.25 75
Nos. 657-661 (5) 2.75 1.97

Issued to commemorate the 50th anniversary of the International Labor Organization.

Souvenir Sheet

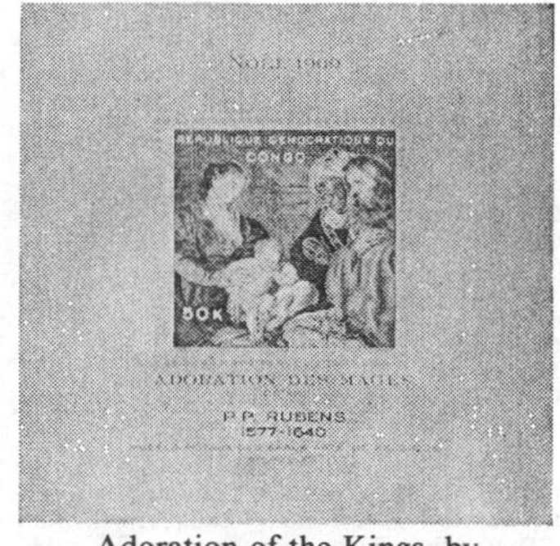

Adoration of the Kings, by Rubens — A129

1969, Dec. Engr. *Perf. 13*
662 A129 50k red lil 2.25 2.25

Issued for Christmas 1969. No. 662 has blue and red lilac marginal inscription. Size: 85x85mm.

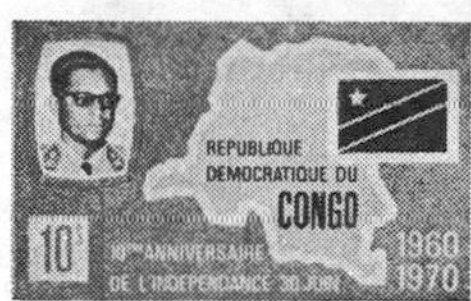

Pres. Mobutu, Map and Flag of Congo A130

1970, June 30 Litho. *Perf. 13½x13*
663 A130 10s multi 5 5
664 A130 90s pur & multi 5 5
665 A130 1k brn & multi 5 5
666 A130 2k multi 9 5
667 A130 7k multi 38 23
668 A130 10k multi 55 35
669 A130 20k multi 1.10 75
Nos. 663-669 (7) 2.27 1.53

10th anniversary of independence.

Issues of 1964-1966 Surcharged

= 0,20 K

Perf. 11½, 12½x13, 13x12½

1970, Sept. 24 Photo.
670 A108 10s on 1fr bl & lil rose (#499) 8 6
671 A108 20s on 2fr brn red & vio (#500) 8 6
672 A117 20s on 2fr dk brn & dk bl (#565) 15 12
673 A108 30s on 3fr emer & red (#501) 8 6
674 A108 40s on 4fr org & vio bl (#502) 10 8
675 A117 40s on 4fr dk brn & org (#566) 15 12
676 A108 60s on 7fr gray ol & red brn (#505) 1.10 80
677 A108 90s on 9fr vio bl & rose red (#507) 1.10 80
678 A115 90s on 9fr ol & brn (#555) 15 12
679 A115 1k on 7fr yel & grn (#554) 15 12
680 A108 1k on 6fr sep & org (#504) 15 12
681 A117 1k on 12fr dk brn & vio (#570) 1.10 80
682 A117 2k on 24fr dk brn & lil rose (#572) 15 12
683 A115 2k on 24fr multi (#586) 15 12
684 A108 3k on 30fr dk car rose & grn (#510) 1.10 80
685 A108 4k on 40fr ultra & dk car rose (#511) 15 12
686 A108 5k on 50fr brn org & grn (#512) 2.50 1.75
687 A108 10k on 100fr sl & ver (#513) 1.10 75
Nos. 670-687 (18) 9.54 6.92

Telecommunications Building, Geneva — A131

Designs: 2k, 6.60k, U.P.U. Headquarters, Bern. 9.80k, 10k, 11k, U.N. Headquarters, New York.

1970, Oct. 24 Photo. *Perf. 11½*

688	A131	1k pink & grn	5	5
689	A131	2k org & grn	10	5
690	A131	6.60k grnsh bl & rose car	35	18
691	A131	9.60k yel & vio bl	45	25
692	A131	9.80k lt ultra & brn	45	25
693	A131	10k lt pur & brn	45	28
694	A131	11k rose & brn	55	32
		Nos. 688-694 (7)	2.40	1.38

Issued for International Telecommunications Day (1k, 9.60k); Inauguration of new Universal Postal Union Headquarters, Bern (2k, 6.60k); 25th anniversary of United Nations (9.80k, 10k, 11k).

Pres. Mobutu, Congolese Flag and Arch — A132

1970, Nov. 24 Litho. *Perf. 13*

695	A132	2k yel & multi	12	8
696	A132	10k bl & multi	60	40
697	A132	20k red & multi	1.25	85

Fifth anniversary of new government.

Apollo 11 in Flight A133

Designs: 2k, Astronaut and spacecraft on moon. 7k, Pres. Mobutu decorating astronauts' wives. 10k, Pres. Mobutu with Neil A. Armstrong, Col. Edwin E. Aldrin, Jr. and Lt. Col. Michael Collins. 30k, Armstrong, Aldrin and Collins in space suits.

1970, Dec. 24 *Perf. 13x13½*

698	A133	1k bl & blk	5	5
699	A133	2k brt pur & blk	12	8
700	A133	7k dl org & blk	45	30
701	A133	10k rose red & blk	50	40
702	A133	30k grn & blk	1.50	1.10
		Nos. 698-702 (5)	2.62	1.93

Visit of U.S. Apollo 11 astronauts and their wives to Kinshasa.

Metopodontus Savagei — A134

Designs: Various insects of Congo.

1971, Jan. 25 Photo. *Perf. 11½*

703	A134	10s dl rose & multi	5	5
704	A134	50s gray & multi	5	5
705	A134	90s multi	8	5
706	A134	1k cit & multi	8	5
707	A134	2k gray grn & multi	12	8
708	A134	3k lt vio & multi	22	15
709	A134	5k bl & multi	60	40
710	A134	10k multi	1.00	65
711	A134	30k grn & multi	2.50	1.50
712	A134	40k ocher & multi	3.25	2.00
		Nos. 703-712 (10)	7.95	4.98

Colotis Protomedia — A135

Designs: Various butterflies and moths of Congo.

1971, Feb. 24

713	A135	10s lt ultra & multi	5	5
714	A135	20s choc & multi	5	5
715	A135	70s dp org & multi	8	5
716	A135	1k vio bl & multi	8	5
717	A135	3k multi	22	15
718	A135	5k dk grn & multi	50	30
719	A135	10k multi	80	50
720	A135	15k emer & multi	1.25	75
721	A135	25k yel & multi	1.75	1.10
722	A135	40k multi	3.25	1.90
		Nos. 713-722 (10)	8.03	4.90

U.N. Emblem, Racial Unity — A136

1971, March 21 Photo. *Perf. 11½*

723	A136	1k lt grn & multi	5	5
724	A136	4k gray & multi	17	10
725	A136	5k lt lil & multi	27	15
726	A136	10k lt bl & multi	50	30

International year against racial discrimination.

Hypericum Bequaertii A137

Flowers: 4k, Dissotis brazzae. 20k, Begonia wollastonii. 25k, Cassia alata.

1971, May 24 Litho. *Perf. 14*

727	A137	1k multi	5	5
728	A137	4k multi	30	18
729	A137	20k multi	1.25	50
730	A137	25k multi	1.65	1.00

Obelisk at N'sele, Pres. Mobutu A138

1971, May 20 Photo. *Perf. 11½*

731	A138	4k gold & multi	22	15

4th anniversary of the People's Revolutionary Movement.

Radar Station A139

Designs: 1k, Waves. 6k, Map of Africa with telecommunications network.

1971, June 25 Photo. *Perf. 11½*

732	A139	1k rose & multi	5	5
733	A139	3k yel & multi	18	10
734	A139	6k lt bl & multi	40	25

Issued for 3rd World Telecommunications Day, May 17 (1k); opening of satellite telecommunications ground station, Kinshasa, June 30 (3k); Pan-African telecommunication system (6k).

Grass Monkeys A140

Designs: 20s, Moustached monkeys (vert.). 70s, De Brazza's monkeys. 1k, Yellow baboons. 3k, Pygmy chimpanzee (vert.). 5k, Mangabeys (vert.). 10k, Owlfaced monkeys. 15k, Diana monkeys. 25k, Black-and-white colobus (vert.). 40k, L'Hoest's monkeys (vert.).

1971, Aug.

735	A140	10s vio & multi	10	5
736	A140	20s lt bl & multi	10	5
737	A140	70s ocher & multi	12	5
738	A140	1k gray & multi	12	5
739	A140	3k rose & multi	25	7
740	A140	5k brn & multi	55	12
741	A140	10k multi	90	25
742	A140	15k multi	1.65	50
743	A140	25k brt bl & multi	2.75	75
744	A140	40k red & multi	3.75	1.00
		Nos. 735-744 (10)	10.29	2.89

Hotel Inter-Continental, Kinshasa — A141

1971, Oct. 2 Photo. *Perf. 13*

745	A141	2k sil & multi	10	5
746	A141	12k gold & multi	65	25

Man Reading A142

Designs: 2.50k, Open book and abacus. 7k, Five letters surrounding symbolic head.

1971, Oct. 24

747	A142	50s gold, red brn, blk & yel	5	5
748	A142	2.50k gold, blk, dk red & tan	15	6
749	A142	7k gold, grn, yel & blk	65	25

Fight against illiteracy.

Succeeding issues are listed in Vol. IV under Zaire.

SEMI-POSTAL STAMPS

Women Carrying Food, Wheat Emblem, and Tractor SP22

1963, Mar. 21 Photo. *Perf. 14x13*

B48	SP22	5fr + 2fr lil, vio & dk bl	18	12
B49	SP22	9fr + 4fr ocher, gray & dk grn	45	25
B50	SP22	12fr + 6fr bl, dk bl & vio	50	35
B51	SP22	20fr + 10fr red, grn & gray	2.50	2.35

"Freedom from Hunger" campaign of the UNFAO.

CONGO PEOPLE'S REPUBLIC

(ex-French)

LOCATION — West Africa at equator.
GOVT. — Republic.
AREA — 132,046 sq. mi.
POP. — 1,740,000 (est. 1984).
CAPITAL — Brazzaville.

The former French colony of Middle Congo became a member state of the French Community on November 28, 1958, and achieved independence on August 15, 1960. For some years before 1958, the colony was joined with three other French territories to form French Equatorial Africa. Issues of Middle Congo (1907-1933) are listed under that heading.

100 Centimes = 1 Franc

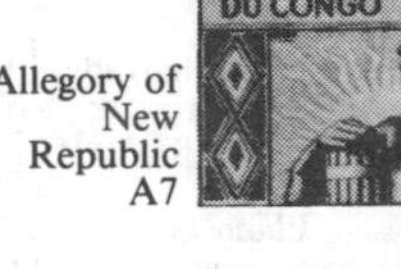

Allegory of New Republic A7

1959 Unwmk. Engr. *Perf. 13*

89	A7	25fr brn, dp cl, org & ol	45	10

Issued to commemorate the first anniversary of the proclamation of the Republic.

Imperforates

Most stamps of the Republic of the Congo exist imperforate in issued and trial colors, and also in small presentation sheets in issued colors.

C.C.T.A. Issue

Common Design Type

1960 Unwmk. *Perf. 13*

90	CD106	50fr dl grn & plum	90	80

President Fulbert Youlou — A8

Flag, Map and U.N. Emblem — A9

1960

91	A8	15fr grn, blk & car	25	17
92	A8	85fr ind & car	1.10	50

1961, March 11 *Perf. 13*

Flag in Green, Yellow & Red

93	A9	5fr vio brn & dk bl	10	6
94	A9	20fr org & dk bl	30	22
95	A9	100fr grn & dk bl	1.50	1.35

Congo's admission to United Nations.

Rainbow Runner A10

Designs (fish): 50c, 3fr, Rainbow runner. 1fr, 2fr, Sloan's viperfish. 5fr, Hatchet fish. 10fr, A deep-sea fish.

1961, Nov. 28 **Engr.**

96 A10 50c brn, ol grn & sal 6 6
97 A10 1fr bl grn & sep 6 6
98 A10 2fr ultra, sep & dk grn 10 10
99 A10 3fr dk bl, grn & sal 10 10
100 A10 5fr red brn, grn & blk 20 15
101 A10 10fr bl & red brn 25 18
Nos. 96-101 (6) 77 65

Brazzaville Market — A11

1962, Mar. 23 **Unwmk.** ***Perf. 13***

102 A11 20fr blk, red & grn 25 12

Abidjan Games Issue

Common Design Type

Designs: 20fr, Boxing. 50fr, Running, finish line.

1962, July 21 **Photo.** ***Perf. 12½x12***

103 CD109 20fr car, brt pink, brn & blk 28 20
104 CD109 50fr car, brt pink, brn & blk 60 45

See No. C7.

Common Design Types pictured in section at front of book.

African-Malgache Union Issue

Common Design Type

1962, Sept. 8

105 CD110 30fr vio, bluish grn, red & gold 55 55

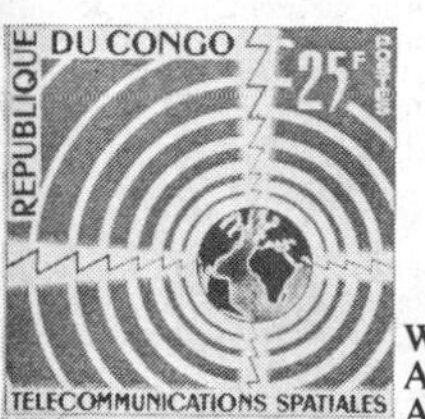

Waves Around Globe A11a

Design: 100fr, Orbit patterns around globe.

1963, Sept. 19 ***Perf. 12½***

106 A11a 25fr org, grn & ultra 40 30
107 A11a 100fr lt red brn, bl & plum 1.40 1.10

Issued to publicize space communications.

King Makoko's Collar — A12

Design: 15fr, Kébékébé mask.

Unwmk.

1963, Oct. 21 **Engr.** ***Perf. 13***

108 A12 10fr blk & ol bis 15 10
109 A12 15fr brn, blk, bl, yel & red 25 12

UNESCO Emblem, Scales and Tree — A12a

1963, Dec. 10 **Unwmk.** ***Perf. 13***

110 A12a 25fr grn, dk bl & brn 35 25

Issued to commemorate the 15th anniversary of the Universal Declaration of Human Rights.

Barograph and WMO Emblem A12b

1964, Mar. 23 **Engr.**

111 A12b 50fr grn, red brn & ultra 65 65

Fourth World Meteorological Day.

Mechanic with Machine — A13

1964, Apr. 8

112 A13 20fr grnsh bl, mag & dk brn 32 20

Training of technicians.

Corn and Tools — A14

1964, Apr. 24 **Unwmk.** ***Perf. 13***

113 A14 80fr brn, grn & brn car 95 50

Importance of manual labor.

Diaboua Ballet — A15

Kebekebe Dance — A16

Carved Figure — A17

1964, May 8 **Engr.**

114 A15 30fr multi 50 30
115 A16 60fr multi 90 60

1964, May 22

116 A17 50fr brn red & sep 65 50

Classroom A18

1964, May 26

117 A18 25fr dk brn, red & bl 32 20

Issued to publicize education.

Type of Air Post Issue, 1963, Inscribed: "Ier ANNIVERSAIRE DE LA REVOLUTION/FETE NATIONALE/15 AOUT 1964"

1964, Aug. 15 **Photo.** ***Perf. 13x12***

118 AP5 20fr lt bl, red, ocher, dk brn & grn 27 15

Issued to commemorate the first anniversary of the revolution and the National Feast Day, Aug. 15.

Fire Squid A19

Design: 15fr, Johnson's deep-sea angler (fish).

1964, Oct. 20 **Engr.** ***Perf. 13***

119 A19 2fr ver, lt grn & brn 10 8
120 A19 15fr vio, lt ol grn & dp cl 35 20

Cooperation Issue

Common Design Type

1964, Nov. 7 **Unwmk.** ***Perf. 13***

121 CD119 25fr car, brt grn & dk brn 35 25

Communications Emblems — A20

1965, Jan. 1 **Litho.** ***Perf. 12½x13***

122 A20 25fr ol, red brn & blk 40 25

Issued to commemorate the establishment of the national postal administration.

Sitatunga A21

Dancer on Stilts A22

Design: 20fr, Elephant (horiz.).

1965, Mar. 15 **Engr.** ***Perf. 13***

123 A21 15fr redsh brn, dl grn & bl 30 15
124 A21 20fr blk, dp bl & sl grn 30 15
125 A22 85fr lil & multi 1.15 90

Pres. Alphonse Massamba-Debat A23

1965-66 **Photo.** ***Perf. 12x12½***

126 A23 20fr dk brn, grn & yel 25 15
127 A23 25fr brn, bl grn, emer & blk ('66) 32 15
128 A23 30fr brn, bl grn, org & blk ('66) 40 20

Soccer Player — A24

Designs: 25fr, Games' emblem (map of Africa and runners). 50fr, Field ball player. 85fr, Runner. 100fr, Bicyclist.

1965, July 17 **Photo.** ***Perf. 12½***

Size: 28x28mm.

129 A24 25fr blk, red, yel & grn 32 20

Size: 34x34mm.

130 A24 40fr yel grn & multi 60 40
131 A24 50fr red & multi 65 40
132 A24 85fr blk & multi 1.10 70
133 A24 100fr yel & multi 1.35 85
a. Min. sheet of 5 4.75 4.75
Nos. 129-133 (5) 4.02 2.55

Issued to commemorate the First African Games, Brazzaville, July 18-25. No. 133a contains one each of Nos. 129-133. Size: 136½x169mm.

Arms of Congo — A25

1965, Nov. 15 **Litho.** ***Perf. 12½x13***

134 A25 20fr multi 28 15

Cooperative Village A26

Design: 30fr, Gymnastic drill team with streamers.

1966, Feb. 18 ***Perf. 12½x13***

135 A26 25fr multi 28 15
136 A26 30fr multi 40 25

Sculptured Mask — A27

Designs: 30fr, Weaver, painting. 85fr, String instrument, painting (horiz.).

Perf. 13x12½, 12½x13

1966, Apr. 9 **Photo.**

137 A27 30fr multi 40 20
138 A27 85fr multi 1.10 65
139 A27 90fr multi 1.25 70

Issued to publicize the International Negro Arts Festival, Dakar, Senegal, Apr. 1-24.

Men and Clocks A28

1966, Apr. 15 *Perf. 12½x12*

140 A28 70fr pale brn, ocher & dk brn 1.10 45

Issued to publicize the introduction of the shorter work day (less lunch time, earlier quitting time).

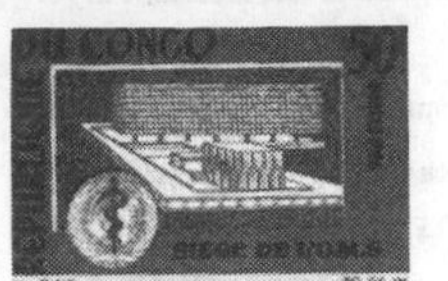

WHO Headquarters, Geneva — A29

1966, May 3 Photo. *Perf. 12½x13*

141 A29 50fr org yel, vio & bl 40 25

Issued to commemorate the inauguration of the World Health Organization Headquarters, Geneva.

Church of St. Peter Claver A30

Women's Basketball A31

1966, June 15 Photo. *Perf. 13x12½*

142 A30 70fr multi 1.10 45

1966, July 15 Engr. *Perf. 13*

Sport: 1fr, Women's volleyball (horiz.). 3fr, Women's field ball (horiz.). 5fr, Athletes of various races. 10fr, Torch bearer. 15fr, Soccer and gold medal of First African Games.

143 A31 1fr ultra, choc & ol 6 6
144 A31 2fr choc, grn & bl 8 6
145 A31 3fr dk grn, dk car & choc 10 8
146 A31 5fr sl, emer & choc 12 10
147 A31 10fr dl bl, dk grn & vio 25 12
148 A31 15fr vio, car & choc 30 18
Nos. 143-148 (6) 91 60

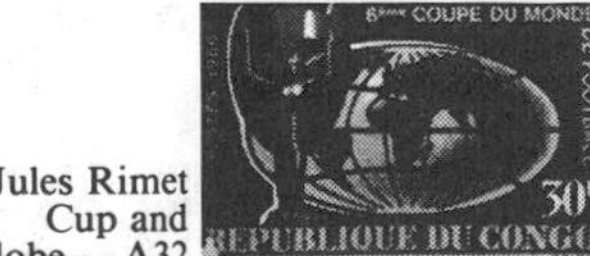

Jules Rimet Cup and Globe — A32

1966, July 15 Photo. *Perf. 12½x12*

149 A32 30fr brt red, gold, blk & bl 50 27

Issued to commemorate the 8th World Soccer Cup Championship, Wembley, England, July 11-30.

Savorgnan de Brazza School A33

1966, Sept. 15 Photo. *Perf. 12½x12*

150 A33 30fr dk pur, grn, yel & blk 40 20

Canceled-to-order stamps are often from remainders. Most collectors of canceled stamps prefer postally used specimens.

Pointe-Noire Railroad Station A34

1966, Oct. 15 Engr. *Perf. 13*

151 A34 60fr grn, red & brn 85 35

Student with Microscope A35

Balumbu Mask A36

1966, Nov. 28 Engr. *Perf. 13*

152 A35 90fr brn, grn & ind 1.20 75

Issued to commemorate the 20th anniversary of UNESCO (United Nations Educational, Scientific and Cultural Organization).

1966, Dec. 12 Engr. *Perf. 13*

Masks: 10fr, Kuyu. 15fr, Bakwele. 20fr, Bateke.

153 A36 5fr car rose & dk brn 12 8
154 A36 10fr Prus bl & brn 20 12
155 A36 15fr sep, dl org & dk bl 25 13
156 A36 20fr dp bl & multi 28 15

Order of the Revolution and Map — A37

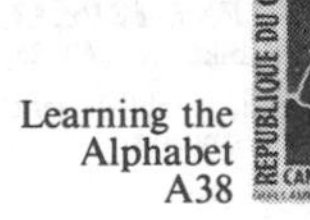

Learning the Alphabet A38

Design: 45fr, Harvesting and loading sugar cane, and sugar mill.

Perf. 12x12½, 12½x12

1967, March 15 **Photo.**

157 A37 20fr org & multi 28 15
158 A38 25fr blk, ocher & dk car 32 20
159 A38 45fr blk, yel grn & lt bl 55 28

Issued to honor the members of the Order of the Revolution (20fr); to publicize the literacy campaign (25fr); to publicize sugar production (45fr).

Mahatma Gandhi A39

Fruit Vendor A40

1967, Apr. 21 Engr. *Perf. 13*

160 A39 90fr bl & blk 1.10 60

Issued in memory of Mohandas K. Gandhi (1869-1948), Hindu nationalist leader.

1967, June Photo. *Perf. 13x12½*

Dolls: 5fr, "Elegant Lady." 25fr, Woman pounding saka-saka. 30fr, Mother and child.

161 A40 5fr gold & multi 12 12
162 A40 10fr yel grn & multi 20 15
163 A40 25fr lt ultra & multi 32 20
164 A40 30fr multi 40 25

ITY Emblem, Village and Waterfall A41

1967, July 5 Engr. *Perf. 13*

165 A41 60fr rose cl, org & ol grn 80 50

Issued for International Tourist Year, 1967.

Symbols of Cooperation A42

Arms of Brazzaville A43

Europafrica Issue, 1967

1967, July 20 Photo. *Perf. 12x12½*

166 A42 50fr multi 65 32

1967, Aug. 15 Litho. *Perf. 12½x13*

167 A43 30fr yel & multi 45 20

Fourth anniversary of the revolution.

U.N. Emblem, Dove and People A44

Boy and UNICEF Emblem A45

1967, Oct. 24 Photo. *Perf. 13x12½*

168 A44 90fr bl, dk brn, red brn & yel 1.35 70

Issued for United Nations Day, Oct. 24.

1967, Dec. 11 Engr. *Perf. 13*

169 A45 90fr mar, blk & ultra 1.20 65

Issued to commemorate the 21st anniversary of UNICEF (United Nations International Children's Emergency Fund).

Albert Luthuli, Dove and Globe A46

1968, Jan. 29 Engr. *Perf. 13*

170 A46 30fr brt grn & ol bis 40 25

Issued in memory of Albert Luthuli (1899-1967) of South Africa, winner of 1960 Nobel Peace Prize.

Arms of Pointe Noire — A47

1968, Feb. 20 Litho. *Perf. 12½x13*

171 A47 10fr brt pink & multi 15 12

Motherhood A48

Mayombe Viaduct A49

1968, May 25 Engr. *Perf. 13*

172 A48 15fr dk car rose, sky bl & blk 25 15

Issued for Mother's Day.

1968, June 24

173 A49 45fr mar, sl grn & bl 50 25

Daimler, 1889 — A50

Antique Cars: 20fr, Berliet, 1897. 60fr, Peugeot, 1898. 80fr, Renault, 1900. 85fr, Fiat, 1902.

1968, July 29 Photo. *Perf. 13x12½*

174 A50 5fr ocher & multi 15 15
175 A50 20fr multi 30 25
176 A50 60fr cit & multi 85 45
177 A50 80fr multi 1.10 60
178 A50 85fr multi 1.20 70
Nos. 174-178 (5) 3.60 2.15

Tanker, Refinery and Map of Area Served — A50a

1968, July 30 *Perf. 12½*

179 A50a 30fr multi 40 18

Issued to commemorate the opening of the Port Gentil (Gabon) Refinery, June 12, 1968.

U.N. Emblem and Tree of Life — A51

1968, Nov. 28 **Engr.** ***Perf. 13***
180 A51 25fr dk grn, red & dp lil 40 18

Issued for the 20th anniversary of the World Health Organization.

Development Bank Issue
Common Design Type

1969, Sept. 10 **Engr.** ***Perf. 13***
181 CD130 25fr car rose, grn & ocher 35 15
182 CD130 30fr bl, grn & ocher 40 15

Issued to commemorate the 5th anniversary of the African Development Bank.

Bicycle A52

Designs (Bicycles and Motorcycles): 75fr, Hirondelle. 80fr, Folding bicycle. 85fr, Peugeot. 100fr, Excelsior Manxman. 150fr, Norton. 200fr, Brough Superior "Old Bill." 300fr, Matchless and N.L.G.-J.A.P.S.

196, Oct. 6 **Engr.** ***Perf. 13***
183 A52 50fr dk ol, org & rose lil 65 32
184 A52 75fr org, rose lake & blk 95 40
185 A52 80fr lil, bl & sl grn 1.00 45
186 A52 85fr dk ol, gray & bl grn 1.10 55
187 A52 100fr blk, vio bl, dk brn & car 1.25 65
188 A52 150fr blk, red brn & brn ol 1.60 90
189 A52 200fr bl grn, sl grn & brt rose lil 2.60 1.10
190 A52 300fr blk, brt rose lil & grn 3.50 1.90
Nos. 183-190 (8) 12.65 6.27

Mayombe Train and Tourist Year Emblem A53

Design: 40fr, Train and Mbamba Tunnel (vert.).

Perf. 13x12½, 12½x13

1969, Oct. 20 **Photo.**
191 A53 40fr multi 55 27
192 A53 60fr multi 70 32

Issued for African Tourist Year.

Loutete Cement Works A54

Designs (Loutete Cement Works): 15fr, Mixing tower (vert.). 25fr, Cable transport (vert.). 30fr, General view of plant.

1969, Dec. 10 **Engr.** ***Perf. 13***
193 A54 10fr dk gray, rose cl & dk ol 13 8
194 A54 15fr Prus bl, red brn & pur 18 13
195 A54 25fr mar, brn & Prus bl 32 18
196 A54 30fr vio brn, ultra & blk 35 22
a. Min. sheet of 4 1.25 1.25

Issued to publicize the cement factory at Loutete. No. 196a contains one each of Nos. 193-196. Size: 170x100mm.

ASECNA ISSUE
Common Design Type

1969, Dec. 12
197 CD132 100fr dl brn 1.35 65

Pineapple Harvest and ILO Emblem A55

Design: 30fr, Worker at lathe and ILO emblem.

1969, Dec. 20 **Engr.** ***Perf. 13***
198 A55 25fr bl, ol & brn 32 18
199 A55 30fr rose red, choc & sl 35 22

Issued to commemorate the 50th anniversary of the International Labor Organization.

SOTEXCO Textile Plant, Kinsoundi A56

Designs: 20fr, Women in spinnery. 25fr, Hand-printing textiles. 30fr, Checking woven cloth.

1970, Jan. 20
200 A56 15fr grn, blk & lil 18 13
201 A56 20fr plum, car & sl grn 22 13
202 A56 25fr bl, sl & brn 32 18
203 A56 30fr gray, car rose & brn 40 18

Hotel Cosmos, Brazzaville A57

1970, Jan. 30
204 A57 90fr sl grn, bl & red brn 1.00 45

Linzolo Church — A58

Diosso Gorge A59

Design: 90fr, Foulakari waterfall.

1970 **Engr.** ***Perf. 13***
205 A58 25fr multi 32 18
206 A59 70fr multi 80 35
207 A59 90fr multi 1.10 45

Issue dates: 25fr, Feb. 10; others, Feb. 25.

Volvaria Esculenta — A60

Mushrooms: 10fr, Termitomyces entolomoides. 15fr, Termitomyces microcarpus. 25fr, Termitomyces aurantiacus. 30fr, Termitomyces mammiformis. 50fr, Tremella fuciformis.

1970, Mar. 31 **Photo.** ***Perf. 13***
208 A60 5fr Prus bl & multi 13 8
209 A60 10fr brt car rose & multi 15 12
210 A60 15fr vio bl & multi 25 18
211 A60 25fr dk grn & multi 45 22
212 A60 30fr pur & multi 50 27
213 A60 50fr brt bl & multi 70 45
Nos. 208-213 (6) 2.18 1.32

Laying Coaxial Cable — A61

Design: 30fr, Full view of rail car; 3 cable layers on railway roadbed.

1970, Apr. 30 **Engr.** ***Perf. 13***
214 A61 25fr dk brn & multi 32 18
215 A61 30fr brn & multi 40 22

Issued to publicize the laying of the coaxial cable linking Brazzaville and Pointe Noire.

U.P.U. Headquarters Issue
Common Design Type

1970, May 20
216 CD133 30fr dk pur, gray & mag 45 22

Mother Feeding Child A62

Dag Hammarskjold and U.N. Emblem A63

Design: 90fr, Mother nursing infant.

1970, May 30 **Photo.**
217 A62 85fr vio bl & multi 1.00 55
218 A62 90fr lil & multi 1.10 60

Issued for Mother's Day.

1970, June 20 **Engr.** ***Perf. 13***

Designs (U.N. Emblem and): No. 220, Trygve Lie (horiz.). No. 221, U Thant (horiz.).

219 A63 100fr scar, dk red & dk pur 1.25 75
220 A63 100fr dk red, ultra & ind 1.25 75
221 A63 100fr grn, emer & dk red 1.25 75
a. Souvenir sheet of 3 4.25 4.25

Issued to commemorate the 25th anniversary of the United Nations and to honor its Secretaries General. No. 221a contains one each of Nos. 219-221; U.N. emblem and scarlet inscriptions in margin. Size: 129½x100mm.

Brillantaisia Vogeliana A64

Sternotomis Variabilis — A65

Designs (Plants and Beetles): 2fr, Plectranthus decurrens. 3fr, Myrianthemum mirabile. 5fr, Connarus griffonianus. 15fr, Chelorrhina polyphemus. 20fr, Metopodontus savagei.

Perf. 12½x12, 12x12½

1970, June 30 **Photo.**
222 A64 1fr dk grn & multi 5 5
223 A64 2fr multi 8 5
224 A64 3fr ind & multi 10 6
225 A64 5fr lem & multi 12 10
226 A65 10fr lil & multi 15 12
227 A65 15fr org & multi 22 12
228 A65 20fr multi 27 18
Nos. 222-228 (7) 99 68

Stegosaurus A66

Prehistoric Fauna: 20fr, Dinotherium (vert.). 60fr, Brachiosaurus (vert.). 80fr, Arsinoitherium.

1970, July 20
229 A66 15fr dl grn, ocher & red brn 25 15
230 A66 20fr lt bl & multi 30 20
231 A66 60fr lt bl & multi 75 28
232 A66 80fr lt bl & multi 1.10 50

Mikado 141, 1932 — A67

Locomotives: 60fr, Steam locomotive 130+032, 1947. 75fr, Alsthom BB 1100, 1962. 85fr, Diesel BB BB 302, 1969.

1970, Aug. 20 **Engr.** ***Perf. 13***
233 A67 40fr mag, bl grn & blk 60 30
234 A67 60fr blk, bl & grn 80 40
235 A67 75fr red, bl & blk 1.00 45
236 A67 85fr car, sl grn & ocher 1.25 55

Cogniauxia Padolaena A68

Green Night Adder A69

Tropical Flowers: 2fr, Celosia cristata. 5fr, Plumeria acutifolia. 10fr, Bauhinia variegata. 15fr, Poinsettia. 20fr, Thunbergia grandiflora.

1971, Feb. 10 **Photo.** ***Perf. 12x12½***
237 A68 1fr lil & multi 8 7
238 A68 2fr yel & multi 8 7
239 A68 5fr ultra & multi 12 8
240 A68 10fr yel & multi 20 13
241 A68 15fr multi 32 18
242 A68 20fr dk red & multi 40 18
Nos. 237-242 (6) 1.20 71

Perf. 12x12½, 12½x12

1971, June 26 **Photo.**

Reptiles: 10fr, African Egg-eating snake (horiz.). 15fr, Flap-necked chameleon. 20fr, Nile crocodile (horiz.). 25fr, Rock python (horiz.). 30fr, Gaboon viper. 40fr, Brown house snake (horiz.). 45fr, Jameson's mamba.

243 A69 5fr multi 8 8
244 A69 10fr multi 15 12
245 A69 15fr multi 25 15
246 A69 20fr red & multi 32 25
247 A69 25fr grn & multi 40 32
248 A69 30fr multi 50 40
249 A69 40fr bis & multi 50 45
250 A69 45fr multi 65 50
Nos. 243-250 (8) 2.85 2.27

Foreign postal stationery (stamped envelopes, postal cards and air letter sheets) lies beyond the scope of this Catalogue, which is limited to adhesive postage stamps.

Pseudimbrasia Deyrollei — A70

Caterpillars: 15fr, Bunaea alcinoe (vert.). 20fr, Epiphora vacuna ploetzi. 25fr, Imbrasia eblis. 30fr, Imbrasia dione (vert.). 40fr, Holocera angulata.

1971, July 3 *Perf. 13*

251 A70 10fr ver, blk & grn 20 15
252 A70 15fr multi 25 20
253 A70 20fr yel grn, blk & ocher 32 28
254 A70 25fr multi 40 32
255 A70 30fr red, blk & yel 50 40
256 A70 40fr bl, blk & org 75 55
Nos. 251-256 (6) 2.42 1.90

Cymothoe Sangaris A71

Butterflies and Moths: 40fr, Papilio dardanus (vert.). 75fr, Iolaus timon. 90fr, Papilio phorcas (vert.). 100fr, Euchloron megaera.

Perf. 12½x12, 12x12½

1971, Oct. 15

257 A71 30fr yel & multi 50 32
258 A71 40fr grn & multi 65 45
259 A71 75fr multi 1.10 65
260 A71 90fr multi 1.35 90
261 A71 100fr ultra & multi 1.75 1.25
Nos. 257-261 (5) 5.35 3.57

Black and White Men Working Together — A72

1971, Oct. 30 *Perf. 13x12½*

262 A72 50fr org & multi 50 25

International Year Against Racial Discrimination.

Nos. 214-215 Surcharged

REPUBLIQUE POPULAIRE DU CONGO 30F

INAUGURATION DE LA LIAISON COAXIALE 18-11-71

1971, Nov. 18 **Engr.** *Perf. 13*

263 A61 30fr on 25fr multi 40 25
264 A61 40fr on 30fr multi 50 32

Inauguration of cable service between Brazzaville and Pointe Noire. Words of surcharge arranged differently on No. 264.

Map of Congo — A73

1971, Dec. 31 **Photo.** *Perf. 12½x13*

265 A73 30fr bl & multi 35 25
266 A73 40fr yel grn & multi 40 20
267 A73 100fr gray & multi 1.10 55

"Labor, Democracy, Peace."

Lion — A74

Animals: 2fr, African elephants. 3fr, Leopard. 4fr, Hippopotamus. 5fr, Gorilla (vert.). 20fr, Potto. 30fr, De Brazza's monkey. 40fr, Pygmy chimpanzee (vert.).

1972, Jan. 31 **Engr.** *Perf. 13*

268 A74 1fr grn & multi 5 5
269 A74 2fr dk red & multi 5 5
270 A74 3fr red brn & multi 10 8
271 A74 4fr vio & multi 10 8
272 A74 5fr brn & multi 12 12
273 A74 20fr org & multi 32 25
274 A74 30fr ocher & multi 50 28
275 A74 40fr Prus bl & multi 65 45
Nos. 268-275 (8) 1.89 1.36

WHO Emblem — A75

Design: 50fr, WHO emblem (horiz.).

Perf. 12½x13, 13x12½

1973, June 30 **Typo.**

276 A75 40fr grn & multi 32 15
277 A75 50fr multi 40 20

World Health Organization, 25th anniversary.

Kronenbourg Brewery — A76

Designs (Brewery Trademark and): 40fr, Laboratory. 75fr, Vats and controls. 85fr, Automatic control room. 100fr, Pressure room. 250fr, Bottling plant.

1973, July 15 **Engr.** *Perf. 13*

278 A76 30fr red & multi 25 15
279 A76 40fr red & multi 32 22
280 A76 75fr red & multi 55 32
281 A76 85fr red & multi 80 40
282 A76 100fr red & multi 1.10 60
283 A76 250fr red & multi 2.10 1.10
Nos. 278-283 (6) 5.12 2.79

Kronenbourg Brewery, Brazzaville.

Golwe Locomotive, 1935 — A77

Locomotives: 40fr, Diesel, 1935. 75fr, Diesel Whithcomb, 1946. 85fr, Diesel CC200.

1973, Aug. 1 **Engr.** *Perf. 13*

284 A77 30fr ind & multi 40 25
285 A77 40fr vio bl & multi 50 25
286 A77 75fr multi 90 40
287 A77 85fr multi 1.00 50

No. 225 Surcharged with New Value, 2 Bars, and Overprinted in Ultramarine: "SECHERESSE SOLIDARITE AFRICAINE"

1973, Aug. 16 **Photo.** *Perf. 12½x12*

288 A64 100fr on 5fr multi 80 55

African solidarity in drought emergency.

African Postal Union Issue

Common Design Type

1973, Sept. 12 **Engr.** *Perf. 13*

289 CD137 100fr bl grn, vio & brn 75 40

Bees, Beehive, Honeycomb A78

1973, Dec. 10 **Engr.** *Perf. 13*

290 A78 30fr sl grn, dk red & bl 27 18
291 A78 40fr sl bl, sl grn & lt grn 35 18

"Work and economy."

Family, UN and FAO Emblems A79

Designs: 40fr, Grain, UN and FAO emblems. 100fr, Grain, UN and FAO emblems (vert.).

1973, Dec. 10

292 A79 30fr dk car & dk brn 27 10
293 A79 40fr dk grn, yel & ind 35 15
294 A79 100fr grn, brn & org 80 50

World Food Program, 10th anniversary.

Amilcar Cabral, Cattle and Child — A80

1974, July 15 **Engr.** *Perf. 13*

295 A80 100fr multi 75 50

First death anniversary of Amilcar Cabral (1924-1973), leader of anti-Portuguese guerrilla activity in Portuguese Guinea.

Félix Eboué, Cross of Lorraine A81

1974, Aug. 31 **Litho.** *Perf. 13*

296 A81 30fr bl & multi 25 15
297 A81 40fr brt pink & multi 35 20

Félix A. Eboué (1884-1944), Governor of Chad, first colonial governor to join Free French in WWII, 30th death anniversary.

Pineapples A82

1974, Nov. 12

298 A82 30fr *shown* 25 15
299 A82 30fr *Bananas* 25 15
300 A82 30fr *Safous* 25 15
301 A82 40fr *Avocados* 35 20
302 A82 40fr *Mangos* 35 20
303 A82 40fr *Papaya* 35 20
304 A82 40fr *Oranges* 35 20
Nos. 298-304 (7) 2.15 1.25

Charles de Gaulle and Conference Building — A83

1974, Nov. 25 **Engr.** *Perf. 13*

305 A83 100fr multi 75 50

Brazzaville Conference, 25th anniversary.

George Stephenson and Various Locomotives — A84

1974, Dec. 15

306 A84 75fr sl grn & ol 55 35

George Stephenson (1781-1848), English inventor and railroad founder.

UDEAC Issue

Presidents and Flags of Cameroun, CAR, Congo, Gabon and Meeting Center — A84a

1974, Dec. 8 **Photo.** *Perf. 13*

307 A84a 40fr gold & multi 35 20

See note after Cameroun No. 595.
See No. C195.

Irish Setter — A85

Designs: Dogs.

1974, Dec. 15 **Photo.** *Perf. 13x13½*

308 A85 30fr *shown* 35 18
309 A85 40fr *Borzoi* 45 22
310 A85 75fr *Pointer* 75 35
311 A85 100fr *Great Dane* 1.00 55

1974, Dec. 15

Designs: Cats.

312 A85 30fr *Havana chestnut* 35 15
313 A85 40fr *Red Persian* 45 18
314 A85 75fr *Blue British* 75 35
315 A85 100fr *African serval* 1.00 55

Labor Party Flags and People A86

Design: 40fr, Hands holding flowers and tools.

1974, Dec. 31 Engr. *Perf. 13x12½*

316 A86 30fr red & multi 25 12
317 A86 40fr red & multi 35 18

5th anniversary of Congolese Labor Party and of introduction of red flag.

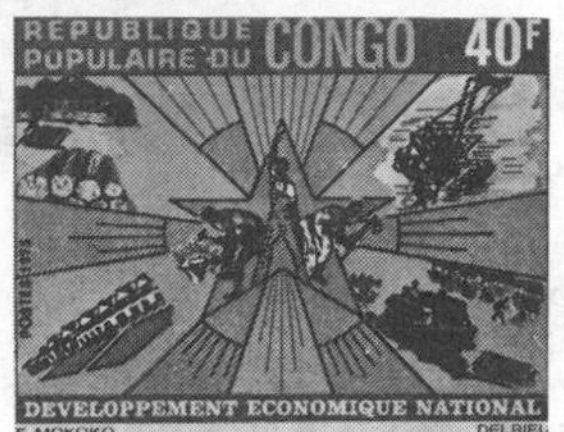

Symbols of Development — A87

U Thant and UN Headquarters — A88

Paul G. Hoffman and UN Emblem A89

Perf. 13x12½, 12½x13

1975, Feb. 28 Litho.

318 A87 40fr multi 32 18
319 A88 50fr lt bl & multi 35 22
320 A89 50fr yel & multi 35 22

National economic development.

Map of China and Mao Tse-tung — A90

1975, Mar. 9 Engr. *Perf. 13*

321 A90 75fr multi 60 40

25th anniversary of the People's Republic of China.

Woman Breaking Bonds, Women's Activities, Map of Congo A91

1975, June 20 Litho. *Perf. 12½*

322 A91 40fr gold & multi 40 20

Revolutionary Union of Congolese Women, URFC, 10th anniversary.

CARA Soccer Team — A92

Design: 40fr, Team captain and manager receiving trophy (vert.).

1975, July 15 Litho. *Perf. 12½*

323 A92 30fr multi 27 18
324 A92 40fr multi 35 22

CARA team, winners of African Soccer Cup 1974.

Citroen, 1935 — A93

Designs: Early autombiles.

1975, July 17 *Perf. 12*

325 A93 30fr *shown* 25 20
326 A93 40fr *Alfa Romeo, 1911* 35 20
327 A93 50fr *Rolls Royce, 1926* 40 30
328 A93 75fr *Duryea, 1893* 60 45

Tipoye Transport — A94

Design: 40fr, Dugout canoe.

1975, Aug. 5

329 A94 30fr multi 22 13
330 A94 40fr multi 32 18

Traditional means of transportation.

Raising Red Flag — A95

Design: 40fr, National Conference.

1975, Aug. 15

331 A95 30fr multi 25 20
332 A95 40fr multi 35 20

2nd anniversary of installation of popular power (30fr) and 3rd anniversary of National Conference (40fr).

Line Fishing — A96

Woman Pounding "Foufou" — A97

Traditional Fishing: 30fr, Trap fishing (horiz.). 60fr, Spear fishing. 90fr, Net fishing (horiz.).

1975, Aug. 31 Litho. *Perf. 12*

333 A96 30fr multi 25 20
334 A96 40fr multi 35 20
335 A96 60fr multi 50 30
336 A96 90fr multi 70 50

1975, Sept. 5

Household Tasks: No. 338, Woman chopping wood. 40fr, Woman preparing manioc (horiz.).

337 A97 30fr multi 25 15
338 A97 30fr multi 25 15
339 A97 40fr multi 35 20

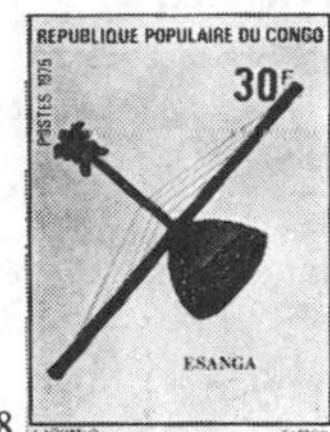

Esanga — A98

Musical Instruments: 40fr, Kalakwa. 60fr, Likembe. 75fr, Ngongui.

1975, Sept. 20 *Perf. 12½*

340 A98 30fr blk & brn 25 15
341 A98 40fr org & multi 35 20
342 A98 60fr grn & multi 50 35
343 A98 75fr multi 60 40

Dzeke (Congolese) Shell Money A99

Ancient Money: No. 346, like No. 344. Nos. 345, 347, Okengo, Congolese, iron bar. 40fr, Gallic coin, c. 60 B.C. 50fr, Roman denarius, 37 B.C. 60fr, Danubian coin, 2nd century B.C. 85fr, Greek stater, 4th century B.C.

1975-76 Engr. *Perf. 13*

344 A99 30fr red & multi 25 20
345 A99 30fr vio & multi 25 20
346 A99 35fr ol & multi 30 20
347 A99 35fr dk car rose & multi 30 20
348 A99 40fr Prus bl & brn 35 20
349 A99 50fr Prus bl & ol 40 25
350 A99 60fr dk grn & brn 50 35
351 A99 85fr mag & sl grn 65 40
Nos. 344-351 (8) 3.00 2.00

Nos. 346-347 inscribed "1976" and issued Mar. 1976; others issued Oct. 5, 1975.

Moschops — A100

Pre-historic Animals: 70fr, Tyrannosaurus. 95fr, Cryptocleidus. 100fr, Stegosaurus.

1975, Oct. 15 Litho. *Perf. 13*

352 A100 55fr multi 45 30
353 A100 75fr multi 60 35
354 A100 95fr multi 75 50
355 A100 100fr multi 80 55

Albert Schweitzer — A101

1975, Oct. 15 Engr.

356 A101 75fr ol, brn & red 60 40

Albert Schweitzer (1875-1965), medical missionary, birth centenary.

Alexander Fleming A102

Designs: No. 358, AndréMarie Ampère. No. 359, Clement Ader.

1975, Nov. 15 Engr. *Perf. 13*

357 A102 60fr brn, grn & blk 50 30
358 A102 95fr blk, red & grn 75 55
359 A102 95fr red, bl & ind 75 55

Alexander Fleming (1881-1955), developer of penicillin, 20th death anniversary; André Marie Ampere (1775-1836), physicist, bicentenary of birth; Clement Ader (1841-1925), aviation pioneer, 50th death anniversary.

U.N. Emblem "ONU" and "30" — A103

1975, Dec. 20 Engr. *Perf. 13*

360 A103 95fr car, ultra & grn 75 55

United Nations, 30th anniversary.

Women's Broken Chain — A104

Design: 60fr, Equality between man and woman, globe, IWY emblem.

1975, Dec. 20 Litho. *Perf. 12½*

361 A104 35fr mag, ocher & gray 30 20
362 A104 60fr ultra, brn & blk 50 35

International Women's Year, 1975.

Pres. Marien Ngouabi, Flag and Workers — A105

Echo of the P.C.T. A106

Perf. 12½x12, 13x12½

1975, Dec. 31 Litho.

363 A105 30fr multi 25 15
364 A106 35fr multi 30 15

6th anniversary of the Congolese Labor Party (P.C.T.). See No. C215.

A.G. Bell and 1876 Telephone A107

1976, Apr. 25 Litho. *Perf. 12½x13*

365 A107 35fr yel, brn & org brn 30 20

Centenary of first telephone call by Alexander Graham Bell, Mar. 10, 1876. See No. C229.

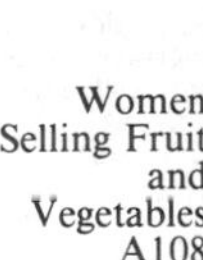

Women Selling Fruit and Vegetables A108

Design: 60fr, Market scene.

1976, Sept. 19 Litho. *Perf. 12½x13*

366 A108 35fr multi 30 20
367 A108 60fr multi 50 30

Congolese Coiffure — A109

Designs: Various women's hair styles.

1976, Oct. 10 Litho. *Perf. 13*

368 A109 35fr multi 30 20
369 A109 60fr multi 50 35
370 A109 95fr multi 75 50
371 A109 100fr multi 80 55

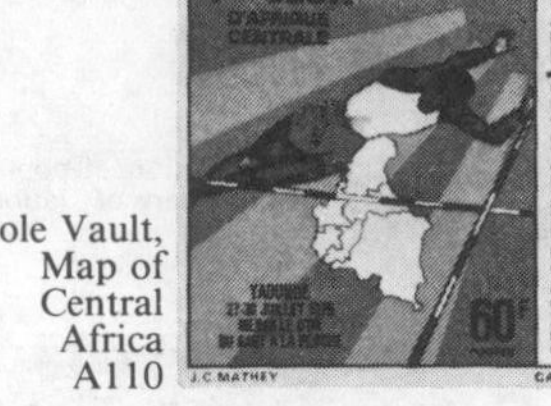

Pole Vault, Map of Central Africa A110

Design: 95fr, Long jump and map of Central Africa.

1976, Oct. 25 *Perf. 12½*

372 A110 60fr yel & multi 50 35
373 A110 95fr yel & multi 75 55

Gold medalists, 1st Central African Games, Yaounde, July 27-30, 1975. See Nos. C230-C231.

Antelope A111

1976, Oct. 27 Litho. *Perf. 12½*

Size: 36x36mm.

374 A111 5fr *shown* 5 5
375 A111 10fr *Buffalos* 10 5
376 A111 15fr *Hippopotamus* 10 7
377 A111 20fr *Wart hog* 15 10
378 A111 25fr *Elephants* 20 13
Nos. 374-378 (5) 60 40

1976, Dec. 8

Designs: Birds.

Size: 26x36mm.

379 A111 5fr *Saddle-bill storks* 5 5

Size: 36x36mm.

380 A111 10fr *Malachite kingfisher* 10 8
381 A111 20fr *Crowned cranes* 15 12

Bicycling, Map of Participants A112

Heliotrope A113

1976, Dec. 21 Photo. *Perf. 12½x13*

Designs (Map and): 60fr, Fieldball. 80fr, Running. 95fr, Soccer.

382 A112 35fr multi 30 20
383 A112 60fr multi 50 35
384 A112 80fr multi 65 50
385 A112 95fr multi 75 55

First Central African Games, Libreville, Gabon, June-July 1976.

1976, Dec. 23 Photo. *Perf. 12½x13*

Flowers: 5fr, Water lilies. 15fr, Bird-of-paradise flower.

386 A113 5fr multi 5 5
387 A113 10fr multi 20 5
388 A113 15fr multi 30 10

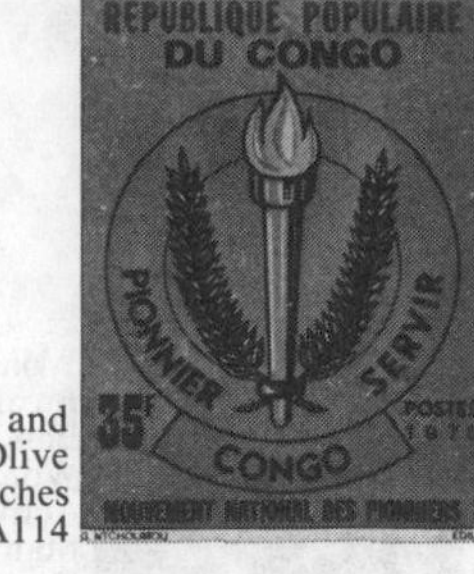

Torch and Olive Branches A114

1976, Dec. 25 Litho. *Perf. 12½x13*

389 A114 35fr multi 20 30

National Pioneer Movement.

The Spirit of '76 A115

Designs: 125fr, Pulling down George III statue. 150fr, Battle of Princeton. 175fr, Generals of Revolutionary War. 200fr, Burgoyne's surrender at Saratoga. 500fr, Battle of Lexington.

1976, Dec. 29 Litho. *Perf. 14*

390 A115 100fr multi 1.00 38
391 A115 125fr multi 1.25 50
392 A115 150fr multi 1.35 55
393 A115 175fr multi 1.65 75
394 A115 200fr multi 1.85 85
Nos. 390-394 (5) 7.10 3.03

Souvenir Sheet

395 A115 500fr multi 4.75 2.00

American Bicentennial.

No. 395 has green and blue margin, black marginal inscription. Size: 114x72mm.

Dugout Canoe Race — A116

Design: 60fr, 2-man dugout canoes.

1977, Mar. 27 Litho. *Perf. 13x13½*

396 A116 35fr multi 35 20
397 A116 60fr multi 55 35

Dugout canoe races on Congo River.

Lilan Goua A117

Fresh-water Fish: 15fr, Liko ko. 25fr, Liyan ga. 35fr, Mbessi. 60fr, Mongandza.

1977, June 15 Litho. *Perf. 12½*

398 A117 10fr multi 10 7
399 A117 15fr multi 18 10
400 A117 25fr multi 25 15
401 A117 35fr multi 35 20
402 A117 60fr multi 55 35
Nos. 398-402 (5) 1.43 87

Traditional Headdress — A118

Design: 60fr, Leopard cap.

1977, June 30 Litho. *Perf. 12½*

403 A118 35fr multi 30 20
404 A118 60fr multi 50 35

See Nos. C234-C235.

Bondjo Wrestling — A119

Designs: 40fr, 50fr, Bondjo wrestling (different). 40fr, horiz.

1977, July 15

405 A119 25fr multi 20 15
406 A119 40fr multi 30 25
407 A119 50fr multi 40 30

"Schwaben" LZ 10, 1911 — A120

Zeppelins: 60fr, "Viktoria Luise." LZ 11, 1913. 100fr, LZ 120. 200fr, LZ 127. 300fr, "Graf Zeppelin II" LZ 130.

1977, Aug. 5 Litho. *Perf. 11*

408 A120 40fr multi 35 18
409 A120 60fr multi 60 30
410 A120 100fr multi 95 35
411 A120 200fr multi 1.90 80
412 A120 300fr multi 3.00 1.20
Nos. 408-412 (5) 6.80 2.83

History of the Zeppelin. Exist imperf. See No. C236.

Coat of Arms and Rising Sun — A121

1977, Aug. 15

413 A121 40fr multi 30 25

14th anniversary of the revolution.

Victor Hugo and The Hunchback of Notre Dame — A122

Designs (Hugo and): 60fr, Les Miserables. 100fr, Les Travailleurs de la Mer (octopus).

1977, Aug. 20 Engr. *Perf. 13*
414 A122 35fr multi 30 20
415 A122 60fr multi 50 35
416 A122 100fr multi 80 60

Victor Hugo (1802-1885), French novelist.

Mao Tse-tung
A123

Lithographed; Gold Embossed
1977, Sept. 9 *Perf. 12x12½*
417 A123 400fr red & gold 3.25 2.50

Chairman Mao Tse-tung (1893-1976), Chinese Communist leader, first death anniversary.

Peter Paul Rubens
A124

1977, Sept. 20 Gold Embossed
418 A124 600fr gold & lt bl 4.75 4.00

Peter Paul Rubens (1577-1640), painter.

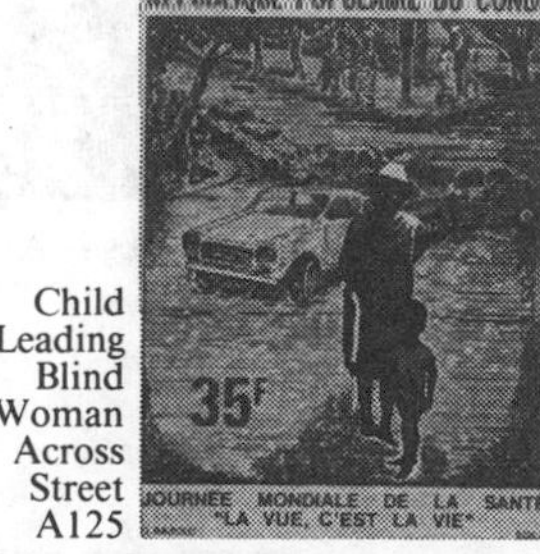

Child Leading Blind Woman Across Street
A125

1977, Oct. 22 Litho. *Perf. 12½x13*
419 A125 35fr multi 30 20

World Health Day: To see is life.

Paul Kamba and Records
A126

1977, Oct. 29
420 A126 100fr multi 80 6

Paul Kamba (1912-1950), musician.

Trajan Vuia and Flying Machine — A127

Designs: 75fr, Louis Bleriot and plane. 100fr, Roland Garros and plane. 200fr, Charles Lindbergh and Spirit of St. Louis. 300fr, Tupolev Tu-144. 500fr, Lindbergh and Spirit of St. Louis over ship in Atlantic.

1977, Nov. 18 Litho. *Perf. 14*
421 A127 60fr multi 60 35
422 A127 75fr multi 70 42
423 A127 100fr multi 95 42
424 A127 200fr multi 1.90 90
425 A127 300fr multi 3.00 1.40
Nos. 421-425 (5) 7.15 3.49

Souvenir Sheet
426 A127 500fr multi 4.00 1.85

History of aviation. No. 426 has multicolored margin showing Spirit of St. Louis at Orly Airport, Paris. Size: 117x91mm.

Elizabeth II and Prince Philip
A128

Design: 300fr, Elizabeth II wearing Crown.

1977, Dec. 21
427 A128 250fr multi 2.40 1.30
428 A128 300fr multi 3.00 1.40

25th anniversary of the reign of Queen Elizabeth II. See No. C239.

King Baudouin
A129

Design: No. 430, Charles de Gaulle.

1977, Dec. 21
429 A129 200fr multi 1.90 95
430 A129 200fr multi 1.90 95

King Baudouin of Belgium and Charles de Gaulle, president of France.

Ambete Sculpture — A130

Design: 85fr, Babembe sculpture.

1978, Feb. 18 Engr. *Perf. 13*
431 A130 35fr lt brn & multi 30 20
432 A130 85fr lt grn & multi 70 50

Congolese art.

St. Simon, by Rubens
A131

Rubens Paintings: 140fr, Duke of Lerma. 200fr, Madonna and Saints. 300fr, Rubens and his Wife Helena Fourment. 500fr, Farm at Laeken.

1978, Mar. 7 Litho. *Perf. 13½x14*
433 A131 60fr gold & multi 60 25
434 A131 140fr gold & multi 1.35 45
435 A131 200fr gold & multi 1.90 70
436 A131 300fr gold & multi 3.00 1.00

Souvenir Sheet
437 A131 500fr gold & multi 4.75 2.00

Peter Paul Rubens (1577-1640), 400th birth anniversary. No. 437 contains one stamp; multicolored margin shows entire painting. Size: 106x123mm.

Pres. Ngouabi and Microphones — A132

Designs: 60fr, Ngouabi at his desk (horiz.). 100fr, Portrait.

Perf. 12½x13, 13x12½
1978, Mar. 18 Litho.
438 A132 35fr multi 30 20
439 A132 60fr multi 50 35
440 A132 100fr multi 80 60

Pres. Marien Ngouabi, first death anniversary.

Ferenc Puskas and Argentina '78 Emblem — A133

Players and Emblem: 75fr, Giacinto Facchetti. 100fr, Bobby Moore. 200fr, Raymond Kopa. 300fr, Pele. 500fr, Franz Beckenbauer.

1978, Apr. 4 *Perf. 14x13½*
441 A133 60fr multi 60 33
442 A133 75fr multi 70 40
443 A133 100fr multi 90 45
444 A133 200fr multi 2.00 95
445 A133 300fr multi 2.85 1.35
Nos. 441-445 (5) 7.05 3.48

Souvenir Sheet
446 A133 500fr multi 4.75 2.00

11th World Cup Soccer Championship, Argentina, June 1-25. No. 446 has light and dark blue margin showing soccer ball and net. Size: 136x100mm.

Pearl S. Buck and Chinese Women — A134

Designs: 75fr, Fridtjof Nansen, refugees and Nansen passport. 100fr, Henri Bergson, book and flame. 200fr, Alexander Fleming and Petri dish. 300fr, Gerhart Hauptmann and book. 500fr, Henri Dunant and Red Cross Station.

1978, Apr. 29
447 A134 60fr multi 60 33
448 A134 75fr multi 70 40
449 A134 100fr multi 90 45
450 A134 200fr multi 2.00 95
451 A134 300fr multi 2.85 1.35
Nos. 447-451 (5) 7.05 3.48

Souvenir Sheet
452 A134 500fr multi 4.75 2.00

Nobel Prize winners. No. 452 has multicolored margin with head of Alfred Nobel and inscribed "Nobel." Size: 119x81mm.

African Buffalos
A135

Animals and Wildlife Fund Emblem: 35fr, Okapi (vert.). 85fr, Rhinoceros. 150fr, Chimpanzee (vert.). 200fr, Hippopotamus. 300fr, Buffon's kob (vert.).

1978 *Perf. 14½*
453 A135 35fr multi 35 25
454 A135 60fr multi 60 30
455 A135 85fr multi 80 42
456 A135 150fr multi 1.40 60
457 A135 200fr multi 2.00 85
458 A135 300fr multi 2.85 1.25
Nos. 453-458 (6) 8.00 3.67

Endangered animals.
Issue dates: 35fr, Aug. 11. Others, July 11.

The lack of a price for a listed item does not necessarily indicate rarity.

Emblem, Young People, Gun and Fist — A136

1978, July 28 *Perf. 12½*
459 A136 35fr multi 30 20

11th World Youth Festival, Havana, July 28-Aug. 5.

Pyramids and Camels — A137

Seven Wonders of the Ancient World: 50fr, Hanging Gardens of Babylon. 60fr, Statue of Zeus, Olympia. 95fr, Colossus of Rhodes. 125fr, Mausoleum of Halicarnassus. 150fr, Temple of Artemis, Ephesus. 200fr, Lighthouse, Alexandria. 300fr, Map of Eastern Mediterranean showing locations. (50fr, 60fr, 95fr, 125fr, 200fr, vertical.)

1978, Aug. 12 **Litho.** *Perf. 14*
460 A137 35fr multi 35 18
461 A137 50fr multi 50 25
462 A137 60fr multi 60 30
463 A137 95fr multi 90 45
464 A137 125fr multi 1.20 55
465 A137 150fr multi 1.50 70
466 A137 200fr multi 1.90 85
467 A137 300fr multi 3.00 1.20
Nos. 460-467 (8) 9.95 4.48

Nos. 427-428 Overprinted in Silver: "ANNIVERSAIRE DU COURONNEMENT 1953-1978"

1978, Sept. **Litho.** *Perf. 14*
468 A128 250fr multi 2.00 75
469 A128 300fr multi 2.40 1.00

25th anniversary of corporation of Queen Elizabeth II. See No. C244.

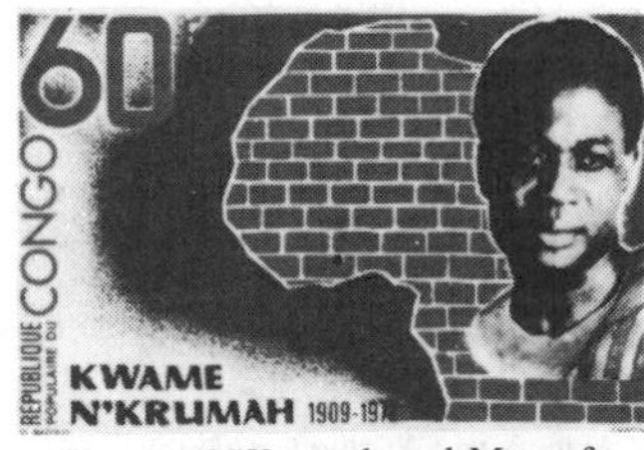

Kwame N'Krumah and Map of Africa — A138

1978, Sept. 23 **Litho.** *Perf. 13x12½*
470 A138 60fr multi 50 25

Kwame N'Krumah (1909-1972), president of Ghana.

Wild Boar Hunt — A139

Designs: 50fr, Fish smoking. 60fr, Hunter with spears and dog (vert.).

1978 **Litho.** *Perf. 12*
471 A139 35fr multi 35 25
472 A139 50fr multi 50 35
473 A139 60fr multi 60 40

Local hunting and fishing.
Issue dates: 35fr, 60fr, Oct. 5; 50fr, Oct. 10.

View of Kalchreut, by Dürer — A140

Paintings by Dürer: 150fr, Elspeth Tucher (vert.). 250fr, "The Great Piece of Turf" (vert.). 350fr, Self-portrait (vert.).

1978, Nov. 23 **Litho.** *Perf. 14*
474 A140 65fr multi 65 42
475 A140 150fr multi 1.50 1.05
476 A140 250fr multi 2.50 1.75
477 A140 350fr multi 3.50 2.50

Albrecht Dürer (1471-1528), German painter.

Basketmaker A141

Productive Labor: 90fr, Woodcarver. 140fr, Women hoeing field.

1978, Nov. 18 **Litho.** *Perf. 12½*
Size: 25x36mm.
478 A141 85fr multi 85 60
479 A141 90fr multi 90 62
Size: 27x48mm.
Perf. 12
480 A141 140fr multi 1.40 1.00

Nos. 441-446 Overprinted in Silver:
a. "1962 VAINQUEUR: BRESIL"
b. "1966 VAINQUEUR: / GRANDE BRETAGNE"
c. "1970 VAINQUEUR: / BRESIL"
d. "1974 VAINQUEUR: / ALLEMAGNE (RFA)"
e. "1978 VAINQUEUR: / ARGENTINE"
f. "ARGENTINE-PAYS BAS 3-1/25 juin 1978"

1978, Nov. *Perf. 14x13½*
481 A133 (a) 60fr multi 60 40
482 A133 (b) 75fr multi 75 50
483 A133 (c) 100fr multi 1.00 70
484 A133 (d) 200fr multi 2.00 1.40
485 A133 (e) 300fr multi 3.00 2.10
Nos. 481-485 (5) 7.35 5.10

Souvenir Sheet
486 A133 (f) 500fr multi 5.25

Winners, World Soccer Cup Championships 1962-1978.

Heart and Charts A142

1978, Dec. 16 **Engr.** *Perf. 13*
487 A142 100fr multi 1.00 70

Fight against hypertension.

Party Emblem and Road — A143

1978, Dec. 31 **Litho.** *Perf. 12½x12*
488 A143 60fr multi 60 40

Congolese Labor Party, 9th anniversary.

Capt. Cook, Polynesians and House — A144

Designs: 150fr, Island scene. 250fr, Polynesian longboats. 350fr, Capt. Cook's ships off Hawaii.

1979, Jan. *Perf. 14½*
489 A144 65fr multi 55 42
490 A144 150fr multi 1.50 1.05
491 A144 250fr multi 2.50 1.75
492 A144 350fr multi 3.50 2.50

Capt. James Cook (1728-1779), 250th birth anniversary.

Pres. Marien Ngouabi — A145

1979, Mar. 18 **Litho.** *Perf. 12*
493 A145 35fr multi 35 22
494 A145 60fr multi 60 40

2nd anniversary of assassination of President Ngouabi.

"1979," IYC Emblem, Child A146

1979, Apr. 30 **Litho.** *Perf. 12½x13*
495 A146 45fr multi 45 30
496 A146 75fr multi 75 50

International Year of the Child.

Pottery Vases and Solanum — A147

Design: 150fr, Mail runner, Concorde, train, UPU emblem, envelope.

1979, June 8 **Litho.** *Perf. 13*
497 A147 60fr multi 60 35

Engr.
498 A147 150fr multi 1.50 90

Philexafrique II, Libreville, Gabon, June 8-17. Nos. 497, 498 each printed in sheets of 10 with 5 labels showing exhibition emblem.

Rowland Hill, Diesel Locomotive, Germany No. 78 — A148

Designs (Rowland Hill and): 100fr, Old steam locomotive and France No. B10. 200fr, Diesel locomotive and US No. 245. 300fr, Steam locomotive and England-Australia First Aerialpost vignette, 1919. 500fr, Electric train, Concorde and Middle Congo No. 75.

1979, June *Perf. 14*
499 A148 65fr multi 65 42
500 A148 100fr multi 1.00 70
501 A148 200fr multi 2.00 1.40
502 A148 300fr multi 3.00 2.10

Souvenir Sheet
503 A148 500fr multi 5.25

Sir Rowland Hill (1795-1879), originator of penny postage. No. 503 has multicolored margin showing locomotive and 19th century woman posting letter in pillar box. Size: 102x77mm.

Salvador Allende, Flags, Demonstrators — A149

1979, July 21 **Litho.** *Perf. 12½*
504 A149 100fr multi 1.00 70

Salvador Allende, president of Chile.

Old Man Telling Stories — A150

1979, July 28
505 A150 45fr multi 45 30

Story telling as education.

Handball Players A151

Designs: 75fr, Players and ball (vert.). 250fr, Pres. Ngouabi, cup on map of Africa, player.

1979, July 31 **Litho.** *Perf. 12½*
Size: 40x30mm, 30x40mm
506 A151 45fr multi 45 30
507 A151 75fr multi 75 50
Size: 22x40mm
Perf. 12x12½
508 A151 250fr multi 2.50 1.75

Marien Ngouabi Handball Cup.

Map and Flag of Congo A152

979, Aug. 15
09 A152 50fr multi 50 35

16th anniversary of revolution.

Souvenir Sheet

Virgin and Child, by Dürer A153

979, Aug. 13 ***Perf. 13½***
10 A153 500fr red brn & lt grn 5.25

Albrecht Dürer (1471-1528), German ngraver and painter. No. 510 has light green nd red brown margin showing entire etching. ize: 90x115mm.

Bach and Contemporary Instruments — A155

Design: No. 512, Albert Einstein, astronauts on moon.

979, Sept. 10 ***Perf. 13½***
11 A155 200fr multi 2.00 1.40
12 A155 200fr multi 2.00 1.40

Yoro Fishing Port — A156

979, Sept. 26 Litho. ***Perf. 12½***
13 A156 45fr *shown* 45 30
14 A156 75fr *Port at night* 75 50

Mukukulu Dam — A157

979, Oct. 5 ***Perf. 12½x12***
15 A157 20fr multi 20 14
16 A157 45fr multi 45 30

Emblem, Control Tower, Jets — A158

1979, Dec. 12 Litho. ***Perf. 12½***
517 A158 100fr multi 1.00 75

ASCENA (Air Safety Board), 20th anniversary.

Congolese Labor Party, 10th Anniversary A159

1979, Dec. 31
518 A159 45fr multi 45 14

Post Office, 15th Anniversary A160

1980, Mar. 30 Litho. ***Perf. 12½***
519 A160 45fr multi 45 34
520 A160 95fr multi 95 70

Visit of Pope John Paul II — A161

1980, May 5
521 A161 100fr multi 80 40

Rotary International, 75th Anniversary — A162

1980, May 10 Litho. ***Perf. 12½***
522 A162 150fr multi 1.50 75

Pointe Noire Foundry A163

1980, June 18 Litho. ***Perf. 12½***
523 A163 30fr *shown* 24 12
524 A163 35fr *Different view* 28 14

Claude Chappe, Tower — A164

1980, June 21 Litho. ***Perf. 12½***
525 A164 200fr multi 1.75 85

Claude Chappe (1763-1805), French engineer.

Mossaka Harbor — A165

1980, June 23
532 A165 45fr *shown* 36 18
533 A165 90fr *Different view* 72 35

Papilio Dardanus (Front and Back) — A167

July 31st Hospital — A168

Human Rights Emblem, People — A169

1980, July 12 Litho. ***Perf. 12½***
534 A167 5fr *shown* 5 5
535 A167 15fr *Kalima aethiops* 16 6
536 A167 20fr *Papilio demodocus* 25 8
537 A167 60fr *Euphaedra* 65 24
538 A167 90fr *Hypolimnas misippus* 1.00 36
Nos. 534-538 (5) 2.11 79

Souvenir Sheet

539 A167 300fr *Charaxes smaragdalis* 3.25

Nos. 539 has multicolored margin showing butterflies. Size: 120x80mm.

1980, July 31
540 A168 45fr multi 36 18

1980, Aug. 2
541 A169 350fr *shown* 3.00 1.50
542 A169 500fr *Man breaking chain* 4.00 4.00

Human Rights Convention, 32nd anniversary.

Citizens and Congolese Arms A170

1980, Aug. 15 ***Perf. 12½***
543 A170 75fr *shown* 60 30
544 A170 95fr *Dove on flag, fists, vert.* 75 38
545 A170 150fr *Dove holding Congolese arms* 1.20 60

August 13-15th Revolution, 17th anniversary.

Coffee and Cocoa Trees on Map of Congo — A171

Coffee and Cocoa Day: 95fr, Branches, map of Congo.

1980, Aug. 18 ***Perf. 13½x13***
546 A171 45fr multi 35 18
547 A171 95fr multi 75 38

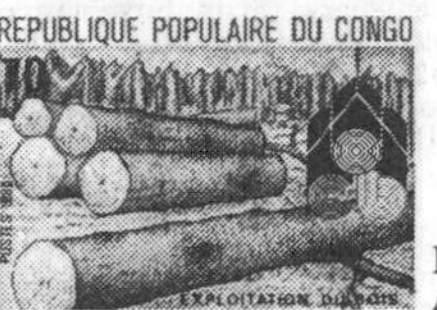

Logging A172

1980, Aug. 28
548 A172 70fr *shown* 56 28
549 A172 75fr *Wood transport* 60 30

President Neto — A173

Lark — A174

1980, Sept. 11
550 A173 100fr multi 80 40

1980, Sept. 17

Designs: Birds.

551 A174 45fr multi, horiz. 45 22
552 A174 75fr multi, horiz. 80 40
553 A174 90fr multi, horiz. 90 45
554 A174 150fr multi 1.50 75
555 A174 200fr multi 2.00 1.00
556 A174 250fr multi 2.50 1.25
a. Souvenir sheet of 6 9.00
Nos. 551-556 (6) 8.15 4.07

No. 556a contains Nos. 551-556. Lilac marginal inscription. Size: 148x105mm.

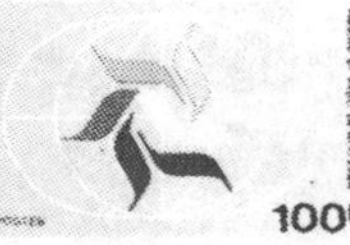

World Tourism Conference, Manila, Sept. 27 — A175

1980, Sept. 27 Litho. ***Perf. 13½x13***
557 A175 100fr multi 80 40

First Day of School Term — A176

1980, Oct. 2 Photo. *Perf. 13*
558 A176 50fr multi 40 20

First House in Brazzaville — A177

Brazzaville Centenary: 65fr, First native village. 75fr, Old Town Hall, 1912. 150fr, View from bank of Bacongo, 1912. 200fr, Meeting of explorer Savorgnan de Brazza and chief Makoko, 1880.

1980, Oct. 3 Litho. *Perf. 12½*
559 A177 45fr multi 36 18
560 A177 65fr multi 52 26
561 A177 75fr multi 60 30
562 A177 150fr multi 1.20 60
563 A177 200fr multi 1.60 80
Nos. 559-563 (5) 4.28 2.14

Boys on Bank of Congo River — A178

1980, Oct. 30
564 A178 80fr *shown* 65 32
565 A178 150fr *Djoue Bridge* 1.20 60

Revolutionary Stadium and Athletes — A179

1980, Nov. 20 *Perf. 13x12½*
566 A179 60fr multi 50 25

Rebuilt Railroad Bridge over Congo River A180

1980, Nov. 29 *Perf. 13x13½*
567 A180 75fr multi 60 30

Mangoes, Loudima Fruit Packing Station A181

1980, Dec. 2 *Perf. 13*
568 A181 10fr *shown* 8 5
569 A181 25fr *Oranges* 20 10
570 A181 40fr *Citrons* 32 16
571 A181 85fr *Mandarins* 70 35

African Postal Union, 5th Anniversary A182

1980, Dec. 24 *Perf. 13½*
572 A182 100fr multi 80 40

Moungouni Earth Satellite Station A183

1980, Dec. 30 *Perf. 12½*
573 A183 75fr multi 60 30

Hertzian Wave Communication, Brazzaville — A184

1980, Dec. 30 *Perf. 12½x12*
574 A184 150fr multi 1.20 60

1980 African Handball Champion Team — A185

Perf. 12½x13, 13x12½
1981, Jan. 26 Litho.
575 A185 100fr Receiving cup, vert. 80 40
576 A185 150fr shown 1.20 60

Pres. Denis Sassou-Nguesso — A186

1981, Feb. 5 Litho. *Perf. 12½*
577 A186 45fr multi 36 18
578 A186 75fr multi 60 30
579 A186 100fr multi 80 40

Columbia Space Shuttle Orbiting Earth — A187

Space Conquest: 100fr, Luna 17, 1970. 200fr, 300fr, 500fr, Columbia space shuttle, 1981.

1981, May 4 Litho. *Perf. 14x13½*
580 A187 100fr multi 80 40
581 A187 150fr multi 1.20 60
582 A187 200fr multi 1.60 80
583 A187 300fr multi 2.40 1.20

Souvenir Sheet
584 A187 500fr multi 4.00 2.00

No. 584 has multicolored margin showing space shuttle orbiting earth. Size: 104x79mm.

Fight Against Apartheid A188

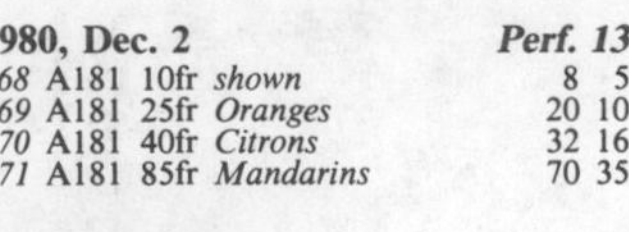

Twin Palm Tree of Louingui A189

1981, May 5 Litho. *Perf. 12½*
585 A188 100fr dp bl 80 40

1981, May 22 *Perf. 12x12½*
586 A189 75fr multi 60 30

13th World Telecommunications Day — A190

1981, June 6 *Perf. 12½*
587 A190 120fr multi 95 45

Rubber Extraction — A191

1981, June 27 *Perf. 13*
588 A191 50fr shown 40 20
589 A191 70fr Sap draining 55 25

Intl. Year of the Disabled A192

1981, June 29 Engr
590 A192 45fr multi 36 1

See No. B7.

Bird Trap — A194

Designs: Animal traps. 10fr vert.

1981, July
596 A194 5fr multi 5
597 A194 10fr multi 10
598 A194 15fr multi 15
599 A194 20fr multi 18
600 A194 30fr multi 26 1
601 A194 35fr multi 30 1
Nos. 596-601 (6) 1.04 5

Mausoleum of King Maloango — A195

1981, July 4 Litho. *Perf. 12½*
602 A195 75fr shown 60 3
603 A195 150fr Mausoleum, portrait 1.20 6

Prince Charles and Lady Diana, Coach A196

Designs: Couple and coaches.

1981, Sept. 1 Litho. *Perf. 14*
604 A196 100fr multi 80 4
605 A196 200fr multi 1.60 8
606 A196 300fr multi 2.40 1.2

Souvenir Sheet
607 A196 400fr multi 3.25 1.7

Royal wedding. No. 607 has multicolore margin showing arms of Prince of Wales Size: 104x78mm.

World Food Day — A197

1981, Oct. 16 Litho. *Perf. 13½x1*
608 A197 150fr multi 1.20 6

12th World UPU Day — A198

1981, Oct. 24 Engr. *Perf. 13x12½*
609 A198 90fr multi 72 3

Royal Guard A199

1981, Oct. 31 Litho. ***Perf. 12½x13***

610 A199 45fr multi 35 18

Eradication of Manioc Beetle — A200

REPUBLIQUE POPULAIRE DU CONGO 10F

Natl. Red Cross — A201

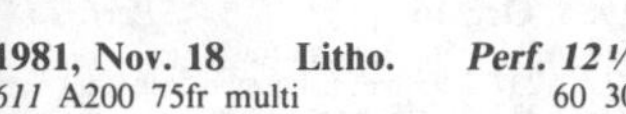

1981, Nov. 18 Litho. ***Perf. 12½***

611 A200 75fr multi 60 30

1981, Nov. 18 ***Perf. 13***

612 A201 10fr Bandaging patient 8 5
613 A201 35fr Treating child 28 15
614 A201 60fr Drawing well water 50 25

Giant Baobab ("Tree of Savorgnan de Brazza") A202

1981, Dec. 19 Litho. ***Perf. 13***

615 A202 45fr multi 35 18
616 A202 65fr multi 60 30

Fetish Figure — A203

Designs: Various carved figures.

1981, Dec. 19 ***Perf. 13x12½***

617 A203 15fr multi 12 6
618 A203 25fr multi 20 10
619 A203 45fr multi 35 18
620 A203 50fr multi 40 20
621 A203 60fr multi 50 25
Nos. 617-621 (5) 1.57 79

Caves of Bangou A204

1981, Dec. 29 ***Perf. 13x13½***

622 A204 20fr multi 16 8
623 A204 25fr multi 20 10

King Makoko and His Queen, Ivory Sculptures by R. Engongodzo A205

Perf. 13½x13, 13x13½

1982, Feb. 27 Litho.

624 A205 25fr Woman, vert. 20 10
625 A205 35fr Woman, diff., vert. 28 14
626 A205 100fr shown 80 40

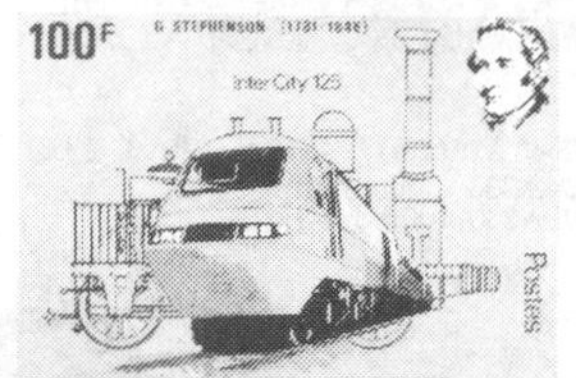

George Stephenson (1781-1848) and Inter City 125, Gt. Britain — A206

Locomotives: 150fr, Sinkansen Bullet Train, Japan. 200fr, Advanced Passenger Train, Gt. Britain. 300fr, TGV-001, France.

1982, Mar. 2 Litho. ***Perf. 12½***

627 A206 100fr multi 80 80
628 A206 150fr multi 1.20 60
629 A206 200fr multi 1.60 80
630 A206 300fr multi 2.40 1.20

Scouting Year A207

1982, Apr. 13 Litho. ***Perf. 13***

631 A207 100fr Looking through binoculars 80 40
632 A207 150fr Reading map 1.20 60
633 A207 200fr Helping woman 1.60 80
634 A207 300fr Crossing rope bridge 2.40 1.25

Souvenir Sheet

635 A207 500fr Hiking, horiz. 4.00 2.00

No. 635 has multicolored margin continuing design. Size: 96x71mm.

Franklin Roosevelt (1882-1945) — A208

1982, June 12 Litho. ***Perf. 13***

636 A208 150fr shown 1.20 60
637 A208 250fr Washington (1732-1799) 2.00 1.00
638 A208 350fr Goethe (1749-1832) 2.80 1.40

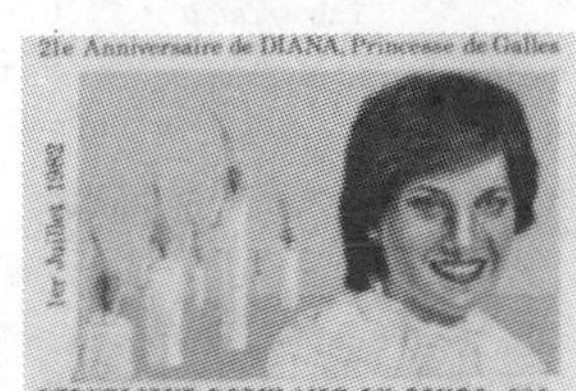

21st Birthday of Princess Diana, July 1 — A209

1982, June 12 ***Perf. 14***

639 A209 200fr Candles 1.60 80
640 A209 300fr "21" 2.40 1.25

Souvenir Sheet

641 A209 500fr Diana 4.00 2.00

No. 641 has multicolored margin showing rose. Size: 112x80mm.

5-Year Plan, 1982-1986 A210

Perf. 13x12½, 12½x13

1982, June 19

642 A210 60fr Road construction 40 20
643 A210 100fr Communications, vert. 60 30
644 A210 125fr Operating room equipment, vert. 75 35
645 A210 150fr Hydroelectric power, vert. 95 45

ITU Plenipotentiary Conference, Nairobi — A211

1982, June 26 ***Perf. 13***

646 A211 300fr multi 2.40 1.25

Nos. 604-607 Overprinted in Blue: "NAISSANCE ROYALE 1982"

1982, July 30 ***Perf. 14½***

647 A196 100fr multi 80 40
648 A196 200fr multi 1.60 80
649 A196 300fr multi 2.40 1.25

Souvenir Sheet

650 A196 400fr multi 3.25 1.75

Birth of Prince William of Wales, June 21.

Nutrition Campaign — A212

1982, July 24 Litho. ***Perf. 12½***

651 A212 100fr multi 80 40

WHO African Headquarters, Brazzaville — A213

1982, July 24 Litho. ***Perf. 12½***

652 A213 125fr multi 1.00 50

TB Bacillus Centenary — A214

1982, Aug. 7 ***Perf. 12½x12***

653 A214 250fr Koch, bacillus 2.00 1.00

Pres. Sassou-Nguesso and 1980 Simba Prize — A215

1982, Oct. 20 Litho. ***Perf. 13***

654 A215 100fr multi 80 40

Turtles — A216

Various turtles and tortoises.

1982, Dec. 1

655 A216 30fr multi 24 12
656 A216 45fr multi 35 18
657 A216 55fr multi 45 22

Boy Gathering Coconuts — A217

REPUBLIQUE POPULAIRE 100F DU CONGO

Nest in Tree Trunk — A218

1982, Dec. 11

658 A217 100fr multi 80 40

1982, Dec. 29 ***Perf. 12½***

659 A218 40fr shown 32 16
660 A218 75fr Nests in palm tree 60 30
661 A218 100fr Woven nest on thron branch 80 40

Hertzian Wave Communication Network — A219

1982, Dec. 30 ***Perf. 13x12½***

662 A219 45fr multi 35 18
663 A219 60fr multi 50 25
664 A219 95fr multi 75 40

30th Anniv. of Customs Cooperation Council — A220

1983, Jan. 26 Litho. *Perf. 12½x13*
665 A220 100fr Headquarters 80 40

Mausoleum of Pres. Marien Ngouabi — A221

1983, Feb. 8 *Perf. 13*
666 A221 60fr multi 50 25
667 A221 80fr multi 65 32

Ironsmiths — A222

1983 *Perf. 12½*
668 A222 45fr shown 35 18
669 A222 150fr Weaver, vert. 1.20 62

Issue dates: 45fr, Mar. 5; 150fr, Feb. 24

Carved Chess Pieces, by R. Engongonzo — A223

Various pieces.

1983, Feb. 26 *Perf. 13*
670 A223 40fr multi 32 15
671 A223 60fr multi 50 25
672 A223 95fr multi 75 38

Easter 1983 A224

Raphael drawings. 200fr, 400fr vert.

1983, Apr. 20 Litho. *Perf. 13*
673 A224 200fr Transfiguration study 1.60 80
674 A224 300fr Deposition from Cross 2.40 1.20
675 A224 400fr Christ in Glory 3.25 1.60

Seashells A225

Seashells. Dated 1982.

1983 Litho. *Perf. 15x14*
676 A225 35fr multi 14 8
677 A225 65fr multi 25 12

Traditional Combs — A226

Various combs.

1983, May *Perf. 14*
678 A226 30fr multi 12 6
679 A226 70fr multi 28 14
680 A226 85fr multi 34 18

20th Anniv. of Revolution A227

Litho & Engr.
1983, Aug. 10 *Perf. 12½x13*
681 A227 60fr multi 24 12
682 A227 100fr multi 40 20

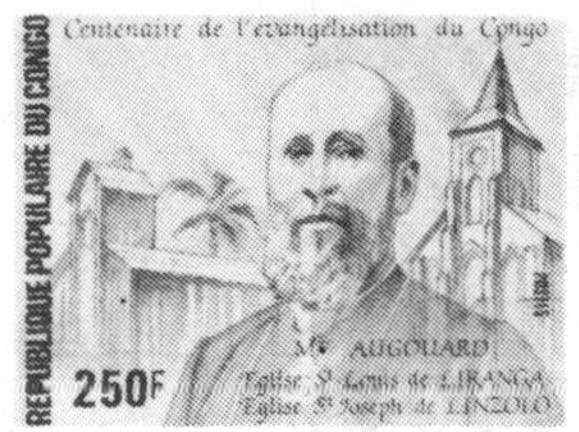
Centenary of the Arrival of Christian Missionaries — A228

Churches and Clergymen: 150fr, A. Carrie, Church of the Sacred Heart, Loango (vert.). 250fr, Msgr. Augouard; St. Louis, Liranga; St. Joseph, Linzolo.

1983, Aug. 23 *Perf. 12½*
683 A228 150fr multi 60 30
684 A228 250fr multi 1.00 50

Local Flowers — A229

1984, Jan. 20 Litho. *Perf. 12½*
685 A229 5fr Liana thunderaie, vert. 5 5
686 A229 15fr Bougainvillea 6 5
687 A229 20fr Anthurium, vert. 8 5
688 A229 45fr Allamanda 18 10
689 A229 75fr Hibiscus, vert. 30 15
Nos. 685-689 (5) 67 40

35th Anniv. of World Peace Council A230

1984, Mar. 31 Litho. *Perf. 13x12½*
690 A230 50fr multi 20 10
691 A230 100fr multi 45 22

Anti-Nuclear Arms Campaign — A231

1984, May 31 Litho. *Perf. 12x12½*
692 A231 200fr Explosion, victims 90 45

Agriculture Day — A232

Perf. 13x13½, 13½x13
1984, June 30 Litho.
693 A232 10fr Rice 5 5
694 A232 15fr Pineapples 6 5
695 A232 60fr Manioc, vert. 25 12
696 A232 100fr Palm tree, map, vert. 48 24

Congress Palace — A233

1984, July 27 *Perf. 13*
697 A233 60fr multi 25 12
698 A233 100fr multi 45 22

Chinese-Congolese cooperation.

CFCO-Congo Railways, 50th Anniv. — A234

1984, July 30 *Perf. 13½*
699 A234 10fr Loulombo Station 5 5
700 A234 25fr Les Bandas Chinese Labor Camp 10 5
701 A234 125fr "50" 60 30
702 A234 200fr Admin. bldg. 90 45

Locomotives — A235

Ships on the Congo River — A236

1984, Aug. 24 *Perf. 12½*
703 A235 100fr CC 203 45 22
704 A236 100fr Tugboat 45 22
705 A235 150fr BB 103 70 35
706 A236 150fr Pusher tugboat 70 35
707 A235 300fr BB-BB 301 1.40 70
708 A236 300fr Dredger 1.40 70
709 A235 500fr BB 420 L'Eclair 2.25 1.10
710 A236 500fr Cargo ship 2.25 1.10
Nos. 703-710 (8) 9.60 4.74

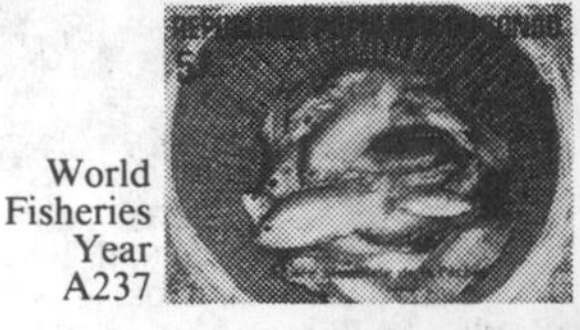
World Fisheries Year A237

1984, Oct. 16 *Perf. 13½*
711 A237 5fr Basket of fish 5 5
712 A237 20fr Net fishermen in boat 8 5
713 A237 25fr School of fish 10 5
714 A237 40fr Net fisherman 16 8
715 A237 55fr Trawler 22 12
Nos. 711-715 (5) 61 35

Anti-polio Campaign A238

M'Bamou Palace Hotel, Brazzaville A239

1984, Oct. 30
716 A238 250fr Disabled men, hand 1.00 50
717 A238 300fr Target, disabled women, horiz. 1.25 65

1984, Dec. 15 *Perf. 14½*
718 A239 60fr multi 25 12
719 A239 100fr multi 40 20

Fauna A240

1984, Dec. *Perf. 15x14½*
720 A240 30fr Pangolin 14 8
721 A240 70fr Bat 30 15
722 A240 85fr Civet cat 35 18

Congo River Logging A241

1984, Dec. *Perf. 13½x13*
723 A241 60fr Log raft, crew hut 25 12
724 A241 100fr Tugboat pushing logs 40 20

Souvenir Sheets
Nos. 584, 635 Ovptd. with Exhibition in Black or Green.

1985, Mar. 8 *Perf. 14x13½, 13*
725 A187 500fr TSUKUBA EXPO '85 2.00 1.00
726 A207 500fr ITALIA '85 emblem, ROME (G) 2.00 1.00

See Nos. C336-C337.

Zonocerus Variegatus — A242

1985, Mar. 15 *Perf. 13*
727 A242 125fr multi 50 25

Burial of a Teke Chief — A243

1985, Apr. 30 *Perf. 12½*
728 A243 225fr multi 95 48

Edible Fruit A244

1985, June 15 *Perf. 13½*
729 A244 5fr Trichoscypha acuminata, vert. 5 5
730 A244 10fr Aframomum africanum 5 5
731 A244 125fr Gambeya lacuurtiana 50 25
732 A244 150fr Landolphia jumelei 60 30

Sizes: No. 729, 22x36mm. No. 731, 36x22mm.

Lions Club Intl., 30th Anniv. — A245

1985, June 25 *Perf. 12½*
733 A245 250fr Flag, District 403B 1.00 50

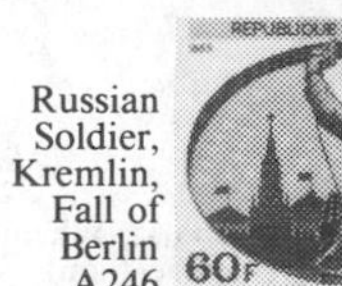

Russian Soldier, Kremlin, Fall of Berlin A246

1985, July 27 *Perf. 12*
734 A246 60fr multi 25 12

Defeat of Nazi Germany, end of World War II, 40th anniv.

Lady Olave Baden-Powell, Girl Guides Founder — A247

Anniversaries and events: 150fr, Girl Guides, 75th anniv. 250fr, Jacob Grimm, fabulist; Sleeping Beauty. 350fr, Johann Sebastian Bach, composer; European Music Year, St. Thomas Church organ, Leipzig. 450fr, Queen Mother, 85th birthday, vert. 500fr, Statue of Liberty, cent., vert.

1985, Aug. 26 *Perf. 13*
735 A247 150fr multi 70 35
736 A247 250fr multi 1.25 60
737 A247 350fr multi 1.65 85
738 A247 450fr multi 1.75 90
739 A247 500fr multi 2.25 1.10
Nos. 735-739 (5) 7.60 3.80

PHILEXAFRICA '85, Lome, Togo, Nov. 16-24 — A248

1985, Oct. 10 *Perf. 13x12½*
740 A248 250fr Silhouettes, cement mixer, skyscrapers 1.40 70
741 A248 250fr Airport, postal van 1.40 70

Nos. 740-741 printed se-tenant with center label picturing map of Africa or UAPT emblem.

Mushrooms — A249

1985, Dec. 14 **Litho.** *Perf. 13*
742 A249 100fr Coprinus, vert. 55 28
743 A249 150fr Cortinarius 82 40
744 A249 200fr Armillariella mellea 1.10 55
745 A249 300fr Dictyophora 1.65 82
746 A249 400fr Crucibulum vulgare 2.25 1.10
Nos. 742-746 (5) 6.37 3.15

Arbor Day — A250

Children's Hoop Races — A251

1986, Mar. 6 *Perf. 13½*
747 A250 60fr Planting sapling 32 16
748 A250 200fr Map, lifecycle diagram 1.10 55

1986, Apr. 30 *Perf. 12½*
749 A251 5fr Two boys 5 5
750 A251 10fr One boy 6 5
751 A251 60fr Three boys, horiz. 32 16
a. Souvenir sheet of 3, #749-751 45 28

No. 751a has blue inscribed margin. Size: 150x100mm.

Intl. Environment Day — A252

1986, June 5 **Litho.** *Perf. 13½*
752 A252 60fr Garbage disposal 32 16
753 A252 125fr Dumping garbage 75 38

Traditional Modes of Transporting Goods — A253

Designs: 5 fr, Basket on head, child in sling carrier. 10fr, Child in carrier on hip, large basket strapped to forehead. 60fr, Man carrying load on shoulder.

1986, July 15 **Litho.** *Perf. 13x12½*
754 A253 5fr multi 5 5
755 A253 10fr multi 6 5
756 A253 60fr multi 32 16

Mission of the Sisters of St. Joseph of Cluny, Cent. A254

1986, Aug. 19 **Litho.** *Perf. 12½x13*
757 A254 230fr multi 1.40 70

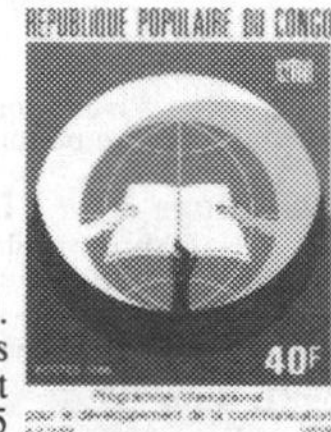

UNESCO Intl. Communications Development Program — A255

1986, Aug. 30 **Litho.** *Perf. 13½*
758 A255 40fr multi 22 10
759 A255 60fr multi 35 18
760 A255 100fr multi 60 30

Intl. Peace Year — A256

1986, Sept. 15 **Litho.** *Perf. 13½*
761 A256 100fr multi 60 30

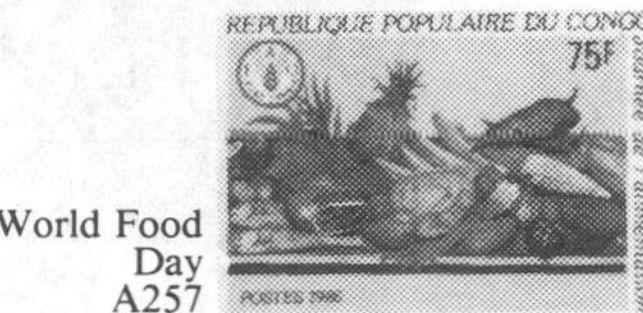

World Food Day A257

1986, Oct. 16
762 A257 75fr Food staples 40 20
763 A257 120fr Mother feeding child 80 40

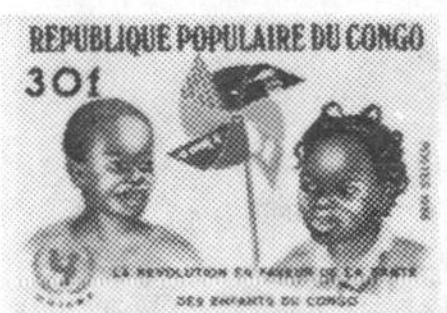

UN Child Survival Campaign A258

Mothers, children and pinwheels in various designs.

1986, Oct. 27
764 A258 15fr multi, vert. 8 5
765 A258 30fr multi 16 8
766 A258 70fr multi, vert. 38 20

27th Soviet Communist Party Congress — A258a

1986, Dec. 5 **Litho.** *Perf. 12x12½*
766A A258a 100fr multi 65 32

Election of President Sassou-Nguesso, Head of the Organization of African States — A259

1987, Feb. 10 Litho. *Perf. 13½*
767 A259 30fr multi 16 8
768 A259 45fr multi 25 12
769 A259 75fr multi 40 20
770 A259 120fr multi 65 32

Traditional Wedding A260

1987, Feb. 18 Litho. *Perf. 12½x13*
771 A260 5fr multi 5 5
772 A260 15fr multi 8 5
773 A260 20fr multi 12 6

The Blue Lake — A261

1987, July 16 *Perf. 12½*
774 A261 5fr multi 5 5
775 A261 15fr multi 8 5
776 A261 75fr multi 42 22
777 A261 120fr multi 68 35

Pres. Marien Ngouabi A262

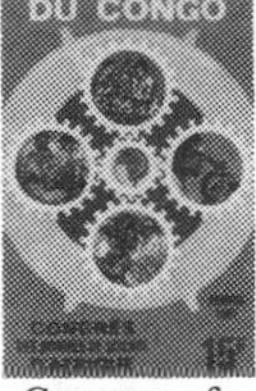

Congress of African Scientists A263

1987, July 16 *Perf. 13*
778 A262 75fr multi 42 22
779 A262 120fr multi 68 35

Tenth death anniv.

1987, Sept. 10 *Perf. 13x12½*
780 A263 15fr multi 10 5
781 A263 90fr multi 60 30
782 A263 230fr multi 1.55 78

4th African Games, Nairobi — A264

1987, Oct. 30 *Perf. 12½*
783 A264 75fr multi 55 28
784 A264 120fr multi 88 45

Raoul Follereau (1903-1977), Philanthropist — A265

1987, Oct. 20 *Perf. 13½*
785 A265 120fr multi 88 45

Cure leprosy.

FAO, 40th Anniv. — A266

1987, Nov. 17 *Perf. 12½*
786 A266 300fr multi 2.15 1.10

SEMI-POSTAL STAMPS

Anti-Malaria Issue
Common Design Type

1962, Apr. 7 Engr. *Perf. 12½x12*
B3 CD108 25fr + 5fr bis 65 65

Issued for the World Health Organization drive to eradicate malaria.

Freedom from Hunger Issue
Common Design Type

1963, Mar. 21 Unwmk. *Perf. 13*
B4 CD112 25fr + 5fr vio bl, bl grn & brn 60 60

Boy Suffering from Sleeping Sickness SP1

Fight Against Communicable Diseases; 40fr + 5fr, Examination, treatment (vert.).

1981, June 6 Litho. *Perf. 13*
B5 SP1 40fr+ 5fr multi 36 18
B6 SP1 65fr+ 10fr multi 60 30

IYD Type of 1981

1981, June 29 *Perf. 12½*
B7 A192 75fr+ 5fr multi 65 32

AIR POST STAMPS

Olympic Games Issue
French Equatorial Africa No. C37 Surcharged in Red Like Chad No. C1.

1960 Unwmk. Engr. *Perf. 13*
C1 AP8 250fr on 500fr grnsh blk, blk & sl 5.50 5.50

Issued to commemorate the 17th Olympic Games, Rome, Aug. 25-Sept. 11.

Helicrysum Mechowiam — AP1

Flowers: 200fr, Cogniauxia podolaena. 500fr, Thesium tencio.

1961, Sept. 28 Engr. *Perf. 13*
C2 AP1 100fr grn, lil & yel 1.35 95
C3 AP1 200fr bl grn, yel & brn 2.65 1.20
C4 AP1 500fr brn red, yel & sl grn 6.00 2.65

Air Afrique Issue
Common Design Type

1961, Nov. 25 Unwmk. *Perf. 13*
C5 CD107 50fr lil rose, sl grn & grn 60 50

Founding of Air Afrique.

Loading Timber, Pointe-Noire Harbor — AP2

1962, June 8 Photo. *Perf. 12½x12*
C6 AP2 50fr multi 60 50

Issued to commemorate the opening of the International Fair and Exhibition, Pointe-Noire, June 8-11.

Abidjan Games Issue

Basketball — AP3

1962, July 21 *Perf. 12x12½*
C7 AP3 100fr multi 1.35 95

Costus Spectabilis — AP4

Design: 250fr, Mountain acanthus.

1963 Unwmk. *Perf. 13*
C8 AP4 100fr multi 1.35 80
C9 AP4 250fr multi 3.50 1.85

Brazzaville City Hall and Pres. Fulbert Youlou — AP4a

1963, Aug. Photo. *Perf. 13x12*
C10 AP4a 100fr multi 60.00 60.00

African Postal Union Issue
Common Design Type

1963, Sept. 8 *Perf. 12½*
C13 CD114 85fr pur, ocher & red 95 65

Air Afrique Issue, 1963
Common Design Type
Perf. 13x12

1963, Nov. 19 Unwmk. Photo.
C14 CD115 50fr multi 65 50

Liberty Place, Brazzaville — AP5

1963, Nov. 28
C15 AP5 25fr multi 32 25

See also No. 118.

Europafrica Issue
Common Design Type

1963, Nov. 30 *Perf. 12x13*
C16 CD116 50fr gray, yel & dk brn 80 55

Timber Industry — AP6

1964, May 12 Engr. *Perf. 13*
C17 AP6 100fr grn, brn red & blk 1.20 70

Chiefs of State Issue

Map and Presidents of Chad, Congo, Gabon and CAR — AP6a

1964, June 23 Photo. *Perf. 12½*
C18 AP6a 100fr multi 1.25 70

See note after Central African Republic No. C19.

Europafrica Issue, 1964

Sunburst, Wheat, Cogwheel and Globe — AP7

1964, July 20 *Perf. 12x13*
C19 AP7 50fr yel, Prus bl & mar 65 40

See note after Cameroun No. 402.

Hammer Thrower, Olympic Flame and Stadium — AP8

Designs (Olympic flame, stadium) and: 50fr, Weight lifter (vert.). 100fr, Volleyball (vert.). 200fr, High jump.

1964, July 30 Engr. *Perf. 13*
C20 AP8 25fr vio bl, org & red brn 32 15
C21 AP8 50fr yel grn, org & red lil 65 45
C22 AP8 100fr sl grn, org & red brn 1.25 95
C23 AP8 200fr crim, org & dp grn 2.50 1.90
a. Min. sheet of 4 5.50 5.50

Issued for the 18th Olympic Games, Tokyo, Oct. 10-25, 1964. No. C23a contains one each of Nos. C20-C23. Size: 191x99mm.

Communications Symbols — AP8a

1964, Nov. 2 Litho. *Perf. 12½x13*
C24 AP8a 25fr dl rose & dk brn 40 30

See note after Chad No. C19.

Town Hall, Brazzaville — AP9

1965, Jan. 30 Photo. *Perf. 12½*
C25 AP9 100fr multi 1.20 65

Coupling Hooks — AP10

1965, Feb. 27 Photo. *Perf. 13x12*
C26 AP10 50fr multi 65 40

Economic Europe-Africa Association.

Breguet Dial Telegraph, ITU Emblem and Telstar — AP11

The Catalogue editors cannot undertake to appraise, identify or judge the genuineness or condition of stamps.

1965, May 17 Engr. *Perf. 13*
C27 AP11 100fr dk bl, ocher & brn 1.35 80

Issued to commemorate the centenary of the International Telecommunication Union.

Pope John XXIII and St. Peter's Cathedral AP12

Perf. 12½x13
1965, June 26 Photo. Unwmk.
C28 AP12 100fr gldn brn & multi 1.20 90

Issued in memory of Pope John XXIII (1881-1963).

Pres. John F. Kennedy AP13

Log Rolling AP14

Portraits: 25fr on 50fr, Patrice Lumumba, premier of Congo Republic (ex-Belgian). 50fr, Sir Winston Churchill. 80fr, Barthelemy Boganda, premier of Central African Republic.

1965, June 25-26 *Perf. 12½*
C29 AP13 25fr on 50fr dk brn & red 40 40
a. Surch. omitted 22.50 22.50
C30 AP13 50fr dk brn & yel grn 90 90
C31 AP13 80fr dk brn & bl 1.20 1.20
C32 AP13 100fr dk brn & org yel 1.50 1.50
a. Min. sheet of 4 6.00 6.00

Issued to honor famous statesmen. No. C32a contains one each of Nos. C29-C32. Size: 106x143 mm.
A second miniature sheet contains one each of Nos. C29a, C30-C32. Price, $30.

1965, Aug. 14 Engr. *Perf. 13*
C33 AP14 50fr grn, brn & red brn 75 40

Issued to publicize national unity.

World Map and Symbols of Agriculture and Industry — AP15

1965, Oct. 18 Engr. *Perf. 13*
C34 AP15 50fr dk bl, blk, brn & org 75 50

International Cooperation Year, 1965.

Abraham Lincoln — AP16

1965, Dec. 15 Photo. *Perf. 13*
C35 AP16 90fr pink & multi 1.10 65

Centenary of death of Abraham Lincoln.

Charles de Gaulle, Torch and Map of Africa — AP17

1966, Feb. 28 Engr. *Perf. 13*
C36 AP17 500fr dk red, dk grn & dk red brn 15.00 12.50

Issued to commemorate the 22nd anniversary of the Brazzaville Conference.

D-1 Satellite over Brazzaville Space Tracking Station — AP18

Grain, Atom Symbol and Map of Africa and Europe — AP19

1966, May 15 Engr. *Perf. 13*
C37 AP18 150fr blk, dl red & bl grn 1.85 95

1966, July 20 Photo. *Perf. 12x13*
C38 AP19 50fr multi 80 50

See note after Gabon No. C46.

Pres. Massamba-Debat and President's Palace — AP20

Designs: 30fr, Robespierre and storming of the Bastille. 50fr, Lenin and storming of the Winter Palace.

1966, Aug. 15 Photo. *Perf. 12x12½*
C39 AP20 25fr multi 28 15
C40 AP20 30fr multi 35 15
C41 AP20 50fr multi 60 28
a. Souv. sheet of 3 1.50 1.50

Issued to commemorate the 3rd anniversary of the revolution. No. C41a contains one each of Nos. C39-C41. Black marginal inscription and control number. Size: 131½x160mm.

Air Afrique Issue, 1966
Common Design Type

1966, Aug. 31 Photo. *Perf. 13*
C42 CD123 30fr lil, lem & blk 45 20

Issued to commemorate the introduction of DC-8F planes by Air Afrique.

Dr. Albert Schweitzer — AP21

1966, Sept. 4 Photo. *Perf. 12½*
C43 AP21 100fr red, blk, bl & lil 1.25 80

Issued to honor Dr. Albert Schweitzer (1875-1965), medical missionary.

Crab, Microscope and Pagoda — AP22

1966, Dec. 26 Photo. *Perf. 13*
C44 AP22 100fr multi 1.20 65

Issued to commemorate the 9th International Anticancer Congress, Tokyo. Oct. 23-29.

Social Weaver — AP23

Birds: 75fr, European Bee-eater. 100fr, Lilac-breasted roller. 150fr, Regal sunbird. 200fr, Crowned cranes. 250fr, Secretary bird. 300fr, Knysna touraco.

1967 Photo. *Perf. 13*
C45 AP23 50fr multi 1.00 40
C46 AP23 75fr multi 1.35 55
C47 AP23 100fr multi 1.65 80
C48 AP23 150fr multi 2.00 1.10
C49 AP23 200fr multi 2.65 1.35
C50 AP23 250fr multi 3.50 1.75
C51 AP23 300fr multi 4.00 2.25
Nos. C45-C51 (7) 16.15 8.20

Issue dates: Nos. C45-C47, Feb. 13. Others, June 20.

Shackled Hands AP24

1967, May 24 Photo. ***Perf. 12½x13***
C52 AP24 500fr multi 7.00 3.00

Issued for African Liberation Day.

Sputnik 1, Explorer 6 and Earth — AP25

Space Craft: 75fr, Ranger 6, Lunik 2 and moon. 100fr, Mars 1, Mariner 4 and Mars. 200fr, Gemini, Vostok and earth.

1967, Aug. 1 Engr. ***Perf. 13***
C53 AP25 50fr pur, bl & org brn 60 32
C54 AP25 75fr dk car & gray 90 50
C55 AP25 100fr red brn, Prus bl & ultra 1.25 80
C56 AP25 200fr car lake, org & bl 2.50 1.60

Space explorations.

African Postal Union Issue, 1967
Common Design Type

1967, Sept. 9 Engr. ***Perf. 13***
C57 CD124 100fr ver, ol & emer 1.20 70

Boy Scouts, Tents and Jamboree Emblem — AP26

Design: 70c, Borah Peak, Idaho; tents, Scout sign and Jamboree emblem.

1967, Sept. 29
C58 AP26 50fr brt bl, brn org & red brn 55 28
C59 AP26 70fr dl bl, sl grn & red brn 80 40

Issued to commemorate the 12th Boy Scout World Jamboree, Farragut State Park, Idaho, Aug. 1-9.

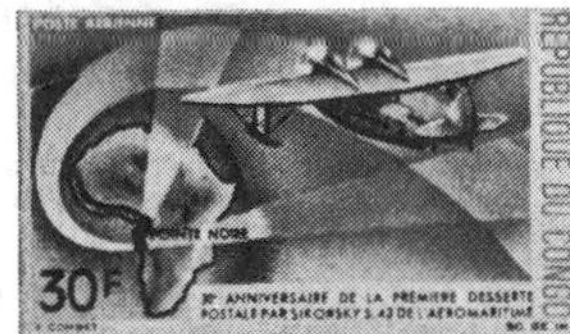

Sikorsky S-43 and Map of Africa — AP27

1967, Oct. 2 Photo. ***Perf. 13***
C60 AP27 30fr multi 45 25

Issued to commemorate the 30th anniversary of the first airmail connection by Aeromaritime Lines from Casablanca to Pointe-Noire.

Men of Four Races Dancing on Globe — AP28

1968, Feb 8 Engr. ***Perf. 13***
C61 AP28 70fr dk brn, ultra & emer 90 50

Friendship among peoples.

The Oath of the Horatii, by Jacques Louis David — AP29

Paintings: 25fr, On the Barricades, by Delacroix. No. C63, Grandfather and Grandson, by Ghirlandajo (vert.). No. C64, The Demolition of the Bastille, by Hubert Robert. 200fr, Negro Woman Arranging Peonies, by Jean F. Bazille.

1968 Photo. ***Perf. 12x12½, 12½x12***
C62 AP29 25fr multi 32 12
C63 AP29 30fr multi 50 32
C64 AP29 30fr multi 35 20
C65 AP29 100fr multi 1.35 80
C66 AP29 200fr multi 3.00 1.75
Nos. C62-C66 (5) 5.52 3.19

Issue dates: Nos. C62, C64, Aug. 15. Nos. C63, C65-C66, Mar. 20.
See also Nos. C78-C81, C111-C115.

Early Automobile Type of Regular Issue

Designs: 150fr, Ford, 1915. 200fr, Citroen, 1922.

1968, July 29 Photo. ***Perf. 13x12½***
C67 A50 150fr multi 2.00 1.00
C68 A50 200fr lil & multi 2.50 1.35

Europafrica Issue

Square Knot — AP30

1968, July 20 Photo. ***Perf. 13***
C69 AP30 50fr multi 55 25

Issued to commemorate the 5th anniversary of the economic agreement between the European Economic Community and the African and Malgache Union.

Martin Luther King, Jr. AP31

Robert F. Kennedy AP32

1968, Aug. 5 ***Perf. 12½***
C70 AP31 50fr lt grn, Prus grn & blk 55 25

Issued in memory of the Rev. Dr. Martin Luther King, Jr. (1929-1968), American civil rights leader.

1968, Sept. 30 Photo. ***Perf. 13x12½***
C71 AP32 50fr dp car, ap grn & blk 65 32

Issued in memory of Robert F. Kennedy (1925-68), U.S. Senator and Attorney General.

Running — AP33

Olympic Rings and: 20fr, Soccer (vert.). 60fr, Boxing (vert.). 85fr, High jump.

1968, Dec. 27 Engr. ***Perf. 13***
C72 AP33 5fr emer, brt bl & choc 7 5
C73 AP33 20fr dk bl, brn & dk grn 25 12
C74 AP33 60fr mar, brt grn & choc 75 40
C75 AP33 85fr blk, car rose & choc 1.00 50

Issued to commemorate the 19th Olympic Games, Mexico City, Oct. 12-27.

PHILEXAFRIQUE Issue

G. De Gueidan, by Nicolas de Largillière AP34

1968, Dec. 30 Photo. ***Perf. 12½***
C76 AP34 100fr pink & multi 1.30 1.10

Issued to publicize PHILEXAFRIQUE, Philatelic Exhibition, in Abidjan, Feb. 14-23. Printed with alternating pink label.
See also Nos. C89-C93.

2nd PHILEXAFRIQUE Issue
Common Design Type

Design: 50fr, Middle Congo No. 72 and Pointe-Noire harbor.

1969, Feb. 14 Engr. ***Perf. 13***
C77 CD128 50fr car rose, sl grn & bis brn 75 65

Issued to commemorate the opening of PHILEXAFRIQUE, Abidjan, Feb. 14.

Painting Type of 1968.

Paintings: 25fr, Battle of Rivoli, by Carle Vernet. 50fr, Battle of Marengo, by Jacques Augustin Pajou. 75fr, Battle of Friedland, by Horace Vernet. 100fr, Battle of Jena, by Charles Thevenin.

1969, May 20 Photo. ***Perf. 12x12½***
C78 AP29 25fr vio bl & multi 40 25
C79 AP29 50fr cop red & multi 75 50
C80 AP29 75fr grn & multi 1.10 50
C81 AP29 100fr brn & multi 1.60 80

Bicentenary of birth of Napoleon I.

Ernesto Ché Guevara — AP35

1969, June 10 Photo. ***Perf. 12½***
C82 AP35 90fr brn, org & blk 1.10 55

Issued in memory of Ernesto ChéGuevara (1928-1967), Cuban revolutionist.

Doll, Train and Space Toy — AP36

1969, June 20 Engr. ***Perf. 13***
C83 AP36 100fr mag, org & gray 1.20 65

Issued to publicize the International Toy Fair, Nuremberg, Germany.

Europafrica Issue, 1969

Ribbon Tied Around Bar — AP37

1969, Aug. 5 Photo. ***Perf. 13x12***
C84 AP37 50fr bl grn, lil & blk 50 30

See note after Chad No. C11.

Armstrong, Aldrin and Collins AP38

Painter, Poto-Poto School AP39

Souvenir Sheet

Design: No. C85b, Blast-off from Moon.

Embossed on Gold Foil

1969, Sept. 15 ***Imperf.***
C85 AP38 Sheet of 2 20.00 20.00
a. 1000fr gold 9.00 9.00
b. 1000fr gold 9.00 9.00

See note after Algeria No. 427. No. C85 contains one each of Nos. C85a and C85b with simulated perforations. Size: 65x52mm.

1970, Feb. 20 Engr. ***Perf. 13***

Designs: 150fr, Sculpture lesson (man, infant and sculpture). 200fr, Potter working on vase.

C86 AP39 100fr multi 1.10 50
C87 AP39 150fr multi 1.60 80
C88 AP39 200fr multi 1.85 1.25

Painting Type (Philexafrique) of 1968

Paintings: 150fr, Child with Cherries, by John Russell. 200fr, Erasmus, by Hans Holbein the Younger. 250fr, "Silence" (head), by Bernardino Luini. 300fr, Scene from the Massacre of Scio, by Delacroix. 500fr, The Capture of Constantinople by the Crusaders, by Delacroix.

1970 Photo. ***Perf. 12½***
C89 AP34 150fr lil & multi 2.00 95
C90 AP34 200fr multi 2.40 1.20
C91 AP34 250fr brn & multi 2.65 1.50
C92 AP34 300fr multi 3.75 1.75
C93 AP34 500fr brn & multi 5.25 2.65
Nos. C89-C93 (5) 16.05 8.05

Aurichalcite — AP40

Design: 15fr, Dioptase.

1970, Mar. 20

C94 AP40 100fr multi 1.10 55
C95 AP40 150fr multi 1.75 80

Lenin — AP41 Karl Marx — AP42

Design: 75fr, Lenin, seated.

1970, June 25 Photo. *Perf. 12½*

C96 AP41 45fr grn, org & brn 50 20
C97 AP41 75fr vio bl, brn lake & dp cl 75 35

Issued to commemorate the centenary of the birth of Lenin (1870-1924), Russian communist leader.

1970, July 10 Engr. *Perf. 13*

Design: No. C99, Friedrich Engels.

C98 AP42 50fr emer, dk brn & dk red 55 28
C99 AP42 50fr ultra, dk brn & dk red 55 28

Issued in memory of Karl Marx (1818-1883) and Friedrich Engels (1820-1895), German socialist writers.

Otto Lilienthal's Glider, 1891 — AP43

Designs: 50fr, "Spirit of St. Louis," Lindbergh's first transatlantic solo flight, 1927. 70fr, Sputnik 1, first satellite in space. 90fr, First man on the moon, Apollo 11, 1969.

1970, Sept. 5 Engr. *Perf. 13*

C100 AP43 45fr dp car, bl & ol bis 55 28
C101 AP43 50fr emer, sl grn & brn 55 32
C102 AP43 70fr brt bl, ol bis & dp car 80 40
C103 AP43 90fr brn, bl & ol gray 1.10 55

Forerunners of space exploration.

Saint on Horseback AP44 Marilyn Monroe and New York AP45

Designs from Stained Glass Windows, Brazzaville Cathedral: 150fr, Saint with staff. 250fr, The Elevation of the Host, from rose window.

1970, Dec. 10 Photo. *Perf. 12½*

C104 AP44 100fr dk vio bl & multi 1.10 55
C105 AP44 150fr dk vio bl & multi 1.75 90
C106 AP44 250fr dk vio bl & multi 3.00 1.60
a. Souvenir sheet of 3 6.00 6.00

Christmas 1970. No. C106a contains one each of Nos. C104-C106. Black marginal inscription. Size: 150x115mm.

1971, Mar. 16 Engr. *Perf. 13*

Portraits: 150fr, Martine Carol and Paris. 200fr, Erich von Stroheim and Vienna. 250fr, Sergei Eisenstein and Moscow.

C107 AP45 100fr brt grn, red brn & ultra 1.00 40
C108 AP45 150fr brn, brt lil & ultra 1.60 60
C109 AP45 200fr choc & ultra 2.00 90
C110 AP45 250fr brt grn, brn vio & ultra 2.40 1.00

History of motion pictures.

Painting Type of 1968

Paintings: 100fr, Christ Carrying Cross, by Paolo Veronese. 150fr, Christ on the Cross, Burgundian School, 1500 (vert.). 200fr, Descent from the Cross, by Rogier van der Weyden. 250fr, Christ Laid in the Tomb, Flemish School, 1500 (vert.). 500fr, Resurrection, by Hans Memling (vert.).

1971, April 26 Photo. *Perf. 13*

C111 AP29 100fr grn & multi 1.00 50
C112 AP29 150fr grn & multi 1.40 65
C113 AP29 200fr grn & multi 2.00 1.00
C114 AP29 250fr grn & multi 2.40 1.20
C115 AP29 500fr grn & multi 4.75 2.40
Nos. C111-C115 (5) 11.55 5.75

Easter 1971.

Map of Africa and Telecommunications System — AP46

1971, June 18 Photo. *Perf. 12½*

C116 AP46 70fr bl, gray & dk brn 65 32
C117 AP46 85fr bl, lil rose & dk brn 75 40
C118 AP46 90fr grn, yel & dk brn 80 45

Pan-African telecommunications system.

Globe and Waves — AP47

1971, June 19

C119 AP47 65fr lt bl & multi 60 27

3rd World Telecommunications Day.

Japanese Mask and Play — AP48 Olympic Torch and Rings — AP49

Design: 150fr, Japanese and African women, symbolic leaves.

1971, June 28 Engr. *Perf. 13*

C120 AP48 75fr lil, blk & mag 80 40
C121 AP48 150fr dk brn, brn red & red lil 1.50 80

PHILATOKYO '71 International Stamp Exhibition, Tokyo, Apr. 20-30.

1971, July 20 Engr. *Perf. 13*

Design: 350fr, Olympic rings and various sports (horiz.).

C122 AP49 150fr brt rose lil, org & sl grn 1.60 90
C123 AP49 350fr bis, brt grn & vio 3.75 1.75

Pre-Olympic Year, 1971.

Scout Emblem, Japanese Dragon and African Carved Canoe — AP50

Designs (Boy Scout Emblem and): 90fr, Japanese mask and African boy (vert.). 100fr, Japanese woman and African drummer (vert.). 250fr, Congolese mask.

1971, Aug. 25

C124 AP50 85fr brt rose lil, Prus bl & brn 1.00 45
C125 AP50 90fr dk car, brn & vio 1.10 50
C126 AP50 100fr ol gray, rose mag & brt grn 1.25 60
C127 AP50 250fr brt grn, choc & car 3.00 1.40

13th Boy Scout World Jamboree, Asagiri Plain, Japan, Aug. 2-10.

Olympic Rings and Running — AP51

Designs (Olympic Rings and): 85fr, Hurdles. 90fr, Weight lifting, boxing, discus, running, javelin. 100fr, Wrestling. 150fr, Boxing.

1971, Sept. 30

C128 AP51 75fr plum, bl & dk brn 70 32
C129 AP51 85fr scar, sl & dk brn 75 35
C130 AP51 90fr vio bl & dk brn 85 45
C131 AP51 100fr brn & sl 1.00 50
C132 AP51 150fr grn, red & dk brn 1.60 80
Nos. C128-C132 (5) 4.90 2.42

75th anniversary of the first modern Olympic Games.

Congo No. C36 and de Gaulle — AP52

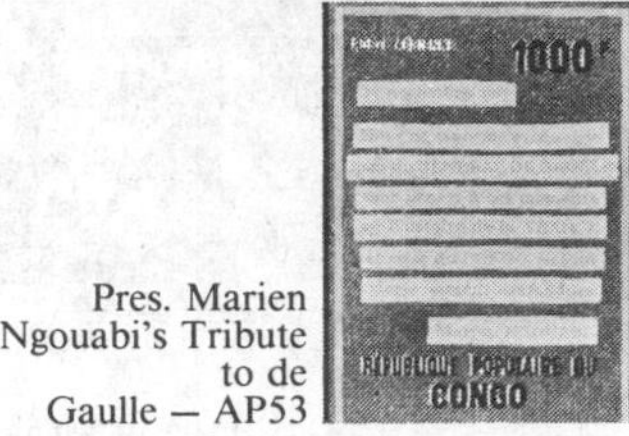

Pres. Marien Ngouabi's Tribute to de Gaulle — AP53

Design: No. C135, Charles de Gaulle.

1971, Nov. 9

C133 AP52 500fr sl grn & multi 6.50 6.50

Lithographed; Gold Embossed
Perf. 12½

C134 AP53 1000fr gold, grn & red 12.00 12.00
C135 AP53 1000fr gold, grn & red 12.00 12.00

Charles de Gaulle (1890-1970), president of France. Nos. C134-C135 printed se-tenant.

African Postal Union Issue, 1971
Common Design Type

Design: 100fr, Allegory of Congo Republic (woman) and UAMPT Building, Brazzaville.

1971, Nov. 13 Photo. *Perf. 13x13½*

C136 CD135 100fr bl & multi 1.10 55

Flag of Congo Republic and "Revolution" — AP54

1971, Nov. 30

C137 AP54 100fr red & multi 1.00 50

8th anniversary of revolution.

Workers and Flag — AP55

Design: 40fr, Flag of Congo Republic and sun.

1971, Dec. 31 Photo. *Perf. 13x12½*

C138 AP55 30fr multi 25 12
C139 AP55 40fr red & multi 35 20

2nd anniversary of founding of Congolese Labor Party (No. C138), and adoption of red flag (No. C139).

Book Year Emblem — AP56

1972, June 3 Litho. *Perf. 12½*
C140 AP56 50fr red, grn & yel 40 20

International Book Year 1972.

Congolese Soccer Team — AP57

Design: No. C142, Captain of winning team and cup (vert.).

1973, Feb. 22 Photo. *Perf. 13*
C141 AP57 100fr ultra, red & blk 1.10 65
C142 AP57 100fr red, yel & blk 1.10 65

Girl Holding Bird, Environment Emblem — AP58

1973, Mar. 5 Engr.
C143 AP58 85fr org, sl grn & bl 65 40

U.N. Conference on Human Environment, Stockholm, Sweden, June 5-16, 1972.

Miles Davis AP59

Designs: 140fr, Ella Fitzgerald. 160fr, Count Basie. 175fr, John Coltrane.

1973, Mar. 5 Photo. *Perf. 13x13½*
C144 AP59 125fr multi 1.00 50
C145 AP59 140fr multi 1.10 55
C146 AP59 160fr multi 1.30 65
C147 AP59 175fr multi 1.50 75

Black American jazz musicians.

Olympic Rings, Hurdling — AP60

Designs (Olympic Rings and): 150fr, Pole vault (vert.). 250fr, Wrestling.

1973, Mar. 15 Engr. *Perf. 13*
C148 AP60 100fr lil rose & vio 1.00 50
C149 AP60 150fr emer & vio 1.50 75
C150 AP60 250fr bl & mag 2.50 1.35

20th Olympic Games, Munich, Aug. 26-Sept. 11, 1972.

Refinery and Storage Tanks, Djeno — AP61

Designs: 230fr, Off-shore drilling platform (vert.). 240fr, Workers assembling drill (vert.). 260fr, Off-shore drilling installation.

1973, Mar. 20
C151 AP61 180fr red, bl & ind 1.60 80
C152 AP61 230fr red, bl & blk 2.00 1.00
C153 AP61 240fr red, ind & brn 2.25 1.20
C154 AP61 260fr red, bl & blk 2.60 1.40

Oil installations, Pointe-Noire.

Astronauts, Landing Module and Lunar Rover on Moon — AP62

1973, Mar. 31
C155 AP62 250fr multi 2.50 1.50

Apollo 17 U.S. moon mission, Dec. 7-19, 1972.

ITU Emblem, Symbols of Communications AP63

1973, May 24 Engr. *Perf. 13*
C156 AP63 120fr multi 80 40

5th International Telecommunications Day.

White Horse, by Delacroix — AP64

Designs: Paintings by Eugene Delacroix.

1973, June 30 Photo. *Perf. 13*
C157 AP64 150fr *shown* 1.35 1.35
C158 AP64 250fr *Lion sleeping* 2.25 1.90
C159 AP64 300fr *Lion and tiger* 2.75 2.25

See Nos. C169-C171.

Copernicus and Heliocentric System — AP65

1973, June 30 Engr.
C160 AP65 50fr multi 45 35

500th anniversary of the birth of Nicolaus Copernicus (1473-1543), Polish astronomer.

Plane, Ship, Rocket, Village, Sun and Clouds — AP66

1973, July
C161 AP66 50fr red & multi 40 28

Centenary of international meteorological cooperation.

Pres. Marien N'Gouabi — AP67

1973, Aug. 12 Photo. *Perf. 13*
C162 AP67 30fr multi 25 10
C163 AP67 40fr aqua & multi 32 15
C164 AP67 75fr red & multi 65 32

10th anniversary of independence.

Stamps, Album, African Woman AP68

Designs: 40fr, No. C167, Stamps in shape of map of Congo, album, globe. No. C168, Like 30fr.

1973, Aug. 12
C165 AP68 30fr pur & multi 25 12
C166 AP68 40fr multi 32 15
C167 AP68 100fr dk brn & multi 75 55
C168 AP68 100fr ocher & multi 75 55

Nos. C165 and C168 commemorate the 10th anniversary of the revolution, Nos. C166-C167 the International Philatelic Exhibition, Brazzaville.

Painting Type of 1973 Inscribed "EUROPAFRIQUE"

Designs: Details from "Earth and Paradise," by Jan Brueghel, the Elder.

1973, Oct. 10 Photo. *Perf. 13*
C169 AP64 100fr *Spotted hyena* 1.00 75
C170 AP64 100fr *Leopard and lion* 1.00 75
C171 AP64 100fr *Elephant and creatures* 1.00 75

U.S. and Russian Spacecraft Docking — AP69

Design: 80fr, US and USSR spacecraft docked in space and emblems of 1975 joint space mission.

1973, Oct. 15 Engr. *Perf. 13*
C172 AP69 40fr bl, red & brn 35 20
C173 AP69 80fr red, grn & bl 65 40

Planned joint United States and Soviet space missions.

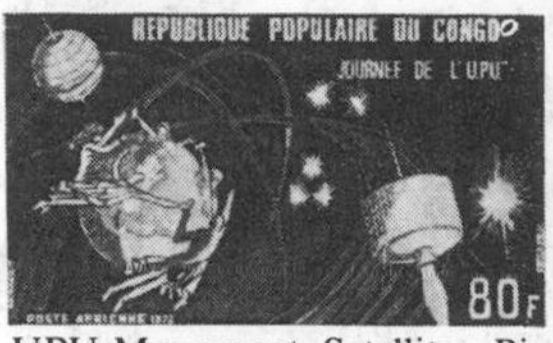
UPU Monument, Satellites, Big Dipper — AP70

1973, Nov. 20 Engr. *Perf. 13*
C174 AP70 80fr vio bl & lt bl 65 35

Universal Postal Union Day.

Astronauts Working in Space — AP71

Design: 40fr, Spacecraft and Skylab docking in space.

1973, Nov. 30
C175 AP71 30fr ultra, sl grn & choc 25 15
C176 AP71 40fr mag, org & sl grn 35 25

Skylab, first space laboratory.

Goalkeeper, Soccer — AP72

Design: 100fr, Soccer player kicking ball.

1973, Dec. 20
C177 AP72 40fr sl grn, sep & brn 32 25
C178 AP72 100fr pur, red & sl grn 1.00 55

World Soccer Cup, Munich, 1974.

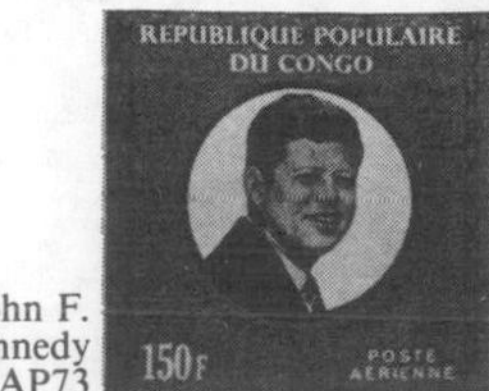
John F. Kennedy AP73

1973, Dec. 20 Photo. *Perf. 12½*
C179 AP73 150fr ultra, gold & blk 1.20 75

10th anniversary of the death of Pres. John F. Kennedy (1917-1963).

Runners — AP74

Flag over Map of Congo — AP75

1973, Dec. 20 Engr. *Perf. 13*
C180 AP74 40fr sl grn, red & brn 32 25
C181 AP74 100fr red, sl grn, & brn 1.00 55

2nd African Games, Lagos, Nigeria.

1973, Dec. 31 Photo.
C182 AP75 40fr dp grn & multi 32 20

4th anniversary of Congolese Labor Party and of the Congo Red Flag.

Soccer and Games Emblem — AP76

1974, June 20 Photo. *Perf. 13*
C183 AP76 250fr multi 2.00 1.30

World Cup Soccer Championship, Munich, June 13-July 7.

Astronauts Yuri A. Gagarin and Alan B. Shepard — AP77

Designs: 30fr, Space, globe, Russian and American flags with names of astronauts who perished in space. 100fr, Alexei Leonov and Neil A. Armstrong in space and on moon.

1974, June 30 Engr. *Perf. 13*
C184 AP77 30fr red, ultra & brn 25 15
C185 AP77 40fr red, bl & brn 35 20
C186 AP77 100fr car, grn & brn 1.00 60

Soccer Game Superimposed on Ball — AP78

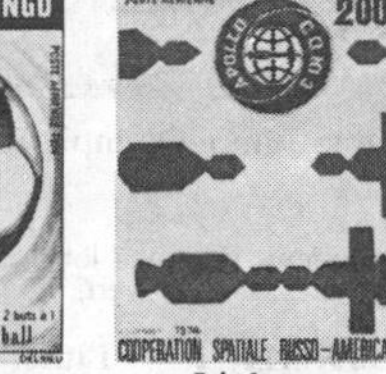

Link-up Emblem, Stages of Link-up — AP79

1974, July 31 Photo. *Perf. 13*
C187 AP78 250fr multi 2.00 1.30

Germany's victory in World Cup Soccer Championship.

1974, Aug. 8 Engr. *Perf. 13*

Design: 300fr, Spacecraft docking over globe (horiz.).

C188 AP79 200fr pur, bl & red 1.60 1.20
C189 AP79 300fr multi 2.40 1.60

Russo-American space cooperation.

Symbols of Communications, UPU Emblem — AP80

1974, Aug. 10
C190 AP80 500fr blk & red 4.00 2.75

Centenary of Universal Postal Union.

Lenin and Pendulum Trace Pattern — AP81

1974, Sept. 16 Engr. *Perf. 13*
C191 AP81 150fr multi 1.20 80

50th death anniversary of Lenin (1870-1924).

Churchill and Order of the Garter AP82

Marconi and Wireless Telegraph AP83

1974, Oct. 1 Litho. *Perf. 13*
C192 AP82 200fr lt grn & multi 1.60 1.00
C193 AP83 200fr lt ultra & multi 1.60 1.00

Birth centenaries of Sir Winston Churchill (1874-1965), statesman; and of Guglielmo Marconi (1874-1937), Italian electrical engineer and inventor.

No. C190 Surcharged in Violet Blue with New Value, 2 Bars and: "9 OCTOBER 1974"

1974, Oct. 9
C194 AP80 300fr on 500fr multi 2.40 1.60

Universal Postal Union Day.

UDEAC Issue

Presidents and Flags of Cameroun, CAR, Gabon and Congo — AP83a

1974, Dec. 8 Photo. *Perf. 13*
C195 AP83a 100fr gold & multi 80 60

See note after Cameroun No. 595.

Regatta at Argenteuil, by Monet — AP84

Impressionist Paintings: 40fr, Seated Dancer, by Degas. 50fr, Girl on Swing, by Renoir. 75fr, Girl with Straw Hat, by Renoir. All vertical.

1974, Dec. 15
C196 AP84 30fr gold & multi 35 25
C197 AP84 40fr gold & multi 40 30
C198 AP84 50fr gold & multi 65 50
C199 AP84 75fr gold & multi 70 55

National Fair — AP85

1974, Dec. 20
C200 AP85 30fr multi 25 15

National Fair, Aug. 24-Sept. 8.

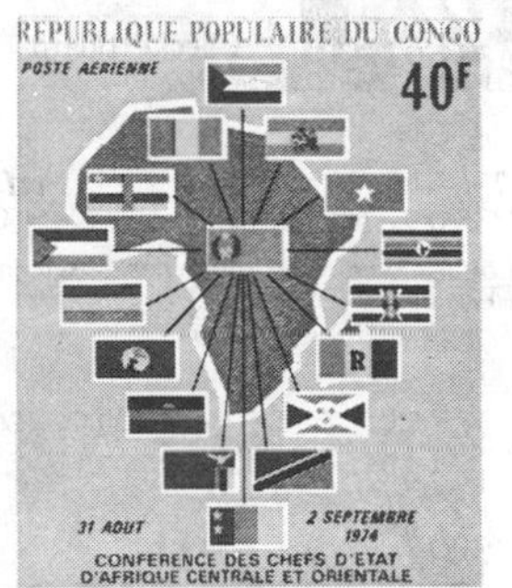

Flags of Participating Nations, Map of Africa — AP86

1974, Dec. 20 *Perf. 13*
C201 AP86 40fr ultra & multi 40 25

Conference of Chiefs of State of Central and East Africa, Brazzaville, Aug. 31-Sept. 2.

"Five Weeks in a Balloon," by Jules Verne AP87

Design: 50fr, "Around the World in 80 Days," by Jules Verne.

1975, June 30 Litho. *Perf. 12½*
C202 AP87 40fr multi 35 20
C203 AP87 50fr multi 40 25

Jules Verne (1828-1905), French science fiction writer, 70th death anniversary.

Paris-Brussels Train, 1890 — AP88

Design: 75fr, Santa Fe, 1880.

1975, June 30
C204 AP88 50fr ocher & multi 40 25
C205 AP88 75fr lt bl & multi 60 35

Soyuz and Apollo-Soyuz Emblem — AP89

Design: 100fr, Apollo and emblem.

1975, July 20 Litho. *Perf. 12½*
C206 AP89 95fr org, blk & mag 75 50
C207 AP89 100fr vio, bl & blk 80 60

Apollo Soyuz space test project (Russo-American space cooperation), launching July 15; link-up, July 17.

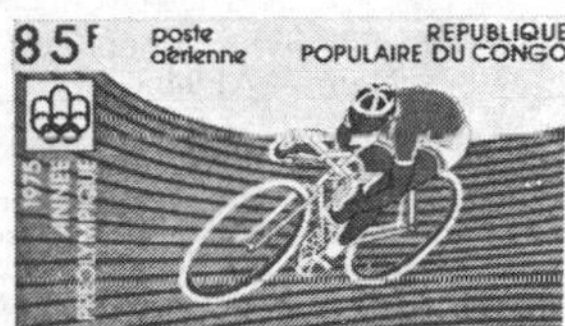

Bicycling and Montreal Olympic Emblem — AP90

Designs (Montreal Olympic Emblem and): 40fr, Boxing (vert.). 50fr, Basketball (vert.). 95fr, High jump. 100fr, Javelin. 150fr, Running.

Perf. 12½x13, 13x12½

1975, Oct. 30 Photo.
C208 AP90 40fr multi 35 20
C209 AP90 50fr red & multi 40 25
C210 AP90 85fr bl & multi 70 50
C211 AP90 95fr org & multi 75 55
C212 AP90 100fr multi 80 60
C213 AP90 150fr multi 1.20 90
Nos. C208-C213 (6) 4.20 3.00

Pre-Olympic Year 1975.

Map of Africa, Sports and Flags — AP91

Workers and Flag — AP92

1975, Dec. 20 Litho. *Perf. 12½*
C214 AP91 30fr multi 25 15

10th anniversary of first African Games, Brazzaville.

1975, Dec. 31 Litho. *Perf. 12½*
C215 AP92 60fr multi 50 30

6th anniversary of the Congolese Labor Party (P.C.T.).

Alphonse Fondere — AP93

Historic Ships: 5fr, like 30fr. 40fr, Hamburg, 1839. 15fr, 50fr, Gomer, 1831. 20fr, 60fr, Great Eastern, 1858. 95fr, J.M. White II, 1878.

1976 Engr. *Perf. 13*

C216	AP93 5fr multi		5	5
C217	AP93 10fr multi		8	6
C218	AP93 15fr multi		12	8
C219	AP93 20fr multi		17	12
C220	AP93 30fr multi		25	15
C221	AP93 40fr multi		30	25
C222	AP93 50fr multi		40	30
C223	AP93 60fr multi		50	35
C224	AP93 95fr multi		75	55
	Nos. C216-C224 (9)		2.62	1.91

Issue dates: Nos. C216-C219, May. Nos. C220-C224, Mar. 7.

Europafrica Issue 1976

Peasant Family, by Louis Le Nain — AP94

Paintings: 80fr, Boy with Top, by Jean B. Chardin. 95fr, Venus and Aeneas, by Nicolas Poussin. 100fr, The Rape of the Sabine Women, by Jacques Louis David.

1976, Mar. 20 Litho. *Perf. 12½*

C225	AP94 60fr gold & multi	50	30
C226	AP94 80fr gold & multi	65	45
C227	AP94 95fr gold & multi	75	55
C228	AP94 100fr gold & multi	80	60

Nos. C225-C228 printed in sheets of 8 stamps and horizontal gutter with commemorative inscription. Black control number in margin.

Telephone Type of 1976

1976, Apr. 25 Litho. *Perf. 12½x13*

C229 A107 60fr pink, mar & crim 50 35

Centenary of first telephone call by Alexander Graham Bell, Mar. 10, 1876.

Sports Type of 1976

Designs: 150fr, Runner and map of Central Africa. 200fr, Discus and map.

1976, Oct. 25 *Perf. 12½*

C230	A110 150fr multi	1.20	90
C231	A110 200fr multi	1.60	1.10

Gold medalists, 1st Central African Games, Yaounde, July 27-30, 1975.

Map of Africa, Flag and OAU Headquarters — AP95

1976, Dec. 16 Typo. *Perf. 13x14*

C232 AP95 60fr multi 50 35

13th anniversary of the Organization for African Unity.

Europafrica Issue

Map of Europe and Africa — AP96

1977, June 28 Litho. *Perf. 13*

C233 AP96 75fr multi 60 50

Headdress Type of 1977

1977, June 30 *Perf. 12½*

Designs: 250fr, Two straw caps. 300fr, Beaded cap.

C234	A118 250fr multi	2.00	1.50
C235	A118 300fr multi	2.40	1.80

Zeppelin Type of 1977
Souvenir Sheet

Design: 500fr, LZ 127 over U.S. Capitol.

1977, Aug. 5 Litho. *Perf. 11*

C236 A120 500fr multi 4.75 2.00

History of the Zeppelin.
No. C236 has multicolored margin showing parts of two Zeppelins. Size: 105x92mm. Exists imperf.

Checkerboard AP97

1977, Aug. 20 Engr. *Perf. 13*

C237 AP97 60fr red & blk 50 35

Lomé Convention on General Agreement on Tariffs and Trade (GATT).

Newton, Intelsat Satellite and Classical "Planets" — AP98

1977, Aug. 25

C238 AP98 140fr multi 1.10 90

Isaac Newton (1642-1727), natural philosopher and mathematician, 250th death anniversary.

Elizabeth II Type of 1977
Souvenir Sheet

Design: 500fr, Royal family on balcony.

1977, Dec. 21 Litho. *Perf. 14*

C239 A128 500fr multi 4.75 2.00

25th anniversary of the reign of Queen Elizabeth II.

Mallard AP99

Birds: 75fr, Purple heron (vert.). 150fr, Reed warbler (vert.). 240fr, Hoopoe (vert.).

Perf. 13x12½, 12½x13

1978, May 22

C240	AP99 65fr multi	50	25
C241	AP99 75fr multi	60	30
C242	AP99 150fr multi	1.20	65
C243	AP99 240fr multi	1.90	1.00

Souvenir Sheet
No. C239 Overprinted in Silver: "ANNIVERSAIRE DU / COURONNEMENT / 1953-1978"

1978, Sept. Litho. *Perf. 14*

C244 A128 500fr multi 4.00 1.85

25th anniversary of coronation of Queen Elizabeth II. Size: 111x92mm.

Philexafrique II-Essen Issue
Common Design Types

Designs: No. C245, Leopard and Congo No. C243. No. C246, Eagle and Wurttemberg No. 1.

1978, Nov. 1 Litho. *Perf. 12½*

C245	CD138 100fr multi	1.00	60
C246	CD139 100fr multi	1.00	60

Nos. C245-C246 printed se-tenant.

Map of Africa Satellites — AP100

1978, Nov. 25 Engr. *Perf. 13*

C247 AP100 100fr multi 1.00 60

Pan-African Telecommunications Network, PANAFEL.

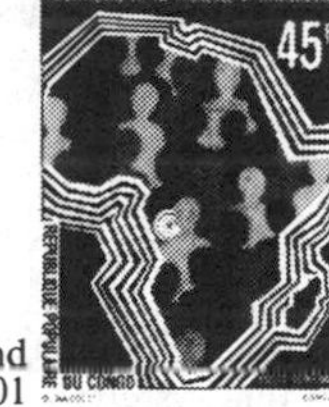
Map of Africa and People — AP101

1979, Aug. 2 Litho. *Perf. 12½*

C248	AP101 45fr multi	45	30
C249	AP101 75fr multi	75	50

5th Conference of Panafrican Youth Movement, Brazzaville, Aug. 2-7.

Abala Peasant Woman AP102

1979, Aug. 20

C250 AP102 150fr multi 1.50 90

Nos. C173, C206-C207, C186, C189 Overprinted "ALUNISSAGE APOLLO XI / JUILLET 1969" and Emblem

Perf. 13, 12½

1979, Nov. 5 Engr., Litho.

C251	AP69 80fr multi	80	52
C252	AP89 95fr multi	95	62
C253	AP89 100fr multi	1.00	65
C254	AP77 100fr multi	1.00	65
C255	AP79 300fr multi	3.00	2.00
	Nos. C251-C255 (5)	6.75	4.44

Apollo 11 moon landing, 10th anniversary.

Runner, Olympic Rings — AP103

Pre-Olympic Year: 100fr, Boxing. 200fr, Fencing (vert.). 300fr, Soccer. 500fr, Moscow '80 emblem (vert.).

1979 Litho. *Perf. 13½*

C256	AP103 65fr multi	60	30
C257	AP103 100fr multi	90	45
C258	AP103 200fr multi	1.75	85
C259	AP103 300fr multi	2.75	1.35
C260	AP103 500fr multi	4.50	2.25
	Nos. C256-C260 (5)	10.50	5.20

Cross-Country Skiing — AP104

Lake Placid '80 Emblem and: 60fr, Slalom. 200fr, Ski jump, 350fr, Downhill skiing (horiz.). 500fr, Woman skier.

1979, Dec *Perf. 14½*
Size: 24x42, 42x24mm.

C261	AP104 40fr multi	40	28
C262	AP104 60fr multi	60	42
C263	AP104 200fr multi	2.00	1.40
C264	AP104 350fr multi	3.50	2.50

Size: 31½x46½mm.
Perf. 14

C265	AP104 500fr multi	5.00	3.50
	Nos. C261-C265 (5)	11.50	8.10

13th Winter Olympic Games, Lake Placid, N.Y., Feb. 12-24, 1980.

Overprinted with Names of Winners

1980, Apr. 28

C266	AP104 40fr Zimiatov	32	16
C267	AP104 60fr Moser-Proell	48	24
C268	AP104 200fr Tomanen	1.60	80
C269	AP104 350fr Stock	2.80	1.40
C270	AP104 500fr Stenmark-Wenzel	4.00	2.00
	Nos. C266-C270 (5)	9.20	4.60

Long Jump, Olympic Rings — AP105

Olympic rings and long jump scenes. Nos. C266, C268-C269 vert.

1980, May 2 Litho. *Perf. 14½*

C271	AP105 75fr multi	60	30
C272	AP105 150fr multi	1.20	60
C273	AP105 250fr multi	2.00	1.00
C274	AP105 350fr multi	2.80	1.40

Souvenir Sheet

C275 AP105 500fr multi 4.00 2.00

22nd Summer Olympic Games, Moscow, July 19-Aug. 3. No. C275 has multicolored margin showing Kremlin and runners. Size: 104x78mm.

Stadium, Mascot, Madrid Club Emblem — AP106

Stadium, Mascot and Club Emblem: 75fr, Zaragoza. 100fr, Madrid Athletic Club. 150fr, Valencia. 175fr, Spain. 250fr, Barcelona.

1980, June 23 Litho. *Perf. 14x13½*

C276	AP106	60fr multi	52	25
C277	AP106	75fr multi	65	32
C278	AP106	100fr multi	90	45
C279	AP106	150fr multi	1.40	70
C280	AP106	175fr multi	1.50	1.25
		Nos. C276-C280 (5)	4.97	2.97

Souvenir Sheet

C281 AP106 250fr multi 2.25 1.25

World Soccer Cup 1982. No. C281 has multicolored margin showing mascot. Size: 104½x79mm.

Adoration of the Shepherds — AP107

Rembrandt Paintings: 100fr, The Burial. 200fr, Christ at Emmaus. 300fr, Annunciation (vert.). 500fr, Crucifixion (vert.).

1980, July 4 *Perf. 12½*

C282	AP107	65fr multi	52	26
C283	AP107	100fr multi	80	40
C284	AP107	200fr multi	1.60	80
C285	AP107	300fr multi	2.40	1.20
C286	AP107	500fr multi	4.00	2.00
		Nos. C283-C286 (4)	8.80	4.40

Albert Camus (1913-1960), Writer — AP108

Design: 150fr, Jacques Offenbach (1819-1880), composer (vert.).

1980, July 5 Engr. *Perf. 13*

C287	AP108	100fr multi	90	45
C288	AP108	150fr multi	1.40	70

Raffia Dancing Skirts — AP109

Traditional Dancing Costumes: 300fr, Tam-tam dancers (vert.). 350fr, Masks.

1980, Aug. 6 Litho. *Perf. 13½*

C289	AP109	250fr multi	2.00	1.00
C290	AP109	300fr multi	2.40	1.20
C291	AP109	350fr multi	2.80	1.40

Nos. C271-C275 Overprinted with Winner and Country

1980, Nov. 14 Litho. *Perf. 14½*

C292	AP105	75fr multi	60	30
C293	AP105	150fr multi	1.20	60
C294	AP105	250fr multi	2.00	1.00
C295	AP105	350fr multi	2.80	1.40

Souvenir Sheet

C296 AP105 500fr multi 4.00 2.00

The Studio by Picasso — AP109a

1981, July 4 *Perf. 12½*

C296A	AP109a	100fr shown	80	40
C296B	AP109a	150fr Landscape	1.20	60
C296C	AP109a	200fr Cannes Studio	1.60	80
C296D	AP109a	300fr Still Life	2.40	1.20
C296E	AP109a	500fr Still Life, diff.	4.00	2.00
		Nos. C296A-C296E (5)	10.00	5.00

1350th Anniv. of Mohamed's Death at Medina — AP110

1982, July 17 Litho. *Perf. 13*

C297 AP110 400fr Medina Mosque minaret 3.25 1.60

Nos. C276-C281 Overprinted with Finalists and/or Scores in Black on Silver.

1982, Oct. 7 Litho. *Perf. 14x13½*

C298	AP106	60fr multi	50	25
C299	AP106	75fr multi	60	30
C300	AP106	100fr multi	80	40
C301	AP106	150fr multi	1.20	60
C302	AP106	175fr multi	1.40	70
		Nos. C298-C302 (5)	4.50	2.25

Souvenir Sheet

C303 AP106 250fr multi 2.00 1.00

30th Anniv. of Amelia Earhart's Transatlantic Flight — AP111

1982, Dec. 4 Engr. *Perf. 13*

C304 AP111 150fr multi 1.20 60

Wind Surfing AP112

Various wind surfing scenes, 1984 Olympic Games, 100fr, 300fr, 400fr vert.

1983, June 4 Litho. *Perf. 13*

C305	AP112	100fr multi	70	35
C306	AP112	200fr multi	1.50	75
C307	AP112	300fr multi	2.25	1.10
C308	AP112	400fr multi	3.00	1.50

Souvenir Sheet

C309 AP112 500fr multi 4.00 2.00

No. C309 has multicolored margin continuing design. Size: 105x80mm.

Manned Flight Bicentenary AP113

Various balloons.

1983, June 7

C310	AP113	100fr Montgolfiere, 1783	70	35
C311	AP113	200fr Flesselles, 1784	1.50	75
C312	AP113	300fr Auguste Piccard, 1931	2.25	1.10
C313	AP113	400fr Don Piccard	3.00	1.50

Souvenir Sheet

C314 AP113 500fr Mail transport balloon, 1870 4.00 2.00

No. C314 has multicolored margin continuing design and showing balloon cover. Size: 78x100mm.

Christmas 1983 AP114

Various Virgin and Child Paintings by Botticelli.

1984, Jan. 21 Litho. *Perf. 13*

C315	AP114	150fr multi	70	35
C316	AP114	350fr multi	1.65	85
C317	AP114	500fr multi	2.50	1.25

Vase of Flowers, by Manet (1832-83) AP115

Paintings: 200fr, Small Holy Family, by Raphael. 300fr, La Belle Jardiniere, by Raphael. 400fr, Virgin of Loretto, by Raphael. 500fr, Portrait of Richard Wagner (1813-83), by Giuseppe Tivoli.

1984, Feb. 24 Litho. *Perf. 13*

C318	AP115	100fr multi	45	22
C319	AP115	200fr multi	90	45
C320	AP115	300fr multi	1.25	60
C321	AP115	400fr multi	1.90	95
C322	AP115	500fr multi	2.25	1.10
		Nos. C318-C322 (5)	6.75	3.32

1984 Summer Olympics — AP116

1984, Mar. 31 *Perf. 13*

C323	AP116	45fr Judo, vert.	18	10
C324	AP116	75fr Judo, diff.	30	15
C325	AP116	150fr Wrestling	70	35
C326	AP116	175fr Fencing	80	40
C327	AP116	350fr Fencing, diff.	1.65	85
		Nos. C323-C327 (5)	3.63	1.85

Souvenir Sheet

C328 AP116 500fr Boxing 2.25 1.10

Size of No. C328: 104x80mm.

1984 Summer Olympic Gold Medalists — AP117

Sailing/yachting: 100fr, Stephan Van Den Berg, Netherlands, Windglider Class, vert. 150fr, US, Soling Class. 200fr, Spain, 470 Class. 500fr, US, Flying Dutchman Class, vert.

1984, Dec. 18 Litho. *Perf. 13*

C329	AP117	100 fr multi	55	28
C330	AP117	150 fr multi	85	42
C331	AP117	200 fr multi	1.10	55
C332	AP117	500 fr multi	2.75	1.40

Virgin and Child, by Giovanni Bellini (c. 1430-1516) — AP118

Religious paintings: 100fr, Holy Family, by Andrea del Sarto (1486-1530), vert. 400fr, Virgin with Angels, by Cimabue (c. 1240-1302), vert.

1985, Feb. 12 Litho. *Perf. 13*

C333	AP118	100fr multi	40	20
C334	AP118	200fr multi	80	40
C335	AP118	400fr multi	1.50	75

Christmas 1984.

Souvenir Sheets
Nos. C309, C314 Ovptd. with Exhibition in Blue or Green.

1985, Mar. 8 *Perf. 13*

C336	AP112	500fr OLYMPHILEX '85/LAUSANNE (B)	2.00	1.00
C337	AP113	500fr MOPHILA '85/HAMBURG (G)	2.00	1.00

Audubon Birth Bicentenary — AP119

Illustrations of North American bird species by Audubon. Nos. C338-C339 vert.

1985, Apr. 11 *Perf. 13½*

C338 AP119 100fr Passiformes fringillidae 40 20
C339 AP119 150fr Eudocimus ruber 60 30
C340 AP119 200fr Buteo jamaicensis 80 40
C341 AP119 350fr Camptorhynchus labradorius 1.40 70

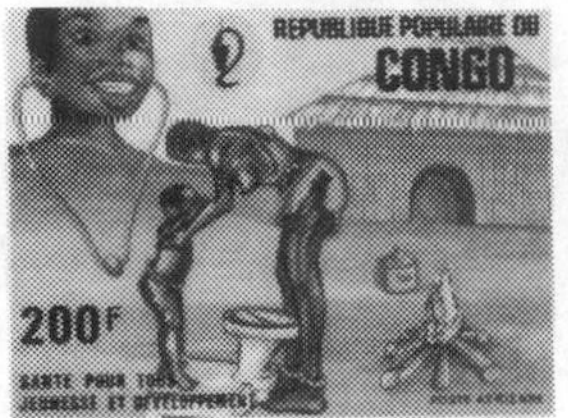

PHILEXAFRICA '85, Lome — AP120

Youths in public service activities.

1985, May 20 *Perf. 13*

C342 AP120 200fr Community health care 80 40
C343 AP120 200fr Agriculture 80 40

Nos. C342-C343 printed se-tenant with center label picturing map of Africa or UAPT emblem.

Admission to UN, 25th Anniv. — AP121

1985, Aug. 13

C344 AP121 190fr multi 85 42

UN, 40th Anniv. — AP122

1985, Oct. 25 *Perf. 12½*

C345 AP122 180fr Rainbow, emblem 95 45

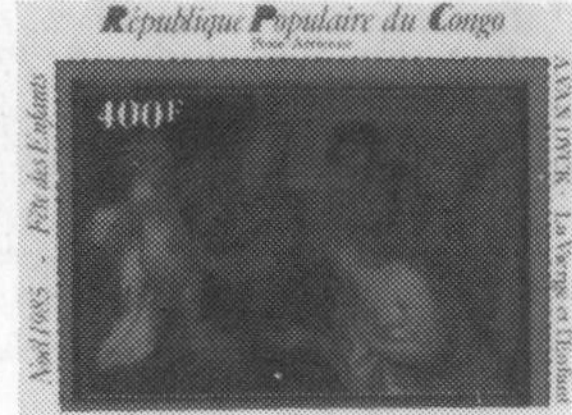

Christmas — AP123

Paintings: 100fr, The Virgin and the Infant Jesus, by David. 200fr, Adoration of the Magi, by Hieronymus Bosch (1450-1516). 400fr, Virgin and Child, by Van Dyck (1599-1641).

1985, Dec. 20 **Litho.** *Perf. 13*

C346 AP123 100fr multi 55 28
C347 AP123 200fr multi 1.10 55
C348 AP123 400fr multi 2.20 1.10

Nos. C346-C347 vert.

Halley's Comet — AP124

1986, Feb. 17

C349 AP124 125fr Halley, comet 68 35
C350 AP124 150fr West's Comet, 1976 82 40
C351 AP124 225fr Ikeya Seki's Comet, 1965 1.25 62
C352 AP124 300fr Trajectory diagram 1.65 82
C353 AP124 350fr Comet, Vega probe 2.00 1.00
Nos. C349-C353 (5) 6.40 3.19

Nos. C350-C351 vert.

Cosmos-Frantel Hotel — AP125

1986, May 1 *Perf. 13½*

C354 AP125 250fr multi 1.40 70

1986 World Cup Soccer Championships, Mexico — AP126

Various soccer plays.

1986, July 22 **Litho.** *Perf. 13*

C355 AP126 150fr multi 90 45
C356 AP126 250fr multi 1.50 75
C357 AP126 440fr multi 2.75 1.40
C358 AP126 600fr multi 3.75 1.90

Air Africa, 25th Anniv. — AP127

1986, Nov. 29 **Litho.** *Perf. 13½*

C359 AP127 200fr multi 1.10 55

1988 Winter Pre-Olympics, Calgary — AP128

1986, Dec. 15 *Perf. 13*

C360 AP128 150fr Downhill skiing 80 40
C361 AP128 250fr Bobsled 1.35 68
C362 AP128 440fr Women's cross-country skiing 2.40 1.20
C363 AP128 600fr Ski jumping 3.25 1.60

Nos. C361-C362 vert.

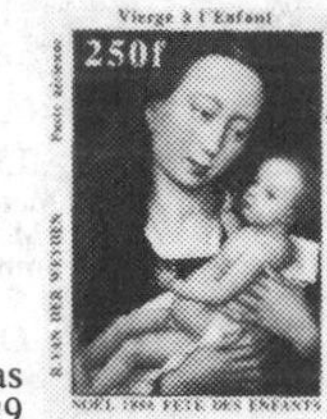

Christmas AP129

Paintings by Rogier van der Weyden (c.1399-1464): 250fr, Virgin and Child. 440fr, The Nativity. 500fr, Virgin with Carnation.

1986, Dec. 23 *Perf. 13½*

C364 AP129 250fr multi 1.35 68
C365 AP129 440fr multi 2.40 1.20
C366 AP129 500fr multi 2.75 1.35

Crocodiles, World Wildlife Fund — AP130

1987, Jan. 22 *Perf. 13*

C367 AP130 75fr Osteolaemus tetraspis 40 20
C368 AP130 100fr Crocodylus cataphractus 55 28
C369 AP130 125fr Osteolaemus tetraspis, diff. 68 35
C370 AP130 150fr Crocodylus cataphractus, diff. 80 40

1988 Summer Olympics, Seoul — AP131

1987, July 11 **Litho.** *Perf. 13*

C371 AP131 100fr Backstroke 70 35
C372 AP131 200fr Freestyle 1.50 75
C373 AP131 300fr Breaststroke 2.25 1.10
C374 AP131 400fr Butterfly 2.75 1.40

Souvenir Sheet

C375 AP131 750fr Start of event 5.25 2.75

No. C375 has multicolored decorative margin continuing the design. Size: 104x80mm.

Launch of Sputnik, First Artificial Satellite, 30th Anniv. — AP132

1987, June 5 *Perf. 12½x12*

C376 AP132 60fr multi 42 20
C377 AP132 240fr multi 1.75 85

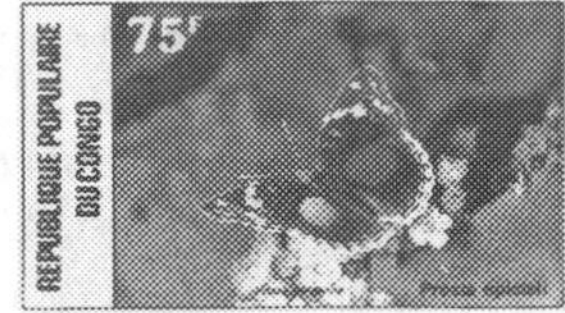

Butterflies — AP133

1987, Sept. 4 *Perf. 12½*

C378 AP133 75fr Precis epicleli 50 25
C379 AP133 120fr Deilephila nerii 80 40
C380 AP133 450fr Euryphene senegalensis 3.00 1.50
C381 AP133 550fr Precis almanta 3.75 1.90

Coubertin, Eternal Flame and Greece No. 125 — AP134

Cameo portrait, athletes and stamps: 120fr, Runners, France No. 198. 350fr, Congo Republic No. C22, hurdler. 600fr, High jump, Congo Republic No. C75.

1987, Nov. 4

C382 AP134 75fr shown 55 28
C383 AP134 120fr multi 88 45
C384 AP134 350fr multi 2.50 1.25
C385 AP134 600fr multi 4.25 2.15

Pierre de Coubertin (1863-1937), promulgator of the modern Olympics.

AIR POST SEMI-POSTAL STAMPS

Hathor Pillar — SPAP1

Unwmk.

1964, March 9 Engr. *Perf. 13*

CB1 SPAP1 10fr + 5fr vio & chnt 28 20
CB2 SPAP1 25fr + 5fr org brn & sl grn 45 35
CB3 SPAP1 50fr + 5fr sl grn & brn red 80 70

Issued to publicize the UNESCO world campaign to save historic monuments in Nubia.

POSTAGE DUE STAMPS

Messenger — D6

Early Transportation: 1fr, Litter. 2fr, Canoe. 5fr, Bicyclist. 10fr, Steam locomotive. 25fr, Seaplane.

Unwmk.

1961, Dec. 4 Engr. *Perf. 11*

J34 D6 50c ultra, ol bis & red 5 5
J35 D6 1fr red brn, red & grn 5 5
J36 D6 2fr grn, ultra & brn 8 8
J37 D6 5fr pur & gray brn 12 12
J38 D6 10fr bl, grn & choc 28 28
J39 D6 25fr bl, dk grn & dk brn 65 65

The two types of each value in Nos. J34-J45 (early and modern transportation) were printed tete beche, se-tenant at the base.

MH. 1521 Broussard Plane — D7

Modern transportation: 1fr, Land Rover. 2fr, River boat transporting barge. 5fr, Trailer-truck. 10fr, Diesel locomotive. 25fr, Boeing 707 jet plane.

J40 D7 50c ultra, ol bis & red 5 5
J41 D7 1fr red & grn 5 5
J42 D7 2fr ultra, grn & brn 8 8
J43 D7 5fr pur & gray brn 12 12
J44 D7 10fr dk grn & choc 28 28
J45 D7 25fr bl, dk grn & sep 65 65
Nos. J34-J45 (11) 2.41 2.41

See note following No. J39.

Flowers — D8

Flowers: 2fr, Phaeomeria magnifica. 5fr, Millettia laurentii. 10fr, Tuberose. 15fr, Pyrostegia venusta. 20fr, Hibiscus.

1971, Mar. 25 Photo. *Perf. 12x12½*

J46 D8 1fr multi 5 5
J47 D8 2fr multi 8 8
J48 D8 5fr pink & multi 10 10
J49 D8 10fr dk grn & multi 12 12
J50 D8 15fr multi 25 25
J51 D8 20fr multi 40 40
Nos. J46-51 (6) 1.00 1.00

Flowers and Fruit — D9

1986, June 5 Litho. *Perf. 13*

J52 D9 5fr Passiflora quadrangulares 5 5
J53 D9 10fr Cannaceae, vert. 6 5
J54 D9 15fr Ananas comosus, vert. 10 5

OFFICIAL STAMPS

Coat of Arms — O1

1968-70 Unwmk. Typo. *Perf. 14x13*

O1 O1 1fr multi ('70) 5 5
O2 O1 2fr multi ('70) 5 5
O3 O1 5fr multi ('70) 10 8
O4 O1 10fr multi ('70) 30 18
O5 O1 25fr emer & multi 25 10
O6 O1 30fr red & multi 30 10
O7 O1 50fr multi ('70) 90 45
O8 O1 85fr multi ('70) 1.60 90
O9 O1 100fr multi ('70) 2.00 1.10
O10 O1 200fr multi ('70) 3.00 2.25
Nos. O1-O10 (10) 8.55 5.26

CORFU

LOCATION — An island in the Ionian Sea opposite the Greek-Albanian border.
GOVT. — A department of Greece.
AREA — 245 sq. mi.
POP. — 114,620 (1938).
CAPITAL — Corfu.

In 1923 Italy occupied Corfu (Kerkyra) during a controversy with Greece over the assassination of an Italian official in Epirus. Italy again occupied Corfu in 1941-43.

100 Centesimi = 1 Lira
100 Lepta = 1 Drachma

Issued under Italian Occupation

Italian Stamps of 1901-23 Overprinted **CORFÙ**

1923, Sept. 20 Wmk. 140 *Perf. 14*

N1 A48 5c green 1.25 1.10
N2 A48 10c claret 3.00 1.10
N3 A48 15c slate 1.25 1.10
N4 A50 20c brn org 1.25 1.10
N5 A49 30c org brn 1.25 1.10
N6 A49 50c violet 1.25 1.10
N7 A49 60c blue 1.25 1.10
N8 A46 1l brn & grn 1.25 1.10
Nos. N1-N8 (8) 11.75 8.80

Italian Stamps of 1901-23 Surcharged **CORFÙ Lepta 25**

1923, Sept. 24

N9 A48 25l on 10c cl 8.00 5.00
N10 A49 60l on 25c bl 3.00
N11 A49 70l on 30c org brn 3.00
N12 A49 1.20d on 50c vio 6.00 5.00
N13 A46 2.40d on 1l brn & grn 6.00 5.00
N14 A46 4.75d on 2l grn & org 3.00

Nos. N10, N11 and N14 were not placed in use.

Issue for Corfu and Paxos.

Nos. N15-N34, NC1-NC12, NJ1-NJ11 and NRA1-NRA3 have been extensively counterfeited, some with forged cancellations.

Stamps of Greece, 1937-38, Overprinted in Black **CORFU**

Perf. 12x13½, 12½x12, 13½x12.

1941, June 5 Wmk. 252

N15 A69 5l brn red & bl 4.00 3.00
N16 A70 10l bl & brn red (On 397) 1.50 1.25
N17 A70 10l bl & brn red (On 413) 75.00 75.00
N18 A71 20l blk & grn 1.00 1.00
N19 A72 40l grn & blk 1.50 1.50
N20 A73 50l brn & blk 4.00 4.00
N21 A74 80l ind & yel brn 2.00 2.00
N22 A67 1d green 2.50 2.00
N23 A84 1.50d green 13.00 12.00
N24 A75 2d ultra 1.65 1.25
N25 A67 3d red brn 2.25 2.00
N26 A76 5d red 3.25 2.00
N27 A77 6d ol brn 3.75 3.00
N28 A78 7d dk brn 6.00 5.00
N29 A67 8d dp bl 4.75 4.00
N30 A79 10d red brn 110.00 65.00
N31 A80 15d green 10.00 9.00
N32 A81 25d dk bl 9.00 8.00
N33 A84 30d org brn 27.50 22.50
N34 A67 100d car lake 52.50 45.00
Nos. N15-N34 (20) 335.15 268.50

AIR POST STAMPS

Greece Nos. C37 and C26 to C35, Overprinted **CORFU**

Perf. 12½x13, 13x12½, 13½x12½.

1941, June 5 Unwmk.

NC1 D3 50l dk brn 6.00 5.00
NC2 AP16 1d red 125.00 75.00
NC3 AP17 2d gray bl 7.00 6.00
NC4 AP18 5d violet 7.00 6.00
NC5 AP19 7d dp ultra 7.00 6.00
NC6 AP20 10d bis brn (On C26) 165.00 72.50
NC7 AP20 10d brn org (On C35) 25.00 22.50
NC8 AP21 25d rose 45.00 37.50
NC9 AP22 30d dk grn 42.50 37.50
NC10 AP23 50d violet 50.00 45.00
a. Double overprint *300.00*
NC11 AP24 100d brown *900.00 475.00*

On No. C36.

Serrate Roulette 13½.

NC12 D3 50l vio brn 25.00 20.00
a. On C36a

POSTAGE DUE STAMPS

Postage Due Stamps of Greece, 1913-35 Overprinted **CORFU**

1941, June 5 Unwmk.

Serrate Roulette 13½.

NJ1 D3 10l carmine 2.00 2.00
NJ2 D3 25l ultra 2.00 2.00
NJ3 D3 80l lil brn 250.00 90.00

Perf. 12½x13, 13½x12½.

NJ4 D3 1d lt bl (On J80) *500.00 275.00*
NJ5 D3 2d lt red 3.00 2.25
NJ6 D3 5d gray 10.00 9.00
NJ7 D3 10d gray grn 6.00 6.00
NJ8 D3 15d red brn 6.00 6.00
NJ9 D3 25d lt red 6.00 6.00
NJ10 D3 50d orange 8.00 8.00
NJ11 D3 100d sl grn 185.00 120.00

POSTAL TAX STAMPS

Greece Nos. RA61 to RA63, Overprinted **CORFU**

1941, June 5 Unwmk. *Perf. 13½x12*

NRA1 PT7 10 l brt rose, *pale rose* 1.50 1.50
NRA2 PT7 50 l gray grn, *pale grn* 1.50 1.00
NRA3 PT7 1d dl bl, *lt bl* 8.00 7.00

Stamps overprinted "CORFU" were replaced by Italian stamps overprinted "Isole Jonie." (See Ionian Islands.)

COSTA RICA

LOCATION — Central America between Nicaragua and Panama.
GOVT. — Republic
AREA — 19,344 sq. mi.
POP. — 2,450,226 (1984)
CAPITAL — San Jose

Coat of Arms — A1

1863 Unwmk. Engr. *Perf. 12*

1 A1 ½r blue 75 1.25
a. ½r lt bl 75 1.75
b. Pair, imperf. btwn. 175.00
2 A1 2r scarlet 1.50 2.25
3 A1 4r green 15.00 17.50
4 A1 1p orange 30.00 35.00

The ½r was printed from two plates. The second is in light blue with little or no sky over the mountains.

Imperforate copies of Nos. 1-2 are corner copies from poorly perforated sheets.

Nos. 1-3 Surcharged in Red or Black:

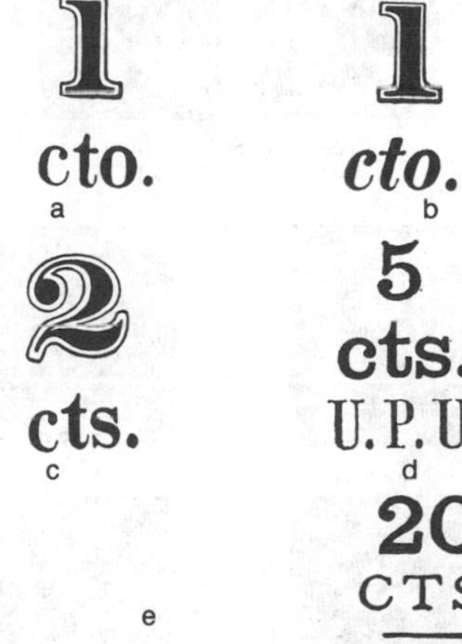

1881-82

Red or Black Surcharge.

7 A1(a) 1c on ½r bl ('82) 3.00 *12.50*
8 A1(b) 1c on ½r bl ('82) 15.00 *22.50*
9 A1(c) 2c on ½r bl 2.50 *6.00*
a. Double surch.
b. "Cts."
12 A1(c) 5c on ½r bl 7.50
a. Double surch.
13 A1(d) 5c on ½r bl ('82) 110.00 *100.00*
14 A1(d) 10c on 2r scar (Bk) ('82) 80.00 *80.00*
15 A1(e) 20c on 4r grn ('82) 185.00 *185.00*

The ½r stamps surcharged "DOS CTS" were never placed in use, and are said to have been surcharged to a dealer's order.

Counterfeits exist of surcharges on Nos. 7-15.

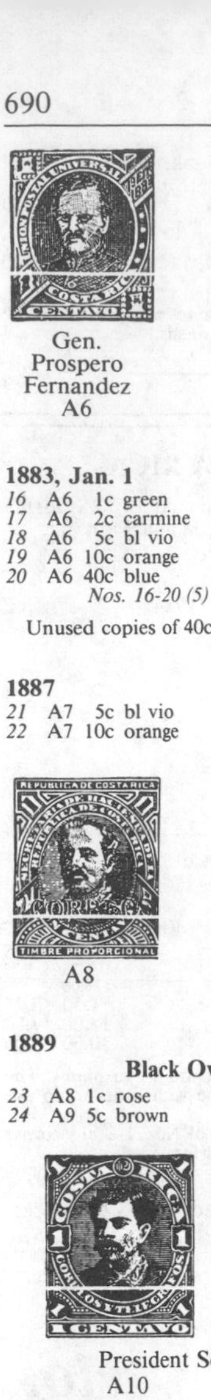

Gen. Prospero Fernandez
A6

President Bernardo Soto Alfaro
A7

1883, Jan. 1

16	A6	1c	green	1.00	60
17	A6	2c	carmine	1.00	70
18	A6	5c	bl vio	15.00	60
19	A6	10c	orange	45.00	7.50
20	A6	40c	blue	1.25	1.25
			Nos. 16-20 (5)	63.25	10.65

Unused copies of 40c usually lack gum.

1887

21	A7	5c	bl vio	8.00	60
22	A7	10c	orange	2.25	85

A8 A9

1889

Black Overprint

23	A8	1c	rose	4.50	1.10
24	A9	5c	brown	4.50	1.10

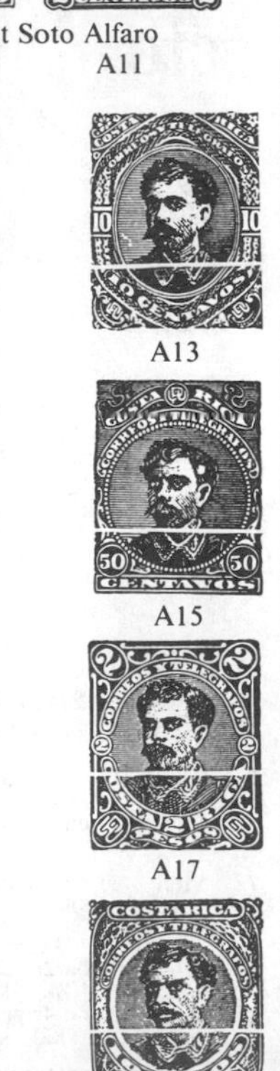

President Soto Alfaro
A10 A11

A12 A13

A14 A15

A16 A17

A18 A19

1889 ***Perf. 14-16 & Compound***

25	A10	1c	brown	40	50
a.			Horiz. pair, imperf. vert	50.00	
b.			Imperf.pair	60.00	
c.			Horiz. or vert. pair, imperf. between	70.00	
26	A11	2c	dk grn	30	50
a.			Imperf., pair	30.00	
b.			Vert. pair, imperf. horiz.	40.00	
c.			Horiz. pair, imperf. btwn.	40.00	
27	A12	5c	orange	60	30
a.			Imperf., pair	75.00	
b.			Horiz. pair, imperf. btwn.	60.00	
28	A13	10c	red brn	50	40
a.			Vert. or horiz. pair, imperf. btwn.	60.00	
29	A14	20c	yel grn	35	30
a.			Vert. pair, imperf. horiz.	50.00	
b.			Horizontal pair, imperf. btwn.	50.00	
30	A15	50c	rose red	1.25	
31	A16	1p	blue	1.75	
32	A17	2p	dl vio	12.00	
a.			2p sl	13.00	
33	A18	5p	ol grn	45.00	
34	A19	10p	black	80.00	
			Nos. 25-34 (10)	142.15	

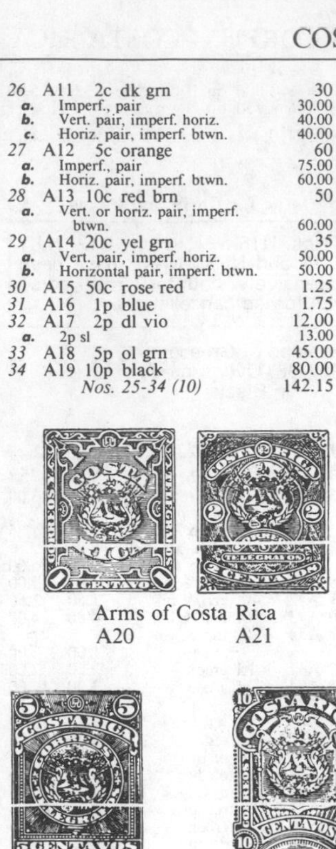

Arms of Costa Rica
A20 A21

A22 A23

A24 A25

A26 A27

A28 A29

1892 ***Perf. 12-15 & Compound***

35	A20	1c	grnsh bl	35	50
36	A21	2c	yellow	35	50
37	A22	5c	red lil	35	20
a.			5c vio	35.00	50
38	A23	10c	lt grn	90	40
a.			Horiz. pair, imperf. btwn.	70.00	
39	A24	20c	scarlet	12.00	40
a.			Horiz. pair, imperf. btwn.		50.00
40	A25	50c	gray bl	8.00	6.00
41	A26	1p	grn, *yel*	1.50	1.10
42	A27	2p	rose red, *pale lil*	3.50	1.50
a.			2p brn red, *lil*	3.50	1.50
43	A28	5p	dk bl, *bl*	3.50	1.50
44	A29	10p	brn, *pale buff*	15.00	6.00
a.			10p brn, *yel*	9.00	9.00
			Nos. 35-44 (10)	45.45	18.10

Imperfs. of Nos. 35-44 are proofs.

Statue of Juan Santamaria
A30

Juan Mora Fernandez
A31

View of Port Limon
A32

Braulio Carillo ("Branlio" on stamp)
A33

National Theater — A34

José M. Castro — A35

Birris Bridge — A36

Juan Rafael Mora — A37

Jesús Jiménez
A38

Coat of Arms
A39

1901, Jan. ***Perf. 12-15½***

45	A30	1c	grn & blk	60	15
a.			Horiz. pair, imperf. btwn.		
46	A31	2c	ver & blk	75	25
47	A32	5c	gray bl & blk	50	20
a.			Vert. pair, imperf. btwn.		150.00
48	A33	10c	ocher & blk	1.50	25
49	A34	20c	lake & blk	6.00	40
a.			Vert. pair, imperf. btwn.	150.00	
50	A35	50c	dl lil & dk bl	5.00	2.00
51	A36	1col	ol bis & blk	60.00	5.00
52	A37	2col	car rose & dk grn	18.00	5.00
53	A38	5col	brn & blk	40.00	5.00
54	A39	10col	yel grn & brn red	30.00	4.00
			Nos. 45-54 (10)	162.35	22.25

The 2c exists with center inverted.

Remainders

In 1914 the government sold a large quantity of stamps at very much less than face value. The lot included most regular issues from 1901 to 1911 inclusive, postage due stamps of 1903 and official stamps of 1901-03. These stamps were cancelled with groups of thin parallel bars. They, of course, sell for much less than the prices quoted which are for stamps with regular postal cancellations.

José M. Canas — A40

Julián Volio — A41

Eusebio Figueroa Oreamuno — A42

1903 ***Perf. 13½, 14, 15***

55	A40	4c	red vio & blk	3.00	1.50
56	A41	6c	ol grn & blk	9.00	4.00
57	A42	25c	gray lil & brn	18.00	50

No. 49 Surcharged in Black:

1905

58	A34	1c on 20c	lake & blk	1.00	1.00
a.			Inverted surcharge	8.50	8.50
b.			Diagonal surcharge	1.00	1.00

Specimens surcharged in other colors are proofs.

Statue of Juan Santamaria
A43

Juan Mora Fernández
A44

José M. Canas
A45

Mauro Fernandez
A46

Braulio Carrillo
A47

Julián Volio
A48

Eusebio Figueroa Oreamuno
A49

José M. Castro
A50

Jesús Jiménez
A51

Juan Rafael Mora
A52

1907 **Unwmk.** ***Perf. 11x14***

59	A43	1c	red brn & ind	75	30
60	A44	2c	yel grn & blk	1.25	30
a.			Perf. 14	1.25	30
61	A45	4c	car & ind	8.00	4.00
a.			Perf. 14	250.00	35.00
62	A46	5c	yel & dl bl perf 14	90	30
a.			Perf. 11x14	20.00	1.50
63	A47	10c	bl & blk	6.00	60
a.			Perf. 14	1.25	60
64	A48	20c	ol grn & blk	9.00	4.00
a.			Perf. 14	7.50	3.00
65	A49	25c	gray lil & blk, perf. 14	3.00	2.00
a.			Perf. 11x14	40.00	7.50
66	A50	50c	red lil & bl	40.00	15.00
a.			Perf. 14	70.00	20.00
67	A51	1col	brn & blk	20.00	15.00
a.			Perf. 14	30.00	15.00

68 A52 2col cl & grn 90.00 65.00
a. Perf. 14 140.00 90.00
Nos. 59-68 (10) 178.90 106.50

Imperforate copies of the above set are either proofs or from unfinished sheets, which were placed on the market in London. The 1c, 2c, 5c, 20c, 50c, 1 col. and 2 col. exist with center inverted. Price, 5c, $300; others each $500.

Nos. 59-68 exist with papermaker's watermark.

Statue of Juan Santamaria A53

Juan Mora Fernandez A54

José M. Canas A55

Mauro Fernandez A56

Braulio Carrillo A57

Julian Volio A58

Euscbio Figueroa Oreamuno A59

Jesus Jimenez A60

1910 *Perf. 12*

69	A53	1c brown	12	10
70	A54	2c dp grn	30	15
71	A55	4c scarlet	30	15
72	A56	5c orange	50	10
73	A57	10c dp bl	20	10
74	A58	20c ol grn	30	25
75	A59	25c dp vio	8.00	1.00
76	A60	1col dk brn	60	75
		Nos. 69-76 (8)	10.32	2.60

Nos. 69a-73a and 72b-72c ("Cafe" ovpts.) are listed after No. 111.

No. 60a Overprinted in Red *1911*

1911 *Perf. 14*

77 A44 2c yel grn & blk 2.00 1.50
a. Inverted overprint 7.00 7.00
b. Double overprint, both inverted 60.00

Stamps of 1901-07 Overprinted in Red or Black * 1911 *

78 A30 1c grn & blk (R) 1.00 50
a. Black overprint 45.00 25.00
b. Inverted overprint
79 A43 1c red brn & ind (Bk) 90 50
a. Inverted overprint 6.00 5.00
b. Double overprint 7.00 7.00
80 A44 2c yel grn & blk (Bk) 90 50
a. Inverted overprint 5.00 5.00
b. Double overprint, one as on No. 77 30.00 30.00
c. Double overprint, one inverted 17.50 17.50
d. Pair, one stamp No. 77 35.00 25.00
e. Perf. 11x14 1.75 50

Habilitado

No. 55 Overprinted in Black

1911

81 A40 4c red vio & blk 1.50 1.00

Habilitado

Stamps of 1907 Overprinted in Blue, Black or Rose

1911

Perf. 14

82 A46 5c yel & bl (Bl) 60 25
a. "Habilitada" 4.50 3.50
b. "2911" 8.00 4.50
c. Roman "I" in "1911" 4.00 3.00
d. Double overprint 6.00 4.50
e. Inverted overprint 8.00 5.50
f. Black overprint 11.00 3.00
g. Triple overprint 8.00
h. Imperf. horizontally (pair) 55.00
83 A47 10c bl & blk (Bk) 2.75 2.00
a. Roman "I" in "1911" 10.00 7.00
c. Double overprint 27.50 16.50
d. Perf. 11x14 1.75 1.00
84 A47 10c bl & blk (R), perf. 11x14 8.00 8.00
a. Roman "I" in "1911" 22.50 20.00
c. Perf. 14 27.50 16.50

Many counterfeits of overprint exist.

A61

A62

A63

Telegraph Stamps Surcharged in Rose, Blue or Black

1911 *Perf. 12, 14, 14x11*

86 A61 1c on 10c bl (R) 30 20
a. "Coereos" 11.00 8.00
b. Inverted surcharge
87 A61 1c on 10c bl (Bk)
88 A61 1c on 25c vio (Bk) 30 20
a. "Coereos" 11.00 8.00
b. Pair, one without surcharge 27.50
c. Double surcharge 11.00
e. Double surcharge, one inverted 16.50
89 A61 1c on 50c red brn (Bl) 60 60
a. Inverted surcharge 7.00 7.00
b. Double surcharge 6.00
90 A61 1c on 1 col brn (R) 60 60
91 A61 1c on 5 col red (Bl) 1.10 85
92 A61 1c on 10 col dk brn (R) 1.35 1.10
93 A62 2c on 5c brn org (Bk) 4.50 3.25
a. Inverted surcharge 11.00 5.50
b. "Correos" inverted 22.50
c. Double surcharge 11.00
94 A62 2c on 10c bl (R) 100.00 70.00
a. Perf. 14 150.00 100.00
b. "Correos" inverted
c. As "b," perf. 14
95 A62 2c on 50c cl (Bk) 60 75
a. Inverted surcharge 5.50 4.50
b. Double surcharge 16.50
96 A62 2c on 1 col brn (Bk) 1.10 1.10
a. Inverted surcharge 16.50
b. Double surcharge 22.50
97 A62 2c on 2 col car (Bk) 85 85
a. Inverted surcharge 10.00 7.00
b. "Correos" inverted 11.00 8.00
c. Double surcharge
d. Perf. 14 20.00 15.00
98 A62 2c on 5 col grn (Bk) 1.10 1.10
a. Inverted surcharge 13.00 10.00
b. "Correos" inverted 22.50 6.00
99 A62 2c on 10 col mar (Bk) 1.35 1.10
a. "Correos" inverted
100 A63 5c on 5c org (Bl) 60 25
a. Double surcharge 8.50 5.50
b. Inverted surcharge 10.00 7.00
c. Pair, one without surcharge 25.00
Nos. 86-100 (14) 114.35 81.95

Counterfeits exist of Nos. 87, 94 and all minor varieties.

Nos. 93-99 exist with papermaker's watermark.

Coffee Plantation — A64

1921, June 17 Litho. *Perf. 11½*

103 A64 5c bl & blk 1.50 1.25
a. Tete beche pair 3.25 3.25
b. Imperf., pair 15.00
c. As "a," imperf. 40.00

Centenary of coffee raising in Costa Rica.

Liberty with Torch of Freedom — A65

1921 Typo. *Perf. 11*

104 A65 5c violet 85 50
a. Imperf. 30.00

Centenary of Central American independence.

Juan Mora and Julio Acosta A66

1921, Sept. 15 *Perf. 11½*

105	A66	2c org & blk	2.00	1.50
106	A66	3c grn & blk	2.00	1.50
107	A66	6c scar & blk	2.50	1.75
108	A66	15c dk bl & blk	6.00	5.00
109	A66	30c org brn & blk	10.00	9.00
		Nos. 105-109 (5)	22.50	18.75

Centenary of Central American independence. Issue requested by Costa Rican Philatelic Society. Authorized by decree calling for 2,000 of 30c and 5,000 each of other values. Many more were printed illegally including imperforates, color changes are inverted centers.

Each sheet of 20 (4x5) contains 5 tête-bêche pairs.

Simon Bolivar — A67

1921 Engr. *Perf. 12*

110 A67 15c dp vio 40 20

CORREOS

No. 104 Overprinted

1922

1922 *Perf. 11*

111 A65 5c violet 60 40
a. Inverted overprint 5.00
b. Double overprint 10.00

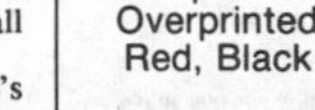

Stamps of 1910-1921 Overprinted in Blue, Red, Black or Gold

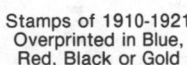

1922 *Perf. 12*

69a	A53	1c brn (Bl)	15	10
70a	A54	2c dp grn (R)	20	15
71a	A55	4c scarlet	25	20
72a	A56	5c orange	40	25
73a	A57	10c dp bl (R)	50	40
110a	A67	15c dp vio (G)	2.00	1.50
		Nos. 69a-110a (6)	3.50	2.60

Inverted overprints occur on all values. Counterfeits exist.

No. 72 Overprinted with Double-Lined Circle, Inscribed: "Compre Ud. Cafe de Costa Rica"

1923

72b A56 5c orange 35 25
c. "VD." for "UD." 60.00 60.00

Jesus Jimenez — A68

1923, June 18 Litho. *Perf. 11½*

112	A68	2c brown	20	20
113	A68	4c green	25	20
114	A68	5c blue	50	20
115	A68	20c carmine	30	30
116	A68	1col violet	50	50
		Nos. 112-116 (5)	1.75	1.40

Issued to commemorate the centenary of the birth of President Jesus Jimenez (1823-1898).

Nos. 112 to 116 exist imperforate but were not regularly issued in that condition.

National Monument A70

Harvesting Coffee A71

Banana Growing A73

General Post Office — A74

Columbus Soliciting Aid of Isabella A75

Christopher Columbus A76

Columbus at Cariari A77

A particular stamp may be scarce, but if few collectors want it, its market value may remain relatively low.

Map of Costa Rica — A78

Manuel M. Gutierrez — A79

1923-26		**Engr.**		***Perf. 12***
117	A70	1c violet	10	10
118	A71	2c yellow	30	20
119	A73	4c dp grn	60	50
120	A74	5c lt bl	1.00	15
121	A74	5c yel grn ('26)	30	10
122	A75	10c red brn	1.75	25
123	A75	10c car rose ('26)	40	10
124	A76	12c car rose	6.00	3.00
125	A77	20c dp bl	8.00	1.00
126	A78	40c orange	7.50	2.50
127	A79	1col ol grn	2.00	1.00
		Nos. 117-127 (11)	27.95	8.90

See Nos. 151-156.

Rodrigo Arias Maldonado — A80

1924				***Perf. 12½***
128	A80	2c dk grn	15	10
a.		Perf. 14	25	10

See No. 162.

Map of Guanacaste A81

Mission at Nicoya A82

1924		**Litho.**		***Perf. 12***
129	A81	1c car rose	50	30
130	A81	2c violet	50	30
131	A81	5c green	50	30
132	A81	10c orange	3.50	75
133	A82	15c lt bl	1.10	65
134	A82	20c gray blk	1.75	1.10
135	A82	25c lt brn	2.50	2.00
		Nos. 129-135 (7)	10.35	5.40

Centenary of annexation of Province of Guanacaste to Costa Rica.

Exist imperf. Price, set, $40.

Stamps of 1923 Surcharged:

a

b

1925				
136	A74(a)	3c on 5c lt bl	30	25
137	A75(a)	6c on 10c red brn	40	40
138	A78(a)	30c on 40c org	75	60
139	A79(b)	45c on 1 col ol grn	1.25	75
a.		Double surcharge	25.00	

No. 124 Surcharged

=10 10=

1926				
140	A76	10c on 12c car rose	1.50	50

College of San Luis, Cartago A83

Chapui Asylum, San Jose — A84

Normal School, Heredia A85

Ruins of Ujarras A86

1926		**Unwmk. Engr.**		***Perf. 12½***
143	A83	3c ultra	25	20
144	A84	6c dk brn	40	30
145	A85	30c dp org	90	40
146	A86	45c blk vio	2.50	1.25

No. 124 Surcharged in Black:

1928, Jan. 7				***Perf. 12***
147	A76	10c on 12c car rose	10.00	7.50

Issued in honor of Col. Charles A. Lindbergh during his Good Will Tour of Central America.

The surcharge has been counterfeited.

No. 110 Surcharged 5 5

1928				
148	A67	5(c) on 15c dp vio	25	15
a.		Inverted surcharge	25.00	

Type I — A88

Type II: CORREOS 5 CENTIMOS

Type III: CORREOS 5 CENTIMOS

Type IV: CORREOS 5 CENTIMOS

Type V: CORREOS 5 CENTIMOS

Surcharge Typographed (I-V) and Lithographed (V)

1929				***Perf. 12½***
149	A88	5c on 2 col car (I)	50	30
a.		Type II	50	30
b.		Type III	50	30
c.		Type IV	50	30
d.		Type V	50	30

Telegraph Stamp Surcharged for Postage as in 1929, Surcharge Lithographed

1929				
150	A88	13c on 40c dp grn	15	10
a.		Inverted surcharge	1.25	1.00

Excellent counterfeits exist of No. 150a.

Types of 1923-26 Issues Dated "1929" Imprint of Waterlow & Sons

1930		**Size: 26x21½mm.**		***Perf. 12½***
151	A70	1c dk vio	10	8
155	A74	5c green	10	8
156	A75	10c car rose	50	8

Juan Rafael Mora — A89

1931				
157	A89	13c car rose	35	25

Seal of Costa Rica Philatelic Society ("Octubre 12 de 1932") — A90

1932, Oct. 12				***Perf. 12***
158	A90	3c orange	25	25
159	A90	5c dk grn	35	35
160	A90	10c car rose	40	40
161	A90	20c dk bl	50	50

Issued to commemorate the Philatelic Exhibition of Oct. 12, 1932. See also Nos. 179-183.

Maldonado Type of 1924

1934				***Perf. 12½***
162	A80	3c dk grn	10	8

Red Cross Nurse — A91

1935, May 31				***Perf. 12***
163	A91	10c rose car	50	25

Issued in commemoration of the 50th anniversary of the founding of the Costa Rican Red Cross Society.

Air View of Cartago A92

Miraculous Statuette and View of Cathedral A93

Vision of 1635 — A94

1935, Aug.				***Perf. 12½***
164	A92	5c green	25	15
165	A93	10c carmine	50	25
166	A92	30c orange	75	35
167	A94	45c dk vio	1.75	60
168	A93	50c bl blk	3.00	1.25
		Nos. 164-168 (5)	6.25	2.60

Issued to commemorate the tercentenary of the Patron Saint, Our Lady of the Angels, of Costa Rica.

Map of Cocos Island — A95

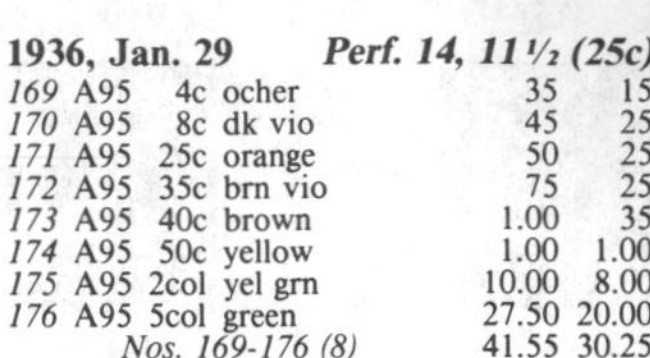

1936, Jan. 29				***Perf. 14, 11½ (25c)***
169	A95	4c ocher	35	15
170	A95	8c dk vio	45	25
171	A95	25c orange	50	25
172	A95	35c brn vio	75	25
173	A95	40c brown	1.00	35
174	A95	50c yellow	1.00	1.00
175	A95	2col yel grn	10.00	8.00
176	A95	5col green	27.50	20.00
		Nos. 169-176 (8)	41.55	30.25

Exist imperf. Price, set, $50.

Map of Cocos Island and Ships of Columbus A96

1936, Dec. 5				***Perf. 12***
177	A96	5c green	20	6
178	A96	10c car rose	20	6

Seal of Costa Rica Philatelic Society ("Diciembre 1937") — A97

1937				
179	A97	2c dk brn	20	20
180	A97	3c black	20	20
181	A97	5c green	25	20
182	A97	10c org red	30	25

Souvenir Sheet

Imperf

183		Sheet of four	80	80
a.	A97	2c dk brn	15	15
b.	A97	3c blk	15	15
c.	A97	5c grn	15	15
d.	A97	10c org red	15	15

Issued to commemorate the Philatelic Exhibition, December, 1937. Size of No. 183: 168x101mm.

Purple Guaria Orchid, National Flower — A98

Tuna
A99

Native with Donkey Carrying Bananas
A101

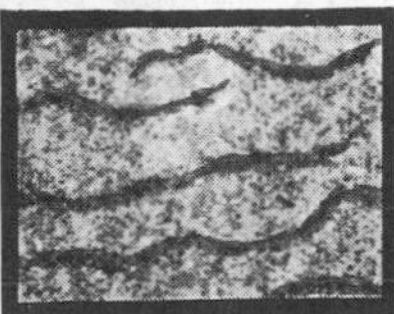

Wmk. 229

Designs: 3c, Cacao pod. 10c, Coffee harvesting.

Wmk. Wavy Lines (229)

1937-38 *Perf. 12½*

No.	Type	Description	Unused	Used
184	A98	1c grn & vio ('38)	50	15
185	A98	3c choc ('38)	25	15

Unwmk. *Perf. 12*

No.	Type	Description	Unused	Used
186	A99	2c ol gray	30	20
187	A101	5c dk grn	35	15
188	A101	10c car rose	50	30
		Nos. 184-188 (5)	1.90	95

Nos. 184-188 were issued to commemorate the National Exposition.

No. 125 Overprinted in Black **1938**

1938 **Unwmk.** *Perf. 12*

No.	Type	Description	Unused	Used
189	A77	20c dp bl	50	25

No. 146 Surcharged in Red:

a

b

c

d

e

1940 *Perf. 12½*

No.	Type	Description	Unused	Used
190	A86(a)	15c on 45c blk vio	60	30
190A	A86(b)	15c on 45c blk vio	60	30
190B	A86(c)	15c on 45c blk vio	60	30
190C	A86(d)	15c on 45c blk vio	80	40
190D	A86(e)	15c on 45c blk vio	60	25
		Nos. 190-190D (5)	3.20	1.55

Allegory
A103

Overprinted "Dia Panamericano de la Salud / 2 Diciembre 1940" and Arc in Black

1940, Dec. 2 **Engr.** *Perf. 12*

No.	Type	Description	Unused	Used
191	A103	5c green	35	20
192	A103	10c rose car	40	25
193	A103	20c dp bl	1.00	30
194	A103	40c brown	2.00	1.50
195	A103	55c org yel	4.00	1.75
		Nos. 191-195 (5)	7.75	4.00

Pan-American Health Day. See Nos. C46-C54.
Exist without overprint.

Stamps of 1936 Surcharged in Black:

15
CENTIMOS
15
◇◇◇◇◇◇◇◇◇◇◇◇◇◇◇

1941 *Perf. 14, 11½*

No.	Type	Description	Unused	Used
196	A95	15c on 25c org	35	30
197	A95	15c on 35c brn vio	35	30
198	A95	15c on 40c brn	35	30
199	A95	15c on 2 col yel grn	35	30
200	A95	15c on 5 col grn	60	55
		Nos. 196-200 (5)	2.00	1.75

Nos. 196-200 exist with surcharge inverted. Price, $5 a set.

National Stadium
A104

Engraved; Flags Typographed in National Colors

1941, May 8 *Perf. 12½*

No.	Type	Description	Unused	Used
201	A104	5c green	1.25	35
a.		Flags omitted	80.00	
202	A104	10c orange	1.00	35
203	A104	15c car rose	1.50	50
204	A104	25c dk bl	2.50	70
205	A104	40c chestnut	6.00	2.00
206	A104	50c purple	8.00	2.50
207	A104	75c red org	15.00	5.00
208	A104	1col dk car	25.00	10.00
		Nos. 201-208 (8)	60.25	21.40

Issued to commemorate the Caribbean and Central American Soccer Championship. See Nos. C57-C66, C121-C123.

No. 157 Surcharged in Black **5 Céntimos 5**

1941 *Perf. 12*

No.	Type	Description	Unused	Used
209	A89	5c on 13c car rose	12	8

Cleto González Viquez — A105

1941-45 **Engr.** *Perf. 12½.*

No.	Type	Description	Unused	Used
210	A105	3c dp org	25	10
210A	A105	3c dp plum ('43)	25	10
210B	A105	3c car ('45)	25	10
211	A105	5c dp vio *(José Rodriguez)*	30	12
211A	A105	5c brn blk ('43)	30	12
		Nos. 210-211A (5)	1.35	54

See No. 256.

Old University of Costa Rica
A106

New National University
A107

1941, Aug. 26 *Perf. 12*

No.	Type	Description	Unused	Used
212	A106	5c green	45	15
213	A107	10c yel org	50	15
214	A106	15c lil rose	70	15
215	A107	25c dl bl	1.00	35
216	A106	50c fawn	4.00	2.00
		Nos. 212-216 (5)	6.65	2.80

National University, founded in 1940. See Nos. C74-C80.

15 CENTIMOS 15

Nos. 144, 189 Surcharged in Black or Red

1942 *Perf. 12½, 12*

No.	Type	Description	Unused	Used
217	A84	5c on 6c dk brn	30	20
218	A77	15c on 20c dp bl (R)	40	25

Torch of Freedom, "Victory" and Flags of American Nations
A108

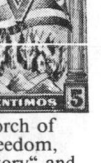

Juan Mora Fernandez
A109

1942, Sept. 25 *Perf. 12*

No.	Type	Description	Unused	Used
219	A108	5c rose	30	15
220	A108	5c yel grn	30	15
221	A108	5c purple	30	15
222	A108	5c dp bl	30	15
223	A108	5c red org	30	15
		Nos. 219-223 (5)	1.50	75

1943-47 **Engr.**

Designs: 2c, Bruno Carranza. 3c, Tomas Guardia. 5c, Manuel Aguilar. 15c, Francisco Morazan. 25c, Jose M. Alfaro. 50c, Francisco M. Oreamuno. 1col, Jose M. Castro. 2col, Juan Rafael Mora.

No.	Type	Description	Unused	Used
224	A109	1c red lil	6	5
225	A109	2c black	6	6
226	A109	3c dp bl	6	6
227	A109	5c brt bl grn	12	8
a.		5c brt grn ('47)	12	10
228	A109	15c scarlet	15	6
229	A109	25c brt ultra	35	20
230	A109	50c dp vio	1.50	75
231	A109	1col blk brn	3.00	2.50
232	A109	2col dp org	5.00	3.50
		Nos. 224-232 (9)	10.30	7.26

See Nos. 344-348, C81-C91A, C124-C127, C154-C158, C179-C185, C768-C772, C790-C794, C854-C858.

View of San Ramon
A118

1944, Jan. 19

No.	Type	Description	Unused	Used
233	A118	5c dk grn	20	10
234	A118	10c orange	25	10
235	A118	15c rose pink	40	12
236	A118	40c gray blk	1.50	75
237	A118	50c dp bl	2.50	1.25
		Nos. 233-237 (5)	4.85	2.32

Issued to commemorate the 100th anniversary of the founding of the City of San Ramón. See Nos. C94-C102.

Nos. 220-223 Overprinted in Red or Black

La entrevista de los Presidentes De la Guardia y Picado contribuirá a afianzar la unidad Continental. 18 setiembre 1944

1944, Sept. 18

No.	Type	Description	Unused	Used
238	A108	5c yel grn (Bk)	15	12
239	A108	5c pur (R)	15	12
240	A108	5c dp bl (R)	15	12
241	A108	5c red org (Bk)	15	12

Issued to commemorate the amicable settlement of a boundary dispute with Panama. This overprint also exists on No. 219.

Mauro Fernandez — A119

Unwmk.

1945, July 21 **Engr.** *Perf. 14*

No.	Type	Description	Unused	Used
242	A119	20c dp grn	25	15

Issued to commemorate the centenary of the birth of Mauro Fernandez (1844-1905), statesman.

Coffee Harvesting — A120

1945, Oct. 9 *Perf. 12*

No.	Type	Description	Unused	Used
243	A120	5c dk grn & blk	15	8
244	A120	10c org & blk	25	12
245	A120	20c car rose & blk	30	20

No. 242 Surcharged in Red Brown

1946 **Unwmk.** *Perf. 14.*

No.	Type	Description	Unused	Used
246	A119	15c on 20c dp grn	20	12

No. O80 Overprinted in Red **CORREOS 1947**

1947, Mar. 19 *Perf. 12*

No.	Type	Description	Unused	Used
247	A96	5c green	15	10

Cervantes — A121

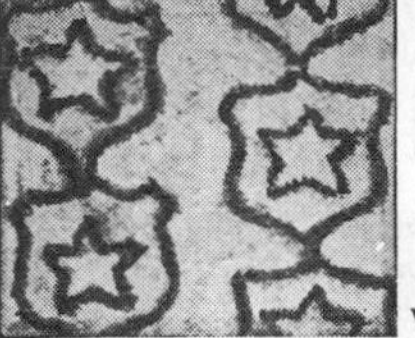

Wmk. 215

Wmk. Small Star in Shield, Multiple. (215)

1947, Nov. 10 Engr. *Perf. 14*

249 A121 30c dp bl 30 15
250 A121 55c dp car 50 35

Issued to commemorate the 400th anniversary of the birth of Miguel de Cervantes Saavedra, novelist, playwright and poet.

Franklin D. Roosevelt — A122

1947, Aug. 26 Unwmk. *Perf. 12*

251 A122 5c brt grn 10 10
252 A122 10c car rose 15 12
253 A122 15c ultra 20 18
254 A122 25c org red 25 25
255 A122 50c lilac 50 35
Nos. 251-255,C160-C167 (13) 9.50 8.95

Small Portrait Type of 1941

Design: 3c, Bishop Bernardo A. Theil.

1948 *Perf. 12½*

256 A105 3c dp ultra 10 8

Old University of Costa Rica A123

1953, June 25 Litho. *Perf. 12*

Black Surcharge

257 A123 5c on 10c grn 12 6

Revenue Stamp Surcharged in Red or Blue — A124

1955-56 Unwmk. Engr. *Perf. 12*

258 A124 5c on 2c emer (R) 8 6
259 A124 15c on 2c emer (Bl) 18 8
260 A124 15c on 2c emer (R) ('56) 18 8
Nos. 258-260,C341-C344 (7) 1.76 1.32

Justo A. Facio A125

Anglo-Costa Rican Bank A126

1960, Apr. 20 Photo. *Perf. 13½*

261 A125 10c brn red 8 6

Centenary of the birth (in 1859) of Prof. Justo A. Facio. Exists imperf.

Nos. RA12-RA15 Surcharged in Red

1963
10
CENTIMOS

1963, Mar.

262 PT3 10c on 5c dk car 25 20
263 PT3 10c on 5c sep 25 20
264 PT3 10c on 5c dl grn 25 20
265 PT3 10c on 5c bl 25 20

1963 Unwmk. *Perf. 13½*

266 A126 10c gray 8 6

Centenary of the Anglo-Costa Rican Bank.

Arms of San Jose — A127

Alberto M. Brenes Mora — A128

Coats of Arms: 35c, Cartago. 50c, Heredia. 55c, Alajuela. 65c, Guanacaste. 1col, Puntarenas. 2col, Limon.

1969, Sept. 14 Litho. *Perf. 14x13½*

267 A127 15c multi 15 10
268 A127 35c multi 15 10
269 A127 50c gray & multi 20 10
270 A127 55c buff & multi 25 20
271 A127 65c multi 35 25
272 A127 1col pink & multi 1.50 25
273 A127 2col multi 1.50 50
Nos. 267-273 (7) 4.10 1.50

1976, March 1 Litho. *Perf. 10½*

274 A128 1col vio bl 25 20
Nos. 274,C653-C657 (6) 3.55 2.73

Prof. Alberto Manuel Brenes Mora, botanist, birth centenary.

Map of Costa Rica, Reader with Book — A129

1978, July 17 Litho. *Perf. 13½*

275 A129 50c multi 12 10

National five-year literacy plan.

World Communications Year — A130

1983, May 17 Litho. *Perf. 13x13½*

276 A130 10c multi 5 5
277 A130 50c multi 5 5
278 A130 10col multi 70 25

First World Congress of Human Rights, 1982 — A131

1983 Litho. *Perf. 10½*

279 A131 20col black 1.40 50

UPU Membership Centenary — A132

1983, June Litho. *Perf. 16*

280 A132 3col No. 17, monument 75 8
281 A132 10col No. 20, headquarters 1.50 28

French Alliance Centenary — A133

1983, July 21 Litho. *Perf. 11*

282 A133 12col Scene in San Jose, by Christina Fournier 85 28

Christmas 1983 — A134

Nativity tableau in continuous design.

1983, Dec. 5 Litho. *Perf. 13½*

283 A134 1.50col multi 10 5
284 A134 1.50col multi 10 5
285 A134 1.50col multi 10 5

Costa Rican Gardens Association.

Fishery Development Administration A135

1983, Dec. 19 Litho. *Perf. 13½*

286 A135 8.50col multi 56 18

Local Birds — A136

1984, Jan. 9 Litho. *Perf. 13½*

287 A136 10c Quetzal 15 5
288 A136 50c Cyanerpes cyaneus 15 5
289 A136 1col Turdus grayi 15 5
290 A136 1.50col Momotus momota 15 5
291 A136 3col Colibri thalassinus 20 5
292 A136 10col Notiochelindon cyanoleuca 1.00 10
Nos. 287-292 (6) 1.80 35

Dated 1983. 10c, 1.50col, 3col vert.

José Joaquin Mora, Hero of 1856 Independence Campaign — A137

Paintings, Juan Santamaria Museum, San Jose: 1.50col, Pancha Carrasco. 3 col, Death of Juan Santamaria (horiz.). 8.50col, Juan Rafael Mora Porras.

1984, Apr. 10 Litho. *Perf. 10½*

293 A137 50c multi 5 5
294 A137 1.50col multi 5 5
295 A137 3col multi 6 5
296 A137 8.50col multi 18 5

Jesus Bonilla Chavarria, Composer — A138

Musicians and Composers: 5col, Benjamin Gutierrez (b. 1937). 12col, Pilar Jimenez (1835-1922). 13col, Jose Daniel Zuniga Zeledon (1889-1981).

1984, May 30 Litho. *Perf. 13½*

297 A138 3.50col blk & lil 8 5
298 A138 5col blk & pink 10 5
299 A138 12col blk & grn 24 6
300 A138 13col blk & yel 26 6

Figurines, Jade Museum A139

1984 Summer Olympics A140

1984, June 27 Litho. *Perf. 13½*

301 A139 4col Man (pendant) 8 5
302 A139 7col Seated man 14 5
303 A139 10col Dish, horiz. 20 5

1984, July 27

304 A140 1col Basketball 5 5
305 A140 8col Swimming 15 5
306 A140 11col Bicycling 22 5
307 A140 14col Running 28 8
308 A140 20col Boxing 40 12
309 A140 30col Soccer 60 16
Nos. 304-309 (6) 1.70 51

Public Street Lighting Centenary A141

1984, Aug. 9 Litho. *Perf. 10½*

310 A141 6col Street scene by Luis Chacon 12 5

10th Natl. Stamp Exhibition, Sept. 10-16 — A142

1984, Sept. 10 Litho. *Perf. 10½*

311 A142 10col Natl. monument 20 5
312 A142 10col Juan Mora Fernandez monument 20 5
a. Miniature sheet of 4 (2 each #311-312) 1.50

Size of No. 312a: 117x87mm.

Natl. Arms — A143

1984, Oct. 29 Engr. *Perf. 14x13½*
313 A143 100col dk grn 4.00 3.00
314 A143 100col yel org 4.00 3.00

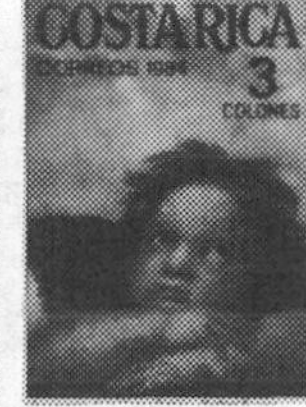

Detail from Sistine Virgin by Raphael
A144 A145

1984, Dec. 7 Litho. *Perf. 10½*
315 A144 3col multi 6 6
316 A145 3col multi 6 6

Nos. 315-316 se-tenant.

20th Intl. Bicycle Race, Costa Rica — A146

1984, Dec. 19 Litho. *Perf. 13½*
317 A146 6col multi 28 28

Intl. Youth Year A147

1985, Jan. 31 *Perf. 10½*
322 A147 11col IYY emblem, No. C476 45 45

Scouting Movement, 75th anniv.

Labor Monument, San Jose — A148

Natl. values: 11col, Freedom of speech - wooden hand printing press. 13col, Neutrality - dove, natl. flag, outline map.

1985, Feb. 28
323 A148 6col shown 28 28
324 A148 11col bl, blk & yel 44 44
325 A148 13col multi 52 52

Size: 68x38mm.

326 A148 30col Nos. 323-325 1.15 1.15

Natl. Red Cross Cent., UN 40th Anniv. A149

1985, Feb. 19 *Perf. 10½*
327 A149 3col No. 163 14 14
328 A149 5col No. C120, vert. 25 25

Club Emblem A150

1st Club Pres., Ricardo Saprissa Ayma A151

Design: No. 330, Hands holding soccer ball.

1985, July 16 *Perf. 10½*
329 A150 3col multi 14 14
330 A150 3col multi 14 14
331 A151 6col multi 28 28

Saprissa Soccer Club, 50th Anniv. Nos. 329-330 printed se-tenant.

Orchids — A152

1985, Nov.
332 A152 6col Brassia arcuigera 28 28
333 A152 6col Encyclia per-altensis 28 28
334 A152 6col Maxillaria es-pecie 28 28
335 A152 13col Oncidium turi-albae 60 60
336 A152 13col Trichopilia marginata 60 60
337 A152 13col Stanhopea ecornuta 60 60
Nos. 332-337 (6) 2.64 2.64

Nos. 332-334 and 335-337 printed se-tenant in sheets of 15.

11th Natl. Philatelic Exposition A153

1985, Dec. 3 Litho. *Perf. 13½*
338 A153 20col No. C41 80 20

Christmas 1985 — A153a

1985 Litho. *Perf. 10½*
338A A153a 3col multi 15 5

Compulsory Education, Cent. — A154

Agriculture Students — A155

Designs: 3col, Primary school, horiz. 30col, Mauro Fernandez Acuna, founder.

1986, Feb. 28 *Perf. 13½*
339 A154 3col pale yel & brn 12 5
340 A154 30col pale pink & brn 1.20 30

1986, Mar. 21 *Perf. 10½*
341 A155 10col shown 40 10
342 A155 10col IDB emblem 40 10
343 A155 10col Capo Bianco fisher-man 40 10

Inter-American Development Bank Annual Governors' Assembly, San Jose. Nos. 341-343 printed se-tenant.

Presidents Type of 1943

Designs: Nos. 344, 349, 354, 359, 364, Francisco J. Orlich Bolmarcich, 1962-1966. Nos. 345, 350, 355, 360, 365, Jose Joaquin Trejos Fernandez, 1966-1970. Nos. 346, 351, 356, 361, 366, Daniel Oduber Quiros, 1974-1978. Nos. 347, 352, 357, 362, 367, Rodrigo Carazo Oido, 1978-1982. Nos. 348, 353, 358, 363, 368, Luis Alberto Monge Alvarez, 1982-1986.

1986, May 8 Litho. *Perf. 10½*
344 A109 3col turq blue 12 5
345 A109 3col turq blue 12 5
346 A109 3col turq blue 12 5
347 A109 3col turq blue 12 5
348 A109 3col turq blue 12 5
a. Strip of 5, Nos. 344-348 60 25
349 A109 6col yel brn 24 6
350 A109 6col yel brn 24 6
351 A109 6col yel brn 24 6
352 A109 6col yel brn 24 6
353 A109 6col yel brn 24 6
a. Strip of 5, Nos. 349-353 1.20 30
354 A109 10col brn org 40 10
355 A109 10col brn org 40 10
356 A109 10col brn org 40 10
357 A109 10col brn org 40 10
358 A109 10col brn org 40 10
a. Strip of 5, Nos. 354-358 2.00 50
359 A109 11col slate gray 45 12
360 A109 11col slate gray 45 12
361 A109 11col slate gray 45 12
362 A109 11col slate gray 45 12
363 A109 11col slate gray 45 12
a. Strip of 5, Nos. 359-363 2.25 60
364 A109 13col olive 52 14
365 A109 13col olive 52 14
366 A109 13col olive 52 14
367 A109 13col olive 52 14
368 A109 13col olive 52 14
a. Strip of 5, Nos. 364-368 2.60 70
Nos. 344-368 (25) 8.65 2.35

1986 World Cup Soccer Championships, Mexico — A156

1986, May 30 Litho. *Perf. 13½*
369 A156 1col Players 5 5
370 A156 1col Character trade-mark, vert. 5 5
371 A156 4col As No. 370 16 5
372 A156 6col As No. 369 24 6
373 A156 11col Players, diff. 45 12
Nos. 369-373 (5) 95 33

Intl. Peace Year — A157

Peace in many languages: No. 374a, "Hoa binh," etc. No. 374b, "Vrede," etc. No. 374c, "Pace," etc.

1986, July Litho. *Perf. 10½*
374 Strip of 3 55 15
a.-c. A157 5col, any single 18 5

Gold Museum, Central Bank of Costa Rica — A158

Designs: Various undescribed works of Pre-Columbian art.

1986, June 3 *Perf. 13½*
375 Strip of 5 1.10 30
a.-e. A158 6col any single 22 6
376 Strip of 5 2.25 60
a.-e. A158 13 col any single 45 12
Nos. 375-376 (2) 3.35 90

A159

Fauna and Flora — A160

1986, Dec. Litho. *Perf. 13x13½*
377 A159 2col Centurio senex 8 5
378 A159 3col Glossophaga soricina 12 5
379 A159 4col Ectophylla alba 14 5
380 A159 5col Ectophylla alba, diff. 18 5
381 A159 6col Agalychnis cal-lidryas 22 6
382 A159 10col Dendrobates pumilio 38 10
383 A159 11col Hyla ebraccata 40 10
384 A159 20col Phyllobates lugubris 75 18
Nos. 377-384 (8) 2.27 64

Souvenir Sheet

Perf. 12½x12

385 A160 50col Agalychnis cal-lidryas, diff. 2.00 50

No. 385 has multicolored margin continuing the design. Size: 60x70mm.

Natl. Science and Technology Day — A161

Mural (detail), by Francisco Amighetti, Clorito Picado Social Security Clinic.

1987, July 31 Litho. *Perf. 10½*
386 A161 8col multi 32 8

Natl. Museum, Cent. A162

Artifacts: No. 387a, Dowel-shaped figure of a man. No. 387b, Ape-like carved stone figurine. No. 387c, Polished stone ritual figure. No. 387d, Carved granite capital. No. 387e, Two-legged pot. No. 388a, Bowl. No. 388b, Sculpture. No. 388c, Water jar.

1987, Aug. 7
387 Strip of 5 1.60 40
a.-e. A162 8col any single 32 8
388 Strip of 3 1.80 45
a.-c. A162 15col any single 60 15
Nos. 387-388 (2) 3.40 85

Horse-drawn Wagon — A163

1987, Oct.
389 A163 20col shown 78 20
390 A163 20col Street in old San Jose 78 20
391 A163 20col Provincial coat of arms 78 20

City of San Jose, 250th anniv. Rotary Club, 60th anniv.

Columbus Day — A164

1987, Oct. *Perf. 10½*
392 A164 30col Map, 16th cent. 1.15 30

Day of the Race; 495th anniv. of Columbus's departure from Palos, Spain, on first journey to the New World.

Discovery of America, 500th Anniv. (in 1992) — A165

Pres. Oscar Arias, 1987 Nobel Peace Prize Winner — A166

Maps of Honduras, Nicaragua, Costa Rica and Panama, believed to be Asia by Columbus: No. 393, Costa Rica, 16th cent. No. 394, Map of "Asia" by Bartholomeu Columbus (1461-1514). Printed se-tenant.

1987, Nov. Litho. *Perf. 13½*
393 A165 4col yel & dk red brn 16 5
394 A165 4col yel & dk red brn 16 5

1987, Dec. *Perf. 10½*
395 A166 10col multi 30 8

Two Houses, a Watercolor by Fausto Pacheco (1899-1966) — A167

1987, Dec. Litho. *Perf. 10½*
396 A167 1col multi 5 5

International Year of Shelter for the Homeless.

SEMI-POSTAL STAMPS

No. 72 Surcharged in Red

1922 Unwmk. *Perf. 12*
B1 A56 5c + 5c org 75 40

Issued for the benefit of the Costa Rican Red Cross Society. In 1928, owing to a temporary shortage of the ordinary 5c stamp, No. B1 was placed on sale as a regular 5c stamp, the surtax being disregarded.

Discus Thrower SP1

Trophy SP2

Parthenon SP3

1924 Litho. *Imperf.*
B2 SP1 5c dk grn 3.00 4.00
B3 SP2 10c carmine 3.00 4.00
B4 SP3 20c dk bl 7.00 6.00
a. Tete beche pair 18.00 20.00

Perf. 12
B5 SP1 5c dk grn 3.00 4.00
B6 SP2 10c carmine 3.00 4.00
B7 SP3 20c dk bl 6.00 7.00
a. Tete beche pair 18.00 20.00
Nos. B2-B7 (6) 25.00 29.00

These stamps were sold at a premium of 10c each, to help defray the expenses of athletic games held at San José in December, 1924.

AIR POST STAMPS

Airplane AP1

Perf. 12½
1926, June 4 Unwmk. Engr.
C1 AP1 20c ultra 2.00 50

No. 123 Overprinted

CORREO AEREO

1930, Mar. 14 *Perf. 12*
C2 A75 10c car rose 85 20

AP3

1930-32 *Perf. 12½*
C3 AP3 5c on 10c dk brn ('32) 25 10
a. Inverted surcharge 6.00
C4 AP3 20c on 50c ultra 25 20
C5 AP3 40c on 50c ultra 50 20

Telegraph Stamp Overprinted

Correo Aereo

1930, Mar. 19
C6 AP3 1col orange 2.50 50

No. O79 Surcharged in Red

1930, Mar. 11
C7 O7 8c on 1col lil & blk 75 60
C8 O7 20c on 1col lil & blk 1.00 75
C9 O7 40c on 1col lil & blk 2.00 1.50
C10 O7 1col on 1col lil & blk 3.00 2.00

AP6

AP7

Red Surcharge on Revenue Stamps

1931-32 *Perf. 12*
C11 AP6 2col on 2col gray grn 27.50 27.50
C12 AP6 3col on 5col lil brn 27.50 27.50
C13 AP6 5col on 10col gray blk 27.50 27.50

There were two printings of this issue which were practically identical in the colors of the stamps and the surcharges.

Nos. C11 and C13 have the date "1929" on the stamp, No. C12 has "1930".

Black Overprint on Telegraph Stamp

1932, Mar. 8 *Perf. 12½*
C14 AP7 40c green 2.50 50
a. Inverted ovpt. 25.00

Mail Plane about to Land — AP8

Allegory of Flight — AP9

1934, Mar. 14 *Perf. 12*
C15 AP8 5c green 25 10
C16 AP8 10c car rose 25 8
C17 AP8 15c chocolate 60 15
C18 AP8 20c dp bl 65 12
C19 AP8 25c dp org 85 10
C20 AP8 40c ol blk 1.50 12
C21 AP8 50c gray blk 1.00 25
C22 AP8 60c org yel 2.00 30
C23 AP8 75c dl vio 3.00 75
C24 AP9 1col dp rose 2.25 25
C25 AP9 2col lt bl 2.50 1.00
C26 AP9 5col black 6.50 6.50
C27 AP9 10col red brn 11.00 11.00
Nos. C15-C27 (13) 32.35 20.72

Stamps Nos. C15 to C27 with holes punched through were for use of government officials.

See Nos. C216-C219.

Airplane over Poas Volcano — AP10

1937, Feb. 10
C28 AP10 1c black 12 10
C29 AP10 2c brown 12 10
C30 AP10 3c dk vio 12 10

First Fair of Costa Rica.

Puntarenas AP11

National Bank AP12

Perf. 12, 12½
1937, Dec. 15 Unwmk.
C31 AP11 2c blk gray 8 8
C32 AP11 5c green 15 12
C33 AP11 20c dp bl 50 40
C34 AP11 1.40col ol brn 5.00 5.00

Wmk. Wavy Lines (229)
1938, Jan. 11 *Perf. 12½*
C35 AP12 1c purple 8 6
C36 AP12 3c red org 10 6
C37 AP12 10c car rose 20 15
C38 AP12 75c brown 3.00 3.00

Nos. C31 to C38 were issued to commemorate the National Products Exposition held at San José in December, 1937.

Airport Administration Building, La Sabana — AP13

1940, May 2 Engr. Unwmk.

No.	Type	Description	Unused	Used
C39	AP13	5c green	15	10
C40	AP13	10c rose pink	20	15
C41	AP13	25c lt bl	25	20
C42	AP13	35c red brn	45	45
C43	AP13	60c red org	70	70
C44	AP13	85c violet	2.00	1.75
C45	AP13	2.35col turq grn	11.00	11.00
		Nos. C39-C45 (7)	14.75	14.35

Issued to commemorate the opening of the International Airport at La Sabana.

Duran Sanatorium AP14

Overprinted "Dia Panamericano de la Salud / 2 Diciembre 1940" and Bar in Black

1940, Dec. 2 ***Perf. 12***

No.	Type	Description	Unused	Used
C46	AP14	10c scarlet	20	15
C47	AP14	15c purple	25	25
C48	AP14	25c lt bl	45	40
C49	AP14	35c bis brn	70	65
C50	AP14	60c pck grn	90	90
C51	AP14	75c olive	2.00	2.25
C52	AP14	1.35col red org	9.00	9.00
C53	AP14	5col sepia	40.00	40.00
C54	AP14	10col red lil	90.00	90.00
		Nos. C46-C54 (9)	143.50	143.60

Pan-American Health Day. Exist without overprint. Few copies of C53-C54 were sold for postal purposes, nearly all having been obtained by philatelic speculators.

No. 174 Surcharged in Black or Blue

AEREO

Aviación Panamericana

Dic. 17 1940

15 CENTIMOS 15

1940, Dec. 17 ***Perf. 14***

No.	Type	Description	Unused	Used
C55	A95	15c on 50c yel (Bk)	75	75
C56	A95	30c on 50c yel (Bl)	75	75

Issued in commemoration of Pan-American Aviation Day, proclaimed by President F. D. Roosevelt.

The 15c surch. exists on No. 171, price $45.

International Soccer Game at National Stadium — AP15

1941, May 8 ***Perf. 12***

No.	Type	Description	Unused	Used
C57	AP15	15c red	1.25	25
C58	AP15	30c dp ultra	1.50	40
C59	AP15	40c red brn	1.50	60
C60	AP15	50c purple	2.00	1.35
C61	AP15	60c brt grn	2.50	1.50
C62	AP15	75c yel org	4.00	2.25
C63	AP15	1col dl vio	7.50	7.50
C64	AP15	1.40col rose	15.00	15.00
C65	AP15	2col bl grn	30.00	30.00
C66	AP15	5col black	65.00	65.00
		Nos. C57-C66 (10)	130.25	123.85

Issued to commemorate the Caribbean and Central American Soccer Championship. See Nos. C121-C123.

Air Post Stamps of 1934 Overprinted or Surcharged in Black with New Values and Bars

Mayo 1941

Tratado Limitrofe

Costa Rica - Panamá

1941, June 2

No.	Type	Description	Unused	Used
C67	AP8	5c on 20c dp bl	30	25
C68	AP8	15c on 20c dp bl	40	30
C69	AP8	40c on 75c dl vio	60	40
C70	AP9	65c on 1col dp rose	1.10	90
C71	AP9	1.40col on 2col lt bl	5.50	5.50
C72	AP9	5col black	20.00	20.00
C73	AP9	10col red brn	22.50	22.50
		Nos. C67-C73 (7)	50.40	49.85

Issued in commemoration of the settlement of the Costa Rica-Panama border dispute.

Nos. C67-C73 are found with hyphen omitted in overprint.

University Types of Regular Issue, 1941

1941, Aug. 26 ***Perf. 12***

No.	Type	Description	Unused	Used
C74	A107	15c salmon	40	20
C75	A106	30c lt bl	60	25
C76	A107	40c orange	70	50
C77	A106	60c turq grn	85	75
C78	A107	1col violet	3.50	3.50
C79	A106	2col black	8.50	8.50
C80	A107	5col sepia	27.50	27.50
		Nos. C74-C80 (7)	42.05	41.20

National University, founded in 1940.

Portrait Type of Regular Issue, 1943-47

Designs: 40c, Manuel Aguilar. No. C83, Francisco Morazan. No. C83A, Jose R. De Gallegos. 50c, Jose M. Alfaro. 60c, Francisco M. Oreamuno. 65c, Jose M. Castro. 85c, Juan Rafael Mora. 1col, Jose M. Montealegre. 1.05col, Braulio Carrillo. 1.15col, Jesus Jimenez. 1.40col, Bruno Carranza. 2col, Tomas Guardia.

1943-45 Engr.

No.	Type	Description	Unused	Used
C81	A109	10c rose pink	15	8
C82	A109	40c blue	35	12
C82A	A109	40c car rose ('45)	35	20
C83	A109	45c magenta	50	40
C83A	A109	45c blk ('45)	30	18
C84	A109	50c turq grn	2.50	30
C84A	A109	50c red org ('45)	45	30
C85	A109	60c brt ultra	65	25
C85A	A109	60c brt grn ('45)	30	20
C86	A109	65c scarlet	1.25	40
C86A	A109	65c brt ultra ('45)	35	30
C87	A109	85c dp org	1.50	55
C87A	A109	85c dl pur ('45)	1.75	70
C88	A109	1col black	1.75	75
C88A	A109	1col scar ('45)	75	30
C88B	A109	1.05col bis brn ('45)	1.00	75
C89	A109	1.15col red brn	2.50	2.50
C89A	A109	1.15col grn ('45)	3.50	2.00
C90	A109	1.40col dp vio	3.75	3.50
C90A	A109	1.40col org yel ('45)	2.25	2.25
C91	A109	2col black	6.00	2.00
C91A	A109	2col ol grn ('45)	1.75	50
		Nos. C81-C91A (22)	33.65	18.53

See Nos. C124-C127, C179-C181.

Nos. C26-C27 Overprinted in Red or Blue

Legislacion Social

15 Setiembre 1943

1943, Sept. 16

No.	Type	Description	Unused	Used
C92	AP9	5col blk (R)	5.00	4.00
C93	AP9	10col red brn (Bl)	10.00	7.50

Mercury and Plane AP31

1944, Jan. 19

No.	Type	Description	Unused	Used
C94	AP31	10c red org	25	20
C95	AP31	15c dk car	30	20
C96	AP31	40c brt ultra	50	40
C97	AP31	45c dp red lil	60	50
C98	AP31	60c turq grn	85	75
C99	AP31	1col dk red brn	1.75	1.50
C100	AP31	1.40col gray blk	10.00	9.00
C101	AP31	5col violet	27.50	27.50
C102	AP31	10col black	50.00	50.00
		Nos. C94-C102 (9)	91.75	90.05

Issued to commemorate the 100th anniversary of the founding of the City of San Ramon.

Very few copies of the 5col or 10col stamps were sold for postal purposes, nearly all having been obtained by philatelic speculators.

No. CO10 With Additional Overprint in Black **1944**

1944, Nov. 22

No.	Type	Description	Unused	Used
C103	AP9	1col dp rose	1.00	60
a.		Blue ovpt.	70.00	

Nos. CO1-13 Overprinted in Carmine or Black

1945, Jan. 12 Unwmk. ***Perf. 12***

No.	Type	Description	Unused	Used
C104	AP8	5c green	1.00	1.00
C105	AP8	10c car rose (Bk)	1.00	1.00
C106	AP8	15c chocolate	1.00	1.00
C107	AP8	20c dp bl	60	60
C108	AP8	25c dp org (Bk)	1.00	1.00
C109	AP8	40c ol blk	60	60
C110	AP8	50c gray blk	1.00	1.00
C111	AP8	60c org yel (Bk)	1.50	60
C112	AP8	75c dl vio	1.25	1.00
C113	AP9	1col dp rose (Bk)	1.25	60
C114	AP9	2col lt bl	8.00	8.00
C115	AP9	5col black	10.00	10.00
C116	AP9	10col red brn (Bk)	15.00	15.00
		Nos. C104-C116 (13)	43.20	41.40

AP32

Telegraph Stamps Overprinted in Black or Carmine

1945, Feb. 28 Unwmk. ***Perf. 12½***

No.	Type	Description	Unused	Used
C117	AP32	40c grn (C)	25	12
C118	AP32	50c ultra (C)	30	12
C119	AP32	1col org (Bk)	65	40

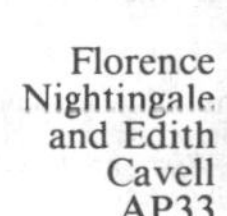

Florence Nightingale and Edith Cavell AP33

1945 Engr.

No.	Type	Description	Unused	Used
C120	AP33	1col blk & car	75	50

Issued to commemorate the 60th anniversary of the Costa Rican Red Cross Society.

Soccer Type of 1941.
Inscribed: "Febrero 1946"

1946, May 13 ***Perf. 12***

No.	Type	Description	Unused	Used
C121	AP15	25c green	1.50	1.10
C122	AP15	30c dl yel	1.50	1.10
C123	AP15	55c dp bl	1.75	1.10

Portrait Type of 1943-47

Designs: 25c, Aniceto Esquivel. 30c, Vicente Herrera. 55c, Prospero Fernandez. 75c, Bernardo Soto.

1946, May 12

No.	Type	Description	Unused	Used
C124	A109	25c blue	20	12
C125	A109	30c red brn	25	20
C126	A109	55c plum	40	30
C127	A109	75c bl grn	60	40

Hospital of St. John of God — AP38

1946, June 24 Unwmk. ***Perf. 12½***

Center in Black.

No.	Type	Description	Unused	Used
C128	AP38	5c yel grn	10	10
C129	AP38	10c dk brn	10	10
C130	AP38	15c carmine	10	10
C131	AP38	25c dk bl	20	20
C132	AP38	30c dp org	40	30
C133	AP38	40c ol grn	20	20
C134	AP38	50c violet	35	35
C135	AP38	60c dk sl grn	75	70
C136	AP38	75c brown	60	50
a.		Horiz. pair, imperf. btwn.	110.00	
C137	AP38	1col blue	75	40
C138	AP38	2col brn org	1.10	90
C139	AP38	3col dk vio brn	2.75	2.75
C140	AP38	5col yellow	3.50	3.50
		Nos. C128-C140 (13)	10.90	10.10

Rafael Iglesias — AP39

Designs: 3col, Ascensión Esquivel. 5col, Cleto Gonzalez Viquez. 10col, Ricardo Jimenez Oreamuno.

1947, Jan. 15 Wmk. 215 ***Perf. 14***

Center in Black

No.	Type	Description	Unused	Used
C141	AP39	2col blue	1.50	1.10
C142	AP39	3col dp car	2.25	1.50
C143	AP39	5col dk grn	3.50	2.25
C144	AP39	10col orange	6.50	4.00

Nos. C121 to C123 Surcharged in Black

Habilitado para

₡ 0.15

Decreto Nº 16 de

28 de abril de 1947

1947, May 5 Unwmk. ***Perf. 12***

No.	Type	Description	Unused	Used
C145	AP15	15c on 25c grn	1.25	1.10
C146	AP15	15c on 30c dl yel	1.25	1.10
C147	AP15	15c on 55c dp bl	1.25	1.10

Nos. C145-C147 exist with inverted surcharge.

Columbus in Cariari AP43

1947, May 19 Engr. ***Perf. 12½***

Center in Black

No.	Type	Description	Unused	Used
C148	AP43	25c green	35	18
C149	AP43	30c dp ultra	35	18
C150	AP43	40c red org	50	20
C151	AP43	45c violet	60	35
C152	AP43	50c brt car	70	30
C153	AP43	65c brn org	2.00	1.00
		Nos. C148-C153 (6)	4.50	2.21

Nos. C84A, C85A, C127, C88A, and C88B Surcharged with New Value in Black or Red

1947, June 3 ***Perf. 12***

No.	Type	Description	Unused	Used
C154	A109	15c on 50c red org	25	25
C155	A109	15c on 60c brt grn (R)	25	25
C156	A109	15c on 75c bl grn (R)	25	25
C157	A109	15c on 1col scar	30	30
C158	A109	15c on 1.05col bis brn	25	25
		Nos. C154-C158 (5)	1.30	1.30

Early Steam Locomotive AP44

Perf. 12½

1947, Nov. 10 Unwmk. Engr.

No.	Type	Description	Unused	Used
C159	AP44	35c bl grn & blk	1.00	50

Issued to commemorate the 50th anniversary of the electric railroad to the Pacific coast.

Roosevelt Type of Regular Issue

1947, Aug. 26 ***Perf. 12***

No.	Type	Description	Unused	Used
C160	A122	15c green	12	10
C161	A122	30c car rose	18	15
C162	A122	45c red brn	35	35
C163	A122	65c org yel	40	40

C164 A122 75c blue 50 40
C165 A122 1col ol grn 75 70
C166 A122 2col black 2.00 1.85
C167 A122 5col scarlet 4.00 4.00
Nos. C160-C167 (8) 8.30 7.95

National Theater
AP46

Rafael Iglesias
AP47

1948, Jan. 26 *Perf. 12½*

Center in Black

C168 AP46 15c brt ultra 20 15
C169 AP46 20c red 25 20
C170 AP47 35c dk grn 35 30
C171 AP46 45c purple 50 35
C172 AP46 50c carmine 50 35
C173 AP46 75c red vio 1.00 1.00
C174 AP46 1col olive 1.85 1.50
C175 AP46 2col red brn 3.00 2.25
C176 AP47 5col org yel 5.00 4.25
C177 AP47 10col brt bl 11.00 8.50
Nos. C168-C177 (10) 23.65 18.85

50th anniversary of National Theater.

No. C150 Surcharged in Carmine

HABILITADO
PARA
₡ 0.35

1948, Apr. 21

C178 AP43 35c on 40c red org & blk 45 45

Exists with surcharge inverted.

Portrait Type of 1943-47

Designs: 5c, Salvador Lara. 15c, Carlos Duran.

1948 **Engr.** *Perf. 12*

C179 A109 5c sepia 50 6
C180 A109 10c ol brn 50 10
C181 A109 15c violet 50 10

Nos. C88B, C120, C89A and C90A Surcharged in Carmine or Black

1824-1949
125 Aniversario
de la Anexión
Guanacaste
₡ 0.55

Perf. 12½, 12

1949, Aug. 28 **Unwmk.**

C182 A109 35c on 1.05col bis brn 25 20
C183 AP33 50c on 1col blk & car 40 35
a. 2nd & 3rd lines both read "125 Aniversario" 7.50 7.50
C184 A109 55c on 1.15col grn 65 55
C185 A109 55c on 1.40col org yel (Bk) 65 50

Issued to commemorate the 125th anniversary of the annexation of the province of Guanacaste.

Overprint differs on No. C183, with "Guanacaste" in capitals, and lower case "a" in "Anexion."

The variety "l" for "i" in "Anexion" is found on Nos. C182, C184 and C185.

Symbols of UPU
AP48

1950, Jan. 11 **Photo.** *Perf. 11½*

C186 AP48 15c lil rose 20 10
C187 AP48 25c chlky bl 25 10
C188 AP48 1col gray grn 50 20

Issued to commemorate the 75th anniversary of the formation of the Universal Postal Union.

Battle of El Tejar, Cartago
AP49

Occupation of Limon — AP50

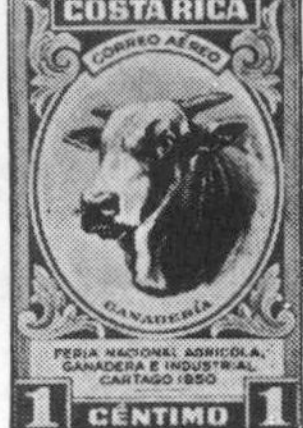

Bull (Cattle Raising) — AP51

Designs: 25c, Lucha ranch. 35c, Trenches of San Isidro Battalion. 55c and 75c, Observation post. 80c and 1col, Dr. Carlos Luis Valverde.

Inscribed: "Guerra de Liberacion Nacional 1948"

Engraved; Center Photogravure

1950, July 20 *Perf. 12½*

Center in Black

C189 AP49 15c brt car 20 10
C190 AP50 20c dl grn 30 20
C191 AP49 25c dl bl 35 25
C192 AP49 35c chestnut 40 25
C193 AP49 55c lilac 80 35
C194 AP49 75c red org 1.25 50
C195 AP50 80c gray 1.25 75
C196 AP50 1col org yel 1.75 85
Nos. C189-C196 (8) 6.30 3.25

Issued to commemorate the second anniversary of the War for National Liberation.

Inscribed: "Feria Nacional Agricola Ganadera e Industrial Cartago 1950"

1950, July 27

Designs: 1c, 10c, 2col, Bull. 2c, 30c and 3col, Tuna fishing. 3c and 65c, Pineapple. 5c, 50c and 5col, Bananas. 45c, 80c and 10col, Coffee picker.

Center in Black

C197 AP51 1c brt grn 10 8
C198 AP51 2c brt bl 10 8
C199 AP51 3c chocolate 10 8
C200 AP51 5c dp ultra 10 8
C201 AP51 10c green 15 8
C202 AP51 30c purple 30 18
C203 AP51 45c vermilion 35 25
C204 AP51 50c bl gray 50 15
C205 AP51 65c dk bl 60 35
C206 AP51 80c dp rose 1.25 1.00
C207 AP51 2col org yel 3.50 3.00
C208 AP51 3col blue 7.50 7.50
C209 AP51 5col carmine 11.00 11.00
C210 AP51 10col dp cl 11.00 11.00
Nos. C197-C210 (14) 36.55 34.83

Issued to publicize the National Agricultural, Livestock and Industrial Fair, Cartago, 1950.

Queen Isabella I and Caravels of Columbus
AP52

Unwmk.

1952, Mar. 4 **Engr.** *Perf. 13*

C211 AP52 15c carmine 25 10
C212 AP52 20c orange 35 15
C213 AP52 25c ultra 50 10
C214 AP52 55c dp grn 1.50 40
C215 AP52 2col violet 3.00 75
Nos. C211-C215 (5) 5.60 1.50

Issued to commemorate the 500th anniversary of the birth of Queen Isabella I of Spain.

Mail Plane Type of 1934

1952-53 *Perf. 12*

C216 AP8 5c blue 25 10
C217 AP8 10c green 25 10
C218 AP8 15c car rose ('53) 30 10
C219 AP8 35c purple 75 20

Nos. C149-C151, C153 Surcharged in Red: "HABILITADO PARA CINCO CENTIMOS 1953"

1953, Apr. 24 *Perf. 12½*

Center in Black

C220 AP43 5c on 30c dp ultra 1.50 1.25
C221 AP43 5c on 40c red org 10 10
C222 AP43 5c on 45c vio 10 10
C223 AP43 5c on 65c brn org 30 25

Nos. C161-C163 Surcharged in Black

1953, Apr. 11 *Perf. 12*

C224 A122 15c on 30c car rose 25 20
C225 A122 15c on 45c red brn 25 15
C226 A122 15c on 65c org yel 25 15

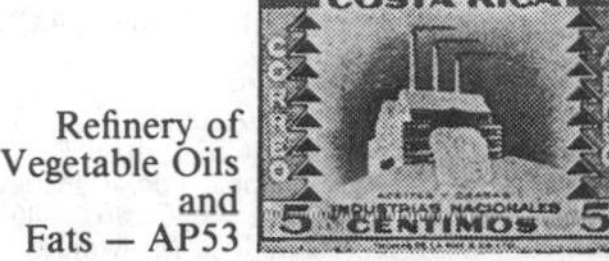

Refinery of Vegetable Oils and Fats — AP53

Industries: 10c, Pottery. 15c, Sugar. 20c, Soap. 25c, Lumber. 30c, Matches. 35c, Textiles. 40c, Leather. 45c, Tobacco. 50c, Preserving. 55c, Canning. 60c, General. 65c, Metals. 75c, Pharmaceuticals. 1col, Paper. 2col, Rubber. 3col, Airplane maintenance. 5col, Marble. 10col, Beer.

Engraved; Center Photogravure

1954 **Unwmk.** *Perf. 13x12½*

Center in Black

C227 AP53 5c red 10 6
C228 AP53 10c dk bl 15 6
C229 AP53 15c green 12 6
C230 AP53 20c violet 15 10
C231 AP53 25c magenta 15 10
C232 AP53 30c purple 45 30
C233 AP53 35c red vio 25 12
C234 AP53 40c black 40 25
C235 AP53 45c dk grn 75 35
C236 AP53 50c vio brn 50 15
C237 AP53 55c yellow 35 12
C238 AP53 60c brown 90 50
C239 AP53 65c carmine 1.10 75
C240 AP53 75c violet 1.65 65
C241 AP53 1col blue 50 30
a. Imperf., pair 110.00
C242 AP53 2col rose pink 1.50 90
C243 AP53 3col ol grn 2.25 1.50
C244 AP53 5col black 3.50 1.25
C245 AP53 10col yellow 10.00 8.50
Nos. C227-C245 (19) 24.77 16.02

See Nos. C252-C255A.

Globe and Rotary Emblem
AP54

Map of Costa Rica
AP55

Designs: 25c, Hand protecting boy. 40c, 2col, Hospital. 45c, Globe and palm leaves. 60c, Lighthouse.

1956, Feb. 7 **Engr.** *Perf. 12*

C246 AP54 10c green 15 6
C247 AP54 25c dk bl 20 18
C248 AP54 40c dk brn 50 40
C249 AP54 45c brt red 35 30
C250 AP54 60c dk red vio 40 35
C251 AP54 2col yel org 1.00 70
Nos. C246-C251 (6) 2.60 1.99

Issued to commemorate the 50th anniversary of Rotary International (in 1955).

Industries Type of 1954

Designs: 80c, Pharmaceuticals. Other designs as in 1954.

Engraved; Center Photogravure

1956-59 *Perf. 12*

Center in Black

C252 AP53 5c ultra 20 6
C253 AP53 10c vio bl 20 6
C254 AP53 15c org yel 20 6
C255 AP53 75c red org 40 25

Perf. 13x12½

C255A AP53 80c pur & gray ('59) 70 60
Nos. C252-C255A (5) 1.70 1.03

1957, June 21 **Engr.** *Perf. 13½x13*

Designs: 10c, Map of Guanacaste. 15c, Inn. 20c, House of Santa Rosa. 25c, Gen. Jose Manuel Quiros. 30c, Old Presidential Palace. 35c, Joaquin Bernardo Calvo. 40c, Luis Molina. 45c, Gen. Jose Joaquin Mora. 50c, Gen. Jose Maria Canas. 55c, Juan Santamaria monument. 60c, National monument. 65c, Antonio Vallerriestra. 70c, Ramon Castilla y Marquesado. 75c, San Carlos fortress. 80c, Francisco Maria Oreamuno. 1col, Pres. Juan Rafael Mora.

C256 AP55 5c lt bl 8 6
C257 AP55 10c green 12 8
C258 AP55 15c dp org 10 8
C259 AP55 20c lt brn 20 12
C260 AP55 25c vio bl 20 15
C261 AP55 30c violet 30 20
C262 AP55 35c car rose 30 20
C263 AP55 40c slate 30 20
C264 AP55 45c rose red 35 25
C265 AP55 50c ultra 35 25
C266 AP55 55c ocher 60 25
C267 AP55 60c brt car 45 35
C268 AP55 65c carmine 50 35
C269 AP55 70c org yel 65 45
C270 AP55 75c emerald 60 40
C271 AP55 80c dk brn 70 50
C272 AP55 1col black 75 50
Nos. C256-C272 (17) 6.55 4.39

Centenary of War of 1856-57.

Cleto Gonzalez Viquez
AP56

Highway and Gonzalez Viquez
AP57

Designs: 10c, Ricardo Jimenez Oreamuno. 20c, Puntarenas wharf and Jimenez. 35c, Post and Telegraph Bldg. and Jimenez. 55c, Pipeline and Gonzalez Viquez. 80c, National Library and Gonzalez Viquez. 1col, Electric train and Jimenez. 2col, Gonzales and Jimenez.

1959 **Engr.** *Perf. 13½*

C274 AP56 5c car & ultra 6 6
C275 AP56 10c red & gray 6 6

Perf. 13½x13

C276 AP57 15c dk bl grn & blk 6 6
C277 AP57 20c car & brn 15 10
C278 AP57 35c rose lil & bl 20 15
C279 AP57 55c ol & vio 40 30
C280 AP57 80c ultra 60 50
C281 AP57 1col org & mar 60 45
C282 AP57 2col gray & mar 1.50 1.25
Nos. C274-C282 (9) 3.63 2.93

Soccer — AP58

Designs: Various soccer scenes.

Perf. 13½

1960, March 7 **Unwmk.** **Photo.**

C283 AP58 10c black 10 8
C284 AP58 25c ultra 20 15
C285 AP58 35c red org 25 20
C286 AP58 50c red brn 30 25
C287 AP58 85c Prus grn 1.00 75
C288 AP58 5col dp cl 3.25 3.25
Nos. C283-C288 (6) 5.10 4.68

Souvenir Sheet

Imperf

C289 AP58 2col blue 1.50 1.50

3rd Pan-American Soccer Games, San José, March, 1960.

Nos. C283-C288 exist imperf.

No. C289 measures 137x80mm. with black marginal inscription.

WRY Uprooted Oak Emblem — AP59

1960, Apr. 7 Unwmk. *Perf. 11½*

Granite Paper

C290 AP59 35c vio bl, blk & yel 30 25
C291 AP59 85c blk & brt pink 60 50

Issued to publicize World Refugee Year, July 1, 1959-June 30, 1960.

Banner and "OEA" AP60

Designs: 35c, "OEA" in oval. 55c, Clasped hands. 2col, "OEA" and map of Americas. 5col, Flags forming bird. 10col, Map of Costa Rica, flags and "OEA."

1960, Aug. 15 Litho. *Perf. 10*

C292 AP60 25c blk & multi 20 15
a. Multi. impression sideways 30.00
C293 AP60 35c multi 50 45
a. Pair, imperf. between 65.00
C294 AP60 55c multi 75 60
C295 AP60 5col multi 4.50 4.00
C296 AP60 10col blk & multi 7.50 6.00
Nos. C292-C296 (5) 13.45 11.20

Souvenir Sheet

Imperf

C297 AP60 2col multi 3.25 3.25

Nos. C292-C297 issued to commemorate the Pan-American Conference, San Jose, Aug. 15.

No. C297 measures 124x76½mm. with flags of American nations forming border.

St. Louisa de Marillac and Orphanage AP61

St. Vincent de Paul — AP62

Designs: 25c, St. Vincent and old seminary. 50c, St. Louisa and sickroom. 1col, St. Vincent and new seminary.

1960, Oct. 26 Engr. *Perf. 14x13½*

C298 AP61 10c green 10 10
C299 AP61 25c carmine 10 10
C300 AP61 50c dk bl 35 25
C301 AP61 1col brn org 60 50
C302 AP62 5col brown 3.00 2.50
Nos. C298-C302 (5) 4.15 3.45

Issued to commemorate the 300th anniversary of the deaths of St. Vincent de Paul (1581?-1660) and St. Louisa de Marillac (1591-1660). Exist imperf.

Runner AP63

Sports: 2c, Woman swimmer. 3c, Bicyclist. 4c, Weight lifter. 5c, Woman tennis player. 10c, Boxers. 25c, Soccer player. 85c, Basketball player. 1col, Baseball batter. 5col, Romulus and Remus statue. 10col, Pistol marksman.

Perf. 13½x14

1960, Dec. 14 Photo. Unwmk.

Designs in Black

C303 AP63 1c brt yel 5 5
C304 AP63 2c lt ultra 5 5
C305 AP63 3c dp rose 5 5
C306 AP63 4c yellow 5 5
C307 AP63 5c brt yel grn 5 5
C308 AP63 10c pink 8 8
C309 AP63 25c lt bl grn 15 15
C310 AP63 85c lilac 1.50 1.25
C311 AP63 1col gray 1.75 1.50
C312 AP63 10col lt vio 15.00 12.00
Nos. C303-C312 (10) 18.73 15.23

Souvenir Sheets

Perf. 14x13½, Imperf.

C313 AP63 5col multi 5.50 5.50

17th Olympic Games, Rome, Aug. 25-Sept. 11.

No. C313 has gold marginal inscription. Size: 100x65mm.

Nos. C303-C312 exist imperf.

No. C255 Surcharged and Overprinted in Blue or Ultramarine: "XV Campeonato Mundial de Beisbol de Aficionados"

Engraved and Photogravure

1961, Apr. 21 *Perf. 12*

Center in Black

C314 AP53 25c on 75c red org (Bl) 30 12
C315 AP53 75c red org (U) 85 35

15th Amateur Baseball Championships.

Alberto Brenes C. AP64

Miguel Obregon AP65

Portraits: No. C317, Manuel Aguilar. No. C318, Agustin Gutierrez L. No. C319, Vicente Herrera.

1961, June 12 Photo. *Perf. 12*

C316 AP64 10c dp cl 10 10
C317 AP64 10c blue 10 10
C318 AP64 25c brt vio 20 15
C319 AP64 25c gray 20 15

First Continental Congress of Lawyers, San Jose, June 11-15. Exist imperf.

See Nos. C330-C333.

1961, July 19 Litho. *Perf. 13½*

C320 AP65 10c Prus grn 8 8

Birth centenary of Prof. Miguel Obregon L. Exists imperf.

U.N. Food and Agriculture Organization AP66

United Nations Organizations: 20c, World Health Organization. 25c, Int. Labor Organization. 30, Int. Telecommunication Union. 35c, World Meteorological Organization. 45c, UNESCO. 85c, Int. Civil Aviation Organization. 5col, "United Nations" holding the world. 10col, Int. Bank for Reconstruction and Development.

Perf. 11½

1961, Oct. 24 Unwmk. Engr.

C321 AP66 10c lt grn 12 12
C322 AP66 20c orange 25 20
C323 AP66 25c Prus grn 30 25
C324 AP66 30c dk bl 30 25
C325 AP66 35c car rose 1.40 35
C326 AP66 45c violet 50 30
C327 AP66 85c blue 1.10 85
C328 AP66 10col dk sl grn 8.00 6.50
Nos. C321-C328 (8) 11.97 8.82

Souvenir Sheet

Imperf

C329 AP66 5col ultra 4.50 4.50

Nos. C321-C329 issued for United Nations Day, Oct. 24.

No. C329 contains one imperf. stamp and has ultramarine border and marginal inscription. Size: 100x65mm.

Portrait Type of 1961

Portraits: No. C330, Dr. José Maria Soto Alfaro. No. C331, Dr. Elias Rojas Roman. No. C332, Dr. Andres Saenz Llorente. No. C333, Dr. Juan José Ulloa Giralt.

1961 Photo. *Perf. 13½*

C330 AP64 10c bl grn 8 8
C331 AP64 10c violet 10 8
C332 AP64 25c dk gray 20 12
C333 AP64 25c dp cl 20 12

Issued to commemorate the ninth Congress of Physicians of Central America and Panama.

Nos. C229, C236 and C280 Surcharged in Black, Orange or Red

Engraved; Center Photogravure

1962 *Perf. 13x12½, 13½x13*

C334 AP53 10c ("10") on 15c grn & blk 10 10
C334A AP53 10c ("c0.10") on 15c grn & blk (R) 10 10
C335 AP53 25c on 15c grn & blk 20 12
C336 AP53 35c on 50c vio brn & blk (O) 30 20

Engr.

C337 AP57 85c on 80c ultra (R) 85 65
Nos. C334-C337 (5) 1.55 1.17

Nos. C324 and C282 Overprinted in Red: "II CONVENCION FILATELICA CENTROAMERICANA SETIEMBRE 1962"

1962, Sept. 12 *Perf. 11½, 13½x13*

C338 AP66 30c dk bl 65 50
C339 AP57 2col gray & mar 2.00 1.40

Issued to commemorate the second Central American Philatelic Convention.

Revenue Stamp Surcharged with New Values and "CORREO AEREO" in Red

1962 Engr. *Perf. 12*

C341 A124 25c on 2c emer 12 10
C342 A124 35c on 2c emer 20 15
C343 A124 45c on 2c emer 35 30
C344 A124 85c on 2c emer 65 55

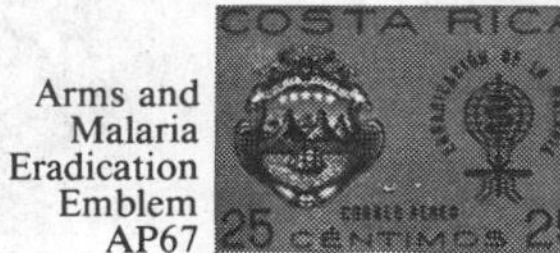

Arms and Malaria Eradication Emblem AP67

1963, Feb. 14 Photo. *Perf. 11½*

C345 AP67 25c brt rose 20 12
C346 AP67 35c brn org 25 20
C347 AP67 45c ultra 40 30
C348 AP67 85c bl grn 65 55
C349 AP67 1col dk bl 85 70
Nos. C345-C349 (5) 2.35 1.87

Issued for the World Health Organization drive to eradicate malaria.

Central American Tapir AP68

Designs: 5c, Paca. 25c, Jaguar. 30c, Ocelot. 35c, Whitetail deer. 40c, Manatee. 85c, White-throated capuchin monkey. 5col, White-lipped peccary.

Perf. 13½

1963, May Unwmk. Photo.

C354 AP68 5c yel ol & brn 8 8
C355 AP68 10c org & sl 8 8
C356 AP68 25c bl & yel 20 10
C357 AP68 30c lt yel grn & brn 35 30
C358 AP68 35c bis & red brn 50 25
C359 AP68 40c emer & sl bl 60 40
C360 AP68 85c grn & blk 90 60
C361 AP68 5col gray grn & choc 5.00 4.00
Nos. C354-C361 (8) 7.71 5.81

Stamp of 1863 and Packet "William Le Lacheur" AP69

Issue of 1863 and: 2col, Recaredo Bonilla Carrillo, Postmaster, 1862-63. 3col, Burros, overland mail transport, 1839. 10col, Burro railway car.

1963, June 26 Litho.

C362 AP69 25c dl rose & chlky bl 20 8
C363 AP69 2col gray bl & org 2.00 1.25
C364 AP69 3col bis & emer 4.00 2.25
C365 AP69 10col dl grn & ocher 10.00 7.00

Centenary of Costa Rica's stamps.

Souvenir Sheets

Stamps of 1863 and San Jose Postmark AP70

Perf. 13½ Imperf.

1963, June 26 Unwmk.

C366 AP70 5col bl, red, grn & org 5.00 5.00

Issued to commemorate the centenary of Costa Rica's stamps. Orange marginal inscription. Size of stamp: 29x50mm. Size of sheet: 60x100mm.

In 1968 copies of No. C366 were overprinted "2-4 Agosto 1968" and "III Exposicion Filatelica Nacional / 'Costa Rica 68'." Price $6.

Animal Type of 1963 Surcharged in Red

Designs: 10c on 1c, Little anteater. 25c on 2c, Gray fox. 35c on 3c, Armadillo. 85c on 4c, Great anteater.

1963, Sept. 14 Photo. *Perf. 13½*

C367 AP68 10c on 1c brt grn & org brn 25 10
C368 AP68 25c on 2c org yel & ol grn 25 10
C369 AP68 35c on 3c bluish grn & brn 35 15
C370 AP68 85c on 4c dp rose & dk brn 65 30

No. C370 exists without surcharge. Price, $50.

President John F. Kennedy AP71

Ancestral Figure AP72

Portraits - Presidents: 25c, Francisco J. Orlich, Costa Rica. 30c, Julio A. Rivera, El Salvador. 35c, Miguel Ydigoras F., Guatemala. 85c, Dr. Ramon Villeda M., Honduras. 1col, Luis A. Somoza, Nicaragua. 3col, Roberto F. Chiari, Panama.

1963, Dec. 7 Unwmk. *Perf. 14*

Portraits in Black Brown

C371	AP71	25c vio brn	15	10
C372	AP71	30c brt lil rose	20	15
C373	AP71	35c ocher	25	20
C374	AP71	85c gray bl	60	40
C375	AP71	1col org brn	60	45
C376	AP71	3col lt ol grn	3.00	2.00
C377	AP71	5col gray	4.00	3.00
		Nos. C371-C377 (7)	8.80	6.30

Issued to commemorate the meeting of Central American Presidents with Pres. John F. Kennedy, San Jose, March 18-20, 1963.

1963-64 Photo. *Perf. 12*

Ancient Art: 5c, Dog (horiz.). 10c, Ornamental stool (horiz.). 25c, Male figure. 30c, Ceremonial dancer. 35c, Ceramic vase. 50c, Frog. 55c, Bell. 75c, Six-limbed figure. 85c, Seated man. 90c, Bird-shaped jug. 1col, Twin human beaker (horiz.). 2col, Alligator (horiz.). 3col, Twin-tailed lizard. 5col, Figure under arch. 10col, Polished stone figure.

C378	AP72	5c lt yel grn & Prus grn	5	5
C379	AP72	10c buff & dk grn	6	6
C380	AP72	25c rose & dk brn	12	9
C381	AP72	30c ocher & Prus grn ('64)	15	8
C382	AP72	35c sal & sl grn	18	12
C383	AP72	45c lt bl & dk brn	20	12
C384	AP72	50c dl bl & dk brn	25	18
C385	AP72	55c yel grn & dk brn	30	18
C386	AP72	75c ocher & dk red brn	30	20
C387	AP72	85c yel & red brn	85	55
C388	AP72	90c cit & red brn	1.10	55
C389	AP72	1col lt bl & dk brn	60	35
C390	AP72	2col buff & dk grn	1.00	65
C391	AP72	3col yel grn & dk brn	1.75	1.10
C392	AP72	5col cit & sep	3.00	2.00
C393	AP72	10col rose lil & sl grn	5.00	4.50
		Nos. C378-C393 (16)	14.91	10.78

Flags of Central American States — AP73

Alfredo Gonzalez F. — AP74

Central American Independence Issue

1964 *Perf. 14*

C394	AP73	30c bl, gray, red & blk	50	40

Nos. C381, C394 and C387 Surcharged **₡ 0.05**

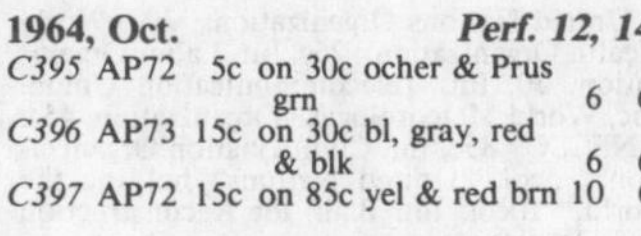

1964, Oct. *Perf. 12, 14*

C395	AP72	5c on 30c ocher & Prus grn	6	6
C396	AP73	15c on 30c bl, gray, red & blk	6	6
C397	AP72	15c on 85c yel & red brn	10	6

No. C388 Surcharged: "C 0.15 / CONFERENCIA POSTAL / DE PARIS - 1864"

1964 *Perf. 12*

C398	AP72	15c on 90c cit & red brn	12	8

Paris Postal Conference.

1965, June Photo. *Perf. 12*

C399	AP74	35c dk bl grn	15	10

Issued to commemorate the 50th anniversary of the National Bank and to honor Alfredo Gonzalez F., first governor of the bank.

No. C390 Overprinted: "75 ANIVERSARIO / ASILO CHAPUI / 1890-1965"

1965, Aug. 14 Unwmk. *Perf. 12*

C400	AP72	2col buff & dk grn	1.25	75

Issued to commemorate the 75th anniversary of Chapui Asylum, San Jose.

Girl, FAO Emblem and Hands Holding Grain AP75

Church of Nicoya AP76

Designs (FAO Emblem and): 15c, Map of Costa Rica and silos (horiz.). 50c, World population chart and children. 1 col, Plane over map of Costa Rica (horiz.).

1965 Litho. *Perf. 14*

C401	AP75	15c lt brn & blk	10	8
C402	AP75	35c blk & yel	20	15
C403	AP75	50c ultra & dk grn	30	20
C404	AP75	1col grn, blk & sil	50	30

Issued for the "Freedom from Hunger" campaign of the U.N. Food and Agriculture Organization.

1965, Dec. 20 *Perf. 13½x14*

Designs: 5c, Leonidas Briceno B. 15c, Scroll dated "25 de Julio de 1964." 35c, Map of Guanacaste and Nicoya peninsula. 50c, Dancing couple. 1col, Map showing local products.

C405	AP76	5c red brn & blk	5	5
C406	AP76	10c bl & gray	5	5
C407	AP76	15c bis & sl	6	6
C408	AP76	35c bl & sl	15	10
C409	AP76	50c gray & vio bl	25	15
C410	AP76	1col buff & sl	60	40
		Nos. C405-C410 (6)	1.16	81

Acquisition of the Nicoya territory.

Runner and Olympic Rings AP77

Pres. Kennedy Speaking in San Jose Cathedral AP78

1965, Dec. 23 *Perf. 13x13½*

Olympic Rings and Emblem: 10c, Bicyclists. 40c, Judo. 65c, Basketball. 80c, Soccer. 1col, Hands holding torches, and Mt. Fuji.

C411	AP77	5c bis & multi	6	6
C412	AP77	10c lt lil & multi	6	6
C413	AP77	40c multi	20	15
C414	AP77	65c lem & multi	35	20
C415	AP77	80c tan & multi	50	30
C416	AP77	1col multi	65	40
a.		Souv. sheet of 2	2.25	2.25
		Nos. C411-C416 (6)	1.82	1.17

Issued to commemorate the 18th Olympic Games, Tokyo, Oct. 10-25, 1964. No. C416a contains two 1col stamps, one like No. C416, the other with gray background replacing yellow orange. Dark brown marginal inscription and red control number. Size: 68x93mm. Sheet also exists imperf.

Perf. 13½x13, 13x13½

1965, Dec. 23 Litho. Unwmk.

Designs: 45c, Friendship 7 capsule circling globe, and Kennedy (horiz.). 85c, Kennedy and John, Jr. 1col, Curtis-Lee Mansion and flame from Kennedy grave, Arlington, Va.

C417	AP78	45c brt bl & lil	25	20
C418	AP78	55c org & brt bl	35	25
C419	AP78	85c gray, dk brn & red brn	55	35
C420	AP78	1col multi	50	40
a.		Souv. sheet of 2	1.50	1.50

Issued in memory of President John F. Kennedy (1917-63). No. C420a contains two 1col stamps, one like No. C420, the other with green background replacing dark blue. Dark gray marginal inscription and red control number. Size: 68x93mm. Sheet also exists imperf.

Firemen with Hoses – AP79

Designs: 5c, Fire engine "Knox" (horiz.). 10c, 1866 fire pump. 35c, Fireman's badge. 50c, Emblem and flags of Confederation of Central American Fire Brigades.

1965, March 12 Litho. *Perf. 11*

C421	AP79	5c blk & red	30	15
C422	AP79	10c bis & red	40	15
C423	AP79	15c blk, red brn & red	60	30
C424	AP79	35c blk & yel	1.00	40
C425	AP79	50c dk bl & red	2.00	60
		Nos. C421-C425 (5)	4.30	1.60

Centenary of San José Fire Brigade.

Nos. C381, C383, C386 and C418-C419 Surcharged

C0.15 a **C 0.50** b

1966 Photo. *Perf. 12*

C426	AP72(a)	15c on 30c ocher & Prus grn	10	8
C427	AP72(a)	15c on 45c lt bl & dk brn	10	8
C428	AP72(a)	35c on 75c ocher & dk red brn	20	12

Litho. *Perf. 13x13½*

C429	AP78(a)	35c on 55c org & brt bl	20	12
C430	AP78(b)	50c on 85c multi	35	20
		Nos. C426-C430 (5)	95	60

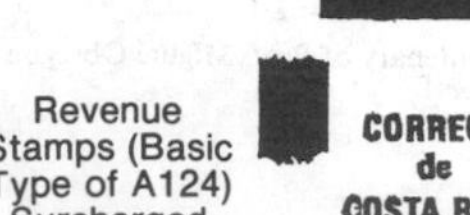

Revenue Stamps (Basic Type of A124) Surcharged

1966, Dec. Engr. *Perf. 12*

C431	A124	15c on 5c bl	10	6
C432	A124	35c on 10c cl	22	12
C433	A124	50c on 20c rose red	35	20

Central Bank of Costa Rica — AP80

1967, Mar. Litho. *Perf. 11*

C434	AP80	5c brt grn	7	5
C435	AP80	15c brown	10	6
C436	AP80	35c scarlet	20	12

Power Lines — AP81

Telecommunications Building, San Pedro — AP82

Designs: 15c, Telephone Central. 25c, La Garita Dam. 35c, Rio Mache Reservoir. 50c, Cachi Dam.

1967, Apr. 24 Litho. *Perf. 11*

C437	AP81	5c dk gray	7	5
C438	AP82	10c brt rose	7	5
C439	AP81	15c brn org	8	6
C440	AP82	25c brt ultra	13	8
C441	AP82	35c brt grn	20	10
C442	AP82	50c red brn	35	20
		Nos. C437-C442 (6)	90	54

Electrification program.

Chondrorhyncha Aromatica AP83

Institute Emblem AP84

Orchids: 10c, Miltonia endresii. 15c, Stanhopea cirrhata. 25c, Trichopilia suavis. 35c, Odontoglossum schlieperianum. 50c, Cattleya skinneri. 1col, Cattleya dowiana. 2col, Odontoglossum chiriquense.

1967, June 15 Engr. *Perf. 13x13½*

Orchids in Natural Colors

C443	AP83	5c multi	15	6
C444	AP83	10c ol & multi	25	6
C445	AP83	15c multi	25	8
C446	AP83	25c multi	50	15
C447	AP83	35c dl vio & multi	50	20
C448	AP83	50c brn & multi	60	25
C449	AP83	1col vio & multi	1.50	50
C450	AP83	2col dk ol bis & multi	2.50	1.00
		Nos. C443-C450 (8)	6.25	2.30

Issued for the University Library.

1967, Oct. 6 Litho. *Perf. 13x13½*

C451	AP84	50c vio bl, lt bl & bl	20	18

Issued to commemorate the 25th anniversary of the Inter-American Agriculture Institute.

Church of Solitude AP85

LACSA Emblem AP86

Costa Rican Churches: 10c, Basilica of Santo Domingo, Heredia. 15c, Cathedral of

Tilaran. 25c, Cathedral of Alajuela. 30c, Mercy Church. 35c, Basilica of Our Lady of Angels. 40c, Church of St. Raphael, Heredia. 45c, Ujarras ruins. 50c, Ruins of parish church, Cartago. 55c, Cathedral of San Jose. 65c, Parish church, Puntarenas. 75c, Church of Orosi. 80c, Cathedral of St. Isidro, the General. 85c, St. Ramon Church. 90c, Church of the Abandonned. 1col, Coronado Church. 2col, Church of St. Teresita. 3col, Parish Church, Heredia. 5col, Carmelite Church. 10col, Limon Cathedral.

1967, Dec. 15 Engr. *Perf. 12½*

C452 AP85 5c green 5 5
C453 AP85 10c blue 5 5
C454 AP85 15c lilac 6 6
C455 AP85 25c dl yel 10 8
C456 AP85 30c org brn 12 10
C457 AP85 35c lt bl 15 12
C458 AP85 40c dp org 15 12
C459 AP85 45c dl bl grn 16 15
C460 AP85 50c olive 18 18
C461 AP85 55c brown 20 18
C462 AP85 65c car rose 35 30
C463 AP85 75c sepia 40 35
C464 AP85 80c yellow 65 50
C465 AP85 85c vio blk 75 50
C466 AP85 90c emerald 75 60
C467 AP85 1col slate 60 35
C468 AP85 2col brt grn 3.00 2.00
C469 AP85 3col orange 4.00 3.00
C470 AP85 5col vio bl 4.00 3.00
C471 AP85 10col carmine 5.00 4.00
Nos. C452-C471 (20) 20.72 15.69

See Nos. C561-C576.

Perf. 13x13½, 13½x13

1967, Dec. 12 Litho. & Engr.

Design: 45c, LACSA emblem and jet (horiz.). 50c, Decorated wheel and anniversary emblem.

C472 AP86 40c ultra, grnsh bl & gold 15 15
C473 AP86 45c blk, pale grn, ultra & gold 18 15
C474 AP86 50c bl & multi 20 18

Issued to commemorate the 20th anniversary (in 1966) of Lineas Aereas Costaricenses, LACSA, Costa Rican Airlines.

Scout Directing Traffic AP87

Runner AP88

Designs: 25c, Campfire under palm tree. 35c, Flag of Costa Rica, Scout flag and emblem. 50c, Encampment (horiz.). 65c, Photograph of first Scout troop (horiz.).

Lithographed and Engraved

1968, Mar. 15 *Perf. 13*

C475 AP87 15c lt bl, blk & lt brn 12 8
C476 AP87 25c lt ultra, vio bl & org 20 12
C477 AP87 35c bl & multi 30 20
C478 AP87 50c multi 35 25
C479 AP87 65c sal, dk bl & brn 50 30
Nos. C475-C479 (5) 1.47 95

Costa Rican Boy Scouts, 50th anniversary.

1968 Litho. *Perf. 10x11*

Sports: 40c, Women's running. 55c, Boxing. 65c, Bicycling. 75c, Weight lifting. 1col, High diving. 3col, Rifle shooting.

C481 AP88 30c multi 15 10
C482 AP88 40c multi 25 15
C483 AP88 55c multi 35 25
C484 AP88 65c lil & multi 45 25
C485 AP88 75c multi 45 25
C486 AP88 1col multi 50 35
C487 AP88 3col multi 2.25 1.25
Nos. C481-C487 (7) 4.40 2.60

Issued to commemorate the 19th Olympic Games, Mexico City, Oct. 12-27.

The only foreign revenue stamps listed in this Catalogue are those authorized for prepayment of postage.

Philatelic Exhibition Emblem — AP89

1969, June 5 Litho. *Perf. 11x10*

C488 AP89 35c multi 15 10
C489 AP89 40c pink & multi 18 12
C490 AP89 50c lt bl & multi 22 15
C491 AP89 2col multi 80 60

Issued to publicize the 4th National Philatelic Exhibition, San Jose, June 5-8.

ILO Emblem AP90

1969, Oct. 29 Litho. *Perf. 10*

C492 AP90 35c bl grn & blk 18 10
C493 AP90 50c scar & blk 27 15

Issued to commemorate the 50th anniversary of the International Labor Organization.

Soccer — AP91

Designs: 65c, Soccer ball, map of North and Central America. 85c, Soccer player. 1 col, Two players in action.

1969, Nov. 23 Litho. *Perf. 11x10*

C494 AP91 65c gray & multi 30 20
C495 AP91 75c multi 30 20
C496 AP91 85c multi 38 25
C497 AP91 1col pink & multi 45 30

Issued to publicize the 4th Soccer Championships (CONCACAF), Nov. 23-Dec. 7.

Stylized Crab — AP92

1970, May 14 Litho. *Perf. 12½*

C498 AP92 10c blk & lil rose 5 5
C499 AP92 15c blk & yel 5 5
C500 AP92 50c blk & brn org 20 10
C501 AP92 1.10col blk & emer 50 20

Issued to publicize the 10th Inter-American Cancer Congress, May 22-29.

Costa Rica No. 124, Magnifying Glass and Stamps — AP93

Design: 2col, Father and son with stamps and album.

1970, Sept. 14 Litho. *Perf. 11*

C502 AP93 1col ultra, brn & car rose 60 20
C503 AP93 2col blk, pink & ultra 70 50

The 5th National Philatelic Exhibition.

EXPO Emblem and Costa Rican Cart — AP94

Designs (EXPO Emblem and): 10c, Japanese floral arrangement (vert.). 35c, Pavilion and Tower of the Sun. 40c, Japanese tea ceremony. 45c, Woman picking coffee (vert.). 55c, Earth seen from moon (vert.).

1970, Oct. 22 Litho. *Perf. 13x13½*

C504 AP94 10c multi 6 5
C505 AP94 15c grn & multi 9 6
C506 AP94 35c bl & multi 15 10
C507 AP94 40c gray & multi 20 12
C508 AP94 45c multi 20 15
C509 AP94 55c blk & multi 20 15
Nos. C504-C509 (6) 90 63

Issued to commemorate EXPO '70 International Exhibition, Osaka, Japan, March 15-Sept. 13.

Escazu Valley, by Margarita Bertheau — AP95

Paintings: 25c, "Irazu," by Rafael A. Garcia (vert.). 80c, Shore landscape, by Teodorico Quiros. 1col, "The Other Face," by Cesar Valverde. 2.50col, Mother and Child, by Luis Daell (vert.).

1970, Nov. 4 Litho. *Perf. 12½*

C510 AP95 25c multi 1.00 50
C511 AP95 45c multi 1.00 50
C512 AP95 80c multi 1.50 80
C513 AP95 1col multi 1.50 90
C514 AP95 2.50col multi 3.00 1.50
Nos. C510-C514 (5) 8.00 4.20

Arms of Costa Rica, 1964 — AP96

Various Coats of Arms, dated: 10c, Nov. 27, 1906. 15c, Sept. 29, 1848. 25c, April 21, 1840. 35c, Nov. 22, 1824. 50c, Nov. 2, 1824. 1col, March 6, 1824. 2col, May 10, 1823.

1971, Feb. 10 Litho. *Perf. 14x13½*

C515 AP96 5c buff & multi 25 10
C516 AP96 10c multi 25 10
C517 AP96 15c yel & multi 30 12
C518 AP96 25c pink & multi 35 15
C519 AP96 35c multi 40 20
C520 AP96 50c rose & multi 45 20
C521 AP96 1col beige & multi 50 25
C522 AP96 2col multi 1.00 50
Nos. C515-C522 (8) 3.50 1.62

National Theater — AP97

1971, Apr. Litho. *Perf. 11*

C523 AP97 2col plum 50 40

Organization of American States meeting.

José Matias Delgado, Manuel Jose Arce AP98

Flag of Costa Rica — AP99

Independence Leaders: 10c, Miguel Larreinaga and Manuel Antonio de la Cerda, Nicaragua. 15c, José Cecilio del Valle, Dionisio de Herrera, Honduras. 35c, Pablo Alvarado and Florencio del Castillo, Costa Rica. 50c, Antonio Larrazabal and Pedro Molina, Guatemala. 2col, Costa Rica coat of arms.

1971, Sept. 14 *Perf. 13*

C524 AP98 5c multi 5 5
C525 AP98 10c multi 5 5
C526 AP98 15c gray, brn & blk 6 5
C527 AP98 35c multi 15 12
C528 AP98 50c multi 15 12
C529 AP99 1col multi 25 15
C530 AP99 2col multi 50 40
Nos. C524-C530 (7) 1.21 94

Sesquicentennial of Central American independence.

Soccer Federation Emblem AP100

Children of the World AP101

1971, Dec.

C531 AP100 50c multi 15 10
C532 AP100 60c multi 15 10

50th anniversary of Soccer Federation of Costa Rica.

1972, Jan. 11 *Perf. 12½*

C533 AP101 50c multi 15 10
C534 AP101 1.10col red & multi 30 25

25th anniversary (in 1971) of the United Nations International Children's Fund (UNICEF).

Tree of Guanacaste AP102

Designs: 40c, Hermitage, Liberia. 55c, Petroglyphs, Rincon Brujo. 60c, Painted head, sculpture from Curubande (vert.).

1972, Feb. 28 *Perf. 11*

C535 AP102 20c brn, ol & brt grn 10 7
C536 AP102 40c brn & ol 15 10
C537 AP102 55c blk & brn 15 12
C538 AP102 60c blk, buff & ver 20 15

Bicentenary of the founding of the city of Liberia, Guanacaste.

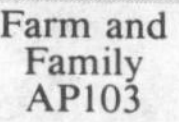

Farm and Family
AP103

Inter-American Exhibitions
AP104

Designs: 45c, Cattle, dairy products and meat (horiz.). 50c, Kneeling figure with plant. 10col, Farmer and map of Americas.

1972, June 30 Litho. *Perf. 12½*
C539 AP103 20c multi 10 7
C540 AP103 45c multi 15 10
C541 AP103 50c dp yel, grn & blk 15 10
C542 AP103 10col brn, org & blk 2.50 1.50

30th anniversary of the Inter-American Institute of Agricultural Sciences.

1972, Aug. 26 Litho. *Perf. 13*
C543 AP104 50c org & brn 15 10
C544 AP104 2col bl & vio 50 40

4th Interamerican Philatelic Exhibition, EXFILBRA, Rio de Janeiro, Aug. 26-Sept. 2.

First Book Printed in Costa Rica — AP105

Design: 50c, 5col, National Library (horiz.).

1972, Dec. 7 Litho. *Perf. 12½*
C545 AP105 20c brt bl 8 7
C546 AP105 50c gold & multi 15 10
C547 AP105 75c multi 20 15
C548 AP105 5col multi 1.25 1.00

International Book Year 1972.

Road to Irazu Volcano
AP106

1972-73 *Perf. 11x11½, 11½x11*
C549 AP106 5c *like 20c* 5 5
C550 AP106 15c *Coco-Culebra Bay* 7 5
C551 AP106 20c *shown* 10 7
C552 AP106 25c *like 15c* 10 8
C553 AP106 40c *Manuel Antonio Beach* 15 10
C554 AP106 45c *Tourist Office emblem* 15 12
C555 AP106 50c *Lindora Lake* 15 12
C556 AP106 60c *San Jose P.O. (vert.).* 20 15
C557 AP106 80c *like 40c* 25 20
C558 AP106 90c *like 45c* 25 20
C559 AP106 1col *like 50c* 25 20
C560 AP106 2col *like 60c* 50 40
Nos. C549-C560 (12) 2.22 1.74

Tourism year of the Americas.
Issue dates: 20c, 25c, 80c, 90c, 1col and 2col, Dec. 26, 1972. Others, Mar. 21, 1973.

Church Type of 1967

Designs as Before.

1973, July 16 Engr. *Perf. 12½*
C561 AP85 5c sl grn 6 5
C562 AP85 10c olive 7 5
C563 AP85 15c orange 8 6
C564 AP85 25c brown 10 8
C565 AP85 30c rose cl 10 8
C566 AP85 35c violet 12 10
C567 AP85 40c brt grn 12 10
C568 AP85 45c dl yel 15 10
C569 AP85 50c rose mag 15 10
C570 AP85 55c blue 15 12
C571 AP85 65c black 20 15
C572 AP85 75c rose red 20 15
C573 AP85 80c yel grn 20 15
C574 AP85 85c lilac 25 20
C575 AP85 90c brt pink 25 20
C576 AP85 1col dk bl 25 20
Nos. C561-C576 (16) 2.45 1.89

Human Rights Flame
AP107

OAS Emblem
AP108

1973 Photo. *Perf. 10½*
C577 AP107 50c blk & red 15 10

25th anniversary of the Universal Declaration of Human Rights.

1973, Dec. 17 Litho. *Perf. 10½*
C578 AP108 20c dk bl & dp car 10 5

25th anniversary of the Organization of American States.

Joaquin Vargas Calvo — AP109

AP110

1974, Jan. 14
C579 AP109 20c *shown* 10 6
C580 AP109 20c *Alejandro Monestel* 10 6
C581 AP109 20c *Julio Mata* 10 6
C582 AP109 60c *Julio Fonseca* 20 15
C583 AP109 2col *Rafael A. Chaves* 50 35
C584 AP109 5col *Manuel M. Gutierrez* 1.25 1.00
Nos. C579-C584 (6) 2.25 1.68

Costa Rican composers honored by the National Symphony Orchestra.

Revenue Stamps Overprinted "Habilitado para Correo Aereo"

1974, Apr. 5 Engr. *Perf. 12*
C585 AP110 50c brown 15 10
C586 AP110 1col violet 25 15
C587 AP110 2col orange 50 30
C588 AP110 5col olive 2.00 1.50

Telephone Building, San Pedro
AP111

EXFILMEX 74 Emblem
AP112

Designs: 65c, Rio Macho Control (horiz.). 85c, Turbines, Rio Macho Center. 1.25col, Cachi Dam and reservoir (horiz.). 2col, I.C.E. Headquarters.

1974, July 30 Litho. *Perf. 10½*
C589 AP111 50c gold & multi 15 10
C590 AP111 65c gold & multi 20 12
C591 AP111 85c gold & multi 25 15
C592 AP111 1.25col gold & multi 30 20
C593 AP111 2col gold & multi 50 30
Nos. C589-C593 (5) 1.40 87

25th anniversary of Costa Rican Electrical Institute (I.C.E.).

1974, Aug. 22 *Perf. 13*
C594 AP112 65c green 20 15
C595 AP112 3col lil rose 75 50

5th Inter-American Philatelic Exhibition, EXFILMEX-74 UPU, Mexico City, Oct. 26-Nov. 3.

Map of Costa Rica, 4-S Emblem
AP113

Design: 50c, Young harvesters and 4-S emblem.

1974, Oct. 7 Litho. *Perf. 12x11*
C596 AP113 20c brt grn 10 5
C597 AP113 50c multi 15 10

25th anniversary of 4-S Clubs of Costa Rica (similar to US 4-H Clubs).

Roberto Brenes Mesen
AP114

"Life Insurance"
AP115

Designs: 85c, "Love and Death," manuscript (horiz.). 5col, Hands of writer.

1974, Oct. 14 Litho. *Perf. 10½*
C598 AP114 20c blk & brn 10 5
C599 AP114 85c blk & red 25 20
C600 AP114 5col blk & red brn 1.25 1.00

Birth centenary of Roberto Brenes Mesen, educator and writer.

1974, Oct. 30 *Perf. 14*

Designs: 20c, Ricardo Jiménez Oreamuno and Tomás Soley Güell (horiz.). 50c, Harvest Insurance (hand holding shovel; horiz.). 85c, Maritime insurance (hand holding paper boat). 1.25col, INS emblem. 2col, Workers rehabilitation (arm with crutch). 2.50col, Workers' Compensation (hand holding wrench). 20col, Fire insurance (hands protecting house).

C601 AP115 20c multi 9 5
C602 AP115 50c multi 15 10
C603 AP115 65c multi 15 10
C604 AP115 85c multi 20 15
C605 AP115 1.25col multi 30 20
C606 AP115 2col multi 50 30
C607 AP115 2.50col multi 65 50
C608 AP115 20col multi 5.00 5.00
Nos. C601-C608 (8) 7.04 6.40

Costa Rican Insurance Institute (Instituto Nacional de Seguros, INS), 50th anniversary.

WPY Emblem
AP116

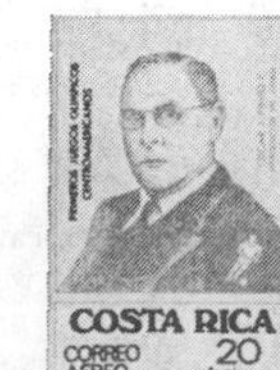

Oscar J. Pinto F.
AP117

1974, Nov. 13 Litho. *Perf. 11x11½*
C609 AP116 2col vio bl & red 50 30

World Population Year.

1974, Dec. 2 *Perf. 13*

Designs: 50c, Alberto Montes de Oca D., champion sharpshooter. 1col, Eduardo Garnier, sports promoter. O. J. Pinto, introducer of soccer.

C610 AP117 20c gray & dk bl 9 5
C611 AP117 50c gray & dk bl 15 10
C612 AP117 1col gray & dk bl 25 15

First Central American Olympic Games, held in Guatemala, 1973.

Mormodes Buccinator
AP118

Masdevallia Ephippium
AP119

Designs: Orchids.

Perf. 10½, 13½
1975, Mar. 7 Litho.
C613 AP118 25c *shown* 30 10
C614 AP118 25c *Gongora claviodora* 30 10
C615 AP119 25c *shown* 30 10
C616 AP119 25c *Encyclia spondiadum* 30 10
C617 AP118 65c *Lycaste skinneri alba* 50 20
C618 AP118 65c *Peristeria elata* 50 20
C619 AP119 65c *Miltonia roezelii* 50 20
C620 AP119 65c *Brassavola digbyana* 50 20
C621 AP118 80c *Epidendrum mirabile* 70 30
C622 AP118 80c *Barkeria lindleyana* 70 30
C623 AP119 80c *Cattleya skinneri* 70 30
C624 AP119 80c *Sobralia macrantha* 70 30
C625 AP118 1.40col *Lycaste cruenta* 90 35
C626 AP118 1.40col *Oncidium obryzatum* 90 35
C627 AP119 1.40col *Gongora armeniaca* 90 35
C628 AP119 1.40col *Sievekingia suavis* 90 35

Perf. 13½
C629 AP118 1.75col *Hexisea imbricata* 1.00 40
C630 AP118 2.15col *Warcewiczella discolor* 1.00 40
C631 AP119 2.50col *Oncidium krameri-anum* 1.25 60
C632 AP119 3.25col *Cattleya dowiana* 2.00 75
Nos. C613-C632 (20) 14.85 5.95

5th National Flower Exhibition.
Stamps of same denominations printed se-tenant. Nos. C613-C628 were printed in both perforations on two different papers: dull finish and shiny. Nos. C629-C632 were printed on shiny paper.

Radio Club Emblem AP120

Members' Flags and Emblem AP121

Design: 2col, Federation emblem.

1975, Apr. 16 Litho. *Perf. 13½*

C633 AP120 1col blk & red lil 50 15
C634 AP121 1.10col multi 60 20
C635 AP120 2col blk & bl 1.00 30

16th Central American Radio Amateurs' Convention, San José, May 2-4.

Nicoya Beach — AP122

Designs: 75c, Driving cattle. 1col, Colonial Church, Nicoya. 3col, Savannah riders (vert.).

1975, Aug. 1 Litho. *Perf. 13½*

C636 AP122 25c gray & multi 6 5
C637 AP122 75c gray & multi 20 20
C638 AP122 1col gray & multi 25 15
C639 AP122 3col gray & multi 75 60

Sesquicentennial of annexation of Nicoya District.

Costa Rica No. 158 AP123

Designs (Type A90 of 1932): No. C641, No. 159. No. C642, No. 160. No. C643, No. 161.

1975, Aug. 14 Litho. *Perf. 12*

C640 AP123 2.20col blk & org 60 50
C641 AP123 2.20col blk & dk grn 60 50
C642 AP123 2.20col blk & car rose 60 50
C643 AP123 2.20col blk & dk bl 60 50

6th National Philatelic Exhibition, San José, Aug. 14-17. Nos. C640-C643 printed se-tenant.

IWY Emblem AP124

1975, Oct. Litho. *Perf. 10½*

C644 AP124 40c vio bl & red 10 8
C645 AP124 1.25col blk & ultra 30 20

International Women's Year 1975.

U.N. Emblem AP125

Designs: 60c, U.N. General Assembly (horiz.). 1.20col, U.N. Headquarters, New York.

1975, Oct. 24 *Perf. 12*

C646 AP125 10c bl & blk 5 5
C647 AP125 60c multi 15 12
C648 AP125 1.20col multi 30 20

30th anniversary of the United Nations.

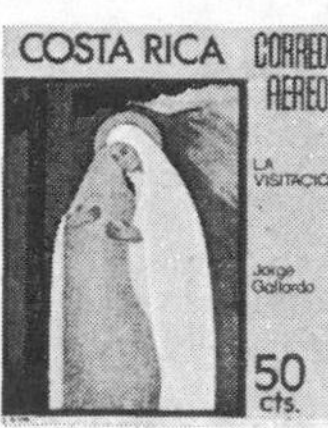

The Visitation, by Jorge Gallardo AP126

"20-30" Club Emblem AP127

Paintings by Jorge Gallardo: 1col, Nativity and Star. 5col, St. Joseph in his Workshop, Virgin and Child.

1975, Nov. *Perf. 10½*

C649 AP126 50c multi 25 10
C650 AP126 1col multi 40 15
C651 AP126 5col multi 1.50 1.00

Christmas 1975.

1976, Jan. 16 Litho. *Perf. 12*

C652 AP127 1col multi 25 15

"20-30" Club of Costa Rica, 20th anniversary.

Quercus Brenessi Trel AP128

"Literary Development" AP129

Plants: 30c, Maxillaria albertii schecht. 55c, Calathea brenesii standl. 2col, Brenesia costaricensis schlecht. 10col, Philodendron brenesii standl.

1976, March 1 *Perf. 10½*

C653 AP128 5c multi 5 5
C654 AP128 30c multi 10 6
C655 AP128 55c multi 15 12
C656 AP128 2col tan & multi 50 30
C657 AP128 10col multi 2.50 2.00
Nos. C653-C657 (5) 3.30 2.53

Prof. Alberto Manuel Brenes Mora, botanist, birth centenary.

1976, Apr. 9 Litho. *Perf. 16*

Designs: 1.10col, Man holding book, stylized. 5col, Costa Rican flag emanating from book (horiz.).

C658 AP129 15c multi 6 5
C659 AP129 1.10col multi 25 20
C660 AP129 5col multi 1.25 1.00

Publishing in Costa Rica.

Postrider, 1839 AP130

Costa Rica No. 13, Post Office AP131

Designs: 65c, Costa Rica No. 14 and Post Office. 85c, Costa Rica No. 15 and Post Office. 2col, UPU Monument, Bern (vert.).

1976, May 24 *Perf. 10½*

C661 AP130 20c ap grn & blk 8 5
C662 AP131 50c bis & multi 15 10
C663 AP131 65c multi 20 15
C664 AP131 85c multi 25 20
C665 AP130 2col blk & lt bl 50 40
Nos. C661-C665 (5) 1.18 90

Centenary of Universal Postal Union (in 1974).

Nos. C662-C664 exist without the surcharges on reproductions of Nos. 13-15.

Telephones, 1876 and 1976 — AP132

Designs: 2col, Wall telephone. 5col, Alexander Graham Bell.

1976, June 28

C666 AP132 1.60col lt bl & blk 40 30
C667 AP132 2col multi 50 30
C668 AP132 5col yel & blk 1.25 1.00

Centenary of first telephone call by Alexander Graham Bell, Mar. 10, 1876.

Inverted Center Stamp of 1901 and Association Emblems — AP133

Design: 5col, 1901 stamp between Costa Rican Philatelic Society and Interamerican Philatelic Federation emblems.

1976, Nov. 11 Litho. *Perf. 10½*

C669 AP133 50c multi 15 10
C670 AP133 1col multi 25 15
C671 AP133 2col multi 50 30

Souvenir Sheet

Perf. 12, Imperf.

C672 AP133 5col multi 1.25 1.25

7th National Philatelic Exhibition and 9th Plenary Assembly of the Interamerican Philatelic Federation (FIAF), San José, Nov. 1976. No. C672 has black marginal inscription. Size: 75x60mm.

"Seeing Eye" and Map of Costa Rica AP134

Amadeo Quiros Blanco — AP135

1976, Nov. 22 *Perf. 16*

C673 AP134 35c blk & bl 10 8
C674 AP135 2col multi 50 30

General Audit Office, 25th anniversary.

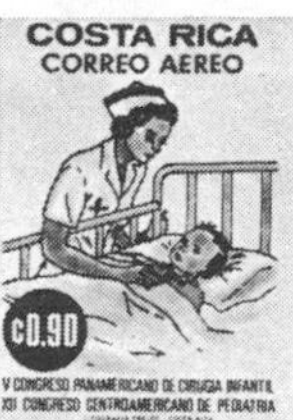

Nurse Attending Child AP136

LACSA Circling Globe AP137

Design: 1.10col, National Children's Hospital (horiz.).

1976, Nov. 29

C675 AP136 90c multi 25 20
C676 AP136 1.10col multi 30 25

5th Panamerican Congress of Pediatric Surgery and 12th Congress of Pediatrics.

1976, Dec. 1 *Perf. 10½*

Designs: 1.20col, Route map. 3col, LACSA emblem and Costa Rican flag.

C677 AP137 1col multi 25 15
C678 AP137 1.20col multi 30 20
C679 AP137 3col multi 75 50

Costa Rican Air Lines (LACSA), 30th anniversary.

Boston Tea Party AP138

Designs: 5col, Declaration of Independence. 10col, Ringing Liberty Bell to announce Independence (vert.).

1976, Dec. 24

C680 AP138 2.20col multi 55 40
C681 AP138 5col multi 1.25 1.00
C682 AP138 10col multi 2.50 2.00

American Bicentennial.

Tree of Guanacaste AP139

Felipe J. Alvarado AP140

Designs (Rotary Emblem and): 60c, Dr. Paul Blanco Cervantes Hospital (horiz.). 3col, Map of Costa Rica (horiz.). 10col, Paul Harris.

1977, Mar. 31 Litho. *Perf. 16*

C683 AP139 40c vio bl & multi 15 8
C684 AP140 50c blk & multi 20 10
C685 AP139 60c vio bl & multi 20 15
C686 AP139 3col vio bl & multi 1.00 60
C687 AP140 10col blk & multi 3.00 2.00
Nos. C683-C687 (5) 4.55 2.93

Rotary Club of San José, 50th anniversary.

Boruca Cloth AP141

Design: 1.50col, Painted wood ornament.

1977, Feb. 22

C688 AP141	75c multi	20	15
C689 AP141	1.50col multi	40	20

National Artisan and Small Industry Program.

Juana Pereira
AP142

Alonso de Anguciana de Gamboa
AP143

Designs: 1col, First Church of Our Lady of the Angels (horiz.). 1.10col, Our Lady of the Angels (gold sculpture). 1.25col, Crown of Our Lady of the Angels.

1977, June 6 Litho. *Perf. 10½*

C690 AP142 50c multi	15	10
C691 AP142 1col multi	25	15
C692 AP142 1.10col multi	30	20
C693 AP142 1.25col multi	35	25

50th anniversary of the coronation of Our Lady of the Angels, patron saint of Costa Rica.

1977, July 4 Litho. *Perf. 10½*

Designs: 75c, Church of Esparza. 1col, Statue of Our Lady of Candlemas. 2col, Statue of Diego de Artieda y Chirino.

C694 AP143 35c multi	10	8
C695 AP143 75c multi	20	15
C696 AP143 1col multi	25	15
C697 AP143 2col multi	50	40

400th anniversary of the founding of Esparza.

CARE Emblem and Child — AP144

Design: 1col, CARE emblem and soybeans (horiz.).

1977, Sept. 14 Litho. *Perf. 16*

C698 AP144 80c multi	20	15
C699 AP144 1col multi	25	15

20th anniversary of CARE (relief organization) in Costa Rica.

Institute's Emblem — AP145

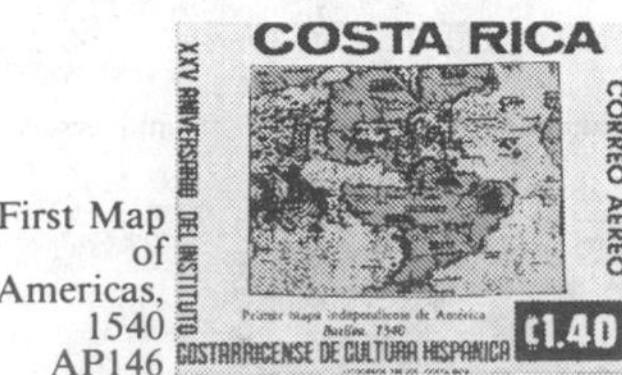

First Map of Americas, 1540
AP146

1977, Oct. 21 Litho. *Perf. 16*

C700 AP145 50c blk & multi	15	10
C701 AP146 1.40col blk & multi	35	30

Hispanic Cultural Institute of Costa Rica, 25th anniversary.

Mercy Church, by Ricardo Ulloa B.
AP147

Health Ministry Emblem
AP148

Paintings: 1col, Christ, by Floria Pinto de Herrero. 5col, St. Francis and the Birds, by Louisa Gonzalez Y Saenz.

1977, Nov. 9 Litho. *Perf. 10½*

C702 AP147 50c multi	15	10
C703 AP147 1col multi	25	15
C704 AP147 5col multi	1.25	1.00

1977, Nov. 16 *Perf. 16*

C705 AP148 1.40col multi	35	30

Creation of Ministry of Health.

Picnic
AP149

José de San Martin
AP150

Designs: 50c, Weaver. 2col, Beach scene. 5col, Fruit and vegetable market. 10col, Swans on lake.

1978, Mar. 21 Litho. *Perf. 10½*

C706 AP149 50c blk & multi	15	10
C707 AP149 1col blk & multi	25	15
C708 AP149 2col blk & multi	50	30
C709 AP149 5col blk & multi	1.25	1.00
C710 AP149 10col blk & multi	2.50	2.00
Nos. C706-C710 (5)	4.65	3.55

Conference of Latin American Tourist Organizations.

1978, Aug. 7 Litho. *Perf. 10½*

C711 AP150 5col multi	1.25	1.00

Gen. José de San Martin (1778-1850), soldier and statesman, fought for South American independence.

Geographical Institute Emblem
AP151

University Federation Emblem
AP152

1978, Aug. 28 Litho. *Perf. 12½*

C712 AP151 5col multi	1.20	90

Pan-American Geography and History Institute, 50th anniversary.

1978, Sept. 18 *Perf. 11*

C713 AP152 80c ultra	20	15

Central American University Federation, 30th anniversary.

Emblems — AP153

1978, Oct. 24 *Perf. 16*

C714 AP153 2col aqua, blk & gold	48	35

6th Interamerican Philatelic Exhibition, Argentina 78, Buenos Aires, Oct. 1978.

Nos. C629-C631 Overprinted: "50 Aniversario del / primer vuelo de PAN AM / en Costa Rica / 1928-1978"

1978, Nov. 1 Litho. *Perf. 13½*

C715 AP118 1.75col multi	42	30
C716 AP118 2.15col multi	50	38
C717 AP119 2.50col multi	60	45

First Pan Am flight in Costa Rica, 50th anniversary.

Nos. C629-C631 Overprinted: "50 Aniversario de la / visita de Lindbergh a / Costa Rica 1928-1978"

1978, Nov. 1

C718 AP118 1.75col multi	42	30
C719 AP118 2.15col multi	50	38
C720 AP119 2.50col multi	60	45

50th anniversary of Lindbergh's visit to Costa Rica.

Nos. C603 and C607 Surcharged with New Value, 4 Bars and: "Centenario del / Asilo Carlos / Maria Ulloa / 1878-1978"

1978, Nov. 8 *Perf. 14*

C721 AP115 50c on 65c multi	12	10
C722 AP115 2col on 2.50col multi	48	35

Asilo Carlos Maria Ulloa, birth centenary.

No. C617-C620, C630-C631 Surcharged with New Value and 4 Bars

Perf. 10½, 13½

1978, Nov. 13 Litho.

C723 AP118 50c on 65c	20	10
C724 AP118 50c on 65c	20	10
C725 AP119 50c on 65c	20	10
C726 AP119 50c on 65c	20	10
C727 AP118 1.20col on 2.15col	50	20
C728 AP119 2col on 2.50col	75	35
Nos. C723-C728 (6)	2.05	95

Nos. C723-C726 printed se-tenant.

Star over Map of Costa Rica
AP154

"Flying Men," Chorotega
AP155

1978, Nov. 13 *Perf. 10½*

C729 AP154 50c bl & blk	12	10
C730 AP154 1col rose lil & blk	24	18
C731 AP154 5col org & blk	1.20	85

Christmas 1978. Nos. C729-C731 printed in sheets of 100 and se-tenant in sheets of 15 (3x5).

1978, Nov. 20 *Perf. 11½*

Designs: 1.20col, Oviedo giving his History of Indies to Duke of Calabria (horiz.). 10col, Lord of Oviedo's coat of arms.

C732 AP155 85c multi	20	15
C733 AP155 1.20col blk & lt bl	30	20
C734 AP155 10col multi	2.40	1.75

500th birth anniversary of Gonzalo Fernandez de Oviedo, first chronicler of Spanish Indies.

Mgr. Domingo Rivas
AP156

San José Cathedral
AP157

1978, Dec. 6 *Perf. 16*

C735 AP156 1col blk & ind	24	18

Perf. 13½

C736 AP157 20col multi	5.00	4.50

Centenary of the Cathedral of San José.

View of Coco Island
AP158

Designs: 2.10, 3, 5 col, various views of Coco Island. 10col, Installation of memorial plaque, people and flag. 5, 10col (vert.).

1979, Apr. 30 Litho. *Perf. 10½*

C737 AP158 90c multi	22	15
C738 AP158 2.10col multi	50	35
C739 AP158 3col multi	72	55
C740 AP158 5col multi	1.20	90
C741 AP158 10col multi	2.40	1.80
a. Souvenir sheet of 3	5.25	5.25
Nos. C737-C741 (5)	5.04	3.75

Visit of Pres. Rodrigo Carazo Odio to Coco Island, June 24, 1978, in the interest of national defense. No. C741a contains Nos. C737-C741. Multicolored margin shows map of Costa Rica. Size: 140x103mm.

Shrimp
AP159

Designs: 85c, Mahogany snapper. 1.80col, Corvina. 3col, Crayfish. 10col, Tuna.

1979, May 14 Litho. *Perf. 13½*

C742 AP159 60c multi	15	10
C743 AP159 85c multi	20	15
C744 AP159 1.80col multi	45	32
C745 AP159 3col multi	72	55
C746 AP159 10col multi	2.40	1.80
Nos. C742-C746 (5)	3.92	2.92

Marine life protection.

Hungry Nestlings, IYC Emblem — AP160

1979, May 24 *Perf. 11*

C747 AP160 1col multi	50	25
C748 AP160 2col multi	1.00	50
C749 AP160 20col multi	6.00	5.00

International Year of the Child.

Catalogue prices for unused stamps up to mid-1953 are for hinged copies matching the condition specified in this volume's introduction.

Microwave Transmitters, Mt. Irazu — AP161

1979, June 28 **Litho.** ***Perf. 14***

Design: 1col, Arenal Dam (horiz.).

C750 AP161 1col multi 25 18
C751 AP161 5col multi 1.25 90

Costa Rican Electricity Institute, 30th anniversary.

Costa Rica No. 1 and Rowland Hill AP162

Design: 10col, Penny Black and Hill.

1979, July 16 ***Perf. 13***

C752 AP162 5col lil rose & bl gray 1.25 90
C753 AP162 10col dl bl & blk 2.00 1.50

Sir Rowland Hill (1795-1879), originator of penny postage.

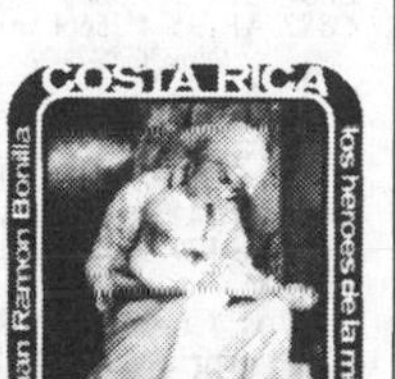

Poverty, by Juan Ramon Bonilla AP163

Sculptures: 60c, Hope, by Hernan Gonzalez. 2.10col, Cattle, by Victor M. Bermudez (horiz.). 5col, Bust of Clorito Picado, by Juan Rafael Chacon. 20col, Mother and Child, by Francisco Zuniga.

1979, July 16 **Litho.** ***Perf. 12***

C754 AP163 60c multi 15 10
C755 AP163 1col multi 25 18
C756 AP163 2.10col multi 45 32
C757 AP163 5col multi 1.25 90
C758 AP163 20col multi 5.00 4.00
Nos. C754-C758 (5) 7.10 5.50

National Sculpture Contest.

Danaus Plexippus — AP164

Butterflies: 1col, Phoebis philea. 1.80col, Rothschildia. 2.10col, Prepona omphale. 2.60col, Marpesia marcella. 4.05col, Morpho cypris.

1979, Aug. 31 **Litho.** ***Perf. 13½***

C759 AP164 60c multi 50 25
C760 AP164 1col multi 1.00 25
C761 AP164 1.80col multi 1.25 50
C762 AP164 2.10col multi 1.50 50
C763 AP164 2.60col multi 1.50 1.00
C764 AP164 4.05col multi 2.50 1.50
Nos. C759-C764 (6) 8.25 4.00

Certain countries cancel stamps in full sheets and sell them (usually with gum) for less than face value. Dealers generally sell "CTO".

SOS Emblem, Houses AP165

Children's Drawings: 5col, 5.50col, Landscapes (diff.).

1979, Sept. 18

C765 AP165 2.50col multi 62 45
C766 AP165 5col multi 1.25 90
C767 AP165 5.50col multi 1.35 1.00

SOS Children's Villages, 30th anniversary.

President Type of 1943

Presidents of Costa Rica: 60c, Rafael Iglesias C. 85c, Ascension Esquivel Ibarra. 1col, Cleto Gonzalez Viquez. 2col, Ricardo Jimenez Oreamuno.

1979, Oct. 8 **Litho.** ***Perf. 13½***

C768 A109 10c dk bl 5 5
C769 A109 60c dl pur 15 10
C770 A109 85c red org 20 15
C771 A109 1col red org 25 18
C772 A109 2col brown 50 35
Nos. C768-C772 (5) 1.15 83

Nos. C768-C772 printed in sheets of 100 and se-tenant in sheets of 25 (5x5).
See Nos. C790-C794.

Holy Family, Creche — AP167

1979, Nov. 16 **Litho.** ***Perf. 12½***

C773 AP167 1col multi 25 18
C774 AP167 1.60col multi 42 30

Christmas 1979.

Reforestation AP168

1980, Jan. 14 **Litho.** ***Perf. 11***

C775 AP168 1col multi 20 15
C776 AP168 3.40col multi 70 50

Anatomy Lesson, by Rembrandt AP169

1980, Feb. 7 **Litho.** ***Perf. 10½***

C777 AP169 10col multi 2.00 1.50

Legal medicine teaching in Costa Rica, 50th anniversary.

Rotary International, 75th Anniversary AP170

1980, Feb. 26 ***Perf. 16***

C778 AP170 2.10col multi 40 30
C779 AP170 5col multi 1.00 75

Gulf of Nicoya, Satellite Photo — AP171

1980, Mar. 10 **Litho.** ***Perf. 12½***

C780 AP171 2.10col *Puerto Limon* 40 30
C781 AP171 5col *shown* 1.00 75

14th International Symposium on Remote Sensing of the Environment, San Jose, Apr. 23-30.

Soccer, Moscow '80 Emblem — AP172

1980, Apr. 16 **Litho.** ***Perf. 10½***

C782 AP172 1col *shown* 20 15
C783 AP172 3col *Bicycling* 60 40
C784 AP172 4.05col *Baseball* 80 60
C785 AP172 20col *Swimming* 4.50 4.00

22nd Summer Olympic Games, Moscow, July 19-Aug. 3.

Poas Volcano AP173

1980, May 14 **Litho.** ***Perf. 10½***

C786 AP173 1col *shown* 20 15
C787 AP173 2.50col *Cahuita Beach* 50 35

National Parks Service, 10th anniversary.

José Maria Zeledon Brenes, Score — AP174

Design: 10col, Manuel Maria Gutierrez.

1980, June 25 **Litho.** ***Perf. 12½***

C788 AP174 1col multi 20 15
C789 AP174 10col multi 2.00 1.50

National anthem composed by Brenes (words) and Gutierrez (music).

President Type of 1943

Presidents of Costa Rica: 1col, Alfredo Gonzalez F. 1.60col, Federico Tinoco G. 1.80col, Francisco Aguilar B. 2.10col, Julio Acosta G. 3col, Leon Cortes C.

1980, Aug. 14 **Litho.** ***Perf. 11***

C790 A109 1col dk red 20 15
C791 A109 1.60col sl bl 30 20
C792 A109 1.80col brown 35 25
C793 A109 2.10col dl grn 40 30
C794 A109 3col dk pur 60 40
Nos. C790-C794 (5) 1.85 1.30

8th National Philatelic Exhibition AP175

Fruits AP176

1980, Sept. 11 ***Perf. 13½***

C795 AP175 5col multi 1.00 75
C796 AP175 20col multi 4.00 3.50

1980, Sept. 24 ***Perf. 10½***

C797 AP176 10c *shown* 5 5
C798 AP176 60c *Cacao* 10 28
C799 AP176 1col *Coffee* 20 15
C800 AP176 2.10col *Bananas* 40 30
C801 AP176 3.40col *Flowers* 70 50
C802 AP176 5col *Sugar cane* 1.00 25
Nos. C797-C802 (6) 2.45 1.53

Giant Tree, by Jorge Carvajal AP177

Virgin and Child, by Raphael AP178

Paintings: 2.10col, Secret Look, by Rolando Cubero. 2.45col, Consuelo, by Fernando Carballo. 3col, Volcano, by Lola Fernandez. 4.05col, attending Mass, by Francisco Amighetti.

1980, Oct. 22 **Litho.** ***Perf. 10½***

C803 AP177 1col multi 20 15
C804 AP177 2.10col multi 40 30

Size: 28x30mm.

C805 AP177 2.45col multi 50 40

Size: 22x36mm.

C806 AP177 3col multi 60 45
C807 AP177 4.05col multi 80 60
Nos. C803-C807 (5) 2.50 1.90

1980, Nov. 11 ***Perf. 13½***

Christmas 1980: 10col, Virgin and Child and St. John, by Raphael.

C808 AP178 1col multi 20 15
C809 AP178 10col multi 2.00 2.00

Juan Santamaria International Airport AP179

1980, Dec. 11 **Litho.** ***Perf. 10½***

Sizes: 30x30mm., 31x25mm. (1.30 col), 25x32mm. (2.60 col)

C810 AP179 1col *Caldera Harbor* 20 15
C811 AP179 1.30col *shown* 25 20
C812 AP179 2.10col *Rio Frio Railroad Bridge* 40 30
C813 AP179 2.60col *Highway to Colon* 50 40
C814 AP179 5col *Huetar post office* 1.00 75
Nos. C810-C814 (5) 2.35 1.80

Paying your taxes means progress.

Repertorio Americano Cover, J. Garcia Monge and Signature — AP180

1981, Jan. 2 Litho. *Perf. 10½*

C815 AP180 1.60col multi 30 20
C816 AP180 3col multi 60 40

Birth centenary of J. Garcia Monge, founder of Repertorio Americano journal.

Arms of Aserri (Site of Cornea Bank) AP181

Harpia Harpyja AP182

1981, Jan. 28 Litho. *Perf. 13½*

C817 AP181 1col shown 20 15
C818 AP181 1.80col Eye 35 25
C819 AP181 5col Rojas 1.00 75

Establishment of human cornea bank, founded by Abelardo Rojas.

1981 *Perf. 11*

C820 AP182 2.10col shown 60 30
C821 AP182 2.50col Ara macao 80 40
C822 AP182 3col Felis concolor 90 45
C823 AP182 5.50col Ateles geoffrovi 2.25 80

Medical and Surgical Clinic AP183

1981, Apr. 8 Litho. *Perf. 10½*

C824 AP183 5c shown 5 5
C825 AP183 10c Physiology class 5 5
C826 AP183 50c Medical school, A. Chavarria (1st dean) 5 5
C827 AP183 1.30col Music school 10 6
C828 AP183 3.40col Carlos Monge Alfaro Library 25 20
C829 AP183 4.05col R.F. Brenes, rector (1952-1961), vert. 30 25
Nos. C824-C829 (6) 80 66

University of Costa Rica, 40th anniversary.

Mail Transport by Horse AP184

1981, May 6 Litho. *Perf. 10½*

C830 AP184 1col shown 20 15
C831 AP184 2.10col Train, 1857 40 30
C832 AP184 10col Mail carriers, 1858 2.00 1.50

Heinrich von Stephan (1831-1897), founder of UPU.

13th World Telecommunications Day — AP185

1981, May 18 *Perf. 11*

C833 AP185 5col multi 1.00 75
C834 AP185 25col multi 5.00 3.50

Bishop Bernardo Thiel AP186

Juan Santamaria AP187

1981, June 8 Litho. *Perf. 10½*

C835 Strip of 5, stained glass windows 50 40
a. AP186 1 col Sts. Peter & Paul 10 6
b. AP186 1 col St. Vincent de Paul 10 6
c. AP186 1 col Death of St. Joseph 10 6
d. AP186 1 col Archangel Michael 10 6
e. AP186 1 col Holy Family 10 6
C836 AP186 2col shown 20 12

Consecration of Bernardo Augusto Thiel as Bishop of San Jose.

1981, June 26 *Perf. 13½*

C837 AP187 1col shown 10 6
C838 AP187 2.45col Alajuela Cathedral, horiz. 25 15

Alajuela province.

Potters — AP188

1981, July 10 Litho. *Perf. 10½*

C839 AP188 15c shown 5 5
C840 AP188 1.60col Bricklayers 15 10
C841 AP188 1.80col Farmers 15 10
C842 AP188 2.50col Fishermen 20 15
C843 AP188 3col Nurse, patient 25 20
C844 AP188 5col Children, traffic policeman 50 30
Nos. C839-C844 (6) 1.30 90

Model of New Natl. Archives AP189

Natl. Archives Centenary: 1.40col, Leon Fernandez Bonilla, founder (vert.). 2col, Arms (vert.). 3col, St. Thomas University, former headquarters.

1981, Aug. 24 Litho. *Perf. 13½*

C845 AP189 1.40col multi 15 10
C846 AP189 2col multi 20 12
C847 AP189 3col multi 25 20
C848 AP189 3.50col multi 30 25

Men Reaching for Sun, Map AP190

1981, Sept. 9 Litho. *Perf. 11*

C849 AP190 1col Man in wheelchair, stairs, vert. 10 6
C850 AP190 2.60col Man reaching for scale, vert. 25 15
C851 AP190 10col shown 90 65

Intl. Year of the Disabled.

World Food Day — AP191

1981, Oct. 16 Litho. *Perf. 10½*

C852 AP191 5col multi 50 30
C853 AP191 10col multi 90 65

President Type of 1943

President of Costa Rica: 1 col, Rafael A. Calderon Guardia, 1940. 2 col, Teodoro Picado Michalski, 1944. 3 col, Jose Figueres Ferrer, 1953. 5 col, Otilio Ulate Blanco, 1949. 10 col, Mario Echandi Jimenez, 1958.

1981, Dec. 7 Litho. *Perf. 13½*

C854 A109 1col pink 10 6
C855 A109 2col orange 20 12
C856 A109 3col green 25 20
C857 A109 5col dk bl 45 30
C858 A109 10col blue 90 65
Nos. C854-C858 (5) 1.90 1.33

Bar Assoc. of Costa Rica Centenary (1981) AP192

1982, Mar. 22 Litho. *Perf. 13½*

C859 AP192 1col Emblem, horiz. 10 5
C860 AP192 2col E. Figueroa, 1st pres. 15 8
C861 AP192 20col Bar building, horiz. 1.50 75

National Progress AP193

1982 *Perf. 10½*

C862 AP193 95c Housing 10 5
C863 AP193 1.15col Agricultural fair 10 6
C864 AP193 1.45col Education 15 8
C865 AP193 1.65col Drinkable water 15 10
C866 AP193 1.80col Rural medical care 15 12
C867 AP193 2.10col Recreational areas 15 12
C868 AP193 2.35col Natl. Theater Square 15 12
C869 AP193 2.60col Communications 15 12
C870 AP193 3col Electric railroad 15 12
C871 AP193 4.05col Irrigation 20 15
Nos. C862-C871 (10) 1.45 1.04

Issue dates: 1.80 col, 2.10 col, 2.60 col, 3 col, 4.05 col, May 5; others, June 16.

City of Alajuela Bicentenary AP194

Perez Zeledon County, 50th Anniv. (1981) AP195

Designs: 5 col, Central Park Fountain. 10 col, Juan Santamaria Historical and Cultural Museum (horiz.). 15 col, Church of Christ of Esquipulas. 20 col, Monsignor Esteban Lorenzo de Tristan, 25 col, Father Juan Manuel Lopez del Corral.

1982, Aug. 9

C872 AP194 5col multi 35 20
C873 AP194 10col multi 70 35
C874 AP194 15col multi 1.05 75
C875 AP194 20col multi 1.40 74
C876 AP194 25col multi 1.75 1.00
Nos. C872-C876 (5) 5.25 3.04

1982, Aug. 30

Designs: 10c, Saint's Stone. 50c, Monument to Mothers. 1 col, Pedro Perz Zeledon. 1.25 col, St. Isidro Labrador Church. 3.50 col, Municipal Building (horiz.). 4.25 col, Arms.

C877 AP195 10c multi 5 5
C878 AP195 50c multi 6 5
C879 AP195 1col multi 10 6
C880 AP195 1.25col multi 12 6
C881 AP195 3.50col multi 25 15
C882 AP195 4.25col multi 30 20
Nos. C877-C882 (6) 88 57

Nos. C695 and C813 Surcharged.

1982, Oct. 28 Litho. *Perf. 10½*

C883 AP143 3col on 75c multi 25 15
C884 AP179 5col on 2.60col multi 40 20

Nos. C640-C643 Surcharged and Overprinted: "IX EXPOSICION FILATELICA - 1982."

1982, Oct. 28 *Perf. 12*

C885 AP123 8.40col on #C640 60 50
C886 AP123 8.40col on #C641 60 50
C887 AP123 8.40col on #C642 60 50
C888 AP123 8.40col on #C643 60 50
C889 AP123 9.70col on #C640 75 60
C890 AP123 9.70col on #C641 75 60
C891 AP123 9.70col on #C642 75 60
C892 AP123 9.70col on #C643 75 60
Nos. C885-C892 (8) 5.40 4.40

9th Natl. Stamp Exhibition.

TB Bacillus Centenary AP196

Pan-American Blood Donors' Society, 7th Congress — AP197

1982, Nov. 19 *Perf. 13½*

C893 AP196 1.50col Koch 10 8
C894 AP196 3col Koch, slide 20 15
C895 AP196 3.30col Health Ministry 25 10

1982, Nov. 25 *Perf. 11*

C896 AP197 30col Natl. Blood Assoc. emblem 2.00 1.25
C897 AP197 50col Congress emblem 3.00 2.00

Inter-Governmental Migration Committee, 30th Anniv. — AP198

St. Francis of Assisi, (1182-1226), by El Greco — AP199

1982, Dec. 13 Litho. *Perf. 10½*

C898 AP198 8.40col Emblem, horiz. 50 25
C899 AP198 9.70col Emblem, diff. 60 30
C900 AP198 11.70col Handshake, horiz. 75 35
C901 AP198 13.05col Emblem, diff., horiz. 80 40

1983, Jan. 3 *Perf. 16*

C902 AP199 4.80col shown 30 10
C903 AP199 7.40col Portrait, diff. 45 15

Visit of Pope John Paul II — AP200

1983, Mar. 1 Litho. *Perf. 10½*

C904 AP200 5col multi 75 20
C905 AP200 10col multi 1.00 50
C906 AP200 15col multi 2.00 75

Simon Bolivar (1783-1830), by Francisco Zuniga Chavarria — AP201

1983, July 22 Litho. *Perf. 16*

C907 AP201 10col multi 70 25

Nos. C902-C903 Surcharged

1983 Litho. *Perf. 16*

C908 AP199 10c on 4.80col 5 5
C909 AP199 50c on 4.80col 5 5
C910 AP199 1.50col on 4.80col 5 5
C911 AP199 3col on 7.40col 6 5

LACSA Costa Rica Airlines, 40th Anniv. — AP202

Various childrens' drawings.

1986, Dec. Litho. *Perf. 13½*

C912 AP202 1col Adriana E. Hidalgo 5 5
C913 AP202 7col Osvaldo A.G. Vega 28 8
C914 AP202 16col David V. Rodriguez 65 18

AIR POST SPECIAL DELIVERY STAMPS

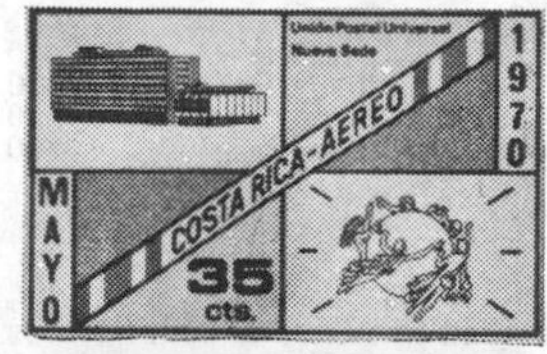

U.P.U. Headquarters and Monument, Bern — APSD1

Perf. 10x11

1970, May 20 Litho. Unwmk.

CE1 APSD1 35c multi 20 10
CE2 APSD1 60c multi 30 15

Issued to commemorate the opening of the new Universal Postal Union Headquarters in Bern. The red and black label attached to the 60c is inscribed "EXPRES". Prices are for stamps with label attached.

Stamps with labels removed were used for regular airmail.

AIR POST OFFICIAL STAMPS

Air Post Stamps of 1934 Overprinted in Red

OFICIAL

1934 Unwmk. *Perf. 12*

CO1	AP8	5c green	35	35
CO2	AP8	10c car rose	35	35
CO3	AP8	15c chocolate	60	60
CO4	AP8	20c dp bl	90	90
CO5	AP8	25c dp org	90	90
CO6	AP8	40c ol blk	1.00	1.00
CO7	AP8	50c gray blk	1.00	1.00
CO8	AP8	60c org yel	1.25	1.25
CO9	AP8	75c dl vio	1.25	1.25
CO10	AP9	1col dp rose	1.75	1.75
CO11	AP9	2col lt bl	6.00	6.00
CO12	AP9	5col black	11.00	11.00
CO13	AP9	10col red brn	13.00	13.00
		Nos. CO1-CO13 (13)	39.35	39.35

SPECIAL DELIVERY STAMPS

Winged Letter SD1

Unwmk.

1972, Mar. 20 Litho. *Perf. 11*

E1 SD1 75c brn & red 25 20
E2 SD1 1.50col bl & red 50 35

1973 *Perf. 11x12*

E3 SD1 75c grn & red 25 20

1973, Nov. 5 Litho. *Perf. 11x11½*

E4 SD1 75c lil & org 1.25 75

Concorde SD2

1976, May 17 Litho. *Perf. 16*

E5 SD2 1col ver & multi 25 20

Concorde — SD3

1979, June 15 Litho. *Perf. 12½*

E6 SD3 2col multi 50 35

Concorde — SD4

1980, Dec. 18 Litho. *Perf. 12½*

E7 SD4 2col multi 50 35

1982, Dec. 20 Litho. *Perf. 11*

E8 SD 4col multi 50 25

POSTAGE DUE STAMPS

D1 D2

1903 Unwmk. Engr. *Perf. 14*

Numerals in Black

J1	D1	5c sl bl	7.50	1.35
J2	D1	10c brn org	7.50	1.00
J3	D1	15c yel grn	3.00	2.75
J4	D1	20c carmine	3.50	2.50
J5	D1	25c sl gray	4.50	2.75
J6	D1	30c brown	7.00	3.75
J7	D1	40c ol bis	7.00	3.75
J8	D1	50c red vio	7.00	3.25
		Nos. J1-J8 (8)	47.00	21.10

1915 Litho. *Perf. 12*

J9	D2	2c orange	12	12
J10	D2	4c dk bl	12	12
J11	D2	8c gray grn	50	50
J12	D2	10c violet	20	20
J13	D2	20c brown	25	25
		Nos. J9-J13 (5)	1.19	1.19

OFFICIAL STAMPS

Official stamps normally were not canceled when affixed to official mail in the 19th century. Occasionally they were canceled in a foreign country of destination. Used prices are for used stamps without cancellation or favor-canceled specimens.

Regular Issues Overprinted

Overprinted in Red, Black, Blue or Green **Oficial**

1883-85 Unwmk. *Perf. 12*

O1	A6	1c grn (R)	2.00	2.00
O2	A6	1c grn (Bk)	2.00	2.00
O3	A6	2c car (Bk)	2.50	2.50
O4	A6	2c car (Bl)	2.75	2.75
O5	A6	5c bl vio (R)	5.25	5.25
O6	A6	10c org (G)	7.00	7.00
O7	A6	40c bl (R)	7.00	7.00
		Nos. O1-O7 (7)	28.50	28.50

Overprinted **OFICIAL**

1886

O8	A6	1c grn (Bk)	2.00	2.00
O9	A6	2c car (Bk)	3.00	3.00
O10	A6	5c bl vio (R)	20.00	20.00
O11	A6	10c org (Bk)	20.00	20.00

Overprinted **OFICIAL**

O12	A6	1c grn (Bk)	1.50	1.50
O13	A6	2c car (Bk)	2.00	2.00
O14	A6	5c bl vio (R)	17.50	17.50
O15	A6	10c org (Bk)	17.50	17.50

Nos. O8-O11 and O12-O15 exist setenant in vertical pairs. Price, each $75.

Overprinted in Black **Oficial**

O16	A6	5c bl vio	50.00	50.00
O17	A6	10c orange	175.00	175.00

Overprinted **OFICIAL.**

1887

O18	A6	1c green	75	75
	a.	"OFICAL"	10.00	10.00
	b.	Without period	90	90
O19	A6	2c carmine	70	70
	a.	"OFICAL"	6.00	6.00
	b.	Without period	90	90
O21	A6	10c orange	6.00	6.00
	c.	Double overprint	10.00	
O22	A7	5c bl vio	3.50	3.50
	a.	"OFICAL"	5.00	
	b.	Without period	3.60	3.60
O23	A7	10c orange	70	70
	a.	"OFICAL"	3.75	3.75
	b.	Without period	1.25	
	c.	Double overprint	12.50	
O24	A6	40c blue	70	70
	a.	"OFICAL"	4.50	4.50
		Nos. O18-O24 (6)	12.35	12.35

Issues of 1889-1901 Overprinted **OFICIAL**

1889 *Perf. 14, 15*

O25	A10	1c brown	30	30
O26	A11	2c dk grn	30	30
O27	A12	5c orange	30	30
O28	A13	10c red brn	30	30
O29	A14	20c yel grn	30	30
O30	A15	50c rose red	1.50	1.50
		Nos. O25-O30 (6)	3.00	3.00

1892

O31	A20	1c grnsh bl	35	35
O32	A21	2c yellow	35	35
O33	A22	5c violet	35	35
O34	A23	10c lt grn	1.50	1.50
O35	A24	20c scarlet	25	22
O36	A25	50c gray bl	70	70
		Nos. O31-O36 (6)	3.50	3.47

1901-02

O37	A30	1c grn & blk	55	55
O38	A31	2c ver & blk	55	55
O39	A32	5c gray bl & blk	55	55
O40	A33	10c ocher & blk	90	90
O41	A34	20c lake & blk	1.20	1.20
O42	A35	50c lil & dk bl	4.25	4.25
O43	A36	1col ol bis & blk	12.00	12.00
		Nos. O37-O43 (7)	20.00	20.00

No. 46 Overprinted in Green **PROVISORIO OFICIAL**

1903

O44	A31	2c ver & blk	3.50	3.50
	b.	"PROVISIORO"	6.00	6.00
	d.	Inverted overprint	6.00	6.00
	f.	Same as "b" inverted	12.00	12.00

Regular Issue of 1903 Overprinted **OFICIAL**

1903 *Perf. 14, 12½ x 14*

O45	A40	4c red vio & blk	1.75	1.75
O46	A41	6c ol grn & blk	2.00	2.00
O47	A42	25c gray lil & brn	12.00	7.00

Regular Issue of 1907 Overprinted **OFICIAL**

1908 *Perf. 14, 11x14*

O48	A43	1c red brn & ind	12	12
O49	A44	2c yel grn & blk	12	12
O50	A45	4c car & ind	15	15
O51	A46	5c yel & dl bl	20	20
O52	A47	10c bl & blk	1.25	1.25
O53	A49	25c gray lil & blk	25	25
O54	A50	50c red lil & bl	40	40
O55	A51	1col brn & blk	1.00	1.00
		Nos. O48-O55 (8)	3.49	3.49

The 5c, 10c and 25c exist with inverted overprint, the 4c with double impression of head.

Imperf examples of Nos. O49 and O53 were found in 1970.

OFICIAL

Regular Issue of 1910 Overprinted in Black

15 VI - 1917

1917

O56	A56	5c orange	30	30
a.		Inverted overprint	3.50	3.50
O57	A57	10c dp bl	25	25
a.		Inverted overprint		

O2

1920 **Red Surcharge** *Perf. 12*

O58	O2	15c on 20c ol grn	50	50

O3

O4

O5 O6

1921 **Black Surcharge** *Perf. 12, 14*

O59	O3	10c on 5c org	50	40
a.		"10 CTS." invert.	22.50	
O60	O4	4c car & ind	45	45
a.		"1291" for "1921"	15.00	
O61	O5	6c on 1c red brn & ind	50	50
O62	O6	20c on 25c gray lil & blk	50	50

Overprinted like No. O60

O63	A50	50c red lil & bl	2.50	2.50
O64	A51	1col brn & blk	4.50	4.50
		Nos. O59-O64 (6)	8.95	8.85

Nos. O60 to O64 exist with date and new values inverted, often in pairs with the normal varieties. These may be printer's waste but probably were deliberately made.

Regular Issue of 1923 Overprinted

OFICIAL

1923 *Perf. 11½*

O65	A68	2c brown	30	30
O66	A68	4c green	15	15
O67	A68	5c blue	30	30
O68	A68	20c carmine	20	20
O69	A68	1col violet	40	40
		Nos. O65-O69 (5)	1.35	1.35

Nos. O65 to O69 exist imperforate but were not regularly issued in that condition.

O7

1926 **Unwmk.** **Engr.** *Perf. 12½*

O70	O7	2c ultra & blk	6	6
O71	O7	3c mag & blk	6	6
O72	O7	4c lt bl & blk	8	8
O73	O7	5c grn & blk	8	8
O74	O7	6c ocher & blk	8	8
O75	O7	10c rose red & blk	8	8
O76	O7	20c ol grn & blk	8	8
O77	O7	30c red org & blk	15	15
O78	O7	45c brn & blk	20	20
O79	O7	1col lil & blk	30	30
		Nos. O70-O79 (10)	1.17	1.17

Regular Issue of 1936 Overprinted in Black

OFICIAL

1936 **Unwmk.** *Perf. 12*

O80	A96	5c green	8	8
O81	A96	10c car rose	8	8

Type of 1926

1937 *Perf. 12½*

O82	O7	2c vio & blk	8	8
O83	O7	3c bis brn & blk	8	8
O84	O7	4c rose car & blk	8	8
O85	O7	5c ol grn & blk	8	
O86	O7	8c blk brn & blk	10	
O87	O7	10c rose lake & blk	10	
O88	O7	20c ind & blk	12	12
O89	O7	40c red org & blk	25	25
O90	O7	55c dk vio & blk	35	
O91	O7	1col brn vio & blk	30	30
O92	O7	2col gray bl & blk	60	60
O93	O7	5col dl yel & blk	3.00	3.00
O94	O7	10col bl & blk	20.00	20.00
		Nos. O82-O94 (13)	25.14	

Nine stamps of this series exist with perforated star (2c, 3c, 4c, 20c, 40c, 1col, 2col, 5col, 10col). These were issued to officials for postal purposes. Unpunched copies were sold to collectors but had no franking power. Prices for unused are for unpunched.

POSTAL TAX STAMPS

Most postal tax issues were to benefit the Children's Village and were obligatory on all mail during December.

No. C198 Surcharged in Red: "Sello de Navidad Pro-Ciudad de Los Ninos 5 5"

Engraved; Center Photogravure

1958 **Unwmk.** *Perf. 12½*

RA1	AP51	5c on 2c brt bl & blk	15	6

Similar Surcharge in Green on Type of 1954

Design: Like No. C228, pottery.

Perf. 12

RA2	AP53	5c on 10c dk bl & blk	40	8
a.		Inverted surch.		

Father Edward J. Flanagan PT1

Father Peralta PT2

Paintings: No. RA4, Boy by El Greco. No. RA5, Boy by Jose Ribera. No. RA6, Girl by Amadeo Modigliani.

Perf. 13½

1959, Nov. 25 **Unwmk.** **Photo.**

RA3	PT1	5c green	30	20
RA4	PT1	5c dl gray vio	30	20
RA5	PT1	5c olive	30	20
RA6	PT1	5c lil rose	30	20

Exist imperf.

1960 **Litho.** *Perf. 14*

Designs: No. RA8, Girl by Renoir. No. RA9, Boys with cups by Velazquez. No. RA10, Singing children, sculpture by F. Zuniga.

RA7	PT2	5c chocolate	30	20
RA8	PT2	5c dp org	30	20
RA9	PT2	5c plum	30	20
RA10	PT2	5c grysh bl	30	20

Exist imperf.

No. C229 Surcharged "Sello de Navidad Pro-Ciudad de los Ninos 5 5"

Engraved; Center Photogravure

1961 *Perf. 13x12½*

RA11	AP53	5c on 15c grn & blk	30	15

Nicolas, Son of Rubens PT3

Boys in Workshop PT4

Designs: No. RA13, Madonna by Bellini. RA14, Angel playing stringed instrument by Melozzo. RA15, Msgr. Ruben Odio H.

1962 **Photo.** *Perf. 13½*

RA12	PT3	5c dk car	30	20
RA13	PT3	5c sepia	30	20
RA14	PT3	5c dl grn	30	20
RA15	PT3	5c blue	30	20

Type of 1962, Inscribed "1963"
Designs as before

Designs: No. RA16, Rubens' son Nicolas. No. RA17, Madonna, Bellini. No. RA18, Angel, Melozzo. No. RA19, Msgr. Ruben Odio H.

1963 **Photo.** *Perf. 13½*

RA16	PT3	5c sepia	30	15
RA17	PT3	5c ultra	30	15
RA18	PT3	5c dk car	30	15
RA19	PT3	5c black	30	15

1964 **Litho.** *Perf. 12½*

Designs: No. RA21, Two playing boys. No. RA22, Teacher and children. No. RA23, Priest with boys.

RA20	PT4	5c brt grn	30	15
RA21	PT4	5c rose lil	30	15
RA22	PT4	5c blue	30	15
RA23	PT4	5c brown	30	15

Brother Casiano de Madrid PT5

Christmas Ornaments PT6

Designs: No. RA25, National Children's Hospital. No. RA26, Poinsettia. No. RA27, Santa Claus with children (diamond).

1965, Dec. 10 **Litho.** *Perf. 10*

RA24	PT5	5c red brn	20	15
RA25	PT5	5c green	20	15
RA26	PT5	5c red	20	15
RA27	PT5	5c ultra	20	15

1966 **Litho.** *Perf. 11*

Designs: No. RA29, Angel. No. RA30, Church. No. RA31, Reindeer.

RA28	PT6	5c red	20	8
RA29	PT6	5c lt ultra	20	8
RA30	PT6	5c brt grn	20	8
RA31	PT6	5c brown	20	8

General Post Office, San José — PT7

1967, March **Litho.** *Perf. 11*

RA32	PT7	10c blue	10	6

No. RA32 was issued as a postal tax stamp to be used by organizations normally allowed free postage. On Dec. 15, 1972, it was authorized for use as an ordinary postage stamp.

Madonna and Child — PT8

Star of Bethlehem, Mother and Child — PT9

1967 **Litho.** *Perf. 11*

RA33	PT8	5c ol grn	15	10
RA34	PT8	5c dp lil rose	15	10
RA35	PT8	5c brt bl	15	10
RA36	PT8	5c grnsh bl	15	10

1968, Dec. **Litho.** *Perf. 12½*

RA37	PT9	5c gray	15	10
RA38	PT9	5c rose red	15	10
RA39	PT9	5c dk rose brn	15	10
RA40	PT9	5c bis brn	15	10

Madonna and Child — PT10

1969, Dec. **Litho.** *Perf. 12½*

RA41	PT10	5c dk bl	5	5
RA42	PT10	5c orange	5	5
RA43	PT10	5c brn red	5	5
RA44	PT10	5c bl grn	5	5

Christ Child and Star — PT11

1970, Dec. **Litho.** *Perf. 12½*

RA45	PT11	5c brt pur	5	5
RA46	PT11	5c lil rose	5	5
RA47	PT11	5c olive	5	5
RA48	PT11	5c ocher	5	5

Christ Child and "PAX" PT12

Madonna and Child PT13

1971, Nov. 29

RA49	PT12	10c dk bl	7	5
RA50	PT12	10c orange	7	5
RA51	PT12	10c brown	7	5
RA52	PT12	10c green	7	5

1972, Nov. 30 *Perf. 11x11½*

RA53	PT13	10c dk bl	7	5

RA54	PT13	10c	brt red	7	5
RA55	PT13	10c	lilac	7	5
RA56	PT13	10c	green	7	5

Madonna and Child PT14

Boys Eating Cake, by Murillo PT15

1973, Nov. 30 Litho. *Perf. 12½*

RA57	PT14	10c	purple	7	5
RA58	PT14	10c	car rose	7	5
RA59	PT14	10c	gray	7	5
RA60	PT14	10c	org brn	7	5

1974, Nov. 25 *Perf. 13*

Paintings: No. RA62, Virgin and Child, with St. John, by Raphael. No. RA63, Maternity, by Juan R. Bonilla. No. RA64, Praying Child, by Reynolds.

RA61	PT15	10c	brt pink	6	5
RA62	PT15	10c	rose lil	6	5
RA63	PT15	10c	dk gray	6	5
RA64	PT15	10c	vio bl	6	5

"Happy Dreams," by Sonia Romero PT16

Virgin and Child, by Hans Memling PT17

Paintings: No. RA66, Virgin with Carnation, by Leonardo da Vinci. No. RA67, Children with Tortoise, by Francisco Amighetti. No. RA68, Boy with Pigeon, by Picasso.

1975, Nov. 25 Litho. *Perf. 10½*

RA65	PT16	10c	gray	5	5
RA66	PT16	10c	red lil	5	5
RA67	PT16	10c	org brn	5	5
RA68	PT16	10c	brt bl	5	5

Obligatory on all mail during December.

1976, Nov. 24 Litho. *Perf. 10½*

Paintings: No. RA70, Boy with Sombrero, by Auguste Renoir. No. RA71, Meditation (Boy), by Floria Pinto de Herrero. No. RA72, Gaston de Mezerville (boy), by Lolita Zeller de Peralta.

RA69	PT17	10c	rose lil	5	5
RA70	PT17	10c	rose car	5	5
RA71	PT17	10c	gray	5	5
RA72	PT17	10c	vio bl	5	5

Obligatory on all mail during December.

Boy's Head, by Amparo Cruz — PT18

Boy with Kite — PT19

Paintings: No. RA74, Girl's head, by Rubens. No. RA75, Girl and infant, by Cristina Fournier. No. RA76, Mariano Goya, by Goya.

1977, Nov. Litho. *Perf. 10½*

RA73	PT18	10c	gray ol	5	5
RA74	PT18	10c	rose red	5	5
RA75	PT18	10c	brt ultra	5	5
RA76	PT18	10c	brt rose lil	5	5

Obligatory on all mail during December.

1978, Nov. 20 Litho. *Perf. 12½*

Designs: No. RA77, like No. RA76. Nos. RA78-RA79, Girl flying kite.

RA77	PT19	10c	magenta	5	5
RA78	PT19	10c	slate	5	5
RA79	PT19	10c	lilac	5	5
RA80	PT19	10c	vio bl	5	5

Obligatory on all mail during December.

Boy Leaning on Tree — PT20

1979, Nov. 19 Litho. *Perf. 12½*

RA81	PT20	10c	blue	5	5
RA82	PT20	10c	orange	5	5
RA83	PT20	10c	magenta	5	5
RA84	PT20	10c	green	5	5

Obligatory on all mail during December.

Boy on Swing — PT21

1980, Nov. 18 Litho. *Perf. 12½*

RA85	PT21	10c	brt bl	5	5
RA86	PT21	10c	brt yel	5	5
RA87	PT21	10c	crim rose	5	5
RA88	PT21	10c	brt grn	5	5

Obligatory on all mail during December.

Boy Riding Toy Car — PT22

1981, Nov. 19 Litho. *Perf. 11*

RA89	PT22	10c	blue	5	5
RA90	PT22	10c	green	5	5
RA91	PT22	10c	red	5	5
RA92	PT22	10c	orange	5	5

Obligatory on all mail during December.

Youth Running Machine — PT23

1982, Nov. 19 Litho. *Perf. 10½*

RA93	PT23	10c	red	5	5
RA94	PT23	10c	gray	5	5
RA95	PT23	10c	purple	5	5
RA96	PT23	10c	grnsh bl	5	5

Obligatory on all mail during December.

Youths Working on Wheelchair — PT24

1983, Nov. 24 Litho. *Perf. 16*

RA97	PT24	10c	red	5	5
RA98	PT24	10c	orange	5	5
RA99	PT24	10c	ultra	5	5
RA100	PT24	10c	green	5	5

Christmas 1983, Children's Village. Obligatory on all mail during December.

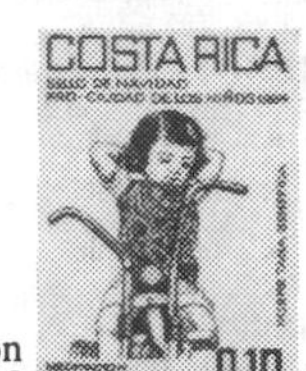

Girl on Bicycle — PT25

1984, Nov. 20 Litho. *Perf. 10½*

RA101	PT25	10c	violet	5	5

Christmas 1984, Children's Village. Obligatory on all mail during December.

Taking a Child in Out of the Cold — PT26

1985, Nov. Litho. *Perf. 13*

RA102	PT26	10c	dull brn	20	5

Christmas 1985. Children's Village. Obligatory on all mail during December.

Depressed Child — PT27

1986, Nov. Litho. *Perf. 10½*

RA103	PT27	10c	lemon	6	5

Christmas stamps, 25th anniv.; Christmas 1986. Children's Village. Obligatory on all mail during December.

Christmas — PT28

1987 Litho. *Perf. 10½*

RA104	PT28	10c	dk ol bis & brt bl	6	5

Chrsitmas 1987. Children's Village. Obligatory on all mail in December.

GUANACASTE

(A province of Costa Rica)

LOCATION — On northwestern coast of Central America.
AREA — 4,000 sq. mi. (approx.).
POP. — 69,531 (estimated).
CAPITAL — Liberia.

Residents of Guanacaste were allowed to buy Costa Rican stamps, overprinted "Guanacaste," at a discount from face value because of the province's isolation and climate, which makes it difficult to keep mint stamps. Use was restricted to the province.

Counterfeits of most Guanacaste overprints are plentiful.

On Issue of 1883
Overprinted Horizontally in Black

16mm. **Guanacaste**

1885 Unwmk. *Perf. 12*

1	A6	1c green		4.00	4.00
	a.	"Gnanacaste"		60.00	
2	A6	2c carmine		4.00	4.00
	a.	"Gnanacaste"		50.00	
3	A6	10c orange		12.00	12.00
	a.	"Gnanacaste"		75.00	

Same Overprint in Red

4	A6	1c green		4.00	4.00
	a.	"Gnanacaste"		45.00	
	b.	Overprinted in blk & red		125.00	
5	A6	5c bl vio		12.50	2.75
	a.	"Gnanacaste"		75.00	
6	A6	40c blue		20.00	20.00

Overprinted Horizontally in Black

17½mm. — b **Guanacaste**

7	A6	1c green	7.50	7.50
8	A6	2c carmine	7.50	7.50
9	A6	5c bl vio	17.50	3.00
10	A6	10c orange	13.50	8.50
11	A6	40c blue	45.00	45.00

Same Overprint in Red

12	A6	5c bl vio	50.00	20.00
13	A6	40c blue	*1,500.*	

Overprinted Horizontally in Black

18½mm. — c **Guanacaste**

14	A6	2c carmine	8.00	8.00
15	A6	10c orange	40.00	30.00

Same Overprint in Red

16	A6	1c green	7.00	7.00
	a.	Double overprint, one in blk	150.00	
17	A6	5c bl vio	32.50	7.00
18	A6	40c blue	50.00	50.00

Same Overprint, Vertically in Black

19	A6	1c green	*2,000.*	*2,000.*
20	A6	2c carmine	800.00	600.00
21	A6	5c bl vio	250.00	100.00
22	A6	10c orange	60.00	50.00

Guanacaste *e* GUANACASTE *f* GUANACASTE *g* GUANACASTE *h* GUANACASTE *i*

Overprinted Type e, Vertically

23	A6	1c green	100.00	100.00
24	A6	2c carmine	110.00	110.00
25	A6	5c bl vio	125.00	62.50
26	A6	10c orange	65.00	60.00

Overprinted Type f, Vertically

27	A6	1c green	275.00	200.00
28	A6	2c carmine	175.00	175.00
29	A6	5c bl vio	200.00	85.00
30	A6	10c orange	75.00	75.00

Overprinted Type g, Vertically

31	A6	1c green	300.00	300.00
32	A6	2c carmine	300.00	300.00
33	A6	5c bl vio	300.00	150.00
34	A6	10c orange	150.00	150.00

Overprinted Type h, Vertically

35	A6	1c green	150.00	150.00
36	A6	2c carmine	90.00	90.00
37	A6	5c bl vio	175.00	85.00
38	A6	10c orange	40.00	40.00

The authenticity of Costa Rica Nos. 16-19 with overprint "i" has not been established.

On Issues of 1883-87

Overprinted Horizontally in Black **Guanacaste**

1888-89

42	A7 5c bl vio	20.00	3.00

Overprinted Horizontally in Black **Guanacaste**

43	A7 5c bl vio	20.00	3.00

Overprinted Horizontally in Black **Guanacaste**

44	A6 2c carmine	3.00
45	A7 10c orange	3.00
a.	Invtd. ovpt.	

On Issue of 1889

Overprinted Type b, Horizontally

1889

47	A8 2c blue	30.00

Vertically

48	A8 2c bl (c)	150.00
49	A8 2c bl (e)	75.00
51	A8 2c bl (f)	90.00
52	A8 2c bl (g)	300.00
54	A8 2c bl (h)	135.00

Nos. 47-54 are overprinted "Correos." Copies without "Correos" are known postally used, and are priced the same as Nos. 47-54, unused.

Dangerous counterfeits exist of Nos. 1-54.

On Nos. 25-33

Overprinted Horizontally in Black **GUANACASTE**

1890 *Perf. 14 and 15*

55	A10	1c brown	10.00	4.00
56	A11	2c dk grn	4.00	2.50
57	A12	5c orange	6.00	2.50
58	A13	10c red brn	6.00	3.00
59	A14	20c yel grn	1.50	1.50
60	A15	50c rose red	2.50	2.50
a.		"GUAGACASTE"	100.00	
61	A16	1p blue	3.50	3.50
a.		"GUAGACASTE"	100.00	100.00
62	A17	2p violet	7.00	7.00
a.		"GUAGACASTE"	100.00	100.00
63	A18	5p ol grn	35.00	35.00
a.		"GUAGACASTE"	100.00	100.00
		Nos. 55-63 (9)	75.50	61.50

Overprinted Horizontally in Black **GUANACASTE**

64	A10	1c brown	2.25	1.75
a.		Vert. pair, imperf. btwn.		
65	A11	2c dk grn	2.25	1.75
66	A12	5c orange	2.25	1.75
67	A13	10c red brn	2.25	1.75

CRETE

LOCATION — An island in the Mediterranean Sea south of Greece.
GOVT. — A department of Greece.
AREA — 3,235 sq. mi.
POP. — 336,150 (1913).
CAPITAL — Canea.

Formerly Crete was a province of Turkey. After an extended period of civil wars, France, Great Britain, Italy and Russia intervened and declaring Crete an autonomy, placed it under the administration of Prince George of Greece as High Commissioner. In October, 1908, the Cretan Assembly voted for union with Greece and in 1913 the union was formally effected.

40 Paras = 1 Piaster
4 Metallik = 1 Grosion (1899)
100 Lepta = 1 Drachma (1900)

Issued Under Joint Administration of France, Great Britain, Italy and Russia

British Sphere of Administration. District of Heraklion (Candia).

A1

A2

Handstamped

1898 **Unwmk.** *Imperf.*

1	A1 20pa violet	500.00	300.00

1898 **Litho.** *Perf. 11½*

2	A2 10pa blue	14.00	5.00
a.	Horizontal pair, imperf. between		
b.	Imperf. pair	500.00	
3	A2 20pa green	14.00	5.00
a.	Imperf. pair	500.00	

1899

4	A2 10pa brown	14.00	5.00
a.	Horizontal pair, imperf. between		
b.	Imperf. pair	500.00	
5	A2 20pa rose	14.00	5.00
a.	Imperf. pair	500.00	

Counterfeits exist of Nos. 1-5.

Reprints exist of Nos. 2-5.

Russian Sphere of Administration. District of Rethymnon.

Coat of Arms
A3 A4

1899 **Handstamped** *Imperf.*

10	A3	1m green	15.00	10.00
11	A3	2m black	15.00	10.00
12	A3	2m rose	95.00	60.00
13	A4	1m blue	45.00	25.00

Nos. 10-13 exist on both wove and laid papers. Counterfeits exist.

Poseidon's Trident
A5 A5a

1899 **Litho.** *Perf. 11½*

With Control Mark Overprinted in Violet.

Without Stars at Sides.

14	A5	1m orange	80.00	70.00
15	A5	2m orange	80.00	70.00
16	A5	1gr orange	80.00	70.00
17	A5	1m green	80.00	70.00
18	A5	2m green	80.00	70.00
19	A5	1gr green	80.00	70.00
20	A5	1m yellow	80.00	70.00
21	A5	2m yellow	80.00	70.00
22	A5	1gr yellow	80.00	70.00
23	A5	1m rose	80.00	70.00
24	A5	2m rose	80.00	72050
25	A5	1gr rose	80.00	70.00
26	A5	1m violet	80.00	70.00
27	A5	2m violet	80.00	70.00
28	A5	1gr violet	80.00	70.00
29	A5	1m blue	80.00	70.00
30	A5	2m blue	80.00	70.00
31	A5	1gr blue	80.00	70.00
32	A5	1m black	1,200	1,050.
33	A5	2m black	1,200.	1,050.
34	A5	1gr black	1,200.	1,050.

With Stars at Sides.

35	A5a	1m blue	30.00	15.00
36	A5a	2m blue	12.00	10.00
37	A5a	1gr blue	9.00	6.00
38	A5a	1m rose	50.00	40.00
39	A5a	2m rose	12.00	10.00
40	A5a	1gr rose	9.00	6.00
41	A5a	1m green	32.50	15.00
42	A5a	2m green	12.00	10.00
43	A5a	1gr green	9.00	6.00
44	A5a	1m violet	32.50	15.00
45	A5a	2m violet	12.00	10.00
46	A5a	1gr violet	9.00	6.00
		Nos. 35-46 (12)	229.00	149.00

Nearly all of Nos. 14 to 46 may be found without control mark, with double control marks and in various colors.

Counterfeits exist of Nos. 14-46.

Issued by the Cretan Government.

Hermes
A6

Hera
A7

Prince George of Greece — A8

Talos — A9

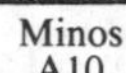
Minos
A10

St. George and the Dragon
A11

1900, Mar. 1 **Engr.** *Perf. 14*

50	A6	1 l vio brn	75	15
51	A7	5 l green	1.50	25
52	A8	10 l red	2.25	20
53	A7	20 l car rose	7.00	1.00

Overprinted **ΠΡΟΣΩΡΙΝΟΝ**

Red Overprint.

54	A8	25 l blue	3.50	1.00
55	A6	50 l lilac	4.00	2.00
56	A9	1d gray vio	9.00	5.00
57	A10	2d brown	30.00	25.00
58	A11	5d grn & blk	110.00	100.00
		Nos. 54-58 (5)	156.50	133.00

Black Overprint.

59	A8	25 l blue	3.50	1.00
60	A6	50 l lilac	4.00	3.00
61	A9	1d gray vio	8.00	4.50
a.		Inverted overprint	*750.00*	*750.00*
62	A10	2d brown	20.00	15.00
63	A11	5d grn & blk	80.00	65.00
		Nos. 59-63 (5)	115.50	88.50

1901

Without Overprint.

64	A6	1 l bister	1.00	50
65	A7	20 l orange	4.00	75
66	A8	25 l blue	14.00	1.00
67	A6	50 l lilac	35.00	15.00
68	A6	50 l ultra	9.00	6.00
69	A9	1d gray vio	40.00	25.00
70	A10	2d brown	10.00	10.00
71	A11	5d grn & blk	27.50	25.00
		Nos. 64-71 (8)	140.50	83.25

No. 64 is a revenue stamp that was used for postage for a short time. Unused, it can only be considered as a revenue.

Types A6 to A8 in olive yellow, and types A9 to A11 in olive yellow and black are revenue stamps.

No. 66 Overprinted in Black **ΠΡΟΣΩΡΙΝΟΝ**

1901

72	A8 25 l blue	35.00	1.00
a.	First letter of overprint inverted	150.00	150.00

No. 65 Surcharged in Black **5** **5**

1904, Dec.

73	A7 5 on 20 l org	4.00	1.00
a.	Without "5" at right	10.00	10.00

Mycenaean Seal — A12

Britomartis (Cortyna Coin) — A13

Prince George
A14

Kydon and Dog (Cydonia Coin)
A15

Triton (Itanos Coin) — A16

Ariadne (Knossos Coin) — A17

Zeus as Bull Abducting Europa (Cortyna Coin)
A18

Palace of Minos Ruins, Knossos
A19

Arkadi Monastery and Mt. Ida — A20

1905, Feb. 15

74	A12	2 l dl vio	2.25	40
75	A13	5 l yel grn	7.50	45
76	A14	10 l red	8.00	65
77	A15	20 l bl grn	9.00	1.25
78	A16	25 l ultra	8.50	1.00
79	A17	50 l yel brn	8.00	5.00
80	A18	1d rose car & dp brn	85.00	60.00
81	A19	3d org & blk	45.00	30.00
82	A20	5d ol grn & blk	30.00	27.50
		Nos. 74-82 (9)	203.25	126.25

The so-called revolutionary stamps of 1905 were issued for sale to collectors and, so far as can be ascertained, were of no postal value whatever.

A. T. A. Zaimis
A21

Prince George Landing at Suda
A22

1907, Aug. 28
83 A21 25 l bl & blk 30.00 1.50
84 A22 1d grn & blk 12.50 10.00

Commemorative of the administration under a High Commissioner.

Stamps of 1900-1907 Overprinted in Black ΕΛΛΑΣ

1908, Sept. 21
85 A6 1 l vio brn 50 25
86 A12 2 l dl vio 50 25
87 A13 5 l yel grn 1.00 38
88 A8 10 l red 1.00 50
89 A15 20 l bl grn 3.00 1.00
90 A21 25 l bl & blk 8.50 1.00
91 A17 50 l yel brn 8.00 4.00
92 A18 1d rose car & dp brn 75.00 55.00
93 A10 2d brown 8.00 8.00
94 A19 3d org & blk 45.00 40.00
95 A20 5d ol grn & blk 40.00 35.00
Nos. 85-95 (11) 190.50 145.38

This overprint exists inverted and double, as well as with incorrect, reversed, misplaced and omitted letters. Similar errors are found on the Postage Due and Official stamps with this overprint.

Hermes by Praxiteles — A23

1908
96 A23 10 l brn red 4.00 1.00
a. Pair, one without overprint 8.00
b. Inverted overprint 15.00
c. Double overprint 15.00

Nos. 96 and 114 were not regularly issued without overprint.

ΕΛΛΑΣ

No. 53 Surcharged

ΠΡΟΣΟΡΙΝΟΝ
5 5

1909
97 A7 5 l on 20 l car rose 150.00 150.00

Forgeries exist of No. 97.

On No. 65

98 A7 5 l on 20 l org 2.00 80
a. Inverted surcharge

ΕΛΛΑΣ

Overprinted on Nos. 64, J1

ΠΡΟΣΟΡΙΝΟΝ

99 A6 1 l bister 1.00 90
100 D1 1 l red 1.50 1.25

ΕΛΛΑΣ

No. J4 Surcharged 2

ΠΡΟΣΩΡΙΝΟΝ

101 D1 2 l on 20 l red 1.50 1.25
a. Double surcharge 10.00
b. Inverted surcharge 10.00
c. Second letter of surch. "D" instead of "P" 30.00 30.00

ΕΛΛΑΣ

No. J4 Surcharged 2

ΠΡΟΣΩΡΙΝΟΝ

102 D1 2 l on 20 l red 1.50 1.25

Overprinted in Black:

ΕΛΛΑΣ a ΕΛΛΑΣ b
c ΕΛΛΑΣ

103 A23(a) 10 l brn red 4.50 50
a. Inverted overprint 40.00
104 A15(a) 20 l bl grn 8.00 1.00
105 A21(c) 25 l bl & blk 10.00 3.00
106 A17(a) 50 l yel brn 7.50 5.00
107 A22(b) 1d grn & blk 10.00 8.00
108 A10(a) 2d brown 8.00 7.50
109 A19(b) 3d org & blk 110.00 100.00
110 A20(b) 5d ol grn & blk 27.50 22.50
Nos. 103-110 (8) 185.50 147.50

Stamps of 1900-08 Overprinted in Red or Black ΕΛΛΑΣ

1909-10
111 A6 1 l vio brn 25 20
112 A12 2 l dl vio 50 25
113 A13 5 l yel grn 50 20
114 A23 10 l brn red (Bk) 70 20
115 A15 20 l bl grn 3.50 50
116 A16 25 l ultra 3.50 75
117 A17 50 l yel brn 7.50 5.00
118 A18 1d rose car & dp brn (Bk) 90.00 80.00
119 A19 3d org & blk 60.00 55.00
120 A20 5d ol grn & blk 40.00 40.00
Nos. 111-120 (10) 206.45 182.10

POSTAGE DUE STAMPS

D1

1901 Unwmk. Litho. *Perf. 14*
J1 D1 1 l red 75 40
J2 D1 5 l red 1.50 50
J3 D1 10 l red 2.00 65
J4 D1 20 l red 3.00 1.75
J5 D1 40 l red 15.00 15.00
J6 D1 50 l red 15.00 15.00
J7 D1 1d red 40.00 40.00
J8 D1 2d red 17.50 17.50
Nos. J1-J8 (8) 94.75 90.80

Surcharged in Black 1 ΔΡΑΧΜΗ

1901
J9 D1 1d on 1d red 18.00 16.00

Overprinted ΕΛΛΑΣ

1908
J10 D1 1 l red 75 65
a. Inverted overprint 10.00 10.00
J11 D1 5 l red 1.75 1.00
J12 D1 10 l red 1.75 1.00
J13 D1 20 l red 5.00 3.00
J14 D1 40 l red 12.50 10.00
J15 D1 50 l red 12.50 10.00
J16 D1 1d red 150.00 140.00
J17 D1 1d on 1d red 12.00 11.00
J18 D1 2d red 20.00 20.00
Nos. J10-J18 (9) 216.25 196.65

Counterfeits of No. J16 exist.

Overprinted ΕΛΛΑΣ

1910
J19 D1 1 l red 60 35
J20 D1 5 l red 3.00 1.00
J21 D1 10 l red 1.65 1.00
J22 D1 20 l red 6.00 4.00
J23 D1 40 l red 12.00 7.00
J24 D1 50 l red 18.00 10.00
J25 D1 1d red 40.00 40.00
J26 D1 2d red 40.00 40.00
Nos. J19-J26 (8) 121.25 103.35

OFFICIAL STAMPS

O1

O2

Unwmk.
1908, Jan. 14 Litho. *Perf. 14*
O1 O1 10 l dl cl 25.00 2.50
O2 O2 30 l blue 45.00 2.75

Nos. O1-O2 exist imperf.

Overprinted ΕΛΛΑΣ

O3 O1 10 l dl cl 27.50 2.25
a. Inverted overprint 42.50
O4 O2 30 l blue 45.00 2.00
a. Inverted overprint 50.00

Overprinted ΕΛΛΑΣ

1910
O5 O1 10 l dl cl 3.00 1.75
O6 O2 30 l blue 3.00 1.75

CROATIA

LOCATION — Southeastern Europe
GOVT. — Independent state
AREA — 44,453 sq. mi.
POP. — 7,000,000 (approx.)
CAPITAL — Zagreb

The Independent Croatian State of 1941-45 became part of the Jugoslav Federation in 1945.

100 Paras = 1 Dinar
100 Banica = 1 Kuna

Jugoslavia Nos. 143 to 148B Overprinted in Black

NEZAVISNA
DRŽAVA
HRVATSKA
IIIIII

Perf. 12½
1941, Apr. 12 Unwmk. Typo.
1 A16 50p orange 1.65 *4.00*
2 A16 1d yel grn 1.65 *4.00*
3 A16 1.50d red 1.65 *2.25*
4 A16 2d dp mag 1.65 *3.25*
5 A16 3d dl red brn 3.25 *8.25*
6 A16 4d ultra 3.25 *9.25*
7 A16 5d dk bl 4.50 *10.00*
8 A16 5.50d dk vio brn 4.50 *11.00*
Nos. 1-8 (8) 22.10 52.00

The overprint exists inverted on Nos. 1-6; double on Nos. 2, 3 and 5.

Jugoslavia Nos. 142 to 154 Overprinted in Black

1941, Apr. 21
9 A16 25p black 22 *55*
10 A16 50p orange 22 *55*
11 A16 1d yel grn 22 *55*
12 A16 1.50d red 22 *55*
13 A16 2d dp mag 22 *1.10*
14 A16 3d dl red brn 22 *1.65*
15 A16 4d ultra 50 *1.90*
16 A16 5d dk bl 80 *1.90*
17 A16 5.50d dk vio brn 80 *2.25*
18 A16 6d sl bl 1.00 *3.25*
19 A16 8d sepia 1.65 *3.25*
20 A16 12d brt vio 2.00 *4.50*
21 A16 16d dl vio 2.25 *5.50*
22 A16 20d blue 2.75 *6.50*
23 A16 30d brt pink 4.00 *10.00*
Nos. 9-23 (15) 17.07 44.00

The overprint exists inverted on Nos. 9-11, 17 and 20; double on Nos. 9, 12 and 17.

Jugoslavia Nos. 147, 148 Surcharged in Black

1941, May 16
24 A16 1d on 3d dl red brn 32 *55*
25 A16 2d on 4d ultra 32 *55*

The overprint exists inverted and double on Nos. 24-25.

Postage Due Stamps of Jugoslavia, Nos. J28, J30 to J32, Overprinted in Black

NEZAVISNA
DRŽAVA
HRVATSKA
FRANCO

1941, May 17
26 D4 50p violet 22 *40*
27 D4 2d dp bl 50 *90*
28 D4 5d orange 50 *90*
29 D4 10d chocolate 75 *1.25*

Counterfeit overprints on Nos. 1-29 are plentiful.

Imperforates

Nearly all Croatian stamps, from No. 30 through 80, B3 through B76, J6 through J25, O1 through O24 and RA1 through RA7 exist imperforate.

Ozalj Castle — A1

Designs: 50b, City of Jajce. 75b, Old Warasdin. 1k, Velebit Mountains. 1.50k, Zelanjak. 2k, Zagreb Cathedral. 3k, Osjek Cathedral. 4k, Drina River. No. 38, Konjica. No. 39, Zemun. 6k, Dubrovnik. 7k, Save River. 8k, Sarajevo. 10k, Plitvice. 12k, Klis Fortress, Split. 20k, Hvar. 30k, Syrmia. 50k, Senj. 100k, Banjaluka (without "F.I.").

1941-43 Unwmk. Photo. *Perf. 11.*

Ordinary Paper.

30 A1 25b henna 5 5
a. Tete beche pair 22 *45*
31 A1 50b sl bl 5 5
a. Tete beche pair 22 *45*
32 A1 75b dk ol grn 5 5
33 A1 1k Prus grn 5 5
a. Tete beche pair 45 *80*
34 A1 1.50k dp grn 5 5
a. Tete beche pair 45 *55*
35 A1 2k car lake 5 5
a. Tete beche pair 30 *45*
36 A1 3k brn red 5 8
37 A1 4k dp ultra 5 8
a. Tete beche pair 30 *55*
38 A1 5k black 90 80
a. Tete beche pair 2.50 *4.50*
39 A1 5k blue 8 8
40 A1 6k lt ol brn 8 8
a. Tete beche pair 30 *55*
41 A1 7k org red 8 8
a. Tete beche pair 30 *55*
42 A1 8k chestnut 18 18
a. Tete beche pair 90 *1.40*
43 A1 10k dk plum 45 18
a. Tete beche pair 1.60 *2.00*
44 A1 12k ol brn 60 45
45 A1 20k gldn brn 45 22
a. Tete beche pair 1.75 *2.25*
46 A1 30k blk brn 60 32
a. Tete beche pair 1.40 *2.25*
47 A1 50k dk sl grn 1.00 45
a. Tete beche pair 6.75 *12.50*
48 A1 100k violet 1.50 *2.75*
Nos. 30-48 (19) 6.32 6.05

Nos. 31, 35 and 43 exist on thin to pelure paper. Shades of all values exist.

Types of 1941 Overprinted in Brown or Green
1941-1942 10-IV

1942, Apr. 9

49 A1 2k dk brn 18 *40*
50 A1 5k dk car 38 *65*
51 A1 10k dk bl grn (G) 55 *1.10*

First anniversary of Croatian independence.

Banjaluka ("F.I." at upper right) — A20

1942, June 13

52 A20 100k violet 2.75 *4.75*

Banjaluka Philatelic Exhibition.

No. 35 Surcharged in Red Brown with New Value and Bar.

1942, June 23

53 A1 25b on 2k car lake 15 *40*
a. Tete beche pair 45 *1.00*

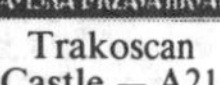

Trakoscan Castle — A21
Catherine Zrinski — A23

Design: 12.50k, Citadel of Veliki Tabor.

1943

Pelure Paper

54 A21 3.50k brn car 55 55
55 A21 12.50k vio blk 55 55

No. 54 exists on ordinary paper.

1943, June 7 Engr. *Perf. 12½*

Designs: 2k, Fran Krsto Frankopan. 3.50k, Peter Zrinski.

Various Frames.

56 A23 1k dk bl 15 *28*
57 A23 2k dk ol grn 15 *28*
58 A23 3.50k dk red 25 *42*

Rugjer Boscovich A26

Ante Pavelich A27

1943, Dec. 13 *Perf. 11*

59 A26 3.50k cop red 22 *42*
60 A26 12.50k dk vio brn 38 *65*

Issued to honor Rugjer Boscovich (1711-1787). Serbo-Croat mathematician and physicist.

1943-44 Litho. *Perf. 12½, 14*

61 A27 25b org ver 10 *18*
62 A27 50b Prus bl 10 *18*
63 A27 75b ol grn 10 *18*
64 A27 1k lt grn 10 *18*
65 A27 1.50k dl gray vio 10 *18*
66 A27 2k rose lake 10 *18*
67 A27 3k rose brn 10 *18*
68 A27 3.50k brt bl 10 *18*
a. 3.50k dk bl, perf. 11½ 1.65 *3.00*
69 A27 4k brt red vio 10 *18*
70 A27 5k ultra 10 *18*
71 A27 8k org brn 10 *18*
72 A27 9k rose pink 18 *28*
73 A27 10k vio brn 18 *28*
74 A27 12k dk ol bis 18 *28*
75 A27 12.50k gray blk 18 *28*
76 A27 18k dl brn 18 *28*
77 A27 32k dk brn 18 *28*
78 A27 50k grnsh bl 18 *28*
79 A27 70k orange 40 *55*
80 A27 100k violet 80 *90*
Nos. 61-80 (20) 3.56 5.39

Nos. 61 and 63 measure 20½x26mm. Nos. 62 and 64-80 measure 22x27½mm.

Issue dates: 2k, 1943; No. 68a, June 13, 1943, Pavelich's birthday; others, 1944.

"Labor Day 1945" — A28

1945 Photo. *Perf. 11½*

81 A28 3.50k red brn 25 *1.65*

SEMI-POSTAL STAMPS

Types of Jugoslavia, 1941, Overprinted in Gold "NEZAVISNA / DRZAVA / HRVATSKA"

Perf. 11½

1941, May 10 Unwmk. Engr.

B1 SP80 1.50d + 1.50d bl blk 13.00 *22.50*
B2 SP81 4d + 3d choc 13.00 *22.50*

Five thousand sets of Jugoslavia Nos. 142-154 were overprinted "NEZAVISNA DRZAVA HRVATSKA 10. IV. 1941" and small shield in red or blue, in 1941. Sold for double face value. Price, set, $225.

Costume of Sinj, Dalmatia — SP1

Soldiers with Arms of the Axis States — SP4

Designs (Costumes): 2k+2k, Travnik, Bosnia. 4k+4k, Turopolje, Croatia.

1941, Oct. 12 Photo. *Perf. 10½x10*

B3 SP1 1.50k + 1.50k Prus bl & red 32 *65*
B4 SP1 2k + 2k ol brn & red 50 *80*
B5 SP1 4k + 4k brn lake & red 80 *2.00*

The surtax aided the Croatian Red Cross. Sheets of 20 stamps and 5 labels.

1941, Dec. 3 *Perf. 11*

B6 SP4 4k + 2k bl 1.65 *3.75*

The surtax was used for Croatian Volunteers in the East.

Model Plane — SP5

Model Plane — SP6

Designs: 3k+3k, Boy with model plane. 4k+4k, Model seaplane in flight.

1942, Mar. 25

B7 SP5 2k + 2k sep 40 *65*
B8 SP6 2.50k + 2.50k dl grn 50 *1.10*
B9 SP5 3k + 3k brn car 60 *1.25*
B10 SP6 4k + 4k dp bl 90 *1.90*

The surtax aided the society of Croatian Wings (Hrvatska Krila).

Nos. B7-B10 were issued in sheets of 25 and in sheets of 24 plus label.

Souvenir Sheets.

SP9

Perf. 11.

B11 SP9 Sheet of two 25.00 *40.00*
a. 2k+8k brn car 9.75 *16.00*
b. 3k+12k dp bl 9.75 *16.00*

Imperf.

B12 SP9 Sheet of two 25.00 *40.00*
a. 2k+8k dp bl 9.75 *16.00*
b. 3k+12k brn car 9.75 *16.00*

The sheets measure 125x110mm.

To commemorate the Aviation Exposition of Zagreb. The surtax aided "Croatian Wings."

Nos. B11 and B12 exist with colors of stamps and inscriptions transposed.

Boy Trumpeters SP10

Triumphal Arch SP11

Mother and Child — SP12

1942, July 5 *Perf. 11½*

B13 SP10 3k + 1k lake 55 *1.10*
B14 SP11 4k + 2k dk brn 70 *1.40*
B15 SP12 5k + 5k dp bl grn 90 *1.65*

The surtax was for national welfare. Sheets of 25.

Matthew Gubec SP13

Ante Starcevich SP14

SP15

1942, Nov. 22 *Perf. 14½*

B16 SP13 3k + 6k dk red 28 *55*
B17 SP14 4k + 7k sep 28 *55*

Souvenir Sheets

Perf. 12, Imperf.

B18 SP15 5k + 20k dl bl 13.00 *15.00*

Issued to commemorate the heroes of Senj, May 9, 1937. Nos. B16-B17 were printed in sheets of 16 plus 9 labels, each bearing a hero's name. Size of No. B18: 80x95mm. The surtax aided the National Youth Society.

Sestine Peasant — SP16

Designs: 3k+1k, Slavonian peasant. 4k+2k, Bosnian peasant. 10k+5k, Dalmatian peasant. 13k+6k, Sestine peasant.

1942, Oct. 4 *Perf. 11½*

B20 SP16 1.50k + 50b org brn & red 75 *1.40*
B21 SP16 3k + 1k dl pur & red 75 *1.40*
B22 SP16 4k + 2k dp bl & red 90 *1.90*
B23 SP16 10k + 5k dk ol bis & red 1.25 *2.75*
B24 SP16 13k + 6k rose lake & red 2.75 *5.50*
Nos. B20-B24 (5) 6.40 *12.9*

The surtax aided the Croatian Red Cross. Issued in sheets of 24 stamps plus label.

Croatian Labor Corpsman — SP20

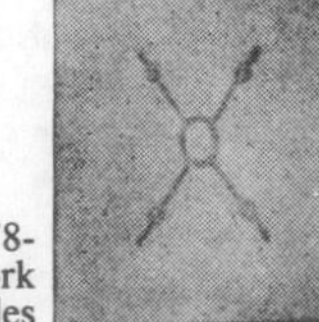
Wmk. 278- Network Connecting Circles

Designs: 3k+3k, Corpsman with wheelbarrow. 7k+4k, Corpsman plowing.

1943, Jan. 17 Wmk. 278 *Perf. 11*

B25 SP20 2(k) + 1(k) ol gray & sep 1.75 *3.50*
B26 SP20 3(k) + 3(k) brn & sep 1.75 *3.50*
B27 SP20 7(k) + 4(k) gray bl & sep 1.75 *3.50*

The surtax aided the State Labor Service (Drzavna Radna Sluzba). Issued in sheets of 9.

Arms of Zagreb and "Golden Bull" – SP23

1943, Mar. 23 Unwmk.

B28 SP23 3.50k (+ 6.50k) bril ultra 1.10 *3.00*

700th anniversary of Zagreb's "Golden Bull," a Magna Carta of civic rights and privileges granted to the city in 1242 by King Bela because the Croats annihilated Tartar hordes at Grobnik.

Issued in sheets of 8 with marginal inscriptions.

Ante Pavelich – SP24

1943, Apr. 10 *Perf. 14*

B29 SP24 5k + 3k cop red 28 *55*
B30 SP24 7k + 5k dk grn 28 *55*

Surtax aided the National Youth Society.

Issued in sheets of 100, and in miniature sheets of 16 stamps and 9 labels.

Souvenir Sheets.

SP25

1943, May 17 *Perf. 12, Imperf.*

B31 SP25 12k + 8k dp ultra 8.25 *13.00*

The sheets measure 79x94mm.

Sailor at Sea of Azov – SP26

Designs: 2k+1k, Flier at Sevastopol and Rzhev. 3.50k+1.50k, Infantrymen at Stalingrad. 9k+4.50k, Panzer Division at Don River.

1943, July 1 *Perf. 11*

B33 SP26 1k + 50b grn 15 *28*
B34 SP26 2k + 1k dk red 15 *28*
B35 SP26 3.50k + 1.50k dk bl 15 *28*
B36 SP26 9k + 4.50k chnt 15 *28*

Issued to honor the Croatian Legion which fought with the Germans in Russia.

Souvenir Sheets.

SP30

Perf. 11, Imperf.

B37 SP30 Sheet of four 1.65 *4.50*
a. 1k+50b dk bl 32 *55*
b. 2k+1k grn 32 *55*
c. 3.50k+1.50k dk red brn 32 *55*
d. 9k+4.50k bluish blk 32 *55*

The sheets measure 105x90mm. The surtax aided the Croatian Legion.

St. Mary's Church and Cistercian Cloister, Zagreb, in 1650 SP31

1943, Sept. 12 Engr. *Perf. 14½*

B39 SP31 18k + 9k dl gray vio 1.50 *3.00*

Souvenir Sheet.

Perf. 12½.

B40 SP31 18k + 9k blk brn 6.50 *11.00*

Nos. B39-B40 were issued in connection with the Croatian Philatelic Society Exhibition at Zagreb. Size of No. B40: 100x131mm.

No. B39 Overprinted in Red

HRVATSKO MORE
8. IX.
1943.

1943, Sept. 12

B41 SP31 18k + 9k dl gray vio 5.50 *9.25*

Return to Croatia of the Dalmatian and Croatian coasts.

Mother and Children SP33

Nurse and Patient SP34

1943, Oct. 3 Litho. *Perf. 11*

B42 SP33 1k + 50b bl grn & red 25 *40*
B43 SP33 2k + 1k bril car & red 25 *40*
B44 SP33 3.50k + 1.50k brt bl & red 25 *40*
B45 SP34 8k + 3k red brn & red 25 *40*
B46 SP34 9k + 4k yel grn & red 32 *55*
B47 SP33 10k + 5k dp vio & red 40 *65*
B48 SP34 12k + 6k brt ultra & red 50 *80*
B49 SP33 12.50k + 6k dk brn & red 75 *1.25*

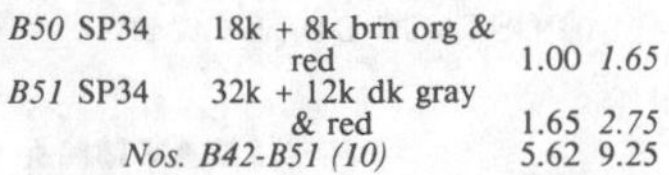

B50 SP34 18k + 8k brn org & red 1.00 *1.65*
B51 SP34 32k + 12k dk gray & red 1.65 *2.75*
Nos. B42-B51 (10) 5.62 9.25

The surtax aided the Croatian Red Cross.

Post Horn and Arms – SP35

Carrier Pigeon and Plane – SP36

Mercury SP37

Winged Wheel SP38

1944, Feb. 3

B52 SP35 7k + 3.50(k) ol bis & red 12 *22*
B53 SP36 16k + 8(k) bl & dk bl 18 *32*
B54 SP37 24k + 12(k) red & rose red 28 *50*
B55 SP38 32k + 16k gray & red 50 *1.00*

The surtax benefited communications and railway employees. Sheets of 9.

St. Sebastian SP39

War Invalids SP40

Statue of Ancient Croatian King – SP41

Death of King Peter Svacic, 1097 – SP42

1944, Feb. 15

B56 SP39 7k + 3.50(k) org red & rose car 20 *38*
B57 SP40 16k + 8k yel grn & dk grn 28 *55*
B58 SP41 24k + 12(k) yel brn & red 28 *55*
B59 SP42 32k + 16k bl & dk bl 55 *1.10*

The surtax aided wounded war victims.

Issued in sheets of eight stamps, with marginal inscriptions and a central label picturing St. Sebastian.

Black Legion in Combat – SP43

Guarding the Drina – SP44

Jure Francetich – SP45

1944, May 22 Photo. *Imperf.*

B60 SP43 3.50(k) + 1.50k brn red 8 15
B61 SP44 12.50(k) + 6.50k sl bl 8 15
B62 SP45 18(k) + 9k ol brn 8 15

Third anniversary of Croatian independence.

The surtax aided the National Youth Society. Sheets of 20.

Perf. 14½.

B63 SP45 12.50(k) + 287.50k int blk 3.25 *16.00*

Issued to commemorate Jure Francetich.

Labor Corpsmen Marching SP46

Corpsman Digging SP47

Designs: 18k+9k, Officer instructing corpsman. 32k+16k, Pavelich reviewing Labor Corps.

Perf. 11, 12½, 14½.

1944, Aug. 20 Engr.

B65 SP46 3.50(k) + 1(k) dk red 10 15
B66 SP47 12.50(k) + 6(k) sep 12 28
B67 SP47 18(k) + 9(k) dk bl 12 32
B68 SP47 32(k) + 16(k) gray grn 18 32

The surtax aided the State Labor Service (Drzavna Radna Sluzba).

Issued in sheets of 8 plus label.

Souvenir Sheet.

SP50

Perf. 12½.

B69 SP50 32(k) + 16(k) dk brn, *cr* 2.25 4.75

The sheet measures 72x99mm. Thesurtax aided the State Labor Service.

Palm Leaf – SP51

1944, Nov. 12 Litho. *Perf. 11*

B70 SP51 2k + 1k dl grn & red 10 22
B71 SP51 3.50k + 1.50k car lake & red 12 28
B72 SP51 12.50k + 6k ind & red 18 32

The surtax aided the Croatian Red Cross. Sheets of 16.

Men of Storm Division – SP52

Designs: 70k+70k, Soldiers of Storm Division in action. 100k+100k, Storm Division emblem.

1944 Unwmk. Litho. *Perf. 11*

B73	SP52	50k + 50k brick red	62.50	*135.00*
B74	SP52	70k + 70k sep	62.50	*135.00*
B75	SP52	100k + 100k chlky bl, pale bl & dp bl	62.50	*135.00*

The surtax aided the First Croatian Storm Division. Sheets of 20.

Souvenir Sheet.

SP54

B76	SP54	Sheet of three	1,000.	*1,750.*
a.		50k + 50k brick red		
b.		70k + 70k sep		
c.		100k + 100k chlky bl, pale bl & dp bl		

Nos. B76a to B76c are inscribed "O. A." in brick red at right below design. The sheet measures 216x132mm. The surtax aided the First Croatian Storm Division. Counterfeits are plentiful.

Postman SP55

Telephone Line Repairman SP56

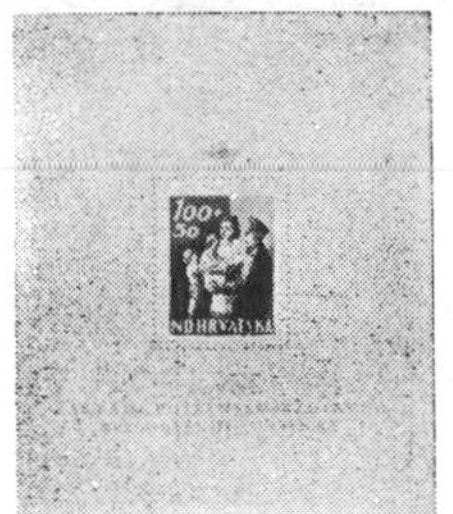
SP59

Designs; 24k+12k, Switchboard operator. 50k+25k, Postman delivering parcel.

1945 Photo.

B77	SP55	3.50(k) + 1.50(k) sl gray	10	*22*
B78	SP56	12.50(k) + 6(k) brn car	12	*28*
B79	SP56	24(k) + 12(k) dk grn	18	*32*
B80	SP56	50(k) + 25(k) brn vio	28	*55*

Sheets of eight.

Souvenir Sheet.

B81	SP59	100(k) + 50(k) dp brn	3.25	*6.50*

The surtax on Nos. B77-B81 aided employees of the P.T.T. Size of No. B81: 100x120mm.

POSTAGE DUE STAMPS

Jugoslavia Nos. J28-J32 Overprinted in Black

1941, Apr. 26 Unwmk. *Perf. 12½*

J1	D4	50p violet	30	*55*
a.		50p rose vio	7.50	*11.00*
J2	D4	1d dp mag	30	*55*
J3	D4	2d dp bl	9.50	*16.00*
J4	D4	5d orange	95	*1.65*
J5	D4	10d chocolate	4.75	*8.25*
		Nos. J1-J5 (5)	15.80	27.00

The overprint on the 50p exists inverted. Counterfeit overprints exist.

Numeral of Value
D1 D2

1941, Sept. 12 Litho. *Perf. 11*

J6	D1	50b car lake	18	*32*
J7	D1	1k car lake	18	*32*
J8	D1	2k car lake	28	*70*
J9	D1	5k car lake	40	*80*
J10	D1	10k car lake	65	*1.10*
		Nos. J6-J10 (5)	1.69	3.24

1943 *Perf. 11½, 12x12½, 12½*

Size: 24x24 mm.

J11	D2	50b lt bl & gray	8	*10*
J12	D2	1k lt bl & gray	8	*10*
J13	D2	2k lt bl & gray	12	*22*
J14	D2	4k lt bl & gray	18	*32*
J15	D2	5k lt bl & gray	22	*40*
J16	D2	6k lt bl & gray	18	*32*
J17	D2	10k bl & ind	28	*50*
J18	D2	15k bl & ind	28	*50*
J19	D2	20k bl & ind	90	*1.50*
		Nos. J11-J19 (9)	2.32	3.96

1942, July 30 *Perf. 10½, 11½*

Size: 25x24¼ mm.

J20	D2	50b lt bl & gray	18	*28*
J21	D2	1k lt bl & gray	12	*28*
J22	D2	2k lt bl & gray	30	*50*
J23	D2	5k lt bl & gray	28	*45*
J24	D2	10k lt bl & bl	60	*95*
J25	D2	20k lt bl & bl	1.00	*1.65*
		Nos. J20-J25 (6)	2.48	4.11

OFFICIAL STAMPS

Croatian Coat of Arms
O1 O2

Perf. 10½, 11½

1942-43 Unwmk. Litho.

Ordinary Paper

O1	O1	25b rose lake	5	*8*
O2	O1	50b sl blk	5	*8*
O3	O1	75b gray grn	8	*8*
O4	O1	1k org brn	5	*8*
O5	O1	2k turq bl	8	*18*
O6	O1	3k vermilion	5	*8*
O7	O1	4k brn vio	5	*8*
O8	O1	5k ultra	18	*35*
a.		Thin paper	7.00	*3.00*
O9	O1	6k brt vio	8	*8*
O10	O1	10k lt grn	5	*8*
O11	O1	12k brn rose	18	*25*
O12	O1	20k dk bl	18	*28*
O13	O2	30k brn vio & gray	12	*18*
O14	O2	40k vio blk & gray	18	*28*
O15	O2	50k brn lake & gray	60	*65*
O16	O2	100k blk & pink	60	*65*
		Nos. O1-O16 (16)	2.58	3.46

1943-44 Thin Paper *Perf. 11½*

O17	O1	25b claret	5	*8*
O18	O1	50b gray	5	*8*
O19	O1	75b dl grn	5	*8*
O20	O1	1k org brn	5	*8*
O21	O1	2k sl bl	5	*8*
O22	O1	3.50k car rose	5	*8*
a.		Ordinary paper	7.00	*13.00*
O23	O1	6k brt red vio	5	*8*
O24	O1	12.50k dp org	5	*8*
a.		Ordinary paper	4.50	*8.25*
		Nos. O17-O24 (8)	40	64

POSTAL TAX STAMPS

Nurse and Soldier – PT1

Wounded Soldier – PT2

Unwmk.

1942, Oct. 4 Litho. *Perf. 11*

RA1	PT1	1k ol grn & red	32	*55*

The tax aided the Croatian Red Cross. Issued in sheets of 24 plus label.

1943, Oct. 3

RA2	PT2	2k bl & red	22	*32*

The tax aided the Croatian Red Cross.

Ruins – PT3

Wounded Soldier – PT4

1944, Jan. 1 Photo. *Perf. 12*

RA3	PT3	1k dk sl grn	12	*18*
RA4	PT4	2k car lake	12	*18*
RA5	PT4	5k black	12	*18*
RA6	PT4	10k dp bl	22	*38*
RA7	PT4	20k brown	50	*80*
		Nos. RA3-RA7 (5)	1.08	1.72

CUBA

LOCATION — The largest island of the West Indies; south of Florida.
GOVT. — Former Spanish possession.
AREA — 44,206 sq. mi.
POP. — 6,743,000 (est. 1960).
CAPITAL — Havana.

Formerly a Spanish possession, Cuba made several unsuccessful attempts to gain her freedom, which finally led to the intervention of the United States in 1898. In that year under the Treaty of Paris, Spain relinquished the island to the U. S. in trust for its inhabitants. In 1902 a republic was established and the Cuban Congress took over the government from the military authorities.

8 Reales Plata = 1 Peso
100 Centesimos = 1 Escudo or Peseta (1867)
1000 Milesimas = 100 Centavos = 1 Peso

> Pen cancellations are common on the earlier stamps of Cuba. Stamps so canceled sell for very much less than those with postmark cancellations.

Issued under Spanish Dominion

Used also in Puerto Rico: Nos. 1-4, 9-14, 18-21, 32-34, 35A-37, 39-41, 43-45, 47-49, 51-53.

Used only in Puerto Rico: Nos. 55-57.

Queen Isabella II — A1

Wmk.104

Blue Paper.
Wmk. Loops. (104)

1855 **Typo.** ***Imperf.***
1 A1 ½r p bl grn 40.00 3.00
2 A1 1r p gray grn 40.00 3.00
3 A1 2r p car 160.00 15.00
4 A1 2r p org red 175.00 15.00

Nos. 2-3 also used in Philippines.

Nos. 3-4 Surcharged **Y ¼**

1855-56
5 A1 ¼r p on 2r p car 825.00 225.00
6 A1 ¼r p on 2r p org red 875.00 325.00

Surcharged **Y ¼**

7 A1 ¼r p on 2r p car 625.00 110.00
a. Without fraction bar 375.00
8 A1 ¼r p on 2r p org red 825.00 225.00
a. Without fraction bar 525.00

The "Y ¼" surcharge met the "Ynterior" rate for delivery within the city of Havana.

Wmk.105

Rough Yellowish Paper.

1856 **Wmk. Crossed Lines. (105)**
9 A1 ½r p on grnsh bl 7.50 1.25
10 A1 1r p grn 425.00 16.00
a. 1r p emer 450.00 22.50
11 A1 2r p org red 225.00 19.00

White Smooth Paper.

1857 **Unwmk.**
12 A1 ½r p bl 6.00 75
13 A1 1r p gray grn 6.00 75
a. 1r p pale yel grn 9.00 1.75
14 A1 2r p dl rose 14.00 3.75

Surcharged **Y ¼**

1860
15 A1 ¼r p on 2r p dl rose 225.00 80.00
a. 1 of ¼ inverted 300.00 160.00

Queen Isabella II
A2 A3

1862-64 ***Imperf.***
16 A2 ¼r p blk 27.50 12.00
17 A3 ¼r p *buff* ('64) 27.50 10.00
18 A3 ½r p grn ('64) 6.00 1.00
19 A3 ½r p grn, *pale rose* ('64) 14.00 4.00
20 A3 1r p bl, *sal* ('64) 6.00 1.20
a. Diagonal half used as ½r on cover 100.00
21 A3 2r p ver, *buff* ('64) 40.00 11.00

No. 17 Overprinted in Black **66**

1866
22 A3 ¼r p *buff* 90.00 27.50

A5 A6

1866
23 A5 5c dl vio 70.00 30.00
24 A5 10c blue 3.00 1.50
25 A5 20c green 2.50 1.50
26 A5 40c rose 17.50 12.00

Stamps Dated "1867".

1867 ***Perf. 14.***
27 A5 5c dl vio 50.00 14.00
28 A5 10c blue 8.00 1.50
a. Imperf. pair 45.00 9.00
29 A5 20c green 8.00 1.50
a. Imperf. pair 65.00 100.00
30 A5 40c rose 17.50 10.00

Stamps Dated "1868".

1868
31 A6 5c dl vio 32.50 10.00
32 A6 10c blue 5.00 2.00
a. Diagonal half used as 5c on cover 100.00
33 A6 20c green 10.00 3.75
a. Diagonal half used as 10c on cover 125.00
34 A6 40c rose 20.00 9.00

Nos. 31 to 34 Overprinted in Black

e **HABILITADO POR LA NACION.**

1868
35 A6 5c dl vio 55.00 25.00
35A A6 10c blue 55.00 25.00
36 A6 20c green 55.00 25.00
37 A6 40c rose 55.00 25.00

1869 **Stamps Dated "1869"**
38 A6 5c rose 55.00 17.50
39 A6 10c red brn 5.00 2.50
a Diagonal half used as 5c on cover 75.00
40 A6 20c orange 10.00 3.00
41 A6 40c dl vio 45.00 10.00

Nos. 38-41 Overprinted type "e."
42 A6 5c rose 180.00 52.50
43 A6 10c red brn 65.00 25.00
44 A6 20c orange 55.00 32.50
45 A6 40c dl vio 80.00 32.50

"Espana"
A8 A9

1870 ***Perf. 14***
46 A8 5c blue 190.00 47.50
47 A8 10c green 3.50 90
a. Diagonal half used as 5c on cover 90.00
48 A8 20c red brn 3.50 90
a. Diagonal half used as 10c on cover 90.00
49 A8 40c rose 170.00 32.50

1871
50 A9 12c red lil 30.00 9.00
a. Imperf. pair 75.00 75.00
51 A9 25c ultra 3.50 1.50
a. Imperf. pair 37.50 37.50
b. Diagonal half used as 12c on cover 125.00
52 A9 50c gray grn 3.50 1.50
a. Imperf. pair 60.00 40.00
b. Diagonal half used as 25c on cover 125.00
53 A9 1p pale brn 35.00 10.00
a. Imperf. pair 60.00 60.00

King Amadeo — A10

1873 ***Perf. 14.***
54 A10 12½c dk grn 47.50 16.00
55 A10 25c gray 3.00 1.50
a. Diagonal half used as 12½c on cover 75.00
56 A10 50c brown 2.00 1.50
a. Imperf. pair 50.00 50.00
b. Half used as 25c on cover 75.00
57 A10 1p red brn 275.00 50.00
a. Diagonal half used as 50c on cover 200.00

Issues for Cuba Only

"Espana" A11

Coat of Arms A12

1874
58 A11 12½c brown 17.50 7.50
59 A11 25c ultra 1.50 1.00
a. Diagonal half used as 12½c on cover 75.00
60 A11 50c dp vio 2.25 1.00
61 A11 50c gray 2.25 1.00
a. Diagonal half used as 25c on cover 75.00
62 A11 1p carmine 100.00 35.00
a. Imperf. pair 225.00 225.00

1875

63 A12 12½c lt vio 1.75 75
a. Imperf. pair 55.00
64 A12 25c ultra 90 60
a. Imperf. pair 55.00
b. Diagonal half used as 12½c on cover 75.00
65 A12 50c bl grn 90 60
a. Imperf. pair 55.00
b. Diagonal half used as 25c on cover 45.00
66 A12 1p brown 13.00 6.00
a. 1p dk brn 13.00 6.00
b. Half used as 50c on cover 85.00

King Alfonso XII
A13 A14

1876

67 A13 12½c green 3.00 60
68 A13 25c gray 1.25 50
a. Diagonal half used as 12½c on cover 75.00
69 A13 50c ultra 1.25 60
a. Imperf. pair 17.50
70 A13 1p black 13.00 5.00
a. Imperf. pair 40.00

1877

71 A14 10c lt grn 55.00 27.50
72 A14 12½c gray 10.00 1.50
a. Imperf. pair 27.50
73 A14 25c dk grn 75 50
a. Imperf. pair 27.50
74 A14 50c black 75 50
a. Imperf. pair 27.50
b. Half used as 25c on cover 75.00
75 A14 1p brown 27.50 15.00
Nos. 71-75 (5) 94.00 45.00

Stamps Dated "1878".

1878

76 A14 5c blue 60 50
a. Imperf. pair 27.50
77 A14 10c black 75.00 37.50
a. Imperf. pair 200.00
78 A14 12½c brn bis 3.50 1.50
a. 12½c gray bis 2.50 1.25
b. Imperf. pair 27.50
79 A14 25c dp grn 50 25
a. Imperf. pair 27.50
b. Diagonal half used as 12½c on cover 60.00
80 A14 50c dk bl grn 50 25
a. Imperf. pair 27.50
81 A14 1p carmine 13.00 7.00
a. Imperf. pair 55.00
Nos. 76-81 (6) 93.10 47.00

Stamps Dated "1879"

1879

82 A14 5c sl blk 1.00 50
83 A14 10c orange 175.00 85.00
84 A14 12½c rose 1.00 50
85 A14 25c ultra 75 50
a. Diagonal half used as 12½c on cover 75.00
b. Imperf. pair 55.00 40.00
86 A14 50c gray 60 40
a. Diagonal half used as 25c on cover 75.00
87 A14 1p ol bis 30.00 15.00
Nos. 82-87 (6) 208.35 101.90

A15

A16

A17

1880

88 A15 5c green 50 15
89 A15 10c lake 85.00 42.50
90 A15 12½c gray 50 15
91 A15 25c gray bl 50 15
a. Diagonal half used as 12½c on cover 75.00
92 A15 50c brown 50 20
a. Half used as 25c on cover 75.00
93 A15 1p yel brn 9.00 3.50
Nos. 88-93 (6) 96.00 46.65

1881

94 A16 1c green 50 15
95 A16 2c lake 45.00 22.50
96 A16 2½c ol bis 90 40
97 A16 5c gray bl 50 15
98 A16 10c yel brn 50 15
99 A16 20c dk brn 9.00 7.00
Nos. 94-99 (6) 56.40 30.35

1882

100 A17 1c green 60 40
101 A17 2c lake 3.50 40
102 A17 2½c dk brn 8.00 2.50
103 A17 5c gray bl 3.50 90
a. Diagonal half used as 2½c on cover 75.00
104 A17 10c ol bis 60 15
105 A17 20c red brn 100.00 35.00
Nos. 100-105 (6) 116.20 39.35

See Nos. 121-131.

Issue of 1882 Surcharged or Overprinted in Black, Blue or Red:

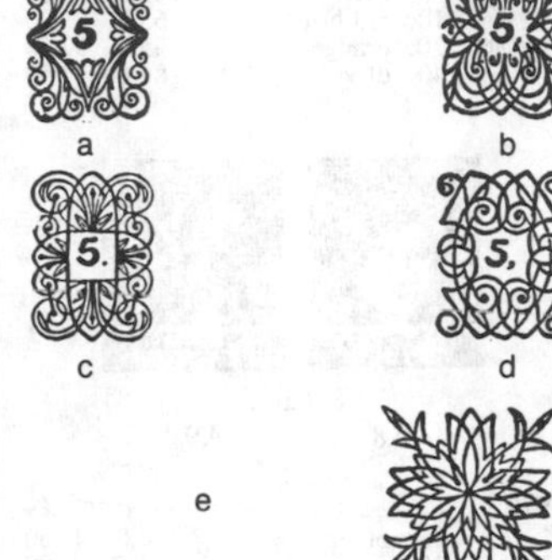

1883

106 A17 (a) 5 on 5c gray bl (R) 2.25 1.25
a. Triple surcharge
b. Double surcharge 4.00 4.00
c. Inverted surcharge 3.00 3.00
d. Without "5" in surcharge 9.00 9.00
e. Double surcharge, types "a" and "d"
107 A17 (a) 10 on 10c ol bis (Bl) 2.50 1.50
a. Inverted surcharge
b. Double surcharge 4.00
108 A17 (a) 20 on 20c red brn (Bk) 35.00 25.00
a. "10" instead of "20" 75.00 75.00
b. Double surcharge
109 A17 (b) 5 on 5c gray bl (R) 2.50 1.25
a. Inverted surcharge 3.50 3.50
b. Double surcharge 5.00
110 A17 (b) 10 on 10c ol bis (Bl) 3.50 1.75
a. Inverted surcharge 4.50 4.50
b. Double surcharge
111 A17 (b) 20 on 20c red brn (Bk) 35.00 25.00
a. Double surcharge
b. Double surcharge, types "b" and "c"
112 A17 (c) 5 on 5c gray bl (R) 2.50 1.50
a. Inverted surcharge
b. Double surcharge, types "c" and "d" 6.00
113 A17 (c) 10 on 10c ol bis (Bl) 6.00 2.50
a. Inverted surcharge
b. Double surcharge
114 A17 (c) 20 on 20c red brn (Bk) 50.00 25.00
a. "10" instead of "20" 120.00 120.00
b. Double surcharge
c. Double surcharge, types "a" and "c"
115 A17 (d) 5 on 5c gray bl (R) 2.50 1.50
a. Inverted surcharge 3.50 3.50
b. Double surcharge
116 A17 (d) 10 on 10c ol bis (Bl) 6.00 2.50
a. Inverted surcharge
b. Double surcharge
117 A17 (d) 20 on 20c red brn (Bk) 80.00 35.00
a. Double surcharge, types "a" and "d"
118 A17 (e) 5c gray bl (R) 3.50 2.00
a. Double overprint 6.00
119 A17 (e) 10c ol bis (Bl) 6.00 5.00
a. Double overprint
120 A17 (e) 20c red brn (Bk) 85.00 40.00
a. Double overprint
Nos. 106-120 (15) 322.25 170.75

No. 120 has been reprinted. The overprint is handstamped instead of being press printed.

Type of 1882

1882

1st retouch

2d retouch

The differences between the stamps of 1882 and the various retouches are as follows:

Original state: The medallion is surrounded by a heavy line of color of nearly even thickness, touching the horizontal line below the word "Cuba" (or "Filipinas", as the case may be); the opening in the hair above the temple is narrow and pointed.

First retouch: The line around the medallion is thin, except at the upper right, and does not touch the horizontal line above it; the opening in the hair is slightly wider and a trifle rounded; the lock of hair above the forehead is shaped like a broad "V" and ends in a point; there is a faint white line below it, which is not found on the stamps in the original state. Owing to wear of the plate the shape of the lock of hair and the width of the white line below it vary.

Second retouch: The opening in the hair forms a semi-circle; the lock above the forehead is nearly straight, having only a slight wave, and the white line is much broader than before.

1883-86

121 A17 1c grn, 2nd retouch 2.00 25
122 A17 2½c ol bis 50 15
124 A17 2½c violet 50 15
a. 2½c red lil ('85) 60 25
b. 2½c ultra 150.00 70.00
125 A17 5c gray bl, 1st retouch 2.00 15
126 A17 5c gray bl, 2nd retouch 6.00 1.50
a. Diagonal half used as 2½c on cover 35.00
127 A17 10c brn, 1st retouch 2.50 75
a. Diagonal half used as 5c on cover 35.00
128 A17 20c ol bis 17.50 4.00
Nos. 121-128 (7) 31.00 6.95

1888

129 A17 2½c red brn 4.00 1.50
130 A17 10c blue 2.25 1.00
a. Diagonal half used as 5c on cover
131 A17 20c brnsh gray 20.00 6.00

King Alfonso XIII
A18 A19

1890-97

132 A18 1c gray brn 16.00 6.00
133 A18 1c ol gray ('91) 10.00 1.25
134 A18 1c ultra ('94) 3.50 50
a. Imperf. pair 75.00
135 A18 1c dk vio ('96) 1.75 25
136 A18 2c sl bl 6.00 1.50
137 A18 2c lil brn ('91) 1.75 50
138 A18 2c rose ('94) 25.00 3.00
a. Imperf. pair 110.00
139 A18 2c cl ('96) 7.50 90
140 A18 2½c emerald 10.00 2.25
141 A18 2½c sal ('91) 30.00 6.00
142 A18 2½c lil ('94) 2.25 35
a. Imperf. pair 100.00
143 A18 2½c rose ('96) 1.00 20
144 A18 5c ol gray 1.00 75
145 A18 5c emer ('91) 1.25 60
a. Imperf. pair 65.00
146 A18 5c sl bl ('96) 50 20
147 A18 10c brn vio 2.50 90
148 A18 10c cl ('91) 1.75 60
a. Imperf. pair 65.00
149 A18 10c emer ('96) 3.50 25
150 A18 20c dk vio 1.00 75
151 A18 20c ultra ('91) 11.00 6.00
152 A18 20c red brn ('94) 25.00 6.00
a. Imperf. pair 160.00
153 A18 20c vio ('96) 25.00 7.00
154 A18 40c org brn ('97) 50.00 15.00
155 A18 80c lil brn ('97) 65.00 20.00
Nos. 132-155 (24) 302.25 80.75

1898

156 A19 1m org brn 25 20
157 A19 2m org brn 25 20
158 A19 3m org brn 25 20
159 A19 4m org brn 6.00 2.00
160 A19 5m org brn 25 20
161 A19 1c blk vio 25 20
162 A19 2c dk bl grn 25 20
163 A19 3c dk brn 25 20
164 A19 4c orange 17.50 5.00
165 A19 5c car rose 1.25 25
a. Imperf. pair 60.00
166 A19 6c dk bl 25 20
a. Imperf. pair 60.00
167 A19 8c gray brn 1.25 50
168 A19 10c vermilion 1.25 50
169 A19 15c sl grn 6.00 50
170 A19 20c maroon 75 25
171 A19 40c dk lil 3.00 50
172 A19 60c black 3.00 50
173 A19 80c red brn 20.00 10.00
174 A19 1p yel grn 20.00 10.00
175 A19 2p sl bl 30.00 10.00
Nos. 156-175 (20) 112.00 41.60

Issued under Administration of the United States.

Puerto Principe Issue.

Issues of Cuba of 1898 and 1896 Surcharged:

HABILITADO 1 cent. — a
HABILITADO 1 cents. — b
HABILITADO 2 cents. — c
HABILITADO 2 cents. — d
HABILITADO 3 cents. — e
HABILITADO 3 cents. — f
HABILITADO 5 cents. — g
HABILITADO 5 cents. — h
HABILITADO 5 cents. — i
HABILITADO 5 cents. — j
HABILITADO 3 cents. — k
HABILITADO 3 cents. — l
HABILITADO 10 cents. — m

Types a, c, d, e, f, g and h are 17½mm. high, the others are 19½mm. high.

Black Surcharge

On Nos. 156, 157, 158 and 160.

1898-99

176 (a) 1c on 1m org brn 55.00 37.50

177 (b) 1c on 1m org brn 45.00 30.00
a. Broken figure "1" 75.00 60.00
b. Inverted surcharge 200.00
d. Same as "a", inverted *250.00*
178 (c) 2c on 2m org brn 22.50 15.00
a. Inverted surcharge 250.00 50.00
179 (d) 2c on 2m org brn 40.00 25.00
a. Inverted surcharge 350.00 100.00
179B (k) 3c on 1m org brn 375.00 150.00
c. Double surcharge 1,500. 750.00
179D (l) 3c on 1m org brn *1,500.* *600.00*
e. Double surcharge
179F (e) 3c on 2m org brn *2,000.*
179G (f) 3c on 2m org brn *2,500.*
180 (e) 3c on 3m org brn 27.50 22.50
a. Inverted surcharge *100.00*
181 (f) 3c on 3m org brn 75.00 50.00
a. Inverted surcharge *300.00*
182 (g) 5c on 1m org brn 700.00 175.00
a. Inverted surcharge *500.00*
183 (h) 5c on 1m org brn *1,500.* *400.00*
a. Inverted surcharge *700.00*
184 (g) 5c on 2m org brn 750.00 200.00
185 (h) 5c on 2m org brn 1,500. 400.00
186 (g) 5c on 3m org brn 165.00
a. Inverted surcharge 700.00
187 (h) 5c on 3m org brn 400.00
a. Inverted surcharge 1,000.
188 (g) 5c on 5m org brn 70.00 55.00
a. Inverted surcharge 400.00 175.00
b. Double surcharge
189 (h) 5c on 5m org brn 350.00 225.00
a. Inverted surcharge 400.00
b. Double surcharge
189C (i) 5c on 5m org brn *4,000.*

Black Surcharge on No. P25.

190 (g) 5c on ½m bl grn 250.00 75.00
a. Inverted surcharge 500.00 150.00
b. Pair, one without surcharge 450.00
191 (h) 5c on ½m bl grn 300.00 90.00
a. Inverted surcharge 200.00
192 (i) 5c on ½m bl grn 550.00 200.00
a. Double surcharge, one diagonal *3,000.*
193 (j) 5c on ½m bl grn 700.00 300.00

Red Surcharge on No. 161.

196 (k) 3c on 1c blk vio 60.00 25.00
a. Inverted surcharge 200.00
197 (l) 3c on 1c blk vio 125.00 45.00
a. Inverted surcharge 300.00
198 (i) 5c on 1c blk vio 20.00 20.00
a. Inverted surcharge 100.00
b. Vertical surcharge *2,000.*
c. Double surcharge *400.00* *600.00*
d. Double inverted surcharge
199 (j) 5c on 1c blk vio 50.00 40.00
a. Inverted surcharge 250.00
b. Vertical surcharge *2,000.*
c. Double surcharge 1,000. 600.00
200 (m) 10c on 1c blk vio 20.00 *50.00*
a. Broken figure "1" 40.00 *100.00*

Black Surcharge on Nos. P26-P30.

201 (k) 3c on 1m bl grn 300.00 200.00
a. Inverted surcharge 400.00
b. "EENTS" 550.00 400.00
c. Same as "b", inverted 850.00
202 (l) 3c on 1m bl grn 500.00 400.00
a. Inverted surcharge 850.00
203 (k) 3c on 2m bl grn 850.00 250.00
a. "EENTS" 1,200. 450.00
b. Inverted surcharge 600.00
c. Same as "a", inverted 750.00
204 (l) 3c on 2m bl grn 1,000. 450.00
a. Inverted surcharge 750.00
205 (k) 3c on 3m bl grn 900.00 250.00
a. Inverted surcharge 500.00
b. "EENTS" 1,200. 375.00
c. Same as "b", inverted 700.00
206 (l) 3c on 3m bl grn 1,200. 375.00
a. Invtd. surch. 700.00
211 (i) 5c on 1m bl grn 1,400.
a. "EENTS" 2,000.
212 (j) 5c on 1m bl grn 2,000.
213 (i) 5c on 2m bl grn 1,250.
a. "EENTS" 1,750.
214 (j) 5c on 2m bl grn 1,750.
215 (i) 5c on 3m bl grn 500.00
a. "EENTS" 900.00
216 (j) 5c on 3m bl grn 900.00
217 (i) 5c on 4m bl grn 2,000. 500.00
a. "EENTS" 2,500. 1,200.
b. Inverted surcharge 900.00
c. Same as "a", inverted 1,400.
218 (j) 5c on 4m bl grn *1,100.*
a. Invtd. surch. *1,400.*
219 (i) 5c on 8m bl grn 2,500. 1,000.
a. Inverted surcharge 1,500.
b. "EENTS" 2,000.
c. Same as "b", inverted 2,500.
220 (j) 5c on 8m bl grn 2,000.
a. Invtd. surch. 2,500.

United States Nos. 279a, 267, 279B, 268, 281a, 282C and 283a Surcharged in Black

1899 Wmk. (191) *Perf. 12.*

221 A87 1c on 1c yel grn 4.25 60
222 A88 2c on 2c car 4.25 50
a. 2c on 2c red 5.00 40
b. "CUPA" 120.00 120.00
c. Invtd. surch. *2,750.* *2,750.*
223 A88 2½c on 2c red 3.00 60
a. 2½c on 2c car 3.50 2.00
224 A89 3c on 3c pur 8.50 1.25
a. Period between "B" and "A" 27.50 27.50
225 A91 5c on 5c bl 8.50 1.25
a. "CUPA" omitted 60.00 50.00
226 A94 10c on 10c brn, type I 22.50 8.00
b. "CUBA" omitted *2,500.* 2,500.
226A A94 10c on 10c brn, type II *4,500.*
Nos. 221-226 (6) 51.00 12.20

The 2½c was sold and used as a 2c stamp.

Excellent counterfeits of this and the preceding issue exist, especially inverted and double surcharges.

Issues of the Republic under U. S. Military Rule.

Statue of Columbus A20

Royal Palms A21

"Cuba" A22

Ocean Liner A23

Cane Field — A24

1899 Engr. Wmk. (191C) *Perf. 12*

227 A20 1c yel grn 3.00 15
228 A21 2c carmine 3.00 15
a. 2c scar 3.00 15
b. Booklet pane of 6 *1,750.*
229 A22 3c purple 3.00 25
230 A23 5c blue 4.50 30
231 A24 10c brown 10.00 75
Nos. 227-231 (5) 23.50 1.60

Issues of the Republic

No. 229 Surcharged in Carmine

HABILITADO
UN CENTAVO 1 OCTUBRE 1902

1902, Sept. 30

232 A22 1c on 3c pur 1.50 75
a. Inverted surcharge 20.00 20.00
b. Surcharge sideways (numeral horizontal)
c. Double surcharge 30.00 30.00

Counterfeits of the errors are plentiful.

Re-engraved.

The re-engraved stamps of 1905-07 may be distinguished from the issue of 1899 as follows:

ORIGINAL RE-ENGRAVED

ORIGINAL RE-ENGRAVED

1c: The ends of the label inscribed "Centavo" are rounded instead of square.

2c: The foliate ornaments, inside the oval disks bearing the numerals of value, have been removed.

5c: Two lines forming a right angle have been added in the upper corners of the label bearing the word "Cuba".

10c: A small ball has been added to each of the square ends of the label bearing the word "Cuba".

1905 Unwmk. *Perf. 12*

233 A20 1c green 2.25 15
234 A21 2c rose 1.50 15
a. Bklt. pane of 6 135.00
236 A23 5c blue 45.00 1.50
237 A24 10c brown 4.00 60

Maj. Gen. Antonio Maceo — A26

1907

238 A26 50c gray bl & blk 1.50 90

Bartolomé Maso A27

Máximo Gomez A28

Julio Sanguily A29

Ignacio Agramonte A30

Calixto Garcia A31

José M. Rodriquez y Rodriquez (Mayia) A32

Carlos Roloff — A33

1910, Feb. 1

239 A27 1c grn & vio 1.10 10
a. Center inverted 200.00 *200.00*
240 A28 2c car & grn 2.25 10
a. Center inverted 450.00 *450.00*
241 A29 3c vio & bl 1.50 25
242 A30 5c bl & grn 20.00 1.00
243 A31 8c ol & vio 1.50 40
244 A32 10c brn & bl 9.00 85
a. Center inverted 1,000.
245 A26 50c vio & blk 2.25 60
246 A33 1p sl & blk 10.00 5.00
Nos. 239-246 (8) 47.60 8.30

1911-13

247 A27 1c green 75 10
248 A28 2c car rose 1.00 8
a. Bklt. pane of 6 ('13) 75.00
250 A30 5c ultra 2.50 10
251 A31 8c ol grn & blk 1.50 75
252 A33 1p black 7.00 2.50
Nos. 247-252 (5) 12.75 3.53

Map of Cuba — A34

1914-15

253 A34 1c green 75 6
a. Booklet pane of 6 80.00
254 A34 2c car rose 90 5
a. Booklet pane of 6 80.00
255 A34 2c red ('15) 1.75 5
a. Booklet pane of 6 80.00
256 A34 3c violet 5.00 50
257 A34 5c blue 7.00 25
258 A34 8c ol grn 6.00 1.00
259 A34 10c brown 11.00 50
260 A34 10c ol grn ('15) 13.00 75
261 A34 50c orange 80.00 15.00
262 A34 1p gray 110.00 30.00
Nos. 253-262 (10) 235.40 48.16

Imperf. pairs, price each $100 to $500.

Gertrudis Gomez de Avellaneda A34a

1914

263 A34a 5c blue 15.00 6.00

Issued to commemorate the centenary of the birth of the Cuban poetess, Gertrudis Gomez de Avellaneda (1814-1873).

José Martí A35

Máximo Gomez A36

José de la Luz Caballero A37

Calixto Garcia A38

Ignacio Agramonte A39

Tomás Estrada Palma A40

Condition is the all-important factor of price. Prices quoted are for stamps in fine condition.

Jose A. Saco A41

Antonio Maceo A42

Carlos Manuel de Cespedes — A43

1917-18 Unwmk. *Perf. 12.*

264 A35 1c bl grn 1.00 5
 a. Booklet pane of 6 37.50
 b. Booklet pane of 30 250.00
265 A36 2c rose 75 5
 a. Booklet pane of 6 50.00
 b. Booklet pane of 30 250.00
266 A36 2c lt red ('18) 75 5
 a. Booklet pane of 6 50.00
267 A37 3c violet 1.25 5
 a. Imperf. pair 325.00
 b. Booklet pane of 6 50.00
268 A38 5c dp bl 2.50 6
269 A39 8c red brn 6.00 15
270 A40 10c yel brn 3.00 10
271 A41 20c gray grn 12.00 1.00
272 A42 50c dl rose 14.00 1.00
273 A43 1p black 14.00 1.00
 Nos. 264-273 (10) 55.25 3.51

Wmk.106

1925-28 Wmk. Star. (106) *Perf. 12.*

274 A35 1c bl grn 1.75 6
 a. Booklet pane of 30 325.00
275 A36 2c brt rose 1.50 5
 a. Booklet pane of 6 70.00
 b. Booklet pane of 30 325.00
276 A38 5c dp bl 3.00 10
277 A39 8c red brn ('28) 6.00 50
278 A40 10c yel brn ('27) 7.00 60
279 A41 20c ol grn 11.00 1.00
 Nos. 274-279 (6) 30.25 2.31

1926 *Imperf.*

280 A35 1c bl grn 2.75 1.75
281 A36 2c brt rose 2.50 1.50
282 A38 5c dp bl 4.00 3.00

See also Nos. 304-310.

Arms of Republic A44

1927, May 20 Unwmk. *Perf. 12*

283 A44 25c violet 12.50 6.00

25th anniversary of the Republic.

Tomás Estrada Palma A45

Designs: 2c, Gen. Gerardo Machado. 5c, Morro Castle. 8c, Havana Railway Station. 10c, Presidential Palace. 13c, Tobacco Plantation. 20c, Treasury Building. 30c, Sugar Mill. 50c, Havana Cathedral. 1p, Galician Clubhouse, Havana.

1928, Jan. 2 Wmk. 106

284 A45 1c dp grn 60 40
285 A45 2c brt rose 60 40
286 A45 5c dp bl 1.75 60
287 A45 8c lt red brn 2.75 1.50
288 A45 10c bis brn 1.50 1.00
289 A45 13c orange 2.25 1.00
290 A45 20c ol grn 2.75 1.25
291 A45 30c dk vio 5.00 1.00
292 A45 50c car rose 8.00 3.50
293 A45 1p gray blk 16.00 8.00
 Nos. 284-293 (10) 41.20 18.65

Sixth Pan-American Conference.

Capitol, Havana A55

1929, May 18

294 A55 1c green 50 40
295 A55 2c car rose 50 35
296 A55 5c blue 75 50
297 A55 10c bis brn 1.50 60
298 A55 20c violet 5.00 2.50
 Nos. 294-298 (5) 8.25 4.35

Opening of the Capitol, Havana.

Hurdler — A56

1930, Mar. 15 Engr.

299 A56 1c green 1.00 50
300 A56 2c carmine 1.00 50
301 A56 5c dp bl 1.50 50
302 A56 10c bis brn 2.25 1.00
303 A56 20c violet 10.00 5.00
 Nos. 299-303 (5) 15.75 7.50

Issued to commemorate the second Central American Athletic Games.

Types of 1917 Portrait Issue.
Flat Plate Printing.

1930-45 Wmk. 106 Engr. *Perf. 10*

304 A35 1c bl grn 1.10 25
 a. Booklet pane of 6 50.00
 b. Booklet pane of 30
305 A36 2c brt rose 200.00 90.00
 a. Booklet pane of 6 1,400.
305B A37 3c dk rose vio ('42) 4.50 60
 c. Booklet pane of 6 50.00.
306 A38 5c dk bl 5.00 40
306A A39 8c red brn ('45) 5.00 50
307 A40 10c brown 5.00 50
 a. 10c yel brn ('35) 7.00 1.00
307B A41 20c ol grn ('41) 8.00 1.00
 Nos. 304-307B (7) 228.60 93.25

Nos. 305 and 305B were printed for booklet panes and all copies have straight edges.

Rotary Press Printing.

308 A35 1c bl grn 1.75 25
309 A36 2c brt rose 1.75 25
 a. Booklet pane of 50
310 A37 3c violet 2.50 25
 a. 3c dl vio ('38) 1.75 25
 b. 3c rose vio ('41) 1.75 25
 c. Bklt. pane of 50

The flat plate stamps measure 18½x21½mm.; those from the rotary press, 19x22mm.

The Mangos of Baragua — A57

Battle of Mal Tiempo A58

Battle of Coliseo A59

Maceo, Gomez and Zayas A60

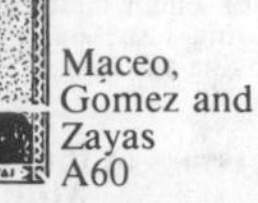

War Memorial — A61

Wmk.229

Wmk. Wavy Lines. (229)

1933, Apr. 23 Photo. *Perf. 12½*

312 A57 3c dk brn 1.00 25
313 A58 5c dk bl 1.00 50
314 A59 10c emerald 3.00 50
315 A60 13c red 3.00 1.25
316 A61 20c black 6.00 4.00
 Nos. 312-316 (5) 14.00 6.50

Issued in commemoration of the War of Independence and the dedication of the "Soldado Invasor" monument.

Types of 1917 Issues with Carmine or Black Overprint Reading Up or Down

GOBIERNO
REVOLUCIONARIO
4-9-1933

Rotary Press Printing.

Wmk. 106

1933, Dec. 23 Engr. *Perf. 10*

317 A35 1c bl grn (C) 1.00 35

With Additional Surcharge of New Value and Bars.

318 A37 2c on 3c vio (Bk) 1.00 35

Nos. 317-318 commemorate the establishment of a revolutionary junta.

Dr. Carlos J. Finlay — A62

Wmk. 106

1934, Dec. 3 Engr. *Perf. 10*

319 A62 2c dk car 1.00 30
320 A62 5c dk bl 2.25 75

Issued to commemorate the centenary of the birth of Dr. Carlos J. Finlay (1833-1915), physician-biologist who found that a mosquito transmitted yellow fever.

Pres. José Miguel Gomez — A63

Gomez Monument — A64

1936, May *Perf. 10*

322 A63 1c green 60 30
323 A64 2c carmine 1.50 30

Issued in commemoration of the unveiling of a monument to Gen. José Miguel Gomez, ex-president.

Matanzas Issue.

Map of Cuba A65

Designs: 2c, Map of Free Zone. 4c, S. S. "Rex" in Matanzas Bay. 5c, Ships in Matanzas Bay. 8c, Caves of Bellamar. 10c, Valley of Yumuri. 20c, Yumuri River. 50c, Ships Leaving Port.

Wmk. Wavy Lines. (229)

1936, May 5 Photo. *Perf. 12½*

324 A65 1c bl grn 40 25
325 A65 2c red 60 30
326 A65 4c claret 1.25 40
327 A65 5c ultra 1.10 40
328 A65 8c org brn 2.50 1.00
329 A65 10c emerald 2.00 1.00
330 A65 20c brown 5.00 3.50
331 A65 50c slate 8.00 5.00
 Nos. 324-331,C18-C21,CE1,E8 (14) 48.10 27.10

Exist imperf. Price 20% more.

"Peace and Work" A73

Máximo Gómez Monument A74

Torch A75

"Independence" — A76

"Messenger of Peace" — A77

1936, Nov. 18 *Perf. 12½*

332 A73 1c emerald 50 25
333 A74 2c crimson 60 20

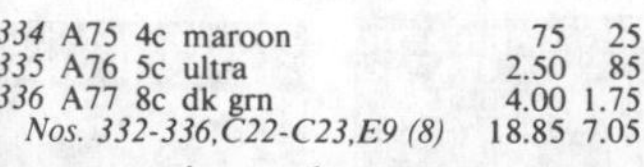

334	A75	4c maroon	75	25
335	A76	5c ultra	2.50	85
336	A77	8c dk grn	4.00	1.75
		Nos. 332-336,C22-C23,E9 (8)	18.85	7.05

Maj. Gen. Máximo Gómez, birth centenary.

Sugar Cane — A78

Primitive Sugar Mill — A79

Modern Sugar Mill — A80

Wmk. Star. (106)

1937, Oct. 2 Engr. *Perf. 10*

337	A78	1c yel grn	1.00	50
338	A79	2c red	70	30
339	A80	5c brt bl	1.00	60

Issued in commemoration of the 400th anniversary of the sugar cane industry in Cuba.

Argentine Emblem A81

Mountain Scene (Bolivia) A82

Arms of Brazil — A83

Canadian Scene — A84

Camilo Henriquez (Chile) A85

Gen, Francisco de Paula Santander (Colombia) A86

National Monument (Costa Rica) — A87

Autograph of Jose Marti (Cuba) — A88

Columbus Lighthouse (Dominican Republic) A89

Juan Montalvo (Ecuador) A90

Abraham Lincoln (United States) A91

Quetzal and Scroll (Guatemala) A92

Arms of Haiti A93

Francisco Morazan (Honduras) A94

Fleet of Columbus — A95

Wmk. 106

1937, Oct. 13 Engr. *Perf. 10*

340	A81	1c dp grn	50	50
341	A82	1c green	50	50
342	A83	2c carmine	50	50
343	A84	2c carmine	50	50
344	A85	3c violet	1.50	1.50
345	A86	3c violet	1.50	1.50
346	A87	4c bis brn	1.75	1.75
347	A88	4c bis brn	3.00	3.00
348	A89	5c blue	1.50	1.50
349	A90	5c blue	1.50	1.50
350	A91	8c citron	10.00	10.00
351	A92	8c citron	2.50	2.50
352	A93	10c maroon	2.50	2.50
353	A94	10c maroon	2.50	2.50
354	A95	25c rose lil	25.00	25.00
		Nos. 340-354,C24-C29,E10-E11 (23)	109.25	102.25

Nos. 340 to 354 were sold by the Cuban Post Office for three days, Oct. 13-15, during which no other stamps were sold. They were postally valid for the full face value. Proceeds from their three-day sale above 30,000 pesos were paid by the Cuban Post Office Department to the Association of American Writers and Artists. Remainders were overprinted "SVP" (Without Postal Value).

1837 1937
PRIMER CENTENARIO
FERROCARRIL EN CUBA

10¢ 10¢

No. 283 Surcharged in Green

1937, Nov. 19 Unwmk. *Perf. 12*

355	A44	10c on 25c vio	10.00	3.00

Centenary of Cuban railroads.

Ciboney Indian and Cigar — A96

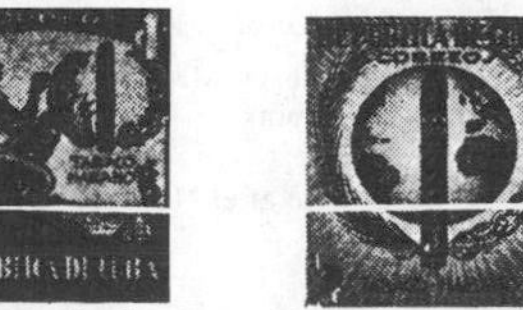

Cigar and Globe — A97

Tobacco Plant and Cigars — A98

Wmk. Star. (106)

1939, Aug. 28 Engr. *Perf. 10*

356	A96	1c yel grn	25	5
357	A97	2c red	50	5
358	A98	5c brt ultra	1.00	20

General Calixto Garcia A99 A100

1939, Nov. 6 *Perf. 10, Imperf.*

359	A99	2c dk red	60	20
360	A100	5c dp bl	1.20	60

Birth centenary of General Garcia.

Gonzalo de Quesada — A101

1940, Apr. 30 Engr. *Perf. 10*

361	A101	2c rose red	1.00	50

Pan American Union, 50th anniversary.

Rotary Club Emblem, Cuban Flag and Tobacco Plant — A102

Lions Emblem, Cuban Flag and Royal Palms — A103

1940, May 18 Wmk. 106 *Perf. 10*

362	A102	2c rose red	2.00	1.00

Issued in commemoration of the Rotary International Convention held at Havana.

1940, July 23

363	A103	2c org ver	2.00	1.00

Lions International Convention, Havana.

Dr. Nicolás J. Gutierrez A104

1940, Oct. 28

364	A104	2c org ver	1.20	50
365	A104	5c blue	1.50	60
a.		Sheet of four, imperf., unwmkd.	5.00	5.00
b.		As "a," blk overprint ('51)	6.00	6.00

Issued in commemoration of the 100th anniversary of the publication of the first Cuban Medical Review, "El Repertorio Medico Habanero".

No. 365a measures 127x177mm, and contains two each of Nos. 364 and 365 imperforate, and upper and lower marginal inscriptions. The sheet sold for 25c.

In 1951 Nos. 365a was overprinted in black: "50 Aniversario Descubrimiento Agente Transmisor de la Flebre Amarilla por el Dr. Carlos J. Finlay Honor a los Martires de la Ciencia 1901 1951." The overprint is illustrated over No. C43A, but does not include the plane and "Correo Aereo."

Major General Guillermo Moncada — A105

Moncada Riding into Battle A106

1941, June 25

366	A105	3c dk brn, *buff*	1.20	40
367	A106	5c brt bl	1.50	75

Issued in commemorate of the centenary of the birth of Maj. Gen. Guillermo Moncada (1841-96).

Globe Showing Western Hemisphere A107

Maceo, Bolivar, Juarez, Lincoln and Arms of Cuba A108

"Labor: Wealth of America" A109

Tree of Fraternity, Havana A110

Statue of Liberty — A111

Perf. 10, Imperf.

1942, Feb. 23 Wmk. 106

368	A107	1c emerald	40	12
369	A108	3c org brn	50	15
370	A109	5c blue	90	30
371	A110	10c red vio	2.00	75
372	A111	13c red	2.50	1.25
		Nos. 368-372 (5)	6.30	2.57

Issued to publicize the spirit of Democracy in the Americas.

The imperforate varieties are without gum.

Ignacio Agramonte Loynaz — A112

Rescue of Sanguily by Agramonte A113

1942, Apr. 10 ***Perf. 10***
373 A112 3c bis brn 90 50
374 A113 5c brt bl, *bluish* 1.75 70

Issued in commemoration of the 100th anniversary of the birth of Ignacio Agramonte Loynaz, patriot.

"Unmask the Fifth Columnists" — A114

"Be Careful, The Fifth Column is Spying on You" — A115

"Destroy it. The Fifth Column is like a Serpent" — A116

"Fulfill your Patriotic Duty by Destroying the Fifth Column" — A117

(A118 illustration)
"Don't be Afraid of the Fifth Column. Attack it" — A118

1943, July 5
375 A114 1c dk bl grn 40 18
376 A115 3c red 60 20
377 A116 5c brt bl 70 20
378 A117 10c dl brn 1.75 60
379 A118 13c dl rose vio 3.50 1.75
Nos. 375-379 (5) 6.95 2.93

General Eloy Alfaro and Flags of Cuba and Ecuador A119

1943, Sept. 20
380 A119 3c green 1.25 40

Issued to commemorate the 100th anniversary of the birth of General Eloy Alfaro of Ecuador.

Retirement Security A120

1943, Nov. 8 **Wmk. 106** ***Perf. 10***
381 A120 1c yel grn 75 30
382 A120 3c vermilion 90 30
383 A120 5c brt bl 1.00 50

1944, Mar. 18
384 A120 1c brt yel grn 75 30
385 A120 3c salmon 90 30
386 A120 5c lt bl 1.50 75

Half the proceeds from the sale of Nos. 381-386 were used for the Communications Ministry Employees' Retirement Fund.

Portrait of Columbus A121

Bartolomé de Las Casas A122

First Statue of Columbus at Cárdenas — A123

Discovery of Tobacco A124

Columbus Sights Land A125

1944, May 19
387 A121 1c dk yel grn 30 20
388 A122 3c brown 50 20
389 A123 5c brt bl 70 30
390 A124 10c dk vio 1.75 1.00
391 A125 13c dk red 3.50 1.75
Nos. 387-391,C36-C37 (7) 8.60 4.00

Issued to commemorate the 450th anniversary of the discovery of America.

Major General Carlos Roloff — A126

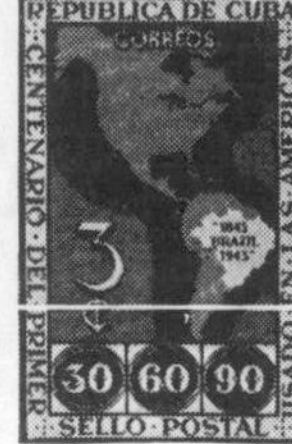

Map of the Americas and First Brazilian Postage Stamps — A127

1944, Aug. 21
392 A126 3c violet 75 35

Issued to commemorate the 100th anniversary of the birth of Maj. Gen. Carlos Roloff.

1944, Dec. 20 **Engr.**
393 A127 3c brn org 1.75 75

Issued to commemorate the centenary of the first postage stamps of the Americas, issued by Brazil in 1843.

Seal of the Society — A128

Luis de las Casas and Luis Maria Penalyer A129

1945, Oct. 5 **Wmk. 106** ***Perf. 10***
394 A128 1c yel grn 30 20
395 A129 2c scarlet 45 20

Issued to commemorate the sesquicentenary of the founding of the Economic Society of Friends of the Country.

Aged Couple A130

1945, Dec. 27
396 A130 1c dk yel grn 25 10
397 A130 2c scarlet 40 15
398 A130 5c cob bl 75 35

1946, Mar. 26
399 A130 1c brt yel grn 50 25
400 A130 2c sal pink 40 25
401 A130 5c lt bl 60 50

See note after No. 386.

Gabriel de la Concepcion Valdés Plácido A131

1946, Feb. 5
402 A131 2c scarlet 90 30

Issued to commemorate the centenary of the death of the poet Gabriel de la Concepcion Valdés.

Manuel Marquez Sterling — A132

Globe and Cross — A133

1946, Apr. 30
403 A132 2c scarlet 90 40

Issued to commemorate the third anniversary of the founding of the Manuel Marquez Sterling Professional School of Journalism.

1946, July 4 **Engr.**
404 A133 2c scar, *pink* 85 40

Issued in honor of the 80th anniversary of the International Red Cross.

Cow and Milkmaid A134

Franklin D. Roosevelt A135

1947, Feb. 20 **Wmk. 106** ***Perf. 10***
405 A134 2c scarlet 75 30

Issued to commemorate the 1947 National Livestock Exposition.

1947, Apr. 12
406 A135 2c vermilion 50 25

Issued to commemorate the second anniversary of the death of Franklin D. Roosevelt.

Antonio Oms Sarret and Aged Couple A136

1947, Oct. 20
407 A136 1c dp yel grn 20 15
408 A136 2c scarlet 35 15
409 A136 5c lt bl 75 40

See note after No. 386.

Marta Abreu Arenabio de Estevez A137

"Charity" A138

A little time given to the study of the arrangement of the Scott Catalogue can make it easier to use effectively.

Marta Abreu Monument, Santa Clara A139

"Patriotism" A140

1947, Nov. 29

410	A137	1c dp yel grn	40	25
411	A138	2c scarlet	60	20
412	A139	5c brt bl	1.00	50
413	A140	10c dk vio	2.00	1.00

Issued to commemorate the centenary of the birth of Marta Abreu Arenabio de Estevez, philanthropist and humanitarian.

Armauer Hansen A141

1948, Apr. 9

414	A141	2c rose car	75	30

International Leprosy Congress, Havana.

Mother and Child — A142

1948, Oct. 15 **Engr.**

415	A142	1c yel grn	30	20
416	A142	2c scarlet	40	20
417	A142	5c brt bl	85	40

See note after No. 386.

Death of José Martí — A143

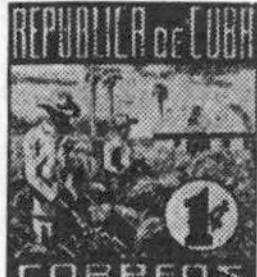

Martí Rowing to Shore — A144

Wmk. 106

1948, Nov. 10 **Engr.** ***Perf. 10***

418	A143	2c scarlet	35	20
419	A144	5c brt bl	80	35

Issued to commemorate (in 1945) the 50th anniversary of the death of José Martí, patriot.

Tobacco Picking A145

Liberty Carrying Flag and Cigars A146

Cigar and Arms of Cuba — A147

1948, Dec. 6

Size: 22½x26mm.

420	A145	1c green	15	5
421	A146	2c rose car	25	10
422	A147	5c brt bl	35	15

Cuba's tobacco industry. See Nos. 445-447.

Equestrian Statue of Gen. Antonio Maceo — A148

Sword Salute to Maceo A149

Designs: 2c, Portrait of Maceo. 5c, Mausoleum, El Cacahual. 10c, East to West invasion. 20c, Battle of Peralejo. 50c, Declaration of Baragua. 1p, Death of Macco at San Pedro.

1948, Dec. 15 **Wmk. 229** ***Perf. 12½***

423	A148	1c bl grn	15	10
424	A148	2c red	25	8
425	A148	5c blue	50	25
426	A149	8c blk & brn	75	50
427	A149	10c brn & bl grn	75	35
428	A149	20c bl & car	3.00	1.50
429	A149	50c car & ultra	5.00	3.50
430	A149	1p blk & vio	10.00	5.00
		Nos. 423-430 (8)	20.40	11.28

Issued to commemorate the centenary (in 1945) of the birth of General Antonio Maceo.

Symbol of Pharmacy A150

Morro Lighthouse A151

1948, Dec. 28 ***Perf. 10***

431	A150	2c rose car	75	30

Issued to commemorate the First Pan-American Congress of Pharmacy, Havana, December 1948.

1949, Jan. 17 **Wmk. 229** ***Perf. 12½***

432	A151	2c carmine	50	25

Issued to commemorate the centenary (in 1944) of the erection of the Morro Lighthouse.

Jagua Castle, Cienfuegos A152

1949, Jan. 27 **Wmk. 106** ***Perf. 10***

433	A152	1c yel grn	40	20
434	A152	2c rose red	80	40

Issued to commemorate the 200th anniversary of the construction of Jagua Castle and the centenary of the publication of the first newspaper in Cienfuegos.

Manuel Sanguily y Garritt — A153

Map of Isle of Pines — A154

1949, Mar. 31

435	A153	2c rose red	35	20
436	A153	5c blue	75	40

Issued to commemorate the centenary of the birth of Manuel Sanguily y Garritt (1848-1925), cabinet member, editor, author.

1949, Apr. 26

437	A154	5c blue	75	35

Issued to commemorate the 20th anniversary of the recognition of Cuban ownership of the Isle of Pines.

Ismael Cespedes — A155

1949, Sept. 28

438	A155	1c yel grn	35	20
439	A155	2c scarlet	35	20
440	A155	5c brt bl	80	40

See note after No. 386.

Gen. Enrique Collazo — A156

Enrique José Varona — A157

1950, Feb. 28 **Engr.** ***Perf. 10***

441	A156	2c scarlet	40	20
442	A156	5c brt bl	80	35

Issued to commemorate the centenary (in 1948) of the birth of General Enrique Collazo.

1950, Feb. 28

443	A157	2c scarlet	40	20
444	A157	5c brt bl	80	40

Issued to commemorate the centenary of the birth of Enrique José Varona, writer and patriot.

Tobacco Types of 1948.

1950, June 20 **Re-engraved**

Size: 21 x 25 mm.

445	A145	1c green	40	10
446	A146	2c rose red	40	10
447	A147	5c blue	60	35

The re-engraved stamps show slight differences in many minor details.

No. 446 Overprinted in Black

BANCO NACIONAL DE CUBA
INAUGURACION 27 ABRIL 1950

1950, Apr. 27

448	A146	2c rose red	75	35

Issued to commemorate the opening of the National Bank of Cuba, April 27, 1950.

Re-engraved Tobacco Types of 1950 Overprinted in Carmine

U.P.U 1874 1949

1950, May 18

449	A145	1c yel grn	25	15
450	A146	2c lil rose	40	20
451	A147	5c lt bl	75	25

75th anniversary (in 1949) of Universal Postal Union.

No. 451 exists with surcharge inverted.

Manuel Balanzategui, Antonio L. Pausa and Train Wreck A158

Fernando Figueredo A159

1950, Sept. 21 **Engr.**

452	A158	1c yel grn	35	20
453	A158	2c scarlet	35	20
454	A158	5c brt bl	75	40

1951, Mar. 17 **Wmk. 106** ***Perf. 10***

455	A159	1c green	40	15
456	A159	2c scarlet	40	15
457	A159	5c brt bl	75	30

Three-fourths of the proceeds from the sale of these stamps were used for the Communication Ministry Employees' Retirement Fund.

See Nos. 474, C51-C56, E15.

Miguel Teurbe Tolon and Flag A160

Narciso Lopez A161

Emilia Teurbe Tolon Sewing Flag — A162

Cuban Flag — A163

Engraved and Lithographed

1951, July 3 **Wmk. 229** ***Perf. 13***

458	A160	1c Prus grn, ultra & red	40	20
459	A161	2c red & gray blk	60	25
460	A162	5c ultra & red	1.25	50
461	A163	10c rose vio, bl & red	2.00	75
		Nos. 458-461,C41-43,E13 (8)	15.50	4.70

Centenary of adoption of Cuba's flag.

Clara Louise Maass and Hospitals A164

Hospitals: Lutheran Memorial, Newark, N.J. and Las Animas, Havana.

Wmk. 106

1951, Aug. 24 Engr. *Perf. 10*

462 A164 2c scarlet 90 40

Issued to commemorate the 75th anniversary of the birth of Clara Louise Maass, (1876-1901), American nurse and martyr in yellow fever fight.

Airmail Type and

José Raul Capablanca — A165

Capablanca Club, Havana A166

Design: 2c, Capablanca making "The Exact Play."

Wmk. 229

1951, Nov. 1 Photo. *Perf. 13*

463 A165 1c bl grn & org 3.50 75
464 AP27 2c rose car & dk brn 4.00 1.50
465 A166 5c blk & dp ultra 8.00 2.50
Nos. 463-465,C44-C46,E14 (7) 53.00 14.50

Jose Raul Capablanca, World Chess titlist (1921). Imperf, set of 7 pairs, $1,500.

Antonio Guiteras Holmes — A167

Guiteras Preparing Social Legislation A168

Fort of the Morrillo A169

Wmk. 106

1951, Oct. 22 Engr. *Perf. 10*

466 A167 1c yel grn 35 15
467 A168 2c rose car 60 20
468 A169 5c dp bl 1.00 30
Nos. 466-468,C47-C49 (6) 6.70 2.55

Issued to commemorate the 16th anniversary of the Action of the Morrillo and to honor Antonio Guiteras Holmes, who was killed there.

Souvenir sheets containing stamps similar to Nos. 466-468, but in different colors, are listed as Nos. C49a-C49b.

Poinsettia A170

Maj. Gen. José Maceo A171

1951, Dec. 1 Engr. and Typo.

469 A170 1c grn & car 3.00 50
470 A170 2c rose car & grn 3.50 75

See note after No. 457. See also Nos. 498-499.

1952, Feb. 6 Engr.

471 A171 2c yel brn 40 20
472 A171 5c indigo 90 30

Issued to commemorate the centenary of the birth of Major General José Maceo.

See note after No. C49.

Queen Isabella I — A172

Receipt of Autonomy — A173

1952, Feb. 22

473 A172 2c brt red 60 20

Issued to commemorate the 500th anniversary of the birth of Queen Isabella I of Spain.

Souvenir sheets containing 2c stamps of type A172 are listed as Nos. C50a-C50b.

Type of 1951 Surcharged in Green.

1952, Mar. 18

474 A159 10c on 2c yel brn 1.25 50

Wmk. 106

1952, May 27 Engr. *Perf. 12½*

Designs: 2c, Tomas Estrada Palma and Luis Estevez Romero. 5c, Barnet, Finlay, Guiteras and Nunez. 8c, Capitol. 20c, Map, Central Highway. 50c, Sugar Mill.

Centers in Black.

475 A173 1c dk grn 40 10
476 A173 2c dk car 50 10
477 A173 5c dk bl 60 20
478 A173 8c dk brn car 1.00 25
479 A173 20c dk ol grn 2.50 75
480 A173 50c dp org 5.00 1.50
Nos. 475-480,C57-C60,E16 (11) 18.25 5.65

Issued to commemorate the 50th anniversary of the foundation of the Republic of Cuba.

Hands Holding Coffee Beans A174

Designs: 2c, Map and man picking coffee beans. 5c, Farmer with pan of beans.

1952, Aug. 22 Wmk. 229 *Perf. 13½*

481 A174 1c green 40 18
482 A174 2c rose red 75 30
483 A174 5c dk vio bl & aqua 1.00 40

Bicentenary of coffee cultivation.

Col. Charles Hernandes y Sandrino A175

Alonso Alvarez de la Campa A176

1952, Oct. 7 Wmk. 106 *Perf. 10*

484 A175 1c yel grn 35 20
485 A175 2c scarlet 65 15
486 A175 5c blue 75 25
487 A175 8c black 2.00 60
488 A175 10c brn red 2.00 60
489 A175 20c brown 7.50 5.00
Nos. 484-489,C63-C72,E17 (17) 47.75 24.55

See note after No. 457.

Frame Engraved; Center in Black.

1952, Nov. 27

Portraits: 2c, Carlos A. Latorre. 3c, Anacleto Bermudez. 5c, Eladio G. Toledo. 8c, Angel Laborde. 10c, Jose M. Medina. 13c, Pascual Rodriguez. 20c, Carlos Verdugo.

490 A176 1c green 25 10
491 A176 2c carmine 50 25
492 A176 3c purple 60 25
493 A176 5c blue 60 25
494 A176 8c bis brn 1.25 60
495 A176 10c org brn 1.00 50
496 A176 13c lil rose 2.00 75
497 A176 20c ol grn 3.00 1.25
Nos. 490-497,C73-C74 (10) 12.85 5.55

Issued to commemorate the 81st anniversary of the execution of eight medical students.

Christmas Type of 1951
Dated "1952-1953."

Frame Engraved; Center Typographed in Black.

1952, Dec. 1

Centers: Tree.

498 A170 1c yel grn & car 4.00 1.25
499 A170 3c vio & dk grn 4.00 1.25

Birthplace of José Marti A177

Marti at St. Lazarus Quarry A178

Designs: No. 501, Court martial. No. 502, artiano house, Havana. No. 504, El Abra ranch, Isle of Pines. No. 505, Symbols, "Marti the Poet." No. 506, Marti and Bolivar statue, Caracas. No. 507, At desk in New York. No. 508, House where revolutionary party was formed. No. 509, First issue of "Patria."

1953 Engr. *Perf. 10.*

500 A177 1c dk grn & red brn 20 10
501 A177 1c dk grn & red brn 20 8
502 A177 3c pur & brn 40 10
503 A178 3c pur & brn 40 8
504 A177 5c dp bl & dk brn 60 25
505 A178 5c ultra & brn 60 25
506 A178 10c red brn & blk 1.50 50
507 A178 10c dk brn & blk 1.50 50
508 A178 13c dk ol grn & dk brn 2.50 1.00
509 A177 13c dk ol grn & brn 2.50 1.25
Nos. 500-509,C79-C89 (21) 29.00 10.95

Centenary of birth of José Marti.

Rafael Montoro Valdez A179

Francisco Carrera Justiz A180

1953, Mar. 5

510 A179 3c dk vio 50 20

Issued to commemorate the centenary of the birth of Rafael Montoro Valdez, statesman.

1953, Mar. 9

511 A180 3c rose red 50 20

Issued to honor Francisco Carrera Justiz, educator and statesman.

No. 446 Surcharged with New Value.

1953, June 16

512 A146 3c on 2c rose red 40 15

Board of Accounts Bldg., Havana — A181

1953, Nov. 3 Engr.

513 A181 3c blue 40 15

Issued to publicize the First International Congress of Boards of Accounts, Havana, November 2-9, 1953.

See also Nos. C90-C91.

Miguel Coyula Llaguno — A182

Communications Association Flag — A183

Designs: 3c, 8c, Enrique Calleja Hensell. 10c, Antonio Ginard Rojas.

1954

Dated 1953.

514 A182 1c green 25 8
515 A182 3c rose red 25 10
516 A182 5c blue 1.00 20
517 A182 8c brn car 1.50 50
518 A182 10c brown 2.50 75
Nos. 514-518,C92-C95,E19 (10) 19.35 9.13

Nos. 515 and 517 show the same portrait, but inscriptions are arranged differently.

See note after No. 457.

José Marti A184

Maximo Gomez A184a

Portraits: 3c, José de la Luz Caballero. 4c, Miguel Aldama. 5c, Calixto Garcia. 8c, Ignacio Agramont. 10c, Tomas Estrada Palma. 13c, Carlos J. Finlay. 14c, Serafin Sanchez. 20c, José Antonio Saco. 50c, Antonio Maceo. 1p, Carlos Manuel de Cespedes.

1954-56 Wmk. 106 *Perf. 10.*

519 A184 1c green 25 5
520 A184a 2c rose car 25 5
521 A184 3c violet 25 5
521A A184 4c red lil ('55) 30 6
522 A184a 5c sl bl 35 8
523 A184a 8c car lake 50 10
524 A184 10c sepia 50 10
525 A184 13c org red 75 15
525A A184a 14c gray ('56) 1.00 15
526 A184 20c olive 1.50 25
527 A184a 50c org yel 2.50 50
528 A184a 1p orange 5.00 75
Nos. 519-528 (12) 13.15 2.29

See Nos. 674-680.

Maj. Gen. José M. Rodriguez — A185

Design: 5c, Gen. Rodriguez on horseback.

1954, June 8 Engr. *Perf. 12½*
Center in Dark Brown

529 A185 2c dk car 50 20
530 A185 5c dp bl 1.00 40

Issued to commemorate the centenary of the birth of Maj. Gen. Jose Maria Rodriguez (in 1851).

Gen. Batista Sanatorium A186

1954, Sept. 21 Wmk. 106 *Perf. 10*

531 A186 3c dp bl 50 20

See also No. C107.

Santa Claus A187

Maria Luisa Dolz A188

1954, Dec. 15

532 A187 2c dk grn & car 4.00 75
533 A187 4c car & dk grn 3.50 75

Christmas 1954.

1954, Dec. 23

534 A188 4c dp bl 50 20

Issued to commemorate the centenary of the birth of Maria Luisa Dolz, educator and defender of women's rights. See also No. C108.

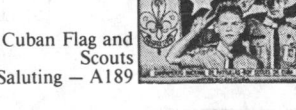

Cuban Flag and Scouts Saluting — A189

1954, Dec. 27 *Perf. 12½*

535 A189 4c dk grn 75 30

Issued to publicize the national patrol encampment of the Boy Scouts of Cuba.

Rotary Emblem and Paul P. Harris — A190

1955, Feb. 23 Engr. Wmk. 106

536 A190 4c blue 75 20

Rotary International, 50th anniversary. See also No. C109.

Maj. Gen. Francisco Carrillo — A191

Portrait: 5c, Gen. Carrillo standing.

1955, Mar. 8 *Perf. 10*

537 A191 2c brt red & dk bl 40 15
538 A191 5c dk bl & dk brn 75 25

Issued to commemorate the centenary of the birth of Maj. Gen. Francisco Carrillo (1851-1926).

Stamp of 1885 and Convent of San Francisco — A192

Designs (including 1855 stamp): 4c, Volanta carriage. 10c, Havana, 19th century. 14c, Captain general's residence.

1955, Apr. *Perf. 12½*

539 A192 2c lil rose & dk grnsh bl 75 25
540 A192 4c ocher & dk grn 1.00 25
541 A192 10c ultra & dk red 2.25 1.25
542 A192 14c grn & dp org 5.50 1.50
Nos. 539-542,C110-C113 (8) 17.75 7.10

Issued to commemorate the centenary of Cuba's first postage stamps.

Maj. Gen. Mario G. Menocal A193

Gen. Emilio Nunez A194

Portraits: 10c, J. G. O. Gomez. 14c, A. Sanchez de Bustamente.

1955, June 22

543 A193 2c dk grn 50 6
544 A194 4c lil rose 60 8
545 A193 10c dp bl 1.00 40
546 A194 14c gray vio 2.00 60
Nos. 543-546,C114-C116,E20 (8) 14.10 6.54

See note after No. 457.

Turkey A195

Gen. Emilio Nunez A196

1955, Dec. 15 Engr.

547 A195 2c sl grn & dk car 3.75 75
548 A195 4c rose lake & brt grn 3.75 60

Christmas 1955.

1955, Dec. 27

549 A196 4c claret 50 20

Issued to commemorate the centenary of the birth of Gen. Emilio Nunez, Cuban revolutionary hero. See also Nos. C127-C128.

Francisco Cagigal de la Vega (1695-1777) A197

Julian del Casal A198

1956, Mar. 27 *Perf. 12½*

552 A197 4c rose brn & sl bl 50 20

Issued to commemorate the bicentenary of the Cuban post. See also No. C129.

1956, May 2

Portraits: 4c, Luisa Perez de Zambrana. 10c, Juan Clemente Zenea. 14c, Jose Joaquin Palma.

Portraits in Black.

553 A198 2c green 40 10
554 A198 4c rose lil 50 12
555 A198 10c blue 1.00 25
556 A198 14c violet 1.25 35
Nos. 553-556,C131-C133,E21 (8) 9.65 3.32

See note after No. 457.

Victor Muñoz A199

Masonic Temple, Havana A200

1956, May 13

557 A199 4c brn & grn 50 20

Issued in honor of Victor Muñoz (1873-1922), founder of Mother's Day in Cuba. See also No. C134.

1956, June 5

558 A200 4c blue 60 20

See also No. C135.

Virgin of Charity, El Cobre — A201

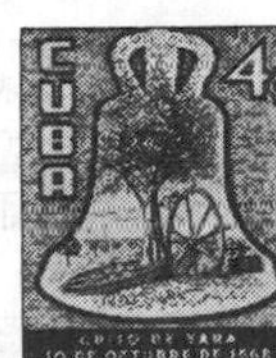

"The Cry of Yara" — A202

1956, Sept. 8 *Perf. 12½*

559 A201 4c brt bl & yel 75 20

Issued in honor of Our Lady of Charity of Cobre, patroness of Cuba. See also No. C149.

1956, Oct. 10

560 A202 4c dk grn & brn 50 20

Issued to commemorate Cuba's independence from Spain.

Raimundo G. Menocal — A203

The Three Wise Men — A204

1956, Dec. 3 Wmk. 106 *Perf. 12½*

561 A203 4c dk brn 50 20

Issued to commemorate the centenary of the birth of Prof. Raimundo G. Menocal, physician.

1956, Dec. 1

562 A204 2c red & sl grn 4.00 1.00
563 A204 4c sl grn & red 4.00 75

Christmas 1956.

Martin Morua Delgado A205

Boy Scouts at Campfire A206

1957, Jan. 30

564 A205 4c dk grn 50 20

Issued to commemorate the centenary of the birth of Martin Morua Delgado, patriot.

1957, Feb. 22 Wmk. 106 *Perf. 12½*

565 A206 4c sl grn & red 90 35

Issued to commemorate the centenary of the birth of Lord Baden-Powell, founder of the Boy Scouts. See also No. C152.

"The Blind," by M. Vega — A207

Paintings: 4c, "The Art Critics" by M. Melero. 10c, "Volanta in Storm" by A. Menocal. 14c, "The Convalescent" by L. Romanach.

1957, Mar. Engr. *Perf. 12½*
Side and Lower Inscriptions in Dark Brown.

566 A207 2c ol grn 40 25
567 A207 4c org red 50 30
568 A207 10c ol grn 75 50
569 A207 14c ultra 1.00 50
Nos. 566-569,C153-C155,E22 (8) 9.60 3.85

See note after No. 457.

Emblem of Philatelic Club of Cuba A208

Juan F. Steegers A209

1957, Apr. 24

570 A208 4c ocher, bl & red 60 20

Issued for Stamp Day, Apr. 24, and the National Philatelic Exhibition. See No. C156.

1957, Apr. 30

571 A209 4c blue 50 20

Issued in honor of the centenary of the birth of Juan Francisco Steegers y Perera (1856-1921), dactyloscopy pioneer. See No. C157.

Victoria Bru Sanchez A210

Joaquin de Aguero in Battle of Jucaral A211

1957, June 3 Wmk. 106 *Perf. 12½*

572 A210 4c indigo 50 20

1957, July 4

573 A211 4c dk grn		50	20

Issued to honor Joaquin de Aguero, Cuban freedom fighter and patriot. See No. C162.

Boy, Dogs and Cat — A212

Col. Rafael Manduley del Rio — A213

1957, July 17

574 A212 4c Prus grn		75	30

Issued in honor of Mrs. Jeanette Ryder, founder of the Humane Society of Cuba. See Nos. C163-C163a.

1957, July 31

575 A213 4c Prus grn		50	15

Issued to honor Col. Manduley del Rio, patriot, on the centenary of his birth (in 1856).

Palace of Justice A214

1957, Sept. 2 Engr. *Perf. 12½*

576 A214 4c bl gray		50	20

Issued to commemorate the opening of the new Palace of Justice in Havana. See also No. C165.

Generals of the Liberation A215

1957, Sept. 26

577 A215 4c dl grn & red brn		50	20
578 A215 4c dl bl & red brn		50	20
579 A215 4c rose & brn		50	20
580 A215 4c org yel & brn		50	20
581 A215 4c lt vio & brn		50	20
Nos. 577-581 (5)		2.50	1.00

Issued to commemorate the Generals of the army of liberation.

First Publication Printed in Cuba — A216

Patio — A217

1957, Oct. 18 Wmk. 106 *Perf. 12½*

582 A216 4c sl bl		50	15

Issued to publicize the José Marti National Library. See Nos. C167-C168.

1957, Nov. 19

583 A217 4c red brn & grn		50	15

Issued to commemorate the centenary of the first Cuban Normal School. See also Nos. C173-C174.

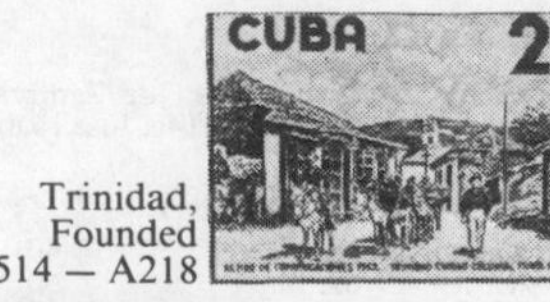

Trinidad, Founded 1514 — A218

Fortifications, Havana, 1611 — A219

Views: 10c, Padre Pico street, Santiago de Cuba. 14c, Church of Our Lady, Camaguey.

1957, Dec. 17 Engr. *Perf. 12½*

584 A218 2c brn & ind		35	6
585 A219 4c sl grn & brn		50	5
586 A219 10c sep & red		1.50	50
587 A219 14c grn & dk red		1.25	25
Nos. 584-587,C175-C177,E23 (8)		8.85	2.81

See note after No. 457.

Nativity — A220

1957, Dec. 20

Center Multicolored.

588 A220 2c dk brn		3.50	1.00
589 A220 4c dk sl grn		3.50	75

Christmas 1957.

Dayton Hedges and Ariguanabo Textile Factory A221

1958, Jan. 30 Wmk. 106 *Perf. 12½*

590 A221 4c blue		50	15

Issued to honor Dayton Hedges, founder of Cuba's textile industry. See No. C178.

Dr. Francisco Dominguez Roldan A222

José Ignacio Rivero y Alonso A223

1958, Feb. 21

591 A222 4c green		50	15

Issued to honor Dr. Francisco Dominguez Roldan (1864-1942), who introduced radiotherapy and physiotherapy to Cuba.

1958, Apr. 1

592 A223 4c lt ol grn		50	15

Issued in honor of José Ignacio Rivero y Alonso, editor of Diario de la Marina, 1919-1944. See also No. C179.

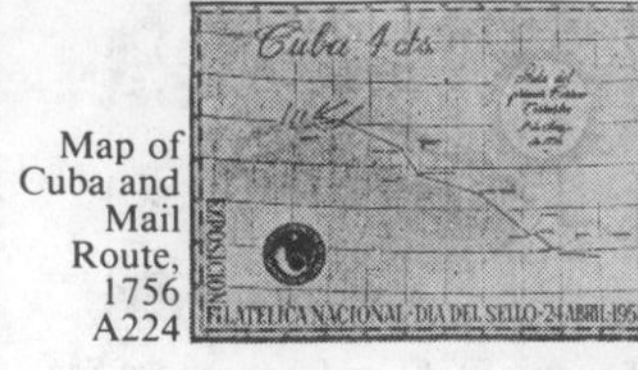

Map of Cuba and Mail Route, 1756 A224

1958, Apr. 24 *Perf. 12½*

593 A224 4c dk grn, aqua & buff		60	20

Issued for Stamp Day, Apr. 24 and the National Philatelic Exhibition. See No. C180.

Maj. Gen. Jose Miguel Gomez A225

Nicolas Ruiz Espadero A226

1958, June 6 Wmk. 106 *Perf. 12½*

594 A225 4c slate		50	15

Issued in honor of Maj. Gen. José Miguel Gomez, President of Cuba, 1909-13. See No. C181.

1958, June 27 *Perf. 12½*

Musicians: 4c, Ignacio Cervantes. 10c, Jose White. 14c, Brindis de Salas.

Indigo Emblem

595 A226 2c brown		50	10
596 A226 4c dk gray		50	20
597 A226 10c ol grn		75	25
598 A226 14c red		1.00	35

Physicians: 2c, Tomas Romay Chacon. 4c, Angel Arturo Aballi. 10c, Fernando Gonzalez del Valle. 14c, Vicente Antonio de Castro.

Green Emblem

599 A226 2c brown		60	10
600 A226 4c gray		1.00	35
601 A226 10c dk car		75	30
602 A226 14c dk bl		1.00	40

Lawyers: 2c, Jose Maria Garcia Montes. 4c, Jose A. Gonzalez Lanuza. 10c, Juan B. Hernandez Barreiro. 14c, Pedro Gonzalez Llorente.

Red Emblem

603 A226 2c sepia		50	10
604 A226 4c gray		75	35
605 A226 10c ol grn		85	25
606 A226 14c sl bl		1.00	35
Nos. 595-606 (12)		9.20	3.10

Carlos de la Torre — A227

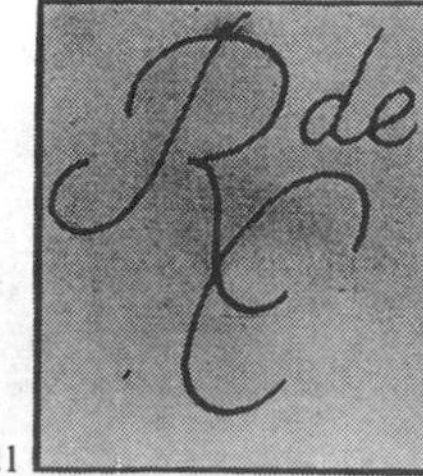

Wmk.321

Wmk. "R de C" (321)

1958, Aug. 29 Engr. *Perf. 12½*

607 A227 4c vio bl		60	20

Issued to commemorate the centenary of the birth of Dr. Carlos de la Torre y Huerta (1858-1950), naturalist. See also Nos. C182-C184.

Poey's "Memorias" Title Page — A228

Felipe Poey — A229

1958, Sept. 26 Wmk. 106

608 A228 2c blk & lt vio		35	15
609 A229 4c brn blk		45	15
Nos. 608-609,C185-C191,E26-E27 (11)		47.30	18.05

Issued in honor of Felipe Poey (1799-1891), naturalist.

Theodore Roosevelt A230

Cattleyopsis Lindenii Orchid A231

1958, Oct. 27 *Perf. 12½*

610 A230 4c gray grn		60	15

Issued to commemorate the centenary of the birth of Theodore Roosevelt. See No. C192.

Engraved and Photogravure

1958, Dec. 16 Wmk. 321 *Perf. 12½*

Design: 4c, Oncidium Guibertianum Orchid.

611 A231 2c multi		3.50	1.00
612 A231 4c multi		4.00	1.00

Christmas 1958.

Flag and Revolutionary A232

Gen. Adolfo Flor Crombet A233

Engraved and Lithographed

1959, Jan. 28 Wmk. 321

613 A232 2c car rose & gray		30	15

Day of Liberation, Jan. 1, 1959.

1959, Mar. 18 Engr. Wmk. 106

614 A233 4c sl grn		40	15

Issued in honor of General Adolfo Flor Crombet (1848-1895).

Maria Teresa Garcia Montes A234

Carlos Manuel de Cespedes A235

1959, Nov. 11 *Perf. 12½*
615 A234 4c brown 40 15

Issued to honor Maria Teresa Garcia Montes (1880-1930), founder of the Musical Arts Society. See No. C198.

1959, Oct. 10 Wmk. 106 *Perf. 12½*

Presidents: No. 617, Salvador Cisneros Betancourt. No. 618, Manuel de Jesus Calvar. No. 619, Bartolomé Maso. No. 620, Juan B. Spotorno. No. 621, Tomas Estrada Palma. No. 622, Francisco Javier de Céspedes. No. 623, Vicente Garcia.

616 A235 2c sl bl	40	10
617 A235 2c green	40	10
618 A235 2c dp vio	40	10
619 A235 2c org brn	40	10
620 A235 4c dk car	50	20
621 A235 4c dp brn	50	20
622 A235 4c dk gray	50	20
623 A235 4c dk vio	50	20
Nos. 616-623 (8)	3.60	1.20

Issued to honor formar Cuban presidents.

No. B3 Surcharged in Red: "HABILITADO PARA / 2¢"

1960 Litho. Wmk. 321
624 SP2 2c on 2c + 1c car & ultra 50 15

See also No. C199.

Rebel Attack on Moncada Barracks A236

Designs: 2c, Rebels disembarking from "Granma." 10c, Battle of the Uvero. 12c, Map of Cuba and rebel ("The Invasion").

Wmk. Interlacing Lines (320)

1960, Jan. 28 Engr. *Perf. 12½*

625 A236 1c gray ol, bl & ver	20	15
626 A236 2c bl, gray ol & brn	25	20
627 A236 10c bl, gray ol & red	50	20
628 A236 12c brt bl, brn & grn	75	30
Nos. 625-628,C200-C202 (7)	6.70	2.85

First anniversary of revolution.

Stamps of 1956-59 Surcharged with New Value in Carmine or Silver

1960, Feb. 3

629 A226 1c on 4c dk gray & ind	40	10
630 A226 1c on 4c gray & grn	60	25
631 A226 1c on 4c gray & red	40	10
632 A227 1c on 4c vio bl	40	10
633 A231 1c on 4c multi (S)	1.00	50
634 A233 1c on 4c sl grn	35	10
635 A234 1c on 4c brn	40	10
636 A184a 1c on 14c gray	50	15
Nos. 629-636,C203-C204 (10)	5.55	2.00

Tomas Estrada Palma Statue, Havana A237

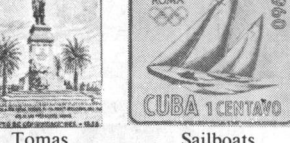

Sailboats A238

Statues: 2c, Mambi Victorioso (Battle of San Juan Hill), Santiago de Cuba. 10c, Marta Abreo de Estevez. 12c, Ignacio Agramonte, Camaguey.

Wmk. 321

1960, Mar. 28 Engr. *Perf. 12½*

637 A237 1c brn & dk bl	20	8
638 A237 2c grn & red	30	8
639 A237 10c choc & red	75	25
640 A237 12c gray ol & vio	1.00	40
Nos. 637-640,C206-C208 (7)	6.10	2.31

See note after No. 386

Nos. 521A, 522 and 525 Surcharged "HABILITADO / PARA / 2¢" in Violet Blue, Red or Black.

1960 Wmk. 106 *Perf. 10*

641 A184 2c on 4c red lil (VB)	50	15
642 A184a 2c on 5c sl bl (R)	60	15
643 A184 2c on 13c org red	75	35

No. 307B Surcharged "HABILITADO / 10¢"

644 A41 10c on 20c ol grn 50 20

Wmk. 321

1960, Sept. 22 Engr. *Perf. 12½*

Design: 2c, Marksman.

645 A238 1c lt vio	30	20
646 A238 2c orange	50	20

Issued to commemorate the 17th Olympic Games, Rome, Aug. 25-Sept. 11.
For souvenir sheet see No. C213a.

Camilo Cienfuegos and View of Escolar A239

1960, Oct. 27 Litho. Unwmk.
647 A239 2c brn, bl, grn & red 25 10

Issued to commemorate the first anniversary of the death of Camilo Cienfuegos, revolutionary hero.

Morning Glory A240

Tobacco and Christmas Hymn A241

1960 Litho. *Perf. 12½*

Flowers in Natural Colors

648 A240 1c red	1.00	50
649 A241 1c blk & red *(Tobacco)*	1.25	75
650 A241 1c blk & red *(Mariposa)*	1.25	75
651 A241 1c blk & red *(Guaiacum)*	1.25	75
652 A241 1c blk & red *(Coffee)*	1.25	75
a. Block of four (1 each, #649-652)	6.50	
653 A240 2c ultra	1.25	75
654 A241 2c blk & ultra *(Tobacco)*	3.50	2.00
655 A241 2c blk & ultra *(Mariposa)*	3.50	2.00
656 A241 2c blk & ultra *(Guaiacum)*	3.50	2.00
657 A241 2c blk & ultra *(Coffee)*	3.50	2.00
a. Block of four (1 each, #654-657)	17.50	
658 A240 10c ocher	4.00	2.00
659 A241 10c blk & ocher *(Tobacco)*	10.00	5.00
660 A241 10c blk & ocher *(Mariposa)*	10.00	5.00
661 A241 10c blk & ocher *(Guaiacum)*	10.00	5.00
662 A241 10c blk & ocher *(Coffee)*	10.00	5.00
a. Block of four (1 each, #659-662)	50.00	
Nos. 648-662 (15)	65.25	34.25

Issued for Christmas 1960.
Nos. 648-602 were printed in three sheets of 25. Nine stamps of type A240 form a center cross, stamps of type A241 form a block of four in each corner with the musical bars joined in an oval around the floral designs.

"Public Capital for Economic Benefit" — A242

Designs: 2c, Chart and symbols of agriculture and industry. 6c, Cogwheels.

Perf. 11½

1961, Jan. 10 Unwmk. Photo.

663 A242 1c yel, blk & org	20	5
664 A242 2c bl, blk & red	20	5
665 A242 6c yel, red org & blk	50	25
Nos. 663-665,C215-C218 (7)	4.40	2.25

Issued to publicize the conference of underdeveloped countries, Havana.

Jesus Menéndez and Sugar Cane — A243

1961, Jan. 22 Litho. *Perf. 12½*
666 A243 2c dk grn & brn 20 10

Jesus Menéndez, leader in sugar industry.

Same Overprinted in Red: "PRIMERO DE MAYO 1961 ESTAMOS VENCIENDO"

1961, May 2
667 A243 2c dk grn & brn 60 40

Issued for May Day, 1961.

Dove and UN Emblem A244

1961, Apr. 12 Litho. *Perf. 12½*

668 A244 2c red brn & yel grn	30	10
669 A244 10c emer & rose lil	50	20
a. Souvenir sheet	2.00	

Issued to commemorate the 15th anniversary (in 1960) of the United Nations.
See also Nos. C222-C223.
No. 669a contains one each of Nos. 668-669, imperf. with red brown marginal inscription. Size: 107x65mm.

Maceo Stamp of 1907 and 1902 Simulated Cancel A245

Designs: 1c, Revolutionary 10c stamp of 1874 and 1868 "cancel." 10c, Stamp of 1959 (No. 613) and "cancel."

1961, Apr. 24 Unwmk.

670 A245 1c dl rose & dk grn	35	25
671 A245 2c sal & dk grn	35	25
672 A245 10c pale grn, car rose & blk	75	40

Issued for Stamp Day, Apr. 24.

Hand Releasing Dove — A246

1961, July 26 *Perf. 12½*
673 A246 2c blk, red, yel & gray 30 10

Issued to commemorate the 26th of July (1953) movement, Castro's revolt against Fulgencio Batista.
Burelage on back consisting of wavy lines and diagonal rows of "CUBA CORREOS" in pale salmon.

Importation Prohibited
Cuban stamps issued after No. 673 have not been priced because the embargo on trade with Cuba, proclaimed Feb. 7, 1962, by President Kennedy, prohibits the importation from any country of stamps of Cuban origin, used or unused.

Portrait Type of 1954

Designs: Same as before. On the 2c, "1833" is replaced by "?".

Wmk. 321 (Nos. 674, 676); Unwmkd.
Perf. 12½ (Nos. 674, 676); Rouletted
1961-69 Engr.

674 A184 1c brown red
675 A184 1c lt blue ('69)
676 A184a 2c slate green
677 A184a 2c yel grn ('69)
678 A184 3c org ('64)
679 A184 13c brn ('64)
680 A184 20c lil ('69)

Issue dates: Nos. 674, 676, Aug. 1, 1961. Nos. 678-679, Dec. 7, 1964. Others, Sept. 1969.

No. 672 Ovptd. in Red

primera exposición filatélica oficial oct. 7-17. 1961

Perf. 12½

1961, Oct. 7 Litho. Unwmk.
681 A245 10c pale grn, car rose & blk

First Official Philatelic Exhibition, Havana, Oct. 7-17.

Education Year — A247

Designs: One letter (per stamp) of "CUBA," book and various quotations by Jose Marti about the virtues of literacy.

1961, Nov. 22

682 A247 1c pale grn, red & blk
683 A247 2c blue, red & blk
684 A247 10c vio, red & blk
685 A247 12c org, red & blk

A248

The first price column gives the catalogue value of an unused stamp, the second that of a used stamp.

Christmas A249

Designs: 1c, Snails. 2c, Birds, vert. 10c, Butterflies.

1961, Dec. 1

686 A248 1c Polymita flammulata
687 A249 1c Polymita fulminata
688 A249 1c Polymita nigrofasciata
689 A249 1c Polymita fuscolimbata
690 A249 1c Polymita roseolimbata
a. Block of 5 + label, Nos. 686-690
691 A248 2c Cuban grassquit
692 A249 2c Cuban macaw
693 A249 2c Cuban trogon
694 A249 2c Bee hummingbird
695 A249 2c Ivory-billed woodpecker
a. Block of 5 + label, Nos. 691-695
696 A248 10c Othreis toddi
697 A249 10c Uranidia boisduvalii
698 A249 10c Phoebis avellaneda
699 A249 10c Phaloe cubana
700 A249 10c Papilio gundlachianus
a. Block of 5 + label, Nos. 696-700

Stamps of the same denomination printed se-tenant in sheets of 20 stamps plus 5 labels picturing bells and star. Stamps of Type A249 are arranged in blocks of 4; Type A248 stamps and labels form a cross in sheet.

See Nos. 760-774, 912-926, 1025-1039, 1179-1193, 1303-1317, 1464-1478 and 1572-1586.

3rd Anniv. of the Revolution A250

1962, Jan. 3

701 A250 1c multi
702 A250 2c multi

See Nos. C226-C228.

Natl. Militia A251

Silhouettes of militiamen and women and their peace-time occupations: 1c, Farmer. 2c, Welder. 3c, Seamstress.

1962, Feb. 26

703 A251 1c blue grn & blk
704 A251 2c deep blue & blk
705 A251 10c brt org & blk

Bay of Pigs, 1st Anniv. — A252

1962, Apr. 17

706 A252 2c multi
707 A252 3c multi
708 A252 10c multi

1st West Indies Packet A253

1962, Apr. 24

709 A253 10c red & gray

Stamp Day. See No. E32.

Intl. Labor Day — A254

1962, May 1

710 A254 2c ocher & blk
711 A254 3c ver & blk
712 A254 10c greenish blue & blk

Natl. Sports Institute (INDER) Emblem and Athletes — A255

1962, July 25 **Wmk. 321**

Buff, Vermilion and Brown

713 A255 1c Judo
714 A255 1c Discus
715 A255 1c Gymnastics
716 A255 1c Wrestling
717 A255 1c Weight lifting

Buff, Green and Carmine

718 A255 2c Roller skating
719 A255 2c Equestrian
720 A255 2c Archery
721 A255 2c Bicycling
722 A255 2c Bowling

Buff, Carmine and Dark Blue

723 A255 3c Power boating
724 A255 3c One-man kayak
725 A255 3c Swimming
726 A255 3c Sculling
727 A255 3c Yachting

Buff, Dark Blue and Maroon

728 A255 9c Soccer
729 A255 9c Volleyball
730 A255 9c Baseball
731 A255 9c Basketball
732 A255 9c Tennis

Buff, Dark Brown and Vermilion

733 A255 10c Boxing
734 A255 10c Underwater fishing
735 A255 10c Model-plane flying
736 A255 10c Pistol shooting
737 A255 10c Water polo

Buff, Red and Black

738 A255 13c Paddleball
739 A255 13c Fencing
740 A255 13c Sports Palace
741 A255 13c Chess
742 A255 13c Jai alai

Stamps of the same denomination printed se-tenant in sheets of 25. Various combinations possible.

9th Anniv. of the Revolution — A256

Attack on Moncada: Abel Santamaria and: 2c, Barracks under seige. 3c, Children at Moncada School.

1962, July 26

743 A256 2c brn car & dark ultra
744 A256 3c dark ultra & brn car

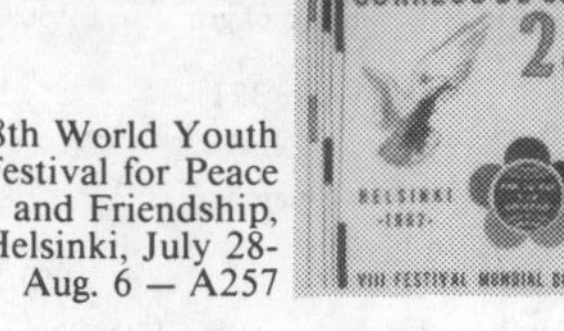
8th World Youth Festival for Peace and Friendship, Helsinki, July 28-Aug. 6 — A257

1962, July 28

745 A257 2c Dove, emblem
746 A257 3c Hand grip, emblem
a. Miniature sheet of 2, Nos. 745-746, imperf.

Size of No. 746a: 100x60mm.

9th Central American and Caribbean Games, Kingston, Jamaica, Aug. 11 - 25 — A258

1962, Aug. 27

747 A258 1c Boxing
748 A258 2c Tennis
749 A258 3c Baseball
750 A258 13c Fencing

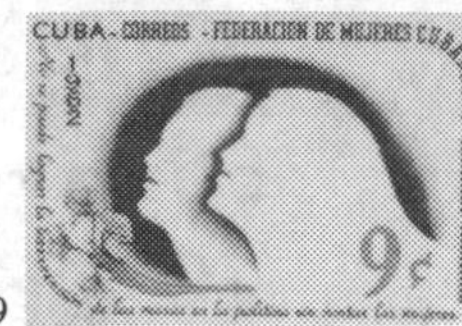
A259

First Natl. Congress of the Federation of Cuban Women — A260

1962, Oct. 1

751 A259 9c rose, blk & grn
752 A260 13c blk, grn & lt blue

Latin American University Games — A261

1962, Oct. 13 **Wmk. 106**

753 A261 1c Running
754 A261 2c Baseball
755 A261 3c Basketball
756 A261 13c World map

World Health Organization Campaign to Eradicate Malaria — A262

Designs: 1c, Magnified specimen of the parasitic protozoa, microscope. 2c, Swamp and mosquito. 3c, Chemist's structural formulas for quinine, cinchona plant.

1962, Dec. 14

757 A262 1c multi
758 A262 2c multi
759 A262 3c multi

Christmas Type of 1961

Designs: 2c, Reptiles. 3c, Insects, vert. 10c, Rodents.

1962, Dec. 21 **Unwmk.**

760 A248 2c Epicrates angulifer
761 A249 2c Cricosaurus typica
762 A249 2c Anolis equestris
763 A249 2c Tropidophis wrighti
764 A249 2c Cyclura macleayi
a. Block of 5 + label, Nos. 760-764
765 A248 3c Cubispa turquino
766 A249 3c Chrysis superba
767 A249 3c Essostruta roberto
768 A249 3c Hortensia conciliata
769 A249 3c Lachnopus argus
a. Block of 5 + label, Nos. 765-769
770 A248 10c Monophyllus cubanus
771 A249 10c Capromys pilorides
772 A249 10c Capromys pre-hensilis
773 A249 10c Atopogale cubana
774 A249 10c Capromys prehensilis
a. Block of 5 + label, Nos. 770-774

Christmas 1962. Stamps of the same denomination printed se-tenant in sheets of 20 stamps and 5 labels picturing bells and star. Stamps of Type A249 are arranged in blocks of four; Type A248 stamps and labels form a cross in sheet.

Soviet Space Flights — A263

Spacecraft and cosmonauts: 1c, Vostok 1, Yuri A. Gagarin, Apr. 12, 1961. 2c, Vostok 2, Gherman S. Titov, Aug. 6-7, 1961. 3c, Vostok 3, Andrian G. Nycolayev, Aug. 11-15, 1962, and Vostok 4, Pavel R. Popovich, Aug. 12-15, 1962. 9c, Vostok 5, Valery F. Bykovsky, June 14-19, 1963. 13c, Vostok 6, Valentina V. Tereshkova, June 16-19, 1963.

1963-1964 **Wmk. 321**

775 A263 1c ultra, red & yel
776 A263 2c grn, yel & rose lake
777 A263 3c yel, vio & ver
778 A263 9c red, dark vio & yel ('64)
779 A263 13c Dark blue green, dull red brown & yel ('64)

Issue dates: 1c, 2c, 3c, Feb. 26. Others, Aug. 15, 1964.

Attack of the Presidential Palace, 6th Anniv. A264

Designs: 9c, Guerillas attacking palace. 13c, Four student leaders. 30c, Jose A. Echeverria, Menelad Mora.

1963, Mar. 13

780 A264 9c dark red & blk
781 A264 13c chalky blue & sep
782 A264 30c org & grn

4th Pan American Games, Sao Paulo, Brazil, Apr. 20-May 5 — A265

1963, Apr. 20

783 A265 1c Baseball
784 A265 13c Boxing

Stamp Day A266

Design: 3c, Mask mailbox, 19th cent. 10c, Mask mailbox at the Plaza de la Catedral, Havana.

1963, Apr. 25

785 A266 3c black & dark org
786 A266 10c black & pur

See Nos. 828-829, 956-957 and 1102-1103.

Labor Day — A267

1963, May 1

787 A267 3c shown
788 A267 13c Four workers

Intl. Children's Week, June 1-7 — A268

1963, June 1

789 A268 3c blue blk & bister brn
790 A268 30c blue blk & red

Ritual Effigy — A269

Broken Chains at Moncada — A270

Taino Civilization artifacts: 3c, Wood-carved throne, horiz. 9c, Stone-carved figurine.

1963, June 29

791 A269 2c org & red brn
792 A269 3c ultra & red brn
793 A269 9c rose & gray

Montane Anthropology Museum, 60th anniv.

1963, July 26

Designs: 2c, Attack on the Presidential Palace. 3c, The insurrection. 7c, Strike of April 9. 9c, Triumph of the revolution. 10c, Agricultural reform and nationalization of industry. 13c, Bay of Pigs victory.

794 A270 1c pink & blk
795 A270 2c lt blue & vio brn
796 A270 3c lt vio & brn
797 A270 7c apple green & rose
798 A270 9c olive bister & rose vio
799 A270 10c beige & sage grn
800 A270 13c pale org & slate blue

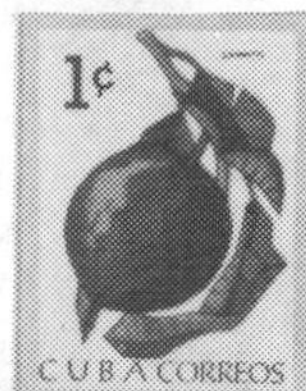

Indigenous Fruit — A271

1963, Aug. 19

801 A271 1c Star apple
802 A271 2c Cherimoya
803 A271 3c Cashew nut
804 A271 10c Custard apple
805 A271 13c Mangoes

Geometric Shapes A272

View of a Town — A273

Designs: No. 806, Circle, triangle, square, vert. No. 807, Roof, window, vert. No. 808, View of a town. No. 809, View of a town in blue. No. 810, View of a town in olive bister and red. No. 811, Circle, triangle, vert. No. 812, House, roof and doorway, vert. No. 813, House, girders.

1963, Sept. 29 **Unwmk.**

806 A272 3c multi
807 A272 3c multi
808 A273 3c multi
809 A273 3c multi
810 A273 13c multi
811 A272 13c multi
812 A272 13c multi
813 A272 13c multi

7th Intl. Congress of the Intl. Union of Architects.

Ernest Hemingway (1899-1961), American Author — A274

Hemingway and: 3c, The Old Man and the Sea. 9c, For Whom the Bell Tolls. 13c, Hemingway Museum (former residence), San Francisco de Paula, near Havana.

1963, Dec. 5 **Wmk. 321**

814 A274 3c brn & lt blue
815 A274 9c sage grn & pink
816 A274 13c blk & yel grn

Natl. Museum, 50th Anniv. — A275

Works of art: 2c, El Zapateo (Dance), by Victor P. Landaluze. 3c, Abduction of the Mulatto Women, by Carlos Enriquez, vert. 9c, Greek Panathean amphora, vert. 13c, My Beloved (bust of a young woman), by Jean Antoine Houdon, vert.

1964, Mar. 19 **Unwmk.**

817 A275 2c multi
818 A275 3c multi
819 A275 9c multi
820 A275 13c multi

General Strike on Apr. 9, 6th Anniv. — A276

Rebel leaders: 2c, Bernardo Juan Borrell. 3c, Marcelo Salado. 10c, Oscar Lucero. 13c, Sergio Gonzalez.

1964, Apr. 9

821 A276 2c blk, yel grn & dull org
822 A276 3c blk, red & dull org
823 A276 10c blk, pur & beige
824 A276 13c blk, brt blue & beige

Bay of Pigs, 3rd Anniv. — A277

Designs: 3c, Fish in net. 10c, Victory Monument. 13c, Fallen eagle, vert.

1964, Apr. 17

825 A277 3c multi
826 A277 10c multi
827 A277 13c multi

Stamp Day Type of 1963

Designs: 3c, Vicente Mora Pera, first postal director. 13c, Unissued provisional stamp, 1871.

1964, Apr. 24

828 A266 3c ocher & dull lil
829 A266 13c dull vio & lt olive grn

Stamp Day 1964.

Labor Day — A278

Diplomatic Relations with China — A279

1964, May 1

830 A278 3c Industry
831 A278 13c Agriculture

1964, May 15

Designs: 1c, China Monument, Havana. 2c, Cuban and Chinese farmers. 3c, Natl. flags.

832 A279 1c multi
833 A279 2c org brn, blk & apple grn
834 A279 3c multi

15th UPU Congress, Vienna, May-June A280

1964, May 29

835 A280 13c Hemispheres on world map
836 A280 30c Heinrich von Stephan
837 A280 50c UPU Monument, Bern

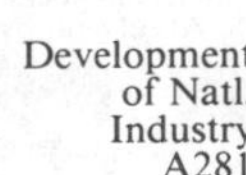

Development of Natl. Industry A281

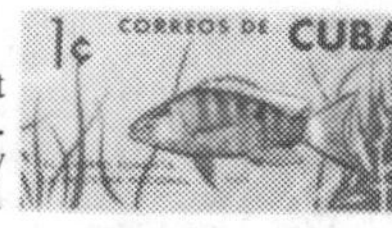

1964, June 16

838 A281 1c Fish
839 A281 2c Cow
840 A281 13c Chickens

Merchant Fleet — A282

1964, June 30

841 A282 1c Rio Jibacoa
842 A282 2c Camilo Cienfuegos
843 A282 3c Sierra Maestra
844 A282 9c Bahia de Siguanea
845 A282 10c Oriente

Unification of Viet Nam — A283

Designs: 2c, Vietnamese guerrilla, American soldier. 3c, Northerner and southerner shaking hands over map of united Viet Nam. 10c, Ox-drawn plow, machinised harvester. 13c, Natl. flags and profiles of Cuban and Vietnamese farmers.

1964, July 20

846 A283 2c multi
847 A283 3c multi
848 A283 10c multi
849 A283 13c multi

11th Anniv. of the Revolution A284

1964 Summer Olympics, Tokyo, Oct. 10-25 A285

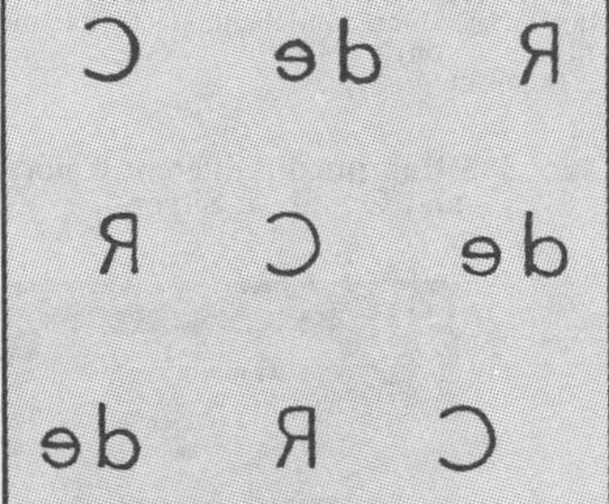

Wmk. 376

Designs: 3c, Raul Gomez Garcia and poem. 13c, Cover of La Historia Me Absolvera, by Fidel Castro.

1964, July 25

850 A284 3c red, tan & blk
851 A284 13c multi

1964, Oct. 10 Wmk. 376 *Perf. 10*

852 A285 1c Gymnastics
853 A285 2c Rowing
854 A285 3c Boxing
855 A285 7c Running, horiz.
856 A285 10c Fencing, horiz.
857 A285 13c Foil, cleats, oar, boxing glove, sun, horiz.

Satellite and Globe A286

Satellite and Partial Globe A287

No. C31 and Partial Globe A288

Various satellites and rockets.

1964, Oct. 15

858 A286 1c shown
859 A287 1c shown
860 A287 1c Globe LL
861 A287 1c Globe UR
862 A287 1c Globe UL
a. Block of 5 + label, Nos. 858-862
863 A286 2c Spacecraft and globe
864 A287 2c Globe LR
865 A287 2c Globe LL
866 A287 2c Globe UR
867 A287 2c Globe UL
a. Block of 5 + label, Nos. 863-867
868 A286 3c Satellite and globe
869 A287 3c Globe LR
870 A287 3c Globe LL
871 A287 3c Globe UR
872 A287 3c Globe UL
a. Block of 5 + label, Nos. 868-872
873 A286 9c Satellite and globe, diff
874 A287 9c Globe LR
875 A287 9c Globe LL
876 A287 9c Globe UR
877 A287 9c Globe UL
a. Block of 5 + label, Nos. 873-877
878 A286 13c Satellite and globe, diff.
879 A287 13c Globe LR
880 A287 13c Globe LL
881 A287 13c Globe UR
882 A287 13c Globe UR
a. Block of 5 + label, Nos. 878-882
883 A288 50c blk & lt grn
a. Souv. sheet of one, litho. & engr., Wmk. 321

Experimental Cuban postal rocket flight, 25th anniv. Stamps of the same denomination printed se-tenant in sheets of 20 stamps and 5 inscribed labels. Stamps of Type A287 arranged in blocks of 4 with a complete globe in center of block; Type A286 stamps and labels form a cross in center of sheet. Inscribed "1939-Cohete Postal Cubano-1964."

No. 883a contains one stamp (size: 46x28mm); black and light green inscribed margin continues the design. Size: 111x74mm.

No. 883 Reprinted (Different Colors) and Ovptd. in Silver

1964, Oct. 17 Unwmk.

884 A288 50c sil on dark red brown & lt grn

No. 884 does not exist without overprint.

40th Death Anniv. of Lenin — A289

Havana Zoo — A290

Designs: 13c, Lenin Mausoleum, horiz. 30c, Lenin, star, hammer and sickle.

1964, Nov. 7 Wmk. 376

885 A289 3c org & blk
886 A289 13c pur, pink & blk
887 A289 30c blue & blk

1964, Nov. 25

888 A290 1c Leopard, horiz.
889 A290 2c Elephant
890 A290 3c Fallow deer
891 A290 4c Kangaroo, horiz.
892 A290 5c Lions, horiz.
893 A290 6c Eland, horiz.
894 A290 7c Zebra, horiz.
895 A290 8c Hyena, horiz.
896 A290 9c Tiger, horiz.
897 A290 10c Guanaco, horiz.
898 A290 13c Chimpanzees, horiz.
899 A290 20c Peccary, horiz.
900 A290 30c Raccoon
901 A290 40c Hippopotamus, horiz.
902 A290 50c Tapir, horiz.
903 A290 60c Dromedary
904 A290 70c Bison, horiz.
905 A290 80c Black bear
906 A290 90c Water buffalo, horiz.

Size: 47x32mm.

907 A290 1p Deer in nature park, horiz.

Heroes of the 1895 War of Independence — A291

1964, Dec. 7

908 A291 1c Jose Marti
909 A291 2c Antonio Maceo
910 A291 3c Maximo Gomez
911 A291 13c Calixto Garcia

Christmas Type of 1961

Designs: 2c, Coral. 3c, Jellyfish. 10c, Starfish and sea-urchins.

1964, Dec. 18

912 A248 2c Dwarf cup coral
913 A249 2c Eusmilia fastigiata
914 A249 2c Acropora palmata
915 A249 2c Acropora profilera
916 A249 2c Diploria labyrinthiformis
a. Block of 5 + label, Nos. 912-916
917 A248 3c Condylactis gigantea
918 A249 3c Physalia physalis
919 A249 3c Aurelia aurita
920 A249 3c Linuche unguiculata
921 A249 3c Cassiopea frondosa
a. Block of 5 + label, Nos. 917-921
922 A248 10c Neocrinus blakei
923 A249 10c Eucidaris tribuloidas
924 A249 10c Tripneutes
925 A249 10c Ophiocoma echinata
926 A249 10c Oreaster celiculatus
a. Block of 5 + label, Nos. 922-926

Christmas 1964. Stamps of the same denomination printed se-tenant in sheets of 20 stamps and 5 labels picturing bells and star. Stamps of Type A249 are arranged in blocks of 4 in a continuous design; Type A248 stamps and labels form a cross in sheet.

Tomas Romay — A292

Romay Monument — A293

Designs: 2c, First vaccination against smallpox. 3c, Portrait and treatise on vaccination.

1964, Dec. 21

927 A292 1c blk & olive brn
928 A292 2c blk & tan
929 A293 3c olive & dark red brown
930 A293 10c bister & blk

Dr. Tomas Romay (1764-1849), physician and scientist.

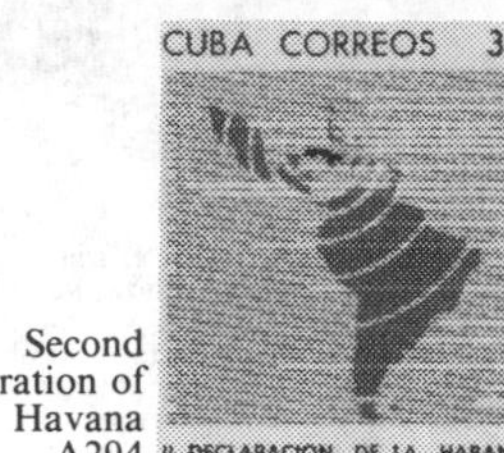

Second Declaration of Havana A294

Map of Latin America and ripples or map of Cuba and peasant breaking shackles under text from the Declaration of Havana: No. 931a, 932a "Visperas de su muerte..." No. 931b, 932b, "Un continente, que juntos suponen representos..." No. 931c, 932c, "Y no se ocultaran ni el gobierna..." No. 931d, 932d, "Millones de mulatos latinamericanos que saben..." No. 931e, "A labran la tierra en condiciones..."

1964, Dec. 23

931 Strip of 5
a.-e. A294 3c any single
932 Strip of 5
a.-e. A294 13c any single

Nos. 931-932 printed in sheets of 25 (5x5).

Cuban Postal Museum Opening — A295

Dioramas.

1965, Jan. 4

Yellow & Black Border

933 A295 13c Maritime Post
934 A295 30c Insurrection Post

Souvenir Sheet

Imperf

935 Sheet of 2
a. A295 13c like No. 933, blue & blk border
b. A295 30c like No. 934, blue & blk border

Stamps in No. 935 have simulated perforations; buff margin is inscribed "PRECIO 50c" LR. Size: 128x75mm.

Fishing Fleet A296

1965, May 1

936 A296 1c Schooner
937 A296 2c Omicron
938 A296 3c Victoria
939 A296 9c Cardenas
940 A296 10c Sigma
941 A296 13c Lambda

Intl. Women's Day — A297

1965, Mar. 8

942 A297 3c Lidia Doce
943 A297 13c Clara Zetkin

Technical Revolution — A298

Designs: 3c, Jose Antonio Echeverria University School. 13c, Stylized symbols of science and research, molecular structure and satellite dish.

1965, Mar. 31

944 A298 3c tan, blk & dark red brn
945 A298 13c multi

Cosmonauts, Rocket — A299

Designs: 30c, Cosmonauts Pavel I. Balyayev, Aleksei A. Leonov taking first space walk.

1965, Apr. 2

946 A299 30c dark blue, blk & brn
947 A299 50c brt pink & blue blk

Flight of Voskhod 2, the first man to walk in space, Mar. 17.

Abstract Wood Carving by Eugenio Rodriguez
A300

Abraham Lincoln
A301

Pintings in the National Museum, Havana: 3c, Garden with Sunflowers, by Victor Manuel. 10c, Abstract, by Wilfredo Lam, horiz. 13c, Children, by Enrique Ponce, horiz.

1965, Apr. 12

948 A300 2c multi

Size: 35x46mm.

949 A300 3c multi

Size: 46x35mm.

950 A300 10c multi

Size: 43x37mm.

951 A300 13c multi

1965, Apr. 15

Designs: 1c, Log cabin, birth site, horiz. 2c, Memorial, Washington, D.C., horiz. 3c, Monument, Washington, D.C. 13c, Portrait, quote.

952 A300 1c yel bister, red brn & gray
953 A300 2c lt blue & dark blue
954 A300 3c reg org, blk & blue blk
955 A300 13c org, blk & blue blk

Stamp Day Type of 1963

Designs: 3c, 19th Cent. postmarks and packet. 13c, No. C16 and airplanes over capital.

1965, Apr. 24

956 A266 3c sep & dark org
957 A266 13c brt blue, sal rose & blk

Stamp Day 1965.

Intl. Quiet Sun Year — A302

Intl. Telecommunications Union, Cent. — A303

1965, May 10

958 A302 1c Sun, Earth's magnetic pole, horiz.
959 A302 2c Sun Year emblem
960 A302 3c Earth's magnetic field, horiz.
961 A302 6c Atmospheric currents, horiz.
962 A302 30c Solar rays on planet surface
963 A302 50c Effect on satellite orbits, horiz.
a. Souv. sheet of one, imperf.
b. As "a," changed colors

Stamps in Nos. 963a-963b have simulated perforations. No. 963a has blue, dark blue and yel margin picturing sun. Size: 94x70mm.

Stamp in No. 963b is blue blk, Prus blue, org yel & red; blue blk and sil margin inscribed "ACADEMIA DE CIENCIAS" pictures stars and Saturn. Issued Oct. 10 for the Philatelic Space Exhibition, Havana, Oct. 10-17. Size: 93x65mm.

1965, May 17

964 A303 1c Station, horiz.
965 A303 2c Satellite
966 A303 3c Telstar, horiz.
967 A303 10c Telstar, receiving station
968 A303 30c ITU emblem, horiz.

9th Communist World Youth and Students Congress — A304

1965, June 10

969 A304 13c Flags of Cuba and Algeria, emblem
970 A304 30c Flags, guerrillas

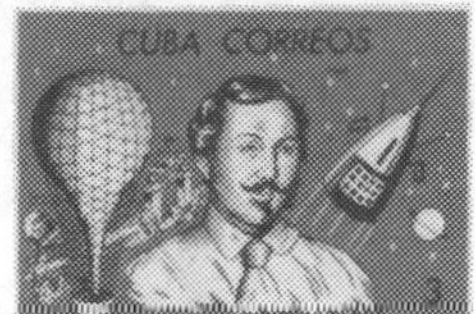

Matias Perez, Cuban Aeronautics Pioneer — A305

1965, June 23

971 A305 3c pink & blk
972 A305 13c dull vio & blk, diff.

Flowers and Maps of Their Locations
A306

1965, July 20

973 A306 1c Rosa canina, Europe
974 A306 2c Chrysanthemum hortorum, Asia
975 A306 3c Strelitzia reginae, Africa
976 A306 4c Dahlia pinnata, No. America
977 A306 5c Cattleya labiata, So. America
978 A306 13c Grevillea banksii, Oceania
979 A306 30c Brunfelsia nitida, Cuba

1st Natl. Games
A307

1965, July 25

980 A307 1c Swimming
981 A307 2c Basketball
982 A307 3c Gymnastics
983 A307 30c Hurdling

Revolution Museum Opening
A308

1965, July 26

984 A308 1c Anti-tank guns
985 A308 2c Tanks
986 A308 3c Bazookas
987 A308 10c Uniform, guerillas
988 A308 13c Compass, yacht Granma

Carlos J. Finlay (1833-1915), Discovered Transmission of Yellow Fever Via Anopheles Monsquito — A309

1965, Aug. 20

989 A309 1c Finlay's signature
990 A309 2c Anopheles mosquito
991 A309 3c Portrait
992 A309 7c Microscope
993 A309 9c Portrait, diff.
994 A309 10c Monument
995 A309 13c Discussing theory with doctors

Nos. 990-995 vert.

Butterflies
A310

1965, Sept. 22 **Unwmk.**

996 A310 2c Dismorphia cubana
997 A310 2c Anetia numidia briarea
998 A310 2c Carathis gortynoides
999 A310 2c Hymenitis cubana
1000 A310 2c Eubaphe heros
a. Strip of 5, Nos. 996-1000
1001 A310 3c Lycorea ceres demeter
1002 A310 3c Eubaphe disparitis
1003 A310 3c Siderone nemesis
1004 A310 3c Syntomidopsis variegata
1005 A310 3c Ctenuchidia virgo
a. Strip of 5, Nos. 1001-1005
1006 A310 13c Prepona antimache crossina
1007 A310 13c Sylepta reginalis
1008 A310 13c Chlosyne perezi perezi
1009 A310 13c Anaea clytemnestra iphigenia
1010 A310 13c Anetia cubana
a. Strip of 5, Nos. 1006-1010

Cuban Mint, 50th Anniv.
A311

Coins (obverse and reverse).

1965, Oct. 13

1011 A311 1c 20 centavos, 1962
1012 A311 2c 1 peso, 1934
1013 A311 3c 40 centavos, 1962
1014 A311 8c 1 peso, 1915
1015 A311 10c Marti peso, 1953
1016 A311 13c 20 pesos, 1915

Tropical Fruit — A312

1965, Nov. 15 ***Perf. 12½***

1017 A312 1c Oranges
1018 A312 2c Custard apples
1019 A312 3c Papayas
1020 A312 4c Bananas
1021 A312 10c Avocado
1022 A312 13c Pineapple
1023 A312 20c Guavas
1024 A312 50c Marmalade plums

Christmas Type of 1961

Birds.

1965, Dec. 1

1025 A248 3c Passerina ciris
1026 A249 3c Icterus galbula
1027 A249 3c Setophaga ruticillar
1028 A249 3c Dendroica tusca
1029 A249 3c Pheucticus ludovicianus
a. Block of 5 + label, Nos. 1025-1029
1030 A248 5c Pyranga olivacea
1031 A249 5c Dendroica dominica
1032 A249 5c Vermivora pinus
1033 A249 5c Protonotaria citrea
1034 A249 5c Wilsonia citrina
a. Block of 5 + label, Nos. 1030-1034
1035 A248 13c Passerina cyanea
1036 A249 13c Anas discors
1037 A249 13c Aix sponsa
1038 A249 13c Spatula clypeata
1039 A249 13c Nycticorax hoactli
a. Block of 5 + label, Nos. 1035-1039

Christmas 1965. Stamps of the same denomination printed se-tenant in sheets of 20 stamps plus 5 labels picturing bells and star. Stamps of Type A249 are arranged in blocks of 4 in a continuous design; labels and stamps of Type A248 form a cross in sheet.

Intl. Athletic Competition, Havana, 7th Anniv. — A313

1965, Dec. 11 **Wmk. 376** ***Perf. 10***

1040 A313 1c Hurdling
1041 A313 2c Discus
1042 A313 3c Shot put
1043 A313 7c Javelin
1044 A313 9c High jump
1045 A313 10c Hammer throw
1046 A313 13c Running

Fish in the Natl. Aquarium
A314

1965, Dec. 5 **Unwmk.** ***Perf. 12½***

1047 A314 1c Echeneis naucrates
1048 A314 2c Katsuwonus pelamis
1049 A314 3c Abudefduf saxatilis
1050 A314 4c Istiophorus
1051 A314 5c Epinephelus striatus
1052 A314 10c Lutianus analis
1053 A314 13c Ocyurus chrysurus
1054 A314 30c Holocentrus ascensionis

Andre Voisin (d. 1964), French Naturalist — A315

1965, Dec. 21 **Wmk. 376**

1055 A315 3c shown
1056 A315 13c Portrait, flags, microscope, plant

Transportation — A316

1965, Dec. 30

1057 A316 1c Skoda bus, Czechoslovakia
1058 A316 2c Ikarus bus, Hungary
1059 A316 3c Leyland bus, G.B.
1060 A316 4c TEM-4 locomotive, USSR
1061 A316 7c BB-69.000 locomotive, France
1062 A316 10c Remolcador tugboat, DDR
1063 A316 13c 15 de Marzo freighter, Spain
1064 A316 20c Ilyushin 18 jet, USSR

A317

7th Anniv. of the Revolution A318

1966, Jan. 2

1065 A317 1c Guerrillas
1066 A317 2c Commander and tank
1067 A317 3c Sailor, patrol boat
1068 A318 10c Jet aircraft
1069 A318 13c Rocket

Conference of Asian, African and South American Countries, Havana — A319

1966, Jan. 3

1070 A319 2c Emblem at R
1071 A319 3c Emblem at L
1072 A319 13c Emblem at center

Guardalabarca Beach — A320

1966, Feb. 10

1073 A320 1c shown
1074 A320 2c Gran Piedra mountain
1075 A320 3c Guama Village
1076 A320 13c Soroa waterfall, vert.

11th Medical and 7th Natl. Dental Congresses A321

1966, Feb. 28 **Wmk. 376**

1077 A321 3c multi
1078 A321 13c multi, diff.

Folk Art A322

1966, Feb. 28 **Unwmk.**

1079 A322 1c Afro-cuban ritual puppet
1080 A322 2c Sombreros
1081 A322 3c Ceramic vase
1082 A322 7c Lanterns, lamp
1083 A322 9c Table lamp
1084 A322 10c Shark, wood sculpture
1085 A322 13c Snail-shell necklace, earrings

Nos. 1079-1083 vert.

Chelsea College, by Canaletto — A323

Ceramics and paintings in the National Museum: 1c, Ming vase. 3c, Portrait of a Lady, by Goya. 13c, Portrait of Fayum, bas-relief. Nos. 1086, 1088-1089 vert.

1966, Mar. 31 **Wmk. 376**

1086 A323 1c multi
1087 A323 2c multi
1088 A323 3c multi
1089 A323 13c multi

First Man in Space, 5th Anniv. A324

Designs: 1c, Konstantin Eduardovich Tsiolkovsky (1857-1935), Soviet rocket and space sciences pioneer. 2c, Cosmonauts in training, vert. 3c, Yuri Gagarin, rocket, Earth. 7c, Cosmonauts Nikolaev and Popovich, vert. 9c, Tereshkova and Bykovsky. 10c, Komarov, Feoktistov and Yegarov. 13c, Leonov taking first space walk.

1966, Apr. 12

1090 A324 1c multi
1091 A324 2c multi
1092 A324 3c multi
1093 A324 7c multi
1094 A324 9c multi
1095 A324 10c multi
1096 A324 13c multi

Bay of Pigs, 5th Anniv. A325

1966, Apr. 17

1097 A325 2c Tank
1098 A325 3c Burning ship, plane crash
1099 A325 9c Tank in ditch
1100 A325 10c Soldier, gunners
1101 A325 13c Operations map

Stamp Day Type of 1963

Designs: 3c, Cuban Postal Museum interior. 13c, No. 613 and stamp collector.

1966, Apr. 24

1102 A266 3c sage grn & sal rose
1103 A266 13c brn, sal rose & blk

Stamp Day 1966. 1st Anniv. of the Cuban Postal Museum (No. 1102); 1st anniv. of the Cuban Philatelic Federation (No. 1103).

Flowers and Symbols of Industry — A326

1966, May 1

1104 A326 2c Anvil
1105 A326 3c Machete
1106 A326 10c Hammer
1107 A326 13c Hemisphere, gearwheel

Labor Day.

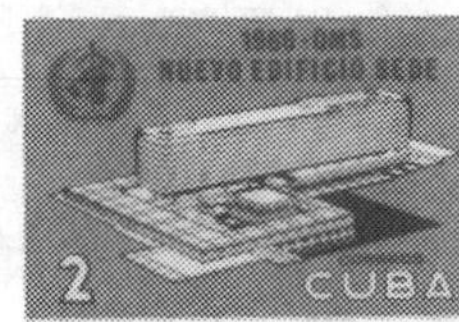

Opening of the World Health Organization Headquarters, Geneva — A327

Views of WHO headquarters and emblem or emblem on flag.

1966, May 3

1108 A327 2c blk & yel org
1109 A327 3c blk, lt blue & yel org
1110 A327 13c blk, lt blue & yel org

10th Central American and Caribbean Games, Puerto Rico, June 11-25 A328

1966, June 11

1111 A328 1c Running, vert.
1112 A328 2c Rifle shooting
1113 A328 3c Baseball, vert.
1114 A328 7c Volleyball, vert.
1115 A328 9c Soccer, vert.
1116 A328 10c Boxing, vert.
1117 A328 13c Basketball, vert.

Progress in Education A329

Designs: 1c, Makarenko School, Playa de Tarara. 2c, Natl. Literacy Campaign Museum. 3c, Lantern, literacy campaign emblem for 1961. 10c, Frank Pais education team in the mountains. 13c, Farmer, factory worker.

1966, June 15

1118 A329 1c grn & blk
1119 A329 2c yel, olive bister & blk
1120 A329 3c brt blue, lt blue & blk
1121 A329 10c golden brn, brn & blk
1122 A329 13c multi

1st Graduating class of Makarenko School (1c), 5th anniv. of the Natl. Literacy Campaign (3c), 4th anniv. of agricultural and industrial trade education (13c).

12th Congress of the Cuban Labor Organization — A330

1966, Aug. 12

1123 A330 3c multi

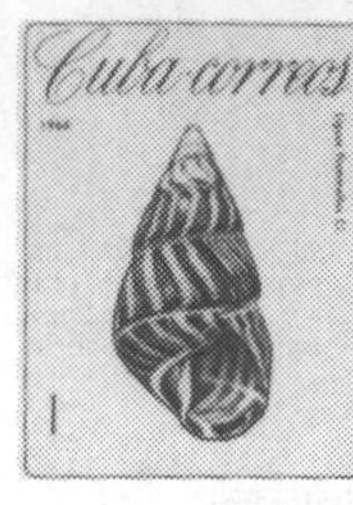

Sea Shells — A331

1966, Aug. 25 **Unwmk.**

1124 A331 1c Liguus flammellus
1125 A331 2c Cypraea zebra
1126 A331 3c Strombus pugilis
1127 A331 7c Aequipecten muscosu
1128 A331 9c Liguus fasciatus crenatus
1129 A331 10c Charonia variegata
1130 A331 13c Liguus fasciatus archeri

Breeding Messenger Pigeons A332

1966, Sept. 18 **Wmk. 376**

1131 A332 1c shown
1132 A332 2c Timer
1133 A332 3c Coops
1134 A332 7c Breeder tending coops
1135 A332 9c Pigeons in yard
1136 A332 10c Two men, message

Size: 47x32mm.

1137 A332 13c Baracoa to Havana championship flight, July 26, 1959

Provincial and Natl. Coats of Arms, Map of Cuba — A333

17th World Chess Olympiad, Havana — A334

1966, Oct. 10

1138 A333 1c Pinar del Rio
1139 A333 2c Havana
1140 A333 3c Matanzas
1141 A333 4c Las Villas
1142 A333 5c Camaguey
1143 A333 9c Oriente

Size: 30x48mm.

1144 A333 13c National arms

1966, Oct. 18

1145 A334 1c Pawn
1146 A334 2c Rook
1147 A334 3c Knight
1148 A334 9c Bishop
1149 A334 10c Queen, games, horiz.
1150 A334 13c King and emblem, horiz.

Canceled-to-order stamps are often from remainders. Most collectors of canceled stamps prefer postally used specimens.

Souvenir Sheet

Imperf

1151 A334 30c Capablanca Vs. Lasker, 1914, horiz.

No. 1151 contains one stamp (size:49.5x31mm); dull gray green margin pictures chessmen on board. Size: 72x61mm.

Cuban-Soviet Diplomatic Relations — A335

1966, Nov. 7

1152 A335 2c Lenin Hospital
1153 A335 3c Oil tanker, world map
1154 A335 10c Workers, gearwheels
1155 A335 13c Agriculture

2nd Song Festival A336

Cuban composers and their compositions.

1966, Nov. 18

1156 A336 1c Amadeo Roldan
1157 A336 2c Eduardo Sanchez de Fuentes
1158 A336 3c Moises Simons
1159 A336 7c Jorge Anckermann
1160 A336 9c Alejandro G. Caturla
1161 A336 10c Eliseo Grenet
1162 A336 13c Ernesto Lecuona

Viet Nam War — A337

Flag of Viet Nam and: 2c, U.S. aircraft discharging bombs, dead cattle. 3c, Gas mask and victims. 13c, U.S. bombs, women and children.

1966, Nov. 23

1163 A337 2c multi
1164 A337 3c multi
1165 A337 13c multi

10th Anniv. of Successful Revolution Campaigns — A338

Revolution leaders and scenes of the insurrection.

1966, Nov. 30

1166 A338 1c Antonio Fernandez
1167 A338 2c Candido Gonzalez
1168 A338 3c Jose Tey
1169 A338 7c Tony Aloma
1170 A338 9c Otto Paralleda
1171 A338 10c Juan Manuel Marquez
1172 A338 13c Frank Pais

Intl. Leisure-time and Recreation Seminar — A339

1966, Dec. 2

1173 A339 3c shown
1174 A339 9c World map, stopwatch, eye
1175 A339 13c Earth, clock, emblem

1st Natl. Telecommunications Forum — A340

1966, Dec. 12

1176 A340 3c shown
1177 A340 10c Satellite in orbit
1178 A340 13c Shell, satellite
a. Souv. sheet of 3, Nos. 1176-1178

No. 1178a has dark blue and maroon margin picturing satellites and communications tower. Sold for 30c. Size: 161x115mm.

Christmas Type of 1961

1966, Dec. 20 **Unwmk.**

1179 A248 1c Cypripedium eurylochus
1180 A249 1c Cattleya speciosissima
1181 A249 1c Cattleya mendelii majestica
1182 A249 1c Cattleya trianae amesiana
1183 A249 1c Cattleya labiata macfarlanei
a. Block of 5 + label, Nos. 1179-1183
1184 A248 3c Cypripedium morganiae burfordense
1185 A249 3c Cattleya Countess of Derby
1186 A249 3c Cypripedium hookerae volunteanum
1187 A249 3c Cattleya warscewiczii reginae burfordense
1188 A249 3c Cypripedium stonei cannartae
a. Block of 5 + label, Nos. 1184-1188
1189 A248 13c Cattleya mendelii Duchess of Montrose
1190 A249 13c Oncidium macranthum
1191 A249 13c Cypripedium stonei platytoenium
1192 A249 13c Cattleya dowiana aurea
1193 A249 13c Laelia anceps
a. Block of 5 + label, Nos. 1189-1193

Christmas 1966. Stamps of the same denomination printed se-tenant in sheets of 20 stamps plus 5 labels picturing bells and star. Stamps of Type A249 are arranged in blocks of 4 in a continuous design; Type A248 stamps and labels form a cross in sheet.

8th Anniv. of the Revolution — A341

1967, Jan. 2

1194 A341 3c Liberation, 1959
1195 A341 3c Agrarian Reform, 1960
1196 A341 3c Education, 1961
1197 A341 3c Agriculture, 1965
1198 A341 13c Rodin's Thinker, Planning, 1962
1199 A341 13c Organization, 1963
1200 A341 13c Economy, 1964
1201 A341 13c Solidarity, 1966

Stamps of the same denomination printed se-tenant in strips of 4. Nos. 1198-1201 vert.

Spring, by Jorge Arche — A342

Paintings in the Natl. Museum: 1c, Coffee Machine, by Angel Acosta Leon, vert. 2c, Country People, by Eduardo Abela, vert. 13c, Still-life, by Amelia Pelaez, vert. 30c, Landscape, by Gonzalo Escalante.

1967, Feb. 27

1202 A342 1c multi
1203 A342 2c multi
1204 A342 3c multi
1205 A342 13c multi
1206 A342 30c multi

Natl. Events, Mar. 13, 1957 A343

1967, Mar. 13 **Wmk. 376**

1207 A343 3c Attack on Presidential Palace

Size: 41x28mm.

1208 A343 13c Landing of Corynthia
1209 A343 30c Cienfuego revolt

Evolution of Man — A344

Prehistoric men: 2c, Australopithecus. 3c, Pithecanthropus erectus. 4c, Sinanthropus pekinensis. 5c, Neanderthal man. 13c, Cro-magnon man carving tusk. 20c, Cro-magnon man painting petroglyph.

1967, Mar. 31 **Unwmk.**

1210 A344 1c multi
1211 A344 2c multi
1212 A344 3c multi
1213 A344 4c multi
1214 A344 5c multi
1215 A344 13c multi
1216 A344 20c multi

Stamp Day A345

Carriages.

1967, Apr. 24

1217 A345 3c Victoria
1218 A345 9c Volante
1219 A345 13c Quitrin

EXPO '67, Montreal, Apr. 28-Oct. 27 A346

1967, Apr. 28

1220 A346 1c Cuban pavilion
1221 A346 2c Space exploration
1222 A346 3c Petroglyph, hieroglyph
1223 A346 13c Agriculture, computer technology
1224 A346 20c Athletes

Botanical Gardens, Sequicentennial A347

Flowering plants.

1967, May 30

1225 A347 1c Eugenia malaccencis
1226 A347 2c Jacaranda filicifolia
1227 A347 3c Coroupita guianensis
1228 A347 4c Spathodea campanulata
1229 A347 5c Cassia fistula
1230 A347 13c Plumieria alba
1231 A347 20c Erythrina poeppigiana

Natl. Ballet — A348

1967, June 15

1232 A348 1c Giselle
1233 A348 2c Swan Lake
1234 A348 3c Don Quixote
1235 A348 4c Calaucan
1236 A348 13c Swan Lake
1237 A348 20c Nutcracker

Intl. Ballet Festival, Havana.

5th Pan American Games, Winnipeg, Canada, July 22-Aug. 7 — A349

1st Conference of Latin American Solidarity Organization (OLAS) — A350

1967, July 22

1238 A349 1c Baseball, horiz.
1239 A349 2c Swimming, horiz.
1240 A349 3c Basketball
1241 A349 4c Gymnastic rings
1242 A349 5c Water polo
1243 A349 13c Weight lifting, horiz.
1244 A349 20c Javelin

1967, July 28 **Wmk. 376**

Portrait of representative, map of South American homeland: No. 1245, Camilo Torres, Colombia. No. 1246, Luis de la Puente Uceda, Peru. No. 1247, Luis A. Turcios Lima, Guatemala. No. 1248, Fabricio Ojeda, Venezuela.

1245 A350 13c pale grn, blk & red
1246 A350 13c lil, blk & red
1247 A350 13c dark chalky blue, blk & red
1248 A350 13c golden brn, blk & red

Portrait of Sonny Rollins, by Alan Davie — A351

Bathers, by Gustave Singier A352

Modern Art: No. 1250, Twelve Selenities, by Felix Labisse. No. 1251, Night of the Drinker, by Fritz Hundertwasser. No. 1252, Figure, by Mariano. No. 1253, All-Souls, by Wilfredo Lam. No. 1254, Darkness and Cracks, by Antonio Tapies. No. 1256, Torso of a Muse, by Jean Arp. No. 1257, Figure, by M.W. Svanberg. No. 1258, Oppenheimer's Information, by Erro. No. 1259, Where Cardinals Are Born, by Max Ernst. No. 1260, Havana Landscape, by Portocarrero. No. 1261, EG 12, by Victor Vasarely. No. 1262, Frisco, by Alexander Calder. No. 1263, The Man with the Pipe, by Picasso. No. 1264, Abstract Composition, by Sergei Poliakoff. No. 1265, Painting, by Bram van Velde. No. 1266, Sower of Fires, by R. Matta. No. 1267, The Art of Living, by Rene Magritte. No. 1268, Poem, by Joan Miro. No. 1269, Young Tigers, by Jean Messagier. No. 1270, Painting, by M. Vieira da Silva. No. 1271, Live Cobra, by Pierre Alechinsky. No. 1272, Stalingrad, by Asger Jorn. No. 1273, Warriors, by Edouard Pignon. No. 1274, Cloister, a mural at the exhibition representing the Salon de Mayo pictures.

1967, July 29 **Unwmk.**

1249 A351 1c shown
1250 A351 1c multi
1251 A351 1c multi
1252 A351 1c multi
1253 A351 1c multi
a. Strip of 5, Nos. 1249-1253

Sizes: 36½x54mm, 36½x53mm, 36½x45mm, 36½x41mm.

1254 A352 2c multi
1255 A352 2c shown
1256 A352 2c multi
1257 A352 2c multi
1258 A352 2c multi
a. Strip of 5, Nos. 1254-1258

Sizes: 36½x54mm, 36½x40mm, 36½x42mm, 36½x49mm.

1259 A352 3c multi
1260 A352 3c multi
1261 A352 3c multi
1262 A352 3c multi
1263 A352 3c multi
a. Strip of 5, Nos. 1259-1263

Sizes: 35x15mm, 35x67mm, 35x46½mm, 35x55mm.

1264 A352 4c multi
1265 A352 4c multi
1266 A352 4c multi
1267 A352 4c multi
1268 A352 4c multi
a. Strip of 5, Nos. 1264-1268

Sizes: 49x32mm, 49x35mm, 49x46mm.

1269 A351 13c multi
1270 A351 13c multi
1271 A351 13c multi
1272 A351 13c multi
a. Strip of 4, Nos. 1269-1272

Size: 54x32mm.

1273 A351 30c multi

Souvenir Sheet

Imperf

1274 A351 50c multi

Salon de Mayo Art Exhibition, Havana. Stamps of the same denomination printed se-tenant. No. 1274 contains one stamp (size: 88x45mm) with simulated perforations and has gray and black inscribed margin. Size: 128x90mm.

World Underwater Fishing Championships — A353

1967, Sept. 5

1275 A353 1c Green moray
1276 A353 2c Octopus
1277 A353 3c Great barracuda
1278 A353 4c Blue shark
1279 A353 5c Spotted jewfish
1280 A353 13c Sting ray
1281 A353 20c Green turtle

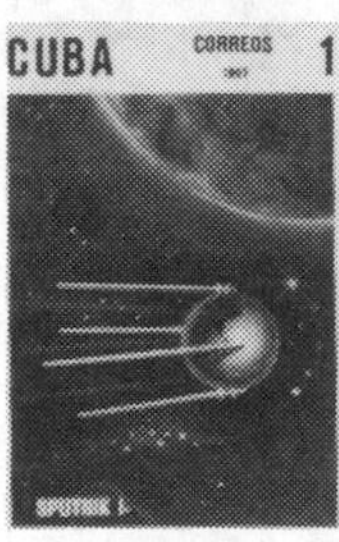

Soviet Space Program — A354

1967, Oct. 4 **Wmk. 376**

1282 A354 1c Sputnik 1
1283 A354 2c Lunik 3
1284 A354 3c Venusik
1285 A354 4c Cosmos
1286 A354 5c Mars 1
1287 A354 9c Electron 1 & 2
1288 A354 10c Luna 9
1289 A354 13c Luna 10
a. Souv. sheet of 8, Nos. 1282-1289, imperf.

Stamps in No. 1289a have simulated perforations. No. 1289a has light blue and black inscribed margin. Size: 163x130mm.

50th Anniv. of the October Revolution, Russia A355

Paintings: 1c, Storming the Winter Palace, by Sokolov, Skalia and Miasnikov. 2c, Lenin Addressing Congress, by W.A. Serov. 3c, Lenin, by H.D. Nalbandian. 4c, Lenin Explaining Electrification Map, by L.A. Schmatko. 5c, Dawn of the Five-Year Plan, by J.D. Romas. 13c, Kusnetzkroi Steel Furnace No. 1, by P. Kotov. 30c, Victory, by A. Krivonogov.

1967, Nov. 7 **Unwmk.**

Sizes: 64x36mm (1c), 48x36mm (2c,4c), 50x36mm (5c, 30c), 36x50mm (13c)

1290 A355 1c multi
1291 A355 2c multi
1292 A355 3c shown
1293 A355 4c multi
1294 A355 5c multi
1295 A355 13c multi
1296 A355 30c multi

Castle of the Royal Forces, Havana A356

Historic architecture: 2c, Iznaga Tower, Trinidad, vert. 3c, Castle of Our Lady of the Angels, Cienfuegos. 4c, St. Francis de Paula Church, Havana. 13c, St. Francis Convent, Havana. 30c, Castle del Morro, Santiago de Cuba.

1967, Nov. 7 **Wmk. 376**

Sizes: 26x47mm (1c), 41x29mm (3c, 4c), 38½x31mm (13c)

1297 A356 1c multi
1298 A356 2c multi
1299 A356 3c multi
1300 A356 4c multi
1301 A356 13c multi
1302 A356 30c multi

Christmas Type of 1961

Birds.

1967, Dec. 20

1303 A248 1c Struthia camelus australis
1304 A249 1c Chysolophus pictus
1305 A249 1c Ciconia ciconia ciconia
1306 A249 1c Balearica pavonina
1307 A249 1c Dromiceius novaehollandiae
a. Block of 5 + label, Nos. 1303-1307
1308 A248 3c Anodorhynchus hyacinthus
1309 A249 3c Psittacus erithacus
1310 A249 3c Domicella garrula
1311 A249 3c Ramphastos sulfuratus
1312 A249 3c Kakatoe galerita galerita
a. Block of 5 + label, Nos. 1308-1312
1313 A248 13c Phoenicopterus ruber
1314 A249 13c Pelecanus erythrorhynchos
1315 A249 13c Alopochen aegyptiacus
1316 A249 13c Dendronessa galericulata
1317 A249 13c Chenopsis atrata
a. Block of 5 + label, Nos. 1313-1317

Christmas 1967. Stamps of the same denomination printed se-tenant in sheets of 20 stamps plus 5 labels picturing bells and star. Stamps of Type A249 are arranged in blocks of 4 in a continuous design; Type A248 stamps and labels form cross in sheet.

Ernesto "Che" Guevara (1928-1967), Revolution Leader — A356a

1968, Jan. 3

1318 A356a 13c blk, dark red & buff

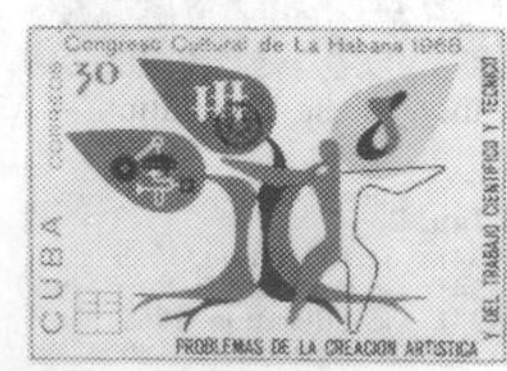

Cultural Congress, Havana — A357

Abstract designs: No. 1319, Independence fostering culture. No. 1320, Integral formation of man. No. 1321, Responsibility of intellectuals. No. 1322, Relationship between culture and the mass media. No. 1323, The arts versus science and technology. Nos. 1319-1322 vert.

1968, Jan. 4

1319 A357 3c multi
1320 A357 3c multi
1321 A357 13c multi
1322 A357 13c multi
1323 A357 30c multi

Canaries and Breeding Cycles — A358

1968, Apr. 13

1324 A358 1c F.C.C. 4016
1325 A358 2c A.C.C. 774
1326 A358 3c A.C.C. 122
1327 A358 4c F.C.C. 4477
1328 A358 5c A.C.C 117
1329 A358 13c A.N.R. 1175
1330 A358 20c A.C.C. 777

Stamp Day — A359

Paintings: 13c, The Village Postman, by J. Harris. 30c, The Philatelist, by G. Sciltian.

1968, Apr. 24 **Unwmk.**

1331 A359 13c multi
1332 A359 30c multi

World Health Organization, 20th Anniv. — A360

1968, May 10 **Wmk. 376**

1333 A360 13c Nurse, mother, child
1334 A360 30c Surgeons

Intl. Children's Day — A361

1968, June 1

1335 A361 3c multi

Prices of premium quality never hinged stamps will be in excess of catalogue price.

Seville Camaguey Flight, 35th Anniv. — A362

1968, June 20

1336 A362 13c Plane Four Winds
1337 A362 30c Capt. Berberan, Lt. Collar, pilots

Natl. Food Production — A363

1968, June 29

1338 A363 1c Yellow tuna, can
1339 A363 2c Cow, dairy products
1340 A363 3c Rooster, eggs
1341 A363 13c Rum, sugar cane
1342 A363 20c Crayfish, box

Attack of Moncada Barracks, 15th Anniv. A364

1968, July 26

Size: 43x29mm (13c)

1343 A364 3c Siboney farmhouse
1344 A364 13c Assault route, Santiago de Cuba
1345 A364 30c Students, school

Committee for the Defense of the Revolution, 8th Anniv. — A365

1968, Sept. 28

1346 A365 3c multi

Guerilla Day A366

Che Guevara and: 1c, Rifleman and "En Cualquier Lugar..." 3c, Machine gunners and "Crear tres muchos Viet Nam." 9c, Silhouette of battalion and "Este Tipo De Lucha..." 10c, Guerillas cheering and "Hoy aquilatamos..." 13c, Map of Caribbean, So. America and "Hasta La Victoria Siempre."

1968, Oct. 8

1347 A366 1c gold, brt blue grn & blk
1348 A366 3c gold, org brn blk
1349 A366 9c multi
1350 A366 10c gold, lt olive grn & blk
1351 A366 13c gold, red org & blk

Cuban War of Independence, Cent. — A367

Independence fighters and scenes.

1968, Oct. 10 **Unwmk.**

1352 A367 1c C.M. de Cespedes, broken wheel
1353 A367 1c E. Betances, horsemen, flag
1354 A367 1c I. Agramonte, Clavellinas Monument
1355 A367 1c A. Maceo, Baragua Protest
1356 A367 1c J. Marti, horsemen
1357 A367 3c M. Gomez, The Invasion
1358 A367 3c J.A. Mella, declaration
1359 A367 3c A. Guiteras, El Morrillo monument
1360 A367 3c A. Santamaria, attack on Moncada Barracks
1361 A367 3c F. Paiz memorial
1362 A367 9c J. Echeverria, student protest
1363 A367 13c C. Cienfuegos, insurrection
1364 A367 30c Che Guevara, 1st Declaration of Havana

Stamps of the same denomination printed se-tenant in strips of 5.

Souvenir Sheet

The Burning of Bayamo, by J.E. Hernandez Giro — A368

1968, Oct. 18 ***Imperf.***

1365 A368 50c multi

Natl. Philatelic Exhibition, independence cent. Stamp in No. 1365 has simulated perforations; pale blue green and black inscribed margin pictures War of Independence battle scenes. Size: 136x83mm.

19th Summer Olympics, Mexico City, Oct. 12-27 — A369

1968, Oct. 21 ***Perf. 12½***

1366 A369 1c Parade of athletes
1367 A369 2c Women's basketball, vert.
1368 A369 3c Hammer throw, vert.
1369 A369 4c Boxing
1370 A369 5c Water polo
1371 A369 13c Pistol shooting

Size: 32x50mm.

1372 A369 30c Mexican flag, calendar stone

Souvenir Sheet

Imperf

1373 A369 50c Running

Stamp in No. 1373 has simulated perforations; multicolored decorative margin pictures flags of participating nations, parade of athletes and statistical data. Size: 125x83mm.

Civilian Activities of the Armed Forces A370

1968, Dec. 2 **Wmk. 376** ***Perf. 12½***

1374 A370 3c Crop dusting
1375 A370 9c Che Guevara's Brigade
1376 A370 10c Road building
1377 A370 13c Plowing, harvesting

San Alejandro School of Painting, Sesquicentennial — A371

Paintings: 1c, Manrique de Lara's Family, by Jean Baptiste Vermay, vert. 2c, Seascape, by Leopoldo Romanach. 3c, Wild Cane, by Antonio Rodriguez, vert. 4c, Self-portrait, by Miguel Melero, vert. 5c, The Lottery List, by Jose Joaquin Tejada. 13c, Portrait of Nina, by Armando B. Menocal, vert. 30c, Landscape, by Esteban B. Chartrand. 50c, Siesta, by Guillermo Collazo.

1968, Dec. 30 **Unwmk.**

Sizes: 38x48mm (1c, 3c), 39x50mm (4c, 13c), 53x36mm (30c)

1378 A371 1c multi
1379 A371 2c multi
1380 A371 3c multi
1381 A371 4c multi
1382 A371 5c multi
1383 A371 13c multi
1384 A371 30c multi

Souvenir Sheet

Imperf

1385 A371 50c multi

No. 1385 contains one stamp (size: 52x41.5mm) that has simulated perforations; multicolored decorative margin pictures easel and curtain. Size: 63x96mm.

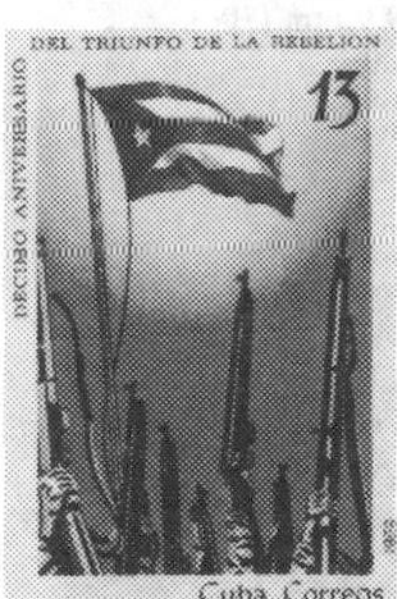

10th Anniv. of the Revolution A372

1969, Jan. 3 **Wmk. 376** ***Perf. 12½***

1386 A372 13c multi

Villaclarenos Rebellion, Cent. — A373

1969, Feb. 6

1387 A373 3c Gutierrez and Sanchez

Women's Day — A374

Design: Mariana Grajales, rose and statue.

1969, Mar. 8

1388 A374 3c multi

Cuban Pioneers and Young Communists Unions — A375

1969, Apr. 4

1389 A375 3c Pioneers
1390 A375 13c Young Communists

Guaimaro Assembly, Cent. — A376

1969, Apr. 10

1391 A376 3c dark brn

The Postman, by Jean C. Cazin A377

Paintings: 30c, Portrait of a Young Man, by George Romney.

1969, Apr. 24 **Unwmk.**

1392 A377 13c multi

Size: 35½x43½mm.

1393 A377 30c multi

Stamp Day.

Agrarian Reform, 10th Anniv. A378

1969, May 17 **Wmk. 376**

1394 A378 13c multi

Marine Life A379

1969, May 20 **Unwmk.**

1395 A379 1c Petrochirus bahamensis
1396 A379 2c Stenopus hispidus
1397 A379 3c Panulirus argus
1398 A379 4c Callinectes sapidus
1399 A379 5c Gecarcinus ruricola
1400 A379 13c Macrobrachium carcinus
1401 A379 30c Carpilius coralinus

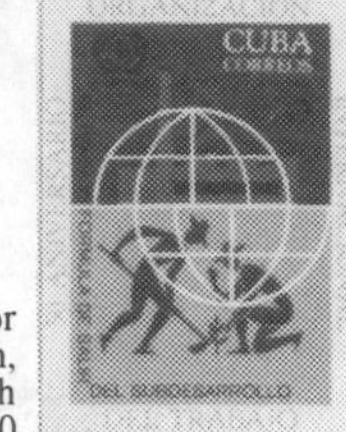

Intl. Labor Organization, 50th Anniv. — A380

1969, June 6 **Wmk. 376**

1402 A380 3c shown
1403 A380 13c Blacksmith breaking chains

Paintings in the Natl. Museum — A381

Designs: 1c, Flowers, by Raul Milian, vert. 2c, Annunciation, by Antonia Eiriz. 3c, Factory, by Marcelo Pogolotti, vert. 4c, Territorial Waters, by Luis Martinez Pedro, vert. 5c, Miss Sarah Gale, by John Hoppner, vert. 13c, Two Women Wearing Mantilla, by Ignacio Zuloaga. 30c, Virgin and Child, by Francisco de Zurburan.

1969, June 15 **Unwmk.**

Sizes: 39x59mm (1c), 39½mm x49mm (3c), 39½x43mm (4c), 39½x45½mm(5c), 38x41½mm (13c), 39x45mm (30c)

1404 A381 1c multi
1405 A381 2c shown
1406 A381 3c multi
1407 A381 4c multi
1408 A381 5c multi
1409 A381 13c multi
1410 A381 30c multi

Broadcasting Institute — A382

1969, July 5 **Wmk. 376**

1411 A382 3c shown
1412 A382 13c Hemispheres, tower
1413 A382 1p Waves on graph

Fish A383

1969, July 20 **Unwmk.**

1414 A383 1c Apogon maculatus
1415 A383 2c Bodianus rufus
1416 A383 3c Microspathodon chrysurus
1417 A383 4c Gramma loreto
1418 A383 5c Chromis marginatus
1419 A383 13c Myripristis jacobus
1420 A383 30c Nomeus gronovii, vert.

Natl. Film Industry, 10th Anniv. — A384

1969, Aug. 5 **Wmk. 376**

1421 A384 1c Poster
1422 A384 3c Documentaries
1423 A384 13c Cartoons
1424 A384 30c Entertainers

Napoleon in Milan, by Andrea Appiani — A385

Paintings in the Napoleon Museum, Havana: 2c, Hortensia de Beauharnais, by Francois Gerard. 3c, Napoleon as First Consul, by J.B. Regnault. 4c, Elisa Bonaparte, by Robert Lefevre. 5c, Napoleon Planning Coronation Ceremony, by J.G. Vibert, horiz. 13c, Napoleon as Cuirassier Corporal, by Jean Meissonier. 30c, Napoleon Bonaparte, by LeFevre.

1969, Aug. 20 **Unwmk.**

Sizes: 41½x55mm (2c), 45½x56mm (3c), 43x62½mm (4c, 13c), 63x47½mm (5c), 45x59½mm (30c).

1425 A385 1c multi
1426 A385 2c multi
1427 A385 3c multi
1428 A385 4c multi
1429 A385 5c multi
1430 A385 13c multi
1431 A385 30c multi

Cuba's Victory at the 17th World Amateur Baseball Championships, Santo Domingo — A386

1969, Sept. 11

1432 A386 13c multi

No. 1432 printed se-tenant with inscribed label listing finalists.

Alexander von Humboldt (1769-1859), German Naturalist — A387

1969, Sept. 14

1433 A387 3c Surinam eel
1434 A387 13c Night ape
1435 A387 30c Condors

World Fencing Championships, Havana — A388

Designs: 1c, Ancient Egyptians in combat. 2c, Roman gladiators. 2c, Viking and Norman. 4c, Medieval tournament. 5c, French musketeers. 13c, Japanese samurai. 30c, Mounted Cubans, War of Independence. 50c, Modern fencers.

1969, Oct. 2

1436 A388 1c multi
1437 A388 2c multi
1438 A388 3c multi
1439 A388 4c multi
1440 A388 5c multi
1441 A388 13c multi
1442 A388 30c multi

Souvenir Sheet

Imperf

1443 A388 50c multi

Stamp in No. 1443 has simulated perforations; multicolored inscribed margin pictures Ramon Fonst, Olympic champion, 1900-1904. Size: 65x98mm.

Natl. Revolutionary Militia, 10th Anniv. — A389

1969, Oct. 26 **Wmk. 376**

1444 A389 3c multi

Disappearance of Maj. Camilo Cienfuegos, 10th Anniv. — A390

1969, Oct. 28

1445 A390 13c multi

Agriculture — A391

1969, Nov. 2 **Unwmk.**

1446 A391 1c Strawberries, grapes
1447 A391 1c Onions, asparagus
1448 A391 1c Rice
1449 A391 1c Banana
1450 A391 3c Pineapple, vert.
1451 A391 3c Tabacco, vert.
1452 A391 3c Citrus fruits, vert.
1453 A391 3c Coffee, vert.
1454 A391 3c Rabbits, vert.
1455 A391 10c Pigs, vert.
1456 A391 13c Sugar cane
1457 A391 30c Bull

Stamps of the same denomination printes se-tenant in strips.

Sporting Events — A392

1969, Nov. 15

1458 A392 1c 2nd Natl. Games
1459 A392 2c 11th Anniv. Games
1460 A392 3c Barrientos Commemorative, vert.
1461 A392 10c 2nd Olympic Trials, vert.
1462 A392 13c 6th Socialist Bicycle Race, vert.
1463 A392 30c 6th Capablanca Memorial Chess Championships, vert.

Christmas Type of 1961

Flowering plants.

1969, Dec. 1

1464 A248 1c Plumbago capensis
1465 A249 1c Petrea volubilis
1466 A249 1c Clitoria ternatea
1467 A249 1c Duranta repens
1468 A249 1c Ruellia tuberosa
a. Block of 5 + label, Nos. 1464-1468
1469 A248 3c Turnera ulmifolia
1470 A249 3c Thevetia peruviana
1471 A249 3c Hibiscus elatus
1472 A249 3c Allamanda cathartica
1473 A249 3c Cosmos sulphureus
a. Block of 5 + label, Nos. 1469-1473
1474 A248 13c Delonix regia
1475 A249 13c Neriun oleander
1476 A249 13c Cordia sebestena
1477 A249 13c Lochnera rosea
1478 A249 13c Jatropha integerrima
a. Block of 5 + label, Nos. 1474-1478

Christmas 1969. Stamps of the same denomination printed se-tenant in sheets of 20 stamps plus 5 labels picturing bells and star. Stamps of Type A249 are arranged in blocks of 4 in a continuous design; Type A248 stamps and labels form a cross in sheet.

Zapata Swamp Fauna A393

1969, Dec. 15

1479 A393 1c Trelanorhynus variabilis
1480 A393 2c Hyla insulsa
1481 A393 3c Atractosteus tristoechus
1482 A393 4c Capromys nana
1483 A393 5c Crocodylus rhombifer
1484 A393 13c Amazona leucocephala
1485 A393 30c Agelaius phoeniceus assimilis

Nos. 1482, 1484-1485 vert.

Tourism A394

1970, Jan. 25 **Wmk. 376**

1486 A394 1c Jibacoa Beach
1487 A394 3c Trinidad City
1488 A394 13c Santiago de Cuba
1489 A394 30c Vinales Valley

Medicinal Plants — A395

1970, Feb. 10 **Unwmk.**

1490 A395 1c Guarea guara
1491 A395 3c Ocimum sanctum
1492 A395 10c Canella winterana
1493 A395 13c Bidens pilosa
1494 A395 30c Turnera ulmifolia
1495 A395 50c Picramnia pentandra

11th Central American and Caribbean Games, Panama, Feb. 28-Mar. 14 — A396

1970, Feb. 28 **Wmk. 376**

1496 A396 1c Weight lifting
1497 A396 3c Boxing
1498 A396 10c Gymnastics
1499 A396 13c Running
1500 A396 30c Fencing

Souvenir Sheet

Imperf

1501 A396 50c Baseball

No. 1501 contains one stamp (size: 50x37mm) that has simulated perforations; black and orange yellow inscribed margin pictures discobolus and baseballs. Size: 86x127mm.

EXPO '70, Osaka, Japan, Mar. 15-Sept. 13 — A397

1970, Mar. 15

1502 A397 1c Enjoying life
1503 A397 2c Improving on nature, vert.
1504 A397 3c Better living standard
1505 A397 13c Intl. cooperation, vert.
1506 A397 30c Cuban pavilion

Speleological Soc., 30th Anniv. — A398

Petroglyphs in Cuban caves: 1c, Ambrosio Cave, Varadero Matanzas. 2c, Cave No. 1, Punta del Este, Isle of Pines. 3c, Pichardo Cave, Cubitas Camaguey Mountains. 4c, Ambrosio Cave, diff. 5c, Cave No. 1, diff. 13c, Garcia Ribiou Cave, Havana. 30c, Cave No. 2, Punta del Este.

1970, Mar. 28 **Unwmk.**

Sizes: 29x45mm (1c, 3c, 4c, 13c)

1507 A398 1c multi
1508 A398 2c shown
1509 A398 3c multi
1510 A398 4c multi
1511 A398 5c multi
1512 A398 13c multi
1513 A398 30c multi

Aviation Pioneers — A399

1970, Apr. 10

1514 A399 3c Jose D. Blino
1515 A399 13c Adolfo Teodore

Lenin Birth Centenary — A400

Paintings and quotes: 1c, Lenin in Kazan, by O. Vishniakov. 2c, Young Lenin, by V. Prager. 3c, Second Socialist Party Congress, by Y. Vinagradov. 4c, First Manifesto, by F. Golubkov. 5c, First Day of Soviet Power, by N. Babasiuk. 13c, Lenin in Smolny, by M. Sokolov. 30c, Autumn in Gorky, by A Varlamov. 50c, Lenin at Gorky, by N. Bashkakov.

1970, Apr. 22

Sizes: 67½x46mm.

1516 A400 1c multi
1517 A400 2c shown
1518 A400 3c multi
1519 A400 4c multi
1520 A400 5c multi
1521 A400 13c multi
1522 A400 30c multi

Souvenir Sheet

Imperf

1523 A400 50c multi

No. 1523 contains one stamp (size: 48x46mm) that has simulated perforations; silver violet and black inscribed margin contains quote. Size: 78x111mm.

Stamp Day — A401

1970, Apr. 24

1524 A401 13c The Letter, by J. Arche

Size: 30x44mm.

1525 A401 30c Portrait of A Cadet, Anonymous

Da Vinci's Anatomical Drawing, Earth, Moon — A402

1970, May 17 **Wmk. 376**

1526 A402 30c multi

World Telecommunications Day.

Ho Chih Minh (b. 1890), President of No. Viet Nam — A403

1970, May 19 **Unwmk.**

1527 A403 1c Vietnamese fisherman

Size: 32x44mm.

1528 A403 3c Two women
1529 A403 3c Plowing field

Size: 33x45mm.

1530 A403 3c Teacher, students in air-raid shelter
1531 A403 3c Nine women in paddy

Size: 34x41½mm.

1532 A403 3c Camouflaged machine shop

Size: 34x39mm.

1533 A403 13c shown

Cuban Cigar Industry A404

1970, July 5

1534 A404 3c Plantation, Eden cigar band
1535 A404 13c Factory, El Mambi band
1536 A404 30c Packing cigars, Lopez Hermanos band

Projected Sugar Production: Over 10 million Tons — A405

1970, July 26

1537 A405 1c Cane-crushing
1538 A405 2c Sowing and crop dusting
1539 A405 3c Cutting sugar cane
1540 A405 10c Transporting cane
1541 A405 13c Modern cutting machine
1542 A405 30c Intl. Brigade, cane cutters, vert.
1543 A405 1p Sugar Warehouse

Pedro Figueredo (d. 1870), Composer — A406

Versions of the Natl. Anthem.

1970, Aug. 17

1544 A406 3c 1868 Version
1545 A406 20c 1898 Version

Women's Federation, 10th Anniv. — A407

1970, Aug. 23

1546 A407 3c multi

Militia, by Servando C. Moreno — A408

Paintings in the Natl. Museum: 2c, Washerwomen, by Aristides Fernandez. 3c, Puerta del Sol, Madrid, by L. Paret Y Alcazar. 4c, Fishermen's Wives, by Joaquin Sorolla. 5c, Portrait of a Woman, by Thomas de Keyser. 13c, Mrs. Edward Foster, by Sir Thomas Lawrence. 30c, Tropical Gypsy, by Victor M. Garcia.

1970, Aug. 31

1547 A408 1c shown

Size: 45x41mm.

1548 A408 2c multi
1549 A408 3c multi

Size: 40x41mm.

1550 A408 4c multi

Size: 38x45½

1551 A408 5c multi
1552 A408 13c multi
1553 A408 30c multi

See Nos. 1640-1646, 1669-1675, 1773-1779.

Havana Declaration, 10th Anniv. — A409

1970, Sept. 2

1554 A409 3c Jose Marti Square

Committee for the Defense of the Revolution, 10th Anniv. A410

1970, Sept. 2

1555 A410 3c multi

39th Sugar Technician's Assoc. (ATAC) Conference — A411

1970, Oct. 11

1556 A411 30c multi

Wildlife — A412

1970, Oct. 20

1557 A412 1c Numida meleagris galeata
1558 A412 2c Dendrocygna arborea
1559 A412 3c Phasianus colchicus torquatus
1560 A412 4c Zenaida macroura macroura
1561 A412 5c Colinus virginianus cubanensis
1562 A412 13c Sus scrofa
1563 A412 30c Odocoileus virginianus

Black-magic Feast, by M. Puente — A413

Afro-Cuban folk paintings: 3c, Hat Dance, by V.P. Landaluze. 10c, Los Hoyos Conga Dance, by Domingo Ravenet. 13c, Climax of the Rumba, by Eduardo Abela.

1970, Nov. 5

1564 A413 1c shown

Sizes: 36x48½mm (3c, 13c), 44½x44mm (10c)

1565 A413 3c multi
1566 A413 10c multi
1567 A413 13c multi

Road Safety Week A414

1970, Nov. 15

1568 A414 3c Zebra, road signs
1569 A414 9c Prudence the Bear

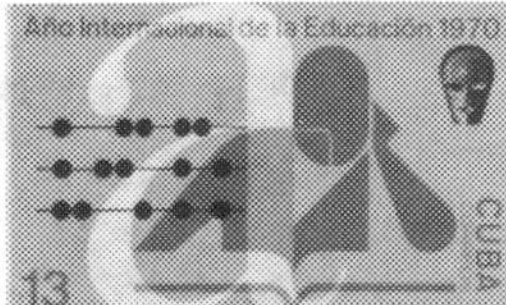

Intl. Education Year — A415

1970, Nov. 20

1570 A415 13c Abacus, "a"
1571 A415 30c Cow, microscope

Christmas Type of 1961

Birds.

1970, Dec. 1

1572 A248 1c Dives atroviolaceus
1573 A249 1c Glaucidium siju siju
1574 A249 1c Todus multicolor
1575 A249 1c Xiphidiopicus percussus percussus
1576 A249 1c Ferminia cerverai
a. Block of 5 + label, Nos. 1572-1576
1577 A248 3c Teretistris fornsi
1578 A249 3c Myadestes elisabeth elisabeth
1579 A249 3c Polioptila lembeyei
1580 A249 3c Vireo gundlachii gundlachii
1581 A249 3c Teretistris fernandinae
a. Block of 5 + label, Nos. 1577-1581
1582 A248 13c Torreornis inexpectata inexpectata
1583 A249 13c Chondrohierax wilsonii
1584 A249 13c Accipiter gundlachi
1585 A249 13c Starnoenas cyanocephala
1586 A249 13c Aratinga euops
a. Block of 5 + label, Nos. 1582-1586

Christmas 1970. Stamps of the same denomination printed se-tenant in sheets of 20 stamps plus 5 labels picturing bells and star. Stamps of Type A249 are arranged in blocks of 4 in a continuous design; Type A248 stamps and labels form a cross in sheet.

Camilo Cienfuegos Military Academy — A416

1970, Dec. 2

1587 A416 3c multi

7th Congress of the Intl. Organization of Journalists — A417

1971, Jan. 4

1588 A417 13c multi

World Meteorology Day — A418

1971, Feb. 16

Size: 39½ x 35½mm (3c).

1589 A418 1c Class, weather chart, computer, vert.
1590 A418 3c Weather map
1591 A418 8c Equipment, vert.
1592 A418 30c shown

6th Pan American Games, Cali, Colombia — A419

1971, Feb. 20

1593 A419 1c Emblem, vert.
1594 A419 2c Women's running, vert.
1595 A419 3c Rifle shooting
1596 A419 4c Gymnastics, vert.
1597 A419 5c Boxing, vert.
1598 A419 13c Water polo
1599 A419 30c Baseball

Porcelain and Mosaics in the Metropolitan Museum, Havana — A420

Designs: 1c, Parisian vase, 19th cent. 3c, Mexican bowl, 17th cent. 10c, Parisian vase, diff. 13c, Colosseum, Italian mosaic, 19th cent. 20c, Mexican bowl, 17th cent. 30c, St. Peter's Square, Italian mosaic, 19th cent.

1971, Mar. 11

Sizes: 34½x53mm (1c, 10c), 46x53mm (3c), 42x48mm (20c)

1600 A420 1c multi
1601 A420 3c multi
1602 A420 10c multi
1603 A420 13c shown
1604 A420 20c multi
1605 A420 30c multi

See Nos. 1699-1705.

Natl. Child Centers, 10th Anniv. — A421

1971, Apr. 10

1606 A421 3c multi

Manned Space Flight 10th Anniv. — A422

Cosmonauts in training.

1971, Apr. 12

1607 A422 1c multi
1608 A422 2c multi, diff.
1609 A422 3c multi, diff.
1610 A422 4c multi, diff.
1611 A422 5c multi, diff.
1612 A422 13c multi, diff.
1613 A422 30c multi, diff.

Souvenir Sheet

Imperf

1614 A422 50c multi

Stamp in No. 1614 has simulated perforations; multicolored inscribed margin pictures spacecraft. Size: 100x63mm.

Cuban Victory at the Bay of Pigs, 10th Anniv. A423

1971, Apr. 17

1615 A423 13c multi

Stamp Day — A424

Packets: 13c, Jeune Richard attacking the Windsor Castle, 1807. 30c, Orinoco.

1971, Apr. 24

1616 A424 13c multi
1617 A424 30c multi

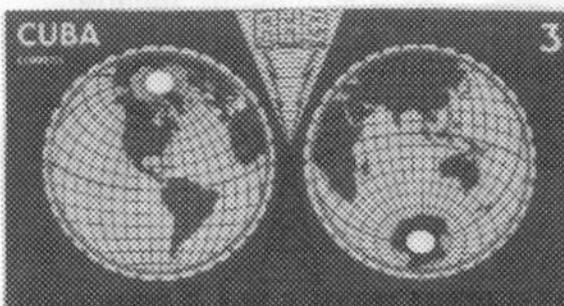

Cuban Intl. Broadcast Service, 10th Anniv. — A425

1971, May 1 **Wmk. 376**

1618 A425 3c multi
1619 A425 50c multi

Orchids A426

1971, May 15

1620 A426 1c Cattleya skinnerii
1621 A426 2c Vanda hibrida
1622 A426 3c Cypripedium collossum
1623 A426 4c Cypripedium gloucophyllum
1624 A426 5c Vanda tricolor
1625 A426 13c Cypripedium mowgh
1626 A426 30c Cypripedium solum

See Nos. 1677-1683 and 1780-1786.

Enrique Loynaz del Castillo (b. 1861), Composer — A427

1971, June 5 **Wmk. 376**

1627 A427 3c Portrait, Invasion Hymn

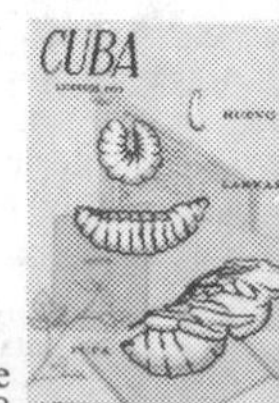

Bee Keeping — A428

1971, June 20 **Unwmk.**

1628 A428 1c Egg, larvae, pupa
1629 A428 3c Worker
1630 A428 9c Drone
1631 A428 13c Defense of hive
1632 A428 30c Queen

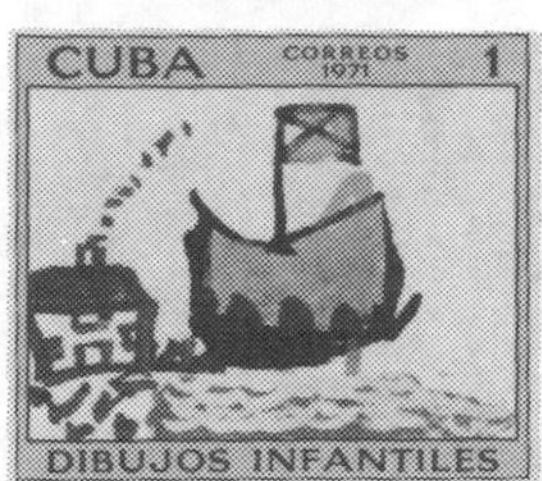
Children's Drawings — A429

1971, Aug. 30
Size: 45x39mm.
1633 A429 1c Sailboat
1634 A429 3c The Little Train
Sizes: 45½x35½mm (9c, 13c), 47x37½mm (10c).
1635 A429 9c Sugar Cane Cutter
1636 A429 10c Return of the Fishermen
1637 A429 13c The Zoo
Size: 47x42mm.
1638 A429 20c House and Garden
Size: 31½x50mm.
1639 A429 30c Landscape

Art Type of 1970

Paintings in the Natl. Museum: 1c, St. Catherine of Alexandria, by F. Zurburan. 2c, The Cart, by Federico Americo. 3c, St. Christopher and Child, by J. Bassano. 4c, Little Devil, by Rene Portocarrero. 5c, Portrait of a Woman, by Nicolas Maes. 13c, Phoenix, by Raul Martinez. 30c, Sir William Pitt, by Thomas Gainsborough.

1971, Sept. 20
Sizes: 31x55mm (1c, 3c), 48x37mm (2c), 37x48mm (4c, 5c), 39x48½mm (13c, 30c)
1640 A408 1c multi
1641 A408 2c multi
1642 A408 3c multi
1643 A408 4c multi
1644 A408 5c multi
1645 A408 13c multi
1646 A408 30c multi

Sport Fishing — A431

1971, Oct. 30
1647 A431 1c Albula vulpes
1648 A431 2c Seriola species
1649 A431 3c Micropterus salmoides
1650 A431 4c Coryphaena hippurus
1651 A431 5c Megalops atlantica
1652 A431 13c Acanthocybium solandri
1653 A431 30c Makaira ampla

19th World Amateur Baseball Championships — A432

1971, Nov. 22 **Wmk. 376**
1654 A432 3c shown
1655 A432 1p Globe as baseball

Execution of Medical Students, Cent. A433

Paintings: 3c, Dr. Fermin Valdez Dominguez, anonymous. 13c, Execution of the Medical Students, by M. Mesa. 30c, Capt. Federico Capdevila, anonymous.

1971, Nov. 27 **Unwmk.**
Size: 61½x46mm (13c).
1656 A433 3c multi
1657 A433 13c multi
1658 A433 30c multi

Spindalis Zena Pretrei — A434

Birds: 1c, Falco sparverius sparverioides vigors. 2c, Glaucidium siju siju. 3c, Priotelus temnurus temnurus. 4c, Saurothera merlini merlini. 5c, Nesoceleus fernandinae. 30c, Mimocichla plumbea rubripes. 50c, Chlorostilbon ricordii ricordii and Archilochus colubris. Nos. 1659-1663 vert.

1971, Dec. 10
1659 A434 1c multi
1660 A434 2c multi
1661 A434 3c multi
1662 A434 4c multi
1663 A434 5c multi
1664 A434 13c shown
1665 A434 30c multi
Size: 55½x29mm.
1666 A434 50c multi

Death centenary of Ramon de la Sagra, naturalist.

Cuba's Victory at the World Amateur Baseball Championships — A435

1971, Dec. 11 **Wmk. 376**
1667 A435 13c multi

UNICEF, 25th Anniv. A436

1971, Dec. 11
1668 A436 13c multi

Art Type of 1970

Paintings in the Natl. Museum: 1c, Arrival of an Ambassador, by Vittore Carpaccio. 2c, Senora Malpica, by G. Collazo. 3c, La Chorrera Tower, by Esteban Chartrand. 4c, Creole Landscape, by Carlos Enriquez. 5c, Sir William Lemon, by George Romney. 13c, Landscape, by Henry Cleenewerk. 30c, Valencia Beach, by Joaquin Sorolla y Bastida.

1972, Jan. 25 **Unwmk.**
Sizes: 50x33mm (1c, 3c), 27½x52mm (2c), 35x43mm (4c, 5c), 43x33mm (13c, 30c)
1669 A408 1c multi
1670 A408 2c multi
1671 A408 3c multi
1672 A408 4c multi
1673 A408 5c multi
1674 A408 13c multi
1675 A408 30c multi

Academy of Sciences, 10th Anniv. — A437

1972, Feb. 2 **Wmk. 376**
1676 A437 13c Capitol Type of 1929

Orchid Type of 1971

1972, Feb. 25 **Unwmk.**
1677 A426 1c Brasso cattleya sindorossiana
1678 A426 2c Cypripedium doraeus
1679 A426 3c Cypripedium exul
1680 A426 4c Cypripedium rosy dawn
1681 A426 5c Cypripedium champolliom
1682 A426 13c Cypripedium bucolique
1683 A426 30c Cypripedium sullanum

Eduardo Agramonte (1849-1872), Physicist A438

1972, Mar. 8
1684 A438 3c Portrait by F. Martinez

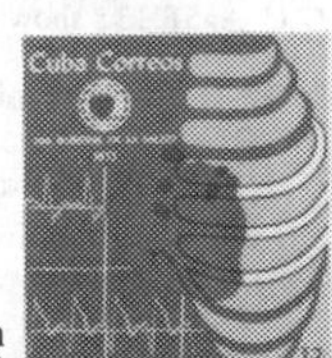
World Health Day — A439

1972, Apr. 7 **Wmk. 376**
1685 A439 13c multi

Soviet Space Program — A440

1972, Apr. 12 **Unwmk.**
1686 A440 1c Sputnik 1
1687 A440 2c Vostok 1
1688 A440 3c Valentina Tereshkova
1689 A440 4c Alexei Leonov
1690 A440 5c Lunokhod 1, moon vehicle
1691 A440 13c Linking Soyuz capsules
1692 A440 30c Victims of Soyuz 11 accident

Stamp Day — A441

Designs: 13c, Postmaster-Gen. Vicente Mora Pera, by Ramon Loy. 30c, Soldier's Letter, Cuba to Venezuela, 1897.

1972, Apr. 24
1693 A441 13c shown
Size: 48x39mm.
1694 A441 30c multi

Labor Day — A442

Jose Marti, Ho Chi Minh — A443

3rd Conference Against War in Indo-China, May 19 — A444

1972, May 1 **Wmk. 376**
1695 A442 3c multi

1972, May 19
1696 A443 3c shown
1697 A444 13c shown
1698 A443 30c Roses, conference emblem

Metropolitan Museum Type of 1971

Portraits: 1c, Salvador del Muro, by J. Del Rio. 2c, Luis de las Casas, by Del Rio. 3c, Cristopher Columbus, anonymous. 4c, Tomas Gamba, by V. Escobar. 5c, Maria Galarraga, by Escobar. 13c, Isabel II, by Federico Madrazo. 30c, Carlos II, by Miguel Melero.

1972, May 25 **Unwmk.**
Size: 34x43½mm.
1699 A420 1c multi
1700 A420 2c multi
1701 A420 3c multi
1702 A420 4c multi
1703 A420 5c multi
Size: 34x51½mm.
1704 A420 13c multi
1705 A420 30c multi

Children's Songs Competition, Natl. Library A445

1972, June 5 **Wmk. 376**
1706 A445 3c multi

Thoroughbred Horses — A446

1972, June 30 **Unwmk.**
1707 A446 1c Tarpan
1708 A446 2c Kertag
1709 A446 3c Creole
1710 A446 4c Andalusian
1711 A446 5c Arabian
1712 A446 13c Quarter horse
1713 A446 30c Pursang

Frank Pais (d. 1957), Educator, Revolutionary — A447

1972, July 26 **Wmk. 376**
1714 A447 13c blk & red

1972 Summer Olympics, Munich, Aug. 26-Sept. 10 — A448

1972, Aug. 26 **Unwmk.**
1715 A448 1c Athlete, emblems, vert.
1716 A448 2c "M," boxing
1717 A448 3c "U," weight lifting
1718 A448 4c "N," fencing
1719 A448 5c "I," rifle shooting
1720 A448 13c "C," running
1721 A448 30c "H," basketball

Souvenir Sheet
Imperf
1722 A448 50c Gymnastics

Stamp in No. 1722 has simulated perforations; gold and dark ultra inscribed margin pictures '72 Summer Games emblem. Size: 64x81mm.

Intl. Hydrological Decade — A449

Landscapes: 1c, Tree Trunks, by Domingo Ramos. 3c, Cyclone, by Tiburcio Lorenzo. 8c, Vinales, by Ramos. 30c, Forest and Brook, by Antonio R. Morey, vert.

1972, Sept. 20
1723 A449 1c multi
1724 A449 3c multi
1725 A449 8c multi
1726 A449 30c multi

Scott's editorial staff cannot undertake to identify, authenticate or appraise stamps and postal markings.

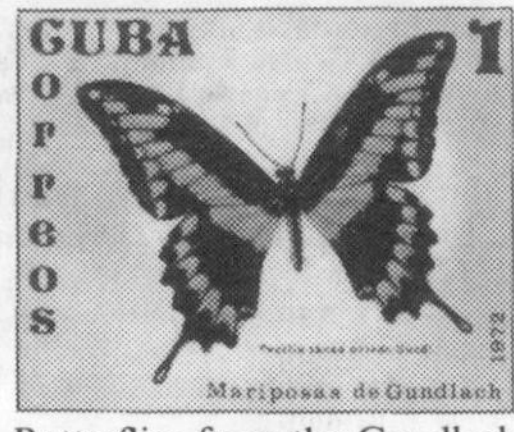
Butterflies from the Gundlach Collection — A450

1972, Sept. 25
1727 A450 1c Papilio thoas oviedo
1728 A450 2c Papilio devilliers
1729 A450 3c Papilio polixenes polixenes
1730 A450 4c Papilio androgeus epidaurus
1731 A450 5c Papilio cayguanabus
1732 A450 13c Papilio andraemon hernandezi
1733 A450 30c Papilio celadon

A451

Miguel de Cervantes Saavedra (1547-1616), Spanish Author — A452

Paintings by A. Fernandez: 3c, In La Mancha, vert. 13c, Battle with Wine Skins. 30c, Don Quixote de La Mancha, vert. 50c, Scene from Don Quixote, by Jose Moreno Carbonero.

1972, Sept. 29
Size: 34½x46mm (3c, 30c)
1734 A451 3c multi
1735 A451 13c shown
1736 A451 30c multi

Souvenir Sheet
Perf. 12½ on 3 Sides
1737 A452 50c shown

No. 1737 has multicolored decorative margin continuing the painting. Size: 120x80mm.

Guerrilla Day, 5th Anniv. — A453

1972, Oct. 8
1738 A453 3c Ernesto "Che" Guevara
1739 A453 13c Tamara "Tania" Bunke
1740 A453 30c Guido "Inti" Peredo

Traditional Musical Instruments A454

1972, Oct. 25
1741 A454 3c Abwe (rattles)
1742 A454 13c Bonko enchemiya (drum)
1743 A454 30c Iya (drum)

MATEX '72, 3rd Natl. Philatelic Exhibition, Matanzas — A455

1972, Nov. 18 **Wmk. 376**
1744 A455 13c No. 467
1745 A455 30c No. C49

Nos. 1744-1745 printed se-tenant with insribed labels picturing Type A232, emblem of the Cuban Philatelic Federation.

Historic Ships A456

1972, Nov. 30 **Unwmk.**
1746 A456 1c Viking long boat, 6th-9th cent.
1747 A456 2c Caravel, 15th cent., vert.
1748 A456 3c Galleass, 16th cent.
1749 A456 4c Galleon, 17th cent., vert.
1750 A456 5c Clipper, 19th cent.
1751 A456 13c Steam packet, 19th cent.

Size: 52½x29mm.
1752 A456 30c Atomic icebreaker Lenin, 20th cent.

UNESCO Save Venice Campaign — A457

1972, Dec. 8
1753 A457 3c Lion of St. Mark
1754 A457 13c Bridge of Sighs, vert.
1755 A457 30c St. Mark's Cathedral

Cuba, World Amateur Baseball Champion in 1972 — A458

Sport Events, 1972 — A459

1972, Dec. 15
1756 A458 3c Umpire

1972, Dec. 22
1757 A459 1c shown
1758 A458 2c Pole vault
1759 A458 3c like No. 1756
1760 A458 4c Wrestling
1761 A458 5c Fencing
1762 A458 13c Boxing
1763 A458 30c Marlin

Barrientos Memorial Athletics Championships, 11th Amateur Baseball Championships, Cerro Pelado Intl. Tournament, Central American and Caribbean Fencing Tournament, Giraldo Cordova Tournament, Ernest Hemingway Natl. Fishing Contest.

No. 1759 inscribed "XI serie nacional de beisbol aficionado."

Medals Won by Cubans at the 1972 Summer Olympics, Munich A460

Designs: 1c, Bronze medal, Women's 100-meter. 2c, Bronze, women's relay. 3c, Gold, 54kg boxing. 4c, Silver, 81kg boxing. 5c, Bronze, 51kg boxing. 13c, Gold, 87kg boxing. 30c, Gold, silver cup, heavy-weight boxing. 50c, Bronze medal, basketball.

1973, Jan. 28
1764 A460 1c multi
1765 A460 2c multi
1766 A460 3c multi
1767 A460 4c multi
1768 A460 5c multi
1769 A460 13c multi
1770 A460 30c multi

Souvenir Sheet
Imperf
1771 A460 50c multi

Stamp in No. 1771 has simulated perforations; lake and sepia margin pictures a photograph of the championship basketball game. Size: 63x88mm.

Portrait by A.M. Esquivel — A461

1973, Feb. 10
1772 A461 13c multi

Gertrudis Gomez de Avellaneda (1814-1873), poet.

Art Type of 1970

Paintings in the Natl. Museum: 1c, Bathers in the Lagoon, by C. Enriquez. 2c, Still-life, by W.C. Heda. 3c, Gallantry, by P. Landaluze. 4c, Return in the Late Afternoon, by C. Troyon. 5c, Elizabetta Mascagni, by F.X. Fabre. 13c, The Picador, by De Lucas

Padilla, horiz. 30c, In the Garden, by Arburu Morell.

1973, Feb. 28
Sizes: 36x46mm, 46x36mm.

1773 A408 1c multi
1774 A408 2c multi
1775 A408 3c multi
1776 A408 4c multi
1777 A408 5c multi
1778 A408 13c multi
1779 A408 30c multi

Orchid Type of 1971

1973, Mar. 26

1780 A426 1c Dendrobium hybrid
1781 A426 2c Cypripedium exul
1782 A426 3c Vanda miss. joaquin rose marie
1783 A426 4c Phalaenopsis schilleriana
1784 A426 5c Vanda gilbert tribulet
1785 A426 13c Dendrobium hybrid, diff.
1786 A426 30c Arachnis catherine

World Health Day — A462

1973, Apr. 7 **Wmk. 376**

1787 A462 10c multi, *buff*

World Health Organization, 25th anniv.

Anti-Polio Campaign — A463

1973, Apr. 9 **Unwmk.**

1788 A463 3c multi

Soviet Space Program A464

1973, Apr. 12

1789 A464 1c Soyuz rocket launch, vert.
1790 A464 2c Luna 1, Moon
1791 A464 3c Luna 16 taking-off from Moon, vert.
1792 A464 4c Venus 7
1793 A464 5c Molnia 1, vert.
1794 A464 13c Mars 3
1795 A464 30c Radar observation ship, Yuri Gagarin

Stamp Day A465

Postmarks: 13c, Santiago de Cuba, 1760. 30c, Havana, 1760.

1973, Apr. 24

1796 A465 13c multi
1797 A465 30c multi

See Nos. 1888-1891.

Portrait by A. Espinosa — A466

1973, May 11

1798 A466 13c multi

Maj.-Gen. Ignacio Agramonte (1841-1873).

Birthplace, Thorn, and Inventions — A467

Copernicus Monument, Warsaw — A468

1973, May 25

1799 A467 3c shown
1800 A467 13c Copernicus, spacecraft
1801 A467 30c Manuscript, Frombork Tower

Souvenir Sheet
Perf. 12½ on 3 Sides.

1802 A468 50c shown

500th anniversary of the birth of Nicolaus Copernicus (1473-1543), Polish astronomer. No. 1802 has multicolored inscribed margin continuing the design. Size: 90x84mm.

Improvement of School Education — A469

1973, June 12 **Wmk. 376**

1803 A469 13c multi

Cattle — A470

1973, June 28 **Unwmk.**

1804 A470 1c Jersey
1805 A470 2c Charolaise
1806 A470 3c Creole
1807 A470 4c Swiss
1808 A470 5c Holstein
1809 A470 13c Santa gertrudis
1810 A470 30c Brahman

10th Communist Festival of Youths and Students, East Berlin — A471

1973, July 10 **Wmk. 376**

1811 A471 13c multi

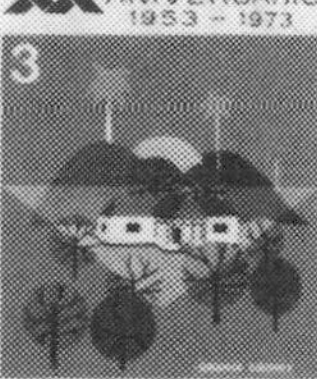

20th Anniv. of the Revolution A472

1973, July 26 **Unwmk.**

1812 A472 3c Siboney Farm, Santiago de Cuba
1813 A472 13c Mocada Barracks
1814 A472 30c Revolution Plaza, Havana

10th Anniv. of the Revolutionary Navy — A473

1973, Aug. 3 **Wmk. 376**

1815 A473 3c Midshipman, missle frigate

Interior, by Manuel Vicens A474

Paintings in the Natl. Museum: 1c, Amalia of Saxony, by J.K. Rossler. 3c, Margarita of Austria, by J. Pantoja de la Cruz. 4c, City Hall Official, anonymous. 5c, View of Santiago de Cuba, by Hernandez Giro. 12c, The Catalan, by J.J. Tejada. 30c, Alley in Guayo, by Tejada.

1973, Aug. 30 **Unwmk.**
Sizes: 26½x41mm (1c, 3c), 28½x39mm (4c, 13c, 30c)

1816 A474 1c multi
1817 A474 2c multi
1818 A474 3c multi
1819 A474 4c multi
1820 A474 5c multi
1821 A474 13c multi
1822 A474 30c multi

WMO Emblem, Paintings by J. Madrazo A475

1973, Sept. 4

1823 A475 8c Spring
1824 A475 8c Summer
1825 A475 8c Fall
1826 A475 8c Winter

World Meteorogical Organization, cent. Nos. 1823-1826 printed se-tenant in strips of 4; frame reversed on 2nd and 4th stamp in strip.

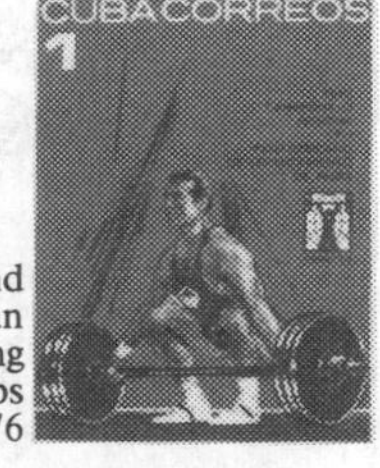

27th World and 1st Pan American Weight Lifting Championships A476

Various weight-lifting positions.

1973, Sept. 12

1827 A476 1c shown
1828 A476 2c multi, diff.
1829 A476 3c multi, diff.
1830 A476 4c multi, diff.
1831 A476 5c multi, diff.
1832 A476 13c multi, diff.
1833 A476 30c multi, diff.

Flowering Plants — A477

1973, Sept. 28

1834 A477 1c Erythrina standleyana
1835 A477 2c Lantana camara
1836 A477 3c Canavalia maritima
1837 A477 4c Dichromena colorata
1838 A477 5c Borrichia arborescens
1839 A477 13c Anguria pedata
1840 A477 30c Cordia sebestena

8th World Trade Union Congress, Varna, Bulgaria — A478

1973, Oct. 5 **Wmk. 376**

1841 A478 13c multi

Cuban Natl. Ballet, 25th Anniv. A479

Sea Shells A480

1973, Oct. 28 **Unwmk.**

1842 A479 13c gold & brt ultra

1973, Oct. 29

1843 A480 1c Liguus fasciatus fasciatus
1844 A480 2c Liguus fasciatus guitarti
1845 A480 3c Liguus fasciatus whartoni
1846 A480 4c Liguus fasciatus angelae

1847 A480 5c Liguus fasciatus trinidadense
1848 A480 13c Liguus blainianus
1849 A480 30c Liguus vittatus

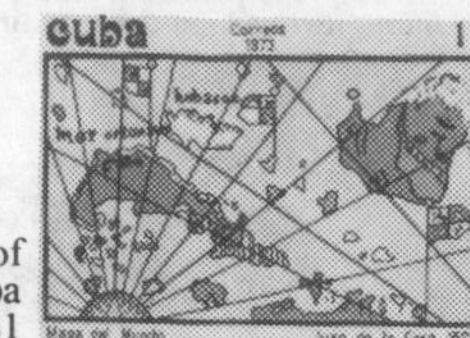

Maps of Cuba A481

1973, Oct. 29
1850 A481 1c Juan de la Cosa, 1502
1852 A481 3c Ortelius, 1572
1853 A481 13c Bellini, 1762
1854 A481 40c 1973

15th Anniversary of the Revolution — A482

1974, Jan. 2
1854 A482 1c No. 625
1855 A482 3c No. 626
1856 A482 13c No. C200
1857 A482 40c No. C201

Woman, by F. Ponce de Leon — A483

Amilcar Cabral — A484

Portraits in the Camaguey Museum: 3c, Mexican Girls, by J. Arche. 8c, Young Woman, by A. Menocal. 10c, Mulatto Woman Drinking from Coconut, by L. Romanach. 13c, Head of an Old Man, by J. Arburu.

1974, Jan. 10
1858 A483 1c multi
1859 A483 3c multi
1860 A483 8c multi
1861 A483 10c multi
1862 A483 13c multi

1974, Jan. 20
1863 A484 13c multi

Amilcar Cabral, Guinea-Bissau freedom fighter, 1st death anniv.

Lenin, by I.V. Kosmin — A485

12th Central American and Caribbean Games, Santo Domingo — A486

1974, Jan. 21
1864 A485 30c multi

50th Death anniv. of Lenin.

1974, Feb. 8
1865 A486 1c Emblem
1867 A487 2c Javelin
1868 A487 3c Boxing
1869 A487 4c Baseball, horiz.
1870 A487 13c Basketball, horiz.
1871 A487 30c Volleyball, horiz.

Portrait by F. Martinez — A487

Portrait of a Man, by J.B. Vermay — A488

1974, Feb. 27
1871 A487 13c multi

Carlos M. de Cespedes (d. 1874), patriot.

1974, Mar. 7

Paintings in the Natl. Museum: 2c, The Wet Nurse, by C.A. Van Loo. 3c, Cattle in River, by R. Morey. 4c, Village, by Morey. 13c, Faun and Bacchus, by Rubens. 30c, Young Woman Playing Cards, by R. Madrazo.

Sizes: 41½x27mm.

1872 A488 1c shown
1873 A488 2c multi
1874 A488 3c multi
1875 A488 4c multi
1876 A488 13c multi
1877 A488 30c multi

Council for Mutual Economic Assistance (COMECON), 25th Anniv. — A489

1974, Mar. 15
1878 A489 30c Comecon building, Moscow

Visit of Leonid I. Brezhnev to Cuba, Jan. 28-Feb.3. — A490

1974, Mar. 28
1879 A490 13c Jose Marti, Lenin, flags
1880 A490 30c Brezhnev, Fidel Castro

Science Fiction A491

Paintings by A. Sokolov.

1974, Apr. 12
1881 A491 1c Martian Crater
1882 A491 2c Fiery Labyrinth
1883 A491 3c Amber Wave
1884 A491 4c Flight Through Space
1885 A491 13c Planet in Nebula
1886 A491 30c World of Two Suns

Cosmonauts Day.

UPU, Cent. A492

1974, Apr. 15
1887 A492 30c Letter, 1874

Stamp Day Type of 1973

Postmarks.

1974, Apr. 24
1888 A465 1c Havana
1889 A465 3c Matanzas
1890 A465 13c Trinidad
1891 A465 20c Guana Vacoa

18th Sports Congress of Friendly Armies — A493

1974, May 5 **Wmk. 376**
1892 A493 3c multi

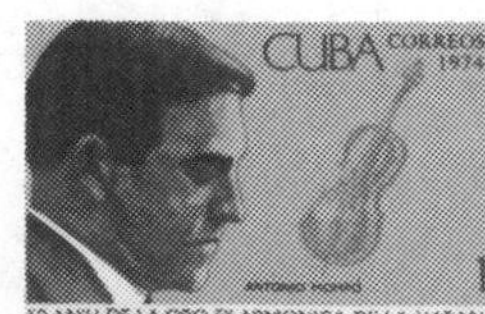

Felipe Poey (1799-1891), Naturalist — A494

Designs: 1c, 4c, Butterflies. 2c, 13c, Sea shells. 3c, 30c, 50c, Fish.

1974, May 26 ***Perf. 12½x12***
1893 A494 1c Eumaeus atala atala
1894 A494 2c Pineria terebra
1895 A494 3c Chaetodon sedentarius
1896 A494 4c Eurema dina dina
1897 A494 13c Hemitrochus fuscolabiata
1898 A494 30c Eupomacentrus partitus

Souvenir Sheet

Imperf

1899 A494 50c Apogon binotatus

Stamp in No. 1899 has simulated perforations; multicolored inscribed margin pictures portrait of Poey. Size: 90x66mm.

Havana Philharmonic Orchestra, 50th Anniv. — A495

Designs: 1c, Antonio Mompo and cello. 3c, Cesar Perez Sentenat and piano. 5c, Pedro Mercado and trumpet. 10c, Pedro Sanjuan and Havana Philharmonic emblem. 13c, Roberto Ondina and flute.

1974, June 8 ***Perf. 12½***
1900 A495 1c multi
1901 A495 3c multi
1902 A495 5c multi
1903 A495 10c multi
1904 A495 13c multi

Garden Flowers — A496

1974, June 12
1905 A496 1c Heliconia humilis
1906 A496 2c Anthurium andraeanum
1907 A496 3c Canna generalis
1908 A496 4c Alpinia purpurata
1909 A496 13c Gladiolus grandiflorus
1910 A496 30c Amomum capitatum

SEMI-POSTAL STAMPS

Pierre and Marie Curie — SP1

Wmk. Star (106)

1938, Nov. 23 **Engr.** ***Perf. 10***
B1 SP1 2c + 1c sal 3.50 1.25
B2 SP1 5c + 1c dp ultra 3.50 1.50

Issued in commemoration of the 40th anniversary of the discovery of radium by Pierre and Marie Curie. The surtax was for the benefit of the International Union for the Control of Cancer.

"Agriculture" Supporting "Industry" SP2

Wmk. 321

1959, May 7 **Litho.** ***Perf. 12½***
B3 SP2 2c + 1c car & ultra 35 15

Agricultural reforms. See Nos. 624, CB1.

Nurse — SP3

Perf. 12½, Imperf.

1959, Sept. 22 **Wmk. 229**
B4 SP3 2c + 1c crim rose 30 15

AIR POST STAMPS

Seaplane over Havana Harbor AP1

Wmk. Star. (106)

1927, Nov. 1 **Engr.** ***Perf. 12***
C1 SP1 5c dk bl 5.00 20

Type of 1927 Issue Overprinted **LINDBERGH FEBRERO 1928**

1928, Feb. 8
C2 AP1 5c car rose 2.50 1.25

No. 283 Surcharged in Red

CORREO AEREO NACIONAL

10¢ 10¢

1930, Oct. 27 **Unwmk.**
C3 A44 10c on 25c vio 2.50 1.25

Airplane and Coast of Cuba — AP3

For Foreign Postage.

1931, Feb. 26 **Wmk. 106** ***Perf. 10***

C4 AP3 5c green	50	5
C5 AP3 10c dk bl	50	5
C6 AP3 15c rose	1.00	30
C7 AP3 20c brown	1.00	6
C8 AP3 30c dk vio	1.50	20
C9 AP3 40c dp org	3.50	40
C10 AP3 50c ol grn	4.00	40
C11 AP3 1p black	6.00	1.00
Nos. C4-C11 (8)	18.00	2.46

See No. C40.

Airplane AP4

For Domestic Postage.

1931-46

C12 AP4 5c rose vio ('32)	40	6
a. 5c brn vio ('36)	40	6
C13 AP4 10c gray blk	40	5
C14 AP4 20c car rose	3.00	85
C14A AP4 20c rose pink ('46)	1.25	20
C15 AP4 50c dk bl	5.00	85
Nos. C12-C15 (5)	10.05	2.01

See also No. C130.

Type of 1931 Surcharged in Black

PRIMER TREN AEREO
INTERNACIONAL. 1935
O'Meara y du Pont + 10 cts.

1935, Apr. 24 ***Perf. 10***
C16 AP3 10c + 10c red 7.50 6.00

Imperf
C17 AP3 10c + 10c red 30.00 30.00

Matanzas Issue.

Air View of Matanzas AP5

Designs: 10c, Airship "Macon." 20c, Airplane "The Four Winds." 50c, Air View of Fort San Severino.

Wmk. Wavy Lines. (229)
1936, May 5 **Photo.** ***Perf. 12½***

C18 AP5 5c violet	75	50
C19 AP5 10c yel org	1.50	75
C20 AP5 20c green	5.00	3.00
C21 AP5 50c grnsh sl	9.00	6.00

Exist imperf. Price 20% more.

"Lightning" AP9

Allegory of Flight AP10

1936, Nov. 18
C22 AP9 5c violet 2.50 50
C23 AP10 10c org brn 3.00 75

Issued in commemoration of the centenary of the birth of Major General Maximo Gomez.

Flat Arch (Panama) AP11

Carlos Antonio Lopez (Paraguay) AP12

Inca Gate, Cuzco (Peru) AP13

Atlacatl (Salvador) AP14

José Enrique Rodó (Uruguay) AP15

Simón Bolívar (Venezuela) AP16

Wmk. 106
1937, Oct. 13 **Engr.** ***Perf. 10***

C24 AP11 5c red	6.00	5.00
C25 AP12 5c red	6.00	5.00
C26 AP13 10c blue	7.00	6.00
C27 AP14 10c blue	7.00	6.00
C28 AP15 20c green	8.00	7.50
C29 AP16 20c green	8.00	7.50
Nos. C24-C29 (6)	42.00	37.00

Issued for the benefit of the Association of American Writers and Artists. See note after No. 354.

Type of 1927 Overprinted in Black

1913 1938
ROSILLO
Key West-Habana

1938, May **Wmk. 106**
C30 AP1 5c dk org 5.00 1.50

Issued in commemoration of the first airplane flight from Key West to Havana, made by Domingo Rosillo, 1913.

Type of 1931-32 Overprinted

EXPERIMENTO DEL COHETE Postal AÑO DE 1939

1939, Oct. 15
C31 AP4 10c emerald 25.00 7.50

Issued in connection with an experimental postal rocket flight held at Havana.

Sir Rowland Hill, Map of Cuba and First Stamps of Britain, Spanish Cuba and Republic of Cuba — AP17

1940, Nov. 28 **Engr.** **Wmk. 106**
C32 AP17 10c brown 4.00 1.50

Souvenir Sheet

Unwmk. ***Imperf.***
C33 AP17 10c lt brn, sheet of four 12.50 10.00
a. Single stamp 2.80 2.00

Centenary of the first postage stamp.

Sheet measures 128x178mm. Sheet sold for 60c.

No. C33 exists with each of the four stamps overprinted in black: "Exposicion de la ACNU/24 de Octubre de 1951/Dia de las Naciones" and "Historia de la Aviacion" in lower margin. Price, $70.

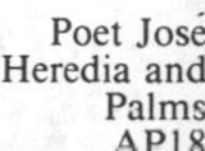

Poet José Heredia and Palms AP18

Heredia and Niagara Falls — AP19

1940, Dec. 30 **Wmk. 106**
C34 AP18 5c emerald 1.50 75
C35 AP19 10c grnsh sl 3.00 1.00

Issued to commemorate the centenary of the death of José Maria Heredia y Campuzano (1803-1839), poet and patriot.

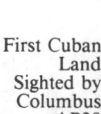

First Cuban Land Sighted by Columbus AP20

Columbus Lighthouse AP21

1944, May 19
C36 AP20 5c ol grn 60 15
C37 AP21 10c sl blk 1.25 40

Issued to commemorate the 450th anniversary of the discovery of America.

Conference of La Mejorana (Meceo, Gomez and Marti) AP22

1948, May 21 **Wmk. 229** ***Perf. 12½***
C38 AP22 8c org yel & blk 2.00 75

Issued to commemorate the 50th anniversary of the start of the War of 1895.

Souvenir Sheet.
No. C33 Overprinted in Ultramarine

1948, May 21 **Unwmk.** ***Imperf.***
C39 AP17 10c sheet of four 8.00 7.00

The overprint is applied in the center of the four stamps, so that a portion falls on each.

Issued in honor of the American Air Mail Society Convention, Havana, May 21 to 23, 1948. The sheets sold for 60c each.

Type of 1931.

1948, June 15 **Wmk. 106** ***Perf. 10***
C40 AP3 8c org brn 1.50 20

Narciso Lopez Landing at Cardenas — AP23

Flag on Cuban Fort — AP24

Flag on Morro Castle, Havana — AP25

Engraved and Lithographed
1951, July 3 **Wmk. 229** ***Perf. 13***

C41 AP23 5c ol grn, ultra & red	1.25	25
C42 AP24 8c red brn, bl & red	2.00	25
C43 AP25 25c gray blk, bl & red	3.00	1.50

Centenary of adoption of Cuba's flag.

Souvenir Sheet.
No. 365a Overprinted in Green.

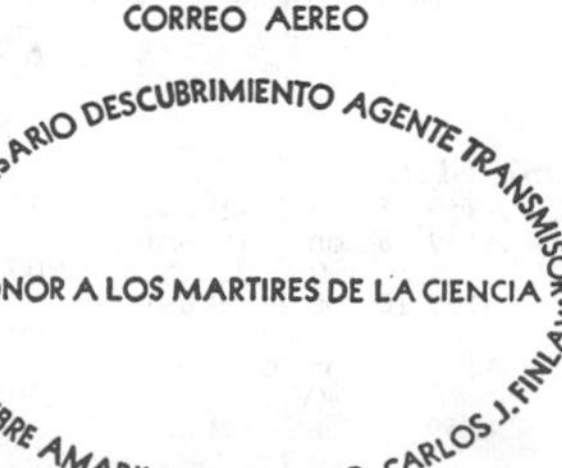

1901 **1951**

(Reduced Illustration of Overprint)

1951, Aug. 24 **Unwmk.** ***Imperf.***
C43A Sheet of four 6.00 5.00

Issued to commemorate the 50th anniversary of the discovery of the cause of yellow fever by Dr. Carlos J. Finlay, and to honor the martyrs of science.

No. C43A measures 127x177 mm. and contains two each of Nos. 364 and 365 imperforate, with upper and lower marginal inscriptions.

Resignation Play of Dr. Lasker AP26

Capablanca Making "The Exact Play" — AP27

Design: 25c, Capablanca.

Wmk. 229

1951, Nov. 1 Photo. *Perf. 13*

C44	AP26	5c bl grn & yel	5.00	1.00
C45	AP27	8c ultra & cl	7.50	1.25
C46	A165	25c brn & dk brn	15.00	4.00

Issued to commemorate the 30th anniversary of the winning of the World Chess title by José Raul Capablanca.

Morrillo Types of Regular Issue, 1951.

Wmk. 106

1951, Nov. 22 Engr. *Perf. 10*

C47	A167	5c violet	1.00	15
C48	A168	8c dp grn	1.25	25
C49	A169	25c dk brn	2.50	1.50
a.		Souvenir sheet of 6, blk brn, perf. 13	25.00	25.00
b.		Souvenir sheet of 6, grn, imperf.	90.00	90.00

Issued to commemorate the 16th anniversary of the Action of the Morrillo and to honor Antonio Guiteras Holmes who was killed there.

Nos. C49a and C49b contain one each of the 1c, 2c and 5c of types A167-A169 and of the 5c, 8c and 25c airmail stamps of types A167-A169. Marginal inscriptions are typographed in black; coat of arms engraved in color of stamps (black brown or green). Sheets are unwatermarked and measure 124x133mm

Isabella Type of Regular Issue, 1952

1952, Feb. 22

C50	A172	25c purple	3.00	1.00
a.		Souvenir sheet of 2, perf. 11	12.50	10.00
b.		Souvenir sheet of 2, imperf.	15.00	15.00

Issued to commemorate the 500th anniversary of the birth of Queen Isabella I of Spain.

Nos. C50a and C50b contain one each of a 2c of type A172 and a 25c air-mail stamp of type A172. In No. C50a, the 2c and marginal inscriptions are brown carmine; the 25c, dark blue. In No. C50b, the 2c and marginal inscriptions are dark blue; the 25c, brown carmine. Sheets measure 108x18mm.

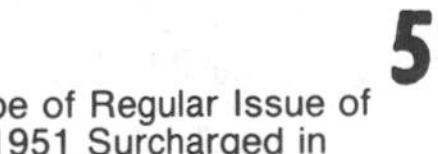

Type of Regular Issue of 1951 Surcharged in Various Colors

1952, Mar. 18

C51	A159	5c on 2c yel brn	50	15
C52	A159	8c on 2c yel brn (C)	1.00	10
C53	A159	10c on 2c yel brn (Bl)	1.00	15
C54	A159	25c on 2c yel brn (V)	1.50	1.00
C55	A159	50c on 2c yel brn (C)	5.00	2.00
C56	A159	1p on 2c yel brn (Bl)	12.50	7.50
		Nos. C51-C56 (6)	21.50	10.90

Country School AP32

Entrance, University of Havana AP33

Designs: 10c, Presidential Mansion, 25c, Banknote.

Wmk. 106

1952, May 27 Engr. *Perf. 12½*

Centers Various Shades of Green.

C57	AP32	5c dk pur	50	10
C58	AP33	8c dk red	75	15
C59	AP32	10c dp bl	1.50	25
C60	AP32	25c dk vio brn	2.50	1.25

Issued to commemorate the 50th anniversary of the foundation of the Republic of Cuba.

Plane and Map AP34

Agustin Parla AP35

1952, July 22 Engr. *Perf. 10*

C61	AP34	8c black	1.25	50
a.		Souv. sheet, 8c dp bl	6.00	6.00
b.		Souv. sheet, 8c dp grn	6.00	6.00
C62	AP35	25c ultra	3.50	1.50
a.		Souv. sheet, 25c dp bl	6.00	6.00
b.		Souv. sheet, 25c dp grn	6.00	6.00

Issued to commemorate the 30th anniversary of the Key West-Mariel flight of Agustin Parla.

The four souvenir sheets are perf. 11, measure 107x95mm. and have marginal inscriptions in the same color as the stamp.

Col. Charles Hernandes y Sandrino — AP36

1952, Oct. 7

C63	AP36	5c orange	75	15
C64	AP36	8c brt yel grn	75	10
C65	AP36	10c dk brn	1.00	25
C66	AP36	15c dk Prus grn	2.00	75
C67	AP36	20c aqua	2.50	1.00
C68	AP36	25c crimson	2.00	1.00
C69	AP36	30c dk vio bl	5.00	2.50
C70	AP36	45c rose lil	5.00	3.50
C71	AP36	50c indigo	3.00	2.50
C72	AP36	1p bister	10.00	5.00
		Nos. C63-C72 (10)	32.00	16.75

Three-fourths of the proceeds from the sale of Nos. C63-C72 were used for the Communications Ministry Employees" Retirement Fund.

Entrance, University of Havana — AP37

F. V. Dominguez, M. Estebanez and F. Capdevila — AP38

Engraved; Centers Typographed

1952, Nov. 27

C73	AP37	5c ind & dk bl	90	35
C74	AP38	25c org & dk grn	2.75	1.25

Issued to commemorate the 81st anniversary of the execution of eight medical students.

AP39

Lockheed Constellation Airliners AP40

1953, May 22 Engr.

C75	AP39	8c org brn	50	6
C76	AP39	15c scarlet	2.00	30

Typographed and Engraved

C77	AP40	2p dp grn & dk brn	30.00	12.50
C78	AP40	5p bl & dk brn	40.00	20.00

See also Nos. C120-C121.

Page of Manifesto of Montecristi AP42

House of Maximo Gomez AP43

Designs: No. C79, Marti in Kingston, Jamaica, No. C80, With Workers in Tampa, Florida. No. C83, Marti addressing liberating army. No. C84, Portrait. No. C85, Dos Rios obelisk. No. C86, Marti's first tomb. No. C87, Present tomb. No. C88, Monument in Havana. No. C89, Martian forge.

1953 Engr. *Perf. 10*

C79	AP42	5c dk car & blk	30	12
C80	AP43	5c dk grn & blk	30	12
C81	AP43	8c dk grn & blk	75	15
C82	AP42	8c dk grn & blk	75	15
C83	AP43	10c dk bl & dk car	1.50	40
C84	AP42	10c dk bl & dk car	1.50	40
C85	AP42	15c vio & gray	1.25	75
C86	AP42	15c vio & gray	1.25	75
C87	AP42	25c brn & car	3.00	1.00
C88	AP42	25c brn & car	3.00	1.00
C89	AP43	50c yel & bl	5.00	2.00
		Nos. C79-C89 (11)	18.60	6.84

Issued to commemorate the centenary of the birth of José Marti.

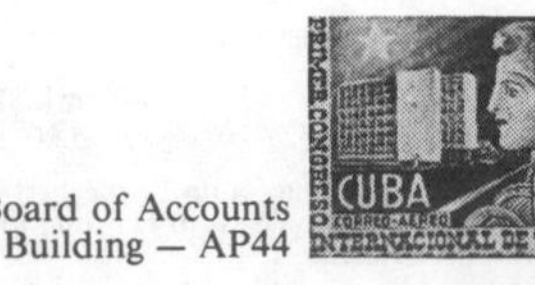

Board of Accounts Building — AP44

Design: 25c, Plane above Board of Accounts Bldg.

1953, Nov. 3

C90	AP44	8c rose car	1.00	25
C91	AP44	25c dk gray grn	2.00	1.00

Issued to publicize the First International Congress of Boards of Account, Havana, November 2-9, 1953.

Miguel Coyula Llaguno AP45

Antonio Ginard Rojas AP46

Designs: 10c, Gregorio Hernandez Saez. 1p, Communications Association Flag.

1954

C92	AP45	5c dk bl	50	15
C93	AP46	8c red vio	60	25
C94	AP46	10c orange	1.25	35
C95	AP45	1p black	8.50	6.00

See note after No. C72.

Four-engine Plane and Cane Field — AP47

Plane and Harvesters Cutting Cane — AP48

Designs in Lower Triangle: 10c, Tractor pulling loaded wagons. 15c, Train of sugar cane. 20c, Modern mill. 25c, Evaporators. 30, Sacks of sugar. 40c, Loading sugar on ship. 45c, Ox cart. 50c, Primitive sugar mill. 1p, Alvaro Reinoso.

1954, Apr. 27 Engr.

C96	AP47	5c yel grn	60	10
C97	AP48	8c brown	1.25	8
C98	AP48	10c dk grn	1.50	15
C99	AP48	15c hn brn	75	35
C100	AP48	20c blue	1.00	50
C101	AP48	25c scarlet	1.50	50
C102	AP48	30c lil rose	2.50	75
C103	AP48	40c dp bl	3.00	1.00
C104	AP48	45c violet	6.00	2.00
C105	AP48	50c brt bl	4.00	1.25
C106	AP47	1p dk gray bl	8.00	2.50
		Nos. C96-C106 (11)	30.10	9.18

Sanatorium Type of Regular Issue, 1954.

1954, Sept. 21 Wmk. 106 *Perf. 10*

C107	A186	9c dp grn	1.00	50

Dolz Type of Regular Issue, 1954.

1954, Dec. 23

C108	A188	12c carmine	1.00	50

Issued to commemorate the centenary of the birth of Maria Luisa Dolz, educator and defender of women's rights.

Rotary Type of Regular Issue, 1955.

1955, Feb. 23

C109	A190	12c carmine	1.25	40

Issued to commemorate the 50th anniversary of the founding of Rotary International.

Stamps of 1855 and 1905, Palace of Fine Arts AP52

Designs (including 2 stamps): 12c, Plaza de la Fraternidad. 24c, View of Havana. 30c, Plaza de la Republica.

1955, Apr. 24 ***Perf. 12½***

C110 AP52 8c dk grnsh bl & grn 1.25 50
C111 AP52 12c dk ol grn & red 1.50 35
C112 AP52 24c dk red & ultra 1.75 1.00
C113 AP52 30c dp org & brn 3.75 2.00

Issued to commemorate the centenary of Cuba's first postage stamps.

Mariel Bay — AP53

Views: 12c, Varadero beach. 1p, Vinales valley.

1955, June 22 **Wmk. 106**

C114 AP53 8c dk car & dk grn 75 30
C115 AP53 12c dk ocher & brt bl 1.00 25
C116 AP53 1p dk grn & ocher 6.00 4.00

See note after No. C72.

Map of Crocier's 1914 Flight — AP54

Design: 30c, Jaime Gonzalez Crocier in plane.

1955, July 4 ***Perf. 10***

C117 AP54 12c red & dk grn 60 20
C118 AP54 30c dk grn & mag 2.25 60

Issued to honor Jaime Gonzalez Crocier, aviation pioneer, on the 35th anniversary of his death.

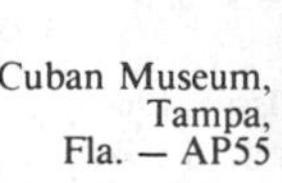

Cuban Museum, Tampa, Fla. — AP55

1955, July 1 **Engr.** ***Perf. 12½***

C119 AP55 12c red & dk brn 1.10 35

Issued to commemorate the centenary of Tampa's incorporation as a town.

Lockheed Type of 1953

Typographed and Engraved

1955, Sept. 21 **Wmk. 106**

C120 AP40 2p bl & ol grn 17.50 8.50
C121 AP40 5p dp rose & ol grn 37.50 16.50

Wright Brothers' Plane and Stamps AP56

Designs: 12c, Spirit of St. Louis. 24c, Graf Zeppelin. 30c, Constellation passenger plane. 50c, Convair jet fighter.

Engraved and Photogravure

1955, Nov. 12 Wmk. 106 ***Perf. 12½***

Inscription and Plane in Black.

C122 AP56 8c car & bl 1.00 35
C123 AP56 12c yel grn & car 2.25 70
C124 AP56 24c vio & car 7.00 2.50
C125 AP56 30c bl & red org 6.00 3.25
C126 AP56 50c ol grn & red org 8.00 4.00
a. Souvenir sheet of 5 40.00 45.00
Nos. C122-C126 (5) 24.25 10.80

Issued to commemorate the International Centenary Philatelic Exhibition in Havana, Nov. 12-19, 1955.

No. C126a is printed on thick paper and measures 140x178mm. It contains one each of Nos. C122-C126 with the background of each stamp printed in a different color from the perforated stamps. The sheet is inscribed in black "Republica de Cuba. Souvenir. Exposition Filatelica Internacional Centenario 1955" and "XXXII Convencion de la American Airmail Society."

"Three Friends" and Gen. Emilio Nunez AP57

Design: 12c, Landing on the Cuban Coast.

1955, Dec. 27 **Engr.** **Unwmk.**

C127 AP57 8c ultra & dk car 1.00 40
C128 AP57 12c grn & dk red brn 1.50 50

Issued to commemorate the centenary of the birth of Gen. Emilio Nuñez, Cuban revolutionary hero.

Post Type of Regular Issue, 1956.

Design: 12c, Bishop P. A. Morell de Santa Cruz (1694-1768).

1956, March 27 **Wmk. 106**

C129 A197 12c dk brn & grn 90 30

Bicentenary of the Cuban post.

Plane Type of 1931-46.

1956 **Engr.** ***Perf. 10***

C130 AP4 50c grnsh bl 2.00 1.00

Portrait Type of Regular Issue, 1956.

1956, May 2 ***Perf. 12½***

Portraits: 8c, Gen. Julio Sanguily. 12c, Gen. Jose Maria Aguirre. 30c, Col. Ernesto Ponts Sterling.

Portraits in Black.

C131 A198 8c brown 75 20
C132 A198 12c dl yel 1.25 20
C133 A198 30c indigo 2.25 1.50

See note after No. C72.

Mother and Child AP60

Masonic Temple Havana AP61

1956, May 13 Wmk. 106 ***Perf. 12½***

C134 AP60 12c ultra & red 80 25

Issued in honor of Mother's Day 1956.

1956, June 5

C135 AP61 12c ol grn 60 20

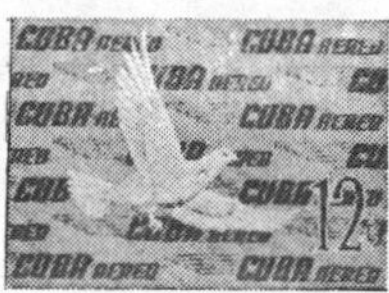

Pigeon AP62

Gundlach Hawk — AP63

Birds: 8c, Wood duck. 19c, Herring gulls. 24c, White pelicans. 29c, Common merganser. 30c, Quail. 50c, Herons (great white, great blue and Wurdemann's). 1p, Northern caracara. 2p, Middle American jacana. 5p, Ivory-billed woodpecker.

1956

C136 AP62 8c blue 50 15
C137 AP62 12c dk bl 7.00 10
C138 AP63 14c green 1.50 25
C139 AP63 19c redsh brn 1.00 50
C140 AP63 24c lil rose 1.25 50
C141 AP62 29c green 1.75 50
C142 AP62 30c dk ol bis 2.00 75
C143 AP63 50c sl blk 4.00 1.00
C144 AP63 1p dk car rose 6.00 2.00
C145 AP62 2p rose vio 12.50 4.00
C146 AP63 5p brt red 30.00 8.00
Nos. C136-C146 (11) 67.50 17.75

See also No. C205.

Inauguración Edificio Club Filatélico de la República de Cuba Julio 13 de 1956.

8¢

Type of 1956 Surcharged

Design: 24c, White pelicans.

1956, July 13

C147 AP63 8c on 24 dp org 1.00 35

Issued to commemorate the opening of the new building of the Cuba Philatelic Club, Havana, July 14, 1956.

Hubert de Blanck AP64

Church of Our Lady of Charity AP65

1956, July 6

C148 AP64 12c ultra 90 25

Issued to commemorate the centenary of the birth of Hubert de Blanck (1856-1932), composer.

1956, Sept. 8

C149 AP65 12c grn & car 90 40
a. Souvenir sheet of 2, imperf. 9.00 8.00

Issued in honor of Our Lady of Charity of Cobre, patroness of Cuba.

No. C149a contains one each of Nos. 559 and C149 with bright blue marginal inscription and coat of arms. Size: 76x77mm. No. C149a exists with yellow of No. 559 omitted.

Benjamin Franklin AP66

1956, Oct. 5 **Engr.** ***Perf. 12½***

C150 AP66 12c red brn 1.00 40

Issued to commemorate the 250th anniversary of the birth of Benjamin Franklin.

Type of 1956 Surcharged in Blue

Design: 2p, Middle American jacana.

1956, Oct. 26 **Wmk. 106**

C151 AP62 12c on 2p dk gray 1.50 75

Issued in honor of the 12th Inter-American Press Association Conference, Havana.

Lord Baden-Powell — AP67

1957, Feb. 22

C152 AP67 12c slate 1.50 35

Issued to commemorate the centenary of the birth of Lord Baden-Powell, founder of the Boy Scouts.

Hanabanilla Waterfall AP68

Designs: 12c, Sierra de Cubitas. 30c, Puerto Boniato.

1957, March 29

C153 AP68 8c bl & red 75 20
C154 AP68 12c grn & red 1.20 25
C155 AP68 30c ol grn & dk pur 2.00 1.00

See note after No. 457.

Philatelic Club, Havana AP69

Fingerprint AP70

1957, Apr. 24 Wmk. 106 ***Perf. 12½***

C156 AP69 12c yel, grn & brn 1.00 25

Issued for Stamp Day, Apr. 24, and the National Philatelic Exhibition.

1957, Apr. 30

C157 AP70 12c cl brn 90 20

Issued in honor of the centenary of the birth (in 1856) of Juan Francisco Steegers y Perera, dactyloscopy pioneer.

Baseball Player — AP71

Designs: 12c, Ballerina. 24c, Girl diver. 30c, Boxers.

1957, May 17 Wmk. 106 *Perf. 12½*

C158	AP71	8c ol grn & brn	1.00	35
C159	AP71	12c pale vio & brn	1.75	40
C160	AP71	24c brt bl & brn	2.50	1.00
C161	AP71	30c org & brn	3.50	1.50

Issued to honor young Cuban athletes.

Joaquin de Aguero AP72

Jeanette Ryder AP73

1957, July 4

C162	AP72	12c indigo	90	25

Issued to honor Joaquin de Aguero, Cuban freedom fighter and patriot.

1957, July 17

C163	AP73	12c dk red brn	90	35
a.		Se-tenant with No. 574	2.00	1.00

Printed in sheets of 40, containing alternate copies of Nos. 574 and C163 to honor Mrs. Jeanette Ryder, founder of the Humane Society of Cuba.

José M. de Heredia y Girard AP74

John Robert Gregg AP75

1957, Aug. 16 Engr. Wmk. 106

C164	AP74	8c dk bl vio	50	25

Issued in honor of the poet José Maria de Heredia y Girard (1842-1905), Cubanborn French poet.

Justice Type of Regular Issue, 1957.

1957, Sept. 2 *Perf. 12½*

C165	A214	12c green	90	50

Opening of Palace of Justice, Havana.

1957, Oct. 1

C166	AP75	12c dk grn	80	35

Issued to commemorate the 90th anniversary of the birth of John Robert Gregg, inventor of the Gregg shorthand system.

D. Figarola Caneda AP76

José Marti National Library AP77

1957, Oct. 18 Wmk. 106 *Perf. 12½*

C167	AP76	8c ultra	50	20
C168	AP77	12c chocolate	90	25

Issued to publicize the José Marti National Library.

Foreign postal stationery (stamped envelopes, postal cards and air letter sheets) lies beyond the scope of this Catalogue, which is limited to adhesive postage stamps.

Map of Cuba and U. N. Emblem AP78

1957, Oct. 24

C169	AP78	8c dk grn & brn	75	25
C170	AP78	12c car rose & grn	1.00	50
C171	AP78	30c ind & brt pink	2.50	1.00

Issued for United Nations Day, 1957.

Map of Cuba and Florida AP79

1957, Oct. 28

C172	AP79	12c dk red brn & bl	85	40

Issued to commemorate the 30th anniversary of airmail service from Key West to Havana.

Type of Regular Issue, 1957 and

Stairway and Bell Tower AP80

Design: 12c, Facade of Normal School.

1957, Nov. 19 Engr. *Perf. 12½*

C173	A217	12c ind & ocher	85	20
C174	AP80	30c dk car & gray	1.25	60

Issued to commemorate the centenary of the first Cuban Normal School.

View Types of Regular Issue, 1957.

Views: 8c, El Viso Fort, El Caney. 12c, Sancti Spiritus Church. 30c, Concordia Bridge, Matanzas.

1957, Dec. 17 *Perf. 12½*

C175	A218	8c dk gray & red	75	25
C176	A219	12c brn & gray	1.00	25
C177	A218	30c red brn & bl gray	1.50	85

See note after No. C72.

Hedges Types of Regular Issue, 1958.

Design: 8c, Dayton Hedges and Matanzas rayon factory.

1958, Jan. 30 Wmk. 106 *Perf. 12½*

C178	A221	8c green	80	40

Issued to honor Dayton Hedges, founder of Cuba's textile industry.

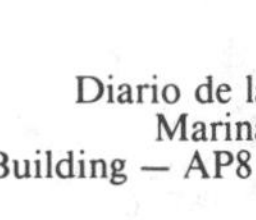

Diario de la Marina Building — AP81

1958, April 1

C179	AP81	29c black	3.00	2.00

Issued in honor of Jose Ignacio Rivero y Alonso, editor of the newspaper, Diario de la Marina.

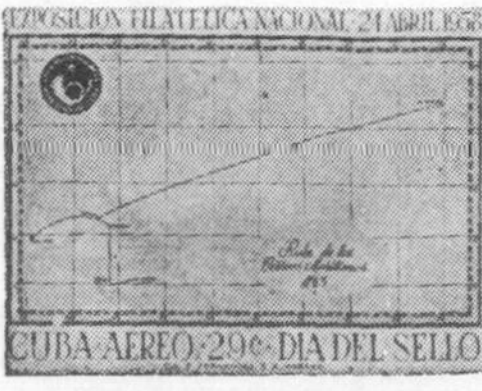

Map Showing Sea Mail Route, 1765 AP82

1958, Apr. 24 Wmk. 106 *Perf. 12½*

C180	AP82	29c dk bl aqua & buff	2.25	1.25

Issued for Stamp Day, Apr. 24, and the National Philatelic Exhibition.

Gen. Gomez in Battle — AP83

Snail (Polymita Picta) — AP84

1958, June 6 Engr.

C181	AP83	12c sl grn	70	25

Issued in honor of Maj. Gen. José Miguel Gomez, President of Cuba, 1909-13.

1958, Aug. 29 Wmk. 321 *Perf. 12½*

Fossils: 12c, Megalocnus Rodens. 30c, Ammonite.

C182	AP84	8c gray, red & yel	1.50	75
C183	AP84	12c brn, *yel grn*	2.50	1.25
C184	AP84	30c grn, *pink*	3.50	1.75

Issued to commemorate the centenary of the birth of Dr. Carlos de la Torre, naturalist.

Papilio Caiguanabus AP85

Cuban Sea Bass AP86

Designs: 12c, Teria gundlachia. 14c, Teria ebriola. 19c, Nathalis felicia. 29c, Butter Hamlet. 30c, Tattler.

1958, Sept. 26 Wmk. 106 *Perf. 12½*

C185	AP85	8c multi	1.75	50
C186	AP85	12c emer, blk & org	2.00	50
C187	AP85	14c multi	3.00	75
C188	AP85	19c bl, blk & yel	3.75	1.00
C189	AP86	24c multi	4.50	1.00
C190	AP86	29c blk, brn & ultra	7.00	1.25
C191	AP86	30c blk, yel grn & sep	8.00	1.75
		Nos. C185-C191 (7)	30.00	6.75

Issued in honor of Felipe Poey (1799-1891), naturalist.

Battle of San Juan Hill, 1898 — AP87

Wmk. 106

1958, Oct. 27 Engr. *Perf. 12½*

C192	AP87	12c blk brn	90	30

Birth centenary of Theodore Roosevelt.

UNESCO Building, Paris — AP88

Design: 30c, "UNESCO" and map of Cuba.

1958, Nov. 7

C193	AP88	12c dk sl grn	1.00	40
C194	AP88	30c dp ultra	2.25	1.35

Issued to commemorate the opening of UNESCO (U. N. Educational, Scientific and Cultural Organization) Headquarters in Paris, Nov. 3.

Postal Notice of 1765 — AP89

Musical Arts Building — AP90

Design: 30c, Administrative postal book of St. Cristobal, Havana, 1765.

1959, Apr. 24 Wmk. 321 *Perf. 12½*

C195	AP89	12c Prus bl & sep	75	25
C196	AP89	30c sep & Prus bl	1.25	85

Issued for Stamp Day, Apr. 24, and the National Philatelic Exhibition.

Type of 1956 Surcharged with New Value, Bar and "ASTA" Emblem in Dark Blue.

1959, Oct. 17 Wmk. 321 *Perf. 12½*

C197	AP63	12c on 1p emer	1.00	40

Issued to publicize the meeting of the American Society of Travel Agents, Oct. 17-23.

Wmk. 106

1959, Nov. 11 Engr. *Perf. 12½*

C198	AP90	12c yel grn	90	25

Issued to commemorate the 40th anniversary of the Musical Arts Society.

No. CB1 Surcharged in Red: "HABILITADO PARA / 12c"

Engraved and Lithographed

1960 Wmk. 321 *Perf. 12½*

C199	SPAP1	12c on 12 + 3c car & grn	1.50	75

Type of Regular Issue, 1960.

Designs: 8c, Battle of Santa Clara. 12c, Rebel forces entering Havana. 29c, Banknote changing hands ("Clandestine activities in the cities").

Wmk. 320

1960, Jan. 28 Engr. *Perf. 12½*

C200	A236	8c bl, gray ol & sal	1.00	25
C201	A236	12c gray ol & ocher	1.50	25
C202	A236	29c gray & car	2.50	1.50

First anniversary of the revolution.

Nos. C9 and C104 Surcharged "12c" in Red

1960, Feb. 3 Wmk. 106

C203	AP3	12c on 40c dp org	75	30
C204	AP48	12c on 45c vio	75	30

Pigeon Type of 1956.

1960, Feb. 12 Wmk. 321

C205	AP62	12c brt bl grn	50	10

Statue Type of Regular Issue, 1960.

Statues: 8c, José Marti, Matanzas. 12c, Heroes of the Cacarajicara, Pinar del Rio. 30c, Cosme de la Torriente, Isle of Pines. (horiz.).

1960, March 28 *Perf. 12½*

C206	A237	8c gray & car	60	25
C207	A237	12c bl & car	1.00	25
C208	A237	30c vio & brn	2.25	1.00

See note after No. 386.

Type of 1956 and No. C33 Overprinted in Dark Blue

1960, Apr. 24 Wmk. 321 *Perf. 12½*

C209	AP62	8c org yel	30	20

C210 AP62 12c cerise 50 20

Souvenir Sheet

C211 AP17 Sheet of four 12.00 12.00

Nos. C209-C211 issued for Stamp Day, Apr. 24, 1960, and to publicize the National Philatelic Exhibition.

No. C211 has added marginal inscription in dark blue commemorating the centenary of the ¼r on 2r (No. 15).

Type of Olympic Games Issue, 1960.

Designs: 8c, Boxer. 12c, Runner.

Wmk. 321

1960, Sept. 22 Engr. *Perf. 12½*

C212 A238 8c ultra	40	20
C213 A238 12c car rose	60	40
a. Souvenir sheet of 4	3.50	

Issued to commemorate the 17th Olympic Games, Rome, Aug. 25-Sept. 11. No. C213a contains one each imperf. of types of Nos. 645-646 and Nos. C212-C213 in dark blue. Red marginal inscription. Size: 78x90mm.

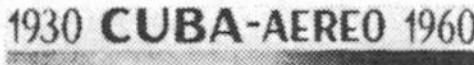

Airmail Stamp of 1930 and Flight Symbols of 1930, 1960
AP91

1960, Oct. 30 Litho. Unwmk.

C214 AP91 8c multi 2.50 1.50

Issued to commemorate the 30th anniversary of national air mail service.

Sword of Sheaf of Wheat — AP92

Designs: 12c, Two workers (horiz.). 30c, Three maps (horiz.). 50c, Hand inscribed "Peace" in 5 languages.

1961, Jan. 10 Photo. *Perf. 11½*

Granite Paper

C215 AP92 8c multi	30	20
C216 AP92 12c multi	45	20
C217 AP92 30c blk & red	1.25	50
C218 AP92 50c blk, bl & red	1.50	1.00

Issued to publicize the Conference of Underdeveloped Countries, Havana.

José Marti and "Declaration of Havana" — AP93

Background in Spanish, English or French

1961, Jan. 28 Litho. *Perf. 12½*

C219 AP93 8c pale grn, blk & red	1.00	60
C220 AP93 12c org yel, blk & pale vio	1.50	1.00
C221 AP93 30c pale bl, blk & pale brn	2.50	1.50
a. Souvenir sheet of 3	7.50	7.50
Nos. C219-C221 (3)	5.00	3.10

Declaration of Havana, Sept. 1, 1960.

Sheets of 25 are imprinted in margin "E" for Spanish, "I" for English or "F" for French.

No. C221a contains one each of Nos. C219-C221, imperf. The 8c has background in Spanish, the 12c in English and the 30c in French. Black marginal inscription. Size: 102x79mm.

U.N. Type of 1961.

1961, Apr. 12 Unwmk. *Perf. 12½*

C222 A244 8c dp car & yel	30	10
C223 A244 12c brt ultra & org	60	30
a. Souvenir sheet of 2	2.00	

Issued to commemorate the 15th anniversary (in 1960) of the United Nations.

No. C223a contains one each of Nos. C222-C223, imperf. with marginal bright ultramarine inscription. Size: 107x65mm.

AIR POST SEMI-POSTAL STAMP

Farm Couple and Factory
SPAP1

Engraved and Lithographed

1959, May 7 Wmk. 321 *Perf. 12½*

CB1 SPAP1 12c + 3c car & grn 1.50 60

Agricultural reforms. See also No. C199.

AIR POST SPECIAL DELIVERY STAMPS

Matanzas Issue.

Matanzas Harbor
APSD1

Wmk. Wavy Lines. (229)

1936, May 5 Photo. *Perf. 12½*

CE1 APSD1 15c lt bl 5.00 2.50

Exists imperf. Price $5 unused, $2.50 used.

SPECIAL DELIVERY STAMPS

Issued under Administration of the United States.

U.S. No. E5 Surcharged in Red

GUBA.
10c.
de PESO

1899 Wmk. 191 *Perf. 12*

E1 SD3 10c on 10c bl	100.00	80.00
a. No period after "CUBA"	350.00	350.00

Issues of the Republic under U. S. Military Rule.

Special Delivery Messenger
SD2

Inscribed: "Immediata".

1899 Wmk. U S-C (191C) Engr.

E2 SD2 10c orange 45.00 10.00

Issues of the Republic

Inscribed: "Inmediata".

1902 Wmk. U S-C (191C) *Perf. 12.*

E3 SD2 10c orange 1.25 60

J. B. Zayas — SD3

1910 Unwmk.

E4 SD3 10c org & bl	11.00	2.50
a. Center inverted	850.00	

Airplane and Morro Castle — SD4

1914, Feb. 24 *Perf. 12*

E5 SD4 10c dk bl 17.50 1.00

1927 Wmk. Star (106)

E6 SD4 10c dp bl 14.00 35

1935 *Perf. 10.*

E7 SD4 10c blue 14.00 30

Matanzas Issue.

Mercury
SD5

Wmk. Wavy Lines. (229)

1936, May 5 Photo. *Perf. 12½*

E8 SD5 10c dp cl 6.00 2.50

Exists imperf. Price $6 unused, $2.50 used.

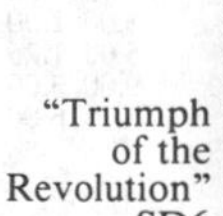

"Triumph of the Revolution"
SD6

1936, Nov. 18

E9 SD6 10c red org 5.00 2.50

Issued in commemoration of the centenary of the birth of Maj. Gen. Maximo Gomez (1836-1905).

Temple of Quetzalcoatl (Mexico)
SD7

Ruben Dario (Nicaragua)
SD8

Wmk. 106

1937, Oct. 13 Engr. *Perf. 10*

E10 SD7 10c dp org	6.00	5.00
E11 SD8 10c dp org	6.00	5.00

Issued for the benefit of the Association of American Writers and Artists. See note after No. 354.

Letter and Symbols of Transportation — SD9

1945, Oct. 30

E12 SD9 10c bl brn 2.00 20

Governor's Building, Cardenas
SD10

Engraved and Lithographed

1951, July 3 Wmk. 229 *Perf. 13*

E13 SD10 10c hn brn, ultra & red 5.00 1.00

Issued to commemorate the centenary of the adoption of Cuba's flag.

Chess Type of Regular Issue, 1951

1951, Nov. 1 Photo.

E14 A166 10c dk grn & rose brn 10.00 3.50

Issued to commemorate the 30th anniversary of the winning of the World Chess title by Jose Raul Capablanca.

Type of Regular Issue of 1951 Surcharged in Red Violet

10¢
E. ESPECIAL

Wmk. 106

1952, Mar. 18 Engr. *Perf. 10*

E15 A159 10c on 2c yel brn 2.25 75

Arms and Bars from National Hymn
SD12

Roseate Tern
SD13

1952, May 27 *Perf. 12½*

E16 SD12 10c dp org & bl 3.00 1.00

Issued to commemorate the 50th anniversary of the founding of the Republic of Cuba.

Type of Air Post Stamps of 1952 Inscribed: "Entrega Especial"

1952, Oct. 7 *Perf. 10*

E17 AP36 10c pale ol grn 2.50 1.00

Three-fourths of the proceeds from the sale of No. E17 were used for the Communications Ministry Employees' Retirement Fund.

1953, July 28

E18 SD13 10c blue 2.50 60

Gregorio Hernandez Saez
SD14

Felix Varela
SD15

1954, Feb. 23

E19 SD14 10c ol grn 3.00 75

1955, June 22 *Perf. 12½*

E20 SD15 10c brn car 2.25 85

See note after No. E17.

Portrait Type of Regular Issue, 1956 Inscribed: "Entrega Especial"

Portrait: 10c, Jose Jacinto Milanes.

1956, May 2 **Wmk. 106**

E21	A198	10c dk car rose & blk	2.25	60

See note after No. E17.

Painting Type of Regular Issue, 1957, Inscribed: "Entrega Especial"

Painting: 10c, "Yesterday" by E. Garcia Cabrera.

1957, Mar. 15 **Engr.** ***Perf. 12½***

E22	A207	10c dk brn & turq bl	3.00	85

See note after No. E17.

View Type of Regular Issue, 1957, Inscribed: "Entrega Especial."

View: 10c, Independence square, Pino del Rio.

1957, Dec. 17

E23	A218	10c dk pur & brn	2.00	60

See note after No. E17.

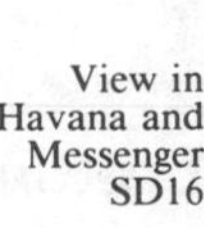

View in Havana and Messenger SD16

1958, Jan. 10 **Engr.**

E24	SD16	10c blue	1.50	50
E25	SD16	20c green	2.00	60

See also Nos. E28, E31.

Fish Type of Air Post Issue, 1958, Inscribed "Entrega Especial."

Fish: 10c, Blackfish snapper. 20c, Mosquitofish.

1958, Sept. 26 **Wmk. 106** ***Perf. 12½***

E26	AP86	10c blk, bl, pink & yel	4.00	2.00
E27	AP86	20c blk, ultra & pink	12.50	9.00

See note after No. C191.

Messenger Type of 1958

1960 **Wmk. 321** ***Perf. 12½***

E28	SD16	10c brt vio	1.50	40

Plane Type of Air Post Issue, of 1931-46, Surcharged in Black or Red: "HABILITADO ENTREGA ESPECIAL 10¢"

1960 **Wmk. 106** ***Perf. 10***

E29	AP4	10c on 20c car rose	1.25	50
E30	AP4	10c on 50c grnsh bl (R)	1.00	50

Messenger Type of 1958

1961, June 28 **Wmk. 321** ***Perf. 12½***

E31	SD16	10c orange	1.50	50

POSTAGE DUE STAMPS

Issued under Administration of the United States

Postage Due Stamps of the United States Nos. J38, J39, J41 and J42 Surcharged in Black Like Regular Issue of Same Date.

1899 **Wmk. 191** ***Perf. 12.***

J1	D2	1c on 1c dp cl	22.50	3.50
J2	D2	2c on 2c dp cl	20.00	3.50
a.		Inverted surcharge		*2,000.*
J3	D2	5c on 5c dp cl	22.50	3.50
a.		"CUPA"	175.00	160.00
J4	D2	10c on 10c dp cl	20.00	1.25

Issues of the Republic.

D1

1914 **Unwmk.** **Engr.** ***Perf. 12***

J5	D1	1c car rose	7.00	1.00
J6	D1	2c car rose	8.00	1.00
J7	D1	5c car rose	14.00	2.00

1927-28

J8	D1	1c rose red	7.00	1.00
J9	D1	2c rose red	11.00	1.00
J10	D1	5c rose red	13.00	1.50

NEWSPAPER STAMPS

Issued under Spanish Dominion.

N1

N2

1888 **Unwmk.** **Typo.** ***Perf. 14***

P1	N1	½m black	25	25
P2	N1	1m black	30	30
P3	N1	2m black	30	30
P4	N1	3m black	2.50	1.00
P5	N1	4m black	3.00	1.75
P6	N1	8m black	12.00	7.50
		Nos. P1-P6 (6)	18.35	11.10

1890

P7	N2	½m red brn	75	60
P8	N2	1m red brn	75	60
P9	N2	2m red brn	1.25	85
P10	N2	3m red brn	1.50	1.00
P11	N2	4m red brn	12.00	5.00
P12	N2	8m red brn	12.00	5.00
		Nos. P7-P12 (6)	28.25	13.05

1892

P13	N2	½m violet	25	25
P14	N2	1m violet	25	25
P15	N2	2m violet	25	25
P16	N2	3m violet	1.50	25
P17	N2	4m violet	6.00	1.50
P18	N2	8m violet	12.00	2.50
		Nos. P13-P18 (6)	20.25	5.00

1894

P19	N2	½m rose	25	25
a.		Imperf. pair	30.00	
P20	N2	1m rose	75	25
P21	N2	2m rose	75	25
P22	N2	3m rose	3.00	1.00
P23	N2	4m rose	5.00	1.25
P24	N2	8m rose	9.00	3.00
		Nos. P19-P24 (6)	18.75	6.00

1896

P25	N2	½m bl grn	25	25
P26	N2	1m bl grn	25	25
P27	N2	2m bl grn	25	25
P28	N2	3m bl grn	4.00	1.25
P29	N2	4m bl grn	9.00	6.00
P30	N2	8m bl grn	16.00	8.00
		Nos. P25-P30 (6)	29.75	16.00

POSTAL TAX STAMPS

Mother and Child PT1

Nurse with Child PT2

Wmk. Star. (106)

1938, Dec. 1 **Engr.** ***Perf. 10***

RA1	PT1	1c brt grn	35	10

The tax benefited the National Council of Tuberculosis fund for children's hospitals. Obligatory on all mail during December and January. This note applies also to Nos. RA2-RA4, RA7-RA10, RA12-RA15, RA17-RA21.

1939, Dec. 1

RA2	PT2	1c org ver	35	10

"Health" Protecting Children PT3

Mother and Child PT4

1940, Dec. 1

RA3	PT3	1c dp bl	35	10

1941, Dec. 1

RA4	PT4	1c ol bis	50	10

Victory — PT5

1942-44

RA5	PT5	½c orange	35	10
RA6	PT5	½c gray ('44)	40	10

Issue dates: No. RA5, July 1, 1942. No. RA6, Oct. 3, 1944.

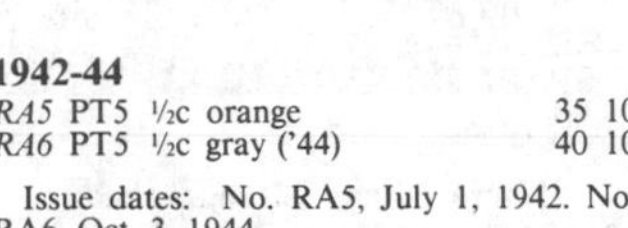

Type of 1941 Overprinted in Black

1942, Dec. 1

RA7	PT4	1c salmon	60	20
a.		Inverted ovpt.	60.00	30.00

"Health" Protecting Children PT6

Mother and Child PT7

1943, Dec. 1

RA8	PT6	1c brown	35	10

1949, Dec. 9

RA9	PT7	1c blue	35	10

Type of 1949 Inscribed: "1950."

1950, Dec. 1 **Engr.**

RA10	PT7	1c rose red	35	10

Model of Proposed Communications Building — PT8

Woman Holding Child Aloft — PT9

1951, June 5 **Wmk. 106** ***Perf. 10***

RA11	PT8	1c violet	50	5

The tax was to help build a new Communications Building. This note applies also to Nos. RA16, RA34, RA43.

1951, Dec. 1

RA12	PT9	1c vio bl	35	5
RA13	PT9	1c brn car	35	5
RA14	PT9	1c ol bis	35	5
RA15	PT9	1c dp grn	35	5

The lack of a price for a listed item does not necessarily indicate rarity.

Proposed Communications Building — PT10

Child — PT11

1952, Feb. 8

RA16	PT10	1c dk bl	20	5

See Nos. RA34, RA43.

1952, Dec. 1

RA17	PT11	1c rose car	50	5
RA18	PT11	1c yel grn	50	5
RA19	PT11	1c blue	50	5
RA20	PT11	1c orange	50	5

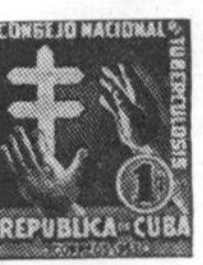

Hands reaching for Lorraine Cross PT12

Child's Head and Lorraine Cross PT13

1953, Dec. 1 ***Perf. 9½***

RA21	PT12	1c rose car	35	5

1954, Nov. 1 ***Perf. 9½x10***

RA22	PT13	1c rose red	35	5
RA23	PT13	1c violet	35	5
RA24	PT13	1c brt bl	35	5
RA25	PT13	1c emerald	35	5

The tax benefited the National Council of Tuberculosis fund for children's hospitals. Obligatory on all mail during November, December, January and February. This note applies also to Nos. RA26-RA33, RA35-RA42.

Rose and Watering Can PT14

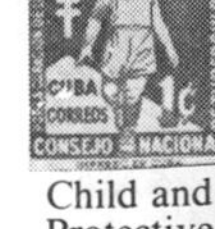

Child and Protective Hands PT15

1955, Nov. 1

RA26	PT14	1c red org	50	10
RA27	PT14	1c red lil	50	10
RA28	PT14	1c brt bl	50	10
RA29	PT14	1c org yel	50	10

1956, Nov. 1

RA30	PT15	1c rose red	35	5
RA31	PT15	1c yel brn	35	5
RA32	PT15	1c brt bl	35	5
RA33	PT15	1c emerald	35	5

Building Type of 1952

1957, Jan. 18 ***Perf. 10***

RA34	PT10	1c rose red	20	5

Mother and Child by Silvia Arrojo Fernandez PT16

National Council of Tuberculosis PT17

Wmk. 321

1957, Nov. 1 Engr. *Perf. 10*

RA35 PT16 1c dl rose 50 5
RA36 PT16 1c brt bl 50 5
RA37 PT16 1c gray 50 5
RA38 PT16 1c emerald 50 5

1958

RA39 PT17 1c rose red 25 5
RA40 PT17 1c red brn 25 5
RA41 PT17 1c gray 25 5
RA42 PT17 1c emerald 25 5

Building Type of 1952

1958 Wmk. 321

RA43 PT10 1c rose red 20 5

CYRENAICA

LOCATION — In northern Africa bordering on the Mediterranean Sea
GOVT. — Former Italian colony
AREA — 75,340 sq. mi.
POP. — 225,000 (approx. 1934)
CAPITAL — Bengasi (Benghazi)

Cyrenaica was incorporated in the kingdom of Libya in 1951.

100 Centesimi = 1 Lira
1000 Milliemes = 1 Pound (1950)

Propaganda of the Faith Issue.

Italy Nos. 143-146 Overprinted **CIRENAICA**

1923 Wmk. Crowns. (140) *Perf. 14*

1 A68 20c ol grn & brn org 1.65 *8.25*
2 A68 30c cl & brn org 1.65 *8.25*
3 A68 50c vio & brn org 1.25 *6.75*
4 A68 1 l bl & brn org 1.25 *6.75*

Fascisti Issue.

Italy Nos. 159-164 Overprinted in Red or Black. **CIRENAICA**

1923 Unwmk. *Perf. 14*

5 A69 10c dk grn (R) 1.50 *6.75*
6 A69 30c dk vio (R) 1.50 *6.75*
7 A69 50c brn car 1.50 *6.75*

Wmk. Crowns. (140)

8 A70 1 l blue 1.50 *6.75*
9 A70 2 l brown 1.50 *6.75*
10 A71 5 l blk & bl (R) 1.50 *11.00*
Nos. 5-10 (6) 9.00 44.75

Manzoni Issue.

Italy Nos. 165-170 Overprinted in Red **CIRENAICA**

1924 *Perf. 14.*

11 A72 10c brn red & blk 75 *7.50*
12 A72 15c bl grn & blk 75 *7.50*
13 A72 30c blk & sl 75 *7.50*
14 A72 50c org brn & blk 75 *7.50*
15 A72 1 l bl & blk 7.50 *50.00*
a. Double overprint 150.00 350.00
16 A72 5 l vio & blk 175.00 *750.00*
Nos. 11-16 (6) 185.50 830.00

Vertical overprints on Nos. 11-14 are essays. On Nos. 15-16 the overprint is vertical at the left.

Victor Emmanuel Issue.

Italy Nos. 175-177 Overprinted **CIRENAICA**

1925-26 Unwmk. *Perf. 11*

17 A78 60c brn car 26 *3.00*
18 A78 1 l dk bl 26 *3.00*
19 A78 1.25 l dk bl ('26) 75 *9.00*
a. Perf. 13½ 82.50 *225.00*

Saint Francis of Assisi Issue.

Italian Stamps of 1926 Overprinted **CIRENAICA**

1926 Wmk. 140 *Perf. 14*

20 A79 20c gray grn 90 *4.50*
21 A80 40c dk vio 90 *4.50*
22 A81 60c red brn 90 *4.50*

Overprinted in Red **Cirenaica**

Unwmk.

23 A82 1.25 l dk bl, perf. 11 90 *4.50*
24 A83 5 l + 2.50 l ol grn 2.25 *8.25*
Nos. 20-24 (5) 5.85 26.25

Volta Issue.

Type of Italy 1927, Overprinted **Cirenaica**

1927 Wmk. 140 *Perf. 14.*

25 A84 20c purple 3.00 *11.00*
26 A84 50c dp org 3.75 *7.50*
27 A84 1.25 l brt bl 4.50 *11.00*

No. 25 exists with overprint omitted. Price $75.

Monte Cassino Issue.

Types of 1929 Issue of Italy, Overprinted in Red or Blue **CIRENAICA**

1929

28 A96 20c dk grn (R) 1.65 *7.50*
29 A96 25c red org (Bl) 1.65 *7.50*
30 A98 50c + 10c crim (Bl) 1.65 *11.00*
31 A98 75c + 15c ol brn (R) 1.65 *11.00*
32 A96 1.25 l + 25c dk vio (R) 3.25 *11.00*
33 A98 5 l + 1 l saph (R) 3.25 *11.00*

Overprinted in Red **Cirenaica**

Unwmk.

34 A100 10 l + 2 l gray brn 3.25 *15.00*
Nos. 28-34 (7) 16.35 74.00

Royal Wedding Issue.

Type of Italian Stamps of 1930 Overprinted **CIRENAICA**

1930 Wmk. 140

35 A101 20c yel grn 75 *3.00*
36 A101 50c + 10c dp org 55 *3.75*
37 A101 1.25 l + 25c rose red 55 *4.50*

No. 35 exists with overprint omitted. Price $750.

Ferrucci Issue.

Types of Italian Stamps of 1930, Overprinted in Red or Blue **Cirenaica**

1930

38 A102 20c vio (R) 55 *2.25*
39 A103 25c dk grn (R) 55 *2.25*
40 A103 50c blk (R) 55 *2.25*
41 A103 1.25 l dp bl (R) 55 *2.25*
42 A104 5 l + 2 l dp car (Bl) 2.25 *4.50*
Nos. 38-42 (5) 4.45 13.50

Virgil Issue.

Types of Italian Stamps of 1930 Overprinted in Red or Blue

CIRENAICA

1930

43 A106 15c vio blk (R) 38 *2.25*
44 A106 20c org brn (Bl) 38 *2.25*
45 A106 25c dk grn (R) 38 *1.90*
46 A106 30c lt brn (Bl) 38 *2.25*
47 A106 50c dl vio (R) 38 *1.90*
48 A106 75c rose red 38 *2.25*
49 A106 1.25 l gray bl (R) 38 *2.25*

Unwmk.

50 A106 5 l + 1.50 l dk vio (R) 2.00 *9.00*
51 A106 10 l + 2.50 l ol brn (Bl) 2.00 *9.00*
Nos. 43-51 (9) 6.66 33.05

Saint Anthony of Padua Issue.

Types of Italian Stamps of 1931 Overprinted in Blue or Red

CIRENAICA

1931 Wmk. 140

52 A116 20c brn (Bl) 75 *3.25*
53 A116 25c grn (R) 75 *3.25*
54 A118 30c gray brn (Bl) 75 *3.25*
55 A118 50c dl vio (Bl) 75 *2.25*
56 A120 1.25 l sl bl (R) 75 *3.25*

Overprinted in Red or Black **Cirenaica**

Unwmk.

57 A121 75c blk (R) 75 *3.25*
58 A122 5 l + 2.50 l dk brn (Bk) 2.25 *11.00*
Nos. 52-58 (7) 6.75 29.50

Carabineer A1

1934 Photo. Wmk. 140

59 A1 5c dk ol grn & brn 1.65 *6.25*
60 A1 10c brn & blk 1.65 *6.25*
61 A1 20c scar & ind 1.65 *6.25*
62 A1 50c pur & brn 1.65 *6.25*
63 A1 60c org brn & ind 1.65 *6.25*
64 A1 1.25 l dk bl & grn 1.65 *6.25*
Nos. 59-64 (6) 9.90 37.50

Issued to commemorate the 2nd Colonial Art Exhibition held at Naples. See also Nos. C24-C29.

Autonomous State

Senussi Warrior
A2 A3

1950 Unwmk. Engr. *Perf. 12½*

65 A2 1m dk brn 8 15
66 A2 2m rose car 8 15
67 A2 3m orange 8 15
68 A2 4m dk grn 65 90
69 A2 5m gray 15 15
70 A2 8m red org 18 45
71 A2 10m purple 22 45
72 A2 12m red 22 55
73 A2 20m dp bl 22 45
74 A3 50m choc & ultra 1.50 *4.50*
75 A3 100m bl blk & car rose 4.50 *13.50*
76 A3 200m vio & pur 6.00 *18.00*
77 A3 500m dk grn & org 20.00 *45.00*
Nos. 65-77 (13) 33.88 84.40

SEMI-POSTAL STAMPS

Many issues of Italy and Italian Colonies include one or more semipostal denominations. To avoid splitting sets, these issues are generally listed as regular postage unless all values carry a surtax.

Holy Year Issue.

Italian Semi-Postal Stamps of 1924 Overprinted in Black or Red

CIRENAICA

1925 Wmk. 140 *Perf. 12*

B1 SP4 20c + 10c dk grn & brn 1.00 *4.50*
B2 SP4 30c + 15c dk brn & brn 1.00 *4.50*
B3 SP4 50c + 25c vio & brn 1.00 *4.50*
B4 SP4 60c + 30c dp rose & brn 1.00 *4.50*
B5 SP8 1 l + 50c dp bl & vio (R) 1.00 *4.50*
B6 SP8 5 l + 2.50 l org brn & vio (R) 1.00 *4.50*
Nos. B1-B6 (6) 6.00 27.00

Colonial Institute Issue.

"Peace" Substituting Spade for Sword — SP1

1926 Typo. *Perf. 14.*

B7 SP1 5c + 5c brn 25 *2.50*
B8 SP1 10c + 5c ol grn 25 *2.50*
B9 SP1 20c + 5c bl grn 25 *2.50*
B10 SP1 40c + 5c brn red 25 *2.50*
B11 SP1 60c + 5c org 25 *2.50*
B12 SP1 1 l + 5c bl 25 *2.50*
Nos. B7-B12 (6) 1.50 15.00

Surtax for Italian Colonial Institute.

Types of Italian Semi-Postal Stamps of 1926 Overprinted **CIRENAICA**

1927 Unwmk. *Perf. 11.*

B13 SP10 40c + 20c dk brn & blk 1.00 *5.25*
B14 SP10 60c + 30c brn red & ol brn 1.00 *5.25*
B15 SP10 1.25 l + 60c dp bl & blk 1.00 *5.25*
B16 SP10 5 l + 2.50 l dk grn & blk 1.50 *6.75*

The surtax on these stamps was for the charitable work of the Voluntary Militia for Italian National Defense.

Allegory of Fascism and Victory — SP2

1928 Wmk. 140 *Perf. 14.*

B17 SP2 20c + 5c bl grn 75 *3.75*
B18 SP2 30c + 5c red 75 *3.75*
B19 SP2 50c + 10c pur 75 *3.75*
B20 SP2 1.25 l + 20c dk bl 75 *3.75*

Issued to commemorate the 46th anniversary of the Societa Africana d'Italia. The surtax aided that society.

Types of Italian Semi-Postal Stamps of 1926 Overprinted **CIRENAICA**

1929 Unwmk. *Perf. 11.*

B21 SP10 30c + 10c red & blk 1.25 *5.50*
B22 SP10 50c + 20c vio & blk 1.25 *5.50*
B23 SP10 1.25 l + 50c brn & bl 1.50 *7.50*
B24 SP10 5 l + 2 l ol grn & blk 1.50 *7.50*

The surtax on Nos. B21-B24 was for the charitable work of the Voluntary Militia for Italian National Defense.

Types of Italian Semi-Postal Stamps of 1926 Overprinted in Black or Red **CIRENAICA**

1930 *Perf. 14.*

B25 SP10 30c + 10c dk grn & bl grn (Bk) 4.00 *15.00*
B26 SP10 50c + 10c dk grn & vio (R) 4.00 *15.00*
B27 SP10 1.25 l + 30c ol brn & red brn (R) 4.00 *15.00*
B28 SP10 5 l + 1.50 l ind & grn (R) 12.00 *47.50*

The surtax on these stamps was for the charitable work of the Voluntary Militia for Italian National Defense.

Sower — SP3

1930 Photo. Wmk. 140
B29 SP3 50c + 20c ol brn 1.10 *6.00*
B30 SP3 1.25 l + 20c dp bl 1.10 *6.00*
B31 SP3 1.75 l + 20c grn 1.10 *6.00*
B32 SP3 2.55 l + 50c pur 1.65 *6.00*
B33 SP3 5 l + 1l dp car 1.65 *6.00*
Nos. B29-B33 (5) 6.60 30.00

Issued in commemoration of the 25th anniversary of the Italian Colonial Agricultural Institute.
The surtax was for the aid of that institution.

AIR POST STAMPS

Air Post Stamps of Tripolitania, 1931, Overprinted in Blue **Cirenaica**

1932 Wmk. 140 *Perf. 14.*
C1 AP1 50c rose car 38 18
C2 AP1 60c dp org 1.65 *11.00*
C3 AP1 80c dl vio 1.65 *11.00*

Air Post Stamps of Tripolitania, 1931, Overprinted in Blue **CIRENAICA**

1932
C4 AP1 50c rose car 55 38
C5 AP1 80c dl vio 2.25 *15.00*

This overprint was also applied to the 60c, Tripolitania No. C9. The overprinted stamp was never used in Cyrenaica, but was sold at Rome in 1943 by the Postmaster General for the Italian Colonies. Price $4.

Arab on Camel — AP2

Airplane in Flight AP3

1932 Photo.
C6 AP2 50c purple 1.10 18
C7 AP2 75c brn rose 2.50 4.00
C8 AP2 80c dp bl 2.50 4.00
C9 AP3 1 l black 38 18
C10 AP3 2 l green 75 *2.25*
C11 AP3 5 l dp car 1.50 *6.75*
Nos. C6-C11 (6) 8.73 17.36

Graf Zeppelin Issue.

Zeppelin and Clouds forming Pegasus AP4

Zeppelin and Ancient Galley AP5

Zeppelin and Giant Bowman AP6

1933, Apr. 15
C12 AP4 3 l dk brn 6.25 *55.00*
C13 AP5 5 l purple 6.25 *55.00*
C14 AP6 10 l dp grn 6.25 *92.50*
C15 AP5 12 l dp bl 6.25 *130.00*
C16 AP4 15 l carmine 6.25 *110.00*
C17 AP6 20 l black 6.25 *150.00*
Nos. C12-C17 (6) 37.50 592.50

North Atlantic Cruise Issue.

Airplane Squadron and Constellations — AP7

1933, June 1
C18 AP7 19.75 l grn & dp bl 15.00 *375.00*
C19 AP7 44.75 l red & ind 15.00 *375.00*

Type of 1932 Overprinted and Surcharged

1934, Jan. 20
C20 AP3 2 l on 5 l org brn 2.25 *40.00*
C21 AP3 3 l on 5 l yel grn 2.25 *40.00*
C22 AP3 5 l ocher 2.25 *40.00*
C23 AP3 10 l on 5 l rose 2.25 *40.00*

For use on mail to be carried on a special flight from Rome to Buenos Aires.

Transport Plane — AP8

Venus of Cyrene AP9

1934, Oct. 9
C24 AP8 25c sl bl & org red 1.65 *6.25*
C25 AP8 50c dk grn & ind 1.65 *6.25*
C26 AP8 75c dk brn & org red 1.65 *6.25*
a. Imperf. 250.00
C27 AP9 80c org brn & ol grn 1.65 *6.25*
C28 AP9 1 l scar & ol grn 1.65 *6.25*
C29 AP9 2 l dk bl & brn 1.65 *6.25*
Nos. C24-C29 (6) 9.90 37.50

Issued in commemoration of the Second Colonial Arts Exhibition held at Naples.

AIR POST SEMI-POSTAL STAMPS

King Victor Emmanuel III SPAP1

1934 Wmk. 104 Photo. *Perf. 14.*
CB1 SPAP1 25c + 10c gray grn 1.90 *7.50*
CB2 SPAP1 50c + 10c brn 1.90 *7.50*
CB3 SPAP1 75c + 15c rose red 1.90 *7.50*
CB4 SPAP1 80c + 15c brn blk 1.90 *7.50*
CB5 SPAP1 1 l + 20c red brn 1.90 *7.50*
CB6 SPAP1 2 l + 20c brt bl 1.90 *7.50*
CB7 SPAP1 3 l + 25c pur 16.00 *60.00*
CB8 SPAP1 5 l + 25c org 16.00 *60.00*
CB9 SPAP1 10 + 30c dp l vio 16.00 *60.00*
CB10 SPAP1 25 + 2 l dp grn l 16.00 *60.00*
Nos. CB1-CB10 (10) 75.40 285.00

Issued in commemoration of the 65th birthday of King Victor Emmanuel III and the non-stop flight from Rome to Mogadiscio.

AIR POST SEMI-POSTAL OFFICIAL STAMP

Type of Air Post Semi-Postal Stamps, 1934, Overprinted Crown and "SERVIZIO DI STATO" in Black.

1934, Nov. 5 Wmk. 140 *Perf. 14*
CBO1 SPAP1 25 l + 2 l cop red *1,400.*

POSTAGE DUE STAMPS

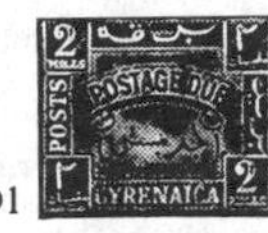

D1

1950 Unwmk. Engr. *Perf. 12½*
J1 D1 2m dk brn 15.00 37.50
J2 D1 4m dp grn 15.00 37.50
J3 D1 8m scarlet 15.00 37.50
J4 D1 10m vermilion 15.00 37.50
J5 D1 20m org yel 15.00 37.50
J6 D1 40m dp bl 15.00 37.50
J7 D1 100m dk gray 15.00 37.50
Nos. J1-J7 (7) 105.00 262.50

CZECHOSLOVAKIA

LOCATION — Central Europe
GOVT. — Republic
AREA — 49,355 sq. mi.
POP. — 15,395,970 (1983)
CAPITAL — Prague

The Czechoslovakian Republic consists of Bohemia, Moravia and Silesia, Slovakia and Ruthenia (Carpatho-Ukraine). In March 1939, a German protectorate was established over Bohemia and Moravia, as well as over Slovakia which had meanwhile declared its independence. Ruthenia was incorporated in the territory of Hungary. These territories were returned to the Czechoslovak Republic in 1945, except for Ruthenia, which was ceded to Russia. Czechoslovakia became a federal state on January 2, 1969.

100 Haleru = 1 Koruna

Stamps of Austria overprinted "Ceskoslovenska Republika", lion and "Cesko Slovensky Stat", "Provisorni Ceskoslovenska Vlada" and Arms, and "Ceskoslovenska Statni Posta" and Arms were made privately. A few of them were passed through the post but all have been pronounced unofficial and unauthorized by the Postmaster General.

During the occupation of part of Northern Hungary by the Czechoslovak forces, stamps of Hungary were overprinted "Cesko Slovenska Posta", "Ceskoslovenska Statni Posta" and Arms, and "Slovenska Posta" and Arms. These stamps were never officially issued though copies have passed the post.

Hradcany at Prague — A1

1918-19 Unwmk. Typo. *Imperf.*
1 A1 3(h) red vio 5 5
2 A1 5(h) yel grn 10 5
3 A1 10(h) rose 10 5
4 A1 20(h) bluish grn 15 5
5 A1 25(h) dp bl 25 5
a. 25(h) ultra 30.00
6 A1 30(h) bister 40 5
7 A1 40(h) red org 40 5
8 A1 100(h) brown 1.25 8
9 A1 200(h) ultra 2.00 10
10 A1 400(h) purple 2.50 20

On the 3(h) to 40(h) the words "Posta Ceskoslovenska" are in white on a colored background; on the higher values the words are in color on a white background.
See Nos. 368, 1554, 1600.

Perf. 11½, 13½
13 A1 5(h) yel grn 50 25
a. Perf. 11½x10½ 1.50 30
14 A1 10(h) rose 35 10
15 A1 20(h) bluish grn 35 10
a. Perf. 11½ 1.50 50
16 A1 25(h) dp bl 40 10
a. Perf. 11½ 2.00 60
20 A1 200(h) ultra 4.00 15
Nos. 1-10,13-16,20 (15) 12.80 1.43

All values of this issue exist with various private perforations and copies have been used on letters.
The 3, 30, 40, 100 and 400h formerly listed are now known to have been privately perforated.

A2

Type II. Sun behind cathedral. Colorless foliage in foreground.
Type III. Without sun. Shaded foliage in foreground.
Type IV. No foliage in foreground. Positions of buildings changed. Letters redrawn.

1919 *Imperf.*
23 A2 1(h) dk brn (II) 5 5
25 A2 5(h) bl grn (IV) 35 5
27 A2 15(h) red (IV) 50 30
29 A2 25(h) dl vio (IV) 35 5
30 A2 50(h) dl vio (II) 35 5
31 A2 50(h) dk bl (IV) 35 5
32 A2 60(h) org (III) 1.25 30
33 A2 75(h) sl (IV) 1.00 15
34 A2 80(h) ol grn (III) 1.25 30
36 A2 120(h) gray blk (IV) 2.00 30
38 A2 300(h) dk grn (III) 7.50 30
39 A2 500(h) red brn (IV) 4.00 30
40 A2 1000(h) vio (III) 16.00 1.50
a. 1000(h) bluish vio 30.00 3.00
Nos. 23-40 (13) 34.95 3.70

1919-20 *Perf. 11½, 13½, 13½x11½*
41 A2 1(h) dk brn (II) 5 5
42 A2 5(h) bl grn (IV), perf. 13½ 15 5
a. Perf. 11½ 20.00 7.50
43 A2 10(h) yel grn (IV) 30 5
a. Imperf. 52.50 40.00
b. Perf. 11½ 15.00 1.25
44 A2 15(h) red (IV) 15 5
a. Perf. 11½x10½ 30.00 5.00
b. Perf. 11½x13½ 40.00 10.00
c. Perf. 13½x10½ 75.00 20.00
45 A2 20(h) rose (IV) 35 5
a. Imperf. 200.00 150.00

46 A2 25(h) dl vio (IV), perf. 11½ 60 18
a. Perf. 11½x10½ 4.50 60
b. Perf. 13½x10½ 22.00 14.00
47 A2 30(h) red vio (IV) 25 5
a. Imperf. 250.00 200.00
b. Perf. 14x13½ 300.00 50.00
c. 30(h) dp vio 25 8
d. As "c," perf. 14x13½ 300.00 50.00
e. As "c," imperf. 225.00 175.00
50 A2 60(h) org (III) 50 15
a. Perf. 14x13½ 20.00 10.00
53 A2 120(h) gray blk (IV) 7.00 3.00
Nos. 41-53 (9) 9.35 3.63

Nos. 43a, 45a and 47a were imperforate by accident and not issued in quantities as were Nos. 23 to 40.

Rouletted stamps of the preceding issues are said to have been made by a postmaster in a branch post office at Prague, or by private firms, but without authority from the Post Office Department.

The 50, 75, 80, 300, 500 and 1000h have been privately perforated.

Unlisted color varieties of types A1 and A2 were not officially released, and some are printer's waste.

Pres. Thomas Garrigue Masaryk — A4

1920 *Perf. 13½*
61 A4 125(h) gray bl 1.65 20
a. 125(h) ultra 40.00 25.00
b. Imperf. (gray bl) 25.00
c. As "a," imperf. 75.00
62 A4 500(h) sl, *grysh* 7.25 3.25
a. Imperf. 35.00
63 A4 1000(h) blk brn, *brnsh* 13.00 6.25
a. Imperf. 50.00

Carrier Pigeon with Letter — A5

Czechoslovakia Breaking Chains to Freedom — A6

Hussite Priest — A7

Agriculture and Science — A8

1920 *Perf. 14*
65 A5 5(h) dk bl 5 5
a. Perf. 13½ 90.00 25.00
b. Imperf. 7.50
66 A5 10(h) bl grn 5 5
a. Perf. 13½ 70.00 30.00
b. Imperf. 8.00
67 A5 15(h) red brn 10 5
a. Imperf. 8.00
68 A6 20(h) rose 5 5
a. Imperf. 10.00
69 A6 25(h) lil brn 8 5
a. Imperf. 12.00
70 A6 30(h) red vio 10 5
a. Imperf. 8.00
71 A6 40(h) red brn 20 5
a. Tete beche pair 3.50 2.00
b. Perf. 13½ 60 20
c. Imperf. 10.00
72 A6 50(h) carmine 40 5
a. Imperf. 6.00
73 A6 60(h) dk bl 50 5
a. Tete beche pair 9.00 5.00
b. Perf. 13½ 4.00 45
c. Imperf. 7.50

Photo.
74 A7 80(h) purple 50 25
a. Imperf. 7.50
75 A7 90(h) blk brn 80 50
a. Imperf. 7.50

Typo.
Perf. 14
76 A8 100(h) dk grn 80 5
a. Imperf. 6.00
77 A8 200(h) violet 1.50 5
a. Imperf. 8.00
78 A8 300(h) vermilion 3.25 5
a. Perf. 14x13½ 10.00 40
b. Imperf. 8.50
79 A8 400(h) brown 10.00 80
a. Imperf. 45.00
80 A8 500(h) dp grn 12.00 80
a. Perf. 14x13½ 80.00 7.50
b. Imperf. 45.00
81 A8 600(h) dp vio 15.00 80
a. Perf. 14x13½ 250.00 10.00
b. Imperf. 45.00
Nos. 65-81 (17) 45.38 3.75

No. 69 has background of horizontal lines.

1920-25 *Perf. 14*
82 A5 5(h) violet 5 5
a. Tete beche pair 2.50 1.75
b. Perf. 13½ 35 20
c. Imperf. 7.50
83 A5 10(h) ol bis 5 5
a. Tete beche pair 3.00 2.00
b. Perf. 13½ 50 20
c. Imperf. 7.50
84 A5 20(h) dp org 10 6
a. Tete beche pair 40.00 15.00
b. Perf. 13½ 8.50 1.25
c. Imperf. 9.00
85 A5 25(h) bl grn 20 5
a. Imperf. 10.00
86 A5 30(h) dp vio ('25) 3.25 6
87 A6 50(h) yel grn 50 5
a. Tete beche pair 60.00 40.00
b. Perf. 13½ 17.50 4.00
c. Imperf. 37.50
88 A6 100(h) dk brn 80 5
a. Perf. 13½ 35.00 40
b. Imperf. 4.00
89 A6 150(h) rose 5.50 1.00
a. Perf. 13½ 90.00 2.00
90 A6 185(h) orange 2.00 20
a. Imperf. 10.00
91 A6 250(h) dk grn 5.50 40
a. Imperf. 20.00
Nos. 82-91 (10) 17.95 1.97

Type of 1920 Issue Redrawn.

Type I. Rib of leaf below "O" of POSTA is straight and extends to tip. White triangle above book is entirely at left of twig. "P" has a stubby, abnormal appendage.

Type II. Rib is extremely bent; does not reach tip. Triangle extends at right of twig. "P" like Type I.

Type III. Rib of top left leaf is broken in two. Triangle like Type II. "P" has no appendage.

1923 *Perf. 14, 14x13½*
92 A8 100(h) red, *yel*, III, perf. 14x13½ 2.25 5
a. Type I, perf. 14 3.25 5
b. Type I, perf. 14x13½ 4.00 5
c. Type II, perf. 14 3.25 5
d. Type II, perf. 14x13½ 3.75 5
e. Type III, perf. 14 20.00 10
93 A8 200(h) bl, *yel*, II, perf. 14 10.50 10
a. Type II, perf. 14x13½ 17.50 35
b. Type III, perf. 14 13.50 40
c. Type III, perf. 14x13½ 75.00 75
94 A8 300(h) vio, *yel*, I, perf. 14 9.00 10
a. Type II, perf. 14 60.00 40
b. Type II, perf. 14x13½ 125.00 80
c. Type III, perf. 14x13½ 15.00 8
d. Type III, perf. 14 35.00 50

President Masaryk
A9 A10

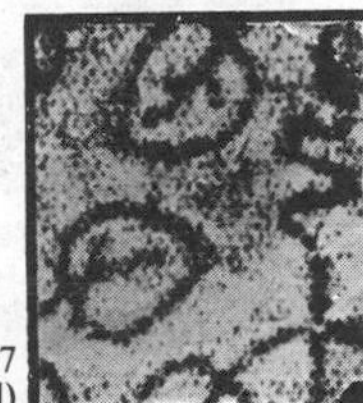
Wmk. 107 (Vertical)

Wmk. Linden Leaves (107)
1925 Photo. ***Perf. 14x13½, 13½***
Size: 19½x23mm.
95 A9 40h brn org 2.00 5
96 A9 50h ol grn 3.50 5
97 A9 60h red vio 4.00 5

Distinctive Marks of the Engravings.

I, II, III: Background of horizontal lines in top and bottom tablets. Inscriptions in Roman letters with serifs.

IV: Crossed horizontal and vertical lines in the tablets. Inscriptions in Antique letters without serifs.

I, II, IV: Shading of crossed diagonal lines on the shoulder at the right.

III. Shading of single lines only.

I: "T" of "Posta" over middle of "V" of "Ceskoslovenska". Three short horizontal lines in lower part of "A" of "Ceskoslovenska".

II: "T" over right arm of "V". One short line in "A".

III: "T" as in II. Blank space in lower part of "A".

IV: "T" over left arm of "V".

Wmk. Horizontally (107)
Engr.
I. First Engraving
Size: 19¾x22½mm.
98 A10 1k carmine 2.25 15
99 A10 2k dp bl 5.50 35
100 A10 3k brown 10.50 90
101 A10 5k bl grn 3.50 60

Wmk. Vertically (107)
Size: 19¼x23mm.
101A A10 1k carmine 200.00 7.50
101B A10 2k dp bl 250.00 25.00
101C A10 3k brown 750.00 25.00
101D A10 5k bl grn 8.00 2.75

II. Second Engraving
Wmk. Horizontally (107)
Size: 19x21½mm.
102 A10 1k carmine 70.00 60
103 A10 2k dp bl 9.00 35
104 A10 3k brown 10.00 70

III. Third Engraving
Size: 19-19½x21½-22mm.
Perf. 10
105 A10 1k car rose 3.00 15
a. Perf. 14 30.00 15

IV. Fourth Engraving
Size: 19-19½x21½-22mm.
1926 *Perf. 10, 14*
106 A10 1k car rose 2.00 10
108 A10 3k brown 11.00 15

See No. 130.

Karlstein Castle — A11

1926, June 1 Engr. *Perf. 10*
109 A11 1.20k red vio 1.40 75
110 A11 1.50k car rose 1.10 5
111 A11 2.50k dk bl 6.00 60

See Nos. 133, 135.

Karlstein Castle A12

Pernstein Castle A13

Orava Castle A14

Masaryk A15

Strahov Monastery A16

Hradcany at Prague A17

Great Tatra — A18

1926-27 Engr. Wmk. 107
114 A13 30h gray grn 2.25 20
115 A14 40h red brn 90 10
116 A15 50h dp grn 90 10
117 A15 60h red vio, *lil* 1.50 5
118 A16 1.20k red vio 7.25 2.50
Perf. 13½
119 A17 2k blue 1.65 15
a. 2k ultra 5.00 75
120 A17 3k dp red 3.25 15
121 A18 4k brn vio ('27) 7.25 70
122 A18 5k dk grn ('27) 30.00 4.50
Nos. 114-122 (9) 54.95 8.45

No. 116 exists in two types. The one with short, straight mustache at left sells for several times as much as that with longer wavy mustache.

See Nos. 137-140.

Coil Stamps
Perf. 10 Vertically
123 A12 20h brick red 1.50 60
a. Vert. pair, imperf. horiz. 150.00
124 A13 30h gray grn 1.00 25
a. Vert. pair, imperf. horiz. 150.00
125 A15 50h dp grn 50 12

See No. 141.

1927-31 Unwmk. ***Perf. 10***
126 A13 30h gray grn 35 5
127 A14 40h dp brn 1.00 5
128 A15 50h dp grn 30 5
129 A15 60h red vio 95 5
130 A10 1k car rose 8.25 20
131 A15 1k dp red 42 5
132 A16 1.20k red vio 60 5
133 A11 1.50k car ('29) 85 5
134 A13 2k dp grn ('29) 70 5
135 A11 2.50k dk bl 8.25 40
136 A14 3k red brn ('31) 85 5
Nos. 126-136 (11) 22.52 1.05

No. 130 exists in two types. The one with longer mustache at left sells for several times as much as that with the short mustache.

1927-28 ***Perf. 13½***
137 A17 2k ultra 1.75 10
138 A17 3k dp red ('28) 4.25 95
139 A18 4k brn vio ('28) 10.00 1.50
140 A18 5k dk grn ('28) 11.50 75

Coil Stamp
1927 ***Perf. 10 Vertically***
141 A12 20h brick red 65 20

Hradec Castle — A19

Town Hall, Levoca — A20

Telephone Exchange, Prague — A21

Town of Jasina — A22

Hluboka Castle — A23

Pilgrims' House at Velehrad — A24

Brno Cathedral
A25

Great Tatra
A26

Masaryk
A27

Old City Square, Prague
A28

1928, Oct. 22 *Perf. 13½*
142 A19 30h black 15 10
143 A20 40h red brn 22 20
144 A21 50h dk grn 25 8
145 A22 60h org red 25 8
146 A23 1k carmine 35 6
147 A24 1.20k brn vio 85 90
148 A25 2k ultra 1.00 35
149 A26 2.50k dk bl 2.50 2.25
150 A27 3k dk brn 1.90 50
151 A28 5k dp vio 3.00 3.00
Nos. 142-151 (10) 10.47 7.52

Tenth anniversary of Czechoslovakian independence.

Coat of Arms — A29

1929-37 *Perf. 10*
152 A29 5h dk ultra ('31) 5 5
153 A29 10h bis brn ('31) 5 5
154 A29 20h red 5 5
155 A29 25h green 8 5
156 A29 30h red vio 8 5
157 A29 40h dk brn ('37) 35 5
a. 40h red brn ('37) 1.25 12

Coil Stamp
Perf. 10 Vertically
158 A29 20h red 30 5
Nos. 152-158 (7) 96 35

St. Wenceslas
A30

Founding St. Vitus' Cathedral
A31

Design: 3k, 5k, St. Wenceslas martyred.

1929, May 14 *Perf. 13½*
159 A30 50h gray grn 40 10
160 A30 60h sl vio 65 10
161 A31 2k dl bl 1.40 60
162 A30 3k brown 1.65 30
163 A30 5k brn vio 8.00 4.00
Nos. 159-163 (5) 12.10 5.10

Millenary of the death of St. Wenceslas.

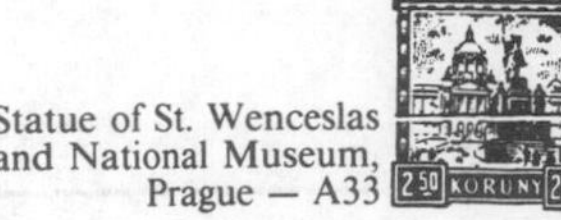
Statue of St. Wenceslas and National Museum, Prague — A33

1929 *Perf. 10*
164 A33 2.50k dp bl 85 5

Brno Cathedral
A34

Tatra Mountain Scene
A35

Design: 5k, Old City Square, Prague.

1929, Oct. 15 *Perf. 13½*
165 A34 3k red brn 3.50 12
166 A35 4k indigo 6.75 85
167 A35 5k gray grn 8.50 50

See No. 183.

A37

Type I

Type II

Two types of 50h:
I. A white space exists across the bottom of the vignette between the coat, shirt and tie and the "HALERU" frame panel.
II. An extra frame line has been added just above the "HALERU" panel which finishes off the coat and tie shading evenly.

1930, Jan. 2 *Perf. 10*
168 A37 50h myr grn (II) 20 5
a. Type I 1.25 5
169 A37 60h brn vio 90 5
170 A37 1k brn red 40 5

See No. 234.

Coil Stamp

1931 *Perf. 10 Vertically*
171 A37 1k brn red 1.75 1.00

President Masaryk
A38

St. Nicholas' Church, Prague
A39

1930, Mar. 1 *Perf. 13½*
175 A38 2k gray grn 1.10 40
176 A38 3k red brn 2.00 38
177 A38 5k sl bl 6.00 2.25
178 A38 10k gray blk 12.00 5.50

Eightieth birthday of President Masaryk.

1931, May 15
183 A39 10k blk vio 12.00 3.75

Krivoklat Castle — A40

Krumlov Castle — A42

Design: 4k, Orlik Castle.

1932, Jan. 2 *Perf. 10*
184 A40 3.50k violet 3.25 1.50
185 A40 4k dp bl 3.75 50
186 A42 5k gray grn 3.25 50

Miroslav Tyrs
A43 A44

1932, Mar. 16
187 A43 50h yel grn 55 8
188 A43 1k brn car 90 8
189 A44 2k dk bl 8.75 35
190 A44 3k red brn 15.00 60

Issued to commemorate the centenary of the birth of Miroslav Tyrs (1832-1884), founder of the Sokol movement, and in connection with the 9th Sokol Congress.

Tyrs — A45

1933, Feb. 1
191 A45 60h dl vio 30 5

First Chirstian Church at Nitra
A46 A47

1933, June 20
192 A46 50h yel grn 50 8
193 A47 1k car rose 5.00 20

Issued in commemoration of Prince Pribina who introduced Christianity into Slovakia and founded there the first Christian church in A. D. 833.
All gutter pairs are vertical.

Bedrich Smetana — A48

1934, Mar. 26 **Engr.** *Perf. 10*
194 A48 50h yel grn 45 5

Issued to commemorate the 50th anniversary of the death of Bedrich Smetana, Czech composer and pianist.

Consecration of Legion Colors at Kiev, Sept. 21, 1914 — A49

Ensign Heyduk with Colors
A51

Legionnaires
A52

Design: 1k, Legion receiving battle flag at Bayonne.

1934, Aug. 15 *Perf. 10*
195 A49 50h green 28 6
196 A49 1k rose lake 45 5
197 A51 2k dp bl 2.25 40
198 A52 3k red brn 4.50 40

Issued in commemoration of the 20th anniversary of the Czechoslovakian Legion which fought in World War I.

Antonin Dvorak — A53

1934, Nov. 22
199 A53 50h green 35 5

Issued to commemorate the 30th anniversary of the death of Antonin Dvorak, (1841-1904), composer.

Pastoral Scene — A54

1934, Dec. 17 *Perf. 10*
200 A54 1k claret 70 12
a. Souvenir sheet of 15 275.00 275.00
b. As "a," single stamp 9.50 8.75
201 A54 2k blue 2.75 60
a. Souvenir sheet of 15 850.00 850.00
b. As "a," single stamp 35.00 35.00

Issued in commemoration of the centenary of the National Anthem.
Nos. 200a & 201a were issued in special souvenir sheets of 15 stamps each on thick paper, darker shades, perf. 13½, no gum. Words and music of the anthem at top and bottom of sheet. Forgeries exist.

President Masaryk
A55 A56

1935, Mar. 1
202 A55 50h grn, *buff* 12 5
203 A55 1k cl, *buff* 28 5
204 A56 2k gray bl, *buff* 2.00 45
205 A56 3k brn, *buff* 3.50 45

85th birthday of President Masaryk.
See No. 235.

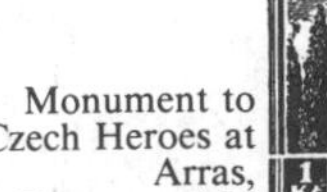

Monument to Czech Heroes at Arras, France — A57

1935, May 4
206 A57 1k rose 65 5
207 A57 2k dl bl 1.75 30

20th anniversary of the Battle of Arras.

General Milan Stefánik
A58

Sts. Cyril and Methodius
A59

1935, May 18
208 A58 50h green 20 5

1935, June 22
209 A59 50h green 15 8
210 A59 1k claret 50 5
211 A59 2k dp bl 1.65 45

Issued in commemoration of the millenary of the arrival in Moravia of the Apostles Cyril and Methodius.

Masaryk
A60

Statue of Macha, Prague
A61

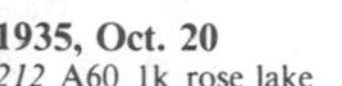

1935, Oct. 20 *Perf. 12½*
212 A60 1k rose lake 10 5

No. 212 exists imperforate. See No. 256.

1936, Apr. 30
213 A61 50h dp grn 20 8
214 A61 1k rose lake 35 8

Issued to commemorate the centenary of the death of Karel Hynek Macha (1810-1836), Bohemian poet.

Jan Amos Komensky
A61a

President Eduard Benes
A62

Gen. Milan Stefanik — A63

1936
215 A61a 40h dk bl 10 5
216 A62 50h dl grn 10 5
217 A63 60h dl vio 10 5

See Nos. 252 and 255.

Castle Palanok near Mukacevo
A64

Town of Banska Bystrica
A65

Castle at Zvikov
A66

Ruins of Castle at Strecno
A67

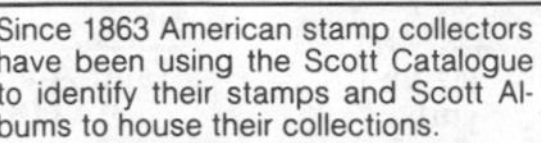

Castle at Cesky Raj
A68

Palace at Slavkov (Austerlitz)
A69

Statue of King George at Podebrad
A70

Town Square at Olomouc
A71

Castle Ruins at Bratislava
A72

1936, Aug. 1
218 A64 1.20k rose lil 12 5
219 A65 1.50k carmine 12 5
220 A66 2k dk bl grn 15 5
221 A67 2.50k dk bl 30 5
222 A68 3k brown 32 6
223 A69 3.50k dk vio 1.50 60
224 A70 4k dk vio 65 10
225 A71 5k green 50 10
226 A72 10k blue 1.75 60
Nos. 218-226 (9) 5.41 1.66

President Benes
A73

Soldiers of the Czech Legion
A74

1937, Apr. 26 **Unwmk.** *Perf. 12½*
227 A73 50h dp grn 10 5

1937, June 15
228 A74 50h dp grn 18 5
229 A74 1k rose lake 32 6

Issued in commemoration of the 20th anniversary of the Battle of Zborov.

Cathedral at Prague
A75

Jan Evangelista Purkyne
A76

1937, July 1
230 A75 2k green 80 15
231 A75 2.50k blue 1.10 50

Issued in commemoration of the 16th anniversary of the founding of the "Little Entente."

1937, Sept. 2
232 A76 50h sl grn 20 5
233 A76 1k dl rose 25 5

Issued in commemoration of the 150th anniversary of the birth of Jan Evangelista Purkyne, Czech physiologist.

Masaryk Types of 1930-35

1937, Sept. *Perf. 12½*
234 A37 50h black 18 5

With date "14.IX. 1937" in design.
235 A56 2k black 45 15

Issued in commemoration of the death of former President Thomas G. Masaryk on Sept. 14, 1937.

International Labor Bureau Issue

Stamps of 1936-37 Overprinted in Violet or Black

B.I.T.1937

1937, Oct. 6 *Perf. 12½*
236 A73 50h dp grn (Bk) 30 40
237 A65 1.50k car (V) 40 50
238 A66 2k dp grn (V) 60 75

Bratislava Philatelic Exhibition Issue Souvenir Sheet

A77

1937, Oct. 24 *Perf. 12½*
239 A77 Sheet of two 1.75 1.75
a. 50h dk bl 75 75
b. 1k brn car 75 75

The sheet measures 149x110mm. The stamps show a view of Poprad Lake (50h) and the tomb of General Milan Stefanik (1k).

No. 239 overprinted "Liberation de la Tchechoslovaquie, 28-X-1945" etc., was sold at a philatelic exhibition in Brussels, Belgium.

St. Barbara's Church, Kutna Hora — A79

Peregrine Falcon, Sokol Emblem — A80

1937, Dec. 4
240 A79 1.60k ol grn 15 5

1938, Jan. 21
241 A80 50h dp grn 35 10
242 A80 1k rose lake 55 15

Issued in commemoration of the 10th International Sokol Games. Imperforate copies of No. 242 are essays. Nos. 241-242 se-tenant with labels sell slightly higher.

Legionnaires
A81

Legionnaires
A82

Legionnaire — A83

1938
243 A81 50h dp grn 15 5
244 A82 50h dp grn 15 5
245 A83 50h dp grn 15 5

Issued to commemorate the 20th anniversary of the Battles of Bachmac, Vouziers and Doss Alto. Nos. 243-245 with label se-tenant sell for more.

Jindrich Fügner, Co-Founder of Sokol Movement — A84

1938, June 18 *Perf. 12½*
246 A84 50h dp grn 10 5
247 A84 1k rose lake 18 5
248 A84 2k sl bl 60 6

Issued to commemorate the 10th Sokol Summer Games. Nos. 246-248 se-tenant with labels sell slightly higher.

View of Pilsen
A85

Cathedral of Kosice
A86

1938, June 24
249 A85 50h dp grn 15 5

Issued in connection with the Provincial Economic Council meeting at Pilsen.

1938, July 15 *Perf. 12½*
250 A86 50h dp grn 15 5

Issued in connection with the Kosice Cultural Exhibition.

Prague Philatelic Exhibition Issue Souvenir Sheet

Vysehrad Castle - Hradcany — A87

1938, June 26 *Perf. 12½*
251 A87 Sheet of two 4.50 4.50
a. 50h dk bl 2.00 2.00
b. 1k dp car 2.00 2.00

Issued in sheets measuring 148½x105mm.

Stefanik Type of 1936

1938, Nov. 21
252 A63 50h dp grn 30 5

Allegory of the Republic — A89

1938, Dec. 19 **Unwmk.**
253 A89 2k lt ultra 65 20
254 A89 3k pale brn 75 25

Issued in commemoration of the 20th anniversary of Independence.

"Wir sind frei!"

Stamps of Czechoslovakia, 1918-37, overprinted with a swastika in black or red and "Wir sind frei!" were issued locally and unofficially in 1938 as Czech authorities were evacuating and German authorities arriving. They appeared in the towns of Asch, Karlsbad, Reichenberg-Maffersdorf, Rumburg, etc.

The overprint, sometimes including a surcharge or the town name (as in Karlsbad), exists on many values of postage, air post, semi-postal, postage due and newspaper stamps.

Stefanik Type of 1936

1939 **Engr.** ***Perf. 12½***
255 A63 60h dk bl 20.00 20.00

Used exclusively in Slovakia.

Masaryk Type of 1935 with hyphen in Cesko-Slovensko

1939, Apr. 23
256 A60 1k rose lake 15 5

Linden Leaves and Buds — A90

1945 **Photo.** ***Perf. 14***
256A A90 10(h) black 5 5
257 A90 30(h) yel brn 5 5
258 A90 50(h) dk grn 5 5
258A A90 60(h) dk bl 5 5

Engr.
(Buds Open)
Perf. 12½

259 A90 60(h) blue 5 5
259A A90 80(h) org ver 6 5
260 A90 1.20(k) rose 5 5
261 A90 3(k) vio brn 5 5
262 A90 5(k) green 5 5
Nos. 256A-262 (9) 46 45

Thomas G. Masaryk A91

Coat of Arms A92

1945-46 **Photo.** ***Perf. 12***
262A A91 5h dl vio ('46) 8 6
262B A91 10h org yel ('46) 8 6
262C A91 20h dk brn ('46) 6 5
263 A91 50h brt grn 10 5
264 A91 1k org red 12 6
265 A91 2k chlky bl 30 30
Nos. 262A-265 (6) 74 58

1945 ***Imperf.***
266 A92 50h ol gray 5 5
267 A92 1k brt red vio 5 5
268 A92 1.50k dk car 6 5
269 A92 2k dp bl 8 5
269A A92 2.40k hn brn 35 20
270 A92 3k brown 6 5
270A A92 4k dk sl grn 10 5
271 A92 6k vio bl 30 8
271A A92 10k sepia 45 10
Nos. 266-271A (9) 1.50 68

Nos. 266 to 217A exist in two printings. Stamps of the first printing are on thin, hard paper in sheets of 100; those of the second printing on thick, soft wove paper in sheets of 200.

Czechoslovakia stamps can be mounted in Scott's annually supplemented Czechoslovakia Album.

Staff Captain Ridky (British Army) A93

Dr. Miroslav Novak (French Army) A94

Captain Otakar Jaros (Russian Army) A95

Staff Captain Stanislav Zimprich (Foreign Legion) A96

Second Lieutenant Jiri Kral (French Air Force) A97

Josef Gabcik (Parachutist) A98

Staff Captain Alois Vasatko (Royal Air Force) A99

Private Frantisek Adamek (British Colonial Service) A100

Perf. 11½x12½
1945, Aug. 18 **Engr.**
272 A93 5h int bl 5 5
273 A94 10h dk brn 5 5
274 A95 20h brick red 5 5
275 A96 25h rose red 5 5
276 A97 30h purple 10 5
277 A98 40h sepia 5 5
278 A99 50h dk ol 5 5
279 A100 60h violet 15 6
280 A93 1k carmine 5 5
281 A94 1.50k lake 6 5
282 A95 2k ultra 8 5
283 A96 2.50k dp vio 10 5
284 A97 3k sepia 10 5
285 A98 4k rose lil 15 6
286 A99 5k myr grn 25 8
287 A100 10k brt ultra 75 20
Nos. 272-287 (16) 2.09 1.00

Flags of Russia, Great Britain, United States and Czechoslovakia A101

View of Banska Bystrica A102

Patriot Welcoming Russian Soldier, Turciansky A103

Ruins of Castle at Sklabina A104

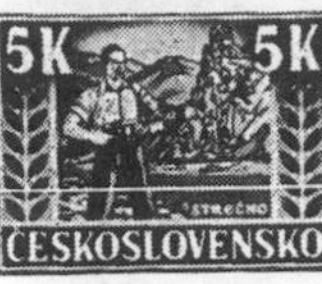

Czech Patriot, Strecno — A105

1945, Aug. 29 **Photo.** ***Perf. 10***
288 A101 1.50k brt car 10 15
289 A102 2k brt bl 10 15
290 A103 4k dk brn 40 30
291 A104 4.50k purple 40 30
292 A105 5k dp grn 1.00 1.00
Nos. 288-292 (5) 2.00 1.90

National uprising against the Germans.

A card contains one each of Nos. 288-292 with multicolored marginal design, on thin cardboard, ungummed. Size: 148x210mm. Sold for 50k.

General Milan Stefanik A106

President Eduard Benes A107

Thomas G. Masaryk — A108

1945-47 **Engr.** ***Perf. 12, 12½***
293 A106 30h rose vio 5 5
294 A107 60h blue 8 5
294A A106 1k red org ('47) 8 5
295 A108 1.20k car rose 10 5
295A A108 1.20(k) rose lil ('46) 8 5
296 A106 2.40(k) rose 10 5
297 A107 3k red vio 22 5
297A A108 4k dk bl ('46) 12 5
298 A108 5k Prus grn 22 5
299 A107 7k gray 25 5
300 A106 10k gray bl 60 5
300A A106 20k sep ('46) 1.25 25
Nos. 293-300A (12) 3.15 80

1945 **Photo.** ***Perf. 14***
301 A108 50h brown 5 5
302 A106 80h dk grn 5 5
303 A107 1.60(k) ol grn 8 5
304 A108 15k red vio 80 10

Kozina and Chod Castle, Taus — A109

Red Army Soldier — A110

1945, Nov. 28 **Engr.** ***Perf. 12½***
305 A109 2.40k rose car 20 16
306 A109 4k blue 25 16

Issued to commemorate the 250th anniversary of the death of Jan Sladky Kozina, peasant leader.

1945, Mar. 26 **Litho.** ***Imperf.***
307 A110 2k crim rose 55 55
308 A110 5k sl blk 2.00 2.00
309 A110 6k ultra 65 65

Souvenir Sheet

A111

1945, July 16
Gray Burelage
310 A111 Sheet of three 3.00 3.00
a. 2k crim rose 35 35
b. 5k sl blk 35 35
c. 6k ultra 35 35

Return of President Benes, April, 1945. Size: 137x120mm.

Clasped Hands A112

Karel Havlicek Borovsky A113

1945 ***Rouletted 12½***
311 A112 1.50k brn red 3.75 3.75
312 A112 9k red org 80 90
313 A112 13k org brn 1.10 1.10
314 A112 20k blue 3.00 3.00

1946, July 5 **Engr.**
315 A113 1.20(k) gray blk 25 25

Issued to commemorate the 90th anniversary of the death of Karel Havlicek Borovsky (1821-1856), editor and writer.

Old Town Hall, Brno A114

Hodonin Square A115

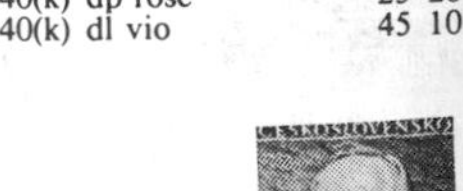

Perf. 12½x12, 12x12½.
1946, Aug. 3 **Engr.** **Unwmk.**
316 A114 2.40(k) dp rose 25 20
317 A115 7.40(k) dl vio 45 10

President Eduard Benes — A116

1946, Oct. 28
318 A116 60h indigo 5 5
319 A116 1.60k dl grn 6 5
320 A116 3k red lil 8 5
321 A116 8k sepia 35 5

Flag and Symbols A117

Saint Adalbert A118

1947, Jan. 1 *Perf. 12½*

322 A117 1.20(k) Prus grn 20 5
323 A117 2.40(k) dp rose 20 5
324 A117 4(k) dp bl 50 15

Issued to publicize Czechoslovakia's two-year reconstruction and rehabilitation program.

1947, Apr. 23

326 A118 1.60(k) gray 60 35
327 A118 2.40(k) rose car 1.00 80
328 A118 5(k) bl grn 1.25 55

Issued to commemorate the 950th anniversary of the death of Saint Adalbert, Bishop of Prague.

Grief — A119

Allegorical Figure — A120

1947, June 10 **Engr.**

329 A119 1.20(k) black 35 30
330 A119 1.60(k) sl blk 45 45
331 A120 2.40(k) brn vio 55 55

Destruction of Lidice, 5th anniversary.

World Federation of Youth Symbol A121

Thomas G. Masaryk A122

1947, July 20

332 A121 1.20(k) vio brn 35 18
333 A121 4k slate 55 22

Issued to commemorate the World Youth Festival held in Prague, July 20th to August 17, 1947.

1947, Sept. 14

334 A122 1.20(k) gray blk, *buff* 25 12
335 A122 4k bl blk, *cr* 65 18

Death of T. G. Masaryk, 10th anniversary.

Msgr. Stefan Moyses — A123

1947, Oct. 24

336 A123 1.20k rose vio 25 8
337 A123 4k dp bl 42 25

Issued to commemorate the 150th anniversary of the birth of Stefan Moyses, first Slovakian chairman of the Slavic movement.

"Freedom from Social Oppression" A124

1947, Oct. 26 **Photo.** *Perf. 14*

338 A124 2.40k brt car 30 30
339 A124 4k brt ultra 60 20

Issued to commemorate the 30th anniversary of the Russian revolution of October, 1917.

President Eduard Benes A125

"Czechoslovakia" Greeting Sokol Marchers A126

1948, Feb. 15 **Photo.**

Size: 17½x21½mm.

340 A125 1.50(k) brown 6 5

Size: 19x23mm.

341 A125 2k dp plum 10 5
342 A125 5k brt ultra 25 5

1948, Mar. 7 **Engr.** *Perf. 12½*

343 A126 1.50(k) brown 15 6
344 A126 3k rose car 15 6
345 A126 5k blue 50 8

The 11th Sokol Congress.

King Charles IV — A127

St. Wenceslas and King Charles IV — A128

1948, Apr. 7

346 A127 1.50(k) blk brn 15 5
347 A128 2(k) dk brn 20 5
348 A128 3(k) brn red 30 12
349 A127 5(k) dk bl 60 25

Issued to commemorate the 600th anniversary of the foundation of Charles University, Prague.

Czech Peasants in Revolt A129

Jindrich Vanicek A130

Unwmk.

1948, May 14 **Photo.** *Perf. 14*

350 A129 1.50k dk ol brn 15 10

Centenary of abolition of serfdom.

1948, June 10 **Engr.** *Perf. 12½*

Designs: 1.50k, 2k, Josef Scheiner.

351 A130 1k dk grn 12 5
352 A130 1.50k sepia 12 5
353 A130 2k gray bl 28 10
354 A130 3k claret 40 15

11th Sokol Congress, Prague, 1948.

Frantisek Palacky and F. L. Rieger — A131

Miloslav Josef Hurban — A132

1948, June 20 **Unwmk.**

355 A131 1.50k gray 20 8
356 A131 3k brn car 30 8

Issued to commemorate the centenary of the Constituent Assembly at Kromeriz.

1948, Aug. 27 *Perf. 12½*

Designs: 3k, Ludwig Stur. 5k, Michael M. Hodza.

357 A132 1.50(k) dk brn 15 8
358 A132 3(k) car lake 25 8
359 A132 5(k) indigo 45 20

Centenary of 1848 insurrection against Hungary.

Eduard Benes A133

Czechoslovak Family A134

1948, Sept. 28

360 A133 8k black 30 10

Issued in tribute to President Eduard Benes, 1884-1948.

1948, Oct. 28 *Perf. 12½x12*

361 A134 1.50k dp bl 10 10
362 A134 3k rose car 30 18

Issued to commemorate the 30th anniversary of Czechoslovakia's Independence.

Pres. Klement Gottwald A135

Gottwald and Presidential Flag A136

1948-49 *Perf. 12½*

Size: 18½x23½mm.

363 A135 1.50(k) dk brn 10 5
364 A135 3(k) car rose 25 5
a. 3(k) rose brn 35 5
365 A135 5(k) gray bl 25 5

Size: 23½x29mm.

366 A135 20(k) purple 1.25 15

See Nos. 373, 564, 600-604.

Souvenir Sheet

1948, Nov. 23 **Unwmk.** ***Imperf.***

367 A136 30k rose brn 4.00 3.00

52nd birthday of Pres. Klement Gottwald (1896-1953). Size: 67x98½mm.

Souvenir Sheet

Hradcany Castle A137

1948, Dec. 18

368 A137 10k dk bl vio 1.50 1.25

30th anniversary of first Czechoslovak postage stamp. Size: 79x90½mm.

Czechoslovak and Russian Workmen Shaking Hands — A138

Lenin — A139

1948, Dec. 12 *Perf. 12½*

369 A138 3k rose car 24 12

Issued to commemorate the fifth anniversary of the treaty of alliance between Czechoslovakia and Russia.

1949, Jan. 21 **Engr.** *Perf. 12½*

370 A139 1.50(k) vio brn 24 10
371 A139 5(k) dp bl 40 16

25th anniversary of the death of Lenin.

Gottwald Type of 1948 Inscribed: "UNOR 1948" and

Gottwald Addressing Meeting — A140

1949, Feb. 25 **Photo.** *Perf. 14*

372 A140 3k red brn 15 5

Perf. 12½

Engr.

Size: 23½x29mm.

373 A135 10k dp grn 65 20

Nos. 372 and 373 were issued to commemorate the first anniversary of Klement Gottwald's speech announcing the appointment of a new government.

P. O. Hviezdoslav A141

Stagecoach and Train A142

Designs (Writers): 80h, V. Vancura. 1k, J. Sverma. 2k, Julius Fucik. 4k, Jiri Wolker. 8k, Alois Jirasek.

1949 **Photo.** *Perf. 14*

374 A141 50h vio brn 5 5
375 A141 80h scarlet 10 5
376 A141 1k dk ol grn 10 5
377 A141 2k brt bl 40 5

Perf. 12½

Engr.

378 A141 4k vio brn 40 5
379 A141 8k brn blk 50 5
Nos. 374-379 (6) 1.55 30

1949, May 20

Designs: 5k, Postrider and post bus. 13k, Sailing ship and plane.

380 A142 3k brn car 2.75 2.25
381 A142 5k dp bl 70 45
382 A142 13k dp grn 1.25 65

Issued to commemorate the 75th anniversary of the formation of the Universal Postal Union.

Reaping — A143

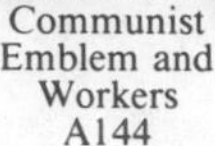

Communist Emblem and Workers
A144

Workman, Symbol of Industry
A145

Perf. 12½x12, 12x12½

1949, May 24 **Unwmk.**

383 A143 1.50k dp grn 75 45
384 A144 3k brn car 40 30
385 A145 5k dp bl 75 45

No. 384 commemorates the ninth meeting of the Communist Party of Czechoslovakia, May 25, 1949.

Friedrich Smetana and National Theater, Prague
A146

Aleksander Pushkin
A147

1949, June 4 ***Perf. 12½x12***

386 A146 1.50k dl grn 30 15
387 A146 5k dp bl 70 40

Issued to commemorate the 125th anniversary of the birth of Friedrich Smetana, composer.

1949, June 6 ***Perf. 12x12½***

388 A147 2k ol gray 35 20

Issued to commemorate the 150th anniversary of the birth of Aleksander S. Pushkin.

Frederic Chopin and Conservatory, Warsaw — A148

1949, June 24 ***Perf. 12½x12***

389 A148 3k dk red 50 30
390 A148 8k vio brn 1.25 60

Issued to commemorate the centenary of the death of Frederic F. Chopin.

Globe and Ribbon — A149

Zvolen Castle — A150

1949, Aug. 20 ***Perf. 12½x12***

391 A149 1.50k vio brn 30 25
392 A149 5k ultra 70 45

Issued to publicize the 50th Prague Sample Fair, September 11-18, 1949.

Starting in 1949, commemorative stamps which are priced in italics were issued in smaller quantities than those in the balance of the set and sold at prices higher than face value.

1949, Aug. 28 ***Perf. 12½***

393 A150 10k rose lake 85 5

Early Miners — A151

Miner of Today — A152

Design: 5k, Mining Machine.

1949, Sept. 11 ***Perf. 12½x12, 12½***

394 A151 1.50k sepia 1.00 90
395 A152 3k car rose *5.25 2.00*
396 A151 5k dp bl *4.25 2.00*

Issued to commemorate the 700th anniversary of the Czechoslovak mining industry and the 150th anniversary of the miner's laws.

Construction Workers
A153

Joseph V. Stalin
A154

Design: 2k, Machinist.

1949, Dec. 11 ***Perf. 12½***

397 A153 1k dk grn 3.50 1.00
398 A153 2k vio brn 2.00 60

2nd Trade Union Congress, Prague, 1949.

1949, Dec. 21 **Unwmk.**

Cream Paper

Design: 3k, Stalin facing left.

399 A154 1.50k grnsh gray *1.75 80*
400 A154 3k claret *2.75 1.25*

70th birthday of Joseph V. Stalin.

Skier — A155

Efficiency Badge — A156

Engraved, 3k Photogravure

1950, Feb. 15 ***Perf. 12½, 13½***

401 A155 1.50k gray bl *2.75 1.00*
402 A156 3k vio brn, *cr* 2.75 1.75
403 A155 5k ultra *3.50 2.50*

Issued to publicize the 51st Ski Championship for the Tatra cup, Feb. 15-26, 1950.

Vladimir V. Mayakovsky — A157

1950, Apr. 14 **Engr.** ***Perf. 12½***

404 A157 1.50k dk brn *3.00 1.75*
405 A157 3k brn red 3.00 1.25

Issued to commemorate the 20th anniversary of the death of V. V. Mayakovsky, poet.

See Nos. 414-417, 422-423, 432-433, 464-465, 477-478.

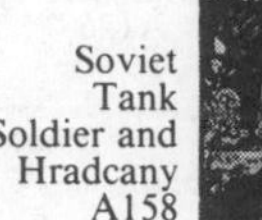

Soviet Tank Soldier and Hradcany
A158

Designs: 2k, Hero of Labor medal. 3k, Two workers (militiamen) and Town Hall, Prague. 5k, Text of government program and heraldic lion.

1950, May 5

406 A158 1.50k gray grn 50 25
407 A158 2k dk brn *1.10 85*
408 A158 3k brn red 40 25
409 A158 5k dk bl 65 20

Issued on the occasion of the fifth anniversary of the Czechoslovak People's Democratic Republic.

Factory and Young Couple with Tools
A159

Designs: 2k, Steam shovel. 3k, Farmer and farm scene. 5k, Three workers leaving factory.

1950, May 9 **Engr.**

410 A159 1.50k dk grn 1.10 1.00
411 A159 2k dk brn *1.50 1.00*
412 A159 3k rose red 55 25
413 A159 5k dp bl 55 25

Canceled to Order

The government philatelic department started about 1950 to sell canceled sets of new issues. Prices in the second ("used") column are for these canceled-to-order stamps. Postally used copies are worth more.

Portrait Type of 1950

Design: S. K. Neumann.

1950, June 5 **Unwmk.** ***Perf. 12½***

414 A157 1.50k dp bl 25 12
415 A157 3k vio brn *1.00 90*

Issued to commemorate the 75th anniversary of the birth of Stanislav Kostka Neumann (1875-1947), journalist and poet.

1950, June 21

Design: Bozena Nemcova.

416 A157 1.50k dp bl *1.50 1.25*
417 A157 7k dk brn 40 30

Issued to commemorate the 130th anniversary of the birth of Bozena Nemcova (1820-1862), writer.

Liberation of Colonies — A160

Designs: 2k, Allegory, Fight for Peace. 3k, Group of Students. 5k, Marching Students with flags.

1950, Aug. 14

418 A160 1.50k dk grn 12 5
419 A160 2k sepia *1.10 80*
420 A160 3k rose car 22 15
421 A160 5k ultra 55 35

Issued to publicize the 2nd International Students World Congress, Prague, August 12-24, 1950.

Portrait Type of 1950

Design: Zdenek Fibich.

1950, Oct. 15

422 A157 3k rose brn *1.10 90*
423 A157 8k gray grn 45 35

Issued to commemorate the centenary of the birth of Zdenek Fibich, musician.

Miner, Soldier and Farmer
A161

Czech and Soviet Soldiers
A162

1950, Oct. 6

424 A161 1.50k slate *75 60*
425 A162 3k car rose 40 20

Issued to publicize Czech Army Day.

Prague Castle, 16th Century
A163

Prague, 1493
A164

Designs: 3k, Prague, 1606. 5k, Prague, 1794.

1950, Oct. 21 ***Perf. 14***

426 A163 1.50k black 4.00 4.00
427 A164 2k chocolate 4.00 4.00
428 A164 3k brn car 4.00 4.00
429 A164 5k gray 4.00 4.00
a. Block of 4 25.00 20.00

Sheets arranged in blocks of four containing one of Nos. 426 to 429. See Nos. 434-435.

Communications Symbols — A165

1950, Oct. 25 ***Perf. 12½***

430 A165 1.50k chocolate 12 5
431 A165 3k brn car *75 40*

Issued to commemorate first anniversary of the foundation of the International League of P.T.T. Employees.

Portrait Type of 1950

Design: J. Gregor Tajovsky.

1950, Oct. 26

432 A157 1.50k brown *1.25 75*
433 A157 5k dp bl *75 50*

Issued to commemorate the 10th anniversary of the death of J. Gregor Tajovsky (1874-1940), Slovakian writer.

Scenic Type of 1950

Design: Prague, 1950.

1950, Oct. 28

434	A164	1.50k	indigo	30	20
a.			Souvenir sheet of 4, imperf.	17.50	15.00
435	A164	3k	brn car	80	75

No. 434a measures 121x100 mm. and contains four copies of No. 434, imperforate, with carmine inscription in top margin.

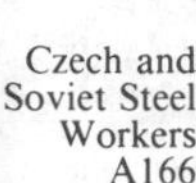

Czech and Soviet Steel Workers A166

1950, Nov. 4 **Unwmk.**

436	A166	1.50k	chocolate	35	20
437	A166	5k	dp bl	85	75

Issued to publicize the 2nd meeting of the Union of Czechoslovak-Soviet Friendship.

Dove by Picasso — A167

1951, Jan. 20 **Photo.** ***Perf. 14***

438	A167	2k	dp bl	5.00	2.50
439	A167	3k	rose brn	2.75	2.00

Issued to commemorate the first Czechoslovak Congress of Fighters for Peace, held in Prague.

Julius Fucik — A168

1951, Feb. 17 **Engr.** ***Perf. 12½***

440	A168	1.50k	gray	670	40
441	A168	5k	gray bl	1.50	1.00

Drop Hammer A169

Installing Gear A170

1951, Feb. 24

442	A169	1.50k	gray blk	8	8
443	A170	3k	vio brn	12	8
444	A169	4k	gray bl	85	65

Women Machinists A171

Apprentice Miners A172

Designs: 3k, Woman tractor operator. 5k, Women of different races.

1951, Mar. 8 **Photo.** ***Perf. 14***

445	A171	1.50k	ol brn	30	10
446	A171	3k	brn car	1.25	75
447	A171	5k	blue	50	20

International Women's Day, Mar. 8.

1951, Apr. 12 **Engr.** ***Perf. 12½***

448	A172	1.50k	gray	50	35
449	A172	3k	red brn	16	10

Plowing — A173

Collective Cattle Breeding — A174

1951, Apr. 28 **Photo.** ***Perf. 14***

450	A173	1.50k	brown	65	50
451	A174	2k	dk grn	1.00	1.00

Tatra Mountain Recreation Center A175

Mountain Recreation Centers: 2k, Beskydy (Beskids). 3k, Krkonose (Carpathians).

1951, May 5 **Engr.** ***Perf. 12½***

452	A175	1.50k	dp grn	20	10
453	A175	2k	dk brn	70	65
454	A175	3k	rose brn	85	35

Issued to publicize the summer opening of trade union recreation centers.

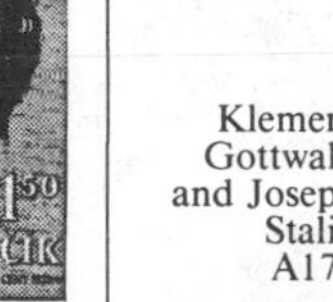

Klement Gottwald and Joseph Stalin A176

Factory Militiaman A177

Red Army Soldier and Partisan A178

Marx, Engels, Lenin and Stalin A179

1951 **Unwmk.** ***Perf. 12½***

455	A176	1.50k	ol gray	70	30
456	A177	2k	red brn	30	8
457	A178	3k	rose brn	50	10
458	A176	5k	dp bl	3.00	2.00
459	A179	8k	gray	1.00	35
			Nos. 455-459 (5)	5.50	2.83

Issued to commemorate the 30th anniversary of the founding of the Czechoslovak Communist Party.

Antonin Dvorák — A180

Design: 1.50k, 3k, Bedrich Smetana.

1951, May 30

460	A180	1k	redsh brn	20	15
461	A180	1.50k	ol gray	90	40
462	A180	2k	dk redsh brn	1.10	90
463	A180	3k	rose brn	20	15

International Music Festival, Prague.

Portrait Type of 1950

1951, June 21

Portrait: Bohumir Smeral (facing right).

464	A157	1.50k	dk gray	55	45
465	A157	3k	rose brn	40	15

Issued to commemorate the 10th anniversary of the death of Bohumir Smeral, political leader.

Gymnast on Rings — A181

Designs: 1.50k, Discus Thrower. 3k, Soccer. 5k, Skier.

1951, June 21

466	A181	1k	dk grn	80	45
467	A181	1.50k	dk brn	80	45
468	A181	3k	brn car	1.40	45
469	A181	5k	dp bl	3.00	2.00

Issued to honor the 9th Congress of the Czechoslovak Sokol Federation.

Scene from "Fall of Berlin" A182

Scene from "The Great Citizen" A183

1951, July 14

470	A182	80h	rose brn	25	20
471	A183	1.50k	dk gray	38	30
472	A182	4k	gray bl	1.50	1.00

Issued on the occasion of the International Film Festival, Karlovy Vary, July 14-29, 1951.

Alois Jirásek — A184

"Fables and Fate" A185

Design: 4k, Scene from "Reign of Tabor."

1951, Aug. 23 **Engr.** ***Perf. 12½***

473	A184	1.50k	gray	22	15
474	A184	5k	dk bl	2.25	1.75

Photo.

Perf. 14

475	A185	3k	dk red	30	20
476	A185	4k	dk brn	45	25

Issued to commemorate the centenary of the birth of Alois Jirasek, author.

Portrait Type of 1950

Design: Josef Hybes.

1951, July 21 **Engr.**

477	A157	1.50k	chocolate	18	8
478	A157	2k	rose brn	80	45

Issued to commemorate the centenary of the birth of Josef Hybes (1850-1921), cofounder of Czech Communist Party.

"Ostrava Region" A186

Mining Iron Ore A187

1951, Sept. 9

479	A186	1.50k	dk brn	12	8
480	A187	3k	rose brn	15	10
481	A186	5k	dp bl	1.50	75

Miner's Day, Sept. 9, 1951.

Soldiers on Parade — A188

Designs: 1k, Gunner and field gun. 1.50k, Klement Gottwald. 3k, Tankman and tank. 5k, Aviators.

Photogravure (80h, 5k), Engraved
1951, Oct. 6 ***Perf. 14 (80h, 5k), 12½***
Inscribed: "Den CS Armady 1951."

482	A188	80h	ol brn	18	15
483	A188	1k	dk ol grn	30	30
484	A188	1.50k	sepia	55	30
485	A188	3k	claret	65	30
486	A188	5k	blue	1.40	1.10
			Nos. 482-486 (5)	3.08	2.15

Issued to publicize Army Day, Oct. 6, 1951.

Joseph Stalin and Klement Gottwald A189

Lenin, Stalin and Soldiers A190

1951, Nov. 3 **Engr.** ***Perf. 12½***

487	A189	1.50k	sepia	15	10
488	A190	3k	red brn	20	8
489	A189	4k	dp bl	1.25	65

Issued to publicize the month of Czechoslovak-Soviet friendship, 1951.

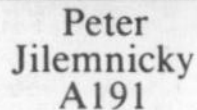

Peter Jilemnicky A191

Ladislav Zapotocky A192

1951, Dec. 5 **Unwmk.**

491 A191 1.50k redsh brn 30 20
492 A191 2k dl bl 60 50

Issued to commemorate the 50th anniversary of the birth of Peter Jilemnicky (1901-1949), writer.

1952, Jan. 12 ***Perf. 11½***

493 A192 1.50k brn red 10 5
494 A192 4k gray 60 45

Issued to commemorate the centenary of the birth of Ladislav Zapotocky, Bohemian socialist pioneer.

Jan Kollar — A193

Lenin and Lenin Hall — A194

1952, Jan. 30 **Unwmk.** ***Perf. 11½***

495 A193 3k dk car 10 5
496 A193 5k vio bl 90 60

Issued to commemorate the centenary of the death of Jan Kollar (1793-1852), poet.

1952, Jan. 30 ***Perf. 12½***

497 A194 1.50k rose car 12 5
498 A194 5k dp bl 60 45

Issued to commemorate the 40th anniversary of the Sixth All-Russian Party Conference.

Emil Holub and African — A195

Klement Gottwald Metallurgical Plant — A196

1952, Feb. 21 ***Perf. 11½***

499 A195 3k red brn 50 35
500 A195 5k gray 1.75 1.50

Issued to commemorate the 50th anniversary of the death of Emil Holub, explorer.

1952, Feb. 25 **Photo.** ***Perf. 14***

Designs: 2k, Foundry. 3k, Chemical plant.

501 A196 1.50k sepia 12 10
502 A196 2k red brn 1.10 95
503 A196 3k scarlet 18 10

Student, Soldier and Worker A197

Youths of Three Races A198

1952, Mar. 21 **Unwmk.** ***Perf. 14***

504 A197 1.50k blue 12 10
505 A198 2k ol blk 25 15
506 A197 3k lake 1.00 80

International Youth Day, Mar. 25, 1952.

Similar to Type of 1951

Portrait: Otakar Sevcik.

1952, Mar. 22 **Engr.** ***Perf. 12½***

507 A184 2k choc, *cr* 70 60
508 A184 3k rose brn, *cr* 20 15

Issued to commemorate the centenary of the birth of Otakar Sevcik, violinist.

Jan A. Komensky A199

Industrial and Farm Women A200

1952, Mar. 28

509 A199 1.50k dk brn, *cr* 1.65 75
510 A199 11k dk bl, *cr* 35 10

Issued to commemorate the 360th anniversary of the birth of Jan Amos Komensky (Comenius), teacher and philosopher.

1952, Mar. 8

511 A200 1.50k dp bl, *cr* 1.25 70

International Women's Day Mar. 8, 1952.

Woman and Children A201

Antifascist A202

1952, Apr. 12

512 A201 2k chocolate, *cr* 90 65
513 A201 3k dp cl, *cr* 20 10

Issued to publicize the International Conference for the Protection of Children, Vienna, April 12-16, 1952.

1952, Apr. 11 **Photo.** ***Perf. 14***

514 A202 1.50k red brn 15 8
515 A202 2k ultra 75 55

Issued to publicize the Day of International Solidarity of Fighters against Fascism, April 11, 1952.

Harvester A203

Design: 3k, Tractor and Seeders.

1952, Apr. 30

516 A203 1.50k dp bl 90 80
517 A203 2k brown 30 22
518 A203 3k brn red 30 22

Youths Carrying Flags A204

1952, May 1

519 A204 3k brn red 75 60
520 A204 4k dk red brn 90 75

Issued to publicize Labor Day, May 1, 1952.

Crowd Cheering Soviet Soldiers A205

1952, May 9

521 A205 1.50k dk red 75 50
522 A205 5k dp bl 1.50 1.25

Liberation of Czechoslovakia from German occupation, 7th anniversary.

Children A206

J. V. Myslbek A207

Design: 3k, "Pioneer" teaching children.

1952, May 31 **Engr.** ***Perf. 12½***

523 A206 1.50k dk brn, *cr* 8 5
524 A206 2k Prus grn, *cr* 1.00 60
525 A206 3k rose brn, *cr* 12 8

International Children's Day May 31, 1952.

1952, June 2

Design: 8k, Allegory, "Music."

526 A207 1.50k red brn 18 6
527 A207 2k dk brn 1.40 1.10
528 A207 8k gray grn 25 10

Issued to commemorate the 30th anniversary of the death of Joseph V. Myslbek (1848-1922), sculptor.

Beethoven A208

House of Artists A209

1952, June 7 **Unwmk.** ***Perf. 11½***

529 A208 1.50k sepia 45 40
530 A209 3k red brn 45 40
531 A208 5k indigo 1.65 1.25

International Music Festival, Prague, 1952.

Lidice, Symbol of a New Life — A210

1952, June 10 ***Perf. 12½***

532 A210 1.50k dk vio brn 20 8
533 A210 5k dk bl 85 65

Destruction of Lidice, 10th anniversary.

Jan Hus — A211

Bethlehem Chapel — A212

1952, July 5

534 A211 1.50k brown 8 6
535 A212 3k red brn 12 8
536 A211 5k black 1.10 80

Issued to commemorate the 550th anniversary of the installation of Jan Hus as pastor of Bethlehem Chapel, Prague.

Doctor Examining Patient — A213

Design: 2k, Doctor, Nurse, Mother and child.

1952, July 31

537 A213 1.50k dk brn 85 60
538 A213 2k bl vio 12 6
539 A213 3k rose brn 22 8

Czechoslovakia's Unified Health Service.

Relay Race — A214

Designs: 2k, Canoeing. 3k, Cycling. 4k, Hockey.

1952, Aug. 2 ***Perf. 11½***

540 A214 1.50k dk brn 70 35
541 A214 2k grnsh blk 1.75 90
542 A214 3k red brn 50 35
543 A214 4k dp bl 3.00 2.25

Issued to publicize Czechoslovakia's Unified Physical Education program.

F. L. Celakovski A215

Mikulas Ales A216

1952, Aug. 5 ***Perf. 12½***

544 A215 1.50k dk brn 12 8
545 A215 2k dk grn 80 60

Issued to commemorate the centenary of the death of Frantisek L. Celakovski, poet and writer.

Perf. 11x11½

1952, Aug. 30 **Engr.** **Unwmk.**

546 A216 1.50k dk gray grn 45 30
547 A216 6k red brn 2.75 2.00

Birth centenary of Mikulas Ales, painter.

The Catalogue editors cannot undertake to appraise, identify or judge the genuineness or condition of stamps.

17th Century Mining Towers — A217

Jan Zizka — A218

Designs: 1.50k, Coal Excavator. 2k, Peter Bezruc mine. 3k, Automatic coaling crane.

1952, Sept. 14 *Perf. 12½*

548	A217	1k sepia	*1.10*	75
549	A217	1.50k dk bl	10	6
550	A217	2k ol gray	18	10
551	A217	3k vio brn	22	8

Issued to publicize Miners' Day, Sept. 14, 1952. No. 550 also commemorates the 85th anniversary of the birth of Peter Bezruc (Vladimir Vasek), poet.

1952, Oct. 5 **Engr.** *Perf. 11½*
Inscribed: ". . . . Armady 1952,"

Designs: 2k, Fraternization with Russians. 3k, Marching with flag.

552	A218	1.50k rose lake	12	6
553	A218	2k ol bis	16	5
554	A218	3k dk car rose	16	10
555	A218	4k gray	*1.50*	*1.10*

Issued to publicize Army Day, Oct. 5, 1952.

Souvenir Sheet

Statues to Bulgarian Partisans and to Soviet Army — A219

1952, Oct. 18 **Unwmk.** *Perf. 12½*

556	A219	Sheet of two	57.50	20.00
a.		2k dp car	22.50	7.50
b.		3k ultra	22.50	7.50

Issued to commemorate the National Philatelic Exhibition, Bratislava, Oct. 18-Nov. 2, 1952.

Danube River, Bratislava A220

1952, Oct. 18

557	A220	1.50k dk brn	25	10

National Philatelic Exhibition, Bratislava.

Conference with Lenin and Stalin — A221

Worker and Nurse Holding Dove and Olive Branch — A222

The indexes in each volume of the Scott Catalogue contain many listings which help to identify stamps.

1952, Nov. 7

558	A221	2k brn blk	*70*	*60*
559	A221	3k carmine	25	10

Issued to commemorate the 35th anniversary of the Russian Revolution and to publicize Czechoslovak-Soviet friendship.

1952, Nov. 15 **Photo.** *Perf. 14*

560	A222	2k brown	*75*	*50*
561	A222	3k red	20	10

Issued to publicize the first State Congress of the Czechoslovak Red Cross.

Matej Louda, Hussite Leader, Painted by Mikulas Ales A223

Design: 3k, Dragon-killer Trutnov, painted by Ales.

1952, Nov. 18 **Engr.** *Perf. 11½*

562	A223	2k red brn	25	8
563	A223	3k grnsh gray	35	15

Issued to commemorate the centenary of the birth of Mikulas Ales, painter.

Gottwald Type of 1948-49

1952, June 2 **Unwmk.** *Perf. 12½*
Size: 19x24mm.

564	A135	1k dk grn	10	5

"Peace" Flags A224

Dove by Picasso A225

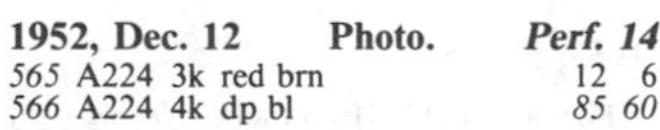

1952, Dec. 12 **Photo.** *Perf. 14*

565	A224	3k red brn	12	6
566	A224	4k dp bl	*85*	*60*

Issued to publicize the Congress of Nations for Peace, Vienna, Dec. 12-19, 1952.

1953, Jan. 17

Design: 4k, Czech Family.

567	A225	1.50k dk brn	10	5
568	A225	4k sl bl	*70*	*40*

2nd Czechoslovak Peace Congress.

Smetana Museum — A226

Design: 4k, Jirásek Museum.

1953, Feb. 10 **Engr.** *Perf. 11½*

569	A226	1.50k dk vio brn	10	6
570	A226	4k dk gray	*1.00*	*75*

Issued to commemorate the 75th anniversary of the birth of Prof. Zdenek Nejedly.

Martin Kukucin A227

Jaroslav Vrchlicky A228

Designs: 2k, Karel Jaromir Erben. 3k, Vaclav Matej Kramerius. 5k, Josef Dobrovsky.

1953, Feb. 28

571	A227	1k gray	10	5
572	A228	1.50k olive	8	5
573	A228	2k rose lake	8	5
574	A228	3k lt brn	25	15
575	A228	5k sl bl	*1.50*	*1.50*
		Nos. 571-575 (5)	2.01	1.80

Issued to honor Czech writers and poets: 1k, 25th anniversary of death of Kukucin. 1.50k, birth centenary of Vrchlicky. 2k, centenary of completion of "Kytice" by Erben. 3k, birth bicentenary of Kramerius. 5k, birth bicentenary of Dobrovsky.

Militia A229

Klement Gottwald A230

Design: 8k, Portraits of Stalin and Gottwald and Peoples Assembly.

Perf. 13½x14

1953, Feb. 25 **Photo.** **Unwmk.**

576	A229	1.50k dp bl	10	10
577	A230	3k red	16	15
578	A229	8k dk brn	*1.25*	*1.00*

Issued to commemorate the 5th anniversary of the defeat of the attempt to reinstate capitalism.

Book and Torch — A231

Design: 3k, Bedrich Vaclavek.

1953, Mar. 5 **Engr.** *Perf. 11½*

579	A231	1k sepia	*75*	*60*
580	A231	3k org brn	20	15

Issued to commemorate the 10th anniversary of the death of Bedrich Vaclavek (1897-1943), socialist writer.

Stalin Type of 1949
Inscribed "21 XII 1879-5 III 1953"

1953, Mar. 12

581	A154	1.50k black	25	15

Death of Joseph Stalin, Mar. 5, 1953.

Mother and Child A232

Girl Revolutionist A233

1953, Mar. 8

582	A232	1.50k ultra	10	5
583	A233	2k brn red	*50*	*40*

International Women's Day.

Klement Gottwald — A234

1953, Mar. 19

584	A234	1.50k black	12	6
585	A234	3k black	12	6

Souvenir Sheet
Imperf

586	A234	5k black	2.75	2.00

No. 586 measures 68x97 mm., with marginal inscriptions and laurel branch.

Nos. 584-586 commemorate the death of President Klement Gottwald, March 14, 1953.

Josef Pecka, Ladislav Zapotocky and Josef Hybes — A236

1953, Apr. 7 **Unwmk.** *Perf. 11½*

587	A236	2k lt vio brn	15	10

Issued to commemorate the 75th anniversary of the first congress of the Czech Social Democratic Party.

Cyclists — A237

1953, Apr. 29

588	A237	3k dp bl	50	30

Issued to commemorate the 6th International Peace Bicycle Race, Prague-Berlin-Warsaw.

Medal of "May 1, 1890" A238

Designs: 1.50k, Lenin and Stalin. 3k, May Day Parade. 8k, Marx and Engels.

Engraved and Photogravure

1953, Apr. 30 *Perf. 11½x11, 14*

589	A238	1k chocolate	*1.40*	*1.35*
590	A238	1.50k dk gray	10	6
591	A238	3k car lake	20	10
592	A238	8k dk gray grn	30	15

Issued to publicize Labor Day, May 1, 1953.

Sowing Grain — A239

Design: 7k, Reaper.

1953, May 8 Photo. *Perf. 14*

593 A239 1.50k brown 40 15
594 A239 7k dp grn *1.25 1.10*

Issued to publicize the socialization of the village.

Dam — A240 Welder — A241

Design: 3k, Iron works.

1953, May 8 *Perf. 11½*

595 A240 1.50k gray *75 60*
596 A241 2k bl gray 15 6
597 A240 3k red brn 15 5

Josef Slavik A242 Leos Janacek A243

1953, June 19

598 A242 75h dp gray bl *40 10*
599 A243 1.60k dk brn 1.10 8

Issued on the occasion of the International Music Festival, Prague, 1953.

Gottwald Type of 1948-49

1953 *Perf. 12½, 11½*

600 A135 15h yel grn 20 5
601 A135 20h dk vio brn 30 5
602 A135 1k purple 90 5
603 A135 3k brn car 10 5
604 A135 3k gray 1.00 5
Nos. 600-604 (5) 2.50 25

Nos. 600-604 vary slightly in size. Nos. 600 and 602 are perf. 12½; Nos. 601, 603-604 are perf. 11½.

Pres. Antonin Zapotocky — A244

1953, June 19 Photo. *Perf. 14*

605 A244 30h vio bl 35 5
606 A244 60h cerise 60 5

Julius Fucik A245 Book and Carnation A246

1953, Sept. 8 Engr. *Perf. 12½*

607 A245 40h dk vio brn 30 5
608 A246 60h pink *65 35*

Issued to commemorate the 10th anniversary of the death of Julius Fucik, Communist leader executed by the Nazis.

Miner and Flag — A247

Design: 60h, Oil field and workers.

1953, Sept. 10 *Perf. 11½*

609 A247 30h gray 22 5
610 A247 60h brn vio *75 50*

Issued to publicize Miner's Day, Sept. 10, 1953.

Volleyball Game A248 Motorcyclist A249

Design: 60h, Woman throwing javelin.

1953, Sept. 15

611 A248 30h brn red *2.50 2.00*
612 A249 40h dk vio brn 4.00 1.25
613 A248 60h rose vio 4.00 1.25

Hussite Warrior A250 Pres. Antonin Zapotocky A251

Designs: 60h, Soldier presenting arms. 1k, Red army soldiers.

1953, Oct. 8

614 A250 30h brown 35 10
615 A250 60h rose lake 80 10
616 A250 1k brn red *1.50 1.25*

Issued to publicize Army Day, Oct. 3, 1953.

1953 Unwmk. *Perf. 11½, 12½*

617 A251 30h vio bl 45 5
618 A251 60h car rose 55 5

No. 617 is perf. 11½ and measures 19x23 mm. No. 618 is perf. 12½ and measures 18½x23½.
See No. 780.

Charles Bridge and Prague Castle — A252 Korean and Czech Girls — A253

1953, Aug. 15 Engr. *Perf. 11½*

619 A252 5k gray 2.75 10

1953, Oct. 11 *Perf. 11x11½*

620 A253 30h dk brn 4.00 2.00

Issued to demonstrate Czechoslovakia's friendship with Korea.

Flags, Hradcany Castle and Kremlin — A254

Designs: 60h, Lomonosov University, Moscow. 1.20k, Lenin Ship Canal.

1953, Nov. 7

621 A254 30h dk gray *1.75 1.10*
622 A254 60h dk brn 2.00 1.25
623 A254 1.20k ultra 3.00 2.00

Issued to publicize the month of Czechoslovak-Soviet friendship.

Emmy Destinn, Opera Singer — A255 National Theater, Prague — A256

Portrait: 2k, Eduard Vojan, actor.

1953, Nov. 18 *Perf. 14*

624 A255 30h bl blk 85 45
625 A256 60h brown 30 6
626 A255 2k sepia *2.50 3.00*

Issued to commemorate the 70th anniversary of the founding of the National Theater.

Josef Manes — A257 Vaclav Hollar — A258

1953, Nov. 28 *Perf. 11x11½*

627 A257 60h brn car 50 10
628 A257 1.20k dp bl *1.50 85*

Issued to honor Josef Manes, painter.

1953, Dec. 5

Portrait: 1.20k, Head framed, facing right.

629 A258 30h brn blk 25 10
630 A258 1.20k dk brn *1.10 75*

Issued to honor Vaclav Hollar, artist and etcher.

Leo N. Tolstoi — A259

1953, Dec. 29 Unwmk.

631 A259 60h dk grn 45 15
632 A259 1k chocolate *1.25 1.00*

Issued to commemorate the 125th anniversary of the birth of Leo N. Tolstoi.

Locomotive — A260

Design: 1k, Plane loading mail.

Engraved, Center Photogravure

1953, Dec. 29 *Perf. 11½x11*

633 A260 60h brn org & gray vio 40 10
634 A260 1k org brn & brt bl *1.65 1.10*

Lenin — A261

Lenin Museum, Prague — A262

1954, Jan. 21 Engr. *Perf. 11½*

635 A261 30h dk brn 65 35
636 A262 1.40k chocolate *1.40 1.40*

Issued to commemorate the 30th anniversary of the death of Lenin.

Klement Gottwald — A263

Design: 2.40k, Revolutionist with flag.

Perf. 11x11½, 14x13½

1954, Feb. 18

637 A263 60h dk brn 50 5
638 A263 2.40k rose lake *4.50 2.00*

Issued to commemorate the 25th anniversary of the fifth congress of the Communist Party in Czechoslovakia.

Gottwald Mausoleum, Prague — A264

Gottwald and Stalin — A265

Design: 1.20k, Lenin & Stalin mausoleum, Moscow.

1954, Mar. 5 *Perf. 11½, 14x13½*

639 A264 30h ol brn 30 10
640 A265 60h dp ultra 40 15
641 A264 1.20k rose brn *1.75 1.35*

Issued to commemorate the first anniversary of the deaths of Joseph V. Stalin and Klement Gottwald.

Two Runners A266 Group of Hikers A267

Design: 1k, Woman swimmer.

1954, Apr. 24 *Perf. 11½*

642 A266 30h dk brn 2.50 1.00
643 A267 80h dk grn *5.50 5.00*
644 A266 1k dk vio bl 3.00 1.00

Nurse — A268

Designs: 15h, Construction worker. 40h, Postwoman. 45h, Ironworker. 50h, Soldier. 75h, Lathe operator. 80h, Textile worker. 1k, Farm woman. 1.20k, Scientist and microscope. 1.60k, Miner. 2k, Physician and baby. 2.40k, Engineer. 3k, Chemist.

1954 ***Perf. 12½x12, 11½x11***

645	A268	15h dk grn	15	5
646	A268	20h lt vio	20	5
647	A268	40h dk brn	30	5
648	A268	45h dk gray bl	25	5
649	A268	50h dk gray grn	40	5
650	A268	75h dp bl	35	5
651	A268	80h vio brn	40	5
652	A268	1k green	60	5
653	A268	1.20k dk vio bl	45	5
654	A268	1.60k brn blk	1.00	5
655	A268	2k org brn	1.25	5
656	A268	2.40k vio bl	1.10	5
657	A268	3k carmine	1.50	8
		Nos. 645-657 (13)	7.95	68

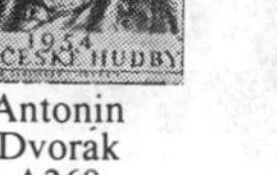
Antonin Dvorak A269

Prokop Divis A270

Portraits: 40h, Leos Janacek. 60h, Bedrich Smetana.

1954, May 22 ***Perf. 11x11½***

658	A269	30h vio brn	1.65	25
659	A269	40h brick red	2.00	25
660	A269	60h dk bl	1.10	25

Issued to publicize the "Year of Czech Music," 1954.

1954, June 15

661	A270	30h gray	15	15
662	A270	75h vio brn	*90*	*75*

Issued to commemorate the 200th anniversary of the invention of a lightning conductor by Prokop Divis.

Slovak Insurrectionist A271

Anton P. Chekhov A272

Design: 1.20k, Partisan woman.

1954, Aug. 28 ***Perf. 11½***

663	A271	30h brn org	15	8
664	A271	1.20k dk bl	*1.10*	*90*

Issued to commemorate the 10th anniversary of the Slovak national uprising.

1954, Sept. 24

665	A272	30h dl gray grn	15	6
666	A272	45h dl gray brn	*1.10*	*95*

Issued to commemorate the 50th anniversary of the death of Anton P. Chekhov, writer.

Czechoslovakia stamps can be mounted in Scott's annually supplemented Czechoslovakia Album.

Soviet Representative Giving Agricultural Instruction — A273

Designs: 60h, Soviet industrial instruction. 2k, Dancers (cultural collaboration).

1954, Nov. 6 ***Perf. 11½x11***

667	A273	30h yel brn	15	5
668	A273	60h dk bl	40	10
669	A273	2k vermilion	*1.50*	*1.50*

Issued to publicize the month of Czechoslovak-Soviet friendship.

Jan Neruda — A274

Portraits: 60h, Janko Jesensky. 1.60k, Jiri Wolker.

1954, Nov. 25 ***Perf. 11x11½***

670	A274	30h dk bl	1.25	15
671	A274	60h dl red	*2.00*	*75*
672	A274	1.60k sepia	1.10	30

Issued to honor Czechoslovak poets.

View of Telc A275

Views: 60h, Levoca. 3k, Ceske Budejovice.

Engraved and Photogravure

1954, Dec. 10

673	A275	30h blk & bis	50	8
674	A275	60h brn & bis	50	8
675	A275	3k blk & bis	*2.75*	*2.25*

Pres. Antonin Zapotocky A276

Attacking Soldiers A278

1954, Dec. 18 **Engr.** ***Perf. 11½***

676	A276	30h blk brn	50	20
677	A276	60h dk bl	40	20

Souvenir Sheet

Imperf

678	A276	2k dp cl	6.25	4.00

No. 678 measures 65 x 99¼mm., with arms and quotation in dark blue on sheet margins.

Nos. 676-678 commemorate the 70th birthday of President Antonin Zapotocky.

See Nos. 829-831.

1954, Oct. 3 ***Perf. 11½***

Design: 2k, Soldier holding child.

679	A278	60h dk grn	50	5
680	A278	2k dk brn	*1.60*	*1.40*

Issued to publicize Army Day, October 6, 1954.

Woman Holding Torch — A279

Comenius University Building — A280

Design: 45h, Ski jumper.

1955, Jan. 20 **Engr.**

681	A279	30h red	2.75	35

Engraved and Photogravure

682	A279	45h blk & bl	2.75	25

Issued to publicize the First National Spartacist Games, 1955.

1955, Jan. 28 **Engr.** ***Perf. 11½***

Design: 75h, Jan A. Komensky medal.

683	A280	60h dp grn	35	10
684	A280	75h chocolate	*90*	*75*

Issued to commemorate the 35th anniversary of the founding of Comenius University, Bratislava.

Czechoslovak Automobile A281

Designs: 60h, Textile worker. 75h, Lathe operator.

1955, Mar. 15 **Unwmk.**

685	A281	45h dl grn	80	75
686	A281	60h dk vio bl	30	5
687	A281	75h sepia	65	10

Woman Decorating Soviet Soldier — A282

Stalin Memorial, Prague — A283

Designs: 35h, Tankman with flowers. 60h, Children greeting soldier.

1955, May 5 **Engr.** ***Perf. 11½***

688	A282	30h blue	20	5
689	A282	35h dk brn	*80*	*60*
690	A282	60h cerise	55	6

Photo.

691	A283	60h sepia	55	8

Issued to commemorate the 10th anniversary of Czechoslovakia's liberation.

Music and Spring A284

Foundry Worker A285

Design: 1k, Woman with lyre.

Engraved and Photogravure

1955, May 12

692	A284	30h blk & pale bl	40	8
693	A284	1k blk & pale rose	*1.50*	*1.25*

Issued on the occasion of the International Music Festival, Prague, 1955.

1955, May 12 **Engr.**

Design: 45h, Farm workers.

694	A285	30h violet	20	5
695	A285	45h green	*80*	*75*

Issued to publicize the third congress of the Trade Union Revolutionary Movement.

Woman Athlete A286

Jakub Arbes A287

Designs: 60h, Dancing couple. 1.60k, Athlete.

1955, June 21

696	A286	20h vio bl	*65*	*60*
697	A286	60h green	35	10
698	A286	1.60k red	90	40

Issued to publicize the first National Spartacist Games, Prague, June-July, 1955.

1955

Portraits: 30h, Jan Stursa. 40h, Elena Marothy-Soltesova. 60h, Josef Vaclav Sladek. 75h, Alexander Stepanovic Popov. 1.40k, Jan Holly. 1.60k, Pavel Josef Safarik.

699	A287	20h brown	35	5
700	A287	30h black	35	5
701	A287	40h gray grn	75	10
702	A287	60h black	35	5
703	A287	75h claret	*1.75*	*1.00*
704	A287	1.40k blk, *cr*	75	25
705	A287	1.60k dk bl	75	15
		Nos. 699-705 (7)	5.05	1.65

Issued to commemorate various anniversaries of prominent Slavs.

Girl and Boy of Two Races A288

Costume of Ocova, Slovakia A289

1955, July 20

706	A288	60h vio bl	40	5

Issued to commemorate the fifth World Festival of Youth in Warsaw, July 31-August 14, 1955.

1955, July 25

Frame and Outlines in Brown

Regional Costumes: 75h, Detva man, Slovakia. 1.60k, Chodsko man, Bohemia. 2k, Hana woman, Moravia.

707	A289	60h org & rose	*10.50*	*6.50*
708	A289	75h org & lil	*3.75*	*2.50*
709	A289	1.60k bl & org	*7.75*	*6.50*
710	A289	2k yel & rose	*10.50*	*7.75*

Carp
A290

Designs: 30h, Beetle. 35h, Gray Partridge. 1.40k, Butterfly. 1.50k, Hare.

Engraved and Photogravure

1955, Aug. 8

No.	Type	Value	Color	Unused	Used
711	A290	20h	sep & lt bl	90	10
712	A290	30h	sep & pink	70	10
713	A290	35h	sep & buff	60	15
714	A290	1.40k	sep & cr	*3.00*	*2.75*
715	A290	1.50k	sep & lt grn	1.25	35
			Nos. 711-715 (5)	6.45	3.45

Tabor
A291

Designs: 45h, Prachatice. 60h, Jindrichuv Hradec.

1955, Aug. 26 **Engr.**

No.	Type	Value	Color	Unused	Used
716	A291	30h	vio brn	20	5
717	A291	45h	rose car	*80*	*75*
718	A291	60h	sage grn	20	5

Issued to publicize the architectural beauty of the towns of Southern Bohemia.

Souvenir Sheet

Various Views of Prague — A292

1955, Sept. 10 Engr. ***Perf. 14x13½***

No.	Type	Value	Color	Unused	Used
719	A292		Sheet of five	30.00	30.00
a.		30h	gray blk	4.75	4.75
b.		45h	gray blk	4.75	4.75
c.		60h	rose lake	4.75	4.75
d.		75h	rose lake	4.75	4.75
e.		1.60k	gray blk	4.75	4.75

Issued to commemorate the International Philatelic Exhibition, Prague, Sept. 10-25, 1955. Size: 145x110mm. Exists imperf., price $45.

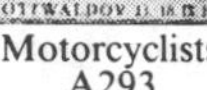
Motorcyclists
A293

Workers, Soldier and Pioneer
A294

1955, Aug. 28

No.	Type	Value	Color	Unused	Used
720	A293	60h	vio brn	3.25	50

Issued to commemorate the 30th International Motorcycle Races at Gottwaldov, Sept. 13-18, 1955.

1955, Oct. 6 Unwmk. ***Perf. 11½***

Design: 60h, Tanks and planes.

No.	Type	Value	Color	Unused	Used
721	A294	30h	vio brn	20	5
722	A294	60h	slate	*1.25*	*1.45*

Army Day, Oct. 6.

Hans Christian Andersen — A295

Portraits: 40h, Friedrich von Schiller. 60h, Adam Mickiewicz. 75h, Walt Whitman.

1955, Oct. 27

No.	Type	Value	Color	Unused	Used
723	A295	30h	brn red	18	10
724	A295	40h	dk bl	*1.10*	*1.00*
725	A295	60h	dp cl	25	8
726	A295	75h	grnsh blk	35	15

Issued in honor of these four poets and to mark the 100th anniversary of the publication of Walt Whitman's "Leaves of Grass".

Railroad Bridge
A296

Designs: 30h, Train crossing bridge. 60h, Train approaching tunnel. 1.60k, Miners' housing project.

Inscribed: "Stavba Socialismu"

1955, Dec. 15

No.	Type	Value	Color	Unused	Used
727	A296	20h	dl grn	12	15
728	A296	30h	vio brn	12	6
729	A296	60h	slate	25	5
730	A296	1.60k	car rose	70	10

Issued to publicize socialist public works.

Hydroelectric Plant
A297

Jewelry
A298

Designs: 10h, Miner with drill. 25h, Building construction. 30h, Harvester. 60h, Metallurgical plant.

Inscribed: "Druhy Petilety Plan 1956-1960."

1956, Feb. 20 ***Perf. 11½x11***

No.	Type	Value	Color	Unused	Used
731	A297	5h	vio brn	15	5
732	A297	10h	gray blk	20	5
733	A297	25h	dk car rose	45	5
734	A297	30h	green	20	5
735	A297	60h	vio bl	25	5
			Nos. 731-735 (5)	1.25	25

Second Five Year Plan.

1956, Mar. 17 ***Perf. 11x11½***

Designs: 45h, Glassware. 60h, Ceramics. 75h, Textiles.

No.	Type	Value	Color	Unused	Used
736	A298	30h	gray grn	42	6
737	A298	45h	dk bl	*4.75*	*2.75*
738	A298	60h	claret	30	6
739	A298	75h	gray	38	8

Products of Czechoslovakian industries.

Karlovy Vary (Karlsbad)
A299

"We Serve our People"
A300

Various Spas: 45h, Marianske Lazne (Marienbad). 75h, Piestany. 1.20k, Tatry Vysne Ruzbachy (Tatra Mountains).

1956, Mar. 17

No.	Type	Value	Color	Unused	Used
740	A299	30h	ol grn	1.10	25
741	A299	45h	brown	1.10	30
742	A299	75h	claret	*7.25*	*5.00*
743	A299	1.20k	ultra	65	20

Issued to publicize Czechoslovakian spas.

1956, Apr. 9 Photo. ***Perf. 11x11½***

Designs: 60h, Russian War Memorial, Berlin. 1(k), Tank crewman with standard.

No.	Type	Value	Color	Unused	Used
744	A300	30h	ol brn	20	5
745	A300	60h	car rose	25	5
746	A300	1k	ultra	*5.25*	*4.50*

Issued to publicize the exhibition: "The Construction and Defense of our Country," Prague, April, '56.

Cyclists
A301

Girl Basketball Players
A302

Athletes and Olympic Rings — A303

Engraved and Photogravure

1956, Apr. 25 Unwmk. ***Perf. 11½***

No.	Type	Value	Color	Unused	Used
747	A301	30h	grn & lt bl	2.00	30
748	A302	45h	dk bl & car	1.25	30
749	A303	75h	brn & lem	1.25	30

Issued to publicize the following: Ninth International Peace Cycling Race, Warsaw-Berlin-Prague, May 1-15, 1956 (No. 747). Fifth European Womens' Basketball Championship (No. 748). Summer Olympics, Melbourne, Nov. 22-Dec. 8, 1956 (No. 749).

Mozart — A304

Home Guard — A305

Designs: 45h, Josef Myslivecek. 60h, Jiri Benda. 1k, Bertramka House, Prague. 1.40k, Xaver Dusek (1731-1799) and wife Josepha. 1.60k, Nostic Theater, Prague.

1956, May 12 **Engr.**

Design in Gray Black

No.	Type	Value	Color	Unused	Used
750	A304	30h	bister	65	35
751	A304	45h	gray grn	*13.00*	*10.00*
752	A304	60h	pale rose lil	65	8
753	A304	1k	salmon	45	15
754	A304	1.40k	lt bl	1.40	50
755	A304	1.60k	lemon	65	10
			Nos. 750-755 (6)	16.80	11.18

Issued to commemorate the 200th anniversary of the birth of Wolfgang Amadeus Mozart and to publicize the International Music Festival in Prague.

1956, May 25

No.	Type	Value	Color	Unused	Used
756	A305	60h	vio bl	40	5

Issued to commemorate the first meeting of the Home Guard, Prague, May 25-27, 1956.

Josef Kajetan Tyl — A306

River Patrol — A307

Portraits: 20h, Ludovit Stur. 30h, Frana Sramek. 1.40k, Karel Havlicek Borovsky.

1956, June 23

No.	Type	Value	Color	Unused	Used
757	A306	20h	dl pur	45	15
758	A306	30h	blue	45	10
759	A306	60h	black	25	6
760	A306	1.40k	claret	*2.75*	*1.75*

Issued to honor various Czechoslovakian writers. See also Nos. 781-784, 873-876.

1956, July 8 ***Perf. 11x11½***

Design: 60h, Guard and dog.

No.	Type	Value	Color	Unused	Used
761	A307	30h	ultra	85	40
762	A307	60h	green	20	5

Issued to honor men of Frontier Guard.

Type of 1956 and

Steeplechase — A308

1956, Sept. 8 Unwmk. ***Perf. 11½***

No.	Type	Value	Color	Unused	Used
763	A308	60h	ind & bis	1.75	50
764	A308	80h	brn vio & vio	1.10	20
765	A303	1.20k	sl & org	90	30

Issued to publicize: Steeplechase, Pardubice, 1956 (No. 763). Marathon race, Kosice, 1956 (No. 764). Olympic Games, Melbourne, Nov. 22-Dec. 8 (No. 765).

Woman Gathering Grapes — A309

Fishermen — A310

Designs: 35h, Women gathering hops. 95h, Logging.

1956, Sept. 20 **Engr.**

No.	Type	Value	Color	Unused	Used
766	A309	30h	brn lake	25	5
767	A309	35h	gray grn	35	20
768	A310	80h	dk bl	30	15
769	A310	95h	chocolate	*1.75*	*1.75*

Issued to publicize natural resources.

Locomotive, 1846 — A311

Locomotive, 1855 – A312

Locomotives: 40h, 1945. 45h, 1952. 60h, 1955. 1k, 1954.

1956, Nov. 9 Unwmk. *Perf. 11½*

770	A311	10h brown	1.75	8
771	A312	30h gray	90	8
772	A312	40h green	2.75	20
773	A312	45h brn car	*12.50*	*10.00*
774	A312	60h indigo	90	5
775	A312	1k ultra	1.40	20
		Nos. 770-775 (6)	20.20	10.61

Issued to commemorate the European Timetable Conference at Prague, Nov. 9-13.

Costume of Moravia – A313

Regional Costumes (women): 1.20k, Blata, Bohemia. 1.40k, Cicmany, Slovakia. 1.60k, Novohradsko, Slovakia.

1956, Dec. 15 *Perf. 13½*

776	A313	30h brn, ultra & car	1.75	75
777	A313	1.20k brn, car & ultra	1.25	45
778	A313	1.40k brn, ocher & ver	*6.25*	*2.50*
779	A313	1.60k brn, car & grn	1.75	60

See Nos. 832-835.

Zapotocky Type of 1953

1956, Oct. 7 Unwmk. *Perf. 12½*

780	A251	30h blue	30	8

Portrait Type of 1956

1957, Jan. 18 Engr. *Perf. 11½*

Portraits: 15h, Ivan Olbracht. 20h, Karel Toman. 30h, F. X. Salda. 1.60k, Terezia Vansova.

781	A306	15h dk red brn, *cr*	38	8
782	A306	20h dk grn, *cr*	12	8
783	A306	30h dk brn, *cr*	12	8
784	A306	1.60k dk bl, *cr*	60	12

Issued in honor of Czechoslovakian writers.

Kolin Cathedral A315

Views: No. 786, Banska Stiavnica. No. 787, Uherske Hradiste. No. 788, Karlstein. No. 789, Charles Bridge, Prague. 1.25k, Moravska Trebova.

1957, Feb. 23

785	A315	30h dk bl gray	18	10
786	A315	30h rose vio	18	10
787	A315	60h dp rose	35	5
788	A315	60h gray grn	35	5
789	A315	60h brown	35	5
790	A315	1.25k gray	*1.65*	*1.50*
		Nos. 785-790 (6)	3.06	1.85

Issued to commemorate anniversaries of various towns and landmarks.

Komensky Mausoleum, Naarden A316

Jan A. Komensky (Comenius) A317

Farm Woman A318

Old Prints: 40h, Komensky teaching. 1k, Sun, moon, stars and earth.

Perf. 11½x11, 14 (A317)

1957, Mar. 28 Engr. Unwmk.

791	A316	30h pale brn	35	10
792	A316	40h dk grn	35	10
793	A317	60h chocolate	*1.65*	*80*
794	A316	1k car rose	55	15

Issued to commemorate the 300th anniversary of the publication of "Didactica Opera Omnia" by J. A. Komensky (Comenius). No. 793 issued in sheets of four.

1957, Mar. 22 *Perf. 11½*

795	A318	30h lt bl grn	35	10

Issued to publicize the 3rd Congress of Agricultural Cooperatives.

Cyclists A319

Woman Archer A320

Boxers – A321

Rescue Team A322

Perf. 11½x11, 11x11½

1957, Apr. 30

796	A319	30h sep & ultra	30	8
797	A319	60h dl grn & bis	*2.00*	*1.75*
798	A320	60h gray & emer	30	10
799	A321	60h sep & org	30	10
800	A322	60h vio & choc	30	5
		Nos. 796-800 (5)	3.20	2.08

Issued to publicize: 10th International Peace Cycling Race, Prague-Berlin-Warsaw (Nos. 796-797). International Archery Championships (No. 798). European Boxing Championships, Prague (No. 799). Mountain Climbing Rescue Service (No. 800).

Jan V. Stamic – A323

Musicians: No. 802, Ferdinand Laub. No. 803, Frantisek Ondricek. No. 804, Josef B. Foerster. No. 805, Vitezslav Novak. No. 806, Josef Suk.

1957, May 12 *Perf. 11½*

801	A323	60h purple	20	6
802	A323	60h black	20	6
803	A323	60h sl bl	20	6
804	A323	60h brown	20	6
805	A323	60h dl red brn	28	6
806	A323	60h bl grn	20	6
		Nos. 801-806 (6)	1.28	36

Spring Music Festival, Prague.

Josef Bozek A324

School of Engineering A325

Portraits: 60h, F. J. Gerstner. 1k, R. Skuhersky.

1957, May 25

807	A324	30h bluish blk	20	6
808	A324	60h gray brn	35	8
809	A324	1k rose lake	40	15
810	A325	1.40k bl vio	75	15

Issued to commemorate the 250th anniversary of the School of Engineering in Prague.

Pioneer and Philatelic Symbols A326

Design: 60h, Girl and carrier pigeon.

Engraved and Photogravure

1957, June 8 *Perf. 11½*

811	A326	30h ol grn & org	60	10

Engr. *Perf. 13½*

812	A326	60h brn & vio bl	*1.75*	*1.60*

Youth Philatelic Exhibition, Pardubice.

"Grief" A327

Motorcyclists A328

Design: 60h, Rose, symbol of new life.

1957, June 10

813	A327	30h black	25	5
814	A327	60h blk & rose red	*75*	*35*

Destruction of Lidice, 15th anniversary.

1957, July 5 *Perf. 11½*

815	A328	60h dk gray & bl	75	8

32nd International Motorcycle Race.

Karel Klic – A329

Josef Ressel – A330

1957, July 5

816	A329	30h gray blk	15	5
817	A330	60h vio bl	25	5

Issued to honor Karel Klic, inventor of photogravure, and Josef Ressel, inventor of the ship screw.

Chamois – A331

Gentian A332

Designs: 30h, Brown bear. 60h, Edelweiss. 1.25k, Tatra Mountains.

1957, Aug. 28 Engr. *Perf. 11½*

818	A331	20h emer & brnsh gray	60	35
819	A331	30h lt bl & brn	30	5
820	A332	40h gldn brn & vio bl	45	5
821	A332	60h yel & grn	35	5
822	A332	1.25k ol grn & bis	*2.50*	*2.00*
		Nos. 818-822 (5)	4.20	2.50

Issued to publicize the Tatra Mountains National Park. No. 822 measures 48x28½mm.

"Marycka Magdonova" A333

Man Holding Banner of Trade Union Congress A334

Engraved and Photogravure

1957, Sept. 15 Unwmk. *Perf. 11½*

823	A333	60h blk & dl red	35	5

Issued to commemorate the 90th birthday of Petr Bezruc, poet and author of "Marycka Magdonova."

1957, Sept. 28 **Engr.**
824 A334 75h rose red 40 10

Issued to publicize the fourth International Trade Union Congress, Leipzig, Oct. 4-15.

Television Transmitter and Antennas — A335

Design: 60h, Family watching television.

1957, Oct. 19 **Engr.** ***Perf. 11½***
825 A335 40h dk bl & car 15 5
826 A335 60h redsh brn & emer 25 5

Issued to publicize the television industry.

Worker, Globe and Lenin A336

Design: 60h, Worker, factory, hammer and sickle.

1957, Nov. 7 ***Perf. 12x11½***
827 A336 30h claret 15 6
828 A336 60h gray bl 25 8

Russian Revolution, 40th anniversary.

Zapotocky Type of 1954 dated: 19 XII 1884-13 XI 1957

1957, Nov. 18 **Unwmk.** ***Perf. 11½***
829 A276 30h black 15 5
830 A276 60h black 30 5

Souvenir Sheet

Imperf

831 A276 2k black 1.40 1.00

Issued to commemorate the death of Pres. Antonin Zapotocky.

No. 831 measures 69x99½mm. Olive branch below stamp; no marginal inscription.

Costume Type of 1956

Regional Costumes: 45h, Pilsen woman, Bohemia. 75h, Slovacko man, Moravia. 1.25k, Hana woman, Moravia. 1.95k, Teshinsko woman, Silesia.

1957, Dec. 18 **Engr.** ***Perf. 13½***
832 A313 45h brn, bl & dk red 3.00 1.25
833 A313 75h dk brn, red & grn 2.50 1.10
834 A313 1.25k dk brn, scar & ocher 3.50 1.00
835 A313 1.95k sep, bl & ver *4.50 2.25*

Radio Telescope and Observatory A337

Meteorological Station in High Tatra — A338

Design: 75h, Sputnik 2 over Earth.

1957, Dec. 20 ***Perf. 11½***
836 A337 30h vio brn & yel 2.25 1.25
837 A338 45h sep & lt bl 60 45
838 A337 75h cl & bl 3.00 1.50

International Geophysical Year, 1957-58. No. 838 also commemorates the launching of Sputnik 2, Nov. 3, 1957.

Girl Skater — A339

Litomysl Castle — A340

Designs: 40h, Canoeing. 60h, Volleyball. 80h, Parachutist. 1.60k, Soccer.

1958, Jan. 25 **Engr.** ***Perf. 11½x12***
839 A339 30h rose vio 50 20
840 A339 40h blue 24 5
841 A339 60h redsh brn 28 5
842 A339 80h vio bl *1.75 85*
843 A339 1.60k brt grn 55 12
Nos. 839-843 (5) 3.32 1.27

Issued to publicize various sports championship events in 1958.

1958, Feb. 10 ***Perf. 11½***

Design: 60h, Bethlehem Chapel.

844 A340 30h green 10 5
845 A340 60h redsh brn 20 5

Issued to commemorate the 80th anniversary of the birth of Zdenek Nejedly, restorer of Bethlehem Chapel.

Giant Excavator A341

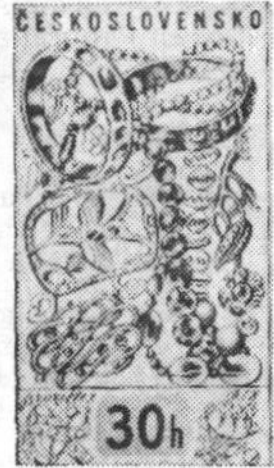

Jewelry A342

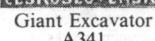

Peace Dove and: 60h, Soldiers, flame and banner (horiz.). 1.60k, Harvester and rainbow (horiz.).

1958, Feb. 25
846 A341 30h gray vio & yel 20 5
847 A341 60h gray brn & car 30 8
848 A341 1.60k grn & dl yel 80 15

Issued to commemorate the 10th anniversary of the "Victorious February."

Engraved and Photogravure

1958 **Unwmk.** ***Perf. 11½***

Designs: 45h, Dolls. 60h, Textiles. 75h, Kaplan turbine. 1.20k, Glass.

849 A342 30h rose car & bl 12 5
850 A342 45h rose red & pale lil 16 5
851 A342 60h vio & aqua 22 5
852 A342 75h ultra & sal *1.90 75*
853 A342 1.20k bl grn & pink 50 10
Nos. 849-853 (5) 2.90 1.00

Issued for the Universal and International Exposition at Brussels.

King George of Podebrad A343

Design: 60h, View of Prague, 1628.

1958, May 19 **Engr.**
854 A343 30h car rose 20 6
855 A343 60h vio bl 30 6

Issued to publicize the National Archives Exhibition, Prague, May 15-Aug. 15.

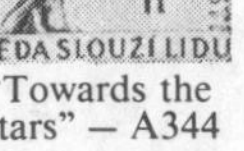

"Towards the Stars" — A344

Women of Three Races — A345

Boy, Girl and Globes A346

1958, May 26
856 A344 30h car rose 75 30
857 A345 45h rose vio 45 15
858 A346 60h blue 22 5

Issued to publicize the following: The Society for Dissemination of Political and Cultural Knowledge (No. 856). The 4th Congress of the International Democratic Women's Federation (No. 857). The First World Trade Union Conference of Working Youths, held in Prague, July 14-20 (No. 858).

Grain, Hammer and Sickle A347

Atomic Reactor A348

Design: 45h, Map of Czechoslovakia, hammer and sickle.

1958, May 26
859 A347 30h dl red 10 5
860 A347 45h green 15 5
861 A348 60h dk bl 25 8

Issued to commemorate the 11th Congress of the Czech Communist Party and the 15th anniversary of the Russo-Czechoslovakian Treaty.

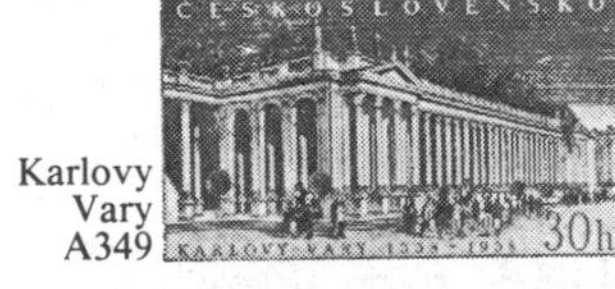

Karlovy Vary A349

Various Spas: 40h, Podebrady. 60h, Marianske Lazne. 80h, Luhacovice. 1.20k, Strbske Pleso. 1.60k, Trencianske Teplice.

1958, June 25
862 A349 30h rose cl 8 5
863 A349 40h redsh brn 12 5
864 A349 60h gray grn 16 5
865 A349 80h sepia 22 5
866 A349 1.20k vio bl 42 8
867 A349 1.60k lt vio *1.65 1.25*
Nos. 862-867 (6) 2.65 1.53

Telephone Operator A350

Pres. Antonin Novotny A351

Design: 45h, Radio transmitter.

1958, June 20
868 A350 30h blk & brn org 25 5
869 A350 45h blk & lt grn 45 12

Issued to commemorate the Conference of Postal Ministers of Communist Countries, Prague, June 30-July 9.

1958-59 ***Perf. 12½, 11½***
870 A351 30h brt vio bl 10 5
870A A351 30h lt vio ('59) 25 5
871 A351 60h car rose 30 5

Perf. 11½

Redrawn

871A A351 60h rose red ('59) 22 5

On No. 871 the top of the "6" turns down; on No. 871A it is open.

Czechoslovak Pavilion, Brussels — A352

Engraved and Photogravure

1958, July 15
872 A352 1.95k lt bl & bis brn 1.10 18

Issued to mark Czechoslovakia Week at the Universal and International Exhibition at Brussels.

Portrait Type of 1956

Portraits: 30h, Julius Fucik. 45h, G. K. Zechenter 60h, Karel Capek. 1.40k, Svatopluk Cech.

1958, Aug. 20 **Engr.** ***Perf. 11½***
873 A306 30h rose red 10 5
874 A306 45h violet *1.50 50*
875 A306 60h dk bl gray 18 5
876 A306 1.40k gray 40 15

Death anniversaries of four famous Czechs.

The Artist and the Muse — A353

1958, Aug. 20 ***Perf. 14***
877 A353 1.60k black 3.25 1.25

Issued to commemorate the 85th birthday of Max Svabinsky, artist and engraver.

A particular stamp may be scarce, but if few collectors want it, its market value may remain relatively low.

Children's Hospital, Brno — A354

Designs: 60h, New Town Hall, Brno. 1k, St. Thomas Church. 1.60k, View of Brno.

1958, Sept. 6 Unwmk. *Perf. 11½*

Size: 40x23mm.

878	A354	30h violet	12	6
879	A354	60h rose red	30	8
880	A354	1k brown	60	15

Perf. 14

Size: 50x28mm.

881	A354	1.60k dk sl grn	*2.50*	*2.25*

Issued to commemorate the National Philatelic Exhibition, Brno, Sept. 9, 1958.

No. 881 sold for 3.10k, including entrance ticket to exhibition. Issued in sheets of four.

Lepiota Procera — A355

Children on Beach — A356

1958, Oct. 6 *Perf. 14*

Mushrooms: 40h, Boletus edulis. 60h, Krombholzia rufescens. 1.40k, Amanita muscaria L. 1.60k, Armillariella mellea.

882	A355	30h dk brn, grn & buff	30	20
883	A355	40h vio brn & brn org	30	20
884	A355	60h blk, red & buff	45	20
885	A355	1.40k brn, scar & grn	60	40
886	A355	1.60k blk, red brn & ol	4.00	*1.75*
		Nos. 882-886 (5)	5.65	2.75

1958, Oct. 24 Unwmk. *Perf. 14*

Designs: 45h, Mother, child and bird. 60h, Skier.

887	A356	30h bl, yel & red	20	5
888	A356	45h ultra & car	35	6
889	A356	60h brn, bl & yel	50	15

Issued to commemorate the opening of UNESCO (U.N. Educational, Scientific and Cultural Organization) Headquarters in Paris, Nov. 3.

Bozek's Steam Car of 1815 A357

Designs: 45h, "Prăsident" car of 1897. 60h, "Skoda" sports car. 80h, "Tatra" sedan. 1k, "Autocar Skoda" bus. 1.25k, Trucks.

Engraved and Photogravure

1958, Dec. 1 *Perf. 11½x11*

890	A357	30h vio blk & buff	50	10
891	A357	45h ol & lt ol grn	35	10
892	A357	60h ol gray & sal	50	10
893	A357	80h cl & bl grn	45	15
894	A357	1k brn & lt yel grn	45	20
895	A357	1.25k grn & buff	*3.00*	*80*
		Nos. 890-895 (6)	5.25	1.45

Issued to honor the automobile industry.

Stamp of 1918 and Allegory — A358

1958, Dec. 18 Engr. *Perf. 11x11½*

896	A358	60h dk bl gray	35	8

Issued to commemorate the 40th anniversary of the first Czechoslovakian postage stamp.

Ice Hockey A359

Sports: 30h, Girl throwing javelin. 60h, Ice hockey. 1k, Hurdling. 1.60k, Rowing. 2k, High jump.

1959, Feb. 14 *Perf. 11½x11*

897	A359	20h dk brn & gray	35	8
898	A359	30h red brn & org brn	35	8
899	A359	60h dk bl & pale grn	25	8
900	A359	1k mar & cit	50	10
901	A359	1.60k dl vio & lt bl	75	10
902	A359	2k red brn & lt bl	*2.50*	*1.25*
		Nos. 897-902 (6)	4.70	1.69

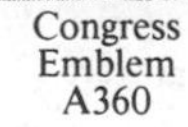

Congress Emblem A360

"Equality of All Races" A361

Design: 60h, Industrial and agricultural workers and emblem.

1959, Feb. 27 *Perf. 11½*

903	A360	30h mar & lt bl	15	5
904	A360	60h dk bl & yel	20	5

Issued to commemorate the 4th Agricultural Cooperative Congress in Prague.

1959, Mar. 23

Designs: 1k, "Peace." 2k, Mother and Child: "Freedom for Colonial People."

905	A361	60h gray grn	25	8
906	A361	1k gray	30	10
907	A361	2k dk gray bl	*1.90*	*75*

Issued to commemorate the 10th anniversary of the signing of the Universal Declaration of Human Rights.

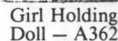

Girl Holding Doll — A362

Frederic Joliot Curie — A363

Designs: 40h, Pioneer studying map. 60h, Pioneer with radio. 80h, Girl pioneer planting tree.

Engraved and Photogravure

1959, Mar. 28

908	A362	30h vio bl & yel	15	5
909	A362	40h ind & ultra	20	5
910	A362	60h blk & lil	20	5
911	A362	80h brn & lt grn	40	15

10th anniversary of the Pioneer organization.

1959, Apr. 17 Engr.

912	A363	60h sepia	90	20

Issued to honor Frederic Joliot Curie and the 10th anniversary of the World Peace Movement.

"Reaching for the Moon" A364

Town Hall Pilsen A365

1959, Apr. 17

913	A364	30h vio bl	1.00	25

Issued to publicize the Second Congress of the Czechoslovak Association for the Propagation of Political and Cultural knowledge.

1959, May 2

Designs: 60h, Part of steam condenser turbine. 1k, St. Bartholomew's Church, Pilsen. 1.60k, Part of lathe.

914	A365	30h lt brn	10	5
915	A365	60h vio & lt grn	20	5
916	A365	1k vio bl	65	15
917	A365	1.60k blk & yel	*2.00*	*1.00*

Issued to publicize the 2nd Pilsen Stamp Exhibition in connection with the centenary of the Skoda (Lenin) armament works.

Factory and Emblem A366

Design: 60h, Dam.

Inscribed: "IV Vseodborovy sjezd, 1959"

1959, May 13

918	A366	30h rose & yel	12	5
919	A366	60h ol gray & bl	25	6

4th Trade Union Congress.

Zvolen Castle A367

1959, June 13

920	A367	60h gray ol & yel	35	8

Regional Stamp Exhibition, Zvolen, 1959.

Frantisek Benda A368

Aurel Stodola A369

Portraits: 30h, Vaclav Kliment Klicpera. 60h, Karel V. Rais. 80h, Antonin Slavicek. 1k, Peter Bezruc.

1959, June 22 *Perf. 11½x11*

921	A368	15h vio bl	5	5
922	A368	30h org brn	10	5
923	A369	40h dl grn	12	5
924	A369	60h dl red brn	22	6
925	A369	80h dl vio	30	8
926	A368	1k dk brn	55	8
		Nos. 921-926 (6)	1.34	37

View of the Fair Grounds A370

Designs: 60h, Fair emblem and world map. 1.60k, Pavilion "Z."

Inscribed: "Mezinarodni Veletrh Brne 6.-20.IX. 1959."

Engraved and Photogravure

1959, July 20 Unwmk. *Perf. 11½*

927	A370	30h lil & yel	16	5
928	A370	60h dl bl	38	5
929	A370	1.60k dk bl & bis	60	15

International Fair at Brno, Sept. 6-20.

Revolutionist and Flag — A371

Slovakian Fighter — A372

Design: 1.60k, Linden leaves, sun and factory.

Perf. 11½

1959, Aug. 29 Unwmk. Engr.

930	A371	30h blk & rose	22	5
931	A372	60h car rose	42	5
932	A371	1.60k dk bl & yel	85	8

Issued to commemorate the 15th anniversary of the national Slovakian revolution and the 40th anniversary of the Slovakian Soviet Republic.

Alpine Marmots A373

Animals: 40h, Bison. 60h, Lynx (vert.). 1k, Wolf. 1.60k, Red deer.

Engraved and Photogravure

1959, Sept. 25

933 A373 30h blk & gray 30 5
934 A373 40h dk brn & bluish grn 45 8
935 A373 60h brn red & yel 35 5
936 A373 1k ol brn & bl *2.50 95*
937 A373 1.60k red brn & pink 75 15
Nos. 933-937 (5) 4.35 1.28

Issued to commemorate the 10th anniversary of the establishment of the Tatra National Park.

Lunik 2 Hitting Moon and Russian Flag
A374

1959, Sept. 23 ***Perf. 11 ½***

938 A374 60h dk red & lt ultra 1.00 20

Issued to commemorate the landing of the Soviet rocket on the moon, Sept. 13, 1959.

Stamp Printing Works, Peking
A375

1959, Oct. 1

939 A375 30h pale grn & red 18 6

Issued to commemorate 10 years of Czechoslovakian-Chinese friendship.

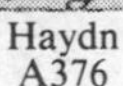

Haydn
A376

Great Spotted Woodpecker
A377

Design: 3k, Charles Darwin.

1959, Oct. 16 **Engr.** ***Perf. 11 ½***

940 A376 60h vio blk 35 5
941 A376 3k dk red brn *1.50 85*

150th anniversary of death of Franz Joseph Haydn, Austrian composer, and 150th anniversary of birth of Charles Darwin, English naturalist.

1959, Nov. 16 ***Perf. 14***

Birds: 30h, Blue tits. 40h, Nuthatch. 60th, Golden oriole. 80h, Goldfinch. 1k, Bullfinch. 1.20k, European kingfisher.

942 A377 20h multi 28 20
943 A377 30h multi 18 20
944 A377 40h multi *3.00 1.50*
945 A377 60h multi 35 15
946 A377 80h multi 45 25
947 A377 1k multi 45 20
948 A377 1.20k multi 75 40
Nos. 942-948 (7) 5.46 2.90

Nikola Tesla
A378

Designs: 30h, Alexander S. Popov. 35h, Edouard Branly. 60h, Guglielmo Marconi. 1k, Heinrich Hertz. 2k, Edwin Howard Armstrong and research tower, Alpine, N. J.

Engraved and Photogravure

1959, Dec. 7 ***Perf. 11 ½***

949 A378 25h blk & pink *70 20*
950 A378 30h blk & org 18 5
951 A378 35h blk & lt vio 22 5
952 A378 60h blk & bl 28 5
953 A378 1k blk & lt grn 35 6
954 A378 2k blk & bis *2.00 60*
Nos. 949-954 (6) 3.73 1.01

Issued to honor inventors in the fields of telegraphy and radio.

Gymnast — A379

Designs: 60h, Skier. 1.60k, Basketball players.

Engraved and Photogravure

1960, Jan. 20 ***Perf. 11 ½***

955 A379 30h sal pink & brn 30 15
956 A379 60h lt bl & blk 38 15
957 A379 1.60k bis & brn 80 20

2nd Winter Spartacist Games.

1960, June 15 **Unwmk.**

Designs: 30h, Two girls in "Red Ball" drill. 60h, Gymnast with stick. 1k, Three girls with hoops.

958 A379 30h lt grn & rose cl 22 5
959 A379 60h pink & blk 42 10
960 A379 1k ocher & vio bl 60 15

Issued to commemorate the 2nd Summer Spartacist Games, Prague, June 23-July 3.

River Dredge Boat
A380

Ships; 60h, River tug. 1k, Tourist steamer. 1.20k, Cargo ship "Lidice."

1960, Feb. 22 ***Perf. 11 ½***

961 A380 30h sl grn & sal 45 8
962 A380 60h mar & pale bl 35 8
963 A380 1k dk vio & yel 65 15
964 A380 1.20k lil & pale grn *1.10 1.00*

Ice Hockey Players — A381

Design: 1.80k, Figure skaters.

1960, Feb. 27

965 A381 60h sep & lt bl 60 25
966 A381 1.80k blk & lt grn *4.50 3.25*

Issued to commemorate the 8th Olympic Winter Games, Squaw Valley, Calif., Feb. 18-29, 1960.

1960, June 15 **Unwmk.**

Designs: 1k, Running. 1.80k, Women's gymnastics. 2k, Rowing.

967 A381 1k blk & org 65 25
968 A381 1.80k blk & sal pink 1.25 40
969 A381 2k blk & bl *3.00 1.50*

Issued to commemorate the 17th Olympic Games, Rome, Aug. 25-Sept. 11.

Trencin Castle
A382

Striped Ovals
Wmk. 341

Castles: 10h, Bezdez. 20h, Kost. 30h, Pernstein. 40h, Kremnica. 50h, Krivoklat castle. 60h, Karlstein. 1k, Smolenice. 1.60k, Kokorin.

1960-63 **Engr.** ***Perf. 11 ½***

970 A382 5h gray vio 8 5
971 A382 10h black 8 5
972 A382 20h brn org 15 5
973 A382 30h green 20 5
974 A382 40h brown 25 5
974A A382 50h blk ('63) 25 5
975 A382 60h rose red 35 5
976 A382 1k lilac 50 5
977 A382 1.60k dk bl 1.00 5
Nos. 970-977 (9) 2.86 45

1961, Oct. **Wmk. 341**

977A A382 30h green 2.00 70

Lenin — A383

Soldier Holding Child — A384

1960, Apr. 22 **Unwmk.**

978 A383 60h gray ol 50 15

90th anniversary of the birth of Lenin.

Engraved and Photogravure

1960, May 5

Designs: No. 980, Child eating pie. No. 981, Soldier helping concentration camp victim. No. 982, Welder and factory (horiz.). No. 983, Tractor driver and farm (horiz.).

979 A384 30h mar & lt bl 20 5
980 A384 30h dl red 20 5
981 A384 30h grn & dl bl 20 5
982 A384 60h dk bl & buff 35 5
983 A384 60h redsh brn & yel grn 40 5
Nos. 979-983 (5) 1.35 25

15th anniversary of liberation.

Steelworker — A385

Design: 60h, Farm woman and child.

1960, May 24

984 A385 30h mar & gray 12 5
985 A385 60h grn & pale bl 25 5

Issued to publicize the 1960 parliamentary elections.

Red Cross Nurse Holding Dove
A386

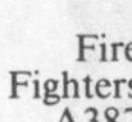

Fire Fighters
A387

1960, May 26 **Unwmk.**

986 A386 30h brn car & bl 20 5
987 A387 60h dk bl & pink 35 5

Issued to commemorate the 3rd Congress of the Czechoslovakian Red Cross (No. 986), and the 2nd Fire Fighters' Congress (No. 987).

Hand of Philatelist with Tongs and Two Stamps
A388

Design: 1k, Globe and 1937 Bratislava stamp (shown in miniature on 60h).

Engraved and Photogravure

1960, July 11 ***Perf. 11 ½***

988 A388 60h blk & dl yel 35 5
989 A388 1k blk & bl 65 8

Issued to publicize the National Stamp Exhibition, Bratislava, Sept. 24-Oct. 9.
See Nos. C49-C50.

Stalin Mine, Ostrava-Hermanovice
A390

Viktorin Cornelius, Lawyer
A391

Designs: 20h, Power station, Hodonin. 30h, Gottwald iron works, Kuncice. 40h, Harvester. 60h, Oil refinery.

1960, July 25

992 A390 10h blk & pale grn 10 5
993 A390 20h mar & lt bl 15 5
994 A390 30h ind & pink 15 5
995 A390 40h grn & pale lil 25 5
996 A390 60h dk bl & yel 35 5
Nos. 992-996 (5) 1.00 25

Issued to publicize the new five-year plan.

1960, Aug. 23 **Engr.**

Portraits: 20h, Karel Matej Capek-Chod, writer. 30h, Hana Kvapilova, actress. 40h, Oskar Nedbal, composer. 60h, Otakar Ostrcil, composer.

997 A391 10h black 15 5
998 A391 20h red brn 20 5
999 A391 30h rose red 25 5
1000 A391 40h dl grn 35 5
1001 A391 60h gray vio 45 8
Nos. 997-1001 (5) 1.40 28

See also Nos. 1037-1041.

Skoda Sports Plane Flying Upside Down
A392

Engraved and Photogravure

1960, Aug. 28

1002 A392 60h vio bl & bl 75 10

Issued to commemorate the first aerobatic world championships, Bratislava.

Constitution and "Czechoslovakia" — A393

1960, Sept. 18

1003	A393	30h vio bl & pink	15	5

Issued to commemorate the proclamation of the new socialist constitution.

Workers Reading Newspaper — A394

Man Holding Newspaper — A395

1960, Sept. 18

1004	A394	30h sl & ver	12	6
1005	A395	60h blk & rose	24	6

Issued for the Day of the Czechoslovak Press, Sept. 21, 1960, and to commemorate the 40th anniversary of the Rude Pravo paper.

Globes and Laurel A396

1960, Sept. 18 **Engr.**

1006	A396	30h dk bl & bis	15	5

Issued to commemorate the 15th anniversary of the World Federation of Trade Unions.

Black-crowned Night Heron A397

Doronicum Clusii (Thistle) A398

Birds: 30h, Great crested grebe. 40h, Lapwing. 60h, Gray heron. 1k, Graylag goose (horiz.). 1.60k, Mallard (horiz.).

Engraved and Photogravure

1960, Oct. 24 **Unwmk.** ***Perf. 11½***

Designs in Black

1007	A397	25h pale vio bl	20	5
1008	A397	30h pale cit	40	6
1009	A397	40h pale bl	25	6
1010	A397	60h pink	40	10
1011	A397	1k pale yel	50	20
1012	A397	1.60k lt vio	*3.25*	*1.10*
		Nos. 1007-1012 (6)	5.00	1.57

1960, Nov. 21 **Engr.** ***Perf. 14***

Flowers: 30h, Cyclamen. 40h, Primrose. 60h, Hen-and-chickens. 1k, Gentian. 2k, Pasqueflower.

1013	A398	20h blk, yel & grn	9	5
1014	A398	30h blk, car rose & grn	15	5
1015	A398	40h blk, yel & grn	20	5
1016	A398	60h blk, pink & grn	25	5
1017	A398	1k blk, bl, vio & grn	45	20
1018	A398	2k blk, lil, yel & grn	*3.00*	*1.25*
		Nos. 1013-1018 (6)	4.14	1.65

Alfons Mucha — A399

1960, Dec. 18 **Engr.** ***Perf. 11½x12***

1019	A399	60h dk bl gray	30	5

Issued for the Day of the Czechoslovak Postage Stamp and to commemorate the centenary of the birth of Alfons Mucha, designer of the first Czechoslovakian stamp (Type A1).

Rolling-mill Control Bridge — A400

Athletes with Flags — A401

Designs: 30h, Turbo generator. 60h, Ditch-digging machine.

1961, Jan. 20 **Unwmk.** ***Perf. 11½***

1020	A400	20h blue	18	5
1021	A400	30h rose	22	5
1022	A400	60h brt grn	35	5

Third Five-Year Plan.

Perf. 11x11½, 11½x11

1961, Feb. 20 **Engr. and Photo.**

Designs: No. 1024, Motorcycle race (horiz.). 40h, Sculling (horiz.). 60h, Ice skater. 1k, Rugby. 1.20k, Soccer. 1.60k, Long-distance runners.

1023	A401	30h rose red & bl	15	5
1024	A401	30h dk bl & car	15	5
1025	A401	40h dk gray & car	40	5
1026	A401	60h lil & bl	35	5
1027	A401	1k ultra & yel	45	10
1028	A401	1.20k grn & buff	65	20
1029	A401	1.60k sep & sal	*2.00*	*1.00*
		Nos. 1023-1029 (7)	4.15	1.50

Various sports events.

Exhibition Emblem A402

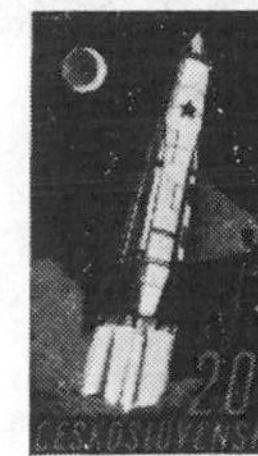

Rocket Launching A403

1961, Mar. 6 **Engr.** ***Perf. 11½***

1030	A402	2k dk bl & red	2.00	8

Issued to publicize the "Praga 1962" International Stamp Exhibition, Prague, Sept. 1962.

Engraved and Photogravure

1961, Mar. 6

Designs: 30h, Sputnik III (horiz.). 40h, As 20h, but inscribed "Start Kosmicke Rakety k Venusi - 12.II.1961". 60h, Sputnik I (horiz.). 1.60k, Interplanetary station (horiz.). 2k, Similar to type A404, without commemorative inscription.

1031	A403	20h vio & pink	40	5
1032	A403	30h dk grn & buff	15	5
1033	A403	40h dk red & yel grn	20	5
1034	A403	60h vio & buff	40	5
1035	A403	1.60k dk bl & pale grn	95	20
1036	A403	2k mar & pale bl	*2.50*	*1.35*
		Nos. 1031-1036 (6)	4.60	1.75

Issued to publicize Soviet space research.

Portrait Type of 1960

Portraits: No. 1037, Jindrich Mosna. No. 1038, Pavol Orszagh Hviezdoslav. No. 1039, Alois Mrstik. No. 1040, Joza Uprka. No. 1041, Josef Hora.

1961, March 27 ***Perf. 11½***

1037	A391	60h green	30	5
1038	A391	60h dk bl	30	5
a.		"ORSZACH" instead of "ORSZAGH"	75	30
1039	A391	60h dl cl	30	5
1040	A391	60h gray	30	5
1041	A391	60h sepia	30	5
		Nos. 1037-1041 (5)	1.50	25

Man Flying into Space A404

Engraved and Photogravure

1961, Apr. 13

1042	A404	60h car & pale bl	50	5
1043	A404	3k ultra & yel	*2.50*	*80*

Issued to commemorate the first man in space, Yuri A. Gagarin, Apr. 12, 1961. See also No. 1036.

Flute Player — A405

Blast Furnace and Mine, Kladno — A406

Designs: No. 1045, Dancer. 60h, Lyre player.

1961, Apr. 24 **Engr.**

1044	A405	30h brn blk	35	5
1045	A405	30h brn red	35	5
1046	A405	60h vio bl	35	8

Issued to commemorate the 150th anniversary of the Prague Conservatory of Music.

1961, Apr. 24

1047	A406	3k dl red	1.50	5

Marching Workers A407

Woman with Hammer and Sickle A408

Klement Gottwald Museum A409

Designs: No. 1050, Lenin Museum. No. 1051, Crowd with flags. No. 1053, Man saluting Red Star.

1961, May 10

1048	A407	30h dl vio	10	5
1049	A409	30h dk bl	10	5
1050	A409	30h redsh brn	10	5
1051	A407	60h vermilion	30	8
1052	A408	60h dk grn	30	8
1053	A408	60h carmine	30	8
		Nos. 1048-1053 (6)	1.20	39

Czech Communist Party, 40th anniversary.

Puppet — A410

Designs: Various Puppets.

Engraved and Photogravure

1961, June 20 **Unwmk.** ***Perf. 11½***

1054	A410	30h ver & yel	15	5
1055	A410	40h sep & bluish grn	15	5
1056	A410	60h vio bl & sal	25	5
1057	A410	1k grn & lt bl	40	6
1058	A410	1.60k mar & pale vio	*1.75*	*45*
		Nos. 1054-1058 (5)	2.70	66

Woman, Map of Africa and Flag of Czechoslovakia — A411

1961, June 26

1059	A411	60h red & bl	35	8

Issued to publicize the friendship between the people of Africa and Czechoslovakia.

Map of Europe and Fair Emblem A412

Designs (Fair emblem and): 60h Horizontal boring machine (vert.). 1k, Scientists' meeting and nuclear physics emblem.

Engraved and Photogravure

1961, Aug. 14 ***Perf. 11½***

1060	A412	30h dk bl & pale grn	15	6

1061	A412	60h grn & pink	25	5
1062	A412	1k vio brn & lt bl	50	8

Issued to publicize the International Trade Fair, Brno, Sept. 10-24.

Sugar Beet, Cup of Coffee and Bags of Sugar A413

Charles Bridge, St. Nicholas Church and Hradcany A414

Designs: 30h, Clover. 40h, Wheat. 60h, Hops. 1.40k, Corn. 2k, Potatoes.

1961, Sept. 18 Unwmk. *Perf. 11½*

1063	A413	20h sl & lil	8	5
1064	A413	30h pale cl & bis	10	5
1065	A413	40h brn & org	15	5
1066	A413	60h sl grn & bis	20	5
1067	A413	1.40k brn & fawn	45	6
1068	A413	2k dl vio & bl	*2.50*	*75*
		Nos. 1063-1068 (6)	3.48	1.01

1961, Sept. 25

1069	A414	60h vio bl & car	1.25	10

Issued to commemorate the 26th session of the Governor's Council of the Red Cross Societies League, Prague.

Orlik Dam and Kaplan Turbine A415

Designs: 30h, View of Prague, flags and stamps. 40h, Hluboka Castle, river and fish. 60h, Karlovy Vary and cup. 1k, Pilsen and beer bottle. 1.20k, North Bohemia landscape and vase. 1.60k, Tatra mountains, boots, ice pick and rope. 2k, Ironworks, Ostrava Kuncice and pulley. 3k, Brno and ball bearing. 4k, Bratislava and grapes. 5k, Prague and flags.

Engraved and Photogravure

1961 Unwmk. *Perf. 11½*

Size: 41x23mm.

1070	A415	20h gray & bl	*42*	*40*
1071	A415	30h vio bl & red	30	22
1072	A415	40h dk bl & lt grn	*55*	*45*
1073	A415	60h dk bl & yel	*38*	*35*
1074	A415	1k mar & grn	85	65
1075	A415	1.20k grn & pink	*90*	*65*
1076	A415	1.60k brn & vio bl	1.25	65
1077	A415	2k blk & ocher	1.90	1.65
1078	A415	3k ultra & yel	*1.90*	*1.75*
1079	A415	4k pur & sal	*3.00*	*3.00*

Perf. 13½

Engr.

Size: 50x29mm.

1080	A415	5k multi	*25.00*	*22.50*
		Nos. 1070-1080 (11)	36.45	32.27

Issued to publicize the "PRAGA 1962 World Exhibition of Postage Stamps," Aug. 18-Sept. 2, 1962. No. 1080 was printed in sheet of four with marginal inscription.

Globe A416

Engraved and Photogravure

1961, Nov. 27 *Perf. 11½*

1081	A416	60h red & ultra	50	10

Issued to publicize the Fifth World Congress of Trade Unions, Moscow, Dec. 4-16.

Orange Tip Butterfly A417

Bicyclists A418

Designs (butterflies): 20h, Zerynthia hypsipyle Sch. 30h, Apollo. 40h, Swallowtail. 60h, Peacock. 80h, Mourning cloak (Camberwell beauty). 1k, Underwing (moth). 1.60k, Red admiral. 2k, Brimstone (sulphur).

1961, Nov. 27 Engr.

Brown Frame and Inscriptions

1082	A417	15h bl, org & yel	10	6
1083	A417	20h bl, yel & red	10	10
1084	A417	30h bl, car & grn	15	10
1085	A417	40h bl, ocher & car	30	10
1086	A417	60h bl, red brn & yel	40	12
1087	A417	80h bl, yel, brn & grn	60	25
1088	A417	1k pale brn, pink & bl	70	35
1089	A417	1.60k multi	90	55
1090	A417	2k bl, yel & red	*5.00*	*2.25*
		Nos. 1082-1090 (9)	8.25	3.88

Printed in sheets of ten.

Engraved and Photogravure

1962, Feb. 5 Unwmk. *Perf. 11½*

Sports: 40h, Woman gymnast. 60h, Figure skaters. 1k, Woman bowler. 1.20k, Goalkeeper, soccer. 1.60k, Discus thrower.

1091	A418	30h blk & vio bl	10	5
1092	A418	40h blk & yel	15	5
1093	A418	60h sl & grnsh bl	20	5
1094	A418	1k blk & pink	50	8
1095	A418	1.20k blk & grn	60	12
1096	A418	1.60k blk & dl grn	*2.00*	*90*
		Nos. 1091-1096 (6)	3.55	1.25

Various 1962 sports events.

No. 1095 does not have the commemorative inscription.

Karel Kovarovic — A419

Frantisek Zaviska and Karel Petr A420

Designs: 20h, Frantisek Skroup. 30h, Bozena Nemcova. 60h, View of Prague and staff of Aesculapius. 1.60k, Ladislav Celakovsky. 1.80k, Miloslav Valouch and Juraj Hronec.

1962, Feb. 26 Engr.

1097	A419	10h red brn	5	5
1098	A419	20h vio bl	8	5
1099	A419	30h brown	12	5
1100	A420	40h claret	15	10
1101	A419	60h black	25	6
1102	A419	1.60k sl grn	60	6
1103	A420	1.80k dk bl	65	15
		Nos. 1097-1103 (7)	1.90	52

Various cultural personalities and events.

Miner and Flag A421

Engraved and Photogravure

1962, Mar. 19

1104	A421	60h ind & rose	35	8

Issued to commemorate the 30th anniversary of the miners' strike at Most.

"Man Conquering Space" — A422

Soviet Spaceship Vostok 2 — A423

Designs: 40h, Launching of Soviet space rocket. 80h, Multi-stage automatic rocket. 1k, Automatic station on moon. 1.60k, Television satellite.

Engraved and Photogravure

1962, Mar. 26

1105	A422	30h dk red & lt bl	30	5
1106	A422	40h dk bl & sal	30	5
1107	A423	60h dk bl & pink	35	8
1108	A423	80h rose vio & lt grn	50	10
1109	A422	1k ind & cit	50	15
1110	A423	1.60k grn & buff	*3.00*	*1.25*
		Nos. 1105-1110 (6)	4.95	1.68

Issued to publicize space research.

Polar Bear — A424

Zoo Animals: 30h, Chimpanzee. 60h, Camel. 1k, African and Indian elephants (horiz.). 1.40k, Leopard (horiz.). 1.60k, Przewalski horse (horiz.).

1962, Apr. 24 Unwmk. *Perf. 11½*

Design and Inscriptions in Black

1111	A424	20h grnsh bl	8	5
1112	A424	30h violet	10	5
1113	A424	60h orange	25	8
1114	A424	1k green	45	10
1115	A424	1.40k car rose	70	25
1116	A424	1.60k lt brn	*2.75*	*1.25*
		Nos. 1111-1116 (6)	4.33	1.78

Child and Grieving Mother — A425

Klary's Fountain, Teplice — A426

Design: 60h, Flowers growing from ruins of Lezaky.

Engraved and Photogravure

1962, June 9

1118	A425	30h blk & red	20	5
1119	A425	60h blk & dl bl	50	5

Issued to commemorate the 20th anniversary of the destruction of Lidice and Lezaky by the Nazis.

1962, June 9

1120	A426	60h dl grn & yel	50	8

Issued to commemorate the 1,200th anniversary of the discovery of the medicinal springs of Teplice.

Malaria Eradication Emblem, Cross and Dove A427

Soccer Goalkeeper A428

Design: 3k, Dove and malaria eradication emblem.

Engraved and Photogravure

1962, June 18

1121	A427	60h blk & crim	28	8
1122	A427	3k dk bl & yel	*2.25*	*80*

Issued for the World Health Organization drive to eradicate malaria.

1962, June 20 Unwmk. *Perf. 11½*

1123	A428	1.60k grn & yel	1.25	18

Issued to commemorate Czechoslovakia's participation in the World Cup Soccer Championship, Chile, May 30-June 17. See No. 1095.

Soldier in Swimming Relay Race A429

"Agriculture" A430

1962, July 20

Designs: 40h, Soldier hurdling. 60h, Soccer player. 1k, Soldier with rifle in relay race.

1124	A429	30h grn & lt ultra	10	5
1125	A429	40h dk pur & yel	12	5
1126	A429	60h brn & grn	25	5
1127	A429	1k dk bl & sal pink	60	15

Issued to publicize the 2nd Summer Spartacist Games of Friendly Armies, Prague, September, 1962.

1962 Engr. *Perf. 13½*

Designs: 60h, Astronaut in capsule. 80h, Boy with flute (horiz.). 1k, Workers of three races (horiz.). 1.40k, Children dancing around tree. 1.60k, Flying bird (horiz.). 5k, View of Prague (horiz.).

1128	A430	30h multi	1.65	1.25
1129	A430	60h multi	80	90
a.		Miniature sheet of 8	*15.00*	*14.00*
1130	A430	80h multi	1.75	1.50
1131	A430	1k multi	3.25	2.75
1132	A430	1.40k multi	3.75	3.75
1133	A430	1.60k multi	*6.25*	*4.00*
		Nos. 1128-1133 (6)	17.45	14.15

Souvenir Sheet

1134 A430 5k multi *16.00 16.00*
a. Imperf. *60.00 60.00*

Issued to commemorate the "PRAGA 1962 World Exhibition of Postage Stamps," Aug. 18-Sept. 2, 1962. No. 1133 also commemorates FIP Day, Sept. 1 (Federation Internationale de Philatelie.) Printed in sheets of 10.

No. 1129a contains four stamps each of Nos. 1128-29 and two labels arranged in two rows of two se-tenant pairs of Nos. 1128-29 with a label between. Size: 170x107mm. Sold for 5k, only with ticket.

No. 1134 contains one large stamp (51x30mm). Black marginal inscription. Size of sheet: 95x74mm. Sold only with ticket.

Children in Day Nursery and Factory A431

Sailboat and Trade Union Rest Home, Zinkovy — A432

Engraved and Photogravure

1962, Oct. 29 Unwmk. *Perf. 11½*

1135 A431 30h blk & lt bl 12 5
1136 A432 60h brn & yel 25 5

Cruiser "Aurora" A433

1962, Nov. 7

1137 A433 30h blk & gray bl 12 5
1138 A433 60h blk & pink 22 5

Issued to commemorate the 45th anniversary of the Russian October revolution.

Cosmonaut and Worker — A434

Lenin — A435

1962, Nov. 7

1139 A434 30h dk red & bl 12 5
1140 A435 60h blk & dp rose 22 5

40th anniversary of the U.S.S.R.

Symbolic Crane — A436

Designs: 40h, Agricultural products (vert.). 60h, Factories.

1962, Dec. 4

1141 A436 30h dk red & yel 10 5
1142 A436 40h gray bl & yel 20 5
1143 A436 60h blk & dp rose 45 15

Issued to commemorate the 12th Congress of the Communist Party of Czechoslovakia.

Ground Beetle — A437

Table Tennis — A438

Beetles: 30h, Cardinal beetle. 60h, Stag beetle (vert.). 1k, Great water beetle. 1.60k, Alpine longicorn (vert.). 2k, Ground beetle (vert.).

1962, Dec. 15 Engr. *Perf. 14*

1144 A437 20h multi 15 5
1145 A437 30h multi 15 5
1146 A437 60h multi 25 8
1147 A437 1k multi 40 20
1148 A437 1.60k multi 1.50 50
1149 A437 2k multi *4.25 1.75*
Nos. 1144-1149 (6) 6.70 2.63

Engraved and Photogravure

1963, Jan. *Perf. 11½*

Sports: 60h, Bicyclist. 80h, Skier. 1k, Motorcyclist. 1.20k, Weight lifter. 1.60k, Hurdler.

1150 A438 30h blk & dp grn 18 5
1151 A438 60h blk & org 22 5
1152 A438 80h blk & ultra 30 8
1153 A438 1k blk & vio 40 22
1154 A438 1.20k blk & pale brn 65 40
1155 A438 1.60k blk & car 1.10 40
Nos. 1150-1155 (6) 2.85 1.20

Various 1963 sports events.

Industrial Plant, Laurel and Star — A439

Symbol of Child Welfare Home — A440

Industrial Plant and Symbol of Growth — A441

1963, Feb. 25 Unwmk. *Perf. 11½*

1156 A439 30h car & lt bl 10 5
1157 A440 60h blk & car 25 5
1158 A441 60h blk & red 25 5

Issued to commemorate the 15th anniversary of the "Victorious February" and to publicize the 5th Trade Union Congress.

Artists' Guild Emblem A442

Juraj Janosik A443

Eduard Urx — A444

National Theater, Prague — A445

Designs: No. 1163, Woman reading to children. No. 1164, Juraj Palkovic. 1.60k, Max Svabinsky.

Engraved and Photogravure; Engraved (A444)

1963, Mar. 25 Unwmk. *Perf. 11½*

1159 A442 20h blk & Prus bl 5 5
1160 A443 30h car & lt bl 10 5
1161 A444 30h carmine 10 5
1162 A445 60h dl red brn & lt bl 20 5
1163 A444 60h green 20 5
1164 A444 60h black 35 5
1165 A444 1.60k brown 75 10
Nos. 1159-1165 (7) 1.75 40

Various cultural personalities and events.

Boy and Girl with Flag A446

Television Transmitter A447

Engraved and Photogravure

1963, Apr. 18 *Perf. 11½*

1166 A446 30h sl & rose red 25 6

The 4th Congress of Czechoslovak Youth.

1963, Apr. 25

Design: 40h, Television camera, mast and set (horiz.).

1167 A447 40h buff & sl 15 5
1168 A447 60h dk red & lt bl 35 5

Czechoslovak television, 10th anniversary.

Rocket to the Sun A448

Designs: 50h, Rockets and Sputniks leaving Earth. 60h, Spacecraft to and from Moon. 1k, 3k, Interplanetary station and Mars 1. 1.60k, Atomic rocket and Jupiter. 2k, Rocket returning from Saturn.

1963, Apr. 25

1169 A448 30h red brn & buff 15 5
1170 A448 50h sl & bluish grn 20 10
1171 A448 60h dk grn & yel 30 5
1172 A448 1k dk gray & sal 50 15
1173 A448 1.60k gray brn & lt grn 80 25
1174 A448 2k dk pur & yel *2.75 1.00*
Nos. 1169-1174 (6) 4.70 1.60

Souvenir Sheet

Imperf

1175 A448 3k Prus grn & org red *4.50 4.50*

No. 1175 issued to commemorate the first Space Research Exhibition, Prague, Apr., 1963. Prussian green and red orange marginal inscription and design. Size: 85x70mm.

Studio and Radio A449

Design: 1k, Globe inscribed "Peace" and aerial mast (vert.).

Engraved and Photogravure

1963, May 18 Unwmk. *Perf. 11½*

1176 A449 30h choc & pale grn 15 5
1177 A449 1k bluish grn & lil 35 5

40th anniversary of Czechoslovak radio.

Tupolev Tu-104B Turbojet A450

Design: 1.80k, Ilyushin Il-18 Moskva.

1963, May 25

1178 A450 80h vio & lt bl 30 6
1179 A450 1.80k dk bl & lt grn 90 6

40th anniversary of Czechoslovak airlines.

Ninth Century Ring and Map of Moravian Settlements A451

Woman Singing A452

Design: 1.60k, Falconer, 9th century silver disk.

1963, May 25

1180 A451 30h lt grn & blk 15 5
1181 A451 1.60k dl yel & blk 60 5

1100th anniversary of Moravian empire.

1963, May 25 Engr.

1182 A452 30h brt red 45 5

Issued to commemorate the 60th anniversary of the founding of the Moravian Teachers' Singing Club.

Kromeriz Castle and Barley — A453

Centenary Emblem, Nurse and Playing Child — A454

Engraved and Photogravure

1963, June 20 Unwmk. *Perf. 11½*

1183 A453 30h sl grn & yel 45 6

Issued to publicize the National Agricultural Exhibition and to commemorate the 700th anniversary of Kromeriz.

1963, June 20

1184 A454 30h dk gray & car 45 5

Centenary of the International Red Cross.

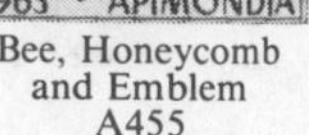

Bee, Honeycomb and Emblem A455

Liberec Fair Emblem A456

1963, June 20

1185 A455 1k brn & yel 55 5

Issued to publicize the 19th International Beekeepers Congress, Apimondia, 1963.

1963, July 13

1186 A456 30h blk & dp rose 45 5

Liberec Consumer Goods Fair.

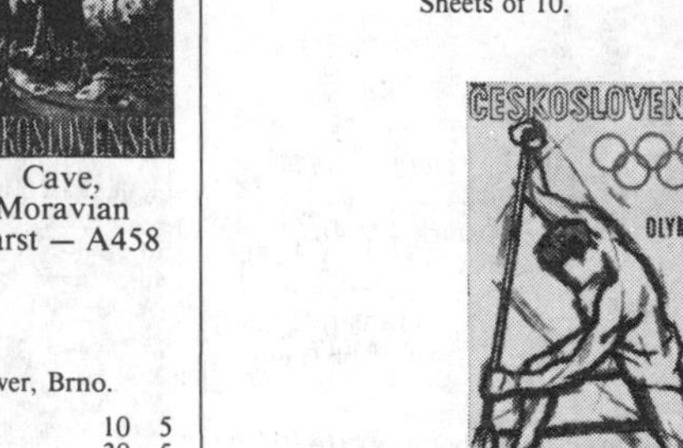

Town Hall, Brno — A457

Cave, Moravian Karst — A458

1963, July 29

Design: 60h, Town Hall tower, Brno.

1187	A457	30h lt bl & mar	10	5
1188	A457	60h pink & dk bl	30	5

International Trade Fair, Brno.

1963, July 29

Designs: No. 1190, Trout, Hornad Valley. 60h, Great Hawk Gorge. 80h, Macocha mountains.

1189	A458	30h brn & lt bl	30	5
1190	A458	30h dk bl & dl grn	35	5
1191	A458	60h grn & bl	30	5
1192	A458	80h sep & pink	30	10

Blast Furnace — A459

Engraved and Photogravure

1963, Aug. 15 Unwmk. *Perf. 11½*

1193 A459 60h blk & bluish grn 35 5

Issued to publicize the 30th International Congress of Iron Founders, Prague.

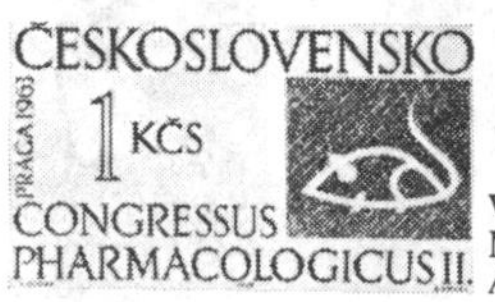

White Mouse A460

1963, Aug. 15

1194 A460 1k blk & car 40 5

Issued to publicize the second International Pharmacological Congress, Prague.

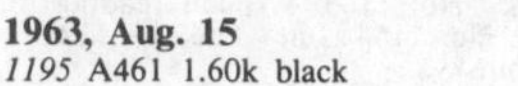

Farm Machinery for Underfed Nations — A461

Wooden Toys — A462

1963, Aug. 15 Engr.

1195 A461 1.60k black 75 8

Issued for the "Freedom from Hunger" campaign of the U.N. Food and Agriculture Organization.

1963, Sept. 2 Engr. *Perf. 13½*

Folk Art (Inscribed "UNESCO"): 80h, Cock and flowers. 1k, Flowers in vase. 1.20k, Janosik, Slovak hero. 1.60k, Stag. 2k, Postilion.

1196	A462	60h red & vio bl	20	10
1197	A462	80h multi	30	15
1198	A462	1k multi	40	20
1199	A462	1.20k multi	50	20
1200	A462	1.60k multi	60	30
1201	A462	2k multi	*4.00*	*1.25*
		Nos. 1196-1201 (6)	6.00	2.20

Sheets of 10.

Canoeing A463

Tree and Star — A464

Sports: 40h, Volleyball. 60h, Wrestling. 80h, Basketball. 1k, Boxing. 1.60k, Gymnastics.

Engraved and Photogravure

1963, Oct. 26 *Perf. 11½*

1202	A463	30h ind & grn	10	5
1203	A463	40h red brn & lt bl	15	5
1204	A463	60h brn red & yel	20	8
1205	A463	80h dk pur & dp org	35	15
1206	A463	1k ultra & dp rose	40	20
1207	A463	1.60k vio bl & ultra	*3.00*	*1.25*
		Nos. 1202-1207 (6)	4.20	1.78

1964 Olympic Games, Tokyo.

1963, Dec. 11 Unwmk. *Perf. 11½*

Design: 60h, Star, hammer and sickle.

1208	A464	30h bis brn & lt bl	10	5
1209	A464	60h car & gray	20	5

Issued to commemorate the 20th anniversary of the Russo-Czechoslovakian Treaty.

Atom Diagrams Surrounding Head A465

Chamois A466

1963, Dec. 12 Engr.

1210 A465 60h dk pur 45 8

Issued to publicize the 3rd Congress of the Association for the Propagation of Scientific Knowledge.

1963, Dec. 14 *Perf. 14*

Animals: 40h, Alpine ibex. 60h, Mouflon. 1.20k, Roe deer. 1.60k, Fallow deer. 2k, Red deer.

1211	A466	30h multi	60	15
1212	A466	40h multi	70	25
1213	A466	60h brn, yel & grn	90	30
1214	A466	1.20k multi	95	30
1215	A466	1.60k multi	1.50	60
1216	A466	2k multi	*5.00*	*2.75*
		Nos. 1211-1216 (6)	9.65	4.35

Figure Skating — A467

Ice Hockey — A468

Designs: 80h, Skiing (horiz.). 1k, Field ball player.

Engraved and Photogravure

1964, Jan. 20 Unwmk. *Perf. 11½*

1217	A467	30h vio bl & yel	16	5
1218	A467	80h dk bl & org	42	8
1219	A467	1k brn & lil	48	20

Issued to commemorate the International University Games (30h and 80h) and the World Field Ball Championships (1k).

1964, Jan. 20

Designs: 1.80k, Toboggan. 2k, Ski jump.

1220	A468	1k pur & pale grn	75	45
1221	A468	1.80k sl grn & bl gray	1.15	1.00
1222	A468	2k dk bl & pale grn	*4.00*	*3.50*

Issued to commemorate the 9th Winter Olympic Games, Innsbruck, Jan. 29-Feb. 9, 1964.

Magura Rest Home, High Tatra — A469

Design: 80h, Slovak National Insurrection Rest Home, Low Tatra.

1964, Feb. 19 Unwmk. *Perf. 11½*

1223	A469	60h grn & yel	25	5
1224	A469	80h vio bl & pink	30	5

Skiers and Ski Lift A470

Designs: 60h, Automobile camp, Telc. 1k, Fishing, Spis Castle. 1.80k, Lake and boats, Cesky Krumlov.

Engraved and Photogravure

1964, Feb. 19

1225	A470	30h dk vio brn & bl	15	5
1226	A470	60h sl & car	25	5
1227	A470	1k brn & ol	50	8
1228	A470	1.80k sl grn & org	75	15

Moses, Day and Night by Michelangelo — A471

Designs: 60th, "A Midsummer Night's Dream," by Shakespeare. 1k, Man, telescope and heaven (vert.). 1.60k, King George of Podebrad (1420-71).

1964, March 20

1229	A471	40h blk & yel grn	20	5
1230	A471	60h sl & car	20	5
1231	A471	1k blk & lt bl	35	8
1232	A471	1.60k blk & yel	75	15

Issued to commemorate the following: 400th anniversary of the death of Michelangelo (40h); 400th anniversary of the birth of Shakespeare (60h); 400th anniversary of the birth of Galileo (1k); 500th anniversary of the pacifist efforts of King George of Podebrad (1.60k).

Yuri A. Gagarin — A472

Astronauts: 60h, Gherman Titov. 80h, John H. Glenn, Jr. 1k, Scott M. Carpenter (vert.). 1.20k, Pavel R. Popovich and Andrian G. Nikolayev. 1.40k, Walter M. Schirra (vert.). 1.60k, Gordon L. Cooper (vert.). 2k, Valentina Tereshkova and Valeri Bykovski (vert.).

Engraved and Photogravure

1964, Apr. 27 Unwmk. *Perf. 11½*

Yellow Paper

1233	A472	30h blk & vio bl	60	10
1234	A472	60h dk grn & dk car	30	10
1235	A472	80h dk car & vio	35	10
1236	A472	1k ultra & rose vio	45	15
1237	A472	1.20k ver & ol gray	1.00	25
1238	A472	1.40k blk & dl grn	1.20	40
1239	A472	1.60k pale pur & Prus grn	*4.00*	*1.75*
1240	A472	2k dk bl & red	1.75	80
		Nos. 1233-1240 (8)	9.65	3.65

World's first 10 astronauts.

Creeping Bellflower A473

Film "Flower" and Karlovy Vary Colonnade A474

Flowers: 80h, Musk thistle. 1k, Chicory. 1.20k, Yellow iris. 1.60k, Gentian. 2k, Corn poppy.

1964, June 15 Engr. *Perf. 14*

1241	A473	60h dk grn, lil & org	1.40	30
1242	A473	80h blk, grn & red lil	1.40	30
1243	A473	1k vio bl, grn & pink	1.40	40
1244	A473	1.20k blk, yel & grn	1.40	40
1245	A473	1.60k vio & grn	1.40	40
1246	A473	2k vio, red & grn	*8.00*	*2.75*
		Nos. 1241-1246 (6)	15.00	4.55

Engraved and Photogravure

1964, June 20 Unwmk. *Perf. 13½*

1247 A474 60h blk, bl & car 1.25 15

Issued to commemorate the 14th International Film Festival at Karlovy Vary, July 4-19.

Silesian Coat of Arms — A475

Young Miner of 1764 — A476

1964, June 20 *Perf. 11½*

1248 A475 30h blk & yel 35 8

Issued to commemorate the 150th anniversary of the Silesian Museum, Opava.

1964, June 20

1249 A476 60h sep & lt grn 35 5

Issued to commemorate the bicentenary of the Mining School at Banska Stiavnica.

Skoda Fire Engine A477

1964, June 20

1250 A477 60h car rose & lt bl 35 5

Issued to commemorate the centenary of voluntary fire brigades in Bohemia.

ČESKOSLOVENSKO

Gulls, Hradcany Castle, Red Cross A478

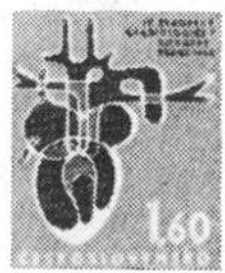

Human Heart A479

1964, July 10

1251 A478 60h car & bluish gray 35 5

Issued to commemorate the 4th Czechoslovak Red Cross Congress at Prague.

1964, July 10

1252 A479 1.60k ultra & car 80 8

Issued to commemorate the 4th European Cardiological Congress at Prague.

Partisans, Girl and Factories A480

Battle Scene, 1944 — A481

Design: 60h, Partisans and flame.

Engraved and Photogravure

1964, Aug. 17 Unwmk. *Perf. 11½*

1253	A480	30h brn & red	10	5
1254	A480	60h dk bl & red	30	5
1255	A481	60h blk & red	30	5

Issued to commemorate the 20th anniversary of the Slovak National Uprising; No. 1255 commemorates the 20th anniversary of the Battles of Dukla Pass.

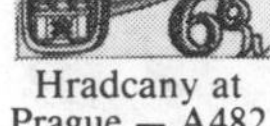

Hradcany at Prague — A482

Discus Thrower and Pole Vaulter — A483

Design: 5k, Charles Bridge and Hradcany.

1964, Aug. 30 *Perf. 11½x12*

1256 A482 60h blk & red 75 10

Souvenir Sheet

Engr. *Imperf.*

1257 A482 5k dp cl 2.75 2.50

Millenium of the Hradcany, Prague.

No. 1257 measures 76x98mm.; stamp size: 30x50mm.

Engraved and Photogravure

1964, Sept. 2 *Perf. 13½*

Designs: 60h, Bicycling (horiz.). 1k, Soccer. 1.20k, Rowing. 1.60k, Swimming (horiz.). 2.80k, Weight lifting (horiz.).

1258	A483	60h multi	30	12
1259	A483	80h multi	40	12
1260	A483	1k multi	50	18
1261	A483	1.20k multi	60	25
1262	A483	1.60k multi	1.00	50
1263	A483	2.80k multi	*5.50*	*3.00*
		Nos. 1258-1263 (6)	8.30	4.17

Issued to commemorate the 18th Olympic Games, Tokyo, Oct. 10-25. Sheets of 10.

Miniature Sheet

Space Ship Voskhod I, Astronauts and Globe — A484

Engraved and Photogravure

1964, Nov. 12 Unwmk. *Perf. 11½*

1264 A484 3k dk bl & dl lil, *buff* 5.50 4.00

Issued to commemorate the Russian three-manned space flight of Vladimir M. Komarov, Boris B. Yegorov and Konstantin Feoktistov, Oct. 12-13. No. 1264 contains one stamp. Size of stamp: 49x30mm.; size of sheet: 92x66mm.

Steam Engine and Atomic Power Plant — A485

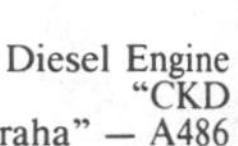

Diesel Engine "CKD Praha" — A486

1964, Nov. 16 Engr.

1265 A485 30h dl red brn 15 5

Engraved and Photogravure

1266 A486 60h grn & sal 25 5

Issued to publicize traditions and development of engineering; No. 1265 commemorates the 150th anniversary of the First Brno Engineering Works, No. 1266 honors the engineering concern CKD Praha.

European Redstart — A487

Birds: 60h, Green woodpecker. 80h, Hawfinch. 1k, Black woodpecker. 1.20k, European robin. 1.60k, European roller.

1964, Nov. 16 Litho. *Perf. 10½*

1267	A487	30h multi	15	5
1268	A487	60h blk & multi	30	5
1269	A487	80h multi	35	10
1270	A487	1k multi	45	20
1271	A487	1.20k lt vio bl & blk	50	25
1272	A487	1.60k yel & blk	1.00	75
		Nos. 1267-1272 (6)	2.75	1.40

Dancer A488

"In the Sun" Pre-school Children A489

Designs: 60h, "Over the Obstacles," teenagers. 1k, "Movement and Beauty," woman flag twirler. 1.60k, Runners at start.

Engraved and Photogravure

1965 Unwmk. *Perf. 11½*

1273 A488 30h red & lt bl 15 5

Perf. 11½x12

1274	A489	30h vio bl & car	10	5
1275	A489	60h brn & ultra	20	5
1276	A489	1k blk & yel	40	6
1277	A489	1.60k mar & gray	75	30
		Nos. 1273-1277 (5)	1.60	51

Issued to publicize the Third National Spartacist Games. Issue dates: No. 1273, Jan. 3. Nos. 1274-1277, May 24.

Mountain Rescue Service — A490

Arms and View, Beroun — A491

1965, Jan. 15 Unwmk. *Perf. 11½*

Designs: No. 1279, Woman gymnast. No. 1280, Bicyclists. No. 1281, Women hurdlers.

1278	A490	60h vio & bl	35	6
1279	A490	60h mar & ocher	35	6
1280	A490	60h blk & car	35	6
1281	A490	60h grn & yel	35	6

Issued to publicize: Mountain Rescue Service (No. 1278); First World Championship in Artistic Gymnastics, Prague, December 1965 (No. 1279); World Championship in Indoor Bicycling, Prague, Oct. 1965 (No. 1280); "Universiada 1965," Brno (No. 1281).

Engraved and Photogravure

1965, Feb. 15

Designs: No. 1283, Town Square, Domazlice. No. 1284, Old and new buildings, Frydek-Mystek. No. 1285, Arms and view, Lipnik. No. 1286, Fortified wall, City Hall and Arms, Policka. No. 1287, View and hops, Zatek. No. 1288, Small fortress and rose, Terezin.

1282	A491	30h vio bl & lt bl	25	5
1283	A491	30h dl pur & yel	25	5
1284	A491	30h sl & gray	25	5
1285	A491	30h grn & bis	25	5
1286	A491	30h brn & tan	25	5
1287	A491	30h dk bl & cit	25	5
1288	A491	30h blk & rose	25	5
		Nos. 1282-1288 (7)	1.75	35

Nos. 1282-87 commemorate the 700th anniversary of the founding of various Bohemian towns; No. 1288 commemorates the 20th anniversary of the liberation of the Theresienstadt (Terezin) concentration camp.

Sun's Corona A492

Space Research: 30h, Sun. 60h, Exploration of the Moon. 1k, Twin space craft (vert.). 1.40k, Space station. 1.60k, Exploration of Mars (vert.). 2k, USSR and USA Meteorological collaboration.

Engraved and Photogravure

Perf. 12x11½, 11½x12

1965, Mar. 15

1289	A492	20th rose & red lil	10	5
1290	A492	30h rose red & yel	12	5
1291	A492	60h bluish blk & yel	22	5
1292	A492	1k pur & pale bl	35	10
1293	A492	1.40k blk & sal	50	15
1294	A492	1.60k blk & pink	65	35
1295	A492	2k bluish blk & lt bl	*1.75*	*1.25*
		Nos. 1289-1295 (7)	3.69	2.00

Issued to publicize space research; Nos. 1289-1290 also commemorate the International Quiet Sun Year, 1964-65.

Frantisek Ventura, Equestrian; Amsterdam, 1928 — A493

Czechoslovakian Olympic Victories: 30h, Discus, Paris, 1900. 60h, Running, Helsinki, 1952. 1k, Weight lifting, Los Angeles, 1932. 1.40k, Gymnastics, Berlin, 1936. 1.60k, Double sculling, Rome, 1960. 2k, Women's gymnastics, Tokyo, 1964.

1965, Apr. 16 *Perf. 11½x12*

1296	A493	20h choc & gold	10	5
1297	A493	30h ind & emer	15	5
1298	A493	60h ultra & gold	25	10
1299	A493	1k red brn & gold	45	25
1300	A493	1.40k dk sl grn & gold	90	50
1301	A493	1.60k blk & gold	1.00	55
1302	A493	2k mar & gold	1.50	75
		Nos. 1296-1302 (7)	4.35	2.25

Astronauts Virgil Grissom and John Young — A494

Designs: No. 1304, Alexei Leonov floating in space. No. 1305, Launching pad at Cape Kennedy, U.S.A. No. 1306, Leonov leaving space ship.

1965, Apr. 17 *Perf. 11x11½*

1303	A494	60h sl bl & lil rose	25	18
1304	A494	60h vio blk & bl	25	18
1305	A494	3k sl bl & lil rose	1.75	1.25
1306	A494	3k vio blk & bl	1.75	1.25

Issued to honor American and Soviet astronauts. Printed in sheets of 25; one sheet contains 20 No. 1303 and 5 No. 1305, the other sheet contains 20 No. 1304 and 5 No. 1306.

Russian Soldier, View of Prague and Guerrilla Fighters A495

Designs: No. 1308, Blast furnace, workers and tank. 60h, Worker and factory. 1k, Worker and new constructions. 1.60k, Woman farmer, new farm buildings and machinery.

1965, May 5 **Engr.** *Perf. 13½*

1307	A495	30h dk red, blk & ol	12	5
1308	A495	30h multi	12	5
1309	A495	60h vio bl, red & blk	25	5
1310	A495	1k dp org, blk & brn	40	15
1311	A495	1.60k yel, red & blk	75	25
		Nos. 1307-1311 (5)	1.64	55

Issued to commemorate the 20th anniversary of liberation from the Nazis.

Slovakian Kopov Dog — A496

Dogs: 40h, German shepherd. 60h, Czech hunting dog with pheasant. 1k, Poodle. 1.60k, Czech terrier. 2k, Afghan hound.

1965, June 10 *Perf. 12x11½*

1312	A496	30h blk & red org	15	5
1313	A496	40h blk & yel	20	5
1314	A496	60h blk & ver	25	8
1315	A496	1k blk & dk car rose	50	10
1316	A496	1.60k blk & org	1.00	20
1317	A496	2k blk & org	2.00	95
		Nos. 1312-1317 (6)	4.10	1.43

Issued to publicize the World Dog Show at Brno and the International Dog Breeders Congress, Prague.

U.N. Headquarters Building, N.Y. — A497

Designs: 60h, U.N. Emblem and inscription. 1.60k, ICY emblem.

1965, June 24 *Perf. 12x11½*

1318	A497	60h dk red brn & yel	25	6
1319	A497	1k ultra & lt bl	40	10
1320	A497	1.60k gold & dk red	75	35

Issued to commemorate the 20th anniversary of the United Nations and for the International Cooperation Year, 1965.

Trade Union Emblem A498

1965, June 24 **Engr.**

1321	A498	60h dk red & ultra	35	5

Issued to commemorate the 20th anniversary of the International Trade Union Federation.

Women and Globe — A499

1965, June 24 *Perf. 11½x12*

1322	A499	60h vio bl	35	5

Issued to commemorate the 20th anniversary of the International Women's Federation.

Children's House (Burgraves' Palace), Hradcany — A500

Matthias Tower — A501

1965, June 25 *Perf. 11½*

1323	A500	30h sl grn	20	5
1324	A501	60h dk brn	40	5

Issued to publicize the Hradcany, Prague.

Marx and Lenin — A502

Engraved and Photogravure

1965, July 1

1325	A502	60h car rose & gold	30	5

Issued to commemorate the 6th conference of Postal Ministers of Communist Countries, Peking, June 21-July 15.

Joseph Navratil A503

Jan Hus A504

Gregor Johann Mendel A505

Costume Jewelry A506

Bohuslav Martinu A507

Seated Woman and University of Bratislava A508

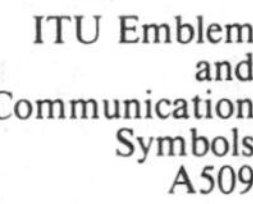

ITU Emblem and Communication Symbols A509

Macromolecular Symposium Emblem A510

Design: No. 1327, Ludwig Stur (diff. frame).

Engraved and Photogravure

1965 **Unwmk.** *Perf. 11½*

1326	A503	30h blk & fawn	18	5
1327	A503	30h blk & dl grn	18	5
1328	A504	60h blk & crim	35	5
1329	A505	60h vio bl & red	35	5
1330	A506	60h pur & gold	35	5
1331	A507	60h blk & org	35	5
1332	A508	60h brn, *yel*	35	5
1333	A509	1k org & bl	55	8
1334	A510	1k blk & dp org	55	8
		Nos. 1326-1334 (9)	3.21	51

No. 1326 commemorates the centenary of the death of Josef Navratil (1798-1865), painter; No. 1327, the sesquicentennial of the birth of Ludwig Stur (1815-56), Slovak author and historian; No. 1328 commemorates the 550th anniversary of the death of Jan Hus, religious reformer;

No. 1329, the centenary of publication of Mendel's laws of inheritance; No. 1330 publicizes the "Jablonec 1965" costume jewelry exhibition; No. 1331, the 75th anniversary of the birth of Bohuslav Martinu (1890-1959), composer; No. 1332, the 500th anniversary of the founding of the University of Bratislava as Academia Istropolitana; No. 1333, the centenary of the International Telecommunication Union; No. 1334, the International Symposium on Macromolecular Chemistry Prague, Sept. 1-8.

"Young Woman at her Toilette," by Titian A512

Help for Flood Victims A513

Rescue of Flood Victims A514

Miniature Sheet

1965, Aug. 12

1336	A512	5k multi	3.75	3.75

Issued to publicize the Hradcany Art Gallery. No. 1336 contains one stamp; size of sheet: 75x97mm.

1965, Sept. 6 **Engr.**

1337	A513	30h vio bl	15	7

Engraved and Photogravure

1338	A514	2k dk ol grn & ol	90	65

Help for Danube flood victims in Slovakia.

Dotterel A515

Mountain Birds: 60h, Wall creeper (vert.). 1.20k, Lesser redpoll. 1.40k, Golden eagle (vert.). 1.60k, Ring ouzel. 2k, Eurasian nutcracker (vert.).

1965, Sept. 20 **Litho.** *Perf. 11*

1339	A515	30h multi	20	5
1340	A515	60h multi	30	5
1341	A515	1.20k multi	65	10
1342	A515	1.40k multi	80	20
1343	A515	1.60k multi	90	25
1344	A515	2k multi	1.40	1.00
		Nos. 1339-1344 (6)	4.25	1.65

Levoca A516

Coltsfoot A517

Views of Towns: 10h, Jindrichuv Hradec. 20h, Nitra. 30h, Kosice. 40h, Hradec Kralove. 50h, Telc. 60h, Ostrava. 1k, Olomouc. 1.20k, Ceske Budejovice. 1.60k, Cheb. 2k, Brno. 3k, Bratislava. 5k, Prague.

Engraved and Photogravure

1965-66 *Perf. 11½x12*

Size: 23x19mm.

1345	A516	5h blk & yle	5	5
1346	A516	10h ultra & ol bis	6	5
1347	A516	20h blk & lt bl	12	5
1348	A516	30h vio bl & lt grn	20	5

1348A A516 40h dk brn & lt bl ('66) 25 5
1348B A516 50h blk & ocher ('66) 30 5
1348C A516 60h red & gray ('66) 40 5
1348D A516 1k pur & pale grn ('66) 60 5

Perf. 11½x11

Size: 30x23mm.

1349 A516 1.20k sl & lt bl 65 8
1350 A516 1.60k ind & yel 75 5
1351 A516 2k sl grn & pale yel 1.25 10
1352 A516 3k brn & yel 1.75 12
1353 A516 5k blk & pink 3.00 15
Nos. 1345-1353 (13) 9.38 90

1965, Dec. 3 Engr. *Perf. 14*

Medicinal Plants: 60h, Meadow saffron. 80h, Corn poppy. 1k, Foxglove. 1.20k, Arnica. 1.60k, Cornflower. 2k, Dog rose.

1354 A517 30h multi 15 8
1355 A517 60h multi 25 12
1356 A517 80h multi 30 15
1357 A517 1k multi 55 20
1358 A517 1.20k multi 75 25
1359 A517 1.60k multi 1.25 40
1360 A517 2k multi *5.00 2.25*
Nos. 1354-1360 (7) 8.25 3.45

Strip of "Stamps" — A518

Engraved and Photogravure

1965, Dec. 18 *Perf. 11½*

1361 A518 1k dk red & gold 3.00 2.50

Issued for Stamp Day, 1965.

Romain Rolland A519

Symbolic Musical Instruments and Names of Composers A520

Portraits: No. 1362, Stanislav Sucharda. No. 1363, Ignac Josef Pesina. No. 1365, Donatello.

1966, Feb. 14 Engr. *Perf. 11½*

1362 A519 30h dp grn 10 5
1363 A519 30h vio bl 10 5
1364 A519 60h rose lake 25 5
1365 A519 60h brown 25 5

Issued to commemorate the following: No. 1362, centenary of birth of Stanislav Sucharda (1866-1916), sculptor; No. 1363, bicentenary of birth of Ignac Josef Pesina (1766-1808), veterinarian. No. 1364, centenary of birth of Romain Rolland (1866-1944), French writer; No. 1365, 500th anniversary of death of Donatello (1386-1466), Italian sculptor.

Engraved and Photogravure

1966, Feb. 15

1366 A520 30h blk & gold 55 20

Issued to commemorate the 70th anniversary of the Czech Philharmonic Orchestra.

Figure Skating Pair A521

Designs: No. 1368, Man skater. No. 1369, Volleyball player, spiking (vert.). 1k, Volleyball player, saving (vert.). 1.60k, Woman skater. 2k, Figure skating pair.

1966, Feb. 17

1367 A521 30h dk car rose 15 5
1368 A521 60h green 30 5
1369 A521 60h car & buff 30 5
1370 A521 1k vio & lt bl 45 5
1371 A521 1.60k brn & yel 60 9
1372 A521 2k bl & grnsh bl *2.50 80*
Nos. 1367-1372 (6) 4.30 1.09

Nos. 1367-68 and 1371-72 commemorate the European Figure Skating Championships, Bratislava; Nos. 1369-70 commemorate the World Volleyball Championships.

Souvenir Sheet

Girl Dancing — A522

1966, Mar. 21 Engr. *Imperf.*

1373 A522 3k sl bl, red & bl 2.25 2.25

Issued to commemorate the centenary of the opera "The Bartered Bride" by Bedrich Smetana. Opening chorus "Why shouldn't we be happy." in margin. Size: 85x105mm.

"Ajax" 1841 A523

Locomotives: 30h, "Karlstejn" 1865. 60h, Steam engine, 1946. 1k, Steam engine with tender, 1946. 1.60k, Electric locomotive, 1964. 2k, Diesel locomotive, 1964.

1966, March 21 *Perf. 11½x11*

Buff Paper

1374 A523 20h sepia 10 5
1375 A523 30h dl vio 12 5
1376 A523 60h dl pur 30 5
1377 A523 1k dk bl 40 7
1378 A523 1.60k dk bl grn 70 30
1379 A523 2k dk red *4.00 1.25*
Nos. 1374-1379 (6) 5.62 1.77

European Perch A524

Fish: 30h, Brown trout (vert.). 1k, Carp. 1.20k, Northern pike. 1.40k, Grayling. 1.60k, Eel.

Perf. 13x13½, 13½x13

1966, Apr. 22 Litho. Unwmk.

1380 A524 30h multi 18 5
1381 A524 60h multi 28 5
1382 A524 1k multi 45 5
1383 A524 1.20k multi 55 15
1384 A524 1.40k multi 65 25
1385 A524 1.60k multi *4.00 1.50*
Nos. 1380-1385 (6) 6.11 2.05

Issued to publicize the International Fishing Championships, Svit, Sept. 3-5.

WHO Headquarters, Geneva — A525

Engraved and Photogravure

1966, Apr. 25 *Perf. 12x11½*

1386 A525 1k dk bl & lt bl 45 10

Issued to commemorate the inauguration of the World Health Organization Headquarters, Geneva.

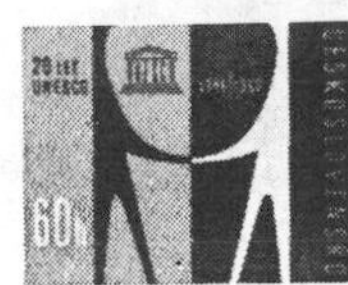

Symbolic Handshake and UNESCO Emblem — A526

1966, Apr. 25 *Perf. 11½*

1387 A526 60h bis & ol gray 25 5

Issued to commemorate the 20th anniversary of UNESCO (U.N. Educational, Scientific and Cultural Organization).

Prague Castle Issue

Belvedere Palace and St. Vitus' Cathedral A527

Crown of St. Wenceslas, 1346 — A528

Design: 60h, Madonna, altarpiece from St. George's Church.

1966, May 9 Engr. *Perf. 11½*

1388 A527 30h dk bl 25 5

Engraved and Photogravure

1389 A527 60h blk & yel bis 55 10

Souvenir Sheet

Engr.

1390 A528 5k multi 3.50 3.50

See Nos. 1537-1539.

Tiger Swallowtail A529

Butterflies and Moths: 60h, Clouded sulphur. 80h, European purple emperor. 1k, Apollo. 1.20k, Burnet moth. 2k, Tiger moth.

1966, May 23 Engr. *Perf. 14*

1391 A529 30h multi 12 8
1392 A529 60h multi 28 10
1393 A529 80h multi 40 12
1394 A529 1k multi 45 15
1395 A529 1.20k multi 65 20
1396 A529 2k multi *4.00 1.50*
Nos. 1391-1396 (6) 5.90 2.15

Sheets of ten.

Flags of Russia and Czechoslovakia — A530

Designs: 60h, Rays surrounding hammer and sickle "sun." 1.60k, Girl's head and stars.

Engraved and Photogravure

1966, May 31 *Perf. 11½*

1397 A530 30h dk bl & crim 12 5
1398 A530 60h dk bl & red 25 15
1399 A530 1.60k red & dk bl 70 15

Issued to commemorate the 13th Congress of the Communist Party of Czechoslovakia.

Dakota Chief — A531

Designs: 20h, Indians, canoe and tepee (horiz.). 30h, Tomahawk. 40h, Haida totem poles. 60h, Kachina, good spirit of the Hopis. 1k, Indian on horseback hunting buffalo (horiz.). 1.20k, Calumet, Dakota peace pipe.

Engraved and Photogravure

1966, June 20

Size: 23x40mm.

1400 A531 20h vio bl & dp org 10 5
1401 A531 30h blk & dl org 10 5
1402 A531 40h blk & lt bl 10 8
1403 A531 60h grn & yel 30 10
1404 A531 1k pur & emer 40 20
1405 A531 1.20k vio bl & rose lil 60 40

Perf. 14

Engr.

Size: 23x37mm.

1406 A531 1.40k multi *2.75 1.25*
Nos. 1400-1406 (7) 4.35 2.13

Issued to commemorate the centenary of the Naprstek Ethnographic Museum, Prague, and in connection with "The Indians of North America" exhibition.

Model of Molecule — A532

Engraved and Photogravure

1966, July 4 Unwmk. *Perf. 11½*

1407 A532 60h blk & lt bl 30 5

Issued to commemorate the centenary of the Czechoslovak Chemical Society.

The only foreign revenue stamps listed in this Catalogue are those authorized for prepayment of postage.

"Guernica" by Pablo Picasso — A533

1966, July 5
Size: 75x30mm.

1408 A533 60k blk & pale bl 2.00 2.00

30th anniversary of International Brigade in Spanish Civil War.

Sheets of 15 stamps and 5 labels inscribed "Picasso-Guernica 1937."

Pantheon, Bratislava — A534

Designs: No. 1410, Devin Castle and Ludwig Stur. No. 1411, View of Nachod. No. 1412, State Science Library, Olomouc.

1966, July 25 **Engr.**

1409 A534 30h dl pur 10 5
1410 A534 60h dk bl 25 5
1411 A534 60h green 25 5
1412 A534 60h sepia 25 5

No. 1409 publicizes the Russian War Memorial, Bratislava; No. 1410, the 9th century Devin Castle as symbol of Slovak nationalism; No. 1411 commemorates the 700th anniversary of the founding of Nachod; No. 1412, the 400th anniversary of the State Science Library, Olomouc.

Atom Symbol and Sun — A535

Engraved and Photogravure
1966, Aug. 29 ***Perf. 11½***

1413 A535 60h blk & red 30 5

Issued to publicize Jachymov (Joachimsthal), where pitchblende was first discovered, "cradle of the atomic age."

Brno Fair Emblem — A536

Olympia Coin and Olympic Rings — A537

1966, Aug. 29

1414 A536 60h blk & red 30 5

8th International Trade Fair, Brno.

1966, Aug. 29

Design: 1k, Olympic flame, Czechoslovak flag and Olympic rings.

1415 A537 60h blk & gold 30 5
1416 A537 1k dk bl & red 55 30

Issued to commemorate the 70th anniversary of the Olympic Committee.

Missile Carrier, Tank and Jet Plane A538

1966, Aug. 31

1417 A538 60h blk & ap grn 35 5

Issued to commemorate the maneuvers of the armies of the Warsaw Pact countries.

Mercury A539

Designs: 30h, Moravian silver thaler, 1620, reverse and obverse (vert.). 1.60k, Old and new buildings of Brno State Theater. 5k, International Trade Fair Administration Tower and postmark (vert.).

1966, Sept. 10

1418 A539 30h dk red & blk 30 5
1419 A539 60h org & blk 30 5
1420 A539 1.60k blk & brt grn 75 35

Souvenir Sheet

1421 A539 5k multi 3.25 3.25

Issued to publicize the Brno Philatelic Exhibition, Sept. 11-25. No. 1421 contains one stamp (size: 30x40mm.). Marginal black inscription and exhibition emblem. Size: 73½x100mm.

First Meeting in Orbit — A540

Designs: 30h, Photograph of far side of Moon and Russian satellite. 60h, Photograph of Mars and Mariner 4. 80th, Soft landing on Moon. 1k, Satellite, laser beam and binary code. 1.20k, Telstar over Earth and receiving station.

Engraved and Photogravure
1966, Sept. 26 ***Perf. 11½***

1422 A540 20h vio & lt grn 10 5
1423 A540 30h blk & sal pink 15 5
1424 A540 60h sl & lil 25 5
1425 A540 80h dk pur & lt bl 40 20
1426 A540 1k blk & vio 50 25
1427 A540 1.20k red & bl *2.00* *75*
Nos. 1422-1427 (6) 3.40 1.35

Issued to publicize American and Russian achievements in space research.

Badger A541

Game Animals: 40h, Red deer (vert.). 60h, Lynx. 80h, Hare. 1k, Red fox. 1.20k, Brown bear (vert.). 2k, Wild boar.

1966, Nov. 28 **Litho.** ***Perf. 13½***

1428 A541 30h multi 15 5
1429 A541 40h multi 20 5
1430 A541 60h multi 28 5
1431 A541 80h multi *(europaens)* 40 12
a. 80h multi *(europaeus)* 3.00 2.00
1432 A541 1k multi 55 20
1433 A541 1.20k multi 65 25
1434 A541 2k multi *4.50* *2.00*
Nos. 1428-1434 (7) 6.73 2.72

The sheet of 50 of the 80h contains 40 with misspelling "europaens" and 10 with "europaeus."

"Spring" by Vaclav Hollar, 1607-77 A542

Paintings: No. 1436, Portrait of Mrs. F. Wussin, by Jan Kupecky (1667-1740). No. 1437, Snow Owl by Karel Purkyne (1834-1868). No. 1438, Tulips by Vaclav Spala (1885-1964). No. 1439, Recruit by Ludovit Fulla (1902-).

1966, Dec. 8 **Engr.** ***Perf. 14***

1435 A542 1k black 3.25 3.25
1436 A542 1k multi 3.25 3.25
1437 A542 1k multi 3.25 3.25
1438 A542 1k multi 3.25 3.25
1439 A542 1k multi *13.00* *10.50*
Nos. 1435-1439 (5) 26.00 23.50

Printed in sheets of 4 stamps and 2 labels. The labels in sheet of No. 1435 are inscribed "Vaclav Hollar 1607-1677" in fancy frame. Other labels are blank.

See also No. 1484.

Symbolic Bird — A543

Engraved and Photogravure
1966, Dec. 17 ***Perf. 11½***

1440 A543 1k dp bl & yel 95 95

Issued for Stamp Day.

Youth — A544

1967, Jan. 16 ***Perf. 11½***

1441 A544 30h ver & lt bl 15 5

Issued to publicize the 5th Congress of the Czechoslovak Youth Organization.

Symbolic Flower and Machinery A545

Engraved and Photogravure
1967, Jan. 16

1442 A545 30h car & yel 15 5

6th Trade Union Congress, Prague.

Parents with Dead Child — A545a

1967, Jan. 16 ***Perf. 11½***

1442A A545a 60h blk & sal 25 6

Issued to publicize "Peace and Freedom in Viet Nam."

View of Jihlava and Tourist Year Emblem A546

Views and Tourist Year Emblem: 40h, Spielberg Castle and churches, Brno. 1.20k, Danube, castle and churches, Bratislava. 1.60k, Vlatava River bridges, Hradcany and churches, Prague.

1967, Feb. 13 **Engr.** ***Perf. 11½***
Size: 40x23mm.

1443 A546 30h brn vio 12 5
1444 A546 40h maroon 18 5

Size: 75x30mm.

1445 A546 1.20k vio bl 65 20
1446 A546 1.60k black *1.75* *75*

International Tourist Year, 1967.

Black-tailed Godwit — A547

Birds: 40h, Shoveler (horiz.). 60h, Purple heron. 80h, Penduline tit. 1k, Avocet. 1.40k, Black stork. 1.60k, Tufted duck (horiz.).

1967, Feb. 20 **Litho.** ***Perf. 13½***

1447 A547 30h multi 10 5
1448 A547 40h multi 12 5
1449 A547 60h multi 20 5
1450 A547 80h multi 30 10
1451 A547 1k multi 40 12
1452 A547 1.40k multi 70 35
1453 A547 1.60k multi *3.00* *1.50*
Nos. 1447-1453 (7) 4.82 2.22

Solar Research and Satellite — A548

Space Research: 40h, Space craft, rocket and construction of station. 60h, Man on moon and orientation system. 1k, Exploration of solar system and rocket. 1.20k, Lunar satellites and moon photograph. 1.60k, Planned lunar architecture and moon landing.

Engraved and Photogravure
1967, March 24 ***Perf. 11½***

1454 A548 30h yel & dk red 12 5
1455 A548 40h vio bl & blk 15 5
1456 A548 60h lil & grn 25 5
1457 A548 1k brt pink & sl 45 15
1458 A548 1.20k lt vio & blk 65 25
1459 A548 1.60k brn lake & blk *2.00* *90*
Nos. 1454-1459 (6) 3.62 1.45

Gothic Painting, by Master Theodoric A549

Designs: 40h, "Burning of Master Hus," from Litomerice Hymnal. 60h, Modern glass sculpture. 80h, "The Shepherdess and the Chimney Sweep," Andersen fairy tale, painting by J. Trnka. 1k, Section of pressure vessel from atomic power station. 1.20k, Three ceramic figurines, by P. Rada. 3k, Montreal skyline and EXPO '67 emblem.

1967, Apr. 10 Engr. *Perf. 14*
Size: 37x23mm.

1460 A549 30h multi 15 5
1461 A549 40h multi 20 10
1462 A549 60h multi 30 15
1463 A549 80h multi 45 20
1464 A549 1k multi 50 30
1465 A549 1.20k multi *1.50 80*
Nos. 1460-1465 (6) 3.10 1.60

Souvenir Sheet
Perf. 11½
Size: 40x30mm.

1466 A549 3k multi 2.25 2.25

Issued to commemorate EXPO '67, International Exhibition, Montreal, Apr. 28-Oct. 27, 1967. No. 1466 contains one stamp with drawing of the Czechoslovakian pavilion in the margin. Size of sheet: 96x74mm.

Canoe Race A550

Women Playing Basketball – A551

Designs: No. 1468, Wheels, dove and emblems of Warsaw, Berlin, Prague. 1.60k, Canoe slalom.

Engraved and Photogravure
Perf. 12x11½, 11½x12
1967, Apr. 17

1467 A550 60h blk & brt bl 20 8
1468 A550 60h blk & sal 20 8
1469 A551 60h blk & grnsh bl 20 8
1470 A551 1.60k blk & brt vio *1.75 70*

Issued to commemorate the following: No. 1467, 5th International Wild-Water Canoeing Championships; No. 1468, 20th Warsaw-Berlin-Prague Bicycle Race: No. 1469, Women's Basketball Championships; No. 1470, 10th International Water Slalom Championships.

"Golden Street" – A552

Designs: 60h, Interior of Hall of King Wenceslas. 5k, St. Matthew, from illuminated manuscript, 11th century.

1967, May 9 *Perf. 11½x11*

1471 A552 30h rose cl 20 5
1472 A552 60h bluish blk 45 15

Souvenir Sheet
Perf. 11½

1473 A552 5k multi 4.00 4.00

Issued to publicize the Castle of Prague. No. 1473 contains one stamp with Latin marginal inscription in gold. Size: 75x95mm.

Stylized Lyre with Flowers A553

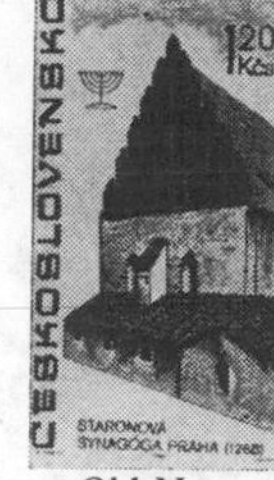

Old-New Synagogue, Prague A554

Engraved and Photogravure
1967, May 10 *Perf. 11½*

1474 A553 60h dl pur & brt grn 35 8

Prague Music Festival.

1967, May 22 *Perf. 11½*

Designs: 30h, Detail from Torah curtain, 1593. 60h, Prague Printer's emblem, 1530. 1k, Mikulov jug, 1804. 1.40k, Memorial for Concentration Camp Victims 1939-45, Pincas Synagogue (menorah and tablet). 1.60k, Tombstone of David Gans, 1613.

1475 A554 30h dl red & lt bl 40 10
1476 A554 60h blk & lt grn 55 10
1477 A554 1k dk bl & rose lil 80 25
1478 A554 1.20k dk brn & mar 1.10 45
1479 A554 1.40k blk & yel 1.40 60
1480 A554 1.60k grn & yel *4.25 2.00*
Nos. 1475-1480 (6) 8.50 3.50

Issued to show Jewish relics. The items shown on the 30h, 60h and 1k are from the State Jewish Museum, Prague.

"Lidice" A555

Prague Architecture A556

1967, June 9 Unwmk. *Perf. 11½*

1481 A555 30h blk & brt rose 20 5

Issued to commemorate the 25th anniversary of the destruction of Lidice by the Nazis.

Engraved and Photogravure
1967, June 10

1482 A556 1k blk & gold 45 30

Issued to publicize the 9th Congress of the International Union of Architects, Prague.

Petr Bezruc A557

1967, June 21

1483 A557 60h dl rose & blk 25 5

Issued to commemorate the centenary of the birth of Petr Bezruc, poet and writer.

Painting Type of 1966

Design: 2k, Henri Rousseau (1844-1910), self-portrait.

1967, June 22 Engr. *Perf. 11½*

1484 A542 2k multi 2.00 1.40

Issued to publicize Praga 68, World Stamp Exhibition, Prague, June 22-July 7, 1968. Printed in sheets of 4 stamps (2x2), separated by horizontal gutter with commemorative inscription and picture of National Gallery, site of Praga 68.

View of Skalitz – A558

Designs: No. 1486, Mining tower and church steeple, Pribram. No. 1487, Hands holding book and view of Presov.

1967, Aug. 21 Engr. *Perf. 11½*

1485 A558 30h vio bl 10 5
1486 A558 30h sl grn 10 5
1487 A558 30h claret 10 5

Issued to commemorate anniversaries of the towns of Skalitz, Pribram and Presov.

Colonnade and Spring, Karlovy Vary and Communications Emblem – A559

Engraved and Photogravure
1967, Aug. 21

1488 A559 30h vio bl & gold 35 15

Issued to commemorate the 5th Sports and Cultural Festival of the Employees of the Ministry of Communications, Karlovy Vary.

Ondrejov Conservatory and Galaxy – A560

1967, Aug. 22 Engr.

1489 A560 60h vio bl, rose lil & sil 95 25

Issued to commemorate the 13th International Congress of the Astronomic Union.

Orchid – A561

Flowers from the Botanical Gardens: 30h, Cobaea scandens. 40h, Lycaste deppei. 60h, Glottiphyllum davisii. 1k, Anthurium. 1.20k, Rhodocactus. 1.40k, Moth orchid.

1967, Aug. 30 Litho. *Perf. 12½*

1490 A561 20h multi 8 5
1491 A561 30h pink & multi 12 5
1492 A561 40h multi 22 5
1493 A561 60h lt bl & multi 22 5
1494 A561 1k multi 50 15
1495 A561 1.20k lt yel & multi 85 18
1496 A561 1.40k multi *2.50 90*
Nos. 1490-1496 (7) 4.49 1.43

Red Squirrel A562

Animals from the Tatra National Park: 60h, Wild cat. 1k, Ermine. 1.20k, Dormouse. 1.40k, Hedgehog. 1.60k, Pine marten.

Engraved and Photogravure
1967, Sept. 25 *Perf. 11½*

1497 A562 30h blk, yel & org 15 5
1498 A562 60h blk & buff 30 6
1499 A562 1k blk & lt bl 50 15
1500 A562 1.20k brn, pale grn & yel 55 18
1501 A562 1.40k blk, pink & yel 70 20
1502 A562 1.60k blk, org & yel *3.75 1.50*
Nos. 1497-1502 (6) 5.95 2.14

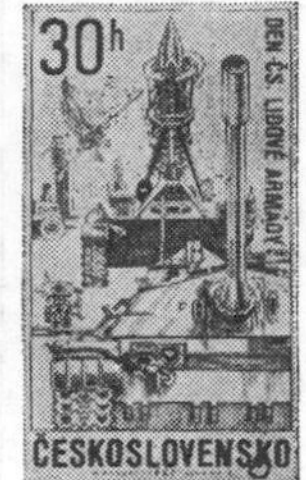

Rockets and Weapons – A563

1967, Oct. 6 Engr. *Perf. 11½*

1503 A563 30h sl grn 30 5

Day of the Czechoslovak People's Army.

Cruiser "Aurora" Firing at Winter Palace A564

Designs: 60h, Hammer and sickle emblems and Red Star (vert.). 1k, Hands reaching for hammer and sickle (vert.).

Engraved and Photogravure
1967, Nov. 7

1504 A564 30h blk & dk car 10 5
1505 A564 60h blk & dk car 20 5
1506 A564 1k blk & dk car 50 10

Issued to commemorate the 50th anniversary of the Russian October Revolution.

The Conjurer, by Frantisek Tichy A565

Paintings: 80h, Don Quixote, by Cyprian Majernik. 1k, Promenade in the Park, by Norbert Grund. 1.20k, Self-portrait, by Peter J. Brandl. 1.60k, Saints from Jan of Jeren Epitaph, by Czech Master of 1395.

1967, Nov. 13 Engr. *Perf. 11½*

1507 A565 60h multi 45 40
1508 A565 80h multi 60 50
1509 A565 1k multi 80 75
1510 A565 1.20k multi 95 80
1511 A565 1.60k multi *4.75 4.25*
Nos. 1507-1511 (5) 7.55 6.70

Sheets of 4. See Nos. 1589-1593, 1658-1662, 1711-1715, 1779-1783, 1847-1851, 1908-1913, 2043-2047, 2090-2093, 2147-2151, 2265-2269, 2335-2339, 2386-2390, 2437-2441, 2534-2538, 2586-2590, 2634-2638.

Pres. Antonin Novotny – A566

1967, Dec. 9 Engr. *Perf. 11½*

1512 A566 2k bl gray 85 5
1513 A566 3k brown 1.25 8

Czechoslovakia Nos. 65, 71 and 81 of 1920 — A567

1967, Dec. 18

1514 A567 1k mar & sil 1.25 1.10

Issued for Stamp Day.

Symbolic Flag and Dates — A568

1968, Jan. 15 Engr. *Perf. 11½*

1515 A568 30h red, dk bl & ultra 45 15

50th anniversary of Czechoslovakia.

Figure Skating and Olympic Rings — A569

Designs (Olympic Rings and): 1k, Ski course. 1.60k, Toboggan chute. 2k, Ice hockey.

Engraved and Photogravure

1968, Jan. 29

1516 A569 60h blk, yel & ocher 30 10
1517 A569 1k ol grn, lt bl & lem 40 20
1518 A569 1.60k blk, lil & bl grn 70 25
1519 A569 2k blk, ap grn & lt bl *2.50* 75

Issued to publicize the 10th WinterOlympic Games, Grenoble, France, Feb. 6-18.

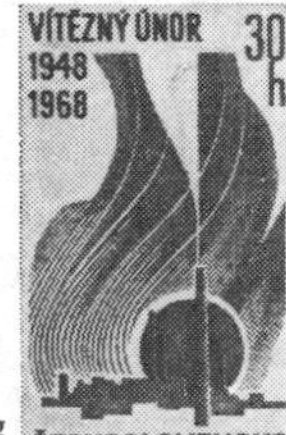

Factories and Rising Sun — A570

Design: 60h, Workers and banner.

Engraved and Photogravure

1968, Feb. 25 *Perf. 11½x12*

1520 A570 30h car & dk bl 10 5
1521 A570 60h car & dk bl 25 5

20th anniversary of February Revolution.

Catalogue prices for unused stamps up to mid-1953 are for hinged copies matching the condition specified in this volume's introduction.

Map of Battle of Sokolow — A571

Human Rights Flame — A572

Engraved and Photogravure

1968, Mar. 8 *Perf. 11½*

1522 A571 30h blk, brt bl & car 35 5

Engr.

1523 A572 1k rose car 55 25

No. 1522 commemorates the 25th anniversary of the Battle of Sokolow, Mar. 8, 1943, against the German Army; No. 1523 commemorates the International Human Rights Year.

Janko Kral and Liptovsky Mikulas — A573

Karl Marx — A574

Girl's Head A575

Arms and Allegory A576

ČESKOSLOVENSKO

1 KČS

Head — A577

1968, Mar. 25 Engr.

1524 A573 30h green 20 5
1525 A574 30h claret 20 5

Engraved and Photogravure

1526 A575 30h dk red & gold 20 5
1527 A576 30h dk bl & dp org 20 5
1528 A577 1k multi 1.10 35
Nos. 1524-1528 (5) 1.90 55

Issued to commemorate the following: The writer Janko Kral and the Slovak town Liptovsky Mikulas (No. 1524); 150th anniversary of the birth of Karl Marx (No. 1525); centenary of the cornerstone laying of the Prague National Theater (No. 1526); 150th anniversary of the Prague National Museum (No. 1527); 20th anniversary of the World Health Organization (1k).

Symbolic Radio Waves A578

Design: No. 1530, Symbolic television screens.

Engraved and Photogravure

1968, Apr. 29 *Perf. 11½*

1529 A578 30h blk, car & vio bl 15 6
1530 A578 30h blk, car & vio bl 15 6

Issued to commemorate the 45th anniversary of Czechoslovak broadcasting (No. 1529), and the 15th anniversary of television (No. 1530).

Olympic Rings, Mexican Sculpture and Gymnast A579

Olympic Rings and: 40h, Runner and "The Sanctification of Quetzalcoatl." 60h, Volleyball and Mexican ornaments. 1k, Czechoslovak and Mexican Olympic emblems and carved altar. 1.60k, Soccer and ornaments. 2k, View of Hradcany, weather vane and key.

1968, Apr. 30

1531 A579 30h blk, bl & car 12 5
1532 A579 40h multi 22 5
1533 A579 60h multi 35 5
1534 A579 1k multi 50 15
1535 A579 1.60k multi 70 20
1536 A579 2k blk & multi *2.75* *95*
Nos. 1531-1536 (6) 4.64 1.45

Issued to publicize the 19th Olympic Games, Mexico City, Oct. 12-27.

Prague Castle Types of 1966

Designs: 30h, Tombstone of Bretislav I. 60h, Romanesque door knocker, St. Wenceslas Chapel. 5k, Head of St. Peter, mosaic from Golden Gate of St. Vitus Cathedral.

Engraved and Photogravure

1968, May 9 *Perf. 11½*

1537 A527 30h multi 20 5
1538 A527 60h blk, red & cit 35 5

Souvenir Sheet

Engr.

1539 A528 5k multi 4.00 4.00

No. 1539 contains one stamp, black ornament in margin. Size: 75x94mm.

Pres. Ludvik Svoboda — A580

1968-70 Engr. *Perf. 11½*

1540 A580 30h ultra 10 5
1540A A580 50h grn ('70) 25 5
1541 A580 60h maroon 20 5
1541A A580 1k rose car ('70) 55 10

Shades exist of No. 1541A.

"Business," Sculpture by Otto Gutfreund A581

Cabaret Performer, by Frantisek Kupka A582

Engr. and Photo.; Engr. (2k)

1968, June 5

Designs (The New Prague): 40h, Broadcasting Corporation Building. 60h, New Parliament. 1.40k, Tapestry by Jan Bauch "Prague 1787." 3k, Presidential standard.

1542 A581 30h blk & multi 10 5
1543 A581 40h blk & multi 15 5
1544 A581 60h dk brn & multi 30 8
1545 A581 1.40k dk brn & multi 65 18
1546 A582 2k ind & multi *2.25* *2.25*
1547 A581 3k blk & multi 1.25 95
Nos. 1542-1547 (6) 4.70 3.56

1968, June 21 *Perf. 11½*

Designs (The Old Prague): 30h, St. George's Basilica. 60h, Renaissance fountain. 1k, Villa America-Dvorak Museum, 18th Century building. 1.60k, Emblem from the House of Three Violins, 18th century. 2k, Josefina, by Josef Manes. 3k, Emblem of Prague, 1475.

1548 A581 30h grn, gray & yel 12 5
1549 A581 60h dk vio, ap grn & gold 28 6
1550 A581 1k blk, lt bl & pink 55 15
1551 A581 1.60k sl grn & multi 70 20
1552 A582 2k brn & multi *2.00* *1.50*
1553 A581 3k blk, yel, bl & pink 1.50 75
Nos. 1548-1553 (6) 5.15 2.71

Nos. 1542-1553 issued to publicize the Praga 68 Philatelic Exhibition. Nos. 1542-1545, 1547-1551 and 1553 issued in sheets of 15 stamps and 15 labels with Praga 68 emblem and inscription. Nos. 1546 and 1552 issued in sheets of 4 (2x2) with one horizontal label between top and bottom rows showing Praga 68 emblem.

Souvenir Sheet

View of Prague and Emblems — A583

Engraved and Photogravure

1968, June 22 *Imperf.*

1554 A583 10k multi 8.50 7.50

Issued for Praga 68 and to commemorate the 50th anniversary of Czechoslovak postage stamps. Type of 1918 issue and commemorative inscription in margin. Size: 75½x110mm. Sold only together with a 5k admission ticket to the Praga 68 philatelic Exhibition.

Madonna with the Rose Garlands, by Dürer A584

1968, July 6 *Perf. 11½*
1555 A584 5k multi 4.50 3.50

Issued to commemorate the FIP Day, July 6 (Fédération Internationale de Philatelie). Issued in sheets of 4 (2x2) with one horizontal label between, showing Praga 68 emblem.

Stagecoach on Rails — A585

Design: 1k, Steam and electric locomotives.

Engraved and Photogravure
1968, Aug. 6
1556 A585 60h multi 55 20
1557 A585 1k multi 75 20

No. 1556 commemorates the 140th anniversary of the horse-drawn railroad Ceské Budejovice to Linz; No. 1557 commemorates the centenary of the Ceské Budejovice to Plzen railroad.

Fanciful "S" — A586

1968, Aug. 7 *Perf. 11½*
1558 A586 30h vio bl & car 25 5

Issued to commemorate the 6th International Slavonic Congress in Prague.

Ardspach Rocks and Ammonite — A587

Designs: 60h, Basalt formation and frog skeleton fossil. 80h, Rocks, basalt veins and polished agate. 1k, Pelecypoda (fossil shell) and Belanske Tatra mountains. 1.60k, Trilobite and Barrande rock formation.

1968, Aug. 8
1559 A587 30h blk & cit 12 5
1560 A587 60h blk & rose cl 30 10
1561 A587 80h blk, lt vio & pink 35 15
1562 A587 1k blk & lt bl 45 20
1563 A587 1.60k blk & bis *2.50 1.00*
Nos. 1559-1563 (5) 3.72 1.50

Issued to publicize the 23rd International Geological Congress, Prague, Aug. 8-Sept. 3.

Certain countries cancel stamps in full sheets and sell them (usually with gum) for less than face value. Dealers generally sell "CTO".

Raising Slovak Flag A588

Design: 60h, Slovak partisans, and mountain.

1968, Sept. 9 **Engr.** *Perf. 11½*
1564 A588 30h ultra 10 5
1565 A588 60h red 20 5

No. 1564 honors the Slovak National Council, No. 1565 commemorates the 120th anniversary of the Slovak national uprising.

Flowerpot, by Jiri Schlessinger (age 10) — A589

Drawings by Children in Terezin Concentration Camp: 30h, Jew and Guard, by Jiri Beutler (age 10). 60h, Butterflies, by Kitty Brunnerova (age 11).

Engraved and Photogravure
1968, Sept. 30 *Perf. 11½*
Size: 30x23mm.
1566 A589 30h blk, buff & rose lil 15 5
1567 A589 60h blk & multi 25 10
Perf. 12x11½
Size: 41x23mm.
1568 A589 1k blk & multi 50 25

30th anniversary of Munich Pact.

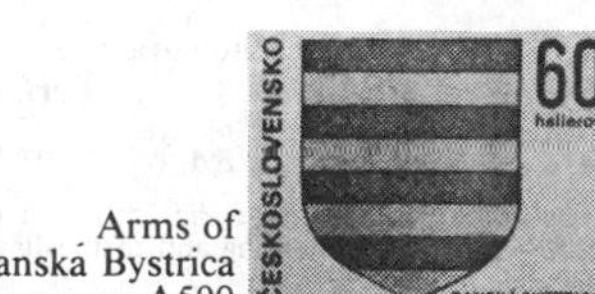

Arms of Banska Bystrica A590

Arms of Prague — A591

Arms of Regional Capitals: No. 1570, Bratislava. No. 1571, Brno. No. 1572, Ceské Budejovice. No. 1573, Hradec Králové. No. 1574, Kosice. No. 1575, Ostrava (horse). No. 1576, Plzen. No. 1577, Usti nad Labem.

1968, Oct. 21 *Perf. 11½*
1569 A590 60h blk, red & sil 25 10
1570 A590 60h blk, red, sil & ultra 25 10
1571 A590 60h blk, red & sil 25 10
1572 A590 60h blk, red, sil & gold 25 10
1573 A590 60h blk, red, sil & gold 25 10
1574 A590 60h blk, bl, red & gold 25 10
1575 A590 60h blk, bl, yel & red 25 10
1576 A590 60h blk, emer, red & gold 25 10
1577 A590 60h blk, red, sil & gold 25 10
Perf. 11½x12
1578 A591 1k multi 75 45
Nos. 1569-1578 (10) 3.00 1.35

No. 1578 issued in sheets of 10. See also Nos. 1652-1657, 1742-1747, 1886-1888, 2000-2001.

Flag and Linden Leaves A592

Bohemian Lion Breaking Chains (Type SP1 of 1919) — A593

Design: 60h, Map of Czechoslovakia, linden leaves, Hradcany in Prague and Castle in Bratislava.

1968, Oct. 28 *Perf. 12x11½*
1579 A592 30h dp bl & mag 20 5
1580 A592 60h blk, gold, red & ultra 25 8

Souvenir Sheet
Engr.
Perf. 11½x12
1581 A593 5k red 3.00 3.00

Issued to commemorate the 50th anniversary of the founding of Czechoslovakia. No. 1581 has violet blue marginal inscription and red ornament. Size: 75x100mm.

Ernest Hemingway A594

Cinderlad A595

Caricatures: 30h, Karel Capek (1890-1938), writer. 40h, George Bernard Shaw, writer. 60h, Maxim Gorki, writer. 1k, Pablo Picasso, painter. 1.20k, Taikan Yokoyama (1868-1958), painter. 1.40k, Charlie Chaplin, actor.

Engraved and Photogravure
1968, Nov. 18 *Perf. 11½x12*
1582 A594 20h blk, org & red 6 5
1583 A594 30h blk & multi 15 5
1584 A594 40h blk, lil & car 15 5
1585 A594 60h blk, sky bl & grn 18 8
1586 A594 1k blk, brn & yel 45 12
1587 A594 1.20k blk, dp car & vio 50 18
1588 A594 1.40k blk, brn & dp org *2.50 85*
Nos. 1582-1588 (7) 3.99 1.38

Issued to honor cultural personalities of the 20th century and UNESCO (United Nations Educational, Scientific and Cultural Organization). See Nos. 1628-1633.

Painting Type of 1967

Czechoslovakian Art: 60h, Cleopatra II, by Jan Zrzavy (1890-). 80h, Black Lake (man and horse), by Jan Preisler (1872-1918). 1.20k, Giovanni Francisci as a Volunteer, by Peter Michal Bohun (1822-1879). 1.60k, Princess Hyacinth, by Alfons Mucha (1860-1939). 3k, Madonna and Child, woodcarving, 1518, by Master Paul of Levoca.

1968, Nov. 29 **Engr.** *Perf. 11½*
1589 A565 60h multi 40 35
1590 A565 80h multi 60 55
1591 A565 1.20k multi 1.00 90
1592 A565 1.60k multi 1.40 1.25
1593 A565 3k multi *5.75 5.25*
Nos. 1589-1593 (5) 9.15 8.30

Sheets of 4.

1968, Dec. 18 **Engr. and Photo.**

Slovak Fairy Tales: 60h, The Proud Lady. 80h, The Ruling Knight. 1k, Good Day, Little Bench. 1.20k, The Spellbound Castle. 1.80k, The Miraculous Hunter. The designs are from illustrations by Ludovit Fulla for "Slovak Stories."

1594 A595 30h multi 10 5
1595 A595 60h multi 25 8
1596 A595 80h multi 30 10
1597 A595 1k multi 35 12
1598 A595 1.20k multi 60 15
1599 A595 1.80k multi *2.50 1.00*
Nos. 1594-1599 (6) 4.10 1.50

Czechoslovakia Nos. 2 and 3 — A596

1968, Dec. 18
1600 A596 1k vio bl & gold 1.25 1.00

Issued to commemorate the 50th anniversary of Czechoslovakian postage stamps.

Crescent, Cross and Lion and Sun Emblems A597

ILO Emblem A598

Design: 60h, 12 crosses in circles forming large cross.

Engraved and Photogravure
1969, Jan. 31 *Perf. 11½*
1601 A597 60h blk, red & gold 25 5
1602 A597 1k blk, ultra & red 45 15

No. 1601 commemorates the 50th anniversary of the Czechoslovak Red Cross; No. 1602 commemorates the 50th anniversary of the League of Red Cross Societies.

1969, Jan. 31
1603 A598 1k blk & gray 35 15

Issued to commemorate the 50th anniversary of the International Labor Organization.

Cheb Pistol A599

Historical Firearms: 40h, Italian pistol with Dutch decorations, c. 1600. 60h, Wheellock rifle from Matej Kubik workshop c. 1720. 1k, Flintlock pistol, Devieuxe workshop, Liege, c. 1760. 1.40k, Duelling pistols, from Lebeda workshop, Prague, c. 1835. 1.60k, Derringer pistols, U.S.A., c. 1865.

1969, Feb. 18
1604 A599 30h blk & multi 10 5
1605 A599 40h blk & multi 15 5
1606 A599 60h blk & multi 20 6

1607	A599	1k blk & multi	45	10
1608	A599	1.40k blk & multi	70	25
1609	A599	1.60k blk & multi	*2.00*	*85*
		Nos. 1604-1609 (6)	3.60	1.36

Bratislava Castle, Muse and Book – A600

Designs: No. 1611, Science symbols and emblem (Brno University). No. 1612, Harp, laurel and musicians' names. No. 1613, Theatrical scene. No. 1614, Arms of Slovakia, banner and blossoms. No. 1615, School, outstretched hands and woman with linden leaves.

1969, Mar. 24 Engr. *Perf. 11 1/2*

1610	A600	60h vio bl	25	8

Engraved and Photogravure

1611	A600	60h blk, gold & sl	25	8
1612	A600	60h gold, bl, blk & red	25	8
1613	A600	60h blk & rose red	25	8
1614	A600	60h rose red, sil & bl	25	8
1615	A600	60h blk & gold	25	8
		Nos. 1610-1615 (6)	1.50	48

Nos. 1610-1614 issued to commemorate the 50th anniversary of: Komensky University in Bratislava (#1610); Brno University (#1611); Brno Conservatory of Music (#1612); Slovak National Theater (#1613); Slovak Soviet Republic (#1614); No. 1615 commemorates the centenary of the Zniev Gymnasium (academic high school).

Baldachin-top Car and Four-seat Coupe of 1900-1905 – A601

Designs: 1.60k, Laurin & Klement Voiturette, 1907, and L & K touring car with American top, 1907. 1.80k, First Prague bus, 1907, and sectionalized Skoda bus, 1967.

Engraved and Photogravure

1969, Mar. 25

1616	A601	30h blk, lil & lt grn	15	5
1617	A601	1.60k blk, org brn & lt bl	65	20
1618	A601	1.80k multi	*2.00*	*1.25*

Peace, by Ladislav Guderna – A602

1969, Apr. 21 *Perf. 11*

1619	A602	1.60k multi	90	55

Issued to commemorate the 20th anniversary of the Peace Movement. Issued in sheets of 15 stamps and 5 tabs.

Horse and Rider, by Vaclav Hollar – A603

Old Engravings of Horses: 30h, Prancing Stallion, by Hendrik Goltzius (horiz.). 80h, Groom Leading Horse, by Matthäus Merian (horiz.). 1.80k, Horse and Soldier, by Albrecht Dürer. 2.40k, Groom and Horse, by Johann E. Ridinger.

Perf. 11x11 1/2, 11 1/2x11

1969, Apr. 24

Yellowish Paper

1620	A603	30h dk brn	12	5
1621	A603	80h vio brn	35	10
1622	A603	1.60k slate	70	20
1623	A603	1.80k sepia	90	30
1624	A603	2.40k multi	*2.75*	*95*
		Nos. 1620-1624 (5)	4.82	1.60

M. R. Stefánik as Astronomy Professor and French General – A604

1969, May 4 Engr. *Perf. 11 1/2*

1625	A604	60h rose cl	35	10

Issued to commemorate the 50th anniversary of the death of Gen. Milan R. Stefánik.

St. Wenceslas Pressing Wine, Mural by the Master of Litomerice – A605

Design: No. 1627, Coronation banner of the Estates, 1723, with St. Wenceslas and coats of arms of Bohemia and Czech Crown lands.

1969, May 9 Engr. *Perf. 11 1/2*

1626	A605	3k multi	2.50	2.00
1627	A605	3k multi	2.50	2.00

Issued to publicize the art treasures of the Castle of Prague. See Nos. 1689-1690.

Caricature Type of 1968

Caricatures: 30h, Pavol Orszagh Hviezdoslav (1849-1921), Slovak writer. 40h, Gilbert K. Chesterton (1874-1936), English writer. 60h, Vladimir Mayakovski (1893-1930), Russian poet. 1k, Henri Matisse (1869-1954), French painter. 1.80k, Ales Hrdlicka (1869-1943), Czech-born American anthropologist. 2k, Franz Kafka (1883-1924), Austrian writer.

Engraved and Photogravure

1969, June 17 *Perf. 11 1/2x12*

1628	A594	30h blk, red & bl	10	5
1629	A594	40h blk, bl & lt vio	15	8
1630	A594	60h blk, rose & yel	20	10
1631	A594	1k blk & multi	45	15
1632	A594	1.80k blk, ultra & ocher	75	25
1633	A594	2k blk, yel & brt grn	*2.00*	*60*
		Nos. 1628-1633 (6)	3.65	1.23

Issued to honor cultural personalities of the 20th century and UNESCO.

"Music," by Alfons Mucha – A606

Paintings by Mucha: 60h, "Painting." 1k, "Dance." 2.40k, "Ruby" and "Amethyst."

1969, July 14 *Perf. 11 1/2x11*

Size: 30x49mm.

1634	A606	30h blk & multi	8	5
1635	A606	60h blk & multi	18	10
1636	A606	1k blk & multi	30	15

Size: 39x51mm.

1637	A606	2.40k blk & multi	*2.25*	*1.75*

Issued to commemorate the 30th anniversary of the death of Alfons Mucha (1860-1930), painter and stamp designer (Type A1).

Pres. Svoboda and Partisans A607

Design: No. 1639, Slovak fighters and mourners.

Engraved and Photogravure

1969, Aug. 29 *Perf. 11*

1638	A607	30h ol grn & red, *yel*	12	5
1639	A607	30h vio bl & red, *yel*	12	5

Issued to commemorate the 25th anniversary of the Slovak uprising and of the Battle of Dukla.

Tatra Mountain Stream and Gentians – A608

Designs: 60h, Various views in Tatra Mountains. No. 1644, Mountain pass and gentians. No. 1645, Houses, Krivan Mountain and autumn crocuses.

1969, Sept. 8 Engr. *Perf. 11*

Size: 71x33mm.

1640	A608	60h gray	35	10
1641	A608	60h dk bl	35	10
1642	A608	60h dl gray vio	35	10

Perf. 11 1/2

Size: 40x23mm.

1643	A608	1.60k multi	75	25
1644	A608	1.60k multi	*1.50*	*60*
1645	A608	1.60k multi	75	25
		Nos. 1640-1645 (6)	4.05	1.40

Issued to commemorate the 20th anniversary of the creation of the Tatra Mountains National Park. Nos. 1640-1642 are printed in sheets of 15 (3x5) with 5 labels showing mountain plants. Nos. 1643-1645 issued in sheets of 10.

Bronze Belt Ornaments A609

Archaeological Treasures from Bohemia and Moravia: 30h, Gilt ornament with 6 masks. 1k, Jeweled earrings. 1.80k, Front and back of lead cross with Greek inscription. 2k, Gilt strap ornament with human figure.

Engraved and Photogravure

1969, Sept. 30 *Perf. 11 1/2x11*

1646	A609	20h gold & multi	10	5
1647	A609	30h gold & multi	10	5
1648	A609	1k red & multi	40	16
1649	A609	1.80k dl org & multi	80	30
1650	A609	2k gold & multi	*1.50*	*50*
		Nos. 1646-1650 (5)	2.90	1.06

"Mail Circling the World" A610

1969, Oct. 1 Engr. *Perf. 12*

1651	A610	3.20k multi	1.50	75

Issued to commemorate the 16th Universal Postal Union Congress, Tokyo, Oct. 1-Nov. 14. Issued in sheets of 4.

Coat of Arms Type of 1968

Engraved and Photogravure

1969, Oct. 25 *Perf. 11 1/2*

1652	A590	50h *Bardejov*	25	8
1653	A590	50h *Hranice*	25	8
1654	A590	50h *Kezmarok*	25	8
1655	A590	50h *Krnov*	25	8
1656	A590	50h *Litomerice*	25	8
1657	A590	50h *Manetin*	25	8
		Nos. 1652-1657 (6)	1.50	48

Painting Type of 1968

Designs: 60h, Requiem, 1944, by Frantisek Muzika. 1k, Resurrection, 1380, by the Master of the Trebon Altar. 1.60k, Crucifixion, 1950, by Vincent Hloznik. 1.80k, Girl with Doll, 1863, by Julius Bencur. 2.20k, St. Jerome, 1357-67, by Master Theodorik.

Engraved and Photogravure

1969, Nov. 25 *Perf. 11 1/2*

1658	A565	60h multi	30	25
1659	A565	1k multi	50	45
1660	A565	1.60k multi	75	65
1661	A565	1.80k multi	1.10	1.00
1662	A565	2.20k multi	*3.50*	*3.25*
		Nos. 1658-1662 (5)	6.15	5.60

Sheets of 4.

Symbolic Sheet of Stamps – A611

1969, Dec. 18 *Perf. 11 1/2x12*

1663	A611	1k dk brn, ultra & gold	65	50

Issued for Stamp Day 1969.

Ski Jump — A612

Designs: 60h, Long distance skier. 1k, Ski jump and slope. 1.60k, Woman skier.

Engraved and Photogravure

1970, Jan. 6 ***Perf. 11½***

No.	Type	Denomination	Unused	Used
1664	A612	50h multi	15	5
1665	A612	60h multi	18	5
1666	A612	1k multi	40	15
1667	A612	1.60k multi	*1.25*	*45*

Issued to publicize the International Ski Championships "Tatra 1970."

Ludwig van Beethoven (1770-1827) — A613

Portraits: No. 1669, Friedrich Engels (1820-1895), German socialist. No. 1670, Maximilian Hell (1720-1792), Slovakian Jesuit and astronomer. No. 1671, Lenin (1870-1924), Russian Communist leader. No. 1672, Josef Manes (1820-1871), Czech painter. No. 1673, John Amos Comenius (1592-1670), theologian and educator.

1970, Feb. 17 **Engr.** ***Perf. 11x11½***

No.	Type	Denomination	Unused	Used
1668	A613	40h black	15	8
1669	A613	40h dl red	15	8
1670	A613	40h yel brn	15	8
1671	A613	40h dl red	15	8
1672	A613	40h brown	15	8
1673	A613	40h black	15	8
		Nos. 1668-1673 (6)	90	48

Issued to commemorate the anniversaries of the birth of Beethoven, Engels, Hell, Lenin and Manes, the 300th anniversary of the death of Comenius, and to honor UNESCO.

Bells A614

Designs: 80h, Machine tools and lathe. 1k, Folklore masks. 1.60k, Angel and Three Wise Men, 17th century icon from Koniec. 2k, View of Orlik Castle, 1787, by F. K. Wolf. 3k, "Passing through Koshu down to Mishima" from Hokusai's 36 Views of Fuji.

Engraved and Photogravure

1970, Mar. 13 ***Perf. 11½x11***

Size: 40x23mm.

No.	Type	Denomination	Unused	Used
1674	A614	50h multi	20	5
1675	A614	80h multi	30	8
1676	A614	1k multi	40	8

Size: 50x40mm.

Perf. 11½

No.	Type	Denomination	Unused	Used
1677	A614	1.60k multi	75	40
1678	A614	2k multi	1.00	50
1679	A614	3k multi	*2.50*	*2.00*
		Nos. 1674-1679 (6)	5.15	3.11

Issued to publicize EXPO '70 International Exhibition, Osaka, Japan, March 15-Sept. 13, 1970. Nos. 1674-1676 issued in sheets of 50, Nos. 1677-1679 in sheets of 4.

Kosice Townhall, Laurel and Czechoslovak Arms — A615

1970, Apr. 5 ***Perf. 11***

No.	Type	Denomination	Unused	Used
1680	A615	60h sl, ver & gold	50	8

Issued to commemorate the 25th anniversary of the government's Kosice Program.

"The Remarkable Horse" by Josef Lada — A616

Lenin — A617

Paintings by Josef Lada: 60h, Autumn, 1955 (horiz.). 1.80k, "The Water Sprite." 2.40k, Children in Winter, 1943 (horiz.).

1970, Apr. 21 ***Perf. 11½***

No.	Type	Denomination	Unused	Used
1681	A616	60h blk & multi	25	10
1682	A616	1k blk & multi	40	15
1683	A616	1.80k blk & multi	75	25
1684	A616	2.40k blk & multi	*1.75*	*1.00*

Engraved and Photogravure

1970, Apr. 22

Design: 60h, Lenin without cap, facing left.

No.	Type	Denomination	Unused	Used
1685	A617	30h dk red & gold	12	5
1686	A617	60h blk & gold	30	6

Issued to commemorate the centenary of the birth of Lenin (1870-1924), Russian communist leader.

Fighters on the Barricades — A618

Design: No. 1688, Lilac, Russian tank and castle.

Engraved and Photogravure

1970, May 5 ***Perf. 11x11½***

No.	Type	Denomination	Unused	Used
1687	A618	30h dl pur, gold & bl	20	6
1688	A618	30h dl grn, gold & red	20	6

No. 1687 commemorates the 25th anniversary of the Prague uprising and No. 1688 the 25th anniversary of the liberation of Czechoslovakia from the Germans.

Prague Castle Art Type of 1969

Designs: No. 1689, Bust of St. Vitus, 1486. No. 1690, Hermes and Athena, by Bartholomy Springer (1546-1611), mural from White Tower.

1970, May 7 **Engr.** ***Perf. 11½***

No.	Type	Denomination	Unused	Used
1689	A605	3k mar & multi	2.50	2.00
1690	A605	3k lt bl & multi	2.50	2.00

Issued to publicize art treasures of the Castle of Prague.

Compass Rose, U.N. Headquarters and Famous Buildings of the World — A619

Engraved and Photogravure

1970, June 26 ***Perf. 11***

No.	Type	Denomination	Unused	Used
1691	A619	1k blk & multi	40	30

Issued to commemorate the 25th anniversary of the United Nations. Issued in sheets of 15 (3x5) and 5 labels showing U.N. emblem.

Cannon from 30 Years' War and Baron Munchhausen — A620

Historical Cannons: 60h, Cannon from Hussite war and St. Barbara. 1.20k, Cannon from Prussian-Austrian war, and legendary cannoneer Javurek. 1.80k, Early 20th century cannon and spaceship "La Colombiad" (Jules Verne). 2.40k, World War I cannon and "Good Soldier Schweik."

1970, Aug. 31 ***Perf. 11½***

No.	Type	Denomination	Unused	Used
1692	A620	30h blk & multi	10	5
1693	A620	60h blk & multi	20	5
1694	A620	1.20k blk & multi	45	10
1695	A620	1.80k blk & multi	80	25
1696	A620	2.40k blk & multi	*2.25*	*1.00*
		Nos. 1692-1696 (5)	3.80	1.45

"Rude Pravo" (Red Truth) A621

1970, Sept. 21 ***Perf. 11½x11***

No.	Type	Denomination	Unused	Used
1697	A621	60h car gold & blk	25	5

Issued to commemorate the 50th anniversary of the Rude Pravo newspaper.

"Great Sun" House Sign and Old Town Tower Bridge, Prague — A622

Designs: 60h, "Blue Lion" and Town Hall Tower, Brno. 1k, Gothic corner stone and Town Hall Tower, Bratislava. 1.40k, Coat of Arms and Gothic Tower, Bratislava, and medallion. 1.60k, Moravian Eagle and Gothic Town Hall Tower, Brno. 1.80k, "Black Sun" and "Green Frog" house signs and New Town Hall, Prague.

Engraved and Photogravure

1970, Sept. 23 ***Perf. 11x11½***

No.	Type	Denomination	Unused	Used
1698	A622	40h blk & multi	12	6
1699	A622	60h blk & multi	18	10
1700	A622	1k blk & multi	35	16
1701	A622	1.40k blk & multi	*2.25*	*75*
1702	A622	1.60k blk & multi	60	24
1703	A622	1.80k blk & multi	75	28
		Nos. 1698-1703 (6)	4.25	1.59

Germany-Uruguay Semifinal Soccer Match — A623

Designs: 20h, Sundisk Games' emblem and flags of participating nations. 60h, England-Czechoslovakia match and coats of arms. 1k, Romania-Czechoslovakia match and coats of arms. 1.20k, Brazil-Italy, final match and emblems. 1.80k, Brazil-Czechoslovakia match and emblems.

1970, Oct. 29 ***Perf. 11½***

No.	Type	Denomination	Unused	Used
1704	A623	20h blk & multi	6	5
1705	A623	40h blk & multi	12	5
1706	A623	60h blk & multi	18	5
1707	A623	1k blk & multi	35	6
1708	A623	1.20k blk & multi	40	15
1709	A623	1.80k blk & multi	*2.00*	*60*
		Nos. 1704-1709 (6)	3.11	96

Issued to commemorate the 9th World Soccer Championships for the Jules Rimet Cup, Mexico City, May 30-June 21.

Congress Emblem — A624

Engraved and Photogravure

1970, Nov. 9

No.	Type	Denomination	Unused	Used
1710	A624	30h blk, gold, ultra & red	30	5

Congress of the Czechoslovak Socialist Youth Federation.

Painting Type of 1967

Paintings: 1k, Seated Mother, by Mikulas Galanda. 1.20k, Bridesmaid, by Karel Svolinsky. 1.40k, Walk by Night, 1944, by Frantisek Hudecek. 1.80k, Banska Bystrica Market, by Dominik Skutecky. 2.40k, Adoration of the Kings, from the Vysehrad Codex, 1085.

1970, Nov. 27 **Engr.** ***Perf. 11½***

No.	Type	Denomination	Unused	Used
1711	A565	1k multi	45	40
1712	A565	1.20k multi	60	55
1713	A565	1.40k multi	80	70
1714	A565	1.80k multi	1.10	90
1715	A565	2.40k multi	*2.75*	*2.50*
		Nos. 1711-1715 (5)	5.70	5.05

Sheets of 4.

Radar A625

Designs: 40h, Interkosmos 3, geophysical satellite. 60h, Molniya meteorological satellite. 1k, Astronaut and Vostok satellite. No. 1720, Interkosmos 4, solar research satellite. No. 1720A, Space satellite (Sputnik) over city. 1.60k, Two-stage rocket on launching pad.

Engraved and Photogravure

1970-71 ***Perf. 11***

No.	Type	Denomination	Unused	Used
1716	A625	20h blk & multi	15	5
1717	A625	40h blk & multi	15	5
1718	A625	60h blk & multi	20	5
1719	A625	1k blk & multi	45	15
1720	A625	1.20k blk & multi	50	15
1720A	A625	1.20k blk & multi ('71)	60	15
1721	A625	1.60k blk & multi	*1.25*	*50*
		Nos. 1716-1721 (7)	3.30	1.10

Issued to publicize "Interkosmos," the collaboration of communist countries in various phases of space research. Issue dates: No. 1720A, Nov. 15, 1971; others, Nov. 30, 1970.

Face of Christ on Veronica's Veil — A626

Slovak Ikons, 16th-18th Centuries: 60h, Adam and Eve in the Garden (vert.). 2k, St. George and the Dragon. 2.80k, St. Michael (vert.).

1970, Dec. 17 Engr. *Perf. 11½*
Cream Paper

1722	A626	60h multi	28	30
1723	A626	1k multi	45	50
1724	A626	2k multi	85	95
1725	A626	2.80k multi	*2.25*	*2.25*

Sheets of 4.

Carrier Pigeon Type of 1920 — A627

Engraved and Photogravure
1970, Dec. 18 *Perf. 11x11½*

1726	A627	1k red, blk & yel grn	50	50

Stamp Day.

Song of the Barricades, 1938, by Karel Stika — A628

Designs (Czech and Slovak Graphic Art): 50h, Fruit Grower's Barge, 1941, by Cyril Bouda. 60h, Moon (woman) Searching for Lilies of the Valley, 1913, by Jan Zrzavy. 1k, At the Edge of Town (working man and woman), 1931, by Koloman Sokol. 1.60k, Summer, 1641, by Vaclav Hollar. 2k, Gamekeeper and Shepherd of Orava Castle, 1847, by Peter M. Bohun.

Engraved (40h, 60h, 1k); Engraved and Photogravure (others)
1971, Jan. 28 *Perf. 11½*

1727	A628	40h brown	15	6
1728	A628	50h blk & multi	18	8
1729	A628	60h slate	18	10
1730	A628	1k black	40	16
1731	A628	1.60k blk & buff	65	24
1732	A628	2k blk & multi	*1.75*	*50*
		Nos. 1727-1732 (6)	3.31	1.14

Saris Church A629 Bell Tower, Hronsek A630

Designs: 1k, Roofs and folk art, Horacko. 2.40k, House, Jicinsko. 3k, House and folk art, Cechy-Melnicko. 3.60k, Chrudimsko Church. 5k, Watch Tower, Cesky-Nachod. 5.40k, Baroque house, Posumavi. 6k, Cottage, Orava. 9k, Cottage, Turnovsko. 10k, Old houses, Liptov. 14k, House and wayside bell stand. 20k, Houses, Slovensko-Cicmany.

Engraved and Photogravure
1971-72 *Perf. 11½x11, 11x11½*

1733	A630	1k blk & multi	40	5
1734	A629	1.60k blk, dk grn & vio	65	6
1735	A630	2k blk & multi	80	5
1736	A629	2.40k blk & multi	95	6
1736A	A630	3k blk & multi ('72)	1.20	8
1737	A629	3.60k blk & multi	1.50	6
1737A	A630	5k blk & multi ('72)	1.75	12
1738	A629	5.40k blk & multi	1.75	6
1739	A630	6k blk & multi	2.10	9
1740	A630	9k blk & multi	3.00	30
1740A	A629	10k blk & multi ('72)	3.75	30
1741	A629	14k blk & multi	5.00	25
1741A	A629	20k blk & multi ('72)	7.50	90
		Nos. 1733-1741A (13)	30.35	2.38

Nos. 1736A, 1738, 1740 are horizontal.

Coat of Arms Type of 1968

1971, Feb. 26 *Perf. 11½*

1742	A590	60h *Zilina*	25	8
1743	A590	60h *Levoca*	25	8
1744	A590	60h *Ceska Trebova*	25	8
1745	A590	60h *Uhersky Brod*	25	8
1746	A590	60h *Trutnov*	25	8
1747	A590	60h *Karlovy Vary*	25	8
		Nos. 1742-1747 (6)	1.50	48

"Fight of the Communards and Rise of the International" — A631

Design: No. 1749, World fight against racial discrimination, and "UNESCO."

1971, March 18 *Perf. 11*

1748	A631	1k multi	50	25
1749	A631	1k multi	50	25

No. 1748 commemorates the centenary of the Paris Commune. No. 1749 publicizes the Year against Racial Discrimination. Issued in sheets of 15 stamps and 5 labels.

Edelweiss, Mountaineering Map and Equipment — A632

Engraved and Photogravure
1971, Apr. 27 *Perf. 11½x11*

1750	A632	30h multi	25	5

50th anniversary of Slovak Alpine Club.

Singer — A633

1971, Apr. 27 *Perf. 11½*

1751	A633	30h multi	20	5

50th anniversary of Slovak Teachers' Choir.

Abbess' Crosier, 16th Century A634

Design: No. 1753, Allegory of Music, 16th century mural.

1971, May 9

1752	A634	3k gold & multi	1.75	1.60
1753	A634	3k blk, dk brn & buff	1.75	1.60

See Nos. 1817-1818, 1884-1885, 1937-1938, 2040-2041, 2081-2082, 2114-2115, 2176-2177, 2238-2239, 2329-2330, 2420-2421.

Lenin A635

Designs: 40h, Hammer and sickle allegory. 60h, Raised fists. 1k, Star, hammer and sickle.

1971, May 14 *Perf. 11*

1754	A635	30h blk, red & gold	12	5
1755	A635	40h blk, ultra, red & gold	18	5
1756	A635	60h blk, ultra, red & gold	25	5
1757	A635	1k blk, ultra, red & gold	50	10

50th anniversary of the Czechoslovak Communist Party.

Star, Hammer-Sickle Emblems — A636

Design: 60h, Hammer-sickle emblem, fist and people vert.).

Engraved and Photogravure
Perf. 11½x11, 11x11½
1971, May 24

1758	A636	30h blk, red, gold & yel	15	5
1759	A636	60h blk, red, gold & bl	30	8

14th Congress of Communist Party of Czechoslovakia.

Ring-necked Pheasant — A637

Designs: 60h, Rainbow trout. 80h, Mouflon. 1k, Chamois. 2k, Stag. 2.60k, Wild boar.

1971, Aug. 17 *Perf. 11½x11*

1760	A637	20h org & multi	6	5
1761	A637	60h lt bl & multi	18	6
1762	A637	80h yel & multi	24	6
1763	A637	1k lt grn & multi	30	10
1764	A637	2k lil & multi	75	30
1765	A637	2.60k bis & multi	*3.00*	*1.00*
		Nos. 1760-1765 (6)	4.53	1.57

World Hunting Exhibition, Budapest, Aug. 27-30.

Diesel Locomotive A638

Gymnasts and Banners A639

1971, Sept. 2 *Perf. 11x11½*

1766	A638	30h lt bl, blk & red	12	5

Centenary of CKD, Prague Machine Foundry.

1971, Sept. 2 *Perf. 11½x11*

1767	A639	30h red brn, gold & ultra	12	5

50th anniversary of Workers' Physical Exercise Federation.

Road Intersections and Bridge — A640

Engraved and Photogravure
1971, Sept. 2

1768	A640	1k blk, gold, red & bl	40	20

14th World Highways and Bridges Congress. Sheets of 25 stamps and 25 labels printed se-tenant with continuous design.

Chinese Fairytale, by Eva Bednarova A641

Designs: 1k, Tiger and other animals, by Mirko Hanak. 1.60k, The Miraculous Bamboo Shoot, by Yasuo Segawa (horiz.).

Perf. 11½x11, 11x11½
1971, Sept. 10

1769	A641	60h multi	30	10
1770	A641	1k multi	60	20
1771	A641	1.60k multi	1.40	60

Bratislava BIB 71 biennial exhibition of illustrations for children's books.

Apothecary Jars and Coltsfoot — A642

Designs: 60h, Jars and dog rose. 1k, Scales and adonis vernalis. 1.20k, Mortars and valerian. 1.80k, Retorts and chicory. 2.40k, Mill, mortar and henbane.

1971, Sept. 20 *Perf. 11½x11*
Yellow Paper

1772	A642	30h multi	9	5
1773	A642	60h multi	18	8
1774	A642	1k multi	35	12
1775	A642	1.20k multi	50	16
1776	A642	1.80k multi	85	30
1777	A642	2.40k multi	*1.75*	*50*
		Nos. 1772-1777 (6)	3.72	1.21

International Pharmaceutical Congress.

Painting Type of 1967

Paintings: 1k, "Waiting" (woman's head), 1967, by Imro Weiner-Kral. 1.20k, Resurrection, by Master of Vyssi Brod, 14th century. 1.40k, Woman with Pitcher, by Milos Bazovsky. 1.80k, Veruna Cudova (in folk costume), by Josef Manes. 2.40k, Detail from "Feast of the Rose Garlands," by Albrecht Dürer.

1971, Nov. 27 ***Perf. 11½***

1779 A565 1k multi 45 40
1780 A565 1.20k multi 65 50
1781 A565 1.40k multi 95 65
1782 A565 1.80k multi 1.25 95
1783 A565 2.40k multi *2.50 2.25*
Nos. 1779-1783 (5) 5.80 4.75

Sheets of 4.

Workers Revolt in Krompachy, by Julius Nemcik — A643

1971, Nov. 28 ***Perf. 11x11½***

1784 A643 60h multi 35 10

History of the Czechoslovak Communist Party.

Wooden Dolls and Birds — A644

Folk Art and UNICEF Emblem: 80h, Jug handles, carved. 1k, Horseback rider. 1.60k, Shepherd carrying lamb. 2k, Easter eggs and rattle. 3k, "Zbojnik," folk hero.

1971, Dec. 11 ***Perf. 11½***

1785 A644 60h multi 25 5
1786 A644 80h multi 35 8
1787 A644 1k multi 50 12
1788 A644 1.60k multi 75 20
1789 A644 2k multi 1.50 55
1790 A644 3k multi 2.75 80
Nos. 1785-1790 (6) 6.10 1.80

25th anniversary of the United Nations International Children's Fund (UNICEF).

Runners, Parthenon, Czechoslovak Olympic Emblem A645

Designs: 40h, Women's high jump, Olympic emblem and plan for Prague Stadium. 1.60k, Cross-country skiers, Sapporo '72 emblem and ski jump in High Tatras. 2.60k, Discus thrower, Discobolus and St. Vitus Cathedral.

Engraved and Photogravure

1971, Dec. 16

1791 A645 30h multi 12 6
1792 A645 40h multi 15 9
1793 A645 1.60k multi 60 45
1794 A645 2.60k multi 1.50 60

75th anniversary of Czechoslovak Olympic Committee (30h, 2.60k); 20th Summer Olympic Games, Munich, Aug. 26-Sept. 10, 1972 (40h); 11th Winter Olympic Games, Sapporo, Japan, Feb. 3-13, 1972 (1.60k).

Post Horns and Lion — A646

1971, Dec. 17 ***Perf. 11x11½***

1795 A646 1k blk, gold, car & bl 55 30

Stamp Day.

Figure Skating A647

"Lezaky" A648

Designs (Olympic Emblems and): 50h, Ski jump. 1k, Ice hockey. 1.60k, Sledding, women's.

1972, Jan. 13 ***Perf. 11½***

1796 A647 40h pur, org & red 15 8
1797 A647 50h dk bl, org & red 20 8
1798 A647 1k mag, org & red 40 18
1799 A647 1.60k bl grn, org & red *1.50 50*

11th Winter Olympic Games, Sapporo, Japan, Feb. 3-13.

Engraved and Photogravure

1972, Feb. 16

Designs: No. 1801, Boy's head behind barbed wire (horiz.). No. 1802, Hand rising from ruins. No. 1803, Soldier and banner (horiz.).

1800 A648 30h blk, dl org & red 18 5
1801 A648 30h blk & brn org 18 5
1802 A648 60h blk, yel & red 25 5
1803 A648 60h sl grn & multi 25 5

30th anniversary of: destruction of Lezaky (No. 1800) and Lidice (1802); Terezin concentration camp (No. 1801); Czechoslovak Army unit in Russia (No. 1803).

Book Year Emblem A649

Steam and Diesel Locomotives A650

1972, Mar. 17 ***Perf. 11½x11***

1804 A649 1k blk & org brn 40 10

International Book Year 1972.

1972, Mar. 17 ***Perf. 11½x11***

1805 A650 30h multi 30 5

Centenary of the Kosice-Bohumin railroad.

"Pasture," by Vojtech Sedlacek — A651

Designs: 50h, Dressage, by Frantisek Tichy. 60th, Otakara Kubina, by Vaclav Fiala. 1k, The Three Kings, by Ernest Zmetak. 1.60k, Woman Dressing, by Ludovit Fulla.

Engraved and Photogravure

1972, Mar. 27 ***Perf. 11½x11***

1806 A651 40h multi 14 5
1807 A651 50h multi 16 6
1808 A651 60h multi 30 8
1809 A651 1k multi 50 20
1810 A651 1.60k multi *1.40 1.25*
Nos. 1806-1810 (5) 2.50 1.64

Czech and Slovak graphic art. 1.60k issued in sheets of 4. See also Nos. 1859-1862, 1921-1924.

Ice Hockey A652

Design: 1k, Two players.

1972, Apr. 7 ***Perf. 11***

1811 A652 60h blk & multi 20 7
1812 A652 1k blk & multi 40 20

World and European Ice Hockey Championships, Prague.

Bicycling, Olympic Rings and Emblem A653

1972, Apr. 7

1813 A653 50h *shown* 20 6
1814 A653 1.60k *Diving* 60 15
1815 A653 1.80k *Canoeing* 75 20
1816 A653 2k *Gymnast* *1.50 75*

20th Olympic Games, Munich, Aug.26-Sept. 11.

Prague Castle Art Type of 1971

Designs: No. 1817, Adam and Eve, column capital, St. Vitus Cathedral. No. 1818, Czech coat of arms (lion), c. 1500.

1972, May 9 ***Perf. 11½***

1817 A634 3k blk & multi *3.50 2.75*
1818 A634 3k blk, red, sil & gold 2.00 1.75

Sheets of 4.

Andrej Sladkovic (1820-1872), Poet — A654

Portraits: No. 1820, Janko Kral (1822-1876), poet. No. 1821, Ludmilla Podjavorinska (1872-1951), writer. No. 1822, Antonin Hudecek (1872-1941), painter. No. 1823, Frantisek Bilek (1872-1941), sculptor. No. 1824, Jan Preisler (1872-1918), painter.

Engraved and Photogravure

1972, June 14 ***Perf. 11***

1819 A654 40h pur, ol & bl 20 8
1820 A654 40h dk grn, bl & yel 20 8
1821 A654 40h blk & multi 20 8
1822 A654 40h brn, grn & bl 20 8
1823 A654 40h choc, grn & org 20 8
1824 A654 40h grn, sl & dp org 20 8
Nos. 1819-1824 (6) 1.20 48

Men with Banners — A655

1972, June 14 ***Perf. 11x11½***

1825 A655 30h dk vio bl, red & yel 12 5

8th Trade Union Congress, Prague.

Art Forms of Wire A656

Ornamental Wirework: 60h, Plane and rosette. 80h, Four-headed dragon and ornament. 1k, Locomotive and loops. 2.60k, Tray and owl.

1972, Aug. 28 ***Perf. 11½x11***

1826 A656 20h sal & multi 8 5
1827 A656 60h multi 25 8
1828 A656 80h pink & multi 35 10
1829 A656 1k multi 50 18
1830 A656 2.60k rose & multi *1.75 60*
Nos. 1826-1830 (5) 2.93 1.01

"Jiskra" A657

Engr. & Photo.

1972, Sept. 27 ***Perf. 11½x11***

Size: 40x22mm.

Multicolored Design on Blue Paper

1831 A657 50h *shown* 18 5
1832 A657 60h *"Mir"* 20 5
1833 A657 80h *"Republika"* 26 6

Size: 48x29mm.

Perf. 11x11½

1834 A657 1k *"Kosice"* 32 10
1835 A657 1.60k *"Dukla"* 55 16
1836 A657 2k *"Kladno"* *2.00 85*
Nos. 1831-1836 (6) 3.51 1.27

Czechoslovak sea-going vessels.

Hussar, 18th Century Tile — A658

1972, Oct. 24 ***Perf. 11½x11***

1837 A658 30h *shown* 15 6
1838 A658 60h *Janissary* 28 8
1839 A658 80h *St. Martin* 35 12
1840 A658 1.60k *St. George* 85 18
1841 A658 1.80k *Nobleman's guard* 1.10 20
1842 A658 2.20k *Slovakian horseman* *2.25 1.00*
Nos. 1837-1842 (6) 4.98 1.64

Horsemen from 18th-19th century tiles or enamel paintings on glass.

Worker, Flag Hoisted on Bayonet A659

Star, Hammer and Sickle A660

1972, Nov. 7 *Perf. 11x11½*

1843 A659 30h gold & multi 12 6
1844 A660 60h rose car & gold 24 8

55th anniversary of the Russian October Revolution (30h); 50th anniversary of the Soviet Union (60h).

Nos. 1811-1812 Overprinted in Violet Blue or Black

CSSR
MAJSTROM
SVETA

1972 *Perf. 11*

1845 A652 60h multi (VBl) 6.50 6.50
1846 A652 1k multi (Bk) 6.50 6.50

Czechoslovakia's victorious ice hockey team. The overprint on the 60h is in Czech and reads CSSR/MISTREM/SVETA; the overprint on the 1k (shown) is in Slovak.

Painting Type of 1967

Designs: 1k, "Nosegay" (nudes and flowers), by Max Svabinsky. 1.20k, Struggle of St. Ladislas with Kuman nomad, anonymous, 14th century. 1.40k, Lady with Fur Hat, by Vaclav Hollar. 1.80k, Midsummer Night's Dream, 1962, by Josef Liesler. 2.40k, Pablo Picasso, self-portrait.

Engraved and Photogravure

1972, Nov. 27

1847 A565 1k multi 65 50
1848 A565 1.20k multi 70 65
1849 A565 1.40k blk & cr 1.40 1.25
1850 A565 1.80k multi 1.25 1.00
1851 A565 2.40k multi *3.50 3.25*
Nos. 1847-1851 (5) 7.50 6.65

Sheets of 4.

Goldfinch A661

Songbirds: 60h, Warbler feeding young cuckoo. 80h, Cuckoo. 1k, Black-billed magpie. 1.60k, Bullfinch. 3k, Song thrush.

1972, Dec. 15

Size: 30x48½mm.

1852 A661 60h yel & multi 24 10
1853 A661 80h multi 32 14
1854 A661 1k lt bl & multi 40 16

Engr.

Size: 30x23mm.

1855 A661 1.60k multi 75 12
1856 A661 2k multi 95 30
1857 A661 3k multi *2.75 1.00*
Nos. 1852-1857 (6) 5.41 1.82

Post Horn and Allegory — A662

Engraved and Photogravure

1972, Dec. 18

1858 A662 1k blk, red lil & gold 55 50

Stamp Day.

Art Type of 1972

1973, Jan. 25 *Perf. 11½x11*

Designs: 30h, Flowers in Window, by Jaroslav Grus. 60h, Quest for Happiness, by Josef Balaz. 1.60k, Balloon, by Kamil Lhotak. 1.80k, Woman with Viola, by Richard Wiesner.

1859 A651 30h multi 12 5
1860 A651 60h multi 24 10
1861 A651 1.60k multi 64 18
1862 A651 1.80k multi *1.50 70*

Czech and Slovak graphic art.

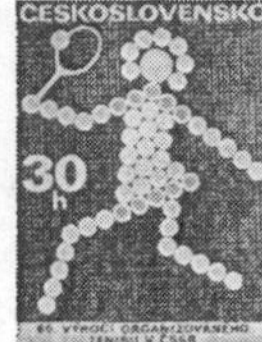
Tennis Player — A663

Figure Skater — A664

Torch and Star — A665

1973, Feb. 22 *Perf. 11*

1863 A663 30h vio & multi 12 5
1864 A664 60h blk & multi 24 10
1865 A665 1k multi 40 18

80th anniversary of the tennis organization in Czechoslovakia (30h); World figure skating championships, Bratislava (60h); 3rd summer army Spartakiad of socialist countries (1k).

Star and Factories — A666

Workers' Militia, Emblem and Flag — A667

Engraved and Photogravure

1973, Feb. 23

1866 A666 30h multi 12 5
1867 A667 60h multi 24 10

25th anniversary of the Communist revolution in Czechoslovakia and of the Militia.

Capt. Jan Nalepka, Major Antonin Sochor and Laurel A668

Designs (Torch and): 40h, Evzen Rosicky, Mirko Nespor and ivy leaves. 60h, Vlado Clementis, Karol Smidke and linden leaves. 80h, Jan Osoha, Josef Molak and oak leaves. 1k, Marie Kuderikova, Jozka Jaburkova and rose. 1.60k, Vaclav Sinkule, Eduard Urx and palm leaf.

1973, Mar. 20 *Perf. 11½x11*

Yellow Paper

1868 A668 30h blk, ver & gold 12 5
1869 A668 40h blk, ver & grn 16 7
1870 A668 60h blk, ver & gold 24 10
1871 A668 80h blk, ver & gold 32 14
1872 A668 1k blk, ver & grn 45 18
1873 A668 1.60k blk, ver & sil *1.00 28*
Nos. 1868-1873 (6) 2.29 82

Fighters against and victims of Fascism and Nazism during German Occupation.

Virgil I. Grissom, Edward H. White, Roger B. Chaffee — A669

Designs: 20h, Soviet planetary station "Vebera." 30h, "Intercosmos" station. 40h, Lunokhod on moon. 3.60k, Vladimir M. Komarov, Georgi T. Dobrovolsky, Vladislav N. Volkov, Victor I. Patsayev. 5k, Yuri A. Gagarin.

Engraved and Photogravure

1973, Apr. 12 *Perf. 11½x11*

Size: 40x22mm.

1874 A669 20h multi 10 5
1875 A669 30h multi 15 5
1876 A669 40h multi 18 8

Engr.

Perf. 11½

Size: 49x30mm.

1877 A669 3k multi 1.50 75
1878 A669 3.60k multi 2.50 1.50
1879 A669 5k multi *4.50 3.50*
Nos. 1874-1879 (6) 8.93 5.93

In memory of American and Russian astronauts.

Radio — A670

Telephone and Map of Czechoslovakia A671

Television A672

1973, May 1 *Perf. 11½x11*

1880 A670 30h blk & multi 12 5
1881 A671 30h lt bl, pink & blk 12 5
1882 A672 30h dp bl & multi 12 5

Czechoslovak anniversaries: 50 years of broadcasting (No. 1880); 20 years of telephone service to all communities (No. 1881); 20 years of television (No. 1882).

Coat of Arms and Linden Branch — A673

1973, May 9 *Perf. 11x11½*

1883 A673 60h red & multi 30 10

25th anniversary of the Constitution of May 9.

Prague Castle Art Type of 1971

Designs: No. 1884, Royal Legate, 14th century. No. 1885, Seal of King Charles IV, 1351.

1973, May 9 *Perf. 11½*

1884 A634 3k bl & multi 1.40 1.10
1885 A634 3k gold, grn & dk brn 1.75 1.65

Sheets of 4.

Coat of Arms Type of 1968

1973, June 20

1886 A590 60h *Mikulov* 24 15
1887 A590 60h *Zlutice* 24 15
1888 A590 60h *Smolenice* 24 15

Coats of arms of Czechoslovakian cities.

Heraldic Colors of Olomouc and Moravia A674

Anthurium A675

Engraved and Photogravure

1973, Aug. 23

1889 A674 30h multi 15 8

400th anniversary of University of Olomouc.

1973, Aug. 23 *Perf. 11½*

Sizes: 60h, 1k, 2k, 30x50mm.; 1.60k, 1.80k, 3.60k, 23x39mm.

1890 A675 60h *Tulips* 30 25
1891 A675 1k *Rose* 40 35
1892 A675 1.60k *shown* 70 35
1893 A675 1.80k *Iris* 90 75
1894 A675 2k *Chrysanthemum* *2.50 2.25*
1895 A675 3.60k *Cymbidium* 1.60 1.35
Nos. 1890-1895 (6) 6.40 5.30

Flower Show, Olomouc, Aug. 18-Sept. 2. 60h, 1k, 2k issued in sheets of 4, others in sheets of 10.

Irish Setter A676

Designs: Hunting dogs.

1973, Sept. 5

1896 A676 20h *shown* 7 5
1897 A676 30h *Czech terrier* 12 5
1898 A676 40h *Bavarian hunting dog* 20 8
1899 A676 60h *German pointer* 35 12
1900 A676 1k *Cocker spaniel* 50 20
1901 A676 1.60k *Dachshund* *1.50 35*
Nos. 1896-1901 (6) 2.74 85

50th anniversary of the Czechoslovak United Hunting Organization.

St. John, the Baptist, by Svabinsky A677

Works by Max Svabinsky: 60h, "August Noon" (woman). 80h, "Marriage of True Minds" (artist and muse). 1k, "Paradise Sonata I" (Adam dreaming of Eve). 2.60k, Last Judgment, stained glass window, St. Vitus Cathedral.

Lithographed and Engraved

1973, Sept. 17

1902 A677 20h blk & pale grn 12 5
1903 A677 60h blk & buff 24 12

Engr.

1904 A677 80h black 45 30
1905 A677 1k sl grn 60 50
1906 A677 2.60k multi *2.25 2.00*
Nos. 1902-1906 (5) 3.66 2.97

Centenary of the birth of Max Svabinsky (1873-1962), artist and stamp designer. 20h and 60h issued in sheets of 25; 80h and 1k se-tenant in sheets of 4 checkerwise; 2.60k in sheets of 4.

Trade Union Emblem A678

Engraved and Photogravure

1973, Oct. 15

1907 A678 1k red, bl & yel 45 18

8th Congress of the World Federation of Trade Unions, Varna, Bulgaria.

Painting Type of 1967

Designs: 1k, Boy from Martinique, by Antonin Pelc. 1.20k, "Fortitude" (mountaineer), by Martin Benka. 1.80k, Rembrandt, self-portrait. 2k, Pierrot, by Bohumil Kubista. 2.40k, Ilona Kubinyiova, by Peter M. Bohun. 3.60k, Virgin and Child (Veveri Madonna), c. 1350.

Engraved and Photogravure

1973, Nov. 27 ***Perf. 11½***

1908 A565 1k multi, vio bl inscriptions *1.65 1.50*
a. 1k multi, blk inscriptions 6.00 5.50
1909 A565 1.20k multi *1.75 1.65*
1910 A565 1.80k multi 65 60
1911 A565 2k multi 70 65
1912 A565 2.40k multi 85 75
1913 A565 3.60k multi 1.25 1.10
Nos. 1908-1913 (6) 6.85 6.25

Sheets of 4. Nos. 1910-1913 printed se-tenant with gold and black inscription on gutter.

Central background bluish gray on No. 1908, light bluish green on No. 1908a.

Postilion — A679

1973, Dec. 18

1914 A679 1k gold & multi 45 30

Stamp Day 1974 and 55th anniversary of Czechoslovak postage stamps. Printed with 2 labels showing telephone and telegraph.

"CSSR" A680

Friedrich Smetana A681

A little time given to the study of the arrangement of the Scott Catalogue can make it easier to use effectively.

Pablo Neruda, Chilean Flag A682

Comecon Building, Moscow A683

1974, Jan. 1

1915 A680 30h red, gold & ultra 12 5

5th anniversary of Federal Government in the Czechoslovak Socialist Republic.

1974, Jan. 4 ***Perf. 11x11½***

Design: No. 1917, Josef Suk.

1916 A681 60h blk, bl & yel 24 12
1917 A681 60h grn & multi 24 12
1918 A682 60h bl, blk & red 24 12

Sesquicentennial of the birth of Friedrich Smetana (1824-1884), composer; centenary of the birth of Josef Suk (1874-1935), composer, and in memory of Pablo Neruda (Neftali Ricardo Reyes, 1904-1973), Chilean poet.

1974, Jan. 23

1919 A683 1k gold, red & vio bl 40 16

25th anniversary of the Council of Mutual Economic Assistance (COMECON).

Symbols of Postal Service — A684

1974, Feb. 20 ***Perf. 11½***

1920 A684 3.60k multi 1.65 60

BRNO '74 National Stamp Exhibition, Brno, June 8-23.

Art Type of 1972

Designs: 60h, Tulips 1973, by Josef Broz. 1k, Structures 1961 (poppy and building), by Orest Dubay. 1.60k, Bird and flowers (Golden Sun-Glowing Day), by Adolf Zabransky. 1.80k, Artificial flowers, by Frantisek Gross.

1974, Feb. 21 ***Perf. 11½x11***

1921 A651 60h multi 24 10
1922 A651 1k multi 50 20
1923 A651 1.60k multi 75 24
1924 A651 1.80k multi 1.25 40

Czech and Slovak graphic art.

Oskar Benes and Vaclav Prochazka — A685

Portraits: 40h, Milos Uher and Anton Sedlacek. 60h, Jan Hajecek and Marie Sedlackova. 80h, Jan Sverma and Albin Grznar. 1k, Jaroslav Neliba and Alois Hovorka. 1.60k, Ladislav Exnar and Ludovit Kukorelli.

Engraved and Photogravure

1974, Mar. 21 ***Perf. 11½x11***

1925 A685 30h ind & multi 12 5
1926 A685 40h ind & multi 16 6
1927 A685 60h ind & multi 24 8
1928 A685 80h ind & multi 32 12
1929 A685 1k ind & multi 40 14
1930 A685 1.60k ind & multi 1.00 35
Nos. 1925-1930 (6) 2.24 80

Partisan commanders and fighters.

"Water, the Source of Energy" A686

Symbolic Designs: 1k, Importance of water for agriculture. 1.20k, Study of the oceans. 1.60k, "Hydrological Decade." 2k, Struggle for unpolluted water.

1974, Apr. 25 **Engr.** ***Perf. 11½***

1931 A686 60h multi 22 20
1932 A686 1k multi 35 30
1933 A686 1.20k multi 55 45
1934 A686 1.60k multi 75 75
1935 A686 2k multi 1.10 1.00
Nos. 1931-1935 (5) 2.97 2.70

Hydrological Decade (UNESCO), 1965-1974. Sheets of 4.

Allegory Holding "Molniya," and Ground Station A687

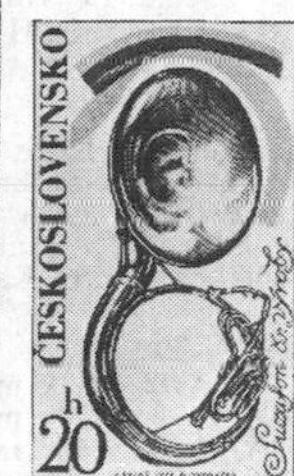

Sousaphone A688

Engraved and Photogravure

1974, Apr. 30

1936 A687 30h vio bl & multi 20 10

"Intersputnik," first satellite communications ground station in Czechoslovakia.

Prague Castle Art Type of 1971

Designs: No. 1937, Golden Cock, 17th century locket. No. 1938, Glass monstrance, 1840.

1974, May 9 **Engr.** ***Perf. 11½***

1937 A634 3k gold & multi 1.75 1.60
1938 A634 3k blk & multi 1.75 1.60

Sheets of 4.

Engraved and Photogravure

1974, May 12 ***Perf. 11x11½***

1939 A688 20h *shown* 10 5
1940 A688 30h *Bagpipe* 12 8
1941 A688 40h *Violin, by Martin Benka* 18 12
1942 A688 1k *Pyramid piano* 40 18
1943 A688 1.60k *Tenor quinton, 1754* 1.25 30
Nos. 1939-1943 (5) 2.05 73

Prague and Bratislava Music Festivals. The 1.60k also commemorates 25th anniversary of Slovak Philharmonic Orchestra.

Child — A689

Engraved and Photogravure

1974, June 1 ***Perf. 11½***

1944 A689 60h multi 30 12

Children's Day. Design is from illustration for children's book by Adolf Zabransky.

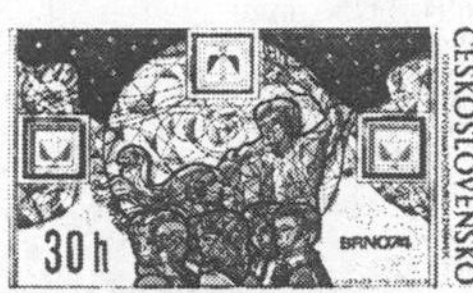

Globe, People and Exhibition Emblems — A690

Design: 6k, Rays and emblems symbolizing "Oneness and Mutuality."

1974, June 1

1945 A690 30h multi 10 6
1946 A690 6k multi 2.25 1.20

BRNO 74 National Stamp Exhibition, Brno, June 8-23. Sheets of 16 stamps and 14 labels.

Resistance Fighter A691

Actress Holding Tragedy and Comedy Masks A692

Engraved and Photogravure

1974, Aug. 29 ***Perf. 11½***

1947 A691 30h multi 12 6

Slovak National Uprising, 30th anniversary.

1974, Aug. 29

1948 A692 30h red, sil & blk 12 6

Bratislava Academy of Music and Drama, 25th anniversary.

Slovak Girl with Flower — A693

1974, Aug. 29

1949 A693 30h multi 12 6

SLUK, Slovak folksong and dance ensemble, 25th anniversary.

Hero and Leander A694

Design: 2.40k, Hero watching Leander swim the Hellespont. No. 1952, Leander reaching shore. No. 1953, Hero mourning over Leander's body. No. 1954, Hermione, Leander's sister. No. 1955, Mourning Cupid. Designs are from 17th century English tapestries in Bratislava Council Palace.

Engraved and Photogravure

1974-76

1950 A694 2k multi 2.50 1.50
1951 A694 2.40k multi 2.50 1.50
1952 A694 3k multi 2.50 1.75
1953 A694 3k multi 1.75 1.60
1954 A694 3.60k multi 2.50 1.75
1955 A694 3.60k multi 1.75 1.50
Nos. 1950-1955 (6) 13.50 9.60

Issue dates: Nos. 1950-1951, Sept. 25, 1974. Nos. 1952, 1954, Aug. 29, 1975. Nos. 1953, 1955, May 9, 1976.

Soldier Standing Guard, Target, 1840 — A695

Painted Folk-art Targets: 60h, Landscape with Pierrot and flags, 1828. 1k, Diana crowning champion marksman, 1832. 1.60k, Still life with guitar, 1839. 2.40k, Salvo and stag in flight, 1834. 3k, Turk and giraffe, 1831.

1974, Sept. 26 ***Perf. 11½***

Size: 30x50mm.

1956 A695 30h blk & multi 12 6
1957 A695 60h blk & multi 24 12
1958 A695 1k blk & multi 40 25

Engr.

Perf. 12

Size: 40x50mm.

1959 A695 1.60k grn & multi 80 60
1960 A695 2.40k sep & multi 1.25 1.00
1961 A695 3k multi 2.10 1.65
Nos. 1956-1961 (6) 4.91 3.68

UPU Emblem and Postilion — A696

Designs (UPU Emblem and): 40h, Mail coach. 60h, Railroad mail coach, 1851. 80h, Early mail truck. 1k, Czechoslovak Airlines mail plane. 1.60k, Radar.

Engraved and Photogravure

1974, Oct. 9 ***Perf. 11½***

1962 A696 30h multi 10 6
1963 A696 40h multi 14 8
1964 A696 60h multi 22 12
1965 A696 80h multi 30 16
1966 A696 1k multi 40 20
1967 A696 1.60k multi 90 32
Nos. 1962-1967 (6) 2.06 94

Centenary of Universal Postal Union.

Post Horn, Old Town Bridge Tower A697

Sealed Letter A698

Stylized Bird A699

Postal Code Symbol A699a

Designs: 40h, Post rider. No. 1971, Carrier pigeon. No. 1979, Map of Czechoslovakia with postal code numbers.

Engraved and Photogravure

1974, Oct. 31 ***Perf. 11½x11***

1968 A697 20h multi 8 5
1969 A698 30h brn, bl & red 12 5
1970 A697 40h multi 16 5
1971 A698 60h bl, yel & red 24 5

See No. 2675.

Coil Stamps

1975 **Photo.** ***Perf. 14***

1976 A699 30h brt bl 18 12
1977 A699 60h carmine 30 18

1976 ***Perf. 11½***

1978 A699a 30h emer 12 5
1979 A699a 60h scar 25 10

Nos. 1976-1979 have black control number on back of every fifth stamp.

Ludvik Kuba, Self-portrait, 1941 — A700

Paintings: 1.20k, Violinist Frantisek Ondricek, by Vaclav Brozik. 1.60k, Vase with Flowers, by Otakar Kubin. 1.80k, Woman with Pitcher, by Janko Alexy. 2.40k, Bacchanalia, c. 1635, by Karel Skreta.

1974, Nov. 27 **Engr.** ***Perf. 11½***

1980 A700 1k multi 40 40
1981 A700 1.20k multi 60 48
1982 A700 1.60k multi 80 70
1983 A700 1.80k multi 1.00 90
1984 A700 2.40k multi 1.35 1.20
Nos. 1980-1984 (5) 4.15 3.68

Czech and Slovak art. Sheets of 4. See Nos. 2209-2211.

Post Horn A701

Engraved and Photogravure

1974, Dec. 18 ***Perf. 11x11½***

1985 A701 1k multi 50 30

Stamp Day.

Still-life with Hare, by Hollar — A702

Designs: 1k, The Lion and the Mouse, by Vaclav Hollar. 1.60k, Deer Hunt, by Philip Galle. 1.80k, Grand Hunt, by Jacques Callot.

Engraved and Photogravure

1975, Feb. 26 ***Perf. 11½x11***

1988 A702 60h blk & buff 24 6
1989 A702 1k blk & buff 40 12
1990 A702 1.60k blk & yel 75 30
1991 A702 1.80k blk & buff 1.00 60

Hunting scenes from old engravings.

Guns Pointing at Family A703

Young Woman and Globe A704

Designs: 1k, Women and building on fire. 1.20k, People and roses. All designs include names of destroyed villages.

Engraved and Photogravure

1975, Feb. 26 ***Perf. 11***

1992 A703 60h multi 30 6
1993 A703 1k multi 50 15
1994 A703 1.20k multi 48 18

Destruction of 14 villages by the Nazis, 30th anniversary.

1975, Mar. 7 ***Perf. 11½x11***

1995 A704 30h red & multi 15 5

International Women's Year 1975.

Little Queens, Moravian Folk Custom A705

Folk Customs: 1k, Straw masks (animal heads and blackened faces), Slovak. 1.40k, The Tale of Maid Dorothea (executioner, girl, king and devil). 2k, Drowning of Morena, symbol of death and winter.

1975, Mar. 26 **Engr.** ***Perf. 11½***

1996 A705 60h blk & multi 60 25
1997 A705 1k blk & multi 50 45
1998 A705 1.40k blk & multi 60 55
1999 A705 2k blk & multi 1.00 90

Sheets of four.

Coat of Arms Type of 1968

Engraved and Photogravure

1975, Apr. 17 ***Perf. 11½***

2000 A590 60h *Nymburk* 24 8
2001 A590 60h *Znojmo* 24 8

Coats of arms of Czechoslovakian cities.

Czech May Uprising — A706

Liberation by Soviet Army — A707

Czechoslovak-Russian Friendship — A708

Engraved and Photogravure

1975, May 9

2002 A706 1k multi 40 15

Engr.

2003 A707 1k multi 40 15

Engraved and Photogravure

2004 A708 1k multi 40 15

30th anniversary of the May uprising of the Czech people and of liberation by the Soviet Army; 5th anniversary of the Czechoslovak-Soviet Treaty of Friendship, Cooperation and Mutual Aid.

Adolescents' Exercises — A709

Designs: 60th, Children's exercises. 1k, Men's and women's exercises.

Engraved and Photogravure

1975, June 15 ***Perf. 12x11½***

2005 A709 30h lil & multi 15 5
2006 A709 60h multi 26 10
2007 A709 1k vio & multi 45 18

Spartakiad 1975, Prague, June 26-29. Nos. 2005-2007 each issued in sheets of 30 stamps and 40 labels, showing different Spartakiad emblems.

Datrioides Microlepis and Sea Horse — A710

Tropical Fish (Aquarium): 1k, Beta splendens regan and pterophyllum scalare. 1.20k, Carassius auratus. 1.60k, Amphiprion percula and chaetodon sp. 2k, Pomacanthodes semicirculatus, pomocanthus maculosus and paracanthorus hepatus.

1975, June 27 ***Perf. 11½***

2008 A710 60h multi 26 8
2009 A710 1k multi 50 10
2010 A710 1.20k multi 65 25
2011 A710 1.60k multi 95 45
2012 A710 2k multi 1.75 50
Nos. 2008-2012 (5) 4.11 1.38

Pelicans, by Nikita Charushin — A711

Book Illustrations: 30h, The Dreamer, by Lieselotte Schwarz. 40h, Hero on horseback, by Val Muntenau. 60h, Peacock, by Klaus Ensikat. 80h, Man on horseback, by Robert Dubravec.

1975, Sept. 5

2013 A711 20h multi 10 6
2014 A711 30h multi 12 8
2015 A711 40h multi 15 10

2016 A711 60h multi 26 12
2017 A711 80h multi 40 20
Nos. 2013-2017 (5) 1.03 56

Bratislava BIB 75 biennial exhibition of illustrations for children's books.

Nos. 2013-2017 issued in sheets of 25 stamps and 15 labels with designs and inscriptions in various languages.

Strakonice, 1951 — A712

Designs: Motorcycles.

Engraved and Photogravure

1975, Sept. 29 ***Perf. 11½***

2018 A712 20h *shown* 8 5
2019 A712 40h *Jawa 250, 1945* 15 5
2020 A712 60h *Jawa 175, 1935* 24 10
2021 A712 1k *ITAR, 1921* 45 25
2022 A712 1.20k *ORION, 1903* 65 30
2023 A712 1.80k *Laurin & Klement, 1898* 1.25 35
Nos. 2018-2023 (6) 2.82 1.10

Study of Shortwave Solar Radiation — A713

Soyuz-Apollo Link-up in Space — A714

Designs: 60h, Study of aurora borealis and Oreol satellite. 1k, Study of ionosphere and cosmic radiation. 2k, Copernicus, radio map of the sun and satellite.

1975, Sept. 30

2024 A713 30h multi 15 5
2025 A713 60h yel, rose red & vio 28 10
2026 A713 1k bl, yel & vio 50 28
2027 A713 2k red, vio & yel 1.10 55

Engr.

2028 A714 5k vio & multi 3.25 2.75
Nos. 2024-2028 (5) 5.28 3.73

International cooperation in space research. No. 2028 issued in sheets of 4.

The design of No. 2026 appears to be inverted.

Slovnaft, Petrochemical Plant — A715

Designs: 60h, Atomic power station. 1k, Construction of Prague subway. 1.20k, Construction of Friendship pipeline. 1.40k, Combine harvesters. 1.60k, Apartment house construction.

Engraved and Photogravure

1975, Oct. 28

2029 A715 30h multi 12 5
2030 A715 60h multi 24 8
2031 A715 1k multi 45 12
2032 A715 1.20k multi 65 15
2033 A715 1.40k multi 70 30
2034 A715 1.60k multi 90 35
Nos. 2029-2034 (6) 3.06 1.05

Socialist construction, 30th anniversary. Nos. 2029-2034 printed se-tenant with labels.

Pres. Gustav Husak — A716

1975, Oct. 28 **Engr.**

2035 A716 30h ultra 12 5
2036 A716 60h rose red 24 15

Prague Castle Art Type of 1971

Designs: 3k, Gold earring, 9th century. 3.60k, Arms of Premysl Dynasty and Bohemia from lid of leather case containing Bohemian crown, 14th century.

1975, Oct. 29

2040 A634 3k blk, grn, pur & gold 1.60 1.40
2041 A634 3.60k red & multi 1.75 1.50

Sheets of 4.

Miniature Sheet

Ludvik Svoboda, Road Map, Buzuluk to Prague, Carnations — A717

1975, Nov. 25

2042 A717 10k multi 17.50 17.50

Pres. Ludvik Svoboda, 80th birthday. Size of No. 2042: 75x95mm. (stamp size: 40x55mm.).

Exists imperf., price $60.

Art Type of 1967

Paintings: 1k, "May 1975" (Woman and doves for 30th anniversary of peace), by Zdenek Sklenar. 1.40k, Woman in national costume, by Eugen Nevan. 1.80k, "Liberation of Prague," by Alena Cermakova (horiz.). 2.40k, "Fire 1938" (woman raising fist), by Josef Capek. 3.40k, Old Prague, 1828, by Vincenc Morstadt.

1975, Nov. 27 **Engr.** ***Perf. 11½***

2043 A565 1k blk, buff & brn 45 40
2044 A565 1.40k multi 70 60
2045 A565 1.80k multi 1.00 80
2046 A565 2.40k multi 1.25 1.00
2047 A565 3.40k multi 2.50 1.70
Nos. 2043-2047 (5) 5.90 4.50

Sheets of 4.

Carrier Pigeon — A718

Engraved and Photogravure

1975, Dec. 18 ***Perf. 11½***

2048 A718 1k red & multi 50 20

Stamp Day 1975.

Frantisek Halas — A719

Wilhelm Pieck — A720

Frantisek Lexa A721

Jindrich Jindrich A722

Ivan Krasko — A723

Engraved and Photogravure

1976, Feb. 25 ***Perf. 11½***

2049 A719 60h multi 24 10
2050 A720 60h multi 24 10
2051 A721 60h multi 24 10
2052 A722 60h multi 24 10
2053 A723 60h multi 24 10
Nos. 2049-2053 (5) 1.20 50

Anniversaries: Frantisek Halas (1901-1949), poet (No. 2049); Wilhelm Pieck (1876-1960), president of German Democratic Republic (No. 2050); Frantisek Lexa (1876-1960), professor of Egyptology (No. 2051); Jindrich Jindrich (1876-1967), composer and writer (No. 2052); Ivan Krasko (1876-1958), Slovak poet (No. 2053). No. 2051 printed in sheets of 10, others in sheets of 50.

Ski Jump, Olympic Emblem A724

Designs (Winter Olympic Games Emblem and): 1.40k, Figure skating, women's. 1.60k, Ice hockey.

Engraved and Photogravure

1976, Mar. 22 ***Perf. 12x11½***

2054 A724 1k gold & multi 45 15
2055 A724 1.40k gold & multi 60 25
2056 A724 1.60k gold & multi 70 30

12th Winter Olympic Games, Innsbruck, Austria, Feb. 4-15.

Javelin and Olympic Rings — A725

Designs (Olympic Rings and): 3k, Relay race. 3.60k, Shot put.

1976, Mar. 22 ***Perf. 11½***

2057 A725 2k multi 90 35
2058 A725 3k multi 1.25 50
2059 A725 3.60k multi 1.65 60

21st Olympic Games, Montreal, Canada, July 17-Aug. 1.

Table Tennis — A726

1976, Mar. 22 ***Perf. 11x12***

2060 A726 1k multi 50 20

European Table Tennis Championship, Prague, Mar. 26-Apr. 4.

Symbolic of Communist Party A727

Worker, Derrick, Emblem A728

1976, Apr. 12 ***Perf. 11x12***

2061 A727 30h gold & multi 12 5
2062 A728 60h gold & multi 24 8

15th Congress of the Communist Party of Czechoslovakia.

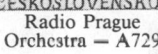

Radio Prague Orchestra — A729

Dancer, Violin, Tragic Mask — A730

Actors — A731

Folk Dancers A732

Film Festival A733

1976, Apr. 26 ***Perf. 11½***

2063 A729 20h gold & multi 8 5
2064 A730 20h pink & multi 8 5
2065 A731 20h lt bl & multi 8 5
2066 A732 30h blk & multi 12 5
2067 A733 30h vio bl, rose & grn 12 5
Nos. 2063-2067 (5) 48 25

Commemorating: Czechoslovak Radio Symphony Orchestra, Prague, 50th anniversary (No. 2063); Academy of Music and Dramatic Art, Prague, 50th anniversary (No. 2064); Nova Scena Theater Company, Bratislava, 30th anniversary (No. 2065); International Folk Song and Dance Festival, Straznice, 30th anniversary (No. 2066); 20th

International Film Festival, Karlovy Vary (No. 2067).

Hammer and Sickle
A734 A735

Design: 6k, Hammer and sickle (horiz.).

1976, May 14

2068 A734 30h gold, red & dk bl 16 5
2069 A735 60h gold, red & dp car 38 15

Souvenir Sheet

2070 A735 6k red & multi 2.60 2.60

Czechoslovak Communist Party, 55th anniversary. No. 2070 contains one stamp (50x30mm.); violet blue marginal inscription and gold emblem. Size: 99x90mm.

Ships in Storm, by Frans Huys (1522-1562)
A736

Old Engravings of Ships: 60h, by Vaclav Hollar (1607-1677). 1k, by Regnier Nooms Zeeman (1623-1668). 2k, by Francois Chereau (1680-1729).

Engraved and Photogravure

1976, July 21 ***Perf. 11x11½***

2071 A736 40h buff & blk 16 6
2072 A736 60h gray, buff & blk 24 8
2073 A736 1k lt grn, buff & blk 45 15
2074 A736 2k lt bl, buff & blk 85 35

"UNESCO"
A737

1976, July 30 ***Perf. 11½***

2075 A737 2k gray & multi 85 50

30th anniversary of UNESCO. Sheets of 10.

Souvenir Sheet

Hands Holding Infant, Globe and Dove
A738

1976, July 30

2076 A738 6k, sheet of 2, multi 10.00 10.00

European Security and Cooperation Conference, Helsinki, Finland, 2nd anniversary. No. 2076 contains 2 stamps, marginal inscription and ornamental designs in blue and black. Size: 115x165mm.

Merino Ram — A739

Couple Smoking, WHO Emblem and Skull — A740

Designs: 40h, Bern-Hana milk cow. 1.60k, Kladruby stallion Generalissimus XXVII.

Engraved and Photogravure

1976, Aug. 28 ***Perf. 11½x12***

2077 A739 30h multi 12 5
2078 A739 40h multi 18 5
2079 A739 1.60k multi 70 25

Bountiful Earth Exhibition, Ceske Budejovice, Aug. 28-Sept. 12.

1976, Sept. 7 ***Perf. 12x11½***

2080 A740 2k multi 85 50

Fight against smoking, World Health Organization drive against drug addiction. Printed in sheets of 10 (2x5) with WHO emblems and inscription in margin.

Prague Castle Art Type of 1971

Designs: 3k, View of Prague Castle, by F. Hoogenberghe, 1572. 3.60k, Faun and Satyr, sculptured panel, 16th century.

1976, Oct. 22 Engr. ***Perf. 11½***

2081 A634 3k multi 1.25 1.10
2082 A634 3.60k multi 1.50 1.40

Sheets of 4.

Guernica 1937, by Imro Weiner-Kral
A741

1976, Oct. 22

2083 A741 5k multi 2.25 90

40th anniversary of the International Brigade in Spain.

Zebras
A742

Designs: 20h, Elephants (vert.). 30h, Cheetah. 40h, Giraffes (vert.). 60h, Rhinoceros. 3k, Bongos (vert.).

Engraved and Photogravure

1976, Nov. 3 ***Perf. 11½x11, 11x11½***

2084 A742 10h multi 6 5
2085 A742 20h multi 8 5
2086 A742 30h multi 12 5
2087 A742 40h multi 16 5
2088 A742 60h multi 24 8
2089 A742 3k multi 1.50 45
Nos. 2084-2089 (6) 2.16 73

African animals in Dvur Kralove Zoo.

Art Type of 1967

Paintings of Flowers: 1k, by Peter Matejka. 1.40k, by Cyril Bouda. 2k, by Jan Breughel. 3.60k, J. Rudolf Bys.

1976, Nov. 27 Engr. ***Perf. 11½***

2090 A565 1k multi 55 55
2091 A565 1.40k multi 75 80
2092 A565 2k multi 1.10 1.10
2093 A565 3.60k multi 1.75 1.85

Sheets of 4. Emblem and name of Praga 1978 on horizontal gutter.

Postrider, 17th Century, and Satellites — A743

Engraved and Photogravure

1976, Dec. 18

2094 A743 1k multi 45 20

Stamp Day 1976.

Ice Hockey
A744

Arms of Vranov
A745

Designs: 1k, Biathlon. 1.60k, Ski jump. 2k, Downhill skiing.

Engraved and Photogravure

1977, Feb. 11 ***Perf. 11½***

2095 A744 60h multi 24 8
2096 A744 1k multi 45 12
2097 A744 1.60k multi 80 25
2098 A744 2k multi 90 35

6th Winter Spartakiad of Socialist Countries' Armies.

1977, Feb. 20

Designs: Coats of Arms of Czechoslovak towns.

2099 A745 60h *shown* 24 10
2100 A745 60h *Kralupy & Vltavou* 24 10
2101 A745 60h *Jicin* 24 10
2102 A745 60h *Valasske Mezirici* 24 10

See Nos. 2297-2300.

Window, Michna Palace — A746

Prague Renaissance Windows: 30h, Michna Palace. 40h, Thun Palace. 60h, Archbishop's Palace, Hradcany. 5k, St. Nicholas Church.

1977, Mar. 10

2103 A746 20h multi 8 5
2104 A746 30h multi 12 5
2105 A746 40h multi 16 5
2106 A746 60h multi 24 8
2107 A746 5k multi 2.25 1.00
Nos. 2103-2107 (5) 2.85 1.23

PRAGA 1978 International Philatelic Exhibition, Prague, Sept. 8-17, 1978.

Children, Auxiliary Police
A747

Engraved and Photogravure

1977, Apr. 21 ***Perf. 11½***

2108 A747 60h multi 24 8

Auxiliary Police, 25th anniversary.

Warsaw, Polish Flag, Bicyclists
A748

Congress Emblem
A749

Designs: 60h, Berlin, DDR flag, bicyclists. 1k, Prague, Czechoslovakian flag, victorious bicyclist. 1.40k, Bicyclists on highways, modern views of Berlin, Prague and Warsaw.

1977, May 7

2109 A748 30h multi 12 5
2110 A748 60h multi 30 15
2111 A748 1k multi 50 25
2112 A748 1.40k multi 60 30

30th International Bicycle Peace Race Warsaw-Prague-Berlin.

Engraved and Photogravure

1977, May 25 ***Perf. 11½***

2113 A749 30h car, red & gold 12 5

9th Trade Union Congress, Prague 1977.

Prague Castle Art Type of 1971

Designs: 3k, Onyx footed bowl, 1350. 3.60k, Bronze horse, 1619.

1977, June 7 **Engr.**

2114 A634 3k multi 1.75 1.20
2115 A634 3.60k multi 1.75 1.50

Sheets of 4.

French Postrider, 19th Century, PRAGA '78 Emblem
A750

Postal Uniforms: 1k, Austrian, 1838. 2k, Austrian, late 18th century. 3.60k, Germany, early 18th century.

Engraved and Photogravure

1977, June 8

2116 A750 60h multi 24 8
2117 A750 1k multi 45 15
2118 A750 2k multi 90 30
2119 A750 3.60k multi 1.50 65

PRAGA 1978 International Philatelic Exhibition, Prague, Sept. 8-17, 1978.
Nos. 2116-2119 issued in sheets of 50 and sheets of 4 with 4 labels and horizontal gutter.

Coffeepots, Porcelain Mark A751

Mlada Boleslav Costume A752

Czechoslovak Porcelain and Porcelain Marks: 30h, Urn. 40h, Vase. 60h, Cup and saucer, jugs. 1k, Candlestick and plate. 3k, Cup and saucer, coffeepot.

1977, June 15

2120 A751 20h multi 8 5
2121 A751 30h multi 12 5
2122 A751 40h multi 16 6
2123 A751 60h multi 24 8
2124 A751 1k multi 45 18
2125 A751 3k multi 1.50 45
Nos. 2120-2125 (6) 2.55 87

1977, Aug. 31 Engr. *Perf. 11½*

PRAGA Emblem and Folk Costumes from: 1.60k, Vazek. 3.60k, Zavadka. 5k, Belkovice.

2126 A752 1k multi 45 40
2127 A752 1.60k multi 70 60
2128 A752 3.60k multi 1.50 1.40
2129 A752 5k multi 2.25 2.00

Issued in sheets of 10 and in sheets of 8 plus 2 labels showing PRAGA '78 emblem.

Old Woman, Devil and Spinner, by Viera Bombova A753

Book Illustrations: 60h, Bear and tiger, by Genadij Pavlisin. 1k, Coach drawn by 4 horses (Hans Christian Andersen), by Ulf Lovgren. 2k, Bear and flamingos (Lewis Carroll), by Nicole Claveloux. 3k, King with keys, and toys, by Jiri Trnka.

Engraved and Photogravure

1977, Sept. 9

2130 A753 40h multi 16 6
2131 A753 60h multi 24 8
2132 A753 1k multi 45 15
2133 A753 2k multi 90 30
2134 A753 3k multi 1.25 45
Nos. 2130-2134 (5) 3.00 1.04

Prize-winning designs, 6th biennial exhibition of illustrations for children's books, Bratislava.

Globe, Violin, Doves, View of Prague — A754

Engraved and Photogravure

1977, Sept. 28 *Perf. 11½*

2135 A754 60h multi 24 8

Congress of International Music Council of UNESCO, Prague and Bratislava.

Souvenir Sheets

"For a Europe of Peace" A755

Designs: 1.60k, "For a Europe of Cooperation." 2.40k, "For a Europe of Social Progress."

1977, Oct. 3

2136 A755 60h, Sheet of 2 55 50
2137 A755 1.60k, Sheet of 2 1.50 1.40
2138 A755 2.40k, Sheet of 2 2.25 2.00

2nd European Security and Cooperation Conference, Belgrade. Nos. 2136-2138 each contain 2 stamps and 2 blue on buff inscriptions and ornaments. Size: 130x80mm.

S. P. Koroljov, Sputnik I Emblem A756

Sailors, Cruiser Aurora A757

Designs: 30h, Yuri A. Gagarin and Vostok I. 40h, Alexei Leonov. 1k, Neil A. Armstrong and footprint on moon. 1.60k, Construction of orbital space station.

1977, Oct. 4

2139 A756 20h multi 8 5
2140 A756 30h multi 12 5
2141 A756 40h multi 16 6
2142 A756 1k multi 45 15
2143 A756 1.60k multi 75 25
Nos. 2139-2143 (5) 1.56 56

Space research, 20th anniversary of first earth satellite.

1977, Nov. 7

2144 A757 30h multi 12 5

60th anniversary of Russian October Revolution.

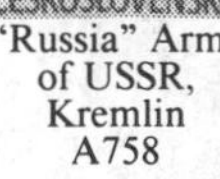

"Russia" Arms of USSR, Kremlin A758

"Science" A759

1977, Nov. 7

2145 A758 30h multi 12 5

55th anniversary of the Union of Soviet Socialist Republics (USSR).

1977, Nov. 17

2146 A759 3k multi 1.10 55

Czechoslovak Academy of Science, 25th anniversary.

Art Type of 1967

Paintings: 2k, "Fear" (woman), by Jan Murdoch. 2.40k, Jan Francisci, portrait by Peter M. Bohun. 2.60k, Vaclav Hollar, self-portrait, 1647. 3k, Young Woman, 1528, by Lucas Cranach. 5k, Cleopatra, by Rubens.

1977, Nov. 27 Engr. *Perf. 11½*

2147 A565 2k multi 75 70
2148 A565 2.40k multi 85 80
2149 A565 2.60k multi 1.00 70
2150 A565 3k multi 1.10 1.00
2151 A565 5k multi 2.00 1.90
Nos. 2147-2151 (5) 5.70 5.10

Sheets of 4.

View of Bratislava, by Georg Hoefnagel — A760

Design: 3.60k, Arms of Bratislava, 1436.

1977, Dec. 6

2152 A760 3k multi 1.25 1.10
2153 A760 3.60k multi 1.50 1.40

Sheets of 4. See Nos. 2174-2175, 2270-2271, 2331-2332, 2364-2365, 2422-2423, 2478-2479, 2514-2515, 2570-2571, 2618-2619.

Stamp Pattern and Post Horn — A761

Engraved and Photogravure

1977, Dec. 18

2154 A761 1k multi 45 15

Stamp Day.

Zdenek Nejedly — A762

Karl Marx — A763

Engraved and Photogravure

1978, Feb. 10 *Perf. 11½*

2155 A762 30h multi 12 5
2156 A763 40h multi 16 6

Zdenek Nejedly (1878-1962), musicologist and historian; Karl Marx (1818-1883), political philosopher.

Civilians Greeting Guardsmen — A764

Intellectual, Farm Woman and Steel Worker, Flag — A765

1978, Feb. 25

2157 A764 1k gold & multi 45 15
2158 A765 1k gold & multi 45 15

30th anniversary of "Victorious February" (No. 2157), and National Front (No. 2158). See note after 2190.

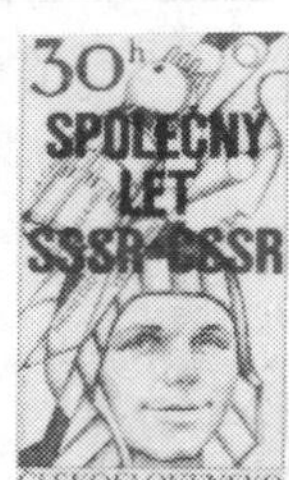

Yuri A. Gagarin and Vostok I — A766

10k Coin, 1964, and 25k Coin, 1965 — A767

Design: 30h, 3.60k, like No. 2140.

Engraved; Overprint Photogravure (Blue and carmine on 30h, green and lilac rose on 3.60k)

1978, Mar. 2 *Perf. 11½x12*

2159 A766 30h dk red 85 65
2160 A766 3.60k vio bl 8.50 6.50

Capt. V. Remek, first Czechoslovakian cosmonaut on Russian spaceship Soyuz 28, Mar. 2-9.

Engraved and Photogravure

1978, Mar. 14

Designs: 40h, Medal for Culture, 1972. 1.40k, Charles University medal, 1948. 3k, Ferdinand I medal, 1568. 5k, Gold florin, 1335.

2161 A767 20h sil & multi 8 5
2162 A767 40h sil & multi 16 6
2163 A767 1.40k gold & multi 70 15
2164 A767 3k gold & multi 1.40 55
2165 A767 5k gold & multi 2.25 1.00
Nos. 2161-2165 (5) 4.59 1.81

650th anniversary of Kremnica Mint.

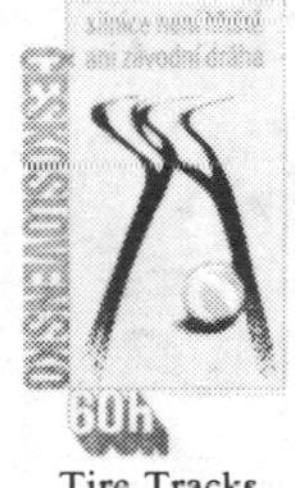

Tire Tracks and Ball A768

Congress Emblem A769

1978, Mar. 15

2166 A768 60h multi 24 8

Road safety.

Engraved and Photogravure

1978, Apr. 16 *Perf. 11½*

2167 A769 1k multi 45 15

9th World Trade Union Congress, Prague 1978.

Shot Put and Praha '78 Emblem A770

Designs: 1k, Pole vault. 3.60k, Women runners.

1978, Apr. 26

2168 A770 40h multi 16 6

2169 A770 1k multi 45 15
2170 A770 3.60k multi 1.50 38

5th European Athletic Championships, Prague 1978.

Ice Hockey — A771

Designs: 30h, Hockey. 2k, Ice hockey play.

1978, Apr. 26
2171 A771 30h multi 12 5
2172 A771 60h multi 25 15
2173 A771 2k multi 90 20

5th European Ice Hockey Championships and 70th anniversary of Bandy hockey.

Bratislava Type of 1977

Designs: 3k, Bratislava, 1955, by Orest Dubay. 3.60k, Fishpound Square, Bratislava, 1955, by Imro Weiner-Kral.

1978, May 9 Engr. *Perf. 11½*
2174 A760 3k multi 1.25 1.10
2175 A760 3.60k multi 1.50 1.40

Sheets of 4.

Prague Castle Art Type of 1971

Designs: 3k, King Ottokar II, detail from tomb. 3.60k, Charles IV, detail from votiv panel by Jan Ocka.

1978, May 9
2176 A634 3k multi 1.25 1.10
2177 A634 3.60k multi 1.75 1.40

Sheets of 4.

Ministry of Post, Prague A772

Engraved and Photogravure
1978, May 29 *Perf. 12x11½*
2178 A772 60h multi 25 8

14th session of permanent COMECOM Commission (Ministers of Post and Telecommunications of Socialist Countries).

Palacky Bridge A773

Prague Bridges and PRAGA '78 Emblem: 40h, Railroad bridge. 1k, Bridge of May 1. 2k, Manes Bridge. 3k, Svatopluk Cech Bridge. 5.40k, Charles Bridge.

1978, May 30
2179 A773 20h blk & multi 8 5
2180 A773 40h blk & multi 16 6
2181 A773 1k blk & multi 45 15
2182 A773 2k blk & multi 90 35
2183 A773 3k blk & multi 1.25 35
2184 A773 5.40k blk & multi 2.25 1.00
Nos. 2179-2184 (6) 5.09 1.96

PRAGA 1978 International Philatelic Exhibition, Prague, Sept. 8-17.

The first price column gives the catalogue value of an unused stamp, the second that of a used stamp.

St. Peter and Apostles, Clock Tower, and Emblem A774

Town Hall Clock, Prague, by Josef Manes, and PRAGA '78 Emblem: 1k, Astronomical clock. 2k, Prague's coat of arms. 3k, Grape harvest (September). 3.60k, Libra. 10k, Arms surrounded by zodiac signs and scenes symbolic of 12 months (horiz.). 2k, 3k, 3.60k show details from design of 10k.

1978, June 20 *Perf. 11½x11*
2185 A774 40h multi 16 6
2186 A774 1k multi 45 15
2187 A774 2k multi 90 30
2188 A774 3k multi 1.65 45
2189 A774 3.60k multi 1.65 70
Nos. 2185-2189 (5) 4.81 1.66

Souvenir Sheet
Perf. 12x12
2190 A774 10k multi 9.50 9.50

PRAGA'78 Intl. Philatelic Exhibition, Prague, Sept. 8-17. No. 1290 contains one stamp (50x40mm.): margin shows black clock tower, red inscription. Size: 90x125mm. Sheet exists imperf.

A non-valid souvenir sheet contains 4 imperf. copies of No. 2157. Blue marginal inscriptions, red PRAGA emblems. Sold only with PRAGA ticket.

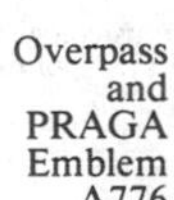

Folk Dancers — A775

Engraved and Photogravure
1978, July 7 *Perf. 11½x12*
2191 A775 30h multi 12 5

25th Folklore Festival, Vychodna.

Overpass and PRAGA Emblem A776

Designs (PRAGA Emblem and): 1k, 2k, Modern office buildings (diff.). 6k, Old and new Prague. 20k, Charles Bridge and Old Town, by Vincent Morstadt, 1828.

1978 *Perf. 12x11½*
2192 A776 60h blk & multi 25 8
2193 A776 1k blk & multi 45 15
2194 A776 2k blk & multi 90 30
2195 A776 6k blk & multi 2.50 75

Souvenir Sheet
Engr.
2196 A776 20k multi 9.50 9.00

PRAGA 1978 International Philatelic Exhibition, Prague, Sept. 8-17. No. 2196 also commemorates 60th anniversary of Czechoslovak postage stamps. Size of No. 2196: 95x76mm. (stamp 61x45mm.).

Issue dates: Nos. 2192-2195, Sept. 8; No. 2196, Sept. 10.

Souvenir Sheet

Apollo's Companion, by Titian — A777

Design: No. 2197b, King Midas. Stamps show details from "Apollo Flaying Marsya" by Titian.

1978, Sept. 12 *Perf. 11½*
2197 Sheet of 2 9.50 9.00
a. A777 10k multi 4.50 4.00
b. A777 10k multi 4.50 4.00

Titian (1488-1576), Venetian painter. Margin of No. 2197 shows painting from which stamp designs were taken, black inscription and red PRAGA emblem. Size: 109x165mm. No. 2197 with dark blue marginal inscription "FIP" was sold only with entrance ticket to PRAGA Philatelic Exhibition.

Exhibition Hall — A778

Engraved and Photogravure
1978, Sept. 13 *Perf. 11½x11*
2198 A778 30h multi 12 5

22nd International Engineering Fair, Brno.

Postal Newspaper Service — A779

TV Screen, Headquarters and Logo — A780

Newspaper, Microphone A781

Engraved and Photogravure
1978, Sept. 21 *Perf. 11½*
2199 A779 30h multi 12 5
2200 A780 30h multi 12 5
2201 A781 30h multi 12 5

25th anniversaries: Postal News Service (No. 2199); Day of the Press (No. 2200); Broadcasting and Television Day (No. 2201).

Sulky Race A782

Pardubice Steeplechase: 10h, Falling horses and jockeys at fence. 30h, Race. 40h, Horses passing post. 1.60k, Hurdling. 4.40k, Winner.

1978, Oct. 6 *Perf. 12x11½*
2202 A782 10h multi 5 5
2203 A782 20h multi 8 5
2204 A782 30h multi 12 5
2205 A782 40h multi 16 6
2206 A782 1.60k multi 70 30
2207 A782 4.40k multi 2.00 55
Nos. 2202-2207 (6) 3.11 1.06

Woman Holding Arms of Czechoslovakia A783

Engraved and Photogravure
1978, Oct. 28 *Perf. 11½*
2208 A783 60h multi 25 10

60th anniversary of independence.

Art Type of 1974

Paintings: 2.40k, Flowers, by Jakub Bohdan (1660-1724). 3k, The Dream of Salas, by Ludovit Fulla (horiz.). 3.60k, Apostle with Censer, Master of the Spissko Capitals (c. 1480-1490).

1978, Nov. 27 Engr.
2209 A700 2.40k multi 1.10 90
2210 A700 3k multi 1.25 1.10
2211 A700 3.60k multi 1.65 1.40

Slovak National Gallery, 30th anniversary.

Musicians, by Jan Könyves — A784

Slovak Ceramics: 30h, Janosik on Horseback, by Jozef Franko. 40h, Woman in Folk Costume by Michal Polasko. 1k, Three Girls Singing, by Ignac Bizmayer. 1.60k, Janosik Dancing, by Ferdis Kostka.

Engraved and Photogravure
1978, Dec. 5 *Perf. 11½x12*
2212 A784 20h multi 8 5
2213 A784 30h multi 12 5
2214 A784 40k multi 16 6
2215 A784 1k multi 45 12
2216 A784 1.60k multi 70 18
Nos. 2212-2216 (5) 1.51 46

Alfons Mucha and his Design for 1918 Issue — A785

1978, Dec. 18 *Perf. 11½*
2217 A785 1k multi 40 12

60th Stamp Day.

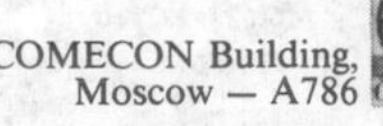
COMECON Building, Moscow — A786

Engraved and Photogravure

1979, Jan. 1 *Perf. 11½*
2218 A786 1k multi 40 10

Council for Mutual Economic Aid (COMECON), 30th anniversary.

Woman's Head and Grain — A787

Woman, Workers, Child, Doves — A788

1979, Jan. 1
2219 A787 30h multi 12 5
2220 A788 60h multi 25 8

Czechoslovakian Federation, 10th anniversary (30h); United Agricultural Production Association, 30th anniversary (60h).

Soyuz 28, Rockets and Capsule — A789

Designs: 60h, Astronauts Aleksei Gubarev and Vladimir Remek on launching pad (vert.). 1.60k, Soviet astronauts J. Romanenko and G. Grecko, Salyut 6 and recovery ship. 2k, Salyut-Soyuz orbital complex, post office in space and Czechoslovakia No. 2153. 4k, Soyuz 28, crew after landing and trajectory map (vert.). 10k, Gubarev and Remek, Intercosmos emblem, arms of Czechoslovakia and USSR.

1979, Mar. 2
2221 A789 30h multi 12 5
2222 A789 60h multi 25 8
2223 A789 1.60k multi 70 18
2224 A789 2k multi 90 30
2225 A789 4k multi 1.75 50
Nos. 2221-2225 (5) 3.72 1.11

Souvenir Sheet
2226 A789 10k multi 5.00 4.75

First anniversary of joint Czechoslovak-Soviet space flight. Size of No. 2226: 76x93mm. (stamp 39x55mm.). No. 2226 exists imperf.

Alpine Bellflowers A790

Stylized Satellite, Dial, Tape A791

Mountain Flowers: 20h, Crocus. 30h, Pinks. 40h, Alpine hawkweed. 3k, Larkspur.

Engraved and Photogravure

1979, Mar. 23 *Perf. 11½*
2227 A790 10h multi 5 5
2228 A790 20h multi 8 5
2229 A790 30h multi 12 5
2230 A790 40h multi 16 6
2231 A790 3k multi 1.25 50
Nos. 2227-2231 (5) 1.66 71

Mountain Rescue Service, 25th anniversary.

1979, Apr. 2
2232 A791 10h multi 12 5

Telecommunications research, 30th anniversary.

Artist and Model, Dove, Bratislava Castle — A792

Cog Wheels, Transformer and Student — A793

Musical Instruments, Bratislava Castle — A794

Pioneer Scarf, IYC Emblem — A795

Red Star, Man, Child and Doves — A796

1979, Apr. 2
2233 A792 20h multi 12 5
2234 A793 20h multi 12 5
2235 A794 30h multi 12 5
2236 A795 30h multi 12 5
2237 A796 60h multi 25 10
Nos. 2233-2237 (5) 73 30

Fine Arts Academy, Bratislava, 30th anniversary; Slovak Technical University, 40th anniversary; Radio Symphony Orchestra, Bratislava, 30th anniversary; Young Pioneers, 30th anniversary and International Year of the Child; Peace Movement, 30th anniversary.

Prague Castle Art Type of 1971

Designs: 3k, Burial crown of King Ottokar II. 3.60k, Portrait of Mrs. Reitmayer, by Karel Purkyne.

Engraved and Photogravure

1979, May 9 *Perf. 11½*
2238 A634 3k multi 1.65 1.25
2239 A634 3.60k multi 1.65 1.35

Sheets of 4.

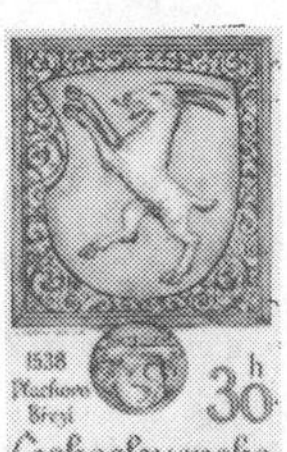

Arms of Vlachovo Brezi, 1538 — A797

Animals in Heraldry: 60h, Jesenik, 1509 (bear and eagle). 1.20k, Vysoke Myto, 1471 (St. George slaying dragon). 1.80k, Martin, 1854 (St. Martin giving coat to beggar). 2k, Zebrak, 1674 (mythological beast).

1979, May 25 *Perf. 11½x12*
2240 A797 30h multi 12 5
2241 A797 60h multi 25 10
2242 A797 1.20k multi 50 20
2243 A797 1.80k multi 75 30
2244 A797 2k multi 85 30
Nos. 2240-2244 (5) 2.47 95

Forest, Thriving and Destroyed A798

Designs: 1.80k, Water. 3.60k, City. 4k, Cattle. All designs show good and bad environment, separated by exclamation point; Man and Biosphere emblem.

1979, June 22 **Engr.** *Perf. 11½*
2245 A798 60h multi 25 12
2246 A798 1.80k multi 75 25
2247 A798 3.60k multi 1.50 70
2248 A798 4k multi 1.65 70

Man and Biosphere Program of UNESCO.

Blast Furnace — A799

Engraved and Photogravure

1979, Aug. 29 *Perf. 11x11½*
2249 A799 30h multi 12 5

Slovak National Uprising, 35th anniversary.

Frog and Goat A800

Book Illustrations (IYC Emblem and): 40h, Knight on horseback. 60h, Maidens. 1k, Boy with sled following rooster. 3k, King riding flying beast.

1979, Aug. 30 *Perf. 11½x11*
2250 A800 20h multi 8 5
2251 A800 40h multi 16 6
2252 A800 60h multi 25 10
2253 A800 1k multi 45 18
2254 A800 3k multi 1.25 50
Nos. 2250-2254 (5) 2.19 89

Prize-winning designs, 7th biennial exhibition of illustrations for children's books, Bratislava; International Year of the Child. Printed with labels showing story characters.

"Bone Shaker" Bicycles, 1870 A801

1979, Sept. 14 *Perf. 12x11½*

Bicycles from: 20h, 1978. 40h, 1910. 60h, 1886. 3.60k, 1820.

2255 A801 20h multi 8 5
2256 A801 40h multi 16 6
2257 A801 60h multi 25 10
2258 A801 2k multi 90 30
2259 A801 3.60k multi 1.50 60
Nos. 2255-2259 (5) 2.89 1.11

Bracket Clock, 18th Century — A802

Designs: 18th century clocks.

Engraved and Photogravure

1979, Oct. 1 *Perf. 11½*
2260 A802 40h multi 16 6
2261 A802 60h multi 25 10
2262 A802 80h multi 32 12
2263 A802 1k multi 45 18
2264 A802 2k multi 90 30
Nos. 2260-2264 (5) 2.08 76

Art Type of 1967

Paintings: 1.60k, Sunday by the River, by Alois Moravec. 2k, Self-portrait, by Gustav Mally. 3k, Self-portrait, by Ilia Yefimovic Repin. 3.60k, Horseback Rider, by Jan Bauch. 5k, Dancing Peasants, by Albrecht Dürer.

1979, Nov. 27 **Engr.** *Perf. 12*
2265 A565 1.60k multi 70 50
2266 A565 2k multi 90 60
2267 A565 3k multi 1.25 70
2268 A565 3.60k multi 1.65 90
2269 A565 5k multi 2.25 1.50
Nos. 2265-2269 (5) 6.75 4.20

Bratislava Type of 1977

Designs: 3k, Bratislava Castle on the Danube, by L. Janscha, 1787. 3.60k, Bratislava Castle, stone engraving by Wolf, 1815.

1979, Dec. 5
2270 A760 3k multi 1.25 60
2271 A760 3.60k multi 1.65 75

Stamp Day — A803

Engraved and Photogravure

1979, Dec. 18 *Perf. 11½x12*
2272 A803 1k multi 45 15

Numeral — A804

1979-80 **Photo.** *Perf. 11½x12*
2273 A804 50h red ('79) 22 8
2274 A804 1k brn ('79) 45 15
2275 A804 2k grn ('80) 90 30
2276 A804 3k lake ('80) 1.25 50

Runners and Dove A805

Engraved and Photogravure

1980, Jan. 29 *Perf. 12x11½*
2289 A805 50h multi 22 8

50th International Peace Marathon, Kosice, Oct. 4.

Canceled-to-order stamps are often from remainders. Most collectors of canceled stamps prefer postally used specimens.

Downhill Skiing — A806

1980, Jan. 29 *Perf. 11½x12*

2290 A806 1k *shown* 40 15
2291 A806 2k *Speed skating* 80 40
2292 A806 3k *Four-man bobsled* 1.25 50

13th Winter Olympic Games, Lake Placid, N.Y., Feb. 12-24.

Basketball — A807

1980, Jan. 29 *Perf. 11½*

2293 A807 40h *shown* 18 6
2294 A807 1k *Swimming* 45 15
2295 A807 2k *Hurdles* 90 30
2296 A807 3.60k *Fencing* 1.65 55

22nd Olympic Games, Moscow, July 19-Aug. 3.

Arms Type of 1977

Engraved and Photogravure

1980, Feb. 20 *Perf. 11½*

2297 A745 50h *Bystrice Nad Pernstejnem* 22 8
2298 A745 50h *Kunstat* 22 8
2299 A745 50h *Rozmital Pod Tremsinem* 22 8
2300 A745 50h *Zlata Idka* 22 8

Theatrical Mask — A808

Slovak National Theater, Actors — A809

1980, Mar. 1

2301 A808 50h multi 22 8
2302 A809 1k multi 45 15

50th Jiraskuv Hronov Theatrical Ensemble Review; Slovak National Theater, Bratislava, 60th anniversary.

Mouse in Space, Satellite A810

Police Corps Banner, Emblem A811

Intercosmos: 1k, Weather map, satellite. 1.60k, Intersputnik television transmission. 4k, Camera, satellite. 5k, Czech satellite station, 1978 (horiz.). 10k, Intercosmos emblem (horiz.).

Perf. 11½x12, 12x11½

1980, Apr. 12

2303 A810 50h multi 22 8
2304 A810 1k multi 45 15
2305 A810 1.60k multi 80 30
2306 A810 4k multi 1.75 60
2307 A810 5k multi 2.25 75
Nos. 2303-2307 (5) 5.47 1.88

Souvenir Sheet

2308 A810 10k multi 4.75 4.50

Intercosmos cooperative space program. No. 2308 has multicolored margin showing emblems, flags of participating countries. Size: 75½x94mm.

1980, Apr. 17 *Perf. 11½*

2309 A811 50h multi 22 8

National Police Corps, 35th anniversary.

Lenin's 110th Birth Anniversary — A812

Design: No. 2311, Engel's 160th birth anniversary.

1980, Apr. 22

2310 A812 1k tan & brn 45 15
2311 A812 1k lt grn & brn 45 15

Old and Modern Prague, Czech Flag, Bouquet A813

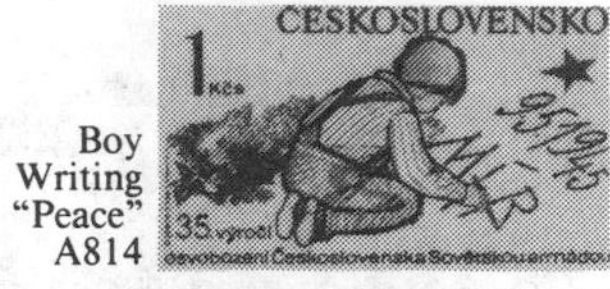
Boy Writing "Peace" A814

Pact Members' Flags, Dove — A815

Czech and Soviet Arms, Prague and Moscow Views A816

1980, May 6 *Perf. 12x11½*

2312 A813 50h multi 22 8
2313 A814 1k multi 45 15
2314 A815 1k multi 45 15
2315 A816 1k multi 45 15

Liberation by Soviet army, 35th anniv.; Soviet victory in WWII, 35th anniv.; Signing of Warsaw Pact (Bulgaria, Czechoslovakia, German Democratic Rep., Hungary, Poland, Romania, USSR), 25th anniv.; Czechoslovak-Soviet Treaty of Friendship, Cooperation and Mutual Aid, 10th anniv.

Souvenir Sheet

United Nations, 35th Anniversary — A817

1980, June 3 **Engr.** *Perf. 12*

2316 A817 4k sheet of 2 4.25 3.50

No. 2316 contains 2 stamps, marginal inscription and symbols of peace and destruction. Size: 111x165½mm.

Athletes Parading Banners in Strahov Stadium, Prague, Spartakiad Emblem — A818

Engraved and Photogravure

1980, June 3 *Perf. 12x11½*

2317 A818 50h *shown* 22 8
2318 A818 1k *Gymnast*, vert. 45 15

Spartakiad 1980, Prague, June 26-29.

Aechmea Fasciata — A819

Engraved and Photogravure

1980, Aug. 13 *Perf. 12*

2319 A819 50h *Gerbera Jamesonii* 22 8
2320 A819 1k *Aechmea fasciata* 45 30
2321 A819 2k *Strelitzia reginae* 90 50
2322 A819 4k *Paphiopedilum* 1.75 1.00

Olomouc and Bratislava Flower Shows.

Chad Girl, Embroidery — A820

Designs: Folktale character embroideries.

Engraved and Photogravure

1980, Sept. 24 *Perf. 11½x12*

2323 A820 50h *shown* 22 8
2324 A820 1k *Punch and dog* 45 15
2325 A820 2k *Dandy and Posy* 90 30
2326 A820 4k *Lion and moon* 1.75 60
2327 A820 5k *Wallachian dance* 2.25 75
Nos. 2323-2327 (5) 5.57 1.88

Prices of premium quality never hinged stamps will be in excess of catalogue price.

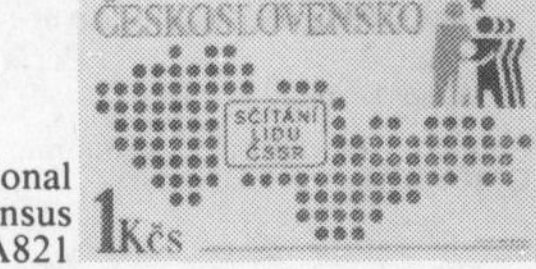
National Census A821

Engraved and Photogravure

1980, Sept. 24 *Perf. 12x11½*

2328 A821 1k multi 45 15

Prague Castle Type of 1971

Designs: 3k, Old Palace gateway. 4k, Armorial lion, 16th century.

1980, Oct. 28 *Perf. 12*

2329 A634 3k multi 1.50 75
2330 A634 4k multi 1.65 1.10

Sheets of 4.

Bratislava Type of 1977

Designs: 3k, View across the Danube, by J. Eder, 1810. 4k, The Old Royal Bridge, by J.A. Lantz, 1820.

1980, Oct. 28

2331 A760 3k multi 1.35 60
2332 A760 4k multi 1.80 90

10th Anniversary of Socialist Youth Federation — A822

1980, Nov. 9 *Perf. 12x11½*

2333 A822 50h multi 22 8

No. 2137 Overprinted in Red: 3. / MEZINARODNI VELETRH ZNAMEK / ESSEN '80

1980, Nov. 18

2334 A755 1.60k multi *20.00 20.00*

Czechoslovak Day/ ESSEN '80, 3rd International Stamp Exhibition, No. 2334 has overprinted red marginal inscription.

Art Type of 1967

Designs: 1k, Pavel Jozef Safarik, by Jozef B. Klemens. 2k, Peasant Revolt mosaic, Anna Podzemma. 3k, St. Lucia, 14th century statue. 4k, Waste Heaps, by Jan Zrzavy (horiz.). 5k, Labor, sculpture by Jan Stursa.

1980, Nov. 27 **Engr.** *Perf. 12*

2335 A565 1k multi 50 30
2336 A565 2k multi 1.00 60
2337 A565 3k multi 1.50 90
2338 A565 4k multi 2.00 1.25
2339 A565 5k multi 2.50 1.50
Nos. 2335-2339 (5) 7.50 4.55

Stamp Day — A823

Engraved and Photogravure

1980, Dec. 18 *Perf. 11½x12*

2340 A823 1k multi 45 15

7th Five-year Plan, 1981-1985 A824

Engraved and Photogravure

1981, Jan. 1 *Perf. 11½*

2341 A824 50h multi 22 8

International Year of the Disabled A825

1981, Feb. 24
2342 A825 1k multi 45 15

Landau, 1800 A826

1981, Feb. 25 *Perf. 12x11½*
2343 A826 50h shown 22 8
2344 A826 1k Mail coach, 1830 45 15
2345 A826 3.60k Mail sled, 1840 1.65 55
2346 A826 5k 4-horse mail coach, 1860 2.25 75
2347 A826 7k Open carriage, 1840 3.25 1.10
a. Sheet of 4 15.00 13.00
Nos. 2343-2347 (5) 7.82 2.63

WIPA '81 Intl. Philatelic Exhibition, Vienna, Austria, May 22-31. No. 2347a has multicolored margin showing exhibition emblems. Size: 150x106mm. Issued May 10.

Wolfgang Amadeus Mozart — A827

Famous Men: No. 2348, Joesph Hlavka (1831-1908). No. 2349, Juraj Hronec (1881-1959). No. 2350, Jan Sverma (1901-1944). No. 2351, Mikulas Schneider-Trnavsky (1881-1958). No. 2352, B. Bolzano (1781-1848). No. 2353, Dimitri Shostakovich (1906-1975), composer. No. 2354, George Bernard Shaw (1856-1950), playwright.

Engraved and Photogravure
1981, Mar. 10 *Perf. 11½*
2348 A827 50h multi 22 8
2349 A827 50h multi 22 8
2350 A827 50h multi 22 8
2351 A827 50h multi 22 8
2352 A827 1k multi 45 15
2353 A827 1k multi 45 15
2354 A827 1k multi 45 15
2355 A827 1k multi 45 15
Nos. 2348-2355 (8) 2.68 92

Souvenir Sheet

Yuri Gagarin A828

1981, Apr. 5 *Perf. 12*
2356 Sheet of 2 6.00 3.50
a. A828 6k multi 2.70 1.75

20th anniversary of first manned space flight. Margin shows satellites orbiting earth, Intercosmos emblem and flags. Size: 108½x166mm.

Scott's editorial staff cannot undertake to identify, authenticate or appraise stamps and postal markings.

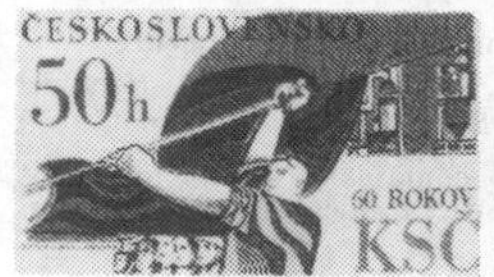
Workers and Banner A829

1981, Apr. 6 *Perf. 12x11½*
2357 A829 50h shown 22 8
2358 A829 1k Hands holding banner 45 15
2359 A829 4k Worker holding banner, vert. 1.75 60

Czechoslovakian Communist Party, 60th anniversary.

Congress Emblem, View of Prague A830

1981, Apr. 6
2360 A830 50h shown 22 8
2361 A830 1k Bratislava 45 15

16th Communist Party Congress.

Agriculture Museum, 90th Anniv. A831

Natl. Assembly Elections A832

1981, May 14 *Perf. 11½x12*
2362 A831 1k multi 45 15

1981, June 1
2363 A832 50h multi 22 8

Bratislava Type of 1977

Designs: 3k, Bratislava Castle, by G.B. Probst, 1760. 4k, Grassalkovic Palace, by C. Bschor, 1815.

1981, June 10 *Perf. 12*
2364 A760 3k multi 1.10 60
2365 A760 4k multi 1.50 90

Uran and Red October Hotels A833

Successes of Socialist Achievements Exhibition: 1k, Brno-Bratislava Highway, Jihlava. 2k, Nuclear power station, Jaslovske Bohunice.

1981, June 10 *Perf. 12x11½*
2366 A833 80h multi 35 12
2367 A833 1k multi 45 15
2368 A833 2k multi 90 30

Border Defense Units, 30th Anniv. A834

Civil Defense, 30th Anniv. A835

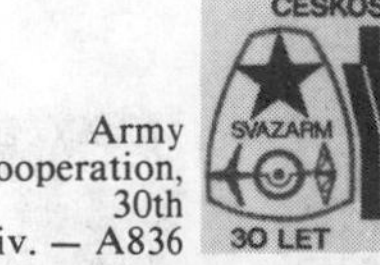
Army Cooperation, 30th Anniv. — A836

Rysy Youth Mountain Climbing Contest — A837

Engraved and Photogravure
1981, July 11 *Perf. 11½*
2369 A834 40h multi 15 6
2370 A835 50h multi 20 8
2371 A836 1k multi 40 15
2372 A837 3.60k multi 1.50 55

30th Natl. Festival of Amateur Puppet Ensembles — A838

Engraved and Photogravure
1981, July 2 *Perf. 11½*
2373 A838 2k Punch and Devil 75 30

Souvenir Sheet

Guernica, by Pablo Picasso — A839

1981, July 2 **Engr.** *Perf. 11½x12*
2374 A839 10k multi 4.75 3.75

Picasso's birth centenary; 45th anniv. of Intl. Brigades in Spain. No. 2374 has multicolored margin showing Picasso drawings. Size: 90x76mm.

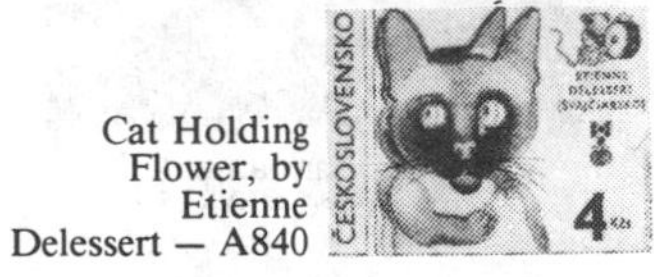
Cat Holding Flower, by Etienne Delessert — A840

8th Biennial Exhibition of Children's Book Illustrations (Designs by): 50h, Albin Brunovsky (vert.). 1k, Adolf Born. 2k, Vive Tolli. 10k, Suekichi Akaba.

Engraved and Photogravure
1981, Sept. 5 *Perf. 11½*
2375 A840 50h multi 22 8
2376 A840 1k multi 45 20
2377 A840 2k multi 90 35
2378 A840 4k multi 1.80 75
2379 A840 10k multi 4.50 1.60
Nos. 2375-2379 (5) 7.87 2.98

Prague Zoo, 50th Anniv. — A841

Engraved and Photogravure
1981, Sept. 28 *Perf. 11½x12*
2380 A841 50h Gorillas 22 8
2381 A841 1k Lions 45 20
2382 A841 7k Przewalski's horses 3.15 1.25

Anti-smoking Campaign A842

Engraved and Photogravure
1981, Oct. 27 *Perf. 12*
2383 A842 4k multi 1.80 90

No. 2383 se-tenant with label.

Prague Castle Art Type of 1971

Designs: 3k, Carved dragon, Palais Lobkovitz, 16th cent. 4k, St. Vitus Cathedral, by J. Sember and G. Dobler, 19th cent.

1981, Oct. 28
2384 A634 3k multi 1.80 90
2385 A634 4k multi 1.80 1.25

Sheets of 4.

Art Type of 1967

Designs: 1k, View of Prague, by Vaclav Hollar (1607-1677). 2k, Czechoslovak Academy medallion, engraved by Otakar Spaniel (1881-1955). 3k, Jihoceska Vysivka, by Zdenek Sklenar (b. 1910). 4k, Still Life, by A.M. Gerasimov (1881-1963). 5k, Standing Woman, by Pablo Picasso (1881-1973).

1981, Nov. 27 **Engr.** *Perf. 12*
2386 A565 1k multi 45 25
2387 A565 2k multi 90 50
2388 A565 3k multi 1.35 80
2389 A565 4k multi 1.80 1.25
2390 A565 5k multi 2.50 1.75
a. Souvenir sheet of 4 10.50 9.50
Nos. 2386-2390 (5) 7.00 4.55

Stamp Day — A843

Engraved and Photogravure
1981, Dec. 18 *Perf. 11½x12*
2391 A843 1k Engraver Edward Karel 45 15

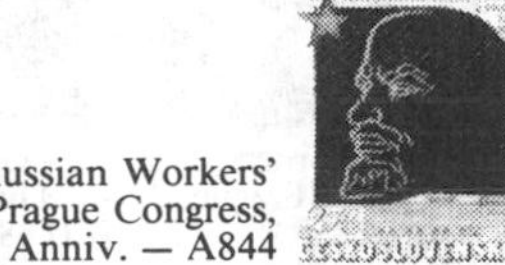
Russian Workers' Party, Prague Congress, 70th Anniv. — A844

Engraved and Photogravure
1982, Jan. 18 *Perf. 12*
2392 A844 2k Lenin 90 40
a. Sheet of 4 3.75 2.25

1982 World Cup Soccer A845

Designs: Various soccer players.

1982, Jan. 29 *Perf. 12x11½*
2393 A845 1k multi 45 18
2394 A845 3.60k multi 1.65 60
2395 A845 4k multi 1.80 70

10th World Trade Union Congress, Havana
A846

Arms of Hrob
A847

1982, Feb. 10 ***Perf. 11½***
2396 A846 1k multi 45 18

1982, Feb. 10 ***Perf. 12x11½***

Arms of various cities.

2397 A847 50h shown 22 8
2398 A847 50h Nove Mesto Nad Metuji 22 8
2399 A847 50h Trencin 22 8
2400 A847 50h Mlada Boleslav 22 8

See Nos. 2499-2502, 2542-2544, 2595-2597.

50th Anniv. of the Great Strike at Most — A848

Engraved and Photogravure

1982, Mar. 23 ***Perf. 11½***
2401 A848 1k multi 45 18

60th Intl. Railway Union Congress
A849

Engraved and Photogravure

1982, Mar. 23 ***Perf. 12x11½***
2402 A849 6k Steam locomotive, 1922, electric, 1982 2.75 1.25

10th Workers' Congress, Prague
A850

George Dimitrov (1882-1947) First Bulgarian Prime Minister
A851

1982, Apr. 15
2403 A850 1k multi 40 15

1982, May 1
2404 A851 50h multi 22 8

The Muse Euterpe Playing a Flute, by Crispin de Passe (1565-1637)
A852

10th Lidice Intl. Children's Drawing Contest
A853

Engravings: 50h, The Lute Player, by Jacob de Gheyn (1565-1629). 1k, Woman Flautist, by Adriaen Collaert (1560-1618). 2k, Musicians in a Hostel, by Rembrandt (1606-1669). 3k, Hurdygurdy Player, by Jacques Callot (1594-1635).

1982, May 18 ***Perf. 11½x12***
2405 A852 40h multi 18 12
2406 A852 50h multi 22 18
2407 A852 1k multi 45 35
2408 A852 2k multi 90 70
2409 A852 3k multi 1.35 90
Nos. 2405-2409 (5) 3.10 2.25

1982, May 18
2410 A853 2k multi 90 80

Issued in sheets of 6.

40th Anniv. of Destruction of Lidice and Lezaky — A854

1982, June 4 ***Perf. 11½***
2411 A854 1k Girl, rose 45 20
2412 A854 1k Hands, barbed wire 45 20

U.N. Disarmament Conference — A855

1982, June 4 ***Perf. 12***
2413 Sheet of 2 6.75 6.00
a. A855 6k Woman holding doves 3.25 2.75

Souvenir Sheet

2nd UN Conference on Peaceful Uses of Outer Space, Vienna, Aug. 9-21 — A856

Foreign postal stationery (stamped envelopes, postal cards and air letter sheets) lies beyond the scope of this Catalogue, which is limited to adhesive postage stamps.

Engraved and Photogravure

1982, Aug. 9 ***Perf. 12***
2414 A856 5k Sheet of 2 6.75 6.00

No. 2414 contains 2 stamps, marginal inscription, space themes. Size: 165x108mm.

Krivoklat Castle
A857

1982, Aug. 31 ***Perf. 12x11½***
2415 A857 50h shown 22 8
2416 A857 1k Statues (Krivoklat) 45 15
2417 A857 2k Nitra Castle 90 30
2418 A857 3k Pottery, lock (Nitra) 1.35 45
a. Souvenir Sheet of 4 4.00 3.50

No. 2418a contains Nos. 2415-2418. Size: 106x126mm.

50th Anniv. of Zizkov Hill Natl. Monument — A858

1982, Sept. 16
2419 A858 1k multi 45 18

Prague Castle Art Type of 1971

Designs: 3k, St. George and the Dragon, 1373. 4k, Tomb of King Vratislav I, 10th cent.

1982, Sept. 28 ***Perf. 12***
2420 A634 3k multi 1.35 60
2421 A634 4k multi 1.80 85

Sheets of 4.

Bratislava Type of 1977

Designs: 3k, Paddle steamer, Parnik, 1818. 4k, View from Bridge, 19th cent.

1982, Sept. 29
2422 A760 3k multi 1.35 60
2423 A760 4k multi 1.80 85

European Danube Commission — A859

1982, Sept. 29 ***Perf. 11½x12***
2424 A859 3k Steamer, Bratislava Bridge 1.35 60
a. Souvenir sheet of 4 7.00 6.00
2425 A859 3.60k Ferry, Budapest 1.65 75
a. Souvenir sheet of 4 7.25 6.00

Nos. 2424a-2425a have multicolored margins showing flags and river map. Size: 129x127mm.

16th Communist Party Congress — A860

1982, Oct. 28 ***Perf. 12x11½***
2426 A860 20h Agriculture 10 5
2427 A860 1k Industry 45 18
2428 A860 3k Engineering 1.35 60

30th Anniv. of Academy of Sciences — A861

1982, Oct. 29 ***Perf. 11½***
2429 A861 6k Emblem 2.50 1.25

65th Anniv. of October Revolution — A862

Design: 1k, 60th anniv. of USSR.

1982, Nov. 7 ***Perf. 12x11½***
2430 A862 50h multi 22 12
2431 A862 1k multi 45 18

Jaroslav Hasek, Writer, Sculpture by Josef Malejovsky — A863

Sculptures: 2k, Jan Zrzavy, freedom fighter, by Jan Simota. 4.40k, Leos Janacek, composer, by Milos Axman. 6k, Martin Kukucin, freedom fighter, by Jan Kulich. 7k, Peaceful Work, by Rudolf Pribis.

Engraved and Photogravure

1982, Nov. 26 ***Perf. 11½x12***
2432 A863 1k multi 45 15
2433 A863 2k multi 90 30
2434 A863 4.40k multi 2.00 68
2435 A863 6k multi 2.75 90
2436 A863 7k multi 3.25 1.05
Nos. 2432-2436 (5) 9.35 3.08

Art Type of 1967

Paintings: 1k, Revolution in Spain, by Josef Sima (1891-1971). 2k, Woman Dressing, by Rudolf Kremlicka (1886-1932). 3k, The Girl Bride, by Dezider Milly (1906-1971). 4k, Performers, by Jan Zelibsky (b. 1907). 5k, The Complaint of the Birds, by Emil Filla (1882-1953).

1982, Nov. 27 ***Perf. 12***
2437 A565 1k multi 50 15
2438 A565 2k multi 1.00 30
2439 A565 3k multi 1.50 45
2440 A565 4k multi 2.00 60
2441 A565 5k multi 2.50 75
Nos. 2437-2441 (5) 7.50 2.25

Stamp Day — A864

Engraved and Photogravure

1982, Dec. 8 ***Perf. 11½***
2442 A864 1k Engraver Jaroslav Goldschmied (1890-1977) 40 15

Pres. Gustav Husak, 70th Birthday — A865

1983, Jan. 10 Engr. *Perf. 12x11½*
2443 A865 50h dk bl 22 8

Jaroslav Hasek (1882-1923), Writer — A866

Designs: 1k, Julius Fucik (1903-1943), antifascist martyr. 2k, Martin Luther (1483-1546). 5k, Johannes Brahms (1833-1897), composer.

Engraved and Photogravure
1983, Feb. 24
2444 A866 50h multi 22 8
2445 A866 1k multi 45 15
2446 A866 2k multi 90 30
a. Souvenir sheet of 4 *18.00 5.00*
2447 A866 5k multi 2.25 75

Nordposta '83 Intl. Stamp Exhibition, Hamburg. Margin shows UNESCO emblem, Prague and Hamburg arms. Size: 110x80mm.

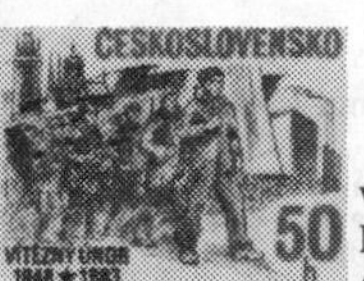

Workers Marching A867

Family — A868

1983, Feb. 25 *Perf. 11½*
2448 A867 50h multi 22 8
2449 A868 1k multi 45 15

35th anniv. of "Victorious February" (50h), and Natl. Front (1k).

World Communications Year — A869

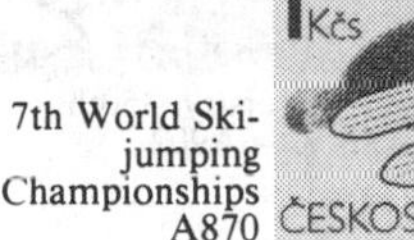

7th World Ski-jumping Championships A870

Engraved and Photogravure
Perf. 11½, 12x11½ (2k)
1983, Mar. 16
2450 A869 40h multi 18 5
2451 A869 1k multi 45 15
2452 A869 2k multi 90 30
2453 A869 3.60k multi 1.65 55

Various wave patterns. 2k, 40x23mm; 3.60k, 49x19mm.

1983, Mar. 16 *Perf. 11½*
2454 A870 1k multi 40 15

Souvenir Sheet

5th Anniv. of Czechoslovak-USSR Intercosmos Cooperative Space Program — A871

1983, Apr. 12 *Perf. 12*
2455 A871 10k Sheet of 2 10.00 3.00

Size: 109x166mm.

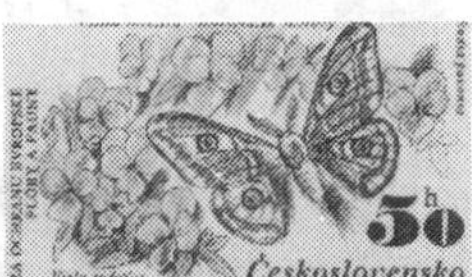

Protected Species — A872

1983, Apr. 28 *Perf. 12x11½*
2456 A872 50h Butterfly, violets 20 8
2457 A872 1k Water lilies, frog 40 15
2458 A872 2k Pine cones, crossbill 80 30
2459 A872 3.60k Herons 1.50 55
2460 A872 5k Gentians, lynx 4.00 1.50
2461 A872 7k Stag 5.00 1.80
Nos. 2456-2461 (6) 11.90 4.38

30th Anniv. of Czechoslovak-Soviet Defense Treaty — A873

Soviet Marshals.

Engraved and Photogravure
1983, May 5 *Perf. 11½*
2462 A873 50h Ivan S. Konev 22 8
2463 A873 1k Andrei I. Sheremenko 45 15
2464 A873 2k Rodion J. Malinovsky 90 30

World Peace and Life Congress, Prague — A874

1983, July 13 *Perf. 12*
2465 A874 2k multi 80 30
a. Souvenir sheet of 4 4.00

No. 2465a has blue control number. Size: 108x83mm.

Emperor Rudolf II by Adrian De Vries (1560-1626) A875

Art treasures of the Prague Castle: 5k, Kinetic relief, Timepiece, Rudolf Svoboda.

Engraved and Photogravure
1983, Aug. 25 *Perf. 11½*
2466 A875 4k multi 1.80 60
2467 A875 5k multi 2.25 75

See Nos. 2518-2519, 2610-2611.

9th Biennial of Illustrations for Children and Youth — A876

Illustrators: 50h, Oleg K. Zotov, USSR. 1k, Zbigniew Rychlicki, Poland. 4k, Lisbeth Zwerger, Austria. 7k, Antonio Dominques, Angola.

Engraved and Photogravure
1983, Sept. 9 *Perf. 11½*
2468 A876 50h multi 22 8
2469 A876 1k multi 45 15
2470 A876 4k multi 1.80 60
2471 A876 7k multi 3.15 1.05
a. Souvenir sheet of 4 5.65 1.90

No. 2471a contains Nos. 2468-2471. Margin shows illustrations by Susan Jeffers, USA and Roald Als, Denmark. Size: 115x134mm.

World Communications Year — A877

Emblems and aircraft.

Engraved and Photogravure
1983, Sept. 30 *Perf. 11½*
2472 A877 50h red & blk 22 8
2473 A877 1k red & blk 45 15
2474 A877 4k red & blk 1.80 60

60th Anniv. of the Czechoslovak Airlines.

16th Party Congress Achievements — A878

Engraved and Photogravure
1983, Oct. 20 *Perf. 12x11½*
2475 A878 50h Civil engineering construction 22 8
2476 A878 1k Chemical industry 45 15
2477 A878 3k Health services 1.35 45

Bratislava Type of 1977

Designs: 3k, Two sculptures, Viktor Tilgner (1844-96). 4k, Mirbachov Palace, 1939, by Julius Schubert (1888-1947).

1983, Oct. 28 *Perf. 12*
2478 A760 3k multi 1.35 45
2479 A760 4k multi 1.80 60

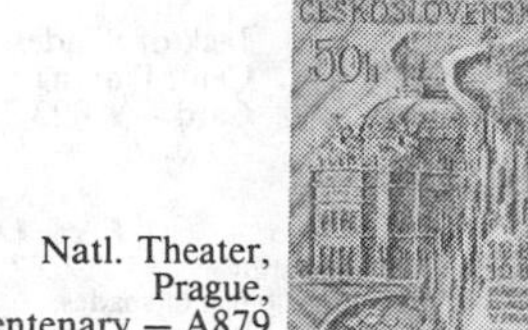

Natl. Theater, Prague, Centenary — A879

1983, Nov. 8 Engr. *Perf. 11½*
2480 A879 50h Natl. Theater building 22 8
2481 A879 2k State Theater, Natl. Theater 90 30

Messenger of Mourning, by Mikolas Ales — A880

Designs: 2k, Genius, theater curtain by Vojtech Hynais (1854-1925). 3k, Music, Lyric drawings by Frantisek Zenisek (1849-1916). 4k, Symbolic figure of Prague, by Vaclav Brozik (1851-1901). 5k, Hradcany Castle, by Julius Marak (1832-1899).

1983, Nov. 18 Engr.
2482 A880 1k multi 60 15
2483 A880 2k multi 1.25 30
2484 A880 3k multi 1.75 45
2485 A880 4k multi 2.25 60
2486 A880 5k multi 3.00 75
Nos. 2482-2486 (5) 8.85 2.25

Warrior with Sword and Shield, Engraving, 17th Cent. — A881

Engravings of Costumes: 50h, Bodyguard of Rudolf II, by Jacob de Gheyn (1565-1629). 1k, Lady with Lace Collar, by Jacques Callot (1592-1635). 4k, Lady, by Vaclav Hollar (1607-77). 5k, Man, by Antoine Watteau (1684-1721).

Engraved and Photogravure
1983, Dec. 2 *Perf. 11½x12*
2487 A881 40h multi 20 6
2488 A881 50h multi 25 8
2489 A881 1k multi 50 15
2490 A881 4k multi 2.00 60
2491 A881 5k multi 2.50 75
Nos. 2487-2491 (5) 5.45 1.64

Stamp Day — A882

1983, Dec. 18
2492 A882 1k Karl Seizinger (1889-1978), #114 40 15

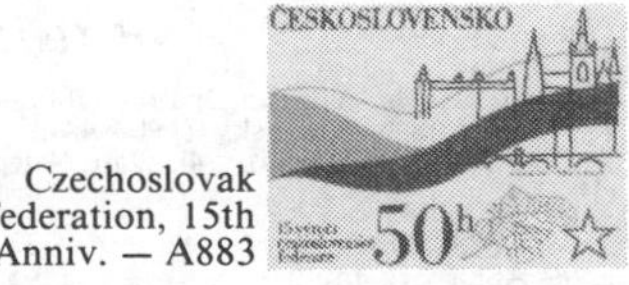

Czechoslovak Federation, 15th Anniv. — A883

1984, Jan. 1 *Perf. 11½*
2493 A883 50h Bratislava, Prague Castles 28 8

35th Anniv. of COMECON A884

1984, Jan. 23

2494 A884 1k Headquarters, Moscow 45 15

1984 Winter Olympics A885

1984, Feb. 7 *Perf. 12x11½*

2495 A885 2k Cross-country skiing 90 30
2496 A885 3k Hockey 1.35 45
a. Souvenir sheet of 4 5.50 5.50
2497 A885 5k Biathlon 2.25 75

No. 2496a contains 4 No. 2496. Size: 110x100m.

Intl. Olympic Committee, 90th Anniv. — A886

Engraved and Photogravure

1984, Feb. 7 *Perf. 11½x12*

2498 A886 7k Rings, runners, torch 3.25 1.05

City Arms Type of 1982

1984, Mar. 1 *Perf. 12x11½*

2499 A847 50h Kutna Hora 22 8
2500 A847 50h Turnov 22 8
2501 A847 1k Martin 45 15
2502 A847 1k Milevsko 45 15

Intercosmos Space Program A887

Resistance Heroes A888

Various satellites. Nos. 2503-2507 se-tenant with labels showing flags.

Engraved and Photogravure

1984, Apr. 12 *Perf. 11½x12*

2503 A887 50h multi 20 8
2504 A887 1k multi 40 15
2505 A887 2k multi 80 30
2506 A887 4k multi 1.65 60
2507 A887 5k multi 3.00 75
Nos. 2503-2507 (5) 6.05 1.88

1984, May 9 *Perf. 11x11½*

Designs: 50h, Vendelin Opatrny (1908-44). 1k, Ladislav Novomesky (1904-44). 2k, Rudolf Jasiok (1919-44). 4k, Jan Nalepka (1912-43).

2508 A888 50h multi 22 8
2509 A888 1k multi 45 15
2510 A888 2k multi 90 30
2511 A888 4k multi 1.80 60

Music Year — A889

1984, May 11 *Perf. 11½*

2512 A889 50h Instruments 22 8
2513 A889 1k Organ pipes, vert. 45 15

Bratislava Type of 1977

Designs: 3k, Vintners' Guild arms, 19th cent. 4k, View of Bratislava (painting commemorating shooting competition, 1827).

Engraved and Photogravure

1984, June 1 *Perf. 12*

2514 A760 3k multi 95 32
2515 A760 4k multi 1.25 42

Issued in sheetlets of 4.

Central Telecommunications Building, Bratislava — A890

1984, June 1 *Perf. 11½*

2516 A890 2k multi 62 20

1984 UPU Congress — A891

1984, June 12 *Perf. 12*

2517 A891 5k UPU emblem, dove, globe 2.00 65

Issued in sheetlets of 4 with and without Philatelic Salon text.

Prague Castle Type of 1983

Designs: 3k, Crowing rooster, St. Vitus Cathedral, 19th cent. 4k, King David from the Roundnice, Book of Psalms illuminated manuscript, Bohemia, 15th cent.

Engraved and Photogravure

1984, Aug. 9 *Perf. 12*

2518 A875 3k multi 90 30
2519 A875 4k multi 1.25 42

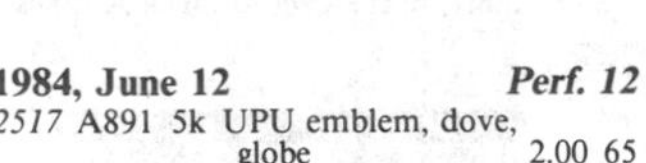

Jack of Spades, 16th Cent. Playing Card — A893

1984, Aug. 28 *Perf. 11½x12*

2520 A893 50h shown 15 5
2521 A893 1k Queen of spades, 17th cent. 30 10
2522 A893 2k 9 of hearts, 18th cent. 60 20
2523 A893 3k Jack of clubs, 18th cent. 90 30
2524 A893 5k King of hearts, 19th cent. 1.50 50
Nos. 2520-2524 (5) 3.45 1.15

Slovak Natl. Uprising, 40th Anniv. — A894

Engraved and Photogravure

1984, Aug. 29 *Perf. 12x11½*

2525 A894 50h Family, factories, flowers 15 5

Battle of Dukla Pass (Carpathians), 40th Anniv. — A895

1984, Sept. 8 *Perf. 11½x12*

2526 A895 2k Soldiers, flag 60 20

1984 Summer Olympics A896

1984, Sept. 9 *Perf. 12x11½*

2527 A896 1k Pole vault 30 10
2528 A896 2k Bicycling 60 20
2529 A896 3k Rowing 90 30
2530 A896 5k Weight lifting 1.50 50
a. Souvenir sheet of 4 4.00 1.40

No. 2530a contains Nos. 2527-2530; margin shows Olympic rings. Size: 108x96mm.

16th Party Congress Goals and Projects A897

Engraved and Photogravure

1984, Oct. 28 *Perf. 12x11½*

2531 A897 1k Communications 30 10
2532 A897 2k Transportation 60 20
2533 A897 3k Transgas pipeline 90 30
a. Souvenir sheet of 3 3.50 1.65

No. 2533a contains 3 Nos. 2533; multicolored margin shows map of Trans-European pipeline, flags. Size: 158x106mm.

Art Type of 1967

Paintings: 1k, The Milevsky River, by Karel Stehlik (b. 1912). 2k, Under the Trees, by Viktor Barvitius (1834-1902). 3k, Landscape with Flowers, by Zolo Palugyay (1898-1935). 4k, King in Palace, Visehrad Codex miniature, 1085. 5k, View of Kokorin Castles, by Antonin Manes. Nos. 2534-2537 horiz.; issued in sheets of 4.

1984, Nov. 16 *Perf. 11½*

2534 A565 1k multi 30 10
2535 A565 2k multi 60 20
2536 A565 3k multi 90 30
2537 A565 4k multi 1.20 40
2538 A565 5k multi 1.50 50
Nos. 2534-2538 (5) 4.50 1.50

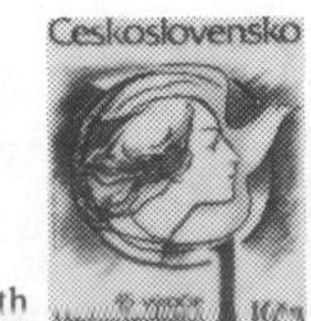

Students' Intl., 45th Anniv. — A898

1984, Nov. 17

2539 A898 1k Head, dove 30 10

Birth Centenary, Antonin Zapotocky — A899

Engraved and Photogravure

1984, Dec. 18 *Perf. 11½*

2540 A899 50h multi 15 8

Stamp Day — A900

Engraved and Photogravure

1984, Dec. 18 *Perf. 11½x12*

2541 A900 1k Engraver Bohumil Heinz (1894-1940) 30 10

City Arms Type of 1982

Engraved and Photogravure

1985, Feb. 5 *Perf. 12x11½*

2542 A847 50h Kamyk nad Vltavou 15 8
2543 A847 50h Havirov 15 8
2544 A847 50h Trnava 15 8

University of Applied Arts, Prague, Centenary — A901

Engraved and Photogravure

1985, Feb. 6 *Perf. 11½x12*

2545 A901 3k Art and Pleasure, sculpture 90 45

Trnava University, 350th Anniv. — A902

Engraved and Photogravure

1985, Feb. 6 *Perf. 11½x12*

2546 A902 2k Town of Trnava 60 30

Military Museum Exposition — A903

Engraved and Photogravure

1985, Feb. 7 *Perf. 11½x12, 12x11½*

2547 A903 50h Armor, crossbow, vert. 15 8
2548 A903 1k Medals, vert. 30 15
2549 A903 2k Biplane, spacecraft 60 30

Vladimir I. Lenin (1870-1924), 1st Chairman of Russia — A904

1985, Mar. 15 Engr. *Perf. 12*
2550 A904 2k multi 60 30

No. 2550 printed in sheets of 6.

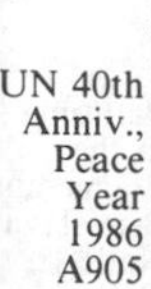

UN 40th Anniv., Peace Year 1986 A905

1985, Mar. 15
2551 A905 6k UN, Peace Year emblems 3.00 1.75

Kosice Govt. Plan, Apr. 5, 1945 — A906

Engraved and Photogravure

1985, Apr. 5 *Perf. 11½*
2552 A906 4k Natl. arms, twig, crowd 1.20 60

Natl. Security Forces, 40th Anniv. — A907

1985, Apr. 5
2553 A907 50h Natl. arms, flag, soldiers 15 8

Halley's Comet, INTERCOSMOS Project Vega — A908

Design: Emblem, space platform, interstellar map, intercept data.

1985, Apr. 12 *Perf. 12x11½*
2554 A908 5k multi 2.25 1.50
a. Souvenir sheet of 2 4.50 3.50

Project Vega, a joint effort of the USSR, France, German Democratic Republic, Austria, Poland, Bulgaria and CSSR, was for the geophysical study of Halley's Comet, Dec. 1984-Mar. 1986. No. 2554a has multicolored margin picturing orbit and intercept data. Size: 106x98mm.

European Ice Hockey Championships, Prague, Apr. 17-May 3 — A909

1985, Apr. 13
2555 A909 1k Hockey players, emblem 30 15

No. 2555 Ovptd. "CSSR MISTREM SVETA" in Violet-Blue

1985, May 31 *Perf. 12x11½*
2556 A909 1k multi 30 15

Natl. Chess Org., 80th Anniv. — A910

1985, Apr. 13 *Perf. 11½*
2557 A910 6k Emblem, game board, chessmen 1.75 90

Anniversaries — A911

1985, May 5 *Perf. 11½x12*
2558 A911 1k May Uprising, 1945 30 15
2559 A911 1k Soviet Army in CSSR, 1945 30 15
2560 A911 1k Warsaw Treaty, 1950 30 15
2561 A911 1k Czech-Soviet Treaty, 1970 30 15

Spartakiad '85, Strahov Stadium, Prague, June 27 — A912

Designs: 50h, Gymnasts warming up with rackets and balls. 1k, Rhythmic gymnastics floor exercise, Prague Castle.

1985, June 3 *Perf. 11½, 11½x12*
2562 A912 50h multi 15 8

Size: 53x22mm.

2563 A912 1k multi 30 15

WW II Anti-Fascist Political Art — A913

Drawings and caricatures: 50h, Fire, and From the Concentration Camp, by Joseph Capek (1887-1945). 2k, The Conference on Disarmament in Geneva, 1927 and The Prophecy of Three Parrots, 1933, by Frantisek Bidlo (1895-1945). 4k, The Unknown Warrior to Order, 1936, and The Almost Peaceful Dove, 1937, by Antonin Pelc (1895-1967).

1985, June 4 *Perf. 12x11½*
2564 A913 50h multi 15 8
2565 A913 2k multi 60 30
2566 A913 4k multi 1.20 60

Helsinki Conference on European Security and Cooperation, 10th Anniv. — A914

Engraved and Photogravure

1985, July 1 *Perf. 12x11½*
2567 A914 7k multi 2.00 1.00
a. Souvenir sheet of 4 8.00 8.00

No. 2567a has multicolored inscribed margin picturing doves, mother and child embracing, Finlandia Hall and map of Europe. Size: 107x136mm.

12th World Youth Festival, Moscow A915

1985, July 2
2568 A915 1k Kremlin, youths 28 14

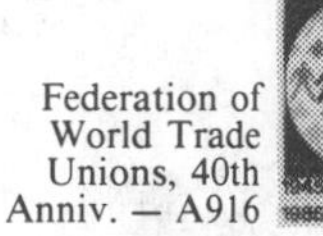

Federation of World Trade Unions, 40th Anniv. — A916

1985, Sept. 3 *Perf. 11½*
2569 A916 50h multi 14 8

Bratislava Type of 1977

Designs: 3k, Castle and river, lace embroidery by Elena Holeczyova (1906-1983). 4k, Pottery cups and mugs, 1600-1500 B.C.

1985, Sept. 4 Engr. *Perf. 12*
2570 A760 3k multi 85 42
2571 A760 4k multi 1.15 58

Issued in sheets of 4.

10th Biennial of Illustrations — A918

Children's book illustrations: 1k, Rocking Horse, by Kveta Pacovska, USSR. 2k, Fairies, by Gennadij Spirin, USSR. 3k, Butterfly and Girl, by Kaarina Kaila, Finland. 4k, Boy and Animals, by Erick Ingraham, USA.

Engraved and Photogravure

1985, Sept. 5 *Perf. 11½*
2572 A918 1k multi 28 14
2573 A918 2k multi 58 30
2574 A918 3k multi 85 42
2575 A918 4k multi 1.15 58
a. Souvenir Sheet of 4, #2572-2575

No. 2575a has black and red decorative margin inscribed in six languages and picturing the BIB '85 emblem and Playing Cards, by Dusan Kallay, Czech. Size: 95x129mm.

5-Year Development Plan — A919

1985, Oct. 28 *Perf. 12x11½*
2576 A919 50h Construction machinery 14 8
2577 A919 1k Prague subway, map 28 14
2578 A919 2k Modern textile spinning 58 30

16th Communist Party Congress goals.

Prague Castle — A920

Engraved, Engraved and Photogravure (3k)

1985, Oct. 28 *Perf. 12*
2579 A920 2k Presidential Palace Gate, 1768 58 30
2580 A920 3k St. Vitus' Cathedral 85 42

Nos. 2579-2580 each issued in sheets of 6.

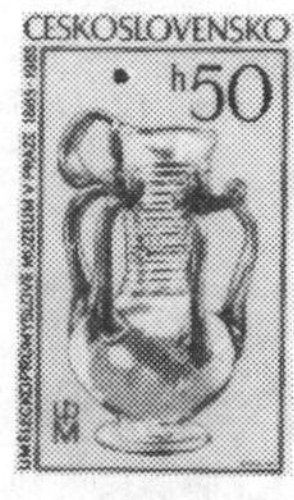

Arts and Crafts Museum, Prague, Cent. — A921

Glassware: 50h, Pitcher, Near East, 4th cent. 1k, Venetian pitcher, 16th cent. 2k, Bohemian goblet, c. 1720. 4k, Harrachov Bohemian vase, 18th cent. 6k, Jablonec Bohemian vase, c. 1900.

Engraved and Photogravure

1985, Nov. 23 *Perf. 11½x12*
2581 A921 50h multi 14 8
2582 A921 1k multi 28 14
2583 A921 2k multi 58 30
2584 A921 4k multi 1.15 58
2585 A921 6k multi 1.75 85
Nos. 2581-2585 (5) 3.90 1.95

Art Type of 1967

Designs: 1k, Young Woman in a Blue Gown, by Jozef Ginovsky (1800-1857). 2k, Lenin on the Charles Bridge, Prague, 1952, by Martin Sladky (b. 1920). 3k, Avenue of Poplars, 1935, by Vaclav Rabas (1885-1954). 4k, The Martyrom of St. Dorothea, 1516, by Hans Baldung Grien (c. 1484-1545). 5k, Portrait of Jasper Schade van Westrum, 1645, by Frans Hals (c. 1581-1666).

1985, Nov. 27 Engr. *Perf. 12*
2586 A565 1k multi 28 14
2587 A565 2k multi 58 30
2588 A565 3k multi 85 42
2589 A565 4k multi 1.15 58
2590 A565 5k multi 1.40 70
Nos. 2586-2590 (5) 4.26 2.14

Nos. 2586-2590 each issued in sheets of 4.

Bohdan Roule (1921-1960), Engraver — A922

Engraved and Photogravure

1985, Dec. 18 *Perf. 11½x12*
2591 A922 1k multi 28 14

Stamp Day 1985.

Intl. Peace Year — A923

1986, Jan. 2
2592 A923 1k multi 28 14

Philharmonic Orchestra, 90th Anniv. — A924

EXPO '86, Vancouver — A925

1986, Jan. 2 *Perf. 11½*
2593 A924 1k Victory Statute, Prague 28 14

1986, Jan. 23 *Perf. 11½*

Design: Z 50 LS monoplane, Cenyerth Prague-Kladno locomotive, Sahara Desert rock drawing, 5th-6th cent. B.C.

2594 A925 4k multi 1.15 58

City Arms Type of 1982

1986, Feb. 10 *Perf. 12x11½*
2595 A847 50h Myjava 14 8
2596 A847 50h Vodnany 14 8
2597 A847 50h Zamberk 14 8

17th Natl. Communist Party Congress, Prague, Mar. 24 — A926

Engraved and Photogravure

1986, Mar. 20 *Perf. 11½*
2598 A926 50h shown 16 8
2599 A926 1k Industry 32 16

Natl. Communist Party, 65th Anniv. — A927

1986, Mar. 20 *Perf. 12x11½*
2600 A927 50h Star, man, woman 16 8
2601 A927 1k Hammer, sickle, laborers 32 16

Natl. Front Election Program A928

1986, Mar. 28
2602 A928 50h multi 16 8

Karlovy Vary Intl. Film Festival, 25th Anniv. — A929

1986, Apr. 3 *Perf. 11½*
2603 A929 1k multi 32 16

Spring of Prague Music Festival — A930

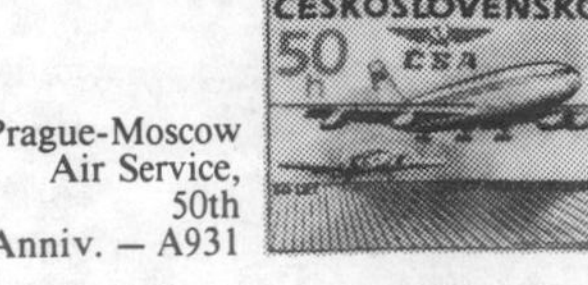

Prague-Moscow Air Service, 50th Anniv. — A931

Engraved and Photogravure

1986, Apr. 8 *Perf. 11½*
2604 A930 1k multi 32 16

1986, Apr. 25
2605 A931 50h multi 16 8

Intl. Olympic Committee, 90th Anniv. — A932

1986, May 12 *Perf. 11½x12*
2606 A932 2k multi 65 32

1986 World Cup Soccer Championships, Mexico — A933

1986, May 15 *Perf. 12x11½*
2607 A933 4k multi 1.30 65

Women's World Volleyball Championships, Prague — A934

1986, May 19
2608 A934 1k multi 32 16

Souvenir Sheet

Intl. Philatelic Federation, FIP, 60th Anniv. — A935

Design: Portrait of Joseph Paar (1654-1725), postmaster, PRAGA '88 emblem, posthorn, covers and hand canceler from the Postal Museum, Prague.

1986, June 3 **Engr.** *Perf. 12*
2609 A935 20k multi 6.50 3.25

No. 2609 has multicolored inscribed margin picturing exhibition emblem and 19th century coach. Size: 110x82mm.

Prague Castle Type of 1983

Designs: 2k, Jewelled funerary pendant, 9th cent. 3k, Allegory of Blossoms, sculpture by Jaroslav Horejc (1886-1983), St. Vitus' Cathedral.

1986, June 6 **Engr.** *Perf. 12*
2610 A875 2k multi 65 32
2611 A875 3k multi 1.00 50

UN Child Survival Campaign — A937

Toys.

Engraved and Photogravure

1986, Sept. 1 *Perf. 11½*
2612 A937 10h Rooster 5 5
2613 A937 20h Horse and rider 6 5
2614 A937 1k Doll 32 16
2615 A937 2k Doll, diff. 65 32
2616 A937 3k Tin omnibus, c. 1910 1.00 50
Nos. 2612-2616 (5) 2.08 1.08

UNICEF, 40th anniv.

Registration, Cent. — A938

1986, Sept. 2 *Perf. 11½x12*
2617 A938 4k Label, mail coach 1.30 65

Bratislava Type of 1977

1986, Sept. 11 **Engr.** *Perf. 12*
2618 A760 3k Sigismund Gate 95 48
2619 A760 4k St. Margaret, bas-relief 1.30 65

Sheets of four.

Owls — A939

Engraved and Photogravure

1986, Sept. 18 *Perf. 11½*
2620 A939 50h Bubo bubo 16 8
2621 A939 2k Asio otus 65 32
2622 A939 3k Strix aluco 95 48
2623 A939 4k Tyto alba 1.30 65
2624 A939 5k Asio flammeus 1.60 80
Nos. 2620-2624 (5) 4.66 2.33

Intl. Brigades in Spain — A940

Theater curtain: Woman Savaged by Horses, 1936, by Vladimir Sychra (1903-1963), Natl Gallery, Prague.

1986, Oct. 1 **Engr.** *Perf. 12*
2625 A940 5k multi 1.60 80

No. 2625 issued in sheets of 2; inscribed margin pictures detail of curtain in black and white. Size: 165x108mm.

Locomotives and Streetcars — A941

Engraved and Photogravure

1986, Oct. 6 *Perf. 12x11½*
2626 A941 50h KT-8 16 8
2627 A941 1k E458.1 32 16
2628 A941 3k T466.2 95 48
2629 A941 5k M152.0 1.60 80

The lack of a price for a listed item does not necessarily indicate rarity.

Paintings in the Prague anc Bratislava Natl. Galleries A942

Designs: 1k, The Circus Rider, 1980, by Ja Bauch (b. 1898). 2k, The Ventriloquist, 1954 by Frantisek Tichy (1896-1961). 3k, In th Circus, 1946, by Vincent Hloznik (b. 1919 6k, Clown, 1985, by Karel Svolinsky (1896 1986).

1986, Oct. 13 **Engr.** *Perf. 1.*
2630 A942 1k multi 32 1
2631 A942 2k multi 65 3.
2632 A942 3k multi 95 4
2633 A942 6k multi 1.90 9.

Art Type of 1967

Designs: 1k, The Czech Lion, May 1918 by Vratislav H. Brunner (1886-1928). 2k Boy with Mandolin, 1945, by Jozef Sturdi (b. 1920). 3k, Metra Building, 1984, by Fran tisek Gross (1909-1985). 4k, Portrait o Maria Maximiliana at Sternberk, 1665, b Karel Skreta (1610-1674). 5k, Adam and Eve 1538, by Lucas Cranach (1472-1553).

1986, Nov. 3 **Engr.** *Perf. 1.*
2634 A565 1k multi 32 1
2635 A565 2k multi 65 3
2636 A565 3k multi 95 4
2637 A565 4k multi 1.30 6
2638 A565 5k multi 1.60 8
Nos. 2634-2638 (5) 4.82 2.4

Sheets of 4.

Stamp Day — A943

Design: V.H. Brunner (1886-1928), stam designer, and No. 88.

Photo. & Engr.

1986, Dec. 18 *Perf. 11½x1.*
2639 A943 1k multi 32 1

World Cyclocross Championships, Jan. 24-25, Central Bohemia — A944

1987, Jan. 22 *Perf. 11½*
2640 A944 6k multi 1.90 9

Czechoslovakian Bowling Union, 50th Anniv. — A945

1987, Jan. 22 *Perf. 11½*
2641 A945 2k multi 65 3

State Decorations — A946

Designs: 50h, Gold Stars of Socialist Labor and Czechoslovakia. 2k, Order of Klement Gottwald. 3k, Order of the Republic. 4k, Order of Victorious February. 5k, Order of Labor.

1987, Feb. 4 *Perf. 12x11½*

2642 A946 50h multi 16 8
2643 A946 2k multi 65 32
2644 A946 3k multi 95 48
2645 A946 4k multi 1.30 65
2646 A946 5k multi 1.60 80
Nos. 2642-2646 (5) 4.66 2.33

Butterflies — A947

1987, Mar. 4

2647 A947 1k Limenitis populi 32 16
2648 A947 2k Smerinthus ocellatus 65 32
2649 A947 3k Pericallia matronula 95 48
2650 A947 4k Saturnia pyri 1.30 65

Natl. Nuclear Power Industry A948

1987, Apr. 6

2651 A948 5k multi 1.60 80

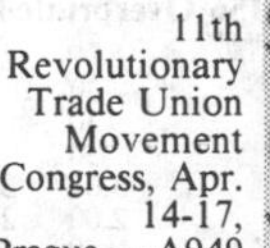

11th Revolutionary Trade Union Movement Congress, Apr. 14-17, Prague — A949

1987, Apr. 7 *Perf. 11½*

2652 A949 1k multi 32 16

Souvenir Sheet

INTERCOSMOS, 10th Anniv. — A950

Design: Cosmonauts Alexei Gubarev of the USSR and Vladimir Remek of Czechoslovakia, rocket and emblem.

1987, Apr. 12 **Engr.** *Perf. 12*

2653 Sheet of 2 6.50 6.50
a. A950 10k multi 3.25 3.25
b. Souv. sheet of 4 (litho. & engr., imperf.) 13.00 13.00

Size of No. 2653: 165x104mm. No. 2653b issued Nov. 15, 1987; inscribed margin pictures PRAGA '88 emblem. Size: 102x100mm.

Prague Castle Art Treasures Type of 1983

Designs: 2k, Three Saints, stained-glass window detail, c. 1870, St. Vitus Cathedral, by Frantisek Sequens (1830-1896). 3k, Coat of Arms, New Land Rolls Hall, 1605.

1987, May 9 *Perf. 11½*

2654 A875 2k multi 65 32
2655 A875 3k dk red, slate gray & yel org 95 48

Nos. 2654-2655 each printed in sheets of 6.

PRAGA '88 A951

Photo. & Engr.

1987, May 12 *Perf. 12x11½*

2656 A951 3k Telephone, 1894 95 48
2657 A951 3k Postal van, 1924 95 48
2658 A951 4k Locomotive tender, 1907 1.30 65
2659 A951 4k Tram, 1900 1.30 65
2660 A951 5k Steam roller, 1936 1.60 80
Nos. 2656-2660 (5) 6.10 3.06

Printed in sheets of 8 + 2 labels picturing telephone or vehicles. Nos. 2657-2658 also printed in sheets of 4 + label picturing vehicles.

Destruction of Lidice and Lezaky, 45th Anniv. — A952

Drawings: No. 2661, When the Fighting Ended, 1945, by Pavel Simon. No. 2662, The End of the game, 1945, by Ludmila Jirincova.

1987, June *Perf. 11½*

2661 A952 1k blk, cerise & vio 32 16
2662 A952 1k blk, gold, pale lil & cerise 32 16

Union of Czechoslovakian Mathematicians and Physicists, 125th Anniv. — A953

Designs: No. 2663, Prague Town Hall mathematical clock, Theory of Functions diagram. No. 2664, J.M. Petzval (1807-1891), J. Strouhal (1850-1922) and V. Jarnik (1897-1970). No. 2665, Geographical measurement from A.M. Malletta;s book, 1672, earth fold and Brownian motion diagrams.

1987, July 6 *Perf. 11½x12*

2663 A953 50h multi 16 8
2664 A953 50h multi 16 8
2665 A953 50h multi 16 8

11th Biennial of Children's Book Illustration, Sept. 11-Oct. 30, Bratislava — A954

Eternal Flame, Flower — A955

Award-winning illustrations.

1987, Sept. 3 *Perf. 11½*

2666 A954 50h Asun Balzola, Spain 16 8
2667 A954 1k Frederic Clement, France 32 16
2668 A954 2k Elzbieta Gaudasinska, Poland 65 32
a. Souv. sheet of 2 + label 1.30
2669 A954 4k Marija Lucija Stupica, Jugoslavia 1.30 65

No. 2668a has inscribed decorative margin Size:

1987, Sept. 23

2670 A955 50h multi 18 10

Theresienstadt Memorial for the victims from 23 European countries who died in the Small Fortress, Terezin, a Nazi concentration camp.

Socialist Communications Organization, 30th Anniv. — A956

1987, Sept. 23

2671 A956 4k Emblem, satellite, dish receiver 1.30 65

Jan Evangelista Purkyne (1787-1869), Physiologist A957

1987, Sept. 30

2672 A957 7k multi 2.25 1.15

Views of Bratislava — A958

Designs: 3k, Male and female figures supporting an oriel, Arkier Palace, c. 1552. 4k, View of Bratislava from Ware Conterfactur de Stadt Presburg, from an engraving by Hans Mayer, 1563.

1987, Oct. 1 **Engr.** *Perf. 12*

2673 A958 3k multi 95 48
2674 A958 4k multi 1.30 65

Printed in sheets of 4 with Bratislava Castle (from Mayer's engraving) between.

Type of 1974

Photo. & Engr.

1987, Nov. 1 *Perf. 12x11½*

2675 A697 1k Post rider 32 16

PRAGA '88, Aug. 26-Sept. 4, 1988. No. 2675 printed se-tenant with label picturing exhibition emblem.

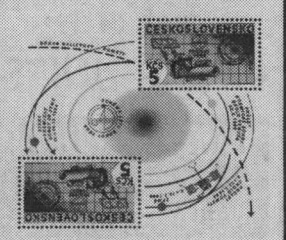

October Revolution, Russia, 70th Anniv. — A959

Establishment of the Union of Soviet Socialist Republics, 65th Anniv. — A960

Photo. & Engr.

1987, Nov. 6 *Perf. 12x11½*

2676 A959 50h multi 16 8
2677 A960 50h multi 16 8

Art Type of 1974

Paintings in national galleries: 1k, Enclosure of Dreams, by Kamil Lhotak (b. 1912). 2k, Tulips, by Ester Simerova-Martincekova (b. 1909). 3k, Triptych with Bohemian Landscape, by Josef Lada (1887-1957). 4k, Accordion Player, by Josef Capek (1887-1945). 5k, Self-portrait, by Jiri Trnka (1912-1969).

1987, Nov. 18 **Engr.** *Perf. 12*

2678 A700 1k ulti 32 16
2679 A700 2k multi 65 32
2680 A700 3k multi 95 48
2681 A700 4k multi 1.30 65
2682 A700 5k multi 1.60 80
Nos. 2678-2682 (5) 4.82 2.41

Czech and Slovak art. Issued in sheets of 4.

69th Stamp Day — A961

Portrait of Jacob Obrovsky (1882-1949), stamp designer, Bohemian Lion (Type SP1), sketch of a lion and PRAGA '88 emblem.

Photo. & Engr.

1987, Dec. 18 *Perf. 11½x12*

2683 A961 1k multi 32 16
a. Pane of 4 + 12 labels 1.30

The eight labels printed se-tenant with stamps in pane are inscribed "100 Years of the National Philatelic Movement in Czechoslovakia" in Czech. Size of No. 2683a: 292x76mm.

Czechoslovak Republic 70th Anniv. A962

1988, Jan. 1 *Perf. 12x11½*

2684 A962 1k Woman, natl. arms, linden branch 32 16

Natl. Front, 40th Anniv. A963

1988, Jan. *Perf. 11½*

2685 A963 50h multi 16 8

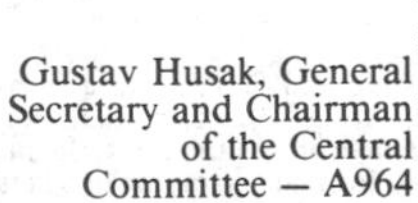

Gustav Husak, General Secretary and Chairman of the Central Committee — A964

Photo. & Engr.

1988, Jan. 10 *Perf. 12x11½*

2686 A964 1k brt rose & dark car 32 16

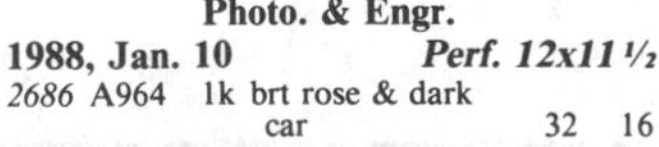

Olympics — A965

1988, Feb. 1 *Perf. 11½x12*

2687 A965 50h Ski jumping, ice hockey 18 10
a. Souv. sheet of 2, imperf. between
2688 A965 1k Basketball, soccer 36 18
a. Souv. sheet of 2, imperf. between
2689 A965 6k Discus, weight lifting 1.95 95
a. Souv. sheet of 2, imperf. between

Nos. 2687a-2689a have black inscribed margins picturing 5-ring Olympic emblem and containing black control number. Exist imperf. Sizes: 79x76mm.

Victorious February, 40th Anniv. — A966

Design: Statue of Klement Gottwald by Rudolf Svoboda.

1988, Feb. 25 *Perf. 11½*

2690 A966 50h multi 18 10
a. Souv. sheet of 2 40 20

No. 2690a has dark brown inscribed margin containing postally invalid copies of No. 637. Exists imperf. Size: 88x100mm.

SEMI-POSTAL STAMPS

Nos. B1-B123 were sold, in sets only, at 1½ times face value at the Philatelists' Window of the Prague P.O. for charity benefit. They were available for ordinary postage.

The overprints of Nos. B1-B123 have been well forged.

Austrian Stamps of 1916-18 Overprinted in Black or Blue

a 

1919 *Perf. 12½*

B1 A37 3h brt vio 30 35
B2 A37 5h lt grn 30 35
B3 A37 6h dp org (Bl) 60 60
B4 A37 6h dp org (Bk) *1,500.* *1,500.*
B5 A37 10h magenta 90 1.00
B6 A37 12h lt bl 90 90
B7 A42 15h dl red 30 35
B8 A42 20h dk grn 30 35
a. 20h grn 160.00 100.00
B9 A42 25h blue 45 55
B10 A42 30h dl vio 45 55
B11 A39 40h ol grn 45 55
B12 A39 50h dk grn 45 55
B13 A39 60h dp bl 45 55
B14 A39 80h org brn 45 55
B15 A39 90h red vio 1.00 1.00
B16 A39 1k car, *yel* (Bl) 70 85
B17 A39 1k car, *yel* (Bk) 175.00 150.00
B18 A40 2k lt bl 3.25 3.25
B18A A40 2k dk bl *3,250.* *2,500.*
B19 A40 3k car rose 80.00 40.00
B19A A40 3k claret 1,200. 1,100.
B20 A40 4k yel grn 22.00 12.00
B20A A40 4k dp grn 57.50 37.50
B21 A40 10k violet 375.00 250.00
B21A A40 10k dp vio 525.00 325.00

The used price of No. B18A is for copies which have only a Czechoslovakian cancellation. Some of the copies of Austria No. 160 which were officially overprinted with type "a" and sold by the post office, had previously been used and lightly canceled with Austrian cancellations. These canceled-before-overprinting copies, which were postally valid, sell for about one-fourth as much.

Granite Paper

B22 A40 2k lt bl 3.00 3.00
B23 A40 3k car rose 11.00 10.00
B24 A40 4k yel grn
B25 A40 10k dp vio

Excellent counterfeits of Nos. B1-B25 exist.

Austrian Newspaper Stamps Overprinted

b 

Imperf.

On Stamp of 1908

B26 N8 10h carmine 2,000. 2,000.

On Stamps of 1916

B27 N9 2h brown 10 10
B28 N9 4h green 40 40
B29 N9 6h dp bl 25 25
B30 N9 10h orange 5.00 5.00
B31 N9 30h claret 2.00 2.00
Nos. B27-B31 (5) 7.75 7.75

Austrian Special Handling Stamps Overprinted in Blue or Black
Stamps of 1916 Overprinted

c
POŠTA
ČESKOSLOVENSKÁ
1919

Perf. 12½

B32 SH1 2h cl, *yel* (Bl) 45.00 35.00
B33 SH1 5h dp grn, *yel* *1,400.* *1,000.*

Stamps of 1917 Overprinted

d
POŠTA
ČESKOSLOVENSKÁ
1919

B34 SH2 2h cl, *yel* (Bl) 40 50
a. Vert. pair, imperf. btwn. *250.00*
B35 SH2 2h cl, *yel* (Bk) 85.00 50.00
B36 SH2 5h grn, *yel* (Bk) 20 20

Austrian Air Post Stamps, Nos. C1-C3, Overprinted Type "c" Diagonally

B37 A40 1.50k on 2k lil 250.00 185.00
B38 A40 2.50k on 3k ocher 250.00 185.00
B39 A40 4k gray 1,000. 800.00

1919

Austrian Postage Due Stamps of 1908-13
Overprinted Type "b"

B40 D3 2h carmine *4,500.* *4,000.*
B41 D3 4h carmine 40.00 27.50
B42 D3 6h carmine 20.00 15.00
B43 D3 14h carmine 125.00 55.00
B44 D3 25h carmine 80.00 40.00
B45 D3 30h carmine 600.00 500.00
B46 D3 50h carmine 1,200. 1,100.

Austria Nos. J49-J56 Overprinted Type "b"

B47 D4 5h rose red 30 45
B48 D4 10h rose red 30 45
B49 D4 15h rose red 30 45
B50 D4 20h rose red 3.00 3.00
B51 D4 25h rose red 2.00 2.00
B52 D4 30h rose red 60 60
B53 D4 40h rose red 3.00 2.50
B54 D4 50h rose red 425.00 375.00

Austria Nos. J57-J59 Overprinted Type "a"

B55 D5 1k ultra 20.00 16.50
B56 D5 5k ultra 80.00 50.00
B57 D5 10k ultra 400.00 375.00

Austria Nos. J47-J48, J60-J63 Overprinted Type "c" Diagonally

B58 A22 1h gray 40.00 25.00
B59 A23 15h on 2h vio 200.00 165.00
B60 A38 10h on 24h bl 140.00 120.00
B61 A38 15h on 36h vio 1.50 1.50
B62 A38 20h on 54h org 140.00 120.00
B63 A38 50h on 42h choc 1.50 1.50

Hungarian Stamps Overprinted Type "b"

Wmk. Double Cross (137)

1919 *Perf. 15*

On Stamps of 1913-16

B64 A4 1f slate 1,650. 1,500.
B65 A4 2f yellow 5.00 4.00
B66 A4 3f orange 80.00 40.00
B67 A4 6f ol grn 8.00 8.00
B68 A4 50f lake, *bl* 2.00 1.50
B69 A4 60f grn, *sal* 80.00 30.00
B70 A4 70f red brn, *grn* 1,850. 1,250.

On Stamps of 1916

B71 A8 10f rose 375.00 275.00
B72 A8 15f violet 200.00 150.00

On Stamps of 1916-18

B73 A9 2f brn org 15 15
B74 A9 3f red lil 30 25
B75 A9 5f green 10 10
B76 A9 6f grnsh bl 1.10 1.00
B77 A9 10f rose red 2.50 3.75
B78 A9 15f violet 42 40

B79 A9 20f gray brn 10.00 8.00
B80 A9 25f dl bl 1.50 1.00
B81 A9 35f brown 12.50 10.00
B82 A9 40f ol grn 3.25 2.75

Overprinted Type "d"

B83 A10 50f red vio & lil 1.50 1.50
B84 A10 75f brt bl & pale bl 1.40 1.40
B85 A10 80f yel grn & pale grn 2.00 2.00
B86 A10 1k red brn & cl 2.50 2.50
B87 A10 2k ol brn & bis 10.00 10.00
B88 A10 3k dk vio & ind 67.50 57.50
B89 A10 5k dk brn & lt brn 225.00 135.00
B90 A10 10k vio brn & vio 1,200. 1,100.

Overprinted Type "b"

On Stamps of 1918

B91 A11 10f scarlet 40 40
B92 A11 20f dk brn 50 50
B93 A11 25f dp bl 2.50 2.50
B94 A12 40f ol grn 2.75 2.75
B95 A12 50f lilac 125.00 40.00

On Stamps of 1919

B96 A13 10f red 10.00 10.00
B97 A13 20f dk brn *4,000.* *4,000.*

Same Overprint On Hungarian Newspaper Stamp of 1914

Imperf

B98 N5 (2f) orange 30 40

Same Overprint On Hungarian Special Delivery Stamp

Perf. 15.

B99 SD1 2f gray grn & red 40 50

Same Overprint On Hungarian Semi-Postal Stamps

B100 SP3 10f + 2f rose red 60 85
B101 SP4 15f + 2f vio 1.00 1.25
B102 SP5 40f + 2f brn car 8.00 5.00
Nos. B98-B102 (5) 10.30 8.00

Hungarian Postage Due Stamps of 1903-18 Overprinted Type "b"

Wmk. Crown in Circle (135)

1919 ***Perf. 11½, 12***

B103 D1 50f grn & blk *750.00* *750.00*

Wmk. Crown (136, 136a)

Perf. 11½x12, 15

B104 D1 1f grn & blk *700.00* *700.00*
B105 D1 2f grn & blk *400.00* *400.00*
B106 D1 12f grn & blk *3,000.* *3,000.*
B107 D1 50f grn & blk 225.00 225.00

Wmk. Double Cross (137)

Perf. 15

On Stamps of 1914

B110 D1 1f grn & blk 600.00 575.00
B111 D1 2f grn & blk 325.00 325.00
B112 D1 5f grn & blk 750.00 750.00
B113 D1 12f grn & blk *2,500.* *2,500.*
B114 D1 50f grn & blk 225.00 225.00

On Stamps of 1915-18

B115 D1 1f grn & red 250.00 200.00
B116 D1 2f grn & red 1.50 1.25
B117 D1 5f grn & red 20.00 16.50
B118 D1 6f grn & red 2.00 2.00
B119 D1 10f grn & red 1.00 1.00
a. Pair, one without overprint
B120 D1 12f grn & red 2.75 2.75
B121 D1 15f grn & red 12.50 9.00
B122 D1 20f grn & red 1.50 1.50
B123 D1 30f grn & red 75.00 55.00
Nos. B115-B123 (9) 366.25 289.00

Bohemian Lion Breaking its Chains — SP1

Mother and Child — SP2

Perf. 11½, 13½ and Compound

1919 **Typo.** **Unwmk.**

Pinkish Paper

B124 SP1 15(h) gray grn 8 10
B125 SP1 25(h) dk brn 8 10
a. 25(h) lt brn 5.00
B126 SP1 50(h) dk bl 8 10

Photo.

Yellowish Paper

B127 SP2 75(h) slate 8 10
B128 SP2 100(h) brn vio 8 10
B129 SP2 120(h) vio, *yel* 8 10
Nos. B124-B129 (6) 48 60

Nos. B124-B129 honor the Czecho-Slovak Legion. Nos. B124-B126 commemorate the first anniversary of Czechoslovak independence. Nos. B127-B129 were sold for the benefit of Legionnaires' orphans. Imperforates exist.

See No. 1581.

Regular Issues of Czechoslovakia Surcharged in Red:

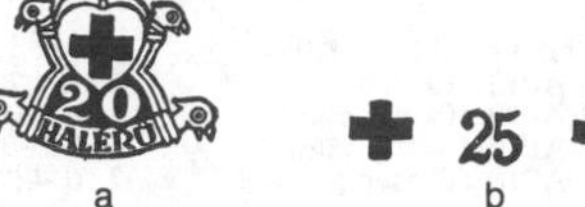

a b

1920 ***Perf. 13½***

B130 A1(a) 40(h) + 20(h) bis 1.75 1.60
B131 A2(a) 60(h) + 20h grn 1.75 1.60
B132 A4(b) 125(h) + 25(h) gray bl 3.50 4.00

President Masaryk — SP3

Wmk. Linden Leaves (107)

1923 **Engr.** ***Perf. 13½x14½***

B133 SP3 50(h) gray grn 95 75
B134 SP3 100(h) carmine 1.90 1.25
B135 SP3 200(h) blue 7.50 6.75
B136 SP3 300(h) dk brn 8.50 6.75

Issued in commemoration of the fifth anniversary of the Republic.

The gum was applied through a screen and shows the monogram "CSP" (Ceskoslovenska Posta). These stamps were sold at double their face values, the excess being given to the Red Cross and other charitable organizations.

International Olympic Congress Issue

Semi-Postal Stamps of 1923 Overprinted in Blue or Red

CONGRES OLYMP. INTERNAT.
PRAHA1925

1925

B137 SP3 50(h) gray grn (Bl) 8.50 8.00
B138 SP3 100(h) car (Bl) 15.00 13.00
B139 SP3 200(h) bl (R) 95.00 90.00

These stamps were sold at double their face values, the excess being divided between a fund for post office clerks and the Olympic Games Committee.

Sokol Issue

Semi-Postal Stamps of 1923 Overprinted in Blue or Red

VIII. SLET VŠESOKOLSKÝ
PRAHA 1926

1926

B140 SP3 50(h) gray grn (Bl) 7.00 6.00
B141 SP3 100(h) car (Bl) 7.00 6.50
B142 SP3 200(h) bl (R) 30.00 26.00
a. Double overprint
B143 SP3 300(h) dk brn (R) 52.50 47.50

These stamps were sold at double their face values, the excess being given to the Congress of Sokols, June, 1926.

Midwife Presenting Newborn Child to its Father; after a Painting by Josef Manes
SP4 SP5

1936 **Unwmk.** **Engr.** ***Perf. 12½***

B144 SP4 50h + 50h grn 60 60
B145 SP5 1k + 50h cl 1.00 1.00
B146 SP4 2k + 50h bl 2.50 2.50

"Lullaby" by Stanislav Sucharda
SP6 SP7

1937 ***Perf. 12½***

B147 SP6 50h + 50h dl grn 50 50
B148 SP6 1k + 50h rose lake 1.00 1.00
B149 SP7 2k + 1k dl bl 2.00 2.00

President Masaryk and Little Girl in Native Costume — SP8

1938 ***Perf. 12½***

B150 SP8 50h + 50h dp grn 48 55
B151 SP8 1k + 50h rose lake 55 65

Souvenir Sheet

Imperf

B152 SP8 2k + 3k blk 4.00 4.50

No. B152 measures 72x90mm. with marginal inscriptions of "TGM" and Masaryk's signature.

Issued to commemorate the 88th anniversary of the birth of President Masaryk (1850-1937).

Souvenir Sheet

Symbol of the Republic SP9

1938 ***Perf. 12½***

B153 SP9 2k (+ 8k) dk bl, sheet 3.25 4.00

Issued to sheets measuring 79x90mm. The surtax was devoted to national relief for refugees.

"Republic" and Congress Emblem SP10

St. George Slaying the Dragon SP11

1945 **Engr.**

B154 SP10 1.50(k) + 1.50(k) car rose 16 10
B155 SP10 2.50(k) + 2.50(k) bl 25 20

Issued to commemorate the Students' World Congress at Prague, Nov. 17, 1945.

1946

B156 SP11 2.40k + 2.60k car rose 22 15
B157 SP11 4k + 6k bl 50 30

Souvenir Sheet

Imperf

B158 SP11 4k + 6k bl 1.00 1.10

No. B158 measures 70x90mm., with marginal inscriptions: "Pravda Vitezi Kveten 1945 1946." Nos. B156-B158 commemorate the 1st anniversary of Czechoslovakia's liberation. The surtax aided World War II orphans.

Souvenir Sheet

SP13

1946, Aug. 3 ***Imperf.***

B159 SP13 2.40k rose brn 90 1.00

Issued for the Brno National Stamp Exhibition, August, 1946.

The sheet measures 70x89mm. It was sold for 10k.

"You Went Away" — SP14

"You Remained Ours" — SP15

"You Came Back" — SP16

1946, Oct. 28 **Photo.** ***Perf. 14***

B160 SP14 1.60k + 1.40k red brn 25 30
B161 SP15 2.40k + 2.60k scar 35 45
B162 SP16 4k + 4k dp bl 60 75

The surtax was for repatriated Slovaks.

Barefoot Boy — SP17

Woman and Child — SP18

Designs: 2k+1k, Mother and child. 3k+1k, Little girl.

Perf. 12½

1948, Dec. 18 **Unwmk.** **Engr.**

B163 SP17 1.50(k) + 1(k) rose lil 22 10
B164 SP17 2(k) + 1(k) dp bl 22 10
B165 SP17 3(k) + 1(k) rose car 30 30

The surtax was for child welfare.

Labels alternate with stamps in sheets of Nos. B163-B165.

Inscribed: "Detem 1949"

1949, Dec. 18 ***Perf. 12½***

Design: 3k+1k, Man lifting child.

B166 SP18 1.50k + 50h gray 3.50 1.75
B167 SP18 3k + 1k cl 4.50 2.25

The surtax was for child welfare.

Dove Carrying Olive Branch
SP19 SP20

1949, Dec. 18
B168 SP19 1.50k + 50h cl 4.00 1.75
B169 SP20 3k + 1k rose red 4.00 1.75

The surtax was for the Red Cross.

AIR POST STAMPS

Stamps of 1918-19 Surcharged in Red, Blue or Green:

1920 Unwmk. *Imperf.*
C1 A1 14k on 200(h) ultra (R) 14.00 16.00
a. Inverted surcharge 75.00
C2 A2 24k on 500(h) red brn (Bl) 37.50 40.00
a. Inverted surcharge 110.00
C3 A2 28k on 1000 (h) vio (G) 37.50 40.00
a. Inverted surcharge 115.00
b. Double surch. 125.00

Perf. 14, 14x13½
C4 A1 14k on 200 (h) ultra (R) 27.50 27.50
a. Perf. 14 x 13½ 80.00 75.00
C5 A2 24k on 500 (h) red brn (Bl) 65.00 65.00
a. Perf. 14 x 13½ 110.00 110.00
C6 A2 28k on 1000(h) vio (G) 47.50 37.50
a. Inverted surcharge 110.00 110.00
b. Perf. 14 600.00 500.00

Excellent counterfeits of the overprint are known.

Stamps of 1920 Surcharged in Black or Violet:

1922, June 15
C7 A8 50(h) on 100(h) dl grn (Bk) 3.00 2.25
a. Inverted surcharge 50.00
b. Double surcharge 45.00
C8 A8 100(h) on 200(h) vio (Bk) 3.75 3.25
a. Inverted surcharge 50.00
C9 A8 250(h) on 400(h) brn (V) 8.25 8.00
a. Inverted surcharge 50.00

Fokker Monoplane AP3

Smolik S 19 AP4

Smolik S 19 — AP5

Fokker over Prague — AP6

1930, Dec. 16 Engr. *Perf. 13½*
C10 AP3 50(h) dp grn 25 25
a. Perf. 12 3.00 3.00
C11 AP3 1k dp red 40 30
a. Perf. 12 30.00 30.00
b. Perf. 12 x 13½ 4.50 4.50
C12 AP4 2k dk grn 90 85
a. Perf. 12 22.50 22.50
b. Perf. 13½ x 12 15.00 15.00
C13 AP4 3k red vio 2.00 1.50
C14 AP5 4k indigo 1.50 1.25
a. Perf. 12 10.00 10.00
C15 AP5 5k red brn 2.25 1.75
a. Perf. 12 *750.00*
C16 AP6 10k vio bl 5.50 5.25
a. 10k ultra 10.00 10.00
C17 AP6 20k gray vio 6.75 5.00
a. Perf. 12 6.75 5.00
b. Perf. 13½x12 *600.00*
Nos. C10-C17 (8) 19.55 16.15

Two types exist of the 50h, 1k and 2k, and three types of the 3k, differing chiefly in the size of the printed area. A "no hill at left" variety of the 3k exists.

Imperforate copies of Nos. C10 to C17 are proofs.

Type of 1930 with hyphen in Cesko-Slovensko

1939, Apr. 22 *Perf. 13½*
C18 AP3 30h rose lil 10 7

Capt. Frantisek Novak — AP7

Plane over Bratislava Castle — AP8

Plane over Charles Bridge Prague — AP9

1946-47 *Perf. 12½*
C19 AP7 1.50k rose red 20 10
C20 AP7 5.50k dk gray bl 48 20
C21 AP7 9k sep ('47) 1.10 20
C22 AP8 10k dl grn 1.00 50
C23 AP7 16k violet 1.40 60
C24 AP8 20k lt bl 1.50 80
C25 AP9 24k dk bl, *cr* 1.10 2.00
C26 AP9 24k rose lake 2.25 1.25
C27 AP9 50k dk gray bl 4.00 2.50
Nos. C19-C27 (9) 13.03 8.15

No. C25 was issued June 12, 1946, for use on the first Prague-New York flight.

Nos. C19 to C24, C26 and C27 Surcharged with New Value and Bars in Various Colors.

1949, Sept. 1 *Perf. 12½*
C28 AP7 1k on 1.50k rose red (Bl) 10 10
C29 AP7 3k on 5.50k dk gray bl (C) 16 12
C30 AP7 6k on 9k sep (Br) 28 20
C31 AP7 7.50k on 16k vio (C) 55 20
C32 AP8 8k on 10k dl grn (G) 65 35
C33 AP8 12.50k on 20k lt bl (Bl) 90 35
C34 AP9 15k on 24k rose lake (Bl) 1.75 50
C35 AP9 30k on 50k dk gray bl (Bl) 2.25 75
Nos. C28-C35 (8) 6.64 2.57

Karlovy Vary (Karlsbad) — AP10

Designs: 10k, Piestany. 15k, Marienbad. 20k, Silac.

1951, Apr. 2 Engr. *Perf. 13½*
C36 AP10 6k sage grn 2.25 70
C37 AP10 10k dp plum 3.00 1.00
C38 AP10 15k dp ultra 4.50 70
C39 AP10 20k sepia *7.50 4.00*

View of Cesky Krumlov — AP11

Views: 1.55k, Olomouc. 2.35k, Banska Bystrica. 2.75k, Bratislava. 10k, Prague.

Perf. 11½
1955, Feb. 20 (10k) and Mar. 28
Cream Paper
C40 AP11 80h ol grn 1.40 8
C41 AP11 1.55k vio brn 1.40 18
C42 AP11 2.35k vio bl 2.25 28
C43 AP11 2.75k rose brn 3.25 1.10
C44 AP11 10k indigo 4.50 2.00
Nos. C40-C44 (5) 12.80 3.64

Airline: Moscow-Prague-Paris — AP12

Design: 2.35k, Airline: Prague-Cairo-Beirut-Damascus.

Engraved and Photogravure
1957, Oct. 15 Unwmk. *Perf. 11½*
C45 AP12 75h ultra & rose 60 15
C46 AP12 2.35k ultra & org yel 1.25 30

Planes at First Czech Aviation School, Pardubice AP13

Design: 1.80k, Jan Kaspar and flight of first Czech plane, 1909.

1959, Oct. 15
C47 AP13 1k gray & yel 35 10
C48 AP13 1.80k blk & pale bl 1.00 18

Issued to commemorate the 50th anniversary of Jan Kaspar's first flight Aug. 25, 1909, at Pardubice.

Mail Coach, Plane and Arms of Bratislava — AP14

Design: 2.80k, Helicopter over Bratislava.

Engraved and Photogravure
1960, Sept. 24 Unwmk. *Perf. 11½*
C49 AP14 1.60k dk bl & gray *2.25 1.50*
C50 AP14 2.80k grn & buff *3.50 2.50*

Issued to publicize the National Stamp Exhibition, Bratislava, Sept. 24-Oct. 9.

Prague Hails Gagarin — AP15

Design: 1.80k, Gagarin, rocket and dove.

1961, June 22
C51 AP15 60h gray & car 25 5
C52 AP15 1.80k gray & bl 1.10 25

No. C51 commemorates Maj. Gagarin's visit to Prague, Apr. 28-29; No. C52 commemorates the first man in space, Yuri A. Gagarin, Apr. 12, 1961.

Dove and Nest of Eggs — AP16

Designs ("PRAGA" emblem and): 1.40k, Dove. 2.80k, Symbolic flower with five petals. 4.20k, Five leaves.

1962, May 14 Engr. *Perf. 14*
C53 AP16 80h multi 75 50
C54 AP16 1.40k blk, dk red & bl 2.00 1.25
C55 AP16 2.80k multi 3.25 2.25
C56 AP16 4.20k multi 4.75 3.00

Issued to publicize the PRAGA 1962 World Exhibition of Postage Stamps, Aug. 18-Sept. 2, 1962.

Vostok 5 and Lt. Col. Valeri Bykovski AP17

Design: 2.80k, Vostok VI and Lt. Valentina Tereshkova.

1963, June 26
C57 AP17 80h sl bl & pink 60 15
C58 AP17 2.80k dl red brn & lt bl 1.25 35

Issued to commemorate the space flights of Valeri Bykovski, June 14-19, and Valentina Tereshkova, first woman astronaut, June 16-19, 1963.

PRAGA 1962 Emblem, View of Prague and Plane — AP18

Designs: 60h, Istanbul '63 (Hagia Sophia). k, Philatec Paris 1964 (Ile de la Cite). 1.40k, VIPA 1965 (Belvedere Palace, Vienna). .60k, SIPEX 1966 (Capitol, Washington). k, Amphilex '67 (harbor and old town, msterdam). 5k, PRAGA 1968 (View of rague).

Engraved and Photogravure

967, Oct. 30 *Perf. 11½*

Size: 30x50mm.

C59	AP18	30h choc, yel & rose	10	5
C60	AP18	60h dk grn, yel & lil	25	15
C61	AP18	1k blk, brick red & lt bl	40	20
C62	AP18	1.40k vio, yel & dp org	55	28
C63	AP18	1.60k ind, tan & lil	65	45
C64	AP18	2k dk grn, org & red	90	60

Size: 40x50mm.

C65	AP18	5k multi	*4.00*	*3.75*
		Nos. C59-C65 (7)	6.85	5.48

Issued to publicize the PRAGA 1968 World Stamp Exhibition, Prague, June 22-July 7, 1968. No. C59-C64 issued in sheets of 15 stamps and 15 bilingual labels. No. C65 issued in sheets of 4 stamps and one center label with commemorative inscription and airplane design.

Glider L-13 AP19

Airplanes: 60th, Sports plane L-40. 80h, Aero taxi L-200. 1k, Crop-spraying plane Z-37. 1.60k, Aerobatics trainer Z-526. 2k, Jet trainer L-29.

Engraved and Photogravure

1967, Dec. 11

C66	AP19	30h multi	10	5
C67	AP19	60h multi	20	10
C68	AP19	80h multi	30	10
C69	AP19	1k multi	35	15
C70	AP19	1.60k multi	55	20
C71	AP19	2k multi	*1.75*	*80*
		Nos. C66-C71 (6)	3.25	1.40

Charles Bridge, Prague, and Balloon AP20

Astronaut, Moon and Manhattan AP21

Designs: 1k, Belvedere, fountain and early plane. 2k, Hradcany, Prague, and airship.

1968, Feb. 5 **Unwmk.** *Perf. 11½*

C72	AP20	60h multi	30	15
C73	AP20	1k multi	45	20
C74	AP20	2k multi	75	35

Issued to publicize the PRAGA 1968 World Stamp Exhibition, Prague, June 22-July 7, 1968.

Engraved and Photogravure

1969, July 21

Design: 3k, Lunar landing module and J. F. Kennedy Airport, New York.

C75	AP21	60h blk, vio, yel & sil	35	10
C76	AP21	3k blk, bl, ocher & sil	1.65	75

Issued to commemorate man's first landing on the moon, July 20, 1969, U. S. astronauts Neil A. Armstrong and Col. Edwin E. Aldrin, Jr., with Lieut. Col. Michael Collins piloting Apollo 11.

Nos. C75-C76 printed with label inscribed with names of astronauts and European date of moon landing.

TU-104A over Bitov Castle AP22

Designs: 60h, IL-62 over Bezdez Castle. 1.40k, TU-13A over Orava Castle. 1.90k, IL-18 over Veveri Castle. 2.40k, IL-14 over Pernstejn Castle. 3.60k, TU-154 over Trencin Castle.

1973, Oct. 24 **Engr.** *Perf. 11½*

C77	AP22	30h multi	10	5
C78	AP22	60h multi	20	8
C79	AP22	1.40k multi	42	15
C80	AP22	1.90k multi	60	22
C81	AP22	2.40k multi	*4.25*	*1.25*
C82	AP22	3.60k multi	80	45
		Nos. C77-C82 (6)	6.37	2.20

50 years of Czechoslovakian aviation.

Old Water Tower and Manes Hall — AP23

Designs (Praga 1978 Emblem, Plane Silhouette and): 1.60k, Congress Hall. 2k, Powder Tower (vert.). 2.40k, Charles Bridge and Old Bridge Tower. 4k, Old Town Hall on Old Town Square (vert.). 6k, Prague Castle and St. Vitus' Cathedral (vert.).

Engraved and Photogravure

1976, June 23 *Perf. 11½*

C83	AP23	60h ind & multi	22	8
C84	AP23	1.60k ind & multi	60	18
C85	AP23	2k ind & multi	80	20
C86	AP23	2.40k ind & multi	90	35
C87	AP23	4k ind & multi	1.65	45
C88	AP23	6k ind & multi	5.50	1.25
		Nos. C83-C88 (6)	9.67	2.51

PRAGA 1978 International Philatelic Exhibition, Prague, Sept. 8-17, 1978.

Zeppelin, 1909 and 1928 — AP24

Designs (PRAGA '78 Emblem and): 1k, Ader, 1890, L'Eole and Dunn, 1914. 1.60k, Jeffries-Blanchard balloon, 1785. 2k, Otto Lilienthal's glider, 1896. 4.40k, Jan Kaspar's plane, Pardubice, 1911.

Engraved and Photogravure

1977, Sept. 15 *Perf. 11½*

C89	AP24	60h multi	20	8
C90	AP24	1k multi	40	10
C91	AP24	1.60k multi	65	20
C92	AP24	2k multi	90	30
C93	AP24	4.40k multi	3.50	1.00
		Nos. C89-C93 (5)	5.65	1.68

History of aviation.

SPECIAL DELIVERY STAMPS

Doves — SD1

1919-20 **Unwmk.** **Typo.** *Imperf.*

E1	SD1	2(h) red vio, *yel*	10	10
E2	SD1	5(h) yel grn, *yel*	10	10
E3	SD1	10(h) red brn, *yel* ('20)	65	65

1921 **White Paper**

E1a	SD1	2(h) red vio	4.75
E2a	SD1	5(h) yel grn	4.00
E3a	SD1	10(h) red brn	80.00

It is doubted that Nos. E1a-E3a were regularly issued.

PERSONAL DELIVERY STAMPS

PD1

Design: No. EX2, "D" in each corner.

1937 **Unwmk.** **Photo.** *Perf. 13½*

EX1	PD1	50h blue	30	40
EX2	PD1	50h carmine	30	40

PD3

1946 *Perf. 13½*

EX3	PD3	2k dp bl	40	30

POSTAGE DUE STAMPS

D1

D2

1918-20 **Unwmk.** **Typo.** *Imperf.*

J1	D1	5(h) dp bis	5	5
J2	D1	10(h) dp bis	8	5
J3	D1	15(h) dp bis	8	5
J4	D1	20(h) dp bis	8	5
J5	D1	25(h) dp bis	30	8
J6	D1	30(h) dp bis	8	5
J7	D1	40(h) dp bis	60	25
J8	D1	50(h) dp bis	65	25
J9	D1	100(h) blk brn	65	10
J10	D1	250(h) orange	12.50	1.75
J11	D1	400(h) scarlet	12.50	1.75
J12	D1	500(h) gray grn	3.75	40
J13	D1	1000(h) purple	5.00	10
J14	D1	2000(h) dk bl	25.00	75
		Nos. J1-J14 (14)	61.32	5.68

1922 **Blue Surcharge**

J15	D2	20(h) on 3(h) red vio	42	25
J16	D2	50(h) on 75(h) sl	1.50	15
J17	D2	60(h) on 80(h) ol grn	50	12
J18	D2	100(h) on 80(h) ol grn	50	10
J19	D2	200(h) on 400(h) pur	1.10	15
		Nos. J15-J19 (5)	4.02	77

1923-26 **Violet Surcharge**

J20	D2	10(h) on 3(h) red vio	10	10
J21	D2	20(h) on 3(h) red vio	10	8
J22	D2	30(h) on 3(h) red vio	15	8
J23	D2	40(h) on 3(h) red vio	30	8
J24	D2	50(h) on 75(h) sl	1.65	8
J25	D2	60(h) on 50(h) dk vio ('26)	3.00	1.50
J26	D2	60(h) on 50(h) dk bl ('26)	3.00	1.40
J27	D2	60(h) on 75(h) sl	1.65	8
J28	D2	100(h) on 80(h) ol grn	55.00	85
J29	D2	100(h) on 120(h) gray blk	2.00	10
J30	D2	100(h) on 400(h) pur ('26)	1.10	15
J31	D2	100(h) on 1000(h) dp vio ('26)	2.50	15
		Nos. J20-J31 (12)	70.55	4.65

Nos. J15, J19, J20, J22, J23 and J30 were surcharged on stamps of type A1; others of the groups J15 to J31 were surcharged on stamps of type A2.

Postage Due Stamp of 1918-20 Surcharged in Violet

1924

J32	D1	50(h) on 400(h) scar	1.75	15
J33	D1	60(h) on 400(h) scar	4.50	1.00
J34	D1	100(h) on 400(h) scar	3.50	25

Postage Due Stamps of 1918-20 Surcharged with New Values in Violet as in 1924

1925

J35	D1	10(h) on 5(h) bis	8	8
J36	D1	20(h) on 5(h) bis	8	8
J37	D1	30(h) on 15(h) bis	40	45
J38	D1	40(h) on 15(h) bis	50	8
J39	D1	50(h) on 250(h) org	1.75	28
J40	D1	60(h) on 250(h) org	2.25	70
J41	D1	100(h) on 250(h) org	5.50	50
		Nos. J35-J41 (7)	10.56	2.17

Stamps of 1918-19 Surcharged with New Values in Violet as in 1922

1926 *Perf. 14, 11½*

J42	D2	30(h) on 15(h) red	1.00	60
J43	D2	40(h) on 15(h) red	75	25

D3

D4

1926 **Violet Surcharge** *Perf. 14*

J44	D3	30(h) on 100(h) dk grn	20	20
J45	D3	40(h) on 200(h) vio	25	15
J46	D3	40(h) on 300(h) ver	95	30
a.		Perf. 14x13½		35.00
J47	D3	50(h) on 500(h) dp grn	70	8
a.		Perf. 14x13½	3.50	
J48	D3	60(h) on 400(h) brn	1.50	20
J49	D3	100(h) on 600(h) dp vio	3.50	20
a.		Perf. 14x13½	35.00	1.50
		Nos. J44-J49 (6)	7.10	1.13

1927 **Violet Surcharge**

J50	D4	100(h) dk brn	1.00	10
a.		Perf. 13½	*275.00*	18.50

Surcharged with New Value in Violet

1927

J51	D4	40(h) on 185(h) org	28	5
J52	D4	50(h) on 20(h) car	35	12
a.		50(h) on 50(h) car (error)		*8,000.*
J53	D4	50(h) on 150(h) rose	45	10
a.		Perf. 13½	12.00	2.50
J54	D4	60(h) on 25(h) brn	65	30
J55	D4	60(h) on 185(h) org	80	20
J56	D4	100(h) on 25(h) brn	90	30
		Nos. J50-J56 (7)	4.43	1.17

No. J52a is known only used.

No. J12 Surcharged in Violet **200**

1927 *Imperf.*

J57	D1	200(h) on 500(h) gray grn	5.50	3.75

D5

D6

1928 *Perf. 14 x 13½*

J58	D5	5h dk red	5	5
J59	D5	10h dk red	5	5
J60	D5	20h dk red	8	5
J61	D5	30h dk red	8	5
J62	D5	40h dk red	8	5
J63	D5	50h dk red	8	5
J64	D5	60h dk red	8	5
J65	D5	1k ultra	25	10
J66	D5	2k ultra	75	10
J67	D5	5k ultra	1.25	10
J68	D5	10k ultra	2.50	15
J69	D5	20k ultra	5.00	15
		Nos. J58-J69 (12)	10.25	95

1946-48 **Photo.** *Perf. 14*

J70	D6	10h dk bl	5	5
J71	D6	20h dk bl	6	5
J72	D6	50h dk bl	10	5
J73	D6	1k car rose	22	5
J74	D6	1.20k car rose	42	5
J75	D6	1.50k car rose ('48)	50	5
J76	D6	1.60k car rose	60	5

J77	D6	2k	car rose ('48)	60	5
J78	D6	2.40k	car rose	1.10	5
J79	D6	3k	car rose	1.50	5
J80	D6	5k	car rose	2.75	5
J81	D6	6k	car rose ('48)	3.00	5
			Nos. J70-J81 (12)	10.90	60

D7

D8

1954-55 Engr. *Perf. 12½, 11½*

J82	D7	5h	gray grn ('55)	5	5
J83	D7	10h	gray grn ('55)	6	5
J84	D7	30h	gray grn	16	5
J85	D7	50h	gray grn ('55)	20	5
J86	D7	60h	gray grn ('55)	25	5
J87	D7	95h	gray grn	50	5
J88	D8	1k	violet	50	5
J89	D8	1.20k	vio ('55)	50	5
J90	D8	1.50k	violet	1.00	5
J91	D8	1.60k	vio ('55)	65	5
J92	D8	2k	violet	1.25	5
J93	D8	3k	violet	1.65	5
J94	D8	5k	vio ('55)	2.00	25
			Nos. J82-J94 (13)	8.77	85

Perf. 11½ stamps are from a 1963 printing which lacks the 95h, 1.60k, and 2k.

Stylized Flower — D9

Designs: Various stylized flowers.

Engraved and Photogravure

1971-72 *Perf. 11½*

J95	D9	10h	vio bl & pink ('72)	8	5
J96	D9	20h	vio & lt bl ('72)	10	5
J97	D9	30h	emer & lil rose ('72)	10	5
J98	D9	60h	pur & emer ('72)	20	5
J99	D9	80h	org & vio bl ('72)	28	5
J100	D9	1k	dk red & emer ('72)	50	5
J101	D9	1.20k	grn & org ('72)	40	5
J102	D9	2k	bl & red ('72)	80	5
J103	D9	3k	blk & yel ('72)	95	10
J104	D9	4k	brn & ultra ('72)	1.65	10
J105	D9	5.40k	red & lil	2.00	25
J106	D9	6k	brick red & org ('72)	2.75	35
			Nos. J95-J106 (12)	9.81	1.20

OFFICIAL STAMPS

Coat of Arms — O1

1945 Unwmk. Litho. *Perf. 10½x10*

O1	O1	50h	dp sl grn	10	5
O2	O1	1k	dp bl vio	15	5
O3	O1	1.20k	plum	30	20
O4	O1	1.50k	crim rose	15	5
O5	O1	2.50k	brt ultra	30	20
O6	O1	5k	dk vio brn	40	30
O7	O1	8k	rose pink	60	50
			Nos. O1-O7 (7)	2.00	1.35

Redrawn

1947 Photo. *Perf. 14*

O8	O1	60h	red	5	5
O9	O1	80h	dk ol grn	5	5
O10	O1	1k	dk lil gray	5	5
O11	O1	1.20k	dp plum	8	5
O12	O1	2.40k	dk car rose	12	6
O13	O1	4k	brt ultra	20	20
O14	O1	5k	dk vio brn	25	25
O15	O1	7.40k	purple	45	40
			Nos. O8-O15 (8)	1.25	1.11

There are many minor changes in design, size of numerals, etc., of the redrawn stamps.

NEWSPAPER STAMPS

Windhover — N1

1918-20 Unwmk. Typo. *Imperf.*

P1	N1	2(h)	gray grn	5	5
P2	N1	5(h)	grn ('20)	5	5
a.		5(h)	dk grn	50	15
P3	N1	6(h)	red	60	40
P4	N1	10(h)	dl vio	5	5
P5	N1	20(h)	blue	10	5
P6	N1	30(h)	gray brn	20	15
P7	N1	50(h)	org ('20)	40	25
P8	N1	100(h)	red brn ('20)	60	40
			Nos. P1-P8 (8)	2.05	1.40

Nos. P1 to P8 exist privately perforated.

Stamps of 1918-20 Surcharged in Violet

1925-26

P9	N1	5(h) on 2 (h) gray grn	1.00	50
P10	N1	5(h) on 6 (h) red ('26)	75	50

Special Delivery Stamps of 1918-20 Overprinted in Violet

NOVINY

1926

P11	SD1	5(h) ap grn, *yel*	35	30
a.		5(h) dl grn, *yel*	75	50
P12	SD1	10(h) red brn, *yel*	25	20

With Additional Surcharge of New Value

P13	SD1	5(h) on 2(h) red vio, *yel*	25	18

Newspaper Stamps of 1918-20 Overprinted in Violet

O.T.

1934

P14	N1	10(h)	dl vio	5	5
P15	N1	20(h)	blue	5	5
P16	N1	30(h)	gray brn	25	25

Overprinted for use by commercial firms only.

Carrier Pigeon — N2

1937 *Imperf.*

P17	N2	2h	bis brn	5	5
P18	N2	5h	dl bl	5	5
P19	N2	7h	red org	5	5
P20	N2	9h	emerald	5	5
P21	N2	10h	hn brn	5	5
P22	N2	12h	ultra	5	5
P23	N2	20h	dk grn	6	5
P24	N2	50h	dk brn	6	5
P25	N2	1k	ol gray	15	10
			Nos. P17-P25 (9)	57	50

Bratislava Philatelic Exhibition Issue Souvenir Sheet

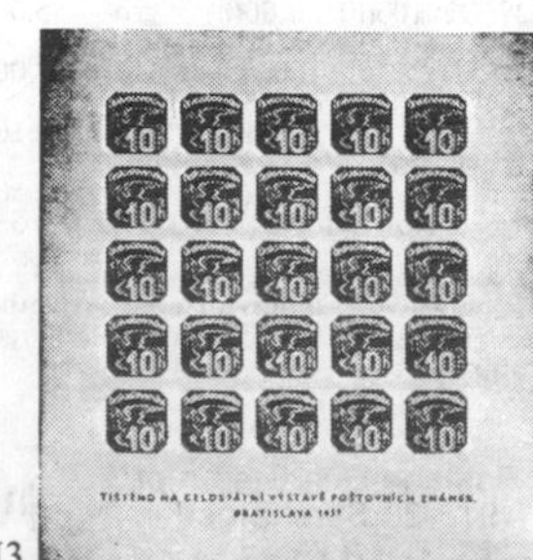
N3

1937 *Imperf.*

P26	N3	10h hn brn, sheet of 25	4.50	4.50

Issued in sheets measuring 150x165mm.

Newspaper Delivery Boy — N4

1945 Unwmk. Typo. *Imperf.*

P27	N4	5h	dl bl	5	5
P28	N4	10h	red	5	5
P29	N4	15h	emerald	5	5
P30	N4	20h	dk sl grn	5	5
P31	N4	25h	brt red vio	5	5
P32	N4	30h	ocher	5	5
P33	N4	40h	red org	5	5
P34	N4	50h	brn red	8	5
P35	N4	1k	sl gray	15	8
P36	N4	5k	dp vio bl	25	15
			Nos. P27-P36 (10)	83	63

CZECHOSLOVAK LEGION POST

The Czechoslovak Legion in Siberia issued these stamps for use on its mail and that of local residents. Forgeries exist.

Urn and Cathedral at Irkutsk — A1

Armored Railroad Car — A2

Sentinel — A3

Lion of Bohemia — A4

1919 Litho. *Perf. 11½*

1	A1	25(k)	carmine	17.00
a.			Imperf.	18.00
2	A2	50(k)	yel grn	17.00
a.			Imperf.	18.00
3	A3	1 (r)	red brn	40.00
a.			Imperf.	45.00

Originals of Nos. 1-3 and 1a-3a have yellowish gum. Ungummed remainders, which were given a white gum, exist imperforate and perforated 11½ and 14. Price per set, $3.

Embossed

Perce en Arc in Blue

4	A4	(25k) bl & rose	3.75

Two types: (I) Six points on star-like mace head at right of goblet; large saber handle; measures 19½x24¾mm. (II) Five points on mace head; small saber handle; measures 20 x 25mm.

No. 4 Overprinted **1920**

1920

5	A4	(25k) bl & rose	10.00

Both types of No. 4 received overprint.

No. 5 Surcharged with New Values in Green **2**

6	A4	2(k) bl & rose	35.00
7	A4	3(k) bl & rose	35.00
8	A4	5(k) bl & rose	35.00
9	A4	10(k) bl & rose	35.00
10	A4	15(k) bl & rose	35.00
11	A4	25(k) bl & rose	35.00
12	A4	35(k) bl & rose	35.00
13	A4	50(k) bl & rose	35.00
14	A4	1r bl & rose	35.00
		Nos. 6-14 (9)	315.00

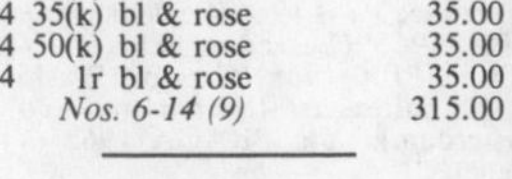

BOHEMIA AND MORAVIA

German Protectorate

Stamps of Czechoslovakia, 1928-39, Overprinted in Black

BÖHMEN u. MÄHREN

ČECHY a MORAVA

Perf. 10, 12½, 12x12½

1939, July 15 Unwmk.

1	A29	5h	dk ultra	12	*30*
2	A29	10h	brown	10	*30*
3	A29	20h	red	10	*30*
4	A29	25h	green	12	*30*
5	A29	30h	red vio	10	*30*
6	A61a	40h	dk bl	3.75	*7.00*
7	A85	50h	dp grn	10	*30*
8	A63	60h	dl vio	3.75	*7.00*
9	A60	1k	rose lake (212)	1.10	*2.50*
10	A60	1k	rose lake (256)	42	*1.25*
11	A64	1.20k	rose lil	4.50	*9.00*
12	A65	1.50k	carmine	3.75	*7.00*
13	A79	1.60k	ol grn	3.75	*7.00*
a.			"Mähnen"	27.50	*40.00*
14	A66	2k	dk bl grn	1.75	*2.50*
15	A67	2.50k	dk bl	4.50	*6.50*
16	A68	3k	brown	4.50	*7.00*
17	A70	4k	dk vio	5.00	*7.50*
18	A71	5k	green	5.00	*8.50*
19	A72	10k	blue	6.75	*14.00*
			Nos. 1-19 (19)	49.16	88.55

The size of the overprint varies with the size of the stamps, Nos. 1 to 10 measure 17½x15½mm., Nos. 11 to 16 measure 19x18mm., Nos. 17 and 19 measure 28x17½ and No. 18 measures 23½x23mm.

Linden Leaves and Closed Buds — A1

1939-41 Photo. *Perf. 14*

20	A1	5h	dk bl	5	5
21	A1	10h	blk brn	5	5
22	A1	20h	crimson	5	5
23	A1	25h	dk bl grn	6	12
24	A1	30h	dp plum	5	8
24A	A1	30h	gldn brn ('41)	5	5
25	A1	40h	org ('40)	5	8
26	A1	50h	sl grn ('40)	8	12
			Nos. 20-26 (8)	44	60

See Nos. 49-51.

Castle at Zvikov A2

Karlstein Castle A3

St. Barbara's Church, Kutna Hora — A4

Cathedral at Prague — A5

Czechoslovak Legion Post stamps can be mounted in Scott's Czechoslovakia Album.

Brno Cathedral — A6

Town Square, Olomouc — A7

1939 Engr. *Perf. 12½*

27	A2	40h dk bl	5	8
28	A3	50h dk bl grn	5	5
29	A4	60h dl vio	5	5
30	A5	1k dp rose	5	5
31	A6	1.20k rose lil	25	*75*
32	A6	1.50k rose car	5	5
33	A7	2k dk bl grn	6	6
34	A7	2.50k dk bl	5	8
		Nos. 27-34 (8)	61	1.17

No. 31 measures 23½x29½mm., while No. 42 measures 18½x23mm.

Zlin — A8

Iron Works at Moravska Ostrava — A9

Prague — A10

1939-40

35	A8	3k dl rose vio	15	15
36	A9	4k sl ('40)	6	8
37	A10	5k green	35	*50*
38	A10	10k lt ultra	25	*85*
39	A10	20k yel brn	75	*1.75*
		Nos. 35-39 (5)	1.56	3.33

Types of 1939 and

Neuhaus A11

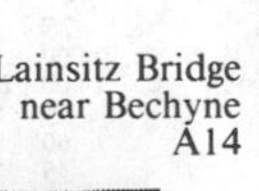
Lainsitz Bridge near Bechyne A14

Pernstein Castle A12

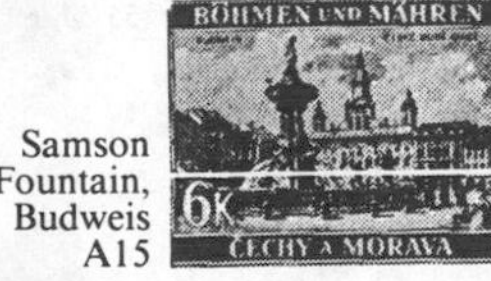

Samson Fountain, Budweis A15

Pardubice Castle A13

Kromeriz A16

Wallenstein Palace, Prague — A17

1940 Engr. *Perf. 12½*

40	A11	50h dk bl grn	5	8
41	A12	80h dp bl	12	*45*
42	A6	1.20k vio brn	28	25
43	A13	2k gray grn	10	8
44	A14	5k dk bl grn	10	10
45	A15	6k brn vio	10	*30*
46	A16	8k sl grn	10	*35*
47	A17	10k blue	30	30
48	A10	20k sepia	70	*1.65*
		Nos. 40-48 (9)	1.85	3.56

No. 42 measures 18½x23mm.; No. 31, 23½x29½mm.

Types of 1939-40

1941

49	A1	60h violet	5	8
50	A1	80h red org	6	8
51	A1	1k brown	6	8
52	A5	1.20k rose red	5	15
53	A4	1.50k lil rose	10	15
53A	A13	2k lt bl	5	15
53B	A6	2.50k ultra	5	8
53C	A12	3k olive	12	15
		Nos. 49-53C (8)	54	92

Nos. 49-51 show buds open. Nos. 52 and 53B measure 18¾x23½mm. and have no inscriptions below design.

Antonin Dvorak — A18

1941, Aug. 25 Engr. *Perf. 12½*

54	A18	60h dl lil	15	*30*
55	A18	1.20k sepia	28	45

Birth centenary of Antonin Dvorak (1841-1904), composer.
Labels alternate with stamps in sheets of Nos. 54-55.

Farming Scene A19

Factories A20

1941, Sept. 7 Photo. *Perf. 13½*

56	A19	30h dk red brn	5	12
57	A19	60h dk grn	5	12
58	A20	1.20k dk plum	15	*30*
59	A20	1.50k sapphire	18	*40*

Issued to publicize the Prague Fair.

Nos. 52 and 53B Overprinted in Blue or Red

1942, Mar. 15 *Perf. 12½*

60	A5	1.20k rose red (Bl)	28	*75*
61	A6	2.50k ultra (R)	45	*75*

Issued to commemorate the third anniversary of the Protectorate of Bohemia and Moravia.

Adolf Hitler A21

17th Century Messenger A22

1942 Photo. *Perf. 14*
Size: 17½x21½mm.

62	A21	10(h) gray blk	5	5
63	A21	30(h) bis brn	5	5
64	A21	40(h) sl bl	5	5
65	A21	50(h) sl grn	5	5
66	A21	60(h) purple	5	5
67	A21	80(h) org ver	5	5

Perf. 12½
Engr.
Size: 18x21mm.

68	A21	1k dl brn	5	5
69	A21	1.20(k) carmine	5	5
70	A21	1.50(k) claret	5	5
71	A21	1.60(k) Prus grn	8	*25*
72	A21	2k lt bl	5	5
73	A21	2.40(k) fawn	8	*30*

Size: 18½x24mm.

74	A21	2.50(k) ultra	5	5
75	A21	3k ol grn	6	5
76	A21	4k brt red vio	6	5
77	A21	5k myr grn	5	5
78	A21	6k cl brn	5	10
79	A21	8k indigo	5	10

Size: 23½x29¾mm.

80	A21	10k dk gray grn	8	10
81	A21	20k gray vio	20	*35*
82	A21	30k red	45	*1.10*
83	A21	50k dp bl	1.00	*2.25*
		Nos. 62-83 (22)	2.71	5.25

1943, Jan. 10 Photo. *Perf. 13½*

84	A22	60(h) dk rose vio	5	8

Stamp Day.

Scene from "Die Meistersinger" A23

Richard Wagner A24

Scene from "Siegfried" — A25

1943, May 22

85	A23	60(h) violet	5	8
86	A24	1.20(k) car rose	6	8
87	A25	2.50(k) dp ultra	6	*25*

130th anniversary of the birth of Richard Wagner (1813-1883).

St. Vitus' Cathedral, Prague A26

Adolf Hitler A27

1944, Nov. 21 Engr. *Perf. 12½*

88	A26	1.50(k) dl rose brn	5	12
89	A26	2.50(k) dl lil bl	8	*30*

1944

90	A27	4.20(k) green	12	*35*

SEMI-POSTAL STAMPS

Nurse and Wounded Soldier — SP1

Red Cross Nurse and Patient — SP2

Perf. 13½
1940, June 29 Photo. Unwmk.

B1	SP1	60h + 40h ind	55	*90*
B2	SP1	1.20k + 80h dp plum	70	*1.10*

Surtax for German Red Cross.

Labels alternate with stamps in sheets of Nos. B1-B2.

1941, Apr. 20

B3	SP2	60h + 40h ind	28	*50*
B4	SP2	1.20k + 80h dp plum	28	*60*

Surtax for German Red Cross.

Labels alternate with stamps in sheets of Nos. B3-B4.

Old Theater, Prague — SP3

Wolfgang Amadeus Mozart — SP4

1941, Oct. 26

B5	SP3	30h + 30h brn	5	10
B6	SP3	60h + 60h Prus grn	5	10
B7	SP4	1.20k + 1.20k scar	15	*45*
B8	SP4	2.50k + 2.50k dk bl	30	*60*

150th anniversary of Mozart's death.

Labels alternate with stamps in sheets of Nos. B5-B8. The labels with Nos. B5-B6 show two bars of Mozart's opera "Don Giovanni." Those with Nos. B7-B8 show Mozart's piano.

Adolf Hitler — SP5

Nurse and Soldier — SP6

1942, Apr. 20 Engr. *Perf. 12½*

B9	SP5	30(h) + 20(h) dl brn vio	8	15
B10	SP5	60(h) + 40(h) dl grn	8	15
B11	SP5	1.20(k) + 80(h) dp cl	8	15
B12	SP5	2.50(k) + 1.50(k) dl bl	12	*28*

Issued to commemorate Hitler's 53rd birthday.

1942, Sept. 4 *Perf. 13½*

B13	SP6	60h + 40h dp bl	5	6
B14	SP6	1.20(k) + 80(h) dp plum	5	8

The surtax aided the German Red Cross.

Emperor Charles IV — SP7

Peter Parler — SP8

John the Blind, King of Bohemia
SP9

Adolf Hitler
SP10

1943, Jan. 29

No.	Type	Denomination	Unused	Used
B15	SP7	60(h) + 40(h) vio	6	8
B16	SP8	1.20(k) + 80(h) car	5	12
B17	SP9	2.50(k) + 1.50(k) vio bl	8	16

The surtax was for the benefit of the German wartime winter relief.

1943, Apr. 20 Engr. *Perf. 12½*

No.	Type	Denomination	Unused	Used
B18	SP10	60(h) + 1.40(k) dl vio	5	12
B19	SP10	1.20(k) + 3.80(k) car	8	25

Issued to commemorate Hitler's 54th birthday.

Deathmask of Reinhard Heydrich
SP11

Eagle and Red Cross
SP12

1943, May 28 Photo. *Perf. 13½*

No.	Type	Denomination	Unused	Used
B20	SP11	60(h) + 4.40(h) blk	22	45

No. B20 exists in a miniature sheet containing a single copy. It was given to officials attending Heydrich's funeral.

1943, Sept. 16 *Perf. 13*

No.	Type	Denomination	Unused	Used
B21	SP12	1.20(k) + 8.80(k) blk & car	7	12

The surtax aided the German Red Cross.

Native Costumes
SP13

Nazi Emblem and Arms of Bohemia, Moravia
SP14

1944, Mar. 15 *Perf. 13½*

No.	Type	Denomination	Unused	Used
B22	SP13	1.20(k) + 3.80(k) rose lake	5	10
B23	SP14	4.20(k) + 10.80(k) gldn brn	5	10
B24	SP13	10k + 20k saph	10	35

Fifth anniversary of protectorate.

Adolf Hitler
SP15

Bedrich Smetana
SP16

1944, Apr. 20

No.	Type	Denomination	Unused	Used
B25	SP15	60(h) + 1.40(k) ol blk	5	8
B26	SP15	1.20(k) + 3.80(k) sl grn	8	12

1944, May 12 Engr. *Perf. 12½*

No.	Type	Denomination	Unused	Used
B27	SP16	60(h) + 1.40(k) dk gray grn	5	8
B28	SP16	1.20(k) + 3.80(k) brn car	8	12

Issued to commemorate the 60th anniversary of the death of Friedrich Smetana (1824-84), Czech composer and pianist.

PERSONAL DELIVERY STAMPS

PD1

1939-40 Unwmk. Photo. *Perf. 13½*

No.	Type	Denomination	Unused	Used
EX1	PD1	50h ind & bl ('40)	60	1.25
EX2	PD1	50h car & rose	75	1.50

POSTAGE DUE STAMPS

D1

1939-40 Unwmk. Typo. *Perf. 14*

No.	Type	Denomination	Unused	Used
J1	D1	5h dk car	6	8
J2	D1	10h dk car	6	8
J3	D1	20h dk car	6	8
J4	D1	30h dk car	6	8
J5	D1	40h dk car	8	10
J6	D1	50h dk car	8	10
J7	D1	60h dk car	8	10
J8	D1	80h dk car	8	10
J9	D1	1k brt ultra	12	40
J10	D1	1.20k brt ultra ('40)	20	40
J11	D1	2k brt ultra	60	1.10
J12	D1	5k brt ultra	65	1.25
J13	D1	10k brt ultra	1.00	2.00
J14	D1	20k brt ultra	2.75	5.00
		Nos. J1-J14 (14)	5.88	10.87

OFFICIAL STAMPS

Numeral
O1

Eagle
O2

Unwmk.

1941, Jan. 1 Typo. *Perf. 14*

No.	Type	Denomination	Unused	Used
O1	O1	30h ocher	12	5
O2	O1	40h indigo	12	5
O3	O1	50h emerald	12	5
O4	O1	60h sl grn	12	5
O5	O1	80h org red	60	25
O6	O1	1k red brn	22	5
O7	O1	1.20k carmine	22	5
O8	O1	1.50k dp plum	40	12
O9	O1	2k brt bl	40	8
O10	O1	3k olive	40	8
O11	O1	4k red vio	70	60
O12	O1	5k org yel	1.75	1.20
		Nos. O1-O12 (12)	5.17	2.63

1943, Feb. 15

No.	Type	Denomination	Unused	Used
O13	O2	30(h) bister	5	5
O14	O2	40(h) indigo	5	5
O15	O2	50(h) yel grn	5	5
O16	O2	60(h) dp vio	5	5
O17	O2	80(h) org red	5	5
O18	O2	1k chocolate	5	5
O19	O2	1.20(k) carmine	5	5
O20	O2	1.50(k) brn red	5	12
O21	O2	2k lt bl	6	12
O22	O2	3k olive	6	12
O23	O2	4k red vio	8	12
O24	O2	5k dk grn	12	30
		Nos. O13-O24 (12)	72	1.13

NEWSPAPER STAMPS

Carrier Pigeon
N1 N2

1939 Unwmk. Typo. *Imperf.*

No.	Type	Denomination	Unused	Used
P1	N1	2h ocher	5	8
P2	N1	5h ultra	5	8
P3	N1	7h red org	5	8
P4	N1	9h emerald	5	8
P5	N1	10h hn brn	5	12
P6	N1	12h dk ultra	5	8
P7	N1	20h dk grn	6	30
P8	N1	50h red brn	10	40
P9	N1	1k grnsh gray	15	40
		Nos. P1-P9 (9)	61	1.62

No. P5 Overprinted in Black **GD-OT**

1940

No.	Type	Denomination	Unused	Used
P10	N1	10h hn brn	12	30

Overprinted for use by commercial firms.

1943, Feb. 15

No.	Type	Denomination	Unused	Used
P11	N2	2(h) ocher	5	5
P12	N2	5(h) lt bl	5	5
P13	N2	7(h) red org	5	5
P14	N2	9(h) emerald	5	5
P15	N2	10(h) hn brn	5	5
P16	N2	12(h) dk ultra	5	5
P17	N2	20(h) dk grn	5	8
P18	N2	50(h) red brn	5	8
P19	N2	1k sl grn	5	30
		Nos. P11-P19 (9)	45	76

CARPATHO-UKRAINE

A former province of Czechoslovakia known as Ruthenia, which in 1938 became an autonomous Czechoslovak state as a result of the Munich Agreement. On Mar. 16, 1939, it was incorporated in the Kingdom of Hungary.

100 Haleru = 1 Koruna

View of Jasina — A1

Perf. 12½

1939, Mar. 15 Engr. Unwmk.

No.	Type	Denomination	Unused	Used
1	A1	3k ultra	9.00	25.00

Issued in commemoration of the inauguration of the Carpatho-Ukraine Diet, March 2, 1939.

SLOVAKIA

LOCATION — Central Europe
GOVT. — Nominally independent republic
AREA — 14,848 sq. mi.
POP. — 2,450,000
CAPITAL — Bratislava

Formerly a province of Czechoslovakia, Slovakia declared its independence in March, 1939. A treaty was immediately concluded with Germany guaranteeing Slovakian independence but providing for German "protection" for 25 years.

In 1945 the republic ended and Slovakia again became a part of Czechoslovakia.

100 Halierov = 1 Koruna

Otvorenie slovenského snemu 18.I. 1939

300 h

Czechoslovakia No. 226 Surcharged in Orange Red

1939, Jan. 18 Unwmk. *Perf. 12½*

No.	Type	Denomination	Unused	Used
1	A72	300h on 10k bl	90	5.00

Issued to commemorate the opening of the Slovakian Parliament.

Stamps of Czechoslovakia, 1928-39, Overprinted in Red or Blue **Slovenský štát 1939**

1939 *Perf. 10, 12½, 12x12½*

No.	Type	Denomination	Unused	Used
2	A29	5h dk ultra (R)	75	1.25
3	A29	10h brn (R)	12	18
4	A29	20h red (Bl)	8	10
5	A29	25h grn (R)	1.50	2.50
6	A29	30h red vio (Bl)	10	18
7	A61a	40h dk bl (R)	12	25
8	A73	50h dp grn (R)	8	8
9	A63	50h dp grn (R)	8	8
10	A63	60h dl vio (R)	10	18
11	A63	60h dl bl (R)	9.00	12.50
12	A60	1k rose lake (Bl) (On No. 212)	8	8

Overprinted Diagonally

No.	Type	Denomination	Unused	Used
13	A64	1.20k rose lil (Bl)	30	45
14	A65	1.50k car (Bl)	30	45
15	A79	1.60k ol grn (Bl)	2.75	3.75
16	A66	2k dk bl grn (R)	2.75	3.75
17	A67	2.50k dk bl (R)	45	75
18	A68	3k brn (R)	60	90
19	A69	3.50k dk vio (R)	27.50	37.50
20	A69	3.50k dk vio (Bl)	32.50	42.50
21	A70	4k dk vio (R)	14.00	17.50
22	A71	5k grn (R)	15.00	20.00
23	A72	10k bl (R)	110.00	140.00
		Nos. 2-23 (22)	218.16	284.93

Excellent counterfeit overprints exist.

Andrej Hlinka
A1 A2

Overprinted in Red or Blue
Perf. 12½

1939, Apr. Unwmk. Photo.

No.	Type	Denomination	Unused	Used
24	A1	50h dk grn (R)	1.75	1.00
a.		Perf. 10½	1.75	1.50
b.		Perf. 10½x12½	4.00	4.50
25	A1	1k dk car rose (Bl)	1.50	1.00
a.		Perf. 10½	70.00	110.00
b.		Perf. 10½x12½	7.50	10.00

1939 Unwmk. *Perf. 12½*

No.	Type	Denomination	Unused	Used
26	A2	5h brt ultra	45	80
27	A2	10h ol grn	75	1.25
a.		Perf. 10½x12½	24.00	8.00
b.		Perf. 10½	24.00	20.00
28	A2	20h org red	75	1.25
a.		Imperf.	60	1.00
29	A2	30h dp vio	75	1.25
a.		Imperf.	90	1.50
b.		Perf. 10½x12½	6.00	9.00
c.		Perf. 10½	9.00	10.00
30	A2	50h dk grn	75	1.25
31	A2	1k dk car rose	90	1.25
32	A2	2.50k brt bl	90	55
33	A2	3k blk brn	2.50	55
		Nos. 26-33 (8)	7.75	8.15

On Nos. 32 and 33 a pearl frame surrounds the medallion. See Nos. 55-57, 69.

Bohemia and Moravia stamps can be mounted in Scott's Czechoslovakia or Germany Part II Albums.

General Stefanik and Memorial Tomb — A3

Rev. Josef Murgas and Radio Towers — A4

1939, May *Perf. 12½*

Size: 25x20mm.

34	A3	40h dk bl	90
35	A3	60h sl grn	90
36	A3	1k gray vio	90

Size: 30x23¾ mm.

37	A3	2k bl vio & sep	90

Prepared to commemorate the 20th anniversary of the death of Gen. Milan Stefanik, but not issued.

1939 **Unwmk.**

38	A4	60h purple	30 45
39	A4	1.20k sl blk	60 30

Issued in commemoration of the 10th anniversary of the death of Rev. Josef Murgas. See No. 65.

Girl Weaving A5

Woodcutter A6

Girl at Spring — A7

Wmk. 263

Wmk. Double-Barred Cross Multiple (263)

1939-44 *Perf. 12½*

40	A5	2k dk bl grn	6.00 55
41	A6	4k cop brn	1.40 1.10
42	A7	5k org red	95 60
a.		Perf. 10 ('44)	85 65

Dr. Josef Tiso A8

Presidential Residence A9

1939-44 **Wmk. 263** *Perf. 12½*

43	A8	50h sl grn	45 50
43A	A8	70h dk red brn ('42)	30 25
b.		Perf. 10½ ('44)	60 35

See No. 88.

1940, Mar. 14

44	A9	10k dp bl	90 1.00

Tatra Mountains A10

Krivan Peak A11

Edelweiss in the Tatra Mountains A12

Chamois A13

Church at Javorina — A14

1940-43 **Wmk. 263** *Perf. 12½*

Size: 17x21mm.

45	A10	5h dk ol grn	15 8
46	A11	10h dp brn	10 8
47	A12	20h bl blk	8 8
48	A13	25h ol brn	65 35
49	A14	30h chnt brn	30 30
a.		Perf. 10½ ('43)	50 35
		Nos. 45-49 (5)	1.28 89

See Nos. 84-87, 103-107.

Hlinka Type of 1939

1940-42 **Wmk. 263** *Perf. 12½*

55	A2	1k dk car rose	75 90
56	A2	2.50k brt bl ('42)	90 1.00
a.		Perf. 10½	60 1.00
57	A2	3k blk brn ('41)	1.25 1.00
a.		Perf. 10½	90 1.00

On Nos. 56 and 57 a pearl frame surrounds the medallion.

Stiavnica A15

Lietava A16

Spissky Hrad A17

Bojnice A18

1941 *Perf. 12½*

58	A15	1.20(k) rose lake	20 30
59	A16	1.50(k) rose pink	20 30
60	A17	1.60(k) ryl bl	30 12
61	A18	2k dk gray grn	20 8

Slovakian Castles.

S. M. Daxner and Stefan Moyses A19

Andrej Hlinka A20

1941, May 26 **Photo.** **Wmk. 263**

62	A19	50h ol grn	2.00 2.50
63	A19	1k sl bl	8.25 10.00
64	A19	2k black	8.25 10.00

Issued in commemoration of the 80th anniversary of the Memorandum of the Slovak Nation.

Murgas Type of 1939

1941 **Wmk. 263**

65	A4	60h purple	35 30

1942

69	A20	1.30k dk pur	45 20

Post Horn and Miniature Stamp A21

Philatelist A22

Philatelist — A23

1942, May 23

70	A21	30h dk grn	1.00 1.50
71	A22	70h dk car rose	1.00 1.50
72	A23	80h purple	1.00 1.50
73	A21	1.30k dk brn	1.00 1.50

Issued to commemorate the National Philatelic Exhibition at Bratislava.

On No. 70 the miniature stamp bears the coat-of-arms of Bratislava; on No. 73 it shows the National arms of Slovakia.

St. Stephen's Cathedral, Vienna — A24

1942, Oct. 12 *Perf. 14*

74	A24	70h bl grn	90 1.50
75	A24	1.30k ol grn	90 1.50
76	A24	2k sapphire	1.75 4.00

Issued to commemorate the European Postal Congress held in Vienna.

Slovakian Educational Society — A25

1942, Dec. 14

77	A25	70h black	12 22
78	A25	1k rose red	30 42
79	A25	1.30k sapphire	12 35
80	A25	2k chnt brn	30 42
81	A25	3k dk grn	45 55
82	A25	4k dl pur	45 65
		Nos. 77-82 (6)	1.74 2.61

Slovakian Educational Society, 150th anniversary.

Andrej Hlinka — A26

1943 **Wmk. 263**

83	A26	1.30k brt ultra	20 20

See Nos. 93-94A.

Types of 1939-40

1943 **Unwmk.** *Perf. 12½*

84	A11	10h dp brn	20 12
85	A12	20h bl blk	55 28
86	A13	25h ol brn	55 28
87	A14	30h chnt brn	35 22
88	A8	70h dk red brn	65 55
		Nos. 84-88 (5)	2.30 1.45

Presov Church A27

Locomotive A28

Railway Tunnel — A29

Viaduct — A30

1943, Sept. 5 *Perf. 14*

89	A27	70h dk rose vio	45 50
90	A28	80h sapphire	45 50
91	A29	1.30k black	45 50
92	A30	2k dk vio brn	60 80

Issued to commemorate the inauguration of the new railroad line between Presov and Strazske.

Hlinka Type of 1943 and

Ludwig Stur A31

Martin Razus A32

1944 **Unwmk.**

93	A31	80h sl grn	18 12
94	A32	1k brn red	24 12
94A	A26	1.30k brt ultra	60 70

Prince Pribina — A33

Designs: 70h, Prince Mojmir. 80h, Prince Ratislav. 1.30k, King Svatopluk. 2k, Prince Kocel. 3k, Prince Mojmir II. 5k, Prince Svatopluk II. 10k, Prince Braslav.

1944, Mar. 14

95	A33	50h dk grn	8 10
96	A33	70h lil rose	8 10
97	A33	80h red brn	8 10
98	A33	1.30k brt ultra	12 12
99	A33	2k Prus bl	12 30
100	A33	3k dk brn	35 45
101	A33	5k violet	75 1.00
102	A33	10k black	2.00 3.00
		Nos. 95-102 (8)	3.58 5.17

Scenic Types of 1940

1944, Apr. 1 *Perf. 14*

Size: 18x23mm.

103	A11	10h brt car	18 35
104	A12	20h brt bl	18 35
105	A13	25h brn red	18 35
106	A14	30h red vio	18 35
107	A10	50h dp grn	18 35
		Nos. 103-107 (5)	90 1.75

Issued to honor the 5th anniversary of Slovakia's independence.

Carpatho-Ukraine and Slovakia stamps can be mounted in Scott's Czechoslovakia or Germany Part II Albums.

Symbolic of National Protection – A41

President Josef Tiso – A42

1944, Oct. 6 **Wmk. 263**

108	A41	2k green	45	60
109	A41	3.80k red vio	45	85

1945 **Unwmk.**

110	A42	1k orange	90	1.00
111	A42	1.50k brown	24	25
112	A42	2k green	30	25
113	A42	4k rose red	90	1.00
114	A42	5k sapphire	90	1.00

Wmk. 263

115	A42	10k red vio	60	50
		Nos. 110-115 (6)	3.84	4.00

To commemorate the sixth anniversary of the Republic of Slovakia's declaration of independence, March 14, 1939.

SEMI-POSTAL STAMPS

Josef Tiso – SP1

Wmk. 263

1939, Nov. 6 **Photo.** ***Perf. 12½***

B1	SP1	2.50k + 2.50k ryl bl	3.50	4.50

The surtax was used for Child Welfare.

Medical Corpsman and Wounded Soldier – SP2

1941, Nov. 10

B2	SP2	50h + 50h dl grn	45	75
B3	SP2	1k + 1k rose lake	60	1.00
B4	SP2	2k + 1k brt bl	2.00	2.50

Mother and Child – SP3

Soldier and Hlinka Youth – SP4

1941, Dec. 10

B5	SP3	50h + 50h dl grn	1.00	1.40
B6	SP3	1k + 1k brn	1.00	1.40
B7	SP3	2k + 1k vio	1.00	1.40

The surtax was for the benefit of child welfare.

1942, Mar. 14

B8	SP4	70h + 1k brn org	45	60
B9	SP4	1.30k + 1k brt bl	60	75
B10	SP4	2k + 1k rose red	1.50	1.75

The surtax aided the Hlinka Youth Society "Hlinkova Mladez."

National Costumes
SP5 SP6 SP7

1943 ***Perf. 14***

B11	SP5	50h + 50h dk sl grn	30	40
B12	SP6	70h + 1k dp car	30	40
B13	SP7	80h + 2k dk bl	30	40

The surtax was for the benefit of children, the Red Cross and winter relief of the Slovakian popular party.

Infantrymen – SP8

Aviator – SP9

Tank and Gun Crew SP10

1943, July 28

B14	SP8	70h + 2k rose brn	70	1.00
B15	SP9	1.30k + 2k saph	70	1.00
B16	SP10	2k + 2k ol grn	85	1.25

The surtax was for soldiers' welfare.

"The Slovak Language Is Our Life" - L. Stur – SP11

Slovakian National Museum – SP12

Slovakian Foundation SP13

Slovakian Peasant SP14

1943, Oct. 16

B17	SP11	30h + 1k brn red	45	60
B18	SP12	70h + 1k sl grn	60	60
B19	SP13	80h + 2k sl bl	45	60
B20	SP14	1.30k + 2k dl brn	45	60

The surtax was for the benefit of Slovakian cultural institutions.

Soccer Player – SP15

Skier – SP16

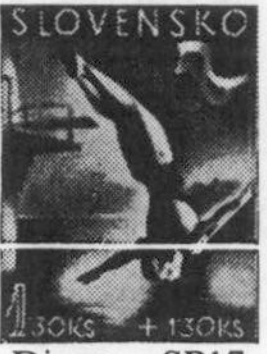

Diver – SP17

Relay Race – SP18

1944, Apr. 30 **Unwmk.**

B21	SP15	70h + 70h sl grn	60	1.40
B22	SP16	1k + 1k vio	75	1.65
B23	SP17	1.30k + 1.30k Prus bl	75	1.65
B24	SP18	2k + 2k chnt brn	90	2.25

Symbolic of National Protection SP19

Children SP20

1944, Oct. 6 **Wmk. 263**

B25	SP19	70h + 4h saph	1.25	2.50
B26	SP19	1.30k + 4k red brn	1.25	2.50

The surtax was for the benefit of social institutions.

1944, Dec. 18

B27	SP20	2k + 4k lt bl	3.50	6.00
a.		Sheet of 8 + Label	45.00	75.00

The surtax was to aid social work for Slovak youth.

AIR POST STAMPS

Planes over Tatra Mountains
AP1 AP2

Perf. 12½

1939, Nov. 20 **Photo.** **Unwmk.**

C1	AP1	30h violet	30	50
C2	AP1	50h dk grn	30	50
C3	AP1	1k vermilion	35	50
C4	AP2	2k grnsh blk	55	60
C5	AP2	3k dk brn	1.00	1.25
C6	AP2	4k sl bl	1.75	2.75
		Nos. C1-C6 (6)	4.25	6.10

See No. C10.

Plane in Flight – AP3

1940, Nov. 30 **Wmk. 263** ***Perf. 12½***

C7	AP3	5k dk vio brn	1.25	2.00
C8	AP3	10k gray blk	1.50	2.50
C9	AP3	20k myr grn	1.75	3.00

Type of 1939

1944, Sept. 15 **Wmk. 263**

C10	AP1	1k vermilion	70	1.00

PERSONAL DELIVERY STAMPS

PD1

1940 **Wmk. 263** **Photo.** ***Imperf***

EX1	PD1	50h ind & bl	90	2.50
EX2	PD1	50h car & rose	90	2.50

POSTAGE DUE STAMPS

D1

Letter, Post Horn – D2

1939 **Unwmk.** **Photo.** ***Perf. 12½***

J1	D1	5h brt bl	35	75
J2	D1	10h brt bl	35	75
J3	D1	20h brt bl	35	75
J4	D1	30h brt bl	1.50	1.25
J5	D1	40h brt bl	70	1.00
J6	D1	50h brt bl	1.75	1.10
J7	D1	60h brt bl	1.50	1.10
J8	D1	1k dk car	15.00	11.00
J9	D1	2k dk car	15.00	3.50
J10	D1	5k dk car	5.00	3.50
J11	D1	10k dk car	40.00	10.00
J12	D1	20k dk car	17.00	12.50
		Nos. J1-J12 (12)	98.50	47.20

1940-41 **Wmk. 263**

J13	D1	5h brt bl ('41)	90	75
J14	D1	10h brt bl ('41)	38	38
J15	D1	20h brt bl ('41)	60	38
J16	D1	30h brt bl ('41)	7.50	6.00
J17	D1	40h brt bl ('41)	75	75
J18	D1	50h brt bl ('41)	90	1.25
J19	D1	60h brt bl	1.10	1.25
J20	D1	1k dk car ('41)	1.10	1.50
J21	D1	2k dk car ('41)	11.25	10.00
J22	D1	5k dk car ('41)	3.00	3.50
J23	D1	10k dk car ('41)	3.75	4.25
		Nos. J13-J23 (11)	31.23	30.01

1942 **Unwmk.** ***Perf. 14***

J24	D2	10h dp brn	5	12
J25	D2	20h dp brn	5	30
J26	D2	40h dp brn	12	30
J27	D2	50h dp brn	1.00	30
J28	D2	60h dp brn	20	30
J29	D2	80h dp brn	26	30
J30	D2	1k rose red	35	30
J31	D2	1.10k rose red	65	80
J32	D2	1.30k rose red	40	30
J33	D2	1.60k rose red	50	30
J34	D2	2k rose red	65	30
J35	D2	2.60k rose red	1.40	1.50
J36	D2	3.50k rose red	8.25	10.00
J37	D2	5k rose red	3.00	3.50
J38	D2	10k rose red	3.25	4.25
		Nos. J24-J38 (15)	20.13	22.87

NEWSPAPER STAMPS

Newspaper Stamps of Czechoslovakia, 1937, Overprinted in Red or Blue

1939, Apr. **Unwmk.** ***Imperf.***

P1	N2	2h bis brn (Bl)	35	55
P2	N2	5h dl bl (R)	35	55

P3 N2 7h red org (Bl) 35 55
P4 N2 9h emer (R) 35 55
P5 N2 10h hn brn (Bl) 35 55
P6 N2 12h ultra (R) 35 55
P7 N2 20h dk grn (R) 75 1.25
P8 N2 50h dk brn (Bl) 2.50 3.75
P9 N2 1k grnsh gray (R) 8.50 15.00
Nos. P1-P9 (9) 13.85 23.30

Excellent counterfeits exist of Nos. P1 to P9.

Arms of Slovakia N1

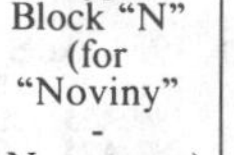

Type Block "N" (for "Noviny" - Newspaper) N2

1939 **Typo.**

P10 N1 2h ocher 12 22
P11 N1 5h ultra 30 50
P12 N1 7h red org 24 35
P13 N1 9h emerald 24 35
P14 N1 10h hn brn 1.40 1.40
P15 N1 12h dk ultra 24 40
P16 N1 20h dk grn 1.25 1.40
P17 N1 50h red brn 1.50 1.65
P18 N1 1k grnsh gray 1.25 1.40
Nos. P10-P18 (9) 6.54 7.67

1940-41 **Wmk. 263**

P20 N1 5h ultra 10 12
P23 N1 10h hn brn 10 20
P24 N1 15h brt pur ('41) 20 20
P25 N1 20h dk grn 45 50
P26 N1 25h lt bl ('41) 35 50
P27 N1 40h red org ('41) 45 50
P28 N1 50h chocolate 75 75
P29 N1 1k grnsh gray ('41) 75 75
P30 N1 2k emer ('41) 1.50 1.75
Nos. P20-P30 (9) 4.65 5.27

1943 **Photo.** **Unwmk.**

P31 N2 10h green 12 25
P32 N2 15h dk brn 12 25
P33 N2 20h ultra 18 25
P34 N2 50h rose red 22 38
P35 N2 1k sl grn 45 60
P36 N2 2k int bl 75 1.25
Nos. P31-P36 (6) 1.84 2.98

DAHOMEY

LOCATION — West coast of Africa
GOVT. — Republic
AREA — 43,483 sq. mi.
POP. — 3,030,000 (est. 1974)
CAPITAL — Porto-Novo

Formerly a native kingdom including Benin, Dahomey was annexed by France in 1894. It became part of the colonial administrative unit of French West Africa in 1895. Stamps of French West Africa superseded those of Dahomey in 1945. The Republic of Dahomey was proclaimed Dec. 4, 1958.

The republic changed its name to the People's Republic of Benin on Nov. 30, 1975. See Benin for stamps issued after that date.

100 Centimes = 1 Franc

Navigation and Commerce — A1

Perf. 14x13½

1899-1905 **Typo.** **Unwmk.**

Name of Colony in Blue or Carmine

1 A1 1c *lil bl* ('01) 40 40
2 A1 2c brn, *buff* ('04) 55 55
3 A1 4c cl, *lav*('04) 85 85
4 A1 5c yel grn ('04) 1.65 1.65
5 A1 10c red ('01) 1.65 1.10
6 A1 15c gray ('01) 1.10 55
7 A1 20c red, *grn*('04) 6.25 6.25
8 A1 25c *rose* ('99) 6.25 4.75
9 A1 25c bl ('01) 6.25 5.00
10 A1 30c brn, *bis*('04) 8.50 6.75
11 A1 40c red, *straw* ('04) 8.50 6.75
12 A1 50c brn, *az* (name in red) ('01) 10.00 7.75
12A A1 50c brn, *az* (name in bl) ('05) 15.00 11.00
13 A1 75c dp vio, *org* ('04) 37.50 27.50
14 A1 1fr brnz grn, *straw* ('04) 20.00 16.00
15 A1 2fr vio, *rose* ('04) 57.50 45.00
16 A1 5fr red lil, *lav* ('04) 75.00 65.00
Nos. 1-16 (17) 256.95 206.85

Gen. Louis Faidherbe — A2

Oil Palm — A3

Dr. Noel Eugene Ballay — A4

1906-07 ***Perf. 13½x14***

Name of Colony in Red or Blue

17 A2 1c slate 70 70
18 A2 2c chocolate 70 70
19 A2 4c choc, *gray bl* 1.25 1.00
20 A2 5c green 4.50 1.00
21 A2 10c car (B) 8.75 1.10
22 A3 20c *azure* 7.00 4.75
23 A3 25c bl, *pnksh* 8.75 5.25
24 A3 30c choc, *pnksh* 8.50 5.25
25 A3 35c *yellow* 52.50 6.25
26 A3 45c choc, *grnsh* ('07) 8.75 7.00
27 A3 50c dp vio 9.50 7.00
28 A3 75c bl, *org* 10.50 8.50
29 A4 1fr blk, *az* 12.00 8.50
30 A4 2fr bl, *pink* 72.50 65.00
31 A4 5fr car, *straw* (B) 60.00 52.50
Nos. 17-31 (15) 265.90 174.50

Stamps of 1901-05 Surcharged in Black or Carmine

05 a **10** b

1912 ***Perf. 14x13½***

32 (a) 5c on 2c brn, *buff* 52 52
33 (a) 5c on 4c cl, *lav*(C) 90 90
a. Double surcharge 160.00
34 (a) 5c on 15c gray (C) 90 90
35 (a) 5c on 20c red, *grn* 90 90
36 (a) 5c on 25c bl (C) 90 90
a. Inverted surcharge 135.00
37 (a) 5c on 30c brn, *bis* (C) 90 90
38 (b) 10c on 40c red, *straw* 90 90
a. Inverted surcharge 210.00
39 (b) 10c on 50c brn, *az,* name in bl (C) 1.00 1.00
40 (b) 10c on 50c brn, *az,* name in red (C) 875.00 950.00
41 (b) 10c on 75c vio,*org* 4.25 4.25
Nos. 32-39,41 (9) 11.17 11.17

Two spacings between the surcharged numerals are found on Nos. 32 to 41.

Man Climbing Oil Palm — A5

1913-39 ***Perf. 13½x14***

42 A5 1c vio & blk 5 5
43 A5 2c choc & rose 5 5
44 A5 4c blk & brn 5 5
45 A5 5c yel grn & bl grn 15 15
46 A5 5c vio brn & vio ('22) 18 18
47 A5 10c org red & rose 60 42
48 A5 10c yel grn & bl grn ('22) 25 25
49 A5 10c red & ol ('25) 6 6
50 A5 15c brn org & dk vio ('17) 18 18
51 A5 20c gray & choc 18 15
52 A5 20c bluish grn & grn ('26) 5 5
53 A5 20c mag & blk ('27) 6 6
54 A5 25c ultra & dp bl 1.00 52
55 A5 25c vio brn & org ('22) 48 48
56 A5 30c choc & vio 1.40 1.10
57 A5 30c red org & rose ('22) 1.40 1.40
58 A5 30c yel & vio ('25) 6 6
59 A5 30c dl grn & grn ('27) 15 15
60 A5 35c brn & blk 60 52
61 A5 35c bl grn & grn ('38) 15 15
62 A5 40c blk & red org 25 18
63 A5 45c gray & ultra 25 25
64 A5 50c choc & brn 2.50 2.00
65 A5 50c ultra & bl ('22) 70 70
66 A5 50c brn red & bl ('26) 6 6
67 A5 55c gray grn & choc ('38) 15 15
68 A5 60c vio, *pnksh* ('25) 6 6
69 A5 65c yel brn & ol grn ('26) 52 52
70 A5 75c bl & vio 48 40
71 A5 80c hn brn & ultra ('38) 15 15
72 A5 85c dk bl & ver ('26) 80 80
73 A5 90c rose & brn red ('30) 48 42
74 A5 90c yel bis & red org ('39) 48 35
75 A5 1fr bl grn & blk 90 52
76 A5 1fr dk bl & ultra ('26) 90 90
77 A5 1fr yel brn & lt red ('28) 95 60
78 A5 1fr dk red & red org ('38) 60 40
79 A5 1.10fr vio & bis ('28) 1.50 1.50
80 A5 1.25fr dp bl & dk brn ('33) 12.00 4.75
81 A5 1.50fr dk bl & lt bl ('30) 60 42
82 A5 1.75fr dk brn & dp buff ('33) 2.25 1.25
83 A5 1.75fr ind & ultra ('38) 52 35
84 A5 2fr yel org & choc 90 70
85 A5 3fr red vio ('30) 1.50 1.10
86 A5 5fr vio & dp bl 1.50 1.25
Nos. 42-86 (45) 38.10 25.81

The 1c gray and yellow green and 5c dull red and black are Togo Nos. 193a, 196a.

Type of 1913 Surcharged **60** **60**

1922-25

87 A5 60c on 75c vio, *pnksh* 42 42
a. Double surcharge 130.00 130.00
88 A5 65c on 15c brn org & dk vio ('25) 90 90
89 A5 85c on 15c brn org & dk vio ('25) 90 90

Common Design Types pictured in section at front of book.

Stamps and Type of 1913-39 Surcharged with New Value and Bars

1924-27

90 A5 25c on 2fr org & choc 42 42
91 A5 90c on 75c cer & brn red ('27) 1.00 1.00
92 A5 1.25fr on 1fr dk bl & ultra (R) ('26) 42 42
93 A5 1.50fr on 1fr dk bl & grnsh bl ('27) 1.10 1.10
94 A5 3fr on 5fr olvn & dp org ('27) 5.50 5.50
95 A5 10fr on 5fr bl vio & red brn ('27) 4.75 4.75
96 A5 20fr on 5fr ver & dl grn ('27) 4.75 4.75
Nos. 90-96 (7) 17.94 17.94

Colonial Exposition Issue

Common Design Types

1931 **Engr.** ***Perf. 12½***

Name of Country in Black

97 CD70 40c dp grn 3.00 3.00
98 CD71 50c violet 3.00 3.00
99 CD72 90c red org 3.00 3.00
100 CD73 1.50fr dl bl 3.00 3.00

Paris International Exposition Issue

Common Design Types

1937 **Engr.** ***Perf. 13***

101 CD74 20c dp vio 55 55
102 CD75 30c dk grn 70 70
103 CD76 40c car rose 70 70
104 CD77 50c dk brn 55 55
105 CD78 90c red 55 55
106 CD79 1.50fr ultra 70 70
Nos. 101-106 (6) 3.75 3.75

Souvenir Sheet

Imperf

107 CD77 3fr dp bl & blk 3.50 3.50

Size of No. 107: 118x99mm.

Caillié Issue

Common Design Type

1939, Apr. 5 **Engr.** ***Perf. 12½x12***

108 CD81 90c org brn & org 95 95
109 CD81 2fr brt vio 1.00 1.00
110 CD81 2.25fr ultra & dk bl 1.10 1.10

New York World's Fair Issue

Common Design Type

1939 **Engr.**

111 CD82 1.25fr car lake 60 60
112 CD82 2.25fr ultra 60 60

Man Poling a Canoe — A7

Pile House — A8

Sailboat on Lake Nokoué A9

Dahomey Warrior A10

1941 ***Perf. 13***

113 A7 2c scarlet 6 6
114 A7 3c dp bl 6 6
115 A7 5c brn vio 30 30
116 A7 10c green 18 18
117 A7 15c black 5 5
118 A8 20c vio brn 5 5
119 A8 30c dk vio 18 18
120 A8 40c scarlet 48 48
121 A8 50c sl grn 48 48
122 A8 60c black 18 18
123 A8 70c brt red vio 18 18
124 A9 80c brn blk 40 40
125 A9 1fr violet 52 52
126 A9 1.30fr brn vio 60 60
127 A9 1.40fr green 75 75
128 A9 1.50fr brt rose 75 75
129 A9 2fr brn org 95 95
130 A10 2.50fr dk bl 75 75
131 A10 3fr scarlet 80 80
132 A10 5fr sl grn 65 65
133 A10 10fr vio brn 1.25 1.25
134 A10 20fr black 1.75 1.75
Nos. 113-134 (22) 11.37 11.37

Stamps of type A8 without "RF" were issued in 1944 by the Vichy Government, but were not placed on sale in the colony.

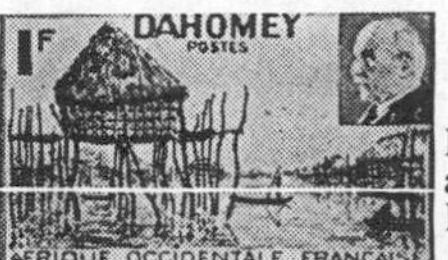

Pile House and Marshal Petain A11

1941 *Perf. 12½x12*
135 A11 1fr green 48
136 A11 2.50fr blue 48

Republic

Village Ganvié — A12

Unwmk.

1960, Mar. 1 Engr. *Perf. 12*
137 A12 25fr dk bl, brn & red 40 10

Imperforates
Most Dahomey stamps from 1960 onward exist imperforate in issued and trial colors, and also in small presentation sheets in issued colors.

C.C.T.A. Issue
Common Design Type

1960, May 16
138 CD106 5fr rose lil & ultra 40 35

Issued to commemorate the 10th anniversary of the Commission for Technical Co-operation in Africa South of the Sahara (C.C.T.A.).

Emblem of the Entente A13

Prime Minister Hubert Maga A14

Council of the Entente Issue

1960, May 29 Photo. *Perf. 13x13½*
139 A13 25fr multi 60 50

Issued to commemorate the first anniversary of the Council of the Entente (Dahomey, Ivory Coast, Niger and Upper Volta).

1960, Aug. Engr. *Perf. 13*
140 A14 85fr dp cl & blk 1.20 35

Issued on the occasion of Dahomey's proclamation of independence, Aug. 1, 1960.

Weaver A15

Doves, U.N. Building and Emblem A16

Designs: 2fr, 10fr, Wood sculptor. 3fr, 15fr, Fisherman and net (horiz.). 4fr, 20fr, Potter (horiz.).

1961, Feb. 17 Engr. *Perf. 13*
141 A15 1fr rose, org & red lil 6 5
142 A15 2fr bis brn & choc 5 5
143 A15 3fr grn & org 8 6
144 A15 4fr ol bis & cl 12 10
145 A15 6fr rose, lt vio & ver 12 10
146 A15 10fr bl & grn 25 12
147 A15 15fr red lil & vio 27 18
148 A15 20fr bluish vio & Prus bl 40 25
Nos. 141-148 (8) 1.35 91

No. 140 Surcharged with New Value, Bars and: "Président de la République"

1961, Aug. 1
149 A14 100fr on 85fr dp cl & blk 1.60 1.50

First anniversary of Independence.

1961, Sept. 20 Unwmk. *Perf. 13*
150 A16 5fr multi 30 20
151 A16 60fr multi 90 80

Issued to commemorate the first anniversary of Dahomey's admission to the United Nations. See No. C16 and souvenir sheet No. C16a.

No. 137 Overprinted: "JEUX SPORTIFS D'ABIDJAN 24 AU 31 DECEMBRE 1961"

1961, Dec. 24
152 A12 25fr dk bl, brn & red 50 40

Abidjan Games, Dec. 24-31.

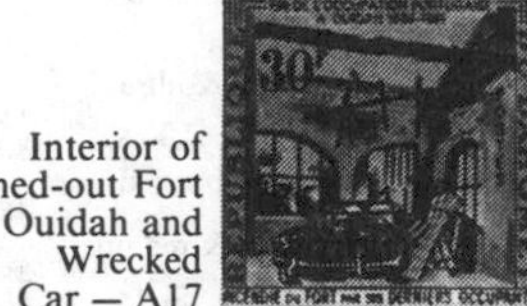

Interior of Burned-out Fort Ouidah and Wrecked Car — A17

1962, July 31 Photo. *Perf. 12½*
153 A17 30fr multi 45 20
154 A17 60fr multi 90 50

Issued to commemorate the first anniversary of the evacuation of Fort Ouidah by the Portuguese, and its occupation by Dahomey.

African and Malgache Union Issue
Common Design Type

1962, Sept. 8 *Perf. 12½x12*
155 CD110 30fr red lil, bluish grn, red & gold 70 30

Issued to commemorate the first anniversary of the African and Malgache Union.

Red Cross Nurses and Map — A18

Unwmk.

1962, Oct. 5 Engr. *Perf. 13*
156 A18 5fr bl, choc & red 10 5
157 A18 20fr bl, dk grn & red 30 25
158 A18 25fr bl, brn & red 40 30
159 A18 30fr bl, blk & red 50 30

Ganvié Woman in Canoe — A19

Peuhl Herdsman and Cattle A20

Designs: 3fr, 65fr, Bariba chief of Nikki. 15fr, 50fr, Ouidah witch doctor, rock python. 20fr, 30fr, Nessoukoue women carrying vases on heads, Abomey. 25fr, 40fr, Dahomey girl. 60fr, Peuhl herdsman and cattle. 85fr, Ganvie woman in canoe.

1963, Feb. 18 Unwmk. *Perf. 13*
160 A19 2fr grnsh bl & vio 5 5
161 A19 3fr bl & blk 6 5
162 A20 5fr brn, blk & grn 10 6
163 A19 15fr brn, bl grn & red brn 25 15
164 A19 20fr grn, blk & car 30 20
165 A20 25fr dk brn, bl & bl grn 35 15
166 A19 30fr brn org, choc & mag 45 20
167 A20 40fr choc, grn & brt bl 60 30
168 A19 50fr blk, grn, brn & red brn 75 35
169 A20 60fr choc, org red & ol 85 40
170 A19 65fr org brn & choc 90 50
171 A19 85fr brt bl & choc 1.25 75
Nos. 160-171 (12) 5.91 3.16

Boxers — A21

Designs: 1fr, 20fr, Soccer goalkeeper (horiz.). 2fr, 5fr, Runners.

1963, Apr. 11 **Engr.**
172 A21 50c grn & bl 5 5
173 A21 1fr ol, blk & brn 5 5
174 A21 2fr ol, bl & brn 6 6
175 A21 5fr brn, crim & blk 10 8
176 A21 15fr dk vio & brn 25 20
177 A21 20fr multi 40 30
Nos. 172-177 (6) 91 74

Friendship Games, Dakar, Apr. 11-21.

President's Palace, Cotonou A22

1963, Aug. 1 Photo. *Perf. 12½x12*
178 A22 25fr multi 40 25

Third anniversary of independence.

Gen. Toussaint L'Ouverture A23

U.N. Emblem, Flame and "15" A24

1963, Nov. 18 Unwmk. *Perf. 12x13*
179 A23 25fr multi 40 25
180 A23 30fr multi 45 30
181 A23 100fr ultra, brn & red 1.50 1.00

Issued to honor Pierre Dominique Toussaint L'Ouverture (1743-1803), Haitian general, statesman and descendant of the kings of Allada (Dahomey).

1963, Dec. 10 *Perf. 12*
182 A24 4fr multi 8 8
183 A24 6fr multi 10 8
184 A24 25fr multi 40 30

Issued to commemorate the 15th anniversary of the Universal Declaration of Human Rights.

Somba Dance — A25

Regional Dances: 3fr, Nago dance, Pobe-Ketou (horiz.). 10fr, Dance of the baton. 15fr, Nago dance, Ouidah (horiz.). 25fr, Dance of the Sakpatassi. 30fr, Dance of the Nessouhouessi (horiz.).

1964, Aug. 8 Engr. *Perf. 13*
185 A25 2fr red, emer & blk 5 5
186 A25 3fr dl red, bl & grn 6 5
187 A25 10fr pur, blk & red 15 10
188 A25 15fr mag, blk & grn 25 15
189 A25 25fr Prus bl, brn & org 40 25
190 A25 30fr dk red, choc & org 45 35
Nos. 185-190 (6) 1.36 95

Runner — A26

Design: 85fr, Bicyclist.

1964, Oct. 20 Photo. *Perf. 11*
191 A26 60fr lt brn & grn 75 55
192 A26 85fr vio bl & red lil 1.25 90

18th Olympic Games, Tokyo, Oct. 10-25.

Cooperation Issue
Common Design Type

1964, Nov. 7 Engr. *Perf. 13*
193 CD119 25fr org, vio & dk brn 40 25

UNICEF Emblem, Mother and Child A27

IQSY Emblem and Apollo Satellite A28

Design: 25fr, Mother holding child in her arms.

1964, Dec. 11 Unwmk. *Perf. 13*
194 A27 20fr yel grn, dk red & blk 30 25
195 A27 25fr bl, dk red & blk 40 25

Issued for the 18th anniversary of the United Nations International Children's Emergency Fund (UNICEF).

1964, Dec. 22 Photo. *Perf. 13x12½*

Design: 100fr, IQSY emblem and Nimbus weather satellite.

196 A28 25fr grn & lt yel 50 20
197 A28 100fr dp plum & yel 1.50 90

International Quiet Sun Year, 1964-65.

Abomey Tapestry — A29

Designs (Abomey tapestries): 25fr, Warrior and fight scenes. 50fr, Birds and warriors (horiz.). 85fr, Animals, ship and plants (horiz.).

1965, Apr. 12 Photo. *Perf. 12½*
198 A29 20fr multi 30 20
199 A29 25fr multi 40 30
200 A29 50fr multi 75 50
201 A29 85fr multi 1.25 90
a. Min. sheet of 4 2.75 2.75

Issued to publicize the local rug weaving industry. No. 201a contains one each of Nos. 198-201. Size: 194x100mm.

Baudot Telegraph Distributor and Ader Telephone A30

1965, May 17 Engr. *Perf. 13*
202 A30 100fr lil, org & blk 1.50 60

Issued to commemorate the centenary of the International Telecommunication Union.

Cotonou Harbor — A31

Design: 100fr, Cotonou Harbor, denomination at left.

1965, Aug. 1 Photo. *Perf. 12½*
203 A31 25fr multi 45 25
204 A31 100fr multi 1.65 1.00

Issued to commemorate the opening of Cotonou Harbor. Nos. 203-204 printed se-tenant show a panoramic view of the harbor.

Cybium Tritor A32

Fish: 25fr, Dentex filosus. 30fr, Atlantic sailfish. 50fr, Blackish tripletail.

1965, Sept. 20 Engr. *Perf. 13*
205 A32 10fr blk & brt bl 15 12
206 A32 25fr brt bl, org & blk 40 30
207 A32 30fr vio bl & grnsh bl 45 30
208 A32 50fr blk, gray bl & org 75 50

Independence Monument — A33

1965, Oct. 28 Photo. *Perf. 12x12½*
209 A33 25fr gray, blk & red 40 20
210 A33 30fr lt ultra, blk & red 45 25

October 28 Revolution, 2nd anniversary.

No. 165 Surcharged

1F

1965, Nov. Engr. *Perf. 13*
211 A20 1fr on 25fr dk brn, bl & bl grn 8 6

Porto Novo Cathedral A34

Designs: 50fr, Ouidah Pro-Cathedral (vert.). 70fr, Cotonou Cathedral.

1966, March 21 Engr. *Perf. 13*
212 A34 30fr Prus bl, vio brn & grn 45 30
213 A34 50fr vio brn, Prus bl & brn 75 45
214 A34 70fr grn, Prus bl & vio brn 1.10 65

Jewelry — A35

Designs: 30fr, Architecture. 50fr, Musician. 70fr, Crucifixion, sculpture.

1966, Apr. 4 Engr. *Perf. 13*
215 A35 15fr dl red brn & blk 25 15
216 A35 30fr dk brn, ultra & brn red 45 25
217 A35 50fr brt bl & dk brn 75 40
218 A35 70fr red brn & blk 1.10 65

Issued to commemorate the International Negro Arts Festival, Dakar, Senegal, Apr. 1-24.

Nos. 203-204 Surcharged

ACCORD DE COOPERATION
FRANCE - DAHOMEY
5e Anniversaire - 24 Avril 1966

15F

1966, Apr. 24 Photo. *Perf. 12½*
219 A31 15fr on 25fr multi 25 15
220 A31 15fr on 100fr multi 25 15

Issued to commemorate the fifth anniversary of the Cooperation Agreement between France and Dahomey.

WHO Headquarters from the East — A36

1966, May 3 *Perf. 12½x13*
Size: 35x22½mm.
221 A36 30fr multi 45 30

Issued to commemorate the inauguration of the World Health Organization Headquarters, Geneva. See No. C32.

Boy Scout Signaling A37

Designs: 10fr, Patrol standard with pennant (vert.). 30fr, Campfire and map of Dahomey (vert.). 50fr, Scouts building foot bridge.

1966, Oct. 17 Engr. *Perf. 13*
222 A37 5fr dk brn, ocher & red 10 5
223 A37 10fr blk, grn & rose cl 15 6
224 A37 30fr org, red brn & pur 40 25
225 A37 50fr vio bl, grn & dk brn 70 40
a. Minature sheet of 4 1.65 1.65

No. 225a contains one each of Nos. 222-225. Size: 168x94mm.

Clappertonia Ficifolia A38

Lions Emblem, Dancing Children and Bird A39

Flowers: 3fr, Hewittia sublobata. 5fr, Butterfly pea. 10fr, Water lily. 15fr, Commelina forskalaei. 30fr, Eremomastax speciosa.

1967, Feb. 20 Photo. *Perf. 12x12½*
226 A38 1fr multi 8 5
227 A38 3fr multi 12 5
228 A38 5fr multi 15 8
229 A38 10fr multi 25 10
230 A38 15fr multi 30 18
231 A38 30fr multi 60 30
Nos. 226-231 (6) 1.50 76

Nos. 170-171 Surcharged with New Value and Heavy Bar

1967, Mar. 1 Engr. *Perf. 13*
232 A19 30fr on 65fr org brn & choc 45 35
a. Double surch. 22.50
233 A19 30fr on 85fr brt bl & choc 45 35
a. Double surch. 35.00
b. Invtd. surch. 35.00

1967, March 20
234 A39 100fr dl vio, dp bl & grn 1.60 50

50th anniversary of Lions International.

EXPO '67 "Man in the City" Pavilion A40

Design: 70fr, "The New Africa" exhibit.

1967, June 12 Engr. *Perf. 13*
235 A40 30fr grn & choc 45 20
236 A40 70fr grn & brn red 1.00 65

Issued to commemorate EXPO '67, International Exhibition, Montreal, Apr. 28-Oct. 27, 1967. See No. C57 and miniature sheet No. C57a.

Europafrica Issue, 1967

Trade (Blood) Circulation, Map of Europe and Africa — A41

1967, July 20 Photo. *Perf. 12x12½*
237 A41 30fr multi 40 20
238 A41 45fr multi 65 25

Scouts Climbing Mountain, Jamboree Emblem A42

Design: 70fr, Jamboree emblem and Scouts launching canoe.

1967, Aug. 7 Engr. *Perf. 13*
239 A42 30fr brt bl, red brn & sl 45 20
240 A42 70fr brt bl, sl grn & dk brn 1.00 65

Issued to commemorate the 12th Boy Scout World Jamboree, Farragut State Park, Idaho, Aug. 1-9. For souvenir sheet see No. C59a.

Rhone River and Olympic Emblems A43

Designs (Olympic Emblems and): 45fr, View of Grenoble (vert.). 100fr, Rhone Bridge, Grenoble, and Pierre de Coubertin.

1967, Sept. 2 Engr. *Perf. 13*
241 A43 30fr bis, dp bl & grn 50 20
242 A43 45fr ultra, grn & brn 85 25
243 A43 100fr choc, grn & brt bl 1.65 90
a. Miniature sheet of 3 3.25 3.25

Issued to publicize the 10th Winter Olympic Games, Grenoble, Feb. 6-18, 1968. No. 243a contains one each of Nos. 241-243. Size: 129x100mm.

Monetary Union Issue
Common Design Type

1967, Nov. 4 Engr. *Perf. 13*
244 CD125 30fr grn, dk car & dk brn 45 25

Issued to commemorate the 5th anniversary of the West African Monetary Union.

Cape Buffalo A45

Animals from the Pendjari Reservation: 30fr, Lion. 45fr, Buffon's kob. 70fr, African slender-snouted crocodile. 100fr, Hippopotamus.

1968, Mar. 18 Photo. *Perf. 12½x13*
245 A45 15fr multi 25 15
246 A45 30fr pur & multi 45 20
247 A45 45fr bl & multi 70 30
248 A45 70fr multi 1.00 45
249 A45 100fr multi 1.50 80
Nos. 245-249 (5) 3.90 1.90

WHO Emblem A46

1968, Apr. 22 Engr. *Perf. 13*

250 A46 30fr dk bl, red brn & brt bl 45 20
251 A46 70fr multi 1.00 55

Issued to commemorate the 20th anniversary of the World Health Organization.

Leopard A47

Animals: 5fr, Warthog. 60fr, Spotted hyena. 75fr, Anubius baboon. 90fr, Hartebeest.

1969, Feb. 10 Photo. *Perf. 12½x12*

252	A47	5fr dk brn & multi	8	5
253	A47	30fr dp ultra & multi	45	20
254	A47	60fr dk grn & multi	90	40
255	A47	75fr dk bl & multi	1.10	55
256	A47	90fr dk grn & multi	1.35	70
		Nos. 252-256 (5)	3.88	1.90

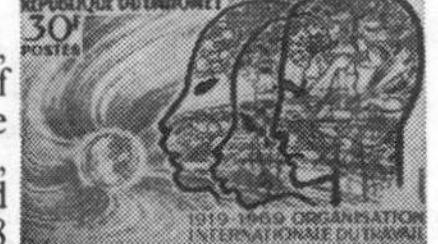

Heads, Symbols of Agriculture and Science, and Globe — A48

1969, Mar. 10 Engr. *Perf. 13*

257 A48 30fr org & multi 45 20
258 A48 70fr mar & multi 1.00 50

Issued to commemorate the 50th anniversary of the International Labor Organization.

Arms of Dahomey — A49

1969, June 30 Litho. *Perf. 13½x13*

259 A49 5fr yel & multi 8 6
260 A49 30fr org red & multi 40 25

See No. C101.

Development Bank Issue

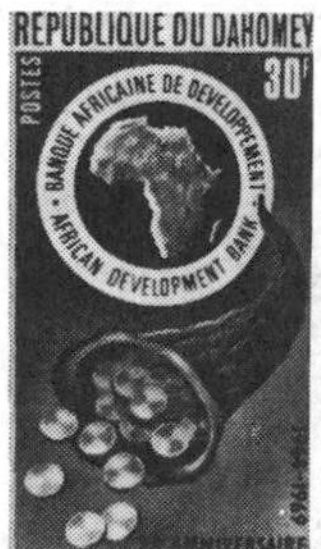

Cornucopia and Bank Emblem — A50

1969, Sept. 10 Photo. *Perf. 13*

261 A50 30fr blk, grn & ocher 50 25

Issued to commemorate the 5th anniversary of the African Development Bank.

Europafrica Issue

Ambary (Kenaf) Industry, Cotonou A51

Design: 45fr, Cotton industry, Parakou.

1969, Sept. 22 Litho. *Perf. 14*

262 A51 30fr multi 40 25
263 A51 45fr multi 60 30

See Nos. C105-C105a.

Sakpata Dance and Tourist Year Emblem — A52

Dances and Tourist Year Emblem: 30fr, Guelede dance. 45fr, Sato dance.

1969, Dec. 15 Litho. *Perf. 14*

264 A52 10fr multi 20 10
265 A52 30fr multi 45 20
266 A52 45fr multi 65 35

See No. C108.

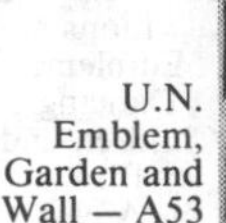

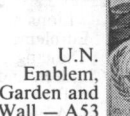

U.N. Emblem, Garden and Wall — A53

1970, Apr. 6 Engr. *Perf. 13*

267 A53 30fr ultra, red org & sl 45 20
268 A53 40fr ultra, brn & sl grn 60 30

25th anniversary of the United Nations.

ASECNA Issue

Common Design Type

1970, June 1 Engr. *Perf. 13*

269 CD132 40fr red & pur 60 35

Mt. Fuji, EXPO '70 Emblem, Monorail Train — A54

1970, June 15 Litho. *Perf. 13½x14*

270 A54 5fr grn, red & vio bl 12 8

Issued to publicize EXPO '70 International Exhibition, Osaka, Japan, Mar. 15-Sept. 13, 1970. See Nos. C124-C125.

Alkemy, King of Ardres — A55

Designs: 40fr, Sailing ships "La Justice" and "La Concorde," Ardres, 1670. 50fr, Matheo Lopes, ambassador of the King of Ardres and his coat of arms. 200fr, Louis XIV and fleur-de-lis.

1970, July 6 Engr. *Perf. 13*

271	A55	40fr brt grn, ultra & brn	65	22
272	A55	50fr dk car, choc & emer	75	27
273	A55	70fr gray, lem & choc	1.00	40
274	A55	200fr Prus bl, dk car & choc	2.75	1.20

Issued to commemorate the 300th anniversary of the mission from the King of Ardres to the King of France, and of the audience with Louis XIV on Dec. 19, 1670.

Star of the Order of Independence A56

Bariba Warrior A57

1970, Aug. 1 Photo. *Perf. 12*

275 A56 30fr multi 35 20
276 A56 40fr multi 50 25

The 10th anniversary of independence.

1970, Aug. 24 *Perf. 12½x13*

Designs: 2fr, 50fr, Two horsemen. 10fr, 70fr, Horseman facing left.

277	A57	1fr yel & multi	6	5
278	A57	2fr gray grn & multi	8	6
279	A57	10fr bl & multi	15	10
280	A57	40fr yel grn & multi	55	30
281	A57	50fr gold & multi	65	30
282	A57	70fr lil rose & multi	1.00	50
		Nos. 277-282 (6)	2.49	1.31

Globe and Heart A58

Design: 40fr, Hands holding heart (vert.).

1971, June 7 Engr. *Perf. 13*

283 A58 40fr red, grn & dk brn 50 30
284 A58 100fr grn, red & bl 1.10 60

International year against racial discrimination.

Ancestral Figures and Lottery Ticket A59

King Behanzin's Emblem (1889-1894) A60

1971, June 24 Litho. *Perf. 14*

285 A59 35fr multi 40 20
286 A59 40fr multi 50 25

4th anniversary of the National Lottery.

Photo.; Litho. (25fr, 135fr)

1971-72 *Perf. 12½*

Emblems of the Kings of Abomey: 25fr, Agoliagbo (1894-1900). 35fr, Ganyehoussou (1620-1645), bird and cup (horiz.). 100fr, Guezo (1818-1858), bull, tree and birds. 135fr, Ouegbadja (1645-1685) (horiz.). 140fr, Glele (1858-1889), lion and sword (horiz.).

287	A60	25fr multi ('72)	30	15
288	A60	35fr grn & multi	45	20
289	A60	40fr grn & multi	50	25
290	A60	100fr red & multi	1.25	45
291	A60	135fr multi ('72)	1.40	70
292	A60	140fr brn & multi	1.75	85
		Nos. 287-292 (6)	5.65	2.60

Issue dates: 25fr, 135fr, July 17, 1972. Others, Aug. 3, 1971.

Kabuki Actor, Long-distance Skiing — A61

Brahms and "Soir d'ete" — A62

1972, Feb. Engr. *Perf. 13*

293 A61 35fr dk car, brn & bl grn 50 25

11th Winter Olympic Games, Sapporo, Japan, Feb. 3-13. See No. C153.

No. 268 Surcharged

1972

294 A53 35fr on 40fr multi 45 25

1972, June 29 Engr. *Perf. 13*

Design: 65fr, Brahms, woman at piano and music (horiz.).

295 A62 30fr red brn, blk & lil 40 25
296 A62 65fr red brn, blk & lil 80 50

75th anniversary of the death of Johannes Brahms (1833-1897), German composer.

The Hare and The Tortoise, by La Fontaine — A63

Fables: 35fr, The Fox and The Stork (vert.). 40fr, The Cat, The Weasel and Rabbit.

1972, Aug. 28 Engr. *Perf. 13*

297 A63 10fr multi 15 10
298 A63 35fr dk red & multi 45 25
299 A63 40fr ultra & multi 50 30

Jean de La Fontaine (1621-1695), French fabulist.

West African Monetary Union Issue

Common Design Type

1972, Nov. 2 Engr. *Perf. 13*

300 CD136 40fr choc, ocher & gray 40 25

10th anniversary of West African Monetary Union.

Dr. Hansen, Microscope, Bacilli — A65

Design: 85 fr, Portrait of Dr. Hansen.

1973, May 14 Engr. *Perf. 13*

301 A65 35fr ultra, vio brn & brn 30 20
302 A65 85fr yel grn, bis & ver 75 50

Centenary of the discovery by Dr. Armauer G. Hansen of the Hansen bacillus, the cause of leprosy.

Arms of Dahomey — A66

1973, June 25 Photo. *Perf. 13*
303 A66 5fr ultra & multi 8 5
304 A66 35fr ocher & multi 30 15
305 A66 40fr red org & multi 35 17

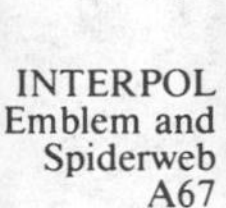

INTERPOL Emblem and Spiderweb A67

Design: 50fr, INTERPOL emblem and communications symbols (vert.).

1973, July Engr.
306 A67 35fr ver, grn & brn 35 20
307 A67 50fr grn, brn & red 50 30

50th anniversary of International Criminal Police Organization (INTERPOL).

Education in Hygiene and Nutrition A68

Design: 100fr, Prenatal examination and care, WHO emblem.

1973, Aug. 2 Photo. *Perf. 12½x13*
308 A68 35fr multi 35 15
309 A68 100fr multi 85 50

World Health Organization, 25th anniversary.

No. 248 Surcharged with New Value, 2 Bars, and Overprinted in Red: "SECHERESSE SOLIDARITE AFRICAINE"

1973, Aug. 16
310 A45 100fr on 70fr multi 1.20 65

African solidarity in drought emergency.

African Postal Union Issue
Common Design Type

1973, Sept. 12 Engr. *Perf. 13*
311 CD137 100fr red, pur & blk 1.00 55

Epinephelus Aeneus — A69

Fish: 15fr, Drepane africana. 35fr, Pragus ehrenbergi.

1973, Sept. 18
312 A69 5fr sl bl & ind 12 7
313 A69 15fr blk & brt bl 12 10
314 A69 35fr emer, ocher & sep 30 15

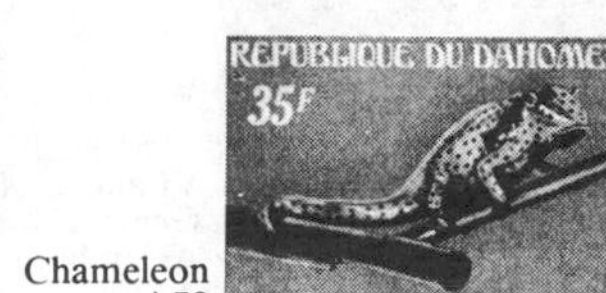
Chameleon A70

Design: 40fr, Emblem over map of Dahomey (vert.).

1973, Nov. 30 Photo. *Perf. 13*
315 A70 35fr ol & multi 35 20
316 A70 40fr multi 40 30

1st anniversary of the Oct. 26 revolution.

The Chameleon in the Tree — A71

Designs: 5fr, The elephant, the hen and the dog (vert.). 10fr, The sparrowhawk and the dog (vert.). 25fr, The chameleon in the tree. 40fr, The eagle, the viper and the hen.

1974, Feb. 14 Photo. *Perf. 13*
317 A71 5fr emer & multi 8 5
318 A71 10fr sl bl & multi 10 7
319 A71 25fr sl bl & multi 20 15
320 A71 40fr lt bl & multi 35 17

Folktales of Dahomey.

German Shepherd — A72

1974, Apr. 25 Photo. *Perf. 13*
321 A72 40fr *shown* 35 20
322 A72 50fr *Boxer* 40 25
323 A72 100fr *Saluki* 85 60

Council Issue

Map and Flags of Members A73

1974, May 29 Photo. *Perf. 13x12½*
324 A73 40fr bl & multi 35 20

15th anniversary of the Council of Accord.

Locomotive 232, 1911 — A74

Designs: Locomotives.

1974, Sept. 2 Photo. *Perf. 13x12½*
325 A74 35fr *shown* 30 20
326 A74 40fr *Freight, 1877* 35 20
327 A74 100fr *Crampton, 1849* 85 60
328 A74 200fr *Stephenson, 1846* 1.65 1.25

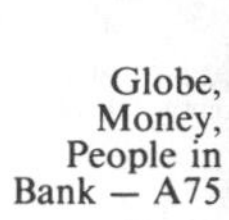

Globe, Money, People in Bank — A75

1974, Oct. 31 Engr. *Perf. 13*
329 A75 35fr multi 35 20

World Savings Day.

Dompago Dance, Hissi Tribe — A76

Flags of Dahomey and Nigeria over Africa — A77

Folk Dances: 25fr, Fetish Dance, Vaudou-Tchinan. 40fr, Bamboo Dance, Agbehoun. 100fr, Somba Dance, Sandoua (horiz.).

1975, Aug. 4 Litho. *Perf. 12*
330 A76 10fr yel & multi 12 6
331 A76 25fr dk grn & multi 20 12
332 A76 40fr red & multi 32 22
333 A76 100fr multi 85 50

1975, Aug. 11 Photo. *Perf. 12½x13*

Design: 100fr, Arrows connecting maps of Dahomey and Nigeria (horiz.).

334 A77 65fr multi 55 35
335 A77 100fr grn & multi 85 55

Year of intensified cooperation between Dahomey and Nigeria.

Map, Pylons, Emblem — A78

Benin Electric Community Emblem and Pylon — A79

1975, Aug. 18
336 A78 40fr multi 35 25
337 A79 150fr multi 1.25 85

Benin Electric Community and Ghana-Togo-Dahomey cooperation.

Map of Dahomey, Rising Sun — A80

Albert Schweitzer, Nurse, Patient — A81

1975, Aug. 25 Photo. *Perf. 12½x13*
338 A80 35fr multi 28 15

Cooperation Year for the creation of a new Dahoman society.

1975, Sept. 22 Engr. *Perf. 13*
339 A81 200fr ol, grn & red brn 1.65 1.10

Birth centenary of Albert Schweitzer (1875-1965), medical missionary and musician.

Woman Speaking on Telephone, IWY Emblem — A82

Design: 150fr, International Women's Year emblem and linked rings.

1975, Oct. 20 Engr. *Perf. 12½x13*
340 A82 50fr Prus bl & lil 40 25
341 A82 150fr emer, brn & org 1.25 65

International Women's Year 1975.
Later issues are listed under Benin.

SEMI-POSTAL STAMPS.

Regular Issue of 1913 Surcharged in Red

1915 Unwmk. *Perf. 14x13½*
B1 A5 10c + 5c org red & rose 75 60

Curie Issue
Common Design Type

1938 *Perf. 13*
B2 CD80 1.75fr + 50c brt ultra 7.00 7.00

French Revolution Issue
Common Design Type

1939 Photo.
Name and Value Typo. in Black
B3 CD83 45(c) + 25(c) grn 4.50 4.50
B4 CD83 70(c) + 30(c) brn 4.75 4.75
B5 CD83 90(c) + 35(c) red org 4.75 4.75
B6 CD83 1.25fr + 1fr rose pink 4.75 4.75
B7 CD83 2.25fr + 2fr bl 4.75 4.75
Nos. B3-B7 (5) 23.50 23.50

Postage Stamps of 1913-38 Surcharged in Black

SECOURS
+ 1 fr.
NATIONAL

1941 *Perf. 13½x14*
B8 A5 50c + 1fr brn red & bl 1.00 1.00
B9 A5 80c + 2fr hn brn & ultra 3.25 3.25
B10 A5 1.50fr + 2fr dk bl & lt bl 4.25 4.25
B11 A5 2fr + 3fr yel org & choc 4.25 4.25

Common Design Type and

Radio Operator — SP1

Senegalese Artillerymen SP2

1941 Photo. *Perf. 13½*
B12 SP1 1fr + 1fr red 1.00
B13 CD86 1.50fr + 3fr cl 1.00
B14 SP2 2.50fr + 1fr bl 1.00

The surtax was for the defense of the colonies.

Stamps of type A11 surcharged "OEUVRES COLONIALES" and new values were issued in 1944 by the Vichy Government, but were not placed on sale in the colony.

Republic
Anti-Malaria Issue
Common Design Type

1962, Apr. 7 Engr. *Perf. 12½x12*
B15 CD108 25fr + 5fr org brn 65 65

Issued for the World Health Organization drive to eradicate malaria.

Freedom from Hunger Issue
Common Design Type

1963, Mar. 21 Unwmk. *Perf. 13*
B16 CD112 25fr + 5fr ol, brn red & brn 65 65

AIR POST STAMPS

Common Design Type

1940 Unwmk. Engr. *Perf. 12½*
C1 CD85 1.90fr ultra 22 22
C2 CD85 2.90fr dk red 30 30
C3 CD85 4.50fr dk gray grn 48 48
C4 CD85 4.90fr yel bis 65 65
C5 CD85 6.90fr dp org 95 95
Nos. C1-C5 (5) 2.60 2.60

Common Design Types

1942
C6 CD88 50c car & bl 18
C7 CD88 1fr brn & blk 22
C8 CD88 2fr dk grn & red brn 30
C9 CD88 3fr dk bl & scar 60
C10 CD88 5fr vio & brn red 60

Frame Engr., Center Typo.
C11 CD89 10fr ultra, ind & org 75
C12 CD89 20fr rose car, mag & gray blk 75
C13 CD89 50fr yel grn, dl grn & dp bl 1.75 2.50
Nos. C6-C13 (8) 5.15

There is doubt whether Nos. C6-C12 were officially placed in use.

Republic

Somba House — AP4

Design: 500fr, Royal Court of Abomey.

Unwmk.
1960, Apr. 1 Engr. *Perf. 13*
C14 AP4 100fr ind, ocher & vio brn 1.50 45
C15 AP4 500fr bis brn, brn red & dk grn 7.00 1.25

Type of Regular Issue, 1961

1961, Sept. 20
C16 A16 200fr multi 2.75 2.00
a. Souvenir sheet of three 4.25 4.25

Issued to commemorate the first anniversary of Dahomey's admission to the United Nations. No. C16a contains one each of Nos. 150-151 and C16. Bistre marginal inscription. Size: 129x85mm.

Air Afrique Issue
Common Design Type

1962, Feb. 17 *Perf. 13*
C17 CD107 25fr ultra, blk & org brn 50 25

Issued to commemorate the founding of Air Afrique (African Airlines).

The indexes in each volume of the Scott Catalogue contain many listings which help to identify stamps.

Palace of the African and Malgache Union, Cotonou — AP5

1963, July 27 Photo. *Perf. 13x12*
C18 AP5 250fr dk & lt bl, ocher & 3.50 2.00

Issued to commemorate the assembly of chiefs of state of the African and Malgache Union held at Cotonou in July.

African Postal Union Issue
Common Design Type

1963, Sept. 8 Unwmk. *Perf. 12½*
C19 CD114 25fr brt bl, ocher & red 45 30

See note after Cameroun No. C47.

Boeing 707 — AP6

Designs (Boeing 707): 200fr, On the ground. 300fr, Over Cotonou airport. 500fr, In the air.

1963, Oct. 25 Engr. *Perf. 13*
C20 AP6 100fr dk pur, grn & bis 1.25 40
C21 AP6 200fr vio, brn org & grn 2.50 1.25
C22 AP6 300fr bl, red brn & brt grn 3.50 1.75
C23 AP6 500fr brn org, dk brn & yel grn 6.00 2.50

Priests Carrying Funerary Boat, Isis Temple, Philae — AP7

1964, March 9 Unwmk. *Perf. 13*
C24 AP7 25fr vio bl & brn 70 50

Issued to publicize the UNESCO world campaign to save historic monuments in Nubia.

Weather Map and Symbols — AP8

1965, Mar. 23 Photo. *Perf. 12½*
C25 AP8 50fr multi 80 50

Fifth World Meteorological Day.

ICY Emblem and Men of Various Races — AP9

1965, June 26 Engr. *Perf. 13*
C26 AP9 25fr dl pur, mar & grn 40 20
C27 AP9 85fr dp bl, mar & sl grn 1.25 80

International Cooperation Year, 1965.

Winston Churchill — AP10

1965, June 15 Photo. *Perf. 12½*
C28 AP10 100fr multi 1.65 1.25

Issued in memory of Sir Winston Churchill (1874-1965), statesman and World War II leader.

Abraham Lincoln — AP11

1965, July 15 *Perf. 13*
C29 AP11 100fr multi 1.65 1.25

Centenary of death of Abraham Lincoln.

John F. Kennedy and Arms of Dahomey — AP12

1965, Nov. 22 Photo. *Perf. 12½*
C30 AP12 100fr dp grn & blk 1.65 1.25

Issued in memory of President John F. Kennedy (1917-63).

Dr. Albert Schweitzer and Patients — AP13

1966, Jan. 17 Photo. *Perf. 12½*
C31 AP13 100fr multi 1.65 1.25

Issued in memory of Dr. Albert Schweitzer (1875-1965), medical missionary, theologian and musician.

WHO Type of Regular Issue

Design: 100fr, WHO Headquarters from the West.

1966, May 3 Unwmk. *Perf. 13*
Size: 47x28mm.
C32 A36 100fr ultra, yel & blk 1.65 1.00

Issued to commemorate the inauguration of the World Health Organization Headquarters, Geneva.

Pygmy Goose — AP14

Broad-billed Rollers — AP15

Birds: 100fr, Firey-breasted bush-shrike. 250fr, Emerald cuckoos. 500fr, Emerald starling.

1966-67 *Perf. 12½*
C33 AP14 50fr multi 1.00 40
C34 AP14 100fr multi 1.75 65
C35 AP15 200fr multi ('67) 3.25 1.35
C36 AP15 250fr multi ('67) 4.00 1.85
C37 AP14 500fr multi 7.00 3.50
Nos. C33-C37 (5) 17.00 7.75

Issue dates: 50fr, 100fr, 500fr, June 13, 1966. Others, Jan. 20, 1967.

Industrial Symbols — AP16

1966, July 21 Photo. *Perf. 12x13*
C38 AP16 100fr multi 1.50 90

3rd anniversary of agreement between European Economic Community and the African and Malagache Union.

Pope Paul VI and St. Peter's, Rome — AP17

Pope Paul VI and U.N. General Assembly AP18

Design: 70fr, Pope Paul VI and view of New York City.

1966, Aug. 22 Engr. *Perf. 13*
C39 AP17 50fr brt grn, rose car & org brn 85 40
C40 AP17 70fr dk bl, sl grn & lake 1.25 60
C41 AP18 100fr dk grn, brn vio & sl bl 1.85 1.00
a. Min. sheet of 3 4.00 4.00

Issued to commemorate Pope Paul's appeal for peace before the U.N. General Assembly, Oct. 4, 1965. No. C41a contains one each of Nos. C39-C41. Size: 178x100mm.

Air Afrique Issue, 1966

Common Design Type

1966, Aug. 31 Photo. *Perf. 12½*
C42 CD123 30fr dk vio, blk & gray 50 25

Issued to commemorate the introduction of DC-8F planes by Air Afrique.

"Science" — AP20

Designs: 45fr, "Art" (carved female statue, vert.). 100fr, "Education" (book and letters).

1966, Nov. 4 Engr. *Perf. 13*
C43 AP20 30fr mag, ultra & vio brn 40 25
C44 AP20 45fr mar & grn 70 40
C45 AP20 100fr blk, mar & brt bl 1.50 90
a. Min. sheet of 3 3.50 3.50

Issued to commemorate the 20th anniversary of UNESCO (United Nations Educational, Scientific and Cultural Organization). No. C45a contains one each of Nos. C43-C45. Size: 169x100mm.

Madonna by Alessio Baldovinetti — AP21

Designs: 50fr, Nativity after 15th century Beaune tapestry. 100fr, Adoration of the Shepherds, by José Ribera.

1966, Dec. 25 Photo. *Perf. 12½x12*
C46 AP21 50fr multi 2.25 1.35
C47 AP21 100fr multi 4.00 2.75
C48 AP21 200fr multi 6.75 5.00

Christmas 1966.

See Nos. C95-C96, C109-C115.

1967, Apr. 10 *Perf. 12½x12*

Paintings by Ingres: No. C49, Self-portrait, 1804. No. C50, Oedipus and the Sphinx.

C49 AP21 100fr multi 2.00 1.50
C50 AP21 100fr multi 2.00 1.50

Issued to commemorate the centenary of the death of Jean Auguste Dominique Ingres (1780-1867), French painter.

Three-master Suzanne — AP22

Windjammers: 45fr, Three-master Esmeralda (vert.). 80fr, Schooner Marie Alice (vert.). 100fr, Four-master Antonin.

1967, May 8 *Perf. 13*
C51 AP22 30fr multi 50 25
C52 AP22 45fr multi 70 45
C53 AP22 80fr multi 1.20 60
C54 AP22 100fr multi 1.50 85

Nos. C29-C30 Surcharged

29 MAI 1967
50e Anniversaire
de la naissance
de
John F. Kennedy
125F

1967, May 29 Photo. *Perf. 13, 12½*
C55 AP11 125fr on 100fr multi 2.00 1.00
a. Surch. invtd. 22.50
C56 AP12 125fr on 100fr dp grn & blk 2.00 1.00
a. Surch. invtd. 25.00

Issued to commemorate the 50th anniversary of the birth of President John F. Kennedy.

EXPO '67 "Man In Space" Pavilion — AP23

1967, June 12 Engr. *Perf. 13*
C57 AP23 100fr dl red & Prus bl 1.50 85
a. Min. sheet of 3 3.25 3.25

Issued to commemorate EXPO '67, International Exhibition, Montreal, Apr. 28-Oct. 27, 1967. No. C57a contains one each of Nos. 235-236 and C57. Size: 149x100mm.

Europafrica Issue, 1967

Konrad Adenauer, by Oscar Kokoschka AP24

1967, July 19 Photo. *Perf. 12½x12*
C58 AP24 70fr multi 1.25 90
a. Souv. sheet of 4 5.00 5.00

Issued in memory of Konrad Adenauer (1876-1967), chancellor of West Germany (1949-1963). No. C58a contains 4 No. C58. Dark gray marginal inscription. Size: 140x158mm.

Jamboree Emblem, Ropes and World Map — AP25

1967, Aug. 7 Engr. *Perf. 13*
C59 AP25 100fr lil, sl grn & dp bl 1.50 90
a. Souv. sheet of 3 3.75 3.50

Issued to commemorate the 12th Boy Scout World Jamboree, Farragut State Park, Idaho, Aug. 1-9. No. C59a contains one each of Nos. 239-240 and C59. Bright blue marginal inscription. Size: 149x100mm.

No. C48 Surcharged in Red

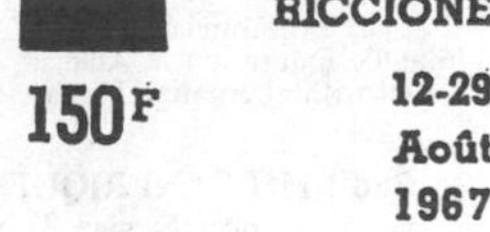

150F **RICCIONE 12-29 Août 1967**

1967, Aug. 12 Photo. *Perf. 12½x12*
C60 AP21 150fr on 200fr multi 2.50 2.00
a. "150F" omitted 125.00 125.00

Issued to publicize the Riccione, Italy, Stamp Exhibition.

African Postal Union Issue, 1967

Common Design Type

1967, Sept. 9 Engr. *Perf. 13*
C61 CD124 100fr red, brt lil & emer 1.50 1.00

Charles de Gaulle AP26

1967, Nov. 21 Photo. *Perf. 12½x13*
C62 AP26 100fr multi 2.50 2.00
a. Souv. sheet of 4 10.00 10.00

Issued to honor Pres. Charles de Gaulle of France on the occasion of Pres. Christophe Soglo's state visit to Paris, Nov. 1967. No. C62a contains 4 No. C62. Black marginal inscription. Size: 140x161mm.

Madonna, by Matthias Grunewald AP27

Paintings: 50fr, Holy Family by the Master of St. Sebastian (horiz.). 100fr, Adoration of the Magi by Ulrich Apt the Elder. 200fr, Annunciation, by Matthias Grunewald.

1967, Dec. 11 Photo. *Perf. 12½*
C63 AP27 30fr multi 35 25
C64 AP27 50fr multi 70 40
C65 AP27 100fr multi 1.50 90
C66 AP27 200fr multi 3.00 1.40

Christmas 1967.

Venus de Milo and Mariner 5 AP28

Gutenberg Monument, Strasbourg Cathedral AP29

Design: No. C68, Venus de Milo and Venus 4 Rocket.

1968, Feb. 17 Photo. *Perf. 13*
C67 AP28 70fr grnsh bl & multi 1.25 60
C68 AP28 70fr dp bl & multi 1.25 60
a. Souv. sheet of 2 2.50 2.50

Issued to commemorate the explorations of the planet Venus, Oct. 18-19, 1967. No. C68a contains one each of Nos. C67-C68. Black marginal inscription. Size: 106x96mm.

1968, May 20 Litho. *Perf. 14x13½*

Design: 100fr, Gutenberg Monument, Mainz, and Gutenberg press.

C69 AP29 45fr grn & org 70 35
C70 AP29 100fr dk & lt bl 1.35 65
a. Souv. sheet of 2 2.25 2.25

Issued to commemorate the 500th anniversary of the death of Johann Gutenberg, inventor of printing from movable type. No. C70a contains one each of Nos. C69-C70. Marginal inscription in green and dark blue. Size: 130x100mm.

Martin Luther King, Jr. — AP30

Designs: 30fr, "We must meet hate with creative love" in French, English and German. 100fr, Full-face portrait.

Perf. 12½, 13½x13

1968, June 17 Photo.

Size: 26x46mm.

C71 AP30 30fr red brn, yel & blk 40 20

Size: 26x37mm.

C72 AP30 55fr multi 70 40
C73 AP30 100fr multi 1.25 65
a. Min. sheet of 3 2.75 2.75

Issued in memory of the Rev. Dr. Martin Luther King, Jr. (1929-1968), American civil rights leader. No. C73a contains one each of Nos. C71-C73. Size: 150x114mm.

Robert Schuman — AP31

Designs: 45fr, Alcide de Gasperi. 70fr, Konrad Adenauer.

1968, July 20 Photo. *Perf. 13*
C74 AP31 30fr dp yel, blk & grn 40 20
C75 AP31 45fr org, dk brn & ol 60 30
C76 AP31 70fr multi 1.00 45

Issued to commemorate the 5th anniversary of the economic agreement between the European Economic Community and the African and Malgache Union.

Battle of Montebello, by Henri Philippoteaux — AP32

Paintings: 45fr, 2nd Zouave Regiment at Magenta, by Riballier. 70fr, Battle of

Magenta, by Louis Eugene Charpentier. 100fr, Battle of Solferino, by Charpentier.

1968, Aug. 12 *Perf. 12½x12*

C77	AP32	30fr multi	45	20
C78	AP32	45fr multi	70	30
C79	AP32	70fr multi	1.00	50
C80	AP32	100fr multi	1.50	75

Issued for the Red Cross.

Mail Truck in Village — AP33

Designs: 45fr, Mail truck stopping at rural post office. 55fr, Mail truck at river bank. 70fr, Mail truck and train.

1968, Oct. 7 **Photo.** *Perf. 13x12½*

C81	AP33	30fr multi	30	20
C82	AP33	45fr multi	60	30
C83	AP33	55fr multi	70	40
C84	AP33	70fr multi	85	50

Aztec Stadium, Mexico City — AP34

Designs (Olympic Rings and); 45fr, Ball player, Mayan sculpture (vert.). 70fr, Wrestler, sculpture from Uxpanapan (vert.). 150fr, Olympic Stadium, Mexico City.

1968, Nov. 20 **Engr.** *Perf. 13*

C85	AP34	30fr dp cl & sl grn	45	20
C86	AP34	45fr ultra & dk rose brn	60	25
C87	AP34	70fr sl grn & dk brn	90	40
C88	AP34	150fr dk car & dk brn	2.10	1.00
a.		Min. sheet of 4	4.50	4.50

Issued to commemorate the 19th Olympic Games, Mexico City, Oct. 12-27.

No. C88a contains one each of Nos. C85-C88. It is folded down the vertical gutter separating Nos. C85-C86 se-tenant at left and Nos. C87-C88 se-tenant at right. Size: 235x102mm.

The Annunciation, by Foujita — AP35

Paintings by Foujita: 30fr, Nativity (horiz.). 100fr, The Virgin and Child. 200fr, The Baptism of Christ.

Perf. 12x12½, 12½x12

1968, Nov. 25 **Photo.**

C89	AP35	30fr multi	50	20
C90	AP35	70fr multi	90	45
C91	AP35	100fr multi	1.50	65
C92	AP35	200fr multi	3.00	1.35

Christmas 1968.

PHILEXAFRIQUE Issue

Painting: 100fr, Diderot, by Louis Michel Vanloo.

1968, Dec. 16 *Perf. 12½x12*

C93	AP35	100fr multi	1.50	1.00

Issued to publicize PHILEXAFRIQUE, Philatelic Exhibition in Abidjan, Feb. 14-23. Printed with alternating bluish violet label.

2nd PHILEXAFRIQUE Issue
Common Design Type

Design: 50fr, Dahomey No. 119 and aerial view of Cotonou.

1969, Feb. 14 **Engr.** *Perf. 13*

C94	CD128	50fr bl, brn & pur	75	60

Issued to commemorate the opening of PHILEXAFRIQUE, Feb. 14.

Type of Painting (Christmas) Issue, 1966

Paintings: No. C95, Virgin of the Rocks, by Leonardo da Vinci. No. C96, Virgin with the Scales, by Cesare da Sesto.

1969, Mar. 17 **Photo.** *Perf. 12½x12*

C95	AP21	100fr vio & multi	1.35	65
C96	AP21	100fr grn & multi	1.35	65

Issued to commemorate the 450th anniversary of the death of Leonardo da Vinci (1452-1519).

General Bonaparte, by Jacques Louis David AP36

Paintings: 60fr, Napoleon I in 1809, by Robert J. Lefevre. 75fr, Napoleon on the Battlefield of Eylau, by Antoine Jean Gros (horiz.). 200fr, Gen. Bonaparte at Arcole, by Gros.

1969, Apr. 14 **Photo.** *Perf. 12½x12*

C97	AP36	30fr multi	1.20	85
C98	AP36	60fr multi	1.75	1.25
C99	AP36	75fr multi	2.50	1.65
C100	AP36	200fr multi	5.50	3.25

Bicentenary of the birth of Napoleon I.

Arms Type of Regular Issue, 1969

1969, June 30 **Litho.** *Perf. 13½x13*

C101	A49	50fr multi	60	30

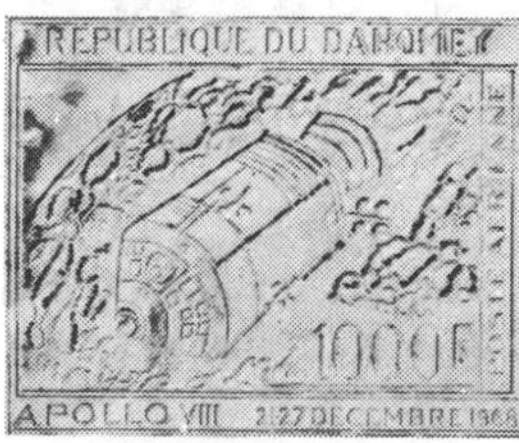

Apollo 8 Trip Around the Moon — AP37

Embossed on Gold Foil

1969, July *Die-cut Perf. 10½*

C102	AP37	1000fr gold	15.00	15.00

Issued to commemorate the U.S. Apollo 8 mission, which put the first men into orbit around the moon, Dec. 21-27, 1968.

ALUNISSAGE
APOLLO XI
JUILLET 1969

Nos. C67-C68 Surcharged

125F

1969, Aug. 1 **Photo.** *Perf. 13*

C103	AP28	125fr on 70fr grnsh bl & multi	2.00	1.00
C104	AP28	125fr on 70fr dp bl & multi	2.00	1.00

Issued to commemorate man's first landing on the moon, July 20, 1969; U. S. astronauts Neil A. Armstrong and Col. Edwin E. Aldrin, Jr., with Lieut. Col. Michael Collins piloting Apollo 11.

Europafrica Issue
Type of Regular Issue, 1969

Design: 100fr, Oil palm industry, Cotonou.

1969, Sept. 22 **Litho.** *Perf. 14*

C105	A51	100fr multi	1.25	65
a.		Souv. sheet of 3	2.25	2.25

No. C105a contains one each of Nos. 262-263 and C105. Black marginal inscription. Size: 107½x148mm.

Dahomey Rotary Emblem — AP38

1969, Sept. 25 *Perf. 14x13½*

C106	AP38	50fr multi	75	40

No. C33 Surcharged 10F

1969, Nov. 15 **Photo.** *Perf. 12½*

C107	AP14	10fr on 50fr multi	12	6

Dance Type of Regular Issue

Design: 70fr, Teke dance and Tourist Year emblem.

1969, Dec. 15 **Litho.** *Perf. 14*

C108	A52	70fr multi	90	40

Painting Type of 1966

Paintings: 30fr, Annunciation, by Vrancke van der Stockt. 45fr, Nativity, Swabian School (horiz.). 110fr, Madonna and Child, by the Master of the Gold Brocade. 200fr, Adoration of the Kings, Antwerp School.

Perf. 12½x12, 12x12½

1969, Dec. 20

C109	AP21	30fr multi	50	35
C110	AP21	45fr red & multi	75	50
C111	AP21	110fr multi	2.00	1.20
C112	AP21	200fr multi	3.50	2.25

Christmas 1969.

1969, Dec. 27 *Perf. 12½x12*

Paintings: No. C113, The Artist's Studio (detail), by Gustave Courbet. No. C114, Self-portrait with Gold Chain, by Rembrandt. 150fr, Hendrickje Stoffels, by Rembrandt.

C113	AP21	100fr red & multi	1.25	75
C114	AP21	100fr grn & multi	1.25	75
C115	AP21	150fr multi	2.00	1.00

A particular stamp may be scarce, but if few collectors want it, its market value may remain relatively low.

Franklin D. Roosevelt AP39

Astronauts, Rocket and U.S. Flag AP40

1970, Feb. **Photo.** *Perf. 12½*

C116	AP39	100fr ultra, yel grn & blk	1.25	50

Issued to commemorate the 25th anniversary of the death of Pres. Franklin Delano Roosevelt (1882-1945).

1970, Mar. 9 **Photo.** *Perf. 12½*

Designs: 50fr, Astronauts riding rocket through space. 70fr, Astronauts in landing module approaching moon. 110fr, Astronauts planting U.S. flag on moon.

C117	AP40	30fr multi	40	25

Souvenir Sheet

C118	AP40	Sheet of 4	3.50	3.50
a.		50fr vio bl & multi	60	60
b.		70fr vio bl & multi	85	85
c.		110fr vio bl & multi	1.25	1.25

See note after No. C104. No. C118 contains one each of Nos. C117, C118a, C118b and C118c; violet blue marginal inscription in French, German and English. Size: 120x157mm.

Walt Whitman and Dahoman Huts — AP41

1970, Apr. 30 **Engr.** *Perf. 13*

C119	AP41	100fr Prus bl, brn & emer	1.25	50

Issued to honor Walt Whitman (1818-1892), American poet.

No. C117 Surcharged in Silver with New Value, Heavy Bar and: "APOLLO XIII / SOLIDARITE / SPATIALE / INTERNATIONALE"

1970, May 15 **Photo.** *Perf. 12½*

C120	AP40	40fr on 30fr multi	65	65

The flight of Apollo 13.

Soccer Players and Globe — AP42

Designs: 50fr, Goalkeeper catching ball. 200fr, Players kicking ball.

1970, May 19

C121	AP42	40fr multi	60	35
C122	AP42	50fr multi	70	40
C123	AP42	200fr multi	3.00	1.40

Issued to publicize the 9th World Soccer Championships for the Jules Rimet Cup, Mexico City, May 30-June 21, 1970.

EXPO '70 Type of Regular Issue

Designs (EXPO '70 Emblems and): 70fr, Dahomey pavilion. 120fr, Mt. Fuji, temple and torii.

1970, June 15 Litho. *Perf. 13½x14*
C124 A54 70fr yel, red & dk vio 85 40
C125 A54 120fr yel, red & grn 1.50 75

Issued to publicize EXPO '70 International Exhibition Osaka, Japan, Mar. 15-Sept. 13, 1970.

No. C123 Surcharged with New Value and Overprinted: "Bresil-Italie / 4-1"

1970, July 13 Photo. *Perf. 12½*
C126 AP42 100fr on 200fr multi 1.50 65

Issued to commemorate Brazil's victory in the 9th World Soccer Championships, Mexico City.

Mercury, Map of Africa and Europe AP43

Ludwig van Beethoven AP44

Europafrica Issue, 1970

1970, July 20 Photo. *Perf. 12x13*
C127 AP43 40fr multi 50 30
C128 AP43 70fr multi 85 40

1970, Sept. 21 Litho. *Perf. 14x13½*
C129 AP44 90fr brt bl & vio blk 1.25 50
C130 AP44 110fr yel grn & dk brn 1.35 70

Issued to commemorate the bicentenary of the birth of Ludwig van Beethoven (1770-1827), composer.

Symbols of Learning — AP45

1970, Nov. 6 Photo. *Perf. 12½*
C131 AP45 100fr multi 1.25 50

Issued to commemorate the laying of the foundation stone for the University at Calavi.

Annunciation, Rhenish School, c.1340 — AP46

Paintings of Rhenish School, circa 1340: 70fr, Nativity. 110fr, Adoration of the Kings. 200fr, Presentation at the Temple.

1970, Nov. 9 *Perf. 12½x12*
C132 AP46 40fr gold & multi 50 25
C133 AP46 70fr gold & multi 90 35
C134 AP46 110fr gold & multi 1.35 60
C135 AP46 200fr gold & multi 2.75 1.10

Christmas 1970.

Charles de Gaulle, Arc de Triomphe and Flag — AP47

Design: 500fr, de Gaulle as old man and Notre Dame Cathedral, Paris.

1971, March 15 Photo. *Perf. 12½*
C136 AP47 40fr multi 60 30
C137 AP47 500fr multi 6.00 3.00

In memory of Gen. Charles de Gaulle (1890-1970), President of France.

L'Indifférent, by Watteau — AP48

Painting: No. C139, Woman playing stringed instrument, by Watteau.

1971, May 3 Photo. *Perf. 13*
C138 AP48 100fr red brn & multi 1.20 80
C139 AP48 100fr red brn & multi 1.20

1971, May 29 Photo. *Perf. 13*

Dürer Paintings: 100fr, Self-portrait, 1498. 200fr, Self-portrait, 1500.

C140 AP48 100fr bl grn & multi 1.20 80
C141 AP48 200fr dk grn & multi 2.75 1.60

500th anniversary of the birth of Albrecht Dürer (1471-1528), German painter and engraver. See Nos. C151-C152, C174-C175.

Johannes Kepler and Diagram — AP49

Designs: 200fr, Kepler, trajectories, satellite and rocket.

1971, July 12 Engr. *Perf. 13*
C142 AP49 40fr brt rose lil, blk & vio bl 50 25
C143 AP49 200fr red, blk & dk bl 2.75 1.20

400th anniversary of the birth of Johannes Kepler (1571-1630), German astronomer.

Europafrica Issue

Jet Plane, Maps of Europe and Africa — AP50

Designs: 100fr, Ocean liner, maps of Europe and Africa.

1971, July 19 Photo. *Perf. 12½x12*
C144 AP50 50fr blk, lt bl & org 60 30
C145 AP50 100fr multi 1.20 60

African Postal Union Issue, 1971
Common Design Type

Design: 100fr, Dahomey coat of arms and UAMPT building, Brazzaville, Congo.

1971, Nov. 13 *Perf. 13x13½*
C146 CD135 100fr bl & multi 1.20 60

Flight into Egypt, by Van Dyke — AP51

Paintings: 40fr, Adoration of the Shepherds, by the Master of the Hausbuch, c. 1500 (vert.). 70fr, Adoration of the Kings, by Holbein the Elder (vert.). 200fr, The Birth of Christ, by Dürer.

1971, Nov. 22 *Perf. 13*
C147 AP51 40fr gold & multi 50 25
C148 AP51 70fr gold & multi 90 45
C149 AP51 100fr gold & multi 1.20 50
C150 AP51 200fr gold & multi 2.40 1.20

Christmas 1971.

Painting Type of 1971 Inscribed: "25e ANNIVERSAIRE DE L'UNICEF"

Paintings: 40fr, Prince Balthazar, by Velasquez. 100fr, Infanta Margarita Maria, by Velazquez.

1971, Dec. 11
C151 AP48 40fr gold & multi 50 30
C152 AP48 100fr gold & multi 1.20 50

25th anniversary of the United Nations International Children's Fund (UNICEF).

Olympic Games Type of Regular Issue

Design: 150fr, Sapporo '72 emblem, ski jump and stork flying.

1972, Feb. Engr. *Perf. 13*
C153 A61 150fr brn, dp rose lil & bl 2.00 1.00

11th Winter Olympic Games, Sapporo, Japan, Feb. 3-13.

Boy Scout and Scout Flag — AP52

Designs: 40fr, Scout playing marimba. 100fr, Scouts doing farm work.

1972, Mar. 19 Photo. *Perf. 13*
Size: 26x35mm.
C154 AP52 35fr multi 30 20
C155 AP52 40fr multi 50 25
Size: 26x46mm.
C156 AP52 100fr yel & multi 1.20 60
a. Souvenir sheet of 3 2.25 2.25

World Boy Scout Seminar, Cotonou, March 1972. No. C156a contains Nos. C154-C156 with perf. 12½. Red marginal inscription and black control number. Size: 150x115mm.

Workers Training Institute and Friedrich Naumann — AP53

Design: 250fr, Workers Training Institute and Pres. Theodor Heuss of Germany.

1972, Mar. 29 Photo. *Perf. 13x12*
C157 AP53 100fr brt rose, blk & vio 1.10 55
C158 AP53 250fr bl, blk & vio 3.00 1.25

Laying of foundation stone for National Workers Training Institute.

Mosaic Floor, St. Mark's, Venice — AP54

12th Century Mosaics from St. Mark's Basilica: 40fr, Roosters carrying fox on a pole. 65fr, Noah sending out dove.

1972, Apr. 10 *Perf. 13*
C159 AP54 35fr gold & multi 50 30
C160 AP54 40fr gold & multi 60 40
C161 AP54 65fr gold & multi 90 60

UNESCO campaign to save Venice.

Neapolitan and Dahoman Dancers — AP55

1972, May 3 *Perf. 13½x13*
C162 AP55 100fr multi 1.20 70

12th Philatelic Exhibition, Naples.

Running, German Eagle, Olympic Rings — AP56

Designs (Olympic Rings and): 85fr, High jump and Glyptothek, Munich. 150fr, Shot put and Propylaeum, Munich.

1972, June 12 **Engr.** ***Perf. 13***

C163	AP56	20fr ultra, grn & brn	25	15
C164	AP56	85fr brn, grn & ultra	90	40
C165	AP56	150fr grn, brn & ultra	1.75	90
a.		Miniature sheet of 3	3.50	3.50

20th Olympic Games, Munich, Aug. 26-Sept. 10. No. C165a contains one each of Nos. C163-C165. Size: 130x99mm.

Louis Blériot and his Plane — AP57

1972, June 26

C166	AP57	100fr vio, cl & brt bl	1.20	65

Birth centenary of Louis Blériot (1872-1936), French aviation pioneer.

Adam, by Lucas Cranach — AP58

Design: 200fr, Eve, by Lucas Cranach.

1972, Oct. 24 **Photo.**

C167	AP58	150fr multi	2.00	1.00
C168	AP58	200fr multi	2.50	1.10

500th anniversary of the birth of Lucas Cranach (1472-1553), German painter.

Pauline Borghese, by Canova — AP59

1972, Nov. 8

C169	AP59	250fr multi	3.00	1.50

Sesquicentennial of the death of Antonio Canova (1757-1822), Italian sculptor.

Nos. C163-C165 Overprinted:
a. 5.00m-10.00m. / VIREN / 2 MEDAILLES D'OR
b. HAUTEUR DAMES / MEYFARTH / MEDAILLE D'OR
c. POIDS / KOMAR / MEDAILLE D'OR

1972, Nov. 13 **Engr.** ***Perf. 13***

C170	AP56(a)	20fr multi	30	20
C171	AP56(b)	85fr multi	1.00	50
C172	AP56(c)	150fr multi	2.00	1.10
a.		Miniature sheet of 3	3.75	3.75

Gold medal winners in 20th Olympic Games: Lasse Viren, Finland, 5,000m. and 10,000m. races (20fr); Ulrike Meyfarth, Germany, women's high jump (85fr); Wladyslaw Komar, Poland, shot put (150fr).

Louis Pasteur — AP60

1972, Nov. 30

C173	AP60	100fr brt grn, lil & brn	1.20	65

Sesquicentennial of the birth of Louis Pasteur (1822-1895), chemist and bacteriologist.

Painting Type of 1971

Paintings by Georges de La Tour: 35fr, Vielle player. 150fr, The Newborn (horiz.).

1972, Dec. 11 **Photo.**

C174	AP48	35fr multi	42	20
C175	AP48	150fr multi	2.00	1.10

320th death anniversary of Georges de La Tour (1593-1652), French painter.

Annunciation, School of Agnolo Gaddi — AP61

Paintings: 125fr, Nativity, by Simone dei Crocifissi. 140fr, Adoration of the Shepherds, by Giovanni di Pietro. 250fr, Adoration of the Kings, by Giotto.

1972, Dec. 15

C176	AP61	35fr gold & multi	40	20
C177	AP61	125fr gold & multi	1.20	60
C178	AP61	140fr gold & multi	1.60	80
C179	AP61	250fr gold & multi	2.60	1.50

Christmas 1972. See Nos. C195-C198, C218, C223, C225-C226.

Statue of St. Teresa, Basilica of Lisieux — AP62

Design: 100fr, St. Teresa, roses, and globe (vert.).

1973, May 14 **Photo.** ***Perf. 13***

C180	AP62	40fr blk, gold & lt ultra	40	25
C181	AP62	100fr gold & multi	1.00	55

Centenary of the birth of St. Teresa of Lisieux (Therese Martin, 1873-97), Carmelite nun.

Scouts, African Scout Emblem — AP63

Designs (African Scout Emblem and): 20fr, Lord Baden-Powell (vert.). 40fr, Scouts building bridge.

1973, July 2 **Engr.** ***Perf. 13***

C182	AP63	15fr bl, grn & choc	15	10
C183	AP63	20fr ol & Prus bl	20	15
C184	AP63	40fr grn, Prus bl & brn	40	20
a.		Souvenir sheet of 3	85	85

24th Boy Scout World Conference, Nairobi, Kenya, July 16-21. No. C184a contains 3 stamps similar to Nos. C182-C184 in changed colors (15fr in ultramarine, slate green and chocolate; 20fr in chocolate, ultramarine and indigo; 40fr in slate green, indigo and chocolate). Ultramarine marginal inscription and border. Size: 180x100 mm.

Copernicus, Venera and Mariner Satellites — AP64

Design: 125fr, Copernicus, sun, earth and moon (vert.).

1973, Aug. 20 **Engr.** ***Perf. 13***

C185	AP64	65fr blk, dk brn & org	80	45
C186	AP64	125fr bl, sl grn & pur	1.25	65

500th anniversary of the birth of Nicolaus Copernicus (1473-1543), Polish astronomer.

Head and City Hall, Brussels — AP64a

1973, Sept. 17 **Engr.** ***Perf. 13***

C187	AP64a	100fr blk, Prus bl & dk grn	90	60

African Weeks, Brussels, Sept. 15-30, 1973.

WMO Emblem, World Weather Map — AP65

1973, Sept. 25

C188	AP65	100fr ol grn & lt brn	1.00	60

Centenary of international meteorological cooperation.

Europafrica Issue

"EUROPAFRIQUE" — AP66

Design: 40fr, similar to 35fr.

1973, Oct. 1 **Engr.** ***Perf. 13***

C189	AP66	35fr multi	35	20
C190	AP66	40fr bl, sep & ultra	40	30

John F. Kennedy — AP67

1973, Oct. 18

C191	AP67	200fr bl grn, vio & sl grn	2.00	1.20
a.		Souvenir sheet	2.50	2.50

10th anniversary of the death of President John F. Kennedy (1917-1963). No. C191a contains one stamp in changed colors (bright blue, magenta & brown). Magenta marginal inscription and border. Size: 140x109mm.

Soccer — AP68

Designs: 40fr, Two soccer players. 100fr, Three soccer players.

1973, Nov. 19 **Engr.** ***Perf. 13***

C192	AP68	35fr multi	30	20
C193	AP68	40fr multi	40	25
C194	AP68	100fr multi	90	65

World Soccer Cup, Munich 1974.

Painting Type of 1972

Designs: 35fr, Annunciation, by Dirk Bouts. 100fr, Nativity, by Giotto. 150fr, Adoration of the Kings, by Botticelli. 200fr, Adoration of the Shepherds, by Jacopo Bassano (horiz.).

1973, Dec. 20 **Photo.** ***Perf. 13***

C195	AP61	35fr gold & multi	35	25
C196	AP61	100fr gold & multi	1.00	60
C197	AP61	150fr gold & multi	1.50	1.00
C198	AP61	200fr gold & multi	2.00	1.30

Christmas 1973.

No C188 Surcharged in Violet with New Value and: "OPERATION SKYLAB / 1973-1974"

1974, Feb. 4 **Engr.** ***Perf. 13***

C199	AP65	200fr on 100fr multi	1.75	1.25

Skylab U.S. space missions, 1973-74.

Skiers, Snowflake, Olympic Rings — AP69

1974, Feb. 25 **Engr.** ***Perf. 13***

C200	AP69	100fr vio bl, brn & brt bl	90	65

50th anniversary of first Winter Olympic Games, Chamonix, France.

Demand, as well as supply, determines a stamp's market value. One is as important as the other.

Marie Curie
AP70

Designs: 50fr, Lenin. 150fr, Churchill.

1974, June 7 Engr. *Perf. 13*

C201 AP70 50fr dk red & brt lil 45 30
C202 AP70 125fr ol & dl red 1.10 75
C203 AP70 150fr brt lil & Prus bl 1.35 90

50th anniversary of the death of Lenin (50fr); 40th anniversary of the death of Marie Sklodowska Curie (125fr); centenary of the birth of Winston Churchill (150fr).

Bishop, Persian, 18th Century — AP71

Frederic Chopin — AP72

Design: 200fr, Queen, Siamese chess piece, 19th century.

1974, June 14 Photo. *Perf. 12½x13*

C204 AP71 50fr org & multi 50 35
C205 AP71 200fr brt grn & multi 1.75 1.25

21st Chess Olympiad, Nice, June 6-30, 1974.

1974, June 24 Engr. *Perf. 13*

Design: No. C207, Ludwig van Beethoven.

C206 AP72 150fr blk & cop red 1.25 90
C207 AP72 150fr blk & cop red 1.25 90

Famous musicians, Frederic Chopin (1810-1849) and Ludwig van Beethoven (1770-1827).

Astronaut on Moon, and Earth
AP73

1974, July 10 Engr. *Perf. 13*

C208 AP73 150fr multi 1.25 1.00

5th anniversary of the first moon walk.

Nos. C182-C183 Surcharged and Overprinted in Black or Red: "XIe JAMBOREE PANARAGE DE BATROUN-LIBAN"

1974, July 19

C209 AP63 100fr on 15fr multi 75 45
C210 AP63 140fr on 20fr multi (R) 1.20 75

11th Pan-Arab Jamboree, Batrun, Lebanon, Aug. 1974. Overprint includes 2 bars over old denomination; 2-line overprint on No. C209, 3 lines on No. C210.

Nos. C193-C194 Overprinted and Surcharged with New Value and Two Bars: "R F A 2 / HOLLANDE 1"

1974, July 26 Engr. *Perf. 13*

C211 AP68 100fr on 40fr 80 35
C212 AP68 150fr on 100fr 1.20 55

World Cup Soccer Championship, 1974, victory of German Federal Republic.

Earth and UPU Emblem — AP74

Designs (UPU Emblem and): 65fr, Concorde in flight. 125fr, French railroad car, c. 1860. 200fr, African drummer and Renault mail truck, pre-1939.

1974, Aug. 5 Engr. *Perf. 13*

C213 AP74 35fr rose cl & vio 30 10
C214 AP74 65fr Prus grn & cl 60 20
C215 AP74 125fr multi 1.10 42
C216 AP74 200fr multi 1.75 70

Centenary of Universal Postal Union.

Painting Type of 1972 and

Lion of Belfort by Frederic A. Bartholdi — AP75

Painting: 250fr, Girl with Falcon, by Philippe de Champaigne.

1974, Aug. 20 Engr. *Perf. 13*

C217 AP75 100fr rose brn 1.00 35
C218 AP61 250fr multi 2.50 1.00

Rhamphorhynchus — AP76

Prehistoric Animals: 150fr, Stegosaurus. 200fr, Tyrannosaurus.

1974, Sept. 23 Photo.

C219 AP76 35fr multi 30 12
C220 AP76 150fr multi 1.20 55
C221 AP76 200fr multi 1.50 70

Europafrica Issue

Globe, Cogwheel, Emblem — AP77

1974, Dec. 20 Typo. *Perf. 13*

C222 AP77 250fr red & multi 2.50 1.00

Printed tête bêche in sheets of 10.

Christmas Type of 1972 and

Nativity, by Martin Schongauer
AP78

Paintings: 35fr, Annunciation, by Schongauer. 100fr, Virgin in Rose Arbor, by Schongauer. 250fr, Virgin and Child, with St. John the Baptist, by Botticelli.

1974, Dec. 23 Photo. *Perf. 13*

C223 AP61 35fr gold & multi 30 15
C224 AP78 40fr gold & multi 40 25
C225 AP61 100fr gold & multi 1.00 35
C226 AP61 250fr gold & multi 2.50 1.00

Apollo and Soyuz Spacecraft
AP79

Designs: 200fr, American and Russian flags, rocket take-off. 500fr, Apollo-Soyuz link-up.

1975, July 16 Litho. *Perf. 12½*

C227 AP79 35fr multi 30 15
C228 AP79 200fr vio bl, red & bl 1.60 70
C229 AP79 500fr vio bl, ind & red 4.00 2.25

Apollo Soyuz space test project (Russo-American cooperation); launching July 15; link-up, July 17.

Nos. C227-C228 Surcharged in Silver or Black: "RENCONTRE / APOLLO-SOYOUZ / 17 Juil. 1975"

1975, July 17 Litho. *Perf. 12½*

C230 AP79 100fr on 35fr (S) 80 35
C231 AP79 300fr on 200fr 2.40 1.00

Apollo-Soyuz link-up in space, July 17, 1975.

ARPHILA Emblem, "Stamps" and Head of Ceres — AP80

1975, Aug. 22 Engr. *Perf. 13*

C232 AP80 100fr blk, bl & lil 90 35

ARPHILA 75, International Philatelic Exhibition, Paris, June 6-16.

Holy Family, by Michelangelo
AP81

Infantry and Stars
AP82

Europafrica Issue

1975, Sept. 29 Litho. *Perf. 12*

C233 AP81 300fr gold & multi 2.75 1.00

1975, Nov. 18 Engr. *Perf. 13*

Designs (Stars and): 135fr, Drummers and fifer. 300fr, Artillery with cannon. 500fr, Cavalry.

C234 AP82 75fr grn car & pur 60 25
C235 AP82 135fr bl, mag & sep 1.10 45
C236 AP82 300fr vio bl, ver & choc 2.40 1.00
C237 AP82 500fr ver, dk grn & brn 4.00 1.75

American bicentennial.

Diving and Olympic Rings
AP83

Design: 250fr, Soccer and Olympic rings.

1975, Nov. 24

C238 AP83 40fr vio, grnsh bl & ol brn 35 15
C239 AP83 250fr red, emer & brn 2.00 90

Pre-Olympic Year 1975.

AIR POST SEMI-POSTAL STAMPS.

V1

V2

V3

V4

Stamps of the preceding designs were issued in 1942 by the Vichy Government, but were not placed in use in the colony.

AIR POST PARCEL POST STAMPS

Nos. C20-C23, C14 Surcharged in Black or Red

COLIS POSTAUX

1967-69 Engr. *Perf. 13*

CQ1	AP6	200fr on 200fr multi	4.00	3.00
CQ2	AP6	300fr on 100fr multi	4.75	4.00
CQ3	AP6	500fr on 300fr multi	9.00	6.25
CQ4	AP6	1000fr on 500fr multi	18.00	15.00
CQ5	AP4	5000fr on 100fr multi (R) ('69)	80.00	80.00
		Nos. CQ1-CQ5 (5)	115.75	108.25

On No. CQ5, "Colis Postaux" is at top, bar at right.

POSTAGE DUE STAMPS.

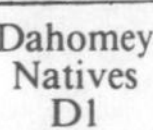
Dahomey Natives D1

Numeral of Value D2

1906 Unwmk. Typo. *Perf. 14x13½*

J1	D1	5c grn, *grnsh*	1.75	1.75
J2	D1	10c red brn	3.00	3.00
J3	D1	15c dk bl	5.75	5.75
J4	D1	20c *yellow*	4.00	4.00
J5	D1	30c red, *straw*	4.75	4.75
J6	D1	50c violet	17.00	17.00
J7	D1	60c *buff*	10.50	10.50
J8	D1	1fr *pinkish*	27.50	27.50
		Nos. J1-J8 (8)	74.25	74.25

1914

J9	D2	5c green	6	6
J10	D2	10c rose	15	15
J11	D2	15c gray	40	40
J12	D2	20c brown	60	60
J13	D2	30c blue	60	60
J14	D2	50c black	95	95
J15	D2	60c orange	1.40	1.40
J16	D2	1fr violet	1.40	1.40
		Nos. J9-J16 (8)	5.56	5.56

Type of 1914 Issue Surcharged **2F.**

1927

J17	D2	2fr on 1fr lil rose	3.50	3.50
J18	D2	3fr on 1fr org brn	3.00	3.00

Carved Mask — D3

1941 Engr. *Perf. 14x13*

J19	D3	5c black	6	6
J20	D3	10c lil rose	6	6
J21	D3	15c dk bl	6	6
J22	D3	20c brt yel grn	18	18
J23	D3	30c orange	30	30
J24	D3	50c vio brn	60	60
J25	D3	60c sl grn	80	80
J26	D3	1fr rose red	1.00	1.00
J27	D3	2fr yellow	1.00	1.00
J28	D3	3fr dk pur	1.40	1.40
		Nos. J19-J28 (10)	5.46	5.46

Stamps of type D3 with value numerals replacing "RF" at upper left corner were issued in 1943-44 by the Vichy Government, but were not placed on sale in the colony.

Republic

Panther and Man — D4

Perf. 14x13½

1963, July 22 Typo. Unwmk.

J29	D4	1fr grn & rose cl	5	5
J30	D4	2fr brn & emer	15	15
J31	D4	5fr org & vio bl	25	25
J32	D4	10fr mag & blk	60	60
J33	D4	20fr vio bl & org	95	95
		Nos. J29-J33 (5)	2.00	2.00

Mail Boat — D5

Designs: No. J35, Heliograph. No. J36, Morse receiver. No. J37, Mailman on bicycle. No. J38, Early telephone. No. J39, Autorail. No. J40, Mail truck. No. J41, Radio tower. No. J42, DC-8F jet plane. No. J43, Early Bird communications satellite.

1967, Oct. 24 Engr. *Perf. 11*

J34	D5	1fr brn, dl pur & bl	8	8
J35	D5	1fr dl pur, brn & bl	8	8
J36	D5	3fr dk brn, dk grn & org	12	12
J37	D5	3fr dk grn, dk brn & org	12	12
J38	D5	5fr ol bis, lil & bl	30	30
J39	D5	5fr lil, ol bis & bl	30	30
J40	D5	10fr brn org, vio & grn	50	50
J41	D5	10fr vio, brn org & grn	50	50
J42	D5	30fr Prus bl, mar & vio	80	80
J43	D5	30fr vio, Prus bl & mar	80	80
		Nos. J34-J43 (10)	3.60	3.60

The two designs of each value in Nos. J34-J43 were printed tete beche, se-tenant at the base.

PARCEL POST STAMPS

Nos. 141-146 and 148 Surcharged

COLIS POSTAUX

1967, Jan. Unwmk. Engr. *Perf. 13*

Q1	A15	5fr on 1fr multi	15	15
Q2	A15	10fr on 2fr multi	30	30
Q3	A15	20fr on 6fr multi	40	40
Q4	A15	25fr on 3fr multi	55	55
Q5	A15	30fr on 4fr multi	65	65
Q6	A15	50fr on 10fr multi	1.00	1.00
a.		"20" instead of "50"	80.00	
Q7	A15	100fr on 20fr multi	2.00	2.00
		Nos. Q1-Q7 (7)	5.05	5.05

The surcharge is arranged to fit the shape of the stamp.

No. Q6a occurred once on the sheet of the 50fr on 10fr.

DALMATIA

LOCATION — A promontory in the northwestern part of the Balkan Peninsula, together with several small islands in the Adriatic Sea.

GOVT. — Part of the former Austro-Hungarian crownland of the same name.

AREA — 113 sq. mi.

POP. — 18,719 (1921)

CAPITAL — Zara.

Stamps were issued during Italian occupation. This territory was subsequently annexed by Italy.

100 Centesimi = 1 Corona = 1 Lira

Issued under Italian Occupation.

Italy No. 87 Surcharged **una corona**

1919, May 1 Wmk. 140 *Perf. 14*

1	A46	1cor on 1 l brn & grn	60	*2.50*

Italian Stamps of 1906-08 Surcharged — a **5 centesimi di corona**

1921-22

2	A48	5c on 5c grn	30	*75*
3	A48	10c on 10c cl	30	*75*
4	A49	25c on 25c bl ('22)	50	*1.25*
5	A49	50c on 50c vio ('22)	75	*2.00*

Italian Stamps of 1901-10 Surcharged — b **1 corona**

6	A46	1cor on 1 l brn & grn ('22)	1.00	*2.50*
7	A46	5cor on 5 l bl & rose ('22)	4.50	*14.00*
8	A51	10cor on 10 l gray grn & red ('22)	7.00	*20.00*
		Nos. 1-8 (8)	14.95	43.75

Surcharges similar to these but differing in style or arrangement of type were used in Austria under Italian occupation.

SPECIAL DELIVERY STAMPS.

Italian Special Delivery Stamp No. E1 Surcharged **25 centesimi di corona**

1921 Wmk. Crowns. (140) *Perf. 14*

E1	SD1	25c on 25c rose red	40	*1.50*
a.		Double surcharge	40.00	

Italian Special Delivery Stamp Surcharged **LIRE 1,20 DI CORONA**

1922

E2	SD2	1.20 l on 1.20 l bl & rose		30.00

No. E2 was not placed in use.

POSTAGE DUE STAMPS.

Italian Postage Due Stamps Surcharged types "a" or "b"

1922 Wmk. Crown. (140) *Perf. 14.*

J1	D3 (a)	50c on 50c buff & mag	1.00	*2.50*
J2	D3 (b)	1cor on 1 l bl & red	1.25	*4.00*
J3	D3 (b)	2cor on 2 l bl & red	4.75	*14.00*
J4	D3 (b)	5cor on 5 l bl & red	7.00	*20.00*

DANISH WEST INDIES

LOCATION — A group of islands in the West Indies, lying east of Puerto Rico

GOVT. — A former Danish colony

AREA — 132 sq. mi.

POP. — 27,086 (1911)

CAPITAL — Charlotte Amalie

The United States bought these islands in 1917 and they became the U. S. Virgin Islands, using U. S. stamps and currency.

100 Cents = 1 Dollar

100 Bits = 1 Franc (1905)

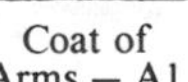
Coat of Arms — A1

Wmk.111

Yellowish Paper.
Yellow Wavy-line Burelage, UL to LR

Wmk. Small Crown (111)

1856 Typo. *Imperf.*

1	A1	3c dk car, brn gum	175.00	200.00
a.		3c dk car, yel gum	275.00	260.00
b.		3c dk car, white gum	2,750.	

White Paper
Yellow Wavy-line Burelage, UR to LL

1866

2	A1	3c rose	80.00	70.00

1872 *Perf. 12½*

3	A1	3c rose	160.00	170.00

1873

Without Burelage.

4	A1	4c dl bl	300.00	350.00
a.		Imperf., (pair)	950.00	1,200.
b.		Horiz. pair, imperf. vert.	750.00	900.00

No. 2 reprints, unwatermarked: 1930, carmine, price $120. 1942, rose carmine, back-printed across each row ("Nytryk 1942 G.A. Hagemann Danmark og Dansk Vestindiens

Frimaerker Bind 2"), price $60. 1981, carmine, back-printed across two stamps ("Reprint by Dansk Post og Telegrafmuseum 1978"), price, pair, $7.

No. 4 reprints, unwatermarked, imperf.: 1930, ultramarine, price $120. 1942, blue, back-printed like 1942 reprint of No. 2, price $60.

Numeral of Value — A2

Normal Frame

Inverted Frame

The arabesques in the corners have a main stem and a branch. When the frame is in normal position, in the upper left corner the branch leaves the main stem half way between two little leaflets. In the lower right corner the branch starts at the foot of the second leaflet. When the frame is inverted the corner designs are, of course, transposed.

Wmk. 112

White Wove Paper, Varying from Thin to Thick.

Wmk. Crown (112)

1874-79 ***Perf. 14x13½***

5 A2 1c grn & brn red 25.00 20.00
 a. 1c grn & rose lil 37.50 37.50
 b. 1c grn & red vio 37.50 37.50
 c. 1c grn & vio 80.00 110.00
 e. Inverted frame 25.00 25.00
6 A2 3c bl & car 27.50 17.00
 d. Imperf., pair 600.00
 e. Inverted frame 27.50 16.00
7 A2 4c brn & dl bl 17.00 17.00
 b. 4c brn & ultra 250.00 175.00
 c. Diagonal half used as 2c on cover 225.00
 d. Inverted frame 1,000. 1,000.
8 A2 5c grn & gray ('76) 30.00 22.50
 b. Inverted frame 30.00 22.50
9 A2 7c lil & org 27.50 *60.00*
 a. 7c lil & yel 70.00 90.00
 b. Inverted frame 65.00 100.00
10 A2 10c bl & brn ('76) 30.00 18.00
 b. Period between "t" & "s" of "cents" 45.00 35.00
 c. Inverted frame 30.00 20.00
11 A2 12c red lil & yel grn ('77) 35.00 47.50
 a. 12c lil & dp grn 100.00 70.00
12 A2 14c lil & grn 700.00 825.00
 a. Inverted frame 2,000. 2,750.
13 A2 50c vio ('79) 120.00 130.00
 a. 50c gray vio 160.00 200.00

Nos. 9 and 13 Surcharged in Black

I CENT
a

10 CENTS 1895
b

1887-95

14 A2 (a) 1c on 7c lil & org 75.00 90.00
 a. 1c on 7c lil & yel 120.00 175.00
 b. Double surcharge 250.00 350.00
 c. Inverted frame 115.00 135.00
15 A2 (b) 10c on 50c vio ('95) 35.00 40.00

Type of 1873

1896-1901 ***Perf. 13***

16 A2 1c grn & red vio ('98) 15.00 15.00
 a. Normal frame 300.00 350.00
17 A2 3c bl & lake ('98) 13.00 13.00
 a. Normal frame 260.00 300.00
18 A2 4c bis & dl bl ('01) 13.00 13.00
 a. Diagonal half used as 2c on cover 45.00
 b. Inverted frame 60.00 60.00
19 A2 5c grn & gray 37.50 32.50
 a. Normal frame 750.00 750.00
20 A2 10c bl & brn ('01) 85.00 100.00
 a. Inverted frame 1,100. 1,600.
 b. Period between "t" and "s" of "cents" 85.00 100.00
 Nos. 16-20 (5) 163.50 173.50

Arms — A5

1900

21 A5 1c lt grn 2.50 2.50
22 A5 5c lt bl 13.00 13.00

See also Nos. 29-30.

Nos. 6, 17, 20 Surcharged:

2 CENTS 1902
c

8 Cents 1902
d

Surcharge "c" in Black

1902 ***Perf. 14x13½***

23 A2 2c on 3c bl & car 500.00 650.00
 a. "2" in date with straight tail 525.00 575.00
 b. Normal frame 1,500.

Perf. 13

24 A2 2c on 3c bl & lake 8.00 10.00
 a. "2" in date with straight tail 13.00 14.00
 b. Dated "1901" 450.00 500.00
 c. Normal frame 225.00 275.00
 d. Dark grn surch. 1,600.
 e. As "d" & "a" 1,700.
 f. As "d" & "c"
25 A2 8c on 10c bl & brn 25.00 35.00
 a. "2" with straight tail 27.50 37.50
 b. On No. 20b 42.50 52.50
 c. Inverted frame 350.00 350.00

Surcharge "d" in Black

27 A2 2c on 3c bl & lake 12.50 25.00
 a. Normal frame 275.00 300.00
28 A2 8c on 10c bl & brn 11.00 11.00
 a. On No. 20b 20.00 20.00
 b. Inverted frame 275.00 275.00

Wmk.113

1903 **Wmk. Crown (113)**

29 A5 2c carmine 13.00 13.00
30 A5 8c brown 27.50 27.50

King Christian IX — A8

St. Thomas Harbor — A9

1905 **Typo.** ***Perf. 13***

31 A8 5b green 7.50 4.00
32 A8 10b red 7.50 4.00
33 A8 20b grn & bl 13.00 13.00
34 A8 25b ultra 13.00 13.00
35 A8 40b red & gray 12.50 12.50
36 A8 50b yel & gray 11.00 13.00

Frame Typographed, Center Engraved
Wmk. Two Crowns. (113)
Perf. 12

37 A9 1fr grn & bl 20.00 30.00
38 A9 2fr org red & brn 42.50 75.00
39 A9 5fr yel & brn 110.00 250.00
 Nos. 31-39 (9) 237.00 414.50

Nos. 18, 22, 30 Surcharged in Black

5 BIT 1905

1905 **Wmk. Crown (112)** ***Perf. 13***

40 A2 5b on 4c bis & dl bl 22.50 45.00
 a. Inverted frame 42.50 75.00
41 A5 5b on 5c lt bl 15.00 27.50

Wmk. Crown (113)

42 A5 5b on 8c brn 14.00 30.00

King Frederik VIII — A10

Frame Typographed, Center Engraved

1907 **Wmk. 113** ***Perf. 13***

43 A10 5b green 2.50 1.50
44 A10 10b red 2.50 1.50
45 A10 15b vio & brn 6.00 6.00
46 A10 20b grn & bl 47.50 20.00
47 A10 25b bl & dk bl 3.25 2.00
48 A10 30b cl & sl 70.00 30.00
49 A10 40b ver & gray 6.50 10.00
50 A10 50b yel & brn 7.00 10.00
 Nos. 43-50 (8) 145.25 81.00

King Christian X — A11

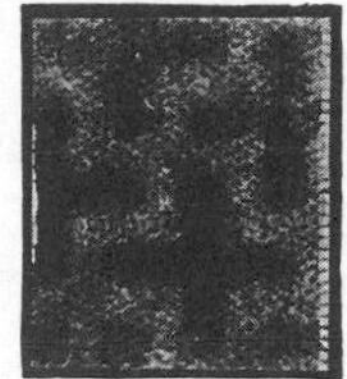
Wmk. 114

Wmk. Multiple Crosses (114)

1915 ***Perf. 14x14½***

51 A11 5b yel grn 3.00 *7.00*
52 A11 10b red 3.00 *60.00*
53 A11 15b lil & red brn 3.00 *60.00*
54 A11 20b grn & bl 3.00 *60.00*
55 A11 25b bl & dk bl 3.00 *15.00*
56 A11 30b cl & blk 3.00 *60.00*
57 A11 40b org & blk 3.00 *60.00*
58 A11 50b yel & brn 3.00 *60.00*
 Nos. 51-58 (8) 24.00 382.00

Forged and favor cancellations exist.

POSTAGE DUE STAMPS

Royal Cipher, "Christian 9 Rex" — D1

1902 **Unwmk.** **Litho.** ***Perf. 11½***

J1 D1 1c dk bl 10.00 15.00
J2 D1 4c dk bl 14.00 20.00
J3 D1 6c dk bl 35.00 60.00
J4 D1 10c dk bl 25.00 35.00

There are five types of each value. On the 4c they may be distinguished by differences in the figures "4"; on the other values the differences are minute.

Counterfeits of Nos. J1-J4 exist.

D2

1905-13 ***Perf. 13***

J5 D2 5b red & gray 7.00 9.00
J6 D2 20b red & gray 14.00 20.00
J7 D2 30b red & gray 8.50 13.00
J8 D2 50b red & gray 12.50 20.00
 a. Perf. 14x14½ ('13) 25.00 125.00
 b. Perf. 11½ 325.00

All values of this issue are known imperforate, but were not regularly issued.

Counterfeits of Nos. J5-J8 exist.

Used prices of Nos. J1-J8 are for canceled copies. Uncanceled examples without gum have probably been used. Price 60% of unused.

DANZIG

LOCATION — In northern Europe bordering on the Baltic Sea
GOVT. — Former free city and state
AREA — 754 sq. mi.
POP. — 407,000 (approx. 1939)
CAPITAL — Danzig

Established as a "Free City and State" under the protection of the League of Nations in 1920, Danzig was seized by Germany in 1939. It became a Polish province in 1945.

100 Pfennig = 1 Gulden (1923)
100 Pfennig = 1 Mark

Used Prices of 1920-23 are for favor-canceled stamps unless otherwise noted. Postally used copies bring higher prices.

German Stamps of 1906-20 Overprinted in Black **Danzig**

Wmk. 125

Perf. 14, 14½, 15x14½

1920 **Wmk. Lozenges. (125)**

1 A16 5pf green 30 25
2 A16 10pf car rose 30 25
3 A22 15pf vio brn 30 25
4 A16 20pf bl vio 30 25
5 A16 30pf org & blk, *buff* 40 30
6 A16 40pf car rose 35 25
7 A16 50pf pur & blk, *buff* 40 30
8 A17 1m red 75 60
9 A17 1.25m green 75 60
10 A17 1.50m yel brn 90 1.10
11 A21 2m blue 1.50 1.50
 a. Double ovpt. *850.*
12 A21 2.50m lil rose 1.90 3.00
13 A19 3m blk vio 6.75 13.00
14 A16 4m blk & rose 5.00 7.25
15 A20 5m sl & car 2.00 2.50
 a. Center inverted *6,000.*
 b. Invtd. ovpt. *10,000.*
 Nos. 1-15 (15) 21.90 31.40

The 5pf brown, 10pf orange and 40pf lake and black with this overprint were not regularly issued. Price for trio, $450.

"Germania" — A1

German Stamps of 1906-20 Surcharged in Violet, Red, Green or Brown.

1920

19 A1 5pf on 30pf org & blk, *buff* (V) 18 20
20 A1 10pf on 20pf bl vio (R) 18 15
 a. Double surch. 175.00 250.00

21 A1 25pf on 30pf org & blk, *buff* (G) 18 20
a. Inverted surcharge 175.00 250.00
22 A1 60pf on 30pf org & blk, *buff* (Br) 70 85
a. Double surch. 175.00 250.00
23 A1 80pf on 30pf org & blk, *buff* (V) 70 85

A2 A3

A4 A5

A6 A7

Surcharged in Black, Red, Blue or Green

Gray Burelage with Points Up.

25 A2 1m on 30pf org & blk, *buff* (Bk) 75 2.00
a. Pair, one without surcharge
26 A3 1¼m on 3pf brn (R) 75 2.00
27 A4 2m on 35pf red brn (Bl) 90 2.00
d. Surch. omitted 90.00 150.00
28 A5 3m on 7½pf org (G) 90 2.00
29 A6 5m on 2pf gray (R) 90 2.00
30 A7 10m on 7½pf org (Bk) 3.00 10.50

Gray Burelage with Points Down.

26a A3 1¼m on 3pf brn 25.00 40.00
27a A4 2m on 35pf red brn 300.00 275.00
28a A5 3m on 7½pf org 11.00 12.50
29a A6 5m on 2pf gray 9.00 22.50
30a A7 10m on 7½pf org 4.50 10.00

Violet Burelage with Points Up.

25b A2 1m on 30pf org & blk, *buff* 35.00 50.00
26b A3 1¼m on 3pf brn 4.00 5.75
27b A4 2m on 35pf red brn 12.00 20.00
28b A5 3m on 7½pf org 1.40 2.25
29b A6 5m on 2pf gray 1.10 2.00
30b A7 10m on 7½pf org 1.10 2.00

Violet Burelage with Points Down.

25c A2 1m on 30pf org & blk, *buff* 1.10 3.50
26c A3 1¼m on 3pf brn 4.00 15.00
27c A4 2m on 35pf red brn 13.00 45.00
28c A5 3m on 7½pf org 35.00 100.00
29c A6 5m on 2pf gray 4.00 8.00
30c A7 10m on 7½pf org 15.00 35.00

Excellent counterfeits of the surcharges are known.

German Stamps of 1906-20 Overprinted in Blue

1920

31 A22 2pf gray 110.00 200.00
32 A22 2½pf gray 140.00 275.00
33 A16 3pf brown 10.00 20.00
a. Dbl. overprint 100.00 100.00
34 A16 5pf green 35 40
a. Dbl. overprint 50.00
35 A22 7½pf orange 27.50 52.50
36 A16 10pf carmine 4.00 7.50
37 A22 15pf dk vio 55 75
b. Dbl. overprint 50.00
38 A16 20pf bl vio 55 75

Overprinted in Carmine or Blue.

39 A16 25pf org & blk, *yel* 55 75
40 A16 30pf org & blk, *buff* 42.50 75.00
42 A16 40pf lake & blk 2.00 4.00
a. Inverted overprint
b. Double ovpt.
43 A16 50pf pur & blk, *buff* 140.00 275.00
44 A16 60pf mag (Bl) 1,650. *3,000.*
45 A16 75pf grn & blk 55 75
46 A16 80pf lake & blk, *rose* 5.50 5.00
47 A17 1m carmine 750.00 *1,200.*
a. Dbl. ovpt. *5,000.*

Overprinted in Carmine

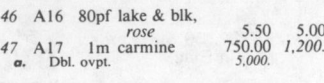

48 A21 2m gray bl 1,150. *1,800.*

Counterfeit overprints of Nos. 31 to 48 exist.

Nos. 44, 47 and 48 were issued in small quantities and usually affixed directly to the mail by the postal clerk.

Hanseatic Trading Ship
A8 A9

Wmk. 108-Honeycomb

Serrate Roulette 13½

1921, Jan. 31 Typo. Wmk. 108

49 A8 5(pf) brn & vio 35 30
50 A8 10(pf) org & dk vio 35 30
51 A8 25(pf) grn & car rose 60 90
52 A8 40(pf) car rose 3.50 3.75
53 A8 80(pf) ultra 45 70
54 A9 1m car rose & blk 1.75 2.25
55 A9 2m dk bl & dk grn 5.50 6.75
56 A9 3m blk & grnsh bl 2.00 2.50
57 A9 5m ind & rose red 2.00 2.50
58 A9 10m dk grn & brn org 3.00 6.00
Nos. 49-58 (10) 19.50 25.95

Issued in commemoration of the Constitution.

Nos. 49 and 50 with center in red instead of violet and Nos. 49, 50 and 54 with center inverted are probably proofs. All values of this issue exist imperforate but are not known to have been regularly issued in that condition.

1921, Mar. 11 ***Perf. 14***

59 A8 25(pf) grn & car rose 75 1.00
60 A8 40(pf) car rose 90 1.10
61 A8 80(pf) ultra 4.50 12.00

No. 45 Surcharged in Black — A10

1921, May 6 Wmk. 125

62 A10 60pf on 75pf grn & blk 60 1.00
a. Double surcharge 90.00 90.00

Arms Coat of Arms
A11 A12

Wmk. Honeycomb. (108) (Vertical or Horizontal.)

1921-22 ***Perf. 14***

63 A11 5(pf) orange 30 30
64 A11 10(pf) dk brn 22 15
65 A11 15(pf) green 22 15
66 A11 20(pf) slate 22 15
67 A11 25(pf) dk grn 22 22
68 A11 30(pf) bl & car 35 30
a. Center inverted 37.50
69 A11 40pf grn & car 22 15
a. Center inverted 37.50
70 A11 50pf dk grn & car 22 15
71 A11 60pf carmine 45 55
72 A11 80pf blk & car 45 70

Paper With Faint Gray Network.

73 A11 1m org & car 22 35
a. Center inverted 37.50
74 A11 1.20m bl vio 1.40 1.25
75 A11 2m gray & car 3.75 4.50
76 A11 3m vio & car 10.00 13.00

Serrate Roulette 13½

77 A12 5m grn, red & blk 1.75 2.75
78 A12 9m rose, red & org ('22) 3.50 7.50
79 A12 10m ultra, red & blk 1.75 2.75
80 A12 20m red & blk 1.75 2.75
Nos. 63-80 (18) 26.99 37.67

In this and succeeding issues the mark values usually have the face of the paper covered with a gray network. This network is often very faint and occasionally is omitted.

Nos. 64, 66, 69-76 exist imperf. Price, each $20-$40.

See Nos. 81-93, 99-105.

Type of 1921 and

Coat of Arms
A13 A13a

1922 Wmk. 108 ***Perf. 14***

81 A11 75(pf) dp vio 20 25
82 A11 80(pf) green 20 25
83 A11 1.25m vio & car 20 25
84 A11 1.50m sl gray 22 35
85 A11 2m car rose 22 25
86 A11 2.40m dk brn & car 1.10 2.25
87 A11 3m car lake 22 35
88 A11 4m dk bl 1.10 1.75
89 A11 5m dp grn 12 30
90 A11 6m car lake 12 38
a. 6m car rose, wmk. 109 horiz. (error) 2,500.
91 A11 8m lt bl 35 1.00
92 A11 10m orange 12 35
93 A11 20m org brn 12 35
94 A13 50m gold & car 1.65 3.75
a. 50m gold & red 10.00 15.00
95 A13a 100m metallic grn & red 3.75 6.00
Nos. 81-95 (15) 9.69 17.83

No. 95 has buff instead of gray network.

Nos. 81-83, 85-86, 88 exist imperf. Price, each $20.

Nos. 94-95 exist imperf. Price, each $50

Nos. 87, 88 and 91 Surcharged in Black or Carmine

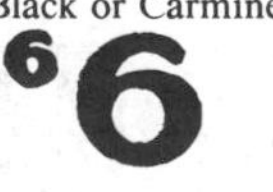

1922

96 A11 6m on 3m car lake 25 45
a. Dbl. surch.
97 A11 8m on 4m dk bl 25 75
a. Dbl. surch. 85.00 85.00
98 A11 20m on 8m lt bl (C) 30 60

Wmk.109

Wmk. Webbing. (109) (Vertical or Horizontal.)

1922-23 ***Perf. 14***

99 A11 4m dk bl 18 38
100 A11 5m dk grn 18 38
102 A11 10m orange 18 38
103 A11 20m org brn 18 38

Paper Without Network.

104 A11 40m pale bl 18 30
105 A11 80m red 18 30
Nos. 99-105 (6) 1.08 2.12

Nos. 104-105 exist imperf. Price, each $15.

A15 A15a

Coat of Arms
A16

1923 ***Perf. 14***

Paper With Gray Network.

106 A15 50m pale bl & red 18 38
107 A15a 100m dk grn & red 18 38
108 A15a 150m vio & red 18 38
109 A16 250m vio & red 22 50
110 A16 500m gray blk & red 22 50
111 A16 1000m brn & red 22 50
112 A16 5000m sil & red 1.50 *6.50*

Paper Without Network.

113 A15 50m pale bl 18 30
114 A15a 100m dp grn 18 30
115 A15 200m orange 18 30
Nos. 106-115 (10) 3.24 10.04

Nos. 109-112 exist imperf. Price, each $25.

Nos. 113-115 exist imperf. Price, each $17.50.

A17

1923 ***Perf. 14***

Paper With Gray Network.

117 A17 250m vio & red 18 35
118 A17 300m bl grn & red 12 40
119 A17 500m gray & red 18 35
120 A17 1000m brn & red 18 35
121 A17 3000m vio & red 18 35
123 A16 10,000m org & red 45 75
124 A16 20,000m pale bl & red 60 1.25
125 A16 50,000m grn & red 45 1.00
Nos. 117-125 (8) 2.34 4.80

Nos. 117-125 exist imperf. Price, each $17.50.

Surcharged in Red 100 000

1923, Aug. 14

No.	Type	Description	Unused	Used
126	A16	100,000m on 20,000m pale bl & red	1.50	6.00

1923 *Perf. 14*

Paper Without Network.

No.	Type	Description	Unused	Used
127	A17	1000m brown	18	32
129	A17	5000m rose	18	32
131	A17	20,000m pale bl	18	32
132	A17	50,000m green	18	32

Paper With Gray Network.

No.	Type	Description	Unused	Used
133	A17	100,000m dp bl	18	32
134	A17	250,000m violet	18	32
135	A17	500,000m slate	18	32
		Nos. 127-135 (7)	1.26	2.24

Nos. 126-135 exist imperf.

Abbreviations: th=(tausend) thousand mil=million

Stamps of Preceding Issues Surcharged

100 Tausend

1923 *Perf. 14*

Paper Without Network.

No.	Type	Description	Unused	Used
137	A15	40th m on 200m org	65	1.75
a.		Double surcharge	87.50	
138	A15	100th m on 200m org	65	1.75
139	A15	250th m on 200m org	6.50	12.00
140	A15a	400th m on 100m dp grn	40	55
141	A17	500th m on 50,000m grn	40	55
142	A17	1 mil m on 10,000m org	3.00	7.25

The surcharges on Nos. 140 to 142 differ in details from those on Nos. 137 to 139.

Type of 1923 Surcharged

10 Millionen

Paper With Gray Network.

No.	Type	Description	Unused	Used
143	A16	10 mil m on 1,000,000m org	45	40
		Nos. 137-143 (7)	12.05	24.25

Nos. 142-143 exist imperf. Price, each $17.50.

Type of 1923 Surcharged

1 Million

Perf. 14.

Paper Without Network.

No.	Type	Description	Unused	Used
144	A17	1 mil m on 10,000m rose	25	45
145	A17	2 mil m on 10,000m rose	25	45
146	A17	3 mil m on 10,000m rose	25	45
147	A17	5 mil m on 10,000m rose	25	45
b.		Dbl. surch.	87.50	
148	A17	10 mil m on 10,000m gray lil	45	60
149	A17	20 mil m on 10,000m gray lil	45	60
150	A17	25 mil m on 10,000m gray lil	35	60
151	A17	40 mil m on 10,000m gray lil	35	60
a.		Double surcharge	75.00	
152	A17	50 mil m on 10,000m gray lil	35	60

Danzig stamps can be mounted in Scott's Germany Part II Album.

Type of 1923 Surcharged in Red

300 Millionen

No.	Type	Description	Unused	Used
153	A17	100 mil m on 10,000m gray lil	35	60
154	A17	300 mil m on 10,000m gray lil	35	60
155	A17	500 mil m on 10,000m gray lil	35	60
		Nos. 144-155 (12)	4.00	6.60

Nos. 144-147 exist imperf. Price, each $17.50.

Nos. 153-155 exist imperf. Price, each $20.

Types of 1923 Surcharged

10 Pfennige

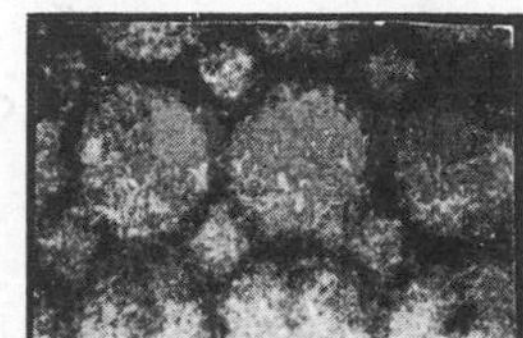

Wmk.110

1923 Wmk. Octagons. (110) *Perf. 14*

No.	Type	Description	Unused	Used
156	A15	5pf on 50m rose	60	52
157	A15	10pf on 50m rose	60	52
158	A15a	20pf on 100m rose	60	52
159	A15	25pf on 50m rose	5.50	9.50
160	A15	30pf on 50m rose	3.25	2.00
161	A15a	40pf on 100m rose	2.50	2.50
162	A15a	50pf on 100m rose	4.00	3.50
163	A15a	75pf on 100m rose	10.00	15.00

Type of 1923 Surcharged

2 Gulden

No.	Type	Description	Unused	Used
164	A16	1g on 1 mil m rose	5.50	6.25
165	A16	2g on 1 mil m rose	15.00	15.00
166	A16	3g on 1 mil m rose	35.00	60.00
167	A16	5g on 1 mil m rose	35.00	62.50
		Nos. 156-167 (12)	117.55	177.81

Coat of Arms — A19

Wmk. Webbing. (109)

1924-37 *Perf. 14*

No.	Type	Description	Unused	Used
168	A19	3(pf) brn, *yelsh* ('36)	1.50	1.10
a.		3(pf) dp brn, *white* ('27)	2.75	1.50
170	A19	5(pf) org, *yelsh* ('36)	4.50	40
a.		White paper	4.75	30
b.		Bklt. pane of 10		
c.		Tete beche pair	750.00	
d.		Syncopated perf., #170 ('37)	12.50	11.00
e.		Syncopated perf., #170a ('32)	21.00	11.00
171	A19	7(pf) yel grn ('33)	1.75	2.25
172	A19	8(pf) yel grn ('37)	2.50	5.00
173	A19	10(pf) grn, *yelsh* ('36)	6.25	30
a.		White paper	6.50	30
b.		Bklt. pane of 10		
c.		10(pf) bl grn, *yelsh* ('37)	5.25	45
d.		Tete beche pair	750.00	
e.		Syncopated perf., #173 ('37)	24.00	12.00
f.		Syncopated perf., #173a ('32)	27.50	18.00
g.		Syncopated perf., #173c ('37)	9.00	14.00
175	A19	15(pf) gray	4.00	70
176	A19	15(pf) red, *yelsh* ('36)	3.50	8
a.		White paper ('25)	3.50	8
b.		Bklt. pane of 10		
177	A19	20(pf) car & red	10.00	45
178	A19	20(pf) gray ('35)	2.25	2.25
179	A19	25(pf) sl & red	17.00	2.25
180	A19	25(pf) car ('35)	17.50	1.00
181	A19	30(pf) grn & red	8.00	75
182	A19	30(pf) dk vio ('35)	1.50	3.75
183	A19	35(pf) ultra ('25)	1.50	90
184	A19	40(pf) dk bl & bl	6.00	75
185	A19	40(pf) yel brn & red ('35)	9.00	20.00
186	A19	40(pf) dk bl ('35)	1.65	2.25
a.		Imperf.	45.00	
187	A19	50(pf) bl & red	11.00	4.50
a.		Yellowish paper ('36)	13.00	6.00
188	A19	55(pf) plum & scar ('37)	5.75	11.00
189	A19	60(pf) dk grn & red ('35)	8.00	18.00
190	A19	70(pf) yel grn & red ('35)	2.75	4.50
191	A19	75(pf) vio & red	6.50	5.25
a.		Yellowish paper ('36)	5.25	6.00
192	A19	80(pf) dk org brn & red ('35)	3.75	6.00
		Nos. 168-192 (23)	136.15	93.43

The 5pf and 10pf with syncopated perforations (Netherlands type C) are coils.

See also Nos. 225-232.

Oliva Castle and Cathedral A20

St. Mary's Church A23

Council Chamber on the Langenmarkt — A24

Designs: 2g, Mottlau River and Krantor. 3g, View of Zoppot.

Wmk. Lozenges. (125)

1924-32 Engr. *Perf. 14.*

No.	Type	Description	Unused	Used
193	A20	1g yel grn & blk	35.00	37.50
		Parcel post cancel		19.00
194	A20	1g org & gray blk ('25)	18.00	2.25
a.		1g red org & blk ('32)	18.00	6.00
		Parcel post cancel		1.65
195	A20	2g red vio & blk	67.50	110.00
		Parcel post cancel		60.00
196	A20	2g rose & blk ('25)	2.75	3.75
		Parcel post cancel		2.75
197	A20	3g dk bl & blk	4.50	6.75
		Parcel post cancel		3.50
198	A23	5g brn red & blk	6.50	8.50
		Parcel post cancel		3.00
199	A24	10g dk brn & blk	42.50	60.00
		Parcel post cancel		30.00
		Nos. 193-199 (7)	176.75	228.75

See also No. 233.

Stamps of 1924-25 Overprinted in Black, Violet or Red

1920 15. November 1930

Wmk. Webbing. (109)

1930, Nov. 15 Typo.

No.	Type	Description	Unused	Used
200	A19	5(pf) orange	3.00	2.75
201	A19	10(pf) yel grn (V)	4.75	3.75
202	A19	15(pf) red	6.75	9.00
203	A19	20(pf) car & red	3.50	4.75
204	A19	25(pf) sl & red	6.00	9.00
205	A19	30(pf) grn & red	12.50	22.50
206	A19	35(pf) ultra (R)	55.00	70.00
207	A19	40(pf) dk bl & bl (R)	15.00	25.00
208	A19	50(pf) dp bl & red	55.00	67.50
209	A19	75(pf) vio & red	55.00	67.50

Wmk. Lozenges. (125)

Engr.

No.	Type	Description	Unused	Used
210	A20	1g org & blk (R)	55.00	67.50
		Nos. 200-210 (11)	271.50	349.25

10th anniversary of the Free State. Counterfeits exist.

Nos. 171 and 183 Surcharged in Red Blue or Green:

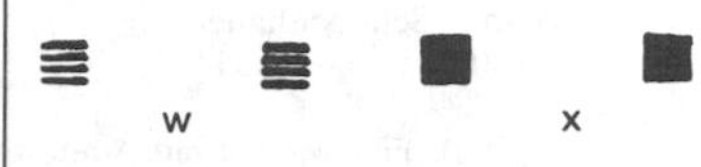

1934-36

No.	Type	Description	Unused	Used
211	A19 (w)	6(pf) on 7(pf) yel grn (R)	1.50	1.75
212	A19 (w)	8(pf) on 7(pf) yel grn (Bl) ('35)	3.75	4.00
213	A19 (w)	8(pf) on 7(pf) yel grn (R) ('36)	2.25	2.50
214	A19 (w)	8(pf) on 7(pf) yel grn (G) ('36)	1.50	1.75
215	A19 (x)	30(pf) on 35(pf) ultra (Bl)	13.00	19.00
		Nos. 211-215 (5)	22.00	29.00

Bathing Beach, Brösen A25

View of Brösen Beach A26

War Memorial at Brösen A27

Skyline of Danzig A28

Wmk. Webbing. (109)

1936, June 23 Typo. *Perf. 14*

No.	Type	Description	Unused	Used
216	A25	10pf dp grn	75	1.50
217	A26	25pf rose red	1.25	2.75
218	A27	40pf brt bl	2.00	4.50

Village of Brösen, 125th anniversary. Exist imperf. Price of set, $150.

1937, Mar. 27

No.	Type	Description	Unused	Used
219	A28	10(pf) dk bl	90	1.50
220	A28	15(pf) vio brn	1.25	2.75

Air Defense League.

Danzig Philatelic Exhibition Issue.

Souvenir Sheet.

St. Mary's Church — A29

1937, June 6 Wmk. 109 *Perf. 14*

No.	Type	Description	Unused	Used
221	A29	50pf dk grn	1.75	5.00

Issued for the Danzig Philatelic Exhibition, June 6-8, 1937. Sheet measures 149x104mm.

Arthur Schopenhauer
A30 A31

Design: 40(pf), Full-face portrait, white hair.

Unwmk.

1938, Feb. 22 Photo. *Perf. 14*

No.	Type	Denomination & color	Unused	Used
222	A30	15(pf) dl bl	1.25	2.75
223	A31	25(pf) sepia	3.25	6.75
224	A31	40(pf) org ver	1.50	4.50

Issued in commemoration of the 150th anniversary of the birth of Schopenhauer.

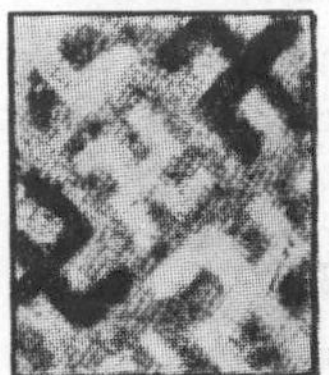
Wmk.237

Type of 1924-35.

Wmk. Swastikas. (237)

1938-39 Typo. *Perf. 14*

No.	Type	Denomination & color	Unused	Used
225	A19	3(pf) brown	85	*6.00*
226	A19	5(pf) orange	85	1.75
a.		Booklet pane of 10		
b.		Syncopated perf.	1.65	*6.75*
227	A19	8(pf) yel grn	5.50	*15.00*
228	A19	10(pf) bl grn	85	1.10
a.		Booklet pane of 10		
b.		Syncopated perf.	2.50	*7.50*
229	A19	15(pf) scarlet	2.50	*6.75*
a.		Booklet pane of 10		
230	A19	25(pf) carmine	2.50	*6.75*
231	A19	40(pf) dk bl	2.50	*8.50*
232	A19	50(pf) brt bl & red ('39)	3.25	*9.25*
		Engr.		
233	A20	1g red org & blk	5.50	*12.00*
		Nos. 225-233 (9)	24.30	67.10

No. 233 measures 32 1/2x21 1/4mm; No. 194, 31x21mm.

Nos. 226b and 228b are coils with Netherlands type C perforation.

Knights in Tournament, 1500 — A33

French Leaving Danzig, 1814 — A35

Designs: 10(pf), Signing of Danzig-Sweden neutrality treaty, 1630. 25(pf), Battle of Weichselmünde, 1577.

Unwmk.

1939, Jan. 7 Photo. *Perf. 14*

No.	Type	Denomination & color	Unused	Used
234	A33	5(pf) dk grn	1.00	*2.25*
235	A33	10(pf) cop brn	1.25	*2.50*
236	A35	15(pf) sl blk	1.50	*3.00*
237	A35	25(pf) brn vio	1.75	*3.75*

Stamp Day.

Scientists Issue.

Gregor Mendel — A37

Designs: 15(pf), Dr. Robert Koch. 25(pf), Wilhelm Roentgen.

1939, Apr. 29 Photo. *Perf. 13x14*

No.	Type	Denomination & color	Unused	Used
238	A37	10(pf) cop brn	40	1.00
239	A37	15(pf) indigo	70	1.25
240	A37	25(pf) dk ol grn	90	2.00

Issued in honor of the achievements of Mendel, Koch and Roentgen.

Issued under German Administration

Stamps of Danzig, 1925-39, Surcharged in Black:

Rpf Deutsches Reich Rpf
a

4 Rpf 4 Deutsches Reich 4 Rpf 4
b

1 Reichsmark Deutsches Reich
c

Wmk. Webbing. (109)

1939 *Perf. 14.*

No.	Type	Denomination & color	Unused	Used
241	A19(b)	4rpf on 35(pf) ultra	1.25	2.25
242	A19(b)	12rpf on 7(pf) yel grn	1.40	2.50
243	A19(a)	20rpf gray	3.75	7.50
		Wmk. 237		
244	A19(a)	3rpf brown	1.25	2.25
245	A19(a)	5rpf orange	1.25	2.25
246	A19(a)	8rpf yel grn	2.00	3.75
247	A19(a)	10rpf bl grn	2.50	4.25
248	A19(a)	15rpf scarlet	3.50	6.00
249	A19(a)	25rpf carmine	3.50	6.00
250	A19(a)	30rpf dk vio	2.25	4.00
251	A19(a)	40rpf dk bl	4.50	6.00
252	A19(a)	50rpf brt bl & red	4.50	8.00
253	A20(c)	1rm on 1g red org & blk	17.50	35.00
		Wmk. 125		
254	A20(c)	2rm on 2g rose & blk	25.00	42.50
		Nos. 241-254 (14)	74.15	132.25

Nos. 241 to 254 were valid throughout Germany.

SEMI-POSTAL STAMPS

St. George and Dragon — SP1

Wmk. Honeycomb. (108)

1921, Oct. 16 Typo. *Perf. 14*

Size: 19x22 mm.

No.	Type	Denomination & color	Unused	Used
B1	SP1	30pf + 30pf grn & org	90	75
B2	SP1	60pf + 60pf rose & org	2.00	2.00
		Size: 25x30 mm.		
		Serrate Roulette 13 1/2.		
B3	SP1	1.20m + 1.20m dk bl & org	3.50	3.50

Aged Pensioner SP2

Wmk. Webbing. (109)

1923, Mar. *Perf. 14*

Paper With Gray Network.

No.	Type	Denomination & color	Unused	Used
B4	SP2	50m + 20m lake	28	50
B5	SP2	100m + 30m red vio	28	50

Philatelic Exhibition Issue.

Neptune Fountain — SP3

Various Frames.

1929, July 7 Engr. Unwmk.

No.	Type	Denomination & color	Unused	Used
B6	SP3	10(pf) yel grn & gray	3.50	3.75
B7	SP3	15(pf) car & gray	3.50	3.75
B8	SP3	25(pf) ultra & gray	11.50	10.00
a.		25(pf) vio bl & blk	50.00	100.00

These stamps were sold exclusively at the Danzig Philatelic Exhibition, June 7th to 14th, 1929. They were sold at double their face values, the excess being for the aid of the exhibition.

Regular Issue of 1924-25 Surcharged in Black

5 W. H. W.

1934, Jan. 15 Wmk. 109

No.	Type	Denomination & color	Unused	Used
B9	A19	5(pf) + 5(pf) org	13.00	21.00
B10	A19	10(pf) + 5(pf) yel grn	37.50	55.00
B11	A19	15(pf) + 5(pf) car	20.00	30.00

Surtax for winter welfare. Counterfeits exist.

Stock Tower — SP4

City Gate, 16th Century SP5

George Hall — SP6

1935, Dec. 16 Typo. *Perf. 14*

No.	Type	Denomination & color	Unused	Used
B12	SP4	5(pf) + 5pf org	70	2.50
B13	SP5	10(pf) + 5pf grn	1.10	2.50
B14	SP6	15(pf) + 10pf scar	1.90	4.00

Surtax for winter welfare.

Milk Can Tower SP7

Frauentor SP8

Krantor — SP9

Langgarter Gate SP10

High Gate SP11

1936, Nov. 25

No.	Type	Denomination & color	Unused	Used
B15	SP7	10pf + 5pf dk bl	1.50	2.50
a.		fImperf.	75.00	
B16	SP8	15pf + 5pf dl grn	1.50	3.25
B17	SP9	25pf + 10pf red brn	1.90	3.50
B18	SP10	40pf + 20pf brn & red brn	3.00	4.50
B19	SP11	50pf + 20pf bl & dk bl	4.50	8.00
		Nos. B15-B19 (5)	12.40	21.75

Surtax for winter welfare.

SP12

SP13

1937, Oct. 30

No.	Type	Denomination & color	Unused	Used
B20	SP12	25(pf) + 25(pf) dk car	3.00	6
B21	SP13	40(pf) + 40(pf) bl & red	3.00	6.00
a.		Souvenir sheet of two	22.50	45.00

Founding of Danzig community at Magdeburg.

No. B21a contains one each of Nos. B20-B21 with marginal inscriptions including "1937." Size: 146x105mm.

Madonna SP14

Mercury SP15

Weather Vane, Town Hall SP16

Neptune Fountain SP17

St. George and Dragon — SP18

1937, Dec. 13

B23 SP14	5pf + 5pf brt vio	2.75	4.75
B24 SP15	10pf + 10pf dk brn	2.75	5.25
B25 SP16	15pf + 5pf bl & yel brn	3.25	7.00
B26 SP17	25pf + 10pf bl grn & grn	3.50	7.75
B27 SP18	40pf + 25pf brt car & bl	6.25	12.50
	Nos. B23-B27 (5)	18.50	37.25

Surtax for winter welfare. Designs are from frieze of the Artushof.

"Peter von Danzig" Yacht Race — SP19

Ships: 10+5pf, Dredger Fu Shing. 15+10pf, S. S. Columbus. 25+10pf, S. S. City of Danzig. 40+15pf, Peter von Danzig, 1472.

1938, Nov. 28 Photo. Unwmk.

B28 SP19	5(pf) + 5(pf) dk bl grn	1.10	2.25
B29 SP19	10(pf) + 5(pf) gldn brn	1.50	3.00
B30 SP19	15(pf) + 10(pf) ol grn	1.65	3.50
B31 SP19	25(pf) + 10(pf) ind	2.25	4.50
B32 SP19	40(pf) + 15(pf) vio brn	2.75	5.75
	Nos. B28-B32 (5)	9.25	19.00

Surtax for winter welfare.

AIR POST STAMPS

AP1

AP2

No. 6 Surcharged in Blue or Carmine.

Wmk. Lozenges. (125)

1920, Sept. 29 *Perf. 14*

C1 AP1	40(pf) on 40pf car rose	1.25	2.50
a.	Double surcharge	300.00	300.00
C2 AP1	60(pf) on 40pf car rose (C)	1.25	2.50
a.	Double surcharge	300.00	300.00
C3 AP2	1m on 40pf car rose	1.25	2.50

Plane faces left on No. C2.

Plane over Danzig
AP3 AP4

Wmk. Honeycomb. (108)

1921-22 Typo. *Perf. 14.*

C4 AP3	40(pf) bl grn	40	75
C5 AP3	60(pf) dk vio	40	75
C6 AP3	1m carmine	40	75
C7 AP3	2m org brn	40	75

Serrate Roulette 13½.

Size: 34½x23mm.

C8 AP4	5m vio bl	1.10	2.25
C9 AP4	10m dp grn ('22)	2.50	4.75
	Nos. C4-C9 (6)	5.20	10.00

Nos. C4-C9 exist imperf. Price, each $50.

Wmk. Webbing. (109)

1923 *Perf. 14.*

C10 AP3	40(pf) bl grn	45	*2.25*
C11 AP3	60(pf) dk vio	45	*2.25*
a.	Double impression	75.00	
C12 AP3	1m carmine	45	*2.75*
C13 AP3	2m org brn	45	*2.75*
C14 AP3	25m pale bl	45	70

Serrate Roulette 13½.

Size: 34½x23mm.

C15 AP4	5m vio bl	45	1.00
C16 AP4	10m dp grn	45	1.00

Paper With Gray Network.

C17 AP4	20m org brn	45	1.00

Size: 40x23mm.

C18 AP4	50m orange	45	80
C19 AP4	100m red	45	80
C20 AP4	250m dk brn	45	80
C21 AP4	500m car rose	45	80
	Nos. C10-C21 (12)	5.40	16.90

Nos. C14, C18-C21 exist imperf. Price, each $35.

Post Horn and Airplanes — AP5

1923, Oct. 18 *Perf. 14*

Paper Without Network.

C22 AP5	250,000m scarlet	42	1.75
C23 AP5	500,000m scarlet	42	1.75

Exist imperf. Price, each $37.50.

Surcharged **2 Millionen**

C24 AP5	2mil m on 100,000m scar	42	1.75
C25 AP5	5mil m on 50,000m scar	42	1.75
b.	Cliché of 10,000m in sheet of 50,000m	30.00	60.00

Exist imperf. Price, each $45.

Nos. C24 and C25 were not regularly issued without surcharge, although copies have been passed through the post. Price, uncanceled, each $7.50.

Plane over Danzig
AP6 AP7

1924

C26 AP6	10(pf) vermilion	18.00	4.00
C27 AP6	20(pf) car rose	2.00	1.75
C28 AP6	40(pf) ol brn	4.00	2.75
C29 AP6	1g dp grn	4.00	2.75
C30 AP7	2½g vio brn	30.00	45.00
	Nos. C26-C30 (5)	58.00	56.25

Exist imperf. Price No. C30, $150, others, each $62.50.

Regular Issue of 1924 Surcharged in Various Colors

10 ▬▬ 10
Luftpost-Ausstellung
1932

1932 Wmk. 125

C31 A20	10(pf) on 1g yel grn & blk (G)	11.00	15.00
C32 A20	15(pf) on 2g red vio & blk (V)	11.00	15.00
C33 A20	20(pf) on 3g dk bl & blk (Bl)	11.00	15.00
C34 A23	25(pf) on 5g brn red & blk (R)	11.00	15.00
C35 A24	30(pf) on 10g dk brn & blk (Br)	11.00	15.00
	Nos. C31-C35 (5)	55.00	75.00

Issued in connection with the International Air Post Exhibition of 1932. The surcharges were variously arranged to suit the shapes and designs of the stamps. The stamps were sold at double their surcharged values, the excess being donated to the exhibition funds.

Airplane
AP8 AP9

1935 Wmk. 109

C36 AP8	10pf scarlet	2.25	1.10
C37 AP8	15pf yellow	2.75	2.00
C38 AP8	25pf dk grn	2.25	2.00
C39 AP8	50pf gray bl	9.00	12.50
C40 AP9	1g magenta	6.25	*14.00*
	Nos. C36-C40 (5)	22.50	31.60

See also Nos. C42-C45.

Souvenir Sheet

St. Mary's Church AP10

1937, June 6 *Perf. 14*

C41 AP10	50pf dk bl	1.50	4.25

Issued for the Danzig Philatelic Exhibition, June 6-8, 1937. Size: 149x104mm.

Type of 1935.

1938-39 Wmk. 237

C42 AP8	10pf scarlet	1.75	*8.00*
C43 AP8	15pf yel ('39)	1.75	*8.75*
C44 AP8	25pf dk grn	1.75	*8.75*
C45 AP8	50pf gray bl ('39)	6.00	*20.00*

POSTAGE DUE STAMPS

Danzig Coat of Arms
D1 D2

Wmk. Honeycomb. (108)

1921-22 Typo. *Perf. 14*

Paper Without Network.

J1 D1	10(pf) dp vio	30	35
J2 D1	20(pf) dp vio	30	35
J3 D1	40(pf) dp vio	30	35
J4 D1	60(pf) dp vio	30	35
J5 D1	75(pf) dp vio ('22)	30	35
J6 D1	80(pf) dp vio	30	35
J7 D1	120(pf) dp vio	30	35
J8 D1	200(pf) dp vio ('22)	1.10	1.10
J9 D1	240(pf) dp vio	30	1.10
J10 D1	300(pf) dp vio ('22)	1.10	1.10
J11 D1	400(pf) dp vio	1.10	1.10
J12 D1	500(pf) dp vio	1.10	1.10
J13 D1	800(pf) dp vio ('22)	1.10	1.10
J14 D1	20m dp vio ('22)	1.10	1.10
	Nos. J1-J14 (14)	9.00	10.15

Nos. J1-J14 exist imperf. Price, each $15.

1923 Wmk. 109

J15 D1	100(pf) dp vio	60	65
J16 D1	200(pf) dp vio	3.50	3.75
J17 D1	300(pf) dp vio	60	60
J18 D1	400(pf) dp vio	60	60
J19 D1	500(pf) dp vio	60	60
J20 D1	800(pf) dp vio	1.00	1.00
J21 D1	10m dp vio	60	70
J22 D1	20m dp vio	60	70
J23 D1	50m dp vio	60	70

Paper With Gray Network.

J24 D1	100m dp vio	60	70
J25 D1	500m dp vio	60	70
	Nos. J15-J25 (11)	9.90	10.70

Nos. J22-J25 exist imperf. Price, each $12.50.

Nos. J22-J23 and type of 1923 Surcharged **10000**

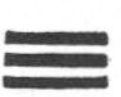

1923, Oct. 1

Paper without Network.

J26 D1	5000(m) on 50m	35	50
J27 D1	10,000(m) on 20m	35	50
J28 D1	50,000(m) on 500m	35	50
J29 D1	100,000(m) on 20m	1.25	1.40

On No. J26 the numerals of the surcharge are all of the larger size.

A 1000(m) on 100m deep violet was prepared but not issued. Price, $110.

Nos. J26-J28 exist imperf. Price, each $25.

1923-28 Wmk. 110

J30 D2	5(pf) bl & blk	1.00	1.00
J31 D2	10(pf) bl & blk	75	75
J32 D2	15(pf) bl & blk	1.50	1.50
J33 D2	20(pf) bl & blk	1.75	2.50
J34 D2	30(pf) bl & blk	8.25	2.50
J35 D2	40(pf) bl & blk	2.25	3.25
J36 D2	50(pf) bl & blk	2.25	3.00
J37 D2	60(pf) bl & blk	15.00	20.00
J38 D2	100(pf) bl & blk	15.00	8.25
J39 D2	3g bl & car	8.25	*45.00*
a.	"Guldeu" instead of "Gulden"	250.00	*500.00*
	Nos. J30-J39 (10)	56.00	87.75

Used prices of Nos. J30-J39 are for postally used copies.

Postage Due Stamps of 1923 Issue Surcharged in Red **5**

1932, Dec. 20

J40 D2	5(pf) on 40(pf) bl & blk	2.25	*10.00*
J41 D2	10(pf) on 60(pf) bl & blk	50.00	7.50
J42 D2	20(pf) on 100(pf) bl & blk	2.50	*8.00*

Type of 1923.

Wmk. Swastikas. (237)

1938-39 *Perf. 14.*

J43 D2	10(pf) bl & blk ('39)	1.40	*18.00*
J44 D2	30(pf) bl & blk	2.00	*20.00*
J45 D2	40(pf) bl & blk ('39)	6.25	*42.50*
J46 D2	60(pf) bl & blk ('39)	7.75	*42.50*
J47 D2	100(pf) bl & blk	9.50	*42.50*
	Nos. J43-J47 (5)	26.90	165.50

OFFICIAL STAMPS

Regular Issues of 1921-22 Overprinted

a **D M**

Wmk. Honeycomb. (108)

1921-22 *Perf. 14x14½.*

O1 A11	5(pf) orange	40	45
O2 A11	10(pf) dk brn	30	35
a.	Invtd. ovpt.	75.00	
O3 A11	15(pf) green	30	35
O4 A11	20(pf) slate	30	35
O5 A11	25(pf) dk grn	30	35
O6 A11	30(pf) bl & car	75	85
O7 A11	40(pf) grn & car	35	40
O8 A11	50(pf) dk grn & car	35	40
O9 A11	60(pf) carmine	35	40
O10 A11	75(pf) dp vio ('22)	15	45
O11 A11	80(pf) blk & car	2.00	2.00
O12 A11	80(pf) grn ('22)	15	45

Paper With Faint Gray Network

O14	A11	1m org & car	30	40
O15	A11	1.20m bl vio	2.00	2.00
O16	A11	1.25m vio & car ('22)	15	45
O17	A11	1.50m sl gray ('22)	18	30
O18	A11	2m gray & car	22.50	15.00
a.		Invtd. ovpt.		
O19	A11	2m car rose ('22)	15	45
O20	A11	2.40m dk brn & car ('22)	1.25	3.25
O21	A11	3m vio & car	15.00	14.00
O22	A11	3m car lake ('22)	18	30
O23	A11	4m dk bl ('22)	1.25	3.25
O24	A11	5m dp grn ('22)	18	30
O25	A11	6m car lake ('22)	18	38
O26	A11	10m org ('22)	18	38
O27	A11	20m org brn ('22)	18	30
		Nos. O1-O27 (26)	49.38	47.56

Double overprints exist on Nos. O1-O2, O5-O7, O10 and O12. Price, each $17.50.

Same Overprint on No. 96

O28	A11	6m on 3m car lake	25	90
a.		Inverted overprint	40.00	

No. 77 Overprinted

1922 *Serrate Roulette 13½*

O29	A12	5m grn, red & blk	4.00	8.50

Nos. 99-103, 106-107 Overprinted Type "a"

1923 Wmk. Webbing. (109) ***Perf. 14***

O30	A11	4m dk bl	20	40
O31	A11	5m dk grn	30	55
O32	A11	10m orange	20	40
O33	A11	20m org brn	20	40
O34	A15	50m pale bl & red	20	38
O35	A15a	100m dk grn & red	20	38

Nos. 113-115, 118-120 Overprinted Type "a"

O36	A15	50m pale bl	22	38
a.		Inverted overprint	30.00	
O37	A15a	100m dk grn	22	38
O38	A15	200m orange	22	38
a.		Inverted overprint	30.00	

Paper With Gray Network.

O39	A17	300m bl grn & red	20	35
O40	A17	500m gray & red	22	38
O41	A17	1000m brn & red	22	38
		Nos. O30-O41 (12)	2.60	4.76

Regular Issue of 1924-25 Overprinted Dienst-marke

1924-25 ***Perf. 14x14½***

O42	A19	5(pf) orange	2.25	1.75
O43	A19	10(pf) yel grn	2.25	1.75
O44	A19	15(pf) gray	2.25	1.75
O45	A19	15(pf) red ('25)	18.00	11.00
O46	A19	20(pf) car & red	2.75	1.75
O47	A19	25(pf) sl & red	18.00	20.00
O48	A19	30(pf) grn & red	3.50	3.00
O49	A19	35(pf) ultra ('25)	50.00	65.00
O50	A19	40(pf) dk bl & dl bl	5.75	9.00
O51	A19	50(pf) dp bl & red	18.00	30.00
O52	A19	75(pf) vio & red	45.00	*100.00*
		Nos. O42-O52 (11)	167.75	245.00

Double overprints exist on Nos. O42-O44, O47, O50-O52. Price, each $65.

DENMARK

LOCATION — northern part of a peninsula which separates the North and Baltic Seas, and includes the surrounding islands.
GOVT. — Kingdom
AREA — 16,631 sq. mi.
POP. — 5,112,130 (1984)
CAPITAL — Copenhagen

96 Skilling = 1 Rigsbank Daler
100 Ore = 1 Krone (1875)

Prices of early Denmark stamps vary according to condition. Quotations for Nos. 1-15 are for fine copies. Very fine to superb specimens sell at much higher prices, and inferior or poor copies sell at reduced prices, depending on the condition of the individual specimen.

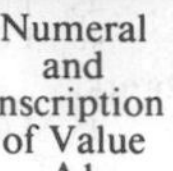

Numeral and Inscription of Value A1

Royal Emblems A2

Wmk.111

Wmk. Small Crown. (111)

1851 **Typo.** ***Imperf.***

With Yellow Brown Burelage.

1	A1	2rs blue	*4,000.*	1,300.
a.		First printing	*7,500.*	*3,000.*
2	A2	4rs brown	800.00	55.00
a.		First printing	1,000.	100.00
b.		4rs yel brn	1,000.	90.00

The first printing of Nos. 1 and 2 had the burelage printed from a copper plate, giving a clear impression with the lines in slight relief. The subsequent impressions had the burelage typographed, with the lines fainter and not rising above the surface of the paper.

Nos. 1-2 were reprinted in 1885 and 1901 on heavy yellowish paper, unwatermarked and imperforate, with a brown burelage. No. 1 was also reprinted without burelage, on both yellowish and white paper. Price for least costly reprint of No. 1, $40.

No. 2 was reprinted in 1951 in 10 shades with "Colour Specimen 1951" printed on the back. It was also reprinted in 1961 in 2 shades without burelage and with "Farve Nytryk 1961" printed on the back. Price for least costly reprint of No. 2, $8.50.

Dotting in Spandrels A3

Wavy Lines in Spandrels A4

1854-57

3	A3	2s bl ('55)	125.00	60.00
4	A3	4s brown	325.00	13.00
a.		4s yel brn	325.00	13.00
5	A3	8s grn ('57)	600.00	100.00
a.		8s yel grn	600.00	100.00
6	A3	16s gray lil ('57)	900.00	275.00

1858-62

7	A4	4s brown	80.00	8.00
a.		4s yel brn	80.00	8.00
b.		Wmk. 112 ('62)	80.00	10.00
8	A4	8s green	550.00	125.00

Nos. 2 to 8 inclusive are known with unofficial perforation 12 or 13, and Nos. 4, 5, 7 and 8 with unofficial roulette 9½.

Nos. 3, 6-8 were reprinted in 1885 on heavy yellowish paper, unwatermarked, imperforate and without burelage. Nos. 4-5 were reprinted in 1924 on white paper, unwatermarked, imperforate, gummed and without burelage. Price for No. 3, $11; Nos. 4-5, each $100; No. 6, $15; Nos. 7-8, each $10.

Wmk. 112- Crown

1863 **Wmk. 112** ***Rouletted 11***

9	A4	4s brown	125.00	22.50
a.		4s dp brn	125.00	22.50
10	A3	16s violet	2,000.	1,200.

Royal Emblems — A5

1864-68 ***Perf. 13.***

11	A5	2s bl ('65)	125.00	60.00
a.		Imperf., (pair)	300.00	300.00
b.		Perf. 12½	475.00	425.00
12	A5	3s red vio ('65)	140.00	90.00
a.		Imperf., (pair)	400.00	
b.		Perf. 12½	500.00	350.00
13	A5	4s red	70.00	8.00
a.		Imperf., (pair)	180.00	300.00
14	A5	8s bis ('68)	550.00	125.00
a.		Imperf., (pair)	1,100.	
b.		Perf. 12½	625.00	350.00
15	A5	16s ol grn	625.00	140.00
a.		Imperf., (pair)	1,400.	
b.		Perf. 12½	1,250.	1,250.

Nos. 11-15 were reprinted in 1886 on heavy yellowish paper, unwatermarked, imperforate and without gum. The reprints of all values except the 4s were printed in two vertical rows of six, inverted with respect to each other, so that horizontal pairs are always tete beche. Price $10 each.

Nos. 13 and 15 were reprinted in 1942 with printing on the back across each horizontal row: "Nytryk 1942. G. A. Hagemann: Danmarks og Vestindiens Frimaerker, Bind 2." Price, $65 each.

A6

NORMAL FRAME

INVERTED FRAME

The arabesques in the corners have a main stem and a branch. When the frame is in normal position, in the upper left corner the branch leaves the main stem half way between two little leaflets. In the lower right corner the branch starts at the foot of the second leaflet. When the frame is inverted the corner designs are, of course, transposed.

1870-71 **Wmk. 112** ***Perf. 14x13½***

Paper Varying from Thin to Thick.

16	A6	2s gray & ultra ('71)	90.00	35.00
a.		2s gray & bl	90.00	30.00
b.		Imperf., (pair)	200.00	
c.		Inverted frame	1,250.	850.00
17	A6	3s gray & brt lil ('71)	200.00	110.00
a.		Imperf., (pair)	550.00	
b.		Inverted frame	2,500.	1,750.
18	A6	4s gray & car	110.00	15.00
a.		Imperf., (pair)	275.00	
b.		Inverted frame	1,100.	170.00
19	A6	8s gray & brn ('71)	300.00	90.00
a.		Imperf., (pair)	600.00	
b.		Inverted frame	2,000.	1,100.
20	A6	16s gray & grn ('71)	450.00	200.00
a.		Imperf., (pair)	900.00	
b.		Inverted frame	1,700.	1,400.

Perf. 12½.

21	A6	2s gray & bl ('71)	2,500.	3,250.
22	A6	4s gray & car	275.00	130.00

24 A6 48s brn & lil 900.00 300.00
a. Imperf., (pair) 1,200.
b. Inverted frame 3,500. 2,500.

Nos. 16-20, 24 were reprinted in 1886 on thin white paper, unwatermarked, imperforate and without gum. These were printed in sheets of 10 in which 1 stamp has the normal frame (price $32.50 each) and 9 the inverted (price $11 each).

1875-79 ***Perf. 14x13½.***
25 A6 3o gray bl & gray 16.00 11.00
a. First "A" of "DANMARK" missing 70.00 150.00
b. Imperf.
c. Inverted frame 16.00 11.00
26 A6 4o sl & bl 14.00 30
a. 4o gray & bl 14.00 30
b. 4o sl & ultra 85.00 13.00
c. 4o gray & ultra 85.00 13.00
d. Imperf., (pair) 225.00
e. Inverted frame 20.00 25
27 A6 5o rose & bl ('79) 45.00 75.00
a. Ball of lower curve of large "5" missing 225.00 325.00
b. Inverted frame 1,500. 2,200.
28 A6 8o sl & car 18.00 30
a. 8o gray & car 50.00 3.00
b. Imperf., (pair) 275.00
c. Inverted frame 22.50 30
29 A6 12o sl & dl lake 13.00 3.50
a. 12o gray & brt lil 60.00 15.00
b. 12o gray & dl mag 13.00 5.00
c. Inverted frame 16.00 3.50
30 A6 16o sl & brn 77.50 4.50
a. 16o lt gray & brn 80.00 13.00
b. Inverted frame 35.00 3.50
31 A6 20o rose & gray 85.00 20.00
a. 20o car & gray 85.00 20.00
b. Inverted frame 85.00 25.00
32 A6 25o gray & grn 80.00 30.00
a. Inverted frame 110.00 60.00
33 A6 50o brn & vio 85.00 25.00
a. 50o brn & bl vio 550.00 125.00
b. Inverted frame 100.00 25.00
34 A6 100o gray & org ('77) 125.00 30.00
a. Imperf., (pair) 450.00
b. Inverted frame 175.00 70.00

The stamps of this issue on thin semitransparent paper are far scarcer than those on thicker paper.

See also Nos. 41-42, 44, 46-47, 50-52.

Arms — A7

Two types of numerals in corners:

⑤ ⑤

1882

Small Corner Numerals.
35 A7 5o green 250.00 125.00
37 A7 20o blue 225.00 40.00

1884-85

Larger Corner Numerals.
38 A7 5o green 14.00 2.00
a. Imperf.
39 A7 10o car ('85) 15.00 1.25
a. Small numerals in corners 650.00 650.00
b. Imperf., pair 250.00
c. Pair, Nos. 39, 39a 750.00 850.00
40 A7 20o blue 25.00 1.25
a. Pair, Nos. 37, 40 500.00 800.00
b. Imperf., pair *2,500.*

Stamps with large corner numerals have white line around crown and lower oval touches frame.

The plate of the 10 ore, No. 39, was damaged and three cliches in the bottom row were replaced by cliches for post cards, which had small numerals in the corners, making the variety No. 39a.

Two cliches with small numerals were inserted in the plate of No. 40.

1895-1901 **Wmk. 112** ***Perf. 13***
41 A6 3o bl & gray 12.00 5.00
b. Inverted frame 14.00 5.50
42 A6 4o sl & bl ('96) 6.00 25
a. Inverted frame 6.00 25
43 A7 5o green 10.00 1.10
44 A6 8o sl & car 6.00 20
a. Inverted frame 6.00 20
45 A7 10o rose car 10.00 1.00
46 A6 12o sl & dl lake 7.00 4.00
a. Inverted frame 16.00 4.00
47 A6 16o sl & brn 25.00 5.00
a. Inverted frame 30.00 5.00
48 A7 20o blue 12.50 2.00
49 A7 24o brn ('01) 14.00 3.50
50 A6 25o gray & grn ('98) 75.00 13.00
a. Inverted frame 65.00 25.00
51 A6 50o brn & vio ('97) 75.00 25.00
a. Inverted frame 90.00 40.00
52 A6 100o sl & org 80.00 35.00
a. Inverted frame 70.00 30.00

1902-04 **Wmk. 113**
41c A6 3o bl & gray 3.75 3.50
d. Invtd. frame 75.00 50.00
42b A6 4o sl & bl 25.00 7.50
c. Invtd. frame 150.00 95.00
43a A7 5o green 2.75 25
44d A6 8o sl & car 600.00 375.00
45a A7 10o rose car 2.75 30
48a A7 20o blue 12.00 2.75
50b A6 25o gray & grn 14.00 6.00
c. Invtd. frame 180.00 55.00
51b A6 50o brn & vio 45.00 18.00
c. Invtd. frame 275.00 125.00
52b A6 100o sl & org 32.50 18.00
c. Invtd. frame 300.00 175.00

Wmk. 113- Crown

1902 **Wmk. 113**
53 A7 1o orange 1.00 50
a. Imperf., pair 275.00
54 A7 15o lilac 15.00 90
a. Imperf., pair

Nos. 44d, 44, 49 Surcharged:

a

15 15
ØRE
b

1904-12 **Wmk. 113**
55 A6(a) 4o on 8o sl & car 3.00 3.00
a. Wmk. 112 ('12) 30.00 60.00
b. As "a", inverted frame

Wmk. 112
56 A7(b) 15o on 24o brn 5.00 5.00
a. Short "15" at right 45.00 60.00

Numeral of Value
A10

King Christian IX
A11

King Frederik VIII — A12

Wmk. Crown. (113)

1905-17 **Typo.** ***Perf. 13.***
57 A10 1o org ('06) 1.75 50
58 A10 2o carmine 2.00 20
a. Perf. 14x14½ ('17) 5.00 4.00
59 A10 3o gray 5.00 45
60 A10 4o dl bl 5.00 20
a. Perf. 14x14½ ('17) 13.00 8.00
61 A10 5o dp grn ('12) 6.00 20
62 A10 10o dp rose ('12) 6.50 20
63 A10 15o lilac 18.00 60
64 A10 20o dk bl ('12) 40.00 1.00
Nos. 57-64 (8) 84.25 3.35

The three wavy lines in design A10 are symbolical of the three waters which separate the principal Danish islands.

See also Nos. 85-96.

1904-05 **Engr.**
65 A11 10o scarlet 5.50 20
66 A11 20o blue 20.00 1.00
67 A11 25o brn ('05) 20.00 3.00
68 A11 50o dl vio ('05) 60.00 60.00
69 A11 100o ocher ('05) 35.00 45.00
Nos. 65-69 (5) 140.50 109.20

1905-06 **Re-engraved.**
70 A11 5o green 6.00 20
71 A11 10o scar ('06) 16.00 25

The re-engraved stamps are much clearer than the originals, and the decoration on the king's left breast has been removed.

1907-12
72 A12 5o green 1.75 12
a. Imperf.
73 A12 10o red 2.75 8
a. Imperf.
74 A12 20o indigo 8.00 40
a. 20o brt bl ('11) 12.00 1.25
75 A12 25o ol brn 15.00 75
76 A12 35o dp org ('12) 11.00 4.50
77 A12 50o claret 45.00 6.00
78 A12 100o bis brn 90.00 3.50
Nos. 72-78 (7) 173.50 15.35

Nos. 47, 31 and O9 Surcharged:

35
ØRE
c

35
ØRE
FRIMÆRKE
d

Dark Blue Surcharge.

1912 **Wmk. 112** ***Perf. 13.***
79 A6(c) 35o on 16o sl & brn 18.00 *55.00*
a. Inverted frame 275.00 500.00

Perf. 14x13½.
80 A6(c) 35o on 20o rose & gray 15.00 *45.00*
a. Inverted frame 85.00 175.00

Black Surcharge.
81 O1(d) 35o on 32o grn 30.00 70.00

General Post Office, Copenhagen
A15

Wmk. Two Crowns. (113)

1912 **Engr.** ***Perf. 13***
82 A15 5k dk red 475.00 125.00

See Nos. 135, 843.

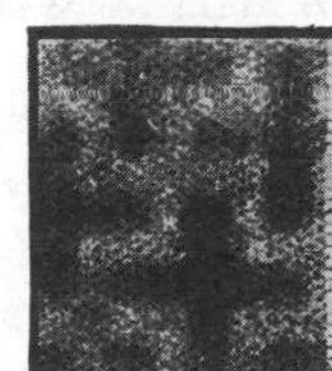
Wmk.114

Wmk. Multiple Crosses. (114)

1913-30 **Typo.** ***Perf. 14x14½***
85 A10 1o dp org ('14) 70 30
a. Booklet pane of 4, (2 No. 85, 2 No. 91 + 2 labels) 25.00
86 A10 2o car ('13) 1.00 15
a. Imperf., (pair) 250.00 400.00
b. Booklet pane, 4 + 2 labels 32.50
87 A10 3o gray ('13) 2.00 20
88 A10 4o bl ('13) 6.00 20
a. Half used as 2o on cover 1,300.
89 A10 5o dk brn ('21) 1.00 10
a. Imperf., pair 350.00
b. Booklet pane, 4 + 2 labels 17.00
90 A10 5o lt grn ('30) 1.50 12
a. Booklet pane, 4 + 2 labels 17.00
b. Booklet pane of 50
91 A10 7o ap grn ('26) 2.00 18
a. Booklet pane, 4 + 2 labels 20.00
92 A10 7o dk vio ('30) 8.00 2.50
93 A10 8o gray ('21) 5.00 75
94 A10 10o grn ('21) 1.00 8
a. Imperf., (pair) 350.00
b. Booklet pane, 4 + 2 labels 45.00
95 A10 10o bis brn ('30) 1.75 12
a. Booklet pane, 4 + 2 labels 18.00
b. Booklet pane of 50
96 A10 12o vio ('26) 14.00 2.00
Nos. 85-96 (12) 43.95 6.70

No. 88a was used with No. 97 in Faroe Islands Jan. 3-23, 1919.

King Christian X
A16 A17

1913-28 **Typo.** ***Perf. 14x14½***
97 A16 5o green 1.50 6
a. Booklet pane of 4 20.00
98 A16 7o org ('18) 2.50 50
99 A16 8o dk gray ('20) 4.50 2.00
100 A16 10o red 1.75 6
a. Imperf., (pair) 350.00
b. Booklet pane of 4 20.00
101 A16 12o gray grn ('18) 11.00 9.00
102 A16 15o violet 2.25 6
103 A16 20o dp bl 7.50 30
104 A16 20o brn ('21) 1.00 6
105 A16 20o red ('26) 2.50 20
106 A16 25o dk brn 9.00 40
107 A16 25o brn & blk ('20) 50.00 3.50
108 A16 25o red ('22) 3.50 50
109 A16 25o yel grn ('25) 3.00 30
110 A16 27o ver & blk ('18) 45.00 60.00
111 A16 30o grn & blk ('18) 11.00 1.50
112 A16 30o org ('21) 3.00 70
113 A16 30o dk bl ('25) 3.00 60
114 A16 35o orange 12.00 3.00
115 A16 35o yel & blk ('19) 10.00 2.25
116 A16 40o vio & blk ('18) 10.00 1.75
117 A16 40o gray bl & blk ('20) 25.00 6.00
118 A16 40o dk bl ('22) 5.00 1.50
119 A16 40o org ('25) 3.25 55
120 A16 50o claret 30.00 2.75
121 A16 50o cl & blk ('19) 65.00 1.50
122 A16 50o lt gray ('22) 6.00 20
a. 50o dk gray ('21) 40.00 2.00
123 A16 60o brn & bl ('19) 35.00 2.75
a. 60o brn & ultra ('19) 130.00 11.00
124 A16 60o grn bl ('21) 9.00 1.00
125 A16 70o brn & grn ('20) 18.00 2.00
126 A16 80o bl grn ('15) 60.00 20.00
127 A16 90o brn & red ('20) 20.00 2.00
128 A16 1k brn & bl ('22) 45.00 1.65
129 A16 2k gray & cl ('25) 75.00 15.00
130 A16 5k vio & brn ('27) 12.00 7.00
131 A16 10k ver & yel grn ('28) 375.00 40.00
Nos. 97-131 (35) 977.25 190.64

No. 97 surcharged "2 ORE" is Faroe Islands No. 1.

Nos. 87 and 98, 89 and 94, 89 and 104, 90 and 95, 97 and 103, 100 and 102 exist se-tenant in coils for use in vending machines.

1913-20 **Engr.**
132 A17 1k yel brn 95.00 1.00
133 A17 2k gray 90.00 4.50
134 A17 5k pur ('20) 22.50 10.00

G.P.O. Type of 1912

Perf. 14x14½

1915 **Wmk. 114** **Engr.**
135 A15 5k dk red ('15) 525.00 125.00

Nos. 46 and O10 Surcharged in Black

DANMARK 80 ØRE POSTFRIM. e

1915 Wmk. 112 Typo. ***Perf. 13***

No.	Type	Description	Unused	Used
136	A6 (c)	80o on 12o sl & dl lake	45.00	125.00
a.		Invtd. frame	550.00	900.00
137	O1 (e)	80o on 8o car	50.00	140.00
a.		"POSTERIM"	85.00	175.00

POSTFRIM.

Newspaper Stamps Surcharged ØRE 27 ØRE

DANMARK

On Issue of 1907.

1918 Wmk. 113 ***Perf. 13***

No.	Type	Description	Unused	Used
138	N1	27o on 1o ol	130.00	250.00
139	N1	27o on 5o bl	130.00	250.00
140	N1	27o on 7o car	130.00	250.00
141	N1	27o on 10o dp lil	130.00	250.00
142	N1	27o on 68o yel brn	8.00	25.00
143	N1	27o on 5k rose & yel grn	9.00	15.00
144	N1	27o on 10k bis & bl	8.00	22.50
		Nos. 138-144 (7)	545.00	1,062.

On Issue of 1914-15.

Wmk. Multiple Crosses. (114)

Perf. 14 x 14½.

No.	Type	Description	Unused	Used
145	N1	27o on 1o ol gray	4.50	11.00
146	N1	27o on 5o bl	9.00	22.50
147	N1	27o on 7o rose	4.00	8.00
148	N1	27o on 8o grn	5.00	14.00
149	N1	27o on 10o dp lil	4.00	9.00
150	N1	27o on 20o grn	4.00	11.00
151	N1	27o on 29o org yel	4.00	9.00
152	N1	27o on 38o org	45.00	85.00
153	N1	27o on 41o yel brn	10.00	*40.00*
154	N1	27o on 1k bl grn & mar	4.00	7.00
		Nos. 145-154 (10)	93.50	216.50

Kronborg Castle — A20

Sonderborg Castle — A21

Roskilde Cathedral — A22

Perf. 14½x14, 14x14½

1920, Oct. 5 **Typo.**

No.	Type	Description	Unused	Used
156	A20	10o red	5.50	50
157	A21	20o slate	5.00	50
158	A22	40o dk brn	20.00	6.00

This issue was to commemorate the reunion of Northern Schleswig with Denmark.

1921

No.	Type	Description	Unused	Used
159	A20	10o green	8.00	50
160	A22	40o dk bl	40.00	7.50

Stamps of 1918 Surcharged in Blue 8 8

1921-22

No.	Type	Description	Unused	Used
161	A16	8o on 7o org ('22)	3.50	2.75
162	A16	8o on 12o gray grn	3.50	5.00

No. 87 Surcharged

1921

No.	Type	Description	Unused	Used
163	A10	8o on 3o gray	2.75	2.75

King Christian X – A23

King Christian IV – A24

A25 A26

1924, Dec. 1 ***Perf. 14x14½***

No.	Type	Description	Unused	Used
164	A23	10o green	5.50	1.75
165	A24	10o green	5.50	1.75
166	A25	10o green	5.50	1.75
167	A26	10o green	5.50	1.75
168	A23	15o violet	5.50	1.75
169	A24	15o violet	5.50	1.75
170	A25	15o violet	5.50	1.75
171	A26	15o violet	5.50	1.75
172	A23	20o dk brn	5.50	1.75
173	A24	20o dk brn	5.50	1.75
174	A25	20o dk brn	5.50	1.75
175	A26	20o dk brn	5.50	1.75
		3 Blocks of 4, #164-175	95.00	110.00
		Nos. 164-175 (12)	66.00	21.00

Issued to commemorate the 300th anniversary of the Danish postal service.

The sheets of each value are composed of stamps of types A23, A24, A25 and A26, arranged in groups of four as illustrated.

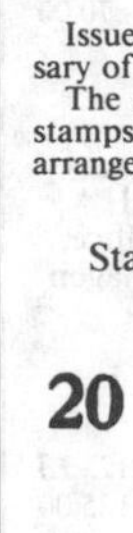

Stamps of 1921-22 Surcharged:

20 k 20

20 ■ l 20 ■

1926

No.	Type	Description	Unused	Used
176	A16 (k)	20o on 30o org	6.00	10.00
177	A16 (l)	20o on 40o dk bl	9.00	14.00

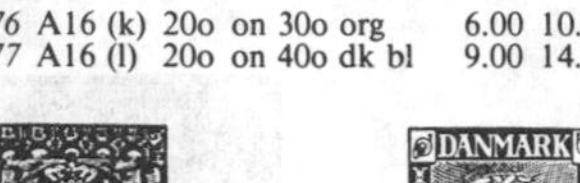

A27

A28

1926, Mar. 11 ***Perf. 14x14½***

No.	Type	Description	Unused	Used
178	A27	10o dl grn	1.50	15
179	A28	20o dk red	2.00	15
180	A28	30o dk bl	9.00	90

Issued in commemoration of the 75th anniversary of the introduction of postage stamps in Denmark.

Stamps of 1913-26 Surcharged in Blue or Black

7 m 7 n 7

1926-27 ***Perf. 14 x 14½.***

No.	Type	Description	Unused	Used
181	A10 (m)	7o on 8o gray (Bl)	1.75	4.00
182	A16 (n)	7o on 27o ver & blk	6.50	15.00
183	A16 (n)	7o on 20o red ('27)	90	80
184	A16 (n)	12o on 15o vio	4.00	6.50

Surcharged on Official Stamps of 1914-23.

No.	Type	Description	Unused	Used
185	O1 (e)	7o on 1o org	4.50	9.00
186	O1 (e)	7o on 3o gray	11.00	25.00
187	O1 (e)	7o on 4o bl	4.50	14.00
188	O1 (e)	7o on 5o grn	80.00	125.00
189	O1 (e)	7o on 10o grn	4.50	11.00
190	O1 (e)	7o on 15o vio	5.50	11.00
191	O1 (e)	7o on 20o ind	22.50	42.50
a.		Double surcharge	*650.00*	*650.00*
		Nos. 181-191 (11)	145.65	263.80

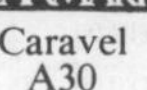

Caravel A30

King Christian X A31

1927 Typo. ***Perf. 14x14½.***

No.	Type	Description	Unused	Used
192	A30	15o red	4.00	6
193	A30	20o gray	6.50	40
194	A30	25o lt bl	70	10
195	A30	30o ocher	70	10
196	A30	35o red brn	15.00	40
197	A30	40o yel grn	15.00	15
		Nos. 192-197 (6)	41.90	1.21

See also Nos. 232-238J.

1930, Sept. 26

No.	Type	Description	Unused	Used
210	A31	5o ap grn	2.50	10
a.		Booklet pane, 4 + 2 labels	32.50	
211	A31	7o violet	9.00	3.00
212	A31	8o dk gray	42.50	10.00
213	A31	10o yel brn	6.50	30
a.		Booklet pane, 4 + 2 labels	45.00	
214	A31	15o red	15.00	15
215	A31	20o lt gray	37.50	3.00
216	A31	25o lt bl	14.00	40
217	A31	30o yel buff	15.00	2.00
218	A31	35o red brn	15.00	4.00
219	A31	40o dp grn	15.00	1.25
		Nos. 210-219 (10)	172.00	24.20

60th birthday of King Christian X.

Wavy Lines and Numeral of Value — A32

Type of 1905-12 Issue.

Engraved, Redrawn

1933-40 Unwmk. ***Perf. 13***

No.	Type	Description	Unused	Used
220	A32	1o gray blk	5	5
221	A32	2o scarlet	10	5
222	A32	4o blue	50	15
223	A32	5o yel grn	1.75	15
a.		5o gray grn	30.00	30.00
b.		Tete beche pair	15.00	15.00
c.		Booklet pane of 4	12.00	
d.		Booklet pane of 4, (1 No. 223a & 3 No. B6)	37.50	
224	A32	5o rose lake ('38)	5	5
a.		Booklet pane of 4	50	
b.		Booklet pane of 10	1.00	
224C	A32	6o org ('40)	40	6
225	A32	7o violet	3.00	25
226	A32	7o yel grn ('38)	2.00	30
226A	A32	7o lt brn ('40)	40	15
227	A32	8o gray	80	15
227A	A32	8o yel grn ('40)	45	10
228	A32	10o yel org	17.50	20
a.		Tete beche pair	60.00	32.50
b.		Booklet pane of 4	87.50	
229	A32	10o lt brn ('37)	15.00	10
a.		Booklet pane of 4	75.00	
b.		Booklet pane of 4, (1 No. 229 & 3 No. B7)	35.00	
230	A32	10o vio ('38)	80	5
a.		Booklet pane of 4	4.00	
b.		Bklt. pane of 4, (2 No. 230 & 2 No. B10)	6.00	
		Nos. 220-230 (14)	42.80	1.81

The stamps of 1905-12 were typographed. They had a solid background with groups of small hearts below the heraldic lions in the upper corners and below "DA" and "RK" of "DANMARK". The numerals of value were enclosed in single-lined ovals.

The 1933-40 stamps are line-engraved and have a background of crossed lines. The hearts have been removed and the numerals of value are now in double-lined ovals. Two types exist of some values.

The 1o, No. 220, was issued on fluorescent paper in 1969.

No. 230 with wide margins is from booklet pane No. 230b.

Of the tete beche pairs, those with gutters are twice as plentiful. Prices are for the less costly.

Surcharges of 20, 50 and 60ore on Nos. 220, 224 and 224C are listed as Faroe Islands Nos. 2-3, 5-6.

See Nos. 318, 333, 382, 416, 437-437A, 493-498, 629, 631, 688-695.

Certain Tête Bêche pairs of 1938-55 issues which reached the market in 1971, and were not regularly issued, are not listed. This group comprises 24 different major-number vertical pairs of types A32, A47, A61 and SP3 (13 with gutters, 11 without), and pairs of some minor numbers and shades. They were removed from booklet pane sheets.

Type of 1927 Issue.

Type I.

Type I-Two columns of squares between sail and left frame line.

1933-34 Engr. ***Perf. 13***

No.	Type	Description	Unused	Used
232	A30	20o gray	17.00	20
233	A30	25o blue	85.00	8.00
234	A30	25o brn ('34)	55.00	15
235	A30	30o org yel	2.50	1.50
236	A30	30o bl ('34)	2.50	15
237	A30	35o violet	1.25	20
238	A30	40o yel grn	6.00	18
		Nos. 232-238 (7)	169.25	10.38

Type II.

Type II-One column of squares between sail and left frame line.

1933-40

No.	Type	Description	Unused	Used
238A	A30	15o dp red	6.00	6
k.		Booklet pane of 4	30.00	
l.		Booklet pane of 4, (1 No. 238A, 3 No. B8)	45.00	
238B	A30	15o yel grn ('40)	14.00	20
238C	A30	20o gray blk ('39)	8.00	20
238D	A30	20o red ('40)	1.50	5
238E	A30	25o dp brn ('39)	1.50	20
238F	A30	30o bl ('39)	6.00	45
238G	A30	30o org ('40)	1.25	10
238H	A30	35o vio ('40)	1.75	55
238I	A30	40o yel grn ('39)	17.00	30
238J	A30	40o bl ('40)	2.00	12
		Nos. 238A-238J (10)	59.00	2.23

Nos. 232-238J, engraved, have crosshatched background. Nos. 192-197, typographed, have solid background.

No. 238A surcharged 20ore is listed as Faroe Islands No. 4.

King Christian X — A33

1934-41 ***Perf. 13***

No.	Type	Description	Unused	Used
239	A33	50o gray	2.50	15
240	A33	60o bl grn	6.00	20
240A	A33	75o dk bl ('41)	1.00	20
241	A33	1k lt brn	6.50	10
242	A33	2k dl red	14.00	75
243	A33	5k violet	22.50	3.25
		Nos. 239-243 (6)	52.50	4.65

Nos. 233, 235 Surcharged in Black

1934, June 9

No.	Type	Description	Unused	Used
244	A30	4o on 25o bl	75	35
245	A30	10o on 30o org yel	5.00	2.25

"The Ugly Duckling" A34

Hans Christian Andersen A35

"The Little Mermaid" — A36

1935, Oct. 4 *Perf. 13*
246 A34 5o lt grn 6.00 12
a. Tete beche pair 20.00 12.00
b. Bklt. pane of 4 27.50
247 A35 7o dl vio 5.00 1.00
248 A36 10o orange 9.00 15
a. Tete beche pair 30.00 20.00
b. Bklt. pane of 4 50.00
249 A35 15o red 22.50 10
a. Tete beche pair 60.00 32.50
b. Bklt. pane of 4 125.00
250 A35 20o gray 20.00 80
251 A35 30o dl bl 6.00 40
Nos. 246-251 (6) 68.50 2.57

Issued to commemorate the centenary of the publication of the earliest installment of Hans Christian Andersen's "Fairy Tales."

Note on tete beche pair prices after No. 230 applies to Nos. 246a, 248a and 249a.

Nikolai Church A37

Hans Tausen A38

Ribe Cathedral — A39

1936 *Perf. 13*
252 A37 5o green 3.00 20
a. Bklt. pane of 4 30.00
253 A37 7o violet 3.00 1.00
254 A38 10o lt brn 4.00 15
a. Bklt. pane of 4 32.50
255 A38 15o dl rose 6.00 10
256 A39 30o blue 25.00 55
Nos. 252-256 (5) 41.00 2.00

Issued in commemoration of the 400th anniversary of the Church Reformation in Denmark.

No. 229 Overprinted in Blue

K.P.K.
17.-26. SEPT.
19 37

1937, Sept. 17
257 A32 10o lt brn 3.00 3.00

Issued in commemoration of the Jubilee Exhibition held by the Copenhagen Philatelic Club on the occasion of their 50th anniversary. The stamps were on sale at the Exhibition only, each holder of a ticket of admission (1kr.) being entitled to purchase 20 stamps at face value, and each holder of a season ticket (5kr.) being entitled to purchase 100 stamps.

Yacht and Summer Palace, Marselisborg A40

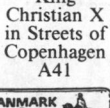

King Christian X in Streets of Copenhagen A41

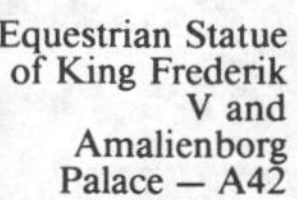

Equestrian Statue of King Frederik V and Amalienborg Palace — A42

1937, May 15 *Perf. 13*
258 A40 5o green 3.00 35
a. Bklt. pane of 4 17.50
259 A41 10o brown 3.00 18
a. Bklt. pane of 4 17.50
260 A42 15o scarlet 3.00 18
a. Bklt. pane of 4 20.00
261 A41 30o blue 25.00 2.00

Issued in commemoration of the 25th anniversary of the accession to the throne of King Christian X.

Emancipation Column, Copenhagen — A43

1938, June 20 *Perf. 13*
262 A43 15o scarlet 1.25 20

Issued to commemorate the 150th anniversary of the abolition of serfdom in Denmark.

No. 223 Overprinted in Red on Alternate Stamps

D.F.U.
FRIM-UDST.
19 38

1938, Sept. 2
263 A32 5o yel grn (pair) 6.00 6.50

10th Danish Philatelic Exhibition.

Bertel Thorvaldsen A44

Statue of Jason A45

1938, Nov. 17 **Engr.** *Perf. 13*
264 A44 5o rose lake 1.00 15
265 A45 10o purple 1.00 12
266 A44 30o dk bl 3.50 55

The return to Denmark in 1838 of Bertel Thorvaldsen, Danish sculptor.

Stamps of 1933-39 Surcharged with New Values in Black:

6
a

15
b

20
c

1940
267 A32 (a) 6o on 7o yel grn 35 35
268 A32 (a) 6o on 8o gray 30 20
269 A30 (b) 15o on 40o yel grn (On No. 238) 2.00 4.50
270 A30 (b) 15o on 40o yel grn (On No. 238I) 2.00 1.00
271 A30 (c) 20o on 15o dp red 2.25 15
272 A30 (b) 40o on 30o bl (On No. 238F) 2.00 35
Nos. 267-272 (6) 8.90 6.55

Bering's Ship — A46

1941, Nov. 27 **Engr.** *Perf. 13*
277 A46 10o dk vio 60 20
278 A46 20o red brn 1.25 40
279 A46 40o dk bl 80 50

Issued in commemoration of the 200th anniversary of the death of Vitus Bering, explorer.

King Christian X — A47

1942-46 **Unwmk.** *Perf. 13*
280 A47 10o violet 25 5
281 A47 15o yel grn 60 6
282 A47 20o red 60 5
283 A47 25o brn ('43) 1.00 6
284 A47 30o org ('43) 75 10
285 A47 35o brt red vio ('44) 75 20
286 A47 40o bl ('43) 75 10
286A A47 45o ol brn ('46) 1.00 20
286B A47 50o gray ('45) 1.50 10
287 A47 60o bluish grn ('44) 1.25 10
287A A47 75o dk bl ('46) 1.00 20
Nos. 280-287A (11) 9.45 1.22

Round Tower — A48

Condor Plane — A49

1942, Nov. 27
288 A48 10o violet 25 20

Issued to commemorate the 300th anniversary of the Round Tower, Copenhagen.

1943, Oct. 29
289 A49 20o red 30 20

Issued to commemorate the 25th anniversary of the Danish Aviation Company (Det Danske Luftfartsselskab).

Ejby Church — A50

Designs: 15ö, Oesterlars Church. 20ö, Hvidbjerg Church.

1944 **Engr.** *Perf. 13*
290 A50 10o violet 30 20
291 A50 15o yel grn 40 60
292 A50 20o red 30 20

Ole Roemer A53

King Christian X A54

1944, Sept. 25
293 A53 20o hn brn 30 20

Issued to commemorate the 300th anniversary of the birth of Ole Roemer, astronomer.

1945, Sept. 26
294 A54 10o lilac 20 10
295 A54 20o red 40 10
296 A54 40o dp bl 90 25

75th birthday of King Christian X.

Small State Seal — A55

Tycho Brahe — A56

1946-47 **Unwmk.** *Perf. 13*
297 A55 1k brown 1.00 5
298 A55 2k red ('47) 80 5
299 A55 5k dl bl 1.50 6

Nos. 297-299 issued on ordinary and fluorescent paper.

See Nos. 395-400, 441A-444D, 499-506, 644-650, 716-720A.

1946, Dec. 14 **Engr.**
300 A56 20(o) dk red 30 10

Issued to commemorate the 400th anniversary of the birth of Tycho Brahe, astronomer.

First Danish Locomotive A57

Modern Steam Locomotive A58

Diesel Locomotive A59

1947, June 27
301 A57 15(o) stl bl 50 40
302 A58 20(o) red 50 20
303 A59 40(o) dp bl 1.75 1.00

Issued to commemorate the centenary of the inauguration of the Danish State Railways.

Jacob C. Jacobsen A60

King Frederik IX A61

1947, Nov. 10 *Perf. 13*
304 A60 20(o) dk red 45 20

Issued to commemorate the 60th anniversary of the death of Jacob Christian Jacobsen, founder of the Glyptothek Art Museum, Copenhagen.

1948-50 **Unwmk.** *Perf. 13*

Three types among 15ö, 20ö, 30ö:

I. Background of horizontal lines. No outline at left for cheek and ear. King's uniform textured in strong lines.

II. Background of vertical and horizontal lines. Contour of cheek and ear at left. Uniform same.

III. Background and facial contour lines as in II. Uniform lines double and thinner.

306 A61 15(o) grn (II) 3.00 6
a. Type III ('49) 2.00 6
307 A61 20(o) dk red (I) 1.25 6
a. Type III ('49) 1.25 6
308 A61 25(o) lt brn 1.75 10
309 A61 30(o) org (II) 18.00 15
a. Type III ('50) 20.00 15
310 A61 40(o) dl bl ('49) 5.00 60
311 A61 45(o) ol ('50) 2.00 10
312 A61 50(o) gray ('49) 2.00 10
313 A61 60(o) grnsh bl ('50) 3.00 10
314 A61 75(o) lil rose ('50) 1.50 10
Nos. 306-314 (9) 37.50 1.37

See also Nos. 319-326, 334-341, 354.

Legislative Assembly, 1849 — A62

Symbol of U.P.U. — A63

1949, June 5
315 A62 20(o) red brn 50 15

Issued to commemorate the centenary of the adoption of the Danish constitution.

1949, Oct. 9
316 A63 40o dl bl 1.25 85

Issued to commemorate the 75th anniversary of the formation of the Universal Postal Union.

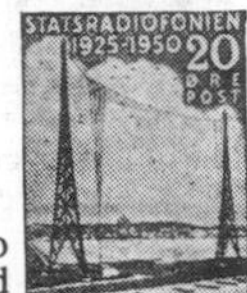
Kalundborg Radio Station and Masts — A64

1950, Apr. 1 Engr. *Perf. 13*
317 A64 20o brn red 60 25

Issued to commemorate the 25th anniversary of radio broadcasting in Denmark.

Types of 1933-50.

1950-51 Unwmk. *Perf. 13*

318	A32 10o green	5	5
319	A61 15(o) lilac	90	5
b.	15(o) gray lil	4.00	5
320	A61 20(o) lt brn	50	5
321	A61 25(o) dk red	4.50	5
322	A61 35(o) gray grn ('51)	1.20	15
323	A61 40(o) gray	1.20	6
324	A61 50(o) dk bl	4.00	20
325	A61 55(o) brn ('51)	22.50	2.50
326	A61 70(o) dp grn	3.75	10
	Nos. 318-326 (9)	38.60	3.21

Warship of 1701 A65

Hans Christian Oersted A66

1951, Feb. 26 Engr. *Perf. 13*
327 A65 25(o) dk red 80 25
328 A65 50(o) dp bl 4.50 1.25

Issued to commemorate the 250th anniversary of the foundation of the Naval Officers' College.

1951, Mar. 9 Unwmk.
329 A66 50(o) blue 2.25 75

Issued to commemorate the centenary of the death of Hans Christian Oersted, physicist.

Post Chaise ("Ball Post") A67

Marine Rescue A68

1951, Apr. 1 *Perf. 13*
330 A67 15(o) purple 1.50 25
331 A67 25(o) hn brn 1.50 25

Issued to commemorate the centenary of Denmark's first postage stamp.

1952, Mar. 26
332 A68 25(o) red brn 80 30

Issued to commemorate the centenary of the foundation of the Danish Lifesaving Service.

Types of 1933-50.

1952-53 *Perf. 13*

333	A32 12(o) lt yel grn	50	5
334	A61 25(o) lt bl	1.60	25
335	A61 30(o) brn red	1.00	5
336	A61 50(o) aqua ('53)	80	6
337	A61 60(o) dp bl ('53)	1.00	6
338	A61 65(o) gray ('53)	1.00	10
339	A61 80(o) org ('53)	1.00	6
340	A61 90(o) ol ('53)	4.00	6
341	A61 95(o) red org ('53)	1.75	35
	Nos. 333-341 (9)	12.65	1.04

Jelling Runic Stone — A69

Designs: 15(ö), Vikings' camp, Trelleborg. 20(ö), Church of Kalundborg. 30(ö), Nyborg castle. 60(ö), Goose tower, Vordinborg.

1953-56 *Perf. 13*

342	A69 10(o) dp grn	15	5
343	A69 15(o) lt rose vio	15	5
344	A69 20(o) brown	20	8
345	A69 30(o) red ('54)	25	8
346	A69 60(o) dp bl ('54)	60	20

Designs: 10(ö), Manor house, Spottrup. 15(ö), Hammershus castle ruins. 20(ö), Copenhagen stock exchange. 30(ö), Statue of Frederik V, Amalienborg. 60(ö), Soldier statue at Fredericia.

347	A69 10(o) grn ('54)	15	5
348	A69 15(o) lil ('55)	15	5
349	A69 20(o) brn ('55)	20	8
350	A69 30(o) red ('55)	25	8
351	A69 60(o) dp bl ('56)	1.10	20
	Nos. 342-351 (10)	3.20	92

Nos. 342-351 were issued to commemorate the 1000th anniversary of the Kingdom of Denmark. Each stamp represents a different century.

Telegraph Equipment of 1854 — A70

King Frederik V — A71

1954, Feb. 2 *Perf. 13*
352 A70 30(o) red brn 80 15

Issued to commemorate the centenary of the telegraph in Denmark.

1954, Mar. 31
353 A71 30(o) dk red 1.00 15

Issued to commemorate the 200th anniversary of the founding of the Royal Academy of Fine Arts.

Type of 1948-50

1955, Apr. 27
354 A41 25(o) lilac 40 5

Nos. 224C and 226A Surcharged with New Value in Black. Nos. 307 and 321 Surcharged with New Value and 4 Bars.

1955-56

355	A32 5o on 6o org	20	20
356	A32 5o on 7o lt brn	20	20
357	A61 30(o) on 20(o) dk red (I)	40	10
a.	Type III	70	15
b.	Double surch.	550.00	550.00
358	A61 30(o) on 25(o) dk red ('56)	90	6
a.	Double surch.		

Sören Kierkegaard — A72

Ellehammer's Plane — A73

1955, Nov. 11 Unwmk.
359 A72 30(o) dk red 60 15

Issued to commemorate the 100th anniversary of the death of Sören Kierkegaard, philosopher and theologian.

1956, Sept. 12 Engr.
360 A73 30o dl red 90 15

Issued to commemorate the 50th anniversary of the first flight made by Jacob Christian Hansen Ellehammer in a heavier-than-air craft.

Northern Countries Issue.

Whooper Swans — A74

1956, Oct. 30 *Perf. 13*
361 A74 30o rose red 5.00 35
362 A74 60o ultra 3.00 1.00

Issued to emphasize the close bonds among the northern countries: Denmark, Finland, Iceland, Norway and Sweden.

Prince's Palace A75

Harvester A76

Design: 60ö, Sun God's Chariot.

1957, May 15 Unwmk.
363 A75 30o dl red 1.75 25
364 A75 60o dk bl 1.75 60

Issued to commemorate the 150th anniversary of the National Museum.

1958, Sept. 4 Engr. *Perf. 13*
365 A76 30o fawn 40 15

Centenary of the Royal Veterinary and Agricultural College.

King Frederik IX A77

Ballet Dancer A78

1959, Mar. 11
366 A77 30o rose red 1.00 15
367 A77 35o rose lil 60 60
368 A77 60o ultra 60 35

King Frederik's 60th birthday.

1959, May 16
369 A78 35o rose lil 40 20

Issued to publicize the Danish Ballet and Music Festival, May 17-31. See also Nos. 401, 422.

No. 319 Surcharged **30 Verdensflygtningeåret 1959-60**

1960, Apr. 7
370 A61 30o on 15o pur 40 20

Issued to publicize World Refugee Year, July 1, 1959-June 30, 1960.

Seeder and Farm — A79

Designs: 30ö, Harvester combine. 60ö, Plow.

1960, Apr. 28 Engr. *Perf. 13*
371 A79 12o green 20 20
372 A79 30o dl red 40 20
373 A79 60o dk bl 85 35

King Frederik IX and Queen Ingrid — A80

1960, May 24 Unwmk.
374 A80 30o dl red 80 20
375 A80 60o blue 80 30

Issued to commemorate the 25th anniversary of the marriage of King Frederik IX and Queen Ingrid.

Bascule Light A81

Niels R. Finsen A82

1960, June 8 Engr.
376 A81 30o dl red 45 15

Issued to commemorate the 400th anniversary of the Lighthouse Service.

1960, Aug. 1 *Perf. 13*
377 A82 30o dk red 45 15

Issued to commemorate the centenary of the birth of Dr. Niels R. Finsen, physician and scientist.

Nursing Mother A83

DC-8 Airliner A84

1960, Aug. 16 Unwmk.
378 A83 60o ultra 1.00 35

Issued to commemorate the 10th meeting of the regional committee for Europe of the World Health Organization, Copenhagen, Aug. 16-20.

Europa Issue, 1960

Common Design Type

1960, Sept. 19 *Perf. 13*

Size: 28x21mm.

379 CD3 60o ultra 1.25 35

SAS Issue

1961, Feb. 24

380 A84 60o ultra 1.00 35

Issued to commemorate the 10th anniversary of the Scandinavian Airlines System, SAS.

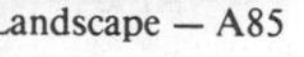

Landscape — A85

Frederik IX — A86

1961, Apr. 21 *Perf. 13*

381 A85 30o cop brn 35 8

Issued to commemorate the 50th anniversary of Denmark's Society of Nature Lovers.

Fluorescent Paper

as well as ordinary paper, was used in printing many definitive and commemorative stamps, starting in 1962. These include No. 220; the 15, 20, 25, 30, 35 (Nos. 386 and 387), 50 and 60ö, 1.20k, 1.50k and 25k definitives of following set, and Nos. 297-299, 318, 318a-b, 333, 380, 401-427, 429-435, 438-439, 493, 543, 548, B30.

Only fluorescent paper was used for Nos. 436-437, 437A and 440 onward; in semipostals from B31 onward.

1961-63 Engr. *Perf. 13*

382 A32 15o grn ('63) 30 5
383 A86 20o brown 80 5
384 A86 25o brn ('63) 40 5
385 A86 30o rose red 1.00 5
386 A86 35o ol grn 1.00 50
387 A86 35o rose red ('63) 40 5
388 A86 40o gray 1.50 5
389 A86 50o aqua 1.00 6
390 A86 60o ultra 1.25 10
391 A86 70o green 2.50 20
392 A86 80o red org 2.50 10
393 A86 90o ol bis 7.00 20
394 A86 95o cl ('63) 1.50 70
Nos. 382-394 (13) 21.15 2.16

See also Nos. 417-419, 438-441.

State Seal Type of 1946-47

1962-65

395 A55 1.10k lil ('65) 6.00 1.00
396 A55 1.20k gray 5.00 8
397 A55 1.25k orange 5.00 12
398 A55 1.30k grn ('65) 6.00 50
399 A55 1.50k red lil 3.00 6
400 A55 25k yel grn 8.00 25
Nos. 395-400 (6) 33.00 2.01

Dancer Type of 1959 Inscribed "15-31 MAJ"

1962, Apr. 26

401 A78 60o ultra 60 25

Issued to publicize the Danish Ballet and Music Festival, May 15-31.

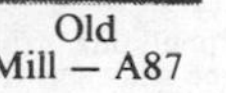

Old Mill — A87

M.S. Selandia — A88

1962, May 10 Unwmk. *Perf. 13*

402 A87 10o red brn 20 10

Issued to commemorate the centenary of the abolition of mill monopolies.

1962, June 14 Engr.

403 A88 60o dk bl 3.00 2.50

Issued to commemorate the 50th anniversary of M.S. Selandia, the first Diesel ship.

Violin Scroll, Leaves, Lights and Balloon A89

1962, Aug. 31

404 A89 35o rose vio 30 10

Issued to commemorate the 150th anniversary of the birth of Georg Carstensen, founder of Tivoli amusement park, Copenhagen.

Cliffs on Moen Island — A90

Germinating Wheat — A91

1962, Nov. 22

405 A90 20o pale brn 20 5

Issued to publicize preservation of natural treasures and landmarks.

1963, Mar. 21 Engr.

406 A91 35o fawn 40 12

Issued for the "Freedom from Hunger" campaign of the U.N. Food and Agriculture Organization.

Railroad Wheel, Tire Tracks, Waves and Swallow — A92

Sailing Vessel, Coach, Postilions and Globe — A93

1963, May 14 Unwmk. *Perf. 13*

407 A92 15o green 30 15

Issued to commemorate the inauguration of the "Bird Flight Line" railroad link between Denmark and Germany.

1963, May 27

408 A93 60o dk bl 80 30

Issued to commemorate the centenary of the first International Postal Conference, Paris, 1863.

Niels Bohr and Atom Diagram — A94

Early Public School Drawn on Slate — A95

1963, Nov. 21 Engr.

409 A94 35o red brn 45 10
410 A94 60o dk bl 90 20

Issued to commemorate the 50th anniversary of Prof. Niels Bohr's (1885-1962) atom theory.

1964, June 19 Unwmk. *Perf. 13*

411 A95 35o red brn 30 10

Issued to commemorate the 150th anniversary of the royal decrees for the public school system.

Fish and Chart A96

Danish Watermarks and Perforations A97

1964, Sept. 7 Engr.

412 A96 60o vio bl 60 30

Issued to commemorate the Conference of the International Council for the Exploration of the Sea, Copenhagen.

1964, Oct. 10 *Perf. 13*

413 A97 35o pink 40 12

Issued for the 25th anniversary of Stamp Day and to publicize the Odense Stamp Exhibition, Oct. 10-11.

Landscape — A98

Calculator, Ledger and Inkwell — A99

1964, Nov. 12 Engr.

414 A98 25o brown 25 10

Issued to publicize preservation of natural treasures and landmarks.

1965, Mar. 8 Unwmk.

415 A99 15o lt ol grn 20 15

Issued to commemorate the centenary of the first Business School in Denmark.

Types of 1933 and 1961

1965, May 15 Engr. *Perf. 13*

416 A32 25o ap grn 35 5
417 A86 40o brown 35 5
418 A86 50o rose red 45 5
419 A86 80o ultra 1.25 10

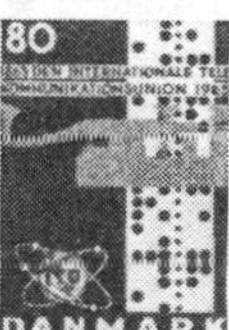

ITU Emblem, Telegraph Key and Teletype Paper A100

Carl Nielsen A101

1965, May 17

420 A100 80o dk bl 60 15

Issued to commemorate the centenary of the International Telecommunication Union.

1965, June 9 Engr.

421 A101 50o brn red 30 10

Issued to commemorate the centenary of the birth of Carl Nielsen (1865-1931), composer.

Dancer Type of 1959 Inscribed "15-31 MAJ"

1965, Sept. 23

422 A78 50o rose red 40 15

Issued to publicize the Danish Ballet and Music Festival, May 15-31.

Denmark stamps can be mounted in Scott's annually supplemented Scandinavia and Finland Album.

Bogo Windmill A102

Mylius Dalgas Surveying Wasteland A103

1965, Nov. 10 Engr. *Perf. 13*

423 A102 40o brown 40 12

Issued to publicize the preservation of natural treasures and landmarks.

1966, Feb. 24

424 A103 25o ol grn 30 15

Issued to commemorate the centenary of the Danish Heath Society (reclamation of wastelands), founded by Enrico Mylius Dalgas.

Christen Kold — A104

1966, March 29 *Perf. 13*

425 A104 50o dl red 40 10

Issued to commemorate the 150th anniversary of the birth of Christen Kold (1816-70), educator.

Poorhouse, Copenhagen A105

Holte Allée, Bregentved A106

Dolmen (Grave) in Jutland — A107

1966 Unwmk.

426 A105 50o dl red 40 10
427 A106 80o dk bl 1.00 20
428 A107 1.50k dk sl grn 1.50 25

Nos. 426-428 issued to publicize preservation of national treasures and ancient monuments. Issue dates: 50ö, May 12; 80ö, June 16; 1.50k, Nov. 24.

George Jensen by Ejnar Nielsen A108

Music Bar and Instruments A109

1966, Aug. 31 Engr. *Perf. 13*

429 A108 80o dk bl 1.00 20

Issued to commemorate the centenary of the birth of George Jensen, silversmith.

1967, Jan. 9
430 A109 50o dk red 40 12

Issued to commemorate the centenary of the Royal Danish Academy of Music.

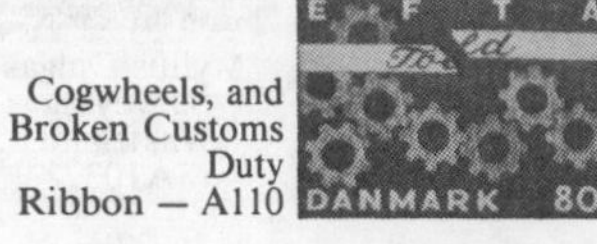

Cogwheels, and Broken Customs Duty Ribbon — A110

1967, Mar. 2
431 A110 80o dk bl 1.10 25

Issued to publicize the European Free Trade Association. Industrial tariffs were abolished Dec. 31, 1966, among EFTA members: Austria, Denmark, Finland, Great Britain, Norway, Portugal, Sweden and Switzerland.

Windmill and Medieval Fortress — A111

Designs: 40ő, Ship's rigging and baroque house front. 50ő, Old Town Hall. 80ő, New building construction.

1967 **Engr.** ***Perf. 13***
432 A111 25o green 60 20
433 A111 40o sepia 50 20
434 A111 50o red brn 50 20
435 A111 80o dk bl 1.50 35

The 800th anniversary of Copenhagen.

Issue dates: Nos. 432-433, Apr. 6; Nos. 434-435, May 11.

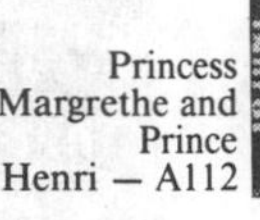

Princess Margrethe and Prince Henri — A112

1967, June 10
436 A112 50o red 60 10

Issued to commemorate the marriage of Crown Princess Margrethe and Prince Henri de Monpezat.

Types of 1933-1961

1967-71		**Engr.**	***Perf. 13***	
437	A32	30o dk grn	35	5
437A	A32	40o org ('71)	35	8
438	A86	50o brown	1.25	6
439	A86	60o rose red	1.25	5
440	A86	80o green	1.25	5
441	A86	90o ultra	1.40	10
441A	A55	1.20k Prus grn ('71)	3.00	30
442	A55	2.20k orange	5.50	10
443	A55	2.80k gray	4.50	20
444	A55	2.90k rose vio	6.50	20
444A	A55	3k dk sl grn ('69)	1.10	10
444B	A55	3.10k plum ('70)	9.00	20
444C	A55	4k gray ('69)	1.50	10
444D	A55	4.10k ol ('70)	9.00	20
		Nos. 437-444D (14)	45.95	1.79

Issue dates: Nos. 437-441, June 30, 1967; Nos. 442-443, July 8, 1967; No. 444, Apr. 29, 1968; Nos. 444A, 444C, Aug. 28, 1969; Nos. 444B, 444D, Aug. 27, 1970; Nos. 437A, 441A, June 24, 1971.

Hans Christian Sonne A113

Cross-anchor and Porpoise A114

1967, Sept. 21
445 A113 60o red 40 10

Issued to commemorate the 150th anniversary of the birth of Hans Christian Sonne, pioneer of the cooperative movement in Denmark.

1967, Nov. 9 **Engr.** ***Perf. 13***
446 A114 90o dk bl 80 40

Issued to commemorate the centenary of the Danish Seamen's Church in Foreign Ports.

Esbjerg Harbor A115

Koldinghus A116

1968, Apr. 24
447 A115 30o dk yel grn 30 15

Centenary of Esbjerg Harbor.

1968, June 13
448 A116 60o cop red 40 12

700th anniversary of Koldinghus Castle.

Shipbuilding Industry A117

Sower A118

Designs: 50ő, Chemical industry. 60ő, Electric power. 90ő, Engineering.

1968, Oct. 24 **Engr.** ***Perf. 13***
449 A117 30o green 35 20
450 A117 50o brown 35 10
451 A117 60o red brn 40 10
452 A117 90o dk bl 60 40

Issued to publicize Danish industries.

1969, Jan. 29
453 A118 30o gray grn 30 12

Issued to commemorate the 200th anniversary of the Royal Agricultural Society of Denmark.

Five Ancient Ships — A119

Frederik IX — A120

Nordic Cooperation Issue

1969, Feb. 28 **Engr.** ***Perf. 13***
454 A119 60o brn red 1.75 25
455 A119 90o blue 2.50 1.00

Issued to commemorate the 50th anniversary of the Nordic Society and to commemorate the centenary of postal cooperation among the northern countries: Denmark, Finland, Iceland, Norway and Sweden. The design is taken from a coin found at the site of Birka, an ancient Swedish town.

1969, Mar. 11
456 A120 50o sepia 35 10
457 A120 60o dl red 35 10

70th birthday of King Frederik IX.

Europa Issue, 1969
Common Design Type

1969, Apr. 28
Size: 28x20mm.
458 CD12 90o chlky bl 1.25 60

Kronborg Castle — A121

Danish Flag — A122

1969, May 22 **Engr.** ***Perf. 13***
459 A121 50o brown 35 10

Issued to commemorate the 50th anniversary of the association of Danes living abroad.

1969, June 12
460 A122 60o bluish blk, red & gray 50 10

Issued to commemorate the 750th anniversary of the fall of the Dannebrog (Danish flag) from heaven.

Martin Andersen Nexo A123

Niels Stensen A124

1969, Aug. 28
461 A123 80o dp grn 60 15

Issued to commemorate the centenary of the birth of Martin Andersen Nexo (1869-1954), novelist.

1969, Sept. 25
462 A124 1k dp brn 65 15

Issued to commemorate the 300th anniversary of the publication of Niels Stensen's geological work "On Solid Bodies."

Abstract Design A125

Symbolic Design A126

1969, Nov. 10 **Engr.** ***Perf. 13***
463 A125 60o rose, red & ultra 40 10

1969, Nov. 20
464 A126 30o ol grn 40 10

Issued to commemorate the centenary of the birth of Valdemar Poulsen (1869-1942), electrical engineer and inventor.

Post Office Bank A127

School Safety Patrol A128

1970, Jan. 15 **Engr.** ***Perf. 13***
465 A127 60o dk red & org 40 10

Issued to commemorate the 50th anniversary of post office banking service.

1970, Feb. 19
466 A128 50o brown 40 10

Issued to publicize road safety.

Candle in Window A129

Deer A130

1970, May 4 **Engr.** ***Perf. 13***
467 A129 50o sl, dl bl & yel 40 10

Issued to commemorate the 25th anniversary of liberation from the Germans.

1970, May 28
468 A130 60o yel grn, red & brn 40 10

Tercentenary of Jaegersborg Deer Park.

Elephant Figurehead, 1741 A131

"The Homecoming" by Povl Christensen A132

1970, June 15 ***Perf. 11½***
469 A131 30o multi 40 35

Royal Naval Museum, tercentenary.

1970, June 15 ***Perf. 13***
470 A132 60o org, dl vio & ol grn 40 10

Issued to commemorate the 50th anniversary of the union of North Schleswig and Denmark.

Electromagnet A133

1970, Aug. 13 **Engr.**
471 A133 80o gray grn 65 12

Issued to commemorate the 150th anniversary of Hans Christian Oersted's discovery of electromagnetism.

Bronze Age Ship A134

Ships: 50ő, Viking shipbuilding, from Bayeux tapestry. 60ő, Thuroe schooner with topgallant. 90ő, Tanker.

1970, Sept. 24
472 A134 30o ocher & brn 40 35
473 A134 50o brn red & rose brn 40 20
474 A134 60o gray ol & red brn 70 20
475 A134 90o bl grn & ultra 1.25 1.00

U.N. Emblem A135

1970, Oct. 22 Engr. *Perf. 13*
476 A135 90o bl, grn & red 1.00 70

25th anniversary of the United Nations.

Bertel Thorvaldsen A136

Mathide Fibiger A137

1970, Nov. 19
477 A136 2k sl bl 1.25 25

Issued to commemorate the bicentenary of the birth of Bertel Thorvaldsen (1768-1844), sculptor.

1971, Feb. 25
478 A137 80o ol grn 60 12

Danish Women's Association centenary.

Refugees A138

Hans Egede A139

1971, March 26 Engr. *Perf. 13*
479 A138 50o brown 40 15
480 A138 60o brn red 60 10

Joint northern campaign for the benefit of refugees.

1971, May 27
481 A139 1k brown 70 15

250th anniversary of arrival of Hans Egede in Greenland and beginning of its colonization.

Swimming A140

Designs: 50ö, Gymnastics. 60ö, Soccer. 90ö, Sailing.

1971, Oct. 14
482 A140 30o bl & grn 40 35
483 A140 50o dk red & brn 40 15
484 A140 60o gray, yel & dk bl 60 15
485 A140 90o ultra, pale grn & vio 1.00 60

Georg Brandes — A141

1971, Nov. 11 Engr. *Perf. 13*
486 A141 90o dk bl 70 25

Centenary of first lectures given by Georg Brandes (1842-1927), writer and literary critic.

Sugar Production A142

1972, Jan. 27
487 A142 80o sl grn 60 15

Centenary of Danish sugar production.

King Frederik IX — A143

1972, Mar. 11 Engr. *Perf. 13*
488 A143 60o red brn 45 10

In memory of King Frederik IX (1899-1972).

Abstract Design A144

1972, Mar. 11
489 A144 1.20k brt rose lil, bl gray & brn 1.00 75

Centenary of the Danish Meteorological Institute.

Nikolai F. S. Grundtvig A145

Locomotive, 1847, Ferry, Travelers A146

1972, May 4 Engr. *Perf. 13*
490 A145 1k sepia 60 30

Centenary of the death of Nikolai Frederik Severin Grundtvig (1783-1872), theologian and poet.

1972, June 26
491 A146 70o rose red 60 20

125th anniversary of Danish State Railways.

Rebild Hills A147

"Tinker Turned Politician" A148

1972, June 26
492 A147 1k bl, sl grn & mar 60 25

Types of 1933-46

1972-78 Engr. *Perf. 13*
493 A32 20o sl bl ('74) 8 5
494 A32 50o sep ('74) 18 5
a. Bklt. pane of 12 (4 #318, 4 #493, 4 #494)('85) 3.25
495 A32 60o ap grn ('76) 2.75 10
496 A32 60o gray ('78) 1.00 50
497 A32 70o red 1.50 5
498 A32 70o ap grn ('77) 25 8
499 A55 2.50k orange 2.50 15
500 A55 2.80k ol ('75) 1.25 30
501 A55 3.50k lilac 3.00 10
502 A55 4.5k olive 7.00 10
503 A55 6k vio blk ('76) 1.75 20
504 A55 7k red lil ('78) 2.00 15
505 A55 9k brn ol ('77) 2.75 15
506 A55 10k lem ('76) 3.00 15
Nos. 493-506 (14) 29.01 2.13

1972, Sept. 14
507 A148 70o dk red 50 10

250th anniversary of the comedies of Ludvig Holberg (1684-1754) on the Danish stage.

WHO Building, Copenhagen A149

1972, Sept. 14
508 A149 2k bl, blk & lt red brn 1.25 50

Opening of World Health Organization Building, Copenhagen.

Bridge Across Little Belt A150

Aeroskobing House c. 1740 A151

Designs (Diagrams): 60ö, Hanstholm Harbor. 70ö, Lim Fjord Tunnel. 90ö, Knudshoved Harbor.

1972, Oct. 19 Engr. *Perf. 13*
509 A150 40o dk grn 35 30
510 A150 60o dk brn 60 10
511 A150 70o dk red 60 10
512 A150 90o dk bl grn 75 35

Highway engineering.

1972, Nov. 23

Danish Architecture: 60ö, East Bornholm farmhouse, 17th century (horiz.). 70ö, House, Christianshavn, c. 1710. 1.20k, Hvide Sande Farmhouse, c. 1810 (horiz.).

Size: 20x28mm., 27x20mm.

513 A151 40o red, brn & blk 60 40
514 A151 60o blk, vio bl & grn 60 40

Size: 18x37mm., 36x20mm.

515 A151 70o red, dk red & blk 70 18
516 A151 1.20k dk brn, red & grn 1.00 90

Johannes V. Jensen A152

Guard Rails and Cogwheels A153

1973, Feb. 22 Engr. *Perf. 13*
517 A152 90o green 50 15

Centenary of the birth of Johannes Vilhelm Jensen (1873-1950), lyric poet and novelist.

1973, Mar. 22
518 A153 50o sepia 40 15

Centenary of first Danish Factory Act for labor protection.

P. C. Abildgaard A154

Rhododendron A155

1973, Mar. 22
519 A154 1k dl bl 60 60

Bicentenary of Royal Veterinary College, Christianshaven, founded by Prof. P. C. Abildgaard.

1973, Apr. 26

Design: 70ö, Dronningen of Denmark rose.

520 A155 60o brn, grn & vio 70 20
521 A155 70o dk red, rose & grn 70 20

Centenary of the founding of the Horticultural Society of Denmark.

Nordic Cooperation Issue 1973

Nordic House, Reykjavik A156

1973, June 26 Engr. *Perf. 13*
522 A156 70o multi 75 30
523 A156 1k multi 3.00 50

A century of postal cooperation among Denmark, Finland, Iceland, Norway and Sweden, and in connection with the Nordic Postal Conference, Reykjavik.

Sextant, Stella Nova and Cassiopeia A157

St. Mark, from 11th Century Book of Dalby A158

1973, Oct. 18 Engr. *Perf. 13*
524 A157 2k dk bl 1.00 30

400th anniversary of the publication of "De Nova Stella," by Tycho Brahe.

1973, Oct. 18 Photo. *Perf. 14x14½*
525 A158 120o buff & multi 1.25 80

300th anniversary of Royal Library.

Devil and Gossips, Fanefjord Church, 1480 — A159

Frescoes: No. 527, Queen Esther and King Ahasuerus, Tirsted Church, c.1400. No. 528, Miraculous Harvest, Jetsmark Church, c.1474. No. 529, Jesus carrying cross, and wearing crown of thorns, Biersted Church, c.1400. No. 530, Creation of Eve, Fanefjord Church, c.1480.

1973, Nov. 28 Engr. *Perf. 13*
Cream Paper
526 A159 70o dk red, yel & grn 1.50 50
527 A159 70o dk red, yel & grn 1.50 50
528 A159 70o dk red, yel & grn 1.50 50

529 A159 70o dk red, yel & grn 1.50 50
530 A159 70o dk red, yel & grn 1.50 50
a. Booklet pane of 10 45.00
Nos. 526-530 (5) 7.50 2.50

Nos. 526-530 printed se-tenant in sheets of 50 (5x10). No. 530a contains 2 each of Nos. 526-530.

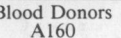

Blood Donors A160

Queen Margrethe A161

1974, Jan. 24
531 A160 90o pur & red 60 20

"Blood Saves Lives."

1974-81 Engr. *Perf. 13*
532 A161 60o brown 60 25
533 A161 60o orange 60 5
534 A161 70o red 60 5
535 A161 70o dk brn 60 5
536 A161 80o green 60 15
537 A161 80o dp brn ('76) 60 25
538 A161 90o red lil 60 5
539 A161 90o dl red 60 5
540 A161 90o sl grn ('76) 60 25
541 A161 100o dp ultra 80 10
542 A161 100o gray ('75) 80 25
543 A161 100o red ('76) 60 5
544 A161 100o brn ('77) 60 25
a. Bklt. pane of 5 (#544, #494, 2 #493, #318) 2.25
545 A161 110o org ('78) 60 25
546 A161 120o slate 80 6
547 A161 120o red ('77) 60 6
548 A161 130o ultra ('75) 2.50 1.00
549 A161 150o vio bl ('78) 1.00 70
550 A161 180o sl grn ('77) 80 50
551 A161 200o bl ('81) 1.25 50
Nos. 532-551 (20) 15.75 4.87

See Nos. 630, 632-643.

Pantomime Theater — A162

1974, May 16
552 A162 100o indigo 70 20

Centenary of the Pantomime Theater, Tivoli.

Hverringe — A163

Views: 60o, Norre Lyndelse, Carl Nielsen's childhood home. 70ö, Odense, Hans Chr. Andersen's childhood home. 90ö, Hesselagergaard (vert.). 120ö, Hindsholm.

1974, June 20 Engr. *Perf. 13*
553 A163 50o brn & multi 70 30
554 A163 60o sl grn & multi 60 35
555 A163 70o red brn & multi 60 35
556 A163 90o dk grn & mar 80 15
557 A163 120o red org & dk grn 1.10 50
Nos. 553-557 (5) 3.80 1.65

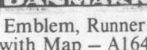

Emblem, Runner with Map — A164

Iris — A165

Design: 80ö, Compass.

1974, Aug. 22 Engr. *Perf. 13*
558 A164 70o dk bl & brn 60 40
559 A164 80o brn & vio bl 60 40

World Orienteering Championships 1974.

1974, Sept. 19

Design: 120ö, Purple orchid.

560 A165 90o brn, vio bl & sl grn 60 20
561 A165 120o ind, lil & sl grn 90 40

Copenhagen Botanical Garden centenary.

Mailman, 1624, and Postilion, 1780 — A166

Carrier Pigeon — A167

Design: 90ö, Balloon and sailing ships.

1974, Oct. 9 Engr. *Perf. 13*
562 A166 70o lem & dk brn 60 40
563 A166 90o dl grn & sep 75 20
564 A167 120o dk bl 1.00 35

350th anniversary of Danish Post Office (70ö, 90ö) and centenary of Universal Postal Union (120ö).

Souvenir Sheet

Ferslew's Essays, 1849 and 1852 A168

Engraved and Photogravure
1975, Feb. 27 *Perf. 13*
565 A168 Sheet of 4 7.00 7.50
a. 70o *Coat of arms* 1.60 1.70
b. 80o *King Frederik VII* 1.60 1.70
c. 90o *King Frederik VII* 1.60 1.70
d. 100o *Mercury* 1.60 1.70

HAFNIA 76 International Stamp Exhibition, Copenhagen, Aug. 20-29, 1976. Size of No. 565: 68x93mm. Sold for 5k.
See No. 585.

Early Radio Equipment A169

Flora Danica Plate A170

1975, Mar. 20 Engr. *Perf. 13*
566 A169 90o dl red 75 18

Danish broadcasting, 50th anniversary.

1975, May 22

Danish China: 90ö, Flora Danica tureen. 130ö, Vase and tea caddy, blue fluted china.

567 A170 50o sl grn 50 18
568 A170 90o brn red 1.00 15
569 A170 130o vio bl 1.50 1.25

Church of Moravian Brethren, Christiansfeld A171

Designs: 120ö, Kongsgaard farmhouse, Lejre. 150ö, Anna Queenstraede, Helsingor (vert.).

1975, June 19
570 A171 70o sepia 50 40
571 A171 120o ol grn 1.50 50
572 A171 150o vio blk 80 20

European Architectural Heritage Year 1975.

Hans Christian Andersen A172

Watchman's Square, Abenra A173

Designs: 70ö, Numbskull Jack, drawing by Vilh. Pedersen. 130ö, The Marshking's Daughter, drawing by L. Frohlich.

1975, Aug. 28 Engr. *Perf. 13*
573 A172 70o brn & blk 1.00 1.00
574 A172 90o brn red & dk brn 1.75 20
575 A172 130o bl blk & sep 2.25 2.25

Hans Christian Andersen (1805-1875), writer, death centenary.

1975, Sept. 25

Designs: 90ö, Haderslev Cathedral (vert.). 100ö, Mögeltönder Polder. 120ö, Mouth of Vidaaen at Höjer Floodgates.

576 A173 70o multi 60 40
577 A173 90o multi 70 20
578 A173 100o multi 70 20
579 A173 120o multi 1.00 50

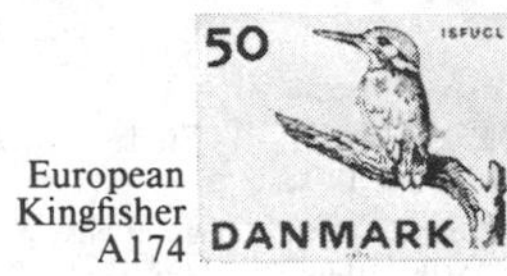

European Kingfisher A174

Designs: 70ö, Hedgehog. 90ö, Cats. 130ö, Avocets. 200ö, Otter.

1975, Oct. 23 Engr. *Perf. 13*
580 A174 50o vio blk 70 35
581 A174 70o black 70 35
582 A174 90o brown 70 20
583 A174 130o bluish blk 1.25 1.10
584 A174 200o brn blk 1.10 25
Nos. 580-584 (5) 4.45 2.25

Protected animals, and for the centenary of the Danish Society for the Prevention of Cruelty to Animals (90ö).

HAFNIA Type of 1974
Souvenir Sheet
Engraved and Photogravure
1975, Nov. 20
585 A168 Sheet of 4 4.50 5.00
a. 50o buff & brn No. 2 1.10 1.25
b. 70o buff, brn & bl, No. 1 1.10 1.25
c. 90o buff, bl & brn, No. 11 1.10 1.25
d. 130o ol, brn & buff, No. 19 1.10 1.25

HAFNIA 76 International Stamp Exhibition, Copenhagen, Aug. 20-29, 1976. Size of No. 585: 68x93mm. Sold for 5k.

Denmark stamps can be mounted in Scott's annually supplemented Scandinavia and Finland Album.

Copenhagen, Center A175

View from Round Tower A176

Copenhagen, Views: 100ö, Central Station, interior. 130ö, Harbor.

1976, Mar. 25 Engr. *Perf. 12½*
586 A175 60o multi 80 30
587 A176 80o multi 80 25
588 A176 100o multi 50 10
589 A175 130o multi 2.25 2.25

Postilion, by Otto Bache A177

Emil Chr. Hansen, Physiologist, in Laboratory A178

1976, June 17 Engr. *Perf. 12½*
590 A177 130o multi 2.00 1.50

Souvenir Sheet
591 A177 130o multi 9.50 11.00

HAFNIA 76 International Stamp Exhibition, Copenhagen, Aug. 20-29. No. 591 contains one stamp similar to No. 590 with design continuous into sheet margin. Sheet shows painting "A String of Horses Outside an Inn" of which No. 590 shows a detail. Black marginal inscription and HAFNIA emblem. Size: 103x81mm. Sheet sold for 15k including exhibition ticket.

1976, Sept. 23 Engr. *Perf. 13*
592 A178 100o org red 50 10

Carlsberg Foundation (art and science), centenary.

Glass Blower Molding Glass A179

Five Water Lilies A180

Danish Glass Production: 80ö, Finished glass removed from pipe. 130ö, Glass cut off from foot. 150ö, Glass blown up in mold.

1976, Nov. 18 Engr. *Perf. 13*
593 A179 60o slate 30 30
594 A179 80o dk brn 40 30
595 A179 130o dk bl 1.10 1.10
596 A179 150o red brn 80 20

Photogravure and Engraved
1977, Feb. 2 *Perf. 12½*
597 A180 100o brt grn & multi 60 35
598 A180 130o ultra & multi 2.00 2.00

Nordic countries cooperation for protection of the environment and 25th Session of Nordic Council, Helsinki, Feb. 19.

Road Accident — A181

1977, Mar. 24 Engr. *Perf. 12½*
599 A181 100o brn red 40 10

Road Safety Traffic Act, May 1, 1977.

Europa Issue 1977

Allinge — A182

Design: 1.30k, View, Ringsted.

1977, May 2 Engr. *Perf. 12½*
600 A182 1k dl red 70 25
601 A182 1.30k dk bl 3.50 3.00

Kongeaen A183

Landscapes, Southern Jutland: 90ö, Skallingen. 150ö, Torskind. 200ö, Jelling.

1977, June 30 Engr. *Perf. 12½*
602 A183 60o multi 1.25 1.25
603 A183 90o multi 60 40
604 A183 150o multi 80 50
605 A183 200o multi 90 30

See Nos. 616-619, 655-658.

Hammers and Horseshoes A184 — Globe Flower A185

Designs: 1k, Chisel, square and plane. 1.30k, Trowel, ceiling brush and folding ruler.

1977, Sept. 22 Engr. *Perf. 12½*
606 A184 80o dk brn 50 40
607 A184 1k red 60 15
608 A184 1.30k vio bl 1.10 50

Danish crafts.

1977, Nov. 17 Engr. *Perf. 12½*

Design: 1.50k, Cnidium dubium.

609 A185 1k multi 60 20
610 A185 1.50k multi 1.25 85

Endangered flora.

Handball — A186

1978, Jan. 19 *Perf. 12½*
611 A186 1.20k red 42 16

Men's World Handball Championships.

The only foreign revenue stamps listed in this Catalogue are those authorized for prepayment of postage.

Christian IV, Frederiksborg Castle A187 — Frederiksborg Museum A188

1978, Mar. 16
612 A187 1.20k brn red 60 16
613 A188 1.80k black 1.00 45

Frederiksborg Museum, centenary.

Europa Issue

Jens Bang's House, Aalborg A189 — Frederiksborg Castle, Ground Plan and Elevation A190

1978, May 11 Engr. *Perf. 12½*
614 A189 1.20k red 42 16
615 A190 1.50k dk bl & vio bl 1.25 1.00

Landscape Type of 1977

Landscapes, Central Jutland: 70ö, Kongenshus Memorial Park. 120ö, Post Office, Old Town in Aarhus. 150ö, Lignite fields, Soby. 180ö, Church wall, Stadil Church.

1978, June 15 Engr. *Perf. 12½*
616 A183 70o multi 35 30
617 A183 120o multi 60 25
618 A183 150o multi 75 75
619 A183 180o multi 85 60

Boats in Harbor A191 — Edible Morel A192

Designs: 1k, Eel traps. 1.80k, Boats in berth. 2.50k, Drying nets.

1978, Sept. 7 Engr. *Perf. 12½*
620 A191 70o ol gray 60 40
621 A191 1k redsh brn 60 25
622 A191 1.80k slate 60 40
623 A191 2.50k sepia 1.25 60

Danish fishing industry.

1978, Nov. 16 Engr. *Perf. 12½*

Design: 1.20k, Satan's mushroom.

624 A192 1k sepia 60 30
625 A192 1.20k dl red 80 30

Telephones — A193

1979, Jan. 25 Engr. *Perf. 12½*
626 A193 1.20k dl red 50 20

Centenary of Danish telephone.

University Seal A194 — Pentagram: University Faculties A195

1979, Apr. 5 Engr. *Perf. 12½*
627 A194 1.30k vermilion 60 20
628 A195 1.60k dk vio bl 80 70

University of Copenhagen, 500th anniversary.

Types of 1933-1974

1979-82 Engr. *Perf. 13*
629 A32 80o green 32 10
630 A161 90o slate 1.50 1.25
631 A32 100o dp grn ('81) 40 15
632 A161 110o brown 45 5
a. Bklt. pane of 5 (#493-494, #632, 2 #318) ('79) 1.00
633 A161 130o red 65 6
a. Bklt. pane of 10, 2 each #494, 629, 632, 4 #633 ('79) 4.00
634 A161 130o brn ('81) 80 35
635 A161 140o red org ('80) 1.25 1.00
636 A161 150o red org ('81) 90 65
637 A161 160o ultra 1.00 80
638 A161 160o red ('81) 75 15
a. Bklt. pane of 14 (2 each #318, 634, 638, 8 #494) 8.00
639 A161 180o ultra ('80) 1.00 90
640 A161 210o gray ('80) 1.25 1.10
641 A161 230o ol grn ('81) 1.25 40
642 A161 250o bl grn ('81) 1.25 50
643 A55 2.80k dl grn 1.00 20
644 A55 3.30k brn red ('81) 1.00 30
645 A55 3.50k grnsh bl ('82) 1.10 60
646 A55 4.30k brn red ('80) 1.75 1.10
647 A55 4.70k rose lil ('81) 1.75 1.25
648 A55 8k orange 2.50 20
649 A55 12k red brn ('81) 3.75 65
650 A55 14k dk red brn ('82) 4.25 85
Nos. 629-650 (22) 29.87 12.61

Europa Issue 1979

Mail Cart, 1785 — A196

Design: 1.60k, Morse key and amplifier.

1979, May 10 *Perf. 12½*
651 A196 1.30k red 45 20
652 A196 1.60k dk bl 1.00 1.00

Gripping Beast Pendant — A197

Viking Art: 2k, Key with gripping beast design.

1979, June 14 Engr. *Perf. 13*
653 A197 1.10k sepia 40 20
654 A197 2k grnsh gray 60 20

Landscape Type of 1977

Landscapes, Northern Jutland: 80ö, Mols Bjerge. 90ö, Orslev Kloster. 200ö, Trans. 280ö, Bovbjerg.

1979, Sept. 6 Engr. *Perf. 12½*
655 A183 80o multi 40 40
656 A183 90o multi 90 80
657 A183 200o multi 70 20
658 A183 280o multi 1.00 75

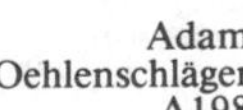

Adam Oehlenschläger A198

1979, Oct, 4 Engr. *Perf. 13*
659 A198 1.30k dk car 45 20

Adam Oehlenschläger (1799-1850), poet and dramatist.

Score, Violin, Dancing Couple — A199 — Ballerina — A200

1979, Nov. 8 Engr. *Perf. 13x12½*
660 A199 1.10k brown 35 25
661 A200 1.60k ultra 65 40

Jacob Gade (b. 1879), composer; August Bournonville (1805-1879), ballet master.

Royal Mail Guards' Office, Copenhagen, 1779 — A201

1980, Feb. 14 Engr. *Perf. 13*
662 A201 1.30k brn red 45 20

National Postal Service, 200th anniversary.

Symbols of Occupation, Health and Education — A202

1980, May 5 Engr. *Perf. 13*
663 A202 1.60k dk bl 80 65

World Conference of the U.N. Decade for Women, Copenhagen, July 14-30.

Europa Issue 1980

Karen Blixen (1885-1962), writer — A203

Design: 1.60k, August Krogh (1874-1949), physiologist.

1980, May 5
664 A203 1.30k red 45 20
665 A203 1.60k blue 80 80

Landscape Type of 1977

Landscapes, Northern Jutland: 80o, Viking ship burial grounds, Lindholm Hoje. 110o, Lighthouse, Skagen (vert.). 200o, Boreglum Monastery. 280o, Fishing boats, Vorupor Beach.

1980, June 19 Engr. *Perf. 13*
666 A183 80o multi 40 40
667 A183 110o multi 40 40
668 A183 200o multi 60 20
669 A183 280o multi 1.00 80

Nordic Cooperation Issue

Silver Tankard, by Borchardt Rollufse, 1641 — A204

1980, Sept. 9 **Engr.** ***Perf. 13***
670 A204 1.30k *shown* 45 20
671 A204 1.80k *Bishop's bowl, Copenhagen faience, 18th century* 1.00 1.00

Frisian Sceat Facsimile, Obverse and Reverse, 9th Century A205

Coins: 1.40k Silver coin of Valdemar the Great and Absalom, 1157-1182, 1.80k, Gold 12-mark coin of Christian VII, 1781.

1980, Oct. 9 **Engr.** ***Perf. 13***
672 A205 1.30k red & redsh brn 45 20
673 A205 1.40k ol gray & sl grn 80 70
674 A205 1.80k dk bl & sl bl 80 70

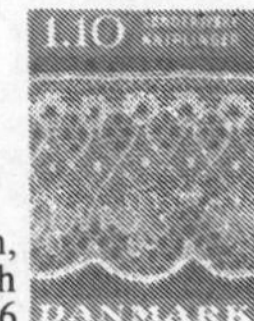

Tonder Lace Pattern, North Schleswig — A206

Designs: Tonder lace patterns.

1980, Nov. 13 **Engr.** ***Perf. 13***
675 A206 1.10k brown 45 35
676 A206 1.30k brn red 52 20
677 A206 2k ol gray 80 30

Nyboder Development, Copenhagen, 350th Anniversary A207

Design: 1.30k, View of Nyboder (diff.).

1981, Mar. 19
678 A207 1.30k dp org & ocher 60 50
679 A207 1.60k dp org & ocher 60 20

Tilting at a Barrel on Shrovetide A208

Design: 2k, Midsummer's Eve bonfire.

1981, May 4 **Engr.** ***Perf. 13***
680 A208 1.60k brn red 60 25
681 A208 2k dk bl 80 45

Soro Lake and Academy, Zealand — A209

Designs: Views of Zealand.

1981, June 18 **Engr.** ***Perf. 13***
682 A209 100o shown 40 15
683 A209 150o Poet N.F.S. Grundtvig's home, Udby 60 35
684 A209 160o Kaj Munk's home, Opager 65 25
685 A209 200o Gronsund 65 40
686 A209 230o Bornholm Isld. 80 50
Nos. 682-686 (5) 3.10 1.65

European Urban Renaissance Year — A210

1981, Sept. 10 **Engr.** ***Perf. 12½x13***
687 A210 1.60k dl red 50 25

Type of 1933

1981-85 **Engr.** ***Perf. 13***
688 A32 30o orange 15 5
a. Bklt. pane 10 (2 #318, 2 #688, 6 #494)('84) 1.75
689 A32 40o purple 16 6
690 A32 80o ol bis ('85) 18 8
691 A32 100o bl ('83) 45 10
b. Bklt. pane of 8 (2 #494, 4 #691, 2 #706) ('83) 6.00
692 A32 150o dk grn ('82) 60 25
693 A32 200o grn ('83) 70 40
694 A32 230o brt yel grn ('84) 45 22
695 A32 250o brt yel grn ('85) 65 22
Nos. 688-695 (8) 3.34 1.38

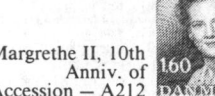

Ellehammer's 18-horsepower Biplane, 1906 — A211

1981, Oct. 8 **Engr.** ***Perf. 13***
696 A211 1k shown 40 40
697 A211 1.30k R-1 Fokker CV reconnaissance plane, 1926 70 60
698 A211 1.60k Bellanca J-300, 1931 50 25
699 A211 2.30k DC-7C, 1957 80 50

Queen Margrethe II, 10th Anniv. of Accession — A212

1982-85 **Engr.** ***Perf. 13***
700 A212 1.60k dl red 75 10
701 A212 1.60k dk ol grn 80 70
702 A212 1.80k sepia 1.00 40
703 A212 2k dl red 1.00 10
b. Bklt. pane of 10 (4 #494, 2 each #493, 702, 703) 10.00
704 A212 2.20k ol grn ('83) 55 40
705 A212 2.30k violet 1.00 10
706 A212 2.50k org red ('83) 1.00 30
707 A212 2.70k dk bl 1.10 35
708 A212 2.70k cop red ('84) 95 25
c. Booklet pane of 8 (3 #688, 2 #494, 3 #708) ('84) 5.00
709 A212 2.80k cop red ('85) 95 25
b. Booklet pane of 8 (3 #493, 2 #494, 3 #709) ('85) 4.00
710 A212 3k vio ('83) 1.25 35
711 A212 3.30k bluish blk ('84) 1.10 28
712 A212 3.50k bl ('83) 1.25 20
713 A212 3.50k dk vio ('85) 1.10 30
714 A212 3.70k dp bl ('84) 1.10 32
715 A212 3.80k dk bl ('85) 1.10 32

Arms Types of 1946

Engr. ***Perf. 13***
716 A55 4.30k dk ol grn ('84) 1.25 38
717 A55 5.50k dk bl grn ('84) 1.65 50
718 A55 16k cop red ('83) 5.00 1.40
719 A55 17k cop red ('84) 5.00 1.50
720 A55 18k brn vio ('85) 4.75 1.50
720A A55 50k dk red ('85) 15.00 4.25
Nos. 700-720A (22) 48.65 14.25

World Figure Skating Championships A213

1982, Feb. 25
721 A213 2k dk bl 60 25

Customs Service Centenary — A214

1982, Feb. 25 **Engr.** ***Perf. 12½***
722 A214 1.60k Revenue schooner Argus 60 18

Europa Issue, 1982 — A215

1982, May 3 **Engr.** ***Perf. 12½***
723 A215 2k Abolition of adscription, 1788 60 15
724 A215 2.70k Women's voting right, 1915 1.00 65

Butter Churn, Barn, Hjedding — A216

Records Office, 400th Anniv. — A217

1982, June 10 **Engr.** ***Perf. 13***
725 A216 1.80k brown 60 30

Cooperative dairy farming centenary.

1982, June 10
726 A217 2.70k green 1.00 25

Steen Steensen Blicher (1782-1848), Poet, by J.V. Gertner — A218

1982, Aug. 26 **Engr.** ***Perf. 13***
727 A218 2k brn red 65 15

Robert Storm Petersen (1882-1949), Cartoonist A219

Printing in Denmark, 500th Anniv. A220

Characters: 1.50k, Three little men and the number man. 2k, Peter and Ping the penguin (horiz.).

1982, Sept. 23 **Engr.** ***Perf. 12½***
728 A219 1.50k dk bl & red 60 40
729 A219 2k red & ol grn 65 30

1982, Sept. 23
730 A220 1.80k Press, text, ink balls 60 30

500th Anniv. of University Library — A221

1982, Nov. 4
731 A221 2.70k Library seal 1.00 40

Catalogue prices for unused stamps up to mid-1953 are for hinged copies matching the condition specified in this volume's introduction.

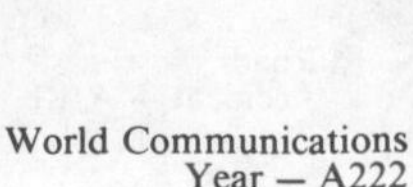

World Communications Year — A222

1983, Jan. 27 **Engr.** ***Perf. 13***
732 A222 2k multi 65 30

Amusement Park, 400th Anniv. A223

Badminton Championship A224

1983, Feb. 24
733 A223 2k multi 65 30

1983, Feb. 24
734 A224 2.70k multi 1.00 35

Nordic Cooperation Issue — A225

1983, Mar. 24
735 A225 2.50k Egeskov Castle 75 30
736 A225 3.50k Troll Church, North Jutland 1.25 80

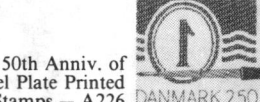

50th Anniv. of Steel Plate Printed Stamps — A226

1983, Mar. 24 **Engr.** ***Perf. 13***
737 A226 2.50k car rose 75 30

Europa 1983 A227

Weights and Measures Ordinance, 300th Anniv. A228

1983, May 5 **Engr.** ***Perf. 13***
738 A227 2.50k Kildekovshallen Recreation Center, Copenhagen 75 30
739 A227 3.50k Salling Sound Bridge 1.25 80

1983, June 16
740 A228 2.50k red 75 30

300th Anniv. of Christian V Danish Law — A229

1983, Sept. 8 **Engr.**
741 A229 5k Codex titlepage 1.65 60

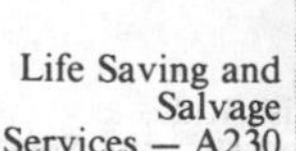

Life Saving and Salvage Services — A230

1983, Oct. 6 Engr. *Perf. 13*

742 A230 1k Car crash, police 40 20
743 A230 2.50k Fire, ambulance service 80 30
744 A230 3.50k Sea rescue 1.25 80

Elderly in Society — A231

1983, Oct. 6

745 A231 2k Stages of life 65 40
746 A231 2.50k Train passengers 80 20

N.F.S. Grundtvig (1783-1872), Poet A232

Street Scene, by C.W. Eckersberg (1783-1853) A233

1983, Nov. 3 Engr.

747 A232 2.50k brn red 80 30
748 A233 2.50k brn red 80 30

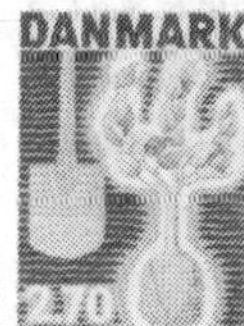

Plant a Tree Campaign — A234

1984 Billiards World Championships, Copenhagen, May 10-13 — A235

Lithographed and Engraved

1984, Jan. 26

749 A234 2.70k Shovel, sapling 85 2

Engr.

750 A235 3.70k Game 1.25 40

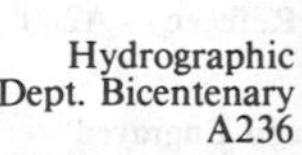

Hydrographic Dept. Bicentenary A236

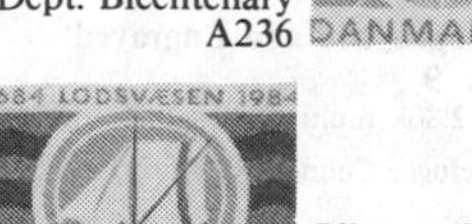

Pilotage Service, 300th Anniv. — A237

1984, Mar. 22 Engr. *Perf. 13*

751 A236 2.30k Compass 75 50
752 A237 2.70k Boat 90 40

Denmark stamps can be mounted in Scott's annually supplemented Scandinavia and Finland Album.

2nd European Parliament Elections A238

Scouts Around Campfire, Emblems A239

Lithographed and Engraved

1984, Apr. 12 *Perf. 13*

753 A238 2.70k org & dk bl 90 22
754 A239 2.70k multi 90 22

Europa (1959-84) — A240

1984, May 3 Engr. *Perf. 12½*

755 A240 2.70k red 90 22
756 A240 3.70k blue 1.25 80

Prince Henrik, 50th Birthday A241

D Day, 40th Anniv. A242

1984, June 6 Engr.

757 A241 2.70k brn red 90 22
758 A242 2.70k War Memorial, Copenhagen 90 22

See Greenland No. 160.

17th Cent. Inn — A243

1984, June 6

759 A243 3k multi 1.00 40

Fishing and Shipping — A244

1984, Sept. 6 Engr.

760 A244 2.30k Research (Herring) 80 60
761 A244 2.70k Sea transport 90 22
762 A244 3.30k Deep-sea fishing 1.10 50
763 A244 3.70k Deep-sea, diff. 1.25 60

Post Bird — A245

Lithographed and Engraved

1984, Oct. 5

764 A245 1k multi 40 15

Holberg Meets with an Officer, by Wilhelm Marstrand (1810-73) — A246

1984, Oct. 5

765 A246 2.70k multi 90 22

Ludvig Holberg (1684-1754), writer.

Jewish Community in Copenhagen, 300th Anniv. A247

1984, Oct. 5

766 A247 3.70k Woman blessing Sabbath candles 1.25 60

Carnival in Rome, by Christoffer W. Eckersberg (1783-1853) — A248

Paintings: 10k, Ymer and Odhumble (Nordic mythology figures), by Nicolai A. Abildgaard (1743-1809) (vert.).

Lithographed and Engraved

Perf. 12½x13, 13x12½

1984, Nov. 22

767 A248 5k multi 1.65 1.40
768 A248 10k multi 3.25 2.50

German and French Reform Church, 300th Anniv. — A249

1985, Jan. 24 Engr. *Perf. 13*

769 A249 2.80k magenta 90 20

Bonn-Copenhagen Declaration, 30th Anniv. — A250

1985, Feb. 21 Litho. *Perf. 14*

770 A250 2.80k Map, flags 90 20

Intl. Youth Year — A251

1985, Mar. 14 *Perf. 13*

771 A251 3.80k multi 1.20 70

Souvenir Sheet

Early Postal Ordinances — A252

Lithographed and Engraved

1985, Mar. 14

772 Sheet of 4 4.75 5.00
a. A252 1k Christian IV's Ordinance on Postmen, 1624 1.10 1.25
b. A252 2.50k Plague Mandate, 1711 1.10 1.25
c. A252 2.80k Ordinance on Prohibition of Mail by Means other than the Post, 1775 1.10 1.25
d. A252 3.80k Act on Postal Articles, 1831 1.10 1.25

HAFNIA '87 philatelic exhibition. Size: 93x68mm. Sold for 15k.

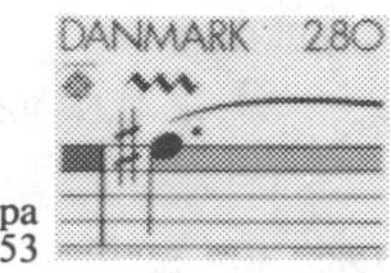

Europa 1985 — A253

1985, May 2

773 A253 2.80k Musical staff 90 40
774 A253 3.80k Musical staff, diff. 1.25 70

Arrival of Queen Ingrid in Denmark, 50th Anniv. — A254

1985, May 21

775 A254 2.80k Queen Mother, chrysanthemums 90 20

See Greenland No. 163.

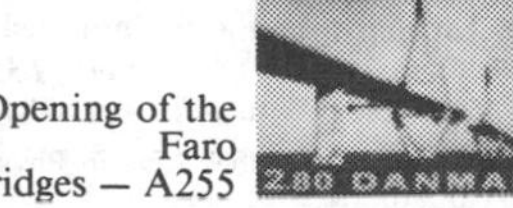

Opening of the Faro Bridges — A255

1985, May 21 Litho. *Perf. 13*

776 A255 2.80k Faro-Falster Bridge 90 20

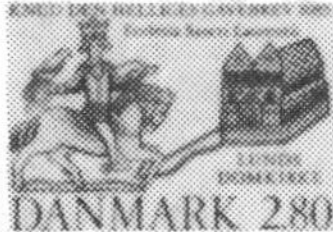

St. Cnut's Land Grant to Lund Cathedral, 900th Anniv. — A256

Seal of King Cnut and: 2.80k, Lund Cathedral. 3k, City of Helsingdorg, Sweden.

1985, May 21 Engr.

777 A256 2.80k multi 90 20
778 A256 3k multi 95 60

See Sweden Nos. 1538-1539.

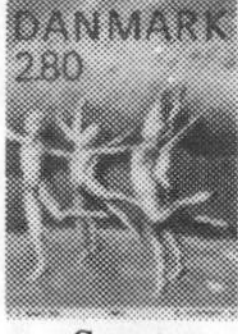

U.N. Decade for Women A257

Sports A258

Lithographed and Engraved

1985, June 27

779 A257 3.80k Cyclist 1.25 60

1985, June 27

780 A258 2.80k Women's floor exercise 90 30
781 A258 3.80k Canoe & kayak 1.25 60
782 A258 6k Cycling 1.75 1.10

Kronborg Castle, Elsinore, 400th Anniv. — A259

Lithographed and Engraved

1985, Sept. 5

783 A259 2.80k multi 90 22

U.N. 40th Anniv. — A260

1985, Sept. 5

784 A260 3.80k Dove, emblem 1.25 60

Niels Bohr (1885-1962), Physicist — A261

Lithographed and Engraved

1985, Oct. 3 *Perf. 13x12½*

785 A261 2.80k With wife Margrethe 90 60

Winner of 1922 Nobel Prize in Physics for theory of atomic structure.

Hand Signing "D" — A262

Boat, by Helge Refn — A263

1985, Nov. 7 **Engr.** *Perf. 13*

786 A262 2.80k multi 90 50

Danish Assoc. for the Deaf, 50th anniv.

1985, Nov. 7 **Litho.**

787 A263 2.80k multi 90 50

Abstract Iron Sculpture by Robert Jacobsen A264

Lithographed and Engraved

1985, Nov. 7 *Perf. 13x12½*

788 A264 3.80k multi 1.25 80

Abstract Painting by Bjorn Wiinblad A265

1986, Jan. 23 **Litho.** *Perf. 13x12½*

789 A265 2.80k multi 95 30

Amnesty Intl., 25th Anniv. A266

Lithographed and Engraved

1986, Jan. 23 *Perf. 13*

790 A266 2.80k multi 95 30

Miniature Sheet

HAFNIA '87 — A267

1986, Feb. 20

791 Sheet of 4 4.25 3.50
a. A267 100o Holstein carriage, c. 1840 95 85
b. A267 250o Iceboat, c. 1880 95 85
c. A267 280o 1st mail van, 1908 95 85
d. A267 380o Airmail service, 1919 95 85

Size: 71x94mm. Sold for 15k.

Changing of the Guard — A268

1986, Mar. 20 *Perf. 13*

792 A268 2.80k multi 95 42

Royal Danish Life Guards barracks and Rosenborg Drilling Ground, bicent.

Types of 1933-82

1986-88 **Engr.** *Perf. 13*

794 A32 270o brt yel grn ('88) 88 8
a. Bklt. pane of 5 (3 No. 318, No. 691, No. 794) 1.50
b. Bklt. pane of 10 (6 No. 318, 2 each Nos. 691, 794) 3.00
797 A212 3k cop red ('88) 95 5
798 A212 3.20k deep vio ('88) 1.00 8
799 A212 3.80k dark vio ('88) 1.20 8
800 A212 4.10k dark blue ('88) 1.30 10
803 A55 4.60k gray ('88) 1.50 15
807 A55 6.50k dp grn 1.50 75
808 A55 6.60k grn ('88) 2.10 30
809 A55 7.10k brn vio ('88) 2.25 35
811 A55 20k dp ultra 4.50 2.25
812 A55 22k hn brn ('87) 6.00 3.00
813 A55 24k dark olive grn ('88) 7.75 2.00
Nos. 794-813 (12) 30.93 9.19

Issue dates: Nos. 807, 811, Jan. 9. No. 812, Jan. 3. Nos. 794, 797-800, 803, 808-809, 813, Jan. 7. Nos. 794a-794b, Jan. 28.

Soro Academy, 400th Anniv. — A269

Lithographed and Engraved

1986, Apr. 28

816 A269 2.80k multi 95 42

Intl. Peace Year — A270

1986, Apr. 28

817 A270 3.80k multi 1.25 65

Crown Prince Frederik, 18th Birthday — A271

1986, May 26 **Litho.**

818 A271 2.80k multi 95 42

Nordic Cooperation Issue 1986 — A272

Sister towns.

1986, May 27 **Engr.**

819 A272 2.80k Aalborg Harbor 95 42
820 A272 3.80k Thisted Church and Town Hall 1.25 65

Hoje Tastrup Train Station Opening, May 31 — A273

1986, May 27 **Litho.**

821 A273 2.80k multi 95 42

Mailbox, Telegraph Lines, Telephone A274

Natl. Bird Candidates A275

1986, June 19 **Litho.** *Perf. 13*

822 A274 2.80k multi 95 42

19th European Intl. PTT Congress, Copenhagen, Aug. 12-16.

Lithographed and Engraved

1986, June 19

Finalists: No. 823a, Corvus corax. No. 823b, Sturnus vulgaris. No. 823c, Cygnus olor (winner). No. 823d, Vanellus vanellus. No. 823e, Alauda arvensis.

823 Strip of 5 4.75 2.25
a.-e. A275 2.80k, any single 95 42

Danish Rifle, Gymnastics and Sports Club, 125th Anniv. — A276

1986, June 19

824 A276 2.80k multi 95 42

Souvenir Sheet

HAFNIA '87 — A277

1986, Sept. 4

825 Sheet of 4 4.75 4.75
a. A277 100o Mailcoach, c. 1841 1.10 1.10
b. A277 250o Postmaster, c. 1840 1.10 1.10
c. A277 280o Postman, c. 1851 1.10 1.10
d. A277 380o Rural postman, c. 1893 1.25 1.25

Sold for 15k.

Europa 1986 — A278

1986, Sept. 4 **Engr.**

826 A278 2.80k Street sweeper 95 42
827 A278 3.80k Garbage truck 1.25 62

Cupid — A279

1986, Oct. 9 **Litho.**

828 A279 3.80k multi 1.25 62

Premiere of The Whims of Cupid and the Ballet Master, by Vincenzo Galeotti, bicent.

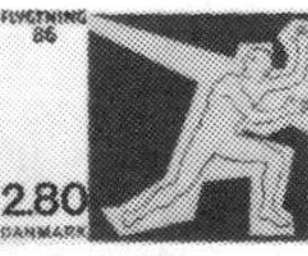

Refugee — A280

Lithographed and Engraved

1986, Oct. 9

829 A280 2.80k multi 95 42

Danish Refugee Council Relief Campaign.

Protestant Reformation in Denmark, 450th Anniv. — A281

Design: Sermon, altarpiece detail, 1561, Thorslunde Church, Copenhagen.

1986, Oct. 9 **Litho.** *Perf. 13*

830 A281 6.50k multi 2.25 1.10

Organization for Economic Cooperation and Development, 25th Anniv. — A282

Lithographed and Engraved

1986, Nov. 6
831 A282 3.80k multi 1.25 62

Abstract by Lin Utzon A283

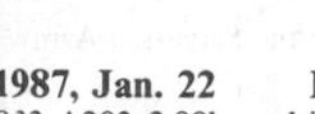
Danish Consumer Council, 40th Anniv. A284

1987, Jan. 22 Litho. *Perf. 13*
832 A283 2.80k multi 82 40

Art appreciation.

1987, Feb. 26 Engr. *Perf. 13*
833 A284 2.80k lake & blk 82 40

Religious Art (Details) from Ribe Cathedral — A285

1987, Apr. 9 Litho. *Perf. 13*
834 A285 3k Fresco 90 45
835 A285 3.80k Stained-glass window 1.15 58
a. Bklt. pane of 10 11.50
836 A285 6.50k Mosaic 1.90 95

Ribe Cathedral redecoration, 1982-1987, by Carl-Henning Pedersen.

Europa 1987 — A286

Modern architecture: 2.80k, Central Library, Gentofte, 1985, vert. 3.80k, Hoje Tastrup High School, 1985.

1987, May 4 Engr. *Perf. 13*
837 A286 2.80k brt ultra 85 42
838 A286 3.80k rose claret 1.15 58

Danish Academy of Technical Sciences (ATV), 50th Anniv. A287

1987, May 4
839 A287 2.50k dark red & blue blk 75 38

8th Gymnaestrada, Herning, July 7-11 — A288

1987, June 18 Litho. & Engr.
840 A288 2.80k multi 80 45

Danish Cooperative Bacon Factories, Cent. — A289

1987, June 18
841 A289 3.80k multi 1.20 60

World Rowing Championships, Aug. 23-30 — A290

1987, Aug. 27 Litho.
842 A290 3.80k Single-sculler 1.10 55

HAFNIA '87, Bella Center, Copenhagen, Oct. 16-25 — A291

1987, Aug. 27 Engr. *Perf. 13x12½*
843 A291 280o Type A15, mail train c. 1912 80 40

Souvenir Sheet

843A A291 280o like No. 843, green lawn and locomotive 12.75 12.75

Purchase of No. 843A included admission to the exhibition. No. 843A has multicolored decorative margin picturing folk and transportation of Copenhagen, c. 1912. Sold for 45k. Size:

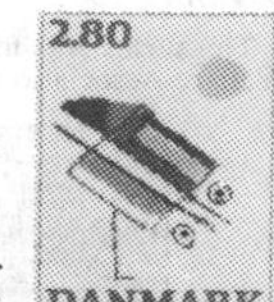

Abstact by Ejler Bille — A292

1987, Sept. 24 Litho. *Perf. 13*
844 A292 2.80k multi 82 40

Rasmus Rask (1787-1832), Linguist — A293

1987, Oct. 15 Engr. *Perf. 13x12½*
845 A293 2.80k dark henna brn 82 40

Clerical Assoc. for the Home Mission in Denmark, 125th Anniv. — A294

Emblem: Miraculous Catch (Luke 5:4-7), New Testament.

1987, Oct. 15 *Perf. 13*
846 A294 3k car lake 88 45

Accession of Christian IV (1577-1648), King of Denmark and Norway (1588-1648), 400th Anniv. — A295

Designs: 3k, Two lions from the gate of Rosenburg Castle around the monogram of Christian IV. 4.10k, Portrait of the monarch painted by P. Isaacsz, vert.

Photo. & Engr., Litho. (4.10k)

1988, Feb. 18 *Perf. 13*
847 A295 3k 95 48
848 A295 4.10k 1.30 65

Ole Worm (1588-1654), Archaeologist, and Runic Artifacts A296

1988, Feb. 18 Engr.
849 A296 7.10k choc 2.25 1.15

SEMI-POSTAL STAMPS

Nos. 159, 157 Surcharged in Red

Wmk. Multiple Crosses. (114)

1921, June 17 *Perf. 14½x14*
B1 A20 10o + 5o grn 25.00 40.00
B2 A21 20o + 10o sl 30.00 47.50

Crown and Staff of Aesculapius SP1

Dybbol Mill SP2

1929, Aug. 1 **Engr.**

B3 SP1 10o yel grn 5.50 5.50
a. Bklt. pane of 2 25.00
B4 SP1 15o brick red 7.00 7.00
a. Bklt. pane of 2 30.00
B5 SP1 25o dp bl 30.00 30.00
a. Bklt. pane of 2 125.00

These stamps were sold at a premium of 5 öre each for benefit of the Danish Cancer Committee.

1937, Jan. 20 **Unwmk.** ***Perf. 13***

B6 SP2 5(o) + 5(o) grn 1.50 1.50
B7 SP2 10(o) + 5(o) lt brn 5.00 5.00
B8 SP2 15(o) + 5(o) car 5.00 5.00

The surtax was for a fund in memory of H. P. Hanssen, statesman.

Nos. 223a and B6, Nos. 229 and B7, Nos. 238A and B8 are found se-tenant in booklets. For booklet panes, see Nos. 223d, 229b and 238e.

Queen Alexandrine SP3

Princesses Ingrid and Margrethe SP4

1939-41 ***Perf. 13***

B9 SP3 5o + 3o rose lake & red ('40) 40 40
a. Booklet pane of 4 2.00 2.00
B10 SP3 10o + 5o dk vio & red 50 35
B11 SP3 15o + 5o scar & red 1.00 1.00

The surtax was for the Danish Red Cross.

Nos. 230 and B10 have been issued se-tenant in booklets. See No. 230b. In this pane No. 230 measures 23½x31mm. from perf. to perf.

1941-43

B12 SP4 10(o) + 5(o) dk vio 40 40
a. Bklt. pane of 10 25.00
B13 SP4 20(o) + 5(o) red ('43) 40 40

The surtax was for the Children's Charity Fund.

No. 288 Surcharged in Red

1944, May 11

B14 A48 10o + 5o vio 30 30
a. Bklt. pane of 10 35.00

The surtax was for the Danish Red Cross.

Symbols of Freedom SP5

Explosions at Rail Junction SP6

Danish Flag SP7

Princess Anne-Marie SP8

1947, May 4 **Engr.** ***Perf. 13***

B15 SP5 15(o) + 5(o) grn 50 50
B16 SP6 20(o) + 5(o) dk red 50 50
B17 SP7 40(o) + 5(o) dp bl 1.25 1.25

Issued in memory of the Danish struggle for liberty and the liberation of Denmark. The surtax was for the Liberty Fund.

1950, Oct. 19 **Unwmk.**

B18 SP8 25o + 5o rose brn 1.00 1.00

The surtax was for the National Children's Welfare Association.

S. S. Jutlandia — SP9

1951, Sept. 13 ***Perf. 13***

B19 SP9 25(o) + 5(o) red 1.25 1.25

The surtax was for the Red Cross.

No. 335 Surcharged in Black **NL ✚ 10**

1953, Feb. 13

B20 A61 30(o) + 10(o) brn red 2.25 2.25

The surtax was for flood relief in the Netherlands.

Stone Memorial — SP10

1953, Mar. 26 ***Perf. 13***

B21 SP10 30(o) + 5(o) dk red 2.25 2.25

The surtax was for cultural work of the Danish Border Union.

Nos. B15 and B16 Surcharged with New Value and Ornamental Screen in Black

1955, Feb. 17

B22 SP5 20(o) + 5 (o) on No. B15 1.75 1.75
B23 SP6 30(o) + 5(o) on No. B16 1.75 1.75

The surtax was for the Liberty Fund.

No. 341 Surcharged **30 + 5 Ungarns-hjælpen**

1957, Mar. 25

B24 A61 30o + 5o on 95o red org 85 85

The surtax went to the Danish Red Cross for aid to Hungary.

No. 335 Surcharged: "Gronlandsfonden + 10"

1959, Feb. 23

B25 A61 30o + 10o brn red 1.50 1.50

The surtax was for the Greenland Fund.

Globe Encircled by Red Cross Flags SP11

Queen Ingrid SP12

1959, June 24 **Engr.** ***Perf. 13***

B26 SP11 30o + 5o rose red 85 65
B27 SP11 60o + 5o lt ultra & car 1.50 1.25

Issued to commemorate the centenary of the International Red Cross idea. The surtax was for the Red Cross. Crosses photogravure on No. B27.

1960, Oct. 25 **Unwmk.**

B28 SP12 30o + 10o dk red 1.50 1.30

Issued to commemorate Queen Ingrid's 25th anniversary as a Girl Scout. The surtax was for the Scouts' fund for needy and sick children.

African Mother and Child SP13

Healthy and Crippled Hands SP14

1962, May 24

B29 SP13 30o + 10o dk red 1.50 1.50

Issued to aid underdeveloped countries.

1963, June 24 ***Perf. 13***

B30 SP14 35o + 10o dk red 1.75 1.75

The surtax was for the benefit of the Cripples' Foundation.

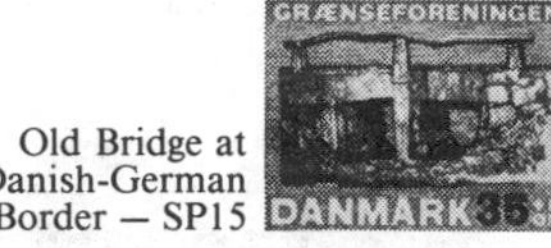
Old Bridge at Danish-German Border — SP15

1964, May 28 **Engr.**

B31 SP15 35o + 10o hn brn 1.00 1.00

The surtax was for the Danish Border Union.

Princesses Margrethe, Benedikte and Anne-Marie SP16

Happy Child SP17

1964, Aug. 24

B32 SP16 35o + 10o dl red 1.25 1.25
B33 SP16 60o + 10o dk bl & red 1.75 1.75

The surtax was for the Red Cross.

1965, Oct. 21 **Engr.** ***Perf. 13***

B34 SP17 50o + 10o brick red 85 85

The surtax was for the National Children's Welfare Association.

"Red Cross" in 32 Languages and Red Cross, Red Lion and Sun, and Red Crescent Emblems SP18

1966, Jan. 20 **Engr.** ***Perf. 13***

B35 SP18 50o + 10o red 75 75

Engraved and Photogravure

B36 SP18 80o + 10o dk bl & red 1.50 1.50

The surtax was for the Red Cross.

"Refugees 66" — SP19

Symbolic Rose — SP20

1966, Oct. 24 **Engr.** ***Perf. 13***

B37 SP19 40o + 10o sep 1.25 1.25
B38 SP19 50o + 10o rose red 1.25 1.25
B39 SP19 80o + 10o bl 1.75 1.75

The surtax was for aid to refugees.

1967, Oct. 12

B40 SP20 60o + 10o brn red 75 75

The surcharge was for the Salvation Army.

Two Greenland Boys in Round Tower — SP21

1968, Sept. 12 **Engr.** ***Perf. 13***

B41 SP21 60o + 10o dk red 1.10 1.10

The surtax was for child welfare work in Greenland.

Princess Margrethe and Prince Henrik with Prince Frederik — SP22

1969, Dec. 11

B42 SP22 50o + 10o brn & red 1.00 1.00
B43 SP22 60o + 10o brn red & red 1.00 1.00

The surtax was for the Danish Red Cross.

Child Seeking Help — SP23

1970, Mar. 13

B44 SP23 60o + 10o brn red 85 85

Surtax for "Save the Children Fund."

Child — SP24

1971, Apr. 29 **Engr.** ***Perf. 13***

B45 SP24 60o + 10o cop red 85 85

Surtax was for the National Children's Welfare Association.

Marsh Marigold — SP25

1972, Aug. 17
B46 SP25 70o + 10o grn & yel 85 85

Centenary of the Society and Home for the Disabled.

Heimaey Town and Volcano — SP26

1973, Oct. 17 Engr. *Perf. 13*
B47 SP26 70o + 20o vio bl & red 85 85

The surtax was for the victims of the eruption of Heimaey Volcano, Jan. 23, 1973.

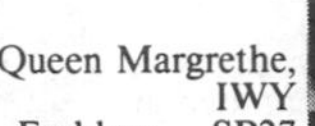

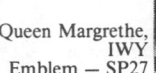

Queen Margrethe, IWY Emblem — SP27

1975, Mar. 20 Engr. *Perf. 13*
B48 SP27 90o + 20o red & buff 1.50 1.50

International Women's Year 1975. Surtax was for a foundation to benefit women primarily in Greenland and Faroe Islands.

Skuldelev I — SP28

Ships: 90ö+20ö, Thingvalla, emigrant steamer. 100ö+20ö, Liner Frederick VIII, c. 1930. 130ö+20ö, Three-master Danmark.

1976, Jan. 22 Engr. *Perf. 13*

B49	SP28	70 + 20o ol brn	1.25	1.25
B50	SP28	90 + 20o brick red	1.25	1.25
B51	SP28	100 + 20o ol grn	1.50	1.50
B52	SP28	130 + 20o vio bl	1.50	1.50

Bicentenary of American Declaration of Independence.

People and Red Cross SP29

Invalid in Wheelchair SP30

1976, Feb. 26 Engr. *Perf. 13*
B53 SP29 100o + 20o red & blk 60 60
B54 SP29 130o + 20o bl, red & blk 85 85

Centenary of Danish Red Cross.

1976, May 6 Engr. *Perf. 13*
B55 SP30 100o + 20o ver & blk 60 60

The surtax was for the Foundation to Aid the Disabled.

Mother and Child SP31

Anti-Cancer Campaign SP32

1977, Mar. 24 Engr. *Perf. 12½*
B56 SP31 1k + 20o multi 60 60

Danish Society for the Mentally Handicapped, 25th anniversary. Surtax was for the Society.

1978, Oct. 12 Engr. *Perf. 13*
B57 SP32 120o + 20o red 60 60

Danish Anti-Cancer Campaign, 50th anniversary. Surtax was for campaign.

Child and IYC Emblem — SP33

1979, Jan. 25 Engr. *Perf. 12½*
B58 SP33 1.20k + 20o red & brn 85 85

International Year of the Child.

Foundation for the Disabled, 25th Anniversary SP34

1980, Apr. 10 Engr. *Perf. 13*
B59 SP34 130o + 20o brn red 60 60

Children Playing Ball — SP35

1981, Feb. 5 Engr. *Perf. 12½x13*
B60 SP35 1.60k + 20o brn red 85 85

Surtax was for child welfare.

Intl. Year of the Disabled — SP36

1981, Sept. 10 Engr. *Perf. 12½x13*
B61 SP36 2k + 20o dk bl 85 85

Stem and Broken Line — SP37

1982, May 3 Engr. *Perf. 13*
B62 SP37 2k + 40o dl red 1.00 1.00

Surtax was for Danish Multiple Sclerosis Society.

Nurse with Patient — SP38

1983, Jan. 27 Engr.
B63 SP38 2k + 40o multi 1.00 1.00

1984 Olympic Games — SP39

Lithographed and Engraved

1984, Feb. 23 *Perf. 13*
B64 SP39 2.70k + 40o multi 1.00 1.00

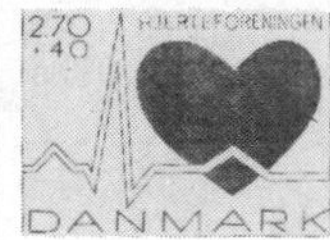

Electrocardiogram Reading, Heart — SP40

1984, Sept. 6 Engr. *Perf. 12½*
B65 SP40 2.70k + 40o red 1.00 1.00

Surtax was for Heart Foundation.

Liberation from German Occupation, 40th Anniv. — SP41

1985, May 2 Litho. *Perf. 13*
B66 SP41 2.80k + 50o multi 1.25 1.25

Surtax for benefit of World War II veterans.

Natl. Society for the Welfare of the Mentally Ill, 25th Anniv. — SP42

Design: Tapestry detail, by Caroline Ebbeson (1852-1936), former patient, St. Hans Hospital, Roskilade.

Lithographed and Engraved

1985, Oct. 3
B67 SP42 2.80k + 40o multi 1.25 1.00

Surtax benefited the mentally ill.

Danish Arthritis Assoc., 50th Anniv. — SP43

1986, Mar. 20 Litho. *Perf. 13*
B68 SP43 2.80k + 50o multi 80 40

Surtax for the Arthritis Assoc.

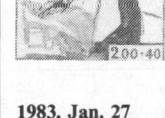

Poul Reichhart (1913-1985), as Papageno in The Magic Flute — SP44

1986, Feb. 6 Litho. *Perf. 13*
B69 SP44 2.80k + 50o multi 85 42

Surtax for the physically handicapped.

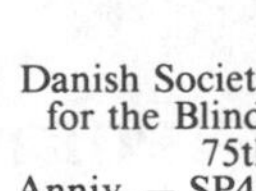

Danish Society for the Blind, 75th Anniv. — SP45

Litho. & Engr.

1986, Feb. 20 *Perf. 13*
B70 SP45 2.80k +50o blk, vio brn & dark red 90 45

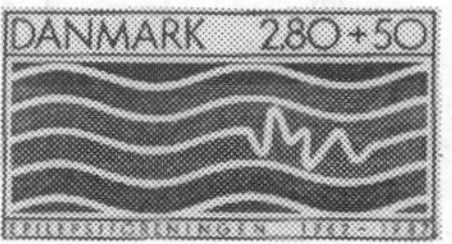

Danish Assoc. of Epileptics, 25th Anniv. SP45

1987, Sept. 24 Engr. *Perf. 13*
B71 SP45 2.80k +50o dark red, brt ultra & dark grn 95 48

AIR POST STAMPS

Airplane and Plowman AP1

Towers of Copenhagen AP2

Wmk. Multiple Crosses. (114)

1925-29 Typo. *Perf. 12x12½*

C1	AP1	10o yel grn	20.00	30.00
C2	AP1	15o vio ('26)	45.00	50.00
C3	AP1	25o scarlet	40.00	45.00
C4	AP1	50o lt gray ('29)	100.00	140.00
C5	AP1	1k choc ('29)	90.00	100.00
		Nos. C1-C5 (5)	295.00	365.00

Unwmk.

1934, June 9 Engr. *Perf. 13*

C6	AP2	10o orange	1.50	1.50
C7	AP2	15o red	5.00	6.00
C8	AP2	20o Prus bl	6.00	6.00
C9	AP2	50o ol blk	5.00	6.00
C10	AP2	1k brown	16.00	17.00
		Nos. C6-C10 (5)	33.50	36.50

LATE FEE STAMPS

Numeral LF1

Coat of Arms LF2

Wmk. Multiple Crosses. (114)

1923 Typo. *Perf. 14x14½*
I1 LF1 10o green 9.00 1.75
a. Double ovpt.

No. I1 was, at first, not a postage stamp but represented a tax for the services of the post office clerks in filling out postal forms and writing addresses. In 1923 it was put into use as a Late Fee stamp.

1926-31
I2 LF2 10o green 3.00 1.75
I3 LF2 10o brn ('31) 2.75 60

1934 Unwmk. Engr. *Perf. 13*
I4 LF2 5o green 40 15
I5 LF2 10o orange 40 20

POSTAGE DUE STAMPS

Regular Issues of 1913-20 Overprinted **PORTO**

Wmk. Multiple Crosses. (114)

1921, May 1 *Perf. 14x14½*
J1 A10 1o dp org 2.00 1.50
J2 A16 5o green 3.25 2.00
J3 A16 7o orange 3.00 2.00
J4 A16 10o red 18.00 9.00
J5 A16 20o dp bl 10.00 5.00
J6 A16 25o brn & blk 15.00 3.25
J7 A16 50o cl & blk 7.00 2.00
Nos. J1-J7 (7) 58.25 24.75

Same Overprint in Dark Blue On Military Stamp of 1917

1921, Nov. 23
J8 A16 10o red 7.00 5.00
a. "S" inverted 140.00 170.00

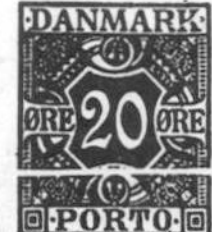

Numeral of Value — D1

Typographed (Solid Panel).

1921-30 *Perf. 14x14½.*
J9 D1 1o org ('22) 60 60
J10 D1 4o bl ('25) 1.75 1.75
J11 D1 5o brn ('22) 1.50 1.00
J12 D1 5o lt grn ('30) 1.00 80
J13 D1 7o ap grn ('27) 16.00 16.00
J14 D1 7o dk vio ('30) 24.00 24.00
J15 D1 10o yel grn ('22) 1.25 60
J16 D1 10o lt brn ('30) 1.10 50
J17 D1 20o grnsh bl ('21) 1.50 75
a. Double impression 1,900.
J18 D1 20o gray ('30) 2.00 1.25
J19 D1 25o scar ('23) 2.50 1.10
J20 D1 25o vio ('26) 2.50 1.40
J21 D1 25o lt bl ('30) 5.00 3.50
J22 D1 1k dk bl ('21) 45.00 7.00
J23 D1 1k brn & dk bl ('25) 15.00 4.25
J24 D1 5k pur ('25) 25.00 8.00
Nos. J9-J24 (16) 145.70 72.50

Engraved (Lined Panel).

1934-55 **Unwmk.** *Perf. 13*
J25 D1 1o slate 18 10
J26 D1 2o carmine 18 10
J27 D1 5o yel grn 18 6
J28 D1 6o dk ol ('41) 60 12
J29 D1 8o mag ('50) 2.00 2.25
J30 D1 10o orange 18 6
J31 D1 12o dp ultra ('55) 45 40
J32 D1 15o vio ('37) 60 10
J33 D1 20o gray 45 10
J34 D1 25o blue 60 18
J35 D1 30o grn ('53) 60 18
J36 D1 40o cl ('49) 75 18
J37 D1 1k brown 1.00 18
Nos. J25-J37 (13) 7.77 4.01

PORTO

No. 96 Surcharged in Black **15**

1934 **Wmk. 114** *Perf. 14x14½*
J38 A10 15o on 12o vio 3.00 1.25

MILITARY STAMPS

Nos. 97 and 100 Overprinted in Blue **S F**

Wmk. Multiple Crosses. (114)

1917 *Perf. 14x14½.*
M1 A16 5o green 22.50 32.50
a. "S" inverted 250.00 375.00
M2 A16 10o red 17.50 27.50
a. "S" inverted 200.00 275.00

The letters "S F" are the initials of "Soldater Frimaerke" (Soldier's Stamp).

OFFICIAL STAMPS

Small State Seal — O1

Wmk. Crown. (112)

1871 **Typo.** *Perf. 14x13½*
O1 O1 2s blue 125.00 90.00
a. 2s ultra 125.00 90.00
b. Imperf., pair 525.00
O2 O1 4s carmine 70.00 16.00
a. Imperf., pair 500.00
O3 O1 16s green 325.00 250.00
a. Imperf., pair 650.00

Perf. 12½.
O4 O1 4s carmine 4,400. 400.00
O5 O1 16s green 350.00 375.00

Nos. O1, O2 and O3 were reprinted in 1886 upon white wove paper, unwatermarked and imperforate. Price $10 each.

1875 *Perf. 14x13½.*
O6 O1 3o violet 3.50 12.00
O7 O1 4o grnsh bl 5.50 3.00
O8 O1 8o carmine 5.50 1.65
a. Imperf., pair
O9 O1 32o green 40.00 35.00

1899-02 *Perf. 13.*
O9A O1 3o red lil ('02) 4.00 4.00
c. Imperf., pair 450.00
O9B O1 4o blue 2.00 1.75
O10 O1 8o carmine 20.00 13.00

1902-06 **Wmk. 113**
O11 O1 1o orange 2.50 2.50
O12 O1 3o red lil ('06) 1.00 1.00
O13 O1 4o bl ('03) 1.75 1.50
O14 O1 5o green 1.50 35
O15 O1 10o carmine 1.50 1.40
Nos. O11-O15 (5) 8.25 6.75

1914-23 **Wmk. 114** *Perf. 14x14½*
O16 O1 1o orange 1.75 1.50
O17 O1 3o gray ('18) 4.50 4.50
O18 O1 4o bl ('16) 32.50 37.50
O19 O1 5o grn ('15) 1.00 35
O20 O1 5o choc ('23) 4.50 *20.00*
O21 O1 10o red ('17) 4.00 1.25
O22 O1 10o grn ('21) 1.50 2.00
O23 O1 15o vio ('19) 32.50 37.50
O24 O1 20o ind ('20) 11.00 7.00
Nos. O16-O24 (9) 93.25 111.60

The use of Official stamps was discontinued April 1, 1924.

NEWSPAPER STAMPS

Numeral of Value — N1

Wmk. Crown. (113)

1907 **Typo.** *Perf. 13*
P1 N1 1o olive 5.00 2.00
P2 N1 5o blue 20.00 12.00
P3 N1 7o carmine 6.50 70
P4 N1 10o dp lil 12.00 3.00
P5 N1 20o green 11.00 1.00
P6 N1 38o orange 16.00 1.00
P7 N1 68o yel brn 32.50 20.00
P8 N1 1k bl grn & cl 12.00 1.50
P9 N1 5k rose & yel grn 90.00 20.00
P10 N1 10k bis & bl 90.00 20.00
Nos. P1-P10 (10) 295.00 81.20

1914-15 **Wmk. 114** *Perf. 14x14½*
P11 N1 1o ol gray 5.00 60
P12 N1 5o blue 14.00 7.00
P13 N1 7o rose 11.00 60
P14 N1 8o grn ('15) 12.00 60
P15 N1 10o dp lil 12.00 60
P16 N1 20o green 140.00 1.75
a. Imperf., pair *600.00*
P17 N1 29o org yel ('15) 18.00 1.40
P18 N1 38o orange 3,250. 160.00
P19 N1 41o yel brn ('15) 18.00 1.25
P20 N1 1k bl grn & mar 30.00 65
Nos. P11-P17,P19-P20 (9) 260.00 14.45

PARCEL POST STAMPS

These stamps were for use on postal packets sent by the Esbjerg-Fano Ferry Service.

Regular Issues of 1913-30 Overprinted **POSTFÆRGE**

1919-41 **Wmk. 114** *Perf. 14x14½*
Q1 A10 10o grn ('22) 16.00 11.00
Q2 A10 10o bis brn ('30) 14.00 6.00
Q3 A16 10o red 60.00 70.00
a. "POSFFAERGE" 225.00 450.00
Q4 A16 15o violet 22.50 27.50
a. "POSFFAERGE" 225.00 *450.00*
Q5 A16 30o org ('22) 16.00 16.00
Q6 A16 30o dk bl ('26) 4.00 4.00
Q7 A16 50o cl & blk ('20) 250.00 275.00
Q8 A16 50o lt gray ('22) 22.50 10.00
a. 50o dk gray ('22) 135.00 160.00
Q9 A16 1k brn & bl ('24) 60.00 18.00
Q9A A16 5k vio & brn ('41) 4.00 3.50
Q10 A16 10k ver & grn ('30) 90.00 90.00

Engr.
Q11 A17 1k yel brn 150.00 150.00
a. "POSFFAERGE" 1,700. 2,750.
Nos. Q1-Q11 (12) 709.00 681.00

1927-30
Q12 A30 15o red ('27) 22.50 14.00
Q13 A30 30o ocher ('27) 22.50 15.00
Q14 A30 40o yel grn ('30) 20.00 8.50

Overprinted on Regular Issues of 1933-40.

1936-42 **Unwmk.** *Perf. 13*
Q15 A32 5o rose lake ('42) 25 20
Q16 A32 10o yel org 35.00 27.50
Q17 A32 10o lt brn ('38) 2.00 2.00
Q18 A32 10o pur ('39) 35 35
Q19 A30 15o dp red 1.25 1.50
Q20 A30 30o bl, I 7.00 6.00
Q21 A30 30o bl, II ('40) 10.00 12.50
Q22 A30 30o org, II ('42) 1.00 90
Q23 A30 40o yel grn, I 7.00 6.00
Q24 A30 40o yel grn, II ('40) 10.00 11.00
Q25 A30 40o bl, II ('42) 1.25 1.25
Q26 A33 50o gray 2.25 2.25
Q27 A33 1k lt brn 1.75 1.50
Nos. Q15-Q27 (13) 79.10 72.95

Overprinted on Nos. 284, 286 and 286B

1945
Q28 A47 30o orange 2.00 1.75
Q29 A47 40o blue 1.75 1.75
Q30 A47 50o gray 2.25 1.75

Overprinted on Nos. 318, 309, 310, 312 and 297.

1949-53
Q31 A32 10o grn ('53) 35 35
Q32 A61 30o orange 2.50 2.00
Q33 A61 40o dl bl 2.50 2.00
Q34 A61 50o gray ('50) 15.00 3.50
Q35 A55 1k brn ('50) 2.00 1.75
Nos. Q31-Q35 (5) 22.35 9.60

Overprinted on Nos. 335, 323, 336, 326 and 397.

1955-65
Q36 A61 30o brn red 1.20 1.10
Q37 A61 40o gray 1.00 1.00
Q38 A61 50o aqua 1.25 1.25
Q39 A61 70o dp grn 1.25 1.25
Q40 A55 1.25k org ('65) 7.00 8.00
Nos. Q36-Q40 (5) 11.70 12.60

Overprinted on Nos. 417 and 419.

1967 **Engr.** *Perf. 13*
Q41 A86 40o brown 1.00 1.00
Q42 A86 80o ultra 1.00 1.00

Nos. 224, 438, 441, 297-299 Overprinted **POSTFÆRGE**

1967-74 **Engr.** *Perf. 13*
Q43 A32 5o rose lake 30 30
Q44 A86 50o brn ('74) 70 70
Q45 A86 90o ultra ('70) 1.40 1.40
Q46 A55 1k brown 1.75 1.50
Q47 A55 2k red ('72) 2.25 2.25
Q48 A55 5k dl bl ('72) 5.00 4.50
Nos. Q43-Q48 (6) 11.40 10.65

Nos. Q44-Q45, Q47-Q48 are on fluorescent paper.

Overprinted on No. 544

1975, Feb. 27
Q49 A161 100o dp ultra 1.25 1.25

DIEGO-SUAREZ

LOCATION — A town at the northern end of Madagascar
GOVT. — Former French colony
POP. — 12,237

From 1885 to 1896 Diego-Suarez, (Antsirane), a French naval base, was a separate colony and issued its own stamps. These were succeeded by stamps of Madagascar.

100 Centimes = 1 Franc

Stamps of French Colonies Handstamp Surcharged in Violet

1890 **Unwmk.** *Perf. 14x13½*
1 A9 15c on 1c *bl* 225.00 70.00
2 A9 15c on 5c grn, *grnsh* 575.00 70.00
3 A9 15c on 10c *lav* 250.00 70.00
4 A9 15c on 20c red, *grn* 575.00 70.00
5 A9 15c on 25c *rose* 95.00 35.00

This surcharge is found inverted, double, etc. Counterfeits exist.

Ship Flying French Flag — A2

Symbolical of Union of France and Madagascar
A3 A4

France — A5

1890 **Litho.** *Imperf.*
6 A2 1c black 950.00 200.00
7 A3 5c black 925.00 150.00
8 A4 15c black 225.00 70.00
9 A5 25c black 250.00 80.00

A6

1891
10 A6 5c black 225.00 87.50

Excellent counterfeits exist of Nos. 6 to 10.

Stamps of French Colonies Surcharged in Red or Black:

a

b

1892 *Perf. 14x13½*

No.	Type	Description	Unused	Used
11	A9 (a)	5c on 10c *lav* (R)	175.00	77.50
a.		Inverted surcharge	350.00	275.00
12	A9 (b)	5c on 20c red, *grn*	160.00	57.50
a.		Inverted surcharge	350.00	275.00

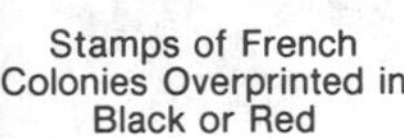
Stamps of French Colonies Overprinted in Black or Red

1892

No.	Type	Description	Unused	Used
13	A9	1c bl (R)	21.00	11.00
a.		Inverted overprint	160.00	130.00
14	A9	2c brn, *buff*	21.00	11.00
a.		Inverted overprint	160.00	130.00
15	A9	4c cl, *lav*	37.50	25.00
16	A9	5c grn, *grnsh*	82.50	60.00
a.		Inverted overprint	160.00	130.00
17	A9	10c *lavender*	25.00	19.00
a.		Inverted overprint	160.00	130.00
18	A9	15c *blue*	21.00	14.00
19	A9	20c red, *grn*	25.00	17.00
20	A9	25c *rose*	19.00	11.00
a.		Inverted overprint	160.00	130.00
21	A9	30c brn, *bis* (R)	1,000.	700.00
a.		Inverted overprint		1,300.
22	A9	35c *yellow*	1,000.	700.00
a.		Inverted overprint		1,300.
23	A9	75c car, *rose*	52.50	32.50
24	A9	1fr brnz grn, *straw* (R)	52.50	32.50
a.		Double overprint	190.00	160.00

Navigation and Commerce
A10 A11

1892 **Typo.**

Name of Colony in Blue or Carmine.

No.	Type	Description	Unused	Used
25	A10	1c *blue*	1.65	1.65
26	A10	2c brn, *buff*	1.75	1.65
27	A10	4c cl, *lav*	1.50	1.50
28	A10	5c grn, *grnsh*	4.00	2.50
29	A10	10c *lavender*	5.50	3.00
30	A10	15c bl, quadrille paper	6.50	5.25
31	A10	20c red, *grn*	12.00	9.50
32	A10	25c *rose*	10.50	7.75
33	A10	30c brn, *bis*	13.00	9.50
34	A10	40c red, *straw*	16.00	11.00
35	A10	50c car, *rose*	32.50	17.50
36	A10	75c vio, *org*	32.50	20.00
37	A10	1fr brnz grn, *straw*	50.00	30.00
		Nos. 25-37 (13)	187.40	120.80

1894

No.	Type	Description	Unused	Used
38	A11	1c *blue*	90	1.00
39	A11	2c brn, *buff*	1.75	1.50
40	A11	4c cl, *lav*	1.75	1.50
41	A11	5c grn, *grnsh*	3.50	2.75
42	A11	10c *lavender*	5.25	3.50
43	A11	15c bl, quadrille paper	5.25	3.50
44	A11	20c red, *grn*	11.00	7.75
45	A11	25c *rose*	6.00	3.50
46	A11	30c brn, *bis*	7.00	4.25
47	A11	40c red, *straw*	7.75	4.25
48	A11	50c car, *rose*	11.00	8.75
49	A11	75c vio, *org*	7.75	4.25
50	A11	1fr brnz grn, *straw*	17.50	14.00
		Nos. 38-50 (13)	86.40	60.50

Bisected stamps of type A11 are mentioned in note after Madagascar No. 62.

POSTAGE DUE STAMPS.

D1

D2

1891 **Unwmk.** **Litho.** ***Imperf.***

No.	Type	Description	Unused	Used
J1	D1	5c violet	130.00	52.50
J2	D2	50c black	130.00	52.50

Excellent counterfeits exist of Nos. J1 and J2.

Postage Due Stamps of French Colonies Overprinted Like Nos. 13-24

1892

No.	Type	Description	Unused	Used
J3	D1	1c black	95.00	37.50
J4	D1	2c black	95.00	37.50
a.		Inverted overprint	350.00	250.00
J5	D1	3c black	95.00	42.50
J6	D1	4c black	95.00	42.50
J7	D1	5c black	95.00	42.50
J8	D1	10c black	26.00	18.00
a.		Inverted overprint	350.00	250.00
J9	D1	15c black	26.00	18.00
a.		Double overprint	525.00	425.00
J10	D1	20c black	160.00	80.00
J11	D1	30c black	82.50	42.50
a.		Inverted overprint	350.00	250.00
J12	D1	60c black	1,100.	700.00
J13	D1	1fr brown	1,750.	1,100.

DJIBOUTI

LOCATION — East Africa
GOVT. — Republic
AREA — 8,880 sq. mi.
POP. — 340,000 (est. 1983)
CAPITAL — Djibouti

The French territory of Afars and Issas became the Republic of Djibouti June 27, 1977. For 1894-1902 issues with "Djibouti" or "DJ," see Somali Coast.

Afars and Issas Issues of 1972-1977 Overprinted and Surcharged with Bars and "REPUBLIQUE DE DJIBOUTI" in Black, Dark Green, Blue or Brown

Printing and Perforations as Before

1977

No.	Type	Description	Unused	Used
439	A63	1fr on 4fr (#358;B)	5	5
440	A81	2fr on 5fr (#433;B)	5	5
441	A75	5fr on 20fr (#421;B)	15	15
442	A70	8fr (#380;B)	22	22
443	A71	20fr (#387;DG)	45	45
444	A81	30fr (#434;B)	60	60
445	A71	40fr (#388;DG)	75	75
446	A71	45fr (#389;Bl)	90	90
447	A78	45fr (#428;B)	90	90
448	A72	50fr (#394;B)	1.10	1.10
449	A71	60fr (#391;Br)	1.25	1.25
450	A79	70fr (#430;B)	1.50	1.50
451	A81	70fr (#435;B)	1.50	1.50
452	A74	100fr (#418;B)	2.00	2.00
453	A72	150fr (#399;B)	3.00	3.00
454	A76	200fr (#422;B)	4.00	4.00
455	A80	200fr (#432;B)	4.00	4.00
456	A74	300fr (#419;B)	6.75	6.75
		Nos. 439-456,C106-108 (21)	41.92	41.17

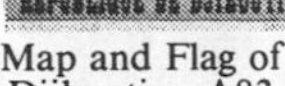
Map and Flag of Djibouti — A83

Water Pipe — A84

Design: 65fr, Map and flag of Djibouti, map of Africa (horiz.).

1977, June 27 **Litho.** ***Perf. 12½***

No.	Type	Description	Unused	Used
457	A83	45fr multi	1.00	60
458	A83	65fr multi	1.50	75

Independence, June 27.

1977, July 4

Designs: 10fr, Headrest (horiz.). 25fr, Pitcher.

No.	Type	Description	Unused	Used
459	A84	10fr multi	22	15
460	A84	20fr multi	45	18
461	A84	25fr multi	60	28

Ostrich — A85

Design: 100fr, Weaver.

1977, Aug. 11 **Litho.** ***Perf. 12½***

No.	Type	Description	Unused	Used
462	A85	90fr multi	1.75	1.25
463	A85	100fr multi	2.25	1.50

Snail — A86

Designs: 15fr, Fiddler crab. 50fr, Klipspringers. 70fr, Green turtle. 80fr, Priacanthus hamrur (fish). 150fr, Dolphinfish.

1977 **Litho.** ***Perf. 12½***

No.	Type	Description	Unused	Used
464	A86	15fr multi	22	18
465	A86	45fr multi	45	38
466	A86	50fr multi	90	55
467	A86	70fr multi	85	50
468	A86	80fr multi	1.00	60
469	A86	150fr multi	3.00	1.75
		Nos. 464-469 (6)	6.42	3.96

Issue dates: 45fr, 70fr, 80fr, Sept. 14. Others, Dec. 5.

Pres. Hassan Gouled Aptidon and Djibouti Flag — A87

1978, Feb. 12 **Litho.** ***Perf. 13***

No.	Type	Description	Unused	Used
470	A87	65fr multi	1.10	60

Charaxes Hansali — A88

Necklace — A89

Butterflies: 20fr, Colias electo. 25fr, Acraea chilo. 150fr, Junonia hierta.

1978, Mar. 13 **Litho.** ***Perf. 12½x13***

No.	Type	Description	Unused	Used
471	A88	5fr multi	5	5
472	A88	20fr multi	22	12
473	A88	25fr multi	45	28
474	A88	150fr multi	2.00	85

1978, May 29 **Litho.** ***Perf. 12½x13***

Design: 55fr, Necklace (different).

No.	Type	Description	Unused	Used
475	A89	45fr pink & multi	60	35
476	A89	55fr bl & multi	70	40

Bougainvillea A90

Flowers: 35fr, Hibiscus schizopetalus. 250fr, Caesalpinia pulcherrima.

1978, July 10 **Photo.** ***Perf. 12½x13***

No.	Type	Description	Unused	Used
477	A90	15fr multi	22	12
478	A90	35fr multi	50	28
479	A90	250fr multi	3.00	1.25

Charonia Nodifera — A91

Sea Shell: 80fr, Charonia variegata.

1978, Oct. 9 **Litho.** ***Perf. 13***

No.	Type	Description	Unused	Used
480	A91	10fr multi	15	6
481	A91	80fr multi	1.10	45

Chaetodon A92

Fish: 30fr, Yellow surgeonfish. 40fr, Harlequinfish.

1978, Nov. 20 **Litho.** ***Perf. 13x12½***

No.	Type	Description	Unused	Used
482	A92	8fr multi	15	6
483	A92	30fr multi	40	15
484	A92	40fr multi	50	22

Alsthom BB 1201 at Dock — A93

Locomotives: 55fr, Steam locomotive 231. 60fr, Steam locomotive 130 and map of route. 75fr, Diesel.

1979, Jan. 29 **Litho.** ***Perf. 13***

No.	Type	Description	Unused	Used
485	A93	40fr multi	60	22
486	A93	55fr multi	75	30
487	A93	60fr multi	90	30
488	A93	75fr multi	1.25	38

Djibouti-Addis Ababa railroad.

Certain countries cancel stamps in full sheets and sell them (usually with gum) for less than face value. Dealers generally sell "CTO".

Children and IYC Emblem — A94

Design: 200fr, Mother and child, IYC emblem.

1979, Feb. 26 Litho. *Perf. 13*

489 A94 20fr multi 30 15
490 A94 200fr multi 2.75 1.75

International Year of the Child.

Plane over Ardoukoba Volcano — A95

Design: 30fr, Helicopter over Ardoukoba Volcano (vert.).

1979, Mar. 19

491 A95 30fr multi 45 38
492 A95 90fr multi 1.35 75

Rowland Hill, Postal Clerks, No. C109 — A96

Designs: 100fr, Somali Coast No. 22, Djibouti No. 457, letters, Rowland Hill. 150fr, Letters hoisted onto ship, smoke signals, Rowland Hill.

1979, Apr. 17 Litho. *Perf. 13x12½*

493 A96 25fr multi 38 15
494 A96 100fr multi 1.40 60
495 A96 150fr multi 2.00 1.00

Sir Rowland Hill (1795-1879), originator of penny postage.

View of Djibouti, Bird and Local Woman — A97

Design: 80fr, Map and flag of Djibouti, UPU emblem, Concorde, train and mail runner.

1979, June 8 Litho. *Perf. 13x12½*

496 A97 55fr multi 1.25 90
497 A97 80fr multi 1.75 1.25

Philexafrique II, Libreville, Gabon, June 8-17. Nos. 496, 497 each printed in sheets of 10 with 5 labels showing exhibition emblem.

Scott's International Album provides spaces for an extensive representative collection of the world's postage stamps.

Solanacea A98

Flowers: 2fr, Opuntia (vert.). 15fr, Trichodesma. 45fr, Acacia etbaica. 50fr, Thunbergia alata (vert.).

Perf. 13x13½, 13½x13

1979, June 18

498 A98 2fr multi 5 5
499 A98 8fr multi 15 8
500 A98 15fr multi 20 8
501 A98 45fr multi 50 18
502 A98 50fr multi 65 18
Nos. 498-502 (5) 1.55 57

Running — A99

Olympic Emblem and: 70fr, Basketball 200fr, Soccer (horiz.).

Perf. 12½x13, 13x12½

1979, Oct. 22 Litho.

503 A99 70fr multi 85 38
504 A99 120fr multi 1.75 75
505 A99 200fr multi 2.75 1.10

Pre-Olympic Year.

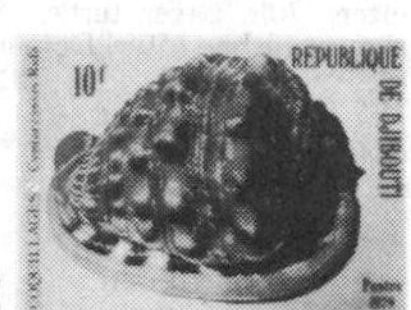

Cypraecassis Rufa — A100

Shells: 40fr, Lambis chiragra arthritica. 300fr, Harpa connaidalis.

1979, Dec. 22 Litho. *Perf. 13*

506 A100 10fr multi 12 8
507 A100 40fr multi 50 22
508 A100 300fr multi 3.75 1.60

Rotary International, 75th Anniversary — A101

1980, Feb. 19 Litho. *Perf. 13x12½*

509 A101 90fr multi 1.50 75

Lions Club of Djibouti — A102

1980, Feb. 19

510 A102 100fr multi 1.65 75

Colotis Danae — A103

1980, Mar. 17 *Perf. 13x13½*

511 A103 5fr *shown* 16 5
512 A103 55fr *Danaus chrysippus* 1.40 30

Chess Players, Knight — A104

Chess Federation Creation: 75fr, Chess Game, Florence, 1493.

1980, June 9 Litho. *Perf. 13*

513 A104 20fr multi 40 12
514 A104 75fr multi 1.25 40

Cribraria A105

1980, Aug. 12 Litho. *Perf. 13*

515 A105 15fr *shown* 20 8
516 A105 85fr *Nautilius pompilius* 1.10 45

Alexander Fleming, Discoverer of Penicillin — A106

Design: 130fr, Jules Verne, French science fiction writer; earth, moon and spacecraft.

1980, Sept. 1

517 A106 20fr multi 30 12
518 A106 130fr multi 1.75 70

Capt. Cook and Endeavor — A107

Capt James Cook Death Bicentenary: 90fr, Ships and Maps of voyages.

1980, Nov. 20 Litho. *Perf. 13*

519 A107 55fr multi 60 30
520 A107 90fr multi 1.10 55

Souvenir sheets of 1 exist, perf. 12½x12.

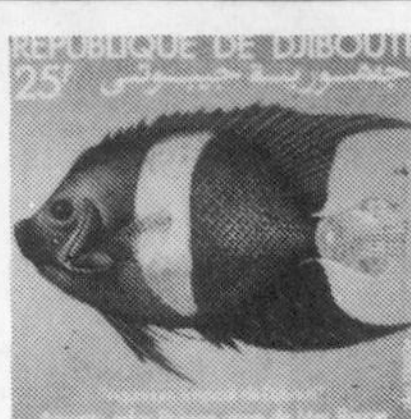

Angel Fish — A108

1981, Apr. 13 Litho. *Perf. 12½*

521 A108 25fr shown 30 12
522 A108 55fr Moorish idol 60 28
523 A108 70fr Scad 75 45

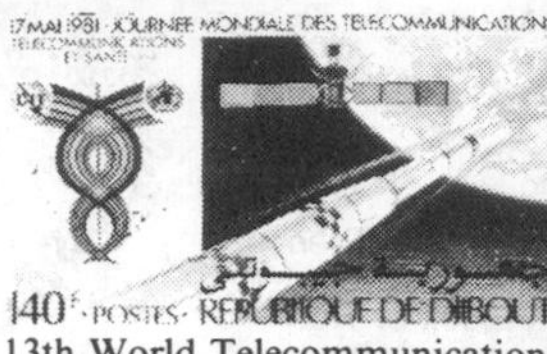

13th World Telecommunications Day — A109

1981, May 17 Litho. *Perf. 13*

524 A109 140fr multi 1.75 75

Type 231 Steam Locomotive, Germany, 1958 and Amtrak, US, 1980 — A110

Locomotives: 55fr, Stephenson and his Rocket, Djibouti Railways 230 engine. 65fr, Type TGV, France, Type 962, Japan.

1981, June 9 Litho. *Perf. 13*

525 A110 40fr multi 45 28
526 A110 55fr multi 60 30
527 A110 65fr multi 75 35

Radio Amateurs Club — A111

1981, June 25

528 A111 250fr multi 3.00 1.50

Prince Charles and Lady Diana — A112

1981, June 29

529 A112 180fr shown 2.25 1.25
530 A112 200fr Couple, diff. 2.50 1.50

Royal Wedding.

Lord Nelson and Victory — A113

1981, July 6 Litho. *Perf. 13x12½*
531 A113 100fr multi 1.25 75
532 A113 175fr multi 2.00 1.25

Lord Horatio Nelson (1758-1805).

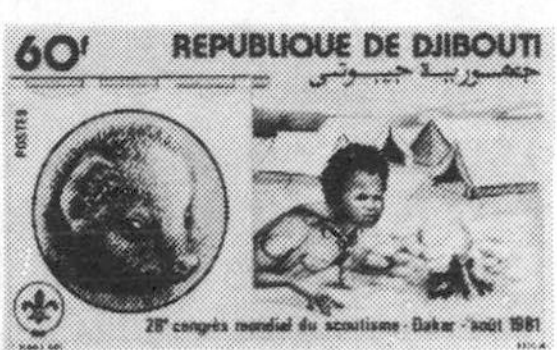

Scout Tending Campfire — A114

1981, July 16 Litho. *Perf. 13*
533 A114 60fr shown 75 45
534 A114 105fr Scout giving sign 1.25 60

28th World Scouting Conference, Dakar, Aug. (60fr); 4th Pan-African Scouting Conference, Abidjan, Aug. (105fr).

Pawn and Queen, Swedish Bone Chess Pieces, 13th Cent. — A115

1981, Oct. 15 Litho. *Perf. 13*
535 A115 50fr shown 60 38
536 A115 130fr Pawn, knight, Chinese, 19th cent. vert. 1.75 1.00

Sheraton Hotel Opening — A116

1981, Nov. 15 Litho. *Perf. 13x12½*
537 A116 75fr multi 90 55

Acacia Mellifera A117

1981, Dec. 21 *Perf. 13*
538 A117 10fr Clitoria ternatea, vert. 12 8
539 A117 30fr shown 38 18
540 A117 35fr Punica granatum 40 28
541 A117 45fr Malvaceous plant, vert. 50 30

Nos. 535-536 Overprinted with Winners' Names.

1981, Dec. Litho. *Perf. 13*
542 A115 50fr multi 60 45
543 A115 130fr multi 1.75 1.10

World Chess Championship.

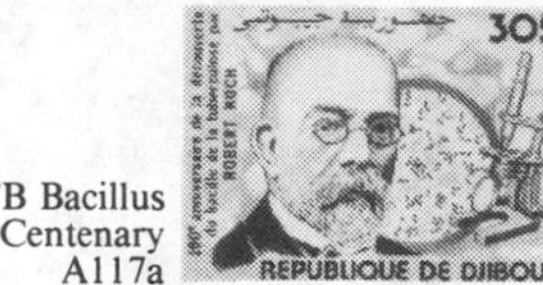

TB Bacillus Centenary A117a

1982 Litho. *Perf. 13*
544 A117a 305fr Koch, slide, microscope 2.25 1.50

1982 World Chess Championship A117b

14th World Telecommunications Day — A118

1982, Apr. 8 Litho. *Perf. 13*
545 A117b 125fr Ivory bishop 1.50 1.00
546 A117b 175fr Queen, pawn, 19th cent. 2.25 1.25

1982, May 17
547 A118 150fr multi 1.75 1.25

Bus and Jeep — A119

1982, July 27 Litho. *Perf. 13*
548 A119 20fr shown 22 15
549 A119 25fr Dhow, ferry 30 22
550 A119 55fr Train, jet 65 45

Shells from the Red Sea — A120

1982, Nov. 20 Litho. *Perf. 12½*
551 A120 10fr Cypraea erythraeensis 12 8
552 A120 15fr Conus sumatrensis 18 12
553 A120 25fr Cypraea pulchra 30 18
554 A120 30fr Conus inscriptus 38 22
555 A120 70fr Casmaria ponderosa 85 55
556 A120 150fr Cypraea exusta 1.75 1.25
Nos. 551-556 (6) 3.58 2.40

See Nos. 563-567.

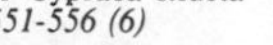

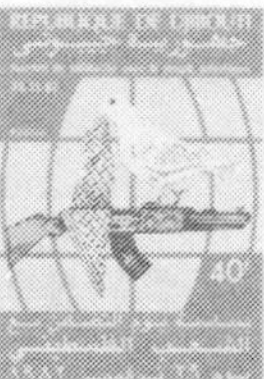

Intl. Palestinian Solidarity Day — A121

1982, Nov. 29 Litho. *Perf. 13*
557 A121 40fr multi 60 40

Local Flowers A122

Various flowers. 5fr, 55fr vert.

1983, Apr. 14 Litho. *Perf. 13*
558 A122 5fr multi 8 6
559 A122 50fr multi 80 60
560 A122 55fr multi 90 65

World Communications Year — A123

1983, June 20 Litho. *Perf. 13*
561 A123 500fr multi 8.00 6.00

Conference of Donors, Nov. 21-23 — A124

1983, Nov. 21 Litho. *Perf. 13x12½*
562 A124 75fr multi 1.10 80

Shell Type of 1982

1983, Dec. 20 Litho. *Perf. 12½*
563 A120 15fr Marginella obtusa 22 16
564 A120 30fr Conus jickelli 42 32
565 A120 55fr Cypraea macandrewi 78 58
566 A120 80fr Conus cuvieri 1.10 90
567 A120 100fr Turbo petholatus 1.40 1.10
Nos. 563-567 (5) 3.92 3.06

Local Butterflies A125

1984, Jan. 24 Litho. *Perf. 13½x13*
568 A125 5fr Colotis chrysonome 8 6
569 A125 20fr Colias erate 28 22
570 A125 30fr Junonia orithyia 42 32
571 A125 75fr Acraea doubledayi 1.10 80
572 A125 110fr Byblia ilithya 1.50 1.10
Nos. 568-572 (5) 3.38 2.50

Landscapes and Animals — A126

1984, Apr. 29 Litho. *Perf. 13*
573 A126 2fr Randa Klipspringer 5 5
574 A126 8fr Ali Sabieh, gazelles 12 10
575 A126 10fr Lake Assal, oryz 14 10
576 A126 15fr Tadjoura, gazelle 22 16
577 A126 40fr Alaila Dada, jackal, vert. 55 42
578 A126 45fr Lake Abbe, warthog 65 50
579 A126 55fr Obock, seagull 80 60
580 A126 125fr Presidential Palace, bird 1.75 1.25
Nos. 573-580 (8) 4.28 3.18

Fire Prevention — A127

1984, Sept. 9 Litho. *Perf. 13*
581 A127 25fr Fire truck 35 28
582 A127 95fr Hook & ladder 1.40 1.00
583 A127 100fr Fire plane 1.40 1.10

International Olympic Committee Membership A128

1984, July 22 Litho. *Perf. 13*
584 A128 45fr Runners 65 50

Motor Carriage, 1886 A128a

1984, Nov. 11 Litho. *Perf. 12½*
585 A128a 35fr shown 50 38
586 A128a 65fr Cabriolet, 1896 90 68
587 A128a 90fr Phoenix, 1900 1.30 1.00

Gottlieb Daimler (1834-1900), pioneer automobile manufacturer.

Marie and Pierre Curie — A129

1984, Dec. 3 Litho. *Perf. 12½*
588 A129 150fr Pierre Curie 2.00 1.65
589 A129 150fr Marie Curie 2.00 1.65

Audubon Bicentenary — A130

1985, Jan. 27 Litho. *Perf. 13*

590 A130 5fr Merops albicollis 8 6
591 A130 15fr Pterocles exustus 22 16
592 A130 20fr Trachyphonus margaritatus somalicus 28 22
593 A130 25fr Coracias garrulus 35 28

Intl. Youth Year — A131

1985, Mar. 26 Litho. *Perf. 13*

594 A131 10fr multi 14 12
595 A131 30fr multi 42 32
596 A131 40fr multi 55 42

German Railways, 150th Anniv. — A132

Designs: 55fr, Engine No. 29, Addis Ababa-Djibouti Railways. 75fr, Adler, museum facsimile of the first German locomotive.

1985, April 22 Litho. *Perf. 13*

597 A132 55fr multi 80 60
598 A132 75fr multi 1.10 80

Scouting — A133

1985, May 23

599 A133 35fr Planting saplings 50 38
600 A133 65fr Hygiene, family health care 90 70

Victor Hugo (1802-1885), Novelist — A134

Authors: 100fr, Arthur Rimbaud (1854-1891), poet.

1985, June 24 Litho.

601 A134 80fr brt bl & sl 1.10 85
602 A134 100fr multi 1.40 1.10

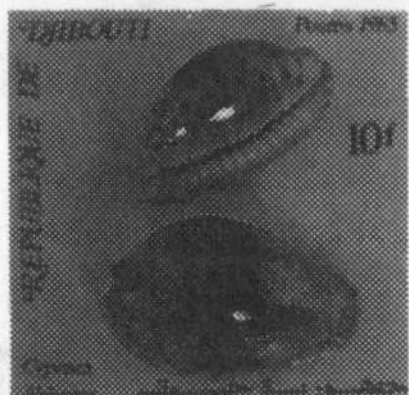

Sea Shells A135

1985, July 15 Litho. *Perf. 12½*

603 A135 10fr Cypraea nebrites 14 12
604 A135 15fr Cypraea turdus 22 16
605 A135 30fr Conus acuminatus 42 32
606 A135 40fr Cypraea camelopardalis 55 42
607 A135 55fr Conus terebra 78 60
Nos. 603-607 (5) 2.11 1.62

1st World Cup Marathon '85, Hiroshima A136

1985, Sept. 2 *Perf. 12½x13*

608 A136 75fr Winners 1.05 80
609 A136 100fr Approaching finish 1.40 1.05

Halley's Comet — A137

Designs: 85fr, Bayeux Tapestry, Comet and Halley. 90fr, Vega I, Giotto space probes, map of planets, comet trajectory.

1986, Jan. 27 Litho. *Perf. 13*

610 A137 85fr multi 1.20 90
611 A137 90fr multi 1.25 95

ISERST Solar Energy Installation — A138

Designs: 50fr, Runners on beach. 150fr, Windmill, headquarters, power control station.

1986, Mar. 20

612 A138 50fr multi 70 52
613 A138 150fr multi 2.10 1.60

Ships from Columbus's Fleet, 1492 — A139

1986, Apr. 14

614 A139 60fr Santa Maria 85 65
615 A139 90fr Nina, Pinta 1.25 95

Fish, Red Sea — A140

1986, June 16 Litho. *Perf. 13½x13*

616 A140 20fr Elagatis bipinnulatus 28 22
617 A140 25fr Valamugil seheli 35 28
618 A140 55fr Lutjanus rivulatus 78 58

Public Buildings — A141

1986, July 21 Litho. *Perf. 13*

619 A141 105fr People's Palace 1.50 1.15
620 A141 115fr Ministry of the Interior, Posts and Telecommunications 1.65 1.25

Sea-Me-We Building, Keyboard — A142

1986, Sept. 8 Litho. *Perf. 13*

621 A142 100fr multi 1.40 1.05

Souvenir Sheet

Perf. 12½

622 A142 250fr multi 3.50 2.65

Southeast Asia, Middle East, Western Europe Submarine Cable System inauguration. No. 622 has multicolored margin picturing map and ship Vercors. Size: 125x95mm.

No. 537 Surcharged "5e ANNIVERSAIRE."

1986, Nov. 15 *Perf. 13x12½*

623 A116 55fr on 75fr multi 78 60

Pasteur Institute, Cent. — A143

1987, Feb. 19 Litho. *Perf. 13*

624 A143 220fr multi 3.25 2.50

Natl. Vaccination Campaign.

Edible Mushrooms A144

1987, Apr. 16 Litho. *Perf. 13x12½*

625 A144 35fr Macrolepiota imbricata 50 38
626 A144 50fr Lentinus squarrosulus 70 52
627 A144 95fr Terfezia boudieri 1.40 1.00

Wildlife A145

1987, May 14 *Perf. 12½x13*

628 A145 5fr Hare 8 6
629 A145 30fr Dromedary 45 35
630 A145 140fr Cheetah 2.00 1.50

1988 Olympics, Seoul and Calgary — A146

Designs: 85fr, Pierre de Coubertin (1863-1937), founder of the modern Olympics, and lighting of the flame. 135fr, Ski jumping. 140fr, Running.

1987, July 16 *Perf. 13*

631 A146 85fr multi 1.20 90
632 A146 135fr multi 1.90 1.40
633 A146 140fr multi 2.00 1.50

AIR POST STAMPS

Afars and Issas Nos. C104-C105, C103 Overprinted with Bars and "REPUBLIQUE DE DJIBOUTI" in Brown or Black

1977 Engr. *Perf. 13*

C106 AP37 55fr multi (Br) 1.50 1.50
C107 AP37 75fr multi 1.75 1.75

Litho. *Perf. 12*

C108 AP36 500fr multi 9.50 8.75

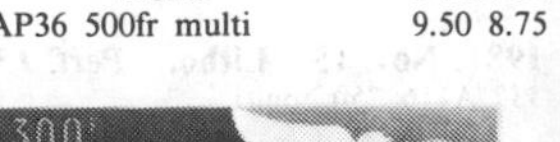

Map of Djibouti, Dove, UN Emblem — AP38

1977, Oct. 19 Photo. *Perf. 13*

C109 AP38 300fr multi 5.25 3.75

Djibouti's admission to the United Nations.

Condition is the all-important factor of price. Prices quoted are for stamps in fine condition.

Marcel Brochet MB 101, 1955 — AP39

Designs: 85fr, Tiger Moth, 1960. 200fr, Rallye-Commodore, 1973.

1978, Feb. 27 Litho. *Perf. 13*

C110 AP39	60fr multi	90	50
C111 AP39	85fr multi	1.25	75
C112 AP39	200fr multi	3.00	1.50

Djibouti Aero Club.

Old Man, by Rubens AP40

Design: 500fr, Hippopotamus Hunt, by Rubens (horiz.).

1978, Apr. 24 Photo. *Perf. 13*

C113 AP40	50fr multi	75	45
C114 AP40	500fr multi	7.50	4.50

Peter Paul Rubens (1577-1640), 400th birth anniversary.

Player Holding Soccer Cup — AP41

Design: 300fr, Soccer player, map of South America with Argentina, Cup and emblem.

1978, June 20 Litho. *Perf. 13*

C115 AP41	100fr multi	1.50	60
C116 AP41	300fr multi	4.50	1.65

11th World Cup Soccer Championship, Argentina, June 1-25.

Nos. C115-C116 Overprinted:
a. ARGENTINE/CHAMPION 1978
b. ARGENTINE/HOLLANDE/3-1

1978, Aug. 20 Litho. *Perf. 13*

C117 AP41 (a)	100fr multi	1.25	55
C118 AP41 (b)	300fr multi	3.75	1.75

Argentina's victory in 1978 Soccer Championship.

Tahitian Women, by Gauguin — AP42

Young Hare, by Dürer AP43

Perf. 13x12½, 12½x13
1978, Sept. 25 Litho.

C119 AP42	100fr multi	1.50	60
C120 AP43	250fr multi	3.75	2.50

Paul Gauguin (1848-1903) and Albrecht Dürer (1471-1528), painters.

Philexafrique II-Essen Issue
Common Design Types

Designs: No. C121, Lynx and Djibouti No. 456. No. C122, Jay and Brunswick No. 3.

1978, Dec. 13 Litho. *Perf. 13x12½*

C121 CD138	90fr multi	1.75	1.50
C122 CD139	90fr multi	1.75	1.50

Nos. C121-C122 printed se-tenant.

UPU Emblem, Map of Djibouti, Dove — AP44

1978, Dec. 18 Engr. *Perf. 13*

C123 AP44	200fr multi	3.00	1.75

Centenary of Congress of Paris.

Junkers JU-52 and Dewoitine D-338 — AP45

Powered Flight, 75th Anniversary: 250fr, Potez P63-11, 1941 and Supermarine Spitfire HF-VII, 1942. 500fr, Concorde, 1969 and Sikorsky S-40 "American Clipper," 1931.

1979, May 21 Litho. *Perf. 13x12½*

C124 AP45	140fr multi	1.75	75
C125 AP45	250fr multi	3.25	1.50
C126 AP45	500fr multi	7.50	2.75

Common Design Types pictured in section at front of book.

The Laundress, by Honore Daumier AP46

1979, July 10 Litho. *Perf. 12½x13*

C127 AP46	500fr multi	6.75	3.75

Olympic Emblem, Skis, Sleds — AP47

1980, Jan. 21 Litho. *Perf. 13*

C128 AP47	150fr multi	2.25	90

13th Winter Olympic Games, Lake Placid, N.Y., Feb. 12-24.

Cathedral of the Archangel, Basketball, Moscow '80 Emblem — AP48

1980, Apr. 10 Litho. *Perf. 13*

C129 AP48	60fr *shown*	75	30
C130 AP48	120fr *Lomonossov Univ., Moscow, Soccer*	1.50	60
C131 AP48	250fr *Cathedral of the Annunciation, Running*	3.00	1.40

22nd Summer Olympic Games, Moscow, July 18-Aug. 3.

Air Djibouti, 1st Anniversary — AP49

1980, Mar. 29 Litho. *Perf. 13x12½*

C132 AP49	400fr multi	4.75	1.75

No. C128 Surcharged in Black and Blue or Purple:
80fr. A.M. MOSER-PROEL / AUTRICHE / DESCENTE DAMES / MEDAILLE D'OR
200fr. HEIDEN / USA / 5 MEDAILLES D'OR / PATINAGE DE VITESSE

1980, Apr. 5 Litho. *Perf. 13*

C133 AP47	80fr on 150fr multi	1.00	60
C134 AP47	200fr on 150fr multi (P)	2.50	1.75

Apollo 11 Moon Landing, 10th Anniversary — AP50

Space Conquests: 300fr, Apollo-Soyuz space project, 5th anniversary.

1980, May 8

C135 AP50	200fr multi	2.75	90
C136 AP50	300fr multi	3.75	1.40

Satellite Earth Station Inauguration — AP51

1980, July 3 Litho. *Perf. 13*

C137 AP51	500fr multi	6.00	2.75

Graf Zeppelin — AP52

1980, Oct. 2 Litho. *Perf. 13*

C138 AP52	100fr *shown*	1.25	60
C139 AP52	150fr *Ferdinand von Zeppelin, blimp*	1.75	90

Zeppelin flight, 80th anniversary.

Voyager Passing Saturn — AP53

1980, Dec. 21 Litho. *Perf. 13*

C140 AP53	250fr multi	3.00	1.50

Soccer Players — AP54

World Cup Soccer Preliminary Games: 200fr, Players (diff.).

1981, Jan. 14

C141 AP54	80fr multi	1.00	45
C142 AP54	200fr multi	2.50	1.10

European-African Economic Convention AP55

1981, Feb. 10 Litho. *Perf. 13*

C143 AP55 100fr multi 1.25 60

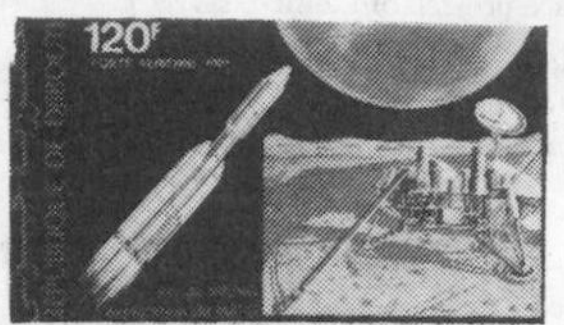

5th Anniversary of Viking I Take-off to Mars — AP56

20th Anniversary of Various Space Flights: 75fr, Vostok I, Yuri Gagarin (vert.). 150fr, Freedom 7, Alan B. Shepard (vert.).

1981, Mar. 9 Litho. *Perf. 13*

C144 AP56 75fr multi 90 45
C145 AP56 120fr multi 1.50 65
C146 AP56 150fr multi 1.75 90

Football Players, by Picasso (1881-1973) — AP57

Design: 400fr Man Wearing a Turban, by Rembrandt (1606-1669) (vert.).

Perf. 13x12½, 12½x13

1981, Aug. 3 Litho.

C147 AP57 300fr multi 3.75 1.75
C148 AP57 400fr multi 4.75 2.75

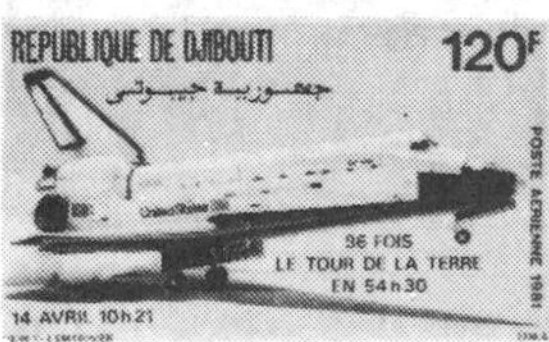

Columbia Space Shuttle — AP58

1981, Sept. 24 Litho. *Perf. 13*

C149 AP58 90fr Shuttle, diff., vert. 1.10 60
C150 AP58 120fr shown 1.50 90

Nos. C149-C150 Overprinted in Brown with Astronauts' Names and Dates.

1981, Nov. 12 Litho. *Perf. 13*

C151 AP58 90fr multi 1.10 75
C152 AP58 120fr multi 1.50 1.10

1982 World Cup Soccer — AP59

Designs: Various soccer players.

1982, Jan. 20

C153 AP59 110fr multi 1.25 75
C154 AP59 220fr multi 2.50 1.50

Space Anniversaries — AP60

Designs: 40fr, Luna 9 moon landing, 15th (vert.). 60fr, John Glenn's flight, 20th (vert.). 180fr, Viking I Mars landing, 5th.

1982, Feb. 15

C155 AP60 40fr multi 45 30
C156 AP60 60fr multi 75 45
C157 AP60 180fr multi 2.10 1.25

21st Birthday of Princess Diana of Wales AP61

1982, Apr. 29 Litho. *Perf. 12½x13*

C158 AP61 120fr Portrait 1.50 1.10
C159 AP61 180fr Portrait, diff. 2.25 1.40

No. 489, Boy Examining Collection — AP62

1982, May 10 *Perf. 13x12½*

C160 AP62 80fr shown 1.00 75
C161 AP62 140fr No. 495 1.75 1.25

PHILEXFRANCE '82 Stamp Exhibition, Paris, June 11-21. Nos. C160-C161 se-tenant with label showing show emblem, dates.

1350th Anniv. of Mohamed's Death at Medina — AP63

1982, June 8 Litho. *Perf. 13*

C162 AP63 500fr Medina Mosque 6.00 3.50

Scouting Year — AP64

1982, June 28

C163 AP64 95fr Baden-Powell 1.25 75
C164 AP64 200fr Camp, scouts 2.50 1.50

2nd UN Conference on Peaceful Uses of Outer Space, Vienna, Aug. 9-21 — AP65

1982, Aug. 19

C165 AP65 350fr multi 4.25 2.25

Nos. C153-C154 Overprinted with Winner's Name and Scores.

1982, July 21 Litho. *Perf. 13*

C166 AP59 110fr multi 1.25 90
C167 AP59 220fr multi 2.50 1.75

Italy's victory in 1982 World Cup.

Nos. C158-C159 Overprinted in Blue or Red with Date, Name, and Title.

1982, Aug. 9 *Perf. 12½x13*

C168 AP61 120fr multi 1.50 1.10
C169 AP61 180fr multi (R) 2.25 1.50

Birth of Prince William of Wales, June 21.

Franklin D. Roosevelt (1882-1945) AP66

1982, Oct. 7 Litho. *Perf. 13*

C170 AP66 115fr shown 1.25 75
C171 AP66 250fr George Washington 3.00 1.50

Manned Flight Bicentenary AP67

Pre-olympic Year AP68

1983, Jan. 20 Litho.

C172 AP67 35fr Montgolfiere, 1783 48 32
C173 AP67 45fr Giffard, Paris Exposition, 1878 68 42
C174 AP67 120fr Double Eagle II, 1978 1.75 1.25

1983, Feb. 15

C175 AP68 75fr Volleyball 1.15 75
C176 AP68 125fr Wind surfing 1.85 1.25

50th Anniv. of Air France — AP69

1983, Mar. 20 Litho. *Perf. 13*

C177 AP69 25fr Bloch 220 38 25
C178 AP69 100fr DC-4 1.50 1.00
C179 AP69 175fr Boeing 747 2.60 1.75

Martin Luther King, Jr. (1929-1968), Civil Rights Leader — AP70

Design: 250fr, Alfred Nobel (1833-1896).

1983, May 18 Litho. *Perf. 13*

C180 AP70 180fr multi 2.90 2.00
C181 AP70 250fr multi 4.00 3.00

Service Clubs — AP71

Designs: 90fr, Rotary Club International, Sailing Show, Toronto, June 5-9. 150fr, Lions Club International, Honolulu Meeting, June 22-24, Djibouti lighthouse.

1983, July 18 Litho. *Perf. 13*

C182 AP71 90fr multi 1.35 90
C183 AP71 150fr multi 2.25 1.50

Printed se-tenant with label showing emblems.

Vintage Motor Cars — AP72

1983, July 18 Litho. *Perf. 13x12½*

C184 AP72 60fr Renault, 1904 90 60
C185 AP72 80fr Mercedes, 1910 1.20 80
C186 AP72 110fr Lorraine-Dietrich, 1912 1.65 1.10

A little time given to the study of the arrangement of the Scott Catalogue can make it easier to use effectively.

Vostok VI — AP74

1983, Oct. 20 Litho. *Perf. 12*
C188 AP74 120fr shown 1.80 1.20
C189 AP74 200fr Explorer I 3.00 2.00

1984 Winter Olympics — AP75

1984, Feb. 14 Litho. *Perf. 13*
C190 AP75 70fr Speed skating 1.00 75
C191 AP75 130fr Figure skating 1.75 1.40

Souvenir Sheet

Ship — AP76

1984, Feb. 14 Litho. *Perf. 12½*
C192 AP76 250fr multi 3.50 2.75

Sea-Me-We (South-east Asia-Middle East-Western Europe) submarine cable construction agreement. Multicolored margin shows map of cable. Size: 127x97mm.

Motorized Hang Gliders — AP77

Various hang gliders.

1984, Mar. 12 *Perf. 13x12½*
C193 AP77 65fr multi 90 70
C194 AP77 85fr multi 1.25 90
C195 AP77 100fr multi 1.40 1.10

Nos. C190-C191 Overprinted with Winners' Names and Country

1984, Mar. 28 *Perf. 13*
C196 AP75 70fr multi 1.00 75
C197 AP75 130fr multi 1.90 1.40

Portrait of Marguerite Matisse, 1910, by Henri Matisse AP78

Design: 200fr, Portrait of Mario Varvogli, by Amedeo Modigliani.

1984, Apr. 15 Litho. *Perf. 12½x13*
C198 AP78 150fr multi 2.25 1.50
C199 AP78 200fr multi 2.75 2.25

1984 Summer Olympics — AP79

1984, May 24 *Perf. 13*
C200 AP79 50fr Running 70 52
C201 AP79 60fr High jump 85 65
C202 AP79 80fr Swimming 1.10 90

Battle Scene AP80

1984, June 16 Litho. *Perf. 13x12½*
C203 AP80 300fr multi 4.25 3.25

125th anniv. of Battle of Solferino and 120th anniv. of Red Cross.

Bleriot's Flight over English Channel, 75th Anniv. — AP81

1984, July 8
C204 AP81 40fr 14-Bis plans 60 45
C205 AP81 75fr Britten-Norman Islander 1.10 80
C206 AP81 90fr Air Djibouti jet 1.25 1.00

375th Anniv., Galileo's telescope — AP82

1984, Oct. 7 Litho. *Perf. 13*
C207 AP82 120fr Telescopes, spacecraft 1.75 1.25
C208 AP82 180fr Galileo, telescopes 2.50 1.90

1984 Soccer Events — AP83

1984, Oct. 20 Litho. *Perf. 13*
C209 AP83 80fr Euro Cup 1.10 90
C210 AP83 80fr Los Angeles Olympics 1.10 90

Issued se-tenant, separated by pictorial label.

Service Clubs — AP84

1985, Feb. 23 Litho. *Perf. 13*
C211 AP84 50fr Lions, World Leprosy Day 70 52
C212 AP84 60fr Rotary, chess board, pieces 85 65

Telecommunications Technology — AP85

Designs: No. C213, Technician, researchist, operator. No. C214, Offshore oil rig, transmission tower, government building.

1985, July 2 *Perf. 13x12½*
C213 AP85 80fr multi 1.15 80
C214 AP85 80fr multi 1.15 80

PHILEXAFRICA '85, Lome. Nos. C213-C214 printed se-tenant with center label picturing map of Africa or UAPT emblem.

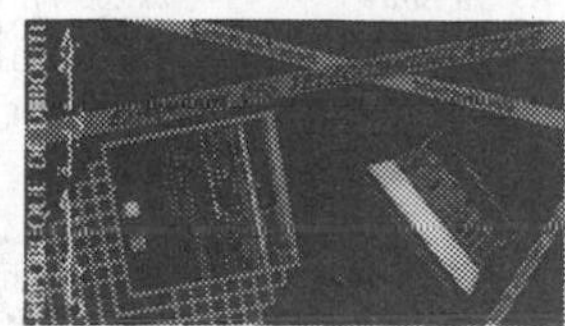
Telecommunications Development — AP86

1985, Oct. 2 *Perf. 13*
C215 AP86 50fr Intl. transmission center 70 52
C216 AP86 90fr Ariane rocket, vert. 1.30 1.00
C217 AP86 120fr ARABSAT satellite 1.70 1.30

Youths Windsurfing, Playing Tennis — AP87

Design: No. C219, Tadjoura Highway construction.

1985, Nov. 13 *Perf. 13x12½*
C218 AP87 100fr multi 1.40 1.05
C219 AP87 100fr multi 1.40 1.05

PHILEXAFRICA '85, Lome, Togo, Nov. 16-24. Nos. C218-C219 printed se-tenant with center label picturing map of Africa or UAPT emblem.

1986 World Cup Soccer Championships, Mexico — AP88

1986, Feb. 24 Litho. *Perf. 13*
C220 AP88 75fr shown 1.05 78
C221 AP88 100fr Players, stadium 1.40 1.05

Statue of Liberty, Cent. — AP89

1986, May 21
C222 AP89 250fr multi 3.50 2.75

Nos. C220-C221 Ovptd. with Winners.

1986, Sept. 15 Litho. *Perf. 13*
C223 AP88 75fr "FRANCE-BELGIQUE/4-2" 1.05 80
C224 AP88 100fr "3-2 ARGENTINE-RFA" 1.40 1.05

1986 World Chess Championships, May 1-19 — AP89a

Malayan animal chess pieces.

1986, Oct. 13 Litho. *Perf. 13*
C225 AP89a 80fr Knight, bishops 1.15 88
C226 AP89a 120fr Rook, king, pawn 1.70 1.30

Yuri Gagarin, Sputnik Spacecraft — AP90

1986, Nov. 27 Litho. *Perf. 13*
C227 AP90 150fr shown 2.15 1.65
C228 AP90 200fr Space rendezvous, 1966 2.85 2.15

First man in space, 25th anniv.; Gemini 8-Agena link-up, 20th anniv.

Historic Flights — AP91

1987, Jan. 22 Litho. *Perf. 13*
C229 AP91 55fr Amiot 370 80 60

C230 AP91 80fr Spirit of St. Louis 1.15 85
C231 AP91 120fr Voyager 1.75 1.30

First flight from Istria to Djibouti, 1942; Lindbergh's Transatlantic flight, 1927; non-stop world circumnavigation without refueling.

Pres. Aptidon, Natl. Crest and Flag
AP92

1987, June 27 Litho. ***Perf. 12½x13***
C232 AP92 250fr multi 3.50 2.60

Natl. independence, 10th anniv.

Telstar, 25th Anniv. — AP93

1987, Oct. 1 ***Perf. 13***
C233 AP93 190fr shown 2.65 2.00
C234 AP93 250fr Samuel Morse, telegraph key 3.50 2.60

Invention of the telegraph, 150th anniv. (250fr).

City of Djibouti, Cent. — AP94

Designs: 100fr, Djibouti Creek and quay, 1887. 150fr, Aerial view of city, 1987. 250fr, Somali Coast Nos. 6, 20, and postmarks of 1898 and 1903.

1987, Nov. 15 Litho. ***Perf. 13x12½***
C235 AP94 100fr blk & buff 1.45 1.10
C236 AP94 150fr multi 2.15 1.60

Souvenir Sheet

C237 AP94 250fr multi 3.55 2.70

Nos. C235-C236 printed se-tenant with center label inscribed "1887/1987" or picturing commemorative emblems. No. C237 has decorative margin like design of 100fr. Size: 119x88mm.

DOMINICAN REPUBLIC

LOCATION — Comprises about two-thirds of the island of Hispaniola in the West Indies
GOVT. — Republic
AREA — 18,700 sq. mi.
POP. — 5,982,000 (est. 1983)

> The first price column gives the catalogue value of an unused stamp, the second that of a used stamp.

CAPITAL — Santo Domingo

8 Reales = 1 Peso
100 Centavos = 1 Peso (1880)
100 Centimos = 1 Franco (1883)
100 Centavos = 1 Peso (1885)

> Prices of early Dominican Republic stamps vary according to condition. Quotations for Nos. 1-31 are for fine copies. Very fine to superb specimens sell at much higher prices, and inferior or poor copies sell at reduced prices, depending on the condition of the individual specimen.

Coat of Arms
A1 A2

1865 Unwmk. Typo. ***Imperf.***
Wove Paper.

1 A1 ½r *rose* 375.00 375.00
2 A1 1r *dp grn* 800.00 800.00

Twelve varieties of each.

Laid Paper.

3 A2 ½r *pale grn* 550.00 500.00
4 A2 1r *straw* 1,000. 925.00

Twelve varieties of the ½r, ten varieties of the 1r.

A3 A4

1866 Laid Paper Unwmk.

5 A3 ½r *straw* 225.00 175.00
6 A3 1r *pale grn* 900.00 900.00
7 A4 1r *pale grn* 175.00 150.00

Nos. 5-8 have 21 varieties (sheets of 21).

Wmk.115

Wmk. Diamonds. (115)

8 A3 1r *pale grn* 2,250. 2,250.

1866-67 Wove Paper. Unwmk.

9 A3 ½r *rose* ('67) 55.00 55.00
10 A3 1r *pale grn* 100.00 90.00
 a. Inscription double, top and bottom *400.00 400.00*
11 A3 1r *bl* ('67) 45.00 35.00
 a. 1r *lt bl* ('67) 45.00 35.00
 b. No space between "Un" and "real" 300.00 250.00
 c. Without inscription at top & bottom 450.00 200.00
 d. Inscription invtd., top & bottom

1867-71 Pelure Paper

13 A3 ½r *rose* 135.00 100.00
15 A3 ½r *lav* ('68) 275.00 275.00
 a. Without inscription at top and bottom 700.00
 b. Double inscriptions, one inverted *550.00*
16 A3 ½r *grnsh gray* ('68) 275.00 275.00
18 A3 ½r *ol* ('69) 2,750. 2,750.
23 A3 1r *lavender* 250.00 225.00
24 A4 1r *rose* ('68) 250.00 225.00
25 A4 1r *mag* ('69) 1,200. 1,200.
26 A4 1r *sal* ('71) 250.00 225.00

1870-73 Ordinary Paper

27 A3 ½r *magenta* 1,000. 1,000.
28 A3 ½r bl,*rose* (blk inscription) ('71) 65.00 55.00
 a. Blue inscription 650.00 650.00
 b. Without inscription at top and bottom
29 A3 ½r *yel* ('73) 40.00 27.50
 a. Without inscription at top and bottom 500.00 500.00
30 A4 1r *vio* ('73) 40.00 27.50
 a. Without inscription at top and bottom 600.00 600.00
31 A4 1r *dk grn* 80.00 65.00

Nos. 9-31 have 21 varieties (sheets of 21). Nos. 29 and 30 are known pin-perforated, unofficially.

Bisects are known of several of the early 1r stamps.

Coat of Arms
A5 A6

1879 ***Perf. 12½x13***

32 A5 ½r violet 4.00 2.00
 a. Imperf., pair 12.00 12.00
 b. Horiz. pair, imperf. vert. 22.50
33 A5 ½r vio,*bluish* 4.00 2.00
 a. Imperf., pair 12.00 10.00
34 A5 1r carmine 4.00 2.00
 a. Imperf., pair 15.00 12.00
 b. Perf. 13 12.00 10.00
 c. Perf. 13x12½ 12.00 10.00
35 A5 1r car, *sal* 4.00 2.00
 a. Imperf., pair 11.00 11.00

In 1891 15 stamps of 1879-83 were surcharged "U P U," new values and crossed diagonal lines.

1880 Typo. ***Rouletted in Color***

36 A6 1c green 1.50 1.00
 b. Laid paper 60.00 60.00
37 A6 2c red 1.00 75
 a. Pelure paper 45.00 45.00
 b. Laid paper 45.00 45.00
38 A6 5c blue 1.50 75
39 A6 10c rose 3.75 1.00
40 A6 20c brown 2.25 1.00
41 A6 25c violet 2.75 1.25
42 A6 50c orange 3.00 1.75
43 A6 75c ultra 6.00 3.00
 a. Laid paper 45.00 45.00
44 A6 1p gold 8.00 5.00
 a. Laid paper 65.00 65.00
 b. Double impression 55.00 55.00
 Nos. 36-44 (9) 29.75 15.50

1881 Network Covering Stamp

45 A6 1c green 1.00 60
46 A6 2c red 1.00 60
47 A6 5c blue 1.50 60
48 A6 10c rose 1.75 75
49 A6 20c brown 1.75 90
50 A6 25c violet 2.25 1.00
51 A6 50c orange 2.50 1.50
52 A6 75c ultra 8.00 4.50
53 A6 1p gold 10.00 7.50
 Nos. 45-53 (9) 29.75 17.95

Preceding Issues Surcharged with Value in New Currency:

5 céntimos. — a
5 céntimos — b
5 céntimos. — c
1 franco. — d
1 Franco. — e
1 franco — f
1 franco, 25 céntimos. — g
5 francos. — h
5 francos — i

1883 Without Network

54 (a) 5c on 1c grn 2.50 1.75
 b. Inverted surcharge 27.50 27.50
 c. Surcharged "25 centimos" 65.00 65.00
 d. Surcharged "10 centimos" 35.00 35.00
55 (b) 5c on 1c grn 30.00 12.00
 b. Double surch. 125.00
 c. Inverted surcharge 75.00 75.00
56 (c) 5c on 1c grn 22.50 12.50
 b. Surcharged "10 centimos" 45.00 45.00
 c. Surcharged "25 centimos" 50.00 50.00
57 (a) 10c on 2c red 6.50 4.00
 a. Inverted surcharge 37.50 37.50
 d. Surcharged "5 centimos" 70.00 70.00
 e. Surcharged "25 centimos" 100.00 100.00
58 (c) 10c on 2c red 6.00 4.00
 a. "Centimso"
 b. Inverted surcharge 50.00 50.00
 c. Surcharged "25 centimos" 80.00 80.00
 d. "10" omitted 80.00
59 (a) 25c on 5c bl 8.00 4.50
 a. Surcharged "5 centimos" 70.00
 b. Surcharged "10 centimos" 70.00 70.00
 c. Surcharged "50 centimos" 100.00 100.00
 d. Inverted surcharge 55.00 55.00
60 (c) 25c on 5c bl 8.00 3.50
 a. Inverted surcharge 60.00 50.00
 b. Surcharged "10 centimos" 60.00 50.00
 e. "25" omitted 100.00
 f. Surcharged on back 100.00
61 (a) 50c on 10c rose 27.50 15.00
 a. Inverted surcharge 65.00 60.00
62 (c) 50c on 10c rose 40.00 22.50
 a. Inverted surcharge 70.00 70.00
63 (d) 1fr on 20c brn 20.00 13.00
64 (e) 1fr on 20c brn 22.50 13.00
 a. Comma after "Franco," 35.00 35.00
65 (f) 1fr on 20c brn 32.50 22.50
 a. Inverted surcharge 100.00
66 (g) 1fr25c on 25c vio 27.50 20.00
 a. Inverted surcharge 85.00 85.00
67 (g) 2fr50c on 50c org 20.00 14.00
 a. Inverted surcharge 45.00 35.00
68 (g) 3fr75c on 75c ultra 35.00 30.00
 b. Inverted surcharge 70.00 70.00
 c. Laid paper 85.00 85.00
70 (i) 5fr on 1p gold 675.00 600.00
 a. "s" of "francos" inverted 900.00 900.00

With Network.

71 (a) 5c on 1c grn 4.00 3.00
 b. Inverted surcharge 30.00 30.00
 c. Double surch. 27.50 27.50
 d. Surcharged "25 centimos" 55.00 55.00
 e. "5" omitted 100.00 100.00
72 (b) 5c on 1c grn 27.50 12.00
 b. Inverted surcharge 65.00 65.00
73 (c) 5c on 1c grn 35.00 15.00
 b. Surcharged "10 centimos" 55.00 50.00
 c. Surcharged "25 centimos" 80.00
74 (a) 10c on 2c red 5.00 3.00
 a. Surcharged "5 centimos" 70.00 60.00
 b. Surcharged "25 centimos" 90.00 90.00
 c. "10" omitted 75.00
75 (c) 10c on 2c red 4.00 2.00
 a. Inverted surcharge 37.50 22.50
76 (a) 25c on 5c bl 9.00 4.00
 a. Surcharged "10 centimos" 100.00
 b. Surcharged "5 centimos" 80.00
 c. Surcharged "50 centimos" 90.00
77 (c) 25c on 5c bl 80.00 40.00
 a. Inverted surcharge
 b. Surcharged on back
78 (a) 50c on 10c rose 32.50 10.00
 a. Inverted surcharge 40.00 25.00
 b. Surcharged "25 centimos" 75.00
79 (c) 50c on 10c rose 37.50 12.50
 a. Inverted surcharge 70.00
80 (d) 1fr on 20c brn 16.00 13.00
81 (e) 1fr on 20c brn 19.00 15.00
 a. Comma after "Franco," 45.00 45.00
 b. Inverted surcharge 100.00
82 (f) 1fr on 20c brn 32.50 25.00
83 (g) 1fr25c on 25c vio 60.00 35.00
 a. Inverted surcharge 85.00
84 (g) 2fr50c on 50c org 25.00 16.50
 a. Inverted surcharge 45.00 35.00
85 (g) 3fr75c on 75c ultra 60.00 55.00
86 (h) 5fr on 1p gold 225.00 225.00
 a. Inverted surcharge
87 (i) 5fr on 1p gold 250.00 250.00

Many minor varieties exist in Nos. 54-87: accent on "i" of "centimos"; "5" with straight top; "1" with straight serif.

Coat of Arms
A7 A7a

1885-91 Engr. *Perf. 12*

88 A7 1c green 1.00 60
89 A7 2c vermilion 1.00 60
90 A7 5c blue 1.50 60
91 A7a 10c orange 2.50 75
92 A7a 20c dk brn 2.50 1.00
93 A7a 50c vio ('91) 8.50 6.50
94 A7 1p car ('91) 24.00 14.00
95 A7 2p red brn ('91) 30.00 16.00
Nos. 88-95 (8) 71.00 40.05

Nos. 93, 94 and 95 were issued without gum.
Imperf. varieties are proofs.

Coat of Arms — A8

1895-97 *Perf. 12½x14*

96 A8 1c green 1.50 60
a. Perf. 14 ('97) 1.75 70
97 A8 2c org red 1.50 60
a. Perf. 14 ('97) 8.00 1.00
98 A8 5c blue 1.50 60
a. Perf. 14 ('97) 1.75 1.00
99 A8 10c orange 3.00 1.75
a. Perf. 14 ('97) 3.50 2.00

Nos. 96 to 99 are known imperforate but were not issued in this condition.

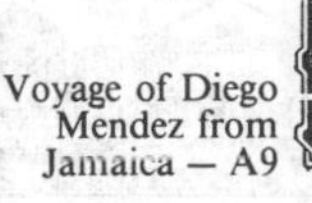

Voyage of Diego Mendez from Jamaica — A9

Enriquillo's Revolt
A10

Sarcophagus of Columbus
A11

"Española" Guarding Remains of Columbus
A12

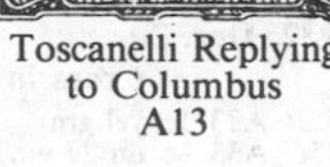

Toscanelli Replying to Columbus
A13

Bartolome de las Casas Defending Indians — A14

Columbus at Salamanca
A15

Columbus' Mausoleum
A16

1899, Feb. 27 Litho. *Perf. 11½*

100 A9 1c brn vio 6.00 5.00
a. Imperf., pair 20.00
102 A10 2c rose red 2.00 1.00
a. Imperf., pair 7.00
103 A11 5c blue 2.25 1.00
a. Imperf., pair 8.00
104 A12 10c orange 5.00 1.75
a. Tete beche pair 60.00 60.00
b. Imperf. pair 12.50
105 A13 20c brown 8.50 5.50
a. Imperf. pair 20.00
106 A14 50c yel grn 9.00 6.50
a. Tete beche pair 80.00 80.00
b. Imperf. pair 25.00
c. as "a," imperf. 175.00
107 A15 1p *gray bl* 22.50 17.50
a. Imperf. pair 60.00
108 A16 2p bis brn 45.00 45.00
a. Imperf. pair 100.00

1900, Jan.

109 A11 ¼c black 1.00 1.00
a. Imperf. pair 3.00 3.50
110 A15 ½c black 1.00 1.00
b. Imperf. pair 3.00 3.50
110A A9 1c gray grn 1.00 75
c. Imperf. pair 5.00
Nos. 100-110A (11) 103.25 86.00

Nos. 100-110A were issued to raise funds for a Columbus mausoleum.

Map of Hispaniola
A17

Coat of Arms
A18

1900, Oct. 21 Unwmk. *Perf. 14*

111 A17 ¼c dk bl 90 60
112 A17 ½c rose 90 60
113 A17 1c ol grn 90 60
114 A17 2c dp grn 90 60
115 A17 5c red brn 90 60
a. Vertical pair, imperf. between 25.00

Perf. 12.

116 A17 10c orange 90 60
117 A17 20c lilac 4.00 3.00
a. 20c rose (error) 8.00 8.00
118 A17 50c black 3.50 3.00
119 A17 1p brown 4.00 3.00
Nos. 111-119 (9) 16.90 12.60

Several varieties in design are known in this issue. They were deliberately made. Counterfeits of Nos. 111-119 abound.

1901-06 Typo. *Perf. 14*

120 A18 ½c car & vio 90 50
121 A18 ½c blk & org ('05) 1.75 1.00
122 A18 ½c grn & blk ('06) 1.00 35
123 A18 1c ol grn & vio 90 25
124 A18 1c blk & ultra ('05) 2.00 1.00
125 A18 1c car & blk ('06) 1.00 40
126 A18 2c dp grn & vio 85 25
127 A18 2c blk & vio ('05) 2.25 75
128 A18 2c org brn & blk ('06) 1.00 20
129 A18 5c org brn & vio 90 30
130 A18 5c blk & cl ('05) 2.75 1.25
131 A18 5c bl & blk ('06) 1.25 40
132 A18 10c org & vio 1.50 50
133 A18 10c blk & grn ('05) 5.00 2.50
134 A18 10c red vio & blk ('06) 1.50 50
135 A18 20c brn vio & vio 3.00 1.00
136 A18 20c blk & ol ('05) 16.00 9.00
137 A18 20c ol grn & blk ('06) 8.00 3.50
138 A18 50c gray blk & vio 10.00 6.00
139 A18 50c blk & red brn ('05) 55.00 35.00
140 A18 50c brn & blk ('06) 10.00 9.00
141 A18 1p brn & vio 22.50 13.50
142 A18 1p blk & gray ('05) 250.00 250.00
143 A18 1p vio & blk ('06) 25.00 15.00
Nos. 120-143 (24) 424.05 352.15

Issue dates: Nov. 15, 1901, May 11, 1905, Aug. 17, 1906.

See also Nos. 172-176.

Francisco Sanchez — A19

Juan Pablo Duarte — A20

Ramon Mella — A21

Ft. Santo Domingo — A22

1902, Feb. 25 Engr. *Perf. 12*

144 A19 1c dk grn & blk 35 35
a. Center inverted 4.50
145 A20 2c scar & blk 35 35
a. Center inverted 4.50
146 A20 5c bl & blk 35 35
a. Center inverted 4.50
147 A19 10c org & blk 35 35
148 A21 12c pur & blk 35 35
a. Center inverted 4.50
149 A21 20c rose & blk 50 50
a. Center inverted 4.50
150 A22 50c brn & blk 75 75
a. Center inverted 4.50
Nos. 144-150 (7) 3.00 3.00

400th anniversary of Santo Domingo.
Imperforate varieties of Nos. 144 to 150 were never sold to the public.

Nos. 138, 141 Surcharged in Black

2
dos cts

1904, Aug.

151 A18 2c on 50c blk & vio 10.00 7.50
a. Inverted surcharge 20.00 20.00
152 A18 2c on 1p brn & vio 15.00 10.00
a. Inverted surcharge 20.00 20.00
b. "2" omitted 70.00 70.00
c. As "b," inverted 100.00 100.00
153 A18 5c on 50c blk & vio 4.50 3.00
a. Inverted surcharge 6.00 5.00
154 A18 5c on 1p brn & vio 5.00 4.00
a. Inverted surcharge 9.00 9.00
155 A18 10c on 50c blk & vio 10.00 8.00
a. Inverted surcharge 20.00 20.00
156 A18 10c on 1p brn & vio 10.00 8.00
a. Inverted surcharge 14.00 14.00
Nos. 151-156 (6) 54.50 40.50

Official Stamps of 1902 Overprinted

16 de Agosto
1904

Red Overprint.

1904, Aug. 16

157 O1 5c dk bl & blk 6.00 3.25
a. Inverted overprint 8.00 7.00

Black Overprint.

158 O1 2c scar & blk 16.00 5.00
a. Inverted overprint 9.00 7.00
159 O1 5c dk bl & blk 800.00 800.00
160 O1 10c yel grn & blk 13.00 10.00
a. Inverted overprint 16.00 16.00

16 de Agosto
1 1904 1

Surcharged

161 O1 1c on 20c yel & blk 5.00 4.00
a. Inverted surcharge 7.50 6.50

Nos. J1-J2 Surcharged or Overprinted

REPUBLICA
DOMINICANA
1
CENTAVOS
CORREOS

Surcharged "CENTAVOS".

1904-05

Black Surcharge.

162 D1 1c on 2c ol gray 135.00 135.00
a. "entavos"
b. "Dominican" 250.00 250.00
c. "Centavo" 250.00 250.00

Carmine Surcharge or Overprint.

163 D1 1c on 2c ol gray 3.00 1.25
a. Inverted surcharge 3.50 3.00
b. "Domihicana" 20.00 20.00
c. Same as "b," inverted 50.00 50.00
d. "Dominican" 15.00 15.00
e. "Centavos" omitted 40.00 40.00
g. "entavos" 35.00
163F D1 1c on 4c ol gray 40.00 8.00
164 D1 2c ol gray 1.00 50
a. "Domihicana" 15.00 15.00
b. Inverted overprint 2.50 2.50
c. Same as "a," inverted 30.00 30.00
d. "Dominican" 8.00 8.00
e. "Centavo" omitted 17.50 14.00
f. "entavos" 15.00 15.00
g. Same as "f," inverted 50.00 50.00
h. Same as "d," inverted 50.00 50.00

Surcharged "CENTAVO".

165 D1 1c on 4c ol gray 1.00 75
a. "Domihicana" 14.00 14.00
c. Inverted surcharge 2.50 2.50
d. "1" omitted 4.00 4.00
e. Same as "a," invtd. 45.00 43.00
f. Same as "d," invtd. 55.00 55.00
g. Double surcharge 35.00 35.00

No. 92 Surcharged in Red

DOS
1905
CENTAVOS

1905, Apr. 4

166 A7a 2c on 20c dk brn 10.00 6.00
a. Inverted surcharge 20.00 20.00
167 A7a 5c on 20c dk brn 5.00 2.00
a. Inverted surcharge 22.50 22.50
b. Double surcharge 35.00 35.00
168 A7a 10c on 20c dk brn 10.00 6.00

Nos. 166-168 exist with inverted "A" for "V" in "CENTAVOS" in surcharge.

Nos. J2, J4, J3 Surcharged:

REPUBLICA
DOMINICANA.
UN
centavo.

REPUBLICA
DOMINICANA.
DOS
centavos.

1906, Jan. 16 *Perf. 14*

Red Surcharge.

169 D1 1c on 4c ol gray 1.00 60
a. Inverted surcharge 15.00 15.00

1906, May 1

Black Surcharge.

170 D1 1c on 10c ol gray 1.25 60
a. Inverted surcharge 15.00 15.00
b. Double surcharge 20.00 20.00
c. "OMINICANA" 27.50 27.50

171 D1 2c on 5c ol gray 1.25 60
a. Inverted surcharge 15.00 15.00

The varieties small "C" or small "A" in "REPUBLICA" are found on Nos. 169, 170 and 171.

Arms Type of 1901-06.

Wmk.116

Wmk. Crosses and Circles. (116)

1907-10

172 A18 ½c grn & blk ('08) 80 25
173 A18 1c car & blk 90 20
174 A18 2c org brn & blk 90 20
175 A18 5c bl & blk 90 30
176 A18 10c red vio & blk ('10) 10.00 1.50
Nos. 172-176 (5) 13.50 2.45

No. O6 Overprinted in Red **HABILITADO 1911**

Perf. 13½x14, 13½x13

1911, July 11

177 O2 2c scar & blk 1.50 75
a. "HABILITAOO" 12.50 8.50
b. Inverted overprint 30.00
c. Double overprint 30.00

Coat of Arms A23

Juan Pablo Duarte A24

1911-13 ***Perf. 14.***

Center in Black

178 A23 ½c org ('13) 35 20
179 A23 1c green 35 15
180 A23 2c carmine 35 15
181 A23 5c gray bl ('13) 75 20
182 A23 10c red vio 1.50 60
183 A23 20c ol grn 10.00 7.00
184 A23 50c yel brn ('12) 4.00 3.50
185 A23 1p vio ('12) 7.00 4.00
Nos. 178-185 (8) 24.30 15.80

See Nos. 230-232.

1914, Apr. 13 ***Perf. 13x14***

Background Red, White and Blue.

186 A24 ½c org & blk 70 55
187 A24 1c grn & blk 70 55
188 A24 2c rose & blk 70 55
189 A24 5c sl & blk 85 60
190 A24 10c mag & blk 1.25 1.00
191 A24 20c ol grn & blk 3.00 3.00
192 A24 50c brn & blk 4.00 4.00
193 A24 1p dl lil & blk 6.50 6.50
Nos. 186-193 (8) 17.70 16.75

To commemorate the centenary of the birth of Juan Pablo Duarte (1813-1876), patriot and revolutionary.

Official Stamps of 1909-12 Surcharged in Violet or Overprinted in Red:

Habilitado 1915 MEDIO CENTAVO
a

Habilitado 1915
b

1915, Feb. ***Perf. 13½x13, 13½x14***

194 O2 (a) ½c on 20c org & blk 75 50
a. Inverted surcharge 8.50 8.50
b. Double surcharge 12.50 12.50
c. "Habilitado" omitted 7.50 7.50
195 O2 (b) 1c bl grn & blk 1.00 35
a. Inverted overprint 8.50 8.50
b. Double overprint 10.00
c. Overprinted "1915" only 17.50
196 O2 (b) 2c scar & blk 1.00 35
a. Inverted overprint 7.50 7.50
b. Double overprint 11.00 11.00
c. Overprinted "1915" only 12.50
d. "1915" double
197 O2 (b) 5c dk bl & blk 1.25 35
a. Inverted overprint 10.00 10.00
b. Double overprint 12.50 12.50
c. Double overprint, one inverted 40.00
d. Overprinted "1915" only 12.00
198 O2 (b) 10c yel grn & blk 3.50 2.75
a. Inverted overprint 12.50
199 O2 (b) 20c org & blk 12.00 9.00
a. "Habilitado" omitted
Nos. 194-199 (6) 19.50 13.30

Nos. 194, 196-198 are known with both perforations. Nos. 195 and 199 are only perf. 13½x13.

The variety capital "I" for "1" in "Habilitado" occurs once in each sheet in all denominations.

A25

Type of 1911-13 Redrawn Overprinted "1915" in Red.

TWO CENTAVOS:
Type I. "DOS" in small letters.
Type II. "DOS" in larger letters with white dot at each end of the word.

1915 Unwmk. Litho. ***Perf. 11½***

200 A25 ½c vio & blk 90 25
a. Imperf., pair 8.00
201 A25 1c yel brn & blk 90 12
a. Imperf., pair 9.00
b. Vert. pair, imperf. horiz. 15.00
c. Horiz. pair, imperf. vert. 15.00
202 A25 2c ol grn & blk (I) 4.50 35
a. Imperf., pair 9.00
203 A25 2c ol grn & blk (II) 7.50 25
a. Center omitted 125.00
b. Frame omitted 125.00
c. Imperf., pair 9.00
d. Horiz. pair, imperf. vert. 15.00
204 A25 5c mag & blk 4.00 35
a. Pair, one without overprint 75.00
b. Imperf., pair 9.00
205 A25 10c gray bl & blk 4.50 50
a. Imperf., pair 11.00
b. Horiz. pair, imperf. vert. 50.00
206 A25 20c rose red & blk 9.00 1.75
a. Imperf., pair 17.50
207 A25 50c grn & blk 12.00 5.00
a. Imperf., pair 35.00
208 A25 1p org & blk 25.00 10.00
a. Imperf., pair 60.00
Nos. 200-208 (9) 68.30 18.57

Type of 1915 Overprinted "1916" in Red.

1916

209 A25 ½c vio & blk 1.50 15
a. Imperf., pair 30.00
210 A25 1c grn & blk 2.50 15
a. Imperf., pair 30.00

Type of 1915 Overprinted "1917" in Red.

1917-19

213 A25 ½c red lil & blk 2.50 40
a. Horizontal pair, imperf. between 60.00 60.00
214 A25 1c yel grn & blk 2.00 10
215 A25 2c ol grn & blk 1.50 10
a. Imperf., pair 45.00
216 A25 5c mag & blk 16.00 1.00

Type of 1915 Overprinted "1919" in Red

1919

219 A25 2c ol grn & blk 11.00 15

Type of 1915 Overprinted "1920" in Red.

1920-27

220 A25 ½c lil rose & blk 70 30
a. Horizontal pair, imperf. between 35.00 35.00
b. Inverted overprint
c. Double overprint
d. Double overprint, one inverted
221 A25 1c yel grn & blk 90 12
a. Overprint omitted 100.00
222 A25 2c ol grn & blk 1.00 8
a. Vertical pair, imperf. between 40.00
223 A25 5c dp rose & blk 11.00 70
224 A25 10c bl & blk 7.00 30
225 A25 20c rose red & blk ('27) 9.00 75
226 A25 50c grn & blk ('27) 75.00 25.00
Nos. 220-226 (7) 104.60 27.25

Type of 1915 Overprinted "1921" in Red.

1921

227 A25 1c yel grn & blk 3.50 40
a. Horizontal pair, imperf. between 60.00 60.00
b. Imperf., pair 60.00 60.00
228 A25 2c ol grn & blk 6.00 45

Redrawn Design of 1915 without Overprint

1922

230 A25 1c green 2.50 15
231 A25 2c car (II) 3.00 15
232 A25 5c blue 5.00 35

Exist imperf.

Arms of Dominican Republic
A26 A27

Second Redrawing.

TEN CENTAVOS:
Type I. Numerals 2 mm. high. "DIEZ" in thick letters with large white dot at each end.
Type II. Numerals 3 mm. high. "DIEZ" in thin letters with white dot with colored center at each end.

1924-27

233 A26 1c green 80 10
a. Vertical pair, imperf. between 50.00 50.00
234 A26 2c red 85 10
235 A26 5c blue 1.25 12
236 A26 10c pale bl & blk (I) ('26) 15.00 2.25
236A A26 10c pale bl & blk (II) 32.50 1.25
236B A26 50c gray grn & blk ('26) 65.00 40.00
237 A26 1p org & blk ('27) 22.50 15.00
Nos. 233-237 (7) 137.90 58.82

In the second redrawing the shield has a flat top and the design differs in many details from the stamps of 1911-13 and 1915-22.

1927

238 A27 ½c lil rose & blk 40 10

Exhibition Pavilion — A28

1927 Unwmk. ***Perf. 12.***

239 A28 2c carmine 1.00 70
240 A28 5c ultra 2.05 70

Issued to commemorate the National and West Indian Exhibition at Santiago de los Caballeros.

Ruins of Columbus' Fortress A29

1928

241 A29 ½c lil rose 80 50
242 A29 1c dp grn 60 15
a. Horizontal pair, imperf. between 35.00
243 A29 2c red 70 15
244 A29 5c dk bl 1.75 40
245 A29 10c lt bl 2.00 40
246 A29 20c rose 3.50 60
247 A29 50c yel grn 15.00 9.00
248 A29 1p org yel 27.50 20.00
Nos. 241-248 (8) 51.85 31.20

Reprints exist of 1c, 2c and 10c.

Issue dates: 1c, 2c, 10c, Oct. 1. Others, Dec.

Horacio Vasquez A30

Convent of San Ignacio de Loyola A31

1929, May-June

249 A30 ½c dl rose 70 35
a. Imperf., pair 17.50
250 A30 1c gray grn 70 20
a. Imperf., pair 17.50
251 A30 2c red 80 20
a. Imperf., pair 17.50
252 A30 5d dk ultra 1.75 40
a. Imperf., pair 20.00
253 A30 10c pale bl 2.50 70
Nos. 249-253 (5) 6.45 1.85

Signing of the "Frontier" treaty with Haiti. 2c issued in May, others in June.

1930, May 1 ***Perf. 11½***

254 A31 ½c red brn 90 65
a. Imperf., pair 75.00 75.00
255 A31 1c dp grn 70 15
256 A31 2c vermilion 70 15
257 A31 5c dp bl 1.75 50
258 A31 10c lt bl 4.00 1.50
Nos. 254-258 (5) 8.05 2.95

Cathedral of Santo Domingo, First Church in America — A32

1931 ***Perf. 12.***

260 A32 1c dp grn 1.00 20
a. Imperf., pair 70.00
261 A32 2c scarlet 75 20
a. Imperf., pair 70.00
262 A32 3c violet 1.00 15
263 A32 7c dk bl 2.75 35
264 A32 8c bister 4.00 1.00
265 A32 10c lt bl 6.00 1.50
a. Imperf., pair 50.00
Nos. 260-265 (6) 15.50 3.40

Issue dates: 3c-7c, Aug. 1. Others, July 11.

A33

Overprinted or Surcharged in Black.

1932, Dec. 20 ***Perf. 12***

Cross in Red

265B A33 1c yel grn 75 60
265C A33 3c on 2c vio 1.00 70
265D A33 5c blue 5.50 4.00
265E A33 7c on 10c turq bl 6.50 6.00

Proceeds of sale given to Red Cross. Valid Dec. 20, to Jan. 5, 1933.

Inverted surcharge or overprint exist on Nos. 265B-265D.

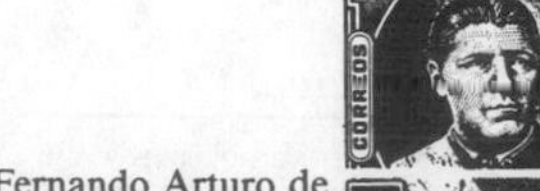

Fernando Arturo de Merino As President — A35

Cathedral of Santo Domingo A36

Designs: ½, 5, 8c, Tomb of Merino. 1, 3, 10c, as Archbishop.

1933, Feb. 27 Engr. *Perf. 14*

266 A35 ½c lt vio 35 35
267 A35 1c yel grn 40 20
268 A35 2c lt red 1.25 1.00
269 A35 3c dp vio 50 20
270 A35 5c dk bl 80 40
271 A35 7c ultra 1.75 60
272 A35 8c dk grn 2.00 1.50
273 A35 10c org yel 1.50 40
274 A35 20c car rose 3.50 2.50
275 A36 50c lemon 15.00 9.00
276 A36 1p dk brn 37.50 25.00
Nos. 266-276 (11) 64.55 41.15

Issued in commemoration of the centenary of the birth of Fernando Arturo de Merino (1833-1906)

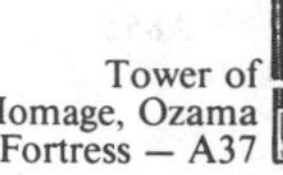

Tower of Homage, Ozama Fortress — A37

1932 Litho. *Perf. 12*

278 A37 1c green 75 20
279 A37 3c violet 75 10

Issue dates: 1c, July 2; 3c, June 22.

"CORREOS" added at left.

1933, May 28

283 A37 1c dk grn 70 20

President Rafael L. Trujillo A38 A39

1933, Aug. 16 Engr. *Perf. 14*

286 A38 1c yel grn & blk 85 60
287 A39 3c dp vio & blk 1.00 30
288 A38 7c ultra & blk 3.00 1.50

Commemorating the 42nd anniversary of the birth of President Rafael Leonidas Trujillo Molina.

San Rafael Bridge — A40

1934 Litho. *Perf. 12.*

289 A40 ½c dl vio 90 40
290 A40 1c dk grn 1.25 25
291 A40 3c violet 2.00 12

Opening of San Rafael Bridge.
Issue dates: ½c, 3c, Mar. 3; 1c, Feb. 17.

Trujillo Bridge A41

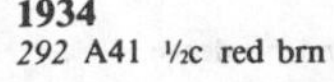

1934

292 A41 ½c red brn 90 35
293 A41 1c green 1.25 12
294 A41 3c purple 1.75 15

Issued in commemoration of the opening of the General Trujillo Bridge near Ciudad Trujillo.
Issue dates: 1c, Aug. 24. Others, Sept. 7.

Ramfis Bridge A42

1935, Apr. 6

295 A42 1c green 65 12
296 A42 3c yel brn 70 12
297 A42 5c brn vio 2.25 1.50
298 A42 10c rose 4.50 2.00

Issued in commemoration of the opening of the Ramfis Bridge over the Higuamo River.

President Trujillo — A43

A44

A45

1935 *Perf. 11*

299 A43 3c yel brn 45 25
300 A44 5c org red, bl, red & bis 55 15
301 A45 7c ultra, bl, red & brn 80 15
302 A44 10c red vio, bl, red & bis 1.25 15

Issue dates: 3c, Oct. 29; 5c, 10c, Nov. 25; 7c, Nov. 8.
Issued in commemoration of the ratification of a treaty setting the frontier between Dominican Republic and Haiti.

National Palace A46

1935, Apr. 1 *Perf. 11½*

303 A46 25c yel org 3.25 25

Issued for obligatory use on all mail addressed to the president and cabinet ministers.

Post Office, Santiago A47

1936

304 A47 ½c brt vio 45 40
305 A47 1c green 45 12

Issue dates: ½c, Jan. 14; 1c, Jan. 4.

George Washington Ave., Ciudad Trujillo — A48

1936, Feb. 22

306 A48 ½c brn & vio brn 60 55
a. Imperf., pair 75.00
307 A48 2c car & brn 60 45
308 A48 3c yel org & red brn 90 25
309 A48 7c ultra, bl & brn 1.75 1.25
a. Imperf., pair 75.00

Issued in commemoration of the dedication of George Washington Avenue, Ciudad Trujillo.

José Nuñez de Caceres — A49 Felix M. del Monte — A55

Proposed National Library — A56

Designs: 1c, Gen. Gregorio Luperon. 2c, Emiliano Tejera. 3c, President Trujillo. 5c, Jose Reyes. 7c, Gen. Antonio Duverge. 25c, Francisco J. Peynado. 30c, Salome Urena. 50c, Gen. Jose M. Cabral. 1p, Manuel de Jesus Galvan. 2p, Gaston F. Deligne.

1936 Unwmk. Engr. *Perf. 13½, 14.*

310 A49 ½c dl vio 50 25
311 A49 1c dk grn 40 15
312 A49 2c carmine 45 25
313 A49 3c violet 45 10
314 A49 5c dp ultra 90 50
315 A49 7c sl bl 1.75 90
316 A55 10c orange 1.75 50
317 A56 20c ol grn 6.00 3.50
318 A55 25c gray vio 8.00 5.00
319 A55 30c scarlet 10.00 7.00
320 A55 50c blk brn 12.00 4.75
321 A55 1p black 40.00 40.00
322 A55 2p yel brn 95.00 90.00
Nos. 310-322 (13) 177.20 152.90

The funds derived from the sale of these stamps were returned to the National Treasury Fund for the erection of a building for the National Library and Archives.
Issue dates: 3c, 7c, Mar. 18; others, May 22.

President Trujillo and Obelisk — A62

1937, Jan. 11 Litho. *Perf. 11½*

323 A62 1c green 30 10
324 A62 3c violet 60 15
325 A62 7c bl & turq bl 1.75 1.50

Issued in commemoration of the first anniversary of naming Ciudad Trujillo.

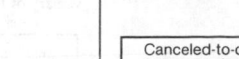

> Canceled-to-order stamps are often from remainders. Most collectors of canceled stamps prefer postally used specimens.

Discus Thrower and Flag — A63

1937, Aug. 14

Flag in Red and Blue.

326 A63 1c dk grn 5.00 1.25
327 A63 3c violet 6.00 75
328 A63 7c dk bl 10.00 5.00

Issued in commemoration of the First National Olympic Games, August 16, 1937.

Symbolical of Peace, Labor and Progress — A64

1937, Sept. 18 *Perf. 12*

329 A64 3c purple 50 12

"8th Year of the Benefactor."

Monument to Father F. X. Billini — A65

1937, Dec. 29

330 A65 ½c dp org 25 12
331 A65 5c purple 70 25

Issued in commemoration of the centenary of the birth of Father Francisco Xavier Billini (1837-1890).

Globe and Torch of Liberty A66

1938, Feb. 22 *Perf. 11½*

332 A66 1c green 60 10
333 A66 3c purple 85 10
334 A66 10c orange 1.75 30

Issued in commemoration of the 150th anniversary of the Constitution of the United States of America.

Pledge of Trinitarians, City Gate and National Flag — A67

1938, July 16 *Perf. 12*

335 A67 1c grn, red & dk bl 60 30
336 A67 3c pur, red & bl 75 25
337 A67 10c org, red & bl 1.50 70

Issued in commemoration of the Trinitarians and patriots, Francisco Del Rosario Sanchez, Ramon Matias Mella and Juan

Pablo Duarte, who helped free their country from foreign domination.

Seal of the University of Santo Domingo — A68

1938, Oct. 28

338 A68 ½c orange 45 30
339 A68 1c dp grn & lt grn 50 15
340 A68 3c pur & pale vio 60 15
341 A68 7c dp bl & lt bl 1.25 65

Issued in commemoration of the fourth centenary of the founding of the University of Santo Domingo, on October 28, 1538.

Trylon and Perisphere, Flag and Proposed Columbus Lighthouse — A69

1939, Apr. 30 Litho. *Perf. 12*

Flag in Blue and Red.

342 A69 ½c red org & org 55 30
343 A69 1c grn & lt grn 60 25
344 A69 3c pur & pale vio 70 18
345 A69 10c org & yel 2.00 85
Nos. 342-345,C33 (5) 5.85 2.58

New York World's Fair.

José Trujillo Valdez — A70

1939, Sept. Typo.

346 A70 ½c blk & pale gray 45 25
347 A70 1c blk & yel grn 60 15
348 A70 3c blk & yel brn 70 15
349 A70 7c blk & dp ultra 1.75 1.25
350 A70 10c blk & brt red vio 2.50 65
Nos. 346-350 (5) 6.00 2.45

Issued in commemoration of the fourth anniversary of the death of José Trujillo Valdez (1863-1935), father of President Trujillo Molina.

Map of the Americas and Flags of 21 American Republics A71

Sir Rowland Hill A72

1940, Apr. 14 Litho. *Perf. 11½*

Flags in National Colors

351 A71 1c dp grn 40 15
352 A71 2c carmine 55 30
353 A71 3c red vio 80 10
354 A71 10c orange 1.60 30
355 A71 1p chestnut 25.00 20.00
Nos. 351-355 (5) 28.35 20.85

Issued in commemoration of the 50th anniversary of the founding of the Pan American Union.

1940, May 6 *Perf. 12*

356 A72 3c brt red vio & rose lil 5.00 60
357 A72 7c dk bl & lt bl 10.00 2.25

Centenary of first postage stamp.

Julia Molina Trujillo A73

1940, May 26

358 A73 1c grn, lt grn & dk grn 45 12
359 A73 2c brt red, buff & dp rose 60 40
360 A73 3c org, dl org & brn org 75 12
361 A73 7c bl, pale bl & dk bl 1.75 65

Issued in commemoration of Mother's Day.

Map of Caribbean A74

1940, June 6 *Perf. 11½*

362 A74 3c brt car & pale rose 60 15
363 A74 7c dk bl & lt bl 1.25 25
364 A74 1p yel grn & pale grn 12.50 9.00

Issued in commemoration of the second Inter-American Caribbean Conference held at Ciudad Trujillo, May 31 to June 6.

Marion Military Hospital — A75

1940, Dec. 24

365 A75 ½c chnt & fawn 40 30

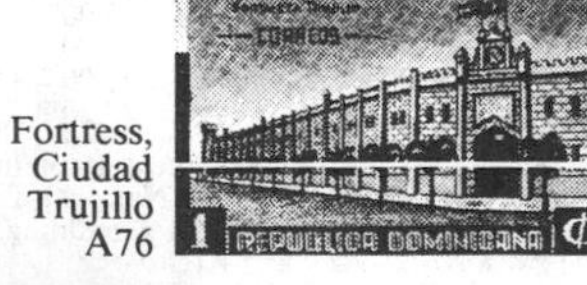

Fortress, Ciudad Trujillo A76

Statue of Columbus, Ciudad Trujillo — A77

1941

366 A76 1c dk grn & lt grn 20 8
367 A77 2c brt red & rose 25 12
368 A77 10c org brn & buff 85 15

Issue dates: 1c, Mar. 27; others, Apr. 7.

Sanchez, Duarte, Mella and Trujillo — A78

1941, May 16

369 A78 3c brt red lil & red vio 35 12
370 A78 4c brt red, crim & pale rose 50 25
371 A78 13c dk bl & lt bl 1.00 30
372 A78 15c org brn & buff 3.50 2.25
373 A78 17c lt bl, bl & pale bl 3.50 2.00
374 A78 1p org, yel brn & pale org 13.00 10.00
375 A78 2p lt gray & pale gray 27.50 12.00
Nos. 369-375 (7) 49.35 26.92

Issued in commemoration of the Trujillo-Hull Treaty signed September 24, 1940 and effective April 1, 1941.

Bastion of February A79

1941, Oct. 20

376 A79 5c brt bl & lt bl 80 30

School, Torch of Knowledge, Pres. Trujillo — A80

1941

377 A80 ½c chnt & fawn 30 12
378 A80 1c dk grn & lt grn 40 15

Education campaign.
Issue dates: ½c, Dec. 12, 1c, Dec. 2.

Reserve Bank of Dominican Republic A81

1942 Unwmk.

379 A81 5c lt brn & buff 60 15
380 A81 17c dp bl & lt bl 1.50 60

Issued to commemorate the founding of the Reserve Bank, October 24, 1941.

Representation of Transportation A82

1942, Aug. 15

381 A82 3c dk brn, grn yel & lt bl 70 10
382 A82 15c pur, grn, yel & lt bl 1.75 60

Issued in commemoration of the 8th anniversary of the Day of Posts and Telegraph.

Prices of premium quality never hinged stamps will be in excess of catalogue price.

Virgin of Altagracia — A83

1942, Aug. 15

383 A83 ½c gray & pale gray 1.25 15
384 A83 1c dp grn & lt grn 2.50 10
385 A83 3c brt red lil & lil 16.00 10
386 A83 5c dk vio brn & vio brn 3.50 15
387 A83 10c rose pink & pink 11.00 40
388 A83 15c dp bl & lt bl 12.00 50
Nos. 383-388 (6) 46.25 1.40

Issued to commemorate the 20th anniversary of the coronation of Our Lady of Altagracia.

Bananas A84

Cows A85

1942-43

389 A84 3c dk brn & grn ('43) 75 15
390 A84 4c ver & blk ('43) 80 45
391 A85 5c dp bl & cop brn 80 15
392 A85 15c dk pur & bl grn 1.25 55

Issue date: 5c, 15c, Aug. 18.

Emblems of Dominican and Trujillista Parties A86

1943, Jan. 15

393 A86 3c orange 60 10
394 A86 4c dk red 80 25
395 A86 13c brt red lil 1.60 30
396 A86 1p lt bl 7.50 2.75

Issued in commemoration of the relection of President Rafael Trujillo Molina, May 16, 1942.

Model Market, Ciudad Trujillo A87

1944

397 A87 2c dk brn & buff 25 15

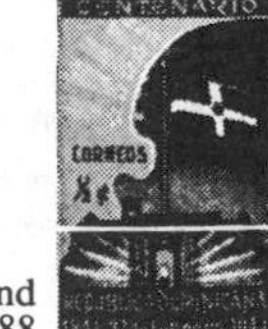

Bastion of Feb. 27 and National Flag — A88

1944, Feb. 27 Unwmk.

Flag in Dark Blue and Carmine.

398 A88 ½c ocher 12 10
399 A88 1c yel grn 12 8
400 A88 2c scarlet 20 12
401 A88 3c brt red vio 25 10
402 A88 5c yel org 30 15
403 A88 7c brt bl 40 35
404 A88 10c org brn 60 50
405 A88 20c ol grn 1.00 80
406 A88 50c lt bl 3.00 2.25
Nos. 398-406,C46-C48 (12) 10.84 7.27

Souvenir Sheet.

Imperf

407 Sheet of 12 150.00 150.00
a.-l. Single stamp 5.00 5.00

Centenary of Independence.

No. 407 contains one each of Nos. 398-406, C46-C48 with simulated perforations. Inscribed in brown: "Serie Conmemorativa del Centenario de la Republica 27 de Febrero." Size: 141x205mm.

Battlefield and Nurse with Child A90

1944, Aug. 1

408 A90 1c dk bl grn, buff & car 25 10
a. Vertical pair, imperf. between 20.00
b. Horiz. pair, imperf. vert. 20.00
409 A90 2c dk brn, buff & car 50 15
410 A90 3c brt bl, buff & car 50 10
411 A90 10c rose car, buff & car 1.00 25

Issued to honor the 80th anniversary of the International Red Cross.

Municipal Building, San Cristobal A91

Emblem of Communications A92

Unwmk.

1945, Jan. 10 Litho. *Perf. 12*

412 A91 ½c bl & lt bl 10 10
413 A91 1c dk grn & grn 15 8
414 A91 2c red org & org 15 10
415 A91 3c dk brn & brn 20 12
416 A91 10c ultra & gray bl 70 20
Nos. 412-416 (5) 1.30 60

Centenary of the constitution.

1945, Sept. 1
Center in Dark Blue and Carmine.

417 A92 3c orange 20 8
418 A92 20c yel grn 1.20 30
419 A92 50c lt bl 2.50 90
Nos. 417-419,C53-C56 (7) 5.90 2.38

Palace of Justice, Ciudad Trujillo A93

1946 *Perf. 11½.*

420 A93 3c dk red brn & buff 30 10

Map of Hispaniola — A94

1946, Aug. 4 *Perf. 12*

421 A94 10c rose brn, yel, lil, bl, red & grn 60 25

Issued to commemorate the 450th anniversary of the founding of Santo Domingo. See also Nos. C62-C63.

Foreign postal stationery (stamped envelopes, postal cards and air letter sheets) lies beyond the scope of this Catalogue, which is limited to adhesive postage stamps.

Waterfall of Jimenoa — A95

1946-47
Center Multicolored

422 A95 1c yel grn ('47) 20 8
423 A95 2c car ('47) 20 10
424 A95 3c dp bl 25 8
425 A95 13c red vio ('47) 70 40
426 A95 20c choc ('47) 1.50 40
427 A95 50c org ('47) 2.75 1.50
Nos. 422-427,C64-C67 (10) 8.15 5.11

Nos. 422-423, 425-427 issued Mar. 18.

Executive Palace — A96

1948, Feb. 27

428 A96 1c yel grn 12 8
429 A96 3c dp bl 18 8

See also Nos. C68-C69.

Church of San Francisco Ruins — A97

1949, Apr. 13 *Perf. 11½*

430 A97 1c dk grn & pale grn 15 6
431 A97 3c dp bl & pale bl 20 8
Nos. 430-431,C70-C73 (6) 2.55 1.46

Gen. Pedro Santana A98

Pigeon and Globe A99

1949, Aug. 10

432 A98 3c dp bl & bl 25 10

Issued to commemorate the centenary of the Battle of Las Carreras. See No. C74.

1949, Sept. 15
Center and Inscriptions in Brown.

433 A99 1c grn & pale grn 18 12
434 A99 2c yel grn & yel 22 8
435 A99 5c bl & pale bl 30 10
436 A99 7c dk vio bl & pale bl 65 25

Issued to commemorate the 75th anniversary of the formation of the Universal Postal Union.

Hotel Jimani A100

Hotels: 1c, 2c, Hamaca. 5c, Montana. 15c, San Cristobal. 20c, Maguana.

1950-52

437 A100 ½c org brn & buff 10 8
438 A100 1c dp grn & grn ('51) 15 8
439 A100 2c red org & sal ('52) 15 8
440 A100 5c bl & lt bl 30 8
441 A100 15c dp org & yel 65 12
442 A100 20c lil & rose lil 1.25 20
443 A100 1p choc & yel 5.00 2.00
Nos. 437-443,C75-C76 (9) 10.75 5.01

Issue dates: 1c, Dec. 1, 1951; 2c, Jan. 11, 1952. Others, Sept. 8, 1950.
The ½c, 15c and 20c exist imperf.

Ruins of Church and Hospital of San Nicolas de Bari — A101

School of Medicine A102

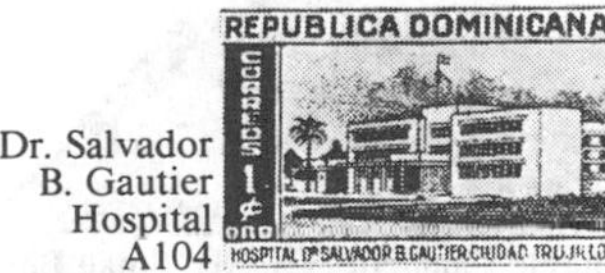

Queen Isabella I A103

1950, Oct. 2

444 A101 2c dk grn & rose brn 30 10
445 A102 5c vio bl & org brn 40 12

13th Pan-American Health Conference. Exist imperf. See No. C77.

1951, Oct. 12

446 A103 5c dk bl & red brn 35 15

500th anniversary of the birth of Queen Isabella I of Spain. Exists imperf.

Dr. Salvador B. Gautier Hospital A104

1952, Aug.

447 A104 1c dk grn 12 6
448 A104 2c red 18 6
449 A104 5c vio bl 35 10
Nos. 447-449,C78-C79 (5) 3.90 2.87

Columbus Lighthouse and Flags of 21 Republics A105

1953, Jan. 6 Engr. *Perf. 13*

450 A105 2c dk grn 25 6
451 A105 5c dp bl 35 8
452 A105 10c dp car 60 30
Nos. 450-452,C80-C86 (10) 5.25 3.49

Miniature sheet containing Nos. 450-452 and C80-C86 is listed as No. C86a.

Treasury Building, Ciudad Trujillo A106

Sugar Industry, "Central Rio Haina" A107

1953 Litho. *Perf. 11½.*

453 A106 ½c brown 8 6
454 A106 2c dk bl 10 8
455 A107 5c bl & vio brn 20 8
456 A106 15c orange 75 25

José Marti A108

Monument to the Peace of Trujillo A109

1954 *Perf. 12½.*

457 A108 10c dp bl & dk brn 45 18

Centenary of the birth of JoséMarti (1853-1895), Cuban patriot.

1954, May 25

458 A109 2c green 8 6
459 A109 7c blue 25 8
460 A109 20c orange 80 15

See also No. 493.

Rotary Emblem A110

1955, Feb. 23 *Perf. 12*

461 A110 7c dp bl 70 25

50th anniversary, Rotary International. See No. C90.

Gen. Rafael L. Trujillo — A111

Designs: 4c, Trujillo in civilian clothes. 7c, Trujillo statue. 10c, Symbols of culture and prosperity.

1955, May 16 Engr. *Perf. 13½x13*

462 A111 2c red 10 6
463 A111 4c lt ol grn 15 8
464 A111 7c indigo 25 12
465 A111 10c brown 50 20
Nos. 462-465,C91-C93 (7) 3.15 1.58

25th anniversary of the Trujillo era.

General Rafael L. Trujillo — A112

Angelita Trujillo — A113

1955, Dec. 20 Unwmk. *Perf. 13*

466 A112 7c dp cl 35 12
467 A112 10c dk bl 55 18

See also No. C94.

1955, Dec. 20 Litho. *Perf. 12½*

468 A113 10c bl & ultra 55 18

Nos. 466-468 were issued to publicize the International Fair of Peace and Brotherhood in Ciudad Trujillo, Dec. 1955.

Airport A114

1956, Apr. 6 *Perf. 12½*

469 A114 1c brown 12 8
470 A114 2c red org 18 8

Issued to commemorate the third Caribbean conference of the International Civil Aviation Organization. See No. C95.

Cedar — A115

1956, Dec. 8 *Perf. 11½x12*

471 A115 5c car rose & grn 30 10
472 A115 6c red vio & grn 35 15

Issued to publicize the reforestation program. See No. C96.

Fair Emblem A116

Fanny Blankers-Koen, Netherlands A117

1957, Jan. 10 *Perf. 12½*

473 A116 7c bl, lt brn & ver 35 15

Issued to publicize the 2nd International Livestock Show, Ciudad Trujillo, Jan. 10-20, 1957. Exists imperf.

Engraved & Lithographed

1957, Jan. 24 *Perf. 11½*

Olympic Winners and Flags: 2c, Jesse Owens, United States. 3c, Kee Chung Sohn, Japan. 5c, Lord Burghley, England. 7c, Bob Mathias, United States.

Flags in National Colors.

474 A117 1c brn, lt bl, vio & mar 5 5
475 A117 2c dk brn, lt bl & vio 5 5
476 A117 3c red lil & red 5 5
477 A117 5c red org & vio 8 8
478 A117 7c grn & vio 10 10
Nos. 474-478,C97-C99 (8) 1.03 73

To commemorate the 16th Olympic Games, Melbourne, Nov. 22-Dec. 8, 1956. Exist imperf.

Miniature sheets of 5 exist, perf. and imperf., containing one each of Nos. 474-478. Sheets measure 169 x 86 mm. and have no marginal inscriptions. Price, 2 sheets, perf. and imperf., $6.

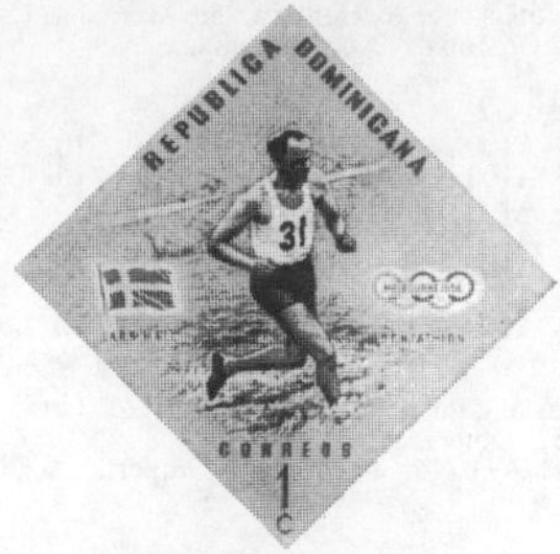

Lars Hall, Sweden, Pentathlon — A118

Olympic Winners and Flags: 2c, Betty Cuthbert, Australia, 100 & 200 meter dash. 3c, Egil Danielsen, Norway, javelin. 5c, Alain Mimoun, France, marathon. 7c, Norman Read, New Zealand, 50 km. walk.

Perf. 13½

1957, July 18 Photo. Unwmk.

Flags in National Colors.

479 A118 1c brn & brt bl 5 5
480 A118 2c org ver & dk bl 5 5
481 A118 3c dk bl 5 5
482 A118 5c ol & dk bl 8 8
483 A118 7c rose brn & dk bl 10 10
Nos. 479-483,C100-C102 (8) 1.03 73

Issued in honor of the 1956 Olympic winners. Exist imperf.

Miniature sheets of 8 exist, perf. and imperf., containing one each of Nos. 479-483 and C100-C102. The center label in these sheets is printed in two forms: Olympic gold medal or Olympic flag. Sheets measure 140x140mm. Price, 4 sheets, perf. and imperf., medal and flag, $18.

A third set of similar miniature sheets (perf. and imperf.) with center label showing an incorrect version of the Dominican Republic flag (colors transposed) was printed. These sheets are said to have been briefly sold on the first day, then withdrawn as the misprint was discovered. Price, 2 sheets, perf. & imperf., $150.

Gerald Ouellette, Canada, Small Bore Rifle, Prone — A119

Ron Delaney, Ireland, 1,500 Meter Run — A120

Olympic Winners and Flags: 3c, Tenley Albright, United States, figure skating. 5c, Joaquin Capilla, Mexico, platform diving. 7c, Ercole Baldini, Italy, individual road race (cycling).

Engraved and Lithographed

1957, Nov. 12 *Perf. 13½*

Flags in National Colors

484 A119 1c red brn 5 5
485 A120 2c gray brn 5 5
486 A119 3c violet 5 5
487 A120 5c red org 8 8
488 A119 7c Prus grn 10 10
Nos. 484-488,C103-C105 (8) 1.03 73

Issued in honor of the 1956 Olympic winners. Exist imperf.

Miniature sheets of 5 exist, perf. and imperf., containing one each of Nos. 484-488. Sheets have no marginal inscriptions. Price, 2 sheets, perf. and imperf., $5.50.

Mahogany Flower — A121

1957-58 Litho. *Perf. 12½*

489 A121 2c grn & mar 12 8

Perf. 12

490 A121 4c lil & rose ('58) 18 12
491 A121 7c ultra & gray grn 35 12
492 A121 25c brn & org ('58) 85 35

Sizes: No. 489, 25x29¼mm.; Nos. 490-492, 24x28¾mm. In 1959, the 2c was reissued in size 24¼x28½mm. with slightly different tones of green and maroon.

Issue dates: 2c, Oct. 24; 7c, Nov. 6; 4c and 25c, Apr. 7, 1958.

Type of 1954, Redrawn

Perf. 12x11½

1957, June 12 Unwmk.

493 A109 7c brt bl 55 20

On No. 493 the cent symbol is smaller, the shading of the sky and steps stronger and the letters in "Coreos" shorter and bolder.

Cervantes, Globe and Book — A122

1958, Apr. 23 Litho. *Perf. 12½*

494 A122 4c yel grn 15 6
495 A122 7c red lil 20 10
496 A122 10c lt ol brn 35 15

Fourth Book Fair, Apr. 23-28. Exist imperf.

Gen. Rafael L. Trujillo — A123

1958, Aug. 16 *Perf. 12*

497 A123 2c red lil & yel 6 6
498 A123 4c grn & yel 15 8
499 A123 7c brn & yel 25 12
a. Souv. sheet of 3 90 75

Issued to commemorate the 25th anniversary of Gen. Trujillo's designation as "Benefactor of his country."

No. 499a measures 152x101mm and contains one each of Nos. 497-499, imperf. Brown marginal inscription.

S. S. Rhadames A124

1958, Oct. 27 *Perf. 12½*

500 A124 7c brt bl 40 18

Day of the Dominican Merchant Marine. Exists imperf.

The lack of a price for a listed item does not necessarily indicate rarity.

Shozo Sasahara, Japan, Featherweight Wrestling — A125

Olympic Winners and Flags: 1c, Gillian Sheen, England, fencing (vert.). 2c, Milton Campbell, United States, decathlon (vert.). 5c, Madeleine Berthod, Switzerland, downhill skiing. 7c, Murray Rose, Australia, 400 & 1,500 meter freestyle.

1958, Oct. 30 Photo. *Perf. 13½*

Flags in National Colors

501 A125 1c rose, ind & ultra 5 5
502 A125 2c brn & bl 5 5
503 A125 3c gray, vio, blk & buff 5 5
504 A125 5c rose, dk bl, brn & red 8 8
505 A125 7c lt brn, dk bl & red 10 10
Nos. 501-505,C106-C108 (8) 1.03 73

To honor 1956 Olympic winners. Exist imperf.

Miniature sheets of 5 exist, perf. and imperf. containing one each of Nos. 501-505. Size: 140x119½mm. Price, 2 sheets, perf. and imperf., $3.

Globe and Symbolic Fire — A126

1958, Nov. 3 Litho. *Perf. 11½*

506 A126 7c bl & dp car 30 15

Issued to commemorate the opening of UNESCO (U. N. Educational, Scientific and Cultural Organization) Headquarters in Paris, Nov. 3.

Dominican Republic Pavilion, Brussels Fair — A127

1958, Dec. 9 Unwmk. *Perf. 12½*

507 A127 7c bl grn 30 15

Issued for the Universal and International Exposition at Brussels. See Nos. C109-C110a.

Gen. Trujillo Placing Wreath on Altar of the Nation — A128

1959, July 10 *Perf. 12*

508 A128 9c brn, grn, red & gold 30 15
a. Souv. sheet 60 60

Issued to commemorate the 29th anniversary of the Trujillo regime.

No. 508a contains one 9c, imperf. Size: 141x90mm.

Lt. Leonidas Rhadames Trujillo, Team Captain — A129

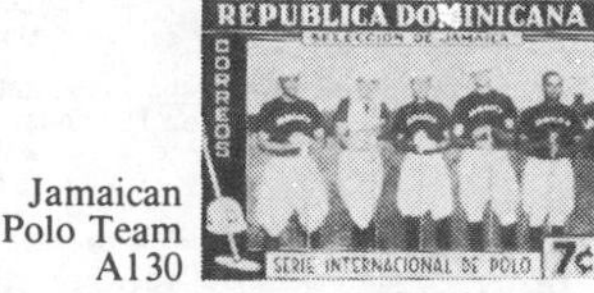

Jamaican Polo Team A130

Design: 10c, Lt. Trujillo on polo pony.

1959, May 15

509	A129	2c violet	20	12
510	A130	7c yel brn	50	25
511	A130	10c green	55	35

Jamaica-Dominican Republic polo match at Ciudad Trujillo.
See also No. C111.

Symbolical of Census A131

1959, Aug. 15 Litho. *Perf. 12½*
Flag in Ultramarine and Red.

512	A131	1c bl & blk	12	10
513	A131	9c grn & blk	30	25
514	A131	13c org & blk	50	35

Issued to publicize the 1960 census.

Trujillo Stadium — A132

1959, Aug. 27

515	A132	9c grn & gray	50	30

Issued to publicize the 3rd Pan American Games Chicago, Aug. 27-Sept. 7.

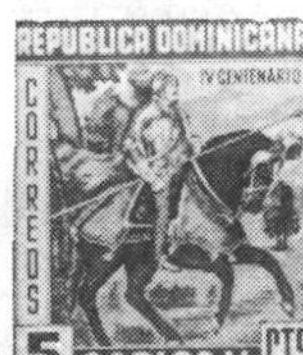

Charles V — A133

1959, Oct. 12 Unwmk. *Perf. 12*

516	A133	5c brt pink	20	10
517	A133	9c vio bl	30	15

Issued to commemorate the 400th anniversary of the death of Charles V (1500-1558), Holy Roman Emperor.

Rhadames Bridge — A134

Designs: 1c and No. 520, Different view of bridge.

1959-60 Litho. *Perf. 12*

518	A134	1c grn & gray ('60)	15	10
519	A134	2c ultra & gray	25	15
520	A134	2c red & gray ('60)	25	10
521	A134	5c brn & dl red brn	35	20

Issue dates: No. 519, Oct. 22; 5c, Nov. 30; 1c and No. 520, Feb. 6, 1960.

Sosua Refugee Settlement and WRY Emblem A135

1960, Apr. 7 *Perf. 12½*
Center in Gray

522	A135	5c red brn & yel grn	15	10
523	A135	9c car & lt bl	30	15
524	A135	13c org & grn	40	25
		Nos. 522-524,C113-C114 (5)	2.05	1.50

Issued to publicize World Refugee Year, July 1, 1959-June 30, 1960.

Sholam Takhti, Iran, Lightweight Wrestling — A136

Olympic Winners: 2c, Mauru Furukawa, Japan, 200 meter breast stroke. 3c, Mildred McDaniel, U.S.A., high jump. 5c, Terence Spinks, England, featherweight boxing. 7c, Carlo Pavesi, Italy, fencing.

Perf. 13½
1960, Sept. 14 Photo. Unwmk.
Flags in National Colors

525	A136	1c red, yel grn & blk	5	5
526	A136	2c org, grnsh bl & brn	5	5
527	A136	3c hn brn & bl	5	5
528	A136	5c brn & ultra	8	8
529	A136	7c grn, bl & rose brn	10	10
		Nos. 525-529,C115-C117 (8)	1.03	73

Issued to commemorate the 17th Olympic Games, Rome, Aug. 25-Sept. 11. Exist imperf.

Miniature sheets of 5 exist, perf. and imperf., containing one each of Nos. 525-529, and a Dominican Republic flag in national colors. Sheet size: 160x121mm. Price, 2 sheets, perf. & imperf., $4.

Post Office, Ciudad Trujillo A137

1960, Aug. 26 Litho. *Perf. 11½x12*

530	A137	2c ultra & gray	18	10

Exists imperf.

Cattle A138

1960, Aug. 30

531	A138	9c car & gray	35	18

Issued to publicize the Agricultural and Industrial Fair, San Juan de la Maguana.

Nos. 518, 490-491, 453, 427 Surcharged in Red, Black or Blue

HABILITADO
PARA
2¢

1960-61 *Perf. 12*

536	A134	2c on 1c grn & gray (R)	20	10
537	A121	9c on 4c lil & rose	70	15
a.		Inverted surcharge	35.00	
538	A121	9c on 7c ultra & gray grn (R) ('61)	70	20
539	A106	36c on ½c brn ('61)	2.25	1.50
a.		Inverted surcharge	30.00	
540	A95	1p on 50c multi (Bl) ('61)	5.00	3.50
		Nos. 536-540 (5)	8.85	5.45

Issue dates: No. 536, Dec. 30, 1960; No. 537, Dec. 20, 1960. Others, Feb. 4, 1961.

Trujillo Memorial A139

Coffee and Cacao A140

1961 Unwmk. *Perf. 11½*

548	A139	1c brown	12	5
549	A139	2c green	15	5
550	A139	4c rose lil	85	85
551	A139	5c lt bl	35	12
552	A139	9c red org	45	30
		Nos. 548-552 (5)	1.92	1.37

Issued in memory of Gen. Rafael L. Trujillo (1891-1961).
Issue dates: 2c, Aug. 7, 4c, Oct. 24, others Aug. 30.

1961, Dec. 30 Litho. *Perf. 12½*

553	A140	1c bl grn	5	5
554	A140	2c org brn	8	5
555	A140	4c violet	15	8
556	A140	5c blue	15	8
557	A140	9c gray	35	8
		Nos. 553-557,C118-C119 (7)	2.03	1.59

Exist imperf.

Dagger Pointing at Mosquito — A141

1962, Apr. 29 Photo. *Perf. 12*

558	A141	10c brt pink & red lil	25	18
559	A141	20c pale brn & brn	50	45
560	A141	25c pale grn & yel grn	65	50
		Nos. 558-560,B39-B40,C120-C121,CB24-CB25 (9)	7.80	6.33

Issued for the World Health Organization drive to eradicate malaria.

Broken Fetters and Laurel A142

"Justice" and Map of Dominican Republic A143

Farm, Factory and Flag A144

Design: 20c, Flag, torch and inscription.

1962, May 30 Litho. *Perf. 12½*

561	A142	1c grn, yel, ultra & red	20	12
562	A143	9c bis ultra & red	45	20
563	A142	20c lt bl, ultra & red	80	45
a.		Souv. sheet of 3	1.00	1.00
564	A143	1p lil, ultra & red	4.00	2.50
		Nos. 561-564,C122-C123 (6)	7.65	4.87

First anniversary of end of Trujillo era. Exist imperf.

No. 563a contains one each of Nos. 561-563, imperf. with ultramarine inscription on pink background. Size: 154x91mm.

1962, May 22

565	A144	1c ultra, red & grn	5	5
566	A144	2c ultra & red	10	5
567	A144	3c ultra, red & brn	12	6
568	A144	5c ultra, red & bl	20	8
569	A144	15c ultra, red & org	40	20
		Nos. 565-569 (5)	87	44

Map and Laurel A145

1962, June 14 Litho.

570	A145	1c black	35	20

Issued to honor the martyrs of June 1959 revolution.

Western Hemisphere and Carrier Pigeon A146

Archbishop Adolfo Alejandro Nouel A147

1962, Oct. 23 Unwmk. *Perf. 12½*

571	A146	2c rose red	12	6
572	A146	9c orange	35	18
573	A146	14c bl grn	22	10
		Nos. 571-573,C124-C125 (5)	1.69	1.14

Issued to commemorate the 50th anniversary of the founding of the Postal Union of the Americas and Spain, UPAE.

1962, Dec. 18

574	A147	2c bl grn & dl bl	8	5
575	A147	9c org & red brn	35	18
576	A147	13c mar & vio brn	45	30
		Nos. 574-576,C126-C127 (5)	2.28	1.53

Issued to commemorate the centenary of the birth of Archbishop Adolfo Alejandro Nouel, President of Dominican Republic in 1911.

Globe, Banner and Emblems
A148

1963, Apr. 15 Unwmk. *Perf. 11½*
Banner in Dark Blue & Red

577 A148 2c green 10 5
578 A148 5c brt rose lil 25 10
579 A148 9c orange 40 18
Nos. 577-579,B41-B43 (6) 1.29 84

Issued for the "Freedom from Hunger" campaign of the U.N. Food and Agriculture Organization.

Juan Pablo Duarte — A149

Designs: 7c, Francisco Sanchez. 9c, Ramon Mella.

1963, July 7 Litho. *Perf. 12x11½*

580 A149 2c ultra 6 5
581 A149 7c dl grn 18 18
582 A149 9c red lil 25 20

Issued to commemorate the 120th anniversary of separation from Haiti. See also No. C128.

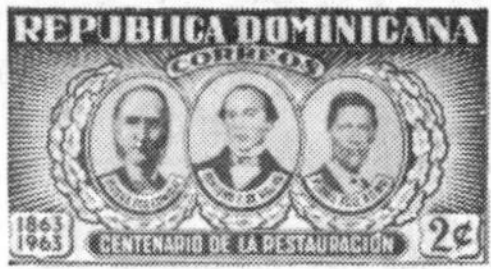

Ulises F. Espaillat, Benigno F. de Rojas and Pedro F. Bono
A150

Designs: 4c, Generals Santiago Rodriguez, José Cabrera and Benito Moncion. 5c, Capotillo monument. 9c, Generals Gaspar Polanco, Gregorio Luperon and JoseA. Salcedo.

1963, Aug. 16 Unwmk. *Perf. 11½*

583 A150 2c green 8 5
584 A150 4c red org 12 10
585 A150 5c brown 15 12
586 A150 9c brt bl 25 20
a. Souv. sheet of 4 75 75

Issued to commemorate the centenary of the Restoration. No. 586a contains 4 imperf. stamps similar to Nos. 583-586. Brown marginal inscription. Size: 229x106½mm.

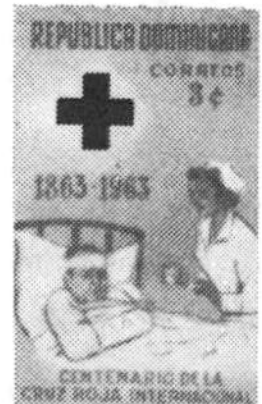

Patient and Nurse — A151

1963, Oct. 25 Unwmk. *Perf. 12½*

587 A151 3c gray & car 12 12
588 A151 6c emer & red 25 15

Centenary of International Red Cross. Exist imperf. See No. C129.

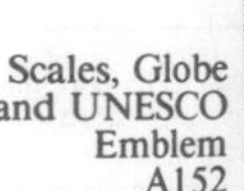

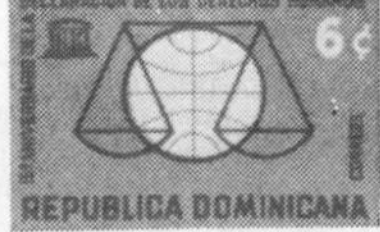

Scales, Globe and UNESCO Emblem
A152

1963, Dec. 10 Litho.

589 A152 6c pink & dp pink 18 12
590 A152 50c lt grn & grn 1.10 85

Universal Declaration of Human Rights, 15th anniversary. Exist imperf. See also Nos. C130-C131.

Ramses II Battling the Hittites (from Abu Simbel)
A153

Design: 6c, Two heads of Ramses II.

1964, March 8 Unwmk. *Perf. 12½*

591 A153 3c pale pink & ver 10 8
592 A153 6c pale bl & ultra 20 15
593 A153 9c pale rose & red brn 30 20
Nos. 591-593,C132-C133 (5) 1.35 1.03

Issued to publicize the UNESCO world campaign to save historic monuments in Nubia.

Maximo Gomez
A154

Palm Chat
A155

1964, Apr. 30 Litho.

594 A154 2c lt bl & bl 6 6
595 A154 6c dl pink & dl cl 18 12

Issued to commemorate the bicentenary of the founding of the town of Bani.

1964, June 8 Unwmk. *Perf. 12½*

Design: 6c, Hispaniolan parrot.

Size: 27x37½mm.

596 A155 3c ultra, brn & yel 20 15
597 A155 6c gray & multi 30 20

See also Nos. 602-604, C134.

Rocket Leaving Earth
A156

Designs: 1c, Launching of rocket (vert.). 3c, Space capsule orbiting earth. 6c, As 2c.

1964, July 28 Litho.

598 A156 1c sky bl 10 8
599 A156 2c emerald 15 10
600 A156 3c blue 20 15
601 A156 6c sky bl 35 18
Nos. 598-601,C135-C136 (6) 1.70 1.16

Issued to commemorate the conquest of space.

Bird Type of 1964

Designs: 1c, Narrow-billed tody. 2c, Hispaniolan emerald hummingbird. 6c, Hispaniolan trogon.

1964, Nov. 7 *Perf. 11½*
Size: 26x37mm.
Birds in Natural Colors

602 A155 1c brt pink 15 10
603 A155 2c dk brn 18 10
604 A155 6c blue 35 20

Universal Postal Union and United Nations Emblems
A157

1964, Dec. 5 Litho. *Perf. 12½*

605 A157 1c red 10 6
606 A157 4c green 20 12
607 A157 5c orange 22 15

Issued to commemorate the 15th Universal Postal Union Congress, Vienna, Austria, May-June 1964. See also No. C138.

International Cooperation Year Emblem
A158

1965, Feb. 16 Unwmk. *Perf. 12½*

608 A158 2c lt bl & ultra 6 5
609 A158 3c emer & dk grn 8 6
610 A158 6c sal pink & red 18 10

Issued to publicize the United Nations International Cooperation Year. See No. C139.

Virgin of Altagracia
A159

Flags of 21 American Nations
A160

Design: 2c, Hands holding lily.

1965, Mar. 18 Unwmk. *Perf. 12½*

611 A159 2c grn, emer & dp rose 15 8
612 A159 6c multi 50 40

Issued to commemorate the Fourth Mariological Congress and the Eleventh International Marian Congress. No. 612 exists imperf. See No. C140.

1965, Apr. 14 Litho. *Perf. 11½*

613 A160 2c brn, yel & multi 8 5
614 A160 6c red lil & multi 20 12

Organization of American States.

Stamp of 1865 (No. 1) — A161

1965, Dec. 28 Litho. *Perf. 12½*

615 A161 1c pink, buff & blk 10 8
616 A161 2c bl, buff & blk 12 10
617 A161 6c emer, buff & blk 20 15
a. Souv. sheet of 2 1.00 1.00
Nos. 615-617,C142-C143 (5) 1.17 98

Issued to commemorate the centenary of the first Dominican postage stamps. No. 617a shows replicas of Nos. 1-2. Bright blue marginal inscription. Size: 100x65mm. Sold for 50c.

The Catalogue editors cannot undertake to appraise, identify or judge the genuineness or condition of stamps.

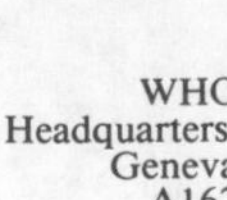

WHO Headquarters, Geneva
A162

1966, May 21 Litho. *Perf. 12½*

618 A162 6c blue 20 10
619 A162 10c red lil 35 20

Issued to commemorate the inauguration of World Health Organization Headquarters, Geneva.

Man Holding Map of Republic — A163

1966, May 23

620 A163 2c blk & brt grn 6 5
621 A163 6c blk & dp org 18 10

Issued to publicize the general elections, June 1, 1966.

Ascia Monuste
A164

National Altar
A165

1966 Litho. *Perf. 12½*
Various Butterflies in Natural Colors

Size: 31x21mm.

622 A164 1c bl & vio bl 12 10
623 A164 2c lt grn & brt grn 18 15
624 A164 3c lt gray & gray 24 20
625 A164 6c pink & mag 35 30
626 A164 8c buff & brn 55 55
Nos. 622-626,C146-C148 (8) 5.79 4.10

Issue dates: 1c, Sept. 7; 3c, Sept. 11; others, Nov. 8.

1967, Jan. 18 Litho. *Perf. 11½*

627 A165 1c brt bl 5 5
628 A165 2c car rose 5 5
629 A165 3c emerald 6 5
630 A165 4c gray 8 6
631 A165 5c org yel 10 8
632 A165 6c orange 12 10
Nos. 627-632,C149-C151 (9) 1.36 1.09

Map of Republic and Emblem
A166

1967, Mar. 30 Litho. *Perf. 12½*

633 A166 2c yel, bl & blk 7 5
634 A166 6c org, bl & blk 20 10
635 A166 10c emer, bl & blk 35 18

Development Year, 1967.

Rook and Knight
A167

1967, June 23 Litho. *Perf. 12½*
636 A167 25c multi 1.00 60

Issued to commemorate the 5th Central American Chess Championships, Santo Domingo. See also Nos. C152-C152a.

Alliance for Progress A168

Institute Emblem A169

1967, Sept. 16 Litho. *Perf. 12½*
637 A168 1c brt grn 6 6

Issued to commemorate the 6th anniversary of the Alliance for Progress. See Nos. C153-C154.

1967, Oct. 7
638 A169 3c brt grn 9 7
639 A169 6c sal pink 18 12

Issued to commemorate the 25th anniversary of the Inter-American Agriculture Institute. See also No. C155.

Globe and Satellite A170

1968, June 15 Typo. *Perf. 12*
640 A170 6c blk & multi 35 25

Issued to commemorate World Meteorological Day, Mar. 23. See Nos. C156-C157.

Boxers A171

1968, June 29
641 A171 6c rose red & dp cl 25 20

Issued to commemorate the fight between Carlos Ortiz, Puerto Rico, and Teo Cruz, Dominican Republic, for the World Lightweight Boxing Championship. See Nos. C158-C159.

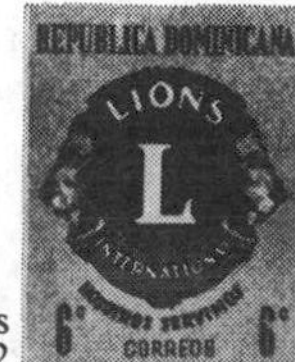

Lions Emblem — A172

1968, Aug. 9 Litho. *Perf. 11½*
642 A172 6c brn & multi 20 12

Issued to commemorate the 50th anniversary (in 1967) of Lions International. See No. C160.

Wrestling and Olympic Emblem A173

Designs (Olympic Emblem and): 6c, Running. 25c, Boxing.

1968, Nov. 12 Litho. *Perf. 11½*
643 A173 1c sky bl & multi 15 8
644 A173 6c pale grn & multi 35 15
645 A173 25c pale lil & multi 1.25 60
Nos. 643-645,C161-C162 (5) 3.20 2.18

Issued to commemorate the 19th Olympic Games, Mexico City, Oct. 12-27.

Map of Americas and House A174

Stool in Human Form A175

1969, Jan. 25 Litho. *Perf. 12½*
646 A174 6c brt bl, lt bl & grn 25 12

Issued to publicize the 7th Inter-American Conference for Savings and Loans, Santo Domingo, Jan. 25-31. See No. C163.

1969, Jan. 31 Litho. *Perf. 12½*

Taino Art: 2c, Wood carved mother figure (vert.). 3c, Face carved on 3-cornered stone. 4c, Stone hatchet (vert.). 5c, Clay pot.

647 A175 1c yel, org & blk 6 5
648 A175 2c lt grn, grn & blk 8 6
649 A175 3c cit, ol & brt grn 12 10
650 A175 4c lt lil, lil & brt grn 18 15
651 A175 5c yel, org & brn 20 18
Nos. 647-651,C164-C166 (8) 1.84 1.42

Taino art flourished in the West Indies at the time of Columbus.

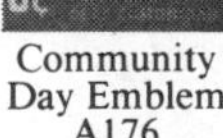

Community Day Emblem A176

COTAL Emblem A177

Headquarters Building and COTAL Emblem — A178

1969, Mar. 25 Litho. *Perf. 12½*
652 A176 6c dl grn & gold 20 10

Issued for Community Development Day, March 22.

1969, May 25 Litho. *Perf. 12½*

Design: 2c, Boy and COTAL emblem.

653 A177 1c lt & dk bl & red 5 5
654 A177 2c emer & dk grn 10 5
655 A178 6c ver & pink 18 10

Issued to publicize the 12th Congress of the Confederation of Latin American Tourist Organizations (COTAL), Santo Domingo, May 25-29.
See No. C167.

ILO Emblem — A179

Sliding into Base — A180

1969, June 27 Litho. *Perf. 12½*
656 A179 6c lt grnsh bl, grnsh bl & blk 40 10

Issued to commemorate the 50th anniversary of the International Labor Organization. See No. C168.

1969, Aug. 15 Litho. *Perf. 12½*

Designs: 1c, Catching a fly ball. 2c, View of Cibao Stadium (horiz.).

Size: 21x31mm. (1c, 3c); 43x30mm. (2c).

657 A180 1c grn & gray 15 8
658 A180 2c grn & lt grn 18 12
659 A180 3c pur & red brn 22 15
Nos. 657-659,C169-C171 (6) 5.05 3.35

Issued to publicize the 17th World Amateur Baseball Championships, Santo Domingo.

Las Damas Dam — A181

Tavera Dam A182

Designs: 2c, Las Damas hydroelectric station (vert.). 6c, Arroyo Hondo substation.

1969 Litho. *Perf. 12*
660 A181 2c grn & multi 6 5
661 A181 3c dk bl & multi 9 5
662 A181 6c brt rose lil 18 10
663 A182 6c multi 25 12
Nos. 660-663,C172-C173 (6) 1.23 67

Issued to publicize the national electrification plan.
Issue dates: Nos. 660-662, Sept. 15. No. 663, Oct. 15.

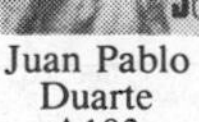

Juan Pablo Duarte A183

Map of Republic, People, Census Emblem A184

1970, Jan. 26 Litho. *Perf. 12*
664 A183 1c emer & dk grn 5 5
665 A183 2c sal pink & dp car 6 5
666 A183 3c brt pink & plum 9 5
667 A183 6c bl & vio bl 18 10
Nos. 664-667,C174 (5) 68 43

Issued for Duarte Day in memory of Juan Pablo Duarte (1813-1876), liberator.

1970, Feb. 6 *Perf. 11*

Design: 6c, Census emblem and inscription.

668 A184 5c emer & blk 15 8
669 A184 6c ultra & bl 18 10

Census of 1970. See No. C175.

Abelardo Rodriguez Urdaneta — A185

"One of Many" A186

1970, Feb. 20 Litho. *Perf. 12½*
670 A185 3c ultra 15 8
671 A185 6c grn & yel grn 25 12

Issued to honor Abelardo Rodriguez Urdaneta, sculptor. See No. C176.

Masonic Symbols — A187

1970, Mar. 2
672 A187 6c green 20 10

Issued to publicize the 8th Inter-American Masonic Conference, Santo Domingo, Mar. 1-7. See No. C177.

Communications Satellite — A188

1970, May 25 Litho. *Perf. 12½*
673 A188 20c ol & gray 80 45

Issued for World Telecommunications Day. See No. C178.

U.P.U. Headquarters, Bern — A189

1970, June 5 *Perf. 11*
674 A189 6c gray & brn 20 12

Issued to commemorate the inauguration of the new Universal Postal Union Headquarters in Bern. See No. C179.

The indexes in each volume of the Scott Catalogue contain many listings which help to identify stamps.

Education Year Emblem A190

Pedro Alejandrino Pina A191

1970, June 26 Litho. *Perf. 12½*
675 A190 4c rose lil 12 6

Issued for International Education Year, 1970. See No. C180.

1970, Aug. 24 Litho. *Perf. 12½*
676 A191 6c lt red brn & blk 18 10

Issued to commemorate the 150th anniversary of the birth and the centenary of the death of Pedro Alejandrino Pina (1820-70), author.

Children Reading — A192

1970, Oct. 12 Litho. *Perf. 12½*
677 A192 5c dl grn 15 10

Issued to publicize the First World Exhibition of Books and Culture Festival, Santo Domingo, Oct. 11-Dec. 11. See Nos. C181-C182.

Virgin of Altagracia A193

Manuel Rodriguez Objio A194

1971, Jan. 20 Litho. *Perf. 12½*
678 A193 3c multi 20 10

Inauguration of the Basilica of Our Lady of Altagracia. See No. C184.

1971, June 18 Litho. *Perf. 11*
679 A194 6c lt bl 20 10

Centenary of the death of Manuel Rodriguez Objio (1838-1871), poet.

Boxing and Canoeing — A195

Design: 5c, Basketball.

1971, Sept. 10
680 A195 2c brn & org 12 8
681 A195 5c brn & lt grn 28 12

2nd National Games. See No. C186.

Goat and Fruit A196

Designs: 2c, Cow and goose. 3c, Cacao and horse. 6c, Bananas, coffee and pig.

1971, Sept. 29 *Perf. 12½*
682 A196 1c brn & multi 6 6
683 A196 2c plum & multi 8 6
684 A196 3c grn & multi 10 8
685 A196 6c bl & multi 20 15
Nos. 682-685,C187 (5) 1.14 85

6th National agriculture and livestock census.

José Nuñez de Caceres — A197

Shepherds and Star — A198

1971, Dec. 1 *Perf. 11*
686 A197 6c lt bl, lil & dk bl 18 10

Sesquicentennial of first national independence. See No. C188.

1971, Dec. 10 *Perf. 12½*
687 A198 6c bl, brn & yel 25 12

Christmas 1971. See No. C189.

UNICEF Emblem, Child on Beach — A199

1971, Dec. 14 Litho. *Perf. 11*
688 A199 6c gray bl & multi 18 10

25th anniversary of the United Nations International Children's Fund (UNICEF). See No. C190.

Book Year Emblem — A200

Taino Mask — A201

1972, Jan. 25 *Perf. 12½*
689 A200 1c grn, ultra & red 5 5
690 A200 2c brn, ultra & red 6 5

International Book Year 1972. See No. C191.

1972, May 10 Litho. *Perf. 11*

Taino Art: 4c, Ladle and amulet. 6c, Human figure.

691 A201 2c pink & multi 12 5
692 A201 4c blk, bl & ocher 18 8
693 A201 6c gray & multi 30 15
Nos. 691-693,C194-C196 (6) 1.90 1.01

Taino art. See note after No. 651.

Globe A202

1972, May 17 *Perf. 12½*
694 A202 6c bl & multi 20 10

4th World Telecommunications Day. See No. C197.

"1972," Stamps and Map of Dominican Republic A203

1972, June 3
695 A203 2c grn & multi 8 5

First National Philatelic Exhibition, Santo Domingo, June 3-17. See No. C198.

Basketball — A204

1972, Aug. 25 Litho. *Perf. 12½*
696 A204 2c bl & multi 15 10

20th Olympic Games, Munich, Aug. 26-Sept. 11. See No. C199.

Club Emblem A205

1972, Sept. 29 Litho. *Perf. 10½*
697 A205 1c lt grn & multi 8 5

50th anniversary of the Club Activo 20-30 International. See No. C200.

Emilio A. Morel A206

1972, Oct. 20 *Perf. 12½*
698 A206 6c brt pink & multi 18 10

Emilio A. Morel (1884-1958), poet and journalist. See No. C201.

Central Bank Building A207

Design: 5c, One peso note.

1972, Oct. 23
699 A207 1c blk & multi 6 5
700 A207 5c red, blk & grn 18 10

25th anniversary of Central Bank. See No. C202.

Holy Family — A208

Poinsettia A209

1972, Nov. 21
701 A208 2c rose lil, pur & gold 12 6
702 A208 6c red & multi 30 12

Christmas 1972. See No. C203.

Mail Box and Student A210

1972, Dec. 15
703 A210 2c rose red 6 5
704 A210 6c blue 18 10
705 A210 10c emerald 30 15

Publicity for correspondence schools.

Tavera Dam A211

1973, Feb. 26 Litho. *Perf. 12½*
706 A211 10c multi 30 15

Inauguration of the Tavera Dam.

Various Sports — A212

1973, Mar. 30 *Perf. 13½x13*
707 A212 2c brn, yel & grn, block of 4 60 35
a. Upper left 15 8
b. Upper right 15 8

c. Lower left 15 8
d. Lower right 15 8
708 A212 25c dk grn & yel grn, block of 4 3.00 1.65
a. Upper left 75 40
b. Upper right 75 40
c. Upper left 75 40
d. Upper right 75 40
Nos. 707-708,C204-C205 (4) 7.60 5.75

Publicity for the 12th Central American and Caribbean Games, Santo Domingo, Summer 1974.

Christ Carrying the Cross A213

Design: 6c, Belfry of Church of Our Lady of Carmen (vert.).

1973, Apr. 18 Litho. *Perf. 10½*
709 A213 2c multi 12 6
710 A213 6c multi 30 15

Holy Week, 1973. See No. C206.

WMO Emblem, Weather Satellite, "Weather" — A214

Mask, Cibao — A215

1973, Aug. 10 Litho. *Perf. 13½x13*
711 A214 6c mag & multi 18 12

Centenary of international meteorological cooperation. See No. C208.

1973, Oct. 12 Litho. *Perf. 10½*
712 A215 1c *Maguey drum* (horiz.) 5 5
713 A215 2c *Carved amber* (horiz.) 6 5
714 A215 4c *shown* 12 8
715 A215 6c *Pottery* 18 12
Nos. 712-715,C210-C211 (6) 92 65

Opening of Museum of Mankind in Santo Domingo.

Nativity A216

Design: 6c, Stained glass window (vert.).

Perf. 13½x13, 13x13½
1973, Nov. 26
716 A216 2c blk, bl & yel 10 8
717 A216 6c rose & multi 25 18

Christmas 1973. See No. C212.
No. 717 exists imperf.

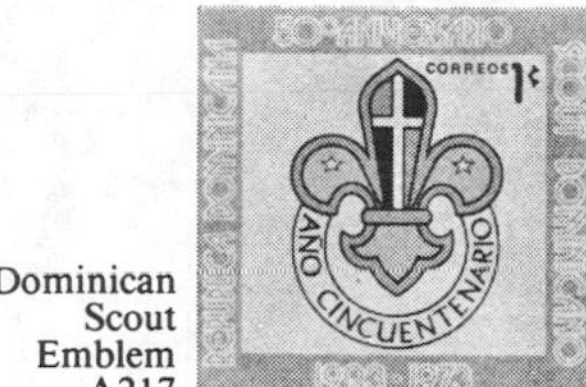
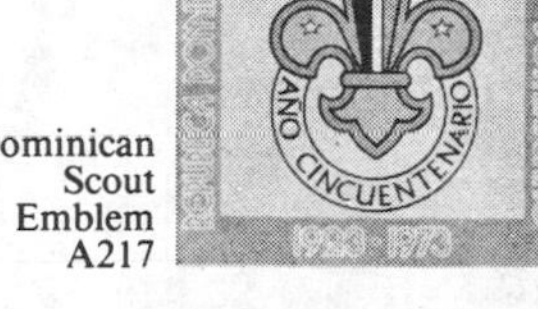

Dominican Scout Emblem A217

Design: 5c, Scouts and flag.

1973, Dec. 7 Litho. *Perf. 12*
Size: 35x35mm.
718 A217 1c ultra & multi 10 5
Size: 26x36mm.
719 A217 5c blk & multi 20 10

50th anniversary of Dominican Republic Boy Scouts. See No. C213.

Sports Palace, Basketball Players A218

Design: 6c, Bicyclist and race track.

1974, Feb. 25 Litho. *Perf. 13½*
720 A218 2c red brn & multi 10 6
721 A218 6c yel & multi 25 15

12th Central American and Caribbean Games, Santo Domingo, 1974. See Nos. C214-C215.

Bell Tower, Cathedral of Santo Domingo A219

Mater Dolorosa A220

1974, June 27 Litho. *Perf. 13½*
722 A219 2c multi 15 8
723 A220 6c multi 35 18

Holy Week 1974. See No. C216.

Francisco del Rosario Sanchez Bridge — A221

1974, July 12 *Perf. 12*
724 A221 6c multi 20 15

See No. C217.

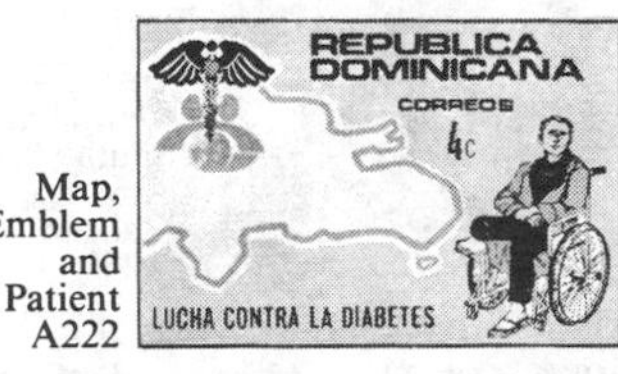

Map, Emblem and Patient A222

Design: 5c, Map of Dominican Republic, diabetics' emblem and pancreas.

1974, Aug. 22 Litho. *Perf. 13*
725 A222 4c bl & multi 14 10
726 A222 5c yel grn & multi 14 12

Fight against diabetes. See Nos. C218-C219.

Train and UPU Emblem A223

Design: 6c, Mail coach and UPU emblem.

1974, Oct. 9 Litho. *Perf. 13½*
727 A223 2c bl & multi 10 5
728 A223 6c brn & multi 20 12

Centenary of Universal Postal Union. See Nos. C220-C221a.

Golfers — A224

Design: 2c, Championship emblem and badge of Dominican Golf Association (horiz.).

Perf. 13x13½, 13½x13
1974, Oct. 24
729 A224 2c yel & blk 15 10
730 A224 6c bl & multi 35 20

World Amateur Golf Championships. See Nos. C222-C223.

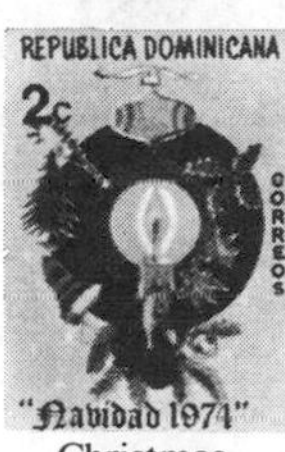

Christmas Decorations A225

Virgin and Child A226

1974, Dec. 3 Litho. *Perf. 12*
731 A225 2c multi 14 8
732 A226 6c multi 30 18

Christmas 1974. See No. C224.

Tomatoes, FAO Emblem — A227

1974, Dec. 5
733 A227 2c *shown* 8 5
734 A227 3c *Avocados* 12 6
735 A227 5c *Coconuts* 20 10

World Food Program, 10th anniversary. See No. C225.

Fernando A. Defillo A228

Tower, Our Lady of the Rosary Convent A229

1975, Feb. 14 Litho. *Perf. 13½x13*
736 A228 1c dl brn 5 5
737 A228 6c dl grn 18 12

Dr. Fernando A. Defillo (1874-1949), physician.

1975, Mar. 26 Litho. *Perf. 13½*

Design: 2c, Jesus saying "I am the Resurrection and the Life."

738 A229 2c brn & multi 15 5
739 A229 6c multi 25 12

Holy Week 1975. See No. C226.

Hands (Steel Beams) with Symbols of Agriculture, Industry A230

1975, May 19 Litho. *Perf. 10½x10*
740 A230 6c dl bl & multi 18 12

16th Assembly of the Governors of the International Development Bank, Santo Domingo, May 1975. See No. C228.

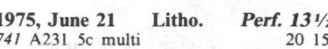

Satellite Tracking Station — A231

1975, June 21 Litho. *Perf. 13½*
741 A231 5c multi 20 15

Opening of first earth satellite tracking station in Dominican Republic. See No. C229.

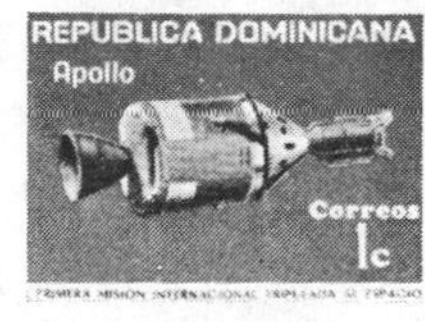

Apollo A232

Design: 4c, Soyuz.

1975, July 24
Size: 35x25mm.
742 A232 1c bl & multi 10 8
743 A232 4c vio bl & multi 25 18

Apollo Soyuz space test project (Russo-American cooperation), launching July 15; link-up, July 17. See No. C230.

Father Rafael C. Castellanos A233

1975, Aug. 6 Litho. *Perf. 12*
744 A233 6c brn & buff 18 12

Father Rafael C. Castellanos (1875-1934), first Apostolic Administrator in Dominican Republic, birth centenary.

Women and Men Around IWY Emblem A234

1975, Aug. 6 *Perf. 13*
745 A234 3c org & multi 12 6

International Women's Year 1975.

Guacanagarix
A235

Basketball
A236

Indian Chiefs: 2c, Guarionex. 3c, Caonabo. 4c, Bohechio. 5c, Cayacoa. 6c, Anacona (woman). 9c, Hatuey.

1975, Sept. 27 **Litho.** *Perf. 12*
746 A235 1c yel & multi 5 5
747 A235 2c sal & multi 6 5
748 A235 3c vio bl & multi 9 6
749 A235 4c grn & multi 12 8
750 A235 5c bl & multi 15 10
751 A235 6c vio & multi 18 12
752 A235 9c rose & multi 20 20
Nos. 746-752,C231-C233 (10) 2.00 1.46

1975, Oct. 24 **Litho.** *Perf. 12*

Design: 6c, Baseball and Games' emblem.

753 A236 2c pink & multi 12 6
754 A236 6c org & multi 30 15

7th Pan-American Games, Mexico City, Oct. 13-26. See Nos. C234-C235.

Carolers
A237

Design: 6c, Dominican nativity with farmers and shepherds.

1975, Dec. 12 **Litho.** *Perf. 13x13½*
755 A237 2c yel & multi 15 6
756 A237 6c bl & multi 25 15

Christmas 1975. See No. C236.

Abudefdul Marginatus — A238

1976, Jan. 23 **Litho.** *Perf. 13*
757 A238 10c *shown* 45 40
758 A238 10c *Doncella* 45 40
759 A238 10c *Carajuelo* 45 40
760 A238 10c *Reina de los Angeles* 45 40
761 A238 10c *Pargo Colorado* 45 40
Nos. 757-761 (5) 2.25 2.00

Nos. 757-761 printed se-tenant.

A particular stamp may be scarce, but if few collectors want it, its market value may remain relatively low.

Ascension, by J. Priego — A239

"Separacion Dominicana" and Adm. Cambiaso — A240

Design: 2c, Mary Magdalene, by Enrique Godoy.

1976, Apr. 14 **Litho.** *Perf. 13½*
762 A239 2c bl & multi 12 10
763 A239 6c yel & multi 30 12

Holy Week 1976. See No. C238.

1976, Apr. 15 *Perf. 13½x13*
764 A240 20c multi 20 20

Naval Battle off Tortuga, Apr. 15, 1844.

Maps of US and Dominican Republic — A241

Design: 9c, Maps within cogwheels.

1976, May 29 **Litho.** *Perf. 13½*
765 A241 6c vio bl & multi 20 10
766 A241 9c vio bl & multi 10 5

American Bicentennial. See Nos. C239-C240.

Flags of Dominican Republic and Spain
A242

1976, May 31
767 A242 6c multi 55 10

Visit of King Juan Carlos I and Queen Sofia of Spain. See No. C241.

Various Telephones
A243

1976, July 15 *Perf. 12x12½*
768 A243 6c multi 20 10

Centenary of first telephone call by Alexander Graham Bell, Mar. 10, 1876. See No. C242.

Vision of Duarte, by Luis Desangles
A244

Juan Pablo Duarte, by Rhadames Mejia — A245

1976, July 20 **Litho.** *Perf. 13x13½*
769 A244 2c multi 10 5

Perf. 13½
770 A245 6c multi 25 8

Juan Pablo Duarte, liberation hero, death centenary. See Nos. C243-C244.

Fire Hydrant — A246

Design: 6c, Firemen's emblem.

1976, Sept. 13 **Litho.** *Perf. 12*
771 A246 4c multi 12 6
772 A246 6c multi 18 8

Honoring firemen. Nos. 771-772 inscribed "Correos". See No. C245.

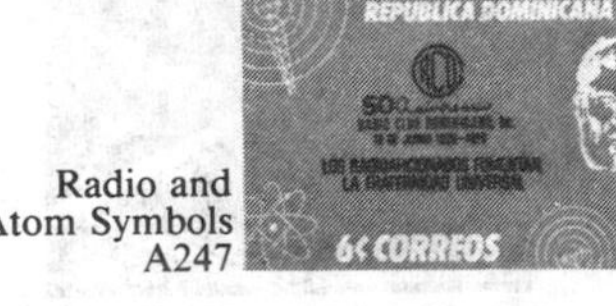

Radio and Atom Symbols
A247

1976, Oct. 8 **Litho.** *Perf. 13½*
773 A247 6c red & blk 20 8

Dominican Radio Club, 50th anniversary. See No. C246.

Spain, Central and South America, Galleon
A248

1976, Oct. 22 **Litho.** *Perf. 13½*
774 A248 6c multi 25 8

Spanish heritage. See No. C247.

Boxing and Montreal Emblem
A249

Design: 3c, Weight lifting.

1976, Oct. 22 *Perf. 12*
775 A249 2c bl & multi 12 5
776 A249 3c multi 12 5

21st Olympic Games, Montreal, Canada July 17-Aug. 1. See Nos. C248-C249.

Virgin and Child
A250

Three Kings
A251

1976, Dec. 8 **Litho.** *Perf. 13½*
777 A250 2c multi 15 8
778 A251 6c multi 30 15

Christmas 1976. See No. C250.

Cable Car and Beach Scenes
A252

1977, Jan. 7
779 A252 6c multi 25 12

Tourist publicity. See Nos. C251-C253.

Championship Emblem — A253

1977, Mar. 4 **Litho.** *Perf. 13½*
780 A253 3c rose & multi 10 6
781 A253 5c yel & multi 18 10

10th Central American and Caribbean Children's and Young People's Swimming Championships, Santo Domingo. See Nos. C254-C255.

Christ Carrying Cross — A254

Design: 6c, Head with crown of thorns.

1977, Apr. 18 **Litho.** *Perf. 13½x13*
782 A254 2c multi 18 8
783 A254 6c blk & rose 35 10

Holy Week 1977. See No. C256.

REPUBLICA DOMINICANA
CORREOS
2c

Doves, Lions Emblem
A255

1977, May 6 *Perf. 13½x13*

784 A255 2c lt bl & multi 8 6
785 A255 6c sal & multi 20 8

12th annual Dominican Republic Lions Convention. See No. C257.

Battle Scene A256

1977, June 15 Litho. *Perf. 13x13½*

786 A256 20c multi 60 40

Dominican Navy.

Water Lily — A257

Designs: 4c, "Flor de Mayo" (orchid). 6c, Sebesten.

1977, Aug. 19 Litho. *Perf. 12*

787 A257 2c multi 12 6
788 A257 4c multi 18 8
789 A257 6c multi 25 10
Nos. 787-789,C259-C260 (5) 1.15 74

National Botanical Garden.

Chart and Computers — A258

1977, Nov. 30 Litho. *Perf. 13*

790 A258 6c multi 25 8

7th Interamerican Statistics Conference. See No. C261.

Solenodon Paradoxus — A259

Design: 20c, Iguana and Congress emblem.

1977, Dec. 29 Litho. *Perf. 13*

791 A259 6c multi 25 8
792 A259 20c multi 70 40

8th Pan-American Veterinary and Zoo-technical Congress. See Nos. C262-C263.

Main Gate, Casa del Cordon, 1503 — A260

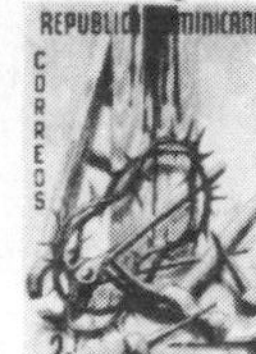

Crown of Thorns, Tools at the Cross — A261

1978, Jan. 19 *Perf. 13x13½*

Size: 26x36mm.

793 A260 6c multi 18 8

Spanish heritage. See No. C264.

1978, Mar. 21 Litho. *Perf. 12*

Design: 6c, Head of Jesus with crown of thorns.

Size: 22x33mm.

794 A261 2c multi 12 5
795 A261 6c slate 30 8

Holy Week 1978. See Nos. C265-C266.

Cardinal Octavio A. Beras Rojas — A262

Pres. Manuel de Troncoso — A263

1978, May 5 Litho. *Perf. 13*

796 A262 6c multi 20 8

First Cardinal from Dominican Republic, consecrated May 24, 1976. See No. C268.

1978, June 12 Litho. *Perf. 13½*

797 A263 2c blk, rose & brn 6 5
798 A263 6c blk, gray & brn 18 8

Manuel de Jesus Troncoso de la Concha (1878-1955), president of Dominican Republic 1940-1942.

Father Juan N. Zegri y Moreno — A264

1978, July 11 Litho. *Perf. 13x13½*

799 A264 6c multi 20 8

Congregation of the Merciful Sisters of Charity, centenary. See No. C273.

Boxing and Games' Emblem A265

Design: 6c, Weight lifting.

1978, July 21 *Perf. 12*

800 A265 2c multi 12 5
801 A265 6c multi 25 8

13th Central American and Caribbean Games, Medellin, Colombia. See Nos. C274-C275.

Sun over Landscape A266

Ships of Columbus, Map of Dominican Republic — A267

Design: 6c, Sun over beach and boat.

1978, Sept. 12 Litho. *Perf. 12*

802 A266 2c multi 8 5
803 A266 6c multi 20 8

Tourist publicity. See Nos. C280-C281.

1978, Oct. 12 Litho. *Perf. 13½*

804 A267 2c multi 10 6

Spanish heritage. See No. C282.

Dove, Lamp, Poinsettia A268

Design: 6c, Dominican family and star (vert.).

1978, Dec. 5 Litho. *Perf. 12*

805 A268 2c multi 18 8
806 A268 6c multi 35 12

Christmas 1978. See No. C284.

Starving Child, ICY Emblem — A269

1979, Feb. 26 Litho. *Perf. 12*

807 A269 2c org & blk 12 5

International Year of the Child. See Nos. C287-C289.

Crucifixion — A270

Design: 3c, Jesus carrying cross (horiz.).

1979, Apr. 9 Litho. *Perf. 13½*

808 A270 2c multi 15 8
809 A270 3c multi 25 8

Holy Week. See No. C290.

Stigmaphyllon Periplocifolium — A271

1979, May 17 Litho. *Perf. 12*

810 A271 50c multi 70 40

"Dr. Rafael M. Moscoso" National Botanical Garden. See Nos. C293-C295.

Heart, Diseased Blood Vessel A272

Design: 1p, Cardiology Institute and heart.

1979, June 2 Litho. *Perf. 13½*

811 A272 3c multi 12 5
812 A272 1p multi 1.10 60

Dominican Cardiology Institute. See No. C296.

Baseball, Games' Emblem A273

Design: 3c, Bicycling and Games' emblem (vert.).

1979, June 20

813 A273 2c multi 10 5
814 A273 3c multi 18 5

8th Pan American Games, Puerto Rico, June 30-July 15. See No. C297.

Soccer — A274

Thomas A. Edison — A275

Design: 25c, Swimming (horiz.).

1979, Aug. 9 Litho. *Perf. 12*

815 A274 2c multi 10 5
816 A274 25c multi 30 20

Third National Games. See No. C298.

1979, Aug. 27 *Perf. 13½*

817 A275 25c multi 80 50

Centenary of invention of electric light. See No. C300.

Demand, as well as supply, determines a stamp's market value. One is as important as the other.

Hand Holding Electric Plug — A276

Design: 6c, Filling automobile gas tank.

1979, Aug. 30

818 A276 2c multi 6 6
819 A276 6c multi 20 12

Energy conservation.

Parrot A277

Birds: 6c, Temnotrogon roseigaster.

1979, Sept. 12 Litho. *Perf. 12*

820 A277 2c multi 10 5
821 A277 6c multi 25 12
Nos. 820-821,C301-C303 (5) 1.50 1.17

Lions Emblem, Map of Dominican Republic — A278

1979, Nov. 13 Litho. *Perf. 12*

822 A278 20c multi 65 35

Lions International Club of Dominican Republic, 10th anniversary. See No. C304.

Holy Family — A279

1979, Dec. 18 Litho. *Perf. 12*

823 A279 2c multi 12 5

Christmas 1979. See No. C305.

Jesus Carrying Cross — A280

1980, Mar. 27 Litho. *Perf. 12*

824 A280 3c multi 18 5

Holy Week. See Nos. C306-C307.

Cacao Harvest (Agriculture Year) — A281

1980, May 15 Litho. *Perf. 13½*

825 A281 1c *shown* 5 5
826 A281 2c *Coffee* 6 5
827 A281 3c *Plantain* 10 5
828 A281 4c *Sugar cane* 12 8
829 A281 5c *Corn* 15 10
Nos. 825-829 (5) 48 33

Cotuf Gold Mine, Pueblo Viejo, Flag of Dominican Republic A282

1980, July 8 Litho. *Perf. 13½*

830 A282 6c multi 20 15

Nationalization of gold mining. See Nos. C310-C311.

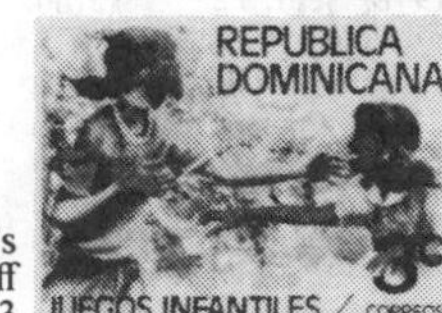

Blind Man's Buff A283

1980, July 21 *Perf. 12*

831 A283 3c *shown* 10 5
832 A283 4c *Marbles* 12 8
833 A283 5c *Drawing in sand* 10 6
834 A283 6c *Hopscotch* 18 12

Iguana A284

1980, Aug. 30 Litho. *Perf. 12*

835 A284 20c multi 70 50
Nos. 835,C314-C317 (5) 2.50 2.20

Dance, by Jaime Colson A285

Perf. 13x13½, 13½x13

1980, Sept. 23 Litho.

836 A285 3c *shown* 10 8
837 A285 50c *Woman, by Gilberto Hernandez Ortega, vert.* 60 40

See Nos. C318-C319.

Three Kings — A286

1980, Dec. 5 Litho. *Perf. 13½*

838 A286 3c *shown* 15 10
839 A286 6c *Carolers* 25 18

Christmas 1980. See No. C327.

Salcedo Province Centenary — A287

1981, Jan. 14 Litho. *Perf. 13½*

840 A287 6c multi 20 15

See No. C328.

Juan Pablo Duarte — A288

1981, Feb. 6 Litho. *Perf. 12*

841 A288 2c sep & dp bis 5 5

Juan Pablo Duarte, liberation hero, 105th anniversary of death.

Gymnast A289

Mother Mazzarello A290

1981, Mar. 31 Litho. *Perf. 13½*

842 A289 1c shown 6 6
843 A289 2c Running 10 5
844 A289 3c Pole vault 15 8
845 A289 6c Boxing 25 15
Nos. 842-845,C331 (5) 74 48

5th National Games. See No. C331.

1981, Apr. 14 *Perf. 12*

846 A290 6c multi 20 15

Mother Maria Mazzarello (1837-1881), founder of Daughters of Mary.

Pedro Henriquez Urena, Historian (1884-1946) A291

1981, May 18 Litho. *Perf. 13½*

847 A291 6c gray vio & lt gray 20 15

Forest Conservation A292

1981, June 30 Litho. *Perf. 12*

848 A292 2c shown 6 5
849 A292 6c River, forest 18 12

Family in House, Census Emblem A293

1981, Aug. 14 Litho. *Perf. 12*

850 A293 3c shown 15 8
851 A293 6c Farmer 25 15

1981 natl. population and housing census.

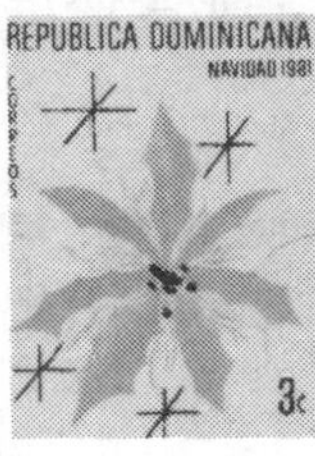

Christmas 1981 — A294

1981, Dec. 23 Litho. *Perf. 13½*

852 A294 2c Bells 10 8
853 A294 3c Poinsettia 15 8

See No. C353

Juan Pablo Duarte — A295

1982, Jan. 29 Litho. *Perf. 13½*

854 A295 2c bl & pale bl 8 5

National Elections A296

Designs: Voters casting votes. 3c, 6c vert.

1982, Mar. 30 Litho. *Perf. 13½*

855 A296 2c multi 8 8
856 A296 3c multi 10 5
857 A296 6c multi 15 10

Energy Conservation A297

Emilio Prud'Homme (1856-1932), Composer A298

Pres. Antonio Guzman Fernandez (1911-1982) A299

Designs: Various forms of energy.

1982, May 10 **Litho.** ***Perf. 12***
858 A297 1c multi 5 5
859 A297 2c multi 6 5
860 A297 3c multi 10 5
861 A297 4c multi 12 5
862 A297 5c multi 10 5
863 A297 6c multi 18 8
Nos. 858-863 (6) 61 33

1982, Aug. 2 ***Perf. 12x12½***
864 A298 6c multi 12 5

1982, Aug. 4 ***Perf. 13x13½***
865 A299 6c multi 15 8

14th Central American and Caribbean Games A300

1982, Aug. 13 ***Perf. 12***
866 A300 3c Baseball 8 5

See Nos. C368-C370. Exist imperf.

San Pedro de Macoris Province Centenary — A301

1982, Aug. 26 ***Perf. 13***
867 A301 1c Wagon 10 10
868 A301 2c Stained-glass window 10 10
869 A301 5c Views 15 15

Size of 1c, 5c, 42x29mm. See No. C375.

St. Teresa of Jesus of Avila (1515-1582) — A302

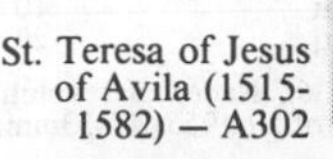

1982, Nov. 17 **Litho.** ***Perf. 13½***
870 A302 6c multi 15 10

Christmas 1982 A303

Environmental Protection A304

Various Christmas balls.

1982, Dec. 8
871 A303 6c multi 15 8

See No. C380.

1982, Dec. 15 ***Perf. 12***
872 A304 2c Bird 8 6
873 A304 3c Water 10 5
874 A304 6c Forest 15 10
875 A304 20c Fish 30 20

Natl. Literacy Campaign A305

1983, Mar. 9 **Litho.** ***Perf. 13½***
876 A305 2c Vowels on blackboard 8 5
877 A305 3c Writing, reading 10 5
878 A305 6c Children, pencil 20 8

Mao City Centenary — A306

1983, Apr. 4 ***Perf. 12***
879 A306 1c multi 10 8
880 A306 5c multi 20 10

Antonio del Monte y Tejada (1780-1861) A307

Famous Men: 3c, Manuel Ubaldo Gomez (1857-1941). 5c, Emiliano Tejera (1841-1923). 6c, Bernardo Pichardo (1877-1924). 7c, Americo Lugo (1870-1952). 10c, Jose Gabriel Garcia (1834-1910). 7c, 10c airmail.

1983, Apr. 25 **Litho.** ***Perf. 12***
881 A307 2c multi 8 5
882 A307 3c multi 8 5
883 A307 5c multi 10 5
884 A307 6c multi 12 5
885 A307 7c multi 15 10
886 A307 10c multi 25 18
Nos. 881-886 (6) 78 48

National Anthem, 100th Anniv. A308

Design: Emilia Prud Homme, Poet, and Jose Reyes, composer.

1983, Sept. 13 **Litho.** ***Perf. 13½***
887 A308 6c cop red & blk 15 8

Free Masons, 125th Anniv. — A309

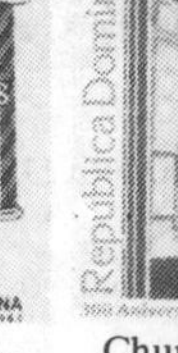

Church of Our Lady of Regla, 300th Anniv. — A310

1983, Oct. 24 **Litho.** ***Perf. 12***
888 A309 4c Emblem 8 5

1983, Nov. 5 ***Perf. 13½***
889 A310 3c Church 6 5
890 A310 6c Statue 12 6

450th Anniv. of Monte Cristi Province — A311

6th Natl. Games — A312

1983, Nov. 25 ***Perf. 12***
891 A311 1c Tower 10 8
892 A311 2c Arms 10 10
893 A311 5c Cuban independence site, horiz. 12 12
894 A311 7c Workers, horiz. 15 15

1983, Dec. 9
895 A312 6c Bicycling, boxing, baseball 12 6
896 A312 10c Gymnast, weight lifting, swimming 20 8

10c airmail.

Restoration of the Republic, 120th Anniv. A313

1983, Dec. 30 **Litho.** ***Perf. 13½***
897 A313 1c Capotillo Heroes Monument 5 5

140th Anniv. of Independence A314

Designs: 6c, Matia Ramon Mella (Patriot), flag. 25c, Mella's Blunderbuss rifle, Gate of Deliverance (independence declaration site).

1984, Feb. 24 **Litho.** ***Perf. 13½***
898 A314 6c multi 10 8
899 A314 25c multi 35 20

Heriberto Pieter (1884-1972), Physician, First Negro Graduate — A315

1984, Mar. 16
900 A315 3c multi 8 6

Battle of Barranquita, 67th Anniv. — A316

1983, Dec. 30 ***Perf. 12***
901 A316 5c multi 10 8

Battle of Santiago, 140th Anniv. A317

1984, Mar. 29 ***Perf. 13½***
902 A317 7c multi 15 8

Coast Guard Ship DC-1, 1934 A318

1984, Apr. 13 **Litho.**
903 A318 10c multi 20 8

Navy Day and 140th anniv. of Battle of Tortuguero.

Birth Centenary of Pedro Henriquez Urena — A319

1984, June 29 **Litho.** ***Perf. 12***
904 A319 7c Salome Urena 12 8
905 A319 10c Text 15 10
906 A319 22c Urena 25 20

The only foreign revenue stamps listed in this Catalogue are those authorized for prepayment of postage.

Monument to Heroes of June 1959
A320

1984, June 20 *Perf. 13½*

907 A320 6c sil & bl 12 5

Gesta de Constanza Maimon and Estero Hondo, 25th anniv.

1984 Summer Olympics
A321

1984, Aug. 1

908 A321 1p Hurdles 2.00 1.00
909 A321 1p Weightlifting 2.00 1.00
910 A321 1p Boxing 2.00 1.00
911 A321 1p Baseball 2.00 1.00

Nos. 908-911 se-tenant.

Protection of Fauna — A322

1984, Oct. 3 **Litho.** *Perf. 12*

912 A322 10c Owl 15 12
913 A322 15c Flamingo 20 18
914 A322 25c Wild Pig 30 30
915 A322 35c Solenodon 40 40

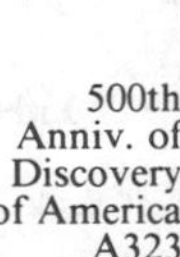

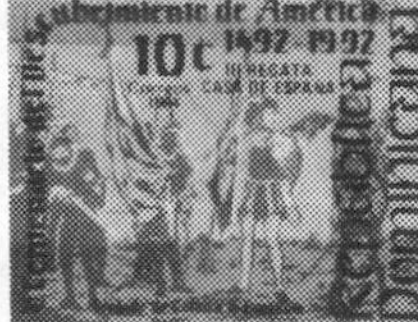

500th Anniv. of Discovery of America
A323

1984, Oct. 10 **Litho.** *Perf. 13½x13*

916 A323 10c Landing on Hispaniola 20 15
917 A323 35c Destruction of Ft. Navidad 60 40
918 A323 65c First Mass in America 1.00 75
919 A323 1p Battle of Santo Cerro 1.65 1.25

Visit of Pope John Paul II — A324

1984, Oct. 11 **Litho.** *Perf. 13x13½*

920 Block of 4 4.25 4.25
a. A324 75c Shown 1.00 1.00
b. A324 75c Pope, map of Caribbean 1.00 1.00
c. A324 75c Pope, globe 1.00 1.00
d. A324 75c Bishop's crozier 1.00 1.00

150th Anniv. of Birth of Maximo Gomez (1986)
A325

1984, Dec. 6 **Litho.** *Perf. 13½*

921 A325 10c Gomez on horseback 15 10
922 A325 20c Maximo Gomez 25 20

Christmas 1984
A326

Perf. 13½x13, 13x13½

1984, Dec. 14 **Litho.**

923 A326 5c multi 8 6
924 A326 10c multi, vert. 15 12

Sacrifice of the Child, by Eligio Pichardo
A327

Paintings and sculpture: 10c, The Pumpkin Sellers, by Gaspar Mario Cruz; 25c, The Market, by Celeste Woss y Gil; 50c, Horses in the Rain, by Dario Suro.

1984, Dec. 19 **Litho.** *Perf. 13½*

925 A327 5c multi 6 6
926 A327 10c multi, vert. 10 8
927 A327 25c multi 25 12
928 A327 50c multi 50 25

Day of Our Lady of Altagracia
A328

1985, Jan. 21

929 A328 5c Old church at Higuey, 1572 10 5
930 A328 10c Our Lady of Altagracia 1514, vert. 20 5
931 A328 25c Basilica of the Protector, Higuey 1971, vert. 50 12

Independence, 141st Anniv. — A329

Painting: The Fathers of Our Country (Duarte, Sanchez and Mella).

1985, Mar. 8 *Perf. 12½*

932 A329 5c multi 8 6
933 A329 10c multi 12 6
934 A329 25c multi 25 12

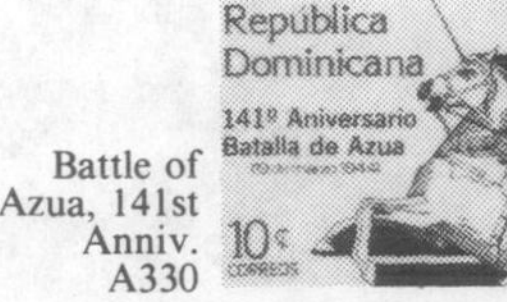

Battle of Azua, 141st Anniv.
A330

1985, Apr. 8 **Litho.** *Perf. 13½*

935 A330 10c Gen. Antonio Duverge, Statue 16 5

Battle of Tortuguero, 141st Anniv. — A331

1985, Apr. 15 **Litho.**

936 A331 25c Santo Domingo Lighthouse, 1853 25 10

American Airforces Cooperation System, 25th Anniv. — A332

1985, Apr. 15 **Litho.** *Perf. 12*

937 A332 35c multi 70 48

Espaillat Province Cent. — A333

1985, May 24 **Litho.** *Perf. 13½*

938 A333 10c Don Carlos M. Rojas, 1st gov. 15 5

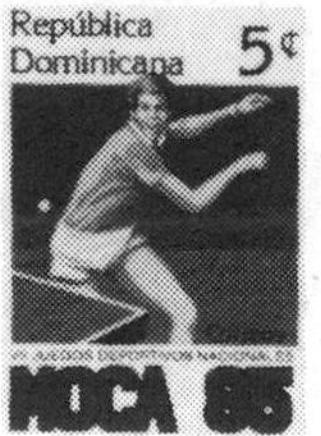

MOCA '85, 7th Natl. Games — A334

1985, July 5 **Litho.** *Perf. 12*

939 A334 5c Table tennis 12 8
940 A334 10c Walking race 25 15

Intl. Youth Year
A335

1985, July 29 *Perf. 13½*

941 A335 5c Youth 10 6
942 A335 25c The Haitises 50 30
943 A335 35c Mt. Duarte summit 70 35
944 A335 2p Mt. Duarte 4.00 2.75

Interamerican Development Bank, 25th Anniv. — A336

Designs: 10c, Haina Harbor. 25c, Map of development sites. 1p, Tavera-Bao-Lopez Hydroelectric Complex.

1985, Aug. 23

945 A336 10c multi 20 14
946 A336 25c multi 50 35
947 A336 1p multi 2.00 1.35

Intl. Decade for Women — A337

15th Central American and Caribbean Games, Santiago — A338

Design: Evangelina Rodriguez (1879-1947), first Dominican woman doctor.

1985, Sept. 26

948 A337 10c multi 20 14

1985, Oct. 9 *Perf. 12*

949 A338 5c multi 10 6
950 A338 25c multi 50 35

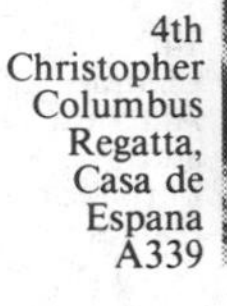

4th Christopher Columbus Regatta, Casa de Espana
A339

Designs: 50c, Founding of Santo Domingo, 1496. 65c, Chapel of Our Lady of the Rosary, 1496, Santo Domingo. 1p, Columbus, American Indian and old Spanish coat of arms.

1985, Oct. 10 *Perf. 13½*

951 A339 35c multi 70 48
952 A339 50c multi 1.00 68
953 A339 65c multi 1.30 88
954 A339 1p multi 2.00 1.35

Discovery of America, 500th anniv. (in 1992).

Cacique Enriquillo
A340

Archbishop Fernando Arturo de Merino
A341

Designs: 5c, Enriquillo in the Bahuroco Mountains, mural detail. 10c, Shown.

1985, Oct. 31

955 A340 5c multi 10 6
956 A340 10c multi 20 14

Enriquillo (d. 1536), leader of revolution against Spain. Size of No. 955: 47x33mm.

1985, Dec. 3 ***Perf. 12***
957 A341 25c multi 50 35

Cent. of holy orders granted to Merino (1833-1906), president of the republic 1880-82.

Mirabal Sisters, Political Martyrs 1960
A342

1985, Dec. 18 ***Perf. 13½***
958 A342 10c multi 20 15

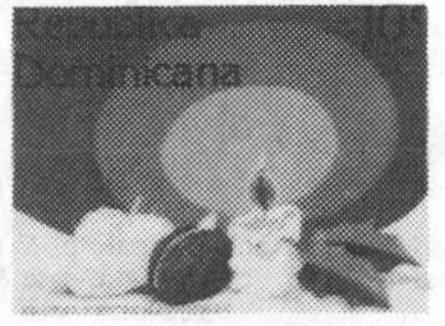
Christmas
A343

1985, Dec. 18
959 A343 10c multi 20 14
960 A343 25c multi 50 35

Day of Independence, Feb. 27 — A344

Design: Mausoleum of founding fathers Duarte, Sanchez and Mella.

1986, Feb. 26 **Litho.** ***Perf. 13½***
961 A344 5c multi 10 6
962 A344 10c multi 20 14

Holy Week
A345

Colonial churches.

1986, Apr. 10
963 A345 5c San Miguel 10 6
964 A345 5c San Andres 10 6
965 A345 10c Santa Barbara 20 14
966 A345 10c San Lazaro 20 14
967 A345 10c San Carlos 20 14
Nos. 963-967 (5) 80 54

Navy Day
A346

Design: Juan Bautista Cambiaso, Juan Bautista Maggiolo and Juan Alejandro Acosta, 1884 independence battle heroes.

1986, Apr. 15
968 A346 10c multi 20 14

Natl. Elections
A347

Natl. Postal Institute Inauguration
A348

1986, Apr. 29
969 A347 5c Voters, map 10 6
970 A347 10c Ballot box 20 14

1986, June 10
971 A348 10c gold, bl & red 20 14
972 A348 25c sil, bl & red 50 35
973 A348 50c blk, bl & red 1.00 68

Central America and Caribbean Games, Santiago — A349

1986, July 17 **Litho.** ***Perf. 13½***
974 A349 10c Weight lifting 20 14
975 A349 25c Gymnastics 50 35
976 A349 35c Diving 70 48
977 A349 50c Equestrian 1.00 68

Historians
A350

Designs: 5c, Ercilia Pepin (b. 1886), vert. 10c, Ramon Emilio Jimenez (b. 1886) and Victor Garrido (1886-1972).

1986, Aug. 1 **Litho.** ***Perf. 13½***
978 A350 5c sil & dl brn 10 6
979 A350 10c sil & dl brn 20 14

A351

A352

Discovery of America, 500th Anniv. (in 1992) — A353

Designs: 25c, Yachts racing, 5th Admiral Columbus Regatta, Casa de Espana. 50c, Columbus founding La Isabela City. 65c, Exploration of the hidalgos. 1p, Columbus returning to the Court of Ferdinand and Isabella. 1.50p, Emblems.

1986, Oct. 10 **Litho.** ***Perf. 13½***
980 A351 25c multi 50 35
981 A352 50c multi 1.00 68
982 A352 65c multi 1.30 88
983 A352 1p multi 2.00 1.35

Textured Paper
Size: 86x58mm.
Imperf

984 A353 1.50p multi 3.00 2.00
Nos. 980-984 (5) 7.80 5.26

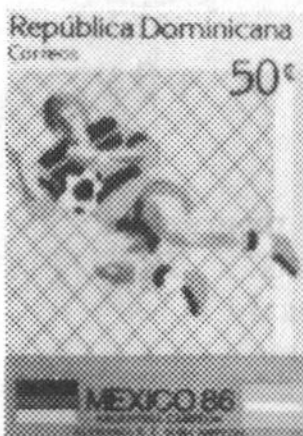

1986 World Cup Soccer Championships, Mexico — A354

Medicinal Plants — A355

Various soccer plays.

1986, Oct. 21 ***Perf. 13½***
985 A354 50c multi 1.00 68
986 A354 75c multi 1.50 1.00

1986, Dec. 15
987 A355 5c Zea mays 10 6
988 A355 10c Bixa orellana 20 14
989 A355 25c Momordica charantia 50 35
990 A355 50c Annona muricata 1.00 68

Second Caribbean Pharmacopeia Seminar.

Christmas
A356

1986, Dec. 19
991 A356 5c Urban scene 10 6
992 A356 25c Rural scene 50 35

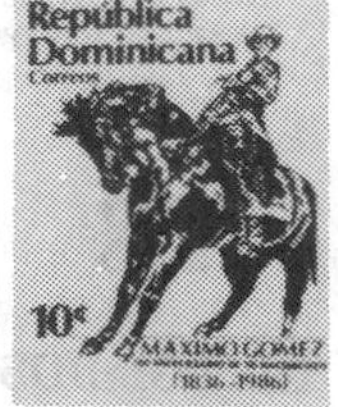

Maximo Gomez y Baez (1836-1905), Revolutionary, Statesman — A357

1986, Dec. 31 **Litho.** ***Perf. 13½***
993 A357 10c shown 20 15
994 A357 25c Portrait, c. 1900 50 35

16th Pan American Ophthalmological Conference, Apr. 5-10 — A358

1987, Mar. 30 **Litho.** ***Perf. 13½***
995 A358 50c brt blue, blk & red 1.00 75

Ascension of Christ to Heaven
A359

Stained-glass window, San Juan Bosco church, Santo Domingo.

1987, May 28
996 A359 35c multi 70 52

Edible Plants — A360

1987, Aug. 2
997 A360 5c Sorghum bicolor 10 8
998 A360 25c Martanta arundinacea 50 38
999 A360 65c Calathaea allouia 1.30 90
1000 A360 1p Voandzeia subterranea 2.00 1.50

Activo 20-30 Intl., 25th Anniv.
A361

1987, Aug. 26
1001 A361 35c multi 70 52

A362

A363

Columbus Memorial, Santo Domingo — A364

1987, Oct. 14
1002 A362 50c shown 1.00 75
1003 A363 75c shown 1.50 1.10

1004 A363 1p Building Ft. Santiago 2.00 1.50
1005 A363 1.50p Columbus imprisoned by Bombadilla 3.00 2.25

Size: 82x70mm.
Imperf

1006 A364 2.50p shown 5.00 3.75
Nos. 1002-1006 (5) 12.50 9.35

Discovery of America, 500th anniv. in 1992.

Junior Olympics, La Vega, 50th Anniv. — A365

1987, Sept. 28
1007 A365 40c multi 80 60

Jose Antonio Hungria 990A366

Historians and authors: 25c, Joaquin Sergio Inchaustegui.

1987, Nov. 10 Litho. *Perf. 13½*
1008 A366 10c buff & brn 20 15
1009 A366 25c pale grn & grn 50 38

SAN CRISTOBAL '87, 8th Natl. Games — A367

1987, Nov. 19
1010 A367 5c Baseball 10 8
1011 A367 10c Boxing 20 15
1012 A367 50c Judo 1.00 75

Fr. Xavier Billini (b. 1837) — A369

1987 Litho. *Perf. 13½*
1015 A369 10c Statue 10 8
1016 A369 25c Portrait 50 38
1017 A369 75c Ana Hernandez de Billini, his mother 1.50 1.10

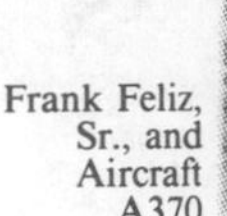

Frank Feliz, Sr., and Aircraft A370

1987
1018 A370 25c shown 50 38

Size: 86x106mm.
Imperf

1019 A370 2p No. C30, map 4.00 2.65

Pan-American goodwill flight to South American countries by the planes Colon, Pinta, Nina and Santa Maria, 50th anniv.

SEMI-POSTAL STAMPS

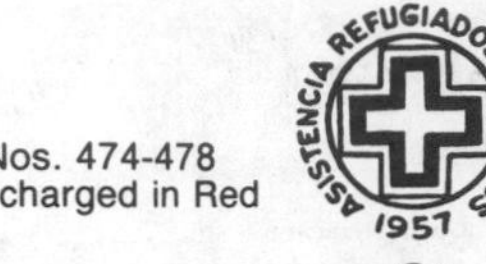

Nos. 474-478 Surcharged in Red

Engraved and Lithographed
1957, Feb. 8 Unwmk. *Perf. 11½*
Flags in National Colors

B1 A117 1c + 2c brn, lt bl, vio & mar 10 10
B2 A117 2c + 2c dk brn, lt bl & vio 10 10
B3 A117 3c + 2c red lil & red 15 15
B4 A117 5c + 2c red org & vio 25 25
B5 A117 7c + 2c grn & vio 35 35
Nos. B1-B5,CB1-CB3 (8) 2.50 2.50

The surtax was to aid Hungarian refugees.

A similar 25c surcharge was applied to the miniature sheets described in the footnote following No. 478. Price, 2 sheets, perf. and imperf., $17.50.

Nos. 479-483 Surcharged in Red Orange

1957, Sept. 9 Photo. *Perf. 13½*
Flags in National Colors

B6 A118 1c + 2c brn & brt bl 25 25
B7 A118 2c + 2c org ver & dk bl 35 35
B8 A118 3c + 2c dk bl 40 40
B9 A118 5c + 2c ol & dk bl 55 55
B10 A118 7c + 2c rose brn & dk bl 65 65
Nos. B6-B10,CB4-CB6 (8) 4.70 4.65

Issued to commemorate the centenary of the birth of Lord Baden Powell and the 50th anniversary of the Scout Movement. The surtax was for the Dominican Republic Boy Scouts.

A similar 5c surcharge was applied to the miniature sheets described in the footnote following No. 483. Price 4 sheets, perf. and imperf., medal and flag, $40.

Types of Olympic Regular Issue, 1957, Surcharged in Carmine

+2¢ +2¢

REFUGIADOS REFUGIADOS
a b

Engraved and Lithographed
1958, May 26
Flags in National Colors
Pink Paper

B11 A119(a) 1c + 2c red brn 25 25
B12 A119(b) 1c + 2c red brn 25 25
B13 A120(a) 2c + 2c gray brn 30 30
B14 A120(b) 2c + 2c gray brn 30 30
B15 A119(a) 3c + 2c vio 30 30
B16 A119(b) 3c + 2c vio 30 30
B17 A120(a) 5c + 2c red org 40 40
B18 A120(b) 5c + 2c red org 40 40
B19 A119(a) 7c + 2c Prus grn 50 50
B20 A119(b) 7c + 2c Prus grn 50 50
Nos. B11-B20,CB7-CB12 (16) 6.50 6.50

The surtax was for the United Nations Relief and Works Agency for Palestine Refugees.

A similar 5c surcharge, plus marginal United Nations emblem and "UNRWA," was applied to the miniature sheets described in the footnote following No. 488. Price, 4 sheets, perf. and imperf., $30.

Nos. 501-505 Surcharged

Perf. 13½
1959, Apr. 13 Photo. Unwmk.
Flags in National Colors

B21 A125 1c + 2c rose, ind & ultra 35 35
B22 A125 1c + 2c brn & bl 45 45
B23 A125 3c + 2c gray, vio, blk & buff 50 50
B24 A125 5c + 2c rose, dk bl, brn & red 60 60
B25 A125 7c + 2c lt brn, dk bl & red 65 65
Nos. B21-B25,CB13-CB15 (8) 5.80 5.80

International Geophysical Year, 1957-58.

A similar 5c surcharge was applied to the miniature sheets described in the footnote following No. 505. Price, 2 sheets, perf. and imperf., $22.50.

Type of 1957 Surcharged in Red

Engraved and Lithographed
1959, Sept. 10 Unwmk. *Imperf.*
Flags in National Colors

B26 A117 1c + 2c brn, lt bl, vio & mar 35 35
B27 A117 2c + 2c dk brn, lt bl & vio 35 35
B28 A117 3c + 2c red lil & red 40 40
B29 A117 5c + 2c red org & vio 45 45
B30 A117 7c + 2c grn & vio 55 55
Nos. B26-B30,CB16-CB18 (8) 4.15 4.15

3rd Pan American Games, Chicago, Aug. 27-Sept. 7, 1959.

World Refugee Year Issue

Nos. 522-524 Surcharged in Red

1960, Apr. 7 Litho. *Perf. 12½*
Center in Gray

B31 A135 5c + 5c red brn & yel grn 25 25
B32 A135 9c + 5c car & lt bl 30 30
B33 A135 13c + 5c org & grn 60 60
Nos. B31-B33,CB19-CB20 (5) 1.50 1.50

Issued to publicize World Refugee Year, July 1, 1959-June 30, 1960. The surtax was for aid to refugees.

Souvenir sheets exist perf. and imperf., containing one each of Nos. B31-B33 and CB19-CB20. Size: 152x99mm. Black marginal inscription. Price, 2 sheets, perf. and imperf., $10.

Nos. 525-529 Surcharged: "XV ANIVERSARIO DE LA UNESCO +2c"

1962, Jan. 8 Photo. *Perf. 13½*
Flags in National Colors

B34 A136 1c + 2c red, yel grn & blk 8 8
B35 A136 2c + 2c org, grnsh bl & brn 10 10
B36 A136 3c + 2c hn brn & bl 12 12
B37 A136 5c + 2c brn & ultra 18 18
B38 A136 7c + 2c grn, bl & rose brn 20 20
Nos. B34-B38,CB21-CB23 (8) 2.08 2.08

Issued to commemorate the 15th anniversary (in 1961) of UNESCO (U.N. Educational, Scientific and Cultural Organization).

A similar 5c surcharge was applied to the miniature sheets described in the footnote following No. 529. Price, 2 sheets, perf. and imperf., $7.50.

Anti-Malaria Type of 1962

1962, Apr. 29 Litho. *Perf. 12*
B39 A141 10c + 2c brt pink & red lil 30 25
B40 A141 20c + 2c pale brn & brn 50 40

Issued for the World Health Organization drive to eradicate malaria.

Freedom from Hunger Type of 1963

1963, Apr. 15 Unwmk. *Perf. 11½*
Banner in Dark Blue & Red

B41 A148 2c + 1c grn 6 6
B42 A148 5c + 2c brt rose lil 18 15
B43 A148 9c + 2c org 30 30

A souvenir sheet contains three imperf. stamps similar to Nos. B41-B43. Dark blue marginal inscription. Size: 172x102mm. Price, $1.25.

Nos. 591-593 Surcharged

1964, March 8 *Perf. 12½*
B44 A153 3c + 2c pale pink & ver 20 20
B45 A153 6c + 2c pale bl & ultra 25 25
B46 A153 9c + 2c pale rose & red brn 40 40
Nos. B44-B46,CB26-CB27 (5) 1.15 1.15

Issued to publicize the UNESCO world campaign to save historic monuments in Nubia.

Nos. 622-626 Surcharged

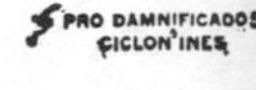

1966, Dec. 9 Litho. *Perf. 12½*
Size: 31x21mm.

B47 A164 1c + 2c multi 10 10
B48 A164 2c + 2c multi 5 5
B49 A164 3c + 2c multi 5 5
B50 A164 6c + 4c multi 10 10
B51 A164 8c + 4c multi 15 15
Nos. B47-B51,CB28-CB30 (8) 2.05 2.05

The surtax was for victims of hurricane Inez.

AIR POST STAMPS

Map of Hispaniola — AP1

Perf. 11½
1928, May 31 Litho. Unwmk.
C1 AP1 10c dp ultra 7.50 4.00

1930
C2 AP1 10c ocher 5.00 4.00
a. Vertical pair imperf. between 1,000.
C3 AP1 15c scarlet 10.00 5.50
C4 AP1 20c dl grn 4.50 85
C5 AP1 30c violet 10.00 6.50

Nos. C2 to C5 have only "CENTAVOS" in lower panel. Dates of issue: 10c, 20c, Jan. 24; 15c, 30c, Feb. 14.

1930
C6 AP1 10c lt bl 2.50 1.00
C7 AP1 15c bl grn 5.00 1.50
C8 AP1 20c yel brn 5.50 75
a. Imperf. vertically (pair) 600.00 600.00
C9 AP1 30c chocolate 9.00 2.50

Dates of issue: 10c, 15c, 20c, Sept.; 30c, Oct.

Batwing Sundial Erected in 1753 — AP2

1931-33 ***Perf. 12***
C10 AP2 10c carmine 5.50 85
C11 AP2 10c lt bl ('32) 2.25 75
C12 AP2 10c dk grn ('33) 9.00 3.50
C13 AP2 15c rose lil 4.00 75
C14 AP2 20c dk bl 9.00 2.75
a. Numerals reading up at left and down at right 10.00 4.00
b. Imperf., pair 400.00
C15 AP2 30c green 3.50 50
C16 AP2 50c red brn 9.00 1.00
C17 AP2 1p dp org 15.00 3.50
Nos. C10-C17 (8) 57.25 13.60

Issue dates: Aug. 16, 1931; July 2, 1932; May 28, 1933.

Airplane and Ozama Fortress AP3

1933, Nov. 20
C18 AP3 10c dk bl 5.50 85

Airplane and Trujillo Bridge AP4

1934, Sept. 20
C19 AP4 10c dk bl 4.50 85

Symbolic of Flight AP5

1935, Apr. 29
C20 AP5 10c lt bl & dk bl 2.25 65

AP6

1936, Feb. 11 ***Perf. 11½***
C21 AP6 10c dk bl & turq bl 3.75 65

Allegory of Flight AP7

1936, Oct. 17
C22 AP7 10c dk bl, bl & turq bl 3.25 50

Macoris Airport AP8

1937, Oct. 22
C23 AP8 10c green 1.50 20

Fleet of Columbus AP9

Air Fleet AP10

Proposed Columbus Lighthouse AP11

1937, Nov. 9 ***Perf. 12***
C24 AP9 10c rose red 2.50 2.00
C25 AP10 15c purple 2.00 1.50
C26 AP11 20c dk bl & lt bl 2.00 1.50
C27 AP10 25c red vio 3.00 1.75
C28 AP11 30c yel grn 2.75 1.50
C29 AP10 50c brown 5.50 2.00
C30 AP11 75c dk ol grn 15.00 15.00
C31 AP9 1p orange 9.00 3.00
Nos. C24-C31 (8) 41.75 28.25

Goodwill flight to all American countries by the planes "Colon", "Pinta", "Nina" and "Santa Maria".

No. C30 was reproduced imperf. on No. 1019.

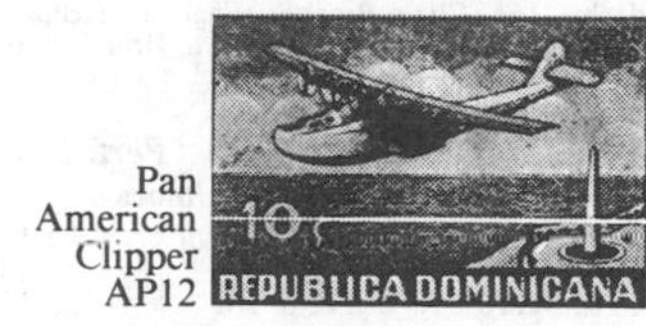

Pan American Clipper AP12

1938, July 30
C32 AP12 10c green 1.50 20

Trylon and Perisphere, Plane and Proposed Columbus Lighthouse — AP13

1939, Apr. 30
C33 AP13 10c grn & lt grn 2.00 1.00

New York World's Fair.

Airplane AP14

1939, Oct. 18
C34 AP14 10c grn & dp grn 2.25 30
a. Pair, imperf. between 750.00

Proposed Columbus Lighthouse, Plane and Caravels — AP15

Christopher Columbus and Proposed Lighthouse — AP16

Proposed Lighthouse — AP17

Christopher Columbus — AP18

Caravel — AP19

1940, Oct. 12
C35 AP15 10c saph & lt bl 75 75
C36 AP16 15c org brn & brn 1.15 1.00
C37 AP17 20c rose red & red 1.15 1.00
C38 AP18 25c brt red lil & red vio 1.15 50
C39 AP19 50c grn & lt grn 2.25 2.00
Nos. C35-C39 (5) 6.45 5.25

Discovery of America by Columbus and proposed Columbus memorial lighthouse in Dominican Republic.

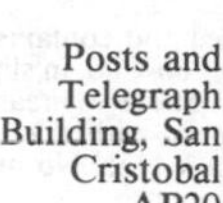

Posts and Telegraph Building, San Cristobal AP20

1941, Feb. 21
C40 AP20 10c brt red lil & pale lil rose 65 25

Globe, Wing and Letter AP21

1942, Feb. 13
C41 AP21 10c dk vio brn 80 8
C42 AP21 75c dp org 5.00 3.00

Plane AP22

1943, Sept. 1
C43 AP22 10c brt red lil 60 12
C44 AP22 20c dp bl & bl 70 18
C45 AP22 25c yel ol 8.00 4.00

Plane, Flag, Coat of Arms and Torch of Liberty — AP23

1944, Feb. 27 ***Perf. 11½***
Flag in Gray, Dark Blue, Carmine
C46 AP23 10c multi 60 12
C47 AP23 20c multi 75 20
C48 AP23 1p multi 3.50 2.50

Centenary of Independence. See No. 407 for souvenir sheet listing.

Communications Building, Ciudad Trujillo — AP24

1944, Nov. 12 **Litho.** ***Perf. 12***
C49 AP24 9c yel grn & bl 30 15
C50 AP24 13c dl brn & rose car 35 10
C51 AP24 25c org & dl red 60 15
b. Vert. pair, imperf. between 75.00
C52 AP24 30c blk & ultra 1.25 1.10

Twenty booklets of 100 (25 panes of 4) of the 25c were issued. Single panes are unknown to experts.

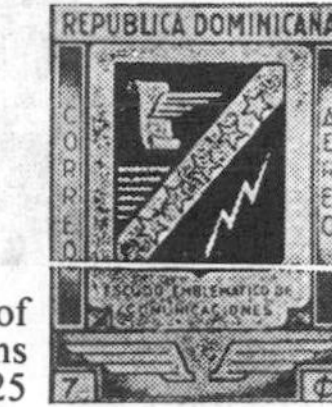

Emblem of Communications AP25

1945, Sept. 1
Center in Dark Blue and Carmine.
C53 AP25 7c dp yel grn 30 35
C54 AP25 12c red org 35 25
C55 AP25 13c dp bl 45 20
C56 AP25 25c org brn 90 30

AP26

Flags and National Anthem AP27

Unwmk.
1946, Feb. 27 **Litho.** ***Perf. 12***
Center in Dark Blue, Deep Carmine and Black.
C57 AP26 10c carmine 70 60
C58 AP26 15c blue 1.75 1.50
C59 AP26 20c chocolate 2.00 1.50
C60 AP26 35c orange 2.00 1.00
C61 AP27 1p grn, yel grn & cit 20.00 17.50
Nos. C57-C61 (5) 26.45 22.10

Nos. C57-C61 exist imperf.

Map of Hispaniola — AP28

1946, Aug. 4
C62 AP28 10c multi 50 20
C63 AP28 13c multi 85 20

See note after No. 421.

Catalogue prices for unused stamps up to mid-1953 are for hinged copies matching the condition specified in this volume's introduction.

Waterfall of Jimenoa — AP29

1947, Mar. 18 **Litho.**
Center Multicolored.
C64 AP29 18c lt bl 60 60
C65 AP29 23c carmine 60 60
C66 AP29 50c red vio 60 60
C67 AP29 75c chocolate 75 75

Executive Palace AP30

1948, Feb. 27
C68 AP30 37c org brn 1.25 1.00
C69 AP30 1p org yel 3.50 2.50

Church of San Francisco Ruins AP31

Las Carreras Monument AP32

1949 **Unwmk.** ***Perf. 11½***
C70 AP31 7c ol grn & pale ol grn 20 15
C71 AP31 10c org brn & buff 25 12
C72 AP31 15c brt rose & pale pink 75 35
C73 AP31 20c grn & pale grn 1.00 70

Issue dates: 10c, Apr. 4; others, Apr. 13.

1949, Aug. 10
C74 AP32 10c red & pink 35 8

Issued to commemorate the centenary of the Battle of Las Carreras.

Hotel Montana AP33

Design: 37c, Hotel San Cristobal.

1950, Sept. 8
C75 AP33 12c dk bl & bl 40 12
C76 AP33 37c car & pink 2.75 2.25

Map, Plane and Caduceus — AP34

1950, Oct. 2
C77 AP34 12c org brn & yel 60 15

The 13th Pan-American Health Conference. Exists imperf.

Dr. Salvador B. Gautier Hospital AP35

1952, Aug.
C78 AP35 23c dp bl 1.00 90
C79 AP35 29c carmine 2.25 1.75

Columbus Lighthouse and Plane AP36

Ano Mariano Initials in Monogram AP37

1953, Jan. 6 **Engr.** ***Perf. 13***
C80 AP36 12c ocher 35 25
C81 AP36 14c dk bl 15 15
C82 AP36 20c blk brn 75 60
C83 AP36 23c dp plum 30 20
C84 AP36 25c dk bl 85 70
C85 AP36 29c dp grn 40 40
C86 AP36 1p red brn 1.25 75
a. Miniature sheet of 10 5.00 5.00
Nos. C80-C86 (7) 4.05 3.05

No. C86a is lithographed and contains one each of Nos. 450-452 and C80-C86, in slightly different shades. Sheet measures 190x130mm. and is imperf. with simulated perforations printed in dark blue. No marginal inscriptions.

A miniature sheet similar to No. C86a, but measuring 200x163mm. and in folder, exists. Price $100

1954, Aug. 5 **Litho.** ***Perf. 11½***
C87 AP37 8c claret 25 15
C88 AP37 11c blue 10 5
C89 AP37 33c brn org 1.00 65

Marian Year. Nos. C87-C89 exist imperf.

Rotary Type of Regular Issue, 1955.

1955, Feb. 23 ***Perf. 12***
C90 A110 11c rose red 45 20

Rotary International, 50th anniversary.

Flags — AP39

Portraits of General Hector B. Trujillo: 25c, In civilian clothes. 33c, In uniform.

1955, May 16 **Engr.** ***Perf. 13½x13***
C91 AP39 11c bl, yel & car 45 12
C92 AP39 25c rose vio 70 40
C93 AP39 33c org brn 1.00 60

The center of No. C91 is lithographed. Issued to commemorate the 25th anniversary of the inauguration of the Trujillo era.

Fair Type of Regular Issue, 1955

1955, Dec. 20 **Unwmk.** ***Perf. 13***
C94 A112 11c vermilion 40 12

Issued to publicize the International Fair of Peace and Brotherhood in Ciudad Trujillo, Dec. 1955.

ICAO Type of Regular Issue, 1956.

1956, Apr. 6 **Litho.** ***Perf. 12½***
C95 A114 11c ultra 35 12

Issued to commemorate the third Caribbean conference of the International Civil Aviation Organization.

Tree Type of Regular Issue, 1956.

Design: 13c, Mahogany tree.

1956, Dec. 8 **Litho.** ***Perf. 11½x12***
C96 A115 13c org & grn 45 18

Issued to publicize the reforestation program.

Type of Regular Issue, 1957.

Olympic Winners and Flags: 11c, Paavo Nurmi, Finland. 16c, Ugo Frigerio, Italy. 17c, Mildred Didrikson ("Didrickson" on stamp), United States.

Engraved and Lithographed
1957, Jan. 24 **Unwmk.** ***Perf. 11½***
Flags in National Colors
C97 A117 11c ultra & red org 20 10
C98 A117 16c car & lt grn 25 15
C99 A117 17c blk, vio & red 25 15

Issued to commemorate the 16th Olympic Games, Melbourne, Nov. 22-Dec. 8, 1956. Exist imperf.

Souvenir sheets of 3 exist, perf. and imperf., containing one each of Nos. C97-C99. Sheets measure 169x86mm., with Olympic flag and motto on left margin.

Price, 2 sheets, perf. & imperf., $7.

Type of Regular Issue, 1957.

Olympic Winners and Flags: 11c, Robert Morrow, United States, 100 & 200 meter dash. 16c, Chris Brasher, England, steeplechase. 17c, A. Ferreira Da Silva, Brazil, hop, step and jump.

1957, July 18 **Photo.** ***Perf. 13½***
Flags in National Colors
C100 A118 11c yel grn & dk bl 20 10
C101 A118 16c lil & dk bl 25 15
C102 A118 17c brn & bl grn 25 15

1956 Olympic winners. Exist imperf.

See note on miniature sheets following No. 483.

Types of Regular Issue, 1957.

Olympic Winners and Flags: 11c, Hans Winkler, Germany, individual jumping. 16c, Alfred Oerter, United States, discus throw. 17c, Shirley Strickland, Australia, 800 meter hurdles.

Engraved and Lithographed
1957, Nov. 12 **Unwmk.** ***Perf. 13½***
Flags in National Colors
C103 A119 11c ultra 20 10
C104 A120 16c rose car 25 15
C105 A119 17c claret 25 15

1956 Olympic winners. Exist imperf.

Miniature sheets of 3 exist, perf. and imperf., containing one each of Nos. C103-C105. Sheets have no marginal inscriptions. Price, 2 sheets, perf. and imperf., $5.50.

Type of Regular Issue, 1958.

Olympic Winners and Flags: 11c, Charles Jenkins, 400 & 800 meter run, and Thomas Courtney, 1,600 meter relay, United States. 16c, Field hockey team, India. 17c, Yachting team, Sweden.

Perf. 13½
1958, Oct. 30 **Unwmk.** **Photo.**
Flags in National Colors
C106 A125 11c bl, ol & brn 20 10
C107 A125 16c lt grn, org & dk bl 25 15
C108 A125 17c ver, bl & yel 25 15

1956 Olympic winners. Exist imperf.

Miniature sheets of 3 exist, perf. and imperf., containing one each of Nos. C106-C108. Size: 140x78½mm. Price, 2 sheets, perf. and imperf., $3.

Fair Type of Regular Issue, 1958.

1958, Dec. 9 **Litho.** ***Perf. 12½***
C109 A127 9c gray 30 20
C110 A127 25c lt vio 75 45
a. Souvenir sheet of 3, imperf. 2.25 1.75

No. C110a contains one each of Nos. C109-C110 and 507 and measures 137x72½mm. Black marginal inscription.

Issued for the Universal and International Exposition at Brussels.

Polo Type of Regular Issue, 1959

Design: 11c, Dominican polo team.

1959, May 15 ***Perf. 12***
C111 A130 11c orange 45 40

Jamaica-Dominican Republic polo match at Ciudad Trujillo.

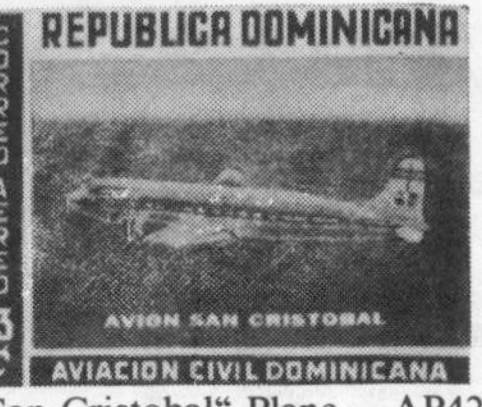

"San Cristobal" Plane — AP42

Perf. 11½
1960, Feb. 25 **Unwmk.** **Litho.**
C112 AP42 13c org, bl, grn & gray 45 25

Dominican Civil Aviation.

Children and WRY Emblem AP43

1960, Apr. 7 ***Perf. 12½***
C113 AP43 10c plum, gray & grn 55 45
C114 AP43 13c gray & grn 65 55

Issued to publicize World Refugee Year, July 1, 1959-June 30, 1960.

Olympic Type of Regular Issue.

Olympic Winners: 11c, Pat McCormick, U.S.A., diving. 16c, Mithat Bayrack, Turkey, welterweight wrestling. 17c, Ursula Happe, Germany, 200 meter breast stroke.

1960, Sept. 14 **Photo.** ***Perf. 13½***
Flags in National Colors
C115 A136 11c bl, gray & brn 20 10
C116 A136 16c red, brn & ol 25 15
C117 A136 17c blk, bl & ocher 25 15

Issued to commemorate the 17th Olympic Games, Rome, Aug. 25-Sept. 11. Exist imperf.

Miniature sheets of 3 exist, perf. and imperf., containing one each of Nos. C115-C117, with no marginal inscription. Size: 160x76mm. Price, 2 sheets, perf. and imperf., $3.75.

Coffee-Cacao Type of Regular Issue, 1961

1961, Dec. 30 **Litho.** ***Perf. 12½***
C118 A140 13c org ver 40 40
C119 A140 33c brt yel 85 85

Exist imperf.

Anti-Malaria Type of Regular Issue, 1962

1962, Apr. 29 **Unwmk.** ***Perf. 12***
C120 A141 13c pink & red 35 30
C121 A141 33c org & dp org 75 75

Issued for the World Health Organization drive to eradicate malaria.

Type of Regular Issue, 1962.

Designs: 13c, Broken fetters and laurel. 50c, Flag, torch and inscription.

1962, May 30 ***Perf. 12½***
C122 A142 13c brn, yel, ol, ultra & red 45 35
C123 A142 50c rose lil, ultra & red 1.75 1.25

First anniversary, end of Trujillo era. No. C122 exists imperf.

UPAE Type of Regular Issue, 1962

1962, Oct. 23 ***Perf. 12½***
C124 A146 13c brt bl 50 30
C125 A146 22c dl red brn 50 50

Issued to commemorate the 50th anniversary of the founding of the Postal Union of the Americas and Spain, UPAE. Exist imperf.

Nouel Type of Regular Issue, 1962

Design: Frame altered with rosary and cross surrounding portrait.

1962, Dec. 18
C126 A147 13c bl & pale bl 60 30
C127 A147 25c vio & pale vio 80 70
a. Souv. sheet 50 50

Birth centenary of Archbishop Adolfo Alejandro Nouel, president of Republic in 1911. Exist imperf.

No. C127a contains one each of Nos. C126-C127 imperf. Pale violet margin with blue inscription. Size: 153x93mm.

Sanchez, Duarte, Mella AP44

1963, July 7 Litho. *Perf. 11½x12*
C128 AP44 15c orange 40 30

Issued to commemorate the 120th anniversary of separation from Haiti.

World Map — AP45

1963, Oct. 25 Unwmk. *Perf. 12½*
C129 AP45 10c gray & car 40 35

Centenary of International Red Cross. Exists imperf.

Human Rights Type of Regular Issue, 1963

1963, Dec. 10 Litho.
C130 A152 7c fawn & red brn 30 25
C131 A152 10c lt bl & bl 35 25

15th anniversary, Universal Declaration of Human Rights. Exist imperf.

Ramses II Battling the Hittites (from Abu Simbel) — AP46

1964, March 8 *Perf. 12½*
C132 AP46 10c brt vio 35 25
C133 AP46 13c yellow 40 35

UNESCO world campaign to save historic monuments in Nubia. Exist imperf.

Striated Woodpecker — AP47

1964, June 8 Litho.
C134 AP47 10c multi 45 30

Type of Space Issue, 1964

Designs: 7c, Rocket leaving earth. 10c, Space capsule orbiting earth.

1964, July 28 Unwmk. *Perf. 12½*
C135 A156 7c brt grn 40 25
C136 A156 10c vio bl 50 40
a. Souv. sheet 5.00 5.00

Issued to commemorate the conquest of space.

No. C136a contains 7c and 10c stamps similar to Nos. C135-C136 with gray border, violet blue inscription and simulated perforation. Size: 149x82mm.

Pres. John F. Kennedy — AP48

1964, Nov. 22 *Perf. 11½*
C137 AP48 10c buff & dk brn 70 40

Issued in memory of President John F. Kennedy (1917-63). Sheets of 10 (5x2) with brown marginal inscription and date and sheets of 50.

U.P.U. Type of Regular Issue

1964, Dec. 5 Litho. *Perf. 12½*
C138 A157 7c blue 20 22

Issued to commemorate the 15th Universal Postal Union Congress, Vienna, Austria, May-June, 1964.

ICY Type of Regular Issue, 1965

1965, Feb. 16 Unwmk. *Perf. 12½*
C139 A158 10c lil & vio 35 30

Issued to publicize the United Nations International Cooperation Year.

Basilica of Our Lady of Altagracia AP49

1965, Mar. 18 Unwmk. *Perf. 12½*
C140 AP49 10c multi 50 35

Issued to commemorate the Fourth Mariological Congress and the Eleventh International Marian Congress.

Abraham Lincoln — AP50

1965, Apr. 15 Litho. *Perf. 12½*
C141 AP50 17c brt bl 55 50

Issued to commemorate the centenary of the death of Abraham Lincoln.

Stamp Centenary Type of Regular Issue, 1965

Design: Stamp of 1865, (No. 2).

1965, Dec. 28 Litho. *Perf. 12½*
C142 A161 7c vio, lt grn & blk 35 30
C143 A161 10c yel, lt grn & blk 40 35

Issued to commemorate the centenary of the first Dominican postage stamps.

ITU Emblem, Old and New Communication Equipment AP51

1966, Apr. 6 Litho. *Perf. 12½*
C144 AP51 28c pink & car 1.00 80
C145 AP51 45c brt grn & grn 1.50 1.50

Issued to commemorate the centenary (in 1965) of the International Telecommunication Union.

Butterfly Type of Regular Issue

1966, Nov. 8 Litho. *Perf. 12½*
Various Butterflies in Natural Colors
Size: 35x24mm.
C146 A164 10c lt vio & vio 60 30
C147 A164 50c org & dp org 2.25 1.25
C148 A164 75c pink & rose red 1.50 1.25

Altar Type of Regular Issue

1967, Jan. 18 Litho. *Perf. 11½*
C149 A165 7c lt ol grn 20 15
C150 A165 10c lilac 25 20
C151 A165 20c yel brn 45 35

Chess Type of Regular Issue

Design: 10c, Pawn and Bishop.

1967, June 23 Litho. *Perf. 12½*
C152 A167 10c ol, lt ol & blk 60 35
a. Souv. sheet 1.25 1.25

Issued to commemorate the 5th Central American Chess Championships, Santo Domingo. No. C152a contains 2 imperf. stamps similar to Nos. 636 and C152. Gray chessboard design in margin with map of Dominican Republic and black inscription. Size: 117x76mm.

Alliance for Progress Type of Regular Issue

1967, Sept. 16 Litho. *Perf. 12½*
C153 A168 8c gray 30 30
C154 A168 10c blue 30 20

Alliance for Progress, 6th anniversary.

Cornucopia and Emblem AP52

Latin American Flags AP53

1967, Oct. 7
C155 AP52 12c multi 35 25

Issued to commemorate the 25th anniversary of the Inter-American Agriculture Institute.

Satellite Type of Regular Issue

1968, June 15 Typo. *Perf. 12*
C156 A170 10c dp bl & multi 40 30
C157 A170 15c pur & multi 60 45

World Meteorological Day, Mar. 23.

Boxing Type of Regular Issue

Designs: Two views of boxing match.

1968, June 29
C158 A171 7c org yel & grn 25 25
C159 A171 10c gray & bl 35 20

See note after No. 641.

Lions Type of Regular Issue

1968, Aug. 9 Litho. *Perf. 11½*
C160 A172 10c ultra & multi 35 25

Issued to commemorate the 50th anniversary (in 1967) of Lions International.

Olympic Type of Regular Issue

Designs (Olympic Emblem and): 10c, Weight lifting. 33c, Pistol shooting.

1968, Nov. 12 Litho. *Perf. 11½*
C161 A173 10c buff & multi 35 35
C162 A173 33c pink & multi 1.10 1.00

Issued to commemorate the 19th Olympic Games, Mexico City, Oct. 12-27.

1969, Jan. 25 Litho. *Perf. 12½*
C163 AP53 10c pink & multi 35 18

Issued to publicize the 7th Inter-American Savings and Loan Conference, Santo Domingo, Jan. 25-31.

Taino Art Type of Regular Issue

Taino Art: 7c, Various spatulas with human heads (vert.). 10c, Female torso forming drinking vessel. 20c, Vase with human head (vert.).

1969, Jan. 31 Litho. *Perf. 12½*
C164 A175 7c lt bl, bl & lem 25 18
C165 A175 10c pink, ver & brn 40 30
C166 A175 20c yel, org & brn 55 40

COTAL Type of Regular Issue

Design: 10c, Airport of the Americas and COTAL emblem.

1969, May 25 Litho. *Perf. 12½*
C167 A178 10c brn & pale fawn 35 20

See note after No. 655.

ILO Type of Regular Issue

1969, June 27 Litho. *Perf. 12½*
C168 A179 10c rose, red & blk 30 18

Issued to commemorate the 50th anniversary of the International Labor Organization.

Baseball Type of Regular Issue

Designs: 7c, Bleachers, Tetelo Vargas Stadium (horiz.). 10c, Batter, catcher and umpire. 1p, Quisqueya Stadium (horiz.).

1969, Aug. 15 Litho. *Perf. 12½*
Size: 43x30mm. (7c, 1p); 21x31mm. (10c).
C169 A180 7c mag & org 40 35
C170 A180 10c mar & rose red 60 40
C171 A180 1p vio bl & brn 3.50 2.25

Issued to publicize the 17th World Amateur Baseball Championships.

Electrification Types of Regular Issue

Design: No. C172, Rio Haina steam plant. No. C173, Valdesa Dam.

1969 Litho. *Perf. 12*
C172 A181 10c org ver 30 15
C173 A182 10c multi 35 20

Issued to publicize the national electrification plan.

Issue dates: No C172, Sept. 15; No. C173, Oct. 15.

Duarte Type of Regular Issue

1970, Jan. 26 Litho. *Perf. 12*
C174 A183 10c brn & dk brn 30 18

Issued for Duarte Day in memory of Juan Pablo Duarte (1813-1876), liberator.

Census Type of Regular Issue

Design: 10c, Buildings and census emblem.

1970, Feb. 6 *Perf. 11*
C175 A184 10c lt bl & multi 35 25

Issued to publicize the 1970 census.

Sculpture Type of Regular Issue

Design: 10c, The Prisoner, by Abelardo Rodriguez Urdaneta (vert.).

1970, Feb. 20 Litho. *Perf. 12½*
C176 A186 10c bluish gray 40 25

Issued to honor Abelardo Rodriguez Urdaneta, sculptor.

Masonic Type of Regular Issue

1970, Mar. 2
C177 A187 10c brown 25 18

The 8th Inter-American Masonic Conference, Santo Domingo, Mar. 1-7.

Satellite Type of Regular Issue

1970, May 25 Litho. *Perf. 12½*
C178 A188 7c bl & gray 30 20

World Telecommunications Day.

U.P.U. Type of Regular Issue

1970, June 5 *Perf. 11*
C179 A189 10c yel & brn 30 20

Inauguration of new Universal Postal Union headquarters, Bern.

Education Year Type of Regular Issue

1970, June 26 Litho. *Perf. 12½*
C180 A190 15c brt pink 35 25

International Education Year, 1970.

Dancers AP54

Album, Globe and Emblem AP55

Design: 10c, U.N. emblem and wheel.

1970, Oct. 12 Litho. *Perf. 12½*
C181 AP54 7c bl & multi 35 20
C182 AP54 10c pink & multi 40 18

Issued to publicize the First World Exhibition of Books and Culture Festival, Santo Domingo, Oct. 11-Dec. 11.

1970, Oct. 26 Litho. *Perf. 11*
C183 AP55 10c multi 40 25

Issued to publicize EXFILCA 70, 2nd Interamerican Philatelic Exhibition, Caracas, Venezuela, Nov. 27-Dec. 6.

Basilica of Our Lady of Altagracia — AP56

1971, Jan. 20 Litho. *Perf. 12½*
C184 AP56 17c multi 65 35

Inauguration of the Basilica of Our Lady of Altagracia.

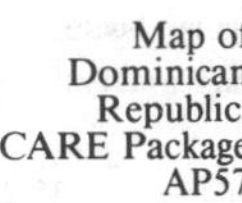

Map of Dominican Republic, CARE Package AP57

1971, May 28 Litho. *Perf. 12½*
C185 AP57 10c bl & grn 25 18

25th anniversary of CARE, a U.S.-Canadian Cooperative for American Relief Everywhere.

Sports Type of Regular Issue

Design: 7c, Volleyball.

1971, Sept. 10 *Perf. 11*
C186 A195 7c lil & gray 30 15

2nd National Games.

Animal Type of Regular Issue

Design: 25c, Cock and grain.

1971, Sept. 29 *Perf. 12½*
C187 A196 25c blk & multi 70 50

6th National agriculture and livestock census.

Independence Type of Regular Issue

Design: 10c, Dominican-Colombian flag of 1821.

1971, Dec. 1 *Perf. 11*
C188 A197 10c vio bl, yel & red 35 18

Sesquicentennial of first national independence.

Christmas Type of Regular Issue

Design: 10c, Bell, 1493.

1971, Dec. 10 *Perf. 12½*
C189 A198 10c red, grn & yel 30 18

Christmas 1971.

UNICEF Type of Regular Issue

Design: 15c, UNICEF emblem and child on beach.

1971, Dec. 14 *Perf. 11*
C190 A199 15c multi 50 40

25th anniversary of the United Nations International Children's Fund (UNICEF).

Book Year Type of Regular Issue

1972, Jan. 25 Litho. *Perf. 12½*
C191 A200 12c lil, dk bl & red 25 20

International Book Year 1972.

Magnifying Glass over Peru on Map of Americas AP58

"Your Heart is your Health" AP59

1972, Mar. 7 Litho. *Perf. 12*
C192 AP58 10c bl & multi 50 35

EXFILIMA '71, 3rd Inter-American Philatelic Exposition, Lima, Peru, Nov. 6-14, 1971.

1972, Apr. 27 Litho. *Perf. 11*
C193 AP59 7c red & multi 20 12

World Health Day.

Taino Art Type of 1972

Taino Art: 8c, Ritual vessel showing human figures. 10c, Trumpet (shell). 25c, Carved vomiting spoons. All horiz.

1972, May 10 Litho. *Perf. 11*
C194 A201 8c multi 15 15
C195 A201 10c lt bl & multi 40 18
C196 A201 25c multi 75 40

Telecommunications Type of Regular Issue

1972, May 17 *Perf. 12½*
C197 A202 21c yel & multi 40 35

4th World Telecommunications Day.

Exhibition Type of Regular Issue

1972, June 3
C198 A203 33c org & multi 1.00 50

First National Philatelic Exhibition, Santo Domingo, June 3-17.

Olympic Type of Regular Issue.

Design: 33c, Running.

1972, Aug. 25 Litho. *Perf. 12½*
C199 A204 33c yel & multi 1.10 65

20th Olympic Games, Munich, Aug. 26-Sept. 11.

Club Type of Regular Issue

1972, Sept. 29 Litho. *Perf. 10½*
C200 A205 20c bl & multi 55 30

50th anniversary of the Club Activo 20-30 Internacional.

Morel Type of Regular Issue

1972, Oct. 20 Litho. *Perf. 12½*
C201 A206 10c multi 25 15

Emilio A. Morel (1884-1958), poet and journalist.

Bank Type of Regular Issue

Design: 25c, Silver coin, 1947, and entrance to the Mint.

1972, Oct. 23
C202 A207 25c ocher & multi 75 35

25th anniversary of the Central Bank.

"La Navidad" Fortress, 1492 AP60

1972, Nov. 21 Litho. *Perf. 12½*
C203 AP60 10c multi 30 12

Christmas 1972.

Sports Type of Regular Issue

Designs: Various sports.

1973, Mar. 30 Litho. *Perf. 13½x13*
C204 A212 8c blk & lt bl, block of 4 1.75 1.75
a. Upper left 40 40
b. Upper right 40 40
c. Lower left 40 40
d. Lower right 40 40
C205 A212 10c dk bl & lil rose, block of 4 2.25 2.00
a. Upper left 50 50
b. Upper right 50 50
c. Lower left 50 50
d. Lower right 50 50

Publicity for the 12th Central American and Caribbean Games, Santo Domingo, Summer 1974.

Easter Type 1973

Design: 10c, Belfry of Church of Our Lady of Help.

1973, Apr. 18 Litho. *Perf. 10½*
C206 A213 10c multi 40 15

Holy Week 1973.

North and South America on Globe — AP61

1973, May 29 Litho. *Perf. 12*
C207 AP61 7c multi 25 15

Pan-American Health Organization, 70th anniversary (in 1972).

WMO Type of Regular Issue

1973, Aug. 10 Litho. *Perf. 13½x13*
C208 A214 7c grn & multi 25 15

Centenary of international meteorological cooperation.

INTERPOL Emblem Police Scientist AP62

1973, Sept. 28 Litho. *Perf. 10½*
C209 AP62 10c vio bl, bl & emer 30 2

50th anniversary of International Criminal Police Organization.

Handicraft Type of Regular Issue

1973, Oct. 12
C210 A215 7c *Sailing ship, mosaic* 21 1
C211 A215 10c *Maracas rattlesif (horiz.)* 30 2

Opening of Museum of Mankind in Santo Domingo.

Christmas Type of Regular Issue

Design: 10c, Angels adoring Christ Child.

1973, Nov. 26 Litho. *Perf. 13½x1*
C212 A216 10c multi 35 2

Christmas 1973.

Scout Type of Regular Issue

Design: 21c, Scouts cooking and Lord Baden-Powell.

1973, Dec. 7 Litho. *Perf. 1*
C213 A217 21c red & multi 30 30

50th anniversary of Dominican Republic Boy Scouts.

Sport Type of Regular Issue

Designs: 10c, Olympic swimming pool and diver. 25c, Olympic Stadium, soccer and discus.

1974, Feb. 25 Litho. *Perf. 13½*
C214 A218 10c bl & multi 10 1
C215 A218 25c multi 30 3

12th Central American and Caribbean Games, Santo Domingo, 1974.

The Last Supper AP63

1974, June 27 Litho. *Perf. 13½*
C216 AP63 10c multi 40 2

Holy Week 1974.

Bridge Type of 1974

Design: 10c, Higuamo Bridge.

1974, July 12 *Perf. 12*
C217 A221 10c multi 35 20

Diabetes Type of 1974

Designs (Map of Dominican Republic Diabetics' Emblem and): 7c, Kidney. 33c Eye and heart.

1974, Aug. 22 Litho. *Perf. 13*
C218 A222 7c yel & multi 25 20
C219 A222 33c lt bl & multi 1.50 85

Fight against diabetes.

UPU Type of 1974

Designs (UPU Emblem and): 7c, Ships 33c, Jet.

1974, Oct. 9 Litho. *Perf. 13½*
C220 A223 7c grn & multi 25 20
C221 A223 33c red & multi 40 40
a. Souvenir sheet of 4 75 75

Centenary of Universal Postal Union. No. C221a contains one each of Nos. 727-728 and C220-C221 forming continuous design. Red marginal inscription. Size: 120x91mm.

Certain countries cancel stamps in full sheets and sell them (usually with gum) for less than face value. Dealers generally sell "CTO".

Golfers and Championship Emblem — AP64

Design: 20c, Golfer and Golf Association emblem.

1974, Oct. 24 Litho. *Perf. 13x13½*
C222 AP64 10c grn & multi 45 30
C223 AP64 20c grn & multi 75 65

World Amateur Golf Championships.

Hand Holding Dove AP65

1974, Dec. 3 Litho. *Perf. 12*
C224 AP65 10c multi 40 20

Christmas 1974.

FAO Type of 1974

Design: 10c, Bee, beehive and barrel of honey.

1974, Dec. 5
C225 A227 10c multi 40 25

World Food Program, 10th anniversary.

Chrismon, Lamb, Candle and Palm — AP66

Spain No. 1, Espana 75 Emblem — AP67

1975, Mar. 26 Litho. *Perf. 13½*
C226 AP66 10c gold & multi 40 20

Holy Week 1975.

1975, Apr. 10
C227 AP67 12c red, yel & blk 22 15

Espa
na 75, International Philatelic Exhibition, Madrid, Apr. 4-13.

Development Bank Type of 1975

1975, May 19 Litho. *Perf. 10½x10*
C228 A230 10c rose car & multi 35 30

16th Assembly of the Governors of the International Development Bank, Santo Domingo, May 1975.

Three Satellites and Globe AP68

1975, June 21 Litho. *Perf. 13½*
C229 AP68 15c multi 55 40

Opening of first earth satellite tracking station in Dominican Republic.

Apollo Type of 1975

Design: 2p, Apollo-Soyuz link-up over earth.

1975, July 24 *Perf. 13*
Size: 42x28mm.
C230 A232 2p multi 2.50 2.50

Apollo Soyuz space test project (Russo-American cooperation), launching July 15; link-up, July 17.

Indian Chief Type of 1975

Designs: 7c, Mayobanex. 8c, Cotubanama and Juan de Esquivel. 10c, Enriquillo and Mencia.

1975, Sept. 27 Litho. *Perf. 12*
C231 A235 7c lt grn & multi 30 20
C232 A235 8c org & multi 40 30
C233 A235 10c gray & multi 45 30

Volleyball AP69

Design: 10c, Weight lifting and Games' emblem.

1975, Oct. 24 Litho. *Perf. 12*
C234 AP69 7c bl & multi 30 20
C235 AP69 10c multi 40 30

7th Pan-American Games, Mexico City, Oct. 13-26.

Christmas Type of 1975

Design: 10c, Dove and peace message.

1975, Dec. 12 Litho. *Perf. 13x13½*
C236 A237 10c yel & multi 40 20

Christmas 1975.

Valdesia Dam AP70

1976, Jan. 26 Litho. *Perf. 13*
C237 AP70 10c multi 30 20

Holy Week Type 1976

Design: 10c, Crucifixion, by Eliezer Castillo.

1976, Apr. 14 Litho. *Perf. 13½*
C238 A239 10c multi 40 30

Holy Week 1976.

Bicentennial Type of 1976 and

George Washington, Independence Hall — AP71

Design: 10c, Hands holding maps of US and Dominican Republic.

1976, May 29 Litho. *Perf. 13½*
C239 A241 10c vio bl, grn & blk 40 25
C240 AP71 75c blk & org 75 60

American Bicentennial; No. C240 also for Interphil 76 International Philatelic Exhibition, Philadelphia, Pa., May 29-June 6.

King Juan Carlos I and Queen Sofia — AP72

1976, May 31
C241 AP72 21c multi 90 50

Visit of King Juan Carlos I and Queen Sofia of Spain.

Telephone Type of 1976

Design: 10c, Alexander Graham Bell and telephones, 1876 and 1976.

1976, July 15
C242 A243 10c multi 35 25

Centenary of first telephone call by Alexander Graham Bell, Mar. 10, 1876.

Duarte Types of 1976

Designs: 10c, Scroll with Duarte letter and Dominican flag. 33c, Duarte leaving for Exile, by E. Godoy.

1976, July 20 Litho. *Perf. 13½*
C243 A245 10c bl & multi 35 20
Perf. 13x13½
C244 A244 33c brn & multi 1.25 75

Juan Pablo Duarte, liberation hero, death centenary.

Fire Engine AP73

1976, Sept. 13 Litho. *Perf. 12*
C245 AP73 10c multi 30 20

Honoring firemen.

Radio Club Type of 1976

1976, Oct. 8 Litho. *Perf. 13½*
C246 A247 10c bl & blk 40 25

Dominican Radio Club, 50th anniversary.

Various People — AP74

1976, Oct. 22 Litho. *Perf. 13½*
C247 AP74 21c multi 30 30

Spanish heritage.

Olympic Games Type of 1976

Design (Montreal Olympic Games Emblem and): 10c, Running. 25c, Basketball.

1976, Oct. 22 *Perf. 12*
C248 A249 10c ocher & multi 30 20
C249 A249 25c grn & multi 45 30

21st Olympic Games, Montreal, Canada, July 17-Aug. 1.

Christmas Type of 1976

Design: 10c, Angel with bells.

1976, Dec. 8 Litho. *Perf. 13½*
C250 A251 10c multi 40 30

Tourist Activities AP75

Designs: 12c, Angling and hotel. 25c, Horseback riding and waterfall (vert.).

1977, Jan. 7
Size: 36x36mm.
C251 AP75 10c multi 30 20
Size: 34x25½, 25½x34mm.
C252 AP75 12c multi 25 15
C253 AP75 25c multi 80 60

Tourist publicity.

Championship Type of 1977

1977, Mar. 4 Litho. *Perf. 13½*
C254 A253 10c yel grn & multi 35 20
C255 A253 25c lt brn & multi 55 25

10th Central American and Caribbean Children's and Young People's Swimming Championships, Santo Domingo.

Holy Week Type 1977

Design: 10c, Belfry and open book.

1977, Apr. 18 Litho. *Perf. 13½x13*
C256 A254 10c multi 40 20

Holy Week 1977.

Lions Type of 1977

1977, May 6 *Perf. 13½x13*
C257 A255 7c lt grn & multi 25 15

12th annual Dominican Republic Lions Convention.

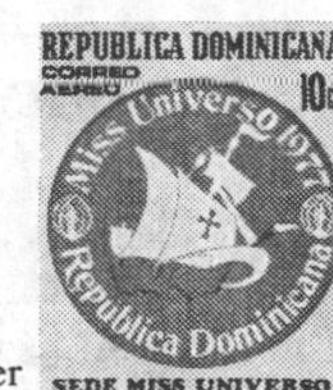

Caravel under Sail — AP76

1977, July 16 Litho. *Perf. 13*
C258 AP76 10c multi 30 20

Miss Universe Contest, held in Dominican Republic.

Melon Cactus — AP77

Design: 33c, Coccothrinax (tree).

1977, Aug. 19 Litho. *Perf. 12*
C259 AP77 7c multi 25 20
C260 AP77 33c multi 35 30

National Botanical Garden.

Chart and Factories — AP78

1977, Nov. 30 Litho. ***Perf. 13x13½***
C261 AP78 28c multi 40 30

7th Interamerican Statistics Conference.

Animal Type of 1977

Designs (Congress Emblem and): 10c, "Dorado," red Roman stud bull. 25c, Flamingo (vert.).

1977, Dec. 29 Litho. ***Perf. 13***
C262 A259 10c multi 35 20
C263 A259 25c multi 75 50

8th Pan-American Veterinary and Zootechnical Congress.

Spanish Heritage Type of 1978

Design: 21c, Window, Casa del Tostado, 16th century.

1978, Jan. 19 ***Perf. 13x13½***
Size: 28x41mm.
C264 A260 21c multi 70 60

Holy Week Type, 1978

Designs: 7c, Facade, Santo Domingo Cathedral. 10c, Facade of Dominican Convent.

1978, Mar. 21 Litho. ***Perf. 12***
Size: 27x36mm.
C265 A261 7c multi 30 25
C266 A261 10c multi 40 30

Holy Week 1978.

Schooner Duarte AP79

1978, Apr. 15 Litho. ***Perf. 13½***
C267 AP79 7c multi 25 14

Dominican naval forces training ship.

Cardinal Type of 1978

1978, May 5 Litho. ***Perf. 13***
C268 A262 10c multi 30 25

Octavio A. Beras Rojas, first Cardinal from Dominican Republic.

Antenna AP80

1978, May 17 Litho. ***Perf. 13½***
C269 AP80 25c sil & multi 75 50

10th World Telecommunications Day.

No. C1 and Map AP81

1978, June 6
C270 AP81 10c multi 40 20

50th anniversary of first Dominican Republic airmail stamp.

Globe, Soccer Ball, Emblem — AP82

Crown, Cross and Rosary Emblem — AP83

Design: 33c, Soccer field, Argentina '78 emblem and globe.

1978, June 29
C271 AP82 12c multi 50 45
C272 AP82 33c multi 40 40

11th World Cup Soccer Championship, Argentina, June 1-25.

1978, July 11 ***Perf. 13x13½***
C273 AP83 21c multi 25 25

Congregation of the Merciful Sisters of Charity, centenary.

Sports Type of 1978

Designs (Games' Emblem and): 7c, Baseball (vert.). 10c, Soccer (vert.).

1978, July 21 Litho. ***Perf. 13½***
C274 A265 7c multi 25 18
C275 A265 10c multi 35 30

13th Central American and Caribbean Games, Medellin, Colombia.

Wright Brothers and Glider, 1902 AP84

Designs: 7c, Diagrams of Flyer I and jet (vert.). 13c, Diagram of air flow over wing. 45c, Flyer I over world map.

1978, Aug. 8 ***Perf. 12***
C276 AP84 7c multi 30 25
C277 AP84 10c multi 45 25
C278 AP84 13c multi 70 45
C279 AP84 45c multi 45 45

75th anniversary of first powered flight.

Tourist Type of 1978

Designs: 7c, Sun and musical instruments. 10c, Sun and plane over Santo Domingo.

1978, Sept. 12 Litho. ***Perf. 12***
C280 A266 7c multi 22 14
C281 A266 10c multi 30 30

Tourist publicity.

People and Globe AP85

1978, Oct. 12 Litho. ***Perf. 13½***
C282 AP85 21c multi 25 25

Spanish heritage.

Dominican Republic and UN Flags AP86

1978, Oct. 23 ***Perf. 12***
C283 AP86 33c multi 35 35

33rd anniversary of the United Nations.

Statue of the Virgin — AP87

1978, Dec. 5 Litho. ***Perf. 12***
C284 AP87 10c multi 45 35

Christmas 1978.

Pope John Paul II — AP88

1979, Jan. 25 Litho. ***Perf. 13½***
C285 AP88 10c multi 4.50 1.00

Visit of Pope John Paul II to the Dominican Republic, Jan. 25-26.

Map of Beata Island AP89

1979, Jan. 25 ***Perf. 12***
C286 AP89 10c multi 30 20

First expedition of radio amateurs to Beata Island.

Year of the Child Type, 1979

Designs (ICY Emblem and): 7c, Children reading book. 10c, Symbolic head and protective hands. 33c, Hands and jars.

1979, Feb. 26
C287 A269 7c multi 25 20
C288 A269 10c multi 35 25
C289 A269 33c multi 35 35

International Year of the Child.

Pope John Paul II Giving Benediction AP90

Adm. Juan Bautista Cambiaso AP91

1979, Apr. 9 Litho. ***Perf. 13½***
C290 AP90 10c multi 50 40

Holy Week.

1979, Apr. 14 ***Perf. 12***
C291 AP91 10c multi 30 20

135th anniversary of the Battle of Tortuguero.

Map of Dominican Rep., Album, Magnifier AP92

1979, Apr. 18
C292 AP92 33c multi 35 30

EXFILNA, 3rd National Philatelic Exhibition, Apr. 18-22.

Flower Type of 1979

Designs: 7c, Passionflower. 10c, Isidorea pungens. 13c, Calotropis procera.

1979, May 17 Litho. ***Perf. 12***
C293 A271 7c multi 20 20
C294 A271 10c multi 45 30
C295 A271 13c multi 30 25

"Dr. Rafael M. Moscoso" National Botanical Garden.

Cardiology Type, 1979

Design: 10c, Figure of man showing blood circulation (vert.).

1979, June 2 Litho. ***Perf. 13½***
C296 A272 10c multi 30 20

Dominican Cardiology Institute.

Sports Type of 1979

Design: 7c, Runner and Games' emblem (vert.).

1979, June 20
C297 A273 7c multi 25 20

8th Pan American Games, Puerto Rico, June 30-July 15.

Soccer Type of 1979

Design: 10c, Tennis (vert.).

1979, Aug. 9 Litho. ***Perf. 12***
C298 A273 10c multi 40 30

Third National Games.

Rowland Hill, Dominican Republic No. 1 — AP93

1979, Aug. 21 ***Perf. 13½***
C299 AP93 2p multi 2.75 2.00

Sir Rowland Hill (1795-1879), originator of penny postage.

Electric Light Type of 1979

Design: 10c, "100" and light bulb (horiz).

1979, Aug. 27 ***Perf. 13½***
C300 A275 10c multi 40 30

Centenary of invention of electric light.

Bird Type of 1979

Birds: 7c, Phaenicophilus palmarum. 10c, Calyptophilus frugivorus tertius. 45c, Icterus dominicensis.

1979, Sept. 12 Litho. ***Perf. 12***
C301 A277 7c multi 30 25

C302 A277 10c multi 40 35
C303 A277 45c multi 45 40

Lions Type of 1979

Design: 10c, Melvin Jones, organization founder.

1979, Nov. 13 Litho. *Perf. 12*
C304 A278 10c multi 40 15

Lions International Club of Dominican Republic, 10th anniversary.

Christmas Type of 1979

Christmas 1979: 10c, Three Kings riding camels.

1979, Dec. 18 Litho. *Perf. 12*
C305 A279 10c multi 40 30

Holy Week Type of 1980

Holy Week: 7c, Crucifixion. 10c, Resurrection.

1980, Mar. 27 Litho. *Perf. 12*
C306 A280 7c multi 25 25
C307 A280 10c multi 35 30

Navy Day — AP94

1980, Apr. 15 Litho. *Perf. 13½*
C308 AP94 21c multi 35 20

Dominican Philatelic Society, 25th Anniversary AP95

1980, Apr. 18
C309 AP95 10c multi 30 20

Gold Type of 1980

1980, July 8 Litho. *Perf. 13½*
C310 A282 10c *Drag line mining* 40 30
C311 A282 33c *Mine* 70 40

Nationalization of gold mining.

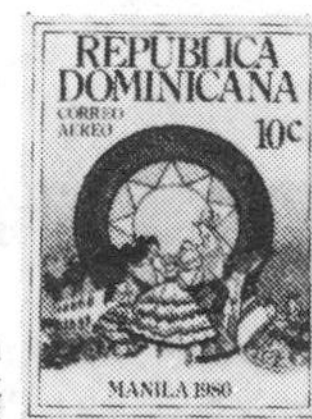

Tourism Secretariat Emblem — AP96

1980, Aug. 26 Litho. *Perf. 13½*
C312 AP96 10c *shown* 45 35
C313 AP96 33c *Conference emblem* 1.50 85

World Tourism Conference, Manila, Sept. 27.

Iguana Type of 1980

1980, Aug. 30 *Perf. 12*
C314 A284 7c *American crocodile* 30 30
C315 A284 10c *Cuban rat* 40 40
C316 A284 25c *Manatee* 50 45
C317 A284 45c *Turtle* 60 55

Painting Type of 1980

1980, Sept. 23 Litho. *Perf. 13½x13*
C318 A285 10c *Abstract, by Paul Guidicelli*, vert. 45 35
C319 A285 17c *Farmer, by Yoryi Morel*, vert. 70 60

Visit of Radio Amateurs to Catalina Island AP97

1980, Oct. 3
C320 AP97 7c multi 25 25

Rotary International, 75th Anniversary AP98

1980, Oct. 23 Litho. *Perf. 12*
C321 AP98 10c *Globe, emblem*, vert. 45 35
C322 AP98 33c *shown* 65 55

Carrier Pigeons, UPU Emblem AP99

1980, Oct. 31 *Perf. 13½*
C323 AP99 33c *shown* 35 35
C324 AP99 45c *Pigeons, diff.* 45 45
C325 AP99 50c *Pigeon, stamp* 70 50

Souvenir Sheet

Imperf

C326 AP99 1.10p *UPU emblem* 1.25 1.25

Universal Postal Union membership centenary. No. C326 contains one stamp (48½x31mm); brown marginal inscription. Size: 102½x70mm.

Christmas Type of 1980

1980, Dec. 5 Litho. *Perf. 13½*
C327 A286 10c *Holy Family* 45 35

Christmas 1980.

Salcedo Type of 1981

Design: Map and arms of Salcedo.

1981, Jan. 14 Litho. *Perf. 13½*
C328 A287 10c multi 40 30

Industrial Symbols, Seminar Emblem — AP100

1981, Feb. 18 Litho. *Perf. 13½*
C329 AP100 10c shown 40 35
C330 AP100 33c Seminar emblem 70 40

CODIA Chemical Engineering Seminar.

National Games Type of 1981

1981, Mar. 31 Litho. *Perf. 13½*
C331 A289 10c Baseball 18 14

Admiral Juan Alejandro Acosta — AP101

1981, Apr. 15
C332 AP101 10c multi 30 25

Battle of Tortuguero anniversary.

13th World Telecommunications Day — AP102

1981, May 16 Litho. *Perf. 12*
C333 AP102 10c multi 35 20

Heinrich von Stephan AP103

Worker in Wheelchair AP104

1981, July 15 Litho. *Perf. 13½*
C334 AP103 33c tan & lt red brn 35 35

Birth sesquicentennial of Universal Postal Union founder.

1981, July 24
C335 AP104 7c Stylized people 25 20
C336 AP104 33c shown 50 40

Intl. Year of the Disabled.

EXPURIDOM '81 Intl. Stamp Show, Santo Domingo, July 31-Aug. 2 — AP105

1981, July 31
C337 AP105 7c multi 25 25

Bullet Holes in Target, Competition Emblem — AP106

1981, Aug. 12
C338 AP106 10c shown 30 25
C339 AP106 15c Riflemen 45 40
C340 AP106 25c Pistol shooting 75 65

2nd World Sharpshooting Championship.

The first price column gives the catalogue value of an unused stamp, the second that of a used stamp.

Exports — AP107

1981, Oct. 16 Litho. *Perf. 12*
C341 AP107 7c Jewelry 30 25
C342 AP107 10c Handicrafts 40 35
C343 AP107 11c Fruit 15 15
C344 AP107 17c Vegetables 70 50

World Food Day — AP108

1981, Oct. 16 Litho. *Perf. 13½*
C345 AP108 10c Fruits 40 30
C346 AP108 50c Vegetables 75 50

5th Natl. Games AP109

1981, Dec. 5 Litho. *Perf. 13½*
C347 AP109 10c Javelin, vert. 40 35
C348 AP109 50c Cycling 1.75 1.50

Orchids AP110

1981, Dec. 14
C349 AP110 7c Encyclia cochleata 25 20
C350 AP110 10c Broughtonia domingensis 35 30
C351 AP110 25c Encyclia truncata 50 25
C352 AP110 75c Elleanthus capitatus 75 60

Christmas Type of 1981

1981, Dec. 23
C353 A294 10c Dove, sun 45 35

Battle of Tortuguero Anniv. AP111

1982, Apr. 15 Litho. *Perf. 13½*
C354 AP111 10c Naval Academy, cadets 25 20

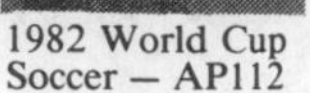

1982 World Cup Soccer — AP112

American Air Forces Cooperation System — AP113

Designs: Various soccer players.

1982, Apr. 19

C355	AP112	10c multi	35	25
C356	AP112	21c multi	25	20
C357	AP112	33c multi	50	35

1982, Apr. 12 ***Perf. 12***

C358	AP113	10c multi	25	25

Scouting Year AP114

1982, Apr. 30 Litho. ***Perf. 13½***

C359	AP114	10c Baden-Powell, vert.	25	20
C360	AP114	15c Globe	40	30
C361	AP114	25c Baden-Powell, scout, vert.	60	35

Dancers — AP115

Espamer '82 Emblem — AP116

1982, June 1 Litho. ***Perf. 13½***

C362	AP115	7c Emblem	20	15
C363	AP115	10c Cathedral, Casa del Tostado, Santo Domingo	30	20
C364	AP115	33c shown	75	50

Tourist Org. of the Americas, 25th Congress (COTAL '82), Santo Domingo.

1982, July 5

Espamer '82 Intl. Stamp Exhibition, San Juan, Oct. 12-17: Symbolic stamps. 7c, 13c horiz.

C365	AP116	7c multi	20	10
C366	AP116	13c multi	35	25
C367	AP116	50c multi	75	50

Sports Type of 1982

1982, Aug. 13 ***Perf. 12***

C368	A300	10c Basketball	20	15
C369	A300	13c Boxing	30	20
C370	A300	25c Gymnast	40	30

Exist imperf.

Condition is the all-important factor of price. Prices quoted are for stamps in fine condition.

Harbor, by Alejandro Bonilla — AP117

Paintings: 10c, Portrait of a Woman, by Leopoldo Navarro. 45c, Amelia Francasci, by Luis Desangles. 2p, Portrait, by Abelardo Rodriguez Urdaneta. 10c, 45c, 2p vert.

1982, Aug. 20 ***Perf. 13***

C371	AP117	7c multi	30	15
C372	AP117	10c multi	35	20
C373	AP117	45c multi	55	30
C374	AP117	2p multi	2.50	2.00

Exist imperf.

San Pedro de Macoris Type of 1982

1982, Aug. 26

Size: 42x29mm.

C375	A301	7c Lake	30	25

35th Anniv. of Central Bank AP118

1982, Oct. 22 Litho. ***Perf. 13½x13***

C376	AP118	10c multi	20	15

490th Anniv. of Discovery of America AP119

1982, Oct. 7 Litho. ***Perf. 13½***

C377	AP119	7c Map	20	15
C378	AP119	10c Santa Maria, vert.	25	20
C379	AP119	21c Columbus, vert.	30	25

Christmas Type of 1982

1982, Dec. 8

C380	A303	10c multi	30	15

French Alliance Centenary AP120

1983, Mar. 31 Litho. ***Perf. 13½***

C381	AP120	33c multi	50	35

Battle of Tortuguero Anniv. AP121

1983, Apr. 15 Litho. ***Perf. 13½***

C382	AP121	15c Frigate Mella-451	35	25

World Communications Year — AP122

1983, May 6 Litho. ***Perf. 13½***

C383	AP122	10c dk bl & bl	30	20

Simon Bolivar (1783-1830) AP123

1983, July 5 Litho. ***Perf. 13½***

C384	AP123	9c multi	20	10

9th Pan American Games, Caracas, Aug. 13-28 — AP124

1983, Aug. 22 Litho. ***Perf. 12***

C385	AP124	7c Gymnast, basketball	15	12
C386	AP124	10c Highjump, boxing	30	15
C387	AP124	15c Baseball, weight lifting, bicycling	35	25

491st Anniv. of Discovery of America AP125

1983, Oct. 11 Litho. ***Perf. 13½***

C388	AP125	10c Columbus' ships, map	22	10
C389	AP125	21c Santa Maria (trophy)	35	15
C390	AP125	33c Yacht Sotavento, vert.	40	20

Size: 103x103mm.

Imperf

C391	AP125	50c Ship models		

10th Anniv. of Latin American Civil Aviation Commission — AP126

1983, Dec. 7

C392	AP126	10c dk bl	20	10

Funeral Procession, by Juan Bautista Gomez — AP127

Designs: 15c, Meeting of Maximo Gomez and Jose Marti in Guayubin, by Enrique Garcia Godoy. 21c, St. Francis, by Angel Perdomo (vert.). 33c, Portrait of a Girl, by Adriana Billini (vert.).

1983, Dec. 26 ***Perf. 13½***

C393	AP127	10c multi	15	10
C394	AP127	15c multi	25	12
C395	AP127	21c multi	40	20
C396	AP127	33c multi	55	20

Christmas 1983 — AP128

1983, Dec. 13 Litho. ***Perf. 13½***

C397	AP128	10c Bells, ornaments	20	10

AIR POST SEMI-POSTAL STAMPS

Nos. C97-C99 Surcharged in Red

Engraved and Lithographed

1957, Feb. 8 Unwmk. ***Perf. 11½***

Flags in National Colors

CB1	A117	11c + 2c ultra & red org	40	40
CB2	A117	16c + 2c car & lt grn	55	55
CB3	A117	17c + 2c blk, vio & red	60	60

The surtax was to aid Hungarian refugees. A similar 25c surcharge was applied to the souvenir sheets described in the footnote following No. C99. Price, 2 sheets, perf. and imperf., $17.50.

Nos. C100-C102 Surcharged in Red Orange

1957, Sept. 9 Photo. ***Perf. 13½***

Flags in National Colors

CB4	A118	11c + 2c yel grn & dk bl	70	65
CB5	A118	16c + 2c lil & dk bl	85	85
CB6	A118	17c + 2c brn & bl grn	95	95

See note after No. B10.

A similar 5c surcharge was applied to the miniature sheets described in the footnote following No. 483. Price, 4 sheets, perf. & imperf., medal and flag, $40.

Types of Olympic Air Post Stamps, 1957, Surcharged in Carmine

+2¢

REFUGIADOS REFUGIADOS

a b

Engraved and Lithographed

1958, May 26 *Perf. 13½*

Flags in National Colors

Pink Paper

CB7 A119(a) 11c + 2c ultra 40 40
CB8 A119(b) 11c + 2c ultra 40 40
CB9 A120(a) 16c + 2c rose car 50 50
CB10 A120(b) 16c + 2c rose car 50 50
CB11 A119(a) 17c + 2c cl 60 60
CB12 A119(b) 17c + 2c cl 60 60
Nos. CB7-CB12 (6) 3.00 3.00

The surtax was for the United Nations Relief and Works Agency for Palestine Refugees.

A similar 5c surcharge, plus marginal United Nations emblem and "UNRWA," was applied to the miniature sheets described in the footnote following No. C105. Price, 4 sheets, perf. and imperf., $30.

Nos. C106-C108 Surcharged

Perf. 13½

1959, Apr. 13 **Unwmk.** **Photo.**

Flags in National Colors

CB13 A125 11c + 2c bl, ol & brn 75 75
CB14 A125 16c + 2c lt grn, org & dk bl 1.00 1.00
CB15 A125 17c + 2c ver bl & yel 1.50 1.50

Issued for the International Geophysical Year.

A similar 5c surcharge was applied to the miniature sheets described in the footnote following No. C108. Price, 2 sheets, perf. and imperf., $25.

Type of Regular Issue 1957 Surcharged in Red

Engraved and Lithographed

1959, Sept. 10 *Imperf.*

Flags in National Colors

CB16 A117 11c + 2c ultra & red org 60 60
CB17 A117 16c + 2c car & lt grn 70 70
CB18 A117 17c + 2c blk, vio & red 75 75

Issued for the 3rd Pan American Games, Chicago, Aug. 27-Sept. 7, 1959.

World Refugee Year Issue.

Nos. C113-C114 Surcharged in Red

+5 ¢

1960, Apr. 7 **Litho.** *Perf. 12½*

CB19 AP43 10c + 5c plum, gray & grn 15 15
CB20 AP43 13c + 5c gray & grn 20 20

For souvenir sheets see note after No. B33.

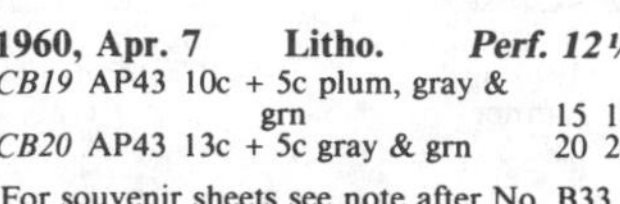

Nos. C115-C117 Surcharged: "XV ANIVERSARIO DE LA UNESCO + 2c"

Perf. 13½

1962, Jan. 8 **Unwmk.** **Photo.**

Flags in National Colors

CB21 A136 11c + 2c bl, gray & brn 35 35
CB22 A136 16c + 2c red, brn & ol 50 50
CB23 A136 17c + 2c blk, bl & ocher 55 55

See note after No. B38.

A similar 5c surcharge was applied to the miniature sheets described in the footnote following No. C117. Price, 2 sheets, perf. and imperf., $7.50.

Anti-Malaria Type of 1962

1962, Apr. 29 **Litho.** *Perf. 12*

CB24 A141 13c + 2c pink & red 15 15
CB25 A141 33c + 2c org & dp org 35 35

Issued for the World Health Organization drive to eradicate malaria. Souvenir sheets exist, perf. and imperf. containing one each of Nos. B39-B40, CB24-CB25 and a 25c+2c pale green and yellow green. Dark brown marginal inscription. Size: 169x102mm.

Nos. C132-C133 Surcharged

1964, March 8

CB26 AP46 10c + 2c brt vio 15 15
CB27 AP46 13c + 2c yel 15 15

Issued to publicize the UNESCO world campaign to save historic monuments in Nubia.

Nos. C146-C148 Surcharged Like Semi-Postal Issue B47-B51

1966, Dec. 9 **Litho.** *Perf. 12½*

Size: 35x24mm.

CB28 A164 10c + 5c multi 15 15
CB29 A164 50c + 10c multi 60 60
CB30 A164 75c + 10c multi 85 85

Surtax for victims of hurricane Inez.

AIR POST OFFICIAL STAMPS

OAP1

Blue Overprint

Unwmk.

1930, Dec. 3 **Typo.** *Perf. 12*

CO1 OAP1 10c lt bl 17.50 15.00
a. Pair, one without overprint *1,500.*
CO2 OAP1 20c orange 17.50 15.00

SPECIAL DELIVERY STAMPS

Biplane — SD1

Perf. 11½.

1920, Apr. **Unwmk.** **Litho.**

E1 SD1 10c dp ultra 9.00 2.00
a. Imperf., pair

Special Delivery Messenger — SD2

1925

E2 SD2 10c dk bl 22.50 7.50

SD3

1927

E3 SD3 10c red brn 9.00 2.00
a. "E EXPRESO" at top 90.00 90.00

Type of 1927.

1941 **Redrawn.**

E4 SD3 10c yel grn 4.00 2.00
E5 SD3 10c dk bl grn 2.50 1.00

The redrawn design differs slightly from SD3.

Issue dates: E4, Mar. 27; E5, Aug. 7.

Emblem of Communications — SD4

1945, Sept. 1 *Perf. 12*

E6 SD4 10c rose car, car & dk bl 75 30

SD5

1950 **Litho.** **Unwmk.**

E7 SD5 10c multi 75 30

Exists imperf.

Modern Communications System — SD6

1956, Aug. 18 *Perf. 11½*

E8 SD6 25c green 1.50 50

Carrier Pigeon SD7

1967 **Litho.** *Perf. 11½*

E9 SD7 25c lt bl 90 40

Carrier Pigeon, Globe — SD8

1978, Aug. 2 **Litho.** *Perf. 13½*

E10 SD8 25c multi 75 50

Messenger and Plane — SD9

1979, Nov. 30 *Perf. 13½*

E11 SD9 25c multi 25 25

INSURED LETTER STAMPS

Merino Issue of 1933 Surcharged in Red or Black

PRIMA
VALORES DECLARADOS
SERVICIO INTERIOR
8
CENTAVOS

1935, Feb. 1 **Unwmk.** *Perf. 14.*

G1 A35 8c on 7c ultra 80 25
a. Invtd. surcharge 30.00
G2 A34 15c on 10c org yel 70 20
a. Invtd. surcharge 30.00
G3 A35 30c on 8c dk grn 2.75 1.25
G4 A35 45c on 20c car rose (Bk) 4.00 1.75
G5 A36 70c on 50c lem 8.50 1.75
Nos. G1-G5 (5) 16.75 5.20

Merino Issue of 1933 Surcharged in Red

PRIMA
VALORES DECLARADOS
SERVICIO INTERIOR
8
CENTAVOS

1940

G6 A35 8c on ½c lt vio 3.50 3.00
G7 A35 8c on 7c ultra 3.50 3.00

Coat of Arms — IL1

1940-45 **Litho.** *Perf. 11½*

Arms in Black

G8 IL1 8c brn red 1.00 10
a. 8c dk red, no shading on inner frame 1.75 12
G9 IL1 15c dp org ('45) 2.00 25
G10 IL1 30c dk grn ('41) 2.50 20
a. 30c yel grn 2.50 20
G11 IL1 45c ultra ('44) 2.50 50
G12 IL1 70c ol brn ('44) 3.00 45
Nos. G8-G12 (5) 11.00 1.50

Redrawn Type of 1940-45.

1952-53

Arms in Black.

G13 IL1 8c car lake ('53) 1.50 70
G14 IL1 15c red org ('53) 2.75 1.25
G15 IL1 70c dp brn car 7.00 2.00

Larger and bolder numerals on 8c and 15c. Smaller and bolder "70." There are many other minor differences in the design.

Type of 1940-45

1954

Arms in Black, 15x16mm.

G16 IL1 10c carmine 1.25 30

A little time given to the study of the arrangement of the Scott Catalogue can make it easier to use effectively.

Coat of Arms — IL2

1955-69 Unwmk. Litho. *Perf. 11½*
Arms in Black, 13½x11½mm.

G17 IL2 10c car rose 60 12
G18 IL2 15c red org ('56) 3.00 2.00
G19 IL2 20c red org ('58) 1.25 50
a. 20c org ('69) 1.50 45
b. 20c org, retouched ('69) 4.00 2.00
G20 IL2 30c dk grn ('55) 2.25 50
G21 IL2 40c dk grn ('58) 2.75 1.50
a. 40c lt yel grn ('62) 2.00 75
G22 IL2 45c ultra ('56) 5.00 3.00
G23 IL2 70c dp brn car ('56) 5.00 3.00
Nos. G17-G23 (7) 19.85 10.62

On No. G19b the horizontal shading lines of shield are omitted.

Type of 1940-45
Second Redrawing
1963 *Perf. 12½*
Arms in Black, 17x16mm.

G24 IL1 10c red org 1.50 40
G25 IL1 20c orange 1.75 75

Third Redrawing
1966 Litho. *Perf. 12½*
Arms in Black, 14x14mm.

G26 IL1 10c violet 60 30
G27 IL1 40c orange 2.25 1.75

Type of 1955-62
1968 Litho. *Perf. 11½*
Arms in Black, 13½x11½mm.

G28 IL2 20c red 2.00 1.25
G29 IL2 60c yellow 1.25 1.00

1973-76 Litho. *Perf. 12½*
Arms in Black, 11x11mm.

G30 IL2 10c car rose ('76) 60 40
G31 IL2 20c yellow 2.00 1.50
G32 IL2 20c org ('76) 1.75 80
G33 IL2 40c yel grn 2.75 1.75
a. 40c grn ('76) 3.25 2.00
G34 IL2 70c blue 1.50 1.50

1973 *Perf. 11½*
Arms in Black, 13½x11½mm.

G35 IL2 10c dk vio 1.50 40

1978, Aug. 9 *Perf. 10½*
Arms in Black, 11x11mm.

G36 IL2 10c rose mag 60 25
G37 IL2 40c brt grn 1.75 1.25

IL3

1982-83 Litho. *Perf. 10½*
Arms in Black.

G38 IL3 10c dp mag 30 8
G39 IL3 20c dp org 60 35
G40 IL3 40c bluish grn 1.25 65

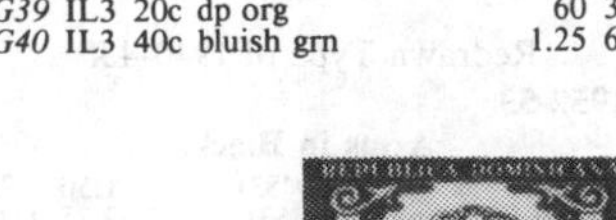

IL4

1986 Litho. *Perf. 10½*
Arms in Black.

G41 IL4 20c brt rose lil 40 28
G42 IL4 60c orange 1.20 80
G43 IL4 1p lt bl 2.00 1.35
G44 IL4 1.25p pink 2.50 1.65
G45 IL4 1.50p vermilion 3.00 2.00
G46 IL4 3p lt grn 6.00 4.00
G47 IL4 3.50p ol bis 7.00 4.65
G48 IL4 4p yellow 8.00 5.35
G49 IL4 4.50p lt bl grn 9.00 6.00
G50 IL4 5p brn ol 10.00 6.75
G51 IL4 6p gray 12.00 8.00
G52 IL4 6.50p lt ultra 13.00 8.65
Nos. G41-G52 (12) 74.10 49.48

Issue dates: Nos. G42-G43, G45, July 6. Nos. G46-G52, Sept. 2. Nos. G41, G44, Nov. 6.

POSTAGE DUE STAMPS

Numeral of Value — D1

1901 Unwmk. Typo. *Perf. 14.*

J1 D1 2 (c) ol gray 1.00 20
J2 D1 4 (c) ol gray 1.25 25
J3 D1 5 (c) ol gray 2.00 40
J4 D1 10 (c) ol gray 3.00 1.00

1909 Wmk. 116

J5 D1 2 (c) ol gray 1.00 30
J6 D1 4 (c) ol gray 1.00 40
J7 D1 6 (c) ol gray 2.50 1.00
J8 D1 10 (c) ol gray 5.00 2.50

1913

J9 D1 2 (c) ol grn 60 20
J10 D1 4 (c) ol grn 70 25
J11 D1 6 (c) ol grn 85 30
J12 D1 10 (c) ol grn 1.25 50

1922 Unwmk. Litho. *Perf. 11½.*

J13 D1 1 (c) ol grn 60 60

Numeral of Value
D2 D3

1942

J14 D2 1c dk red & pale pink 20 10
J15 D2 2c dk bl & pale bl 20 15
J16 D2 4c dk grn & pale grn 20 20
J17 D2 6c grn & buff 30 25
J18 D2 8c yel org & pale yel 30 30
J19 D2 10c mag & pale pink 40 40
Nos. J14-J19 (6) 1.60 1.40

1959
Size: 20½x25mm.

J20 D2 2c dk bl 2.00 1.50

1960-66 Litho. *Perf. 11½*
Size: 21x25½mm.

J21 D3 1c dk car rose 2.00 2.00
J22 D3 2c dk bl ('66) 2.00 2.00
J23 D3 4c green 5.00 5.00

OFFICIAL STAMPS

Bastion of February 27 — O1

Unwmk.
1902, Feb. 25 Litho. *Perf. 12*

O1 O1 2c scar & blk 70 25
O2 O1 5c dk bl & blk 90 30
O3 O1 10c yel grn & blk 1.00 60
O4 O1 20c yel & blk 1.50 70
a. Imperf., pair 15.00

Bastion of February 27 — O2

Columbus Lighthouse — O3

Wmk. Crosses and Circles. (116)
Perf. 13½x13, 13½x14
1909-12 Typo.

O5 O2 1c bl grn & blk 20 20
O6 O2 2c scar & blk 25 25
O7 O2 5c dk bl & blk 60 30
O8 O2 10c yel grn & blk ('12) 1.25 75
O9 O2 20c org & blk ('12) 2.00 1.25
Nos. O5-O9 (5) 4.30 2.75

The 2c and 5c are found in both perforations; 1c and 20c only perf. 13½x13; 10c only perf. 13½x14.

1928 Unwmk. *Perf. 12.*

O10 O3 1c green 10 8
O11 O3 2c red 15 15
O12 O3 5c ultra 25 25
O13 O3 10c lt bl 35 35
O14 O3 20c orange 50 50
Nos. O10-O14 (5) 1.35 1.33

Proposed Columbus Lighthouse O4

1937 Litho. *Perf. 11½.*

O15 O4 3c dk pur 60 20
O16 O4 7c ind & bl 70 40
O17 O4 10c org yel 90 60

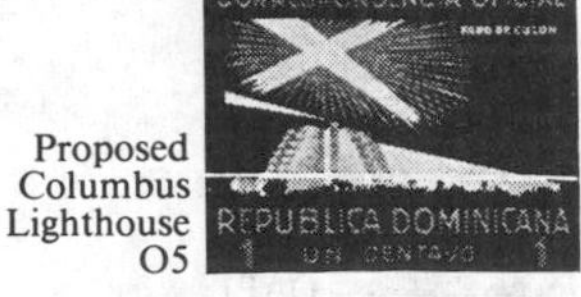
Proposed Columbus Lighthouse O5

1939-41

O18 O5 1c dp grn & lt grn 10 6
O19 O5 2c crim & pale pink 12 8
O20 O5 3c pur & lt vio 15 8
O21 O5 5c dk bl & lt bl ('40) 35 18
O21A O5 5c lt bl ('41) 1.00 30
O22 O5 7c brt bl & lt bl ('41) 40 15
O23 O5 10c yel org & pale org ('41) 60 25
O24 O5 20c brn org & buff ('41) 1.50 40
O25 O5 50c brt red lil & pale lil ('41) 3.00 1.25
Nos. O18-O25 (9) 7.22 2.75

Type of 1939.
1950 Redrawn.

O26 O5 50c dp car & rose 2.00 1.25

The numerals "50" measure 3mm., and are close to left and right frames; numerals measure 4mm. on No. O25. There are other minor differences.

Denominations in "Centavos Oro."
1950

O27 O5 5c lt bl 30 15
O28 O5 10c yel & pale yel 60 25
O29 O5 20c dl org brn & buff 90 60

Letters of top inscription are 1½mm. high.

Type of 1939-41.
Second Redrawing.
Denominations in "Centavos Oro."
1956 Unwmk. *Perf. 11½*

O30 O5 7c bl & lt bl 25 15
O31 O5 20c yel brn & buff 60 40
O32 O5 50c red lil & brt pink 1.50 1.00

The letters of top inscription are 2mm. high, the trees at base of monument have been redrawn, etc. On No. O32 the numerals are similar to No. O26.

POSTAL TAX STAMPS

Santo Domingo after Hurricane PT1
Hurricane's Effect on Capital PT2

1930, Dec. Unwmk. Litho. *Perf. 12.*

RA1 PT1 1¢ grn & rose 25 15
a. Tete Beche pair 3.00 3.00
RA2 PT1 2¢ red rose 30 25
a. Tete Beche pair 3.00 2.50
RA3 PT2 5¢ ultra & rose 50 25
a. Tete Beche pair 3.00 3.50
RA4 PT2 10¢ yel & rose 60 50
a. Tete Beche pair 3.50 3.50

Imperf

RA5 PT1 1¢ grn & rose 70 50
a. Tete Beche pair 3.00 3.00
RA6 PT1 2¢ red & rose 80 55
a. Tete Beche pair 3.00 3.00
RA7 PT2 5¢ ultra & rose 1.00 80
a. Tete Beche pair 3.50 3.50
RA8 PT2 10¢ yel & rose 1.50 1.25
a. Tete Beche pair 3.50 3.50
Nos. RA1-RA8 (8) 5.65 4.25

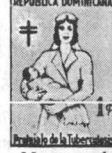

Dr. Martos Sanatorium PT3

Nurse and Child PT4

1944, Apr. 1 Litho. *Perf. 11½*

RA9 PT3 1c dp bl, sl bl & red 35 15

1947, Apr. 1 Unwmk.

RA10 PT4 1c dp bl, pale bl & car 35 15

Sanatorium of the Holy Help — PT5

1949, Apr. 1

RA11 PT5 1c dp bl, pale bl & car 30 15

Youth Holding Banner PT6

"Suffer Little Children to Come Unto Me" PT7

1950, Apr. 1 *Perf. 11½*

RA12 PT6 1c dp bl, pale bl & car 30 15

1950, Dec. 1 *Perf. 12, 12½*
Size: 22½ x 32mm.

RA13 PT7 1c lt bl & pale bl 75 15

Vertical line centering side borders merges into dots toward the bottom. See also Nos. RA13A, RA17, RA19, RA26, RA32, RA35. The tax was for child welfare.

1951, Dec. 1 **Redrawn**
RA13A PT7 1c lt bl & pale bl 2.25 25

In the redrawn stamp, the standing child, a blonde in No. RA13, is changed to a brunette; more foliage has been added above child's head and to branches showing in upper right corner. Vertical dashes in side borders.

Tuberculosis Sanatorium, Santiago — PT8

1952, Apr. 1 **Litho.** ***Perf. 11½***
RA14 PT8 1c lt bl & car 30 15

Sword, Serpent and Crab — PT9

1953, Feb. 1 **Unwmk.** ***Perf. 12.***
RA15 PT9 1c carmine 45 15

The tax was for the Dominican League Against Cancer. See Nos. RA18, RA21, RA43, RA46, RA51, RA56, RA61, RA67, RA72, RA76, RA82, RA88, RA93, RA96.

Tuberculosis Dispensary for Children — PT10

1953, Apr. 1 **Litho.** ***Perf. 12½***
RA16 PT10 1c dp bl, pale bl & red 30 15

See No. RA22.

Jesus Type of 1950
Second Redrawing

1953, Dec. 1 ***Perf. 11½***
Size: 22x31mm.
RA17 PT7 1c blue 60 15

Solid shading in sky reduced to a few scattered dots. Girl's left arm indicated. Rough white dots in side borders.

Cancer Type of 1952

1954, Oct. 1 **Redrawn** ***Perf. 12½***
RA18 PT9 1c rose car 35 12
a. 1c red org ('58) 50 15
b. 1c car ('70) 1.00 30

Upper right serif of numeral "1" eliminated; diagonal line added through "C" and period removed; sword extended, placing top on a line with top of "1." Dots of background screen arranged diagonally. Many other differences.

The tax was for the Dominican League Against Cancer. No. RA18a exists imperf.

On No. RA18b background screen eliminates white outline of crab.

Jesus Type of 1950

1954, Dec. 1 **Third Redrawing**
Size: 23x32¾mm.
RA19 PT7 1c brt bl 40 15
a. 1c pale bl ('59) 20 10

Center completely screened. Tiny white horizontal rectangles in side borders.

Lorraine Cross as Bell Clapper — PT11

1955, Apr. 1 **Litho.** ***Perf. 11½x12***
RA20 PT11 1c blk, yel & red 25 12

Cancer Type of 1952
Second Redrawing.

1956, Oct. 1 ***Perf. 12½***
RA21 PT9 1c carmine 50 20
a. 1c red org ('64) 1.50 75

Similar to No. RA18, but dots of background screen arranged in vertical and horizontal rows. Outlines of central device, lettering and frame clearly delineated. "C" of centsign smaller. Upper claw in solid color.

TB Dispensary Type of 1953

1954, Apr. 1 **Redrawn**
RA22 PT10 1c bl & red 35 15
a. Red (cross) omitted 80.00

No. RA22 has third color omitted; clouds added; bolder letters and numerals.

Angelita Trujillo PT12

Lorraine Cross PT13

1955, Dec. 1 **Unwmk.** ***Perf. 12½***
RA23 PT12 1c violet 25 15

The tax was for child welfare.

1956, Apr. 1 **Litho.** ***Perf. 11½***
RA24 PT13 1c blk, grn, lem & red 25 12

The tax was for the Anti-Tuberculosis League. Inscribed: B.C.G. (Bacillus Calmette-Guerin).

Children PT14

Lorraine Cross PT15

1957, Apr. 1
RA25 PT14 1c red, blk, yel, grn & bl 25 12

Jesus Type of 1950
Fourth Redrawing.

1956, Dec. 1 **Unwmk.** ***Perf. 12***
Size: 21¾x31¼mm.
RA26 PT7 1c blue 30 12

Thin white lines around numeral boxes. Girl's bouquet touches Jesus' sleeve. Tiny white squares or rectangles in side borders. Foliage at either side of "Era de Trujillo" panel.

1958, Apr. 1 **Litho.** ***Perf. 12½***
RA27 PT15 1c brn car & red 20 12

Inscribed "1959"

1959, Apr. 1
RA28 PT15 1c brn car & red 20 12

Lorraine Cross PT16

Lorraine Cross PT17

1960, Apr. 1 **Litho.** ***Perf. 12***
RA29 PT16 1c bl, pale yel & red 30 20

The tax was for the Anti-Tuberculosis League.

1961, Apr. 1 **Unwmk.** ***Perf. 11½***
RA30 PT17 1c bl & red 15 12

The tax was for the Anti-Tuberculosis League.

See No. RA33.

Maria de los Angeles M. de Trujillo and Housing Project PT18

1961, Aug. 1 **Litho.** ***Perf. 12***
RA31 PT18 1c car rose 30 12

The tax was for aid to the needy.
Nos. RA31-RA33 exist imperf.

Jesus Type of 1950
Fifth Redrawing

1961, Dec. 1 **Unwmk.** ***Perf. 12½***
RA32 PT7 1c blue 25 15

No. RA32 is similar to No. RA19, but "Era de Trujillo" has been replaced by a solid color panel.

Type of 1961 Dated "1962"

1962, Apr. 1 ***Perf. 12½***
RA33 PT17 1c bl & red 15 12

The tax was for the Anti-Tuberculosis League.

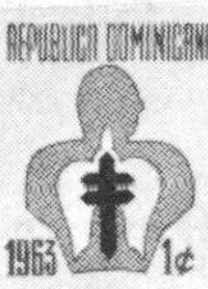

Man's Chest and Lorraine Cross PT19

Hibiscus PT20

1963, Apr. 1 ***Perf. 12x11½***
RA34 PT19 1c ultra & red 25 12

Jesus Type of 1950
Sixth Redrawing

1963, Dec. 1 ***Perf. 11½***
Size: 21¾x32mm.
RA35 PT7 1c blue 20 12
a. 1c dp bl ('64) 20 12

No. RA35 is similar to No. RA26, but "Era de Trujillo" panel has been omitted.

1966, Apr. 1 **Litho.** ***Perf. 11½***
RA36 PT20 1c emer & car 25 12

The tax was for the Anti-Tuberculosis League.

Domingoa Nodosa PT21

Civil Defense Emblem PT22

1967, Apr. 1 **Litho.** ***Perf. 12½***
RA37 PT21 1c lil & red 25 12

The tax was for the Anti-Tuberculosis League.

1967, July 1 **Litho.** ***Rouletted 13***
RA38 PT22 1c multi 30 18

The tax was for the Civil Defense Organization.

Boy, School and Yule Bells PT23

Hand Holding Invalid PT24

1967, Dec. 1 **Litho.** ***Perf. 12½***
RA39 PT23 1c rose red & pink 35 12

1968 ***Perf. 11***
RA40 PT23 1c vermilion 45 20

No. RA40 has screened background; No. RA39, smooth background.

The tax was for child welfare.

See Nos. RA49A, RA52, RA57, RA62, RA68, RA73, RA77, RA81.

1968, Mar. 19 **Litho.** ***Perf. 12½***
RA41 PT24 1c grn & yel 15 8
a. 1c ol grn & dp yel, perf. 11½x12 ('69) 15 8

The tax was for the rehabilitation of the handicapped. See Nos. RA47, RA50, RA54.

Dogbane PT25

Schoolyard and Torch PT26

1968, Apr. 25 **Litho.** ***Perf. 12½***
RA42 PT25 1c emer, yel & red 10 5

The tax was for the Anti-Tuberculosis League. See Nos. RA45, RA49.

Redrawn Cancer Type of 1955

1968, Oct. 1 **Litho.** ***Perf. 12***
RA43 PT9 1c emerald 15 8

The tax was for the Dominican League against Cancer.

1969, Feb. 1 **Litho.** ***Perf. 12½***
RA44 PT26 1c lt bl 8 5

Issued for Education Year 1969.

Flower Type of 1968

Design: No. RA45, Violets.

1969, Apr. 25 **Litho.** ***Perf. 12½***
RA45 PT25 1c emer, lil & red 20 8

The tax was for the Anti-Tuberculosis League.

Redrawn Cancer Type of 1955

1969, Oct. 1 **Litho.** ***Perf. 11***
RA46 PT9 1c brt rose lil 20 5

The tax was for the Dominican League against Cancer.

Invalid Type of 1968

1970, Mar. 2 ***Perf. 12½***
RA47 PT24 1c blue 18 12

The tax was for the rehabilitation of the handicapped.

Book, Sun and Education Year Emblem — PT27

Communications Emblem — PT28

1970, Feb. 6 ***Perf. 11***
RA48 PT27 1c brt pink 8 5

International Education Year.

Flower Type of 1968

Design: 1c, Eleanthus capitatus; cross in upper left corner, denomination in lower right.

1970, Apr. 30 ***Perf. 11***
RA49 PT25 1c emer, red & yel 15 8

Tax for Anti-Tuberculosis League.

Boy Type of 1967

1970, Dec. 1 ***Perf. 12½***
RA49A PT23 1c orange 40 20

1971, Jan. 2 Litho. ***Perf. 11***
Size: 17½x20½mm.
RA49B PT28 1c vio bl & red (white frame) 35 10

Tax was for Postal and Telegraph Communications School.

See Nos. RA53, RA58, RA63, RA69, RA78, RA91.

Invalid Type of 1968

1971, Mar. 1 Litho. ***Perf. 11***
RA50 PT24 1c brt rose lil 20 8

Tax was for rehabilitation of the handicapped.

Cancer Type of 1952
Third Redrawing

1971, Oct. 1 ***Perf. 11½***
RA51 PT9 1c dp yel grn 25 10

Background of No. RA51 appears white and design stands out. No. RA43 has greenish background and design appears faint. Numeral "1" on No. RA51 is 3½mm. high, on No. RA43 it is 3mm.

Boy Type of 1967

1971, Dec. 1 Litho. ***Perf. 11***
RA52 PT23 1c green 35 10

Communications Type of 1971

1972, Jan. 3 Litho. ***Perf. 12½***
Size: 19x22mm.
RA53 PT28 1c dk bl & red (bl frame) 20 8

Tax was for the Postal and Telegraph Communications School.

Invalid Type of 1968

1972, Mar. 1 Litho. ***Perf. 11½***
RA54 PT24 1c brown 20 10

Orchid — PT29

1972, Apr. 2 ***Perf. 11***
RA55 PT29 1c lt grn, red & yel 25 10

Tax was for the Anti-Tuberculosis League.

Redrawn Cancer Type of 1954-58

1972, Oct. 2 ***Perf. 12½***
RA56 PT9 1c brange 18 10

Tax was for Dominican League against Cancer.

Boy Type of 1967

1972, Dec. 1 ***Perf. 12***
RA57 PT23 1c violet 25 10

Tax was for child welfare.

Communications Type of 1971

1973, Jan. 2 ***Perf. 10½***
Size: 19x22mm.
RA58 PT28 1c dk bl & red (red frame) 10 8

Tax was for Postal and Telegraph Communications School.

Invalid
PT30

Hibiscus
PT31

1973, Mar. 1 Litho. ***Perf. 12½***
Size: 21x25mm.
RA59 PT30 1c olive 15 8

Tax was for the Dominican Rehabilitation Association. See Nos. RA66, RA70, RA74, RA79, RA86.

1973, Apr. 17 Litho. ***Perf. 10½***
RA60 PT31 1c multi 20 10

Tax was for Anti-Tuberculosis League. Exists imperf.

Cancer Type of 1952 Redrawn and "1973" Added

1973, Oct. 1 ***Perf. 13½***
RA61 PT9 1c ol grn 15 8

Tax was for Dominican League Against Cancer.

Boy Type of 1967

1973, Dec. 1 Litho. ***Perf. 13x13½***
RA62 PT23 1c blue 25 15

Communications Type of 1971

1973, Nov. 3 ***Perf. 10½***
Size: 19x22mm.
RA63 PT28 1c bl & red (lt grn frame) 10 6

Tax was for Postal and Telegraph Communications School. Exists imperf.

Invalid Type of 1972

1974, Mar. 1 Litho. ***Perf. 10½***
Size: 22x27½mm.
RA66 PT30 1c lt ultra 25 15

See note after No. RA59.

Cancer Type of 1952 Redrawn and "1974" Added

1974, Oct. 1 ***Perf. 12***
RA67 PT9 1c orange 15 8

Tax was for Dominican League Against Cancer.

Boy Type of 1967

1974, Dec. 2 Litho. ***Perf. 11½***
RA68 PT23 1c dk brn & buff 15 8

Communications Type of 1971

1974, Nov. 13 ***Perf. 10½***
RA69 PT28 1c bl & red (yel frame) 15 8

Invalid Type of 1972 Dated "1975"

1975, Mar. 1 ***Perf. 13½x13***
Size: 21x32mm.
RA70 PT30 1c ol brn 15 8

See note after No. RA59.

Catteyopsis Rosea
PT32

Oncidium Colochilum
PT33

1975, Apr. 1 ***Perf. 12***
RA71 PT32 1c bl & multi 15 8

Tax was for Anti-Tuberculosis League.

Cancer Type of 1952 Redrawn and "1975" Added

1975, Oct. 1 Litho. ***Perf. 12***
RA72 PT9 1c vio bl 15 8

Tax was for Dominican League Against Cancer. Exists imperf.

Boy Type of 1967

1975, Dec. 1 Litho. ***Perf. 12***
RA73 PT23 1c red org 15 8

Tax was for child welfare.

Invalid Type of 1973 Dated "1976"

1976, Mar. 1 Litho. ***Perf. 12***
Size: 21x31mm.
RA74 PT30 1c ultra 15 8

See note after No. RA59.

1976, Apr. 6 ***Perf. 13x13½***
RA75 PT33 1c grn & multi 15 8

Tax was for Anti-Tuberculosis League. See No. RA80, RA84.

Cancer Type of 1952 Redrawn and "1976" Added

1976, Oct. 1 Litho. ***Perf. 13½***
RA76 PT9 1c green 15 8

Tax was for Dominican League Against Cancer.

Boy Type of 1967

1976, Dec. 1 Litho. ***Perf. 13½***
RA77 PT23 1c purple 20 8

Tax was for child welfare.

Communications Type of 1971

1977, Jan. 7 Litho. ***Perf. 10½***
Size: 19x22mm.
RA78 PT28 1c bl & red (lil frame) 15 8

Tax was for Postal and Telegraph Communications School.

Invalid Type of 1973 Dated "1977"

1977, Mar. 11 ***Perf. 12***
Size: 21x31mm.
RA79 PT30 1c ultra 15 8

See note after No. RA59.

Orchid Type of 1976 Dated "1977"

Orchid: Oncidium variegatum.

1977, Apr. 22 Litho. ***Perf. 13½***
RA80 PT33 1c multi 20 8

Tax was for Anti-Tuberculosis League.

Boy Type of 1967

1977, Dec. 27 Litho. ***Perf. 12***
RA81 PT23 1c emerald 15 8

Tax was for child welfare.

Cancer Type of 1952 Redrawn and "1977" Added

1978, Oct. 2 Litho. ***Perf. 13½***
RA82 PT9 1c lil rose 15 8

Tax was for Dominican League Against Cancer.

Mother, Child and Holly — PT34

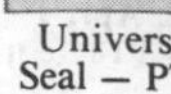

University Seal — PT35

1978, Dec. 1 Litho. ***Perf. 13½***
RA83 PT34 1c green 15 8

Tax was for child welfare.

See Nos. RA89, RA92, RA97.

Orchid Type of 1973 Dated "1978"

Flower: Yellow alder.

1979, Apr. Litho. ***Perf. 13½***
RA84 PT33 1c lt bl & multi 20 8

Tax was for Anti-Tuberculosis League.

1979, Feb. 10 Litho. ***Perf. 13½***
RA85 PT35 2c ultra & gray 20 5

450th anniversary of University of Santo Domingo.

Invalid Type of 1973 Dated "1978"

1979, Mar. 1 Litho. ***Perf. 12***
RA86 PT30 1c emerald 8 5

See note after No. RA59.

Invalid
PT36

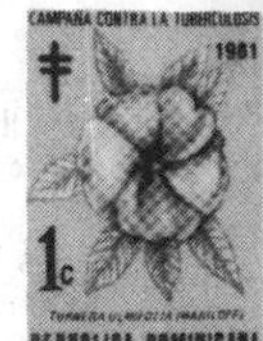

Turnera Ulmifolia (Marilope)
PT37

1980, Mar. 28 Litho. ***Perf. 13½***
RA87 PT36 1c ol & cit 8 5

Cancer Type of 1952 Redrawn and "1980" Added

1980, Oct. 1
RA88 PT9 1c vio & dk pur 8 5

Mother and Child Type of 1978

1980, Dec. 1 Litho. ***Perf. 13½***
RA89 PT34 1c brt bl 8 5

1981, Apr. 27 Litho. ***Perf. 12***
RA90 PT37 1c multi 10 5

Tax was for Anti-Tuberculosis League. See Nos. RA98-RA99.

Communications Type of 1971

1981 Litho. ***Perf. 10½***
RA91 PT28 1c bl & red (lt bl frame) 8 5

Mother and Child Type of 1978

1982, Dec. 1 Litho. ***Perf. 12x12½***
RA92 PT34 1c lt bluish grn 8 5

Inscribed 1981.

Cancer Type of 1952 Redrawn and "1981" Added.

1982 Litho. ***Perf. 13½***
RA93 PT9 1c bl & dp bl 10 6

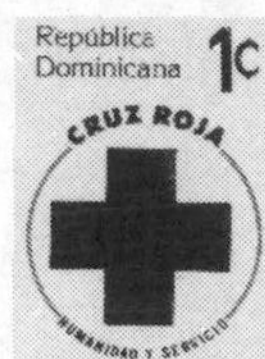

PT38

Disabled — PT39

1983, Apr. 29 Litho. *Perf. 12*

RA94 PT38 1c multi 10 6

Tax was for Red Cross.

1984 Litho. *Perf. 13½*

RA95 PT39 1c sky bl 10 6

Cancer Type of 1952 Redrawn and "1983" Added.

1983, Oct. 1 Litho. *Perf. 13½*

RA96 PT9 1c lt bluish grn & dk grn 10 6

Mother and Child Type of 1978

1983, Dec. 1 Litho. *Perf. 12*

RA97 PT34 1c lt grn 8 5

Inscribed 1983.

Flower Type of 1981 Dated "1983" or "1984"

1983-85 Litho. *Perf. 12x12½*

RA98 PT37 1c 1983 5 5
RA99 PT37 1c 1984 5 5

Issue dates: No. RA98, Apr. 19, 1983. No. RA99, Apr. 1, 1985.

POSTAL TAX AIR POST STAMPS

Postal Tax Stamps Surcharged in Red or Gold

HABILITADO PARA
CORREO AEREO
+5

1930, Dec. 3 Unwmk. *Perf. 12*

RA1 PT2 5c + 5c blk & rose (R) 30.00 30.00
a. Tête bêche pair 200.00
b. "Habilitado Para" missing 85.00
RA2 PT2 10c + 10c blk & rose (R) 30.00 30.00
a. Tête bêche pair 200.00
b. "Habilitado Para" missing 85.00
c. Gold surch. 225.00 225.00
d. As "c," tete beche pair 750.00
e. As "c," "Habilitado Para" missing 400.00

Nos. RAC1-RAC2 were on sale only on Dec. 3, 1930.

RA4 PT2 5c + 5c ultra & rose (R) 10.00 10.00
a. Tête bêche pair 75.00
b. Inverted surcharge 70.00
c. Tete beche pair, inverted surcharge 1,000.
d. Pair, one without surcharge 300.00
e. "Habilitado Para" missing 25.00
RA5 PT2 10c + 10c yel & rose (G) 7.50 7.50
a. Tête bêche pair 70.00
b. "Habilitado Para" missing 30.00

Imperf

RA6 PT2 5c + 5c ultra & rose (R) 10.00 10.00
a. Tête bêche pair 85.00
b. "Habilitado Para" missing 30.00

Eastern Silesia stamps can be mounted in Scott's Czechoslovakia Album.

RA7 PT2 10c + 10c yel & rose (G) 10.00 10.00
a. Tete bêche pair 85.00
b. "Habilitado Para" missing 30.00

It was obligatory to use Nos. RA1 to RA8 and RAC1 and RAC7 on all postal matter, in amounts equal to the ordinary postage.

This surtax was for the aid of sufferers from the hurricane of Sept. 3rd, 1930.

No. 261 Overprinted in Green CORREO AEREO INTERNO

1933, Oct. 11

RA8 A32 2c scarlet 60 45
a. Double overprint 15.00
b. Pair, one without ovpt. 600.00

By official decree a copy of this stamp, in addition to the regular postage, had to be used on every letter, etc., sent by the internal air post service.

EASTERN RUMELIA

(South Bulgaria)

LOCATION — In southern Bulgaria
GOVT. — A former autonomous unit of the Turkish Empire.
CAPITAL — Philippopolis (Plovdiv)

In 1885 the province of Eastern Rumelia revolted against Turkish rule and united with Bulgaria, adopting the new name of South Bulgaria. This union was assured by the Treaty of Bucharest in 1886, following the war between Serbia and Bulgaria.

40 Paras = 1 Piastre

Counterfeits of all overprints are plentiful.

A1

A2

A3

Stamps of Turkey, 1876-84, Overprinted in Blue.

1880 Unwmk. *Perf. 13½*

1 A1 ½pi on 20pa yel grn 35.00 35.00
2 A1 2pi on 2pi yel brn
3 A2 10pa blk & rose 40.00
4 A2 20pa vio & grn 37.50 37.50
5 A2 1pi blk & bl
6 A2 2pi blk & buff 75.00 75.00
7 A2 5pi red & bl 250.00 250.00
8 A3 10pa blk & red lil 25.00

Nos. 2, 3, 5 & 8 were not placed in use.

Inverted and double overprints of all values exist.

Same, with Extra Overprint "R. O."

9 A3 10pa blk & red lil 40.00 40.00

Crescent and Turkish Inscriptions of Value — A4

1881 Typo. *Perf. 13½*

10 A4 5pa blk & ol 2.00 60
11 A4 10pa blk & grn 7.00 60
12 A4 20pa blk & rose 30 60
13 A4 1pi blk & bl 3.00 2.50
14 A4 5pi rose & bl 25.00 35.00

Tête bêche pairs, imperforates and all perf. 11½copies of Nos. 10 to 14 were not placed in use, and were found only in the remainder stock. This is true also of a 10pa cliche in the 20pa plate, and of a cliche of Turkey No. 63 in the 1pi plate.

1884 *Perf. 11½, 13½*

15 A4 5pa lil & pale lil 20 20
16 A4 10pa grn & pale grn 10 20
17 A4 20pa car & pale rose 20
18 A4 1pi bl & pale bl 20
19 A4 5pi brn & pale brn 150.00

No. 17-19 were not placed in use.

Nos. 15 to 19 imperf. are from the remainder stock.

South Bulgaria.

Counterfeits of all overprints are plentiful.

Nos. 10 to 14 Overprinted in Two Types:

a

b

Type a: Four toes on each foot.
Type b: Three toes on each foot.

1885 Unwmk. *Perf. 13½.*

Blue Overprint.

20 A4 5pa blk & ol 100.00 100.00
21 A4 10pa blk & grn 350.00 350.00
22 A4 20pa blk & rose 100.00 100.00
23 A4 1pi blk & bl 20.00 22.50
24 A4 5pi rose & bl 300.00 325.00

Black Overprint.

25 A4 1pi blk & bl 16.50 20.00
26 A4 5pi rose & bl 400.00 400.00

Same Overprint on Nos. 15 to 17.

Perf. 11½, 13½

Blue Overprint.

27 A4 5pa lil & pale lil, perf. 11½ 9.00 14.00
a. Perf. 13½ 22.50 27.50
28 A4 10pa grn & pale grn 9.00 14.00
29 A4 20pa car & pale rose 80.00 90.00

Black Overprint.

30 A4 5pa lil & pale lil 16.00 20.00
31 A4 10pa grn & pale grn 16.00 20.00
32 A4 20pa car & pale rose 14.00 20.00

Nos. 10 to 14 Handstamped in Black in Two Types:

a

b

Type a: First letter at top circular.
Type b: First letter at top oval.

1885 *Perf. 13½*

33 A4 5pa blk & ol 300.00
34 A4 10pa blk & grn 300.00
35 A4 20pa blk & rose 55.00 65.00
36 A4 1pi blk & bl 40.00 45.00
a. On Turkey No. 63 (error)
37 A4 5pi rose & bl 500.00 600.00

Same Handstamp in Black on Nos. 15 to 17.

Perf. 11½, 13½.

38 A4 5pa lil & pale lil, perf. 13½ 11.00 11.00
a. Perf. 11½ 100.00 125.00
39 A4 10pa grn & pale grn 10.00 11.00
40 A4 20pa car & pale rose 10.00 15.00

Nos. 20 to 40 exist with inverted and double handstamps. Overprints in unlisted colors are proofs.

The stamps of South Bulgaria were superseded in 1886 by those of Bulgaria.

EASTERN SILESIA

LOCATION — In central Europe
GOVT. — Former Austrian crownland
AREA — 1,987 sq. mi.
POP. — 680,422 (estimated 1920)
CAPITAL — Troppau

After World War I, this territory was occupied by Czechoslovakia and eventually was divided between Poland and Czechoslovakia, the dividing line running through Teschen.

100 Heller = 1 Krone
100 Fennigi = 1 Marka

Plebiscite Issues.

Stamps of Czechoslovakia 1918-20, Overprinted in Black, Blue, Violet or Red SO 1920

1920 Unwmk. *Imperf.*

1 A2 1(h) dk brn 35 35
2 A1 3(h) red vio 12 12
3 A2 5(h) bl grn 40.00 30.00
4 A2 15(h) red 20.00 10.00
5 A1 20(h) bl grn 15 15
6 A2 25(h) dl vio 1.25 1.25
7 A1 30(h) bis (R) 25 25
8 A1 40(h) red org 25 25
9 A2 50(h) dl vio 50 50
10 A2 50(h) dk bl 1.75 1.75
11 A2 60(h) org (Bl) 75 75
12 A2 75(h) sl (R) 50 50
13 A2 80(h) ol grn (R) 50 50
14 A1 100(h) brown 70 70
15 A2 120(h) gray blk (R) 1.75 1.75
16 A1 200(h) ultra (R) 1.75 1.75
17 A2 300(h) grn (R) 2.50 2.50
18 A1 400(h) pur (R) 2.00 2.00
20 A2 500(h) red brn (Bl) 6.00 4.75
a. Black overprint 12.00 10.00
21 A2 1000(h) vio (Bl) 16.00 10.00
a. Black ovpt. 200.00 125.00
Nos. 1-21 (20) 97.07 69.82

Perf. 11½, 14

22 A2 1(h) dk brn 5 5
23 A2 5(h) bl grn 25 25
24 A2 10(h) yel grn 15 15
a. Imperf. 400.00 400.00
25 A2 15(h) red 15 15
26 A2 20(h) rose 35 35
a. Imperf. 300.00 300.00
27 A2 25(h) dl vio 35 35
28 A2 30(h) red vio (Bl) 35 35
29 A2 60(h) org (Bl) 50 50
30 A1 200(h) ultra (R) 3.75 3.75
Nos. 22-30 (9) 5.90 5.90

The letters "S. O." are the initials of "Silésie Orientale".

Forged cancellations are found on Nos. 1-30.

Overprinted 19 SO 20

31 A4 500(h) sl, *grysh* (C) 120.00
32 A4 1000(h) blk brn, *brnsh* (V) 120.00

Excellent counterfeits of this overprint exist.

Stamps of Poland, 1919, Overprinted S. O. 1920.

1920 *Perf. 11½*

41 A10 5f green 6 8
42 A10 10f red brn 6 8
43 A10 15f lt red 6 8
44 A11 25f ol grn 6 8
45 A11 50f bl grn 6 8

Overprinted S. O. 1920.

46 A17 1k dp grn 6 8
47 A17 1.50k brown 6 8
48 A17 2k dk bl 6 8
49 A18 2.50k dl vio 10 15
50 A19 5k sl bl 12 20
Nos. 41-50 (10) 70 99

SPECIAL DELIVERY STAMPS

Czechoslovakia Special Delivery Stamps Overprinted

S O
19 20

1920 **Unwmk.** ***Imperf.***

Blue Overprint.

E1 SD1 2(h) red vio, *yel*		8	8
a. Black overprint		1.00	80
E2 SD1 5(h) yel grn, *yel*		8	10
a. Black overprint		6.00	5.00

POSTAGE DUE STAMPS

Czechoslovakia Postage Due Stamps Overprinted In Blue or Red

SO
1920

1920 **Unwmk.** ***Imperf.***

J1	D1	5(h) dp bis (Bl)	12	12
a.		Black ovpt.	55.00	45.00
J2	D1	10(h) dp bis	20	12
J3	D1	15(h) dp bis	20	12
J4	D1	20(h) dp bis	40	20
J5	D1	25(h) dp bis	40	25
J6	D1	30(h) dp bis	40	25
J7	D1	40(h) dp bis	60	50
J8	D1	50(h) dp bis	60	50
J9	D1	100(h) blk brn (R)	1.25	85
J10	D1	500(h) gray grn (R)	5.00	3.75
J11	D1	1000(h) pur (R)	9.50	8.50
		Nos. J1-J11 (11)	18.67	15.16

Forged cancellations exist.

NEWSPAPER STAMPS

Czechoslovakia Newspaper Stamps Overprinted in Black

SO
1920

1920 **Unwmk.** ***Imperf.***

P1	N1	2(h) gray grn	40	40
P2	N1	6(h) red	10	10
P3	N1	10(h) dl vio	30	30
P4	N1	20(h) blue	40	40
P5	N1	30(h) gray brn	40	40
		Nos. P1-P5 (5)	1.60	1.60

ECUADOR

LOCATION — On the northwest coast of South America, bordering on the Pacific Ocean
GOVT. — Republic
AREA — 116,270 sq. mi.
POP. — 8,420,000 (est. 1984)
CAPITAL — Quito

The Republic of Ecuador was so constituted on May 11, 1830, after the Civil War which separated the original members of the Republic of Colombia, founded by Simon Bolivar by uniting the Presidency of Quito with the Viceroyalty of New Grenada and the Captaincy of Venezuela. The Presidency of Quito became the Republic of Ecuador.

8 Reales = 1 Peso
100 Centavos = 1 Sucre (1881)

Coat of Arms
A1 A2

1865-72 Unwmk. Typo. *Imperf.*
Quadrille Paper.

1 A1 1r yel ('72) 37.50 35.00

Wove Paper

2 A1 ½r ultra 16.00 12.00
a. ½r gray bl ('67) 16.00 12.00
b. Batonne paper ('70) 32.50 20.00
c. Blue paper ('72) 165.00 110.00
3 A1 1r buff 25.00 15.00
a. 1r org buff 30.00 17.50
4 A1 1r yellow 17.50 12.50
a. 1r ol yel ('66) 25.00 15.00
b. Laid paper 160.00 110.00
c. Diagonal half used as ½r on cover 300.00
d. Batonne paper 32.50 25.00
5 A1 1r green 250.00 55.00
a. Diagonal half used as ½r on cover 300.00
6 A2 4r red ('66) 275.00 135.00
a. 4r red brn ('66) 275.00 135.00
b. Arms in circle 275.00 135.00
c. Printed on both sides 700.00
d. Half used as 2r on cover 1,500.

Letter paper embossed with arms of Ecuador was used in printing a number of sheets of Nos. 2, 4-6.

Papermakers' watermarks are known on No. 2 ("Bath" and crown) and No. 4 ("Roland Freres").

On the 4r the oval holding the coat of arms is usually 13½-14mm. wide, but on about one-fifth of the stamps in the sheet it is 15-15½mm. wide, almost a circle.

The 2r, 8r and 12r, type A1, are bogus.

Proofs of the ½r, type A1, are known in black and green.

An essay of type A2 shows the condor's head facing right.

1871-72

Blue-surface Paper

7 A1 ½r ultra 30.00 19.00
8 A1 1r yellow 165.00 60.00

Unofficial reprints of types A1-A2 differ in color, have a different sheet makeup and lack gum. Type A1 reprints usually have a double frameline at left. All stamps on blue paper with horiz. blue lines are reprints.

A3 A4

1872 White Paper Litho. *Perf. 11*

9 A3 ½r blue 17.50 4.00
10 A4 1r yellow 20.00 6.00
11 A3 1p rose 4.00 *12.00*

The 1r surcharged 4c is fraudulent.

A5 A6

A7 A8

A9 A10

1881, Nov. 1 Engr. *Perf. 12*

12 A5 1c yel brn 10 10
13 A6 2c lake 15 15
14 A7 5c blue 3.00 50
15 A8 10c orange 15 15
16 A9 20c gray vio 20 20
17 A10 50c bl grn 1.00 *3.00*
Nos. 12-17 (6) 4.60 4.10

The 1c surcharged 3c, and 20c surcharged 5c are fraudulent.

No. 17 Surcharged in Black

DIEZ
CENTAVOS

1883, April

18 A10 10c on 50c bl grn 25.00 20.00
a. Double surcharge

A12 A13

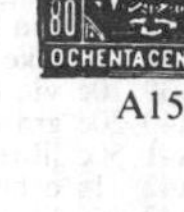

A14 A15

1887

19 A12 1c bl grn 30 15
20 A13 2c vermilion 50 15
21 A14 5c blue 1.50 30
22 A15 80c ol grn 3.00 *7.50*

President Juan Flores — A16

1892

23 A16 1c orange 15 10
24 A16 2c dk brn 15 10
25 A16 5c vermilion 15 10
26 A16 10c green 15 10
27 A16 20c red brn 15 10
28 A16 50c maroon 15 *40*
29 A16 1s blue 25 *1.00*
30 A16 5s purple 75 *1.50*
Nos. 23-30 (8) 1.90 3.40

The issues of 1892, 1894, 1895 and 1896 were printed by the Hamilton Bank Note Co., New York, to the order of N. F. Seebeck, who held a contract for stamps with the government of Ecuador.

No. 30 in green is said to be an essay or color trial.

Nos. 29 and 30 Surcharged in Black

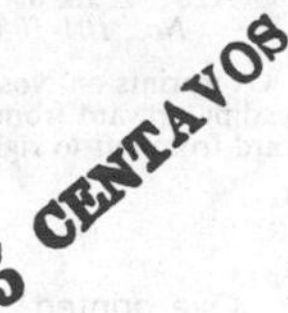

1893

Surcharge Measures 25½x2½ mm.

31 A16 5c on 1s bl 2.50 2.00
32 A16 5c on 5s pur 7.00 5.00
a. Double surcharge

Surcharge Measures 24x2¼ mm.

33 A16 5c on 1s bl 1.75 1.50
a. Double surcharge, one inverted
34 A16 5c on 5s pur 7.50 6.00
a. Double surcharge, one inverted

Nos. 28-30 Surcharged in Black

35 A16 5c on 50c mar 75 65
a. Inverted surch. 2.50
36 A16 5c on 1s bl 1.25 1.00
37 A16 5c on 5s pur 6.00 5.00

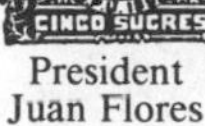

President Juan Flores A19 — President Vicente Rocafuerte A20

38 A19 5c on 5s lake 1.00 75

It is stated that No. 38 was used exclusively as a postage stamp and not for telegrams.

1894 Dated 1894. *Perf. 12.*
Various Frames

39 A20 1c blue 30 30
40 A20 2c yel brn 30 30
41 A20 5c green 30 30
b. Perf. 14 4.00 1.50
42 A20 10c vermilion 50 40
43 A20 20c black 75 50
44 A20 50c orange 4.00 1.50
45 A20 1s carmine 6.00 3.00
46 A20 5s dk bl 8.00 6.00
Nos. 39-46 (8) 20.15 12.30

1895 Same, Dated "1895".

47 A20 1c blue 60 50
48 A20 2c yel brn 60 50
49 A20 5c green 50 35
50 A20 10c vermilion 50 30
51 A20 20c black 75 65
52 A20 50c orange 2.50 1.25
53 A20 1s carmine 12.50 5.00
54 A20 5s dk bl 6.00 2.50
Nos. 47-54 (8) 23.95 11.05

Reprints of the 2c, 10c, 50c, 1s and 5s of the 1894-95 issues are generally on thick paper. Original issues are on thin to medium thick paper. To distinguish reprints from originals, a comparison of paper thickness, paper color, gum, printing clarity and direction of paper weave is necessary. Price 10 cents each.

A21 A22

A23 A24

A25 A26

A27 A28

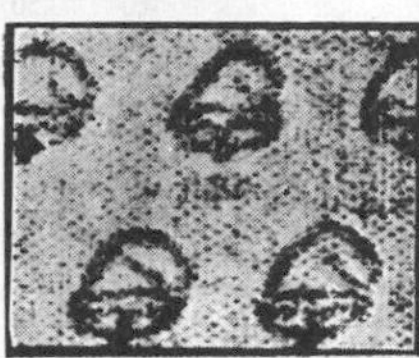

Wmk. 117- Liberty Cap

1896 Wmk. d. Liberty Cap. (117)

55 A21 1c dk grn 50 45
56 A22 2c red 50 20
57 A23 5c blue 50 20
58 A24 10c bis brn 40 *50*
59 A25 20c orange 70 *1.00*
60 A26 50c dk bl 1.25 *2.00*
61 A27 1s yel brn 2.50 *2.00*
62 A27 5s violet 5.00 *4.00*
Nos. 55-62 (8) 11.35 10.35

Unwmk.

62A A21 1c dk grn 60 20
62B A22 2c red 60 20
62C A23 5c blue 60 20
62D A24 10c bis brn 50 *1.00*
62E A25 20c orange 3.75 *4.00*
62F A26 50c dk bl 50 *2.00*
62G A27 1s yel brn 3.50 *6.00*
62H A28 5s violet 3.75 *4.00*
Nos. 62A-62H (8) 13.80 17.60

Reprints of Nos. 55-62H are on very thick paper, with paper weave direction vertical. Price 10 cents each.

Vicente Roca, Diego Noboa and Jose Olmedo A28a — General Juan Francisco Elizalde A28b

Perf. 11½

1896, Oct. 9 Unwmk. Litho.

63 A28a 1c rose 50 50
64 A28b 2c blue 50 50
65 A28a 5c green 60 60
66 A28b 10c ocher 60 60
67 A28a 20c red 75 *1.25*
68 A28b 50c violet 1.00 *2.00*
69 A28a 1s orange 2.00 *2.50*
Nos. 63-69 (7) 5.95 7.95

Issued in commemoration of the success of the Liberal Party in 1845 and 1895.

Canceled-to-order stamps are often from remainders. Most collectors of canceled stamps prefer postally used specimens.

A29

A30

Black Surcharge.

1896, Nov. ***Perf. 12***

70 A29 1c on 1c ver, "1893-1894" 60 40
a. Inverted surcharge 1.75 1.50
b. Double surcharge 6.00 5.00
71 A29 2c on 2c bl, "1893-1894" 1.50 1.25
a. Invtd. surcharge 3.00 2.50
72 A29 5c on 10c org, "1887-1888" 60 40
a. Inverted surcharge 1.50 1.25
b. Double surcharge 3.50 3.00
c. Surcharged "2cts" 75 60
d. "1893-1894" 4.00 3.50
73 A29 10c on 4c brn, "1887-1888" 1.00 75
a. Inverted surcharge 1.50 1.25
b. Double surcharge 3.00 2.50
c. Double surcharge, one inverted
d. Surcharged "1 cto" 2.25 2.00
e. "1891-1892" 12.50 10.00

Similar surcharges of type A29 include: Dated "1887-1888"-1c on 1c blue green, 1c on 2c red, 1c on 4c brown, 1c on 10c yellow; 2c on 2c red, 2c on 10c yellow; 10c on 1c green. Dated "1891-1892"- 1c on 1c blue green, 1c on 4c brown. Dated "1893-1894"-2c on 10c yellow; 10c on 1c vermilion, 10c on 10s black.

Surcharge in Black or Red

Wmk. Liberty Cap. (117)

1896, Oct.

74 A30 5c on 20c org 25.00 25.00
76 A30 10c on 50c dk bl (R) 25.00 25.00
a. Double surcharge

The surcharge is diagonal, horizontal, or vertical.

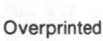

Overprinted

On Issue of 1894.

1897 **Unwmk.**

77 A20 1c blue 1.50 1.00
78 A20 2c yel brn 1.25 65
79 A20 5c green 60 40
80 A20 10c vermilion 1.75 1.25
81 A20 20c black 2.00 1.50
82 A20 50c orange 4.50 1.25
83 A20 1s carmine 13.00 3.00
84 A20 5s dk bl 55.00 40.00
Nos. 77-84 (8) 79.60 49.05

On Issue of 1895.

85 A20 1c blue 4.00 3.50
86 A20 2c yel brn 1.50 1.25
87 A20 5c green 1.25 75
88 A20 10c vermilion 4.50 4.00
89 A20 20c black 1.25 1.25
90 A20 50c orange 22.50 9.00
91 A20 1s carmine 10.00 5.00
92 A20 5s dk bl 10.00 8.00
Nos. 85-92 (8) 55.00 32.75

Overprinted

On Issue of 1894.

93 A20 1c blue 1.00 60
94 A20 2c yel brn 75 50
95 A20 5c green 40 20
96 A20 10c vermilion 2.25 1.25
97 A20 20c black 2.50 1.25
98 A20 50c orange 4.50 1.75
99 A20 1s carmine 8.00 4.50
100 A20 5s dk bl 55.00 45.00
Nos. 93-100 (8) 74.40 55.05

On Issue of 1895.

101 A20 1c blue 2.25 80
102 A20 2c yel brn 1.00 80
103 A20 5c green 1.25 70
104 A20 10c vermilion 4.00 2.50
105 A20 20c black 3.50 80
106 A20 50c orange 1.30 85
107 A20 1s carmine 6.00 4.00
108 A20 5s dk bl 7.00 5.00
Nos. 101-108 (8) 26.30 15.45

Overprints on Nos. 77-108 are to be found reading upward from left to right and downward from left to right, as well as inverted.

Overprinted **1897 Y 1898**

On Issue of 1894.

1897

109 A20 10c vermilion *60.00 55.00*

On Issue of 1895.

110 A20 2c yel brn *50.00 45.00*
111 A20 1s carmine *60.00 55.00*
112 A20 5s dk bl *60.00 45.00*

Nos. 56, 59 Overprinted

1897, June **Wmk. 117**

113 A22 2c red 50.00 40.00
114 A25 20c orange 60.00 45.00

Many forged overprints on Nos. 77-114 exist, made on original stamps and reprints.

Same Overprint on Stamps or Types of 1896.

1897 **Unwmk.** ***Perf. 11 ½.***

115 A28a 1c rose 1.75 1.50
116 A28b 2c blue 1.50 1.25
117 A28b 10c ocher 1.50 1.25
118 A28a 1s yellow 4.50 4.00

No. 63 Overprinted

1897

119 A28a 1c rose 90 75

Nos. 63-66 Overprinted in Black

1897

122 A28a 1c rose 3.50 3.00
a. Inverted overprint 4.50 4.00
123 A28b 2c blue 3.50 3.00
a. Inverted overprint 4.50 4.00
124 A28a 5c green 3.50 3.00
a. Inverted overprint 4.50 4.00
125 A28b 10c ocher 3.50 3.00
a. Double overprint 8.00 7.00
b. Inverted overprint 4.00 4.00

The 20c, 50c and 1s with this overprint in black and all values of the issue overprinted in blue are reprints.

Coat of Arms — A33

1897, June 23 **Engr.** ***Perf. 14-16***

127 A33 1c dk yel grn 15 15
128 A33 2c org red 20 15
129 A33 5c lake 20 20
130 A33 10c dk brn 20 25
131 A33 20c yellow 40 *60*
132 A33 50c dl bl 40 *1.00*
133 A33 1s gray 50 *1.25*
134 A33 5s dk lil 75 *1.75*
Nos. 127-134 (8) 2.80 5.35

A34

A35

1899, May

135 A34 1c on 2c org red 2.25 75
136 A35 5c on 10c brn 1.75 50
a. Double surcharge

Luis Vargas Torres A36

Abdón Calderon A37

Juan Montalvo A38

José Mejia A39

Santa Cruz y Espejo — A40

Pedro Carbo — A41

José Joaquin Olmedo A42

Pedro Moncayo A43

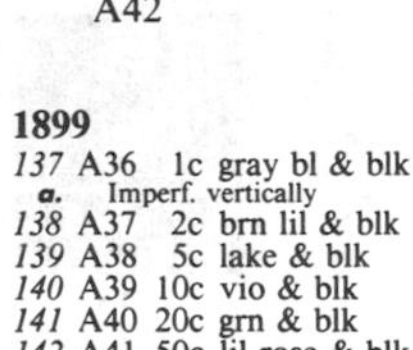

1899 ***Perf. 12½-16***

137 A36 1c gray bl & blk 25 12
a. Imperf. vertically
138 A37 2c brn lil & blk 25 10
139 A38 5c lake & blk 35 12
140 A39 10c vio & blk 35 10
141 A40 20c grn & blk 35 12
142 A41 50c lil rose & blk 1.25 60
143 A42 1s ocher & blk 6.00 2.00
144 A43 5s lil & blk 10.00 5.00
Nos. 137-144 (8) 18.80 8.16

1901

145 A36 1c scar & blk 15 10
146 A37 2c grn & blk 20 10
147 A38 5c gray lil & blk 20 10
148 A39 10c dp bl & blk 20 15
149 A40 20c gray & blk 25 15
150 A41 50c lt bl & blk 1.10 65
151 A42 1s brn & blk 4.50 2.25
152 A43 5s gray blk & blk 6.75 4.50
Nos. 145-152 (8) 13.35 8.00

In July, 1902, following the theft of a quantity of stamps during a fire at Guayaquil, the Government authorized the governors of the provinces to handstamp their stocks. Many varieties of these handstamps exist.

Other control marks were used in 1907.

A44

Surcharged on Revenue Stamp Dated 1901-1902.

1903-06 ***Perf. 14, 15.***

153 A44 1c on 5c gray lil ('06) 30 25
154 A44 1c on 20c gray ('06) 4.50 3.00
155 A44 1c on 25c yel 60 25
a. Double surcharge
156 A44 1c on 1s bl ('06) 37.50 25.00
157 A44 3c on 5c gray lil ('06) 4.50 2.50
158 A44 3c on 20c gray ('06) 11.00 7.50
159 A44 3c on 25c yel ('06) 11.00 7.50
159A A44 3c on 1s bl ('06) 1.25 1.00
Nos. 153-159A (8) 70.65 47.00

Counterfeits are plentiful. See Nos. 191-197.

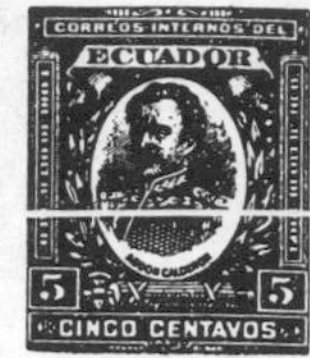
Capt. Abdón Calderón
A45 A46

1904, July 31 ***Perf. 12***

160 A45 1c red & blk 45 35
161 A45 2c bl & blk 45 35
162 A46 5c yel & blk 1.75 1.20
163 A45 10c red & blk 3.50 1.20
164 A45 20c bl & blk 9.00 3.00
165 A46 50c yel & blk 75.00 50.00
Nos. 160-165 (6) 90.15 56.10

Issued in commemoration of the centenary of the birth of Abdón Calderon, 1804-1904.

President Vicente Roca A47

President Diego Noboa A48

President Francisco Robles A49

President Jose M. Urvina A50

President Garcia Moreno A51

President Jeronimo Carrion A52

President Javier Espinoza A53

President Antonio Borrero A54

1907, July ***Perf. 14, 15***

166 A47 1c red & blk 25 15
167 A48 2c pale bl & blk 35 20
168 A49 3c org & blk 50 20
169 A50 5c lil rose & blk 60 15
170 A51 10c dp bl & blk 2.00 25
171 A52 20c yel grn & blk 2.50 30

No.	Type	Denom.	Color	Unused	Used
172	A53	50c	vio & blk	6.00	75
173	A54	1s	grn & blk	8.50	2.00
			Nos. 166-173 (8)	20.70	4.00

The stamps of the 1907 issue frequently have control marks similar to those found on the 1899 and 1901 issues. These marks were applied to distinguish the stamps issued in the various provinces and to serve as a check on local officials.

Locomotive — A55

Garcia Moreno — A56

Gen. Eloy Alfaro A57

Abelardo Moncayo — A58

Archer Harman A59

James Sivewright — A60

Mt. Chimborazo A61

1908, June 25

No.	Type	Denom.	Color	Unused	Used
174	A55	1c	red brn	90	90
175	A56	2c	bl & blk	1.50	1.20
176	A57	5c	cl & blk	3.00	2.50
177	A58	10c	ocher & blk	1.75	1.50
178	A59	20c	grn & blk	1.75	1.75
179	A60	50c	gray & blk	1.75	1.75
180	A61	1s	black	3.75	3.75
			Nos. 174-180 (7)	14.40	13.35

Issued in commemoration of the opening of the Guayaquil-Quito Railway.

José Mejía Vallejo A62

Francisco J. E. Santa Cruz y Espejo A63

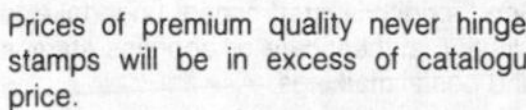

Prices of premium quality never hinged stamps will be in excess of catalogue price.

Francisco Ascásubi A64

Juan Salinas A65

Juan Pío de Montúfar A66

Carlos de Montúfar A67

Juan de Dios Morales A68

Manuel R. de Quiroga A69

Principal Exposition Building — A70

1909, Aug. 10 *Perf. 12.*

No.	Type	Denom.	Color	Unused	Used
181	A62	1c	green	35	60
182	A63	2c	blue	35	60
183	A64	3c	orange	35	75
184	A65	5c	claret	35	75
185	A66	10c	yel brn	40	75
186	A67	20c	gray	40	1.10
187	A68	50c	vermilion	40	1.10
188	A69	1s	ol grn	40	1.50
189	A70	5s	violet	1.20	3.00
			Nos. 181-189 (9)	4.20	10.15

National Exposition of 1909.

Surcharged CINCO CENTAVOS

1909

No.	Type	Description	Unused	Used
190	A68	5c on 50c ver	85	75

Revenue Stamps Surcharged as in 1903.

1910 *Perf. 14, 15*

Stamps Dated 1905-1906.

No.	Type	Description	Unused	Used
191	A44	1c on 5c grn	1.50	1.00
192	A44	5c on 20c bl	5.00	1.25
193	A44	5c on 25c vio	8.00	2.25

Stamps Dated 1907-1908.

No.	Type	Description	Unused	Used
194	A44	1c on 5c grn	30	15
195	A44	5c on 20c bl	9.00	6.00
196	A44	5c on 25c vio	30	25

Stamp Dated 1909-1910

No.	Type	Description	Unused	Used
197	A44	5c on 20c bl	*45.00*	*37.50*

President Roca A71

President Noboa A72

President Robles A73

President Urvina A74

President Moreno A75

President Borrero A76

1911-28 *Perf. 12.*

No.	Type	Denom.	Color	Unused	Used
198	A71	1c	scar & blk	15	8
199	A71	1c	org ('16)	15	8
200	A71	1c	lt bl ('25)	15	8
201	A72	2c	bl & blk	35	8
202	A72	2c	grn ('16)	15	8
203	A72	2c	dk vio ('25)	15	8
204	A73	3c	org & blk ('13)	1.25	35
205	A73	3c	blk ('15)	15	8
206	A74	5c	scar & blk	60	8
207	A74	5c	vio ('15)	25	8
208	A74	5c	rose ('25)	25	8
209	A74	5c	dk brn ('28)	30	8
210	A75	10c	dp bl & blk	1.00	8
211	A75	10c	dp bl ('15)	1.00	20
212	A75	10c	yel grn ('25)	25	8
213	A75	10c	blk ('28)	75	10
214	A76	1s	grn & blk	5.00	1.50
215	A76	1s	org & blk ('27)	3.00	30
			Nos. 198-215 (18)	14.90	3.49

A77

1912 *Perf. 14, 15*

No.	Type	Description	Unused	Used
216	A77	1c on 1s grn	60	60
217	A77	2c on 2s car	90	90
218	A77	2c on 5s dl bl	90	90
219	A77	2c on 10s yel	2.00	1.50
a.		Inverted surcharge	4.00	3.50

No. 216 exists with narrow "V" and small "U" in "UN" and Nos. 217, 218 and 219 with "D" with serifs or small "O" in "DOS".

Enrique Valdez A78

Jerónimo Carrión A79

Javier Espinoza — A80

1915-17 *Perf. 12*

No.	Type	Denom.	Color	Unused	Used
220	A78	4c	red & blk	20	8
221	A79	20c	grn & blk ('17)	2.00	25
222	A80	50c	dp vio & blk	3.50	50

Olmedo A86

Monument to "Fathers of the Country" A95

Laurel Wreath and Star — A104

Designs: 2c, Rafael Ximena. 3c, Roca. 4c, Luis F. Viviero. 5c, Luis Febres Cordero. 6c, Francisco Lavayen. 7c, Jorge Antonio de Elizalde. 8c, Baltazar Garcia. 9c, Jose de Antepara. 15c, Luis Urdaneta. 20c, Jose M. Villamil. 30c, Miguel Letamendi. 40c, Gregorio Escobedo. 50c, Gen. Antonio Jose de Sucre. 60c, Juan Illingworth. 70c, Roca. 80c, Rocafuerte. 1s, Simon Bolivar.

1920

No.	Type	Denom.	Color	Unused	Used
223	A86	1c	yel grn	30	10
224	A86	2c	carmine	25	15
225	A86	3c	yel brn	25	15
226	A86	4c	myr grn	40	20
227	A86	5c	pale bl	40	10
228	A86	6c	red org	75	40
229	A86	7c	brown	1.75	75
230	A86	8c	ap grn	1.00	50
231	A86	9c	lake	3.50	1.50
232	A95	10c	lt bl	1.50	20
233	A86	15c	dk gray	1.75	50
234	A86	20c	dk vio	1.75	25
235	A86	30c	brt vio	3.50	1.25
236	A86	40c	dk brn	4.50	2.00
237	A86	50c	dk grn	4.00	50
238	A86	60c	dk bl	6.00	2.25
239	A86	70c	gray	10.00	5.00
240	A86	80c	org yel	9.00	5.00
241	A104	90c	green	10.00	5.00
242	A86	1s	pale bl	15.00	8.00
			Nos. 223-242 (20)	75.60	33.80

Nos. 223 to 242 were issued in commemoration of the centenary of the independence of Guayaquil.

Postal Tax Stamp of 1924 Overprinted POSTAL

1925

No.	Type	Denom.	Color	Unused	Used
259	PT6	20c	bis brn	1.50	50

Stamps of 1915-25 Overprinted in Black or Red (Upright or Inverted)

1926

No.	Type	Denom.	Color	Unused	Used
260	A71	1c	lt bl	3.50	3.00
261	A72	2c	dk vio	3.50	3.00
262	A73	3c	blk (R)	3.50	3.00
263	A86	4c	myr grn	3.50	3.00
264	A74	5c	rose	3.50	3.00
265	A75	10c	yel grn	3.50	3.00
			Nos. 260-265 (6)	21.00	18.00

Quito-Esmeraldas railway opening.

Postal Tax Stamps of 1920-24 Overprinted POSTAL

1927

No.	Type	Denom.	Color	Unused	Used
266	PT6	1c	ol grn	15	8
a.			"POSTAI"	2.00	1.25
b.			Double overprint	2.00	1.25
c.			Inverted overprint	2.00	1.25
267	PT6	2c	dp grn	15	8
a.			"POSTAI"	2.00	1.25
b.			Double overprint	2.00	1.25
268	PT6	20c	bis brn	1.00	15
a.			"POSTAI"	12.50	7.50

Quito Post Office — A109

1927, June

269 A109 5c orange 20 10
270 A109 10c dk grn 25 15
271 A109 20c violet 50 25

Opening of new Quito P.O.

Postal Tax Stamp of 1924 Overprinted in Dark Blue

POSTAL

1928

273 PT6 20c bis brn 30 10
a. Double overprint, one inverted 2.00 1.00

A110

Nos. 235, 239-240 Overprinted in Red Brown and Surcharged in Dark Blue.

1928, July 8

274 A110 10c on 30c vio 3.00 3.00
a. Surch. invtd.
275 A110 50c on 70c gray 4.00 4.00
276 A110 1s on 80c org yel 5.00 5.00
a. Surch. invtd.

Quito-Cayambe railway opening.

Stamps of 1920 Surcharged

ASAMBLEA NCNAL. 1928 5 CTVOS.

1928, Oct. 9

277 A86 1c on 1c yel grn 12.00 10.00
278 A86 1c on 2c car 20 15
279 A86 2c on 3c yel brn 1.25 1.00
a. Double surcharge, one reading up 6.00 6.00
280 A86 2c on 4c myr grn 90 75
281 A86 2c on 5c lt bl 50 35
a. Double surcharge 6.00 6.00
282 A86 2c on 7c brn 16.00 12.50
283 A86 5c on 6c red org 25 20
a. "5 ctvos." omitted 20.00 20.00
284 A86 10c on 7c brn 75 60
285 A86 20c on 8c ap grn 25 20
a. Double surcharge
286 A95 40c on 10c bl 3.50 3.00
287 A86 40c on 15c dk gray 60 50
288 A86 50c on 20c dk vio 11.00 9.00
289 A86 1s on 40c dk brn 2.25 2.00
290 A86 5s on 50c dk grn 3.00 2.25
291 A86 10s on 60c dk bl 13.00 9.00

With Additional Surcharge in Red **0.10**

292 A86 10c on 2c on 7c brn 20 20
a. Red surcharge double 6.00 6.00
Nos. 277-292 (16) 65.65 51.70

National Assembly of 1928.

Counterfeit overprints exist of Nos. 277-291.

A111

A112

Surcharged in Various Colors

1928, Oct. 31 ***Perf. 14***

293 A111 5c on 20c gray lil (Bk) 1.25 1.00
294 A111 10c on 20c gray lil (R) 1.25 1.00
295 A111 20c on 1s grn (O) 1.25 1.00
296 A111 50c on 1s grn (Bl) 1.50 75
297 A111 1s on 1s grn (V) 2.00 1.00
298 A111 5s on 2s red (G) 6.00 5.00
299 A111 10s on 2s red (Br) 7.50 7.50
a. Black surcharge 8.00 8.00
Nos. 293-299 (7) 20.75 17.25

Quito-Otavalo railway opening.

Postal Tax Stamp of 1924 Overprinted in Red

POSTAL

1929 ***Perf. 12.***

302 PT6 2c dp grn 10 10

There are two types of overprint on No. 302 differing slightly.

1929

Red Overprint.

303 A112 1c dk bl 10 10
a. Overprint reading down 10 10

See also Nos. 586-587.

Plowing — A113

Cultivating Cacao — A114

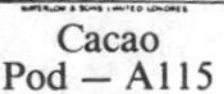
Cacao Pod — A115

Growing Tobacco — A116

Exportation of Fruits — A117

Landscape — A118

Loading Sugar Cane — A119

Scene in Quito A120

Scene in Quito A121

Olmedo — A122

Sucre — A123

Bolivar — A124

Monument to Simón Bolivar — A125

1930, Aug. 1 ***Perf. 12½***

304 A113 1c yel & car 20 10
305 A114 2c yel & grn 20 10
306 A115 5c dp grn & vio brn 25 15
307 A116 6c yel & red 30 25
308 A117 10c org & ol grn 35 15
309 A118 16c red & yel grn 50 40
310 A119 20c ultra & yel 50 18
311 A120 40c org & sep 60 18
312 A121 50c org & sep 75 18
313 A122 1s dp grn & blk 2.50 25
314 A123 2s dk bl & blk 5.00 50
315 A124 5s dk vio & blk 9.00 75
316 A125 10s car rose & blk 25.00 6.00
Nos. 304-316 (13) 45.15 9.19

Centenary of founding of republic.

A126

A127

Red Overprint.

1933 ***Perf. 15.***

317 A126 10c ol brn 25 15

Blue Overprint.

318 A127 10c ol brn 25 10
a. Inverted overprint 5.00 5.00

Nos. 307, 309 Surcharged in Black

1933 ***Perf. 12½***

319 A116 5c on 6c yel & red 30 15
320 A118 10c on 16c red & yel grn 40 15
a. Inverted ovpt. 4.00 4.00

Landscape A128

Mt. Chimborazo A129

1934-45 ***Perf. 12.***

321 A128 5c violet 15 8
322 A128 5c blue 15 8
323 A128 5c dk brn 15 8
323A A128 5c sl blk ('45) 15 8
324 A128 10c rose 15 8
325 A128 10c dk grn 15 8
326 A128 10c brown 15 8
327 A128 10c orange 15 8
328 A128 10c ol grn 15 8
329 A128 10c gray blk ('35) 20 8
329A A128 10c red lil ('44) 15 8

Perf. 14.

330 A129 1s car rose 1.50 60
Nos. 321-330 (12) 3.20 1.48

Stamps of 1930 Surcharged or Overprinted in various colors similar to:

INAUGURACION MONUMENTO A BOLIVAR

QUITO, 24 DE JULIO DE 1935

1935 ***Perf. 12½.***

331 A116 5c on 6c yel & red (Bl) 30 15
332 A116 10c on 6c yel & red (G) 35 15
333 A119 20c ultra & yel (R) 40 20
334 A120 40c org & sep (G) 50 30
335 A121 50c org & sep (G) 70 50
336 A124 1s on 5s dk vio & blk (Gold) 2.00 90
337 A124 2s on 5s dk vio & blk (Gold) 3.00 1.35
338 A125 5s on 10s car rose & blk (Bl) 5.00 3.25
Nos. 331-338,C35-C38 (12) 32.25 26.80

Unveiling of a monument to Bolivar at Quito, July 24, 1935.

The five-stamp Sociedad Colombista Panamericana series of 1935 and five airmail stamps of a similar design are not recognized by this Catalogue as having been issued primarily for postal purposes.

Telegraph Stamp Overprinted Diagonally in Red **POSTAL**

1935 *Perf. 14½*

339 A126 10c ol brn 12 8

Map of Galapagos Islands A130

Galapagos Land Iguana A131

Galapagos Tortoise A132

Charles R. Darwin A133

Columbus A134

Island Scene A135

1936 *Perf. 14.*

340	A130	2c black	25	10
341	A131	5c ol grn	35	15
342	A132	10c brown	60	15
343	A133	20c dk vio	60	20
344	A134	1s dk car	1.25	50
345	A135	2s dk bl	2.25	1.00
		Nos. 340-345 (6)	5.30	2.10

Issued to commemorate the centenary of the visit of Charles Darwin to the Galapagos Islands, September 17, 1835.

Tobacco Stamp Overprinted in Black

P O S T A L

1936 *Rouletted 7.*

346 PT7 1c rose red 12 8
- *a.* Horiz. pair, imperf. vertical
- *b.* Double surcharge

No. 346 is similar to type PT7 but does not include "CASA CORREOS".

Louis Godin, Charles M. de la Condamine and Pierre Bouguer A136

Portraits: 5c, 20c, Antonio Ulloa, La Condamine and Jorge Juan.

1936 **Engr.** *Perf. 12½*

347	A136	2c dp bl	8	8
348	A136	5c dk grn	10	8
349	A136	10c dp org	12	8
350	A136	20c violet	30	15
351	A136	50c dk red	60	35
		Nos. 347-351,C39-C42 (9)	2.80	1.41

Bicentenary of Geodesical Mission to Quito.

Independence Monument — A137

1936 *Perf. 13½x14.*

352	A137	2c green	1.75	30
353	A137	5c dk vio	1.75	30
354	A137	10c car rose	1.75	35
355	A137	20c black	1.75	50
356	A137	50c blue	3.00	1.50
357	A137	1s dk red	3.50	1.75
		Nos. 352-357,C43-C50 (14)	45.30	36.20

Issued to commemorate the first International Philatelic Exhibition at Quito.

Coat of Arms — A138

Overprint in Black or Red

1937 *Perf. 12½*

359	A138	5c ol grn	25	10
360	A138	10c dk bl (R)	25	10

Andean Landscape A139

Atahualpa, the Last Inca A140

Hat Weavers A141

Coast Landscape A142

Gold Washing — A143

1937, Aug. 19 *Perf. 11½*

361	A139	2c green	15	8
362	A140	5c dp rose	20	8
363	A141	10c blue	25	5
364	A142	20c dp rose	60	25
365	A143	1s ol grn	85	35
		Nos. 361-365 (5)	2.05	81

"Liberty" Carrying Flag of Ecuador — A144

Engraved and Lithographed

1938, Feb. 22 *Perf. 12*

Center Multicolored

366	A144	2c blue	20	10
367	A144	5c violet	25	10
368	A144	10c black	30	10
369	A144	20c brown	40	15
370	A144	50c black	60	15
371	A144	1s ol blk	1.00	25
372	A144	2s dk brn	2.00	40
		Nos. 366-372,C57-C63 (14)	10.40	2.85

U.S. Constitution, 150th anniversary.

Winged Figure Holding Globe A145

Cactus and Winged Wheel A146

"Communications" A147

"Construction" A148

Perf. 13, 13x13½

1938, Oct. 30 **Engr.**

373	A145	10c brt ultra	10	5
374	A146	50c dp red vio	20	10
375	A147	1s cop red	40	10
376	A148	2s dk grn	60	10

Progress of Ecuador Exhibition.

Parade of Athletes A149

Runner A150

Basketball A151

Wrestlers A152

Diver — A153

1939, Mar. *Perf. 12*

377	A149	5c car rose	2.50	50
378	A150	10c dp bl	3.00	60
379	A151	50c gray ol	3.50	75
380	A152	1s dl vio	6.50	75
381	A153	2s dl ol grn	9.00	1.00
		Nos. 377-381,C65-C69 (10)	46.25	5.75

First Bolivarian Games (1938), La Paz.

Dolores Mission A154

Trylon and Perisphere A155

1939, June 16 *Perf. 12½x13*

382	A154	2c bl grn	5	5
383	A154	5c rose red	10	5
384	A154	10c ultra	10	5
385	A154	50c yel brn	30	20
386	A154	1s black	50	20
387	A154	2s purple	1.00	20
		Nos. 382-387,C73-C79 (13)	3.30	1.40

Golden Gate International Exposition.

1939, June 30

388	A155	2c lt ol grn	10	5
389	A155	5c red org	10	5
390	A155	10c ultra	15	10
391	A155	50c sl gray	50	20
392	A155	1s rose car	75	25
393	A155	2s blk brn	1.25	30
		Nos. 388-393,C80-C86 (13)	4.65	1.87

New York World's Fair.

Flags of the 21 American Republics A156

Francisco J. E. Santa Cruz y Espejo A157

1940 *Perf. 12.*

394	A156	5c dp rose & blk	12	10
395	A156	10c dk bl & blk	18	10
396	A156	50c Prus grn & blk	45	14
397	A156	1s dp vio & blk	65	28
		Nos. 394-397,C87-C90 (8)	3.75	1.72

Pan American Union, 50th anniversary.

1941, Dec. 15

398	A157	30c blue	25	10
399	A157	1s red org	60	20

Issued to commemorate the Exposition of Journalism held under the auspices of the National Newspaper Men's Union. See Nos. C91-C92.

Francisco de Orellana A158

Gonzalo Pizarro A159

View of Guayaquil A160

View of Quito — A161

1942, Jan. 30

400	A158	10c sepia	15	10
401	A159	40c dp rose	30	10

No.	Type	Description	Unused	Used
402	A160	1s violet	50	20
403	A161	2s dk bl	90	40
		Nos. 400-403,C93-C96 (8)	5.25	1.90

Issued to commemorate the 400th anniversary of the discovery and exploration of the Amazon River by Francisco de Orellana.

Remigio Crespo Toral A162

Alfredo Baquerizo Moreno A163

1942 *Perf. 13½*

No.	Type	Description	Unused	Used
404	A162	10c green	10	6
405	A162	50c brown	25	10

See also No. C97.

1942

No.	Type	Description	Unused	Used
406	A163	10c green	10	6

Mt. Chimborazo A164

1942-47 *Perf. 12*

No.	Type	Description	Unused	Used
407	A164	30c red brn	20	8
407A	A164	30c lt bl ('43)	20	8
407B	A164	30c red org ('44)	20	8
407C	A164	30c grn ('47)	20	8

View of Guayaquil — A165

1942-44

No.	Type	Description	Unused	Used
408	A165	20c red	15	10
408A	A165	20c dp bl ('44)	15	10

Gen. Eloy Alfaro A166

Devil's Nose A167

Designs: 30c, Military College. 1s, Montecristi, Alfaro's birthplace.

1942

No.	Type	Description	Unused	Used
409	A166	10c dk rose & blk	20	8
410	A167	20c ol blk & red brn	20	10
411	A167	30c ol gray & grn	30	12
412	A167	1s sl & sal	60	25
		Nos. 409-412,C98-C101 (8)	5.30	2.80

Issued to commemorate the centenary of the birth of President Alfaro (1842-1903).

Nos. 370-372 Overprinted in Red Brown

BIENVENIDO — WALLACE
Abril 15 — 1943

1943, Apr. 15 *Perf. 11½*

No.	Type	Description	Unused	Used
413	A144	50c multi	50	30
414	A144	1s multi	1.00	1.00
415	A144	2s multi	1.50	1.50
		Nos. 413-415,C102-C104 (6)	7.75	5.25

Visit of Vice-President Henry A. Wallace of the United States.

"30 Centavos" — A170

Black Surcharge.

1943 *Perf. 12½*

No.	Type	Description	Unused	Used
416	A170	30c on 50c red brn	20	10
a.		Without bars	20	10

Map Showing United States and Ecuador — A171

1943, Oct. 9 *Perf. 12*

No.	Type	Description	Unused	Used
417	A171	10c dl vio	25	20
418	A171	20c red brn	25	20
419	A171	30c orange	35	25
420	A171	50c ol grn	40	25
421	A171	1s dp vio	50	40
422	A171	10s ol bis	5.00	3.00
		Nos. 417-422,C114-C118 (11)	16.10	11.90

Issued to commemorate the good will tour of President Arroyo del Rio in 1942.

1944, Feb. 7

No.	Type	Description	Unused	Used
423	A171	10c yel grn	15	10
424	A171	20c rose pink	20	15
425	A171	30c dk gray brn	25	20
426	A171	50c dp red lil	40	30
427	A171	1s ol gray	50	40
428	A171	10s red org	5.00	3.00
		Nos. 423-428,C119-C123 (11)	11.50	7.85

No. 385 Surcharged in Black

30
Centavos

1944 **Unwmk.** *Perf. 12½x13*

No.	Type	Description	Unused	Used
429	A154	30c on 50c yel brn	20	10

Archbishop Federico Gonzalez Suarez A172

Government Palace, Quito A173

1944 *Perf. 12*

No.	Type	Description	Unused	Used
430	A172	10c dp bl	15	8
431	A172	20c green	20	8
432	A172	30c dk vio brn	25	6
433	A172	1s dl vio	50	20
		Nos. 430-433,C124-C127 (8)	4.55	2.57

Birth centenary of Archbishop Federico Gonzalez Suarez.

Air Post Stamps Nos. C76 and C83 Surcharged in Black

POSTAL
30
Centavos

1944 *Perf. 12½x13*

No.	Type	Description	Unused	Used
434	AP15	30c on 50c rose vio	20	10
435	AP16	30c on 50c sl grn	20	10

Nos. 382 and 388 Surcharged in Black

CINCO
Centavos

1944-45

No.	Type	Description	Unused	Used
436	A154	5c on 2c bl grn	15	12
a.		Double surcharge		
437	A155	5c on 2c lt ol grn ('45)	15	12

1944 **Engr.** *Perf. 11*

No.	Type	Description	Unused	Used
438	A173	10c dk grn	15	10
439	A173	30c blue	15	10

Symbol of the Red Cross — A174

1945, Apr. 25 *Perf. 12*

Cross in Rose.

No.	Type	Description	Unused	Used
440	A174	30c bis brn	60	25
441	A174	1s red brn	75	30
442	A174	5s turq grn	1.50	1.00
443	A174	10s scarlet	4.00	2.50
		Nos. 440-443,C131-C134 (8)	15.85	10.55

International Red Cross, 80th anniversary.

Nos. 370 to 372 Overprinted in Dark Blue and Gold

LOOR A CHILE
OCTUBRE 2 1945

1945, Oct. 2 *Perf. 11½*

Center Multicolored.

No.	Type	Description	Unused	Used
444	A144	50c black	25	20
a.		Double overprint		
445	A144	1s ol blk	40	30
446	A144	2s dk brn	90	75
		Nos. 444-446,C139-C141 (6)	3.45	3.15

Visit of Pres. Juan Antonio Rios of Chile.

General Antonio Jose de Sucre — A175

1945, Nov. 14 **Engr.** *Perf. 12*

No.	Type	Description	Unused	Used
447	A175	10c olive	5	5
448	A175	20c red brn	10	8
449	A175	40c ol gray	12	10
450	A175	1s dk grn	25	20
451	A175	2s sepia	60	35
		Nos. 447-451,C142-C146 (10)	4.67	2.98

150th anniversary of birth of Gen. Antonio José de Sucre.

No. 438 Surcharged in Blue

VEINTE
CENTAVOS

1945 *Perf. 11*

No.	Type	Description	Unused	Used
452	A173	20c on 10c dk grn	15	10
a.		Fancy bar omitted		

Map of Pan-American Highway and Arms of Loja — A176

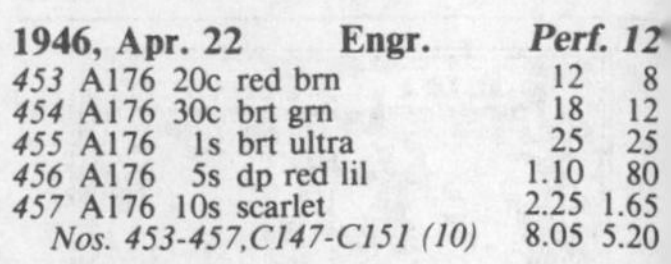

1946, Apr. 22 **Engr.** *Perf. 12*

No.	Type	Description	Unused	Used
453	A176	20c red brn	12	8
454	A176	30c brt grn	18	12
455	A176	1s brt ultra	25	25
456	A176	5s dp red lil	1.10	80
457	A176	10s scarlet	2.25	1.65
		Nos. 453-457,C147-C151 (10)	8.05	5.20

Torch of Democracy A177

Popular Suffrage A178

Flag of Ecuador A179

Pres. José M. Velasco Ibarra A180

1946, Aug. 9 **Unwmk.** *Perf. 12½*

No.	Type	Description	Unused	Used
458	A177	5c dk bl	5	5
459	A178	10c Prus grn	10	5
460	A179	20c carmine	25	10
461	A180	30c chocolate	40	15
		Nos. 458-461,C152-C155 (8)	2.05	1.15

Issued to commemorate the 2nd anniversary of the Revolution of May 28, 1944.

"30 Ctvs." — A181

Black Surcharge.

1948

No.	Type	Description	Unused	Used
462	A181	30c on 50c red brn	10	10

Nos. CO13-CO14 With Additional Overprint in Black

POSTAL

1946 *Perf. 11½*

No.	Type	Description	Unused	Used
463	AP7	10c chestnut	10	10
464	AP7	20c ol blk	10	10

Instructor and Student — A182

1946, Sept. 16 *Perf. 12½*

No.	Type	Description	Unused	Used
465	A182	10c dp bl	15	10
466	A182	20c chocolate	15	10
467	A182	30c dk grn	20	15
468	A182	50c bluish blk	40	20
469	A182	1s dk red	60	20
470	A182	10s dk vio	4.00	1.00
		Nos. 465-470,C156-C160 (11)	11.15	3.95

Campaign for adult education.

Mariana de Jesus Paredes y Flores — A183

Urn — A184

1946, Nov. 28

No.	Type	Description	Unused	Used
471	A183	10c blk brn	20	10
472	A183	20c green	20	10
473	A183	30c purple	25	15
474	A184	1s rose brn	50	35
		Nos. 471-474,C161-C164 (8)	4.20	2.90

Issued to commemorate the 300th anniversary of the death of the Blessed Mariana de Jesus Paredes y Flores.

Pres. Vicente Rocafuerte A185

Jesuits' Church Quito A186

F.J.E. de Santa Cruz y Espejo — A187

1947, Nov. 27 *Perf. 12*

No.	Type	Description	Unused	Used
475	A185	5c redsh brn	10	5
476	A185	10c sepia	10	5
477	A185	15c gray blk	12	5
478	A186	20c redsh brn	20	5
479	A186	30c red vio	20	8
480	A186	40c brt ultra	25	15
481	A187	45c dk sl grn	30	15
482	A187	50c ol blk	40	20
483	A187	80c org red	50	15
		Nos. 475-483,C165-C171 (16)	3.62	1.63

Type of 1946, Overprinted "POSTAL" in Black but Without Additional Surcharge.

1948 **Engr.**

No.	Type	Description	Unused	Used
484	A181	10c orange	60	10

Andrés Bello A188

Flagship of Columbus A189

1948, Apr. 21 *Perf. 13*

No.	Type	Description	Unused	Used
485	A188	20c lt bl	20	10
486	A188	30c rose car	25	10
487	A188	40c bl grn	30	15
488	A188	1s blk brn	60	20
		Nos. 485-488,C172-C174 (7)	2.25	1.05

83rd anniversary of the death of Andrés Bello (1781-1865), educator.

No. 480 Overprinted in Black

CONFERENCIA
ECONOMICA
GRANCOLOMBIANA
MAYO 24 DE 1948

1948, May 24 *Perf. 12*

No.	Type	Description	Unused	Used
489	A186	40c brt ultra	25	20

See also No. C175.

1948 *Perf. 14*

No.	Type	Description	Unused	Used
490	A189	10c dk bl grn	15	6
491	A189	20c brown	25	8
492	A189	30c dk pur	30	8
493	A189	50c dp cl	40	10
494	A189	1s ultra	50	15
495	A189	5s carmine	1.75	35
		Nos. 490-495,C176-C180 (11)	6.95	2.32

Issued to publicize the proposed Columbus Memorial Lighthouse near Ciudad Trujillo. Dominican Republic.

No. 483 Overprinted in Blue

Feria Nacional
1948
ECUADOR de hoy y del MAÑANA

1948 *Perf. 12*

"MANANA" Reading Down.

No.	Type	Description	Unused	Used
496	A187	80c org red	40	35

Issued to publicize the National Fair of Today and Tomorrow, 1948. See No. C181.

Telegrafo I in Flight A190

Book and Pen A191

1948 **Engr.** *Perf. 12½*

No.	Type	Description	Unused	Used
497	A190	30c red org	20	8
498	A190	40c rose lil	20	8
499	A190	60c vio bl	20	10
500	A190	1s brn red	25	10
501	A190	3s brown	90	25
502	A190	5s gray blk	1.00	40
		Nos. 497-502,C182-C187 (12)	5.50	3.11

25th anniversary (in 1945) of the first postal flight in Ecuador.

1948, Oct. 12 **Unwmk.** *Perf. 14*

No.	Type	Description	Unused	Used
503	A191	10c dp cl	10	6
504	A191	20c brown	15	8
505	A191	30c dk grn	20	10
506	A191	50c red	25	12
507	A191	1s purple	35	15
508	A191	5s dl bl	3.00	50
		Nos. 503-508,C188-C192 (11)	6.70	2.46

Campaign for adult education.

Franklin D. Roosevelt and Two of "Four Freedoms"
A192 A193

1948, Oct. 24 *Perf. 12½*

No.	Type	Description	Unused	Used
509	A192	10c rose brn & gray	25	18
510	A192	20c brn ol & bl	30	18
511	A193	30c ol bis & car rose	35	22
512	A193	40c red vio & sep	45	22
513	A193	1s org brn & car	55	45
		Nos. 509-513,C193-C197 (10)	4.05	2.25

Issued in tribute to Franklin D. Roosevelt (1882-1945).

Maldonado and Map — A194

Riobamba Aqueduct A195

Maldonado on Bank of Riobamba A196

Pedro V. Maldonado A197

1948, Nov. 17 **Engr.** **Unwmk.**

No.	Type	Description	Unused	Used
514	A194	5c gray blk & ver	20	8
515	A195	10c car & gray blk	25	8
516	A196	30c bis brn & ultra	35	12
517	A195	40c sage grn & vio	40	12
518	A194	50c grn & car	50	15
519	A197	1s brn & sl bl	60	20
		Nos. 514-519,C198-C201 (10)	3.60	1.35

Bicentenary of the death of Pedro Vicente Maldonado, geographer.

A198

Miguel de Cervantes Saavedra A199

1949, May 2 *Perf. 12½x12*

No.	Type	Description	Unused	Used
520	A198	30c dk car rose & dp ultra	20	12
521	A199	60c bis & brn vio	40	20
522	A198	1s grn & rose car	50	25
523	A199	2s gray blk & red brn	1.25	40
524	A198	5s choc & aqua	2.25	75
		Nos. 520-524,C202-C206 (10)	10.85	4.12

Issued to commemorate the 400th anniversary of the birth of Miguel de Cervantes Saavedra, novelist, playwright and poet.

II CONGRESO
Junio 1949

No. 480 Surcharged in Carmine

0.10
Eucarístico Ncl.

1949, June 15 *Perf. 12*

No.	Type	Description	Unused	Used
525	A186	10c on 40c brt ultra	25	10
526	A186	20c on 40c brt ultra	35	15
a.		Double surcharge		
527	A186	30c on 40c brt ultra	40	20
		Nos. 525-527,C207-C209 (6)	1.60	1.05

Issued to commemorate the Second National Eucharistic Congress, Quito, June, 1949.

No. 526 exists se-tenant with No. 527

Monument on Equator A200

Arms of Ecuador R1

1949, June **Engr.** *Perf. 12½x12*

No.	Type	Description	Unused	Used
528	A200	10c dp plum	30	12

No. 542 Surcharged in Black and Carmine

0.30
75 ANIVERSARIO
U.
P.
U.

1949 *Perf. 12x12½*

No.	Type	Description	Unused	Used
529	A203	10c on 50c grn	15	10
530	A203	20c on 50c grn	20	10
531	A203	30c on 50c grn	30	10
		Nos. 529-531,C210-C213 (7)	3.30	1.80

Universal Postal Union, 75th anniversary.

Consular Service Stamps Surcharged in Black

POSTAL
20 ctvs.

1949 *Perf. 12*

No.	Type	Description	Unused	Used
532	R1	20c on 25c red brn	10	5
533	R1	30c on 50c gray	10	5

Nos. RA49A and RA55 Overprinted in Black

a **POSTAL**

1950 **Unwmk.** *Perf. 12*

No.	Type	Description	Unused	Used
534	PT18	5c green	10	5
535	PT21	5c blue	10	5

Overprint 15 mm. on No. 534.

Nos. 528 and 517 to 519 Overprinted or Surcharged in Black or Carmine.

ALFABETIZACION

1950, Feb. 10 *Perf. 12½x12*

No.	Type	Description	Unused	Used
536	A200	10c dp plum	10	10

Perf. 12½

No.	Type	Description	Unused	Used
537	A195	20c on 40c sage grn & vio	10	10
538	A195	30c on 40c sage grn & vio	15	15
539	A194	50c grn & car	20	15
540	A197	1s brn & sl bl (C)	25	15

No. C220 Overprinted Type "a" in Carmine.

Perf. 11

Overprint 15 mm. long.

No.	Type	Description	Unused	Used
541	AP28	10s violet	2.00	75
		Nos. 536-541,C216-C220 (11)	6.15	3.00

Nos. 536 to 541 were issued to publicize adult education.

Foreign postal stationery (stamped envelopes, postal cards and air letter sheets) lies beyond the scope of this Catalogue, which is limited to adhesive postage stamps.

San Pablo Lake — A203

Perf. 12x12½

1950, May **Engr.** **Unwmk.**
542 A203 50c green 20 15

Consular Service Stamp Surcharged "CORREOS" and New Value Vertically in Black.

1950 ***Perf. 12***
544 R1 30c on 50c gray 15 5

Coat of Arms — R2

Consular Service Stamps Overprinted or Surcharged in Black.

POSTAL 20 Ctvs. 20
b

POSTAL 50 ctvs.
c

CORREOS
d

POSTAL
e

1951 **Unwmk.** ***Perf. 12***
545 R1 (b) 5c on 10c car rose 10 5
546 R1 (c) 10c car rose 10 5
547 R1 (d) 10c car rose 10 5
548 R1 (b) 20c on 25c red brn 10 5
549 R1 (b) 30c on 50c gray 15 5
550 R2 (b) 40c on 25c bl 15 10
551 R2 (e) 50c on 25c bl 20 10
Nos. 545-551 (7) 90 45

Surcharge on No. 545 expressed: "5 ctvs." Small (lower case) "c" in "ctvs." on No. 550.

Consular Service Stamps Surcharged in Black

CAMPAÑA Alfabetización 20 Ctvs. 20

1951
552 R2 20c on 25c bl 20 10
553 R2 30c on 25c bl 20 10

Adult education. See Nos. C225-C226.

Consular Service Stamp Surcharged Type "e" in Black.

1951
554 R2 $0.30 on 50c car rose 20 10

Reliquary of St. Mariana and Vatican — A204

Perf. 12½x12

1952, Feb. **Engr.** **Unwmk.**
555 A204 10c emer & red brn 10 5
556 A204 20c dp bl & pur 15 10
557 A204 30c car & bl grn 25 10
Nos. 555-557,C227-C230 (7) 2.30 95

Issued to publicize the canonization of Mariana de Jesus Paredes y Flores.

Presidents Galo Plaza and Harry Truman A205

Design: 2s, Pres. Plaza addressing U. S. Congress.

1952, Mar. 26 ***Perf. 12***
558 A205 1s rose car & gray blk 30 20
559 A205 2s dl bl & sep 60 25

Issued to commemorate the 1951 visit of Pres. Galo Plaza y Lasso to the United States. See Nos. C231-C232.

R3

Fiscal Stamps Surcharged or Overprinted Type "c" Horizontally in Carmine or Black.

1952 **Unwmk.** **Engr.** ***Perf. 12.***
560 R3 20c on 30c dp bl (C) 10 5
561 R3 30c dp bl 10 5

Diagonal Overprint.
562 A138 50c purple 10 5

Pres. José M. Urvina, Slave and "Liberty" A206

Hyphen-hole Perf. 7x6½

1952 **Litho.**
563 A206 20c red & grn 15 5
564 A206 30c red & vio bl 20 5
565 A206 50c bl & car 35 10
Nos. 563-565,C236-C239 (7) 4.70 1.35

Centenary of abolition of slavery in Ecuador. Counterfeits exist.

Consular Service Stamps Surcharged in Black

POSTAL 10 Centavos
f

1952-53 **Unwmk.** ***Perf. 12.***
566 R1 10c on 20s bl ('53) 10 5
567 R1 20c on 10s gray ('53) 10 5
568 R1 20c on 20s bl 10 5
569 R1 30c on 10s gray ('53) 10 5
570 R1 30c on 20s bl 15 5
Nos. 566-570 (5) 55 25

Similar surcharges of 60c and 90c on the 20s blue are said to be bogus.

Teacher and Students A207

New Citizens Voting A208

Designs: 10c, Instructor with student. 30c, Teaching the alphabet.

1953, Apr. 13 **Engr.**
571 A207 5c lt bl 15 5
572 A207 10c dk car rose 20 5
573 A208 20c brt brn org 28 5
574 A208 30c dp red lil 35 10
Nos. 571-574,C240-C241 (6) 2.23 45

1952 adult education campaign.

A209

Cuicocha Lagoon — A210

Black Surcharge.

1953
575 A209 40c on 50c pur 40 20

1953 **Engr.** ***Perf. 13x12½.***

Designs: 10c, Equatorial Line monument. 20c, Quininde countryside. 30c, Tomebamba river. 40c, La Chilintosa rock. 50c, Iliniza Mountains.

Frames in Black.
576 A210 5c brt bl 6 6
577 A210 10c brt grn 6 6
578 A210 20c purple 10 8
579 A210 30c brown 10 8
580 A210 40c orange 12 12
581 A210 50c dp car 35 12
Nos. 576-581 (6) 79 52

Carlos Maria Cardinal de la Torre and Arches — A211

1954, Jan. **Photo.** ***Perf. 8½***
582 A211 30c blk & ver 15 5
583 A211 50c blk & rose lil 20 8
Nos. 582-583,C253-C255 (5) 1.15 58

Issued to commemorate the first anniversary of the elevation of Archbishop de la Torre to Cardinal.

Queen Isabella I — A212

1954, Apr. 22
584 A212 30c blk & gray 20 8
585 A212 50c blk brn & yel 20 10
Nos. 584-585,C256-C260 (7) 1.65 1.18

Issued to commemorate the 500th anniversary of the birth of Queen Isabella I (1451-1504) of Spain.

Type of 1929; "POSTAL" Overprint Larger, No Letterspacing.

1954-55 **Unwmk.** ***Perf. 12***
586 A112 5c ol grn ('55) 15 5
587 A112 10c orange 20 5

The normal overprint on Nos. 586-587 reads up. It also exists reading down.

Indian Messenger A213

Products of Ecuador A214

1954, Aug. 2 **Litho.** ***Perf. 11***
588 A213 30c dk brn 15 10

Issued to publicize the Day of the Postal Employee. See also No. C263.

1954, Sept. 24 **Photo.**
589 A214 10c orange 8 5
590 A214 20c vermilion 10 5
591 A214 30c rose pink 15 5
592 A214 40c dk gray grn 20 8
593 A214 50c yel brn 30 10
Nos. 589-593 (5) 83 33

José Abel Castillo A215

Babahoyo River Los Rios A216

Perf. 11½x11

1955, Oct. 19 **Engr.** **Unwmk.**
594 A215 30c ol bis 10 10
595 A215 50c dk gray 15 10
Nos. 594-595,C282-C286 (7) 2.60 1.35

Issued to commemorate the 30th anniversary of the first flight of the "Telegrafo I" and to honor José Abel Castillo, aviation pioneer.

1955-56 **Photo.** ***Perf. 13***

Designs: 5c, Palms, Esmeraldas. 10c, Fishermen, Manabi. 30c, Guayaquil, Guayas. 50c, Pital River, El Oro. 70c, Cactus, Galapagos Isls. 80c, Orchids, Napo-Pastaza. 1s, Aguacate Mission, Zamora-Chinchipe. 2s, Jibaro Indian, Morona-Santiago.

596 A216 5c yel grn ('56) 5 5
597 A216 10c bl ('56) 10 5
598 A216 20c brown 10 5
599 A216 30c dk gray 10 5
600 A216 50c bl grn 15 5
601 A216 70c ol ('56) 20 5
602 A216 80c dp vio ('56) 40 10
603 A216 1s org ('56) 30 10
604 A216 2s rose red ('56) 60 20
Nos. 596-604 (9) 2.00 70

See also Nos. 620-630, 670, C288-C297, C310-C311.

Brother Juan Adam Schwarz, S. J. — A217

1956, Aug. 27 **Engr.** ***Perf. 13½***
605 A217 5c yel grn 5 5
606 A217 10c org red 5 5
607 A217 20c lt vio 5 5
608 A217 30c dk grn 5 5

609 A217 40c blue 10 5
610 A217 50c dp ultra 15 5
611 A217 70c orange 20 5
Nos. 605-611,C302-C305 (11) 1.65 1.10

Issued to commemorate the bicentennial of printing in Ecuador and in honor of Brother Juan Adam Schwarz, S.J.

Andres Hurtado de Mendoza — A218

Gil Ramirez Davalos A219

Designs: 20c, Brother Vincent Solano.

1957, Apr. 7 Unwmk. *Perf. 12*
612 A218 5c dk bl, *pink* 10 5
613 A219 10c grn, *grnsh* 10 5
614 A218 20c choc, *buff* 15 5
a. Souvenir sheet of 4 50 50
Nos. 612-614,C312-C314 (6) 80 45

Issued to commemorate the fourth centenary of the founding of Cuenca.

No. 614a contains two 5c gray and two 20c brown red stamps in designs similar to Nos. 612 and 614. It was printed on white ungummed paper, is imperf. and is inscribed "II Exposicion Filatelica Nacional, Cuenca, 11 al 20 de Abril de 1957." Size: 140x120mm.

Francisco Marcos, Gen. Pedro Alcantara Herran and Santos Michelena A220

1957, Sept. 5 Engr. *Perf. 14½x14*
615 A220 40c yellow 15 5
616 A220 50c ultra 15 5
617 A220 2s dk red 50 20

7th Postal Congress of the Americas and Spain (in 1955).

Souvenir Sheets

Various Railroad Scenes — A221

1957 Litho. *Perf. 10½x11*
618 A221 Sheet of five 20c 80 80
619 A221 Sheet of five 30c 60 50

Issued to commemorate the opening of the Quito-Ibarra-San Lorenzo railroad.

Nos. 618-619 measure 118x110mm. with ultramarine inscriptions and contain 2 orange yellow, 1 ultramarine and 2 carmine stamps, each in a different design.

Scenic Type of 1955-56.

Designs as before, except: 40c, Cactus, Galapagos Islands. No. 629, San Pablo, Imbabura.

1957-58 Photo. *Perf. 13*
620 A216 5c lt bl 10 5
621 A216 10c brown 10 5
622 A216 20c crim rose 10 5
623 A216 20c yel grn 10 5
624 A216 30c rose red 15 5
625 A216 40c chlky bl 40 5
626 A216 50c lt vio 15 5
627 A216 90c brt ultra 40 5
628 A216 1s dk brn 20 10
629 A216 1s gray blk ('58) 20 10
630 A216 2s brown 50 20
Nos. 620-630 (11) 2.40 80

Blue and Yellow Macaw — A222

Birds: 20c, Red-breasted toucan. 30c, Condor. 40c, Black-tailed and sword-tailed hummingbirds.

Perf. 13½x13
1958, Jan. 7 Litho. Unwmk.
Birds in Natural Colors.
634 A222 10c red brn 20 5
635 A222 20c dk gray 20 10
636 A222 30c brt yel grn 45 12
637 A222 40c red org 45 12

Carlos Sanz de Santamaria — A223

Richard M. Nixon and Flags — A224

Design: No. 640, Dr. Ramon Villeda Morales and flags. 2.20s, Jose Carlos de Macedo Soares and horizontal flags.

1958 *Perf. 12*
Flags in Red, Blue, Yellow & Green.
638 A223 1.80s dl vio 50 15
639 A224 2s dk grn 50 20
640 A223 2s dk brn 50 20
641 A223 2.20s blk brn 50 20

No. 638 commemorates the visit of Colombia's Foreign Minister Dr. Carlos Sanz de Santamaria to Ecuador.

No. 639 commemorates the visit of U. S. Vice President Richard M. Nixon to Ecuador, May 9-10.

No. 640 commemorates the visit of President Ramon Villeda Morales of Honduras.

No. 641 commemorates the visit of Brazil's Foreign Minister Jose Carlos de Macedo Soares to Ecuador. See Nos. C419-C421.

Locomotive of 1908 — A225

Garcia Moreno, Jose Caamano, L. Plaza and Eloi Alfaro — A226

Design: 50c, Diesel locomotive.

Perf. 13½x14, 14
1958, Aug. 9 Photo. Unwmk.
642 A225 30c brn blk 12 8
643 A225 50c dk car 20 10
644 A226 5s dk brn 85 60

Issued to commemorate the 50th anniversary of the Guayaquil-Quito railroad.

Cardinal — A227

Birds: 30c, Andean cock-of-the-rock. 50c, Glossy cowbird. 60c, Red-fronted Amazon.

1958 Litho. *Perf. 13½x13*
Birds in Natural Colors.
645 A227 20c bluish grn, blk & red 15 8
646 A227 30c buff, blk & brt bl 15 8
647 A227 50c org, blk & grn 20 14
648 A227 60c pale rose, blk & bluish grn 30 15

UNESCO Building and Eiffel Tower, Paris — A228

1958, Nov. 3 Engr. *Perf. 12½*
649 A228 80c brown 25 15

Issued to commemorate the opening of UNESCO (U. N. Educational, Scientific and Cultural Organization) Headquarters in Paris, Nov. 3.

Globe and Satellites A229

Virgin of Quito A230

1958, Dec. 20 Photo. *Perf. 14x13½*
650 A229 1.80s dk bl 1.25 50

Issued to commemorate the International Geophysical Year, 1957-58.

1959, Sept. 8 Unwmk. *Perf. 13*
651 A230 5c ol grn 6 6
652 A230 10c yel brn 6 6
653 A230 20c purple 6 6
654 A230 30c ultra 12 6
655 A230 80c dk car rose 20 10
Nos. 651-655 (5) 50 34

See also No. C290.

Uprooted Oak Emblem — A231

1960, Apr. 7 Litho. *Perf. 14x13*
656 A231 80c rose car & grn 20 10

Issued to publicize World Refugee Year, July 1, 1959-June 30, 1960.

Great Anteater and Arms — A232

Animals: 40c, Tapir and map. 80c, Spectacled bear and arms. 1s, Puma and map.

1960, May 14 Photo. *Perf. 13*
657 A232 20c org, grn & blk 10 10
658 A232 40c yel grn, bl grn & brn 15 10
659 A232 80c bl, blk & red brn 28 16
660 A232 1s Prus bl, plum & ocher 55 28

Issued to commemorate the 4th centenary of the founding of the city of Baeza.

See also Nos. 676-679.

Hotel Quito A233

Designs: No. 662, Dormitory, Catholic University. No. 663, Dormitory, Central University. No. 664, Airport, Quito. No. 665, Overpass on Highway to Quito. No. 666, Security Bank. No. 667, Ministry of Foreign Affairs. No. 668, Government Palace. No. 669, Legislative Palace.

Perf. 11x11½
1960, Aug. 8 Engr. Unwmk.
661 A233 1s dk pur & redsh brn 20 14
662 A233 1s dk bl & brn 20 14
663 A233 1s blk & red 20 14
664 A233 1s dk bl & ultra 20 14
665 A233 1s dk pur & dk car rose 20 14
666 A233 1s blk & ol bis 20 14
667 A233 1s dk pur & turq 20 14
668 A233 1s dk bl & grn 20 14
669 A233 1s blk & vio 20 14
Nos. 661-669 (9) 1.80 1.26

11th Inter-American Conference, Quito.

Souvenir Sheet

Type of Regular Issue, 1955-56.

Design: Orchids, Napo-Pastaza.

1960 Photo. *Perf. 13*
Yellow Paper.
670 A216 Sheet of two 30 30
a. 80c dp vio 10 10
b. 90c dp grn 10 10

Issued to commemorate the 25th anniversary of Asociacion Filatelica Ecuatoriana. Marginal inscription in silver. Size: 85x55mm. Exists with silver inscription omitted.

"Freedom of Expression" A234

Manabi Bridge A235

Designs: 10c, "Freedom to vote." 20c, "Freedom to work." 30c, Coins, "Monetary stability."

1960, Aug. 29 Litho. *Perf. 13*
671 A234 5c dk bl 6 6
672 A234 10c lt vio 6 6
673 A234 20c orange 12 6
674 A234 30c bluish grn 12 6
675 A235 40c brn & bluish grn 20 6
Nos. 671-675 (5) 56 30

Issued to publicize the achievements of President Camilo Ponce Enriquez. See Nos. C370-C374.

Animal Type of 1960.

Animals: 10c, Collared peccary. 20c, Kinkajou. 80c, Jaguars. 1s, Mountain coati.

Unwmk.

1961, July 13 Photo. *Perf. 13*

676 A232 10c grn, rose red & blk 5 5
677 A232 20c vio, grnsh bl & brn 15 8
678 A232 80c red org, dl yel & blk 30 15
679 A232 1s brn, brt grn & org 35 20

Issued to commemorate the 400th anniversary of the founding of the city of Tena.

Graphium Pausianus — A236

Butterflies: 30c, Papilio torquatus leptalea. 50c, Graphium molops molops. 80c, Battus lycidas.

1961, July 13 Litho. *Perf. 13½*

680 A236 20c pink & multi 12 6
681 A236 30c lt ultra & multi 12 6
682 A236 50c org & multi 20 14
683 A236 80c bl grn & multi 25 12

See also Nos. 711-713.

1961

Galapagos Islands Nos. L1-L3 Overprinted in Black or Red

Estación de Biología Marítima de Galápagos

XXXXXXXXXXX

1961, Oct. 31 Photo. *Perf. 12*

684 A1 20c dk brn 25 12
685 A2 50c violet 25 12
686 A1 1s dk ol grn (R) 45 22
Nos. 684-686,C389-C391 (6) 2.45 1.59

Establishment of maritime biological stations on Galapagos Islands by UNESCO. Overprint arranged differently on 20c, 1s. See Nos. C389-C391.

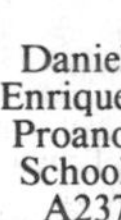

Daniel Enrique Proano School A237

Designs: 60c, Loja-Zamora highway (vert.). 80c, Aguirre Abad College, Guayaquil. 1s, Army quarters, Quito.

Perf. 11x11½, 11½x11

1962, Jan. 10 Engr. Unwmk.

687 A237 50c dl bl & blk 10 5
688 A237 60c ol grn & blk 10 5
689 A237 80c org red & blk 20 10
690 A237 1s rose lake & blk 25 10

Pres. Arosemena, Flags of Ecuador, U.S. — A238

Protection for The Family — A239

Designs (Arosemena and): 10c, Flags of Ecuador. 20c, Flags of Ecuador and Panama.

1963, July 1 Litho. *Perf. 14*

691 A238 10c buff & multi 5 5
692 A238 20c multi 15 8
693 A238 60c multi 20 8
Nos. 691-693,C409-C411 (6) 1.73 91

Issued to commemorate Pres. Carlos J. Arosemena's friendship trip, July 1962.

1963, July 9 Unwmk. *Perf. 14*

694 A239 10c ultra, red, gray & blk 10 5

Issued to commemorate the 25th anniversary of Social Insurance. See No. C413.

No. 655 Overprinted or Surcharged in Black or Blue

1961 DIA DEL EMPLEADO POSTAL 10

1963 Photo. *Perf. 13*

695 A230 10c on 80c dk car rose 5 5
696 A230 20c on 80c dk car rose 10 5
697 A230 50c on 80c dk car rose 10 10
698 A230 60c on 80c dk car rose (Bl) 15 10
699 A230 80c dk car rose 25 10
Nos. 695-699 (5) 65 40

Nos. 661-669 Surcharged **0,10** **XXXXX**

1964, Apr. 20 Engr. *Perf. 11x11½*

700 A233 10c on 1s dk pur & redsh brn 5 5
701 A233 10c on 1s dk pur & turq 5 5
702 A233 20c on 1s dk bl & brn 5 5
703 A233 20c on 1s dk bl & grn 5 5
704 A233 30c on 1s dk pur & dk car rose 10 5
705 A233 40c on 1s blk & ol bis 10 5
706 A233 60c on 1s blk & red 15 10
707 A233 80c on 1s dk bl & ultra 20 10
708 A233 80c on 1s blk & vio 20 10
Nos. 700-708 (9) 95 60

No. 656 Overprinted in Black or Light Ultramarine

1964 Litho. *Perf. 14x13*

709 A231 80c rose car & grn 2.00 60

Butterfly Type of 1961

Butterflies: Same as on Nos. 680, 682-683.

1964, June Litho. *Perf. 13½*

711 A236 20c brt grn & multi 5 5
712 A236 50c sal pink & multi 10 5
713 A236 80c lt red brn & multi 15 10

Alliance for Progress Emblem, Agriculture and Industry A240

Designs: 50c, Emblem, gear wheels, mountain and seashore. 80c, Emblem, banana worker, fish, factory and ship.

1964, Aug. 26 Unwmk. *Perf. 12*

715 A240 40c bis brn & vio 10 5
716 A240 50c red org & blk 15 5
717 A240 80c bl & dk brn 20 10

Issued to publicize the Alliance for Progress which aims to stimulate economic growth and raise living standards in Latin America.

No. 650 Overprinted in Red

FARO DE COLON

1964 Photo. *Perf. 14x13½*

718 A229 1.80s dk bl 2.50 1.25

No. 656 Overprinted

(Reduced Size)
Overprint covers four stamps

1964, July Litho. *Perf. 14x13*

719 A231 80c block of 4 2.75 1.10

Organization of American States.

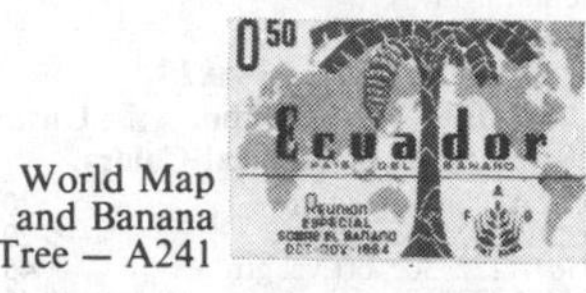

World Map and Banana Tree — A241

1964, Oct. 26 *Perf. 12½x12*

720 A241 50c dk brn, gray & gray ol 5 5
721 A241 80c blk, org & gray ol 10 5

Issued to publicize the Banana Conference, Oct.-Nov. 1964. See Nos. C427-C428a.

King Philip II of Spain and Map of Upper Amazon River A242

Designs (Map and): 20c, Juan de Salinas de Loyola. 30c, Hernando de Santillan.

1964, Dec. 6 Litho. *Perf. 13½*

722 A242 10c rose, blk & buff 5 5
723 A242 20c bl grn, blk & buff 14 8
724 A242 30c bl, blk & buff 14 8

Issued to commemorate the 4th centenary of the establishment of the Royal High Court in Quito.

Pole Vaulting A243

1964, Dec. 16 *Perf. 14x13½*

725 A243 80c vio bl, yel grn & brn 15 10

Issued to commemorate the 18th Olympic Games, Tokyo, Oct. 10-25. See also Nos. C432-C434.

Peter Fleming and Two-toed Sloth — A244

Designs: 20c, James Elliot and armadillo. 30c, T. Edward McCully, Jr., and squirrel. 40c, Roger Youderian and deer. 60c, Nathaniel (Nate) Saint and plane over Napo River.

1965 Unwmk. *Perf. 13½*

726 A244 20c emer & multi 5 5
727 A244 30c yel & multi 5 5
728 A244 40c lil & multi 5 5
729 A244 60c multi 10 10
730 A244 80c multi 15 10
Nos. 726-730 (5) 40 35

Issued in memory of five American Protestant missionaries, killed by the Auca Indians, Jan. 8, 1956. Issue dates: 80c, May 11; others, July 8.

Juan B. Vázquez and Benigno Malo College — A245

1965, June 6 Litho. *Perf. 14*

731 A245 20c blk, yel & vio bl 5 5
732 A245 60c blk, red, yel & vio bl 14 8
733 A245 80c blk, emer, yel & vio bl 14 14

Issued to commemorate the centenary (in 1964) of the founding of Benigno Malo National College.

National Anthem, Juan Leon Mera and Antonio Neumane A246

1965, Aug. 10 Litho. *Perf. 13½*

734 A246 50c pink & blk 5 5
735 A246 80c lt grn & blk 10 10
736 A246 5s bis & blk 50 40
737 A246 10s lt ultra & blk 90 75

Issued to commemorate the centenary of the national anthem. The name of the poet Juan Leon Mera is misspelled on the stamps.

Torch and Athletes (Shot Put, Discus, Javelin and Hammer Throw) — A247

Torch and Athletes: 50c, 1s, Runners. 60c, 1.50s, Soccer.

1965, Nov. 20 *Perf. 12x12½*

738 A247 40c org, gold, & blk 5 5
739 A247 50c org ver, gold & blk 5 5
740 A247 60c bl, gold & blk 12 6
741 A247 80c brt yel grn, gold & blk 12 12
742 A247 1s lt vio, gold & blk 20 8
743 A247 1.50s brt pink, gold & blk 25 18
Nos. 738-743,C435-C440 (12) 2.54 1.99

Issued to publicize the 5th Bolivarian Games, held at Guayaquil and Quito.

Stamps of 1865 — A248

1965, Dec. 30 Litho. *Perf. 13½*

Stamps of 1865 in Yellow, Ultramarine & Green

744 A248 80c rose red 20 14
745 A248 1.30s rose lil 25 12
746 A248 2s chocolate 35 18
747 A248 4s black 55 28
a. Souv. sheet of 4 1.50 1.50

Issued to commemorate the centenary of Ecuadorian postage stamps. No. 747a contains four imperf. stamps similar to Nos. 744-747. Dark blue marginal inscription and black control number. Size: 140x125mm.

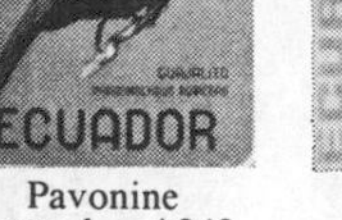

Pavonine Quetzal — A249

Bust of Penaherrera, Central University, Quito — A250

Birds: 50c, Blue-crowned motmot. 60c, Paradise tanager. 80c, Wire-tailed manakin.

1966, June 17 Litho. *Perf. 13½*

Birds in Natural Colors

No.	Type	Description	Unused	Used
748	A249	40c dl rose & blk	5	5
749	A249	50c sal & blk	5	5
750	A249	60c lt ocher & blk	10	10
751	A249	80c lt bl & blk	10	10
		Nos. 748-751,C441-C448 (12)	2.92	2.33

Various Surcharges on Issues of 1956-66

1967-68

No.	Type	Description	Unused	Used
752	AP72	30c on 1.10s multi (C337)	5	5
753	AP66	40c on 1.70s yel brn (C292)	5	5
754	A247	40c on 3.50s lt vio, gold & blk (C438)	5	5
755	A246	50c on 5s bis & blk (736) ('68)	10	5
756	A247	80c on 1.50s brt pink, gold & blk (743)	15	5
757	A249	80c on 2.50s lt yel grn & multi (C445)	15	5
758	A249	1s on 4s gray & multi (C447)	15	5
759	AP66	1.30s on 1.90s ol (C293)	20	15
760	A246	2s on 10s lt ultra & blk (737) ('68)	30	15
		Nos. 752-760,C449-C450 (11)	1.40	75

The surcharge on Nos. 754-755, 757 and 759-760 includes "Resello." The obliteration of old denomination and arrangement of surcharges differ on each stamp.

Perf. 12x12½, 12½x12

1967, Dec. 29 Litho.

Designs: 50c, Law books. 80c, Open book and laurel (horiz.).

No.	Type	Description	Unused	Used
761	A250	50c brt grn & blk	5	5
762	A250	60c rose & blk	5	5
763	A250	80c rose lil & blk	10	5
		Nos. 761-763,C451-C452 (5)	50	35

Issued to commemorate the centenary (in 1964) of the birth of Dr. Victor Manuel Penaherrera (1864-1932), author of the civil and criminal codes of Ecuador.

Otto Arosemena Gomez — A251

Lions Emblem — A252

1968, May 9 Litho. *Perf. 13½x14*

Design: 1s, Page from the Constitution.

No.	Type	Description	Unused	Used
764	A251	80c lil & multi	5	5
765	A251	1s multi	10	5

First anniversary of the administration of Pres. Otto Arosemena Gomez. See Nos. C453-C454.

1968, May 24 Litho. *Perf. 13½x14*

No.	Type	Description	Unused	Used
766	A252	80c multi	10	10
767	A252	1.30s multi	15	10
768	A252	2s pink & multi	20	15
a.		Souv. sheet of 1	3.00	3.00

Issued to commemorate the 50th anniversary (in 1967) of Lions International.

No. 768a contains one 5s stamp (size: 39x49mm.). Violet blue marginal inscriptions and red control numbers. Size: 71x104mm. Exists imperf.

Nos. C331 and C326 Surcharged in Violet and Dark Blue

RESELLO

a

$ 0,40

$ 0,50

b

RESELLO

1969, Jan. 10 *Perf. 11½, 14x13½*

No.	Type	Description	Unused	Used
769	AP79 (a)	40c on 1.30s grn & brn red (V)	5	5
770	AP76 (b)	50c on 1.30s dk grn & lt brn (DBl)	5	5

Type of 1958 Surcharged and Overprinted in Plum and Black

RESELLO

$ 0,50

Design: Ignacio Luis Arcaya, Foreign Minister of Venezuela.

1969, Mar. Litho. *Perf. 12*

Flags in Red, Blue and Yellow.

No.	Type	Description	Unused	Used
771	A223	50c on 2s sep	5	5
772	A223	80c on 2s sep	10	5
773	A223	1s on 2s sep	10	10
774	A223	2s sepia	20	15
		Nos. 771-774,C455-C457 (7)	75	65

Nos. 771-774 were not issued without overprint. The obliteration of old denomination on No. 772 is a small square around a star. Overprint is plum, except for the black small coat of arms on right flag.

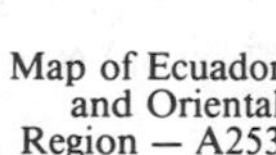

Map of Ecuador and Oriental Region — A253

Surcharge typographed in Dark Blue, Red Brown, Black or Lilac

1969 Litho. *Perf. 14*

No.	Type	Description	Unused	Used
775	A253	20c on 30c multi (DBl)	5	5
776	A253	40c on 30c multi (RBr)	5	5
777	A253	50c on 30c multi (DBl)	5	5
778	A253	60c on 30c multi (DBl)	5	5
779	A253	80c on 30c multi (Bk)	10	10
780	A253	1s on 30c multi (L)	10	10
781	A253	1.30s on 30c multi (Bk)	15	10
782	A253	1.50s on 30c multi (Bk)	20	15
783	A253	2s on 30c multi (DBl)	25	20
784	A253	3s on 30c multi (DBl)	35	25
785	A253	4s on 30c multi (Bk)	25	15
786	A253	5s on 30c multi (Bk)	30	20
		Nos. 775-786 (12)	1.90	1.45

Not issued without surcharge.

M. L. King, John and Robert Kennedy — A254

Thecla Coronata — A255

1969-70 Typo. *Perf. 12½*

No.	Type	Description	Unused	Used
787	A254	4s blk, bl, grn & buff	40	15

Perf. 13½

No.	Type	Description	Unused	Used
788	A254	4s blk, lt bl & grn ('70)	40	15

In memory of John F. Kennedy, Robert F. Kennedy and Martin Luther King, Jr.

1970 Litho. *Perf. 12½*

Butterflies: 20c, Papilio zabreus. 30c, Heliconius chestertoni. 40c, Papilio pausanias. 50c, Pereute leucodrosime. 60c, Metamorpha dido. 80c, Morpho cypris. 1s, Catagramma astarte.

No.	Type	Description	Unused	Used
789	A255	10c buff & multi	5	5
790	A255	20c lt grn & multi	5	5
791	A255	30c pink & multi	5	5
792	A255	40c lt bl & multi	5	5
793	A255	50c gold & multi	5	5
794	A255	60c sal & multi	10	5
795	A255	80c sil & multi	10	5
796	A255	1s lt grn & multi	10	5
		Nos. 789-796,C461-C462 (10)	75	60

Same, White Background

1970 *Perf. 13½*

No.	Type	Description	Unused	Used
797	A255	10c multi	5	5
798	A255	20c multi	5	5
799	A255	30c multi	5	5
800	A255	40c multi	5	5
801	A255	50c multi	5	5
802	A255	60c multi	5	5
803	A255	80c multi	10	5
804	A255	1s multi	10	5
		Nos. 797-804,C463-C464 (10)	70	60

Surcharged Revenue Stamps

A256 A257

1970, June 16 Litho. *Perf. 14*

Red Surcharge

No.	Type	Description	Unused	Used
805	A256	1s on 1s lt bl	10	5
806	A256	1.30s on 1s lt bl	15	5
807	A256	1.50s on 1s lt bl	20	10
808	A256	2s on 1s lt bl	20	10
809	A256	5s on 1s lt bl	50	20
810	A256	10s on 1s lt bl	1.00	40
		Nos. 805-810 (6)	2.15	90

1970 Typo. *Perf. 12*

Black Surcharge

No.	Type	Description	Unused	Used
811	A257	60c on 1s vio	10	5
812	A257	80c on 1s vio	10	5
813	A257	1s on 1s vio	10	5
814	A257	1.10s on 1s vio	10	5
815	A257	1.30s on 1s vio	10	5
816	A257	1.50s on 1s vio	15	5
817	A257	2s on 1s vio	20	5
818	A257	2.20s on 1s vio	30	5
819	A257	3s on 1s vio	40	10
		Nos. 811-819 (9)	1.55	50

1970

No.	Type	Description	Unused	Used
820	A257	1.10s on 2s grn	10	10
821	A257	1.30s on 2s grn	15	10
822	A257	1.50s on 2s grn	15	10
823	A257	2s on 2s grn	20	10
824	A257	3.40s on 2s grn	35	10
825	A257	5s on 2s grn	50	15
826	A257	10s on 2s grn	90	20
827	A257	20s on 2s grn	1.50	40
828	A257	50s on 2s grn	4.00	1.00
		Nos. 820-828 (9)	7.85	2.25

1970

No.	Type	Description	Unused	Used
829	A257	3s on 5s bl	30	5
830	A257	5s on 5s bl	50	10
831	A257	10s on 40s org	75	20

Arms of Zamora Chinchipe A258

Flags of Ecuador and Chile A259

Design: 1s, Arms and flag of Esmeraldas.

1971 Litho. *Perf. 10½*

No.	Type	Description	Unused	Used
832	A258	50c pale yel & multi	5	5
833	A258	1s sal & multi	10	5
		Nos. 832-833,C465-C469 (7)	1.75	1.35

1971, Sept. *Perf. 12½*

No.	Type	Description	Unused	Used
840	A259	1.30s blk & multi	10	10

Visit of Pres. Salvador Allende of Chile, Aug. 24. See Nos. C481-C482.

Ismael Perez Pazmino — A260

1971, Sept. 16 *Perf. 12x11½*

No.	Type	Description	Unused	Used
841	A260	1s grn & multi	10	5

50th anniversary of "El Universo," newspaper founded by Ismael Perez Pazmino. See Nos. C485-C486.

CARE Package A261

Flags of Ecuador and Argentina A262

1971-72 *Perf. 12½*

No.	Type	Description	Unused	Used
842	A261	30c lil ('72)	5	5
843	A261	40c emer ('72)	5	5
844	A261	50c blue	5	5
845	A261	60c carmine	5	5
846	A261	80c lt brn ('72)	10	5
		Nos. 842-846 (5)	30	25

25th anniversary of CARE, a U.S.-Canadian Cooperative for American Relief Everywhere.

1972 *Perf. 11½*

No.	Type	Description	Unused	Used
847	A262	1s blk & multi	10	5

Visit of Lt. Gen. Alejandro Agustin Lanusse, president of Argentina, Jan. 25. See Nos. C491-C492.

Jesus Giving Keys to St. Peter, by Miguel de Santiago — A263

Ecuadorian Paintings: 1.10s, Virgin of Mercy, Quito School. 2s, Virgin Mary, by Manuel Samaniego.

1972, Apr. 24 Litho. *Perf. 14x13½*

848	A263	50c blk & multi	5	5
849	A263	1.10s blk & multi	10	10
850	A263	2s blk & multi	20	15
a.		Souv. sheet of 3	40	40
		Nos. 848-850,C494-C495 (5)	1.30	95

No. 850a contains 3 imperf. stamps similar to Nos. 848-850. Blue marginal inscription. Size: 129x110mm.

1972, May 4

Ecuadorian Statues: 50c, Our Lady of Sorrow, by Caspicara. 1.10s, Nativity. Quito School (horiz.). 2s, Virgin of Quito, anonymous.

851	A263	50c blk & multi	5	5
852	A263	1.10s blk & multi	10	10
853	A263	2s blk & multi	20	10
a.		Souv. sheet of 3	40	40
		Nos. 851-853,C496-C497 (5)	1.35	95

Letters of "Ecuador" 3mm. high on Nos. 851-853, 7mm. high on Nos. 848-850. No. 853a contains 3 imperf. stamps similar to Nos. 851-853. Blue marginal inscription. Size: 129x110mm.

Gen. Juan Ignacio Pareja — A264

Designs: 40c, Juan José Flores. 50c, Leon de Febres Cordero. 60c, Ignacio Torres. 70c, Francisco de Paula Santander. 1s, José M. Cordova.

1972, May 24 *Perf. 12½*

854	A264	30c bl & multi	5	5
855	A264	40c bl & multi	5	5
856	A264	50c bl & multi	5	5
857	A264	60c bl & multi	5	5
858	A264	70c bl & multi	10	5
859	A264	1s bl & multi	10	5
		Nos. 854-859,C498-C503 (12)	3.70	2.60

Sesquicentennial of the Battle of Pichincha and the liberation of Quito.

Woman Wearing Poncho — A265

Designs: 3s, Striped poncho. 5s, Embroidered poncho. 10s, Metal vase.

1972, July Photo. *Perf. 13*

860	A265	2s multi	20	10
861	A265	3s multi	25	20
862	A265	5s multi	50	15
863	A265	10s dp bl & multi	1.00	40
a.		Souvenir sheet of 4	2.00	2.00
		Nos. 860-863,C504-C507 (8)	3.45	1.90

Handicraft of Ecuador. No. 863a contains 4 imperf. stamps similar to Nos. 860-863. Gray green marginal inscription and ornament. Black control number. Size 104x164mm.

Sucre Statue, Santo Domingo A266 — Radar Station A267

Wmk.367

Wmk. Liberty Cap, Emblem and Inscription (367)

1972, Dec. 6 Litho. *Perf. 11½*

Designs: 1.80s, San Agustin Convent. 2.30s, Plaza de la Independencia. 2.50s, Bolivar statue, La Alameda. 4.75s, Chapel door.

864	A266	1.20s yel & multi	15	10
865	A266	1.80s yel & multi	15	10
866	A266	2.30s yel & multi	20	15
867	A266	2.50s yel & multi	30	20
868	A266	4.75s yel & multi	50	25
		Nos. 864-868,C518-C524 (12)	4.50	3.30

Sesquicentennial of the Battle of Pichincha.

1973, Apr. 5 Litho. *Perf. 11½*

869	A267	1s multi	20	10

Inauguration of earth telecommunications station, Oct. 19, 1972.

Blue-footed Boobies A268

1973 Litho. *Perf. 11½x12*

870	A268	30c *shown*	5	5
871	A268	40c *Blue-faced booby*	5	5
872	A268	50c *Oyster-catcher*	5	5
873	A268	60c *California sea lions*	10	10
874	A268	70c *Galapagos giant tortoise*	15	10
875	A268	1s *California sea lion*	20	10
		Nos. 870-875,C527-C528 (8)	1.00	65

Elevation of Galapagos Islands to a /province of Ecuador.

Issue dates: 50c, Oct. 3; others Aug. 16.

Black-chinned Mountain Tanager — A269

Birds of Ecuador: 2s, Moriche oriole. 3s, Toucan barbet (vert.). 5s, Masked crimson tanager (vert.). 10s, Blue-necked tanager (vert.).

Perf. 11x11½, 11½x11

1973, Dec. 6 Litho. Unwmk.

876	A269	1s brick red & multi	15	10
877	A269	2s lt bl & multi	25	10
878	A269	3s lt grn & multi	25	10
879	A269	5s pale lil & multi	60	25
880	A269	10s pale yel grn & multi	1.25	60
		Nos. 876-880 (5)	2.50	1.15

Two souvenir sheets exist: one contains 2 imperf. stamps similar to Nos. 876-877 with yellow margin and black inscription; the other 3 stamps similar to Nos. 878-880; gray margin and black inscription including "Aereo." Both sheets dated "1972." Size: 143x84mm.

Marco T. Varea, Botanist — A270

Portraits: 60c, Pio Jaramillo Alvarado, writer. 70c, Prof. Luciano Andrade M. No. 883, Marco T. Varea, botanist. No. 884, Dr. Juan Modesto Carbo Noboa, medical researcher. No. 885, Alfredo J. Valenzuela. No. 886, Capt. Edmundo Chiriboga G. 1.20s, Francisco Campos R., scientist. 1.80s, Luis Vernaza Lazarte, philanthropist.

1974 Unwmk. *Perf. 12x11½*

881	A270	60c crim rose	5	5
882	A270	70c lilac	5	5
883	A270	1s ultra	10	5
884	A270	1s orange	10	5
885	A270	1s emerald	10	5
886	A270	1s brown	10	5
887	A270	1.20s ap grn	15	10
889	A270	1.80s lt bl	25	15
		Nos. 881-889 (8)	90	55

Arcade A271

Designs: 30c, Monastery, entrance. 40c, Church. 50c, View of Church through gate (vert.). 60c, Chapel (vert.). 70c, Church and cemetery (vert.).

Perf. 11½x12, 12x11½

1975, Feb. 4 Litho.

896	A271	20c yel & multi	5	5
897	A271	30c yel & multi	5	5
898	A271	40c yel & multi	5	5
899	A271	50c yel & multi	5	5
900	A271	60c yel & multi	10	5
901	A271	70c yel & multi	10	5
		Nos. 896-901 (6)	40	30

Colonial Monastery, Tilipulo, Cotopaxi Province.

Angel Polibio Chaves, Founder of Bolivar Province — A272

Portrait: No. 903, Emilio Estrada Ycaza (1916-1961), archeologist.

1975 Litho. *Perf. 12x11½*

902	A272	80c vio bl & lt bl	10	10
903	A272	80c ver & pink	10	10

Issue dates: No. 902, Feb. 21; No. 903, Mar. 25.

R. Rodriguez Palacios and A. Duran Quintero — A273

"Woman of Action" — A274

1975, Apr. 1 Litho. *Perf. 12x11½*

910	A273	1s multi	10	10

Meeting of the Ministers for Public Works of Ecuador and Colombia, July 27, 1973. See Nos. C547-C548.

1975, June

Design: No. 912, 1s, "Woman of Peace."

911	A274	1s yel & multi	10	10
912	A274	1s bl & multi	10	10

International Women's Year 1975.

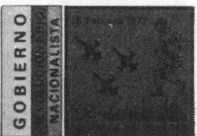

Planes, Soldier and Ship — A275

1975, July 9 *Perf. 11½x12*

913	A275	2s multi	20	15

Three years of National Revolutionary Government.

Hurdling — A276

Designs: Modern sports drawn Inca style.

1975, Sept. 11 Litho. *Perf. 11½*

914	A276	20c *shown*	5	5
915	A276	20c *Chess*	5	5
916	A276	30c *Basketball*	5	5
917	A276	30c *Boxing*	5	5
918	A276	40c *Bicycling*	5	5
919	A276	40c *Steeplechase*	5	5
920	A276	50c *Soccer*	5	5
921	A276	50c *Fencing*	5	5
922	A276	60c *Golf*	5	5
923	A276	60c *Vaulting*	5	5
924	A276	70c *Judo (standing)*	10	5
925	A276	70c *Wrestling*	10	5
926	A276	80c *Swimming*	10	5
927	A276	80c *Weight lifting*	10	5
928	A276	1s *Table Tennis*	10	5
929	A276	1s *Paddle ball*	10	5
		Nos. 914-929,C554-C558 (21)	2.30	1.30

3rd Ecuadorian Games.

Genciana A277

Designs: Ecuadorian plants.

Perf. 12x11½, 11½x12

1975, Nov. 18 Litho.

930	A277	20c *Orchid* (vert.)	5	5
931	A277	30c *shown*	5	5
932	A277	40c *Bromeliaceae cactaceae (vert.)*	5	5
933	A277	50c *Orchid*	5	5
934	A277	60c *Orchid*	5	5

935 A277 80c *Flowering cactus* 10 5
936 A277 1s *Orchid* 10 5
Nos. 930-936,C559-C563 (12) 1.70 1.05

Venus, Chorrera Culture — A278

Female Mask, Tolita Culture — A279

Designs: 30c, Venus, Valdivia Culture. 40c, Seated man, Chorrera Culture. 50c, Man with poncho, Panzaleo Culture (late). 60c, Mythical head, Cashaloma Culture. 80c, Musician, Tolita Culture. No. 943, Chief Priest, Mantefia Culture. No. 945, Ornament, Tolita Culture. No. 946, Angry mask, Tolita Culture.

1976, Feb. 12 Litho. *Perf. 11½*
937 A278 20c multi 5 5
938 A278 30c multi 5 5
939 A278 40c multi 5 5
940 A278 50c multi 5 5
941 A278 60c multi 5 5
942 A278 80c multi 10 5
943 A278 1s multi 10 5
944 A279 1s multi 10 5
945 A279 1s multi 10 5
946 A279 1s multi 10 5
Nos. 937-946,C568-C572 (15) 1.90 1.10

Archaeological artifacts.

Strawberries A280

Carlos Amable Ortiz (1859-1937) A281

1976, Mar. 30
947 A280 1s bl & multi 10 5

25th Flower and Fruit Festival, Ambato. See Nos. C573-C574.

1976, Mar. 15 Litho. *Perf. 11½*

Portraits: No. 949, Sixto Maria Duran (1875-1947). No. 950, Segundo Cueva Celi (1901-1969). No. 951, Cristobal Ojeda Davila (1910-1952). No. 952, Luis Alberto Valencia (1918-1970).

948 A281 1s ver & multi 10 5
949 A281 1s org & multi 10 5
950 A281 1s lt grn & multi 10 5
951 A281 1s bl & multi 10 5
952 A281 1s lt brn & multi 10 5
Nos. 948-952 (5) 50 25

Ecuadorian composers and musicians.

Institute Emblem A282

1977, Aug. 15 Litho. *Perf. 11½x12*
953 A282 2s multi 20 10

11th General Assembly of Pan-American Institute of Geography and History, Quito, Aug. 15-30. See Nos. C597-C597a.

Hands Holding Rotary Emblem — A283

José Peralta — A284

1977, Aug. 31 Litho. *Perf. 12*
954 A283 1s multi 10 5
955 A283 2s multi 20 10

Souvenir Sheets
Imperf
956 A283 5s multi 50 30
957 A283 10s multi 1.00 60

Rotary Club of Guayaquil, 50th anniversary. Nos. 956-957 have black control numbers. Size: 90x115mm.

1977 Litho. *Perf. 11½*
Design: 2.40s, Peralta statue.
958 A284 1.80s multi 15 10
959 A284 2.40s multi 20 10

José Peralta (1855-1937), writer, 40th death anniversary. See No. C609.

Blue-faced Booby — A285

Galapagos Birds: 1.80s, Red-footed booby. 2.40s, Blue-footed boobies. 3.40s, Gull. 4.40s, Galapagos hawk. 5.40s, Map of Galapagos Islands and boobies (vert.).

Perf. 11½x12, 12x11½
1977, Nov. 29 Litho.
960 A285 1.20s multi 10 5
961 A285 1.80s multi 15 10
962 A285 2.40s multi 20 10
963 A285 3.40s multi 25 15
964 A285 4.40s multi 35 20
965 A285 5.40s multi 50 20
Nos. 960-965 (6) 1.55 80

Dr. Corral Moscoso Hospital, Cuenca A286

1978, Apr. 12 Litho. *Perf. 11½x12*
966 A286 3s multi 25 15

Inauguration (in 1977) of Dr. Vicente Corral Moscoso Regional Hospital, Cuenca. See Nos. C613-C614.

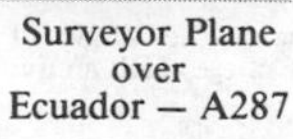

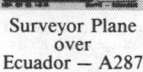

Surveyor Plane over Ecuador — A287

Latin-American Lions Emblem — A288

1978, Apr. 12 Litho. *Perf. 11½*
967 A287 6s multi 50 30

Military Geographical Institute, 50th anniversary. See Nos. C619-C620.

1978
968 A288 3s multi 25 15
969 A288 4.20s multi 40 20

7th meeting of Latin American Lions, Jan. 25-29. See Nos. C621-C623.

70th Anniversary Emblem — A289

1978, Sept. Litho. *Perf. 11½*
970 A289 4.20s gray & multi 40 20

70th anniversary of Filanbanco (Philanthropic Bank). See No. C626.

Goalmouth and Net — A290

Designs: 1.80s, "Gauchito" and Games emblem (vert.). 4.40s, "Gauchito" (vert.).

1978, Nov. 1 Litho. *Perf. 12*
971 A290 1.20s multi 10 5
972 A290 1.80s multi 15 10
973 A290 4.40s multi 35 20
Nos. 971-973,C627-C629 (6) 2.20 1.20

11th World Cup Soccer Championship, Argentina, June 1-25.

Symbols for Male and Female — A291

1979, Feb. 15 Litho. *Perf. 12x11½*
974 A291 3.40s multi 30 15

Inter-American Women's Commission, 50th anniversary.

Emblem A292

1979, June 21 Litho. *Perf. 11½x12*
975 A292 4.40s multi 40 20
976 A292 5.40s multi 50 20

Ecuadorian Mortgage Bank, 16th anniversary.

The lack of a price for a listed item does not necessarily indicate rarity.

Street Scene, Quito — A293

Perf. 12x11½
1979, Aug. 3 Litho. Unwmk.
977 A293 3.40s multi 30 15

National heritage: Quito and Galapagos Islands. See Nos. C651-C653.

Jose Joaquin de Olmedo (1780-1847), Physician A294

Chief Enriquillo, Dominican Republic A295

1980, Apr. 29 Litho. *Perf. 12x11½*
978 A294 3s multi 25 10
979 A294 5s multi 40 20

First President of Free State of Guayaquil, 1820. See No. C662.

1980, May 12

Indo-American Tribal Chiefs: 3.40s, Guaycaypuro, Venezuela. No. 982, Abayuba, Uruguay. No. 983, Atlacatl, Salvador.

980 A295 3s multi 25 10
981 A295 3.40s multi 35 15
982 A295 5s multi 50 25
983 A295 5s multi 50 25
Nos. 980-983,C663-C678 (20) 18.90 9.40

King Juan Carlos and Queen Sofia, Visit to Ecuador A296

1980, May 18 *Perf. 11½x12*
984 A296 3.40s multi 30 15

See No. C679.

Cofan Indian, Napo Province — A297

1980, June 10 Litho. *Perf. 12x11½*
985 A297 3s *shown* 25 10
986 A297 3.40s *Zuleta woman, Imbabura* 30 15
987 A297 5s *Chota woman, Imbabura* 50 25
Nos. 985-987,C681-C684 (7) 4.75 2.35

Basilica, Our Lady of Mercy Church, Quito A298

1980, July 7 Litho. *Perf. 11½*
988 A298 3.40s *shown* 30 15
989 A298 3.40s *Balcony* 30 15

989A A298 3.40s *Dome and cupolas* 30 15

Sizes: 91x116mm, 116x91mm.

Imperf

990 A298 5s multi 50 25
990A A298 5s multi, horiz. 50 25
990B A298 5s multi 50 25
Nos. 988-990B,C685-C691 (13) 8.70 4.35

Virgin of Mercy, patron saint of Ecuadorian armed forces. No. 990 contains designs of Nos. C686, C685, 989. No. 990A contains designs of Nos. C688, C691, C690. No. 990B contains designs of Nos. C689, C687, 989A, 988. All have black control number.

Olympic Torch and Rings — A299

1980, July 19 *Perf. 12x11½*

991 A299 5s multi 40 20
992 A299 7.60s multi 60 30

Souvenir Sheet

Imperf

993 A299 30s multi 2.50 1.25

22nd Summer Olympic Games, Moscow, July 19-Aug. 3. See Nos. C695-C696.

No. 993 contains vignettes in designs of Nos. 991 and C695, black control number. Size: 116x90mm.

Coronation of Virgin of Cisne, 50th Anniversary A300

1980 Litho. *Perf. 11½*

994 A300 1.20s *shown* 10 5
995 A300 3.40s *Different statue* 30 15

J.J. Olmeda, Father de Velasco, Flags of Ecuador and Riobamba, Constitution A301

1980, Sept. 20 Litho. *Perf. 11½*

996 A301 3.40s multi 30 15
997 A301 5s multi 50 20

Souvenir Sheet

Imperf

998 A301 30s multi 3.00 1.25

Constitutional Assembly of Riobamba sesquicentennial. No. 998 contains vignettes in designs of Nos. 996-997, black control number. Size: 116x90mm. See Nos. C700-C702.

First Lady Mrs. Aguilera — A302

Perf. 12x11½

1980, Oct. 9 Litho. Wmk. 367

999 A302 1.20s multi 10 5
1000 A302 3.40s multi 30 15

Democratic government, 1st anniversary. See Nos. C703-C705.

OPEC Emblem A303

1980, Nov. 8 *Perf. 11½x12*

1001 A303 3.40s multi 30 15

20th anniversary of OPEC. See No. C706.

Decorative Hedges, Capitol Gardens, Carchi A304

1980, Nov. 21 *Perf. 13*

1002 A304 3s multi 25 10

Carchi province centennial. See Nos. C707-C708.

Cattleya Maxima A305

Designs: Orchids.

1980, Nov. 22 *Perf. 11½x12*

1003 A305 1.20s *shown* 10 5
1004 A305 3s *Comparattia speciosa* 25 10
1005 A305 3.40s *Cattleya iricolor* 30 15
Nos. 1003-1005,C709-C712 (7) 5.75 3.60

Souvenir Sheet

Imperf

1006 A305 20s multi 2.00 1.00

No. 1006 contains vignettes in designs of Nos. 1003-1005; black control number. Size: 115x90mm.

Pope John Paul II and Children — A306

1980, Dec. 27 *Perf. 12*

1007 A306 3.40s multi 30 15

Christmas 1980/visit of Pope John Paul II. See Nos. C715-C716.

Carlos and Jorge Ortega, Editors of El Comercio — A307

El Comercio Newspaper, 75th Anniversary: 3.40s, Editors Cesar and Carlos Jacome.

1981, Jan. 6

1008 A307 2s multi 15 10
1009 A307 3.40s multi 25 15

Soldier on Map of Ecuador A308

National Defense (Map of Ecuador and): No. 1011, Pres. Roldos.

1981, Mar. 10 Litho. *Perf. 13*

1010 A308 3.40s multi 25 15
1011 A308 3.40s multi 25 15

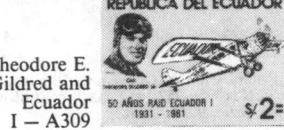

Theodore E. Gildred and Ecuador I — A309

1981, Mar. 31 Litho. *Perf. 13*

1012 A309 2s lt bl & blk 15 10

Ecuador-U.S. flight, 50th anniv.

Octavio Cordero Palacios (1870-1930), Humanist — A310

1981, Apr. 10

1013 A310 2s multi 15 10

Radio Station HCJB 50th Anniv. — A311

1981 Litho. *Perf. 13*

1014 A311 2s multi 15 10

See Nos. C721-C722.

Virgin of Dolorosa A312

1981, Apr. 30 Litho. *Perf. 12*

1015 A312 2s shown 15 10
1016 A312 2s San Gabriel College Church 15 10

Miracle of the painting of the Virgin of Dolorosa at San Gabriel College, 75th anniv.

Dr. Rafael Mendoza Aviles Bridge Inauguration A313

1981, July 25 *Perf. 13*

1017 A313 2s multi 15 10

Pablo Picasso (1881-1973), Painter — A313a

1981, Oct. 26 Litho. *Imperf.*

1017A A313a 20s multi 1.75 90

No. 1017A contains design of No. C728, additional portrait; black control number. See Nos. C728-C731.

World Food Day — A314

1981, Dec. 31 Litho. *Perf. 13½x13*

1018 A314 5s multi 50 20

See No. C732

Transnave Shipping Co. 10th Anniv. A315

Intl. Year of the Disabled A316

1982, Jan. 21 Litho. *Perf. 13*

1019 A315 3.50s Freighter Isla Salango 35 15

1982, Feb. 25

1020 A316 3.40s Man in wheelchair 30 15

See Nos. C733-C734.

Arch A317

Juan Montalvo Birth Sesquicentennial A318

1982, May Litho. *Perf. 13*

1021 A317 3s shown 15 10
1022 A317 3s Houses 25 10

Souvenir Sheet

1023 Sheet of 4, 18th cent. map of Quito 2.50 1.00
a.-d. A317 6s multi 60 25

QUITEX '82, 4th Natl. Stamp Exhibition, Quito, Apr. 16-22. No. 1023 contains 4 stamps (48x31mm., perf. 12½); black control number, inscription. Size: 109x89mm.

1982

1024 A318 2s Portrait 15 10
1025 A318 3s Mausoleum 20 10

See No. C735.

American Air Forces Cooperation System — A319

4th World Swimming Champ., Guayaquil — A320

1982

1026 A319 5s Emblem 40 20

1982, July 30

1027 A320 1.80s Stadium 15 10
1028 A320 3.40s Water polo 25 15

See Nos. C736-C737.

Juan L. Mera (1832-?), Writer, by Victor Mideros — A321

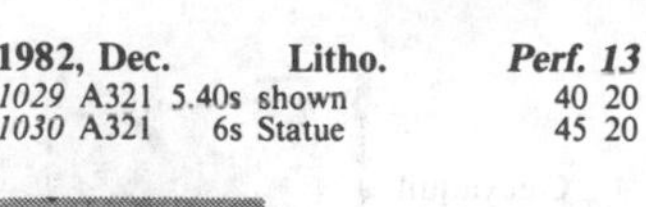

1982, Dec. **Litho.** ***Perf. 13***

1029 A321 5.40s shown 40 20
1030 A321 6s Statue 45 20

St. Teresa of Jesus of Avila (1515-1582) — A322

1983, Mar. 28 **Litho.** ***Perf. 13***

1031 A322 2s multi 15 10

Sea Lions A323

Flamingoes A324

1983, June 17 **Litho.** ***Perf. 13***

1032 A323 3s multi 15 5
1033 A324 5s multi 20 10

Sesquicentennial of Ecuadorian rule over Galapagos Islds (3s); Charles Darwin (1809-1882).

The Catalogue editors cannot undertake to appraise, identify or judge the genuineness or condition of stamps.

Pres. Vicente Rocafuerte Birth Bicentenary A325

Simon Bolivar A326

Perf. 13x13½

1983, Aug. 26 **Litho.** **Wmk. 367**

1034 A325 5s Statue 20 10
1035 A325 20s Portrait 75 35
1036 A326 20s Portrait 75 35

Vicente Rocafuerte Bejarano, president, 1833-39 (Nos. 1034-1035).

Paute Hydroelectric Plant Opening — A327

1983, Sept. 3

1037 A327 5s River 15 10
1038 A327 10s Dam 30 20

Souvenir Sheet

Imperf

1039 A327 20s Dam, river 1.00 60

No. 1039 has black control number, airmail. Size: 110x90mm.

World Communications Year — A328

Wmk. 367

1983, Nov. 10 **Litho.** ***Perf. 13***

1040 A328 2s multi 10 5

Centenary of Bolivar and El Oro Provinces (1984) — A329

Wmk. 367

1983, Sept. **Litho.** ***Perf. 13***

1041 A329 3s multi 6 5

Atahualpa (1497-1529), Last Incan Rulers — A330

1984, Mar. **Litho.** ***Perf. 13***

1042 A330 15s Engraving 30 15

Christmas 1983 — A331

Creche figures.

Perf. 13½x13, 13x13½

1984, July 7 **Litho.**

1043 A331 5s Jesus and lawyers 10 5
1044 A331 5s Three kings 10 5
1045 A331 5s Holy Family 10 5
1046 A331 6s Priest, vert. 12 6

Foreign Policy of Pres. Hurtado A332

State visits.

1984, July 10 ***Perf. 13½x13***

1047 A332 8s Brazil 16 8
1048 A332 9s People's Rep. of China 18 10
1049 A332 24s U.N. 48 24
1050 A332 28s U.S. 56 28
1051 A332 29s Venezuela 58 30
1052 A332 37s Latin-American Economic Conference, Quito 75 38
Nos. 1047-1052 (6) 2.71 1.38

Miguel Diaz Cueva (1884-1942), Lawyer A333

1984, Aug. 8 **Litho.** ***Perf. 13½x13***

1053 A333 10s Cueva, arms 35 18

1984 Winter Olympics A334

Manned Flight Bicentenary A335

Perf. 13x13½, 12x11½ (6s)

1984, Aug. 15

1054 A334 2s Emblem 8 5
1055 A334 4s Ice skating 14 8
1056 A334 6s Skating, diff. 22 12
1057 A334 10s Skiing 35 18

1984, Aug. 15 ***Perf. 13x13½***

1058 A335 3s Montgolfier 10 5
1059 A335 6s Charlier's balloon, Paris, 1789 22 12

Souvenir Sheet

1060 A335 20s Graf Zeppelin, Montgolfier 75 50

No. 1060 is airmail and contains one stamp (50x37mm., imperf.); multicolored margin shows balloons, plane; red control number. Size: 110x90mm.

SAN MATEO '83, Esmeraldas A336

1984 **Litho.** ***Perf. 13***

1061 A336 8s La Marimba folk dance 35 18

Size: 89x110mm.

Imperf

1061A A336 15s La Marimba, diff. 40 20

No. 1061A airmail, has bronze control number. Size: 90x110mm.

Jose Maria de Jesus Yerovi (b. 1824), 4th Archbishop of Quito — A337

1984

1062 A337 5s multi 25 14

Canonization of Brother Miguel A338

1984 **Litho.** ***Perf. 13***

1063 A338 9s Academy of Languages 35 20
1064 A338 24s Vatican City, vert. 75 45
1065 A338 28s Home of Brother Miguel 80 50

No. 1065, airmail, has black control number. Size: 110x90mm.

State Visit of Pope John Paul II — A339

Beatification of Mercedes de Jesus Molina — A340

1985, Jan. 23 **Litho.** ***Perf. 13x13½***

1066 A339 1.60s Papal arms 5 5
1067 A339 5s Blessing crowd 12 6
1068 A339 9s World map, itinerary 24 12
1069 A339 28s Pope waving 70 35
1070 A339 29s Portrait 75 38
Nos. 1066-1070 (5) 1.86 96

Size: 90x109mm.

Imperf

1071 A339 30s Pope holding crosier 2.75 1.40

No. 1071 has black control number.

1985, Jan. 23

Paintings, sculpture.

1072 A340 1.60s Portrait 5 5
1073 A340 5s Czestochowa Madonna 12 6
1074 A340 9s Alborada Madonna 15 8

Size: 90x110mm.

Imperf

1075 A340 20s Mercedes de Jesus, children 2.00 1.00

Visit of Pope John Paul II, birth bimillennium of the Virgin Mary. No. 1075 has red control number.

Samuel Valarezo Delgado, Naturalist, Politician — A341

1985, Feb.

1076 A341 2s Bird 6 6
1077 A341 3s Swordfish, tuna 6 6
1078 A341 6s Portrait 25 12

ESPANA '84, Madrid A342

1985, Apr. 25 *Perf. 13½x13*

1079 A342 6s Emblem 15 8
1080 A342 10s Spanish royal family 35 18

Size: 110x90mm.

Imperf

1081 A342 15s Retiro Park, exhibition site 1.00 50

No. 1081 has black control number.

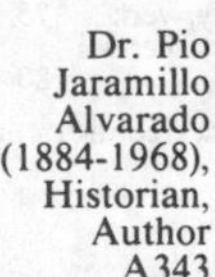

Dr. Pio Jaramillo Alvarado (1884-1968), Historian, Author A343

1985, May 17

1082 A343 6s multi 25 12

Ingenio Valdez Sugar Refinery — A344

Designs: 50s, Sugar cane, emblem. 100s, Rafael Valdez Cervantes, founder.

1985, June **Litho.** *Perf. 13*

1082A A344 50s multi 1.00 50
1082B A344 100s multi 2.00 1.00

Size: 110x90mm.

Imperf

1083 A344 30s multi 60 30

No. 1083 has red control number.

Chamber of Commerce, 10th Anniv. A345

Design: 50s, Natl. and American Statues of Liberty.

1985, Aug. 15 *Perf. 13½x13*

1084 A345 24s multi 65 32
1085 A345 28s multi 75 38

Size: 110x90mm.

Imperf

1086 A345 50s multi 1.10 55

No. 1086 has black control number.

Natl. Philatelic Assoc., AFE, 50th Anniv. A346

1985, Aug. 25 *Perf. 12*

1087 A346 25s AFE emblem 52 25
1088 A346 30s No. 357, horiz. 65 32

Guayaquil Fire Dept., 150th Anniv. A347

1985, Oct. 10 *Perf. 13½x13*

1089 A347 6s Steam fire pump, 1882 12 6
1090 A347 10s Fire Wagon, 1899 20 10
1091 A347 20s Anniv. emblem, natl. flag 38 20

Natl. Infant Survival Campaign A348

1st Natl. Philatelic Congress, Quito, Nov. 25-28 A349

1985, Oct. *Perf. 13x13½*

1092 A348 10s Boy, girl, tree 30 15

1985, Nov. *Perf. 13x13½, 13½x13*

20th century illustrations, natl. cultural collection: 5s, Supreme Court, Quito, by J. M. Roura. 10s, Riobamba Cathedral, by O. Munaz. 15s, House of 100 Windows, by J. M. Roura, horiz. 20s, Rural cottage near Cuenca, by J. M. Roura. No. 1097a, Stampless cover, 1779, Riobamba. No. 1097b, Hand press, 1864, Quito. No. 1097c, Postrider, 1880, Cuenca. No. 1097d, Monoplane, 1st airmail flight, 1919, Guayaquil.

1093 A349 5s multi 15 8
1094 A349 10s multi 25 12
1095 A349 15s multi 30 15
1096 A349 20s multi 50 20

Souvenir Sheet

1097 Sheet of 4 1.00 50
a.-d. A349 5s, any single 25 14

AFE, 50th anniv. No. 1097 contains 4 stamps (size: 53x42mm, perf. 13x12½ on 2 sides); black control number. Size: 109x90mm.

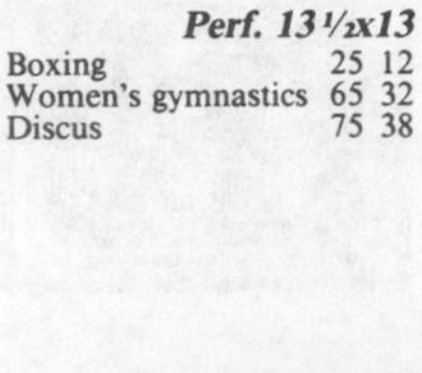

10th Bolivarian Games, Cuenca A350

1985, Nov. *Perf. 13½x13*

1098 A350 10s Boxing 25 12
1099 A350 25s Women's gymnastics 65 32
1100 A350 30s Discus 75 38

BAE Calderon, Navy Cent. — A351

Military anniversaries: No. 1102, Fighter plane, Air Force 65th anniv. No. 1103, Army and paratroops emblems, Special Forces 30th anniv.

1985, Dec. *Perf. 13x13½*

1101 A351 10s multi 25 12
1102 A351 10s multi 25 12
1103 A351 10s multi 25 12

UN, 40th Anniv. A352

1985, Oct. **Litho.** *Perf. 13*

1104 A352 10s UN flag 30 15
1105 A352 20s Natl. flag 45 18

Size: 110x90mm.

Imperf

1106 A352 50s UN Building 1.00 50

No. 1106 bears black control number.

Christmas A353

Indigenous Flowers A354

1985, Nov.

1107 A353 5s Child riding donkey 15 8
1108 A353 10s Baked goods 25 12
1109 A353 15s Riding donkey, diff. 35 18

Size: 90x110mm.

Imperf

1110 A353 30s like 5s 60 30

No. 1110 bears green control number.

1986, Feb.

1111 A354 24s Embotrium grandiforum 50 25
1112 A354 28s Topobea sp. 55 28
1113 A354 29s Befaria resinosa mutis 60 30

Size: 110x90mm.

Imperf

1114 A354 15s multi 28 14

No. 1114 contains designs of Nos. 1111, 1113, 1112; black control number.

Discovery of the Galapagos Isls., 450th Anniv. A355

Map of the Islands — A356

1986, Feb. 12

1115 A355 10s Land iguana 20 12
1116 A355 20s Sea lion 38 20
1117 A355 30s Frigate birds 55 28
1118 A355 40s Penguins 75 38
1119 A355 50s Sea turtle 1.00 50
1120 A355 100s Charles Darwin 2.00 1.00
1121 A355 200s Bishop Tomas de Berlenga, discoverer 4.00 2.00

Perf. 12½

1122 Sheet of 4 3.50 1.75
a.-d. A356 50s, Map of the islands 85 42
Nos. 1115-1122 (8) 12.38 6.23

No. 1122 contains 4 stamps (size: 53x42mm, perf. 12½ on 2 sides); red control number. Size: 110x90mm.

Inter-American Development Bank, 25th Anniv. — A357

Designs: 5s, Antonio Ortiz Mena, president 1971- . 10s, Felipe Herrera, president 1960-1971. 50s, Emblem.

1986, Mar. 6

1123 A357 5s multi 10 8
1124 A357 10s multi 22 12
1125 A357 50s multi 95 48

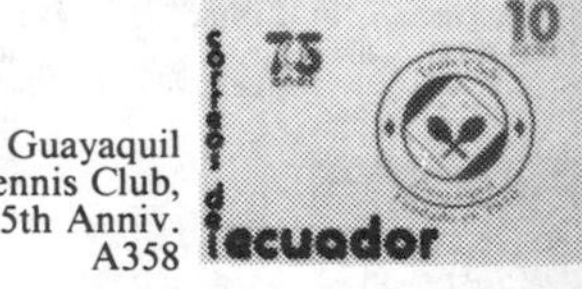

Guayaquil Tennis Club, 75th Anniv. A358

1986, Mar. 7

1126 A358 10s Emblem 18 10
1127 A358 10s Francisco Segura Cano, vert. 18 10
1128 A358 10s Andres Gomez Santos, vert. 18 10

1986 World Cup Soccer Championships, Mexico — A359

1986, May 5

1129 A359 5s shot 10 8
1130 A359 10s Block 18 10

An imperf. stamp exists picturing flags, player and emblem. Black control number.

Meeting of Presidents Cordero and Betancourt of Colombia, Feb. 1985 — A360

1986 Litho. *Perf. 13½x13*
1131 A360 20s Presidents 35 18
1132 A360 20s Embracing 35 18

Exports A361

Designs: 35s, 1137c, Shrimp. 40s, No. 1137b, Tuna. 45s, No. 1137a, Sardines. No. 1137d, MICIP emblem.

1986, Apr. 12
1133 A361 35s ultra & ver 60 30
1134 A361 40s red & yel grn 65 32
1135 A361 45s car & dk yel 75 38

Perf. 12½ on 2 Sides
1137 Sheet of 4 60 32
a.-d. A361 10s, any single 14 8

No. 1137 contains 4 stamps (Size: 53x42mm); black control number. Size: 110x90mm.

A362

La Condamine's First Geodesic Mission, 250th Anniv. — A363

Designs: No. 1141a, Triangulation map for determining equatorial meridian, 1736. No. 1141b, Partial map of the Maranon and Amazon Rivers, by Samuel Fritz, 1743-1744. No. 1141c, Base of measurement, Yaruqui plains. No. 1141d, Caraburo and Dyambaru Pyramids near Quito. Nos. 1141c-1141d printed se-tenant in a continuous design.

1986, July 10 Litho. *Perf. 13½x13*
1138 A362 10s La Condamine 18 10
1139 A362 15s Maldonado 25 12
1140 A362 20s Middle of the World, Quito 30 15

Souvenir Sheet
Perf. 12½ on 2 Sides
1141 Sheet of 4 60 32
a.-d. A363 10s, any single 14 8

No. 1141 has black control number. Size: 110x90mm.

Chambers of Commerce A364

1986 Litho. *Perf. 13½x13*
1142 A364 10s Pichincha 18 10
1143 A364 10s Cuenca 18 10
1144 A364 10s Guayaquil 18 10

Civil Service and Communications Ministry, 57th Anniv. — A365

Organization emblems.

1986, Dec. Litho. *Perf. 13x13½*
1145 A365 5s State railway 10 5
1146 A365 10s Post office 20 10
1147 A365 15s Communications 30 15
1148 A365 20s Ministry of Public Works 40 20

Chamber of Agriculture of the 1st Zone, 50th Anniv. — A366

1987, Feb. 16 Litho. *Perf. 13x13½*
1149 A366 5s multi 15 8

Col. Luis Vargas Torres (d. 1887) — A367

Designs: 50s, Portrait. No. 1151, Combat unit, c. 1885. No. 1152a, Torres and his mother, Delfina. No. 1152b, Letter to Delfina written by Torres during imprisonment, 1882. No. 1152c, Arms of Ecuador and combat unit.

1987, Jan. 6 Litho. & Typo. *Perf. 13*
1150 A367 50s yel grn, blk & gold 65 32
1151 A367 100s ver, gold & ultra 1.30 65

Size: 95x140mm.
Perf. 12 on One or Two Sides.
1152 Block of 3 3.90 1.95
a.-c. A367 100s any single 1.30 65

Sizes: Nos. 1152a, 1152c, 95x28mm. No. 1152b, 95x83mm. No. 1152b contains black control number.

SEMI-POSTAL STAMPS

Nos. 423-428 Surcharged in Carmine or Blue:

Hospital
Méndez + $ 0,50

1944, May 9 Unwmk. *Perf. 12*
B1 A171 10c + 10c yel grn (C) 50 35
B2 A171 20c + 20c rose pink 50 40
B3 A171 30c + 20c dk gray brn 50 50
B4 A171 50c + 20c dp red lil 1.00 75
B5 A171 1s + 50c ol gray (C) 1.50 1.25
B6 A171 10s + 2s red org 6.00 3.50
Nos. B1-B6 (6) 10.00 6.75

The surtax aided Mendez Hospital.

AIR POST STAMPS

In 1928-30, the internal airmail service of Ecuador was handled by the Sociedad Colombo-Alemana de Transportes Aereos ("SCADTA") under government sanction. During this period SCADTA issued stamps which were the only legal franking for airmail service except that handled under contract with Pan American-Grace Airways. SCADTA issues are Nos. C1-C6, C16-C25.

Colombia Air Post Stamps of 1923 Surcharged in Carmine

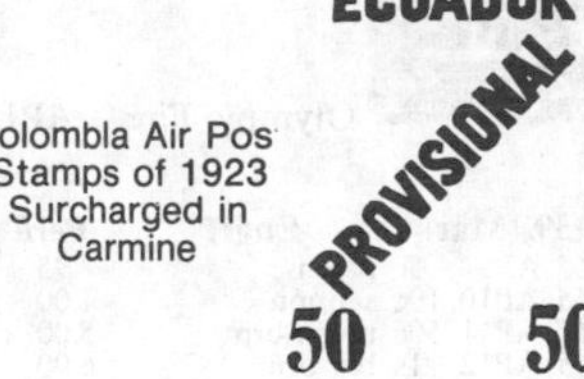

"Provisional" at 45 degree Angle.
Perf. 14x14½
1928, Aug. 28 Wmk. 116
C1 AP6 50c on 10c grn 150.00 100.00
C2 AP6 75c on 15c car 300.00 200.00
C3 AP6 1s on 20c gray 100.00 60.00
C4 AP6 1½s on 30c bl 75.00 50.00
C5 AP6 3s on 60c brn 125.00 75.00
Nos. C1-C5 (5) 750.00 485.00

"Provisional" at 41 degree Angle.
1929, Mar. 20
C1a AP6 50c on 10c grn 165.00 150.00
C2a AP6 75c on 15c car 200.00 175.00
C3a AP6 1s on 20c gray 165.00 175.00

Same with "Cts." Between Surcharged Numerals
C6 AP6 50c on 10c grn *1,250. 1,000.*

A 75c on 15c carmine with "Cts." between the surcharged numerals exists. There is no evidence that it was regularly issued or used.

Plane over River Guayas — AP1

Unwmk.
1929, May 5 Engr. *Perf. 12*
C8 AP1 2c black 20 10
C9 AP1 5c car rose 20 10
C10 AP1 10c dp brn 25 6
C11 AP1 20c dk vio 40 8
C12 AP1 50c dp grn 1.25 35
C13 AP1 1s dk bl 3.50 1.75
C14 AP1 5s org yel 10.00 5.00
C15 AP1 10s org red 50.00 40.00
Nos. C8-C15 (8) 65.80 47.44

Issued to commemorate the establishing of commercial air service in Ecuador. The stamps were available for all forms of postal service and were largely used for franking ordinary letters.

Nos. C13-C15 show numerals in color on white background. Counterfeits of No. C15 exist.

See Nos. C26-C31.

Quito Cathedral AP2

Mount Chimborazo AP3

Wmk. 127
1929, Apr. 1 Litho. *Perf. 14*
C16 AP2 50c red brn 2.50 2.50
C17 AP2 75c green 2.50 2.50
C18 AP2 1s rose 3.50 2.50
C19 AP2 1½s gray bl 3.50 3.00
C20 AP2 2s violet 12.50 10.00
C21 AP2 3s brown 12.50 10.00
C22 AP3 5s lt bl 40.00 30.00
C23 AP3 10s lt red 85.00 65.00
C24 AP3 15s violet 150.00 125.00
C25 AP3 25s ol grn 200.00 150.00
Nos. C16-C25 (10) 512.00 400.50

Plane Type of 1929

1930-44 Unwmk. Engr. *Perf. 12.*
C26 AP1 1s car lake 3.50 50
C27 AP1 1s grn ('44) 60 12
C28 AP1 5s ol grn 5.00 4.00
C29 AP1 5s pur ('44) 1.25 12
C30 AP1 10s black 15.00 5.00
C31 AP1 10s brt ultra ('44) 2.25 12
Nos. C26-C31 (6) 27.60 9.86

Nos. C26-C31 show numerals in color on white background.

Overprinted in Various Colors.

AP4

1930, June 4
C32 AP4 1s car lake (Bk) 30.00 30.00
a. Double overprint (R Br + Bk) 100.00
C33 AP4 5s ol grn (Bl) 30.00 30.00
C34 AP4 10s blk (R Br) 30.00 30.00

Issued to commemorate the flight of Capt. Benjamin Mendez from Bogota to Quito, bearing a crown of flowers for the tomb of Grand Marshal Sucre.

Air Post Official Stamps of 1929-30 Overprinted in Various Colors or Surcharged Similarly in Upper & Lower Case

INAUGURACION
MONUMENTO
A BOLIVAR
QUITO, 24 DE
JULIO DE 1935

1935, July 24
C35 AP1 50c dp grn (Bl) 5.00 5.00
C36 AP1 50c ol brn (R) 5.00 5.00
C37 AP1 1s on 5s ol grn (Bk) 5.00 5.00
a. Double surcharge 100.00
C38 AP1 2s on 10s blk (R) 5.00 5.00

Issued to commemorate the unveiling of a monument to Bolivar at Quito, July 24th, 1935.

Geodesical Mission Issue

Nos. 349-351 Overprinted in Blue or Black **AÉREO**

1936, July 3 *Perf. 12½*
C39 A136 10c dp org (Bl) 25 10
C40 A136 20c vio (Bk) 25 10
C41 A136 50c dk red (Bl) 40 12

Charles M. de la Condamine and Pedro Maldonado AP5

C42 AP5 70c black 70 35

Bicentenary of Geodesical Mission visit to Quito.

Philatelic Exhibition Issue
Type of Regular Issue Overprinted "AEREA"

1936, Oct. 20 *Perf. 13½x14*
C43 A137 2c rose 5.00 5.00
C44 A137 5c brn org 5.00 5.00
C45 A137 10c brown 5.00 5.00
C46 A137 20c ultra 5.00 5.00
C47 A137 50c red vio 5.00 5.00
C48 A137 1s green 5.00 5.00
Nos. C43-C48 (6) 30.00 30.00

Condor and Plane — AP6

Perf. 13½

C49	AP6	70c org brn	90	65
C50	AP6	1s dl vio	90	85

Nos. C43-C50 were issued to commemorate the first Internationl Philatelic Exhibition at Quito.

Condor over "El Altar" — AP7

1937-46 *Perf. 11½, 12*

C51	AP7	10c chestnut	10	5
C52	AP7	20c ol blk	20	6
C53	AP7	40c rose car ('46)	20	6
C54	AP7	70c blk brn	25	15
C55	AP7	1s gray blk	35	25
C56	AP7	2s dk vio	75	35
		Nos. C51-C56 (6)	1.85	92

Issue dates: 40c, Oct. 7, 1946; others, Aug. 19, 1937.

Portrait of Washington, American Eagle and Flags — AP8

1938, Feb. 9 Engr. Litho. *Perf. 12*

Center Multicolored.

C57	AP8	2c brown	20	10
C58	AP8	5c black	20	10
C59	AP8	10c brown	25	10
C60	AP8	20c dk bl	50	10
C61	AP8	50c violet	75	20
C62	AP8	1s black	1.25	25
C63	AP8	2s violet	2.50	75
		Nos. C57-C63 (7)	5.65	1.60

Issued in commemoration of the 150th anniversary of the Constitution of the United States of America.

In 1947, Nos. C61 to C63 were overprinted in dark blue: "Primero la Patria!" and plane. These revolutionary propaganda stamps were later renounced by decree.

AEREO
SEDTA

No. RA35 Surcharged in Red

0,65

1938, Nov. 16 *Perf. 13½*

C64	PT12	65c on 3c ultra	15	10

A national airmail concession was given to the Sociedad Ecuatoriano de Transportes Aereos (SEDTA) in July, 1938. No. RA35 was surcharged for SEDTA postal requirements. SEDTA operated through 1940.

Army Horseman AP9

Woman Runner AP10

Tennis AP11

Boxing AP12

Olympic Fire — AP13

1939, Mar. Engr. *Perf. 12*

C65	AP9	5c lt grn	75	15
C66	AP10	10c salmon	1.00	25
C67	AP11	50c redsh brn	5.00	25
C68	AP12	1s blk brn	6.00	50
C69	AP13	2s rose car	9.00	1.00
		Nos. C65-C69 (5)	21.75	2.15

First Bolivarian Games (1938), La Paz.

Plane over Chimborazo AP14

1939, May 1 *Perf. 13x12½*

C70	AP14	1s yel brn	25	15
C71	AP14	2s rose vio	50	15
C72	AP14	5s black	1.25	15

Golden Gate Bridge and Mountain Peak — AP15

Empire State Building and Mountain Peak — AP16

1939 *Perf. 12½x13*

C73	AP15	2c black	5	5
C74	AP15	5c rose red	5	5
C75	AP15	10c indigo	5	5
C76	AP15	50c rose vio	10	10
C77	AP15	1s chocolate	15	10
C78	AP15	2s yel brn	25	10
C79	AP15	5s emerald	60	20
		Nos. C73-C79 (7)	1.25	65

Golden Gate International Exposition.

1939

C80	AP16	2c brn org	5	5
C81	AP16	5c dk car	5	5
C82	AP16	10c indigo	5	5
C83	AP16	50c sl grn	15	15
C84	AP16	1s dp org	25	12
C85	AP16	2s dk red vio	45	28
C86	AP16	5s dk gray	80	22
		Nos. C80-C86 (7)	1.80	92

New York World's Fair.

Map of the Americas and Airplane AP17

Francisco J. E. Santa Cruz y Espejo AP18

1940, July 9

C87	AP17	10c red org & bl	20	10
C88	AP17	70c sep & bl	25	10
C89	AP17	1s cop brn & bl	40	15
C90	AP17	10s blk & bl	1.50	75

Pan American Union, 50th anniversary.

1941, Dec. 15

C91	AP18	3s rose car	1.25	20
C92	AP18	10s yel org	2.50	30

See note after No. 399.

Old Map of South America Showing Amazon River AP19

Panoramic View of Amazon River AP20

Designs: 70c, Gonzalo de Pineda. 5s, Painting of the expedition.

1942, Jan. 30

C93	AP19	40c blk & buff	40	15
C94	AP19	70c olive	75	10
C95	AP20	2s dk grn	75	25
C96	AP19	5s rose	1.50	60

See note after No. 403.

Remigio Crespo Toral — AP21

1942, Sept. 1 *Perf. 13½*

C97	AP21	10c dl vio	25	10

Gen. Eloy Alfaro AP22

Devil's Nose AP23

Designs: 3s, Military College. 5s, Montecristi, Alfaro's birthplace.

1943, Feb. 16 *Perf. 12*

C98	AP22	70c dk rose & blk	50	20
C99	AP23	1s ol blk & red brn	75	40
C100	AP23	3s ol gray & grn	1.00	75
C101	AP23	5s sl & sal	1.75	90

Issued to commemorate the centenary of the birth of President Alfaro (1842-1903).

Nos. C61-C63 Overprinted in Red Brown

BIENVENIDO — WALLACE

Abril 15 — 1943

1943, Apr. 15 *Perf. 11½*

Center Multicolored.

C102	AP8	50c violet	1.25	50
C103	AP8	1s black	1.50	75
C104	AP8	2s violet	2.00	1.00

Issued to commemorate the visit of Vice-President Henry A. Wallace of the United States.

Nos. 374-376 Overprinted "AEREO LOOR A BOLIVIA JUNIO 11-1943" (like Nos. C111-C113)

1943, June 11 *Perf. 13*

C105	A146	50c dp red vio	20	20
C106	A147	1s cop red	40	30
C107	A148	2s dk grn	60	35

Issued to commemorate the visit of President Eurique Penaranda of Bolivia.

Vertical overprints on Nos. C105-C106.

Nos. 374-376 Overprinted "AEREO LOOR A PARAGUAY JULIO 5-1943" (like Nos. C111-C113)

1943, July 5

C108	A146	50c dp red vio	20	20
a.		Double ovpt.	40.00	
C109	A147	1s cop red	40	30
C110	A148	2s dk grn	60	35

Issued to commemorate the visit of President Higinio Morinigo of Paraguay.

Vertical overprints on Nos. C108-C109.

Nos. 374-376 Overprinted in Black

A E R E O

LOOR A VENEZUELA

JULIO 23 — 1943

1943, July 23

C111	A146	50c dp red vio	20	20
C112	A147	1s cop red	40	30
C113	A148	2s dk grn	60	35

Issued to commemorate the visit of President Isaias Medina Angarita of Venezuela.

Vertical overprint on Nos. C111-C112.

See Nos. C105-C110.

President Arroyo del Rio Addressing U.S. Congress — AP26

1943, Oct. 9 *Perf. 12*

C114	AP26	50c dk brn	50	40
C115	AP26	70c brt rose	60	60
C116	AP26	3s dk bl	75	60
C117	AP26	5s dk grn	1.50	1.00
C118	AP26	10s ol blk	6.00	5.00
		Nos. C114-C118 (5)	9.35	7.60

Issued to commemorate the good will tour of President Arroyo del Rio in 1942.

1944, Feb. 7

C119	AP26	50c dp red lil	50	40
C120	AP26	70c red brn	75	40
C121	AP26	3s turq grn	75	40
C122	AP26	5s brt ultra	1.25	1.00
C123	AP26	10s scarlet	1.75	1.50
		Nos. C119-C123 (5)	5.00	3.70

Church of San Francisco, Quito — AP27

1944, Feb. 13

C124	AP27	70c turq grn	60	40
C125	AP27	1s olive	60	40
C126	AP27	3s red org	1.00	60
C127	AP27	5s car rose	1.25	75

See note after No. 433.

Government Palace, Quito — AP28

1944 Engr. *Perf. 11*

C128	AP28	3s orange	50	10

C129	AP28	5s dk brn	75	10
C130	AP28	10s dk red	1.50	20

See also No. C221.

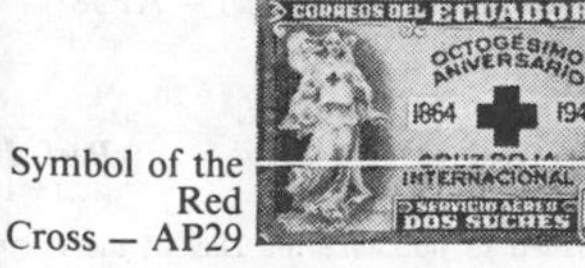
Symbol of the Red Cross — AP29

1945, Apr. 25 Unwmk. *Perf. 12*

Cross in Rose.

C131	AP29	2s dp bl	75	75
C132	AP29	3s green	1.25	75
C133	AP29	5s dk vio	2.00	1.25
C134	AP29	10s car rose	5.00	3.75

Issued to commemorate the 80th anniversary of the founding of the International Red Cross.

No. RA55 Surcharged in Black

AEREO 40 Ctvs.

1945, June 8

C135	PT21	40c on 5c bl	20	10
a.		Double surcharge	10.00	

Counterfeits exist.

Nos. C128 to C130 Overprinted in Green

V SETIEMBRE 5 1945

1945, Sept. 6 *Perf. 11*

C136	AP28	3s orange	60	60
a.		Inverted ovpt.	30.00	
b.		Double ovpt.	30.00	
C137	AP28	5s dk brn	75	75
C138	AP28	10s dk red	2.50	2.50

Nos. C61-C63 Overprinted in Dark Blue and Gold

LOOR A CHILE OCTUBRE 2 1945

1945, Oct. 2 *Perf. 12*

Center Multicolored.

C139	AP8	50c violet	60	60
C140	AP8	1s black	65	65
C141	AP8	2s violet	65	65

Visit of Pres. Juan Antonio Rios of Chile.

Monument to Liberty AP30

Map of Pan-American Highway and Arms of Cuenca AP31

1945, Nov. 14 Engr.

C142	AP30	30c blue	20	10
C143	AP30	40c rose car	25	10
C144	AP30	1s dl vio	60	25
C145	AP30	3s gray blk	1.00	75
C146	AP30	5s pur brn	1.50	1.00
		Nos. C142-C146 (5)	3.55	2.20

Issued to commemorate the 150th anniversary of the birth of General Antonio Josede Sucre.

1946, Apr. 22 Unwmk.

C147	AP31	1s car rose	40	30
C148	AP31	2s violet	50	40
C149	AP31	3s turq grn	75	50
C150	AP31	5s red org	1.00	60
C151	AP31	10s dk bl	1.50	50
		Nos. C147-C151 (5)	4.15	2.30

Revolution Types of Regular Issue

1946, Aug. 9 *Perf. 12½*

C152	A177	40c dp cl	10	10
C153	A178	1s sepia	15	10
C154	A179	2s indigo	40	20
C155	A180	3s ol grn	60	40

Issued to commemorate the 2nd anniversary of the Revolution of May 28, 1944.

National Union of Periodicals, Initials and Quill Pen — AP36

1946, Sept. 16

C156	AP36	50c dl pur	40	25
C157	AP36	70c dk grn	50	30
C158	AP36	3s red	75	40
C159	AP36	5s indigo	1.00	50
C160	AP36	10s chocolate	3.00	75
		Nos. C156-C160 (5)	5.65	2.20

Issued to publicize a campaign for adult education.

The Blessed Mariana Teaching Children AP37

"Lily of Quito" AP38

1946, Nov. 28 Unwmk.

C161	AP37	40c chocolate	30	10
C162	AP37	60c dp bl	40	35
C163	AP38	3s org yel	85	75
C164	AP38	5s green	1.50	1.00

Issued to commemorate the 30th anniversary of the death of the Blessed Mariana de Jesus Paredes y Flores.

Juan de Velasco AP39

Riobamba Irrigation Canal AP40

1947, Nov. 27 *Perf. 12*

C165	AP39	60c dk grn	10	5
C166	AP39	70c purple	15	5
C167	AP39	1s blk brn	15	5
C168	AP39	1.10s car rose	15	10
C169	AP40	1.30s dp bl	20	15
C170	AP40	1.90s ol bis	35	20
C171	AP40	2s ol grn	35	10
		Nos. C165-C171 (7)	1.45	70

Andrés Bello AP41

Christopher Columbus AP42

1948, Apr. 21 *Perf. 13*

C172	AP41	60c magenta	20	10
C173	AP41	1.30s dk bl grn	40	20
C174	AP41	1.90s dk rose car	30	20

No. C166 Overprinted in Black

CONFERENCIA ECONOMICA GRANCOLOMBIANA MAYO 24 DE 1.948

1948, May 24 *Perf. 12*

C175	AP39	70c purple	50	30

1948, May 26 *Perf. 14*

C176	AP42	50c ol grn	15	15
C177	AP42	70c rose car	20	20
C178	AP42	3c ultra	50	40
C179	AP42	5s brown	1.00	35
C180	AP42	10s dp vio	1.75	40
		Nos. C176-C180 (5)	3.60	1.50

See note after No. 495.

No. C169 Overprinted in Carmine

Feria Nacional 1948 ECUADOR de hoy y del MAÑANA

1948, Aug. 26 Unwmk. *Perf. 12*

C181	AP40	1.30s dp bl	50	35

Issued to publicize the National Fair of Today and Tomorrow, 1948.

Elia Liut and Telegrafo I — AP43

Teacher and Pupils — AP44

1948, Sept. 10 *Perf. 12½*

C182	AP43	60c rose red	30	25
C183	AP43	1s green	30	25
C184	AP43	1.30s dp cl	30	30
C185	AP43	1.90s dp vio	35	30
C186	AP43	2s dk brn	50	40
C187	AP43	5s blue	1.00	60
		Nos. C182-C187 (6)	2.75	2.10

Issued to commemorate the 25th anniversary (in 1945) of the first postal flight in Ecuador.

1948, Oct. 12 *Perf. 14*

C188	AP44	50c violet	25	20
C189	AP44	70c dp bl	25	20
C190	AP44	3s dk grn	40	30
C191	AP44	5s red	50	25
C192	AP44	10s brown	1.25	50
		Nos. C188-C192 (5)	2.65	1.45

Campaign for adult education.

Franklin D. Roosevelt and Two of "Four Freedoms"
AP45 AP46

1948, Oct. 24 *Perf. 12½*

C193	AP45	60c emer & org brn	15	15
C194	AP45	1s car rose & sl	15	15
C195	AP46	1.50s grn & red brn	25	20
C196	AP46	2s red & blk	60	25
C197	AP46	5s ultra & blk	1.00	25
		Nos. C193-C197 (5)	2.15	1.00

Issued in tribute to Franklin D. Roosevelt, 1882-1945.

Maldonado Types of Regular Issue

1948, Nov. 17

C198	A196	60c dp org & rose car	25	10
C199	A197	90c red & gray blk	25	10
C200	A196	1.30s pur & dp org	40	20
C201	A197	2s dp bl & dl grn	40	20

See note after No. 519.

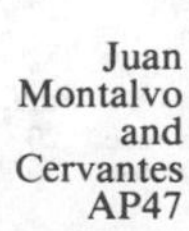

Juan Montalvo and Cervantes AP47

Don Quixote — AP48

1949, May 2 Engr. *Perf. 12½x12*

C202	AP47	1.30s ol brn & ultra	2.00	1.50
C203	AP48	1.90s grn & rose car	50	30
C204	AP47	3s vio & org brn	50	30
C205	AP48	5s red & gray blk	1.25	15
C206	AP47	10s red lil & aqua	2.00	15
		Nos. C202-C206 (5)	6.25	2.40

Issued to commemorate the 400th anniversary of the birth of Miguel de Cervantes Saavedra, novelist, playwright and poet, and the 60th anniversary of the death of Juan Montalvo (1832-1889), Ecuadorean writer.

No. C168 Surcharged in Blue

II CONGRESO Junio 1949 Eucarístico Ncl. 50 —— 50

1949, June 15 *Perf. 12*

C207	AP39	50c on 1.10s car rose	15	15
C208	AP39	60c on 1.10s car rose	20	20
C209	AP39	90c on 1.10s car rose	25	25

Issued to commemorate the Second Eucharistic Congress, Quito, June 1949.

No. C128 Surcharged in Black

75 Aniversario U. P. U. 60 centavos 60

1949, Oct. 11 *Perf. 11*
C210 AP28 60c on 3s org 50 40
a. Double surcharge 20.00
C211 AP28 90c on 3s org 40 25
C212 AP28 1s on 3s org 50 35
C213 AP28 2s on 3s org 1.25 50

"SUCRE(S)" in capitals on Nos. C212-C213.
Issued to commemorate the 75th anniversary of the formation of the Universal Postal Union.

AP49

Black Surcharge.

1950 **Unwmk.** *Perf. 12*
C214 AP49 60c on 50c gray 15 5
a. Double surcharge 20.00

No. C170 Surcharged with New Value in Black.

C215 AP40 90c on 1.90s ol bis 40 15

Nos. C168, C128-C129 and Type of 1944 Surcharged or Overprinted in Black or Carmine.

ALFABETIZACION

1950, Feb. 10 *Perf. 12*
C216 AP39 50c on 1.10s car rose 20 15
C217 AP39 70c on 1.10s car rose 25 20

Perf. 11

C218 AP28 3s orange 50 40
C219 AP28 5s dk brn (C) 90 50
C220 AP28 10s vio (C) 1.50 35
Nos. C216-C220 (5) 3.35 1.60

Issued to publicize adult education.

Govt. Palace Type of 1944

1950, May 15 **Engr.** *Perf. 11*
C221 AP28 10s violet 1.00 10

No. C169 Surcharged with New Value in Black.

1950 *Perf. 12*
C222 AP40 90c on 1.30s dp bl 20 10

See No. C235.

Nos. C128-C129 Overprinted in Black

20.000 Cruce
Línea Ecuatorial
PANAGRA
26-Julio-1951

1951, July 28 **Unwmk.** *Perf. 11*
C223 AP28 3s orange 60 60
C224 AP28 5s dk brn 1.00 75

Issued to commemorate the 20,000th crossing of the equator by Pan American-Grace Airways planes.

Nos. C202-C203 Surcharged in Black

CAMPANA
●
Alfabetización
60 Ctvs. 60

CAMPAÑA
ALFABETIZACION
1,00 Sucre 1,00

1951 **Unwmk.** *Perf. 12½x12*
C225 AP47 60c on 1.30s ol brn & ultra 25 10
C226 AP48 1s on 1.90s grn & rose car 25 10
a. Inverted surcharge 17.50

Issued to publicize adult education.

St. Mariana de Jesus — AP50

1952, Feb. 15 **Engr.**
C227 AP50 60c plum & aqua 40 20
C228 AP50 90c dk grn & lt ultra 40 15
C229 AP50 1s car & dk grn 50 20
C230 AP50 2s ind & rose lil 50 15

Issued to publicize the canonization of Mariana de Jesus Paredes y Flores.

Presidents Galo Plaza and Harry Truman AP51

Design: 5s, Pres. Plaza addressing U. S. Congress.

1952, Mar. 26 *Perf. 12*
C231 AP51 3s lil & bl grn 50 40
C232 AP51 5s red brn & ol gray 1.00 75
a. Souvenir sheet 3.00 3.00

No. C232a measures 126 x 61 mm., and contains one each of Nos. C231 and C232, with marginal inscriptions in lilac and red brown.
Issued to commemorate the 1951 visit of Pres. Galo Plaza y Lasso to the United States.

Consular Service Stamps Surcharged "AEREO" and New Value in Black.

1952 **Unwmk.** *Perf. 12*
C233 R2 60c on 1s grn 10 5
C234 R2 1s on 1s grn 15 5

Type R2 illustrated above No. 545.

No. C169 Surcharged with New Value in Carmine.

C235 AP40 90c on 1.30s dp bl 10 5

See No. C222.

Pres. José M. Urvina and Allegory of Freedom AP52

Torch of Knowledge AP53

Hyphen-hole Perf. 7x6½

1952, Nov. 18 **Litho.**
C236 AP52 60c rose red & bl 1.00 30
C237 AP52 90c lil & red 1.00 40
C238 AP52 1s org & grn 1.00 20
C239 AP52 2s red brn & bl 1.00 25

Centenary of abolition of slavery in Ecuador. Counterfeits exist.

Unwmk.

1953, Apr. 13 **Engr.** *Perf. 12*

Design: 2s, Aged couple studying alphabet.

C240 AP53 1s dk bl 50 10
C241 AP53 2s red org 75 10

1952 adult education campaign.

Globe Showing Part of Western Hemisphere AP54

1953, June 5 *Perf. 12½x12*
C242 AP54 60c org yel 30 30
C243 AP54 90c dk bl 35 30
C244 AP54 3s carmine 75 50

Issued to publicize the crossing of the equator by the Pan-American highway.

Consular Service Stamps Surcharged in Black

AEREO
1
SUCRE
a
245a

AEREO
1 SUCRE
b
245b

1953-54 *Perf. 12.*
C245 R1 (a) 60c on 2s brn 20 10
C246 R2 (a) 60c on 5s sep ('54) 20 10
C247 R2 (a) 70c on 5s sep ('54) 25 15
C248 R2 (a) 90c on 50c car rose ('54) 35 10
C249 R1 (b) 1s on 2s brn 35 15
C250 R1 (a) 1s on 2s brn ('54) 35 10
C251 R1 (a) 2s on 2s brn ('54) 40 20
C252 R1 (a) 3s on 5s vio ('54) 75 20
Nos. C245-C252 (8) 2.85 1.10

The surcharge reads upward on Nos. C250-C252.

Carlos Maria Cardinal de la Torre — AP55

Queen Isabella I — AP56

1954, Jan. 13 **Photo.** *Perf. 8½.*
Center in Black.
C253 AP55 60c rose lil 20 10
C254 AP55 90c green 25 10
C255 AP55 3s orange 35 25

Issued to commemorate the first anniversary of the elevation of Archbishop de la Torre to Cardinal.

1954, Apr. 22
C256 AP56 60c dk grn & grn 10 10
C257 AP56 90c lil rose 15 15
C258 AP56 1s blk & pale lil 15 15
C259 AP56 2s blk brn & pale bl 25 20
C260 AP56 5s blk brn & buff 60 40
Nos. C256-C260 (5) 1.25 1.00

See note after No. 585.

Post Office, Guayaquil AP57

1954, May 19 **Engr.** *Perf. 12½x12.*
Black Surcharge
C261 AP57 80c on 20c red 20 15
C262 AP57 1s on 20c red 25 15

Issued to commemorate the 25th anniversary of Pan American-Grace Airways' operation in Ecuador.

Plane, Gateway and Wheel — AP58

Unwmk.

1954, Aug. 2 **Litho.** *Perf. 11*
C263 AP58 80c blue 15 10

Issued to publicize the Day of the Postal Employee.

San Pablo Lagoon — AP59

1954, Sept. 24 **Photo.**
C264 AP59 60c orange 10 5
C265 AP59 70c rose pink 10 5
C266 AP59 90c dp grn 15 5
C267 AP59 1s dk gray grn 20 5
C268 AP59 2s blue 30 10
C269 AP59 3s yel brn 40 15
Nos. C264-C269 (6) 1.25 45

Glorification of Abdon Calderon Garaicoa AP60

Capt. Calderon — AP61

1954, Oct. 1
C270 AP60 80c rose pink 25 15
C271 AP61 90c blue 25 15

Issued to commemorate the 150th anniversary of the birth of Capt. Abdon Calderon Garaicoa.

El Cebollar College — AP62

Brother Miguel Instructing Boys — AP63

Designs: 90c, Francisco Febres Cordero (Brother Miguel). 2.50s, Tomb of Brother Miguel. 3s, Monument to Brother Miguel.

1954, Dec. 3 **Unwmk.** *Perf. 11*
C272 AP62 70c dk grn 10 10
C273 AP63 80c dk brn 15 10
C274 AP63 90c dk gray bl 15 10
C275 AP63 2.50s indigo 25 20
C276 AP62 3s lil rose 50 35
Nos. C272-C276 (5) 1.15 85

Issued to commemorate the centenary of the birth of Francisco Febres Cordero (Brother Miguel).

No. C221 Surcharged in Various Colors

E. M. P. 1955

$ 1,00

1955, May 25

C277	AP28	1s on 10s vio (Bk)	25	10
C278	AP28	1.70s on 10s vio (C)	40	15
C279	AP28	4.20s on 10s vio (Br)	75	50

Denomination in larger type on No. C279.

Issued to publicize the National Exhibition of Daily Periodicals.

"La Rotonda," Guayaquil, and Rotary Emblem AP64

Design: 90c, Eugenio Espejo hospital, Quito, and Rotary emblem.

1955, July 9 Engr. *Perf. 12½*

C280	AP64	80c dk brn	40	30
C281	AP64	90c dk grn	40	35

Issued to commemorate the 50th anniversary of the founding of Rotary International.

José Abel Castillo AP65

Design: 2s, 5s, Jose Abel Castillo and Map of Ecuador.

1955, Oct. 19 *Perf. 11x11½*

C282	AP65	60c chocolate	40	15
C283	AP65	90c lt ol grn	40	15
C284	AP65	1s lilac	40	15
C285	AP65	2s vermilion	40	20
C286	AP65	5s ultra	75	50
		Nos. C282-C286 (5)	2.35	1.15

See note after No. 595.

No. C29 Surcharged in Black

1

X SUCRE X

1955, Oct. 24 *Perf. 12*

C287	AP1	1s on 5s pur	25	20

A similar surcharge on No. C29, set in two lines with letters 5mm. high and no X's or black-out line of squares, was privately applied.

San Pablo, Imbabura — AP66

Designs: 50s, Rumichaca Caves. 1.30s, Virgin of Quito. 1.50s, Cotopaxi Volcano. 1.70s, Tungurahua Volcano, Tungurahua. 1.90s, Guanacos. 2.40s, Mat market. 2.50s, Ruins at Incapirca. 4.20s, El Carmen, Cuenca, Azuay. 4.80s, Santo Domingo Church.

1956, Jan. 2 Photo. *Perf. 13*

C288	AP66	50c sl bl	30	10
C289	AP66	1s ultra	30	10
C290	AP66	1.30s crimson	35	15
C291	AP66	1.50s dp grn	25	10
C292	AP66	1.70s yel brn	20	10
C293	AP66	1.90s olive	30	25
C294	AP66	2.40s red org	35	25
C295	AP66	2.50s violet	35	25
C296	AP66	4.20s black	40	30
C297	AP66	4.80s yel org	60	50
		Nos. C288-C297 (10)	3.40	2.10

See also Nos. C310-C311.

Honorato Vazquez AP67

Title Page of First Book AP68

1956, May 28 Engr.

Various Portraits.

C298	AP67	1s yel grn	20	15
C299	AP67	1.50s red	25	20
C300	AP67	1.70s brt bl	20	20
C301	AP67	1.90s sl bl	25	20

Birth centenary (in 1955) of Honorato Vazquez, statesman.

1956, Aug. 27 Unwmk. *Perf. 13½*

C302	AP68	1s black	15	10
C303	AP68	1.70s sl bl	20	15
C304	AP68	2s blk brn	30	20
C305	AP68	3s redsh brn	35	30

Bicentenary of printing in Ecuador.

Hands Reaching for U.N. Emblem AP69

1956, Oct. 24 *Perf. 14*

C307	AP69	1.70s red org	50	20

Issued to commemorate the tenth anniversary of the United Nations (in 1955).

See also No. C319.

Coat of Arms and Basketball Player — AP70

Designs: 1.70s, Map of South America with flags and girl basketball players.

1956, Dec. 28 Photo. *Perf. 14½x14*

C308	AP70	1s red lil	25	10
C309	AP70	1.70s dp grn	40	20

Issued to commemorate the 6th South American Women's Basketball Championship, August 1956.

Scenic Type of 1956.

1957, Jan. 2 *Perf. 13*

C310	AP66	50c bl grn	25	10
C311	AP66	1s orange	30	15

Type of Regular Issue, 1957

Designs: 50c, Map of Cuenca, 16th century. 80c, Cathedral of Cuenca. 1s, Modern City Hall.

Unwmk.

1957, Apr. 7 Photo. *Perf. 12*

C312	A219	50c brn, *cr*	10	5
a.		Souvenir sheet of 4	75	75
C313	A219	80c red, *bluish*	15	15
C314	A219	1s pur, *yel*	20	10
a.		Souvenir sheet of 3	1.25	1.25

Issued to commemorate the fourth centenary of the founding of Cuenca.

No. C312a contains four imperf. 50c stamps similar to No. 613, but inscribed "AEREO" and printed in green. The sheet measures 140x120mm. and is printed on white ungummed paper. It is inscribed "IV Reunion de Consulta de la Comision del Instituto Panamericano de Geografia e Historia, Cuenca 4 al 12 de Abril de 1957."

No. C314a contains three imperf. stamps in designs similar to Nos. C312-C314, but with colors changed to orange (50c), brown (80c), violet (1s). The sheet measures 140x120mm. and is printed on white ungummed paper. It is inscribed "III Congreso de Ingenieros y Arquitectos del Ecuador, Cuenca, 6 al 9 de Abril de 1957."

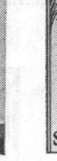

Gabriela Mistral AP71

Arms of Espejo, Carchi AP72

Unwmk.

1957, Sept. 18 Litho. *Perf. 14*

C315	AP71	2s lt bl, blk & red	30	20

Issued to honor Gabriela Mistral (1889-1957), Chilean poet and educator.

See also Nos. C406-C407.

Province of Carchi.

1957, Nov. 16 *Perf. 14½x13½*

Arms of Cantons: 2s, Montufar. 4.20s, Tulcan.

Coat of Arms Multicolored

C316	AP72	1s carmine	20	10
C317	AP72	2s black	25	15
C318	AP72	4.20s ultra	60	40

See Nos. C334-C337, C355-C364, C392-C395.

Redrawn UN Type of 1956.

1957, Dec. 10 Engr. *Perf. 14*

C319	AP69	2s grnsh bl	50	35

Issued to honor the United Nations. Dates, as on No. C307, are omitted; inscribed: "Homenaje a las Naciones Unidas."

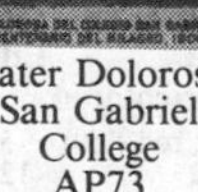

Mater Dolorosa, San Gabriel College AP73

Rafael Maria Arizaga AP74

Design: Nos. C321 & 1s, Door of San Gabriel College, Quito.

1958, Apr. 27 Engr. *Perf. 14*

C320	AP73	30c rose cl, *dp rose*	20	10
C321	AP73	30c rose cl, *dp rose*	20	10
C322	AP73	1s dk bl, *lt bl*	20	10
C323	AP73	1.70s dk bl, *lt bl*	25	20

Issued to commemorate the 50th anniversary of the miracle of San Gabriel College, Quito.

Issued in 2 sheets of 50. One sheet contains alternate copies of Nos. C320-C321, the other Nos. C322-C323.

1958, July 21 Litho.

C324	AP74	1s multi	15	10

Issued to commemorate the centenary of the birth of Rafael Maria Arizaga (1858-1933), writer.

See also Nos. C343, C350, C412.

Daule River Bridge AP75

1958, July 25 Engr. *Perf. 13½x14*

C325	AP75	1.30s green	25	15

Issued to commemorate the opening of the River Daule bridge in Guayas province.

See also Nos. C367-C369.

Basketball Player AP76

Symbolical of the Eucharist AP77

1958, Sept. 1 Photo. *Perf. 14x13½*

C326	AP76	1.30s dk grn & lt brn	50	40

South American basketball championships.

1958, Sept. 25 Litho. Unwmk.

Design: 60c, Cathedral of Guayaquil.

C327	AP77	10c vio & buff	10	10
C328	AP77	60c org & vio brn	10	10
C329	AP77	1s brn & lt bl	20	10

Souvenir Sheet

Symbolical of the Eucharist — AP78

***Perf.* 13½x14**

C330	AP78	Sheet of four	75	75
a.		40c dk bl (any position)	15	15

Nos. C327-C330 issued to commemorate the 3rd National Eucharistic Congress.

No. C330 measures 115 x 88½mm.

Stamps of 1865 and 1920 — AP79

Designs: 2s, Stamps of 1920 and 1948. 4.20s, Municipal museum and library.

Perf. 11½

1958, Oct. 8 Unwmk. Photo.

Granite Paper

C331	AP79	1.30s grn & brn red	25	20
C332	AP79	2s bl & vio	50	30
C333	AP79	4.20s dk brn	90	60

Issued to publicize the National Philatelic Exposition (EXFIGUA), Guayaquil, Oct. 4-14.

Coat of Arms Type of 1957.

Province of Imbabura.

Arms of Cantons: 50c, Cotacachi. 60c, Antonio Ante. 80c, Otalvo. 1.10s, Ibarra.

1958, Nov. 9 Litho. *Perf. 14½x13½*
Coats of Arms Multicolored.

C334 AP72	50c blk & red	10	10
C335 AP72	60c blk, bl & red	10	10
C336 AP72	80c blk & yel	15	10
C337 AP72	1.10s blk & red	20	10

Charles V — AP80

Paul Rivet — AP81

Perf. 14x13½
Unwmk.
1958, Dec. 12 Engr. Photo.

C338 AP80	2s brn red & dk brn	30	15
C339 AP80	4.20s dk gray & red brn	60	50

Issued to commemorate the 400th anniversary of the death of Charles V, Holy Roman Emperor.

1958, Dec. 29 Photo. *Perf. 11½*
Granite Paper.

C340 AP81 1s brown 15 10

Issued in honor of Paul Rivet (1876-1958), French anthropologist.

1959, May 6

Portrait: 2s, Alexander von Humboldt.

C341 AP81 2s slate 20 10

Issued to commemorate the centenary of the death of Alexander von Humboldt, German naturalist and geographer.

Front Page of "El Telegrafo" AP82

1959, Feb. Litho. *Perf. 13½*

C342 AP82 1.30s bl grn & blk 20 15

Issued to commemorate the 75th anniversary of Ecuador's oldest newspaper.

Portrait Type of 1958

Portrait: José Luis Tamayo.

1959, June 26 Unwmk. *Perf. 14*
Portrait Multicolored.

C343 AP74 1.30s lt grn, bl & sal 20 15

Issued to commemorate the centenary of the birth of José Luis Tamayo (1858-1947), lawyer.

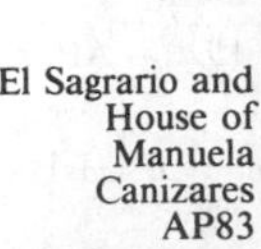

El Sagrario and House of Manuela Canizares AP83

Condor — AP84

Designs: 80c, Hall at San Agustin. 1s, First words of the constitutional act. 2s, Entrance to Cuartel Real. 4.20s, Allegory of Liberty.

Unwmk.
1959, Aug. 28 Photo. *Perf. 14*

C344 AP83	20c ultra & lt brn	10	5
C345 AP83	80c brt bl & dp org	10	5
C346 AP83	1s dk red & dk ol	15	10
C347 AP84	1.30s brt bl & org	25	10
C348 AP84	2s ultra & org brn	25	15
C349 AP84	4.20s scar & brt bl	60	40
	Nos. C344-C349 (6)	1.45	85

Sesquicentennial of the revolution.

Portrait Type of 1958

Portrait: 1s, Alfredo Baquerizo Moreno.

1959, Sept. 26 Litho. *Perf. 14*

C350 AP74 1s gray, red & sal 15 10

Issued to commemorate the centenary of the birth of Alfredo Baquerizo Moreno (1859-1951), statesman.

Pope Pius XII — AP85

1959, Oct. 9 Unwmk. *Perf. 14½*

C351 AP85 1.30s multi 30 25

Issued in memory of Pope Plus XII.

Flags of Argentina, Bolivia, Brazil, Guatemala, Haiti, Mexico and Peru — AP86

Flags of: 80c, Chile, Costa Rica, Cuba, Dominican Republic, Panama, Paraguay, United States. 1.30s, Colombia, Ecuador, Honduras, Nicaragua, Salvador, Uruguay, Venezuela.

1959, Oct. 12 *Perf. 13½.*

C352 AP86	50c multi	15	10
C353 AP86	80c yel, red & bl	20	15
C354 AP86	1.30s multi	25	20

Organization of American States.

Coat of Arms Type of 1957 Province of Pichincha.

Arms of Cantons: 10c, Rumiñahui. 40c, Pedro Moncayo. 1s, Mejia. 1.30s, Cayambe. 4.20s, Quito.

Perf. 14½x13½
1959-60 Unwmk. Litho.
Coat of Arms Multicolored.

C355 AP72	10c blk & dk red ('60)	5	5
C356 AP72	40c blk & yel	12	6
C357 AP72	1s blk & brn ('60)	12	12
C358 AP72	1.30s blk & grn ('60)	22	12
C359 AP72	4.20s blk & org	45	35
	Nos. C355-C359 (5)	96	70

Province of Cotopaxi.

Arms of Cantons: 40c, Pangua. 60c, Pujili. 70c, Saquisili. 1s, Salcedo. 1.30s, Latacunga.

1960
Coat of Arms Multicolored

C360 AP72	40c blk & car	6	6
C361 AP72	60c blk & bl	12	6
C362 AP72	70c blk & turq	25	12
C363 AP72	1s blk & red org	25	12
C364 AP72	1.30s blk & org	30	18
	Nos. C360-C364 (5)	98	54

The indexes in each volume of the Scott Catalogue contain many listings which help to identify stamps.

Flags of American Nations — AP87

1960, Feb. 23 *Perf. 13x12½*

C365 AP87	1.30s multi	15	10
C366 AP87	2s multi	25	20

Issued to commemorate the 11th Inter-American Conference, Feb. 1960.

Bridge Type of 1958.

Bridges: No. C367, Juntas. No. C368, Saracay. 2s, Railroad bridge, Ambato.

1960 Litho. *Perf. 13½*

C367 AP75 1.30s chocolate 18 12

Photo. *Perf. 12½*

C368 AP75	1.30s emerald	18	12
C369 AP75	2s brown	28	18

Building of three new bridges.

Bahia-Chone Road — AP88

Pres. Camilo Ponce Enriquez AP89

Designs: 4.20s, Public Works Building, Cuenca. 5s, El Coca airport. 10s, New Harbor, Guayaquil.

1960, Aug. Litho. *Perf. 14*

C370 AP88	1.30s blk & dl yel	20	10
C371 AP88	4.20s rose car & lt grn	40	40
C372 AP88	5s dk brn & yel	60	50
C373 AP88	10s dk bl & bl	1.25	1.00

Perf. 11x11½

C374 AP89	2s org brn & blk	2.00	40
	Nos. C370-C374 (5)	4.45	2.40

Nos. C370-C374 issued to publicize the achievements of Pres. Camilo Ponce Enriquez (1956-1960).

Issue dates: Nos. C370-C373, Aug. 24. No. C374, Aug. 31.

Red Cross Building, Quito and Henri Dunant AP90

1960, Oct. 5 Unwmk. *Perf. 13x14*

C375 AP90 2s rose vio & car 45 22

Centenary (in 1959) of Red Cross idea.

El Belen Church, Quito — AP91

1961, Jan. 14 *Perf. 12½*

C376 AP91 3s multi 55 28

Issued to commemorate Ecuador's participation in the 1960 Barcelona Philatelic Congress.

Map of Ecuador and Amazon River System AP92

1961, Feb. 27 Litho. *Perf. 10½*

C377 AP92	80c sal, cl & grn	25	18
C378 AP92	1.30s gray, sl & grn	30	25
C379 AP92	2s beige, red & grn	35	30

Issued to commemorate Amazon Week, and the 132nd anniversary of the Battle of Tarqui against Peru.

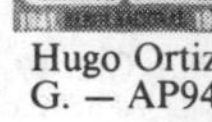

Juan Montalvo, Juan Leon Mera, Juan Benigno Vela — AP93

Hugo Ortiz G. — AP94

1961, Apr. 13 Unwmk. *Perf. 13*

C380 AP93 1.30s sal & blk 30 10

Centenary of Tungurahua province.

1961, May 25 *Perf. 14x14½*

Design: No. C382, Ortiz monument.

C381 AP94	1.30s grnsh bl, blk & yel	22	12
C382 AP94	1.30s grnsh bl, pur, ol & brn	22	12

Issued in memory of Lieutenant Hugo Ortiz G., killed in battle Aug. 2, 1941.

Condor and Airplane Stamp of 1936 AP95

Designs: 1.30s, Map of South America and stamp of 1865. 2s, Bolivar monument stamp of 1930.

Perf. 10½
1961, May 25 Litho. Unwmk.
Size: 41x28mm.

C383 AP95 80c org & vio 25 15

Size: 41x34mm.

C384 AP95 1.30s bl, yel, ol & car 40 20

Size: 40½x37mm.

C385 AP95 2s car rose & blk 50 30

Issued to publicize the Third National Philatelic Exhibition, Quito, May 25-June 3, 1961.

Arms of Los Rios and Egret — AP96

1961, May 27 ***Perf. 14½x13½***
Coat of Arms Multicolored

C386 AP96 2s bl & blk 40 25

Centenary (in 1960) of Los Rios province.

Gabriel Garcia Moreno AP97

Remigio Crespo Toral AP98

1961, Sept. 24 **Unwmk.** ***Perf. 12***

C387 AP97 1s bl, brn & buff 20 10

Issued to commemorate the centenary of the restoration of national integrity.

1961, Nov. 3 **Unwmk.** ***Perf. 14***

C388 AP98 50c multi 10 10

Issued to commemorate the centenary of the birth of Remigio Crespo Toral, poet laureate of Ecuador.

Galapagos Islands Nos. LC1-LC3 Overprinted in Black or Red: "Estacion de Biologia Maritima de Galapagos" and "UNESCO 1961" (Similarly to Nos. 684-686).

1961, Oct. 31 **Photo.** ***Perf. 12***

C389 A1 1s dp bl 35 25
 a. "de Galapagos" on top line 1.25 1.25
C390 A1 1.80s rose vio 45 28
 a. UNESCO emblem omitted 75 75
C391 A1 4.20s blk (R) 70 60

Issued to commemorate the establishment of maritime biological stations on Galapagos Islands by UNESCO.

Coat of Arms Type of 1957.
Province of Tungurahua.

Arms of Cantons: 50c, Pillaro. 1s, Pelileo. 1.30s, Banos. 2s, Ambato.

Perf. 14½x13½

1962, Mar. 30 **Litho.** **Unwmk.**
Coats of Arms Multicolored

C392 AP72 50c black 12 6
C393 AP72 1s black 18 12
C394 AP72 1.30s black 22 12
C395 AP72 2s black 35 25

Pres. Arosemena and Prince Philip, Arms of Ecuador and Great Britain and Equator Monument AP99

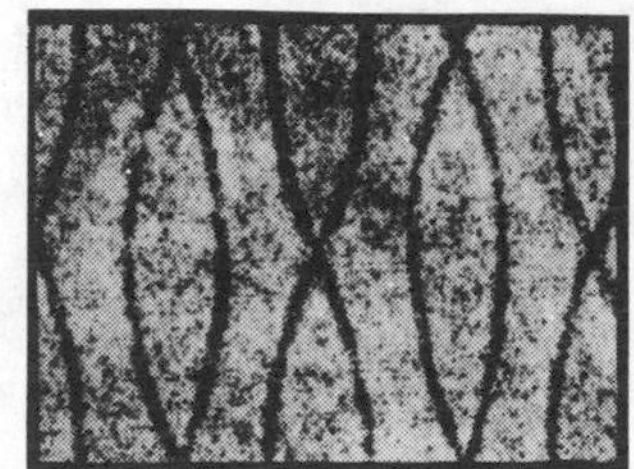
Wmk. 340- Alternating Interlaced Wavy Lines

Perf. 14x13½

1962, Feb. 17 **Wmk. 340**

C396 AP99 1.30s bl, sep, red & yel 22 18
C397 AP99 2s multi 28 22

Issued to commemorate the visit of Prince Philip, Duke of Edinburgh, to Ecuador, Feb. 17-20, 1962.

Mountain Farming — AP100

Perf. 12½

1963, Mar. 21 **Unwmk.** **Litho.**

C398 AP100 30c emer, yel & blk 15 15
C399 AP100 3s dl red, grn & org 50 30
C400 AP100 4.20s bl, blk & yel 70 50

Issued for the "Freedom from Hunger" campaign of the U.N. Food and Agriculture Organization.

Mosquito and Malaria Eradication Emblem AP101

1963, Apr. 17 **Unwmk.** ***Perf. 12½***

C401 AP101 50c dl yel, car rose & blk 12 12
C402 AP101 80c brt grn, car rose & blk 12 12
C403 AP101 2s brt pink, dp cl & blk 28 28

Issued for the World Health Organization drive to eradicate malaria.

Stagecoach and Jet Plane AP102

1963, May 7 **Litho.**

C404 AP102 2s org & car rose 40 20
C405 AP102 4.20s cl & ultra 60 40

Issued to commemorate the centenary of the first International Postal Conference, Paris, 1863.

Type of 1957 Inscribed "Islas Galapagos," Surcharged with New Value and Overprinted "Ecuador" in Black or Red.

1963, June 19 **Unwmk.** ***Perf. 14***

C406 AP71 5s on 2s gray, dk bl & red 45 35
C407 AP71 10s on 2s gray, dk bl & red (R) 1.10 80

The basic 2s exists without surcharge and overprint. No. C407 exists with "ECUADOR" omitted, and with both "ECUADOR" and "10 SUCRES" double.

No. C375 Overprinted: "1863-1963/Centenario/de la Fundacion/ de la Cruz Roja/Internacional"

1963, June 21 **Photo.** ***Perf. 13x14***

C408 AP90 2s rose vio & car 30 20

Issued to commemorate the centenary of the founding of the International Red Cross.

Type of Regular Issue, 1963.

Designs (Arosemena and): 70c, Flags of Ecuador. 2s, Flags of Ecuador and Panama. 4s, Flags of Ecuador and U.S.

1963, July 1 **Litho.** ***Perf. 14***

C409 A238 70c pale bl & multi 18 12
C410 A238 2s pink & multi 35 18
C411 A238 4s lt bl & multi 80 40

Issued to commemorate Pres. Arosemena's friendship trip, July 1962.

Portrait Type of 1958

Portrait: 2s, Dr. Mariano Cueva.

Unwmk.

1963, July 4 **Litho.** ***Perf. 14***

C412 AP74 2s lt grn & multi 30 18

Issued to commemorate the 150th anniversary of the birth of Dr. Mariano Cueva (1812-1882).

Social Insurance Symbol AP103

Mother and Child AP104

1963, July 9 **Litho.**

C413 AP103 10s brn, bl, gray & ocher 90 70

25th anniversary of Social Insurance.

1963, July 28 ***Perf. 12½***

C414 AP104 1.30s org, dk bl & blk 30 18
C415 AP104 5s gray, red & brn 60 42

Issued to publicize the 7th Pan-American and South American Pediatrics Congresses, Quito.

Simon Bolivar Airport, Guayaquil AP105

1963, July 25 ***Perf. 14***

C416 AP105 60c gray 12 6
C417 AP105 70c dl grn 18 12
C418 AP105 5s brn vio 55 38

Issued to commemorate the opening of Simon Bolivar Airport, Guayaquil, July 15, 1962.

Nos. 638, 640-641 Overprinted "AEREO"

1964 ***Perf. 12***
Flags in National Colors

C419 A223 1.80s dl vio 50 35
C420 A224 2s dk brn 50 35
C421 A223 2.20s blk brn 50 35

On 1.80s and 2.20s, "AEREO" is vertical, reading down.

No. 650 Overprinted in Gold: "FARO DE COLON / AEREO"

1964 **Photo.** ***Perf. 14x13½***

C422 A229 1.80s dk bl 2.50 1.50

Nos. C352-C354 Overprinted **1961**

1964 **Litho.** ***Perf. 13½***

C423 AP86 50c bl & multi 60 30
C424 AP86 80c yel & multi 60 30
C425 AP86 1.30s pale grn & multi 60 30

No. C307 Overprinted: "DECLARACION / DERECHOS HUMANOS / 1964 / XV-ANIV"

Unwmk.

1964, Sept. 29 **Engr.** ***Perf. 14***

C426 AP69 1.70s red org 40 20

Issued to commemorate the 15th anniversary (in 1963) of the Universal Declaration of Human Rights.

Banana Type of Regular Issue

1964, Oct. 26 **Litho.** ***Perf. 12½x12***

C427 A241 4.20s blk, bis & gray ol 40 30
C428 A241 10s blk, scar & gray ol 75 60
 a. Souv. sheet of 4 1.50 1.50

Issued to publicize the Banana Conference, Oct.-Nov. 1964. No. C428a contains four imperf. stamps similar to Nos. 720-721 and C427-C428. Pale blue margin with black inscription and red control number. Size: 120x95mm.

John F. Kennedy, Flag-draped Coffin and John Jr. — AP106

1964, Nov. 22 **Litho.** ***Perf. 14***

C429 AP106 4.20s multi 1.00 80
C430 AP106 5s multi 1.25 95
C431 AP106 10s multi 1.75 1.10
 a. Souv. sheet of 3 6.00 6.00

Issued in memory of President John F. Kennedy (1917-63).

No. C431a contains stamps similar to Nos. C429-C431, imperf. Pale lilac margin with brown and white inscriptions. Red control number. Size: 114x130mm.

Olympic Type of Regular Issue

Designs: 1.30s, Gymnast (vert.). 1.80s, Hurdler. 2s, Basketball.

Perf. 13½x14, 14x13½

1964, Dec. 16 **Unwmk.**

C432 A243 1.30s vio bl, ver & brn 25 15
C433 A243 1.80s vio bl & multi 25 20
C434 A243 2s red & multi 35 25
 a. Souv. sheet of 4 3.00 3.00

18th Olympic Games, Tokyo, Oct. 10-25.

No. C434a contains stamps similar to Nos. 725 and C432-C434, imperf. Pale olive margin with black and white inscriptions and red control number. Size: 139x107mm.

Sports Type of Regular Issue, 1965

Torch and Athletes: 2s, 3s, Diver, gymnast, wrestlers and weight lifter. 2.50s, 4s, Bicyclists. 3.50s, 5s, Jumpers.

1965, Nov. 20 **Litho.** ***Perf. 12x12½***

C435 A247 2s bl, gold & blk 20 15
C436 A247 2.50s org, gold & blk 25 20
C437 A247 3s brt pink, gold & blk 25 20
C438 A247 3.50s lt vio, gold & bl 30 25
C439 A247 4s brt yel grn, gold & blk 35 30
C440 A247 5s red org, gold & blk 40 35
 a. Souv. sheet of 12 4.00 4.00
 Nos. C435-C440 (6) 1.75 1.45

Issued to commemorate the 5th Bolivarian Games, held at Guayaquil and Quito. No. C440a contains 12 imperf. stamps similar to Nos. 738-743 and C435-C440. Black and red inscriptions. Size: 215x129mm.

Bird Type of Regular Issue

Birds: 1s, Yellow grosbeak. 1.30s, Black-headed parrot. 1.50s, Scarlet tanager. 2s, Sapphire quail-dove. 2.50s, Violet-tailed sylph. 3s, Lemon-throated barbet. 4s, Yellow-tailed oriole. 10s, Collared puffbird.

1966, June 17 Litho. *Perf. 13½*
Birds in Natural Colors
C441 A249 1s lt red brn & blk 14 8
C442 A249 1.30s pink & blk 14 8
C443 A249 1.50s pale grn & blk 14 14
C444 A249 2s sal & blk 20 12
C445 A249 2.50s lt yel grn & blk 25 18
C446 A249 3s sal & blk 35 28
C447 A249 4s gray & blk 40 35
C448 A249 10s beige & blk 1.00 80
Nos. C441-C448 (8) 2.62 2.03

Nos. C436 and C443 Surcharged

1967
C449 A247 80c on 2.50s org, gold & blk 10 5
C450 A249 80c on 1.50s multi 10 5

Old denomination on No. C449 is obliterated with heavy bar; the surcharge on No. C450 includes "Resello" and an ornament over old denomination.

Peñaherrera Monument, Quito — AP107

Design: 2s, Peñaherrera statue.

1967, Dec. 29 Litho. *Perf. 12x12½*
C451 AP107 1.30s blk & org 15 10
C452 AP107 2s blk & lt ultra 15 10

See note after No. 763.

Arosemena Type of Regular Issue

Designs: 1.30s, Inauguration of Pres. Arosemena. 2s, Pres. Arosemena speaking in Punta del Este.

1968, May 9 Litho. *Perf. 13½x14*
C453 A251 1.30s multi 15 15
C454 A251 2s multi 20 20

First anniversary of administration of Pres. Otto Arosemena Gomez.

No. C448 Surcharged in Plum, Dark Blue or Green

RESELLO

$ 0,80

1969, Jan. 9 Litho. *Perf. 13½*
Bird in Natural Colors
C455 A249 80c on 10s beige (P) 5 5
C456 A249 1s on 10s beige (DBl) 10 10
C457 A249 2s on 10s beige (G) 15 15

"Operation Friendship" AP108

1969-70 Typo. *Perf. 13½*
C458 AP108 2s yel, blk, red & lt bl 15 15
a. Perf. 12½ 15 15
C459 AP108 2s bl, blk, car & yel ('70) 15 15

Friendship campaign. Medallion background on Nos. C458 and C458a is blue; on No. C459, yellow.

No. 639 Surcharged in Gold "S/. 5 AEREO" and Bar

1969, Nov. 25 Litho. *Perf. 12*
C460 A224 5s on 2s multi 1.25 75

Butterfly Type of Regular Issue

Butterflies: 1.30s, Morpho peleides. 1.50s, Anartia amathea.

1970 Litho. *Perf. 12½*
C461 A255 1.30s multi 10 10
C462 A255 1.50s pink & multi 10 10

Same, White Background

1970 *Perf. 13½*
C463 A255 1.30s multi 10 10
C464 A255 1.50s multi 10 10

Arms Type of Regular Issue

Provincial Arms and Flags: 1.30s, El Oro. 2s, Loja. 3s, Manabi. 5s, Pichincha. 10s, Guayas.

1971 Litho. *Perf. 10½*
C465 A258 1.30s pink & multi 10 10
C466 A258 2s multi 15 10
C467 A258 3s multi 20 15
C468 A258 5s multi 40 30
C469 A258 10s multi 75 60
Nos. C465-C469 (5) 1.60 1.25

Presentation of the Virgin AP109

Pres. Allende and Chilean Flag AP110

Art of Quito: 1.50s, Blessed Anne at Prayer. 2s, St. Theresa de Jesus. 2.50s, Altar of Carmen (horiz.). 3s, Descent from the Cross. 4s, Christ of St. Mariana de Jesus. 5s, Shrine of St. Anthony. 10s, Cross of San Diego.

1971 *Perf. 11½*
Inscriptions in Black
C473 AP109 1.30s multi 15 10
C474 AP109 1.50s multi 20 10
C475 AP109 2s multi 25 10
C476 AP109 2.50s multi 30 15
C477 AP109 3s multi 40 20
C478 AP109 4s multi 60 25
C479 AP109 5s multi 60 30
C480 AP109 10s multi 1.20 60
Nos. C473-C480 (8) 3.70 1.80

Design: 2.10s, Pres. José M. Velasco Ibarra of Ecuador, Pres. Salvador Allende of Chile and national flags.

1971, Aug. 24 *Perf. 12½*
C481 AP110 2s multi 15 10
C482 AP110 2.10s multi 15 10

Visit of Pres. Salvador Allende of Chile, Aug. 24.

Globe and Emblem AP111

1971
C483 AP111 5s black 60 35
C484 AP111 5.50s dl pur & blk 60 40

Opening of Postal Museum, Aug. 24, 1971.

Pazmino Type of Regular Issue

1971, Sept. 16 *Perf. 12x11½*
C485 A260 1.50s grn & multi 10 10
C486 A260 2.50s grn & multi 20 15

50th anniversary of "El Universo," newspaper founded by Ismael Pérez Pazmino.

Map of Americas — AP112

Designs: 10s, Converging roads and map. 20s, Map of Americas and Equator. 50s, Mountain road and monument on Equator.

1971 *Perf. 11½*
C487 AP112 5s org & multi 70 40
C488 AP112 10s org & blk 1.10 80
C489 AP112 20s blk, bl & brt rose 1.75 1.50
C490 AP112 50s bl, blk & gray 2.75 2.50

11th Pan-American Road Congress.
Issue dates: 5s, 10s, 50s, Nov. 15; 20s, Nov. 22.

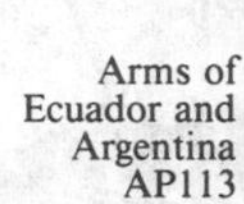

Arms of Ecuador and Argentina AP113

Design: 5s, Presidents José M. Velasco Ibarra and Alejandro Agustin Lanusse.

1972
C491 AP113 3s blk & multi 25 20
C492 AP113 5s blk & multi 40 30

Visit of Lt. Gen. Alejandro Agustin Lanusse, president of Argentina, Jan. 25.

Flame, Scales, Map of Americas AP114

1972, Apr. 24 Litho. *Perf. 12½*
C493 AP114 1.30s bl & red 10 10

17th Conference of the Interamerican Federation of Lawyers, Quito, Apr. 24.

Religious Paintings Type of Regular Issue

Ecuadorian Paintings: 3s, Virgin of the Flowers, by Miguel de Santiago. 10s, Virgin of the Rosary, by Quito School.

1972, Apr. 24 *Perf. 14x13½*
C494 A263 3s blk & multi 20 15
C495 A263 10s blk & multi 75 50
a. Souv. sheet of 2 1.00 1.00

No. C495a contains one each of Nos. C494-C495. Blue marginal inscription. Size: 98x110½mm.

1972, May 4

Ecuadorian Statues: 3s, St. Dominic, Quito School. 10s, St. Rosa of Lima, by Bernardo de Legarda.

C496 A263 3s blk & multi 25 20
C497 A263 10s blk & multi 75 50
a. Souv. sheet of 2 1.00 1.00

No. C497a contains one each of Nos. C496-C497. Blue marginal inscription. Size: 98x110½mm. Letters of "Ecuador" 3mm. high on Nos. C496-C497, 7mm. high on Nos. C494-C495.

Portrait Type of Regular Issue

Designs (Generals, from Paintings): 1.30s, Jose Maria Saenz. 3s, Tomas Wright. 4s, Antonio Farfan. 5s, Antonio José de Sucre. 10s, Simon Bolivar. 20s, Arms of Ecuador.

1972, May 24
C498 A264 1.30s bl & multi 10 10
C499 A264 3s bl & multi 25 20
C500 A264 4s bl & multi 30 20
C501 A264 5s bl & multi 40 30
C502 A264 10s bl & multi 75 50
C503 A264 20s bl & multi 1.50 1.00
Nos. C498-C503 (6) 3.30 2.30

Sesquicentennial of the Battle of Pichincha and the liberation of Quito.

Artisan Type of Regular Issue

Designs: 2s, Woman wearing flowered poncho. 3s, Striped poncho. 5s, Poncho with roses. 10s, Gold sunburst sculpture.

1972, July Photo. *Perf. 13*
C504 A265 2s multi 15 10
C505 A265 3s multi 20 15
C506 A265 5s multi 40 30
C507 A265 10s org red & multi 75 50
a. Souvenir sheet of 4 1.75 1.75

Handicraft of Ecuador. No. C507a contains one each of Nos. C504-C507. Pale claret marginal inscription and ornament. Black control number. Size 104x164mm.

Epidendrum Orchid — AP115

1972 Photo. *Perf. 12½*
C508 AP115 4s *shown* 40 25
C509 AP115 6s *Canna* 50 30
C510 AP115 10s *Jimson weed* 1.00 60
a. Souv. sheet of 3 2.25 2.25

No. C510a contains one each of Nos. C508-C510. Blue marginal inscription and ornaments. Black control number. Size: 166x106mm. Exists imperf.

Oil Drilling Towers AP116

Coat of Arms AP117

1972, Oct. 17 Litho. *Perf. 11½*
C511 AP116 1.30s bl & multi 15 10

Ecuadorian oil industry.

1972, Nov. 18 Litho. *Perf. 11½*
Arms Multicolored
C512 AP117 2s black 20 15
C513 AP117 3s black 30 20
C514 AP117 4s black 40 25
C515 AP117 4.50s black 40 25
C516 AP117 6.30s black 75 40
C517 AP117 6.90s black 75 40
Nos. C512-C517 (6) 2.80 1.65

Pichincha Type of Regular Issue

Designs: 2.40s, Corridor, San Agustin. 4.50s, La Merced Convent. 5.50s, Column base. 6.30s, Chapter Hall, San Agustin. 6.90s, Interior, San Agustin. 7.40s, Crucifixion, Cantuna Chapel. 7.90s, Decorated ceiling, San Agustin.

1972, Dec. 6 Wmk. 367
C518 A266 2.40s yel & multi 20 15
C519 A266 4.50s yel & multi 35 25
C520 A266 5.50s yel & multi 40 30
C521 A266 6.30s yel & multi 50 40
C522 A266 6.90s yel & multi 50 40

C523 A266 7.40s yel & multi 60 50
C524 A266 7.90s yel & multi 65 50
Nos. C518-C524 (7) 3.20 2.50

Sesquicentennial of the Battle of Pichincha.

UN Emblem AP118

OAS Emblem AP119

1973, Mar. 23 Litho. Unwmk.
Perf. 11½

C525 AP118 1.30s lt bl & blk 20 10

25th anniversary of the Economic Committee for Latin America (CEPAL).

Wmk. 367

1973, Apr. 14 Litho. *Perf. 11½*

C526 AP119 1.50s multi 20 10
a. Unwatermarked

Day of the Americas and "Philately for Peace."

Bird Type of Regular Issue

1973 Unwmk. *Perf. 11½x11*

C527 A268 1.30s *Blue-footed booby* 20 10
C528 A268 3s *Brown pelican* 20 10

Elevation of Galapagos Islands to a province of Ecuador.

Presidents Lara and Caldera AP120

1973, June 15 Wmk. 367

C529 AP120 3s multi 40 20

Visit of Pres. Rafael Caldera of Venezuela, Feb. 5-7.

Silver Coin, 1934 AP121

Globe, OPEC Emblem, Oil Derrick AP122

Ecuadorian Coins: 10s, Silver coin, obverse. 50s, Gold coin, 1928.

Unwmk.

1973, Dec. 14 Photo. *Perf. 14*

C530 AP121 5s multi 40 20
C531 AP121 10s multi 75 40
C532 AP121 50s multi 3.75 2.00
a. Souvenir sheet of 3 5.00 5.00

No. C532a contains one each of Nos. C530-C532; light blue margin with gold and black inscription, coat of arms and control numbers. Dated "1972." Size: 115x88mm. Exists imperf.

A gold marginal overprint was applied in 1974 to No. C532a (perf. and imperf.): "X Campeonato Mundial de Football / Munich - 1974".

A carmine overprint was applied in 1974 to No. C532a (perf. and imperf.): "Seminario de Telecommunicaciones Rurales, / Septiembre-1974 / Quito-cuador" and ITU emblem.

1974, June 15 Litho. *Perf. 11½*

C533 AP122 2s multi 20 10

Meeting of Organization of Oil Exporting Countries, Quito, June 15-24.

Ecuadorian Flag, UPU Emblem — AP123

1974, July 15 Litho. *Perf. 11½*

C534 AP123 1.30s multi 15 10

Centenary of Universal Postal Union.

Teodoro Wolf AP124

Capt. Edmundo Chiriboga AP125

1974 Litho. *Perf. 12x11½*

C535 AP124 1.30s blk & ultra 10 5
C536 AP125 1.50s gray 10 5

Teodoro Wolf, geographer; Edmundo Chiriboga, national hero. Issue dates, No. C535, Nov. 29; No. C536, Dec. 4.

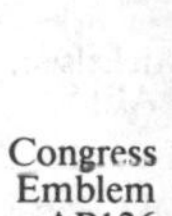
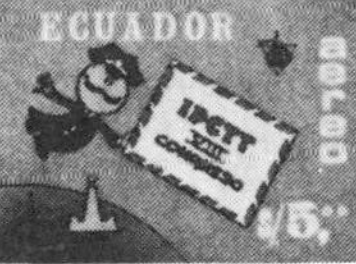

Congress Emblem AP126

1974, Dec. 8 Litho. *Perf. 11½x12*

C537 AP126 5s bl & multi 40 20

8th Inter-American Postmasters' Congress, Quito.

Map of Americas and Coat of Arms AP127

Manuel J. Calle, Journalist AP128

1975, Feb. 1 *Perf. 12x11½*

C538 AP127 3s bl & multi 25 15

EXFIGUA Stamp Exhibition and 5th General Assembly of Federation Inter-Americana de Filatelia, Guayaquil, Nov. 1973.

1975 *Perf. 12x11½*

Portraits: No. C540, Leopoldo Benites V., president of U.N. General Assembly, 1973-74; No. C541, Adofo H. Simmonds G. (1892-1969), journalists; No. C542, Juan de Dios Martinez Mera, President of Ecuador, birth centenary.

C539 AP128 5s lil rose 40 20
C540 AP128 5s gray 40 20
C541 AP128 5s violet 40 20
C542 AP128 5s blk & rose red 40 20

Pres. Guillermo Rodriguez Lara — AP129

1975 Unwmk. *Perf. 12*

C546 AP129 5s ver & blk 50 20

State visit of Pres. Guillermo Rodriguez Lara to Algeria, Romania and Venezuela.

Meeting Type of 1975

Designs: 1.50s, Rafael Rodriguez Palacio and Argelino Duran Quintero meeting at border in Ruichacha. 2s, Signing border agreement.

1975, Apr. 1 Litho. *Perf. 12x11½*

C547 A273 1.50s multi 15 15
C548 A273 2s multi 25 12

Meeting of the Ministers for Public Works of Ecuador and Colombia, July 27, 1973.

Sacred Heart (Painting) AP130

Quito Cathedral AP131

Design: 2s, Monstrance.

1975, Apr. 28 Litho. *Perf. 12x11½*

C549 AP130 1.30s yel & multi 15 5
C550 AP130 2s bl & multi 20 10
C551 AP131 3s multi 30 10

3rd Bolivarian Eucharistic Congress, Quito, June 9-16, 1974.

J. Delgado Panchana with Trophy — AP132

J. Delgado Panchana Swimming AP133

Perf. 12x11½, 11½x12

1975, June 12 Unwmk.

C552 AP132 1.30s bl & multi 20 5
C553 AP133 3s blk & multi 30 10

Jorge Delgado Panchana. South American swimming champion, 1971 and 1974.

Sports Type of 1975

1975, Sept. 11 Litho. *Perf. 11½*

C554 A276 1.30s *Tennis* 10 5
C555 A276 2s *Target shooting* 20 10
C556 A276 2.80s *Volleyball* 25 10
C557 A276 3s *Raft with sails* 25 10
C558 A276 5s *Mask* 40 15
Nos. C554-C558 (5) 1.20 50

3rd Ecuadorian Games.

Flower Type of 1975

1975, Nov. 18 Litho. *Perf. 11½x12*

C559 A227 1.30s *Pitcairnia pungens* 10 5
C560 A227 2s *Scaret sage* 20 10
C561 A227 3s *Amaryllis* 25 15
C562 A227 4s *Opuntia quitense* 30 20
C563 A227 5s *Amaryllis* 40 20
Nos. C559-C563 (5) 1.25 70

Tail Assemblies and Emblem AP134

Planes over Map of Ecuador AP135

1975, Dec. 17 Litho. *Perf. 11½*

C564 AP134 1.30s bl & multi 15 5
C565 AP135 3s multi 25 10

TAME, Military Transport Airline, 13th anniversary.

Benalcázar Statue — AP136

1976, Feb. 6 Litho. *Perf. 11½*

C566 AP136 2s multi 20 10
C567 AP136 3s multi 30 10

Sebastián de Benalcázar (1495-1550), Spanish conquistador, founder of Quito.

Archaeology Type of 1975

Designs: 1.30s, Seated man, Carchi Culture. 2s, Funerary urn, Tuncahuan Culture. 3s, Priest, Bahia de Caraquez Culture. 4s, Snail's shell, Cuasmal Culture. 5s, Bowl supported by figurines, Guangala Culture.

1976, Feb. 12 Litho. *Perf. 11½*

C568 A278 1.30s multi 10 5
C569 A278 2s multi 15 10
C570 A278 3s multi 20 10
C571 A278 4s multi 30 15
C572 A278 5s multi 40 20
Nos. C568-C572 (5) 1.15 60

Archaeological artifacts.

Fruit Type of 1976

1976, Mar. 30

C573 A280 2s Apples 15 10
C574 A280 5s Rose 40 20

25th Flower and Fruit Festival, Ambato.

Lufthansa Jet — AP137

1976, June 25 Litho. *Perf. 12*

C575 AP137 10s bl & multi 90 50

Lufthansa, 50th anniversary.

An imperf. 20s miniature sheet exists, similar to No. C575 enlarged, with overprinted black bar covering line below "Lufthansa." Size: 90x115mm.

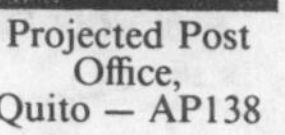

Projected Post Office, Quito — AP138

Fruit Peddler — AP139

1976, Aug. 10 Litho. *Perf. 12*
C576 AP138 5s blk & multi 40 20

Design for new General Post Office, Quito.

1976, July 25

Designs: No. C578, Longshoreman. No. C579, Cerros del Carmen and Santa Ana, hills of Guayaquil (horiz.). No. C580, Sebastian de Belalcazar. No. C581, Francisco de Orellana. No. C582, Chief Guayas and his wife Quila.

C577 AP139 1.30s red & multi 10 5
C578 AP139 1.30s red & multi 10 5
C579 AP139 1.30s red & multi 10 5
C580 AP139 2s red & multi 15 10
C581 AP139 2s red & multi 15 10
C582 AP139 2s red & multi 15 10
Nos. C577-C582 (6) 75 45

Founding of Quayaquil, 441st anniversary.

Emblem and Laurel AP140

1976, Aug. 9
C583 AP140 1.30s yel & multi 10 5

Bolivarian Society of Ecuador, 50th anniversary.

Western Hemisphere and Equator Monument AP141

Congress Emblem AP142

1976, Sept. 6
C584 AP141 2s multi 15 10

Souvenir Sheet
Imperf
C585 AP141 5s multi 2.50 2.50

3rd Conference of Pan-American Transport Ministers, Quito, Sept. 6-11. No. C585 contains design similar to No. C584 with black denomination and red control number in margin. Size: 95x114mm.

1976, Sept. 27 Litho. *Perf. 11½*
C586 AP142 1.30s bl & multi 10 5
C587 AP142 3s bl & multi 20 10

Souvenir Sheet
Imperf
C588 AP142 10s bl & multi 1.00 1.00

10th Inter-American Congress of the Construction Industry, Quito, Sept. 27-30. No. C588 has black control number. Size: 89x115mm.

George Washington AP143

Design: 5s, Naval battle, Sept. 23, 1779, in which the Bonhomme Richard, commanded by John Paul Jones, defeated and captured the Serapis, British man-of-war, off Yorkshire coast (horiz.).

1976, Oct. 18 Litho. *Perf. 12*
C589 AP143 3s blk & multi 50 15
C590 AP143 5s red brn & yel 70 25

American Bicentennial.

Dr. Hideyo Noguchi AP144

Luis Cordero AP145

1976 Litho. *Perf. 11½*
C591 AP144 3s yel & multi 25 10

Dr. Hideyo Noguchi (1876-1928), bacteriologist (at Rockefeller Institute), birth centenary. A 10s imperf. miniature sheet in same design exists with red control number and without "Aereo." Size: 95x114mm.

1976, Dec. Litho. *Perf. 11½*
C592 AP145 2s multi 15 10

Luis Cordero (1833-1912), president of Ecuador.

Mariuxi Febres Cordero — AP146

1976, Dec. *Perf. 11½*
C593 AP146 3s multi 25 10

Mariuxi Febres Cordero, South American swimming champion.

Flags and Monument AP147

1976, Nov. 9 *Perf. 12*
C594 AP147 3s, multi 25 10

Miniature Sheet
Imperf
C595 AP147 5s multi 50 50

2nd Meeting of the Agriculture Ministers of the Andean Countries, Quito, Nov. 8-10. No. C595 has red control number. Size: 95x115mm.

Sister Catalina AP148

Congress Hall, Quito AP149

1977, June 17 Litho. *Perf. 12x11½*
C596 AP148 1.30s blk & pale sal 10 5

Sister Catalina de Jesus Herrera (1717-1795), writer.

1977, Aug. 15 Litho. *Perf. 12x11½*
C597 AP149 5s multi 40 20
a. 10s souvenir sheet 1.00 1.00

11th General Assembly of Pan-American Institute of Geography and History, Quito, Aug. 15-30. No. C597a contains the designs of types A282 and AP149 without denominations and with simulated perforations; black and blue inscriptions, black control number. Size: 90x115mm.

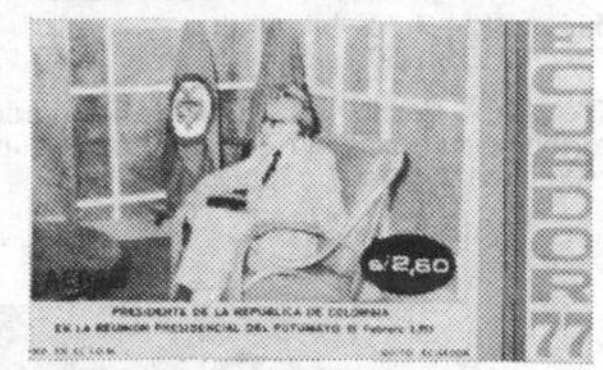

Pres. Alfonso Lopez Michelsen, Flag of Colombia — AP150

Designs: 5s, Pres. Lopez M. of Colombia, Pres. Alfredo Povedo B. of Ecuador and aide. 7s, as 5s (vert.). 9s, 10s, Presidents with aides.

1977 *Perf. 12*
C598 AP150 2.60s multi 30 10
C599 AP150 5s multi 60 20
C600 AP150 7s multi 60 30
C601 AP150 9s multi 90 45

Imperf
C602 AP150 10s multi 1.00 1.00

Meeting of the Presidents of Ecuador and Colombia and Declaration of Putumayo, Feb. 25, 1977. Nos. C598-C602 are overprinted in multiple fluorescent, colorless rows: INSTITUTO GEOGRAFICO MILITAR GOBIERNO DEL ECUADOR. No. C602 has black control number. Size: 115x91mm.

Ceramic Figure, Tolita Culture AP151

Designs: 9s, Divine Shepherdess, sculpture by Bernardo de Legarda. 11s, The Fruit Seller, sculpture by Legarda. 20s, Sun God, pre-Columbian gold mask.

1977, Aug. 31 *Perf. 12*
C603 AP151 7s gold & multi 60 20
C604 AP151 9s gold & multi 80 40
C605 AP151 11s gold & multi 1.00 50

Souvenir Sheet
Gold Embossed
Imperf
C606 AP151 20s vio, bl, blk & gold 2.00 2.00

Central Bank of Ecuador, 50th anniversary. No. C606 has black control number. Size: 89x115mm. Nos. C603-C605 overprinted like Nos. C598-C602.

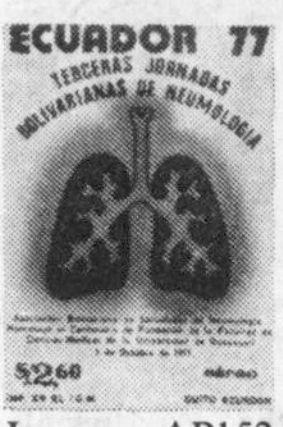

Lungs — AP152

Brother Miguel, St. Peter's, Rome — AP153

1977, Oct. 5 Litho. *Perf. 12x11½*
C607 AP152 2.60s multi 30 15

3rd Congress of the Bolivarian Pneumonic Society and centenary of the founding of the medical faculty of the University of Guayaquil.

1977
C608 AP153 2.60s multi 30 15

Beatification of Brother Miguel.

Peralta Type of 1977

Design: 2.60s, Titles of works by Peralta and his bookmark.

1977 *Perf. 11½*
C609 A284 2.60s multi 30 15

José Peralta (1855-1937), writer, 40th death anniversary.

Broadcast Tower AP154

Remigio Romero y Cordero AP155

1977, Dec. 2 Litho. *Perf. 12x11½*
C610 AP154 5s multi 40 20

9th World Telecommunications Day.

1978, Mar. 2 Litho. *Perf. 12½x11½*
C611 AP155 3s multi 20 10
C612 AP155 10.60s multi 80 40

Imperf
C612A AP155 10s multi 80 40

Remigio Romero y Cordero (1895-1967), poet.

No. C612A contains a vignette similar to Nos. C611-C612, poem and black control number. Size: 90x114mm.

Dr. Vicente Corral Moscoso AP156

Faces AP157

Design: 5s, Hospital emblem with Caduceus.

1978, Apr. 12 Litho. *Imperf.*
C613 AP156 5s multi 40 20

Perf. 12x11½
C614 AP156 7.60s multi 60 30

Inauguration (in 1977) of Dr. Vicente Corral Moscoso Regional Hospital, Cuenca.
No. C613 has black control number. Size: 89x114mm.

1978, Mar. 17

Designs: 9s, Emblems and flags of Ecuador. 10s, 11s, Hands reaching for light.

C615 AP157 7s multi 60 30
C616 AP157 9s multi 80 40
C617 AP157 11s multi 90 45

Imperf
C618 AP157 10s multi 80 40

Ecuadorian Social Security Institute, 50th anniversary.
No. C618 has black control number. Size: 89x114mm.

Geographical Institute Type of 1978

Design: 7.60s, Plane over map of Ecuador with mountains.

1978, Apr. 12 Litho. *Perf. 11½*
C619 A287 7.60s multi 60 30

Imperf
C620 A287 10s multi 90 45

Military Geographical Institute, 50th anniversary. No. C620 contains 2 vignettes with simulated perforations in designs of Nos. 967 and C619, Institute emblem, black control number. Size: 115x89mm.

Lions Type of 1978

1978 *Perf. 11½*
C621 A288 5s multi 40 20
C622 A288 6.20s multi 50 25

Imperf
C623 A288 10s multi 80 40

7th meeting of Latin American Lions, Jan. 25-29. No. C623 contains a vignette similar to Nos. C621-C622, inscriptions and black control number. Size: 115x90mm.

San Martin — AP158

1978, Apr. 13 Litho. *Perf. 12*
C624 AP158 10.60s multi 90 45

Imperf
C625 AP158 10s multi 80 40

Gen. José de San Martin (1778-1850), soldier and statesman. No. C625 contains a vignette similar to No. C624, inscriptions and black control number. Size: 115x90mm.

Bank Type of 1978

Design: 5s, Bank emblem.

1978, Sept. Litho. *Perf. 11½*
C626 A289 5s gray & multi 40 20

70th anniversary of Filanbanco (Philanthropic Bank).

Soccer Type of 1978

Designs: 2.60s, "Gauchito" and Games' emblem. 5s, "Gauchito." 7s, Soccer ball. 9s, Games' emblem (vert.). 10s, Games' emblem.

1978, Nov. 1 *Perf. 12*
C627 A290 2.60s multi 20 15
C628 A290 7s multi 60 30
C629 A290 9s multi 80 40

Imperf
C630 A290 5s blk & bl 40 20
C631 A290 10s blk & bl 80 40

11th World Cup Soccer Championship, Argentina, June 1-25. Nos. C630-C631 have black control numbers. Size: 115x90mm.

Bernadro O'Higgins AP159

Old Men of Vilcabamba AP160

1978, Nov. 11 Litho. *Perf. 12x11½*
C632 AP159 10.60s multi 90 45

Imperf
C633 AP159 10s multi 80 40

Gen. Bernardo O'Higgins (1778-1842), Chilean soldier and statesman. No. C633 contains a vignette similar to No. C632, inscriptions and black control number. Size: 115x99mm.

1978, Nov. 11 *Perf. 12x11½*
C634 AP160 5s multi 40 20

Vilcabamba, valley of longevity.

Hubert H. Humphrey AP161

Virgin and Child AP162

1978, Nov. 27 Litho. *Perf. 12x11½*
C635 AP61 5s multi 40 20

Hubert H. Humphrey (1911-1978), Vice President of the U.S.

1978

Children's Drawings: 4.60s, Holy Family. 6.20s, Candle and children.

C636 AP162 2.20s multi 20 10
C637 AP162 4.60s multi 40 20
C638 AP162 6.20s multi 60 25

Christmas 1978.

Village, by Anibal Villacis AP163

Ecuadorian Painters: No. C640, Mountain Village, by Gilberto Almeida. No. C641, Bay, by Roura Oxandaberro. No. C642, Abstract, by Luis Molinari. No. C643, Statue, by Oswaldo Viteri. No. C644, Tools, by Enrique Tabara.

1978, Dec. 9 *Perf. 12*
C639 AP163 5s multi 40 20
C640 AP163 5s multi 40 20
C641 AP163 5s multi 40 20
C642 AP163 5s multi 40 20
C643 AP163 5s multi 40 20
C644 AP163 5s multi 40 20
Nos. C639-C644 (6) 2.40 1.20

House and Monument AP164

Design: 3.40s, Monument (vert.).

1979, Feb. 27 Litho. *Perf. 12*
C645 AP164 2.40s multi 20 10
C646 AP164 3.40s multi 25 10

Imperf
C647 AP164 10s multi 90

Sesquicentennial of Battle of Portete and Tarqui. No. C647 contains vignettes similar to Nos. C645-C646; inscriptions and black control number. Size: 115x90mm.

Fish and Ship — AP165

Flags of Ecuador and U.S. — AP166

Designs: 7s, Map of Ecuador and Galapagos showing territorial waters (horiz.). 9s, Map of South America with west-coast territorial waters.

Perf. 12x11½, 11½x12

1979, July 23 Litho. Wmk. 367
C648 AP165 5s multi 40 20
C649 AP165 7s multi 60 30
C650 AP165 9s multi 80 40

Declaration of 200-mile territorial limit, 25th anniversary.

1979, Aug. 3 *Perf. 12x11½*

Designs: 10.60s, Bells in Quito clock tower (horiz.). 13.60s, Aerial view of Galapagos coast.

C651 A293 10.60s multi 90 45
C652 A293 13.60s multi 1.00 50

Souvenir Sheet
Imperf
Unwmk.
C653 A293 10s multi 90 45

National heritage: Quito and Galapagos Islands. No. C653 contains vignettes similar to Nos. 977, C651-C652; black control number, black and blue inscriptions. Size: 115x90mm.

1979, Aug. Wmk. 367 *Perf. 11½x12*
C654 AP166 7.60s multi 60 30
C655 AP166 10.60s multi 90 45

Souvenir Sheet
Unwmk. *Imperf.*
C656 AP166 10s multi 90 45

5th anniversary of Ecuador-U.S. Chamber of Commerce. No. C656 contains vignettes similar to Nos. C654-C655; black control number and marginal inscription. Size: 115x90mm.

Smiling Girl, IYC Emblem — AP167

1979, Sept. 7 Litho. *Perf. 12x11½*
C657 AP167 10s multi 90 45

International Year of the Child.

Citizens and Flag of Ecuador AP168

Design: 10.60s, Pres. Jaime Roldas Aguilera, flag of Ecuador (vert.).

Perf. 11½

1979, Sept. 27 Litho. Unwmk.
C658 AP168 7.60s multi 75 40

Wmk. 367
C659 AP168 10.60s multi 90 45

Restoration of democracy to Ecuador.

Ecuador Coat of Arms, Olympic Rings and Eagle — AP169

1979, Nov. 23 Litho. *Perf. 12x11½*
C660 AP169 28s multi 2.25 1.10

5th National Games, Cuenca.

CIESPAL Building, Quito AP170

1979, Dec. 26 *Perf. 11½x12½*
C661 AP170 10.60s multi 90 45

Opening of Ecuadorian Institute of Engineers building.

Olmedo Type of 1980

1980, Apr. 29 Litho. *Perf. 12x11½*
C662 A294 10s multi 90 45

Tribal Chief Type of 1980

1980, May 12

Indo-American Tribal Chiefs: No. C663, Cuauhtemoc, Mexico. No. C664, Lempira, Honduras. No. C665, Nicaragua. No. C666, Lambare, Paraguay. No. C667, Urraca, Panama. No. C668, Anacoana, Haiti No. C669, Caupolican, Chile. No. C670, Tacun-Uman, Guatemala. No. C671, Calarca, Colombia. No. C672. Garabito, Costa Rica. No. C673, Hatuey, Cuba. No. C674, Cmarao, Brazil. No. C675, Tehuelche, Argentina. No. C676, Tupaj Katri, Bolivia. 17.80s, Sequoya, U.S. 22.80s, Ruminahui, Ecuador.

C663 A295 7.60s multi 70 35
C664 A295 7.60s multi 70 35
C665 A295 7.60s multi 70 35
C666 A295 10s multi 90 45
C667 A295 10s multi 90 45
C668 A295 10.60s multi 90 45
C669 A295 10.60s multi 90 45
C670 A295 10.60s multi 90 45
C671 A295 12.80s multi 1.20 60
C672 A295 12.80s multi 1.20 60
C673 A295 12.80s multi 1.20 60
C674 A295 13.60s multi 1.20 60
C675 A295 13.60s multi 1.20 60
C676 A295 13.60s multi 1.20 60
C677 A295 17.80s multi 1.50 75
C678 A295 22.80s multi 2.00 1.00
Nos. C663-C678 (16) 17.30 8.65

Royal Visit Type of 1980

1980, May 18 *Perf. 11½x12*
C679 A296 10.60s multi 90 45

Pichincha Provincial Development Council Building — AP171

1980, June 1 *Perf. 12x11½*

C680 AP171 10.60s multi 90 45

Progress in Pichincha Province.

Indian Type of 1980

1980, June 10 Litho. *Perf. 12x11½*

C681 A297 7.60s *Salasaca boy, Tungurahua* 70 35

C682 A297 10s *Amula woman, Chimborazo* 90 45

C683 A297 10.60s *Canar woman, Canar* 90 45

C684 A297 13.60s *Colorado Indian, Pichincha* 1.20 60

Virgin of Mercy Type of 1980

1980, July 7 Litho. *Perf. 11½*

C685 A298 7.60s *Cupola, cloisters* 70 35

C686 A298 7.60s *Gold screen* 70 35

C687 A298 7.60s *Quito from basilica tower* 70 35

C688 A298 10.60s *Retable* 90 45

C689 A298 10.60s *Pulpit* 90 45

C690 A298 13.60s *Cupola* 1.20 60

C691 A298 13.60s *Statue of Virgin* 1.20 60

Nos. C685-C691 (7) 6.30 3.15

Virgin of Mercy, patron saint of Ecuadorian armed forces.

U.P.U. Monument AP172

Marshal Sucre, by Marco Sales AP173

Design: 17.80s, Mail box, 1880.

1980, July 7 *Perf. 12*

C692 AP172 10.60s multi 90 45

C693 AP172 17.80s multi 1.50 75

Souvenir Sheet

C694 AP172 25s multi 2.50 1.25

Universal Postal Union membership centenary. No. C694 contains designs of C692 and C693 (horiz.), perf. 11½. Black control number. Size: 116x91mm.

Olympic Type of 1980.

Design: 10.60s, 13.60s, Moscow '80 emblem, Olympic rings.

1980, July 19 *Perf. 12x11½*

C695 A299 10.60s multi 90 45

C696 A299 13.60s multi 1.20 60

Souvenir Sheet

C697 A299 30s multi 2.50 1.25

22nd Summer Olympic Games, Moscow, July 19-Aug. 3.

No. C697 contains vignettes in designs of Nos. 991 and C695, black control number. Size: 116x90mm.

1980

C698 AP173 10.60s multi 90 45

Marshal Antonio Jose de Sucre, death sesquicentennial.

A particular stamp may be scarce, but if few collectors want it, its market value may remain relatively low.

Rotary International, 75th Anniversary AP174

1980, Aug. 4 *Perf. 11½*

C699 AP174 10s multi 90 45

Riobamba Type of 1980

Design: 7.60s, 10.60s, Monstrance, Riobamba Cathedral (vert.).

1980, Sept. 20 Litho. *Perf. 11½*

C700 A301 7.60s multi 70 35

C701 A301 10.60s multi 90 45

Souvenir Sheet

Imperf

C702 A301 30s multi 2.50 1.25

Constitutional Assembly of Riobamba sesquicentennial. No. C702 contains vignettes in designs of Nos. 996-997, black control number. Size: 116x90mm.

Democracy Type of 1980

Designs: 7.60s, 10.60s, Pres. Aguilera and voter.

Perf. 12x11½

1980, Oct. 9 Litho. Wmk. 367

C703 A302 7.60s multi 70 35

C704 A302 10.60s multi 90 45

Souvenir Sheet

Imperf

C705 A302 15s multi 1.30 65

No. C705 contains vignettes in designs of Nos. 999 and C703; control number.

OPEC Type of 1980

20th Anniversary of OPEC: 7.60s, Men holding OPEC emblem (vert.).

1980, Nov. 8 *Perf. 11½x12*

C706 A303 7.60s multi 70 35

Carchi Province Type of 1980

Designs: 10.60s, Governor's Palace (vert.). 17.80s, Victory Museum, Central Square (vert.).

1980, Nov. 21 *Perf. 13*

C707 A304 10.60c multi 90 45

C708 A304 17.80s multi 1.50 75

Orchid Type of 1980

Perf. 12x11½, 11½x12

1980, Nov. 22

C709 A305 7.60s *Anguloa uniflora* 70 35

C710 A305 10.60s *Scuticaria salesiana* 90 45

C711 A305 50s *Helcia sanguinolenta, vert.* 1.50 1.00

C712 A305 100s *Anguloa virginalis* 2.00 1.50

Souvenir Sheets

Imperf

C713 A305 20s multi 1.75 85

C714 A305 20s multi 1.75 85

Nos. C713-C714 contain vignettes in designs of Nos. C709-C710 and C711-C712 respectively; blue control numbers: 115 x 90 mm.

Christmas Type of 1980

Designs: 7.60s, Pope blessing crowd (vert.). 10.60s, Portrait (vert.).

1980, Dec. 27 *Perf. 12*

C715 A306 7.60s multi 70 35

C716 A306 10.60s multi 90 45

Isidro Cueva — AP175

Simon Bolivar, by Marco Salas — AP176

1980, Nov. 20 *Perf. 13*

C717 AP175 18.20s multi 1.75 85

Dr. Isidro Ayora Cueva, former president, birth centenary.

1980, Dec. 17 *Perf. 11½*

C718 AP176 13.60s multi 1.50 75

Simon Bolivar death sesquicentennial.

Turtle, Galapagos Islands AP177

Design: 100s, Oldest Ecuadorian mail box, 1793 (vert.).

1981, Feb. 12 Litho. *Perf. 13*

C719 AP177 50s multi 3.50 1.75

C720 AP177 100s multi 5.00 3.50

HCJB Type of 1981

1981 Litho. *Perf. 13*

C721 A311 7.60s Emblem, horiz. 70 35

C722 A311 10.60s Emblem, diff. 90 45

Soccer Players — AP178

1981, July 8

C723 AP178 7.60s Emblem 70 35

C724 AP178 10.60s shown 90 45

C725 AP178 13.60s World Cup 1.20 60

Souvenir Sheets

C726 AP178 20s multi 1.75 85

C727 AP178 20s multi 1.75 85

1982 World Cup Soccer Championship. Nos. C726-C727 contain vignettes in designs of Nos. C723 and C724 respectively; black control numbers. Size: 115x90mm.

Picasso Type of 1981

1981, Oct. 26 Litho. *Perf. 13*

C728 A313a 7.60s Still-life 65 32

C729 A313a 10.60s First Communion, vert. 90 45

C730 A313a 13.60s Las Meninas, vert. 1.15 58

Size: 110x90mm.

Imperf

C731 A313a 20s multi 1.75 90

No. C731 contains designs of Nos. C730, C729; black control number.

World Food Day Type of 1981

1981, Dec. 31 Litho. *Perf. 13x13½*

C732 A314 10s Farming, vert. 90 45

IYD Type of 1982

1982, Feb. 25 Litho. *Perf. 13*

C733 A316 7.60s Emblem 70 35

C734 A316 10.60s Man with crutch 90 45

Montalvo Type of 1982

1982 Litho. *Perf. 13*

C735 A318 5s Home, horiz. 40 20

Swimming Type of 1982

1982, July 30

C736 A320 10.20s Emblem, vert. 90 45

C737 A320 14.20s Diving, vert. 1.20 60

Pres. Jaime Roldos, (1940-81), Mrs. Martha Roldos, Independence Monument, Quito — AP179

1983, May 25 Litho. *Perf. 12*

C738 AP179 13.60s multi 65 30

Souvenir Sheet

Imperf

C739 AP179 20s multi 1.00 50

AIR POST SEMI-POSTAL STAMPS

Nos. C119-C123 Surcharged in Blue or Red:

Hospital
Méndez + $ 0,50

1944, May 9 Unwmk. *Perf. 12*

CB1 AP26 50c + 50c dp red lil 5.00 5.00

CB2 AP26 70c + 30c red brn 5.00 5.00

CB3 AP26 3s + 50c turq grn (R) 5.00 5.00

CB4 AP26 5s + 1s brt ultra (R) 5.00 5.00

CB5 AP26 10s + 2s scar 5.00 5.00

Nos. CB1-CB5 (5) 25.00 25.00

The surtax aided Mendez Hospital.

AIR POST REGISTRATION STAMPS

Issued by Sociedad Colombo-Alemana de Transportes Aereos (SCADTA)

Nos. C3 and C3a Overprinted "R" in Carmine.

1928-29 Wmk. 116 *Perf. 14x14½*

CF1 AP6 1s on 20c gray (C3) 200.00 175.00

a. 1s on 20c gray (C3a) ('29) 225.00 200.00

No. C18 Overprinted "R" in Black.

1929, Apr. 1 Wmk. 127 *Perf. 14*

CF2 AP2 1s rose 90.00 75.00

AIR POST OFFICIAL STAMPS

in Red or Black **OFICIAL**

1929, May Unwmk. *Perf. 12*

CO1 AP1 2c blk (R) 60 60

CO2 AP1 5c car rose 60 60

CO3 AP1 10c dp brn 60 60

CO4 AP1 20c dk vio 60 60

CO5 AP1 50c dp grn 2.00 1.50

CO6 AP1 1s dk bl 2.00 1.75

a. Invtd. ovpt. 425.00

CO7 AP1 5s org yel 7.50 7.50

CO8 AP1 10s org red 100.00 75.00

Nos. CO1-CO8 (8) 113.90 88.15

Establishment of commercial air service in Ecuador.

Counterfeits of No. CO8 exist.

1930, Jan. 9

CO9 AP1 50c ol brn 1.50 1.35

CO10 AP1 1s car lake 2.50 2.00

CO11 AP1 5s ol grn 5.00 5.00

CO12 AP1 10s black 10.00 10.00

Air Post Stamps of 1937 Overprinted in Black **OFICIAL**

1937, Aug. 19

CO13	AP7	10c chestnut	25	20
CO14	AP7	20c ol blk	35	20
CO15	AP7	70c blk brn	35	20
CO16	AP7	1s gray blk	50	20
CO17	AP7	2s dk vio	60	40
		Nos. CO13-CO17 (5)	2.05	1.20

No. C79 Overprinted in Black **OFICIAL**

1940, Aug. 1 *Perf. 12½x13*

CO18	AP15	5s emerald	1.25	90

Nos. C352-C354 Overprinted: "1961 oficial"

1964 *Perf. 13½*

CO19	AP86	50c bl & multi	1.00	1.00
CO20	A86	80c yel & multi	1.00	1.00
CO21	A86	1.30s pale grn & multi	1.00	1.00

SPECIAL DELIVERY STAMPS

SD1

1928 **Unwmk.** *Perf. 12.*

E1	SD1	2c on 2c bl	4.50	6.00
E2	SD1	5c on 2c bl	4.00	6.00
E3	SD1	10c on 2c bl	4.50	4.00
a.		10 CTVOS inverted	14.00	17.50
E4	SD1	20c on 2c bl	6.00	6.00
E5	SD1	50c on 2c bl	6.00	6.00
		Nos. E1-E5 (5)	25.00	28.00

No. RA49A Surcharged in Red **EXPRESO 20 Ctvs.**

1945

E6	PT18	20c on 5c grn	25	10

LATE FEE STAMP

No. RA49A Surcharged in Black **U. H. 10 Ctvs.**

1945 **Unwmk.** *Perf. 12.*

I1	PT18	10c on 5c grn	15	12

POSTAGE DUE STAMPS

Numeral D1

Coat of Arms D2

Wmk. Liberty Cap. (117)

1896 **Engr.** *Perf. 12*

J1	D1	1c bl grn	1.25	2.00
J2	D1	2c bl grn	40	1.00
J3	D1	5c bl grn	1.25	1.25
J4	D1	10c bl grn	85	1.50
J5	D1	20c bl grn	35	2.00
J6	D1	50c bl grn	30	2.50
J7	D1	100c bl grn	60	5.00
		Nos. J1-J7 (7)	5.00	15.25

Reprints are on very thick paper with distinct watermark and vertical paper-weave direction. Price 5c each.

Unwmk.

J8	D1	1c bl grn	1.75	4.00
J9	D1	2c bl grn	1.75	4.00
J10	D1	5c bl grn	1.75	4.00
J11	D1	10c bl grn	1.75	4.00
J12	D1	20c bl grn	2.25	5.00
J13	D1	50c bl grn	3.00	7.00
J14	D1	100c bl grn	4.00	10.00
		Nos. J8-J14 (7)	16.25	38.00

1929

J15	D2	5c dp bl	15	8
J16	D2	10c org yel	20	12
J17	D2	20c red	30	25

Numeral — D3

Perf. 13½

1958, Nov. **Unwmk.** **Litho.**

J18	D3	10c brt lil	5	5
J19	D3	50c emerald	10	6
J20	D3	1s maroon	20	15
J21	D3	2s red	30	25

OFFICIAL STAMPS

Regular Issues of 1881 and 1887 Handstamped in Black

1886 **Unwmk.** *Perf. 12*

O1	A5	1c yel brn	50	50
O2	A6	2c lake	75	75
O3	A7	5c blue	1.25	1.25
O4	A8	10c orange	1.00	1.00
O5	A9	20c gray vio	1.00	1.00
O6	A10	50c bl grn	4.00	3.50
		Nos. O1-O6 (6)	8.50	8.00

1887

O7	A12	1c green	75	75
O8	A13	2c vermilion	75	75
O9	A14	5c blue	1.00	1.00
O10	A15	80c ol grn	4.00	3.00

Nos. O1 to O10 are known with red handstamp but these are believed to be speculative.

The overprint on the 1886-87 issues is handstamped and is found in various positions.

Flores — O1 Arms — O1a

1892

Carmine Overprint.

O11	O1	1c ultra	12	25
O12	O1	2c ultra	12	25
O13	O1	5c ultra	12	25
O14	O1	10c ultra	12	20
O15	O1	20c ultra	12	10
O16	O1	50c ultra	12	50
O17	O1	1s ultra	40	50
		Nos. O11-O17 (7)	1.12	2.05

1894

O18	O1a	1c sl grn (R)	10.00	
O19	O1a	2c lake (Bk)	10.00	

Nos. O18 and O19 were not placed in use.

Rocafuerte — O2

Dated 1894.

1894

Carmine Overprint

O20	O2	1c gray blk	25	50
O21	O2	2c gray blk	25	25
O22	O2	5c gray blk	25	25
O23	O2	10c gray blk	10	20
O24	O2	20c gray blk	30	25
O25	O2	50c gray blk	1.50	1.50
O26	O2	1s gray blk	2.00	2.00
		Nos. O20-O26 (7)	4.65	4.95

Dated 1895

1895

Carmine Overprint.

O27	O2	1c gray blk	2.25	2.25
O28	O2	2c gray blk	3.00	3.00
O29	O2	5c gray blk	50	50
O30	O2	10c gray blk	3.00	3.00
O31	O2	20c gray blk	5.00	5.00
O32	O2	50c gray blk	*12.50*	*12.50*
O33	O2	1s gray blk	1.50	1.50
		Nos. O27-O33 (7)	27.75	27.75

Reprints of 1894-95 issues are on very thick paper with paper weave found both horizontal and vertical for all denominations. Generally they are blacker than originals.

Overprinted in Carmine.

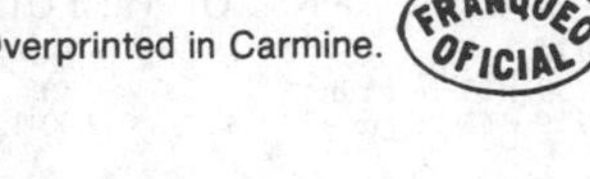

1896 **Wmk. d. Liberty Cap. (117)**

O34	A21	1c ol bis	35	35
O35	A22	2c ol bis	35	35
O36	A23	5c ol bis	35	35
O37	A24	10c ol bis	35	35
O38	A25	20c ol bis	35	35
O39	A26	50c ol bis	35	35
O40	A27	1s ol bis	1.00	75
O41	A28	5s ol bis	1.75	1.65
		Nos. O34-O41 (8)	4.85	4.50

Reprints of Nos. O34-O41 are on thick paper with vertical paper weave direction.

Unwmk.

O42	A21	1c ol bis	1.00	1.00
O43	A22	2c ol bis	1.00	1.00
O44	A23	5c ol bis	1.00	70
O45	A24	10c ol bis	75	60
O46	A25	20c ol bis	1.00	1.00
O47	A26	50c ol bis	1.00	1.50
O48	A27	1s ol bis	2.00	1.25
O49	A28	5s ol bis	3.00	2.25
		Nos. O42-O49 (8)	10.75	9.30

Reprints of Nos. O42-O49 all have overprint in black. Price 10 cents each.

Issue of 1894 Overprinted

1897-98

O50	O2	1c gray blk	*5.00*	*5.00*
O51	O2	2c gray blk	*6.00*	*6.00*
O52	O2	5c gray blk	*50.00*	*50.00*
O53	O2	10c gray blk	*6.00*	*6.00*
O54	O2	20c gray blk	*2.75*	*1.75*
O55	O2	50c gray blk	*10.00*	*10.00*
O56	O2	1s gray blk	*15.00*	*15.00*
		Nos. O50-O56 (7)	94.75	93.75

Issue of 1894 Overprinted

O57	O2	1c gray blk	*1.50*	*1.50*
O58	O2	2c gray blk	*3.50*	*1.25*
O59	O2	5c gray blk	*6.00*	*6.00*
O60	O2	10c gray blk	*50.00*	*50.00*
O61	O2	20c gray blk	*1.50*	*1.50*
O62	O2	50c gray blk	*6.00*	*5.00*
O63	O2	1s gray blk	*65.00*	*65.00*
		Nos. O57-O63 (7)	133.50	130.25

Issue of 1894 Overprinted **1897 Y 1898**

O64	O2	1c gray blk	*12.00*	*12.00*
O65	O2	2c gray blk	*12.00*	*12.00*
O66	O2	5c gray blk	*12.00*	*12.00*
O67	O2	10c gray blk	*12.00*	*12.00*
O68	O2	20c gray blk	*12.00*	*12.00*
O69	O2	50c gray blk	*12.00*	*12.00*
O70	O2	1s gray blk	*12.00*	*12.00*
		Nos. O64-O70 (7)	84.00	84.00

Issue of 1895 Overprinted in Black

O71	O2	1c gray blk	*3.00*	*3.00*
O72	O2	2c gray blk	*2.00*	*2.00*
O73	O2	5c gray blk	*3.00*	*3.00*
O74	O2	10c gray blk	*3.00*	*3.00*
O75	O2	20c gray blk	*5.00*	*5.00*
O76	O2	50c gray blk	*22.50*	
O77	O2	1s gray blk	*45.00*	*45.00*
		Nos. O71-O77 (7)	83.50	

Issue of 1895 Overprinted

O78	O2	1c gray blk	*1.25*	*1.25*
O79	O2	2c gray blk	*90*	*90*
O80	O2	5c gray blk	*2.50*	*2.50*
O81	O2	10c gray blk	*90*	*90*
O82	O2	20c gray blk	*1.00*	*60*
O83	O2	50c gray blk	*2.00*	*75*
O84	O2	1s gray blk	*7.50*	*7.50*
		Nos. O78-O84 (7)	16.05	14.40

Issue of 1895 Overprinted **1897 Y 1898**

O85	O2	1c gray blk	*45.00*	*45.00*
O86	O2	2c gray blk	*1.50*	*1.50*
O87	O2	5c gray blk	*1.10*	*85*
O88	O2	10c gray blk	*40.00*	*40.00*
O89	O2	20c gray blk	*65.00*	*65.00*
O90	O2	50c gray blk	*16.00*	*16.00*
O91	O2	1s gray blk	*82.50*	*82.50*
		Nos. O85-O91 (7)	251.10	250.85

Many forged overprints of Nos. O50-O91 exist, made on the original stamps and reprints.

O3

Black Surcharge.

1898-99 *Perf. 15, 16*

O92	O3	5c on 50c lil	30	30
a.		Inverted surcharge	1.50	1.50
O93	O3	10c on 20s org	85	85
a.		Double surcharge	2.25	2.25
O94	O3	10c on 50c lil	*80.00*	*80.00*
O95	O3	20c on 50c lil	2.50	2.50
O96	O3	20c on 50s grn	2.25	2.25
		Nos. O92-O96 (5)	85.90	85.90

Green Surcharge.

O97	O3	5c on 50c lil	1.25	1.25
a.		Double surcharge	2.00	
b.		Double surcharge, blk and grn	6.50	
c.		Same as "b", blk surcharge inverted	2.00	

Red Surcharge.

1899

O98	O3	5c on 50c lil	1.25	1.25
a.		Double surcharge	2.00	
b.		Double surcharge, blk and red	2.50	
O99	O3	20c on 50s grn	2.50	2.50
a.		Inverted surcharge	5.00	
b.		Double surcharge, red and blk	8.00	

Similar Surcharge, Value in Words in Two Lines. Black Surcharge.

O100	O3	1c on 5c bl	*30.00*	

Red Surcharge

O101	O3	2c on 5c bl	*65.00*
O102	O3	4c on 20c bl	*55.00*

Types of Regular Issue of 1899 Overprinted in Black OFICIAL

1899			*Perf. 14, 15*	
O103	A37	2c org & blk	40	1.00
O104	A39	10c org & blk	40	1.00
O105	A40	20c org & blk	30	1.50
O106	A41	50c org & blk	30	2.00

OFICIAL

The above overprint was applied to remainders of the postage stamps of 1904 with the idea of increasing their salability. They were never regularly in use as official stamps.

Regular Issue of 1911-13 Overprinted in Black OFICIAL

1913			*Perf. 12.*	
O107	A71	1c scar & blk	75	75
O108	A72	2c bl & blk	75	75
O109	A73	3c org & blk	40	35
O110	A74	5c scar & blk	1.00	75
O111	A75	10c bl & blk	1.00	30
		Nos. O107-O111 (5)	3.90	2.90

Regular Issue of 1911-13 Overprinted

OFICIAL

Overprint 22x3½ mm.

1916-17				
O112	A72	2c bl & blk	7.50	7.50
O113	A74	5c scar & blk	7.50	7.50
O114	A75	10c bl & blk	4.50	4.50

Overprint 25x4 mm.

O115	A71	1c scar & blk	75	75
O116	A72	2c bl & blk	1.00	1.00
a.		Invtd. ovpt.	1.50	1.50
O117	A73	3c org & blk	60	60
O118	A74	5c scar & blk	1.00	1.00
O119	A75	10c bl & blk	1.00	50
		Nos. O115-O119 (5)	4.35	3.85

Same Overprint On Regular Issue of 1915-17.

O120	A71	1c orange	30	30
O121	A72	2c green	30	30
O122	A73	3c black	50	40
O123	A78	4c red & blk	50	50
a.		Invtd. ovpt.	1.00	
O124	A74	5c violet	30	25
O125	A75	10c blue	55	55
O126	A79	20c grn & blk	3.50	3.50
		Nos. O120-O126 (7)	5.95	5.80

Regular Issues of 1911-17 Overprinted in Black or Red

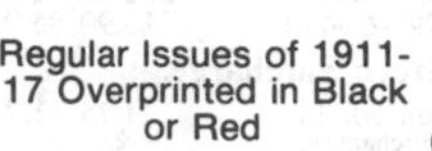

OFICIAL

O127	A71	1c orange	20	15
O128	A72	2c green	20	20
O129	A73	3c blk (Bk)	15	10
O130	A73	3c blk (R)	20	20
a.		Inverted overprint		
O131	A78	4c red & blk	20	10
O132	A74	5c violet	35	20
O133	A75	10c bl & blk	1.00	50
O134	A75	10c blue	20	20
O135	A79	20c grn & blk	1.00	40
		Nos. O127-O135 (9)	3.50	2.05

Regular Issue of 1920 Overprinted OFICIAL

1920				
O136	A86	1c green	50	40
a.		Inverted overprint	6.00	6.00
O137	A86	2c carmine	40	30
O138	A86	3c yel brn	50	40
O139	A86	4c dk grn	75	60
a.		Inverted overprint	6.00	10.00
O140	A86	5c blue	75	60
O141	A86	6c orange	50	40
O142	A86	7c brown	75	60
O143	A86	8c yel grn	1.00	75
O144	A86	9c red	1.25	1.00
O145	A95	10c blue	75	60
O146	A86	15c gray	4.00	3.00
O147	A86	20c dp vio	5.00	3.50
O148	A86	30c violet	6.00	4.00
O149	A86	40c dk brn	8.00	4.00
O150	A86	50c dk grn	5.00	4.00
O151	A86	60c dk bl	6.00	5.00
O152	A86	70c gray	6.00	5.00
O153	A86	80c yellow	7.50	6.00
O154	A104	90c green	8.00	7.00
O155	A86	1s blue	15.00	12.00
		Nos. O136-O155 (20)	77.65	59.15

Nos. O136 to O155 were issued in commemoration of the centenary of the independence of Guayaquil.

Stamps of 1911 Overprinted OFICIAL

1922				
O156	A71	1c scar & blk	2.00	75
O157	A72	2c bl & blk	1.00	75

Revenue Stamps of 1919-1920 Overprinted like Nos. O156 and O157

1924				
O158	PT3	1c dk bl	40	30
O159	PT3	2c green	2.00	1.25

Regular Issues of 1911-17 Overprinted

1924				
O160	A71	1c orange	1.50	1.50
a.		Inverted overprint	2.50	

Overprinted in Black or Red OFICIAL

O161	A72	2c green	25	25
O162	A73	3c blk (R)	30	30
O163	A78	4c red & blk	60	60
O164	A74	5c violet	75	40
O165	A75	10c dp bl	60	50
O166	A76	1s grn & blk	2.00	2.00
		Nos. O160-O166 (7)	6.00	5.55

No. O106 with Additional Overprint Acuerdo No 4.228

1924			*Perf. 14, 15*	
O167	A41	50c org & blk	1.25	1.25

Nos. O160 to O167 inclusive exist with inverted overprint.

No. 199 Overprinted

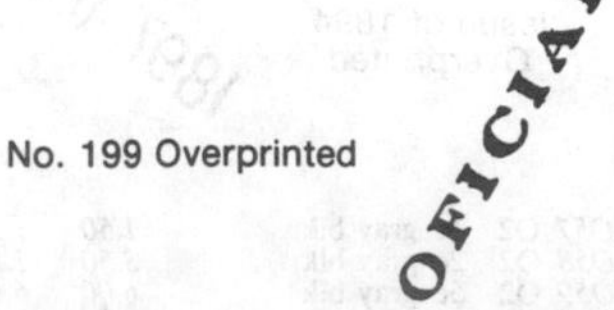

1924			*Perf. 12*	
O168	A71	1c orange	1.00	1.00

Regular Issues of 1911-25 Overprinted

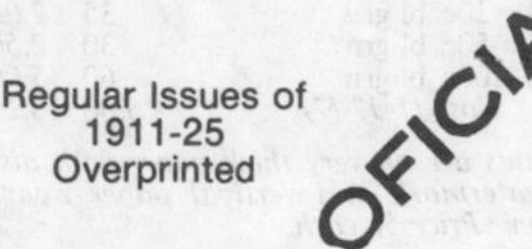

1925				
O169	A71	1c scar & blk	1.50	70
a.		Invtd. ovpt.	1.50	
O170	A71	1c orange	20	15
a.		Invtd. ovpt.	1.00	
O171	A72	2c green	15	15
a.		Invtd. ovpt.	1.00	
O172	A73	3c blk (Bk)	25	25
O173	A73	3c blk (R)	30	30
O174	A78	4c red & blk	15	15
O175	A74	5c violet	25	25
O176	A74	5c rose	25	25
O177	A75	10c dp bl	15	15
		Nos. O169-O177 (9)	3.20	2.35

Regular Issues of 1916-25 Overprinted Vertically Up or Down OFICIAL

1927, Oct.				
O178	A71	1c orange	40	30
O179	A86	2c carmine	40	30
O180	A86	3c yel brn	40	30
O181	A86	4c myr grn	40	30
O182	A86	5c pale bl	40	30
O183	A75	10c yel grn	40	30
		Nos. O178-O183 (6)	2.40	1.80

Regular Issues of 1920-27 Overprinted OFICIAL

1928				
O184	A71	1c lt bl	15	12
O185	A86	2c carmine	15	12
O186	A86	3c yel brn	15	15
a.		Invtd. ovpt.	1.00	
O187	A86	4c myr grn	15	15
O188	A86	5c lt bl	15	15
O189	A75	10c yel grn	15	15
O190	A109	20c violet	2.00	50
a.		Ovpt. reading up	50	50
		Nos. O184-O190 (7)	2.90	1.34

The overprint is placed vertically reading down on No. O190.

Regular Issue of 1936 Overprinted in Black OFICIAL

1936			*Perf. 14.*	
O191	A131	5c ol grn	8	6
O192	A132	10c brown	10	12
O193	A133	20c dk vio	12	10
O194	A134	1s dk car	30	25
O195	A135	2s dk bl	50	40
		Nos. O191-O195 (5)	1.10	93

Regular Postage Stamps of 1937 Overprinted in Black OFICIAL

1937			*Perf. 11½*	
O196	A139	2c green	5	5
O197	A140	5c dp rose	10	10
O198	A141	10c blue	10	10
O199	A142	20c dp rose	10	10
O200	A143	1s ol grn	25	20
		Nos. O196-O200 (5)	60	55

Tobacco Stamp, Overprinted in Black

CORRESPONDENCIA OFICIAL

1946	**Unwmk.**		*Rouletted.*	
O201	PT7	1c rose red	6	6

Communications Building, Quito — O4

1947	**Unwmk.**	**Litho.**	*Perf 11*	
O202	O4	30c brown	15	15
O203	O4	30c grnsh bl	15	10
a.		Imperf., pair		
O204	O4	30c purple	15	10

Nos. O202 to O204 overprinted "Primero la Patria!" and plane in dark blue are said to be essays.

No. 719 with Additional Diagonal Overprint:

oficial

1964			*Perf. 14x13*	
O205	A231	80c block of 4	3.00	3.00

The "OEA" overprint covers four stamps, the "oficial" overprint is applied to every stamp.

A set of 20 imperforate items in the above Roosevelt design, some overprinted with the initials of various government ministries, was released in 1949. Later that year a set of eight miniature sheets, bearing the same design plus a marginal inscription, "Presidencia (or Vicepresidencia) de la Republica," and a frame-line were released. In the editors' opinion, information justifying the listing of these issues has not been received.

POSTAL TAX STAMPS

Roca — PT1

1920	**Unwmk.**		*Perf. 12.*	
RA1	PT1	1c orange	35	15

PT2 PT3

RA2	PT2	1c red & bl	25	15
a.		"de" inverted	2.00	2.00
b.		Double overprint	2.00	60
c.		Inverted overprint	2.00	60
RA3	PT3	1c dp bl	30	10
a.		Inverted ovpt.	1.25	1.00
b.		Double ovpt.	1.25	1.00

PT4 PT5

Red or Black Surcharge or Overprint.

Stamp Dated 1911-1912

RA4	PT4	20c dp bl	27.50	12.00

Stamp Dated 1913-1914.

RA5	PT4	20c dp bl (R)	1.50	50

Stamp Dated 1917-1918.

RA6	PT4	20c ol grn (R)	2.00	75
a.		Dated 1919-20	*9.00*	
RA7	PT5	1c on 2c grn	30	12

Stamp Dated 1911-1912.

RA8 PT5 1c on 5c grn 25 10
a. Double surcharge

Stamp Dated 1913-1914.

RA9 PT5 1c on 5c grn 2.50 50
a. Double surcharge 3.00 2.00

On Nos. RA7, RA8 and RA9 the surcharge is found reading upward or downward.

Post Office — PT6

1920-24 **Engr.**

RA10 PT6 1c ol grn 15 10
RA11 PT6 2c dp grn 20 10
RA12 PT6 20c bis brn ('24) 75 20
RA13 PT6 2s violet 3.00 3.00
RA14 PT6 5s blue 5.00 5.00
Nos. RA10-RA14 (5) 9.10 8.40

Revenue Stamps of 1917-18 Surcharged Vertically in Red reading up or down

Casa de Correos
VEINTE CTS.
1921—1922

1921-22

RA15 PT5 20c on 1c dk bl 20.00 3.00
RA16 PT5 20c on 2c grn 20.00 3.00

No. RA12 Surcharged in Green

DOS
CENTAVOS
—2—

1924

RA17 PT6 2c on 20c bis brn 20 10
a. Invtd. surch. 2.00 2.00
b. Dbl. surch. 3.00 3.00

PT7

1924 ***Rouletted 7***

RA18 PT7 1c rose red 25 15
a. Inverted overprint 1.50

Similar Design, Eagle at left

Perf. 12

RA19 PT7 2c blue 30 12
a. Inverted overprint 1.50 1.00

PT8

Inscribed "Timbre Fiscal".

1924

RA20 PT8 1c yellow 1.00 75
RA21 PT8 2c dk bl 40 20

Inscribed "Region Oriental".

RA22 PT8 1c yellow 35 15
RA23 PT8 2c dk bl 35 30

Overprint on No. RA22 reads down or up.

Revenue Stamp Overprinted in Blue

CASA
de
Correos y
Telegrafos
de
Guayaquil

1934

RA24 2c green 15 10
a. Blue overprint inverted 2.00 1.50
b. Blue overprint double, one inverted 2.50 1.50

Postage Stamp of 1930 Overprinted in Red

Perf. 12½.

RA25 A119 20c ultra & yel 25 20

Telegraph Stamp Overprinted in Red, like No. RA24, and Surcharged diagonally in Black

1934 ***Perf. 14***

RA26 2c on 10c ol brn 20 15
a. Double surcharge 2.00

Overprint Blue, Surcharge Red.

RA27 2c on 10c ol brn 25 15

PT9

PT10

Symbols of Post and Telegraph Service PT11

Wmk. 233- "Harrison & Sons, London" in Script Letters

1934-36 ***Perf. 12.***

RA28 PT9 2c green 15 10
a. Both overprints in red ('36) 15 10

Postal Tax stamp of 1920-24, overprinted in red "POSTAL" has been again overprinted "CASA de Correos y Teleg. de Guayaquil" in black.

Perf. 14½x14

1934 **Photo.** **Wmk. 233**

RA29 PT10 2c yel grn 15 10

Issued to pay a postal tax of 2c for the rebuilding of the General Post Office at Guayaquil.

1935

RA30 PT11 20c claret 15 10

Issued to pay a postal tax of 20c for the rebuilding of the General Post Office at Guayaquil.

No. RA29 Surcharged in Red and Overprinted in Black

3 ctvs,
Seguro
Social del
Campesino
Quito, 16 de
Otbre-1935

1935

RA31 PT10 3c on 2c yel grn 15 10
a. Double surcharge

Issued for the Social and Rural Workers' Insurance Fund.

Tobacco Stamp Surcharged in Black

Seguro Social 3
del Campesino ctvs

1936 **Unwmk.** ***Rouletted 7***

RA32 PT7 3c on 1c rose red 15 10
a. Lines of words reversed 18 12
b. Imperf. vertically (pair)

Issued for the Social and Rural Workers' Insurance Fund.

No. 310 Overprinted in Black

Casa de Correos
y Telégrafos
de Guayaquil

1936 ***Perf. 12½***

RA33 A119 20c ultra & yel 15 8
a. Double overprint

Tobacco Stamp Surcharged in Black

SEGURO SOCIAL 3
DEL CAMPESINO ctvs.

1936 ***Rouletted 7***

RA34 PT7 3c on 1c rose red 15 10

Issued for the Social and Rural Workers' Insurance Fund.

Worker

PT12 PT13

1936 **Engr.** ***Perf. 13½***

RA35 PT12 3c ultra 10 5

Issued for the Social and Rural Workers' Insurance Fund.

Surcharged in Black.

1936

RA36 PT13 5c on 3c ultra 15 12

This combines the 2c for the rebuilding of the post office with the 3c for the Social and Rural Workers' Insurance Fund.

National Defense Issue.

Tobacco Stamp, Surcharged in Black.

TIMBRE PATRIOTICO
DIEZ CENTAVOS

1936 ***Rouletted 7.***

RA37 PT7 10c on 1c rose 20 12
a. Double surch.

Symbolical of Defense — PT14

1937-42 ***Perf. 13½***

RA38 PT14 10c dp bl 20 10

A 1s violet and 2s green exist in type PT14.

PT15

Overprinted or Surcharged in Black.

Engraved and Typographed

1937-42 ***Perf. 13½***

RA39 PT15 5c lt brn & red 50 20
d. Invert. ovpt. 5.00

Perf. 12, 11½.

RA39A PT15 20c on 5c rose pink & red ('42) 35.00
RA39B PT15 20c on 1s yel brn & red ('42) 35.00
RA39C PT15 20c on 2s grn & red ('42) 35.00

A 50c dark blue and red exists in type PT15.

5 5

No. RA38 Surcharged in Red

POSTAL
ADICIONAL

1937 **Engr.** ***Perf. 12½***

RA40 PT14 5c on 10c dp bl 25 12

Map of Ecuador — PT16

1938 ***Perf. 14x13½.***

RA41 PT16 5c car rose 18 10

Issued for the Social and Rural Workers' Insurance Fund.

No. C42 Surcharged in Red

20 20
CASA DE CORREOS
Y TELEGRAFOS
DE GUAYAQUIL
20 20

1938 ***Perf. 12½.***

RA42 AP5 20c on 70c blk 30 10

No. 307 Surcharged in Red

CAMPAÑA
CONTRA
EL CANCER
5 5

1938

RA43 A116 5c on 6c yel & red 15 6

This stamp was obligatory on all mail from Nov. 23rd to 30th, 1938. The tax was for the International Union for the Control of Cancer.

Tobacco Stamp, Surcharged in Black

POSTAL ADICIONAL
CINCO CENTAVOS

1939 ***Rouletted***

RA44 PT7 5c on 1c rose 12 10
a. Double surcharge
b. Triple surcharge

Tobacco Stamp, Surcharged in Blue

CASAS DE CORREOS
Y TELEGRAFOS
CINCO CENTAVOS

1940

RA45 PT7 5c on 1c rose red 15 10
a. Double surcharge 1.00 1.00

No. 370 Surcharged in Carmine

CASA DE
CORREOS y TELEGRAFOS
DE GUAYAQUIL

20 20

1940 *Perf. 11½.*
RA46 A144 20c on 50c blk & multi 15 12
a. Double surcharge, one inverted

Tobacco Stamp, Surcharged in Black

TIMBRE PATRIOTICO
VEINTE CENTAVOS

1940 *Rouletted*
RA47 PT7 20c on 1c rose red 15 7

Farmer Plowing
PT17

Communication Symbols
PT18

1940 *Perf. 13x13½.*
RA48 PT17 5c car rose 25 10

1940-43 *Perf. 12.*
RA49 PT18 5c cop brn 15 10
RA49A PT18 5c grn ('43) 15 10

Pursuit Planes — PT19

1941 *Perf. 11½x13*
RA50 PT19 20c ultra 25 6

The tax was used for national defense.

Warrior Shielding Women — PT20

1942-46 **Engr.** *Perf. 12*
RA51 PT20 20c dk bl 25 10
RA51A PT20 40c blk brn ('46) 25 10

The tax was used for national defense.

A 20c carmine, 20c brown and 30c gray exist lithographed in type PT20.

No. 370 Surcharged in Carmine

CASA DE
CORREOS y TELEGRAFOS
DE GUAYAQUIL
VEINTE CENTAVOS

1942 *Perf. 11½*
RA52 A144 20c on 50c blk & multi 25 15
a. Double surch. 2.50

No. RA35 Surcharged in Red

ADICIONAL
CINCO
CENTAVOS

1943 *Perf. 13½.*
RA53 PT12 5c on 3c ultra 10 5

No. RA35 with Additional Surcharge in Black

5 Centavos
CASA DE
CORREOS
DE GQUIL.
y

1943
RA54 PT12 5c on 5c on 3c ultra 10 5

Peons — PT21

1943 *Perf. 12*
RA55 PT21 5c blue 20 10

The tax was for farm workers.

Revenue Stamp (as No. RA64) Overprinted in Black

TIMBRE
PATRIOTICO

1943 *Perf. 12½*
RA56 20c red org 60.00 1.00

Revenue Stamp (as No. RA64) Surcharged in Black

TIMBRE PATRIOTICO
VEINTE CENTAVOS

1943 *Perf. 12*
RA57 20c on 10c org 55 10
a. Double surch.

Coat of Arms — PT22

1943 *Perf. 12½*
RA58 PT22 20c org red 12 10

The tax was for national defense.

No. RA58 Surcharged in Black

30
Centavos

1944
RA59 PT22 30c on 20c org red 15 10
a. Double surcharge

Consular Service Stamps Surcharged in Black

TIMBRE
ESCOLAR
20 ctvs. 20

1951 **Unwmk.** *Perf. 12.*
RA60 R1 20c on 1s red 15 8
RA61 R1 20c on 2s brn 15 8
RA62 R1 20c on 5s vio 15 8

Teacher and Pupils in Schoolyard — PT23

PT24

1952 **Engr.** *Perf. 13*
RA63 PT23 20c bl grn 15 8

Revenue Stamp Overprinted "PATRIOTICO / SANITARIO"

1952 *Perf. 12*
RA64 PT24 40(c) ol grn 20 10

Woman Holding Flag — PT25

PT26

1953 *Perf. 12½.*
RA65 PT25 40c ultra 30 10

Telegraph Stamp Surcharged "ESCOLAR 20 Centavos" in Black

1954 **Unwmk.** *Perf. 13*
RA66 PT26 20c on 30c red brn 30 12

Revenue Stamps Surcharged or Overprinted Horizontally in Black "PRO TURISMO 1954"

1954 **Unwmk.** *Perf. 12*
RA67 R2 10c on 25c bl 25 10
RA68 R3 10c on 50c org red 25 10
RA69 R3 10c carmine 25 10

PT27

Telegraph Stamp Surcharged "Pro-Turismo 1954 10 ctvs. 10" in Black

1954 *Perf. 13*
RA70 PT27 10c on 30c red brn 35 12

Revenue Stamp Overprinted in Black

ESCOLAR

1954 *Perf. 12*
RA71 R3 20c ol blk 35 12

Consular Service Stamp Surcharged in Black

0,20 0,20
ESCOLAR
Veinte centavos

1954
RA72 R1 20c on 10s gray 35 12

Young Student at Desk
PT28

Globe, Ship and Plane
PT29

Imprint: "Heraclio Fournier.-Vitoria"

1954 **Photo.** *Perf. 11*
RA73 PT28 20c rose pink 35 12

See also No. RA76.

1954 **Engr.** *Perf. 12*
RA74 PT29 10c dp mag 35 12

Soldier Kissing Flag — PT30

1955 **Photo.** *Perf. 11*
RA75 PT30 40c blue 35 12

See also No. RA77.

Types of 1954-55 Redrawn.
Imprint: "Thomas de la Rue & Co. Ltd.'

1957 **Unwmk.** *Perf. 13*
RA76 PT28 20c rose pink 15 8
Perf. 14x14½
RA77 PT30 40c blue 40 20

No. RA77 is inscribed "Republica del Ecuador."

AIR POST POSTAL TAX STAMPS

No. 438 Surcharged in Black or Carmine

FOMENTO-AERO-
COMUNICACIONES
20 Ctvs.

1945 **Unwmk.** *Perf. 11.*
RAC1 A173 20c on 10c dk grn 35 15
a. Pair, one without surch. 45.00
RAC2 A173 20c on 10c dk grn (C) 35 15

Obligatory on letters and parcel post carried on planes in the domestic service.

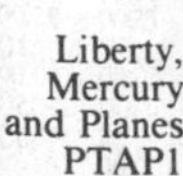

Liberty, Mercury and Planes
PTAP1

1946	Engr.	*Perf. 12.*	
RAC3 PTAP1 20c org brn		25	15

GALAPAGOS ISLANDS

(Columbus Archipelago)

Issued for use in the Galapagos Islands, a province of Ecuador, but were commonly used throughout the country.

Sea Lions — A1

Map — A2

Design: 1s, Marine iguana.

Unwmk.

1957, July 15	Photo.	*Perf. 12*	
L1 A1 20c dk brn		30	15
L2 A2 50c violet		20	15
L3 A1 1s dl ol grn		1.00	40

Issued to commemorate the 125th anniversary of Ecuador's possession of the Galapagos Islands, and to publicize the islands.

AIR POST STAMPS

Type of Regular Issue, 1957.

Designs: 1s, Santa Cruz Island. 1.80s, Map of Galapagos archipelago. 4.20s, Galapagos giant tortoise.

Unwmk.

1957, July 19	Photo.	*Perf. 12*	
LC1 A1 1s dp bl		25	15
LC2 A1 1.80s rose vio		50	25
LC3 A1 4.20s black		1.50	60

Issued to commemorate the 125th anniversary of Ecuador's possession of the Galapagos Islands and to publicize the islands.

Redrawn Type of Ecuador, 1956

1959, Jan. 3	Engr.	*Perf. 14*	
LC4 AP69 2s lt ol grn		75	50

Issued to honor the United Nations. See note after No. C407.

EGYPT

LOCATION — Northern Africa, bordering on the Mediterranean and the Red Sea.
GOVT. — Republic
AREA — 386,900 sq. mi.
POP. — 46,000,000 (est. 1984)
CAPITAL — Cairo

Modern Egypt was a part of Turkey until 1914 when a British protectorate was declared over the country and the Khedive was deposed in favor of Hussein Kamil under the title of sultan. In 1922 the protectorate ended and the reigning sultan was declared king of the new monarchy. Egypt became a republic on June 18, 1953. Egypt merged with Syria in 1958 to form the United Arab Republic. Syria left this union in 1961. In 1971 Egypt took the name of Arab Republic of Egypt.

40 Paras = 1 Piastre
1000 Milliemes = 100 Piastres = 1 Pound (1888)
1000 Milliemes = 1 Pound

Turkish Suzerainty

Turkish Inscriptions — A1

A2

A3

A4

A5

A6

A7

Wmk.118

Surcharged in Black

Wmk. Pyramid and Star. (118)

1866, Jan. 1	**Litho.**	***Perf. 12½***	
1	A1 5pa sl grn	35.00	25.00
a.	Imperf. pair	275.00	
b.	Pair, imperf. btwn.	350.00	
c.	Perf. 12½x13	50.00	50.00
d.	Perf. 13	350.00	450.00
2	A2 10pa brown	45.00	30.00
a.	Imperf. pair	250.00	
b.	Pair, imperf. btwn.	250.00	
c.	Perf. 13	250.00	
d.	Perf. 12½x15	325.00	350.00
3	A3 20pa blue	70.00	35.00
a.	Imperf. pair	350.00	
b.	Pair, imperf. btwn.	500.00	
c.	Perf. 12½x13	125.00	125.00
d.	Perf. 13	600.00	350.00
4	A4 2pi yellow	90.00	45.00
a.	Imperf.	125.00	75.00
b.	Imperf. vert or horiz. pair	350.00	350.00
c.	Perf. 12½x15	150.00	
d.	Diagonal half used as 1 pi on cover		1,500.
e.	Perf. 12½x13, 13x12½	120.00	50.00
5	A5 5pi rose	250.00	200.00
a.	Imperf.	300.00	300.00
b.	Imperf. vert. or horiz. pair	*1,000.*	
d.	Inscription of 10 pi, imperf.	500.00	
e.	Perf. 12½x13, 13x12½	300.00	300.00
f.	As "d" perf. 12½x15	600.00	600.00
6	A6 10pi sl bl	275.00	250.00
a.	Imperf.	275.00	275.00
b.	Pair, imperf. btwn.	*2,000.*	
c.	Perf. 12½x13, 13x12½	500.00	500.00
d.	Perf. 13	*2,000.*	

Unwmk.

Typo.

7	A7 1pi rose lil	50.00	5.00
a.	Imperf.	100.00	
b.	Pair, imperf. vert.	350.00	
c.	Perf. 12½x13, 13x12½	100.00	35.00
d.	Perf. 13	350.00	200.00

Single imperforates of types A1-A10 are sometimes simulated by trimming wide-margined copies of perforated stamps.

Proofs of Nos. 1-7 are on smooth white paper, unwatermarked and imperforate. Proofs of No. 7 are on thinner paper than No. 7a.

Sphinx and Pyramid — A8

Wmk.119

Wmk. Crescent and Star. (119)

1867	**Litho.**	***Perf. 15x12½***	
8	A8 5pa orange	13.00	10.00
a.	Imperf.	50.00	50.00
b.	Imperf. vert. or horiz. pair	200.00	
9	A8 10pa lilac	37.50	10.00
a.	10pa vio	35.00	10.00
b.	Half used as 5pa on newspaper piece		600.00
11	A8 20pa bl grn	37.50	15.00
a.	20pa yel grn	40.00	15.00
13	A8 1pi rose red	6.00	1.25
a.	Imperf.	60.00	
b.	Pair, imperf. btwn.	200.00	
c.	Half used as 20pa on cover		700.00
d.	Rouletted	50.00	
14	A8 2pi blue	75.00	12.00
a.	Imperf.	150.00	
b.	Imperf. vert., pair	500.00	
c.	Diagonal half used as 1pi on cover		
d.	Perf. 12½	300.00	
15	A8 5pi brown	200.00	150.00

There are four types of each value, so placed that any block of four contains all four types.

A9

A10

Clear Impressions.
Thick Opaque Paper.

Typographed by the Government at Boulac

Perf. 12½x13½, Clean-cut.

1872		**Wmk. 119**	
19	A9 5pa brown	9.00	4.50
20	A9 10pa lilac	8.00	3.00
21	A9 20pa blue	25.00	3.50
22	A9 1pi rose red	25.00	60
h.	Half used as 20pa on cover		300.00
23	A9 2pi dl yel	50.00	5.00
24	A9 2½pi dl vio	45.00	5.00
25	A9 5pi green	200.00	30.00
i.	Tete beche pair		

Perf. 13½, Clean-cut.

19a	A9 5pa brown	20.00	12.00
20a	A9 10pa dl lil	8.00	3.00
21a	A9 20pa blue	45.00	15.00
22a	A9 1pi rose red	50.00	2.75
23a	A9 2pi dl yel	20.00	3.50
24a	A9 2½pi dl vio	800.00	250.00
25a	A9 5pi green	300.00	75.00

Litho.

21m	A9 20pa bl, perf. 12½x13½	120.00	40.00
21n	A9 20pa bl, perf. 13½	200.00	75.00
21p	A9 20pa bl, imperf.	200.00	
22m	A9 1pi rose red, perf. 12½x13½	250.00	3.00
22n	A9 1pi rose red, perf. 13½		5.00

Typographed

Blurred Impressions.
Thinner Paper.

Wmk. Crescent and Star. (119)

1874-75		***Perf. 12½, Rough.***	
26	A10 5pa brn ('75)	6.00	2.50
e.	Imperforate		40.00
f.	Imperforate horiz., pair	150.00	150.00
g.	Tete beche pair	50.00	50.00
20b	A9 10pa gray lil	6.00	3.00
g.	Tete beche pair	200.00	200.00
21b	A9 20pa gray bl	40.00	3.00
k.	Half used as 10pa on cover		400.00
22b	A9 1pi vermilion	4.00	85
f.	Imperforate	8.00	7.00
g.	Tete beche pair	75.00	75.00
23b	A9 2pi yellow	30.00	4.00
i.	Tete beche pair	500.00	500.00
24b	A9 2½pi dp vio	5.00	2.50
e.	Imperforate	22.50	22.50
f.	Tete beche pair	400.00	400.00

25b A9 5pi yel grn 35.00 10.00
e. Imperforate 25.00

No. 26f normally occurs tête-bêche.

Perf. 13½x12½, Rough.

26c A10 5pa brown 4.00 2.50
i. Tete beche pair 35.00 35.00
20c A9 10pa gray lil 6.00 2.50
i. Tete beche pair 200.00 200.00
21c A9 20pa gray bl 4.00 2.75
h. Pair, imperf. between 250.00
22c A9 1pi vermilion 11.00 1.00
i. Tete beche pair 300.00 300.00
23c A9 2pi yellow 5.00 4.00
g. Tete beche pair 400.00 400.00
k. Half used as 1pi on cover 850.00

Perf. 12½x13½, Rough.

23d A9 2pi yel ('75) 16.50 5.00
h. Tete beche pair
24d A9 2½pi dp vio ('75) 15.00 9.00
i. Tete beche pair 700.00 700.00
25d A9 5pi yel grn ('75) 250.00 150.00

Stamp of 1872-75 Surcharged in Black

PARAS 5

Perf. 12½, 12½x13½, Rough

1879, Jan. 1

27 A9 5pa on 2½pi dl vio 6.00 6.00
a. Imperf. 35.00 35.00
b. Tete beche pair 3,000.
c. Inverted surcharge 60.00 60.00
d. Perf. 12½x13½ 6.00 6.50
e. As "d," tete beche pair
f. As "c," perf. 12½x13½ 110.00 110.00
28 A9 10pa on 2½pi dl vio 6.00 6.00
a. Imperf.
b. Tete beche pair 1,500.
c. Inverted surcharge 70.00 70.00
d. Perf. 12½x13½ 10.00 10.00
e. As "c," perf. 12½x13½ 90.00 90.00

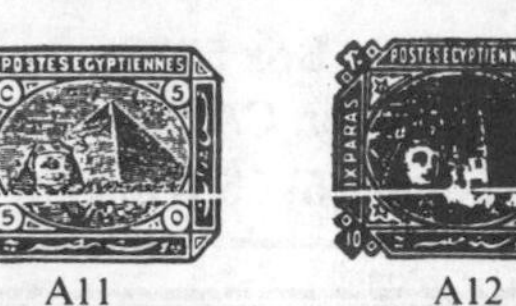

A11 A12

A13 A14

A15 A16

1879-93 Typo. *Perf. 14x13½*

29 A11 5pa brown 30 15
30 A12 10pa violet 27.50 3.00
31 A12 10pa lil rose ('81) 45.00 4.00
32 A12 10pa gray ('82) 12.50 75
33 A12 10pa grn ('84) 30 12
34 A13 20pa ultra 60.00 1.25
35 A13 20pa rose ('84) 10.00 40
36 A14 1pi rose 15.00 25
37 A14 1pi ultra ('84) 1.75 10
38 A15 2pi org yel 18.00 35
39 A15 2pi org brn 10.00 35
40 A16 5pi green 80.00 5.50
41 A16 5pi gray ('84) 12.50 40
Nos. 29-41 (13) 292.85 16.62

Imperf. examples of Nos. 29-31, 35-38 and 40 are proofs.

A17

1884, Feb. 1

42 A17 20pa on 5pi grn 10.00 1.00
a. Inverted surcharge 45.00 35.00

A18

A19

A20

1888

43 A18 1m brown 25 5
44 A19 2m green 50 6
45 A20 5m car rose 1.00 5

Imperf. examples of Nos. 43-45 are proofs.

A21

A22

1889-93

46 A21 3m mar ('92) 2.50 80
47 A21 3m org ('93) 1.25 15
48 A22 10pi purple 21.00 50

Nos. 37, 39, 41, 43 to 45, 47 and 48 exist on both ordinary and chalky paper.

A23

1906 Chalk-surfaced Paper.

49 A23 4m brn red 1.50 60

Boats on Nile
A24

Cleopatra
A25

Ras-el-Tin Palace
A26

Giza Pyramids
A27

Sphinx
A28

Colossi of Thebes
A29

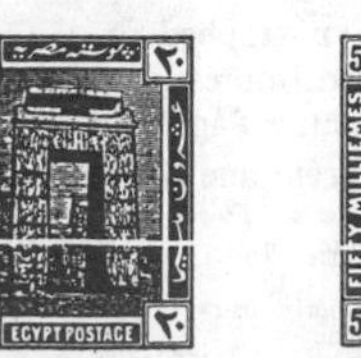

Pylon of Karnak and Temple of Khonsu
A30

Citadel at Cairo
A31

Rock Temple of Abu Simbel — A32

Aswan Dam — A33

Perf. 13½x14

1914, Jan. 8 Wmk. 119

Chalk-surfaced Paper

50 A24 1m ol brn 12 8
51 A25 2m dp grn 30 12
52 A26 3m orange 50 15
53 A27 4m red 1.00 50
54 A28 5m lake 60 5
a. Bklt. pane of 6
55 A29 10m dk bl 1.25 8

Perf. 14

56 A30 20m ol grn 3.00 15
57 A31 50m red vio 5.00 50
58 A32 100m black 10.00 50
59 A33 200m plum 25.00 85
Nos. 50-59 (10) 46.77 2.98

All values of this issue exist imperforate on both watermarked and unwatermarked paper but are not known to have been issued in that condition.

See Nos. 61-72.

British Protectorate

No. 52 Surcharged

2 Milliemes

1915, Oct. 15

60 A26 2m on 3m org 1.00 75
a. Inverted surcharge 150.00 150.00

Scenic Types of 1914 and Statue of Ramses II
A34 A35

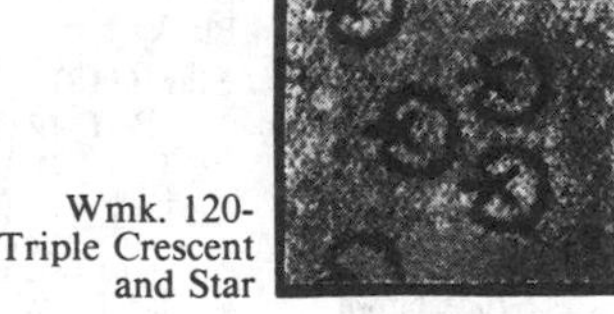

Wmk. 120-
Triple Crescent and Star

1921-22 Wmk. 120 *Perf. 13½x14*

Chalk-surfaced Paper

61 A24 1m ol brn 15 7
62 A25 2m dp grn 1.50 1.00
63 A25 2m red ('22) 40 20
64 A26 3m orange 1.75 35
65 A27 4m grn ('22) 1.50 1.25
66 A28 5m lake 50 6
67 A28 5m pink 1.00 6
68 A29 10m dp bl 2.00 10
69 A29 10m lake ('22) 1.50 25
70 A34 15m ind ('22) 1.25 15
71 A35 15m ind ('22) 12.50 1.00

Perf. 14

72 A30 30m ol grn 3.50 15
73 A31 50m maroon 7.00 30
74 A32 100m black 30.00 3.00
Nos. 61-74 (14) 64.55 7.94

Independent Kingdom

Stamps of 1921-22 Overprinted

1922, Oct. 10

78 A24 1m ol brn 30 15
a. Inverted overprint 60.00 60.00
b. Double overprint 75.00 75.00
79 A25 2m red 50 10
a. Double overprint 60.00 60.00
80 A26 3m orange 1.00 50
81 A27 4m green 75 50
a. Double ovpt. 100.00
b. Inverted ovpt.
82 A28 5m pink 60 5
83 A29 10m lake 1.00 6
84 A34 15m indigo 2.50 10
85 A35 15m indigo 1.25 25

Perf. 14

86 A30 20m ol grn 2.25 20
a. Inverted overprint 200.00 200.00
b. Double overprint 125.00 125.00
87 A31 50m maroon 3.00 20
a. Inverted overprint 425.00 400.00
b. Double overprint
88 A32 100m black 10.00 60
a. Inverted overprint 225.00 225.00
b. Double overprint 225.00 225.00
Nos. 78-88 (11) 23.15 2.71

Same Overprint on Nos. 58-59

Wmk. Crescent and Star (119)

90 A32 100m black 75.00 40.00
91 A33 200m plum 10.00 60
a. Inverted overprint 375.00

Nos. 78-91 were issued to commemorate the proclamation of the Egyptian monarchy.

The overprint signifies "The Egyptian Kingdom, March 15, 1922". It exists in four types, one lithographed and three typographed on Nos 78-87, but lithographed only on Nos. 88-91.

King Fuad
A36 A37

Wmk. Triple Crescent and Star. (120)

1923-24 Photo. *Perf. 13½*

Size 18x22½ mm.

92 A36 1m orange 25 6
93 A36 2m black 40 6
94 A36 3m brown 75 18
a. Imperf., pair 225.00
95 A36 4m yel grn 75 15
96 A36 5m org brn 40 5
a. Imperf., pair 30.00
97 A36 10m rose 60 5
98 A36 15m ultra 75 5
a. Imperf., pair 225.00

Perf. 14

Size 22x28 mm.

99 A36 20m dk grn 1.50 10
100 A36 50m myr grn 5.00 10
101 A36 100m red vio 8.00 25
102 A36 200m vio ('24) 15.00 1.00
a. Imperf., pair 375.00
103 A37 £1 ultra & dk vio ('24) 100.00 10.00
a. Imperf., pair 900.00
Nos. 92-103 (12) 133.40 12.05

Thoth Carving Name of King Fuad — A38

1925, Apr. Litho. *Perf. 11*

105 A38 5m brown 4.00 4.00
106 A38 10m rose 5.50 5.50
107 A38 15m ultra 8.00 8.00

International Geographical Congress, Cairo.

Nos. 106-107 exist with both white and yellowish gum.

Oxen Plowing A39

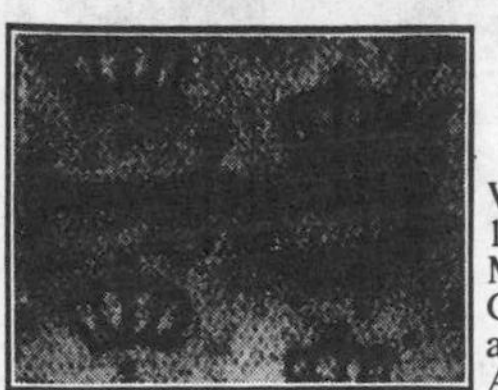

Wmk. 195- Multiple Crown and Arabic F

1926 Wmk. 195 *Perf. 13x13½*

108 A39	5m lt brn	1.00	70
109 A39	10m brt rose	1.00	70
110 A39	15m dp bl	1.00	70
111 A39	50m Prus grn	5.00	4.00
112 A39	100m brn vio	11.00	7.00
113 A39	200m brt vio	15.00	12.00
	Nos. 108-113 (6)	34.00	25.10

Issued to commemorate the 12th Agricultural and Industrial Exhibition at Gezira.
"F" in watermark stands for Fuad.

King Fuad — A40

Perf. 14x14½

1926, Apr. 2 Photo. Wmk. 120

114 A40 50pi brn vio & red vio 70.00 10.00

58th birthday of King Fuad.

Nos. 111-113 Surcharged

5 MILLIEMES

Perf. 13x13½

1926, Aug. 24 Wmk. 195

115 A39	5m on 50m Prus grn	1.50	1.25
116 A39	10m on 100m brn vio	1.50	1.25
117 A39	15m on 200m brt vio	1.50	1.25
a.	Dbl. surcharge	200.00	

Ship of Hatshepsut — A41

1926, Dec. 9 Litho. *Perf. 13x13½*

118 A41	5m brn & blk	2.00	1.00
119 A41	10m dp red & blk	2.50	1.25
120 A41	15m dp bl & blk	2.50	1.25

International Navigation Congress, Cairo.

Nos. 118-120, 114 Overprinted

PORT FOUAD *a* PORT FOUAD *b*

1926, Dec. 21

121 A41 (a)	5m brn & blk	100.00	75.00
122 A41 (a)	10m dp red & blk	100.00	75.00
123 A41 (a)	15m dp bl & blk	100.00	75.00

Perf. 14x14½

Wmk. 120

124 A40 (b) 50pi brn vio & red vio 1,300. 1,100.

Inauguration of Port Fuad opposite Port Said.
Nos. 121-123 have a block over "Le Caire" at lower left.
Forgeries of Nos. 121-124 exist.

Branch of Cotton A42

Perf. 13x13½

1927, Jan. 25 Wmk. 195

125 A42	5m dk brn & sl grn	1.00	1.00
126 A42	10m dp red & sl grn	2.50	1.50
127 A42	15m dp bl & sl grn	2.50	1.50

International Cotton Congress, Cairo.

King Fuad
A43 A44

A45

A46

Perf. 13x13½

1927-37 Wmk. 195 Photo.

128 A43	1m orange	10	5
129 A43	2m black	15	5
130 A43	3m ol brn	15	8
131 A43	3m dp grn ('30)	25	6
132 A43	4m yel grn	45	15
133 A43	4m brn ('30)	50	20
134 A43	4m dp grn ('34)	1.00	25
135 A43	5m dk red brn ('29)	25	5
b.	5m chnt	30	5
136 A43	10m dk red ('29)	60	5
a.	10m org red	90	6
137 A43	10m pur ('34)	1.75	8
138 A43	13m car rose ('32)	50	12
139 A43	15m ultra	1.00	5
140 A43	15m dk vio ('34)	2.00	5
141 A43	20m ultra ('34)	3.50	8

Early printings of Nos. 128, 129, 130, 132, 135, 136 and 139 were from plates with screen of vertical dots in the vignette; later printings show screen of diagonal dots.

Perf. 13½x14

142 A44	20m ol grn	1.00	5
143 A44	20m ultra ('32)	2.25	6
144 A44	40m ol brn ('32)	1.25	6
145 A44	50m Prus grn	1.00	5
a.	50m grnsh bl	1.50	5
146 A44	100m brn vio	4.00	6
a.	100m cl	4.00	8
147 A44	200m dp vio	5.00	25

Printings of Nos. 142, 145 and 146, made in 1929 and later, were from new plates with stronger impressions and darker colors.

Litho.; Center Photo.

Perf. 13x13½

148 A45	500m choc & Prus bl ('32)	40.00	6.00
a.	Entirely photogravure	50.00	8.00
149 A46	£1 dk grn & org brn ('37)	50.00	5.00
a.	Entirely photogravure	50.00	5.00
	Nos. 128-149 (22)	116.70	12.85

Statue of Amenhotep, Son of Hapu — A47

1927, Dec. 29 Photo. *Perf. 13½x13*

150 A47	5m org brn	50	40
151 A47	10m cop red	1.00	55
152 A47	15m dp bl	2.00	65

Statistical Congress, Cairo.

Imhotep A48 Mohammed Ali Pasha A49

1928, Dec. 15

153 A48	5m org brn	75	35
154 A49	10m cop red	75	35

Issued to commemorate the International Congress of Medicine at Cairo and the centenary of the Faculty of Medicine at Cairo.

Prince Farouk — A50

1929, Feb. 11 Litho.

155 A50	5m choc & gray	1.00	1.00
156 A50	10m dl red & gray	2.00	1.00
157 A50	15m ultra & gray	2.00	1.00
158 A50	20m Prus bl & gray	2.00	1.00

Ninth birthday of Prince Farouk.
Nos. 155-158 with black or brown centers are trial color proofs. They were sent to the Universal Postal Union, but were never placed on sale to the public, although some are known used.

Tomb Fresco at El-Bersheh A51

1931, Feb. 15 *Perf. 13x13½*

163 A51	5m brown	70	60
164 A51	10m cop red	1.50	60
165 A51	15m dk bl	2.00	75

Issued to commemorate the 14th Agricultural and Industrial Exhibition, Cairo.

Nos. 114 and 103 Surcharged with Bars and

MILLS 50 ملليما ٥٠ *a* MILLS 100 ملليم ١٠٠ *b*

1932 Wmk. 120 *Perf. 14x14½*

166 A40 50m on 50pi brn vio & red vio 7.50 1.25

Perf. 14

167 A37 100m on £1 ultra & dk vio 135.00 100.00

Locomotive of 1852 — A52

Designs (Locomotives): 13m, Of 1859. 15m, Of 1862. 20m, Of 1932.

Perf. 13x13½

1933, Jan. 19 Litho. Wmk. 195

168 A52	5m brn & blk	2.50	1.50
169 A52	13m dl red & blk	10.00	7.50
170 A52	15m pur & blk	10.00	7.50
171 A52	2m dp bl & blk	10.00	7.50

International Railroad Congress, Heliopolis.

Commercial Passenger Airplane — A56

Dornier Do-X A57

Graf Zeppelin A58

1933, Dec. 20 Photo.

172 A56	5m brown	3.25	1.50
173 A56	10m brt vio	10.00	6.00
174 A57	13m brn car	12.00	6.00
175 A57	15m violet	12.00	6.00
176 A58	20m blue	18.00	12.50
	Nos. 172-176 (5)	55.25	32.00

International Aviation Congress, Cairo.

Khedive Ismail Pasha
A59 A60

1934, Feb. 1 *Perf. 13½*

177 A59	1m dp org	15	15
178 A59	2m black	20	15
179 A59	3m brown	20	20
180 A59	4m bl grn	30	30
181 A59	5m red brn	30	15
182 A59	10m violet	60	25
183 A59	13m cop red	90	60
184 A59	15m dl vio	70	25
185 A59	20m ultra	1.00	40
186 A59	50m Prus bl	3.00	40
187 A59	100m ol grn	6.50	60
188 A59	200m dp vio	15.00	3.00

Perf. 13½x13

189 A60 50pi brown 75.00 42.50
190 A60 £1 Prus bl 140.00 65.00
Nos. 177-190 (14) 243.85 113.95

10th Congress of Universal Postal Union, Cairo.

King Fuad — A61

1936-37 *Perf. 13½*

191 A61 1m dl org 12 5
192 A61 2m black 25 5
193 A61 4m dk grn 30 10
194 A61 5m chestnut 25 5
195 A61 10m pur ('37) 1.00 10
196 A61 15m brn vio 1.50 8
197 A61 20m sapphire 2.00 10
Nos. 191-197 (7) 5.42 53

Entrance to Agricultural Building — A62

Agricultural Building — A63

Design: 15m, 20m, Industrial Building.

1936, Feb. 15 *Perf. 13½x13*

198 A62 5m brown 55 50

Perf. 13x13½

199 A63 10m violet 80 75
200 A63 13m cop red 1.75 1.25
201 A63 15m dk vio 1.00 75
202 A63 20m blue 2.00 2.00
Nos. 198-202 (5) 6.10 5.25

Issued to commemorate the 15th Agricultural and Industrial Exhibition, Cairo.

Signing of Treaty — A65

1936, Dec. 22 *Perf. 11*

203 A65 5m brown 50 40
204 A65 15m dk vio 75 50
205 A65 20m sapphire 1.50 70

Signing of Anglo-Egyptian Treaty, Aug. 26, 1936.

King Farouk A66

Medal for Montreux Conference A67

1937-44 **Wmk. 195** *Perf. 13x13½*

206 A66 1m brn org 5 5
207 A66 2m vermilion 5 5
208 A66 3m brown 5 5
209 A66 4m green 10 5
210 A66 5m red brn 10 5
211 A66 6m lt yel grn ('40) 20 5
212 A66 10m purple 20 5
213 A66 13m rose car 20 12
214 A66 15m dk vio brn 25 5
215 A66 20m blue 30 5
216 A66 20m lil gray ('44) 35 6
Nos. 206-216 (11) 1.85 63

1937, Oct. 15 *Perf. 13½x13*

217 A67 5m red brn 50 30
218 A67 15m dk vio 85 50
219 A67 20m sapphire 1.00 60

Issued in commemoration of the International Treaty signed at Montreux, Switzerland, under which foreign privileges in Egypt were to end in 1949.

Eye of Re — A68

1937, Dec. 8 *Perf. 13x13½*

220 A68 5m brown 60 55
221 A68 15m dk vio 1.00 60
222 A68 20m sapphire 1.40 60

15th Ophthalmological Congress, Cairo, December, 1937.

King Farouk, Queen Farida — A69

1938, Jan. 20 *Perf. 11*

223 A69 5m red brn 10.00 2.50

Royal wedding of King Farouk and Farida Zulficar.

Inscribed: "11 Fevrier 1938"

1938, Feb. 11

224 A69 £1 grn & sep 125.00 100.00

King Farouk's 18th birthday.

Cotton Picker — A70

1938, Jan. 26 *Perf. 13½x13*

225 A70 5m red brn 65 60
226 A70 15m dk vio 2.00 1.25
227 A70 20m sapphire 1.50 1.00

Issued to commemorate the 18th International Cotton Congress at Cairo.

Pyramids of Giza and Colossus of Thebes A71

1938, Feb. 1 *Perf. 13x13½*

228 A71 5m red brn 80 75
229 A71 15m dk vio 1.50 1.00
230 A71 20m sapphire 2.00 1.00

International Telecommunication Conference, Cairo.

Branch of Hydnocarpus — A72

1938, Mar. 21 *Perf. 13x13½*

231 A72 5m red brn 85 50
232 A72 15m dk vio 1.50 70
233 A72 20m sapphire 1.50 70

International Leprosy Congress, Cairo.

King Farouk and Pyramids — A73

King Farouk
A74 A75

Backgrounds: 40m, Hussan Mosque. 50m, Cairo Citadel. 100m, Aswan Dam. 200m, Cairo University.

1939-46 **Photo.** *Perf. 14x13½*

234 A73 30m gray 35 5
a. 30m sl gray 30 5
234B A73 30m ol grn ('46) 35 5
235 A73 40m dk brn 50 5
236 A73 50m Prus grn 55 5
237 A73 100m brn vio 80 5
238 A73 200m dk vio 2.50 8

Perf. 13½x13

239 A74 50pi grn & sep 5.00 50
240 A75 £1 dp bl & dk brn 10.00 70
Nos. 234-240 (8) 20.05 1.53

For £1 with A77 portrait, see No. 269D. See Nos. 267-269D.

King Fuad A76

King Farouk A77

1944, Apr. 28 *Perf. 13½x13*

241 A76 10m dk vio 25 20

Issued to commemorate the eighth anniversary of the death of King Fuad.

1944-50 **Wmk. 195** *Perf. 13x13½*

242 A77 1m yel brn ('45) 6 5
243 A77 2m red org ('45) 6 5
244 A77 3m sep ('46) 25 15
245 A77 4m dp grn ('45) 25 20
246 A77 5m red brn ('46) 10 5
247 A77 10m dp vio 18 5
247A A77 13m rose red ('50) 1.50 75
248 A77 15m dk vio ('45) 20 5
249 A77 17m ol grn 25 8
250 A77 20m dk gray ('45) 30 6
251 A77 22m dp bl ('45) 40 10
Nos. 242-251 (11) 3.55 1.59

King Farouk — A78

Khedive Ismail Pasha — A79

1945, Feb. 10 *Perf. 13½x13*

252 A78 10m dp vio 25 20

25th birthday of King Farouk.

1945, Mar. 2 **Photo.**

253 A79 10m dk ol 25 20

50th anniversary of death of Khedive Ismail Pasha.

Flags of Arab Nations — A80

1945, July 29

254 A80 10m violet 12 12
255 A80 22m dp yel grn 30 30

League of Arab Nations Conference, Cairo, Mar. 22, 1945.

Flags of Egypt and Saudi Arabia A81

Perf. 13x13½

1946, Jan. 10 **Wmk. 195**

256 A81 10m dp yel grn 15 15

Visit of King Ibn Saud, Jan., 1946.

Citadel, Cairo A82

1946, Aug. 9

257 A82 10m yel brn & dp yel grn 25 25

Withdrawal of British troops from Cairo Citadel, Aug. 9, 1946.

King Farouk and Inchas Palace, Cairo A83

Portraits: 2m, Prince Abdullah, Yemen. 3m, Pres. Bechara el-Khoury, Lebanon. 4m, King Abdul Aziz ibn Saud, Saudi Arabia. 5m, King Faisal II, Iraq. 10m, Amir Abdullah ibn Hussein, Jordan. 15m, Pres. Shukri el Kouatly, Syria.

1946, Nov. 9

258 A83 1m dp yel grn 8 8
259 A83 2m sepia 8 8
260 A83 3m dp bl 10 10
261 A83 4m brn org 12 12
262 A83 5m brn red 15 15

263 A83 10m dk gray 18 18
264 A83 15m dp vio 20 20
Nos. 258-264 (7) 91 91

Issued to commemorate the Arab League Congress at Cairo, May 28, 1946.

Parliament Building, Cairo — A84

1947, Apr. 7 **Photo.**
265 A84 10m green 18 18

Issued to commemorate the 36th conference of the Interparliamentary Union, April, 1947.

Raising Egyptian Flag over Kasr-el-Nil Barracks A85

King Farouk A85a

1947, May 6 ***Perf. 13½x13***
266 A85 10m dp plum & yel grn 15 15

Issued to commemorate the withdrawal of British troops from the Nile Delta.

Farouk Types 1939 Redrawn

1947-51 **Wmk. 195** ***Perf. 14x13½***

267	A73	30m ol grn	30	5
268	A73	40m dk brn	40	5
269	A73	50m Prus grn ('48)	55	5
269A	A73	100m dk brn vio ('49)	1.65	8
269B	A73	200m dk vio ('49)	5.00	20
		Perf. 13½x13		
269C	A85a	50pi grn & sep ('51)	15.00	3.75
269D	A75	£1 dp bl & dk brn ('50)	30.00	2.00
		Nos. 267-269D (7)	52.90	6.18

The king faces slightly to the left and clouds have been added in the sky on Nos. 267-269B. Backgrounds as in 1939-46 issue. Portrait on £1 as on type A77.

Field and Branch of Cotton — A86

Map and Infantry Column — A87

Perf. 13½x13
1948, Apr. 1 **Wmk. 195**
270 A86 10m ol grn 30 25

International Cotton Congress held at Cairo in April, 1948.

1948, June 15 ***Perf. 11½x11***
271 A87 10m green 35 35

Arrival of Egyptian troops at Gaza, May 15, 1948.

Ibrahim Pasha A88

1948, Nov. 10 ***Perf. 13x13½***
272 A88 10m brn red & dp grn 25 25

Issued to commemorate the centenary of the death of Ibrahim Pasha (1789-1848).

Statue, "The Nile" A89

Protection of Industry and Agriculture — A90

Perf. 13x13½
1949, Mar. 1 **Photo.** **Wmk. 195**

273	A89	1m dk grn	10	10
274	A89	10m purple	20	20
275	A89	17m crimson	25	25
276	A89	22m dp bl	30	30
		Perf. 11½x11		
277	A90	30m dk brn	40	40
		Nos. 273-277 (5)	1.25	1.25

Souvenir Sheets.
Photogravure and Lithographed
Imperf

278	A89	Sheet of 4	1.25	1.25
a.		1m red brn	25	25
b.		10m dk brn	25	25
c.		17m brn org	25	25
d.		22m dk Prus grn	25	25
279	A90	Sheet of 2	1.75	1.75
a.		10m vio gray	75	75
b.		30m red org	75	75

Nos. 273-279 were issued to publicize the 16th Agricultural and Industrial Exposition, Cairo.

No. 278 has frame and marginal inscriptions in dark green. Size: 127x104½mm.

No. 279 has frame and marginal inscriptions in dark violet. Size: 108x123mm.

Mohammed Ali and Map — A93

Globe — A94

Perf. 11½x11
1949, Aug. 2 **Photo.** **Wmk. 195**
280 A93 10m org brn & grn 25 25

Centenary of death of Mohammed Ali.

1949, Oct. 9 ***Perf. 13½x13***

281	A94	10m rose brn	35	30
282	A94	22m violet	60	50
283	A94	30m dl bl	80	70

75th anniversary of the formation of the Universal Postal Union.

Scales of Justice A95

1949, Oct. 14 ***Perf. 13x13½***
284 A95 10m dp ol grn 20 20

Issued to commemorate the end of the Mixed Judiciary System, Oct. 14, 1949.

Desert Scene A96

1950, Dec. 27
285 A96 10m vio & red brn 25 25

Issued to commemorate the opening of the Fuad I Institute of the Desert.

Fuad I University A97

1950, Dec. 27
286 A97 22m dp grn & cl 35 35

Issued to commemorate the 25th anniversary of the founding of Fuad I University.

Globe and Khedive Ismail Pasha A98

1950, Dec. 27
287 A98 30m cl & dp grn 40 40

75th anniversary of Royal Geographic Soviety of Egypt.

Picking Cotton — A99

1951, Feb. 24
290 A99 10m ol grn 25 20

International Cotton Congress, 1951.

King Farouk and Queen Narriman — A100

1951, May 6 **Photo.** ***Perf. 11x11½***
291 A100 10m grn & red brn 1.00 1.00
a. Souvenir sheet 1.50 1.50

Issued to commemorate the marriage of King Farouk and Narriman Sadek, May 6, 1951.

No. 291a was issued in sheets measuring 129x112mm., with ornamental border and inscriptions in gray and black.

Stadium Entrance A101

Arms of Alexandria and Olympic Emblem — A102

King Farouk A103

1951, Oct. 5 ***Perf. 13x13½, 13½x13***

292	A101	10m brown	50	50
293	A102	22m dp grn	90	90
294	A103	30m bl & dp grn	1.00	1.00
a.		Souvenir sheet	5.00	5.00

Issued to publicize the first Mediterranean Games, Alexandria, Oct. 5-20, 1951.

No. 294a measures 189x117mm., and contains one each of Nos. 292-294 with ornamental frame and background in buff.

Winged Figure and Map — A105

Designs: 22m, King Farouk and Map. 30m, King Farouk and Flag.

Dated "16 Oct. 1951"

1952, Feb. 11 ***Perf. 13½x13***

296	A105	10m dp grn	50	50
297	A105	22m plum & dp grn	90	90
298	A105	30m grn & brn	1.00	1.00
a.		Souvenir sheet	5.00	5.00

Issued to commemorate the abrogation of the Anglo-Egyptian treaty.

No. 298a measures 134 x 113mm., and contains one each of Nos. 296 to 298, with ornamental border and Arabic inscriptions in gray.

Stamps of 1937-51 Overprinted in Various Colors

ملك مصر والسودان
١٦ اكتوبر سنة ١٩٥١

Perf. 13x13½

1952, Jan. 17 **Wmk. 195**

299 A77 1m yel brn 10 8
300 A77 2m red org (Bl) 10 8
301 A66 3m brn (Bl) 12 10
302 A77 4m dp grn (RV) 12 8
303 A66 6m lt yel grn (RV) 60 15
304 A77 10m dp vio (C) 20 5
305 A77 13m rose red (Bl) 75 15
306 A77 15m dk vio (C) 60 22
307 A77 17m ol grn (C) 90 15
308 A77 20m dk gray (RV) 1.00 15
309 A77 22m dp bl (C) 1.50 80

No. 244, the 3m sepia, exists with this overprint but was not regularly issued or used.

Same Overprint, 24½mm. Wide on Nos. 267 to 269B.

Perf. 14x13½

310 A73 30m ol grn 55 8
a. Dark bl overprint 35 6
311 A73 40m dk brn (G) 50 18
312 A73 50m Prus grn (C) 65 10
313 A73 100m dk brn vio (C) 1.00 25
314 A73 200m dk vio (C) 2.50 30

Same Overprint, 19mm. Wide, on Nos. 269C-269D.

Perf. 13½x13.

315 A85a 50pi grn & sep (C) 12.00 3.50
316 A75 £1 dp bl & dk brn (Bl) 25.00 3.75
Nos. 299-316 (18) 48.19 10.17

The overprint translates: King of Egypt and the Sudan, Oct. 16, 1951.

Egyptian Flag — A106

Perf. 13½x13

1952, May 6 **Photo.** **Wmk. 195**

317 A106 10m org yel, dp bl & dp grn 25 25
a. Souvenir sheet 1.25 1.25

Issued to commemorate the birth of Crown Prince Ahmed Fuad, January 16, 1952.

No. 317a measures 115¼ x 137¼mm., with ornamental border and Arabic inscriptions in deep blue, salmon and green.

"Dawn of New Era" A107

Symbolical of Egypt Freed — A108

Designs: 10m, "Egypt" with raised sword. 22m, Citizens marching with flag.

Perf. 13x13½, 13½x13

1952, Nov. 23

Dated: "23 Juillet 1952."

318 A107 4m dp grn & org 10 10
319 A107 10m dp grn & cop brn 15 15
320 A108 17m brn org & dp grn 25 25
321 A108 22m choc & dp grn 35 35

Change of government, July 23, 1952.

Demand, as well as supply, determines a stamp's market value. One is as important as the other.

Republic

Farmer A109

Soldier A110

Mosque of Sultan Hassan A111

Queen Nefertiti A112

1953-56 ***Perf. 13x13½***

322 A109 1m red brn 5 5
323 A109 2m dk lil 6 5
324 A109 3m brt bl 6 5
325 A109 4m dk grn 6 5
326 A110 10m dk brn *("Defence")* 12 6
327 A110 10m dk brn *("Defense")* 8 5
328 A110 15m gray 15 5
329 A110 17m dk grnsh bl 18 6
330 A110 20m purple 18 6

Perf. 13½.

331 A111 30m dl grn 20 5
332 A111 32m brt bl 25 10
333 A111 35m vio ('55) 50 5
334 A111 37m gldn brn ('56) 1.75 15
335 A111 40m red brn 30 5
336 A111 50m vio brn 45 5
337 A112 100m hn brn 1.00 10
338 A112 200m dk grnsh bl 2.50 20
339 A112 500m purple 5.00 90
340 A112 £1 dk grn, blk & red 12.00 1.00
Nos. 332-340 (9) 23.75 2.60

Nos. 327-330 are inscribed "Defense." See No. 490.

Nos. 206, 208 and 211 Overprinted in Black with Three Bars to Obliterate Portrait.

1953 ***Perf. 13x13½***

342 A66 1m brn org 5.00 5.00
343 A66 3m brown 1.00 1.00
344 A66 6m lt yel grn 25 25

Same Overprint on Stamps of 1939-51

Perf. 13x13½, 13½x13.

345 A77 1m yel brn 6 6
346 A77 2m red org 6 6
347 A77 3m sepia 6 6
348 A77 4m dp grn 8 6
349 A77 10m dp vio 12 10
350 A77 13m rose red 35 25
351 A77 15m dk vio 18 10
352 A77 17m ol grn 20 15
353 A77 20m dk gray 25 12
354 A77 22m dp bl 30 25
355 A73 30m ol grn (#267) 35 18
356 A73 50m Prus grn (#269) 50 20
357 A73 100m dk brn vio (#269A) 75 25
358 A73 200m dk vio (#269B) 3.00 1.00
359 A85a 50pi grn & sep 6.00 2.00
360 A75 £1 dp bl & dk brn (#269D) 15.00 5.00
Nos. 345-360 (16) 27.26 9.84

Same Overprint on Nos. 299-309, 311 and 314.

360A A77 1m yel brn 2.00 2.00
360B A77 2m red org 25 20
360C A66 3m brown 2.00 2.00
360D A77 4m dp grn 2.00 2.00
360E A66 6m lt yel grn 2.50 2.50
361 A77 10m dp vio 1.00 1.00
362 A77 13m rose red 50 30
362A A77 15m dk vio 7.00 7.00
362B A77 17m ol grn 7.00 7.00
362C A77 20m dk gray 7.00 7.00
362D A77 22m dp bl 25.00 25.00
363 A73 40m dk brn 60 35
364 A73 200m dk vio 3.00 50
Nos. 360A-364 (13) 59.85 56.85

Practically all values of Nos. 342-364 exist with double overprint.

Symbols of Electronic Progress — A113

1953, Nov. 23 **Photo.** ***Perf. 13x13½***

365 A113 10m brt bl 30 25

Electronics Exposition, Cairo, Nov. 23.

Crowd Acclaiming the Republic A114

Farmer A115

Design: 30m, Crowd, flag and eagle.

Perf. 13½x13

1954, June 18 **Wmk. 195**

366 A114 10m brown 15 15
367 A114 30m dp bl 35 35

Issued to commemorate the first anniversary of the proclamation of the republic.

1954-55 ***Perf. 13x13½.***

368 A115 1m red brn 5 5
369 A115 2m dk lil 5 5
370 A115 3m brt bl 6 5
371 A115 4m dk grn ('55) 6 6
372 A115 5m dp car ('55) 12 8
Nos. 368-372 (5) 34 29

Egyptian Flag and Map — A116

Globe — A117

Design: 35m, Bugler, soldier and map.

1954, Nov. 4 ***Perf. 13½x13***

373 A116 10m rose vio & grn 15 15
374 A116 35m ver, blk & bl grn 50 50

Issued to commemorate the agreement of Oct. 19, 1954, with Great Britain for the evacuation of the Suez Canal zone by British troops.

Arab Postal Union Issue.

1955, Jan. 1

375 A117 5m yel brn 10 10
376 A117 10m green 20 20
377 A117 37m violet 60 60

Issued to commemorate the founding of the Arab Postal Union, July 1, 1954.

Paul P. Harris and Rotary Emblem — A118

Design: 35m, Globe, wings and Rotary emblem.

Perf. 13½x13

1955, Feb. 23 **Wmk. 195**

378 A118 10m claret 30 15
379 A118 35m blue 60 40

Issued to commemorate the 50th anniversary of the founding of Rotary International.

Nos. 375-377 Overprinted

مؤتمر البريد العربي
القاهرة ١٩٥٥/٣/١٥

1955, Nov. 1

381 A117 5m yel brn 10 10
382 A117 10m green 20 20
383 A117 37m violet 55 55

Issued to commemorate the Arab Postal Union Congress held at Cairo, March 15, 1955.

Map of Africa and Asia, Olive Branch and Rings A119

Globe, Torch, Dove and Olive Branch — A120

Perf. 13x13½, 13½x13

1956, July 29

384 A119 10m chnt & grn 20 15
385 A120 35m org yel & dl pur 45 40

Afro-Asian Festival, Cairo, July, 1956.

Map of Suez Canal and Ship A121

Queen Nefertiti A122

Perf. 11½x11

1956, Sept. 26 **Wmk. 195**

386 A121 10m bl & buff 50 25

Nationalization of the Suez Canal, July 26, 1956. See also No. 393.

956, Oct. 15 ***Perf. 13½x13***
87 A122 10m dk grn 1.50 45

Issued to publicize the International Iuseum Week (UNESCO), Oct. 8-14.

Egyptians Defending Port Said — A123

956, Dec. 20 Litho. ***Perf. 11x11½***
88 A123 10m brn vio 30 20

Issued in honor of the defenders of Port aid.

No. 388 Overprinted in Carmine Rose EVACUATION 22·12·56

957, Jan. 14
89 A123 10m brn vio 50 20

Issued to commemorate the evacuation of ort Said by British and French troops, Dec. 2, 1956.

Old and New Trains A124

1957, Jan. 30 Photo. ***Perf. 13x13½***
90 A124 10m red vio & gray 25 15

Issued to commemorate the 100th anniversary of the Egyptian Railway System (in 956).

Mother and Children A125

1957, Mar. 21
391 A125 10m crimson 25 15

Mother's Day, 1957.

Battle Scene A126

Perf. 13x13½
1957, Mar. 28 Wmk. 195
392 A126 10m brt bl 25 15

Issued to commemorate the 150th anniversary of the victory over the British at Rosetta.

Type of 1956; New Inscriptions in English

1957, Apr. 15 ***Perf. 11½x11***
393 A121 100m bl & yel grn 1.00 65

Issued to commemorate the reopening of the Suez Canal.
No. 393 is inscribed: "Nationalisation of Suez Canal Co. Guarantees Freedom of Navigation" and "Reopening 1957".

The only foreign revenue stamps listed in this Catalogue are those authorized for prepayment of postage.

Map of Gaza Strip — A127

Perf. 13½x13
1957, May 4 Photo. Wmk. 195
394 A127 10m Prus bl 50 18

"Gaza Part of Arab Nation."

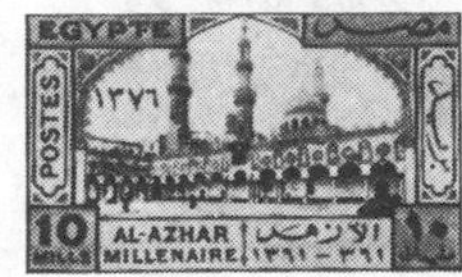

Al Azhar University A128

1957, Apr. 27 ***Perf. 13x13½***
New Arabic Date in Red.
395 A128 10m brt vio 25 15
396 A128 15m vio brn 30 20
397 A128 20m dk gray 40 25

Millenary of Al Azhar University, Cairo.

Shepheard's Hotel, Cairo — A129 Gate, Palace and Eagle — A130

Perf. 13½x13
1957, July 20 Wmk. 195
398 A129 10m brt vio 25 12

Reopening of Shepheard's Hotel, Cairo.

Wmk.315

Wmk. Multiple Eagle (315)
1957, July 22 ***Perf. 11½x11***
399 A130 10m yel & brn 25 12

First meeting of New National Assembly.

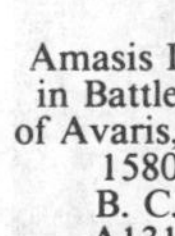

Amasis I in Battle of Avaris, 1580 B. C. A131

Designs: No. 401, Sultan Saladin, Hitteen, 1187 A. D. No. 402, Louis IX of France in chains, Mansourah, 1250 (vertical). No. 403, Map of Middle East, Ein Galout, 1260. No. 404, Port Said, 1956.

Inscribed:
"Egypt Tomb of Aggressors 1957"
Perf. 13x13½, 13½x13
1957, July 26
400 A131 10m car rose 30 10
401 A131 10m dk ol grn 30 10
402 A131 10m brn vio 30 10
403 A131 10m grnsh bl 30 10
404 A131 10m yel brn 30 10
Nos. 400-404 (5) 1.50 50

No. 400 exists with Wmk. 195.

Ahmed Arabi Speaking to the Khedive A132

Perf. 13x13½
1957, Sept. 16 Wmk. 315
405 A132 10m dp vio 25 12

75th anniversary of Arabi Revolution.

Hafez Ibrahim — A133

Portrait: No. 407, Ahmed Shawky.

1957, Oct. 14 ***Perf. 13½x13***
406 A133 10m dl red brn 15 12
407 A133 10m ol grn 15 12

Nos. 406-407 are printed se-tenant in sheets of 50. Issued to commemorate the 25th anniversary of the deaths of Hafez Ibrahim and Ahmed Shawky, poets.

MiG and Ilyushin Planes A134

Design: No. 409, Viscount plane.

1957, Dec. 19 ***Perf. 13x13½***
408 A134 10m ultra 25 15
409 A134 10m green 25 15

Issued to commemorate the 25th anniversaries of the Egyptian Air Force and of Misrair, the Egyptian airline. Nos. 408-409 printed se-tenant.

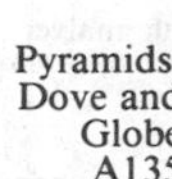

Pyramids, Dove and Globe A135

1957, Dec. 26 Photo. Wmk. 315
410 A135 5m brn org 12 8
411 A135 10m green 18 12
412 A135 15m brt vio 25 20

Issued to publicize the Afro-Asian Peoples Conference, Cairo, Dec. 26-Jan. 2.

Farmer's Wife — A136 Ramses II — A137

1957-58 Wmk. 315 ***Perf. 13½***
413 A136 1m bl grn ('58) 5 5
414 A137 10m violet 12 8

"Industry" — A138

Wmk. 318- Multiple Eagle and "Misr"

1958 Wmk. 318
415 A136 1m lt bl grn 5 5
416 A138 5m brown 6 5
417 A137 10m violet 12 5

See also Nos. 438-444, 474-488.

Cyclists — A139 Mustafa Kamel — A140

Perf. 13½x13
1958, Jan. 12 Wmk. 315
418 A139 10m lt red brn 25 15

Issued to publicize the fifth International Bicycle Race, Egypt, Jan. 12-26.

1958, Feb. 10 Photo. Wmk. 318
419 A140 10m bl gray 25 15

Issued to commemorate the 50th anniversary of the death of Mustafa Kamel, orator and politician.

United Arab Republic

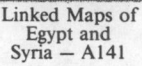

Linked Maps of Egypt and Syria — A141

Cotton — A142

Perf. 11½x11

1958, Mar. 22 **Wmk. 318**
436 A141 10m yel & grn 15 12

Birth of United Arab Republic. See No. C90.

1958, Apr. 5 *Perf. 13½x13*
437 A142 10m Prus bl 15 12

Issued for the International Fair for Egyptian Cotton, April, 1958.

Types of 1957-58 Inscribed "U.A.R. EGYPT" and

Princess Nofret — A143

Designs: 1m, Farmer's wife. 2m, Ibn-Tulun's Mosque. 4m, 14th century glass lamp (design lacks "1963" of A217). 5m. "Industry" (factories and cogwheel). 10m, Ramses II. 35m, "Commerce" (eagle, ship and cargo).

1958 *Perf. 13½x14*
438 A136 1m crimson 5 5
439 A138 2m blue 5 5
440 A143 3m dk red brn 5 5
441 A217 4m green 5 5
442 A138 5m brown 6 5
443 A137 10m violet 12 5
444 A138 35m lt ultra 80 5
Nos. 438-444 (7) 1.18 35

See Nos. 474-488, 532-535.

Qasim Amin — A144

Doves, Broken Chain and Globe — A145

1958, Apr. 23 *Perf. 13½x13*
445 A144 10m dp bl 18 12

50th anniversary of the death of Qasim Amin, author of "Emancipation of Women."

1958, June 18
446 A145 10m violet 15 10

Issued on the fifth anniversary of the republic to publicize the struggle of peoples and individuals for freedom.

Cement Industry — A146

Industries: No. 448, Textile. No. 449, Iron & steel. No. 450, Petroleum (Oil). No. 451, Electricity and fertilizers.

Perf. 13½x13

1958, July 23 **Photo.** **Wmk. 318**
447 A146 10m red brn 15 10
448 A146 10m bl grn 15 10
449 A146 10m brt red 15 10
450 A146 10m ol grn 15 10
451 A146 10m dk bl 15 10
Nos. 447-451 (5) 75 50

Nos. 447-451 are printed in one sheet of 25 in vertical rows of five.

Souvenir Sheet

U. A. R. Flag — A147

1958, July 23 *Imperf.*
452 A147 50m grn, dp car & blk 10.00 10.00

No. 452 measures 80½x75½mm. with black marginal inscription. Nos. 447-452 issued on the 6th anniversary of the Revolution of July 23, 1952.

Sayed Darwich A148

Hand Holding Torch, Broken Chain and Flag A149

1958, Sept. 15 *Perf. 13½x13*
453 A148 10m vio brn 12 10

Issued to commemorate the 35th anniversary of the death of Sayed Darwich, Arab composer.

1958, Oct. 14 **Photo.** **Wmk. 318**
454 A149 10m car rose 12 10

Establishment of the Republic of Iraq.

Maps and Cogwheels A150

1958, Dec. 8 *Perf. 13x13½*
455 A150 10m blue 18 10

Issued to publicize the Economic Conference of Afro-Asian Countries, Cairo, Dec. 8.

Overprinted in Red in English and Arabic in 3 Lines: "Industrial and Agricultural Production Fair."

1958, Dec. 9
456 A150 10m lt red brn 18 10

Issued to publicize the Industrial and Agricultural Production Fair, Cairo, Dec. 9.

Dr. Mahmoud Azmy and U.N. Emblem — A151

1958, Dec. 10
457 A151 10m dl vio 20 15
458 A151 35m green 55 45

Tenth anniversary of the signing of the Universal Declaration of Human Rights.

University Building, Sphinx, "Education" and God Thoth — A152

1958, Dec. 21 **Photo.** **Wmk. 318**
459 A152 10m grnsh blk 12 10

50th anniversary of Cairo University.

الجمهورية العربية المتحدة
٥٥

No. 337 Surcharged

UAR
55

1959, Jan. 20 **Wmk. 195** *Perf. 13½*
460 A112 55m on 100m hn brn 45 30

Emblem A153

1959, Feb. 2 *Perf. 13x13½*
461 A153 10m lt ol grn 12 10

Afro-Asian Youth Conference, Cairo, Feb. 2.

Arms of U.A.R. — A154

Perf. 13½x13

1959, Feb. 22 **Photo.** **Wmk. 318**
462 A154 10m grn, blk & red 12 10

First anniversary, United Arab Republic.

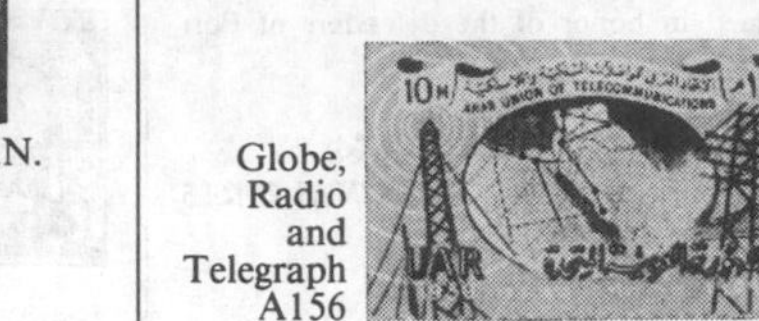
Nile Hilton Hotel A155

1959, Feb. 22 *Perf. 13x13½*
463 A155 10m dk gray 12 10

Opening of the Nile Hilton Hotel, Cairo.

Globe, Radio and Telegraph A156

1959, Mar. 1
464 A156 10m violet 12 10

Arab Union of Telecommunications.

United Arab States Issue

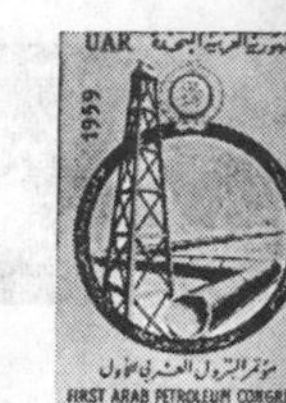
Flags of U. A. R. and Yemen A157

1959, Mar. 8
465 A157 10m sl grn, car & blk 12 10

First anniversary of United Arab States.

Oil Derrick and Pipe Line — A158

Perf. 13½x13

1959, Apr. 16 **Litho.** **Wmk. 318**
466 A158 10m lt bl & dk bl 12 8

First Arab Petroleum Congress, Cairo.

Railroad A159

Designs: No. 468, Bus on highway. No. 469, River barge. No. 470, Ocean liner. No. 471, Telecommunications on map. No. 472, Stamp printing building, Heliopolis.

1959, July 23 **Photo.** *Perf. 13x13½*
Frame in Gray.
467 A159 10m maroon 7 7
468 A159 10m green 7 7
469 A159 10m violet 7 7
470 A159 10m dk bl 8 8
471 A159 10m dl pur 8 8
472 A159 10m scarlet 8 8
Nos. 467-472 (6) 45 45

An imperf. souvenir sheet, issued with this set, commemorates the seventh anniversary of the Egyptian revolution of 1952. The sheet carries a single 50m green and red stamp, 57x32mm., picturing a ship, train, plane and motorcycle mail carrier. Marginal Arabic inscriptions in black; size: 80x74mm. The government printed 140,000 of this sheet and sold it only if the buyer also bought five sets of Nos. 467-472.

Globe, Swallows and Map — A160

1959, Aug. 8 *Perf. 13½x13*
473 A160 10m maroon 10 8

Issued to commemorate the convention of the Association of Arab Emigrants in the United States.

Types of 1953-58 without "Egypt" and

St. Simon's Gate, Bosra, Syria — A161

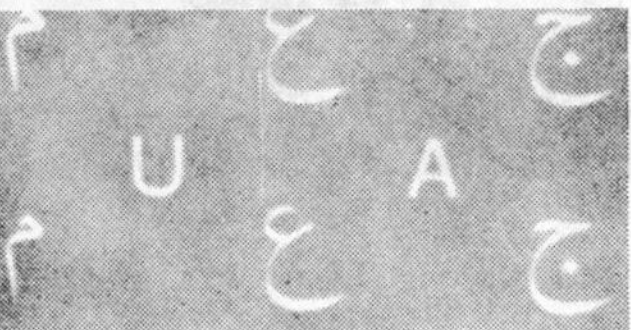

Wmk.328

Designs: 1m, Farmer's wife. 2m, Ibn-Tulun's Mosque. 3m, Princess Nofret. 4m, 14th century glass lamp (design lacks "1963" of A217). 5m, "Industry" (factories and cogwheel). 10m, Ramses II. 15m, Omayyad Mosque, Damascus. 20m, Lotus vase, Tutankhamen treasure. 35m, Eagle, ship and cargo. 40m, Scribe statue. 45m, Saladin's citadel, Aleppo. 55m, Eagle, cotton and wheat. 60m, Dam and factory. 100m, Eagle, hand, cotton and grain. 200m, Palmyra ruins, Syria. 500m, Queen Nefertiti, inscribed "UAR" (no ovpt.).

Perf. 13½x14, 14x13½.
Wmk. U A R. (328)

1959-60 **Photo.**
474 A136 1m vermilion 5 5
475 A138 2m dp bl ('60) 5 5
476 A143 3m maroon 5 5
477 A217 4m grn ('60) 5 5
478 A138 5m blk ('60) 5 5
479 A137 10m dk ol grn 10 5
480 A138 15m dp cl 15 5
481 A138 20m crim ('60) 20 5
482 A161 30m brn vio 30 6
483 A138 35m lt vio bl ('60) 40 6
484 A143 40m sepia 60 8
485 A161 45m lil gray ('60) 1.00 8
486 A138 55m brt bl grn 1.00 8
487 A138 60m dp pur ('60) 60 8
488 A138 100m org & sl grn ('60) 2.00 10
489 A161 200m lt bl & mar 3.50 10
490 A112 500m dk gray & red ('60) 6.00 30
Nos. 474-490 (17) 16.10 1.34

Shield and Cogwheel — A162

Perf. 13½x13
1959, Oct. 20 Photo. Wmk. 328
491 A162 10m brt car rose 12 8

Issued for Army Day, 1959.

Cairo Museum A163

1959, Nov. 18 *Perf. 13x13½*
492 A163 10m ol gray 12 8

Centenary of Cairo museum.

Abu Simbel Temple of Ramses II — A164

1959, Dec. 22 *Perf. 11x11½*
493 A164 10m lt red brn, *pnksh* 25 20

Issued as propaganda to save historic monuments in Nubia threatened by the construction of Aswan High Dam.

Postrider, 12th century A165

1960, Jan. 2 *Perf. 13x13½*
494 A165 10m dk bl 12 8

Issued for Post Day, Jan. 2.

Hydroelectric Power Station, Aswan Dam — A166

1960, Jan. 9
495 A166 10m vio blk 15 8

Issued to commemorate the inauguration of the Aswan Dam hydroelectric power station, Jan. 9.

Arabic and English Description of Aswan High Dam — A167

Architect's Drawing of Aswan High Dam — A168

1960, Jan. 9 *Perf. 11x11½*
496 A167 10m claret 15 8
497 A168 35m claret 45 25

Issued to commemorate the start of work on the Aswan High Dam. Nos. 496-497 printed se-tenant vertically in sheet.

Symbols of Agriculture and Industry A169

Arms and Flag A170

1960, Jan. 16 *Perf. 13½x13*
498 A169 10m gray grn & sl grn 12 8

Industrial and Agricultural Fair, Cairo.

1960, Feb. 22 Photo. Wmk. 328
499 A170 10m grn, blk & red 12 8

Issued to commemorate the 2nd anniversary of the proclamation of the United Arab Republic.

No. 340 Overprinted "UAR" in English and Arabic in Red

1960 Wmk. 195 *Perf. 13½*
500 A112 £1 dk grn, blk & red 10.00 1.00
a. Double ovpt. 50.00

"Art" — A171

Perf. 13½x13
1960, Mar. 1 Wmk. 328
501 A171 10m brown 12 8

Issued to publicize the 3rd Biennial Exhibition of Fine Arts in Alexandria.

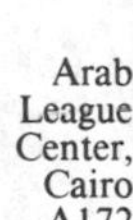

Arab League Center, Cairo A172

1960, Mar. 22 Photo. *Perf. 13x13½*
502 A172 10m dl grn & blk 12 8

Opening of Arab League Center and Arab Postal Museum, Cairo.

Refugees Pointing to Map of Palestine A173

1960, Apr. 7
503 A173 10m org ver 25 8
504 A173 35m Prus bl 50 25

Issued to publicize World Refugee Year, July 1, 1959-June 30, 1960.

Weight Lifter — A174

Stadium, Cairo — A175

Sports: No. 506, Basketball. No. 507, Soccer. No. 508, Fencing. No. 509, Rowing. 30m, Steeplechase (horiz.). 35m, Swimming (horiz.)

Perf. 13½x13
1960, July 23 Photo. Wmk. 328
505 A174 5m gray 5 5
506 A174 5m brown 5 5
507 A174 5m dp cl 10 5
508 A174 10m brt car 15 5
509 A174 10m gray grn 15 5
510 A174 30m purple 35 15
511 A174 35m dk bl 45 20
Nos. 505-511 (7) 1.30 60

Souvenir Sheet
Imperf
512 A175 100m car & brn 1.25 75

Nos. 505-511 issued to commemorate the 17th Olympic Games, Rome, Aug. 25-Sept. 11.

Nos. 505-509 are printed in one sheet of 25 in vertical rows of five.

No. 512 measures 80x75mm. with black marginal inscription.

Dove and U.N. Emblem — A176

Design: 35m, Lights surrounding U.N. emblem (horiz.).

Perf. 13½x13
1960, Oct. 24 Wmk. 328
513 A176 10m purple 10 8
514 A176 35m brt rose 30 25

15th anniversary of United Nations.

Abu Simbel Temple of Queen Nefertari — A177

Perf. 11x11½
1960, Nov. 14 Photo. Wmk. 328
515 A177 10m ocher, *buff* 30 20

Issued as propaganda to save historic monuments in Nubia and in connection with the UNESCO meeting, Paris, Nov. 14.

Catalogue prices for unused stamps up to mid-1953 are for hinged copies matching the condition specified in this volume's introduction.

Model Post Office A178

1961, Jan. 2 *Perf. 13x13½*
516 A178 10m brt car rose 12 8

Issued for Post Day, Jan. 2.

Eagle, Fasces and Victory Wreath — A179

Wheat and Globe Surrounded by Flags — A180

1961, Feb. 22 *Perf. 13½x13*
517 A179 10m dl vio 12 8

3rd anniversary of United Arab Republic.

1961, March 21 **Wmk. 328**
518 A180 10m vermilion 12 8

Issued to publicize the International Agricultural Exhibition, Cairo, March 21-April 20.

Patrice Lumumba and Map A181

Reading Braille and WHO Emblem A182

1961, March 30 *Perf. 13½x13*
519 A181 10m black 12 8

Issued for Africa Day, Apr. 15 and to commemorate the 3rd Conference of Independent African States, Cairo, March 25-31.

1961, Apr. 6 **Photo.**
520 A182 10m red brn 12 8

World Health Organization Day. See No. B21.

Tower of Cairo — A183

Arab Woman and Son, Palestine Map — A184

1961, Apr. 11 *Perf. 13½x13*
521 A183 10m grnsh bl 12 8

Issued to commemorate the opening of the 600-foot Tower of Cairo, on island of Gizireh. See also No. C95.

1961, May 15 **Wmk. 328**
522 A184 10m brt grn 45 8

Issued for Palestine Day.

Symbols of Industry and Electricity A185

Chart and Workers — A186

Designs: No. 524, New buildings and family. No. 525, Ship, train, bus and radio. No. 526, Dam, cotton and field. No. 527, Hand holding candle and family.

1961, July 23 **Photo.** *Perf. 13x13½*

523 A185	10m dp car	8	5
524 A185	10m brt bl	8	5
525 A185	10m dk vio brn	8	5
526 A185	35m dk grn	28	5
527 A185	35m brt pur	28	6
	Nos. 523-527 (5)	80	26

Souvenir Sheet

Imperf

528 A186 100m red brn 1.25 1.25

Nos. 523-528 issued to commemorate the ninth anniversary of the revolution. No. 528 has pale brown border with black inscription. Size: 82x75mm.

Map of Suez Canal and Ships — A187

Perf. 11½x11

1961, July 26 **Unwmk.**
529 A187 10m olive 12 8

Fifth anniversary of the nationalization of the Suez Canal Company.

Various Enterprises of Misr Bank A188

Perf. 13x13½

1961, Aug. 22 **Wmk. 328**
530 A188 10m red brn, *pnksh* 12 8

The 41st anniversary of Misr Bank.

Flag, Ship's Wheel and Battleship — A189

1961, Aug. 29 **Photo.** *Perf. 13½x13*
531 A189 10m dp bl 12 8

Issued for Navy Day.

Eagle of Saladin over Cairo — A190

U.N. Emblem, Book, Cogwheel and Corn — A191

Type A143 of 1958 Redrawn and Type A190

1961, Aug. 31 **Unwmk.** *Perf. 11½*

Designs: 1m, Farmer's wife. 4m, 14th century glass lamp. 35m, "Commerce."

532 A143	1m blue	5	5
533 A143	4m olive	5	5
534 A190	10m purple	10	5
535 A143	35m sl bl	30	6

Smaller of two Arabic inscriptions in new positions: 1m, at right above Egyptian numeral; 4m, upward to spot beside waist of lamp; 35m, upper left corner below "UAR." On 4m, "UAR" is 2mm. deep instead of 1mm. "Egypt" omitted as in 1959-60.

Perf. 13½x13

1961, Oct. 24 **Photo.** **Wmk. 328**

Design: 35m, Globe and cogwheel (horiz.).

536 A191	10m blk & ocher	10	8
537 A191	35m bl grn & brn	30	25

Issued to honor the United Nations' Technical Assistance Program and to commemorate the 16th anniversary of the United Nations.

Trajan's Kiosk, Philae — A192

1961, Nov. 4 **Unwmk.** *Perf. 11½*
Size: 60x27mm.
538 A192 10m dp vio bl 35 20

Issued to commemorate the 15th anniversary of UNESCO, and to publicize UNESCO's help in safeguarding the monuments of Nubia.

Palette, Brushes and Map of Mediterranean A193

Atom and Educational Symbols A194

1961, Dec. 14 **Wmk. 328** *Perf. 13½*
539 A193 10m dk red brn 12 8

Issued to publicize the 4th Biennial Exhibition of Fine Arts in Alexandria.

1961, Dec. 18
540 A194 10m dl pur 12 8

Issued to publicize Education Day.

Arms of U.A.R. A195

1961, Dec. 23 **Unwmk.** *Perf. 11½*
541 A195 10m brt pink, brt grn & blk 20 8

Issued to commemorate Victory Day.

Sphinx at Giza — A196

1961, Dec. 27 *Perf. 11x11½*
542 A196 10m black 12 8

Issued to publicize the "Sound and Light" Project, the installation of floodlights and sound equipment at the site of the Pyramids and Sphinx.

Post Office Printing Plant, Nasser City A197

1962, Jan. 2 **Photo.** *Perf. 11½x11*
543 A197 10m dk brn 12 8

Issued for Post Day, Jan. 2.

Map of Africa, King Mohammed V of Morocco and Flags — A198

1962, Jan. 4 *Perf. 11x11½*

544 A198 10m indigo 12 8

Issued to commemorate the first anniversary of the African Charter, Casablanca.

Girl Scout Saluting and Emblem A199

Perf. 13x13½

1962, Feb. 22 **Wmk. 328**

545 A199 10m brt bl 25 15

Egyptian Girl Scouts' 25th anniversary.

Arab Refugees, Flag and Map — A200

Mother and Child — A201

1962, Mar. 7 *Perf. 13½x13*

546 A200 10m dk sl grn 12 8

Issued to commemorate the 5th anniversary of the liberation of the Gaza Strip.

1962, Mar. 21 **Photo.**

547 A201 10m dk vio brn 12 8

Issued for Arab Mother's Day, March 21.

Map of Africa and Post Horn — A202

1962, Apr. 23 **Wmk. 328**

548 A202 10m crim & ocher 12 8
549 A202 50m dp bl & ocher 40 30

Establishment of African Postal Union.

Cadets on Parade and Academy Emblem — A203

1962, June 18 *Perf. 13x13½*

550 A203 10m green 12 8

Issued to commemorate the 150th anniversary of the Egyptian Military Academy.

Certain countries cancel stamps in full sheets and sell them (usually with gum) for less than face value. Dealers generally sell "CTO".

Malaria Eradication Emblem A204

Theodor Bilharz A205

1962, June 20 *Perf. 13½x13*

551 A204 10m dk brn & red 12 8
552 A204 35m dk grn & bl 30 28

Issued for the World Health Organization drive to eradicate malaria.

1962, June 24 *Perf. 11x11½*

553 A205 10m brn org 12 8

Issued to commemorate the centenary of the death of Dr. Theodor Bilharz (1825-1862), German physician who first described bilharziasis, an endemic disease in Egypt.

Patrice Lumumba and Map of Africa — A206

Hand on Charter — A207

Wmk.342

1962, July 1 **Photo.**

554 A206 10m rose & red 25 10

Issued in memory of Patrice Lumumba (1925-61), Premier of Congo.

1962, July 10 *Perf. 11x11½*

555 A207 10m brt bl & dk brn 12 8

Proclamation of the National Charter.

"Birth of the Revolution" A208

Symbolic Designs: No. 557, Proclamation (Scroll and book). No. 558, Agricultural Reform (Farm and crescent). No. 559, Bandung Conference (Dove, globe and olive branch). No. 560, Birth of UAR (Eagle and flag). No. 561, Industrialization (cogwheel, factory, ship and bus). No. 562, Aswan High Dam. No. 563, Social Revolution (Modern buildings and emblem). 100m, Arms of UAR, emblems of Afro-Asian and African countries and United Nations emblem.

1962, July 23 *Perf. 11½*

556 A208 10m brn, dk red brn & pink 15 8
557 A208 10m dk bl & sep 15 8
558 A208 10m sep & brt bl 15 8
559 A208 10m ol & dk ultra 15 8
560 A208 10m grn, blk & red 15 8
561 A208 10m brn org & ind 15 8
562 A208 10m brn org & vio blk 15 8
563 A208 10m org & blk 15 8
Nos. 556-563 (8) 1.20 64

Souvenir Sheets

Perf. 11½, Imperf.

564 A208 100m grn, pink, red & blk 1.25 1.00

Issued to commemorate the tenth anniversary of the revolution. No. 564 contains one stamp; green marginal inscription. Size: 71x79mm.

Mahmoud Moukhtar, Museum and Sculpture — A209

1962, July 24 *Perf. 11½x11*

565 A209 10m lt vio bl & ol 12 8

Issued to commemorate the opening of the Moukhtar Museum, Island of Gezireh. The sculpture is "La Vestale de Secrets" by Moukhtar.

Flag of Algeria and Map of Africa Showing Algeria — A210

1962, Aug. 15 *Perf. 11x11½*

566 A210 10m multi 12 8

Algeria's independence, July 1, 1962.

Rocket, Arms of U.A.R. and Atom Symbol — A211

1962, Sept. 1 **Photo.** **Wmk. 342**

567 A211 10m brt grn, red & blk 12 8

Launching of U.A.R. rockets.

Rifle and Target — A212

Map of Africa, Table Tennis Paddle, Net and Ball — A213

1962, Sept. 18 *Perf. 11½*

568 A212 5m grn, blk & red 5 5
569 A213 5m grn, blk & red 6 5
570 A212 10m bis, bl & dk grn 12 10
571 A213 10m bis, bl & dk grn 12 10
572 A212 35m dp ultra, red & blk 40 30
573 A213 35m dp ultra, red & blk 40 30
Nos. 568-573 (6) 1.15 90

Issued to commemorate the 38th World Shooting Championships and the First African Table Tennis Tournament. Types A212 and A213 are printed se-tenant at the base in sheets of 70.

Dag Hammarskjold and U.N. Emblem — A214

Perf. 11½x11

1962, Oct. 24 **Photo.** **Wmk. 342**

Portrait in Slate Blue

574 A214 5m dp lil 5 5
575 A214 10m olive 15 8
576 A214 35m dp ultra 30 30

Issued to honor Dag Hammarskjold, Secretary General of the United Nations, 1953-61, and to commemorate the 17th anniversary of the United Nations.

Queen Nefertari Crowned by Isis and Hathor — A215

1962, Oct. 31 *Perf. 11½*

577 A215 10m bl & ocher 25 15

Issued to publicize the UNESCO campaign to safeguard the monuments of Nubia.

Jet Trainer, Hawker Hart Biplane and College Emblem A216

1962, Nov. 2 *Perf. 11½x11*

578 A216 10m bl, dk bl & crim 12 8

25th anniversary of Air Force College.

14th Century Glass Lamp and "1963" — A217

Yemen Flag and Hand with Torch — A218

1963, Feb. 20 *Perf. 11x11½*
579 A217 4m dk brn, grn & car 6 5

Issued for use on greeting cards. See also nos. 441, 477.

1963, Mar. 14 Photo. Wmk. 342
580 A218 10m ol & brt car 12 8

Establishment of Yemen Arab Republic.

Tennis Player, Pyramids and Globe A219

Perf. 11½x11
1963, Mar. 20 Unwmk.
581 A219 10m gray, blk & brn 12 8

Issued to commemorate the International Lawn Tennis Championships, Cairo.

Cow, U.N. and F.A.O. Emblems A220

Designs: 10m, Corn, wheat and emblems (vert.). 35m, Wheat, corn and emblems.

Perf. 11½x11, 11x11½
1963, Mar. 21 Wmk. 342
582 A220 5m vio & dp org 10 5
583 A220 10m ultra & yel 15 10
584 A220 35m bl, yel & blk 35 30

Issued for the "Freedom from Hunger" campaign of the U.N. Food and Agriculture Organization.

Centenary Emblem — A221

Design: 35m, Globe and emblem.

1963, May 8 Unwmk. *Perf. 11x11½*
585 A221 10m lt bl, red & mar 10 8
586 A221 35m lt bl & red 30 25

Centenary of the Red Cross.

Arab Socialist Union Emblem A222

Design: 50m, Tools, torch and symbol of National Charter.

Wmk. 342
1963, July 23 Photo. *Perf. 11½*
587 A222 10m sl & rose pink 10 8

Souvenir Sheets
Perf. 11½, Imperf.
588 A222 50m vio bl & org yel 1.00 1.00

Issued to commemorate the 11th anniversary of the revolution and to publicize the Arab Socialist Union. No. 588 contains one stamp, violet blue marginal inscription. Size: 69x80mm.

Television Station, Cairo, and Screen — A223

1963, Aug. 1 *Perf. 11½x11*
589 A223 10m dk bl & yel 12 8

Issued to publicize the 2nd International Television Festival, Alexandria, Sept. 1-10.

Queen Nefertari A224

Swimmer and Map of Suez Canal A225

Designs: 10m, Great Hypostyle Hall, Abu Simbel. 35m, Ramses in moonlight.

Wmk. 342
1963, Oct. 1 Photo. *Perf. 11*
Size: 25x42mm. (5m, 35m); 28x61mm. (10m)
590 A224 5m brt vio bl & yel 5 5
591 A224 10m gray, blk & red org 10 8
592 A224 35m org yel & blk 30 28

Issued to publicize the UNESCO world campaign to save historic monuments in Nubia.

1963, Oct. 15
593 A225 10m bl & sal rose 10 8

Issued to commemorate the International Suez Canal Swimming Championship.

Ministry of Agriculture — A226

Perf. 11½x11
1963, Nov. 20 Wmk. 342
594 A226 10m multi 10 8

Issued to commemorate the 50th anniversary of the Ministry of Agriculture.

Modern Building and Map of Africa and Asia A227

1963, Dec. 7
595 A227 10m multi 10 8

Afro-Asian Housing Congress, Dec. 7-12.

Scales, Globe, UN Emblem A228

1963, Dec. 10
596 A228 5m dk grn & yel 8 5
597 A228 10m bl, gray & blk 15 8
598 A228 35m rose red, pink & red 40 28

Issued to commemorate the 15th anniversary of the Universal Declaration of Human Rights.

Sculpture, Arms of Alexandria and Palette with Flags — A229

1963, Dec. 12 *Perf. 11x11½*
599 A229 10m pale bl, dk bl & brn 10 8

Issued to publicize the 5th Biennial Exhibition of Fine Arts in Alexandria.

Lion and Nile Hilton Hotel A230

Vase, 13th Century A231

Pharaoh Userkaf (5th Dynasty) A232

Designs: 1m, Vase, 14th century. 2m, Ivory headrest. 3m, Pharaonic calcite boat. 4m, Minaret and gate. 5m, Nile and Aswan High Dam. 10m, Eagle of Saladin over pyramids. 15m, Window, Ibn Tulun's mosque. No 608, Mitwalli Gate, Cairo. 35m, Nefertari. 40m, Tower Hotel. 55m, Sultan Hassan's Mosque. 60m, Courtyard, Al Azhar University. 200m, Head of Ramses II. 500m, Funerary mask of Tutankhamen.

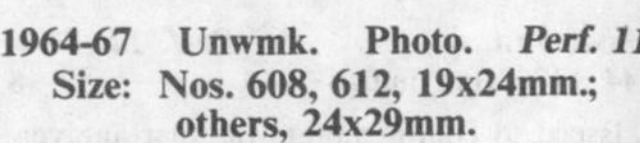

1964-67 Unwmk. Photo. *Perf. 11*
Size: Nos. 608, 612, 19x24mm.; others, 24x29mm.
600 A231 1m cit & ultra 5 5
601 A230 2m mag & bis 10 5
602 A230 3m sal, org & bl 10 5
603 A235 4m ocher, blk & ultra 30 10
604 A230 5m brn & brt bl 10 10
a. 5m brn & dk bl 50 10
605 A231 10m grn, dk brn & lt brn 10 10
606 A230 15m ultra & yel 10 8
607 A230 20m brn org & blk 25 8
608 A231 20m lt ol grn ('67) 25 8
609 A231 30m yel & brn 35 10
610 A231 35m sal, ocher & ultra 30 10
611 A231 40m ultra & yel 45 10
612 A231 55m brt red lil ('67) 75 20
613 A231 60m grnsh bl & yel brn 60 20

Wmk. 342
614 A232 100m dk vio brn & sl 1.50 25
615 A232 200m bluish blk & yel brn 3.50 50
616 A232 500m ultra & dp org 6.00 1.00
Nos. 600-616 (17) 14.80 3.14

Nos. 603 and N107 lack the vertically arranged dates which appear at lower right on No. 619.

HSN Commission Emblem — A233

Perf. 11x11½
1964, Jan. 10 Wmk. 342
617 A233 10m dl bl, dk bl & yel 10 5

Issued to commemorate the first conference of the Commission of Health, Sanitation and Nutrition.

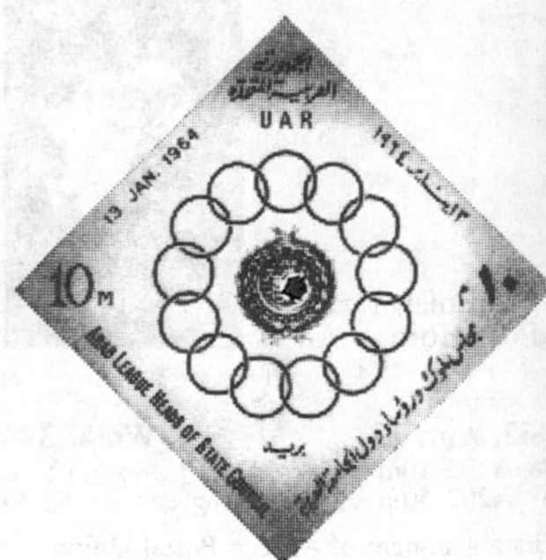

Arab League Emblem — A234

1964, Jan. 13 *Perf. 11*
618 A234 10m brt grn & blk 20 10

Issued to commemorate the first meeting of the Heads of State of the Arab League, Cairo, January.

Minaret at Night — A235

1964 Unwmk. *Perf. 11*
619 A235 4m emer, blk & red 8 5

Issued for use on greeting cards. See also No. 603.

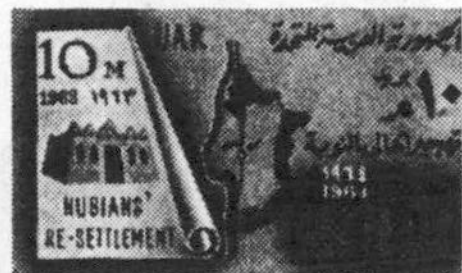

Old and New Dwellings and Map of Nubia A236

Perf. 11½x11

1964, Feb. 27 Photo. Wmk. 342

620 A236 10m dl vio & yel 10 8

Resettlement of Nubian population.

Map of Africa and Asia and Train A237

1964, March 21

621 A237 10m dl bl, dk bl & yel 8 8

Asian Railway Conference, Cairo, Mar. 21.

Ikhnaton and Nefertiti with Children — A238

1964, Mar. 21 ***Perf. 11x11½***

622 A238 10m dk brn & ultra 8 8

Issued for Arab Mother's Day, March 21.

Arab Postal Union Emblem A239

World Health Organization Emblem A240

1964, Apr. 1 Photo. Wmk. 342

623 A239 10m org brn & bl, *sal* 8 8

Issued to commemorate the 10th anniversary of the Permanent Office of the Arab Postal Union.

1964, Apr. 7

624 A240 10m dk bl & red 8 8

World Health Day (Anti-Tuberculosis).

Statue of Liberty, World's Fair Pavilion and Pyramids A241

1964, Apr. 22 ***Perf. 11½x11***

625 A241 10m brt grn & ol, *grysh* 25 15

New York World's Fair, 1964-65.

Nile and Aswan High Dam A242

1964, May 15 Unwmk. ***Perf. 11½***

626 A242 10m blk & bl 8 8

The diversion of the Nile.

"Land Reclamation" — A243

Design: No. 628, "Electricity," Aswan High Dam hydroelectric station.

1964, July 23 ***Perf. 11½***

627 A243 10m yel & emer 25 8

628 A243 10m grn & blk 25 8

Issued to publicize land reclamation and hydroelectric power due to the Aswan High Dam.

An imperf. souvenir sheet, issued July 23, contains two 50m black and blue stamps showing Aswan High Dam before and after diversion of the Nile. Black portrait of President Nasser and blue inscription in margin. Size of stamps: 42x26mm.; size of sheet: 104x81mm. Price $2.25.

Map of Africa and 34 Flags — A244

1964, July 17 Photo.

629 A244 10m brn, brt bl & blk 8 8

Issued to commemorate the Assembly of Heads of State and Government of the Organization for African Unity at Cairo in July.

Jamboree Emblem — A245

Design: No. 631, Emblem of Air Scouts.

1964, Aug. 28 Unwmk. ***Perf. 11½***

630 A245 10m red, grn & blk 25 8

631 A245 10m grn & red 25 8

The 6th Pan Arab Jamboree, Alexandria.

Flag of Algeria A246

1964, Sept. 5 ***Perf. 11½x11***

Flags in Original Colors

632 A246 10m grn *(Algeria)*	25	12
633 A246 10m grn *(Iraq)*	25	12
634 A246 10m grn *(Jordan)*	25	12
635 A246 10m grn *(Kuwait)*	25	12
636 A246 10m grn *(Lebanon)*	25	12
637 A246 10m grn *(Libya)*	25	12
638 A246 10m grn *(Morocco)*	25	12
639 A246 10m grn *(Saudi Arabia)*	25	12
640 A246 10m bl *(Sudan)*	25	12
641 A246 10m grn *(Syria)*	25	12
642 A246 10m grn *(Tunisia)*	25	12
643 A246 10m grn *(U.A.R.)*	25	12
644 A246 10m grn *(Yemen)*	25	12
Nos. 632-644 (13)	3.25	1.56

Issued to commemorate the second meeting of the Heads of State of the Arab League, Alexandria, Sept. 1964.

World Map, Dove, Olive Branches and Pyramids — A247

1964, Oct. 5 ***Perf. 11½***

645 A247 10m sl bl & yel 8 8

Issued to commemorate the Conference of Heads of State of Non-Aligned Countries, Cairo, Oct. 1964.

Pharaonic Athletes — A248

Designs from ancient decorations: 10m, Four athletes (vert.). 35m, Wrestlers (vert.). 50m, Pharaoh in chariot hunting.

Perf. 11½x11, 11x11½

1964, Oct. 10 Photo. Unwmk.

Sizes: 39x22mm., 22x39mm.

646 A248 5m lt grn & org 5 5

647 A248 10m sl bl & lt brn 8 8

648 A248 35m dl vio & lt brn 38 35

Size: 58x24mm.

649 A248 50m ultra & brn org 40 40

18th Olympic Games Tokyo, Oct. 10-25.

Emblem, Map of Africa and Asia A249

Map of Africa, Communication Symbols A250

1964, Oct. 10 ***Perf. 11x11½***

650 A249 10m vio & yel 8 8

First Afro-Asian Medical Congress.

1964, Oct. 24

651 A250 10m grn & blk 8 8

Issued to commemorate the Pan-African and Malagasy Posts and Telecommunications Congress, Cairo, Oct. 24-Nov. 6.

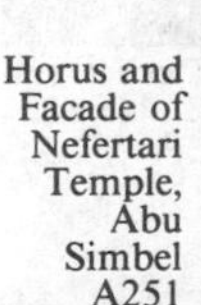

Horus and Facade of Nefertari Temple, Abu Simbel A251

Ramses II — A252

Designs: 35m, A god holding rope of life, Abu Simbel. 50m, Isis of Kalabsha (horiz.).

1964, Oct. 24 ***Perf. 11½, 11x11½***

652 A251 5m grnsh bl & yel brn 15 15

653 A252 10m sep & brt yel 30 15

654 A251 35m brn org & ind 75 50

Souvenir Sheet

Imperf

655 A252 50m ol & vio blk 1.00 1.00

Issued to publicize the "Save the Monuments of Nubia" campaign. No. 655 contains one horizontal stamp; violet black and olive marginal inscription. Size: 106x63mm.

Emblems of Cooperation, Rural Handicraft and Women's Work — A253

Perf. 11½x11

1964, Dec. 8 Photo. Unwmk.

656 A253 10m yel & dk bl 8 8

Issued to commemorate the 25th anniversary of the Ministry of Social Affairs.

United Nations and UNESCO Emblems, Pyramids A254

Minaret, Mardani Mosque A255

1964, Dec. 24 ***Perf. 11x11½***

657 A254 10m ultra & yel 8 8

Issued for UNESCO Day.

1965, Jan. 20 Photo. *Perf. 11*
658 A255 4m bl & dk brn 5 5

Issued for use on greeting cards.

Police Emblem over City A256

Oil Derrick and Emblem A257

Perf. 11x11½
1965, Jan. 25 Wmk. 342
659 A256 10m blk & yel 8 8

Issued for Police Day.

1965, Mar. 16 Photo.
660 A257 10m dk brn & yel 8 8

Issued to publicize the 5th Arab Petroleum Congress and the 2nd Arab Petroleum Exhibition.

Flags and Emblem of the Arab League A258

Red Crescent and WHO Emblem A259

Design: 20m, Arab League emblem (horiz.).

1965, Mar. 22 Wmk. 342
661 A258 10m grn, red & blk 15 15
662 A258 20m ultra & brn 16 15

20th anniversary of the Arab League.

1965, Apr. 7 Photo.
663 A259 10m bl & crim 8 8

Issued to commemorate World Health Day (Smallpox: Constant Alert).

Dagger in Map of Palestine — A260

1965, Apr. 9 *Perf. 11x11½*
664 A260 10m blk & red 50 25

Deir Yassin massacre, Apr. 9, 1948.

ITU Emblem, Old and New Communication Equipment — A261

1965, May 17 *Perf. 11½x11*
665 A261 5m vio blk & yel 5 5
666 A261 10m red & yel 8 5
667 A261 35m dk bl, ultra & yel 28 25

Issued to commemorate the centenary of the International Telecommunication Union.

Library Aflame and Lamp A262

1965, June 7 Photo. Wmk. 342
668 A262 10m blk, grn & red 8 5

Issued to commemorate the burning of the Library of Algiers, June 7, 1962.

Sheik Mohammed Abdo — A263

1965, July 11 *Perf. 11x11½*
669 A263 10m Prus bl & bis brn 6 5

Issued to commemorate the 60th anniversary of the death of Mohammed Abdo (1850-1905), Mufti of Egypt.

Pouring Ladle (Heavy Industry) A264

President Gamal Abdel Nasser and Emblems of Arab League, African Unity Organization, Afro-Asian Countries and United Nations — A265

1965, July 23 *Perf. 11½*

Designs: No. 670, Search for off-shore oil. No. 672, Housing, construction in Nassar City (diamond shaped).

670 A264 10m ind & lt bl 15 10
671 A264 10m brn & yel 15 10
672 A264 10m yel brn & blk 15 10
673 A265 100m lt grn & blk 2.50 1.75

13th anniversary of the revolution.
The 100m was printed in sheets of six, consisting of two singles and two vertical pairs. Margins and gutters contain multiple UAR coat of arms in light green. Size: 240x330mm.

A little time given to the study of the arrangement of the Scott Catalogue can make it easier to use effectively.

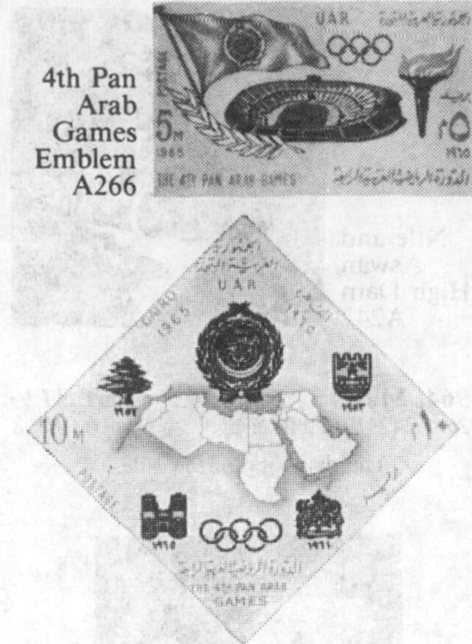

4th Pan Arab Games Emblem A266

Map and Emblems of Previous Games — A267

Designs: No. 675, Swimmers Zeitun and Abd el Gelil and arms of Alexandria. 35m, Race horse "Saadoon."

Perf. 11½x11; 11½ (#676)
1965, Sept. 2 Photo. Wmk. 342
674 A266 5m bl & red 5 5
675 A266 10m dp bl & dk brn 25 10
676 A267 10m org brn & dp bl 25 10
677 A266 35m grn & brn 45 25

Issued to publicize the 4th Pan Arab Games, Cairo, Sept. 2-11. No. 675 commemorates the long-distance swimming competition at Alexandria, a part of the Games.

Map of Arab Countries, Emblem of Arab League and Broken Chain A268

1965, Sept. 13 Photo. *Perf. 11½*
678 A268 10m brn & yel 6 5

Issued to commemorate the Third Arab Summit Conference, Casablanca, Sept. 13.

Land Forces Emblem and Sun — A269

Perf. 11x11½
1965, Oct. 20 Wmk. 342
679 A269 10m bis brn & blk 6 5

Issued for Land Forces Day.

Map of Africa, Torch and Olive Branches — A270

1965, Oct. 21 *Perf. 11½*
680 A270 10m dl pur & car rose 6 5

Issued to commemorate the Assembly of Heads of State of the Organization for African Unity.

Ramses II, Abu Simbel, and ICY Emblem A271

Pillars, Philae, and U.N. Emblem — A272

Designs: 35m, Two Ramses II statues, Abu Simbel and UNESCO emblem. 50m, Cartouche of Ramses II and ICY emblem (horiz.).

Wmk. 342
1965, Oct. 24 Photo. *Perf. 11½*
681 A271 5m yel & sl grn 10 10
682 A272 10m bl & blk 35 15
683 A271 35m dk vio & yel 75 25

Souvenir Sheet
Imperf
684 A272 50m brt ultra & dk brn 1.25 1.00

Issued to publicize the international cooperation in saving the Nubian monuments. No. 684 also commemorates the 20th anniversary of the United Nations. No. 684 contains one stamp (42x25m.) and has marginal inscription in bright ultramarine and dark brown. Size: 105x63mm.

Al-Maqrizi, Buildings and Books — A273

Perf. 11½x11
1965, Nov. 20 Photo. Wmk. 342
685 A273 10m ol & dk sl grn 6 5

Issued to commemorate the 600th anniversary of the birth of Ahmed Al-Maqrizi (1365-1442), historian.

Flag of U.A.R., Arms of Alexandria and Art Symbols — A274

1965, Dec. 16 **Perf. 11x11½**
686 A274 10m multi 6 5

Issued to publicize the 6th Biennial Exhibition of Fine Arts in Alexandria, Dec. 16, 1965-March 31, 1966.

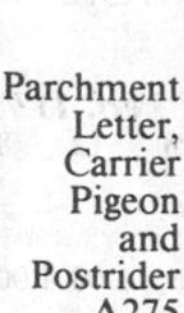

Parchment Letter, Carrier Pigeon and Postrider A275

1966, Jan. 2 **Wmk. 342** **Perf. 11½**
687 A275 10m multi 10 10

Post Day, Jan. 2. See Nos. CB1-CB2.

Lamp and Arch — A276

Exhibition Poster — A277

1966, Jan. 10 **Unwmk.** **Perf. 11**
688 A276 4m vio & dp org 5 5

Issued for use on greeting cards.

Perf. 11x11½

1966, Jan. 27 **Wmk. 342**
689 A277 10m lt bl & blk 6 5

Industrial Exhibition, Jan. 29-Feb.

Arab League Emblem A278

Printed Page and Torch A279

1966, March 22 **Photo.** **Wmk. 342**
690 A278 10m brt yel & pur 6 5

Arab Publicity Week, March 22-28.

1966, March 25 **Perf. 11x11½**
691 A279 10m dp org & sl bl 6 5

Centenary of the national press.

The first price column gives the catalogue value of an unused stamp, the second that of a used stamp.

Traffic Signal at Night — A280

Hands Holding Torch, Flags of U.A.R. and Iraq — A281

1966, May 4 **Photo.** **Wmk. 342**
692 A280 10m grn & red 6 5

Issued for Traffic Day.

1966, May 26 **Perf. 11x11½**
693 A281 10m dp cl, rose red & brt grn 6 5

Friendship between U.A.R. and Iraq.

Workers and U.N. Emblem A282

Perf. 11½x11

1966, June 1 **Photo.** **Wmk. 342**
694 A282 5m bl grn & blk 5 5
695 A282 10m brt rose lil & grn 10 5
696 A282 35m org & blk 35 25

50th session of the ILO.

Mobilization Dept. Emblem, People and City — A283

1966, June 30 **Perf. 11x11½**
697 A283 10m dl pur & brn 10 5

Population sample, May 31-June 16.

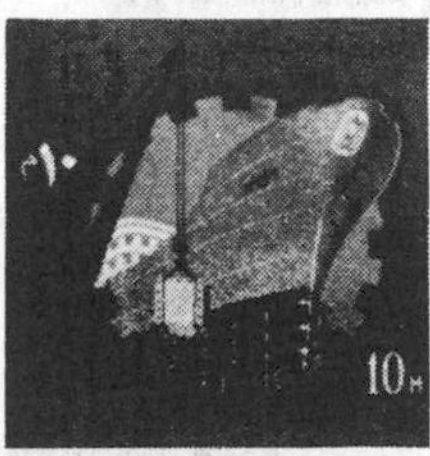

"Salah el Din," Crane and Cogwheel A284

Present-day Basket Dance and Pharaonic Dance — A285

Designs: No. 699, Transfer of first stones of Abu Simbel. No. 700, Development of Sinai (map of Red Sea area and Sinai Peninsula). No. 701, El Maadi Hospital and nurse with patient.

Wmk. 342

1966, July 23 **Photo.** **Perf. 11½**
698 A284 10m org & multi 12 10
699 A284 10m brt grn & multi 12 10
700 A284 10m yel & multi 12 10
701 A284 10m lt bl & multi 12 10

Souvenir Sheet

Imperf

702 A285 100m multi 2.50 2.00

Issued to commemorate the 14th anniversary of the revolution. No. 702 contains one stamp. Size: 115x67mm.

Suez Canal Headquarters, Ships and Map of Canal — A286

1966, July 26 **Perf. 11½**
703 A286 10m bl & crim 20 10

Issued to commemorate the 10th anniversary of the nationalization of the Suez Canal.

Cotton, Farmers with Plow and Tractor A287

Designs: 10m, Rice. 35m, Onions.

Perf. 11½x11

1966, Sept. 9 **Photo.** **Wmk. 342**
704 A287 5m pur & lt bl 5 5
705 A287 10m emer & yel brn 10 10
706 A287 35m bl & org 28 25

Issued for Farmer's Day.

WHO Headquarters, Geneva — A288

Designs: 10m, U.N. refugee emblem. 35m, UNICEF emblem.

Perf. 11½x11

1966, Oct. 24 **Wmk. 342**
707 A288 5m ol & brt pur 10 5
708 A288 10m org & brt pur 20 10
709 A288 35m lt bl & brt pur 55 25

21st anniversary of the United Nations.

World Map and Festival Emblem A289

1966, Nov. 8 **Photo.**
710 A289 10m brt pur & yel 6 5

Issued to publicize the 5th International Television Festival, Nov. 1-10.

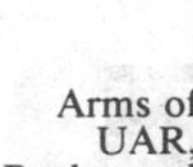

Arms of UAR, Rocket and Pylon A290

1966, Dec. 23 **Wmk. 342** **Perf. 11½**
711 A290 10m brt grn & car rose 25 10

Issued for Victory Day.

Jackal A291

Design: 35m, Alabaster head from Tutankhamen treasure.

1967, Jan. 2 **Photo.**
712 A291 10m sl, yel & brn 75 20
713 A291 35m bl, dk vio & ocher 1.40 45

Issued for Post Day, Jan. 2.

Carnations A292

Workers Planting Tree A293

1967, Jan. 10 **Unwmk.** **Perf. 11**
714 A292 4m cit & pur 5 5

Issued for use on greeting cards.

Perf. 11x11½

1967, Mar. 15 **Wmk. 342**
715 A293 10m brt grn & blk vio 10 5

Issued to publicize the Tree Festival.

Gamal el-Dine el-Afaghani and Arab League Emblem — A294

1967, Mar. 22 **Photo.** **Wmk. 342**
716 A294 10m dp grn & dk brn 10 5

Arab Publicity Week, March 22-28.

Census Emblem, Man, Woman and Factory A295

1967, Apr. 23 ***Perf. 11½x11***
717 A295 10m blk & dp org 10 5

First industrial census.

Brickmaking Fresco, Tomb of Rekhmire, Thebes, 1504-1450 B.C. — A296

1967, May 1 **Photo.** **Wmk. 342**
718 A296 10m ol & org 10 5

Issued for Labor Day, 1967.

Ramses II and Queen Nefertari — A297

Design: 35m, Shooting geese, frieze from tomb of Atet at Meidum, c. 2724 B. C.

Perf. 11½x11

1967, June 7 **Photo.** **Wmk. 342**
719 A297 10m multi 50 20
720 A297 35m dk grn & org 75 45
Nos. 719-720,C113-C115 (5) 4.25 1.85

Issued for International Tourist Year, 1967.

President Nasser, Crowd and Map of Palestine A298

1967, June 22 ***Perf. 11½***
721 A298 10m dp org, yel & ol 45 30

Issued to publicize Arab solidarity for "the defense of Palestine."

Souvenir Sheet

National Products — A299

1967, July 23 **Wmk. 342** ***Imperf.***
722 A299 100m multi 2.00 90

15th anniv.of the revolution. No. 722 contains one stamp with yellow, green and brown margin. Size: 111½x66mm.

Salama Higazi — A300

Perf. 11x11½

1967, Oct. 14 **Photo.** **Wmk. 342**
723 A300 20m brn & dk bl 12 8

50th anniv. of the death of Salama Higazi, pioneer of Egyptian lyric stage.

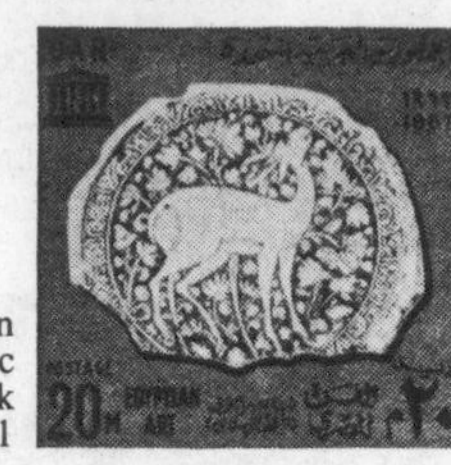

Stag on Ceramic Disk A301

Design: 55m, Apse showing Christ in Glory, Madonna and Saints, Coptic Museum, and UNESCO Emblem.

1967, Oct. 24 ***Perf. 11½***
724 A301 20m dl rose & dk bl 15 10
725 A301 55m dk sl grn & yel 50 30

22nd anniv. of the UN. See No. C117.

Savings Bank and Postal Authority Emblems A302

1967, Oct. 31 ***Perf. 11½x11***
726 A302 20m sal pink & dk bl 12 8

International Savings Day.

Rose — A303

Unwmk.

1967, Dec. 15 **Photo.** ***Perf. 11***
727 A303 5m grn & rose lil 5 5

Issued for use on greeting cards.

Pharaonic Dress — A304

Aswan High Dam and Power Lines — A305

Designs: Various pharaonic dresses from temple decorations.

Perf. 11x11½

1968, Jan. 2 **Wmk. 342**
728 A304 20m brn, grn & buff 50 15
729 A304 55m lt grn, yel & sep 1.10 35
730 A304 80m dk brn, bl & brt rose 1.50 75

Issued for Post Day, Jan. 2.

1968, Jan. 9
731 A305 20m yel, bl & dk brn 10 8

Issued to commemorate the first electricity generated by the Aswan Hydroelectric Station.

Alabaster Vessel, Tutankhamen Treasure — A306

Capital of Coptic Limestone Pillar A307

Girl, Moon and Paint Brushes — A308

Perf. 11x11½, 11½

1968, Jan. 20 **Photo.** **Wmk. 342**
732 A306 20m dk ultra, yel & brn 15 10
733 A307 80m lt grn, dk pur & ol grn 40 35

2nd International Festival of Museums.

1968, Feb. 15 ***Perf. 11x11½***
734 A308 20m brt bl & blk 10 8

Issued to publicize the 7th Biennial Exhibition of Fine Arts, Alexandria, Feb. 15.

Cattle and Veterinarian — A309

Perf. 11½x11

1968, May 4 **Photo.** **Wmk. 342**
735 A309 20m brn, yel & grn 10 8

8th Arab Veterinary Congress, Cairo.

Human Rights Flame — A310

Perf. 11x11½

1968, July 1 **Photo.** **Wmk. 342**
736 A310 20m cit, crim & grn 15 8
737 A310 60m sky bl, crim & grn 40 30

International Human Rights Year, 1968.

Open Book with Symbols of Science, Victory Election Result A311

Workers, Cogwheel with Coat of Arms and Open Book — A312

1968, July 23 ***Perf. 11½***
738 A311 20m rose red & sl grn 12 8

Souvenir Sheet

Imperf

739 A312 10m lt grn, org & pur 1.00 1.00

16th anniversary of the revolution.
No. 739 has orange marginal inscription and the ornaments. Size: 116x68mm.

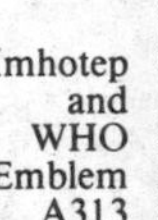

Imhotep and WHO Emblem A313

Design: No. 741, Avicenna and WHO emblem.

Perf. 11½x11

1968, Sept. 1 **Photo.** **Wmk. 342**
740 A313 20m bl, yel & brn 30 10
741 A313 20m yel, bl & brn 30 10

Issued to commemorate the 20th anniversary of the World Health Organization. Nos. 740-741 printed in checkerboard sheets of 50 (5x10).

Table Tennis — A314

Perf. 11x11½

1968, Sept. 20 **Photo.** **Wmk. 342**
742 A314 20m lt grn & dk brn 12 8

First Mediterranean Table Tennis Tournament, Alexandria, Sept. 20-27.

Factories and Fair Emblem A315

1968, Oct. 20 **Wmk. 342** ***Perf. 11½***
743 A315 20m bl gray, red & sl bl 12 8

Cairo International Industrial Fair.

Canceled-to-order stamps are often from remainders. Most collectors of canceled stamps prefer postally used specimens.

Temples of Philae — A316

Refugees, Map of Palestine, Refugee Year Emblem
A317

Design: 55m, Temple at Philae and UNESCO emblem.

1968, Oct. 24 **Photo.**
744 A316 20m multi 12 8
745 A317 30m multi 1.00 20
746 A317 55m lt bl, yel & blk 50 26

Issued for United Nations Day, Oct. 24.

Egyptian Boy Scout Emblem — A318

1968, Nov. 1
747 A318 10m dl org & vio bl 25 10

50th anniversary of Egyptian Boy Scouts.

Pharaonic Sports
A319

Design: 30m, Pharaonic sports (different).

1968, Nov. 1
748 A319 20m pale ol, pale sal & blk 20 8
749 A319 30m pale bl, buff & pur 30 15

Issued to commemorate the 19th Olympic Games, Mexico City, Oct. 12-27.

Aly Moubarak
A320

Lotus
A321

1968, Nov. 9 ***Perf. 11½***
750 A320 20m grn, brn & bis 25 8

Issued to honor Aly Moubarak (1823-1893), founder of the modern educational system in Egypt.

1968, Dec. 11 **Photo.** **Wmk. 342**
751 A321 5m brt bl, grn & yel 30 15

Issued for use on greeting cards.

Son of Ramses III
A322

Hefni Nassef
A323

Pharaonic Dress: No. 753, Ramses III. No. 754, Girl carrying basket on her head. 55m, Queen of the New Empire in transparent dress.

1969, Jan. 2 **Photo.** ***Perf. 11½***
752 A322 5m bl & multi 50 25
753 A322 20m bl & multi 75 50
754 A322 20m bl & multi 1.00 75
755 A322 55m bl & multi 70 35

Issued for Post Day, Jan. 2.

Perf. 11x11½
1969, Mar. 2 **Photo.** **Wmk. 342**

Portrait: No. 757, Mohammed Farid.

756 A323 20m pur & brn 30 10
757 A323 20m emer & brn 30 10

Issued to commemorate the 50th anniversaries of the death of Hefni Nassef (1860-1919) writer and government worker, and of Mohammed Farid (1867-1919), lawyer and Speaker of the Nationalist Party. Nos. 756-757 printed setenant in sheets of 50 (10x5).

Teacher and Children
A324

ILO Emblem and Factory Chimneys
A325

1969, Mar. 2 ***Perf. 11x11½***
758 A324 20m multi 25 8

Arab Teacher's Day.

1969, Apr. 11 **Photo.** **Wmk. 342**
759 A325 20m brn, ultra & car 25 8

Issued to commemorate the 50th anniversary of the International Labor Organization.

Flag of Algeria, Africa Day and Tourist Year Emblems
A326

Perf. 11½x11
1969, May 25 **Litho.** **Wmk. 342**
760 A326 10m grn *(Algeria)* 50 30
761 A326 10m grn *(Botswana)* 50 30
762 A326 10m grn *(Burundi)* 50 30
763 A326 10m grn *(Cameroun)* 50 30
764 A326 10m bl *(Cent. Afr. Rep.)* 50 30
765 A326 10m bl *(Chad)* 50 30
766 A326 10m bl *(Congo, ex-Belgian)* 50 30
767 A326 10m grn *(Congo, ex-French)* 50 30
768 A326 10m grn *(Dahomey)* 50 30
769 A326 10m bl *(Equatorial Guinea)* 50 30
770 A326 10m bl *(Ethiopia)* 50 30
771 A326 10m bl *(Gabon)* 50 30
772 A326 10m grn *(Gambia)* 50 30
773 A326 10m grn *(Ghana)* 50 30
774 A326 10m grn *(Guinea)* 50 30
775 A326 10m grn *(Ivory Coast)* 50 30
776 A326 10m grn *(Kenya)* 50 30
777 A326 10m grn *(Lesotho)* 50 30
778 A326 10m bl *(Liberia)* 50 30
779 A326 10m grn *(Libya)* 50 30
780 A326 10m grn *(Malagasy)* 50 30
781 A326 10m grn *(Malawi)* 50 30
782 A326 10m grn *(Mali)* 50 30
783 A326 10m grn *(Mauritania)* 50 30
784 A326 10m bl *(Mauritius)* 50 30
785 A326 10m grn *(Morocco)* 50 30
786 A326 10m grn *(Niger)* 50 30
787 A326 10m grn *(Nigeria)* 50 30
788 A326 10m grn *(Rwanda)* 50 30
789 A326 10m grn *(Senegal)* 50 30
790 A326 10m grn *(Sierra Leone)* 50 30
791 A326 10m grn *(Somalia)* 50 30
792 A326 10m bl *(Sudan)* 50 30
793 A326 10m vio *(Swaziland)* 50 30
794 A326 10m bl *(Tanzania)* 50 30
795 A326 10m grn *(Togo)* 50 30
796 A326 10m grn *(Tunisia)* 50 30
797 A326 10m blk *(Uganda)* 50 30
798 A326 10m grn *(U.A.R.)* 50 30
799 A326 10m grn *(Upper Volta)* 50 30
800 A326 10m bl *(Zambia)* 50 30
Nos. 760-800 (41) 20.50 12.30

El Fetouh Gate, Cairo
A327

Sculptures from the Egyptian Museum, Cairo — A328

Millenary of Cairo — A329

Designs: No. 802, Al Azhar University. No. 803, The Citadel. No. 805, Sculptures, Coptic Museum. No. 806, Glass plate and vase, Fatimid dynasty, Islamic Museum. No. 807a, Islamic coin. No. 807b, Fatimist era jewelry. No. 807c, Copper vase. No. 807d, Coins and plaque.

Perf. 11½x11
1969, July 23 **Photo.** **Wmk. 342**
801 A327 10m dk brn & multi 50 25
802 A327 10m grn & multi 50 25
803 A327 10m bl & multi 50 25

Perf. 11½
804 A328 20m yel grn & multi 80 40
805 A328 20m dp ultra & multi 80 40
806 A328 20m brn & multi 80 40
Nos. 801-806 (6) 3.90 1.95

Souvenir Sheet
807 A329 Sheet of 4 5.00 5.00
a. 20m dk bl & multi 1.00 1.00
b. 20m lil & multi 1.00 1.00
c. 20m yel & multi 1.00 1.00
d. 20m dk grn & multi 1.00 1.00

Issued to commemorate the millenium of the founding of Cairo. No. 807 has pale lilac margin and dark blue inscription. Size: 128x70mm.

African Development Bank Emblem — A330

Perf. 11x11½
1969, Sept. 10 **Photo.** **Wmk. 342**
808 A330 20m emer, yel & vio 25 8

Issued to publicize the 5th anniversary of the African Development Bank.

Pharaonic Boat and UN Emblem
A331

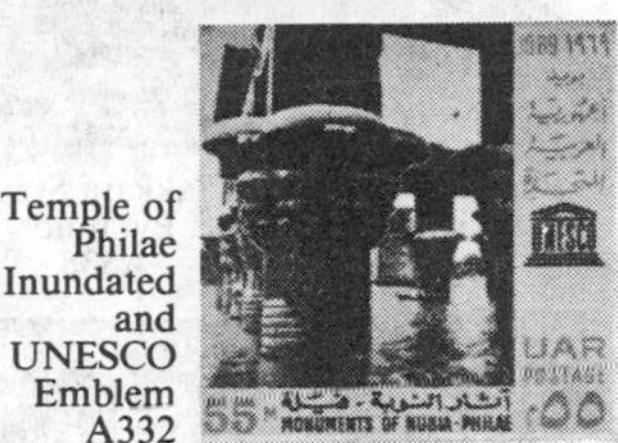

Temple of Philae Inundated and UNESCO Emblem
A332

Design: 5m, King and Queen from Abu Simbel Temple and UNESCO Emblem (size: 21x38mm.).

Perf. 11x11½, 11½x11
1969, Oct. 24 **Photo.** **Wmk. 342**
809 A332 5m brn & multi 8 5
810 A331 20m yel & ultra 60 25

Perf. 11½
811 A332 55m yel & multi 50 25

Issued for United Nations Day.

Ships of 1869 and 1967 and Maps of Africa and Suez Canal — A333

1969, Nov. 15 ***Perf. 11½x11***
812 A333 20m lt bl & multi 25 8

Centenary of the Suez Canal.

Cairo Opera House and Performance of Aida — A334

1969, Nov. 15
813 A334 20m multi 25 8

Centenary of the Cairo Opera House.

Crowd with Egyptian and Revolutionary Flags — A335

1969, Nov. 15 *Perf. 11½x11*

814 A335 20m brt grn, dl lil & red 25 8

Revolution of 1919.

Ancient Arithmetic and Computer Cards — A336

Perf. 11½x11

1969, Dec. 17 Photo. Wmk. 342

815 A336 20m multi 25 8

Issued to publicize the International Congress for Scientific Accounting, Cairo, Dec. 17-19.

Poinsettia A337

Sakkara Step Pyramid A338

El Fetouh Gate, Cairo — A339

Fountain, Sultan Hassan Mosque, Cairo — A340

King Khafre (Ruled c. 2850 B.C.) A341

1969, Dec. 24 Unwmk. Perf. 11

816 A337 5m yel, grn & car 5 5

Issued for use on greeting cards.

Photo.; Engr. (20,55m)
Wmk. 342 (2m, £1)

1969-70 *Perf. 11*

Designs: 5m, Al Azhar Mosque. 10m, Luxor Temple. 50m, Qaitbay Fort, Alexandria.

817	A338	1m multi ('70)	10	5
818	A338	5m multi ('70)	15	5
819	A338	10m multi ('70)	25	5
820	A339	20m dk brn	50	8
821	A338	50m multi ('70)	75	20
822	A340	55m sl grn	1.00	22

Perf. 11½

Photo. & Engr.

823	A341	£1 org & sl grn ('70)	8.50	4.00
		Nos. 817-823 (7)	11.25	4.65

See Nos. 889-891, 893-897, 899, 901-902, 904.

Veiled Women, by Mahmoud Said — A342

Perf. 11x11½

1970, Jan. 2 Photo. Wmk. 342

Size: 45x89mm.

824 A342 100m bl & multi 1.75 45

Post Day, Jan. 2. Sheet of 8 with two panes of 4.

Parliament, Scales, Globe and Laurel — A343

1970, Feb. 2 *Perf. 11½x11*

825 A343 20m bl, vio bl & ocher 25 8

Issued to publicize the International Conference of Parliamentarians on the Middle East Crisis, Cairo, Feb. 2-5.

Map of Arab League Countries, Flag and Emblem A344

Perf. 11½x11

1970, Mar. 22 Photo. Wmk. 342

826 A344 30m brn org, grn & dk pur 25 12

Issued to commemorate the 25th anniversary of the Arab League. See No. B42.

Mena House and Sheraton Hotel — A345

1970, Mar. 23

827 A345 20m ol, org & bl 25 8

Issued to commemorate the centenary of Mena House and the inauguration of the Cairo Sheraton Hotel.

Manufacture of Medicine — A346

1970, Apr. 20

828 A346 20m brn, yel & bl 25 8

Issued to commemorate the 30th anniversary of the production of medicines in Egypt.

Mermaid — A347

1970, Apr. 20 *Perf. 11x11½*

829 A347 20m org, blk & ultra 25 8

Issued to publicize the 8th Biennial Exhibition of Fine Arts, Alexandria, March 12.

Misr Bank and Talaat Harb A348

ITU Emblem A349

1970, May 7 Photo. Wmk. 342

830 A348 20m multi 25 8

50th anniversary of Misr Bank.

1970, May 17 *Perf. 11x11½*

831 A349 20m dk brn, yel & dl bl 25 8

World Telecommunications Day.

U.P.U. Headquarters, Bern — A350

1970, May 20 *Perf. 11½x11*

832 A350 20m multi 25 8

Issued to commemorate the inauguration of the new Universal Postal Union Headquarters in Bern. See No. C128.

Basketball Player and Map of Africa — A351

U.P.U., U.N. and U.P.A.F. Emblems A352

Designs: No. 834, Soccer player, map of Africa and cup (horiz.).

Perf. 11x11½, 11½x11

1970, May 25 Photo. Wmk. 342

833	A351	20m lt bl, yel & brn	30	8
834	A351	20m yel & multi	30	8
835	A352	20m ocher, grn & blk	30	8

Issued for Africa Day. No. 833 also commemorates the 5th African basketball championship for men; No. 834 the annual African Soccer championship and No. 835 publicizes the African Postal Union seminar.

Fist and Freed Bird — A353

1970, July 23 Photo. *Perf. 11*

836 A353 20m lt grn, org & blk 25 8

Souvenir Sheet

Imperf

837 A353 100m lt bl, dp org & blk 1.00 45

Issued to commemorate the 18th anniversary of the revolution. No. 837 contains one stamp; U.N. emblem, Scales of Justice and orange commemorative inscription in margin. Size: 110x70mm.

Al Aqsa Mosque on Fire — A354

1970, Aug. 21 Wmk. 342 *Perf. 11*

838 A354 20m multi 50 8

839 A354 60m brt bl & multi 1.00 24

First anniversary of the burning of Al Aqsa Mosque, Jerusalem.

Standardization Emblems — A355

1970, Oct. 14 Wmk. 342 *Perf. 11*

840 A355 20m yel, ultra & grn 25 8

Issued to commemorate World Standards Day and the 25th anniversary of the International Standardization Organization, ISO.

U.N. Emblem, Scales and Dove — A356

Temple at Philae A357

Child, Education Year and U.N. Emblems A358

Designs: 10m, U.N. emblem. No. 845, Second Temple at Philae (denomination at left).

Perf. 11 (5m), 11 ½ (others)

1970, Oct. 24 Photo. Wmk. 342

841 A356	5m lt bl, rose lil & sl	10	10
842 A357	10m yel, brn & lt bl	18	10
843 A358	20m sl & multi	30	20
844 A357	55m brn, bl & ocher	55	35
845 A357	55m brn, bl & ocher	55	35
	Strip of 3 (#842, 844-845)	1.40	85
	Nos. 841-845,B43 (6)	3.18	1.85

Issued to commemorate the 25th anniversary of the United Nations. No. 843 also commemorates International Education Year; Nos. 842, 844-845 commemorate the work of UNESCO in saving the Temples of Philae; Nos. 842, 844-845 printed se-tenant in sheets of 35 (15 No. 842 and 10 each Nos. 844-845). Nos. 844-845 show continuous picture of the Temples at Philae.

Gamal Abdel Nasser — A359

1970, Nov. 6 Wmk. 342 *Perf. 11*

846 A359	5m sky bl & blk	10	5
847 A359	20m gray grn & blk	25	8

Issued in memory of Gamal Abdel Nasser (1918-1970), President of Egypt. See Nos. C129-C130.

Medical Association Building A360

Designs: No. 849, Old and new National Library. No. 850, Egyptian Credo (Nasser quotation). No. 851, Engineering Society, old and new buildings. No. 852, Government Printing Offices, old and new buildings.

1970, Dec. 20 Photo. *Perf. 11*

848 A360	20m yel, grn & brn	30	8
849 A360	20m grn & multi	30	8
850 A360	20m lt bl & brn	30	8
851 A360	20m bl, yel & brn	30	8
852 A360	20m bl, yel & brn	30	8
	Nos. 848-852 (5)	1.50	40

Nos. 848-852 printed se-tenant in sheets of 50 (5x10) commemorate: 50th anniversary of Egyptian Medical Association (No. 848); centenary of National Library (No. 849); Egyptian Engineering Association (No. 851) sesquicentennial of Government Printing Offices (No. 852).

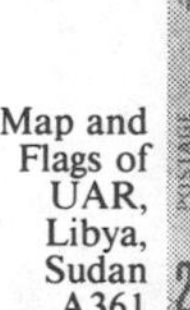

Map and Flags of UAR, Libya, Sudan A361

1970, Dec. 27 *Perf. 11 ½*

853 A361	20m lt grn, car & blk	25	8

Signing of the Charter of Tripoli affirming the unity of UAR, Libya and the Sudan, Dec. 27, 1970.

Qalawun Minaret — A362

Designs (Minarets): 10m, As Saleh. 20m, Isna. 55m, Al Hakim.

1971, Jan. 2 Wmk. 342 *Perf. 11*

854 A362	5m grn & multi	45	25
855 A362	10m grn & multi	1.25	50
856 A362	20m grn & multi	2.50	1.00
857 A362	55m grn & multi	4.25	2.00
	Strip of 4 (#854-857) + label	10.00	4.00

Post Day, 1971. Nos. 854-857 printed se-tenant in sheets of 40 stamps and 10 blue and yellow labels.

See Nos. 905-908, 932-935.

Gamal Abdel Nasser A363

Photogravure and Engraved

1971 Wmk. 342 *Perf. 11 ½*

858 A363	200m brn vio & dk bl	2.50	1.00
859 A363	500m bl & blk	6.00	2.75

Souvenir Sheet

Design: Portrait facing right.

Imperf

860 A363	Sheet of 2	6.00	3.75
a.	100m lt grn & blk	3.00	1.00
b.	200m bl & blk	2.25	1.75

No. 860 commemorates inauguration of the Aswan High Dam, which is shown in margin. Green and blue marginal inscription. Size: 134x79mm.

Issue dates: No. 860, Jan. 15; Nos. 858-859, Feb. 1.

See No. 903.

Cotton and Globe A364

1971, Mar. 6 Photo. *Perf. 11 ½x11*

861 A364	20m lt grn, bl & brn	25	10

Egyptian cotton.

Arab Countries, and Arab Postal Union Emblem A365

1971, Mar. 6 Wmk. 342

862 A365	20m lt bl, org & sl grn	25	10

9th Arab Postal Congress, Cairo, March 6-25. See No. C131.

Cairo Fair Emblem — A366

1971, Mar. 6 *Perf. 11x11 ½*

863 A366	20m plum, blk & org	25	10

Cairo International Fair, March 2-23.

Nesy Ra, Apers Papyrus and WHO Emblem A367

Perf. 11 ½x11

1971, Apr. 30 Photo. Wmk. 342

864 A367	20m yel bis & pur	25	10

World Health Organization Day.

Gamal Abdel Nasser — A368

1971, May 1 *Perf. 11*

865 A368	20m pur & bl gray	15	8
866 A368	55m bl & pur	45	20

Map of Africa, Telecommunications Symbols — A369

1971, May 17 *Perf. 11 ½x11*

867 A369	20m bl & multi	25	10

Pan-African telecommunications system.

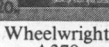

Wheelwright A370

Hand Holding Wheat and Laurel A371

Candle Lighting Africa A372

Perf. 11x11 ½

1971, July 23 Photo. Wmk. 342

868 A370	20m yel & multi	25	8
869 A371	20m tan, grn & ocher	25	8

Souvenir Sheet

Imperf

870 A372	100m bl & multi	1.00	60

19th anniversary of the July Revolution. No. 870 contains one stamp with simulated perforations in gold and with blue marginal inscription. Portrait of Pres. Nasser in margin. Size: 115x70mm.

Arab Postal Union Emblem A373

1971, Aug. 3 *Perf. 11 ½*

871 A373	20m blk, yel & grn	25	8

25th anniversary of the Conference of Sofar, Lebanon, establishing the Arab Postal Union. See No. C135.

Arab Republic of Egypt

Three Links A374

Perf. 11 ½x11

1971, Sept. 28 Photo. Wmk. 342

872 A374	20m gray, org brn & blk	50	40

Confederation of Arab Republics (Egypt, Syria and Libya). See No. C136.

Gamal Abdel Nasser A375

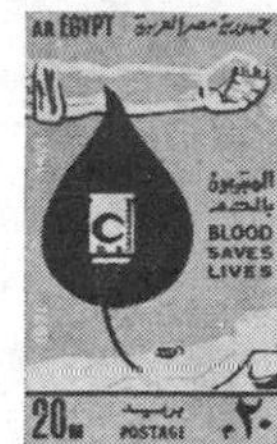

Blood Donation A376

1971, Sept. 28 *Perf. 11x11 ½*

873 A375	5m sl grn & vio brn	8	8
874 A375	20m vio brn & ultra	20	10
875 A375	30m ultra & brn	30	15
876 A375	55m brn & emer	50	25

First anniversary of the death of President Gamal Abdel Nasser.

1971, Oct. 24

877 A376	20m grn & car	25	8

"Blood Saves Lives."

Princess Nursing Child, UNICEF Emblem — A377

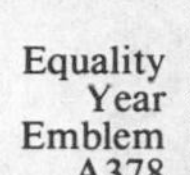

Equality Year Emblem A378

Submerged Pillar, Philae, UNESCO Emblem — A379

Perf. 11x11½, 11½x11

1971, Oct. 24 Photo. Wmk. 342

878 A377 5m buff, blk & org brn 5 5
879 A378 20m red brn, grn, yel & blk 25 8
880 A379 55m blk, lt bl, yel & brn 50 20

United Nations Day. No. 878 honors U.N. International Children's Fund; No. 879 for International Year Against Racial Discrimination; No. 880 honors U.N. Educational, Scientific and Cultural Organization. See No. C137.

Postal Traffic Center, Alexandria A380

1971, Oct. 31 ***Perf. 11½x11***

881 A380 20m bl & bis 25 8

Opening of Postal Traffic Center in Alexandria.

Sunflower A381

Abdalla El Nadim A382

1971, Nov. 13 ***Perf. 11***

882 A381 5m lt bl & multi 10 5

For use on greeting cards.

1971, Nov. 14 ***Perf. 11x11½***

883 A382 20m grn & brn 25 10

Abdalla El Nadim (1845-1896), journalist, publisher, connected with Orabi Revolution.

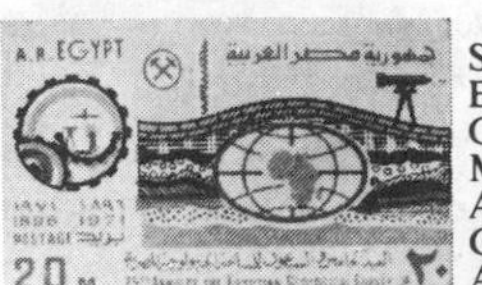

Section of Earth's Crust, Map of Africa on Globe A383

1971, Nov. 27 ***Perf. 11½x11***

884 A383 20m ultra, yel & brn 25 10

75th anniversary of Egyptian Geological Survey and International Conference, Nov. 27-Dec. 1.

Postal Union Emblem, Letter and Dove A384

Design: 55m, African Postal Union emblem and letter.

1971, Dec. 2

885 A384 5m multi 5 5
886 A384 20m ol, blk & org 25 8
887 A384 55m red, blk & bl 50 20

10th anniversary of African Postal Union. See No. C138.

Money and Safe Deposit Box — A385

1971, Dec. 23 ***Perf. 11½***

888 A385 20m rose, brn & grn 25 8

70th anniversary of Postal Savings Bank.

Types of 1969-70, 1971 Inscribed "A. R. Egypt" and

Ramses II — A385a

Designs as before and: No. 894, King Citi I. No. 897, Queen Nefertari. No. 900, Sphinx and Middle Pyramid. 100m, Cairo Mosque. 200m, Head of Pharaoh Userkaf.

Wmk. 342 (#892A, 901-904)

1972-76 Photo. Unwmk. ***Perf. 11***

889	A338	1m	multi	5	5
890	A338	1m	dk brn ('73)	5	5
891	A338	5m	multi	5	5
892	A385a	5m	ol ('73)	5	5
892A	A385a	5m	bis ('76)	5	5
893	A338	10m	multi	7	5
894	A338	10m	lt brn ('73)	5	5
895	A339	20m	olive	40	20
896	A339	20m	pur ('73)	10	5
897	A338	50m	multi	33	22
898	A385a	50m	dl bl ('73)	25	15
899	A340	55m	red lil	36	24
900	A340	55m	grn ('74)	75	40
901	A339	100m	lt bl, dp org & blk	50	35

Perf. 11½

Photo. & Engr.

902	A341	200m	yel grn & brn	1.25	70
903	A363	500m	bl & choc	7.50	5.00
904	A341	£1	org & sl grn	10.00	7.50
			Nos. 889-904 (17)	21.81	15.16

Minaret Type of 1971

Designs: 5m, West Minaret, Nasser Mosque. 20m, East Minaret, Nasser Mosque. 30m, Minaret, Al Gawli Mosque. 55m, Minaret, Ibn Tulun Mosque.

Wmk. 342

1972, Jan. 2 Photo. ***Perf. 11***

905 A362 5m dk grn & multi 45 15
906 A362 20m dk grn & multi 1.40 20
907 A362 30m dk grn & multi 3.00 30
908 A362 55m dk grn & multi 4.25 60
Strip of 4 (#905-908) + label 11.00 1.75

Post Day, 1972. Nos. 905-908 printed se-tenant in sheets of 40 stamps and 10 blue and yellow labels.

Police Emblem and Activities — A386

1972, Jan. 25 ***Perf. 11½***

909 A386 20m dl bl, brn & yel 25 9

Police Day 1972.

UNESCO, U.N. and Book Year Emblems — A387

1972, Jan. 25 ***Perf. 11x11½***

910 A387 20m lt yel grn, vio bl & yel 25 9

International Book Year 1972.

Alexandria Biennale A388

1972, Feb. 15 Wmk. 342 ***Perf. 11½***

911 A388 20m blk, brt rose & yel 14 9

9th Biennial Exhibition of Fine Arts, Alexandria, March, 1972.

Fair Emblem A389

Abdel Moniem Riad A390

1972, March 5 ***Perf. 11x11½***

912 A389 20m bl, org & yel grn 25 9

International Cairo Fair.

1972, Mar. 21 Photo. Wmk. 342

913 A390 20m bl & brn 50 9

In memory of Brig. Gen. Abdel Moniem Riad (1919-1969), military hero.

Bird Feeding Young A391

1972, Mar. 21 ***Perf. 11½***

914 A391 20m yel & multi 25 9

Mother's Day.

Tutankhamen — A392

Design: 55m, Back of chair with king's name and symbols of eternity.

1972, May 22 Unwmk

915 A392 20m gray, blk & ocher 75 2
916 A392 55m pur & yel 1.50 4

50th anniversary of the discovery of the tomb of Tutankhamen by Howard Carter and Lord Carnarvon. See Nos. C142-C144.

Queen Nefertiti A393

Wmk. 342

1972, May 22 Photo. ***Perf. 11½***

917 A393 20m red, blk & gold 10 7

50th anniversary of the Society of the Friends of Art.

Map of Africa — A394

1972, May 25 ***Perf. 11x11½***

918 A394 20m pur, bl & brn 25 7

Africa Day.

Atom Symbol, "Faith and Science" A395

Design: No. 920, Egyptian coat of arms.

1972, July 23 ***Perf. 11½***

919 A395 20m bl, cl & blk 15 7
920 A395 20m ol grn, gold & blk 15 7

20th anniversary of the revolution.

Boxing, Olympic and Motion Emblems — A396

Designs (Olympic and Motion Emblems and): 10m, Wrestling. 20m, Basketball.

1972, Aug. 17 ***Perf. 11½x11***

921 A396 5m bl & multi 5 5
922 A396 10m yel & multi 25 5
923 A396 20m ver & multi 45 7
Nos. 921-923,C149-C152 (7) 2.20 69

20th Olympic Games, Munich, Aug. 26-Sept. 11.

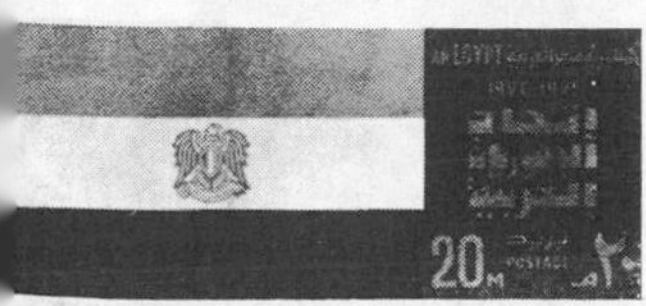
Flag of Confederation of Arab Republics — A397

1972, Sept. 1 Wmk. 342 *Perf. 11 1/2*
924 A397 20m car, bis & blk 25 15

First anniversary of Confederation of Arab Republics.

Red Crescent, TB and UN Emblems — A398

Refugees, UNRWA Emblem, Map of Palestine — A400

Design: 55m, Inundated Temple of Philae, UNESCO emblem.

1972, Oct. 24 Photo. *Perf. 11x11 1/2*
925 A398 10m brn org, red & bl 25 10

Perf. 11 1/2
926 A399 20m grn, yel & blk 50 15

Perf. 11
927 A400 30m lt bl, pur & lt brn 1.50 50

Perf. 11 1/2
928 A399 55m brn, gold & bluish gray 1.40 55

United Nations Day. No. 925 commemorates the 14th Regional Tuberculosis Conference, Cairo, 1972; No. 926 is for World Health Month; No. 927 publicizes aid to refugees and No. 928 the U.N. campaign to save the Temples at Philae.

Morning Glory — A401

1972, Oct. 24 *Perf. 11*
929 A401 10m yel, lil & grn 5 5

For use on greeting cards.

"Seeing Eye" — A402

1972, Nov. 30 *Perf. 11 1/2*
930 A402 20m multi 15 7

Social Work Day.

Sculling Race, View of Luxor — A403

1972, Dec. 17 Wmk. 342 *Perf. 11*
931 A403 20m bl & brn 10 7

Third Nile International Rowing Festival, Dec. 1972.

Minaret Type of 1971

Minarets: 10m, Al Maridani, 1338. 20m, Bashtak, 1337. 30m, Qusun, 1330. 55m, Al Gashankir, 1306.

1973, Jan. 2
Frame in Brt. Yel. Green

932	A362	10m multi	90	20
933	A362	20m multi	1.40	30
934	A362	30m multi	3.00	50
935	A362	55m multi	4.25	1.25
		Strip of 4 (#932-935) + Label	10.00	4.00

Post Day, 1973. Nos. 932-935 printed se-tenant in sheets of 40 stamps and 10 yellow and green labels.

Cairo Fair Emblem A404

Perf. 11 1/2x11
1973, Mar. 21 Photo. Wmk. 342
936 A404 20m gray & multi 10 7

International Cairo Fair.

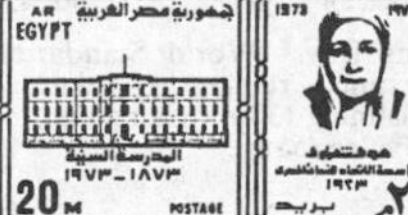
Sania Girls' School and Hoda Sharawi A406

Family — A405

1973, Mar. 21 *Perf. 11x11 1/2*
937 A405 20m multi 10 7

Family planning.

Scott's editorial staff cannot undertake to identify, authenticate or appraise stamps and postal markings.

Perf. 11 1/2x11
1973, July 15 Photo. Wmk. 342
938 A406 20m ultra, grn 10 7

Centenary of education for girls and 50th anniversary of the Egyptian Women's Union, founded by Hoda Sharawi.

Rifaa el Tahtawi — A407

1973, July 15 *Perf. 11x11 1/2*
939 A407 20m brt grn, ol & brn 25 7

Centenary of the death of Rifaa el Tahtawi, champion of democracy and principal of language school.

Omar Makram A408

Abdel Rahman al Gabarti, Historian A409

"Reconstruction and Battle" — A410

Design: No. 941, Mohamed Korayem, martyr.

1973, July 23

940	A408	20m yel grn, bl & brn	10	7
941	A408	20m lt grn, bl & brn	10	7
942	A409	20m ocher & brn	10	7

Souvenir Sheet
Imperf
943 A410 110m gold, bl & blk 1.00 1.00

21st anniversary of the revolution establishing the republic. No. 943 contains one stamp and has gold marginal inscription. Size: 97x102mm.

Grain, Cow, FAO Emblem A411

Perf. 11 1/2x11
1973, Oct. 24 Wmk. 342
944 A411 10m brn, dk bl & yel grn 5 5

10th anniversary of the World Food Organization.

Inundated Temples at Philae A412

1973, Oct. 24 *Perf. 11 1/2*
945 A412 55m bl, pur & org 40 25

UNESCO campaign to save the temples at Philae.

Bank Building A413

1973, Oct. 24
946 A413 20m brn org, grn & blk 10 8

75th anniversary of the National Bank of Egypt.

Rose — A414

1973, Oct. 24 *Perf. 11*
947 A414 10m bl & multi 5 5

For use on greeting cards.

Human Rights Flame A415

Taha Hussein A416

Perf. 11x11 1/2
1973, Dec. 8 Photo. Wmk. 342
948 A415 20m yel grn, dk bl & car 10 8

25th anniversary of the Universal Declaration of Human Rights.

1973, Dec. 10
949 A416 20m dk bl, brn & emer 10 8

In memory of Dr. Taha Hussein (1893-1973), "Father of Education" in Egypt, writer, philosopher.

Pres. Sadat, Flag and Battle of Oct. 6 — A417

1973, Dec. 23 *Perf. 11x11½*
950 A417 20m yel, blk & red 2.50 1.00

Crossing of Suez Canal by Egyptian forces, Oct. 6, 1973.

WPY Emblem and Chart A418

Cairo Fair Emblem A419

1974, Mar. 21 Wmk. 342 *Perf. 11*
951 A418 55m org, grn & dk bl 30 18

World Population Year.

1974, Mar. 21 Photo.
952 A419 20m bl & multi 15 8

Cairo International Fair.

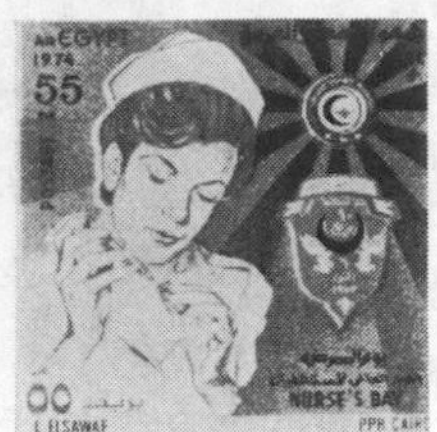
Nurse and Medal of Angels of Ramadan 10 — A420

1974, May 15 *Perf. 11½*
953 A420 55m multi 28 18

Nurses' and World Hospital Day.

Workers, Relief Carving from Queen Tee's Tomb, Sakhara — A421

1974, May 15 *Perf. 11*
954 A421 20m yel, bl & brn 25 10

Workers' Day.

Pres. Sadat, Troops Crossing Suez Canal — A422

"Reconstruction," Map of Suez Canal and New Building — A423

Sheet of Aluminum A424

Design: 110m, Pres. Sadat's "October Working Paper," symbols of science and development.

1974, July 23 Photo. *Perf. 11x11½*
955 A422 20m multi 75 25
956 A423 20m bl, gold & blk 75 25

Perf. 11½
957 A424 20m plum & sil 45 15

Souvenir Sheet
Imperf
958 A424 110m grn & multi 1.00 75

22nd anniversary of the revolution establishing the republic and for the end of the October War. No. 958 contains one stamp (52x59mm.). Gold and green marginal inscription. Size: 72½x108mm.

Pres. Sadat and Flag — A425

Perf. 11x11½
1974, Oct. 6 Wmk. 342
959 A425 20m yel, blk & red 1.50 75

First anniversary of Battle of Oct. 6.

Palette and Brushes A426

1974, Oct. 6 *Perf. 11½*
960 A426 30m pur, yel & blk 15 12

6th Exhibition of Plastic Art.

Teachers and Pupils — A427

1974, Oct. 6 *Perf. 11x11½*
961 A427 20m multi 10 8

Teachers' Day.

Souvenir Sheet

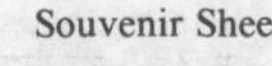

UPU Monument, Bern — A428

1974, Oct. 6 *Imperf.*
962 A428 110m gold & multi 1.75 1.00

Centenary of Universal Postal Union. No. 962 contains one stamp, yellow green marginal inscription. Size: 75x100mm.

Emblems, Cogwheel and Calipers — A429

Refugee Camp under Attack and UN Refugee Organization Emblem A430

Child and UNICEF Emblem A431

Temple of Philae — A432

1974, Oct. 24 *Perf. 11½, 11x11½*
963 A429 10m blk, bl & yel 25 15
964 A430 20m dp org, bl & blk 75 50
965 A430 30m grn, bl & brn 60 30
966 A430 55m blk, bl & yel 90 45

United Nations Day. World Standards Day (10m); Palestinian refugee repatriation (20m); Family Planning (30m); Campaign to save Temple of Philae (55m).

Foreign postal stationery (stamped envelopes, postal cards and air letter sheets) lies beyond the scope of this Catalogue, which is limited to adhesive postage stamps.

Calla Lily — A433

1974, Nov. 7 *Perf. 1*
967 A433 10m ultra & multi 5

For use on greeting cards.

10m-coins, Smokestacks and Grain — A434

1974, Nov. 7 *Perf. 11½x1*
968 A434 20m yel grn, dk bl & sil 10

International Savings Day.

Organizatio Emblem an Medical Services A435

1974, Nov. 7 *Perf. 11*
969 A435 30m vio, red & gold 15 1

Health Insurance Organization, 10t anniversary.

Mustafa Lutfy El Manfalouty A436

Abbas Mahmoud El Akkad A437

Perf. 11x11½
1974, Dec. 8 Photo. Wmk. 34
970 A436 20m bl blk & brn 15
971 A437 20m brn & bl blk 15

Arab writers; Mustafa Lutfy El Manfalout (1876-1924) and Abbas Mahmoud El Akka (1889-1964). Nos. 970-971 printed se-tenan in sheets of 50.

Goddess Maat Facing God Thoth — A438

Fish-shaped Vase — A439

Pharaonic Golden Vase — A440

Sign of Life, Mirror — A441

Wmk. 342

1975, Jan. 2 Photo. *Perf. 11½*

972	A438	20m sil & multi	25	15
973	A439	30m multi	30	25
974	A440	55m multi	40	30
975	A441	110m bl & multi	1.00	65

Post Day 1975. Egyptian art works from 12th-5th centuries B.C.

Om Kolthoum A442

Perf. 11½

1975, Mar. 3 Photo. Unwmk.

976	A442	20m brown	20	12

In memory of Om Kolthoum, singer.

Crescent, Globe, Al Aqsa and Kaaba A443

Cairo Fair Emblem A444

1975, Mar. 25

977	A443	20m multi	50	25

Mohammed's Birthday.

Perf. 11x11½

1975, Mar. 25 Wmk. 342

978	A444	20m multi	10	8

International Cairo Fair.

Kasr El Ainy Hospital WHO Emblem A445

Perf. 11½x11

1975, May 7 Photo. Wmk. 342

979	A445	20m dk brn & bl	10	8

World Health Organization Day.

Children Reading Book A446

Children and Line Graph A447

1975, May 7 *Perf. 11x11½*

980	A446	20m multi	10	8
981	A447	20m multi	10	8

Science Day.

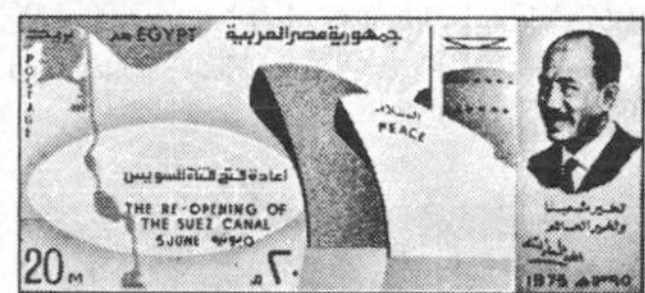
Suez Canal, Globe, Ships, Pres. Sadat — A448

1975, June 5 *Perf. 11½*

982	A448	20m bl, brn & blk	70	30

Reopening of the Suez Canal, June 5. See Nos. C166-C167.

Belmabgoknis Flowers — A449

1975, July 30 Photo. Wmk. 342

983	A449	10m grn & bl	5	5

For use on greeting cards.

Sphinx and Pyramids Illuminated A450

Rural Electrification — A451

Map of Egypt with Tourist Sites — A452

1975, July 23

984	A450	20m blk, org & grn	15	8
985	A451	20m dk bl & brn	15	8

Perf. 11

986	A452	110m multi	1.75	1.50

23rd anniversary of the revolution establishing the republic. No. 986 printed in sheets of 6 (2x3). Size: 71x80mm.

Volleyball — A453

1975, Aug. 2 Photo. *Perf. 11x11½*

987	A453	20m *shown*	20	10
988	A453	20m *Running*	20	10
989	A453	20m *Torch and flag bearers*	20	10
990	A453	20m *Basketball*	20	10
991	A453	20m *Soccer*	20	10
		Nos. 987-991 (5)	1.00	50

6th Arab School Tournament. Nos. 987-991 printed se-tenant in sheets of 50.

Egyptian Flag and Tanks A454

1975 Photo. Unwmk. *Perf. 11½*

992	A454	20m multi	1.00	25

Two-line Arabic Inscription in Bottom Panel, "M" over "20"

992A	A454	20m multi	1.00	25

No. 992 commemorates 2nd anniversary of Battle of Oct. 6, "The Spark;" No. 992A, the International Symposium on War of October 1973, Cairo University, Oct. 27-31.

Issue dates: No. 992, Oct. 6. No. 992A, Oct. 24.

Arrows Pointing to Fluke, and Emblems A455

Submerged Wall and Sculpture, UNESCO Emblem A456

Perf. 11x11½

1975, Oct. 24 Wmk. 342

993	A455	20m multi	15	10
994	A456	55m multi	85	30

United Nations Day. 20m publicizes International Conference on Schistosomiasis (Bilharziasis); 55m commemorates UNESCO help in saving temples at Philae. See Nos. C169-C170.

Pharaonic Gate, University Emblem A457

Al Biruni A458

1975, Nov. 15 Photo. Wmk. 342

995	A457	20m multi	25	15

Ain Shams University, 25th anniversary.

1975, Dec. 23 Photo. *Perf. 11x11½*

Designs: No. 997, Al Farabi and lute. No. 998, Al Kanady, book and compass.

996	A458	20m bl, brn & grn	45	8
997	A458	20m bl, brn & grn	45	8
998	A458	20m bl, brn & grn	45	8

Arab philosophers.

Ibex (Prow) — A459

Designs (from Tutankhamen's Tomb): 30m, Lioness. 55m, Cow's head (Goddess Hawthor). 110m, Hippopotamus' head (God Horus).

1976, Jan. 2 Unwmk. *Perf. 11½*

999	A459	20m multi	35	15

Wmk. 342

1000	A459	30m brn, gold & ultra	65	30
1001	A459	55m multi	85	35
1002	A459	110m multi	1.25	75

Post Day 1976.

Lake, Aswan Dam, Industry and Agriculture — A460

Perf. 11½x11

1976, Jan. 27 Photo. Wmk. 342

1003	A460	20m multi	10	8

Filling of lake formed by Aswan High Dam.

Fair Emblem — A461

The lack of a price for a listed item does not necessarily indicate rarity.

Commemorative Medal — A462

1976, Mar. 15 *Perf. 11x11½*
1004 A461 20m org & pur 10 8

9th International Cairo Fair, Mar. 8-27.

1976, Mar. 15 **Wmk. 342**
1005 A462 20m ol, yel & blk 10 8

11th Biennial Exhibition of Fine Arts, Alexandria.

Hands Shielding Invalid A463

1976, Apr. 7 **Photo.** *Perf. 11½*
1006 A463 20m dk grn, lt grn & yel 10 8

Founding of Faithfulness and Hope Society.

Eye and WHO Emblem A464

1976, Apr. 7
1007 A464 20m dk brn, yel & grn 10 8

World Health Day: "Foresight prevents blindness."

Pres. Sadat, Legal Department Emblem — A465

Perf. 11½x11
1976, May 15 **Photo.** **Wmk. 342**
1008 A465 20m ol & multi 25 15

Centenary of State Legal Department.

Scales of Justice — A466

1976, May 15 *Perf. 11x11½*
1009 A466 20m car, blk & grn 10 8

5th anniversary of Rectification Movement.

Al-Ahram Front Page, First Issue A467

Perf. 11½x11
1976, June 25 **Photo.** **Wmk. 342**
1010 A467 20m bis & multi 10 8

Centenary of Al-Ahram newspaper.

World Map, Pres. Sadat and Emblems — A468

1976, July 23 *Perf. 11x11½*
1011 A468 20m bl, blk & yel 75 35

Souvenir Sheet

Imperf

1012 A468 110m bl, blk & yel 2.50 1.00

24th anniversary of the revolution. No. 1012 shows design of No. 1011 enlarged to fill entire area. Size: 85x76mm.

Scarborough Lily — A469

1976, Sept. 10 **Photo.** *Perf. 11*
1013 A469 10m multi 5 5

For use on greeting cards.

Reconstruction of Sinai by Irrigation — A470

Abu Redice Oil Wells and Refinery — A471

Unknown Soldier, Memorial Pyramid for October War — A472

1976, Oct. 6 *Perf. 11x11½*
1014 A470 20m multi 50 15
1015 A471 20m multi 50 15
1016 A472 110m grn, bl & blk 2.00 1.00

October War (crossing of Suez Canal), 3rd anniversary. Size of No. 1016: 65x77mm.

Papyrus with Children's Animal Story — A473

Al Aqsa Mosque, Palestinian Refugees A474

Designs: 55m, Isis, from Philae Temple, UNESCO emblem (vert.). 110m, UNESCO emblem and "30".

Perf. 11½, 11½x11
1976, Oct. 24 **Photo.** **Wmk. 342**
1017 A473 20m dk bl, bis & brn 25 10
1018 A474 30m brn, grn & blk 90 25
1019 A473 55m dk bl & bis 75 35
1020 A474 110m lt grn, vio bl & red 1.50 60

30th anniversary of UNESCO.

Census Chart A475

1976, Nov. 22 **Photo.** *Perf. 11½x11*
1021 A475 20m multi 15 8

10th General Population and Housing Census.

Nile and Commemorative Medal — A476

Ikhnaton — A477

1976, Nov. 22 *Perf. 11x11½*
1022 A476 20m grn & brn 15 8

Geographical Society of Egypt, centenary (in 1975).

1977, Jan. 2 **Photo.** *Perf. 11x11½*

Designs: 30m, Ikhnaton's daughter. 55m, Nefertiti, Ikhnaton's wife. 110m, Ikhnaton, front view.

1023 A477 20m multi 35 15
1024 A477 30m multi 30 20
1025 A477 55m multi 75 30
1026 A477 110m multi 1.50 75

Post Day 1977.

Policeman, Emblem and Emergency Car — A478

Perf. 11½x11
1977, Feb. 25 **Photo.** **Wmk. 342**
1027 A478 20m multi 20 8

Police Day.

Map of Africa, Arab League Emblem — A479

1977, Mar 7 *Perf. 11x11½*
1028 A479 55m multi 40 20

First Afro-Arab Summit Conference, Cairo.

Fair Emblem, Pharaonic Ship A480

1977, Mar. 7 *Perf. 11½x11*
1029 A480 20m grn, blk & red 20 8

10th International Cairo Fair.

King Faisal — A481

1977, Mar. 22 Photo. ***Perf. 11x11½***
1030 A481 20m ind & brn 50 25

King Faisal Ben Abdel-Aziz Al Saud of Saudi Arabia (1906-1975).

Healthy and Crippled Children — A482

1977, Apr. 12 **Wmk. 342**
1031 A482 20m multi 10 8

National campaign to fight poliomyelitis.

APU Emblem, Members' Flags A483

1977, Apr. 12 ***Perf. 11½***
1032 A483 20m bl & multi 15 10
1033 A483 30m gray & multi 20 15

25th anniv. of Arab Postal Union (APU).

Children's Village A484

Perf. 11½x11
1977, May 7 Photo. Wmk. 342
1034 A484 20m multi 10 8
1035 A484 55m multi 30 18

Inauguration of Children's Village, Cairo.

Loom, Spindle and Factory A485

1977, May 7
1036 A485 20m multi 10 8

Egyptian Spinning and Weaving Company, El Mehalla el Kobra, 50th anniversary.

Satellite, Globe, ITU Emblem — A486

1977, May 17 ***Perf. 11x11½***
1037 A486 110m dk bl & multi 1.00 75

World Telecommunications Day.

Flag and "25" A487

Egyptian Flag and Eagle — A488

Perf. 11½x11
1977, July 23 Photo. Wmk. 342
1038 A487 20m sil, car & blk 20 8
Perf. 11x11½
1039 A488 110m multi 1.25 75

25th anniversary of July 23rd Revolution. No. 1039 printed in sheets of six. Size: 75x83mm.

Saad Zaghloul A489

Archbishop Capucci, Map of Palestine A490

Perf. 11x11½
1977, Aug. 23 Photo. Wmk. 342
1040 A489 20m dk grn & dk brn 20 8

Saad Zaghloul, leader of 1919 Revolution, 50th death anniversary.

1977, Sept. 1
1041 A490 45m emer & bl 45 18

Palestinian Archbishop Hilarion Capucci, jailed by Israel in 1974.

Bird-of-Paradise Flower — A491

1977, Sept. 3
1042 A491 10m multi 10 5

For use on greeting cards.

Proclamation Greening the Land — A492

Perf. 11x11½
1977, Sept. 25 Photo. Wmk. 342
1043 A492 20m multi 20 8

Agraian Reform Law, 25th anniversary.

Soldier, Tanks, Medal of Oct. 6 — A493

Anwar El Sadat — A494

1977, Oct. 6 ***Perf. 11½x11***
1044 A493 20m multi 50 25
Unwmk.
Perf. 11
1045 A494 140m dk brn, gold & red 5.00 2.75

Crossing of Suez Canai, 4th anniversary. No. 1045 printed in sheets of 16.

Refugees Looking at Al Aqsa Mosque A495

Goddess Taueret and Spirit of Flight (Horus) A496

Mural Relief, Temple of Philae — A497

Wmk. 342
1977, Oct. 24 Photo. ***Perf. 11***
1046 A495 45m grn, red & blk 25 20
1047 A496 55m dp bl & yel 30 25
1048 A497 140m ol bis & dk brn 70 50

United Nations Day.

Electric Trains, First Egyptian Locomotive — A498

1977, Oct. 22
1049 A498 20m multi 25 8

125th anniversary of Egyptian railroads.

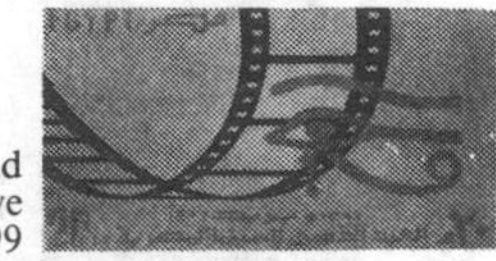

Film and Eye A499

1977, Nov. 16 ***Perf. 11½x11***
1050 A499 20m gray, blk & gold 12 8

50th anniversary of Egyptian cinema.

Natural Gas Well and Refinery — A500

1977, Nov. 17 **Photo.**
1051 A500 20m multi 25 15

National Oil Festival, celebrating the acquisition of Sinai oil wells.

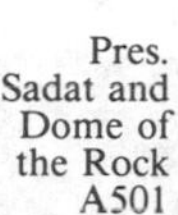

Pres. Sadat and Dome of the Rock A501

Perf. 11½x11
1977, Dec. 31 Photo. Wmk. 342
1052 A501 20m grn, brn & blk 25 15
1053 A501 140m grn, blk & brn 1.15 75

Pres. Sadat's peace mission to Israel.

Ramses II — A502

Design: 45m, Queen Nefertari, bas-relief.

1978, Jan. 2 ***Perf. 11½***
1054 A502 20m grn, blk & gold 10 8
1055 A502 45m org, blk & ol 25 16

Post Day 1978.

Water Wheels, Fayum — A503

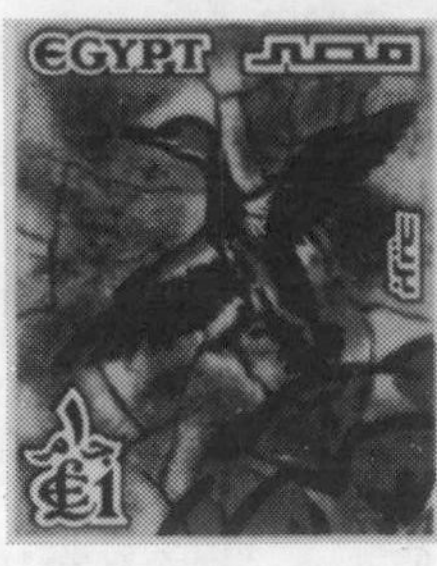

Flying Duck, from Floor in Ikhnaton's Palace
A504

Designs: 5m, Birdhouse. 10m, Statue of Horus. 20m, Al Rifa'i Mosque, Cairo. 50m, Monastery, Wadi al-Natrun. 55m, Ruins of Edfu Temple. 70m, Bridge of Oct. 6. 85m, Medum pyramid. 100m, Facade, El Morsi Mosque, Alexandria. 200m, Column, Alexandria, and Sphinx. 500m, Arabian stallion.

1978-82 Wmk. 342 *Perf. 11½*

1056	A503	1m sl bl	5	5
1057	A503	5m bis brn	5	5
1058	A503	10m brt grn	5	5
1059	A503	20m dk brn	10	8
1059A	A503	30m sepia	15	15
1060	A503	50m brt bl	25	15
1061	A503	55m olive	28	18
1062	A503	70m ol ('79)	35	20
1062A	A503	80m like #1062 ('82)	40	40
1063	A503	85m dp pur	42	30
1064	A503	100m brown	50	40
1065	A503	200m bl & ind	1.00	80
1066	A504	500m multi	2.50	1.25
1067	A504	£1 multi	5.00	2.50
		Nos. 1056-1067 (14)	11.10	6.56

Issue dates: 500m, £1, Feb. 27. Others, July 23, 70m, Aug. 22, 1979.

Fair Emblem and Wheat
A505

1978, Mar. 15 *Perf. 11½*

1072	A505	20m multi	10	8

11th Cairo International Fair, Mar. 11-25.

Emblem, Kasr El Ainy School
A506

1978, Mar. 18 *Perf. 11½x11*

1073	A506	20m lt bl, blk & gold	10	8

Kasr El Ainy School of Medicine, 150th anniversary.

Soldiers and Emblem
A507

Youssef El Sebai
A508

1978, Mar. 30 *Perf. 11x11½*

1074	A507	20m multi	10	8
1075	A508	20m bis brn	10	8

Nos. 1069-1070 printed se-tenant.

Youssef El Sebai, newspaper editor, assassinated on Cyprus and in memory of the commandos killed in raid on Cyprus.

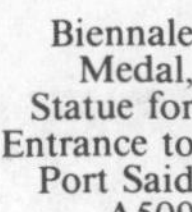

Biennale Medal, Statue for Entrance to Port Said
A509

1978, Apr. 1 *Perf. 11½*

1076	A509	20m bl, grn & blk	10	8

12th Biennial Exhibition of Fine Arts, Alexandria.

Child with Smallpox, UN Emblem
A510

1978, Apr. 7 Photo. *Perf. 11½*

1077	A510	20m multi	10	8

Eradication of smallpox.

Heart and Arrow, UN Emblem
A511

Anwar El Sadat
A512

1978, Apr. 7 Wmk. 342

1078	A511	20m multi	10	8

Fight against hypertension.

1978, May 15 Photo. *Perf. 11½x11*

1079	A512	20m grn, brn & gold	25	15

7th anniversary of Rectification Movement.

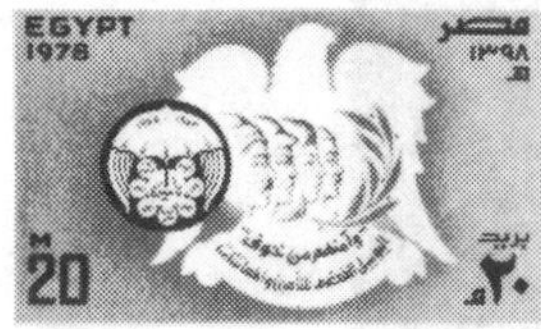

Social Security Emblem — A513

1978, May 16 *Perf. 11*

1080	A513	20m lt grn & dk brn	10	8

General Organization of Insurance and Pensions (Social Security), 25th anniversary.

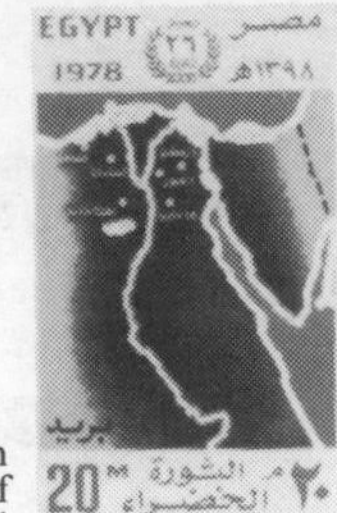

New Cities on Map of Egypt — A514

Map of Egypt and Sudan, Wheat — A515

Wmk. 342

1978, July 23 Photo. *Perf. 11½*

1081	A514	20m multi	35	8
1082	A515	45m multi	60	16

26th anniversary of July 23rd revolution.

Symbols of Egyptian Ministries
A516

1978, Aug. 28 Photo. *Perf. 11½x11*

1083	A516	20m multi	10	8

Centenary of Egyptian Ministerial System.

Pres. Nasser and "Spirit of Egypt" Showing Way — A517

1978, Oct. 6 Photo. *Perf. 11x11½*

1084	A517	20m multi	25	15

Crossing of Suez Canal, 5th anniversary.

Human Rights Emblem — A518

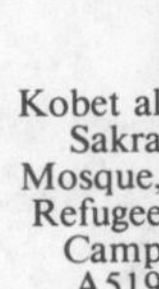

Kobet al Sakra Mosque, Refugee Camp
A519

Dove and Human Rights Emblem — A520

Design: 55m, Temple at Biga and UNESCO emblem (horiz.).

Perf. 11, 11½ (45m)

1978, Oct. 24 Photo. Wmk. 342

1085	A518	20m multi	10	8
1086	A519	45m multi	75	50
1087	A518	55m multi	28	18
1088	A520	140m multi	70	48

United Nations Day.

Pilgrims, Mt. Arafat and Holy Kaaba — A521

1978, Nov. 7 Photo. *Perf. 11*

1089	A521	45m multi	25	16

Pilgrimage to Mecca.

Tahtib Horse Dance — A522

1978, Nov. 7

1090	A522	10m multi	5	5
1091	A522	20m multi	10	8

U.N. Emblem, Globe and Grain
A523

1978, Nov. 11 Photo. *Perf. 11½*

1092	A523	20m grn, dk bl & yel	10	8

Technical Cooperation Among Developing Countries Conference, Buenos Aires, Argentina, Sept. 1978.

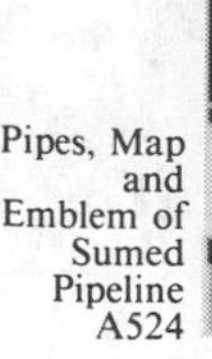

Pipes, Map and Emblem of Sumed Pipeline A524

1978, Nov. 11
1093 A524 20m brn, bl & yel 10 8

Inauguration of Sumed pipeline from Suez to Alexandria, 1st anniversary.

Mastheads A525

Abu el Walid A526

1978, Dec. 24 ***Perf. 11x11½***
1094 A525 20m brn & blk 10 8

150th anniversary of the newspaper El Wakea el Masriya.

1978, Dec. 24
1095 A526 45m brt grn & ind 22 18

800th death anniversary of Abu el Walid ibn Rashid.

Helwan Observatory and Sky — A527

1978, Dec. 30 **Wmk. 342**
1096 A527 20m multi 10 8

Helwan Observatory, 75th anniversary.

Second Daughter of Ramses II — A528

Ramses Statues, Abu Simbel, and Cartouches — A529

1979, Jan. 2 **Photo.** ***Perf. 11***
1097 A528 20m brn & yel 10 8

Perf. 11½x11
1098 A529 140m multi 70 48

Post Day 1978.

Book, Reader and Globe A530

Perf. 11½x11
1979, Feb. 1 **Photo.** **Wmk. 342**
1099 A530 20m yel grn & brn 10 10

Cairo 11th International Book Fair.

Wheat, Globe, Fair Emblem — A531

Perf. 11x11½
1979, Mar. 17 **Photo.** **Unwmk.**
1100 A531 20m bl, org & blk 10 10

12th Cairo International Fair, March-Apr.

Skull, Poppy, Agency Emblem — A532

1979, Mar. 20 ***Perf. 11***
1101 A532 70m multi 40 35

Anti-Narcotics General Administration, 50th anniversary.

Isis Holding Horus — A533

1979, Mar. 21
1102 A533 140m multi 80 70

Mother's Day.

World Map and Book — A534

Perf. 11x11½
1979, Mar. 22 **Wmk. 342**
1103 A534 45m yel, bl & brn 25 20

Cultural achievements of the Arabs.

Pres. Sadat's Signature, Peace Doves A535

Wmk. 342
1979, Mar. 31 **Photo.** ***Perf. 11½***
1104 A535 70m brt grn & red 50 35
1105 A535 140m yel grn & red 90 70

Signing of Peace Treaty between Egypt and Israel, Mar. 26.

1979, May 26 **Photo.** ***Perf. 11½***
1106 A535 20m yel & dk brn 35 10

Return of Al Arish to Egypt.

Honeycomb with Food Symbols A536

1979, May 15
1107 A536 20m multi 12 10

8th anniversary of movement to establish food security.

Coins, 1959, 1979 A537

Perf. 11½x11
1979, June 1 **Wmk. 342** **Photo.**
1108 A537 20m yel & gray 12 10

25th anniversary of the Egyptian Mint.

Egypt No. 1104 under Magnifying Glass — A538

1979, June 1 ***Perf. 11***
1109 A538 20m grn, blk & brn 25 10

Philatelic Society of Egypt, 50th anniversary.

Book, Atom Symbol, Rising Sun — A539

"23 July," "Revolution" and "Peace" — A540

Perf. 11½x11
1979, July 23 **Wmk. 342**
1110 A539 20m multi 10 10

Miniature Sheet

Imperf
1111 A540 140m multi 85 85

27th anniversary of July 23rd revolution. Size of No. 1111: 50x62mm.

Musicians — A541

1979, Aug. 22 ***Perf. 11½***
1112 A541 10m multi 8 6

For use on greeting cards.

Dove over Map of Suez Canal A542

Wmk. 342
1979, Oct. 6 **Photo.** ***Perf. 11½***
1113 A542 20m bl & brn 15 12

Crossing of Suez Canal, 6th anniversary.

Dinosaur Skeleton, Map of Africa A543

Perf. 11½x11
1979, Oct. 9 **Photo.** **Wmk. 342**
1114 A543 20m multi 12 10

Egyptian Geological Museum, 75th anniversary.

T Square on Drawing Board — A544

1979, Oct. 11 *Perf. 11*
1115 A544 20m multi 12 10

Engineers Day.

Human Rights Emblem Over Globe — A545

Boy Balancing IYC Emblem — A546

Perf. 11½
1979, Oct. 24 Photo. Unwmk.
1116 A545 45m multi 30 25
1117 A546 140m multi 90 70

United Nations Day and International Year of the Child.

International Savings Day — A547

1979, Oct. 31
1118 A547 70m multi 45 35

Shooting Championship Emblem — A548

1979, Nov. 16
1119 A548 20m multi 15 10

20th International Military Shooting Championship, Cairo.

International Palestinian Solidarity Day — A549

1979, Nov. 29 *Perf. 11x11½*
1120 A549 140m multi 85 70

Dove Holding Grain, Rotary Emblem, Globe A550

1979, Dec. 3 Photo. *Perf. 11½*
1121 A550 45m multi 30 25

Rotary International, 75th anniversary; Cairo Rotary Club, 50th anniversary.

Arms Factories, 25th Anniversary — A551

Perf. 11½x11
1979, Dec. 23 Photo. Wmk. 342
1122 A551 20m lt ol grn & brn 10 10

Aly El Garem (1881-1949) A552

Pharaonic Capital A553

Poets: No. 1124, Mahmoud Samy El Baroudy (1839-1904).

1979, Dec. 25 *Perf. 11x11½*
1123 A552 20m dk brn & yel brn 25 10
1124 A552 20m brn & dk brn 25 10

Nos. 1123-1124 printed se-tenant.

1980, Jan. 2 Unwmk. *Perf. 11½*

Post Day: Various Pharaonic capitals. Printed se-tenant.

1125 A553 20m multi 25 10
1126 A553 45m multi 40 20
1127 A553 70m multi 65 35
1128 A553 140m multi 1.00 70

Golden Goddess of Writing, Fair Emblem — A554

Exhibition Catalogue and Medal — A555

1980, Feb. 2 Photo. *Perf. 11½*
1129 A554 20m multi 25 15

12th Cairo International Book Fair, Jan. 24-Feb. 4.

1980, Feb. 2
1130 A555 20m multi 10 10

13th Biennial Exhibition of Fine Arts, Alexandria.

13th Cairo International Fair — A556

1980, Mar. 8 Photo. *Perf. 11x11½*
1131 A556 20m multi 10 10

Kiosk of Trajan — A557

1980, Mar. 10 *Perf. 11½*
1132 Strip of 4 plus label 2.75 2.75
a. A557 70m, single stamp 45 45

UNESCO campaign to save Nubian monuments, 20th anniversary. Shown on stamps are Temples of Philae, Kalabsha, Korasy.

Physicians' Day — A558

1980, Mar. 18 *Perf. 11x11½*
1133 A558 20m multi 10 10

Rectification Movement, 9th Anniversary — A559

Perf. 11½x11
1980, May 15 Photo. Wmk. 342
1134 A559 20m multi 25 15

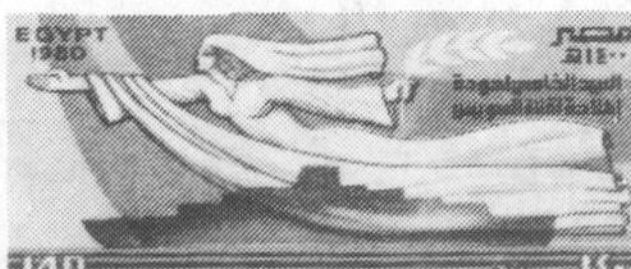
Re-opening of Suez Canal, 5th Anniversary — A560

1980, June 5 *Perf. 11½*
1135 A560 140m multi 70 70

Prevention of Cruelty to Animals Week A561

1980, June 5
1136 A561 20m lt yel grn & gray 10 10

Industry Day A562

Perf. 11½x11
1980, July 12 Photo. Wmk. 342
1137 A562 20m multi 10 10

Leaf with Text A563

Family Protection Emblem A564

1980, July 23 *Perf. 11½*
1138 A563 20m multi 10 10

Souvenir Sheet

Imperf

1139 A564 140m multi 75 75

July 23rd Revolution, 28th anniversary; Social Security Year. Size of No. 1139: 51x67mm.

Erksous Seller and Nakrazan Player — A565

Perf. 11½
1980, Aug. 8 Unwmk. Photo.
1140 A565 10m multi 5 5

For use on greeting cards.

The indexes in each volume of the Scott Catalogue contain many listings which help to identify stamps.

7th Anniversary of Suez Canal Crossing — A566

1980, Oct. 6 **Litho.**
1141 A566 20m multi 10 10

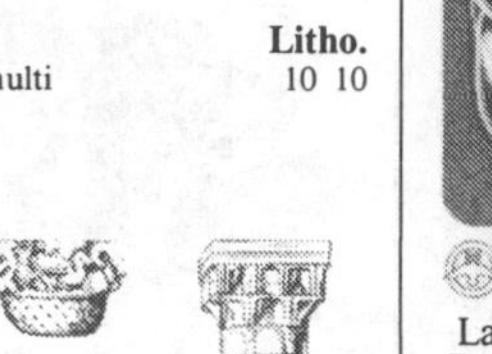

Islamic and Coptic Columns A567

International Telecommunications Union Emblem — A568

Wmk. 342
1980, Oct. 24 **Photo.** ***Perf. 11½***
1142 A567 70m multi 35 35
1143 A568 140m multi 70 70

United Nations Day. Campaign to save Egyptian monuments (70m), International Telecommunications Day (140m).

Hegira (Pilgrimage Year) A569

1980, Nov. 9 **Litho.** ***Perf. 11x11½***
1144 A569 45m multi 22 22

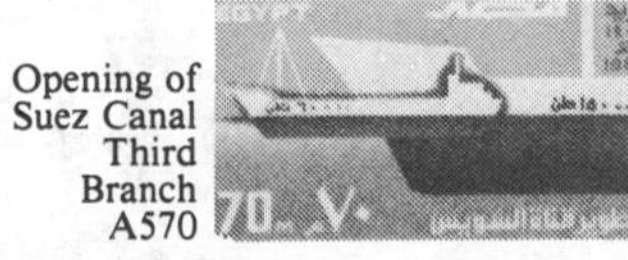

Opening of Suez Canal Third Branch A570

Perf. 11½x11
1980, Dec. 16 **Photo.** **Wmk. 342**
1145 A570 70m multi 35 35

Mustafa Sadek El-Rafai (1880-1927), Writer — A571

Famous Men: No. 1147, Ali Mustafa Mousharafa (1898-1950), mathematician, No. 1148, Ali Ibrahim (1880-1947), surgeon Nos. 1146-1148 se-tenant.

1980, Dec. 23 ***Perf. 11x11½***
1146 A571 20m grn & brn 25 15
1147 A571 20m grn & brn 25 15
1148 A571 20m grn & brn 25 15

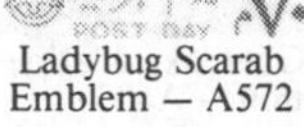

Ladybug Scarab Emblem — A572

Heinrich von Stephan, UPU — A573

Perf. 11½
1981, Jan. 2 **Photo.** **Unwmk.**
1149 A572 70m *shown* 35 35
1150 A572 70m *Scarab, reverse* 35 35

Post Day.

Perf. 11x11½
1981, Jan. 7 **Wmk. 342**
1151 A573 140m grnsh bl & dk brn 70 70

Heinrich von Stephan (1831-1897), founder of Universal Postal Union, birth sesquicentennial.

13th Cairo International Book Fair — A574

1981, Feb. 1 ***Perf. 11½x11***
1152 A574 20m multi 10 10

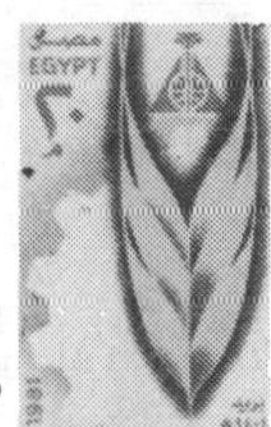

14th Cairo International Fair, Mar. 14-28 — A575

Perf. 11x11½
1981, Mar. 14 **Photo.** **Wmk. 342**
1153 A575 20m multi 10 10

Rural Electrification Authority, 10th Anniversary — A576

1981, Mar. 18
1154 A576 20m multi 10 10

Veterans' Day — A577

1981, Mar. 26
1155 A577 20m multi 10 10

International Dentistry Conference, Cairo — A578

Perf. 11x11½
1981, Apr. 14 **Photo.** **Wmk. 342**
1156 A578 20m red & ol 10 10

Trade Union Emblem A579

Nurses' Day A580

Perf. 11x11½
1981, May 1 **Photo.** **Wmk. 342**
1157 A579 20m brt bl & dk brn 10 10

International Confederation of Arab Trade Unions, 25th anniv.

1981, May 12
1158 A580 20m multi 10 10

Irrigation Equipment (Electrification Movement) — A581

1981, May 15 ***Perf. 11½***
1159 A581 20m multi 10 10

Air Force Day — A582

Perf. 11x11½
1981, June 30 **Photo.** **Wmk. 342**
1160 A582 20m multi 10 10

Flag Surrounding Map of Suez Canal — A583

Wmk. 342
1981, July 23 **Photo.** ***Perf. 11½***
1161 A583 10m multi 5 5
1162 A583 20m Emblems 10 10

July 23rd Revolution, 29th anniv.; Social Defense Year.

1981 Feasts — A584

Wmk. 342
1981, July 29 **Photo.** ***Perf. 11***
1163 A584 10m multi 5 5

Kemal Ataturk — A585

1981, Aug. 10 ***Perf. 11x11½***
1164 A585 140m dk grn & brn 70 70

Arabi Pasha, Leader of Egyptian Force A586

Athlete, Pyramids, Sphinx A587

Perf. 11x11½
1981, Sept. 9 **Photo.** **Wmk. 342**
1165 A586 20m dk grn & brn 10 10

Orabi Revolution centenary.

1981, Sept. 14
1166 A587 45m multi 22 22

World Muscular Athletics Championships, Cairo.

Ministry of Industry and Mineral Resources, 25th Anniv. — A588

Perf. 11x11½

1981, Sept. 26 Photo. Wmk. 342

1167 A588 45m multi 22 22

20th Intl. Occupational Health Congress, Cairo — A589

1981, Sept. 28 *Perf. 11½x11*

1168 A589 20m multi 10 10

8th Anniv. of Suez Canal Crossing A590

1981, Oct. 6

1169 A590 20m multi 25 10

World Food Day A591

13th World Telecommunications Day — A592

Intl. Year of the Disabled — A593

Fight Against Apartheid A594

Perf. 11½x11, 11x11½

1981, Oct. 24 Photo. Wmk. 342

1170 A591 10m multi 5 5
1171 A592 20m multi 10 10
1172 A593 45m multi 22 22
1173 A594 230m multi 1.15 1.15

United Nations Day.

Pres. Anwar El-Sadat (1917-1981) — A595

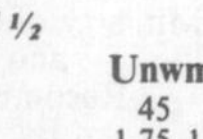

Perf. 11x11½

1981, Nov. 14 Unwmk.

1174 A595 30m multi 45 35
1175 A595 230m multi 1.75 1.50

Establishment of Shura Family Council — A596

Perf. 11½x11

1981, Dec. 12 Photo. Wmk. 342

1176 A596 45m pur & yel 22 22

Agricultural Credit and Development Bank, 50th Anniv. — A597

1981, Dec. 15 *Perf. 11x11½*

1177 A597 20m multi 10 10

Famous Men Type of 1980

Designs: 30m, Ali el-Ghayati (1885-1956), journalist. 60m, Omar Ebn sl-Fared (1181-1234), Sufi poet. Nos. 1178-1179 se-tenant.

Perf. 11x11½

1981, Dec. 21 Photo. Wmk. 342

1178 A571 30m grn & brn 15 15
1179 A571 60m grn & brn 30 30

20th Anniv. of African Postal Union A598

1981, Dec. 21 *Perf. 11½x11*

1180 A598 60m multi 30 30

14th Cairo Intl. Book Fair A599

Arab Trade Union of Egypt, 25th Anniv. A600

1982, Jan. 28

1181 A599 3p brn & yel 15 15

1982, Jan. 30

1182 A600 3p multi 15 15

Khartoum Branch of Cairo University, 25th Anniv. — A601

Perf. 11½x11

1982, Mar. 4 Wmk. 342

1183 A601 6p bl & grn 30 30

15th Cairo Intl. Fair — A602

1982, Mar. 13 *Perf. 11x11½*

1184 A602 3p multi 15 15

50th Anniv. of Al-Ghardaka Marine Biological Station — A603

Fish of the Red Sea. Nos. 1185-1188 se-tenant in continuous design.

1982, Apr. 24 Litho. *Perf. 11½x11*

1185 A603 10m Blue-banded sea perch 5 5
1186 A603 30m Lined butterfly fish 15 15
1187 A603 60m Batfish 30 30
1188 A603 230m Blue-spotted boxfish 1.15 1.15

Liberation of the Sinai — A604

1982, Apr. 25 Photo. *Perf. 11x11½*

1189 A604 3p multi 15 15

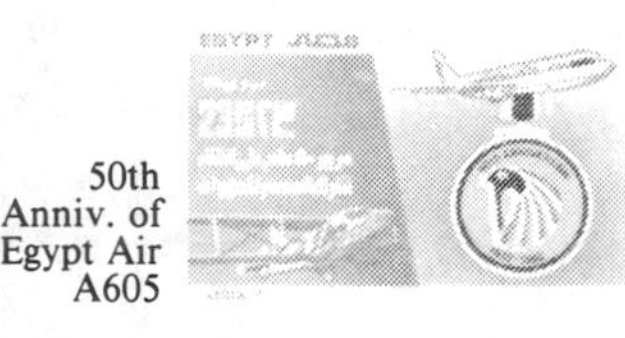

50th Anniv. of Egypt Air A605

1982, May 7 Photo. *Perf. 11½x11*

1190 A605 23p multi 1.15 1.15

Minaret — A606

Al Azhar Mosque — A607

Perf. 11x11½

1982, June 28 Photo. Wmk. 342

1191 Strip of 4 plus label 1.25 1.25
a. A606 6p, any single multi 30 30

Souvenir Sheet

Unwmk. ***Imperf.***

1192 A607 23p multi 1.25 1.25

Al Azhar Mosque millennium. Size of No. 1192: 61x60mm.

No. 1192 is airmail.

Dove — A608

Flower in Natl. Colors — A609

Perf. 11x11½

1982, July 23 Photo. Wmk. 342

1193 A608 3p multi 15 15

Souvenir Sheet

Imperf

1194 A609 23p multi 1.25 1.25

30th anniv. of July 23rd Revolution. Size of No. 1194: 55x74mm.

World Tourism Day A610

Perf. 11½x11

1982, Sept. 27 Photo. Wmk. 342

1195 A610 23p Sphinx, pyramid of Cheops, St. Catherine's Tower 1.25 1.25

10th Anniv. of Suez Canal Crossing A611

1982, Oct. 6

1196 A611 3p Memorial, map 15 15

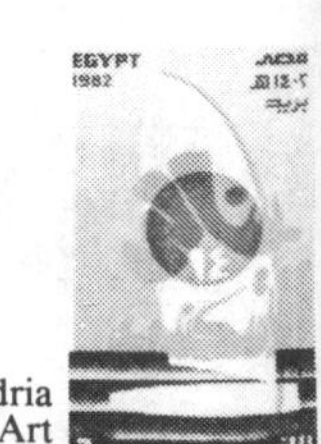

Biennale of Alexandria Art Exhibition — A612

1982, Oct. 17 *Perf. 11x11½*

1197 A612 3p multi 15 15

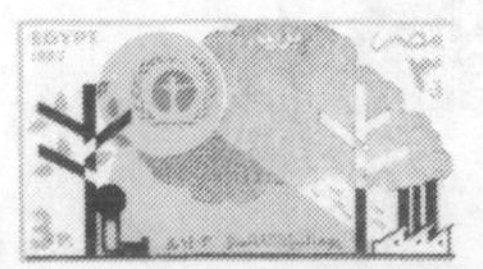

10th Anniv. of UN Conference on Human Environment — A613

2nd UN Conference on Peaceful Uses of Outer Space, Vienna, Aug. 9-21
A614

Scouting Year — A615

TB Bacillus Centenary
A616

Perf. 11½x11, 11½ (A615)

1982, Oct. 24

1198 A613 3p multi	15	15
1199 A614 6p multi	30	30
1200 A615 6p multi	30	30
1201 A616 8p multi	40	40

United Nations Day.

50th Anniv. of Air Force
A617

1982, Nov. 2 *Perf. 11½x11*
1202 A617 3p Jet, plane 15 15

Ahmed Chawki (1868-1932) and Hafez Ibrahim (1871-1932), Poets — A618

Perf. 11½x11

1982, Nov. 25 Photo. Wmk. 342
1203 A618 6p multi 30 30

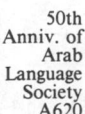

Natl. Research Center, 25th Anniv. — A619

1982, Dec. 12 Photo. *Perf. 11x11½*
1204 A619 3p red & bl 15 15

50th Anniv. of Arab Language Society
A620

1982, Dec. 25 *Perf. 11½x11*
1205 A620 6p multi 30 30

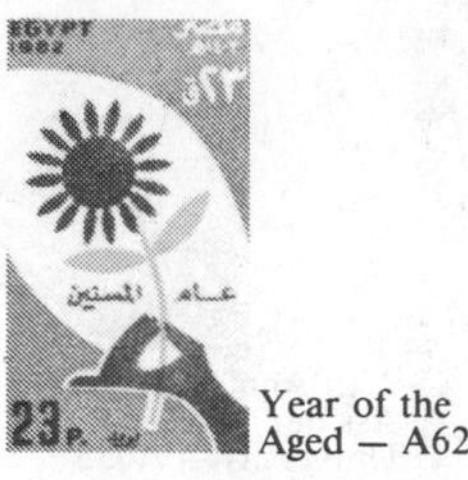

Year of the Aged — A621

Post Day — A622

1982, Dec. 25 *Perf. 11x11½*
1206 A621 23p multi 1.15 1.15

1983, Jan. 2 *Perf. 11½*
1207 A622 3p multi 15 15

15th Cairo Intl. Book Fair — A623

Perf. 11x11½

1983, Jan. 25 Photo. Wmk. 342
1208 A623 3p bl & red 15 15

Police Day
A624

1983, Jan. 25 *Perf. 11½x11*
1209 A624 3p multi 15 15

16th Cairo Intl. Fair — A625

5th UN African Map Conference, Cairo — A626

Perf. 11x11½

1983, Mar. 2 Photo. Wmk. 342
1210 A625 3p multi 15 15

1983, Mar. 2
1211 A626 3p lt grn & bl 15 15

African Ministers of Transport, Communications and Planning, 3rd Conference — A627

1983, Mar. 8 *Perf. 11½x11*
1212 A627 23p grn & bl 1.15 1.15

Victory in African Soccer Cup — A628

1983, Mar. 20 *Perf. 11x11½*

1213 A628 3p Heading	15	15
1214 A628 3p Kick	15	15

World Health Day and Natl. Blood Donation Campaign — A629

Perf. 11x11½

1983, Apr. 2 Photo. Wmk. 342
1215 A629 3p ol & red 15 15

Org. of African Trade Union Unity
A630

Perf. 11½x11

1983, Apr. 21 Photo. Wmk. 342
1216 A630 3p multi 15 15

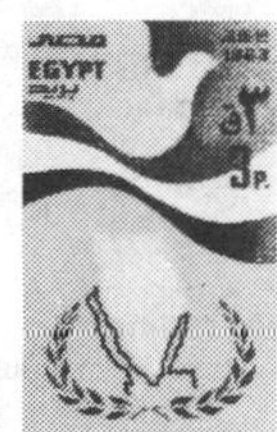

First Anniv. of Sinai Liberation — A631

1983, Apr. 25 *Perf. 11x11½*
1217 A631 3p multi 15 15

75th Anniv. of Entomology Society — A632

1983, May 23
1218 A632 3p Emblem (Holy Scarab) 15 15

Flowers — A633

1983, June 11 Photo. *Perf. 11½x11*
1219 A633 20m grn & org red 10 6

5th African Handball Championship, Cairo — A634

Perf. 11½x11

1983, July 22 Photo. Wmk. 342
1220 A634 6p brn & dk grn 30 30

31st Anniv. of Revolution
A635

Simon Bolivar (1783-1830)
A636

1983, July 23 *Perf. 11½*
1221 A635 3p multi 15 15

1983, Aug. *Perf. 11x11½*
1222 A636 23p brn & dl grn 1.15 1.15

Centenary of Arrival of Natl. Hero Orabi in Ceylon
A637

Perf. 11½x11

1983, Aug. 25 Photo. Wmk. 342
1223 A637 3p Map, Orabi, El-Zahra School 15 15

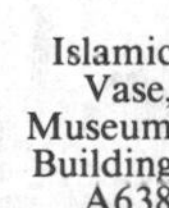

Islamic Vase, Museum Building
A638

1983, Sept. 14 Photo. *Perf. 11½x11*
1224 A638 3p yel brn & dk brn 15 15

Reopening of Islamic Museum.

10th Anniv., Sinai Crossing
A639

2nd Pharaonic Race
A640

1983, Oct. 6 *Perf. 11½*
1225 A639 3p multi 15 15

1983, Oct. 17 *Perf. 11½*
1226 A640 23p multi 1.15 1.15

A particular stamp may be scarce, but if few collectors want it, its market value may remain relatively low.

United Nations Day — A641

1983, Oct. 24 Photo. *Perf. 11*

1227 A641 3p IMO, ships 15 15
1228 A641 6p ITU, UPU 30 30
1229 A641 6p FAO, UN, grain 30 30
1230 A641 23p UN, ocean 1.15 1.15

4th World Karate Championship, Cairo — A642

1983, Nov. Photo. *Perf. 13*

1231 A642 3p multi 15 15

Intl. Palestinian Cooperation Day — A643

1983, Nov. 29 Photo. *Perf. 13x13½*

1232 A643 6p Dome of the Rock 30 30

75th Anniv. of Faculty of Fine Arts, Cairo A644

1983, Nov. 30 *Perf. 13*

1233 A644 3p multi 15 15

75th Anniv. of Cairo University — A645

1983, Nov. 30 *Perf. 11x11½*

1234 A645 3p multi 15 15

Intl. Egyptian Society of Mother and Child Care A646

1983, Nov. 30 *Perf. 11½x11*

1235 A646 3p multi 15 15

Org. of African Unity, 20th Anniv. A647

World Heritage Convention, 10th Anniv. A648

Perf. 11x11½

1983, Dec. 20 Photo. Wmk. 342

1236 A647 3p multi 15 15

1983, Dec. 24

1237 Strip of 3 45 45
a. A648 3p Wood carving, Islamic 15 15
b. A648 3p Coptic tapestry 15 15
c. A648 3p Ramses II Thebes 15 15

Post Day A649

Restored Forts: 6p, Quatbay. 23p, Mosque, Salah El-Din.

1984, Jan. 2 *Perf. 13*

1238 A649 6p multi 30 30
1239 A649 23p multi 1.15 1.15

Misr Insurance Co., 50 Anniv. A650

1984, Jan. 14 *Perf. 11½x11*

1240 A650 3p multi 15 15

16th Cairo Intl. Book Fair — A651

Perf. 13½x13

1984, Jan. 26 Photo. Wmk. 342

1241 A651 3p multi 15 15

17th Cairo Intl. Fair A652

Perf. 11½x11

1984, Mar. 10 Photo. Wmk. 342

1242 A652 3p multi 15 15

25th Anniv. of Assiout University — A653

1984, Mar. 10 *Perf. 11x11½*

1243 A653 3p multi 15 15

75th Anniv. of Cooperative Unions — A654

1984, Mar. 17

1244 A654 3p multi 15 15

World Theater Day — A655

Mahmoud Mokhtar (1891-1934), Sculptor — A656

Perf. 11x11½, 11½x11

1984, Mar. 27 Photo. Wmk.

1245 A655 3p Masks 15 15
1246 A656 3p Pride of the Nile 15 15

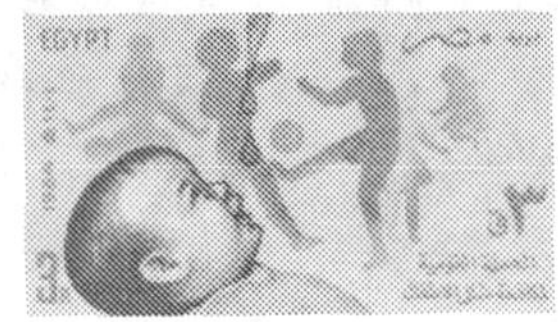

World Health Day and Fight Against Polio — A657

Perf. 11½x11

1984, Apr. 7 Photo. Wmk. 342

1247 A657 3p Polio vaccine 15 15

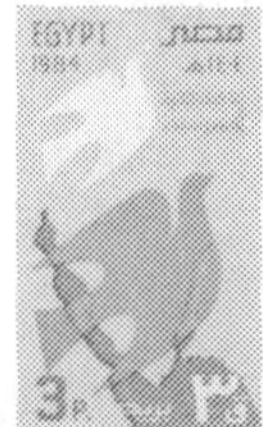

2nd Anniv. of Sinai Liberation — A658

1984, Apr. 25

1248 A658 3p Doves, map 15 15

Demand, as well as supply, determines a stamp's market value. One is as important as the other.

Africa Day A659

Perf. 12½x13½

1984, May 25 Photo. Wmk. 342

1249 A659 3p Map, UN emblem 15 15

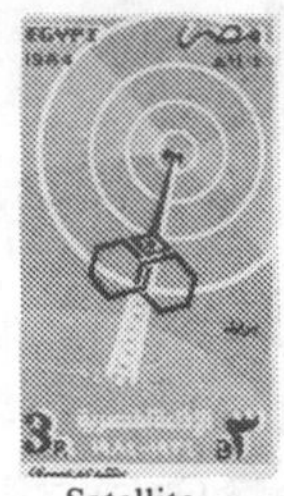

Satellite, Waves A660

Flower A661

1984, May 31 *Perf. 11x11½*

1250 A660 3p multi 15 15

Radio broadcasting in Egypt, 50th anniv.

1984, June 1

1251 A661 2p red & grn 10 10

Intl. Cairo Arab Arts Biennale — A662

1984, June 1 *Perf. 13½x12½*

1252 A662 3p multi 15 15

July Revolution, 32nd Anniv. — A663

Wmk. 342

1984, July 23 Photo. *Perf. 11*

1253 A663 3p Atomic energy, agriculture 15 15

1984 Summer Olympics — A664

Designs: a. Boxing. b. Basketball. c. Volleyball. d. Soccer.

1984, July 28

1254 Strip of 4 + label 60 60
a.-d. A664 3p, any single 15 15

Imperf

1255 A664 30p Like #1254 1.50 1.50

Size of No. 1255: 130x80mm.

2nd Genl. Conference of Egyptians Abroad, Aug. 11-15, Cairo — A665

Wmk. 342

1984, Aug. 13 Photo. *Perf. 11*

1256 A665 3p bl & multi 15 15
1257 A665 23p grn & multi 1.15 1.15

Youth Hostels, 30th Anniv. A666

Egypt Tour Co., 50th Anniv. A667

Perf. 11x11 1/2

1984, Sept. 22 Photo. Wmk. 342

1258 A666 3p Youths, emblem 15 15

1984, Sept. 27

1259 A667 3p Emblem, sphinx 15 15

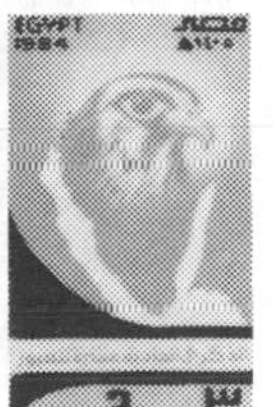

Sinai Crossing, 11th Anniv. A668

Egypt-Sudan Unity A669

1984, Oct. 6

1260 A668 3p Map, eagle 15 15

1984, Oct. 12

1261 A669 3p Map of Nile, arms 15 15

UN Day — A670

Perf. 13 1/2x12 1/2

1984, Oct. 24 Photo. Wmk. 342

1262 A670 3p UNICEF Emblem, child 15 15

UN campaign for infant survival.

The only foreign revenue stamps listed in this Catalogue are those authorized for prepayment of postage.

Tanks, Emblem — A671

1984, Nov. 10

1263 A671 3p multi 15 15

Military Equipment Exhibition, Cairo, Nov. 10-14.

Tolon Mosque, Egypt A672

1984, Dec. 23 Photo. *Perf. 11 1/2x11*

1264 A672 3p multi 15 15

Ahmed Ebn Tolon (A.D. 835-884), Gov. of Egypt, founder of Kataea City.

Kamel el-Kilany (1897-1959), Author — A673

1984, Dec. 23 *Perf. 11x11 1/2*

1265 A673 3p multi 15 15

Globe and Congress Emblem — A674

Perf. 11x11 1/2

1984, Dec. 26 Photo. Wmk. 342

1266 A674 3p lt bl, ver & blk 15 15

29th Intl. Congress on the History of Medicine, Dec. 27, 1984-Jan. 1, 1985, Cairo.

Academy of the Arts, 25th Anniv. A675

1984, Dec. 31 *Perf. 13*

1267 A675 3p Emblem in spotlights 15 15

Pharaoh Receiving Message, Natl. Postal Museum, Cairo A676

1985, Jan. 2 *Perf. 11 1/2x11*

1268 A676 3p brn, lt bl & ver 15 15

Postal Museum, 50th anniv.

Intl. Union of Architects, 15th Conference, Jan. 14-Feb. 15 — A677

1985, Jan. 20

1269 A677 3p multi 15 15

Seated Pharaonic Scribe A678

Wheat, Cogwheels, Fair Emblem A679

1985, Jan. 22 *Perf. 11x11 1/2*

1270 A678 3p brt org & dk bl grn 15 15

17th Intl. Book Fair, Jan. 22-Feb. 3, Cairo.

1985, Mar. 9 *Perf. 13 1/2x13*

1271 A679 3p multi 15 15

18th Intl. Fair, Mar. 9-22, Cairo.

Return of Sinai to Egypt, 3rd Anniv. A680

Ancient Artifacts A681

1985, Apr. 25 Wmk. 342 Litho.

1272 A680 5p multi 25 25

Wmk. 342

1985-86 Photo. *Perf. 11 1/2*

Designs: 1p, God Mout, limestone sculpture, 360-340 B.C. 2p, 20p, Five wading birds, bas-relief. 3p, 5p, Seated statue, Ramses II, Temple of Luxor. 8p, 15p, Slave bearing votive fruit offering, mural. 11p, Sculpted head of woman. 35p, Temple of Karnak carved capitals.

1273	A681	1p brn ol	5	5
1274	A681	2p brt grnsh bl	10	10
1275	A681	3p yel brn	15	15
1276	A681	5p dk vio	25	25
1277	A681	8p pale ol grn, sep & brn	40	40
1279	A681	11p dk vio	55	55
1282	A681	15p pale yel, sep & brn	75	75
1283	A681	20p yel grn ('86)	1.00	1.00
1285	A681	35p sep & pale yel	1.75	1.75
		Nos. 1273-1285 (9)	5.00	5.00

Issue dates: 1p, 2p, 3p, 5p, 8p, 11p, 15p, May 1. 35p, July 7. 20p, Apr. 1.

Helwan University School of Music, 50th Anniv. A682

1985, May 15

1287 A682 5p multi 25 25

El-Moulid Bride, Folk Doll — A683

1985

1288 A683 2p org & multi 10 10
1289 A683 5p red & multi 25 25

Festivals 1985. Issue dates: 2p, June 11. 5p, Aug. 10.

1985 Africa Cup Soccer Championships A684

Designs and winning teams: Nos. 1287a, 1287b, Cairo Sports Stadium. No. 1287c, El-Mokawiloon Club, white uniform, 1983. No. 1287d, Natl. Club, red uniform, 1984. No. 1287e, El-Zamalek Club, orange uniform, 1984.

1985, June 17 *Perf. 13 1/2x13*

1290 Strip of 5 1.25 1.25
a.-e. A684 5p, Any single 25 25

Cairo Sports Stadium, 25th anniv. Nos. 1287a-1287b se-tenant in a continuous design.

Egyptian Television, 25th Anniv. — A685

1985, July 23 *Perf. 11 1/2x11*

1291 A685 5p bl, brn & yel 25 25

Egyptian Revolution, 33rd anniv.

Suez Canal Reopening, 10th Anniv. — A686

Perf. 13x13 1/2

1985, July 23 Litho. Wmk. 342

1292 A686 5p multi 25 25

Egyptian Revolution, 33rd anniv.

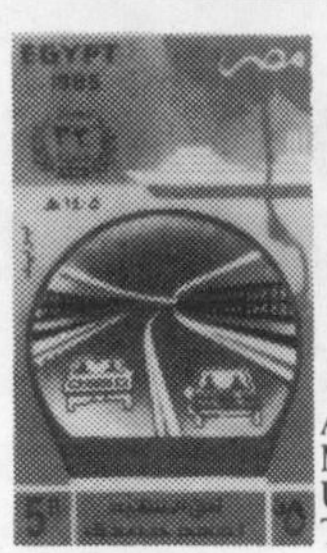

Ahmed Hamdi Memorial Underwater Tunnel — A687

1985, July 23 *Perf. 13½x13*
1293 A687 5p bl, vio & org 25 25

Egyptian Revolution, 33rd anniv.

Souvenir Sheet

Aswan High Dam, 25th Anniv. — A688

Wmk. 342
1985, July 23 Photo. ***Imperf.***
1294 A688 30p multi 1.50 1.50

No. 1294 has multicolored margin. Size: 97x79m.

Heart, Map, Olive Laurel, Conference Emblem — A689

1985, Aug. 10 Litho. *Perf. 13½x13*
1295 A689 15p multi 75 75

Egyptian Emigrants, 3rd general conference, Aug. 10-14, Cairo.

Natl. Tourism Ministry, 50th Anniv. — A690

1985, Sept. 10 *Perf. 13x13½*
1296 A690 5p multi 25 25

Sinai Crossing, 12th Anniv. — A691

1985, Oct. 6
1297 A691 5p multi 25 25

Air Scouts Assoc., 30th Anniv. — A692

1985, Oct. 15 Photo. *Perf. 11½*
1298 A692 5p Emblem 25 25

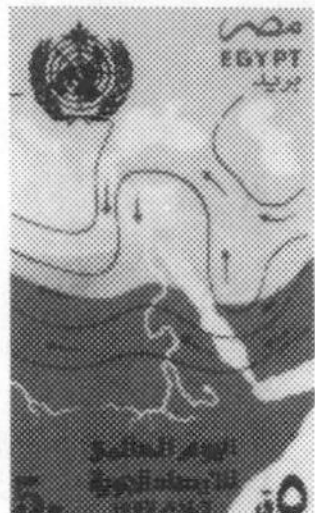

UN Day, Meteorology Day — A693

1985, Oct. 24
1299 A693 5p UN emblem, weather map 25 25

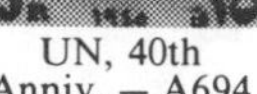

UN, 40th Anniv. — A694

Intl. Youth Year — A695

1985, Oct. 24
1300 A694 15p multi 75 75

1985, Oct. 24
1301 A695 5p multi 25 25

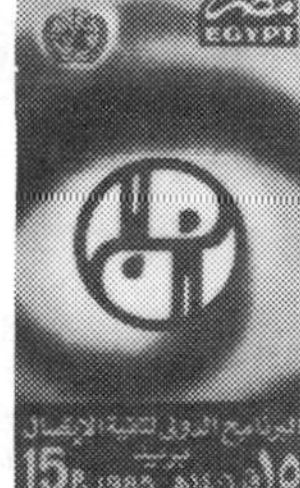

Intl. Communications Development Program A696

2nd Intl. Dentistry Conference A697

1985, Oct. 24
1302 A696 15p bl & int bl 75 75

1985, Oct. 29 *Perf. 11x11½*

Emblem, hieroglyphics of Hassi Raa, 1st known dentist.

1303 A697 5p beige & pale bl vio 25 25

Emblem, Squash Player — A698

1985, Nov. 18 Photo. *Perf. 11½*
1304 A698 5p dl org yel, grn & sep 25 25

1985 World Squash Championships, Nov. 18-Dec. 4.

4th Intl. Conference on the Biography and Sunna of Mohammed A699

1st Conference on the Development of Vocational Training A700

1985, Nov. 2 Litho. *Perf. 13½x13*
1305 A699 5p multi 25 25

1985, Dec. 1 Photo. *Perf. 11x11½*
1306 A700 5p multi 25 25

Natl. Olympic Committee, 75th Anniv. A701

18th Intl. Book Fair, Cairo A702

1985, Dec. 28 Photo. *Perf. 13x13½*
1307 A701 5p multi 25 25

1986, Jan. 21 *Perf. 11x11½*
1308 A702 5p Pharaonic scribe 25 25

CODATU III — A703

1986, Jan. 26 *Perf. 11½*
1309 A703 5p lt ol grn, ver & grnsh bl 25 25

3rd Intl. Conference on Urban Transportation in Developing Countries, Cairo.

Central Bank, 25th Anniv. — A704

1986, Jan. 30 *Perf. 13x13½*
1310 A704 5p multi 25 25

Cairo Postal Traffic Center Inauguration — A705

1986, Jan. 30 *Perf. 11½x11*
1311 A705 5p bl & dk brn 25 25

Pharaonic Mural, Btah Hotteb's Tomb at Saqqara A706

1986, Feb. 27 Photo. *Perf. 11½x11*
1312 A706 5p yel, gldn brn & brn 25 25

Faculty of Commerce, Cairo University, 75th anniv.

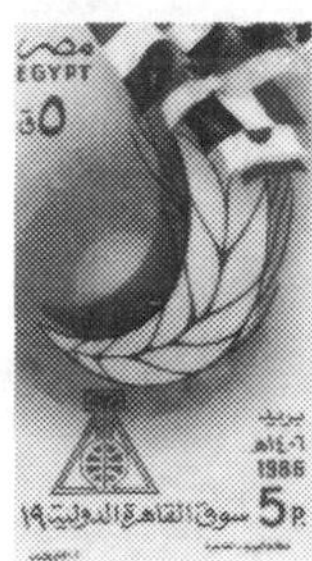

Cairo Intl. Fair, Mar. 8-21 — A707

1986, Mar. 8 Litho. *Perf. 13½x13*
1313 A707 5p multi 25 25

Queen Nefertiti, Sinai — A708

Perf. 13x13½
1986, Mar. 25 Litho. Wmk. 342
1314 A708 5p multi 25 25

Return of the Sinai to Egypt, 4th anniv.

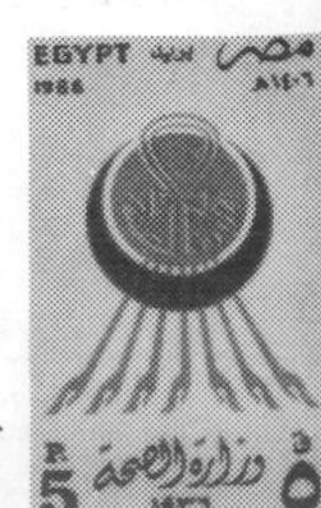

Ministry of Health, 50th Anniv. — A709

1986, Apr. 10 *Perf. 13½x13*
1315 A709 5p multi 25 25

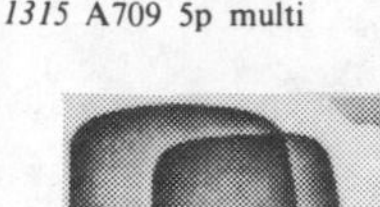

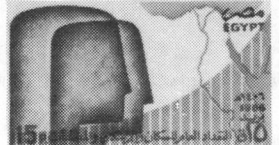

1986 Census — A710

1986, May 26 Photo. *Perf. 11½*
1316 A710 15p brn, grnsh bl & yel bis 75 75

Egypt, Winner of African Soccer Cup — A711

Festivals, Roses — A712

1986, May 31 *Perf. 13½x13*
1317 A711 5p English inscription below cup 25 25
1318 A711 5p Arabic 25 25

Nos. 1317-1318 printed se-tenant.

1986, June 2 *Perf. 11½*
1319 A712 5p multi 25 25

World Environment Day — A713

1986, June 5 *Perf. 13½x13*
1320 A713 15p Emblem, smokestacks 75 75

July 23rd Revolution, 34th Anniv. A714

1986, July 23 Litho. *Perf. 13*
1321 A714 5p gray grn, scar & yel bis 25 25

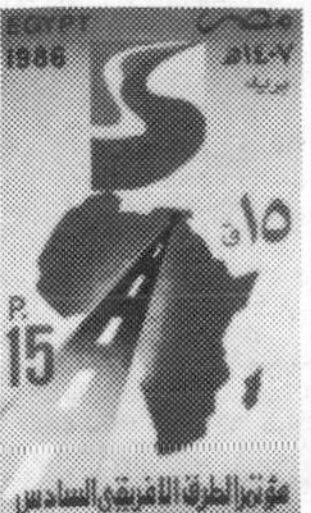

6th African Roads Conference, Cairo, Sept. 22-26 — A715

Perf. 13½x13
1986, Sept. 21 Litho. Wmk. 342
1322 A715 15p multi 75 75

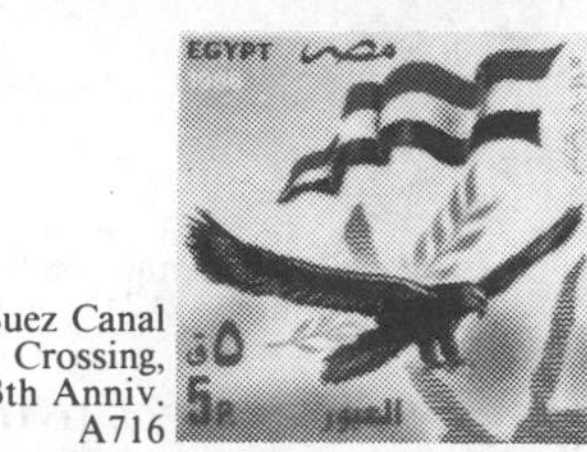

Suez Canal Crossing, 13th Anniv. A716

1986, Oct. 6 Litho. *Perf. 13*
1323 A716 5p multi 25 25

Engineers' Syndicate, 40th Anniv. A717

1986, Oct. 11 Photo. *Perf. 11½*
1324 A717 5p lt bl, brn & pale grn 25 25

Workers' Cultural Education Assoc., 25th Anniv. A718

Intl. Peace Year A719

1986, Oct. 11 *Perf. 11x11½*
1325 A718 5p org & rose vio 25 25

1986, Oct. 24
1326 A719 5p bl, grn & pale sal 25 25

First Oil Well in Egypt, Cent. — A720

1986, Nov. 7 Photo. *Perf. 11½*
1327 A720 5p dl grn, blk & pale yel 25 25

UN Child Survival Campaign A721

1986, Nov. 20 Litho. *Perf. 13*
1328 A721 5p multi 25 25

Ahmed Amin, Philosopher A722

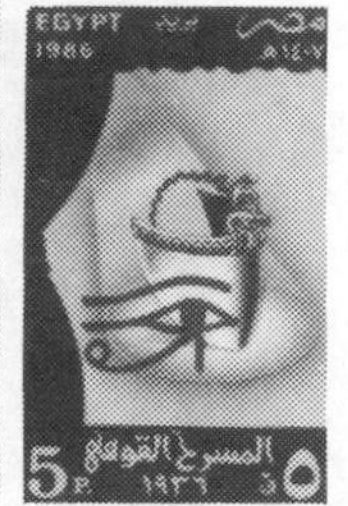

National Theater, 50th Anniv. A723

1986, Dec. 20 *Perf. 11½*
1329 A722 5p pale grn, pale yel & brn 25 25

1986, Dec. 20 *Perf. 13½x13*
1330 A723 5p multi 25 25

Post Day A724

Design: Step Pyramid, Saqqara, King Zoser.

Perf. 13x13½
1987, Jan. 2 Litho. Wmk. 342
1331 A724 5p multi 25 25

19th Intl. Book Fair, Cairo A725

1987, Jan. 25 Litho. *Perf. 13*
1332 A725 5p multi 25 25

5th World Conference on Islamic Education A726

Wmk. 342
1987, Mar. 8 Litho. *Perf. 13*
1333 A726 5p multi 25 25

20th Intl. Fair, Cairo — A727

1987, Mar. 21 Photo. *Perf. 11½*
1334 A727 5p Good workers medal 25 25

Veteran's Day — A728

1987, Mar. 26
1335 A728 5p multi 25 25

Intl. Gardens Inauguration, Nasser City — A729

1987, Mar. 30 Litho. *Perf. 13*
1336 A729 15pmulti 75 75

World Health Day — A730

Perf. 11½, 13 (No. 1338)
Photo., Litho. (No. 1338)
1987, Apr. 7
1337 A730 5p Mother feeding child 25 25
1338 A730 5p Oral rehydration therapy 25 25

A731

Natl. Team Victory at 1986 Intl. Soccer Championships — A732

Trophies: No. 1339a, Al Ahly Cup. No. 1339b, National Cup. No. 1339c, Al Zamalek Cup. No. 1340, Natl. flag, Cairo Stadium and trophies pictured on No. 1339.

1987, Apr. 19 Litho. *Perf. 13½x13*
1339 Strip of 3 75 75
a.-c. A731 5p any single 25 25

Size: 115x85mm.
Imperf

1340 A732 30pmulti 1.50 1.50

Salah El Din Citadel, Pharoah's Is., Sinai — A733

1987, Apr. 25
1341 A733 5p sky blue & lt brn 25 25

Return of the Sinai to Egypt, 5th anniv.

Festivals — A734

1987, May 21 Photo. ***Perf. 11½***
1342 A734 5p Dahlia 25 25

Cultural Heritage Exhibition — A735

1987, June 17 Litho. ***Perf. 13x13½***
1343 A735 15pmulti 75 75

Tourism Year — A736

Designs: No. 1344a, Columb and Sphinx, Alexandria. No. 1344b, St. Catherine's Monastery, Mt. Sinai. No. 1344c, Colossi of Thebes. No. 1344d, Temple of Theban Triad, Luxor.

1987, June 18
1344 Block of 4 3.00 3.00
a.-d. A736 15p any single 75 75

See No. C187.

National Day — A737

1987, June 26 ***Perf. 13***
1345 A737 5p multi 25 25

Industry-Agriculture Exhibition — A738

1987, July 23 Photo. ***Perf. 11½***
1346 A738 5p grn, dull org & blk 25 25

Intl. Year of Shelter for the Homeless A739

1987, Sept. 2 Litho. ***Perf. 13***
1347 A739 5p multi 25 25

World Architects' Day.

Aida, Performed at Al Ahram Pyramid, Giza A740

Design: Radamis and troops returning from Ethiopia.

1987, Sept. 21
1348 A740 15pmulti 75 75

Size: 70x70mm.
Imperf

1349 A740 30pmulti 1.50 1.50

No. 1349 has blue and gold decorative margin containing denomination in gold.

Greater Cairo Subway Inauguration — A741

1987, Sept. 27 ***Perf. 13x13½***
1350 A741 5p multi 25 25

Industry Day — A742

1987, Oct. 1 ***Perf. 13***
1351 A742 5p multi 25 25

Battle Hettin, 700th Anniv. — A743

1987, Oct. 6 Photo. ***Perf. 11x11½***
1352 A743 5p multi 25 25

UPU Emblem A744

Perf. 11½
1987, Oct. 24 Unwmk. Photo.
1353 A744 5p multi 25 25

UN Executive Council, 40th anniv.; UPU Consultative Council, 30th anniv.

16th Art Biennial of Alexandria A745

1987, Nov. 7 Litho. ***Perf. 13½x13***
1354 A745 5p multi 25 25

Second Intl. Defense Equipment Exhibition, Cairo, Nov. 9-13 — A746

Perf. 13x13½
1987, Nov. 9 Litho. Unwmk.
1355 A746 5p multi 25 25

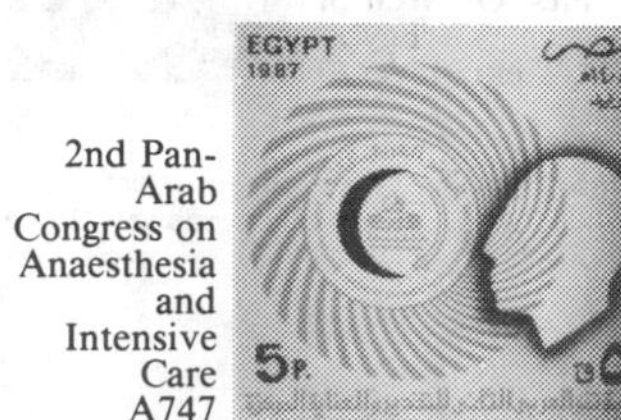
2nd Pan-Arab Congress on Anaesthesia and Intensive Care A747

Unwmk.
1987, Dec. 1 Litho. ***Perf. 13***
1356 A747 5p multi 25 25

Intl. Orthopedic and Traumatology Conference A748

1987, Dec. 1 ***Perf. 13½x13***
1357 A748 5p gray, red brn & bl 25 25

Selim Hassan (1887-1961), Egyptologist, and Hieroglyphs A749

Abdel Hamid Badawi (1887-1965), Jurist, and Scales of Justice A750

Perf. 13½x13
1987, Dec. 30 Litho. Unwmk.
1358 A749 5p multi 25 25
1359 A750 5p multi 25 25

Stamp Day 1988 — A751

Pyramids of the Pharaohs and: No. 1360a, Cheops. No. 1360b, Chefren. No. 1360c, Mycerinus. Printed se-tenant in a continuous design.

1988, Jan. 2
1360 Strip of three 2.25 2.25
a.-c. A751 15p any single 75 75

Afro-Asian Peoples Solidarity Organization, 30th Anniv. — A752

1988, Jan. 10 ***Perf. 13x13½***
1361 A752 15pmulti 75 75

Catalogue prices for unused stamps up to mid-1953 are for hinged copies matching the condition specified in this volume's introduction.

20th Intl. Book Fair, Cairo — A753

1988, Jan. 26 *Perf. 13½x13*
1362 A753 5p multi 25 25

SEMI-POSTAL STAMPS

Princess Ferial — SP1

Perf. 13½x14

1940, May 17 Photo. Wmk. 195
B1 SP1 5m + 5m cop brn 50 45

No. B1 Overprinted in Green **1943** ١٩٤٣

1943, Nov. 17
B2 SP1 5m + 5m cop brn 5.00 4.00
a. Arabic date "1493" 175.00 175.00

The surtax on Nos. B1 and B2 was for the children's fund.

First Postage Stamp of Egypt SP2

Khedive Ismail Pasha SP3

Designs: 17m+17m, King Fuad. 22m+22m, King Farouk.

Perf. 13x13½

1946, Feb. 28 Wmk. 195
B3 SP2 1m + 1m gray 10 10
B4 SP3 10m + 10m vio 15 15
B5 SP3 17m + 17m brn 25 25
B6 SP3 22m + 22m yel grn 30 30
a. Souvenir sheet, perf. 8½ 40.00 35.00
b. As "a," imperf. 40.00 35.00

Issued to commemorate the 80th anniversary of Egypt's first postage stamp.
Nos. B6a and B6b measure 129x171mm. and contain one each of Nos. B3 to B6, with inscriptions in top and bottom margins.

Goddess Hathor, King Men-kau-Re (Mycerinus) and Jackalheaded Goddess — SP7

Ramesseum, Thebes — SP8

Queen Nefertiti SP9

Funerary Mask of King Tutankhamen SP10

Perf. 13½x13

1947, Mar. 9 Wmk. 195
B9 SP7 5m + 5m sl 25 25
B10 SP8 15m + 15m dp bl 50 40
B11 SP9 30m + 30m hn brn 70 70
B12 SP10 50m + 50m brn 1.00 1.00

Issued to commemorate the International Exposition of Contemporary Art, Cairo.

Boy Scout Emblem — SP11

Scout Emblems: 20m+10m, Sea Scouts. 35m+15m, Air Explorers.

1956, July 25 Photo. *Perf. 13½x13*
B13 SP11 10m + 10m grn 35 30
B14 SP11 20m + 10m ultra 50 45
B15 SP11 35m + 15m bl 70 65

Issued to commemorate the 2nd Arab Scout Jamboree, Alexandria-Aboukir, 1956.
Souvenir sheets, perf. and imperf., contain one each of Nos. B13-B15. Size: 118x158mm. Price $500 each.

Ambulance — SP12

1957, May 13 *Perf. 13x13½*
B16 SP12 10m + 5m rose red 20 18

Issued to commemorate the 50th anniversary of the Public Aid Society.

United Arab Republic

Eye and Map of Africa, Europe and Asia SP13

Postal Emblem SP14

Perf. 13½x13

1958, Mar. 1 Photo. Wmk. 318
B17 SP13 10m + 5m org 60 60

Issued to commemorate the First Afro-Asian Congress of Ophthalmology, Cairo.
The surtax was for centers to aid the blind.

1959, Jan. 2
B18 SP14 10m + 5m bl grn, red & blk 20 12

Issued for Post Day, Jan. 2. The surtax went to the social fund for postal employees.

Children, UN Emblem SP15

Arab League Building, Cairo, and Emblem SP16

1959, Oct. 24 Wmk. 328
B19 SP15 10m + 5m brn lake 20 12
B20 SP15 35m + 10m dk bl 40 35

Issued for International Children's Day and to honor UNICEF.

Braille Type of Regular Issue, 1961.

1961, Apr. 6 *Perf. 13½x13*
B21 A182 35m + 15m yel & brn 50 50

World Health Organization Day.

1962, Mar. 22 Photo. Wmk. 328
B22 SP16 10m + 5m gray 25 25

Arab Publicity Week, Mar. 22-28.

Postal Emblem — SP17

Stamp of 1866 — SP18

1963, Jan. 2 Wmk. 342 *Perf. 11½*
B23 SP17 20m + 10m brt grn, red & blk 60 60
B24 SP18 40m + 20m blk & brn org 90 90
B25 SP18 40m + 20m brn org & blk 90 90

Issued for Post Day, Jan. 2 and to publicize the 1966 exhibition of the Federation International de Philatelie. Nos. B24-B25 printed se-tenant.

Arms of U.A.R. and Pyramids SP19

1964, Jan. 2 Wmk. 342 *Perf. 11*
B26 SP19 10m + 5m org yel & grn 1.00 75
B27 SP19 80m + 40m grnsh bl & blk 2.00 1.50
B28 SP19 115m + 55m org brn & blk 2.50 2.00

Issued for Post Day. Jan. 2.

Type of 1963 and

Postal Emblem — SP20

Designs: No. B30, Emblem of Postal Secondary School. 80m+40m, Postal emblem, gearwheel and laurel wreath.

Perf. 11½

1965, Jan. 2 Unwmk. Photo.
B29 SP20 10m + 5m lt grn & car 12 12
B30 SP20 10m + 5m ultra, car & blk 12 12
B31 SP18 80m + 40m rose, brt grn & blk 95 95

Issued for Post Day, Jan. 2. No. B31 also publicizes the Stamp Centenary Exhibition.

Souvenir Sheet

Stamps of Egypt, 1866 — SP21

1966, Jan. 2 Wmk. 342 *Imperf.*
B32 SP21 140m + 60m blk, sl bl & rose 2.50 2.50

Issued for Post Day, 1966, and to commemorate the centenary of the first Egyptian postage stamps. Size: 105x62mm.

Pharaonic "Mediator" SP22

Design: 115m+40m, Pharaonic guard.

1967, Jan. 2 Wmk. 342 *Perf. 11½*
B33 SP22 80m + 20m multi 1.50 1.25
B34 SP22 115m + 40m multi 2.75 1.75

Issued for Post Day, Jan. 2.

Grand Canal, Doges' Palace, Venice, and Santa Maria del Fiore, Florence — SP23

Design: 115m+30m, Piazzetta and Campanile, Venice, and Palazzo Vecchio, Florence.

Perf. 11½x11

1967, Dec. 9 Photo. Wmk. 342

B35 SP23 80m + 20m grn, yel & brn 65 65
B36 SP23 115m + 30m ol, yel & sl bl 1.00 1.00

The surtax was to help save the cultural monuments of Venice and Florence, damaged in the 1966 floods.

Boy and Girl SP24

Emblem and Flags of Arab League SP25

Design: No. B38, Five children and arch.

Wmk. 342

1968, Dec. 11 Photo. *Perf. 11*

B37 SP24 20m + 10m car, bl & lt brn 25 20
B38 SP24 20m + 10m vio bl, sep & lt grn 25 20

Issued for Children's Day and to commemorate the 22nd anniversary of UNICEF (United Nations Children's Fund).

1969, Mar. 22 *Perf. 11x11½*

B39 SP25 20m + 10m multi 35 18

Arab Publicity Week, March 22-28.

Refugee Family SP26

Wmk. 342

1969, Oct. 24 Photo. *Perf. 11½*

B40 SP26 30m + 10m multi 75 50

Issued for United Nations Day.

Men of Three Races, Human Rights Emblem SP27

1970, Mar. 21 *Perf. 11½x11*

B41 SP27 20m + 10m multi 25 18

Issued to publicize the International Day for the Elimination of Racial Discrimination.

Arab League Type of Regular Issue

1970, Mar. 22 Wmk. 342

B42 A344 20m + 10m bl, grn & brn 75 50

25th anniversary of Arab League.

Map of Palestine and Refugees SP28

Perf. 11½x11

1970, Oct. 24 Photo. Wmk. 342

B43 SP28 20m + 10m multi 1.50 75

Issued to commemorate the 25th anniversary of the United Nations and to draw attention to the plight of the Palestinian refugees.

Arab Republic of Egypt

Blind Girl, WHO and Society Emblems — SP29

1973, Oct. 24 Photo. *Perf. 11x11½*

B44 SP29 20m + 10m bl & gold 25 15

25th anniversary of the World Health Organization and for the Light and Hope Society, which educates and helps blind girls.

Map of Africa, OAU Emblem SP30

Social Work Day Emblem SP31

Perf. 11x11½

1973, Dec. 8 Photo. Wmk. 342

B45 SP30 55m + 20m multi 1.50 1.50

10th anniversary of the Organization for African Unity.

1973, Dec. 8

B46 SP31 20m + 10m multi 25 15

Social Work Day.

Jihan al Sadat Consoling Wounded Man — SP32

1974, Mar. 21 Wmk. 342 *Perf. 11*

B47 SP32 20m + 10m multi 50 25

Faithfulness and Hope Society.

Afghan Solidarity SP33

Wmk. 342

1981, July 15 Photo. *Perf. 11½*

B48 SP33 20m + 10m multi 15 15

Size: 30x25mm

1981 Photo. *Perf. 11½*

B49 SP33 20m + 10m multi 15 15

Map of Sudan, Dunes, Dead Tree — SP34

1986, Mar. 25 Photo. *Perf. 13x13½*

B50 SP34 15p + 5p multi 50 50

Fight against drought and desertification of the Sudan. Surtax for drought relief.

AIR POST STAMPS

Mail Plane in Flight AP1

Perf. 13x13½

1926, Mar. 10 Wmk. 195 Photo.

C1 AP1 27m dp vio 14.00 8.00

1929, July 17

C2 AP1 27m org brn 5.00 3.00

Zeppelin Issue.

No. C2 Surcharged in Blue or Violet

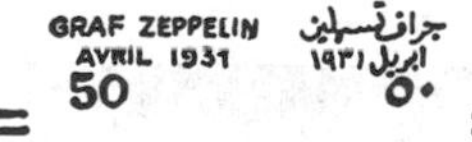

1931, Apr. 6

C3 AP1 50m on 27m org brn (Bl) 37.50 32.50
a. "1951" instead of "1931" 70.00 70.00
C4 AP1 100m on 27m org brn (V) 37.50 32.50

Airplane over Giza Pyramids AP2

1933-38 Litho. *Perf. 13x13½*

C5 AP2 1m org & blk 10 8
C6 AP2 2m gray & blk 1.00 55
C7 AP2 2m org red & blk ('38) 80 75
C8 AP2 3m ol brn & blk 20 20
C9 AP2 4m grn & blk 50 45
C10 AP2 5m dp brn & blk 35 10
C11 AP2 6m dk grn & blk 70 65
C12 AP2 7m dk bl & blk 45 45
C13 AP2 8m vio & blk 25 15
C14 AP2 9m dp red & blk 80 80
C15 AP2 10m vio & brn 50 15
C16 AP2 20m dk grn & brn 35 10
C17 AP2 30m dl bl & brn 50 20
C18 AP2 40m dp red & brn 10.00 20
C19 AP2 50m org & brn 7.25 20
C20 AP2 60m gray & brn 2.75 20
C21 AP2 70m dk bl & bl grn 1.50 20
C22 AP2 80m ol brn & bl grn 1.50 20
C23 AP2 90m org & bl grn 2.50 20
C24 AP2 100m vio & bl grn 3.00 25
C25 AP2 200m dp red & bl grn 6.00 50
Nos. C5-C25 (21) 41.00 6.58

Type of 1933.

1941-43 Photo.

C34 AP2 5m cop brn ('43) 15 12
C35 AP2 10m violet 40 20
C36 AP2 25m dk vio brn ('43) 40 20
C37 AP2 30m green 50 20

No. C37 Overprinted in Black

مؤتمر الملاحة الجوية الدولى للشرق الأوسط

Le Caire 1946 - ١٩٤٦ القاهرة

1946, Oct. 1

C38 AP2 30m green 40 20
a. Double overprint 125.00 125.00
b. Inverted overprint 200.00 200.00

Issued to commemorate the Middle East International Air Navigation Congress, Cairo, October 1946.

King Farouk, Delta Dam and DC-3 Plane AP3

Perf. 13x13½

1947, Feb. 19 Photo. Wmk. 195

C39 AP3 2m red org 10 5
C40 AP3 3m dk brn 10 10
C41 AP3 5m red brn 10 10
C42 AP3 7m dp yel org 12 12
C43 AP3 8m green 15 10
C44 AP3 10m violet 15 8
C45 AP3 20m brt bl 25 15
C46 AP3 30m brn vio 35 18
C47 AP3 40m car rose 50 20
C48 AP3 50m Prus grn 60 25
C49 AP3 100m ol grn 1.50 45
C50 AP3 200m dk gray 2.50 1.25
Nos. C39-C50 (12) 6.42 3.03

Nos. C49 and C50 Surcharged in Black

Mills 13 مليم ١٣
سعيدة
S. A. I. D. E.
23-8-1948 ١٩٤٨-٨-٢٣

1948, Aug. 23

C51 AP3 13m on 100m ol grn 45 45
C52 AP3 22m on 200m dk gray 55 55
a. Date omitted

Issued to commemorate the inaugural flights of "Services Aeriens Internationaux d'Egypte" from Cairo to Athens and Rome, August 23, 1948.

Nos. C39 to C50 Overprinted in Various Colors

ملك مصر والسودان
١٦ اكتوبر سنة ١٩٥١

Overprint 27mm. Wide.

1952, Jan. Wmk. 195 *Perf. 13x13½*

C53 AP3 2m red org (Bl) 8 8
C54 AP3 3m dk brn (RV) 10 10
C55 AP3 5m red brn 12 10
C56 AP3 7m dp yel org (Bl) 25 25
C57 AP3 8m grn (RV) 18 18
C58 AP3 10m vio (G) 45 45
C59 AP3 20m brt bl (RV) 1.25 1.00
C60 AP3 30m brn vio (G) 50 40
C61 AP3 40m car rose 2.50 80
C62 AP3 50m Prus grn (RV) 1.50 1.50
C63 AP3 100m ol grn 3.00 2.50
C64 AP3 200m dk gray (RV) 4.25 4.00
Nos. C53-C64 (12) 14.18 11.36

See note after No. 316.

Certain countries cancel stamps in full sheets and sell them (usually with gum) for less than face value. Dealers generally sell "CTO".

Delta Dam and Douglas DC-3 AP4

1953 **Photo.**
C65 AP4 5m red brn 15 8
C66 AP4 15m ol grn 45 15

Nos. C39-C49 Overprinted in Black with Three Bars to Obliterate Portrait.

1953

C67	AP3	2m red org	20	20
C68	AP3	3m dk brn	40	40
C69	AP3	5m red brn	10	10
C70	AP3	7m dp yel org	50	35
C71	AP3	8m green	20	20
C72	AP3	10m violet	10.00	8.00
C73	AP3	20m brt bl	25	20
C74	AP3	30m brn vio	40	35
C75	AP3	40m car rose	45	45
C76	AP3	50m Prus grn	60	55
C77	AP3	100m ol grn	1.75	1.50
C77A	AP3	200m gray	20.00	17.50
		Nos. C67-C77A (12)	34.85	29.80

Nos. C53-C64 Overprinted in Black with Three Bars to Obliterate Portrait.

1953

C78	AP3	2m red org	8	8
C79	AP3	3m dk brn	12	12
C80	AP3	5m red brn	8	8
C81	AP3	7m dp yel org	4.50	4.50
C82	AP3	8m green	35	35
C83	AP3	10m violet	25	25
C84	AP3	20m brt bl	20.00	20.00
C85	AP3	30m brn vio	35	35
C86	AP3	40m car rose	20.00	20.00
C87	AP3	50m Prus grn	50	45
C88	AP3	100m ol grn	75	75
C89	AP3	200m dk gray	7.50	2.75
		Nos. C78-C89 (12)	54.48	49.68

Practically all values of Nos. C67-C89 exist with double overprint.

United Arab Republic
Type of Regular Issue
Perf. 11½x11

1958, March 22 Photo. Wmk. 318
C90 A141 15m ultra & red brn 30 20

Birth of United Arab Republic

Pyramids at Giza AP5

Al Azhar University – AP6

Designs: 15m, Colossi of Memnon, Thebes. 90m, St. Catherine Monastery, Mt. Sinai.

1959-60 Wmk. 328 *Perf. 13x13½*

C91	AP5	5m brt red	5	5
C92	AP5	15m dk dl vio	15	15
C93	AP6	60m dk grn	50	50
C94	AP5	90m brn car ('60)	1.00	40

Nos. C91-C93 exist imperf. See also Nos. C101, C105.

Type of Regular Issue, Redrawn (Tower of Cairo)

1961, May 1 *Perf. 13½x13*
C95 A183 50m brt bl 40 35

Top inscription has been replaced by two airplanes.

Scott's International Album provides spaces for an extensive representative collection of the world's postage stamps.

Weather Vane, Anemometer and U.N. World Meteorological Organization Emblem – AP7

Perf. 11½x11
1962, Mar. 23 Photo. Unwmk.
C96 AP7 60m yel & dp bl 50 50

2nd World Meteorological Day, Mar. 23.

Patrice Lumumba and Map of Africa – AP8

Perf. 13½x13
1962, July 1 Wmk. 328
C97 AP8 35m multi 30 30

Issued in memory of Patrice Lumumba (1925-61), Premier of Congo.

Maritime Station, Alexandria – AP9

Designs: 30m, International Airport, Cairo. 40m, Railroad Station, Luxor.

1963, Mar. 18 *Perf. 13x13½*

C98	AP9	20m dk brn	16	12
C99	AP9	30m car rose	25	20
C100	AP9	40m black	35	30

Type of 1959-60 and

Temple of Queen Nefertari, Abu Simbel AP10

Arch and Tower of Cairo – AP11

Designs: 80m, Al Azhar University seen through arch. 140m, Ramses II, Abu Simbel.

Perf. 11½x11, 11x11½
1963, Oct. 24 Photo. Wmk. 342

C101	AP6	80m vio blk & brt bl	3.00	50
C102	AP10	115m brn & yel	95	70
C103	AP10	140m pale vio, blk & org red	1.15	90

Unwmk.

C104	AP11	50m yel brn & brt bl ('64)	50	40
C105	AP6	80m vio bl & lt bl ('65)	2.50	50

Weather Vane, Anemometer and WMO Emblem – AP12

Perf. 11½x11
1965, Mar. 23 Wmk. 342
C106 AP12 80m dk bl & rose lil 65 50

Fifth World Meteorological Day.

Game Board from Tomb of Tutankhamen – AP13

1965, July 1 Photo. Unwmk.
C107 AP13 10m yel & dk bl 50 25

Temples at Abu Simbel – AP14

1966, Apr. 28 Wmk. 342 *Perf. 11½*
C108 AP14 20m multi 12 10
C109 AP14 80m multi 60 35

Issued to commemorate the transfer of the temples of Abu Simbel to a hilltop, 1963-66.

Scout Camp and Jamboree Emblem AP15

1966, Aug. 10 *Perf. 11½x11*
C110 AP15 20m ol & rose 25 10

Issued to commemorate the 7th Pan-Arab Boy Scout Jamboree, Good Daim, Libya, Aug. 12.

St. Catherine Monastery, Mt. Sinai – AP16

1966, Nov. 30 Photo. Wmk. 342
C111 AP16 80m multi 60 35

Issued to commemorate the 1400th anniversary of St. Catherine Monastery, Sinal.

Cairo Airport AP17

1967, Apr. 26 *Perf. 11½x11*
C112 AP17 20m sky bl, sl grn & lt brn 12 10

Hotel El Alamein and Map of Nile Delta AP18

Designs: 80m, The Virgin's Tree, Virgin Mary and Child. 115m, Fishing in the Red Sea.

1967, June 7 Wmk. 342 *Perf. 11½*

C113	AP18	20m dl pur, sl grn & dl org	25	10
C114	AP18	80m bl & multi	1.00	35
C115	AP18	115m brn, org & bl	1.75	75

Issued for International Tourist Year, 1967.

Oil Derricks, Map of Egypt AP19

1967, July 23 Photo.
C116 AP19 50m org & bluish blk 45 26

15th anniversary of the revolution.

Type of Regular Issue, 1967

Design: 80m, Back of Tutankhamen's throne and UNESCO emblem.

1967, Oct. 24 Wmk. 342 *Perf. 11½*
C117 A301 80m bl & yel 50 35

22nd anniversary of the United Nations.

Koran – AP20

1968, Mar. 25 Wmk. 342 *Perf. 11½*
C118 AP20 30m lil, bl & yel 75 50
C119 AP20 80m lil, bl & yel 1.50 1.00

Issued to commemorate the 1400th anniversary of the Koran. Nos. C118-C119 are printed in miniature sheets of 4 containing 2 each of Nos. C118-C119, decorative border and gutters. Size: 240x158mm.

St. Mark and St. Mark's Cathedral – AP21

1968, June 25 Wmk. 342 *Perf. 11½*
C120 AP21 80m brt grn, dk brn & dp car 60 35

Issued to commemorate the 1900th anniversary of the martyrdom of St. Mark and to commemorate the consecration of St. Mark's Cathedral, Cairo.

Map of United Arab Airlines and Boeing 707
AP22

Design: No. C122, Ilyushin 18 and routes of United Arab Airlines.

1968-69 Photo. ***Perf. 11½x11***
C121 AP22 55m bl, ocher & car 35 25
C122 AP22 55m bl, yel & vio blk ('69) 35 25

Issued to commemorate the first flights of a Boeing 707 (No. C121) and an Ilyushin 18 (No. C122) for United Arab Airlines.

Mahatma Gandhi, Arms of India and UAR
AP23

Imam El Boukhary
AP24

1969, Sept. 10 ***Perf. 11x11½***
C123 AP23 80m lt bl, ocher & brn 65 35

Issued to commemorate the centenary of the birth of Mohandas K. Gandhi (1869-1948), leader in India's fight for independence.

1969, Dec. 27 Photo. Wmk. 342
C124 AP24 30m lt ol & dk brn 20 15

Issued to commemorate the 1100th anniversary of the death of the Imam El Boukhary (824-870), philosopher and writer.

Azzahir Beybars Mosque
AP25

1969, Dec. 27 Engr. ***Perf. 11½x11***
C125 AP25 30m red lil 18 15

700th anniversary of the founding of the Azzahir Beybars Mosque, Cairo.

Lenin — AP26

Perf. 11x11½
1970, Apr. 22 Photo. Wmk. 342
C126 AP26 80m lt grn & brn 50 35

Issued to commemorate the centenary of the birth of Lenin (1870-1924).

Phantom Fighters and Destroyed Factory — AP27

1970, May 1 ***Perf. 11½x11***
C127 AP27 80m yel, grn & dk vio brn 75 35

Issued to commemorate the destruction of the Abu-Zaabal factory by Israeli planes.

U.P.U. Type of Regular Issue
1970, May 20 Photo. Wmk. 342
C128 A350 80m multi 50 35

Issued to commemorate the inauguration of the new Universal Postal Union Headquarters in Bern.

Nasser and Burial Mosque — AP28

1970, Nov. 6 Wmk. 342 ***Perf. 11***
C129 AP28 30m ol & blk 35 15
C130 AP28 80m brn & blk 75 35

Issued in memory of Gamal Abdel Nasser (1918-1970), President of Egypt.

Postal Congress Type of Regular Issue
Perf. 11½x11
1971, Mar. 6 Photo. Wmk. 342
C131 A365 30m lt ol, org & sl grn 25 15

9th Arab Postal Congress, Cairo, March 6-25.

Nasser, El Rifaei and Sultan Hussein Mosques
AP29

Designs: 85m, Nasser and Ramses Square, Cairo. 110m, Nasser, Sphinx and pyramids.

Perf. 11½x11
1971, July 1 Photo. Wmk. 342
C132 AP29 30m multi 50 15
C133 AP29 85m multi 1.25 35
C134 AP29 110m multi 1.75 50

APU Type of Regular Issue
1971, Aug. 3 Wmk. 342 ***Perf. 11½***
C135 A373 30m brn, yel & bl 18 15

25th anniversary of the Conference of Sofar, Lebanon, establishing the Arab Postal Union.

Arab Republic of Egypt
Confederation Type of Regular Issue
Perf. 11½x11
1971, Sept. 28 Photo. Wmk. 342
C136 A374 30m gray, sl grn & dk pur 18 12

Confederation of Arab Republics (Egypt, Syria and Libya).

Al Aqsa Mosque and Woman
AP30

Wmk. 342
1971, Oct. 24 Photo. ***Perf. 11½***
C137 AP30 30m bl, yel, brn & grn 75 50

25th anniversary of the United Nations (in 1970) and for the return of Palestinian refugees.

Postal Union Type of Regular Issue

Design: 30m, African Postal Union emblem and letter.

1971, Dec. 2 ***Perf. 11½x11***
C138 A384 30m grn, blk & bl 18 12

10th anniversary of African Postal Union.

Aida, Triumphal March
AP31

1971, Dec. 23 Wmk. 342 ***Perf. 11½***
C139 AP31 110m dk brn, yel & sl grn 80 40

Centenary of the first performance of the opera Aida, by Giuseppe Verdi.

Globe, Glider, Rocket Club Emblem
AP32

St. Catherine's Monastery on Fire
AP33

1972, Feb. 11 ***Perf. 11x11½***
C140 AP32 30m bl, ocher & yel 18 12

International Aerospace Education Conference, Cairo, Jan. 11-13.

Perf. 11½x11
1972, Feb. 15 Unwmk.
C141 AP33 110m dp car, org & blk 70 40

The burning of St. Catherine's Monastery in Sinai Desert, Nov. 30, 1971.

Tutankhamen in Garden — AP34

Tutankhamen, from 2nd Sarcophagus — AP35

Design: No. C143, Ankhesenamun.

1972, May 22 Photo. ***Perf. 11½***
C142 AP34 110m brn org, bl & grn 2.50 75
C143 AP34 110m brn org, bl & grn 2.50 75

Souvenir Sheet
Imperf

C144 AP35 200m gold & multi 5.00 5.00

50th anniversary of the discovery of the tomb of Tutankhamen. Nos. C142-C143 printed se-tenant in sheets of 50. The continuous design is from a painted ivory plaque on lid of a coffer.

No. C144 has blue inscription and gold scarab ornaments in margin. Size: 97x102mm.

Souvenir Sheet

Flag of Confederation of Arab Republics — AP36

1972, July 23 Photo. ***Imperf.***
C145 AP36 110m gold, dp car & blk 1.75 1.50

20th anniversary of the revolution. No. C145 has gold commemorative inscription and black portraits of Presidents Nasser and Anwar El Sadat in margin. Size: 107x69mm.

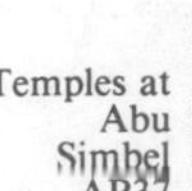

Temples at Abu Simbel
AP37

Designs: 30m, Al Azhar Mosque and St. George's Church. 110m, Pyramids at Giza.

1972 Wmk. 342 *Perf. 11½x11*
C146 AP37 30m bl brn & buff 25 10
C147 AP37 85m bl, brn & ocher 65 30
C148 AP37 110m multi 90 32

Issue dates: Nos. C146, C148, Nov. 22; No. C147, Aug. 1.

Olympic Type of Regular Issue

Designs (Olympic and Motion Emblems and): No. C149, Handball. No. C150, Weight lifting. 50m, Swimming. 55m, Gymnastics. All vertical.

1972, Aug. 17 *Perf. 11x11½*
C149 A396 30m multi 25 10
C150 A396 30m yel & multi 25 10
C151 A396 50m bl & multi 45 16
C152 A396 55m multi 50 16

Champollion, Rosetta Stone, Hieroglyphics — AP38

1972, Oct. 16
C153 AP38 110m gold, grn & blk 1.25 50

Sesquicentennial of the deciphering of Egyptian hieroglyphics by Jean-François Champollion.

World Map, Telephone, Radar, ITU Emblem — AP39

1973, Mar. 21 Photo. *Perf. 11*
C154 AP39 30m lt bl, dk bl & blk 15 10

5th World Telecommunications Day.

Karnak Temple, Luxor — AP40

Hand Dripping Blood and Falling Plane — AP41

1973, Mar. 21
C155 AP40 110m dp ultra, blk & rose 1.00 70

Sound and light at Karnak.

1973, May 1 *Perf. 11x11½*
C156 AP41 110m multi 3.00 1.00

Israeli attack on Libyan civilian plane, Feb. 1973.

WMO Emblem, Weather Vane — AP42

1973, Oct. 24 *Perf. 11x11½*
C157 AP42 110m bl, gold & pur 1.00 50

Centenary of international meteorological cooperation.

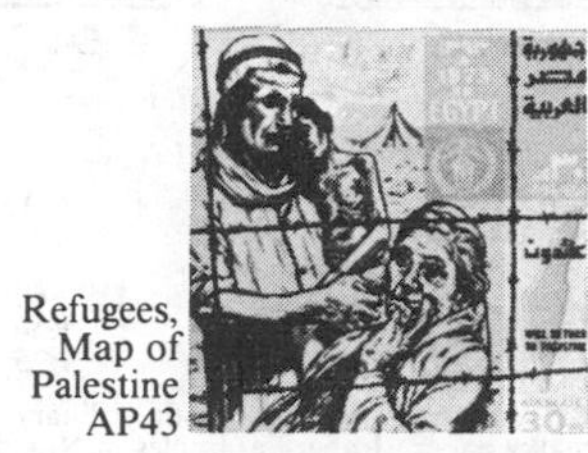
Refugees, Map of Palestine AP43

1973, Oct. 24 *Perf. 11½*
C158 AP43 30m dk brn, yel & bl 1.00 35

Plight of Palestinian refugees.

INTERPOL Emblem AP44

Postal and UPU Emblems AP45

Perf. 11x11½
1973, Dec. 8 Photo. Wmk. 342
C159 AP44 110m blk & multi 75 35

50th anniversary of the International Criminal Police Organization.

1974, Jan. 2 Unwmk. *Perf. 11*

Designs (UPU Emblems and): 30m, Arab Postal Union emblem. 55m, African Postal Union emblem. 110m, Universal Postal Union emblem.

Size: 26x46½mm.

C160 AP45 20m gray, red & blk 10 8
C161 AP45 30m sal, blk & pur 15 10
C162 AP45 55m emer, blk & brt mag 70 25

Size: 37x37½mm.

Perf. 11½

C163 AP45 110m lt bl, blk & gold 1.00 50

Post Day 1974.

Solar Bark of Khufu (Cheops) — AP46

Wmk. 342
1974, Mar. 21 Photo. *Perf. 11½*
C164 AP46 110m bl, gold & brn 1.00 50

Solar Bark Museum.

Hotel Meridien AP47

1974, Oct. 6 *Perf. 11½x11*
C165 AP47 110m multi 1.00 50

Opening of Hotel Meridien, Cairo.

Suez Canal Type of 1975

1975, June 5 *Perf. 11½*
C166 A448 30m bl, yel grn & ind 60 25
C167 A448 110m ind & bl 1.50 50

Reopening of the Suez Canal, June 5.

Irrigation Commission Emblem — AP48

1975, July 20
C168 AP48 110m org & dk grn 1.00 50

9th International Congress on Irrigation and Drainage, Moscow, and 25th anniversary of the International Commission on Irrigation and Drainage.

Refugees and UNWRA Emblem — AP49

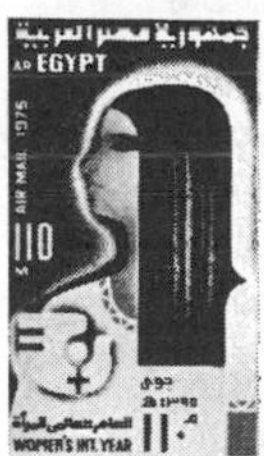

Woman and IWY Emblem — AP50

Perf. 11x11½
1975, Oct. 24 Photo. Wmk. 342
C169 AP49 30m multi 75 50

Unwmk.

C170 AP50 110m ol, org & blk 1.10 65

United Nations Day. 30m publicizes U.N. help for refugees; 110m is for International Women's Year 1975.

Step Pyramid, Sakhara, and Entrance Gate AP51

Designs: 45m, 60m, Plane over Giza Pyramids. 140m, Plane over boats on Nile.

Perf. 11½x11
1977-84 Photo. Wmk. 342
C171 AP51 45m yel & brn 22 16
C171A AP51 60m olive ('82) 30 30
C172 AP51 115m bl & brn 60 30
C173 AP51 140m bl & pur 70 48
C173A AP51 185m bl, sep & gray brn ('84) 1.00 1.00
Nos. C171-C173A (5) 2.82 2.24

Flyer and U.N. ICAO Emblem — AP52

Perf. 11x11½
1978, Dec. 30 Photo. Wmk. 342
C174 AP52 140m bl, blk & brn 70 55

75th anniversary of 1st powered flight.

Seeing Eye Medallion AP53

Perf. 11½x11
1981, Oct. 1 Photo. Wmk. 342
C175 AP53 230m multi 1.15 60

Hilton Ramses Hotel Opening — AP54

Perf. 11x11½
1982, Mar. 15 Photo. Wmk. 342
C176 AP54 18½p multi 90 50

Temple of Horus, Edfu AP55

Designs: 15p, like 6p. 18½p, 25p, Statue of Akhnaton, Thebes, hieroglyphics, vert. 23p, 30p, Gizeh pyramids.

1985 Photo. *Perf. 11½x11, 11x11½*
C177 AP55 6p lt bl & dk bl grn 30 25
C178 AP55 15p grnsh bl & brn 75 60
C179 AP55 18½p grn, sep & dp yel 90 75
C180 AP55 23p grnsh bl, sep & yel bis 1.15 90
C181 AP55 25p lt bl, sep & yel bis 1.25 95
C182 AP55 30p grnsh bl, sep & org yel 1.50 1.10
Nos. C177-C182 (6) 5.85 4.55

Issue dates: 6p, 18½p, 23p, Mar. 1. 15p, 25p, 30p, May. 1.

Post Day — AP56

Narmer Board, oldest known hieroglyphic inscriptions: No. C183a, Tablet obverse. No. C183b, Reverse.

1986, Jan. 2 Photo. *Perf. 13½x13*
C183 Pair 1.50 1.50
a.-b. AP56 15p any single 75 75

Map, Jet, AFRAA Emblem AP57

1986, Apr. 7 Photo. *Perf. 11½*
C184 AP57 15p bl, yel & blk 38 38

African Airlines Assoc., 18th General Assembly, Cairo, Apr. 7-10.

World Food Day AP58

UNESCO, 40th Anniv. — AP59

Perf. 13½x13, 13x13½
1986, Oct. 24 Litho.
C185 AP58 15p multi 75 75
C186 AP59 15p multi 75 75

UN Day.

Tourism Year — AP60

Design: Column and Sphinx in Alexandria, St. Catherine's Monastery in Mt. Sinai, Colossi of Thebes and Temple of Theban Triad in Luxor.

Unwmk.
1987, Sept. 30 Litho. *Imperf.*
Size: 140x90mm.
C187 AP60 30p multi 1.50 1.50

AIR POST SEMI-POSTAL STAMPS

United Arab Republic

Pharaonic Mail Carriers and Papyrus Plants SPAP1

Design: 115m+55m, Jet plane, world map and stamp of Egypt, 1926 (No. C1).

Wmk. 342
1966, Jan. 2 Photo. *Perf. 11½*
CB1 SPAP1 80m + 40m yel, grn, brn, lil & bl 90 70
CB2 SPAP1 115m + 55m bl, yel & lil 1.10 85

Issued for Post Day, Jan. 2. Nos. CB1-CB2 printed se-tenant in sheets of 28.

SPECIAL DELIVERY STAMPS

Motorcycle Postman — SD1

Perf. 13x13½
1926, Nov. 28 Photo. Wmk. 195
E1 SD1 20m dk grn 6.50 2.00

1929, Sept.
E2 SD1 20m brn red & blk 75 40

Inscribed "Postes Expres."

1943-44 Litho.
E3 SD1 26m brn red & gray blk 1.00 90
E4 SD1 40m dl brn & pale gray ('44) 75 30

No. E4 Overprinted in Black

Overprint 27mm. Wide.

1952, Jan.
E5 SD1 40m dl brn & pale gray 1.00 45

See note after No. 316.

POSTAGE DUE STAMPS

D1

D2

Wmk. Crescent and Star. (119)
1884, Jan. 1 Litho. *Perf. 10½*
J1 D1 10pa red 10.00 2.00
a. Imperf. vert., pair 125.00
J2 D1 20pa red 22.50 4.00
J3 D1 1pi red 35.00 7.50
J4 D1 2pi red 50.00 4.00
J5 D1 5pi red 12.50 10.00

1886, Aug. 1 Unwmk.
J6 D1 10pa red 3.00 1.00
a. Imperf. vert., pair 75.00 60.00
J7 D1 20pa red 75.00 10.00
J8 D1 1pi red 2.50 1.00
J9 D1 2pi red 2.50 50

1888, Jan. 1 *Perf. 11½*
J10 D2 2m green 1.50 75
a. Horiz. pair, imperf. between 75.00
J11 D2 5m rose red 2.50 75
J12 D2 1pi blue 25.00 8.50
J13 D2 2pi yellow 20.00 3.50
J14 D2 5pi gray 75.00 50.00
a. Period after "PIASTRES" 100.00 75.00
Nos. J10-J14 (5) 124.00 63.50

Excellent counterfeits of J1 to J14 are plentiful.

There are four types of each of Nos. J1 to J14, so placed that any block of four contains all four types.

D3

D4

Perf. 14x13½
1889 Wmk. 119 Typo.
J15 D3 2m green 90 10
a. Half used as 1m on cover 5.00
J16 D3 4m maroon 60 8
J17 D3 1pi ultra 1.50 8
J18 D3 2pi orange 1.75 25

Nos. J15-J18 exist on both ordinary and chalky paper. Imperf. examples of Nos. J15-J17 are proofs.

Black Surcharge.

1898
J19 D4 3m on 2pi org 30 25
a. Inverted surch. 30.00 30.00
b. Double surcharge 100.00 100.00
c. Pair, one without surcharge 175.00

There are two types of this surcharge. In one type, the spacing between the last two Arabic characters at the right is 2mm. In the other type, this spacing is 3mm., and there is an added sign on top of the second character from the right.

D5

D6

Wmk. Triple Crescent and Star. (120)
1921 *Perf. 14x13½*
J20 D5 2m green 40 35
J21 D5 4m vermilion 1.50 75
J22 D6 10m dp bl 1.50 1.00

1921-22
J23 D5 2m vermilion 35 15
J24 D5 4m green 35 15
J25 D6 10m lake ('22) 50 10

Nos. J18, J23-J25 Overprinted

1922, Oct. 10 Wmk. 119
J26 D3 2pi orange 4.00 1.00
a. Ovpt. right side up 8.00 5.00

Wmk. 120
J27 D5 2m vermilion 50 25
J28 D5 4m green 75 50
J29 D6 10m lake 1.25 60

Overprint on Nos. J26-J29 is inverted.

Arabic Numeral — D7

Wmk. Multiple Crown and Arabic F. (195)
1927-56 Litho. *Perf. 13x13½*
Size: 18x22½ mm.
J30 D7 2m slate 50 15
J31 D7 2m org ('38) 25 15
J32 D7 4m green 40 15
J33 D7 4m ol brn ('32) 1.50 20
J34 D7 5m brown 1.00 30
J35 D7 6m gray grn ('41) 50 20
J36 D7 8m brn vio 50 25
J37 D7 10m brick red ('29) 65 25
a. 10m dp red 75 35
J38 D7 12m rose lake ('41) 90 25
J38A D7 20m dk red ('56) 1.50 75

Perf. 13½x14
Size: 22x28 mm.
J39 D7 30m purple 3.50 1.50
Nos. J30-J39 (11) 11.20 4.15

Postage Due Stamps and Type of 1927 Overprinted in Various Colors

1952, Jan. 16 *Perf. 13x13½*
J40 D7 2m org (Bl) 15 15
J41 D7 4m green 30 30
J42 D7 6m gray grn (RV) 45 35
J43 D7 8m brn vio (Bl) 40 35
J44 D7 10m dl rose (Bl) 1.00 35
a. 10m brn red (Bk) 65 40
J45 D7 12m rose lake (Bl) 50 30

Perf. 14
J46 D7 30m pur (C) 1.50 55
Nos. J40-J46 (7) 4.30 2.35

See note after No. 316.

United Arab Republic

1960 Wmk. 318 *Perf. 13x13½*
Size: 18x22½ mm.
J47 D7 2m orange 45 15
J48 D7 4m lt grn 55 20
J49 D7 6m green 75 25
J50 D7 8m brn vio 55 35
J51 D7 12m rose brn 1.00 50
J52 D7 20m dl rose brn 1.50 50

Perf. 14
Size: 22x28 mm.
J53 D7 30m violet 5.00 1.00
Nos. J47-J53 (7) 9.80 2.95

1962 Wmk. 328 *Perf. 13x13½*
Size: 18x22½mm.
J54 D7 2m salmon 35 25
J55 D7 4m lt grn 70 35
J56 D7 10m red brn 1.00 50
J57 D7 12m rose brn 1.75 75
J58 D7 20m dl rose brn 2.50 1.50

Perf. 14
Size: 22x28mm.
J59 D7 30m lt vio 3.25 2.25
Nos. J54-J59 (6) 9.55 5.60

D8

1965 Unwmk. Photo. *Perf. 11*
J60 D8 2m org & vio blk 15 10
J61 D8 8m lt bl & dk bl 20 15
J62 D8 10m yel & emer 25 15
J63 D8 20m lt bl & vio blk 30 15
J64 D8 40m org & emer 60 20
Nos. J60-J64 (5) 1.50 75

MILITARY STAMPS

From November 1, 1932 to February 29, 1936 members of the British Forces in Egypt were permitted to send letters to Great Britain at reduced rates. Special seals were used in place of Egyptian stamps. These seals were replaced by special stamps March 1, 1936.

Fuad Type of 1927.
Inscribed "Army Post".

Perf. 13½x14

1936, Mar. 1 Photo. Wmk. 195

No.	Type	Description	Unused	Used
M1	A44	3m green	50	15
M2	A44	10m carmine	1.50	30

King Farouk — M1

1939, Dec. 16 ***Perf. 13x13½***

No.	Type	Description	Unused	Used
M3	M1	3m green	50	3.00
M4	M1	10m car rose	1.50	20

United Arab Republic

Arms of UAR and Military Emblems — M2

Perf. 11x11½

1971, Apr. 15 Photo. Wmk. 342

No.	Type	Description	Unused	Used
M5	M2	10m purple	12	12

OFFICIAL STAMPS

O1

Wmk. Crescent and Star. (119)

1893, Jan. 1 Typo. ***Perf. 14x13½***

No.	Type	Description	Unused	Used
O1	O1	org brn	30	15

No. O1 exists on ordinary and chalky paper. Imperf. examples of No. O1 are proofs.

Regular Issues of 1884-93 Overprinted — O.H.H.S. اميري

1907

No.	Type	Description	Unused	Used
O2	A18	1m brown	15	6
O3	A19	2m green	20	6
a.		Double ovpt.		
O4	A21	3m orange	20	6
O5	A20	5m car rose	35	5
O6	A14	1pi ultra	60	6
O7	A16	5pi gray	3.50	20
		Nos. O2-O7 (6)	5.00	49

Imperf. examples of Nos. O2-O3, O5-O7 are proofs.

Overprinted — O.H.H.S.

1913

No.	Type	Description	Unused	Used
O8	A20	5m car rose	30	15
a.		Inverted overprint	100.00	50.00
b.		No period after "S"	6.50	3.50

Regular Issues Overprinted — O.H.H.S. اميرى

1914-15

On Issues of 1888-1906

No.	Type	Description	Unused	Used
O9	A19	2m green	30	20
a.		Inverted ovpt.	20.00	20.00
b.		Dbl. ovpt.	250.00	250.00
c.		No period after "S"	6.00	6.00
O10	A23	4m brn red	50	20
a.		Inverted ovpt.	140.00	110.00

On Issue of 1914.

No.	Type	Description	Unused	Used
O11	A24	1m ol brn	20	12
a.		No period after "S"	2.50	2.50
O12	A26	3m orange	25	15
a.		No period after "S"	5.00	5.00
O13	A28	5m lake	50	8
a.		No period after "S"	4.00	4.00
b.		Two periods after "S"	4.00	4.00
		Nos. O9-O13 (5)	1.75	75

Regular Issues Overprinted — O.H.H.S. أميرى

On Issues of 1888-1906

1915, Oct.

No.	Type	Description	Unused	Used
O14	A19	2m green	75	12
a.		Inverted overprint	10.00	10.00
b.		Double overprint	15.00	
O15	A23	4m brn red	1.00	15

On Issue of 1914.

No.	Type	Description	Unused	Used
O16	A28	5m lake	60	18
a.		Pair, one without ovpt.	200.00	

On Issue of 1921-22.

1922 Wmk. 120

No.	Type	Description	Unused	Used
O17	A24	1m ol brn	5.00	2.00
a.		Two periods after "S"	300.00	
O18	A25	2m red	5.00	2.00
O19	A26	3m orange	100.00	85.00
O20	A28	5m pink	5.00	3.00
a.		Double ovpt.	100.00	

Regular Issues of 1921-22 Overprinted — O.H.E.M.S. الحكومة الملكية المصرية

1922

No.	Type	Description	Unused	Used
O21	A24	1m ol brn	35	35
a.		Two periods after "S"	35.00	
O22	A25	2m red	40	30
O23	A26	3m orange	1.75	1.25
O24	A27	4m green	2.50	1.50
a.		Two periods after "H" none after "S"	100.00	100.00
O25	A28	5m pink	60	25
a.		Two periods after "H" none after "S"	50.00	50.00
O26	A29	10m dp bl	1.75	1.00
O27	A34	15m indigo	2.00	1.25
O28	A35	15m indigo	125.00	75.00
a.		Two periods after "H" none after "S"	300.00	300.00
O29	A31	50m maroon	10.00	3.75
		Nos. O21-O29 (9)	144.35	84.65

1923

No.	Type	Description	Unused	Used
O30	A29	10m lake	3.00	1.25
a.		Two periods after "H" none after "S"	75.00	75.00

Regular Issue of 1923 Overprinted in Black or Red — أميرى

1924 ***Perf. 13½x14***

No.	Type	Description	Unused	Used
O31	A36	1m orange	60	50
O32	A36	2m gray (R)	75	60
O33	A36	3m brown	2.00	1.10
O34	A36	4m yel grn	2.50	1.25
O35	A36	5m org brn	75	30
O36	A36	10m rose	2.25	45
O37	A36	15m ultra	2.50	90

Perf. 14

No.	Type	Description	Unused	Used
O38	A36	50m myr grn	6.00	2.50
		Nos. O31-O38 (8)	17.35	7.60

O2

O3

Wmk. Multiple Crown and Arabic F. (195)

1926-35 Litho. ***Perf. 13x13½***

Size 18½x22mm.

No.	Type	Description	Unused	Used
O39	O2	1m lt org	6	6
O40	O2	2m black	6	6
O41	O2	3m ol brn	8	8
O42	O2	4m lt grn	12	8
O43	O2	5m brown	18	6
O44	O2	10m dl red	55	8
O45	O2	10m brt vio ('34)	28	8
O46	O2	15m dp bl	85	10
O47	O2	15m brn vio ('34)	35	8
O48	O2	20m dp bl ('35)	45	10

Perf. 13½

Size 22½x27½ mm.

No.	Type	Description	Unused	Used
O49	O2	20m ol grn	2.25	20
O50	O2	50m myr grn	1.65	15
		Nos. O39-O50 (12)	6.88	1.13

1938, Dec. Size 22½x19mm.

No.	Type	Description	Unused	Used
O51	O3	1m orange	5	5
O52	O3	2m red	6	6
O53	O3	3m ol brn	10	8
O54	O3	4m yel grn	12	8
O55	O3	5m brown	12	6
O56	O3	10m brt vio	15	8
O57	O3	15m rose vio	22	10
O58	O3	20m blue	30	12

Perf. 14x13½.

Size 26½x22 mm.

No.	Type	Description	Unused	Used
O59	O3	50m myr grn	65	15
		Nos. O51-O59 (9)	1.77	78

Nos. O51 to O59 Overprinted in Various Colors — ملك مصر والسودان ١٦ اكتوبر سنة ١٩٥١

Overprint 19mm. Wide.

1952, Jan. ***Perf. 13x13½***

No.	Type	Description	Unused	Used
O60	O3	1m org (Br)	5	5
O61	O3	2m red	5	5
O62	O3	3m ol brn (Bl)	10	10
O63	O3	4m yel grn (Bl)	12	12
O64	O3	5m brn (Bl)	12	12
O65	O3	10m brt vio (Bl)	18	12
O66	O3	15m rose vio (Bl)	25	18
O67	O3	20m blue	35	35

Overprint 24½mm. Wide.

Perf. 14x13½.

No.	Type	Description	Unused	Used
O68	O3	50m myr grn (RV)	95	75
		Nos. O60-O68 (9)	2.17	1.84

See note after No. 316.

United Arab Republic

Numeral O4

Arms of U.A.R. O5

Perf. 13x13½

1959 Litho. Wmk. 318

No.	Type	Description	Unused	Used
O69	O4	10m brn vio	50	8
O70	O4	35m chlky bl	1.00	12

1962-63 Wmk. 328

No.	Type	Description	Unused	Used
O71	O4	1m org ('63)	5	5
O72	O4	4m yel grn ('63)	5	5
O73	O4	5m brown	5	5
O74	O4	10m dk brn	5	5
O75	O4	35m dk bl	35	35
O76	O4	50m green	50	50
O77	O4	100m vio ('63)	1.00	50
O78	O4	200m rose red ('63)	2.00	1.00
O79	O4	500m gray ('63)	5.00	3.00
		Nos. O71-O79 (9)	9.05	5.55

Perf. 11½x11

1966-68 Unwmk. Photo.

No.	Type	Description	Unused	Used
O80	O5	1m ultra	5	5
O81	O5	4m brown	5	5
O82	O5	5m olive	5	5
O83	O5	10m brn blk	10	10
O84	O5	20m magenta	15	15
O85	O5	35m dk pur	30	30
O86	O5	50m orange	35	35
O87	O5	55m dk pur	40	40

Wmk. 342

No.	Type	Description	Unused	Used
O88	O5	100m brt grn & brick red	1.00	75
O89	O5	200m bl & brick red	1.75	1.00
O90	O5	500m ol & brick red	4.00	2.50
		Nos. O80-O90 (11)	8.20	5.70

1969 Wmk. 342

No.	Type	Description	Unused	Used
O91	O5	10m magenta	8	8

Arab Republic of Egypt

Arms of Egypt — O6

Wmk. 342

1972, June 30 Photo. ***Perf. 11***

No.	Type	Description	Unused	Used
O92	O6	1m blk & vio bl	5	5
a.		1m blk & lt bl ('75)	5	5
O93	O6	10m blk & car	8	8
a.		10m blk & rose red ('76)	8	8
O94	O6	20m blk & ol	15	15
O95	O6	50m blk & org	30	30
O96	O6	55m blk & pur	35	35
		Nos. O92-O96 (5)	93	93

1973

No.	Type	Description	Unused	Used
O97	O6	20m lil & sep	15	15
a.		20m pur & lt brn ('76)	15	15
O98	O6	70m blk & grn ('79)	50	50

1982 Photo. Unwmk. ***Perf. 11***

No.	Type	Description	Unused	Used
O99	O6	30m pur & brn	15	15
O100	O6	60m blk & org	30	30
O101	O6	80m blk & grn	40	40

Issue dates: 30m, Feb. 12; 60m, Feb. 24; 80m, Feb. 18.

Arms of Egypt — O7

1985, May 1 Photo. ***Perf. 11½***

No.	Type	Description	Unused	Used
O102	O7	1p vermilion	5	5
O103	O7	3p sepia	15	15
O104	O7	5p org yel	25	25
O105	O7	8p green	40	40
O106	O7	15p dl vio	75	75
		Nos. O102-O106 (5)	1.60	1.60

OCCUPATION STAMPS

For Use in Palestine.

فلسطين

Nos. 208, 211 and 213 Overprinted in Green or Black — a

PALESTINE

Perf. 13x13½

1948, May 15 Wmk. 195

No.	Type	Description	Unused	Used
N1	A66	3m brown	15	15
N2	A66	6m lt yel grn (Bk)	20	20
N3	A66	13m rose car	25	25

Same Overprint in Red, Green or Black on Stamps of Egypt, 1939-46.

Perf. 13x13½, 13½x13

No.	Type	Description	Unused	Used
N4	A77	1m yel brn (G)	15	15
N5	A77	2m red org (G)	15	15
N6	A77	4m dp grn	15	15
N7	A77	5m red brn (Bk)	15	15
N8	A77	10m dp vio	20	20
N9	A77	15m dk vio	20	20
N10	A77	17m ol grn	25	25
N11	A77	20m dk gray	25	25
N12	A77	22m dp bl	35	35
N13	A74	50pi grn & sep	6.00	5.00
N14	A75	£1 dp bl & dk brn	12.00	10.00

The two lines of the overprint are more widely separated on Nos. N13 and N14.

Nos. 267-269, 237 and 238 Overprinted in Red

فلسطين

b

PALESTINE

Perf. 14x13½

No.	Type	Description	Unused	Used
N15	A73	30m ol grn	75	75
N16	A73	40m dk brn	1.00	75
N17	A73	50m Prus grn	1.50	1.00
N18	A73	100m brn vio	1.75	1.50
N19	A73	200m dk vio	5.00	5.00
		Nos. N1-N19 (19)	30.45	26.45

Overprint arranged to fit size of stamps.

Nos. N1-N19 Overprinted in Black with Three Bars to Obliterate Portrait

Perf. 13x13½, 13½x13, 14x13½

1953 **Wmk. 195**

No.	Type	Description	Unused	Used
N20	A77	1m yel brn	8	8
N21	A77	2m red org	8	8
N22	A66	3m brown	15	15
N23	A77	4m dp grn	15	15
N24	A77	5m red brn	15	15
N25	A66	6m lt yel grn	25	25
N26	A77	10m dp vio	30	30
N27	A66	13m rose car	35	35
N28	A77	15m dk vio	35	35
N29	A77	17m ol grn	40	40
N30	A77	20m dk gray	40	40
N31	A77	22m dp bl	60	60
N32	A73	30m ol grn	70	70
N33	A73	40m dk brn	1.10	1.10
N34	A73	50m Prus grn	1.50	1.50
N35	A73	100m brn vio	3.50	3.50
N36	A73	200m dk vio	7.25	7.25
N37	A74	50pi grn & sep	21.00	21.00
N38	A75	£1 dp bl & dk brn	35.00	35.00
		Nos. N20-N38 (19)	73.31	73.31

Regular Issue of 1953-55 Overprinted Type "a" in Blue or Red

1954-55 ***Perf. 13x13½***

No.	Type	Description	Unused	Used
N39	A115	1m red brn	5	5
N40	A115	2m dk lil	5	5
N41	A115	3m brt bl (R)	8	8
N42	A115	4m dk grn (R)	10	10
N43	A115	5m dp car	10	10
N44	A110	10m dk brn	15	15
N45	A110	15m gray (R)	15	15
N46	A110	17m dk grnsh bl (R)	20	20
N47	A110	20m pur (R) ('54)	20	20

فلسطين

Nos. 331-333 and 335-340 Overprinted in Blue or Red — c

PALESTINE

1955-56 ***Perf. 13½.***

No.	Type	Description	Unused	Used
N48	A111	30m dl grn (R)	35	35
N49	A111	32m brt bl (R)	40	40
N50	A111	35m vio (R)	45	45
N51	A111	40m red brn	70	70
N52	A111	50m vio brn	75	75
N53	A112	100m hn brn	1.75	1.75
N54	A112	200m dk grnsh bl (R)	3.50	3.50
N55	A112	500m pur (R)	15.00	15.00
N56	A112	£1 dk grn, blk & red (R) ('56)	24.00	24.00
		Nos. N39-N56 (18)	47.98	47.98

Type of 1957 Overprinted in Red — d

فلسطين
PALESTINE

1957 **Wmk. 195** ***Perf. 13½x13***

No.	Type	Description	Unused	Used
N57	A127	10m bl grn	1.25	1.25

Nos. 414-417 Overprinted Type "d" in Red.

1957-58 **Wmk. 315** ***Perf. 13½***

No.	Type	Description	Unused	Used
N58	A137	10m violet	20	20

Wmk. 318

No.	Type	Description	Unused	Used
N59	A136	1m lt bl grn ('58)	8	8
N60	A138	5m brn ('58)	10	10
N61	A137	10m vio ('58)	15	15

United Arab Republic

Nos. 438-444 Overprinted Type "d" in Red or Green

Perf. 13½x14

1958 **Wmk. 318** **Photo.**

No.	Type	Description	Unused	Used
N62	A136	1m crimson	5	5
N63	A138	2m blue	5	5
N64	A143	3m dk red brn (G)	5	5
N65	A217	4m green	6	6
N66	A138	5m brown	10	10
N67	A137	10m violet	10	10
N68	A138	35m lt ultra	40	40
		Nos. N62-N68 (7)	81	81

Same Overprint in Red on Freedom Struggle Type of 1958

1958 ***Perf. 13½x13***

No.	Type	Description	Unused	Used
N69	A145	10m dk brn	1.00	1.00

Same Overprint in Green on Declaration of Human Rights Type of 1958.

1958 ***Perf. 13x13½***

No.	Type	Description	Unused	Used
N70	A151	10m rose vio	1.00	1.00
N71	A151	35m red brn	1.50	1.50

No. 460 Overprinted Type "d" in Green

1959 **Wmk. 195** ***Perf. 13½***

No.	Type	Description	Unused	Used
N72	A112	55m on 100m hn brn	75	75

"PALESTINE" Added in English and Arabic to Stamps of Egypt

World Refugee Year Type

1960 **Wmk. 328** ***Perf. 13x13½***

No.	Type	Description	Unused	Used
N73	A173	10m org brn	10	10
N74	A173	35m dk bl gray	35	35

Type of Regular Issue 1959-60

1960 ***Perf. 13½x14***

No.	Type	Description	Unused	Used
N75	A136	1m brn org	5	5
N76	A217	4m ol gray	5	5
N77	A138	5m dk dl pur	10	10
N78	A137	10m dk ol grn	15	15

Palestine Day Type

1961, May 15 ***Perf. 13½x13***

No.	Type	Description	Unused	Used
N79	A184	10m purple	15	15

WHO Day Type

1961 **Wmk. 328** ***Perf. 13½x13***

No.	Type	Description	Unused	Used
N80	A182	10m blue	20	20

U.N.T.A.P. Type

1961, Oct. 24

No.	Type	Description	Unused	Used
N81	A191	10m dk bl & org	10	10
N82	A191	35m vert & blk	30	30

Education Day Type

1961, Dec. 18 **Photo.** ***Perf. 13½***

No.	Type	Description	Unused	Used
N83	A194	10m red brn	10	10

Victory Day Type

1961, Dec. 23 **Unwmk.** ***Perf. 11½***

No.	Type	Description	Unused	Used
N84	A195	10m brn org & brn	15	15

Gaza Strip Type

Perf. 13½x13

1962, March 7 **Wmk. 328**

No.	Type	Description	Unused	Used
N85	A200	10m red brn	10	10

Arab Publicity Week Type

1962, March 22 ***Perf. 13½x13***

No.	Type	Description	Unused	Used
N86	SP16	10m dk pur	10	10

Anti-Malaria Type

1962, June 20 **Photo.**

No.	Type	Description	Unused	Used
N87	A204	10m brn & dk car rose	15	15
N88	A204	35m blk & yel	40	40

Hammarskjold Type

Perf. 11½x11

1962, Oct. 24 **Wmk. 342**

Portrait in Slate Blue

No.	Type	Description	Unused	Used
N89	A214	5m brt rose	10	10
N90	A214	10m brown	20	20
N91	A214	35m blue	40	40

Lamp Type of Regular Issue

Perf. 11x11½

1963, Feb. 20 **Unwmk.**

No.	Type	Description	Unused	Used
N92	A217	4m dk brn, org & ultra	10	10

"Freedom from Hunger" Type

Perf. 11½x11, 11x11½

1963, Mar. 21 **Wmk. 342**

No.	Type	Description	Unused	Used
N93	A220	5m lt grn & dp org	5	5
N94	A220	10m ol & yel	10	10
N95	A220	35m dl pur, yel & blk	35	35

Red Cross Centenary Type

Designs: 10m, Centenary emblem, bottom panel added. 35m, Globe and emblem, top and bottom panels added.

1963, May 8 **Unwmk.** ***Perf. 11x11½***

No.	Type	Description	Unused	Used
N96	A221	10m dk bl & crim	10	10
N97	A221	35m crim & dk bl	35	35

"Save Abu Simbel" Type, 1963

1963, Oct. 15 **Wmk. 342** ***Perf. 11***

No.	Type	Description	Unused	Used
N98	A224	5m blk & yel	5	5
N99	A224	10m gray, blk & yel	10	10
N100	A224	35m org yel & vio	35	35

Human Rights Type, 1963

1963, Dec. 10 **Photo.** ***Perf. 11½x11***

No.	Type	Description	Unused	Used
N101	A228	5m dk brn & yel	5	5
N102	A228	10m dp cl, gray & blk	10	10
N103	A228	35m lt grn, pale grn & blk	35	35

Types of Regular Issue, 1964

1964 **Unwmk.** ***Perf. 11***

No.	Type	Description	Unused	Used
N104	A231	1m cit & lt vio	10	10
N105	A230	2m org & sl	10	10
N106	A230	3m bl & ocher	10	10
N107	A235	4m ol gray, ol, brn & rose	10	10
N108	A230	5m rose & brt bl	15	15
a.		5m rose & dk bl	1.50	1.50
N109	A231	10m ol, rose & brn	20	20
N110	A230	15m lil & yel	35	35
N111	A230	20m brn blk & ol	20	20
N112	A231	30m dp org & ind	35	35
N113	A231	35m buff, ocher & emer	50	50
N114	A231	40m ultra & emer	50	50
N115	A231	60m grnsh bl & brn org	1.00	1.00

Wmk. 342

No.	Type	Description	Unused	Used
N116	A232	100m bluish blk & yel brn	1.00	1.00
		Nos. N104-N116 (13)	4.65	4.65

Arab League Council Type, 1964

1964, Jan. 13 **Photo.**

No.	Type	Description	Unused	Used
N117	A234	10m ol & blk	5	5

Minaret Type, 1964

1964 **Unwmk.** ***Perf. 11***

No.	Type	Description	Unused	Used
N118	A235	4m ol, red brn & red	5	5

Arab Postal Union Type, 1964

1964, Apr. 1 **Wmk. 342** ***Perf. 11***

No.	Type	Description	Unused	Used
N119	A239	10m emer & ultra, *lt grn*	10	10

WHO Type, 1964

1964, Apr. 7

No.	Type	Description	Unused	Used
N120	A240	10m vio blk & red	10	10

Minaret Type, 1965

1965, Jan. 20 **Unwmk.** ***Perf. 11***

No.	Type	Description	Unused	Used
N121	A255	4m grn & dk brn	6	6

Arab League Type, 1965

1965, Mar. 22 **Wmk. 342** ***Perf. 11***

No.	Type	Description	Unused	Used
N122	A258	10m grn, red & blk	10	10
N123	A258	20m grn & brn	20	20

World Health Day Type, 1965

1965, Apr. 7 **Wmk. 342** ***Perf. 11***

No.	Type	Description	Unused	Used
N124	A259	10m brt grn & crim	10	10

Massacre Type, 1965

1965, Apr. 9 **Photo.**

No.	Type	Description	Unused	Used
N125	A260	10m sl bl & red	15	15

ITU Type, 1965

1965, May 17 **Wmk. 342** ***Perf. 11***

No.	Type	Description	Unused	Used
N126	A261	5m sl grn, sl bl & yel	5	5
N127	A261	10m car, rose red & gray	10	10
N128	A261	35m vio bl, ultra & yel	30	30

United Nations Type, 1966

Designs: 5m, WHO Headquarters Building, Geneva. 10m, U.N. Refugee emblem. 35m, UNICEF emblem.

1966, Oct. 24 **Wmk. 342** ***Perf. 11***

No.	Type	Description	Unused	Used
N129	A288	5m rose & brt pur	5	5
N130	A288	10m yel brn & brt pur	6	6
N131	A288	35m brt grn & brt pur	30	30

Victory Day Type, 1966

Wmk. 342

1966, Dec. 23 **Photo.** ***Perf. 11½***

No.	Type	Description	Unused	Used
N132	A290	10m ol & car rose	6	6

Arab Publicity Week Type, 1967

Perf. 11x11½

1967, Mar. 22 **Photo.** **Wmk. 342**

No.	Type	Description	Unused	Used
N133	A294	10m vio bl & brn	6	6

Labor Day Type, 1967

Perf. 11½x11

1967, May 1 **Photo.** **Wmk. 342**

No.	Type	Description	Unused	Used
N134	A296	10m ol & sep	6	6

OCCUPATION AIR POST STAMPS

Nos. C39-C50 Overprinted Type "b" in Black, Carmine or Red.

Perf. 13x13½

1948, May 15 **Wmk. 195**

No.	Type	Description	Unused	Used
NC1	AP3	2m red org (Bk)	15	15
NC2	AP3	3m dk brn (C)	15	15
NC3	AP3	5m red brn (Bk)	15	15
NC4	AP3	7m dp yel org (Bk)	15	15
NC5	AP3	8m grn (C)	15	15
NC6	AP3	10m violet	20	20
NC7	AP3	20m brt bl	35	35
NC8	AP3	30m brn vio (Bk)	50	50
NC9	AP3	40m car rose (Bk)	65	65
NC10	AP3	50m Prus grn	90	90
NC11	AP3	100m ol grn	1.50	1.50
NC12	AP3	200m dk gray	5.00	5.00
		Nos. NC1-NC12 (12)	9.85	9.85

Nos. NC1-NC12 Overprinted in Black with Three Bars to Obliterate Portrait

1953

No.	Type	Description	Unused	Used
NC13	AP3	2m red org	90	90
NC14	AP3	3m dk brn	15	15
NC15	AP3	5m red brn	3.50	3.50
NC16	AP3	7m dp yel org	50	50
NC17	AP3	8m green	75	75
NC18	AP3	10m violet	25	25
NC19	AP3	20m brt bl	60	60
NC20	AP3	30m brn vio	75	75
NC21	AP3	40m car rose	75	75
NC22	AP3	50m Prus grn	4.00	4.00
NC23	AP3	100m ol grn	20.00	20.00
NC24	AP3	200m dk gray	10.00	10.00
		Nos. NC13-NC24 (12)	42.15	42.15

Nos. NC1-NC3, NC6, NC10, NC11 with Additional Overprint in Various Colors Overprinted in Black with Three Bars to Obliterate Portrait

ملك مصر والسودان
١٦ اكتوبر سنة ١٩٥١

No.	Type	Description	Unused	Used
NC25	AP3	2m red org (Bk + Bl)	15	15
NC26	AP3	3m dk brn (Bk + RV)	2.50	2.50
NC27	AP3	5m red brn (Bk)	15	10
NC28	AP3	10m vio (R + G)	5.00	5.00
NC29	AP3	50m Prus grn (R + RV)	3.25	3.25
NC30	AP3	100m ol grn (R + Bk)	15.00	15.00
		Nos. NC25-NC30 (6)	26.05	26.00

Nos. C65-C66 Overprinted Type "b" in Black or Red

1955 **Wmk. 195** ***Perf. 13x13½***

No.	Type	Description	Unused	Used
NC31	AP4	5m red brn	90	90
NC32	AP4	15m ol grn (R)	1.25	1.25

United Arab Republic

"PALESTINE" Added in Arabic and English to Air Post Stamps.

Type of 1963

Perf. 11½x11

1963, Oct. 24 **Photo.** **Wmk. 342**

No.	Type	Description	Unused	Used
NC33	AP6	80m blk & brt bl	1.25	75
NC34	AP10	115m blk & yel	1.75	1.00
NC35	AP10	140m bl, ultra & org red	2.25	1.25

Cairo Tower Type, 1964

1964, Nov. 2 **Unwmk.** ***Perf. 11x11½***

No.	Type	Description	Unused	Used
NC36	AP11	50m dl vio & lt bl	50	50

World Meteorological Day Type

1965, Mar. 23 **Wmk. 342** ***Perf. 11***

No.	Type	Description	Unused	Used
NC37	AP12	80m dk bl & org	1.00	1.00

Type of Regular Issue, 1965 (Game Board)

1965, July 1 **Photo.** ***Perf. 11***

No.	Type	Description	Unused	Used
NC38	AP13	10m brn org & brt grn	45	45

OCCUPATION SPECIAL DELIVERY STAMP

No. E4 Overprinted Type "b" in Carmine.

1948 **Wmk. 195** ***Perf. 13x13½***

No.	Type	Description	Unused	Used
NE1	SD1	40m dl brn & pale gray	1.50	1.50

OCCUPATION POSTAGE DUE STAMPS

Postage Due Stamps of Egypt, 1927-41, Overprinted Type "a" in Black or Rose.

1948 Wmk. 195 *Perf. 13x13½.*

NJ1	D7	2m orange	15	15
NJ2	D7	4m grn (R)	15	15
NJ3	D7	6m gray grn	20	20
NJ4	D7	8m brn vio	30	30
NJ5	D7	10m brick red	30	30
NJ6	D7	12m rose lake	45	45

Overprinted Type "b" in Red.

Perf. 14.

Size: 22x28mm.

NJ7	D7	30m purple	1.10	1.10
		Nos. NJ1-NJ7 (7)	2.65	2.65

ELOBEY, ANNOBON AND CORISCO

LOCATION — A group of islands near the Guinea Coast of western Africa

GOVT. — Spanish colonial possessions administered as part of the Continental Guinea District. A second district under the same governor-general included Fernando Po.

AREA — 13¾ sq. mi.

POP. — 2,950 (estimated 1910)

CAPITAL — Santa Isabel

100 Centimos = 1 Peseta

King Alfonso XIII — A1

1903 Unwmk. Typo. *Perf. 14*

Control Numbers on Back

1	A1	¼c carmine	55	25
2	A1	½c dk vio	55	25
3	A1	1c black	55	25
4	A1	2c red	55	25
5	A1	3c dk grn	55	25
6	A1	4c dk bl grn	55	25
7	A1	5c violet	55	25
8	A1	10c rose lake	1.10	75
9	A1	15c org buff	3.25	75
10	A1	25c dk bl	5.50	2.25
11	A1	50c red brn	7.75	3.50
12	A1	75c blk brn	7.75	4.50
13	A1	1p org red	11.50	6.50
14	A1	2p chocolate	30.00	17.50
15	A1	3p dp ol grn	45.00	22.50
16	A1	4p claret	90.00	32.50
17	A1	5p bl grn	110.00	32.50
18	A1	10p dl bl	200.00	47.50
		Nos. 1-18 (18)	515.70	172.50

Same as A1, Dated "1905".

1905 Control Numbers on Back

19	A1	1c carmine	1.00	30
20	A1	2c dp vio	4.50	30
21	A1	3c black	1.00	30
22	A1	4c dl red	1.00	30
23	A1	5c dp grn	1.00	30
24	A1	10c bl grn	3.50	45
25	A1	15c violet	4.50	2.00
26	A1	25c rose lake	4.50	2.00
27	A1	50c org buff	8.00	2.75
28	A1	75c dk bl	8.00	2.75
29	A1	1p red brn	16.00	6.50
30	A1	2p blk brn	17.50	9.00
31	A1	3p org red	17.50	9.00
32	A1	4p dk brn	120.00	37.50
33	A1	5p brnz grn	120.00	37.50
34	A1	10p claret	325.00	110.00
		Nos. 19-34 (16)	653.00	220.95

Nos. 19-22 Surcharged in Black or Red

1906

35	A1	10c on 1c rose (Bk)	9.00	6.75
	a.	Inverted surcharge	9.00	6.75
	b.	Value omitted	32.50	17.50
	c.	Frame omitted	17.00	8.00
	d.	Double surcharge	9.00	6.75
	e.	Surcharged "15 cents"	32.50	17.50
	f.	Surcharged "25 cents"	50.00	25.00
	g.	Surcharged "50 cents"	50.00	25.00
	h.	"1906" omitted	17.50	8.00
36	A1	15c on 2c dp vio (R)	9.00	6.75
	a.	Frame omitted	12.00	6.50
	b.	Surcharged "25 cents"	17.00	10.00
	c.	Inverted surcharge	9.00	6.75
	d.	Double surcharge	9.00	6.75
36E	A1	15c on 2c dp vio (Bk)	17.00	10.00
37	A1	25c on 3c blk (R)	9.00	6.75
	a.	Inverted surcharge	9.00	6.75
	b.	Double surcharge	9.00	6.75
	c.	Surcharged "15 cents"	17.00	10.00
	d.	Surcharged "50 cents"	25.00	12.00
37E	A1	25c on 3c blk (Bk)	17.00	10.00
	f.	Inverted surcharge	17.00	10.00
	g.	Surcharged "15 cents"	17.00	11.50
	h.	Surcharged "10 cents"	25.00	11.00
38	A1	50c on 4c red (Bk)	9.00	6.75
	a.	Inverted surcharge	9.00	6.75
	b.	Value omitted	40.00	20.00
	c.	Frame omitted	17.50	8.50
	e.	Double surcharge	9.00	6.75
	f.	"1906" omitted	17.50	8.50
	g.	Surcharged "10 cents"	35.00	17.50
	h.	Surcharged "25 cents"	35.00	17.50
		Nos. 35-38 (6)	70.00	47.00

Eight other surcharges were prepared but not issued: 10c on 50c, 75c, 1p, 2p and 3p; 15c on 50c and 5p; 50c on 5c.

King Alfonso XIII — A2

1907 Control Numbers on Back

39	A2	1c dk vio	50	40
40	A2	2c black	50	40
41	A2	3c red org	50	40
42	A2	4c dk grn	50	40
43	A2	5c bl grn	50	40
44	A2	10c violet	4.25	2.25
45	A2	15c carmine	1.50	75
46	A2	25c orange	1.50	75
47	A2	50c blue	1.50	75
48	A2	75c brown	4.50	1.25
49	A2	1p blk brn	7.50	2.25
50	A2	2p org red	11.00	3.75
51	A2	3p dk brn	10.00	3.75
52	A2	4p brnz grn	11.00	3.25
53	A2	5p claret	15.00	3.75
54	A2	10p rose	37.50	11.00
		Nos. 39-54 (16)	107.75	35.50

Stamps of 1907 Surcharged

HABILITADO
PARA
05CTMS

1908-09 Black Surcharge

55	A2	5c on 3c red org ('09)	3.25	1.50
56	A2	5c on 4c dk grn ('09)	3.25	1.50
57	A2	5c on 10c vio	6.75	6.00
58	A2	25c on 10c vio	32.50	17.00

1910 Red Surcharge

59	A2	5c on 1c dk vio	3.25	1.50
60	A2	5c on 2c blk	3.25	1.50

Nos. 55-60 exist with surcharge inverted (price each $10 unused, $7.50 used); with double surcharge, one black, one red (price $15 each); with "PARA" omitted (price each $15 unused, $7.50 used).

The same 5c surcharge was also applied to Nos. 45-54, but these were not issued. Price $10 each.

In 1909, stamps of Spanish Guinea replaced those of Elobey, Annobon and Corisco.

1909
CORREOS
10 cen de peseta

Revenue stamps surcharged as above were unauthorized although some were postally used.

EPIRUS

LOCATION — Southeastern Europe comprising parts of Greece and Albania.

This territory formerly belonged to Turkey but is now divided between Greece and Albania. The northern part of the Greek section, now a part of Albania, set up a provisional government during 1912-13 and issued postage stamps but it collapsed in 1916, following Greek occupation. The name "Epirus" is taken from the Greek word meaning "Mainland."

100 Lepta = 1 Drachma

Chimarra Issue.

Double-headed Eagle, Skull and Crossbones — A1

Handstamped

1914 (Feb.) Unwmk. *Imperf.*

Control Mark in Blue.

Without Gum

1	A1	1 l blk & bl		
2	A1	5 l bl & red		
3	A1	10 l red & blk		
4	A1	25 l bl & red		
		Nos. 1-4 (4)	400.00	360.00

All values exist without control mark. This mark is a solid blue oval, about 12x8mm., containing the colorless Greek letters "SP," the first two letters of Spiromilios, the Chimarra commander.

All four exist with value inverted and the 1, 5 and 10 l with value double.

Some students question the official character of this issue. Counterfeits are plentiful.

Provisional Government Issues

Infantryman with Rifle
A2 A3

Serrate Roulette 13½

1914 (March) Litho.

5	A2	1 l orange	50	50
6	A2	5 l green	50	50
7	A3	10 l carmine	50	50
8	A3	25 l dp bl	50	50
9	A2	50 l brown	1.10	1.10
10	A2	1d violet	3.50	3.50
11	A2	2d blue	16.00	16.00
12	A2	5d gray grn	22.50	19.00
		Nos. 5-12 (8)	45.10	41.60

Turkish stamps surcharged "Epirus Autonomous" and new values in Greek were on sale for a few days in Argyrokastron (Gjinokaster).

Flag of Epirus — A5

1914 (Aug.)

15	A5	1 l brn & bl	90	90
16	A5	5 l grn & bl	90	90
17	A5	10 l rose red & bl	90	90
18	A5	25 l dk bl & bl	1.00	1.00
19	A5	50 l vio & bl	1.25	1.25
20	A5	1d car & bl	6.00	6.00
21	A5	2d org & bl	1.25	1.25
22	A5	5d dk grn & bl	5.00	5.00
		Nos. 15-22 (8)	17.20	17.20

Koritsa Issue.

A7

1914

26	A7	25 l dk bl & bl	4.00	4.00
27	A7	50 l vio & bl	6.00	6.00

Chimarra Issue.

1911-23 Issues of Greece Overprinted

ΕΛΛΗΝΙΚΗ
1914
ΧΕΙΜΑΡΡΑ

1914 (Aug.)

34	A24	1 l green	*12.00*	*10.00*
35	A25	2 l carmine	*10.50*	*12.00*
36	A24	3 l vermilion	*14.00*	*16.00*
37	A26	5 l green	*22.00*	*20.00*
38	A24	10 l carmine	*26.00*	*17.00*
39	A25	20 l slate	*42.00*	*37.50*
40	A25	25 l blue	*55.00*	*50.00*
41	A26	50 l vio brn	*70.00*	*65.00*
		Nos. 34-41 (8)	251.50	227.50

The 2 l and 3 l are engraved stamps of the 1911-21 issue, the others are lithographed stamps of the 1912-23 issue.

Overprint reads: "Greek Chimarra 1914".

Stamps of this issue are with or without a black monogram (S.S., for S. Spiromilios) in manuscript. Counterfeits are plentiful.

Stamps of the following designs were not regularly issued for postal purposes in the opinion of the editors.

Three varieties, 1914

Six varieties, 1914

Seven varieties, 1914.

Fifteen varieties, 1914

Four varieties, 1920.

OCCUPATION STAMPS

Issued under Greek Occupation.

Greek Occupation Stamps of 1913 Overprinted Horizontally

Β. ΗΠΕΙΡΟΣ

Serrate Roulette 13½

1914-15			**Black Overprint**	**Unwmk.**	
N1	O1	1 l	brown	75	75
N2	O2	2 l	red	75	75
b.		2 l	rose	75	75
N4	O2	3 l	orange	75	75
N5	O1	5 l	green	1.00	75
N6	O1	10 l	rose red	2.00	1.00
N7	O1	20 l	violet	5.00	3.00
N8	O2	25 l	pale bl	4.00	3.00
N9	O1	30 l	gray grn	17.50	12.50
N10	O2	40 l	indigo	20.00	15.00
N11	O1	50 l	dk bl	22.50	17.50
N12	O2	1d	vio brn	75.00	75.00
			Nos. N1-N12 (11)	149.25	130.00

The overprint exists double on 4 denominations (1 l, 2 l red, 3 l and 1d); inverted on 7 (1 l, 2 l red, 3 l, 5 l, 10 l, 20 l and 1d). Prices twice or triple normal copies.

Red Overprint.

N1a	1 l brown	5.00
N2a	2 l red	5.00
N4a	3 l orange	5.00
N5a	5 l green	5.00

Nos. N1a-N5a were not issued. Exist canceled.

Regular Issues of Greece, 1911-23, Overprinted

Β. ΗΠΕΙΡΟΣ

On Issue of 1911-21

1916				**Engr.**	
N17	A24	3 l	vermilion	1.00	1.00
N18	A26	30 l	car rose	60.00	60.00
N19	A27	1d	ultra	50.00	45.00
N20	A27	2d	vermilion	80.00	80.00
N21	A27	3d	car rose	90.00	90.00
N22	A27	5d	ultra	325.00	325.00
a.			Double overprint	325.00	325.00
			Nos. N17-N22 (6)	606.00	601.00

On Issue of 1912-23.

1916				**Litho.**	
N23	A24	1 l	green	1.00	1.00
N24	A25	2 l	carmine	1.00	1.00
N25	A24	3 l	vermilion	1.10	1.10
N26	A26	5 l	green	1.25	1.25
N27	A24	10 l	carmine	2.25	2.25
N28	A25	20 l	slate	3.25	3.25
N29	A25	25 l	blue	5.00	5.00
N30	A26	30 l	rose	10.00	10.00
N31	A25	40 l	indigo	15.00	15.00
N32	A26	50 l	vio brn	17.50	17.50
			Nos. N23-N32 (10)	57.35	57.35

In each sheet there are two varieties in the overprint: the "I" in "Epirus" omitted and an inverted "L" in place of the first letter of the word.

Counterfeits exist of Nos. N1-N32.

Postage stamps issued in 1940-41, during Greek occupation, are listed under Greece.

EQUATORIAL GUINEA

LOCATION — Gulf of Guinea, West Africa
GOVT. — Republic
AREA — 10,832 sq. mi.
POP. — 310,000 (est. 1974)
CAPITAL — Malabo

The Spanish provinces Fernando Po and Rio Muni united and became independent as the Republic of Equatorial Guinea, Oct. 12, 1968.

100 Centimos = 1 Peseta
100 centimos = 1 ekuele, bipkwele is plural (1973)
100 centimes = 1 CFA franc (1985)

Clasped Hands and Laurel — A1

Pres. Francisco Macias Nguema — A2

Unwmk.

1968, Oct. 12			**Photo.**	***Perf. 13***	
1	A1	1p	dp bl, gold & sep	8	8
2	A1	1.50p	dk grn, gold & brn	8	8
3	A1	6p	cop red, gold & brn	20	10

Issued to commemorate the attainment of independence, Oct. 12, 1968.

1970, Jan. 27				***Perf. 13x12½***	
4	A2	50c	dl org, brn & crim	8	8
5	A2	1p	pink, grn & lil	8	8
6	A2	1.50p	pale ol, brn & bl grn	8	8
7	A2	2p	buff, grn & ol	10	8
8	A2	2.50p	pale grn, dk grn & dk bl	10	10
9	A2	10p	bis, Prus bl & vio brn	1.00	15
10	A2	25p	gray, blk & brn	1.75	25
			Nos. 4-10 (7)	3.19	82

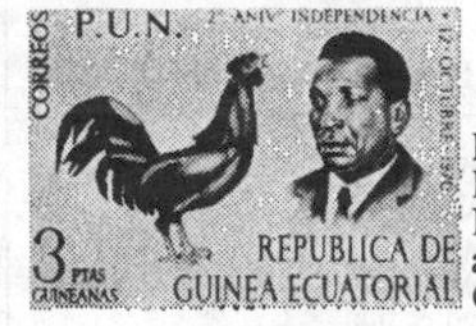

Pres. Macias Nguema and Cock — A3

1971, Apr.			**Photo.**	***Perf. 13***	
11	A3	3p	lt bl & multi	10	10
12	A3	5p	buff & multi	20	10
13	A3	10p	pale lil & multi	40	10
14	A3	25p	pale grn & multi	60	30

2nd anniversary of independence, Oct. 12, 1970.

Torch, Bow and Arrows — A4

1972			**Photo.**	***Perf. 11½***	
15	A4	50p	ocher & multi	1.75	65

"3rd Triumphal Year."

United Natl. Workers' Party Emblem — A5

1973			**Litho.**	***Perf. 13½x13***	
16	A5	1p	multi	10	8
17	A5	1.50p	multi	14	10
18	A5	2p	multi	18	12
19	A5	4p	multi	22	15
20	A5	5p	multi	35	24
			Nos. 16-20 (5)	99	69

Natl. Independence, 4th Anniv. — A6

Pres. Macias Nguena and: 1.50p, Agriculture. 2p, 4p, Education. 3p, 5p, Natl. defense.

1973				***Perf. 13½***	
21	A6	1.50p	multi	14	10
22	A6	2p	multi	18	12
23	A6	3p	multi	20	14
24	A6	4p	multi	22	15
25	A6	5p	multi	40	28
			Nos. 21-25 (5)	1.14	79

Natl. Independence, 5th Anniv. (in 1973) — A7

1979				***Perf. 13x13½***	
26	A7	1e	Ekuele coin	50	35

Natl. Independence, 5th Anniv. (in 1973) — A8

1979					
27	A8	1e	Port Bata	50	35
28	A8	1.50e	State Palace	75	50
29	A8	2e	Central Bank, Bata	1.00	68
30	A8	2.50e	Nguema Biyogo Bridge	1.25	85
31	A8	3e	Port, palace, bank, bridge	1.50	1.00
			Nos. 27-31 (5)	5.00	3.38

Pres. Nguema — A9

Independence Martyrs — A10

1979				***Perf. 13½x13***	
32	A9	1.50e	multi	75	50

United Natl. Workers's Party (PUNT), 3rd Congress.

1979					
33	A10	1e	Enrique Nvo	50	35
34	A10	1.50e	Salvador Ndongo Ekang	75	50
35	A10	2e	Acacio Mane	1.00	68

Agricultural Experiment Year — A11

1979				***Perf. 13x13½***	
36	A11	1e	multi	50	35
37	A11	1.50e	multi, diff.	75	50

Independence Martyrs — A12

Natl. Coat of Arms — A13

1981, Mar.			**Photo.**	***Perf. 13½x12½***	
38	A12	5b	Obiang Esono Nguema	10	8
39	A12	15b	Fernando Nvara Engonga	30	20
40	A12	25b	Ela Edjodjomo Mangue	50	35
41	A12	35b	Obiang Nguema Moasogo, president	70	48
42	A12	50b	Hipolito Micha Eworo	1.00	68
43	A13	100b	multi	2.00	1.35
			Nos. 38-43 (6)	4.60	3.14

Dated 1980.

Christmas 1980 A14

1981, Mar. 30				***Perf. 13½***	
44	A14	8b	Cathedral, infant	25	16
45	A14	25b	Bells, youth	75	50

Dated 1980.

Souvenir Sheet

Pres. Obiang Nguema Mbasogo — A15

1981, Aug. 30			**Litho.**	***Imperf.***	
46	A15	400b	multi	6.00	6.00

No. 46 has inscribed multicolored margin continuing the design and picturing natl. flag, black control number. Size: 140x110mm.

State Visit of King Juan Carlos of Spain — A16

Perf. 13x13½, 13½x13

1981, Nov. 30

47 A16 50b Government reception 68 45
48 A16 100b Arrival at airport 1.35 90
49 A16 150b King, Pres. Mbasogo, vert. 2.00 1.35

State Visit of Pope John Paul II — A17

1982, Feb. 18

50 A17 100b Papal and natl. arms
51 A17 200b Pres. Mbasogo greeting Pope
52 A17 300b Pope, vert.

Christmas 1981 A18

1982, Feb. 25 **Photo.**

53 A18 100b Carolers, vert. 1.75 1.20
54 A18 150b Magi, African youth 2.50 1.75

Dated 1981.

1982 World Cup Soccer Championships, Spain — A19

1982, June 13 ***Perf. 13½***

55 A19 40b Emblem 50 35
56 A19 60b Naranjito character trademark 75 50
57 A19 100b World Cup trophy 1.25 85
58 A19 200b Players, palm tree, emblem 2.50 1.75

Fauna A20

1983, Feb. 4 **Litho.**

59 A20 40b Gorilla 45 30
60 A20 60b Hippopotamus 70 48
61 A20 80b Atherurus africanus 95 65
62 A20 120b Felis pardus 1.40 95

Dated 1982.

Christmas 1982 A21

1983, Feb. 25 **Photo.**

63 A21 100b Stars 1.25 85
64 A21 200b King offering frankincense 2.25 1.50

Dated 1982.

World Communications Year — A22

1983, July 18 **Litho.**

65 A22 150b Postal runner 1.00 68
66 A22 200b Microwave station, drimmer 2.25 1.50

Banana Trees A23

1983, Oct. 8

67 A23 300b shown 2.50 1.75
68 A23 400b Forest, vert. 3.50 2.40

Christmas 1983 A24

1984

69 A24 80b Folk dancer, musical instruments 1.00 68
70 A24 100b Holy Family 1.25 85

Dated 1983.

Constitution of State Powers — A25

Scales of justice, fundamental lawbook and various maps.

1984, Feb. 15

71 A25 50b Annobon and Bioko 62 42
72 A25 100b Mainland regions 1.25 85

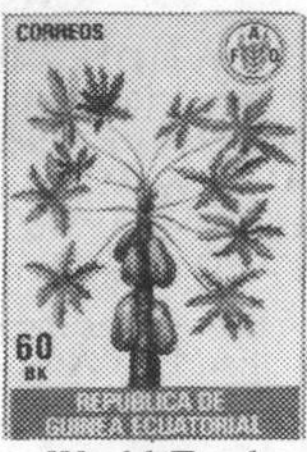

Turtle hunting, Rio Muni — A26

World Food Day — A27

1984, May 1

73 A26 125b Hunting Whales, horiz. 1.15 78
74 A26 150b shown 1.40 95

1984, Sept.

75 A27 60b Papaya 88 60
76 A27 80b Malanga 1.15 78

Abstract Wood-Carved Figurines and Art — A28

Designs: 25b, *Black Gazelle* and *Anxiety.* 30b, *Black Gazelle,* diff., and *Woman.* 60b, *Man and woman,* vert. 75b, *Poster,* vert. 100b, *Mother and Child,* vert. 150b, *Man and Woman,* diff., and *Bust of a Woman.*

1984, Nov. 15

77 A28 25b multi 25 16
78 A28 30b multi 30 20
79 A28 60b multi 60 40
80 A28 75b multi 75 50
81 A28 100b multi 1.00 68
82 A28 150b multi 1.50 1.00
Nos. 77-82 (6) 4.40 2.94

Christmas A29

1984, Dec. 24

83 A29 60b Mother and child, vert. 58 40
84 A29 100b Musical instruments 95 65

Immaculate Conception Missions, Cent. — A30

Designs: 50fr, Emblem, vert. 60fr, Map, nun and youths, vert. 80fr, First Guinean nuns. 125fr, Missionaries landing at Bata Beach, 1885.

1985, Apr. ***Perf. 14***

85 A30 50fr multi 28 29
86 A30 60fr multi 35 24
87 A30 80fr multi 45 30
88 A30 125fr multi 70 48

A little time given to the study of the arrangement of the Scott Catalogue can make it easier to use effectively.

Jose Mavule Ndjong, First Postmaster A31

1985, July ***Perf. 13½***

89 A31 50fr Postal emblem, vert. 48 32
90 A31 80fr shown 75 50

Equatorial Guinea Postal Service.

Christmas A32

1985, Dec.

91 A32 40fr Nativity 48 32
92 A32 70fr Folk band, dancers, mother and child 75 50

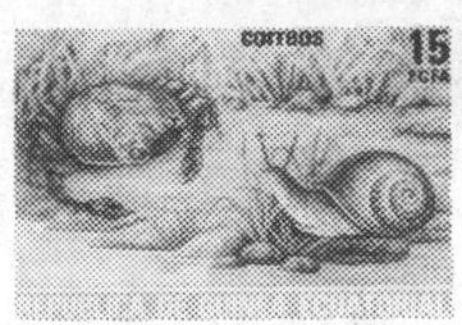

Nature Conservation — A33

1985

93 A33 15fr Crab, snail 10 8
94 A33 35fr Butterflies, bees, birds 22 14
95 A33 45fr Flowering plants 28 18
96 A33 65fr Spraying and harvesting cacao 40 28

Folklore — A34

1986 World Cup Soccer Championships, Mexico — A35

1986, Apr. 15

97 A34 10fr Ndowe dance, Mekuyo, horiz. 6 5
98 A34 50fr Fang dance, Mokom 30 20
99 A34 65fr Cacha Bubi, Bisila 40 28
100 A34 80fr Fang dance, Ndong-Mba 50 35

1986, June 25

Various soccer plays. Nos. 101-102 horiz.

101 A35 50fr multi 30 20
102 A35 100fr multi 60 40
103 A35 150fr multi 90 60
104 A35 200fr multi 1.20 90

Christmas — A36

Conference of the Union of Central African States — A37

1986, Dec. 12
105 A36 100fr Musical instruments, horiz. 60 40
106 A36 150fr Holy Family, lamb 90 60

1986, Dec. 29
107 A37 80fr Flags, map 50 35
108 A37 100fr Emblem, map, horiz. 60 40

Campaign Against Hunger A38

1987, June 5
109 A38 60fr Chicken 35 24
110 A38 80fr Fish 50 35
111 A38 100fr Wheat 60 40

Intl. Peace Year A39

1987, July 15 Litho. *Perf. 13½*
112 A39 100fr shown 75 50
113 A39 200fr Hands holding dove 1.50 1.00

Stamp Day 1987 — A40

1987, Oct. 5 Litho. *Perf. 13½*
114 A40 150fr shown 1.05 70
115 A40 300fr posting envelope 2.15 1.45

SPECIAL DELIVERY STAMPS

Archer with Crossbow — SD1

1971, Oct. 12 Photo. *Perf. 12½x13*
E1 SD1 4p bl & multi 15 10
E2 SD1 8p rose & multi 25 10

3rd anniversary of independence.

ERITREA

LOCATION — In northeast Africa, bordering on the Red Sea
GOVT. — Former Italian Colony
AREA — 15,754 sq. mi. (1936)
POP. — 600,573 (1931)
CAPITAL — Asmara

Eritrea was incorporated as a State of Italian East Africa in 1936.

100 Centesimi = 1 Lira

Stamps of Italy Overprinted

Colonia Eritrea
a

b

Wmk.140

1892 Wmk. Crown (140) *Perf. 14.*
Overprinted Type "a" in Black.
1 A6 1c brnz grn 1.50 90
a. Invtd. overprint 185.00 130.00
b. Double ovpt. 400.00
2 A7 2c org brn 55 45
a. Invtd. overprint 300.00 185.00
b. Double ovpt. 400.00
3 A33 5c green 19.00 1.65
a. Invtd. overprint 2,750. 1,250.

Overprinted Type "b" in Black.
4 A17 10c claret 7.50 1.25
5 A17 20c orange 47.50 1.25
6 A17 25c blue 150.00 6.75
7 A25 40c brown 3.00 3.25
8 A26 45c sl grn 3.25 4.75
9 A27 60c violet 3.25 5.50
10 A28 1 l brn & yel 5.50 7.50
11 A38 5 l bl & rose 120.00 62.50

1895-99
Overprinted type "a" in Black.
12 A39 1c brn ('99) 3.00 4.50
13 A40 2c org brn ('99) 45 75
14 A41 5c green 45 60
a. Inverted ovpt. 300.00 850.00

Overprinted type "b" in Black.
15 A34 10c cl ('98) 55 75
16 A35 20c orange 75 80
17 A36 25c blue 95 1.25
18 A37 45c ol grn 3.00 6.25

1903-28
Overprinted type "a" in Black.
19 A42 1c brown 15 45
a. Inverted ovpt. 26.00 45.00
20 A43 2c org brn 15 38
21 A44 5c bl grn 12.00 45
22 A45 10c claret 16.00 45
23 A45 20c orange 38 45
24 A45 25c blue 82.50 4.50
a. Double ovpt. 110.00 110.00
25 A45 40c brown 67.50 6.75
26 A45 45c ol grn 75 3.25
27 A45 50c violet 37.50 4.25
28 A46 75c dk red & rose ('28) 9.00 4.50
29 A46 1 l brn & grn 75 38
30 A46 1.25 l bl & ultra ('28) 7.50 3.00
31 A46 2 l dk grn & org ('25) 10.50 26.00
32 A46 2.50 l dk grn & org ('28) 26.00 16.00
33 A46 5 l bl & rose 9.00 5.50
Nos. 19-33 (15) 279.68 76.31

Surcharged in Black

Colonia Eritrea
C. 15

1905
34 A45 15c on 20c org 7.50 1.25

1908-28
Overprinted type "a" in Black
35 A48 5c green 30 22
36 A48 10c cl ('09) 30 22
37 A48 15c sl ('20) 2.50 1.50
38 A49 20c grn ('25) 2.25 3.75
39 A49 20c lil brn ('28) 2.25 3.25
40 A49 25c bl ('09) 90 65
41 A49 30c gray ('25) 2.25 3.75
42 A49 40c brn ('16) 11.00 19.00
43 A49 50c vio ('16) 75 75
44 A49 60c brn car ('18) 5.50 6.75
45 A49 60c brn org ('28) 22.50 62.50
46 A51 10 gray grn & red 1 ('16) 92.50 250.00
Nos. 35-46 (12) 143.00 352.34

See also No. 53.

Government Building at Massaua
A1 A2

1910-29 Unwmk. Engr. *Perf. 13½*
47 A1 15c slate 42.50 4.00
a. Perf. 11 ('29) 26.00 16.00
48 A2 25c dk bl 1.10 1.50
a. Perf. 12

Farmer Plowing
A3 A4

1914-28
49 A3 5c green 38 38
a. Perf. 11 ('28) 100.00 20.00
50 A4 10c carmine 1.10 1.50
a. Perf. 11 ('28) 19.00 16.00
b. Perf. 13½x14 15.00 30.00

No. 47 Surcharged in Red or Black

Cent. 5

CENT. 20

1916
51 A1 5c on 15c sl (R) 2.25 6.75
52 A1 20c on 15c sl 75 75
a. "CEN" for "CENT" 11.00 22.50
b. "CENT" omitted 45.00 90.00
c. "ENT" 15.00 30.00

Italy No. 113 Overprinted in Black — f ERITREA

1921 Wmk. 140 *Perf. 14.*
53 A50 20c brn org 1.25 4.50

Victory Issue.
Italian Victory Stamps of 1921 Overprinted type "f" 13mm. long.

1922
54 A64 5c ol grn 55 2.25
55 A64 10c red 55 2.25
56 A64 15c sl grn 75 3.75
57 A64 25c ultra 75 3.00

Somalia Nos. 10-16 Overprinted in Black and Bars over Original Values, — g ERITREA

1922 Wmk. 140
58 A1 2c on 1b brn 2.50 5.50
59 A1 5c on 2b bl grn 2.50 3.75
60 A2 10c on 1a cl 2.50 75
61 A2 15c on 2a brn org 2.50 90
62 A2 25c on 2½a bl 2.50 90
63 A2 50c on 5a yel 3.25 2.25
a. "ERITREA" double 375.00
64 A2 1 l on 10a lil 4.00 5.75
a. "ERITREA" double 225.00 300.00
Nos. 58-64 (7) 19.75 19.80

See Nos. 81-87.

Propagation of the Faith Issue.
Italy Nos. 143-146 Overprinted ERITREA

1923
65 A68 20c ol grn & brn org 1.65 8.25
66 A68 30c cl & brn org 1.65 8.25
67 A68 50c vio & brn org 1.25 6.75
68 A68 1 l bl & brn org 1.25 6.75

Fascisti Issue.
Italy Nos. 159-164 Overprinted in Red or Black — j ERITREA

1923 Unwmk. *Perf. 14*
69 A69 10c dk grn (R) 1.50 6.75
70 A69 30c dk vio (R) 1.50 6.75
71 A69 50c brn car 1.50 6.75
Wmk. 140
72 A70 1 l blue 1.50 6.75
73 A70 2 l brown 1.50 6.75
74 A71 5 l blk & bl (R) 1.50 11.50
Nos. 69-74 (6) 9.00 45.25

Manzoni Issue.
Italy Nos. 165-170 Overprinted in Red. ERITREA

1924 *Perf. 14.*
75 A72 10c brn red & blk 75 7.50
76 A72 15c bl grn & blk 75 7.50
77 A72 30c blk & sl 75 7.50
78 A72 50c org brn & blk 75 7.50
79 A72 1 l bl & blk 12.00 82.50
80 A72 5 l vio & blk 275.00 1,200.
Nos. 75-79 (5) 15.00 112.50

On Nos. 79 and 80 the overprint is placed vertically at the left side.

Somalia Nos. 10-16 Overprinted type "g" in Blue or Red.

1924
Bars over Original Values.
81 A1 2c on 1b brn 6.00 15.00
82 A1 5c on 2b bl grn (R) 3.75 9.00
83 A2 10c on 1a rose red 2.25 4.50
84 A2 15c on 2a brn org 2.25 4.50
a. Pair, one without "ERITREA" 550.00
85 A2 25c on 2½a bl (R) 2.25 4.50
a. Double surch. 225.00
86 A2 50c on 5a yel 3.75 8.25
87 A2 1 l on 10a lil (R) 4.00 10.50
Nos. 81-87 (7) 24.25 56.25

Stamps of Italy, 1901-08 Overprinted type "j" in Black.

1924
88 A42 1c brown 1.50 3.75
a. Inverted ovpt. 110.00
89 A43 2c org brn 1.10 3.75
90 A48 5c green 1.90 3.75

Victor Emmanuel Issue.
Italy Nos. 175-177 Overprinted — k ERITREA

1925-26 Unwmk. *Perf. 11*
91 A78 60c brn car 25 2.25
a. Perf. 13½ 1.90 11.00
92 A78 1 l dk bl 30 2.25
a. Perf. 13½ 6,750. 1,400.
Perf. 13½
93 A78 1.25l dk bl ('26) 75 10.00
a. Perf. 11 1.25 10.00

Saint Francis of Assisi Issue.
Italian Stamps of 1926 Overprinted ERITREA

1926 Wmk. 140 *Perf. 14*
94 A79 20c gray grn 90 4.50
95 A80 40c dk vio 90 4.50
96 A81 60c red vio 90 4.50

Overprinted in Red **Eritrea**

Unwmk. *Perf. 11*
97 A82 1.25 l dk bl 90 4.50

		Perf. 14		
98	A83	5 l + 2.50 l ol grn	2.25	*8.00*
		Nos. 94-98 (5)	5.85	26.00

Italian Stamps of 1926 Overprinted type "f" in Black.

1926 **Wmk. 140** ***Perf. 14.***

99	A46	75c dk red & rose	11.00	5.25
a.		Double ovpt.	125.00	
100	A46	1.25 l bl & ultra	7.50	2.25
101	A46	2.50 l dk grn & org	26.00	15.00

Volta Issue.

Type of Italy, 1927, Overprinted — o   Eritrea

1927

102	A84	20c purple	3.00	*11.00*
103	A84	50c dp org	3.75	*7.50*
a.		Double overprint	19.00	
104	A84	1.25 l brt bl	4.50	*11.00*

Italian Stamps of 1925-28 Overprinted type "a" in Black.

1928-29

105	A86	7½c lt brn ('29)	5.50	*19.00*
106	A86	50c brt vio	11.00	15.00

Italian Stamps of 1927-28 Overprinted type "f."

1928-29

107	A86	50c brt vio	13.00	*22.50*
		Unwmk. ***Perf. 11.***		
107A	A85	1.75 l dp brn	9.00	7.50

Italy No. 192 Overprinted type "o."

1928 **Wmk. 140** ***Perf. 14***

108	A85	50c brn & sl	3.75	1.50

Monte Cassino Issue.

Types of 1929 Issue of Italy Overprinted in Red or Blue   ERITREA

1929 ***Perf. 14.***

109	A96	20c dk grn (R)	1.65	*7.50*
110	A96	25c red org (Bl)	1.65	*7.50*
111	A98	50c + 10c crim (Bl)	1.65	*11.00*
112	A98	75c + 15c ol brn (R)	1.65	*11.00*
113	A96	1.25 l + 25c dl vio (R)	3.25	*11.00*
114	A98	5 l + 1 l saph (R)	3.25	*11.00*

Overprinted in Red   **Eritrea**

Unwmk.

115	A100	10 l + 2 l gray brn	3.25	*15.00*
		Nos. 109-115 (7)	16.35	74.00

Royal Wedding Issue.

Type of Italian Stamps of 1930 Overprinted   ERITREA

1930 **Wmk. 140**

116	A101	20c yel grn	75	*3.00*
117	A101	50c + 10c dp org	55	*3.75*
118	A101	1.25 l + 25c rose red	55	*4.50*

Lancer — A5

Scene in Massaua A6

Designs: 2c, 35c, Lancer. 5c, 10c, Postman. 15c, Lineman. 25c, Askari (infantryman). 2 l, Railroad viaduct. 5 l, Asmara Deghe Selam. 10 l, Camels.

1930 **Wmk. 140** **Litho.** ***Perf. 14***

119	A5	2c brt bl & blk	55	*1.50*
120	A5	5c dk vio & blk	75	65
121	A5	10c yel brn & blk	75	38
122	A5	15c dk grn & blk	75	55
123	A5	25c gray grn & blk	75	38
124	A5	35c red brn & blk	2.25	*4.50*
125	A6	1 l dk bl & blk	90	22
126	A6	2 l choc & blk	1.75	*4.50*
127	A6	5 l ol grn & blk	3.00	*7.50*
128	A6	10 l dl bl & blk	3.25	*10.00*
		Nos. 119-128 (10)	14.70	30.18

Ferrucci Issue.

Types of Italian Stamps of 1930 Overprinted type "f" in Red or Blue.

1930

129	A102	20c vio (R)	55	*2.25*
130	A103	25c dk grn (R)	55	*2.25*
131	A103	50c blk (R)	55	*2.25*
132	A103	1.25 l dp bl (R)	55	*2.25*
133	A104	5 l + 2 l dp car (Bl)	2.25	*4.50*
		Nos. 129-133 (5)	4.45	13.50

Virgil Issue.

Types of Italian Stamps of 1930 Overprinted in Red or Blue

ERITREA

1930 **Photo.**

134	A106	15c vio blk	38	*2.25*
135	A106	20c org brn	38	*2.25*
136	A106	25c dk grn	38	*1.90*
137	A106	30c lt brn	38	*2.25*
138	A106	50c dl vio	38	*1.90*
139	A106	75c rose red	38	*2.25*
140	A106	1.25 l gray bl	38	*2.25*
		Unwmk. **Engr.**		
141	A106	5 l + 1.50 l dk vio	2.00	*9.00*
142	A106	10 l + 2.50 l ol brn	2.00	*9.00*
		Nos. 134-142 (9)	6.66	33.05

Saint Anthony of Padua Issue.

Types of Italian Stamps of 1931 Overprinted type "f" in Blue, Red or Black

1931 **Photo.** **Wmk. 140**

143	A116	20c brn (Bl)	75	*3.25*
144	A116	25c grn (R)	75	*3.25*
145	A118	30c gray brn (Bl)	75	*3.25*
146	A118	50c dl vio (Bl)	75	*2.25*
147	A120	1.25 l sl bl (R)	75	*3.25*
		Unwmk. **Engr.**		
148	A121	75c blk (R)	75	*3.25*
149	A122	5 l + 2.50 l dk brn (Bk)	2.25	*11.00*
		Nos. 143-149 (7)	6.75	29.50

King Victor Emmanuel III — A13

1931 **Photo.** **Wmk. 140**

150	A13	7½c ol brn	38	75
151	A13	20c sl bl & car	30	12
152	A13	30c ol grn & brn vio	38	12
153	A13	40c bl & yel grn	30	12
154	A13	50c bis brn & ol	15	12
155	A13	75c car rose	75	18
156	A13	1.25 l vio & ind	90	12
157	A13	2.50 l dl grn	1.25	90
		Nos. 150-157 (8)	4.41	2.43

Camel A14

Temple Ruins — A18

Designs: 2c, 10, Camel. 5c, 15c, Shark fishery. 25c, Baobab tree. 35c, Pastoral scene. 2 l, African elephant. 5 l, Eritrean man. 10 l, Eritrean woman.

1934 **Photo.** **Wmk. 140**

158	A14	2c dp bl	45	90
159	A14	5c black	55	55
160	A14	10c brown	75	38
161	A14	15c org brn	90	80
162	A14	25c gray grn	55	25
163	A14	35c purple	1.65	3.25
164	A18	1 l dk bl gray	25	12
165	A14	2 l ol blk	4.50	1.10
166	A18	5 l car rose	2.50	1.50
167	A18	10 l red org	3.25	2.00
		Nos. 158-167 (10)	15.35	10.85

Abruzzi Issue.

Types of 1934 Issue Overprinted in Black or Red   ONORANZE AL DUCA DEGLI ABRUZZI

1934

168	A14	10c dl bl (R)	3.00	*11.00*
169	A14	15c blue	3.00	*11.00*
170	A14	35c grn (R)	1.90	*11.00*
171	A18	1 l cop red	1.90	*11.00*
172	A14	2 l rose red	4.50	*11.00*
173	A18	5 l pur (R)	2.25	*11.00*
174	A18	10 l ol grn (R)	2.25	*11.00*
		Nos. 168-174 (7)	18.80	77.00

Grant's Gazelle A22

1934 **Photo.**

175	A22	5c ol grn & brn	1.65	*6.25*
176	A22	10c yel brn & blk	1.65	*6.25*
177	A22	20c scar & ind	1.65	*6.25*
178	A22	50c dk vio & brn	1.65	*6.25*
179	A22	60c org brn & ind	1.65	*6.25*
180	A22	1.25 l dk bl & grn	1.65	*6.25*
		Nos. 175-180 (6)	9.90	37.50

Second Colonial Arts Exhibition, Naples. See also Nos. C1-C6.

SEMI-POSTAL STAMPS

Many issues of Italy and Italian Colonies include one or more semipostal denominations. To avoid splitting sets, these issues are generally listed as regular postage, airmail, etc., unless all values carry a surtax.

Italy Nos. B1-B3 Overprinted type "f."

1915-16 **Wmk. 140** ***Perf. 14.***

B1	SP1	10c + 5c rose	1.50	*3.25*
a.		"EPITREA"	9.00	13.00
b.		Inverted ovpt.	130.00	185.00
B2	SP2	15c + 5c sl	3.75	*9.00*
B3	SP2	20c + 5c org	2.25	*4.75*
a.		"EPITREA"	13.00	21.00
b.		Inverted overprint	75.00	110.00
c.		Pair, one without ovpt.		*925.00*

No. B2 Surcharged   **20**

1916

B4	SP2	20c on 15c+5c sl	3.75	*9.00*
a.		"EPITREA"	22.50	32.50
b.		Pair, one without overprint	200.00	

Counterfeits exist of the minor varieties of Nos. B1, B3-B4.

Holy Year Issue.

Italy Nos. B20-B25 Overprinted in Black or Red

ERITREA

1925 ***Perf. 12***

B5	SP4	20c + 10c dk grn & brn	1.00	*4.50*
B6	SP4	30c + 15c dk brn & brn	1.00	*4.50*
a.		Double overprint		
B7	SP4	50c + 25c vio & brn	1.00	*4.50*
B8	SP4	60c + 30c dp rose & brn	1.00	*4.50*
a.		Inverted overprint		
B9	SP8	1 l + 50c dp bl & vio (R)	1.00	*4.50*
B10	SP8	5 l + 2.50 l org brn & vio (R)	1.00	*4.50*
		Nos. B5-B10 (6)	6.00	27.00

Colonial Institute Issue.

"Peace" Substituting Spade for Sword — SP1

1926 **Typo.** ***Perf. 14***

B11	SP1	5c + 5c brn	25	*2.50*
B12	SP1	10c + 5c ol grn	25	*2.50*
B13	SP1	20c + 5c bl grn	25	*2.50*
B14	SP1	40c + 5c brn red	25	*2.50*
B15	SP1	60c + 5c org	25	*2.50*
B16	SP1	1 l + 5c bl	25	*2.50*
		Nos. B11-B16 (6)	1.50	15.00

The surtax of 5c on each stamp was for the Italian Colonial Institute.

Types of Italian Semi-Postal Stamps of 1926 Overprinted type "k."

1927 **Unwmk.** ***Perf. 11½***

B17	SP10	40c + 20c dk brn & blk	1.00	*5.25*
B18	SP10	60c + 30c brn red & ol brn	1.00	*5.25*
B19	SP10	1.25 l + 60c dp bl & blk	1.00	*5.25*
B20	SP10	5 l + 2.50 l dk grn & blk	1.50	*6.75*

The surtax on these stamps was for the charitable work of the Voluntary Militia for Italian National Defense.

Fascism and Victory — SP2

1928 **Wmk. 140** **Typo.** ***Perf. 14.***

B21	SP2	20c + 5c bl grn	75	*3.75*
B22	SP2	30c + 5c red	75	*3.75*
B23	SP2	50c + 10c pur	75	*3.75*
B24	SP2	1.25 l + 20c dk bl	75	*3.75*

The surtax was for the Society Africana d'Italia, whose 46th anniversary was commemorated by the issue.

Types of Italian Semi-Postal Stamps of 1928 Overprinted type "f."

1929 **Unwmk.** ***Perf. 11.***

B25	SP10	30c + 10c red & blk	1.25	*5.50*
B26	SP10	50c + 20c vio & blk	1.25	*5.50*
B27	SP10	1.25 l + 50c brn & bl	1.50	*7.50*
B28	SP10	5 l + 2 l ol grn & blk	1.50	*7.50*

The surtax was for the charitable work of the Voluntary Militia for Italian National Defense.

Types of Italian Semi-Postal Stamps of 1929 Overprinted type "f" in Black or Red.

1930 ***Perf. 14.***

B29	SP10	30c + 10c dk grn & bl grn (Bk)	4.00	*15.00*
B30	SP10	50c + 10c dk grn & vio (R)	4.00	*15.00*
B31	SP10	1.25 l + 30c ol brn & red brn (R)	4.00	*15.00*

B32 SP10 5 l + 1.50 l ind & grn (R) 12.00 *47.50*

The surtax was for the charitable work of the Voluntary Militia for Italian National Defense.

Agriculture — SP3

1930 Photo. Wmk. 140
B33 SP3 50c + 20c ol brn 1.10 *6.00*
B34 SP3 1.25 l + 20c dp bl 1.10 *6.00*
B35 SP3 1.75 l + 20c grn 1.10 *6.00*
B36 SP3 2.55 l + 50c pur 1.65 *6.00*
B37 SP3 5 l + 1 l dp car 1.65 *6.00*
Nos. B33-37 (5) 6.60 30.00

Italian Colonial Agricultural Institute, 25th anniversary. The surtax aided that institution.

AIR POST STAMPS

Desert Scene — AP1

Design: 80c, 1 l, 2 l, Plane and globe.

Wmk. Crowns. (140)

1934 Photo. Perf. 14.
C1 AP1 25c sl bl & org red 1.65 *6.25*
C2 AP1 50c grn & ind 1.65 *6.25*
C3 AP1 75c brn & org red 1.65 *6.25*
C4 AP1 80c org brn & ol grn 1.65 *6.25*
C5 AP1 1 l scar & ol grn 1.65 *6.25*
C6 AP1 2 l dk bl & brn 1.65 *6.25*
Nos. C1-C6 (6) 9.90 37.50

Second Colonial Arts Exhibition, Naples.

Plowing AP3

Plane and Cacti — AP6

Designs: 25c, 1.50 l, Plowing. 50c, 2 l, Plane over mountain pass. 60c, 5 l, Plane and trees. 75c, 10 l, Plane and cacti. 1 l, 3 l, Bridge.

1936 Photo.
C7 AP3 25c dp grn 75 1.50
C8 AP3 50c dk brn 45 30
C9 AP3 60c brn org 1.10 3.75
C10 AP6 75c org brn 90 75
C11 AP3 1 l dp bl 22 12
C12 AP3 1.50 l purple 65 40
C13 AP3 2 l gray bl 90 75
C14 AP3 3 l cop red 7.50 6.75
C15 AP3 5 l green 3.75 1.25
C16 AP6 10 l rose red 10.00 2.25
Nos. C7-C16 (10) 26.22 17.82

AIR POST SEMI-POSTAL STAMPS

King Victor Emmanuel III SPAP1

1934 Wmk. 140 Photo. Perf. 14
CB1 SPAP1 25c + 10c gray grn 1.90 1.90
CB2 SPAP1 50c + 10c brn 1.90 1.90
CB3 SPAP1 75c + 15c rose red 1.90 1.90
CB4 SPAP1 80c + 15c blk brn 1.90 1.90
CB5 SPAP1 1 l + 20c red brn 1.90 1.90
CB6 SPAP1 2 l + 20c brt bl 1.90 1.90
CB7 SPAP1 3 l + 25c pur 17.50 17.50
CB8 SPAP1 5 l + 25c org 17.50 17.50
CB9 SPAP1 10 l + 30c dp vio 17.50 17.50
CB10 SPAP1 25 l + 2 l dp grn 17.50 17.50
Nos. CB1-CB10 (10) 81.40 81.40

Issued in commemoration of the 65th birthday of King Victor Emmanuel III and the nonstop flight from Rome to Mogadiscio. Used prices are for stamps canceled to order.

AIR POST SEMI-POSTAL OFFICIAL STAMP

Type of Air Post Semi-Postal Stamps, 1934, Overprinted Crown and "SERVIZIO DI STATO" in Black.

1934 Wmk. 140 Perf. 14.
CBO1 SPAP1 25 l + 2 l cop red *1,400.*

SPECIAL DELIVERY STAMPS

Special Delivery Stamps of Italy, Overprinted type "a."

1907 Wmk. 140 Perf. 14
E1 SD1 25c rose red 5.50 5.50
a. Double ovpt.

1909
E2 SD2 30c bl & rose 30.00 *62.50*

1920
E3 SD1 50c dl red 1.90 5.50

"Italia" SD1

1924 Engr. Unwmk.
E4 SD1 60c dk red & brn 3.25 *7.50*
a. Perf. 13½ 9.00 *19.00*
E5 SD1 2 l dk bl & red 4.00 *11.00*

Nos. E4 and E5 Surcharged in Dark Blue or Red:

v 70 ٧٠

w 2,50 ٢,٥٠

1926
E6 SD1 (v) 70c on 60c dk red & brn (Bl) 3.25 *7.50*
E7 SD1 (w) 2.50 l on 2 l dk bl & red (R) 4.00 *11.00*

Type of 1924 Surcharged in Blue or Black:

LIRE
1,25

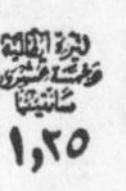

1927-35 Perf. 11
E8 SD1 1.25 l on 60c dk red & brn (Bl) 3.00 75
a. Perf. 14 (Bl) ('35) 60.00 5.50
b. Perf. 11 (Bk) ('35) *3,000.* 165.00
c. Perf. 14 (Bk) ('35) 165.00 9.00

AUTHORIZED DELIVERY STAMP

Authorized Delivery Stamp of Italy, No. EY2, Overprinted Type "f" in Black.

1939-41 Wmk. 140 Perf. 14
EY1 AD2 10c dk brn ('41) 25
a. 10c redsh brn 17.00 21.00

On No. EY1a, which was used in Eritrea, the overprint hits the figures "10." On No. EY1, which was sold in Rome, the overprint falls above the 10's.

POSTAGE DUE STAMPS

Postage Due Stamps of Italy Overprinted type "a" at Top

1903 Wmk. 140 Perf. 14
J1 D3 5c buff & mag 6.75 9.00
a. Double overprint 75.00
J2 D3 10c buff & mag 4.50 7.50
J3 D3 20c buff & mag 4.50 7.50
J4 D3 30c buff & mag 6.75 9.00
J5 D3 40c buff & mag 16.00 22.50
J6 D3 50c buff & mag 19.00 26.00
J7 D3 60c buff & mag 6.75 13.00
J8 D3 1 l bl & mag 4.50 2.25
J9 D3 2 l bl & mag 19.00 26.00
J10 D3 5 l bl & mag 62.50 100.00
J11 D3 10 l bl & mag 600.00 62.50

Same with Overprint at Bottom

1920-22
J1b D3 5c buff & mag 38 1.90
c. Numeral and ovpt. inverted 75.00
J2a D3 10c buff & mag 75 2.25
J3a D3 20c buff & mag 82.50 92.50
J4a D3 30c buff & mag 6.75 11.00
J5a D3 40c buff & mag 4.50 11.00
J6a D3 50c buff & mag 4.50 11.00
J7a D3 60c buff & mag 6.75 15.00
J8a D3 1 l bl & mag 10.50 11.00
J9a D3 2 l bl & mag 550.00 400.00
J10a D3 5 l bl & mag 75.00 130.00
J11a D3 10 l bl & mag 3.75 19.00

1903 Wmk. 140
J12 D4 50 l yellow 130.00 82.50
J13 D4 100 l blue 75.00 22.50

1927
J14 D3 60c buff & brn 18.00 *45.00*

Postage Due Stamps of Italy, 1934, Overprinted type "j" in Black.

1934
J15 D6 5c brown 30 *1.10*
J16 D6 10c blue 30 *1.10*
J17 D6 20c rose red 1.25 *1.50*
a. Inverted ovpt. 62.50
J18 D6 25c green 1.25 *1.50*
J19 D6 30c red org 1.25 *2.50*
J20 D6 40c blk brn 1.25 *3.25*
J21 D6 50c violet 1.25 55
J22 D6 60c black 2.00 *4.50*
J23 D7 1 l red org 2.00 75
J24 D7 2 l green 16.00 22.50
J25 D7 5 l violet 21.00 26.00
J26 D7 10 l blue 21.00 26.00
J27 D7 20 l car rose 24.00 35.00
Nos. J15-J27 (13) 92.85 126.25

PARCEL POST STAMPS

These stamps were used by affixing them to the way bill so that one half remained on it following the parcel, the other half staying on the receipt given the sender. Most used halves are right halves. Complete stamps were obtainable canceled, probably to order. Both unused and used prices are for complete stamps.

Parcel Post Stamps of Italy, 1914-17, Overprinted type "j" in Black on Each Half.

1916 Wmk. 140 Perf. 13½.
Q1 PP2 5c brown 32.50 *60.00*
Q2 PP2 10c dp bl *1,100.* *1,500.*
Q3 PP2 25c red 45.00 *90.00*
Q4 PP2 50c orange 16.00 *30.00*
Q5 PP2 1 l violet 16.00 *30.00*
Q6 PP2 2 l green 13.00 *30.00*
Q7 PP2 3 l bister 90.00 *150.00*
Q8 PP2 4 l slate 90.00 *150.00*

Halves Used
Q1, Q7-Q8 2.00
Q2 30.00
Q3 1.00
Q4 25
Q5-Q6 30

Overprinted type "f" on Each Half.

1917-24
Q9 PP2 5c brown 1.10 *3.00*
Q10 PP2 10c dp bl 1.10 *3.00*
Q11 PP2 20c black 1.10 *3.00*
Q12 PP2 25c red 1.10 *3.00*
Q13 PP2 50c orange 1.10 *3.00*
Q14 PP2 1 l violet 1.10 *3.00*
Q15 PP2 2 l green 1.10 *3.00*
Q16 PP2 3 l bister 1.50 *3.75*
Q17 PP2 4 l slate 2.25 *4.50*
Q18 PP2 10 l rose lil ('24) 26.00 *45.00*
Q19 PP2 12 l red brn ('24) 55.00 *100.00*
Q20 PP2 15 l ol grn ('24) 55.00 *100.00*
Q21 PP2 20 l brn vio ('24) 55.00 *100.00*
Nos. Q9-Q21 (13) 202.45 374.25

Halves Used
Q9-Q16 10
Q17 12
Q18 40
Q19 75
Q20 25
Q21 2.00

Parcel Post Stamps of Italy, 1927-39, Overprinted type "f" on Each Half.

1927-37
Q21A PP3 10c dp bl ('37) *2,500.* 150.00
Q22 PP3 25c red ('37) 200.00 7.50
Q23 PP3 30c ultra ('29) 18 1.50
Q24 PP3 50c org ('36) 200.00 7.50
Q25 PP3 60c red ('29) 18 1.50
Q26 PP3 1 l brn vio ('36) 110.00 3.75
a. 1 l lil 150.00 3.75
Q27 PP3 2 l grn ('36) 30.00 6.00
Q28 PP3 3 l bister 45 3.75
Q29 PP3 4 l gray 55 6.00
Q30 PP3 10 l rose lil ('36) 130.00 190.00
Q31 PP3 20 l lil brn ('36) 150.00 225.00
Nos. Q22-Q31 (10) 821.36 452.50

Halves Used
Q21A 8.00
Q22-Q25, Q27-Q28 20
Q26, Q26a, Q27 30
Q30 75
Q31 1.50

ESTONIA

LOCATION — In Northern Europe, bordering on the Baltic Sea and the Gulf of Finland.
GOVT. — Former independent republic
AREA — 18,353 sq. mi.
POP. — 1,126,413 (1940)
CAPITAL — Tallinn

Formerly a part of Russia, Estonia declared its independence in 1918. In 1940 it was incorporated in the Union of Soviet Socialist Republics.

100 Kopecks = 1 Ruble
100 Penni = 1 Mark (1919)
100 Sents = 1 Kroon (1928)

A1

A2

1918-19 Unwmk. Litho. Imperf.
1 A1 5k pale red 75 .75

2 A1 15k brt bl 75 75
3 A2 35p brn ('19) 1.50 1.50
a. Printed on both sides *100.00*
b. olive 20.00 20.00
4 A2 70p ol grn ('19) 2.00 2.00

Nos. 1-4 exist privately perforated.

Russian Stamps of 1909-17 Handstamped in Violet or Black

1919 ***Perf. 14, 14½x15, 13½***

8 A14 1k orange *2,500. 2,500.*
9 A14 2k green 35.00 40.00
10 A14 3k red 40.00 40.00
11 A14 5k claret 30.00 35.00
12 A15 10k dk bl (Bk) 45.00 45.00
13 A15 10k dk bl 110.00 110.00
14 A14 10k on 7k lt bl *400.00 400.00*
15 A11 15k red brn & bl 40.00 40.00
16 A11 25k grn & vio 45.00 45.00
17 A11 35k red brn & grn *1,200. 1,200.*
18 A8 50k vio & grn 100.00 100.00
19 A9 1r pale brn, brn & org 150.00 150.00
20 A13 10r scar, yel & gray *3,000. 3,000.*

Imperf

21 A14 1k orange 40.00 50.00
22 A14 2k green *400.00 400.00*
23 A14 3k red 75.00 75.00
24 A9 1r pale brn, brn & red org *300.00 300.00*
25 A12 3½r mar & grn *400.00 400.00*
26 A13 5r dk bl, grn & pale bl *500.00 500.00*

This overprint has been extensively counterfeited.
No. 20 is always creased.

Gulls — A3

1919, May 13 ***Imperf.***

27 A3 5p yellow 2.00 2.00

A4

A5

A6

A7

Viking Ship — A8

1919-20 ***Perf. 11½***

28 A4 10p green 50 50

Imperf

29 A4 5p orange 20 20
30 A4 10p green 20 20
31 A5 15p rose 20 20
32 A6 35p blue 40 40
33 A7 70p dl vio ('20) 40 40
34 A8 1m bl & blk brn 1.00 50
a. Gray granite paper ('20) 60 35
35 A8 5m yel & blk 2.50 1.00
a. Gray granite paper ('20) 1.50 50
36 A8 15m yel grn & vio ('20) 4.50 1.00
37 A8 25m ultra & blk brn ('20) 6.75 3.00
Nos. 28-37 (10) 16.65 7.40

See Nos. 76-77. The 5m exists with inverted center. Not a postal item.

Skyline of Tallinn — A9

1920-24 ***Imperf.***

Pelure Paper

39 A9 25p green 40 20
40 A9 25p yel ('24) 65 50
41 A9 35p rose 40 15
42 A9 50p grn ('21) 40 15
43 A9 1m vermilion 75 15
44 A9 2m blue 1.00 15
45 A9 2m ultra 75 15
46 A9 2.50m blue 60 30
Nos. 39-46 (8) 4.95 1.75

Nos. 39 to 46 with sewing machine perforation are unofficial.

Stamps of 1919-20 Surcharged

1 Mk. 2 Mk.

1920 ***Imperf.***

55 A5 1m on 15p rose 35 35
56 A9 1m on 35p rose 35 35
57 A7 2m on 70p dl vio 35 35

Weaver A10

Blacksmith A11

1922-23 **Typo.** ***Imperf.***

58 A10 ½m org ('23) 2.50 3.25
59 A10 1m brn ('23) 3.00 3.00
60 A10 2m yel grn 3.00 3.00
61 A10 2½m claret 3.50 3.00
62 A11 5m rose 5.00 3.00
63 A11 9m red ('23) 9.00 6.00
64 A11 10m dp bl 5.50 3.50
Nos. 58-64 (7) 31.50 24.75

1922-25 ***Perf. 14.***

65 A10 ½m org ('23) 1.00 15
66 A10 1m brn ('23) 1.50 15
67 A10 2m yel grn 2.50 15
68 A10 2½m claret 2.50 15
69 A10 3m bl grn ('24) 2.75 15
70 A11 5m rose 4.00 15
71 A11 9m red ('23) 2.75 1.25
72 A11 10m dp bl 4.50 15
73 A11 12m red ('25) 5.00 1.75
74 A11 15m plum ('25) 4.00 50
75 A11 20m ultra ('25) 12.00 30
Nos. 65-75 (11) 42.50 4.85

See also No. 89.

Viking Ship Type of 1920.

1922, June 8 ***Perf. 14x13½***

76 A8 15m yel grn & vio 5.00 60
77 A8 25m ultra & blk brn 7.50 2.25

Map of Estonia — A13

1923-24

Paper with Lilac Network.

78 A13 100m ol grn & bl 20.00 2.00

Paper with Buff Network.

79 A13 300m brn & bl ('24) 40.00 9.00

National Theater, Tallinn — A14

1924, Dec. 9 ***Perf. 14x13½.***

Paper with Blue Network.

81 A14 30m vio & blk 8.50 3.00

Paper with Rose Network.

82 A14 70m car rose & blk 12.50 3.50

Vanemuine Theater, Tartu — A15

1927, Oct. 25

Paper with Lilac Network.

83 A15 40m dp bl & ol brn 7.50 1.00

Stamps of 1922-25 Surcharged in New Currency in Red or Black

1918 24/II 1928

S. S.

1928 ***Perf. 14.***

84 A10 2s yel grn 1.00 20
85 A11 5s rose red 1.00 15
86 A11 10s dp bl 1.25 15
a. Perf. pair *500.00 500.00*
87 A11 15s plum 3.50 50
88 A11 20s ultra 3.00 60
Nos. 84-88 (5) 9.75 1.60

10th anniversary of independence.

3rd Philatelic Exhibition Issue

Blacksmith Type of 1922-23.

1928, July 6

89 A11 10m gray 5.00 5.50
a. Perf. pair

Sold only at Tallinn Philatelic Exhibition.

Arms — A16

Paper with Network in Parenthesis.

1928-40 ***Perf. 14, 14½x14***

90 A16 1s dk gray (bl) 60 15
a. Thick gray-toned laid paper ('40) 8.25 9.00
91 A16 2s yel grn (org) 75 10
92 A16 4s grn (brn) ('29) 1.00 15
93 A16 5s red (grn) 75 10
a. 5 feet on lowest lion 20.00 25.00
94 A16 8s vio (buff) ('29) 3.25 15
95 A16 10s lt bl (lil) 2.00 10
96 A16 12s crim (grn) 3.00 20
97 A16 15s yel (bl) 3.00 20
98 A16 15s car (gray) ('35) 10.00 90
99 A16 20s sl bl (red) 4.50 20
100 A16 25s red vio (grn) ('29) 11.00 30
101 A16 25s bl (brn) ('35) 10.00 75
102 A16 40s red org (bl) ('29) 7.50 50
103 A16 60s gray (brn) ('29) 8.00 60
104 A16 80s brn (bl) ('29) 15.00 2.00
Nos. 90-104 (15) 80.35 6.40

Types of 1924 Issues Surcharged:

KROON 1 KROON
a
2 KROONI 2
b
3 KROONI 3
c

1930, Sept. 1 ***Perf. 14x13½.***

Paper with Green Network.

105 A14 1k on 70m car & blk 8.50 5.00

Paper with Rose Network.

106 A13 2k on 300m brn & bl 15.00 8.50

Paper with Blue Network.

107 A13 3k on 300m brn & bl 37.50 22.50

University Observatory A17

University of Tartu A18

Paper with Network as in Parenthesis.

1932, June 1 ***Perf. 14.***

108 A17 5s red (yel) 6.50 60
109 A18 10s lt bl (lil) 2.00 20
110 A17 12s car (bl) 9.50 1.75
111 A18 20s dk bl (grn) 8.00 35

University of Tartu tercentenary.

Narva Falls A19

Ancient Bard Playing Harp A20

1933, Apr. 1 **Photo.** ***Perf. 14x13½.***

112 A19 1k gray blk 7.50 60

See also No. 149.

Paper with Network as in Parenthesis.

1933, May 29 **Typo.** ***Perf. 14***

113 A20 2s grn (org) 3.00 40
114 A20 5s red (grn) 4.00 40
115 A20 10s bl (lil) 5.00 25

Tenth National Singing Festival.

The first price column gives the catalogue value of an unused stamp, the second that of a used stamp.

Woman Harvester A21

President Konstantin Päts A22

1935, Mar. 1 **Engr.** ***Perf. 13½.***

116 A21 3k blk brn	90	1.50

1936-40 **Typo.** ***Perf. 14.***

117 A22 1s chocolate	75	20
118 A22 2s yel grn	75	20
119 A22 3s dp org ('40)	7.50	5.50
120 A22 4s rose vio	1.40	35
121 A22 5s lt bl grn	1.40	20
122 A22 6s rose lake	1.25	35
123 A22 6s dp grn ('40)	27.50	22.50
124 A22 10s grnsh bl	1.50	20
125 A22 15s crim rose ('37)	2.50	30
126 A22 15s dp bl ('40)	8.00	50
127 A22 18s dp car ('39)	20.00	9.00
128 A22 20s brt vio	2.50	25
129 A22 25s dk bl ('38)	8.25	35
130 A22 30s bis ('38)	8.50	30
131 A22 30s ultra ('39)	15.00	2.50
132 A22 50s org brn	8.00	1.00
133 A22 60s brt pink	12.00	2.00
Nos. 117-133 (17)	126.80	45.70

St. Brigitta Convent Entrance A23

Ruins of Convent, Pirita River A24

Front View of Convent A25

Seal of Convent A26

Paper with Network as in Parenthesis.

1936, June 10 ***Perf. 13½***

134 A23 5s grn (buff)	70	25
135 A24 10s bl (lil)	90	25
136 A25 15s red (org)	1.50	2.25
137 A26 25s ultra (brn)	2.00	2.75

St. Brigitta Convent, 500th anniversary.

Harbor at Tallinn — A27

1938, Apr. 11 **Engr.** ***Perf. 14***

138 A27 2k blue	1.00	2.00

Friedrich R. Faehlmann A28

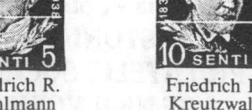

Friedrich R. Kreutzwald A29

1938 **Typo.** ***Perf. 13½.***

139 A28 5s dk grn	1.00	1.00
140 A29 10s dp brn	1.00	1.00
141 A29 15s dk car	1.25	1.75
142 A28 25s ultra	2.25	2.75
a. Sheet of four	13.00	22.50

Society of Estonian Scholars centenary.

No. 142a contains one each of Nos. 139-142, with inscription in top margin. Size: 89x138mm.

Hospital at Pärnu — A30

Seashore Hotel — A31

1939, June 20 **Typo.**

144 A30 5s dk grn	1.40	75
145 A31 10s dp red vio	1.00	75
146 A30 18s dk car	3.00	3.00
147 A31 30s dp bl	3.50	3.50
a. Sheet of four	20.00	40.00

Centenary of health resort and baths at Pärnu.

No. 147a contains one each of Nos. 144-147, with inscription at left. Size: 137x90mm.

Narva Falls Type of 1933.

1940, Apr. 15 **Engr.**

149 A19 1k sl grn	1.00	2.50

The sky consists of heavy horizontal lines and the background consists of horizontal and vertical lines.

Carrier Pigeon and Plane — A32

1940, July 30 **Typo.**

150 A32 3s red org	20	15
151 A32 10s purple	20	15
152 A32 15s rose brn	25	15
153 A32 30s dk bl	2.00	1.25

Centenary of the first postage stamp.

SEMI-POSTAL STAMPS.

Assisting Wounded Soldier SP1

Offering Aid to Wounded Hero SP2

1920, June **Unwmk.** **Litho.** ***Imperf.***

B1 SP1 35p + 10p red & ol grn	40	65
B2 SP2 70p + 15p dp bl & brn	40	65

Surcharged **2 Mk**

1920

B3 SP1 1m on 35p + 10p red & ol grn	50	50
B4 SP2 2m on 70p + 15p dp bl & brn	50	50

Nurse and Wounded Soldier — SP3

1921, Aug. 1 ***Imperf.***

B5 SP3 2½ (3½)m org, brn & car	1.00	1.40
B6 SP3 5 (7)m ultra, brn & car	1.00	1.40

1922, Apr. 26 ***Perf. 13½x14***

B7 SP3 2½ (3½)m org, brn & car	1.50	2.00
a. Vert. pair, imperf. horiz.	15.00	20.00
B8 SP3 5 (7)m ultra, brn & car	1.50	2.00
a. Vert. pair, imperf. horiz.	15.00	20.00

Nos. B5-B8 Overprinted **Aita hädalist.**

1923 ***Imperf.***

B9 SP3 2½ (3½)m	25.00	35.00
B10 SP3 5 (7)m	30.00	40.00

Perf. 13½x14.

B11 SP3 2½ (3½)m	35.00	45.00
a. Vert. pair, imperf. horiz.	125.00	175.00
B12 SP3 5 (7)m	40.00	50.00
a. Vert. pair, imperf. horiz.	125.00	175.00

Excellent forgeries are plentiful.

Nos. B7 and B8 Surcharged **5 5** **6 6**

1926, June 15

B13 SP3 5 (6)m on 2½(3½)m	2.50	4.00
a. Vert. pair, imperf. horiz.	15.00	20.00
B14 SP3 10 (12)m on 5(7)m	2.50	4.00
a. Vert. pair, imperf. horiz.	15.00	20.00

Nos. B5-B14 had the franking value of the lower figure. They were sold for the higher figure, the excess going to the Red Cross Society.

Kuressaare Castle SP4

Tartu Cathedral SP5

Tallinn Castle SP6

Narva Fortress SP7

View of Tallinn — SP8

Wmk. 207- Arms of Finland in the Sheet

Reduced illustration. Watermark covers a large part of sheet.

Laid Paper.

Perf. 14½x14

1927, Nov. 19 **Typo.** **Wmk. 207**

B15 SP4 5m + 5m bl grn & ol, *grysh*	65	1.00
B16 SP5 10m + 10m dp bl & brn, *cr*	65	1.00
B17 SP6 12m + 12m rose red & ol grn, *bluish*	65	1.50

Perf. 14x13½

B18 SP7 20m + 20m bl & choc, *gray*	1.25	2.25
B19 SP8 40m + 40m org brn & sl, *buff*	1.25	2.25
Nos. B15-B19 (5)	4.45	8.00

The money derived from the surtax was donated to the Committee for the commemoration of War for Liberation.

Red Cross Issue.

Symbolical of Succor to Injured SP9

Symbolical of "Light of Hope" SP10

1931, Aug. 1 **Unwmk.** ***Perf. 13½***

B20 SP9 2s + 3s grn & car	8.50	10.00
B21 SP10 5s + 3s red & car	8.50	10.00
B22 SP10 10s + 3s lt bl & car	8.50	10.00
B23 SP9 20s + 3s dk bl & car	13.00	15.00

Nurse and Child SP11

Taagepera Sanatorium SP12

Lorraine Cross and Flower — SP13

Paper with Network as in Parenthesis.

1933, Oct. 1 ***Perf. 14, 14½.***

B24 SP11 5s + 3s ver (grn)	8.50	8.50
B25 SP12 10s + 3s lt bl & red (vio)	8.50	8.50
B26 SP13 12s + 3s rose & red (grn)	9.50	9.50
B27 SP12 20s + 3s dk bl & red (org)	15.00	15.00

The surtax was for a fund to combat tuberculosis.

Arms of Narva SP14

Arms of Pärnu SP15

Arms of Tartu SP16

Arms of Tallinn SP17

Paper with Network as in Parenthesis.

1936, Feb. 1 *Perf. 13½*

B28	SP14 10s + 10s grn & ultra (gray)	6.25	7.50
B29	SP15 15s + 15s car & bl (gray)	6.25	7.50
B30	SP16 25s + 25s gray bl & red (brn)	9.00	10.00
B31	SP17 50s + 50s blk & dl org (ol)	20.00	27.50

Arms of Paide SP18

Arms of Rakvere SP19

Arms of Valga SP20

Arms of Viljandi SP21

Paper with Network as in Parenthesis.

1937, Jan. 2

B32	SP18 10s + 10s grn (gray)	5.50	7.50
B33	SP19 15s + 15s red brn (gray)	5.50	7.50
B34	SP20 25s + 25s dk bl (lil)	8.00	10.00
B35	SP21 50s + 50s dk vio (gray)	15.00	20.00

Arms of Baltiski SP22

Arms of Võru SP23

Arms of Haapsalu SP24

Arms of Kuressaare SP25

Designs are the armorial bearings of various cities.

1938, Jan. 21

Paper with Gray Network.

B36	SP22 10s + 10s dk brn	5.00	6.50
B37	SP23 15s + 15s car & grn	6.00	7.00
B38	SP24 25s + 25s dk bl & car	8.00	10.00
B39	SP25 50s + 50s blk & org yel	12.00	17.50
a.	Sheet of four	35.00	55.00

Annual charity ball, Tallinn, Jan. 2, 1938. No. B39a contains one each of Nos. B36-B39. Size: 106x150mm.

Arms of Viljandi SP27

Arms of Pärnu SP28

Arms of Tartu SP29

Arms of Harju SP30

Designs are the armorial bearings of various districts.

1939, Jan. 10

Paper with Gray Network.

B41	SP27 10s + 10s dk bl grn	5.00	6.00
B42	SP28 15s + 15s car	6.00	7.00
B43	SP29 25s + 25s dk bl	8.00	9.50
B44	SP30 50s + 50s brn lake	12.50	20.00
a.	Sheet of four	40.00	55.00

No. B44a measures 90x138mm., and contains one each of Nos. B41 to B44, with marginal inscriptions.

Arms of Võru — SP32

Arms of Järva — SP33

Arms of Lääne SP34

Arms of Saare SP35

Designs are the armorial bearings of various districts.

1940, Jan. 2 **Typo.** *Perf. 13½*

Paper with Gray Network.

B46	SP32 10s + 10s dp grn & ultra	4.50	6.00
B47	SP33 15s + 15s dk car & ultra	4.50	6.00
B48	SP34 25s + 25s dk bl & scar	5.50	10.00
B49	SP35 50s + 50s ocher & ultra	7.50	16.00

AIR POST STAMPS.

Airplane AP1

Unwmk.

1920, Mar. 13 **Typo.** *Imperf.*

C1	AP1 5m yel, blk & lt grn	2.25	3.00

No. C1 Overprinted "1923" in Red.

1923, Oct. 1

C2	AP1 5m multi	7.00	10.00

No. C1 Surcharged in Red

1923, Oct. 1

C3	AP1 15m on 5m multi	10.00	12.00

Pairs of No. C1 Surcharged in Black or Red

45 Marka

1923

1923, Oct.

C4	AP1 10m on 5m + 5m (B)	10.00	*14.00*
C5	AP1 20m on 5m + 5m (R)	22.50	30.00
C6	AP1 45m on 5m + 5m (R)	75.00	90.00
	Rough Perf. 11½.		
C7	AP1 10m on 5m + 5m (B)	*250.00*	*300.00*
C8	AP1 20m on 5m + 5m (R)	*150.00*	*200.00*

The pairs comprising Nos. C7 and C8 are imperforate between. Forged surcharges and perforations abound.

Monoplane in Flight — AP2

Designs: Various views of planes in flight.

1924, Feb. 12 ***Imperf.***

C9	AP2 5m yel & blk	2.75	4.25
C10	AP2 10m bl & blk	2.75	4.25
C11	AP2 15m red & blk	2.75	4.25
C12	AP2 20m grn & blk	2.75	4.25
C13	AP2 45m vio & blk	2.75	4.25
	Nos. C9-C13 (5)	13.75	21.25

The paper is covered with a faint network in pale shades of the frame colors. There are four varieties of the frames and five of the pictures.

1925, July 15 ***Perf. 13½.***

C14	AP2 5m yel & blk	2.00	3.00
C15	AP2 10m bl & blk	2.00	3.00
C16	AP2 15m red & blk	2.00	3.00
C17	AP2 20m grn & blk	2.00	3.00
C18	AP2 45m vio & blk	2.00	3.00
	Nos. C14-C18 (5)	10.00	15.00

Counterfeits of Nos. C1 to C18 are plentiful.

OCCUPATION STAMPS.

Issued under German Occupation.
For Use in Tartu (Dorpat)

Russian Stamps of 1909-12 Surcharged **20 Pfg.**

1918 **Unwmk.** ***Perf. 14x14½***

N1	A15 20pf on 10k dk bl	40.00	*60.00*
N2	A8 40pf on 20k bl & car	40.00	*60.00*

Forged overprints exist.

Estonian Arms and Swastika — OS1

Perf. 11½

1941, Aug. **Typo.** **Unwmk.**

N3	OS1 15k brown	15.00	15.00
N4	OS1 20k green	11.00	11.00
N5	OS1 30k dk bl	11.00	11.00

Exist imperf. Price, set, $60.

Nos. N3-N5 were issued on both ordinary paper with colorless gum and thick chalky paper with yellow gum. Same prices.

SEMI-POSTAL STAMPS

Castle Tower, Tallinn — OSP1

Designs: 20k+20k, Stone Bridge, Tartu (horiz.). 30k+30k, Narva Castle (horiz.). 50k+50k, Tallinn view (horiz.). 60k+60k, Tartu University. 100k+100k, Narva Castle, close view.

Paper with Gray Network

Perf. 11½

1941, Sept. 29 **Photo.** **Unwmk.**

NB1	OSP1 15k + 15k dk brn	45	*5.00*
NB2	OSP1 20k + 20k red lil	45	*5.00*
NB3	OSP1 30k + 30k dk bl	45	*5.00*
NB4	OSP1 50k + 50k bluish grn	45	*5.00*
NB5	OSP1 60k + 60k car	65	*5.00*
NB6	OSP1 100k + 100k gray	1.40	*6.00*
	Nos. NB1-NB6 (6)	3.80	5.10

Nos. NB1-NB6 exist imperf. Price, set unused $20, used $40.

A miniature sheet containing one each of Nos. NB1-NB6, imperf., exists in various colors. It was not postally valid.

ETHIOPIA

(Abyssinia)

LOCATION — Northeastern Africa
GOVT. — Provisional military
AREA — 471,800 sq. mi.
POP. — 40,000,000 (est. 1984)
CAPITAL — Addis Ababa

16 Guerche = 1 Menelik Dollar or 1 Maria Theresa Dollar
100 Centimes = 1 Franc (1905)
40 Paras = 1 Piastre (1908)
16 Mehalek = 1 Thaler or Talari (1928)
100 Centimes = 1 Thaler (1936)
100 Cents = 1 Ethiopian Dollar (1946)
100 Cents = 1 Birr (1978)

Excellent forgeries of Nos. 1-86 exist.

Menelik II — A1

Lion of Judah — A2

1894 **Unwmk.** **Typo.** ***Perf. 14x13½***

1	A1 ¼g green	2.00	2.00
2	A1 ½g red	1.50	1.50
3	A1 1g blue	1.50	1.50
4	A1 2g dk brn	1.50	1.50
5	A2 4g lil brn	1.50	1.50
6	A2 8g violet	1.50	1.50
7	A2 16g black	1.75	1.75
	Nos. 1-7 (7)	11.25	11.25

For 4g, 8g and 16g stamps of type A1, see Nos. J3a, J4a, and J7a.

Nos. 1-7 Handstamped in Violet, Blue or Black **Ethiopie**

1901

8 A1 ¼g green 8.00 8.00
9 A1 ½g red 8.00 8.00
10 A1 1g blue 8.00 8.00
11 A1 2g dk brn 8.00 8.00
12 A2 4g lil brn 11.00 11.00
13 A2 8g violet 14.00 14.00
14 A2 16g black 15.00 15.00
Nos. 8-14 (7) 72.00 72.00

Two types of overprint on Nos. 8-14: 9½mm. and 8½mm. wide.

Handstamped in Violet, Blue or Black ቦስጣ።

1902

15 A1 ¼g green 5.00 5.00
16 A1 ½g red 6.00 5.00
17 A1 1g blue 7.50 7.50
18 A1 2g dk brn 7.50 7.50
19 A2 4g lil brn 12.50 12.50
20 A2 8g violet 17.50 17.50
21 A2 16g black 30.00 30.00
Nos. 15-21 (7) 86.00 85.00

The handstamp reads "Bosta" (Post).

Handstamped in Violet, Blue or Black መልክት።

1903

22 A1 ¼g green 5.00 5.00
a. On stamp No. 15
23 A1 ½g red 5.00 5.00
24 A1 1g blue 7.50 7.50
a. On stamp No. 17
25 A1 2g dk brn 10.00 10.00
26 A2 4g lil brn 10.00 10.00
27 A2 8g violet 22.50 22.50
28 A2 16g black 30.00 30.00
Nos. 22-28 (7) 90.00 90.00

The handstamp reads "Malekt." (Message).

Handstamped in Violet or Blue ምልክት

1904

36 A1 ¼g green 10.00 10.00
37 A1 ½g red 10.00 10.00
38 A1 1g blue 12.00 12.00
39 A1 2g dk brn 15.00 15.00
40 A2 4g lil brn 20.00 20.00
41 A2 8g violet 32.50 32.50
42 A2 16g black 47.50 47.50
Nos. 36-42 (7) 147.00 147.00

The handstamp reads "Malekt." (Message).

Preceding Issues Surcharged with New Values in French Currency in Blue, Violet, Rose or Black:

05 — a   1,60 — b

1905

On Nos. 1 to 7.

43 A1 (a) 5c on ¼g grn 6.00 6.00
44 A1 (a) 10c on ½g red 6.00 6.00
45 A1 (a) 20c on 1g bl 6.00 6.00
46 A1 (a) 40c on 2g dk brn 8.00 8.00
47 A2 (a) 80c on 4g lil brn 13.00 13.00
48 A2 (b) 1.60fr on 8g vio 12.50 17.50
49 A2 (b) 3.20fr on 16g blk 25.00 25.00
Nos. 43-49 (7) 76.50 81.50

On No. 8.

50 A1 (a) 5c on ¼g grn 75.00 75.00

On Nos. 15 to 20.

51 A1 (a) 5c on ¼g grn 15.00 15.00
51B A1 (a) 10c on ½g red *275.00 275.00*
51C A1 (a) 20c on 1g bl *20.00*
51D A1 (a) 40c on 2g dk brn *67.50*
51E A2 (a) 80c on 4g lil brn *110.00*
51F A2 (b) 1.60fr on 8g vio *140.00*

On Nos. 22, 24 & 26.

52 A1 (a) 5c on ¼g grn 32.50 32.50
52B A1 (a) 20c on 1g bl *52.50*
52D A2 (a) 80c on 4g lil brn *140.00*

On No. 36.

53 A1 (a) 5c on ¼g grn 35.00 35.00

The status of Nos. 51C-51F, 52B-52D is questioned.

5% — c   5 centimes. — d

On No. 2.

54 A1 (c) 5c on half of ½g red 3.50 3.50

On Nos. 15 & 21.

54B A1(c) 5c on ¼g grn 50.00 50.00
55 A2(d) 5c on 16g blk 90.00 90.00

On No. 28.

56 A2(d) 5c on 16g blk 90.00 90.00

The overprints and surcharges on Nos. 8 to 56 inclusive were handstamped, the work being very roughly done. Apparently any color of ink that was at hand was used. It is not at all improbable that other varieties may exist.

As is usual with handstamped overprints and surcharges there are many inverted and double.

Surcharged with New Values in Various Colors

and in Violet: ምኒልክ

1906, Jan. 1

57 A1 5c on ¼g grn 6.00 6.00
58 A1 10c on ½g red 8.00 8.00
59 A1 20c on 1g bl 8.00 8.00
60 A1 40c on 2g dk brn 8.00 8.00
61 A2 80c on 4g lil brn 10.00 10.00
62 A2 1.60fr on 8g vio 14.00 14.00
63 A2 3.20fr on 16g blk 37.50 37.50
Nos. 57-63 (7) 91.50 91.50

Two types of the 4-character overprint ("Menelik"): 15x3½mm. and 16½x4½mm.

Surcharged with New Values

and in Violet: ምኒልክ።

1906, July 1

64 A1 5c on ¼g grn 6.00 6.00
a. Surcharged "20" 40.00 40.00
65 A1 10c on ½g red 7.00 7.00
66 A1 20c on 1g bl 10.00 10.00
67 A1 40c on 2g dk brn 10.00 10.00
68 A2 80c on 4g lil brn 14.00 14.00
69 A2 1.60fr on 8g vio 14.00 14.00
70 A2 3.20fr on 16g blk 35.00 35.00
Nos. 64-70 (7) 96.00 96.00

The control overprint reads "Menelik."

Surcharged in Violet:

ዳግማዊ።   ዳግማዊ።

☆1/2☆ — e   ✳ 1. ✳ — f

1907, July 1

71 A1(e) ¼ on ¼g grn 6.00 6.00
72 A1(e) ½ on ½g red 6.00 6.00
73 A1(f) 1 on 1g bl 7.50 7.50
74 A1(f) 2 on 2g dk brn 9.00 9.00
a. Surcharged "40" 45.00
75 A2(f) 4 on 4g lil brn 9.00 9.00
a. Surcharged "80" 42.50
76 A2(f) 8 on 8g vio 18.00 18.00
77 A2(f) 16 on 16g blk 25.00 25.00
Nos. 71-77 (7) 80.50 80.50

Nos. 71-72 are also found with stars farther away from figures.

The control overprint reads "Dagmawi" ("Second"), meaning Emperor Menelik II.

Nos. 2, 23 Surcharged in Blue **PIASTRE**

1908, Mar. 25

78 A1 1pi on ½g red (#2) 6.00 6.00
79 A1 1pi on ½g red (#23) *250.00 250.00*

The surcharges on Nos. 57 to 79 are handstamped and are found double, inverted, etc.

Surcharged in Black 1/4 piastre

1908, Nov. 1

80 A1 ¼p on ¼g grn 1.25 1.25
81 A1 ½p on ½g red 1.25 1.25
82 A1 1p on 1g bl 2.00 2.00
83 A1 2p on 2g dk brn 3.00 3.00
84 A2 4p on 4g lil brn 4.75 4.75
85 A2 8p on 8g vio 10.00 10.00
86 A2 16p on 16g blk 16.00 16.00
Nos. 80-86 (7) 38.25 38.25

Surcharges on Nos. 80-85 are found double, inverted, etc.

King Solomon's Throne
A3

Menelik in Native Costume
A4

Menelik in Royal Dress — A5

1909, Mar. 27 *Perf. 11½*

87 A3 ¼g bl grn 60 50
88 A3 ½g rose 60 50
89 A3 1g grn & org 3.25 1.25
90 A4 2g blue 2.50 1.50
91 A4 4g grn & car 3.75 3.00
92 A5 8g ver & dp grn 6.25 4.50
93 A5 16g ver & car 9.00 7.50
Nos. 87-93 (7) 25.95 18.75

Nos. 1-7 Handstamped and Surcharged in ms.

AFF EXCEP FAUTE TIMB

1911, Oct. 1 *Perf. 14x13½*

94 A1 ¼g on ¼g grn 90.00 40.00
95 A1 ½g on ½g red 90.00 40.00
96 A1 1g on 1g bl 90.00 40.00
97 A1 2g on 2g dk brn 90.00 40.00
98 A2 4g on 4g lil brn 90.00 40.00
99 A2 8g on 8g vio 90.00 40.00
100 A2 16g on 16g blk 90.00 40.00
Nos. 94-100 (7) 630.00 280.00

Nos. 94-100 are provisionals used at Dire-Dawa for 5 days. The overprint is abbreviated from "Affranchissement Exceptionnel Faute Timbres" (Special Franking Lacking Stamps). Nos. 94-100 exist without ms. surcharge. Forgeries exist.

Stamps of 1909 Handstamped in Violet or Black:

g — 11·2·1917   h — 11·2·1917

1917, Mar. 30 *Perf. 11½*

101 A3(g) ¼g bl grn (V) 3.00 3.00
102 A3(g) ½g rose (V) 3.00 3.00
104 A4(h) 2g bl (Bk) 4.00 4.00
105 A4(h) 4g grn & car (Bk) 7.00 7.00
106 A5(h) 8g ver & dp grn (Bk) 12.00 12.00
107 A5(h) 16g ver & car (Bk) 25.00 25.00
Nos. 101-107 (6) 54.00 54.00

Coronation of Empress Zauditu.

Nos. 101-107 exist with overprint inverted and Nos. 101-106 with it double.

Stamps of 1909 Overprinted in Blue, Black or Red:

11/2/1917 — i   11/2/1917 — j

1917, Apr. 5

108 A3(i) ¼g bl grn (bl) 25 25
109 A3(i) ½g rose (Bl) 25 25
110 A3(i) 1g grn & org (Bl) 1.75 1.75
111 A4(i) 2g bl (R) 67.50 75.00
112 A4(j) 2g bl (Bk) 30 25
113 A4(j) 4g grn & car (Bl) 75 75
a. Black ovpt. 10.00 10.00
114 A5(j) 8g ver & dp grn (Bl) 60 60
115 A5(j) 16g ver & car (Bl) 1.00 1.00
Nos. 108-115 (8) 72.40 79.85

Coronation of Empress Zauditu.

Nos. 108-115 all exist with double overprint and inverted overprint. Nos. 108, 112, 113, 114 and 115 exist with double overprint, one inverted, and various combinations.

Preceding Issue with Additional Surcharge

1/4 — *k*   1/2 — *l*   1 — *m*   2 — *n*

1917, May 28

116 A5(k) ¼g on 8g ver & dp grn 2.50 2.50
117 A5(l) ½g on 8g ver & dp grn 2.50 2.50
118 A5(m) 1g on 16g ver & car 6.50 6.50
119 A5(n) 2g on 16g ver & car 6.50 6.50

Nos. 116 to 119 all exist with the numerals double and inverted and No. 116 with the Amharic surcharge double.

Sommering's Gazelle — A6

Ras Tafari — A9

Cathedral of St. George A12

Empress Waizeri Zauditu — A18

Designs: 1/4g, Giraffes. 1/2g, Leopard. 2g, Ras Tafari. 4g, Regent Tafari. 8g, White rhinoceros. 12g, Somali ostriches. 1t, African elephant. 2t, Water buffalo. 3t, Lions. 5t, 10t, Empress Zauditu.

1919, June 16 Typo. *Perf. 11 1/2.*

No.	Type	Description	Unused	Used
120	A6	1/8g vio & brn	10	6
121	A6	1/4g bl grn & db	10	6
122	A6	1/2g scar & ol grn	10	6
123	A9	1g rose lil & gray grn	8	5
124	A9	2g dp ultra & fawn	8	6
125	A9	4g turq bl & org	10	10
126	A12	6g lt bl & org	10	10
127	A12	8g ol grn & blk brn	25	12
128	A12	12g red vio & gray	40	20
129	A12	1t rose & gray blk	70	30
130	A12	2t blk & brn	1.75	1.10
131	A12	3t grn & dp org	2.00	1.40
132	A18	4t brn & lil rose	2.25	2.00
133	A18	5t car & gray	3.00	3.00
134	A18	10t gray grn & bis	6.00	4.00
		Nos. 120-134 (15)	17.01	12.61

Reprints differ slightly in color from originals. Reprints exist imperf. and some values with inverted centers. Price for set, unused or canceled, $1.50.

No. 132 Surcharged in Blue

4guerches

1919, Oct.

No.	Type	Description	Unused	Used
135	A18	4g on 4t brn & lil rose	90	90

The Amharic surcharge indicates the new value and, therefore, varies on Nos. 135 to 154. There are numerous defective letters and figures, several types of the "2" of "1/2," the errors "guerhce," "gnerche," etc.

Stamps of 1919 Surcharged

አንድ ፡
ግርሽ ፡፡
1 guerche

1921-22

No.	Type	Description	Unused	Used
136	A6	1/2g on 1/8g vio & brn ('22)	50	50
137	A6	1g on 1/4g grn & db	50	50
138	A9	2g on 1g lil brn & gray grn ('22)	75	75
139	A18	2g on 4t brn & lil rose ('22)	27.50	27.50
140	A6	2 1/2g on 1/2g scar & ol grn	75	75
141	A9	4g on 2g ultra & fawn ('22)	75	75
		Nos. 136-141 (6)	30.75	30.75

Stamps and Type of 1919 Surcharged

1 guerche

1925-28

No.	Type	Description	Unused	Used
142	A12	1/2g on 1t rose & gray blk ('26)	75	75
a.		Without colon ('28)	10.00	10.00
143	A18	1/2g on 5t car & gray ('26)	40	40
144	A12	1g on 6g bl & org	40	40
145	A12	1g on 12g lil & gray	80.00	80.00
146	A12	1g on 3t grn & org ('26)	17.50	17.50
147	A18	1g on 10t gray grn & bis ('26)	50	50
		Nos. 142-147 (6)	99.55	99.55

On No. 142 the surcharge is at the left side of the stamp, reading upward. On No. 142a it is at the right, reading downward. The two surcharges are from different, though similar, settings. On No. 146 the surcharge is at the right, reading upward. See note following No. 154.

There are also many irregularly produced settings in imitation of Nos. 136-154 which differ slightly from the originals.

Type of 1919 Surcharged

= 1 guerche =

1926

No.	Type	Description	Unused	Used
147A	A12	1g on 12g lil & gray	55.00	55.00
b.		Vertical bars at lower right corner		65.00

Stamps of 1919 Surcharged

አንድ ፡ ግርሽ ፡

1 guerche

1926

No.	Type	Description	Unused	Used
148	A12	1/2g on 8g ol grn & blk brn	1.00	1.00
149	A12	1g on 6g bl & org	22.50	22.50
150	A12	1g on 12g lil & gray	65.00	65.00

Stamps of 1919 Surcharged

የግርሽ ፡ አላድ ፡

1/2 guerche

1927

No.	Type	Description	Unused	Used
151	A12	1/2g on 8g ol grn & blk brn	75	75
152	A12	1g on 6g bl & org	35.00	35.00
153	A12	1g on 12g lil & gray	1.00	1.00
154	A12	1g on 3t grn & org	80.00	80.00

Many varieties of surcharge, such as double, inverted, lines transposed or omitted, and inverted "2" in "1/2," exist on Nos. 136-154.

Ras Tafari A22

Empress Zauditu A23

1928, Sept. 5 Typo. *Perf. 13 1/2x14*

No.	Type	Description	Unused	Used
155	A22	1/8m org & lt bl	50	40
156	A23	1/4m ind & red org	30	30
157	A22	1/2m gray grn & blk	50	40
158	A23	1m dk car & blk	30	25
159	A22	2m dk bl & blk	30	25
160	A23	4m yel & ol	30	25
161	A22	8m vio & ol	80	60
162	A23	1t org brn & vio	1.00	80
163	A22	2t grn & bis	1.40	1.40
164	A23	3t choc & grn	2.00	1.50
		Nos. 155-164 (10)	7.40	6.15

Preceding Issue Overprinted in Black, Violet or Red

1928, Sept. 1

No.	Type	Description	Unused	Used
165	A22	1/8m org & lt bl (Bk)	1.00	1.00
166	A23	1/4m ind & red org (V)	1.00	1.00
167	A22	1/2m gray grn & blk (V)	1.00	1.00
168	A23	1m dk car & blk (V)	1.00	1.00
169	A22	2m dk bl & blk (R)	1.00	1.00
170	A23	4m yel & ol (Bk)	1.00	1.00
171	A22	8m vio & ol (R)	1.00	1.00
172	A23	1t org brn & vio (Bk)	1.00	1.00
173	A22	2t grn & bis (R)	1.50	1.50
174	A23	3t choc & grn (R)	2.00	2.00
		Nos. 165-174 (10)	11.50	11.50

Opening of General Post Office, Addis Ababa.

Stamps of 1928 Issue Handstamped in Violet, Red or Black

NEGOUS TEFERI

1928, Oct. 7

No.	Type	Description	Unused	Used
175	A22	1/8m org & lt bl (V)	1.00	1.00
176	A22	1/2m gray grn & blk (R)	1.00	1.00
177	A22	2m dk bl & blk (R)	1.00	1.00
178	A22	8m vio & ol (Bk)	1.00	1.00
179	A22	2t grn & bis (V)	1.00	1.00
		Nos. 175-179 (5)	5.00	5.00

Crowning of Regent Tafari Makonen as Negus on Oct. 7, 1928.

Nos. 175-177 exist with overprint vertical.

Stamps of 1928 Overprinted in Red or Green

HAYLE SELASSIE 1er
3 Avril 1930

1930, Apr. 3

No.	Type	Description	Unused	Used
180	A22	1/8m org & lt bl (R)	20	15
181	A23	1/4m ind & red org (G)	25	20
182	A22	1/2m gray grn & blk (R)	20	15
183	A23	1m dk car & blk (G)	25	20
184	A22	2m dk bl & blk (R)	25	20
185	A23	4m yel & ol (R)	40	30
186	A22	8m vio & ol (R)	75	75
187	A23	1t org brn & vio (R)	1.75	1.75
188	A22	2t grn & bis (R)	2.25	2.25
189	A23	3t choc & grn (R)	3.00	3.00
		Nos. 180-189 (10)	9.30	8.95

Issued in commemoration of the proclamation of the Negus Tafari as King of Kings of Abyssinia under the name "Haile Selassie I."

A similar overprint, set in four vertical lines, was printed on all denominations of the 1928 issue. It was not considered satisfactory and was rejected. The trial impressions were not placed on sale to the public, but some copies reached private hands and have been passed through the post.

Stamps of 1928 Overprinted in Red or Olive Brown

HAILE SELASSIE 1er
3 Avril 1930

1930, Apr. 3

No.	Type	Description	Unused	Used
190	A22	1/8m org & lt bl	25	20
191	A23	1/4m ind & red org (OB)	25	25
192	A22	1/2m gray grn & blk	25	20
193	A23	1m dk car & blk (OB)	25	25
194	A22	2m dk bl & blk	25	25
195	A23	4m yel & ol	50	50
196	A22	8m vio & ol	75	75
197	A23	1t org brn & vio	1.75	1.75
198	A22	2t grn & bis	2.25	2.25
199	A23	3t choc & grn	3.00	3.00
		Nos. 190-199 (10)	9.50	9.40

Issued in commemoration of the proclamation of the Negus Tafari as Emperor Haile Selassie I.

All stamps of this series exist with "H" of "HAILE" omitted.

Stamps of 1928 Handstamped in Violet or Red

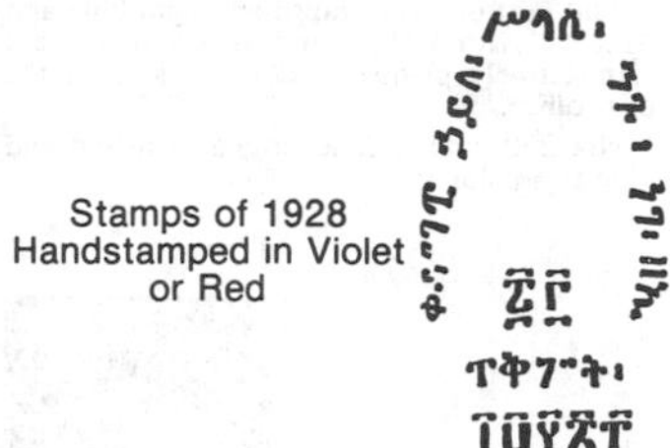

1930, Nov. 2

No.	Type	Description	Unused	Used
200	A22	1/8m org & lt bl (V)	30	25
201	A23	1/4m ind & red org (V)	30	25
202	A22	1/2m gray grn & blk (R)	30	25
203	A23	1m dk car & blk (V)	30	25
204	A22	2m dk bl & blk (R)	30	25
205	A23	4m yel & ol (V)	30	25
206	A22	8m vio & ol (V or R)	75	75
207	A23	1t org brn & vio (V)	1.00	1.00
208	A22	2t grn & bis (V or R)	1.50	1.50
209	A23	3t choc & grn (V or R)	2.25	2.25
		Nos. 200-209 (10)	7.30	7.00

Issued in commemoration of the cornation of the Emperor Haile Selassie I, November 2nd, 1930.

Haile Selassie Coronation Monument, Symbols of Empire — A24

1930, Nov. Engr. *Perf. 12 1/2*

No.	Type	Description	Unused	Used
210	A24	1g orange	20	20
211	A24	2g ultra	20	20
212	A24	4g violet	20	20
213	A24	8g dl grn	35	30
214	A24	1t brown	50	50
215	A24	3t green	75	75
216	A24	5t red brn	75	75
		Nos. 210-216 (7)	2.95	2.90

Coronation of Emperor Haile Selassie I.

Reprints of Nos. 210 to 216 exist. Paper is thinner and gum whiter than the originals. Price 7c each.

Stamps of 1928 Surcharged in Green, Red or Blue

1/8 Mehalek

Type I   Type II

1931, Mar. 20 *Perf. 13 1/2x14.*

No.	Type	Description	Unused	Used
217	A23	1/8m on 1m dk car & blk (G)	30	30
218	A22	1/8m on 2m dk bl & blk (R)	30	30

219 A23 ⅛m on 4m yel & ol (G) 30 30
220 A23 ¼m on 1m dk car & blk (Bl) 30 30
221 A22 ¼m on 2m dk bl & blk (R) 75 75
222 A23 ¼m on 4m yel & ol (G) 75 75
225 A23 ½m on 1m dk car & blk (Bl) 75 75
226 A22 ½m on 2m dk bl & blk (R) 75 75
227 A23 ½m on 4m yel & ol (G) (II) 75 75
a. ½m on 4m yel & ol (I) 7.50 7.50
228 A23 ½m on 3t choc & grn (R) 6.00 6.00
230 A22 1m on 2m dk bl & blk (R) 1.00 1.00
Nos. 217-230 (11) 11.95 11.95

The ½m on ⅛m orange and light blue and ½m on ¼m indigo and red orange were clandestinely printed and never sold at the post office.

No. 230 with double surcharge in red and blue is a color trial.

Ras Makonnen — A25

View of Hawash River and Railroad Bridge A26

Empress Menen — A27

Designs: 2g, 8g, Haile Selassie (profile). 4g, 1t, Statue of Menelik II. 3t, Empress Menen (full face). 5t, Haile Selassie (full face).

Perf. 12½, 12x12½, 12½x12.

1931, June 27 Engr.

232 A25 ⅛g red 15 15
233 A26 ¼g ol grn 15 15
234 A25 ½g dk vio 20 15
235 A27 1g red org 20 20
236 A27 2g ultra 25 25
237 A25 4g violet 35 35
238 A27 8g bl grn 1.10 1.10
239 A25 1t chocolate 2.00 2.00
240 A27 3t yel grn 3.25 3.25
241 A27 5t red brn 6.00 5.00
Nos. 232-241 (10) 13.65 12.60

Reprints of Nos. 232 to 241 are on thinner and whiter paper than the originals. Price 5c each.

Stamps of 1931 Surcharged in Blue or Carmine similar to cut

2 c

1936 *Perf. 12x12½, 12½x12.*

242 A25 1c on ⅛g red 1.10 75
243 A26 2c on ¼g ol grn (C) 1.10 75
244 A25 3c on ½g dk vio 1.10 85
245 A27 5c on 1g red org 2.00 1.25
246 A27 10c on 2g ultra (C) 2.50 1.50
Nos. 242-246 (5) 7.80 5.10

Haile Selassie
A32 A33

1942, Mar. 23 Litho. *Perf. 14x13½*

247 A32 4c lt bl grn, ind & blk 30 25
248 A32 10c rose, ind & blk 1.00 50
249 A32 20c dp ultra, ind & blk 2.00 90

1942-43 Unwmk.

250 A33 4c lt bl grn & ind 20 15
251 A33 8c yel org & ind 25 15
252 A33 10c rose & ind 40 20
253 A33 12c dl vio & ind 45 25
254 A33 20c dp ultra & ind 65 40
255 A33 25c dl grn & ind ('43) 1.10 60
256 A33 50c dl brn & ind ('43) 1.50 1.00
257 A33 60c lil & ind ('43) 2.50 1.25
Nos. 250-257 (8) 7.05 4.00

ኦብሊስክ ፡
OBELISK
3 Nov. 1943

Nos. 250-254 Surcharged in Black or Brown

3

1943, Nov. 3

258 A33 5c on 4c lt bl grn & ind 30.00 30.00
259 A33 10c on 8c yel org & ind 30.00 30.00
260 A33 15c on 10c rose & ind 30.00 30.00
261 A33 20c on 12c dl vio & ind (Br) 30.00 30.00
262 A33 30c on 20c dp ultra & ind (Br) 30.00 30.00
Nos. 258-262 (5) 150.00 150.00

Restoration of the Obelisk in Myazzia Place, Addis Ababa, and the 14th anniversary of the coronation of Emperor Haile Selassie.

On No. 262, "3" is surcharged on "2" of "20" to make "30."

Palace of Menelik II — A34

Menelik II — A35

Statue — A36

Designs: 50c, Mausoleum. 65c, Menelik II (with scepter).

1944, Dec. 31 Litho. *Perf. 10½*

263 A34 5c green 1.50 75
264 A35 10c red lil 2.00 1.00
265 A36 20c dp bl 3.50 2.00
266 A34 50c dl pur 4.00 2.00
267 A35 65c bis brn 7.50 3.00
Nos. 263-267 (5) 18.50 8.75

Issued to commemorate the centenary of the birth of Emperor Menelik II, August 18, 1844.

Unissued Semi-Postal Stamps Overprinted in Carmine:

Nurse and Baby — A39

Various Designs Inscribed "Croix Rouge".

1945, Aug. 7 Photo. *Perf. 11½*

268 A39 5c brt grn 40 40
269 A39 10c brt red 40 40
270 A39 25c brt bl 40 40
271 A39 50c dk yel brn 2.25 1.75
272 A39 1t brt vio 3.50 2.50
Nos. 268-272 (5) 6.95 5.45

Nos. 268 to 272 without overprint were ordered printed in Switzerland before Ethiopia fell to the invading Italians, so were not delivered to Addis Ababa. After that country's liberation, the set was overprinted "V" and issued for ordinary postage. These stamps exist without overprint, but were not so issued. Price $1.25.

See Nos. B36-B40.

Lion of Judah — A44

Menelik II — A45

Mail Transport, Old and New A46

Designs: 50c, Old Post Office, Addis Ababa. 70c, Menelik II and Haile Selassie.

1947, Apr. 18 Engr. *Perf. 13*

273 A44 10c yel org 1.75 60
274 A45 20c dp bl 2.25 75
275 A46 30c org brn 3.50 1.25
276 A46 50c dk sl grn 8.00 2.50
277 A46 70c red vio 15.00 5.00
Nos. 273-277 (5) 30.50 10.10

Issued to commemorate the 50th anniversary of Ethiopia's postal system.

Haile Selassie and Franklin D. Roosevelt — A49

Design: 65c, Roosevelt and U. S. Flags.

Engraved and Photogravure

1947, May 23 Unwmk. *Perf. 12½*

278 A49 12c car lake & bl grn 35 20
279 A49 25c dk bl & rose 75 40
280 A49 65c blk, red & dp bl 1.50 1.00
Nos. 278-280,C21-C22 (5) 37.60 36.60

Negus Sahle Selassie A50

Negus Sahle Selassie — A52

Design: 30c, View of Ankober.

1947, May 1 Engr. *Perf. 13*

281 A50 20c dp bl 1.50 75
282 A50 30c dk pur 2.50 1.00
283 A52 $1 dp grn 6.00 3.00

150th anniversary of Selassie dynasty.

No. 255 Surcharged in Orange

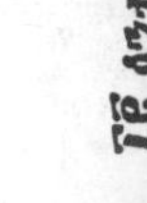

1947, July 14 *Perf. 14x13½*

284 A33 12c on 25c dl grn & ind 40.00 40.00

Amba Alaguie A53

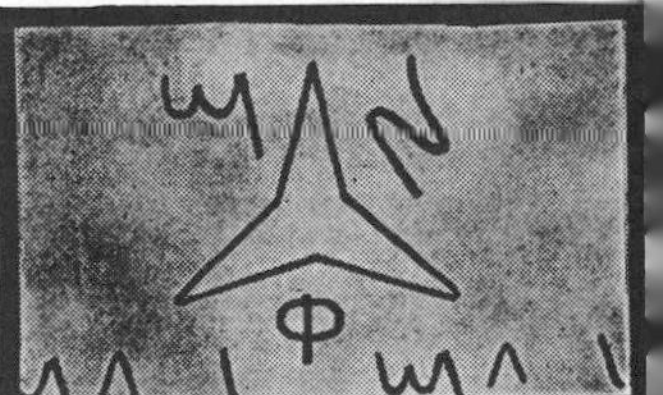

Wmk. 282- Ethiopian Star and Amharic Characters, Multiple

Designs: 2c, Trinity Church. 4c, Debra Sina. 5c, Mecan, near Achanguie. 8c, Lake Tana. 12c, 15c, Parliament Building, Addis Ababa. 20c, Aiba, near Mai Cheo. 30c, Bahr Bridge over Blue Nile. 60c, 70c, Canoe on Lake Tana. $1, Omo Falls. $3, Mt. Alamata. $5, Ras Dashan Mountains.

Perf. 13x13½

1947-53 Engr. Wmk. 282

285 A53 1c rose vio 10 5
286 A53 2c bl vio 15 8
287 A53 4c green 25 12
288 A53 5c dk grn 25 12
289 A53 8c dp org 40 20
290 A53 12c red 50 20
290A A53 15c dk ol brn ('53) 45 20
291 A53 20c blue 75 30
292 A53 30c org brn 1.25 40
292A A53 60c red ('51) 1.50 70
293 A53 70c rose lil 2.00 50
294 A53 $1 dk car rose 3.50 50

295 A53 $3 brt bl 9.00 2.00
296 A53 $5 olive 15.00 4.00
Nos. 285-296 (14) 35.10 9.37

Issue dates: 15c, May 25, 1953; 60c, Feb. 10, 1951; others, Aug. 23, 1947.

Empress Waizero Menen and Haile Selassie A54

1949, May 5 Wmk. 282 ***Perf. 13***
297 A54 20c blue 1.00 50
298 A54 30c yel org 1.00 65
299 A54 50c purple 2.50 1.25
300 A54 80c green 3.00 1.50
301 A54 $1 red 5.50 2.50
Nos. 297-301 (5) 13.00 6.40

Central ornaments differ on each denomination.
Issued to commemorate the eighth anniversary of Ethiopia's liberation from Italian occupation.

Dejach Balcha Hospital A55

Abuna Petros — A56

Designs: 20c, Haile Selassie raising flag. 30c, Lion of Judah statue. 50c, Empress Waizero Menen, Haile Selassie and building.

Perf. 13x13½, 13½x13.
1950, Nov. 2 Engr. Wmk. 282
302 A55 5c purple 60 30
303 A56 10c dp plum 1.50 60
304 A56 20c dp car 2.00 75
305 A56 30c green 3.50 1.50
306 A55 50c dp bl 6.00 3.00
Nos. 302-306 (5) 13.60 6.15

Issued to commemorate the 20th anniversary of the coronation of Emperor Haile Selassie and Empress Menen.

Abbaye Bridge — A57

1951, Jan. 1 Unwmk. ***Perf. 14***
308 A57 5c dk grn & dk brn 3.50 30
309 A57 10c dp org & blk 5.00 35
310 A57 15c dp bl & org brn 7.00 50
311 A57 30c ol & lil rose 12.50 65
312 A57 60c brn & dp bl 17.50 1.50
313 A57 80c pur & grn 22.50 2.25
Nos. 308-313 (6) 68.00 5.55

Issued to commemorate the opening of the Abbaye Bridge over the Blue Nile.

Tomb of Ras Makonnen A58

1951, Mar. 2
Center in Black.
314 A58 5c dk grn 1.75 25
315 A58 10c dp ultra 1.75 35
316 A58 15c blue 2.50 35
317 A58 30c claret 6.00 1.35
318 A58 80c rose car 8.00 2.00
319 A58 $1 org brn 10.00 2.00
Nos. 314-319 (6) 30.00 6.30

55th anniversary of the Battle of Adwa.

Haile Selassie — A59

1952, July 23 ***Perf. 13½***
320 A59 5c dk grn 35 20
321 A59 10c red org 60 25
322 A59 15c black 85 35
323 A59 25c ultra 1.25 35
324 A59 30c violet 1.50 60
325 A59 50c rose red 2.25 85
326 A59 65c chocolate 3.75 1.50
Nos. 320-326 (7) 10.55 4.10

60th birthday of Haile Selassie.

Open Road to Sea — A60

Designs: 25c, 50c, Road and broken chain. 65c, Map. 80c, Allegory: Reunion. $1, Haile Selassie raising flag. $2, Ethiopian flag and seascape. $3, Haile Selassie addressing League of Nations.

Wmk. 282
1952, Sept. 11 Engr. ***Perf. 13***
327 A60 15c brn car 75 30
328 A60 25c red brn 1.00 50
329 A60 30c yel brn 1.75 75
330 A60 50c purple 2.25 90
331 A60 65c gray 3.00 1.10
332 A60 80c bl grn 3.50 75
333 A60 $1 rose car 7.00 1.75
334 A60 $2 dp bl 13.00 3.00
335 A60 $3 magenta 27.50 5.00
Nos. 327-335 (9) 59.75 14.05

Issued to celebrate Ethiopia's federation with Eritrea, effected Sept. 11, 1952.

Haile Selassie and New Ethiopian Port A61

Design: 15c, 30c, Haile Selassie on deck of ship.

1953, Oct. 4
337 A61 10c red & dk brn 1.25 75
338 A61 15c bl & dk grn 1.50 75
339 A61 25c org & dk brn 2.50 1.25
340 A61 30c red brn & dk grn 4.50 1.50
341 A61 50c pur & dk brn 8.50 3.25
Nos. 337-341 (5) 18.25 7.50

Issued to commemorate the first anniversary of the federation of Ethiopia and Eritrea.

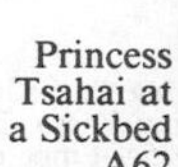

Princess Tsahai at a Sickbed A62

Canceled-to-order stamps are often from remainders. Most collectors of canceled stamps prefer postally used specimens.

Perf. 13x13½
1955, July 8 Engr. Wmk. 282
Cross Typo. in Red
342 A62 15c choc & ultra 1.00 50
343 A62 20c grn & org 1.50 60
344 A62 30c ultra & grn 2.50 75

Issued to commemorate the 20th anniversary of the founding of the Ethiopian Red Cross.

Promulgating the Constitution — A63

Bishops' Consecration by Archbishop — A64

Designs: 25c, Kagnew Battalion. 35c, Reunion with the Motherland. 50c, "Progress." 65c, Empress Waizero Menen and Haile Selassie.

Perf. 12½
1955, Nov. 3 Unwmk. Engr.
345 A63 5c grn & choc 50 25
346 A64 20c car & brn 1.10 35
347 A64 25c mag & gray 1.50 50
348 A63 35c brn & red org 2.00 65
349 A64 50c dk brn & ultra 3.00 1.00
350 A64 65c vio & car 4.25 1.50
Nos. 345-350 (6) 12.35 4.25

Issued to commemorate the silver jubilee of the coronation of Emperor Haile Selassie and Empress Waizero Menen.

Emperor Haile Selassie and Fair Emblem — A65

1955, Nov. 5 Wmk. 282
351 A65 5c grn & ol grn 60 15
352 A65 10c car & dp ultra 90 25
353 A65 15c vio blk & grn 1.25 35
354 A65 50c mag & red brn 1.75 90

Silver Jubilee Fair, Addis Ababa.

Nos. 291 and [illegible]2A Overprinted

የዓለም ስደተኞች፡ዓመት።
World Refugee Year
1959-1960

1960, Apr. 7 ***Perf. 13x13½***
355 A53 20c blue 35 25
356 A53 60c red 75 50

Issued to publicize World Refugee Year, July 1, 1959-June 30, 1960.

Map of Africa, "Liberty" and Haile Selassie — A66

Emperor Haile Selassie — A67

Perf. 13½
1960, June 14 Engr. Unwmk.
357 A66 20c org & grn 60 60
358 A66 80c org & vio 1.50 60
359 A66 $1 org & mar 1.75 80

Issued to commemorate the 2nd Conference of Independent African States at Tunis. Issued in sheets of 10.

1960, Nov. 2 Wmk. 282 ***Perf. 14***
360 A67 10c brn & bl 40 20
361 A67 25c vio & emer 80 25
362 A67 50c dk bl & org yel 1.50 1.00
363 A67 65c sl grn & sal pink 2.00 1.00
364 A67 $1 ind & rose vio 3.00 1.50
Nos. 360-364 (5) 7.70 3.95

Issued to commemorate the 30th anniversary of the coronation of Emperor Haile Selassie.

Africa Hall, U.N. Economic Commission for Africa — A68

1961, Apr. 15 Wmk. 282 ***Perf. 14***
365 A68 80c ultra 1.00 50

Issued for Africa Freedom Day, Apr. 15. Issued in sheets of 10.

Map of Ethiopia, Olive Branch and Emperor Haile Selassie A69

1961, May 5 ***Perf. 13x13½***
366 A69 20c green 20 15
367 A69 30c vio bl 30 20
368 A69 $1 brown 1.25 60

Issued to commemorate the 20th anniversary of Ethiopia's liberation from Italian occupation.

African Wild Ass — A70

Designs: 15c, Eland. 25c, Elephant. 35c, Giraffe. 50c, Beisa. $1, Lion.

1961, June 16 Wmk. 282 ***Perf. 14***
369 A70 5c blk & emer 15 5
370 A70 15c red brn & grn 20 5
371 A70 25c sep & emer 30 15
372 A70 35c lt red brn & grn 40 20
373 A70 50c brn red & emer 50 35
374 A70 $1 red brn & grn 1.50 85
Nos. 369-374 (6) 3.05 1.65

Issued in sheets of 10.

Emperor Haile Selassie and Empress Waizero Menen
A71

1961, July 27 Unwmk. *Perf. 11*
375 A71 10c green 50 25
376 A71 50c vio bl 1.00 50
377 A71 $1 car rose 1.75 1.00

Issued to commemorate the golden wedding anniversary of the Emperor and Empress.

Warlike Horsemanship (Guks) — A72

Designs: 15c, Hockey. 20c, Bicycling. 30c, Soccer. 50c, Marathon runner, Olympic winner, 1960.

Photogravure and Engraved

1962, Jan. 14 *Perf. 12x11½*
378 A72 10c yel grn & car 15 5
379 A72 15c pink & dk brn 20 6
380 A72 20c red & blk 25 10
381 A72 30c ultra & dl pur 35 15
382 A72 50c yel & grn 75 25
Nos. 378-382 (5) 1.70 61

Issued to commemorate the Third Africa Football (soccer) Cup, Addis Ababa, Jan. 14-22.

Malaria Eradication Emblem, World Map and Mosquito — A73

Wmk. 282

1962, Apr. 7 Engr. *Perf. 13½*
383 A73 15c black 20 10
384 A73 30c purple 40 25
385 A73 60c red brn 1.00 60

Issued for the World Health Organization drive to eradicate malaria.

Abyssinian Ground Hornbill
A74

Birds: 15c, Abyssinian roller. 30c, Bataleur (vert.). 50c, Double-toothed barbet (vert.). $1, Didric cuckoo.

Perf. 11½

1962, May 5 Unwmk. Photo.

Granite Paper

386 A74 5c multi 20 10
387 A74 15c emer, brn & ultra 40 15
388 A74 30c lt brn, blk & red 75 25
389 A74 50c multi 1.50 60
390 A74 $1 multi 3.00 1.25
Nos. 386-390 (5) 5.85 2.35

See also Nos. C77-C81, C97-C101, C107-C111.

Assab Hospital
A75

Designs: 15c, School at Assab. 20c, Church at Massawa. 50c, Mosque at Massava. 60c, Assab port.

Wmk. 282

1962, Sept. 11 Engr. *Perf. 13½*
391 A75 3c purple 15 5
392 A75 15c dk bl 20 10
393 A75 20c green 25 10
394 A75 50c brown 50 25
395 A75 60c car rose 75 35
Nos. 391-395 (5) 1.85 85

Issued to commemorate the tenth anniversary of the Federation of Ethiopia and Eritrea.

King Bazen, Madonna and Stars over Bethlehem — A76

Designs: 15c, Ezana, obelisks and temple. 20c, Kaleb and sailing fleet. 50c, Lalibela, rock-church and frescoes (vert.). 60c, Yekuno Amlak and priests preaching in village. 75c, Zara Yacob and procession around tree. $1, Lebna Dengel and tournament.

Perf. 14½

1962, Nov. 2 Unwmk. Photo.
396 A76 10c multi 15 10
397 A76 15c multi 25 10
398 A76 20c multi 30 10
399 A76 50c multi 50 20
400 A76 60c multi 55 30
401 A76 75c multi 90 50
402 A76 $1 multi 1.25 75
Nos. 396-402 (7) 3.90 2.05

Issued on the 32nd anniversary of the coronation of Emperor Haile Selassie and to commemorate ancient kings and saints.

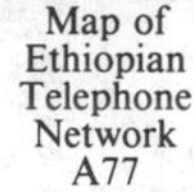
Map of Ethiopian Telephone Network
A77

Wheat Emblem
A78

Designs: 50c, Radio mast and waves. 60c, Telegraph pole and rising sun.

Perf. 13½x14

1963, Jan. 1 Engr. Wmk. 282
403 A77 10c dk red 40 10
404 A77 50c ultra 1.00 40
405 A77 60c brown 1.25 50

Issued to commemorate the 10th anniversary of the Imperial Board of Telecommunications.

1963, Mar. 21 Unwmk. *Perf. 13½*
406 A78 5c dp rose 10 5
407 A78 10c rose car 15 10
408 A78 15c vio bl 20 10
409 A78 30c emerald 30 20

Issued for the "Freedom from Hunger" campaign of the U.N. Food and Agriculture Organization.

Abuna Salama — A79

Queen of Sheba — A80

Spiritual Leaders: 15c, Abuna Aregawi. 30c, Abuna Tekle Haimanot. 40c. Yared. 60c, Zara Yacob.

1964, Jan. 3 Unwmk. *Perf. 13½*
410 A79 10c blue 25 10
411 A79 15c dk grn 35 15
412 A79 30c brn red 60 35
413 A79 40c dk bl 1.00 60
414 A79 60c brown 1.50 1.10
Nos. 410-414 (5) 3.70 2.30

1964, March 2 Photo. *Perf. 11½*

Ethiopian Queens: 15c, Helen. 50c, Seble Wongel. 60c, Mentiwab. 80, Taitu, consort of Menelik II.

Granite Paper

415 A80 10c multi 50 15
416 A80 15c multi 60 20
417 A80 50c multi 1.25 55
418 A80 60c multi 2.00 85
419 A80 80c multi 2.50 1.25
Nos. 415-419 (5) 6.85 3.00

Priest Teaching Alphabet to Children
A81

Eleanor Roosevelt
A82

Designs: 10c, Classroom. 15c, Woman learning to read (vert.). 40c, Students in chemistry laboratory (vert.). 60c, Graduation procession (vert.).

1964, June 1 Unwmk. *Perf. 11½*

Granite Paper

420 A81 5c brown 15 7
421 A81 10c emerald 15 10
422 A81 15c rose vio 20 14
423 A81 40c vio bl 60 25
424 A81 60c dk pur 1.00 50
Nos. 420-424 (5) 2.10 1.06

Issued to publicize education.

1964, Oct. 11 Photo.

Granite Paper

Portrait in Slate Blue

425 A82 10c yel bis 15 8
426 A82 60c org brn 80 50
427 A82 80c grn & gold 1.00 70

Issued to honor Eleanor Roosevelt (1884-1962).

King Serse Dengel and View of Gondar, 1563
A83

Ethiopian Leaders: 10c, King Fasiladas and Gondar in 1632. 20c, King Yassu the Great and Gondar in 1682. 25c, Emperor Theodore II and map of Ethiopia. 60c, Emperor John IV and Battle of Gura, 1876. 80c, Emperor Menelik II and Battle of Adwa, 1896.

1964, Dec. 12 Photo. *Perf. 14½x14*
428 A83 5c multi 10 5
429 A83 10c multi 15 6
430 A83 20c multi 30 15
431 A83 25c multi 50 20
432 A83 60c multi 1.00 55
433 A83 80c multi 1.25 75
Nos. 428-433 (6) 3.30 1.76

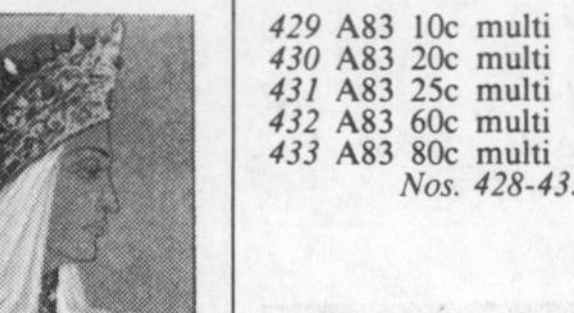

Ethiopian Rose — A84

Flowers: 10c, Kosso tree. 25c, St.-John's-wort. 35c, Parrot's-beak. 60c, Maskal daisy.

1965, Mar. 30 *Perf. 12x13½*
434 A84 5c multi 10 5
435 A84 10c multi 15 5
436 A84 25c multi 50 15
437 A84 35c multi 90 30
438 A84 60c grn, yel & org 1.25 50
Nos. 434-438 (5) 2.90 1.05

ITU Emblem, Old and New Communication Symbols — A85

Perf. 13½x14½

1965, May 17 Litho. Unwmk.
439 A85 5c bl, ind & yel 15 6
440 A85 10c bl, ind & org 25 10
441 A85 60c bl, ind & lil rose 90 50

Issued to commemorate the centenary of the International Telecommunication Union.

Laboratory
A86

Designs: 5c, Textile spinning mill. 10c, Sugar factory. 20c, Mountain road. 25c, Autobus. 30c, Diesel locomotive and bridge. 35c, Railroad station, Addis Ababa.

1965, July 19 Photo. *Perf. 11½*

Granite Paper

Portrait in Black

442 A86 3c sepia 8 5
443 A86 5c dl pur & buff 10 5
444 A86 10c blk & gray 12 5
445 A86 20c grn & pale yel 25 10
446 A86 25c dk brn & yel 35 15
447 A86 30c mar & gray 55 25
448 A86 35c dk bl & gray 65 35
Nos. 442-448 (7) 2.10 1.00

ICY Emblem
A87

1965, Oct. 24 Unwmk. *Perf. 11½*

Granite Paper

449 A87 10c bl & red brn 20 10
450 A87 50c dp bl & red brn 75 40
451 A87 80c vio bl & red brn 1.00 60

International Cooperation Year, 1965.

National Bank Emblem
A88

Designs: 10c, Commercial Bank emblem. 60c, National and Commercial Bank buildings.

1965, Nov. 2 Photo. *Perf. 13*

452 A88 10c dp car, blk & ind 35 10
453 A88 30c ultra, blk & ind 65 30
454 A88 60c blk, yel & ind 95 50

Issued to publicize the National and Commercial Banks of Ethiopia.

"Light and Peace" Press Building A89

1966, Apr. 5 Engr. *Perf. 13*

455 A89 5c pink & blk 8 5
456 A89 15c lt yel grn & blk 35 12
457 A89 30c org yel & blk 60 30

Issued to commemorate the opening of the "Light and Peace" Printing Press building.

Kebero Drum — A90

Musical Instruments: 10c, Begena harp. 35c, Mesenko guitar. 50c, Krar lyre. 60c, Washent flutes.

1966, Sept. 9 Photo. *Perf. 13½*

458 A90 5c brt grn & blk 10 5
459 A90 10c dl bl & blk 15 8
460 A90 35c org & blk 55 25
461 A90 50c yel & blk 80 35
462 A90 60c rose car & blk 1.00 60
Nos. 458-462 (5) 2.60 1.33

Emperor Haile Selassie — A91

1966, Nov. 1 Unwmk. *Perf. 12*

463 A91 10c blk, gold & grn 15 5
464 A91 15c blk, gold & dp car 30 10
465 A91 40c blk & gold 90 60

Issued to commemorate 50 years of leadership of Emperor Haile Selassie.

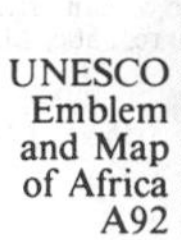
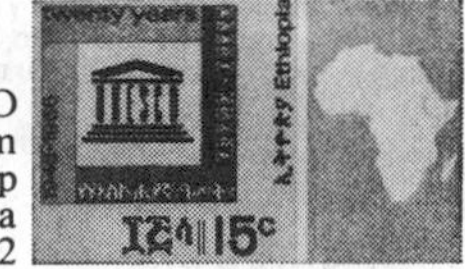

UNESCO Emblem and Map of Africa A92

Wmk. 282

1966, Nov. 30 Litho. *Perf. 13½*

466 A92 15c bl car & blk 35 10
467 A92 60c ol, brn & dk bl 90 45

Issued to commemorate the 20th anniversary of UNESCO (United Nations Educational, Scientific and Cultural Organization).

WHO Headquarters, Geneva — A93

1966, Nov. 30

468 A93 5c ol, ultra & brn 20 5
469 A93 40c brn, pur & emer 65 35

Issued to commemorate the opening of World Health Organization Headquarters, Geneva.

Expo '67 Ethiopian Pavilion and Columns of Axum (Replica) — A94

Perf. 12x13½

1967, May 2 Photo. Unwmk.

470 A94 30c brt bl & multi 60 25
471 A94 45c multi 75 35
472 A94 80c gray & multi 1.50 60

Issued to commemorate EXPO '67, International Exhibition, Montreal, Apr. 28-Oct. 27, 1967.

Diesel Train and Map A95

1967, June 7 Photo. *Perf. 12*

473 A95 15c multi 35 15
474 A95 30c multi 75 30
475 A95 50c multi 1.25 35

Issued to commemorate the 50th anniversary of the Djibouti-Addis Ababa railroad.

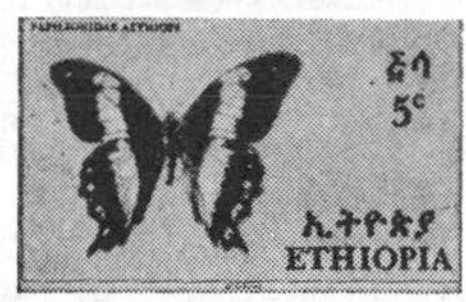

Papilionidae Aethiops — A96

Various Butterflies.

Perf. 13½x13

1967, June 30 Photo. Unwmk.

476 A96 5c buff & multi 10 5
477 A96 10c lil & multi 25 6
478 A96 20c multi 50 15
479 A96 35c bl & multi 1.00 35
480 A96 40c multi 1.25 40
Nos. 476-480 (5) 3.10 1.01

Emperor Haile Selassie and Lion of Judah A97

1967, July 21 *Perf. 11½*

Granite Paper

481 A97 10c dk brn, emer & gold 25 12
482 A97 15c dk brn, yel & gold 40 15
483 A97 $1 dk brn, red & gold 1.75 75

Souvenir Sheet

484 A97 $1 dk brn, pur & gold 4.00 3.75

Issued to commemorate the 75th birthday of Emperor Haile Selassie. No. 484 contains one stamp; brown marginal inscription. Size 120x75mm.

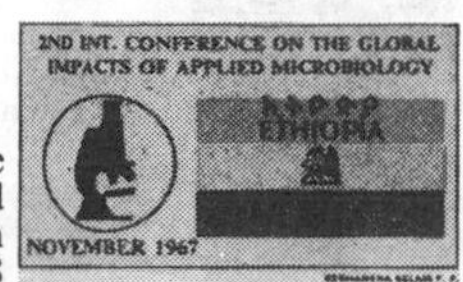

Microscope and Ethiopian Flag — A98

1967, Nov. 6 Litho. *Perf. 13*

Flag in Grn., Yel., Red & Blk.

485 A98 5c blue 15 5
486 A98 30c ocher 50 25
487 A98 $1 violet 1.75 80

Issued to commemorate the 2nd International Conference on the Global Impact of Applied Microbiology, Addis Ababa, Nov. 6-12.

Wall Painting from Debre Berhan Selassie Church, Gondar, 17th Century — A99

Designs (ITY Emblem and): 25c, Votive throne from Atsbe Dera, 4th Century B.C. (vert.). 35c, Prehistoric cave painting, Harar Provincc. 50c, Prehistoric stone tools, Melke Kontoure (vert.).

1967, Nov. 20 Photo. *Perf. 14½*

488 A99 15c multi 50 20
489 A99 25c yel grn, buff & blk 70 30
490 A99 35c grn, brn & blk 80 50
491 A99 50c yel & blk 1.00 75

International Tourist Year, 1967.

Processional Bronze Cross, Biet-Maryam Church A100

Emperor Theodore A101

Crosses of Lalibela: 10c, Processional copper cross. 15c, Copper cross, Biet-Maryam church. 20c, Lalibela-style cross. 50c, Chiseled copper cross, Madhani Alem church.

1967, Dec. 7 Photo. *Perf. 14½*

Crosses in Silver

492 A100 5c yel & blk 8 5
493 A100 10c red org & blk 15 6
494 A100 15c vio & blk 25 10
495 A100 20c brt rose & blk 30 15
496 A100 50c org yel & blk 1.10 50
Nos. 492-496 (5) 1.88 86

Perf. 14x13½

1968, Apr. 18 Litho. Unwmk.

Designs: 20c, Emperor Theodore and lions (horiz.). 50c, Imperial crown.

497 A101 10c lt vio, ocher & brn 15 6
498 A101 20c lil, brn & dk vio 35 15
499 A101 50c dk grn, org & rose cl 1.00 40

Issued to commemorate the centenary of the death of the Emperor Theodore (1818?-1868).

Human Rights Flame A102

1968, May 31 Unwmk. *Perf. 14½*

500 A102 15c pink, red & blk 30 30
501 A102 $1 lt bl, brt bl & blk 1.50 1.50

International Human Rights Year, 1968.

Shah Riza Pahlavi, Emperor and Flags A103

1968, June 3 Litho. *Perf. 13½*

502 A103 5c multi 12 12
503 A103 15c multi 25 25
504 A103 30c multi 85 85

Issued to commemorate the visit of Shah Mohammed Riza Pahlavi of Iran.

Emperor Haile Sclassie Appcaling to League of Nations, 1935 — A104

Designs: 35c, African Unity Building and map of Africa. $1, World map, symbolizing international relations.

1968, July 22 Photo. *Perf. 14x13½*

505 A104 15c bl, red, blk & gold 25 25
506 A104 35c blk, emer, red & gold 55 55
507 A104 $1 dk bl, lil, blk & gold 1.75 1.75

Ethiopia's struggle for peace.

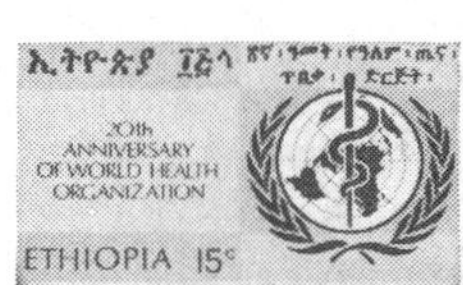

WHO Emblem A105

Perf. 14x13½

1968, Aug. 30 Litho. Unwmk.

508 A105 15c brt grn & blk 25 25
509 A105 60c red lil & blk 90 90

Issued to commemorate the 20th anniversary of the World Health Organization.

Running A106

Designs: 15c, Soccer. 20c, Boxing. 40c, Basketball. 50c, Bicycling.

1968, Oct. 12 *Perf. 11½*

510 A106 10c lt grn & multi 15 15
511 A106 15c brt vio & multi 25 25
512 A106 20c bl & multi 30 30

513 A106 40c multi 60 60
514 A106 50c beige & multi 90 90
Nos. 510-514 (5) 2.20 2.20

Issued to commemorate the 19th Olympic Games, Mexico City, Oct. 12-27.

Arrussi Woman — A107

Regional Costumes: 15c, Man from Gemu Gefa. 20c, Gojam man. 30c, Kefa man. 35c, Harer woman. 50c, Ilubabor grass coat. 60c, Woman from Eritrea.

Perf. 13½x13

1968, Dec. 10 Photo. Unwmk.
515 A107 5c sil & multi 7 7
516 A107 15c sil & multi 15 15
517 A107 20c sil & multi 20 20
518 A107 30c sil & multi 30 30
519 A107 35c sil & multi 35 35
520 A107 50c sil & multi 60 60
521 A107 60c sil & multi 85 85
Nos. 515-521 (7) 2.52 2.52

See Nos. 575-581.

Message Stick and Amharic Postal Emblem A108

1969, Mar. 10 Litho. *Perf. 14*
522 A108 10c emer, blk & brn 20 20
523 A108 15c yel, blk & brn 30 30
524 A108 35c multi 75 75

Issued to commemorate the 75th anniversary of Ethiopian postal service.

ILO Emblem A109

1969, Apr. 11 Litho. *Perf. 14½*
525 A109 15c org & blk 30 30
526 A109 60c emer & blk 1.25 1.25

Issued to commemorate the 50th anniversary of the International Labor Organization.

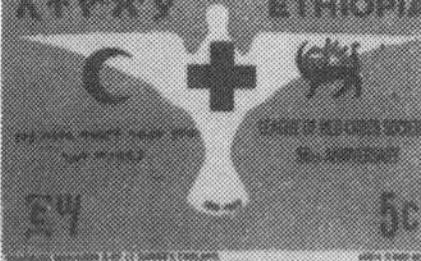

Dove, Red Cross, Crescent, Lion and Sun Emblems A110

1969, May 8 Wmk. 282 *Perf. 13*
527 A110 5c lt ultra, blk & red 8 8
528 A110 15c lt ultra, grn & red 30 30
529 A110 30c lt ultra, vio bl & red 60 60

Issued to commemorate the 50th anniversary of the League of Red Cross Societies.

Endybis Silver Coin, 3rd Century — A111

Ancient Ethiopian Coins: 10c, Gold coin of Ezana, 4th century. 15c, Gold coin of Kaleb, 6th century. 30c, Bronze coin of Armah, 7th century. 40c, Bronze coin of Wazena, 7th century. 50c, Silver coin of Gersem, 8th century.

1969, June 19 Photo. *Perf. 14½*
530 A111 5c ultra, blk & sil 10 10
531 A111 10c brt red, blk & gold 18 18
532 A111 15c brn, blk & gold 30 30
533 A111 30c dp car, blk & brnz 60 60
534 A111 40c dk grn, blk & brnz 70 70
535 A111 50c dp vio, blk & sil 90 90
Nos. 530-535 (6) 2.78 2.78

Zebras and Tourist Year Emblem A112

Designs: 10c, Camping. 15c, Fishing. 20c, Water skiing. 25c, Mountaineering (vert.).

Perf. 13x13½, 13½x13

1969, Aug. 29 Litho. Unwmk.
536 A112 5c multi 10 10
537 A112 10c multi 15 15
538 A112 15c multi 25 25
539 A112 20c multi 40 40
540 A112 25c multi 50 50
Nos. 536-540 (5) 1.40 1.40

International Year of African Tourism.

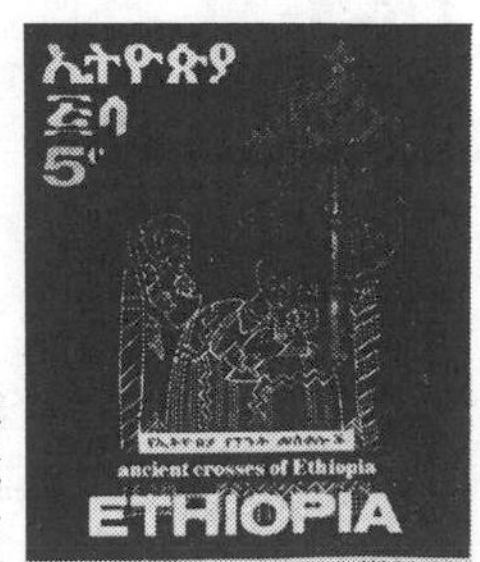

Stylized Bird and U.N. Emblem A113

Designs: 30c, Stylized flowers, U.N. and peace emblems (vert.). 60c, Stylized bird, U.N. emblem and plane.

1969, Oct. 24 Unwmk. *Perf. 11½*
541 A113 10c lt bl & multi 15 15
542 A113 30c lt bl & multi 45 45
543 A113 60c lt bl & multi 1.00 1.00

25th anniversary of the United Nations.

Ancient Cross and Holy Family A114

Designs: Various ancient crosses.

Perf. 14½x13½

1969, Dec. 10 Photo.
544 A114 5c blk, yel & dk bl 10 10
545 A114 10c blk & yel 15 15
546 A114 25c blk, yel & grn 50 50
547 A114 60c blk & ocher 1.25 1.25

Ancient Figurines — A115

Ancient Ethiopian Pottery: 20c, Vases, Yeha period, 4th-3rd centuries B.C. 25c, Vases and jugs, Axum, 4th-6th centuries A.D. 35c, Bird-shaped jug and jugs, Matara, 4th-6th centuries A.D. 60c, Decorated pottery, Adulis, 6th-7th centuries A.D.

1970, Feb. 6 Photo. *Perf. 14½*
548 A115 10c blk & multi 15 15
549 A115 20c blk & multi 30 30
550 A115 25c blk & multi 35 35
551 A115 35c blk & multi 60 60
552 A115 60c blk & multi 1.10 1.10
Nos. 548-552 (5) 2.50 2.50

Medhane Alem Church — A116

Rock Churches of Lalibela, 12th-13th Centuries: 10c, Bieta Emmanuel. 15c, The four Rock Churches of Lalibela. 20c, Bieta Mariam. 50c, Bieta Giorgis.

1970, Apr. 15 Unwmk. *Perf. 13*
553 A116 5c brn & multi 8 8
554 A116 10c brn & multi 15 15
555 A116 15c brn & multi 30 30
556 A116 20c brn & multi 50 50
557 A116 50c brn & multi 1.15 1.15
Nos. 553-557 (5) 2.18 2.18

Sailfish Tang A117

Tropical Fish: 10c, Undulate triggerfish. 15c, Orange butterflyfish. 25c, Butterflyfish. 50c, Imperial Angelfish.

1970, June 19 Photo. *Perf. 12½*
558 A117 5c multi 10 10
559 A117 10c multi 15 15
560 A117 15c multi 25 25
561 A117 25c multi 60 60
562 A117 50c multi 1.25 1.25
Nos. 558-562 (5) 2.35 2.35

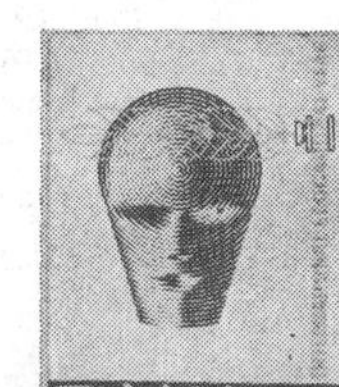

Education Year Emblem — A118

1970, Aug. 14 Unwmk. *Perf. 13½*
563 A118 10c multi 15 15
564 A118 20c gold, ultra & emer 35 35
565 A118 50c gold, emer & org 85 85

Issued for International Education Year.

Map of Africa — A119

Designs: 30c, Flag of Organization of African Unity. 40c, OAU Headquarters, Addis Ababa.

1970, Sept. 21 Photo. *Perf. 13½*
566 A119 20c multi 27 27
567 A119 30c multi 40 40
568 A119 40c grn & multi 75 75

Organization of African Unity.

Emperor Haile Selassie — A120

1970, Oct. 30 Unwmk. *Perf. 14½*
569 A120 15c Prus bl & multi 18 18
570 A120 50c multi 65 65
571 A120 60c multi 1.25 1.25

Issued to commemorate the 40th anniversary of the coronation of Emperor Haile Selassie I.

Posts, Telecommunications and G.P.O. Buildings — A121

1970, Dec. 30 Litho. *Perf. 13½*
572 A121 10c ver & multi 18 18
573 A121 50c brn & multi 1.00 1.00
574 A121 80c multi 1.25 1.25

Opening of new Posts, Telecommunications and General Post Office buildings.

Costume Type of 1968

Regional Costumes: 5c, Warrior from Begemedir and Semain. 10c, Woman from Bale. 15c, warrior from Wolega. 20c, Woman from Showa. 25c, Man from Sidamo. 40c, Woman from Tigre. 50c, Man from Wello.

1971, Feb. 17 Photo. *Perf. 11½*
Granite Paper
575 A107 5c gold & multi 8 8
576 A107 10c gold & multi 15 15
577 A107 15c gold & multi 25 25
578 A107 20c gold & multi 30 30
579 A107 25c gold & multi 40 40
580 A107 40c gold & multi 50 50
581 A107 50c gold & multi 1.00 1.00
Nos. 575-581 (7) 2.68 2.68

Plane's Tail with Emblem — A122

Designs: 10c, Ethiopian scenes. 20c, Nose of Boeing 707. 60c, Pilots in cockpit, and engine. 80c, Globe with routes shown.

1971, Apr. 8 ***Perf. 14½x14***

582 A122 5c multi 8 8
583 A122 10c multi 15 15
584 A122 20c multi 30 30
585 A122 60c multi 1.00 1.00
586 A122 80c multi 1.35 1.35
Nos. 582-586 (5) 2.88 2.88

Ethiopian Airlines, 25th anniversary.

Fountain of Life, 15th Century Gospel Book — A123

Ethiopian Paintings: 10c, King David, 15th century manuscript. 25c, St. George, 17th century painting on canvas. 50c, King Lalibela, 18th century painting on wood. 60c, Yared singing before King Kaleb. mural in Axum Cathedral,

1971, June 15 **Photo.** ***Perf. 11½***
Granite Paper

587 A123 5c tan & multi 8 8
588 A123 10c pale sal & multi 15 15
589 A123 25c lem & multi 30 30
590 A123 50c yel & multi 80 80
591 A123 60c gray & multi 1.25 1.25
Nos. 587-591 (5) 2.58 2.58

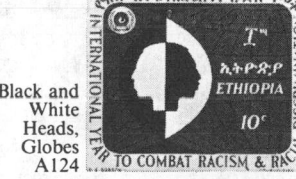

Black and White Heads, Globes A124

Designs: 60c, Black and white hand holding globe. 80c, Four races, globes.

1971, Aug. 31 **Unwmk.**

592 A124 10c org, red brn & blk 20 20
593 A124 60c grn, bl & blk 75 75
594 A124 80c bl, org, yel & blk 1.25 1.25

International Year Against Racial Discrimination.

Emperor Menelik II and Reading of Treaty of Ucciali A125

Contemporary Paintings: 30c, Menelik II on horseback gathering the tribes. 50c, Ethiopians and Italians in Battle of Adwa. 60c, Menelik II at head of his army.

1971, Oct. 20 **Litho.** ***Perf. 13½***

595 A125 10c multi 20 20
596 A125 30c multi 50 50
597 A125 50c multi 75 75
598 A125 60c multi 1.25 1.25

75th anniversary of victory of Adwa over the Italians, March 1, 1896.

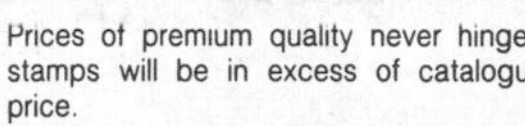
Prices of premium quality never hinged stamps will be in excess of catalogue price.

Haile Selassie Broadcasting and Map of Ethiopia — A126

Designs: 5c, Two telephones, 1897, Menelik II and Ras Makonnen. 30c, Ethiopians around television set. 40c, Telephone microwave circuits. 60c, Map of Africa on globe and telephone dial.

1971, Nov. 2

599 A126 5c bry & multi 6 6
600 A126 10c yel & multi 12 12
601 A126 30c vio bl & multi 40 40
602 A126 40c blk & multi 55 55
603 A126 60c vio bl & multi 1.10 1.10
Nos. 599-603 (5) 2.23 2.23

75th anniversary of telecommunications in Ethiopia.

UNICEF Emblem, Mother and Child — A127

Designs (UNICEF Emblem and): 10c, Children drinking milk. 15c, Man holding sick child. 30c, Kindergarten class. 50c, Father and son.

1971, Dec. 15 **Unwmk.**

604 A127 5c yel & multi 8 8
605 A127 10c pale brn & multi 15 15
606 A127 15c rose & multi 22 22
607 A127 30c vio & multi 45 45
608 A127 50c grn & multi 75 75
Nos. 604-608 (5) 1.65 1.65

25th anniversary of the United Nations International Children's Fund (UNICEF).

Nos. 445-448 Overprinted

U.N. SECURITY COUNCIL FIRST MEETING IN AFRICA 1972

1972, Jan. 28 **Photo.** ***Perf. 11***
Portrait in Black

609 A86 20c grn & pale yel 30 30
610 A86 25c dk brn & yel 45 45
611 A86 30c mar & gray 65 65
612 A86 35c dk bl & gray 80 80

First meeting of U.N. Security Council in Africa.

River Boat on Lake Haik — A128

1972, Feb. 7 **Litho.** ***Perf. 11½***
Granite Paper

613 A128 10c *shown* 15 15
614 A128 20c *Boats on Lake Abaya* 30 30
615 A128 30c *on Lake Tana* 60 60
616 A128 60c *on Baro River* 1.25 1.25

Proclamation of Cyrus the Great — A129

1972, Mar. 28 **Photo.** ***Perf. 14x14½***

617 A129 10c red & multi 15 15
618 A129 60c emer & multi 90 90
619 A129 80c gray & multi 1.25 1.25

2500th anniversary of the founding of the Persian empire by Cyrus the Great.

Houses, Sidamo Province A130

Ethiopian Architecture: 10c, Tigre Province. 20c, Eritrea Province. 40c, Addis Ababa. 80c, Shoa Province.

1972, Apr. 11 **Litho.** ***Perf. 13½***

620 A130 5c blk & multi 8 8
621 A130 10c blk, gray & brn 15 15
622 A130 20c blk & multi 30 30
623 A130 40c blk, bl grn & brn 60 60
624 A130 80c blk, brn & red brn 1.35 1.35
Nos. 620-624 (5) 2.48 2.48

Hands Holding Map of Ethiopia — A131

Designs: 10c, Hands shielding Ethiopians. 25c, Map of Africa, hands reaching for African Unity emblem. 50c, Brown and white hands clasped, U.N. emblem. 60c, Hands protecting dove. Each denomination shows different portrait of the Emperor.

Perf. 14½x14
1972, July 21 **Litho.** **Unwmk.**

625 A131 5c scar & multi 7 7
626 A131 10c ultra & multi 13 13
627 A131 25c vio bl & multi 33 33
628 A131 50c lt bl & multi 65 65
629 A131 60c brn & multi 80 80
Nos. 625-629 (5) 1.98 1.98

80th birthday of Emperor Haile Selassie.

Running, Flags of Mexico, Japan, Italy — A132

1972, Aug. 25 ***Perf. 13½x13***

630 A132 10c *shown* 13 13
631 A132 30c *Soccer* 40 40
632 A132 50c *Bicycling* 80 80
633 A132 60c *Boxing* 1.10 1.10

20th Olympic Games, Munich, Germany, Aug. 26-Sept. 11.

Open Bible, Cross and Orbit A133

Designs: 50c, First and 1972 headquarters of the British and Foreign Bible Society (vert.). 80c, First Amharic Bible.

1972, Sept. 25 **Photo.** ***Perf. 13½***

634 A133 20c dp red & multi 27 27
635 A133 50c dp red & multi 65 65
636 A133 80c dp red & multi 1.25 1.25

United Bible Societies World Assembly, Addis Ababa, Sept. 1972.

Security Council Meeting A134

Designs: 60c, Building where Security Council met. 80c, Map of Africa with flags of participating members.

1972, Nov. 1 **Litho.** ***Perf. 13½***

637 A134 10c lt bl & vio bl 13 13
638 A134 60c multi 75 75
639 A134 80c multi 1.50 1.50

First United Nations Security Council meeting, Addis Ababa, Jan. 28-Feb. 4, 1972.

Fish in Polluted Sea A135

Designs: 30c, Fisherman, beacon, family. 80c, Polluted seashore.

1973, Feb. 23 **Photo.** ***Perf. 13½***

640 A135 20c gold & multi 30 30
641 A135 30c gold & multi 45 45
642 A135 80c gold & multi 1.25 1.25

World message from the sea, Ethiopian anti-pollution campaign.

INTERPOL and Ethiopian Police Emblems — A136

Designs: 50c, INTERPOL emblem and General Secretariat, Paris. 60c, INTERPOL emblem.

1973, Mar. 20 **Photo.** ***Perf. 13½***

643 A136 40c dl org & blk 65 65
644 A136 50c bl, blk & yel 85 85
645 A136 60c dk car & blk 1.00 1.00

50th anniversary of International Criminal Police Organization (INTERPOL).

Virgin of Emperor Zara Yaqob A137

Ethiopian Art: 15c, Crucifixion, Zara Yaqob period. 30c, Virgin and Child, from Entoto Mariam Church. 40c, Christ, contemporary mosaic. 80c, The Evangelists, contemporary bas-relief.

1973, May 15 Photo. *Perf. 11½*
Granite Paper

646 A137 5c brn & multi 7 7
647 A137 15c dp bl & multi 20 20
648 A137 30c gray grn & multi 55 55
649 A137 40c multi 60 60
650 A137 80c sl & multi 1.50 1.50
Nos. 646-650 (5) 2.92 2.92

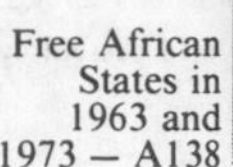

Free African States in 1963 and 1973 — A138

Designs (Map of Africa and): 10c, Flags of OAU members. 20c, Symbols of progress. 40c, Dove and people. 80c, Emblems of various UN agencies.

1973 May 25 *Perf. 14½x14*

651 A138 5c red & multi 8 8
652 A138 10c ol gray & multi 17 17
653 A138 20c grn & multi 33 33
654 A138 40c sep & multi 65 65
655 A138 80c lt bl & multi 1.75 1.75
Nos. 651-655 (5) 2.98 2.98

Organization for African Unity, 10th anniversary.

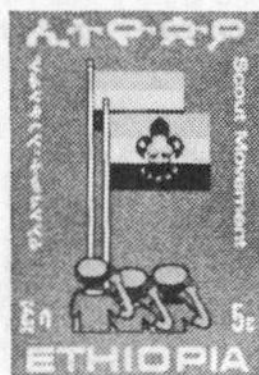

Scouts Saluting Ethiopian and Scout Flags — A139

Designs: 15c, Road and road sign. 30c, Girl Scout reading to old man. 40c, Scout and disabled people. 60c, Ethiopian Boy Scout.

1973, July 10 Photo. *Perf. 11½*
Granite Paper

656 A139 5c bl & multi 7 7
657 A139 15c lt grn & multi 20 20
658 A139 30c yel & multi 42 42
659 A139 40c crim & multi 60 60
660 A139 60c vio & multi 1.10 1.10
Nos. 656-660 (5) 2.39 2.39

24th Boy Scout World Conference, Nairobi, Kenya, July 16-21.

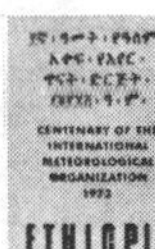

WMO Emblem A140

Designs: 50c, WMO emblem and anemometer. 60c, Weather satellite over earth, and WMO emblem.

1973, Sept. 4 Photo. *Perf. 13½*

661 A140 40c blk, bl & dl bl 55 55
662 A140 50c dl bl & blk 65 65
663 A140 60c dl bl & multi 1.00 1.00

Centenary of international meteorological cooperation.

Prince Makonnen, Duke of Harer — A141

Human Rights Flame — A142

Designs: 5c, Old wall of Harer. 20c, Operating room. 40c, Boy Scouts learning first aid, and hospital. 80c, Prince Makonnen and hospital.

1973, Nov. 1 Unwmk. *Perf. 14½*

664 A141 5c gray & multi 5 5
665 A141 10c red brn & multi 10 10
666 A141 20c grn & multi 30 30
667 A141 40c brn red & multi 65 65
668 A141 80c ultra & multi 1.35 1.35
Nos. 664-668 (5) 2.45 2.45

Opening of Prince Makonnen Memorial Hospital.

Perf. 11½
1973, Nov. 16 Photo. Unwmk.
Granite Paper

669 A142 40c yel, gold & dk grn 60 60
670 A142 50c lt grn, gold & dk grn 75 75
671 A142 60c org, gold & dk grn 1.00 1.00

25th anniversary of the Universal Declaration of Human Rights.

Emperor Haile Selassie — A143

1973, Nov. 5 Photo. *Perf. 11½*

672 A143 5c yel & multi 5 5
673 A143 10c brt bl & multi 12 5
674 A143 15c grn & multi 18 7
675 A143 20c dl yel & multi 25 10
676 A143 25c multi 30 13
677 A143 30c multi 35 15
678 A143 35c multi 42 17
679 A143 40c ultra & multi 48 20
680 A143 45c multi 55 22
681 A143 50c org & multi 60 25
682 A143 55c mag & multi 75 50
683 A143 60c multi 90 65
684 A143 70c red org & multi 1.00 70
685 A143 90c brt vio & multi 1.20 85
686 A143 $1 multi 1.60 1.10
687 A143 $2 org & multi 3.00 2.00
688 A143 $3 multi 4.50 3.00
689 A143 $5 multi 7.50 5.00
Nos. 672-689 (18) 23.75 15.19

Wicker Furniture A144

Designs: Various wicker baskets, wall hangings, dinnerware.

1974, Jan. 31 Photo. *Perf. 11½*
Granite Paper

690 A144 5c vio bl & multi 5 5
691 A144 10c vio bl & multi 10 10
692 A144 30c vio bl & multi 30 30
693 A144 50c vio bl & multi 60 60
694 A144 60c vio bl & multi 75 75
Nos. 690-694 (5) 1.80 1.80

Cow, Calf, Syringe — A145

Designs: 15c, Inoculation of cattle. 20c, Bullock and syringe. 50c, Laboratory technician, cow's head, syringe. 60c, Map of Ethiopia, cattle, syringe.

1974, Feb. 20 Litho. *Perf. 13½x13*

695 A145 5c sep & multi 5 5
696 A145 15c ultra & multi 15 15
697 A145 20c ultra & multi 20 20
698 A145 50c org & multi 75 75
699 A145 60c gold & multi 1.00 1.00
Nos. 695-699 (5) 2.15 2.15

Campaign against cattle plague.

Umbrella Makers A146

Designs: 30c, Weaving. 50c, Child care. 60c, Foundation headquarters.

1974, Apr. 17 Photo. *Perf. 14½*

700 A146 10c lt lil & multi 10 10
701 A146 30c multi 30 30
702 A146 50c multi 60 60
703 A146 60c bl & multi 75 75

20th anniversary of Haile Selassie I Foundation.

Ceremonial Robe — A147

Designs: Ceremonial robes.

1974, June 26 Litho. *Perf. 13*

704 A147 15c multi 15 15
705 A147 25c ocher & multi 25 25
706 A147 35c grn & multi 50 50
707 A147 40c lt brn & multi 60 60
708 A147 60c gray & multi 85 85
Nos. 704-708 (5) 2.35 2.35

World Population Statistics A148

Designs: 50c, "Larger families-lower living standard." 60c, Rising population graph.

1974, Aug. 19 Photo. *Perf. 14½*

709 A148 40c yel & multi 50 50
710 A148 50c vio & multi 60 60
711 A148 60c grn & multi 75 75

World Population Year 1974.

UPU Emblem, Letter Carrier's Staff — A149

Celebration Around "Damara" Pillar — A150

Designs (UPU Emblem and): 50c, Letter and flags. 60c, Globe. 70c, Headquarters Bern.

1974, Oct. 9 Photo. *Perf. 11½*
Granite Paper

712 A149 15c yel & multi 15 1
713 A149 50c multi 60 6
714 A149 60c ultra & multi 75 7
715 A149 70c multi 85 8

Centenary of Universal Postal Union.

1974, Dec. 17 Photo. *Perf. 14x14½*

Designs: 5c, Site of Gishen Mariam Monastery. 20c, Cross and festivities. 80c, Torch (Chibos) Parade.

716 A150 5c yel & multi 5
717 A150 10c yel & multi 10 1
718 A150 20c yel & multi 25 2
719 A150 80c yel & multi 1.00 1.0

Meskel Festival, Sept. 26-27, commemorating the finding in the 4th century of the True Cross, of which a fragment is kept at Gishen Mariam Monastery in Wollo Province.

Precis Clelia — A151

Adoration of the Kings — A152

Butterflies: 25c, Charaxes achaemenes. 45c, Papilio dardanus. 50c, Charaxes druceanus. 60c, Papilio demodocus.

1975, Feb. 18 Photo. *Perf. 12x12½*

720 A151 10c sil & multi 10 10
721 A151 25c gold & multi 25 2
722 A151 45c pur & multi 65 6
723 A151 50c grn & multi 85 8
724 A151 60c brt bl & multi 1.00 1.0
Nos. 720-724 (5) 2.85 2.8

1975, Apr. 23 Photo. *Perf. 11½*

Designs: 10c, Baptism of Jesus. 15c, Jesus teaching in the Temple. 30c, Jesus giving sight to the blind. 40c, Crucifixion. 80c, Resurrection.

Granite Paper

725 A152 5c brn & multi 5 5
726 A152 10c blk & multi 10 10
727 A152 15c dk brn & multi 15 15
728 A152 30c dk brn & multi 30 30
729 A152 40c blk & multi 60 60
730 A152 80c sl & multi 1.10 1.10
Nos. 725-730 (6) 2.30 2.30

Murals from Ethiopian churches.

Warthog A153

Designs: Wild animals.

975, May 27 Photo. *Perf. 11½*

Granite Paper

No.	Type	Denom.	Description	Unused	Used
31	A153	5c	*shown*	5	5
32	A153	10c	*Aardvark*	10	10
33	A153	20c	*Semien wolf*	20	20
34	A153	40c	*Gelada baboon*	50	50
35	A153	80c	*Civet*	1.10	1.10
			Nos. 731-735 (5)	1.95	1.95

"Peace," Dove, Globe, IWY Emblem — A154

Designs (IWY Emblem and): 50c, Symbols f development. 90c, Equality between men nd women.

975, June 30 Litho. *Perf. 14x14½*

No.	Type	Denom.	Description	Unused	Used
36	A154	40c	bl & blk	50	50
37	A154	50c	sal & multi	60	60
'38	A154	90c	multi	1.25	1.25

International Women's Year 1975.

Postal Museum A155

Designs: Various interior views of Postal Auseum.

1975, Aug. 19 Photo. *Perf. 13x12½*

No.	Type	Denom.	Description	Unused	Used
'39	A155	10c	ocher & multi	10	10
'40	A155	30c	pink & multi	30	30
'41	A155	60c	multi	75	75
'42	A155	70c	lt grn & multi	85	85

Ethiopian National Postal Museum, opening.

Map of Ethiopia and Sun — A156

1975, Sept. 11 Photo. *Perf. 11½*

Granite Paper

No.	Type	Denom.	Description	Unused	Used
743	A156	5c	lil & multi	5	5
744	A156	10c	ultra & multi	10	10
745	A156	25c	brn & multi	25	25
746	A156	50c	yel & multi	60	60
747	A156	90c	brt grn & multi	1.10	1.10
			Nos. 743-747 (5)	2.10	2.10

1st anniversary of Ethiopia Tikdem (Socialism).

U.N. Emblem A157

1975, Oct. 24 Photo. *Perf. 11½*

No.	Type	Denom.	Description	Unused	Used
748	A157	40c	lil & multi	50	50
749	A157	50c	multi	60	60
750	A157	90c	bl & multi	1.10	1.10

United Nations, 30th anniversary.

Scott's editorial staff cannot undertake to identify, authenticate or appraise stamps and postal markings.

Ilubabor Hair Style A158

Delphinium Wellbyi A159

Regional Hair Styles: 15c, Arusi. 20c, Eritrea. 30c, Bale. 35c, Kefa. 50c, Begemdir. 60c, Shewa.

1975, Dec. 15 Photo. *Perf. 11½*

No.	Type	Denom.	Description	Unused	Used
751	A158	5c	multi	5	5
752	A158	15c	multi	15	15
753	A158	20c	multi	25	25
754	A158	30c	multi	35	35
755	A158	35c	multi	50	50
756	A158	50c	multi	60	60
757	A158	60c	multi	75	75
			Nos. 751-757 (7)	2.65	2.65

See Nos. 832-838.

1976, Jan. 15 Photo. *Perf. 11½*

Flowers: 10c, Plectocephalus varians. 20c, Brachystelma asmarensis (horiz.). 40c, Ceropegia inflata. 80c, Erythrina brucei.

No.	Type	Denom.	Description	Unused	Used
758	A159	5c	multi	5	5
759	A159	10c	multi	10	10
760	A159	20c	multi	25	25
761	A159	40c	multi	50	50
762	A159	80c	multi	1.00	1.00
			Nos. 758-762 (5)	1.90	1.90

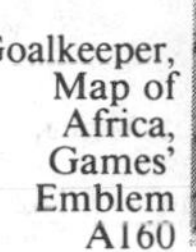

Goalkeeper, Map of Africa, Games' Emblem A160

Designs; Various scenes from soccer, map of Africa and ball.

1976, Feb. 27 Photo. *Perf. 14½*

No.	Type	Denom.	Description	Unused	Used
763	A160	5c	org & multi	5	5
764	A160	10c	yel & multi	10	10
765	A160	25c	lil & multi	30	30
766	A160	50c	grn & multi	60	60
767	A160	90c	brt grn & multi	1.10	1.10
			Nos. 763-767 (5)	2.15	2.15

10th African Cup of Nations, Addis Ababa and Dire Dawa, Feb. 29-Mar. 14.

Telephones, 1876 and 1976 A161

Ethiopian Jewelry A162

Designs: 60c, Alexander Graham Bell. 90c, Transmission tower.

1976, Mar. 10 Litho. *Perf. 12x13½*

No.	Type	Denom.	Description	Unused	Used
768	A161	30c	lt ocher & multi	35	35
769	A161	60c	emer & multi	75	75
770	A161	90c	ver, blk & buff	1.10	1.10

Centenary of first telephone call by Alexander Graham Bell, Mar. 10, 1876.

1976, May 14 Photo. *Perf. 11½*

Designs: Women wearing various kinds of Ethiopian jewelry.

Granite Paper

No.	Type	Denom.	Description	Unused	Used
771	A162	5c	bl & multi	5	5
772	A162	10c	plum & multi	10	10
773	A162	20c	gray & multi	30	30
774	A162	40c	grn & multi	60	60
775	A162	80c	org & multi	1.10	1.10
			Nos. 771-775 (5)	2.15	2.15

Boxing A163

Hands Holding Map of Ethiopia A164

Designs (Montreal Olympic Emblem and): 80c, Runner and maple leaf. 90c, Bicycling.

1976, July 15 Litho. *Perf. 12½x12*

No.	Type	Denom.	Description	Unused	Used
776	A163	10c	multi	10	10
777	A163	80c	brt red, blk & grn	1.00	1.00
778	A163	90c	brt red & multi	1.10	1.10

21st Olympic Games, Montreal, Canada, July 17-Aug. 1.

1976, Aug. 5 Photo. *Perf. 14½*

No.	Type	Denom.	Description	Unused	Used
779	A164	5c	rose & multi	5	5
780	A164	10c	ol & multi	10	10
781	A164	25c	org & multi	25	25
782	A164	50c	multi	60	60
783	A164	90c	dk bl & multi	1.10	1.10
			Nos. 779-783 (5)	2.10	2.10

Development through cooperation.

Revolution Emblem: Eye and Map — A165

1976, Sept. 9 Photo. *Perf. 13½*

No.	Type	Denom.	Description	Unused	Used
784	A165	5c	multi	5	5
785	A165	10c	multi	10	10
786	A165	25c	multi	25	25
787	A165	50c	yel & multi	60	60
788	A165	90c	grn & multi	1.10	1.10
			Nos. 784-788 (5)	2.10	2.10

2nd anniversary of the revolution (Tikdem).

Sunburst Around Crest A166

Plane Over Man with Donkey A167

1976, Sept. 13 Photo. *Perf. 11½*

No.	Type	Denom.	Description	Unused	Used
789	A166	5c	grn gold & blk	5	5
790	A166	10c	org, gold & blk	10	5
791	A166	15c	grnsh bl, gold & blk	15	8
792	A166	20c	lil, gold & blk	20	10
793	A166	25c	brt grn, gold & blk	25	12
794	A166	30c	car, gold & blk	30	15
795	A166	35c	yel, gold & blk	35	18
796	A166	40c	ol, gold & blk	40	20
797	A166	45c	brt grn, gold & blk	45	22
798	A166	50c	car rose, gold & blk	50	25
799	A166	55c	ultra, gold & blk	55	28
800	A166	60c	fawn, gold & blk	60	30
801	A166	70c	rose, gold & blk	70	35
802	A166	90c	bl, gold & blk	90	45
803	A166	$1	dl grn, gold & blk	1.00	50
804	A166	$2	gray, gold & blk	2.00	1.00
805	A166	$3	brn vio, gold & blk	3.00	1.50
806	A166	$5	sl bl, gold & blk	5.00	2.50
			Nos. 789-806 (18)	16.50	8.28

A high value has been seen with denomination expressed as "birr" instead of "$". Information on these is needed.

1976, Oct. 28 Litho. *Perf. 12x12½*

Designs: 10c, Globe showing routes. 25c, Crew and passengers forming star. 50c, Propeller and jet engine. 90c, Airplanes surrounding map of Ethiopia.

No.	Type	Denom.	Description	Unused	Used
807	A167	5c	dl bl & multi	5	5
808	A167	10c	lil & multi	10	10
809	A167	25c	multi	25	25
810	A167	50c	org & multi	50	50
811	A167	90c	ol & multi	90	90
			Nos. 807-811 (5)	1.80	1.80

Ethiopian Airlines, 30th anniversary.

Tortoises A168

Hand Holding Makeshift Hammer A169

Reptiles: 20c, Chameleon. 30c, Python. 40c, Monitor lizard. 80c, Nile crocodiles.

1976, Dec. 15 Photo. *Perf. 14½*

No.	Type	Denom.	Description	Unused	Used
812	A168	10c	multi	10	10
813	A168	20c	multi	20	20
814	A168	30c	multi	30	30
815	A168	40c	multi	40	40
816	A168	80c	multi	80	80
			Nos. 812-816 (5)	1.80	1.80

1977, Jan. 20 Litho. *Perf. 12½*

Designs: 5c, Hands holding bowl and plane dropping food. 45c, Infant with empty bowl, and bank note. 60c, Map of affected area, footprints and tire tracks. 80c, Film strip, camera and Ethiopian sitting between eggshells.

No.	Type	Denom.	Description	Unused	Used
817	A169	5c	multi	5	5
818	A169	10c	multi	10	10
819	A169	45c	multi	45	45
820	A169	60c	multi	60	60
821	A169	80c	multi	80	80
			Nos. 817-821 (5)	2.00	2.00

Ethiopian Relief and Rehabilitation Commission for drought and disaster areas.

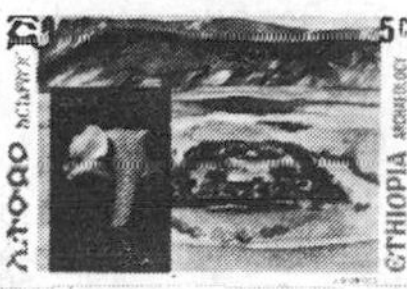

Elephant and Ruins, Axum, 7th Century A170

Designs: 10c, Ibex and temple, 5th century, B.C., Yeha. 25c, Megalithic dolmen and pottery, Sourre Kabanawa. 50c, Awash Valley, stone axe, Acheulean period. 80c, Omo Valley, hominid jawbone.

1977, Mar. 15 Photo. *Perf. 13½*

No.	Type	Denom.	Description	Unused	Used
822	A170	5c	gold & multi	5	5
823	A170	10c	gold & multi	10	10
824	A170	25c	gold & multi	25	25
825	A170	50c	gold & multi	50	50
826	A170	80c	gold & multi	80	80
			Nos. 822-826 (5)	1.70	1.70

Archaeological sites and finds in Ethiopia.

Map of Africa with Trans-East Highway — A171

1977, Mar. 30 *Perf. 14*

No.	Type	Denom.	Description	Unused	Used
827	A171	10c	gold & multi	10	10
828	A171	20c	gold & multi	20	20
829	A171	40c	gold & multi	40	40

830 A171 50c gold & multi 50 50
831 A171 60c gold & multi 60 60
Nos. 827-831 (5) 1.80 1.80

Addis Ababa to Nairobi Highway and projected highways to Cairo, Egypt, and Gaborone, Botswana.

Hairstyle Type of 1975

Regional Hairstyles: 5c, Wollega. 10c, Gojjam. 15c, Tigre. 20c, Harrar. 25c, Gemu Gofa. 40c, Sidamo. 50c, Wollo.

1977, Apr. 28 Photo. *Perf. 11½*
832 A158 5c multi 5 5
833 A158 10c multi 10 10
834 A158 15c multi 15 15
835 A158 20c multi 20 20
836 A158 25c multi 25 25
837 A158 40c multi 45 45
838 A158 50c multi 60 60
Nos. 832-838 (7) 1.80 1.80

Addis Ababa
A172

Towns of Ethiopia: 10c, Asmara. 25c, Harer. 50c, Jima. 90c, Dese.

1977, June 20 Photo. *Perf. 14½*
839 A172 5c sil & multi 5 5
840 A172 10c sil & multi 10 10
841 A172 25c sil & multi 25 25
842 A172 50c sil & multi 50 50
843 A172 90c sil & multi 90 90
Nos. 839-843 (5) 1.80 1.80

Terebratula Abyssinica
A173

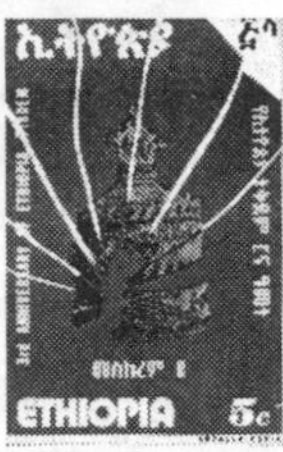
Fractured Imperial Crown
A174

Fossil Shells: 10c, Terebratula subalata. 25c, Cuculloea lefeburiaua. 50c, Ostrea plicatissima. 90c, Trigonia cousobrina.

1977, Aug. 15 Photo. *Perf. 14x13½*
844 A173 5c multi 5 5
845 A173 10c multi 10 10
846 A173 25c multi 25 25
847 A173 50c multi 50 50
848 A173 90c multi 90 90
Nos. 844-848 (5) 1.80 1.80

1977, Sept. 9 Litho. *Perf. 15*

Designs: 10c, Symbol of the Revolution (spade, axe, torch). 25c, Warriors, hammer and sickle, map of Ethiopia. 60c, Soldier, farmer and map. 80c, Map and emblem of revolutionary government.

849 A174 5c multi 5 5
850 A174 10c multi 10 10
851 A174 25c multi 25 25
852 A174 60c multi 60 60
853 A174 80c multi 80 80
Nos. 849-853 (5) 1.80 1.80

Third anniversary of the revolution.

Cicindela Petitii
A175

Lenin, Globe, Map of Ethiopia and Emblem
A176

Insects: 10c, Heliocopris dillonii. 25c, Poekilocerus vignaudii. 50c, Pepsis heros. 90c, Pepsis dedjaz.

1977, Sept. 30 Photo. *Perf. 14x13½*
854 A175 5c multi 5 5
855 A175 10c multi 10 10
856 A175 25c multi 25 25
857 A175 50c multi 50 50
858 A175 90c multi 90 90
Nos. 854-858 (5) 1.80 1.80

1977, Nov. 15 Litho. *Perf. 12*
859 A176 5c org & multi 5 5
860 A176 10c multi 10 10
861 A176 25c sal & multi 25 25
862 A176 50c lt bl & multi 50 50
863 A176 90c yel & multi 90 90
Nos. 859-863 (5) 1.80 1.80

60th anniversary of Russian October Revolution.

Chondrostoma Dilloni
A177

Salt-water Fish: 10c, Ostracion cubicus. 25c, Serranus summana. 50c, Serranus luti. 90c, Tetraodon maculatus.

1978, Jan. 20 Litho. *Perf. 15½*
864 A177 5c multi 5 5
865 A177 10c multi 10 10
866 A177 25c multi 25 25
867 A177 50c multi 50 50
868 A177 90c multi 90 90
Nos. 864-868 (5) 1.80 1.80

Cattle — A178

Domestic Animals: 10c, Mules. 25c, Goats. 50c, Dromedaries. 90c, Horses.

1978, Mar. 27 Litho. *Perf. 13½x14*
869 A178 5c yel & multi 5 5
870 A178 10c multi 10 10
871 A178 25c grn & multi 25 25
872 A178 50c ver & multi 50 50
873 A178 90c ultra & multi 90 90
Nos. 869-873 (5) 1.80 1.80

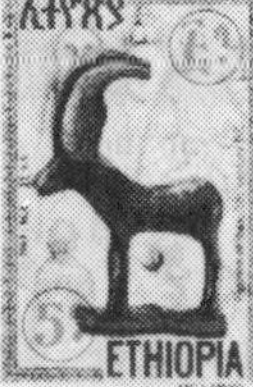
Weapons and Shield, Map of Ethiopia
A179

Bronze Ibex, 5th Century B.C.
A180

Designs: (Map of Ethiopia and): 10c, Civilian fighters. 25c, Map of Africa. 60c, Soldiers. 80c, Red Cross nurse and wounded man.

1978, May Litho. *Perf. 15½*
874 A179 5c multi 5 5
875 A179 10c multi 10 10
876 A179 25c multi 25 25
877 A179 60c multi 60 60
878 A179 80c multi 80 80
Nos. 874-878 (5) 1.80 1.80

"Call of the Motherland."

1978, June 21 Litho. *Perf. 15½*

Ancient Bronzes: 10c, Lion, Yeha, 5th century B.C. (horiz.). 25c, Lamp with ibex attacked by dog, Matara, 1st century B.C. 50c, Goat, Axum, 3rd century A.D. (horiz.). 90c, Ax, chisel and sickle, Yeha, 5th-4th centuries B.C.

879 A180 5c multi 5 5
880 A180 10c multi 10 10
881 A180 25c multi 25 25
882 A180 50c multi 50 50
883 A180 90c multi 90 90
Nos. 879-883 (5) 1.80 1.80

Globe and Argentina '78 Emblem
A181

Designs (Argentina '78 Emblem and): 20c, Soccer player kicking ball. 30c, Two players embracing, net and ball. 55c, World map and ball. 70c, Soccer field (vert.).

Perf. 14x13½, 13½x14
1978, July 19 Litho.
884 A181 5c multi 5 5
885 A181 20c multi 20 20
886 A181 30c multi 30 30
887 A181 55c multi 55 55
888 A181 70c multi 70 70
Nos. 884-888 (5) 1.80 1.80

11th World Cup Soccer Championship, Argentina, June 1-25.

Map of Africa, Oppressed African — A182

Designs (Map of Africa and): 10c, Policeman pointing gun. 25c, Sniper with gun. 60c, African caught in net. 80c, Head of free man.

1978, Aug. 25 *Perf. 12½x13½*
889 A182 5c multi 5 5
890 A182 10c multi 10 10
891 A182 25c multi 25 25
892 A182 60c multi 60 60
893 A182 80c multi 80 80
Nos. 889-893 (5) 1.80 1.80

Namibia Day.

Soldiers, Guerrilla and Jets
A183

Design: 1b, People looking toward sun, crushing snake, flags.

1978, Sept. 8 Photo. *Perf. 14*
894 A183 80c multi 80 80
895 A183 1b multi 1.00 1.00

4th anniversary of revolution.

Hand and Globe with Tools
A184

Designs: 15c, Symbols of energy, communications, education, medicine, agriculture and industry. 25c, Cogwheels and world map. 60c, Globe and hands passing wrench. 70c, Flying geese and turtle over globe.

1978, Nov. 10 Litho. *Perf. 12x12½*
896 A184 10c multi 10 10
897 A184 15c multi 15 15
898 A184 25c multi 25 2
899 A184 60c multi 60 6
900 A184 70c multi 70 7
Nos. 896-900 (5) 1.80 1.8

Technical Cooperation Among Developin Countries Conference, Buenos Aires, Argen tina, Sept. 1978.

Human Rights Emblem — A185

1978, Dec. 7 Photo. *Perf. 12½x13½*
901 A185 5c multi 5
902 A185 15c multi 15 1
903 A185 25c multi 25 2
904 A185 35c multi 35 3
905 A185 1b multi 1.00 1.0
Nos. 901-905 (5) 1.80 1.8

Declaration of Human Rights, 30t anniversary.

Broken Chain, Anti-Apartheid Emblem
A186

Stele from Osole
A187

1978, Dec. 28 Litho. *Perf. 12½x1*
906 A186 5c multi 5
907 A186 20c multi 20 2
908 A186 30c multi 30 3
909 A186 55c multi 55 5
910 A186 70c multi 70 7
Nos. 906-910 (5) 1.80 1.8

Anti-Apartheid Year.

1979, Jan. 25 *Perf. 1*

Ancient Carved Stones, Soddo Region: 10c Anthropomorphous stele, Gorashino. 25c Leaning stone, Wado. 60c, Round stones Ambeut. 80c, Bas-relief, Tiya.

911 A187 5c multi 5 5
912 A187 10c multi 10 1
913 A187 25c multi 25 2
914 A187 60c multi 60 6
915 A187 80c multi 80 8
Nos. 911-915 (5) 1.80 1.8

Cotton and Shemma Valley
A188

Shemma Industry: 10c, Women spinning cotton yarn. 20c, Man reeling cotton. 65c Weaver. 80c, Cotton garments.

1979, Mar. 15 Litho. *Perf. 15½*
916 A188 5c multi 5 5
917 A188 10c multi 10 1
918 A188 20c multi 20 20
919 A188 65c multi 65 65
920 A188 80c multi 80 80
Nos. 916-920 (5) 1.80 1.80

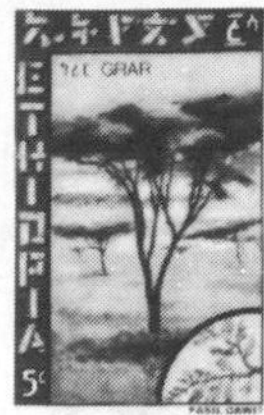

"Grar" Tree — A189

Designs: Ethiopian trees.

1979, Apr. 26 Photo. ***Perf. 13½x14***

921 A189 5c multi 5 5
922 A189 10c multi 10 10
923 A189 25c multi 25 25
924 A189 50c multi 50 50
925 A189 90c multi 90 90
Nos. 921-925 (5) 1.80 1.80

Agricultural Development A190

Revolutionary Development Campaign: 15c, Industry. 25c, Transportation and communication. 60c, Education and health. 70c, Commerce.

1979, July 3 Litho. ***Perf. 12x12½***

926 A190 10c multi 10 10
927 A190 15c multi 15 15
928 A190 25c multi 25 25
929 A190 60c multi 60 60
930 A190 70c multi 70 70
Nos. 926-930 (5) 1.80 1.80

IYC Emblem — A191

Designs: 15c, Adults leading children. 25c, Adult helping child. 60c, IYC emblem surrounded by children. 70c, Adult and children embracing.

1979, Aug. 16 Litho. ***Perf. 12x12½***

931 A191 10c multi 10 10
932 A191 15c multi 15 15
933 A191 25c multi 25 25
934 A191 60c multi 60 60
935 A191 70c multi 70 70
Nos. 931-935 (5) 1.80 1.80

International Year of the Child.

Guerrilla Fighters — A192

Designs: 15c, Soldiers. 25c, Map of Africa within cogwheel and star. 60c, Students with book and torch. 70c, Family, hammer and sickle emblem.

1979, Sept. 11 Photo. ***Perf. 14***

936 A192 10c multi 10 10
937 A192 15c multi 15 15
938 A192 25c multi 25 25
939 A192 60c multi 60 60
940 A192 70c multi 70 70
Nos. 936-940 (5) 1.80 1.80

Fifth anniversary of revolution.

Telephone Receiver — A193

Telecom Emblem and: 5c, Symbolic waves. 35c, Satellite beaming to earth. 45c, Dish antenna. 65c, Television cameraman.

1979, Sept. Photo. ***Perf. 11½***

941 A193 5c multi 5 5
942 A193 30c multi 30 30
943 A193 35c multi 35 35
944 A193 45c multi 45 45
945 A193 65c multi 65 65
Nos. 941-945 (5) 1.80 1.80

3rd World Telecommunications Exhibition, Geneva, Sept. 20-26.

Incense Container — A194

1979, Nov. 15 Litho. ***Perf. 15***

946 A194 5c *shown* 5 5
947 A194 10c *Vase* 10 10
948 A194 25c *Earthenware cover* 25 25
949 A194 60c *Milk container* 60 60
950 A194 80c *Storage container* 80 80
Nos. 946-950 (5) 1.80 1.80

Wooden Grain Bowl A195

Lappet-faced Vulture A196

1980, Jan. Litho. ***Perf. 13½x13***

951 A195 5c *shown* 5 5
952 A195 30c *Chair, stool* 30 30
953 A195 35c *Mortar, pestle* 35 35
954 A195 45c *Buckets* 45 45
955 A195 65c *Storage jars* 65 65
Nos. 951-955 (5) 1.80 1.80

1980, Feb. 12 ***Perf. 13½x14***

Birds of Prey: 15c, Long-crested hawk eagle. 25c, Secretary bird. 60c, Abyssinian long-eared owl. 70c, Lanner falcon.

956 A196 10c multi 10 10
957 A196 15c multi 22 22
958 A196 25c multi 35 35
959 A196 60c multi 90 90
960 A196 70c multi 1.00 1.00
Nos. 956-960 (5) 2.57 2.57

Fight Against Cigarette Smoking — A197

1980, Apr. 7 Photo. ***Perf. 13x13½***

961 A197 20c *shown* 20 20
962 A197 60c *Cigarette* 60 60
963 A197 1b *Respiratory system* 1.00 1.00

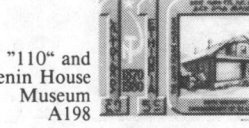

"110" and Lenin House Museum A198

Lenin, 110th "Birthday" (Paintings): 15c, In hiding. 20c, As a young man. 40c, Returning to Russia. 1b, Speaking on the Goelro Plan.

1980, Apr. 22 Litho. ***Perf. 12x12½***

964 A198 5c multi 5 5
965 A198 15c multi 15 15
966 A198 20c multi 20 20
967 A198 40c multi 40 40
968 A198 1b multi 1.00 1.00
Nos. 964-968 (5) 1.80 1.80

Grévy's Zebras A199

1980, June 10 Litho. ***Perf. 12½x12***

969 A199 10c *shown* 10 10
970 A199 15c *Gazelles* 22 22
971 A199 25c *Wild hunting dogs* 35 35
972 A199 60c *Swayne's hartebeests* 90 90
973 A199 70c *Cheetahs* 1.00 1.00
Nos. 969-973 (5) 2.57 2.57

Runner, Moscow '80 Emblem — A200

1980, July 19 Photo. ***Perf. 11½x12***

974 A200 30c *shown* 30 30
975 A200 70c *Gymnast* 70 70
976 A200 80c *Boxing* 80 80

22nd Summer Olympic Games, Moscow, July 19-Aug. 3.

Removing Blindfold — A201

1980, Sept. 11 Photo. ***Perf. 14x13½***

977 A201 30c *shown* 30 30
978 A201 40c *Revolutionary* 40 40
979 A201 50c *Woman breaking chain* 50 50
980 A201 70c *Russian and Ethiopian flags* 70 70

6th anniversary of revolution.

Bamboo Food Basket — A202

1980, Oct. 23 Litho. ***Perf. 14***

981 A202 5c *shown* 5 5
982 A202 15c *Hand basket* 15 15
983 A202 25c *Stool* 25 25
984 A202 35c *Fruit basket* 35 35
985 A202 1b *Lamp shade* 1.00 1.00
Nos. 981-985 (5) 1.80 1.80

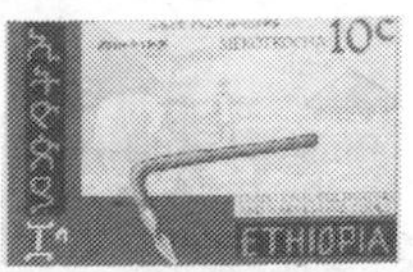

Mekotkocha (Used in Weeding) A203

Traditional Harvesting Tools: 15c, Layda (grain separater). 40c, Mensh (fork). 45c, Medekdekia (soil turner). 70c, Plow and yoke.

1980, Dec. 18 Litho. ***Perf. 12½x12***

986 A203 10c multi 10 10
987 A203 15c multi 15 15
988 A203 40c multi 40 40
989 A203 45c multi 45 45
990 A203 70c multi 70 70
Nos. 986-990 (5) 1.80 1.80

Baro River Bridge Opening A204

Perf. 13½ x 13

1981, Feb. 28 Photo.

991 A204 15c *Canoes and ferry* 15 15
992 A204 65c *Bridge construction* 65 65
993 A204 1b *shown* 1.00 1.00

Simion National Park — A205

World Heritage Year: 5c, Wawel Castle, Poland. 15c, Quito Cathedral, Ecuador. 20c, Old Slave Quarters, Goree Island, Senegal. 30c, Mesa Verde Indian Village, US. 1b, L'Anse aux Meadows excavation, Canada.

Perf. 11x11½, 11½x11

1981, Mar. 10 Photo.

994 A205 5c multi 5 5
995 A205 15c multi 15 15
996 A205 20c multi 20 20
997 A205 30c multi 30 30
998 A205 80c multi 80 80
999 A205 1b multi 1.00 1.00

1981, June 16 Photo.

Designs: 10c, Biet Medhami Alem Church, Ethiopia. 15c, Nahenni National Park, Canada. 20c, Yellowstone River Lower Falls, U.S. 30c, Aachen Cathedral, Germany. 80c, Kicker Rock, San Cristobal Island, Ecuador. 1b, The Lizak corridor, Holy Cross Chapel, Cracow, Poland (vert.).

1000 A205 10c multi 10 10
1001 A205 15c multi 15 15
1002 A205 20c multi 20 20
1003 A205 30c multi 30 30
1004 A205 80c multi 80 80
1005 A205 1b multi 1.00 1.00
Nos. 994-1005 (12) 5.05 5.05

Ancient Drinking Vessel — A206

1981, May 5 Litho. ***Perf. 12½x12***

1006 A206 20c shown 20 20
1007 A206 25c Spice container 25 25
1008 A206 35c Jug 35 35
1009 A206 40c Cooking pot holder 40 40
1010 A206 60c Animal figurine 60 60
Nos. 1006-1010 (5) 1.80 1.80

Intl. Year of the Disabled — A207

7th Anniv. of Revolution A208

1981, July 16 Photo. *Perf. 11½x12*
1011 A207 5c Prostheses 5 5
1012 A207 15c Boys writing 15 15
1013 A207 20c Activities 20 20
1014 A207 40c Knitting 40 40
1015 A207 1b Weaving 1.00 1.00
Nos. 1011-1015 (5) 1.80 1.80

1981, Sept. 10 *Perf. 14*
1016 A208 20c Children's Center 20 20
1017 A208 60c Heroes' Center 60 60
1018 A208 1b Serto Ader (state newspaper) 1.00 1.00

World Food Day — A209

Perf. 13½x12½
1981, Oct. 15 Litho.
1019 A209 5c Wheat airlift 5 5
1020 A209 15c Plowing 15 15
1021 A209 20c Malnutrition 20 20
1022 A209 40c Agriculture education 40 40
1023 A209 1b Cattle, corn 1.00 1.00
Nos. 1019-1023 (5) 1.80 1.80

Ancient Bronze Type of 1978

1981, Dec. 15 Litho. *Perf. 14x13½*
1024 A180 15c Pitcher 15 15
1025 A180 45c Tsenatsil (musical instrument) 45 45
1026 A180 50c Pitcher, diff. 50 50
1027 A180 70c Pot 70 70

Horn Artifacts — A210

1982, Feb. 18 Photo. *Perf. 12x12½*
1028 A210 10c Tobacco containers 10 10
1029 A210 15c Cup 15 15
1030 A210 40c Container, diff. 40 40
1031 A210 45c Goblet 45 45
1032 A210 70c Spoons 70 70
Nos. 1028-1032 (5) 1.80 1.80

Coffee Cultivation — A211

1982, Apr. 20 Photo. *Perf. 13½*
1033 A211 5c Plants 5 5
1034 A211 15c Bushes 15 15
1035 A211 25c Mature bushes 25 25
1036 A211 35c Picking beans 35 35
1037 A211 1b Drinking coffee 1.00 1.00
Nos. 1033-1037 (5) 1.80 1.80

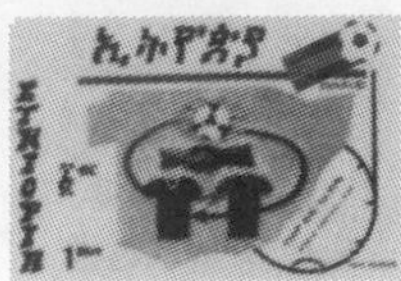
1982 World Cup — A212

Perf. 13½x12½
1982, June 10 Litho.
1038 A212 5c multi 5 5
1039 A212 15c multi 15 15
1040 A212 20c multi 20 20
1041 A212 40c multi 40 40
1042 A212 1b multi 1.00 1.00
Nos. 1038-1042 (5) 1.80 1.80

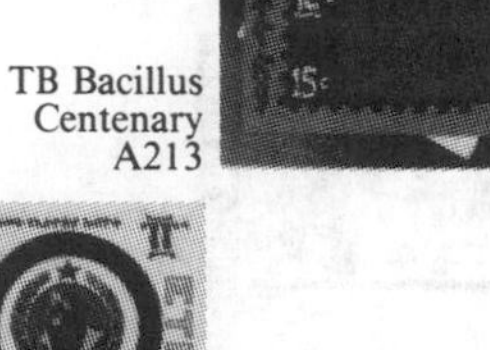
TB Bacillus Centenary A213

8th Anniv. of Revolution — A214

Perf. 13½x12½
1982, July 12 Litho.
1043 A213 15c Cow 15 15
1044 A213 20c Magnifying glass 30 30
1045 A213 30c Koch, microscope 45 45
1046 A213 35c Koch 50 50
1047 A213 80c Man coughing 1.25 1.25
Nos. 1043-1047 (5) 2.65 2.65

1982, Sept. 10 *Perf. 12½x13½*
Designs: Symbols of justice.
1048 A214 80c multi 80 80
1049 A214 1b multi 1.00 1.00

World Standards Day — A215

Perf. 13½x12½
1982, Oct. 14 Litho.
1050 A215 5c Hand, foot, square 5 5
1051 A215 15c Scales 15 15
1052 A215 20c Rulers 20 20
1053 A215 40c Weights 40 40
1054 A215 1b Emblem 1.00 1.00
Nos. 1050-1054 (5) 1.80 1.80

10th Anniv. of UN Conference on Human Environment A216

1982, Dec. 13 Litho. *Perf. 12*
1055 A216 5c Wildlife conservation 5 5
1056 A216 15c Environmental health and settlement 15 15
1057 A216 20c Forest protection 20 20
1058 A216 40c Natl. literacy campaign 40 40
1059 A216 1b Soil and water conservation 1.00 1.00
Nos. 1055-1059 (5) 1.80 1.80

Cave of Sof Omar A217

Various views.

1983, Feb. 10 Photo. *Perf. 13½*
1060 A217 5c multi 5 5
1061 A217 10c multi 10 10
1062 A217 15c multi 15 15
1063 A217 70c multi 70 70
1064 A217 80c multi 80 80
Nos. 1060-1064 (5) 1.80 1.80

25th Anniv. of Economic Commission for Africa — A218

1983, Apr. 29 Photo. *Perf. 14*
1065 A218 80c multi 80 80
1066 A218 1b multi 1.00 1.00

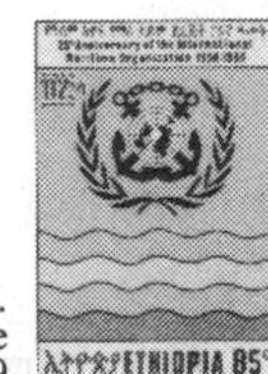

25th Anniv. of Intl. Maritime Org. — A219

Perf. 12½x11½
1983, June 3 Photo.
1067 A219 85c Emblem 85 85
1068 A219 1b Lighthouse, ship 1.00 1.00

World Communications Year — A220

1983, July 22 Litho.
1069 A220 25c UPU emblem 25 25
1070 A220 55c Dish antenna, emblems 55 55
1071 A220 1b Bridge, tunnel 1.00 1.00

9th Anniv. of Revolution — A221

1983, Sept. 10 Litho. *Perf. 14½*
1072 A221 25c Dove 25 25
1073 A221 55c Star 55 55
1074 A221 1b Emblems 1.00 1.00

Musical Instruments — A222

Perf. 12½x13½
1983, Oct. 17 Litho.
1075 A222 5c Hura 5 5
1076 A222 15c Dinke 15 15
1077 A222 20c Meleket 20 20
1078 A222 40c Embilta 40 40
1079 A222 1b Tom 1.00 1.00
Nos. 1075-1079 (5) 1.80 1.80

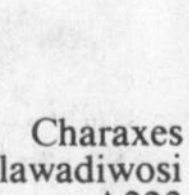

Charaxes Galawadiwosi A223

1983, Dec. 13 Photo. *Perf. 14*
1080 A223 10c shown 10 10
1081 A223 15c Epiphora elianae 20 20
1082 A223 55c Batuana rougeoti 70 70
1083 A223 1b Achaea saboeareginae 1.25 1.25

Intl. Anti-Apartheid Year (1983) — A224

Perf. 13½x12½
1984, Feb. 10 Litho.
1084 A224 5c multi 5 5
1085 A224 15c multi 15 15
1086 A224 20c multi 20 20
1087 A224 40c multi 40 40
1088 A224 1b multi 1.00 1.00
Nos. 1084-1088 (5) 1.80 1.80

Local Flowers — A225

1984, Apr. 13 Litho. *Perf. 13½*
1089 A225 5c Protea gaguedi 5 5
1090 A225 25c Sedum epidendrum 25 25
1091 A225 50c Echinops amplexicaulis 50 50
1092 A225 1b Canarina eminii 1.00 1.00

Traditional Houses — A226

1984, Aug. 3 Photo.
1093 A226 15c Konso 15 15
1094 A226 65c Dorze 65 65
1095 A226 $1 Harer 1.00 1.00

10th Anniv. of the Revolution A227

1984, Sept. 10 Photo. *Perf. 11½*
1096 A227 5c September 12, 1974 5 5
1097 A227 10c March 4, 1975 10 10
1098 A227 15c April 20, 1976 15 15
1099 A227 20c February 11, 1977 20 20
1100 A227 25c March 1978 25 25
1101 A227 40c July 8, 1980 40 40
1102 A227 45c December 17, 1980 45 45
1103 A227 50c September 15, 1980 50 50
1104 A227 70c September 18, 1981 70 70
1105 A227 1b June 6, 1983 1.00 1.00
Nos. 1096-1105 (10) 3.80 3.80

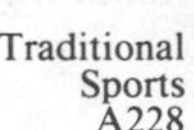

Traditional Sports A228

1984, Dec. 7 Photo. *Perf. 14*

1106 A228 5c Gugs 5 5
1107 A228 25c Tigil 25 25
1108 A228 50c Genna 50 50
1109 A228 1b Gebeta 1.00 1.00

Birds — A229

1985, Jan. 4 Photo. *Perf. 14½*

1110 A229 5c Francolinus harwoodi 5 5
1111 A229 15c Rallus rougetti 15 15
1112 A229 80c Merops pusillus 80 80
1113 A229 85c Malimbus rubriceps 85 85

Indigenous Fauna — A230

1985, Feb. 4 Litho. *Perf. 12½x12*

1114 A230 20c Hippopotamus amphibius 20 20
1115 A230 25c Litocranius walleri 25 25
1116 A230 40c Sylivicapra grimmia 40 40
1117 A230 1b Rhynchotragus guentheri 1.00 1.00

Freshwater Fish A231

1985, Apr. 3 *Perf. 13½*

1118 A231 10c Barbus degeni 10 10
1119 A231 20c Labeo cylindricus 20 20
1120 A231 55c Protopterus annectens 55 55
1121 A231 1b Alestes dentex 1.00 1.00

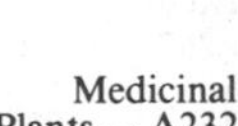

Medicinal Plants — A232

1985, May 23 *Perf. 11½x12½*

1122 A232 10c Securidaca longependunculata 10 10
1123 A232 20c Plumbago zeylanicum 20 20
1124 A232 55c Brucea antidysenteric 55 55
1125 A232 1b Dorstenia barminiana 1.00 1.00

Ethiopian Red Cross Soc., 50th Anniv. — A233

1985, Aug. 6 Litho. *Perf. 13½x13*

1126 A233 35c multi 35 35
1127 A233 55c multi 55 55
1128 A233 1b multi 1.00 1.00

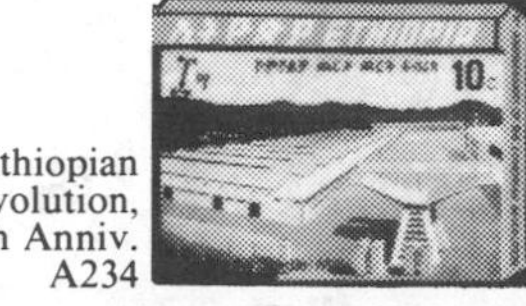

Ethiopian Revolution, 11th Anniv. A234

Designs: 10c, Kombolcha Mills, Wollo Region. 80c, Muger Cement Factory, Mokoda, Shoa. 1b, Relocating famine and drought victims.

1985, Sept. 10 Litho. *Perf. 13½*

1129 A234 10c multi 10 10
1130 A234 80c multi 80 80
1131 A234 1b multi 1.00 1.00

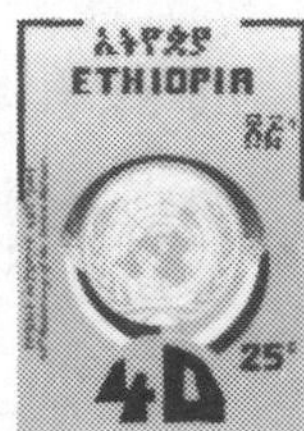

U.N. 40th Anniv. — A235

1985, Nov. 22 Litho. *Perf. 13½x14*

1132 A235 25c multi 25 25
1133 A235 55c multi 55 55
1134 A235 1b multi 1.00 1.00

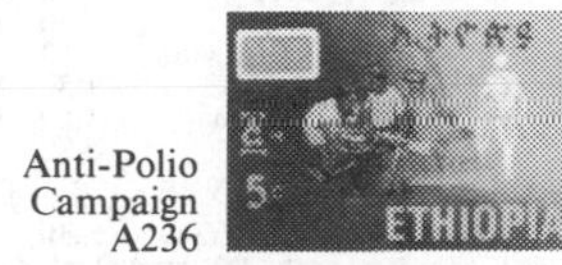

Anti-Polio Campaign A236

Perf. 11½x12½

1986, Jan. 10 Litho.

1135 A236 5c Boy, prosthesis 5 5
1136 A236 10c Boy on crutches 10 10
1137 A236 20c Nurse, boy 20 20
1138 A236 55c Man, sewing machine 55 55
1139 A236 1b Nurse, mother, child 1.00 1.00
Nos. 1135-1139 (5) 1.90 1.90

Indigenous Trees A237

1986, Feb. 10 *Perf. 13½x14½*

1140 A237 10c Millettia ferruginea 10 10
1141 A237 30c Syzyigum guineense 30 30
1142 A237 50c Cordia africana 50 50
1143 A237 1b Hagenia abyssinica 1.00 1.00

Spices — A238

1986, Mar. 10 *Perf. 13½*

1144 A238 10c Zingiber officinale rosc 10 10
1145 A238 15c Ocimum bacilicum 15 15
1146 A238 55c Sinapsis alba 55 55
1147 A238 1b Cuminum cyminum 1.00 1.00

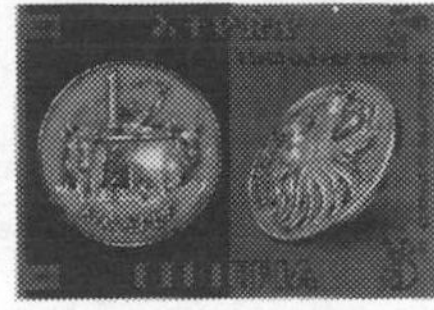

Current Coins, Obverse and Reverse A239

1986, May 9 Litho. *Perf. 13½x14*

1148 A239 5c 1-cent 5 5
1149 A239 10c 25-cent 10 10
1150 A239 35c 5-cent 35 35
1151 A239 50c 50-cent 50 50
1152 A239 1b 10-cent 1.00 1.00
Nos. 1148-1152 (5) 2.00 2.00

Discovery of 3.5 Million Year-old Hominid Skeleton, Dinkinesh — A240

1986, July 4 *Perf. 13½*

1153 A240 2b multi 2.00 2.00

Ethiopian Revolution, 12th Anniv. — A241

Designs: 20c, Military service. 30c, Tiglachin monument. 55c, Delachin Exhibition emblem. 85c, Food processing plant, Merti.

1986, Sept. 10 Litho. *Perf. 14*

1154 A241 20c multi 20 20
1155 A241 30c multi 30 30
1156 A241 55c multi 52 52
1157 A241 85c multi 82 82

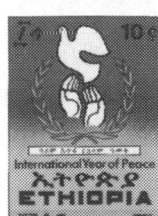

Ethiopian Airlines, 40th Anniv. — A242

Intl. Peace Year — A243

1986, Oct. 14

1158 A242 10c DC-7 10 10
1159 A242 20c DC-3 20 20
1160 A242 30c Personnel, jet tail 30 30
1161 A242 40c Engine 38 38
1162 A242 1b DC-7, map 95 95
Nos. 1158-1162 (5) 1.93 1.93

1986, Nov. 13 *Perf. 13½*

1163 A243 10c multi 10 10
1164 A243 80c multi 78 78
1165 A243 1b multi 95 95

UN Child Survival Campaign — A244

1986, Dec. 11 *Perf. 12½*

1166 A244 10c Breast feeding 10 10
1167 A244 35c Immunization 35 35
1168 A244 50c Hygiene 48 48
1169 A244 1b Growth monitoring 95 95

Umbrellas — A245

1987, Feb. 10 *Perf. 13½*

1170 A245 35c Axum 35 35
1171 A245 55c Negele-Borena 52 52
1172 A245 1b Jimma 95 95

Artwork by Afewerk Tekle (b. 1932) — A246

Designs: 50c, Defender of His Country - Afar, stained glass window. 2b, Defender of His Country - Adwa, painting.

1987, Mar. 19 Litho. *Perf. 13½*

1173 A246 50c multi 48 48
1174 A246 2b multi 1.90 1.90

Stained Glass Windows by Afewerk Tekle — A247

1987, June 16 Photo. *Perf. 11½x12*

Granite Paper

1175 A247 50c multi 48 48

Size: 26x38mm.

1176 A247 80c multi 75 75
1177 A247 1b multi 95 95

Struggle of the African People. Nos. 1176-1177 vert.

Simien Fox — A248

1987, June 29 Litho. *Perf. 13½*

1178 A248 5c multi 5 5
1179 A248 10c multi 10 10
1180 A248 15c multi 15 15
1181 A248 20c multi 20 20
1182 A248 25c multi 25 25
1183 A248 45c multi 45 45
1184 A248 55c multi 52 52
Nos. 1178-1184 (7) 1.72 1.72

Ethiopian Revolution, 13th Anniv. — A249

1987, Sept. 10 *Perf. 12½*

1185 A249 5c Constitution, freedom of press 5 5
1186 A249 10c Popular elections 10 10
1187 A249 80c Referendum 75 75
1188 A249 1b Bahir Dar Airport, map 95 95

Addis Ababa, Cent. A251

"100" and views: 5c, Emperor Menelik, Empress Taitu and city. 10c, Traditional buildings. 80c, Central Addis Ababa. 1b, Aerial view of city.

1987, Sept. 7 *Perf. 13½*

1193 A251 5c multi 5 5
1194 A251 10c multi 10 10
1195 A251 80c multi 75 75
1196 A251 1b multi 95 95

Wooden Spoons A252

1987, Nov. 30

1197 A252 85c Hurso, Harerge 80 80
1198 A252 1b Borena, Sidamo 95 95

SEMI-POSTAL STAMPS

Types of 1931, Overprinted in Red at Upper Left

Perf. 12x12½, 12½x12.

1936, Feb. 25 **Unwmk.**

B1 A27 1g lt grn 35 30
B2 A27 2g rose 35 30
B3 A25 4g blue 35 30
B4 A27 8g brown 50 50
B5 A25 1t purple 50 50
Nos. B1-B5 (5) 2.05 1.90

Nos. B1-B5 were sold at twice face value, the surtax going to the Red Cross.

Nos. 289, 290 and 292 to 294 Surcharged in Blue

EXPOSITION
1949
+8c

Perf. 13x13½

1949, June 13 **Wmk. 282**

B6 A53 8c + 8c dp org 1.25 1.25
B7 A53 12c + 5c red 1.25 1.25
B8 A53 30c + 15c org brn 2.50 2.50
B9 A53 70c + 70c rose lil 16.50 16.50
B10 A53 $1 + 80c dk car rose 20.00 20.00
Nos. B6-B10 (5) 41.50 41.50

Type A39 Surcharged Carmine

+ 10 ct.

Perf. 11½

1950, May 8 **Unwmk.** **Photo.**

Various Designs

Inscribed "Croix Rouge"

B11 A39 5c + 10c brt grn 1.00 1.00
B12 A39 10c + 10c brt red 1.50 1.50
B13 A39 25c + 10c brt bl 2.50 2.50
B14 A39 50c + 10c dk yel brn 7.00 7.00
B15 A39 1t + 10c brt vio 11.00 11.00
Nos. B11-B15 (5) 23.00 23.00

The surtax was for the Red Cross.

Nos. B6-B10 Overprinted in Black

1951

Perf. 13x13½

1951, Nov. 17 **Wmk. 282**

B16 A53 8c + 8c dp org 75 75
B17 A53 12c + 5c red 75 75
B18 A53 30c + 15c org brn 1.10 1.10
B19 A53 70c + 70c rose lil 10.00 10.00
B20 A53 $1 + 80c dk car rose 15.00 15.00
Nos. B16-B20 (5) 27.60 27.60

Tree, Staff and Snake — SP1

Wmk. 282

1951, Nov. 25 **Engr.** *Perf. 13*

Lower Panel in Red.

B21 SP1 5c + 2c dp bl grn 30 15
B22 SP1 10c + 3c org 50 25
B23 SP1 15c + 3c dp bl 60 40
B24 SP1 30c + 5c red 1.35 1.00
B25 SP1 50c + 7c red brn 3.00 2.00
B26 SP1 $1 + 10c pur 5.25 3.00
Nos. B21-B26 (6) 11.00 6.80

The surtax was for anti-tuberculosis work.

1958, Dec. 1

Lower Panel in Red

B27 SP1 20c + 3c dl pur 40 30
B28 SP1 25c + 4c emer 50 35
B29 SP1 35c + 5c rose vio 75 40
B30 SP1 60c + 7c vio bl 1.50 80
B31 SP1 65c + 7c vio 3.00 1.75
B32 SP1 80c + 9c car rose 5.00 3.00
Nos. B27-B32 (6) 11.15 6.60

The surtax was for anti-tuberculosis work.
Nos. B27-B32 were the only stamps on sale from Dec. 1-25, 1958.

Type of Regular Issue, 1955, Surcharged

RED CROSS CENTENARY
1859 1959 + 2c

Engraved; Cross Typographed in Red

1959, May 30 **Wmk. 282**

B33 A62 15c + 2c ol bis & rose red 60 60
B34 A62 20c + 3c vio & emer 75 75
B35 A62 30c + 5c rose car & grnsh bl 1.25 1.25

Issued to commemorate the centenary of the International Red Cross idea. The surtax was for the Red Cross.

Type A39 Surcharged

Silver Jubilee
1960
+ 5 ct.

Perf. 11½

1960, May 7 **Photo.** **Unwmk.**

B36 A39 5c + 1c brt grn 35 25
B37 A39 10c + 2c brt red 50 30
B38 A39 25c + 3c brt bl 1.10 75
B39 A39 50c + 4c dk yel brn 1.75 1.50
B40 A39 1t + 5c brt vio 3.00 2.75
Nos. B36-B40 (5) 6.70 5.55

25th anniversary of Ethiopian Red Cross.

Foreign postal stationery (stamped envelopes, postal cards and air letter sheets) lies beyond the scope of this Catalogue, which is limited to adhesive postage stamps.

Crippled Boy on Crutches — SP2

Wmk. 282

1963, July 23 **Engr.** *Perf. 13½*

B41 SP2 10c + 2c ultra 25 25
B42 SP2 15c + 3c red 35 30
B43 SP2 50c + 5c brt grn 1.10 1.00
B44 SP2 60c + 5c red lil 1.75 1.25

The surtax was to aid the disabled.

AIR POST STAMPS

Regular Issue of 1928 Handstamped in Violet, Red, Black or Green

Perf. 13½x14

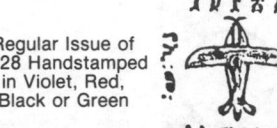

1929, Aug. 17 **Unwmk.**

C1 A22 ⅛m org & lt bl 75 90
C2 A23 ¼m ind & red org 75 90
C3 A22 ½m gray grn & blk 75 90
C4 A23 1m dk car & blk 75 90
C5 A22 2m dk bl & blk 90 1.10
C6 A23 4m yel & ol 90 1.10
C7 A22 8m vio & ol 90 1.10
C8 A23 1t org brn & vio 1.10 1.10
C9 A22 2t grn & bis 1.50 1.75
C10 A23 3t choc & grn 1.50 1.75
Nos. C1-C10 (10) 9.80 11.50

The overprint signifies "16 August 1929 - Airplane of the Ethiopian Government." The stamps commemorate the arrival at Addis Ababa of the first air mail carried by an airplane of the Ethiopian Government. There are three types of the overprint: (I) 19½mm. high; "colon" at right of bottom word. (II) 20mm. high; same "colon." (III) 19½-mm. high; no "colon." Many errors exist.

Symbols of Empire, Airplane and Map — AP1

1931, June 17 **Engr.** *Perf. 12½*

C11 AP1 1g org red 20 30
C12 AP1 2g ultra 25 35
C13 AP1 4g violet 30 50
C14 AP1 8g bl grn 70 1.00
C15 AP1 1t ol brn 1.75 1.25
C16 AP1 2t carmine 3.00 4.50
C17 AP1 3t yel grn 4.50 6.00
Nos. C11-C17 (7) 10.70 13.90

Nos. C11 to C17 exist imperforate.

Reprints of C11 to C17 exist. Paper is thinner and gum whiter than the originals. Reprints usually sell at about one-tenth of above prices.

Nos. 250, 255 and 257 Surcharged in Black

a: 20 - 4 - 39
b: AERIENNE REPRISE POSTE ETHIOPIENNE 29/12/46 Eth. Doll. 0,50

Perf. 14x13½

1947, Mar. 20 **Unwmk.**

C18 A33 (a) 12c on 4c lt bl grn & ind 30.00 30.00
C19 A33 (b) 50c on 25c dl grn & ind 30.00 30.00
a. "26-12-46" 125.00
C20 A33 (b) $2 on 60c lil & ind 50.00 50.00
a. "26-12-46" 125.00

Resumption of airmail service, Dec. 29, 1946.

Franklin D. Roosevelt AP2

Design: $2, Haile Selassie.

Engraved and Photogravure

1947, May 23 *Perf. 12½*

C21 AP2 $1 dk pur & sep 4.00 3.50
C22 AP2 $2 car & dp bl 6.00 5.00

Farmer Plowing AP3

Designs: 10c, 25c, Zoquala, extinct volcano. 30c, 35c, Tesissat Falls, Abai River. 65c, 70c, Amba Alaguie. $1, Sacala, source of Nile. $3, Gorgora and Dembia, Lake Tana. $5, Magdala, former capital. $10, Ras Dashan, mountain peak.

Perf. 13x13½

1947-55 **Wmk. 282** **Engr.**

C23 AP3 8c pur brn 20 10
C24 AP3 10c brt grn 20 10
C25 AP3 25c dl pur ('52) 35 20
C26 AP3 30c org yel 50 15
C27 AP3 35c bl ('55) 50 25
C28 AP3 65c pur ('51) 60 40
C29 AP3 70c red 90 40
C30 AP3 $1 dp bl 1.00 50
C31 AP3 $3 rose lil 4.00 2.50
C32 AP3 $5 red brn 7.50 3.50
C33 AP3 $10 rose vio 15.00 9.00
Nos. C23-C33 (11) 30.75 17.10

U. P. U. Monument, Bern — AP4

1950, Apr. 3 **Unwmk.** *Perf. 12½*

C34 AP4 5c grn & red 20 15
C35 AP4 15c dk sl grn & car 25 25

C36 AP4 25c org yel & grn 30 25
C37 AP4 50c car & ultra 75 60

Issued to commemorate the 75th anniversary of the formation of the Universal Postal Union.

Convair Plane over Mountains AP5

Engraved and Lithographed
1955, Dec. 30 Unwmk. *Perf. 12½*
Center Multicolored

C38 AP5 10c gray grn 40 20
C39 AP5 15c carmine 50 25
C40 AP5 20c violet 75 40

10th anniversary of Ethiopian Airlines.

Promulgating the Constitution — AP6

Perf. 14x13½
1956, July 16 Engr. Wmk. 282

C41 AP6 10c redsh brn & ultra 30 20
C42 AP6 15c dk car rose & ol grn 40 25
C43 AP6 20c bl & org red 60 40
C44 AP6 25c pur & grn 75 50
C45 AP6 30c dk grn & red brn 1.00 75
Nos. C41-C45 (5) 3.05 2.10

25th anniversary of the constitution.

Aksum AP7

Ancient Capitals: 10c, Lalibela. 15c, Gondar. 20c, Mekele. 25c, Ankober.

1957, Feb. 7 *Perf. 14*
Centers in Green.

C46 AP7 5c red brn 50 25
C47 AP7 10c rose car 50 25
C48 AP7 15c red org 60 30
C49 AP7 20c ultra 85 45
C50 AP7 25c claret 1.25 65
Nos. C46-C50 (5) 3.70 1.90

Amharic "A" — AP8

Designs: Various Amharic characters and views of Addis Ababa. The characters, arranged by values, spell Addis Ababa.

1957, Feb. 14 Engr.
Amharic Letters in Scarlet.

C51 AP8 5c ultra, *sal pink* 15 10
C52 AP8 10c ol grn, *pink* 25 15
C53 AP8 15c dl pur, *yel* 35 15
C54 AP8 20c grn, *buff* 50 25
C55 AP8 25c plum, *pale bl* 75 30
C56 AP8 30c red, *pale grn* 90 35
Nos. C51-C56 (6) 2.90 1.30

70th anniversary of Addis Ababa.

Map, Rock Church at Lalibela and Obelisk AP9

1958, April 15 Wmk. 282 *Perf. 13½*

C57 AP9 10c green 20 10
C58 AP9 20c rose red 30 20
C59 AP9 30c brt bl 50 25

Issued to commemorate the conference of Independent African States, Accra, April 15-22.

Map of Africa and U. N. Emblem AP10

1958, Dec. 29 *Perf. 13*

C60 AP10 5c emerald 15 5
C61 AP10 20c car rose 25 20
C62 AP10 25c ultra 30 25
C63 AP10 50c pale pur 60 40

Issued to commemorate the first session of the United Nations Economic Conference for Africa, opened in Addis Ababa Dec. 29.

Nos. C23-29 Overprinted

የአየር ፖስታ ፴ኛ ዓመት
30th Airmail Ann.
1929 - 1959

Perf. 13x13½
1959, Aug. 16 Engr. Wmk. 282

C64 AP3 8c pur brn 30 25
C65 AP3 10c brt grn 40 30
C66 AP3 25c dl pur 60 35
C67 AP3 30c org yel 65 50
C68 AP3 35c blue 85 55
C69 AP3 65c purple 1.25 85
C70 AP3 70c red 1.60 1.10
Nos. C64-C70 (7) 5.65 3.90

30th anniversary of Ethiopian airmail service.

Ethiopian Soldier and Map of Congo — AP11

Globe with Map of Africa — AP12

Perf. 11½
1962, July 23 Unwmk. Photo.
Granite Paper

C71 AP11 15c org, bl, brn & grn 20 10
C72 AP11 50c pur, bl, brn & grn 40 30
C73 AP11 60c red, bl, brn & grn 70 35

Issued to commemorate the second anniversary of the Ethiopian contingent of the United Nations forces in the Congo and in honor of the 70th birthday of Emperor Haile Selassie.

1963, May 22
Granite Paper

C74 AP12 10c mag & blk 20 10
C75 AP12 40c emer & blk 40 25
C76 AP12 60c bl & blk 70 35

Issued to commemorate the conference of African heads of state for African Unity, Addis Ababa.

Bird Type of Regular Issue, 1962

Birds: 10c, Black-headed forest oriole. 15c, Broad-tailed paradise whydah (vert.). 20c, Lammergeier (vert.). 50c, White-checked touraco. 80c, Purple indigo bird.

1963, Sept. 12 *Perf. 11½*
Granite Paper

C77 A74 10c multi 20 12
C78 A74 15c multi 25 18
C79 A74 20c bl, blk & ocher 45 25
C80 A74 50c lem & multi 75 45
C81 A74 80c ultra, blk & brn 1.50 75
Nos. C77-C81 (5) 3.15 1.75

Swimming AP13

Sport: 10c, Basketball (vert.). 15c, Javelin. 80c, Soccer game in stadium.

Perf. 14x13½
1964, Sept. 15 Litho. Unwmk.

C82 AP13 5c multi 10 15
C83 AP13 10c multi 15 15
C84 AP13 15c multi 30 30
C85 AP13 80c multi 1.25 60

18th Olympic Games, Tokyo, Oct. 10-25.

Queen Elizabeth II and Emperor Haile Selassie — AP14

1965, Feb. 1 Photo. *Perf. 11½*
Granite Paper

C86 AP14 5c multi 12 5
C87 AP14 35c multi 50 30
C88 AP14 60c multi 85 50

Issued to commemorate the visit of Queen Elizabeth II of Great Britain, Feb. 1-8.

Koka Dam and Power Plant — AP15

Designs: 15c, Sugar cane field. 50c, Blue Nile bridge. 60c, Gondar castles. 80c, Coffee tree. $1, Cattle at water hole. $3, Camels at well. $5, Ethiopian Air Lines jet plane.

1965, July 19 Unwmk. *Perf. 11½*
Granite Paper
Portrait in Black

C89 AP15 15c vio brn & buff 20 15
C90 AP15 40c vio bl & lt bl 50 30
C91 AP15 50c grn & lt bl 60 35
C92 AP15 60c cl & yel 75 45
C93 AP15 80c grn, yel & red 90 50
C94 AP15 $1 brn & lt bl 1.10 60
C95 AP15 $3 cl & pink 3.50 1.65
C96 AP15 $5 ultra & lt bl 7.50 3.00
Nos. C89-C96 (8) 15.05 7.00

Bird Type of Regular Issue, 1962

Birds: 10c, White-collared kingfisher. 15c, Blue-breasted bee-eater. 25c, African paradise flycatcher. 40c, Village weaver. 60c, White-collared pigeon.

1966, Feb. 15 Photo. *Perf. 11½*
Granite Paper

C97 A74 10c dl yel & multi 20 15
C98 A74 15c lt bl & multi 30 15
C99 A74 25c gray & multi 65 35
C100 A74 40c pink & multi 1.25 50
C101 A74 60c multi 1.50 75
Nos. C97-C101 (5) 3.90 1.90

Black Rhinoceros AP16

Animals: 10c, Leopard. 20c, Black-and-white colobus (monkey). 30c, Mountain nyala. 60c, Nubian ibex.

1966, June 20 Litho. *Perf. 13*

C102 AP16 5c dp grn, blk & gray 15 7
C103 AP16 10c grn, blk & ocher 20 10
C104 AP16 20c cit, blk & grn 40 15
C105 AP16 30c yel grn, blk & ocher 60 18
C106 AP16 60c yel grn, blk & dk brn 1.25 30
Nos. C102-C106 (5) 2.60 80

Bird Type of Regular Issue, 1962

Birds: 10c, Blue-winged goose (vert.). 15c, Yellow-billed duck. 20c, Wattled ibis. 25c, Striped swallow. 40c, Black-winged lovebird (vert.).

1967, Sept. 29 Photo. *Perf. 11½*
Granite Paper

C107 A74 10c lt ultra & multi 20 15
C108 A74 15c grn & multi 25 15
C109 A74 20c yel & multi 30 15
C110 A74 25c sal & multi 50 15
C111 A74 40c pink & multi 1.00 40
Nos. C107-C111 (5) 2.25 1.00

SPECIAL DELIVERY STAMPS

Motorcycle Messenger — SD1

Addis Ababa Post Office SD2

Unwmk.
1947, Apr. 24 Engr. *Perf. 13*

E1 SD1 30c org brn 60 50
E2 SD2 50c blue 2.00 1.50

1954-62 Wmk. 282

E3 SD1 30c org brn ('62) 1.00 75
E4 SD2 50c blue 90 50

POSTAGE DUE STAMPS

Menelik II — D1

Perf. 14x13½
1896, June 10 Unwmk.
Black Overprint.

J1 D1 ¼g green 1.00
J2 D1 ½g red 1.00
J3 D1 4g lil brn 75
a. Without overprint 75
J4 D1 8g violet 75
a. Without overprint 75

Red Overprint.

J5 D1 1g blue 1.00
J6 D1 2g dk brn 1.00
J7 D1 16g black 75
a. Without overprint 75
Nos. J1-J7 (7) 6.25

Regular Issue of 1894 Handstamped in Various Colors:

T a T b

1905, Jan. 1

No.	Type	Description	Unused	Used
J8	A1 (a)	¼g green	14.00	14.00
J9	A1 (a)	½g red	14.00	14.00
J10	A1 (a)	1g blue	14.00	14.00
J11	A1 (a)	2g dk brn	14.00	14.00
J12	A2 (a)	4g lil brn	14.00	14.00
J13	A2 (a)	8g violet	20.00	20.00
J14	A2 (a)	16g black	40.00	40.00
J15	A1 (b)	¼g green	14.00	14.00
J16	A1 (b)	½g red	14.00	14.00
J17	A1 (b)	1g blue	14.00	14.00
J18	A1 (b)	2g dk brn	14.00	14.00
J19	A2 (b)	4g lil brn	14.00	14.00
J20	A2 (b)	8g violet	20.00	20.00
J21	A2 (b)	16g black	40.00	40.00
		Nos. J8-J21 (14)	260.00	260.00

Excellent forgeries of Nos. J8-J42 exist.

Regular Issue of 1894 Handstamped in Blue or Violet

TAXE A PERCEVOIR T

1906, July 1

No.	Type	Description	Unused	Used
J22	A1	¼g green	9.00	9.00
J23	A1	½g red	9.00	9.00
J24	A1	1g blue	9.00	9.00
J25	A1	2g dk brn	9.00	9.00
J26	A2	4g lil brn	9.00	9.00
J27	A2	8g violet	14.00	14.00
J28	A2	16g black	20.00	20.00
		Nos. J22-J28 (7)	79.00	79.00

Nos. J22, J24, J25 and J26 exist with inverted overprint, also No. J22 with double overprint.

With Additional Surcharge of Value Handstamped as on Regular Issue of 1907.

1907, July 1

No.	Type	Description	Unused	Used
J29	A1(e)	¼ on ¼g grn	15.00	15.00
J30	A1(e)	½ on ½g red	15.00	15.00
J31	A1(f)	1 on 1g bl	15.00	15.00
J32	A1(f)	2 on 2g dk brn	15.00	15.00
J33	A2(f)	4 on 4g lil brn	15.00	15.00
J34	A2(f)	8 on 8g vio	15.00	15.00
J35	A2(f)	16 on 16g blk	25.00	25.00
		Nos. J29-J35 (7)	115.00	115.00

Nos. J30, J31, J32 and J33 exist with inverted surcharge.

Regular Issue of 1894 Handstamped in Black

1908, Dec. 1

No.	Type	Description	Unused	Used
J36	A1	¼g green	1.00	75
J37	A1	½g red	1.00	75
J38	A1	1g blue	1.00	75
J39	A1	2g dk brn	1.25	1.00
J40	A2	4g lil brn	1.75	1.50
J41	A2	8g violet	4.00	4.00
J42	A2	16g black	12.00	12.00
		Nos. J36-J42 (7)	22.00	20.75

Nos. J36 to J42 exist with inverted overprint and Nos. J36, J37, J38 and J40 with double overprint.

Same Handstamp on Regular Issue of 1909.

1912, Dec. 1 — *Perf. 11½*

No.	Type	Description	Unused	Used
J43	A3	¼g bl grn	1.00	75
J44	A3	½g rose	1.50	1.00
J45	A3	1g grn & org	3.50	2.50
J46	A4	2g blue	4.00	3.50
J47	A4	4g grn & car	6.00	4.00
J48	A5	8g ver & dp grn	8.00	6.50
J49	A5	16g ver & car	20.00	15.00
		Nos. J43-J49 (7)	44.00	33.25

Nos. J43 to J49, all exist with inverted overprint.

Same Handstamp on Regular Issue of 1919 in Blue Black

1925-27 — *Perf. 11½*

No.	Type	Description	Unused	Used
J50	A6	⅛g vio & brn	22.50	22.50
J51	A6	¼g bl grn & db	22.50	22.50
J52	A6	½g scar & ol grn	25.00	25.00
J53	A9	1g rose lil & gray grn	3.00	3.00
J54	A9	2g dp ultra & fawn	25.00	25.00

Same Handstamp on Nos. 110 and 112.

1930 (?)

No.	Type	Description	Unused	Used
J55	A3(i)	1g grn & org	25.00	25.00
J56	A4(j)	2g blue	25.00	25.00

D2

Perf. 11½

1951, Apr. 2 — **Unwmk.** — **Litho.**

No.	Type	Description	Unused	Used
J57	D2	1c emerald	25	10
J58	D2	5c rose red	35	15
J59	D2	10c violet	50	20
J60	D2	20c ocher	75	55
J61	D2	50c brt ultra	1.50	1.10
J62	D2	$1 rose lil	3.00	1.75
		Nos. J57-J62 (6)	6.35	3.85

OCCUPATION STAMPS

Issued under Italian Occupation.

100 Centesimi = 1 Lira

Victor Emmanuel III — OS1

Emperor Victor Emmanuel — OS2

Wmk. 140- Crowns

1936 — **Wmk. 140** — *Perf. 14*

No.	Type	Description	Unused	Used
N1	OS1	10c org brn	40	40
N2	OS1	20c purple	75	75
N3	OS2	25c dk grn	50	50
N4	OS2	30c dk brn	50	50
N5	OS2	50c rose car	50	50
N6	OS1	75c dp org	75	75
N7	OS1	1.25l dp bl	1.50	1.50
		Nos. N1-N7 (7)	4.90	4.90

For later issues see Italian East Africa.

FAR EASTERN REPUBLIC

LOCATION — In Siberia east of Lake Baikal
GOVT. — Republic
AREA — 900,745 sq. mi.
POP. — 1,560,000 (approx. 1920)
CAPITAL — Chita

A short-lived independent government was established here in 1920.

100 Kopecks = 1 Ruble

Vladivostok Issue.

Russian Stamps Surcharged or Overprinted:

a b c

On Stamps of 1909-17.

Perf. 14, 14½x15, 13½.

1920 — **Unwmk.**

No.	Type	Description	Unused	Used
2	A14(a)	2k green	13.00	20.00
3	A14(a)	3k red	11.00	14.00
4	A11(b)	3k on 35k red brn & grn	14.00	20.00
5	A15(a)	4k carmine	11.00	14.00
6	A11(b)	4k on 70k brn & org	9.00	9.00
8	A11(b)	7k on 15k red brn & bl	4.00	5.50
a.		Inverted surcharge	50.00	
b.		Pair, one overprinted "DBP" only		
9	A15(a)	10k dk bl	80.00	110.00
a.		Overprint on back	150.00	
10	A12(c)	10k on 3½r mar & lt grn	30.00	35.00
11	A11(a)	14k bl & rose	30.00	35.00
12	A11(a)	15k red brn & bl	14.00	16.00
13	A8(a)	20k bl & car	85.00	110.00
14	A11(b)	20k on 14k bl & rose	9.00	10.00
a.		Surch. on back	60.00	
15	A11(a)	25k grn & vio	17.50	22.50
16	A11(a)	35k red brn & grn	50.00	60.00
17	A8(a)	50k brn vio & grn	16.50	22.50
18	A9(a)	1r pale brn, dk brn & org	400.00	500.00

On Stamps of 1917.

Imperf.

No.	Type	Description	Unused	Used
21	A14(a)	1k orange	12.50	14.00
22	A14(a)	2k gray grn	5.50	5.50
23	A14(a)	3k red	16.00	20.00
25	A11(b)	7k on 15k red brn & dp bl	5.50	5.50
a.		Pair, one without surcharge		
b.		Pair, one overprinted "DBP" only		
26	A12(c)	10k on 3½r mar & lt grn	16.00	20.00
27	A9(a)	1r pale brn, brn & red org	20.00	22.50

On Stamps of Siberia 1919.

Perf. 14, 14½x15.

No.	Type	Description	Unused	Used
30	A14(a)	35k on 2k grn	6.00	7.50
a.		"DBP" on back	40.00	80.00

Imperf

No.	Type	Description	Unused	Used
31	A14(a)	35k on 2k grn	14.00	15.00
32	A14(a)	70k on 1k org	7.50	9.00

Counterfeit surcharges and overprints abound.

Postal Savings Stamps Surcharged for Postal Use.

A1 Wmk.171

Wmk. Diamonds. (171)

Perf. 14½x15.

No.	Type	Description	Unused	Used
35	A1(b)	1k on 5k grn, *buff*	15.00	20.00
36	A1(b)	2k on 10k brn, *buff*	20.00	25.00

The letters on these stamps resembling "DBP," are the Russian initials of "Dalni Vostochini Respoublika" (Far Eastern Republic).

Chita Issue.

A2

A2a

1921 — **Unwmk.** — **Typo.** — *Imperf.*

No.	Type	Description	Unused	Used
38	A2	2k gray grn	1.50	1.75
39	A2a	4k rose	1.50	1.75
40	A2	5k claret	2.00	3.00
41	A2a	10k blue	3.00	3.50

Blagoveshchensk Issue.

A3

1921 — **Litho.** — *Imperf.*

No.	Type	Description	Unused	Used
42	A3	2r red	4.00	5.00
43	A3	3r dk grn	4.00	5.00
44	A3	5r dk bl	4.00	5.00
a.		Tete beche pair	40.00	50.00
45	A3	15r dk brn	4.00	5.00
46	A3	30r dk vio	4.00	5.00
a.		Tete beche pair	40.00	50.00
		Nos. 42-46 (5)	20.00	25.00

Remainders of Nos. 42-46 were canceled in colored crayon or by typographed bars. These sell for half of foregoing prices.

Chita Issue.

A4

A5

1922 — **Litho.** — *Imperf.*

No.	Type	Description	Unused	Used
49	A4	1k orange	90	1.50
50	A4	3k dl red	50	90
51	A5	4k dp rose & buff	50	90
52	A4	5k org brn	1.25	90
53	A4	7k lt bl	1.25	2.50
a.		Perf. 11½	1.25	2.50
b.		Rouletted 9	2.25	4.00
c.		Perf. 11½x rouletted	4.00	6.00
54	A5	10k dk bl & red	60	1.25
55	A4	15k dl rose	90	1.50
56	A5	20k bl & red	90	1.50
57	A5	30k grn & red org	1.00	2.00
58	A5	50k blk & red org	1.75	3.00
		Nos. 49-58 (10)	9.55	15.95

The 4k exists with "4" omitted.

Vladivostok Issue.

Stamps of 1921 Overprinted in Red

1917
7-XI
1922

1922 — *Imperf.*

No.	Type	Description	Unused	Used
62	A2	2k gray grn	12.50	17.50
a.		Inverted overprint	42.50	
63	A2a	4k rose	12.50	17.50
a.		Inverted overprint	75.00	
b.		Double overprint	60.00	
64	A2	5k claret	15.00	22.50
a.		Inverted overprint	75.00	
b.		Double overprint	60.00	
65	A2a	10k blue	15.00	22.50
a.		Inverted overprint	150.00	

Issued to commemorate the fifth anniversary of the Russian revolution of November, 1917.

Once in the setting the figures "22" of 1922 have the bottom stroke curved instead of straight. Price $15 apiece.

Vladivostok Issue.

Russian Stamps of 1922-23 Surcharged in Black or Red

Д. В.
коп. 1 коп.
ЗОЛОТОМ

1923 *Imperf.*
66 A50 1k on 100r red 60 1.50
a. Invtd. surch. 55.00
67 A50 2k on 70r vio 60 1.50
68 A49 5k on 10r bl (R) 60 1.50
69 A50 10k on 50r brn 1.00 2.50
a. Invtd. surch. 37.50

Perf. 14½x15.
70 A50 1k on 100r red 1.00 2.50
Nos. 66-70 (5) 3.80 9.50

OCCUPATION STAMPS

Issued under Occupation of General Semenov.
Chita Issue.
Russian Stamps of 1909-12 Surcharged:

р. 1 р. — a
2р.50к. — b
Р. 5 Р. — c

1920 Unwmk. *Perf. 14, 14x15½*
N1 A15 (a) 1r on 4k car 30.00 40.00
N2 A8 (b) 2r50k on 20k bl & car 30.00 40.00
N3 A14 (c) 5r on 5k cl 17.50 27.50
a. Double surch. 35.00
N4 A11 (a) 10r on 70k brn & org 30.00 40.00

FAROE ISLANDS

(The Faroes)

LOCATION — North Atlantic Ocean
GOVT. — Self-governing part of Kingdom of Denmark.
AREA — 540 sq. mi.
POP. — 52,347 (1984)
CAPITAL — Thorshavn

100 Ore = 1 Krone

Denmark No. 97 Handstamp Surcharged

2
ØRE

1919, Jan. Typo. *Perf. 14x14½*
1 A16 2o on 5ö grn 1,200. 600.00

Counterfeits of surcharge exist.
Denmark No. 88a, the bisect, was used with Denmark No. 97 in Faroe Islands Jan. 3-23, 1919.

Denmark Nos. 220, 224, 238A, 224C Surcharged in Blue or Black

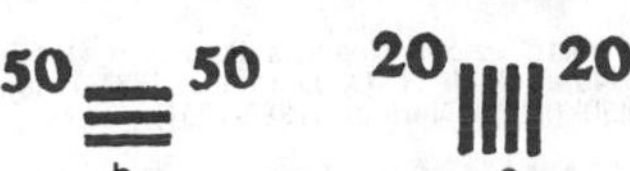

b c

d 20

1940-41 Engr. *Perf. 13*
2 A32 (b) 20(o) on 1ö gray blk (Bl) ('41) 70.00 115.00
3 A32 (c) 20(o) on 5ö rose lake (Bl) ('41) 52.50 35.00
4 A30 (d) 20(o) on 15ö dp red (Bk) 70.00 20.00
5 A32 (b) 50(o) on 5ö rose lake (Bk) 325.00 90.00
6 A32 (b) 60(o) on 6ö org (Bk) 140.00 240.00
Nos. 2-6 (5) 657.50 500.00

Nos. 2-6 were issued during British administration.

Map of Islands, 1673 — A1

Map of North Atlantic, 1573 — A2

West Coast, Sandoy — A3

Vidoy and Svinoy, by Eyvindur Mohr — A4

Designs: 50ö, 90ö, like 5ö. 60ö, 80ö, 120ö, like 10ö. 200ö, like 70ö. 250ö, 300ö, View of Streymoy and Vagar. 450ö, Houses, Nes, by Ruth Smith. 500ö, View of Hvitanes and Skalafjordur, by S. Joensen-Mikines.

Unwmk.
1975, Jan. 30 Engr. *Perf. 13*
7 A1 5o sepia 5 5
8 A2 10o emer & dk bl 5 5
9 A1 50o grysh grn 18 18
10 A2 60o brn & dk bl 2.00 2.00
11 A3 70o vio bl & sl grn 2.00 2.00
12 A2 80o ocher & dk bl 1.00 1.00
13 A1 90o red brn 2.00 2.00
14 A2 120o brt bl & dk bl 1.00 70
15 A3 200o vio bl & sl grn 1.00 1.00
16 A3 250o multi 90 90
17 A3 300o multi 10.00 3.00

Photo. *Perf. 12½x13*
18 A4 350o multi 1.25 1.25
19 A4 450o multi 1.50 1.50
20 A4 500o multi 1.50 1.50
Nos. 7-20 (14) 24.43 17.13

Faroe Boat — A5

Faroe Flag — A6

Faroe Mailman — A7

Perf. 12½x13, 12 (A6)
1976, Apr. 1 Engr.; Litho. (A6)
21 A5 125o cop red 4.00 2.00
22 A6 160o multi 60 60
23 A7 800o olive 1.75 1.50

Faroe Islands independent Postal service, Apr. 1, 1976.

Faroe Islands stamps can be mounted in Scott's annually supplemented Scandinavia and Finland Album.

Motor Fishing Boat — A8

Faroese Fishing Vessels and Map of Islands: 125ö, Inland fishing cutter. 160ö, Modern seine fishing vessel. 600ö, Deep-sea fishing trawler.

1977, Apr. 28 Photo. *Perf. 14½x14*
24 A8 100o grn & blk 11.00 8.00
25 A8 125o car & blk 3.00 3.00
26 A8 160o bl & blk 1.00 1.00
27 A8 600o brn & blk 1.50 1.25

Common Snipe — A9

Birds: 180ö, Oystercatcher. 250ö, Whimbrel.

Photogravure & Engraved
1977, Sept. 29 *Perf. 14½x14*
28 A9 70o multi 30 30
29 A9 180o multi 60 60
30 A9 250o multi 90 90

North Coast, Puffins A10

Mykines Village A11

Mykines Island: 140ö, Tilled fields and coast. 150ö, Aerial view. 180ö, Map.

Perf. 13x13½, 13½x13
1978, Jan. 26 Photo.
Size: 21x28mm., 28x21mm.
31 A10 100o multi 35 35
32 A11 130o multi 45 45
33 A11 140o multi 90 90
34 A10 150o multi 60 60

Size: 37x26mm.
Perf. 14½x14
35 A11 180o multi 60 60
Nos. 31-35 (5) 2.90 2.90

Gannets A12

Old Library A13

Sea Birds: 180ö, Puffins. 400ö, Guillemots.

Lithographed and Engraved
1978, Apr. 13 *Perf. 12x12½*
36 A12 140o multi 1.25 1.25
37 A12 180o multi 1.65 1.65
38 A12 400o multi 1.25 1.25

1978, Dec. 7 *Perf. 13*
Design: 180ö, New Library.

39 A13 140o gray grn & lt grn 1.25 1.25
40 A13 180o brn & buff 1.25 85

Completion of New Library Building.

Girl Guide, Tent and Fire — A14

1978, Dec. 7 Photo. *Perf. 13½*
41 A14 140o multi 1.65 1.65

Faroese Girl Guides, 50th anniversary.

Ram — A15

Lithographed and Engraved
1979, Mar. 19 *Perf. 12*
42 A15 25k multi 7.50 6.00

Europa Issue 1979

Denmark No. 88a — A16

Design: 180ö, Faroe Islands No. 1.

Lithographed and Engraved
1979, May 7 *Perf. 12½*
43 A16 140o yel & bl 1.25 1.25
44 A16 180o rose, grn & blk 1.25 1.25

Girl Wearing Festive Costume — A17

Children's Drawings and IYC Emblem: 150ö, Fisherman. 200ö, Two friends.

Lithographed and Engraved
1979, Oct. 1 *Perf. 12*
45 A17 110o multi 35 35
46 A17 150o multi 50 50
47 A17 200o multi 65 65

International Year of the Child.

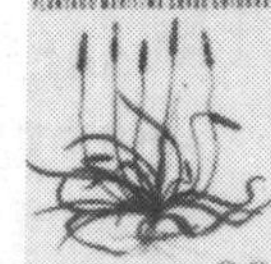

Sea Plantain — A18

1980, Mar. 17 Photo. *Perf. 12x11½*
48 A18 90o *shown* 30 30
49 A18 110o *Glacier buttercup* 35 35
50 A18 150o *Purple saxifrage* 50 50
51 A18 200o *Starry saxifrage* 70 70
52 A18 400o *Lady's mantle* 1.25 1.25
Nos. 48-52 (5) 3.10 3.10

Jakob Jakobsen (1864-1918), Linguist — A19

Coat of Arms, Virgin and Child, Gothic Pew Gable — A20

Europa Issue 1980

Design: 200ö, Vensel Ulrich Hammershaimb (1819-1909), theologian, linguist and folklorist.

1980, Oct. 6 Engr. *Perf. 11½*
53 A19 150o dl grn 60 60
54 A19 200o dl red brn 80 80

Photo. & Engr.
1980, Oct. 6 *Perf. 13½*

Kirkjubour Pew Gables, 15th Century: 140ö, Norwegian coat of arms, John the Baptist. 150ö, Christ's head, St. Peter. 200ö, Hand in halo, Apostle Paul.

55 A20 110o multi 30 30
56 A20 140o multi 50 50
57 A20 150o multi 50 50
58 A20 200o multi 65 65

See Nos. 102-105.

Fishing Boats, Old Torshavn A21

Designs: Sketches of Old Torshavn by Ingalzur Reyni.

1981, Mar. 2 Engr.
59 A21 110o dk grn 30 30
60 A21 140o black 55 55
61 A21 150o dk brn 55 55
62 A21 200o dk bl 75 75

Europa Issue 1981

The Ring Dance A22

Design: 200o, The garter dance.

1981, June 1 Engr. *Perf. 13x14*
63 A22 150o pale rose & grn 70 70
64 A22 200o pale yel grn & dk brn 80 80

Rune Stones, 800-1000 AD — A23

Historic Writings: 1k, Folksong, 1846. 3k, Sheep Letter excerpt, 1298. 6k, Seal and text, 1533. 10k, Titlepage from Faeroae et Faeroa, by Lucas Jacobson Debes, library.

Photo. & Engr.
1981, Oct. 19 *Perf. 11½*
65 A23 10o multi 10 10
69 A23 1k multi 34 34
72 A23 3k multi 90 90
75 A23 6k multi 1.75 1.75
78 A23 10k multi 3.25 3.25
Nos. 65-78 (5) 6.34 6.34

Europa 1982 — A24

1982, Mar. 15 Engr. *Perf. 13½*
81 A24 1.50k Viking North Atlantic routes 70 70
82 A24 2k Viking house foundation 80 80

View of Gjogv, by Ingalvur av Reyni A25

1982, June 7 Litho. *Perf. 12½x13*
83 A25 180o shown 60 60
84 A25 220o Hvalvik 3.00 1.10
85 A25 250o Kvivik 80 80

Ballad of Harra Paetur and Elinborg — A26

Designs: Scenes from the medieval ballad of chivalry.

1982, Sept. 27 Litho.
86 A26 220o multi 85 85
87 A26 250o multi 85 85
88 A26 350o multi 1.25 1.25
89 A26 450o multi 1.65 1.65

Cargo Ships — A27

1983, Feb. 21 Litho. *Perf. 14x14½*
90 A27 220o Arcturus, 1856 85 85
91 A27 250o Laura, 1882 85 85
92 A27 700o Thyra, 1866 2.25 2.25

Chessmen, by Pol i Buo (1791-1857) — A28

1983, May 2 Engr. *Perf. 13 Vert.*
93 A28 250o King 1.00 1.25
94 A28 250o Queen 1.00 1.25
a. Bklt. pane of 6 (3 each #93-94) 6.00

Nos. 93-94 issued only in booklets.

Europa 1983 — A29

Nobel Prizewinners in Medicine: 250o, Niels R. Finsen (1860-1903), ultraviolet radiation pioneer. 400o, Alexander Fleming (1881-1955), discoverer of penicillin.

1983, June 6 Engr. *Perf. 12x11½*
95 A29 250o dk bl 75 75
96 A29 400o red brn 1.40 1.40

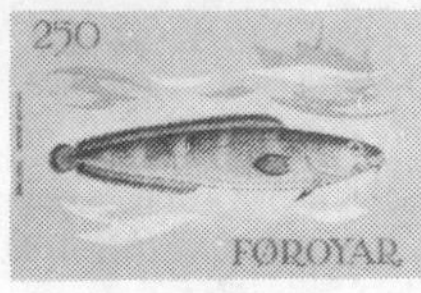

Haddock A30

1983, Sept. 19 Litho. *Perf. 12½x13*
97 A30 250o Tusk 80 80
98 A30 280o shown 1.00 1.00
99 A30 500o Halibut 1.50 1.50
100 A30 900o Catfish 2.75 2.75

Souvenir Sheet

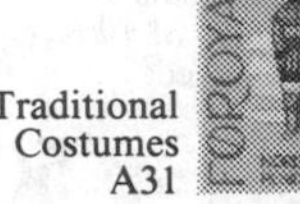

Traditional Costumes A31

Various national costumes.

1983, Nov. 4 Litho. *Perf. 12*
101 Sheet of 3 7.00 7.50
a. A31 250o multi 2.25 2.50
b. A31 250o multi 2.25 2.50
c. A31 250o multi 2.25 2.50

Nordic House Cultural Center opening. Margin shows Scandinavian flags. Size: 120x67mm.

Pew Gables Type of 1980

Designs: 250o, John, shield with three crowns. 300o, St. Jacob, shield with crossed keys. 350o, Thomas, shield with crossbeam. 400o, Judas Taddeus, Toulouse cross halo.

Photo. & Engr.
1984, Jan. 30 *Perf. 14x13½*
102 A20 250o lil, pur & dk brn 75 75
103 A20 300o red brn, dk buff & dk brn 90 90
104 A20 350o blk, lt gray & dk brn 1.05 1.05
105 A20 400o ol grn, pale yel & dk brn 1.20 1.20

Europa (1959-84) A33

1984, Apr. 2 Engr. *Perf. 13½*
106 A33 250o red 75 75
107 A33 500o dk bl 2.00 2.00

Sverri Patursson (1871-1960), Writer — A34

Poets: 2.50k, Joannes Patursson (1866-1946). 3k, J. H. O. Djurhuus (1881-1948). 4.50k, H.A. Djurhuus (1883-1951).

1984, May 28 Engr. *Perf. 13½*
108 A34 2k ol grn 60 60
109 A34 2.50k red 75 75
110 A34 3k dk bl 90 90
111 A34 4.50k violet 1.35 1.35

Faroese Smack (Fishing Boat) — A35

Perf. 12½x13, 13x12½

1984, Sept. 10 **Engr.**
112 A35 280o shown 90 90
113 A35 300o Fishermen, vert. 90 90
114 A35 12k Helmsman, vert. 3.60 3.60

Fairytale Illustrations by Elinborg Lutzen — A36

1984, Oct. 29 **Litho.** ***Perf. 13 Vert.***
115 A36 140o Beauty of the Veils 1.10 1.10
116 A36 280o Veils, diff. 1.10 1.10
117 A36 280o Girl Shy Prince 1.10 1.10
118 A36 280o The Glass Sword 1.10 1.10
119 A36 280o Little Elin 1.10 1.10
120 A36 280o The Boy and the Ox 1.10 1.10
a. Bklt. pane of 6 (#115-120) 6.75
Nos. 115-120 (6) 6.60 6.60

View of Torshavn and the Forts, by Edward Dayes A37

Dayes' Landscapes, 1789: 280o, Skaeling. 550o, View Towards the North Seen from the Hills Near Torshavn in Stremoy, Faroes. 800o, The Moving Stones in Eysturoy, Faroes. Nos. 121-124 se-tenant.

Litho. & Engr.

1985, Feb. 4 ***Perf. 13***
121 A37 250o multi 75 75
122 A37 280o multi 1.75 1.75
123 A37 550o multi 1.65 1.65
124 A37 800o multi 2.50 2.50

Europa 1985 — A38

Children taking music lessons.

1985, Apr. 1 **Litho.** ***Perf. 13½x14½***
125 A38 280o multi 90 90
126 A38 550o multi 1.65 1.65

Paintings, Faroese Museum of Art — A39

Designs: 550o, Winter's Day in Nolsoy, 1959, by Steffan Danielsen (1922-1976). 450o, Self-Portrait, 1952, by Ruth Smith (1913-1958). 280o, The Garden, Hoyvik, 1973, by Thomas Arge (1942-1978).

Litho. & Engr.

1985, June 3 ***Perf. 12½***
127 A39 280o multi 90 90
128 A39 450o multi, vert. 1.40 1.40
129 A39 550o multi 1.65 1.65

Lighthouses — A40

1985, Sept. 23 **Litho.** ***Perf. 13½x14***
130 A40 270o Nolsoy, 1893 85 85
131 A40 320o Thorshavn, 1909 95 95
132 A40 350o Mykines, 1909 1.10 1.10
133 A40 470o Map of locations 1.40 1.40

Passenger Aviation in the Faroes, 22nd Anniv. A41

Perf. 13½ Horiz.

1985, Oct. 28 **Photo.**
134 A41 300o Douglas DC-3 90 90
135 A41 300o Fokker Friendship 90 90
136 A41 300o Boeing 737 90 90
137 A41 300o Interisland LM-IKB 90 90
138 A41 300o Helicopter Snipan 90 90
a. Bklt. pane of 5, #134-138 4.50 4.50

Nos. 134-138 printed in booklets only.

Skrimsla, Ancient Folk Ballad — A42

1986, Feb. 3 **Litho.** ***Perf. 12½x13***
139 A42 300o Peasant in woods 90 90
140 A42 420o Meets Giant 1.25 1.25
141 A42 550o Giant loses game 1.65 1.65
142 A42 650o Giant grants Peasant's wish 2.00 2.00

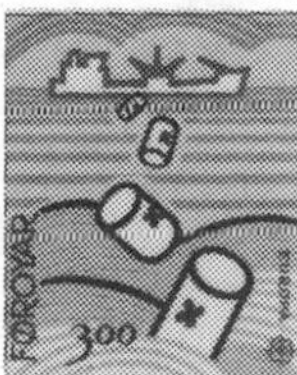

Europa 1986 — A43

Amnesty Intl., 25th Anniv. — A44

1986, Apr. 7 **Litho.** ***Perf. 13½***
143 A43 300o shown 90 90
144 A43 550o Sea pollution 1.65 1.65

1986, June 2 ***Perf. 14x13½***

Winning design competition artwork.

145 A44 300o Olivur vid Neyst 90 90
146 A44 470o Eli Smith 1.40 1.40
147 A44 550o Ranna Kunoy 1.65 1.65

Nos. 145-146 horiz.

Souvenir Sheet

HAFNIA '87, Copenhagen — A45

Design: East Bay of Torshavn, watercolor, 1782, by Christian Rosenmeyer (1728-1802).

1986, Aug. 29 **Litho.** ***Perf. 13x13½***
148 Sheet of 3 6.00 6.00
a. A45 3k multi 2.00 2.00
b. A45 4.70k multi 2.00 2.00
c. A45 6.50k multi 2.00 2.00

No. 148 has multicolored inscribed margin continuing the painting. Sold for 20k.

Old Stone Bridges A46

Designs: 2.70k, Glyvrar on Eysturoy. 3k, Leypanagjogv on Vagar, vert. 13k, Skaelinger on Streymoy.

Perf. 13½x14½, 14½x13½

1986, Oct. 13 **Engr.**
149 A46 2.70k dp brn vio 80 80
150 A46 3k bluish blk 90 90
151 A46 13k gray grn 4.00 4.00

Farmhouses A47

Traditional architecture: 300o, Depil on Borooy, 1814. 420o, Depil, diff. 470o, Frammi vio Gjonna on Streymoy, c. 1814. 650o, Frammi, diff.

1987, Feb. 9 **Engr.** ***Perf. 13x14½***
152 A47 300o pale bl & bl 72 72
153 A47 420o buff & brn 1.00 1.00
154 A47 470o pale grn & dp grn 1.15 1.15
155 A47 650o pale gray & blk 1.55 1.55

Europa 1987 — A48

Nordic House: 300o, Exterior. 550o, Interior.

1987, Apr. 6 ***Perf. 13x14***
156 A48 300o dk bl 90 90
157 A48 550o dk brn 1.65 1.65

Fishing Trawlers A49

1987, June 1 **Litho.** ***Perf. 14x13½***
158 A49 3k Joannes Patursson 90 90
159 A49 5.50k Magnus Heinason 1.65 1.65
160 A49 8k Sjurdarberg 2.40 2.40

Hestur (Horse) Island A50

Litho. & Engr.

1987, Sept. 7 ***Perf. 13***
161 A50 270o Map 75 75
162 A50 300o Seaport 85 85
163 A50 420o Bird cliff 1.20 1.20
164 A50 470o Pasture, sheep 1.35 1.35
165 A50 550o Seashore 1.55 1.55
Nos. 161-165 (5) 5.70 5.70

Nos. 161, 163 and 165 vert.

Abstract Collages by Zacharias Heinesen A51

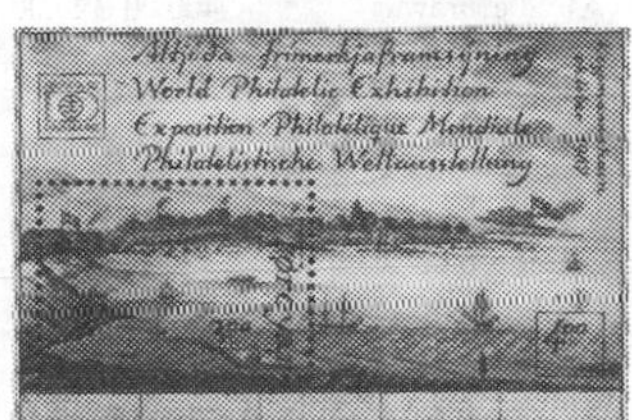

West Bay of Torshavn, Watercolor by Rosenmeyer — A52

1987, Oct. 16 **Litho.** ***Perf. 13½x14***
166 A51 4.70k Eystaravag 1.40 1.40
167 A51 6.50k Vestarvag 1.90 1.90

Souvenir Sheet

Perf. 13½x13

168 A52 3k multi 1.20 1.20

HAFNIA '87. No. 168 has inscribed multicolored margin continuing the painting and picturing the artist at LR wearing greatcoat and tricorner hat, easel in hand. Sold for 4k. Size: 76x54mm.

FERNANDO PO

LOCATION — An island in the Gulf of Guinea off west Africa.
GOVT. — Province of Spain
AREA — 800 sq. mi.
POP. — 62,612 (1960)
CAPITAL — Santa Isabel

Together with the islands of Elobey, Annobon and Corisco, Fernando Po came under the administration of Spanish Guinea. Postage stamps of Spanish Guinea were used until 1960.

The provinces of Fernando Po and Rio Muni united Oct. 12, 1968, to form the Republic of Equatorial Guinea.

100 Centimos = 1 Escudo = 2.50 Pesetas
100 Centimos = 1 Peseta
1000 Milesimas = 100 Centavos = 1 Peso (1882)

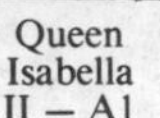

Queen Isabella II — A1

King Alfonso XII — A2

1868 Unwmk. Typo. *Perf. 14*

1 A1 20c brown 400.00 125.00

Forgeries exist.

1879 Centimos de Peseta.

2 A2 5c green 35.00 6.75
3 A2 10c rose 35.00 6.75
4 A2 50c blue 45.00 6.75

1882-89 Centavos de Peso.

5 A2 1c green 8.00 2.75
6 A2 2c rose 12.50 4.75
7 A2 5c gray bl 30.00 4.00
8 A2 10c dk brn ('89) 47.50 4.00

Nos. 5-7 Handstamp Surcharged in Blue, Black or Violet — a

1884-95

9 A2 50c on 1c grn ('95) 55.00 12.00
11 A2 50c on 2c rose 20.00 4.50
12 A2 50c on 5c bl ('87) 80.00 17.50

Inverted and double surcharges exist.

King Alfonso XIII — A4

1894-97 *Perf. 14*

13 A4 1/8c sl ('96) 17.50 2.50
14 A4 2c rose ('96) 12.50 2.00
15 A4 5c bl grn ('97) 12.50 2.00
16 A4 6c dk vio ('96) 10.00 2.25
17 A4 10c brn vio ('94) 100.00 20.00
18 A4 10c lake ('95) 27.50 5.00
19 A4 10c org brn ('96) 10.00 2.00
20 A4 12½c dk brn ('96) 10.00 2.25
21 A4 20c sl bl ('96) 10.00 2.25
22 A4 25c cl ('96) 17.50 2.25
Nos. 13-22 (10) 227.50 42.50

Stamps of 1894-97 Handstamped in Blue, Black or Red

b

c

Type "b" Surcharge

1896-98

23 A4 5c on 2c rose (Bl) 22.50 4.00
24 A4 5c on 10c brn vio (Bl) 75.00 10.00
25 A4 5c on 12½c brn (Bl) 17.50 4.25
a. Black surcharge 17.50 4.25

Type "c" Surcharge

26 A4 5c on 1/8c sl (Bk) 15.00 3.75
27 A4 5c on 2c rose (Bl) 15.00 3.75
a. Black surcharge 15.00 3.75
28 A4 5c on 5c grn (R) 80.00 15.00
29 A4 5c on 6c dk vio (R) 11.00 7.50
a. Violet surcharge 12.00 11.50
30 A4 5c on 10c org brn (Bk) 80.00 18.00
31 A4 5c on 12½c brn (R) 30.00 6.00
32 A4 5c on 20c sl bl (R) 20.00 5.50
33 A4 5c on 25c cl (Bk) 20.00 5.50
a. Blue surcharge 22.50 7.25

Type "a" Surcharge

1898-99

34 A4 50c on 2c rose (Bl) 40.00 7.00
35 A4 50c on 10c brn vio (Bl) 110.00 20.00
36 A4 50c on 10c lake (Bl) 120.00 20.00
37 A4 50c on 10c org brn (Bl) 110.00 20.00
38 A4 50c on 12½c brn (Bk) 85.00 15.00

The "a" surcharge also exists on 1/8c, 5c and 25c.

Arms
A5 A6

Revenue Stamps Handstamped in Blue

1897-98 *Imperf.*

39 A5 5c on 10c rose 40.00 20.00
40 A6 10c rose 40.00 17.50

A7

Arms — A8

A9

A9a

Revenue Stamps Handstamped in Black or Red

1899 *Imperf.*

41 A7 15c on 10c grn 42.50 27.50
a. Blue surcharge, vertical 42.50 27.50
42 A8 10c on 25c grn 135.00 80.00
43 A9 15c on 25c grn 200.00 135.00
43A A9a 15c on 25c grn (R) *4,000. 2,250.*
b. Black surcharge *4,000. 2,250.*

Surcharge on No. 41 is either horizontal, inverted or vertical.

On No. 42 "CORREOS" is overprinted in red.

King Alfonso XIII — A10

1899 *Perf. 14*

44 A10 1m org brn 2.00 50
45 A10 2m org brn 2.00 50
46 A10 3m org brn 2.00 50
47 A10 4m org brn 2.00 50
48 A10 5m org brn 2.00 50
49 A10 1c blk vio 2.00 50
50 A10 2c dk bl grn 2.00 50
51 A10 3c dk brn 2.00 50
52 A10 4c orange 11.00 1.00
53 A10 5c car ros 2.00 50
54 A10 6c dk bl 2.00 50
55 A10 8c gray brn 6.00 50
56 A10 10c vermilion 3.50 50
57 A10 15c sl grn 3.50 50
58 A10 20c maroon 11.50 1.00
59 A10 40c violet 72.50 13.50
60 A10 60c black 72.50 13.50
61 A10 80c red brn 72.50 13.50
62 A10 1p yel grn 250.00 65.00
63 A10 2p sl bl 265.00 65.00
Nos. 44-63 (20) 788.00 179.00

Nos. 44-63 exist imperf. Price for set, $1,400.

1900 Surcharged type "a".

64 A10 50c on 20c mar 16.00 3.25
a. Blue surcharge 30.00 6.50

Surcharged type "b".

64B A10 5c on 20c mar 160.00 9.00

Surcharged type "c".

65 A10 5c on 20c mar 10.00 3.25

Dated "1900"

1900

66 A10 1m black 2.25 50
67 A10 2m black 2.25 50
68 A10 3m black 2.25 50
69 A10 4m black 2.25 50
70 A10 5m black 2.25 50
71 A10 1c green 2.25 50
72 A10 2c violet 2.25 50
73 A10 3c rose 2.25 50
74 A10 4c blk brn 2.25 50
75 A10 5c blue 2.25 50
76 A10 6c orange 2.25 1.50
77 A10 8c brnz grn 2.25 1.50
78 A10 10c claret 2.25 50
79 A10 15c dk vio 2.25 50
80 A10 20c ol brn 2.25 50
81 A10 40c brown 6.75 1.50
82 A10 60c green 16.00 1.50
83 A10 80c dk bl 16.00 2.75
84 A10 1p red brn 85.00 17.50
85 A10 2p orange 135.00 37.50
Nos. 66-85 (20) 292.50 70.25

Nos. 66-85 exist imperf.

A11 A12

Revenue Stamps Overprinted or Surcharged with Handstamp in Red or Black

1900 *Imperf.*

86 A11 10c bl (R) 50.00 12.50
87 A12 5c on 10c bl 125.00 42.50

Nos. 52 and 80 Surcharged type "a" in Violet or Black.

1900

88 A10 50c on 4c org (V) 20.00 5.75
a. Green surcharge 32.50 16.00
88B A10 50c on 20c ol brn 12.50 5.00

A13 A14

1901 *Perf. 14*

89 A13 1c black 2.00 50
90 A13 2c org brn 2.00 50
91 A13 3c dk vio 2.00 50
92 A13 4c lt vio 2.00 50
93 A13 5c org red 1.25 50
94 A13 10c vio brn 1.25 50
95 A13 25c dp bl 1.25 50
96 A13 50c claret 2.00 50
97 A13 75c dk brn 1.50 50
98 A13 1p bl grn 37.50 3.50
99 A13 2p red brn 25.00 5.50
100 A13 3p ol grn 25.00 7.25
101 A13 4p dl red 25.00 7.25
102 A13 5p dk grn 30.00 7.25
103 A13 10p buff 62.50 17.50
Nos. 89-103 (15) 220.25 52.75

Dated "1902"

1902 Control Numbers on Back.

104 A13 5c dk grn 2.00 30
105 A13 10c slate 2.00 30
106 A13 25c claret 5.00 75
107 A13 50c vio brn 12.00 2.25
108 A13 75c lt vio 12.00 2.25
109 A13 1p car rose 15.00 3.50
110 A13 2p ol grn 30.00 8.00
111 A13 5p org red 45.00 18.00
Nos. 104-111 (8) 123.00 35.35

Nos. 104-111 exist imperf. Price for set, $425.

1903 *Perf. 14*

Control Numbers on Back

112 A14 1/4c dk vio 30 20
113 A14 1/2c black 30 20
114 A14 1c scarlet 30 20
115 A14 2c dk grn 30 20
116 A14 3c bl grn 30 20
117 A14 4c violet 30 20
118 A14 5c rose lake 40 20
119 A14 10c org buff 50 25
120 A14 15c bl grn 2.00 75
121 A14 25c red brn 2.25 1.00
122 A14 50c blk brn 3.75 1.75
123 A14 75c carmine 13.00 3.00
124 A14 1p dk brn 19.00 4.50
125 A14 2p dk ol grn 25.00 6.25
126 A14 3p claret 25.00 6.25
127 A14 4p dk bl 32.50 10.00
128 A14 5p dp dl bl 45.00 12.00
129 A14 10p dl red 90.00 18.00
Nos. 112-129 (18) 260.20 65.15

Dated "1905"

1905 Control Numbers on Back.

136 A14 1c dp vio 30 25
137 A14 2c black 30 25
138 A14 3c vermilion 30 25
139 A14 4c dp grn 30 25

The lack of a price for a listed item does not necessarily indicate rarity.

140	A14	5c bl grn	40	25
141	A14	10c violet	1.25	40
142	A14	15c car lake	1.25	40
143	A14	25c org buff	9.00	1.10
144	A14	50c green	6.75	1.65
145	A14	75c red brn	8.00	5.25
146	A14	1p dp gray brn	9.00	5.25
147	A14	2p carmine	17.00	7.50
148	A14	3p dp brn	26.00	8.75
149	A14	4p brnz grn	30.00	10.00
150	A14	5p claret	47.50	16.00
151	A14	10p dp bl	75.00	22.50
		Nos. 136-151 (16)	232.35	80.05

King Alfonso XIII — A15

1907 Control Numbers on Back.

152	A15	1c bl blk	20	25
153	A15	2c car rose	20	6
154	A15	3c dp vio	20	6
155	A15	4c black	20	6
156	A15	5c org buff	25	20
157	A15	10c maroon	1.20	35
158	A15	15c brnz grn	40	20
159	A15	25c dk brn	17.50	6.50
160	A15	50c bl grn	25	15
161	A15	75c vermilion	30	15
162	A15	1p dl bl	1.75	35
163	A15	2p brown	6.75	2.50
164	A15	3p lake	6.75	2.50
165	A15	4p violet	6.75	2.50
166	A15	5p blk brn	6.75	2.50
167	A15	10p org brn	6.75	2.50
		Nos. 152-167 (16)	56.20	20.83

No. 157 Handstamp Surcharged in Black or Blue

HABILITADO PARA 05CTMS

1908

168	A15	5c on 10c mar (Bk)	3.50	2.50
169	A15	5c on 10c mar (Bl)	12.50	6.75

The surcharge on Nos. 168-169 exists inverted, double and otherwise.

Seville-Barcelona Issue of Spain, 1929, Overprinted in Blue or Red

170

1929 *Perf. 11.*

170	A52	5c rose lake	15	15
171	A53	10c grn (R)	15	15
a.		Perf. 14	60	50
172	A50	15c Prus bl (R)	15	15
173	A51	20c pur (R)	15	15
174	A50	25c brt rose	15	15
175	A52	30c blk brn	15	15
176	A53	40c dk bl (R)	30	30
177	A51	50c dp org	50	45
178	A52	1p bl blk (R)	1.50	1.00
179	A53	4p dp rose	7.50	6.00
180	A53	10p brown	8.50	7.50
		Nos. 170-180 (11)	19.20	16.15

Virgin Mary — A16

1960 Unwmk. Photo. *Perf. 13x12½*

181	A16	25c dl gray vio	6	6
182	A16	50c brn ol	6	6
183	A16	75c vio brn	6	6
184	A16	1p org ver	15	6
185	A16	1.50p lt bl grn	15	6
186	A16	2p red lil	15	6
187	A16	3p dk bl	3.75	1.10
188	A16	5p lt red brn	35	12
189	A16	10p lt ol grn	65	20
		Nos. 181-189 (9)	5.38	1.78

Tricorn and Windmill from "The Three-Cornered Hat" by Falla — A17

Manuel de Falla A18

1960 *Perf. 13x12½, 12½x13*

190	A17	35c sl grn	10	5
191	A18	80c Prus grn	10	6

Issued to honor Manuel de Falla (1876-1946), Spanish composer.

See Nos. B1-B2.

Map of Fernando Po — A19

General Franco A20

Designs: 70c, Santa Isabel Cathedral.

Perf. 13x12½, 12½x13

1961, Oct. 1 Photo. Unwmk.

192	A19	25c gray vio	12	5
193	A20	50c ol brn	12	6
194	A19	70c brt grn	12	6
195	A20	1p red org	12	6

Issued to commemorate the 25th anniversary of the nomination of Gen. Francisco Franco as Chief of State.

Ocean Liner A21

Design: 50c, S.S. San Francisco.

1962, July 10 *Perf. 12½x13*

196	A21	25c dl vio	15	5
197	A21	50c gray ol	15	5
198	A21	1p org brn	15	6

Mailman — A22

Mail Transport Symbols A23

Perf. 13x12½, 12½x13

1962, Nov. 23 Unwmk.

199	A22	15c dk grn	15	5
200	A23	35c lil rose	15	5
201	A22	1p brown	15	6

Issued for Stamp Day.

Fetish — A24

1963, Jan. 29 *Perf. 13x12½*

202	A24	50c ol gray	10	5
203	A24	1p dp mag	10	6

Issued to help the victims of the Seville flood.

Nuns A25

Design: 50c, Nun and child (vert.).

Perf. 12½x13, 13x12½

1963, July 6 Photo. Unwmk.

204	A25	25c brt lil	10	5
205	A25	50c dl grn	10	5
206	A25	1p red org	10	6

Issued for child welfare.

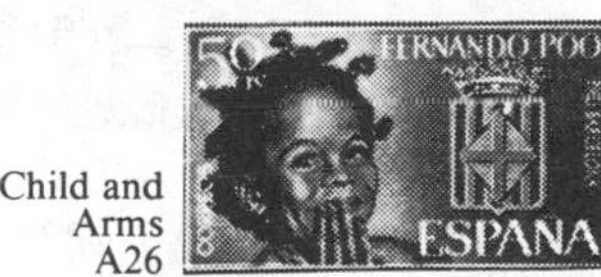

Child and Arms A26

1963, July 12 *Perf. 12½x13*

207	A26	50c brn ol	6	6
208	A26	1p car rose	6	6

Issued for Barcelona flood relief.

Governor Chacon A27

Orange Blossoms A28

Men in Dugout Canoe A29

1964, Mar. 6 *Perf. 12½x13, 13x12½*

209	A27	25c vio blk	12	5
210	A28	50c dk ol	12	5
211	A27	1p brn red	12	6

Issued for Stamp Day 1963.

1964, June 1 Photo. *Perf. 13x12½*

Design: 50c, Pineapple.

212	A29	25c purple	12	6
213	A28	50c dl ol	12	6
214	A29	1p dp cl	12	5

Issued for child welfare.

Ring-necked Francolin — A30

1964, July 1

Designs: 15c, 70c, 3p, Ring-necked francolin. 25c, 1p, 5p, Two mallards. 50c, 1.50p, 10p, Head of great blue touraco.

215	A30	15c chestnut	6	5
216	A30	25c dl vio	6	5
217	A30	50c dk ol grn	6	5
218	A30	70c green	6	5
219	A30	1p brn org	12	5
220	A30	1.50p grnsh bl	15	6
221	A30	3p vio bl	1.00	15
222	A30	5p dl pur	2.25	25
223	A30	10p brt grn	3.00	1.00
		Nos. 215-223 (9)	6.76	1.71

The Three Kings A31

Designs: 50c, 1.50p, Caspar (vert.).

Perf. 13x12½, 12½x13

1964, Nov. 23 Unwmk.

224	A31	50c green	5	5
225	A31	1p org ver	5	5
226	A31	1.50p dp grn	25	6
227	A31	3p ultra	2.25	1.10

Issued for Stamp Day, 1964.

Boy — A32

Woman Fruit Picker — A33

Design: 1.50p, Girl learning to write, and church.

1964, Mar. 1 Photo. *Perf. 13x12½*

228	A32	50c indigo	5	5
229	A33	1p dk red	6	6
230	A33	1.50p grnsh bl	15	6

Issued to commemorate 25 years of peace.

Plectrocnemia Cruciata — A34

Design: 1p, Metopodontus savagei (horiz.).

Perf. 13x12½, 12½x13

1965, June 1 Photo. Unwmk.

231	A34	50c sl grn	5	5

232 A34 1p rose red 6 6
233 A34 1.50p Prus bl 15 6

Issued for child welfare.

Pole Vault A35

Arms of Fernando Po — A36

Perf. 12½x13, 13x12½

1965, Nov. 23 Photo. Unwmk.
234 A35 50c yel grn 5 5
235 A36 1p brt org brn 6 6
236 A35 1.50p brt bl 15 6

Issued for Stamp Day, 1965.

Children Reading A37

Design: 1.50p, St. Elizabeth of Hungary (vert.).

Perf. 12½x13, 13x12½

1966, June 1 Photo. Unwmk.
237 A37 50c dk grn 5 5
238 A37 1p brn red 6 6
239 A37 1.50p dk bl 15 6

Issued for child welfare.

White-nosed Monkey — A38

Designs: 40c, 4p, Head of moustached monkey (vert.).

1966, Nov. 23 Photo. *Perf. 13*
240 A38 10c dk bl & yel 5 5
241 A38 40c lt brn, bl & blk 5 5
242 A38 1.50p ol bis, brn org & blk 10 6
243 A38 4p sl grn, brn org & blk 20 15

Issued for Stamp Day, 1966.

Flowers — A39

Designs: 40c, 4p, Six flowers.

1967, June 1 Photo. *Perf. 13*
244 A39 10c brt car & pale grn 5 5
245 A39 40c red brn & org 5 5
246 A39 1.50p red lil & lt red brn 10 6
247 A39 4p dk bl & lt grn 20 15

Issued for child welfare.

Linsang — A40

Designs: 1.50p, Needle-clawed galago (vert.). 3.50p, Fraser's scaly-tailed flying squirrel.

1967, Nov. 23 Photo. *Perf. 13*
248 A40 1p blk & bis 15 6
249 A40 1.50p brn & ol 15 10
250 A40 3.50p rose lake & dl grn 25 20

Issued for Stamp Day 1967.

Stamp of 1868, No. 1, and Arms of San Carlos A41

Designs: 1.50p, Fernando Po No. 1 and arms of Santa Isabel. 2.50p, Fernando Po No. 1 and arms of Fernando Po.

1968, Feb. 4 Photo. *Perf. 13*
251 A41 1p brt plum & brn org 15 10
252 A41 1.50p dp bl & brn org 15 10
253 A41 2.50p brn & brn org 20 15

Centenary of the first postage stamp.

Zodiac Issue

Libra — A42

Signs of the Zodiac: 1.50p, Leo. 2.50p, Aquarius.

1968, Apr. 25 Photo. *Perf. 13*
254 A42 1p brt mag, *lt yel* 15 10
255 A42 1.50p brn, *pink* 15 10
256 A42 2.50p dk vio, *yel* 20 15

Issued for child welfare.

SEMI-POSTAL STAMPS

Types of Regular Issue, 1960

Designs: 10c+5c, Manuel de Falla. 15c+5c, Dancers from "Love, the Magician."

Perf. 12½x13, 13x12½

1960 Photo. Unwmk.
B1 A18 10c + 5c mar 10 5
B2 A17 15c + 5c dk brn & bis 10 5

The surtax was for child welfare.

Whale SP1

Design: 20c+5c, 50c+20c, Harpooning whale.

1961 *Perf. 12½x13*
B3 SP1 10c + 5c rose brn 6 5
B4 SP1 20c + 5c dk sl grn 6 5
B5 SP1 30c + 10c ol brn 6 5
B6 SP1 50c + 20c dk brn 20 6

Issued for Stamp Day, 1960.

Hand Blessing Woman — SP2

Design: 25c+10c, Boy making sign of the cross, and crucifix.

1961, June 21 *Perf. 13x12½*
B7 SP2 10c + 5c rose brn 10 5
B8 SP2 25c + 10c gray vio 10 5
B9 SP2 80c + 20c dk grn 10 5

The surtax was for child welfare.

Ethiopian Tortoise SP3

Design: 25c+10c, 1p+10c, Native carriers, palms and shore.

1961, Nov. 23 *Perf. 12½x13*
B10 SP3 10c + 5c rose red 10 5
B11 SP3 25c + 10c dk pur 10 5
B12 SP3 30c + 10c vio brn 10 5
B13 SP3 1p + 10c red org 10 6

Issued for Stamp Day 1961.

FINLAND

(Suomi)

LOCATION — Northern Europe bordering on the Gulfs of Bothnia and Finland.
GOVT. — Republic
AREA — 130,119 sq. mi.
POP. — 4,869,858 (1984)
CAPITAL — Helsinki

Finland was a Grand Duchy of the Russian Empire from 1809 until December 1917, when it declared its independence.

100 Kopecks = 1 Ruble
100 Pennia = 1 Markka (1866)

Issues under Russian Empire.

> Prices of early Finland stamps vary according to condition. Quotations for Nos. 1-3B are for fine copies. Used prices are for pen-canceled copies. Very fine to superb specimens sell at much higher prices, and inferior or poor copies sell at reduced prices, depending on the condition of the individual specimen.

Coat of Arms — A1

1856 Unwmk. Typo. *Imperf.*
Small Pearls in Post Horns.
Wove Paper.

1 A1 5k blue *8,000.* 1,600.
Pen and town cancellation 2,200.
Town cancellation 3,300.
a. Tete beche pair *25,000.*
As "a," pen and town cancellation *44,000.*
2 A1 10k rose 9,500. 350.00
Pen and town cancellation 800.00
Town cancellation 1,050.
a. Tete beche pair *20,000.*
As "a," pen and town cancellation *27,500.*

1858
Wide Vertically Laid Paper

2C A1 10k rose 1,400.
Pen and town cancellation 1,900.
Town cancellation 2,500.
d. Tete beche pair

The wide vertically laid paper has 13-14 distinct lines per 2 cm. The 10k rose also exists on a narrow laid paper with lines sometimes indistinct. Price, 60 per cent of that for a wide laid paper example.

A 5k blue with small pearls exists on narrow vertically laid paper.

Stamps on diagonally laid paper are envelope cut squares.

Large Pearls in Post Horns.
Wove Paper

3 A1 5k blue *8,000.* 1,400.
Pen and town cancellation 1,800.
Town cancellation 2,750.
a. Tete beche pair *35,000.*
As "a," pen and town cancellation *44,000.*

1859 Wide Vertically Laid Paper

3B A1 5k blue *12,000.*
Pen and town cancellation *17,500.*

Reprints of Nos. 2 and 3, made in 1862, are on brownish paper, on vertically laid paper, and in tete beche pairs on normal and vertically laid paper. Reprints of 1871, 1881 and 1893 are on yellowish or white paper. Price for least costly of each, $85.

In 1956, Nos. 2 and 3 were reprinted for the Centenary with post horn watermark and gum. Price, $85 each.

Coat of Arms — A2

1860 *Serpentine Roulette 7½, 8*

Nos. 4-13, with serpentine roulette, are seldom in perfect condition. Usually some of the "teeth" are missing. In average condition, one or two teeth are gone. Prices are for average specimens. Copies with all teeth intact sell for many times more.

Four types of indentation are noted:

I. Depth 1-1¼mm.

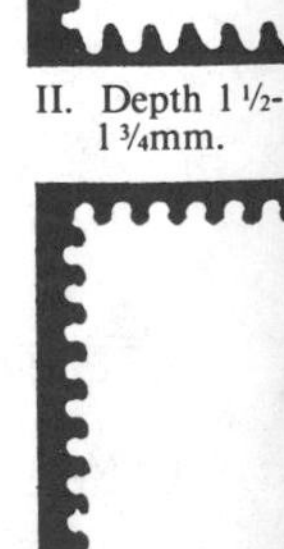
II. Depth 1½-1¾mm.

III. Depth 2-2¼mm.

IV. Shovel-shaped teeth. Depth 1¼-1½mm.

Wove Paper.

4 A2 5k bl, *bluish*, roulette I 450.00 110.00
a. Roulette II 600.00 120.00
b. Perf. vert.
5 A2 10k rose, *pale rose*, roulette I 325.00 40.00
a. Roulette II 700.00 65.00

A3

A4

1866-74 ***Serpentine Roulette***

6 A3 5p pur brn, *lil,* roulette I ('73) 180.00 65.00
a. Roulette II 1,400.
b. 5p red brn, *lil,* roulette III ('71) 180.00 65.00
7 A3 8p *grn,* roulette III ('67) 175.00 80.00
a. Ribbed paper, roulette III ('72) 750.00 250.00
b. Roulette II ('74) 180.00 80.00
c. As "b," ribbed paper ('74) 250.00 90.00
d. Roulette I ('73) 275.00 110.00
e. As "d," ribbed paper 750.00 250.00
f. Serp. roulette 10½ ('67) *8,750.*
8 A3 10p *yel,* roulette III ('70) 260.00 85.00
a. 10p *buff,* roulette II 450.00 140.00
b. 10p *buff,* roulette I ('73) 325.00 140.00
9 A3 20p bl, *bl,* roulette III 250.00 22.50
a. Roulette II 250.00 22.50
b. Roulette I ('73) 350.00 45.00
c. Roulette IV ('74) *1,100.* *650.00*
d. Perf. horiz. *300.00*
e. Printed on both sides (40p bl on back) *6,500.*
10 A3 40p rose, *lil rose,* roulette III 250.00 30.00
a. Ribbed paper, roulette III ('73) 325.00 40.00
b. Roulette II 250.00 30.00
c. As "b," ribbed paper ('73) 325.00 45.00
d. Roulette I 525.00 47.50
e. As "d," ribbed paper 375.00 47.50
f. Roulette IV *1,200.*
g. As "f," ribbed paper *1,500.*
h. Serp. roulette 10½ *4,500.*
11 A4 1m yel brn, roulette III ('67) 1,000. 400.00
a. Roulette II 1,800. 700.00

Nos. 7f and 10h are also known in compound serpentine roulette 10½ and 7½.

Nos. 4 to 11 were reprinted in 1893 on thick wove paper. Colors differ from originals. Roulette type IV. Price for Nos. 4-5, each $40, Nos. 6-10, each $50, No. 11, $55.

Thin or Thick Laid Paper

12 A3 5p red brn, *lil,* roulette III 180.00 65.00
a. Roulette II 180.00 65.00
b. Roulette I 180.00 70.00
d. 5p *buff,* roul. III (error) *7,500.*
e. Tete beche pair *10,000.*
13 A3 10p *buff,* roulette III 275.00 90.00
a. 10p *yel,* roulette II 325.00 90.00
b. 10p *yel,* roulette I 1,000. 150.00
c. 10p red brn, *lil,* roul. III (error) *6,000.* *3,500.*

A5

A6

1875 ***Perf. 14x13½***

16 A5 32p lake 2,250. 700.00

1875-81 ***Perf. 11***

17 A5 2p gray 60.00 60.00
18 A5 5p orange 175.00 15.00
a. 5p yel 175.00 15.00
19 A5 8p bl grn 250.00 95.00
a. 8p yel grn 250.00 80.00
20 A5 10p brn ('81) 475.00 80.00
21 A5 20p ultra 175.00 4.50
a. 20p bl 175.00 4.50
b. 20p Prus bl 225.00 25.00
c. Tete beche pair 3,000. 2,500.
22 A5 25p car ('79) 200.00 18.00
a. 25p rose 200.00 27.50
23 A5 32p carmine 375.00 45.00
a. 32p rose 375.00 50.00
24 A5 1m vio ('77) 600.00 200.00

A souvenir card was issued in 1974 for NORDIA 1975 reproducing a block of four of the unissued "1 MARKKAA" design.

Nos. 19 and 23 were reprinted in 1893, perf. 12½. Price $25 each.

1881-83 ***Perf. 12½***

25 A5 2p gray 20.00 20.00
a. Perf. pair 150.00
26 A5 5p orange 55.00 7.50
a. Tete beche pair 3,500. 3,000.
b. Perf. vert., pair 150.00 150.00
c. Perf. horiz., pair 175.00
27 A5 10p brown 130.00 20.00
28 A5 20p ultra 65.00 2.25
a. 20p bl 65.00 2.25
b. Tete beche pair 1,800. 2,250.
c. Perf. pair 100.00
29 A5 25p rose 65.00 11.00
a. 25p car 65.00 11.00
b. Tete beche pair 4,000. 4,500.
30 A5 1m vio ('82) 425.00 65.00

Nos. 27-29 were reprinted in 1893 in deeper shades, perf. 12½. Price $45 each.

1881 ***Perf. 11x12½***

26d A5 5p orange 375.00 80.00
27a A5 10p brown 1,200. 300.00
28d A5 20p ultra 550.00 50.00
28e A5 20p blue 550.00 50.00
29c A5 25p rose 525.00 140.00
29d A5 25p carmine 525.00 140.00
30a A5 1m violet 1,500.

1881 ***Perf. 12½x11***

26e A5 5p orange 375.00 80.00
27b A5 10p brown 1,200. 300.00
28f A5 20p ultra 550.00 50.00
28g A5 20p blue 550.00 50.00
29e A5 25p rose 525.00 140.00
29f A5 25p carmine 525.00 140.00

1885 ***Perf. 12½.***

31 A5 5p emerald 25.00 50
a. 5p yel grn 25.00 50
b. Tete beche pair 5,750. 4,750.
32 A5 10p carmine 35.00 3.50
a. 10p rose 35.00 3.50
33 A5 20p orange 35.00 50
a. 20p yel 40.00 3.25
b. Tete beche pair 3,250. 2,750.
34 A5 25p ultra 65.00 2.50
a. 25p bl 65.00 2.50
35 A5 1m gray & rose 37.50 20.00
36 A5 5m grn & rose 600.00 450.00
37 A5 10m brn & rose 925.00 800.00

1889-92 ***Perf. 12½***

38 A6 2p sl ('90) 1.00 1.00
39 A6 5p grn ('90) 35.00 35
40 A6 10p car ('90) 60.00 65
a. 10p rose ('90) 60.00 65
41 A6 20p org ('92) 55.00 30
a. 20p yel ('90) 60.00 1.50
42 A6 25p ultra ('91) 60.00 65
a. 25p bl 60.00 70
43 A6 1m sl & rose ('92) 8.00 5.50
a. 1m brnsh gray & rose ('90) 40.00 5.50
44 A6 5m grn & rose ('90) 55.00 70.00
45 A6 10m brn & rose ('90) 90.00 120.00

The 2p slate, perf. 14x13, is believed to be an essay.
See also Nos. 60-63.

Imperial Arms of Russia
A7 A8 A9

A10

A11

Wmk. 168- Wavy Lines and Letters

Laid Paper.

1891-92 **Wmk. 168** ***Perf. 14½x15***

46 A7 1k org yel 8.50 11.00
47 A7 2k green 8.50 11.00
48 A7 3k carmine 15.00 18.00
49 A8 4k rose 16.00 18.00
50 A7 7k dk bl 9.00 3.00
51 A8 10k dk bl 22.50 18.00
52 A9 14k bl & rose 30.00 25.00
53 A8 20k bl & car 22.50 20.00
54 A9 35k vio & grn 35.00 50.00
55 A8 50k vio & grn 50.00 40.00

Perf. 13½.

56 A10 1r brn & org 130.00 100.00
57 A11 3½r blk & gray 525.00 550.00
a. 3½r blk & yel *(error)* *7,000.* *5,500.*
58 A11 7r blk & yel 350.00 300.00
Nos. 46-58 (13) 1,222. 1,164.

Forgeries of Nos. 57, 57a, 58 exist.

Type of 1889-90.
Wove Paper.

1895-96 **Unwmk.** ***Perf. 14x13***

60 A6 5p green 75 25
61 A6 10p rose 1.00 25
a. Imperf. 125.00 125.00
62 A6 20p orange 1.00 25
a. Imperf 110.00 125.00
63 A6 25p ultra 2.00 50
a. 25p bl 2.00 50
b. Imperf 125.00 125.00

A12

A13

A14

A15

1901 **Litho.** ***Perf. 14½x15***
Chalky Paper.

64 A12 2p yellow 5.00 4.00
65 A12 5p green 15.00 70
66 A13 10p carmine 25.00 1.25
67 A12 20p dk bl 50.00 55
68 A14 1m vio & grn 225.00 7.50

Perf. 13½

69 A15 10m blk & gray 350.00 300.00
Nos. 64-69 (6) 670.00 314.00

Imperf sheets of 10p and 20p, stolen during production, were privately perforated 11½ to defraud the P.O. Uncanceled imperfs. of Nos. 65-68 are believed to be proofs.

Types of 1901 Redrawn.

No. 64.

No. 70.

2p. On No. 64, the "2" below "II" is shifted slightly leftward. On No. 70, the "2" is centered below "II."

No. 65. No. 71.

5p. On No. 65, the frame lines are very close. On No. 71, a clear white space separates them.

Nos. 66, 67. Nos. 72, 73.

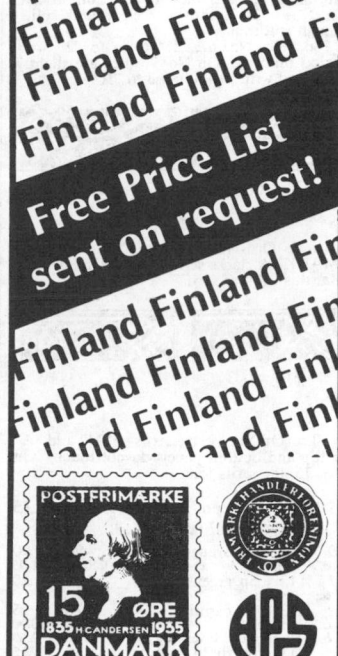

10p, 20p. On Nos. 66-67, the horizontal central background lines are faint and broken. On Nos. 72-73, they are clear and solid, though still thin.

20p. On No. 67, "H" close to "2" with period midway. On No. 73 they are slightly separated with period close to "H".

No. 68.

Nos. 74, 74a.

1m. On No. 68, the "1" following "MARKKA" lacks serif at base. On Nos. 74-74a, this "1" has serif.

No. 69.

No. 75.

10m. On No. 69, the serifs of "M" and "A" in top and bottom panels do not touch. On No. 75, the serifs join.

1901-14 Typo. *Perf. 14, 14½x15*

Ordinary Paper.

No.	Type	Description	Unused	Used
70	A12	2p orange	90	90
a.		Imperf.	250.00	*275.00*
71	A12	5p green	2.25	20
b.		Imperf.	100.00	140.00
72	A13	10p carmine	70	25
a.		Imperf.	100.00	110.00
b.		Background inverted	22.50	2.50
73	A12	20p dk bl	60	25
a.		Imperf.	100.00	110.00
74	A14	1m lil & grn, perf. 14 ('14)	1.50	50
a.		1m vio & bl grn, perf. 14½x15 ('02)	11.00	50
b.		Imperf.	125.00	150.00
		Nos. 70-74 (5)	5.95	2.10

Perf. 13½

No.	Type	Description	Unused	Used
75	A15	10m blk & db ('03)	160.00	62.50

Prices of premium quality never hinged stamps will be in excess of catalogue price.

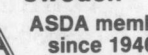

A16

A17

A18

1911-16 *Perf. 14, 14½x15*

No.	Type	Description	Unused	Used
77	A16	2p orange	25	25
78	A16	5p green	40	25
a.		Imperf.	100.00	100.00
b.		Perf. 14½x15	275.00	50.00
79	A17	10p rose	30	25
a.		Imperf.	60.00	80.00
b.		Perf. 14½x15	1.65	1.10
80	A16	20p dp bl	30	25
a.		Imperf.	60.00	60.00
81	A18	40p vio & bl	20	20
a.		Perf. 14½x15	2,000.	2,000.
		Nos. 77-81 (5)	1.45	1.20

There are three minor types of No. 79.

Perf. 14½

No.	Type	Description	Unused	Used
82	A15	10m blk & grnsh gray ('16)	200.00	225.00
a.		Horiz. pair, imperf. vert.	1,250.	

Republic.

Helsinki Issue.

Arms of the Republic — A19

Two types of the 40p.
Type I-Thin figures of value.
Type II-Thick figures of value.

1917-29 Unwmk. *Perf. 14, 14½x15*

No.	Type	Description	Unused	Used
83	A19	5p green	15	8
84	A19	5p gray ('19)	15	8
85	A19	10p rose	25	8
a.		Imperf., pair	275.00	325.00
86	A19	10p grn ('19)	1.75	10
a.		Perf. 14½x15		1,600.
87	A19	10p lt bl ('21)	15	8
88	A19	20p buff	25	10
89	A19	20p rose ('20)	50	10
90	A19	20p brn ('24)	50	35
91	A19	25p blue	30	10
92	A19	25p lt brn ('19)	18	10
93	A19	30p grn ('23)	40	25
94	A19	40p vio (I)	25	8
a.		Perf. 14½x15	180.00	15.00
95	A19	40p bl grn (II) ('29)	25	50
a.		Type I ('24)	10.00	4.50
96	A19	50p org brn	25	8
97	A19	50p dp bl ('19)	4.00	12
a.		Perf. 14½x15		550.00
98	A19	50p grn ('21)	30	20
99	A19	60p red vio ('21)	50	8
a.		Imperf., pair	100.00	135.00
100	A19	75p yel ('21)	25	30
101	A19	1m dl rose & blk	14.00	10
102	A19	1m red org ('25)	40	*14.00*
103	A19	1½m bl grn & red vio ('29)	20	20
104	A19	2m grn & blk ('21)	3.00	60
105	A19	2m dk bl & ind ('22)	1.00	12
106	A19	3m bl & blk ('21)	110.00	30
107	A19	5m red vio & blk	25.00	15
108	A19	10m brn & gray blk, perf. 14	85	85
a.		10m lt brn & blk, perf. 14½x15 ('29)	8.00	*450.00*
110	A19	25m dl red & yel ('21)	1.00	*20.00*
		Nos. 83-108,110 (27)	165.83	39.10

Copies of a 2½p gray of this type exist. They are proofs from the original die which were distributed through the Universal Postal Union. No plate was made for this denomination.

See also Nos. 127-140, 143-152.

Vasa Issue

A20

1918 Litho. *Perf. 11½.*

No.	Type	Description	Unused	Used
111	A20	5p green	40	60
112	A20	10p red	35	55
113	A20	30p slate	1.00	2.00
114	A20	40p brn vio	30	60
115	A20	50p org brn	50	1.40
116	A20	70p gray brn	2.25	13.00
117	A20	1m red & gray	50	1.00
118	A20	5m red vio & gray	100.00	140.00
		Nos. 111-118 (8)	105.30	159.15

Nos. 111-118 exist imperforate but were not regularly issued in that condition.

Sheet margin copies, perf. on 3 sides, imperf. on margin side, were sold by post office.

Stamps and Type of 1917-29 Surcharged 50 50 50

1919 *Perf. 14*

No.	Type	Description	Unused	Used
119	A19	10p on 5p grn	40	40
120	A19	20p on 10p rose	40	40
121	A19	50p on 25p bl	90	40
122	A19	75p on 20p org	40	40

Stamps and Type of 1917-29 Surcharged:

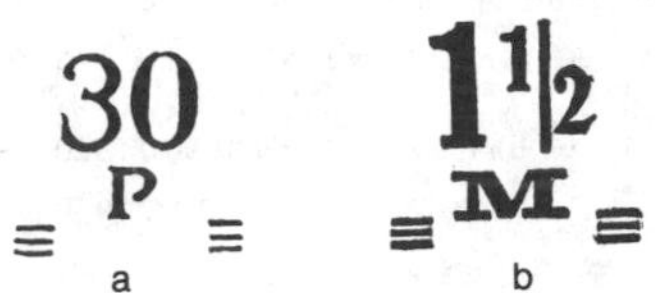

a b

1921

No.	Type	Description	Unused	Used
123	A19 (a)	30p on 10p grn	80	40
124	A19 (a)	60p on 40p red vio	4.00	60
125	A19 (a)	90p on 20p rose	25	25
126	A19 (b)	1½m on 50p bl	1.75	20
a.		Thin "2" in "½"	8.00	4.50
b.		Imperf., pair	200.00	400.00

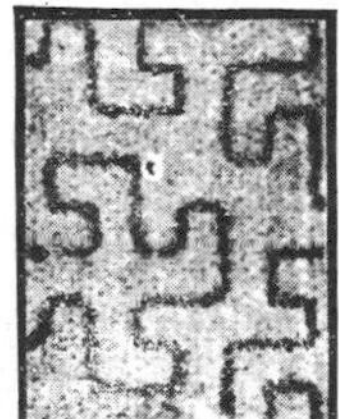

Wmk.121

Arms Type of 1917-29.

Wmk. Multiple Swastika. (121)

1925-29 *Perf. 14, 14½x15*

No.	Type	Description	Unused	Used
127	A19	10p ultra ('27)	60	1.00
128	A19	20p brown	60	80
129	A19	25p brn org ('29)	1.00	*40.00*
130	A19	30p yel grn	25	25
131	A19	40p bl grn (I)	3.00	25
a.		Type II	3.00	25
132	A19	50p gray grn ('27)	50	25
133	A19	60p red vio	25	25
134	A19	1m dp org	5.00	25
135	A19	1½m bl grn & red vio	8.50	25
136	A19	2m dk bl & ind	40	50
137	A19	3m chlky bl & blk	1.25	25
138	A19	5m red vio & blk	35	25
139	A19	10m lt brn & blk ('27)	5.00	11.00
140	A19	25m dp org & yel ('27)	30.00	*275.00*
		Nos. 127-140 (14)	56.70	

A21

Wmk.208

Wmk. Post Horn. (208)

1927, Dec. 6 Typo. *Perf. 14*

No.	Type	Description	Unused	Used
141	A21	1½m dp vio	25	50
142	A21	2m dp bl	40	1.50

Issued in commemoration of the tenth anniversary of Finnish independence.

Arms Type of 1917-29.

1927-29 Wmk. 208 *Perf. 14½x15*

No.	Type	Description	Unused	Used
143	A19	20p lt brn ('29)	1.75	*7.00*
144	A19	40p bl grn (II) ('28)	25	25
145	A19	50p gray grn ('28)	25	25
146	A19	1m dp org	25	25
a.		Imperf., pair	160.00	200.00
b.		Perf. 14	1.50	25
147	A19	1½m bl grn & red vio ('28)	3.25	15
a.		Perf. 14	675.00	15.00
148	A19	2m dk bl & ind ('28)	50	50
149	A19	3m chlky bl & blk	50	50
a.		Perf. 14	2.75	2.75
150	A19	5m red vio & blk ('28)	50	50
151	A19	10m lt brn & blk	1.50	*37.50*
152	A19	25m brn org & yel	1.75	*140.00*
		Nos. 143-152 (10)	10.50	

Philatelic Exhibition Issue.

A22

Overprint in Black

1928, Nov. 10 Litho. Wmk. 208

No.	Type	Description	Unused	Used
153	A22	1m dp org	11.00	18.00
154	A22	1½m bl grn & red vio	11.00	18.00

Nos. 153 and 154 were sold exclusively at the Helsinki Philatelic Exhibition, Nov. 10-18, 1928, and were valid only during that period.

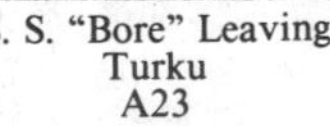

S. S. "Bore" Leaving Turku
A23

Turku Cathedral
A24

Turku Castle — A25

Wmk. 208

1929, May 22 Typo. *Perf. 14*

No.	Type	Description	Unused	Used
155	A23	1m ol grn	1.75	4.00
156	A24	1½m chocolate	3.00	3.50
157	A25	2m dk gray	1.00	4.00

Issued to commemorate the 700th anniversary of the founding of the city of Turku (Abo).

A26

1930-46 Unwmk. *Perf. 14*

158 A26 5p chocolate 10 10
159 A26 10p dl vio 10 10
160 A26 20p yel grn 40 50
161 A26 25p yel brn 15 10
162 A26 40p bl grn 3.50 25
163 A26 50p yellow 60 50
164 A26 50p bl grn ('32) 15 6
b. Imperf., pair 160.00 175.00
165 A26 60p dk gray 50 60
165A A26 75p dp org ('42) 15 10
166 A26 1m red org 60 8
a. Booklet pane of 4 2.75
166B A26 1m yel grn ('42) 25 10
167 A26 1.20m crimson 50 75
168 A26 1.25m yel ('32) 30 10
169 A26 1½m red vio 3.50 10
170 A26 1½m car ('32) 20 10
170A A26 1½m sl ('40) 20 8
170B A26 1.75m org yel ('40) 75 15
171 A26 2m indigo 40 15
172 A26 2m dp vio ('32) 10.00 10
173 A26 2m car ('36) 25 8
173B A26 2m yel org ('42) 40 10
173C A26 2m bl grn ('45) 25 10
174 A26 2½m brt bl ('32) 3.00 15
174A A26 2½m car ('42) 20 8
174B A26 2.75m rose vio ('40) 20 10
175 A26 3m ol blk 40.00 15
175B A26 3m car ('45) 30 10
175C A26 3m yel ('45) 50 60
176 A26 3½m brt bl ('36) 8.00 15
176A A26 3½m ol ('42) 20 8
176B A26 4m ol ('45) 50 8
176C A26 4½m saph ('42) 20 20
176D A26 5m saph ('45) 50 10
176E A26 5m pur ('45) 50 15
j. Imperf., pair 160.00 175.00
176F A26 5m yel ('46) 1.00 10
k. Imperf., pair 140.00 160.00
176G A26 6m car ('45) 50 15
m. Imperf., pair 160.00 175.00
176H A26 8m pur ('46) 20 10
176I A26 10m saph ('45) 1.00 10
Nos. 158-176I (38) 80.05 6.69

See also Nos. 257 262, 270-274, 291-296, 302-304.

Stamps of types A26-A29 overprinted "ITA KARJALA" are listed under Karelia, Nos. N1-N15.

Castle in Savonlinna
A27

Lake Saima — A28

Woodchopper
A29

1930 Engr.

177 A27 5m blue 30 6
178 A28 10m gray lil 120.00 4.75
179 A29 25m blk brn 1.25 25

See also Nos. 205 and 305.

Elias Lönnrot
A30

Seal of Finnish Literary Society
A31

Finland stamps can be mounted in Scott's annually supplemented Scandinavia and Finland Album.

1931, Jan. 1 Typo.

180 A30 1m ol brn 4.00 4.00
181 A31 1½m dl bl 15.00 4.00

Centenary of Finnish Literary Society.

A32

1931, Feb. 28

182 A32 1½m red 3.50 5.00
183 A32 2m blue 3.50 6.00

75th anniversary of first use of postage stamps in Finland.

Nos. 162-163 Surcharged

50 PEN.

1931, Dec.

195 A26 50p on 40p bl grn 1.50 30
196 A26 1.25m on 50p yel 4.00 70

President P. E. Svinhufvud
A33

Alexis Kivi
A34

1931, Dec. 15

197 A33 2m gray bl & blk 2.25 2.50

Issued to commemorate the 70th birthday of President Pehr Eyvind Svinhufvud.

Lake Saima Type of 1930.

1932-43 Re-engraved

205 A28 10m red vio ('43) 75 10
a. 10m dk vio 25.00 70

On Nos. 205 and 205a the lines of the islands, the clouds and the foliage are much deeper and stronger than on No. 178.

1934, Oct. 10 Typo.

206 A34 2m red vio 2.75 3.50

Issued in commemoration of the centenary of the birth of Alexis Kivi, Finnish poet (1834-1872).

Bards Reciting the "Kalevala"
A35

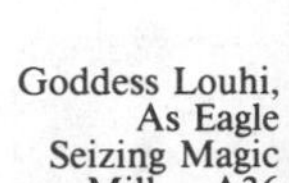

Goddess Louhi, As Eagle Seizing Magic Mill — A36

Kullervo
A37

1935, Feb. 28 Engr.

207 A35 1¼m brn lake 1.50 1.50
208 A36 2m black 4.50 1.25
209 A37 2½m blue 4.50 2.50

Issued to commemorate the centenary of the publication of the "Kalevala" (Finnish National Epic).

No. 170 Surcharged in Black

2 MARKKAA

1937, Feb.

212 A26 2m on 1½m car 5.50 65

Field Marshal Gustaf Mannerheim
A38

Swede-Finn Co-operation in Colonization
A39

1937, June 4 Photo. *Perf. 14*

213 A38 2m ultra 85 1.25

Issued in commemoration of the 70th birthday of Field Marshal Baron Carl Gustaf Mannerheim, June 4th, 1937.

1938, June 1

214 A39 3½m dk brn 1.80 3.00

Tercentenary of the colonization of Delaware by Swedes and Finns.

Early Post Office — A40

Designs: 1¼m, Mail delivery in 1700. 2m, Modern mail plane. 3½m, Helsinki post office.

1938, Sept. 6 Photo. *Perf. 14*

215 A40 50p green 45 90
216 A40 1¼m dk bl 1.75 3.50
217 A40 2m scarlet 2.00 1.00
218 A40 3½m sl blk 7.00 9.00

Issued in commemoration of the 300th anniversary of the Finnish Postal System.

Post Office, Helsinki — A44

1939-42 Photo.

219 A44 4m brn blk 25 15

Engr.

219A A44 7m blk brn ('42) 75 15
219B A44 9m rose lake ('42) 75 15

See also No. 248.

University of Helsinki — A45

1940, May 1 Photo.

220 A45 2m dp bl & bl 80 1.00

Issued in commemoration of the 300th anniversary of the founding of the University of Helsinki.

Nos. 168 and 173 Surcharged in Black

mk 1:75

1940, June 16 Typo.

221 A26 1.75m on 1.25m yel 1.10 1.40
222 A26 2.75m on 2m car 3.25 40

President Kallio Reviewing Military Band — A46

1941, May 24 Engr.

223 A46 2.75m black 80 1.00

Issued in memory of President Kyösti Kallio (1873-1940).

Castle at Viborg — A47

1941, Aug. 30 Typo.

224 A47 1.75m yel org 50 1.00
225 A47 2.75m rose vio 50 1.00
226 A47 3.50m blue 1.00 2.00

Field Marshal Mannerheim — A48

Wmk.273

Wmk. Roses. (273)

1941, Dec. 31 Engr. *Perf. 14*

227 A48 50p dl grn 80 1.25
228 A48 1.75m dp brn 80 1.25
229 A48 2m dk red 80 1.25
230 A48 2.75m dl vio brn 80 1.25
231 A48 3.50m dp bl 80 1.25
232 A48 5m sl bl 80 1.25
Nos. 227-232 (6) 4.80 7.50

President Risto Ryti — A49

233 A49 50p dl grn 80 1.25
234 A49 1.75m dp brn 80 1.25
235 A49 2m dk red 80 1.25
236 A49 2.75m dl vio brn 80 1.25
237 A49 3.50m dp bl 80 1.25
238 A49 5m sl bl 80 1.25
Nos. 233-238 (6) 4.80 7.50

Types A48-A49 overprinted "ITA KARJALA" are listed under Karelia, Nos. N16-N27.

Häme Bridge, Tampere — A50

South Harbor, Helsinki — A51

1942 **Unwmk.**
239 A50 50m dl brn vio 2.00 12
240 A51 100m indigo 2.50 20

See No. 350.

Altar and Open Bible A52 — 17th Century Printer A53

1942, Oct. 10
241 A52 2.75m dk brn 50 1.00
242 A53 3.50m vio bl 1.00 1.75

Issued to commemorate the 300th anniversary of the printing of the first Bible in Finnish, 1642.

No. 174B Surcharged in Black **3½mk**

1943, Feb. 1
243 A26 3.50m on 2.75m rose vio 20 20

Minna Canth — A54

1944, Mar. 20
244 A54 3.50m dk ol grn 60 1.00

Issued to commemorate the centenary of the birth of Minna Canth (1844-96), author and playwright.

President P. E. Svinhufvud A55 — K. J. Stahlberg A56

1944, Aug. 1
245 A55 3.50m black 60 1.00

Death of President Svinhufvud (1861-1944).

1945, May 16 **Engr.** ***Perf. 14***
246 A56 3.50m brn vio 30 80

80th birthday of Dr. K. J. Stahlberg.

Castle in Savonlinna A57 — Jean Sibelius A58

1945, Sept. 4
247 A57 15m lil rose 1.25 15
248 A44 20m sepia 1.50 8

For a 35m of type A57, see No. 280.

1945, Dec. 8
249 A58 5m dk sl grn 25 50

80th birthday of Jean Sibelius (1865-1957), composer.

No. 176E Surcharged with New Value and Bars in Black.

1946, Mar. 16
250 A26 8(m) on 5m pur 20 20

Victorious Athletes A59 — Lighthouse at Uto A60

1946, June 1 **Engr.** ***Perf. 13½***
251 A59 8m brn vio 50 80

Issued to commemorate the 3rd Sports Festival, Helsinki, June 27-30, 1946.

1946, Sept. 19
252 A60 8m dp vio 50 80

Issued to commemorate the 250th anniversary of the Finnish Department of Pilots and Lighthouses.

Post Bus — A61

1946-47 **Unwmk.** ***Perf. 14***
253 A61 16m gray blk 50 90
253A A61 30m gray blk ('47) 1.75 20

Old Town Hall, Porvoo A62 — Cathedral, Porvoo A63

1946, Dec. 3
254 A62 5m gray blk 30 45
255 A63 8m dp cl 50 65

Issued to commemorate the 600th anniversary of the founding of the city of Porvoo (Borga).

Waterfront, Tammisaari A64

1946, Dec. 14
256 A64 8m grnsh blk 50 65

Issued to commemorate the 400th anniversary of the founding of the town of Tammisaari (Ekenas).

Lion Type of 1930.

1947 **Typo.** ***Perf. 14***
257 A26 2½m dk grn 40 10
258 A26 3m sl gray 20 8
259 A26 6m dp org 1.00 12
260 A26 7m carmine 40 10
261 A26 10m purple 2.50 8
262 A26 12m dp bl 1.25 8
Nos. 257-262 (6) 5.75 56

Pres. Juho K. Paasikivi A65 — Postal Savings Emblem A66

1947, Mar. 15 **Engr.**
263 A65 10m gray blk 50 65

1947, Apr. 1
264 A66 10m brn vio 50 65

Issued to commemorate the 60th anniversary of the foundation of the Finnish Postal Savings Bank.

Ilmarinen, the Plowman A67 — Girl and Boy Athletes A68

1947, June 2
265 A67 10m gray blk 50 65

Issued to mark the second year of peace following World War II.

1947, June 2
266 A68 10m brt bl 50 65

Issued to commemorate the Finnish Athletic Festival, Helsingfors, June 29-July 3, 1947.

Wheat and Savings Bank Association Emblem A69 — Sower A70

1947, Aug. 21
267 A69 10m red brn 50 65

Issued to commemorate the 125th anniversary of the Finnish Savings Bank Association.

1947, Nov. 1
268 A70 10m gray blk 50 65

150th anniv. of Finnish Agricultural Societies.

Koli Mountain and Lake Pielisjärvi A71 — Statue of Michael Agricola A72

1947, Nov. 1
269 A71 10m indigo 50 65

Issued to commemorate the 60th anniversary of the Finnish Touring Association.

Lion Type of 1930.

1948 **Typo.** ***Perf. 14***
270 A26 3m dk grn 2.00 15
271 A26 6m yel grn 60 50
272 A26 9m carmine 45 8
273 A26 15m dk bl 4.00 8
274 A26 24m brn lake 1.25 30
Nos. 270-274 (5) 8.30 1.11

No. 261 Surcharged with New Value and Bars in Black.

1948, Feb. 9
275 A26 12(m) on 10m pur 1.00 18

1948, Oct. 2 **Engr.** ***Perf. 14***

Design: 12m, Agricola translating New Testament.

276 A72 7m rose vio 1.25 1.75
277 A72 12m gray bl 1.25 1.75

Issued to commemorate the 400th anniversary of publication of the Finnish translation of the New Testament, by Michael Agricola.

Sveaborg Fortress — A73 — Post Rider — A74

1948, Oct. 15
278 A73 12m dp grn 1.75 1.75

Issued to commemorate the 200th anniversary of the construction of Sveaborg Fortress on the Gulf of Finland.

1948, Oct. 27
279 A74 12m green 22.50 32.50

Issued to commemorate the Helsinki Philatelic Exhibition. Sold only at exhibition, for 62m of which 50m was entrance fee.

Castle Type of 1945.

1949
280 A57 35m violet 5.50 15

Sawmill and Cellulose Plant — A75

Pine Tree and Globe A76

Woman with Torch A77

1949, June 15

281 A75	9m brown	3.00	3.00
282 A76	15m dl grn	3.00	3.00

Issued to publicize the Third World Forestry Congress, Helsinki, July 10-20, 1949.

1949, July 16 Engr. *Perf. 14*

283 A77	5m dl grn	5.50	*12.00*
284 A77	15m red *(Worker)*	5.50	*12.00*

Issued to commemorate the 50th anniversary of the Finnish labor movement.

Harbor of Lappeenranta (Willmanstrand) A78

Raahe (Brahestad) A79

1949

285 A78	5m dk bl grn	1.00	90
286 A79	9m brn car	1.25	1.25
287 A78	15m brt bl*(Kristiinankaupunki)*	2.00	2.00

Issued to commemorate the 300th anniversary of the founding of Willmanstrand, Brahestad and Kristinestad (Kristiinankaupunki).

Issue dates: 5m, Aug. 6; 9m, Aug. 13; 15m, July 30.

Technical High School Badge A80

Hannes Gebhard A81

1949, Sept. 13

288 A80	15m ultra	1.00	1.00

Issued to commemorate the centenary of the founding of the technical school.

1949, Oct. 2

289 A81	15m dl grn	1.00	1.00

Issued to commemorate the 50th anniversary of the establishment of Finnish cooperatives.

Finnish Lake Country — A82

1949, Oct. 8

290 A82	15m blue	2.00	1.50

Issued to commemorate the 75th anniversary of the formation of the Universal Postal Union.

Lion Type of 1930

1950 Typo. *Perf. 14.*

291 A26	8m brt grn	65	1.00
292 A26	9m red org	1.00	50
293 A26	10m vio brn	4.50	10
294 A26	12m scarlet	65	15
295 A26	15m plum	12.00	10
296 A26	20m dp bl	4.50	10
	Nos. 291-296 (6)	23.30	1.95

Forsell's Map of Old Helsinki — A83

J. A. Ehrenstrom and C. L. Engel — A84

City Hall — A85

1950, June 11 Engr.

297 A83	5m emerald	90	90
298 A84	9m brown	1.50	1.50
299 A85	15m dp bl	1.00	1.00

Issued to commemorate the 400th anniversary of the founding of Helsinki.

J. K. Paasikivi A86

View of Kajaani A87

1950, Nov. 27

300 A86	20m dp ultra	90	65

80th birthday of Pres. J. K. Paasikivi.

1951, July 7 Unwmk. *Perf. 14*

301 A87	20m red brn	1.00	90

Tercentenary of Kajaani.

Lion and Chopper Types of 1930

1952 Typo.

302 A26	10m emerald	2.25	15
303 A26	15m red	3.25	12
304 A26	25m blue	4.00	10

Engr.

305 A29	40m blk brn	3.00	12

Arms of Pietarsaari A88

Rooftops of Vaasa A89

1952, June 19 Unwmk. *Perf. 14*

306 A88	25m blue	1.25	1.00

Issued to commemorate the 300th anniversary of the founding of Pietarsaari (Jacobstad).

1952, Aug. 3

307 A89	25m brown	1.25	1.00

Centenary of the burning of Vaasa.

Chess Symbols — A90

1952, Aug. 10

308 A90	25m gray	3.00	3.00

Issued to publicize the 10th Chess Olympics, Helsinki, Aug. 10-31, 1952.

Torch Bearers — A91

1953, Jan. 27

309 A91	25m blue	1.50	1.00

Issued to commemorate the centenary of the temperance movement in Finland.

Air View of Hamina (Fredrikshamn) A92

Ivar Wilskman A93

1953, June 20

310 A92	25m dk gray grn	1.00	90

Tercentenary of Hamina.

1954, Feb. 26

311 A93	25m blue	1.00	65

Issued to commemorate the centenary of the birth of Prof. Ivar Wilskman, "father of gymnastics in Finland."

Arms of Finland A94

"In the Outer Archipelago" A95

1954-59 *Perf. 11½*

312	A94	1m red brn ('55)	60	8
313	A94	2m grn ('55)	60	8
314	A94	3m dp org	60	8
314A	A94	4m gray ('58)	50	8
315	A94	5m vio bl	1.00	8
316	A94	10m bl grn	1.50	5
a.		Bklt. pane of 5 (vert. strip)	30.00	
317	A94	15m rose red	4.50	5
318	A94	15m yel org ('57)	10.00	8
319	A94	20m rose lil	12.00	10
320	A94	20m rose red ('56)	4.00	5
321	A94	25m dp bl	5.00	5
322	A94	25m rose lil ('59)	18.00	8
323	A94	30m lt ultra ('56)	4.00	5
		Nos. 312-323 (13)	62.30	91

See Nos. 398, 400-405A, 457-459, 461A-462, 464-464B.

1954, July 21 *Perf. 14*

324 A95	25m black	1.00	75

Issued to commemorate the centenary of the birth of Albert Edelfelt, painter.

J. J. Nervander A96

Composite of Finnish Public Buildings A97

1955, Feb. 23

325 A96	25m blue	1.50	1.00

Issued to commemorate the 150th anniversary of the birth of J. J. Nervander, astronomer and poet.

1955, Mar. 20 Engr. *Perf. 14*

326 A97	25m gray	22.50	27.50

Sold for 125m, which included the price of admission to the National Postage Stamp Exhibition, Helsinki, March 30 to April 3, 1955.

Bishop Henrik with Foot on Lalli, his Murderer A98

Conference Hall, Helsinki A99

Design: 25m, Arrival of Bishop Henrik and monks.

1955, May 19

327 A98	15m rose brn	1.50	1.00
328 A98	25m green	1.50	1.00

Issued to commemorate the 800th anniversary of the adoption of Christianity in Finland.

1955, Aug. 25

329 A99	25m bluish grn	2.00	1.50

Issued to commemorate the 44th conference of the Interparliamentarian Union, Helsinki, Aug. 25-31, 1955.

Sailing Vessel and Merchant A100

1955, Sept. 2

330 A100	25m sepia	2.00	1.50

350th anniversary of founding of Oulu.

Town Hall, Lahti A101

Radio Sender and Map of Finland A102

1955, Nov. 1 *Perf. 14x13½*

331 A101	25m vio bl	1.75	1.25

50th anniversary of founding of Lahti.

1955, Dec. 10 *Perf. 14*

Designs: 15m, Otto Nyberg. 25m, Telegraph wires and pines under snow.
Inscribed: Lennatin 1855-1955 Telegrafen.

332 A102 10m green 1.75 1.65
333 A102 15m dl vio 1.75 80
334 A102 25m lt ultra 1.75 80

Issued to commemorate the centenary of the telegraph in Finland.

Lighthouse and Porkkala Peninsula — A103

1956, Jan. 26 **Unwmk.** *Perf. 14*
335 A103 25m grnsh bl 1.25 80

Issued to commemorate the return of the Porkkala Region to Finland by Russia, Jan. 1956.

Church at Lammi — A104

Designs: 40m, House of Parliament. 60m, Fortress of Olavinlinna (Olofsborg).

1956-57 *Perf. 11½*
336 A104 30m gray ol 1.00 15
337 A104 40m dl pur 4.00 20
338 A104 50m gray ol ('57) 7.00 20
338A A104 60m pale pur ('57) 16.00 20

See Nos. 406-408A.

Johan V. Snellman A105

Gymnast and Athletes A106

1956, May 12 **Engr.** *Perf. 14*
339 A105 25m dk vio brn 1.25 80

Issued to commemorate the 150th anniversary of the birth of Johan V. Snellman (1806-1881), statesman.

1956, June 28
340 A106 30m vio bl 1.50 1.00

Issued to commemorate the Finnish Gymnastic and Sports Games, Helsinki, June 28-July 1, 1956.

A107

Wmk. 208

1956, July 7 **Typo.** ***Rouletted***
341 A107 30m dp ultra 5.00 7.00
a. Tete beche pair 10.00 15.00
b. Pane of 10 55.00 80.00

Issued to publicize the FINLANDIA Philatelic Exhibition, Helsinki, July 7-15, 1956.
Printed in sheets containing four 2x5 panes, with white margins around each group. The stamps in each double row are printed tete-beche, making the position of the watermark differ in the vertical row of each pane of ten.
Sold for 155m, price including entrance ticket to exhibition.

Town Hall at Vasa — A108

Unwmk.

1956, Oct. 2 **Engr.** *Perf. 14*
342 A108 30m brt bl 1.25 80

350th anniversary of Vasa.

Northern Countries Issue.

Whooper Swans — A108a

1956, Oct. 30 *Perf. 12½*
343 A108a 20m rose red 5.00 2.50
344 A108a 30m ultra 16.00 2.25

See footnote after Denmark No. 362.

University Clinic, Helsinki A109

Scout Sign, Emblem and Globe A110

1956, Dec. 17 *Perf. 11½*
345 A109 30m dl grn 1.50 80

Issued to commemorate the bicentenary of public health service in Finland.

1957, Feb. 22 *Perf. 14*
346 A110 30m ultra 2.50 1.50

50th anniversary of Boy Scouts.

Arms Holding Hammers and Laurel A111

"Lex" from Seal of Parliament A112

Design: 20m, Factories and cogwheel.

1957 **Engr.** *Perf. 13½*
347 A111 20m dk bl 1.25 75
348 A111 30m carmine 1.25 1.00

50th anniv.: Central Fed. of Finnish Employers (20m, issued 9/27); Finnish Trade Union Movement (30m, issued 4/15).

1957, May 23 *Perf. 14*
349 A112 30m ol gray 1.25 1.00

Issued to commemorate the 50th anniversary of the Finnish parliament.

Harbor Type of 1942.

1957 **Unwmk.** *Perf. 14*
350 A51 100m grnsh bl 9.00 20

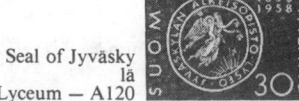

Finland stamps can be mounted in Scott's annually supplemented Scandinavia and Finland Album.

Ida Aalberg A114

Arms of Finland A115

1957, Dec. 4 *Perf. 14*
351 A114 30m vio gray & mar 1.25 80

Issued to commemorate the centenary of the birth of Ida Aalberg, Finnish actress.

1957, Dec. 6 *Perf. 11½*
352 A115 30m blue 1.25 80

Issued to commemorate the 40th anniversary of Finland's independence.

Jean Sibelius A116

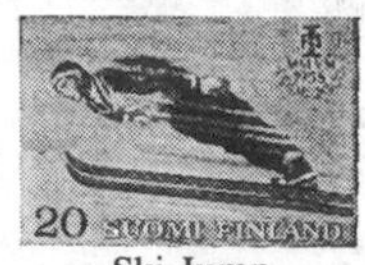

Ski Jump A117

1957, Dec. 8 *Perf. 14*
353 A116 30m black 1.25 80

Issued in memory of Jean Sibelius (1865-1957), composer.

1958, Feb. 1 **Engr.** *Perf. 11½*

Design: 30m, Skier (vertical).

354 A117 20m sl grn 1.25 1.25
355 A117 30m blue 1.50 75

Issued to publicize the Nordic championships of the International Ski Federation, Lahti.

"March of the Bjorneborgienses," by Edelfelt — A118

South Harbor, Helsinki — A119

1958, Mar. 8
356 A118 30m vio gray 2.00 1.00

Issued to commemorate the 400th anniversary of the founding of Pori (Bjorneborg).

1958, June 2 **Unwmk.** *Perf. 11½*
357 A119 100m bluish grn 25.00 15

See No. 410.

Seal of Jyväskylä Lyceum — A120

1958, Oct. 1 *Perf. 11½*
358 A120 30m rose car 2.00 1.25

Issued to commemorate the centenary of the founding of the first Finnish secondary school.

Chrismon and Globe — A121

Diet at Porvoo, 1809 — A122

1959, Jan. 19
359 A121 30m dl vio 1.40 60

Issued to commemorate the centenary of the Finnish Missionary Society.

1959, Mar. 22 *Perf. 11½*
360 A122 30m dk bl gray 1.40 60

Issued to commemorate the 150th anniversary of the inauguration of the Diet at Porvoo.

Saw Cutting Log — A123

Pyhakoski Power Station — A124

Design: 30m, Forest.

1959, May 13 **Engr.**
361 A123 10m redsh brn 80 60
362 A123 30m green 1.00 1.00

No. 361 commemorates the centenary of the establishment of the first steam saw-mill in Finland; No. 362, the centenary of the Department of Forestry.

1959, May 24
363 A124 75m gray 6.00 25

See No. 409.

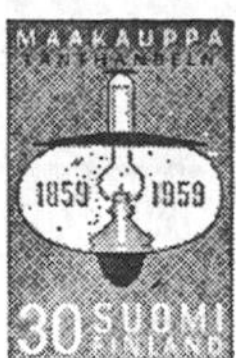

Oil Lamp A125

Woman Gymnast A126

1959, Dec. 19
364 A125 30m blue 1.00 65

Issued to commemorate the centenary of the liberation of the country trade.

1959, Nov. 14 **Unwmk.**
365 A126 30m rose lil 1.00 65

Issued to honor Finnish women's gymnastics and the centenary of the birth of Elin Oihonna Kallio, pioneer of Finnish women's physical education.

Arms of Six New Towns — A127

1960, Jan. 2 *Perf. 14*
366 A127 30m lt vio 1.00 65

Issued to commemorate the founding of new towns in Finland: Hyvinkaa, Kouvola, Riihimaki, Rovaniemi, Salo and Seinajoki.

Type of 1860 Issue A128

1960, Mar. 25 Typo. *Rouletted 4½*
367 A128 30m bl & gray 11.00 12.50

Issued to commemorate the centenary of Finland's serpentine roulette stamps, and in connection with HELSINKI 1960, 40th anniversary exhibition of the Federation of Philatelic Societies of Finland, March 25-31. Sold only at the exhibition for 150m including entrance ticket.

Mother and Child, Waiting Crowd and Uprooted Oak Emblem — A129

1960, Apr. 7 Engr. *Perf. 11½*
368 A129 30m rose cl 90 60
369 A129 40m dk bl 90 60

Issued to publicize World Refugee Year, July 1, 1959-June 30, 1960.

Johan Gadolin A130

Hj. Nortamo A131

1960, June 4 *Perf. 11½*
370 A130 30m dk brn 1.25 85

Issued to commemorate the bicentennary of the birth of Johan Gadolin, chemist.

1960, June 13 Unwmk.
371 A131 30m gray grn 1.25 60

Issued to commemorate the centenary of the birth of Hj. Nortamo (Hjalmar Nordberg), writer.

Symbolic Tree and Cuckoo — A132

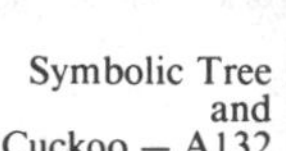

1960, June 18
372 A132 30m vermilion 1.25 60

Karelian National Festival, Helsinki, June 18-19.

Geodetic Instrument A133

Urho Kekkonen A134

Design: 30m, Aurora borealis and globe.

1960, July 26 Unwmk. *Perf. 13½*
373 A133 10m bl & pale brn 80 60
374 A133 30m ver & rose car 1.50 75

Issued to publicize the 12th General Assembly of the International Union of Geodesy and Geophysics, Helsinki.

1960, Sept. 3 Engr. *Perf. 11½*
375 A134 30m vio bl 1.25 60

Issued to honor President Urho Kekkonen on his 60th birthday.

Europa Issue, 1960
Common Design Type

1960, Sept. 19 *Perf. 13½*
Size: 30½x21mm.
376 CD3 30m dk bl & Prus bl 75 60
377 CD3 40m dk brn & plum 1.00 75

A 30m gray similar to No. 376 was printed with simulated perforations in a non-valid souvenir sheet privately released in London for STAMPEX 1961.

Uno Cygnaeus A135

"Pommern" and Arms of Mariehamn A136

1960, Oct. 13 *Perf. 11½*
378 A135 30m dl vio 1.25 60

Issued to commemorate the 150th anniversary of the birth of Pastor Uno Cygnaeus, founder of elementary schools.

1961, Feb. 21 *Perf. 11½*
379 A136 30m grnsh bl 4.25 1.75

Centenary of the founding of Mariehamn.

Lake and Rowboat A137

Turku Castle — A138

1961 Engr. Unwmk.
380 A137 5m green 50 20
381 A138 125m sl grn 35.00 60

See also Nos. 399, 411.

Postal Savings Bank Emblem A139

Symbol of Standardization A140

1961, May 24
382 A139 30m Prus grn 1.25 60

Issued to commemorate the 75th anniversary of Finland's Postal Savings Bank.

1961, June 5 Litho. *Perf. 14x13½*
383 A140 30m dk sl grn & org 1.25 60

Issued to commemorate the meeting of the International Organization for Standardization, ISO, Helsinki, June 5.

Juhani Aho — A141

Perf. 11½
1961, Sept. 11 Unwmk. Engr.
384 A141 30m red brn 1.25 60

Issued to commemorate the centenary of the birth of Juhani Aho (1861-1921), writer.

Various Buildings — A142

1961, Oct. 16 *Perf. 11½*
385 A142 30m slate 1.25 60

Issued to commemorate 150 years of the Central Board of Buildings.

Arvid Jarnefelt — A143

1961, Nov. 16
386 A143 30m dp cl 1.25 60

Issued to commemorate the centenary of the birth of Arvid Jarnefelt, writer.

Bank of Finland A144

First Finnish Locomotive A145

1961, Dec. 12 Engr. *Perf. 11½*
387 A144 30m brn vio 1.25 60

150th anniversary of Bank of Finland.

1962, Jan. 31 Unwmk. *Perf. 11½*

Designs: 30m, Steam locomotive and timber car. 40m, Diesel locomotive and passenger train.

388 A145 10m gray grn 1.25 60
389 A145 30m vio bl 1.50 60
390 A145 40m dl red brn 4.00 80

Centenary of the Finnish State Railways.

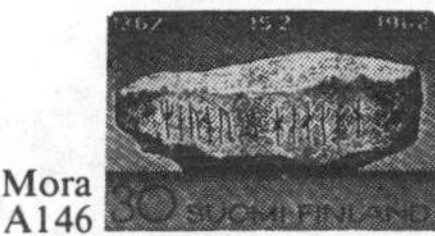
Mora Stone — A146

1962, Feb. 15
391 A146 30m gray brn 1.25 60

Issued to commemorate 600 years of political rights of the Finnish people.

Senate Place, Helsinki — A147

1962, Apr. 8 Unwmk. *Perf. 11½*
392 A147 30m vio brn 1.25 60

Issued to commemorate the sesquicentennial of the proclamation of Helsinki as capital of Finland.

Common Design Types pictured in section at front of book.

Customs Emblem A148

Staff of Mercury A149

1962, Apr. 11
393 A148 30m red 1.25 60

Issued to commemorate the sesquicentennial of the Finnish Board of Customs.

1962, May 21 Engr.
394 A149 30m bluish grn 1.25 60

Issued to commemorate the centenary of the first commercial bank in Finland.

Santeri Alkio A150

Finnish Labor Emblem and Conveyor Belt A151

1962, June 17 Unwmk. *Perf. 11½*
395 A150 30m brn car 1.25 60

Issued to commemorate the centenary of the birth of Santeri Alkio, writer and pioneer of the young people's societies in Finland.

1962, Oct. 19
396 A151 30m chocolate 1.25 60

National production progress.

Survey Plane and Compass — A152

1962, Nov. 14
397 A152 30m yel grn 1.25 60

Issued to commemorate the 150th anniversary of the Finnish Land Survey Board.

Types of 1954-61 and

Log Floating — A153

Parainen Bridge — A154

Farm on Lake Shore — A155

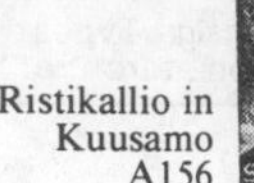

Ristikallio in Kuusamo A156

Designs: 40p, House of Parliament. 50p, Church at Lammi. 60p, 65p, Fortress of Olavinlinna. 2.50m, Aerial view of Punkaharju.

1963-67 Engr. *Perf. 11½*

No.	Type	Denom.	Color	Unused	Used
398	A94	5p	vio bl	40	6
a.		Booklet pane of 2 (vert. pair)		27.50	
b.		Bklt. pane of 2 (horiz. pair)		35.00	
399	A137	5p	green	30	8
400	A94	10p	bl grn	50	6
a.		Booklet pane of 2 (vert. pair)		27.50	
401	A94	15p	yel org	1.40	6
402	A94	20p	rose red	90	6
a.		Booklet pane of 1		27.50	
b.		Bklt. pane of 3 (2 No. 400, 1 No. 402 + label; horiz. strip)		50.00	
c.		Bklt. pane of 5 (2 No. 398, 2 No. 400, 1 No. 402; horiz. strip)		7.50	
403	A94	25p	rose lil	60	6
404	A94	30p	lt ultra	8.00	6
404A	A94	30p	bl gray ('65)	75	6
405	A94	35p	blue	1.50	6
405A	A94	40p	ultra ('67)	2.00	6
406	A104	40p	dl pur	2.00	10
407	A104	50p	gray ol	2.00	10
408	A104	60p	pale pur	6.00	10
408A	A104	65p	pale pur ('67)	1.50	10
409	A124	75p	gray	2.00	10
410	A119	1m	bluish grn	55	5
411	A138	1.25m	sl grn	2.25	10
412	A153	1.50m	dk grnsh gray	1.10	8
413	A154	1.75m	blue	1.75	10
414	A155	2m	grn ('64)	2.25	20
414A	A155	2.50m	ultra & yel ('67)	3.00	25
415	A156	5m	dk sl grn ('64)	8.00	60
			Nos. 398-415 (22)	48.75	2.50

Pennia denominations expressed: "0.05", "0.10", etc.

Four stamps of type A94 (5p, 10p, 20p, 25p) come in two types: I. Four vertical lines in "O" of SUOMI. II. Three lines in "O."

See Nos. 457-464B.

Mother and Child — A157

1963, Mar. 21 Unwmk. *Perf. 11½*
416 A157 40p red brn 1.00 60

Issued for the "Freedom from Hunger" campaign of the U.N. Food and Agriculture Organization.

"Christ Today" — A158

Design: 10p, Crown of thorns and medieval cross of consecration.

1963, July 30 Engr. *Perf. 11½*
417 A158 10p maroon 60 60
418 A158 30p dk grn 1.00 60

Issued to commemorate the 4th assembly of the Lutheran World Federation, Helsinki, July 30-Aug. 8.

Europa Issue, 1963
Common Design Type

1963, Sept. 16
Size: 30x20mm.
419 CD6 40p red lil 1.50 60

Assembly Building, Helsinki — A159

1963, Sept. 18
420 A159 30p vio bl 1.25 60

Issued to commemorate the centenary of the Representative Assembly of Finland.

Convair Metropolitan A160

M. A. Castren A161

Design: 40p, Caravelle jetliner.

1963, Nov. 1
421 A160 35p sl grn 1.25 60
422 A160 40p brt ultra 1.25 60

40th anniversary of Finnish air traffic.

1963, Dec. 2 Unwmk.
423 A161 35p vio bl 1.25 60

Issued to commemorate the 150th anniversary of the birth of Matthias Alexander Castren (1813-52), ethnologist and philologist.

Stone Elk's Head, 2000 B.C. A162

Emil Nestor Setälä A163

1964, Feb. 5 Litho. *Perf. 11½*
424 A162 35p ocher & sl grn 1.25 60

Issued to commemorate the centenary of the Finnish Artists' Association. The soapstone sculpture was found at Huittinen.

1964, Feb. 27 Engr.
425 A163 35p dk red brn 1.25 60

Centenary of the birth of Emil Nestor Setälä (1864-1946), philologist, minister of education and foreign affairs and chancellor of Abo University.

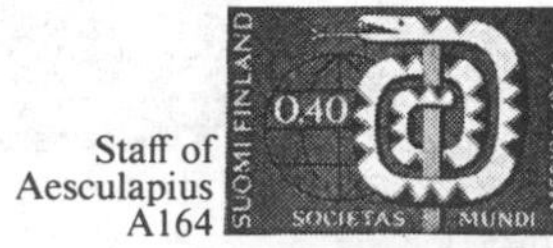
Staff of Aesculapius A164

1964, June 13 Unwmk. *Perf. 11½*
426 A164 40p sl grn 1.25 60

Issued to commemorate the 18th General Assembly of the World Medical Association, Helsinki, June 13-19, 1964.

Ice Hockey — A165

1965, Jan. 4 Engr.
427 A165 35p dk bl 1.25 60

Issued to publicize the World Ice Hockey Championships, Finland, March 3-14, 1965.

Design from Centenary Medal — A166

1965, Feb. 6 Unwmk. *Perf. 11½*
428 A166 35p ol gray 1.25 60

Issued to commemorate the centenary of communal self-government in Finland.

K. J. Stahlberg and "Lex" by W. Runeberg A167

1965, Mar. 22 Engr.
429 A167 35p brown 1.25 60

Issued to commemorate the centenary of the birth of Kaarlo Juho Stahlberg (1865-1952), first President of Finland.

International Cooperation Year Emblem — A168

1965, Apr. 2 Litho. *Perf. 14*
430 A168 40p bis, dl red, blk & grn 1.25 60

U. N. International Cooperation Year.

"Fratricide" by Gallen-Kallela A169

Sibelius, Piano and Score A170

Design: 35p, Girl's Head by Akseli Gallen-Kallela.

1965, Aug. 26 *Perf. 13½x14*
431 A169 25p multi 1.50 65
432 A169 35p multi 1.50 65

Issued to commemorate the centenary of the birth of the painter Aksell Gallen-Kallela.

1965, May 15 Engr. *Perf. 11½*
Design: 35p, Musical score and bird.

433 A170 25p violet 1.25 55
434 A170 35p dl grn 1.25 55

Issued to commemorate the centenary of the birth of Jean Sibelius (1865-1957), composer.

Antenna for Satellite Telecommunication A171

"Winter Day" by Pekka Halonen A172

1965, May 17
435 A171 35p blue 1.25 60

Issued to commemorate the centenary of the International Telecommunication Union.

Perf. 14x13½
1965, Sept. 23 Litho. Unwmk.
436 A172 35p gold & multi 1.25 60

Issued to commemorate the centenary of the birth of the painter Pekka Halonen.

Europa Issue, 1965
Common Design Type
Engraved and Lithographed

1965, Sept. 27 *Perf. 13½x14*
437 CD8 40p bis, red brn, dk bl & grn 1.25 60

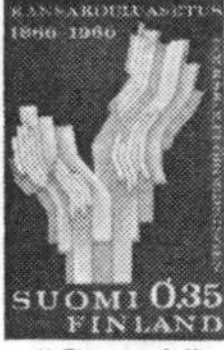
"Growth" A173

Old Post Office A174

1966, May 11 Litho. *Perf. 14*
438 A173 35p vio bl & bl 1.00 45

Issued to commemorate the centenary of the promulgation of the Elementary School Decree.

1966, June 11 Litho. *Perf. 14*
439 A174 35p ocher, yel, dk bl & blk 11.00 12.50

Issued to commemorate the centenary of the first postage stamps in Finnish currency, and in connection with the NORDIA Stamp Exhibition, Helsinki, June 11-15. The stamp was sold only to buyers of a 1.25m exhibition entrance ticket.

UNESCO Emblem and World Map A175

Finnish Police Emblem A176

Lithographed and Engraved

1966, Oct. 9 *Perf. 14*
440 A175 40p grn, yel, blk & brn org 1.25 45

20th anniv. of UNESCO.

1966, Oct. 15
441 A176 35p dp ultra, blk & sil 1.25 45

Issued to honor the Finnish police.

Insurance Sesquicentennial Medal — A177

Engraved and Photgravure

1966, Oct. 28 *Perf. 14*

442 A177 35p mar, ol & blk 1.25 45

Issued to commemorate the 150th anniversary of the Finnish insurance system.

UNICEF Emblem — A178

1966, Nov. 14

443 A178 15p lt ultra, pur & grn 75 40

Issued to publicize the activities of UNICEF (United Nations Children's Emergency Fund).

"FINEFTA," Finnish Flag and Circle — A179

1967, Feb. 15 **Engr.** *Perf. 14*

444 A179 40p ultra 1.25 40

Issued to publicize the European Free Trade Association, EFTA. See note after Denmark No. 431.

Windmill and Arms of Uusikaupunki A180

Mannerheim Monument by Aimo Tukiainen A181

Lithographed and Engraved

1967, Apr. 19 *Perf. 14*

445 A180 40p multi 1.25 40

Issued to commemorate the 350th anniversary of Uusikaupunki (Nystad).

1967, June 4 *Perf. 14*

446 A181 40p vio & multi 1.25 40

Issued to commemorate the centenary of the birth of Field Marshal Carl Gustav Emil Mannerheim.

Double Mortise Corner — A182

Watermark of Thomasböle Paper Mill — A183

Lithographed and Photogravure

1967, June 16

447 A182 40p multi 1.25 40

Issued to honor Finnish settlers in Sweden.

Lithographed and Photogravure

1967, Sept. 6 *Perf. 14*

448 A183 40p ol & blk 1.25 40

Issued to commemorate the 300th anniversary of the Finnish paper industry.

Martin Luther, by Lucas Cranach — A184

Photogravure and Engraved

1967, Nov. 4 *Perf. 14*

449 A184 40p bis & brn 1.25 40

450th anniversary of the Reformation.

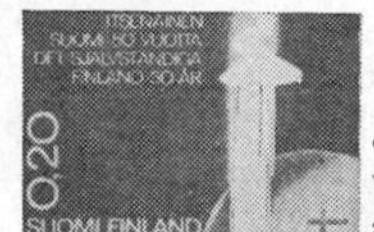

"Wood and Water" Globe and Flag — A185

Designs (Globe, Flag and): 25p, Flying swan. 40p, Ear of wheat.

1967, Dec. 5 *Perf. 11 ½*

450 A185 20p grn & bl 1.25 40
451 A185 25p ultra & bl 1.25 40
452 A185 40p mag & bl 1.25 40

Issued to commemorate the 50th anniversary of Finland's independence.

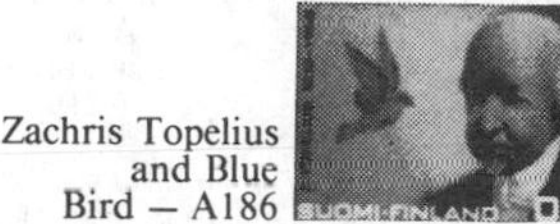

Zachris Topelius and Blue Bird — A186

1968, Jan. 14 **Litho.** *Perf. 14*

453 A186 25p bl & multi 1.25 40

Issued to commemorate the 150th anniversary of the birth of Zachris Topelius (1818-1898), writer and educator.

Skiers and Ski Lift — A187

1968, Feb. 19 **Photo.** *Perf. 14*

454 A187 25p multi 1.25 40

Issued to publicize winter Tourism in inland.

Paper Making, by Hannes Autere — A188

Wmk. Tree Stump (363)

1968, Mar. 12 **Litho.**

455 A188 45p dk red, brn & org 1.25 40

Issued to publicize the Finnish paper industry and to commemorate the 150th anniversary of the oldest Finnish paper mill, Tervakoski, whose own watermark was used for this stamp.

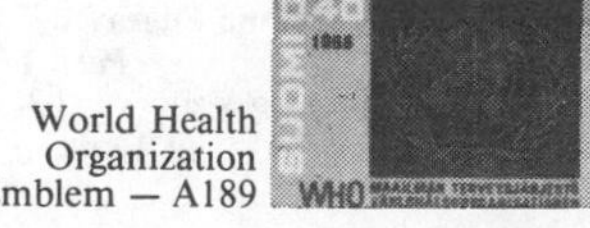

World Health Organization Emblem — A189

Lithographed and Photogravure

1968, Apr. 6 **Unwmk.** *Perf. 14*

456 A189 40p red org, dk bl & gold 1.25 40

To honor World Health Organization.

Lion Type of 1954-58 and

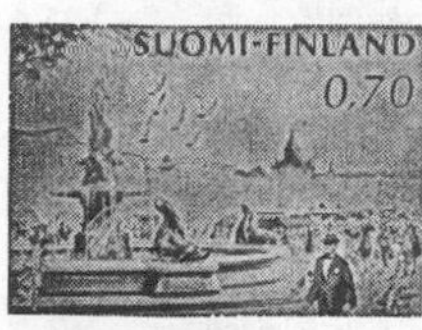

Market Place and Mermaid Fountain, Helsinki A190

Keuru Wooden Church, 1758 — A191

Häme Bridge, Tampere — A192

Finnish Arms from Grave of King Gustav Vasa, 1581 — A194

Designs: 25p, Post bus. 30p, Aquarium-Planetarium, Tampere. No. 463, P.O., Tampere. No. 465, National Museum, Helsinki (vert.). No. 467A, like 70p. 1.30m, Helsinki railroad station.

Engr. (type A94); Litho. (#465 & type A190); Engr. & Litho. (others).
Perf. 11 ½; 12 ½ (type A190); 14 (#465, 470A); 13 ½ (#470).

1968-78

457	A94	1p lt red brn	50	10
458	A94	2p gray grn	50	10
459	A94	4p gray	50	10
460	A192	25p multi ('71)	50	10
461	A191	30p multi ('71)	1.25	15
461A	A94	35p dl org ('74)	50	6
b.		Bklt. pane of 4 (#398, #461A, #400, #464A) + label	4.00	
462	A94	40p org ('73)	75	10
a.		Bklt. pane of 3 (2 #404A, #462) + 2 labels	10.00	
463	A192	40p multi ('73)	1.25	10
464	A94	50p lt ultra ('70)	1.25	5
c.		Bklt. pane of 5 (#401, #403, #464, 2 #398) + 5 labels	12.00	
464A	A94	50p rose lake ('74)	1.00	5
d.		Bklt. pane of 4 (#400, 2 #402, #464A) + label	3.00	
464B	A94	60p bl ('73)	75	5
465	A191	60p multi ('73)	60	10
466	A190	70p multi ('73)	1.00	10
467	A191	80p multi ('70)	3.00	10
467A	A190	80p multi ('76)	60	10
468	A192	90p multi	2.50	10
469	A191	1.30m multi ('71)	1.25	12
470	A194	10m multi ('74)	4.00	60
470A	A194	20m multi ('78)	8.00	1.50
		Nos. 457-470A (19)	29.70	3.68

Infantry Monument, Vaasa A195

Camping Ground A196

Designs: 25p, War Memorial (cross), Hietaniemi Cemetery. 40p, Soldier, 1968.

1968, June 4 **Photo.** *Perf. 14*

471 A195 20p lt vio & multi 1.50 45
472 A195 25p lt bl & multi 1.50 45
473 A195 40p org & multi 1.50 45

To honor Finnish national defense.

1968, June 10 **Litho.**

474 A196 25p multi 1.25 40

Issued to publicize Finland for summer vacations.

Paper, Pulp and Pine — A197

Mustola Lock, Saima Canal — A198

Lithographed and Embossed

1968, July 2 **Unwmk.** *Perf. 14*

475 A197 40p multi 1.25 40

Finnish wood industry.

1968, Aug. 5 **Litho.** *Perf. 14*

476 A198 40p multi 1.25 40

Opening of the Saima Canal.

Oskar Merikanto and Pipe Organ — A199

1968, Aug. 5 **Unwmk.**

477 A199 40p vio, sil & lt brn 1.25 40

Issued to commemorate the centenary of the birth of Oskar Merikanto, composer.

Ships in Harbor and Emblem of Central Chamber of Commerce A200

Welder A201

1968, Sept. 13 **Litho.** *Perf. 14*

478 A200 40p lt bl, brt bl & blk 1.25 40

Issued to publicize economic development and to commemorate the 50th anniversary of the Central Chamber of Commerce of Finland.

1968, Oct. 11 **Litho.** *Perf. 14*

479 A201 40p bl & multi 1.25 40

Finnish metal industry.

Lyre, Students' Emblem A202

Five Ancient Ships A203

Lithographed and Engraved

1968, Nov. 24 *Perf. 14*

480 A202 40p ultra, vio bl & gold 1.25 40

Issued to publicize the work of the student unions in Finnish social life.

Nordic Cooperation Issue

1968, Feb. 28 Engr. *Perf. 11½*

481 A203 40p lt ultra 3.00 45

See footnote after Denmark No. 455.

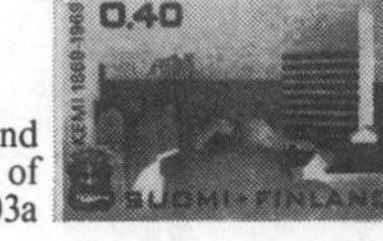

Town Hall and Arms of Kemi — A203a

1969, Mar. 5 Photo. *Perf. 14*

482 A203a 40p multi 1.25 40

Centenary of the town of Kemi.

Europa Issue, 1969

Common Design Type

1969, Apr. 28 Photo. *Perf. 14*

Size: 30x20mm.

483 CD12 40p dl rose, vio bl & dk bl 3.25 70

I.L.O. Emblem A204

Armas Järnefelt A205

Lithographed and Engraved

1969, June 2 *Perf. 11½*

484 A204 40p dp rose & vio bl 1.25 40

Issued to commemorate the 50th anniversary of the International Labor Organization.

1969, Aug. 14 Photo. *Perf. 14*

485 A205 40p multi 1.25 40

Centenary of the birth of Armas Järnefelt (1869-1958), composer and conductor. Portrait on stamp by Vilho Sjöström.

Emblems and Flag A206

Johannes Linnankoski A207

1969, Sept. 19 Photo. *Perf. 14*

486 A206 40p lt bl, blk, grn & lil 1.25 40

Issued to publicize the importance of National and International Fairs in Finnish economy.

1969, Oct. 18 **Litho.**

487 A207 40p dk brn red & multi 1.25 40

Issued to commemorate the centenary of the birth of Johannes Linnankoski (1869-1913), writer.

Educational Symbols A208

Lithographed and Engraved

1969, Nov. 24 *Perf. 11½*

488 A208 40p gray, vio & grn 1.25 40

Centenary of the Central School Board.

DC-8-62 CF Plane and Helsinki Airport — A209

1969, Dec. 22 Photo. *Perf. 14*

489 A209 25p sky bl & multi 1.25 40

Golden Eagle — A210

1970, Feb. 10 Litho. *Perf. 14*

490 A210 30p multi 4.00 1.00

Year of Nature Conservation, 1970.

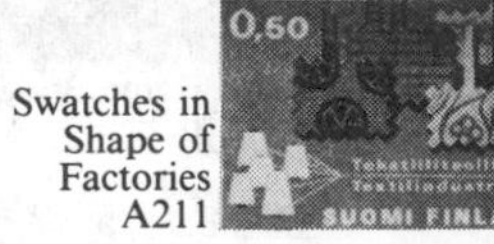

Swatches in Shape of Factories A211

1970, Mar. 9 Litho. *Perf. 14*

491 A211 50p multi 1.25 40

Finnish textile industry.

Molecule Diagram and Factories A212

UNESCO Emblem and Lenin A213

Atom Diagram and Laurel A214

U.N. Emblem and Globe A215

1970, Mar. 26 Photo. *Perf. 14*

492 A212 50p multi 1.25 40

Finnish chemical industry.

1970 **Litho. and Engraved**

493 A213 30p gold & multi 1.25 40

494 A214 30p red & multi 1.25 40

Photogravure and Gold Embossed

495 A215 50p bl, vio bl & gold 1.25 40

Issued to commemorate the 25th anniversary of the United Nations. No. 493 also publicizes the UNESCO-sponsored Lenin Symposium, Tampere, Apr. 6-10. No. 494 also publicizes the Nuclear Data Conference of the Atomic Energy Commission, Otaniemi (Helsinki), June 15-19.

Issue dates: No. 493, Apr. 6; No. 494, June 15; No. 495, Oct. 24.

Handicapped Volleyball Player A216

Meeting of Auroraseura Society A217

1970, June 27 Litho. *Perf. 14*

496 A216 50p org, red & blk 1.50 40

Issued to publicize the position of handicapped civilians and war veterans in society and their potential contributions to it.

1970, Aug. 15 Photo. *Perf. 14*

497 A217 50p multi 1.25 40

Issued to commemorate the 200th anniversary of the Auroraseura Society, dedicated to the study of Finnish history, geography, economy and language. The design of the stamp is after a painting by Eero Jarnefelt.

Uusikaarlepyy Arms, Church and 17th Century Building A218

Urho Kekkonen, Medal by Aimo Tukiainen A219

Design: No. 499, Arms of Kokkola, harbor, Sports Palace and 17th century building.

1970 *Perf. 14*

498 A218 50p multi 1.25 40

499 A218 50p multi 1.25 40

Issued to commemorate the 350th anniversaries of the towns of Uusikaarlepyy and Kokkola. Issue dates: No. 498, Aug. 21; No. 499, Sept. 17.

1970, Sept. 3 **Litho. & Engr.**

500 A219 50p ultra, sil & blk 1.25 40

70th birthday of Pres. Urho Kekkonen.

Globe, Maps of U.S., Finland, U.S.S.R. A220

Pres. Paasikivi by Essi Renavall A221

Lithograped and Gold Embossed

1970, Nov. 2

501 A220 50p blk, bl, pink & gold 1.25 40

Issued to publicize the Strategic Arms Limitation Talks (SALT) between the U.S. and U.S.S.R., Helsinki, Nov. 2-Dec. 18.

1970, Nov. 27 Photo. *Perf. 14*

502 A221 50p gold, brt bl & sl 1.75 40

Centenary of the birth of Juho Kusti Paasikivi (1870-1956), President of Finland.

Cogwheels A222

1971, Jan. 28 Litho. *Perf. 14*

503 A222 50p multi 1.25 40

Finnish industry.

Europa Issue, 1971

Common Design Type

1971, May 3 Litho. *Perf. 14*

Size: 30x20mm.

504 CD14 50p dp rose, yel & blk 2.75 60

Tornio Church A223

Front Page, January 15, 1771 A224

1971, May 12 Litho. *Perf. 14*

505 A223 50p multi 1.25 40

350th anniversary of the town of Tornio.

1971, June 1 Litho. *Perf. 14*

506 A224 50p multi 1.25 40

Bicentenary of the Finnish press.

Athletes in Helsinki Stadium — A225

Design: 50p, Running and javelin in Helsinki Stadium.

1971, July 5 Litho. *Perf. 14*

507 A225 30p multi 1.25 60

508 A225 50p multi 2.75 60

European Athletic Championships.

Sailboats A226

1971, July 14

509 A226 50p multi 1.50 60

International Lightning Class Championships, Helsinki, July 14-Aug. 1.

Silver Tea Pot, Guild's Emblem, Tools — A227

1971, Aug. 6

510 A227 50p lil & multi 1.25 40

600th anniversary of Finnish goldsmiths' art.

"Plastic Buttons and Houses" A228

Photogravure and Embossed

1971, Oct. 20 *Perf. 14*
511 A228 50p multi 1.25 40

Finnish plastics industry.

Europa Issue 1972
Common Design Type

1972, May 2 Litho. *Perf. 14*
Size: 20x30mm.
512 CD15 30p dk red & multi 2.00 60
513 CD15 50p lt brn & multi 3.00 60

Finnish National Theater — A229

1972, May 22. Litho. *Perf. 14*
514 A229 50p lt vio & multi 1.25 40

Centenary of the Finnish National Theater, founded by Kaarlo and Emilie Bergbom.

Globe, U.S. and U.S.S.R. Flags — A230

1972, June 2
515 A230 50p multi 1.75 50

Strategic Arms Limitation Talks (SALT), final meeting, Helsinki, Mar. 28-May 26; treaty signed, Moscow, May 26.

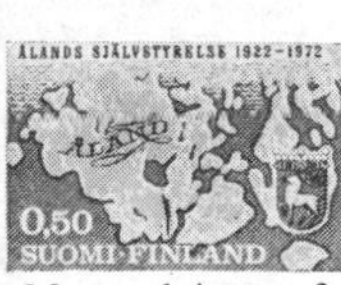
Map and Arms of Aland A231

Training Ship Suomen Joutsen A232

1972, June 9
516 A231 50p multi 5.50 1.25

50th anniversary of first Provincial Meeting of Aland.

1972, June 19
517 A232 50p org & multi 1.50 50

Tall Ship'" Race 1972, Helsinki, Aug. 20.

Costume from Perni, 12th Century A233

Circle Surrounding Map of Europe A234

1972, Nov. 19 Litho. *Perf. 13*
518 A233 50p *shown* 1.75 40
519 A233 50p *Couple, Tenhola, 18th cent.* 1.75 40
520 A233 50p *Girl, Nastola, 19th century* 1.75 40
521 A233 50p *Man, Voyni, 19th century* 1.75 40
522 A233 50p *Lapps, Inari, 19th century* 1.75 40
a. Booklet pane of 10 20.00
Nos. 518-522 (5) 8.75 2.00

Regional costumes. Nos. 518-522 printed se-tenant.
No. 522a contains 2 each of Nos. 518-522.
See Nos. 533-537.

1972, Dec. 11 *Perf. 14x13½*
523 A234 50p multi 4.00 75

Preparatory Conference on European Security and Cooperation.

Book, Finnish and Soviet Colors — A235

Litho.; Gold Embossed

1973, Apr. 6 *Perf. 14*
524 A235 60p multi 1.50 40

25th anniversary of the Soviet-Finnish Treaty of Friendship.

Pres. Kyösti Kallio — A236

1973, Apr. 10 Litho. *Perf. 13*
525 A236 60p multi 1.50 40

Centenary of the birth of Kyösti Kallio (1873-1940), president of Finland.

Europa Issue 1973
Common Design Type

1973, Apr. 30 Photo. *Perf. 14*
Size: 31x21mm.
526 CD16 60p bl, brt bl & emer 1.25 50

Nordic Cooperation Issue

Nordic House, Reykjavik A236a

1973, June 26 Engr. *Perf. 12½*
527 A236a 60p multi 1.50 50
528 A236a 70p multi 1.50 50

A century of postal cooperation among Denmark, Finland, Iceland, Norway and Sweden, and in connection with the Nordic Postal Conference, Reykjavik.

Map of Europe, "EUROPA" as a Maze — A237

Litho., Embossed

1973, July 3 *Perf. 13*
529 A237 70p multi 1.25 40

Conference for European Security and Cooperation, Helsinki, July 1973.

Paddling A238

Radiosonde, WMO Emblem A239

1973, July 18 Litho. *Perf. 14*
530 A238 60p multi 1.25 40

Canoeing World Championships, Tampere, July 26-29.

1973, Aug. 6 Litho. *Perf. 14*
531 A239 60p multi 1.25 40

Centenary of international meteorological cooperation.

Eliel Saarinen and Design for Parliament, Helsinki A240

1973, Aug. 20 *Perf. 12½x13*
532 A240 60p multi 1.25 40

Centenary of the birth of Eliel Saarinen (1873-1950), architect.

Costume Type of 1972

1973, Oct. 10 Litho. *Perf. 13*
533 A233 60p *Woman, Kaukola* 3.75 40
534 A233 60p *Woman, Jaaski* 3.75 40
535 A233 60p *Married couple, Koivisto* 3.75 40
536 A233 60p *Mother and son, Sakyla* 3.75 40
537 A233 60p *Girl, Hainavesi* 3.75 40
Nos. 533-537 (5) 18.75 2.00

Regional costumes. Nos. 533-537 printed se-tenant.

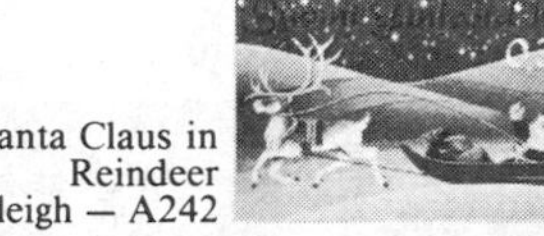
DC10-30 Jet — A241

1973, Nov. 1 Litho. *Perf. 14*
538 A241 60p multi 1.25 40

50th anniversary of regular air service, Finnair.

Santa Claus in Reindeer Sleigh — A242

1973, Nov. 15 Litho. *Perf. 14*
539 A242 30p multi 1.00 25

Christmas 1973.

"The Barber of Seville" — A243

1973, Nov. 21
540 A243 60p multi 1.25 40

Centenary of opera in Finland.

Production of Porcelain Jug A244

Nurmi, by Waino Aaltonen A245

1973, Nov. 23
541 A244 60p bl & multi 1.25 40

Finnish porcelain.

1973, Dec. 11
542 A245 60p multi 1.25 40

Paavo Nurmi (1897-1973), runner, Olympic winner, 1920-1924-1928.

Arms, Map and Harbor of Hanko — A246

1974, Jan. 10 Litho. *Perf. 14*
543 A246 60p bl & multi 1.25 40

Centenary of the town of Hanko.

Ice Hockey A247

1974, Mar. 5 Litho. *Perf. 14*
544 A247 60p multi 1.25 40

European and World Ice Hockey Championships, held in Finland.

Seagulls (7 Baltic States) A248

1974, Mar. 18 *Perf. 12½*
545 A248 60p multi 1.25 40

Protection of marine environment of the Baltic Sea.

Goddess of Freedom, by Waino Aaltonen A249

Ilmari Kianto and Old Pine A250

Europa Issue, 1974

1974, Apr. 29 Litho. *Perf. 13x12½*
546 A249 70p multi 1.25 40

1974, May 7 *Perf. 13*
547 A250 60p multi 1.25 40

Ilmari Kianto (1874-1970), writer.

Society Emblem, Symbol — A251

Lithographed and Embossed

1974, June 12 *Perf. 13½x14*
548 A251 60p gold & multi 1.25 40

Centenary of Adult Education.

Grid
A252

UPU Emblem
A253

1974, June 14 Litho. *Perf. 14x13½*
549 A252 60p multi 1.25 40

Rationalization Year in Finland, dedicated to economic and business improvements.

1974, Oct. 10 Litho. *Perf. 13½x14*
550 A253 60p multi 1.25 40
551 A253 70p multi 1.25 40

Centenary of Universal Postal Union.

Elves Distributing Gifts
A254

Concrete Bridge and Granite Bridge, Aunessilta
A255

1974, Nov. 16 Litho. *Perf. 14x13½*
552 A254 35p multi 1.00 40

Christmas 1974.

Lithographed and Engraved

1974, Dec. 17 *Perf. 14*
553 A255 60p multi 1.25 40

Royal Finnish Directorate of Roads and Waterways, 175th anniversary.

Coat of Arms, 1581
A256

Chimneyless Log Sauna
A256a

Cheese Frames
A257

Carved Wooden Distaffs
A238

Kirvu Weather Vane — A258a

Design: 1.50m, Wood-carved high drinking bowl, 1542.

1975-87 Engr. *Perf. 11½; 14 (2m)*
555 A256 10p red lil ('78) 6 5
a. Bklt. pane of 4 (#555, 2 #556, #559) + label 3.00
b. Bklt. pane of 5 (2 #555, #557, #563, #564) 2.25
c. As #555a, no label 60
556 A256 20p ol ('77) 12 5
a. yel bister ('87) 12 5
557 A256 30p car ('77) 18 5
558 A256 40p orange 22 5
559 A256 50p grn ('76) 28 5
560 A256 60p blue 35 5
561 A256 70p sepia 40 5
562 A256 80p dl red & bl grn ('76) 45 5
563 A256 90p vio ('77) 50 5
564 A256 1.10m yel ('79) 55 8
565 A256 1.20m dk bl ('79) 60 10
566 A258 1.50m multi ('76) 70 10
567 A256a 2m multi, litho. ('77) 90 25

Lithographed and Engraved

568 A257 2.50m multi ('76) 1.10 25
569 A258 4.50m multi ('76) 2.00 25
570 A258a 5m multi ('77) 2.25 25
Nos. 555-570 (16) 10.66 1.73

No 556a issue only in booklet No. 716a.

Finland No. 16 — A259

Girl Combing Hair, by Magnus Enckell — A260

Lithographed and Typographed

1975, Apr. 26 *Perf. 13*
571 A259 70p multi 5.00 5.50

Nordia 75 Philatelic Exhibition, Helsinki, Apr. 26-May 1. Sold only at exhibition for 3m including entrance ticket.

Europa Issue 1975

Design: 90p, Washerwoman, by Tyko Sallinen (1879-1955).

1975, Apr. 28 Litho. *Perf. 13x12½*
572 A260 70p gray & multi 1.25 40
573 A260 90p tan & multi 1.25 40

Balance of Justice, Sword of Legality
A261

Rescue Boat and Sinking Ship
A262

1975, May 7 *Perf. 14*
574 A261 70p vio bl & multi 1.00 40

Sesquicentennial of State Economy Comptroller's Office.

1975, June 2 Litho. *Perf. 14*
575 A262 70p multi 1.25 40

12th International Salvage Conference, Finland, stressing importance of coordinating sea, air and communications resources in salvage operations.

Safe and Unsafe Levels of Drugs — A263

1975, July 21 Litho. *Perf. 14*
576 A263 70p multi 1.00 40

Importance of pharmacological studies and for the 6th International Pharmacology Congress, Helsinki.

Olavinlinna Castle — A264

1975, July 29 *Perf. 13*
577 A264 70p multi 1.00 40

500th anniversary of Olavinlinna Castle.

Swallows over Finlandia Hall — A265

"Men and Women Working for Peace" — A266

1975, July 30
578 A265 90p multi 1.25 40

European Security and Cooperation Conference, Helsinki, July 30-Aug. 1. (The swallows of the design represent freedom, mobility and continuity.) See No. 709

1975, Oct. 24 Litho. *Perf. 13x12½*
579 A266 70p multi 1.00 40

International Women's Year 1975.

"Continuity and Growth"
A267

Boys as Three Kings and Herod
A268

1975, Oct. 29 *Perf. 13*
580 A267 70p brn & multi 1.00 40

Industrial Art and for the centenary of the Finnish Society of Industrial Art.

1975, Nov. 8 *Perf. 14*
581 A268 40p bl & multi 1.00 25

Christmas 1975.

Top Border of State Debenture
A269

Lithographed and Engraved

1976, Jan. 9 *Perf. 11½*
582 A269 80p multi 1.00 40

Centenary of State Treasury.

Glider over Lake Region — A270

1976, Jan. 13 Litho. *Perf. 14*
583 A270 80p multi 1.50 40

15th World Glider Championships, Rayskala, June 13-27.

Heikki Klemetti
A271

1976, Feb. 14 Litho. *Perf. 13*
584 A271 80p grn & multi 1.00 40

Prof. Heikki Klemetti (1876-1953), musician and writer, birth centenary.

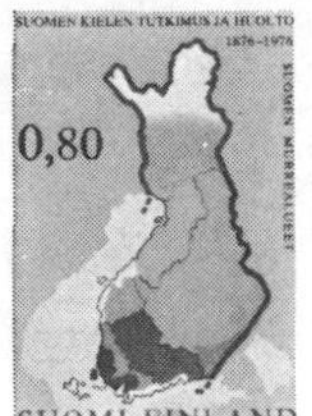

Map with Areas of Different Dialects — A272

Aino Ackté, by Albert Edelfelt — A273

1976, Mar. 10 Litho. *Perf. 13*
585 A272 80p multi 1.00 40

Finnish Language Society, centenary.

1976, Apr. 23
586 A273 70p yel & multi 1.00 40

Aino Ackté (1876-1944), opera singer, birth centenary.

Europa Issue 1976

Knife from Voyri, Sheath and Belt — A274

1976, May 3 Litho. *Perf. 13*
587 A274 80p vio bl & multi 3.00 50

Radio and Television
A275

1976, Sept. 9 Litho. *Perf. 13*
588 A275 80p multi 1.00 40

Radio broadcasting in Finland, 50th anniversary.

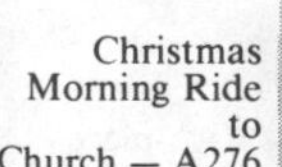
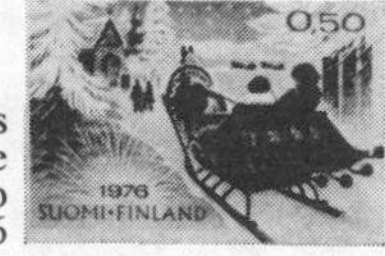
Christmas Morning Ride to Church — A276

1976, Oct. 23 Litho. *Perf. 14*
589 A276 50p multi 1.00 30

Christmas 1976.

Turku Chapter Seal (Virgin and Child) A277

1976, Nov. 1 Litho. *Perf. 12½*
590 A277 80p buff, brn & red 1.00 40

700th anniversary of the Cathedral Chapter of Turku.

Alvar Aalto, Finlandia Hall, Helsinki A278

1976, Nov. 4
591 A278 80p multi 1.00 40

Hugo Alvar Henrik Aalto (1898-1976), architect.

Ice Dancers — A280

Five Water Lilies — A281

1977, Jan. 25 Litho. *Perf. 13*
592 A280 90p multi 1.00 40

European Figure Skating Championships, Finland, Jan. 25-29.

Photogravure and Engraved

1977, Feb. 2 *Perf. 12½*
593 A281 90p brt grn & multi 1.50 55
594 A281 1m ultra & multi 1.50 55

Nordic countries cooperation for protection of the environment and 25th Session of Nordic Council, Helsinki, Feb. 19.

Icebreaker Rescuing Merchantman A282

1977, Mar. 2 Litho. *Perf. 13*
595 A282 90p multi 1.00 40

Winter navigation between Finland and Sweden, centenary.

Nuclear Reactor A283

1977, Mar. 3 *Perf. 12½x13*
596 A283 90p multi 1.00 40

Opening of nuclear power station on Hästholmen Island.

Europa Issue 1977

Autumn Landscape, Northern Finland A284

1977, May 2 Litho. *Perf. 12½x13*
597 A284 90p multi 1.25 40

Tree, Birds and Nest A285

Orthodox Church, Valamo Cloister A286

1977, May 4 *Perf. 13x12½*
598 A285 90p multi 1.00 40

75th anniversary of cooperative banks.

1977, May 31 Litho. *Perf. 14*
599 A286 90p multi 1.00 40

Consecration festival of new Orthodox Church at Valamo Cloister, Heinävesi; 800th anniversary of introduction of orthodoxy in Karelia and of founding of Valamo Cloister.

Paavo Ruotsalainen A287

1977, July 8 Litho. *Perf. 13*
600 A287 90p multi 1.00 40

Paavo Ruotsalainen (1777-1852), lay leader of Pietists in Finland.

People Fleeing Fire and Water A288

Volleyball A289

1977, Sept. 14 Litho. *Perf. 14*
601 A288 90p multi 1.00 40

Civil defense for security.

1977, Sept. 15
602 A289 90p multi 1.00 40

European Women's Volleyball Championships, Finland, Sept. 29-Oct. 2.

Children Bringing Water for Sauna — A290

1977, Oct. 25
603 A290 50p multi 1.00 25

Christmas 1977.

Finnish Flag A291

Wall Telephone, 1880, New Telephone A292

1977, Dec. 5 Litho. *Perf. 14*
Size: 31x21mm.
604 A291 80p multi 1.00 40
Size: 37x25mm.
Perf. 13
605 A291 1m multi 1.40 40

60th anniversary of Finland's declaration of independence.

1977, Dec. 9 *Perf. 14*
606 A292 1m multi 1.00 40

Centenary of first telephone in Finland.

Harbor, Sunila Factory, Kotka Arms — A293

1978, Jan. 2 Litho. *Perf. 14*
607 A293 1m multi 1.00 40

Centenary of founding of Kotka.

Europa Issue 1978

Paimio Sanitarium by Alvar Aalto — A294

Design: 1.20m, Hvittrask studio house, 1902 (horiz.).

1978, May 2 Litho. *Perf. 13*
608 A294 1m multi 3.00 75
609 A294 1.20m multi 6.00 5.50

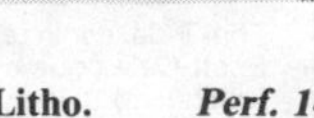
Rural Bus Service — A295

1978, June 8 Litho. *Perf. 14*
610 A295 1m multi 1.00 40

Eino Leino and Eagle — A296

1978, July 6 Litho. *Perf. 13*
611 A296 1m multi 1.00 40

Eino Leino (1878-1926), poet.

Function Theory and Rhythmical Lines — A297

1978, Aug. 15 Litho. *Perf. 14*
612 A297 1m multi 1.00 40

ICM 78, International Congress of Mathematicians, Helsinki, Aug. 15-23.

Child Feeding Birds — A298

1978, Oct. 23 Litho. *Perf. 14*
613 A298 50p multi 1.00 25

Christmas 1978.

Child, Flowers, IYC Emblem A299

1979, Jan. 2 Litho. *Perf. 13*
614 A299 1.10m multi 3.50 50

International Year of the Child.

Runner — A300

1979, Feb. 7 Litho. *Perf. 14*
615 A300 1.10m multi 1.40 40

8th Orienteering World Championships, Finland, Sept. 1-4.

Old School, Hamina, Academy Flag — A301

1979, Mar. 20 Litho. *Perf. 14*
616 A301 1.10m multi 1.00 40

200th anniversary of Finnish Military Academy.

Turku Cathedral and Castle, Prinkkala House, Brahe Statue — A302

1979, Mar. 31
617 A302 1.10m multi 1.00 40

Streetcar, Helsinki — A303

1979, May 2 Litho. *Perf. 14*
618 A303 1.10m multi 1.00 40

Non-polluting urban transportation.

View of Tampere, 1779 — A304

View of Tampere, 1979 — A305

1979, May 2
619 A304 90p multi 1.00 40

1979, Oct. 1 Litho. *Perf. 13*
620 A305 1.10m multi 1.00 40

Bicentenary of founding of Tampere.

Europa Issue 1979

Optical Telegraph, 1796, Map of Islands A306

Design: 1.10m, Letter of Queen Christina to Per Brahe, 1638, establishing postal service (vert.).

1979, May 2 *Perf. 13*
621 A306 1.10m multi 1.00 40
622 A306 1.30m multi 1.65 1.00

Shops and Merchants' Signs — A307

1979, Sept. 26 *Perf. 14*
623 A307 1.10m multi 1.00 40

Business and industry regulation centenary.

Old and New Cars, Street Crossing A308

1979, Oct. 1
624 A308 1.10m multi 1.00 40

Road safety.

Elves Feeding Horse — A309

1979, Oct. 24
625 A309 60p multi 80 25

Christmas 1979.

Korppi House, Lapinjarvi A310

Farm houses, First Row: Syrjala House, Tammela, 2 stamps in continuous design; Murtovaara House, Valtimo; Antila House, Lapua. Second row: Lofts, Pohjanmaa; Courtyard gate, Kanajarvi House, Kalvola; Main door, Havuselka House, Kauhajoki; Maki-Rasinpera House and dinner bell tower; Gable and eaves, Rasula Kuortane granary.

1979, Oct. 27 Litho. *Perf. 13*
626 A310 Bklt. pane of 10 9.00
a.-j. 1.10m, single stamp 90 50

See Nos. 672, 737.

Type of 1975

Kauhaneva Swamp A315

Hame Castle, Hameenlinna A316

Windmill, Harrstrom A318

Multiharju Forest, Seitseminen Natl. Park A319

Shuttle, Raanu Designs A322

Kaspaikka Towel Design A323

The indexes in each volume of the Scott Catalogue contain many listings which help to identify stamps.

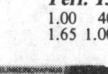

Bridal Rug, Teisko, 1815 A324

Iron-forged Door, Hollola Church A325

Iron Fish Spear c. 1100 — A326

Litho. & Engr., Litho., Engr.

1979-85 *Perf. 11½, 14*

No.	Type	Value	Color	Unused	Used
627	A315	70p	multi ('81)	40	18
628	A316	90p	brn red ('82)	45	25
629	A256	1m	red brn ('81)	50	20
630	A318	1m	bl & red brn ('83)	50	20
631	A256	1.30m	dk grn ('83)	60	20
632	A256	1.40m	pur ('84)	65	20
633	A256	1.50m	grnsh bl ('85)	70	20
634	A319	1.60m	multi	75	30
635	A315	1.80m	Eastern Gulf natl. park ('83)	80	30
636	A322	3m	multi	1.40	25
637	A323	6m	multi ('80)	2.75	40
638	A324	7m	multi ('82)	3.25	50
639	A325	8m	multi ('83)	3.50	60
640	A326	9m	blk & dk bl ('84)	4.00	60
			Nos. 627-640 (14)	20.25	4.38

Coil Stamp

Perf. 11½ Vert.
641 A316 90p brn red ('82) 45 30

Perf. 12½ Horiz.
642 A318 1m bl & red brn ('83) 50 32

Maria Jotuni (1880-1943), Writer — A327

1980, Apr. 9 Litho.
643 A327 1.10m multi 80 30

Europa Issue 1980

Frans Eemil Sillanpaa (1888-1964), Writer — A328

Design: 1.30m, Artturi Ilmari Virtanen (1895-1973), chemist (vert.).

1980, Apr. 28 *Perf. 13*
644 A328 1.10m multi 1.25 40
645 A328 1.30m multi 1.25 50

Pres. Urho Kekkonen, 80th Birthday — A329

1980, Sept. 3 Litho. *Perf. 13*
646 A329 1.10m multi 80 35

Nordic Cooperation Issue

Back-piece Harness, 19th century A330

1980, Sept. 9 *Perf. 14*
647 A330 1.10m *shown* 1.00 40
648 A330 1.30m *Collar harness, vert.* 1.00 50

Biathlon A331

1980, Oct. 17 Litho. *Perf. 14*
649 A331 1.10m multi 80 35

World Biathlon Championship, Lahti, Feb. 10-15, 1981.

Pull the Roller, Weighing out the Salt — A332

Christmas 1980 (Traditional Games): 1.10m, Putting out the shoemaker's eye.

1980, Oct. 27
650 A332 60p multi 35 16
651 A332 1.10m multi 1.00 25

Boxing Match A333

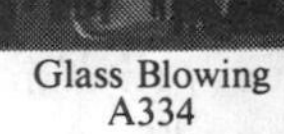

Glass Blowing A334

1981, Feb. 28 Litho. *Perf. 14*
652 A333 1.10m multi 60 30

European Boxing Championships, Tampere, May 2-10.

1981, Mar. 12
653 A334 1.10m multi 60 30

Glass industry, 300th anniversary.

Mail Boat Furst Menschikoff, 1836 — A335

Litho & Engr.

1981, May 6 *Perf. 13*
654 A335 1.10m brn & tan 4.50 5.00

Nordia '81 Stamp Exhibition, Helsinki, May 6-10. Sold only at exhibition for 3m including entrance ticket.

Europa Issue 1981

Rowing to Church A336

1981, May 18 Litho. *Perf. 13*

655 A336 1.10m shown 1.00 38
656 A336 1.50m Midsummer's Eve dance 1.00 52

Traffic Conference Emblem A337

Boy and Girl Riding Pegasus A338

1981, May 26 Litho. *Perf. 14*

657 A337 1.10m multi 60 30

European Conference of Ministers of Transport, May 25-28.

1981, June 11

658 A338 1m multi 55 30

Youth associations centenary.

Intl. Year of the Disabled — A339

1981, Sept. 2 Litho. *Perf. 13*

659 A339 1.10m multi 60 30

Christmas 1981 — A340

1981, Oct. 27 Litho. *Perf. 14*

660 A340 70p Children, Christmas tree 40 22
661 A340 1.10m Decorating tree, vert. 60 40

"Om Konsten att Ratt Behaga" First Issue (Periodicals Bicentenary) A341

1982, Jan. 15

662 A341 1.20m multi 65 30

Kuopio Bicentenary A343

Score, String Instrument Neck A344

1982, Mar. 4 Litho. *Perf. 14*

664 A343 1.20m multi 65 30

1982, Mar. 11 *Perf. 13*

665 A344 1.20m multi 65 30

Centenaries of Sibelius Academy of Music and Helsinki Orchestra.

Electric Power Plant Centenary A345

1982, Mar. 15 *Perf. 14*

666 A345 1.20m multi 65 30

Gardening A346

1982, Apr. 16 Litho. *Perf. 14*

667 A346 1.10m multi 65 30

Europa Issue 1982 — A347

Designs: 1.20m, Publication of Abckiria (first Finnish book), 1543. (Sculpture of Mikael Agricola, printer, by Oskari Jauhiainen, 1951). 1.50m, Turku Academy, first Finnish university (Turku Academy Inaugural Procession, 1640, after Albert Edelfelt).

1982, Apr. 29 Litho. *Perf. 13x12½*

668 A347 1.20m multi 65 35

Size: 47x31mm.

Perf. 12½

669 A347 1.50m multi 70 60

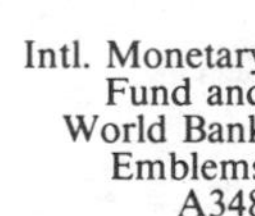

Intl. Monetary Fund and World Bank Emblems A348

1982, May 12 *Perf. 14*

670 A348 1.60m multi 72 30

IMF Interim Committee and IMF-WB Joint Development Committee Meeting, Helsinki, May 12-14.

75th Anniv. of Unicameral Parliament A349

1982, May 25

671 A349 2.40m Future, by Waino Aaltonen, Parliament 1.10 50

House Type of 1979

Manor Houses, First Row: a, Kuitia, Parainen, 1490. b, Louhisaari, Askainen, 1655. c, Frugard, Joroinen, 1780. d, Jokioinen, 1798. e, Moisio, Elimaki, 1820. Second Row: f, Sjundby, Siuntio, 1560. g, Fagervik, Inkoo, 1773. h, Mustio, Karjaa, 1792. i, Fiskars, Pohja, 1818. j, Kotkaniemi, Vihti, 1836.

1982, June 14 Litho. *Perf. 13x13½*

672 A310 Bklt. pane of 10 7.50
a.-j. 1.20m, single stamp 75 40

Christmas 1982 — A350

1982, Oct. 25

673 A350 90p Feeding forest animals 60 30
674 A350 1.20m Children eating porridge 60 30

Nordic Cooperation A351

1983, Mar. 24 Litho. *Perf. 14*

675 A351 1.20m Panning for gold 60 30
676 A351 1.30m Kitkajoki River rapids 65 30

World Communications Year — A352

1983, Apr. 9 Litho. *Perf. 13*

677 A352 1.30m Postal services 65 30
678 A352 1.70m Sound waves, optical cables 85 50

Europa 1983 A353

1983, May 2 Litho. *Perf. 12½x13*

679 A353 1.30m Flash smelting method 65 30
680 A353 1.70m Temppeliaukio Church 85 50

Pres. Lauri Kristian Relander (1883-1942) A354

Running A355

1983, May 31 Litho. *Perf. 14*

681 A354 1.30m multi 65 30

1983, June 6

682 A355 1.20m Javelin, horiz. 60 40
683 A355 1.30m shown 65 30

First World Athletic Championships, Helsinki, Aug. 7-14.

Toivo Kuula (1883-1918), Composer — A356

1983, July 7 *Perf. 14*

684 A356 1.30m multi 65 30

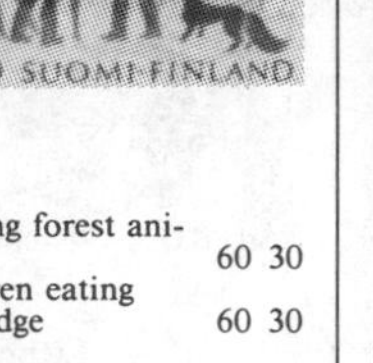

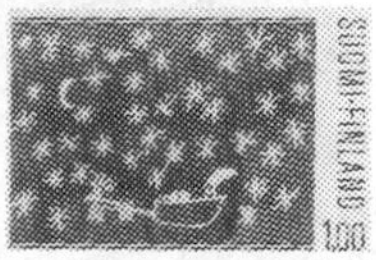

Christmas 1983 — A357

Childrens drawings: 1m, Santa, reindeer, sled and gifts by Eija Myllyviita. 1.30m, Two candles by Camilla Lindberg.

Engr., Litho.

1983, Nov. 4 *Perf. 12, 14*

685 A357 1m dk bl 50 30
686 A357 1.30m multi, vert. 65 30

President Mauno Henrik Koivisto, 60th Birthday A358

1983, Nov. 25 Litho. *Perf. 14*

687 A358 1.30m brt bl & blk 65 30

Inauguration of Nordic Postal Rates — A360

1984, Mar. 1 Engr. *Perf. 12*

689 A360 1.10m Letters (2nd class rate) 50 20

Photo. & Engr.

690 A360 1.40m Automated sorting (1st class rate), vert. 65 20

Museum Pieces A361

Work and Skill A362

Designs: No. 691, Pottery, 3200 B.C.; Silver chalice, 1416; Crossbow, 16th cent. No. 692, Kaplan hydraulic turbine.

1984, Apr. 30 Litho. *Perf. 13½*

691 A361 1.40m multi 65 32
692 A362 1.40m multi 65 32

Europa (1959-84) A363

1984, May 7 *Perf. 12½x13*

693 A363 1.40m multi 65 32
694 A363 2m multi 90 50

Dentistry — A364

1984, Aug. 27 Litho. *Perf. 14*

695 A364 1.40m Dentist, teeth 65 32

Astronomy A365

1984, Sept. 12
696 A365 1.10m Observatory, planets, sun 50 25

Aleksis Kivi (1934-72), Writer — A366

1984, Oct. 10 **Litho.** ***Perf. 14***
697 A366 1.40m Song of my Heart 65 32

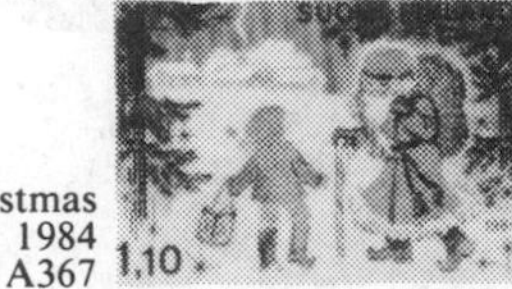
Christmas 1984 A367

Litho. & Engr.
1984, Nov. 30 ***Perf. 12***
698 A367 1.10m Father Christmas, brownie 50 25

Common Law of 1734 — A368

1984, Dec. 6 ***Perf. 14***
699 A368 2m Statute Book 90 40

25th Anniv. of EFTA — A369

1985, Feb. 2 **Litho.**
700 A369 1.20m multi 55 25

100th Anniv. of Society of Swedish Literature in Finland A370

1985, Feb. 5 **Litho.**
701 A370 1.50m Johan Ludvig Runeberg 70 30

100th Anniv. of Order of St. Sergei and St. Herman — A371

1985, Feb. 18 **Litho.** ***Perf. 11½x12***
702 A371 1.50m Icon 70 30

150th Anniv. of Kalevala — A372

Litho. & Engr.
1985, Feb. 28 ***Perf. 13x12½***
703 A372 1.50m Pedri Semeikka 70 30
704 A372 2.10m Larin Paraske 95 45

NORDIA 1985 — A373

Litho. & Engr.
1985, May 15 ***Perf. 13***
705 A373 1.50m Mermaid and sea lions 6.50 8.00

NORDIA 1985 philatelic exhibition, May 15-19. Sold for 10m, which included admission ticket.

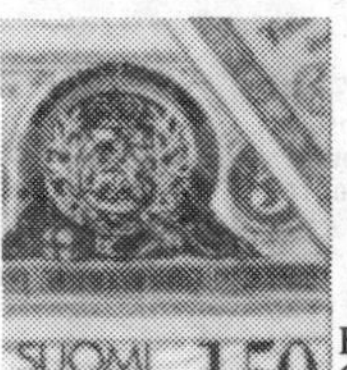
Finnish Banknote Centenary A374

Designs: Finnish banknotes of 1886, 1909, 1922, 1945 and 1955.

Photo. & Engr.
1985, May 18 ***Perf. 11½***
706 Booklet pane of 8 6.00 6.00
a.-h. A374 1.50m Any single 70 30

Europa 1985 — A375

Designs: 1.50m, Children playing the recorder. 2.10m, Excerpt "Ramus Virens Olivarum" from the "Piae Cantiones," 1582.

1985, June 17 **Litho.** ***Perf. 13***
707 A375 1.50m multi 70 30
708 A375 2.10m multi 95 45

Security Conference Type of 1975

1985, June 19 **Litho.**
709 A265 2.10m multi 95 45

European Security and Cooperation Conference, 10th Anniv.

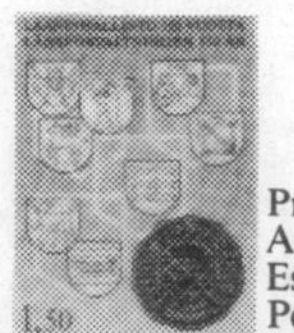
Provincial Administration Established by Count Per Brahe, 350th Anniv. — A376

1985, Sept. 5 **Litho.** ***Perf. 14***
710 A376 1.50m Provincial arms, Count's seal 70 30

Arms Type of 1975 and

Kerimaki Church A376a

Urho Kekkonen Natl. Park A376b

1986-88 **Engr.** ***Perf. 11½***
715 A256 1.60m ver 75 20
716 A256 1.70m gray blk ('87) 75 20
a. Bklt pane of 8 + 2 labels (2 #555, 2 #556a, #558, #560, 2 #716) 2.50

Perf. 12½
717 A256 1.80m olive grn('88) 90 90

Litho.
Perf. 14
719 A376a 2.20m multi ('88) 1.10 1.10
720 A376b 2.40m multi ('88) 1.20 1.20

Issue dates: 1.80m, Jan. 4. 2.20m, 2.40m, Jan. 20.

No. 716a contains 2 labels publicizing FINLANDIA '88.

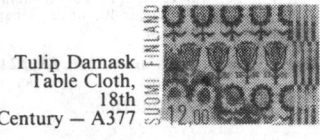

Tulip Damask Table Cloth, 18th Century — A377

1985, Sept. 13 **Litho.** ***Perf. 14***
723 A377 12m multi 5.50 1.25

Miniature Sheet

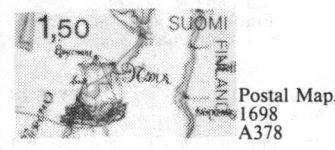

Postal Map, 1698 A378

Designs: No. 728a, Postman on foot. No. 728c, Sailing vessel, diff. No. 728d, Postrider, vert.

Litho. & Engr.
1985, Oct. 16 ***Perf. 14***
728 Sheet of 4 4.00 4.00
a.-d. A378 1.50m, Any single 1.00 1.00

FINLANDIA '88, 350th anniv. of Finnish Postal Service, founded in 1638 by Gov.-Gen. Per Brahe. Sheet sold for 8m. Size: 135x90mm.

Intl. Youth Year — A379

Christmas 1985 — A380

1985, Nov. 1 **Litho.** ***Perf. 13***
729 A379 1.50m multi 70 30

1985, Nov. 29 ***Perf. 14***
730 A380 1.20m Bird, tulips 55 30
731 A380 1.20m Cross of St. Thomas, hyacinths 55 30

Natl. Geological Society, Cent. A390

1986, Feb. 8 **Litho.** ***Perf. 14***
732 A390 1.30m Orbicular granite 60 30
733 A390 1.60m Rapaviki 75 50
734 A390 2.10m Veined gneiss 95 50

Europa 1986 A391

1986, Apr. 10 ***Perf. 12½x13***
735 A391 1.60m Saimaa ringed seal 75 50
736 A391 2.20m Environmental conservation 1.00 50

Conference Palace, Baghdad, 1982 — A392

Natl. Construction Year. No. 737b, Lahti Theater, 1983. No. 737c, Kuusamo Municipal Offices, 1978. No. 737d, Hamina Court Building, 1983. No. 737e, Finnish Embassy, New Delhi, 1986. No. 737f, Western Sakyla Daycare Center, 1980.

1986, Apr. 19 ***Perf. 14***
737 Bklt. pane of 6 4.50
a.-f. A392 1.60m, any single 75 30

Nordic Cooperation Issue 1986 — A393

Sister towns.

1986, May 27 **Litho.** ***Perf. 14***
738 A393 1.60m Joensuu 75 40
739 A393 2.20m Jyvaskyla 1.00 50

Souvenir Sheet

FINLANDIA '88 — A394

Postal ships: No. 740a, Iron paddle steamer Aura, Stockholm-St. Petersburg, 1858. No. 740b, Screw vessel Alexander, Helsinki-Tallinn-Lubeck, 1859. No. 740c, Steamship Nicolai, Helsinki-Tallinn-St. Petersburg, 1858. No. 740d, 1st Ice steamship Express II, Helsinki-Stockholm, 1877-98, vert.

Litho. & Engr.
1986, Aug. 29 ***Perf. 13***
740 Sheet of 4 5.00 5.75
a.-b. A394 1.60m, any single 1.25 1.40
c.-d. A394 2.20m, any single 1.25 1.40

No. 740 has multicolored margin picturing map of Sweden, Aland Isls., Germany, Finland and Russia, showing postal ship routes. Sold for 10m. Size: 135x90mm.

Pierre-Louis Moreau de Maupertuis (1698-1759) — A395

1986, Sept. 5 Litho. *Perf. 12½x13*
741 A395 1.60m multi 75 30

Lapland Expedition, 250th anniv., proved Earth's poles are flattened.
See France No. 2016.

Urho Kaleva Kekkonen (1900-1986), President A396

Intl. Peace Year A397

1986, Sept. 30 Engr. *Perf. 14*
742 A396 5m black 2.25 2.25

1986, Oct. 13 Litho. *Perf. 13*
743 A397 1.60m multi 75 30

A398

Christmas A399

Photo. & Engr.

1986, Oct. 31 *Perf. 12*
744 A398 1.30m shown 60 30
745 A398 1.30m Denomination at right 60 30
746 A399 1.60m Elves 75 40

Nos. 744-745 printed se-tenant in a continuous design.

Postal Savings Bank, Cent. — A400

1987, Jan. 2 Litho. *Perf. 14*
747 A400 1.70m multi 75 38

Natl. Tourism, Cent. — A401

1987, Feb. 4 Litho. *Perf. 14*
748 A401 1.70m Winter 75 38
749 A401 2.30m Summer 1.05 52

Metric System in Finland, Cent. — A402

1987, Feb. 4 *Perf. 14*
750 A402 1.40m multi 65 32

Leevi Madetoja (1887-1947), Composer A403

1987, Feb. 17 Litho. *Perf. 14*
751 A403 2.10m multi 90 45

European Wrestling Championships A404

1987 World Bowling Championships A405

1987, Feb. 17
752 A404 1.70m multi 75 38

1987, Apr. 13
753 A405 1.70m multi 75 38

Mental Health A406

1987, Apr. 13
754 A406 1.70m multi 75 38

Souvenir Sheet

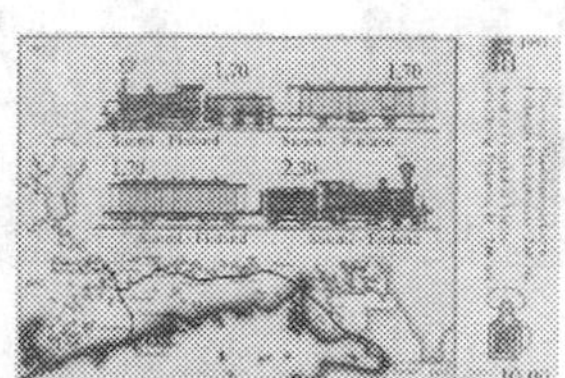

FINLANDIA '88 — A407

Locomotives and mail cars: No. 755a, Steam locomotive, six-wheeled tender. No. 755b, Four-window mail car. No. 755c, Seven-window mail car.

Litho. & Engr.

1987, May 8 *Perf. 12½x13*
755 Sheet of 4 5.00 5.00
a.-c. A407 1.70m any single 1.25 1.25
d. A407 2.30m multi 1.25 1.25

No. 755 has inscribed multicolored margin picturing maps of railroad routes in 1987, 1862 and 1870. Sold for 10m. Size: 135x91mm.

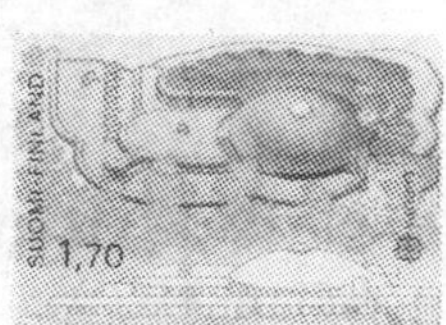

Europa 1987 A408

Modern architecture: 1.70m, Tampere Main Library, 1986, designed by Raili and Reima Pietila. 2.30m, Stoa Monument, Helsinki, c. 1981, by sculptor Hannu Siren.

1987, May 15 Litho. *Perf. 13*
756 A408 1.70m multi 80 40
757 A408 2.30m multi 1.10 55

Booklet Stamps

Natl. Art Museum, Ateneum, Cent. — A409

Paintings: No. 758a, Strawberry Girl, by Nils Schillmark (1745-1804). No. 758b, Still-life on a Lady's Work Table, by Ferdinand von Wright (1822-1906). No. 758c, Old Woman with Basket, by Albert Edelfelt (1854-1906). No. 758d, Boy and Crow, by Akseli Gallen-Kallela (1865-1931). NO. 758e, Late Winter, by Tyko Sallinen (1879-1955).

1987, May 15
758 Bklt. pane of 5 4.00
a.-e. A409 1.70m any single 80 40

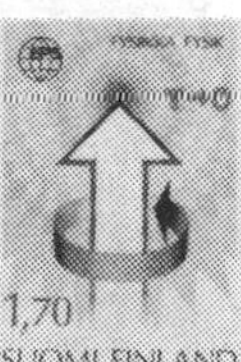

European Physics Soc. 7th General Conference, Helsinki, Aug. 10-14 — A410

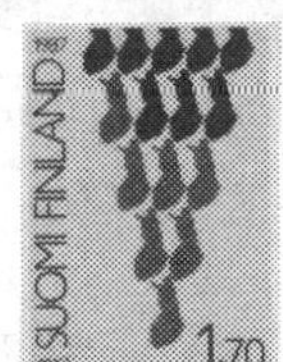

Natl. Independence, 70th Anniv. — A411

1987, Aug. 12 *Perf. 14*
759 A410 1.70m multi 78 78

1987, Oct. 12
760 A411 1.70m ultra, sil & pale lt gray 75 75

Size: 30x41mm.

761 A411 10m dark ultra, lt blue & sil 4.50 4.50

Ylppo, Child and Lastenlinna Children's Hospital A412

1987, Oct. 27
762 A412 1.70m multi 75 75

Avro Ylppo (b. 1887), pediactrics pioneer.

Finland stamps can be mounted in Scott's annually supplemented Scandinavia and Finland Album.

Christmas A413

Finnish News Agency (STT), Cent. A414

1987, Oct. 30
763 A413 1.40m Santa Claus, youths, horiz. 65 65
764 A413 1.70m shown 75 75

1987, Nov. 1
765 A414 2.30m multi 1.05 1.05

Lauri "Tahko" Pihkala (1888-1981), Promulgator of Sports and Physical Education A415

1988, Jan. 5 Litho. *Perf. 14*
766 A415 1.80m blk, chalky bl & brt bl 90 90

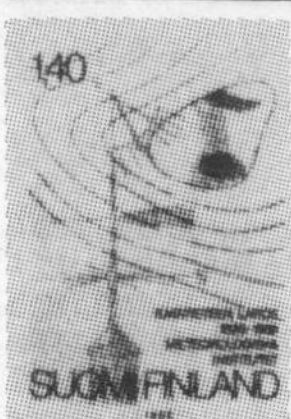

Meteorological Institute, 150th Anniv. — A416

1988, Mar. 23 **Litho.**
767 A416 1.40m multi 70 70

Settlement of New Sweden in America, 350th Anniv. — A417

Design: 17th Century European settlers negotiating with 3 American Indians, map of New Sweden, the Swedish ships Kalmar Nyckel and Fogel Grip, based on an 18th cent. illustration from a Swedish book about the American Colonies.

Litho. & Engr.

1988, Mar. 29 ***Perf. 13***
768 A417 3m multi 1.50 1.50

See US No. C117 and Sweden No. 1672.

SEMI-POSTAL STAMPS

Arms — SP1

Unwmk.

1922, May 15 **Typo.** ***Perf. 14***
B1 SP1 1m + 50p gray & red 1.00 *10.00*
a. Perf. 13x13½ 7.00

Red Cross Standard SP2

Symbolic SP3

Ship of Mercy — SP4

1930, Feb. 6
B2 SP2 1m + 10p red org & red 2.00 *10.00*
B3 SP3 1½m + 15p grysh grn & red 1.25 *10.00*
B4 SP4 2m + 20p dk bl & red 3.50 *40.00*

The surtax on this and subsequent similar issues was for the benefit of the Red Cross Society of Finland.

Church in Hattula — SP5

SP8

Designs: 1½m+15p, Castle of Hameenlinna. 2m+20p, Fortress of Viipuri.

1931, Jan. 1 **Engr.**

Cross in Red.
B5 SP5 1m + 10p gray grn 2.00 *8.00*
B6 SP5 1½m + 15p lil brn 11.00 11.00
B7 SP5 2m + 20p dl bl 1.85 *15.00*

1931, Oct. 15 **Typo.** ***Rouletted 4, 5***
B8 SP8 1m + 4m blk 32.50 *60.00*

The surtax was to assist the Postal Museum of Finland in purchasing the Richard Granberg collection of entire envelopes.

Helsinki University Library SP9

Nikolai Church at Helsinki SP10

Design: 2½m+25p, Parliament Building, Helsinki.

1932, Jan. 1 ***Perf. 14***
B9 SP9 1¼m + 10p ol bis & red 2.00 *12.50*
B10 SP10 2m + 20p dp vio & red 1.00 *6.00*
B11 SP9 2½m + 25p lt bl & red 1.50 *20.00*

Bishop Magnus Tawast SP12

Michael Agricola SP13

Design: 2½m+25p, Isacus Rothovius.

1933, Jan. 20 **Engr.**
B12 SP12 1¼m + 10p blk brn & red 2.50 6.50
B13 SP13 2m + 20p brn vio & red 75 2.00
B14 SP13 2½m + 25p ind & red 1.00 3.00

Evert Horn — SP15

Designs: 2m+20p, Torsten Stalhandske. 2½m+25p, Jakob (Lazy Jake) de la Gardie.

1934, Jan.

Cross in Red.
B15 SP15 1¼m + 10p brn 1.00 2.00
B16 SP15 2m + 20p gray lil 1.80 3.50
B17 SP15 2½m + 25p gray 1.00 2.50

Mathias Calonius SP18

Robert Henrik Rehbinder SP21

Designs: 2m+20p, Henrik C. Porthan. 2½m+25p, Anders Chydenius.

1935, Jan. 1

Cross in Red.
B18 SP18 1¼m + 15p brn 1.00 2.00
B19 SP18 2m + 20p gray lil 1.50 3.00
B20 SP18 2½m + 25p gray bl 75 2.50

1936, Jan. 1

Designs: 2m+20p, Count Gustaf Mauritz Armfelt. 2½m+25p, Count Arvid Bernard Horn.

Cross in Red.
B21 SP21 1¼m + 15p dk brn 75 2.00
B22 SP21 2m + 20p vio brn 4.00 5.50
B23 SP21 2½m + 25p bl 75 3.00

The "Uusimaa" SP24

The "Turunmaa" SP25

Design: 3½m+35p, The "Hameenmaa."

1937, Jan. 1

Cross in Red.
B24 SP24 1¼m + 15p brn 1.00 2.50
B25 SP25 2m + 20p brn lake 18.50 6.75
B26 SP24 3½m + 35p ind 1.00 3.00

Aukuste Makipeska SP27

Skiing SP31

Designs: 1¼m+15p, Robert Isidor Orn. 2m+20p, Edward Bergenheim. 3½m+35p, Johan Mauritz Nordenstam.

1938, Jan. 5 **Engr.**

Cross in Red
B27 SP27 50p + 5p dk grn 70 1.00
B28 SP27 1¼m + 15p dk brn 1.00 2.00
B29 SP27 2m + 20p rose lake 9.00 7.00
B30 SP27 3½m + 35p dk bl 90 3.50

1938, Jan. 18

Designs: 2m+1m, Skijumper. 3.50m+1.50m, Skier.

B31 SP31 1.25m + 75p sl grn 6.00 11.00
B32 SP31 2m + 1m dk car 6.00 11.00
B33 SP31 3.50m + 1.50m dk bl 6.00 11.00

Issued to commemorate the ski championships held at Lahti.

Soldier — SP34

1938, May 16
B34 SP34 2m + ½m bl 2.00 4.00

Issued to commemorate the victory of the White Army over the Red Guards. The surtax was for the benefit of the members of the Union of the Finnish Front.

Battlefield at Solferino SP35

1939, Jan. 2

Cross in Scarlet.
B35 SP35 50p + 5p dk grn 1.00 1.50
B36 SP35 1¼m + 15p dk brn 1.00 2.50
B37 SP35 2m + 20p lake 18.50 10.00
B38 SP35 3½m + 35p dk bl 80 3.50

Issued in commemoration of the 75th anniversary of the founding of the International Red Cross Society.

Soldiers with Crossbows SP36

Arms of Finland SP40

Designs: 1¼m+15p, Cavalryman. 2m+20p, Soldier of Charles XII of Sweden. 3½m+35p, Officer and soldier of War with Russia, 1808-1809.

1940, Jan. 3

Cross in Red.
B39 SP36 50p + 5p dk grn 70 1.50
B40 SP36 1¼m + 15p dk brn 1.50 2.50
B41 SP36 2m + 20p lake 2.00 2.50
B42 SP36 3½m + 35p dp ultra 2.00 3.50

The surtax aided the Finnish Red Cross.

1940, Feb. 15 **Litho.**
B43 SP40 2m + 2m ind 60 1.10

The surtax was given to a fund for the preservation of neutrality.

Mason SP41

Soldier's Emblem SP45

Designs: 1.75m+15p, Farmer plowing. 2.75m+25p, Mother and child. 3.50m+35p, Finnish flag.

1941, Jan. 2 **Engr.**

Cross in Red.
B44 SP41 50p + 5p grn 50 1.10
B45 SP41 1.75m + 15p brn 1.25 2.00
B46 SP41 2.75m + 25p brn car 6.50 10.00
B47 SP41 3.50m + 35p dp ultra 1.25 3.00

See also Nos. B65-B68.

1941, May 24 **Unwmk.**
B48 SP45 2.75m + 25p brt ultra 1.00 1.25

The surtax was for the aid of the soldiers who fought in the Russo-Finnish War.

Aaland Arms SP46

Lapland Arms SP51

Designs: Coats of Arms-1.75m+15p, Nyland. 2.75m+25p, Finland's first arms. 3.50m+35p, Karelia. 4.75m+45p, Satakunta.

1942, Jan. 2 ***Perf. 14***
Cross in Red.

B49 SP46	50p + 5p grn	1.00	1.50
B50 SP46	1.75m + 15p brn	1.25	2.25
B51 SP46	2.75m + 25p dk red	1.25	2.25
B52 SP46	3.50m + 35p dp ultra	1.25	2.25
B53 SP46	4.75m + 45p dk sl grn	1.00	2.25
	Nos. B49-B53 (5)	5.75	10.50

The surtax aided the Finnish Red Cross.

1943, Jan. 6 **Inscribed "1943"**

Designs: Coats of Arms-2m+20p, Hame. 3.50m+35p, Eastern Bothnia. 4.50m+45p, Savo.

Cross in Red

B54 SP51	50p + 5p grn	50	1.25
B55 SP51	2m + 20p brn	1.00	2.00
B56 SP51	3.50m + 35p dk red	1.00	2.00
B57 SP51	4.50m + 45p brt ultra	1.50	5.00

The surtax aided the Finnish Red Cross.

Soldier's Helmet and Sword SP55

Mother and Children SP56

1943, Feb. 1 ***Perf. 13***
B58 SP55 2m + 50p dk brn 75 1.00
B59 SP56 3.50m + 1m brn red 75 1.00

The surtax was for national welfare.

Red Cross Train — SP57

Designs: 2m+50p, Ambulance. 3.50m+75p, Red Cross Hospital, Helsinki. 4.50m+1m, Hospital plane.

1944, Jan. 2 ***Perf. 14***
Cross in Red.

B60 SP57	50p + 25p grn	50	50
B61 SP57	2m + 50p sep	70	1.00
B62 SP57	3.50m + 75p ver	70	1.00
B63 SP57	4.50m + 1m brt ultra	1.50	2.50

The surtax aided the Finnish Red Cross.

Symbols of Peace SP61

Wrestling SP62

1944, Dec. 1
B64 SP61 3.50m dk red brn + 1.50m 65 1.00

The surtax was for national welfare.

Types of 1941 Inscribed "1945"

1945, May 2 **Photo. and Engr.**
Cross in Red.

B65 SP41	1m + 25p grn	20	50
B66 SP41	2m + 50p brn	40	80
B67 SP41	3.50m + 75p brn car	40	80
B68 SP41	4.50m + 1m dp ultra	80	1.50

The surtax was for the Finnish Red Cross.

1945, Apr. 16 **Engr.** ***Perf. 13½***

Designs: 2m+1m, Gymnast. 3.50m+1.75m, Runner. 4.50m+2.25m, Skier. 7m+3.50m, Javelin thrower.

B69 SP62	1m + 50p bluish grn	30	1.00
B70 SP62	2m + 1m dp red	30	1.00
B71 SP62	3.50m + 1.75m dl vio	30	1.00
B72 SP62	4.50m + 2.25m ultra	60	1.25
B73 SP62	7m + 3.50m dl brn	90	2.00
	Nos. B69-B73 (5)	2.40	6.25

Fishing SP67

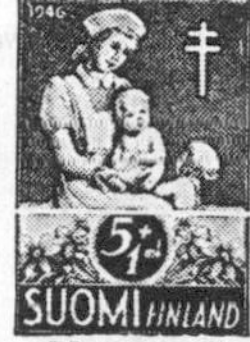
Nurse and Children SP71

Designs: 3m+75p, Churning. 5m+1.25m, Reaping. 10m+2.50m, Logging.

Engraved; Cross Typo. in Red
1946, Jan. 7

B74 SP67	1m + 25p dl grn	60	75
B75 SP67	3m + 75p lil brn	45	50
B76 SP67	5m + 1.25m rose red	60	75
a.	Red cross omitted	*600.00*	
B77 SP67	10m + 2.50m ultra	75	1.00

The surtax was for the Finnish Red Cross.

1946, Sept. 2 **Engr.**

Design: 8m+2m, Doctor examining infant.

B78 SP71 5m + 1m grn 60 80
B79 SP71 8m + 2m brn vio 60 80

The surtax was for the prevention of tuberculosis.

Nos. B78 and B79 Surcharged with New Values in Black.

1947, Apr. 1
B80 SP71 6m + 1m on 5m + 1m grn 60 1.00
B81 SP71 10m + 2m on 8m + 2m brn vio 60 1.00

The surtax was for the prevention of tuberculosis.

Medical Examination of Infants
SP73 SP74

Designs: 10m+2.50m, Infant held by the feet. 12m+3m, Mme. Alli Paasikivi and a child. 20m+5m, Infant standing.

1947, Sept. 15 **Engr.**

B82 SP73	2.50mm + 1m grn	60	1.00
B83 SP74	6m + 1.50m dk red	80	1.00
B84 SP74	10m + 2.50m red brn	1.00	1.00
B85 SP73	12m + 3m dp bl	1.25	1.50
B86 SP74	20m + 5m dk red vio	1.50	2.00
	Nos. B82-B86 (5)	5.15	6.50

The surtax was for the prevention of tuberculosis.

Zachris Topelius — SP78

Designs: 7m+2m, Fredrik Pacius. 12m+3m, Johan L. Runeberg. 20m+5m, Fredrik Cygnaeus.

Engraved; Cross Typo. in Red
1948, May 10 **Unwmk.** ***Perf. 14***

B87 SP78	3m + 1m grn	80	1.00
B88 SP78	7m + 2m rose red	1.00	1.10
B89 SP78	12m + 3m brt bl	1.10	1.25
B90 SP78	20m + 5m dk vio	1.25	1.50

The surtax was for the Finnish Red Cross.

Nos. B83, B84 and B86 Surcharged with New Values and Bars in Black.

1948, Sept. 13 **Engr.** ***Perf. 13½***

B91 SP74	7m + 2m on 6m + 1.50m dk red	1.75	2.50
B92 SP74	15m + 3m on 10m + 2.50m red brn	1.75	2.50
B93 SP74	24m + 6m on 20m + 5m dk red vio	2.00	2.50

The surtax was for the prevention of tuberculosis.

Tying Birch Boughs SP79

Wood Anemone SP83

Designs: 9m+3m, Bathers in Sauna house. 15m+5m, Rural bath house. 30m+10m, Cold plunge in lake.

Engraved; Cross Typo. in Red
1949, May 5 ***Perf. 13½x14***

B94 SP79	5m + 2m dl grn	60	85
B95 SP79	9m + 3m dk car	1.00	1.25
B96 SP79	15m + 5m dp bl	1.00	1.25
B97 SP79	30m + 10m dk vio brn	1.75	3.00

The surtax was for the Finnish Red Cross.

1949, June 2 **Engr.**

Designs: 9m+3m, Wild rose. 15m+5m, Coltsfoot.

Inscribed: "1949"

B98 SP83	5m + 2m grn	80	1.25
B99 SP83	9m + 3m car	1.00	1.25
B100 SP83	15m + 5m ol bis	1.25	1.75

The surtax was for the prevention of tuberculosis.

Similar to Type of 1949.

Designs: 5m+2m, Water lily. 9m+3m, Pasqueflower. 15m+5m, Bell flower cluster.

1950, Apr. 1
Inscribed: "1950."

B101 SP83	5m + 2m emer	2.00	2.00
B102 SP83	9m + 3m rose car	1.75	1.75
B103 SP83	15m + 5m bl	1.75	1.75

The surtax was for the prevention of tuberculosis.

Hospital Entrance, Helsinki SP84

Blood Donor's Medal SP86

Design: 12m+3m, Giving blood.

Engraved; Cross Typo. in Red
1951, Mar. 17 **Unwmk.** ***Perf. 14***

B104 SP84	7m + 2m choc	1.75	1.75
B105 SP84	12m + 3m bl vio	1.75	1.75
B106 SP86	20m + 5m car	3.25	3.25

The surtax was for the Finnish Red Cross.

Capercaillie — SP87

Designs: 12m+3m, European cranes. 20m+5m, Caspian terns.

1951, Oct. 26 **Engr.**

B107 SP87	7m + 2m dk grn	2.50	2.75
B108 SP87	12m + 3m rose brn	2.50	2.75
B109 SP87	20m + 5m bl	2.50	2.75

The surtax was for the prevention of tuberculosis.

Diver SP88

Soccer Players SP89

Designs: 20m+3m, Stadum, Helsinki. 25m+4m, Runners.

1951-52

B110 SP88	12m + 2m rose car	1.25	1.50
B111 SP89	15m + 2m grn ('52)	1.25	1.50
B112 SP88	20m + 3m dp bl	1.25	1.50
B113 SP89	25m + 4m brn ('52)	1.25	1.50

Issued to publicize the XV Olympic Games, Helsinki, 1952. The surtax was to help finance the games.

Margin blocks of four of each denomination were cut from regular or perf.-through-margin sheets and pasted by the selvage, overlapping, in a printed folder to create a kind of souvenir booklet. Price $35.

Field Marshal Mannerheim SP90

Great Titmouse SP91

Engraved; Cross Typo. in Red

1952, Mar. 4

B114 SP90 10m + 2m gray 2.25 2.25
B115 SP90 15m + 3m rose vio 2.25 2.25
B116 SP90 25m + 5m bl 2.25 2.25

The surtax was for the Red Cross.

1952, Dec. 4 **Engr.**

Designs: 15m+3m, Spotted flycatchers and nest. 25m+5m, Swift.

B117 SP91 10m + 2m grn 2.50 2.50
B118 SP91 15m + 3m plum 2.50 2.50
B119 SP91 25m + 5m dp bl 2.50 2.50

The surtax was for the prevention of tuberculosis.

European Red Squirrel SP92

Children Receiving Parcel from Welfare Worker SP93

Designs: 15m+3m, Brown bear. 25m+5m, European elk.

Unwmk.

1953, Nov. 16 **Engr.** ***Perf. 14***

B120 SP92 10m + 2m red brn 2.50 2.50
B121 SP92 15m + 3m vio 2.50 2.50
B122 SP92 25m + 5m dk grn 2.50 2.50

The surtax was for the prevention of tuberculosis.

Engraved; Cross Typo. in Red

1954, Mar. 8 ***Perf. 11½***

Designs: 15m+3m, Aged woman knitting. 25m+5m, Blind basket-maker and dog.

B123 SP93 10m + 2m dk ol grn 1.75 1.75
B124 SP93 15m + 3m dk bl 1.75 1.75
B125 SP93 25m + 5m dk brn 1.75 1.75

The surtax was for the Finnish Red Cross.

Bumblebees and Dandelions SP94

European Perch SP95

Designs: 15m+3m, Butterfly. 25m+5m, Dragonfly.

Engraved; Cross Typo. in Red

1954, Dec. 7 ***Perf. 14***

B126 SP94 10m + 2m brn 1.75 1.75
B127 SP94 15m + 3m car 1.75 1.75
B128 SP94 25m + 5m bl 1.75 1.75

The surtax was for the prevention of tuberculosis.

Engraved; Cross Typo. in Red

1955, Sept. 26 ***Perf. 14***

Designs: 15m+3m, Northern pike. 25m+5m, Atlantic salmon.

B129 SP95 10m + 2m dl grn 1.75 1.75
B130 SP95 15m + 3m vio brn 1.75 1.75
B131 SP95 25m + 5m dk bl 1.75 1.75

The surtax was for the Anti-Tuberculosis Society.

Gen. von Dobeln in Battle of Juthas, 1808 SP96

Waxwing SP97

Illustrations by Albert Edelfelter from J. L. Runeberg's "Tales of Ensign Stal": 15(m)+3(m), Col. J. Z. Duncker holding flag. 25(m)+5(m), Son of fallen Soldier.

Engraved; Cross Typo. in Red.

1955, Nov. 24

B132 SP96 10m + 2m dp ultra 1.75 1.75
B133 SP96 15m + 3m dk red brn 1.75 1.75
B134 SP96 25m + 5m grn 1.75 1.75

The surtax was for the Red Cross.

Birds: 20m+3m, Eagle owl. 30m+5m, Mute swan.

Engraved; Cross Typo. in Red.

1956, Sept. 25 ***Perf. 11½***

B135 SP97 10m + 2m dl red brn 1.65 1.65
B136 SP97 20m + 3m bl grn 1.75 1.75
B137 SP97 30m + 5m bl 1.75 1.75

The surtax was for the Anti-Tuberculosis Society.

Pekka Aulin SP98

Wolverine (Glutton) SP99

Portraits: 10m+2m, Leonard von Pfaler. 20m+3m, Gustaf Johansson. 30m+5m, Viktor Magnus von Born.

Engraved; Cross Typo. in Red

1956, Nov. 26 **Unwmk.**

B138 SP98 5m + 1m grysh grn 1.25 1.25
B139 SP98 10m + 2m brn 1.50 1.50
B140 SP98 20m + 3m mag 1.75 1.75
B141 SP98 30m + 5m lt ultra 1.75 1.75

The surtax was for the Red Cross.

Engraved; Cross Typo. in Red

1957, Sept. 5 ***Perf. 11½***

Designs: 20m+3m, Lynx. 30m+5m, Reindeer.

B142 SP99 10m + 2m dl pur 1.50 1.50
B143 SP99 20m + 3m sep 1.75 1.75
B144 SP99 30m + 5m dk bl 1.75 1.75

The surtax was for the Anti-Tuberculosis Society. See also Nos. B160-B165.

Red Cross Flag SP100

Raspberry SP101

1957, Nov. 25 **Engr.** ***Perf. 14***

Cross in Red.

B145 SP100 10m + 2m ol grn 2.25 2.25
B146 SP100 20m + 3m mar 2.25 2.25
B147 SP100 30m + 5m dl bl 2.25 2.25

Issued to commemorate the 80th anniversary of the Finnish Red Cross.

Type of 1952.

Flowers: 10m+2m, Lily of the valley. 20m+3m, Red clover. 30m+5m, Hepatica.

Engraved; Cross Typo. in Red

1958, May 5 **Unwmk.** ***Perf. 14***

B148 SP91 10m + 2m grn 1.50 1.50
B149 SP91 20m + 3m lil rose 1.75 1.75
B150 SP91 30m + 5m ultra 1.75 1.75

The surtax was for the Anti-Tuberculosis Society.

Engraved; Cross Typo. in Red

1958, Nov. 20 ***Perf. 11½***

Designs: 20m+3m, Cowberry. 30m+5m, Blueberry.

B151 SP101 10m + 2m org 1.25 1.25
B152 SP101 20m + 3m red 1.75 1.75
B153 SP101 30m + 5m dk bl 1.75 1.75

The surtax was for the Red Cross.

Daisy SP102

Reindeer SP103

Designs: 20m+5m, Primrose. 30m+5m, Cornflower.

Engraved; Cross Typo. in Red

1959, Sept. 7 **Unwmk.**

B154 SP102 10m + 2m grn 3.25 1.75
B155 SP102 20m + 3m lt brn 4.00 2.25
B156 SP102 30m + 5m bl 4.00 2.25

The surtax was for the Anti-Tuberculosis Society.

Engraved; Cross Typo. in Red

1960, Nov. 24 ***Perf. 11½***

Designs: 20m+3m, Lapp and lasso. 30m+5m, Mountains.

B157 SP103 10m + 2m dk gray 1.50 1.50
B158 SP103 20m + 3m gray vio 2.25 2.25
B159 SP103 30m + 5m rose vio 2.25 2.25

The surtax was for the Red Cross.

Animal Type of 1957.

Designs: 10m+2m, Muskrat. 20m+3m, Otter. 30m+5m, Seal.

Engraved; Cross at right, Typo. in Red

1961, Sept. 4

B160 SP99 10m + 2m brn car 1.50 1.50
B161 SP99 20m + 3m sl bl 2.25 2.25
B162 SP99 30m + 5m bl grn 2.25 2.25

The surtax was for the Anti-Tuberculosis Society.

Animal Type of 1957.

Designs: 10m+2m, Hare. 20m+3m, Pine marten. 30m+5m, Ermine.

Engraved; Cross Typo. in Red

1962, Oct. 1

B163 SP99 10m + 2m gray 1.50 1.50
B164 SP99 20m + 3m dl red brn 2.00 2.00
B165 SP99 30m + 5m vio bl 2.00 2.00

The surtax was for the Anti-Tuberculosis Society.

Cross and Outstretched Hands — SP104

Engraved; Cross Typo. in Red

1963, May 8 **Unwmk.** ***Perf. 11½***

B166 SP104 10p + 2p red brn 1.25 1.25
B167 SP104 20p + 3p vio 1.50 1.50
B168 SP104 30p + 5p grn 1.50 1.50

The surtax was for the Red Cross.

Attending the Wounded SP105

Red Cross Activities: 25p+4p, Hospital ship. 35p+5p, Prisoner-of-war health examination. 40p+7p, Gift parcel distribution.

Engraved; Cross Typo. in Red

1964, May 26 ***Perf. 11½***

B169 SP105 15p + 3p vio bl 1.10 1.10
B170 SP105 25p + 4p grn 1.50 1.25
B171 SP105 35p + 5p vio brn 1.50 1.25
B172 SP105 40p + 7p dk ol grn 1.50 1.25

The surtax was for the Red Cross.

Finnish Spitz SP106

Artificial Respiration SP107

Designs: 25p+4p, Karelian bear dog. 35p+5p, Finnish hunting dog.

Engraved; Cross Typo. in Red

1965, May 10 ***Perf. 11½***

B173 AP106 15p + 3p org brn 1.50 1.50
B174 AP106 25p + 4p blk 1.75 1.75
B175 AP106 35p + 5p gray brn 1.75 1.75

Surtax for Anti-Tuberculosis Society.

1966, May 7 **Litho.** ***Perf. 14***

First Aid: 25p+4p, Skin diver rescuing occupants of submerged car. 35p+5p, Helicopter rescue in winter.

B176 SP107 15p + 3p multi 1.50 1.50
B177 SP107 25p + 4p multi 1.50 1.50
B178 SP107 35p + 5p multi 1.50 1.50

The surtax was for the Red Cross.

Birch SP108

Horse-drawn Ambulance SP109

Trees: 25p+4p, Pine. 40p+7p, Spruce.

1967, May 12 **Litho.** ***Perf. 14***

B179 SP108 20p + 3p multi 1.25 1.25

B180 SP108 25p + 4p multi 1.25 1.25
B181 SP108 40p + 7p multi 1.25 1.25

Surtax for Anti-Tuberculosis Society. See Nos. B185-B187.

1967, Nov. 24 Litho. *Perf. 14*

Designs: 25p+4p, Ambulance, 1967. 40p+7p, Red Cross.

Cross in Red

B182 SP109 20p + 3p dl yel, grn & blk 1.25 1.25
B183 SP109 25p + 4p vio & blk 1.25 1.25
B184 SP109 40p + 7p dk grn, blk & dk ol 1.25 1.25

The surtax was for the Red Cross.

Tree Type of 1967

Trees: 20p+3p, Juniper. 25+4p, Aspen. 40p+7p, Chokecherry.

1969, May 12 Litho. *Perf. 14*

B185 SP108 20p + 3p multi 1.25 1.25
B186 SP108 25p + 4p multi 1.25 1.25
B187 SP108 40p + 7p multi 1.25 1.25

Surtax for Anti-Tuberculosis Society.

"On the Lapp's Magic Rock" — SP110

Designs: 30p+6p, Juhani blowing horn on Impivaara Rock (vert.). 50+10p, The Pale Maiden. The designs are from illustrations by Askeli Gallen-Kallelas for "The Seven Brothers" by Aleksis Kivi.

1970, May 8 Litho. *Perf. 14*

B188 SP110 25p + 5p multi 1.00 1.00
B189 SP110 30p + 6p multi 1.00 1.00
B190 SP110 50p + 10p multi 1.00 1.00

The surtax was for the Red Cross.

Cutting and Loading Timber SP111

Designs: 30p+6p, Floating logs downstream. 50p+10p, Sorting logs at sawmill.

1971, Apr. 25 Litho. *Perf. 14*

B191 SP111 25p + 5p multi 1.00 1.00
B192 SP111 30p + 6p multi 1.00 1.00
B193 SP111 50p + 10p multi 1.00 1.00

Surtax for Anti-Tuberculosis Society.

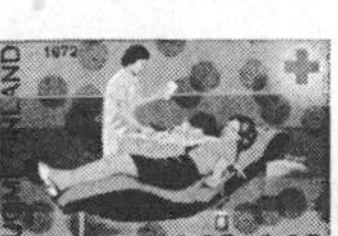

Blood Donor and Nurse — SP112

Designs: 30p+6p, Blood research (microscope, slides; vert.). 50p+10p, Blood transfusion.

1972, Oct. 23

B194 AP112 25p + 5p multi 1.00 1.00
B195 AP112 30p + 6p multi 1.00 1.00
B196 AP112 50p + 10p multi 1.00 1.00

Surtax was for the Red Cross.

Girl with Lamb, by Hugo Simberg — SP113

Paintings: 40p+10p, Summer Evening, by Vilho Sjöström. 60p+15p, Woman at Mountain Foun ain, by Juho Rissanen.

1973, Sept. 12 Litho. *Perf. 13x12½*

B197 SP113 30p + 5p multi 1.00 1.00
B198 SP113 40p + 10p multi 1.50 1.50
B199 SP113 60p + 15p multi 1.50 1.50

Surtax for the Finnish Anti-Tuberculosis Assoc. Birth centenaries of featured artists.

Morel SP114

Mushrooms: 50p+10p, Chanterelle. 60p+15p, Boletus edulis.

1974, Sept. 24 Litho. *Perf. 12½x13*

B200 SP114 35p + 5p multi 1.50 1.25
B201 SP114 50p + 10p multi 1.50 1.25
B202 SP114 60p + 15p multi 1.50 1.25

Finnish Red Cross.

Echo, by Ellen Thesleff (1869-1954) SP115

Paintings: 60p+15p, Hilda Wiik, by Maria Wiik (1853-1928). 70p+20p, At Home (old woman in chair), by Helene Schjerfbeck (1862-1946).

1975, Sept. 30 Litho. *Perf. 13x12½*

B203 SP115 40p + 10p multi 1.00 1.00
B204 SP115 60p + 15p multi 1.25 1.25
B205 SP115 70p + 20p multi 1.25 1.25

Finnish Red Cross. In honor of International Women's Year paintings by women artists were chosen.

Disabled Veterans' Emblem SP116

Lithographed and Photogravure

1976, Jan. 15 *Perf. 14*

B206 SP116 70p + 30p multi 2.00 1.40

The surtax was for hospitals for disabled war veterans.

Wedding Procession SP117

Designs: 70p+15p, Wedding dance (vert.). 80p+20p, Bride, groom, matron and pastor at wedding dinner.

1976, Sept. 15 Litho. *Perf. 13*

B207 SP117 50p + 10p multi 75 75
B208 SP117 70p + 15p multi 1.00 1.00
B209 SP117 80p + 20p multi 1.10 1.10

Surtax for Anti-Tuberculosis Society.

Aland stamps can be mounted in Scott's annual Scandinavia and Finland Supplement.

Disaster Relief — SP118

Designs: 80p+15p, Community work. 90p+20p, Blood transfusion service.

1977, Jan. 19 Litho. *Perf. 14*

B210 SP118 50p + 10p multi 75 75
B211 SP118 80p + 15p multi 1.10 1.10
B212 SP118 90p + 20p multi 1.10 1.10

Finnish Red Cross centenary.

Long-distance Skiing SP119

Design: 1m+50p, Ski jump.

1977, Oct. 5 Litho. *Perf. 13*

B213 SP119 80p + 40p multi 3.25 3.25
B214 SP119 1m + 50p multi 2.25 2.25

Surtax was for World Ski Championships, Lahti, Feb. 17-26, 1978.

Saffron Milkcap SP120

Edible Mushrooms: 80p+15p, Parasol mushrooms (vert.). 1m+20p, Gypsy mushrooms.

1978, Sept. 13 Litho. *Perf. 13*

B215 SP120 50p + 10p multi 75 75
B216 SP120 80p + 15p multi 1.10 1.10
B217 SP120 1m + 20p multi 1.10 1.10

Surtax was for Red Cross. See Nos. B221-B223.

Pehr Kalm, 1716-1779 SP121

Finnish Scientists: 90p + 15p, Title page of Pehr Adrian Gadd's (1727-1797) book (vert.). 1.10m+20p, Petter Forsskal (1732-1763).

Perf. 12½x13, 13x12½

1979, Sept. 26 Litho.

B218 SP121 60p + 10p multi 70 70
B219 SP121 90p + 15p multi 1.10 1.10
B220 SP121 1.10m + 20p multi 1.10 1.10

Surtax was for the Finnish Anti-Tuberculosis Association.

Mushroom Type of 1978

Edible Mushrooms: 60p+10p, Woolly milkcap. 90p+15p, Orange-cap boletus (vert.). 1.10m+20p, Russula paludosa.

1980, Apr. 19 Litho. *Perf. 13*

B221 SP120 60p + 10p multi 60 60
B222 SP120 90p + 15p multi 90 90
B223 SP120 1.10m + 20p multi 90 90

Surtax was for Red Cross.

Fuchsia — SP122

1981, Aug. 24 Litho. *Perf. 13*

B224 SP122 70p + 10p shown 45 45
B225 SP122 1m + 15p African violet 60 60
B226 SP122 1.10m + 20p Geranium 75 75

Surtax was for Red Cross.

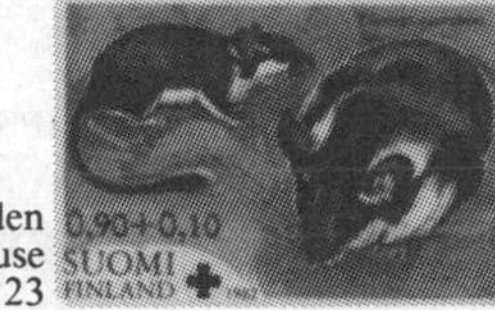

Garden Dormouse SP123

1982, Aug. 16 Litho. *Perf. 13*

B227 SP123 90p + 10p shown 50 50
B228 SP123 1.10m + 15p Flying squirrels 65 65
B229 SP123 1.20m + 20p European minks 70 70

Surtax was for Red Cross. No. B228 vert.

Forest and Wetland Plants SP124

Designs: 1m + 20p, Chickweed wintergreen. 1.20m + 25p, Marsh violet. 1.30m + 30p, Marsh marigold. Surtax was for Finnish Anti-Tuberculosis Assoc.

1983, July 7 Litho. *Perf. 13*

B230 SP124 1m + 20p multi 60 60
B231 SP124 1.20m + 25p multi 80 80
B232 SP124 1.30m + 30p multi 80 80

Globe Puzzle — SP125

Design: 2m + 40p, Symbolic world communication. Surtax was for Red Cross.

1984, May 28 Litho. *Perf. 13*

B233 SP125 1.40m + 35p multi 80 80
B234 SP125 2m + 40p multi 1.10 1.10

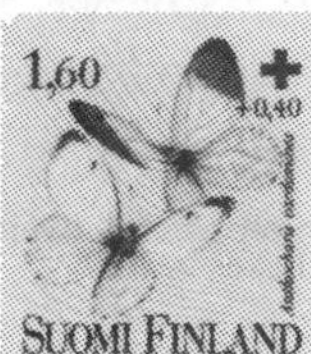

Butterflies SP126

1986, May 22 Litho. *Perf. 13*

B235 SP126 1.60m + 40p Anthocharis carda- mines 1.00 1.00
B236 SP126 2.10m + 45p Nymphalis antiopa 1.40 1.40
B237 SP126 5m + 50p Parnassius apollo 2.50 2.50

Surtax for Red Cross.

Festivals SP127

1988, Mar. 14 Litho. *Perf.*

B238 SP127 1.40m +40p Christmas 90 90
B239 SP127 1.80m +45p Easter 1.10 1.10
B240 SP127 2.40m +50p Midsummer 1.45 1.45

Surtax for the Red Cross.

AIR POST STAMPS

No. 178 Overprinted in Red

ZEPPELIN
1930

1930, Sept. 24 Unwmk. *Perf. 14*

C1 A28 10m gray lil 175.00 280.00
a. 1830 for 1930 2,750. 4,250.

Issued Sept. 24, 1930; overprinted expressly for use on mail carried in "Graf Zeppelin" on her return flight from Finland to Germany on Sept. 24, 1930, after which trip the stamps ceased to be valid for postage. Forgeries of Nos. C1 and C1a are almost always on No. 205, rather than No. 178.

Douglas DC-2 — AP1

1944 Engr.

C2 AP1 3.50m dk brn 70 *1.10*

Issued to commemorate the 20th anniversary of Air Transport Service, 1923-43.

Douglas DC-6 Over Winter Landscape — AP2

1950, Feb. 13

C3 AP2 300m blue 20.00 10.00

Available also for ordinary postage.

Type of 1950 Redrawn

1958, Jan. 20 *Perf. 11½*

C4 AP2 300 (m) bl 27.50 1.10

On No. C4 "mk" is omitted.

Convair 440 over Lakes — AP3

1958, Oct. 31 Unwmk. *Perf. 11½*

C5 AP3 34m blue 1.30 55

See Nos. C7-C8, C10.

No. C5 Surcharged with New Value and Bars

1959, Apr. 5

C6 AP3 45m on 34m bl 3.00 3.00

1959, Nov. 2

C7 AP3 45m blue 3.00 75

1963, Feb. 15

C8 AP3 45p blue 2.00 20

DC-6 Type, Comma After "3"

Type I- 16 lines in "0"

Type II- 13 lines in "0"

1963, Oct. 10

C9 AP2 3m bl, Type II ('73) 2.50 35
a. Type I

Convair Type of 1958

1970, July 15

C10 AP3 57p ultra 2.00 80

MILITARY STAMPS

Unwmk.

1941, Nov. 1 Typo. *Imperf.*

M1 M1 (4m) *dk org* 40 *80*

No. M1 has simulated roulette printed in black.

Type of 1930-46 Overprinted in Black

KENTTÄ-
POSTI
FÄLTPOST

1943, Oct. 16 *Perf. 14*

M2 A26 2m dp org 40 *60*
M3 A26 3½m grnsh bl 40 *60*

Post Horn and Sword — M2

1943

Size: 29½x19½mm.

M4 M2 (2m) green 30 *60*
M5 M2 (3m) rose vio 30 *60*

1944

Size: 20x16mm.

M6 M2 (2m) green 25 30
M7 M2 (3m) rose vio 25 30

Post Horns and Arms of Finland — M3

1963, Sept. 26 Litho. *Perf. 14*

M8 M3 vio bl *250.00 225.00*

Used during maneuvers Sept. 30-Oct. 5, 1963. Valid from Sept. 26.

No. M8 with overprint "1983" was issued in that year.

PARCEL POST STAMPS

PP1

Wmk. Rose & Triangles Multiple

Rouletted 6 on 2 or 3 Sides

1949-50 Typo.

Q1 PP1 1m brt grn & blk 2.00 4.50
Q2 PP1 5m red & blk 16.00 14.00
Q3 PP1 20m org & blk 30.00 22.50
Q4 PP1 50m bl & blk ('50) 11.00 11.00
Q5 PP1 100m brn & blk ('50) 12.50 11.00
Nos. Q1-Q5 (5) 71.50 63.00

Mail Bus — PP2

1952-58 Unwmk. Engr. *Perf. 14*

Q6 PP2 5m car rose 4.00 5.00
Q7 PP2 20m orange 10.00 7.00
Q8 PP2 50m bl ('54) 25.00 10.00
Q9 PP2 100m brn ('58) 30.00 15.00

Mail Bus — PP3

1963 *Perf. 12*

Q10 PP3 5p red & blk 3.00 3.00
Q11 PP3 20p org & blk 2.75 1.50
Q12 PP3 50p bl & blk 5.00 2.00
Q13 PP3 1m brn & blk 1.25 1.50

Nos. Q1-Q13 were issued only in booklets: panes of 6 for Nos. Q1-Q5, 10 for Nos. Q6-Q9 and 5 for Nos. Q10-Q13.

Used prices are for regular postal or mail-bus cancels. Pen strokes, cutting or other cancels sell for half as much.

1981 SISU Bus — PP4

Photo. & Engr.

1981, Dec. 7 *Perf. 12 Horiz.*

Q14 PP4 50p dk bl & blk 50 *3.00*
Q15 PP4 1m dk brn & blk 75 *3.00*
Q16 PP4 5m grn & blk 3.00 *6.50*
Q17 PP4 10m red & blk 6.00 *13.00*

Parcel post stamps invalid after Jan. 9, 1985.

ALAND ISLANDS

Gaff-rigged Sloop — A1

Aland Flag — A2

Midsummer Pole — A3

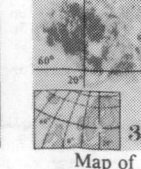

Landscapes A4

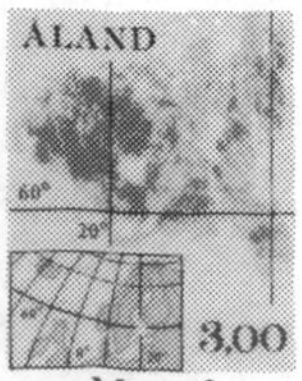

Map of Scandinavia A5

Seal of St. Olaf and Aland Province, 1326 — A6

Artifacts A7

Sea Birds — A8

Designs: 1.60m, Burial site, clay hands. 1.70m, Somateria mollissima. 2m, Grove. 2.20m, Bronze Staff of Finby, apostolic decoration. 2.30m, Aythya fuligula. 5m, Outer Aland Archipelago. 8m, Farm and windmill. 12m, Melantha fusca. 20m, Ancient court site, contemporary monument.

1984-87 Engr. *Perf. 12*

1 A1 10p mag ('85) 5 5
2 A1 20p brn ol 8 8
4 A1 50p brt grn 18 18
6 A1 1.10m dp bl 38 38
7 A1 1.20m blk ('85) 42 42
8 A1 1.30m ('86) 45 45

Litho. *Perf. 14*

10 A2 1.40m multi 48 48
11 A3 1.50m multi ('85) 52 52

Litho. *Perf. 13*

12 A7 1.60m multi, vert. ('86) 62 62
13 A8 1.70m multi ('87) 70 70
14 A4 2m multi ('85) 70 70
15 A7 2.20m multi, vert. ('86) 85 85
15A A8 2.30m multi ('87) 95 95
16 A5 3m multi 1.00 1.00
18 A4 5m multi, horiz. ('85) 1.75 1.75
20 A4 8m multi, horiz. ('85) 2.75 2.75

Litho. & Engr.

21 A6 10m multi 3.50 3.50

Litho.

21A A8 12m multi ('87) 5.00 5.00
22 A7 20m multi ('86) 7.75 7.75
Nos. 1-22 (19) 28.13 28.13

Issue dates: Nos. 1, 7, 11, Jan. 2. Nos. 2, 4, 6, 10, 16, 21, Mar. 1. No. 8, Jan. 2. Nos. 14, 18, 20, Sept. 16. Nos. 12, 15, 22, Apr. 4. Nos. 13, 15A, 21A, Jan. 2.

Bark Pommern and Car Ferries, Mariehamn West Harbor — A10

1984, Mar. 1 Litho. *Perf. 14*

23 A10 2m multi 3.00 3.00

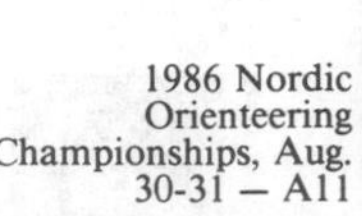

1986 Nordic Orienteering Championships, Aug. 30-31 — A11

1986, Jan. 2 Litho. *Perf. 14*

24 A11 1.60m multi 58 58

Onningeby Artists' Colony, Cent. — A12

Design: Pallette, pen and ink drawing of Onningeby landscape, 1891, by Victor Westerholm (1860-1919), founder.

1986, Sept. 1 **Litho.**

25	A12	3.70m multi	1.50	1.50

Mariehamn Volunteer Fire Brigade, Cent. A13

1987, Apr. 27 **Litho.** ***Perf. 14***

26	A13	7m ulti	3.25	3.25

Farjsund Bridge, 50th Anniv., Rebuilt in 1980 — A14

1987, Apr. 27 **Engr.** ***Perf. 13x13½***

27	A14	1m greenish blk	45	45

Municipal Meeting, Finstrom, 1917 A15

1987, Aug. 20 **Litho.** ***Perf. 14***

28	A15	1.70m multi	78	78

Movement for reunification with Sweden, 70th anniv.

Loading of Mail Barrels on Sailboat, Post Office, Eckero — A16

1988, Jan. 4 **Litho.** ***Perf. 14***

29	A16	1.80m multi	90	90

Postal Service, 350th anniv. From Feb. 1 to May 31, Alanders were entitled to buy 20 stamps for 28m with a discount coupon.

FIUME

LOCATION — A city and surrounding territory on the Adriatic Sea.
GOVT. — Formerly a part of Italy.
AREA — 8 sq. mi.
POP. — 44,956 (estimated 1924)

Formerly a port of Hungary, Fiume was claimed by Jugoslavia and Italy following World War I. During the discussion, the poet, Gabriele d'Annunzio, organized his legionnaires and seized Fiume, together with the islands of Arbe, Carnaro and Veglia, in the name of Italy. Jugoslavia recognized Italy's claim and the city was annexed in January, 1924.

100 Filler = 1 Korona
100 Centesimi = 1 Corona (1919)
100 Centesimi = 1 Lira

Hungarian Stamps of 1916-18 Overprinted **FIUME**

1918, Dec. 2 **Wmk. 137** ***Perf. 15***

On Stamps of 1916.

White Numerals.

1	A8	10f rose	25.00	7.50
2	A8	15f violet	12.00	5.00

Nos. 1-2 overprints are handstamped.

On Stamps of 1916-18.
Colored Numerals.

3	A9	2f brn org	35	20
4	A9	3f red vio	45	20
5	A9	5f green	45	20
6	A9	6f grnsh bl	45	20
7	A9	10f rose red	22.50	7.50
8	A9	15f violet	45	20
9	A9	20f gray brn	45	20
10	A9	25f dp bl	50	40
11	A9	35f brown	60	60
12	A9	40f ol grn	9.00	2.00

White Numerals

13	A10	50f red vio & lil	50	40
14	A10	75f brt bl & pale bl	1.75	60
15	A10	80f grn & pale grn	1.25	40
16	A10	1k red brn & cl	7.00	1.75
17	A10	2k ol brn & bis	60	40
18	A10	3k dk vio & ind	5.50	1.75
19	A10	5k dk brn & lt brn	8.50	3.50
20	A10	10k vio brn & vio	60.00	35.00

Inverted or double overprints exist on most of Nos. 4-15.

On Stamps of 1918.

21	A11	10f scarlet	50	25
22	A11	20f dk brn	50	25
23	A12	40f ol grn	2.00	1.00

The overprint on Nos. 3-23 was applied both by press and handstamp. Prices are for the less costly. Prices of Nos. 7, 12, 20 and 23 are for handstamps.
Forgeries of Nos. 1-23 abound.

A1

A2

Postage Due Stamps of Hungary, 1915-20 Overprinted and Surcharged in Black.

1919, Jan.

24	A1	45f on 6f grn & red	1.75	75
25	A1	45f on 20f grn & red	1.75	75

Hungarian Savings Bank Stamp Surcharged in Black.

1919, Jan. 29

26	A2	15f on 10f dk vio	1.75	75

"Italy" — A3

Italian Flag on Clock-Tower in Fiume — A4

"Revolution" A5

Sailor Raising Italian Flag at Fiume (1918) A6

1919 **Unwmk.** **Litho.** ***Perf. 11½***

27	A3	2c dl bl	20	30
28	A3	3c gray brn	20	30
29	A3	5c yel grn	20	30
30	A4	10c rose	20	30
31	A4	15c violet	20	30
32	A4	20c green	20	30
33	A5	25c dk bl	20	30
34	A6	30c dp vio	20	30
35	A5	40c brown	25	40
36	A5	45c orange	20	30
37	A6	50c yel grn	20	30
38	A6	60c claret	20	30
39	A6	1cor brn org	25	40
40	A6	2cor brt bl	30	45
41	A6	3cor org red	30	45
42	A6	5cor dp brn	30	45
43	A6	10cor ol grn	1.10	1.75
		Nos. 27-43 (17)	4.70	7.20

The earlier printings of January and February are on thin grayish paper and in sheets of 70. A March printing is on semi-transparent white paper, also in sheets of 70. An April printing is on white paper of medium thickness and in sheets of 100. Part-perforate examples of most of this series are known.

A7

A8

A9

A10

1919, July 28 ***Perf. 11½***

46	A7	5c yel grn	15	15
47	A8	10c rose	15	15
48	A9	30c violet	20	15
49	A10	40c yel brn	85	85
50	A10	45c orange	20	20
51	A9	50c yel grn	22	22
52	A9	60c claret	22	22
a.		Perf. 13x12½	30.00	30.00
53	A9	10cor ol grn	1.00	1.00
a.		Perf. 13x12½	30.00	30.00
b.		Perf. 10½	30.00	30.00
		Nos. 46-53 (8)	2.99	2.94

Five other denominations-25c, 1cor, 2cor, 3cor and 5cor-were not officially issued. Some copies of the 25c are known canceled.

Stamps of 1919 Handstamp Surcharged **FRANCO 5**

1919-20

58	A4	5c on 20c grn ('20)	15	20
59	A10	5c on 25c bl	15	20
60	A5	10c on 45c org	15	20
61	A9	15c on 30c vio ('20)	15	20
62	A10	15c on 45c org	15	20
63	A9	15c on 60c cl ('20)	15	30
64	A6	25c on 50c yel grn ('20)	1.00	1.10
65	A9	25c on 50c yel grn ('20)	25	30
66	A6	55c on 1cor brn org	1.00	1.10
67	A6	55c on 2cor brt bl	1.00	1.10
68	A6	55c on 3cor org red	1.00	1.10
69	A6	55c on 5cor dp brn	1.00	1.10
70	A9	55c on 10cor ol grn	1.35	1.25
		Nos. 58-70 (13)	7.50	8.35

Semi-Postal Stamps of 1919 Surcharged:

Valore globale Cent. 5
a

Valore globale Cent. 45
b

1919-20

73	SP6(a)	5c on 5c grn	15	15
74	SP6(a)	10c on 10c rose	15	15
75	SP6(a)	15c on 15c gray	15	15
76	SP6(a)	20c on 20c org	20	20
77	SP9(a)	25c on 25c bl ('20)	25	25
78	SP7(b)	45c on 45c ol grn	25	25
79	SP7(b)	60c on 60c rose	25	25
80	SP7(b)	80c on 80c vio	30	30
81	SP7(b)	1cor on 1cor sl	30	30
82	SP8(a)	2cor on 2cor red brn	40	40
83	SP8(a)	3cor on 3cor blk brn	85	85
84	SP8(a)	5cor on 5cor yel brn	1.00	1.00
85	SP8(a)	10cor on 10cor dk vio ('20)	50	50
		Nos. 73-85 (13)	4.75	4.75

Double or inverted surcharges, or imperf. varieties, exist on most of Nos. 73-85.
There were three settings of the surcharges on Nos. 73-85 except No. 77 which is known only with one setting.

Gabriele d'Annunzio A11

Severing the Gordian Knot A12

1920, Sept. 12 **Typo.** ***Perf. 11½***

Pale Buff Background.

86	A11	5c green	20	20
87	A11	10c carmine	20	20
88	A11	15c dk gray	30	30
89	A11	20c orange	30	30
90	A11	25c dk bl	50	50
91	A11	30c red brn	50	50
92	A11	45c ol gray	75	75
93	A11	50c lilac	75	75
94	A11	55c bister	75	75
95	A11	1 l black	1.20	1.20
96	A11	2 l red vio	2.50	2.50
97	A11	3 l dk grn	2.50	2.50
98	A11	5 l brown	2.50	2.50
99	A11	10 l gray vio	3.00	3.00
		Nos. 86-99 (14)	15.95	15.95

Counterfeits of Nos. 86 to 99 are plentiful.

1920, Sept. 12

Designs: 10c, Ancient emblem of Fiume. 20c Head of "Fiume." 25c, Hands holding daggers.

100	A12	5c green	7.50	7.50
101	A12	10c dp rose	1.50	1.50
102	A12	20c brn org	2.00	1.50
103	A12	25c dk bl	15.00	11.00

These stamps were issued to mark the anniversary of the occupation of Fiume by d'Annunzio. They were available for franking the correspondence of the legionnaires on the day of issue only, Sept. 12, 1920.
Counterfeits of Nos. 100 to 103 are plentiful.

Commemorative Stamps of 1920 Overprinted in Black or Red and New Values **Reggenza Italiana del Carnaro**

1920, Nov. 20

104	A12	1c on 5c grn	20	20
105	A12	2c on 25c bl (R)	20	20
106	A12	5c green	20	20
107	A12	10c rose	30	30
108	A12	15c on 10c rose	30	30
109	A12	15c on 20c brn org	30	30
110	A12	15c on 25c bl (R)	40	40
111	A12	20c brn org	40	40
112	A12	25c bl (R)	40	40
113	A12	25c bl (Bk)	40.00	32.50
114	A12	25c on 10c rose	1.35	1.35
115	A12	50c on 20c brn org	50	50
116	A12	55c on 5c grn	50	50
117	A12	1 l on 10c rose	2.00	2.00
118	A12	1 l on 25c bl (R)	150.00	90.00
119	A12	2 l on 5c grn	4.00	4.00
120	A12	5 l on 10c rose	25.00	13.00
121	A12	10 l on 20c brn org	90.00	32.50
		Nos. 104-121 (18)	316.05	179.05

The Fiume Legionnaires of d'Annunzio occupied the islands of Arbe and Veglia in the Gulf of Carnaro from Nov. 13, 1920, until Jan. 5, 1921.
Varieties of overprint or surcharge exist for most of Nos. 104-121.

Same Overprinted at top with **ARBE**

1920, Nov. 18

122	A12	5c green	1.25	1.00
123	A12	10c rose	1.50	1.25

124 A12 20c brn org 2.00 1.50
125 A12 25c dp bl 8.00 5.00
126 A12 50c on 20c brn org 2.75 1.75
127 A12 55c on 5c grn 2.75 1.75
Nos. 122-127 (6) 18.25 12.25

The overprint on Nos. 122-125 comes in two widths: 11mm. and 14mm. Prices are for the 11mm. width.

Same Overprinted at top with **VEGLIA**

1920, Nov. 18
128 A12 5c green 1.25 1.00
129 A12 10c rose 1.50 1.25
130 A12 20c brn org 2.00 1.50
131 A12 25c dp bl 8.00 5.00
132 A12 50c on 20c brn org 2.75 1.75
133 A12 55c on 5c grn 2.75 1.75
Nos. 128-133 (6) 18.25 12.25

The overprint on Nos. 128-131 comes in two widths: 17mm. and 19mm. Prices are for the 17mm. width.

Nos. 122-133 exist with double and inverted overprints.

Counterfeits of these overprints exist.

Stamps of 1920 Overprinted **Governo Provvisorio**

1921, Feb. 2
Pale Buff Background.
134 A11 5c green 20 20
135 A11 10c carmine 20 20
136 A11 15c dk gray 30 30
137 A11 20c orange 30 30
138 A11 25c dk bl 40 40
139 A11 30c red brn 40 40
140 A11 45c ol gray 50 50
141 A11 50c lilac 50 50
142 A11 55c bister 50 50
143 A11 1 l black 20.00 22.50
144 A11 2 l red vio 1.00 75
145 A11 3 l dk grn 1.50 1.50
146 A11 5 l brown 2.00 75
147 A11 10 l gray vio 2.25 2.00

With Additional Surcharge **LIRE UNA**

148 A11 1 l on 30c red brn 50 30
Nos. 134-148 (15) 30.55 31.10

Most of Nos. 134-143, 148 and E10-E11 exist with inverted or double overprint.

See Nos. E10-E11.

First Constituent Assembly.

Semi-Postal Stamps of 1919 Overprinted

1921, Apr. 24
149 SP6 5c bl grn 40 25
150 SP6 10c rose 30 25
151 SP6 15c gray 30 25
152 SP6 20c orange 30 25
153 SP7 45c ol grn 50 35
154 SP7 60c car rose 60 50
155 SP7 80c brt vio 75 60

With Additional Overprint "L".
156 SP7 1 l on 1cor dk sl 1.00 85
157 SP8 2 l on 2cor red brn 3.00 50
158 SP8 3 l on 3cor blk brn 5.00 6.00
159 SP8 5 l on 5cor yel brn 9.00 50
160 SP8 10 l on 10cor dk vio 9.00 10.00
Nos. 149-160 (12) 30.15 20.30

The overprint exists inverted on several denominations.

Second Constituent Assembly.
"Constitution" Issue of 1921 With Additional Overprint "1922".

1922
161 SP6 5c bl grn 1.50 40
162 SP6 10c rose 15 20
163 SP6 15c gray 3.00 60
164 SP6 20c orange 15 20
165 SP7 45c ol grn 20 25
166 SP7 60c car rose 20 25
167 SP7 80c brt vio 20 25
168 SP7 1 l on 1cor dk sl 20 25
169 SP8 2 l on 2cor red brn 20 35
170 SP8 3 l on 3cor blk brn 25 50
171 SP8 5 l on 5cor yel brn 30 75
Nos. 161-171 (11) 6.35 4.00

Nos. 161-171 have the overprint in heavier type than Nos. 149-160 and "IV" in Roman instead of sans-serif numerals.

The overprint exists inverted or double on almost all values.

Venetian Ship — A16

Roman Arch — A17

St. Vitus A18

Rostral Column A19

1923, Mar. 23 *Perf. 11½*
Pale Buff Background.
172 A16 5c bl grn 20 20
173 A16 10c violet 20 20
174 A16 15c brown 20 20
175 A17 20c org red 20 20
176 A17 25c dk gray 20 20
177 A17 30c dk grn 20 20
178 A18 50c dl bl 20 20
179 A18 60c rose 30 30
180 A18 1 l dk bl 30 30
181 A19 2 l vio brn 1.50 1.00
182 A19 3 l ol bis 8.00 6.00
183 A19 5 l yel brn 3.50 3.00
Nos. 172-183 (12) 15.00 12.00

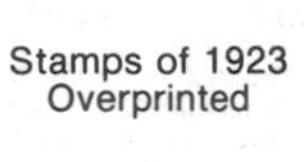
Stamps of 1923 Overprinted

1924, Feb. 22
Pale Buff Background.
184 A16 5c bl grn 15 30
185 A16 10c violet 15 30
186 A16 15c brown 15 30
187 A17 20c org red 15 30
188 A17 25c dk gray 15 30
189 A17 30c dk grn 15 30
190 A18 50c dl bl 15 30
191 A18 60c red 15 30
192 A18 1 l dk bl 15 30
193 A19 2 l vio brn 50 1.00
194 A19 3 l olive 1.75 3.50
195 A19 5 l yel brn 1.75 3.50
Nos. 184-195 (12) 5.35 10.70

The overprint exists inverted on almost all values.

Stamps of 1923 Overprinted

22 Febb. 1924

1924, Mar. 1
Pale Buff Background.
196 A16 5c bl grn 15 30
197 A16 10c violet 15 30
198 A16 15c brown 15 30
199 A17 20c org red 15 30
200 A17 25c dk gray 15 30
201 A17 30c dk grn 15 30
202 A18 50c dl bl 15 30
203 A18 60c red 15 30
204 A18 1 l dk bl 15 30
205 A19 2 l vio brn 75 1.50
206 A19 3 l olive 75 1.50
207 A19 5 l yel brn 75 1.50
Nos. 196-207 (12) 3.60 7.20

Postage stamps of Fiume were superseded by stamps of Italy.

SEMI-POSTAL STAMPS

Semi-Postal Stamps of Hungary, 1916-17. Overprinted **FIUME**

Wmk. Double Cross. (137)
1918, Dec. 2 *Perf. 15*
B1 SP3 10f + 2f rose 85 30
a. Inverted overprint 25.00 7.50
B2 SP4 15f + 2f dl vio 90 30
a. Inverted overprint 25.00 6.00
B3 SP5 40f + 2f brn car 1.25 90
a. Inverted overprint 25.00 6.00

Examples of Nos. B1-B3 with overprint hand-stamped sell for higher prices.

Statue of Romulus and Remus Being Suckled by Wolf — SP6

Venetian Galley — SP7

Church of St. Mark's, Venice — SP8

Perf. 11½
1919, May 18 **Unwmk.** **Typo.**
B4 SP6 5c + 5 l bl grn 1.35 1.40
B5 SP6 10c + 5 l rose 1.35 1.40
B6 SP6 15c + 5l dk gray 1.35 1.40
B7 SP6 20c + 5 l org 1.35 1.40
B8 SP7 45c + 5 l ol grn 1.35 1.40
B9 SP7 60c + 5 l car rose 1.35 1.40
B10 SP7 80c + 5 l brt vio 1.35 1.40
B11 SP7 1cor + 5 l dk sl 1.35 1.40
B12 SP8 2cor + 5 l red brn 1.35 1.40
B13 SP8 3cor + 5 l blk brn 1.35 1.40
B14 SP8 5cor + 5 l yel brn 1.35 1.40
B15 SP8 10cor + 5 l dk vio 1.35 1.40
Nos. B4-B15 (12) 16.20 16.80

Nos. B4 to B15 were issued in commemoration of the 200th day of peace. The surtax aided Fiume students in Italy. "Posta di Fiume" is printed on the back of Nos. B4-B16.

Dr. Antonio Grossich — SP9

1919, Sept. 20
B16 SP9 25c + 2 l bl 15 15

The surtax benefited the Dr. Grossich Foundation.

SPECIAL DELIVERY STAMPS

Special Delivery Stamp of Hungary, 1916, Overprinted **FIUME**

1918, Dec. 2 **Wmk. 137** *Perf. 15*
E1 SD1 2f gray grn & red 40 25

No. E1 with overprint handstamped sells for more.

SD3

Perf. 11½
1920, Sept. 12 **Unwmk.** **Typo.**
E2 SD3 30c sl bl 1.00 1.00
E3 SD3 50c rose 1.00 1.00

Nos. 102 and 100 Surcharged **Reggenza Italiana del Carnaro 50 50 ESPRESSO**

1920, Nov.
E4 A12 30c on 20c brn org 30.00 20.00
E5 A12 50c on 5c grn 10.00 5.00

Same Surcharge on Nos. 124, 122
E6 A12 30c on 20c brn org 35.00 17.50
E7 A12 50c on 5c grn 10.00 11.50

Overprint on Nos. E6-E7 is 11mm. wide.

Same Surcharge on Nos. 130, 128
E8 A12 30c on 20c brn org 35.00 17.50
E9 A12 50c on 5c grn 10.00 11.50

Overprint on Nos. E8-E9 is 17mm. wide.

Nos. E2 and E3 Overprinted

Governo Provvisorio

1921, Feb. 2
E10 SD3 30c sl bl 1.00 1.00
E11 SD3 50c rose 1.00 1.00

Fiume in 16th Century SD4

1923, Mar. 23 *Perf. 11, 11½*
E12 SD4 60c rose & buff 50 50
E13 SD4 2 l dk bl & buff 50 50

Stamps of 1923 Overprinted

1924, Feb. 22
E14 SD4 60c car & buff 50 1.00
E15 SD4 2 l dk bl & buff 50 1.00

Stamps of 1923 Overprinted

1924, Mar. 1
E16 SD4 60c car & buff 50 1.00
E17 SD4 2 l dk bl & buff 50 1.10

POSTAGE DUE STAMPS

Postage Due Stamps of Hungary, 1915-1916, Overprinted FIUME

1918, Dec. **Wmk. 137** ***Perf. 15***

J1	D1	6f grn & blk	70.00	22.50
J2	D1	12f grn & blk	55.00	22.50
J3	D1	50f grn & blk	30.00	11.50
J4	D1	1f grn & red	9.00	5.50
J5	D1	2f grn & red	30	20
J6	D1	5f grn & red	4.00	1.50
J7	D1	6f grn & red	30	20
J8	D1	10f grn & red	5.00	2.00
J9	D1	12f grn & red	30	20
J10	D1	15f grn & red	7.50	5.00
J11	D1	20f grn & red	30	20
J12	D1	30f grn & red	6.00	4.00

The overprint on Nos. J1-J12 was applied both by press and handstamp. Prices are for the less costly. Inverted and double overprints exist. Excellent forgeries exist.

Eagle — D2

Perf. 11½

1919, July 28 **Unwmk.** **Typo.**

J13	D2	2c brown	15	15
J14	D2	5c brown	15	15

Semi-Postal Stamps of 1919 with Overprint "Valore Globale" Surcharged:

a

L. 0.02

1921, Mar. 21

J15	SP6	2c on 15c gray	25	30
J16	SP6	4c on 10c rose	15	20
J17	SP9	5c on 25c bl	15	20
J18	SP6	6c on 20c org	15	20
J19	SP6	10c on 20c org	40	50

Surcharged:

b

L. 0.20

J20	SP7	20c on 45c ol grn	30	40
J21	SP7	30c on 1cor dk sl	30	45
J22	SP7	40c on 80c vio	20	30
J23	SP7	50c on 60c car	25	40
J24	SP7	60c on 45c ol grn	30	40
J25	SP7	80c on 45c ol grn	30	45

Surcharged type "a."

J26	SP8	1 l on 2cor red brn	50	75
		Nos. J15-J26 (12)	3.25	4.55

See note below No. 85 regarding settings of "Valore Globale" overprint.

NEWSPAPER STAMPS

Newspaper Stamp of Hungary, 1914, Overprinted FIUME

1918, Dec. 2 **Wmk. 137** ***Imperf.***

P1	N5	(2f) orange	45	30

No. P1 with overprint handstamped sells for more.

Eagle — N1

1919 **Unwmk.** ***Perf. 11½***

P2	N1	2c dp buff	45	75

Re-engraved

P3	N1	2c dp buff	75	1.40

In the re-engraved stamp the top of the "2" is rounder and broader, the feet of the eagle show clearly and the diamond at bottom has six lines instead of five.

Steamer N2

1920, Sept. 12

P4	N2	1c gray grn	22	38

No. P4 exists imperf.

See note on FIUME-KUPA Zone, Italian Occupation, after Jugoslavia No. NJ22.

FRANCE

LOCATION — Western Europe
GOVT. — Republic
AREA — 210,033 sq. mi.
POP. — 54,539,000 (est. 1984)
CAPITAL — Paris

100 Centimes = 1 Franc

> Prices of early French stamps vary according to condition. Quotations for Nos. 1-48 are for fine copies. Very fine to superb specimens sell at much higher prices, and inferior or poor copies sell at reduced prices, depending on the condition of the individual specimen.

Ceres — A1

FORTY CENTIMES.

Type I 4

Type II 4

1849-50 Unwmk. Typo. *Imperf.*

No.			Unused	Used
1	A1	10c bis, *yelsh* ('50)	1,400.	350.00
a.		10c dk bis, *yelsh*	1,650.	400.00
b.		10c grnsh bis	2,750.	550.00
c.		Tete beche pair	*57,500.*	*12,000.*
2	A1	15c yel grn, *grnsh* ('50)	*12,000.*	1,250.
a.		15c grn, *grnsh*	*13,500.*	1,350.
b.		Tete beche pair		*135,000.*
3	A1	20c blk, *yelsh*	275.00	52.50
a.		20c blk	500.00	60.00
b.		20c blk, *buff*	1,650.	375.00
c.		Tete beche pair	*6,000.*	*6,000.*
4	A1	20c dk bl	*1,500.*	
a.		20c bl, *bluish*	*1,650.*	
b.		20c bl, *yelsh*	*2,000.*	
c.		Tete beche pair	*30,000.*	
6	A1	25c lt bl, *bluish*	*3,750.*	37.50
a.		25c bl, *bluish* ('50)	*4,500.*	50.00
b.		25c bl, *yelsh*	*3,750.*	52.50
c.		Tete beche pair	*100,000.*	*9,000.*
7	A1	40c org, *yelsh* (I)('50)	*2,250.*	525.00
a.		40c org ver, *yelsh* (I)	2,750.	675.00
b.		40c org, *yelsh* (II)	*15,000.*	*3,750.*
c.		Pair, types I and II	*22,500.*	*8,000.*
8	A1	1fr dl org red	*30,000.*	*13,500.*
a.		1fr ver, *yelsh*	*55,000.*	*20,000.*
b.		Tete beche pair	*225,000.*	*165,000.*
c.		1fr pale ver ("Vervelle")	*18,000.*	
9	A1	1fr dk car, *yelsh*	*6,750.*	900.00
a.		Tete beche pair	*100,000.*	*21,000.*
b.		1fr brn car	*9,000.*	1,350.
c.		1fr lt car	*7,000.*	1,000.

No. 4, which lacks gum, was not issued due to a rate change to 25c after the stamps were prepared.

An ungummed sheet of No. 8c was found in 1895 among the effects of Anatole A. Hulot, the printer. It was sold to Ernest Vervelle, a Parisian dealer, by whose name the stamps are known.

Nos. 1, 4, 6, 7 and 13 are of similar designs and colors to French Colonies Nos. 9, 11, 12, 14, and 8. There are numerous shades of each. They can seldom be correctly allocated except by the cancellations.

See Nos. 329-329e, 612-613, 624.

1862 Re-issue

No.			Price
1d	A1	10c bister	250.00
2d	A1	15c yel grn	350.00
3d	A1	20c blk, *yelsh*	225.00
4d	A1	20c blue	225.00
6d	A1	25c blue	225.00
7d	A1	40c org (I)	350.00
7e	A1	40c org (II)	*10,000.*
9d	A1	1fr pale lake	375.00

The re-issues are in lighter colors and on whiter paper than the originals. An official imitation of the essay, 25c on 20c blue, was made at the same time as the re-issues.

President Louis Napoleon — A2

Emperor Napoleon III — A3

1852

No.			Unused	Used
10	A2	10c pale bis, *yelsh*	*22,500.*	600.00
a.		10c dk bis, *yelsh*	*25,000.*	675.00
11	A2	25c bl, *bluish*	*2,500.*	52.50

1862 Re-issue

No.			Price
10b	A2	10c bister	300.00
11a	A2	25c blue	240.00

The re-issues are in lighter colors and on whiter paper than the originals.

1853-60 *Imperf.*

Die I. The curl above the forehead directly below "R" of "EMPIRE" is made up of two lines very close together, often appearing to form a single thick line. There is no shading across the neck.

Die II. The curl is made of two distinct, more widely separated lines. There are lines of shading across the upper neck.

No.			Unused	Used
12	A3	1c ol grn, *pale bl* (II) ('60)	140.00	70.00
a.		1c brnz grn, *pale bluish*	165.00	80.00
13	A3	5c grn, *grnsh* (I) ('54)	600.00	70.00
14	A3	10c bis, *yelsh* (I)	300.00	8.25
a.		10c yel, *yelsh* (I)	1,800.	82.50
b.		10c bis brn, *yelsh* (I)	450.00	25.00
c.		10c bis, *yelsh* (II) ('60)	450.00	30.00
15	A3	20c bl, *bluish* (I) ('54)	165.00	1.00
a.		20c dk bl, *bluish* (I)	250.00	1.65
b.		20c mlky bl (I)	275.00	15.00
c.		20c bl, *lil* (I)	*3,500.*	90.00
d.		20c bl, *bluish* (II) ('60)	375.00	5.25
e.		As "d," tete beche pair	*100,000.*	
16	A3	20c bl, *grnsh* (I)	*4,000.*	180.00
a.		20c bl, *grnsh* (II)	*4,000.*	225.00
17	A3	25c bl, *bluish* (I)	1,900.	275.00
18	A3	40c org, *yelsh* (I)	1,900.	13.50
a.		40c org ver, *yelsh*	2,000.	22.50
19	A3	80c lake, *yelsh* (I) ('54)	1,500.	52.50
a.		Tete beche pair	*165,000.*	*11,000.*
20	A3	80c rose *pnksh* (I) ('60)	1,350.	57.50
a.		Tete beche pair	*30,000.*	*8,000.*
21	A3	1fr lake, *yelsh* (I)	*4,000.*	*3,000.*
a.		Tete beche pair	*180,000.*	*85,000.*

Most values of the 1853-60 issue are known unofficially rouletted, pin-perf., perf. 7 and percé en scie.

1862 Re-issue

No.			Price
17c	A3	25c bl (I)	250.00
20c	A3	80c rose (I)	1,350.
21c	A3	1fr lake (I)	1,100.
d.		Tete beche pair	*13,500.*

The re-issues are in lighter colors and on whiter paper than the originals.

1862-71 *Perf. 14x13½*

No.			Unused	Used
22	A3	1c ol grn, *pale bl* (II)	100.00	40.00
a.		1c brnz grn, *pale bl* (II)	100.00	42.50
23	A3	5c yel grn, *grnsh*(I)	150.00	9.00
a.		dp grn, *grnsh* (I)	185.00	12.50
24	A3	5c grn, *pale bl* ('71) (I)	900.00	75.00
25	A3	10c bis, *yelsh* (II)	900.00	4.00
a.		10c yel brn, *yelsh* (II)	1,000.	5.00
26	A3	20c bl, *bluish* (II)	160.00.	75
a.		Tete beche pair (II)	3,250.	1,000.
27	A3	40c org, *yelsh* (I)	1,000.	6.50
28	A3	80c rose, *pnksh* (I)	850.00	42.50
a.		80c brt rose, *pnksh* (I)	1,000.	65.00
b.		Tete beche pair (I)	*11,000.*	*4,250.*

Napoleon III
A4 A5

Napoleon III — A6

1863-70 *Perf. 14x13½*

No.			Unused	Used
29	A4	1c brnz grn, *pale bl* ('70)	21.00	12.50
a.		1c ol grn, *pale bl*	24.00	15.00
b.		Imperf.	1,000.	
30	A4	2c red brn, *yelsh*	57.50	27.50
a.		Imperf.	185.00	
31	A4	4c gray	135.00	52.50
a.		Tete beche pair	*10,000.*	*7,500.*
b.		Imperf.	150.00	
32	A5	10c bis, *yelsh* ('67)	225.00	5.00
a.		Imperf.	150.00	
33	A5	20c bl, *bluish* ('67)	165.00	1.25
a.		Imperf.	225.00	
34	A5	30c brn, *yelsh* ('67)	575.00	18.00
a.		30c dk brn, *yelsh*	825.00	37.50
c.		Imperf.	150.00	
35	A5	40c org, *yelsh* ('68)	650.00	11.00
a.		40c pale org, *yelsh*	675.00	13.00
b.		Imperf.	200.00	
36	A5	80c rose, *pnksh* ('68)	600.00	20.00
a.		80c car, *yelsh*	775.00	32.50
b.		Imperf.	350.00	
37	A6	5fr gray lil, *lav* ('69)	*5,000*	850.00
a.		"5" and "F" omitted		*45,000.*
b.		Imperf.	*7,500.*	

No. 33 exists in two types, differing in the size of the dots at either side of POSTES.

On No. 37, the "5" and "F" vary in height from 3¾mm. to 4½mm. All known copies of No. 37a are more or less damaged.

The imperforate varieties of Nos. 29-36 constitute the "Rothschild Issue," said to have been authorized exclusively for the banker to use on his correspondence. Used copies exist.

No. 29 was reprinted in 1887 by authority of Granet, Minister of Posts. The reprints show a yellowish shade under the ultraviolet lamp. Price $850.

Ceres
A7 A8

Type I — A9

Type II — A10

Type III — A11

Bordeaux Issue

On the lithographed stamps, except for type I of the 20c, the shading on the cheek and neck is in lines or dashes, not in dots. On the typographed stamps the shading is in dots. The 2c, 10c and 20c (types II and III) occur in two or more types. The most easily distinguishable are:

2c--Type A. To the left of and within the top of the left "2" are lines of shading composed of dots.

2c--Type B. These lines of dots are replaced by solid lines.

10c--Type A. The inner frame lines are of the same thickness as all other frame lines.

10c--Type B. The inner frame lines are much thicker than the others.

Three Types of the 20c.

A9--Type I. The inscriptions in the upper and lower labels are small and there is quite a space between the upper label and the circle containing the head. There is also very little shading under the eye and in the neck.

A10--Type II. The inscriptions in the labels are similar to those of the first type, the shading under the eye and in the neck is heavier and the upper label and circle almost touch.

A11--Type III. The inscriptions in the labels are much larger than those of the two preceding types, and are similar to those of the other values of the same type in the set.

1870-71 Litho. *Imperf.*

No.			Unused	Used
38	A7	1c ol grn, *pale bl*	60.00	90.00
a.		1c brnz grn, *pale bl*	120.00	125.00

39 A7 2c red brn, *yelsh* (B) 175.00 240.00
a. 2c brick red, *yelsh* (B) 1,000. 850.00
b. 2c mar, *yelsh* (B) 1,350. 900.00
c. 2c choc, *yelsh* (A) 900.00 875.00
40 A7 4c gray 250.00 250.00
41 A8 5c grn, *grnsh* 250.00 150.00
a. 5c yel grn, *grnsh* 225.00 165.00
b. 5c emer, *grnsh* 2,500. 1,000.
42 A8 10c bis, *yelsh* (A) 700.00 75.00
a. 10c bis, *yelsh* (B) 825.00 87.50
43 A9 20c bl, *bluish*(I) *10,000.* 675.00
a. 20c dk bl, *bluish*(I) *11,000.* 850.00
44 A10 20c bl, *bluish* (II) 850.00 57.50
a. 20c dk bl, *bluish* (II) 1,150. 85.00
b. 20c ultra, *bluish* (II) *16,500.* *3,000.*
45 A11 20c bl, *bluish* (III) ('71) 850.00 18.00
a. 20c ultra, *bluish* (III) 2,250. 675.00
46 A8 30c brn, *yelsh* 375.00 200.00
a. 30c blk brn, *yelsh* 1,500. 825.00
47 A8 40c org, *yelsh* 400.00 125.00
a. 40c yel org, *yelsh* 400.00 125.00
b. 40c red org, *yelsh* 600.00 180.00
c. 40c scar, *yelsh* *5,250.* *1,900.*
48 A8 80c rose, *pnksh* 575.00 275.00
a. 80c dl rose, *pnksh* 625.00 275.00

All values of the 1870 issue are known rouletted, pin-perf. and perf. 14, unofficially.

A12

Blue Surcharge

1871 Typo. *Perf. 14x13½*
49 A12 10(c) on 10c bis 1,500.

No. 49 was never placed in use. Counterfeits exist.

Ceres
A13 A14

Two types of the 40c as in the 1849-50 issue.

1870-73 Typo. *Perf. 14x13½*
50 A7 1c ol grn, *pale bl* 30.00 12.00
a. 1c brnz grn, *pale bl* ('72) 37.50 12.50
51 A7 2c red brn, *yelsh* ('72) 67.50 12.00
52 A7 4c gray ('72) 300.00 37.50
53 A7 5c yel grn,*pale bl*('72) 120.00 7.50
a. 5c grn 125.00 9.00
54 A13 10c bis, *yelsh* 400.00 50.00
a. Tete beche pair *4,000.* 2,000.
55 A13 10c bis, *rose*('73) 300.00 8.75
a. Tete beche pair 3,000. 1,500.
56 A13 15c bis, *yelsh* ('71) 300.00 3.75
a. Tete beche pair *27,500.* *7,000.*
57 A13 20c dl bl, *bluish* 225.00 6.00
a. 20c brt bl, *bluish* 240.00 9.00
b. Tete beche pair 2,750. 1,350.
58 A13 25c bl, *bluish* ('71) 95.00 90
a. 25c dk bl, *bluish* 100.00 1.00
b. Tete beche pair *5,000.* *2,500.*
59 A13 40c org, *yelsh* (I) 450.00 4.50
a. 40c org yel, *yelsh* (I) 575.00 6.00
b. 40c org, *yelsh* (II) 2,250. 150.00
c. 40c org yel, *yelsh* (II) 2,250. 150.00
d. Pair, types I and II *4,000.* 500.00

No. 58 exists in three main plate varieties, differing in one or another of the flower-like corner ornaments.

Nos. 54, 57 and 58 were reprinted imperf. in 1887. See note after No. 37.

1872-75

Larger Numerals
60 A14 10c bis, *rose* ('75) 250.00 8.75
a. Cliche of 15c in plate of 10c *3,250.* *3,750.*
b. As "a," se-tenant with #60 *4,500.* *4,750.*
61 A14 15c bis ('73) 250.00 4.50
62 A14 30c brn, *yelsh* 475.00 6.00
63 A14 80c rose, *pnksh* 550.00 12.50

Peace and Commerce ("Type Sage") — A15

Type I. The "N" of "INV" is under the "B" of "REPUBLIQUE".
Type II. The "N" of "INV" is under the "U" of "REPUBLIQUE".

1876-78

Type I
64 A15 1c grn, *grnsh* 115.00 52.50
a. Imperf. 165.00
65 A15 2c grn, *grnsh* 1,150. 275.00
a. Imperf. 1,100.
66 A15 4c grn, *grnsh* 100.00 45.00
a. Imperf. 165.00
67 A15 5c grn, *grnsh* 475.00 45.00
a. Imperf. 525.00
68 A15 10c grn, *grnsh* 625.00 25.00
a. Imperf. 600.00
69 A15 15c gray lil, *grysh* 575.00 18.00
a. Imperf. 600.00
70 A15 20c red brn, *straw* 425.00 17.00
a. Imperf. 400.00
71 A15 20c bl, *bluish* *13,500.*
72 A15 25c ultra, *bluish* *5,250.* 52.50
73 A15 30c brn, *yelsh* 300.00 8.25
a. Imperf. 275.00
74 A15 40c red, *straw* ('78) 300.00 30.00
a. Imperf. 275.00
75 A15 75c car, *rose* 450.00 11.00
a. Imperf. 400.00
76 A15 1fr brnz grn, *straw* 525.00 10.00
a. Imperf. 450.00

No. 71 was never put into use.

The reprints of No. 71 are of the second type. They are imperforate or with forged perforation.

1876-77

Type II
77 A15 2c grn, *grnsh* 82.50 19.00
78 A15 5c grn, *grnsh* 18.50 30
a. Imperf. 185.00
79 A15 10c grn, *grnsh* 850.00 250.00
80 A15 15c gray lil, *grysh* 450.00 1.25
81 A15 25c ultra, *bluish* 350.00 30
a. 25c bl, *bluish* 375.00 50
b. Pair, types I & II *32,500.* *10,000.*
c. Imperf. 350.00
82 A15 30c yel brn, *yelsh* 32.50 65
a. 30c brn, *yelsh* 37.50 75
b. Imperf. 525.00
83 A15 75c car, *rose* ('77) 1,800. 85.00
84 A15 1fr brnz grn, *straw* ('77) 65.00 5.25
a. Imperf. 525.00

1877-80
86 A15 1c *lil bl* 2.25 60
a. 1c *gray bl* 2.50 65
b. Imperf. 67.50
87 A15 1c *Prus bl* ('80) *9,000.* *4,000.*
88 A15 2c brn, *straw* 3.25 75
a. 2c brn, *yel* 4.50 1.50
b. Imperf. 67.50
89 A15 3c yel, *straw* ('78) 190.00 45.00
a. Imperf. 120.00
90 A15 4c cl, *lav* 3.25 1.65
a. 4c vio brn, *lav* 5.25 3.00
b. Imperf. 67.50
91 A15 10c *lavender* 30.00 85
a. 10c *rose lil* 32.50 1.25
b. 10c *lil* 32.50 1.25
c. Imperf. 75.00
92 A15 15c bl ('78) 18.00 30
a. Imperf. 95.00
b. 15c bl, *bluish* 325.00 3.75
93 A15 25c *red* ('78) 650.00 22.50
a. Imperf. 600.00
94 A15 35c *yel* ('78) 400.00 35.00
a. 35c *yel org* 450.00 37.50
b. Imperf. 400.00
95 A15 40c red, *straw* ('80) 52.50 1.25
a. Imperf. 250.00
96 A15 5fr vio, *lav* 500.00 85.00
a. 5fr red lil, *lav* 525.00 90.00
b. Imperf. 800.00

1879-90
97 A15 3c gray, *grysh* ('80) 2.25 1.00
a. Imperf. 67.50
98 A15 20c red, *yel grn* 30.00 2.25
a. 20c red, *dp grn* ('84) 40.00 4.50
b. Imperf. 82.50
99 A15 25c yel, *straw* 275.00 4.00
a. Imperf. 285.00
100 A15 25c *pale rose* ('86) 32.50 45
a. Imperf. 120.00
101 A15 50c rose, *rose* ('90) 125.00 1.00
a. 50c car, *rose* 125.00 1.00
102 A15 75c dp vio, *org* ('90) 185.00 30.00
a. 75c dp vio, *yel* 190.00 37.50

1892 Quadrille Paper
103 A15 15c blue 11.00 28
a. Imperf. 135.00

1898-1900 Ordinary Paper
104 A15 5c yel grn 12.00 28
a. Imperf. 90.00

Type I
105 A15 5c yel grn 9.00 65
a. Imperf. 325.00
106 A15 10c *lavender* 15.00 2.00
a. Imperf. 180.00
107 A15 50c car, *rose* 125.00 30.00

108 A15 2fr brn, *az* ('00) 110.00 37.50
b. Imperf. *2,100.*

See No. 226.

Reprints of A15, type II, were made in 1887 and left imperf. See note after No. 37. Price for set of 27, $2,750.

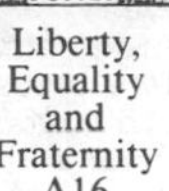
Liberty, Equality and Fraternity
A16

"The Rights of Man"
A17

Liberty and Peace
A18

1900-29 *Perf. 14x13½*
109 A16 1c gray 70 15
a. Imperf. 37.50
110 A16 2c vio brn 80 10
a. Imperf. 55.00
111 A16 3c orange 90 15
a. 3c red 20.00 5.00
b. Imperf. 40.00
112 A16 4c yel brn 3.50 75
a. Imperf. 180.00
113 A16 5c green 3.00 8
a. Imperf. 75.00
b. Bklt. pane of 10 35.00
114 A16 7½c lil ('26) 75 32
115 A16 10c lil ('29) 5.00 15
116 A17 10c carmine 26.00 75
a. Numerals printed separately 30.00 10.00
b. Imperf., #116 or 116a 300.00 *200.00*
117 A17 15c orange 9.00 30
a. Imperf. 225.00 *165.00*

118 A17 20c brn vio 75.00 5.75
119 A17 25c blue 110.00 90
a. Numerals printed separately 135.00 7.00
b. Imperf. #119 or 119a 650.00 *400.00*
120 A17 30c violet 75.00 5.50
121 A18 40c red & pale bl 17.50 50
a. Imperf. 225.00 150.00
122 A18 45c grn & bl ('06) 22.50 90
a. Imperf. 225.00 165.00
123 A18 50c bis brn & lav 125.00 1.00
a. Imperf. 350.00 275.00
124 A18 60c vio & ultra ('20) 1.40 45
a. Imperf. 525.00 375.00
125 A18 1fr cl & ol grn 35.00 30
a. Imperf. 210.00 165.00
126 A18 2fr gray vio & yel 950.00 55.00
a. Imperf. *2,500.* *1,500.*
127 A18 2fr org & pale bl ('20) 50.00 32
a. Imperf. 600.00 450.00
128 A18 3fr vio & bl ('25) 25.00 5.25
129 A18 3fr brt vio & rose ('27) 62.50 1.10
a. Imperf. 450.00
130 A18 5fr dk bl & buff 100.00 2.75
a. Imperf. 1,100. 600.00
131 A18 10fr grn & red ('26) 150.00 12.00
132 A18 20fr mag & grn ('26) 225.00 26.00
Nos. 109-132 (24) 2,073. 120.47

In the 10c and 25c values, the first printings show the numerals to have been impressed by a second operation, whereas, in later printings, the numerals were inserted in the plates. Two operations were used for all 20c and 30c, and one operation for the 15c.

No. 114 was issued precanceled only. Prices for precanceled stamps in first column are for those which have not been through the post and have original gum. Prices in the second column are for postally used, gumless stamps.

See No. P7.

Flat Plate & Rotary Press

The following stamps were printed by both flat plate and rotary press: Nos. 109-113, 144-146, 163, 166, 168, 170, 177-178, 185, 192 and P7.

"Rights of Man" A19

Sower A20

1902
133 A19 10c rose red 27.50 45
a. Imperf., without gum 225.00
134 A19 15c pale red 11.00 30
a. Imperf., without gum 400.00
135 A19 20c brn vio 110.00 15.00
a. Imperf., without gum 450.00
136 A19 25c blue 125.00 1.65
137 A19 30c lilac 300.00 11.00
a. Imperf., without gum 750.00
Nos. 133-137 (5) 573.50 28.40

1903-38
138 A20 10c rose 10.00 22
a. Imperf. 120.00 75.00
139 A20 15c sl grn 3.75 5
a. Imperf. 110.00 70.00
b. Booklet pane of 10 50.00
140 A20 20c vio brn 70.00 1.35
a. Imperf. 200.00 110.00
141 A20 25c dl bl 100.00 1.25
a. Imperf. 225.00 110.00
142 A20 30c violet 175.00 4.25
a. Imperf. 600.00 300.00
143 A20 45c lt vio ('26) 5.50 65
144 A20 50c dl bl ('21) 27.50 60
a. Imperf. 110.00
145 A20 50c gray grn ('26) 6.75 30
a. Imperf. 135.00
146 A20 50c ver ('26) 45 5
a. Booklet pane of 10 9.00
b. Imperf. 90.00
147 A20 50c grnsh bl ('38) 1.50 15
a. Imperf. 60.00
148 A20 60c lt vio ('24) 6.75 80
149 A20 65c rose ('24) 3.25 60
a. Imperf. 185.00
150 A20 65c gray grn ('27) 9.00 90
151 A20 75c rose lil ('26) 5.25 30
a. Imperf. 475.00
152 A20 80c ver ('26) 40.00 5.25
153 A20 85c ver ('24) 16.00 60
154 A20 1fr dl bl ('26) 6.25 22
Nos. 138-154 (17) 486.95 17.54

See Nos. 941, 942A.

Sower, Ground under Feet — A21

Sower, no Ground under Feet — A22

1906

With Ground Under Feet of Figure
155 A21 10c red 4.00 60
a. Imperf., pair, without gum 225.00

1906-37 No Ground Under the Feet

TEN AND THIRTY-FIVE CENTIMES.
Type I. Numerals and letters of the inscriptions thin.
Type II. Numerals and letters thicker.

156 A22 1c ol bis ('33) 15 15
157 A22 2c dk grn ('33) 22 10
158 A22 3c ver ('33) 15 10
159 A22 5c green 2.75 5
a. Imperf., pair 27.50
b. Bklt. pane of 10 42.50
160 A22 5c org ('21) 2.25 15
a. Bklt. pane of 10 40.00
161 A22 5c cer ('34) 22 15
162 A22 10c red (II) 2.75 5
a. Imperf., pair 27.50
b. 10c red (I) ('06) 11.00 30
c. Booklet pane of 10 (I) 140.00
d. Booklet pane of 10 (II) 85.00
e. Booklet pane of 6 (II) 275.00
163 A22 10c grn (II) ('21) 75 10
a. 10c grn (I) ('27) 35.00 30.00
b. Booklet pane of 10 (II) 17.50
c. Booklet pane of 10 (I) 475.00
164 A22 10c ultra ('32) 1.40 22
165 A22 15c red brn ('26) 32 5
a. Booklet pane of 10 27.50
166 A22 20c brown 4.50 30
a. Imperf., pair 45.00
167 A22 20c red vio ('26) 32 10
a. Bklt. pane of 10 7.50
168 A22 25c blue 2.75 10
a. Bklt. pane of 10 35.00
b. Imperf., pair 45.00
169 A22 25c brn ('27) 22 10
170 A22 30c orange 18.00 90
a. Imperf., pair 140.00
171 A22 30c red ('21) 12.00 1.65
172 A22 30c cer ('25) 1.40 30
a. Booklet pane of 10 14.00
173 A22 30c lt bl ('25) 3.25 22
a. Bklt. pane of 10 40.00
174 A22 30c cop red ('37) 45 10
a. Booklet pane of 10 9.00
175 A22 35c vio (II) ('26) 12.50 50
a. Imperf., pair 140.00
b. 35c vio (I) ('06) 225.00 5.25
176 A22 35c grn ('37) 85 20
177 A22 40c ol ('25) 1.50 30
b. Bklt. pane of 10 37.50
178 A22 40c ver ('26) 2.50 22
a. Bklt. pane of 10 30.00
179 A22 40c vio ('27) 2.75 22
180 A22 40c lt ultra ('28) 1.75 15
181 A22 1.05fr ver ('25) 10.00 2.75
182 A22 1.10fr cer ('27) 12.50 1.50
183 A22 1.40fr cer ('26) 20.00 14.00
184 A22 2fr Prus grn ('31) 15.00 45
Nos. 156-184 (29) 133.20 25.18

The 10c and 35c, type I, were slightly retouched by adding thin white outlines to the sack of grain, the underside of the right arm and the back of the skirt. It is difficult to distinguish the retouches except on clearly-printed copies. The white outlines were made stronger on the stamps of type II.

Stamps of types A16, A18, A20 and A22 were printed in 1916-20 on paper of poor quality, usually grayish and containing bits of fiber. This is called G. C. (Grande Consommation) paper.

Nos. 160, 162b, 163, 175b and 176 also exist imperf.

See Nos. 241-241b, P8.

Louis Pasteur — A23

1923-26
185 A23 10c green 80 22
a. Booklet pane of 10 11.00
186 A23 15c grn ('24) 2.25 22
187 A23 20c grn ('26) 3.50 45
188 A23 30c red 50 32
189 A23 30c grn ('26) 90 22
190 A23 45c red ('24) 2.25 1.00
191 A23 50c blue 4.50 15
192 A23 75c bl ('24) 4.00 30
a. Imperf., pair 275.00
193 A23 90c red ('26) 10.50 2.00
194 A23 1fr bl ('25) 22.50 15
195 A23 1.25fr bl ('26) 22.50 5.50
196 A23 1.50fr bl ('26) 5.75 15
Nos. 185-196 (12) 79.95 10.68

Nos. 185, 188 and 191 were issued to commemorate the centenary of the birth of Pasteur.

No. 125 Overprinted in Blue

CONGRES PHILATELIQUE
DE
BORDEAUX
1923

1923, June 15
197 A18 1fr cl & ol grn 400.00 400.00

Allegory of Olympic Games at Paris — A24

The Trophy A25

Milo of Crotona A26

Victorious Athlete A27

1924, Apr. 1 ***Perf. 14x13½, 13½x14***
198 A24 10c gray grn & yel grn 1.50 50
199 A25 25c rose & dk rose 2.25 28
200 A26 30c brn red & blk 8.00 6.00
201 A27 50c ultra & dk bl 18.00 3.25

8th Olympic Games, Paris. Exist imperf.

Pierre de Ronsard — A28

1924, Oct. 6 ***Perf. 14x13½***
219 A28 75c bl, *bluish* 1.25 75

Issued to commemorate the 400th anniversary of the birth of Pierre de Ronsard, poet (1524-1585).

"Light and Liberty" Allegory A29

Majolica Vase — A30

Potter Decorating Vase — A31

Terrace of Chateau
A32

1924-25 *Perf. 14x13½, 13½x14*

220 A29 10c dk grn & yel ('25) 75 45
221 A30 15c ind & grn ('25) 75 45
a. Imperf. 225.00
222 A31 25c vio brn & garnet 90 22
223 A32 25c gray bl & vio ('25) 1.40 50
a. Imperf. 400.00
224 A31 75c ind & ultra 3.75 1.40
225 A29 75c dk bl & lt bl ('25) 15.00 6.00
a. Imperf. 300.00
Nos. 220-225 (6) 22.55 9.02

Issued to commemorate the International Exhibition of Decorative Modern Arts at Paris, 1925.

Philatelic Exhibition Issue
Souvenir Sheet

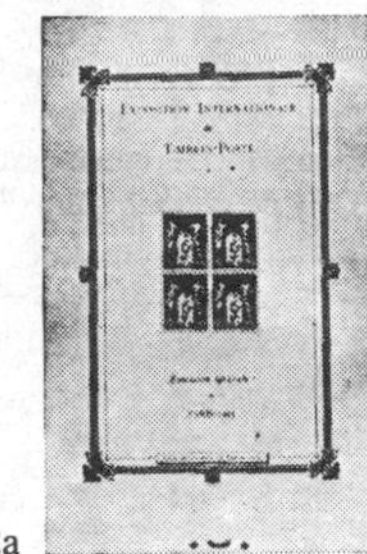
A32a

1925, May 2 *Perf. 14x13½*

226 A32a 5fr car (A15, type II) sheet of four 1,000. 1,000.
a. Imperf. sheet 4,750.
b. Single stamp, perf. 120.00 110.00
c. Single stamp, imperf. 900.00

Issued in sheets measuring 140x220 mm. These were not on sale at post offices but solely at the International Philatelic Exhibition, Paris, May, 1925.

Stamps of 1907-26 Surcharged **=25c**

1926-27

227 A22 25c on 30c lt bl 38 22
228 A22 25c on 35c vio 38 30
a. Double surcharge 300.00
229 A20 50c on 60c lt vio ('27) 1.50 60
230 A20 50c on 65c rose ('27) 1.25 30
231 A23 50c on 75c bl 3.25 30
232 A20 50c on 80c ver ('27) 1.50 60
233 A20 50c on 85c ver ('27) 2.50 30
234 A22 50c on 1.05fr ver ('27) 2.00 45
235 A23 50c on 1.25fr bl 2.00 30
236 A20 55c on 60c lt vio 125.00 52.50
238 A22 90c on 1.50fr ver 4.00 2.75
240 A22 1.10fr on 1.40fr cer 1.40 45
Nos. 227-240 (12) 145.16 59.07

No. 236 is known only precanceled. See second note after No. 132.

Nos. 229, 230, 234, 238 and 240 have three bars instead of two. The 55c surcharge has thinner, larger numerals and a rounded "c." Width, including bars, is 17mm., instead of 13mm.

Strasbourg Exhibition Issue
Souvenir Sheet

A32b

1927, June 4

241 A32b Sheet of two 950.00 950.00
a. 5fr lt ultra (A22) 190.00 190.00
b. 10fr car rose (A22) 190.00 190.00

Issued in sheets measuring 111x140mm. Sold at the Strasbourg Philatelic Exhibition as souvenirs.

Marcelin Berthelot — A33

1927, Sept. 7

242 A33 90c dl rose 1.75 32

Issued to commemorate the centenary of the birth of Marcelin Berthelot (1827-1907), chemist and statesman.

Lafayette, Washington, S. S. Paris and Airplane "Spirit of St. Louis"
A34

1927, Sept. 15

243 A34 90c dl red 90 65
a. Value omitted 1,250.
244 A34 1.50fr dp bl 2.50 90
a. Value omitted 1,100.

Visit of American Legionnaires to France, September, 1927. Exist imperf.

Joan of Arc — A35

1929, Mar.

245 A35 50c dl bl 1.50 18
a. Booklet pane of 10 160.00
b. Imperf. 135.00

Issued in commemoration of the 500th anniversary of the relief of Orleans by the French forces led by Joan of Arc.

Le Havre Exhibition Issue

A36

Blue Overprint

1929, May 18

246 A36 2fr org & pale bl 525.00 525.00

No. 246 was sold exclusively at the International Philatelic Exhibition, Le Havre, May, 1929. Sold for 7fr, which included a 5fr admission ticket.

Excellent counterfeits of No. 246 exist.

Reims Cathedral — A37

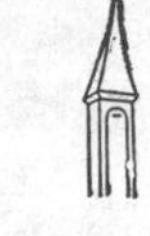
Dies I, II & III

Die IV

Die I

Die II

Die III

3fr—Die I. The window of the first turret on the left is made of two lines. The horizontal line of the frame surrounding 3F is not continuous.

3fr—Die II. Same as Die I but the line under 3F is continuous.

3fr—Die III. Same as Die II but there is a deeply cut line separating 3 and F.

3fr—Die IV. The window of the first turret on the left is made of three lines.

Mont-Saint-Michel — A38

Die I

Die II

5fr—Die I. The line at the top of the spire is broken.

5fr—Die II. The line is unbroken.

Port of La Rochelle
A39

Dies I & II

Die III

10fr—Die I. The top of the "E" of "POSTES" has a serif. The oval of shading inside the "0" of "10 fr" and the outer oval are broken at their bases.

10fr—Die II. The same top has no serif. Interior and exterior of "0" broken as in Die I.

10fr—Die III. Top of "E" has no serif. Interior and exterior of "0" complete.

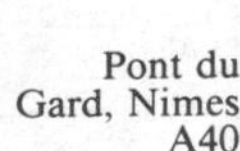

Pont du Gard, Nimes
A40

Dies I & II

Die III

20fr—Die I. Shading of the first complete arch in the left middle tier is made of horizontal lines. Size 36 x 20¾ mm. Perf. 13½.

20fr—Die II. Same, size 35½ x 21 mm. Perf. 11.

20fr—Die III. Shading of same arch is made of three diagonal lines. Thin paper. Perf. 13.

1929-33 **Engr.** *Perf. 11, 13, 13½*

247 A37 3fr dk gray ('30) (I) 95.00 2.50
247A A37 3fr dk gray ('30) (II) 150.00 4.00
247B A37 3fr dk gray ('30) (III) 425.00 20.00
248 A37 3fr bluish sl ('31) (IV) 95.00 2.50
249 A38 5fr brn ('30) (I) 25.00 1.90
250 A38 5fr brn ('31) (II) 22.50 38
251 A39 10fr lt ultra (I) 135.00 13.00
251A A39 10fr ultra (II) 150.00 22.50
252 A39 10fr dk ultra ('31) (III) 100.00 6.75
253 A40 20fr red brn (I) 325.00 32.50
254 A40 20fr brt red brn ('33) (II) 900.00 250.00
254A A40 20fr org brn ('31) (III) 275.00 32.50

View of Algiers
A41

1929, Jan. 1 **Typo.**
255 A41 50c bl & rose red 2.25 32

Issued in commemoration of the centenary of the first French settlement in Algeria.

Nos. 146 and 196 Overprinted

CONGRÈS DU B. I. T. 1930

1930, Apr. 23 ***Perf. 14x13½***
256 A20 50c vermilion 2.75 1.50
257 A23 1.50fr blue 18.00 13.00

International Labor Bureau, 48th Congress, Paris.

Colonial Exposition Issue

Fachi Woman A42

French Colonials A43

1930-31 **Typo.** ***Perf. 14x13½***
258 A42 15c gray blk 65 22
259 A42 40c dk brn 1.50 22
260 A42 50c dk red 60 5
a. Booklet pane of 10 12.00
261 A42 1.50fr dp bl 9.00 30

Perf. 13½
Photo.
262 A43 1.50fr dp bl ('31) 37.50 1.10
Nos. 258-262 (5) 49.25 1.89

Arc de Triomphe A44

Peace with Olive Branch A45

1931 **Engr.** ***Perf. 13***
263 A44 2fr red brn 27.50 45

1932-39 **Typo.** ***Perf. 14x13½***
264 A45 30c dp grn 1.00 38
265 A45 40c brt vio 38 6
266 A45 45c yel brn 2.75 60
267 A45 50c rose red 15 5
a. Imperf., pair 110.00
b. Booklet pane of 10 7.50
268 A45 55c dl vio ('37) 1.00 28
269 A45 60c ocher ('37) 30 28
270 A45 65c vio brn 50 22
271 A45 65c brt ultra ('37) 45 10
a. Booklet pane of 10 10.00
272 A45 75c ol grn 22 15
273 A45 80c org ('38) 18 18
274 A45 90c dk red 37.50 1.75
275 A45 90c brt grn ('38) 10 6
276 A45 90c ultra ('38) 80 5
a. Booklet pane of 10 12.50
277 A45 1fr orange 2.00 15
278 A45 1fr rose pink ('38) 2.25 15
279 A45 1.25fr brn ol 87.50 2.75
280 A45 1.25fr rose car ('39) 2.00 90
281 A45 1.40fr brt red vio ('39) 8.50 4.00
282 A45 1.50fr dp bl 30 22
283 A45 1.75fr magenta 6.25 22
Nos. 264-283 (20) 154.13 12.55

The 50c is found in 4 types, differing in the lines below belt and size of "c."

Le Puy-en-Velay A46

1933 **Engr.** ***Perf. 13***
290 A46 90c rose 3.25 45

Aristide Briand A47

Paul Doumer A48

Victor Hugo — A49

1933, Dec. 11 **Typo.** ***Perf. 14x13½***
291 A47 30c bl grn 19.00 7.50
292 A48 75c red vio 21.00 75
293 A49 1.25fr claret 5.50 75

Dove and Olive Branch A50

Joseph Marie Jacquard A51

1934, Feb. 20
294 A50 1.50fr ultra 70.00 13.00

1934, Mar. 14 **Engr.** ***Perf. 14x13***
295 A51 40c blue 3.00 75

Issued to commemorate the centenary of the death of Joseph Marie Jacquard (1752-1834), inventor of an improved loom for figured weaving.

Jacques Cartier A52

1934, July 18 ***Perf. 13***
296 A52 75c rose lil 19.00 1.50
297 A52 1.50fr blue 42.50 2.75

Issued to commemorate the 400th anniversary of Cartier's discovery of Canada.

No. 279 Surcharged

=
50c

1934, Nov. ***Perf. 14x13½***
298 A45 50c on 1.25fr brn ol 4.75 28

Breton River Scene A53

1935, Feb. **Engr.** ***Perf. 13***
299 A53 2fr bl grn 40.00 50

S. S. Normandie A54

1935, April
300 A54 1.50fr dk bl 16.00 1.10
a. 1.50fr bl ('36) 75.00 15.00
b. 1.50fr bl grn ('36) *4,000.*

Issued in commemoration of the maiden voyage of the transatlantic steamship, the "Normandie".

Benjamin Delessert A55

1935, May 20
301 A55 75c bl grn 20.00 75

Issued in commemoration of the opening of the International Savings Bank Congress, May 20, 1935.

View of St. Trophime at Arles A56

Victor Hugo A57

1935, May 3
302 A56 3.50fr dk brn 30.00 2.00

1935, May 30 ***Perf. 14x13***
303 A57 1.25fr magenta 5.00 1.25

Victor Hugo (1802-1885), 50th anniversary of death.

Cardinal Richelieu A58

Jacques Callot A59

1935, June 12 ***Perf. 13***
304 A58 1.50fr dp rose 20.00 1.25

Issued in commemoration of the tercentenary of the founding of the French Academy by Cardinal Richelieu.

1935, Nov. ***Perf. 14x13***
305 A59 75c red 15.00 38

Issued in commemoration of the 300th anniversary of the death of Jacques Callot, engraver.

André Marie Ampère — A60

1936, Feb. 27 ***Perf. 13***
306 A60 75c brown 20.00 90

Issued to commemorate the centenary of the death of Andre Marie Ampere (1775-1836), scientist. (Portrait by Louis Boilly.)

Windmill at Fontvielle, Immortalized by Daudet — A61

1936, Apr. 27
307 A61 2fr ultra 2.00 22

Issued in commemoration of the 70th anniversary of the publication, in 1866, of Alphonse Daudet's "Lettres de mon Moulin".

Pilâtre de Rozier and his Balloon A62

1936, June 4
308 A62 75c Prus bl 20.00 1.75

Issued in commemoration of the 150th anniversary of the death of Jean Joseph Pilatre de Rozier, balloonist.

Rouget de Lisle — A63

"La Marseillaise" — A64

1936, June 27
309 A63 20c Prus grn 3.00 75
310 A64 40c dk brn 6.00 2.00

Centenary of the death of Claude Joseph Rouget de Lisle, composer of "La Marseillaise."

Canadian War Memorial at Vimy Ridge A65

1936, July 26
311 A65 75c hn brn 7.75 1.50
312 A65 1.50fr dl bl 14.00 7.00

Issued to commemorate the unveiling of the Canadian War Memorial at Vimy Ridge, July 26, 1936.

Jean Léon Jaures — A66

Jean Jaurès A67

1936, July 30

313	A66	40c red brn	2.75	48
314	A67	1.50fr ultra	11.00	1.75

Issued in commemoration of the assassination of Jean Léon Jaurès (1859-1914), socialist and politician.

Herald A68

Allegory of Exposition A69

1936, Sept. 15 Typo. *Perf. 14x13½*

315	A68	20c brt vio	45	30
316	A68	30c Prus grn	2.50	95
317	A68	40c ultra	1.10	30
318	A68	50c red org	90	15
319	A69	90c carmine	12.50	7.00
320	A69	1.50fr ultra	27.50	2.00
		Nos. 315-320 (6)	44.95	10.70

Publicity for the 1937 Paris Exposition.

"Peace" A70

1936, Oct. 1 Engr. *Perf. 13*

321	A70	1.50fr blue	16.00	2.25

Skiing A71

1937, Jan. 18

322	A71	1.50fr dk bl	9.00	1.00

Issued in commemoration of the International Ski Meet at Chamonix-Mont Blanc.

Pierre Corneille, Portrait by Charles Le Brun — A72

1937, Feb. 15

323	A72	75c brn car	2.25	90

Issued to commemorate the 300th anniversary of the publication of "Le Cid."

Paris Exposition Issue

Exposition Allegory A73

1937, Mar. 15

324	A73	1.50fr turq bl	1.75	70

Jean Mermoz A74

Memorial to Mermoz — A75

1937, Apr. 27

325	A74	30c dk sl grn	65	40
326	A75	3fr dk vio	6.25	2.75
a.		3fr vio	8.00	3.75

Issued in honor of aviator Jean Mermoz (1901-36).

Electric Train A76

Streamlined Locomotive A77

1937, May 31

327	A76	30c dk grn	1.75	1.10
328	A77	1.50fr dk ultra	10.00	7.00

13th International Railroad Congress.

International Philatelic Exhibition Issue

Souvenir Sheet

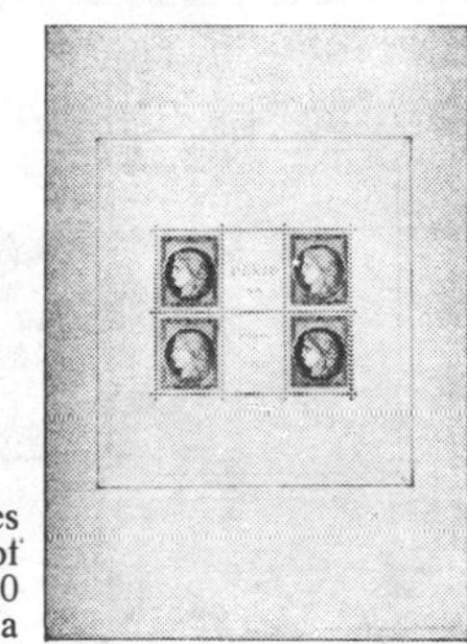

Ceres Type of 1849-50 A77a

1937, June 18 Typo. *Perf. 14x13½*

329	A77a	Sheet of four (A1)	200.00	200.00
a.		5c ultra & dk brn	40.00	40.00
b.		15c red & rose red	40.00	40.00
c.		30c ultra & rose red	40.00	40.00
d.		50c red & dk brn	40.00	40.00
e.		Imperf. sheet of four	1,500.	

Issued in sheets measuring 150x220mm.

The sheets were sold only at the exhibition in Paris, a ticket of admission being required for each sheet purchased.

René Descartes, by Frans Hals — A78

1937, June Engr. *Perf. 13*

Inscribed: "Discours sur la Méthode."

330	A78	90c cop red	1.25	90

Inscribed "Discours de la Méthode"

331	A78	90c cop red	4.00	90

Issued in commemoration of the third centenary of the publication of "Discours de la Méthode" by René Descartes.

France Congratulating U.S.A. — A79

1937, Sept. 17

332	A79	1.75fr ultra	2.00	1.00

Issued to commemorate the 150th anniversary of the Constitution of the United States of America.

No. 277 Surcharged in Red

80c

1937, Oct. *Perf. 14x13½*

333	A45	80c on 1fr org	45	30
a.		Inverted surch.	600.00	

Mountain Road at Iseran — A80

1937, Oct. 4 Engr. *Perf. 13*

334	A80	90c dk grn	90	18

Issued in commemoration of the opening of the mountain road at Iseran, Savoy.

Ceres — A81

1938-40 Typo. *Perf. 14x13½*

335	A81	1.75fr dk ultra	1.25	22
336	A81	2fr car rose ('39)	30	15
337	A81	2.25fr ultra ('39)	11.00	38
338	A81	2.50fr grn ('39)	2.75	22
339	A81	2.50fr vio bl ('40)	1.00	45
340	A81	3fr rose lil ('39)	1.00	22
		Nos. 335-340 (6)	17.30	1.64

Léon Gambetta — A82

1938, Apr. 2 Engr. *Perf. 13*

341	A82	55c dk vio	50	38

Issued in commemoration of the centenary of the birth of Léon Gambetta (1838-1882), lawyer and statesman.

Arc de Triomphe of Orange A82a

Miners — A83

Palace of the Popes, Avignon A84

Medieval Walls of Carcassonne A85

Keep and Gate of Vincennes — A86

Port of St. Malo — A87

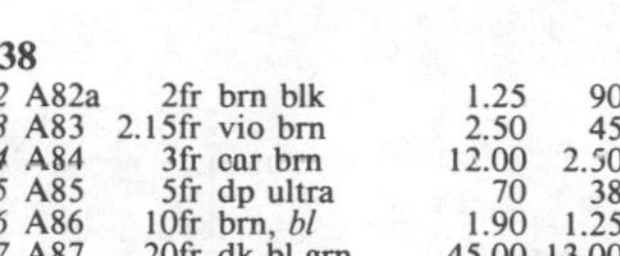

1938

342	A82a	2fr brn blk	1.25	90
343	A83	2.15fr vio brn	2.50	45
344	A84	3fr car brn	12.00	2.50
345	A85	5fr dp ultra	70	38
346	A86	10fr brn, *bl*	1.90	1.25
347	A87	20fr dk bl grn	45.00	13.00
		Nos. 342-347 (6)	63.35	18.48

Clément Ader — A88

1938, June 16

348	A88	50fr ultra (thin paper)	100.00	60.00
a.		50fr dk ultra (thick paper)	110.00	80.00

Issued in honor of Clément Ader, air pioneer.

Soccer Players A89

1938, June 1

349	A89	1.75fr dk ultra	10.00	6.00

World Cup Soccer Championship.

Costume of Champagne Region
A90

Jean de La Fontaine
A91

1938, June 13

350	A90	1.75fr dk ultra	4.00	2.50

Issued in commemoration of the tercentenary of the birth of Dom Pierre Perignon, discoverer of the champagne process.

1938, July 8

351	A91	55c dk bl grn	55	40

Issued to honor Jean de La Fontaine (1621-1695), the fabulist.

Seal of Friendship and Peace, Victoria Tower and Arc de Triomphe
A92

1938, July 19

352	A92	1.75fr ultra	1.00	60

Issued in honor of the visit of King George VI and Queen Elizabeth of Great Britain to France.

Mercury
A93

Paul Cézanne, Self-portrait
A95

1938-42 Typo. *Perf. 14x13½*

353	A93	1c dk brn ('39)	5	5
354	A93	2c sl grn ('39)	5	5
355	A93	5c rose	5	5
356	A93	10c ultra	5	5
357	A93	15c red org	5	5
358	A93	15c org brn ('39)	85	30
359	A93	20c red vio	5	5
360	A93	25c bl grn	15	5
361	A93	30c rose red ('39)	5	5
362	A93	40c dk vio ('39)	5	5
363	A93	45c lt grn ('39)	80	30
364	A93	50c dp bl ('39)	3.50	15
365	A93	50c dk grn ('41)	75	15
366	A93	50c grnsh bl ('42)	15	10
367	A93	60c red org ('39)	22	10
368	A93	70c mag ('39)	25	8
369	A93	75c dk org brn ('39)	6.25	1.65
		Nos. 353-369 (17)	13.32	3.28

No. 366 exists imperforate. See Nos. 455-458.

1939, Mar. 15 Engr. *Perf. 13*

370	A95	2.25fr Prus bl	4.25	2.00

Issued in commemoration of the centenary of the birth of Paul Cezanne (1839-1906), painter.

Georges Clemenceau and Battleship Clemenceau
A96

1939, Apr. 18

371	A96	90c ultra	50	42

Issued to commemorate the laying of the keel of the warship "Clemenceau" January 17, 1939.

Statue of Liberty, French Pavilion, Trylon and Perisphere
A97

1939-40

372	A97	2.25fr ultra	5.00	2.50
373	A97	2.50fr ultra ('40)	3.00	2.00

New York World's Fair.

Joseph Nicéphore Niepce and Louis Jacques Mandé Daguerre
A98

1939, Apr. 24

374	A98	2.25fr dk bl	5.25	3.50

Centenary of photography.

Iris — A99

Pumping Station at Marly — A100

1939-44 Typo. *Perf. 14x13½*

375	A99	80c red brn ('40)	30	22
376	A99	80c yel grn ('44)	6	5
377	A99	1fr green	75	5
378	A99	1fr crim ('40)	22	5
a.		Bklt. pane of 10	7.50	
379	A99	1fr grnsh bl ('44)	6	6
380	A99	1.20fr vio ('44)	6	5
381	A99	1.30fr ultra ('40)	22	22
382	A99	1.50fr red org ('41)	30	30
383	A99	1.50fr hn brn ('44)	6	6
384	A99	2fr vio brn ('44)	15	15
385	A99	2.40fr car rose ('44)	15	15
386	A99	3fr org ('44)	22	8
387	A99	4fr ultra ('44)	30	22
		Nos. 375-387 (13)	2.85	1.66

1939 Engr. *Perf. 13*

388	A100	2.25fr brt ultra	6.25	2.00

Issued in commemoration of France's participation in the International Water Exposition at Liege.

St. Gregory of Tours — A101

1939, June 10

389	A101	90c red	75	60

Issued to commemorate the 14th centenary of the birth of St. Gregory of Tours, historian and bishop.

"The Oath of the Tennis Court" by Jacques David
A102

1939, June 20

390	A102	90c dp sl grn	1.25	75

150th anniversary of French Revolution.

Cathedral of Strasbourg — A103

1939, June 23

391	A103	70c brn car	95	65

Issued to commemorate the 500th anniversary of the completion of Strasbourg Cathedral.

Porte Chaussée, Verdun
A104

1939, June 23

392	A104	90c blk brn	1.00	90

Issued to commemorate the 23rd anniversary of the Battle of Verdun.

View of Pau — A105

1939, Aug. 25

393	A105	90c brt rose, *gray bl*	1.10	50

Maid of Languedoc
A106

Bridge at Lyons
A107

1939

394	A106	70c blk, *bl*	50	45
395	A107	90c dl brn vio	75	45

Imperforates
Nearly all French stamps issued from 1940 onward exist imperforate. Officially 20 sheets, ranging from 25 to 100 subjects, were left imperforate.

Georges Guynemer — A108

1940, Nov. 7

396	A108	50fr ultra	13.00	8.50

Issued in honor of Georges Guynemer (1894-1917), World War I ace.

Stamps of 1938-39 Surcharged in Carmine 1F

1940-41 *Perf. 14x13½*

397	A81	1fr on 1.75fr dk ultra	18	18
398	A81	1fr on 2.25fr ultra ('41)	18	18
399	A81	1fr on 2.50fr grn ('41)	55	55

Stamps of 1932-39 Surcharged in Carmine, Red or Black

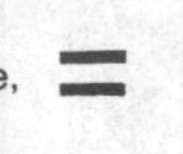

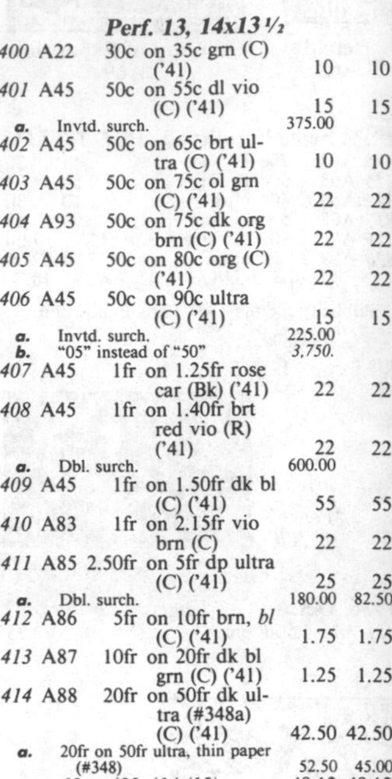

Perf. 13, 14x13½

400	A22	30c on 35c grn (C) ('41)	10	10
401	A45	50c on 55c dl vio (C) ('41)	15	15
a.		Invtd. surch.	375.00	
402	A45	50c on 65c brt ultra (C) ('41)	10	10
403	A45	50c on 75c ol grn (C) ('41)	22	22
404	A93	50c on 75c dk org brn (C) ('41)	22	22
405	A45	50c on 80c org (C) ('41)	22	22
406	A45	50c on 90c ultra (C) ('41)	15	15
a.		Invtd. surch.	225.00	
b.		"05" instead of "50"	*3,750.*	
407	A45	1fr on 1.25fr rose car (Bk) ('41)	22	22
408	A45	1fr on 1.40fr brt red vio (R) ('41)	22	22
a.		Dbl. surch.	600.00	
409	A45	1fr on 1.50fr dk bl (C) ('41)	55	55
410	A83	1fr on 2.15fr vio brn (C)	22	22
411	A85	2.50fr on 5fr dp ultra (C) ('41)	25	25
a.		Dbl. surch.	180.00	82.50
412	A86	5fr on 10fr brn, *bl* (C) ('41)	1.75	1.75
413	A87	10fr on 20fr dk bl grn (C) ('41)	1.25	1.25
414	A88	20fr on 50fr dk ultra (#348a) (C) ('41)	42.50	42.50
a.		20fr on 50fr ultra, thin paper (#348)	52.50	45.00
		Nos. 400-414 (15)	48.12	48.12

Marshal Pétain
A109

Fréderic Mistral
A110

1941 *Perf. 13*

415	A109	40c red brn	40	38
416	A109	80c turq bl	65	50
417	A109	1fr red	20	22
418	A109	2.50fr dp ultra	1.25	90

1941, Feb. 20 *Perf. 14x13*

419	A110	1fr brn lake	15	15

Issued in honor of Fréderic Mistral, poet and Nobel prize winner for literature in 1904.

Beaune Hospital
A111

View of Angers
A112

Ramparts of St. Louis, Aiguesmortes
A113

1941

420	A111	5fr brn blk	30	22
421	A112	10fr dk vio	45	30
422	A113	20fr brn blk	60	50

1942

Inscribed "Postes Francaises", Imprinted: "FELTESSE" at right

423	A111	15fr brn lake	50	30

Marshal Pétain
A114 A115

Marshal Pétain
A116 A117

Marshal Pétain — A118

1941-42 Typo. *Perf. 14x13½*

427	A114	20c lil ('42)	5	5
428	A114	30c rose red	5	5
429	A114	40c ultra	10	6
431	A115	50c dp grn	5	5
432	A115	60c vio ('42)	8	8
433	A115	70c saph ('42)	8	8
434	A115	70c org ('42)	8	6
435	A115	80c brown	10	10
436	A115	80c emer ('42)	8	8
437	A115	1fr rose red	6	6
438	A115	1.20fr red brn ('42)	5	5
439	A116	1.50fr rose	15	10
440	A116	1.50fr dl red brn ('42)	5	5
a.		Booklet pane of 10	3.50	
441	A116	2fr bl grn ('42)	5	5
443	A116	2.40fr rose red ('42)	15	15
444	A116	2.50fr ultra	90	45
445	A116	3fr orange	8	6
446	A115	4fr ultra ('42)	15	15
447	A115	4.50fr dk grn ('42)	90	25
		Nos. 427-447 (19)	3.21	1.98

Nos. 431 to 438 measure 16½x20½mm.

No. 440 was forged by the French Underground ("Defense de la France") and used to frank clandestine journals, etc., from February to June, 1944. The forgeries were ungummed, both perforated 11½ and imperforate, with a back handstamp covering six stamps and including the words: "Atelier des Faux."

1942 Engr. *Perf. 14x13*

448	A115	4fr brt ultra	25	20
449	A115	4.50fr dk grn	25	10
450	A117	5fr Prus grn	15	15

Perf. 13

451	A118	50fr black	3.50	2.50

Nos. 448 and 449 measure 18x21½mm.

Jules Massenet A119

Stendhal (Marie Henri Beyle) A120

1942, June 22 *Perf. 14x13*

452	A119	4fr Prus grn	22	18

Issued to commemorate the centenary of the birth of Jules Massenet (1842-1912), composer.

1942, Sept. 14 *Perf. 13*

453	A120	4fr blk brn & org red	32	32

Issued to commemorate the centenary of the death of Stendhal (1783-1842), writer.

André Blondel A121

Town-Hall Belfry, Arras A122

1942, Sept. 14

454	A121	4fr dl bl	32	32

Issued in honor of André Eugène Blondel (1863-1938), physicist.

Mercury Type of 1938-42
Inscribed "Postes Françaises"

1942 *Perf. 14x13½*

455	A93	10c ultra	6	6
456	A93	30c rose red	6	6
457	A93	40c dk vio	6	6
458	A93	50c turq bl	6	6

1942, Dec. 8 Engr. *Perf. 13*

459	A122	10fr green	22	22

Coats of Arms

Lyon A123

Brittany A124

Provence A125

Ile de France A126

1943 Typo. *Perf. 14x13½*

460	A123	5fr vio bl, org, red	32	22
461	A124	10fr ocher & blk	40	30
462	A125	15fr vio bl, org, red & blk	1.75	1.25
463	A126	20fr vio bl, org, & dl brn	1.25	75

Antoine Lavoisier — A127

1943, July 5 Engr. *Perf. 14x13*

464	A127	4fr ultra	15	15

Issued to commemorate the 200th anniversary of the birth of Lavoisier (1743-94), French scientist.

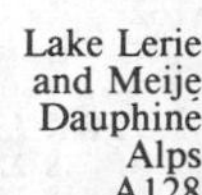

Lake Lerie and Meije Dauphine Alps A128

1943, July 5 *Perf. 13*

465	A128	20fr dl gray grn	45	45

Nicolas Rolin, Guigone de Salins and Hospital of Beaune A129

1943, July 21

466	A129	4fr blue	25	25

Issued to commemorate the 500th anniversary of the founding of the Hospital of Beaune.

Coats of Arms

Flanders A130

Languedoc A131

Orleans A132

Normandy A133

1944, Mar. 27 Typo. *Perf. 14x13½*

467	A130	5fr ver, org & blk	15	15
468	A131	10fr brn, blk, dl red & yel	22	22
469	A132	15fr brn, brt ultra & org	60	40
470	A133	20fr ultra, dl red org & blk	75	55

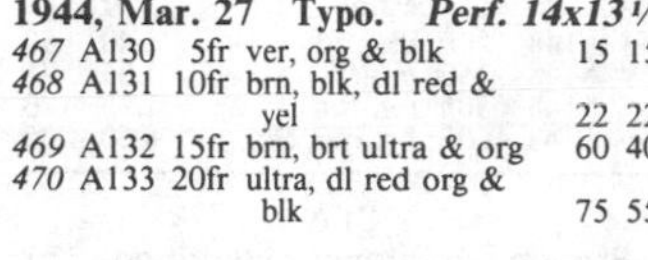

Edouard Branly A134

Early Postal Car A135

1944, Feb. 21 Engr. *Perf. 14x13*

471	A134	4fr ultra	18	15

Issued to commemorate the centenary of the birth of Edouard Branly, electrical inventor.

1944, June 10 *Perf. 13*

472	A135	1.50fr dk bl grn	40	30

Issued to commemorate the centenary of France's traveling postal service.

Chateau de Chenonceaux A136

Claude Chappe A137

1944, June 10

473	A136	15fr lil brn	50	50
a.		15fr blk brn	7.50	1.75
b.		15fr blk	47.50	

1944, Aug. 14 *Perf. 14x13*

474	A137	4fr dk ultra	15	15

Issued to commemorate the 150th anniversary of the invention of an optical telegraph by Claude Chappe (1763-1805).

Gallic Cock A138

Marianne A139

1944 Litho. *Perf. 12*

477	A138	10c yel grn	10	10
478	A138	30c dk rose vio	22	22
479	A138	40c blue	10	10
480	A138	50c dk red	6	6
481	A139	60c ol brn	10	10
482	A139	70c rose lil	12	12
483	A139	80c yel grn	65	65
484	A139	1fr violet	8	8
485	A139	1.20fr dp car	10	10
486	A139	1.50fr dp bl	8	8
487	A138	2fr indigo	10	10
488	A139	2.40fr red org	1.25	1.25
489	A139	3fr dp bl grn	22	22
490	A139	4fr grnsh bl	22	22
491	A139	4.50fr black	18	18
492	A139	5fr vio bl	4.00	4.00
493	A138	10fr violet	4.50	4.50
494	A138	15fr ol brn	4.50	4.50
495	A138	20fr dk sl grn	4.50	4.50
		Nos. 477-495 (19)	21.08	21.08

Nos. 477-495 were issued first in Corsica after the Allied landing, and released in Paris Nov. 15, 1944.

Chateau de Chenonceaux — A140

1944, Oct. 30 Engr. *Perf. 13*

496	A140	25fr black	55	55

Thomas Robert Bugeaud — A141

1944, Nov. 20

497	A141	4fr myr grn	18	18

Issued to commemorate the 100th anniversary of the Battle of Isly, August 14th, 1844.

Church of St. Denis A142

1944, Nov. 20

498	A142	2.40fr brn car	15	15

Issued to commemorate the 800th anniversary of the Church of St. Denis.

Type of 1938-42, Overprinted in Black Inscribed "Postes Francaises" **RF**

1944 *Perf. 14x13½*

499	A93	10c ultra	5	5
500	A93	30c rose red	15	15
501	A93	40c dk vio	15	15
502	A93	50c grnsh bl	15	15

The overprint "RF" in various forms, with or without Lorraine Cross, was also applied to stamps of the French State at Lyon and fourteen other cities.

Scott's editorial staff cannot undertake to identify, authenticate or appraise stamps and postal markings.

French Forces of the Interior and Symbol of Liberation — A143

1945, Jan.

503 A143 4fr dk ultra 35 30

Issued to commemorate the Liberation.

Stamps of the above design, and of one incorporating "FRANCE" in the top panel, were printed by photogravure in England during World War II upon order of the Free French Government. They were not issued. There are three values in each design; 25c green, 1fr red, 2.50fr blue. Price: set, above design, $135; set inscribed "FRANCE," $525.

Marianne — A144

Perf. 11½x12½

1944-45 Engr. Unwmk.

505	A144	10c ultra	5	5
506	A144	30c bister	5	5
507	A144	40c indigo	5	5
508	A144	50c red org	5	5
509	A144	60c chlky bl	5	5
510	A144	70c sepia	5	5
511	A144	80c dp grn	5	5
512	A144	1fr lilac	5	5
513	A144	1.20fr dk ol grn	5	5
514	A144	1.50fr rose ('44)	5	5
515	A144	2fr dk brn	6	5
516	A144	2.40fr red	6	6
517	A144	3fr brt ol grn	6	5
518	A144	4fr brt ultra	5	5
519	A144	4.50fr sl gray	15	15
520	A144	5fr brt org	22	22
521	A144	10fr yel grn	32	30
522	A144	15fr lake	32	30
523	A144	20fr brn org	1.00	95
523A	A144	50fr dp pur	2.00	2.00
		Nos. 505-523A (20)	4.74	5.13

The 2.40fr exists imperf. in a miniature sheet of 4 which was not issued.

Coat of Arms A145

Ceres A146

Marianne — A147

1945-47 Typo. Perf. 14x13½

524	A145	10c brn blk	5	5
525	A145	30c dk bl grn	10	10
526	A145	40c lil rose	10	10
527	A145	50c vio bl	5	5
528	A146	60c brt ultra	10	10
530	A146	80c brt grn	5	5
531	A146	90c dl grn ('46)	75	35
532	A146	1fr rose red	10	6
533	A146	1.20fr brn blk	18	15
534	A146	1.50fr rose lil	10	6
535	A147	1.50fr rose pink	15	15
536	A147	2fr myr grn	10	6
536A	A146	2fr lt bl grn ('46)	18	10
537	A147	2.40fr scarlet	38	30
538	A146	2.50fr brn ('46)	18	15
539	A147	3fr sepia	10	6
540	A147	3fr dp rose ('46)	15	6
541	A147	4fr ultra	15	15
541A	A147	4fr vio ('46)	15	12
541B	A147	4.50fr ultra ('47)	10	5
542	A147	5fr lt grn	15	5
542A	A147	5fr rose pink ('47)	6	5
543	A147	6fr brt ultra	38	30
544	A147	6fr crim rose ('46)	25	8
545	A147	10fr red org	38	15
546	A147	10fr ultra ('46)	1.25	42
547	A147	15fr brt red vio	2.00	85
		Nos. 524-547 (27)	7.69	4.17

No. 531 is known only precanceled. See second note after No. 132.

Due to a reduction of the domestic postage rate, No. 542A was sold for 4.50fr.

See Nos. 576 to 580, 594 to 602, 614, 615, 650 to 654.

1945-46 Engr. Perf. 14x13

548	A147	4fr dk bl	18	15
549	A147	10fr dp bl ('46)	48	22
550	A147	15fr brt red vio ('46)	4.50	1.00
551	A147	20fr bl grn ('46)	95	22
552	A147	25fr red ('46)	3.50	80
		Nos. 548-552 (5)	9.61	2.39

Marianne — A148

1945 Engr. Perf. 13

553	A148	20fr dk grn	1.40	50
554	A148	25fr violet	1.65	75
555	A148	50fr red brn	1.75	70
556	A148	100fr brt rose car	8.50	4.00

CFA

French stamps inscribed or surcharged "CFA" and new value are listed under Réunion in Vol. IV.

Arms of Metz A149

Arms of Strasbourg A150

1945, Mar. 3 Perf. 14x13

557 A149 2.40fr dl bl 18 18
558 A150 4fr blk brn 18 18

Liberation of Metz and Strasbourg.

Costumes of Alsace and Lorraine and Cathedrals of Strasbourg and Metz A151

1945, May 16 Perf. 13

559 A151 4fr hn brn 18 18

Liberation of Alsace and Lorraine.

World Map Showing French Possessions A152

1945, Sept. 17

560 A152 2fr Prus bl 18 18

No. B193 Surcharged with New Value in Black

1946 Perf. 14x13½

561 SP147 3fr on 2fr+1fr red org 15 15

Coats of Arms

Corsica A153

Alsace A154

Lorraine A155

County of Nice A156

1946 Unwmk. Typo. Perf. 14x13½

562	A153	10c dp ultra & blk	5	5
563	A154	30c blk, red org & yel	6	5
564	A155	50c brn, yel & red	6	5
565	A156	60c red, ultra & blk	6	6

Reaching for "Peace" A157

Holding the Dove of Peace A158

1946, July 29 Engr. Perf. 13

566 A157 3fr Prus grn 18 18
567 A158 10fr dk bl 18 18

Peace Conference of Paris, 1946.

Vézelay A159

Luxembourg Palace A160

Rocamadour — A161

Pointe du Raz, Finistère A162

1946 Unwmk. Perf. 13

568 A159 5fr rose vio 18 22
569 A160 10fr dk bl 18 15
570 A161 15fr dk vio brn 70 22
571 A162 20fr sl gray 24 15

See Nos. 591-592.

Globe and Wreath — A163

1946, Nov.

572 A163 10fr dk bl 25 25

Issued to honor the general conference of the United Nations Educational, Scientific and Cultural Organization, Paris, 1946.

Cannes A164

Stanislas Square, Nancy A165

1946-48 Engr. Perf. 13

573 A164 6fr rose red 38 30
574 A165 25fr blk brn 75 15
575 A165 25fr dk bl ('48) 3.75 80

Ceres & Marianne Types of 1945

1947 Unwmk. Typo. Perf. 14x13½

576	A146	1.30fr dl bl	30	30
577	A147	3fr green	70	15
578	A147	3.50fr brn red	50	25
579	A147	5fr blue	22	10
580	A147	6fr carmine	40	40
		Nos. 576-580 (5)	2.12	1.20

Colonnade of the Louvre A166

La Conciergerie, Paris Prison — A167

La Cité, Oldest Section of Paris A168

Place de la Concorde A169

1947, May 7 Engr. Perf. 13

581 A166 3.50fr chocolate 38 38
582 A167 4.50fr dk sl gray 38 38
583 A168 6fr red 70 70
584 A169 10fr brt ultra 70 70

Issued to commemorate the 12th Congress of the Universal Postal Union, Paris, May 7 to July 7, 1947.

Auguste Pavie
A170

Francois Fenelon
A171

1947, May 30
585 A170 4.50fr sepia 18 18

Issued to commemorate the centenary of the birth of Auguste Pavie, French pioneer in Laos.

1947, July 12
586 A171 4.50fr chocolate 18 18

Issued to honor Francois de Salignac de la Mothe-Fenelon, prelate and writer.

Fleur-de-Lis and Double Carrick Bend — A172

1947, Aug. 2 **Unwmk.**
587 A172 5fr brown 18 18

Issued to commemorate the 6th World Boy Scout Jamboree held at Moisson, August 9th to 18th, 1947.

Captured Patriot
A173

View of Conques
A174

1947, Nov. 10 **Engr.** ***Perf. 13***
588 A173 5fr sepia 55 55

No. 576 Surcharged in Carmine

1947, Nov. **Typo.** ***Perf. 14x13½***
589 A146 1fr on 1.30fr dl bl 15 15

1947, Dec. 18 **Engr.** ***Perf. 13***
590 A174 15fr hn brn 50 25

Types of 1946-47

1948 **Re-engraved**
591 A160 12fr rose car 30 20
592 A160 15fr brt red 20 18
593 A174 18fr dk bl 50 20

"FRANCE" substituted for inscriptions "RF" and "REPUBLIQUE FRANCAISE."

Marianne Type of 1945

1948-49 **Typo.** ***Perf. 14x13½***

594	A147	2.50fr brown	2.50	1.50
595	A147	3fr lil rose	22	10
596	A147	4fr lt bl grn	30	10
597	A147	4fr brn org	1.10	45
598	A147	5fr lt bl grn	60	5
599	A147	8fr blue	32	15
600	A147	10fr brt vio	20	5
601	A147	12fr ultra ('49)	1.10	15
602	A147	15fr crim rose ('49)	50	5
a.		Bklt. pane of 10	80.00	
		Nos. 594-602 (9)	6.84	2.60

No. 594 known only precanceled. See second note after No. 132.

François Rene de Chateaubriand — A175

1948, July 3 **Engr.** ***Perf. 13***
603 A175 18fr dk bl 30 30

Issued to commemorate the centenary of the death of Vicomte de Chateaubriand (1768-1848).

Philippe François M. de Hautecloque (Gen. Jacques Leclerc)
A176

1948, July 3
604 A176 6fr gray blk 38 32

See Nos. 692-692A.

Chaillot Palace
A177

A178

1948, Sept. 21
605 A177 12fr car rose 38 38
606 A178 18fr indigo 45 45

Issued to commemorate the meeting of the United Nations General Assembly, Paris, 1948.

Genissiat Dam
A179

Paul Langevin
A180

1948, Sept. 21
607 A179 12fr car rose 48 45

1948, Nov. 17 ***Perf. 14x13***

Design: 8fr, Jean Perrin.

608 A180 5fr dk brn car 18 18
609 A180 8fr dk grnsh bl 18 18

Issued to commemorate the placing of the ashes of physicists Paul Langevin (1872-1946) and Jean Perrin (1870-1942) in the Pantheon.

No. 580 Surcharged with New Value and Bars in Black

1949, Jan. ***Perf. 14x13½***
610 A147 5fr on 6fr carmine 15 15

Arctic Scene — A181

1949, May 2 ***Perf. 13***
611 A181 15fr indigo 38 38

Issued to publicize French polar explorations.

Types of 1849 and 1945

1949, May 9 **Engr.** ***Imperf.***
612 A1 15fr red 4.00 4.00
a. Strip of 4 (1 each Nos. 612 to 615) + label 18.00 18.00
613 A1 25fr dp bl 4.00 4.00

Perf. 14x13
614 A147 15fr red 4.00 4.00
615 A147 25fr dp bl 4.00 4.00

Printed in sheets containing a horizontal row of ten each of Nos. 612 to 615, the imperforate and perforated stamps separated by a row of labels.

Nos. 612 to 615 were issued to commemorate the centenary of the first French postage stamps.

Arms of Burgundy — A182

Designs (Arms): 50c, Guyenne (Aquitania). 1fr, Savoy. 2fr, Auvergne. 4fr, Anjou.

1949, May 11 **Typo.** ***Perf. 14x13½***
616 A182 10c bl, red & yel 6 6
617 A182 50c bl, red & yel 10 10
618 A182 1fr brn & red 15 15
619 A182 2fr grn, yel & red 22 15
620 A182 4fr bl, red & yel 42 38
Nos. 616-620 (5) 95 84

See Nos. 659-663, 694-699, 733-739, 782-785.

Collegiate Church of St. Barnard and Dauphine Arms
A183

1949, May 14 **Engr.** ***Perf. 13***
621 A183 12fr red brn 32 30

Issued to commemorate the 600th anniversary of France's acquisition of the Dauphine region.

U.S. and French Flags, Plane and Steamship
A184

1949, May 14
622 A184 25fr bl & car 55 48

Issued to publicize Franco-American friendship.

Cloister of St. Wandrille Abbey
A185

1949, May 18
623 A185 25fr dp ultra 30 15

See No. 649.

Type of 1849 Inscribed "1849-1949" in Lower Margin

1949, June 1
624 A1 10fr brn org 60.00 52.50
a. Sheet of 10 600.00 600.00

Issued to commemorate the centenary of the first French postage stamp.

No. 624 has wide margins, measuring 40 x 52mm., from perforation to perforation. Sold for 110 francs which included cost of admission to the Centenary International Exhibition, Paris, June 1949.

Claude Chappe
A186

Jean Racine
A187

Designs: 15fr, François Arago and André M. Ampere. 25fr, Emile Baudot. 50fr, Gen. Gustave A. Ferrie.

Inscribed: "C.I.T.T. PARIS 1949".

1949, June 13 **Unwmk.** ***Perf. 13***
625 A186 10fr vermilion 65 60
626 A186 15fr sepia 1.00 75
627 A186 25fr dp cl 3.00 2.25
628 A186 50fr dp bl 4.75 2.25

Issued to publicize the International Telegraph and Telephone Conference, Paris, May-July 1949.

1949
629 A187 12fr sepia 38 38

Issued to commemorate the 250th anniversary of the death of Jean Racine, dramatist.

Abbey of St. Bertrand de Comminges
A188

Meuse Valley, Ardennes
A189

Mt. Gerbier de Jonc, Vivarais
A190

1949 **Engr.**
630 A188 20fr dk red 20 15
631 A189 40fr Prus grn 7.75 22
632 A190 50fr sepia 1.50 15

A191

1949, Oct. 18
633 A191 15fr dp car 30 30

Issued to commemorate the 50th anniversary of the Assembly of Presidents of Chambers of Commerce of the French Union.

U.P.U. Allegory
A192

1949, Nov. 7
634 A192 5fr dk grn 32 30

635 A192 15fr dp car 40 30
636 A192 25fr dp bl 1.25 1.00

Issued to commemorate the 75th anniversary of the formation of the Universal Postal Union.

Raymond Poincaré — A193

Charles Péguy and Cathedral at Chartres A194

François Rabelais — A195

1950, May 27 Unwmk. *Perf. 13*
637 A193 15fr indigo 32 30

1950, June
638 A194 12fr dk brn 32 32
639 A195 12fr red brn 40 40

Chateau of Chateaudun A196

1950, Nov. 25
640 A196 8fr choc & bis brn 32 32

Madame Recamier A197

Marie de Sévigné A198

1950
641 A197 12fr dk grn 38 38
642 A198 15fr ultra 30 30

Palace of Fontainebleau A199

1951, Jan. 20
643 A199 12fr dk brn 38 38

France stamps can be mounted in Scott's annually supplemented France Album.

Jules Ferry — A200

Hands Holding Shuttle A201

Jean-Baptiste de la Salle — A202

1951, Mar. 17
644 A200 15fr brt red 40 35

1951, Apr. 9
645 A201 25fr dp ultra 1.00 90

Issued to publicize the International Textile Exposition at Lille, April-May, 1951.

1951, Apr. 28
646 A202 15fr chocolate 38 38

Issued to commemorate the 300th anniversary of the birth of Jean-Baptiste de la Salle, educator and saint.

Map and Anchor A203

1951, May 12
647 A203 15fr dp ultra 50 45

Issued to commemorate the 50th anniversary of the creation of the French colonial troops.

Vincent d'Indy A204

1951, May 15
648 A204 25fr dp grn 1.75 1.25

Issued to commemorate the centenary of the birth of Vincent d'Indy, composer.

Abbey Type of 1949

1951
649 A185 30fr brt bl 4.75 3.75

Marianne Type of 1945-47

1951 Typo. *Perf. 14x13½*
650 A147 5fr dl vio 50 5
651 A147 6fr green 4.50 45
652 A147 12fr red org 90 15
653 A147 15fr ultra 22 6
a. Booklet pane of 10 22.50
654 A147 18fr cerise 12.00 1.00
Nos. 650-654 (5) 18.12 1.71

Professors Nocard, Bouley and Chauveau; Gate at Lyons School A205

1951, June 8 Engr. *Perf. 13*
655 A205 12fr red vio 60 50

Issued to honor Veterinary Medicine.

Gen. Picqué, Cols. Roussin and Villemin; Val de Grace Dome A206

1951, June 17 Unwmk.
656 A206 15fr red brn 65 50

Issued to honor Military Medicine.

St. Nicholas, by Jean Didier — A207

1951, June 23
657 A207 15fr ind, dp cl & org 55 50

Chateau Bontemps, Arbois A208

1951, June 23
658 A208 30fr indigo 65 22

Arms Type of 1949

Arms of: 10c, Artois. 50c, Limousin. 1fr, Bearn. 2fr, Touraine. 3fr, Franche-Comté.

1951, June Typo. *Perf. 14x13½*
659 A182 10c red, vio bl & yel 6 5
660 A182 50c grn, red & blk 15 15
661 A182 1fr bl, red & yel 22 15
662 A182 2fr vio bl, red & yel 65 22
663 A182 3fr red, vio bl & yel 80 30
Nos. 659-663 (5) 1.88 87

Seal of Paris — A209

Maurice Nogues and Globe — A210

Unwmk.
1951, July 7 Engr. *Perf. 13*
664 A209 15fr dp bl, dk brn & red 45 38

Issued to commemorate the 2,000th anniversary of the founding of Paris.

1951, Oct. 13
665 A210 12fr ind & bl 75 50

Issued to honor Maurice Nogues, aviation pioneer.

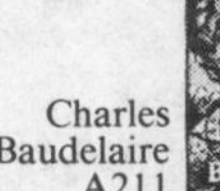

Charles Baudelaire A211

Poets: 12fr, Paul Verlaine. 15fr, Arthur Rimbaud.

1951, Oct. 27
666 A211 8fr purple 40 40
667 A211 12fr gray 55 55
668 A211 15fr dp grn 65 65

Georges Clemenceau — A212

1951, Nov. 11
669 A212 15fr blk brn 30 30

Issued to commemorate the centenary of the birth of Georges Clemenceau.

Chateau du Clos, Vougeot A213

1951, Nov. 17
670 A213 30fr blk brn & brn 3.00 1.65

Chaillot Palace and Eiffel Tower A214

1951, Nov. 6
671 A214 18fr red 65 60
672 A214 30fr dp ultra 1.10 75

Issued to publicize the opening of the Geneva Assembly of the United Nations, Paris, Nov. 6, 1951.

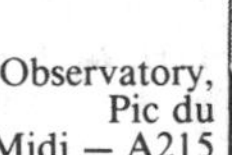

Observatory, Pic du Midi — A215

Abbaye aux Hommes, Caen — A216

1951, Dec. 22
673 A215 40fr violet 4.00 22
674 A216 50fr blk brn 3.00 22

Marshal Jean de Lattre de Tassigny A217

1952, May 8 Unwmk. *Perf. 13*
675 A217 15fr vio brn 90 45

Issued to honor Marshal Jean de Lattre de Tassigny, 1890-1952.
See No. 717.

Gate of France, Vaucouleurs — A218

1952, May 11
676 A218 12fr brn blk 1.65 1.00

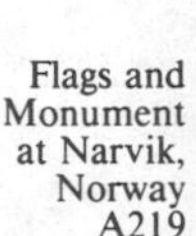

Flags and Monument at Narvik, Norway A219

1952, May 28
677 A219 30fr vio bl 2.25 1.65

Issued to commemorate the 12th anniversary of the Battle of Narvik, May 27, 1940.

Chateau de Chambord A220

1952, May 30
678 A220 20fr dk pur 50 22

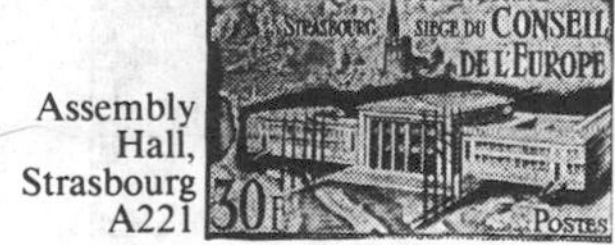

Assembly Hall, Strasbourg A221

1952, May 31
679 A221 30fr dk grn 10.00 6.00

Issued to honor the Council of Europe.

Monument, Bir-Hacheim Cemetery A222

1952, June 14
680 A222 30fr rose lake 3.75 2.25

Issued to commemorate the 10th anniversary of the defense of Bir-Hacheim.

Abbey of the Holy Cross, Poitiers — A223

1952, June 21
681 A223 15fr brt red 40 38

Issued to commemorate the 14th centenary of the foundation of the Abbey of the Holy Cross at Poitiers.

Leonardo da Vinci, Amboise Chateau and La Signoria, Florence
A224

1952, July 9
682 A224 30fr dp ultra 8.50 5.50

Issued to commemorate the 500th anniversary of the birth of Leonardo da Vinci.

Garabit Viaduct A225

1952, July 5
683 A225 15fr dk bl 60 45

Sword and Military Medals, 1852-1952 A226

Dr. René Laennec A227

1952, July 5
684 A226 15fr choc, grn & yel 48 40

Issued to commemorate the centenary of the creation of the Military Medal.

1952, Nov. 7
685 A227 12fr dk grn 50 45

Versailles Gate, Painted by Utrillo A228

1952, Dec. 20
686 A228 18fr vio brn 2.00 1.50

Publicity for the restoration of Versailles Palace. See No. 728.

Mannequin — A229

1953, Apr. 24 Unwmk. *Perf. 13*
687 A229 30fr bl blk & rose vio 90 45

Issued to publicize the dressmaking industry of France.

Gargantua of François Rabelais A230

Célimène from The Misanthrope A231

Figaro, from the Barber of Seville A232

Hernani of Victor Hugo A233

1953
688 A230 6fr dp plum & car 30 30
689 A231 8fr ind & ultra 22 18
690 A232 12fr vio brn & dk grn 22 15
691 A233 18fr vio brn & blk brn 65 45

Type of 1948
Inscribed "Général Leclerc Maréchal de France"

1953-54
692 A176 8fr red brn 65 50
692A A176 12fr dk grn & gray grn ('54) 2.25 1.50

Issued to honor the memory of General Jacques Leclerc.

Map and Cyclists, 1903-1953 A234

1953, July 26
693 A234 12fr red brn, ultra & blk 1.50 1.00

Issued to commemorate the 50th anniversary of the inauguration of the Bicycle Tour of France.

Arms Type of 1949

Coats of Arms: 50c, Picardy. 70c, Gascony. 80c, Berri. 1fr, Poitou. 2fr, Champagne. 3fr, Dauphine.

1953 Typo. *Perf. 14x13½*
694 A182 50c bl, yel & red 28 28
695 A182 70c red, bl & yel 25 25
696 A182 80c bl, red & yel 25 25
697 A182 1fr blk, red & yel 28 22
698 A182 2fr brn, bl & yel 28 22
699 A182 3fr red, bl & yel 50 25
Nos. 694-699 (6) 1.84 1.47

Swimming A235

Sports: 25fr, Track. 30fr, Fencing. 40fr, Canoe racing. 50fr, Rowing. 75fr, Equestrian.

1953, Nov. 28 Engr. *Perf. 13*
700 A235 20fr car & dk brn 2.00 22
701 A235 25fr dk grn & dk brn 7.75 50
702 A235 30fr ultra & dk brn 2.00 30
703 A235 40fr choc & ind 7.25 30
704 A235 50fr bl grn & dk brn 4.25 22
705 A235 75fr org & cl 27.50 12.00
Nos. 700-705 (6) 50.75 13.54

No. 654 Surcharged with New Value and Bars in Black

1954 *Perf. 14x13½*
706 A147 15fr on 18fr cer 75 18

Farm Woman A236

Gallic Cock A237

1954 Typo.
707 A236 4fr blue 38 15
708 A236 8fr brn red 6.00 1.00
709 A237 12fr cerise 4.00 45
710 A237 24fr bl grn 17.50 4.75

Nos. 707-710 are known only precanceled. See Nos. 833-834, 840-844, 910-913, 939 and 952-955. See second note after No. 132.

Tapestry and Gobelin Workshop A238

Entrance to Exhibition Park A239

Designs: 30fr, Book manufacture. 40fr, Porcelain and glassware. 50fr, Jewelry and metalsmith's work. 75fr, Flowers and perfumes.

1954, May 6 Engr. *Perf. 13*
711 A238 25fr red brn car & blk brn 6.75 30
712 A238 30fr dk grn & lil gray 1.25 10
713 A238 40fr dk brn, vio brn & org brn 2.00 10
714 A238 50fr brt ultra, dl grn & org brn 1.40 6
715 A238 75fr dp car & mag 8.00 45
Nos. 711-715 (5) 19.40 1.01

1954, May 22
716 A239 15fr bl & dk car 48 45

Issued to commemorate the 50th anniversary of the founding of the Fair of Paris.

De Lattre Type of 1952

1954, June 5
717 A217 12fr vio bl & ind 2.00 1.40

Allied Landings A240

1954, June 5
718 A240 15fr scar & ultra 1.00 65

The 10th anniversary of the liberation.

View of Lourdes A241

Foreign postal stationery (stamped envelopes, postal cards and air letter sheets) lies beyond the scope of this Catalogue, which is limited to adhesive postage stamps.

Street Corner, Quimper — A242

Views: 8fr, Seine valley, Les Andelys. 10fr, Beach at Royan. 18fr, Cheverny Chateau. 20fr, Beach, Gulf of Ajaccio.

1954

719	A241	6fr ultra, ind & dk grn	32	30
720	A241	8fr brt bl & dk grn	32	15
721	A241	10fr aqua & org brn	32	12
722	A242	12fr rose vio & dk vio	32	6
723	A241	18fr bl, dk grn & ind	2.00	60
724	A241	20fr blk brn, bl grn & red brn	1.65	15
		Nos. 719-724 (6)	4.93	1.38

See No. 873.

Abbey Ruins, Jumièges A243

St. Philibert Abbey, Tournus A244

1954, June 13
725 A243 12fr vio bl, ind & dk grn 1.50 1.10

13th centenary of Abbey of Jumièges.

1954, June 18
726 A244 30fr ind & bl 6.00 3.75

Issued to publicize the first conference of the International Center of Romance Studies.

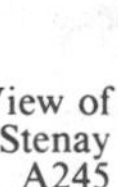

View of Stenay A245

1954, June 26
727 A245 15fr dk brn & org brn 1.00 75

Issued to commemorate the 300th anniversary of the acquisition of Stenay by France.

Versailles Type of 1952

1954, July 10
728 A228 18fr dp bl, ind & vio brn 5.75 3.50

Villandry Chateau A246

1954, July 17
729 A246 18fr dk bl & dk bl grn 4.00 3.50

Napoleon Awarding Legion of Honor Decoration A247

1954, Aug. 14
730 A247 12fr scarlet 1.65 1.00

Issued to commemorate the 150th anniversary of the first Legion of Honor awards at Camp de Boulogne.

Cadets Marching Through Gateway A248

1954, Aug. 1
731 A248 15fr vio gray, dk bl & car 1.65 1.00

Issued to commemorate the 150th anniversary of the founding of the Military School of Saint-Cyr.

Allegory A249

Duke de Saint-Simon A250

1954, Oct. 4
732 A249 30fr ind & choc 6.50 5.50

Issued to publicize the fact that the metric system was first introduced in France.

Arms Type of 1949

Arms: 50c, Maine. 70c, Navarre. 80c, Nivernais. 1fr, Bourbonnais. 2fr, Angoumois. 3fr, Aunis. 5fr, Saintonge.

1954 Typo. *Perf. 14x13½*

733	A182	50c multi	15	15
734	A182	70c grn, red & yel	25	25
735	A182	80c bl, red & yel	25	25
736	A182	1fr red, bl & yel	18	15
737	A182	2fr blk, red & yel	6	5
738	A182	3fr brn, red & yel	5	5
739	A182	5fr bl & yel	6	5
		Nos. 733-739 (7)	1.00	95

1955, Feb. 5 Engr. *Perf. 13*
740 A250 12fr dk brn & vio brn 70 50

Issued to commemorate the 200th anniversary of the death of Louis de Rouvroy, Duke de Saint-Simon (1675-1755).

Allegory and Rotary Emblem A251

Marianne A252

1955, Feb. 23
741 A251 30fr vio bl, bl & org 1.25 1.00

Issued to commemorate the 50th anniversary of the founding of Rotary International.

1955-59 Typo. *Perf. 14x13½*

751	A252	6fr fawn	3.00	2.25
752	A252	12fr green	2.50	1.50
a.		Bklt. pane of 10 + 2 labels	27.50	
753	A252	15fr carmine	30	5
a.		Bklt. pane of 10	8.50	
754	A252	18fr ultra ('58)	30	15
755	A252	20fr ultra ('57)	45	5
756	A252	25fr rose red ('59)	1.00	5
a.		Bklt. pane of 8	10.00	
b.		Bklt. pane of 10	11.00	
		Nos. 751-756 (6)	7.55	4.05

No. 751 was issued in coils of 1,000.
No. 752 was issued in panes of 10 stamps and two labels with marginal instructions for folding to form a booklet.

Nos. 754-755 are found in two types, distinguished by the numerals. On the 18fr there is no serif at base of "1" on the earlier type.

Philippe Lebon, Inventor of Illuminating Gas — A253

Inventors: 10fr, Barthélemy Thimonnier, sewing machine. 12fr, Nicolas Appert, canned foods. 18fr, Dr. E. H. St. Claire Deville, aluminum. 25fr, Pierre Martin, steel making. 30fr, Bernigaud de Chardonnet, rayon.

1955, Mar. 5 Engr.

757	A253	5fr dk vio bl & bl	85	55
758	A253	10fr dk brn & org brn	85	65
759	A253	12fr dk grn	1.25	75
760	A253	18fr dk vio bl & ind	2.75	2.50
761	A253	25fr dk brnsh pur & vio	2.75	2.25
762	A253	30fr rose car & scar	2.75	2.25
		Nos. 757-762 (6)	11.20	8.95

St. Stephen Bridge, Limoges A254

1955, Mar. 26 Unwmk. *Perf. 13*
763 A254 12fr yel brn & dk vio brn 1.50 1.10

Gloved Model in Place de la Concorde — A255

1955, Mar. 26
764 A255 25fr blk brn, vio bl & blk 80 22

Issued to publicize French glove manufacturing.

Jean Pierre Claris de Florian A256

1955, Apr. 2
765 A256 12fr bl grn 70 50

200th anniversary of the birth of Jean Pierre Claris de Florian, fabulist.

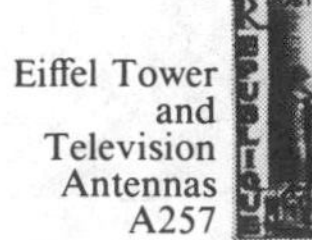

Eiffel Tower and Television Antennas A257

1955, Apr. 16
766 A257 15fr ind & ultra 65 40

Issued to publicize French advancement in television.

Wire Fence and Guard Tower A258

1955, Apr. 23
767 A258 12fr dk gray bl & brn blk 65 50

Issued to commemorate the 10th anniversary of the liberation of concentration camps.

Electric Train A259

1955, May 11
768 A259 12fr blk brn & sl bl 1.65 80

Issued to publicize the electrification of the Valenciennes-Thionville railroad line.

Jacquemart of Moulins — A260

1955, May 28
769 A260 12fr blk brn 1.00 70

Jules Verne and Nautilus A261

1955, June 3
770 A261 30fr indigo 6.00 5.00

Issued to commemorate the 50th anniversary of the death of Jules Verne.

Auguste and Louis Lumière and Motion Picture Projector A262

1955, June 12
771 A262 30fr rose brn 4.25 3.50

Issued to commemorate the 60th anniversary of the invention of motion pictures.

Jacques Coeur and His Mansion at Bourges A263

1955, June 18
772 A263 12fr violet 2.00 1.50

Issued to commemorate the 5th centenary of the death of Jacques Coeur (1395?-1456), French merchant.

Corvette "La Capricieuse" A264

1955, July 9
773 A264 30fr aqua & dk bl 5.00 3.75

Issued to commemorate the centenary of the voyage of La Capricieuse to Canada.

Bordeaux
A265

Designs: 8fr, Marseilles. 10fr, Nice. 12fr, Valentre bridge, Cahors. 18fr, Uzerche. 25fr, Fortifications, Brouage.

1955, Oct. 15

774 A265 6fr car lake 25 22
775 A265 8fr indigo 35 15
776 A265 10fr dp ultra 30 6
777 A265 12fr vio & brn 30 6
778 A265 18fr bluish grn & ind 80 18
779 A265 25fr org brn & red brn 1.00 12
Nos. 774-779 (6) 3.00 79

See Nos. 838-839.

Mount Pelée, Martinique
A266

1955, Nov. 1

780 A266 20fr dk & lt pur 2.00 15

Gérard de Nerval — A267

1955, Nov. 11

781 A267 12fr lake & sep 50 32

Issued to commemorate the centenary of the death of Gérard de Nerval (Labrunie), author.

Arms Type of 1949

Arms of: 50c, County of Foix. 70c, Marche. 80c, Roussillon. 1fr, Comtat Venaissin.

Perf. 14x13½

1955, Nov. 19 Typo. Unwmk.

782 A182 50c multi 6 6
783 A182 70c red, bl & yel 15 15
784 A182 80c brn, yel & red 15 15
785 A182 1fr bl, red & yel 6 5

Concentration Camp Victim and Monument
A268

Belfry at Douai
A269

1956, Jan. 14 Engr. *Perf. 13*

786 A268 15fr brn blk & red brn 75 75

No. 786 shows the national memorial for Nazi deportation victims erected at the Natzwiller Struthof concentration camp in Alsace.

1956, Feb. 11

787 A269 15fr ultra & ind 38 38

The lack of a price for a listed item does not necessarily indicate rarity.

Col. Emil Driant
A270

1956, Feb. 21

788 A270 15fr dk bl 32 32

Issued to commemorate the 40th anniversary of the death of Col. Emil Driant during the battle of Verdun.

Trench Fighting — A271

1956, Mar. 3

789 A271 30fr ind & dk ol 1.75 1.00

40th anniversary of Battle of Verdun.

Jean Henri Fabre, Entomology
A272

Scientists: 15fr, Charles Tellier, Refrigeration. 18fr, Camille Flammarion, Popular Astronomy. 30fr, Paul Sabatier, Catalytic Chemistry.

1956, Apr. 7

790 A272 12fr vio brn & org brn 65 45
791 A272 15fr vio bl & int blk 1.00 65
792 A272 18fr brt ultra 2.25 1.50
793 A272 30fr Prus grn & dk grn 3.25 2.50

Grand Trianon, Versailles
A273

1956, Apr. 14

794 A273 12fr vio brn & gray grn 1.25 95

Symbols of Latin American and French Culture
A274

1956, Apr. 21

795 A274 30fr brn & red brn 1.75 1.10

Issued in recognition of the friendship between France and Latin America.

"The Smile of Reims" and Botticelli's "Spring"
A275

1956, May 5

796 A275 12fr blk & grn 75 50

Issued to emphasize the cultural and artistic kinship of Reims and Florence.

Leprosarium and Maltese Cross — A276

1956, May 12

797 A276 12fr sep, red brn & red 40 35

Issued in honor of the Knights of Malta.

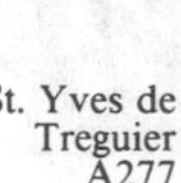

St. Yves de Treguier
A277

1956, May 19

798 A277 15fr bluish gray & blk 38 32

Issued in honor of St. Yves, patron saint of lawyers.

Marshal Franchet d'Esperey
A278

Miners Monument
A279

1956, May 26

799 A278 30fr dp cl 2.00 1.10

Issued to commemorate the centenary of the birth of Marshal Louis Franchet d'Esperey.

1956, June 2

800 A279 12fr vio brn 40 35

Issued to commemorate the 100th anniversary of the town Montceau-les-Mines.

Basketball
A280

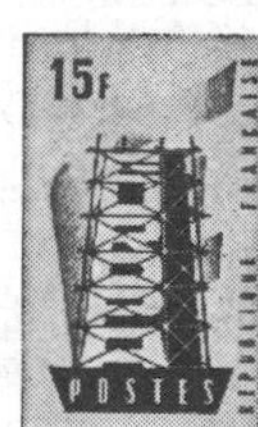

"Rebuilding Europe"
A281

Sports: 40fr, Pelota (Jai alai). 50fr, Rugby. 75fr, Mountain climbing.

1956, July 7

801 A280 30fr gray vio & blk 80 18
802 A280 40fr brn & vio brn 2.50 28
803 A280 50fr rose vio & vio 1.65 15
804 A280 75fr ind, grn & bl 5.00 1.50

Europa Issue

Perf. 13½x14

1956, Sept. 15 Typo. Unwmk.

805 A281 15fr rose & rose lake 1.10 25

Perf. 13

Engr.

806 A281 30fr lt bl & vio bl 5.75 1.00

Issued to symbolize the cooperation among the six countries comprising the Coal and Steel Community.

No. 805 measures 21x35½mm., No. 806 measures 22x35½mm.

Dam at Donzère-Mondragon — A282

Cable Railway to Pic du Midi — A283

Rhine Port of Strasbourg
A284

1956, Oct. 6 Engr. *Perf. 13*

807 A282 12fr gray vio & vio brn 1.10 75
808 A283 18fr indigo 1.75 1.10
809 A284 30fr ind & dk bl 5.50 2.25

French technical achievements.

Antoine-Augustin Parmentier — A285

1956, Oct. 27

810 A285 12fr brn red & brn 40 35

Issued in honor of A. A. Parmentier, nutrition chemist, who popularized the potato in France.

Petrarch — A286

Portraits: 12fr, J. B. Lully. 15fr, J. J. Rousseau. 18fr, Benjamin Franklin. 20fr, Frederic Chopin. 30fr, Vincent van Gogh.

1956, Nov. 10

811 A286 8fr green 60 50
812 A286 12fr claret 60 50
813 A286 15fr dk red 90 60
814 A286 18fr ultra 2.50 1.75
815 A286 20fr brt vio 3.00 1.40
816 A286 30fr brt grnsh bl 3.75 2.75
Nos. 811-816 (6) 11.35 7.50

Issued in honor of famous men who lived in France.

Pierre de Coubertin and Olympic Stadium
A287

1956, Nov. 24

817 A287 30fr dk bl gray & pur 1.25 80

Issued in honor of Baron Pierre de Coubertin, founder of the modern Olympic Games.

Homing Pigeon
A288

1957, Jan. 12
818 A288 15fr dp ultra, ind & red brn 30 28

Victor Schoelcher — A289

1957, Feb. 16 **Engr.**
819 A289 18fr lil rose 40 35

Issued in honor of Victor Schoelcher, who freed the slaves in the French Colonies.

Sèvres Porcelain
A290

1957, Mar. 23 **Unwmk.** ***Perf. 13***
820 A290 30fr ultra & vio bl 60 45

Issued to commemorate the the bicentenary of the porcelain works at Sèvres (in 1956).

Gaston Planté and Storage Battery
A291

Designs: 12fr, Antoine Béclère and X-ray apparatus. 18fr, Octave Terrillon, autoclave, microscope and surgical instruments. 30fr, Etienne Oemichen and early helicopter.

1957, Apr. 13
821 A291 8fr gray blk & dp cl 35 35
822 A291 12fr dk bl, blk & emer 40 40
823 A291 18fr rose red & mag 1.25 1.25
824 A291 30fr grn & sl grn 1.90 1.90

Uzès Chateau
A292

1957, Apr. 27
825 A292 12fr sl bl & bis brn 30 30

Jean Moulin A293 — Le Quesnoy A294

Portraits: 10fr, Honoré d'Estienne d'Orves. 12fr, Robert Keller. 18fr, Pierre Brossolette. 20fr, Jean-Baptiste Lebas.

1957, May 18
826 A293 8fr vio brn 45 35
827 A293 10fr blk & vio bl 42 35
828 A293 12fr brn & sl grn 45 30
829 A293 18fr pur & blk 1.40 80
830 A293 20fr Prus bl & dk bl 80 45
Nos. 826-830 (5) 3.52 2.25

Issued in honor of the heroes of the French Underground of World War II.
See Nos. 879-882, 915-919, 959-963, 990-993.

1957, June 1
831 A294 8fr dk sl grn 18 18

See No. 837.

Symbols of Justice
A295

1957, June 1
832 A295 12fr sep & ultra 30 30

Issued to commemorate the 150th anniversary of the French Cour des Comptes.

Farm Woman Type of 1954

1957-59 ***Perf. 14x13½***
833 A236 6fr orange 10 10
833A A236 10fr brt grn ('59) 60 6
834 A236 12fr red lil 18 15

Nos. 833-834 issued without precancellation.

Symbols of Public Works
A296

1957, June 20 **Engr.** ***Perf. 13***
835 A296 30fr sl grn, brn & ocher 1.00 60

Brest
A297

1957, July 6
836 A297 12fr gray grn & brn ol 50 35

Scenic Types of 1955, 1957

Designs: 15fr, Le Quesnoy. 35fr, Bordeaux. 70fr, Valentre bridge, Cahors.

1957, July 19 **Unwmk.**
837 A294 15fr dk bl grn & sep 18 5
838 A265 35fr dk bl grn & sl grn 1.25 40
839 A265 70fr blk & dl grn 5.50 1.25

Gallic Cock Type of 1954

1957 **Typo.** ***Perf. 14x13½***
840 A237 5fr ol bis 38 30
841 A237 10fr brt bl 90 38
842 A237 15fr plum 2.00 60
843 A237 30fr brt red 4.75 1.25
844 A237 45fr green 30.00 15.00
Nos. 840-844 (5) 38.03 17.53

Nos. 840-844 are known only precanceled. See second note after No. 132.

Leo Lagrange and Stadium
A298

1957, Aug. 31 **Engr.** ***Perf. 13***
845 A298 18fr lil gray & blk 35 28

Issued to commemorate the International University Games, Paris, Aug. 31-Sept. 8.

"United Europe" A299 — Auguste Comte A300

1957, Sept. 16
846 A299 20fr red brn & grn 40 25
847 A299 35fr dk brn & bl 1.25 50

Issued to publicize a united Europe for peace and prosperity.

1957, Sept. 14
848 A300 35fr brn red & sep 50 50

Issued to commemorate the centenary of the death of Auguste Comte, mathematician and philosopher.

Roman Amphitheater, Lyon — A301

1957, Oct. 5 ***Perf. 13***
849 A301 20fr brn org & brn vio 40 30

Issued to commemorate the 2,000th anniversary of the founding of Lyon.

Sens River, Guadeloupe
A302

Beynac-Cazenac, Dordogne A303 — Nicolaus Copernicus A304

Designs: 10fr, Elysee Palace. 25fr, Chateau de Valencay, Indre. 35fr, Rouen Cathedral. 50fr, Roman Ruins, Saint-Remy. 65fr, Evian-les-Bains.

1957, Oct. 19
850 A302 8fr grn & lt brn 15 15
851 A302 10fr dk ol bis & vio brn 15 12
852 A303 18fr ind & dk brn 28 15
853 A302 25fr bl gray & vio brn 38 15
854 A303 35fr car rose & lake 38 6
855 A302 50fr ol grn & ol bis 55 6
856 A302 65fr dk bl & ind 90 18
Nos. 850-856 (7) 2.79 87

See Nos. 907-909.

1957, Nov. 9 **Engr.** ***Perf. 13***

Portraits: 10fr, Michelangelo. 12fr, Miguel de Cervantes. 15fr, Rembrandt. 18fr, Isaac Newton. 25fr, Mozart. 35fr, Johann Wolfgang von Goethe.

857 A304 8fr dk brn 60 45
858 A304 10fr dk grn 65 45
859 A304 12fr dk pur 75 45
860 A304 15fr brn & org brn 95 40
861 A304 18fr dp bl 1.25 90
862 A304 25fr lil & cl 1.25 45
863 A304 35fr blue 1.50 1.10
Nos. 857-863 (7) 6.95 4.20

Louis Jacques Thenard
A305

1957, Nov. 30 **Unwmk.**
864 A305 15fr ol bis & grnsh blk 40 40

Issued to commemorate the centenary of the death of L. J. Thenard, chemist, and the founding of the Charitable Society of the Friends of Science.

Dr. Philippe Pinel A306 — Joseph Louis Lagrange A307

Doctors' Portraits: 12fr, Fernand Widal. 15fr, Charles Nicolle. 35fr, Rene Leriche.

1958, Jan. 25
865 A306 8fr brn ol 65 50
866 A306 12fr brt vio bl 65 50
867 A306 15fr dp bl 1.10 60
868 A306 35fr black 1.50 1.00

Issued in honor of famous French physicians.

1958, Feb. 15 ***Perf. 13***

Portraits: 12fr, Urbain Jean Joseph Leverrier. 15fr, Jean Bernard Leon Foucault. 35fr, Claude Louis Berthollet.

869 A307 8fr bl grn & vio bl 80 55
870 A307 12fr sep & gray 95 70
871 A307 15fr sl grn & grn 1.90 95
872 A307 35fr mar & cop red 2.00 1.10

Issued to honor French scientists.

Lourdes Type of 1954

1958
873 A241 20fr grnsh bl & ol 38 22

Le Havre
A308

Maubeuge — A309

Designs: 18fr, Saint-Die. 25fr, Sete.

1958, Mar. 29 **Engr.** ***Perf. 13***
874 A308 12fr ol grn & car rose 55 45
875 A309 15fr brt pur & brn 60 40
876 A309 18fr ultra & ind 95 75
877 A308 25fr dk bl, bl grn & brn 1.25 75

Reconstruction of war-damaged cities.

French Pavilion, Brussels
A310

1958, Apr. 12
878 A310 35fr brn, dk grn & bl 38 32

Issued for the Universal and International Exposition at Brussels.

Heroes Type of 1957

Portraits: 8fr, Jean Cavaillès. 12fr, Fred Scamaroni. 15fr, Simone Michel-Levy. 20fr, Jacques Bingen.

1958, Apr. 19
879 A293 8fr vio & blk 38 30
880 A293 12fr ultra & grn 38 30
881 A293 15fr brn & gray 1.10 90
882 A293 20fr ol & ultra 1.00 65

Issued in honor of the heroes of the French Underground in World War II.

Bowling A311

Sports: 15fr, Naval joust. 18fr, Archery (vert.). 25fr, Breton wrestling (vert.).

1958, Apr. 26
883 A311 12fr rose & brn 75 38
884 A311 15fr bl, ol gray & grn 95 55
885 A311 18fr grn & brn 1.65 95
886 A311 25fr brn & ind 2.25 1.25

Senlis Cathedral — A312

1958, May 17
887 A312 15fr ultra & ind 35 35

Bayeux Tapestry Horsemen A313

1958, June 21
888 A313 15fr bl & car 35 30

Europa Issue, 1958
Common Design Type

1958, Sept. 13 Engr. *Perf. 13*
Size: 22x36mm.
889 CD1 20fr rose red 35 20
890 CD1 35fr ultra 65 40

Foix Chateau A314

1958, Oct. 11
891 A314 15fr ultra, grn & ol brn 18 18

City Halls, Paris and Rome A315

1958, Oct. 11
892 A315 35fr gray, grnsh bl & rose red 40 35

Issued to publicize the cultural ties between Rome and Paris and the need for European unity.

Common Design Types pictured in section at front of book.

UNESCO Building, Paris A316

Design: 35fr, Different view of building.

1958, Nov. 1 ***Perf. 13***
893 A316 20fr grnsh bl & ol bis 15 15
894 A316 35fr dk sl grn & red org 25 25

Issued to commemorate the opening of UNESCO (U.N. Educational, Scientific and Cultural Organization) Headquarters in Paris, Nov. 3.

Soldier's Grave in Wheat Field A317

Arms of Marseilles A318

1958, Nov. 11
895 A317 15fr dk grn & ultra 18 18

Issued to commemorate the 40th anniversary of the World War I armistice.

1958-59 Typo. *Perf. 14x13½*

Arms (Cities): 70c, Lyon. 80c, Toulouse. 1fr, Bordeaux. 2fr, Nice. 3fr, Nantes. 5fr, Lille. 15fr, Algiers.

896 A318 50c dk bl & ultra 5 5
897 A318 70c multi 5 5
898 A318 80c red, bl & yel 5 5
899 A318 1fr dk bl, yel & red 6 5
900 A318 2fr dk bl, red & grn 6 5
901 A318 3fr multi 10 10
902 A318 5fr dk brn & red 10 5
903 A318 15fr multi ('59) 18 15
Nos. 896-903 (8) 65 55

See Nos. 938, 940, 973, 1040-1042, 1091-1095, 1142-1144.

Arc de Triomphe and Flowers — A319

1959, Jan. 17 Engr. *Perf. 13*
904 A319 15fr brn, bl, grn, cl & red 30 25

Paris Flower Festival.

Symbols of Learning and Medal A320

1959, Jan. 24 ***Perf. 13***
905 A320 20fr lake, blk & vio 25 25

Issued to commemorate the sesquicentennial of the Palm Leaf Medal of the French Academy.

Charles de Foucauld A321

1959, Jan. 31
906 A321 50fr dp brn, bl & mar 65 55

Issued to honor Father Charles de Foucauld, explorer and missionary of the Sahara.

Type of 1957

Designs: 30fr, Elysee Palace. 85fr, Evian-les- Bains. 100fr, Sens River, Guadeloupe.

1959, Feb. 10
907 A302 30fr dk sl grn 80 15
908 A302 85fr dp cl 1.65 18
909 A302 100fr dp vio 8.75 30

Gallic Cock Type of 1954

1959 Typo. *Perf. 14x13½*
910 A237 8fr violet 60 22
911 A237 20fr yel grn 1.75 65
912 A237 40fr hn brn 3.75 2.25
913 A237 55fr emerald 17.00 10.00

Nos. 910-913 were issued with precancellation. See second note after No. 132.

Miners' Tools and School A322

1959, Apr. 11 Engr. *Perf. 13*
914 A322 20fr red, blk & bl 18 18

Issued to commemorate the 175th anniversary of the National Mining School.

Heroes Type of 1957

Portraits: No. 915, The five martyrs of the Buffon school. No. 916, Yvonne Le Roux. No. 917, Mederic-Vedy. No. 918, Louis Martin-Bret. 30fr, Gaston Moutardier.

1959, Apr. 25 Engr. *Perf. 13*
915 A293 15fr blk & vio 38 30
916 A293 15fr mag & rose vio 45 40
917 A293 20fr grn & grnsh bl 48 40
918 A293 20fr org brn & brn 70 55
919 A293 30fr mag & vio 80 55
Nos. 915-919 (5) 2.81 2.20

Dam at Foum el Gherza A323

Marcoule Atomic Center — A324

Designs: 30fr, Oil field at Hassi Messaoud, Sahara. 50fr, C. N. I. T. Building (Centre National des Industries et des Techniques).

1959, May 23
920 A323 15fr ol & grnsh bl 38 30
921 A324 20fr brt car & red brn 50 38
922 A324 30fr dk bl, brn & grn 75 38
923 A323 50fr ol grn & sl bl 1.40 60

Issued to publicize French technical achievements.

Marceline Desbordes-Valmore — A325

1959, June 20
924 A325 30fr bl, brn & grn 32 32

Issued to commemorate the centenary of the death of Marceline Desbordes-Valmore, poet.

Pilots Goujon and Rozanoff A326

1959, June 13
925 A326 20fr lt bl & org brn 32 32

Issued in honor of Charles Goujon and Col. Constantin Rozanoff, test pilots.

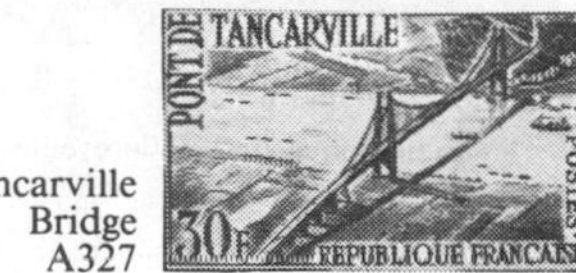

Tancarville Bridge A327

1959, Aug. 1 Engr. *Perf. 13*
926 A327 30fr dk bl, brn & ol 32 25

Marianne and Ship of State A328

Jean Jaures A329

1959, July Typo. *Perf. 14x13½*
927 A328 25fr blk & red 40 6

See No. 942.

1959, Sept. 12 Engr. *Perf. 13*
928 A329 50fr chocolate 50 40

Issued to commemorate the centenary of the birth of Jean Jaures, socialist leader.

Europa Issue, 1959
Common Design Type

1959, Sept. 19 Size: 22x36mm
929 CD2 25fr brt grn 45 30
930 CD2 50fr brt vio 90 45

Blood Donors A330

1959, Oct. 17 Engr.
931 A330 20fr mag & gray 30 25

French-Spanish Handshake — A331

1959, Oct. 24 *Perf. 13*

932 A331 50fr bl, rose car & org 60 45

Issued to commemorate the 300th anniversary of the signing of the Treaty of the Pyrenees.

Polio Victim Holding Crutches A332

Henri Bergson A333

1959, Oct. 31

933 A332 20fr dk bl 22 15

Vaccination against poliomyelitis.

1959, Nov. 7

934 A333 50fr lt red brn 48 40

Issued to commemorate the centenary of the birth of Henri Bergson, philosopher.

Avesnes-sur-Helpe — A334

Design: 30fr, Perpignan.

1959, Nov. 14

935 A334 20fr sep & bl 30 25
936 A334 30fr brn, dp cl & bl 38 30

New NATO Headquarters, Paris — A335

1959, Dec. 12

937 A335 50fr grn, brn & ultra 95 65

Issued to commemorate the 10th anniversary of the North Atlantic Treaty Organization.

Types of 1958-59 and

Farm Woman A336

Sower A337

Designs: 5c, Arms of Lille. 15c, Arms of Algiers. 25c, Marianne and Ship of State.

Perf. 14x13½

1960-61 **Unwmk.** **Typo.**

938 A318 5c dk brn & red 10.00 22
939 A336 10c brt grn 38 5
940 A318 15c red, ultra, yel & grn 75 18
941 A337 20c grnsh bl & car rose 25 10
942 A328 25c ver & ultra 3.00 15
b. Bklt. pane of 8 27.50
c. Bklt. pane of 10 32.50
942A A337 30c gray & ultra ('61) 2.50 45
Nos. 938-942A (6) 16.88 1.15

Earlier stamps of Farm Woman type (A336), but with no decimals in denominations, are listed as Nos. 707-708, 833-834 (A236). Nos. 938-942A are in the New Franc currency (100 old francs equal 1 New Franc).

Laon Cathedral A338

Kerrata Gorge — A339

Designs: 30c, Fougères Chateau. 50c, Mosque, Tlemcen. 65c, Sioule Valley. 85c, Chaumont Viaduct. 1fr, Cilaos Church, Reunion.

1960, Jan. 16 **Engr.** *Perf. 13*

943 A338 15c bl & ind 22 22
944 A338 30c bl, sep & grn 2.25 15
945 A339 45c brt vio & ol gray 75 12
946 A339 50c sl grn & lt cl 75 5
947 A338 65c sl grn, bl & blk brn 90 18
948 A338 85c bl, sep & grn 2.25 18
949 A339 1fr vio bl, bl & grn 1.50 12
Nos. 943-949 (7) 8.62 1.02

Pierre de Nolhac A340

1960, Feb. 13

950 A340 20c blk & gray 75 50

Issued to commemorate the centenary of the birth of Pierre de Nolhac, curator of Versailles and historian.

Museum of Art and Industry, Saint-Etienne A341

1960, Feb. 20

951 A341 30c brn, car & sl 75 50

Gallic Cock Type of 1954

1960 **Typo.** *Perf. 14x13½*

952 A237 8c violet 1.10 6
953 A237 20c yel grn 3.75 45
954 A237 40c hn brn 9.25 2.75
955 A237 55c emerald 35.00 17.00

Nos. 952-955 were issued only precanceled. See second note after No. 132.

View of Cannes A342

1960, Mar. 5 **Engr.** *Perf. 13*

956 A342 50c red brn & lt grn 1.00 80

Issued to commemorate the meeting of European municipal administrators, Cannes, March, 1960.

Woman of Savoy and Alps — A343

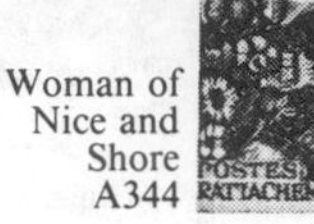

Woman of Nice and Shore A344

1960 **Unwmk.** *Perf. 13*

957 A343 30c sl grn 55 55
958 A344 50c brn, yel & rose 60 45

Issued to commemorate the centenary of the annexation of Nice and Savoy.

Heroes Type of 1957

Portraits: No. 959, Edmund Debeaumarché. No. 960, Pierre Massé. No. 961, Maurice Ripoche. No. 962, Leonce Vieljeux. 50c, Abbé René Bonpain.

1960, Mar. 26

959 A293 20c bis & blk 2.50 1.65
960 A293 20c pink & rose cl 2.50 1.65
961 A293 30c vio & brt vio 2.50 1.65
962 A293 30c sl bl & brt bl 2.75 2.50
963 A293 50c sl grn & red brn 3.50 3.00
Nos. 959-963 (5) 13.75 10.45

Issued in honor of the heroes of the French Underground of World War II.

"Education" and Children A345

1960, May 21 **Engr.** *Perf. 13*

964 A345 20c rose lil, pur & blk 32 30

Issued to commemorate the 150th anniversary of the first secondary school in Strasbourg.

Blois Chateau A346

View of La Bourboule A347

1960, May

965 A346 30c dk bl, sep & grn 75 45
966 A347 50c ol brn, car & grn 90 60

Lorraine Cross A348

Marianne A349

1960, June 18

967 A348 20c red brn, dk brn & yel grn 45 30

Issued to commemorate the 20th anniversary of the French Resistance Movement in World War II.

1960, June 18 **Typo.** *Perf. 14x13½*

968 A349 25c lake & gray 18 5
a. Bklt. pane of 8 6.00
b. Bklt. pane of 10 4.50

Jean Bouin and Stadium A350

1960, July 9 **Engr.** *Perf. 13*

969 A350 20c bl, mag & ol gray 32 30

Issued to commemorate the 17th Olympic Games, Rome, Aug. 25-Sept. 11.

Europa Issue, 1960

Common Design Type

1960, Sept. 17 *Perf. 13*

Size: 36x22mm.

970 CD3 25c grn & bluish grn 18 18
971 CD3 50c mar & red lil 40 30

Lisieux Basilica A351

1960, Sept. 24 *Perf. 13*

972 A351 15c bl, gray & blk 30 30

Arms Type of 1958-59

Design: Arms of Oran.

1960, Oct. 15 **Typo.** *Perf. 14x13½*

973 A318 5c red, bl, yel & emer 25 5

Madame de Stael by François Gerard — A352

1960, Oct. 22 **Engr.** *Perf. 13*

974 A352 30c dl cl & brn 32 30

Issued to honor Madame de Stael (1766-1817), writer.

Gen. J. B. E. Estienne A353

1960, Nov. 5

975 A353 15c lt lil & blk 22 22

Issued to commemorate the centenary of the birth of Gen. Jean Baptiste Eugene Estienne.

Marc Sangnier and Youth Hostel at Bierville A354

1960, Nov. 5
976 A354 20c bl, blk & lil 22 18

Issued to honor Marc Sangnier, founder of the French League for Youth Hostels.

Badge of Order of Liberation — A355

1960, Nov. 14 Engr. *Perf. 13*
977 A355 20c blk & brt grn 38 30

Order of Liberation, 20th anniversary.

Lapwings A356

Birds: 30c, Puffin. 45c, European teal. 50c, European bee-eaters.

1960, Nov. 12
978 A356 20c multi 38 30
979 A356 30c multi 38 38
980 A356 45c multi 1.25 75
981 A356 50c multi 80 38

Issued to publicize wildlife protection.

André Honnorat A357

1960, Nov. 19
982 A357 30c bl, blk & grn 38 30

Issued to honor André Honnorat, statesman, fighter against tuberculosis and founder of the University City of Paris, an international students' community.

St. Barbara and Medieval View of School A358

1960, Dec. 3 Engr.
983 A358 30c red, bl & ol brn 40 40

Issued to commemorate the 500th anniversary of St. Barbara School, Paris.

"Mediterranean" by Aristide Maillol — A359

Marianne by Cocteau — A360

1961, Feb. 18 Unwmk. *Perf. 13*
984 A359 20c car & ind 30 25

Issued to commemorate the centenary of the birth of Aristide Maillol, sculptor.

1961, Feb. 23
985 A360 20c bl & car 25 5

A second type has an extra inverted V-shaped mark (a blue flag top) at right of hair tip. Price unused $2.50, used 50 cents.

Paris Airport, Orly A361

1961, Feb. 25
986 A361 50c blk, dk bl, & bluish grn 55 45

Issued to commemorate the inauguration of new facilities at Orly airport.

George Melies and Motion Picture Screen A362

1961, March 11
987 A362 50c pur, ind & ol bis 90 50

Issued to commemorate the centenary of the birth of George Melies, motion picture pioneer.

Jean Baptiste Henri Lacordaire — A363

1961, Mar. 25 *Perf. 13*
988 A363 30c lt brn & blk 30 30

Issued to commemorate the centenary of the death of the Dominican monk Lacordaire, orator and liberal Catholic leader.

A364

1961, Mar. 25
989 A364 30c grn, red brn & red 30 30

Introduction of tobacco use into France, fourth centenary. By error stamp portrays Jan Nicquet instead of Jean Nicot.

Heroes Type of 1957

Portraits: No. 990, Jacques Renouvin. No. 991, Lionel Dubray. No. 992, Paul Gateaud. No. 993, Mère Elisabeth.

1961, Apr. 22
990 A293 20c bl & lil 90 60
991 A293 20c gray grn & bl 90 65
992 A293 30c brn org & blk 1.25 80
993 A293 30c vio & blk 1.50 90

Bagnoles-de-l'Orne — A365

1961, May 6
994 A365 20c ol, ocher, bl & grn 30 25

Dove, Olive Branch and Federation Emblem — A366

1961, May 6
995 A366 50c brt bl, grn & mar 40 38

World Federation of Ex-Service Men.

Deauville in 19th Century A367

1961, May 13 Engr.
996 A367 50c rose cl 1.75 1.25

Centenary of Deauville.

La Champmeslé A368

Mont-Dore, Snowflake and Cable Car A369

French actors: No. 998, Talma. No. 999, Rachel. No. 1000, Gérard Philipe. No. 1001, Raimu.

1961, June 10 Unwmk. *Perf. 13*
Dark Carmine Frame
997 A368 20c choc & yel grn 45 30
998 A368 30c brn & crim 50 38
999 A368 30c yel brn & sl grn 50 38
1000 A368 50c ol & choc 90 60
1001 A368 50c bl grn & red brn 90 45
Nos. 997-1001 (5) 3.25 2.11

Issued to honor great French actors and in connection with the Fifth World Congress of the International Federation of Actors.

1961, July 1
1002 A369 20c org & rose lil 32 25

Pierre Fauchard A370

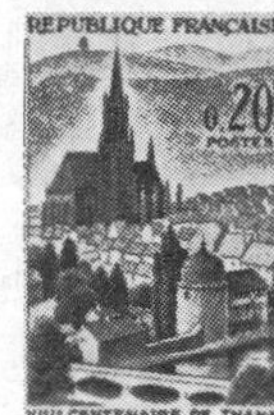
St. Theobald's Church, Thann A371

1961, July 1
1003 A370 50c dk grn & blk 60 45

Issued to commemorate the bicentenary of the death of Pierre Fauchard, first surgeon dentist.

1961, July 1
1004 A371 20c sl grn, vio & brn 75 45

800th anniversary of Thann.

Europa Issue, 1961
Common Design Type

1961, Sept. 16 *Perf. 13*
Size: 35x22mm.
1005 CD4 25c vermilion 18 15
1006 CD4 50c ultra 38 30

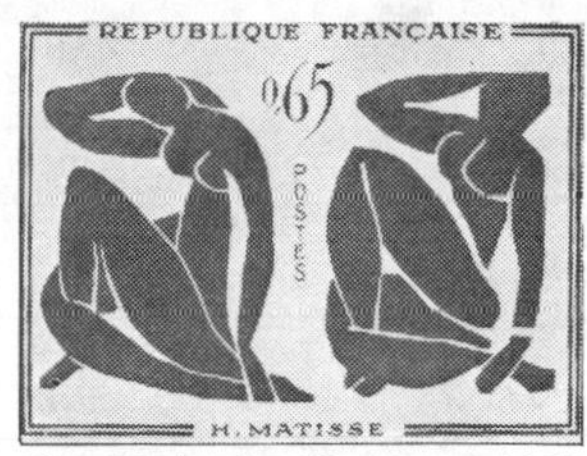
Saint-Paul, Maritime Alps — A372

Designs: 30c, Beach and sailboats, Arcachon. 45c, Sully-sur-Loire Chateau. 50c, View of Cognac. 65c, Rance Valley and Dinan. 85c, City hall and Rodin's Burghers, Calais. 1fr, Roman gates of Lodi, Medea, Algeria.

1961, Oct. 9 Engr. *Perf. 13*
1007 A372 15c bl & pur 15 15
1008 A372 30c ultra, sl grn & lt brn 25 15
1009 A372 45c vio bl, red brn & grn 32 5
1010 A372 50c grn, Prus bl & sl 48 12
1011 A372 65c red brn, sl grn & bl 48 10
1012 A372 85c sl grn, sl & red brn 75 16
1013 A372 1fr dk bl, sl & bis 2.75 15
Nos. 1007-1013 (7) 5.18 88

Blue Nudes, by Matisse — A373

Paintings: 50c, "The Messenger," by Braque. 85c, "The Cardplayers," by Cézanne. 1fr, "The 14th July," by Roger de La Fresnaye.

1961, Nov. 10 *Perf. 13x12*
1014 A373 50c dk brn, bl, blk & gray 3.75 2.25
1015 A373 65c grn, vio, & ultra 4.50 3.00
1016 A373 85c blk, brn, red & ol 3.50 2.50
1017 A373 1fr multi 5.50 3.75

Liner France A374

1962, Jan. 11 Engr. *Perf. 13*
1018 A374 30c dk bl, blk & car 75 48

New French liner France.

Skier Going Downhill A375

Maurice Bourdet A376

Design: 50c, Slalom.

1962, Jan. 27 *Perf. 13*
1019 A375 30c ultra & dk vio bl 30 30
1020 A375 50c dk grn, bl & lil 50 38

Issued to publicize the World Ski Championships, Chamonix, Feb. 1962.

1962, Feb. 17
1021 A376 30c slate 30 30

Issued to commemorate the 60th anniversary of the birth of Maurice Bourdet, radio commentator and resistance hero.

Pierre-Fidele Bretonneau A377

1962, Feb. 17
1022 A377 50c brt lil & bl 45 32

Issued to commemorate the centenary of the death of Pierre-Fidele Bretonneau, physician.

Chateau and Bridge, Laval, Mayenne A378

Gallic Cock A379

1962, Feb. 24
1023 A378 20c bis brn & sl grn 30 25

1962-65 ***Perf. 13***
1024 A379 25c ultra, car & brn 30 10
a. Bklt. pane of 4 (horiz. strip) 3.25
1024B A379 30c gray grn, red & brn ('65) 1.40 5
c. Bklt. pane of 5 8.00
d. Bklt. pane of 10 16.00

No. 1024 was also issued on experimental luminescent paper in 1963.

Ramparts of Vannes A380

Dunkirk — A381

Paris Beach, Le Touquet A381a

1962 **Engr.** ***Perf. 13***
1025 A380 30c dk bl 65 60
1026 A381 95c grn, bis & red lil 1.50 22
1027 A381a 1fr grn, red brn & bl 60 5

No. 1026 commemorates the 300th anniversary of Dunkirk.

Stage Setting and Globe — A382

1962, Mar. 24 **Unwmk.**
1028 A382 50c sl grn, ocher & mag 50 45

International Day of the Theater, Mar. 27.

Memorial to Fighting France, Mont Valerien A383

Resistance Heroes' Monument, Vercors — A384

Design: 50c, Ile de Sein monument.

1962, Apr. 7
1029 A383 20c ol & sl grn 75 38
1030 A384 30c bluish blk 60 45
1031 A384 50c bl & ind 1.00 60

Issued to publicize memorials for the French Underground in World War II.

Malaria Eradication Emblem and Swamp A385

Nurses with Child and Hospital A386

1962, Apr. 14 **Engr.**
1032 A385 50c dk bl & dk red 45 38

Issued for the World Health Organization drive to eradicate malaria.

1962, May 5 **Unwmk.** ***Perf. 13***
1033 A386 30c bl grn, gray & red brn 22 22

National Hospital Week, May 5-12.

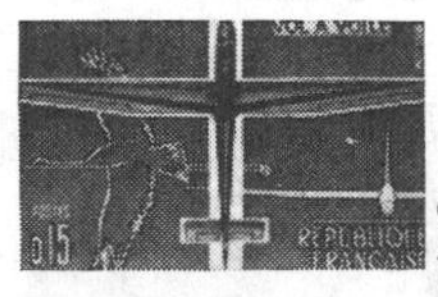

Glider A387

Design: 20c, Planes showing development of aviation.

1962, May 12
1034 A387 15c org red & brn 45 45
1035 A387 20c lil rose & rose cl 50 50

Issued to publicize sports aviation.

School Emblem — A388

1962, May 19 **Engr.**
1036 A388 50c mar, ocher & dk vio 50 50

Issued to commemorate the centenary of the Watchmaker's School at Besançon.

Louis XIV and Workers Showing Modern Gobelin A389

1962, May 26 **Unwmk.** ***Perf. 13***
1037 A389 50c ol, sl grn & car 50 45

Issued to commemorate the 300th anniversary of the Gobelin tapestry works, Paris.

Blaise Pascal A390

1962, May 26
1038 A390 50c sl grn & dp org 60 50

Issued to commemorate 300th anniversary of the death of Blaise Pascal (1623-1662), mathematician, scientist and philosopher.

Palace of Justice, Rennes A391

1962, June 12
1039 A391 30c blk, grysh bl & grn 1.50 90

Arms Type of 1958-59

Arms: 5c, Amiens. 10c, Troyes. 15c, Nevers.

1962-63 **Typo.** ***Perf. 14x13½***
1040 A318 5c ver, ultra & yel 7 6
1041 A318 10c red, ultra & yel ('63) 5 5
1042 A318 15c yer, ultra & yel 10 5

Phosphor Tagging

In 1970 France began to experiment with luminescence. Phosphor bands have been added to Nos. 1041, 1143, 1231, 1231C, 1292A-1294B, 1494-1498, 1560-1579B, etc.

Rose — A392

Design: 30c, Old-fashioned rose.

1962, Sept. 8 **Engr.** ***Perf. 13***
1043 A392 20c ol, grn & brt car 50 30
1044 A392 30c dk sl grn, ol & car 65 45

Europa Issue, 1962

Common Design Type

1962, Sept. 15 **Size: 36x22mm.**
1045 CD5 25c violet 18 15
1046 CD5 50c hn brn 38 30

Space Communications Center, Pleumeur-Bodou, France — A394

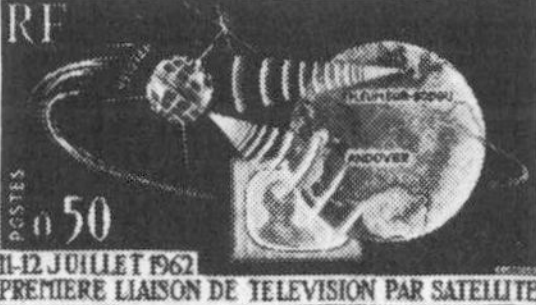

Telstar, Earth and Television Set — A395

1962, Sept. 29 **Engr.** ***Perf. 13***
1047 A394 25c gray, yel & grn 22 15
1048 A395 50c dk bl, grn & ultra 40 38

Issued to commemorate the first television connection of the United States and Europe through the Telstar satellite, July 11-12.

"Bonjour Monsieur Courbet" by Gustave Courbet — A396

Paintings: 65c, "Madame Manet on Blue Sofa," by Edouard Manet. 1fr, "Guards officer on horseback," by Theodore Gericault (vert.).

1962, Nov. 9 ***Perf. 13x12, 12x13***
1049 A396 50c multi 4.75 2.50
1050 A396 65c multi 3.50 2.50
1051 A396 1fr multi 6.75 4.00

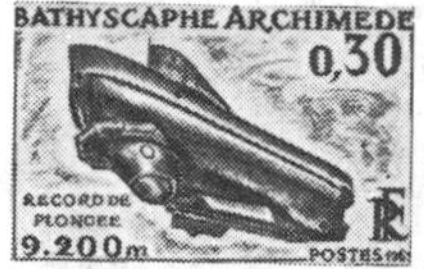

Bathyscaph "Archimede" A397

1963, Jan. 26 **Unwmk.** ***Perf. 13***
1052 A397 30c dk bl & blk 40 35

French deep-sea explorations.

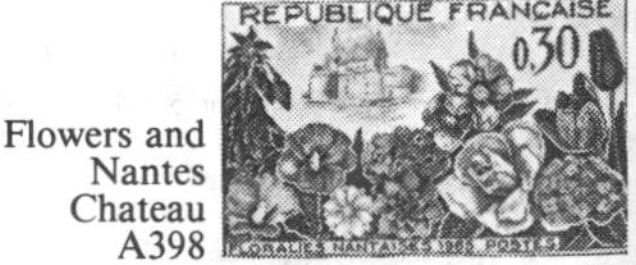

Flowers and Nantes Chateau A398

1963, Feb. 11
1053 A398 30c vio bl, car & sl grn 40 35

Nantes flower festival.

St. Peter, Window at St. Foy de Conches A399

Design: 50c, Jacob Wrestling with the Angel, by Delacroix.

1963, Mar. 2 *Perf. 12x13*
1054 A399 50c multi 4.50 3.00
1055 A399 1fr multi 7.00 5.00

See Nos. 1076-1077.

Hungry Woman and Wheat Emblem A400

1963, Mar. 21 **Engr.** *Perf. 13*
1056 A400 50c sl grn & brn 40 32

Issued for the "Freedom from Hunger" campaign of the U.N. Food and Agriculture Organization.

Cemetery and Memorial, Glieres — A401

Design: 50c, Memorial, Ile de la Cite, Paris.

1963, Mar. 23 **Unwmk.** *Perf. 13*
1057 A401 30c dk brn & ol 40 40
1058 A401 50c indigo 48 48

Issued to commemorate the heroes of the resistance against the Nazis.

Beethoven, Birthplace at Bonn and Rhine A402

Designs: No. 1060, Emile Verhaeren, memorial at Roisin and residence. No. 1061, Giuseppe Mazzini, Marcus Aurelius statue and Via Appia, Rome. No. 1062, Emile Mayrisch, Colpach Chateau and blast furnace, Esch. No. 1063, Hugo de Groot, Palace of Peace, The Hague and St. Agatha Church, Delft.

1963, Apr. 27 **Unwmk.** *Perf. 13*
1059 A402 20c ocher, sl & brt grn 38 38
1060 A402 20c pur, blk & mar 38 38
1061 A402 20c mar, sl & ol 38 38
1062 A402 20c mar, dk brn & ocher 38 38
1063 A402 30c dk brn, vio & ocher 38 38
Nos. 1059-1063 (5) 1.90 1.90

Issued to honor famous men of the European Common Market countries.

Hotel des Postes and Stagecoach, 1863 — A403

1963, May 4
1064 A403 50c grysh blk 45 38

Issued to commemorate the first International Postal Conference, Paris, 1863.

Lycée Louis-le-Grand, Belvedere, Pantheon and St. Etienne du Mont Church — A404

1963, May 18
1065 A404 30c sl grn 32 30

Issued to commemorate the 400th anniversary of the Jesuit Clermont secondary school, named after Louis XIV.

St. Peter's Church and Ramparts, Caen A405

1963, June 1 **Unwmk.** *Perf. 13*
1066 A405 30c gray bl & brn 32 32

Radio Telescope, Nançay — A406

1963, June 8 **Engr.**
1067 A406 50c dk bl & dk brn 40 38

Amboise Chateau A407

Saint-Flour — A408

Designs: 50c, Cote d'Azur Varoise. 85c, Vittel. 95c, Moissac.

1963, June 15
1068 A407 30c sl, grn & bis 30 15
1069 A407 50c dk grn, dk bl & hn brn 45 5
1070 A408 60c ultra, dk grn & hn brn 50 32
1071 A407 85c dk grn, yel grn & brn 1.40 18
1072 A408 95c dk brn & blk 90 30
Nos. 1068-1072 (5) 3.55 1.00

Water Skiing Slalom A409

1963, Aug. 31 **Unwmk.** *Perf. 13*
1073 A409 30c sl grn, blk & car 32 30

Issued to commemorate the World Water Skiing Championships, Vichy.

Europa Issue, 1963
Common Design Type

1963, Sept. 14 **Size: 36x22mm.**
1074 CD6 25c red brn 25 15
1075 CD6 50c green 40 30

Type of 1963

Designs: 85c, "The Married Couple of the Eiffel Tower" by Marc Chagall. 95c, "The Fur Merchants," window, Chartres Cathedral.

1963, Nov. 9 **Engr.** *Perf. 12x13*
1076 A399 85c multi 1.90 1.40
1077 A399 95c multi 1.00 75

Philatec Issue
Common Design Type

1963, Dec. 14 **Unwmk.** *Perf. 13*
1078 CD118 25c dk gray, sl grn & dk car 22 15

Radio and Television Center, Paris A411

1963, Dec. 15 **Engr.**
1079 A411 20c org brn, sl & ol 20 15

Fire Brigade Insignia, Symbols of Fire, Water and Civilian Defense A412

1964, Feb. 8 **Engr.** *Perf. 13*
1082 A412 30c bl, org & red 38 30

Issued to honor the fire brigades and civilian defense corps.

Handicapped Laboratory Technician — A413

1964, Feb. 22 **Unwmk.** *Perf. 13*
1083 A413 30c grn, red brn & brn 30 25

Rehabilitation of the handicapped.

John II the Good (1319-64) by Girard d'Orleans A414

1964, Apr. 25 *Perf. 12x13*
1084 A414 1fr multi 2.75 1.90

Stamp of 1900 A415

Mechanized Mail Handling A416

Designs: No. 1086, Stamp of 1900, Type A17. No. 1088, Telecommunications.

1964, May 9 *Perf. 13*
1085 A415 25c bis & dk car 30 30
1086 A415 25c bis & bl 30 30
1087 A416 30c blk, bl & org brn 30 30
1088 A416 30c blk, car rose & bluish grn 30 30
a. Strip of 4 (1 each Nos. 1085-1088 + label) 1.50 1.50

Printed in sheets of 20 stamps, containing five No. 1088a. The label shows the Philatec emblem in green.

Type of Semi-Postal Issue, 1959 with "25e ANNIVERSAIRE" Added

1964, May 9
1089 SP208 25c multi 30 18

25th anniversary, night airmail service.

Madonna and Child from Rose Window of Notre Dame A417

1964, May 23 *Perf. 12x13*
1090 A417 60c multi 60 60

Issued to commemorate the 800th anniversary of Notre Dame Cathedral, Paris.

Arms Type of 1958-59

Arms: 1c, Niort. 2c, Gueret. 12c, Agen. 18c, Saint-Denis, Reunion. 30c, Paris.

1964-65 **Typo.** *Perf. 14x13½*
1091 A318 1c vio bl & yel 6 6
1092 A318 2c emer, vio bl & yel 6 6
1093 A318 12c blk, red & yel 10 5
1094 A318 18c multi 22 22
1095 A318 30c vio, bl & red ('65) 45 5
a. Bklt. pane of 10 8.50
Nos. 1091-1095 (5) 89 44

Gallic Coin — A418

Perf. 13½x14
1964-66 **Typo.** **Unwmk.**
1096 A418 10c emer & bis 1.40 15
1097 A418 15c org & bis ('66) 45 15
1098 A418 25c lil & brn 75 32
1099 A418 50c brt bl & brn 1.50 65

Nos. 1096-1099 are known only precanceled. See second note after No. 132. See Nos. 1240-1242, 1315-1318, 1421-1424.

Postrider, Rocket and Radar Equipment — A419

1964, June 5 **Engr.** *Perf. 13*
1100 A419 1fr brn, dk red & dk bl 32.50 27.50

Sold for 4fr, including 3fr admission to PHILATEC. Issued in sheets of 8 stamps and 8 labels (2x8 subjects with labels in horizontal rows 1, 4, 5, 8; stamps in rows 2, 3, 6, 7). Commemorative inscriptions on side margins.

Caesar's Tower, Provins — A420

Chapel of Notre Dame du Haut, Ronchamp A421

1964-65
1101 A421 40c sl grn, dk brn & brn ('65) 30 10
1102 A420 70c sl, grn & car 45 6
1103 A421 1.25fr brt bl, sl grn & ol 90 38

The 40c was issued in vertical coils in 1971. Every 10th coil stamp has a red control number printed twice on the back.

Georges Mandel A422

Judo A423

1964, July 4 Unwmk. *Perf. 13*
1104 A422 30c vio brn 22 22

Issued to commemorate the 20th anniversary of the death of Georges Mandel (1885-1944), Cabinet minister, executed by the Nazis.

1964, July 4
1105 A423 50c dk bl & vio brn 38 30

Issued to publicize the 18th Olympic Games, Tokyo, Oct. 10-25, 1964.

Champlevé Enamel from Limoges, 12th Century A424

Design: No. 1107, The Lady (Claude Le Viste ?) with the Unicorn, 15th century tapestry.

1964 *Perf. 12x13*
1106 A424 1fr multi 2.00 1.25
1107 A424 1fr multi 75 60

No. 1106 shows part of an enamel sepulchral plate portraying Geoffrey IV, Count of Anjou and Le Maine (1113-1151), who was called Geoffrey Plantagenet.

Issue dates: No. 1106, July 4. No. 1107, Oct. 31.

Paris Taxis Carrying Soldiers to Front, 1914 — A425

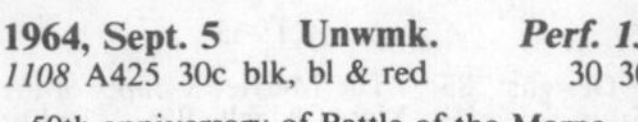
1964, Sept. 5 Unwmk. *Perf. 13*
1108 A425 30c blk, bl & red 30 30

50th anniversary of Battle of the Marne.

Europa Issue, 1964
Common Design Type

1964, Sept. 12 Engr.
Size: 22x36mm.
1109 CD7 25c dk car, dp ocher & grn 18 15
1110 CD7 50c vio, yel grn & dk car 32 30

Cooperation Issue
Common Design Type

1964, Nov. 6 Unwmk. *Perf. 13*
1111 CD119 25c red brn, dk brn & dk bl 22 22

Joux Chateau — A427

1965, Feb. 6 Engr.
1112 A427 1.30fr redsh brn, brn red & dk brn 1.00 20

"The English Girl from the Star" by Toulouse-Lautrec — A428

St. Paul on the Damascus Road, Window, Cathedral of Sens — A429

Leaving for the Hunt — A430

Apocalypse Tapestry, 14th Century A431

"The Red Violin" by Raoul Dufy — A432

Designs: No. 1115, "August" miniature of Book of Hours of Jean de France, Duc de Berry ("Les Tres Riches Heures du Duc de Berry"), painted by Flemish brothers, Pol, Hermant and Jannequin Limbourg, 1411-16. No. 1116, Scene from oldest existing set of French tapestries, showing the Winepress of the Wrath of God (Revelations 14: 19-20).

1965 *Perf. 12x13, 13x12*
1113 A428 1fr multi 60 60
1114 A429 1fr multi 55 55
1115 A430 1fr multi 55 55
1116 A431 1fr multi 55 55
1117 A432 1fr blk, pink & car 55 55
Nos. 1113-1117 (5) 2.80 2.80

No. 1114 issued to commemorate the 800th anniversary of the Cathedral of Sens.

Dates of issue: No. 1113, Mar. 12. No. 1114, June 5. No. 1115, Sept. 25. No. 1116, Oct. 30. No. 1117, Nov. 6.

Paris Parade of Returning Deportees, 1945 — A433

1965, Apr. 1 Unwmk. *Perf. 13*
1118 A433 40c Prus grn 60 50

Issued to commemorate the 20th anniversary of the return of people deported during World War II.

House of Youth and Culture, Troyes A434

1965, Apr. 10 Engr.
1119 A434 25c ind, brn & dk grn 32 25

Issued to publicize the 20th anniversary of the establishment of recreational cultural centers for young people.

Woman Carrying Flowers A435

Flags of France, USA, USSR and Great Britain Crushing Swastika A436

1965, Apr. 24 Unwmk. *Perf. 13*
1120 A435 60c dk grn, dp org & ver 40 38

Issued to publicize the tourist Campaign of Welcome and Amiability.

1965, May 8
1121 A436 40c blk, car & ultra 40 30

Issued to commemorate the 20th anniversary of victory in World War II.

Telegraph Key, Syncom Satellite and Pleumeur-Bodou Station — A437

1965, May 17
1122 A437 60c dk bl, brn & blk 40 38

Issued to commemorate the centenary of the International Telecommunication Union.

Croix de Guerre — A438

1965, May 22 Engr.
1123 A438 40c red, brn & brt grn 48 38

Issued to commemorate the 50th anniversary of the Croix de Guerre medal.

Cathedral of Bourges — A439

Moustiers-Sainte-Marie — A440

Views: 30c, Road and tunnel, Mont Blanc. 60c, Aix-les-Bains, sailboat. 75c, Tarn Gorge, Lozere mountains. 95c, Vendee River, man poling boat, and windmill. 1fr, Prehistoric stone monuments, Carnac.

1965, June-July
1124 A439 30c bl, vio bl & brn vio 25 22
1125 A439 40c gray bl & redsh brn 30 25
1126 A440 50c grn, bl gray & bis 32 10
1127 A439 60c bl & red brn 40 15
1128 A439 75c brn, bl & grn 1.00 48
1129 A440 95c brn, grn & bl 2.00 22
1130 A440 1fr gray grn & brn 90 6
Nos. 1124-1130 (7) 5.17 1.48

No. 1124 was issued July 17 to commemorate the opening of the Mont Blanc Tunnel. No. 1125 (Bourges Cathedral) was issued in connection with the French Philatelic Societies Federation Congress, held at Bourges.

Europa Issue, 1965
Common Design Type

1965, Sept. 25 *Perf. 13*
Size: 36x22mm.
1131 CD8 30c red 22 15
1132 CD8 60c gray 38 38

Planting Seedling A441

Etienne Regnault, "Le Taureau" and Coast of Reunion A442

1965, Oct. 2

1133 A441 25c sl grn, yel grn & red brn 22 22

National reforestation campaign.

1965, Oct. 2

1134 A442 30c ind & dk car 22 18

Tercentenary of settlement of Reunion.

Atomic Reactor and Diagram, Symbols of Industry, Agriculture and Medicine — A443

1965, Oct. 9

1135 A443 60c brt bl & blk 75 60

Issued to commemorate the 20th anniversary of the Atomic Energy Commission.

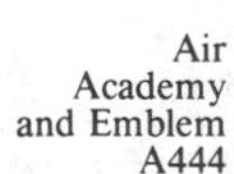

Air Academy and Emblem A444

1965, Nov. 6 *Perf. 13*

1136 A444 25c dk bl & grn 25 22

Issued to commemorate the 50th anniversary of the Air Academy, Salon-de-Provence.

French Satellite A-1 Issue

Common Design Type

Design: 60c, A-1 satellite.

1965, Nov. 30 Engr. *Perf. 13*

1137 CD121 30c Prus bl, brt bl & blk 22 22

1138 CD121 60c blk, Prus bl & brt bl 32 30

a. Strip of 2 + label 70 70

Issued to commemorate the launching of France's first satellite, Nov. 26, 1965. No. 1138a contains one each of Nos. 1137-1138 and bright blue label with commemorative inscription. Each sheet contains 16 triptychs (2x8).

Arms of Auch — A446

Arms (Cities): 20c, Saint-Lô. 25c, Mont-de-Marsan.

Typographed; Photogravure (20c)

1966 *Perf. 14x13; 14 (20c)*

1142 A446 5c bl & red 5 5

1143 A446 20c vio bl, sil, gold & red 18 5

1144 A446 25c red brn & ultra 38 15

The 5c and 20c were issued in sheets and in vertical coils. In the coils, every 10th stamp has a red control number on the back.

French Satellite D-1 Issue

Common Design Type

1966, Feb. 18 Engr. *Perf. 13*

1148 CD122 60c bl blk, grn & cl 32 30

Launching of the D-1 satellite at Hammaguir, Algeria, Feb. 17, 1966.

Horses from Bronze Vessel of Vix — A448

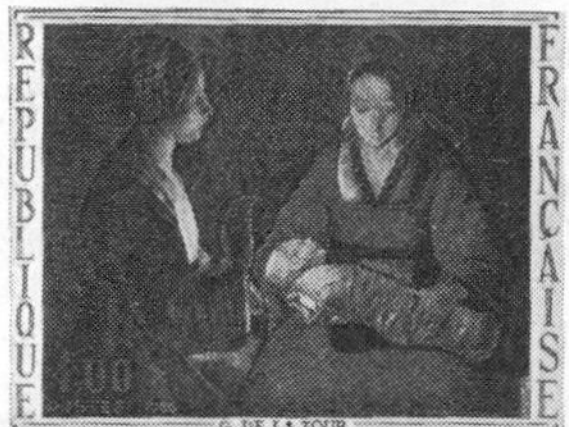
"The Newborn" by Georges de La Tour — A449

The Baptism of Judas (4th Century Bishop of Jerusalem) — A450

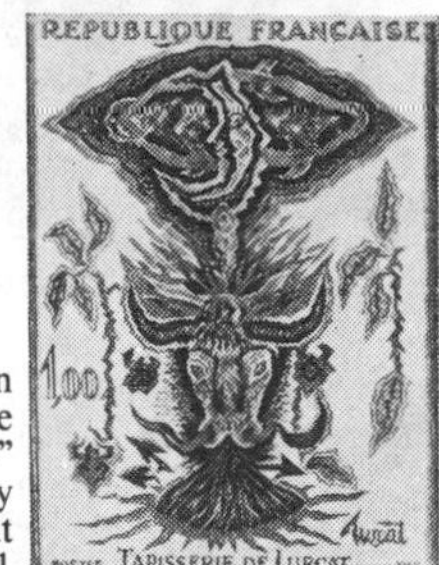
"The Moon and the Bull" Tapestry by Jean Lurçat A451

"Crispin and Scapin" by Honoré Daumier — A452

1966 *Perf. 13x12, 12x13*

1149 A448 1fr multi 45 45

1150 A449 1fr multi 45 45

1151 A450 1fr multi 50 50

1152 A451 1fr multi 50 50

1153 A452 1fr multi 50 50

Nos. 1149-1153 (5) 2.40 2.40

The design of No. 1149 is a detail from a 6th century B.C. vessel, found in 1953 in a grave near Vix, Cote d'Or.

The design of No. 1151 is from a stained glass window in the 13th century Sainte-Chapelle, Paris.

Issue dates: No. 1149, Mar. 26. No. 1150, June 25. No. 1151, Oct. 22. No. 1152, Nov. 19. No. 1153, Dec. 10.

Chessboard, Knight, Emblems for King and Queen — A453

Rhone Bridge, Pont-Saint-Esprit — A454

St. Michael Slaying the Dragon — A455

1966, Apr. 2 Engr. *Perf. 13*

1154 A453 60c sep, gray & dk vio bl 60 50

Issued to publicize the Chess Festival.

1966, Apr. 23 Unwmk. *Perf. 13*

1155 A454 25c blk & dl bl 22 18

Lithographed and Engraved

1966, Apr. 30

1156 A455 25c multi 22 18

Millenium of Mont-Saint-Michel.

Stanislas Leszczynski, Luneville Chateau A456

1966, May 6 Engr.

1157 A456 25c sl, grn & brn 22 18

Issued to commemorate the 200th anniversary of the reunion of Lorraine and Bar (Barrois) with France.

St. Andrew's and Sevre River, Niort — A457

1966, May 28 Engr. *Perf. 13*

1158 A457 40c brt bl, ind & grn 30 25

Bernard Le Bovier de Fontenelle and 1666 Meeting Room A458

1966, June 4

1159 A458 60c dk car rose & brn 40 38

300th anniversary, Académie des Sciences.

William the Conqueror, Castle and Norman Ships — A459

1966, June 4

1160 A459 60c brn red & dp bl 45 45

900th anniversary of Battle of Hastings.

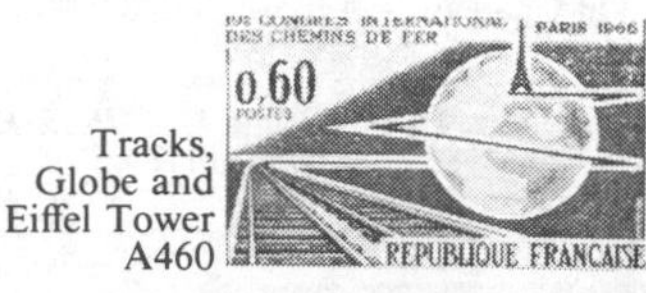
Tracks, Globe and Eiffel Tower A460

1966, June 11

1161 A460 60c dk brn, car & dl bl 80 50

19th International Railroad Congress.

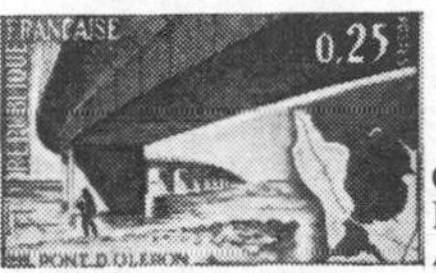
Oleron Bridge A461

1966, June 20

1162 A461 25c Prus bl, brn & bl 22 18

Issued to commemorate the opening of Oleron Bridge, connecting Oleron Island in the Bay of Biscay with the French mainland.

Europa Issue, 1966

Common Design Type

1966, Sept. 24 Engr. *Perf. 13*

Size: 22x36mm.

1163 CD9 30c Prus bl 18 15

1164 CD9 60c red 40 38

Vercingetorix at Gergovie, 52 B.C. — A462

Bishop Remi Baptizing King Clovis, 496 A.D. — A463

Design: 60c, Charlemagne attending school (page holding book for crowned king).

1966, Nov. 5 *Perf. 13*

1165 A462 40c choc, grn & gray bl 25 25

1166 A463 40c dk red brn & blk 25 25

1167 A463 60c pur, rose car & brn 38 30

Map of Pneumatic Post and Tube
A464

1966, Nov. 11
1168 A464 1.60fr mar & ind 90 50

Centenary of Paris pneumatic post system.

Val Chateau — A465

1966, Nov. 19 **Engr.** ***Perf. 13***
1169 A465 2.30fr dk bl, sl grn & brn 2.25 18

Rance Power Station
A466

1966, Dec. 3
1170 A466 60c dk bl, sl grn & brn 45 30

Issued to publicize the tidal power station in the estuary of the Rance River on the English Channel.

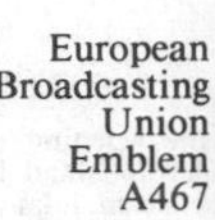

European Broadcasting Union Emblem
A467

1967, Mar. 4 **Engr.** ***Perf. 13***
1171 A467 40c dk bl & rose brn 30 30

Issued to publicize the 3rd International Congress of the European Broadcasting Union, Paris, March 8-22.

"Father Juniet's Gig" by Henri Rousseau — A468

Francois I by Jean Clouet
A469

The Catalogue editors cannot undertake to appraise, identify or judge the genuineness or condition of stamps.

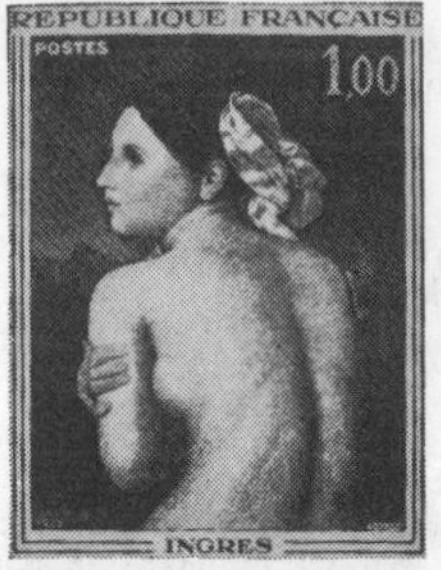

The Bather, by Jean-Dominique Ingres — A470

St. Eloi, the Goldsmith, at Work — A471

1967 **Engr.** ***Perf. 13x12, 12x13***
1172 A468 1fr multi 50 50
1173 A469 1fr multi 50 50
1174 A470 1fr multi 48 45
1175 A471 1fr multi 48 45

The design of No. 1175 is from a 16th century stained glass window in the Church of Sainte Madeleine, Troyes.

Issue dates: No. 1172, Apr. 15. No. 1173, July 1. No. 1174, Sept. 9. No. 1175, Oct. 7.

Snow Crystal and Olympic Rings — A472

1967, Apr. 22 **Photo.** ***Perf. 13***
1176 A472 60c brt & lt bl & red 45 30

Issued to publicize the 10th Winter Olympic Games, Grenoble, Feb. 6-18, 1968.

French Pavilion, EXPO '67 — A473

1967, Apr. 22 **Engr.**
1177 A473 60c dl bl & bl grn 40 30

Issued to commemorate the International Exhibition EXPO '67, Montreal, Apr. 28-Oct. 27, 1967.

Europa Issue, 1967
Common Design Type

1967, Apr. 29 **Size: 22x36mm.**
1178 CD10 30c bl & gray 18 15
1179 CD10 60c brn & lt bl 32 30

Great Bridge, Bordeaux
A474

1967, May 8
1180 A474 25c ol, blk & brn 30 22

Nungesser, Coli and "L'Oiseau Blanc"
A475

1967, May 8
1181 A475 40c sl, dk & lt brn 45 30

Issued to commemorate the 40th anniversary of the attempted transatlantic flight of Charles Nungesser and François Coil, French aviators.

Goüin House, Tours — A476

1967, May 13 **Engr.** ***Perf. 13***
1182 A476 40c vio bl, red brn & red 32 30

Issued to publicize the Congress of the Federation of French Philatelic Societies in Tours.

Ramon and Alfort Veterinary School
A477

1967, May 27
1183 A477 25c brn, dp bl & yel grn 20 15

Issued to commemorate the 200th anniversary of the Alfort Veterinary School and to honor Professor Gaston Ramon (1886-1963).

Robert Esnault-Pelterie, Diamant Rocket and A-1 Satellite — A478

1967, May 27
1184 A478 60c sl & vio bl 45 38

Issued to honor Robert Esnault-Pelterie (1881-1957), aviation and space expert.

City Hall, Saint-Quentin
A479

Saint-Germain-en-Laye — A480

Views: 60c, Clock Tower, Vire. 75c, Beach, La Baule, Brittany. 95c, Harbor, Boulogne-sur-Mer. 1fr, Rodez Cathedral. 1.50fr, Morlaix; old houses, grotesque carving, viaduct.

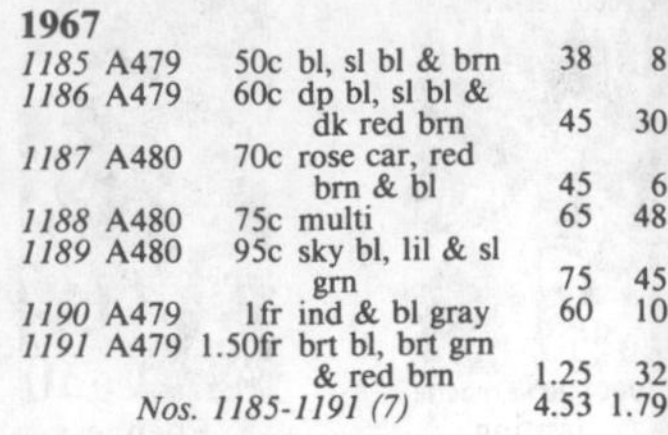
1967
1185 A479 50c bl, sl bl & brn 38 8
1186 A479 60c dp bl, sl bl & dk red brn 45 30
1187 A480 70c rose car, red brn & bl 45 6
1188 A480 75c multi 65 48
1189 A480 95c sky bl, lil & sl grn 75 45
1190 A479 1fr ind & bl gray 60 10
1191 A479 1.50fr brt bl, brt grn & red brn 1.25 32
Nos. 1185-1191 (7) 4.53 1.79

Issue Dates: 1fr, 1.50fr, June 10; 70c, June 17; 50c, 60c, 95c, July 8; 75c, July 24.

Orchids — A481

Scales of Justice, City and Harbor
A482

Cross of Lorraine, Soldiers and Sailors — A483

1967, July 29 **Engr.** ***Perf. 13***
1192 A481 40c dp car, brt pink & pur 45 30

Orleans flower festival.

1967, Sept. 4
1193 A482 60c dk plum, dl bl & ocher 38 30

Issued to publicize the 9th International Accountancy Congress, Paris, Sept. 6-12.

1967, Oct. 7 **Engr.** ***Perf. 13***
1194 A483 25c brn, dp ultra & bl 22 18

Issued to commemorate the 25th anniversary of the Battle of Bir Hacheim.

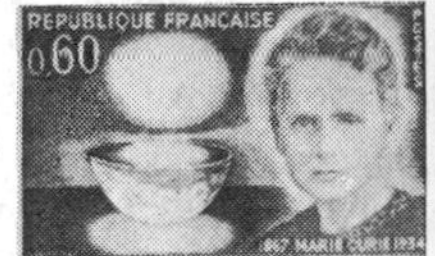

Marie Curie, Bowl Glowing with Radium
A484

1967, Oct. 23 **Engr.** ***Perf. 13***
1195 A484 60c dk bl & ultra 45 32

Issued to commemorate the centenary of the birth of Marie Curie (1867-1934), scientist who discovered radium and polonium, Nobel prize winner for physics and chemistry.

Lions Emblem
A485

Marianne (by Cheffer)
A486

1967, Oct. 28
1196 A485 40c dk car & vio bl 38 28

50th anniversary of Lions International.

1967, Nov. 4 **Engr.**
1197 A486 25c dk bl 60 30
1198 A486 30c brt lil 65 5
a. Bklt. pane of 5 5.00
b. Bklt. pane of 10 11.00

Coils (vertical) of Nos. 1197 and 1231 show a red number on the back of every 10th stamp.
See Nos. 1230-1231C.

King Philip II (Philip Augustus) at Battle of Bouvines — A487

Designs: No. 1200, Election of Hugh Capet as King (horiz.). 60c, King Louis IX (St. Louis) holding audience for the poor.

1967, Nov. 13 **Engr.** ***Perf. 13***
1199 A487 40c gray & blk 32 30
1200 A487 40c stl bl & ultra 32 30
1201 A487 60c grn & dk red brn 45 30

Commemorative Medal — A488

1968, Jan. 6 **Engr.** ***Perf. 13***
1202 A488 40c dk sl grn & bis 30 30

Issued to commemorate the 50th anniversary of postal checking service.

Various Road Signs — A489

1968, Feb. 24
1203 A489 25c lil, red & dk bl grn 22 18

Issued to publicize road safety.

Prehistoric Paintings, Lascaux Cave — A490

The indexes in each volume of the Scott Catalogue contain many listings which help to identify stamps.

"Arearea" (Merriment) by Paul Gauguin — A491

The Dance, by Emile Antoine Bourdelle A492

Portrait of the Model, by Auguste Renoir A493

1968 **Engr.** ***Perf. 13x12, 12x13***
1204 A490 1fr multi 50 45
1205 A491 1fr multi 60 50
1206 A492 1fr car & gray ol 60 50
1207 A493 1fr multi 60 50

Issue dates: No. 1204, Apr. 13. No. 1205, Sept. 21. No. 1206, Oct. 26. No. 1207, Nov. 9.

Audio-visual Institute, Royan A494

1968, Apr. 13 ***Perf. 13***
1208 A494 40c sl grn, brn & Prus bl 30 30

Issued to publicize the 5th Conference for World Cooperation with the theme of teaching living languages by audio-visual means.

Europa Issue, 1968
Common Design Type

1968, Apr. 27
Size: 36x22mm
1209 CD11 30c brt red lil & ocher 22 15
1210 CD11 60c brn & lake 38 30

Alain René Le Sage — A495

1968, May 4
1211 A495 40c bl & rose vio 30 22

Issued to commemorate the 300th anniversary of the birth of Alain René Le Sage (1668-1747), novelist and playwright.

Chateau de Langeais A496

1968, May 4
1212 A496 60c sl bl, grn & red brn 45 38

Pierre Larousse A497

1968, May 11 **Engr.** ***Perf. 13***
1213 A497 40c rose vio & brn 30 22

Issued to honor Pierre Larousse (1817-1875), grammarian, lexicographer and encyclopedist.

Gnarled Trunk and Fir Tree — A498

1968, May 18 **Engr.** ***Perf. 13***
1214 A498 25c grnsh bl, brn & grn 22 22

Issued to commemorate the twinning of Rambouillet Forest in France and the Black Forest in Germany.

Map of Papal Enclave, Valréas, and John XXII Receiving Homage A499

1968, May 25
1215 A499 60c brn, bis brn & pur 40 38

Issued to commemorate the 650th anniversary of the papal enclave at Valreas.

Louis XIV, Arms of France and Flanders A500

1968, June 29
1216 A500 40c rose car, gray & lem 30 22

Issued to commemorate the 300th anniversary of the Treaty of Aachen which reunited Flanders with France.

Martrou Bridge, Rochefort A501

1968, July 20
1217 A501 25c sky bl, blk & dk red brn 20 20

Letord Lorraine Bimotor Plane over Map of France A502

1968, Aug. 17 **Engr.** ***Perf. 13***
1218 A502 25c brt bl, ind & red 55 30

Issued to commemorate the 50th anniversary of the first regularly scheduled air mail route in France from Paris to St. Nazaire.

Tower de Constance, Aigues-Mortes A503

1968, Aug. 31
1219 A503 25c red brn, sky bl & ol bis 30 22

Bicentenary of the release of Huguenot prisoners from the Tower de Constance, Aigues-Mortes.

Cathedral and Pont Vieux, Beziers A504

1968, Sept. 7 **Engr.** ***Perf. 13***
1220 A504 40c ind, bis & grn 28 15

"Victory" over White Tower of Salonika — A505

1968, Sept. 28
1221 A505 40c red lil & plum 32 30

Issued to commemorate the 50th anniversary of the armistice on the eastern front in World War I, Sept. 29, 1918.

Louis XV, Arms of France and Corsica A506

1968, Oct. 5 ***Perf. 13***
1222 A506 25c ultra, grn & blk 22 15

Issued to commemorate the 200th anniversary of the return of Corsica to France.

Relay Race A507

1968, Oct. 12
1223 A507 40c ultra, brt grn & ol brn 38 30

Issued to commemorate the 19th Olympic Games, Mexico City, Oct. 12-27.

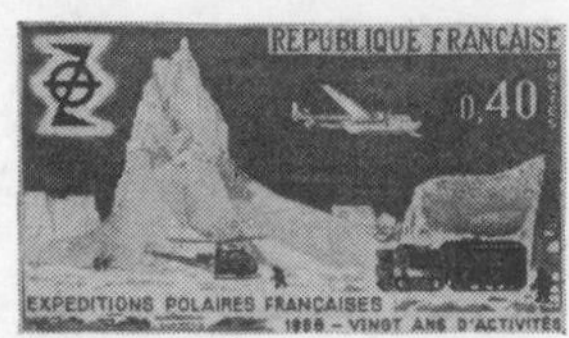
Polar Camp with Helicopter, Plane and Snocat Tractor — A508

1968, Oct. 19
1224 A508 40c Prus bl, lt grnsh bl & brn red 38 30

20 years of French Polar expeditions.

Leon Bailby, Paris Opera Staircase and Hospital Beds — A509

"Victory" over Arc de Triomphe and Eternal Flame — A510

1968, Oct. 26
1225 A509 40c ocher & mar 30 25

Issued to publicize the 50th anniversary of the "Little White Beds" children's hospital fund.

1968, Nov. 9 Engr. *Perf. 13*
1226 A510 25c dk car rose & dp bl 22 18

Issued to commemorate the 50th anniversary of the armistice which ended World War I.

Death of Bertrand Du Guesclin at Chateauneuf-de-Randon, 1380 — A511

1968, Nov. 16

Designs: No. 1228, King Philip IV (the Fair) and first States-General assembly, 1302 (horiz.). 60c, Joan of Arc leaving Vaucouleurs, 1429.

1227 A511 40c cop red, grn & gray 30 30
1228 A511 40c grn, ultra & brn 30 30
1229 A511 60c vio bl, sl bl & bis 40 30

See also No. 1260.

Marianne Type of 1967

1969-70 Engr. *Perf. 13*
1230 A486 30c green 25 15
a. Bklt. pane of 10 4.00
1231 A486 40c dp car 40 5
a. Bklt. pane of 5 (horiz. strip) 3.50
b. Bklt. pane of 10 5.75
d. With label ('70) 60 38

Typo. *Perf. 14x13*
1231C A486 30c bl grn 22 5

No. 1231d was issued in sheets of 50 with alternating labels showing coat of arms of Perigueux, arranged checkerwise, to commemorate the inauguration of the Perigueux stamp printing plant.

The 40c coil is noted after No. 1198.

Church of Brou, Bourg-en-Bresse — A512

Views: 80c, Vouglans Dam, Jura. 85c, Chateau de Chantilly. 1.15fr, Sailboats in La Trinite-sur-Mer harbor.

1969 Engr. *Perf. 13*
1232 A512 45c ol, bl & red brn 32 22
1233 A512 80c ol bis, brn red & dk brn 60 10
1234 A512 85c sl grn, dl bl & gray 70 65
1235 A512 1.15fr brt bl, gray grn & brn 75 45

"February" Bas-relief from Amiens Cathedral A513

Philip the Good, by Roger van der Weyden A514

Sts. Savin and Cyprian before Ladicius, Mural, St. Savin, Vienne — A515

The Circus, by Georges Seurat A515a

1969 *Perf. 12x13*
1236 A513 1fr dk grn & brn 60 50
1237 A514 1fr multi 60 50
1238 A515 1fr multi 60 50
1239 A515a 1fr multi 60 50

Issue dates: No. 1236, Feb. 22; No. 1237, May 3; No. 1238, June 28; No. 1239, Nov. 8.

Gallic Coin Type of 1964-66

1969 Typo. *Perf. 13½x14*
1240 A418 22c brt grn & vio 1.25 25
1241 A418 35c red & ultra 2.50 70
1242 A418 70c ultra & red brn 9.50 3.75

Nos. 1240-1242 are known only precanceled. See note after No. 132.

Hautefort Chateau A516

1969, Apr. 5 Engr. *Perf. 13*
1243 A516 70c bl, sl & bis 50 45

Irises A517

1969, Apr. 12 Photo.
1244 A517 45c multi 38 38

Issued to publicize the 3rd International Flower Show, Paris, Apr. 23-Oct. 5.

Europa Issue, 1969
Common Design Type

1969, Apr. 26 Engr. *Perf. 13*
Size: 36x22mm.
1245 CD12 40c car rose 25 15
1246 CD12 70c Prus bl 40 38

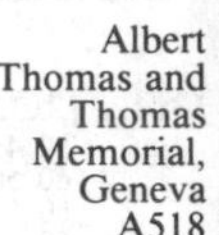

Albert Thomas and Thomas Memorial, Geneva A518

1969, May 10 Engr. *Perf. 13*
1247 A518 70c brn, ol bis & ind 50 45

Issued to commemorate the 50th anniversary of the International Labor Organization and to honor Albert Thomas (1878-1932), director of the ILO 1920-1932.

Garigliano Battle Scene, 1944 — A519

1969, May 10
1248 A519 45c blk & vio 38 30

Issued to commemorate the 25th anniversary of the Battle of the Garigliano against the Germans.

Chateau du Marché, Chalons-sur-Marne A520

Parachutists over Normandy Beach A521

1969, May 24
1249 A520 45c bis, dl bl & grn 45 32

Federation of French Philatelic Societies, 42nd congress.

1969, May 31
1250 A521 45c dk bl & vio bl 60 45

Issued to commemorate the 25th anniversary of the landing of Special Air Service and Free French commandos in Normandy, June 6, 1944.

Monument of the French Resistance, Mt. Mouchet — A522

1969, June 7
1251 A522 45c dk grn, sl & ind 60 45

Issued to commemorate the 25th anniversary of the battle of Mt. Mouchet between French resistance fighters and the Germans, June 2 and 10, 1944.

French Troops Landing in Provence — A523

1969, Aug. 23 Engr. *Perf. 13*
1252 A523 45c sl & blk brn 60 45

Issued to commemorate the 25th anniversary of the landing of French and American forces in Provence, Aug. 15, 1944.

Russian and French Aviators — A524

1969, Oct. 18 Engr. *Perf. 13*
1253 A524 45c sl, dp bl & car 60 45

Issued to honor the French aviators of the Normandy-Neman Squadron who fought on the Russian Front, 1942-45.

Kayak on Isere River A525

1969, Aug. 2 Engr. *Perf. 13*
1254 A525 70c org brn, ol & dk bl 55 45

Issued to commemorate the International Canoe and Kayak Championships, Bourg-Saint-Maurice, Savoy, July 31-Aug. 6.

Napoleon as Young Officer and his Birthplace, Ajaccio — A526

1969, Aug. 16
1255 A526 70c brt grnsh bl, ol & rose vio 55 45

Issued to commemorate the 200th anniversary of the birth of Napoleon Bonaparte (1769-1821).

Drops of Water and Diamond A527

Mediterranean Mouflon A528

1969, Sept. 27
1256 A527 70c blk, dp bl & brt grn 60 45

European Water Charter.

1969, Oct. 11
1257 A528 45c ol, blk & org brn 45 45

Issued to publicize wildlife protection.

Central School of Arts and Crafts A529

1969, Oct. 18
1258 A529 70c dk grn, yel grn & org 45 38

Issued to commemorate the inauguration of the Central School of Arts and Crafts at Chatenay-Malabry.

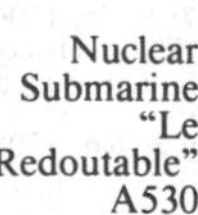

Nuclear Submarine "Le Redoutable" A530

1969, Oct. 25
1259 A530 70c dp bl, grn & sl grn 50 45

Type of 1968 and

Henri IV and Edict of Nantes — A531

Designs: No. 1260, Pierre Terrail de Bayard wounded at Battle of Brescia (after a painting in Versailles). No. 1262, Louis XI, Charles the Bold and map of France.

1969, Nov. 8 Engr. *Perf. 13*
1260 A511 80c brn, bis & blk 50 38
1261 A531 80c blk & vio bl 60 38
1262 A531 80c ol, dp grn & dk red brn 50 38

"Firecrest" and Alain Gerbault — A532

1970, Jan. 10 Engr. *Perf. 13*
1263 A532 70c ind, brt bl & gray 60 45

Issued to commemorate the 40th anniversary of the completion of Alain Gerbault's trip around the world aboard the "Firecrest," 1923-29.

Gendarmery Emblem, Mountain Climber, Helicopter, Motorcyclists and Motorboat — A533

1970, Jan. 31
1264 A533 45c sl grn, dk bl & brn 50 38

Issued to honor the National Gendarmery, founded 1791.

Field Ball Player — A534

1970, Feb. 21 Engr. *Perf. 13*
1265 A534 80c sl grn 60 32

Issued to publicize the 7th International Field Ball Games, Feb. 26-March 8.

Alphonse Juin and Church of the Invalides — A535

1970, Feb. 28
1266 A535 45c gray bl & dk brn 38 30

Issued to honor Marshal Alphonse Pierre Juin (1888-1967), military leader.

Aerotrain A536

1970, Mar. 7
1267 A536 80c pur & gray 60 32

Issued to publicize the introduction of the aerotrain, which reaches a speed of 320 miles per hour.

Pierre Joseph Pelletier, Joseph Bienaimé Caventou, Quinine Formula and Cell — A537

1970, Mar. 21 Engr. *Perf. 13*
1268 A537 50c sl grn, sky bl & dp car 45 30

Discovery of quinine, 150th anniversary.

Pink Flamingos A538

Diamant B Rocket and Radar A539

1970, Mar. 21
1269 A538 45c ol, gray & pink 40 30

European Nature Conservation Year, 1970.

1970, Mar. 28
1270 A539 45c brt grn 45 30

Issued to publicize the space center in Guyana and the launching of the Diamant B rocket, Mar. 10, 1970.

Europa Issue, 1970
Common Design Type
1970, May 2 Engr. *Perf. 13*
Size: 36x22mm.
1271 CD13 40c dp car 25 15
1272 CD13 80c sky bl 48 38

Annunication, by Primitive Painter of Savoy, 1480 — A540

The Triumph of Flora, by Jean Baptiste Carpeaux — A541

Diana Returning from the Hunt, by François Boucher — A542

Dancer with Bouquet, by Edgar Degas A543

1970 *Perf. 12x13, 13x12*
1273 A540 1fr multi 75 55
1274 A541 1fr red brn 75 55
1275 A542 1fr multi 75 65
1276 A543 1fr multi 75 65

Issue dates: No. 1273, May 9. No. 1274, July 4. No. 1275, Oct. 10. No. 1276, Nov. 14.

Arms of Lens, Miner's Lamp and Pit Head A544

1970, May 16 Engr. *Perf. 13*
1277 A544 40c scarlet 30 22

Issued to publicize the 43rd National Congress of the Federation of French Philatelic Societies, Lens, May 14-21.

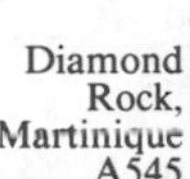

Diamond Rock, Martinique A545

Haute Provence Observatory and Spiral Nebula — A546

Designs: 95c, Chancelade Abbey, Dordogne. 1fr, Gosier Islet, Guadeloupe.

1970, June 20 Engr. *Perf. 13*
1278 A545 50c sl grn, brt bl & plum 40 15
1279 A545 95c lt ol, car & brn 1.25 65
1280 A545 1fr sl grn, brt bl & dk car rose 65 6
1281 A546 1.30fr dk bl, vio bl & dk grn 2.00 1.00

Hand Reaching for Freedom A547

Handicapped Javelin Thrower A548

1970, June 27
1282 A547 45c vio bl, bl & bis 50 30

Liberation of concentration camps, 25th anniversary.

1970, June 27
1283 A548 45c rose car, ultra & emer 50 38

Issued to publicize the International Games of the Handicapped, St. Etienne, June 1970.

Pole Vault — A549

1970, Sept. 11 **Engr.** ***Perf. 13***
1284 A549 45c car, bl & ind 50 38

Issued to publicize the First European Junior Athletic Championships, Colombes, Sept. 11-13.

Royal Salt Works, Arc-et-Senans — A550

1970, Sept. 26
1285 A550 80c bl, brn & dk grn 65 45

Issued to publicize the restoration of the 18th century Royal Salt Works buildings, by Claude Nicolas Ledoux (1736-1806) at Arc-et-Senans, for use as a center for studies of all aspects of future human life.

Armand Jean du Plessis, Duc de Richelieu — A551

Designs: No. 1287, Battle of Fontenoy, 1745. No. 1288, Louis XIV and Versailles.

1970, Oct. 17 **Engr.** ***Perf. 13***
1286 A551 45c blk, sl & car rose 38 30
1287 A551 45c org, brn & ind 38 30
1288 A551 45c sl grn, lem & org brn 38 30

U.N. Headquarters in New York and Geneva — A552

1970, Oct. 24 **Engr.** ***Perf. 13***
1289 A552 80c ol, dp ultra & dk pur 50 45

25th anniversary of the United Nations.

View of Bordeaux and France No. 43 — A553

1970, Nov. 7
1290 A553 80c vio bl & gray bl 50 45

Centerary of the Bordeaux issue.

Col. Denfert-Rochereau and Lion of Belfort, by Frederic A. Bartholdi — A554

1970, Nov. 14
1291 A554 45c dk bl, ol & red brn 40 30

Centenary of the siege of Belfort during Franco-Prussian War.

Marianne (by Bequet) — A555

1971-74 **Typo.** ***Perf. 14x13***
1292 A555 45c sky bl 45 10
1292A A555 60c grn ('74) 1.40 5

Engr.
Perf. 13

1293 A555 50c rose car 50 5
a. Bklt. pane of 5 (horiz. strip) 3.75
b. Bklt. pane of 10 6.00
1294 A555 60c grn ('74) 6.75 15
a. Booklet pane of 10 75.00
1294B A555 80c car rose ('74) 75 5
c. Booklet pane of 5 6.00
d. Booklet pane of 10 12.00

Nos. 1294 and 1294B issued also in vertical coils with control number on back of every 10th stamp.
No. 1293 issued only in booklets and in vertical coils with red control number on back of every 10th stamp.
See Nos. 1494-1498.

St. Matthew, Sculpture from Strasbourg Cathedral A556

Winnower, by François Millet A557

The Dreamer, by Georges Rouault A558

1971 **Engr.** ***Perf. 12x13***
1295 A556 1fr dk red brn 75 65
1296 A557 1fr multi 75 55
1297 A558 1fr multi 75 55

Issue dates: No. 1295, Jan. 23; No. 1296, Apr. 3; No. 1297, June 5.

Figure Skating Pair A560

1971, Feb. 20 **Engr.** ***Perf. 13***
1299 A560 80c vio bl, sl & aqua 60 38

World Figure Skating Championships, Lyons, Feb. 23-28.

Underwater Exploration — A561

1971, March 6
1300 A561 80c bl blk & bl grn 60 38

International Exhibition of Ocean Exploration, Bordeaux, March 9-14.

Cape Horn Clipper "Antoinette" and Solidor Castle, Saint-Malo — A562

1971, Apr. 10 **Engr.** ***Perf. 13***
1301 A562 80c bl, pur & sl 55 50

Pyrenean Chamois — A563

1971, Apr. 24 **Engr.** ***Perf. 13***
1302 A563 65c bl, dk brn & brn ol 55 32

National Park of Western Pyrenees.

Europa Issue, 1971
Common Design Type and

Santa Maria della Salute, Venice A564

1971, May 8 **Engr.** ***Perf. 13***
1303 A564 50c bl gray & ol bis 38 15

Size: 36x22mm.

1304 CD14 80c rose lil 50 45

Cardinal, Nobleman and Lawyer — A565

Storming of the Bastille — A566

Design: No. 1306, Battle of Valmy.

1971
1305 A565 45c bl, rose red & pur 40 30
1306 A565 45c bl, ol bis & brn red 40 38
1307 A566 65c dk brn, gray bl & mag 60 45

No. 1305 commemorates the opening of the Estates General, May 5, 1789; No. 1306, Battle of Valmy (Sept. 20, 1792) between French and Prussian armies; 65c, Storming of the Bastille, Paris, July 14, 1789.
Issue dates: No. 1305, May 8; No. 1306, Sept. 18; 65c, July 10.

Grenoble A568

1971, May 29 **Engr.** ***Perf. 13***
1308 A568 50c ocher, lil & rose red 30 15

44th National Congress of the Federation of French Philatelic Societies, Grenoble, May 30-31.

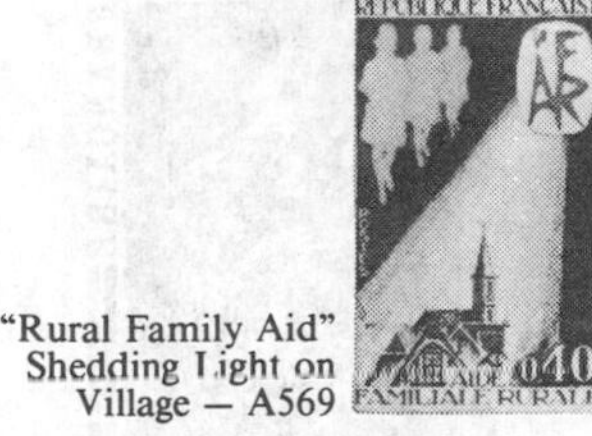

"Rural Family Aid" Shedding Light on Village — A569

1971, June 5

1309 A569 40c vio, bl & grn 30 22

Aid for rural families.

Chateau and Fort de Sedan A570

Pont d'Arc, Ardeche Gorge — A571

Views: 60c, Sainte Chapelle, Riom. 65c, Fountain and tower, Dole. 90c, Tower and street, Riquewihr.

1971	Engr.	*Perf. 13*	
1310 A571	60c blk, grn & bl	32	18
1311 A571	65c lil, ocher & blk	45	18
1312 A571	90c grn, vio brn & red brn	60	15
1313 A570	1.10fr sl grn, Prus bl & brn	80	30
1314 A571	1.40fr sl grn, bl & dk brn	1.00	22
	Nos. 1310-1314 (5)	3.17	1.03

Issue dates: 60c, June 19; 65c, 90c, July 3; 1.10fr, 1.40fr, June 12.

Gallic Coin Type of 1964-66

1971, July 1	Typo.	*Perf. 13½x14*	
1315 A418	26c lil & brn	90	22
1316 A418	30c lt brn & brn	1.50	30
1317 A418	45c dl grn & brn	3.00	45
1318 A418	90c red & brn	3.75	75

Nos. 1315-1318 are known only precanceled. See second paragraph after No. 132.

Bourbon Palace A572

1971, Aug. 28 Engr. *Perf. 13*

1319 A572 90c vio bl 60 38

59th Conference of the Interparliamentary Union.

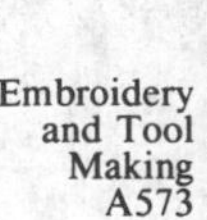

Embroidery and Tool Making A573

1971, Oct. 16

1320 A573 90c brn red, brt lil & cl 75 45

40th anniversary of the first assembly of presidents of artisans' guilds.

Reunion Chameleon A574

1971, Nov. 6 Photo. *Perf. 13*

1321 A574 60c brn, yel, grn & blk 1.50 48

Nature protection.

De Gaulle Issue

Common Design Type and

De Gaulle in Brazzaville, 1944 — A576

Designs: No. 1324, De Gaulle entering Paris, 1944. No. 1325, Pres. de Gaulle, 1970.

1971, Nov. 9		Engr.	
1322 CD134	50c black	80	45
1323 A576	50c ultra	80	45
1324 A576	50c rose red	80	45
1325 CD134	50c black	80	45
a.	Strip of 4 + label	3.00	2.75

First anniversary of the death of Charles de Gaulle (1890-1970). Nos. 1322-1325 printed se-tenant in sheets of 20 containing 5 strips of 4 plus label with Cross of Lorraine and inscription.

Antoine Portal and first Session of Academy — A577

1971, Nov. 13

1326 A577 45c dk pur & mag 38 30

Sesquicentennial of the founding of the National Academy of Medicine; Baron Antoine Portal was first president.

L'Etude, by Jean Honoré Fragonard A578

Women in Garden, by Claude Monet A579

St. Peter Presenting Pierre de Bourbon, by Maitre de Moulins A580

Boats, by André Derain — A581

1972	Engr.	*Perf. 12x13, 13x12*	
1327 A578	1fr blk & multi	75	50
1328 A579	1fr sl grn & multi	1.10	50
1329 A580	2fr dk brn & multi	2.75	1.25
1330 A581	2fr yel & multi	4.00	1.40

Issue dates: No. 1327, Jan. 22; No. 1328, June 17; No. 1329, Oct. 14; No. 1330, Dec. 16.

Map of South Indian Ocean, Penguin and Ships — A582

1972, Jan. 29 *Perf. 13*

1331 A582 90c blk, bl & ocher 90 60

Bicentenary of discovery of the Crozet and Kerguelen Islands.

Slalom and Olympic Emblems A583

1972, Feb. 7

1332 A583 90c dk ol & dp car 75 45

11th Winter Olympic Games, Sapporo, Japan, Feb. 3-13.

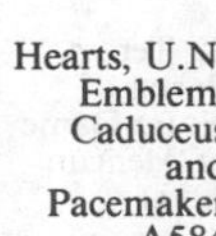

Hearts, U.N. Emblem, Caduceus and Pacemaker A584

1972, Apr. 8 Engr. *Perf. 13*

1333 A584 45c dk car, org & gray 45 30

"Your heart is your health," world health month.

Red Deer, Sologne Plateau — A585

Charlieu Abbey A585a

Bazoches-du-Morvand Chateau — A586

Saint-Just Cathedral, Narbonne A587

1972		*Perf. 13*	
1334 A585	1fr ocher & red brn	80	15
1335 A585a	1.20fr sl & dl brn	70	18
1336 A586	2fr sl grn, blk & red brn	1.40	15
1337 A587	3.50fr bl, gray ol & car rose	2.00	32

Issue dates: 1fr, Sept. 10; 1.20fr, Apr. 29; 2fr, Sept. 9; 3.5fr, Apr. 8.

Eagle Owl — A588

Design: 60c, Salmon (horiz.).

1972			
1338 A588	60c grn, ind & brt bl	2.25	90
1339 A588	65c sl, ol brn & sep	1.40	48

Nature protection. Issue dates: 60c, May 27; 65c, Apr. 15.

Europa Issue 1972

Common Design Type and

Aix-la-Chapelle Cathedral — A589

1972, Apr. 22 Engr. *Perf. 13*

1340 A589 50c yel, vio brn & dk ol 32 15

Photo.

Size: 22x36mm.

1341 CD15 90c red org & multi 60 45

Bouquet Made of Hearts and Blood Donors' Emblem
A590

Newfoundlander "Cote d'Emeraude"
A591

1972, May 5 **Engr.**

1342 A590 40c red 40 30

20th anniversary of the Blood Donors Association of Post and Telecommunications Employees.

1972, May 6

1343 A591 90c org, vio bl & sl grn 70 50

Cathedral, Saint-Brieuc
A592

1972, May 20

1344 A592 50c lil rose 38 22

45th Congress of the Federation of French Philatelic Societies, Saint-Brieuc, May 21-22.

Hand Holding Symbol of Postal Code
A593

1972, June 3 **Typo.** ***Perf. 14x13***

1345 A593 30c grn, blk & car 22 10
1346 A593 50c car, blk & yel 38 6

Introduction of postal code system.

Old and New Communications
A594

1972, July 1 **Engr.** ***Perf. 13***

1347 A594 45c sl & vio bl 32 30

21st International Congress of P.T.T. (Post, Telegraph and Telephone) Employees, Paris, July 1-7.

Hurdler and Olympic Rings
A595

1972, July 8

1348 A595 1fr dp ol 75 32

20th Olympic Games, Munich, Aug. 26-Sept. 11.

Hikers and Mt. Aigoual
A596

Bicyclist
A597

1972, July 15 **Photo.** ***Perf. 13***

1349 A596 40c brt rose & multi 2.00 90

International Year of Tourism and 25th anniversary of the National Hikers Association.

1972, July 22 **Engr.**

1350 A597 1fr gray, brn & lil 2.25 90

World Bicycling Championships, Marseille, July 29-Aug. 2.

"Incroyables and Merveilleuse," 1794 — A598

Designs: 60c, Bonaparte at the Arcole Bridge. 65c, Egyptian expedition (soldiers and scientists finding antiquities; pyramids in background).

1972 **Engr.** ***Perf. 13***

1351 A598 45c ol, dk grn & car rose 45 30
1352 A598 60c red, blk & ind 50 38
1353 A598 65c ocher, ultra & choc 50 45

French history. Issue dates: 45c, Oct. 7; 60c, 65c, Nov. 11.

Champollion, Rosetta Stone with Key Inscription — A599

1972, Oct. 14

1354 A599 90c vio bl, brn red & blk 75 50

Sesquicentennial of the deciphering of hieroglyphs by Jean-François Champollion.

St. Teresa, Portal of Notre Dame of Alençon
A600

1973, Jan. 6 **Engr.** ***Perf. 13***

1355 A600 1fr Prus bl & ind 90 45

Centenary of the birth of St. Teresa of Lisieux, the Little Flower (Therese Martin, 1873-1897), Carmelite nun.

A particular stamp may be scarce, but if few collectors want it, its market value may remain relatively low.

Anthurium (Martinique) — A601

1973, Jan. 20 **Photo.**

1356 A601 50c gray & multi 38 30

Colors of France and Germany Interlaced — A602

1973, Jan. 22

Size: 48x27mm.

1357 A602 50c multi 38 30

10th anniversary of the Franco-German Cooperation Treaty. See Germany No. 1101.

Polish Immigrants — A603

1973, Feb. 3 **Engr.** ***Perf. 13***

1358 A603 40c sl grn, dp car & brn 30 30

50th anniversary of Polish immigration into France, 1921-1923.

Last Supper, St. Austremoine Church, Issoire — A604

Kneeling Woman, by Charles Le Brun
A605

Angel, Wood, Moutier-D'Ahun — A606

Lady Playing Archlute, by Antoine Watteau
A607

1973 **Engr.** ***Perf. 12x13***

1359 A604 2fr brn & multi 2.25 1.25
1360 A605 2fr dk red & yel 2.25 1.25
1361 A606 2fr ol brn & vio brn 2.25 1.25
1362 A607 2fr blk & multi 2.25 1.25

Issue dates: No. 1359, Feb. 10; No. 1360, Apr. 28; No. 1361, May 26; No. 1362, Sept. 22.

Tuileries Palace, Telephone Relays
A608

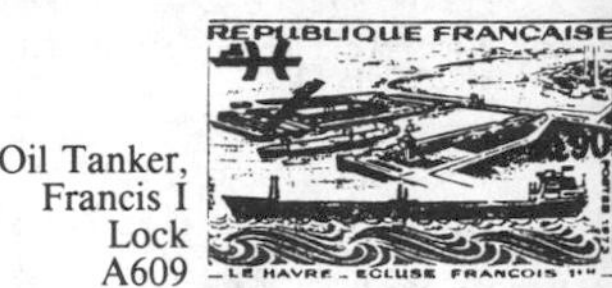

Oil Tanker, Francis I Lock
A609

Airbus A300-B
A610

1973

1363 A608 45c ultra, sl grn & bis 45 22
1364 A609 90c plum, blk & bl 75 25
1365 A610 3fr dk brn, bl & blk 2.50 1.25

French technical achievements.

Issue dates: 45c, May 15; 90c, Oct. 27; 3fr, Apr. 7.

Europa Issue 1973

Common Design Type and

City Hall, Brussels, CEPT Emblem — A611

1973, Apr. 14 **Engr.** ***Perf. 13***

1366 A611 50c brt pink & choc 45 15

Photo.

Size: 36x22mm.

1367 CD16 90c sl grn & multi 1.00 45

Masonic Lodge Emblem A612

1973, May 12 **Engr.** ***Perf. 13***
1368 A612 90c mag & vio bl 75 45

Bicentenary of the Free Masons of France.

Guadeloupe Raccoon A613

White Storks A614

1973
1369 A613 40c lil, sep & ol 45 30
1370 A614 60c blk, aqua & org red 65 38

Nature protection.
Issue dates: 40c, June 23; 60c, May 12.

Tourist Issue

Doubs Waterfall — A615

Palace of Dukes of Burgundy, Dijon A616

Clos-Lucé, Amboise — A617

Design: 90c, Gien Chateau.

1973 **Engr.** ***Perf. 13***
1371 A615 60c multi 30 20
1372 A616 65c red & pur 45 20
1373 A616 90c Prus bl, ind & brn 50 20
1374 A617 1fr ocher, bl & sl grn 50 18

Issue dates: 60c, Sept. 8; 65c, May 19; 90c, Aug. 18; 1fr, June 23.

Academy Emblem — A618

1973, May 26
1375 A618 1fr lil, sl grn & red 60 38

50th anniversary of the Academy of Overseas Sciences.

Racing Car and Clocks A619

1973, June 2
1376 A619 60c dk brn & bl 75 60

50th anniversary of the 24-hour automobile race at Le Mans.

Five-master France II — A620

1973, June 9
1377 A620 90c ultra, Prus bl & ind 60 38

Tower and Square, Toulouse — A621

1973, June 9
1378 A621 50c pur & red brn 38 22

46th Congress of the Federation of French Philatelic Societies, Toulouse, June 9-12.

Dr. Armauer G. Hansen A622

Ducretet and his Transmission Diagram A623

1973, Sept. 29 **Engr.** ***Perf. 13***
1379 A622 45c grn, dk ol & ocher 40 30

Centenary of the discovery of the Hansen bacillus, the cause of leprosy.

1973, Oct. 6
1380 A623 1fr yel grn & mag 60 30

75th anniversary of the first transmission of radio signals from the Eiffel Tower to the Pantheon by Eugene Ducretet (1844-1915).

Molière as Sganarelle — A624

1973, Oct. 20
1381 A624 1fr dk red & ol brn 60 32

Tercentenary of the death of Molière (Jean-Baptiste Poquelin; 1622-1673), playwright and actor.

Pierre Bourgoin and Philippe Kieffer A625

1973, Oct. 27
1382 A625 1fr red, rose cl & vio bl 75 38

Pierre Bourgoin (1907-70), and Philippe Kieffer (1899-1963), heroes of the Free French forces in World War II.

Napoleon, Jean Portalis and Palace of Justice, Paris — A626

Exhibition Halls — A627

The Coronation of Napoleon, by Jean Louis David — A628

1973 **Engr.** ***Perf. 13***
1383 A626 45c bl, choc & gray 30 30
1384 A627 60c ol, sl grn & brn 45 30
1385 A628 1fr sl grn, ol & cl 65 32

History of France. No. 1383 commemorates the preparation of the Code Napoleon; No. 1384, Napoleon's encouragement of industry and No. 1385 his coronation. Issue dates: 45c, Nov. 3; 60c, Nov. 24; 1fr, Nov. 12.

Eternal Flame, Arc de Triomphe A629

Weather Vane A630

1973, Nov. 10
1386 A629 40c pur, vio bl & red 32 30

50th anniversary of the Eternal Flame at the Arc de Triomphe, Paris.

1973, Dec. 1
1387 A630 65c ultra, blk & grn 40 30

50th anniversary of the Department of Agriculture.

Human Rights Flame and Man A631

Postal Museum A632

1973, Dec. 8 **Engr.** ***Perf. 13***
1388 A631 45c car, org & blk 30 22

25th anniversary of the Universal Declaration of Human Rights.

1973, Dec. 19
1389 A632 50c mar & bis 30 15

Opening of new post and philately museum, Paris.

ARPHILA 75 Emblem A633

1974, Jan. 19 **Engr.** ***Perf. 13***
1390 A633 50c brn, bl & brt lil 38 18

ARPHILA 75 Philatelic Exhibition, Paris, June 1975.

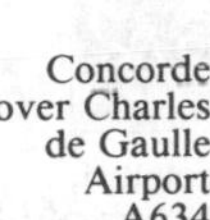

Concorde over Charles de Gaulle Airport A634

Turbotrain T.G.V. 001 — A635

Phenix Nuclear Power Station A636

1974 **Engr.** ***Perf. 13***
1391 A634 60c pur & ol gray 60 38
1392 A635 60c multi 1.50 60
1393 A636 65c multi 45 30

French technical achievements.
Issue dates: No. 1391, Mar. 18; No. 1392, Aug. 31; 65c, Sept. 21.

Cardinal Richelieu, by Philippe de Champaigne — A637

Painting by Joan Miró — A638

Canal du Loing, by Alfred Sisley — A639

"In Honor of Nicolas Fouquet," Tapestry by Georges Mathieu — A640

Engr.; Photo. (#1395, 1397)

1974 ***Perf. 12x13, 13x12***

1394 A637 2fr multi 1.75 1.10
1395 A638 2fr multi 1.75 1.10
1396 A639 2fr multi 2.25 1.10
1397 A640 2fr multi 2.25 1.10

Nos. 1394-1397 are printed in sheets of 25 with alternating labels publicizing "ARPHILA 75," Paris, June 6-16, 1975.

Issue dates: No. 1394, Mar. 23; No. 1395, Sept. 14; No. 1396, Nov. 9; No. 1397, Nov. 16.

French Alps and Gentian A641

1974, Mar. 30 **Engr.** ***Perf. 13***

1398 A641 65c vio bl & gray 50 38

Centenary of the French Alpine Club.

Europa Issue 1974

"Age of Bronze," by Auguste Rodin — A642

"Air," by Aristide Maillol A643

1974, Apr. 20 ***Perf. 13***

1399 A642 50c brt rose lil & blk 45 22
1400 A643 90c ol & brn 90 38

Sea Rescue — A644

1974, Apr. 27

1401 A644 90c multi 50 38

Reorganized sea rescue organization.

Council Building, View of Strasbourg and Emblem — A645

1974, May 4 **Engr.** ***Perf. 13***

1402 A645 45c ind, bis & bl 32 22

25th anniversary of the Council of Europe.

Tourist Issue

View of Salers A646

Basilica of St. Nicolas de Porte — A647

Seashell over Corsica — A648

Design: 1.10fr, View of Lot Valley.

1974 **Engr.** ***Perf. 13***

1403 A646 65c yel grn & choc 38 30
1404 A646 1.10fr choc & sl grn 65 38
1405 A647 2fr gray & lil 1.25 25
1406 A648 3fr multi 1.50 45

Issue dates: 65c, June 22; 1.10fr, Sept. 7; 2fr, Oct. 12; 3fr, May 11.

Bison A649

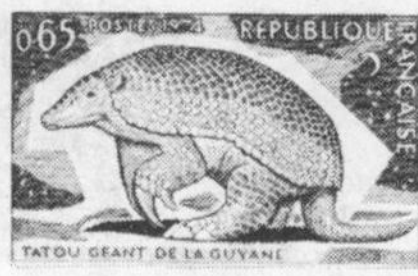

Giant Armadillo of Guyana A650

1974

1407 A649 40c bis, choc & bl 45 22
1408 A650 65c sl, ol & grn 45 30

Nature protection.

Issue dates: No. 1407, May 25; No. 1408, Oct. 19.

Americans Landing in Normandy and Arms of Normandy — A651

General Marie-Pierre Koenig — A652

Order of the French Resistance — A653

1974

1409 A651 45c grn, rose & ind 50 30
1410 A652 1fr multi 75 30
1411 A653 1fr multi 60 30

30th anniversary of the liberation of France from the Nazis. Design of No. 1410 includes diagram of battle of Bir-Hakeim and Free French and Bir-Hakeim memorials.

Issue dates, 45c, June 8; No. 1410, May 25. No. 1411, Nov. 23. See No. B478.

Pfister House, 16th Century, Colmar — A654

1974, June 1

1412 A654 50c multi 30 15

47th Congress of the Federation of French Philatelic Societies, Colmar, May 30-June 4.

Chess A655

1974, June 8

1413 A655 1fr dk brn & multi 80 50

21st Chess Olympiad, Nice, June 6-30.

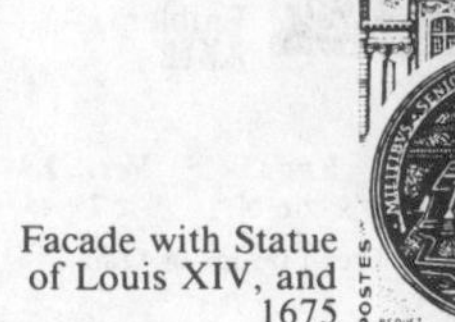

Facade with Statue of Louis XIV, and 1675 Medal — A656

1974, June 15

1414 A656 40c ind, bl & brn 30 22

300th anniversary of the founding of the Hotel des Invalides (Home for poor and sick officers and soldiers).

Peacocks Holding Letter, and Globe — A657

1974, Oct. 5 **Engr.** ***Perf. 13***

1415 A657 1.20fr ultra, dp grn & dk car 65 48

Centenary of Universal Postal Union.

Copernicus and Heliocentric System — A658

1974, Oct. 12

1416 A658 1.20fr multi 60 45

500th anniversary of the birth of Nicolaus Copernicus (1473-1543), Polish astronomer.

Tourist Issue

Palace of Justice, Rouen A659

Saint-Pol-de-Leon A660

Chateau de Rochechouart — A661

1975 **Engr.** ***Perf. 13***

1417 A659 85c multi 50 18
1418 A660 1.20fr bl, bis & choc 60 22
1419 A661 1.40fr brn, ind & grn 75 22

Issue dates: 85c, Jan. 25; 1.20fr, Jan. 18; 1.40fr, Jan. 11.

Snowy Egret — A662

Gallic Coin — A663

1975, Feb. 15 Engr. *Perf. 13*

1420	A662	70c brt bl & bis	48	38

Nature protection.

1975, Feb. 16 Typo. *Perf. 13½x14*

1421	A663	42c org & mag	2.00	38
1422	A663	48c lt bl & red brn	2.50	38
1423	A663	70c brt pink & red	4.00	75
1424	A663	1.35fr lt grn & brn	4.75	1.10

Nos. 1421-1424 are known only precanceled. See second note after No. 132. See Nos. 1460-1463, 1487-1490.

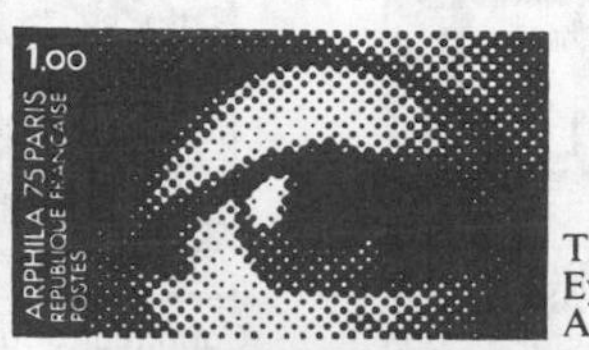
The Eye A664

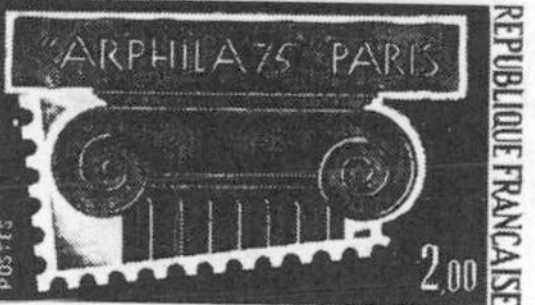
Ionic Capital — A665

Graphic Art — A666

Ceres — A667

1975 Engr. *Perf. 13*

1425	A664	1fr red, pur & org	65	30
1426	A665	2fr grn, sl grn & mag	1.00	45
1427	A666	3fr dk car & ol grn	1.50	65
1428	A667	4fr red, sl grn & bis	2.00	90

Souvenir Sheet

1429	Sheet of 4	12.00	12.00
a.	A664 2fr dp car & sl bl	1.75	1.75
b.	A665 3fr brt bl, sl bl & dp car	2.25	2.25
c.	A666 4fr sl bl, brt bl & plum	3.25	3.25
d.	A667 6fr brt bl, sl bl & plum	4.25	4.00

ARPHILA 75, International Philatelic Exhibition, Paris, June 6-16. No. 1429 has ornamental border and commemorative inscription. Size: 150x143mm. Issue dates: 1fr, Mar. 1; 2fr, Mar. 22; 3fr, Apr. 19; 4fr, May 17; souvenir sheet, Apr. 2.

Pres. Georges Pompidou A668

Paul as Harlequin, by Picasso A669

1975, Apr. 3 Engr. *Perf. 13*

1430	A668	80c blk & gray	45	15

Georges Pompidou (1911-74), President of France, 1969-74.

Europa Issue 1975

1975, Apr. 26 Photo. *Perf. 13*

Design: 1.20fr, Woman on Balcony, by Kees van Dongen (horiz.).

1431	A669	80c multi	60	22
1432	A669	1.20fr multi	90	38

Machines, Globe, Emblem A670

1975, May 3 Engr.

1433	A670	1.20fr bl, blk & red	60	45

World Machine Tool Exhibition, Paris, June 17-26.

Senate Assembly Hall — A671

1975, May 24 Engr. *Perf. 13*

1434	A671	1.20fr ol & dk car	60	45

Centenary of the Senate of the Republic.

Meter Convention Document, Atom Diagram and Waves — A672

1975, May 31

1435	A672	1fr multi	50	32

Centenary of International Meter Convention, Paris, 1875.

Metro Regional Train A673

"Gazelle" Helicopter A674

1975

1436	A673	1fr ind & brt bl	1.25	38
1437	A674	1.30fr vio bl & grn	95	60

French technical achievements. Issue dates: 1fr, June 21; 1.30fr, May 31.

Youth and Flasks, Symbols of Study and Growth — A675

1975, June 21

1438	A675	70c red pur & blk	38	30

Student Health Foundation.

People's Theater, Bussang, and Maurice Pottecher A676

1975, Aug. 9 Engr. *Perf. 13*

1439	A676	85c multi	45	30

80th anniversary of the People's Theater at Bussang, founded by Maurice Pottecher.

Regions of France

Central France A677

Aquitaine A678

Limousin A679

Picardy A680

Burgundy A681

Loire A682

Guyana A683

Auvergne A684

Poitou-Charentes A685

Southern Pyrenees A686

Pas-de-Calais — A687

1975-76 Engr. *Perf. 13*

1440	A677	25c bl & yel grn	30	22
1441	A678	60c multi	32	25
1442	A679	70c multi	65	25
1443	A680	85c bl, grn & org	95	30
1444	A681	1fr red, yel & mar	90	30
1445	A682	1.15fr bl, bis & grn	90	38
1446	A683	1.25fr multi	75	45
1447	A684	1.30fr dk bl & red	75	30
1448	A685	1.90fr sl, ol & Prus bl	1.25	30
1449	A686	2.20fr multi	1.40	75
1450	A687	2.80fr car, bl & blk	2.00	80
		Nos. 1440-1450 (11)	10.17	4.30

Issue dates—1975: 85c, Nov. 15; 1fr, Oct. 25; 1.15fr, Sept. 6; 1.30fr, Oct. 4; 1.90fr, Dec. 6; 2.80fr, Dec. 13. 1976: 25c, Jan. 31; 2.20fr, Jan. 10; 60c, May 22; 70c, May 29; 125fr, Oct. 16.

French Flag, F.-H. Manhes, Jean Verneau, Pierre Kaan — A690

1975, Sept. 27

1453	A690	1fr multi	50	38

Liberation of concentration camps, 30th anniversary. F.-H. Manhes (1889-1959), Jean Verneau (1890-1944) and Pierre Kaan (1903-1945) were French resistance leaders, imprisoned in concentration camps.

Monument, by Joseph Riviere — A691

1975, Oct. 11

1454	A691	70c multi	38	30

Land Mine Demolition Service, 30th anniversary. Monument was erected in Alsace to honor land mine victims.

The only foreign revenue stamps listed in this Catalogue are those authorized for prepayment of postage.

Symbols of Suburban Living
A692

1975, Oct. 18
1455 A692 1.70fr brn, bl & grn 1.00 75

Creation of new towns.

Women and Rainbow — A693

1975, Nov. 8 **Photo.**
1456 A693 1.20fr sil & multi 65 45

International Women's Year 1975.

Saint-Nazaire Bridge — A694

1975, Nov. 8 **Engr.**
1457 A694 1.40fr bl, ind & grn 90 32

French and Russian Flags
A695

Frigate Melpomene
A696

1975, Nov. 22
1458 A695 1.20fr bl, red & ocher 65 45

Franco-Soviet diplomatic relations, 50th anniversary.

1975, Dec. 6
1459 A696 90c multi 50 30

Gallic Coin Type of 1975

1976, Jan. 1 **Typo.** ***Perf. 13½x14***
1460 A663 50c lt grn & brn 2.00 45
1461 A663 60c lil & brn 3.00 45
1462 A663 90c org & brn 3.75 1.00
1463 A663 1.60fr vio & brn 6.75 3.00

Nos. 1460-1463 are known only precanceled. See second note after No. 132.

Lintel, St. Genis des Fontaines Church
A697

Venus of Brassempouy (Paleolithic) — A698

"The Joy of Life," by Robert Delaunay
A699

Ramses II, from Abu Simbel Temple, Egypt — A700

Still Life, by Maurice de Vlaminck — A701

1976 **Engr.** ***Perf. 13***
1464 A697 2fr bl & sl bl 1.25 90
1465 A698 2fr dk brn & yel 1.25 90

Photo.

Perf. 12½x13

1466 A699 2fr multi 1.25 90

Engr.

Perf. 13x12½

1467 A700 2fr multi 1.10 75

Perf. 13

1468 A701 2fr multi 1.10 75
Nos. 1464-1468 (5) 5.95 4.20

Issue dates: No. 1464, Jan. 24; No. 1465, Mar. 6; No. 1466, July 24; No. 1467, Sept. 4; No. 1468, Dec. 18.

Tourist Issue

Chateau Fort de Bonaguil
A702

Lodeve Cathedral
A703

Biarritz
A704

Thiers — A705

Ussel — A706

Chateau de Malmaison
A707

1976 **Engr.** ***Perf. 13***
1469 A702 1fr multi 45 15
1470 A703 1.10fr vio bl 55 30
1471 A704 1.40fr multi 60 22
1472 A705 1.70fr multi 75 18
1473 A706 2fr multi 1.25 22
1474 A707 3fr multi 1.40 32
Nos. 1469-1474 (6) 5.00 1.39

Issue dates: 1fr, 2fr, July 10; 1.10fr, Nov. 13; 1.40fr, Sept. 25; 1.70fr, Oct. 9; 3fr, Apr. 10.

Destroyers, Association Emblem
A708

1976, Apr. 24
1475 A708 1fr vio bl, mag & lem 75 32

Naval Reserve Officers Association, 50th anniversary.

Gate, Rouen — A709

Young Person — A710

1976, Apr. 24
1476 A709 80c ol gray & sal 45 18

49th Congress of the Federation of French Philatelic Societies, Rouen, Apr. 23-May 2.

1976, Apr. 27
1477 A710 60c bl grn, ind & car 50 18

JUVAROUEN 76, International Youth Philatelic Exhibition, Rouen, Apr. 25-May 2.

Europa Issue 1976

Ceramic Pitcher, Strasbourg, 18th Century
A711

Design: 1.20fr, Sevres porcelain plate and CEPT emblem.

1976, May 8 **Photo.** ***Perf. 13***
1478 A711 80c multi 48 22
1479 A711 1.20fr multi 75 32

Count de Vergennes and Benjamin Franklin — A712

1976, May 15 **Engr.** ***Perf. 13***
1480 A712 1.20fr multi 60 45

American Bicentennial.

Battle of Verdun Memorial
A713

Communication
A714

1976, June 12 **Engr.**
1481 A713 1fr multi 60 32

Battle of Verdun, 60th anniversary.

1976, June 12 **Photo.**
1482 A714 1.20fr multi 60 38

Troncais Forest
A715

Cross of Lorraine
A716

1976, June 19 **Engr.**
1483 A715 70c grn & multi 40 30

Protection of the environment.

1976, June 19
1484 A716 1fr multi 50 30

Association of Free French, 30th anniversary.

Symphonie Communications Satellite — A717

1976, June 26 **Photo.**
1485 A717 1.40fr multi 80 38

French technical achievements.

Gallic Coin Type of 1975

1976, July 1 **Typo.** ***Perf. 13½x14***
1487 A663 52c ver & dk brn 1.00 30
1488 A663 62c vio & dk brn 2.00 60

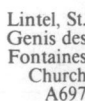

1489 A663 95c tan & dk brn 2.50 90
1490 A663 1.70fr dk bl & dk brn 4.50 2.25

Nos. 1487-1490 are known only precanceled. See second note after No. 132.

Paris Summer Festival — A719

1976, July 10 **Engr.**
1491 A719 1fr multi 75 32

Summer festival in Tuileries Gardens, Paris.

Emblem and Soldiers A720

1976, July 8
1492 A720 1fr blk, dp bl & mag 55 30

Officers Reserve Corps, centenary.

Sailing A721

1976, July 17
1493 A721 1.20fr bl, blk & vio 60 45

21st Olympic Games, Montreal, Canada, July 17 Aug. 1.

Marianne Type of 1971-74

1976 **Typo.** ***Perf. 14x13***
1494 A555 80c green 50 5

Engr.

Perf. 13

1495 A555 80c green 60 15
a. Booklet pane of 10 6.00
1496 A555 1fr car rose 60 5
a. Booklet pane of 5 5.00
b. Booklet pane of 10 9.00

No. 1495 issued in booklets only. "POSTES" 6mm. long on Nos. 1292A and 1494; 4mm. on others.

Nos. 1494 and 1496 were issued untagged in 1977.

Coil Stamps

1976, Aug. 1 **Engr.** ***Perf. 13 Horiz.***
1497 A555 80c green 60 38
1498 A555 1fr car rose 60 30

Red control number on back of every 10th stamp.

Woman's Head, by Jean Carzou — A722

1976, Sept. 18 **Engr.** ***Perf. 13x12½***
1499 A722 2fr multi 1.10 65

Old and New Telephones A723

1976, Sept. 25 **Engr.** ***Perf. 13***
1500 A723 1fr multi 55 22

Centenary of first telephone call by Alexander Graham Bell, Mar. 10, 1876.

Festival Emblem and Trophy, Pyrenees, Hercules and Pyrene A724

Police Emblem A725

1976, Oct. 2
1501 A724 1.40fr multi 75 45

10th International Tourist Film Festival, Tarbes, Oct. 4-10.

1976, Oct. 9 **Engr.** ***Perf. 13***
1502 A725 1.10fr ultra, red & ol 65 30

National Police, help and protection.

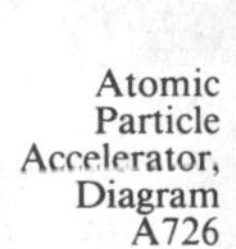
Atomic Particle Accelerator, Diagram A726

1976, Oct. 22 **Photo.**
1503 A726 1.40fr multi 90 38

European Center for Nuclear Research (CERN).

"Exhibitions" — A727

1976, Nov. 20 **Engr.** ***Perf. 13***
1504 A727 1.50fr multi 75 45

Trade Fairs and Exhibitions.

Abstract Design A728

1976, Nov. 27 **Photo.**
1505 A728 1.10fr multi 65 32

Customs Service.

Atlantic Museum, Port Louis — A729

1976, Dec. 4 **Engr.**
1506 A729 1.45fr grnsh bl & ol 75 45

Regions of France

Réunion A730

Martinique A731

Franche-Comte A732

Brittany A733

Rhône-Alps A735

Languedoc-Roussillon A734

Champagne-Ardennes A736

Alsace A737

Photogravure (1.45fr, 1.50fr, 2.50fr); Engraved

1977 ***Perf. 13***
1507 A730 1.45fr grn & lil rose 75 30
1508 A731 1.50fr multi 80 38
1509 A732 2.10fr multi 1.10 50
1510 A733 2.40fr multi 1.50 32
1511 A734 2.50fr multi 1.50 50
1512 A735 2.75fr Prus bl 1.75 48
1513 A736 3.20fr multi 1.90 80
1514 A737 3.90fr multi 2.50 90
Nos. 1507-1514 (8) 11.80 4.18

Issue dates: 1.45fr, Feb. 5; 1.50fr, Jan. 29; 2.10fr, Jan. 8; 2.40fr, Feb. 19; 2.50fr, Jan. 15; 2.75fr, Jan. 22; 3.20fr, Apr. 16; 3.90fr, Feb. 26.

Pompidou Cultural Center — A738

1977, Feb. 5 **Engr.** ***Perf. 13***
1515 A738 1fr multi 55 22

Inauguration of the Georges Pompidou National Center for Art and Culture, Paris.

Dunkirk Harbor A739

1977, Feb. 12
1516 A739 50c multi 32 18

Expansion of Dunkirk harbor facilities.

Bridge at Mantes, by Corot — A740

Virgin and Child, by Rubens A741

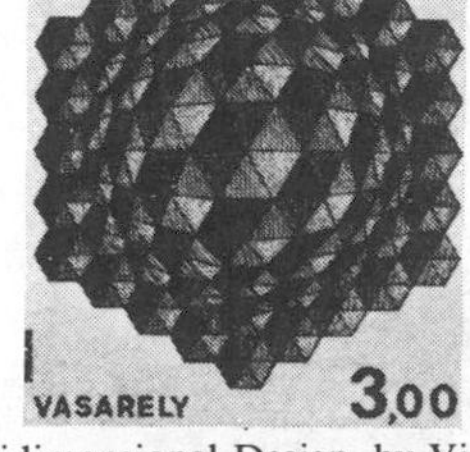

Tridimensional Design, by Victor Vasarely — A742

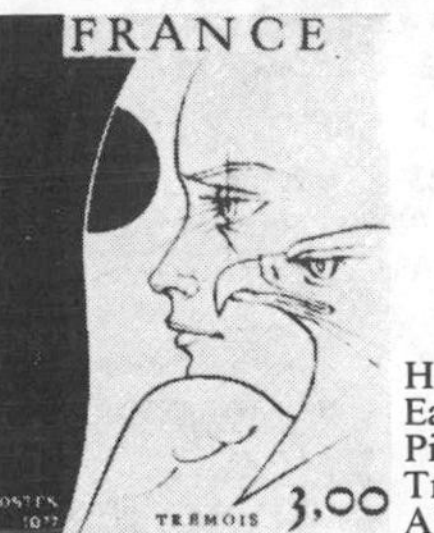

Head and Eagle, by Pierre-Yves Tremois A743

1977 **Engr.** ***Perf. 13x12½***
1517 A740 2fr multi 1.10 75

Perf. 12x13

1518 A741 2fr multi 1.10 75

Perf. 12½x13

1519 A742 3fr ultra & sl grn 1.50 75

Photo.

1520 A743 3fr dk red & blk 1.90 90

Issue dates: No. 1517, Feb. 12; No. 1518, Nov. 5; No. 1519, Apr. 7; No. 1520, Sept. 17.

Hand Holding Torch and Sword — A744

Pisces — A745

1977, Mar. 5 Engr. *Perf. 13*

1521 A744 80c ultra & multi 55 22

"France remembers its dead."

1977-78 Engr. *Perf. 13*

Zodiac Signs: 58c, Cancer. 61c, Sagittarius. 68c, Taurus. 73c, Aries. 78c, Libra. 1.05fr, Scorpio. 1.15fr, Capricorn. 1.25fr, Leo. 1.85fr, Aquarius. 2fr, Virgo. 2.10fr, Gemini.

1522 A745 54c vio bl 1.00 45
1523 A745 58c emerald 1.50 50
1524 A745 61c brt bl 80 45
1525 A745 68c dp brn 1.25 60
1526 A745 73c rose car 2.25 95
1527 A745 78c vermilion 1.00 60
1528 A745 1.05fr brt lil 2.25 1.25
1529 A745 1.15fr orange 3.50 1.90
1530 A745 1.25fr lt ol grn 1.75 1.00
1531 A745 1.85fr sl grn 4.00 1.50
1532 A745 2fr bl grn 4.50 3.00
1533 A745 2.10fr lil rose 2.50 1.65
Nos. 1522-1533 (12) 26.30 13.85

Issue dates: 54c, 68c, 1.05fr, 1.85fr, Apr. 1, 1977. Others, 1978.

Nos. 1522-1533 are known only precanceled. See second note after No. 132.

Europa Issue

Village in Provence A746

Design: 1.40fr, Brittany port.

1977, Apr. 23

1534 A746 1fr multi 50 15
1535 A746 1.40fr multi 75 30

Flowers and Gardening A747

1977, Apr. 23 Engr. *Perf. 13*

1536 A747 1.70fr multi 90 45

National Horticulture Society, centenary.

Symbolic Flower A748

1977, May 7

1537 A748 1.40fr multi 70 60

International Flower Show, Nantes, May 12-23.

Battle of Cambray A749

1977, May 14

1538 A749 80c multi 50 30

300th anniversary of the capture of Cambray and the incorporation of Cambresis District into France.

Carmes Church, School, Map of France A750

Modern Constructions A751

1977, May 14

1539 A750 1.10fr multi 60 30

Catholic Institutes in France.

1977, May 21

1540 A751 1.10fr multi 60 38

European Federation of the Construction Industry.

Annecy Castle A752

1977, May 28

1541 A752 1fr multi 50 22

Congress of the Federation of French Philatelic Societies, Annecy, May 28-30.

Tourist Issue

Abbey, Pont-a-Mousson — A753

Abbey Tower, Saint-Amand-les-Eaux A754

Collegiate Church of Dorat A755

Fontenay Abbey A756

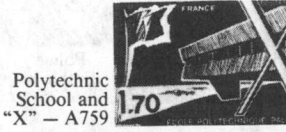

Bayeux Cathedral A757

Chateau de Vitre A758

1977 Engr. *Perf. 13*

1542 A753 1.25fr multi 60 22
1543 A754 1.40fr multi 65 22
1544 A755 1.45fr multi 65 25
1545 A756 1.50fr multi 75 30
1546 A757 1.90fr blk & yel 90 38
1547 A758 2.40fr blk & yel 1.10 30
Nos. 1542-1547 (6) 4.65 1.67

Issue dates: 1.25fr, Oct. 1; 1.40fr, Sept. 17; 1.45fr, July 16; 1.50fr, June 4; 1.90fr, July 9; 2.40fr, Sept. 24.

Polytechnic School and "X" — A759

1977, June 4 Engr. *Perf. 13*

1548 A759 1.70fr multi 80 32

Relocation at Palaiseau of Polytechnic School, founded 1794.

Soccer and Cup — A760

1977, June 11

1549 A760 80c multi 80 32

Soccer Cup of France, 60th anniversary.

De Gaulle Memorial A761

Stylized Map of France A762

Photogravure and Embossed

1977, June 18

1550 A761 1fr gold & multi 75 18

5th anniversary of dedication of De Gaulle memorial at Colombey-les-Deux-Eglises.

1977, June 18 Engr. *Perf. 13*

1551 A762 1.10fr ultra & red 65 30

French Junior Chamber of Commerce.

Catalogue prices for unused stamps up to mid-1953 are for hinged copies matching the condition specified in this volume's introduction.

Battle of Nancy A763

Arms of Burgundy A764

1977, June 25

1552 A763 1.10fr bl & sl 1.40 60

Battle of Nancy between the Dukes of Burgundy and Lorraine, 500th anniversary.

1977, July 2

1553 A764 1.25fr ol brn & sl grn 75 32

Annexation of Burgundy by the French Crown, 500th anniversary.

Association Emblem A765

1977, July 8

1554 A765 1.40fr ultra, ol & red 75 38

French-speaking Parliamentary Association.

Red Cicada — A766

1977, Sept. 10 Photo. *Perf. 13*

1555 A766 80c multi 55 25

Nature protection.

French Handicrafts A767

1977, Oct. 1 Engr. *Perf. 13*

1556 A767 1.40fr multi 65 30

French craftsmen.

Industry and Agriculture — A768

1977, Oct. 22

1557 A768 80c brn & ol 45 30

Economic and Social Council, 30th anniversary.

Table Tennis A769

1977, Dec. 17 Engr. *Perf. 13*
1558 A769 1.10fr multi 1.25 38

French Table Tennis Federation, 50th anniversary, and French team, gold medal winner, Birmingham.

Abstract, by Roger Excoffon — A770

1977, Dec. 17 *Perf. 13x12½*
1559 A770 3fr multi 1.75 75

Sabine, after David — A771

1977-78 Engr. *Perf. 13*
1560 A771 1c slate 10 5
1561 A771 2c brt vio 10 5
1562 A771 5c sl grn 10 5
1563 A771 10c red brn 10 5
1564 A771 15c Prus bl 15 15
1565 A771 20c brt grn 15 6
1566 A771 30c orange 15 6
1567 A771 50c red lil 22 15
1568 A771 80c green ('77) 1.65 25
a. Bklt. pane of 10 16.00
1569 A771 80c olive 40 5
1570 A771 1fr red ('77) 1.75 5
a. Bklt. pane of 5 12.00
b. Bklt. pane of 10 21.00
1571 A771 1fr green 80 5
a. Bklt. pane of 10 8.00
1572 A771 1.20fr red 80 5
a. Bklt. pane of 5 6.00
b. Bklt. pane of 10 11.00
1573 A771 1.40fr brt bl 2.75 25
1574 A771 1.70fr grnsh bl 1.00 30
1575 A771 2fr emerald 1.00 6
1576 A771 2.10fr lil rose 1.10 10
1577 A771 3fr dk brn 1.40 40
Nos. 1560-1577 (18) 13.72 2.18

Coil Stamps

1978 *Perf. 13 Horiz.*
1578 A771 80c brt grn 1.75 60
1579 A771 1fr brt grn 1.40 45
1579A A771 1fr brt red 1.75 60
1579B A771 1.20fr brt red 1.40 45

See Nos. 1658-1677.

Percheron, by Jacques Birr — A772

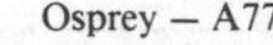
Osprey — A773

1978 Photo. *Perf. 13*
1580 A772 1.70fr multi 1.25 60

Engr.
1581 A773 1.80fr multi 1.00 32

Nature protection.
Issue dates: 1.70fr, Jan. 7; 1.80fr, Oct. 14.

Tournament, 1662, Etching — A774

Institut de France and Pont des Arts, Paris, by Bernard Buffet — A776

Horses, by Yves Brayer — A777

1978 Engr. *Perf. 12x13*
1582 A774 2fr black 2.00 90

Perf. 13x12
1584 A776 3fr multi 2.25 60
1585 A777 3fr multi 1.65 60

Issue dates: 2fr, Jan. 14; No. 1584, Feb. 4; No. 1585, Dec. 9.

Communications School and Tower — A778

1978, Jan. 19 Engr. *Perf. 13*
1586 A778 80c Prus bl 40 22

National Telecommunications School, centenary.

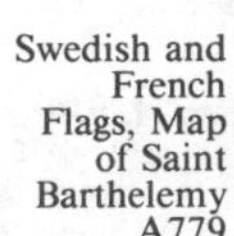

Swedish and French Flags, Map of Saint Barthelemy A779

1978, Jan. 19
1587 A779 1.10fr multi 60 25

Centenary of the reunion with France of Saint Barthelemy Island, West Indies.

Regions of France

Ile de France — A780

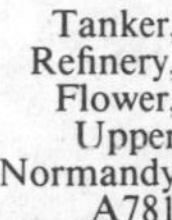

Tanker, Refinery, Flower, Upper Normandy A781

Lower Normandy A782

1978 Photo. *Perf. 13*
1588 A780 1fr red, bl & blk 60 30

Engr.
1589 A781 1.40fr multi 65 30

Photo.
1590 A782 1.70fr multi 1.10 45

Issue dates. 1fr, Mar. 4; 1.40fr, Jan. 21; 1.70fr, Mar. 31.

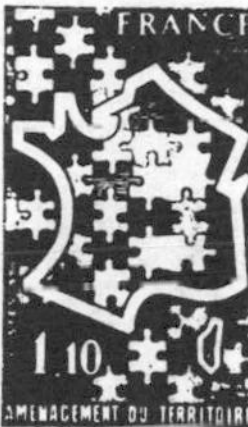

Stylized Map of France A788

Young Stamp Collector A789

1978, Feb. 11 Engr. *Perf. 13*
1596 A788 1.10fr vio & grn 60 25

Program of administrative changes, 15th anniversary.

1978, Feb. 25
1597 A789 80c multi 45 22

JUVEXNIORT, Youth Philatelic Exhibition, Niort, Feb. 25-March 5.

Tourist Issue

Verdon Gorge — A790

Pont Neuf, Paris A791

Saint-Saturnin Church — A792

Our Lady of Bec-Hellouin Abbey — A793

Chateau D'Esquelbecq — A794

Aubazine Abbey A795

Fontevraud Abbey A796

1978 Engr. *Perf. 13*
1598 A790 50c multi 25 15
1599 A791 80c multi 50 22
1600 A792 1fr black 55 15
1601 A793 1.10fr multi 70 22
1602 A794 1.10fr multi 55 32
1603 A795 1.25fr car & brn 70 30
1604 A796 1.70fr multi 1.00 32
Nos. 1598-1604 (7) 4.25 1.68

Issue dates: 1.25fr, Feb. 18; 50c, Mar. 6; No. 1601, Mar. 26; 80c, May 27; 1fr, June 10; 1.70fr, June 3; No. 1602, June 17.

Fish and Underwater Flora A797

1978, Apr. 15 Photo. *Perf. 13*
1605 A797 1.25fr multi 80 60

Port Cros National Park, 15th anniversary.

Flowers, Butterflies and Houses — A798

1978, Apr. 22 Engr. *Perf. 13*
1606 A798 1.70fr multi 3.00 45

50th anniversary of the beautification of France campaign.

Hands Shielding Source of Heat and Light A799

1978, Apr. 22
1607 A799 1fr multi 80 18

Energy conservation.

World War I Memorial near Lens — A800

Fountain of the Innocents, Paris — A801

1978, May 6
1608 A800 2fr lem & mag 1.25 45

Colline Notre Dame de Lorette memorial of World War I.

Europa Issue 1978

Design: 1.40fr, Flower Park Fountain, Paris.

1978, May 6
1609 A801 1fr multi 55 15
1610 A801 1.40fr multi 70 30

Maurois Palace, Troyes — A802

1978, May 13
1611 A802 1fr multi 55 22

51st Congress of the Federation of French Philatelic Societies, Troyes, May 13-15.

Roland Garros Tennis Court and Player — A803

1978, May 27
1612 A803 1fr multi 1.40 38

Roland Garros Tennis Court, 50th anniversary.

Hand and Plant A804

Printing Office Emblem A805

1978, Sept. 9 **Engr.** ***Perf. 13***
1613 A804 1.30fr brn, red & grn 65 32

Encouragement of handicrafts.

1978, Sept. 23
1614 A805 1fr multi 55 22

National Printing Office, established 1538.

Fortress, Besançon, and Collegiate Church, Dole — A806

Valenciennes and Maubeuge — A807

1978
1615 A806 1.20fr multi 65 22
1616 A807 1.20fr multi 65 22

Reunion of Franche-Comté and Valenciennes and Maubeuge with France, 300th anniversary.
Issue dates: No. 1615, Sept. 23, No. 1616, Sept. 30.

Sower Type of 1906-1937 and Academy Emblem A808

Gymnasts, Strasbourg Cathedral, Storks A809

1978, Oct. 7
1617 A808 1fr multi 55 25

Academy of Philately, 50th anniversary.

1978, Oct. 21
1618 A809 1fr multi 65 25

19th World Gymnastics Championships, Strasbourg, Oct. 23-26.

Various Sports A810

Polish Veterans' Monument A811

1978, Oct. 21
1619 A810 1fr multi 1.10 45

Sports for all.

1978, Nov. 11
1620 A811 1.70fr multi 80 38

Polish veterans of World War II.

Railroad Car and Monument, Compiegne Forest, Rethondes A812

1978, Nov. 11 **Engr.** ***Perf. 13***
1621 A812 1.20fr indigo 75 22

60th anniversary of World War I armistice.

Handicapped People A813

1978, Nov. 18
1622 A813 1fr multi 55 22

Rehabilitation of the handicapped.

Human Rights Emblem A814

1978, Dec. 9 **Engr.** ***Perf. 13***
1623 A814 1.70fr dk brn & bl 90 45

30th anniversary of Universal Declaration of Human Rights.

Child and IYC Emblem A815

1979, Jan. 6 **Engr.** ***Perf. 13***
1624 A815 1.70fr multi 5.25 2.25

International Year of the Child.

"Music," 15th Century Miniature — A816

1979, Jan. 13 ***Perf. 13x12½***
1625 A816 2fr multi 1.50 75

Diana Taking a Bath, d'Ecouen Castle A817

Church at Auvers-on-Oise, by Vincent Van Gogh — A818

Head of Marianne, by Salvador Dali A819

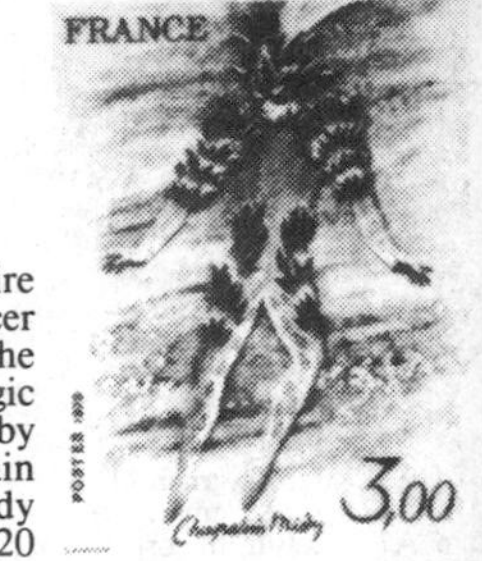
Fire Dancer from The Magic Flute, by Chaplain Midy A820

1979 **Photo.** ***Perf. 12½x13***
1626 A817 2fr multi 1.25 60
1627 A818 2fr multi 2.25 60
1628 A819 3fr multi 1.65 60
1629 A820 3fr multi 1.65 75

Issue dates: No. 1626, Sept. 22; No. 1627, Oct. 27; No. 1628, Nov. 19; No. 1629, Nov. 26.

Orange Agaric — A821

Mushrooms: 83c, Death trumpet. 1.30fr, Olive wood pleurotus. 2.25fr, Cauliflower claveria.

1979, Jan. 15 **Engr.** ***Perf. 13***
1630 A821 64c orange 50 38
1631 A821 83c brown 80 45
1632 A821 1.30fr yel bis 1.25 65
1633 A821 2.25fr brn pur 2.00 1.10

Nos. 1630-1633 are known only precanceled. See second note after No. 132.

Certain countries cancel stamps in full sheets and sell them (usually with gum) for less than face value. Dealers generally sell "CTO".

Victor Segalen A822

1979, Jan. 20
1634 A822 1.50fr multi 65 30

Victor Segalen (1878-1919), physician, explorer and writer.

Hibiscus and Palms — A823

1979, Feb. 3
1635 A823 35c multi 20 15

International Flower Festival, Martinique.

Buddha, Stupas, Temple of Borobudur A824

1979, Feb. 24
1636 A824 1.80fr ol & sl grn 90 45

Save the Temple of Borobudur, Java, campaign.

Boy, by Poulbot — A825

1979, Mar. 24 **Photo.**
1637 A825 1.30fr multi 65 22

Francisque Poulbot (1879-1946).

Tourist Issue

Chateau de Maisons, Laffitte A826

Bernay and St. Pierre sur Dives Abbeys A827

View of Auray A827a

Scott's International Album provides spaces for an extensive representative collection of the world's postage stamps.

Steenvorde Windmill — A828

Wall Painting, Niaux Cave A829

Royal Palace, Perpignan A830

1979 **Engr.** ***Perf. 13***
1638 A826 45c multi 25 15
1639 A827 1fr multi 50 22
1640 A827a 1fr multi 50 22
1641 A828 1.20fr multi 65 18
1642 A829 1.50fr multi 70 30
1643 A830 1.70fr multi 80 30
Nos. 1638-1643 (6) 3.40 1.37

Issue dates: 45c, Oct. 6; No. 1639, June 16; No. 1640, June 30; 1.20fr, May 12; 1.50fr, July 9; 1.70fr, Apr. 21.

Honey Bee — A831

1979, Mar. 31 **Engr.** ***Perf. 13***
1644 A831 1fr multi 55 18

Nature protection.

St. Germain des Pres Abbey A832

1979, Apr. 21
1645 A832 1.40fr multi 60 30

Europa Issue 1979

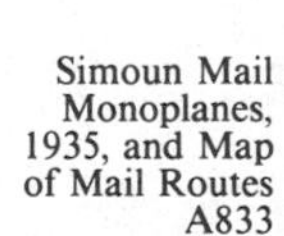

Simoun Mail Monoplanes, 1935, and Map of Mail Routes A833

Design: 1.70fr, Floating spheres used on Seine during siege of Paris, 1870.

1979, Apr. 28
1646 A833 1.20fr multi 60 22
1647 A833 1.70fr multi 75 38

Ship and View of Nantes A834

1979, May 5 **Engr.** ***Perf. 13***
1648 A834 1.20fr multi 55 22

52nd National Congress of French Philatelic Societies, Nantes, May 5-7.

Royal Palace, 1789 — A835

1979, May 19
1649 A835 1fr car rose & pur 55 30

European Elections A836

1979, May 19 **Photo.** ***Perf. 13***
1650 A836 1.20fr multi 60 18

European Parliament, first direct elections, June 10.

Joan of Arc Monument A837

1979, May 24 **Engr.**
1651 A837 1.70fr brt lil rose 1.00 45

Joan of Arc, the Maid of Orleans (1412-1431).

Felix Guyon and Catheters A840

1979, June 23
1652 A840 1.80fr sep & bl 75 30

Felix Guyon (1831-1920), urologist.

Lantern Tower, La Rochelle A841

Telecom '79 A842

Towers: 88c, Chartres Cathedral. 1.40fr, Bourges Cathedral. 2.35fr, Amiens Cathedral.

1979, Aug. 13 **Engr.** ***Perf. 13***
1653 A841 68c vio brn & blk 50 45
1654 A841 88c ultra & blk 65 45
1655 A841 1.40fr gray grn & blk 1.00 80
1656 A841 2.35fr dl brn & blk 1.50 95

Nos. 1653-1656 are known only precanceled. See second note after No. 132.
See Nos. 1684-1687.

1979, Sept. 22
1657 A842 1.10fr multi 55 18

3rd World Telecommunications Exhibition.

Sabine Type of 1977-78

1979-81 **Engr.** ***Perf. 13***
1658 A771 40c brn ('81) 18 15
1659 A771 60c red brn ('81) 25 18
1660 A771 70c vio bl 30 15
1661 A771 90c brt lil ('81) 38 22
1662 A771 1fr gray ol 38 5
1663 A771 1.10fr green 1.10 5
1664 A771 1.20fr grn ('80) 70 5
1665 A771 1.30fr rose red 1.10 5
1666 A771 1.40fr rose red ('80) 80 5
1667 A771 1.60fr purple 1.50 15
1668 A771 1.80fr ocher 1.10 18
1669 A771 3.50fr lt ol grn ('81) 1.50 22
1670 A771 4fr brt car ('81) 1.75 30
1671 A771 5fr brt grnsh bl ('81) 2.25 15
Nos. 1658-1671 (14) 13.29 1.95

Coil Stamps

1979-80 ***Perf. 13 Horiz.***
1674 A771 1.10fr green 1.65 30
1675 A771 1.20fr grn ('80) 70 30
1676 A771 1.30fr rose red 1.65 30
1677 A771 1.40fr rose red ('80) 80 30

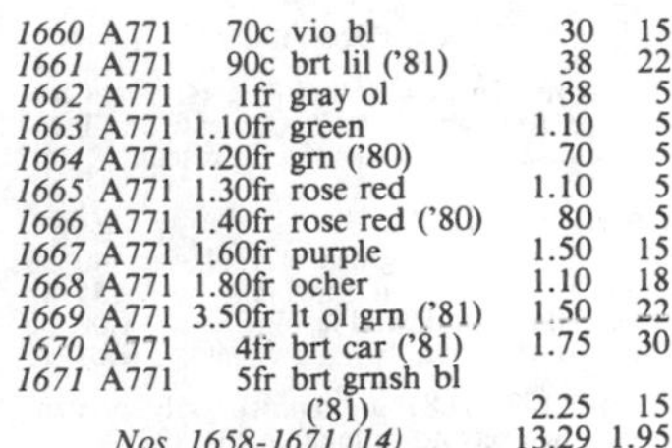

Lorraine Region — A845

1979, Nov. 10
1678 A845 2.30fr multi 1.00 32

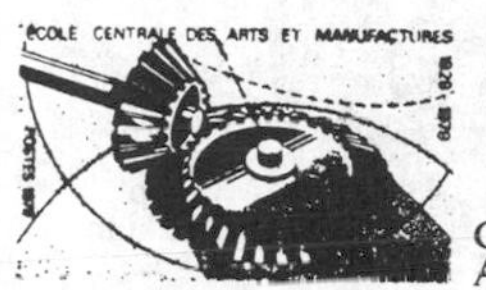
Gears A847

1979, Nov. 17 ***Perf. 13***
1680 A847 1.80fr multi 90 45

Central Technical School of Paris, 150th anniv.

Judo Throw A848

1979, Nov. 24 **Engr.**
1681 A848 1.60fr multi 75 38

World Judo Championships, Paris, Dec.

Violins — A849

1979, Dec. 10
1682 A849 1.30fr multi 75 22

Eurovision A850

1980, Jan. 12 **Engr.** ***Perf. 13x13½***
1683 A850 1.80fr multi 1.25 60

Tower Type of 1979

Designs: 76c, Chateau d'Angers. 99c, Chateau de Kerjean. 1.60fr, Chateau de Pierrefonds. 2.65fr, Chateau de Tarascon.

1980, Jan. 21 **Engr.**

1684	A841	76c grnsh bl & blk	40	38
1685	A841	99c sl grn & blk	55	45
1686	A841	1.60fr red & blk	1.00	80
1687	A841	2.65fr brn org & blk	1.65	95

Nos. 1684-1687 are known only precanceled. See second note after No. 132.

Self-portrait, by Albrecht Dürer, Philexfrance '82 Emblem — A851

Woman Holding Fan, by Ossip Zadkine A852

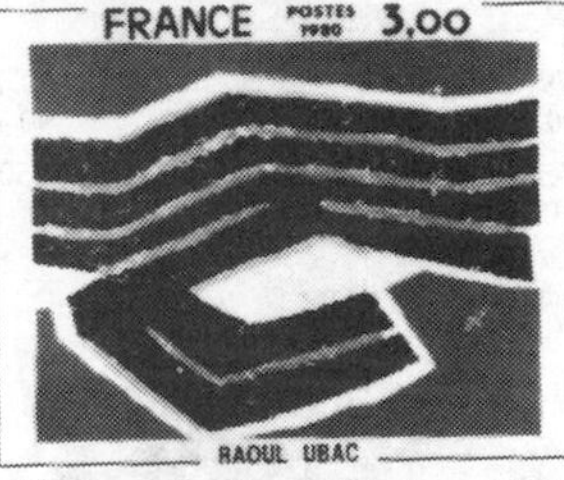

Abstract, by Raoul Ubak — A853

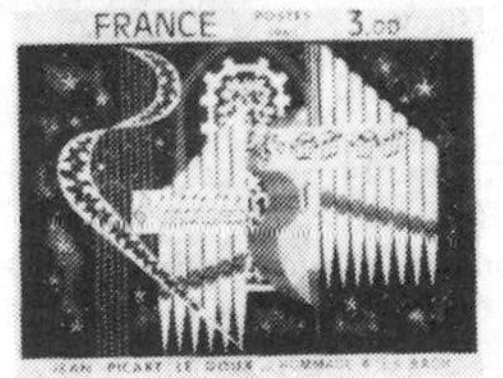

Hommage to J.S. Bach, by Jean Picart Le Doux — A854

Peasant, by Louis Le Nain A855

Woman with Blue Eyes, by Modigliani A856

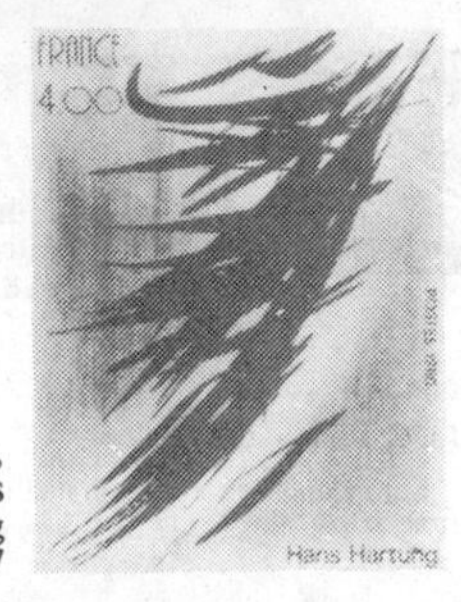

Abstract, by Hans Hartung A857

Engraved, Engraved & Photogravure

1980 ***Perf. 12½x13, 13x12½***

1688	A851 2fr multi	90	60
1689	A852 3fr multi	1.65	60
1690	A853 3fr multi	1.65	60
1691	A854 3fr multi	1.65	65
1692	A855 3fr multi	1.65	50
1693	A856 4fr multi	2.25	50
1694	A857 4fr ultra & blk	2.25	50
	Nos. 1688-1694 (7)	12.00	3.95

Issue dates: #1688, June 7; #1689, Jan. 19; #1690, Feb. 2; #1691, Sept. 20; #1693, Oct. 26; #1692, Nov. 10; #1694, Dec. 20.

Giants of the North Festival — A858

1980, Feb. 16 ***Perf. 13***

1695	A858 1.60fr multi	75	45

French Cuisine — A859

1980, Feb. 23

1696	A859 90c red & lt brn	40	22

Woman Embroidering A860

Fight Against Cigarette Smoking A861

Photogravure and Engraved

1980, Mar. 29 ***Perf. 13***

1697	A860 1.10fr multi	60	22

1980, Apr. 5 **Photo.** ***Perf. 13***

1698	A861 1.30fr multi	60	22

Europa Issue

Aristide Briand — A862

Design: 1.80fr, St. Benedict.

1980, Apr. 26 **Engr.** ***Perf. 13***

1699	A862 1.30fr multi	50	15
1700	A862 1.80fr red & red brn	80	25

Aristide Briand (1862-1932), prime minister, 1909-1911, 1921-1922; St. Benedict, patron saint of Europe.

Liancourt, College, Map of Northwestern France — A863

1980, May 19 **Engr.** ***Perf. 13***

1701	A863 2fr dk grn & pur	75	30

National College of Arts and Handicrafts (founded by Larochefoucauld Liancourt) bicentenary.

Cranes, Town Hall Tower, Dunkirk — A864

1980, May 24

1702	A864 1.30fr multi	60	18

53rd National Congress of French Federation of Philatelic Societies, Dunkirk, May 24-26.

Tourist Issue

Cordes — A865

Chateau de Maintenon A866

Montauban A867

St. Peter's Abbey, Solesmes A868

Puy Cathedral — A869

1980 **Engr.** ***Perf. 13***

1703	A865 1.50fr multi	70	22
1704	A866 2fr multi	85	18
1705	A867 2.30fr multi	1.00	30
1706	A868 2.50fr multi	1.10	15
1707	A869 3.20fr multi	1.40	38
	Nos. 1703-1707 (5)	5.05	1.23

Issue dates: #1703, Apr. 5; #1704, June 7; #1705, May 7; #1706, Sept. 20; #1707, May 12.

Graellsia Isabellae A870

1980, May 31 **Photo.**

1708	A870 1.10fr multi	75	30

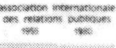

Association Emblem — A871

Marianne, French Architecture A872

1980, June 10 **Photo.**

1709	A871 1.30fr red & bl	55	22

International Public Relations Association, 25th anniversary.

1980, June 21 **Engr.**

1710	A872 1.50fr bluish & gray blk	75	32

Heritage Year.

Earth Sciences A873

1980, July 5

1711	A873 1.60fr dk brn & red	70	38

International Geological Congress.

Rochambeau's Landing — A874

1980, July 15
1712 A874 2.50fr multi 1.25 48

Rochambeau's landing at Newport, R.I. (American Revolution), bicentenary.

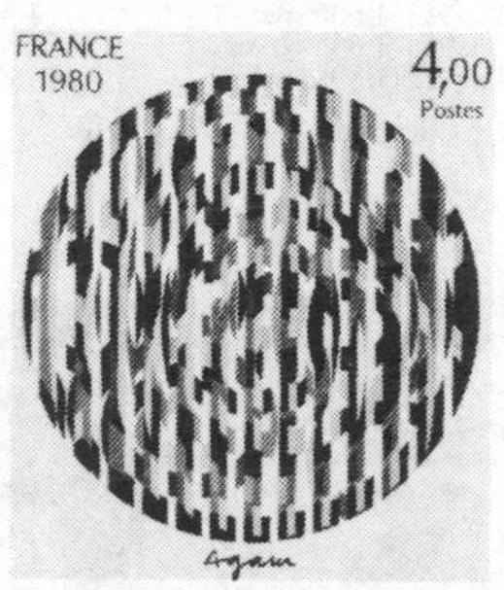

Message of Peace, by Yaacov Agam — A875

1980, Oct. 4 Photo. *Perf. 11½x13*
1713 A875 4fr multi 2.50 90

French Golf Federation A876

1980, Oct. 18 Engr.
1714 A876 1.40fr multi 70 22

Comedie Francaise, 300th Anniversary — A877

1980, Oct. 18
1715 A877 2fr multi 80 30

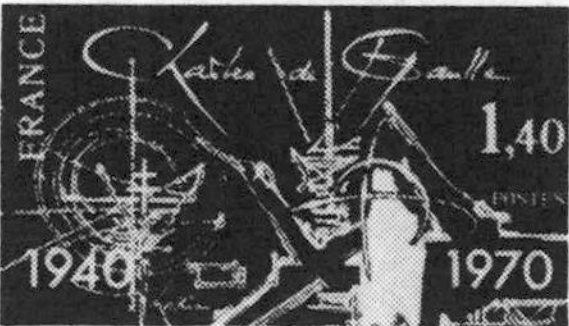

Charles de Gaulle — A878

1980, Nov. 10 Photo. *Perf. 13*
1716 A878 1.40fr multi 80 15

40th anniversary of De Gaulle's appeal of June 18, and 10th anniversary of his death.

A little time given to the study of the arrangement of the Scott Catalogue can make it easier to use effectively.

Guardsman — A879

1980, Nov. 24 Engr. *Perf. 13*
1717 A879 1.70fr multi 70 45

Rambouillet Chateau A880

1980, Dec. 6 Engr. *Perf. 13*
1718 A880 2.20fr multi 90 22

Tower Type of 1979

Designs: 88c, Imperial Chapel, Ajaccio. 1.14fr, Astronomical Clock, Besancon. 1.84fr, Coucy Castle ruins. 3.05fr, Font-de-Gaume cave drawing, Les Eyzies de Tayac.

1981, Jan. 11 Engr. *Perf. 13*
1719 A841 88c dp mag & blk 45 30
1720 A841 1.14fr ultra & blk 60 38
1721 A841 1.84fr dk grn & blk 90 60
1722 A841 3.05fr brn red & blk 1.50 95

Nos. 1719-1722 are known only precanceled. See second note after No. 132.

Microelectronics — A881

1981 Photo.
1723 A881 1.20fr shown 1.00 18
1724 A881 1.20fr Biology 55 25
1725 A881 1.40fr Energy 70 32
1726 A881 1.80fr Marine exploration 90 45
1727 A881 2fr Telemetry 1.10 25
Nos. 1723-1727 (5) 4.25 1.45

Issue dates: No. 1723, Feb. 5; others, Mar. 28.

Abstract, by Albert Gleizes A882

1981, Feb. 28 *Perf. 12½x13*
1728 A882 4fr multi 1.65 65

The Footpath by Camille Pissaro A883

1981, Apr. 18 Engr. *Perf. 13x12½*
1729 A883 2fr multi 1.00 45

Child Watering Smiling Map of France — A884

1981, Mar. 14 Engr. *Perf. 13*
1730 A884 1.40fr multi 55 18

Sully Chateau, Rosny-sur-Seine — A885

1981, Mar. 21
1731 A885 2.50fr multi 1.25 15

Tourist Issue

Roman Temple, Nimes — A886

1981, Apr. 11 *Perf. 13*
1732 A886 1.70fr multi 70 30

Church of St. Jean, Lyon A887

St. Anne d'Auray Basilica A888

1981 Engr. *Perf. 13*
1733 A887 1.40fr dk red & dk brn 50 18
1734 A888 2.20fr bl & blk 90 30

Issue dates: 1.40fr, May 30; 2.20fr, July 4.

Vaucelles Abbey A889

Notre Dame of Louviers A890

1981
1735 A889 2fr red & blk 70 22
1736 A890 2.20fr red brn & dk brn 85 38

Issue dates: 2fr, Sept. 19; 2.20fr, Sept. 26.

Europa Issue 1981

Bouree A891

Folkdances: 2fr, Sardane.

1981, May 4 *Perf. 13*
1737 A891 1.40fr multi 55 15
1738 A891 2fr multi 90 25

Bookbinding A892

Cadets A893

1981, Apr. 4 *Perf. 13*
1739 A892 1.50fr ol & car rose 65 30

1981, May 16
1740 A893 2.50fr multi 1.10 22

Military College at St. Maixent centenary.

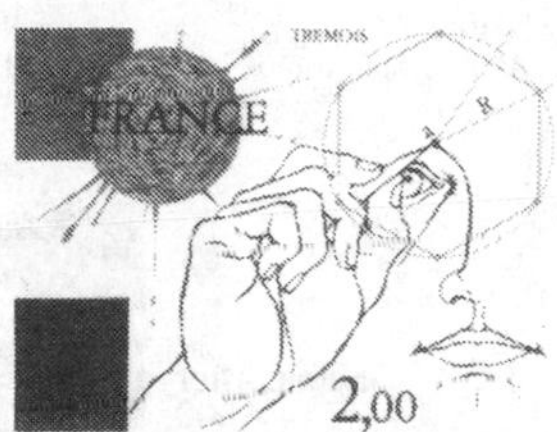

Man Drawing Geometric Diagram — A894

1981, May 23 Photo.
1741 A894 2fr shown 1.75 60
1742 A894 2fr Faces 1.75 60

PHILEXFRANCE '82 Stamp Exhibition, Paris, June 11-21, 1982. Nos. 1741-1742 se-tenant with label showing exhibition emblem.

Theophraste Renaudot and Emile de Girardin A895

Public Gardens, Vichy A896

1981, May 30 Engr.
1743 A895 2.20fr blk & red 90 45

350th anniversary of La Gazette (founded by Renaudot), and death centenary of founder of Le Journal (de Girardin).

1981, June 6
1744 A896 1.40fr multi 50 22

54th National Congress of French Federation of Philatelic Societies, Vichy.

Higher National College for Commercial Studies Centenary
A897

1981, June 20 *Perf. 13*
1745 A897 1.40fr multi 55 22

Sea Shore Conservation — A898

1981, June 20
1746 A898 1.60fr multi 75 25

World Fencing Championship, Clermont-Ferrand, July 2-13 — A899

1981, June 27
1747 A899 1.80fr multi 80 32

Sabine, after David — A900

1981, Sept. 1 **Engr.**
1755 A900 1.40fr green 50 6
1756 A900 1.60fr red 60 6
1757 A900 2.30fr blue 80 30

Coil Stamps

1981 **Engr.** *Perf. 13 Horiz.*
1758 A900 1.40fr green 75 30
1759 A900 1.60fr red 80 22

Highway Safety ("Drink or Drive") A901

1981, Sept. 5 *Perf. 13*
1768 A901 1.60fr multi 60 15

45th Intl. PEN Club Congress A902

Jules Ferry, Statesman A903

1981, Sept *Perf. 13*
1769 A902 2fr multi 90 32

1981, Sept. 28 *Perf. 12½x13*
1770 A903 1.60fr multi 75 22

Free compulsory public school centenary.

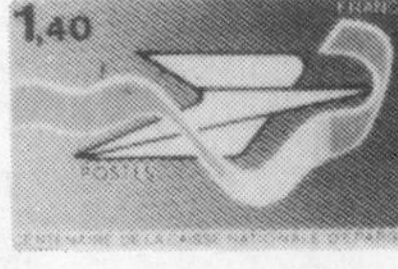

Natl. Savings Bank Centenary A904

1981, Sept. 21 **Photo.** *Perf. 13*
1771 A904 1.40fr multi 55 22
1772 A904 1.60fr multi 65 22

The Divers, by Edouard Pignon — A905

1981, Oct. 3 *Perf. 13x12½*
1773 A905 4fr multi 2.00 45

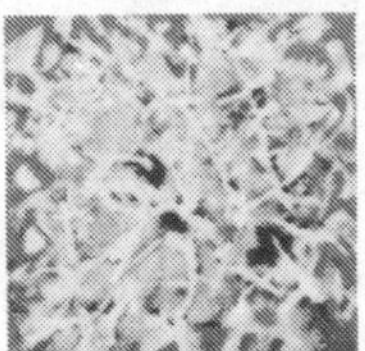

Alleluia, by Alfred Manessier A906

1981, Dec. 19 **Photo.** *Perf. 12x13*
1774 A906 4fr multi 2.00 45

Tourist Issue

Saint-Emilion — A907

Crest — A908

Perf. 13x12½, 13 (2.90fr)

1981 **Engr.**
1775 A907 2.60fr dk red & lt ol grn 1.25 18
1776 A908 2.90fr dk grn 1.40 10

Issue dates: #1775, Oct. 10; #1776, Nov. 28.

150th Anniv. of Naval Academy A909

1981, Oct. 17 *Perf. 13*
1777 A909 1.40fr multi 65 22

St. Hubert Kneeling Before the Stag, 15th Cent. Sculpture — A910

1981, Oct. 24
1778 A910 1.60fr multi 65 18

Museum of hunting and nature.

V. Schoelcher, J. Jaures, J. Moulin and the Pantheon — A911

1981, Nov. 2
1779 A911 1.60fr bl & dl pur 65 22

Intl. Year of the Disabled A912

1981, Nov. 7
1780 A912 1.60fr multi 65 15

Men Leading Cattle, 2nd Cent. Roman Mosaic — A913

1981, Nov. 14 *Perf. 13x12*
1781 A913 2fr multi 1.00 45

Virgil's birth bimillennium.

Martyrs of Chateaubriant A914

1981, Dec. 12 **Engr.** *Perf. 13*
1782 A914 1.40fr multi 65 18

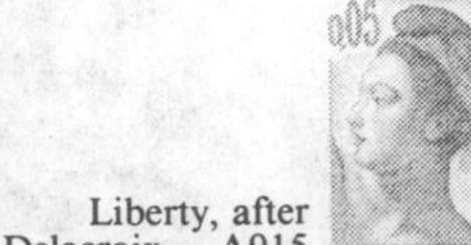

Liberty, after Delacroix — A915

1982-87 **Engr.** *Perf. 13*
1783 A915 5c dk grn 5 5
1784 A915 10c dl red 5 5
1785 A915 15c brt rose lil 5 5
1786 A915 20c brt grn 6 6
1787 A915 30c orange 8 5
1788 A915 40c brown 10 10
a. Bklt. pane of 5, 4 No. 1784, No. 1788 ('87) 30
1789 A915 50c lilac 12 8
1790 A915 60c lt red brn 18 10
1791 A915 70c ultra 20 10
1792 A915 80c lt ol grn 24 10
1793 A915 90c brt lil 28 20
1794 A915 1fr ol grn 30 6
1795 A915 1.40fr green 75 10
1796 A915 1.60fr green 55 6
1797 A915 1.60fr red 85 6
1798 A915 1.80fr red 70 6
1799 A915 2fr brt yel grn 70 6
1800 A915 2.30fr blue 75 35
1801 A915 2.60fr blue 85 35
1802 A915 3fr chocolate 85 6
1803 A915 4fr brt car 1.25 18
1804 A915 5fr gray bl 1.50 18
Nos. 1783-1804 (22) 10.46 2.46

Perf. 13 Horiz.
Coil Stamps
1805 A915 1.40fr green 1.40 38
1806 A915 1.60fr red 1.65 38
1807 A915 1.60fr green 65 22
1807A A915 1.80fr red 80 18

See Nos. 1881-1896, 2070.

Tourist Issue

St. Pierre and Miquelon A916

Corsica A917

1982, Jan. 9 **Engr.** *Perf. 12½*
1808 A916 1.60fr dk bl & blk 55 15
1809 A917 1.90fr bl & red 70 30

Renaissance Fountain, Aix-en Provence — A918

Collonges-la-Rouge — A919

Castle of Henry IV, Pau A920

1982 *Perf. 13*
1810 A918 2fr multi 75 15
1811 A919 3fr multi 1.10 22
1812 A920 3fr ultra & dk bl 1.10 15

Issue dates, Aix-en-Provence, June 21, Collonges-la-Rouge, July 5, Pau, May 15.

Lille — A921

Chateau Ripaille, Haute-Savoie — A921a

1982 ***Perf. 13x12½***
1813 A921 1.80fr dl red & ol 60 15
1813A A921a 2.90fr multi 1.00 10

Issue dates: 1.80fr, Oct. 16; 2.90fr, Sept. 4.

Tower Type of 1979

Designs: 97c, Tanlay Castle, Yonne. 1.25fr, Salses Fort, Pyrenees-Orientales. 2.03fr, Montlhery Tower, Essonne. 3.36fr, Chateau d'If Bouches-du-Rhone.

1982, Jan. 11 **Engr.** ***Perf. 13***
1814 A841 97c ol grn & blk 60 32
1815 A841 1.25fr red & blk 70 40
1816 A841 2.03fr sep & blk 1.10 60
1817 A841 3.36fr ultra & blk 1.75 95

Nos. 1814-1817 are known only precanceled. See second note after No. 132.

800th Birth Anniv. of St. Francis of Assisi A922

Photogravure and Engraved

1982, Feb. 6
1818 A922 2fr blk & bl 90 30

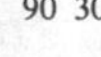

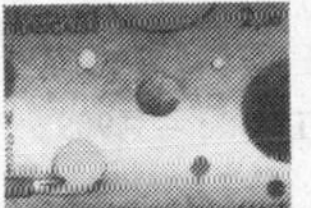

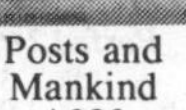

Posts and Mankind A923

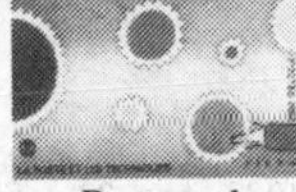

Posts and Technology A924

1982, Feb. 13 **Photo.**
1819 A923 2fr multi 3.50 75
1820 A924 2fr multi 3.50 75

PHILEXFRANCE '82 Stamp Exhibition, Paris, June 11-21. Nos. 1819-1820 se-tenant with label showing emblem.

Souvenir Sheet

Marianne, by Jean Cocteau — A925

1982, June 11
1821 Sheet of 2 27.50 27.50
a. A925 4fr red & bl 12.00 12.00
b. A925 6fr bl & red 13.00 13.00

No. 1821 has gray marginal inscription, show emblem. Size: 100x71mm. Sold only with 20fr show admission ticket.

Scouting Year A926

1982, Feb. 20 **Engr.**
1822 A926 2.30fr yel grn & blk 1.00 45

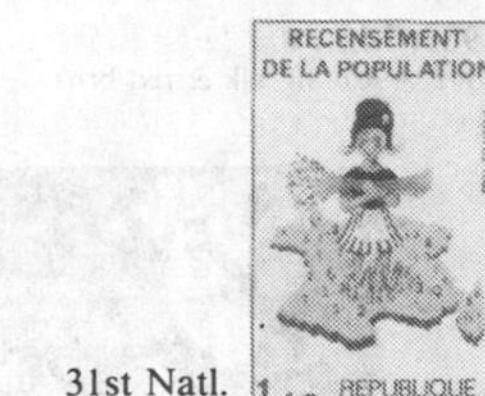

31st Natl. Census — A927

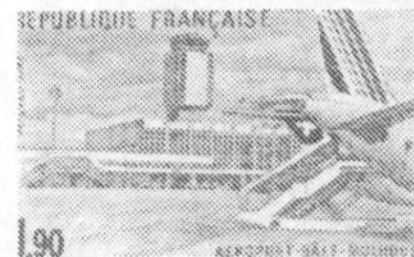

Bale-Mulhouse Airport Opening — A928

1982, Feb. 27 **Photo.**
1823 A927 1.60fr multi 65 22

1982, Mar. 15 **Engr.** ***Perf. 13***
1824 A928 1.90fr multi 90 38

Fight Against Racism A929

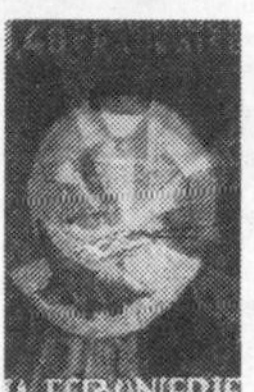

Blacksmith — A930

1982, Mar. 20
1825 A929 2.30fr brn & red org 90 45

1982, Apr. 17
1826 A930 1.40fr multi 65 30

Europa 1982 A931

1982, Apr. 24
1827 A931 1.60fr Treaty of Rome, 1957 60 15
1828 A931 2.30fr Treaty of Verdun, 843 85 25

1982 World Cup A932

1982, Apr. 28
1829 A932 1.80fr multi 75 18

Young Greek Soldier, Hellenic Sculpture, Agude A933

1982, May 15 ***Perf. 12½x13***
1830 A933 4fr multi 1.65 50

Embarkation for Ostia, by Claude Gellee — A934

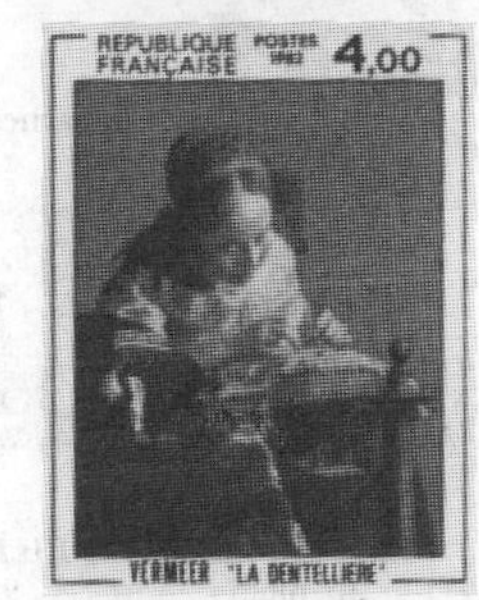

The Lacemaker, by Vermeer — A935

Turkish Chamber, by Balthus — A936

1982 **Photo.** ***Perf. 13x12½, 12½x13***
1831 A934 4fr multi 1.40 50
1832 A935 4fr multi 1.40 50
1833 A936 4fr multi 1.40 45

Issue dates: No. 1831, June 19; No. 1832, Sept. 4; No. 1833, Nov. 6.

35th Intl. Film Festival, Cannes — A937

Natl. Space Studies Center, 20th Anniv. — A938

1982, May 15 **Photo.** ***Perf. 13***
1834 A937 2.30fr multi 90 45

1982, May 15 **Engr.**
1835 A938 2.60fr multi 1.10 45

Industrialized Countries' Summit Meeting, Versailles, June 4-6 — A939

1982, June 4 **Photo.**
1836 A939 2.60fr multi 1.10 45

Jules Valles (1832-1885), Writer — A940

1982, June 4 **Engr.** ***Perf. 13***
1837 A940 1.60fr ol grn & dk grn 90 18

Frederic and Irene Curie, Radiation Diagrams A941

1982, June 26
1838 A941 1.80fr multi 75 22

Electric Street Lighting Centenary A942

1982, July 10
1839 A942 1.80fr dk bl & vio 90 22

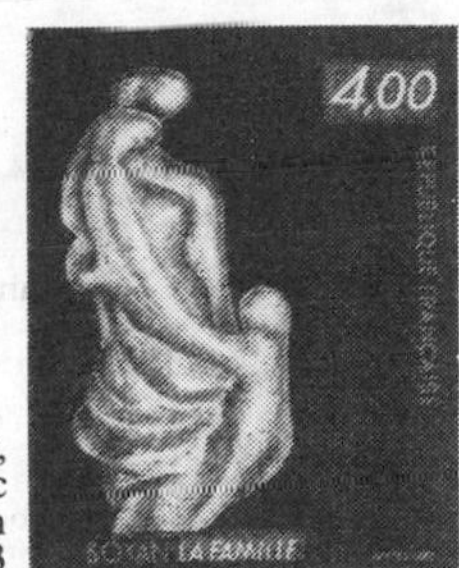

The Family, by Marc Boyan A943

Photogravure and Engraved

1982, Sept. 18 ***Perf. 12½x13***
1840 A943 4fr multi 1.65 45

Natl. Federation of Firemen Centenary A944

Marionettes A945

1982, Sept. 18 **Engr.** ***Perf. 13***
1841 A944 3.30fr red & sep 1.50 25

1982, Sept. 25
1842 A945 1.80fr multi 60 15

Rugby A946

1982, Oct. 9
1843 A946 1.60fr multi 65 22

Higher Education A947

1982, Oct. 16
1844 A947 1.80fr red & blk 75 18

TB Bacillus Centenary A948

1982, Nov. 13
1845 A948 2.60fr red & blk 90 38

St. Teresa of Avila (1515-1582) — A949

1982, Nov. 20
1846 A949 2.10fr multi 75 30

Leon Blum (1872-1950), Politician — A950

1982, Dec. 18 Engr. *Perf. 13*
1847 A950 1.80fr dk brn & brn 60 18

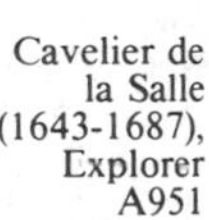

Cavelier de la Salle (1643-1687), Explorer A951

1982, Dec. 18 *Perf. 13x12½*
1848 A951 3.25fr multi 1.40 30

Spring — A952

1983, Jan. 17 Engr. *Perf. 13*
1849 A952 1.05fr shown 50 25
1850 A952 1.35fr Summer 65 32
1851 A952 2.19fr Autumn 90 50
1852 A952 3.63fr Winter 1.65 90

Nos. 1849-1852 known only pre-canceled. See second note after No. 132.

Provence-Alpes-Cote d'Azur — A953

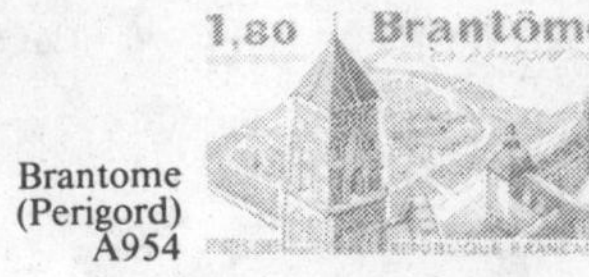

Brantome (Perigord) A954

Photogravure, Engraved
1983 *Perf. 13, 13x12½*
1853 A953 1fr multi 42 10
1854 A954 1.80fr multi 65 8

Issue dates: 1fr, Jan. 8; 1.80fr, Feb. 5.

Concarneau A955

Noirlac Abbey A956

1983 Engr. *Perf. 13, 13x12½*
1855 A955 3fr multi 95 22
1856 A956 3.60fr multi 1.10 30

Issue dates: No. 1855, June 11; No. 1856, July 2.

Jarnac A957

Charleville-Mezieres — A958

1983 Engr. *Perf. 13x12½*
1857 A957 2fr multi 65 10
1858 A958 3.10fr multi 1.10 75

Issue dates: No. 1857, Oct. 8; No. 1858, Sept. 17.

Martin Luther (1483-1546) — A959

1983, Feb. 12 Engr. *Perf. 13*
1859 A959 3.30fr dk brn & tan 1.25 30

Alliance Francaise Centenary A960

1983, Feb. 19
1860 A960 1.80fr multi 70 22

Danielle Casanova (d. 1942), Resistance Leader A961

1983, Mar. 8
1861 A961 3fr blk & red brn 1.10 30

World Communications Year — A962

1983, Mar. 12 **Photo.**
1862 A962 2.60fr multi 90 30

Manned Flight Bicentenary — A963

1983, Mar. 19 **Photo.** *Perf. 13*
1863 A963 2fr Hot air balloon 85 45
1864 A963 3fr Hydrogen balloon 1.25 60

Se-tenant with label.

Female Nude, by Raphael A964

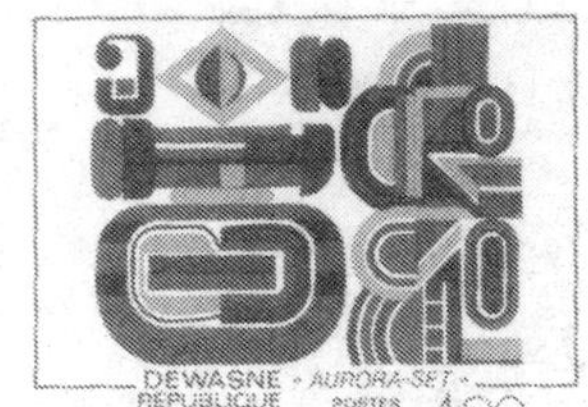

Aurora-Set, by Dewasne — A965

Engraved, Photogravure
1983 *Perf. 13*
1865 A964 4fr multi 1.50 60
1866 A965 4fr multi 1.50 60

Issue dates: No. 1866, Mar. 19; No. 1865, Apr. 9.

Illustration from Perrault's Folk Tales, by Gustave Dore A966

1983, June 18 Engr. *Perf. 13*
1867 A966 4fr red & blk 1.40 60

The first price column gives the catalogue value of an unused stamp, the second that of a used stamp.

Homage to Jean Effel — A967

1983, Oct. 15
1868 A967 4fr multi 1.40 45

Le Lapin Agile, by Utrillo — A968

1983, Dec. 3 *Perf. 13x12½*
1869 A968 4fr multi 1.40 60

Thistle — A969

1983, Apr. 23 Engr. *Perf. 12½x12*
1870 A969 1fr shown 35 15
1871 A969 2fr Martagon lily 1.00 15
1872 A969 3fr Aster 1.10 25
1873 A969 4fr Aconite 1.50 45

Europa 1983 — A970

1983, Apr. 29 *Perf. 13*
1874 A970 1.80fr Symbolic shutter 1.75 22
1875 A970 2.60fr Lens-to-screen diagram 2.00 38

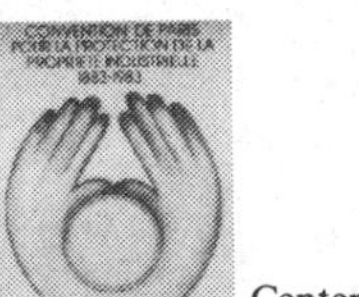

Centenary of Paris Convention for the Protection of Industrial Property — A971

1983, May 14 **Photo.** *Perf. 13*
1876 A971 2fr multi 65 18

French Philatelic Societies Congress, Marseilles A972

1983, May 21 Engr. *Perf. 13*
1877 A972 1.80fr multi 75 18

Liberty Type of 1982

1983-87 Engr. *Perf. 13*

No.	Type	Value	Color	Unused	Used
1881	A915	1.70fr	grn ('84)	50	8
1882	A915	1.80fr	grn ('85)	48	8
1882B	A915	1.90fr	grn ('86)	60	12
1883	A915	2fr	red	65	6
1883A	A915	2fr	grn ('87)	68	6
1884	A915	2.10fr	red ('84)	65	8
1885	A915	2.20fr	red ('85)	65	10
a.		Bklt. pane of 10 ('86)		5.25	
b.		Bklt. pane of 5, No. 1788, 4 No. 1885 ('87)		2.50	
c.		With label ('87)		65	10
1887	A915	2.80fr	blue	85	30
1888	A915	3fr	blue ('84)	1.00	22
1889	A915	3.20fr	blue ('85)	90	10
1890	A915	3.40fr	blue ('86)	1.10	20
1890A	A915	3.60fr	blue ('87)	1.20	8
1891	A915	10fr	purple	2.75	10
1892	A915	(1.90fr)	grn ('86)	60	12
1892A	A915	(2fr)	grn ('87)	68	6
		Nos. 1881-1892A (15)		13.29	1.76

No. 1892 is inscribed "A." No. 1892A is inscribed "B."

1885c was issued in sheets of 50 plus 50 alternating labels picturing the PHILEX-FRANCE '89 emblem to publicize the international philatelic exhibition.

Issue dates: No. 1883A, Oct. 15. No. 1885b, Apr. 21. No. 1885c, Mar. 9. Nos. 1890A, 1892A, Aug. 1.

Coil Stamps

Engr. *Perf. 13 Horiz.*

No.	Type	Value	Color	Unused	Used
1893	A915	1.70fr	grn ('84)	50	8
1894	A915	1.80fr	grn ('85)	52	8
1894A	A915	1.90fr	grn ('86)	58	12
1895	A915	2fr	red	75	22
1895A	A915	2.10fr	red ('84)	90	30
1896	A915	2.20fr	red ('85)	65	10

50th Anniv. of Air France A973

1983, June 18
1898 A973 3.45fr multi 1.40 50

Treaties of Versailles and Paris Bicentenary — A974

1983, Sept. 2 *Perf. 13x12½*
1899 A974 2.80fr multi 1.10 45

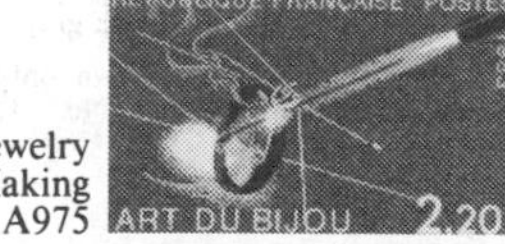

Jewelry Making A975

1983, Sept. 10 Photo. *Perf. 13*
1900 A975 2.20fr multi 80 30

30th Anniv. of Customs Cooperation Council — A976

1983, Sept. 22 Engr. *Perf. 13x12½*
1901 A976 2.30fr multi 85 30

Michaux's Bicycle A977

1983, Oct. 1 Engr. *Perf. 13*
1902 A977 1.60fr multi 70 22

Natl. Weather Forecasting — A978

1983, Oct. 22 Engr. *Perf. 12½x13*
1903 A978 1.50fr multi 60 15

Berthie Albrecht (1893-1943) A979

1983, Nov. 5
1904 A979 1.60fr dk brn & ol 55 15
1905 A979 1.60fr Rene Levy (1906-1943) 55 15

Resistance heroines.

Pierre Mendes France (1907-1982), Premier — A980

1983, Dec. 16
1906 A980 2fr dk gray & red 70 15

Trade Union Centenary — A981

1984, Mar. 22 *Perf. 13*
1907 A981 3.60fr Union leader Waldeck-Rousseau 1.25 38

Homage to the Cinema, by Cesar A982

1984, Feb. 4 Engr. *Perf. 12½x13*
1908 A982 4fr multi 1.40 60

Four Corners of the Sky, by Jean Messagier — A983

1984, Mar. 31 Photo. *Perf. 13x12½*
1909 A983 4fr multi 1.40 60

Dining Room Corner, at Cannet, by Pierre Bonnard — A984

Photogravure and Engraved

1984, Apr. 14 *Perf. 12½x12*
1910 A984 4fr multi 1.40 60

Pythia, by Andre Masson A985

Painter at the Feet of His Model, by Helion A986

1984 Photo. *Perf. 12x13*
1911 A985 5fr multi 1.65 45
1912 A986 5fr multi 1.65 45

Issue dates: No. 1911, Oct. 13; No. 1912, Dec. 1.

Guadeloupe A987

1984, Feb. 25 *Perf. 13*
1913 A987 2.30fr Map, West Indian dancers 85 22

Vauban Citadel, Belle Ile-en-Mer A988

Phare de Cordouan — A989

1984 Engr. *Perf. 13*
1914 A988 2.50fr multi 90 22
1915 A989 3.50fr multi 1.25 22

Issue dates: No. 1914, May 26; No. 1915, June 23.

La Grande Chartreuse Monastery, 900th Anniv. A990

Palais Ideal, Hauterives-Drome — A991

Montsegur Chateau A992

1984 Engr. *Perf. 13*
1916 A990 1.70fr multi 55 15
1917 A991 2.10fr multi 90 10
1917A A992 3.70fr multi 1.25 18

Issue dates: 1.70fr, July 7; 2.10fr, June 30; 3.70fr, Sept. 15.

Flora Tristan (1803-44), Feminist A992a

1984, Mar. 8
1918 A992a 2.80fr multi 90 30

Playing Card Suits — A993

1984, Apr. 11 Engr.
1919 A993 1.14fr Hearts 45 25
1920 A993 1.47fr Spades 50 32
1921 A993 2.38fr Diamonds 80 60
1922 A993 3.95fr Clubs 1.50 1.00

Nos. 1919-1922 known only precanceled. See second note after No. 132.

450th Anniv. of Cartier's Landing in Quebec A994

Photogravure and Engraved

1984, Apr. 20
1923 A994 2fr multi 75 15

See Canada No. 1011.

Philex '84, Dunkirk A995

1984, Apr. 21 *Perf. 13x12½*
1924 A995 1.60fr multi 55 22

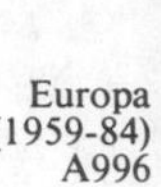

Europa (1959-84) A996

1984, Apr. 28 Engr. *Perf. 13*
1925 A996 2fr red brn 60 15
1926 A996 2.80fr blue 90 38

2nd European Parliament Election A997

1984, Mar. 24 Photo. *Perf. 13*
1927 A997 2fr multi 75 10

Foreign Legion A998

1984, Apr. 30 Engr. *Perf. 13x12½*
1928 A998 3.10fr multi 1.10 38

40th Anniv. of Liberation A999

Photogravure and Engraved
1984, May 8 *Perf. 12½x13*
1929 A999 2fr Resistance 75 30
1930 A999 3fr Landing 1.10 45

Se-tenant with label showing Order of Liberation emblem.

Olympic Events — A1000

1984, June 1 *Perf. 13*
1931 A1000 4fr multi 1.65 75

Intl. Olympic Committee, 90th anniv. and 1984 Summer Olympics.

Engraving — A1001

1984, June 8 Engr.
1932 A1001 2fr multi 75 15

Bordeaux A1002

1984, June 9 *Perf. 13x12½*
1933 A1002 2fr red 75 15

French Philatelic Societies Congress, Bordeaux.

Natl. Telecommunications College, 40th Anniv. — A1003

1984, June 16 Photo. *Perf. 13*
1934 A1003 3fr Satellite, phone, keyboard 1.00 30

25th Intl. Geography Congress, Paris — A1004

1984, Aug. 25 Engr. *Perf. 13x12½*
1935 A1004 3fr Alps 1.10 30

Telecom I Satellite A1005

1984, Sept. 1 Photo. *Perf. 13*
1936 A1005 3.20fr multi 1.25 30

High-speed Train Mail Transport A1006

1984, Sept. 8
1937 A1006 2.10fr Electric train, Paris-Lyon 85 22

Local Birds A1007

Marx Dormoy (1888-1941) A1008

Photogravure and Engraved
1984, Sept. 22 *Perf. 12½x12*
1938 A1007 1fr Gypaetus barbatus 35 22
1939 A1007 2fr Circaetus gallicus 85 22
1940 A1007 3fr Accipiter nisus 1.00 30
1941 A1007 5fr Peregrine falcon 1.65 45

1984, Sept. 22 Engr. *Perf. 13*
1942 A1008 2.40fr multi 85 18

100th Anniv. of the Automobile — A1009

1984, Oct. 6 Engr. *Perf. 12½x13*
1943 A1009 3fr Automobile plans 1.10 18

Pres. Vincent Auriol (1884-1966) — A1010

1984, Nov. 3
1944 A1010 2.10fr multi 75 10

9th 5-Year Plan A1011

1984, Dec. 8 Photo. *Perf. 13*
1945 A1011 2.10fr dk bl & scar 75 10

French Language Promotion — A1012

1985, Jan. 15 Engr. *Perf. 12½x13*
1946 A1012 3fr multi 1.10 18

Tourism Issue

View of Vienne A1013

Cathedral at Montpelier A1014

St. Michel de Cuxa (Codalet) Abbey — A1015

Talmont Church, Saintonge Romane A1016

Solutre A1017

1985 *Perf. 13x12½*
1947 A1013 1.70fr ol blk & dk grn 55 8
1948 A1014 2.10fr sep & org 70 10
1949 A1015 2.20fr multi 70 10
1950 A1016 3fr multi 85 12
1951 A1017 3.90fr multi 1.10 18
Nos. 1947-1951 (5) 3.90 58

Issue dates: 1.70fr, Jan. 19; 2.10fr, Mar. 30; 2.20fr, July 6; 3fr, June 15; 3.90fr, Sept. 28.

French TV, 50th Anniv. A1018

1985, Jan. 26 Photo. *Perf. 13*
1952 A1018 2.50fr multi 85 10

Months of the Year — A1019

Designs: 1.22fr, January. 1.57fr, February. 2.55fr, March. 4.23fr, April.

1985, Feb. 11 Engr.
1953 A1019 1.22fr brt pur & blk 45 5
1954 A1019 1.57fr dp bl & sl bl 50 6
1955 A1019 2.55fr dk ol grn & dk brn 80 10
1956 A1019 4.23fr org brn & dk ol grn 1.50 18

1986, Feb. 10 Engr. *Perf. 13*

Designs: 1.28fr, May. 1.65fr, June. 2.67fr, July. 4.44fr, August.

1957 A1019 1.28fr sage grn & lil rose 35 8
1958 A1019 1.65fr Prus bl & brt yel grn 45 10
1959 A1019 2.67fr dk red & saph 75 15
1960 A1019 4.44fr dk ol bis & org 1.25 25

1987, Feb. 16 Engr.

Designs: 1.31fr, September. 1.69fr, October. 2.74fr, November. 4.56fr, December.

1961 A1019 1.31fr org & lake 45 10
1962 A1019 1.69fr red vio & brn org 58 12
1963 A1019 2.74fr bl & bl gray 92 18
1964 A1019 4.56fr pur & dk gray 1.55 32

Nos. 1953-1964 are known only precanceled. See second note after No. 132.

St. Valentine, by Raymond Peynet A1020

1985, Feb. 14 Photo. *Perf. 13x12½*
1965 A1020 2.10fr multi 65 10

Pauline Kergomard (1838-1925) A1021

1985, Mar. 8 Engr. *Perf. 13x12½*
1966 A1021 1.70fr int bl & cop red 55 8

Art Issue

Stained Glass Window, Strasbourg Cathedral A1022

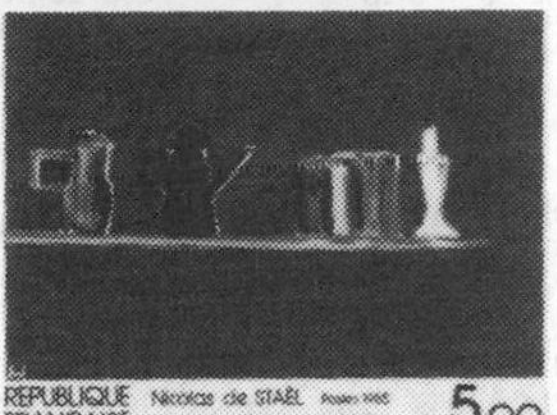

Still-life with Candle, Nicolas de Stael — A1023

Engraved, Photogravure (#1968)

1985 ***Perf. 12x13, 13x12***

1967 A1022 5fr multi 1.65 22
1968 A1023 5fr multi 1.65 22

Issue dates: No. 1967, Apr. 13; No. 1968, June 1.

Untitled Abstract by Jean Dubuffet — A1024

Octopus Overlaid on Manuscript, by Pierre Alechinsky A1025

Photogravure; Engraved (#1970)

1985 ***Perf. 13x12½***

1969 A1024 5fr multi 1.50 24
1970 A1025 5fr multi 1.50 24

Issue dates: No. 1969, Sept. 14; No. 1970, Oct. 12.

The Dog, Abstract by Alberto Giacometti (1901-1966) — A1026

1985, Dec. 7 **Engr.** ***Perf. 13x12½***

1971 A1026 5fr grnsh blk & lt lem 1.25 25

Housing in Givors A1027

Contemporary architecture by Jean Renaude.

1985, Apr. 20 **Engr.** ***Perf. 13***

1972 A1027 2.40fr blk, yel org & ol grn 65 12

Landevennec Abbey, 1500th Anniv. — A1028

1985, Apr. 20 ***Perf. 13x12½***

1973 A1028 1.70fr grn & brn vio 50 8

Europa 1985 A1029

Liberation of France from German Occupation Forces, 40th Anniv. A1030

Designs: 2.10 fr, Adam de la Halle (1240-1285), composer. 3fr, Darius Milhaud (1892-1974), composer.

1985, Apr. 27 ***Perf. 12½x13***

1974 A1029 2.10fr dk bl, blk & brt bl 55 10
1975 A1029 3fr dk bl, brt bl & blk 75 14

1985, May 8 ***Perf. 13x12½***

1976 A1030 2fr Return of peace 60 10
1977 A1030 3fr Return of liberty 80 14
a. Pair with label 1.40

Nos. 1976-1977 se-tenant with central label inscribed for 40th anniv. of the victory.

Natl. Philatelic Congress, Tours — A1031

1985, May 25 ***Perf. 12½x13***

1978 A1031 2.10fr Tours Cathedral 55 10

Rabies Vaccine Cent. A1032

1985, June 1 ***Perf. 13x12½***

1979 A1032 1.50fr Pasteur inoculating patient 45 6

Mystere Falcon-900 A1033

1985, June 1 ***Perf. 13***

1980 A1033 10fr blue 2.50 45

Lake Geneva Life-Saving Society Cent. A1034

1985, June 15

1981 A1034 2.50fr blk, red & brt ultra 65 12

United Nations, 40th Anniv. — A1035

1985, June 26 ***Perf. 13x12½***

1982 A1035 3fr multi 80 14

Huguenot Cross — A1036

1985, Aug. 31 **Engr.** ***Perf. 12½x13***

1983 A1036 2.50fr dp vio, dk red brn & dk red 65 12

King Louis XIV revoked the Edict of Nantes on Oct. 18, 1685, dispossessing French Protestants of religious and civil liberty.

Trees — A1037

Trees, leaves and fruit of the beech, elm, oak and spruce varieties.

1985, Sept. 21 **Engr.** ***Perf. 12½***

1984 A1037 1fr shown 30 5
1985 A1037 2fr Ulmus montana 60 10
1986 A1037 3fr Quercus pedunculata 90 15
1987 A1037 5fr Picea abies 1.50 25

La France Mourning the Dead, Eternal Flame A1038

Charles Dullin, 1885-1949, Impressario, Theater A1039

1985, Nov. 2 **Engr.** ***Perf. 12½x13***

1988 A1038 1.80fr brn, org & lake 55 10

Memorial Day.

1985, Nov. 9 **Engr.**

1989 A1039 3.20fr blk & bl 90 16

National Information System — A1040

1985, Nov. 16 **Engr.** ***Perf. 13x12½***

1990 A1040 2.20fr red & blk 65 12

Thai Ambassadors at the Court of King Louis XIV, Painting — A1041

1986, Jan. 25 **Engr.** ***Perf. 13***

1991 A1041 3.20fr rose lake & blk 85 18

Normalization of diplomatic relations with Thailand, 300th anniv.

Leisure, by Fernand Leger A1042

1986, Feb. 1 **Photo.** ***Perf. 13***

1992 A1042 2.20fr multi 60 12

1936 Popular Front, 50th anniv.

Venice Carnival, Paris — A1043

1986, Feb. 12 ***Perf. 12½x13***

1993 A1043 2.20fr multi 60 12

La Marianne, Typograph by Raymond Gid A1044

Photogravure & Engraved

1986, Mar. 3 *Perf. 12½x13½*

1994 A1044 5fr blk & dk red 1.50 30

Tourism Series

Filitosa, South Corsica A1045

Loches Chateau A1046

Norman Manor, St. Germain de Livet A1047

Notre-Dame-en-Vaux Monastery, Marne — A1048

Market Square, Bastide de Monpazier, Dordogne — A1049

Perf. 13, 13x12½ (#1999)

1986 **Engr.**

1995 A1045 1.80fr multi 52 10
1996 A1046 2fr int bl & blk 60 12
1997 A1047 2.20fr grnsh bl, brn & grn 65 14
1998 A1048 2.50fr henna brn & sep 75 15
1999 A1049 3.90fr blk & yel org 1.10 22

Issue dates: 2fr, June 14; 2.50fr, June 9. 1.80fr, 3.90fr, July 5.

Louise Michel (1830-1905), Anarchist — A1050

1986, Mar. 10 **Engr.**

2000 A1050 1.80fr dk red & gray blk 38 8

> Canceled-to-order stamps are often from remainders. Most collectors of canceled stamps prefer postally used specimens.

City of Science and Industry, La Villette — A1051

1986, Mar. 17

2001 A1051 3.90fr multi 85 18

Center for Modern Asia-Africa Studies A1052

1986, Apr. 12 **Photo.** *Perf. 13*

2002 A1052 3.20fr Map 90 18

Art Series

Skibet, Abstract by Maurice Esteve — A1053

1986, Apr. 14 **Photo.** *Perf. 12½x13*

2003 A1053 5fr multi 1.10 22

Virginia, Abstract by Alberto Magnelli — A1054

1986, June 25 **Photo.** *Perf. 13x12½*

2004 A1054 5fr multi 1.40 28

Abstract, by Pierre Soulages — A1055

1986, Dec. 22 **Engr.** *Perf. 13x12½*

2005 A1055 5fr brt vio, blk & brn gray 1.55 32

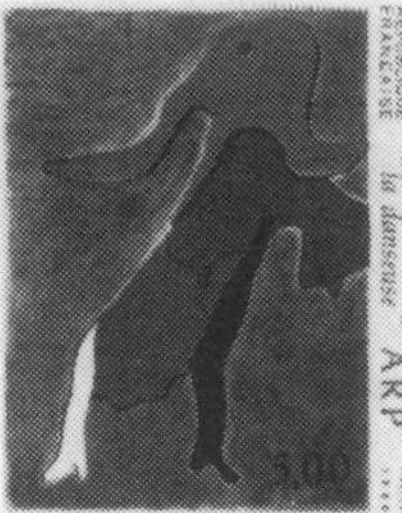

The Dancer, by Jean Arp A1056

1986, Nov. 10 **Photo.** *Perf. 12½x13*

2006 A1056 5fr multi 1.50 30

Isabelle d'Este, by Leonardo da Vinci A1057

1986, Nov. 10 **Engr.**

2007 A1057 5fr blk, red brn & grnsh yel 1.60 32

Victor Basch (1863-1944), IPY Emblem — A1058

1986, Apr. 28 **Engr.** *Perf. 13*

2008 A1058 2.50fr blk & yel grn 55 12

International Peace Year.

Europa 1986 A1059

1986, Apr. 28 *Perf. 13x12½*

2009 A1059 2.20fr Civet cat 48 10
2010 A1059 3.20fr Bat 68 14

St. Jean-Marie Vianney, Curé of Ars A1060

1986, May 3 **Engr.** *Perf. 13x12½*

2011 A1060 1.80fr sep, brn org & brn 52 10

Philatelic Societies Federation Congress, Nancy — A1061

1986, May 17 *Perf. 13*

2012 A1061 2.20fr Exposition Center 62 12

Men's World Volleyball Championships A1062

Statue of Liberty, Cent. A1063

1986, May 24 **Engr.** *Perf. 13*

2013 A1062 2.20fr dk vio, brn vio & scar 62 12

1986, July 4 *Perf. 13*

2014 A1063 2.20fr scar & dk bl 62 12

See US No. 2224.

1st Ascent of Mt. Blanc, 1786 A1064

1986, Aug. 8 **Engr.** *Perf. 13x12½*

2015 A1064 2fr J. Balmat, M.G. Paccard 60 12

Pierre-Louis Moreau de Maupertuis (1698-1759), La Condamine and Sextant — A1065

1986, Sept. 5

2016 A1065 3fr lt bl, int bl & brt ultra 88 18

Lapland Expedition, 250th anniv., proved Earth's poles are flattened.
See Finland No. 741.

Marcassite A1066

1986, Sept. 13 *Perf. 12½*

2017 A1066 2fr shown 60 12
2018 A1066 3fr Quartz 88 18
2019 A1066 4fr Calcite 1.20 24
2020 A1066 5fr Fluorite 1.50 30

Souvenir Sheet

Natl. Film Industry, 50th Anniv. A1067

Personalities and film scenes: No. 2021a, Louis Feuillade, The Vampires. No. 2021b, Max Linder. No. 2021c, Sacha Guitry,

Romance of the Trickster. No. 2021d, Jean Renoir, The Great Illusion. No. 2021e, Marcel Pagnol, The Baker's Woman. No. 2021f, Jean Epstein, The Three-Sided Mirror. No. 2021g, Rene Clair, Women of the Night. No. 2021h, Jean Gremillon, Talk of Love. No. 2021i, Jacques Becker, Helmet of Gold. No. 2021j, Francois Truffaut, The Young Savage.

1986, Sept. 20 Photo. *Perf. 13x12½*
2021 Sheet of 10 6.50 6.50
a.-j. A1067 2.20fr, any single 65 65

No. 2021 has a multicolored inscribed margin picturing film clips. Size: 142x180mm.

Scene from Le Grand Meaulnes, by Henry Alain-Fournier (b. 1886), Novelist A1068

Professional Education, Cent. A1069

1986, Oct. 4 Engr. *Perf. 12½x13*
2022 A1068 2.20fr blk & dk red 68 14

1986, Oct. 4
2023 A1069 1.90fr brt vio & dp lil rose 58 12

World Energy Conference, Cannes — A1070

1986, Oct. 5 Photo. *Perf. 13*
2024 A1070 3.40fr multi 1.10 22

Mulhouse Technical Museum — A1071

1986, Dec. 1 Engr.
2025 A1071 2.20fr int bl, dk red & blk 70 14

Museum at Orsay, Opening — A1072

1986, Dec. 10 Photo.
2026 A1072 3.70fr bluish blk & pck bl 1.15 24

Fulgence Bienvenue (1852-1934), and the Metro — A1073

1987, Jan. 17 Engr. *Perf. 13*
2027 A1073 2.50fr vio brn, brn & dk grn 80 16

Raoul Follereau (1903-1977), Care for Lepers — A1074

1987, Jan. 24
2028 A1074 1.90fr grn & grnsh blk 60 12

Cutlery Industry, Thiers — A1075

1987, Mar. 7 Engr. *Perf. 12½x13*
2029 A1075 1.90fr blk & red 65 14

Tourism Series

Redon, Ille et Vilaine A1076

1987, Mar. 7 Engr. *Perf. 13*
2030 A1076 2.20fr dp rose lil, blk & brn ol 75 20

Azay-le-Rideau Chateau — A1077

Meuse District — A1078

De Gaulle's Home, Etretat A1079

Les Baux-de-Provence — A1080

1987 *Perf. 13, 12½ (No. 2032)*
2031 A1077 2.50fr Prus blue & olive grn 85 22
2032 A1078 3.70fr brn lake, dark vio & dark chalky blue 1.25 32

Issue dates: 2.50fr, May 9. 3.70fr, May 30.

Photo. (No. 2033), Engr.
1987 *Perf. 13*
2033 A1079 2.20fr multi 75 18
2034 A1080 3fr dark olive bister & deep vio 1.05 25

Issue dates: 2.20fr, June 12. 3fr, June 27.

Jean Jenneret Le Corbusier (1887-1965), Architect A1081

1987, Apr. 11 Photo. *Perf. 13x12½*
2035 A1081 3.70fr Abstract 1.25 32

Europa 1987 A1082

Modern architecture: 2.20fr, Metal factory at Boulogne-Billancourt, by architect Claude Vasconi. 3.40fr, Rue Mallet-Stevens housing, by Rob Mallet-Stevens.

1987, Apr. 25 Engr. *Perf. 13x12½*
2036 A1082 2.20fr dk bl & grn 75 20
2037 A1082 3.40fr brn & dk grn 1.15 30

Art Series

Abstract Painting, by Bram van Velde — A1083

Woman under Parasol, by Eugene Boudin (1824-1898) — A1084

Precambrien, by Camille Bryen — A1085

World, Bronze Sculpture by Antoine Pevsner — A1086

Perf. 12½x13, 13x12½ (Nos. 2039, 2041)
Photo., Engr. (Nos. 2039, 2041)
1987
2038 A1083 5fr multi 1.75 45
2039 A1084 5fr multi 1.75 45
2040 A1085 5fr multi 1.65 42
2041 A1086 5fr bister & blk 1.70 35

Issue dates: No. 2038, Apr. 25. No. 2039, May 23. No. 2040, Sept. 12. No. 2041, Nov. 14.

Gaspard de Montagnes, from a Manuscript Illustration — A1087

1987, May 9 Engr. *Perf. 13*
2042 A1087 1.90fr deep grn & sepia 65 16

Henri Pourrat (1887-1959), novelist.

Natl. Philatelic Societies Congress, Lens A1088

1987, June 6 *Perf. 13x13½*
2043 A1088 2.20fr choc & red 75 18

Involvement of U.S. Forces in World War I, 70th Anniv. A1089

Design: Stars and Stripes, troops, Gen. John J. Pershing (1860-1948), American army commander.

1987, June 13 *Perf. 13*
2044 A1089 3.40fr olive grn, sapphire & ver 1.15 28

6th Intl. Cable Car Transport Congress, Grenoble — A1090

1987, June 17 Photo.
2045 A1090 2fr multi 68 16

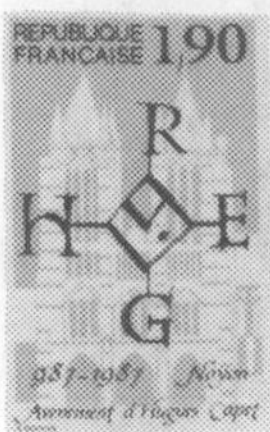

Accession of Hugh Capet (c. 938-996), First King of France, Millenary A1091

La Fleche Natl. Military School A1092

1987, June 20 **Litho.**
2046 A1091 1.90fr pale chalky blue & blk 65 16

1987, June 20 **Engr.** ***Perf. 12½x13***
2047 A1092 2.20fr blue grn, grnh blk & brt red 75 18

World Assembly of Expatriate Algerians, Nice — A1093

1987, June 27 **Photo.** ***Perf. 13***
2048 A1093 1.90fr multi 65 16

World Wrestling Championships — A1094

1987, Aug. 21 **Engr.**
2049 A1094 3fr brt pur, vio gray & brt olive grn 1.00 25

Mushrooms A1095

William the Conqueror (c. 1027-1087) A1096

1987, Sept. 5 ***Perf. 12½***
2050 A1095 2fr Gyroporus cyanescens 65 16
2051 A1095 3fr Gomphus clavatus 1.00 25
2052 A1095 4fr Morchella conica 1.30 32
2053 A1095 5fr Russula virescens 1.65 42

1987, Sept. 5 ***Perf. 13***
2054 A1096 2fr Bayeux Tapestry detail 65 16

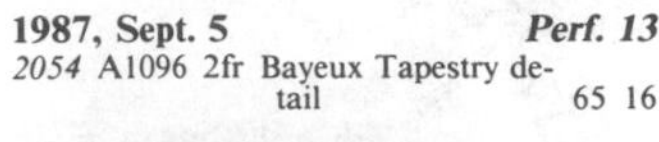

Montbenoit Le Saugeais A1097

Design: Abbey of Medieval Knights, cloisters, winter scene.

1987, Sept. 19
2055 A1097 2.50fr sapphire, blk & scarlet 82 20

Pasteur Institute, Cent. — A1098

1987, Oct. 3
2056 A1098 2.20fr deep blue & dark red 75 18

Blaise Cendrars (1887-1961), Poet and Novelist A1099

Treaty of Andelot, 1400th Anniv. A1100

Pen and ink portrait by Modigliani.

1987, Nov. 6 ***Perf. 12½***
2057 A1099 2fr brt grn, buff & blk 68 14

1987, Nov. 28 ***Perf. 12½x13***
2058 A1100 3.70fr brt blue, blue blk & dark blue 1.25 25

Gen. Leclerc (1902-1947), Marshal of France A1101

1987, Nov. 28 ***Perf. 13x12½***
2059 A1101 2.20fr brn blk, blk & dark olive bister 75 15

Liberty Type of 1982

1987, Nov. 16 ***Perf. 13***
2070 A915 3.70fr brt lil rose 1.35 8

Franco-German Cooperation Treaty, 25th Anniv. — A1102

1988, Jan. 15 ***Perf. 13***
2086 A1102 2.20fr Adenauer, De Gaulle 80 16

See Fed. Rep. of Germany No. 1546.

Marcel Dassault (1892-1986), Aircraft Designer — A1103

1988, Jan. 23 **Photo.**
2087 A1103 3.60fr 1.35 28

Communications A1104

Angouleme Festival prize-winning cartoons.

Booklet Stamps

1988, Jan. 29 **Photo.** ***Perf. 13½x13***
2088 A1104 2.20fr Pellos 80 16
2089 A1104 2.20fr Reiser 80 16
2090 A1104 2.20fr Marijac 80 16
2091 A1104 2.20fr Fred 80 16
2092 A1104 2.20fr Moebius 80 16
2093 A1104 2.20fr Gillon 80 16
2094 A1104 2.20fr Bretecher 80 16
2095 A1104 2.20fr Forest 80 16
2096 A1104 2.20fr Mezieres 80 16
2097 A1104 2.20fr Tardi 80 16
2098 A1104 2.20fr Lob 80 16
2099 A1104 2.20fr Bilal 80 16
a. Bklt. pane of 12, Nos. 2088-2099 9.75
Nos. 2088-2099 (12) 9.60 1.92

Issued in booklets only.

Great Synagogue, Rue Victoire, Paris — A1105

1988, Feb. 7 **Litho.** ***Perf. 13***
2100 A1105 2fr blk & gold 75 15

INDEX OF COMMEMORATIVE ISSUES

SEMI-POSTAL STAMPS

SP1

SP2

Red Surcharge on No. B1

1914 Unwmk. Typo. ***Perf. 14x13½***
B1 SP1 10c + 5c red 6.25 5.50
B2 SP2 10c + 5c red 37.50 3.75
a. Bklt. pane of 10 575.00

Issue dates: No. B1, Aug. 11; No. B2, Sept. 10.

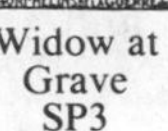
Widow at Grave SP3

War Orphans SP4

Woman Plowing — SP5

"Trench of Bayonets" SP6

Lion of Belfort SP7

"La Marseillaise" SP8

1917-19
B3 SP3 2c + 3c vio brn 4.50 4.50
B4 SP4 5c + 5c grn ('19) 10.00 6.75
B5 SP5 15c + 10c gray grn 22.50 22.50
B6 SP5 25c + 15c dp bl 85.00 47.50
B7 SP6 35c + 25c sl & vio 140.00 110.00
B8 SP7 50c + 50c pale brn & dk brn 225.00 175.00
B9 SP8 1fr + 1fr cl & mar 425.00 325.00
B10 SP8 5fr + 5fr dp bl & blk 1,800. 1,250.
Nos. B3-B10 (8) 2,712. 1,941.

Hospital Ship and Field Hospital SP9

1918, Aug.
B11 SP9 15c + 5c sl & red 165.00 62.50

Semi-Postal Stamps of 1917-19 Surcharged **+5c**

1922, Sept. 1
B12 SP3 2c + 1c vio brn 45 45
B13 SP4 5c + 2½c grn 75 75
B14 SP5 15c + 5c gray grn 1.25 1.25
B15 SP5 25c + 5c dp bl 2.50 2.50
B16 SP6 35c + 5c sl & vio 11.00 11.00
B17 SP7 50c + 10c pale brn & dk brn 17.00 17.00
a. Pair, one without surcharge
B18 SP8 1fr + 25c cl & mar 25.00 25.00
B19 SP8 5fr + 1fr bl & blk 140.00 140.00
Nos. B12-B19 (8) 197.95 197.95

Style and arrangement of surcharge differs for each denomination.

Types of 1917-19

1926-27
B20 SP3 2c + 1c vio brn 1.10 1.10
B21 SP7 50c + 10c ol brn & dk brn 30.00 11.00
B22 SP8 1fr + 25c dp rose & red brn 47.50 30.00
B23 SP8 5fr + 1fr sl bl & blk 110.00 80.00

Sinking Fund Issues

Types of Regular Issues of 1903-07 Surcharged in Red or Blue **Caisse d'Amortissement +10c**

1927, Sept. 26
B24 A22 40c + 10c lt bl (R) 4.50 4.50
B25 A20 50c + 25c grn (Bl) 6.50 6.50

Type of Regular Issue of 1923 Surcharged in Black **C A +50c**

B26 A23 1.50fr + 50c org 10.00 10.00

Industry and Agriculture SP10

1928, May Engr. ***Perf. 13½***
B27 SP10 1.50fr + 8.50fr dl bl 140.00 140.00
a. bl grn 400.00 400.00

Types of 1903-23 Issues Surcharged as in 1927

1928, Oct. 1 ***Perf. 14x13½***
B28 A22 40c + 10c gray lil (R) 11.00 11.00
B29 A20 50c + 25c org brn (Bl) 30.00 25.00
B30 A23 1.50fr + 50c rose lil (Bk) 42.50 35.00

Types of 1903-23 Issues Surcharged as in 1927

1929, Oct. 1
B31 A22 40c + 10c grn 19.00 16.00
B32 A20 50c + 25c lil rose 30.00 25.00
B33 A23 1.50fr + 50c chnt 52.50 50.00

"The Smile of Reims" SP11

1930, Mar. 15 Engr. ***Perf. 13***
B34 SP11 1.50fr + 3.50fr red vio 67.50 67.50
a. Bklt. pane of 4 325.00 325.00

Types of 1903-07 Issues Surcharged **Caisse d'Amortissement +10c**

1930 Oct. 1 ***Perf. 14x13½***
B35 A22 40c + 10c cer 20.00 17.50
B36 A20 50c + 25c gray brn 37.50 25.00
B37 A22 1.50fr + 50c vio 65.00 55.00

Allegory, French Provinces SP12

1931, Mar. 1 ***Perf. 13***
B38 SP12 1.50fr + 3.50fr grn 150.00 150.00

Types of 1903-07 Issues Surcharged **Caisse d'Amortissement +10c**

1931, Oct. 1 ***Perf. 14x13½***
B39 A22 40c + 10c ol grn 27.50 25.00
B40 A20 50c + 25c gray vio 87.50 65.00
B41 A22 1.50fr + 50c dp red 87.50 80.00

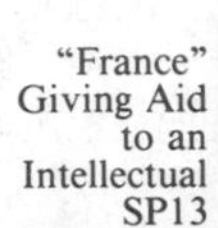

"France" Giving Aid to an Intellectual SP13

Symbolic of Music SP14

1935, Dec. 9 Engr. ***Perf. 13***
B42 SP13 50c + 10c ultra 3.25 1.75
B43 SP14 50c + 2fr dl red 52.50 35.00

The surtax was for the aid of distressed and exiled intellectuals.

Statue of Liberty SP15

Children of the Unemployed SP16

1936-37
B44 SP15 50c + 25c dk bl ('37) 3.50 2.50
B45 SP15 75c + 50c vio 8.50 6.00

The surtax was for the aid of political refugees.

1936, May
B46 SP16 50c + 10c cop red 5.50 4.50

The surtax was for the aid of children of the unemployed.

Type of 1935 Semi-Postal Surcharged in Black **+20c**

1936, Nov.
B47 SP14 20c on 50c + 2fr dl red 3.75 3.00

Jacques Callot SP17

Anatole France (Jacques Anatole Thibault) — SP18

Hector Berlioz SP19

Victor Hugo — SP20

Auguste Rodin SP21

Louis Pasteur SP22

1936-37 Engr.
B48 SP17 20c + 10c brn car 2.50 2.25
B49 SP18 30c + 10c emer ('37) 2.75 1.65
B50 SP19 40c + 10c emer 3.00 2.50
B51 SP20 50c + 10c cop red 4.50 2.50
B52 SP21 90c + 10c rose red ('37) 6.00 4.00
B53 SP22 1.50fr + 50c dp ultra 24.00 15.00
Nos. B48-B53 (6) 42.75 27.90

The surtax was used for relief of unemployed intellectuals.

1938
B54 SP18 30c + 10c brn car 1.50 1.50
B55 SP17 35c + 10c dl grn 2.50 2.00
B56 SP19 55c + 10c dl vio 4.50 2.50
B57 SP20 65c + 10c ultra 4.50 2.75
B58 SP21 1fr + 10c car lake 4.50 2.75
B59 SP22 1.75fr + 25c dp bl 12.50 7.00
Nos. B54-B59 (6) 30.00 18.50

Tug of War — SP23

Foot Race SP24

Hiking — SP25

1937, June 16
B60 SP23 20c + 10c brn 2.50 1.75
B61 SP24 40c + 10c red brn 2.50 1.75
B62 SP25 50c + 10c blk brn 2.50 1.75

The surtax was for the Recreation Fund of the employees of the Post, Telephone and Telegraph.

Pierre Loti (Louis Marie Julien Viaud) SP26

1937, Aug.
B63 SP26 50c + 20c rose car 3.75 2.75

The surtax was for the Pierre Loti Monument Fund.

"France" and Infant SP27

1937-39
B64 SP27 65c + 25c brn vio 2.75 2.00
B65 SP27 90c + 30c pck bl ('39) 1.75 1.25

The surtax was used for public health work.

Winged Victory of Samothrace SP28

Jean Baptiste Charcot SP29

1937, Aug.
B66 SP28 30c bl grn 65.00 32.50
B67 SP28 55c red 65.00 32.50

On sale at the Louvre for 2.50 fr. The surtax of 1.65 fr. was for the benefit of the Louvre Museum.

1938-39
B68 SP29 65c + 35c dk bl grn 1.50 1.50
B69 SP29 90c + 35c brt red vio ('39) 9.00 7.50

The surtax was for the benefit of French seamen.

Palace of Versailles SP30

1938, May 9
B70 SP30 1.75fr + 75c dp bl 18.00 14.00

Issued in commemoration of the National Exposition of Painting and Sculpture at Versailles.

The surtax was for the benefit of the Versailles Concert Society.

French Soldier SP31

Monument SP32

1938, May 16
B71 SP31 55c + 70c brn vio 3.75 2.75
B72 SP31 65c + 1.10fr pck bl 3.75 2.75

The surtax was for a fund to erect a monument to the glory of the French Infantrymen.

1938, May 25
B73 SP32 55c + 45c ver 10.00 7.50

The surtax was for a fund to erect a monument in honor of the Army Medical Corps.

Reims Cathedral SP33

"France" Welcoming Her Sons SP34

1938, July 10
B74 SP33 65c + 35c ultra 10.00 8.50

Issued to commemorate the completion of the reconstruction of Reims Cathedral, July 10, 1938.

1938, Aug. 8
B75 SP34 65c + 60c rose car 5.00 4.00

The surtax was for the benefit of French volunteers repatriated from Spain.

Curie Issue
Common Design Type

1938, Sept. 1
B76 CD80 1.75fr + 50c dp ultra 9.00 8.00

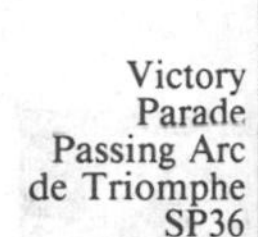

Victory Parade Passing Arc de Triomphe SP36

1938, Oct. 8
B77 SP36 65c + 35c brn car 5.00 4.00

20th anniversary of the Armistice.

Student and Nurse — SP37

1938, Dec. 1
B78 SP37 65c + 60c pck bl 5.50 4.00

The surtax was for Student Relief.

Blind Man and Radio SP38

1938, Dec.
B79 SP38 90c + 25c brn vio 6.00 4.50

The surtax was used to help provide radios for the blind.

Prices of premium quality never hinged stamps will be in excess of catalogue price.

Civilian Facing Firing Squad — SP39

Red Cross Nurse — SP40

1939, Feb. 1
B80 SP39 90c + 35c blk brn 6.00 4.75

The surtax was used to erect a monument to civilian victims of World War I.

1939, Mar. 24
B81 SP40 90c + 35c dk sl grn, turq bl & red 5.50 4.50

Issued in commemoration of the 75th anniversary of the founding of the International Red Cross Society.

Army Engineer SP41

1939, Apr. 3
B82 SP41 70c + 50c ver 5.50 4.50

Issued in honor of the Army Engineering Corps. The surtax was used to erect a monument to those members who died in World War I.

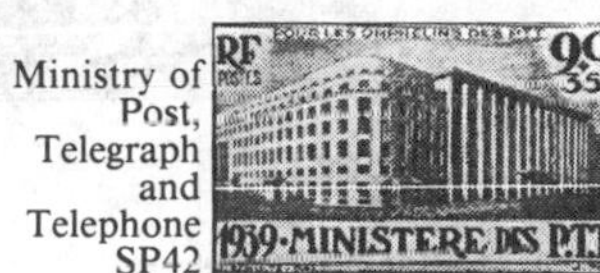

Ministry of Post, Telegraph and Telephone SP42

1939, Apr. 8
B83 SP42 90c + 35c turq bl 13.00 8.50

The surtax was used to aid orphans of employees of the postal system. Issued to commemorate the opening of the new building for the Ministry of Post, Telegraph and Telephones.

Mother and Child — SP43

Eiffel Tower — SP44

1939, Apr. 24
B84 SP43 90c + 35c red 2.75 2.00

The surtax was used to aid children of the unemployed.

1939, May 5
B85 SP44 90c + 50c red vio 6.75 5.00

Issued in commemoration of the 50th anniversary of the Eiffel Tower. The surtax was used for celebration festivities.

Puvis de Chavannes — SP45

Claude Debussy SP46

Honoré de Balzac SP47

Claude Bernard SP48

1939-40

B86	SP45	40c + 10c ver	1.00	85
B87	SP46	70c + 10c brn vio	1.25	1.10
B87A	SP46	80c + 10c brn vio ('40)	2.00	2.00
B88	SP47	90c + 10c brt red vio	2.00	1.65
B88A	SP47	1fr + 10c brt red vio ('40)	2.00	2.00
B89	SP48	2.25fr + 25c brt ultra	6.00	3.25
B89A	SP48	2.50fr + 25c brt ultra ('40)	2.00	2.00
		Nos. B86-B89A (7)	16.25	12.85

The surtax was used to aid unemployed intellectuals.

Mothers and Children SP49 SP50

1939, June 15
B90 SP49 70c + 80c bl, grn & vio 2.75 2.50
B91 SP50 90c + 60c dk brn, dl vio & brn 3.50 3.00

The surtax was used to aid France's repopulation campaign.

"The Letter" by Jean Honore Fragonard SP51

Statue of Widow and Children SP52

1939, July 6
B92 SP51 40c + 60c brn, sep & pur 3.50 2.75

The surtax was used for the Postal Museum.

1939, July 20
B93 SP52 70c + 30c brn vio 6.00 4.50

The surtax was for the benefit of French seamen.

French Soldier SP53

Colonial Trooper SP54

1940, Feb. 15

B94	SP53	40c + 60c sep	1.25	80
B95	SP54	1fr + 50c turq bl	1.25	80

The surtax was used to assist the families of mobilized men.

World Map Showing French Possessions SP55

1940, Apr. 15
B96 SP55 1fr + 25c scar 2.25 1.75

Marshal Joseph J. C. Joffre SP56

Marshal Ferdinand Foch — SP57

Gen. Joseph S. Gallieni SP58

Woman Plowing SP59

1940, May 1

B97	SP56	80c + 45c choc	2.25	2.25
B98	SP57	1fr + 50c dk vio	2.50	2.50
B99	SP58	1.50fr + 50c brn red	2.50	2.50
B100	SP59	2.50fr + 50c ind & dl bl	3.00	3.00

The surtax was used for war charities.

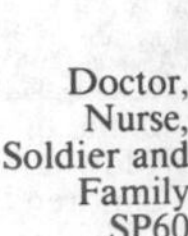

Doctor, Nurse, Soldier and Family SP60

Scott's editorial staff cannot undertake to identify, authenticate or appraise stamps and postal markings.

Nurse and Wounded Soldier SP61

1940, May 12

B101	SP60	80c + 1fr dk grn & red	5.00	3.25
B102	SP61	1fr + 2fr sep & red	5.00	3.25

The surtax was used for the Red Cross.

Nurse with Injured Children — SP62

1940, Nov. 12
B103 SP62 1fr + 2fr sep 1.10 90

The surtax was used for victims of the war.

Wheat Harvest SP63

Sowing SP64

Picking Grapes SP65

Grazing Cattle SP66

1940, Dec. 2

B104	SP63	80c + 2fr brn blk	1.40	1.25
B105	SP64	1fr + 2fr chnt	1.40	1.25
B106	SP65	1.50fr + 2fr brt vio	1.40	1.25
B107	SP66	2.50fr + 2fr dp grn	1.65	1.25

The surtax was for national relief.

Prisoners of War
SP67 SP68

1941, Jan. 1

B108	SP67	80c + 5fr dk grn	1.00	1.00
B109	SP68	1fr + 5fr rose brn	1.00	1.00

The surtax was for prisoners of war.

Science Fighting Cancer SP69

1941, Feb. 20
B110 SP69 2.50fr + 50c sl blk & brn 1.10 1.10

The surtax was used for the control of cancer.

Type of 1941 Surcharged "+10c" in Blue.

1941, Mar. 4
B111 A109 1fr + 10c crim 18 18

Men Hauling Coal SP70

"France" Aiding Needy Man SP71

1941

B112	SP70	1fr + 2fr sep	75	60
B113	SP71	2.50fr + 7.50fr dk bl	2.75	2.00

The surtax was for Marshal Pétain's National Relief Fund.

Liner Pasteur SP72

Red Surcharge

1941, July 17
B114 SP72 1fr + 1fr on 70c dk bl grn 18 18

World Map, Mercator Projection SP73

1941
B115 SP73 1fr + 1fr multi 50 45

Fisherman — SP74

1941, Oct. 23
B116 SP74 1fr + 9fr dk bl grn 1.00 1.00

Surtax for benefit of French seamen.

Arms of Various Cities

Nancy SP75 Lille SP76

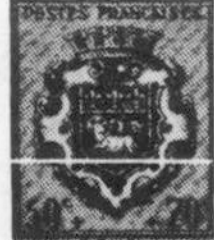
Rouen SP77

Bordeaux SP78

Toulouse SP79

Clermont-Ferrand SP80

Marseilles SP81

Lyon SP82

Rennes SP83

Reims SP84

Montpellier SP85

Paris SP86

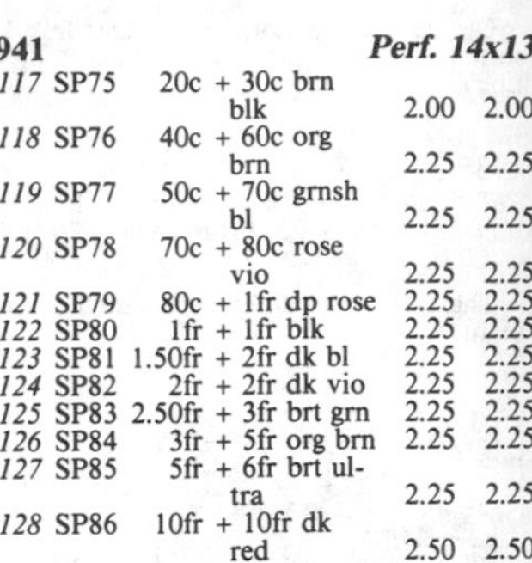

1941 *Perf. 14x13*

B117	SP75	20c + 30c brn blk	2.00	2.00
B118	SP76	40c + 60c org brn	2.25	2.25
B119	SP77	50c + 70c grnsh bl	2.25	2.25
B120	SP78	70c + 80c rose vio	2.25	2.25
B121	SP79	80c + 1fr dp rose	2.25	2.25
B122	SP80	1fr + 1fr blk	2.25	2.25
B123	SP81	1.50fr + 2fr dk bl	2.25	2.25
B124	SP82	2fr + 2fr dk vio	2.25	2.25
B125	SP83	2.50fr + 3fr brt grn	2.25	2.25
B126	SP84	3fr + 5fr org brn	2.25	2.25
B127	SP85	5fr + 6fr brt ultra	2.25	2.25
B128	SP86	10fr + 10fr dk red	2.50	2.50
		Nos. B117-B128 (12)	27.00	27.00

Count de La Perouse SP87

1942, Mar. 23 *Perf. 13*
B129 SP87 2.50fr + 7.50fr ultra 1.00 1.00

Issued to commemorate the 200th anniversary of the birth of Jean Francois de Galaup de La Perouse, (1741-1788), French navigator and explorer. The surtax was for National Relief.

Planes over Fields SP88

1942, Apr. 4
B130 SP88 1.50fr + 3.50fr lt vio 50 50

The surtax was for the benefit of French airmen and their familes.

Alexis Chabrier
SP89

1942, May 18

B131	SP89	2fr + 3fr sep	90	90

Emmanuel Chabrier (1841-1894), composer, birth centenary. The surtax was for works of charity among musicians.

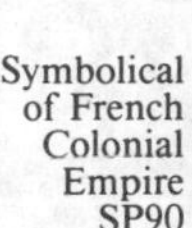

Symbolical of French Colonial Empire
SP90

1942, May 18

B132	SP90	1.50fr + 8.50fr blk	60	60

The surtax was for National Relief.

Jean de Vienne
SP91

1942, June 16

B133	SP91	1.50fr + 8.50fr sep	90	90

Issued in commemoration of the 600th anniversary of the birth of Jean de Vienne, first admiral of France. The surtax was for the benefit of French seamen.

+ 50

S N

Type of Regular Issue, 1941 Surcharged in Carmine

1942, Sept. 10 ***Perf. 14x13½***

B134	A116	1.50fr + 50c brt ultra	15	15

The surtax was for national relief ("Secours National").

Arms of Various Cities

Chambery
SP92

La Rochelle
SP93

Poitiers
SP94

Orleans
SP95

Grenoble
SP96

Angers
SP97

Dijon
SP98

Limoges
SP99

Le Havre
SP100

Nantes
SP101

Nice
SP102

St. Etienne
SP103

Perf. 14x13

1942, Oct. **Unwmk.** **Engr.**

B135	SP92	50c + 60c blk	2.25	2.25
B136	SP93	60c + 70c grnsh bl	2.25	2.25
B137	SP94	80c + 1fr rose	2.25	2.25
B138	SP95	1fr + 1.30fr dk grn	2.50	2.50
B139	SP96	1.20fr + 1.50fr rose vio	2.50	2.50
B140	SP97	1.50fr + 1.80fr sl bl	2.50	2.50
B141	SP98	2fr + 2.30fr dp rose	2.50	2.50
B142	SP99	2.40fr + 2.80fr sl grn	2.50	2.50
B143	SP100	3fr + 3.50fr dp vio	2.50	2.50
B144	SP101	4fr + 5fr lt ultra	2.50	2.50
B145	SP102	4.50fr + 6fr red	2.50	2.50
B146	SP103	5fr + 7fr brt red vio	2.50	2.50
		Nos. B135-B146 (12)	29.25	29.25

The surtax was for national relief.

Tricolor Legion
SP104

1942, Oct. 12 ***Perf. 13***

B147	SP104	1.20 + 8.80fr dk bl	5.50	5.50
a.		Vert. strip of 3 (1 each Nos. B147, B148 + albino impression)	11.00	11.00
B148	SP104	1.20 + 8.80fr crim	5.50	5.50

These stamps were printed in sheets of 20 stamps and 5 albino impressions arranged: 2 horizontal rows of 5 dark blue stamps, 1 row of 5 albino impressions, and 2 rows of 5 crimson stamps.

Marshal Henri Philippe Petain
SP105 SP106

1943, Feb. 8

B149	SP105	1fr + 10fr rose red	2.50	2.50
a.		Strip of 4 (1 each Nos. B149-B152 + label)	11.00	11.00
B150	SP105	1fr + 10fr bl	2.50	2.50
B151	SP106	2fr + 12fr rose red	2.50	2.50
B152	SP106	2fr + 12fr bl	2.50	2.50

The surtax was for national relief. Printed in sheets of 20, the 10 blue stamps at left, the 10 rose red at right, separated by a vertical row of five white labels bearing a tri-colored battle-ax.

Marshal Petain
SP107

"Work"
SP108

"Family"
SP109

"State"
SP110

Marshal Petain — SP111

1943, June 7

B153	SP107	1.20fr + 1.40fr dl vio	11.00	11.00
a.		Strip of 5 (1 each Nos. B153 to B157)	60.00	60.00
B154	SP108	1.50fr + 2.50fr red	11.00	11.00
B155	SP109	2.40fr + 7fr brn	11.00	11.00
B156	SP110	4fr + 10fr dk vio	11.00	11.00
B157	SP111	5fr + 15fr red brn	11.00	11.00
		Nos. B153-B157 (5)	55.00	55.00

Issued to commemorate Pétain's 87th birthday.

The surtax was for national relief.

Printed in sheets of 25 (5x5). Each horizontal strip includes the five values, arranged by denomination.

Civilians Under Air Attack
SP112

Civilians Doing Farm Work
SP113

Prisoner's Family Doing Farm Work
SP114

1943, Aug. 23

B158	SP112	1.50fr + 3.50fr blk	55	55

Surtax was for bomb victims at Billancourt, Dunkirk, Lorient, Saint-Nazaire.

1943, Sept. 27

B159	SP113	1.50fr + 8.50fr sep	80	80
B160	SP114	2.40fr + 7.60fr dk grn	80	80

The surtax was for families of war prisoners.

Michel de Montaigne
SP115

Picardy Costume
SP121

Designs: 1.20fr+1.50fr, Francois Clouet. 1.50fr+3fr, Ambrose Pare. 2.40fr+4fr, Chevalier Pierre de Bayard. 4fr+6fr, Duke of Sully. 5fr+10fr, Henri IV.

1943, Oct. 2

B161	SP115	60c + 80c Prus grn	1.40	1.40
B162	SP115	1.20fr + 1.50fr blk	1.40	1.40
B163	SP115	1.50fr + 3fr dp ultra	1.40	1.40
B164	SP115	2.40fr + 4fr red	1.40	1.40
B165	SP115	4fr + 6fr dl brn red	1.75	1.75
B166	SP115	5fr + 10fr dl grn	1.75	1.75
		Nos. B161-B166 (6)	9.10	9.10

The surtax was for national relief. Issued to honor famous 16th century Frenchmen.

1943, Dec. 27

Designs: 18th Century Costumes: 1.20fr+2fr, Brittany. 1.50fr+4fr, Ile de France. 2.40+5fr, Burgundy. 4fr+6fr, Auvergne. 5fr+7fr, Provence.

B167	SP121	60c + 1.30fr sep	1.65	1.65
B168	SP121	1.20fr + 2fr lt vio	1.65	1.65
B169	SP121	1.50fr + 4fr turq bl	1.65	1.65
B170	SP121	2.40fr + 5fr rose car	1.65	1.65
B171	SP121	4fr + 6fr chlky bl	2.25	2.25
B172	SP121	5fr + 7fr red	2.25	2.25
		Nos. B167-B172 (6)	11.10	11.10

The surtax was for national relief.

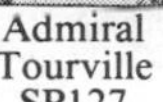
Admiral Tourville
SP127

Charles Gounod
SP128

1944, Feb. 21

B173	SP127	4fr + 6fr dl red brn	55	55

Issued to commemorate the 300th anniversary of the birth of Admiral Anne-Hilarion de Cotentin Tourville (1642-1701).

1944, Mar. 27 ***Perf. 14x13***

B174	SP128	1.50fr + 3.50fr sep	30	30

Issued to commemorate the 50th anniversary of the death of Charles Gounod, composer (1818-1893).

Marshal Petain
SP129

Farming
SP130

Industry
SP131

1944, Apr. 24 ***Perf. 13***

B175 SP129 1.50fr + 3.50fr sep 3.00 3.00
B176 SP130 2fr + 3fr dp ultra 60 60
B177 SP131 4fr + 6fr rose red 60 60

Marshal Henri Pétain's 88th birthday.

Modern Streamliner and 19th Century Train
SP132

Molière (Jean-Baptiste Poquelin)
SP133

1944, Aug. 14

B178 SP132 4fr + 6fr blk 1.25 1.25

Issued to commemorate the centenary of the Paris-Rouen, Paris-Orléans railroad.

1944, July 31

Designs: 80c+2.20fr, Jules Hardouin Mansart. 1.20fr+2.80fr, Blaise Pascal. 1.50fr+3.50fr, Louis II of Bourbon. 2fr+4fr, Jean-Baptiste Colbert. 4fr+6fr, Louis XIV.

B179 SP133 50c + 1.50fr rose car 95 95
B180 SP133 80c + 2.20fr dk grn 95 95
B181 SP133 1.20fr + 2.80fr blk 95 95
B182 SP133 1.50fr + 3.50fr brt ultra 95 95
B183 SP133 2fr + 4fr dl brn red 95 95
B184 SP133 4fr + 6fr red 95 95
Nos. B179-B184 (6) 5.70 5.70

Noted 17th century Frenchmen.

French Cathedrals

Angoulême
SP139

Chartres
SP140

Amiens
SP141

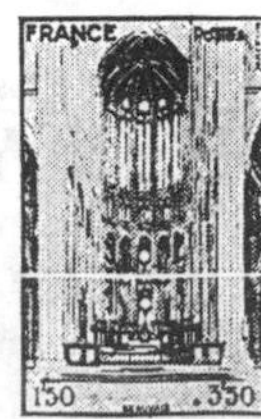
Beauvais
SP142

Albi — SP143

1944, Nov. 20

B185 SP139 50c + 1.50fr blk 22 22
B186 SP140 80c + 2.20fr rose vio 35 35
B187 SP141 1.20fr + 2.80fr brn car 48 48
B188 SP142 1.50fr + 3.50fr dp bl 48 48
B189 SP143 4fr + 6fr org red 48 48
Nos. B185-B189 (5) 2.01 2.01

Coat of Arms of Renouard de Villayer
SP144

Sarah Bernhardt
SP145

1944, Dec. 9 **Engr.**

B190 SP144 1.50fr + 3.50fr dp brn 18 15

Stamp Day.

1945, May 16 **Unwmk.** ***Perf. 13***

B191 SP145 4fr + 1fr dk vio brn 30 30

Issued to commemorate the 100th anniversary of the birth of Sarah Bernhardt, actress.

War Victims
SP146

Tuberculosis Patient
SP147

1945, May 16

B192 SP146 4fr + 6fr dk vio brn 15 15

The surtax was for war victims of the P.T.T.

1945, May 16 **Typo.** ***Perf. 14x13½***

B193 SP147 2fr + 1fr red org 15 10

The surtax was for the aid of tuberculosis victims.

Boy and Girl
SP148

Burning of Oradour Church
SP149

1945, July 9 **Engr.** ***Perf. 13***

B194 SP148 4fr + 2fr Prus grn 18 18

The surtax was used for child welfare.

1945, Oct. 13

B195 SP149 4fr + 2fr sep 18 18

Destruction of Oradour, June, 1944.

Louis XI and Post Rider
SP150

1945, Oct. 13

B196 SP150 2fr + 3fr dp ultra 22 22

Stamp Day.

Ruins of Dunkirk
SP151

Ruins of Rouen
SP152

Ruins of Caen
SP153

Ruins of Saint-Malo
SP154

1945, Nov. 5

B197 SP151 1.50fr + 1.50fr red brn 18 18
B198 SP152 2fr + 2fr vio 18 18
B199 SP153 2.40fr + 2.60fr bl 18 18
B200 SP154 4fr + 4fr blk 18 18

The surtax was to aid the suffering residents of Dunkirk, Rouen, Caen and Saint Malo.

Alfred Fournier
SP155

Henri Becquerel
SP156

1946, Feb. 4 **Engr.** ***Perf. 13***

B201 SP155 2fr + 3fr red brn 18 18
B202 SP156 2fr + 3fr vio 18 18

Issued to raise funds for the fight against venereal disease (B201) and for the struggle against cancer (B202).

No. B202 commemorated the 50th anniversary of the discovery of radio-activity by Henri Becquerel.

See No. B221.

Church of the Invalides, Paris — SP157

1946, Mar. 11

B203 SP157 4fr + 6fr red brn 22 22

The surtax was to aid disabled war veterans.

French Warships
SP158

1946, Apr. 8

B204 SP158 2fr + 3fr gray blk 18 18

The surtax was for naval charities.

"The Letter" by Jean Simeon Chardin
SP159

Fouquet de la Varane
SP160

1946, May 25

B205 SP159 2fr + 3fr brn red 38 38

The surtax was used for the Postal Museum.

1946, June 29

B206 SP160 3fr + 2fr sep 38 38

Stamp Day.

François Villon — SP161

Designs: 3fr+1fr, Jean Fouquet. 4fr+3fr, Philippe de Commynes. 5fr+4fr, Joan of Arc. 6fr+5fr, Jean de Gerson. 10fr+6fr, Charles VII.

1946, Oct. 28

B207 SP161 2fr + 1fr dk Prus grn 1.25 1.25
B208 SP161 3fr + 1fr dk bl vio 1.25 1.25
B209 SP161 4fr + 3fr hn brn 1.25 1.25
B210 SP161 5fr + 4fr ultra 1.25 1.25
B211 SP161 6fr + 5fr sep 1.25 1.25
B212 SP161 10fr + 6fr red 1.40 1.40
Nos. B207-B212 (6) 7.65 7.65

Church of St. Sernin, Toulouse
SP167

Notre Dame du Port, Clermont-Ferrand
SP168

Cathedral of St. Front, Perigueux
SP169

Foreign postal stationery (stamped envelopes, postal cards and air letter sheets) lies beyond the scope of this Catalogue, which is limited to adhesive postage stamps.

Cathedral of St. Julien, Le Mans
SP170

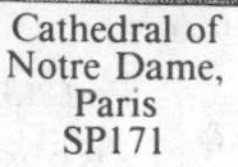
Cathedral of Notre Dame, Paris
SP171

François Michel le Tellier de Louvois
SP172

1947 **Engr.**

B213	SP167	1fr + 1fr car rose	42	42
B214	SP168	3fr + 2fr dk bl vio	60	60
B215	SP169	4fr + 3fr hn brn	85	85
B216	SP170	6fr + 4fr dp bl	1.10	1.10
B217	SP171	10fr + 6fr dk gray grn	2.50	2.50
		Nos. B213-B217 (5)	5.47	5.47

1947, Mar. 15

B218	SP172	4.50fr + 5.50fr car rose	1.10	1.10

Stamp Day, March 15, 1947.

Submarine Pens, Shipyard and Monument
SP173

1947, Aug. 2

B219	SP173	6fr + 4fr bluish blk	30	30

Issued to commemorate the British commando raid on the Nazi U-boat base at St. Nazaire, 1942.

Liberty Highway Marker
SP174

Louis Braille
SP175

1947, Sept. 5

B220	SP174	6fr + 4fr dk grn	45	45

The surtax was to help defray maintenance costs of the Liberty Highway.

Fournier Type of 1946

1947, Oct. 20

B221	SP155	2fr + 3fr ind	25	25

1948, Jan. 19

B222	SP175	6fr + 4fr pur	30	30

Etienne Arago
SP176

Alphonse de Lamartine
SP177

1948, Mar. 6

B223	SP176	6fr + 4fr blk brn	45	45

Stamp Day, March 6-7, 1948.

1948, Apr. 5 **Engr.** ***Perf. 13***

Designs: 3fr+2fr, Alexandre A. Ledru-Rollin. 4fr+3fr, Louis Blanc. 5fr+4fr, Albert (Alexandre Martin). 6fr+5fr, Pierre J. Proudhon. 10fr+6fr, Louis Auguste Blanqui. 15fr+7fr, Armand Barbès. 20fr+8fr, Dennis A. Affre.

B224	SP177	1fr + 1fr dk grn	1.10	1.10
B225	SP177	3fr + 2fr hn brn	1.25	1.25
B226	SP177	4fr + 3fr vio brn	1.25	1.25
B227	SP177	5fr + 4fr lt bl grn	1.50	1.50
B228	SP177	6fr + 5fr ind	1.50	1.50
B229	SP177	10fr + 6fr car rose	1.50	1.50
B230	SP177	15fr + 7fr sl blk	2.50	2.50
B231	SP177	20fr + 8fr pur	2.75	2.75
		Nos. B224-B231 (8)	13.35	13.35

Centenary of the Revolution of 1848.

Dr. Léon Charles Albert Calmette
SP178

1948, June 18

B232	SP178	6fr + 4fr dk grnsh bl	25	25

Issued to mark the first International Congress on the Calmette-Guerin bacillus vaccine.

Farmer — SP179

Designs: 5fr+3fr, Fisherman. 8fr+4fr, Miner. 10fr+6fr, Metal worker.

1949, Feb. 14

B233	SP179	3fr + 1fr cl	60	45
B234	SP179	5fr + 3fr dk bl	65	65
B235	SP179	8fr + 4fr ind	70	55
B236	SP179	10fr + 6fr dk red	1.10	80

Etienne François de Choiseul and Post Cart
SP180

Baron de la Brede et de Montesquieu
SP181

1949, Mar. 26

B237	SP180	15fr + 5fr dk grn	95	95

Stamp Day, March 26-27, 1949.

1949, Nov. 14

Designs: 8fr+2fr, Voltaire. 10fr+3fr, Antoine Watteau. 12fr+4fr, Georges de Buffon. 15fr+5fr, Joseph F. Dupleix. 25fr+10fr, A. R. J. Turgot.

B238	SP181	5fr + 1fr dk grn	3.50	3.50
B239	SP181	8fr + 2fr ind	3.50	3.50
B240	SP181	10fr + 3fr brn red	3.50	3.50
B241	SP181	12fr + 4fr pur	3.50	3.50
B242	SP181	15fr + 5fr rose car	4.50	4.50
B243	SP181	25fr + 10fr ultra	4.50	4.50
		Nos. B238-B243 (6)	23.00	23.00

"Spring"
SP182

Designs: 8fr+2fr, Summer. 12fr+3fr, Autumn. 15fr+4fr, Winter.

1949, Dec. 19

B244	SP182	5fr + 1fr grn	1.50	1.50
B245	SP182	8fr + 2fr yel org	1.50	1.50
B246	SP182	12fr + 3fr pur	2.00	2.00
B247	SP182	15fr + 4fr dp bl	2.25	2.25

Postman — SP183

1950, Mar. 11

B248	SP183	12fr + 3fr dp bl	2.75	2.00

Stamp Day, March 11-12, 1950.

André de Chenier
SP184

Alexandre Brongniart, Bust by Houdon
SP185

Portraits: 8fr+3fr, J. L. David. 10fr+4fr, Lazare Carnot. 12fr+5fr, G. J. Danton. 15fr+6fr, Maximilian Robespierre. 20fr+10fr, Louis Hoche.

1950, July 10 **Engr.** ***Perf. 13***
Frames in Indigo

B249	SP184	5fr + 2fr brn vio	6.75	6.75
B250	SP184	8fr + 3fr blk brn	6.75	6.75
B251	SP184	10fr + 4fr lake	6.75	6.75
B252	SP184	12fr + 5fr red brn	7.25	7.25
B253	SP184	15fr + 6fr dk grn	8.50	8.50
B254	SP184	20fr + 10fr dk vio bl	8.50	8.50
		Nos. B249-B254 (6)	44.50	44.50

1950, Dec. 22

Design: 15fr-3fr, "L'Amour" by Etienne M. Falconet.

B255	SP185	8fr + 2fr ind & car	3.00	3.00
B256	SP185	15fr + 3fr red brn & car	3.00	3.00

The surtax was for the Red Cross.

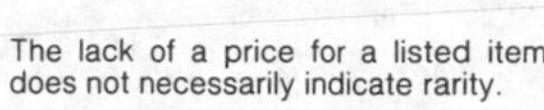
The lack of a price for a listed item does not necessarily indicate rarity.

Mail Car Interior
SP186

Alfred de Musset
SP187

1951, Mar. 10 **Unwmk.** ***Perf. 13***

B257	SP186	12fr + 3fr lil gray	2.50	2.50

Stamp Day, March 10-11, 1951.

1951, June 2
Frames in Dark Brown

Designs: 8fr+2fr, Eugène Delacroix. 10fr+3fr, J.-L. Gay-Lussac. 12fr+4fr, Robert Surcouf. 15fr+5fr, C. M. Talleyrand. 30fr+10fr, Napoleon I.

B258	SP187	5fr + 1fr dk grn	6.25	6.25
B259	SP187	8fr + 2fr vio brn	6.75	6.75
B260	SP187	10fr + 3fr grnsh blk	7.00	7.00
B261	SP187	12fr + 4fr dk vio brn	7.00	7.00
B262	SP187	15fr + 5fr brn car	7.25	7.25
B263	SP187	30fr + 10fr ind	10.50	10.50
		Nos. B258-B263 (6)	44.75	44.75

Child at Prayer by Le Maitre de Moulins
SP188

18th Century Child by Quentin de la Tour
SP189

1951, Dec. 15 **Cross in Red**

B264	SP188	12fr + 3fr dk brn	3.75	3.75
B265	SP189	15fr + 5fr dp ultra	3.75	3.75

The surtax was for the Red Cross.

Stagecoach of 1844
SP190

1952, Mar. 8 ***Perf. 13***

B266	SP190	12fr + 3fr dp grn	2.75	2.75

Stamp Day, March 8, 1952.

Gustave Flaubert — SP191

Portraits: 12fr+3fr, Edouard Manet. 15fr+4fr, Camille Saint-Saens. 18fr+5fr, Henri Poincaré. 20fr+6fr, Georges-Eugene Haussmann. 30fr+7fr, Adolphe Thiers.

1952, Oct. 18
Frames in Dark Brown

B267	SP191	8fr + 2fr ind	5.50	5.50
B268	SP191	12fr + 3fr vio bl	5.50	5.50
B269	SP191	15fr + 4fr dk grn	5.50	5.50
B270	SP191	18fr + 5fr dk brn	5.50	5.50

B271 SP191 20fr + 6fr car 7.25 7.25
B272 SP191 30fr + 7fr pur 7.25 7.25
Nos. B267-B272 (6) 36.50 36.50

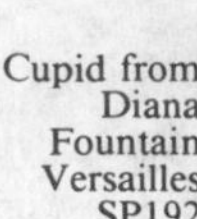

Cupid from Diana Fountain Versailles SP192

Design: 15fr+5fr, Similar detail, cupid facing left.

1952, Dec. 13 **Cross in Red**

B273 SP192 12fr + 3fr dk grn 4.50 4.50
B274 SP192 15fr + 5fr ind 4.50 4.50
a. Bklt. pane of 10 60.00

The surtax was for the Red Cross.

Count d'Argenson SP193

St. Bernard SP194

1953, Mar. 14

B275 SP193 12fr + 3fr dp bl 2.25 2.25

Issued to commemorate the Day of the Stamp. The surtax was for the Red Cross.

1953, July 9

Portraits: 12fr+3fr, Olivier de Serres. 15fr+4fr, Jean Philippe Rameau. 18fr+5fr, Gaspard Monge. 20fr+6fr, Jules Michelet. 30fr+7fr, Marshal Hubert Lyautey.

B276 SP194 8fr + 2fr ultra 4.75 4.75
B277 SP194 12fr + 3fr dk grn 4.75 4.75
B278 SP194 15fr + 4fr brn car 6.25 6.25
B279 SP194 18fr + 5fr dk bl 6.25 6.25
B280 SP194 20fr + 6fr dk pur 6.25 6.25
B281 SP194 30fr + 7fr brn 7.25 7.25
Nos. B276-B281 (6) 35.50 35.50

The surtax was for the Red Cross.

Madame Vigee-Lebrun and her Daughter SP195

Count Antoine de La Vallette SP196

Design: 15fr+5fr, "The Return from Baptism," by Louis Le Nain.

1953, Dec. 12 **Cross in Red**

B282 SP195 12fr + 3fr red brn 6.75 6.75
a. Bklt. pane (4 # B282, 4 # B283 with gutter btwn.) 75.00
B283 SP195 15fr + 5fr ind 8.00 8.00

The surtax was for the Red Cross.

1954, Mar. 20 **Engr.** ***Perf. 13***

B284 SP196 12fr + 3fr dp grn & choc 3.75 3.75

Stamp Day, March 20, 1954.

Louis IX SP197

"The Sick Child," by Eugene Carriere SP198

Portraits: 15fr+5fr, Jacques Benigne Bossuet. 18fr+6fr, Sadi Carnot. 20fr+7fr, Antoine Bourdelle. 25fr+8fr, Dr. Emile Roux. 30fr+10fr, Paul Valery.

1954, July 10

B285 SP197 12fr + 4fr dp bl 17.00 17.00
B286 SP197 15fr + 5fr pur 18.00 18.00
B287 SP197 18fr + 6fr dk brn 18.00 18.00
B288 SP197 20fr + 7fr crim 22.50 22.50
B289 SP197 25fr + 8fr ind 22.50 22.50
B290 SP197 30fr + 10fr dp cl 22.50 22.50
Nos. B285-B290 (6) 120.50 120.50

See Nos. B303-B308 and B312-B317.

1954, Dec. 18 **Cross in Red**

Design: 15fr+5fr, "Young Girl with Doves," by Jean Baptiste Greuze.

B291 SP198 12fr + 3fr vio gray & ind 8.20 8.20
a. Bklt. pane (4 # B291, 4 # B292 with gutter btwn.) 75.00
B292 SP198 15fr + 5fr dk brn & org brn 8.00 8.00

No. B291a was issued to commemorate the 90th anniversary of the Red Cross. The gutter between panes is inscribed in red.
The surtax was for the Red Cross.

Balloon Post, 1870 SP199

1955, Mar. 19 **Unwmk.** ***Perf. 13***

B293 SP199 12fr + 3fr dk grnsh bl, vio brn & ol grn 5.00 3.75

Stamp Day, March 19-20, 1955.

King Philip II SP200

Child with Cage by Pigalle SP201

Portraits: 15fr+6fr, Francois de Malherbe. 18fr+7fr, Sebastien de Vauban. 25fr+8fr, Charles G. de Vergennes. 30fr+9fr, Pierre S. de Laplace. 50fr+15fr, Pierre Auguste Renoir.

1955, June 11

B294 SP200 12fr + 5fr brt pur 13.00 13.00
B295 SP200 15fr + 6fr dp bl 13.00 13.00
B296 SP200 18fr + 7fr dp grn 15.00 15.00
B297 SP200 25fr + 8fr gray 20.00 20.00
B298 SP200 30fr + 9fr rose brn 21.00 21.00
B299 SP200 50fr + 15fr bl grn 24.00 24.00
Nos. B294-B299 (6) 106.00 106.00

See Nos. B321-B326.

1955, Dec. 17 **Cross in Red**

Design: 15fr+5fr, Child with Goose, by Boethus of Chalcedon.

B300 SP201 12fr + 3fr cl 4.75 4.75
B301 SP201 15fr + 5fr dk bl 4.75 4.75
a. Booklet pane of 10 57.50

The surtax was for the Red Cross.

Francois of Taxis SP202

1956, Mar. 17 **Engr.** ***Perf. 13***

B302 SP202 12fr + 3fr ultra, grn & dk brn 2.00 2.00

Stamp Day, March 17-18, 1956.

Portrait Type of 1954

Portraits: No. 303, Guillaume Budé. No. B304, Jean Goujon. No. B305, Samuel de Champlain. No. B306, Jean Simeon Chardin. No. B307, Maurice Barrès. No. B308, Maurice Ravel.

1956, June 9 ***Perf. 13***

B303 SP197 12fr + 3fr saph 5.00 5.00
B304 SP197 12fr + 3fr lil gray 5.00 5.00
B305 SP197 12fr + 3fr brt red 6.25 6.25
B306 SP197 15fr + 5fr grn 6.25 6.25
B307 SP197 15fr + 5fr vio brn 6.75 6.75
B308 SP197 15fr + 5fr dp vio 7.25 7.25
Nos. B303-B308 (6) 36.50 36.50

Peasant Boy by Le Nain — SP203

Design: 15fr+5fr, Gilles by Watteau.

1956, Dec. 8 **Unwmk.**
Cross in Red

B309 SP203 12fr + 3fr ol gray 2.75 2.75
a. Bklt. pane (4 # B309, 4 # B310 with gutter btwn.) 25.00
B310 SP203 15fr + 5fr rose lake 2.75 2.75

The surtax was for the Red Cross.

Genoese Felucca, 1750 SP204

1957, Mar. 16 ***Perf. 13***

B311 SP204 12fr + 3fr bluish gray & brn blk 1.65 1.40

Issued to commemorate the Day of theStamp, March 16, 1957, and to honor the Maritime Postal Service.

Portrait Type of 1954

1957, June 15

Portraits: No. B312, Jean de Joinville. No. B313, Bernard Palissy. No. B314, Quentin de la Tour. No. B315, Hugues Félicité Robert de Lamennais. No. B316, George Sand. No. B317, Jules Guesde.

B312 SP197 12fr + 3fr ol gray & ol grn 2.50 2.50
B313 SP197 12fr + 3fr grnsh blk & grnsh bl 2.75 2.75
B314 SP197 15fr + 5fr cl & brt red 3.25 3.25
B315 SP197 15fr + 5fr ultra & ind 3.50 3.50
B316 SP197 18fr + 7fr grnsh blk & dk grn 3.75 3.75
B317 SP197 18fr + 7fr dk vio brn & red brn 4.50 4.50
Nos. B312-B317 (6) 20.25 20.25

Blind Man and Beggar, Engraving by Jacques Callot — SP205

Design: 20fr+8fr, Women beggars.

1957, Dec. 7 **Engr.** ***Perf. 13***

B318 SP205 15fr + 7fr ultra & red 2.75 2.75
a. Bklt. pane (4 # B318, 4 # B319 with gutter btwn.) 27.50
B319 SP205 20fr + 8fr dk vio brn & red 2.75 2.75

The surtax was for the Red Cross.

Motorized Mail Distribution SP206

1958, Mar. 15

B320 SP206 15fr + 5fr ol gray, ol grn & red brn 1.40 1.10

Stamp Day, Mar. 15.

Portrait Type of 1955

Portraits: No. B321, Joachim du Bellay. No. B322, Jean Bart. No. B323, Denis Diderot. No. B324, Gustave Courbet. 20fr+8fr, J. B. Carpeaux. 35fr+15fr, Toulouse-Lautrec.

1958, June 7 **Engr.** ***Perf. 13***

B321 SP200 12fr + 4fr yel grn 1.90 1.90
B322 SP200 12fr + 4fr dk bl 1.90 1.90
B323 SP200 15fr + 5fr dl cl 2.00 2.00
B324 SP200 15fr + 5fr ultra 2.00 2.00
B325 SP200 20fr + 8fr brt red 2.50 2.50
B326 SP200 35fr + 15fr grn 2.50 2.50
Nos. B321-B326 (6) 12.80 12.80

St. Vincent de Paul — SP207

Portrait: 20fr+8fr, J. H. Dunant.

1958, Dec. 6 **Unwmk.**
Cross in Carmine

B327 SP207 15fr + 7fr grysh grn 1.10 1.10
a. Bklt. pane (4 # B327, 4 # B328 with gutter btwn.) 10.50
B328 SP207 20fr + 8fr vio 1.10 1.10

The surtax was for the Red Cross.

Plane Landing at Night SP208

1959, Mar. 21

B329 SP208 20fr + 5fr sl grn, blk & rose 55 55

Issued for the Day of the Stamp, March 21, and to publicize night air mail service.
The surtax was for the Red Cross.
See No. 1089.

Geoffroi de Villehardouin and Ships — SP209

Designs: No. B331, André Le Nôtre and formal garden. No. B332, Jean Le Rond d'Alembert, books and wheel. No. B333, David d'Angers, statue and building. No. B334, M. F. X. Bichat and torch. No. B335, Frederic Auguste Bartholdi, Statue of Liberty and Lion of Belfort.

1959, June 13 Engr. *Perf. 13*

B330 SP209 15fr + 5fr vio bl 1.25 1.25
B331 SP209 15fr + 5fr dk sl grn 1.25 1.25
B332 SP209 20fr + 10fr ol bis 1.40 1.40
B333 SP209 20fr + 10fr dk gray 1.40 1.40
B334 SP209 30fr + 10fr dk car rose 1.90 1.90
B335 SP209 30fr + 10fr org brn 1.90 1.90
Nos. B330-B335 (6) 9.10 9.10

The surtax was for the Red Cross.

No. 927 Surcharged **FREJUS +5f**

1959, Dec. Typo. *Perf. 14x13½*

B336 A328 25fr + 5fr blk & red 38 38

The surtax was for the flood victims at Frejus.

Charles Michel de l'Epee — SP210

Design: 25fr+10fr, Valentin Hauy.

1959, Dec. 5 Engr. *Perf. 13*
Cross in Carmine

B337 SP210 20fr + 10fr blk & cl 1.00 1.00
a. Bklt. pane (4 # B337, 4 # B338 with gutter btwn.) 9.50
B338 SP210 25fr + 10fr dk bl & blk 1.00 1.00

The surtax was for the Red Cross.

Ship Laying Underwater Cable SP211

1960, Mar. 12

B339 SP211 20c + 5c grnsh bl & dk bl 1.65 1.65

Issued for the Day of the Stamp. The surtax went to the Red Cross.

Refugee Girl Amid Ruins — SP212

1960, Apr. 7

B340 SP212 25c + 10c grn, brn & ind 38 32

Issued to publicize World Refugee Year, July 1, 1959-June 30, 1960. The surtax was for aid to refugees.

Michel de L'Hospital SP213

Designs: No. B342, Henri de la Tour D'Auvergne, Viscount of Turenne. No. B343, Nicolas Boileau (Despreaux). No. B344, Jean-Martin Charcot, M.D. No. B345, Georges Bizet. 50c+15c, Edgar Degas.

1960, June 11 Engr. *Perf. 13*

B341 SP213 10c + 5c pur & rose car 2.50 2.50
B342 SP213 20c + 10c ol & vio brn 2.75 2.75
B343 SP213 20c + 10c Prus grn & dp yel grn 3.25 3.25
B344 SP213 30c + 10c rose car & rose red 3.25 3.25
B345 SP213 30c + 10c dk bl & vio bl 4.00 4.00
B346 SP213 50c + 15c sl bl & gray 4.50 4.50
Nos. B341-B346 (6) 20.25 20.25

The surtax was for the Red Cross.
See Nos. B350-B355.

Staff of the Brotherhood of St. Martin SP214

Letter Carrier, Paris 1760 SP215

Design: 25c+10c, St. Martin, 16th century wood sculpture.

1960, Dec. 3 Unwmk. *Perf. 13*

B347 SP214 20c + 10c rose cl & red 3.00 3.00
a. Bklt. pane (4# B347, 4# B348 with gutter btwn.) 30.00
B348 SP214 25c + 10c lt ultra & red 3.00 3.00

The surtax was for the Red Cross.

1961, March 18 *Perf. 13*

B349 SP215 20c + 5c sl grn, brn & red 1.00 80

Stamp Day. Surtax for Red Cross.

Famous Men Type of 1960

Designs: 15+5c, Bertrand Du Guesclin. No. B351, Pierre Puget. No. B352, Charles Coulomb. 30+10c, Antoine Drouot. 45c+10c, Honoré Daumier. 50+15c, Guillaume Apollinaire.

1961, May 20 Engr.

B350 SP213 15c + 5c red brn & blk 2.00 2.00
B351 SP213 20c + 10c dk grn & lt bl 2.00 2.00
B352 SP213 20c + 10c ver & rose car 2.00 2.00
B353 SP213 30c + 10c blk & brn org 2.00 2.00
B354 SP213 45c + 10c choc & dk grn 3.00 3.00
B355 SP213 50c + 15c dk car rose & vio 3.00 3.00
Nos. B350-B355 (6) 14.00 14.00

"Love" by Rouault SP216

Medieval Royal Messenger SP217

Designs from "Miserere" by Georges Rouault: 25c+10c, "The Blind Consoles the Seeing."

1961, Dec. 2 *Perf. 13*

B356 SP216 20c + 10c brn, blk & red 2.50 2.50
a. Bklt. pane (4 # B356, 4 # B357 with gutter btwn.) 22.50
B357 SP216 25c + 10c brn, blk & red 2.50 2.50

The surtax was for the Red Cross.

1962, March 17

B358 SP217 20c + 5c rose red, bl & sep 90 65

Stamp Day. Surtax for Red Cross.

Denis Papin, Scientist SP218

Rosalie Fragonard by Fragonard SP219

Portraits: No. B360, Edme Bouchardon, sculptor. No. B361, Joseph Lakanal, educator. 30c+10c, Gustave Charpentier, composer. 45c+15c, Edouard Estaunie, writer. 50c+20c, Hyacinthe Vincent, physician and bacteriologist.

1962, June 2 Engr.

B359 SP218 15c + 5c bluish grn & dk gray 3.00 3.00
B360 SP218 20c + 10c cl brn 3.00 3.00
B361 SP218 20c + 10c gray & sl 3.00 3.00
B362 SP218 30c + 10c brt bl & ind 3.75 3.75
B363 SP218 45c + 15c org brn & choc 4.00 4.00
B364 SP218 50c + 20c grnsh bl & blk 4.00 4.00
Nos. B359-B364 (6) 20.75 20.75

The surtax was for the Red Cross.

1962, Dec. 8 Cross in Red

Design: 25c+10c, Child dressed as Pierrot.

B365 SP219 20c + 10c redsh brn 1.25 1.25
a. Bklt. pane (4# B365, 4# B366 with gutter btwn.) 11.00
B366 SP219 25c + 10c dl grn 1.25 1.25

The surtax was for the Red Cross.

Jacques Amyot, Classical Scholar SP220

Portraits: 30c+10c, Pierre de Marivaux, playwright. 50c+20c, Jacques Daviel, surgeon.

1963, Feb. 23 Unwmk. *Perf. 13*

B367 SP220 20c + 10c mar, gray & pur 1.50 1.50
B368 SP220 30c + 10c Prus grn & mar 1.40 1.40
B369 SP220 50c + 20c ultra, ocher & ol 1.50 1.50

The surtax was for the Red Cross.

Roman Chariot SP221

1963, March 16 Engr.

B370 SP221 20c + 5c brn org & vio brn 32 32

Stamp Day. Surtax for Red Cross.

Etienne Méhul, Composer SP222

Designs: 30c+10c, Nicolas-Louis Vauquelin, chemist. 50c+20c, Alfred de Vigny, poet.

1963, May 25 Unwmk. *Perf. 13*

B371 SP222 20c + 10c dp bl, dk brn & dp org 1.75 1.75
B372 SP222 30c + 10c mag, gray ol & blk 1.40 1.40
B373 SP222 50c + 20c sl, blk & brn 2.25 2.25

The surtax was for the Red Cross.

"Child with Grapes" by David d'Angers and Centenary Emblem — SP223

Design: 25c+10c, "The Fifer," by Edouard Manet.

1963, Dec. 9 Unwmk. *Perf. 13*

B374 SP223 20c + 10c blk & red 70 70
a. Bklt. pane (4# B374, 4# B375 with gutter btwn.) 5.75
B375 SP223 25c + 10c sl grn & red 70 70

Issued to commemorate the centenary of the International and the French Red Cross. The surtax was for the Red Cross.

Post Rider, 18th Century SP224

1964, March 14 Engr.

B376 SP224 20c + 5c Prus grn 30 25

Issued for Stamp Day.

Resistance Memorial by Watkin, Luxembourg Gardens — SP225

De Gaulle's 1940 Poster "A Tous les Francais" SP226

Allied Troops Landing in Normandy and Provence SP227

Designs: 20c+5c, "Deportation," concentration camp with watchtower and barbed wire. No. B380, Street fighting in Paris and Strasbourg.

1964 Engr. *Perf. 13*

B377 SP225 20c + 5c sl blk 75 75

Perf. 12x13

B378 SP226 25c + 5c dk red, bl, red & blk 1.00 1.00

Perf. 13

B379 SP227 30c + 5c blk, bl & org brn 75 75
B380 SP227 30c + 5c org brn, cl & blk 90 90
B381 SP225 50c + 5c dk grn 1.00 1.00
Nos. B377-B381 (5) 4.40 4.40

Issued to commemorate the 20th anniversary of liberation from the Nazis.

Issue dates: Nos. B377, B381, Mar. 21; No. B378, June 18; No. B379, June 6; No. B380, Aug. 22.

President Rene Coty SP229

Jean Nicolas Corvisart SP230

Portraits: No. B383, John Calvin. No. B384, Pope Sylvester II (Gerbert).

1964 Unwmk. *Perf. 13*

B382 SP229 30c + 10c dp cl & blk 32 32
B383 SP229 30c + 10c dk grn, blk & brn 32 32
B384 SP229 30c + 10c sl & cl 32 32

The surtax was for the Red Cross.

Issue dates: No. B382, Apr. 25; No. B383, May 25; No. B384, June 1.

1964, Dec. 12 Engr.

Cross in Carmine

Portrait; 25c+10c, Dominique Larrey.

B385 SP230 20c + 10c blk 38 30
a. Bklt. pane (4# B385, 4# B386 with gutter btwn.) 3.75
B386 SP230 25c + 10c blk 38 30

Issued to honor Jean Nicolas Corvisart (1755-1821), physician of Napoleon I, and Dominique Larrey (1766-1842), Chief Surgeon of the Imperial Armies. The surtax was for the Red Cross.

Paul Dukas, Composer — SP231

Portraits: No. B387, Duke François de La Rochefoucauld, writer. No. B388, Nicolas Poussin, painter. No. B389, Duke Charles of Orleans, poet.

1965, Feb. Engr. *Perf. 13*

B387 SP231 30c + 10c org brn & dk bl 48 48
B388 SP231 30c + 10c car & dk red brn 48 48
B389 SP231 40c + 10c dk red brn, dk red & Prus bl 60 60
B390 SP231 40c + 10c dk brn & sl bl 60 60

The surtax was for the Red Cross.

Nos. B387 and B390 were issued Feb. 13; Nos. B388-B389 were issued Feb. 20.

Packet "La Guienne" SP232

1965, Mar. 29 Unwmk. *Perf. 13*

B391 SP232 25c + 10c ultra, blk & sl grn 55 55

Issued for Stamp Day, 1965. "La Guienne" was used for transatlantic mail service. Surtax was for the Red Cross.

Infant with Spoon by Auguste Renoir — SP233

Design: 30c+10c, Coco Writing (Renoir's daughter Claude).

1965, Dec. 11 Engr. *Perf. 13*

Cross in Carmine

B392 SP233 25c + 10c sl 25 25
a. Bklt. pane (4# B392, 4# B393 with gutter btwn.) 3.00
B393 SP233 30c + 10c dl red brn 32 32

The surtax was for the Red Cross.

Francois Mansart and Carnavalet Palace, Paris SP234

Designs: No. B395, St. Pierre Fourier and Basilica of St. Pierre Fourier, Mirecourt. No. B396, Marcel Proust and St. Hilaire Bridge, Illiers. No. B397, Gabriel Faure, monument and score of "Penelope." No. B398, Elie Metchnikoff, microscope and Pasteur Institute. No. B399, Hippolyte Taine and birthplace.

1966 Engr. *Perf. 13*

B394 SP234 30c + 10c dk red brn & grn 38 38
B395 SP234 30c + 10c blk & gray grn 38 38
B396 SP234 30c + 10c ind, sep & grn 38 38
B397 SP234 30c + 10c bis brn & ind 38 38
B398 SP234 30c + 10c blk & dl brn 38 38
B399 SP234 30c + 10c grn & ol brn 38 38
Nos. B394-B399 (6) 2.28 2.28

The surtax was for the Red Cross.

Issue dates: Nos. B394-B396, Feb. 12. Others, June 25.

Engraver Cutting Die and Tools SP235

1966, March 19 Engr. *Perf. 13*

B400 SP235 25c + 10c sl, dk brn & dp org 45 45

Stamp Day. Surtax for Red Cross.

Angel of Victory, Verdun Fortress, Marching Troops SP236

First Aid on Battlefield, 1859 SP237

1966, May 28 *Perf. 13*

B401 SP236 30c + 5c Prus bl, ultra & dk bl 32 32

Victory of Verdun, 50th anniversary.

1966, Dec. 10 Engr. *Perf. 13*

Cross in Carmine

Design: 30c+10c, Nurse giving first aid to child, 1966.

B402 SP237 25c + 10c grn 38 38
a. Bklt pane (4 #B402, 4 #B403 with gutter btwn.) 3.75
B403 SP237 30c + 10c sl 38 38

The surtax was for the Red Cross.

Emile Zola — SP238

Letter Carrier, 1865 — SP239

Portraits: No. B405, Beaumarchais (pen name of Pierre Augustin Caron). No. B406, St. Francois de Sales (1567-1622). No. B407, Albert Camus (1913-1960).

1967 Engr. *Perf. 13*

B404 SP238 30c + 10c sl bl & bl 42 42
B405 SP238 30c + 10c rose brn & lil 42 42
B406 SP238 30c + 10c dl vio & pur 42 42
B407 SP238 30c + 10c brn & dl cl 42 42

The surtax was for the Red Cross.

Issue dates: Nos. B404-B405, Feb. 4. Others, June 24.

1967, Apr. 8

B408 SP239 25c + 10c ind, grn & red 32 32

Issued for Stamp Day.

Ivory Flute Player SP240

Ski Jump and Long Distance Skiing SP241

Design: 30c+10c, Violin player, ivory carving.

1967, Dec. 16 Engr. *Perf. 13*

Cross in Carmine

B409 SP240 25c + 10c dl vio & lt brn 38 38
a. Bklt. pane (4 #B409, 4 #B410 with gutter btwn.) 3.75
B410 SP240 30c + 10c grn & lt brn 38 38

The surtax was for the Red Cross.

1968, Jan. 27

Designs: 40c+10c, Ice hockey. 60c+20c, Olympic flame and snowflakes. 75c+25c, Woman figure skater. 95c+35c, Slalom.

B411 SP241 30c + 10c ver, gray & brn 25 25
B412 SP241 40c + 10c lil, lem & brt mag 32 32
B413 SP241 60c + 20c dk grn, org & brt vio 45 45
B414 SP241 75c + 25c brt pink, yel grn & blk 60 60
B415 SP241 95c + 35c bl, brt pink & red brn 75 75
Nos. B411-B415 (5) 2.37 2.37

Issued for the 10th Winter Olympic Games, Grenoble, Feb. 6-18.

Rural Mailman, 1830 — SP242

1968, Mar. 16 Engr. *Perf. 13*

B416 SP242 25c + 10c bl gray, ultra & red 30 30

Issued for Stamp Day.

François Couperin, Composer, and Instruments SP243

Portraits: No. B418, Gen. Louis Desaix de Veygoux (1768-1800) and scene showing his death at the Battle of Marengo, Italy. No. B419, Saint-Pol-Roux (pen name of Paul-Pierre Roux, 1861-1940), Christ on the Cross and ruins of Camaret-sur-Mer. No. B420, Paul Claudel (poet and diplomat, 1868-1955) and Joan of Arc at the stake.

1968 Engr. *Perf. 13*

B417 SP243 30c + 10c pur & rose lil 30 30
B418 SP243 30c + 10c dk grn & brn 30 30
B419 SP243 30c + 10c cop red & ol bis 30 30
B420 SP243 30c + 10c dk brn & lil 30 30

Issue dates: Nos. B417-B418, Mar. 23; Nos. B419-B420, July 6.

Spring, by Nicolas Mignard — SP244

Designs (Paintings by Nicolas Mignard); 30c+10c, Fall. No. B423, Summer. No. B424, Winter.

1968-69 Engr. *Perf. 13*
Cross in Carmine

B421 SP244 25c + 10c pur & sl bl 32 32
a. Bklt. pane (4 #B421, 4 #B422 with gutter btwn.) 3.00
B422 SP244 30c + 10c brn & rose car 32 32
B423 SP244 40c + 15c dk brn & brn ('69) 40 40
a. Bklt. pane (4 #B423, 4 #B424 with gutter btwn.) 3.75
B424 SP244 40c + 15c pur & Prus bl ('69) 40 40

The surtax was for the Red Cross.

Mailmen's Omnibus, 1881 SP245

1969, Mar. 15 Engr. *Perf. 13*
B425 SP245 30c + 10c brn, grn & blk 30 30

Issued for Stamp Day.

Gen. Francois Marceau — SP246

Portraits: No. B427, Charles Augustin Sainte-Beuve (1804-1869), writer. No. B428, Albert Roussel (1869-1937), musician. No. B429, Marshal Jean Lannes (1769-1809). No. B430, Georges Cuvier (1769-1832), naturalist. No. B431, André Gide, (1869-1951), writer.

1969
B426 SP246 50c + 10c brn red 60 60
B427 SP246 50c + 10c sl bl 60 60
B428 SP246 50c + 10c dp vio bl 60 60
B429 SP246 50c + 10c choc 60 60
B430 SP246 50c + 10c dp plum 60 60
B431 SP246 50c + 10c bl grn 60 60
Nos. B426-B431 (6) 3.60 3.60

The surtax was for the Red Cross.
Issue dates: Nos. B426-B428, Mar. 24. No. B429, May 10, Nos. B430-B431, May 17.

Gen. Jacques Leclerc, La Madeleine and Battle — SP247

1969, Aug. 23 Engr. *Perf. 13*
B432 SP247 45c + 10c sl & ol 65 65

Issued to commemorate the 25th anniversary of the liberation of Paris, Aug. 25, 1944.

Same Inscribed "Liberation de Strasbourg"

1969, Nov. 22 Engr. *Perf. 13*
B433 SP247 70c + 10c brn, choc & ol 1.25 1.25

Issued to commemorate the 25th anniversary of the liberation of Strasbourg.

Philibert Delorme, Architect, and Chateau d'Anet SP248

Designs: No. B435, Louis Le Vau (1612-1670), architect, and Vaux-le-Vicomte Chateau, Paris. No. B436, Prosper Merimee (1803-1870), writer, and Carmen. No. B437, Alexandre Dumas (1820-1870), writer, and Three Musketeers. No. B438, Edouard Branly (1844-1940), physicist, electric circuit and convent of the Carmes, Paris. No. B439, Maurice de Broglie (1875-1960), physicist, and X-ray spectrograph.

1970 Engr. *Perf. 13*
B434 SP248 40c + 10c sl grn 60 60
B435 SP248 40c + 10c dk car 60 60
B436 SP248 40c + 10c Prus bl 60 60
B437 SP248 40c + 10c vio bl 60 60
B438 SP248 40c + 10c dp brn 60 60
B439 SP248 40c + 10c dk gray 60 60
Nos. B434-B439 (6) 3.60 3.60

The surtax was for the Red Cross.
Issue dates: No. B434-B436, Feb. 14; Nos. B437-B439, Apr. 11.

City Mailman, 1830 SP249

"Life and Death" SP250

1970, Mar. 14
B440 SP249 40c + 10c blk, ultra & dk car rose 45 45

Issued for Stamp Day.

1970, Apr. 4
B441 SP250 40c + 10c brt bl, ol & car rose 40 40

Issued to publicize the fight against cancer in connection with Health Day, Apr. 7.

Marshal de Lattre de Tassigny — SP251

1970, May 8 Engr. *Perf. 13*
B442 SP251 40c + 10c sl & vio bl 65 45

Issued to commemorate the 25th anniversary of the entry into Berlin of French troops under Marshal Jean de Lattre de Tassigny, May 8, 1945.

Lord and Lady, Dissay Chapel Fresco — SP252

Design: No. B444, Angel holding whips, from fresco in Dissay Castle Chapel, Vienne, c. 1500.

1970, Dec. 12 Engr. *Perf. 13*
Cross in Carmine

B443 SP252 40c + 15c grn 80 75
a. Bklt. pane (4 #B443, 4 #B444 with gutter btwn.) 8.50
B444 SP252 40c + 15c cop red 80 75

The surtax was for the Red Cross.

Daniel-Francois Auber and "Fra Diavolo" Music — SP253

Designs: No. B446, Gen. Charles Diego Brosset (1898-1944), and Basilica of Fourviere. No. B447, Victor Grignard (1871-1935), chemist, and Nobel Prize medal. No. B448, Henri Farman (1874-1958) and plane. No. B449, Gen. Charles Georges Delestraint (1879-1945) and scroll. No. B450, Jean Eugene Robert-Houdin (1805-1871) and magician's act.

1971 Engr. *Perf. 13*
B445 SP253 50c + 10c brn vio & brn 1.25 1.00
B446 SP253 50c + 10c dk sl grn & ol gray 1.25 1.00
B447 SP253 50c + 10c brn red & ol 1.25 1.00
B448 SP253 50c + 10c vio bl & vio 1.25 1.00
B449 SP253 50c + 10c pur & cl 1.40 1.25
B450 SP253 50c + 10c sl grn & bl grn 1.40 1.25
Nos. B445-B450 (6) 7.80 6.50

The surtax was for the Red Cross.
Issue dates: Nos. B445-B446, Mar. 6. No. B447, May 8. No. B448, May 29. Nos. B449-B450, Oct. 16.

Army Post Office, 1914-1918 SP254

1971, March 27 Engr. *Perf. 13*
B451 SP254 50c + 10c ol, brn & bl 55 48

Stamp Day, 1971.

Girl with Dog, by Greuze SP255

Aristide Bergès (1833-1904) SP256

Design: 50c+10c, "The Dead Bird," by Jean-Baptiste Greuze (1725-1805).

1971, Dec. 11
Cross in Carmine

B452 SP255 30c + 10c vio bl 80 80
a. Bklt. pane (4 #B452, 4 #B453 with gutter btwn.) 7.50
B453 SP255 50c + 10c dp car 80 80

The surtax was for the Red Cross.

1972 Engr. *Perf. 13*

Portraits: No. B455, Paul de Chomedey (1612-1676), founder of Montreal, and arms of Neuville-sur-Vanne. No. B456, Edouard Belin (1876-1963), inventor. No. B457, Louis Blériot (1872-1936), aviation pioneer. No. B458, Adm. François Joseph, Count de Grasse (1722-1788), hero of the American Revolution. No. B459, Théophile Gautier (1811-1872), writer.

B454 SP256 50c + 10c blk & grn 1.25 1.25
B455 SP256 50c + 10c blk & bl 1.25 1.25
B456 SP256 50c + 10c blk & lil rose 1.25 1.25
B457 SP256 50c + 10c red & blk 1.25 1.25
B458 SP256 50c + 10c org & blk 1.65 1.65
B459 SP256 50c + 10c blk & brn 1.65 1.65
Nos. B454-B459 (6) 8.30 8.30

The surtax was for the Red Cross.
Issue dates: Nos. B454-B455, Feb. 19; No. B456, June 24; No. B457, July 1; Nos. B458-B459, Sept. 9.

Rural Mailman, 1894 SP257

Nicolas Desgenettes SP258

1972, Mar. 18 Engr. *Perf. 13*
B460 SP257 50c + 10c bl, yel & ol gray 75 60

Stamp Day 1972.

1972, Dec. 16 Engr. *Perf. 13*

Designs: 30c+10c, ReneNicolas Dufriche, Baron Desgenettes, M.D. (1762-1837). 50c+10c, François Joseph Broussais, M.D. (1772-1838).

B461 SP258 30c + 10c sl grn & red 95 80
a. Bklt. pane (4 #B461, 4 #B462 with gutter btwn.) 9.25
B462 SP258 50c + 10c red 95 80

The surtax was for the Red Cross.

Gaspard de Coligny — SP259

Portraits: No. B463, Gaspard de Coligny (1519-1572), admiral and Huguenot leader. No. B464, Ernest Renan (1823-1892), philologist and historian. No. B465, Alberto Santos Dumont (1873-1932), Brazilian aviator. No. B466, Gabrielle-Sidonie Colette (1873-1954), writer. No. B467, Rene Duguay-Trouin (1673-1736), naval commander. No. B468, Louis Pasteur (1822-1895), chemist, bacteriologist. No. B469, Tony Garnier (1869-1948), architect.

1973 Engr. *Perf. 13*
B463 SP259 50c + 10c multi 1.25 1.00
B464 SP259 50c + 10c multi 1.25 1.00
B465 SP259 50c + 10c multi 1.25 1.00
B466 SP259 50c + 10c multi 1.25 1.00
B467 SP259 50c + 10c multi 1.25 1.00
B468 SP259 50c + 10c multi 1.25 1.10
B469 SP259 50c + 10c multi 1.25 1.10
Nos. B463-B469 (7) 8.75 7.20

Issue dates: No. B463, Feb. 17; No. B464, Apr. 28; No. B465, May 26; No. B466, June 2;

No. B467, June 9; No. B468, Oct. 6; No. B469, Nov. 17.

Mail Coach, 1835
SP260

1973, Mar. 24 **Engr.** ***Perf. 13***

B470 SP260 50c + 10c grnsh bl 55 50

Stamp Day, 1973.

Mary Magdalene
SP261

St. Louis-Marie de Montfort
SP262

Design: 50c+10c, Mourning woman. Designs are from 15th century Tomb of Tonnerre.

1973, Dec. 1

B471 SP261 30c + 10c sl grn & red 60 60
a. Bklt. pane (4 #B471, 4 #B472 with gutter btwn.) 6.00
B472 SP261 50c + 10c dk gray & red 75 75

Surtax was for the Red Cross.

1974, Feb. 23 **Engr.** ***Perf. 13***

Portraits: No. B474, Francis Poulenc (1899-1963), composer. No. B475, Jules Barbey d'Aurevilly (1808-1889), writer. No. B476, Jean Giraudoux (1882-1944), writer.

B473 SP262 50c + 10c multi 1.65 1.65
B474 SP262 50c + 10c multi 1.10 1.10
B475 SP262 80c + 15c multi 1.25 1.25
B476 SP262 80c + 15c multi 1.25 1.25

Issue dates: No. B473, Mar. 9; No. B474, July 20; Nos. B475-B476, Nov. 16.

Automatically Sorted Letters — SP263

1974, Mar. 9 **Engr.** ***Perf. 13***

B477 SP263 50c + 10c multi 38 32

Stamp Day 1974. Automatic letter sorting center, Orleans-la-Source, opened Jan. 30, 1973.

Order of Liberation and 5 Honored Cities — SP264

1974, June 15 **Engr.** ***Perf. 13***

B478 SP264 1fr + 10c multi 75 60

30th anniversary of liberation from the Nazis.

"Summer"
SP265

"Winter"
SP266

Designs: B481, "Spring" (girl on swing). B482, "Fall" (umbrella and rabbits).

1974, Nov. 30 **Engr.** ***Perf. 13***

B479 SP265 60c + 15c multi 65 60
a. Bklt. pane (4 #B479, 4 #B480 with gutter btwn.) 6.00
B480 SP266 80c + 15c multi 80 75

1975, Nov. 29

B481 SP265 60c + 15c multi 55 45
a. Booklet pane (4 #B481, 4 #B482 with gutter btwn.) 6.00
B482 SP266 80c + 20c multi 85 75

Surtax was for the Red Cross.

Dr. Albert Schweitzer
SP267

Edmond Michelet
SP268

André Siegfried and Map
SP269

Portraits: No. B483, Albert Schweitzer (1875-1965), medical missionary, birth centenary. No. B484, Edmond Michelet (1899-1970), Resistance hero, statesman. No. B485, Robert Schuman (1886-1963), promoter of United Europe. No. B486, Eugene Thomas (1903-1969), minister of PTT. No. B487, Andre Siegfried (1875-1959), political science professor, writer, birth centenary.

1975 **Engr.** ***Perf. 13***

B483 SP267 80c + 20c multi 60 60
B484 SP268 80c + 20c bl & ind 60 60
B485 SP268 80c + 20c blk & ind 60 60
B486 SP268 80c + 20c blk & sl 60 60
B487 SP269 80c + 20c blk & bl 65 65
Nos. B483-B487 (5) 3.05 3.05

Issue dates: No. B483, Jan. 11; No. B484, Feb. 22; No. B485, May 10; No. B486, June 28; No. B487, Nov. 15.

Second Republic Mailman's Badge — SP270

1975, Mar. 8 **Photo.**

B488 SP270 80c + 20c multi 55 52

Stamp Day.

The Catalogue editors cannot undertake to appraise, identify or judge the genuineness or condition of stamps.

"Sage" Type of 1876
SP271

Marshal A. J. de Moncey
SP272

1976, Mar. 13 **Engr.** ***Perf. 13***

B489 SP271 80c + 20c blk & lil 60 50

Stamp Day 1976.

1976 **Engr.** ***Perf. 13***

Designs: No. B491, Max Jacob (1876-1944), Dadaist writer, by Picasso. No. B492, Jean Mounet-Sully (1841-1916), actor. No. B493, Gen. Pierre Daumesnil (1776-1832). No. B494, Eugene Fromentin (1820-1876), painter.

B490 SP272 80c + 20c multi 65 65
B491 SP272 80c + 20c red brn & ol 65 65
B492 SP272 80c + 20c multi 65 65
B493 SP272 1fr + 20c multi 75 75
B494 SP272 1fr + 20c multi 75 75
Nos. B490-B494 (5) 3.45 3.45

Issue dates: No. B490, May 22; No. B491, July 22. No. B492, Aug. 28; No. B493, Sept. 4; No. B494, Sept. 25.

Anna de Noailles
SP273

St. Barbara
SP274

1976, Nov. 6 **Engr.** ***Perf. 13***

B495 SP273 1fr + 20c multi 75 75

Anna de Noailles (1876-1933), writer and poet.

1976, Nov. 20

Design: 1fr+25c, Cimmerian Sibyl. Sculptures from Brou Cathedral.

Cross in Carmine

B496 SP274 80c + 20c vio 75 65
a. Booklet pane (4 #B496, 4 #B497 with gutter between) 7.50
B497 SP274 1fr + 25c dk brn 90 80

Surtax was for the Red Cross.

Marckolsheim Relay Station Sign — SP275

1977, Mar. 26 **Engr.** ***Perf. 13***

B498 SP275 1fr + 20c multi 65 65

Stamp Day.

Edouard Herriot, Statesman and Writer
SP276

Christmas Figurine, Provence
SP277

Designs: No. B500, AbbéBreuil (1877-1961), archaeologist. No. B501, Guillaume de Machault (1305-1377), poet and composer. No. B502, Charles Cross (1842-1888).

1977 **Engr.** ***Perf. 13***

B499 SP276 1fr + 20c multi 80 80
B500 SP276 1fr + 20c multi 80 80
B501 SP276 1fr + 20c multi 80 80
B502 SP276 1fr + 20c multi 80 80

Issue dates: No. B499, Oct. 8; No. B500, Oct. 15; No. B501, Nov. 12; No. B502, Dec. 3.

1977, Nov. 26

Design: 1fr+25c, Christmas figurine (woman), Provence.

B503 SP277 80c + 20c red & ind 65 65
a. Booklet pane (4 #B503, 4 #B504 with gutter between) 6.50
B504 SP277 1fr + 25c red & sl grn 80 80

Surtax was for the Red Cross.

Marie Noel, Writer
SP278

Mail Collection, 1900
SP279

Designs: No. B506, Georges Bernanos (1888-1948), writer. No. B507, Leo Tolstoi (1828-1910), Russian writer. No. B508, Charles Marie Leconte de Lisle (1818-1894), poet. No. B509, Voltaire (1694-1778) and Jean Jacques Rousseau (1712-1778). No. B510, Claude Bernard (1813-1878), physiologist.

1978 **Engr.** ***Perf. 13***

B505 SP278 1fr + 20c multi 75 75
B506 SP278 1fr + 20c multi 75 75
B507 SP278 1fr + 20c multi 75 75
B508 SP278 1fr + 20c multi 75 75
B509 SP278 1fr + 20c multi 75 75
B510 SP278 1fr + 20c multi 75 75
Nos. B505-B510 (6) 4.50 4.50

Issued dates: No. B505, Feb. 11; No. B506, Feb. 18; No. B507, Apr. 15; No. B508, Mar. 26; No. B509, July 1; No. B510, Sept. 16.

1978, Apr. 8 **Engr.** ***Perf. 13***

B511 SP279 1fr + 20c multi 65 60

Stamp Day 1978.

The Hare and the Tortoise — SP280

Design: 1.20fr+30c, The City Rat and the Country Rat.

1978, Dec. 2 Engr. Perf. 13

B512 SP280 1fr + 25c multi 75 60
a. Booklet pane (4 #B512,4 #B513 with gutter between) 7.50
B513 SP280 1.20fr + 30c multi 90 75

Surtax was for the Red Cross.

Ladislas Marshal de Bercheny (1689-1778) — SP281

Design: No. B515, Leon Jouhaux (1879-1954), labor leader. No. B516, Peter Abelard (1079-1142), theologian and writer. No. B517, Georges Courteline (1860-1929), humorist. No. B518, Simone Weil (1909-1943), social philosopher. No. B519, André Malraux (1901-1976), novelist.

1979 Engr. Perf. 13

B514 SP281 1.20fr + 30c multi 80 80
B515 SP281 1.20fr + 30c multi 95 95
B516 SP281 1.20fr + 30c multi 80 80
B517 SP281 1.20fr + 30c multi 80 80
B518 SP281 1.30fr + 30c multi 90 90
B519 SP281 1.30fr + 30c multi 90 90
Nos. B514-B519 (6) 5.15 5.15

Issue dates: Nos. B514, Jan. 13; B515, May 12; B516, June 9; B517, June 25; B518, Nov. 12; B519, Nov. 26.

General Post Office, from 1908 Post Card SP282

1979, Mar. 10 Engr. Perf. 13

B520 SP282 1.20fr + 30c multi 75 52

Stamp Day 1979.

Woman, Stained-Glass Window — SP283

Stained-glass windows, Church of St. Joan of Arc, Rouen: 1.30fr + 30c, Simon the Magician.

1979, Dec. 1

B521 SP283 1.10fr + 30c multi 65 60
a. Bklt. pane (4# B521, 4# B522 with gutter between) 6.00
B522 SP283 1.30fr + 30c multi 80 65

Surtax was for the Red Cross.

Eugene Viollet le Duc (1814-1879), Architect SP284

Jean-Marie de Le Mennais (1780-1860), Priest and Educator — SP285

Designs No. B524, Jean Monnet (1888-1979), economist and diplomat. No. B526, Frederic Mistral (1830-1914), poet. No. B527, Saint-John Perse (Alexis Leger, 1887-1975), poet and diplomat. No. B528, Pierre Paul de Riquet (1604-1680), canal builder.

1980 Engr. Perf. 13

B523 SP284 1.30fr + 30c multi 85 75
B524 SP284 1.30fr + 30c multi 95 95
B525 SP285 1.40fr + 30c bl 95 90
B526 SP285 1.40fr + 30c blk 95 90
B527 SP285 1.40fr + 30c multi 95 90
B528 SP284 1.40fr + 30c multi 95 90
Nos. B523-B528 (6) 5.60 5.30

Issue dates: No. B523, Feb. 16; No. B524, Nos. B525-B526, Sept. 6; Nos. B527-B528, Oct. 11.

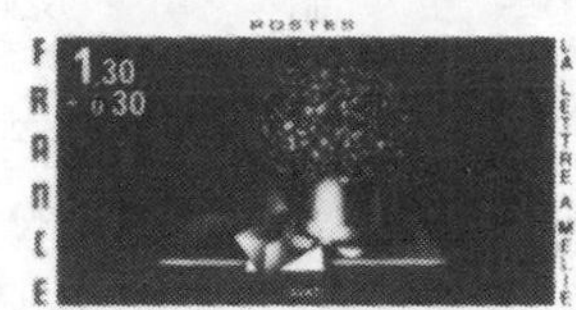

The Letter to Melie, by Avati, Stamp Day, 1980 — SP286

1980, Mar. 8 Photo.

B529 SP286 1.30fr + 30c multi 80 65

Filling the Granaries, Choir Stall Detail, Amiens Cathedral — SP287

Design: 1.40fr + 30c, Grapes from the Promised Land.

1980, Dec. 6 Engr. Perf. 13

B530 SP287 1.20fr + 30c red & dk red brn 65 55
B531 SP287 1.40fr + 30c red & dk red brn 75 65
a. Bklt. pane (4 #B530, 4 #B531 with gutter between) 5.25

Sister Anne-Marie Javouhey (1779-1851), Founded Congregation of St. Joseph of Cluny — SP288

Designs: No. B532, Louis Armand (1905-1971), railway engineer. B533, Louis Jouvet (1887-1951), theater director. B534, Marc Boegner (1881-1970), peace worker. No. B536, Jacques Offenbach (1819-1880), composer. No. B537, Pierre Teilhard de Chardin (1881-1955), philosopher.

1981 Engr. Perf. 13

B532 SP288 1.20 + 30c multi 70 70
B533 SP288 1.20 + 30c multi 70 70
B534 SP288 1.40 + 30c multi 1.10 75
B535 SP288 1.40 + 30c multi 85 75
B536 SP288 1.40 + 30c multi 85 75
B537 SP288 1.40 + 30c multi 85 75
Nos. B532-B537 (6) 5.05 4.40

Issue dates: #B532, May 23; #B533, June 13; #B534, Nov. 14; #B535, Feb. 7; #B536, Feb. 14; #B537, May 23.

The Love Letter, by Goya — SP289

1981, Mar. 7 Perf. 13x12½

B538 SP289 1.40 + 30c multi 75 50

Stamp Day 1981.

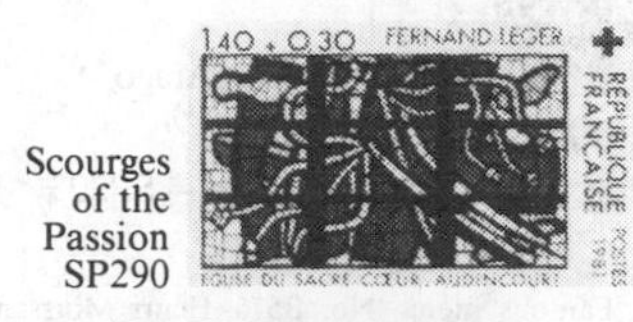

Scourges of the Passion SP290

Guillaume Postel (1510-1581), Theologian — SP291

Stained-glass Windows, Church of the Sacred Heart, Audincourt: 1.60fr + 30c, "Peace."

1981, Dec. 5 Photo. Perf. 13

B539 SP290 1.40 + 30c multi 70 65
B540 SP290 1.60 + 30c multi 80 70
a. Bklt. pane (4 #B539, 4 #B540 with gutter between) 6.00

1982 Engr. Perf. 13

Designs: No. B542, Henri Mondor (1885-1962), physician. No. B543, Andre Chantemesse (1851-1919), Scientist. No. B544, Louis Pergaud (1882-1915), writer. No. B545, Robert Debre (1882-1978), writer. No. B546, Gustave Eiffel (1832-1923), engineer.

B541 SP291 1.40 + 30c multi 90 75
B542 SP291 1.40 + 30c dk brn & dk bl 75 60
B543 SP291 1.60 + 30c multi 85 80
B544 SP291 1.60 + 40c multi 1.10 75
B545 SP291 1.60 + 40c dk bl 90 75
B546 SP291 1.80 + 40c sep 90 90
Nos. B541-B546 (6) 5.40 4.55

Woman Reading, by Picasso — SP292

1982, Mar. 27 Perf. 13x12½

B547 SP292 1.60 + 40c multi 1.25 65

Stamp Day.

Five Weeks in a Balloon, by Jules Verne — SP293

Design: 20,000 Leagues under the Sea.

1982, Nov. 20 Perf. 13

B548 SP293 1.60 + 30c multi 90 80
B549 SP293 1.80 + 40c multi 90 80
a. Bklt. pane (4 #B548, 4 #B549 with gutter between) 6.50

Surtax was for Red Cross.

Andre Messager (1853-1929) — SP294

Designs: No. B551, J.A. Gabriel (1698-1782), architect. No. B552, Hector Berlioz (1803-1869), composer. No. B553, Max Fouchet (1913-1980). No. B554, Rene Cassin (1887-1976). No. B555, Stendhal (Marie Henri Beyle, 1783-1842).

1983 Engr. Perf. 12½x13

B550 SP294 1.60 + 30c multi 75 75
B551 SP294 1.60 + 30c multi 75 75
B552 SP294 1.80 + 40c dp lil & blk 85 85
B553 SP294 1.80 + 40c multi 85 85
B554 SP294 2fr + 40c multi 90 90
B555 SP294 2fr + 40c multi 90 90
Nos. B550-B555 (6) 5.00 5.00

Issue dates: No. B550, Jan. 15; No. B551, Apr. 16; No. B552, Jan. 22; No. B553, Apr. 30; No. B554, June 25; No. B555, Nov. 12.

Man Dictating a Letter, by Rembrandt — SP295

Perf. 13x12½

1983, Feb. 26 Photo. Engr.

B556 SP295 1.80 + 40c multi 80 45

Stamp Day.

Virgin with Child, Baillon, 14th Cent. — SP296

Design: No. B558, Virgin with Child, Genainville, 16th Cent.

1983, Nov. 26 Engr. Perf. 13

B557 SP296 1.60 + 40c shown 60 50
B558 SP296 2fr + 40c multi 75 60
a. Bklt pane (4 #B557, 4 #B558 with gutter between) 6.50

Emile Littre (1801-1881), Physician SP297

Designs: No. B560, Jean Zay (1904-44). No. B561, Pierre Corneille (1606-1684). No. B562, Gaston Bachelard (1884-1962). No. B563, Jean Paulhan (1884-1968). No. B564, Evariste Galois (1811-1832).

1984 Engr. Perf. 13

B559 SP297 1.60fr + 40c plum & blk 65 65
B560 SP297 1.60fr + 40c dk grn & blk 65 65

B561 SP297 1.70fr + 40c dp vio & blk 52 52
B562 SP297 2fr + 40c gray & blk 56 56
B563 SP297 2.10fr + 40c dk brn & blk 58 58
B564 SP297 2.10fr + 40c ultra & blk 58 58

Diderot Holding a Letter, by L.M. Van Loo — SP298

1984, Mar. 17 Engr. *Perf. 12½x13*
B565 SP298 2fr + 40c multi 1.00 60

The Rose Basket, by Caly — SP299

1984, Nov. 24 Photo. *Perf. 12½x13*
B566 SP299 2.10fr + 50c pnksh (basket) & multi 60 60
a. Sal (basket) & multi, perf. 13½x13 60 60
b. Bklt pane of #B566a + 2 labels 6.00

Surtax was for the Red Cross.

Jules Romains (1885-1972) — SP300

Authors: No. B568, Jean-Paul Sartre (1905-1980). No. B569, Romain Rolland (1866-1944). No. B570, Roland Dorgeles (1885-1973). No. B571, Victor Hugo (1802-1885). No. B572, Francois Mauriac (1885-1970).

1985, Feb. 23 Engr. *Perf. 13*
B567 SP300 1.70fr + 40c vio & dp vio *1.65 1.65*
B568 SP300 1.70fr + 40c dp vio & brn vio *1.65 1.65*
B569 SP300 1.70fr + 40c brn vio & dp vio *1.65 1.65*
B570 SP300 2.10fr + 50c brn vio & vio *2.00 2.00*
B571 SP300 2.10fr + 50c vio & brn vio *2.00 2.00*
B572 SP300 2.10fr + 50c dp vio & vio *2.00 2.00*
a. Bklt. pane of 6, #B567-B572 + 2 labels, perf. 15x15½

Stamp Day — SP301

Design: Canceling apparatus invented by Eugene Daguin (1849-1888).

1985, Mar. 16 Engr. *Perf. 12½x13*
B573 SP301 2.10fr + 50c brn blk & bluish gray 58 58

Issenheim Altarpiece Retable — SP302

1985, Nov. 23 Photo.
B574 SP302 2.20fr + .50fr multi 70 70
a. Bklt. pane of 10, perf. 13½x13 7.00

Surtaxed for the Red Cross.

Francois Arago (1786-1853), Physician, Politician — SP303

Famous men: No. B576, Henri Moissan (1852-1907), chemist. No. B577, Henri Fabre (1882-1984), engineer. No. B578, Marc Seguin (1786-1875), engineer. No. B579, Paul Heroult (1863-1914), chemist.

1986, Feb. 22 Engr. *Perf. 13*
B575 SP303 1.80fr + 40c multi 60 12
B576 SP303 1.80fr + 40c multi 60 12
B577 SP303 1.80fr + 40c multi 60 12
B578 SP303 2.20fr + 50c multi 72 14
B579 SP303 2.20fr + 50c multi 72 14
a. Bklt. pane of 5, #B575-B579, + 3 labels 4.00

Pierre Cot (1895-1977) — SP304

1986, Mar. 1 Engr. *Perf. 13x12½*
B580 SP304 2.20fr + 50c brn blk 80 16

Mail Britzska SP305

1986, Apr. 5 *Perf. 13*
B581 SP305 2.20fr + 60c pale tan & dk vio brn 85 18

Engr. *Perf. 13*
B582 SP305 2.20fr + 60c buff & blk 85 18
a. Bklt. pane of 6 + label 5.10

No. B582 issued in booklets only. See Nos. B590-B591.

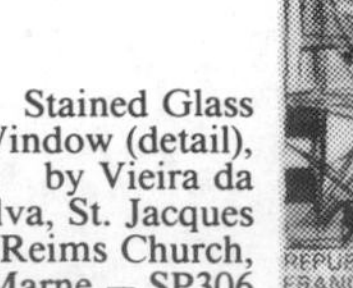

Stained Glass Window (detail), by Vieira da Silva, St. Jacques of Reims Church, Marne — SP306

1986, Nov. 24 Photo. *Perf. 12½x13*
B583 SP306 2.20fr + 60c multi 88 18
a. Bklt. pane of 10, perf. 13½x13 8.80

Surtaxed to benefit the natl. Red Cross.

Physicians and Biologists SP307

Designs: No. B584, Charles Richet (1850-1935). No. B585, Eugene Jamot (1879-1937). No. B586, Bernard Halpern (1904-1978). No. B587, Alexandre Yersin (1863-1943). No. B588, Jean Rostand (1894-1977). No. B589, Jacques Monod (1910-1976).

1987, Feb. 21 Engr. *Perf. 13*
B584 SP307 1.90fr + 50c dp ultra 78 15
B585 SP307 1.90fr + 50c dl lil 78 15
B586 SP307 1.90fr + 50c grnish gray 78 15
B587 SP307 2.20fr + 50c grnish gray 88 18
B588 SP307 2.20fr + 50c dp ultra 88 18
B589 SP307 2.20fr + 50c dl lil 88 18
a. Bklt. pane of 6, # B584-B589 5.00
Nos. B584-B589 (6) 4.98 99

Stamp Day Type of 1986

Design: Berline carriage.

1987, Mar. 14 Engr.
B590 SP305 2.20fr + 60c buff & sepia 95 20

Booklet Stamp

B591 SP305 2.20fr + 60c pale & dk bl 95 20
a. Bklt. pane of 6 + 2 labels 5.75

Stamp Day 1987. No. B591 issued in booklets only.

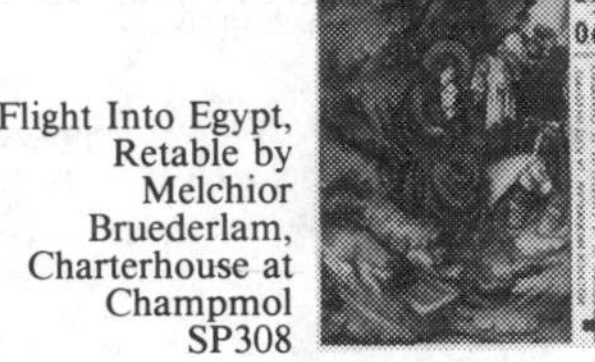

Flight Into Egypt, Retable by Melchior Bruederlam, Charterhouse at Champmol SP308

1987, Nov. 21 Photo. *Perf. 12½x13*
B592 SP308 2.20fr +60c multi 95 18
a. Bklt. pane of 10 + 2 labels 9.50

Surtaxed to benefit the Red Cross.

Explorers SP309

Profiles and maps: No. B593, Marquis Abraham Duquesne (1610-1688), naval commander. No. B594, Pierre Andre de Suffren (1729-1788). No. B595, Jean-Francois de La Perouse (1741-1788). No. B596, Mahe de La Bourdonnais (1699-1753). No. B597, Louis-Antoine de Bougainville (1729-1811). No. B598, Jules Dumont d'Urville (1790-1842).

1988, Feb. 20 Engr. *Perf. 13*
B593 SP309 2fr + 50c multi 92 18
B594 SP309 2fr + 50c multi 92 18
B595 SP309 2fr + 50c multi 92 18
B596 SP309 2.20fr + 50c multi 1.00 20
B597 SP309 2.20fr + 50c multi 1.00 20
B598 SP309 2.20fr + 50c multi 1.00 20
a. Bklt. pane of 6, Nos. B593-B598 5.75
Nos. B593-B598 (6) 5.76 1.14

AIR POST STAMPS

Nos. 127, 130 Overprinted in Dark Blue or Black

Perf. 14x13½

1927, June 25 Unwmk.
C1 A18 2fr org & bl (DB) 165.00 140.00
C2 A18 5fr dk bl & buff (Bk) 165.00 140.00

These stamps were on sale only at the International Aviation Exhibition at Marseilles, June, 1927. One set could be purchased by each holder of an admission ticket. Excellent counterfeits exist.

Nos. 242, 196 Surcharged

10 FR.

1928, Aug. 23
C3 A33 10fr on 90c dl rose 1,500. 1,500.
a. Inverted surcharge *12,000. 12,000.*
b. Space between "10" and bars 6½mm *3,000. 3,000.*
C4 A23 10fr on 1.50fr bl *8,000. 8,000.*
a. Space between "10" and bars 6½mm *10,000. 10,000.*

Nos. C3-C4 received their surcharge in New York by order of the French consulgeneral. They were for use in paying the 10fr fee for letters leaving the liner Ile de France on a catapulted hydroplane when the ship was one day off the coast of France on its eastward voyage.

The normal space between "10" and bars is 4½mm., but on 10 stamps in each pane of 50 the space is 6½mm. Counterfeits exist.

View of Marseille, Church of Notre Dame at Left — AP1

1930-31 Engr. *Perf. 13*
C5 AP1 1.50fr dp car 20.00 2.00
C6 AP1 1.50fr dk bl ('31) 18.00 1.65
a. 1.50fr ultra 40.00 12.00
b. With perf. initials (EIPA 30) 500.00 375.00

No. C6a was sold at the International Air Post Exhibition, Paris, Nov. 6-20, 1930, at face value plus 5 francs, the price of admission. Most of the stamps of the first printing were perforated "EIPA30".

Blériot's Monoplane AP2

1934, Sept. 1 *Perf. 13*
C7 AP2 2.25fr violet 17.00 6.00

Issued in commemoration of the first flight across the English Channel, by Louis Blériot.

Plane over Paris — AP3

1936
C8 AP3 85c dp grn 2.75 1.00
C9 AP3 1.50fr blue 10.00 3.25
C10 AP3 2.25fr violet 20.00 5.50
C11 AP3 2.50fr rose 30.00 6.00
C12 AP3 3fr ultra 18.00 65
C13 AP3 3.50fr org brn 62.50 15.00
C14 AP3 50fr emerald 750.00 250.00
a. 50fr dp grn 1,100. 500.00
Nos. C8-C14 (7) 893.25 281.40

Monoplane over Paris — AP4

Paper with Red Network Overprint

1936, July 10 *Perf. 12½*
C15 AP4 50fr ultra 700.00 275.00

Airplane and Galleon — AP5

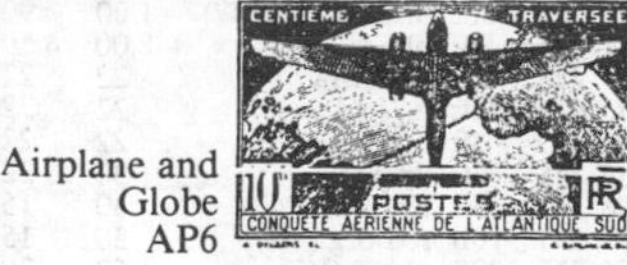

Airplane and Globe AP6

1936, Aug. 17 *Perf. 13*
C16 AP5 1.50fr dk ultra 17.00 2.25
C17 AP6 10fr Prus grn 325.00 100.00

Issued in commemoration of the 100th air mail flight across the South Atlantic Ocean.

Centaur and Plane — AP7

Iris — AP8

Zeus Carrying Hebe — AP9

Chariot of the Sun — AP10

1946-47 **Engr.** **Unwmk.**
C18 AP7 40fr dk grn 50 22
C19 AP8 50fr rose pink 50 22
C20 AP9 100fr dk bl ('47) 4.25 50
C21 AP10 200fr red 3.75 75

Ile de la Cité, Paris, and Gull — AP11

1947, May 7
C22 AP11 500fr dk Prus grn 42.50 27.50

Universal Postal Union 12th Congress, Paris, May 7-July 7, 1947.

View of Lille — AP12

Air View of Paris — AP13

Designs: 200fr, Bordeaux. 300fr, Lyon. 500fr, Marseille.

1949-50 **Unwmk.** *Perf. 13.*
C23 AP12 100fr sepia 90 22
C24 AP12 200fr dk bl grn 8.00 55
C25 AP12 300fr purple 17.50 9.00
C26 AP12 500fr brt red 40.00 3.50
C27 AP13 1000fr sep & blk, *bl* ('50) 80.00 17.50
Nos. C23-C27 (5) 146.40 30.77

Alexander III Bridge and Petit Palais, Paris — AP14

1949, June 13
C28 AP14 100fr brn car 8.00 5.75

Issued to publicize the International Telegraph and Telephone Conference, Paris, May-July 1949.

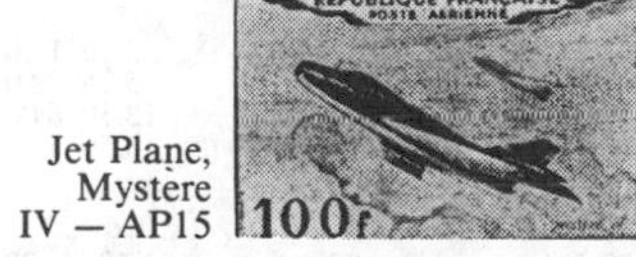

Jet Plane, Mystere IV — AP15

Planes: 200fr, Noratlas. 500fr, Miles Magister. 1000fr, Provence.

1954, Jan. 16
C29 AP15 100fr red brn & bl 1.50 15
C30 AP15 200fr blk brn & vio bl 5.25 22
C31 AP15 500fr car & org 60.00 8.50
C32 AP15 1000fr vio brn, bl grn & ind 70.00 11.00

Maryse Bastie and Plane AP16

1955, June 4 **Unwmk.** *Perf. 13*
C33 AP16 50fr dp plum & rose pink 6.75 4.75

Issued to honor Maryse Bastie, 1898-1952.

Caravelle AP17

Designs: 300fr, Morane Saulnier 760 "Paris." 1000fr, Alouette helicopter.

1957-59 **Engr.** *Perf. 13*
C34 AP17 300fr sl grn, grnsh bl & sep ('59) 4.00 2.00
C35 AP17 500fr dp ultra & blk 32.50 1.75
C36 AP17 1000fr lil, ol blk & blk ('58) 50.00 20.00

Types of 1954-59.

Planes: 2fr, Noratlas. 3fr, MS760, Paris. 5fr, Caravelle. 10fr, Alouette helicopter.

1960, Jan. 11
C37 AP15 2fr vio bl & ultra 2.25 10
a. 2fr ultra 3.75 22
C38 AP17 3fr sl grn, grnsh bl & sep 1.90 5
C39 AP17 5fr dp ultra & blk 3.25 30
C40 AP17 10fr lil, ol blk & blk 18.00 1.50

Type of 1957-59.

Design: 2fr, Jet plane, Mystere 20.

1965, June 12 **Engr.** *Perf. 13*
C41 AP17 2fr sl bl & ind 1.40 6

Concorde Issue
Common Design Type

1969, Mar. 2 **Engr.** *Perf. 13*
C42 CD129 1fr ind & brt bl 1.90 38

Issued to commemorate the first flight of the prototype Concorde plane at Toulouse, March 1, 1969.

Jean Mermoz, Antoine de Saint-Exupery and Concorde — AP19

1970, Sept. 19 **Engr.** *Perf. 13*
C43 AP19 20fr bl & ind 7.00 45

Issued to honor Jean Mermoz (1901-1936) and the writer Antoine de Saint-Exupery (1900-1944), aviators and air mail pioneers.

Balloon, Gare d'Austerlitz, Paris — AP20

1971, Jan. 16 **Engr.** *Perf. 13*
C44 AP20 95c bl, vio bl, org & sl grn 1.25 90

Centenary of the balloon post from besieged Paris, 1870-71.

Didier Daurat, Raymond Vanier and Plane Landing at Night — AP21

1971, Apr. 17 **Engr.** *Perf. 13*
C45 AP21 5fr Prus bl, blk & lt grn 2.00 10

Honoring Didier Daurat (1891-1969) and Raymond Vanier (1895-1965), aviation pioneers.

Hélène Boucher, Maryse Hilsz and Caudron-Renault and Moth-Morane Planes — AP22

Design: 15fr, Henri Guillaumet, Paul Codos, Latecoere 521, Guillaumet's crashed plane in Andes, skyscrapers.

1972-73 **Engr.** *Perf. 13*
C46 AP22 10fr plum, red & sl 4.00 15
C47 AP22 15fr dp car, gray & brn ('73) 6.75 45

Hélène Boucher (1908-1934) and Maryse Hilsz (1901-1946), aviation pioneers.

Henri Guillaumet (1902-1940) and Paul Codos (1896-1960), aviation pioneers.

Issue dates: 10fr, June 10, 1972; 15fr, Feb. 24, 1973.

Concorde AP23

1976, Jan. 10 **Engr.** *Perf. 13*
C48 AP23 1.70fr brt bl, red & blk 1.00 50

First flight of supersonic jet Concorde from Paris to Rio de Janeiro, Jan. 21.

Planes over the Atlantic, New York-Paris — AP24

1977, June 4 **Engr.** *Perf. 13*
C49 AP24 1.90fr multi 1.00 60

First transatlantic flight by Charles A. Lindbergh from New York to Paris, 50th anniversary, and first attempted westbound flight by French aviators Charles Nungesser and Francois Coli.

Plane over Flight Route AP25

1978, Oct. 14 **Engr.** *Perf. 13*
C50 AP25 1.50fr multi 1.50 45

75th anniversary of first airmail route from Villacoublay to Pauillac, Gironde.

Rocket, Concorde, Exhibition Hall — AP26

1979, June 9 Engr. *Perf. 13*
C51 AP26 1.70fr ultra, org & brn 1.10 50

33rd International Aerospace and Space Show, Le Bourget, June 11-15.

First Nonstop Transatlantic Flight, Paris-New York — AP27

1980, Aug. 30 Engr. *Perf. 13*
C52 AP27 2.50fr vio brn & ultra 90 32

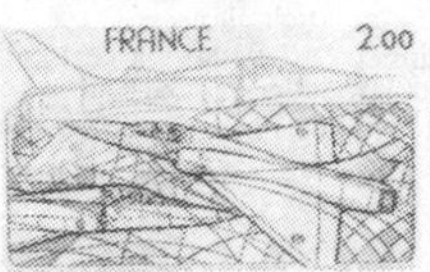

34th Intl. Space and Aeronautics Exhibition, June 5-14 AP28

1981, June 6 Engr. *Perf. 13*
C53 AP28 2fr multi 2.50 45

Dieudonné Costes and Joseph Le Brix and their Breguet Bi-plane AP29

1981, Sept. 12 Engr.
C54 AP29 10fr dk brn & red 4.50 22

First South Atlantic crossing, Oct. 14-15, 1927.

Seaplane Late-300 — AP30

Planes: 15fr, Farman F-60 Goliath. 20fr, CAMS-53 seaplane. 30fr, Wibault 283 Monoplane. 50fr, Dewoitine 338.

1982-87 Engr.
C55 AP30 1.60fr multi 60 45
C56 AP30 15fr dk bl ('84) 5.00 45
C57 AP30 20fr dp org ('85) 6.75 60
C58 AP30 30fr brt vio ('86) 10.00 1.80
C59 AP30 50fr grn ('87) 17.00 3.00
Nos. C55-C59 (5) 39.35 6.30

Issue dates: 1.60fr, Dec. 4. 15fr, Mar. 3. 20fr, Mar. 2. 30fr, Oct. 11. 50fr, Apr. 11.

AIR POST SEMI-POSTAL STAMPS

Antoine de Saint-Exupéry — SPAP1

Col. Jean Dagnaux SPAP2

1948 Unwmk. Engr. *Perf. 13*
CB1 SPAP1 50fr + 30fr vio brn 1.75 1.75
CB2 SPAP2 100fr + 70fr dk bl 2.75 2.75

Modern Plane and Ader's "Eole" SPAP3

1948, Feb.
CB3 SPAP3 40fr + 10fr dk bl 1.40 1.10

Issued to commemorate the 50th anniversary of the flight of Clement Ader's plane, the Eole, in 1897.

POSTAGE DUE STAMPS

D1

D2

1859-70 Unwmk. Litho. *Imperf.*
J1 D1 10c black *11,000.* 210.00
J2 D1 15c blk ('70) 125.00 225.00

In the lithographed stamps the central bar of the "E" of "CENTIMES" is very short, and the accent on "a" slants at an angle of 30 degree, for the 10c and 17 degree for the 15c, while on the typographed the central bar of the "E" is almost as wide as the top and bottom bars and the accent on the "a" slants at an angle of 47 degree.

No. J2 is known rouletted unofficially.

1859-78 Typo.
J3 D1 10c black 21.00 16.50
J4 D1 15c blk ('63) 25.00 13.50
J5 D1 20c blk ('77) *2,250.*
J6 D1 25c blk ('71) 110.00 37.50
J7 D1 30c blk ('78) 185.00 120.00
J8 D1 40c bl ('71) 300.00 400.00
a. 40c ultra *5,250.* *6,000.*
b. 40c Prus bl *2,500.*
J9 D1 60c yel ('71) 500.00 *1,200.*
J10 D1 60c bl ('78) 50.00 80.00
a. 60c dk bl 550.00 650.00
J10B D1 60c black *2,250.*

The 20c and 60c black were never put into use.

Nos. J3, J4, J6, J8 and J9 are known rouletted unofficially and Nos. J4, J6, J7 and J10 pin-perf. unofficially.

1882-92 *Perf. 14x13½*
J11 D2 1c black 75 75
J12 D2 2c black 11.00 9.00
J13 D2 3c black 12.00 11.00
J14 D2 4c black 20.00 14.00
J15 D2 5c black 42.50 11.00
J16 D2 10c black 40.00 1.50
J17 D2 15c black 22.50 4.00
J18 D2 20c black 125.00 57.50
J19 D2 30c black 80.00 1.50
J20 D2 40c black 50.00 25.00
J21 D2 50c blk ('92) 225.00 67.50
J22 D2 60c blk ('84) 225.00 25.00
J23 D2 1fr black 300.00 200.00
J24 D2 2fr blk ('84) 525.00 375.00
J25 D2 5fr blk ('84) 1,100. 850.00

Excellent counterfeits exist of Nos. J23-J25.

1884
J26 D2 1fr brown 200.00 50.00
J27 D2 2fr brown 120.00 80.00
J28 D2 5fr brown 225.00 170.00

1893-1941
J29 D2 5c bl ('94) 45 22
J30 D2 10c brown 45 15
J31 D2 15c lt grn ('94) 18.00 1.35
J32 D2 20c ol grn ('06) 3.00 22
J33 D2 25c rose ('23) 3.75 2.65
J34 D2 30c red ('94) 45 15
J35 D2 30c org red ('94) 400.00 55.00
J36 D2 40c rose ('25) 6.75 2.65
J37 D2 45c grn ('24) 5.00 3.50
J38 D2 50c brn vio ('95) 45 15
a. 50c lil 45 15
J39 D2 60c bl grn ('25) 55 20
J40 D2 1fr rose, *straw* ('96) 450.00 375.00
J41 D2 1fr red brn, *straw* ('20) 3.75 15
J42 D2 1fr red brn ('35) 75 18
J43 D2 2fr red org ('10) 150.00 40.00
J44 D2 2fr brt vio ('26) 55 30
J45 D2 3fr mag ('26) 55 30
J45A D2 5fr red org ('41) 1.50 1.50

D3

D4

1908-25
J46 D3 1c ol grn 90 45
J47 D3 10c violet 1.00 30
a. Imperf., pair 180.00
J48 D3 20c bis ('19) 18.00 50
J49 D3 30c bis ('09) 9.50 30
J50 D3 50c red ('09) 210.00 52.50
J51 D3 60c red ('25) 2.25 1.10
Nos. J46-J51 (6) 241.65 55.15

"Recouvrements" stamps were used to recover charges due on undelivered or refused mail which was returned to the sender.

Nos. J49-J50 Surcharged **20 c.**

1917
J52 D3 20c on 30c bis 9.00 2.40
J53 D3 40c on 50c red 9.00 2.10
a. Double surch. 165.00

In Jan. 1917 several values of the current issue of postage stamps were handstamped "T" in a triangle and used as postage due stamps.

Recouvrements Stamps of 1908-25 Surcharged **50**

1926
J54 D3 50c on 10c lil 3.50 1.50
J55 D3 60c on 1c ol grn 5.25 2.50
J56 D3 1fr on 60c red 13.50 6.00
J57 D3 2fr on 60c red 13.50 6.75

1927-31
J58 D4 1c ol grn ('28) 1.10 38
J59 D4 10c rose ('31) 16.50 38
J60 D4 30c bister 3.75 22
J61 D4 60c red 3.25 30
J62 D4 1fr violet 12.00 2.40
J63 D4 1fr Prus grn ('31) 13.50 45
J64 D4 2fr blue 40.00 25.00
J65 D4 2fr ol brn ('31) 125.00 18.00
Nos. J58-J65 (8) 215.10 47.13

Nos. J62 to J65 have the numerals of value double-lined.

Nos. J64, J62 Surcharged in Red or Black **1F20**

1929
J66 D4 1.20fr on 2fr bl 30.00 4.50
J67 D4 5fr on 1fr vio (Bk) 37.50 6.00

No. J61 Surcharged **UN FRANC**

1931
J68 D4 1fr on 60c red 15.00 1.50

D5

Sheaves of Wheat — D6

Perf. 14x13½.
1943-46 Unwmk. Typo.
J69 D5 10c sepia 15 15
J70 D5 30c brt red vio 15 15
J71 D5 50c bl grn 15 15
J72 D5 1fr brt ultra 15 15
J73 D5 1.50fr rose red 30 30
J74 D5 2fr turq bl 35 30
J75 D5 3fr brn org 35 30
J76 D5 4fr dp vio ('45) 3.00 2.50
J77 D5 5fr brt pink 45 30
J78 D5 10fr red org ('45) 2.75 30
J79 D5 20fr ol bis ('46) 5.00 2.00
Nos. J69-J79 (11) 12.80 6.60

Type of 1943. Inscribed "Timbre Taxe"

1946-53
J80 D5 10c sep ('47) 1.35 1.00
J81 D5 30c brt red vio ('47) 1.00 90
J82 D5 50c bl grn ('47) 8.00 4.50
J83 D5 1fr brt ultra ('47) 22 22
J85 D5 2fr turq bl 22 22
J86 D5 3fr brn org 22 22
J87 D5 4fr dp vio 30 22
J88 D5 5fr brt pink ('47) 30 15
J89 D5 10fr red org ('47) 30 15
J90 D5 20fr ol bis ('47) 1.50 30
J91 D5 50fr dk grn ('50) 9.50 30
J92 D5 100fr dp grn ('53) 40.00 4.75
Nos. J80-J92 (12) 62.91 12.93

1960 Typo. *Perf. 14x13½*
J93 D6 5c brt pink 1.65 30
J94 D6 10c red org 2.10 30
J95 D6 20c ol bis 3.75 30
J96 D6 50c dk grn 12.00 1.20
J97 D6 1fr dp grn 45.00 1.65
Nos. J93-J97 (5) 64.50 3.75

Corn Poppy — D7

Flowers: 5c, Centaury. 10c, Gentian. 20c, Violets. 30c, Forget-me-not. 40c, Columbine. 50c, Clover. 1fr, Soldanel.

1964-71 Typo. *Perf. 14x13½*
J98 D7 5c car rose, red & grn ('65) 5 5
J99 D7 10c car rose, brt bl & grn ('65) 10 5
J100 D7 15c brn, grn & red 15 15
J101 D7 20c dk grn, grn & vio ('71) 15 10
J102 D7 30c brn, ultra & grn 18 6
J103 D7 40c dk grn, scar & yel ('71) 27 15
J104 D7 50c vio bl, car & grn ('65) 27 6
J105 D7 1fr vio bl, lil & grn ('65) 45 12
Nos. J98-J105 (8) 1.62 74

Ampedus Cinnabarinus — D8

1982-83 Engr. *Perf. 13*
J106 D8 10c shown 5 5
J107 D8 20c Dorcadion fuliginator 6 5
J108 D8 30c Leptura cordigera 12 5
J109 D8 40c Paederus littoralis 12 6
J110 D8 50c Pyrochroa coccinea 15 5
J111 D8 1fr Scarites laevigatus 30 5
J112 D8 2fr Trichius gallicus 55 5
J113 D8 3fr Adalia alpina 90 6
J114 D8 4fr Apoderus coryli 1.20 5
J115 D8 5fr Trichodes alvearius 1.50 10
Nos. J106-J115 (10) 4.95 57

MILITARY STAMPS

Regular Issue Overprinted in Black or Red **F. M.**

1901-39 Unwmk. *Perf. 14x13½*
M1 A17 15c org ('01) 55.00 7.50
a. Inverted overprint 140.00 60.00
b. Imperf., pair 325.00
M2 A19 15c pale red ('03) 50.00 5.25
M3 A20 15c sl grn ('04) 40.00 6.00
a. No period after "M" 100.00 40.00
b. Imperf., pair 210.00

M4 A20 10c rose ('06) 25.00 6.00
a. No period after "M" 85.00 40.00
b. Imperf., pair 200.00
M5 A22 10c red ('07) 60 30
a. Inverted overprint 65.00 37.50
b. Imperf., pair 175.00
M6 A20 50c ver ('29) 3.00 90
a. No period after "M" 40.00 15.00
b. Period in front of F 40.00 15.00
M7 A45 50c rose red ('34) 1.50 30
a. No period after "M" *20.00 12.50*
b. Invtd. ovpt. 95.00 45.00
M8 A45 65c brt ultra (R) ('38) 38 22
a. No period after "M" 27.50 22.50
M9 A45 90c ultra (R) ('39) 45 38

"F. M." are initials of Franchise Militaire (Military Frank). See No. S1.

M1

Flag — M2

1946-47 **Typo.**
M10 M1 dk grn 1.40 65
M11 M1 rose red ('47) 22 10

Nos. M10-M11 were valid also in the French colonies.

1964, July 20 ***Perf. 13x14***
M12 M2 multi 30 22

OFFICIAL STAMPS

FOR THE COUNCIL OF EUROPE.

For use only on mail posted in the post office in the Council of Europe Building, Strasbourg.

France No. 854 Overprinted: "CONSEIL DE L'EUROPE"

Unwmk.

1958, Jan. 14 **Engr.** ***Perf. 13***
1O1 A303 35fr car rose & lake 1.50 3.00

Council of Europe Flag — O1

1958-59
Flag in Ultramarine.
1O2 O1 8fr red org & brn vio 22 22
1O3 O1 20fr yel & lt brn 45 38
1O4 O1 25fr lil rose & sl grn ('59) 90 50
1O5 O1 35fr red 70 70
1O6 O1 50fr lil rose ('59) 1.65 1.50
Nos. 1O2-1O6 (5) 3.92 3.30

1963, Jan. 3
Flag in Ultramarine
1O7 O1 20c yel & lt brn 1.90 75
1O8 O1 25c lil rose & sl grn 3.00 1.65
1O9 O1 50c lil rose 3.00 2.50

1965-71
Flag in Ultramarine & Yellow
1O10 O1 25c ver, yel & sl grn 1.25 95
1O11 O1 30c ver & yel 1.25 95
1O12 O1 40c ver, yel & gray ('69) 1.90 95
1O13 O1 50c red, yel & grn ('71) 3.80 1.75
1O14 O1 60c ver, yel & vio 1.50 95
1O15 O1 70c ver, yel & dk brn ('69) 5.50 3.75
Nos. 1O10-1O15 (6) 15.20 9.30

Issue dates: 25c, 30c, 60c, Jan. 16, 1965. 50c, Feb. 20, 1971. Others, Mar. 24, 1969.

Type of 1958 Inscribed "FRANCE"

1975-76 **Engr.** ***Perf. 13***
Flag in Ultramarine & Yellow
1O16 O1 60c org, yel & emer 1.50 1.00
1O17 O1 80c yel & mag 2.25 1.65
1O18 O1 1fr car, yel & gray ol ('76) 5.00 4.50
1O19 O1 1.20fr org, yel & bl 6.25 3.75

Issue dates: 1fr, Oct. 16, 1976. Others, Nov. 22, 1975.

New Council Headquarters, Strasbourg — O2

1977, Jan. 22 **Engr.** ***Perf. 13***
1O20 O2 80c car & multi 1.25 75
1O21 O2 1fr brn & multi 1.25 75
1O22 O2 1.40fr gray & multi 2.50 1.50

Human Rights Emblem in Upper Left Corner

1978, Oct. 14
1O23 O2 1.20fr red lil & multi 70 60
1O24 O2 1.70fr bl & multi 1.10 80

30th anniversary of the Universal Declaration of Human Rights.

Council Headquarters Type of 1977

1980, Nov. 24 **Engr.** ***Perf. 13***
1O25 O2 1.40fr olive 75 65
1O26 O2 2fr bl gray 90 80

New Council Headquarters, Strasbourg — O3

1981-84 **Engr.**
1O27 O3 1.40fr multi 60 60
1O28 O3 1.60fr multi 60 60
1O29 O3 1.70fr emerald 40 40
1O30 O3 1.80fr multi 90 80
1O31 O3 2fr multi 1.10 90
1O32 O3 2.10fr red 45 45
1O33 O3 2.30fr multi 95 95
1O34 O3 2.60fr multi 1.10 95
1O35 O3 2.80fr multi 1.25 1.10
1O36 O3 3fr brt bl 65 65
Nos. 1O27-1O36 (10) 8.00 7.40

Issue dates: 1.40, 1.60, 2.30fr, Nov. 21. 1.80, 2.60fr, Nov. 13, 1982. 2, 2.80fr, Nov. 21, 1983. 1.70, 2.10, 3fr, Nov. 5, 1984.

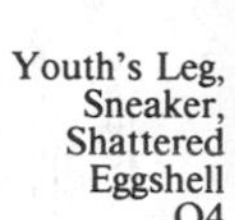

Youth's Leg, Sneaker, Shattered Eggshell O4

1985, Aug. 31 **Engr.** ***Perf. 13***
1O37 O4 1.80fr brt grn 42 8
1O38 O4 2.20fr vermilion 52 10
1O39 O4 3.20fr brt bl 75 15

New Council Headquarters, Strasbourg — O5

1986, Dec. 13 **Engr.**
1O40 O5 1.90fr green 70 12
1O41 O5 2.20fr red 80 14
1O42 O5 3.40fr blue 1.25 22

1987, Oct. 10 **Litho.**
1O43 O5 2fr brt yel grn 68 14
1O44 O5 3.60fr brt blue 1.20 24

FOR THE UNITED NATIONS EDUCATIONAL, SCIENTIFIC AND CULTURAL ORGANIZATION

For use only on mail posted in the post office in the UNESCO Building, Paris.

Khmer Buddha and Hermes by Praxiteles O1

1961-65 **Unwmk.** **Engr.** ***Perf. 13***
2O1 O1 20c dk gray, ol bis & bl 40 38
2O2 O1 25c blk, lake & grn 55 45
2O3 O1 30c choc & bis brn ('65) 90 90
2O4 O1 50c blk, red & vio bl 2.25 1.90
2O5 O1 60c grnsh bl, red brn & rose lil ('65) 2.00 1.90
Nos. 2O1-2O5 (5) 6.10 5.53

Book and Globe — O2

1966, Dec. 17
2O6 O2 25c gray 75 75
2O7 O2 30c dk red 95 95
2O8 O2 60c green 1.65 1.65

20th anniversary of UNESCO.

Human Rights Flame — O3

1969-71 **Engr.** ***Perf. 13***
2O9 O3 30c sl grn, red & dp brn 90 60
2O10 O3 40c dk car rose, red & dp brn 1.40 90
2O11 O3 50c ultra, car & brn ('71) 3.00 2.25
2O12 O3 70c pur, red & sl 4.50 3.75

Universal Declaration of Human Rights.

Type of 1969 Inscribed "FRANCE"

1975, Nov. 15 **Engr.** ***Perf. 13***
2O13 O3 60c grn, red & dk brn 1.65 1.00
2O14 O3 80c ocher, red & red brn 2.50 1.65
2O15 O3 1.20fr ind, red & brn 6.25 4.50

O4

1976-78 **Engr.** ***Perf. 13***
2O16 O4 80c multi 1.25 1.00
2O17 O4 1fr multi 1.25 1.00
2O18 O4 1.20fr multi ('78) 70 65
2O19 O4 1.40fr multi 3.25 2.00
2O20 O4 1.70fr multi ('78) 1.10 90
Nos. 2O16-2O20 (5) 7.55 5.55

Issue dates: 1.20fr, 1.70fr, Oct. 14, 1978. Others, Oct. 23, 1976.

Slave Quarters, Senegal O5

Designs: 1.40fr, Mohenjo-Daro excavations, Pakistan. 2fr, Sans-Souci Palace, Haiti.

1980, Nov. 17 **Engr.** ***Perf. 13***
2O21 O5 1.20fr multi 65 55
2O22 O5 1.40fr multi 75 60
2O23 O5 2fr multi 1.00 80

Fort St. Elmo, Malta — O6

Designs: 1.40fr, Building, Fez, Morocco (vert.). 1.60fr, Seated deity, Sukhotai, Thailand (vert.).

1981, Dec. 12
2O24 O6 1.40fr multi 65 60
2O25 O6 1.60fr multi 65 60
2O26 O6 2.30fr multi 1.00 90

Hue, Vietnam — O7

1982, Oct. 23 **Engr.**
2O27 O7 1.80fr shown 80 80
2O28 O7 2.60fr St. Michael Church ruins, Brazil 1.00 1.00

Mosque, Chinguetti, Mauritania O8

Architecture: 1.70fr, Church, Lalibela, Ethiopia. 1.80fr, Roman Theater and female standing sculpture, Carthage, Tunisia. 2.10fr, San'a, Yemen. 2.20fr, Old Town Square and wrought iron latticework, Havana. 2.80fr, Enclosure wall interior, Istanbil. 3fr, Church, Kotor, Jugoslavia. 3.20fr, Temple of Anuradhapura and bas-relief of two women, Sri Lanka.

1983-85 **Engr.**
2O29 O8 1.70fr multi 40 40
2O30 O8 1.80fr multi 42 8
2O31 O8 2fr shown 1.00 1.00
2O32 O8 2.10fr multi 45 45
2O33 O8 2.20fr multi 52 10
2O34 O8 2.80fr multi 1.25 1.25
2O35 O8 3fr multi 65 65
2O36 O8 3.20fr multi 75 15
Nos. 2O29-2O36 (8) 5.44 4.08

Issue dates: 2, 2.80fr, Oct. 10, 1983. 1.70, 2.10, 3fr, Oct. 22, 1984. 1.80, 2.20. 3.20fr, Oct. 26, 1985.

Tikal Temple, Guatemala — O9

1986, Dec. 6 **Engr.** ***Perf. 13***
2O37 O9 1.90fr shown 60 12
2O38 O9 3.40fr Bagerhat Mosque, Bangladesh 1.05 22

France Council of Europe and UNESCO stamps can be mounted in Scott's France Album.

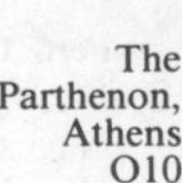
The Parthenon, Athens O10

1987, Dec. 5 Engr. *Perf. 13x12½*

2O39	O10	2fr shown	75	15
2O40	O10	3.60fr Temple of Philae, Egypt	1.30	25

NEWSPAPER STAMPS

Coat of Arms — N1

1868 Unwmk. Typo. *Imperf.*

P1	N1	2c lilac	250.00	45.00
P2	N1	2c (+ 2c) bl	525.00	250.00

Perf. 12½.

P3	N1	2c lilac	37.50	20.00
P4	N1	2c (+ 4c) rose	135.00	90.00
P5	N1	2c (+ 2c) bl	62.50	30.00
P6	N1	5c lilac	1,000.	650.00

Nos. P2, P4, and P5 were sold for face plus an added fiscal charge indicated in parenthesis. Nos. P1, P3 and P6 were used simply as fiscals.

The 2c rose and 5c lilac imperforate and the 5c rose and 5c blue, both imperforate and perforated, were never put into use.

Nos. P1-P6 were reprinted for the 1913 Ghent Exhibition and the 1937 Paris Exhibition (PEXIP).

No. 109 Surcharged in Red

1/2 centime

1919 *Perf. 14x13½*

P7	A16	½c on 1c gray	30	22
a.		Inverted surcharge	1,000.	450.00

No. 156 Surcharged.

1933

P8	A22	½c on 1c ol bis	45	38

FRANCHISE STAMP

No. 276 Overprinted "F"

1939 Unwmk. *Perf. 14x13½*

S1	A45	90c ultra	2.25	2.25
a.		Period after "F"	27.50	22.50

No. S1 was for the use of Spanish refugee soldiers in France. "F" stands for "Fugitives."

OCCUPATION STAMPS

Issued under German Occupation. (Alsace and Lorraine)

O1

1870 Typo. Unwmk. *Perf. 13½x14.*

Network with Points Up.

N1	O1	1c ol grn	52.50	100.00
N2	O1	2c red brn	100.00	125.00
a.		2c dk brn	120.00	160.00
N3	O1	4c gray	92.50	60.00
N4	O1	5c yel grn	60.00	10.00
N5	O1	10c yel brn	30.00	3.50
a.		10c bis brn	55.00	4.75
b.		Network lem yel	72.50	8.00
N6	O1	20c ultra	65.00	10.00
N7	O1	25c brown	120.00	65.00
a.		25c blk brn	160.00	95.00

There are three varieties of the 4c and two of the 10c, differing in the position of the figures of value, and several other setting varieties.

Network with Points Down.

N8	O1	1c ol grn	325.00	*750.00*
N9	O1	2c red brn	150.00	*675.00*
N10	O1	4c gray	160.00	120.00
N11	O1	5c yel grn	2,400.	325.00
N12	O1	10c bister	80.00	9.50
a.		Network lem yel	265.00	80.00
N13	O1	20c ultra	225.00	110.00
N14	O1	25c brown	475.00	240.00

Official imitations have the network with points downward. The "P" of "Postes" is 2½mm. from the border in the imitations and 3mm. in the originals. The word "Postes" measures 12¾ to 13mm. on the imitations, and from 11 to 12½mm. on the originals.

The imitations are perf. 13½x14½; originals, perf. 13½x14¼.

The stamps for Alsace and Lorraine were replaced by stamps of the German Empire on Jan. 1, 1872.

German Stamps of 1905-16 Surcharged:

3 Cent. a — 1 F b — c ✱ 1 F. 25 Cent. ✱

1916 Wmk. 125 *Perf. 14, 14½*

N15	A16(a)	3c on 3pf brn	50	50
N16	A16(a)	5c on 5pf grn	50	75
N17	A22(a)	8c onn 7½pf org	60	1.00
N18	A16(a)	10c on 10pf car	50	50
N19	A22(a)	15c on 15pf yel brn	50	50
N20	A16(a)	25c on 20pf bl	75	75
a.		25c on 20pf ultra	1.25	2.50
N21	A16(a)	40c on 30pf org & blk, *buff*	1.00	2.00
N22	A16(a)	50c on 40pf lake & blk	1.00	2.00
N23	A16(a)	75c on 60pf mag	5.00	6.00
N24	A16(b)	1fr on 80pf lake & blk, *rose*	5.00	9.00
N25	A17	1fr25c on 1m car	22.50	25.00
a.		Double surcharge	100.00	
N26	A21	2fr50c on 2m gray bl	22.50	20.00
a.		Double surcharge	100.00	
		Nos. N15-N26 (12)	60.35	68.00

These stamps were also used in parts of Belgium occupied by the German forces.

Alsace.

Issued under German Occupation.

Stamps of Germany 1933-36 Overprinted in Black — Elsass

1940 Wmk. 237 *Perf. 14*

N27	A64	3pf ol bis	28	50
N28	A64	4pf dl bl	45	1.00
N29	A64	5pf brt grn	28	50
N30	A64	6pf dk grn	28	50
N31	A64	8pf vermilion	28	50
N32	A64	10pf chocolate	28	90
N33	A64	12pf dp car	30	60
N34	A64	15pf maroon	45	1.00
N35	A64	20pf brt bl	45	1.00
N36	A64	25pf ultra	60	1.35
N37	A64	30pf ol grn	1.15	1.60
N38	A64	40pf red vio	1.15	1.60
N39	A64	50pf dk grn & blk	1.65	2.50
N40	A64	60pf cl & blk	2.00	3.50
N41	A64	80pf dk bl & blk	2.25	5.00
N42	A64	100pf org & blk	3.25	3.00
		Nos. N27-N42 (16)	15.10	25.05

Lorraine

Issued under German Occupation.

Stamps of Germany 1933-36 Overprinted in Black — Lothringen

Wmk. Swastikas. (237)

1940 *Perf. 14.*

N43	A64	3pf ol bis	50	*1.00*
N44	A64	4pf dl bl	50	*1.00*
N45	A64	5pf brt grn	50	*1.00*
N46	A64	6pf dk grn	50	50
N47	A64	8pf vermilion	50	*1.00*
N48	A64	10pf chocolate	50	75
N49	A64	12pf dp car	50	75
N50	A64	15pf maroon	50	*1.25*
a.		Inverted surcharge	125.00	
N51	A64	20pf brt bl	50	*1.40*
N52	A64	25pf ultra	65	*1.40*
N53	A64	30pf ol grn	70	*1.50*
N54	A64	40pf red vio	70	*1.50*
N55	A64	50pf dk grn & blk	1.00	*2.50*
N56	A64	60pf cl & blk	1.00	*3.00*
N57	A64	80pf dk bl & blk	1.25	*3.75*
N58	A64	100pf org & blk	1.50	*6.00*
		Nos. N43-N58 (16)	11.30	28.30

Besetztes Gebiet Nordfrankreich

These three words, in a rectangular frame covering two stamps, were handstamped in black on Nos. 267, 367 and 369 and used in the Dunkerque region in July-August, 1940. The German commander of Dunkerque authorized the overprint.

ISSUED JOINTLY BY THE

Allied Military Government of the United States and Great Britain, for civilian use.

Arc de Triomphe — OS2

1944 Unwmk. Litho. *Perf. 11*

2N1	OS2	5c brt red vio	5	5
2N2	OS2	10c lt gray	5	5
2N3	OS2	25c brown	5	5
2N4	OS2	50c ol bis	5	5
2N5	OS2	1fr pck grn	10	10
2N6	OS2	1.50fr rose pink	15	15
2N7	OS2	2.50fr purple	15	15
2N8	OS2	4fr ultra	15	15
2N9	OS2	5fr black	15	15
2N10	OS2	10fr yel org	21.50	18.50
		Nos. 2N1-2N10 (10)	22.40	19.40

1945

Denominations in Black.

2N11	OS2	30c orange	6	6
2N12	OS2	40c pale gray	6	6
2N13	OS2	50c ol bis	6	6
2N14	OS2	60c violet	10	10
2N15	OS2	80c emerald	10	10
2N16	OS2	1.20fr brown	15	15
2N17	OS2	1.50fr vermilion	15	15
2N18	OS2	2fr yellow	15	15
2N19	OS2	2.40fr dk rose	15	15
2N20	OS2	3fr brt red vio	15	15
		Nos. 2N11-2N20 (10)	1.13	1.13

FRENCH OFFICES ABROAD OFFICES IN CHINA

Prior to 1923 several of the world powers maintained their own post offices in China for the purpose of sending and receiving overseas mail. French offices were maintained in Canton, Hoi Hao (Hoihow), Kwangchowan (Kouang-tcheou-wan), Mongtseu (Mong-tseu), Packhoi (Pakhoi), Tong King (Tchongking), Yunnan Fou (Yunnanfu).

100 Centimes = 1 Franc

100 Cents = 1 Piaster

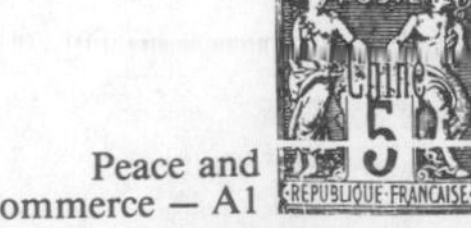

Peace and Commerce — A1

Stamps of France Overprinted in Red or Black

1894-1900 Unwmk. *Perf. 14x13½*

1	A1	5c grn, *grnsh* (R)	1.10	1.00
2	A1	5c yel grn, I (R) ('00)	1.25	70
a.		Type II	25.00	12.50
3	A1	10c *lav*, I (R)	2.50	90
a.		Type II	10.00	6.75
4	A1	15c bl (R)	3.00	1.00
5	A1	20c red, *grn*	2.50	1.25
6	A1	25c *rose* (R)	2.50	90
7	A1	30c brn, *bis*	2.50	1.75
8	A1	40c red, *straw*	3.00	2.00
9	A1	50c car, *rose*, I	7.00	4.75
a.		Red overprint	30.00	
b.		Type II (Bk)	7.50	3.75
10	A1	75c dp vio, *org* (R)	42.50	30.00
11	A1	1fr brnz grn, *straw*	5.00	2.00
a.		Double overprint	225.00	
12	A1	2fr brn, *az* ('00)	16.00	10.00
12A	A1	5fr red lil, *lav*	37.50	25.00
b.		Red overprint	265.00	

Surcharged in Black — Chine 25

13	A1	25c on 1fr brnz, grn, *straw*	47.50	20.00

Surcharged in Red — Chine 2 Cents

1901

14	A1	2c on 25c *rose*	775.00	190.00
15	A1	4c on 25c *rose*	650.00	190.00
16	A1	6c on 25c *rose*	750.00	325.00
17	A1	16c on 25c *rose*	210.00	150.00
a.		Black surcharge		*5,750.*

Stamps of Indo-China Surcharged in Black — CHINE 二之五仙

1902-04

18	A3	1c *lil bl*	1.25	1.00
19	A3	2c brn, *buff*	2.00	1.90
20	A3	4c cl, *lav*	1.40	1.25
21	A3	5c yel grn	1.50	1.40
22	A3	10c red	2.00	1.90
23	A3	15c gray	3.00	2.75
24	A3	20c red, *grn*	3.50	3.00
25	A3	25c *rose*	4.75	4.50
26	A3	25c bl ('04)	4.00	3.75
27	A3	30c brn, *bis*	2.25	2.25
28	A3	40c red, *straw*	10.00	8.00
29	A3	50c car, *rose*	30.00	25.00
30	A3	50c brn, *az* ('04)	3.50	3.00
31	A3	75c vio, *org*	16.00	12.50
32	A3	1fr brnz grn, *straw*	20.00	16.00
33	A3	5fr red lil, *lav*	50.00	45.00
		Nos. 18-33 (16)	155.15	133.20

The Chinese characters surcharged on Nos. 18-33 are the Chinese equivalents of the French values and therefore differ on each denomination. Another printing of these stamps was made in 1904 which differs from the first onc principally in the size and shape of the letters in "CHINE", particularly the "H" which is much thinner in the second printing. Prices are for the less expensive variety. Many varieties of surcharge exist.

Liberty, Equality and Fraternity A3

"Rights of Man" A4

A5

1902-03 **Typo.**
34 A3 5c green 1.00 90
35 A4 10c rose red ('03) 1.00 90
36 A4 15c pale red 1.50 1.00
37 A4 20c brn vio ('03) 2.50 2.50
38 A4 25c bl ('03) 2.50 1.40
39 A4 30c lil ('03) 2.75 2.75
40 A5 40c red & pale bl 5.50 5.00
41 A5 50c bis brn & lav 6.50 5.50
42 A5 1fr cl & ol grn 10.00 6.00
43 A5 2fr gray vio & yel 32.50 22.50
44 A5 5fr dk bl & buff 47.50 30.00
Nos. 34-44 (11) 113.25 78.45

Surcharged in Black **5**

1903
45 A4 5c on 15c pale red 9.50 5.25
a. Invtd. surcharge 60.00 60.00

Stamps of Indo-China, 1904-06, Surcharged as Nos. 18 to 33 in Black

1904-05
46 A4 1c ol grn 70 70
47 A4 2c vio brn, *buff* 70 70
47A A4 4c cl, *bluish* 775.00 575.00
48 A4 5c dp grn 1.00 1.00
49 A4 10c carmine 1.00 1.00
50 A4 15c org brn, *bl* 1.00 1.00
51 A4 20c red, *grn* 5.50 5.00
52 A4 25c dp bl 2.25 1.25
53 A4 40c *bluish* 3.25 2.50
54 A4 1fr pale grn 275.00 210.00
55 A4 2fr brn, *org* 15.00 11.50
56 A4 10fr org brn, *grn* 110.00 95.00
Nos. 46-56 (12) 1,190. 904.65

Many varieties of the surcharge exist on Nos. 46-55.

Stamps of 1902-03 Surcharged in Black **2 CENTS 仙二**

1907
57 A3 2c on 5c grn 60 52
58 A4 4c on 10c rose red 60 52
a. Pair, one without surcharge 35.00
59 A4 6c on 15c pale red 75 55
60 A4 8c on 20c brn vio 2.25 1.75
a. "8" inverted 35.00 35.00
61 A4 10c on 25c bl 30 30
62 A5 20c on 50c bis brn & lav 1.50 1.00
a. Double surcharge
b. Triple surch. 225.00 225.00
63 A5 40c on 1fr cl & ol grn 10.00 5.50
64 A5 2pi on 5fr dk bl & buff 10.00 6.00
a. Double surcharge *1,000.* *1,000.*
Nos. 57-64 (8) 26.00 16.14

Stamps of 1902-03 Surcharged in Black **2 CENTS 分二**

1911-22
65 A3 2c on 5c grn 40 30
66 A4 4c on 10c rose red 55 30
67 A4 6c on 15c org 1.00 40
68 A4 8c on 20c brn vio 80 40
69 A4 10c on 25c bl ('21) 80 40
70 A4 20c on 50c bl ('22) 30.00 20.00
71 A5 40c on 1fr cl & ol grn 1.65 1.10

No. 44 Surcharged **2 $ 圓二**

73 A5 $2 on 5fr bl & buff ('22) 95.00 75.00
Nos. 65-73 (8) 130.20 97.90

Types of 1902-03 Surcharged in Black **2 CENTS 分二**

1922
75 A3 1c on 5c org 1.90 1.00
76 A4 2c on 10c grn 3.25 2.75
77 A4 3c on 15c org 4.75 3.75
78 A4 4c on 20c red brn 6.50 4.50
79 A4 5c on 25c dk vio 3.50 1.75
80 A4 6c on 30c red 4.75 3.25
82 A4 10c on 50c bl 4.75 3.25
83 A5 20c on 1fr cl & ol grn 22.50 18.00
84 A5 40c on 2fr org & pale bl 22.50 18.00
85 A5 $1 on 5fr dk bl & buff 100.00 100.00
Nos. 75-85 (10) 174.40 156.25

POSTAGE DUE STAMPS

Postage Due Stamps of France Handstamped in Red or Black **Chine**

1901-07 **Unwmk.** ***Perf. 14x13½***
J1 D2 5c lt bl (R) 2.25 1.50
J2 D2 10c choc (R) 4.00 3.00
J3 D2 15c lt grn (R) 4.00 3.00
J4 D2 20c ol grn (R) ('07) 4.75 3.50
J5 D2 30c carmine 7.00 5.00
J6 D2 50c lilac 7.50 5.00
Nos. J1-J6 (6) 29.50 21.00

Stamps of 1894-1900 Handstamped in Carmine **A PERCEVOIR**

1903
J7 A1 5c yel grn *2,100.* 700.00
a. pur handstamp *2,100.* 700.00
b. 5c grn, *grnsh* *4,750.*
J8 A1 10c *lavender* *5,250.* *4,250.*
a. pur handstamp *5,250.* *4,250.*
J9 A1 15c blue *2,100.* 650.00
a. pur handstamp *2,100.* 700.00
J10 A1 30c brn, *bis* *1,200.* 75.00
a. pur handstamp *1,200.* 75.00

Same Handstamp on Stamps of 1902-03 in Carmine

1903
J14 A3 5c green *1,200.* 700.00
a. pur handstamp *1,200.* 700.00
J15 A4 10c rose red 575.00 110.00
a. pur handstamp 575.00 110.00
J16 A4 15c pale red 600.00 110.00
a. pur handstamp 600.00 110.00

Stamps of 1894-1900 Handstamped in Carmine **A PERCEVOIR**

1903
J20 A1 5c yel grn *1,400.* 175.00
a. pur handstamp *1,400.* 240.00
b. 5c grn, *grnsh* *4,750.*
J21 A1 10c *lavender* *6,500.* *5,250.*
a. pur handstamp *6,500.* *5,250.*
J22 A1 15c blue 875.00 75.00
a. pur handstamp 875.00 75.00
J23 A1 30c brn, *bis* 450.00 57.50
a. pur handstamp 450.00 57.50

Same Handstamp on Stamps of 1902-03 in Carmine or Purple

1903
J27 A3 5c grn (C) 950.00 425.00
a. pur handstamp 950.00 425.00
J28 A4 10c rose red (C) 260.00 37.50
a. pur handstamp 260.00 37.50
J29 A4 15c pale red (C) 575.00 42.50
a. pur handstamp 575.00 42.50
J30 A4 30c lil (P) *6,500.* *5,250.*

The handstamps on Nos. J7-J30 are found inverted, double, etc.

The cancellations on these stamps should have dates between Sept. 1, and Nov. 30, 1903, to be genuine.

Postage Due Stamps of France 1893-1910 Surcharged in Black **2 CENTS 分二**

1911
J33 D2 2c on 5c bl 90 70
a. Double surch. 70.00 70.00
J34 D2 4c on 10c choc 90 70
a. Double surch. 70.00 70.00
J35 D2 8c on 20c ol grn 1.00 1.00
a. Double surch. 70.00 70.00
J36 D2 20c on 50c lil 1.25 1.00

1922
J37 D2 1c on 5c bl 52.50 47.50
J38 D2 2c on 10c brn 70.00 65.00
J39 D2 4c on 20c ol grn 70.00 65.00
J40 D2 10c on 50c brn vio 70.00 65.00

CANTON

Stamps of Indo-China, 1892-1900, Overprinted in Red **CANTON 州廣**

1901 **Unwmk.** ***Perf. 14x13½***
1 A3 1c *lil bl* 1.00 1.00
1A A3 2c brn, *buff* 1.00 1.00
2 A3 4c cl, *lav* 1.25 1.25
2A A3 5c grn, *grnsh* 425.00 425.00
3 A3 5c yel grn 1.10 1.10
4 A3 10c *lavender* 2.25 2.25
5 A3 15c bl, quadrille paper 1.40 1.40
6 A3 15c gray 2.25 2.25
a. Dbl. overprint 20.00
7 A3 20c red, *grn* 4.00 4.00
8 A3 25c *rose* 4.00 4.00
9 A3 30c brn, *bis* 9.00 9.00
10 A3 40c red, *straw* 10.00 10.00
11 A3 50c car, *rose* 17.50 17.50
12 A3 75c dp vio, *org* 27.50 27.50
13 A3 1fr brnz grn, *straw* 20.00 20.00
14 A3 5fr red lil, *lav* 150.00 150.00
Nos. 1-14 (16) 677.25 677.25

The Chinese characters in the overprint on Nos. 1-14 read "Canton." On Nos. 15-64, they restate the denomination of the basic stamp.

Surcharged in Black **CANTON 仙六**

1903-04
15 A3 1c *lil bl* 1.40 1.40
16 A3 2c brn, *buff* 1.40 1.25
17 A3 4c cl, *lav* 1.40 1.25
18 A3 5c yel grn 1.40 1.10
19 A3 10c rose red 1.25 1.10
20 A3 15c gray 2.00 1.65
21 A3 20c red, *grn* 8.00 7.75
22 A3 25c blue 3.75 2.75
23 A3 25c *rose* ('04) 3.75 2.75
24 A3 30c brn, *bis* 10.00 9.00
25 A3 40c red, *straw* 25.00 20.00
26 A3 50c car, *rose* 225.00 200.00
27 A3 50c brn, *az* ('04) 42.50 37.50
28 A3 75c dp vio, *org* 42.50 37.50
a. "INDO-CHINE" inverted *22,500.*
29 A3 1fr brnz grn, *straw* 35.00 30.00
30 A3 5fr red lil, *lav* 45.00 35.00
Nos. 15-30 (16) 449.35 390.00

Many varieties of the surcharge exist on Nos. 15-30.

Stamps of Indo-China, 1892-1906, Surcharged in Red or Black **CANTON 花銀八厘**

A second printing of the 1906 surcharges of Canton, Hoi Hao, Kwangchowan, Mongtseu, Packhoi, Tong King and Yunnan Fou was made in 1908. The inks are grayish instead of full black and vermilion instead of carmine. Prices are for the cheaper variety which usually is the second printing.

The 4c and 50c of the 1892 issue of Indo-China are known with this surcharge and similarly surcharged for other cities in China. The surcharges on these two stamps are always inverted. It is stated that they were irregularly produced and never issued.

1906
31 A4 1c ol grn (R) 1.00 1.00
32 A4 2c vio brn, *buff* 1.00 1.00
33 A4 4c cl, *bluish* (R) 1.00 1.00
34 A4 5c dp grn (R) 1.25 1.25
35 A4 10c carmine 1.50 1.40
36 A4 15c org brn, *bl* 1.90 1.90
37 A4 20c red, *grn* 1.50 1.50
38 A4 25c dp bl 1.50 1.50
39 A4 30c pale brn 2.75 2.50
40 A4 35c *yel* (R) 1.50 1.40
41 A4 40c *bluish* (R) 3.25 3.00
42 A4 50c bis brn 3.75 3.25
43 A3 75c dp vio, *org* (R) 30.00 27.50
44 A4 1fr pale grn 8.25 7.75
45 A4 2fr brn, *org* (R) 22.50 21.00
46 A3 5fr red lil, *lav* 50.00 40.00
47 A4 10fr org brn, *grn* 42.50 42.50
Nos. 31-47 (17) 175.15 159.45

The surcharge exists inverted on 1c, 25c and 1fr.

Stamps of Indo-China, 1907, Surcharged "CANTON", and Chinese Characters, in Red or Blue

1908
48 A5 1c ol brn & blk 65 65
49 A5 2c brn & blk 65 65
50 A5 4c bl & blk 1.00 1.00
51 A5 5c grn & blk 1.00 1.00
52 A5 10c red & blk (Bl) 1.00 1.00
53 A5 15c vio & blk 1.50 1.50
54 A6 20c vio & blk 1.50 1.50
55 A6 25c bl & blk 1.50 1.50
56 A6 30c brn & blk 3.00 2.75
57 A6 35c ol grn & blk 3.00 2.75
58 A6 40c brn & blk 4.50 3.00
59 A6 50c car & blk (Bl) 5.00 3.50
60 A7 75c ver & blk (Bl) 5.00 4.00
61 A8 1fr car & blk (Bl) 7.50 6.00
62 A9 2fr grn & blk 24.00 22.50
63 A10 5fr bl & blk 32.50 25.00
64 A11 10fr pur & blk 52.50 45.00
Nos. 48-64 (17) 145.80 123.30

Nos. 48-64 Surcharged with New Values in Cents or Piasters in Black, Red or Blue

1919
65 A5 ⅖c on 1c 60 60
66 A5 ⅘c on 2c 60 60
67 A5 1⅗c on 4c (R) 80 75
68 A5 2c on 5c 80 75
69 A5 4c on 10c (Bl) 80 70
a. Chinese "2" instead of "4" 21.00 21.00
70 A5 6c on 15c 1.25 95
71 A6 8c on 20c 1.25 1.10
72 A6 10c on 25c 1.40 95
73 A6 12c on 30c 1.40 95
a. Double surcharge 87.50 87.50
74 A6 14c on 35c 1.40 95
a. Closed "4" 7.00 7.00
75 A6 16c on 40c 1.40 1.10
76 A6 20c on 50c (Bl) 1.40 1.10
77 A7 30c on 75c (Bl) 1.40 95
78 A8 40c on 1fr (Bl) 5.50 3.75
79 A9 80c on 2fr (R) 7.00 5.00
80 A10 2pi on 5fr (R) 7.75 7.00
81 A11 4pi on 10fr (R) 9.00 8.50
Nos. 65-81 (17) 43.75 35.70

HOI HAO

Stamps of Indo-China Overprinted in Red **HOI HAO 州瓊**

1901 **Unwmk.** ***Perf. 14x13½***
1 A3 1c *lil bl* 1.65 1.65
2 A3 2c brn, *buff* 1.65 1.65
3 A3 4c cl, *lav* 1.65 1.65
4 A3 5c yel grn 1.65 1.65
5 A3 10c *lavender* 2.00 2.00
6 A3 15c blue 1,150. 425.00
7 A3 15c gray 1.40 1.40
8 A3 20c red, *grn* 8.00 8.00
9 A3 25c *rose* 3.75 2.25
10 A3 30c brn, *bis* 12.50 11.00
11 A3 40c red, *straw* 12.50 11.00
12 A3 50c car, *rose* 20.00 17.00
13 A3 75c dp vio, *org* 100.00 90.00
14 A3 1fr brnz grn, *straw* 500.00 450.00
15 A3 5fr red lil, *lav* 400.00 375.00
Nos. 1-15 (15) 2,216. 1,399.

The Chinese characters in the overprint on Nos. 1-15 read "Hoi Hao." On Nos. 16-66, they restate the denomination of the basic stamp.

Surcharged in Black **HOI HAO 仙六**

1903-04
16 A3 1c *lil bl* 70 70
17 A3 2c brn, *buff* 70 70
18 A3 4c cl, *lav* 1.65 1.65
19 A3 5c yel grn 1.65 1.65
20 A3 10c red 1.65 1.65
21 A3 15c gray 1.65 1.65
22 A3 20c red, *grn* 4.25 4.25
23 A3 25c blue 1.90 1.90
24 A3 25c *rose* ('04) 1.90 1.90
25 A3 30c brn, *bis* 2.00 2.00
26 A3 40c red, *straw* 20.00 20.00

27 A3 50c car, *rose* 20.00 20.00
28 A3 50c brn, *az* ('04) 67.50 67.50
29 A3 75c dp vio, *org* 27.50 27.50
a. "INDO-CHINE" inverted 22,000.
30 A3 1fr brnz grn, *straw* 30.00 30.00
31 A3 5fr red lil, *lav* 125.00 125.00
Nos. 16-31 (16) 308.05 308.05

Many varieties of the surcharge exist on Nos. 1-31.

HOI HAO

Stamps of Indo-China, 1892-1906, Surcharged in Red or Black

HOI HAO
花銀八厘

1906

32 A4 1c ol grn (R) 1.10 1.10
33 A4 2c vio brn, *buff* 1.10 1.10
34 A4 4c cl, *bluish* (R) 1.65 1.65
35 A4 5c dp grn (R) 1.90 1.90
36 A4 10c carmine 1.90 1.90
37 A4 15c org brn, *bl* 1.90 1.90
38 A4 20c red, *grn* 3.25 3.25
39 A4 25c dp bl 4.50 4.50
40 A4 30c pale brn 4.50 4.50
41 A4 35c *yel* (R) 7.50 7.50
42 A4 40c *bluish* (R) 7.75 7.75
43 A4 50c gray brn 8.00 8.00
44 A3 75c dp vio, *org* (R) 20.00 20.00
45 A4 1fr pale grn 20.00 20.00
46 A4 2fr brn, *org* (R) 20.00 20.00
47 A3 5fr red lil, *lav* 75.00 75.00
48 A4 10fr org brn, *grn* 92.50 92.50
Nos. 32-48 (17) 272.55 272.55

Stamps of Indo-China, 1907, Surcharged "HOI HAO" and Chinese Characters, in Red or Blue

1908

49 A5 1c ol brn & blk 65 65
50 A5 2c brn & blk 65 65
51 A5 4c bl & blk 95 95
52 A5 5c grn & blk 1.25 1.25
53 A5 10c red & blk (Bl) 1.75 1.75
54 A5 15c vio & blk 2.50 2.50
55 A6 20c vio & blk 3.25 3.25
56 A6 25c bl & blk 3.25 3.25
57 A6 30c brn & blk 3.25 3.25
58 A6 35c ol grn & blk 3.25 3.25
59 A6 40c brn & blk 3.00 3.00
61 A6 50c car & blk (Bl) 3.75 3.75
62 A7 75c ver & blk (Bl) 4.25 4.25
63 A8 1fr car & blk (Bl) 9.50 9.50
64 A9 2fr grn & blk 20.00 20.00
65 A10 5fr bl & blk 40.00 40.00
66 A11 10fr pur & blk 57.50 57.50
Nos. 49-66 (17) 158.75 158.75

Issue of 1908 Surcharged with New Values in Cents or Piasters in Black, Red or Blue

1919

67 A5 ⅖c on 1c ol brn & blk 45 45
68 A5 ⅘c on 2c yel brn & blk 45 45
69 A5 1⅗c on 4c bl & blk (R) 70 70
70 A5 2c on 5c grn & blk 45 45
71 A5 4c on 10c red & blk (Bl) 70 70
a. Chinese "2" instead of "4" 4.25 4.25
72 A5 6c on 15c vio & blk 70 70
73 A6 8c on 20c vio & blk 1.25 1.25
a. "S" of "CENTS" omitted 65.00 65.00
74 A6 10c on 25c bl & blk 2.75 2.75
75 A6 12c on 30c brn & blk 1.00 1.00
76 A6 14c on 35c ol grn & blk 1.00 1.00
a. Closed "4" 9.50 9.50
77 A6 16c on 40c yel brn & blk 1.00 1.00
79 A6 20c on 50c car & blk (Bl) 1.25 1.25
80 A7 30c on 75c ver & blk (Bl) 1.90 1.90
81 A8 40c on 1fr car & blk (Bl) 4.25 4.25
82 A9 80c on 2fr grn & blk (R) 12.00 12.00
83 A10 2pi on 5fr bl & blk (R) 35.00 35.00
a. Triple surcharge of new value 350.00
84 A11 4pi on 10fr pur & blk (R) 110.00 110.00
Nos. 67-84 (17) 174.85 174.85

KWANGCHOWAN

A Chinese Territory leased to France, 1898 to 1945.

Stamps of Indo-China, 1892-1906, Surcharged in Red or Black

Kouang
Tchéou-Wan
花銀八厘

1906 **Unwmk.** ***Perf. 14x13½***

1 A4 1c ol grn (R) 1.25 1.25
2 A4 2c vio brn, *buff* 1.25 1.25
3 A4 4c cl, *bluish* (R) 2.00 2.00
4 A4 5c dp grn (R) 2.00 2.00
5 A4 10c carmine 2.00 2.00
6 A4 15c org brn, *bl* 4.75 4.75
7 A4 20c red, *grn* 2.00 2.00
8 A4 25c dp bl 2.00 2.00
9 A4 30c pale brn 2.50 2.50
10 A4 35c *yel* (R) 3.50 3.50
11 A4 40c *bluish* (R) 2.50 2.50
12 A4 50c bis brn 9.50 9.50
13 A3 75c dp vio, *org* (R) 13.00 13.00
14 A4 1fr pale grn 16.00 16.00
15 A4 2fr brn, *org* (R) 16.00 16.00
16 A3 5fr red lil, *lav* 110.00 110.00
17 A4 10fr org brn, *grn* 150.00 150.00
Nos. 1-17 (17) 340.25 340.25

Various varieties of the surcharge exist on Nos. 2-10.

Stamps of Indo-China, 1907, Surcharged "KOUANG-TCHEOU" and Value in Chinese in Red or Blue

1908

18 A5 1c ol brn & blk 25 25
19 A5 2c brn & blk 25 25
20 A5 4c bl & blk 25 25
21 A5 5c grn & blk 25 25
22 A5 10c red & blk (Bl) 25 25
23 A5 15c vio & blk 80 80
24 A6 20c vio & blk 1.65 1.65
25 A6 25c bl & blk 2.50 2.50
26 A6 30c brn & blk 4.50 4.50
27 A6 35c ol grn & blk 5.50 5.50
28 A6 40c brn & blk 5.50 5.50
30 A6 50c car & blk (Bl) 6.25 6.25
31 A7 75c ver & blk (Bl) 6.25 6.25
32 A8 1fr car & blk (Bl) 7.75 7.75
33 A9 2fr grn & blk 18.00 18.00
34 A10 5fr bl & blk 37.50 37.50
35 A11 10fr pur & blk 55.00 55.00
a. Double surch. 575.00 575.00
b. Triple surch. 575.00 575.00
Nos. 18-35 (17) 152.45 152.45

The Chinese characters overprinted on Nos. 1 to 35 repeat the denomination of the basic stamp.

Issue of 1908 Surcharged with New Values in Cents or Piasters in Black, Red or Blue

1919

36 A5 ⅖c on 1c ol grn & blk 25 25
37 A5 ⅘c on 2c yel brn & blk 25 25
38 A5 1⅗c on 4c bl & blk (R) 35 35
39 A5 2c on 5c grn & blk 35 35
a. "2 CENTS" inverted 47.50
40 A5 4c on 10c red & blk (Bl) 1.10 75
41 A5 6c on 15c vio & blk 35 25
42 A6 8c on 20c vio & blk 1.90 1.75
43 A6 10c on 25c bl & blk 4.75 4.50
44 A6 12c on 30c brn & blk 60 48
45 A6 14c on 35c ol grn & blk 1.00 90
a. Closed "4" 21.00 17.50
46 A6 16c on 40c yel brn & blk 80 65
48 A6 20c on 50c car & blk (Bl) 80 65
49 A7 30c on 75c ver & blk (Bl) 3.00 2.75
50 A8 40c on 1fr car & blk (Bl) 3.75 3.50
a. "40 CENTS" inverted
51 A9 80c on 2fr grn & blk (R) 4.00 3.50
52 A10 2pi on 5fr bl & blk (R) 90.00 80.00
53 A11 4pi on 10fr pur & blk (R) 11.00 10.00
Nos. 36-53 (17) 124.25 110.88

Stamps of Indo-China, 1922-23, Overprinted in Black, Red or Blue

KOUANG-TCHEOU

1923

54 A12 ⅒c blk & sal (Bl) 8 8
55 A12 ⅕c dp bl & blk (R) 8 8
a. Black ovpt. 65.00
56 A12 ⅖c ol brn & blk (R) 18 18
57 A12 ⅘c brt rose & blk 22 22
58 A12 1c yel brn & blk (Bl) 22 22
59 A12 2c gray grn & blk (R) 35 35
60 A12 3c vio & blk (R) 35 35
61 A12 4c org & blk 35 35
62 A12 5c car & blk 35 35
63 A13 6c dl red & blk 45 45
64 A13 7c ol grn & blk 35 35
65 A13 8c blk (R) 60 60
66 A13 9c yel & blk 60 60
67 A13 10c bl & blk 60 60
68 A13 11c vio & blk 60 60
69 A13 12c brn & blk 60 60
70 A13 15c org & blk 80 80
71 A13 20c bl & blk, *straw* (R) 60 60
72 A13 40c ver & blk, *bluish* (Bl) 1.25 1.25
73 A13 1pi bl grn & blk, *grnsh* 3.50 3.50
74 A13 2pi vio brn & blk, *pnksh* (Bl) 6.00 6.00
Nos. 54-74 (21) 18.13 18.13

Indo-China Stamps of 1927 Overprinted in Black or Red

KOUANG-TCHÉOU

1927

75 A14 ⅒c lt ol grn (R) 6 6
76 A14 ⅕c yellow 18 18
77 A14 ⅖c lt bl (R) 22 22
78 A14 ⅘c dp brn 22 22
79 A14 1c orange 25 25
80 A14 2c bl grn (R) 35 35
81 A14 3c ind (R) 35 35
82 A14 4c lil rose 35 35
83 A14 5c dp vio 35 35
84 A15 6c dp red 35 35
85 A15 7c lt brn 35 35
86 A15 8c gray grn (R) 35 35
87 A15 9c red vio 45 45
88 A15 10c lt bl (R) 45 45
89 A15 11c orange 45 45
90 A15 12c myr grn (R) 45 45
91 A16 15c dl rose & ol brn 90 90
92 A16 20c vio & sl (R) 95 95
93 A17 25c org brn & lil rose 95 95
94 A17 30c dp bl & ol gray (R) 90 90
95 A18 40c ver & lt bl 90 90
96 A18 50c lt grn & sl (R) 90 90
97 A19 1pi dk bl, blk & yel (R) 2.00 2.00
98 A19 2pi red, dp bl & org (R) 2.00 2.00
a. Double ovpt. 75.00
Nos. 75-98 (24) 14.68 14.68

Stamps of Indo-China, 1931-41, Overprinted in Black or Red

KOUANG-TCHÉOU

1937-41 ***Perf. 13, 13½***

99 A20 ⅒c Prus bl 5 5
100 A20 ⅕c lake 6 6
101 A20 ⅖c org red 8 8
102 A20 ½c red brn 8 8
103 A20 ⅘c dk vio 18 18
104 A20 1c blk brn 18 18
105 A20 2c dk grn 18 18
a. Inverted ovpt. 75.00
106 A21 3c dk grn 52 52
107 A21 3c yel brn ('41) 8 8
108 A21 4c dk bl (R) 35 35
109 A21 4c dk grn ('41) 18 18
110 A21 4c yel org ('41) 1.10 1.10
111 A21 5c dp vio 35 35
112 A21 5c dp grn ('41) 20 20
113 A21 6c org red 25 25
114 A21 7c blk (R) ('41) 25 25
115 A21 8c rose lake ('41) 25 25
116 A21 9c blk, *yel* (R) ('41) 25 25
d. Black ovpt. 5.50 5.50
117 A22 10c dk bl (R) 85 85
118 A22 10c ultra, *pink* (R) ('41) 35 35
119 A22 15c dk bl (R) 25 25
120 A22 18c bl (R) ('41) 8 8
121 A22 20c rose 25 25
122 A22 21c ol grn 25 25
123 A22 22c grn ('41) 20 20
124 A22 25c dp vio 1.65 1.65
125 A22 25c dk bl (R) ('41) 25 25
126 A22 30c org brn 25 25
127 A23 50c dk brn 70 70
128 A23 60c dl vio 70 70
129 A23 70c lt bl (R) ('41) 25 25
130 A23 1pi yel grn 95 95
131 A23 2pi red 1.00 1.00
Nos. 99-131 (33) 12.57 12.57

Colonial Arts Exhibition Issue
Common Design Type
Souvenir Sheet

1937 **Engr.** ***Imperf.***
132 CD79 30c grn & sep 2.75 2.75

Sheet size: 118x99mm.

New York World's Fair Issue
Common Design Type

1939 **Unwmk.** ***Perf. 12½x12***
133 CD82 13c car lake 65 65
134 CD82 23c ultra 65 65

Petain Issue
Indo-China Nos. 209-209A Overprinted "KOUANG TCHEOU" in Blue or Red

1941 **Engr.** ***Perf. 12½x12***
135 A27a 10c car lake (B) 35
136 A27a 25c bl (R) 35

Nos. 135-136 were issued by the Vichy government, and were not placed on sale in Kwangchowan. This is also true of 16 stamps of Indo-China types A20-A23 without "RF" and overprinted "KOUANG-TCHEOU."

SEMI-POSTAL STAMPS

French Revolution Issue
Common Design Type

1939 **Unwmk.** **Photo.** ***Perf. 13***
Name and Value Typo. in Black

B1 CD83 6c + 2c grn 3.00 3.00
B2 CD83 7c + 3c brn 3.00 3.00
B3 CD83 9c + 4c red org 3.00 3.00
B4 CD83 13c + 10c rose pink 3.00 3.00
B5 CD83 23c + 20c bl 3.00 3.00
Nos. B1-B5 (5) 15.00 15.00

Indo-China Nos. B19A and B19C Overprinted "KOUANG-TCHEOU" in Blue or Red, and Common Design Type

1941 **Photo.** ***Perf. 13½***
B6 SP1 10c + 10c red (B) 35
B7 CD86 15c + 30c mar & car 35
B8 SP2 25c + 10c bl (R) 45

Nos. B6-B8 were issued by the Vichy government, and were not placed on sale in Kwangchowan.

Nos. 135-136 were surcharged "OEUVRES COLONIALES" and surtax (including change of denomination of the 25c to 5c). These were issued in 1944 by the Vichy government, and not placed on sale in Kwangchowan.

AIR POST SEMI-POSTAL STAMPS

Stamps of Indo-China types V4, V5 and V6 overprinted "KOUANG-TCHEOU" and type of Cameroons V10 inscribed "KOUANG-TCHEOU" were issued in 1942 by the Vichy Government, but were not placed on sale in the territory.

MONGTSEU (MENGTSZ)

Stamps of Indo-China Surcharged in Black

MONGTZE
仙 六

1903-04 **Unwmk.** ***Perf. 14x13½***

1 A3 1c *lil bl* 3.25 3.25
2 A3 2c brn, *buff* 1.90 1.90
3 A3 4c cl, *lav* 3.25 3.25
4 A3 5c yel grn 2.50 2.50
5 A3 10c red 3.50 3.50
6 A3 15c gray 4.25 4.25
7 A3 20c red, *grn* 4.50 4.50
7C A3 25c *rose* 375.00 375.00
8 A3 25c blue 5.00 5.00
9 A3 30c brn, *bis* 4.25 4.25
10 A3 40c red, *straw* 30.00 30.00
11 A3 50c car, *rose* 175.00 175.00
12 A3 50c brn, *az* ('04) 52.50 52.50
13 A3 75c dp vio, *org* 52.50 52.50
a. "INDO-CHINE" inverted 31,000.

14 A3 1fr brnz grn, *straw* 52.50 52.50
15 A3 5fr red lil, *lav* 52.50 52.50
Nos. 1-15 (16) 822.40 822.40

Many varieties of the surcharge exist on Nos. 1-15.

Common Design Types pictured in section at front of book.

Stamps of Indo-China, 1892-1906, Surcharged in Red or Black

Mong-Tseu
花銀八厘

1906

16 A4 1c ol grn (R) 80 80
17 A4 2c vio brn, *buff* 80 80
18 A4 4c cl, *bluish*(R) 80 80
19 A4 5c dp grn (R) 80 80
20 A4 10c carmine 1.00 1.00
21 A4 15c org brn, *bl* 1.00 1.00
22 A4 20c red, *grn* 2.00 2.00
23 A4 25c dp bl 2.00 2.00
24 A4 30c pale brn 3.50 3.50
25 A4 35c *yel* (R) 2.50 2.50
26 A4 40c *bluish* (R) 3.00 3.00
27 A4 50c bis brn 8.25 8.25
28 A3 75c dp vio, *org* (R) 20.00 20.00
a. "INDO-CHINE" inverted 31,000.
29 A4 1fr pale grn 9.50 9.50
30 A4 2fr brn, *org* (R) 25.00 25.00
31 A3 5fr red lil, *lav* 55.00 55.00
32 A4 10fr org brn, *grn* 75.00 75.00
a. Chinese characters inverted 1,400. 1,750.
Nos. 16-32 (17) 210.95 210.95

Inverted varieties of the surcharge exist on Nos. 19, 22 and 32.

Stamps of Indo-China, 1907, Surcharged "MONGTSEU" and Value in Chinese in Red or Blue

1908

33 A5 1c ol brn & blk 30 30
34 A5 2c brn & blk 30 30
35 A5 4c bl & blk 48 48
36 A5 5c grn & blk 60 60
37 A5 10c red & blk (Bl) 80 80
38 A5 15c vio & blk 80 80
39 A6 20c vio & blk 2.50 2.50
40 A6 25c bl & blk 3.25 3.25
41 A6 30c brn & blk 2.00 2.00
42 A6 35c ol grn & blk 2.00 2.00
43 A6 40c brn & blk 2.00 2.00
45 A6 50c car & blk (Bl) 2.00 2.00
46 A7 75c ver & blk (Bl) 5.25 5.25
47 A8 1fr car & blk (Bl) 6.25 6.25
48 A9 2fr grn & blk 7.50 7.50
49 A10 5fr bl & blk 55.00 55.00
50 A11 10fr pur & blk 67.50 67.50
Nos. 33-50 (17) 158.53 158.53

The Chinese characters overprinted on Nos. 1 to 50 repeat the denomination of the basic stamp.

Issue of 1908 Surcharged with New Values in Cents or Piasters in Black, Red or Blue

1919

51 A5 ⅖c on 1c ol brn & blk 30 30
52 A5 ⅘c on 2c yel brn & blk 30 30
53 A5 1⅗c on 4c bl & blk (R) 75 75
54 A5 2c on 5c grn & blk 45 45
55 A5 4c on 10c red & blk (Bl) 95 95
56 A5 6c on 15c vio & blk 95 95
57 A6 8c on 20c vio & blk 1.65 1.65
58 A6 10c on 25c bl & blk 1.40 1.40
59 A6 12c on 30c brn & blk 1.40 1.40
60 A6 14c on 35c ol grn & blk 1.40 1.40
a. Closed "4" 8.00 8.00
61 A6 16c on 40c yel brn & blk 1.90 1.90
63 A6 20c on 50c car & blk (Bl) 1.90 1.90
64 A7 30c on 75c ver & blk (Bl) 1.65 1.65
65 A8 40c on 1fr car & blk (Bl) 4.00 4.00
66 A9 80c on 2fr grn & blk (R) 2.50 2.50
a. Triple surcharge, one inverted 275.00 275.00
67 A10 2pi on 5fr bl & blk (R) 65.00 65.00
a. Triple surcharge, one inverted 275.00 275.00
b. Double surch. 275.00 275.00
68 A11 4pi on 10fr pur & blk (R) 11.00 11.00
Nos. 51-68 (17) 97.50 97.50

PAKHOI

Stamps of Indo-China Surcharged in Black

PACKHOI
仙六

1903-04 Unwmk. *Perf. 14x13½*

1 A3 1c *lil bl* 3.50 3.50
2 A3 2c brn, *buff* 2.50 2.50
3 A3 4c cl, *lav* 2.00 2.00
4 A3 5c yel grn 2.00 2.00
5 A3 10c red 1.65 1.65
6 A3 15c gray 1.65 1.65
7 A3 20c red, *grn* 3.50 3.50
8 A3 25c blue 3.50 3.50
9 A3 25c *rose*('04) 2.50 2.50
10 A3 30c brn, *bis* 3.50 3.50
11 A3 40c red, *straw* 25.00 25.00
12 A3 50c car, *rose* 225.00 225.00
13 A3 50c brn, *az* ('04) 27.50 27.50
14 A3 75c dp vio, *org* 27.50 27.50
a. "INDO-CHINE" inverted 22,000.
15 A3 1fr brnz grn, *straw* 30.00 30.00
16 A3 5fr red lil, *lav* 55.00 55.00
Nos. 1-16 (16) 416.30 416.30

Many varieties of the surcharge exist on Nos. 1-16.

Stamps of Indo-China 1892-1906, Surcharged in Red or Black

PAK-HOI
花銀八厘

1906

17 A4 1c ol grn (R) 75 75
18 A4 2c vio brn, *buff* 75 75
19 A4 4c cl, *bluish* (R) 75 75
20 A4 5c dp grn (R) 75 75
21 A4 10c carmine 75 75
22 A4 15c org brn, *bl* 2.50 2.50
23 A4 20c red, *grn* 1.75 1.75
24 A4 25c dp bl 1.75 1.75
25 A4 30c pale brn 1.75 1.75
26 A4 35c *yel* (R) 1.75 1.75
27 A4 40c *bluish* (R) 1.75 1.75
28 A4 50c bis brn 3.50 3.50
29 A3 75c dp vio, *org* (R) 22.50 22.50
30 A4 1fr pale grn 14.00 14.00
31 A4 2fr brn, *org* (R) 22.50 22.50
32 A3 5fr red lil, *lav* 57.50 57.50
33 A4 10fr org brn, *grn* 70.00 70.00
Nos. 17-33 (17) 205.00 205.00

Various varieties of the surcharge exist on Nos. 17-24.

Stamps of Indo-China, 1907, Surcharged "PAKHOI" and Value in Chinese in Red or Blue

1908

34 A5 1c ol brn & blk 30 30
35 A5 2c brn & blk 42 42
36 A5 4c bl & blk 42 42
37 A5 5c grn & blk 70 70
38 A5 10c red & blk (Bl) 70 70
39 A5 15c vio & blk 90 90
40 A6 20c vio & blk 90 90
41 A6 25c bl & blk 1.00 1.00
42 A6 30c brn & blk 1.50 1.50
43 A6 35c ol grn & blk 1.50 1.50
44 A6 40c brn & blk 1.50 1.50
46 A6 50c car & blk (Bl) 1.50 1.50
47 A7 75c ver & blk (Bl) 3.25 3.25
48 A8 1fr car & blk (Bl) 4.00 4.00
49 A9 2fr grn & blk 9.00 9.00
50 A10 5fr bl & blk 52.50 52.50
51 A11 10fr pur & blk 82.50 82.50
Nos. 34-51 (17) 162.59 162.59

The Chinese characters overprinted on Nos. 1 to 51 repeat the denomination of the basic stamps.

Issue of 1908 Surcharged with New Values in Cents or Piasters in Black, Red or Blue

1919

52 A5 ⅖c on 1c ol brn & blk 42 42
a. "PAK-HOI" and Chinese double 125.00 125.00
53 A5 ⅘c on 2c yel brn & blk 42 42
54 A5 1⅗c on 4c bl & blk (R) 42 42
55 A5 2c on 5c grn & blk 60 60
56 A5 4c on 10c red & blk (Bl) 1.50 1.50
57 A5 6c on 15c vio & blk 60 60
58 A6 8c on 20c vio & blk 1.50 1.50
59 A6 10c on 25c bl & blk 1.90 1.90
60 A6 12c on 30c brn & blk 80 80
a. "12 CENTS" double 100.00 100.00
61 A6 14c on 35c ol grn & blk 42 42
a. Closed "4" 5.50 5.50
62 A6 16c on 40c yel brn & blk 1.25 1.25
64 A6 20c on 50c car & blk (Bl) 80 80
65 A7 30c on 75c ver & blk (Bl) 1.25 1.25
66 A8 40c on 1fr car & blk (Bl) 5.50 5.50
67 A9 80c on 2fr grn & blk (R) 2.50 2.50
68 A10 2pi on 5fr bl & blk (R) 5.75 5.75
69 A11 4pi on 10fr pur & blk (R) 11.00 11.00
Nos. 52-69 (17) 36.63 36.63

TCHONGKING (CHUNGKING)

Stamps of Indo-China Surcharged in Black

TCHONGKING
仙六

1903-04 Unwmk. *Perf. 14x13½*

1 A3 1c *lil bl* 1.40 1.40
2 A3 2c brn, *buff* 1.40 1.40
3 A3 4c cl, *lav* 1.40 1.40
4 A3 5c yel grn 1.40 1.40
5 A3 10c red 1.40 1.40
6 A3 15c gray 1.40 1.40
7 A3 20c red, *grn* 1.40 1.40
8 A3 25c blue 20.00 20.00
9 A3 25c *rose* ('04) 3.50 3.50
10 A3 30c brn, *bis* 5.00 5.00
11 A3 40c red, *straw* 20.00 20.00
12 A3 50c car, *rose* 125.00 125.00
13 A3 50c brn, *az* ('04) 70.00 70.00
14 A3 75c vio, *org* 20.00 20.00
15 A3 1fr brnz grn, *straw* 27.50 27.50
16 A3 5fr red lil, *lav* 50.00 50.00
Nos. 1-16 (16) 350.80 350.80

Many varieties of the surcharge exist on Nos. 1-14.

Stamps of Indo-China and French China, issued in 1902 with similar overprint, but without Chinese characters, were not officially authorized.

Stamps of Indo-China, 1892-1906, Surcharged in Red or Black

Tch'ong K'ing
花銀八厘

1906

17 A4 1c ol grn (R) 90 90
18 A4 2c vio brn, *buff* 90 90
19 A4 4c cl, *bluish* (R) 90 90
20 A4 5c dp grn (R) 90 90
21 A4 10c carmine 90 90
22 A4 15c org brn, *bl* 3.25 3.25
23 A4 20c red, *grn* 90 90
24 A4 25c dp bl 2.00 2.00
25 A4 30c pale brn 1.75 1.75
26 A4 35c *yellow* (R) 1.75 1.75
27 A4 40c *bluish* (R) 3.25 3.25
28 A4 50c bis brn 3.25 3.25
29 A3 75c dp vio, *org* (R) 16.00 16.00
30 A4 1fr pale grn 13.00 13.00
31 A4 2fr brn, *org* (R) 13.00 13.00
32 A3 5fr red lil, *lav* 65.00 65.00
33 A4 10fr org brn, *grn* 70.00 70.00
Nos. 17-33 (17) 197.65 197.65

Variety "T" omitted in surcharge occurs once in each sheet of Nos. 17-33. Other surcharge varieties exist, such as inverted surcharge on 1c and 2c.

Stamps of Indo-China, 1907, Surcharged "TCHONGKING" and Value in Chinese in Red or Blue

1908

34 A5 1c ol brn & blk 14 14
35 A5 2c brn & blk 25 25
36 A5 4c bl & blk 30 30
37 A5 5c grn & blk 55 55
38 A5 10c red & blk (Bl) 70 70
39 A5 15c vio & blk 85 85
40 A6 20c vio & blk 1.65 1.65
41 A6 25c bl & blk 1.65 1.65
42 A6 30c brn & blk 1.75 1.75
43 A6 35c ol grn & blk 3.00 3.00
44 A6 40c brn & blk 6.50 6.50
45 A6 50c car & blk (Bl) 4.50 4.50
46 A7 75c ver & blk (Bl) 4.50 4.50
47 A8 1fr car & blk (Bl) 6.25 6.25
48 A9 2fr grn & blk 50.00 50.00
49 A10 5fr bl & blk 17.00 17.00
50 A11 10fr pur & blk 140.00 140.00
Nos. 34-50 (17) 239.59 239.59

The Chinese characters overprinted on Nos. 1 to 50 repeat the denomination of the basic stamp.

Issue of 1908 Surcharged with New Values in Cents or Piasters in Black, Red or Blue

1919

51 A5 ⅖c on 1c ol brn & blk 52 52
52 A5 ⅘c on 2c yel brn & blk 60 60
53 A5 1⅗c on 4c bl & blk (R) 80 80
54 A5 2c on 5c grn & blk 70 52
55 A5 4c on 10c red & blk (Bl) 52 52
56 A5 6c on 15c vio & blk 52 52
57 A6 8c on 20c vio & blk 52 52
58 A6 10c on 25c bl & blk 80 70
59 A6 12c on 30c brn & blk 1.00 70
60 A6 14c on 35c ol grn & blk 1.00 60
a. Closed "4" 8.00 8.00
61 A6 16c on 40c yel brn & blk 1.25 1.00
a. "16 CENTS" dbl. 65.00 65.00
62 A6 20c on 50c car & blk (Bl) 4.75 4.75
63 A7 30c on 75c ver & blk (Bl) 1.25 1.25
64 A8 40c on 1fr car & blk (Bl) 1.90 1.25
65 A9 80c on 2fr grn & blk (R) 2.75 2.25
66 A10 2pi on 5fr bl & blk (R) 3.50 3.00
67 A11 4pi on 10fr pur & blk (R) 5.50 4.50
Nos. 51-67 (17) 27.88 24.00

YUNNAN FOU

(Formerly Yunnan Sen, later known as Kunming)

Stamps of Indo-China Surcharged in Black

YUNNANSEN
仙六

1903-04 Unwmk. *Perf. 14x13½*

1 A3 1c *lil bl* 2.75 2.25
2 A3 2c brn, *buff* 2.25 2.25
3 A3 4c cl, *lav* 2.25 2.25
4 A3 5c yel grn 2.25 2.25
5 A3 10c red 2.25 2.25
6 A3 15c gray 3.50 2.75
7 A3 20c red, *grn* 4.00 3.00
8 A3 25c blue 2.75 3.00
9 A3 30c brn, *bis* 4.50 3.00
10 A3 40c red, *straw* 42.50 27.50
11 A3 50c car, *rose* 215.00 200.00
12 A3 50c brn, *az* ('04) 100.00 100.00
13 A3 75c dp vio, *org* 27.50 25.00
a. "INDO-CHINE" inverted 22,000.
14 A3 1fr brnz grn, *straw* 30.00 27.50
15 A3 5fr red lil, *lav* 62.50 60.00
Nos. 1-15 (15) 504.00 463.00

The Chinese characters overprinted on Nos. 1 to 15 repeat the denomination of the basic stamp.

Many varieties of the surcharge exist on Nos. 1-15.

Stamps of Indo-China, 1892-1906, Surcharged in Red or Black

Yunnan-Fou
花銀八厘

1906 Unwmk. *Perf. 14 x 13½*

17 A4 1c ol grn (R) 1.10 1.10
18 A4 2c vio brn, *buff* 1.25 1.25
19 A4 4c cl, *bluish* (R) 1.50 1.50
20 A4 5c dp grn (R) 1.50 1.50
21 A4 10c carmine 1.50 1.50

22 A4 15c org brn, *bl* 3.00 3.00
23 A4 20c red, *grn* 2.00 2.00
24 A4 25c dp bl 2.75 2.75
25 A4 30c pale brn 2.00 2.00
26 A4 35c *yel* (R) 3.50 3.50
27 A4 40c *bluish* (R) 2.75 2.75
28 A4 50c bis brn 3.50 3.50
29 A3 75c dp vio, *org* (R) 27.50 27.50
30 A4 1fr pale grn 10.00 10.00
31 A4 2fr brn, *org* (R) 10.00 10.00
32 A3 5fr red lil, *lav* 42.50 42.50
33 A4 10fr org brn, *grn* 47.50 47.50
Nos. 17-33 (17) 163.85 163.85

Various varieties of the surcharge exist on Nos. 18, 20, 21 and 27.

Stamps of Indo-China, 1907, Surcharged "YUNNANFOU", and Value in Chinese in Red or Blue

1908

34 A5 1c ol brn & blk 60 60
35 A5 2c brn & blk 60 60
36 A5 4c bl & blk 60 60
37 A5 5c grn & blk 90 90
38 A5 10c red & blk (Bl) 60 60
39 A5 15c vio & blk 2.25 1.75
40 A6 20c vio & blk 2.50 2.00
41 A6 25c bl & blk 2.50 2.00
42 A6 30c brn & blk 3.50 2.75
43 A6 35c ol grn & blk 3.50 2.75
44 A6 40c brn & blk 3.75 3.75
45 A6 50c car & blk (Bl) 3.75 3.75
46 A7 75c ver & blk (Bl) 4.50 3.75
47 A8 1fr car & blk (Bl) 7.75 5.50
48 A9 2fr grn & blk 12.50 10.00
a. "YUNANNFOU" *1,600. 1,600.*
49 A10 5fr bl & blk 30.00 25.00
a. "YUNANNFOU" *1,600. 1,600.*
50 A11 10fr pur & blk 45.00 45.00
a. "YUNANNFOU" *1,600. 1,600.*
Nos. 34-50 (17) 124.80 111.30

The Chinese characters overprinted on Nos. 17 to 50 repeat the denomination of the basic stamp.

Issue of 1908 Surcharged with New Values in Cents or Piasters in Black, Red or Blue

1919

51 A5 ⅖c on 1c ol brn & blk 52 52
a. New value double 65.00
52 A5 ⅘c on 2c yel brn & blk 80 70
53 A5 1⅗c on 4c bl & blk (R) 90 80
54 A5 2c on 5c grn & blk 80 70
a. Triple surcharge 110.00
55 A5 4c on 10c red & blk (Bl) 80 70
56 A5 6c on 15c vio & blk 80 70
57 A6 8c on 20c vio & blk 1.00 90
58 A6 10c on 25c bl & blk 1.40 1.25
59 A6 12c on 30c brn & blk 1.25 1.00
60 A6 14c on 35c ol grn & blk 2.25 2.00
a. Closed "4" 60.00 60.00
61 A6 16c on 40c yel brn & blk 2.50 2.00
62 A6 20c on 50c car & blk (Bl) 1.40 1.40
63 A7 30c on 75c ver & blk (Bl) 2.50 2.50
64 A8 40c on 1fr car & blk (Bl) 3.25 3.00
65 A9 80c on 2fr grn & blk (R) 3.75 3.75
a. Triple surch., one inverted 175.00
66 A10 2pi on 5fr bl & blk (R) 22.50 22.50
67 A11 4pi on 10fr pur & blk (R) 7.50 7.00
Nos. 51-67 (17) 53.92 51.42

OFFICES IN CRETE

Austria, France, Italy and Great Britain maintained their own post offices in Crete during the period when that country was an autonomous state.

100 CENTIMES = 1 FRANC

Liberty, Equality and Fraternity A1

"Rights of Man" A2

Liberty and Peace (Symbolized by Olive Branch) — A3

Perf. 14x13½

1902-03 Unwmk. Typo.

1 A1 1c gray 95 95
2 A1 2c vio brn 1.00 1.00
3 A1 3c red org 1.00 1.00
4 A1 4c yel brn 1.00 1.00
5 A1 5c green 90 60
6 A2 10c rose red 1.25 90
7 A2 15c pale red ('03) 1.25 95
8 A2 20c brn vio ('03) 1.75 1.40
9 A2 25c bl ('03) 2.25 1.75
10 A2 30c lil ('03) 3.25 3.00
11 A3 40c red & pale bl 5.00 4.00
12 A3 50c bis brn & lav 8.00 7.50
13 A3 1fr cl & ol grn 10.00 8.00
14 A3 2fr gray vio & yel 17.50 16.00
15 A3 5fr dk bl & buff 27.50 24.00
Nos. 1-15 (15) 82.60 72.05

A4

A5

Black Surcharge

1903

16 A4 1pi on 25c bl 20.00 18.00
17 A5 2pi on 50c bis brn & lav 37.50 27.50
18 A5 4pi on 1fr cl & ol grn 55.00 47.50
19 A5 8pi on 2fr gray vio & yel 62.50 62.50
20 A5 20pi on 5fr dk bl & buff 100.00 90.00
Nos. 16-20 (5) 275.00 245.50

OFFICES IN EGYPT

French post offices formerly maintained in Alexandria and Port Said.

100 CENTIMES = 1 FRANC

ALEXANDRIA

A1

French Stamps Overprinted in Red, Blue or Black

1899-1900 Unwmk. *Perf. 14x13½*

1 A1 1c *lil bl* (R) 65 65
a. Double overprint 67.50
b. Triple overprint 67.50
2 A1 2c brn, *buff* (Bl) 95 95
3 A1 3c gray, *grysh* (Bl) 1.25 1.00
4 A1 4c cl, *lav*(Bl) 1.10 90
5 A1 5c yel grn, (I) (R) 2.00 1.25
a. Type II (R) 95.00 67.50
6 A1 10c *lav,* (I) (R) 4.50 3.75
a. Type II (R) 37.50 18.00
7 A1 15c bl (R) 3.75 2.50
8 A1 20c red, *grn* 7.50 3.75
a. Double ovpt.
9 A1 25c *rose* (R) 3.00 1.90
a. Inverted overprint 47.50
b. Double overprint, one inverted 82.50
10 A1 30c brn, *bis* 8.50 6.00
11 A1 40c red, *straw* 6.75 6.75
12 A1 50c car, *rose* (II) 13.00 7.00
a. Type I 110.00 9.50
13 A1 1fr brnz grn, *straw* 13.00 8.50
14 A1 2fr brn, *az* ('00) 60.00 42.50
15 A1 5fr red lil, *lav* 77.50 67.50
Nos. 1-15 (15) 203.45 154.90

A2

A3

A4

1902-03

16 A2 1c gray 38 15
17 A2 2c vio brn 38 22
18 A2 3c red org 38 18
19 A2 4c yel brn 52 30
20 A2 5c green 70 38
21 A3 10c rose red 85 38
22 A3 15c orange 70 45
a. 15c pale red ('03) 1.00 52
23 A3 20c brn vio ('03) 1.10 60
24 A3 25c bl ('03) 52 22
25 A3 30c vio ('03) 2.75 1.25
26 A4 40c red & pale bl 2.25 80
27 A4 50c bis brn & lav 3.50 1.10
28 A4 1fr cl & ol grn 4.50 1.40
29 A4 2fr gray vio & yel 8.50 4.75
30 A4 5fr dk bl & buff 11.00 7.50
Nos. 16-30 (15) 38.03 19.68

The 2c, 5c, 10c, 20c and 25c exist imperf. Price, each $15.

See Nos. 77-86.

Stamps of 1902-03 Surcharged Locally in Black **4 Mill.**

1921

31 A2 2m on 5c grn 3.00 2.25
32 A2 3m on 3c red org 3.25 2.25
a. Larger numeral 47.50 40.00
33 A3 4m on 10c rose 2.50 2.25
34 A2 5m on 1c dk gray 3.75 3.00
35 A2 5m on 4c yel brn 3.75 3.00
36 A3 6m on 15c org 1.75 1.75
a. Larger numeral 45.00 45.00
37 A3 8m on 20c brn vio 3.00 2.25
a. Larger numeral 21.00 19.00
38 A3 10m on 25c bl 1.10 1.10
a. Inverted surcharge 22.50 22.50
b. Double surcharge 22.50 22.50
39 A3 12m on 30c vio 8.25 8.25
40 A2 15m on 2c vio brn 3.25 3.25

Surcharged **15 Mill.**

41 A4 15m on 40c red & pale bl 9.00 8.25
42 A4 15m on 50c bis brn & lav 3.75 3.75
43 A4 30m on 1fr cl & ol grn 110.00 100.00
44 A4 60m on 2fr gray vio & yel 150.00 150.00
a. Larger numeral 400.00 400.00
45 A4 150m on 5fr dk bl & buff 225.00 225.00

Port Said Nos. 20 and 19 Surcharged like Nos. 32 and 40

45A A2 3m on 3c red org 67.50 67.50
46 A2 15m on 2c vio brn 67.50 67.50

Alexandria No. 28 Surcharged with Two New Values

1921

46A A4 30m on 15m on 1fr cl & ol grn 750.00 750.00

The surcharge "15 Mill." was made in error and is cancelled by a bar.

The surcharges were lithographed on Nos. 31, 33, 38, 39 and 42 and typographed on the other stamps of the 1921 issue. Nos. 34, 36 and 37 were surcharged by both methods.

Alexandria Stamps of 1902-03 Surcharged in Paris **2 MILLIEMES**

1921-23

47 A2 1m on 1c gray 90 90
48 A2 2m on 5c grn 85 85
49 A3 4m on 10c rose 1.50 1.40
50 A3 4m on 10c grn ('23) 1.00 85
51 A2 5m on 3c red org ('23) 3.25 3.00
52 A3 6m on 15c org 90 80
53 A3 8m on 20c brn vio 70 52
54 A3 10m on 25c bl 70 48
55 A3 10m on 30c vio 2.00 1.65
56 A3 15m on 50c bl ('23) 1.25 85

Surcharged **15 MILLIÈMES**

57 A4 15m on 50c bis brn & lav 2.00 1.65
58 A4 30m on 1fr cl & ol grn 1.25 1.10
59 A4 60m on 2fr gray vio & yel *1,300. 1,300.*
60 A4 60m on 2fr org & pale bl ('23) 5.00 3.00
61 A4 150m on 5fr bl & buff 6.00 3.00
Nos. 47-58,60-61 (14) 27.30 20.05

Stamps and Types of 1902-03 Surcharged with New Values and Bars in Black

1925

62 A2 1m on 1c gray 45 45
63 A2 2m on 5c org 38 38
64 A2 2m on 5c grn 85 85
65 A3 4m on 10c grn 60 45
66 A2 5m on 3c red org 45 45
67 A3 6m on 15c org 60 45
68 A3 8m on 20c brn vio 60 52
69 A3 10m on 25c bl 38 38
70 A3 15m on 50c bl 85 70
71 A4 30m on 1fr cl & ol grn 95 75
72 A4 60m on 2fr org & pale bl 1.90 1.65
73 A4 150m on 5fr dk bl & buff 2.50 2.00
Nos. 62-73 (12) 10.51 9.03

Types of 1902-03 Issue

1927-28

77 A2 3m org ('28) 75 70
81 A3 15m sl bl 75 70
82 A3 20m rose lil ('28) 2.25 1.65
84 A4 50m org & bl 5.50 4.50
85 A4 100m sl bl & buff 7.00 5.50
86 A4 250m gray grn & red 13.00 9.25
Nos. 77-86 (6) 29.25 22.30

SEMI-POSTAL STAMPS

Regular Issue of 1902-03 Surcharged in Carmine **+5c**

1915 Unwmk. *Perf. 14 x 13½*

B1 A3 10c + 5c rose 45 45

Sinking Fund Issue

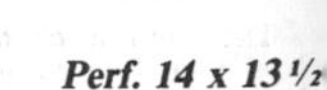

Type of 1902-03 Issue Surcharged in Blue or Black **+5 Mm Caisse d'Amortissement**

1927-30

B2 A3 15m + 5m dp org 1.50 1.50
B3 A3 15m + 5m red vio ('28) 2.25 2.25
a. 15m + 5m vio ('30) 5.25 5.25

Type of 1902-03 Issue Surcharged as in 1927-28

1929

B4 A3 15m + 5m fawn 3.75 3.75

POSTAGE DUE STAMPS

Postage Due Stamps of France, 1893-1920, Surcharged in Paris in Black **2 MILLIEMES**

1922 Unwmk. *Perf. 14 x 13½*

J1 D2 2m on 5c bl 1.25 1.25
J2 D2 4m on 10c brn 1.25 1.25

J3 D2 10m on 30c rose red 1.50 1.50
J4 D2 15m on 50c brn vio 1.65 1.65
J5 D2 30m on 1fr red brn, *straw* 2.75 2.75
Nos. J1-J5 (5) 8.40 8.40

D3

1928 **Typo.**
J6 D3 1m slate 90 90
J7 D3 2m lt bl 75 75
J8 D3 4m lil rose 1.00 1.00
J9 D3 5m gray grn 70 70
J10 D3 10m lt red 90 90
J11 D3 20m vio brn 75 75
J12 D3 30m green 2.50 2.50
J13 D3 40m lt vio 2.25 2.25
Nos. J6-J13 (8) 9.75 9.75

Nos. J6 to J13 were also available for use in Port Said.

PORT SAID

A1

Stamps of France Overprinted in Red, Blue or Black

1899-1900 **Unwmk.** ***Perf. 14 x 13½***
1 A1 1c *lil bl* (R) 75 52
2 A1 2c brn, *buff* (bl) 90 70
3 A1 3c gray, *grysh* (Bl) 1.00 85
4 A1 4c cl, *lav* (Bl) 1.00 85
5 A1 5c yel grn (I) (R) 5.00 2.50
a. Type II (R) 27.50 7.50
6 A1 10c *lav* (I) (R) 6.75 6.75
a. Type II (R) 30.00 20.00
7 A1 15c bl (R) 6.75 4.25
8 A1 20c red, *grn* 7.50 4.25
9 A1 25c *rose* (R) 7.00 1.50
a. Double overprint 110.00
10 A1 30c brn, *bis* 7.50 4.25
a. Inverted overprint 110.00
11 A1 40c red, *straw* 8.25 4.50
12 A1 50c car, *rose* (II) 11.00 5.75
a. Type I 200.00 57.50
b. Dbl. ovpt. (II) 150.00
13 A1 1fr brnz grn, *straw* 15.00 7.50
14 A1 2fr brn, *az* ('00) 40.00 30.00
15 A1 5fr red lil, *lav* 65.00 45.00
Nos. 1-15 (15) 183.40 119.17

Regular Issue Surcharged in Red

1899
16 A1 25c on 10c *lav* 82.50 19.00

With Additional Surcharge "25"
17 A1 25c on 10c *lav* 300.00 120.00

A2

A3

A4

1902-03 **Typo.**
18 A2 1c gray 38 30
19 A2 2c vio brn 38 30
20 A2 3c red org 45 30
21 A2 4c yel brn 52 38
22 A2 5c bl grn 52 45
a. 5c yel grn 1.75 1.50
23 A3 10c rose red 90 52
24 A3 15c pale red ('03) 90 90
a. 15c org 1.00 90
25 A3 20c brn vio ('03) 90 60
26 A3 25c bl ('03) 1.00 75
27 A3 30c vio ('03) 2.50 1.90
28 A4 40c red & pale bl 2.50 1.90
29 A4 50c bis brn & lav 3.50 2.50
30 A4 1fr cl & ol grn 4.25 3.00
31 A4 2fr gray vio & yel 6.75 6.00
32 A4 5fr dk bl & buff 15.00 13.00
Nos. 18-32 (15) 40.45 32.80

See Nos. 83-92.

Stamps of 1902-03 Surcharged Locally — **2 Milliemes**

1921
33 A2 2m on 5c grn 3.75 3.75
a. Inverted surcharge 24.00 24.00
34 A3 4m on 10c rose 3.75 3.75
a. Inverted surcharge 24.00 24.00
35 A2 5m on 1c gray 5.25 5.25
a. Inverted surcharge 45.00 45.00
c. Surcharged "2 Milliemes" 30.00 30.00
36 A2 5m on 2c vio brn 6.75 6.75
a. Surcharged "2 Milliemes" 37.50 37.50
b. Sames as "a," inverted 62.50 62.50
37 A2 5m on 3c red org 5.25 5.25
a. Inverted surcharge 26.00 26.00
b. On Alexandria #18 190.00 190.00
38 A2 5m on 4c yel brn 5.25 5.25
a. Inverted surcharge 45.00 45.00
39 A2 10m on 2c vio brn 6.75 6.75
40 A2 10m on 4c yel brn 10.50 10.50
a. Inverted surcharge 45.00 45.00
41 A3 10m on 25c bl 3.25 3.25
a. Inverted surcharge 45.00 45.00
42 A3 12m on 30c vio 19.00 19.00
43 A2 15m on 4c yel brn 4.00 4.00
a. Inverted surcharge 45.00 45.00
44 A3 15m on 15c pale red 30.00 30.00
a. Inverted surcharge 60.00 60.00
45 A3 15m on 20c brn vio 30.00 30.00
a. Inverted surcharge 60.00 60.00
46 A4 30m on 50c bis brn & lav 200.00 200.00
47 A4 60m on 50c bis brn & lav 225.00 225.00
48 A4 150m on 50c bis brn & lav 275.00 275.00

Nos. 46, 47 and 48 have a bar between the numerals and "Milliemes", which is in capital letters.

Same Surcharge on Stamps of French Offices in Turkey, 1902-03
49 A2 2m on 2c vio brn 47.50 47.50
50 A2 5m on 1c gray 42.50 42.50
a. "5" inverted 475.00 475.00

Stamps of 1902-03 Surcharged — **15 MILLIEMES**

51 A4 15m on 40c red & pale bl 27.50 27.50
a. "MILLtEMES" 70.00 67.50
52 A4 15m on 50c bis brn & lav 37.50 37.50
a. "MILLtEMES" 180.00 180.00
b. Bar below 15 30.00 30.00
53 A4 30m on 1fr cl & ol grn 150.00 150.00
a. "MILLtEMES" 450.00 425.00
54 A4 60m on 2fr gray vio & yel 52.50 52.50
a. "MILLtEMES" 190.00 150.00
55 A4 150m on 5fr dk bl & buff 190.00 190.00
a. "MILLtEMES" 525.00 450.00

Stamps of 1902-03 Surcharged in Paris — **2 MILLIEMES**

1921-23
56 A2 1m on 1c gray 52 52
57 A2 2m on 5c grn 52 52
58 A3 4m on 10c rose 1.00 1.00
59 A2 5m on 3c red org 4.00 4.00
60 A3 6m on 15c org 1.25 1.25
a. 6m on 15c pale red 5.50 5.50
61 A3 8m on 20c brn vio 1.00 1.00
62 A3 10m on 25c bl 1.75 1.75
63 A3 10m on 30c vio 3.50 3.50
64 A3 15m on 50c bl 2.75 2.75

Surcharged — **15 MILLIÈMES**

65 A4 15m on 50c bis brn & lav 2.75 2.75
66 A4 30m on 1fr cl & ol grn 3.25 3.25
67 A4 60m on 2fr gray vio & yel 67.50 67.50
68 A4 60m on 2fr org & pale bl 4.75 4.75
69 A4 150m on 5fr bl & buff 4.00 4.00
Nos. 56-69 (14) 98.54 98.54

Stamps and Types of 1902-03 Surcharged with New Values and Bars

1925
70 A2 1m on 1c gray 38 38
71 A2 2m on 5c grn 45 45
72 A3 4m on 10c rose red 45 45
73 A2 5m on 3c red org 45 45
74 A3 6m on 15c org 70 70
75 A3 8m on 20c brn vio 45 45
76 A3 10m on 25c bl 75 75
77 A3 15m on 50c bl 75 75
78 A4 30m on 1fr cl & ol grn 85 85
79 A4 60m on 2fr org & pale bl 1.00 1.00
80 A4 150m on 5fr dk bl & buff 1.25 1.25
Nos. 70-80 (11) 7.48 7.48

Types of 1902-03 Issue

1927-28
83 A2 3m org ('28) 75 75
87 A3 15m sl bl 85 85
88 A3 20m rose lil ('28) 95 95
90 A4 50m org & bl 1.75 1.75
91 A4 100m sl bl & buff 2.25 2.25
92 A4 250m gray grn & red 4.00 4.00
Nos. 83-92 (6) 10.55 10.55

SEMI-POSTAL STAMPS

Regular Issue of 1902-03 Surcharged in Carmine — **+5c**

1915 **Unwmk.** ***Perf. 14x13½***
B1 A3 10c + 5c rose 85 85

Sinking Fund Issue

Type of 1902-03 Issue Surcharged in Blue or Black — **+5 Mm Caisse d'Amortissement**

1927-30
B2 A3 15m + 5m dp org (Bl) 1.40 1.40
B3 A3 15m + 5m red vio ('28) 1.40 1.40
a. 15m + 5m vio ('30) 2.50 2.50
B4 A3 15m + 5m fawn ('29) 1.50 1.50

POSTAGE DUE STAMPS

Postage Due Stamps of France, 1893-1906, Surcharged Locally in Black — **15 Millièmes**

1921 **Unwmk.** ***Perf. 14 x 13½***
J1 D2 12m on 10c brn 30.00 30.00
J2 D2 15m on 5c bl 32.50 32.50
J3 D2 30m on 20c ol grn 37.50 37.50
a. Invtd. surch. 375.00 375.00
J4 D2 30m on 50c red vio *2,250. 2,250.*

Same Surcharged in Red or Blue — **4 MILLIÈMES**

1921
J5 D2 2m on 5c bl (R) 30.00 30.00
a. Blue surcharge 180.00 180.00
J6 D2 4m on 10c brn (Bl) 32.50 32.50
a. Surcharged "15 Millièmes" 450.00 450.00
J7 D2 10m on 30c red (Bl) 30.00 30.00
a. Inverted surcharge 75.00 75.00
J8 D2 15m on 50c brn vio (Bl) 40.00 40.00
a. Inverted surcharge 77.50 77.50

Nos. J5-J8 exist with second "M" in "Milliemes" inverted, also with final "S" omitted.
Alexandria Nos. J6-J13 were also available for use in Port Said.

FRENCH OFFICES IN MOROCCO See French Morocco.

FRENCH OFFICES IN TURKISH EMPIRE (LEVANT)

Various powers maintained post offices in the Turkish Empire before World War I by authority of treaties which ended with the signing of the Treaty of Lausanne in 1923. The foreign post offices were closed Oct. 27, 1923.

100 Centimes = 1 Franc
25 Centimes = 40 Paras = 1 Piaster

A1

Stamps of France Surcharged in Black or Red

1885-1901 **Unwmk.** ***Perf. 14 x 13½***
1 A1 1pi on 25c yel, *straw* ('85) 300.00 5.50
a. Inverted surch. 1,400. 1,400.
2 A1 1pi on 25c *rose* (R) ('86) 1.10 52
a. Inverted surch. 165.00 150.00
3 A1 2pi on 50c car, *rose* (II) ('90) 9.00 1.25
a. Type I ('01) 190.00 22.50
4 A1 3pi on 75c car, *rose* ('85) 11.00 5.50
5 A1 4pi on 1fr brnz grn, *straw* ('85) 8.50 3.50
6 A1 8pi on 2fr brn, *az* ('00) 22.50 12.50
7 A1 20pi on 5fr red lil, *lav* ('90) 55.00 24.00

A2

A3

A4

A5

A6

1902-07 **Typo.** ***Perf. 14x13½***
21 A2 1c gray 30 22
22 A2 2c vio brn 45 30
23 A2 3c red org 45 30
24 A2 4c yel brn 90 52
a. Imperf., pair 47.50
25 A2 5c grn ('06) 45 22
26 A3 10c rose red 55 18
27 A3 15c pale red ('03) 1.00 70
28 A3 20c brn vio ('03) 1.00 70
29 A3 25c bl ('07) 30.00 25.00
a. Imperf., pair 275.00
30 A3 30c lil ('03) 2.50 1.40
31 A4 40c red & pale bl 2.50 1.40
32 A4 50c bis brn & lav ('07) 110.00 95.00
a. Imperf., pair 600.00

33 A4 1fr cl & ol grn ('07) 275.00 275.00
a. Imperf., pair 675.00

Black Surcharge

34 A5 1pi on 25c bl ('03) 55 18
a. Second "I" omitted 12.00 10.00
b. Double surch. 37.50 27.50
35 A6 2pi on 50c bis brn & lav 1.25 45
36 A6 4pi on 1fr cl & ol grn 1.65 60
a. Imperf., pair 500.00
37 A6 8pi on 2fr gray vio & yel 10.50 5.50
38 A6 20pi on 5fr dk bl & buff 3.75 1.65
Nos. 21-38 (18) 442.80 409.32

Nos. 29, 32-33 were used during the early part of 1907 in the French Offices at Harrar and Diredawa, Ethiopia. Djibouti and Port Said stamps were also used.

No. 27 Surcharged in Green

1 Piastre
Beyrouth

1905

39 A3 1pi on 15c pale red 1,200. 165.00
a. "Piastte" 3,750. 675.00

Stamps of France 1900-21 Surcharged:

1 PIASTRE
30 PARAS — a
20 PARAS — b
15 PIASTRES — c

1921-22

40 A22 (a) 30pa on 5c grn 45 30
41 A22 (a) 30pa on 5c org 45 30
42 A22 (b) 1pi 20pa on 10c red 45 30
43 A22 (b) 1pi 20pa on 10c grn 45 30
44 A22 (b) 3pi 30pa on 25c bl 45 30
45 A22 (b) 4pi 20pa on 30c org 45 30
a. "4" omitted 550.00
46 A20 (b) 7pi 20pa on 50c bl 45 30
47 A18 (c) 15pi on 1fr car & ol grn 75 52
48 A18 (c) 30pi on 2fr org & pale bl 6.50 4.00
49 A18 (c) 75pi on 5fr dk bl & buff 4.00 2.50
Nos. 40-49 (10) 14.40 9.12

Stamps of France, 1903-07, Handstamped

3 PIASTRES
30 PARAS

1923

52 A22 1pi 20pa on 10c red 30.00 30.00
54 A20 3pi 30pa on 15c gray grn 10.00 10.00
55 A22 7pi 20pa on 35c vio 12.00 12.00
a. 1pi 20pa on 35c vio 475.00 475.00

CAVALLE (CAVALLA)

A1

A2

Stamps of France Overprinted or Surcharged in Red, Blue or Black

1893-1900 Unwmk. *Perf. 14 x 13½*

1 A1 5c grn, *grnsh* (R) 8.00 7.00
2 A1 5c yel grn (I) ('00) (R) 8.75 5.50
3 A1 10c *lav* (II) (Bl) 9.00 6.50
a. 10c *lav* (I) 95.00 82.50
4 A1 15c bl (R) 14.00 10.00
5 A2 1pi on 25c *rose* (Bl) 15.00 11.00
6 A2 2pi on 50c car, *rose* (Bl) 40.00 30.00
7 A2 4pi on 1fr brnz grn, *straw* (R) 40.00 35.00
8 A2 8pi on 2fr brn, *az* ('00) (Bk) 60.00 55.00
Nos. 1-8 (8) 194.75 160.00

A3

A4

A5

A6

1902-03

9 A3 5c green 75 75
10 A4 10c rose red ('03) 90 90
11 A4 15c orange 1.00 1.00
a. 15c pale red ('03) 4.50 4.50

Surcharged in Black

12 A5 1pi on 25c bl 1.65 1.50
13 A6 2pi on 50c bis brn & lav 4.00 3.25
14 A6 4pi on 1fr cl & ol grn 5.75 5.00
15 A6 8pi on 2fr gray vio & yel 8.25 7.75
Nos. 9-15 (7) 22.30 20.15

DEDEAGH (DEDEAGATCH)

A1

A2

Stamps of France Overprinted or Surcharged in Red, Blue or Black

1893-1900 Unwmk. *Perf. 14 x 13½*

1 A1 5c grn, *grnsh* (II) (R) 6.75 6.00
2 A1 5c yel grn (I) ('00) (R) 6.75 6.00
3 A1 10c *lav* (II) (Bl) 10.00 9.00
a. Type I 24.00 12.50
4 A1 15c bl (R) 14.00 12.00
5 A2 1pi on 25c *rose* (Bl) 14.00 12.00
6 A2 2pi on 50c car, *rose* (Bl) 30.00 22.50
7 A2 4pi on 1fr brnz grn, *straw* (R) 35.00 27.50
8 A2 8pi on 2fr brn, *az* ('00) (Bk) 55.00 42.50
Nos. 1-8 (8) 171.50 137.50

A3

A4

A5

A6

1902-03

9 A3 5c green 60 60
10 A4 10c rose red ('03) 85 60
11 A4 15c orange 1.25 90

Black Surcharge

15 A5 1pi on 25c bl ('03) 1.50 90
16 A6 2pi on 50c bis brn & lav 4.00 3.25
a. Double surcharge 95.00
17 A6 4pi on 1fr cl & ol grn 7.50 6.00
18 A6 8pi on 2fr gray vio & yel 11.00 10.00
Nos. 9-18 (7) 26.70 22.25

PORT LAGOS

A1

A2

Stamps of France Overprinted or Surcharged in Red or Blue

1893 Unwmk. *Perf. 14x13½*

1 A1 5c grn, *grnsh* (R) 13.00 6.75
2 A1 10c *lav* (Bl) 27.50 13.00
3 A1 15c bl (R) 50.00 27.50
4 A2 1pi on 25c *rose* 35.00 22.50
5 A2 2pi on 50c car, *rose* (Bl) 110.00 45.00
6 A2 4pi on 1fr brnz grn, *straw* (R) 60.00 35.00

VATHY (SAMOS)

A1

A2

Stamps of France Overprinted or Surcharged in Red, Blue or Black

1894-1900 Unwmk. *Perf. 14x13½*

1 A1 5c grn, *grnsh* (R) 4.25 3.50
2 A1 5c yel grn (I) ('00) (R) 4.25 3.50
a. Type II 52.50 50.00
3 A1 10c *lav* (I) (Bl) 6.00 5.00
a. Type II 32.50 18.00
4 A1 15c bl (R) 5.50 5.50
5 A2 1pi on 25c *rose* (Bl) 6.00 4.75
6 A2 2pi on 50c car, *rose* (Bl) 14.00 14.00
7 A2 4pi on 1fr brnz grn, *straw* (R) 16.00 15.00
8 A2 8pi on 2fr brn, *az* ('00) (Bk) 50.00 37.50
9 A2 20pi on 5fr lil, *lav* ('00) (Bk) 65.00 60.00
Nos. 1-9 (9) 171.00 148.75

OFFICES IN ZANZIBAR

Until 1906 France maintained post offices in the Sultanate of Zanzibar, but in that year Great Britain assumed direct control over this protectorate and the French withdrew their postal system.

16 Annas = 1 Rupee

A1

A2

Stamps of France Surcharged in Red, Blue or Black

1894-96 Unwmk. *Perf. 14x13½*

1 A1 ½a on 5c grn, *grnsh* (R) 3.50 3.00
2 A1 1a on 10c *lav* (Bl) 7.00 5.25
3 A1 1½a on 15c bl ('96) (R) 11.00 10.50
a. "ANNAS" 55.00 55.00
4 A1 2a on 20c red, *grn* ('96) (Bk) 7.00 5.25
5 A1 2½a on 25c *rose* (Bl) 5.75 3.75
a. Double surcharge 100.00
6 A1 3a on 30c brn, *bis* ('96) (Bk) 11.00 9.50
7 A1 4a on 40c red, *straw* ('96) (Bk) 11.00 9.50
8 A1 5a on 50c car, *rose* (Bl) 18.00 15.00
9 A1 7½a on 75c vio, *org* ('96) (R) 285.00 250.00
10 A1 10a on 1fr brnz grn, *straw* (R) 30.00 24.00
11 A1 50a on 5fr red lil, *lav* ('96) (Bk) 210.00 175.00

1894

12 A2 ½a & 5c on 1c *lil bl* (R) 100.00 100.00
13 A2 1a & 10c on 3c gray, *grysh* (R) 95.00 95.00
14 A2 2½a & 25c on 4c cl, *lav* (Bk) 135.00 135.00
15 A2 5a & 50c on 20c red, *grn* (Bk) 135.00 135.00
16 A2 10a & 1fr on 40c red, *straw* (Bk) 275.00 275.00

There are two distinct types of the figures 5c, four of the 25c and three of each of the others of this series.

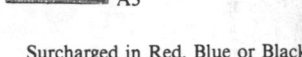

A3

Surcharged in Red, Blue or Black

1896-1900

17 A3 ½a on 5c grn, *grnsh* (R) 4.00 3.00
18 A3 ½a on 5c yel grn (I) (R) 4.00 3.00
a. Type II 4.00 3.25
19 A3 1a on 10c *lav* (II) (Bl) 4.50 3.25
a. Type I 8.25 7.50
20 A3 1½a on 15c bl (R) 4.00 3.00
21 A3 2a on 20c red, *grn* (Bk) 4.00 3.75
a. "ZANZIBAR" double 62.50
b. "ZANZIBAR" triple 70.00
22 A3 2½a on 25c *rose* (Bl) 5.50 4.50
23 A3 3a on 30c brn, *bis* (Bk) 5.00 4.50
24 A3 4a on 40c red, *straw* (Bk) 5.00 4.50
25 A3 5a on 50c rose, *rose* (II) (Bl) 21.00 16.00
a. Type I 40.00 35.00
26 A3 10a on 1fr brnz grn, *straw* (R) 11.00 8.25
27 A3 20a on 2fr brn, *az* (Bk) 15.00 9.50
a. "ZANZIBAS" 400.00 400.00
28 A3 50a on 5fr lil, *lav* (Bk) 40.00 26.00
a. "ZANZIBAS" *1,800.*
Nos. 17-28 (12) 123.00 89.25

A4

A5

1897

29 A4 2½a & 25c on ½a on 5c grn, *grnsh* 700.00 100.00
30 A4 2½a & 25c on 1a on 10c *lav* *2,750.* 625.00
31 A4 2½a & 25c on 1½a on 15c bl *2,750.* 525.00
32 A5 5a & 50c on 3a on 30c brn, *bis* *2,750.* 450.00
33 A5 5a & 50c on 4a on 40c red, *straw* *2,750.* 550.00

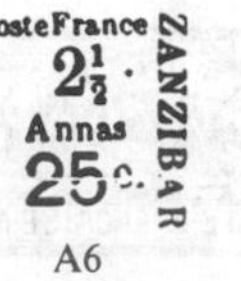

A6

PosteFrance
5
Annas
50c.
ZANZIBAR
A7

Printed on the Margins of Sheets of French Stamps

1897

No.	Type	Description	Unused	Used
34	A6	2½a & 25c grn, *grnsh*	675.00	
35	A6	2½a & 25c *lav*	1,900.	
36	A6	2½a & 25c bl	*1,900.*	
37	A7	5a & 50c brn, *bis*	*1,500.*	
38	A7	5a & 50c red, *straw*	*1,900.*	

There are several varieties of figures in the above surcharges.

A8

A9

A10

Surcharged in Red or Black

1902-03

No.	Type	Description	Unused	Used
39	A8	½a on 5c grn (R)	2.50	1.90
40	A9	1a on 10c rose red ('03)	3.00	2.75
41	A9	1½a on 15c pale red ('03)	6.00	5.25
42	A9	2a on 20c brn vio ('03)	7.50	6.25
43	A9	2½a on 25c bl ('03)	7.50	6.25
44	A9	3a on 30c lil ('03)	6.00	4.50
a.		5a on 30c (error)	190.00	190.00
45	A10	4a on 40c red & pale bl	10.00	9.00
46	A10	5a on 50c bis brn & lav	8.00	6.75
47	A10	10a on 1fr cl & ol grn	13.00	12.00
48	A10	20a on 2fr gray vio & yel	30.00	27.50
49	A10	50a on 5fr dk bl & buff	50.00	50.00
		Nos. 39-49 (11)	143.50	132.15

Nos. 23-24 Surcharged in Black:

25 ▬ 2½
a

50 ▬ 5
b

c

1 fr ▬ 10

1904

No.	Type	Description	Unused	Used
50	A3	25(c) & 2½(a) on 4a on 40c red, *straw*	600.00	
51	A3	50(c) & 5(a) on 3a on 30c brn, *bis*	750.00	
52	A3	50(c) & 5(a) on 4a on 40c red, *straw*	750.00	
53	A3	1fr & 10(a) on 3a on 30c brn, *bis*	1,250.	
54	A3	1fr & 10(a) on 4a on 40c red, *straw*	1,250.	

Stamps of 1902-03 Issue Surcharged in Red or Black:

2
25
d

25c
2½
e

50c
cinq
f

1 fr
dix
g

No.	Type	Description	Unused	Used
55	A8 (d)	25(c) & 2(a) on ½a on 5c grn (R)	*1,650.*	67.50
56	A9 (e)	25c & 2½(a) on 1a on 10c rose red	*3.250.*	77.50
a.		Inverted surcharge		750.00
57	A9 (e)	25c & 2½(a) on 3c on 30c lil		*2,000.*
a.		Inverted surcharge		*2,000.*
b.		Double surcharge, both inverted		*2,500.*
58	A9 (f)	50c & 5(a) on 3a on 30c lil	675.00	
59	A9 (g)	1fr & 10(a) on 3a on 30c lil	900.00	

Postage Due Stamps of 1897 Issue With Various Surcharges

Overprinted "Timbre" in Red

No.	Type	Description	Unused	Used
60	D1	½a on 5c bl	250.00	

Overprinted "Affrancht" in Black

No.	Type	Description	Unused	Used
61	D1	1a on 10c brn	250.00	

With Red Bars Across "CHIFFRE" and "TAXE"

No.	Type	Description	Unused	Used
62	D1	1½a on 15c grn	550.00	

The illustrations are not exact reproductions of the new surcharges but are merely intended to show their relative positions and general styles.

POSTAGE DUE STAMPS

D1

Stamps of France Surcharged in Red, Blue or Black

1897 Unwmk. *Perf. 14 x 13½*

No.	Type	Description	Unused	Used
J1	D1	½a on 5c bl (R)	8.00	4.75
J2	D1	1a on 10c brn (Bl)	8.00	4.75
a.		Inverted surcharge	75.00	75.00
J3	D1	1½a on 15c grn (R)	11.00	6.50
J4	D1	3a on 30c car (Bk)	13.00	9.50
J5	D1	5a on 50c lil (Bl)	13.00	9.50
a.		2½a on 50c lil (Bl)	575.00	550.00
		Nos. J1-J5 (5)	53.00	35.00

FRENCH COLONIES

From 1859 to 1906 and in 1944 and 1945 special stamps were issued for use in all French Colonies which did not have stamps of their own.

100 CENTIMES = 1 FRANC

Perforations: Nos. 1-45 are known variously perforated unofficially.
Gum: Many of Nos. 1-45 were issued without gum. Some were gummed locally.

Reprints: Nos. 1-7, 9-12, 24, 26-42, 44 and 45 were reprinted officially in 1887. These reprints are ungummed and the colors of both design and paper are deeper or brighter than the originals. Price for Nos. 1-6, $30 each.

Prices of early French Colonies stamps vary according to condition. Quotations for Nos. 1-23 are for fine copies. Very fine to superb specimens sell at much higher prices, and inferior or poor copies sell at reduced prices, depending on the condition of the individual specimen.

Eagle and Crown — A1

1859-65 Unwmk. Typo. *Imperf.*

No.	Type	Description	Unused	Used
1	A1	1c ol grn, *pale bl* ('62)	11.00	14.00
2	A1	5c yel grn, *grnsh* ('62)	12.50	10.00
3	A1	10c bis, *yel*	18.00	6.75
a.		Pair, one sideways	700.00	400.00
4	A1	20c bl, *bluish* ('65)	22.50	12.00
5	A1	40c org, *yelsh*	15.00	8.25
6	A1	80c car rose, *pnksh* ('65)	55.00	47.50

Napoleon III
A2 A3

Ceres — A4

Napoleon III — A5

1871-72 *Imperf.*

No.	Type	Description	Unused	Used
7	A2	1c ol grn, *pale bl* ('72)	55.00	55.00
8	A3	5c yel grn, *grnsh* ('72)	700.00	450.00
9	A4	10c bis, *yelsh*	265.00	120.00
a.		Tete beche pair	*24,000.*	*18,000.*
10	A4	15c bis, *yelsh* ('72)	210.00	10.00
11	A4	20c bl, *bluish*	450.00	120.00
a.		Tete beche pair		*12,500.*
12	A4	25c bl, *bluish* ('72)	120.00	8.00
13	A5	30c brn, *yelsh*	100.00	35.00
14	A4	40c org, *yelsh* (I)	210.00	12.00
a.		Type II	*3,000.*	*600.00*
b.		Pair, types I & II	*6,250.*	*1,600.*
15	A5	80c rose, *pnksh*	750.00	95.00

For types I and II of 40c see illustrations over No. 1 of France.

Ceres
A6 A7

1872-77 *Imperf.*

No.	Type	Description	Unused	Used
16	A6	1c ol grn, *pale bl* ('73)	12.50	13.00
17	A6	2c red brn, *yelsh* ('76)	450.00	750.00
18	A6	4c gray ('76)	*9,000.*	600.00
19	A6	5c grn, *pale bl*	12.50	7.50
20	A7	10c bis, *rose* ('76)	165.00	12.00
21	A7	15c bis ('77)	475.00	95.00
22	A7	30c brn, *yelsh*	80.00	14.00
23	A7	80c rose, *pnksh* ('73)	375.00	135.00

No. 17 was used only in Cochin China, 1876-77. Excellent forgeries of Nos. 17 and 18 exist.

With reference to the stamps of France and French Colonies in the same designs and colors see the note after France No. 9.

Peace and Commerce
A8

Commerce
A9

1877-78 Type I. *Imperf.*

No.	Type	Description	Unused	Used
24	A8	1c grn, *grnsh*	25.00	30.00
25	A8	4c grn, *grnsh*	15.00	11.00
26	A8	30c brn, *yelsh* ('78)	32.50	32.50
27	A8	40c ver, *straw*	22.50	19.00
28	A8	75c car, *rose* ('78)	67.50	55.00
29	A8	1fr brnz grn, *straw*	30.00	16.00

Type II.

No.	Type	Description	Unused	Used
30	A8	2c grn, *grnsh*	11.00	9.50
31	A8	5c grn, *grnsh*	15.00	4.50
32	A8	10c grn, *grnsh*	80.00	9.50
33	A8	15c gray, *grnsh*	225.00	67.50
34	A8	20c red brn, *straw*	47.50	6.00
35	A8	25c ultra, *bluish*	32.50	8.00
a.		25c bl, *bluish* ('78)	*4,750.*	165.00
36	A8	35c vio blk, *org* ('78)	40.00	25.00

1878-80

Type II.

No.	Type	Description	Unused	Used
38	A8	1c *lil bl*	16.00	16.00
39	A8	2c brn, *buff*	15.00	11.00
40	A8	4c cl, *lav*	20.00	20.00
41	A8	10c *lav* ('79)	90.00	18.00
42	A8	15c bl ('79)	25.00	11.00
43	A8	20c red, *grn* ('79)	75.00	11.00
44	A8	25c *red* ('79)	475.00	300.00
45	A8	25c yel, *straw* ('80)	525.00	25.00

No. 44 was used only in Mayotte, Nossi-Bé and New Caledonia. Forgeries exist.

The 3c yellow, 3c gray, 15c yellow, 20c blue, 25c rose and 5fr lilac were printed together with the reprints, and were never issued.

1881-86 *Perf. 14x13½.*

No.	Type	Description	Unused	Used
46	A9	1c *lil bl*	2.50	1.75
47	A9	2c brn, *buff*	3.00	2.50
48	A9	4c cl, *lav*	3.00	2.50
49	A9	5c grn, *grnsh*	3.00	1.25
50	A9	10c *lavender*	6.00	3.50
51	A9	15c blue	9.00	1.25
52	A9	20c red, *yel grn*	22.50	11.00
53	A9	25c yel, *straw*	5.75	1.60
54	A9	25c *rose* ('86)	5.75	1.50
55	A9	30c brn, *bis*	16.00	11.00
56	A9	35c vio blk, *yel org*	20.00	13.00
a.		35c vio blk, *yel*	37.50	19.00
57	A9	40c ver, *straw*	22.50	14.00
58	A9	75c car, *rose*	57.50	27.50
59	A9	1fr brnz grn, *straw*	37.50	19.00

Nos. 46-59 exist imperforate. They are proofs and were not used for postage, except the 10c.

For stamps of type A9 surcharged with numerals see: Cochin China, Diego Suarez, Gabon, Madagascar, Nossi Be, New Caledonia, Reunion, Senegal, Tahiti.

SEMI-POSTAL STAMPS

Resistance Fighters — SP1

1943 Unwmk. Litho. *Rouletted*

No.	Type	Description	Unused	Used
B1	SP1	1.50fr + 98.50fr ind & gray	16.00	18.00

The surtax was for the benefit of patriots and the French Committee of Liberation.

No. B1 was printed in sheets of 10 (5x2) with adjoining labels for each stamp. The label shows the Lorraine cross in indigo in a gray frame.

Colonies Offering Aid to France SP2

1943 *Perf. 12*

No.	Type	Description	Unused	Used
B2	SP2	9fr + 41fr red vio	1.10	1.25

The surtax was for the benefit of French Patriots.

Patriots and Map of France — SP3

1943

No.	Type	Description	Unused	Used
B3	SP3	50c + 4.50fr yel grn	75	90
B4	SP3	1.50fr + 8.50fr cer	75	90
B5	SP3	3fr + 12fr grnsh bl	75	90
B6	SP3	5fr + 15fr ol gray	75	90

The surtax was for the aid of combatants and patriots.

The indexes in each volume of the Scott Catalogue contain many listings which help to identify stamps.

Refugee Family SP4

1943

B7 SP4 10fr + 40fr dl bl 3.25 3.75

The surtax was for refugee relief work.

Woman and Child with Wing — SP5

1944

B8 SP5 10fr + 40fr grnsh blk 3.75 4.00

The surtax was for the general benefit of aviation.

Nos. B1-B8 were originally prepared for use in the French Colonies, but after the landing of Free French troops in Corsica they were used there and later also in Southern France. They became valid throughout France in November 1944.

POSTAGE DUE STAMPS

D1

1884-85 Unwmk. Typo. *Imperf.*

J1 D1 1c black 1.40 1.40
J2 D1 2c black 1.40 1.40
J3 D1 3c black 1.40 1.40
J4 D1 4c black 2.25 1.75
J5 D1 5c black 2.75 2.25
J6 D1 10c black 4.00 3.00
J7 D1 15c black 6.50 5.00
J8 D1 20c black 6.50 5.75
J9 D1 30c black 8.50 4.25
J10 D1 40c black 11.00 4.25
J11 D1 60c black 17.00 10.00
J12 D1 1fr brown 15.00 10.00
a. 1fr blk 190.00
J13 D1 2fr brown 12.50 8.50
a. 2fr blk 190.00
J14 D1 5fr brown 55.00 30.00
a. 5fr blk 250.00

Nos. J12a, J13a and J14a were not regularly issued.

1894-1906

J15 D1 5c pale bl 50 50
J16 D1 10c gray brn 50 50
J17 D1 15c pale grn 50 50
J18 D1 20c ol grn ('06) 50 50
J19 D1 30c carmine 90 75
J20 D1 50c lilac 90 75
J21 D1 60c brn, *buff* 2.00 1.50
a. 60c dk vio, *buff* 2.50 1.50
J22 D1 1fr red, *buff* 3.00 2.50
a. 1fr rose, *buff* 15.00 13.00
Nos. J15-J22 (8) 8.80 7.50

D2

1945 Litho. *Perf. 12*

J23 D2 10c sl bl 5 5
J24 D2 15c yel grn 5 5
J25 D2 25c dp org 12 12
J26 D2 50c grnsh blk 38 38
J27 D2 60c cop brn 38 38
J28 D2 1fr dp red lil 18 18
J29 D2 2fr red 38 38
J30 D2 4fr sl gray 1.40 1.40
J31 D2 5fr brt ultra 1.40 1.40
J32 D2 10fr purple 8.00 6.00
J33 D2 20fr dl brn 1.65 1.65
J34 D2 50fr dp grn 3.00 3.00
Nos. J23-J34 (12) 16.99 14.99

FRENCH CONGO

LOCATION — Central Africa
GOVT. — French possession

French Congo was originally a separate colony, but was joined in 1888 to Gabon and placed under one commissioner-general with a lieutenant-governor presiding in Gabon and another in French Congo. In 1894 the military holdings in Ubangi were attached to French Congo, and in 1900 the Chad military protectorate was added. Postal service was not established in Ubangi or Chad, however, at that time. In 1906 Gabon and Middle Congo were separated and French Congo ceased to exist as such. Chad and Ubangi remained attached to Middle Congo as the joint dependency of "Ubangi-Chari-Chad," and Middle Congo stamps were used there.

Issues of the Republic of the Congo are listed under Congo Republic (ex-French).

100 Centimes = 1 Franc

Stamps of French Colonies Surcharged Horizontally in Red or Black

Congo français
5c.

1891 Unwmk. *Perf. 14x13½.*

1 A9 5c on 1c *lil bl* (R) 6,000. 3,000.
2 A9 5c on 1c *lil bl* 110.00 65.00
a. Double surcharge 500.00 250.00
3 A9 5c on 15c bl 250.00 100.00
a. Double surcharge 500.00 250.00
5 A9 5c on 25c *rose* 100.00 26.00
a. Inverted surcharge

First "O" of "Congo" is a Capital, "Francais" with Capital "F".

1891-92

6 A9 5c on 20c red, *grn* 1,000. 350.00
7 A9 5c on 25c *rose* 130.00 57.50
a. Surch. vert. 190.00 57.50
8 A9 10c on 25c *rose* 140.00 37.50
a. Inverted surcharge 265.00 87.50
b. Surch. vert. 150.00 65.00
c. First "o" of "Congo" small
d. Double surcharge 300.00 95.00
9 A9 10c on 40c red, *straw* 2,000. 325.00
10 A9 15c on 25c *rose* 130.00 27.50
a. Surch. vert. 190.00 57.50
b. Inverted surcharge
c. Double surch. 265.00 82.50

First "O" of Congo small. Surcharge Vertical, Reading Down or Up. No period.

11 A9 5c on 25c *rose*
12 A9 10c on 25c *rose*
13 A9 15c on 25c *rose*

Postage Due Stamps of French Colonies Surcharged in Red or Black Reading Down or Up

Congo français
Timbres poste
10 c

1892 *Imperf.*

14 D1 5c on 5c blk (R) 110.00 95.00
15 D1 5c on 20c blk (R) 120.00 92.50
16 D1 5c on 30c blk (R) 160.00 110.00
17 D1 10c on 1fr brn 130.00 92.50
a. Double surcharge
b. Surch. horiz. 1,400.

Excellent counterfeits of Nos. 1-17 exist.

Navigation and Commerce — A3

1892-1900 Typo. *Perf. 14x13½*
Colony Name in Blue or Carmine

18 A3 1c *lil bl* 1.25 1.00
19 A3 2c brn, *buff* 1.50 1.25
a. Name double 100.00 87.50
20 A3 4c cl, *lav* 1.65 1.40
a. Name in blk and in bl 100.00 87.50
21 A3 5c grn, *grnsh* 3.50 3.00
22 A3 10c *lavender* 11.00 8.50
a. Name double 425.00 350.00
23 A3 10c red ('00) 1.50 1.00
24 A3 15c bl, quadrille paper 35.00 9.00
25 A3 15c gray ('00) 4.75 3.50
26 A3 20c red, *grn* 15.00 9.50
27 A3 25c *rose* 11.00 8.50
28 A3 25c bl ('00) 5.75 4.75
29 A3 30c brn, *bis* 17.00 10.00
30 A3 40c red, *straw* 27.50 15.00
31 A3 50c car, *rose* 27.50 15.00
32 A3 50c brn, *az* ('00) 5.75 4.75
a. Name double 475.00 475.00
33 A3 75c dp vio, *org* 20.00 15.00
34 A3 1fr brnz grn, *straw* 35.00 17.50
Nos. 18-34 (17) 224.65 128.65

Leopard — A4

Bakalois Woman — A5

Coconut Grove — A6

Wmk. 122- Thistle Branch

1900 Wmk. 122 *Perf. 11*

35 A4 1c brn vio & gray lil 42 42
a. Background inverted 40.00 40.00
36 A4 2c brn & org 42 42
a. 2c dk red & red 100.00
b. Imperf., pair 42.50 42.50
37 A4 4c scar & gray bl 60 42
a. 4c dk red & red 600.00
b. Background inverted 47.50 47.50
38 A4 5c grn & gray grn 1.00 42
a. Imperf., pair 87.50 87.50
39 A4 10c dk red & red 3.50 1.50
a. Imperf., pair 87.50 87.50
40 A4 15c dl vio & ol grn 1.25 52
a. Imperf. pair 50.00 50.00

Wmk.123

Wmk. Rose Branch. (123)

41 A5 20c yel grn & org 1.25 80
42 A5 25c bl & pale bl 1.75 95
43 A5 30c car rose & org 2.00 1.00
44 A5 40c org brn & brt grn 3.00 1.40
a. Imperf., pair 60.00 60.00
b. Center inverted 92.50 92.50
45 A5 50c gray vio & lil 3.50 2.75
46 A5 75c red vio & org 5.50 4.50
a. Imperf., pair 60.00 60.00

Wmk.124

Wmk. Olive Branch. (124)

47 A6 1fr gray lil & ol 11.00 8.00
a. Center inverted 200.00 200.00
b. Imperf., pair 87.50 87.50
48 A6 2fr car & brn 20.00 11.00
a. Imperf., pair 175.00 175.00
49 A6 5fr brn org & gray 55.00 35.00
a. 5fr ocher & gray 600.00 600.00
b. Center inverted 290.00 290.00
c. Wmk. 123 190.00
d. Imperf., pair 400.00 400.00
Nos. 35-49 (15) 110.19 69.10

Nos. 26 and 29 Surcharged in Black

Valeur
15

1900 Unwmk. *Perf. 14x13½*

50 A3 5c on 20c red, *grn* 17,500. 5,750.
a. Dbl. surch. 11,000.
51 A3 15c on 30c brn, *bis* 9,500. 2,400.
a. Dbl. surch. 4,750.

Nos. 43 and 48 Surcharged in Black:

5c
0,10

1903 Wmk. 123 *Perf. 11*

52 A5 5c on 30c car rose & org 200.00 110.00
a. Inverted surcharge 1,750.

Wmk. 124

53 A6 10c on 2fr car & brn 300.00 100.00
a. Inverted surcharge 1,750.
b. Double surcharge 2,000.

Counterfeits of the preceding surcharges are known.

FRENCH EQUATORIAL AFRICA

LOCATION — North of Belgian Congo and south of Libya.
GOVT. — Former French Colony
AREA — 959,256 square miles
POP. — 4,491,785
CAPITAL — Brazzaville

In 1910 Gabon and Middle Congo, with its military dependencies, were politically united as French Equatorial Africa. The component colonies were granted administrative autonomy. In 1915 Ubangi-Chari-Chad was made an autonomous civilian colony and in 1920 Chad was made a civil colony. In 1934 the four colonies were administratively united as one colony, but this federation was not completed until 1936. Each colony had its own postal administration until 1936 when they were united. The postal issues of the former colonial subdivisions are listed under the names of those colonies.

In 1958, French Equatorial Africa was divided into four republics: Chad,

Congo, Gabon and Central African Republic (formerly Ubangi-Chari).

100 Centimes = 1 Franc

Stamps of Gabon, 1932, Overprinted "Afrique Equatoriale Francaise" and Bars Similar to "a" and "b" in Black

Perf. 13x13½, 13½x13.

1936 **Unwmk.**

No.	Type	Description	Unused	Used
1	A16	1c brn vio	6	6
2	A16	2c blk, *rose*	6	6
3	A16	4c green	42	30
4	A16	5c grnsh bl	40	30
5	A16	10c red, *yel*	40	35
6	A17	40c brn vio	1.00	80
7	A17	50c red brn	1.00	60
8	A17	1fr yel grn, *bl*	16.00	5.50
9	A18	1.50fr dl bl	1.75	90
10	A18	2fr brn red	9.50	5.25
		Nos. 1-10 (10)	30.59	14.12

Stamps of Middle Congo, 1933 Overprinted in Black:

a — AFRIQUE ÉQUATORIALE FRANÇAISE

b — AFRIQUE ÉQUATORIALE FRANÇAISE

c — AFRIQUE EQUATORIALE FRANÇAISE

1936

No.	Type	Description	Unused	Used
11	A4 (b)	1c lt brn	6	6
12	A4 (b)	2c dl bl	6	6
13	A4 (b)	4c ol grn	35	22
14	A4 (b)	5c red vio	42	30
15	A4 (b)	10c slate	80	52
16	A4 (b)	15c dk vio	90	52
17	A4 (b)	20c red, *pink*	70	42
18	A4 (b)	25c orange	1.90	1.40
19	A5 (a)	40c org brn	2.00	1.50
20	A5 (c)	50c blk vio	1.75	1.25
21	A5 (c)	75c blk, *pink*	3.00	2.00
22	A5 (a)	90c carmine	1.75	1.40
23	A5 (c)	1.50fr dk bl	1.00	65
24	A6 (a)	5fr sl bl	37.50	22.50
25	A6 (a)	10fr black	20.00	16.00
26	A6 (a)	20fr dk brn	20.00	17.50
		Nos. 11-26 (16)	92.19	66.30

Paris International Exposition Issue.

Common Design Types

1937, Apr. 15 **Engr.** ***Perf. 13.***

No.	Type	Description	Unused	Used
27	CD74	20c dk vio	1.40	1.40
28	CD75	30c dk grn	1.40	1.40
29	CD76	40c car rose	1.50	1.50
30	CD77	50c dk brn & bl	1.25	1.25
31	CD78	90c red	1.50	1.50
32	CD79	1.50fr ultra	1.50	1.50
		Nos. 27-32 (6)	8.55	8.55

Logging on Loeme River — A1

People of Chad — A2

Pierre Savorgnan de Brazza A3

Emile Gentil A4

Paul Crampel A5

Governor Victor Liotard A6

Two types of 25c:
I. Wide numerals (4mm.).
II. Narrow numerals (3½mm.).

1937-40 **Photo.** ***Perf. 13½x13***

No.	Type	Description	Unused	Used
33	A1	1c brn & yel	5	5
34	A1	2c vio & grn	6	6
35	A1	3c bl & yel ('40)	14	14
36	A1	4c mag & bl	6	6
37	A1	5c dk & lt grn	5	5
38	A2	10c mag & bl	5	5
39	A2	15c bl & buff	14	5
40	A2	20c brn & yel	22	14
41	A2	25c cop red & bl (I)	35	6
a.		Type II	90	55
42	A3	30c gray grn & grn	25	25
43	A3	30c chlky bl, ind & buff ('40)	14	14
44	A2	35c dp grn & yel ('38)	70	48
45	A3	40c cop red & bl	14	5
46	A3	45c dk bl & lt grn	3.25	2.25
47	A3	45c dp grn & yel grn ('40)	25	25
48	A3	50c brn & yel	14	5
49	A3	55c pur & bl ('38)	42	25
50	A3	60c mar & gray bl ('40)	25	25
51	A4	65c dk bl & lt grn	25	5
52	A4	70c dp vio & buff ('40)	25	25
53	A4	75c ol blk & dl yel	4.25	2.75
54	A4	80c brn & yel ('38)	25	14
55	A4	90c cop red & buff	25	14
56	A4	1fr dk vio & lt grn	95	40
57	A3	1fr cer & dl org ('38)	1.75	40
58	A4	1fr bl grn & sl grn ('40)	25	25
59	A5	1.25fr cop red & buff	70	60
60	A5	1.40fr dk brn & pale grn ('40)	40	40
61	A5	1.50fr dk & lt bl	1.10	42
62	A5	1.60fr dp vio & buff ('40)	40	40
63	A5	1.75fr brn & yel	1.10	52
64	A4	1.75fr bl & lt bl ('38)	25	22
65	A5	2fr dk & lt grn	95	42
66	A6	2.15fr brn, vio & yel ('38)	42	30
67	A6	2.25fr bl & lt bl ('39)	95	95
68	A6	2.50fr rose lake & buff ('40)	42	42
69	A6	3fr dk bl & buff	52	25
70	A6	5fr dk & lt grn	1.00	55
71	A6	10fr dk vio & bl	2.50	1.25
72	A6	20fr ol blk & dl yel	3.25	1.90
		Nos. 33-72 (40)	28.82	17.61

Colonial Arts Exhibition Issue

Souvenir Sheet.

Common Design Type

1937 ***Imperf.***

No.	Type	Description	Unused	Used
73	CD79	3fr red brn	4.00	4.00

Sheet size: 111x99mm.

Count Louis Edouard Bouet-Willaumez and His Ship "La Malouine" — A7

1938, Dec. 5 ***Perf. 13½.***

No.	Type	Description	Unused	Used
74	A7	65c gray brn	60	60
75	A7	1fr dp rose	60	60
76	A7	1.75fr blue	1.00	1.00
77	A7	2fr dl vio	1.25	1.25

Issued in commemoration of the centenary of Gabon.

New York World's Fair Issue.

Common Design Type

1939, May 10 **Engr.** ***Perf. 12½x12***

No.	Type	Description	Unused	Used
78	CD82	1.25fr car lake	80	80
79	CD82	2.25fr ultra	80	80

Common Design Types pictured in section at front of book.

Libreville View and Marshal Petain A7a

1941 **Engr.** ***Perf. 12½x12***

No.	Type	Description	Unused	Used
79A	A7a	1fr bluish grn	1.00	
79B	A7a	2.50fr blue	1.00	

Nos. 79A-79B were issued by the Vichy government, and were not placed on sale in the colony. This is also true of four stamps of types A2, A3 and A5 without "RF" monogram released in 1943-44.

Stamps of 1936-40, Overprinted in Carmine or Black:

a — AFRIQUE FRANÇAISE LIBRE

b — LIBRE

1940-41 ***Perf. 13½x13***

No.	Type	Description	Unused	Used
80	A1 (a)	1c brn & yel (C)	60	60
81	A1 (a)	2c vio & grn (C)	70	70
82	A1 (a)	3c bl & yel (C)	70	70
83	A4 (b)	4c ol grn (Bk) (No. 13)	5.50	5.50
84	A1 (a)	5c dk grn & lt grn (C)	80	80
85	A2 (a)	10c mag & bl (Bk)	95	95
86	A2 (a)	15c bl & buff (C)	95	95
87	A2 (a)	20c brn & yel (C)	1.25	1.25
88	A2 (a)	25c cop red & bl (Bk)	4.50	4.50
89	A3 (b)	30c gray grn & grn (C)	7.00	6.00
90	A3 (b)	30c gray grn & grn (Bk) ('41)	1.25	95
91	A3 (b)	30c chlky bl, ind & buff (C) ('41)	6.50	5.50
92	A3 (b)	30c chlky bl, ind & buff (Bk) ('41)	3.50	3.50
93	A2 (a)	35c dp grn & yel (C)	1.00	1.00
94	A3 (b)	40c cop red & bl (Bk)	42	42
a.		Double overprint	22.50	
95	A3 (b)	45c dp grn & yel grn (C)	80	52
96	A3 (b)	45c dp grn & yel grn (Bk) ('41)	42	42
a.		Double overprint	5.75	5.75
97	A3 (b)	50c brn & yel (C)	4.00	2.75
98	A3 (b)	50c brn & yel (Bk) ('41)	2.25	2.25
a.		Double overprint	40.00	
99	A3 (b)	55c pur & bl (C)	80	52
100	A3 (b)	55c pur & bl (Bk) ('41)	42	42
a.		Double overprint	7.00	7.00
b.		Double, one inverted	22.50	
101	A3 (b)	60c mar & gray bl (Bk)	42	40
102	A4 (b)	65c dk bl & lt grn (Bk)	42	40
a.		Double overprint	22.50	
103	A4 (b)	70c dp vio & buff (Bk)	42	40
a.		Double overprint	5.75	5.75
104	A4 (b)	75c ol blk & dl yel (Bk)	25.00	25.00
105	A4 (b)	80c brn & yel (Bk)	42	42
a.		Double overprint	22.50	
106	A4 (b)	90c cop red & buff (Bk)	70	70
a.		Double overprint	22.50	
b.		Double, one inverted	22.50	
107	A4 (b)	1fr bl grn & sl grn (Bk)	3.25	2.75
108	A4 (b)	1fr bl grn & sl grn (C) ('41)	4.00	3.00
109	A3 (b)	1fr cer & dl org (Bk)	95	90
110	A5 (b)	1.40fr dk brn & pale grn (Bk)	42	40
a.		Double overprint	4.75	4.75
111	A5 (b)	1.50fr dk bl & lt bl (Bk)	42	40
a.		Double overprint	7.00	7.00
112	A5 (b)	1.60fr dp vio & buff (Bk)	42	40
113	A5 (b)	1.75fr brn & yel (Bk)	90	60
114	A6 (b)	2.15fr brn, vio & yel (Bk)	70	60
a.		Double overprint	4.75	4.75
115	A6 (b)	2.25fr bl & lt bl (C)	80	65
a.		Double overprint	7.00	7.00
116	A6 (b)	2.25fr bl & lt bl (Bk) ('41)	1.25	1.10
a.		Double overprint	22.50	
117	A6 (b)	2.50fr rose lake & buff (Bk)	60	60
a.		Double overprint	22.50	
118	A6 (b)	3fr dk bl & buff (C)	80	65
119	A6 (b)	3fr dk bl & buff (Bk) ('41)	1.40	1.10
a.		Double overprint	6.25	6.25
120	A6 (b)	5fr dk grn & lt grn (C)	2.50	2.25
121	A6 (b)	5fr dk grn & lt grn (Bk) ('41)	75.00	40.00
122	A6 (b)	10fr dk vio & bl (C)	1.25	1.10
123	A6 (b)	10fr dk vio & bl (Bk) ('41)	50.00	40.00
a.		Double overprint		
124	A6 (b)	20fr ol blk & dl yel (C)	1.25	1.10
125	A6 (b)	20fr ol blk & dl yel (Bk) ('41)	7.25	7.25
		Nos. 80-125 (46)	224.85	172.37

Nos. 48, 51 Surcharged in Black or Carmine — LIBRE 75c

1940

No.	Type	Description	Unused	Used
126	A3	75c on 50c brn & yel (Bk)	35	35
a.		Double surcharge		
127	A4	1fr on 65c dk bl & lt grn (C)	35	35
a.		Double surcharge	6.00	

Middle Congo No. 67 Overprinted in Carmine:

AFRIQUE FRANÇAISE LIBRE

Perf. 13½

No.	Type	Description	Unused	Used
128	A4	4c ol grn	30.00	27.50

Stamps of 1940 With Additional Overprint in Black — 24-10-40

1940 ***Perf. 13½x13***

No.	Type	Description	Unused	Used
129	A4	80c brn & yel	9.50	7.50
a.		Overprint without "2"	25.00	
130	A4	1fr bl grn & sl grn	9.00	7.50
131	A3	1fr cer & dl org	9.50	7.50
132	A5	1.50fr dk bl & lt bl	9.50	7.50

These stamps were sold affixed to post cards and at a slight increase over face value to cover the cost of the cards.

Issued to commemorate the arrival of General de Gaulle in Brazzaville, capital of Free France, October 24, 1940.

Stamps of 1937-40 Overprinted in Black

Afrique Française Libre

1941

No.	Type	Description	Unused	Used
133	A1	1c brn & yel	75	75
134	A1	2c vio & grn	75	75
135	A1	3c bl & yel	75	75
136	A1	5c dk & lt grn	75	75
137	A2	10c mag & bl	75	75
138	A2	15c bl & buff	75	75
139	A2	20c brn & yel	75	75
140	A2	25c cop red & bl	2.25	2.25
141	A2	35c dp grn & yel	1.75	1.75
a.		Double overprint	14.00	
		Nos. 133-141 (9)	9.25	9.25

There are two settings of the overprint on Nos. 133 to 141 and C10. The first has a space of 1 mm. between lines of the overprint, the second has space of 2 mm.

Phoenix — A8

1941		Photo.	*Perf. 14x14½*	
142	A8	5c brown	5	5
143	A8	10c dk bl	5	5
144	A8	25c emerald	5	5
145	A8	30c dp org	6	6
146	A8	40c dk sl grn	25	22
147	A8	80c red brn	8	6
148	A8	1fr dp red lil	10	6
149	A8	1.50fr brt red	6	6
150	A8	2fr gray	18	18
151	A8	2.50fr brt ultra	42	40
152	A8	4fr dl vio	48	40
153	A8	5fr yel bis	48	40
154	A8	10fr dp brn	55	52
155	A8	20fr dp grn	90	52
		Nos. 142-155 (14)	3.71	3.03

Eboue Issue.

Common Design Type

1945	Unwmk.	Engr.	*Perf. 13.*	
156	CD91	2fr black	25	25
157	CD91	25fr Prus grn	1.25	1.25

Nos. 156 and 157 exist imperforate.

Nos. 142, 144 and 151 Surcharged with New Values and Bars in Red, Carmine or Black.

1946			*Perf. 14x14½*	
158	A8	50c on 5c brn (R)	42	42
159	A8	60c on 5c brn (R)	42	42
160	A8	70c on 5c brn (R)	35	35
161	A8	1.20fr on 5c brn (C)	35	35
162	A8	2.40fr on 25c emer	65	65
163	A8	3fr on 25c emer	90	90
164	A8	4.50fr on 25c emer	90	90
165	A8	15fr on 2.50fr brt ultra (C)	90	90
		Nos. 158-165 (8)	4.89	4.89

Black Rhinoceros and Rock Python A9

Jungle Scene — A10

Mountainous Shore Line — A11

Gabon Forest — A12

Niger Boatman — A13

A particular stamp may be scarce, but if few collectors want it, its market value may remain relatively low.

Young Bacongo Woman — A14

1946	Unwmk.	Engr.	*Perf. 12½*	
166	A9	10c dp bl	5	5
167	A9	30c vio blk	5	5
168	A9	40c dp org	5	5
169	A10	50c vio blk	5	5
170	A10	60c dk car	35	25
171	A10	80c dk ol grn	40	25
172	A11	1fr dp org	40	25
173	A11	1.20fr dp cl	52	40
174	A11	1.50fr dk grn	80	65
175	A12	2fr dk vio brn	10	6
176	A12	3fr rose car	8	5
177	A12	3.60fr red brn	1.40	1.10
178	A12	4fr dp bl	25	18
179	A13	5fr dk brn	48	14
180	A13	6fr dp bl	40	18
181	A13	10fr black	48	18
182	A14	15fr brown	90	18
183	A14	20fr dp cl	90	18
184	A14	25fr black	1.10	25
		Nos. 166-184 (19)	8.76	4.50

Imperforates

Most French Equatorial Africa stamps from 1951 onward exist imperforate in issued and trial colors, and also in small presentation sheets in issued colors.

Pierre Savorgnan de Brazza — A15

1951, Nov. 5			*Perf. 13*	
185	A15	10fr ind & dk grn	80	25

Issued to commemorate the centenary of the birth of Pierre Savorgnan de Brazza, explorer.

Military Medal Issue.

Common Design Type

Engraved and Typographed

1952, Dec. 1			*Perf. 13*	
186	CD101	15fr multi	4.25	3.50

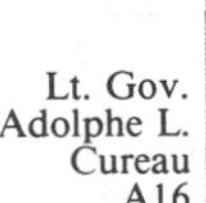

Lt. Gov. Adolphe L. Cureau A16

1954, Sept. 20			Engr.	
187	A16	15fr ol grn & red brn	1.00	48

Savannah Monitor A17

1955, May 2			Unwmk.	
188	A17	8fr dk grn & cl	1.25	60

Issued in connection with the International Exhibition for Wildlife Protection, Paris, May 1955.

FIDES Issue.

Boali Waterfall and Power Plant, Ubangi-Chari — A18

Designs: 10fr, Cotton, Chad. 15fr, Brazzaville Hospital, Middle Congo. 20fr, Libreville Harbor, Gabon.

1956, Apr. 25			*Perf. 13x12½*	
189	A18	5fr dk brn & cl	25	18
190	A18	10fr blk & bluish grn	35	25
191	A18	15fr ind & gray vio	40	14
192	A18	20fr dk red & red org	48	25

See note after Common Design Type CD103.

Coffee Issue.

Coffee A19

1956, Oct.		Engr.	*Perf. 13*	
193	A19	10fr brn vio & vio bl	60	22

Leprosarium at Mayumba and Maltese Cross — A20

1957, Mar. 11				
194	A20	15fr grn, bl grn & red	1.10	52

Issued in honor of the Knights of Malta.

Giant Eland — A21

Animals: 2fr, Lions. 3fr, Elephant. 4fr, Greater kudu. (3fr and 4fr vertical.)

1957, Nov. 4				
195	A21	1fr grn & brn	22	18
196	A21	2fr Prus grn & ol grn	22	18
197	A21	3fr grn, gray & bl	25	22
198	A21	4fr mar & gray	25	25

WHO Building, Brazzaville A22

1958, May 19		Engr.	*Perf. 13*	
199	A22	20fr dk grn & org brn	70	52

Issued to commemorate the 10th anniversary of the World Health Organization.

Flower Issue

Common Design Type

Design: 10fr, Euadania. 25fr, Spathodea.

1958, July 7		Photo.	*Perf. 12x12½*	
200	CD104	10fr dk vio, yel & grn	42	35
201	CD104	25fr grn, yel & red	80	42

Human Rights Issue

Common Design Type

1958, Dec. 10		Engr.	*Perf. 13*	
202	CD105	20fr Prus grn & dk bl	90	80

SEMI-POSTAL STAMPS

Common Design Type

1938, Oct. 24			Engr.	
B1	CD80	1.75fr + 50c brt ultra	11.00	11.00

Stamps of 1937-38 Surcharged in Black or Red **+35c**

1938, Nov. 7			*Perf. 13x13½*	
B2	A4	65c + 35c dk bl & lt grn (R)	1.40	1.25
B3	A4	1.75fr + 50c bl & lt bl (Bk)	1.40	1.25

The surtax was for welfare.

French Revolution Issue

Common Design Type

Name and Value Typo. in Black.

1939, July 5			Photo.	
B4	CD83	45(c) + 25(c) grn	7.50	7.50
B5	CD83	70(c) + 30(c) brn	7.50	7.50
B6	CD83	90(c) + 35(c) red org	7.50	7.50
B7	CD83	1.25fr + 1fr rose pink	7.50	7.50
B8	CD83	2.25fr + 2fr bl	7.50	7.50
		Nos. B4-B8 (5)	37.50	37.50

Issued to commemorate the 150th anniversary of the French Revolution. The surtax was used for the defense of the colonies.

Common Design Type and

Native Artilleryman SP1

Gabon Infantryman SP2

1941		Photo.	*Perf. 13½*
B8A	SP1	1fr + 1fr red	1.75
B8B	CD86	1.50fr + 3fr mar	1.75
B8C	SP2	2.50fr + 1fr bl	1.75

Nos. B8A-B8C were issued by the Vichy government and not placed on sale in the colony.

Nos. 79A-79B were surcharged "OEUVRES COLONIALES" and surtax (including change of denomination of the 2.50fr to 50c). These were issued in 1944 by the Vichy government and not placed on sale in the colony.

Brazza and Stanley Pool — SP3

1941		Photo.	*Perf. 14½x14.*	
B9	SP3	1fr + 2fr dk brn & red	60	60

The surtax was for a monument to Pierre Savorgnan de Brazza.

Regular Stamps of 1937-39 Surcharged in Red

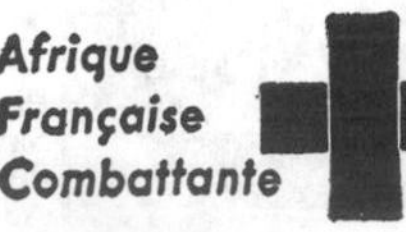

1943, June 28			*Perf. 13½x13*	
B10	A6	2.25fr + 50fr bl & lt bl	7.50	7.50
B11	A6	10fr + 100fr dk vio & bl	22.50	22.50

Nos. 129 and 132 with additional Surcharge in Carmine

LIBÉRATION
+ 10 fr.

1944
B12 A4 80c + 10fr brn & yel 10.00 10.00
B13 A5 1.50fr + 15fr dk bl & lt bl 10 00

Same surcharge printed Vertically on Stamps of 1941.
Perf. 14x14½.

B14 A8 5c + 10fr brn 4.00 4.00
B15 A8 10c + 10fr dk bl 4.00 4.00
B16 A8 25c + 10fr emer 4.00 4.00
B17 A8 30c + 10fr dp org 4.00 4.00
B18 A8 40c + 10fr dk sl grn 4.00 4.00
B19 A8 1fr + 10fr dp red lil 4.00 4.00
B20 A8 2fr + 20fr gray 4.50 4.50
B21 A8 2.50fr + 25fr brt ultra 4.50 4.50
Nos. B12-B21 (10) 43.10 43.00

Nos. 129 and 132 with additional Surcharge in Carmine

RÉSISTANCE
+ 10 fr.

1944 ***Perf. 13½x13***
B22 A4 80c + 10fr brn & yel 11.00 11.00
B23 A5 1.50fr + 15fr dk bl & lt bl 11.00 11.00

Same Surcharge printed Vertically on Stamps of 1941.
Perf. 14x14½

B24 A8 5c + 10fr brn 3.25 3.25
B25 A8 10c + 10fr dk bl 3.25 3.25
B26 A8 25c + 10fr emer 3.25 3.25
B27 A8 30c + 10fr dp org 3.25 3.25
B28 A8 40c + 10fr dk sl grn 3.25 3.25
B29 A8 1fr + 10fr dp red lil 3.25 3.25
B30 A8 2fr + 20fr gray 3.25 3.25
B31 A8 2.50fr + 25fr brt ultra 3.25 3.25
B32 A8 4fr + 40fr dl vio 3.25 3.25
B33 A8 5fr + 50fr yel bis 3.25 3.25
B34 A8 10fr + 100fr dp brn 5.50 5.50
B35 A8 20fr + 200fr dp grn 5.50 5.50
Nos. B22-B35 (14) 65.50 65.50

Nos. B12 to B35 were issued to raise funds for the Committee to Aid the Fighting Men and Patriots of France.

Red Cross Issue
Common Design Type

1944 **Photo.** ***Perf. 14½x14***
B38 CD90 5fr + 20fr ryl bl 80 80

The surtax was for the French Red Cross and national relief.

Tropical Medicine Issue
Common Design Type

1950, May 15 **Engr.** ***Perf. 13***
B39 CD100 10fr + 2fr dk bl grn & vio brn 3.00 3.00

The surtax was for charitable work.

AIR POST STAMPS

Hydroplane over Pointe-Noire — AP1

Trimotor over Stanley Pool — AP2

1937 **Unwmk.** **Photo.** ***Perf. 13½***
C1 AP1 1.50fr ol blk & yel 18 18
C2 AP1 2fr mag & bl 25 25
C3 AP1 2.50fr grn & buff 25 25
C4 AP1 3.75fr brn & lt grn 52 52
C5 AP2 4.50fr cop red & bl 52 52
C6 AP2 6.50fr bl & lt grn 75 75
C7 AP2 8.50fr red brn & yel 75 75
C8 AP2 10.75fr vio & lt grn 75 75
Nos. C1-C8 (8) 3.97 3.97

V4

Stamps of types AP1 and AP2 without "R F" and stamp of the design shown above were issued in 1943 and 1944 by the Vichy Government, but were not placed on sale in the colony.

Nos. C1, C3-C7 Overprinted in Black

Afrique Française Libre

1940-41
C9 AP1 1.50fr ('41) 125.00 125.00
a. Double overprint
C10 AP1 2.50fr 90 90
a. Double overprint 50.00
C11 AP1 3.75fr ('41) 125.00 125.00
95 95
C12 AP2 4.50fr
a. Double overprint 50.00 50.00
C13 AP2 6.50fr 1.25 1.25
90 90
C14 AP2 8.50fr

No. C8 Surcharged in Carmine

Afrique Française Libre
50 fr.

C15 AP2 50fr on 10.75fr 5.75 5.75

No. C3 Surcharged in Black

Afrique Française Libre

C16 AP1 10fr on 2.50fr ('41) 55.00 55.00
Nos. C9-C16 (8) 314.75 314.75

Counterfeits of Nos. C9 and C11 exist. See note following No. 141.

Common Design Type

1941 **Photo.** ***Perf. 14½x14***
C17 CD87 1fr dk org 42 30
C18 CD87 1.50fr brt red 42 30
C19 CD87 5fr brn red 90 42
C20 CD87 10fr black 90 60
C21 CD87 25fr ultra 80 52
C22 CD87 50fr dk grn 52 52
C23 CD87 100fr plum 80 65
Nos. C17-C23 (7) 4.76 3.31

Victory Issue
Common Design Type
Perf. 12½

1946, May 8 **Unwmk.** **Engr.**
C24 CD92 8fr lil rose 80 65

Chad to Rhine Issue
Common Design Types

1946, June 6
C25 CD93 5fr dk vio 60 60
C26 CD94 10fr sl grn 60 60
C27 CD95 15fr dp bl 80 80
C28 CD96 20fr red org 1.00 1.00
C29 CD97 25fr sepia 1.10 1.10
C30 CD98 50fr brn car 1.10 1.10
Nos. C25-C30 (6) 5.20 5.20

Palms and Village — AP3

Village and Waterfront — AP4

Bearers in Jungle — AP5

1946 **Engr.** ***Perf. 13.***
C31 AP3 50fr red brn 1.50 60
C32 AP4 100fr grnsh blk 2.50 95
C33 AP5 200fr dp bl 4.75 1.50

UPU Issue
Common Design Type

1949, July 4
C34 CD99 25fr green 6.50 6.50

Brazza Holding Map — AP6

1951, Nov. 5
C35 AP6 15fr brn, ind & red 1.00 52

Issued to commemorate the centenary of the birth of Pierre Savorgnan de Brazza, explorer.

Archbishop Augouard and St. Anne Cathedral, Brazzaville — AP7

1952, Dec. 1
C36 AP7 15fr ol grn, dk brn & vio brn 3.00 2.00

Issued to commemorate the centenary of the birth of Archbishop Philippe-Prosper Augouard.

Anhingas — AP8

1953, Feb. 16
C37 AP8 500fr grnsh blk, blk & sl 25.00 4.75

Liberation Issue
Common Design Type

1954, June 6
C38 CD102 15fr vio & vio brn 2.75 2.75

Log Rafts — AP9

Designs: 100fr, Fishing boats and nets, Lake Chad. 200fr, Age of mechanization.

1955, Jan. 24 **Engr.**
C39 AP9 50fr ind, brn & dk grn 1.10 60
C40 AP9 100fr aqua, dk grn & blk brn 3.75 60
C41 AP9 200fr red & dp plum 5.00 1.75

Gov. Gen. Félix Eboué, View of Brazzaville and the Pantheon — AP10

1955, Apr. 30 **Unwmk.** ***Perf. 13***
C42 AP10 15fr sep, brn & sl bl 2.75 1.50

Gen. Louis Faidherbe and African Sharpshooter AP11

1957, July 20
C43 AP11 15fr sep & org ver 1.50 1.10

Centenary of French African Troops.

AIR POST SEMI-POSTAL STAMPS

French Revolution Issue
Common Design Type

1939 **Unwmk.** **Photo.** ***Perf. 13.***
Name and Value Typo. in Orange.
CB1 CD83 4.50fr + 4fr brn blk 16.00 16.00

V5

V6

V7

Stamps of the designs shown above and stamp of Cameroun type V10 inscribed "Afrique Equatoriale Frcaise" were issued in 1942 by the Vichy Government, but were not placed on sale in the colony.

No. C8 Surcharged in Red

Afrique
Française
Combattante
+ 200 fr.

1943, June 28 *Perf. 13½*
CB2 AP2 10.75fr + 200fr vio & lt grn 100.00 100.00

Counterfeits exist.

POSTAGE DUE STAMPS

Numeral of Value on Equatorial Butterfly
D1 D2

1937 Unwmk. Photo. *Perf. 13*
J1 D1 5c redsh pur & lt bl 5 5
J2 D1 10c cop red & buff 6 6
J3 D1 20c dk grn & grn 6 6
J4 D1 25c red brn & buff 6 6
J5 D1 30c cop red & lt bl 14 14
J6 D1 45c mag & yel grn 40 40
J7 D1 50c dk ol grn & buff 35 35
J8 D1 60c redsh pur & yel 50 50
J9 D1 1fr brn & yel 60 60
J10 D1 2fr dk bl & buff 80 80
J11 D1 3fr red brn & lt grn 80 80
Nos. J1-J11 (11) 3.82 3.82

1947 **Engr.**
J12 D2 10c red 6 6
J13 D2 30c dp org 6 6
J14 D2 50c grnsh bl 6 6
J15 D2 1fr carmine 18 18
J16 D2 2fr emerald 18 18
J17 D2 3fr dp red lil 35 35
J18 D2 4fr dp ultra 40 40
J19 D2 5fr red brn 60 60
J20 D2 10fr pck bl 80 80
J21 D2 20fr sepia 90 90
Nos. J12-J21 (10) 3.59 3.59

FRENCH GUIANA

LOCATION — On the northeast coast of South America bordering on the Atlantic Ocean.
GOVT. — Former French colony
AREA — 34,740 sq. mi.
POP. — 28,537 (1946)
CAPITAL — Cayenne

Formerly a colony, French Guiana became an overseas department of France in 1946.

100 Centimes = 1 Franc

Stamps of French Colonies Surcharged in Black

Déc. 1886.
GUY. FRANÇ.
0f 05

1886, Dec. Unwmk. *Imperf.*
1 A8 5c on 2c grn, *grnsh* 350.00 350.00
b. No "f" after "O" 475.00 475.00

Perf. 14x13½.
2 A9 5c on 2c brn, *buff* 350.00 350.00
b. No "f" after "O" 250.00 225.00

Two types of No. 1: Surcharge 12mm. high, and surcharge 10½mm. high.

Avril 1887.
—
GUY FRANÇ
0f 20

Avril 1887.
—
GUY FRANÇ.
0f 25

"Av" of Date Line Inverted-Reversed
1887, Apr. *Imperf.*
4 A8 20c on 35c *org* 27.50 25.00

Date Line Reads "Avril 1887"
5 A8 5c on 2c grn, *grnsh* 72.50 65.00
6 A8 20c on 35c *org* 200.00 150.00
7 A7 25c on 30c brn, *yelsh* 18.00 16.00

Variety "small 'f' omitted" occurs on Nos. 5-7.

French Colonies Nos. 22 and 26 Surcharged:

DÉC. 1887.
GUY. FRANÇ.
5c

8 A7 5c on 30c brn, *yelsh* 80.00 67.50
a. Double surcharge 425.00 425.00
b. Inverted surcharge 550.00 550.00
c. Pair, one without surcharge 700.00 700.00
9 A8 5c on 30c brn, *yelsh* 825.00 825.00

French Colonies Nos. 22 and 28 Surcharged:

Février 1888
—
GUY. FRANÇ
5

Février 1888
—
GUY. FRANÇ
10

1888
10 A7 5c on 30c brn, *yelsh* 75.00 67.50
b. Double surcharge 275.00 275.00
c. Inverted surcharge 275.00 275.00
11 A8 10c on 75c car, *rose* 125.00 125.00

Stamps of French Colonies Overprinted in Black

1892, Feb. 20 *Imperf.*
12 A8 2c grn, *grnsh* 450.00 450.00
13 A7 30c brn, *yelsh* 80.00 80.00
14 A8 35c *orange* 1,700. 1,400.
15 A8 40c red, *straw* 60.00 55.00
16 A8 75c car, *rose* 62.50 55.00
a. Inverted overprint 250.00 250.00
17 A8 1fr brnz grn, *straw* 80.00 80.00
a. Inverted overprint 325.00 325.00

1892 *Perf. 14x13½*
18 A9 1c *lil bl* 22.50 15.00
19 A9 2c brn, *buff* 18.00 15.00
20 A9 4c cl, *lav* 18.00 15.00
21 A9 5c grn, *grnsh* 18.00 15.00
a. Inverted overprint 55.00 55.00
b. Double overprint 55.00
22 A9 10c *lavender* 27.50 16.00
a. Inverted overprint 27.50 16.00
23 A9 15c blue 25.00 15.00
24 A9 20c red, *grn* 22.50 15.00
25 A9 25c *rose* 30.00 15.00
26 A9 30c brn, *bis* 18.00 14.00
27 A9 35c *orange* 110.00 110.00
28 A9 40c red, *straw* 65.00 60.00
a. Inverted overprint 100.00 87.50
29 A9 75c car, *rose* 60.00 52.50
30 A9 1fr brnz grn, *straw* 125.00 110.00

French Colonies No. 51 Surcharged

GUYANE.
DÉC. 92.
0f05

1892, Dec.
31 A9 5c on 15c bl 21.00 14.00

Navigation and Commerce — A12

1892-1904 **Typo.**
Name of Colony in Blue or Carmine.
32 A12 1c *lil bl* 1.00 95
33 A12 2c brn, *buff* 70 75
34 A12 4c cl, *lav* 95 75
a. "GUYANE" double 125.00 125.00
35 A12 5c grn, *grnsh* 6.50 5.25
36 A12 5c yel grn ('04) 80 42
37 A12 10c *lavender* 6.00 3.00
38 A12 10c red ('00) 2.25 80
39 A12 15c bl, quadrille paper 15.00 1.50
40 A12 15c gray, *lt gray* ('00) 55.00 42.50
41 A12 20c red, *grn* 9.00 6.00
42 A12 25c *rose* 7.50 2.25
43 A12 25c bl ('00) 7.00 6.50
44 A12 30c brn, *bis* 8.00 6.00
45 A12 40c red, *straw* 9.20 6.00
46 A12 50c car, *rose* 15.00 6.00
47 A12 50c brn, *az* ('00) 10.00 8.25
48 A12 75c dp vio,*org* 16.00 9.00
49 A12 1fr brn grn, *straw* 6.75 6.00
50 A12 2fr vio, *rose* ('02) 100.00 6.50
Nos. 32-50 (19) 276.65 118.42

Great Anteater
A13

Washing Gold
A14

Palm Grove at Cayenne
A15

1905-28
51 A13 1c black 5 5
52 A13 2c blue 6 6
53 A13 4c red brn 6 6
54 A13 5c green 60 48
55 A13 5c org ('22) 5 5
56 A13 10c rose 18 14
57 A13 10c grn ('22) 14 14
58 A13 10c red, *bluish* ('25) 14 6
59 A13 15c violet 90 60
60 A14 20c red brn 18 14
61 A14 25c blue 1.10 42
62 A14 25c vio ('22) 52 18
63 A14 30c black 80 42
64 A14 30c rose ('22) 18 18
65 A14 30c red org ('25) 18 14
66 A14 30c dk grn, *grnsh* ('28) 65 65
67 A14 35c *yel* ('06) 18 14
68 A14 40c rose 18 14
69 A14 40c blk ('22) 30 18
70 A14 45c ol ('07) 52 18
71 A14 50c violet 1.25 95
72 A14 50c bl ('22) 18 18
73 A14 50c gray ('25) 52 22
74 A14 60c lil, *rose* ('25) 22 18
75 A14 65c myr grn ('26) 22 18
76 A14 75c green 70 42
77 A14 85c mag ('26) 42 18
78 A15 1fr rose 48 18
79 A15 1fr bl, *bluish* ('25) 52 18
80 A15 1fr bl, *yel grn* ('28) 1.25 1.25
81 A15 1.10fr lt red ('28) 85 85
82 A15 2fr blue 60 42
83 A15 2fr org red, *yel* ('26) 1.10 90
84 A15 5fr black 3.75 2.25
85 A15 10fr grn, *yel* ('24) 7.50 7.25
a. Printed on both sides 30.00 30.00
86 A15 20fr brn lake ('24) 10.50 8.50
Nos. 51-86 (36) 37.03 28.50

Issue of 1892 Surcharged in Black or Carmine

05
10

1912
87 A12 5c on 2c brn, *buff* 52 52
88 A12 5c on 4c cl, *lav* (C) 48 48
89 A12 5c on 20c red, *grn* 52 52
90 A12 5c on 25c *rose* (C) 1.75 1.75
91 A12 5c on 30c brn, *bis* (C) 80 80
92 A12 10c on 40c red, *straw* 48 48
93 A12 10c on 50c car, *rose* 1.00 1.00
a. Double surcharge 325.00
Nos. 87-93 (7) 5.55 5.55

Two spacings between the surcharged numerals are found on Nos. 87 to 93.

No. 59 Surcharged in Various Colors

0,01 =

1922
94 A13 1c on 15c vio (Bk) 22 22
95 A13 2c on 15c vio (Bl) 22 22
a. Inverted surch. 52.50
96 A13 4c on 15c vio (G) 22 22
a. Double surch. 52.50
97 A13 5c on 15c vio (R) 22 22

Type of 1905-28 Surcharged in Blue

VINGT
FRANCS

VINGT
FRANCS

1923
98 A15 10fr on 1fr grn, *yel* 7.50 7.50
99 A15 20fr on 5fr lil, *rose* 7.50 7.50

Stamps and Types of 1905-28 Surcharged with New Value and Bars in Black or Red.

1924-27
100 A13 25c on 15c vio ('25) 22 22
101 A15 25c on 2fr bl ('24) 22 22
a. Double surcharge 75.00
b. Triple surcharge 87.50
102 A14 65c on 45c ol (R) ('25) 60 60
103 A14 85c on 45c ol (R) ('25) 60 60
104 A14 90c on 75c red ('27) 60 60
105 A15 1.05fr on 2fr lt yel brn ('27) 60 60
106 A15 1.25fr on 1fr ultra (R) ('26) 60 60
107 A15 1.50fr on 1fr lt bl ('27) 75 75
108 A15 3fr on 5fr vio ('27) 75 75
a. No period after "F" 6.00 6.00
Nos. 100-108 (9) 4.94 4.94

Carib Archer — A16

Shooting Rapids, Maroni River
A17

Government Building, Cayenne
A18

1929-40 *Perf. 13½x14.*

109	A16	1c gray lil & grnsh bl	6	6
110	A16	2c dk red & bl grn	5	5
111	A16	3c gray lil & grnsh bl ('40)	5	5
112	A16	4c ol brn & red vio	18	18
113	A16	5c Prus bl & red org	6	6
114	A16	10c mag & brn	6	6
115	A16	15c yel brn & red org	6	6
116	A16	20c dk bl & ol grn	14	14
117	A16	25c dk red & dk brn	18	18

Perf. 14x13½.

118	A17	30c dl & lt grn	35	18
119	A17	30c grn & brn ('40)	5	5
120	A17	35c Prus grn & ol grn ('38)	48	48
121	A17	40c org brn & ol gray	14	14
122	A17	45c grn & dk brn	48	48
123	A17	45c ol grn & lt grn ('40)	18	18
124	A17	50c dk bl & ol gray	14	14
125	A17	55c vio bl & car ('38)	60	60
126	A17	60c sal & grn ('40)	18	18
127	A17	65c sal & grn	52	52
128	A17	70c ind & sl bl ('40)	55	55
129	A17	75c ind & sl bl	75	75
130	A17	80c blk & vio bl ('38)	40	35
131	A17	90c dk red & ver	52	52
132	A17	90c red vio & brn ('39)	55	55
133	A17	1fr lt vio & brn	52	52
134	A17	1fr car & lt red ('38)	1.10	1.00
135	A17	1fr blk & vio bl ('40)	18	18
136	A18	1.05fr ver & olvn	3.00	2.50
137	A18	1.10fr ol brn & red vio	3.00	2.50
138	A18	1.25fr blk brn & bl grn ('33)	52	52
139	A18	1.25fr rose & lt red ('39)	30	30
140	A18	1.40fr ol brn & red vio ('40)	55	55
141	A18	1.50fr dk bl & lt bl	6	6
142	A18	1.60fr ol brn & bl grn ('40)	30	30
143	A18	1.75fr brn red & blk brn ('33)	1.10	1.00
144	A18	1.75fr vio bl ('38)	52	52
145	A18	2fr dk grn & rose red	18	18
146	A18	2.25fr vio bl ('39)	55	55
147	A18	2.50fr cop red & brn ('40)	55	55
148	A18	3fr brn red & red vio	48	48
149	A18	5fr dl vio & yel grn	48	48
150	A18	10fr ol gray & dp ultra	70	70
151	A18	20fr ind & ver	1.00	90
		Nos. 109-151 (43)	21.82	20.30

Colonial Exposition Issue.
Common Design Types

1931 **Engr.** *Perf. 12½.*
Name of Country Printed in Black

152	CD70	40c dp grn	2.25	2.25
153	CD71	50c violet	2.25	2.25
154	CD72	90c red org	2.50	2.50
155	CD73	1.50fr dl bl	2.50	2.50

Recapture of Cayenne by d'Estrees, 1676 — A19

Products of French Guiana
A20

1935, Oct. 21 *Perf. 13*

156	A19	40c gray brn	2.50	2.25
157	A19	50c dl red	6.00	3.00
158	A19	1.50fr ultra	2.50	2.25
159	A20	1.75fr lil rose	7.75	6.25
160	A20	5fr brown	6.00	4.00
161	A20	10fr bl grn	6.00	4.00
		Nos. 156-161 (6)	30.75	21.75

Issued to commemorate the tercentenary of the founding of French possessions in the West Indies.

Paris International Exposition Issue.
Common Design Types

1937, Apr. 15

162	CD74	20c dp vio	45	45
163	CD75	30c dk grn	45	45
164	CD76	40c car rose	45	45
165	CD77	50c dk brn	45	45
166	CD78	90c red	50	50
167	CD79	1.50fr ultra	50	50
		Nos. 162-167 (6)	2.80	2.80

Colonial Arts Exhibition Issue
Souvenir Sheet.
Common Design Type

1937 *Imperf.*

168	CD75	3fr violet	2.75 2.75

Sheet size: 118x99mm.

New York World's Fair Issue
Common Design Type

1939, May 10 **Engr.** *Perf. 12½x12*

169	CD82	1.25fr car lake	45	45
170	CD82	2.25fr ultra	45	45

View of Cayenne and Marshal Petain
A21a

1941 **Engr.** *Perf. 12½x12*

170A	A21a	1fr dp lil	48
170B	A21a	2.50fr blue	48

Nos. 170A-170B were issued by the Vichy government and were not placed on sale in the colony. This is also true of three stamps of types A16-A18 without "RF" released in 1944.

Common Design Types pictured in section at front of book.

Eboue Issue.
Common Design Type

1945 **Engr.** *Perf. 13.*

171	CD91	2fr black	48	48
172	CD91	25fr Prus grn	75	75

This issue exists imperforate.

Arms of Cayenne
A22

1945 **Litho.** *Perf. 12*

173	A22	10c dp pray vio	6	6
174	A22	30c brn org	6	6
175	A22	40c lt bl	6	6
176	A22	50c vio brn	6	6
177	A22	60c org yel	6	6
178	A22	70c pale brn	18	18
179	A22	80c lt grn	18	18
180	A22	1fr blue	14	14
181	A22	1.20fr brt vio	18	12
182	A22	1.50fr dp org	40	40
183	A22	2fr black	40	40
184	A22	2.40fr red	45	45
185	A22	3fr pink	45	45
186	A22	4fr dp ultra	45	45
187	A22	4.50fr dp yel grn	45	45
188	A22	5fr org brn	45	45
189	A22	10fr dk vio	45	45
190	A22	15fr rose car	65	65
191	A22	20fr ol grn	70	70
		Nos. 173-191 (19)	5.83	5.77

Hammock — A23

Maroni River Bank — A24

Inini Scene
A25

Guiana Girl — A26

Toucans
A27

Parrots
A28

Perf. 13.

1947, June 2 **Unwmk.** **Engr.**

192	A23	10c dk bl grn	6	6
193	A23	30c brt red	6	6
194	A23	50c dk vio brn	6	6
195	A24	60c grnsh blk	6	6
196	A24	1fr red brn	18	18
197	A24	1.50fr blk brn	18	18
198	A25	2fr dp yel grn	35	18
199	A25	2.50fr dp ultra	35	30
200	A25	3fr red brn	48	42
201	A26	4fr blk brn	1.00	60
202	A26	5fr dp bl	85	60
203	A26	6fr red brn	90	60
204	A27	10fr dp ultra	2.50	1.75
205	A27	15fr blk brn	2.50	2.50
206	A27	20fr red brn	3.00	2.75
207	A28	25fr brt bl grn	4.00	3.00
208	A28	40fr blk brn	4.00	3.00
		Nos. 192-208 (17)	20.53	16.30

SEMI-POSTAL STAMPS

Regular Issue of 1905-28 Surcharged in Red

1915 **Unwmk.** *Perf. 13½x14.*

B1	A13	10c + 5c rose	6.75	6.75
a.		Inverted surcharge	100.00	100.00
b.		Double surcharge	87.50	87.50

Regular Issue of 1905-28 Surcharged in Rose

B2	A13	10c + 5c rose	52	52

Curie Issue
Common Design Type

1938 *Perf. 13.*

B3	CD80	1.75fr + 50c brt ultra	5.50	5.50

French Revolution Issue
Common Design Type

1939 **Photo.**
Name and Value in Black.

B4	CD83	45c + 25c grn	4.50	4.50
B5	CD83	70c + 30c brn	4.50	4.50
B6	CD83	90c + 35c red org	4.50	4.50
B7	CD83	1.25fr + 1fr rose pink	4.50	4.50
B8	CD83	2.25fr + 2fr bl	6.00	6.00
		Nos. B4-B8 (5)	24.00	24.00

Common Design Type and

Colonial Infantryman — SP1

Colonial Policeman
SP2

1941 **Photo.** *Perf. 13½*

B9	SP1	1fr + 1fr red	70
B10	CD86	1.50fr + 3fr mar	95
B11	SP2	2.50fr + 1fr bl	70

Nos. B9-B11 were issued by the Vichy government, and were not placed on sale in the colony.

Nos. 170A-170B were surcharged "OEUVRES COLONIALES" and surtax (including change of denomination of the 2.50fr to 50c). These were issued in 1944 by the Vichy government, and not placed on sale in the colony.

Red Cross Issue
Common Design Type

1944 *Perf. 14½x14.*

B12	CD90	5fr + 20fr dk cop brn	65	65

The surtax was for the French Red Cross and national relief.

AIR POST STAMPS

Cayenne
AP1

Perf. 13½

1933, Nov. 20 **Unwmk.** **Photo.**

C1	AP1	50c org brn	22	22
C2	AP1	1fr yel grn	22	22
C3	AP1	1.50fr dk bl	22	22
C4	AP1	2fr orange	22	22
C5	AP1	3fr black	65	65
C6	AP1	5fr violet	30	30
C7	AP1	10fr ol grn	55	55
C8	AP1	20fr scarlet	65	65
		Nos. C1-C8 (8)	3.03	3.03

Demand, as well as supply, determines a stamp's market value. One is as important as the other.

V4

V5

Stamp of type AP1 without "RF" and stamps of the designs shown above were issued in 1942 and 1944 by the Vichy Government, but were not placed on sale in the colony.

Common Design Type

1945 Photo. *Perf. 14½x14*

C9 CD87 50fr dk grn 60 60
C10 CD87 100fr plum 1.00 1.00

Victory Issue
Common Design Type

1946, May 8 Engr. *Perf. 12½.*

C11 CD92 8fr black 75 75

Issued to commemorate the European victory of the Allied Nations in World War II.

Chad to Rhine Issue
Common Design Types

1946, June 6

C12 CD93 5fr dk sl bl 65 65
C13 CD94 10fr lil rose 75 75
C14 CD95 15fr dk vio brn 75 75
C15 CD96 20fr dk sl grn 85 85
C16 CD97 25fr vio brn 90 90
C17 CD98 50fr brt lil 1.25 1.25
Nos. C12-C17 (6) 5.15 5.15

Eagles — AP2

Tapir — AP3

Toucans — AP4

1947, June 2 Engr. *Perf. 13*

C18 AP2 50fr dp grn 8.00 8.00
C19 AP3 100fr red brn 8.00 8.00
C20 AP4 200fr dk gray bl 15.00 15.00

AIR POST SEMI-POSTAL STAMP

French Revolution Issue
Common Design Type
Unwmk.

1939, July 5 Photo. *Perf. 13*
Name & Value Typo. in Orange

CB1 CD83 5fr + 4fr brn blk 10.00 10.00

V6

Stamps of the design shown above and stamp of Cameroun type V10 inscribed "Guyane Francaise" were issued in 1942 by the Vichy Government, but were not placed on sale in the colony.

POSTAGE DUE STAMPS

Postage Due Stamps of France, 1893-1926, Overprinted **GUYANE FRANÇAISE**

1925-27 Unwmk. *Perf. 14x13½.*

J1 D2 5c lt bl 14 14
J2 D2 10c brown 22 22
J3 D2 20c ol grn 22 22
J4 D2 50c vio brn 55 42
J5 D2 3fr mag ('27) 4.50 4.00

Surcharged in Black **GUYANE FRANÇAISE 25 centimes à percevoir**

J6 D2 15c on 20c ol grn 22 22
a. Blue surcharge 30.00
J7 D2 25c on 5c lt bl 52 35
J8 D2 30c on 20c ol grn 65 42
J9 D2 45c on 10c brn 40 30
J10 D2 60c on 5c lt bl 55 42
J11 D2 1fr on 20c ol grn 80 70
J12 D2 2fr on 50c vio brn 1.00 80
Nos. J1-J12 (12) 9.77 8.21

Royal Palms — D3

Guiana Girl — D4

1929, Oct. 14 Typo. *Perf. 13½x14*

J13 D3 5c ind & Prus bl 14 14
J14 D3 10c bis brn & Prus grn 14 14
J15 D3 20c grn & rose red 14 14
J16 D3 30c ol brn & rose red 14 14
J17 D3 50c vio & ol brn 42 42
J18 D3 60c brn red & ol brn 65 65
J19 D4 1fr dp bl & org brn 95 95
J20 D4 2fr brn red & bluish grn 1.10 1.10
J21 D4 3fr vio & blk 2.00 2.00
Nos. J13-J21 (9) 5.68 5.68

D5

1947, June 2 Engr. *Perf. 14x13*

J22 D5 10c dk car rose 5 5
J23 D5 30c dl grn 5 5
J24 D5 50c black 8 8
J25 D5 1fr brt ultra 22 22
J26 D5 2fr dk brn red 22 22
J27 D5 3fr dp vio 35 35
J28 D5 4fr red 45 45
J29 D5 5fr brn vio 60 60
J30 D5 10fr bl grn 1.00 1.00
J31 D5 20fr lil rose 1.25 1.25
Nos. J22-J31 (10) 4.27 4.27

FRENCH GUINEA

LOCATION — On the coast of West Africa, between Portuguese Guinea and Sierra Leone.
GOVT. — Former French colony
AREA — 89,436 sq. mi.
POP. — 2,058,442 (est. 1941)
CAPITAL — Conakry

French Guinea stamps were replaced by those of French West Africa around 1944-45. French Guinea became the Republic of Guinea Oct. 2, 1958. See "Guinea" for issues of the republic.

100 Centimes = 1 Franc

Navigation and Commerce
A1

Fulah Shepherd
A2

Perf. 14x13½.
1892-1900 Typo. Unwmk.
Name of Colony in Blue or Carmine

1 A1 1c *lil bl* 90 90
2 A1 2c brn, *buff* 1.00 1.00
3 A1 4c cl, *lav* 1.25 1.25
4 A1 5c grn, *grnsh* 3.50 2.25
5 A1 10c *lavender* 3.25 2.25
6 A1 10c red ('00) 20.00 16.00
7 A1 15c bl, quadrille paper 3.50 2.25
8 A1 15c gray, *lt gray* ('00) 62.50 52.50
9 A1 20c red, *grn* 9.00 6.25
10 A1 25c *rose* 5.00 3.75
11 A1 25c bl ('00) 12.00 8.00
12 A1 30c brn, *bis* 18.00 11.00
13 A1 40c red, *straw* 18.00 11.00
a. "GUINEE FRANCAISE" double 375.00 375.00
14 A1 50c car, *rose* 22.00 11.00
15 A1 50c brn, *az* ('00) 15.00 11.00
16 A1 75c dp vio, *org* 30.00 22.50
17 A1 1fr brnz grn, *straw* 22.50 15.00
Nos. 1-17 (17) 247.40 177.90

1904

18 A2 1c *yel grn* 60 42
19 A2 2c vio brn, *buff* 60 60
20 A2 4c car, *bl* 95 70
21 A2 5c grn, *grnsh* 95 70
22 A2 10c carmine 1.75 1.00
23 A2 15c vio, *rose* 3.75 2.00
24 A2 20c car, *grn* 6.00 5.00
25 A2 25c blue 6.75 5.00
26 A2 30c brown 11.00 9.50
27 A2 40c red, *straw* 14.00 12.50
28 A2 50c brn, *az* 14.00 12.50
29 A2 75c grn, *org* 18.00 17.00
30 A2 1fr brnz grn, *straw* 24.00 21.00
31 A2 2fr red, *org* 52.50 45.00
32 A2 5fr grn, *yel grn* 70.00 60.00
Nos. 18-32 (15) 224.85 192.92

Gen. Louis Faidherbe — A3

Oil Palm — A4

Dr. Noel Eugene Ballay — A5

1906-07
Name of Colony in Red or Blue.

33 A3 1c gray 52 52
34 A3 2c brown 65 52
35 A3 4c brn, *bl* 85 70
36 A3 5c green 1.90 1.25
37 A3 10c car (B) 8.25 1.40
38 A4 20c *blue* 2.75 2.00
39 A4 25c bl, *pnksh* 3.25 2.50
40 A4 30c brn, *pnksh* 3.00 2.00
41 A4 35c *yellow* 1.75 1.25
42 A4 45c choc, *grnsh gray* 2.50 2.00
43 A4 50c dp vio 5.75 4.75
44 A4 75c bl, *org* 2.75 2.00
45 A5 1fr blk, *az* 10.50 9.50
46 A5 2fr bl, *pink* 22.50 20.00
47 A5 5fr car, *straw* (B) 32.50 30.00
Nos. 33-47 (15) 99.42 80.39

Regular Issues Surcharged in Black or Carmine

05 a **10** b

1912

On Issue of 1892-1900

48 A1 5c on 2c brn, *buff* 70 70
49 A1 5c on 4c cl, *lav* (C) 52 52
50 A1 5c on 15c bl (C) 52 52
51 A1 5c on 20c red, *grn* 1.75 1.75
52 A1 5c on 30c brn, *bis* (C) 1.75 1.75
53 A1 10c on 40c red, *straw* 1.00 1.00
54 A1 10c on 75c dp vio, *org* 3.00 3.00
a. Double surcharge, inverted 160.00

On Issue of 1904.

55 A2 5c on 2c vio brn, *buff* 60 60
a. Pair, one without surcharge 425.00
56 A2 5c on 4c car, *bl* 60 60
57 A2 5c on 15c vio, *rose* 60 60
58 A2 5c on 20c car, *grn* 60 60
59 A2 5c on 25c bl (C) 60 60
60 A2 5c on 30c brn (C) 85 85
61 A2 10c on 40c red, *straw* 90 90
62 A2 10c on 50c brn, *az* (C) 1.75 1.75
Nos. 48-62 (15) 15.74 15.74

Two spacings between the surcharged numerals are found on Nos. 48 to 62.

Ford at Kitim — A6

1913-33 *Perf. 13½x14*

63 A6 1c vio & bl 5 5
64 A6 2c brn & vio brn 5 5
65 A6 4c gray & blk 5 5
66 A6 5c yel grn & bl grn 18 18
67 A6 5c brn vio & grn ('22) 5 5
68 A6 10c red org & rose 18 18
69 A6 10c yel grn & bl grn ('22) 5 5
70 A6 10c vio & ver ('25) 6 5
71 A6 15c vio brn & rose ('16) 5 5
72 A6 15c gray grn & yel grn ('25) 5 5
73 A6 15c red brn & rose lil ('27) 15 5
74 A6 20c brn & vio 5 5
75 A6 20c grn & bl grn ('26) 60 40
76 A6 20c brn red & brn ('27) 15 6
77 A6 25c ultra & bl 80 70
78 A6 25c blk & vio ('22) 52 35
79 A6 30c vio brn & grn 45 42
80 A6 30c red org & rose ('22) 18 18
81 A6 30c rose red & grn ('25) 5 5
82 A6 30c dl grn & bl grn ('28) 95 80
83 A6 35c bl & rose 18 18

84 A6 40c grn & gray 65 52
85 A6 45c brn & red 85 65
86 A6 50c ultra & blk 2.50 1.75
87 A6 50c ultra & bl ('22) 48 22
88 A6 50c yel brn & ol ('25) 6 5
89 A6 60c vio, *pnksh* ('25) 15 15
90 A6 65c yel brn & sl bl ('26) 90 80
91 A6 75c red & ultra 80 60
92 A6 75c ind & dl bl ('25) 48 35
93 A6 75c mag & yel grn ('27) 95 70
94 A6 85c ol grn & red brn ('26) 55 42
95 A6 90c brn red & rose ('30) 2.50 2.25
96 A6 1fr vio & blk 90 52
97 A6 1.10fr vio & ol brn ('28) 2.50 2.00
98 A6 1.25fr vio & yel brn ('33) 80 60
99 A6 1.50fr dk bl & lt bl ('30) 2.25 1.40
100 A6 1.75fr ol brn & vio ('33) 90 75
101 A6 2fr org & vio brn 1.25 75
102 A6 3fr red vio ('30) 4.00 3.50
103 A6 5fr blk & vio 6.00 5.00
104 A6 5fr dl bl & blk ('22) 90 85
Nos. 63-104 (42) 35.22 27.83

Nos. 66 and 68 exist on both ordinary and chalky paper, No. 71 on chalky paper only.

Type of 1913-33 Surcharged **60 = 60**

1922
105 A6 60c on 75c vio, *pnksh* 42 42

Stamps and Type of 1913-33 Surcharged with New Value and Bars.

1924-27
106 A6 25c on 2fr org & brn (R) 8 8
107 A6 25c on 5fr dl bl & blk ('24) 6 6
108 A6 65c on 75c rose & ultra ('25) 90 90
109 A6 85c on 75c rose & ultra ('25) 90 90
110 A6 90c on 75c brn red & cer ('27) 95 95
111 A6 1.25fr on 1fr dk bl & ultra ('26) 42 42
112 A6 1.50fr on 1fr dp bl & lt bl ('27) 95 95
113 A6 3fr on 5fr mag & sl ('27) 1.75 1.75
114 A6 10fr on 5fr bl & bl grn, *bluish* ('27) 3.50 3.50
115 A6 20fr on 5fr rose lil & brn ol, *pnksh* ('27) 9.00 9.00
Nos. 106-115 (10) 18.51 18.51

Colonial Exposition Issue.
Common Design Types

1931 Engr. *Perf. 12½.*
Name of Country in Black.
116 CD70 40c dp grn 2.25 2.25
117 CD71 50c violet 2.25 2.25
118 CD72 90c red org 2.25 2.25
119 CD73 1.50fr dl bl 1.75 1.75

Paris International Exposition Issue.
Common Design Types

1937 *Perf. 13.*
120 CD74 20c dp vio 75 75
121 CD75 30c dk grn 75 75
122 CD76 40c car rose 85 85
123 CD77 50c dk brn 85 85
124 CD78 90c red 90 90
125 CD79 1.50fr ultra 90 90
Nos. 120-125 (6) 5.00 5.00

Colonial Arts Exhibition Issue.
Souvenir Sheet.
Common Design Type

1937 *Imperf.*
126 CD76 3fr Prus grn 3.00 3.00

Sheet size: 118x99mm.

Guinea Village A7

Hausa Basket Workers A8

Forest Waterfall A9

Guinea Women — A10

1938-40 *Perf. 13*
128 A7 2c vermilion 5 5
129 A7 3c ultra 5 5
130 A7 4c green 5 5
131 A7 5c rose car 5 5
132 A7 10c pck bl 5 5
133 A7 15c vio brn 5 5
134 A8 20c dk car 5 5
135 A8 25c pck bl 18 14
136 A8 30c ultra 14 14
137 A8 35c green 35 35
138 A8 40c blk brn ('40) 14 14
139 A8 45c dk grn ('40) 18 18
140 A8 50c red brn 15 15
141 A9 55c dk ultra 52 40
142 A9 60c dk ultra ('40) 65 65
143 A9 65c green 55 35
144 A9 70c grn ('40) 65 65
145 A9 80c rose vio 35 35
146 A9 90c rose vio ('39) 65 65
147 A9 1fr org red 1.10 90
148 A9 1fr brn blk ('40) 42 42
149 A9 1.25fr org red ('39) 85 85
150 A9 1.40fr brn ('40) 85 85
151 A9 1.50fr brown 1.10 90
152 A10 1.60fr org red ('40) 85 85
153 A10 1.75fr ultra 45 42
154 A10 2fr magenta 75 42
155 A10 2.25fr brt ultra ('39) 1.00 1.00
156 A10 2.50fr brn blk ('40) 85 85
157 A10 3fr pck bl 42 22
158 A10 5fr rose vio 52 42
159 A10 10fr sl grn 90 65
160 A10 20fr chocolate 1.10 90
Nos. 128-160 (33) 16.02 14.15

Caillié Issue
Common Design Type

1939 Engr. *Perf. 12½x12*
161 CD81 90c org brn & org 50 50
162 CD81 2fr brt vio 50 50
163 CD81 2.25fr ultra & dk bl 50 50

Issued to commemorate the centenary of the death of René Caillié, French explorer.

New York World's Fair Issue.
Common Design Type

1939
164 CD82 1.25fr car lake 50 50
165 CD82 2.25fr ultra 50 50

Ford at Kitim and Marshal Petain — A11

1941 *Perf. 12x12½.*
166 A11 1fr green 42
167 A11 2.50fr dp bl 42

Nos. 166-167 were issued by the Vichy government. Seven stamps of types A7-A10 without "RF" are also Vichy issues (1943-44), but are believed not to have been placed on sale in the colony.

Stamps of French Guinea were followed by those of French West Africa.

SEMI-POSTAL STAMPS

Regular Issue of 1913 Surcharged in Red **✚ 5c**

1915 Unwmk. *Perf. 13½x14.*
B1 A6 10c + 5c org & rose 90 52

No. B1 exists on both ordinary and chalky paper.

Curie Issue
Common Design Type

1938 Engr. *Perf. 13.*
B2 CD80 1.75fr + 50c brt ultra 4.75 4.75

French Revolution Issue
Common Design Type

1939 Photo.
Name and Value Typo. in Black
B3 CD83 45c + 25c grn 3.00 3.00
B4 CD83 70c + 30c brn 3.00 3.00
B5 CD83 90c + 35c red org 3.00 3.00
B6 CD83 1.25fr + 1fr rose pink 3.00 3.00
B7 CD83 2.25fr + 2fr bl 3.00 3.00
Nos. B3-B7 (5) 15.00 15.00

Stamps of 1938, Surcharged in Black **SECOURS + 1 fr. NATIONAL**

1941 Unwmk. *Perf. 13.*
B8 A8 50c + 1fr red brn 90 90
B9 A9 80c + 2fr rose vio 2.50 2.25
B10 A9 1.50fr + 2fr brn 2.50 2.25
B11 A10 2fr + 3fr mag 2.50 2.25

Common Design Type and

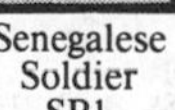
Senegalese Soldier SP1

Colonial Infantryman SP2

1941 Unwmk. *Perf. 13*
B12 SP1 1fr + 1fr red 70
B13 CD86 1.50fr + 3fr mar 70
B14 SP2 2.50fr + 1fr bl 70

Nos. B12-B14 were issued by the Vichy government, and were not placed on sale in the colony.

Nos. 166-167 were surcharged "OEUVRES COLONIALES" and surtax (including change of denomination of the 2.50fr to 50c). These were issued in 1944 by the Vichy government and not placed on sale in the colony.

AIR POST STAMPS

Common Design Type

1940 Unwmk. Engr. *Perf. 12½x12*
C1 CD85 1.90fr ultra 20 20
C2 CD85 2.90fr dk red 25 25
C3 CD85 4.50fr dk gray grn 30 30
C4 CD85 4.90fr yel bis 45 45
C5 CD85 6.90fr dp org 60 60
Nos. C1-C5 (5) 1.80 1.80

Common Design Types

1942 Engr.
C6 CD88 50c car & bl 5
C7 CD88 1fr brn & blk 14
C8 CD88 2fr dk grn & red brn 14
C9 CD88 3fr dk bl & scar 25
C10 CD88 5fr vio & brn red 25

Frame Engraved, Center Typographed
C11 CD89 10fr ultra, ind & vio 30
C12 CD89 20fr rose car, mag & gray bl 30
C13 CD89 50fr yel grn, dl grn & gray blk 50 1.50
Nos. C6-C13 (8) 1.93

There is doubt whether Nos. C6-C12 were officially placed in use.

AIR POST SEMI-POSTAL STAMPS

Stamps of types of Dahomey V1, V2 and V3, and of Cameroun V10, inscribed "Guinée", "Guinee Frcaise" or "Guinee Francaise," were issued in 1942 by the Vichy Government, but were not placed on sale in the colony.

POSTAGE DUE STAMPS

Fulah Woman D1

Heads and Coast D2

1905 Unwmk. Typo. *Perf. 14x13½*
J1 D1 5c blue 70 80
J2 D1 10c brown 70 80
J3 D1 15c green 2.75 2.00
J4 D1 30c rose 2.75 2.00
J5 D1 50c black 5.75 4.75
J6 D1 60c dl org 7.50 5.50
J7 D1 1fr violet 22.50 20.00
Nos. J1-J7 (7) 42.65 35.85

1906-08
J8 D2 5c grn, *grnsh* ('08) 9.50 8.00
J9 D2 10c vio brn ('08) 3.50 3.75
J10 D2 15c dk bl ('08) 2.50 3.75
J11 D2 20c *yellow* 2.50 2.50
J12 D2 30c red, *straw* ('08) 15.00 12.50
J13 D2 50c vio ('08) 12.00 10.50
J14 D2 60c blk, *buff* ('08) 11.00 9.75
J15 D2 1fr *pnksh* ('08) 7.25 6.25
Nos. J8-J15 (8) 63.25 57.00

D3

D4

1914
J16 D3 5c green 6 6
J17 D3 10c rose 6 6
J18 D3 15c gray 30 30
J19 D3 20c brown 30 30
J20 D3 30c blue 30 30
J21 D3 50c black 60 60
J22 D3 60c orange 60 90
J23 D3 1fr violet 1.00 1.00
Nos. J16-J23 (8) 3.52 3.52

Type of 1914 Issue Surcharged **2F.**

1927
J24 D3 2fr on 1fr lil rose 3.25 3.25
J25 D3 3fr on 1fr org brn 3.75 3.75

1938 Engr.
J26 D4 5c dk vio 5 5
J27 D4 10c carmine 5 5
J28 D4 15c green 5 5
J29 D4 20c red brn 5 5
J30 D4 30c rose vio 30 30
J31 D4 50c chocolate 45 45
J32 D4 60c pck bl 75 75
J33 D4 1fr vermilion 75 75
J34 D4 2fr ultra 80 80
J35 D4 3fr black 90 90
Nos. J26-J35 (10) 4.15 4.15

A 10c of type D4 without "RF" was issued in 1944 by the Vichy Government, but was not placed on sale in the colony.

FRENCH INDIA

LOCATION — East coast of India bordering on Bay of Bengal.
GOVT. — Former French Territory
AREA — 196 sq. mi.
POP. — 323,295 (1941)
CAPITAL — Pondichery

French India was an administrative unit comprising the five settlements of Chandernagor, Karikal, Mahe, Pondichery and Yanaon. These united with India in 1949 and 1954.

100 Centimes = 1 Franc
24 Caches = 1 Fanon (1923)
8 Fanons = 1 Rupie

Navigation and Commerce — A1

A2

Perf. 14x13½.

1892-1907 Typo. Unwmk.
Colony Name in Blue or Carmine

No.	Type	Description	Unused	Used
1	A1	1c *lil bl*	90	70
2	A1	2c brn, *buff*	1.00	90
3	A1	4c cl, *lav*	1.10	1.00
4	A1	5c grn, *grnsh*	3.00	1.90
5	A1	10c *lavender*	4.00	1.90
6	A1	10c red ('00)	2.00	1.50
7	A1	15c bl, quadrille paper	4.00	3.00
8	A1	15c gray, *lt gray* ('00)	15.00	13.00
9	A1	20c red, *grn*	4.50	3.25
10	A1	25c *rose*	2.00	1.50
11	A1	25c bl ('00)	6.50	4.75
12	A1	30c brn, *bis*	30.00	27.50
13	A1	35c *yel* ('06)	6.50	4.50
14	A1	40c red, *straw*	3.75	3.00
15	A1	45c *gray grn* ('07)	3.25	2.25
16	A1	50c car, *rose*	3.75	3.00
17	A1	50c brn, *az* ('00)	5.50	4.00
18	A1	75c dp vio, *org*	4.25	4.25
19	A1	1fr brnz grn, *straw*	5.50	5.50
		Nos. 1-19 (19)	106.50	87.40

Nos. 10 and 16 Surcharged in Carmine or Black **0,05**

1903

No.	Type	Description	Unused	Used
20	A1	5c on 25c *rose*	190.00	125.00
21	A1	10c on 25c *rose*	190.00	125.00
22	A1	15c on 25c *rose*	62.50	62.50
23	A1	40c on 50c car, *rose* (B)	325.00	275.00

Counterfeits of Nos. 20-23 abound.

1903

No.	Type	Description	Unused	Used
24	A2	5c gray bl & blk	12.00	12.00

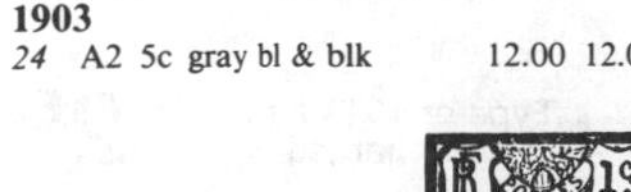

Brahma — A5

Kali Temple near Pondichery A6

1914-22 *Perf. 13½x14, 14x13½*

No.	Type	Description	Unused	Used
25	A5	1c gray & blk	6	6
26	A5	2c brn vio & blk	6	6
27	A5	2c grn & brn vio ('22)	18	18
28	A5	3c brn & blk	15	15
29	A5	4c org & blk	18	18
30	A5	5c bl grn & blk	35	35
31	A5	5c vio brn & blk ('22)	18	18
32	A5	10c dp rose & blk	42	42
33	A5	10c grn & blk ('22)	30	30
34	A5	15c vio & blk	48	48
35	A5	20c org red & blk	70	70
36	A5	25c bl & blk	70	70
37	A5	25c ultra & fawn ('22)	42	42
38	A5	30c ultra & blk	75	75
39	A5	30c rose & blk ('22)	52	52
40	A6	35c choc & blk	75	75
41	A6	40c org red & blk	75	75
42	A6	45c bl grn & blk	75	75
43	A6	50c dp rose & blk	65	65
44	A6	50c ultra & bl ('22)	65	65
45	A6	75c bl & blk	1.00	1.00
46	A6	1fr yel & blk	1.00	1.00
47	A6	2fr vio & blk	2.25	2.25
48	A6	5fr ultra & blk	95	95
49	A6	5fr rose & blk ('22)	1.40	1.40
		Nos. 25-49 (25)	15.60	15.60

No. 34 Surcharged in Various Colors. **0,01 ≡**

1922

No.	Type	Description	Unused	Used
50	A5	1c on 15c (Bk)	42	42
51	A5	2c on 15c (Bl)	42	42
53	A5	5c on 15c (R)	42	42

Stamps and Types of 1914-22 Surcharged with New Values in Caches, Fanons and Rupies in Black, Red or Blue:

1 FANON

2 CACHES

12 CACHES

3 ROUPIES

1923-28

No.	Type	Description	Unused	Used
54	A5	1ca on 1c gray & blk (R)	6	6
55	A5	2ca on 5c vio brn & blk	18	18
a.		Horizontal pair, imperf. between		
56	A5	3ca on 3c brn & blk	30	30
57	A5	4ca on 4c org & blk	48	40
58	A5	6ca on 10c grn & blk	55	55
59	A6	6ca on 45c bl grn & blk (R)	42	42
60	A5	10ca on 20c dp red & bl grn ('28)	1.00	1.00
61	A5	12ca on 15c vio & blk	60	60
62	A5	15ca on 20c org & blk	85	85
63	A6	16ca on 35c lt bl & yel brn ('28)	1.00	1.00
64	A5	18ca on 30c rose & blk	85	85
65	A6	20ca on 45c grn & dl red ('28)	95	75
66	A5	1fa on 25c dp grn & rose red ('28)	1.40	1.40
67	A6	1fa3ca on 35c choc & blk (Bl)	85	85
68	A6	1fa6ca on 40c org & blk (R)	95	70
69	A6	1fa12ca on 50c ultra & bl (Bl)	85	85
70	A6	1fa12ca on 75c bl & blk (Bl)	85	85
a.		Double surch.	95.00	
71	A6	1fa16ca on 75c brn red & grn ('28)	1.50	1.25
72	A5	2fa9ca on 25c ultra & fawn (Bl)	95	75
73	A6	2fa12ca on 1fr vio & dk brn ('28)	1.25	1.25
74	A6	3fa3ca on 1fr yel & blk (R)	1.10	1.00
a.		Double surch.	95.00	
75	A6	6fa6ca on 2fr vio & blk (Bl)	2.75	2.00
76	A6	1r on 1fr grn & dp bl (R) ('26)	3.00	2.75
77	A6	2r on 5fr rose & blk (R)	3.00	2.75
a.		Double surch.	95.00	
78	A6	3r on 2fr gray & bl vio (R) ('26)	7.50	6.00
79	A6	5r on 5fr rose & blk, *grnsh* ('26)	9.50	8.25
		Nos. 54-79 (26)	42.69	37.61

Nos. 60, 63, 66 and 73 have the original value obliterated by bars.

A7

A8

1929

No.	Type	Description	Unused	Used
80	A7	1ca dk gray & blk	6	6
81	A7	2ca vio brn & blk	6	6
82	A7	3ca brn & blk	6	6
83	A7	4ca org & blk	6	6
84	A7	6ca gray grn & grn	22	22
85	A7	10ca brn, red & grn	22	22
86	A8	12ca grn & lt grn	42	35
87	A7	16ca brt bl & blk	60	52
88	A7	18ca brn red & ver	60	52
89	A7	20ca dk bl & grn, *bluish*	48	42
90	A8	1fa gray grn & rose red	42	35
91	A8	1fa6ca red org & blk	42	35
92	A8	1fa12ca dp bl & ultra	42	35
93	A8	1fa16ca rose red & grn	65	60
94	A8	2fa12ca brt vio & brn	75	60
95	A8	6fa6ca dl vio & blk	75	60
96	A8	1r gray grn & dp bl	52	42
97	A8	2r rose & blk	1.00	52
98	A8	3r lt gray & gray lil	1.50	1.10
99	A8	5r rose & blk, *grnsh*	2.25	1.90
		Nos. 80-99 (20)	11.46	9.28

Colonial Exposition Issue.
Common Design Types

1931 Engr. *Perf. 12½.*

No.	Type	Description	Unused	Used
100	CD70	10ca dp grn	1.50	1.50
101	CD71	12ca violet	1.50	1.50
102	CD72	18ca red org	1.50	1.50
103	CD73	1fa12ca dl bl	1.50	1.50

Paris International Exposition Issue.
Common Design Types

1937 *Perf. 13.*

No.	Type	Description	Unused	Used
104	CD74	8ca dp vio	80	80
105	CD75	12ca dk grn	80	80
106	CD76	16ca car rose	80	80
107	CD77	20ca dk brn	80	80
108	CD78	1fa12ca red	80	80
109	CD79	2fa12ca ultra	80	80
		Nos. 104-109 (6)	4.80	4.80

Colonial Arts Exhibition Issue.
Souvenir Sheet.
Common Design Type

1937 *Imperf.*

No.	Type	Description	Unused	Used
110	CD79	5fa red vio	3.50	3.50

Sheet size: 118x99mm.

New York World's Fair Issue.
Common Design Type

1939 Engr. *Perf. 12½x12*

No.	Type	Description	Unused	Used
111	CD82	1fa12ca car lake	95	95
112	CD82	2fa12ca ultra	1.10	1.10

Temple near Pondichery and Marshal Petain — A9

1941 Engr. *Perf. 12½x12*

No.	Type	Description	Unused	Used
112A	A9	1fa16ca car & red	42	
112B	A9	4fa4ca blue	42	

Nos. 112A-112B were issued by the Vichy government, and were not placed on sale in French India.

Stamps of 1923 Overprinted in Carmine or Blue:

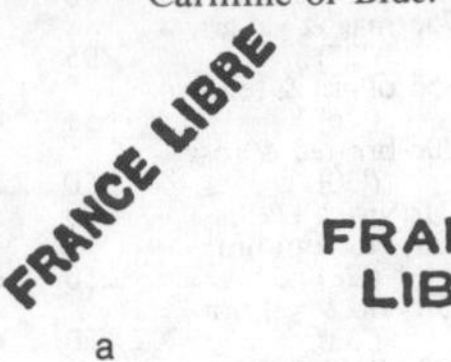

Perf. 13½x14, 14x13½

1941 Unwmk.

No.	Type	Description	Unused	Used
113	A5 (a)	15ca on 20c org & blk	37.50	37.50
114	A5 (a)	18ca on 30c rose & blk	1.10	1.10
115	A6 (a)	1fa3ca on 35c choc & blk	45.00	45.00
a.		Horiz. ovpt.	50.00	50.00
116	A5 (b)	2fa9ca on 25c ultra & fawn (Bl)	875.00	775.00
a.		Ovpt. "a" (Bl)	875.00	775.00
b.		Ovpt. "b" (C)	*1,400.*	

Common Design Types pictured in section at front of book.

Stamps of 1929 Overprinted Type "a" in Carmine or Blue

No.	Type	Description	Unused	Used
117	A7	2ca vio brn & blk	4.50	4.50
118	A7	3ca brn & blk	1.10	1.10
119	A7	4ca org & blk	2.75	2.50
120	A7	6ca gray grn & grn	75	75
121	A7	10ca brn red & grn (Bl)	95	80
122	A8	12ca grn & lt grn	95	80
123	A7	16ca brt bl & blk	1.25	95
123A	A7	18ca brn red & ver (Bl)	575.00	525.00
124	A7	20ca dk bl & grn, *bluish*	95	80
125	A8	1fa gray grn & rose red (Bl)	80	80
126	A8	1fa6ca red org & blk	1.00	95
127	A8	1fa12ca dp bl & ultra	2.25	1.90
128	A8	1fa16ca rose red & grn	95	80
129	A8	2fa12ca brt vio & brn	95	80
130	A8	6fa6ca dl vio & blk	95	95
131	A8	1r gray grn & dp bl	95	95
132	A8	2r rose & blk	95	95
133	A8	3r lt gray & gray lil	1.10	1.10
134	A8	5r rose & blk, *grnsh*	4.50	5.25
		Nos. 113-115,117-123,124-134 (21)	111.20	110.25

Same Overprints on Paris Exposition Issue of 1937.

Perf. 13.

No.	Type	Description	Unused	Used
135	CD74 (b)	8ca dp vio (C)	3.50	3.50
135A	CD74 (b)	8ca dp vio (Bl)	140.00	140.00
135B	CD74 (a)	8ca dp vio (C)	85.00	85.00
135C	CD74 (a)	8ca dp vio (Bl)	125.00	125.00
136	CD75 (a)	12ca dk grn (C)	2.00	2.00
137	CD76 (a)	16ca car rose (Bl)	2.00	2.00

138 CD78 (a) 1fa12ca red (Bl) 2.00 2.00
139 CD79 (a) 2fa12ca ultra (C) 2.00 2.00
Nos. 135-139 (8) 361.50 361.50

Inverted overprints exist.

Souvenir Sheet
No. 110 Overprinted "FRANCE LIBRE" Diagonally in Blue Violet

Two types of overprint:
I. Overprint 37mm. With serifs.
II. Overprint 24mm., as type "a" shown above No. 113. No serifs.

1941 **Unwmk.** ***Imperf.***
140 CD79 5fa red vio (I) 425.00 400.00
a. Type II 600.00 600.00

Overprinted on New York World's Fair Issue, 1939.
Perf. 12½x12.
141 CD82 (a) 1fa12ca car lake (Bl) 2.00 2.00
142 CD82 (a) 2fa12ca ultra (C) 2.00 2.00

Lotus Flowers — A10

1942 **Unwmk.** **Photo.** ***Perf. 14x14½***

143	A10	2ca brown	18	18
144	A10	3ca dk bl	18	18
145	A10	4ca emerald	18	18
146	A10	6ca dk org	18	18
147	A10	12ca grnsh blk	18	18
148	A10	16ca rose vio	18	18
149	A10	20ca dk red brn	52	52
150	A10	1fa brt red	52	42
151	A10	1fa18ca sl blk	80	52
152	A10	6fa6ca brt ultra	90	75
153	A10	1r dl vio	80	75
154	A10	2r bister	90	90
155	A10	3r chocolate	1.25	1.00
156	A10	5r dk grn	1.75	1.25
		Nos. 143-156 (14)	8.52	7.19

Stamps of 1923-39 Overprinted in Blue or Carmine

c

FRANCE LIBRE

d

1942-43 ***Perf. 13½x14, 14x13½.***

Overprinted on No. 64
156A A5 (c) 18ca on 30c rose & blk (B) 160.00 125.00

Overprinted on Stamps of 1929

157	A7 (c)	2ca vio brn & blk (C)	65	65
a.		Black overprint	19.00	19.00
158	A7 (c)	3ca brn & blk (C)	75	75
159	A7 (c)	6ca gray grn & grn (Bl)	85	85
160	A8 (d)	12ca grn & lt grn (Bl)	1.65	1.65
161	A7 (c)	16ca brt bl & blk (C)	85	85
162	A7 (c)	18ca brn red & ver (Bl)	85	85
163	A7 (c)	20ca dk bl & grn, *bluish* (Bl) ('43)	3.00	2.50
164	A7 (c)	20ca dk bl & grn, *bluish* (C)	85	85
165	A8 (d)	1fa gray grn & rose red (Bl)	85	85
166	A8 (d)	1fa6ca red org & blk (C)	1.10	1.10
167	A8 (d)	1fa12ca dp bl & ultra (C)	1.00	1.00
168	A8 (d)	1fa16ca rose red & grn (Bl)	85	85
169	A8 (d)	2fa12ca brt vio & brn (Bl)	27.50	27.50
170	A8 (d)	2fa12ca brt vio & brn (C)	1.00	1.00
171	A8 (d)	6fa6ca dl vio & blk (C)	1.65	1.65
172	A8 (d)	1r gray grn & dp bl (C)	4.00	4.00
173	A8 (d)	2r rose & blk (C)	3.25	3.25
174	A8 (d)	3r lt gray & gray lil (C)	4.00	4.00
175	A8 (d)	3r lt gray & gray lil (Bl) ('43)	80.00	75.00
176	A8 (d)	5r rose & blk, *grnsh* (C)	4.25	4.25
		Nos. 156A-176 (21)	298.90	258.40

Same Overprints on Paris International Exposition Issue of 1937.
Perf. 13.

177	CD74 (c)	8ca dp vio (Bl)	4.75	4.25
178	CD75 (d)	12ca dk grn (Bl)	4.25	4.25
179	CD76 (d)	16ca car rose (Bl)	850.00	750.00
180	CD78 (d)	1fa12ca red (Bl)	90	90
181	CD79 (d)	2fa12ca ultra (C)	2.25	2.25

Same Overprint on New York World's Fair Issue, 1939.
Perf. 12½x12.
182 CD82 (d) 1fa12ca car lake (Bl) 1.50 1.50
183 CD82 (d) 2fa12ca ultra (C) 2.50 2.50

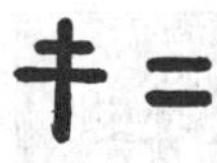

No. 87 Surcharged in Carmine

FRANCE LIBRE

2 fa 9 ca

1942-43 ***Perf. 13½x14***

184	A7	1ca on 16ca	37.50	22.50
185	A7	4ca on 16ca ('43)	37.50	22.50
186	A7	10ca on 16ca	24.00	9.50
187	A7	15ca on 16ca	21.00	9.50
188	A7	1fa3ca on 16ca ('43)	37.50	19.00
189	A7	2fa9ca on 16ca ('43)	32.50	30.00
190	A7	3fa3ca on 16ca ('43)	26.00	30.00
		Nos. 184-190 (7)	216.00	126.00

The only foreign revenue stamps listed in this Catalogue are those authorized for prepayment of postage.

Nos. 95-99 Surcharged in Carmine

1943 ***Perf. 14x13½.***

191	A8	1ca on 6fa6ca	5.25	4.50
192	A8	4ca on 6fa6ca	6.25	5.50
193	A8	10ca on 6fa6ca	1.25	1.10
194	A8	15ca on 6fa6ca	2.50	1.25
195	A8	1fa3ca on 6fa6ca	3.75	1.75
196	A8	2fa9ca on 6fa6ca	3.00	2.50
197	A8	3fa3ca on 6fa6ca	4.50	2.75
198	A8	1ca on 1r	2.50	2.25
199	A8	2ca on 1r	95	95
200	A8	4ca on 1r	95	90
201	A8	6ca on 2r	90	75
202	A8	10ca on 2r	1.10	1.10
203	A8	12ca on 2r	90	75
204	A8	15ca on 3r	80	80
205	A8	16ca on 3r	80	80
206	A8	1fa3ca on 3r	90	90
207	A8	1fa6ca on 5r	1.10	1.10
208	A8	1fa12ca on 5r	1.10	1.00
209	A8	1fa16ca on 5r	1.10	1.00
		Nos. 191-209 (19)	39.60	31.65

In 1943, twenty-seven stamps were overprinted in red or dark blue, "FRANCE TOUJOURS" and a Lorraine Cross within a circle measuring 17½mm. in diameter. The stamps overprinted were 19 denominations of the regular 1929 postage series, plus Nos. 104 to 109 and Nos. 111 and 112. Of each stamp, 200 were overprinted.

No. 95 Surcharged in Carmine with New Value and Bars.

1943 **Unwmk.** ***Perf. 14x13½.***

209A	A8	1ca on 6fa6ca	16.00	10.00
209B	A8	4ca on 6fa6ca	16.00	10.00
209C	A8	10ca on 6fa6ca	5.00	3.50
209D	A8	15ca on 6fa6ca	5.00	3.50
209E	A8	1fa3ca on 6fa6ca	13.00	11.50
209F	A8	2fa9ca on 6fa6ca	13.00	11.50
209G	A8	3fa3ca on 6fa6ca	15.00	12.50
		Nos. 209A-209G (7)	83.00	62.50

Eboue Issue.
Common Design Type

1945 **Engr.** ***Perf. 13.***
210 CD91 3fa8ca black 42 42
211 CD91 5r 1fa 16ca Prus grn 90 90

Nos. 210 and 211 exist imperforate.

Apsaras
A11

Brahman Ascetic
A12

Designs: 6ca, 8ca, 10ca, Dvarabalagar. 12ca, 15ca, 1fa, Vishnu. 1fa 6ca, 2fa, 2fa 2ca, Dvarabalagar (foot raised). 2fa 12ca, 3fa, 5fa, Temple Guardian. 7fa 12ca, 1r 2fa, 1r 4fa 12ca, Tigoupalagar.

1948 **Photo.** ***Perf. 13x13½***

212	A11	1ca dk ol grn	5	5
213	A11	2ca org brn	6	6
214	A11	4ca vio, *cr*	6	6
215	A11	6ca yel org	60	30
216	A11	8ca gray blk	70	60
217	A11	10ca dl yel grn, *pale grn*	70	60
218	A11	12ca vio brn	30	22
219	A11	15ca Prus grn	30	22
220	A11	1fa vio, *pale rose*	85	42
221	A11	1fa6ca brn red	60	60
222	A11	2fa dk grn	60	42
223	A11	2fa 2ca bl, *cr*	1.00	70
224	A11	2fa12ca brown	1.00	80
225	A11	3fa dp org	1.25	85
226	A11	5fa red vio, *rose*	1.10	85
227	A11	7fa12ca dk brn	90	85
228	A11	1r2fa brn blk	2.50	2.00
229	A11	1r 4fa 12ca ol grn	2.75	2.50
		Nos. 212-229 (18)	15.32	12.10

1952

230	A12	18ca rose red	90	90
231	A12	1fa15ca vio bl	1.25	1.25
232	A12	4fa ol grn	1.75	1.75

Military Medal Issue.
Common Design Type

1952 **Engr. and Typo.** ***Perf. 13***
233 CD101 1fa multi 2.50 2.50

SEMI-POSTAL STAMPS

Regular Issue of 1914 Surcharged in Red ✚ 5c

1915 **Unwmk.** ***Perf. 14x13½***
B1 A5 10c + 5c rose & blk 70 70
a. Inverted surch. 52.50 52.50

There were two printings of this surcharge; in the first it was placed at the bottom of the stamp, in the second it was near the top.

Regular Issue of 1914 Surcharged in Red 5 ✠

1916
B2 A5 10c + 5c rose & blk 9.50 9.50
a. Inverted surch. 52.50 52.50
b. Double surch. 47.50 47.50

Surcharged ✚ 5 C

B3 A5 10c + 5c rose & blk 1.75 1.75

Surcharged 5 c

B4 A5 10c + 5c rose & blk 90 90

Surcharged ✚ 5c

B5 A5 10c + 5c rose & blk 90 90

Curie Issue
Common Design Type

1938 **Engr.** ***Perf. 13.***
B6 CD80 2fa12ca + 20ca brt ultra 7.00 7.00

French Revolution Issue
Common Design Type

1939 **Photo.**
Name and Value Typo. in Black

B7	CD83	18ca + 10ca grn	3.25	3.25
B8	CD83	1fa6ca + 12ca brn	3.25	3.25
B9	CD83	1fa12ca + 16ca red org	3.25	3.25
B10	CD83	1fa16ca + 1fa16ca rose pink	3.25	3.25
B11	CD83	2fa12ca + 3fa bl	3.25	3.25
		Nos. B7-B11 (5)	16.25	16.25

Common Design Type and

Non-Commissioned Officer, Native Guard — SP1

Sepoy SP2

1941	**Photo.**	***Perf. 13½***
B12 SP1	1fa16ca + 1fa16ca red	75
B13 CD86	2fa12ca + 5fa mar	75
B13A SP2	4fa4ca + 1fa16ca bl	75

Nos. B12-B13A were issued by the Vichy government, and were not placed on sale in French India.

Nos. 112A-112B were surcharged "OEUVRES COLONIALES" and surtax (including change of denomination of the 4fa 4ca to 20ca). These were issued in 1944 by the Vichy government and were not placed on sale in French India.

Red Cross Issue
Common Design Type

1944	**Photo.**	***Perf. 14½x14.***
B14 CD90	3fa + 1r4fa dk ol brn	80 80

The surtax was for the French Red Cross and national relief.

Tropical Medicine Issue
Common Design Type

1950	**Engr.**	***Perf. 13.***
B15 CD100	1fa + 10ca ind & dp bl	1.25 1.25

The surtax was for charitable work.

AIR POST STAMPS

Common Design Type
Perf. 14½x14.

1942	**Unwmk.**		**Photo.**
C1 CD87	4fa dk org	48	48
C2 CD87	1r brt red	48	48
C3 CD87	2r brn red	85	85
C4 CD87	5r black	1.00	1.00
C5 CD87	8r ultra	1.25	1.25
C6 CD87	10r dk grn	1.40	1.40
	Nos. C1-C6 (6)	5.46	5.46

Victory Issue
Common Design Type

1946	**Engr.**	***Perf. 12½***
C7 CD92	4fa dk bl grn	70 70

Issued to commemorate the European Victory of the Allied Nations in World War II.

Chad to Rhine Issue
Common Design Types

1946, June 6			
C8 CD93	2fa12ca ol bis	65	65
C9 CD94	5fa dk bl	65	65
C10 CD95	7fa12ca dk pur	85	85
C11 CD96	1r2fa green	85	85
C12 CD97	1r4fa12ca dk car	95	95
C13 CD98	3r1fa vio brn	95	95
	Nos. C8-C13 (6)	4.90	4.90

A 3r ultramarine and red, picturing the Temple of Chindambaram, was sold at Paris June 7 to July 8, 1948, but not placed on sale in the colony.

Bas-relief Figure of Goddess — AP1

Wing and Temple — AP2
Bird over Palms — AP3

Perf. 12x13, 13x12.

1949	**Photo.**	**Unwmk.**	
C14 AP1	1r yel & plum	2.50	1.50
C15 AP2	2r grn & dk grn	3.25	3.00
C16 AP3	5r lt bl & vio brn	11.00	7.50

UPU Issue
Common Design Type

1949	**Engr.**	***Perf. 13***
C17 CD99	6fa lil rose	3.75 3.75

Issued to commemorate the 75th anniversary of the formation of the Universal Postal Union.

Liberation Issue
Common Design Type

1954, June 6		
C18 CD102	1fa sep & vio brn	3.00 3.00

AIR POST SEMI-POSTAL STAMPS

V4

Stamps of the above design and of Cameroun type V10 inscribed "Etabts Frcais dans l'Inde" were issued in 1942 by the Vichy Government, but were not placed on sale in French India.

POSTAGE DUE STAMPS

Postage Due Stamps of France, 1893-1941. Surcharged like Regular Issue in Black, Blue or Red.

6 CACHES

1923	**Unwmk.**	***Perf. 14x13½.***	
J1 D2	6ca on 10c brn (Bl)	70	70
J2 D2	12ca on 25c rose (Bk)	70	70
J3 D2	15ca on 20c ol grn (R)	85	85
J4 D2	1fa6ca on 30c red (Bl)	85	85
J5 D2	1fa12a on 50c brn vio (Bl)	1.10	1.10
J6 D2	1fa15ca on 5c bl (Bk)	1.25	1.25
J7 D2	3fa3ca on 1fr red brn, *straw* (Bl)	1.50	1.50
	Nos. J1-J7 (7)	6.95	6.95

Types of Postage Due Stamps of French Colonies, 1884-85, Surcharged with New Values as in 1923 in Red or Black. Bars over Original Values.

1928			
J8 D1	4ca on 20c gray lil	70	70
J9 D1	1fa on 30c org	1.00	1.00
J10 D1	1fa16ca on 5c bl blk (R)	1.10	1.10
J11 D1	3fa on 1 fr lt grn	1.40	1.40

D3 D4

1929		**Typo.**	
J12 D3	4ca dp red	42	42
J13 D3	6ca blue	52	52
J14 D3	12ca green	52	52
J15 D3	1fa brown	85	85
J16 D3	1fa12ca lil gray	85	85
J17 D3	1fa16ca buff	95	95
J18 D3	3fa lilac	1.10	1.10
	Nos. J12-J18 (7)	5.21	5.21

Perf. 13x13½.

1948	**Unwmk.**	**Photo.**	
J19 D4	1ca dk vio	5	5
J20 D4	2ca dk brn	5	5
J21 D4	6ca bl grn	15	15
J22 D4	12ca dp org	35	35
J23 D4	1fa dk car rose	42	42
J24 D4	1fa12ca brown	60	60
J25 D4	2fa dk sl bl	80	80
J26 D4	2fa12ca hn brn	95	95
J27 D4	5fa dk ol grn	1.25	1.25
J28 D4	1r dk bl vio	1.65	1.65
	Nos. J19-J28 (10)	6.27	6.27

FRENCH MOROCCO

LOCATION — Northwest coast of Africa
GOVT. — Former French Protectorate
AREA — 153,870 sq. mi.
POP. — 8,340,000 (estimated 1954)
CAPITAL — Rabat

French Morocco was a French Protectorate from 1912 until 1956 when it, along with the Spanish and Tangier zones of Morocco, became the independent country, Morocco.

Stamps inscribed "Tanger" were for use in the international zone of Tangier in northern Morocco.

100 Centimos = 1 Peseta
100 Centimes = 1 franc (1917)

French Offices in Morocco

A1

A2

Stamps of France Surcharged in Red or Black.

1891-1900	**Unwmk.**	***Perf. 14 x 13½.***	
1 A1	5c on 5c grn, *grnsh* (R)	4.00	1.50
a.	Imperf., pair	87.50	
2 A1	5c on 5c yel grn (I) (R) ('99)	15.00	12.00
a.	Type II	15.00	15.00
3 A1	10c on 10c *lav* (II) (R)	12.00	1.65
a.	Type I	22.50	5.50
b.	10c on 25c *rose*	450.00	
4 A1	20c on 20c red, *grn*	17.50	12.00
5 A1	25c on 25c *rose* (R)	12.00	80
a.	Double surcharge	140.00	
b.	Imperf., pair	95.00	
6 A1	50c on 50c car, *rose* (II)	45.00	14.00
a.	Type I	300.00	240.00
7 A1	1p on 1fr brnz grn, *straw*	45.00	40.00
8 A1	2p on 2fr brn, *az* (Bk) ('00)	175.00	145.00
	Nos. 1-8 (8)	325.50	226.95

No. 3b was never sent to Morocco.

France Nos. J15-J16 Overprinted in Carmine.

1893			
9 A2	5c black	1,900.	650.00
10 A2	10c black	1,600.	400.00

Counterfeits exist.

A3

A4

A5

Surcharged in Red or Black.

1902-10			
11 A3	1c on 1c gray (R)('08)	50	25
a.	Surcharge omitted		
12 A3	2c on 2c vio brn ('08)	60	50
13 A3	3c on 3c red org ('08)	70	50
14 A3	4c on 4c yel brn ('08)	5.00	3.00
15 A3	5c on 5c grn (R)	2.75	60
a.	Double surch.	140.00	
16 A4	10c on 10c rose red ('03)	2.00	60
a.	Surcharge omitted		
17 A4	20c on 20c brn vio ('03)	12.00	7.00
18 A4	25c on 25c bl ('03)	12.00	1.00
19 A4	35c on 35c vio ('10)	17.50	10.00
20 A5	50c on 50c bis brn & lav ('03)	22.50	5.50
21 A5	1p on 1fr cl & ol grn ('03)	60.00	40.00
22 A5	2p on 2fr gray vio & yel ('03)	75.00	40.00
	Nos. 11-22 (12)	210.55	108.95

Nos. 11-14 exist spelled CFNTIMOS or GENTIMOS.

The 25c on 25c with surcharge omitted is listed as No. 81a.

Postage Due Stamps Nos. J1-J2 Handstamped

1903			
24 D2	5c on 5c lt bl	1,200.	875.00
25 D2	10c on 10c choc	2,400.	1,750.

Nos. 24 and 25 were used only on Oct. 10, 1903. Used copies were not canceled, the overprint serving as a cancellation.

Counterfeits exist.

Types of 1902-10 Issue Surcharged in Red or Blue

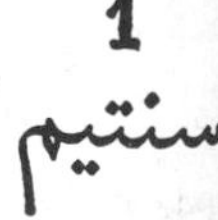

1911-17			
26 A3	1c on 1c gray (R)	30	15
27 A3	2c on 2c vio brn	48	30
28 A3	3c on 3c org	52	30
29 A3	5c on 5c grn (R)	55	15
30 A4	10c on 10c rose	18	6
a.	Imperf. pair	180.00	
31 A4	15c on 15c org ('17)	1.00	80
32 A4	20c on 20c brn vio	2.25	1.50
33 A4	25c on 25c bl (R)	1.25	60
34 A4	35c on 35c vio (R)	3.75	1.50
35 A5	40c on 40c red & pale bl ('17)	3.75	3.00
36 A5	50c on 50c bis brn & lav (R)	15.00	7.50
37 A5	1p on 1fr cl & ol grn	10.00	3.00
	Nos. 26-37 (12)	39.03	18.86

Catalogue prices for unused stamps up to mid-1953 are for hinged copies matching the condition specified in this volume's introduction.

Stamps of this design were issued by the Cherifien posts in 1912-13. The Administration Cherifienne des Postes, Telegraphes et Telephones was formed in 1911 under French guidance.

French Protectorate

A6

A7

A8

Issue of 1911-17
Overprinted "Protectorat Francais"

1914-21

No.	Type	Description	Unused	Used
38	A6	1c on 1c gray	30	30
39	A6	2c on 2c vio brn	30	22
40	A6	3c on 3c org	60	42
41	A6	5c on 5c grn	15	5
a.		New value omitted	190.00	190.00
42	A7	10c on 10c rose	15	5
a.		New value omitted	350.00	350.00
43	A7	15c on 15c org ('17)	18	5
a.		New value omitted	70.00	70.00
44	A7	20c on 20c brn vio	2.25	1.10
a.		"Protectorat Francais" double	225.00	225.00
45	A7	25c on 25c bl	75	5
a.		New value omitted	225.00	225.00
46	A7	25c on 25c vio ('21)	60	6
a.		"Protectorat Francais" omitted	42.50	42.50
b.		"Protectorat Francais" double	110.00	110.00
c.		"Protectorat Francais" double (R + Bk)	100.00	100.00
47	A7	30c on 30c vio ('21)	6.75	5.75
48	A7	35c on 35c vio	2.25	75
49	A8	40c on 40c red & pale bl	7.75	4.25
a.		New value omitted	225.00	225.00
50	A8	45c on 45c grn & bl ('21)	22.50	19.00
51	A8	50c on 50c bis brn & lav	52	18
a.		"Protectorat Francais" inverted	110.00	110.00
b.		"Protectorat Francais" double		
52	A8	1p on 1fr cl & ol grn	1.00	18
a.		"Protectorat Francais" inverted	250.00	250.00
b.		New value double	110.00	110.00
c.		New value double, one inverted	110.00	110.00
53	A8	2p on 2fr gray vio & yel	2.00	75
a.		New value omitted	125.00	125.00
b.		"Protectorat Francais" omitted	75.00	75.00
c.		New value double		
d.		New value double, one inverted		
54	A8	5p on 5fr dk bl & buff	7.50	2.50
		Nos. 38-54 (17)	55.55	35.66

Tower of Hassan, Rabat — A9

Mosque of the Andalusians, Fez — A10

City Gate, Chella
A11

Koutoubiah, Marrakesh
A12

Bab Mansour, Meknes
A13

Roman Ruins, Volubilis
A14

1917 Engr. *Perf. 13½x14, 14x13½*

No.	Type	Description	Unused	Used
55	A9	1c grnsh gray	18	18
56	A9	2c brn lil	35	30
57	A9	3c org brn	30	22
a.		Imperf., pair	42.50	42.50
58	A10	5c yel grn	22	6
59	A10	10c rose red	22	6
60	A10	15c dk gray	22	10
a.		Imperf., pair	35.00	35.00
61	A11	20c red brn	1.75	1.75
62	A11	25c dl bl	1.50	48
63	A11	30c gray vio	2.00	1.65
64	A12	35c orange	1.75	1.50
65	A12	40c ultra	95	48
66	A12	45c gray grn	10.00	6.50
67	A13	50c dk brn	3.25	2.00
a.		Imperf., pair	37.50	37.50
68	A13	1fr slate	4.00	2.50
a.		Imperf., pair	32.50	32.50
69	A14	2fr blk brn	110.00	55.00
70	A14	5fr dk gray grn	22.50	18.00
71	A14	10fr black	22.50	20.00
		Nos. 55-71 (17)	181.69	110.78

See note following No. 115.
See Nos. 93-105.

Types of the 1902-10 Issue Overprinted **TANGER**

1918-24 ***Perf. 14x13½.***

No.	Type	Description	Unused	Used
72	A3	1c gray	15	15
73	A3	2c vio brn	18	18
74	A3	3c red org	30	30
75	A3	5c green	42	35
76	A3	5c org ('23)	85	80
77	A4	10c rose	42	42
78	A4	10c grn ('24)	42	35
79	A4	15c orange	95	70
80	A4	20c vio brn	1.25	1.25
81	A4	25c blue	1.40	1.00
a.		"TANGER" omitted	300.00	225.00
82	A4	30c red org ('24)	1.40	1.40
83	A4	35c violet	1.40	1.25
84	A5	40c red & pale bl	1.50	1.25
85	A5	50c bis brn & lav	9.00	5.00
86	A4	50c blue	7.00	3.75
87	A5	1fr cl & ol grn	4.50	2.50
88	A5	2fr org & pale bl ('24)	45.00	37.50
89	A5	5fr dk bl & buff ('24)	37.50	35.00
		Nos. 72-89 (18)	113.64	93.15

Types of 1917 and

Tower of Hassan, Rabat
A15

Bab Mansour, Meknes
A16

Roman Ruins, Volubilis
A17

1923-27 Photo. *Perf. 13½*

No.	Type	Description	Unused	Used
90	A15	1c ol grn	5	5
91	A15	2c brn vio	5	5
92	A15	3c yel brn	5	5
93	A10	5c orange	6	6
94	A10	10c yel grn	6	5
95	A10	15c dk gray	6	5
96	A11	20c red brn	6	5
97	A11	20c red vio ('27)	42	40
98	A11	25c ultra	6	6
99	A11	30c dp red	6	6
100	A11	30c turq bl ('27)	70	40
101	A12	35c violet	70	60
102	A12	40c org red	5	5
103	A12	45c dp grn	6	6
104	A16	50c dl turq	10	10
105	A12	50c dk ol grn ('27)	48	10
106	A16	60c lilac	35	22
107	A16	75c red vio ('27)	65	35
108	A16	1fr dp brn	48	30
109	A16	1.05fr red brn ('27)	1.00	75
110	A16	1.40fr dl rose ('27)	52	40
111	A16	1.50fr turq bl ('27)	75	10
112	A17	2fr ol brn	90	60
113	A17	3fr dp red ('27)	90	70
114	A17	5fr dk gray grn	2.50	1.65
115	A17	10fr black	7.50	4.75
		Nos. 90-115 (26)	18.57	12.01

Nos. 90-110, 112-115 exist imperf.

The stamps of 1917 were line engraved. Those of 1923-27 were printed by photogravure and have in the margin at lower right the imprint "Helio Vaugirard".

No. 102 Surcharged in Black

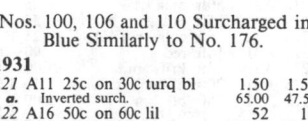

1930

No.	Type	Description	Unused	Used
120	A12	15c on 40c org red	1.00	1.00

Nos. 100, 106 and 110 Surcharged in Blue Similarly to No. 176.

1931

No.	Type	Description	Unused	Used
121	A11	25c on 30c turq bl	1.50	1.50
a.		Inverted surch.	65.00	47.50
122	A16	50c on 60c lil	52	18
a.		Inverted surch.	75.00	70.00
123	A16	1fr on 1.40fr rose	1.90	1.00
a.		Inverted surch.	75.00	70.00

Old Treasure House and Tribunal, Tangier
A18

Roadstead at Agadir
A19

Post Office at Casablanca
A20

Moulay Idriss of the Zehroun
A21

Kasbah of the Oudayas, Rabat — A22

Court of the Medersa el Attarine at Fez — A23

Kasbah of Si Madani el Glaoui at Ouarzazat
A24

Saadiens' Tombs at Marrakesh — A25

1933-34 Engr. *Perf. 13*

No.	Type	Description	Unused	Used
124	A18	1c ol blk	6	5
125	A18	2c red vio	6	6
126	A19	3c dk brn	6	6
127	A19	5c brn red	6	6
128	A20	10c bl grn	15	6
129	A20	15c black	6	6
130	A20	20c red brn	18	10
131	A21	25c dk bl	18	6
132	A21	30c cmcrald	30	5
133	A21	40c blk brn	30	10
134	A22	45c brn vio	35	35
135	A22	50c dk bl grn	30	5
a.		Booklet pane of 10		
136	A22	65c brn red	6	6
a.		Booklet pane of 10		
137	A23	75c red vio	30	6
138	A23	90c org red	30	5
139	A23	1fr dp brn	60	5
140	A23	1.25fr blk ('34)	85	40
141	A24	1.50fr ultra	35	5
142	A24	1.75fr myr grn ('34)	30	5
143	A24	2fr yel brn	1.75	5
144	A24	3fr car rose	37.50	4.00
145	A25	5fr red brn	3.50	75
146	A25	10fr black	5.50	3.75
147	A25	20fr bluish gray	6.75	3.75
		Nos. 124-147 (24)	59.82	14.08

No. 135 Surcharged in Red

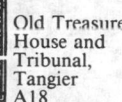

1939

No.	Type	Description	Unused	Used
148	A22	40c on 50c dk bl grn	42	18

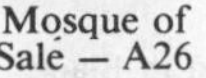
Mosque of Sale — A26

Sefrou — A27

Cedars — A28

Goatherd A29

Ramparts of Sale — A30

Scimitar-horned Oryxes — A31

Valley of Draa — A32

Fez — A33

1939-42

149	A26	1c	rose vio	5	5
150	A27	2c	emerald	5	5
151	A27	3c	ultra	5	5
152	A26	5c	dk bl grn	6	5
153	A27	10c	brt red vio	6	5
154	A28	15c	dk grn	6	5
155	A28	20c	blk grn	6	5
156	A29	30c	dp bl	6	5
157	A29	40c	chocolate	6	5
158	A29	45c	Prus grn	42	30
159	A30	50c	rose red	1.25	60
159A	A30	50c	Prus grn ('40)	18	6
160	A30	60c	turq bl	1.25	60
160A	A30	60c	choc ('40)	18	5
161	A31	70c	dk vio	6	5
162	A32	75c	grnsh blk	30	30
163	A32	80c	pck bl ('40)	10	5
163A	A32	80c	dk grn ('42)	10	5
164	A30	90c	ultra	10	5
165	A28	1fr	chocolate	10	5
165A	A32	1.20fr	rose vio ('42)	30	10
166	A32	1.25fr	hn brn	85	42
167	A32	1.40fr	rose vio	30	10
168	A30	1.50fr	cop red ('40)	6	6
168A	A30	1.50fr	rose ('42)	6	6
169	A33	2fr	Prus grn	6	6
170	A33	2.25fr	dk bl	25	25
170A	A26	2.40fr	red ('42)	10	5
171	A26	2.50fr	scarlet	85	42
171A	A26	2.50fr	dp bl ('40)	75	42
172	A33	3fr	blk brn	22	18
172A	A26	4fr	dp ultra ('42)	18	5
172B	A32	4.50fr	grnsh blk ('42)	42	18
173	A31	5fr	dk bl	42	18
174	A31	10fr	red	70	48
174A	A31	15fr	Prus grn ('42)	3.50	3.00
175	A31	20fr	dk vio brn	1.25	1.25
			Nos. 149-175 (37)	14.82	9.87

See also Nos. 197-219.

No. 136 Surcharged in Black

1940

176	A22	35c on 65c brn red		1.25	80
a.		Pair, one without surcharge		2.25	1.50

The surcharge was applied on alternate rows in the sheet, making pairs, one stamp with a surcharge and one without. This was done to make a pair equal 1 franc, the new rate.

One Aim Alone-Victory A34

Tower of Hassan, Rabat A35

1943 **Litho.** ***Perf. 12.***

177	A34	1.50fr	dp bl	18	5

1943

178	A35	10c	rose lil	5	5
179	A35	30c	blue	5	5
180	A35	40c	lake	5	5
181	A35	50c	bl grn	5	5
182	A35	60c	dk vio brn	5	5
183	A35	70c	rose vio	5	5
184	A35	80c	gray grn	5	5
185	A35	1fr	car lake	5	5
186	A35	1.20fr	violet	5	5
187	A35	1.50fr	red	5	5
188	A35	2fr	lt bl grn	18	5
189	A35	2.40fr	car rose	6	5
190	A35	3fr	ol brn	10	5
191	A35	4fr	dk ultra	10	5
192	A35	4.50fr	sl blk	6	5
193	A35	5fr	dl bl	50	18
194	A35	10fr	org brn	30	6
195	A35	15fr	sl grn	1.00	22
196	A35	20fr	dp plum	1.40	35
			Nos. 178-196 (19)	4.20	1.56

Types of 1939-42.

Perf. 13½ x 14, 14 x 13½.

1945-47 **Typo.** **Unwmk.**

197	A27	10c	red vio	6	6
199	A29	40c	chocolate	8	6
200	A30	50c	Prus grn	6	6
203	A28	1fr	choc ('46)	6	6
204	A32	1.20fr	vio brn ('46)	6	6
205	A27	1.30fr	bl ('47)	35	22
206	A30	1.50fr	dp red	28	25
207	A33	2fr	Prus grn	6	6
209	A33	3fr	blk brn	6	6
210	A29	3.50fr	dk red ('47)	50	42
212	A31	4.50fr	mag ('47)	25	6
214	A31	5fr	indigo	55	30
215	A32	6fr	chlky bl ('46)	25	6
216	A31	10fr	red	90	65
217	A31	5fr	Prus grn	1.00	55
218	A31	20fr	dk vio brn	1.50	1.00
219	A31	25fr	blk brn	2.00	1.50
			Nos. 197-219 (17)	8.02	5.43

The Terraces A37

Fortress A38

Mountain District A39

Marrakesh A40

Gardens of Fez — A41

Ouarzazat District — A42

1947-48 **Unwmk.** **Engr.** ***Perf. 13***

221	A37	10c	blk brn	5	5
222	A37	30c	brt red	10	6
223	A37	50c	brt grnsh bl	6	5
224	A37	60c	brt red vio	6	5
225	A38	1fr	black	6	5
226	A38	1.50fr	blue	6	5
227	A39	2fr	brt grn	22	18
228	A39	3fr	brn red	6	6
229	A40	4fr	dk bl vio	8	6
230	A41	5fr	dk grn	42	22
231	A40	6fr	crimson	8	5
232	A41	10fr	dp bl ('47)	15	6
233	A42	15fr	dk grn ('47)	90	65
234	A42	20fr	hn brn ('47)	60	6
235	A42	25fr	pur ('47)	1.50	65
			Nos. 221-235 (15)	4.40	2.30

1948-49

236	A37	30c	purple	5	5
237	A38	2fr	vio brn ('49)	6	5
238	A40	4fr	green	8	5
239	A41	8fr	org ('49)	35	12
240	A41	10fr	blue	35	18
241	A42	10fr	car rose	35	22
242	A38	12fr	red	50	18
243	A42	18fr	dp bl	95	75
			Nos. 236-243 (8)	2.69	1.60

No. 175 Surcharged with New Value and Wavy Lines in Carmine.

1948

244	A31	8fr on 20fr dk vio brn		60	42

Fortified Oasis — A43

Walled City — A44

1949

245	A43	5fr	bl grn	15	5
246	A44	15fr	red	90	5
247	A44	25fr	ultra	95	10

See also No. 300.

Detail, Gate of Oudayas, Rabat A45

Nejjarine Fountain, Fez A46

Garden, Meknes — A47

1949 ***Perf. 14x13***

248	A45	10c	black	6	5
249	A45	50c	rose brn	10	8
250	A45	1fr	bl vio	6	6
251	A46	2fr	dk car rose	6	6
252	A46	3fr	dk bl	6	6
253	A46	5fr	brt grn	18	5
254	A47	8fr	dk bl grn	60	5
255	A47	10fr	brt red	80	15
			Nos. 248-255 (8)	1.92	56

Postal Administration Building, Meknes — A48

1949, Oct. ***Perf. 13***

256	A48	5fr	dk grn	1.25	1.25
257	A48	15fr	dp car	1.40	1.40
258	A48	25fr	dp bl	1.75	1.75

Issued to commemorate the 75th anniversary of the formation of the Universal Postal Union.

Todra Valley A49

1950

259	A49	35fr	red brn	1.00	18
260	A49	50fr	indigo	1.00	8

See also No. 270.

Nos. 204 and 205 Surcharged in Black or Blue

1950 ***Perf. 14x13½, 13½x14***

261	A32	1fr on 1.20fr vio brn (Bk)		10	10
262	A27	1fr on 1.30fr bl (Bl)		10	10

The surcharge is transposed and spaced to fit the design on No. 262.

No. 231 Surcharged with New Value and Wavy Lines in Black.

1951 ***Perf. 13***

263	A40	5fr on 6fr crim		18	15

Statue of Gen. Jacques Leclerc — A50

1951, Apr. 28 **Engr.**

264	A50	10fr	bl grn	1.25	1.25
265	A50	15fr	dp car	1.50	1.50
266	A50	25fr	indigo	1.50	1.50

Issued to commemorate the unveiling of a monument to Gen. Leclerc at Casablanca. April 28, 1951. See No. C39.

Loustau Hospital, Oujda — A51

Designs: 15fr, New Hospital, Meknes. 25fr, New Hospital, Rabat.

1951

267	A51	10fr	ind & pur	1.00	1.00
268	A51	15fr	Prus grn & red brn	1.00	1.00
269	A51	25fr	dk brn & ind	1.50	1.50

Todra Valley Type of 1950.

1951

270	A49	30fr	ultra	90	42

Pigeons at Fountain A52

Karaouine Mosque, Fez A53

Patio, Oudayas A54

Oudayas Point, Rabat A55

Patio of Old House — A56

Type I (No. 275)

Type II (No. 276)

Perf. 14x13, 13.

1951-53		Engr.	Unwmk.	
271	A52	5fr mag ('52)	6	5
272	A53	6fr bl grn ('52)	22	22
273	A52	8fr brn ('52)	18	18
273A	A53	10fr rose red ('53)	22	5
274	A53	12fr dp ultra ('52)	42	6
275	A54	15fr red brn (I)	2.00	6
276	A54	15fr red brn (II)	48	5
277	A55	15fr pur ('52)	60	5
278	A55	18fr red ('52)	1.00	50
279	A56	20fr dp grnsh bl ('52)	70	48
		Nos. 271-279 (10)	5.88	1.70

See also Nos. 297-299.

8th-10th Century Capital A57

Casablanca Monument A58

Capitals: 20fr, XIIth Century. 25fr, XIIIth-XVIth Century. 50fr, XVIIth Century.

1952, Apr. 5			*Perf. 13*	
280	A57	15fr dp bl	2.25	2.50
281	A57	20fr red	2.25	2.50
282	A57	25fr purple	2.25	2.50
283	A57	50fr dp grn	2.50	2.75

1952, Sept. 22			**Engr. & Typo.**	
284	A58	15fr multi	2.00	1.50

Issued to commemorate the centenary of the creation of the French Military Medal.

Daggers of South Morocco A59

Post Rider and Public Letter-writer A60

Designs: 20fr and 25fr, Antique brooches.

1953, Mar. 27			**Engr.**	
285	A59	15fr dk car rose	2.25	2.25
286	A59	20fr vio brn	2.25	2.25
287	A59	25fr dk bl	2.25	2.25

See No. C46.

1953, May 16				
288	A60	15fr vio brn	1.25	1.25

Stamp Day, May 16, 1953.

Bine el Ouidane Dam — A61

1953, Nov. 3			*Perf. 13*	
290	A61	15fr indigo	1.25	1.25

See also No. 295.

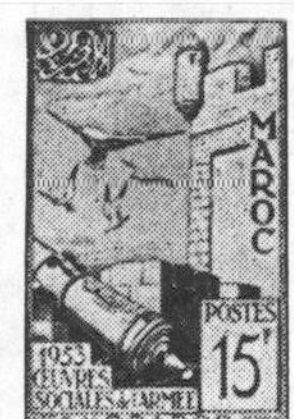
Mogador Fortress — A62

Design: 30fr, Moorish knights.

1953, Dec. 4				
291	A62	15fr green	1.25	1.25
292	A62	30fr red brn	1.25	1.25

Issued to aid Army Welfare Work.

Nos. 226 and 243 Surcharged with New Value and Wavy Lines in Black.

1954				
293	A38	1fr on 1.50fr bl	10	10
294	A42	15fr on 18fr dp bl	52	52

Dam Type of 1953.

1954, Mar. 8				
295	A61	15fr red brn & ind	75	30

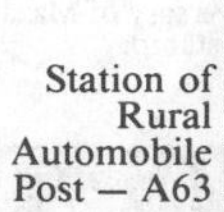

Station of Rural Automobile Post — A63

1954, Apr. 10				
296	A63	15fr dk bl grn	70	70

Stamp Day, April 10, 1954.

Types of 1951-53

1954		**Engr.**	*Perf. 14x13*	
297	A52	15fr dk bl grn	45	5
		Typo.		
298	A52	5fr magenta	30	22
299	A55	15fr rose vio	60	35

Walled City Type of 1949

1954		**Engr.**	*Perf. 13*	
300	A44	25fr purple	60	35

Marshal Lyautey at Rabat — A64

Lyautey, Builder of Cities — A65

Designs: 15fr, Marshal Lyautey at Khenifra. 50fr, Hubert Lyautey, Marshal of France.

1954, Nov. 17				
301	A64	5fr indigo	2.25	2.25
302	A64	15fr dk grn	2.25	2.25
303	A65	30fr rose brn	2.75	2.75
304	A65	50fr dk red brn	2.75	2.75

Issued to commemorate the centenary of the birth of Marshal Hubert Lyautey.

Franco-Moslem Education — A66

Moslem Student at Blackboard — A67

Designs: 30fr, Moslem school at Camp Boulhaut. 50fr, Moulay Idriss College at Fez.

1955, Apr. 16		**Unwmk.**	*Perf. 13*	
305	A66	5fr indigo	1.00	1.00
306	A67	15fr rose lake	1.25	1.25
307	A66	30fr chocolate	1.65	1.65
308	A67	50fr dk bl grn	1.75	1.75

Issued to publicize Franco-Moslem solidarity.

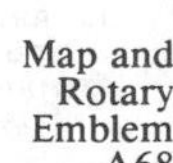

Map and Rotary Emblem A68

1955, June 11				
309	A68	15fr bl & org brn	1.25	1.00

Issued to commemorate the 50th anniversary of the founding of Rotary International.

Post Office, Mazagan A69

1955, May 24				
310	A69	15fr red	65	65

Stamp Day.

Bab el Chorfa, Fez A70

Mahakma (Courthouse), Casablanca A71

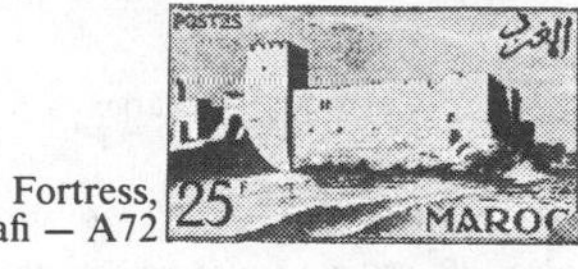
Fortress, Safi — A72

Designs: 50c, 1fr, 2fr, Mrissa Gate, Salé. 10fr, 12fr, 15fr, Minaret at Rabat. 30fr, Menara Garden, Marrakesh. 40fr, Tafraout Village. 50fr, Portuguese cistern, Mazagan. 75fr, Garden of Oudaya, Rabat.

1955		*Perf. 13½x13, 13x13½, 13*		
311	A70	50c brn vio	6	5
312	A70	1fr blue	6	5
313	A70	2fr red lil	6	5
314	A70	3fr bluish blk	8	5
315	A70	5fr vermilion	75	30
316	A70	6fr green	18	18
317	A70	8fr org brn	65	40
318	A70	10fr vio brn	1.10	18
319	A70	12fr grnsh bl	30	5
320	A70	15fr magenta	95	5
321	A71	18fr dk grn	1.25	65
322	A71	20fr brn lake	52	5
323	A72	25fr brt ultra	1.65	18
324	A72	30fr green	1.65	42
325	A72	40fr org red	85	10
326	A72	50fr blk brn	5.00	30
327	A71	75fr grnsh bl	1.25	75
		Nos. 311-327 (17)	16.36	3.81

Succeeding issues, released under the Kingdom, are listed under Morocco in Vol. III.

SEMI-POSTAL STAMPS

French Protectorate

No. 30 Surcharged in Red

1914		**Unwmk.**	*Perf. 14x13½*	
B1	A4	10c + 5c on 10c rose	*22,500.*	*22,500.*

No. B1 is known only with inverted surcharge.

Same Surcharge on No. 42 with "Protectorat Francais".

B2	A7	10c + 5c on 10c rose	2.00	2.00
a.		Double surcharge	87.50	87.50
b.		Inverted surcharge	110.00	110.00
c.		"c" omitted	52.50	52.50

On Nos. B1 and B2 the cross is set up from pieces of metal (quads), the horizontal bar being made from two long pieces, the vertical bar from two short pieces. Each cross in the setting of twenty-five differs from the others.

No. 30 Handstamp Surcharged in Red

B3	A4	10c + 5c on 10c rose	*1,500.*	*1,100.*

No. B3 was issued at Oujda. The surcharge ink is water-soluble.

No. 42 Surcharged in Vermilion or Carmine

B4	A7	10c + 5c on 10c rose (V)	11.00	11.00
a.		Double surcharge	100.00	100.00
b.		Inverted surcharge	120.00	120.00
c.		Double surcharge, one inverted	120.00	120.00

B5 A7 10c + 5c on 10c rose (C) 265.00 300.00

On Nos. B4 and B5 the horizontal bar of the cross is single and not as thick as on Nos. B1 and B2.

No. B5 was sold largely at Casablanca.

SP1

SP2

Carmine Surcharge.

1915

B6	SP1 5c + 5c grn	1.10	90
a.	Inverted surcharge	160.00	160.00

No. B6 was not issued without the Red Cross surcharge.

B7	SP2 10c + 5c rose	1.40	1.40

No. B7 was used in Tangier.

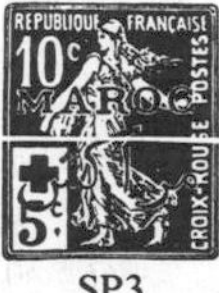
SP3

SP4

France No. B2 Overprinted in Black.

B8	SP3 10c + 5c red	3.00	3.00

Carmine Surcharge.

1917

B9	SP4 10c + 5c on 10c rose	1.25	1.25

On No. B9 the horizontal bar of the cross is made from a single, thick piece of metal.

Marshal Hubert Lyautey — SP5

1935, May 15 Photo. *Perf. 13x13½*

B10	SP5 50c + 50c red	5.50	5.50
B11	SP5 1fr + 1fr dk grn	5.50	5.50
B12	SP5 5fr + 1fr blk brn	27.50	27.50

Stamps of 1933-34 Surcharged in Blue or Red **O.S.E. +3c**

1938 *Perf. 13.*

B13	A18	2c + 2c red vio (Bl)	3.75	3.75
B14	A19	3c + 3c dk brn (Bl)	3.75	3.75
B15	A20	20c + 20c red brn (Bl)	3.75	3.75
B16	A21	40c + 40c blk brn (R)	3.75	3.75
B17	A22	65c + 65c brn red (Bl)	3.75	3.75
B18	A23	1.25fr + 1.25fr blk (R)	3.75	3.75
B19	A24	2fr + 2fr yel brn (Bl)	3.75	3.75
B20	A25	5fr + 5fr red brn (Bl)	3.75	3.75
		Nos. B13-B20 (8)	30.00	30.00

Stamps of 1939 Surcharged in Black

+2f Enfants de France au Maroc

1942

B21	A29	45c + 2fr Prus grn	3.00	3.00
B22	A30	90c + 4fr ultra	3.00	3.00
B23	A32	1.25fr + 6fr hn brn	3.00	3.00
B24	A26	2.50fr + 8fr scar	3.00	3.00

The arrangement of the surcharge differs slightly on each denomination.

No. 207 Surcharged in Black **AIDEZ LES TUBERCULEUX +1f**

1945 Unwmk. *Perf. 13½x14*

B26	A33 2fr + 1fr Prus grn	22	22

Mausoleum of Marshal Lyautey SP7

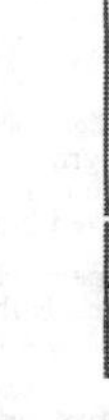

Statue of Marshal Lyautey SP8

1945 Litho. *Perf. 11½*

B27	SP7 2fr + 3fr dk bl	18	18

The surtax was for French works of solidarity.

No. B26 Surcharged in Red

1946 *Perf. 13½x14*

B28	A33 3fr (+ 1fr) on 2fr + 1fr Prus grn	10	6

Perf. 13½x14, 13

1946, Dec. 16 Engr.

B29	SP8 2fr + 10fr blk	1.00	1.00
B30	SP8 3fr + 15fr cop red	1.25	1.25
B31	SP8 10fr + 20fr brt bl	1.90	1.90

The surtax was for works of solidarity.

No. 212 Surcharged in Rose Violet **JOURNÉE DU TIMBRE 1947 +5F50**

1947, Mar. 15 *Perf. 13½x14*

B32	A31 4.50fr + 5.50fr mag	1.00	1.00

Stamp Day, 1947.

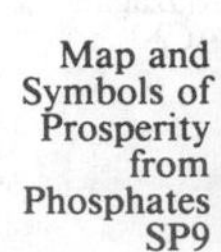

Map and Symbols of Prosperity from Phosphates SP9

1947 *Perf. 13*

B33	SP9 4.50fr + 5.50fr grn	65	65

Issued to commemorate the 25th anniversary of the exploitations of the Cherifien Office of Phosphates.

Power SP10

Health SP11

1948, Feb. 9

B34	SP10 6fr + 9fr red brn	1.75	1.75
B35	SP11 10fr + 20fr dp ultra	1.75	1.75

The surtax was for combined works of Franco-Moroccan solidarity.

Type of Regular Issue of 1923, Inscribed: "Journée du Timbre 1948."

1948, Mar. 6

B36	A16 6fr + 4fr red brn	60	60

Stamp Day, Mar. 6, 1948.

Battleship off Moroccan Coast SP12

1948, Aug.

B37	SP12 6fr + 9fr pur	1.25	1.25

The surtax was for naval charities.

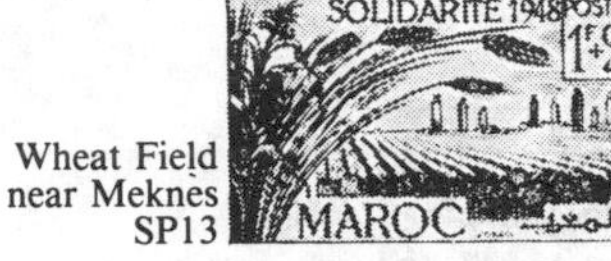

Wheat Field near Meknes SP13

Designs: 2fr+5fr, Olive grove, Taroudant. 3fr+7fr, Net and coastal view. 5fr+10fr, Aguedal Gardens, Marrakesh.

1949, Apr. 12 Engr. Unwmk.

Inscribed: "SOLIDARITÉ 1948."

B38	SP13 1fr + 2fr org	1.00	1.00
B39	SP13 2fr + 5fr car	1.00	1.00
B40	SP13 3fr + 7fr pck bl	1.00	1.00
B41	SP13 5fr + 10fr dk brn vio	1.00	1.00
a.	Sheet of four	11.00	11.00
	Nos. B38-B41,CB31-CB34 (8)	8.13	8.03

No. B41a contains one each of Nos. B38-B41. Size: 120x96mm.

Gazelle Hunter, from 1899 Local Stamp SP14

1949, May 1

B42	SP14 10fr + 5fr choc & car rose	90	90

Stamp Day and 50th anniversary of Mazagan-Marrakesh local postage stamp.

Moroccan Soldiers and Flag SP15

Rug Weaving SP16

1949

B43	SP15 10fr + 10fr brt red	75	75

The surtax was for Army Welfare Work.

1950, Apr. 11

Designs: 2fr+5fr, Pottery making. 3fr+7fr, Bookbinding. 5fr+10fr, Copper work.

Inscribed: "SOLIDARITE 1949."

B44	SP16 1fr + 2fr dp car	1.50	1.50
B45	SP16 2fr + 5fr dk grnsh bl	1.50	1.50
B46	SP16 3fr + 7fr dk pur	1.50	1.50
B47	SP16 5fr + 10fr red brn	1.50	1.50
a.	Sheet of four	11.00	11.00
	Nos. B44-B47,CB36-CB39 (8)	11.00	11.00

No. B47a contains one each of Nos. B44-B47. Size: 95½x120½mm.

Ruins of Sala Colonia at Chella SP17

1950, Sept. 25 Engr. *Perf. 13*

B48	SP17 10fr + 10fr dp mag	90	90
B49	SP17 15fr + 15fr ind	90	90

The surtax was for Army Welfare Work.

AIR POST STAMPS

French Protectorate

Biplane over Casablanca AP1

1922-27 Unwmk. Photo. *Perf. 13½*

C1	AP1	5c dp org ('27)	18	18
a.		Imperf., pair	47.50	
C2	AP1	25c dp ultra	65	22
a.		Imperf., pair	57.50	
C3	AP1	50c grnsh bl	18	18
a.		Imperf., pair	47.50	
C4	AP1	75c dp bl	50.00	6.00
a.		Imperf., pair	525.00	
C5	AP1	75c dp grn	18	12
a.		Imperf., pair	62.50	
C6	AP1	80c vio brn ('27)	1.25	30
a.		Imperf., pair	50.00	
C7	AP1	1fr vermilion	18	12
a.		Imperf., pair	57.50	
C8	AP1	1.40fr brn lake ('27)	1.00	75
C9	AP1	1.90fr dp bl ('27)	1.25	1.25
C10	AP1	2fr blk vio	95	70
a.		2fr dp vio	1.25	90
b.		Imperf., pair	190.00	
C11	AP1	3fr gray blk ('27)	1.00	80
		Nos. C1-C11 (11)	56.82	10.62

The 25c, 50c, 75c deep green and 1fr each were printed in two or three types, differing in frameline thickness, or hyphen in "Helio-Vaugirard" imprint.

Nos. C8-C9 Surcharged in Blue or Black

1fr

1931, Apr. 10

C12	AP1 1fr on 1.40fr (B)	1.25	1.25
a.	Inverted surcharge	250.00	250.00
C13	AP1 1.50fr om 1.90fr (Bk)	1.25	1.25

Rabat and Tower of Hassan AP2

Casablanca AP3

1933, Jan. **Engr.**

C14	AP2	50c dk bl	65	35
C15	AP2	80c org brn	42	30
C16	AP2	1.50fr brn red	52	22
C17	AP3	2.50fr car rose	3.50	42
C18	AP3	5fr violet	1.50	1.00
C19	AP3	10fr bl grn	75	75
		Nos. C14-C19 (6)	7.34	3.04

Storks and Minaret, Chella — AP4

Plane and Map of Morocco AP5

1939-40 ***Perf. 13***

C20	AP4	80c Prus grn	5	5
C21	AP4	1fr dk red	5	5
C22	AP5	1.90fr ultra	5	6
C23	AP5	2fr red vio ('40)	6	5
C24	AP5	3fr chocolate	6	6
C25	AP4	5fr violet	75	52
C26	AP5	10fr turq bl	60	35
		Nos. C20-C26 (7)	1.62	1.14

Plane over Oasis — AP6

1944 **Litho.** ***Perf. 11½***

C27	AP6	50c Prus grn	6	5
C28	AP6	2fr ultra	15	15
C29	AP6	5fr scarlet	15	15
C30	AP6	10fr violet	52	52
C31	AP6	50fr black	85	85
C32	AP6	100fr dp bl & red	2.50	2.50
		Nos. C27-C32 (6)	4.23	4.22

Plane — AP7

1945 **Engr.** ***Perf. 13***

C33	AP7	50fr sepia	60	50

Moulay Idriss — AP8

La Medina AP9

1947-48

C34	AP8	9fr dk rose car	18	18
C35	AP8	40fr dk bl	55	30
C36	AP8	50fr dp cl ('47)	55	18
C37	AP9	100fr dp grnsh bl	1.50	60
C38	AP9	200fr hn brn	2.75	1.25
		Nos. C34-C38 (5)	5.53	2.51

Leclerc Type of Regular Issue

1951, Apr. 28

C39	A50	50fr purple	1.75	1.75

Issued to commemorate the unveiling of a monument to Gen. Leclerc at Casablanca, April 28, 1951.

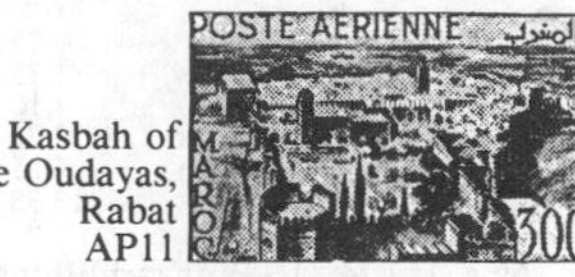

Kasbah of the Oudayas, Rabat AP11

1951, May 22

C40	AP11	300fr purple	10.50	7.50

Ben Smine Sanatorium AP12

1951, June 4

C41	AP12	50fr pur & Prus grn	2.25	2.25

Fortifications, Chella — AP13

Plane Near Marrakesh AP14

Fort, Anti-Atlas Mountains AP15

View of Fez AP16

1952, Apr. 19 **Unwmk.** ***Perf. 13***

C42	AP13	10fr bl grn	50	18
C43	AP14	40fr red	70	42
C44	AP15	100fr brown	1.90	42
C45	AP16	200fr purple	5.75	3.00

Antique Brooches — AP17

1953, Mar. 27

C46	AP17	50fr dk grn	2.25	2.25

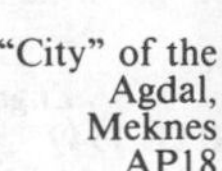
"City" of the Agdal, Meknes AP18

Designs: 20fr, Yakoub el Mansour, Rabat. 40fr, Ainchock, Casablanca. 50fr, El Aliya, Fedala.

1954, Mar. 8

C47	AP18	10fr ol brn	1.50	1.75
C48	AP18	20fr purple	1.50	1.75
C49	AP18	40fr red brn	1.50	1.75
C50	AP18	50fr dp grn	1.50	1.75

Franco-Moroccan solidarity.

Naval Vessel and Sailboat AP19

Village in the Anti-Atlas AP20

"Ksar es Souk," Rabat and Plane AP21

1954, Oct. 18

C51	AP19	15fr dk bl grn	1.25	1.25
C52	AP19	30fr vio bl	1.50	1.50

1955, July 25 **Engr.** ***Perf. 13***

Designs: 200fr, Estuary of Bou Regreg, Rabat and Plane.

C53	AP20	100fr brt vio	1.50	30
C54	AP20	200fr brt car	2.25	70
C55	AP21	500fr grnsh bl	6.50	3.25

AIR POST SEMI-POSTAL STAMPS

French Protectorate

Moorish Tribesmen SPAP1

Designs: 25c, Moor plowing with camel and burro. 50c, Caravan nearing Saffi. 75c, Walls, Marrakesh. 80c, Sheep grazing at Azrou. 1fr, Gate at Fez. 1.50fr, Aerial view of Tangier. 2fr, Aerial view of Casablanca. 3fr, Storks on old wall, Rabat. 5fr, Moorish fete.

Perf. 13½

1928, July 26 **Photo.** **Unwmk.**

CB1	SPAP1	5c dp bl	2.50	2.50
CB2	SPAP1	25c brn org	2.50	2.50
CB3	SPAP1	50c red	2.50	2.50
CB4	SPAP1	75c org brn	2.50	2.50
CB5	SPAP1	80c ol grn	2.50	2.50
CB6	SPAP1	1fr orange	2.50	2.50
CB7	SPAP1	1.50fr Prus bl	2.50	2.50
CB8	SPAP1	2fr dp brn	2.50	2.50
CB9	SPAP1	3fr dp vio	2.50	2.50
CB10	SPAP1	5fr brn blk	2.50	2.50
		Nos. CB1-CB10 (10)	25.00	25.00

These stamps were sold in sets only and at double their face value. The money received for the surtax was divided among charitable and social organizations. The stamps were not sold at post offices but solely by subscription to the Moroccan Postal Administration.

Stamps of 1928 Overprinted in Red or Blue. **Tanger**

1929, Feb. 1

CB11	SPAP1	5c dp bl (R)	2.50	2.50
CB12	SPAP1	25c brn org (Bl)	2.50	2.50
CB13	SPAP1	50c red (Bl)	2.50	2.50
CB14	SPAP1	75c org brn (Bl)	2.50	2.50
CB15	SPAP1	80c ol grn (R)	2.50	2.50
CB16	SPAP1	1fr org (Bl)	2.50	2.50
CB17	SPAP1	1.50fr Prus bl (R)	2.50	2.50
CB18	SPAP1	2fr dp brn (R)	2.50	2.50
CB19	SPAP1	3fr dp vio (R)	2.50	2.50
CB20	SPAP1	5fr brn blk (R)	2.50	2.50
		Nos. CB11-CB20 (10)	25.00	25.00

These stamps were sold at double their face values and only in Tangier. The surtax benefited various charities.

Marshal Hubert Lyautey SPAP10

1935, May 15 ***Perf. 13½***

CB21	SPAP10	1.50fr + 1.50fr bl	12.50	11.00

Nos. C14, C19 Surcharged in Red **O.S.E. +50c**

1938 ***Perf. 13***

CB22	AP2	50c + 50c dk bl	3.25	3.25
CB23	AP3	10fr + 10fr bl grn	3.25	3.25

Plane over Oasis SPAP11

Statue of Marshal Lyautey SPAP12

1944 **Litho.** ***Perf. 11½***

CB23A	SPAP11	1.50fr + 98.50fr red, dp bl & blk	1.25	1.25

The surtax was for charity among the liberated French.

No. C29 Surcharged in Black

+ 5F
18 Juin 1940
‡
18 Juin 1946

1946, June 18 ***Perf. 11***

CB24	AP6	5fr + 5fr scar	60	60

Issued to commemorate the 6th anniversary of the appeal made by Gen. Charles de Gaulle, June 18, 1940. The surtax was for the Free French Association of Morocco.

1946, Dec. **Engr.** ***Perf. 13***

CB25	SPAP12	10fr + 30fr dk grn	1.50	1.50

The surtax was for works of solidarity.

Replenishing Stocks of Food SPAP13

Agriculture SPAP14

1948, Feb. 9 **Unwmk.**

CB26 SPAP13 9fr + 16fr dp grn 1.25 1.25
CB27 SPAP14 20fr + 35fr brn 1.25 1.25

The surtax was for combined works of Franco-Moroccan solidarity.

Tomb of Marshal Hubert Lyautey – SPAP15

1948, May 18 ***Perf. 13***

CB28 SPAP15 10fr + 25fr dk grn 1.00 1.00

Lyautey Exposition, Paris, June, 1948.

P. T. T. Clubhouse SPAP16

1948, June 7 **Engr.**

CB29 SPAP16 6fr + 34fr dk grn 1.50 1.50
CB30 SPAP16 9fr + 51fr red brn 1.65 1.65

The surtax was used for the Moroccan P. T. T. employees vacation colony at Ifrane.

View of Agadir SPAP17

Plane over Globe SPAP18

Designs: 6fr+9fr, Fez. 9fr+16fr, Atlas Mountains. 15fr+25fr, Valley of Draa.

1949, Apr. 12 ***Perf. 13***
Inscribed: "SOLIDARITÉ 1948."

CB31 SPAP17 5fr + 5fr dk grn 1.25 1.25
CB32 SPAP17 6fr + 9fr org red 1.25 1.25
CB33 SPAP17 9fr + 16fr blk brn 1.25 1.25
CB34 SPAP17 15fr + 25fr ind 1.25 1.25
a. Sheet of four 7.50 7.50

No. CB34a contains one each of Nos. CB31-CB34. Size: 96x120mm.

1950, Mar. 11 **Engr. and Typo.**

CB35 SPAP18 15fr + 10fr bl grn & car 52 52

Issued to commemorate the "Day of the Stamp," March 11-12, 1950, and to mark the 25th anniversary of the first air post link between Casablanca and Dakar.

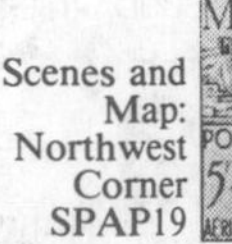

Scenes and Map: Northwest Corner SPAP19

Designs (quarters of map): 6fr+9fr, Northeast. 9fr+16fr, Southwest. 15fr+25fr, Southeast.

1950, Apr. 11 **Engr.**
Inscribed: "SOLIDARITÉ 1949."

CB36 SPAP19 5fr + 5fr dp ultra 1.25 1.25
CB37 SPAP19 6fr + 9fr Prus grn 1.25 1.25
CB38 SPAP19 9fr + 16fr dk brn 1.25 1.25
CB39 SPAP19 15fr + 25fr brn red 1.25 1.25
a. Sheet of four 7.50 7.50

No. CB39a contains one each of Nos. CB36-CB39. Size: 120½x95½mm.

Arch of Triumph of Caracalla at Volubilis SPAP20

1950, Sept. 25 **Unwmk.**

CB40 SPAP20 10fr + 10fr sep 1.00 1.00
CB41 SPAP20 15fr + 15fr bl grn 1.00 1.00

The surtax was for Army Welfare Work.

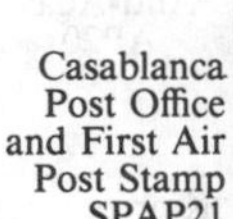

Casablanca Post Office and First Air Post Stamp SPAP21

1952, Mar. 8 ***Perf. 13***

CB42 SPAP21 15fr + 5fr red brn & dp grn 3.00 3.00

Issued to publicize the "Day of the Stamp," March 8, 1952, and to commemorate the 30th anniversary of French Morocco's first air post stamp.

POSTAGE DUE STAMPS

French Offices in Morocco

Postage Due Stamps and Types of France Surcharged in Red or Black — 5 CENTIMOS

1896 **Unwmk.** ***Perf. 14x13½.***
On Stamps of 1891-93.

J1 D2 5c on 5c lt bl (R) 3.00 1.75
J2 D2 10c on 10c choc (R) 5.00 1.75
J3 D2 30c on 30c car 12.00 8.25
a. Pair, one without surcharge
J4 D2 50c on 50c lil 12.50 7.50
a. "S" of "CENTIMOS" omitted 15.00
J5 D2 1p on 1fr lil brn 275.00 250.00

1909-10
On Stamps of 1908-10.

J6 D3 1c on 1c ol grn (R) 80 80
J7 D3 10c on 10c vio 18.00 15.00
J8 D3 30c on 30c bis 22.50 21.00
J9 D3 50c on 50c red 35.00 35.00

Postage Due Stamps of France Surcharged in Red or Blue — 5

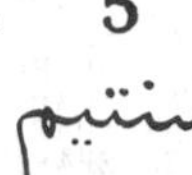

1911
On Stamps of 1893-96.

J10 D2 5c on 5c bl (R) 1.50 1.50
J11 D2 10c on 10c choc (R) 5.00 5.00
a. Double surch. 87.50 87.50
J12 D2 50c on 50c lil (Bl) 6.25 6.25

On Stamps of 1908-10.

J13 D3 1c on 1c ol grn (R) 70 70
J14 D3 10c on 10c vio (R) 2.00 2.00
J15 D3 30c on 30c bis (R) 3.00 3.00
J16 D3 50c on 50c red (Bl) 5.50 5.50
Nos. J10-J16 (7) 23.95 23.95

French Protectorate

D4

D5

Type of 1911 Issue Overprinted "Protectorat Francais".

1915-17

J17 D4 1c on 1c blk 18 18
a. New value double 100.00
J18 D4 5c on 5c bl 85 75
J19 D4 10c on 10c choc 1.25 1.00
J20 D4 20c on 20c ol grn 1.10 1.00
J21 D4 30c on 30c rose red 3.75 3.50
J22 D4 50c on 50c vio brn 6.25 3.00
Nos. J17-J22 (6) 13.38 9.43

Nos. J13 to J16 With Additional Overprint "Protectorat Francais".

1915

J23 D3 1c on 1c ol grn 60 60
J24 D3 10c on 10c vio 1.25 1.00
J25 D3 30c on 30c bis 1.65 1.25
J26 D3 50c on 50c red 1.65 1.40

1917-26 **Typo.**

J27 D5 1c black 5 5
J28 D5 5c dp bl 15 5
J29 D5 10c brown 18 10
J30 D5 20c ol grn 1.25 75
J31 D5 30c rose 18 6
J32 D5 50c lil brn 18 8
J33 D5 1fr red brn, *straw* ('26) 90 28
J34 D5 2fr vio ('26) 1.10 65
Nos. J27-J34 (8) 3.99 2.02

Postage Due Stamps of France, 1882-1906 Overprinted — TANGER

1918

J35 D2 1c black 30 30
J36 D2 5c blue 52 52
J37 D2 10c chocolate 85 85
J38 D2 15c green 1.65 1.65
J39 D2 20c ol grn 2.50 2.50
J40 D2 30c rose red 5.75 5.75
J41 D2 50c vio brn 9.50 9.50
Nos. J35-J41 (7) 21.07 21.07

Postage Due Stamps of France, 1908-19 Overprinted — TANGER

1918

J42 D3 1c ol grn 40 40
J43 D3 10c violet 65 65
J44 D3 20c bister 3.50 3.50
J45 D3 40c red 7.50 7.50

Nos. J31 and J29 Surcharged — 50c

1944 **Unwmk.** ***Perf. 14x13½***

J46 D5 50c on 30c rose 1.90 1.90
J47 D5 1fr on 10c brn 2.75 2.50
J48 D5 3fr on 10c brn 7.50 5.75

Type of 1917-1926

1945-52 **Typo.**

J49 D5 1fr brn lake ('47) 60 52
J50 D5 2fr rose lake ('47) 80 60
J51 D5 3fr ultra 30 18
J52 D5 4fr red org 30 22
J53 D5 5fr green 65 15
J54 D5 10fr yel brn 65 18
J55 D5 20fr car ('50) 1.00 75
J56 D5 30fr dl brn ('52) 1.75 1.25
Nos. J49-J56 (8) 6.05 3.85

PARCEL POST STAMPS

French Protectorate

PP1

1917 **Unwmk.** ***Perf. 13½x14***

Q1 PP1 5c green 48 22
Q2 PP1 10c carmine 52 30
Q3 PP1 20c lil brn 55 35
Q4 PP1 25c blue 95 48
Q5 PP1 40c dk brn 1.65 70
Q6 PP1 50c red org 1.75 60
Q7 PP1 75c pale sl 2.50 1.50
Q8 PP1 1f ultra 3.50 42
Q9 PP1 2f gray 5.25 60
Q10 PP1 5f violet 6.50 60
Q11 PP1 10f black 11.00 60
Nos. Q1-Q11 (11) 34.65 6.37

FRENCH POLYNESIA

(French Oceania)

LOCATION – South Pacific Ocean
GOVT. – French Overseas Territory
AREA – 1,522 sq. mi.
POP. – 172,000 (est. 1984)
CAPITAL – Papeete

In 1903 various French Establishments in the South Pacific were united to form a single colony. Most important of the island groups are the Society Islands, Marquesas Islands, the Tuamotu group and the Gambier, Austral, and Rapa Islands. Tahiti, largest of the Society group, ranks first in importance.

100 Centimes = 1 Franc

Navigation and Commerce – A1

Perf. 14x13½.
1892-1907 **Typo.** **Unwmk.**
Name of Colony in Blue or Carmine.

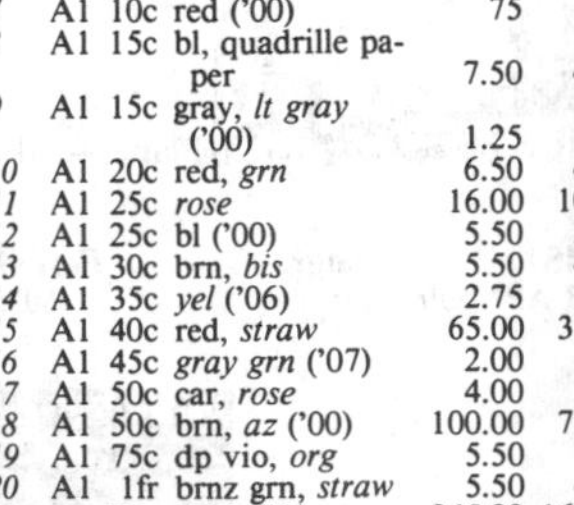

1 A1 1c *lil bl* 80 70
2 A1 2c brn, *buff* 1.00 90
3 A1 4c cl, *lav* 1.75 1.40
4 A1 5c grn, *grnsh* 4.00 4.25
5 A1 5c yel grn ('06) 90 60
6 A1 10c *lavender* 9.00 5.50
7 A1 10c red ('00) 75 60
8 A1 15c bl, quadrille paper 7.50 4.75
9 A1 15c gray, *lt gray* ('00) 1.25 1.40
10 A1 20c red, *grn* 6.50 4.25
11 A1 25c *rose* 16.00 10.00
12 A1 25c bl ('00) 5.50 3.75
13 A1 30c brn, *bis* 5.50 4.75
14 A1 35c *yel* ('06) 2.75 1.90
15 A1 40c red, *straw* 65.00 35.00
16 A1 45c *gray grn* ('07) 2.00 1.50
17 A1 50c car, *rose* 4.00 3.00
18 A1 50c brn, *az* ('00) 100.00 75.00
19 A1 75c dp vio, *org* 5.50 3.75
20 A1 1fr brnz grn, *straw* 5.50 4.75
Nos. 1-20 (20) 245.20 167.75

Tahitian Girl A2

Kanakas A3

Fautaua Valley — A4

1913-30

No.	Type	Description	Unused	Used
21	A2	1c vio & brn	14	14
22	A2	2c brn & blk	14	14
23	A2	4c org & bl	18	18
24	A2	5c grn & yel grn	18	18
25	A2	5c bl & blk ('22)	18	18
26	A2	10c rose & org	52	35
27	A2	10c bl grn & yel grn ('22)	30	30
28	A2	10c org red & brn red, *bluish* ('26)	60	60
29	A2	15c org & blk ('15)	18	18
a.		Imperf., pair	26.00	
30	A2	20c blk & vio	18	18
a.		Imperf., pair	35.00	
31	A2	20c grn & bl grn ('26)	25	25
32	A2	20c brn red & dk brn ('27)	60	60
33	A3	25c ultra & bl	40	18
34	A3	25c vio & rose ('22)	18	18
35	A3	30c gray & brn	1.50	1.25
a.		Imperf., pair	95.00	
36	A3	30c rose & red org ('22)	52	52
37	A3	30c blk & red org ('26)	18	18
38	A3	30c sl bl & bl grn ('27)	60	60
39	A3	35c grn & rose	40	18
40	A3	40c blk & grn	40	30
41	A3	45c org & red	40	35
42	A3	50c dk brn & blk	7.00	6.00
43	A3	50c ultra & bl ('22)	40	40
44	A3	50c gray & bl vio ('26)	40	40
45	A3	60c grn & blk ('26)	40	40
46	A3	65c ol brn & red vio ('27)	1.00	1.00
47	A3	75c vio brn & vio	95	65
48	A3	90c brn red & rose ('30)	8.25	8.25
49	A4	1fr rose & blk	1.10	80
50	A4	1.10fr vio & dk brn ('28)	90	90
51	A4	1.40fr bis brn & vio ('29)	2.25	2.25
52	A4	1.50fr ind & bl ('30)	8.25	8.25
53	A4	2fr dk brn & grn	2.25	1.25
54	A4	5fr vio & bl	5.75	4.75
		Nos. 21-54 (34)	46.93	42.32

No. 7 Overprinted **EFO 1915**

1915

No.	Type	Description	Unused	Used
55	A1	10c red	1.75	1.75
a.		Inverted overprint	52.50	52.50

No. 29 Surcharged **10**

1916

No.	Type	Description	Unused	Used
56	A2	10c on 15c org & blk	70	70

Nos. 22, 41 and 29 Surcharged **05 1921**

1921

No.	Type	Description	Unused	Used
57	A2	5c on 2c brn & blk	12.50	12.50
58	A3	10c on 45c org & red	12.50	12.50
59	A2	25c on 15c org & blk	3.00	3.00

On No. 58 the new value and date are set wide apart and without bar.

Types of 1913-30 Issue Surcharged **60**

1923-27

No.	Type	Description	Unused	Used
60	A3	60c on 75c bl & brn	18	18
61	A4	65c on 1fr dk bl & ol (R) ('25)	60	60
62	A4	85c on 1fr dk bl & ol (R) ('25)	65	65
63	A3	90c on 75c brn red & cer ('27)	65	65

No. 26 Surcharged **45 c. 1924**

1924

No.	Type	Description	Unused	Used
64	A2	45c on 10c rose & org	1.00	1.00
a.		Inverted surch.	350.00	350.00

Stamps and Type of 1913-30 Surcharged with New Value and Bars

1924-27

No.	Type	Description	Unused	Used
65	A4	25c on 2fr dk brn & grn	52	52
66	A4	25c on 5fr vio & bl	60	60
67	A4	1.25fr on 1fr dk bl & ultra (R) ('26)	60	60
68	A4	1.50fr on 1fr dk bl & lt bl ('27)	1.00	1.00
69	A4	20fr on 5fr org & brt vio ('27)	10.00	7.75
		Nos. 65-69 (5)	12.72	10.47

Surcharged **TROIS FRANCS**

1926

No.	Type	Description	Unused	Used
70	A4	3fr on 5fr gray & bl (Bk)	90	70
71	A4	10fr on 5fr grn & blk (R)	2.25	1.75

Papetoai Bay, Moorea A5

1929, Mar. 25

No.	Type	Description	Unused	Used
72	A5	3fr grn & dk brn	3.00	3.00
73	A5	5fr lt bl & dk brn	5.25	5.25
74	A5	10fr lt red & dk brn	18.00	18.00
75	A5	20fr lil & dk brn	21.00	21.00

Colonial Exposition Issue.
Common Design Types

1931, Apr. 13 Engr. *Perf. 12½*
Name of Country Printed in Black.

No.	Type	Description	Unused	Used
76	CD70	40c dp grn	2.50	2.50
77	CD71	50c violet	2.50	2.50
78	CD72	90c red org	2.50	2.50
79	CD73	1.50fr dl bl	2.75	2.75

Spear Fishing A12

Tahitian Girl — A13

Idols — A14

1934-39 Photo. *Perf. 13½, 13½x13*

No.	Type	Description	Unused	Used
80	A12	1c gray blk	6	6
81	A12	2c claret	8	8
82	A12	3c lt bl ('39)	8	8
83	A12	4c orange	22	22
84	A12	5c violet	42	42
85	A12	10c dk brn	8	8
86	A12	15c green	18	18
87	A12	20c red	6	6
88	A13	25c gray bl	18	18
89	A13	30c yel grn	60	60
90	A13	30c org brn ('39)	18	18
91	A14	35c dp grn ('38)	1.75	1.75
92	A13	40c red vio	18	18
93	A13	45c brn org	4.75	4.75
94	A13	45c dk grn ('39)	48	48
95	A13	50c violet	6	6
96	A13	55c bl ('38)	2.00	2.00
97	A13	60c blk ('39)	18	18
98	A13	65c brown	1.50	1.50
99	A13	70c brt pink ('39)	40	40
100	A13	75c ol grn	3.00	3.00
101	A13	80c vio brn ('38)	60	60
102	A13	90c rose red	40	40
103	A14	1fr red brn	18	18
104	A14	1.25fr brn vio	4.25	4.25
105	A14	1.25fr rose red ('39)	40	40
106	A14	1.40fr org yel ('39)	40	40
107	A14	1.50fr blue	40	40
108	A14	1.60fr dl vio ('39)	40	40
109	A14	1.75fr olive	3.00	3.00
110	A14	2fr red	40	40
111	A14	2.25fr dp bl ('39)	35	35
112	A14	2.50fr blk ('39)	48	48
113	A14	3fr brn org ('39)	48	48
114	A14	5fr red vio ('39)	48	48
115	A14	10fr dk grn ('39)	1.50	1.50
116	A14	20fr dk brn ('39)	1.75	1.75
		Nos. 80-116 (37)	31.91	31.91

Paris International Exposition Issue.
Common Design Types

1937 Engr. *Perf. 13.*

No.	Type	Description	Unused	Used
117	CD74	20c dp vio	1.00	1.00
118	CD75	30c dk grn	1.00	1.00
119	CD76	40c car rose	1.00	1.00
120	CD77	50c dk brn & bl	1.25	1.25
121	CD78	90c red	1.50	1.50
122	CD79	1.50fr ultra	1.75	1.75
		Nos. 117-122 (6)	7.50	7.50

Common Design Types pictured in section at front of book.

Colonial Arts Exhibition Issue.
Souvenir Sheet.
Common Design Type

1937 *Imperf.*

No.	Type	Description	Unused	Used
123	CD78	3fr emerald	4.00	4.00

Sheet size: 118x99mm.

New York World's Fair Issue.
Common Design Type

1939, May 10 Engr. *Perf. 12½x12*

No.	Type	Description	Unused	Used
124	CD82	1.25fr car lake	1.00	1.00
125	CD82	2.25fr ultra	1.00	1.00

Fautaua Valley and Marshal Petain A15

1941 Engr. *Perf. 12½x12*

No.	Type	Description	Unused	Used
125A	A15	1fr bluish grn	40	
125B	A15	2.50fr dp bl	40	

Nos. 125A-125B were issued by the Vichy government, and were not placed on sale in the colony. This is also true of five stamps of types A12-A14 without "RF" released in 1942-44.

Stamps of 1929-39 Overprinted in Black or Red **FRANCE LIBRE**

1941 *Perf. 14x13½, 13½x13*

No.	Type	Description	Unused	Used
126	A14	1fr red brn (Bk)	2.00	2.00
127	A14	2.50fr blk (R)	2.75	2.75
128	A5	3fr grn & dk brn (R)	2.75	2.75
129	A14	3fr brn org (Bk)	2.75	2.75
130	A5	5fr lt bl & dk brn (R)	2.75	2.75
131	A14	5fr red vio (Bk)	2.75	2.75
132	A5	10fr lt red & dk brn (R)	7.00	7.00
133	A14	10fr dk grn (R)	27.50	27.50
134	A5	20fr lil & dk brn (R)	47.50	47.50
135	A14	20fr dk brn (R)	24.00	24.00
		Nos. 126-135 (10)	121.75	121.75

Ancient Double Canoe A16

1942 Photo. *Perf. 14½x14*

No.	Type	Description	Unused	Used
136	A16	5c dk brn	5	5
137	A16	10c dk gray bl	6	6
138	A16	25c emerald	6	6
139	A16	30c red org	6	6
140	A16	40c dk sl grn	6	6
141	A16	80c red brn	14	14
142	A16	1fr rose vio	14	14
143	A16	1.50fr brt red	25	22
144	A16	2fr gray blk	25	25
145	A16	2.50fr brt ultra	1.00	1.00
146	A16	4fr dl vio	42	40
147	A16	5fr bister	60	55
148	A16	10fr dp brn	60	55
149	A16	20fr dp grn	1.00	90
		Nos. 136-149 (14)	4.69	4.44

Eboue Issue.
Common Design Type

1945 Engr. *Perf. 13*

No.	Type	Description	Unused	Used
150	CD91	2fr black	25	25
151	CD91	25fr Prus grn	1.00	1.00

Nos. 150 and 151 exist imperforate.

Nos. 136, 138 and 145 Surcharged with New Values and Bars in Carmine or Black.

1946 *Perf. 14½x14.*

No.	Type	Description	Unused	Used
152	A16	50c on 5c (C)	18	18
153	A16	60c on 5c (C)	18	18
154	A16	70c on 5c (C)	22	22
155	A16	1.20fr on 5c (C)	22	22
156	A16	2.40fr on 25c (Bk)	70	70
157	A16	3fr on 25c (Bk)	42	42
158	A16	4.50fr on 25c (Bk)	1.00	1.00
159	A16	15fr on 2.50fr (C)	1.25	1.25
		Nos. 152-159 (8)	4.17	4.17

Coast of Moorea A17

Fisherman and Catch — A18

House at Faa — A19

Tahitian Girl — A20

Island of Borabora A21

Island Women A22

1948 Unwmk. Engr. *Perf. 13*

No.	Type	Description	Unused	Used
160	A17	10c brown	6	6
161	A17	30c bl grn	6	6
162	A17	40c dp bl	6	6
163	A18	50c red brn	8	8
164	A18	60c dk brn ol	10	10
165	A18	80c brt bl	10	10
166	A19	1fr red brn	14	8
167	A19	1.20fr slate	25	18
168	A19	1.50fr dp ultra	35	25
169	A20	2fr sepia	60	48
170	A20	2.40fr red brn	80	80
171	A20	3fr purple	6.00	1.75
172	A20	4fr bl blk	70	70
173	A21	5fr sepia	80	70
174	A21	6fr stl bl	85	70
175	A21	10fr dk brn ol	1.40	60
176	A22	15fr vermilion	2.50	1.50
177	A22	20fr slate	2.75	1.50
178	A22	25fr sepia	3.00	1.90
		Nos. 160-178 (19)	20.60	11.60

Imperforates
Most French Polynesia stamps from 1948 onward exist imperforate in issued and trial colors, and also in small presentation sheets in issued colors.

Military Medal Issue.
Common Design Type
Engraved and Typographed

1952, Dec. 1
179 CD101 3fr blk, grn, yel & pur 4.00 4.00

Girl of Borabora A23

Girl Playing Guitar A24

1955, Sept. 26 **Engr.**
180 A23 9fr dk brn, blk & red 9.00 7.50

FIDES Issue.
Common Design Type
Design: 3fr, Dry dock at Papeete.

1956, Oct. 22 **Engr.** ***Perf. 13x12½***
181 CD103 3fr grnsh bl 1.00 75

1958, Nov. 3 **Unwmk.** ***Perf. 13***
Design: 4fr, 7fr, 9fr, Man with headdress. 10fr, 20fr, Girl with shells on beach.

182	A24	10c grn & redsh brn	38	38
183	A24	25c sl grn, cl & car	38	38
184	A24	1fr brt bl, brn & red org	52	52
185	A24	2fr brn, vio brn & vio	52	52
186	A24	4fr sl grn & org yel	70	70
187	A24	7fr red brn, grn & org	1.10	90
188	A24	9fr vio brn, grn & org	2.00	1.65
189	A24	10fr dk bl, brn & car	2.25	1.75
190	A24	20fr pur, rose red & brn	4.50	3.00
		Nos. 182-190 (9)	12.35	9.80

See Nos. 302-304.

Human Rights Issue
Common Design Type

1958, Dec. 10
191 CD105 7fr dk gray & dk bl 6.75 6.00

Flower Issue
Common Design Type
Design: 4fr, Breadfruit.

1959, Jan. **Photo.** ***Perf. 12½x12***
192 CD104 4fr multi 3.25 2.50

Spear Fishing — A25

Tahitian Dancers A26

1960, May 16 **Engr.** ***Perf. 13***
193 A25 5fr grn, brn & lil 70 70
194 A26 17fr ultra, brt grn & red brn 3.50 1.50

Post Office, Papeete A27

1960, Dec. 15 **Unwmk.** ***Perf. 13***
195 A27 16fr grn, bl & cl 4.00 2.25

Saraca Indica — A28

Design: 25fr, Hibiscus.

1962, July 12 **Photo.** ***Perf. 13***
196 A28 15fr multi 8.00 6.75
197 A28 25fr multi 11.00 10.00

Map of Australia and South Pacific — A29

1962, July 18 ***Perf. 13x12***
198 A29 20fr multi 7.50 6.00

Issued to commemorate the Fifth South Pacific Conference, Pago Pago, July 1962.

Spined Squirrelfish A30

Fish: 10fr, One-spot butterflyfish. 30fr, Radiate lionfish. 40fr, Horned boxfish.

1962, Dec. 15 **Engr.** ***Perf. 13***
199 A30 5fr blk, mag & bis 2.25 90
200 A30 10fr multi 3.00 1.65
201 A30 30fr multi 7.50 4.50
202 A30 40fr multi 11.00 7.00

South Pacific Games Issue

Soccer A30a

Design: 50fr, Throwing the javelin.

1963, Aug. 29 **Photo.** ***Perf. 12½***
203 A30a 20fr brt ultra & brn 6.75 5.25
204 A30a 50fr brt car rose & ultra 10.50 7.50

Issued to publicize the South Pacific Games, Suva, Aug. 29-Sept. 7.

Red Cross Centenary Issue
Common Design Type

1963, Sept. 2 **Engr.** ***Perf. 13***
205 CD113 15fr vio brn, gray & car 10.00 8.00

International Red Cross centenary.

Human Rights Issue
Common Design Type

1963, Dec. 10 **Unwmk.** ***Perf. 13***
206 CD117 7fr grn & vio bl 8.25 7.00

Philatec Issue
Common Design Type

1964, Apr. 9 **Unwmk.** ***Perf. 13***
207 CD118 25fr grn, dk sl grn & red 10.50 7.50

Tahitian Dancer A31

1964, May 14 **Engr.** ***Perf. 13***
208 A31 1fr multi 38 38
209 A31 3fr dp cl, blk & org 75 75

Soldiers, Truck and Battle Flag — A32

1964, July 10 **Photo.** ***Perf. 12½***
210 A32 5fr multi 4.50 2.25

Issued to honor the Tahitian Volunteers of the Pacific Battalion. See No. C31.

Tuamotu Scene — A33

Views: 4fr, Borabora. 7fr, Papeete Harbor. 8fr, Paul Gauguin's tomb, Marquesas. 20fr, Mangareva, Gambier Islands.

1964, Dec. 1 **Litho.** ***Perf. 12½x13***

211	A33	2fr multi	45	38
212	A33	4fr multi	85	38
213	A33	7fr multi	1.40	80
214	A33	8fr multi	1.75	80
215	A33	20fr multi	4.50	2.00
		Nos. 211-215,C32 (6)	14.20	6.86

Painting from a School Dining Room — A34

1965, Nov. 29 **Engr.** ***Perf. 13***
216 A34 20fr dk brn, sl grn & dk car 12.00 9.00

Issued to publicize the School Canteen Program. See No. C38.

Outrigger Canoe on Lagoon A35

Ships: 11fr, Large cruising yacht (vert.). 12fr, Motorboat for sport fishing. 14fr, Outrigger canoes with sails. 19fr, Schooner (vert.). 22fr, Modern coaster "Oiseau des Isles II."

1966, Aug. 30 Engr. Perf. 13

217 A35 10fr brt ultra, emer & mar 1.25 60
218 A35 11fr mar, dk bl & sl grn 1.50 1.10
219 A35 12fr emer, dk bl & red lil 2.25 1.40
220 A35 14fr brn, bl & sl grn 2.75 1.50
221 A35 19fr scar, sl grn & dp bl 3.75 1.50
222 A35 22fr multi 5.00 3.00
Nos. 217-222 (6) 16.50 9.10

High Jump A36

Designs: 20fr, Pole vault (vert.). 40fr, Women's basketball (vert.). 60fr, Hurdling.

1966, Dec. 15 Engr. Perf. 13

223 A36 10fr dk red, lem & blk 1.40 1.00
224 A36 20fr bl, emer & blk 3.25 1.50
225 A36 40fr emer, brt pink & blk 6.50 4.25
226 A36 60fr dl yel, bl & blk 11.00 7.50

Issued to commemorate the Second South Pacific Games, Nouméa, New Caledonia, Dec. 8-18.

Poi Pounder A37

Javelin Throwing A38

1967, June 15 Engr. Perf. 13

227 A37 50fr org & blk 10.50 7.50

Issued to commemorate the 50th anniversary of the Society for Oceanic Studies.

1967, July 11

Designs: 5fr, Spring dance (horiz.). 15fr, Horse race (horiz.). 16fr, Fruit carriers' race. 21fr, Canoe race (horiz.).

228 A38 5fr multi 80 70
229 A38 13fr multi 1.65 1.10
230 A38 15fr multi 1.75 1.40
231 A38 16fr multi 3.00 2.25
232 A38 21fr multi 5.50 3.50
Nos. 228-232 (5) 12.70 8.95

Issued to publicize the July Festival.

Earring — A39

Art of the Marquesas Islands: 10fr, Carved mother-of-pearl. 15fr, Decorated canoe paddle. 23fr, Oil vessel. 25fr, Carved stilt stirrups. 30fr, Fan handles. 35fr, Tattooed man. 50fr, Tikis.

1967-68 Engr. Perf. 13

233 A39 10fr dp cl, dl red & ultra ('68) 1.25 70
234 A39 15fr blk & emer ('68) 1.75 95
235 A39 20fr ol gray, dk car & lt bl 2.25 1.65
236 A39 23fr dk brn, ocher & bl ('68) 3.25 2.75
237 A39 25fr dk brn, dk bl & lil 4.00 2.75
238 A39 30fr brn & red lil 5.50 3.00
239 A39 35fr ultra & dk brn ('68) 7.50 5.00
240 A39 50fr brn, sl grn & lt bl 8.00 5.50
Nos. 233-240 (8) 33.50 22.30

Issue dates: 20fr, 25fr, 30fr, 50fr, Dec. 19, 1967; others Feb. 28, 1968.

WHO Anniversary Issue
Common Design Type

1968, May 4 Engr. Perf. 13

241 CD126 15fr bl grn, mar & dp vio 5.50 2.50
242 CD126 16fr org, lil & bl grn 6.50 3.25

Issued for the 20th anniversary of the World Health Organization.

Human Rights Year Issue
Common Design Type

1968, Aug. 10 Engr. Perf. 13

243 CD127 15fr bl, red & brn 5.00 3.75
244 CD127 16fr brn, brt pink & ultra 6.00 5.25

Tiare Apetahi A40

Flower: 17fr, Tiare Tahiti.

1969, Mar. 27 Photo. Perf. 12½x13

245 A40 9fr multi 1.75 90
246 A40 17fr multi 2.75 1.40

Runner — A41

Designs: 9fr, Boxer (horiz.). 17fr, High jump. 22fr, Long jump.

1969, Aug. 13 Engr. Perf. 13

247 A41 9fr bl, vio & sep 1.50 75
248 A41 17fr red, sep & cl 2.25 1.50
249 A41 18fr bl, brn ol & cl 3.75 2.25
250 A41 22fr brt grn & choc 5.50 3.75

Issued to publicize the 3rd South Pacific Games, Port Moresby, Papua and New Guinea, Aug. 13-23.

ILO Issue
Common Design Type

1969, Nov. 24 Engr. Perf. 13

251 CD131 17fr org, emer & ol 5.00 3.25
252 CD131 18fr org, dk brn & vio bl 6.00 4.00

Territorial Assembly A42

Buildings: 14fr, Governor's Residence. 17fr, House of Tourism. 18fr, Maeva Hotel. 24fr, Taharaa Hotel.

1969, Dec. 22 Photo. Perf. 12½x12

253 A42 13fr blk & multi 1.40 90
254 A42 14fr blk & multi 2.00 1.40
255 A42 17fr blk & multi 3.00 2.25
256 A42 18fr blk & multi 4.50 2.25
257 A42 24fr blk & multi 7.00 4.50
Nos. 253-257 (5) 17.90 11.30

Stone Figure with Globe — A43

Designs: 40fr, Globe, plane, map of Polynesia and men holding "PATA" sign (horiz.). 60fr, Polynesian carrying globe.

1970, Apr. 7 Engr. Perf. 13

258 A43 20fr dp plum, gray & bl 2.75 2.25
259 A43 40fr emer, rose lil & ultra 6.00 4.50
260 A43 60fr red brn, bl & dk brn 10.50 8.25

Issued to publicize the 1970 Pacific Area Travel Association Congress (PATA).

U.P.U. Headquarters Issue
Common Design Type

1970, May 20 Engr. Perf. 13

261 CD133 18fr mar, pur & brn 5.00 3.75
262 CD133 20fr lil rose, ol & ind 6.50 4.50

Night Fishing — A44

1971, May 11 Photo. Perf. 13

263 A44 10fr multi 6.00 3.00

See Nos. C71-C73.

Flowers — A45

Designs: Various flowers. 12fr is horiz.

Perf. 12½x13, 13x12½

1971, Aug. 27

264 A45 8fr multi 1.10 75
265 A45 12fr multi 2.25 1.10
266 A45 22fr multi 4.00 2.25

Day of a Thousand Flowers.

Water-skiing Slalom — A46

Designs: 20fr, Water-skiing, jump (vert.). 40fr, Figure water-skiing.

1971, Oct. 11 Engr. Perf. 13

267 A46 10fr grnsh bl, dk red & brn 2.00 1.50
268 A46 20fr car, emer & brn 4.75 3.00
269 A46 40fr brn, grn & lil 9.50 7.50

World water-skiing championships, Oct. 1971.

De Gaulle Issue
Common Design Type

Designs: 30fr, Gen. de Gaulle, 1940. 50fr, Pres. de Gaulle, 1970.

1971, Nov. 9 Engr. Perf. 13

270 CD134 30fr red lil & blk 5.25 4.50
271 CD134 50fr red lil & blk 8.00 6.75

First anniversary of the death of Charles de Gaulle (1890-1970), president of France.

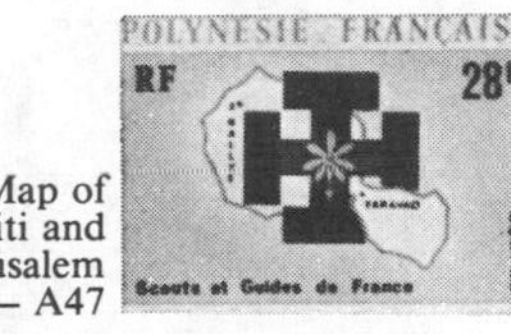

Map of Tahiti and Jerusalem Cross — A47

1971, Dec. 18 Photo. Perf. 13x12½

272 A47 28fr lt bl & multi 7.50 6.00

2nd rally of French Boy Scouts and Guides, Taravao, French Polynesia.

"Alcoholism" A48

Mother and Child A49

1972, Mar. 24 Photo. Perf. 13

273 A48 20fr brn & multi 4.00 2.50

Fight against alcoholism.

1973, Sept. 26 Photo. Perf. 12½x13

274 A49 28fr pale yel & multi 4.50 2.50

Day nursery.

Polynesian Golfer — A50

Design: 24fr, Atimaono Golf Course.

1974, Feb. 27 Photo. Perf. 13

275 A50 16fr multi 3.50 1.50
276 A50 24fr multi 4.25 2.25

Atimaono Golf Course.

Hand Throwing Life Preserver to Puppy — A51

1974, May 9 Photo. Perf. 13

277 A51 21fr brt bl & multi 6.00 3.00

Society for the Protection of Animals.

Around a Fire, on the Beach A52

Polynesian Views: 2fr, Lagoons and mountains. 6fr, Pebble divers. 10fr, Lonely Mountain and flowers (vert.). 15fr, Sailing ship at sunset. 20fr, Lagoon and mountain.

1974, May 22

278 A52 2fr multi	30	30
279 A52 5fr multi	60	52
280 A52 6fr multi	75	55
281 A52 10fr multi	90	65
282 A52 15fr multi	1.90	95
283 A52 20fr multi	3.00	1.50
Nos. 278-283 (6)	7.45	4.47

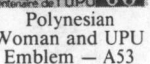

Polynesian Woman and UPU Emblem — A53

Lion, Sun and Emblem — A54

1974, Oct. 9 Engr. *Perf. 13*
284 A53 65fr multi 7.50 5.25

Centenary of Universal Postal Union.

1975, June 17 Photo.
285 A54 26fr multi 5.50 2.00

15th anniversary of Lions International in Tahiti.

Fish and Leaf A55

1975, July 9 Litho. *Perf. 12*
286 A55 19fr dp ultra & grn 4.00 2.50

Polynesian Association for the Protection of Nature.

Pompidou Type of France 1975

1976, Feb. 16 Engr. *Perf. 13*
287 A668 49fr dk vio & blk 6.75 5.25

Georges Pompidou (1911-74), President of France (1965-74).

Alain Gerbault and Sailboat A56

1976, May 25 Photo. *Perf. 13*
288 A56 90fr multi 7.50 6.75

50th anniversary of Alain Gerbault's arrival in Bora Bora.

Turtle — A57

Design: 42fr, Hand protecting bird.

1976, June 24 Litho. *Perf. 12½*

289 A57 18fr multi	4.00	1.90
290 A57 42fr multi	6.50	5.00

World Ecology Day.

A. G. Bell, Telephone, Radar and Satellite — A58

1976, Sept. 15 Engr. *Perf. 13*
291 A58 37fr multi 5.00 2.50

Centenary of first telephone call by Alexander Graham Bell, Mar. 10, 1876.

Marquesas Dugout Canoe — A59

Dugout Canoes from: 30fr, Raiatea. 75fr, Tahiti. 100fr, Tuamotu.

1976, Dec. 16 Litho. *Perf. 13x12½*

292 A59 25fr multi	1.50	1.10
293 A59 30fr multi	2.25	1.50
294 A59 75fr multi	5.25	2.75
295 A59 100fr multi	7.50	5.25

Sailing Ship A60

Designs: Various sailing vessels.

1977, Dec. 22 Litho. *Perf. 13*

296 A60 20fr multi	1.50	1.10
297 A60 50fr multi	3.00	1.50
298 A60 85fr multi	4.50	2.75
299 A60 120fr multi	6.00	4.50

Hibiscus — A61

Girl with Shells on Beach — A62

Designs: 10fr, Vanda orchids. 16fr, Pua (fagraea berteriana). 22fr, Gardenia.

1978-79 Photo. *Perf. 12½x13*

300 A61 10fr multi	45	30
301 A61 13fr multi	1.10	70
302 A61 16fr multi	1.50	70
303 A61 22fr multi	75	52

Issue dates: Nos. 301-302, Aug. 23, 1978; Nos. 300, 303, Jan. 25, 1979.

1978, Nov. 3 Engr. *Perf. 13*

Designs (as type A24 with "1958 1978" added): 28fr, Man with headdress. 36fr, Girl playing guitar.

304 A62 20fr multi	1.10	52
305 A62 28fr multi	1.65	95
306 A62 36fr multi	2.25	1.50
a. Souvenir sheet of 3	7.50	7.50

20th anniv. of stamps inscribed: Polynesie Francaise. No. 306a contains Nos. 304-306 in changed colors. Size: 130x100mm.

Tahiti — A63

Ships: 30fr, Monowai. 75fr, Tahitien. 100fr, Mariposa.

1978, Dec. 29 Litho. *Perf. 13x12½*

307 A63 15fr multi	1.10	90
308 A63 30fr multi	1.50	1.25
309 A63 75fr multi	3.75	2.00
310 A63 100fr multi	5.50	3.00

Porites Coral — A64

Design: 37fr, Montipora coral.

1979, Feb. 15 *Perf. 13x12½*

311 A64 32fr multi	1.50	75
312 A64 37fr multi	2.25	1.10

Raiatea A65

Landscapes: 1fr, Moon over Bora Bora. 2fr, Mountain peaks, Ua Pou. 3fr, Sunset over Motu Tapu. 5fr, Motu Beach. 6fr, Palm and hut, Tuamotu.

1979, Mar. 8 *Perf. 13x13½*

313 A65 1fr multi	6	6
314 A65 2fr multi	6	6
315 A65 3fr multi	15	5
316 A65 4fr multi	22	6
317 A65 5fr multi	38	15
318 A65 6fr multi	45	38
Nos. 313-318 (6)	1.32	76

See Nos. 438-443.

Dance Costumes, Fetia — A66

Dance Costumes: 51fr, Teanuanua. 74fr, Temaeva.

1979, July 14 Litho. *Perf. 12½*

319 A66 45fr multi	1.40	90
320 A66 51fr multi	2.00	1.00
321 A66 74fr multi	2.75	1.75

Hill, Great Britain No. 53, Tahiti No. 28 — A67

1979, Aug. 1 Engr. *Perf. 13*
322 A67 100fr multi 3.75 3.00

Sir Rowland Hill (1795-1879), originator of penny postage.

Hastula Strigilata — A68

Shells: 28fr, Scabricola variegata. 35fr, Fusinus undatus.

1979, Aug. 21 Litho. *Perf. 12½*

323 A68 20fr multi	75	60
324 A68 28fr multi	95	60
325 A68 35fr multi	1.65	1.25

Statue Holding Rotary Emblem — A69

1979, Nov. 30 Litho. *Perf. 13*
326 A69 47fr multi 2.50 1.65

Rotary International, 75th anniversary; Papeete Rotary Club, 20th anniversary.

A little time given to the study of the arrangement of the Scott Catalogue can make it easier to use effectively.

Myripristis Murdjan A70

Fish: 8fr, Napoleon fish. 12fr, Emperor fish.

1980, Jan. 21 Litho. Perf. 12½
327 A70 7fr multi 45 18
328 A70 8fr multi 45 18
329 A70 12fr multi 75 45

No. 326 Overprinted and Surcharged in Gold: "75eme / ANNIVERSAIRE / 1905-1980"

1980, Feb. 23 Litho. Perf. 13
330 A69 77fr on 47fr multi 3.25 2.25

Rotary International, 75th anniversary.

CNEXO Fish Hatchery A71

1980, Mar. 17 Photo. Perf. 13x13½
331 A70 15fr *shown* 75 45
332 A70 22fr *Crayfish* 90 60

Papeete Post Office Building Opening A72

1980, May 5 Photo. Perf. 13x12½
333 A71 50fr multi 1.90 1.50

Tiki and Festival Emblem — A73

1980, June 30 Photo. Perf. 13½
334 A73 34fr *shown* 90 70
335 A73 39fr *Drum (pahu)* 1.40 1.00
336 A73 49fr *Ax (to'i)* 2.25 1.65
a. Souvenir sheet of 3 5.50 5.50

South Pacific Arts Festival, Port Moresby, Papua New Guinea. No. 336a contains Nos. 334-336; multicolored margin shows festival emblem. Size: 136x100mm.

Titmouse henparrot — A74

CHARLES DE GAULLE 1890 1970 100F POSTES RF POLYNESIE FRANÇAISE

Charles de Gaulle — A75

Perf. 13x12½, 12½x13

1980, Oct. 20 Photo.
337 A74 25fr *White sea-swallow, horiz.* 85 52
338 A74 35fr *shown* 90 75
339 A74 45fr *Minor frigate bird, horiz.* 1.25 95

1980, Nov. 9 Engr. Perf. 12½x13
340 A75 100fr multi 3.25 2.50

Naso Vlamingi (Karaua) A76

1981, Feb. 5 Litho. Perf. 12½
341 A76 13fr shown 45 38
342 A76 16fr Lutjanus vaigensis (toau) 60 38
343 A76 24fr Plectropomus leopardus (tonu) 90 45

POLYNESIE FRANÇAISE RF 23F

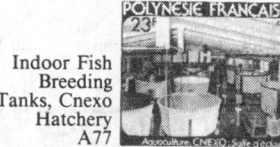

Indoor Fish Breeding Tanks, Cnexo Hatchery A77

1981, May 14 Photo. Perf. 13x13½
344 A77 23fr shown 80 60
345 A77 41fr Mussels 1.25 90

Folk Dancers A78

Perf. 13x13½, 13½x13

1981, July 10 Litho.
346 A78 26fr shown 70 45
347 A78 28fr Dancer 75 60
348 A78 44fr Dancers, vert. 1.40 90

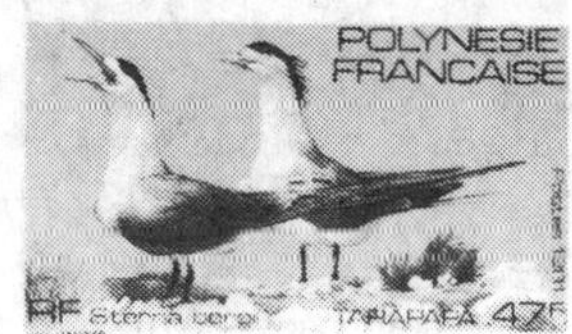

Sterna Bergii — A79

1981, Sept. 24 Litho. Perf. 13
349 A79 47fr shown 1.10 75
350 A79 53fr Ptilinopus purpuratus, vert. 1.40 90
351 A79 65fr Estrilda astrild, vert. 1.65 1.40

See Nos. 370-372

POLYNESIE FRANÇAISE 34F HUAHINE RF

Huahine Island A80

1981, Oct. 22 Litho. Perf. 12½
352 A80 34fr shown 75 52
353 A80 134fr Maupiti 2.25 1.50
354 A80 136fr Bora-Bora 2.25 1.50

The first price column gives the catalogue value of an unused stamp, the second that of a used stamp.

A81

1982, Feb. 4 Photo. Perf. 13x13½
355 A81 30fr Parrotfish 60 52
356 A81 31fr Regal angel 60 52
357 A81 45fr Spotted bass 90 75

Pearl Industry A82

1982, Apr. 22 Photo. Perf. 13x13½
358 A82 7fr Pearl beds 14 6
359 A82 8fr Extracting pearls 18 14
360 A82 10fr Pearls 22 18

Tahiti "No. 1A," Emblem — A83

1982, May 12 Engr. Perf. 13
361 A83 150fr multi 4.50 3.75
a. Souvenir sheet 8.00 8.00

PHILEXFRANCE Stamp Exhibition, Paris, June 11-21. No. 361a contains No. 361 in changed colors; blue marginal inscription. Size: 122x95mm.

King Holding Carved Scepter — A84

Designs: Coronation ceremony.

1982, July 14 Photo. Perf. 13½x13
362 A84 12fr shown 30 18
363 A84 13fr King, priest 30 18
364 A84 17fr Procession 38 30

Championship Emblem — A85

1982, Aug. 13 Perf. 13
365 A85 90fr multi 2.25 1.90

4th Hobie-Cat 16 World Catamaran Sailing Championship, Tahiti, Aug. 15-21.

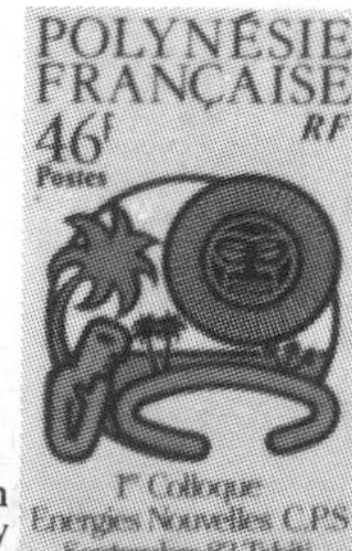

First Colloquium on New Energy Sources — A86

1982, Sept. 29 Litho.
366 A86 46fr multi 1.10 90

Motu, Tuamotu Islet — A87

1982, Oct. 12 Litho. Perf. 13
367 A87 20fr shown 55 30
368 A87 33fr Tupai Atoll 65 45
369 A87 35fr Gambier Islds. 85 60

Bird Type of 1981

1982, Nov. 17 Litho. Perf. 13
370 A79 37fr Sacred egret 75 45
371 A79 39fr Pluvialis dominica, vert. 85 60
372 A79 42fr Lonchura castaneothorax 95 60

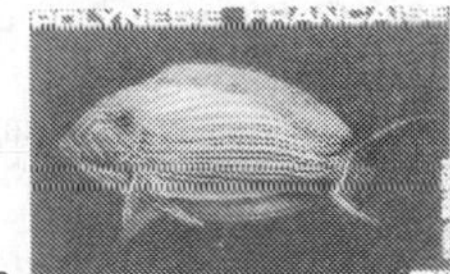

Fish — A88

1983, Feb. 9 Litho. Perf. 13x13½
373 A88 8fr Acanthurus lineatus 15 12
374 A88 10fr Caranx melampygus 22 12
375 A88 12fr Carcharhinus melanopterus 30 18

The Way of the Cross, Sculpture by Damien Haturau — A89

1983, Mar. 9 Litho. Perf. 13
376 A89 7fr shown 15 6
377 A89 21fr Virgin and Child 42 18
378 A89 23fr Christ 48 30

Traditional Hats — A90

1983, May 24 Litho. Perf. 13x12½
379 A90 11fr Acacia 22 18
380 A90 13fr Niau 30 18
381 A90 25fr Ofe 52 32
382 A90 35fr Ofe, diff. 75 45

See Nos. 393-396

Chieftain in Traditional Costume, Sainte-Christine Isld. — A91

Traditional Costumes, Marquesas Islds.

1983, July 12 Photo. *Perf. 13*
383 A91 15fr shown 30 22
384 A91 17fr Man 38 30
385 A91 28fr Woman 52 38

See Nos. 397-399

Polynesian Crowns — A92

Various flower garlands.

1983, Oct. 19 Litho. *Perf. 13*
386 A92 41fr multi 90 75
387 A92 44fr multi 1.00 75
388 A92 45fr multi 1.00 75

See Nos. 400-402

Martin Luther (1483-1546), 500th Birth Anniv. — A93

1983, Nov. 19 Engr. *Perf. 13*
389 A93 90fr blk, brn & lil gray 1.90 1.50

Tiki Carvings — A94

Various carvings.

1984, Feb. 8 Litho. *Perf. 12½x13*
390 A94 14fr multi 30 22
391 A94 16fr multi 38 25
392 A94 19fr multi 45 25

Hat Type of 1983

1984, June 20 Litho. *Perf. 13x12½*
393 A90 20fr Aeho ope 38 30
394 A90 24fr Paeore 45 30
395 A90 26fr Ofe fei 52 38
396 A90 33fr Hua 70 45

Costume Type of 1983

1984, Aug. 21 Litho. *Perf. 13*
397 A91 34fr Tahitian playing nose flute 70 45
398 A91 35fr Priest, Oei-eitia 70 45
399 A91 39fr Tahitian adult and child 75 52

Garland Type of 1983

1984, Oct. 24 Litho. *Perf. 13x12½*
400 A92 46fr Moto'i Lei 85 52
401 A92 47fr Pitate Lei 90 60
402 A92 53fr Bougainvillea Lei 1.00 75

4th Pacific Arts Festival, Noumea, New Caledonia, Dec. 8-22 — A95

1984, Nov. 20 Litho. *Perf. 13*
403 A95 150fr Statue, headdress 2.50 2.00

See No. C213.

Paysage D'Anaa, by Jean Masson — A96

Paintings: 50fr, Sortie Du Culte, by Jacques Boulaire. 75fr, La Fete, by Robert Tatin. 85fr, Tahitiennes Sur La Plage, by Pierre Heyman.

Perf. 12½x13, 13x12½
1984, Dec. 12 Litho.
404 A96 50fr multi, vert. 85 60
405 A96 65fr multi 1.00 60
406 A96 75fr multi 1.25 90
407 A96 85fr multi 1.50 1.10

Tiki Carvings — A97

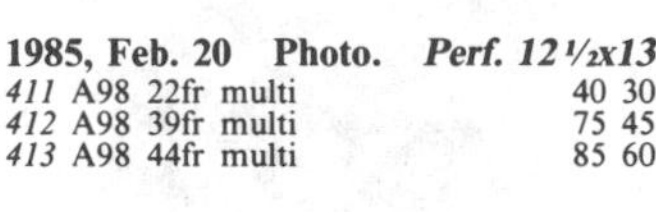

Polynesian Faces — A98

1985, Jan. 23 Litho. *Perf. 13½*
408 A97 30fr multi 52 38
409 A97 36fr multi 60 45
410 A97 40fr multi 70 52

1985, Feb. 20 Photo. *Perf. 12½x13*
411 A98 22fr multi 40 30
412 A98 39fr multi 75 45
413 A98 44fr multi 85 60

Early Tahiti — A99

Perf. 13x12½, 12½x13
1985, Apr. 24 Litho.
414 A99 42fr Entrance to Papeete 70 45
415 A99 45fr Girls, vert. 75 52
416 A99 48fr Papeete market 80 52

5th Intl. Congress on Coral Reefs, Tahiti A100

1985, May 28 Litho. *Perf. 13½*
417 A100 140fr Local reef formation 2.25 1.90

Printed se-tenant with label picturing congress emblem.

National Flag — A101

1985, June 28
418 A101 9fr Flag, natl. arms 20 15

18th-19th Century Prints, Beslu Collection A102

1985, July 17 *Perf. 13*
419 A102 38fr Tahitian dancer 70 45
420 A102 55fr Man and woman from Otahiti, 1806 90 70
421 A102 70fr Traditional chief 1.25 90

Local Foods — A103

1985-86 Litho. *Perf. 13*
422 A103 25fr Roasted pig 45 30
423 A103 35fr Pit fire 60 45
423A A103 80fr Fish in coconut milk ('86) 1.50 90
423B A103 110fr Fafaru ('86) 2.00 1.40

Issue dates: 25fr, 35fr, Nov. 14. 80fr, 110fr, May 20.

See Nos. 458-459, 474-475.

Catholic Churches — A104

1985, Dec. 11 Litho. *Perf. 13*
424 A104 90fr St. Anne's, Otepipi 1.50 1.10
425 A104 100fr St. Michael's Cathedral, Rikitea 1.65 1.25
426 A104 120fr Cathedral, exterior 2.00 1.50

Nos. 424-426 printed se-tenant with labels picturing local religious art.

Crabs A105

1986, Jan. 22 *Perf. 13½*
427 A105 18fr Fiddler 35 22
428 A105 29fr Hermit 55 35
429 A105 31fr Coconut 60 38

Faces of Polynesia A106

Perf. 12½x13, 13x12½
1986, Feb. 19
430 A106 43fr Boy, fish 75 50
431 A106 49fr Boy, coral 85 55
432 A106 51fr Boy, turtle, vert. 90 58

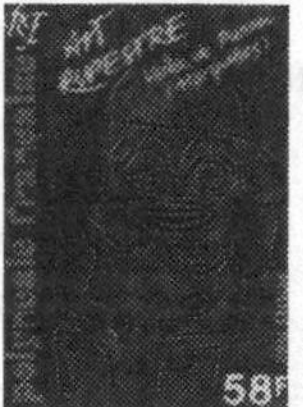

Old Tahiti — A107

1986, Mar. 18 *Perf. 13x12½*
433 A107 52fr Papeete 90 60
434 A107 56fr Harpoon fishing 95 65
435 A107 57fr Royal Palace, Papeete 95 68

Tiki Rock Carvings — A108

1986, Apr. 16
436 A108 58fr Atuona, Hiva Oa 1.10 68
437 A108 59fr Ua Huka Hill, Hane Valley 1.10 70

Landscapes Type of 1979 Redrawn.

1986-87 *Perf. 13½*
438 A65 1fr multi ('87) 6 5
439 A65 2fr multi 5 5
440 A65 3fr multi 5 5
442 A65 5fr multi 8 6
443 A65 6fr multi 10 8
Nos. 438-443 (5) 34 29

Nos. 439-440, 442-443 printed in sharper detail, box containing island name is larger and margin inscribed "CARTOR" instead of "DELRIEU."

No. 438 printed in sharper detail, box containing island name is larger and margin is without "CARTOR" or "DELRIEU" inscription.

Traditional Crafts A109

Perf. 13x12½, 12½x13
1986, July 17 Litho.
444 A109 8fr Quilting, vert. 15 12
445 A109 10fr Baskets, hats 18 15
446 A109 12fr Grass skirts 22 16

Building a Pirogue (Canoe) A110

1986, Oct. 21 Litho. Perf. 13½

447 A110 46fr Boat-builders 70 52
448 A110 50fr Close-up 75 58

Medicinal Plants — A111

1986, Nov. 19 Perf. 13

449 A111 40fr Phymatosorus 60 45
450 A111 41fr Barringtonia asiatica 62 45
451 A111 60fr Ocimum bacilicum 90 68

Polynesians A112

1987, Jan. 21 Litho. Perf. 13½

452 A112 28fr Old man 42 32
453 A112 30fr Mother and child 45 35
454 A112 37fr Old woman 55 42

Crustaceans A113

1987, Feb. 18 Perf. 12½x13

455 A113 34fr Carpilius maculatus 52 40
456 A113 35fr Parribacus antarticus 55 42
457 A113 39fr Justitia longimana 58 30

Local Foods Type of 1985

1987, Mar. 19 Litho. Perf. 13

458 A103 33fr Papaya poe 50 38
459 A103 65fr Chicken fafa 1.00 75

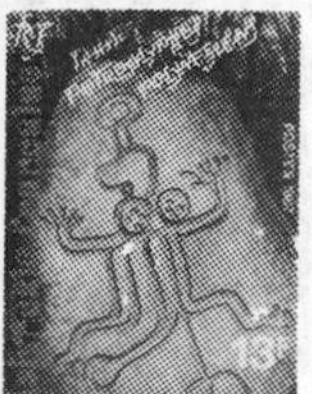
Polynesian Petroglyphs A114

1987, May 13 Perf. 12½

460 A114 13fr Tipaerui, Tahiti 20 15
461 A114 21fr Turtle, Raiatea Is. 32 24

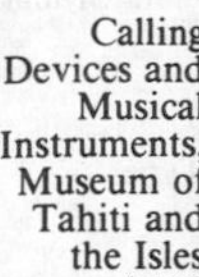
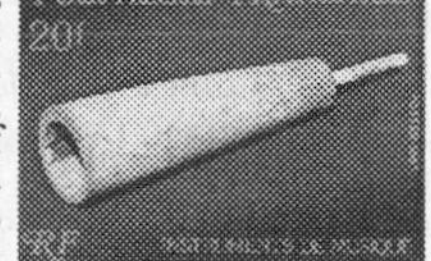
Calling Devices and Musical Instruments, Museum of Tahiti and the Isles A115

1987, July 1 Perf. 13½

462 A115 20fr Wood horn 30 24
463 A115 26fr Triton's conch 40 30
464 A115 33fr Nose flutes 50 38

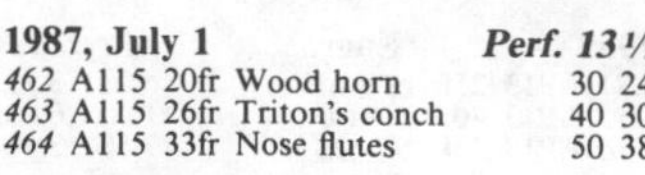

Medicinal Plants — A116

1987, Sept. 16 Perf. 12½x13

465 A116 46fr Thespesia populnea 70 52
466 A116 53fr Ophioglossum reticulatum 80 60
467 A116 54fr Dicrocephala latifolia 82 62

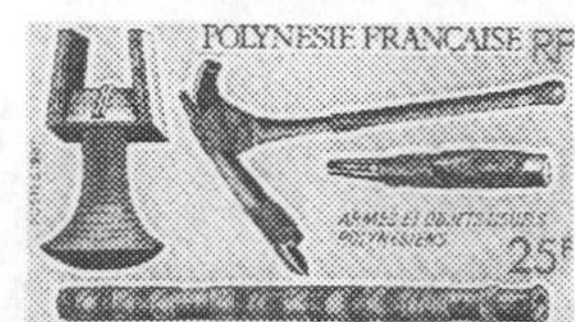
Ancient Weapons and Tools — A117

Designs: 25fr, Adze, war club, chisel, flute. 27fr, War clubs, tatooing comb, mallet. 32fr, Headdress, necklaces, nose flute.

1987, Oct. 14 Engr. Perf. 13

468 A117 25fr lt olive grn & blk 55 42
469 A117 27fr Prus grn & int blue 58 45
470 A117 32fr brt olive bister & brn blk 70 52

Catholic Missionaries — A118

Monsignors: 95fr, Rene Ildefonse Dordillon (1808-1888), biship of the Marquesas Isls. 105fr, Tepano Jaussen (1815-1891), first bishop of Polynesia. 115fr, Paul Laurent Maze (1885-1976), archbishop of Papeete.

1987, Nov. 9 Litho. Perf.

471 A118 95fr multi 2.00 1.50
472 A118 105frmulti 2.25 1.70
473 A118 115frmulti 2.50 1.90

Local Foods Type of 1985

1988, Jan. 12 Litho. Perf. 13

474 A103 40fr Crayfish (varo) 78 58
475 A103 75fr Bananas in coconut milk 1.50 1.15

Nos. 474-475 are vert.

Authors — A119

1988, Feb. 10

476 A119 62fr James Norman Hall (1887-1951) 1.20 90
477 A119 85fr Charles Bernard Nordhoff (1887-1947) 1.70 2.25

SEMI-POSTAL STAMPS

Nos. 55 and 26 Surcharged in Red

1915 Unwmk. Perf. 14x13½

B1 A1 10c + 5c red 13.00 13.00
a. "e" instead of "c" 24.00 24.00
b. Inverted surcharge 65.00 55.00
B2 A2 10c + 5c rose & org 3.75 3.75
a. "e" instead of "c" 19.00 19.00
b. "c" inverted 19.00 19.00
c. Inverted surcharge 65.00 65.00

Surcharged in Carmine

B3 A2 10c + 5c rose & org 1.25 1.25
a. "e" instead of "c" 11.00 11.00
b. Inverted surcharge 65.00 65.00

Surcharged in Carmine

1916

B4 A2 10c + 5c rose & org 1.25 1.25

Curie Issue
Common Design Type

1938 Engr. Perf. 13

B5 CD80 1.75fr + 50c brt ultra 8.75 8.75

French Revolution Issue
Common Design Type

1939 Photo.
Name and Value Typo. in Black.

B6 CD83 45(c) + 25(c) grn 6.00 6.00
B7 CD83 70(c) + 30(c) brn 6.00 6.00
B8 CD83 90(c) + 35(c) red org 6.00 6.00
B9 CD83 1.25fr + 1fr rose pink 6.00 6.00
B10 CD83 2.25fr + 2fr bl 6.00 6.00
Nos. B6-B10 (5) 30.00 30.00

Common Design Type and

Marine Officer — SP1

"L'Astrolabe" — SP2

1941 Photo. Perf. 13½

B11 SP1 1fr + 1fr red 1.00
B12 CD86 1.50fr + 3fr mar 1.00
B12A SP2 2.50fr + 1fr bl 1.00

Nos. B11-B12A were issued by the Vichy government, and were not placed on sale in the colony.

Nos. 125A-125B were surcharged "OEUVRES COLONIALES" and surtax (including change of denomination of the 2.50fr to 50c). These were issued in 1944 by the Vichy government and not placed on sale in the colony.

Red Cross Issue
Common Design Type

1944 Photo. Perf. 14½x14.

B13 CD90 5fr + 20fr pck bl 60 60

The surtax was for the French Red Cross and national relief.

Tropical Medicine Issue
Common Design Type

1950 Engr. Perf. 13.

B14 CD100 10fr + 2fr dk bl grn & dk grn 2.50 2.50

The surtax was for charitable work.

AIR POST STAMPS

Seaplane in Flight — AP1

Perf. 13½

1934, Nov. 5 Unwmk. Photo.

C1 AP1 5fr green 25 25

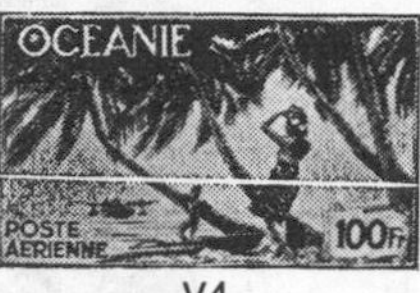
V4

Stamps of type AP1 without "RF" monogram and stamp of the above design were issued in 1944 by the Vichy Government, but were not placed on sale in the colony.

No. C1 Overprinted in Red **FRANCE LIBRE**

1941

C2 AP1 5fr green 2.00 2.00

Common Design Type

1942 Perf. 14½x14.

C3 CD87 1fr dk org 35 35
C4 CD87 1.50fr brt red 42 42
C5 CD87 5fr brn red 52 52
C6 CD87 10fr black 80 80
C7 CD87 25fr ultra 1.00 1.00
C8 CD87 50fr dk grn 1.00 1.00
C9 CD87 100fr plum 1.00 1.00
Nos. C3-C9 (7) 5.09 5.09

Victory Issue
Common Design Type

1946, May 8 Engr. Perf. 12½

C10 CD92 8fr dk grn 1.00 1.00

Issued to commemorate the European Victory of the Allied Nations in World War II.

Chad to Rhine Issue
Common Design Types

1946, June 6

C11 CD93 5fr red org 90 90
C12 CD94 10fr dk ol bis 90 90
C13 CD95 15fr dk yel grn 90 90
C14 CD96 20fr carmine 1.40 1.40
C15 CD97 25fr dk rose vio 1.40 1.40
C16 CD98 50fr black 2.25 2.25
Nos. C11-C16 (6) 7.75 7.75

Shearwater and Moorea Landscape — AP2

Fishermen — AP3

Shearwater over Maupiti Shoreline — AP4

1948, Mar. 1 Unwmk. Perf. 13

C17 AP2 50fr red brn	11.00	8.50
C18 AP3 100fr purple	8.75	7.00
C19 AP4 200fr bl grn	22.50	15.00

UPU Issue
Common Design Type

1949

C20 CD99 10fr dp bl	8.00	8.00

Gauguin's "Nafea faaipoipo" — AP5

1953, Sept. 24

C21 AP5 14fr dk brn, dk gray grn & red	60.00	60.00

Issued to commemorate the 50th anniversary of the death of Paul Gauguin.

Liberation Issue
Common Design Type

1954, June 6

C22 CD102 3fr dk grnsh bl & bl grn	2.00	2.00

Bahia Peak, Borabora — AP6

1955, Sept. 26 Unwmk. Perf. 13

C23 AP6 13fr ind & bl	5.50	4.25

Mother-of-Pearl Artist — AP7

Designs: 50fr, "Women of Tahiti," Gauguin (horiz.). 100fr, "The White Horse," Gauguin. 200fr, Night fishing at Moorea (horiz.).

1958, Nov. 3 Engr. Perf. 13

C24 AP7 13fr multi	3.25	2.50
C25 AP7 50fr multi	5.75	4.00
C26 AP7 100fr multi	9.50	6.75
C27 AP7 200fr lil & sl	25.00	18.00

Airport, Papeete — AP8

1960, Dec. 15

C28 AP8 13fr rose lil, vio, & yel grn	2.50	1.75

Telstar Issue
Common Design Type

1962, Dec. 5 Perf. 13

C29 CD111 50fr red lil, mar & vio bl	10.00	7.50

Tahitian Dancer — AP10

1964, May 14 Photo. Perf. 13

C30 AP10 15fr multi	2.50	1.75

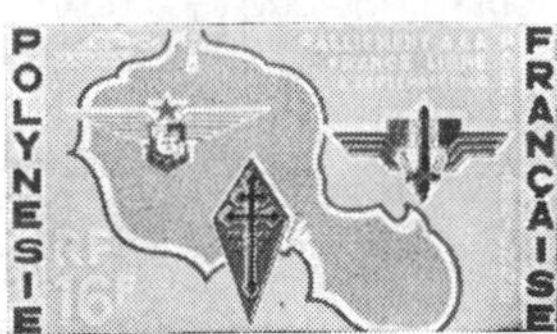

Map of Tahiti and Free French Emblems — AP11

1964, July 10 Unwmk.

C31 AP11 16fr multi	8.00	5.25

Issued to commemorate the rallying of French Polynesia to the Free French cause.

Moorea Scene — AP12

1964, Dec. 1 Litho. Perf. 13

C32 AP12 23fr multi	5.25	2.50

ITU Issue
Common Design Type

1965, May 17 Engr. Perf. 13

C33 CD120 50fr vio, red brn & bl	70.00	45.00

Issued to commemorate the centenary of the International Telecommunication Union.

Paul Gauguin — AP13

Design: 25fr, Gauguin Museum (stylized). 40fr, Primitive statues at Gauguin Museum.

1965 Engr. Perf. 13

C34 AP13 25fr ol grn	6.00	3.75
C35 AP13 40fr bl grn	11.00	6.00
C36 AP13 75fr brt red brn	17.50	12.50

Opening of Gauguin Museum, Papeete.

Skin Diver with Spear Gun — AP14

1965, Sept. 1 Engr. Perf. 13

C37 AP14 50fr red brn, dl bl & dk grn	62.50	52.50

World Championships in Underwater Fishing, Tuamotu Archipelago, Sept. 1965.

Painting from a School Dining Room — AP15

Radio Tower, Globe and Palm — AP16

1965, Nov. 29

C38 AP15 80fr brn, bl, dl bl & red	18.00	13.00

School Canteen Program.

1965, Dec. 29 Engr. Perf. 13

C39 AP16 60fr org, grn & dk brn	15.00	12.50

50th anniversary of the first radio link between Tahiti and France.

French Satellite A-1 Issue
Common Design Type

Designs: 7fr, Diamant Rocket and launching installations. 10fr, A-1 satellite.

1966, Feb. 7

C40 CD121 7fr choc, dp grn & lil	4.75	4.75
C41 CD121 10fr lil, dp grn & dk brn	6.00	6.00
a. Strip of 2 + label	10.00	10.00

Issued to commemorate the launching of France's first satellite, Nov. 26, 1965. No. C41a contains one each of Nos. C40-C41 and dark brown label with commemorative inscription. Each sheet contains 16 triptychs (2x8).

French Satellite D-1 Issue
Common Design Type

1966, May 10 Engr. Perf. 13

C42 CD122 20fr brn, brt grn & cl	6.50	4.50

Papeete Harbor — AP17

1966, June 30 Photo. Perf. 13

C43 AP17 50fr multi	13.00	10.50

"Vive Tahiti" by A. Benichou — AP18

1966, Nov. 28 Photo. Perf. 13

C44 AP18 13fr multi	7.50	4.00

Explorer's Ship and Canoe — AP19

Designs: 60fr, Polynesian costume and ship. 80fr, Louis Antoine de Bougainville (vert.).

1968 Engr. Perf. 13

C45 AP19 40fr grn, bl & ocher	5.00	3.00
C46 AP19 60fr brt bl, org & blk	9.25	5.25
C47 AP19 80fr red lil, sal & lake	9.50	6.75
a. Souv. sheet of 3	62.50	62.50

Issued to commemorate the 200th anniversary of the discovery of Tahiti by Louis Antoine de Bougainville. No. C47a contains one each of Nos. C45-C47. Ocher marginal inscription. Size: 174x99mm.

The Meal, by Paul Gauguin — AP20

1968, July 30 Photo. Perf. 12x12½

C48 AP20 200fr multi	32.50	26.00

See also Nos. C63-C67, C78-C82, C89-C93, C98.

Shot Put — AP21

PATA 1970 Poster — AP22

1968, Oct. 12 Engr. Perf. 13

C49 AP21 35fr dk car rose & brt grn	10.50	6.75

Issued to commemorate the 19th Olympic Games, Mexico City, Oct. 12-27.

Concorde Issue
Common Design Type

1969, Apr. 17

C50 CD129 40fr red brn & car rose	47.50	32.50

1969, July 9 Photo. *Perf. 12½x13*
C51 AP22 25fr bl & multi 7.50 5.25

Issued to publicize PATA 1970 (Pacific Area Travel Association Congress), Tahiti.

Underwater Fishing — AP23

Design: 52fr, Hand holding fish made up of flags (vert.).

1969, Aug. 5 Photo. *Perf. 13*
C52 AP23 48fr blk, grnsh bl & red lil 8.00 6.00
C53 AP23 52fr bl, blk & red 12.50 11.00

Issued to publicize the World Underwater Fishing Championships.

Gen. Bonaparte as Commander of the Army in Italy, by Jean Sebastien Rouillard AP24

1969, Oct. 15 Photo. *Perf. 12½x12*
C54 AP24 100fr car & multi 82.50 67.50

Bicentenary of the birth of Napoleon Bonaparte (1769-1821).

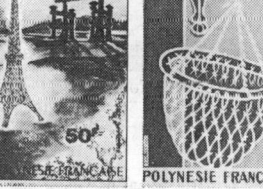

Eiffel Tower, Torii and EXPO Emblem — AP25

Pearl Diver Descending, and Basket — AP26

Design: 30fr, Mount Fuji, Tower of the Sun and EXPO emblem (horiz.).

1970, Sept. 15 Photo. *Perf. 13*
C55 AP25 30fr multi 6.00 4.50
C56 AP25 50fr multi 9.00 6.75

EXPO '70 International Exposition, Osaka, Japan, Mar. 15-Sept. 13.

1970, Sept. 30 Engr. *Perf. 13*

Designs: 5fr, Diver collecting oysters. 18fr, Implantation into oyster (horiz.). 27fr, Open oyster with pearl. 50fr, Woman with mother of pearl jewelry.

C57 AP26 2fr sl, grnsh bl & red brn 1.00 75
C58 AP26 5fr grnsh bl, ultra & org 1.75 1.10
C59 AP26 18fr sl, mag & org 3.00 2.25
C60 AP26 27fr brt pink, brn & dl lil 5.00 4.00
C61 AP26 50fr gray, red brn & org 9.00 6.75
Nos. C57-C61 (5) 19.75 14.85

Pearl industry of French Polynesia.

The Thinker, by Auguste Rodin and Education Year Emblem — AP27

1970, Oct. 15 Engr. *Perf. 13*
C62 AP27 50fr bl, ind & fawn 9.50 7.50

International Education Year.

Painting Type of 1968

Paintings by Artists Living in Polynesia: 20fr, Woman on the Beach, by Yves de Saint-Front. 40fr, Abstract, by Frank Fay. 60fr, Woman and Shells, by Jean Guillois. 80fr, Hut under Palms, by Jean Masson. 100fr, Polynesian Girl, by Jean-Charles Bouloc (vert.).

Perf. 12x12½, 12½x12
1970, Dec. 14 Photo.
C63 AP20 20fr brn & multi 5.25 4.50
C64 AP20 40fr brn & multi 9.00 6.75
C65 AP20 60fr brn & multi 13.00 9.00
C66 AP20 80fr brn & multi 19.00 13.00
C67 AP20 100fr brn & multi 27.50 22.50
Nos. C63-C67 (5) 73.75 55.75

South Pacific Games Emblem — AP28

1971, Jan. 26 *Perf. 12½*
C68 AP28 20fr ultra & multi 5.50 4.50

Publicity for 4th South Pacific Games, held in Papeete, Sept. 8-19, 1971.

Memorial Flame — AP29

1971, March 19 Photo. *Perf. 12½*
C69 AP29 5fr multi 3.25 2.25

In memory of Charles de Gaulle.

Soldier and Badge — AP30

1971, Apr. 21
C70 AP30 25fr multi 7.50 6.00

30th anniversary of departure of Tahitian volunteers to serve in World War II.

Water Sports Type of Regular Issue

Designs: 15fr, Surfing (vert.). 16fr, Skin diving (vert.). 20fr, Water-skiing with kite.

1971, May 11 Photo. *Perf. 13*
C71 A44 15fr multi 3.00 2.00
C72 A44 16fr multi 3.75 2.75
C73 A44 20fr multi 5.50 4.75

Sailing AP31

Designs: 18fr, Golf. 27fr, Archery. 53fr, Tennis.

1971, Sept. 8 *Perf. 12½*
C74 AP31 15fr multi 2.25 1.50
C75 AP31 18fr multi 3.00 2.25
C76 AP31 27fr multi 6.00 4.50
C77 AP31 53fr multi 9.50 6.75
a. Souvenir sheet of 4 47.50 47.50

4th South Pacific Games, Papeete, Sept. 8-19. No. C77a contains one each of Nos. C74-C77. Black marginal inscription. Size: 136x169mm.

Painting Type of 1968

Paintings by Artists Living in Polynesia: 20fr, Hut and Palms, by Isabelle Wolf. 40fr, Palms on Shore, by André Dobrowolski. 60fr, Polynesian Woman, by Françoise Seli (vert.). 80fr, Holy Family, by Pierre Heymann (vert.). 100fr, Crowd, by Nicolai Michoutouchkine.

1971, Dec. 15 Photo. *Perf. 13*
C78 AP20 20fr multi 4.00 3.75
C79 AP20 40fr multi 7.50 6.00
C80 AP20 60fr multi 11.00 9.00
C81 AP20 80fr multi 15.00 11.00
C82 AP20 100fr multi 25.00 22.50
Nos. C78-C82 (5) 62.50 52.25

Papeete Harbor — AP32

1972, Jan. 13
C83 AP32 28fr vio & multi 7.50 6.00

Free port of Papeete, 10th anniversary.

Figure Skating and Dragon AP33

1972, Jan. 25 Engr. *Perf. 13*
C84 AP33 20fr ultra, lake & brt grn 7.00 4.00

11th Winter Olympic Games, Sapporo, Japan, Feb. 3-13.

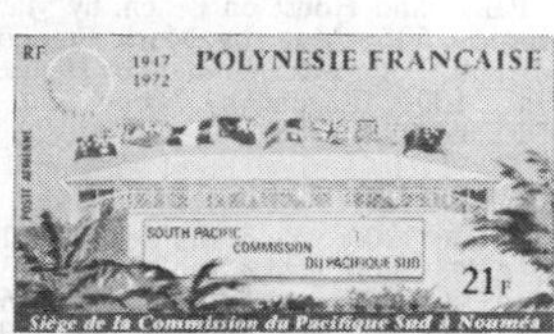

South Pacific Commission Headquarters, Noumea — AP34

1972, Feb. 5 Photo. *Perf. 13*
C85 AP34 21fr bl & multi 6.50 3.00

South Pacific Commission, 25th anniversary.

Festival Emblem — AP35

1972, May 9 Engr. *Perf. 13*
C86 AP35 36fr org, bl & grn 6.00 5.25

South Pacific Festival of Arts, Fiji, May 6-20.

Kon Tiki and Route, Callao to Tahiti — AP36

1972, Aug. 18 Photo. *Perf. 13*
C87 AP36 16fr dk & lt bl, blk & org 4.75 2.50

25th anniversary of the arrival of the raft Kon Tiki in Tahiti.

Charles de Gaulle and Memorial — AP37

1972, Dec. 9 Engr. *Perf. 13*
C88 AP37 100fr slate 25.00 20.00

Gen. Charles de Gaulle (1890-1970), president of France.

Painting Type of 1968

Paintings by Artists Living in Polynesia; 20fr, Horses, by Georges Bovy. 40fr, Sailboats, by Ruy Juventin (vert.). 60fr, Harbor, by André Brooke. 80fr, Farmers, by Daniel Adam (vert.). 100fr, Dancers, by Aloysius Pilioko (vert.).

1972, Dec. 14 Photo.
C89 AP20 20fr gold & multi 4.50 3.00
C90 AP20 40fr gold & multi 7.50 4.50
C91 AP20 60fr gold & multi 12.50 7.50
C92 AP20 80fr dk grn, buff & dk brn 19.00 10.50
C93 AP20 100fr gold & multi 24.00 19.00
Nos. C89-C93 (5) 67.50 44.50

St. Teresa and Lisieux Basilica AP38

1973, Jan. 23 Engr. *Perf. 13*
C94 AP38 85fr multi 20.00 15.00

Centenary of the birth of St. Teresa of Lisieux (1873-1897), Carmelite nun.

Nicolaus Copernicus — AP39

1973, Mar. 7	Engr.	Perf. 13
C95 AP39 100fr brn, vio bl & red lil		20.00 15.00

500th anniversary of the birth of Nicolaus Copernicus (1473-1543), Polish astronomer.

Plane over Tahiti — AP40

1973, Apr. 3	Photo.	Perf. 13
C96 AP40 80fr ultra, gold & lt grn		15.00 12.00

Air France's World Tour via Tahiti.

DC-10 at Papeete Airport — AP41

1973, May 18	Engr.	Perf. 13
C97 AP41 20fr bl, ultra & sl grn		7.50 3.00

Start of DC-10 service.

Painting Type of 1968

Design: 200fr, "Ta Matete" (seated women), by Paul Gauguin.

1973, June 7	Photo.	Perf. 13
C98 AP20 200fr multi		22.50 15.00

70th anniversary of the death of Paul Gauguin (1848-1903), painter.

Pierre Loti and Characters from his Books — AP42

1973, July 4	Engr.	Perf. 13
C99 AP42 60fr multi		15.00 11.00

50th anniversary of the death of Pierre Loti (1850-1923), French naval officer and writer.

"Sun," by Jean Francois Favre AP43

Paintings by Artists Living in Polynesia: 40fr, Woman with Flowers, by Eliane de Gennes. 60fr, Seascape, by Alain Sidet. 80fr, Crowded Bus, by Francois Ravello. 100fr, Stylized Boats, by Jackie Bourdin (horiz.).

1973, Dec. 13	Photo.	Perf. 13
C100 AP43 20fr gold & multi	3.00	2.25
C101 AP43 40fr gold & multi	6.75	3.75
C102 AP43 60fr gold & multi	9.00	6.75
C103 AP43 80fr gold & multi	15.00	12.00
C104 AP43 100fr gold & multi	22.50	16.00
Nos. C100-C104 (5)	56.25	40.75

Bird, Fish, Flower and Water — AP44

1974, June 12	Photo.	Perf. 13
C105 AP44 12fr bl & multi		5.50 2.50

Nature protection.

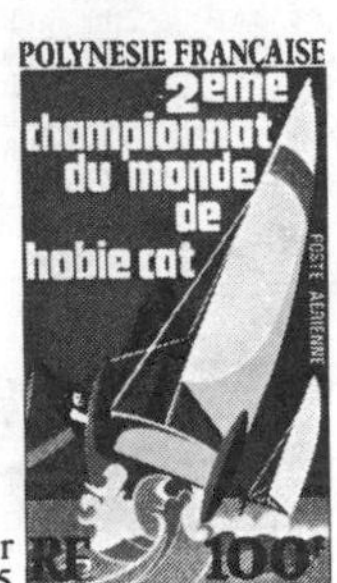

Catamaran under Sail — AP45

1974, July 22	Engr.	Perf. 13
C106 AP45 100fr multi		16.00 12.00

2nd Catamaran World Championships.

Still-life, by Rosine Temarui-Masson — AP46

Paintings by Artists Living in Polynesia: 40fr, Palms and House on Beach, by Marcel Chardon. 60fr, Man, by Marie-Françoise Avril. 80fr, Polynesian Woman, by Henriette Robin. 100fr, Lagoon by Moon-light, by David Farsi (horiz.).

1974, Dec. 12	Photo.	Perf. 13
C107 AP46 20fr gold & multi	3.75	2.25
C108 AP46 40fr gold & multi	5.50	3.75
C109 AP46 60fr gold & multi	8.75	6.00
C110 AP46 80fr gold & multi	14.00	9.00
C111 AP46 100fr gold & multi	22.50	16.00
Nos. C107-C111 (5)	54.50	37.00

See also Nos. C122-C126.

Polynesian Gods of Travel — AP47

Designs: 75fr, Tourville hydroplane, 1929. 100fr, Passengers leaving plane.

1975, Feb. 7	Engr.	Perf. 13
C112 AP47 50fr sep, pur & brn	4.50	3.75
C113 AP47 75fr grn, bl & red	6.75	5.25
C114 AP47 100fr grn, sep & car	11.00	9.00

Fifty years of Tahitian aviation.

French Ceres Stamp and Woman — AP48

1975, May 29	Engr.	Perf. 13
C115 AP48 32fr ver, brn & blk		5.50 3.75

ARPHILA 75 International Philatelic Exhibition, Paris, June 6-16.

Shot Put and Games' Emblem AP50

Designs: 30fr, Volleyball. 40fr, Women's swimming.

1975, Aug. 1	Photo.	Perf. 13
C117 AP50 25fr dk red & multi	3.00	2.25
C118 AP50 30fr emer & multi	3.75	2.25
C119 AP50 40fr vio bl & multi	5.25	3.75

5th South Pacific Games, Guam, Aug. 1-10.

Flowers, Athlete, View of Montreal — AP51

1975, Oct. 15	Engr.	Perf. 13
C120 AP51 44fr brt bl, ver & blk		6.00 3.75

Pre-Olympic Year 1975.

U.P.U. Emblem, Jet and Letters — AP52

1975, Nov. 5	Engr.	Perf. 13
C121 AP52 100fr brn, bl & ol		12.50 9.00

World Universal Postal Union Day.

Paintings Type of 1974

Paintings by Artists Living in Polynesia: 20fr, Beach Scene, by R. Marcel Marius (horiz.). 40fr, Roofs with TV antennas, by M. Anglade (horiz.). 60fr, Street scene with bus, by J. Day (horiz.). 80fr, Tropical waters (fish), by J. Steimetz. 100fr, Women, by A. van der Heyde.

1975, Dec. 17	Litho.	Perf. 13
C122 AP46 20fr gold & multi	2.50	1.50
C123 AP46 40fr gold & multi	3.25	1.90
C124 AP46 60fr gold & multi	5.75	3.25
C125 AP46 80fr gold & multi	7.75	6.00
C126 AP46 100fr gold & multi	13.00	7.50
Nos. C122-C126 (5)	32.25	20.15

Concorde — AP53

1976, Jan. 21	Engr.	Perf. 13
C127 AP53 100fr car, bl & ind		15.00 11.00

First commercial flight of supersonic jet Concorde from Paris to Rio de Janeiro, Jan. 21.

Adm. Rodney, Count de la Perouse, "Barfleur" and "Triomphant" in Battle — AP54

Design: 31fr, Count de Grasse and Lord Graves, "Ville de Paris" and "Le Terible" in Chesapeake Bay Battle.

1976, Apr. 15	Engr.	Perf. 13
C128 AP54 24fr grnsh bl, lt brn & blk	3.00	1.90
C129 AP54 31fr mag, red & lt brn	3.75	2.25

American Bicentennial.

King Pomaré I — AP55

Portraits: 21fr, King Pomaré II. 26fr, Queen Pomaré IV. 30fr, King Pomaré V.

1976, Apr. 28	Litho.	Perf. 12½
C130 AP55 18fr ol & multi	1.10	60
C131 AP55 21fr multi	1.50	90

C132 AP55 26fr gray & multi 1.90 1.10
C133 AP55 30fr plum & multi 2.25 1.50

Pomaré Dynasty. See Nos. C141-C144.

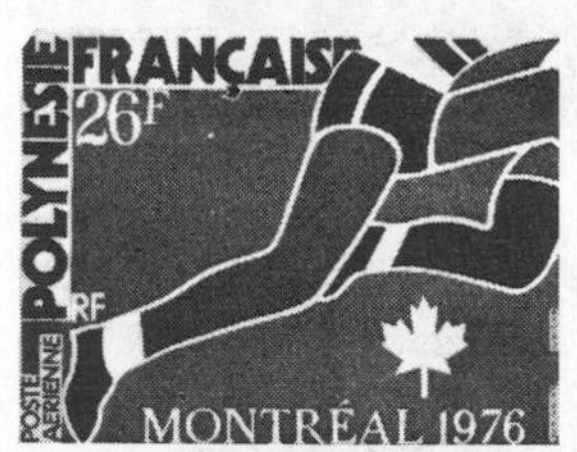

Running and Maple Leaf — AP56

Designs: 34fr, Long jump (vert.). 50fr, Olympic flame and flowers.

1976, July 19 Engr. *Perf. 13*
C134 AP56 26fr ultra & multi 2.50 1.90
C135 AP56 34fr ultra & multi 3.25 2.50
C136 AP56 50fr ultra & multi 6.00 4.50
a. Miniature sheet of 3 26.00 26.00

21st Olympic Games, Montreal, Canada, July 17-Aug. 1. No. C136a contains one each of Nos. C134-C136. Size: 180x100mm.

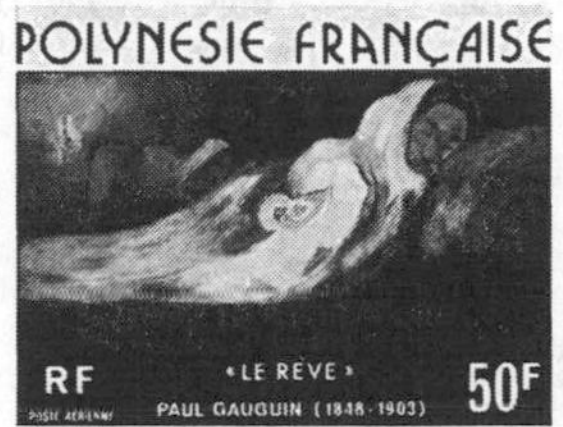

The Dream, by Paul Gauguin — AP57

1976, Oct. 17 Photo. *Perf. 13*
C137 AP57 50fr multi 6.50 4.50

Murex Steeriae AP58

Pocillopora AP59

Sea Shells: 27fr, Conus Gauguini. 35fr, Conus marchionatus.

1977, Mar. 14 Photo. *Perf. 12½x13*
C138 AP58 25fr vio bl & multi 1.50 85
C139 AP58 27fr ultra & multi 1.90 95
C140 AP58 35fr bl & multi 2.50 1.25

See Nos. C156-C158.

Royalty Type of 1976

Portraits: 19fr, King Maputeoa, Mangareva. 33fr, King Camatoa V, Raiatea. 39fr, Queen Vaekehu, Marquesas. 43fr, King Teurarii III, Rurutu.

1977, Apr. 19 Litho. *Perf. 12½*
C141 AP55 19fr dl red & multi 95 70
C142 AP55 33fr dk bl & multi 1.25 95
C143 AP55 39fr ultra & multi 1.50 1.10
C144 AP55 43fr grn & multi 1.90 1.40

Polynesian rulers.

Perf. 13x12½, 12½x13
1977, May 23 Photo.

Design: 25fr, Acropora (horiz.).

C145 AP59 25fr multi 1.40 75
C146 AP59 33fr multi 2.00 1.10

3rd Symposium on Coral Reefs, Miami, Fla. See Nos. C162-C163.

De Gaulle Memorial AP60

Tahitian Dancer AP61

Photogravure and Embossed
1977, June 18 *Perf. 13*
C147 AP60 40fr gold & multi 2.75 2.25

5th anniversary of dedication of De Gaulle memorial at Colombey-les-Deux-Eglises.

1977, July 14 Litho. *Perf. 12½*
C148 AP61 27fr multi 1.90 95

Charles A. Lindbergh and Spirit of St. Louis — AP62

1977, Aug. 18 Litho. *Perf. 12½*
C149 AP62 28fr multi 3.00 2.25

Charles A. Lindbergh's solo transatlantic flight from New York to Paris, 50th anniversary.

Mahoe — AP63

Palms on Shore — AP64

Design: 12fr, Frangipani.

1977, Sept. 15 Photo. *Perf. 12½x13*
C150 AP63 8fr multi 60 38
C151 AP63 12fr multi 80 52

1977, Nov. 8 Photo. *Perf. 12½x13*
C152 AP64 32fr multi 2.25 1.75

Ecology, protection of trees.

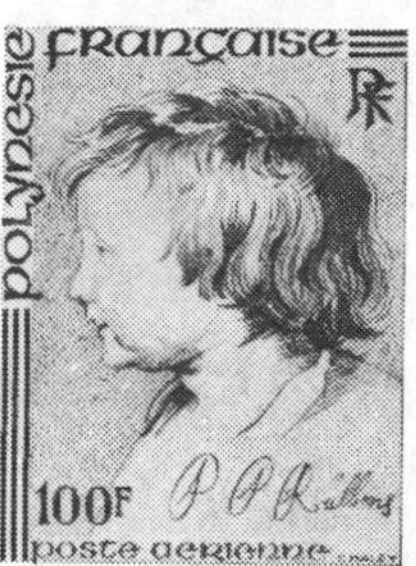

Rubens' Son Albert AP65

1977, Nov. 28 Engr. *Perf. 13*
C153 AP65 100fr grnsh blk & rose cl 6.25 4.75

Peter Paul Rubens (1577-1640), painter, 400th birth anniversary.

Capt. Cook and "Discovery" — AP66

Design: 39fr, Capt. Cook and "Resolution."

1978, Jan. 20 Engr. *Perf. 13*
C154 AP66 33fr multi 2.25 1.50
C155 AP66 39fr multi 3.00 1.90

Bicentenary of Capt. James Cook's arrival in Hawaii.

Shell Type of 1977

Sea Shells: 22fr, Erosaria obvelata. 24fr, Cypraea ventriculus. 31fr, Lambis robusta.

1978, Apr. 13 Photo. *Perf. 13½x13*
C156 AP58 22fr brt bl & multi 1.40 75
C157 AP58 24fr brt bl & multi 1.50 75
C158 AP58 31fr brt bl & multi 2.00 1.10

Tahitian Woman and Boy, by Gauguin AP67

1978, May 7 *Perf. 13*
C159 AP67 50fr multi 5.00 3.75

Paul Gauguin (1848-1903), 75th death anniversary.

Antenna and ITU Emblem AP68

1978, May 17 Litho. *Perf. 13*
C160 AP68 80fr gray & multi 5.00 3.75

10th World Telecommunications Day.

Soccer and Argentina '78 Emblem — AP69

1978, June 1
C161 AP69 28fr multi 1.90 1.40

11th World Cup Soccer Championship, Argentina, June 1-25.

Coral Type of 1977

Designs: 26fr, Fungia (horiz.). 34fr, Millepora.

Perf. 13x12½, 12½x13
1978, July 13 Photo.
C162 AP59 26fr multi 1.00 85
C163 AP59 34fr multi 1.40 95

Radar Antenna, Polynesian Woman — AP70

1978, Sept. 5 Engr. *Perf. 13*
C164 AP70 50fr bl & blk 3.00 2.25

Papenoo earth station.

Bird and Rainbow over Island — AP71

1978, Oct. 5 Photo.
C165 AP71 23fr multi 1.65 1.00

Nature protection.

Nos. C154-C155 Overprinted in Black or Violet Blue: "'1779-1979 / BICENTENAIRE / DE LA / MORT DE"

1979, Feb. 14 Engr. *Perf. 13*
C166 AP66 33fr multi 2.00 1.10
C167 AP66 39fr multi (VBl) 2.50 1.90

Bicentenary of Capt. Cook's death. On No. C167 date is last line of overprint.

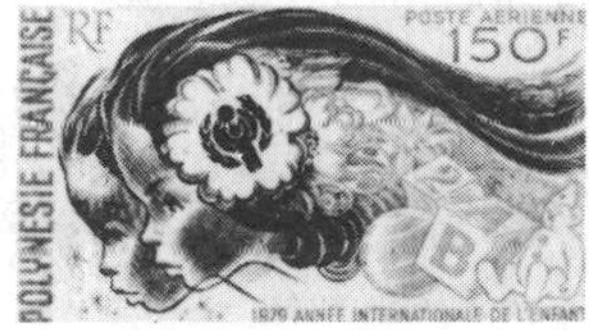

Children, Toys and IYC Emblem — AP72

1979, May 3 Engr. *Perf. 13*
C168 AP72 150fr multi 7.50 6.00

International Year of the Child.

"Do you expect a letter?" by Paul Gauguin — AP73

1979, May 20 Photo. *Perf. 13*
C169 AP73 200fr multi 8.50 6.50

Canceled-to-order stamps are often from remainders. Most collectors of canceled stamps prefer postally used specimens.

Shell and Carved Head — AP74

1979, June 30 Engr. *Perf. 13*
C170 AP74 44fr multi 2.25 1.90

Museum of Tahiti and the Islands.

Conference Emblem over Island AP75

1979, Oct. 6 Photo. *Perf. 13*
C171 AP75 23fr multi 1.50 1.00

19th South Pacific Conference, Tahiti, Oct. 6-12.

Flying Boat "Bermuda" — AP76

Planes Used in Polynesia: 40fr, DC-4 over Papeete. 60fr, Britten-Norman "Islander." 80fr, Fairchild F-27A. 120fr, DC-8 over Tahiti.

1979, Dec. 19 Litho. *Perf. 13*
C172 AP76 24fr multi 90 60
C173 AP76 40fr multi 1.50 1.10
C174 AP76 60fr multi 2.50 1.65
C175 AP76 80fr multi 3.25 2.25
C176 AP76 120fr multi 5.25 3.25
Nos. C172-C176 (5) 13.40 8.85

See Nos. C180-C183.

Window on Tahiti, by Henri Matisse AP77

1980, Feb. 18 Photo.
C177 AP77 150fr multi 6.00 4.50

Marshi Metua No Tehamana, by Gauguin AP78

1980, Aug. 18 Photo. *Perf. 13*
C178 AP78 500fr multi 15.00 12.50

Sydpex '80, Philatelic Exhibition, Sydney Town Hall — AP79

1980, Sept. 29 Photo. *Perf. 13*
C179 AP79 70fr multi 3.00 2.25

Aviation Type of 1979

1980, Dec. 15 Litho. *Perf. 13*
C180 AP76 15fr *Catalina* 45 45
C181 AP76 26fr *Twin Otter* 75 60
C182 AP76 30fr *CAMS 55* 1.00 75
C183 AP76 50fr *DC-6* 1.50 1.25

And The Gold of their Bodies, by Gauguin — AP80

1981, Mar. 15 Photo. *Perf. 13*
C184 AP80 100fr multi 3.25 2.25

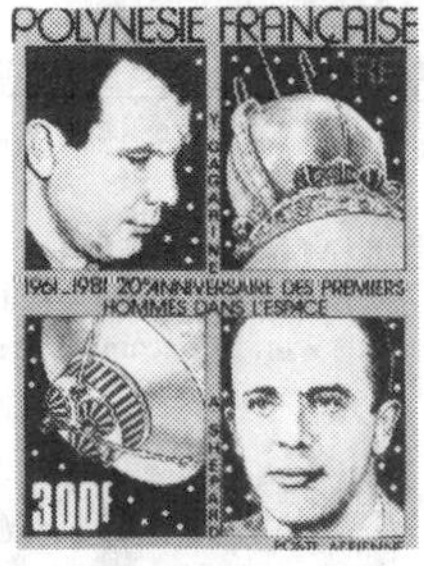

20th Anniv. of Manned Space Flight AP81

1981, June 13 Litho. *Perf. 12½*
C185 AP81 300fr multi 7.00 5.50

First Intl. Pirogue (6-man Canoe) Championship — AP82

1981, July 25 Litho. *Perf. 13x12½*
C186 AP82 200fr multi 5.50 4.50

Matavai Bay, by William Hodges — AP83

Paintings: 60fr, Poedea, by John Weber (vert.). 80fr, Omai, by Joshua Reynolds (vert.). 120fr, Point Venus, by George Tobin.

1981, Dec. 10 Photo. *Perf. 13*
C187 AP83 40fr multi 90 75
C188 AP83 60fr multi 1.40 1.10
C189 AP83 80fr multi 2.00 1.50
C190 AP83 120fr multi 2.75 2.25

See Nos. C194-C197, C202-C205.

TB Bacillus Centenary — AP84

1982, Mar. 24 Engr. *Perf. 13*
C191 AP84 200fr multi 4.50 3.25

1982 World Cup — AP85

1982, May 18 Litho. *Perf. 13*
C192 AP85 250fr multi 6.25 5.25

French Overseas Possessions' Week, Sept. 18-25 — AP86

1982, Sept. 17 Engr.
C193 AP86 110fr multi 2.50 1.90

Painting Type of 1981

Designs: 50fr, The Tahitian, by M. Radiguet (vert.). 70fr, Souvenir of Tahiti, by C. Giraud. 100fr, Beating Cloth Lengths, by Atlas JL the Younger. 160fr, Papeete Harbor, by C.F. Gordon Cumming.

1982, Dec. 15 Photo. *Perf. 13*
C194 AP83 50fr multi 1.10 75
C195 AP83 70fr multi 1.50 1.10
C196 AP83 100fr multi 2.25 1.90
C197 AP83 160fr multi 3.75 2.50

Wood Cutter, by Gauguin AP87

Photo. & Engr.
1983, May 8 *Perf. 12½x13*
C198 AP87 600fr multi 14.00 9.00

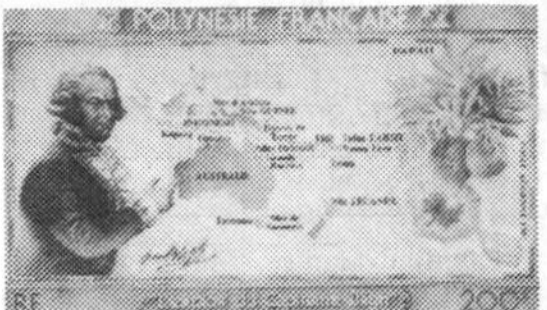

Voyage of Capt. Bligh — AP88

1983, June 9 Litho. *Perf. 13*
C199 AP88 200fr Map, fruit 4.00 3.00

BRASILIANA '83 Intl. Stamp Exhibition, Rio de Janeiro, July 29-Aug. 7 — AP89

1983, July 29 Litho. *Perf. 13x12½*
C200 AP89 100fr multi 2.25 1.75
a. Souvenir sheet 2.75 2.75

Size of No. C200a: 132x93mm.

1983, Aug. 4 Litho. *Perf. 13x12½*
C201 AP89 110fr Bangkok '83 2.25 1.75
a. Souvenir sheet 3.00 3.00

Size of No. C201a: 93x132mm.

Painting Type of 1981

20th Century Paintings: 40fr, View of Moorea, by William Alister MacDonald (1861-1956). 60fr, The Fruit Carrier, by Adrian Herman Gouwe (1875-1965, vert.). 80fr, Arrival of the Destroyer Escort, by Nicolas Mordvinoff (1911-1977, vert.). 100fr, Women on a Veranda, by Charles Alfred Le Moine (1872-1918).

1983, Dec. 22 Photo. *Perf. 13*
C202 AP83 40fr multi 75 60
C203 AP83 60fr multi 1.10 90
C204 AP83 80fr multi 1.50 1.10
C205 AP83 100fr multi 2.25 1.50

ESPANA '84 — AP90

Design: Maori canoers.

1984, Apr. 27 Engr. *Perf. 13*
C206 AP90 80fr brn red & dk bl 1.75 1.40

Souvenir Sheet

C207 AP90 200fr dk bl & dk red 5.25 5.25

Margin of No. C207 continues design. Size: 144x101mm.

Woman with Mango, by Gauguin AP91

Photo. & Engr.

1984, May 27 ***Perf. 12½x13***

C208 AP91 400fr multi 7.50 6.00

Ausipex '84 — AP92

Details from Human Sacrifice of the Maori in Tahiti, 18th cent. engraving.

1984, Sept. 5 **Litho.** ***Perf. 13x12½***

C209 AP92 120fr Worshippers 2.75 1.75
C210 AP92 120fr Preparation 2.75 1.75

Souvenir Sheet

C211 AP92 200fr Entire 9.00 9.00

Nos. C209-C210 se-tenant with label showing exhibition emblem. Size of No. C211: 128x94mm.

Painting by Gaugin (1848-1903) — AP93

Design: Where have we come from? What are we? Where are we going?

1985, Mar. 17 **Litho.** ***Perf. 13½x13***

C212 AP93 550fr multi 9.00 7.50

No. C212 printed se-tenant with label showing self-portrait.

4th Pacific Arts Festival Type of 1984

1985, July 3 **Litho.** ***Perf. 13***

C213 A95 200fr Islander, tiki, artifacts 3.25 2.25

Intl. Youth Year — AP95

1985, Sept. 18 **Litho.**

C214 AP95 250fr Island youths, frigate bird 4.00 3.00

ITALIA '85 — AP96

Designs: Ship sailing into Papeete Harbor, 19th century print.

1985, Oct. 22 **Engr.**

C215 AP96 130fr dk grn 2.50 1.75

Souvenir Sheet

C216 AP96 240fr dk bl 4.50 2.00

No. C216 has multicolored margin continuing the design and picturing the exhibition emblem.
No. C215 exists with exhibition label.

1st Intl. Marlin Fishing Contest, Feb. 27-Mar. 5 — AP97

1986, Feb. 27 **Litho.** ***Perf. 12½***

C217 AP97 300fr multi 5.25 3.25

Arrival of a Boat, c. 1880 — AP98

1986, June 24 **Engr.** ***Perf. 13***

C218 AP98 400fr int bl 6.75 4.50

STOCKHOLMIA '86 — AP99

Design: Dr. Karl Solander and Anders Sparrmann, Swedish scientists who accompanied Capt. Cook, and map of Tahiti.

1986, Aug. 28 **Engr.** ***Perf. 13***

C219 AP99 150fr brt bl, dk bl & emer grn 2.50 2.25

Souvenir Sheet

C220 AP99 210fr brt ultra, Prus bl & emer grn 4.50 4.50

STOCKHOLMIA '86, Aug. 28-Sept. 7. No. 448 has bright ultramarine and emerald green margin picturing sea chart. Size: 143x106mm.

Protestant Churches — AP100

1986, Dec. 17 **Litho.** ***Perf. 13***

C221 AP100 80fr Tiva, 1955 1.20 90
C222 AP100 200fr Avera, 1880 3.00 2.25
C223 AP100 300fr Papetoai, 1822 4.50 3.40

Broche Barracks, 120th Anniv. — AP101

1987, Apr. 21 **Litho.** ***Perf. 12½x12***

C224 AP101 350fr multi 5.25 4.00

CAPEX '87 — AP102

Design: George Vancouver (1757-1798), English navigator and cartographer, chart and excerpt from ship's log.

1987, June 15 **Engr.** ***Perf. 13***

C225 AP102 130fr 2.00 1.50

Imperf

Size: 143x100mm.

C226 AP102 260fr 4.00 3.00

No. C225 printed se-tenant with label picturing exhibition emblem.

Soyez Mysterieuses, from a 5-Panel Sculpture by Paul Gauguin, Gauguin Museum — AP103

1987, Nov. 15 ***Perf. 13***

Size: 77x23mm

C227 AP103 600fr multi 13.25 10.00

Prices of premium quality never hinged stamps will be in excess of catalogue price.

AIR POST SEMI-POSTAL STAMP

French Revolution Issue

Common Design Type

Unwmk.

1939, July 5 **Photo.** ***Perf. 13***

Name and Value Typo. in Orange

CB1 CD83 5fr + 4fr brn blk 14.00 14.00

V5

Stamps of the above design and of Cameroun type V10 inscribed "Etabts Frcais de l'Oceanie" were issued in 1942 by the Vichy Government, but were not placed on sale in the colony.

POSTAGE DUE STAMPS

Postage Due Stamps of French Colonies, 1894-1906, Overprinted

Établissements Français de l'Océanie

1926-27 **Unwmk.** ***Perf. 14x13½***

J1	D1	5c lt bl	25	25
J2	D1	10c brown	40	40
J3	D1	20c ol grn	60	60
J4	D1	30c dl red	60	60
J5	D1	40c rose	1.25	1.25
J6	D1	60c bl grn	90	90
J7	D1	1fr red brn, *straw*	1.10	1.10
J8	D1	3fr mag ('27)	5.25	5.25

With Additional Surcharge of New Value

J9 D1 2fr on 1fr org red 1.75 1.75
Nos. J1-J9 (9) 12.10 12.10

Fautaua Falls, Tahiti — D2

Tahitian Youth — D3

1929 **Typo.** ***Perf. 13½x14***

J10	D2	5c lt bl & dk brn	42	42
J11	D2	10c ver & grn	42	42
J12	D2	30c dk brn & dk red	90	90
J13	D2	50c yel grn & dk brn	42	42
J14	D2	60c dl vio & yel grn	2.00	2.00
J15	D3	1fr Prus bl & red vio	90	90
J16	D3	2fr brn red & dk brn	60	60
J17	D3	3fr bl vio & bl grn	90	90
		Nos. J10-J17 (8)	6.56	6.56

D4

Polynesian Club — D5

1948 **Engr.** ***Perf. 14x13.***

J18 D4 10c brt bl grn 6 6

J19 D4 30c blk brn 6 6
J20 D4 50c dk car rose 6 6
J21 D4 1fr ultra 25 25
J22 D4 2fr dk bl grn 52 52
J23 D4 3fr red 70 70
J24 D4 4fr violet 75 75
J25 D4 5fr lil rose 90 90
J26 D4 10fr slate 1.75 1.75
J27 D4 20fr red brn 2.50 2.50
Nos. J18-J27 (10) 7.55 7.55

1958 **Unwmk.** ***Perf. 14x13***
J28 D5 1fr dk brn & grn 30 30
J29 D5 3fr bluish blk & hn brn 45 45
J30 D5 5fr brn & ultra 75 75

Tahitian Bowl — D6

1984-87 **Litho.** ***Perf. 13***
J31 D6 1fr Mother-of-pearl fish hook, vert. 5 5
J32 D6 3fr shown 6 5
J33 D6 5fr Marquesan fan 18 15
J34 D6 10fr Lamp stand, vert. 28 22
J35 D6 20fr Wood headrest ('87) 30 22
J36 D6 50fr Wood scoop ('87) 75 58
Nos. J31-J36 (6) 1.62 1.27

Issue dates: Nos. J31-J34, Mar. 16. Nos. J35-J36, Aug. 18.

OFFICIAL STAMPS

Breadfruit O1

Polynesian Fruits: 2fr, 3fr, 5fr, like 1fr. 7fr, 8fr, 10fr, 15fr, "Vi Tahiti." 19fr, 20fr, 25fr, 35fr, Avocados. 50fr, 100fr, 200fr, Mangos.

1977, June 9 **Litho.** ***Perf. 12½***
O1 O1 1fr ultra & multi 5 5
O2 O1 2fr ultra & multi 6 6
O3 O1 3fr ultra & multi 8 8
O4 O1 5fr ultra & multi 12 12
O5 O1 7fr red & multi 18 18
O6 O1 8fr red & multi 18 18
O7 O1 10fr red & multi 22 22
O8 O1 15fr red & multi 30 30
O9 O1 19fr blk & multi 45 45
O10 O1 20fr blk & multi 45 45
O11 O1 25fr blk & multi 52 52
O12 O1 35fr blk & multi 70 70
O13 O1 50fr blk & multi 90 90
O14 O1 100fr red & multi 2.75 2.75
O15 O1 200fr ultra & multi 6.25 6.25
Nos. O1-O15 (15) 13.21 13.21

FRENCH SOUTHERN AND ANTARCTIC TERRITORIES

AREA — 9,000 sq. mi.
POP. — 168 (1983)

Formerly dependencies of Madagascar, these areas, comprising the Kerguelen Archipelago; St. Paul, Amsterdam and Crozet Islands and Adelle Land in Antarctica achieved territorial status on August 6, 1955.

100 Centimes = 1 Franc

Madagascar No. 289 Overprinted in Red:

TERRES AUSTRALES ET
ANTARCTIQUES FRANÇAISES

Unwmk.

1955, Oct. 28 **Engr.** ***Perf. 13***
1 A25 15f dk grn & dp ultra 14.00 17.50

Rockhopper Penguins, Crozet Archipelago — A1

New Amsterdam A2

Design: 10fr, 15fr, Elephant seal.

1956, Apr. 25 **Engr.** ***Perf. 13***
2 A1 50c dk bl, sep & yel 45 52
3 A1 1fr ultra, org & gray 45 52
4 A2 5fr bl & dp ultra 1.00 1.25
5 A2 8fr gray vio & dk brn 8.50 9.00
6 A2 10fr indigo 2.25 2.50
7 A2 15fr ind & brn vio 2.50 2.75
Nos. 2-7 (6) 15.15 16.54

Polar Observation A3

1957, Oct. 11
8 A3 5fr blk & vio 3.00 3.00
9 A3 10fr rose red 3.50 3.50
10 A3 15fr dk bl 3.50 3.50

International Geophysical Year, 1957-58.

Imperforates
Most stamps of this French possession exist imperforate in issued and trial colors, and also in small presentation sheets in issued colors.

Flower Issue
Common Design Type

Design: Pringlea (horiz.).

1959 **Photo.** ***Perf. 12½x12***
11 CD104 10fr sal, grn & yel 3.00 3.50

Common Design Types pictured in section at front of book.

Light-mantled Sooty Albatross A4

Coat of Arms A5

Designs: 40c, Skua (horiz.). 12fr, King shag.

1959, Sept. 14 **Engr.** ***Perf. 13***
12 A4 30c bl, grn & red brn 40 40
13 A4 40c blk, dl red brn & bl 40 40
14 A4 12fr lt bl & blk 6.75 6.75

Typo. ***Perf. 13x14***
15 A5 20fr ultra, lt bl & yel 15.00 15.00

Sheathbills — A6

Designs: 4fr, Sea leopard (horiz.). 25fr, Weddell seal at Kerguelen (horiz.). 85fr, King penguin.

1960, Dec. 15 **Engr.** ***Perf. 13***
16 A6 2fr grnsh bl, gray & choc 1.25 1.25
17 A6 4fr bl, dk brn & dk grn 4.50 4.50
18 A6 25fr sl grn, bis brn & blk 40.00 30.00
19 A6 85fr grnsh bl, org & blk 24.00 24.00

Yves-Joseph de Kerguelen-Tremarec — A7

1960, Nov. 22
20 A7 25fr red org, dk bl & brn 20.00 19.00

Issued to honor Yves-Joseph de Kerguelen-Tremarec, discoverer of the Kerguelen Archipelago.

Charcot, Compass Rose and "Pourquoi-pas?" — A8

1961, Dec. 26 **Unwmk.** ***Perf. 13***
21 A8 25fr brn, grn & red 20.00 19.00

25th anniv. of the death of Commander Jean Charcot (1867-1936), Antarctic explorer.

Elephant Seals Fighting A9

1963, Feb. 11 **Engr.** ***Perf. 13***
22 A9 8fr dk bl, blk & cl 7.50 7.50

See No. C4.

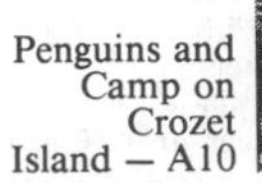

Penguins and Camp on Crozet Island — A10

Design: 20fr, Research station and IQSY emblem.

1963, Dec. 16 **Unwmk.** ***Perf. 13***
23 A10 5fr blk, red brn & Prus bl 27.50 18.00
24 A10 20fr vio, sl & red brn 67.50 50.00

Issued to publicize the International Quiet Sun Year, 1964-65. See No. C6.

Great Blue Whale A11

Black-browed Albatross A12

Aurora Australis, Map of Antarctica and Rocket A13

Designs: 10fr, Cape pigeons. 12fr, Phylica trees, Amsterdam Island. 15fr, Killer whale (orca).

1966-69 **Engr.** ***Perf. 13***
25 A11 5fr brt bl & ind 7.50 7.50
26 A12 10fr sl, ind & ol brn ('69) 30.00 27.50
27 A11 12fr brt bl, sl grn & lem ('69) 15.00 12.00
27A A11 15fr ol, dk bl & ind ('69) 7.50 7.50
28 A12 20fr sl, ol & org ('68) 400.00 325.00
Nos. 25-28 (5) 460.00 379.50

Issue dates: 5fr, Dec. 12, 1966; 20fr, Jan. 31, 1968; 10fr, 12fr, Jan. 6, 1969; 15fr, Dec. 21, 1969.

1967, March 4 **Engr.** ***Perf. 13***
29 A13 20fr mag, bl & blk 27.50 27.50

Issued to commemorate the launching of the first space rocket from Adelie Land, January, 1967.

Dumont d'Urville A14

1968, Jan. 20
30 A14 30fr lt ultra, dk bl & dk brn 110.00 110.00

Jules Sebastien Cesar Dumont d'Urville (1790-1842), French naval commander and South Seas explorer.

WHO Anniversary Issue
Common Design Type

1968, May 4 **Engr.** ***Perf. 13***
31 CD126 30fr red, yel & bl 60.00 52.50

Issued for the 20th anniversary of the World Health Organization.

Human Rights Year Issue
Common Design Type

1968, Aug. 10 **Engr.** ***Perf. 13***
32 CD127 30fr grnsh bl, red & brn 60.00 52.50

Polar Camp with Helicopter, Plane and Snocat Tractor — A15

1969, Mar. 17 **Engr.** ***Perf. 13***
33 A15 25fr Prus bl, lt grnsh bl & brn red 17.00 15.00

20 years of French Polar expeditions.

ILO Issue

Common Design Type

1970, Jan. 1 Engr. *Perf. 13*

35 CD131 20fr org, dk bl & brn 15.00 12.50

U.P.U. Headquarters Issue

Common Design Type

1970, May 20 Engr. *Perf. 13*

36 CD133 50fr bl, plum & ol bis 30.00 27.50

Ice Fish A16

Fish: Nos. 38-43, Antarctic cods, various species. 135fr, Zanchlorhynchus spinifer.

1971 Engr. *Perf. 13*

37 A16 5fr brt grn, ind & org 75 75
38 A16 10fr redsh brn & dp vio 90 90
39 A16 20fr dp cl, brt grn & org 1.40 1.40
40 A16 22fr pur, brn ol & mag 2.25 1.50
41 A16 25fr grn, ind & org 2.25 2.25
42 A16 30fr sep, gray & bl vio 3.75 3.75
43 A16 35fr sl grn, dk brn & ocher 3.00 2.25
44 A16 135fr Prus bl, dp org & ol grn 5.25 4.50
Nos. 37-44 (8) 19.55 17.30

Issue dates: Nos. 37-39, 41-42, Jan. 1; Nos. 40, 43-44, Dec. 22.

Map of Antarctica A17

Microzetia Mirabilis A18

1971, Dec. 22

45 A17 75fr red 27.50 27.50

Tenth anniversary of the Antarctic Treaty pledging peaceful uses of and scientific cooperation in Antarctica.

1972

Insects: 15fr, Christiansenia dreuxi. 22f, Phtirocoris antarcticus. 30fr, Antarctophytosus atriceps. 40fr, Paractora drenxi. 140fr, Pringleophaga Kerguelenensis.

46 A18 15fr cl, org & brn 3.00 2.25
47 A18 22fr vio bl, sl grn & yel 3.00 2.25
48 A18 25fr grn, rose lil & pur 3.00 2.50
49 A18 30fr bl & multi 3.75 3.00
50 A18 40fr dk brn, ocher & blk 3.00 2.50
51 A18 140fr bl, emer & brn 7.50 7.50
Nos. 46-51 (6) 23.25 20.00

Issue dates: Nos. 48, 50-51, Jan. 3; Nos. 46-47, 49, Dec. 16.

De Gaulle Issue

Common Design Type

Designs: 50fr, Gen. de Gaulle, 1940. 100fr, Pres. de Gaulle, 1970.

1972, Feb. 1 Engr. *Perf. 13*

52 CD134 50fr brt grn & blk 12.50 10.50
53 CD134 100fr brt grn & blk 20.00 17.00

First anniversary of death of Charles de Gaulle (1890-1970), president of France.

Kerguelen Cabbage — A19

Designs: 61fr, Azorella selago (horiz.). 87fr, Acaena ascendens (horiz.).

1972-73

54 A19 45fr dl red, ultra & sl grn 4.00 3.75
55 A19 61fr multi ('73) 2.25 2.25
56 A19 87fr multi ('73) 3.00 3.00

Issue dates: 45fr, Dec. 18, 1972; others, Dec. 13, 1973.

Mailship Sapmer and Map of Amsterdam Island — A20

1974, Dec. 31 Engr. *Perf. 13*

57 A20 75fr bl, blk & dk brn 6.00 6.00

25th anniversary of postal service.

Antarctic Tern — A21

Designs: 50c, Antarctic petrel. 90c, Sea lioness. 1fr, Weddell seal. 1.20fr, Kerguelen cormorant (vert.). 1.40fr, Gentoo penguin (vert.).

1976, Jan. Engr. *Perf. 13*

58 A21 40c multi 2.25 1.50
59 A21 50c multi 3.00 2.25
60 A21 90c multi 4.50 3.75
61 A21 1fr multi 11.00 9.50
62 A21 1.20fr multi 11.00 11.00
63 A21 1.40fr multi 15.00 15.00
Nos. 58-63 (6) 46.75 43.00

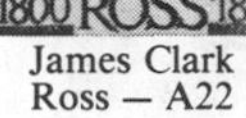

James Clark Ross — A22

James Cook — A23

Design: 30c, Climbing Mount Ross.

1976, Dec. 16 Engr. *Perf. 13*

64 A22 30c multi 3.75 3.00
65 A22 3fr multi 4.25 4.25

First climbing of Mount Ross, Kerguelen Island, by James Clark Ross, Jan. 5, 1875.

1976, Dec. 16

66 A23 70c multi 13.00 13.00

Bicentenary of Capt. Cook's voyage past Kerguelen Island. See No. C46.

Commerson's Dolphins — A24

Design: 1.10fr, Blue whale.

1977, Feb. 1 Engr. *Perf. 13*

67 A24 1.10fr bl & ind 3.00 2.25
68 A24 1.50fr multi 4.00 4.00

Macrocystis Algae — A25

Salmon Hatchery — A26

Magga Dan — A27

Designs: 70c, Durvillea algae. 90c, Albatross. 1fr, Underwater sampling and scientists (vert.). 1.40fr, Thala Dan and penguins.

1977, Dec. 20 Engr. *Perf. 13*

69 A25 40c ol brn & bis 45 38
70 A26 50c dk bl & pur 1.00 75
71 A25 70c blk, grn & brn 60 60
72 A26 90c grn, brt bl & brn 75 75
73 A27 1fr slate 90 90
74 A27 1.20fr multi 1.40 95
75 A27 1.40fr multi 1.65 1.25
Nos. 69-75 (7) 6.75 5.58

See Nos. 77-79.

Explorer with French and Expedition Flags — A28

1977, Dec. 24

76 A28 1.90fr multi 3.00 3.00

French Polar expeditions, 1947-48, 30th anniversary.

Types of 1977

Designs: 40c, Forbin, destroyer. 50c Jeanne d'Arc, helicopter carrier. 1.40fr, Kerguelen cormorant.

1979, Jan. 1 Engr. *Perf. 13*

77 A27 40c blk & bl 1.25 1.25
78 A27 50c blk & bl 1.40 1.40
79 A26 1.40fr multi 1.40 1.25

Scott's editorial staff cannot undertake to identify, authenticate or appraise stamps and postal markings.

R. Rallier du Baty — A29

1979, Jan. 1
80 A29 1.20fr cit & ind 1.25 1.25

French Navigators Monument, Hobart — A30

1979, Jan. 1
81 A30 1fr multi 85 85

French navigators and explorers.

Petrel — A31

1979 **Engr.** ***Perf. 13***
82 A31 70c *Rockhopper penguins, vert.* 1.00 75
83 A31 1fr *shown* 1.00 75

Commandant Bourdais — A32

1979
84 A32 1.10fr *Doudart de Lagree, vert.* 70 70
85 A32 1.50fr *shown* 95 95

Admiral Antoine d'Entrecasteaux A33

Sebastian de el Cano A34

1979
86 A33 1.20fr multi 1.25 1.00

1979

Discovery of Amsterdam Island, 1522: 4fr, Victoria, horiz.

87 A34 1.40fr multi 85 75
88 A34 4fr multi 1.90 1.90

Adelie Penguins — A35

Adelie Penguin — A36

Sea Leopard A37

1980, Dec. 15 **Engr.** ***Perf. 13***
89 A35 50c rose vio 1.40 1.50
90 A36 60c multi 1.00 95
91 A35 1.20fr multi 1.40 1.25
92 A37 1.30fr multi 95 85
93 A37 1.80fr multi 1.00 95
Nos. 89-93 (5) 5.75 5.50

20th Anniv. of Antarctic Treaty — A38

1981, June 23 **Engr.** ***Perf. 13***
94 A38 1.80fr multi 6.75 6.75

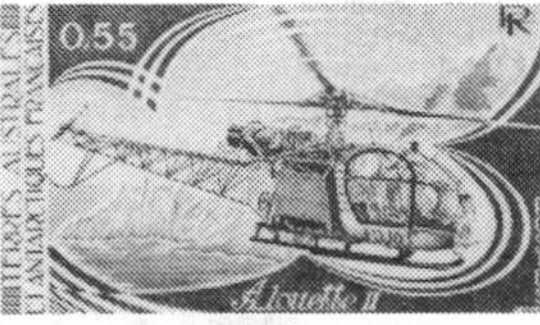
Alouette II — A39

1981-82 **Engr.** ***Perf. 13***
95 A39 55c brn & multi 50 30
96 A39 65c bl & multi 50 30

Jean Loranchet — A40

1981
97 A40 1.40fr multi 75 60

Landing Ship Le Gros Ventre, Kerguelen — A41

1983, Jan. 3 **Engr.** ***Perf. 13***
98 A41 55c multi 45 45

Our Lady of the Winds Statue and Church, Kerguelen A42

Martinde Vivies, Navigator A43

1983, Jan. 3
99 A42 1.40fr multi 1.10 90
100 A43 1.60fr multi 1.00 75

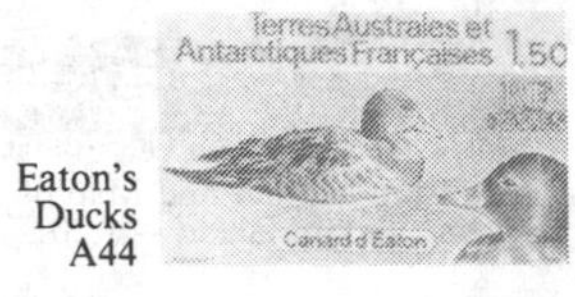
Eaton's Ducks A44

1983, Jan. 3
101 A44 1.50fr multi 75 75
102 A44 1.80fr multi 1.10 75

Trawler Austral — A45

1983, Jan. 3
103 A45 2.30fr multi 1.40 1.10

Freighter Lady Franklin — A46

1983, Aug. 4 **Engr.** ***Perf. 13***
104 A46 5fr multi 5.25 3.75

Glaciology — A47

Design: Scientists examining glacier, base.

1984, Jan. 1 **Engr.** ***Perf. 13***
105 A47 15c multi 38 38
106 A47 1.70fr multi 70 70

Foreign postal stationery (stamped envelopes, postal cards and air letter sheets) lies beyond the scope of this Catalogue, which is limited to adhesive postage stamps.

Crab-eating Seal — A48

Penguins — A49

1984, Jan. 1
107 A48 60c multi 50 50
108 A49 70c multi 50 50
109 A49 2fr multi 1.10 1.00
110 A48 5.90fr multi 2.00 2.00

Alfred Faure, Explorer — A50

1984, Jan. 1
111 A50 1.80fr multi 90 75

Biomass — A51

1985, Jan. 1 **Engr.** ***Perf. 13***
112 A51 1.80fr multi 75 75
113 A51 5.20fr multi 2.00 2.00

Emperor Penguins — A52

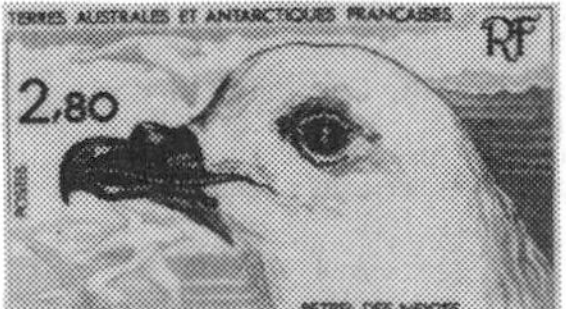
Snowy Petrel — A53

1985, Jan. 1 **Engr.** ***Perf. 13***
114 A52 1.70fr multi 60 60
115 A53 2.80fr multi 1.40 1.40

Port Martin — A54

Andre-Frank Liotard — A55

1985, Jan. 1 Engr. *Perf. 13*
116 A54 2.20fr multi 90 75

1985, Jan. 1 Engr. *Perf. 13*
117 A55 2fr multi 75 60

Antarctic Fulmar — A56

1986, Jan. 1 Engr. *Perf. 13*
118 A56 1fr shown 30 30
119 A56 1.70fr Giant petrels 52 52

See No. C91.

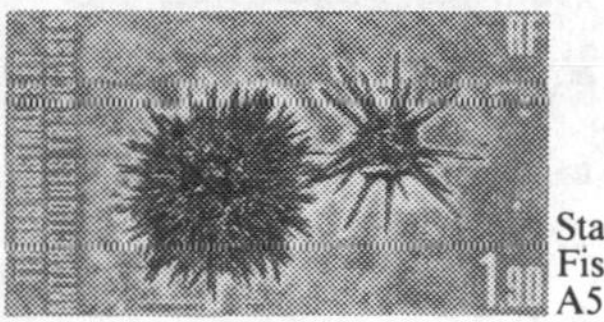

Star Fish A57

1986, Jan. 1
120 A57 1.90fr shown 60 60

Cotula Plumosa — A58

Shipping — A59

1986, Jan. 1
121 A58 2.30fr shown 75 75
122 A58 6.20fr Lycopodium. saururus 1.90 1.90

1986, Jan. 1
123 A59 2.10fr Var research ship 90 90
124 A59 3fr Polarbjorn support ship 1.40 1.40

Marine Life — A60

Flora — A61

Marret Base, Adelie Land — A62

Adm. Mouchez — A63

Reindeer — A64

Transport Ship Eure — A65

Macaroni Penguins — A66

1987, Jan. 1 Engr. *Perf. 13½x13*
125 A60 50c dk bl & org 16 16

1987, Jan. 1
126 A61 1.80fr Poa cookii 58 58
127 A61 6.50fr Lichen, Neuropogon taylori 2.10 2.10

1987, Jan. 1
128 A62 2fr yel brn, dk ultra & lake 65 65

1987, Jan. 1
129 A63 2.20fr blk, brn & dk bl 72 72

1987, Jan. 1
130 A64 2.50fr black 80 80

1987, Jan. 1
131 A65 3.20fr dk ultra, Prus grn & dk grn 1.05 1.05

1987, Jan. 1 *Perf. 13x12½*
132 A66 4.80fr multi 1.55 1.55

Elephant Grass — A67

Rev.-Father Lejay, Explorer A68

Robert Gessain (1907-1986), Explorer A69

Le Gros Ventre, 18th Cent. — A70

Mermaid and B.A.P. Jules Verne, Research Vessel — A71

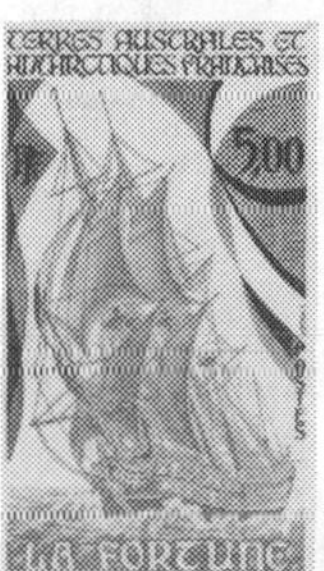

La Fortune, Early 19th Cent. — A72

Wilson's Petrel — A73

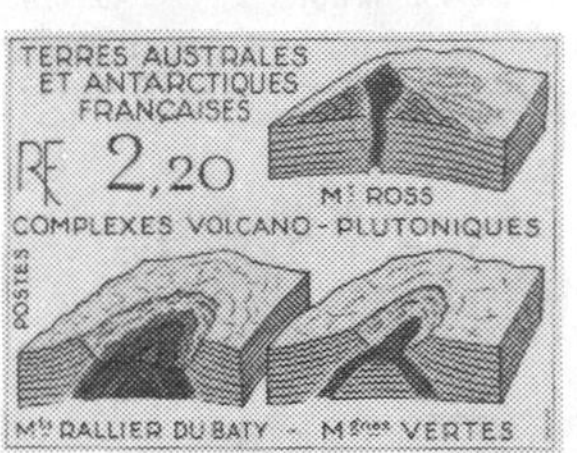

Mt. Ross Campaign (in 1987) — A74

1988, Jan. 1 Engr. *Perf. 13*
133 A67 1.70fr Prus grn, emer & olive 62 62

1988, Jan. 1
134 A68 2.20fr vio, ultra & blk 80 80

1988, Jan. 1
135 A69 3.40fr gray, dk red & blk 1.25 1.25

1988, Jan. 1
136 A70 3.50fr dp ultra, bl grn & brn 1.30 1.30

1988, Jan. 1
137 A71 4.90fr gray & dk bl 1.75 1.75

1988, Jan. 1
138 A72 5fr blk & dl bl grn 1.80 1.80

1988, Jan. 1
139 A73 6.80fr blk, sepia & dl bl grn 2.45 2.45

1988, Jan. 1 *Perf. 13x12½*
140 A74 2.20fr Volcanic rock cross-sections 80 80
141 A74 15.10fr Kerguelen Is. 5.40 5.40

Darrieus System Wind Vane Electric Generator — A75

1988, Jan. 1 Engr. *Perf. 13*
142 A75 1fr dark blue & blue 36 36

AIR POST STAMPS

Emperor Penguins and Map of Antarctica — AP1

Unwmk.
1956, April 25 Engr. *Perf. 13*
C1 AP1 50fr lt ol grn & dk grn 30.00 30.00
C2 AP1 100fr dl bl & ind 27.50 27.50

Wandering Albatross — AP2

1959, Sept. 14
C3 AP2 200fr brn red, bl & blk 27.50 25.00

Adélie Penguins — AP3

1963, Feb. 11 Unwmk. *Perf. 13*
C4 AP3 50fr blk, dk bl & dp cl 47.50 45.00

Telstar Issue
Common Design Type

1963, Feb. 11
C5 CD111 50fr dp bl, ol & grn 30.00 26.00

Radio Towers, Adelie Penguins and IQSY Emblem — AP4

1963, Dec. 16 **Engr.**
C6 AP4 100fr bl, ver & blk 125.00 120.00

International Quiet Sun Year, 1964-65.

Discovery of Adelie Land — AP5

1965, Jan. 20 **Engr.** ***Perf. 13***
C7 AP5 50fr bl & ind 125.00 125.00

125th anniversary of the discovery of Adelie Land by Dumont d'Urville.

ITU Issue
Common Design Type

1965, May 17 **Unwmk.** ***Perf. 13***
C8 CD120 30fr Prus bl, sep & dk car rose 300.00 275.00

Issued to commemorate the centenary of the International Telecommunication Union.

French Satellite A-1 Issue
Common Design Type

Designs: 25fr, Diamant rocket and launching installations. 30fr, A-1 satellite.

1966, Mar. 2 **Engr.** ***Perf. 13***
C9 CD121 25fr dk grn, choc & sl 15.00 12.50
C10 CD121 30fr choc, sl & dk grn 15.00 12.50
a. Strip of 2 + label 30.00 25.00

Issued to commemorate the launching of France's first satellite, Nov. 26, 1965. No. C10a contains one each of Nos. C9-C10 and label with dark green commemorative inscription. Each sheet contains 16 triptychs (2x8).

French Satellite D-1 Issue
Common Design Type

1966, Mar. 27
C11 CD122 50fr dk pur, lil & org 40.00 32.50

Issued to commemorate the launching of the D-1 satellite at Hammaguir, Algeria, Feb. 17, 1966.

Ionospheric Research Pylon, Adelie Land — AP6

1966, Dec. 12
C12 AP6 25fr plum, bl & dk brn 21.00 18.00

Port aux Français, Emperor Penguin and Explorer — AP7

Design: 40fr, Aerial view of Saint Paul Island.

1968-69 **Engr.** ***Perf. 13***
C13 AP7 40fr brt bl & dk gray ('69) 40.00 37.50
C14 AP7 50fr lt ultra, dk grn & blk 140.00 135.00

Kerguelen Island and Rocket — AP8

Design: 30fr, Adelie Land.

1968, Apr. 22 **Engr.** ***Perf. 13***
C15 AP8 25fr sl grn, dk brn & Prus bl 18.00 15.00
C16 AP8 30fr dk brn, sl grn & Prus bl 18.00 15.00
a. Strip of 2 + label 37.50 30.00

Issued to commemorate space explorations with Dragon rockets, 1967-68. No. C16a contains one each of Nos. C15-C16 and label with slate green and dark brown commemorative inscription.

Eiffel Tower, Antarctic Research Station, Ship from Paris Arms and Albatross AP9

1969, Jan. 13
C17 AP9 50fr brt bl 40.00 40.00

Issued to commemorate the 5th Consultative Meeting of the Antarctic Treaty Powers, Paris, Nov. 18, 1968.

Concorde Issue
Common Design Type

1969, Apr. 17
C18 CD129 85fr ind & bl 45.00 45.00

Map of Amsterdam Island AP10

Map of Kerguelen Island — AP11

Coat of Arms AP12

Designs: 50fr, Possession Island. 200fr, Point Geology Archipelago.

1969-71 **Engr.** ***Perf. 13***
C19 AP10 30fr brn ('70) 8.50 6.00
C20 AP11 50fr sl grn, bl & dk red ('70) 16.00 15.00
C21 AP11 100fr bl & blk 25.00 15.00
C22 AP10 200fr sl grn, brn & Prus bl ('71) 52.50 37.50
C23 AP12 500fr pck bl 15.00 13.00
Nos. C19-C23 (5) 117.00 86.50

The 30fr commemorates the 20th anniversary of the Amsterdam Island Meteorological Station.

Issue dates: 30fr, Mar. 27, 1970; 50fr, Dec. 22, 1970; 100fr, 500fr, Dec. 21, 1969; 200fr, Jan. 1, 1971.

Port-aux-Français, 1970 — AP13

Design: 40fr, Port-aux-Français, 1950.

1971, Mar. 9 **Engr.** ***Perf. 13***
C24 AP13 40fr bl, ocher & sl grn 9.00 7.50
C25 AP13 50fr bl, grn ol & sl grn 9.00 7.50
a. Strip of 2 + label 19.00 16.00

20th anniversary of Port-aux-Français on Kerguelen Island. No. C25a contains one each of Nos. C24-C25 and label with blue and brown olive commemorative inscription.

Marquis de Castries Taking Possession of Crozet Island, 1772 — AP14

Design: 250fr, Fleur-de-lis flag raising on Kerguelen Island.

1972 **Engr.** ***Perf. 13***
C26 AP14 100fr black 16.00 13.00
C27 AP14 250fr blk & dk brn 27.50 24.00

Bicentenary of the discovery of the Crozet and Kerguelen Islands. Issue dates: 100fr, Jan. 24; 250fr, Feb. 23.

M. S. Gallieni — AP15

1973, Jan. 25 **Engr.** ***Perf. 13***
C28 AP15 100fr blk & bl 18.00 15.00

Exploration voyages of the Gallieni.

"Le Mascarin," 1772 — AP16

Sailing Ships: 145fr, "L'Astrolabe," 1840. 150fr, "Le Rolland," 1774. 185fr, "La Victoire," 1522.

1973, Dec. 13 **Engr.** ***Perf. 13***
C29 AP16 120fr brn ol 3.75 3.00
C30 AP16 145fr brt ultra 3.75 3.25
C31 AP16 150fr slate 4.50 4.50
C32 AP16 185fr ocher 6.00 5.25

Ships used in exploring Antarctica. See Nos. C37-C38.

Alfred Faure Base — AP17

Design: Nos. C33-C35 show panoramic view of Alfred Faure Base.

1974, Jan. 7 **Engr.** ***Perf. 13***
C33 AP17 75fr Prus bl, ultra & brn 4.50 3.75
C34 AP17 110fr Prus bl, ultra & brn 6.75 4.50
C35 AP17 150fr Prus bl, ultra & brn 6.75 6.00
Triptych (Nos. C33-C35) 19.00 16.00

10th anniversary of the Alfred Faure Antarctic Base. Nos. C33-C35 printed se-tenant.

Penguin, Map of Antarctica, Letters — AP18

1974, Oct. 9 **Engr.** ***Perf. 13***
C36 AP18 150fr multi 6.75 6.00

Centenary of Universal Postal Union.

Ship Type of 1973

Designs: 100fr, "Le Français." 200fr, "Pourquoi-pas?"

1974, Dec. 16 **Engr.** ***Perf. 13***
C37 AP16 100fr brt bl 3.75 2.50
C38 AP16 200fr dk car rose 5.25 4.00

Ships used in exploring Antarctica.

Rockets over Kerguelen Islands — AP19

Design: 90fr, Northern lights over map of northern coast of Russia.

1975, Jan. 26 Engr. *Perf. 13*

C39 AP19 45fr pur & multi 3.75 3.00
C40 AP19 90fr pur & multi 3.75 3.00
a. Strip of 2 + label 8.25 6.75

Franco-Soviet magnetosphere research. No. C40a contains one each of Nos. C39-C40, and label with red inscription and indigo design. Sheets contain 5 No. C40a.

"La Curieuse" — AP20

Ships: 2.70fr, Commandant Charcot. 4fr, Marion-Dufresne.

1976, Jan. Engr. *Perf. 13*

C41 AP20 1.90fr multi 2.25 1.50
C42 AP20 2.70fr multi 3.75 3.00
C43 AP20 4fr red & multi 4.50 3.75

Dumont d'Urville Base, 1956 — AP21

Design: 4fr, Dumont d'Urville Base, 1976, Adelie Land.

1976, Jan.

C44 AP21 1.20fr multi 3.00 2.25
C45 AP21 4fr multi 6.00 4.50
a. Strip of 2 + label 10.00 8.25

20th anniversary of the Dumont d'Urville Antarctic Base. No. C45a contains one each of Nos. C44-C45 and label with map of Antarctica and penguins.

Capt. Cook's Ships Passing Kerguelen Island — AP22

1976, Dec. 31 Engr. *Perf. 13*

C46 AP22 3.50fr sl & bl 10.50 9.00

Bicentenary of Capt. Cook's voyage past Kerguelen Island.

Sea Lion and Cub AP23

1977-79 Engr. *Perf. 13*

C47 AP23 4fr dk bl & grn ('79) 2.75 2.25
C48 AP23 10fr multi 12.00 9.50

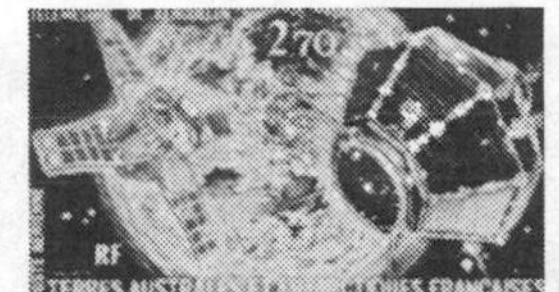

Satellite Survey, Kerguelen — AP24

Designs: 70c, Geophysical laboratory. 1.90fr, Satellite and Kerguelen tracking station. 3fr, Satellites, Adelie Land.

1977-79 Engr. *Perf. 13*

C49 AP24 50c multi ('79) 75 75
C50 AP24 70c multi ('79) 75 70
C51 AP24 1.90fr multi ('79) 1.50 1.40
C52 AP24 2.70fr multi ('78) 2.25 2.25
C53 AP24 3fr multi 3.75 3.00
Nos. C49-C53 (5) 9.00 8.10

Elephant Seals — AP25

1979, Jan. 1

C54 AP25 10fr blk & bl 5.25 5.25

Challenger — AP26

1979, Jan. 1

C55 AP26 2.70fr blk & bl 2.00 2.00

Antarctic expeditions to Crozet and Kerguelen Islands, 1972-1976.

La Recherche and L'Esperance — AP27

1979

C56 AP27 1.90fr dp bl 1.10 1.00

Arrival of d'Entrecasteaux and Kermadec at Amsterdam Island, Mar. 28, 1792.

Lion Rock — AP28

1979

C57 AP28 90c multi 75 75

Natural Arch, Kerguelen Island, 1840 — AP29

1979

C58 AP29 2.70fr multi 1.25 1.25

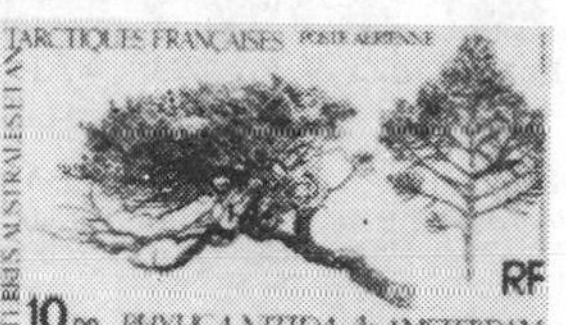

Phylica Nitida, Amsterdam Island — AP30

1979

C59 AP30 10fr multi 4.50 4.50

Charles de Gaulle, 10th Anniversary of Death AP31

1980, Nov. 9 Engr. *Perf. 13*

C60 AP31 5.40fr multi 11.00 11.00

HB-40 Castor Truck and Trailer — AP32

1980, Dec. 15

C61 AP32 2.40fr multi 1.00 1.00

The lack of a price for a listed item does not necessarily indicate rarity.

Supply Ship Saint Marcouf — AP33

1980, Dec. 15

C62 AP33 3.50fr *shown* 1.50 1.40
C63 AP33 7.30fr *Icebreaker Norsel* 3.00 2.75

Glacial Landscape, Dumont d'Urville Sea — AP34

Chionis — AP35

Adele Dumont d'Urville (1798-1842) AP36

Arcad III — AP37

25th Anniv. of Charcot Station — AP38

Antares — AP39

1981 Engr. *Perf. 13, 12½x13 (2fr)*

C64 AP34 1.30fr multi 70 52
C65 AP35 1.50fr black 75 70
C66 AP36 2fr blk & lt brn 1.10 1.10
C67 AP37 3.85fr multi 1.50 1.50
C68 AP38 5fr multi 2.25 2.00
C69 AP39 8.40fr multi 3.00 3.00
Nos. C64-C69 (6) 9.30 8.82

PHILEXFRANCE '82 Stamp Exhibition, Paris, June 11-21 — AP40

1982, June 11 **Engr.** ***Perf. 13***
C70 AP40 8fr multi 7.00 7.00

French Overseas Possessions Week, Sept. 18-25 — AP41

1982, Sept. 17 **Engr.** ***Perf. 13***
C71 AP41 5fr Commandant Charcot 2.25 2.25

Apotres Islands — AP42

1983, Jan. 3 **Engr.** ***Perf. 13***
C72 AP42 65c multi 45 30

Sputnik I — AP43

Orange Bay Base, Cape Horn, 1883 — AP44

Intl. Polar Year Centenary and 24th Anniv. of Intl. Geophysical Year: 5.20fr, Scoresby Sound Base, Greenland, 1983. Nos. C73-C75 se-tenant.

1983, Jan. 3
C73 AP43 1.50fr multi 52 52
C74 AP44 3.30fr multi 1.50 1.50
C75 AP44 5.20fr multi 2.00 2.00

AP45

1983, Jan. 3
C76 AP45 4.55fr dk bl 3.00 2.50

Abstract, by G. Mathieu — AP46

Illustration reduced

1983, Jan. 3 **Photo.** ***Perf. 13x13½***
C77 AP46 25fr multi 9.50 9.50

Erebus off Antarctic Ice Cap, 1842 — AP47

Port of Joan of Arc, 1930 — AP48

1984, Jan. 1 **Engr.** ***Perf. 13***
C78 AP47 2.60fr ultra & dk bl 1.40 90
C79 AP48 4.70fr multi 2.00 1.50

Aurora Polaris — AP49

1984, Jan. 1 **Photo.**
C80 AP49 3.50fr multi 2.00 1.50

Manned Flight Bicentenary (1983) — AP50

Various balloons and airships. Se-tenant with label showing anniv. emblem.

1984, Jan. 1 **Engr.**
C81 AP50 3.50fr multi 2.00 2.00
C82 AP50 7.80fr multi 3.00 3.00

Patrol Boat Albatros — AP51

1984, July 2 **Engr.** ***Perf. 13***
C83 AP51 11.30fr multi 4.50 4.50

NORDPOSTA Exhibition — AP52

1984, Nov. 3 **Engr.** ***Perf. 13***
C84 AP52 9fr Scientific Vessel Gauss 3.50 3.50

Issued se-tenant with label.

Corsican Sheep — AP53 Amsterdam Albatross — AP54

1985, Jan. 1 **Engr.** ***Perf. 13***
C85 AP53 70c Mouflons 30 30
C86 AP54 3.90fr Diomedia amsterdam- ensis 1.50 1.25

La Novara, Frigate AP55

1985, Jan. 1 **Engr.** ***Perf. 13***
C87 AP55 12.80fr La Novara at St. Paul 5.25 5.25

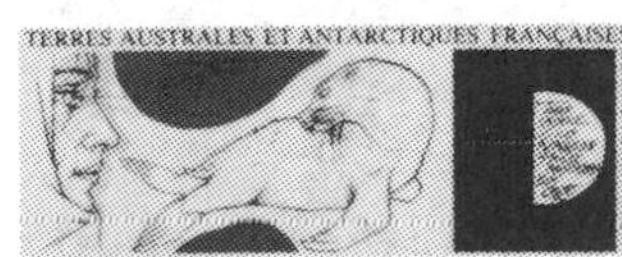
Explorer and Seal, by Tremois — AP56

1985, Jan. 1 **Photo.** ***Perf. 13x12½***
C88 AP56 30fr Explorer, seal, names of territories 10.00 10.00

Issued se-tenant with label containing artist's signature.

Sailing Ships, Ropes, Flora & Fauna — AP57

1985, Aug. 6 **Engr.** ***Perf. 13***
C89 AP57 2fr blk, brt bl & ol grn 75 75
C90 AP57 12.80fr blk, ol grn & brt bl 4.00 4.00

French Southern & Antarctic Territories, 30th anniv. Nos. C89-C90 printed se-tenant in continuous design with center label.

Bird Type of 1986

1986, Jan. 1 **Engr.** ***Perf. 13½x13***
C91 A56 4.60fr Sea Gulls 1.75 1.75

Antarctic Atmospheric Research, 10th Anniv. — AP58

1986, Jan. 1
C92 AP58 14fr blk, dk red & brt org 4.25 4.25

Jean Charcot (1867-1936), Explorer — AP59

1986, Jan. 1
C93 AP59 2.10fr Ship Pourquoi Pas 60 60
C94 AP59 14fr Ship in storm 4.25 4.25

Nos. C93-C94 printed se-tenant with center label.

SPOT Satellite over the Antarctic — AP60

1986, May 26 **Engr.** ***Perf. 13***
C95 AP60 8fr dp ultra, sep & dk ol grn 2.50 2.50

J.B. Charcot — AP61

1987, Jan. 1 **Engr.** ***Perf. 13x13½***
C96 AP61 14.60fr dk bl, rose lake & rose brn 4.75 4.75

Marine Oil Drilling Program — AP62

1987, Jan. 1 ***Perf. 13½x13***

C97 AP62 16.80fr lem, dk ultra & bluish blk 5.50 5.50

INMARSAT — AP63

1987, Mar. 2 **Engr.** ***Perf. 13***

C98 AP63 16.80fr multi 5.50 5.50

French Polar Expeditions, 40th Anniv. — AP64

1988, Jan. 1

C99 AP64 20fr lake, ol grn & plum 7.25 7.25

Views of Penguin Is. — AP65

1988, Jan. 1

C100 AP65 3.90fr dk bl & sepia 1.40 1.40
C101 AP65 15.10fr dp grn, choc brn & dk bl 5.40 5.40

FRENCH SUDAN

LOCATION — In northwest Africa, north of French Guinea and Ivory Coast.
GOVT. — Former French Colony.
AREA — 590,966 sq. mi.
POP. — 3,794,270 (1941).
CAPITAL — Bamako.

In 1899 French Sudan was abolished as a separate colony and was divided among Dahomey, French Guinea, Ivory Coast, Senegal and Senegambia and Niger. Issues for French Sudan were resumed in 1921.

From 1906 to 1921 a part of this territory was known as Upper Senegal and Niger. A part of Upper Volta was added in 1933. See Mali.

100 Centimes = 1 Franc

Navigation and Commerce
A1 A2

Stamps of French Colonies, Surcharged in Black.

1894 **Unwmk.** ***Perf. 14x13½***

1 A1 15c on 75c car, *rose* *3,250. 1,900.*
2 A1 25c on 1fr brnz grn, *straw* *4,000. 1,400.*

The imperforate stamp like No. 1 was made privately in Paris from a fragment of the lithographic stone which had been used in the Colony for surcharging No. 1.

Counterfeit surcharges exist.

1894-1900 **Typo.**
Name of colony in Blue or Carmine.

3 A2 1c *lil bl* 1.10 90
4 A2 2c brn, *buff* 1.25 1.10
5 A2 4c cl, *lav* 3.00 2.00
6 A2 5c grn, *grnsh* 3.50 3.50
7 A2 10c *lavender* 8.50 6.50
8 A2 10c red ('00) 2.00 2.50
9 A2 15c bl, quadrille paper 2.50 1.65
10 A2 15c gray, *lt gray* ('00) 3.50 3.75
11 A2 20c red, *grn* 13.00 11.00
12 A2 25c *rose* 13.00 11.00
13 A2 25c bl ('00) 3.50 3.50
14 A2 30c brn, *bis* 27.50 17.50
15 A2 40c red, *straw* 16.00 11.00
16 A2 50c car, *rose* 30.00 25.00
17 A2 50c brn, *az* ('00) 6.00 6.00
18 A2 75c dp vio, *org* 21.00 18.00
19 A2 1fr brnz grn, *straw* 5.00 5.00
Nos. 3-19 (17) 160.35 129.90

Camel and Rider — A3

Stamps of Upper Senegal and Niger Overprinted in Black.

1921-30 ***Perf. 13½x14***

21 A3 1c brn vio & vio 6 6
22 A3 2c dk gray & dl vio 6 6
23 A3 4c blk & bl 6 6
24 A3 5c ol brn & dk brn 8 8
25 A3 10c yel grn & bl grn 8 8
26 A3 10c red vio & bl ('25) 8 8
27 A3 15c red brn & org 6 6
28 A3 15c yel grn & dp grn ('25) 8 8
29 A3 15c org brn & vio ('27) 65 65
30 A3 20c brn vio & blk 8 8
31 A3 25c blk & bl grn 35 35
a. Booklet pane of 4
32 A3 30c red org & rose 35 35
33 A3 30c bl grn & blk ('26) 18 18
34 A3 30c dl grn & bl grn ('28) 1.00 1.00
35 A3 35c rose & vio 8 8
36 A3 40c gray & rose 52 35
37 A3 45c bl & ol brn 35 30
38 A3 50c ultra & bl 48 40
39 A3 50c red org & bl ('26) 55 35
40 A3 60c vio, *pnksh* ('26) 35 22
41 A3 65c bis & pale bl ('28) 95 95
42 A3 75c org & ol brn 42 40
43 A3 90c brn red & pink ('30) 3.25 3.25
44 A3 1fr dk brn & dl vio 75 65
45 A3 1.10fr gray lil & red vio ('28) 1.75 1.75
46 A3 1.50fr dp bl & bl ('30) 3.25 3.25
47 A3 2fr grn & bl 1.50 1.25
48 A3 3fr red vio ('30) 5.50 5.50
a. Double overprint 100.00
49 A3 5fr vio & blk 3.50 2.75
Nos. 21-49 (29) 26.37 24.62

Type of 1921 Surcharged **60 = 60**

1922

50 A3 60c on 75c vio, *pnksh* 35 35

Stamps and Type of 1921-30 Surcharged with New Values and Bars.

1925-27

51 A3 25c on 45c bl & ol brn ('25) 35 35
52 A3 65c on 75c org & ol brn ('25) 90 70
53 A3 85c on 2fr grn & bl ('25) 1.10 1.00
54 A3 85c on 5fr vio & blk ('25) 1.10 1.00
55 A3 90c on 75c brn red & sal pink ('27) 2.00 1.25
56 A3 1.25fr on 1fr dp bl & lt bl (R) ('26) 60 70
57 A3 1.50fr on 1fr dp bl & ultra ('27) 60 70
58 A3 3fr on 5fr dl red & brn org ('27) 2.00 1.75
59 A3 10fr on 5fr brn red & bl grn ('27) 10.00 8.00
60 A3 20fr on 5fr vio & ver ('27) 15.00 12.00
Nos. 51-60 (10) 33.65 27.45

Sudanese Woman — A4

Entrance to the Residency at Djenne — A5

Sudanese Boatman — A6

1931-40 **Typo.** ***Perf. 13x14.***

61 A4 1c dk red & blk 5 5
62 A4 2c dp bl & org 6 6
63 A4 3c dk red & blk ('40) 6 6
64 A4 4c gray lil & rose 6 6
65 A4 5c ind & grn 8 8
66 A4 10c ol grn & rose 6 6
67 A4 15c blk & brt vio 8 8
68 A4 20c hn brn & lt bl 8 8
69 A4 25c red vio & lt red 8 6
70 A5 30c grn & lt grn 30 8
71 A5 30c dk bl & red org ('40) 15 15
72 A5 35c ol grn & grn ('38) 8 6
73 A5 40c ol grn & pink 8 8
74 A5 45c dk bl & red org 42 35
75 A5 45c ol grn & grn ('40) 18 18
76 A5 50c red & blk 6 6
77 A5 55c ultra & car ('38) 30 30
78 A5 60c brt bl & brn ('40) 55 55
79 A5 65c brt vio & blk 10 8
80 A5 70c vio bl & car rose ('40) 18 18
81 A5 75c brt bl & ol brn 1.25 90
82 A5 80c car & brn ('38) 10 8
83 A5 90c dp red & red org 42 35
84 A5 90c brt vio & sl blk ('39) 30 30
85 A5 1fr ind & grn 4.75 80
86 A5 1fr rose red ('38) 2.50 55
87 A5 1fr car & brn ('40) 18 18
88 A6 1.25fr vio & dl vio ('33) 42 35
89 A6 1.25fr red ('39) 30 30
90 A6 1.40fr brt vio & blk ('40) 30 30
91 A6 1.50fr dk bl & ultra 22 10
92 A6 1.60fr brn & dp bl ('40) 30 30
93 A6 1.75fr dk brn & dp bl ('33) 30 30
94 A6 1.75fr vio bl ('38) 30 30
95 A6 2fr org brn & grn 42 8
96 A6 2.25fr vio bl & ultra ('39) 48 48
97 A6 2.50fr lt brn ('40) 60 60
98 A6 3fr Prus grn & brn 42 8
99 A6 5fr red & blk 1.00 55
100 A6 10fr dl bl & grn 1.40 90
101 A6 20fr red vio & brn 1.90 1.10
Nos. 61-101 (41) 20.87 11.56

Colonial Exposition Issue.
Common Design Types

1931 **Engr.** ***Perf. 12½***
Name of Country Printed in Black.

102 CD70 40c dp grn 1.25 1.25
103 CD71 50c violet 1.25 1.25
104 CD72 90c red org 1.25 1.25
105 CD73 1.50fr dl bl 1.25 1.25

Paris International Exposition Issue.
Common Design Types

1937 ***Perf. 13.***

106 CD74 20c dp vio 70 70
107 CD75 30c dk grn 70 70
108 CD76 40c car rose 70 70
109 CD77 50c dk brn 70 70
110 CD78 90c red 70 70
111 CD79 1.50fr ultra 70 70
Nos. 106-111 (6) 4.20 4.20

Colonial Arts Exhibition Issue.
Souvenir Sheet.
Common Design Type

1937 **Engr.** ***Imperf.***

112 CD77 3fr mag & blk 3.25 3.25

Sheet size: 118x99mm.

Caillie Issue
Common Design Type

1939 ***Perf. 12½x12.***

113 CD81 90c org brn & org 52 52
114 CD81 2fr brt vio 52 52
115 CD81 2.25fr ultra & dk bl 52 52

Centenary of the death of René Caillié (1799-1838), French explorer.

New York World's Fair Issue.
Common Design Type

1939, May 10

116 CD82 1.25fr car lake 65 65
117 CD82 2.25fr ultra 65 65

Entrance to the Residency at Djenné and Marshal Petain — A7

1941 **Engr.** ***Perf. 12x12½.***

118 A7 1fr green 35 35
119 A7 2.50fr blue 35 35

Stamps of types A4 and A5 without "RF" were issued in 1943 and 1944 by the Vichy Government, but were not placed on sale in the colony.

Stamps of French Sudan were superseded by those of French West Africa.

SEMI-POSTAL STAMPS.

Curie Issue
Common Design Type

1938 **Unwmk.** **Engr.** ***Perf. 13***

B1 CD80 1.75fr + 50c brt ultra 7.00 7.00

French Revolution Issue
Common Design Type

1939 **Photo.**
Name and Value Typo. in Black

B2 CD83 45(c) + 25(c) grn 4.50 4.50
B3 CD83 70(c) + 30(c) brn 4.50 4.50
B4 CD83 90(c) + 35(c) red org 4.50 4.50
B5 CD83 1.25fr + 1fr rose pink 4.50 4.50
B6 CD83 2.25fr + 2fr bl 4.50 4.50
Nos. B2-B6 (5) 22.50 22.50

Stamps of 1931-40, Surcharged in Black or Red

SECOURS
+ 1 fr.
NATIONAL

1941			***Perf. 13x14***	
B7	A5	50c + 1fr red & blk (R)	1.00	1.00
B8	A5	80c + 2fr car & brn (Bk)	5.00	5.00
B9	A6	1.50fr + 2fr dk bl & ultra (Bk)	5.00	5.00
B10	A6	2fr + 3fr org brn & grn (Bk)	5.00	5.00

Common Design Type and

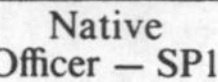

Native Officer — SP1

Aviation Officer — SP2

1941		**Photo.**	***Perf. 13½***
B11	SP1	1fr + 1fr red	65
B12	CD86	1.50fr + 3fr cl	65
B13	SP2	2.50fr + 1fr bl	65

The surtax was for the defense of the colonies.

Nos. B11-B13 were issued by the Vichy government and were not placed on sale in the colony.

Stamps of type A7, surcharged "OEUVRES COLONIALES" and new values, were issued in 1944 by the Vichy Government, but were not placed on sale in the colony.

AIR POST STAMPS.

Common Design Type

1940	**Unwmk.**	**Engr.** ***Perf. 12½x12.***		
C1	CD85	1.90fr ultra	22	22
C2	CD85	2.90fr dk red	30	30
C3	CD85	4.50fr dk gray grn	60	60
C4	CD85	4.90fr yel bis	60	60
C5	CD85	6.90fr dp org	65	65
		Nos. C1-C5 (5)	2.37	2.37

Common Design Types

1942				
C6	CD88	50c car & bl	6	40
C7	CD88	1fr brn & blk	15	
C8	CD88	2fr dk grn & red brn	22	
C9	CD88	3fr dk bl & scar	30	
C10	CD88	5fr vio & brn red	30	
		Frame Engr., Center Typo.		
C11	CD89	10fr ultra, ind & gray blk	30	
C12	CD89	20fr rose car, mag & lt vio	35	
C13	CD89	50fr yel grn, dl grn & dl bl	80	1.50
		Nos. C6-C13 (8)	2.48	

There is doubt whether Nos. C7-C12 were officially placed in use.

AIR POST SEMI-POSTAL STAMPS

Stamps of type of Dahomey V1, V2, V3 and V4 inscribed "Soudan Frcais", "Soudan" or "Soudan Francais" were issued in 1942 by the Vichy Government, but were not placed on sale in the colony.

POSTAGE DUE STAMPS.

D1

D2

Postage Due Stamps of Upper Senegal and Niger Overprinted in Black.

1921		**Unwmk. Typo.** ***Perf. 14x13½***		
J1	D1	5c green	30	30
J2	D1	10c rose	42	42
J3	D1	15c gray	42	42
J4	D1	20c brown	60	60
J5	D1	30c blue	60	60
J6	D1	50c black	90	90
J7	D1	60c orange	1.10	1.25
J8	D1	1fr violet	1.40	1.50
		Nos. J1-J8 (8)	5.74	5.99

Type of 1921 Issue Surcharged **2F.**

1927				
J9	D1	2fr on 1fr lil rose	4.00	4.00
J10	D1	3fr on 1fr org brn	4.00	4.00

1931				
J11	D2	5c green	6	6
J12	D2	10c rose	6	6
J13	D2	15c gray	5	5
J14	D2	20c dk brn	6	6
J15	D2	30c dk bl	10	10
J16	D2	50c black	15	15
J17	D2	60c dp org	30	30
J18	D2	1fr violet	60	60
J19	D2	2fr lil rose	80	80
J20	D2	3fr red brn	80	80
		Nos. J11-J20 (10)	2.98	2.98

FRENCH WEST AFRICA

LOCATION — Northwestern Africa.
GOVT. — Former French colonial administrative unit.
AREA — 1,821,768 sq. mi.
POP. — 18,777,163 (est.).
CAPITAL — Dakar.

French West Africa comprised the former colonies of Senegal, French Guinea, Ivory Coast, Dahomey, French Sudan, Mauritania, Niger and Upper Volta.

In 1958, these former colonies became republics, eventually issuing their own stamps. Until the republic issues appeared, stamps of French West Africa continued in use. The Senegal and Sudanese Republics issued stamps jointly as the Federation of Mali, starting in 1959.

Senegal No. 156 Surcharged in Red **50 fr. =**

1943		**Unwmk.** ***Perf. 12½x12.***		
1	A30	1.50fr on 65c dk vio	48	48
2	A30	5.50fr on 65c dk vio	50	55
3	A30	50fr on 65c dk vio	1.75	1.25

Mauritania No. 91 Surcharged in Red

5 fr. =

1944		***Perf. 13***		
4	A7	3.50fr on 65c dp grn	18	18
5	A7	4fr on 65c dp grn	40	22
6	A7	5fr on 65c dp grn	65	65
7	A7	10fr on 65c dp grn	70	52
		Nos. 1-7 (7)	4.66	3.85

Senegal Nos. 143, 148 and 188 Surcharged with New Values in Black or Orange.

1944		***Perf. 12½x12***		
8	A29	1.50fr on 15c blk (O)	40	40
9	A29	4.50fr on 15c blk (O)	50	50
10	A29	5.50fr on 2c brn	90	90
11	A29	10fr on 15c blk (O)	1.25	1.10
12	CD81	20fr on 90c org brn & org	85	60
13	CD81	50fr on 90c org brn & org	2.00	1.75
		Mauritania No. 109 Surcharged in Black.		
14	CD81	15fr on 90c org brn & org	70	60
		Nos. 8-14 (7)	6.60	5.85

Eboue Issue.
Common Design Type

1945		**Engr.** ***Perf. 13***		
15	CD91	2fr black	52	52
16	CD91	25fr Prus grn	1.25	1.25

Nos. 15 and 16 exist imperforate.

Colonial Soldiers — A1

1945		**Litho.** ***Perf. 12***		
17	A1	10c ind & buff	6	5
18	A1	30c ol & yel	6	5
19	A1	40c bl & buff	30	30
20	A1	50c red org & gray	6	6
21	A1	60c ol brn & bl	6	6
22	A1	70c mag & cit	35	35
23	A1	80c bl grn & pale lem	30	30
24	A1	1fr brn vio & cit	5	5
25	A1	1.20fr gray brn & cit	2.50	1.75
26	A1	1.50fr choc & pink	30	18
27	A1	2fr ocher & gray	52	30
28	A1	2.40fr red & gray	80	60
29	A1	3fr brn red & yelsh	18	5
30	A1	4fr ultra & pink	18	6
31	A1	4.50fr org brn & yelsh	18	15
32	A1	5fr dk pur & yelsh	18	6
33	A1	10fr ol grn & pink	95	15
34	A1	15fr org & yel	1.25	75
35	A1	20fr sl grn & grnsh	1.40	1.00
		Nos. 17-35 (19)	9.68	6.27

Rifle Dance, Mauritania — A2

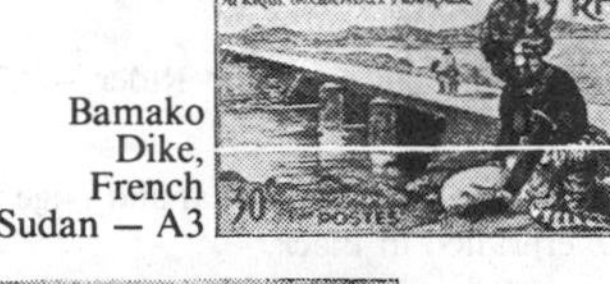

Bamako Dike, French Sudan — A3

Trading Canoe, Niger River — A4

Oasis of Bilma, Niger — A5

Shelling Coconuts, Togo — A6

Kouande Weaving, Dahomey A7

Donkey Caravan, Senegal A8

Crocodile and Hippopotamus, Ivory Coast — A9

Gathering Coconuts, French Guinea — A10

Bamako Fountain, French Sudan A11

Peul Woman of Djenne — A12

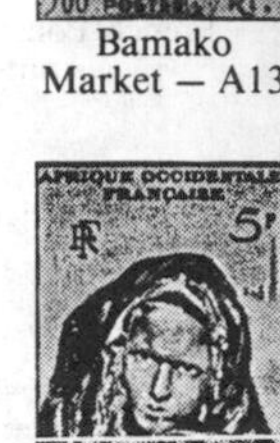

Bamako Market — A13

Dahomey Laborer A14

Woman of Mauritania A15

Fula Woman, French Guinea — A16

Djenne Mosque, French Sudan A17

Monorail Train, Senegal A18

Agni Woman, Ivory Coast — A19

Azwa Women at Niger River — A20

1947 Unwmk. Engr. *Perf. 12½*

36	A2	10c blue	5	5
37	A3	30c red brn	5	5
38	A4	40c gray grn	5	5
39	A5	50c red brn	5	5
40	A6	60c gray blk	40	35
41	A7	80c brn vio	55	52
42	A8	1fr maroon	6	6
43	A9	1.20fr dk bl grn	80	52
44	A10	1.50fr ultra	1.00	70
45	A11	2fr red org	6	6
46	A12	3fr chocolate	40	18
47	A13	3.60fr brn red	1.10	80
48	A14	4fr dp bl	22	15
49	A15	5fr dk gray grn	22	15
50	A16	6fr dk bl	30	15
51	A17	10fr brn red	80	18
52	A18	15fr sepia	95	5
53	A19	20fr chocolate	80	18
54	A20	25fr grnsh blk	1.50	22
		Nos. 36-54 (19)	9.36	4.47

Types of 1947.

1948 Re-engraved.

55	A6	60c brn ol	52	35
56	A12	3fr chocolate	42	18

Nos. 40 and 46 are inscribed "TOGO" in lower margin. Inscription omitted on Nos. 55 and 56.

Imperforates

Most stamps of French West Africa from 1949 onward exist imperforate in issued and trial colors, and also in small presentation sheets in issued colors.

Military Medal Issue.

Common Design Type

Engraved and Typographed

1952, Dec. 1 *Perf. 13*

57 CD101 15fr blk, grn, yel & blk brn 4.25 4.25

Treich Laplene and Map — A21

1952, Dec. 1 Engr.

58 A21 40fr brn lake 1.25 18

Issued to honor Marcel Treich Laplene, a leading contributor to the development of Ivory Coast.

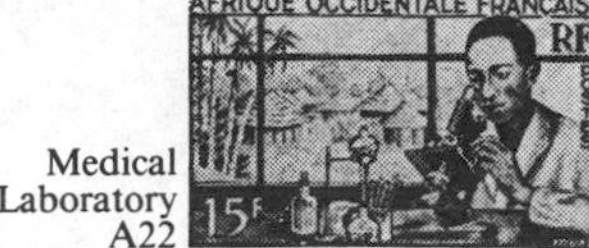

Medical Laboratory A22

1953, Nov. 18

59 A22 15fr brn, dk bl grn & blk brn 80 5

Couple Feeding Antelopes A23

1954, Sept. 20

60 A23 25fr multi 1.00 18

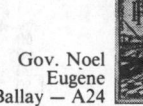

Gov. Noel Eugene Ballay — A24

1954, Nov. 29

61 A24 8fr ind & brn 1.00 42

Chimpanzee — A25

Giant Pangolin A26

1955, May 2 Unwmk. *Perf. 13*

62	A25	5fr dk gray & dk brn	1.00	52
63	A26	8fr dk brn & bl grn	1.00	52

Issued in connection with the International Exhibition for Wildlife Protection, Paris, May 1955.

Map, Symbols of Industry, Rotary Emblem A27

1955, July 4

64 A27 15fr dk bl 1.00 60

Issued to commemorate the 50th anniversary of the founding of Rotary International.

FIDES Issue

Mossi Railroad Upper Volta — A28

Designs: 1fr, Date grove, Mauritania. 2fr, Milo Bridge, French Guinea. 4fr, Cattle raising, Niger. 15fr, Farm machinery and landscape, Senegal. 17fr, Woman and Sansanding River, French Sudan. 20fr, Palm oil production, Dahomey. 30fr, Road construction, Ivory Coast.

1956 Engr. *Perf. 13x12½*

65	A28	1fr dk grn & dk bl grn	42	35
66	A28	2fr dk bl grn & bl	42	35
67	A28	3fr dk brn & red brn	70	60
68	A28	4fr dk car rose	70	60
69	A28	15fr ind & ultra	80	35
70	A28	17fr dk bl & ind	90	42
71	A28	20fr rose lake	90	42
72	A28	30fr dk pur & cl	1.00	80
		Nos. 65-72 (8)	5.84	3.89

See note after Cameroun No. 329.

Coffee Issue.

Coffee A28a

1956, Oct. 22 *Perf. 13*

73 A28a 15fr dk bl grn 42 18

Mobile Leprosy Clinic and Maltese Cross — A29

1957, Mar. 11

74 A29 15fr dl red brn, pur & red 1.10 52

Issued in honor of the Knights of Malta.

Map of Africa — A30

1958, Feb. Unwmk. *Perf. 13*

75 A30 20fr grnsh bl, blk & dl red brn 1.00 60

Issued to publicize the sixth International Congress for African Tourism at Dakar.

"Africa" and Communications Symbols — A31

1958, Mar. 15 Engr.

76 A31 15fr org, ultra & choc 1.00 52

Stamp Day. See No. 86.

Abidjan Bridge A32

1958, Mar. 15

77 A32 20fr dk sl grn & grnsh bl 1.00 52

Bananas A33

1958, May 19 *Perf. 13*

78 A33 20fr rose lil, dk grn & ol 70 25

Flower Issue

Common Design Type

Designs: 10fr, Gloriosa. 25fr, Adenopus. 30fr, Cyrtosperma. 40fr, Cistanche. 65fr, Crinum Moorei.

1958-59 Photo. *Perf. 12x12½*

79	CD104	10fr multi	52	22
80	CD104	25fr red, yel & grn ('59)	60	35
81	CD104	30fr multi	75	55
82	CD104	40fr blk brn, grn & yel ('59)	1.25	90
83	CD104	65fr multi	1.65	90
		Nos. 79-83 (5)	4.77	2.92

Moro Naba Sagha and Map — A34

1958, Nov. 1 Engr. *Perf. 13*

84 A34 20fr ol brn, car & vio 90 52

Issued to commemorate the 10th anniversary of the reestablishment of the Upper Volta territory.

Human Rights Issue

Common Design Type

1958, Dec. 10

85 CD105 20fr mar & dk bl 1.40 1.40

Type of 1958 Redrawn.

1959, Mar. 21 Engr. *Perf. 13*

86 A31 20fr red, grnsh bl & sl grn 1.75 1.25

Name of country omitted on No. 86; "RF" replaced by "CF," inscribed "Dakar-Abidjan."

Stamp Day.

SEMI-POSTAL STAMPS.

Red Cross Issue

Common Design Type

1944 Unwmk. Photo. *Perf. 14½x14*

B1 CD90 5fr + 20fr plum 3.75 3.75

The surtax was for the French Red Cross and national relief.

Type of France, 1945, Overprinted in Black **A O F**

1945 Engr. *Perf. 13.*

B2 SP150 2fr + 3fr org red 60 60

Tropical Medicine Issue

Common Design Type

1950, May 15 *Perf. 13*

B3 CD100 10fr + 2fr red brn & sep 4.00 4.00

The surtax was for charitable work.

AIR POST STAMPS.

Common Design Type

1945 Unwmk. Photo. *Perf. 14½x14*

C1	CD87	5.50fr ultra	60	52
C2	CD87	50fr dk grn	2.00	52
C3	CD87	100fr plum	2.00	52

Victory Issue

Common Design Type

1946, May 8 Engr. *Perf. 12½*

C4 CD92 8fr violet 65 60

Chad to Rhine Issue

Common Design Types

1946, June 6

C5	CD93	5fr brn car	90	90
C6	CD94	10fr dp bl	90	90
C7	CD95	15fr brt vio	1.10	1.10
C8	CD96	20fr dk sl grn	1.40	1.40
C9	CD97	25fr ol brn	2.00	2.00
C10	CD98	50fr brown	2.75	2.75
		Nos. C5-C10 (6)	9.05	9.05

Antoine de Saint-Exupery, Map and Natives — AP1

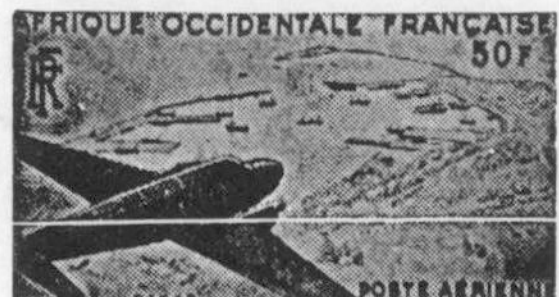

Plane over Dakar — AP2

Great White Egrets in Flight — AP3

Natives and Phantom Plane — AP4

1947, Mar. 24 **Engr.**

C11	AP1	8fr red brn	35	35
C12	AP2	50fr rose vio	1.40	35
C13	AP3	100fr ultra	4.75	3.00
C14	AP4	200fr sl gray	7.25	2.00

UPU Issue
Common Design Type

1949, July 4 ***Perf. 13***

C15	CD99	25fr multi	4.50	4.50

Vridi Canal, Abidjan — AP5

1951, Nov. 5 **Unwmk.** ***Perf. 13***

C16	AP5	500fr red org, bl grn & dp ultra	16.00	4.25

Liberation Issue
Common Design Type

1954, June 6

C17	CD102	15fr ind & ultra	3.50	2.25

Logging — AP6

Designs: 100fr, Radiotelephone exchange. 200fr, Baobab trees.

1954, Sept. 20

C18	AP6	50fr ol grn & org brn	1.65	52
C19	AP6	100fr ind, dk brn & dk grn	2.25	75
C20	AP6	200fr bl grn, grnsh blk & brn lake	7.00	2.25

Gen. Louis Faidherbe and African Sharpshooter
AP7

1957, July 20 **Unwmk.** ***Perf. 13***

C21	AP7	15fr ind & bl	1.25	1.25

Centenary of French African troops.

Gorée Island and Woman — AP8

Designs: 20fr, Map with planes and ships. 25fr, Village and modern city. 40fr, Seat of Council of French West Africa. 50fr, Worker, ship and peanut plant. 100fr, Bay of N'Gor.

1958, March 15 **Engr.**

C22	AP8	15fr blk brn, grn & vio	70	55
C23	AP8	20fr blk brn, dk bl & red brn	70	55
C24	AP8	25fr blk vio, bis & grn	70	55
C25	AP8	40fr dk bl, brn & grn	70	55
C26	AP8	50fr vio, brn & grn	1.10	80
C27	AP8	100fr brn, bl & grn	3.50	1.25
a.		Souvenir sheet	10.00	10.00
		Nos. C22-C27 (6)	7.40	4.25

Issued to commemorate the centenary of Dakar.

No. C27a measures 185x125mm. and contains one each of Nos. C22-C27, with picture of old Dakar in center and inscribed: "Centenaire de Dakar."

Woman Playing Native Harp — AP9

1958, Dec. 1 **Unwmk.** ***Perf. 13***

C28	AP9	20fr red brn, blk & gray	1.00	70

Issued in connection with the inauguration of Nouakchot as capital of Mauritania.

POSTAGE DUE STAMPS.

D1

1947 **Unwmk.** **Engr.** ***Perf. 13***

J1	D1	10c red	6	6
J2	D1	30c dp org	6	6
J3	D1	50c grnsh blk	18	18
J4	D1	1fr carmine	18	18
J5	D1	2fr emerald	18	18
J6	D1	3fr red lil	22	22
J7	D1	4fr dp ultra	40	40
J8	D1	5fr red brn	90	90
J9	D1	10fr pck bl	1.40	1.40
J10	D1	20fr sepia	3.25	3.25
		Nos. J1-J10 (10)	6.83	6.83

OFFICIAL STAMPS

Mask — O1

Designs: Various masks.

1958 **Unwmk.** **Typo.** ***Perf. 14x13***

O1	O1	1fr dk brn red	40	40
O2	O1	3fr brt grn	40	40
O3	O1	5fr crim rose	25	6
O4	O1	10fr lt ultra	35	6
O5	O1	20fr brt red	60	6
O6	O1	25fr purple	60	6
O7	O1	30fr green	90	70
O8	O1	45fr gray blk	1.00	90
O9	O1	50fr dk red	1.50	70
O10	O1	65fr brt ultra	2.25	90
O11	O1	100fr ol bis	4.00	70
O12	O1	200fr dp grn	7.75	2.50
		Nos. O1-O12 (12)	20.00	7.44

FUNCHAL

LOCATION — A city and administrative district in the Madeira island group in the Atlantic Ocean northwest of Africa

GOVT. — A part of the Republic of Portugal

POP. — 150,574 (1900)

Postage stamps of Funchal were superseded by those of Madeira. These, in turn, were displaced by the stamps of Portugal.

1000 Reis = 1 Milreis

King Carlos
A1 A2

Perf. 11½, 12½, 13½

1892-93 **Typo.** **Unwmk.**

1	A1	5r yellow	1.50	1.00
a.		Half used as 2½r on cover		25.00
b.		Perf. 11½	6.00	4.00
2	A1	10r red vio	1.50	1.10
3	A1	15r chocolate	2.75	1.50
4	A1	20r lavender	3.25	1.75
a.		Perf. 13½	6.50	4.50
5	A1	25r dk grn	2.50	1.25
6	A1	50r ultra	3.75	1.00
a.		Perf. 13½	7.50	2.00
7	A1	75r carmine	7.50	6.00
8	A1	80r yel grn	10.00	8.00
a.		Perf. 13½	13.00	11.00
9	A1	100r brn, *yel* ('93)	5.00	3.75
a.		Diagonal half used as 50r on cover		
10	A1	150r car, *rose* ('93)	32.50	22.50
11	A1	200r dk bl, *bl* ('93)	35.00	27.50
12	A1	300r dk bl, *sal* ('93)	40.00	30.00

The reprints of this issue have shiny white gum and clean-cut perforation 13½. The shades differ from those of the originals and the uncolored paper is thin. Price $4 each.

1897-1905 ***Perf. 12***

Name and Value in Black except Nos. 25 and 34.

13	A2	2½r gray	20	20
14	A2	5r orange	25	22
15	A2	10r lt grn	25	22
16	A2	15r brown	4.00	3.00
17	A2	15r gray grn ('99)	2.50	2.00
18	A2	20r gray vio	60	40
19	A2	25r sea grn	1.75	50
20	A2	25r car rose ('99)	75	25
a.		Booklet pane of 6		
21	A2	50r dk bl	3.00	1.10
a.		Perf. 12½	10.00	5.00
22	A2	50r ultra ('05)	60	40
23	A2	65r sl bl ('98)	60	40
24	A2	75r rose	90	70
25	A2	75r brn & red, *yel* ('05)	1.00	1.50
26	A2	80r violet	75	60
27	A2	100r dk bl, *bl*	75	60
a.		Diagonal half used as 50r on cover		
28	A2	115r org brn, *pink* ('98)	1.25	1.25
29	A2	130r gray brn, *buff* ('98)	1.25	1.25
30	A2	150r lt brn, *buff*	1.25	1.00
31	A2	180r sl, *pnksh* ('98)	1.25	1.25
32	A2	200r red vio, *pale lil*	2.25	2.25
33	A2	300r bl, *rose*	2.25	2.00
34	A2	500r blk & red, *bl*	2.25	1.75
a.		Perf.12½	7.00	5.50
		Nos. 13-34 (22)	29.65	22.84

ADDENDA

BENIN

Locust Control A206

1987, Dec. 7 Litho. ***Perf. 12½x13***
646 A206 100fr multi 72 72

Christmas 1987 A207

1987, Dec. 21 ***Perf. 13***
647 A207 150fr multi 1.10 1.10

BRAZIL

Spanish Galleons Anchored in Recife Port, 1537 A1135

1987, Nov. 12 Litho. ***Perf. 11½x12***
2115 A1135 5cz Harbor entrance 18 14

Recife City, 450th anniv.

Thanksgiving A1136

1987, Nov. 26 ***Perf. 12x11½***
2116 A1136 5cz multi 18 14

Christmas 1987 A1137

1987, Nov. 30 ***Perf. 11½x12***
2117 A1137 6cz Shepherd and flock 20 15
2118 A1137 6cz Christmas pageant 20 15
2119 A1137 6cz Six angels 20 15

Pedro II College, 150th Anniv. — A1138

Gold pen Emperor Pedro II used to sign edict establishing the school, and Senator Bernardo Pereira de Vasconcellos, founder.

1987, Dec. 2
2120 A1138 6cz multi 20 15

Natl. Orchid Growers' Soc., 50th Anniv. A1139

1987, Dec. 3
2121 A1139 6cz Laelia lobata veitch 20 15
2122 A1139 6cz Cattleya guttata lindley 20 15

Marian Year — A1140

Statue of Our Lady and Basilica at Fatima, Portugal.

1987, Dec. 20 ***Perf. 12x11½***
2123 A1140 50cz multi 1.50 1.15

Exhibit of the Statue of Our Lady of Fatima in Brazil.

CONGO REPUBLIC

Anti-Apartheid Campaign A267

Nelson Mandela A268

Perf. 13½x15, 14½x15
1987, Sept. 21 Litho.
787 A267 60fr multi 42 20
788 A268 240fr multi 1.75 88

Natl. UNICEF Vaccination Campaign A269

Africa Fund A270

Perf. 13½x14½, 14½x13½
1987, Sept. 28
789 A269 30fr Inoculating adults, horiz. 22 10
790 A269 45fr shown 32 16
791 A269 500fr Inoculating children, horiz. 3.50 1.75

Size of No. 789: 51x32mm. No. 791 is airmail.

1987, Sept. 28 ***Perf. 13½x15***
792 A270 25fr multi 18 10
793 A270 50fr multi 36 18
794 A270 70fr multi 50 25

Self-sufficiency in Food Production by the Year 2000 — A271

1987, Nov. 20 Litho. ***Perf. 13½***
795 A271 20fr multi 15 8
796 A271 55fr multi 40 20
797 A271 100fr multi 72 35

Simon Kimbangu (b. 1887), Founder of the Church of Christ on Earth A272

1987, Nov. 28 ***Perf. 12½***
798 A272 75fr Kimbangu, vert. 55 28
799 A272 120fr Kimbangu, parrot, vert. 85 42
800 A272 240fr Kimbanguist Church, Nkamba 1.70 85
a. Souv. sheet of 3, Nos. 798-800 3.10 1.55

No. 800a has dark blue green inscribed margin. Size: 160x100mm.

FOR THE RECORD

The items recorded here appeared on the stamp market in the 1960's and '70s, and have not been listed in the *Scott Standard Postage Stamp Catalogue*. They are arranged chronologically and briefly described. Completeness is not claimed.

Contents

AFGHANISTAN
Sets exist perf., imperf.

1963
GANEFO Games, Djakarta. *Sept. 3.* 2, 3, 4, 5, 10p, 9af; airmail, 300, 500p (8v). 2 souvenir sheets, 250, 300p.
Red Cross centenary. *Oct. 9.* 2, 3, 4, 5, 10p; airmail, 100, 200p, 4, 6af (9v). 2 souvenir sheets, 3, 4af.
Nubian Monuments Protection. *Nov. 16.* 100, 150, 200, 250, 500p; airmail, 5, 7.50, 10af (8v).

1964
Women's Day. *Jan. 5.* 2, 3, 4, 5, 10p (5v).
Afghan Boy and Girl Scouts. *Jan. 5.* 2, 3, 4, 5, 10p; airmail, 2af x 2, 2.50, 3, 4, 5, 12af (12v). 4 souvenir sheets, 5, 6x2, 10 af.
Children and Young People. *Jan. 22.* 2, 3, 4, 5, 10p; airmail, 200, 300p (7v).
Afghan Red Crescent Society. *Feb. 8.* 100, 200p, 2.50, 3.50af; airmail, 100p, 5, 7.50af (7v).
Teacher's Day. *Mar. 3.* 2, 3, 4, 5, 10p; airmail, 1.50, 2, 3, 3.50af (9v). 2 souvenir sheets, 4, 6af.
United Nations Day. *Mar. 9.* 2, 3, 4, 5, 10p; airmail, 100p, 2, 3af (8v). 2 souvenir sheets, 4, 5af, imperf.
Declaration of Human Rights, 15th anniversary. *May. 9.* Same values and sheets as United Nations Day set, each with 50p surcharge (8v).
UNICEF (United Nations Children's Fund). *Mar. 15.* 100, 150, 200, 250p; airmail, 5, 7.50, 10af (7v).
Fight Against Malaria. *Mar. 15.* 2, 3, 4, 5p, semi-postal, 4p+10p; airmail, 2, 5, 10af (8v). 2 souvenir sheets, 2af, perf; 5af, imperf.

BHUTAN
1966
King Jigme Wangchuk, Coins, 40th anniversary of accession. *July 1.* Gold foil embossed. 10, 25, 50ch, 1, 1.30, 2, 3, 4, 5nu (9v).
Abominable Snowman (Yeti). *Oct. 12.* 1, 2, 3, 4, 5, 15, 30, 40, 50ch. *Nov. 15.* 1.25, 2.50, 3, 5, 6, 7nu (15v).

1967
Nos. 19-21, 38-39, 63-67 overprinted "Air Mail" in straight or curved lines. *Jan. 10.* (20v).
Flowers, *Feb. 9.* 3, 5, 7, 10, 50ch, 1, 2.50, 4, 5nu (9v).
Boy Scouts of Bhutan. *Mar. 28,* Perf., imperf. 5, 10, 15, 50ch, 1.25, 4nu (6v). Souvenir sheet of 2 (1.25, 4nu).
EXPO '67. *May 15.* Nos. 50-52 overprinted (3v). Souvenir sheet of 2 (1.50, 2.50nu) perf., imperf.
Churchill and Battle of Britain. *June 26.* Perf., imperf. 45ch, 2, 4nu (3v). Souvenir sheet of 2 (2, 4nu).
World Boy Scout Jamboree, Idaho. *Aug. 1.* Boy Scouts of Bhutan issue overprinted "World Jamboree/Idaho, U.S.A./Aug. 1-9/67." (6v and sheet).
Girl Scouts of Bhutan. *Sept. 18.* Perf., imperf. 5, 10, 15ch, 1.50, 2.50, 5nu (6v). Souvenir sheet of 2 (2.50, 5nu).
Astronauts. *Oct. 30.* Imperf., tridimensional. 3, 5, 7, 10, 15, 30, 50ch, 1.25nu; airmail, 2.50, 4, 5, 9nu (12v). 3 souvenir sheets of 4 (3, 5, 7, 10ch; 15, 30, 50ch. 1.25nu; 2.50, 4, 5, 9nu).

1968
Pheasants. *Jan. 20.* Perf., imperf. 1, 2, 4, 8, 15ch, 2, 4nu; *Apr. 23.* 5, 7, 9nu (10v).
10th Winter Olympics, Grenoble. Abominable Snowman issue of 1966 overprinted (2 types). *Feb. 16.* Perf., imperf. 40ch. 1.25, 3, 6nu (4v).
Mythological Creatures. *Mar. 14.* 2, 3, 4, 5, 15, 20, 30, 50ch. 1.25, 2nu; airmail, 1.50, 2.50, 4, 5, 10nu (15v).
Butterflies, *May 20.* Imperf., tridimensional, 15, 50ch, 1.25, 2nu; airmail, 3, 4, 5, 6nu (8v). 2 souvenir sheets of 4 (15, 50ch, 1.25, 2nu; 3, 4, 5, 6nu).
Paintings (relief printed). *July 8.* Imperf. 2, 4, 5, 10, 45, 80ch, 1.05, 1.40, 2, 3, 4, 5nu; *Aug. 28;* airmail, 1.50, 2.50, 6, 8nu (16v). (van Gogh, Millet, Monet, Corot). 4 souvenir sheets of 4 (2, 4, 5, 10ch; 45, 80ch, 1.05, 1.40nu; 2, 3, 4, 5nu; 1.50, 2.50, 6, 8nu).
19th Summer Olympics, Mexico City. *Oct. 1.* Perf., imperf. 5, 45, 60, 80ch, 1.05, 2, 3, 5nu (8v). Souvenir sheet of 2 (1.05, 5nu).
International Human Rights Year. *Nov. 12.* (Black and gold overprint on unissued gold foil coin set, 3 sizes) 15, 35ch, 9nu (3v).
Flood Relief. *Dec. 7.* Summer Olympics issue surcharged 5ch+5ch, 80ch+25ch, 2nu+50ch (3v).
Birds of Bhutan. *Dec. 7.* 2, 3, 4, 5, 15ch; *Dec. 28;* 20, 30, 50ch 1.25, 2nu; *Jan. 29, 1969;* Airmail, 1.50, 2.50, 4, 5, 10nu (15v).

1969
Fish. *Feb. 27.* Imperf., tridimensional. 15, 20, 30ch; airmail, 5, 6, 7nu (6v). Souvenir sheet of 4 (30ch, 5, 6, 7nu).
Insects. *Apr. 10.* Imperf., tridimensional. 10, 75ch, 1.25, 2nu; airmail, 3, 4, 5, 6nu (8v). 2 Souvenir sheets of 4 (10, 75ch, 1.25, 2nu; 3, 4, 5, 6nu).
Universal Postal Union, admission of Bhutan. *May 2.* Perf., imperf. 5, 10, 15, 45, 60ch, 1.05, 1.40, 4nu (8v).
History of Steel Making (printed on steel foil), Imperf. *June 2;* 2, 5, 15, 45, 75ch. 1.50, 1.75, 2nu; airmail, 3, 4, 5, 6nu (12v). *June 30.* 6 souvenir sheets of 2 (2, 45ch; 5, 15ch; 75ch, 2nu, 1.50, 1.7nu; 3, 6nu; 4, 5nu).
Birds, *Aug. 5.* Imperf., tridimensional. 15, 50ch, 1.25, 2nu; airmail, 3, 4, 5, 6nu (8v). *Aug. 28;* 2 souvenir sheets of 4 (15, 50ch, 1.25, 2nu; 3, 4, 5, 6nu).
Buddhist Prayer Banners (printed on silk). *Sept. 30.* Imperf. 15, 75ch, 2, 5, 6nu (5v). Souvenir sheet of 3 (75ch, 5, 6nu) perf., imperf.
Apollo 11 Moon Landing. *Nov. 3.* Imperf., tridimensional, 3, 5, 15, 20, 25, 45, 50ch, 1.75nu; airmail, 3, 4, 5, 6nu (12v). *Nov. 20.* 3 souvenir sheets of 4 (3, 5, 15, 20ch; 25, 45, 50ch, 1.75nu; 3, 4, 5, 6nu).

1970
Paintings. *Jan. 19.* Imperf., tridimensional. 5, 10, 15ch., 2.75nu; airmail, 3, 4, 5, 6nu (8v). (Clouet, van Eyck, David, Homer, Rubens, Gentileschi, Ghirlandaio, Raphael). 2 souvenir sheets of 4 (5, 10, 15ch, 2.75nu; 3, 4, 5, 6nu).
Flowers, paintings (relief printed). *May 6,* Imperf. 2, 3, 5, 10, 15, 75ch, 1, 1.40nu; *May 28.* Amrial, 80, 90ch, 1.10, 1.40, 1.60, 1.70, 3, 3.50nu (16v). (van Gogh, Redon, Kiyoteru Kuroda, Renoir, Monet, La Tour, Oudot). 4 souvenir sheets of 4 (2, 3, 5, 10ch; 15, 75ch, 1, 1.40nu; 80, 90ch, 1.10, 1.40nu; 1.60, 1.70, 3, 3.50nu).

Preceding Issues Surcharged, *June.*
Mythological Creatures issue of 1968. 5ch x 6; 20ch x 3.
No. 14 (Freedom from Hunger). 20ch.
Nos. 63-67 (Animals). 20ch x 5.
Abominable Snowman issue of 1966. 20ch x 6.
Flower issue of 1967. 20ch x 2.
Boy Scout issue of 1967. 20ch x 2.
Churchill. Battle of Britain issue of 1967. 20ch x 2.
Pheasant issue of 1968. 20ch x 3.
Birds issue of 1968. 20ch x 9.
UPU issue of 1969. 20ch x 3.
Animals, Imperf., tridimensional. *Sept. 17;* 5, 10, 20, 25, 30, 40, 65, 75, 85ch; *Oct. 15;* airmail. 2, 3, 4, 5nu (13v).
Space Conquest. Imperf., tridimensional. *Nov. 9;* 2, 5, 15, 25, 30, 50, 75ch, 1.50nu; *Nov. 30;* airmail, 2, 3, 6, 7nu (12v). 3 souvenir sheets of 4 (2, 5, 15, 25ch; 30, 50, 75ch, 1.50nu; 2, 3, 6, 7nu).

1971
History of Sculpture (plastic bas-relief sculptures from antiquity to Modigliani). *Mar.* Imperf. 10, 75ch, 1.25, 2nu; airmail, 3, 4, 5, 6nu (8v). 2 souvenir sheets of 4 (10, 75ch, 1.25, 2nu; 3, 4, 5, 6nu).
Apollo 15 and Lunokhod 1. *Mar. 20.* Imperf., tridimensional. 10ch, 1.70nu; airmail, 2.50, 4nu (4v). Souvenir sheet of 4 (10ch. 1.70, 2.50, 4nu).
Antique Cars. Imperf. *May 20;* 2, 5, 10, 15, 20, 30, 60chg; *June 10;* 75, 85ch, 1, 1.20, 1.55, 1.80, 2, 2.50nu; *July 5;* 4, 6, 7, 9, 10nu (20v).
Preceding Issues Surcharged. *July 1.*
Nos. 22-23, 55ch on 1.30nu, 90ch on 2nu.
Nos. 65-66, 55ch on 3nu, 90ch on 4nu.
Boy Scout issue of 1967, 90ch on 4nu.
Pheasant issue of 1968, 55ch on 5nu, 90ch on 9nu.
Mythology issue of 1968, 55ch on 4nu.
Olympic issue of 1968, 90ch on 1.05nu.
Birds issue of 1968, 90ch on 2nu.
UPU issue of 1969, 55ch on 60ch.
UPU issue of 1970, 90ch on 2.50nu.
Space issue of 1971 (Apollo 15), 90ch on 1.70nu.

1972
Paintings (relief printed). Imperf. *Jan. 29;* 15, 20, 90ch, 2.50nu; *Feb. 28;* airmail, 1.70, 4.60, 5.40, 6nu (8v). (Renoir, Manet, da Vinci, Millet, Rousseau, Gauguin, Degas, Guillaumin) 2 souvenir sheets of 4 (15, 20, 90ch, 2.50nu; 1.70, 4.60, 5.40, 6nu).
Famous Men (plastic bas-reliefs). *Apr. 22.* Imperf. 10, 15, 55ch; airmail; 2, 6, 8nu (6v). (Gandhi, J.F. Kennedy, Churchill, de Gaulle, Pope John XXIII, Eisenhower). Souvenir sheet of 4 (55ch, 2, 6, 8nu).
International Book Year. *May 15.* 2, 3, 5, 20ch (4v).
20th Summer Olympics. Munich. *June 6.* 10, 15, 20, 30, 45ch; airmail, 35ch. 1.35, 7nu (8v). Souvenir sheet of 3 (35ch, 1.35, 7nu) perf., imperf.
Apollo 16 (rockets and astronauts). *Sept. 1.* Imperf., tridimensional. 15, 20, 90ch, 2.50nu; airmail, 1.70, 4.60, 5.40, 6nu (8v). 2 souvenir sheets of (15, 20, 90ch, 2.50nu; 1.70, 4.60, 5.40, 6nu).
Dogs. *Oct. 5.* Perf., imperf. 5, 10, 15, 25, 55ch, 8nu, souvenir sheet of 2 (55ch, 8nu); *Jan. 1, 1973.* 2, 3, 15, 20, 30, 99ch, 2.50, 4nu, souvenir sheet of 3 (99ch, 2.50, 4nu); *Jan. 15.* Airmail souvenir sheet, 18nu. (14v).

1973
Roses (scented paper). *Jan. 30.* 15, 25, 30ch, 3nu; airmail, 6, 7nu (6v). Souvenir sheet of 2 (6, 7nu) perf., imperf.
Apollo 17 (astronauts on moon). *Feb. 23.* Imperf., tridimensional. 10, 15, 55ch, 2nu; airmail, 7, 9nu (6v). Souvenir sheet of 4 (10, 15, 55ch, 2nu); circular souvenir sheet of 2 (7, 9nu).
Folk Songs, on Record. *Apr. 15.* 10, 25ch, 1.25, 7, 8nu; airmail, 3, 9nu (7v).
King Jigme Dorji Wangchuk, memorial. *May 2.* Gold foil, 10, 25ch, 3nu; airmail, 6, 8nu (5v). Souvenir sheet of 2 (6, 8nu).
Mushrooms. *Sept. 25.* Imperf., tridimensional. 15, 25, 30ch, 3nu; airmail, 6, 7nu (6v). Souvenir sheet of 4 (15, 25, 30ch, 3nu) and of 2 (6, 7nu).
INDIPEX Philatelic Exhibition (Bhutanese mail service scenes). *Nov. 14.* 5, 10, 15, 25ch. 1.25, 3nu, airmail, 5, 6nu (8v). Souvenir sheet of 2 (5, 6nu).

1974
Reading and Writing, paintings. *Feb. 15.* 1, 2, 3, 5, 10, 15, 25, 50, 60, 80ch, 1, 1.25nu (12v). (Fragonard, Carpaccio, Liotard, Holbein, Terborch).

CAMBODIA (Khmer)
1972
20th Summer Olympics, Munich. *Nov. 2.* Gold foil, airmail, 900r x 4 (4v). 2 souvenir sheets of 2, 900r x 2.
Apollo 16. *Nov. 2.* Gold foil, airmail 900r x 2. (2v). Souvenir sheet of 2 (900r x 2) perf., imperf.

1973
World Cup Soccer Championships. Gold foil, airmail, 900r x 4 (4v).

1974
John F. Kennedy and Apollo 11 Astronauts on Moon. Goil foil, airmail, 110r x 2 (2v). Souvenir sheet of 2 (110r x 2).
Copernicus, 500th birth anniversary. Gold foil, airmail, 1200r. Souvenir sheet, 1200r.
UPU Centenary. Gold foil, airmail, 1200r x 2 (2v). Souvenir sheet, 1200r.

1975
World Cup Soccer Championships. *Feb.* 1, 5, 10, 25r; airmail, 50, 100, 150, 200, 250r (9v). 9 imperf. souvenir sheets; same with simulated perforations; 2 sheets, 200, 250r, perf. Gold foil, airmail, 1200r, same, souvenir sheet.
21st Summer Olympics, Montreal, 1976 (ancient and modern sports). 1, 5, 10, 25r; airmail, 50, 100, 150, 200, 250r (9v). 9 imperf. souvenir sheets; same with simulated perforations. 2 souvenir sheets, 200, 250r, perf. Gold foil, airmail, 1200r.
UPU Centenary. *April 12.* (Second issue) 15, 20, 70, 160, 180, 235r, airmail 500, 1000, 2000r (9v). 9 imperf. souvenir sheets; same with simulated perforations. 2 souvenir sheets, 1000, 2000r. Gold foil embossed, airmail, perf., imperf. 1000r x 2 (train & plane). Same, souvenir sheet, 1200r (Chinese junks).

CAMEROUN
1977
Winter Olympics, 1976, Innsbruck. *Aug. 10.* 40, 50fr; airmail, 140, 200, 350fr (5v). Airmail souvenir sheet, 500fr.
Apollo-Soyuz Project. *Aug. 10.* 40, 60fr; airmail, 100, 250, 350fr (5v). Airmail souvenir sheet, 500fr.

CHAD
1970
Apollo Program. *May.* 40fr; airmail, 15, 25fr (3v). Souvenir sheet, 50fr.
Napoleon. *June 12.* Perf., imperf. airmail, 10, 25, 32fr, se-tenant in sheets of 6 (3v). Souvenir sheet, 40fr. Gold foil, 10fr and souvenir sheet.
World Cup Soccer Championships, Mexico. *July 2.* Perf., imperf. 1, 4, 5fr x 2 (4v). Souvenir sheet; 15fr.
EXPO '70, Osaka, Japan (Japanese prints). *July.* Perf., imperf. 50c, 1, 2fr, se-tenant in sheets of 6 (3v).
19th Summer Olympics and 1970 Soccer Cup, Mexico. *July 1.* Airmail 5fr. Souvenir sheet, 15fr. Gold foil, 5 fr. Souvenir sheet, 5fr.

Christmas, paintings. *Aug. 19.* Perf., imperf. 3, 25fr; airmail, 32fr (3v). (Virgin and Child by Solario, Durer, Fouquet).
Paintings, flowers and woman (Iba N'Diaye). *Aug. 28.* Airmail, 250 fr x 2.
20th Summer Olympics, Munich, 1972. *Sept.* 3, 8, 20fr; airmail, 10, 35fr (5v). Souvenir sheet, 40fr.
Apollo 11 and 12. *Sept.* Imperf. airmail gold foil, 25fr and souvenir sheet.
20th Summer Olympics, Munich, *Oct. 14.* Imperf. gold foil, 10fr and airmail souvenir sheet.
Napoleon II. *July 23.* 10fr, se-tenant with label. Souvenir sheet, 40fr. Embossed gold foil, 10fr perf., imperf. Same, 2 souvenir sheets. 10fr., perf., imperf.
French Royalty. *1970-71.* Perf., imperf. About 70 stamps and souvenir sheets showing paintings against gold background. Various denominations, both postage and airmail, printed se-tenant.

1971
11th Winter Olympics, Sapporo, 1972 (Kiyonaga paintings). *Feb. 16.* Perf., imperf. 50c, 1, 2fr (3v).
Flowers, paintings. *Apr. 28.* Perf., imperf. 1, 4, 5fr, printed setenant (3v). (Rubens, Van Os, Brueghel).
Space Exploration and John F. Kennedy. *Feb. 16.* Perf., imperf. 8, 10fr; airmail, 35fr (3v). Souvenir sheet, 40fr.
Olympic Games (sport and culture). *Apr. 28.* Perf., imperf. 15, 20fr; airmail, 25fr (3v). Airmail souvenir sheet, 50fr.
Peace and Sciences. *July 5.* Embossed gold foil. Perf. and imperf., 10fr and souvenir sheet, 10fr.
Christmas. *July 17.* Nos. 205-210 overprinted "Noel/1971" in gold (6v).
20th Summer Olympics, Munich. Soccer Cup issue of 1970 overprinted in gold. Airmail souvenir sheets; 15fr, 5fr x 2 and 2 labels.
11th Winter Olympics, Sapporo. *July 17.* EXPO '70 and Winter Olympic issues of 1971 overprinted in gold (6v).

1972-73
Soccer World Champion, Great Britain, 1966. Gold foil, 5fr and souvenir sheet, 5fr.
Summer Olympics, Munich. *June 24.* Nos. 181-204 overprinted (24v).
Wild Animals. *Nov.* Airmail, 20, 30, 100, 130, 150fr (5v). Souvenir sheet, 200fr.
20th Summer Olympics, Munich.
Olympic Flame and Athletes: *1973.* 20, 30, 50fr; airmail, 100, 130, 150fr (6v), souvenir sheet, 200 fr.
Athletes and Abstract White Drawings of Athletes in Background: *1973.* 25, 40, 50, 75fr; airmail, 100, 150fr (6v). Souvenir sheet, 250fr.
Music, paintings. *Apr.* 30, 70, 100fr; airmail, 125, 150fr (5v). (Costa, Oudry, Saraceni, Metsu). Souvenir sheet, 300fr.
Easter. *Apr.* 60, 120fr; airmail, 40, 150, 250fr (5v). Souvenir sheet, 400fr.
Modern Trains. 10, 40, 50, 150, 200fr (5v). Souvenir sheet, 300fr.
Domestic Animals (sheep, dromedaries, cats, dogs, horses). 20, 30fr; airmail, 100, 130, 150fr (5v).
Horses, paintings. 20, 60, 100, 150fr (4v). (Gericault, Potter, Stubbs, Vernet). Souvenir sheet, 500fr.
Aircraft, Airmail, 5, 25, 70, 150, 200fr (5v). Souvenir sheet, 350fr.
Christmas, paintings. 30, 40, 55fr; airmail, 60, 250fr (5v). (Lotto, Tintoretto, Schongauer, Barocci, Lochner, Memling). Souvenir sheet, 400fr.

COMORO ISLANDS
Most sets exist perf., imperf.
1975
Apollo-Soyuz Space Issue. 10, 30, 50fr; airmail 100, 200, 400fr (6v). Souvenir sheet, 500fr. Embossed gold foil, airmail, 1500fr. same souvenir sheet, 1500fr.

1976
American Bicentennial. *Jan. 15.* 15, 25, 35, 40, 75fr; airmail, 500fr (6v). Airmail souvenir sheet, 400fr. Embossed on gold foil, airmail, 1000fr, same, souvenir sheet, 1500fr.
12th Winter Olympics, Innsbruck. *Mar. 30.* 5, 30, 35, 50fr; airmail, 200, 400fr (6v). Airmail souvenir sheet, 500fr. Embossed on gold foil, airmail, 1000fr, same airmail souvenir sheet, 1000fr.
21st Summer Olympics, Montreal. *Mar. 30.* 20, 25, 40, 75fr; airmail, 100, 500fr (6v). Airmail souvenir sheet, 400fr.
Telephone Centenary. *July 1.* 10, 25, 75fr; airmail, 100, 200, 500fr (6v). 2 airmail souvenir sheets, 400, 500fr.
American Bicentennial, Project Viking III. *Nov. 23.* 5, 10, 25, 35, 100fr; airmail, 500fr (6v). **Project Viking IV.** Embossed on gold foil, airmail, 1500fr (Pioneer and rocket). Same; airmail souvenir sheet, 1500fr (Mars landing vehicle).
United Nations Postal Administration, 25th anniversary. *Nov. 25.* 15, 30, 50, 75fr; airmail, 200, 400fr (6v). Airmail souvenir sheet, 500fr.
American Bicentennial, Civil War Battles. *Dec. 30.* 10, 30, 50fr; airmail, 100, 200, 400fr (6v). Airmail souvenir sheet, 500fr. Embossed on gold foil, airmail, 1500fr (Kennedy, moon landing). Same, airmail souvenir sheet, 1000fr (Abraham Lincoln).
Endangered Species. *Dec. 30.* 15, 20, 35, 40, 75fr; airmail, 400fr (6v). Airmail souvenir sheet, 500fr.

1977
Endangered Species. *Apr. 14.* 10, 30, 40, 50fr; airmail, 200, 400fr (6v). Airmail souvenir sheet, 500fr.
Airships and Railroads. *Apr. 14.* 20, 25, 50, 75fr; airmail, 200, 500fr (6v). Airmail souvenir sheet, 500fr.
Nobel Prize, 75th anniversary. *July 7.* 30, 40, 50, 100fr; airmail, 200, 400fr (6v). Airmail souvenir sheet, 500fr.
Peter Paul Rubens, 400th birth anniversary. *July 7.* 20, 25, 50, 75fr; airmail, 200, 500fr (6v). Airmail souvenir sheet, 500fr (self-portrait).
Silver Jubilee QEII. *July 7.* Embossed on gold foil, airmail, 500fr. Same, 2 airmail souvenir sheets, 500, 1000fr.
Fish, various local species. 30, 40, 50, 100fr; airmail, 200, 400fr (6v). Airmail souvenir sheet, 500fr.
Space Ships and Vehicles. 30, 50, 75, 100fr; airmail, 200, 400fr (6v). Airmail souvenir sheet, 500fr.
Concord, "Paris-New-York-22 nov, 1977" overprinted in gold on UNPA 25th anniversary, 200fr airmail.
Fairy Tales. 15, 30, 35, 40, 50fr; airmail, 400fr (6v) (Hansel & Gretel, Alice in Wonderland, Pinocchio, Good Little Henri, Peter and the Wolf, 1001 Nights).

1978
Birds. *Feb. 6.* 15, 20, 35, 40, 75fr; airmail, 400fr (6v). Airmail souvenir sheet, 500fr.
World Cup Soccer, Argentina '78. *Feb. 6.* 30, 50, 75, 100fr; airmail, 200, 400fr (6v). Airmail souvenir sheet, 500fr. Embossed in gold foil, airmail, 1000fr. Same, airmail souvenir sheet, 1000fr.
Famous Composers. *Apr. 5.* 30, 40, 50, 100fr; airmail, 200, 400fr (6v). Airmail souvenir sheet, 500fr.
Albrecht Durer, 450th death anniversary. *Apr. 5.* 20, 25, 50, 75fr; airmail, 200, 500fr (6v). Airmail souvenir sheet, 500fr.
Aug. 20, 30, 40fr; airmail, 100, 200, 400fr (6v). 3 airmail souvenir sheets, 500, 1000, 1500fr.
QE II Coronation, 25th anniversary. *May 25.* 10, 25, 40, 100fr; airmail, 200, 500fr (6v). Airmail souvenir sheet, 500fr. Embossed on gold foil, airmail, 500, 1000fr. Same, 2 souvenir sheets, 1000fr.
Butterflies. *May 8.* 15, 20, 30, 50, 75fr; airmail, 400fr (6v). Airmail souvenir sheet, 500fr.
World Telecommuniations, 10th anniversary. *June.* 30, 50, 75, 100fr; airmail, 200, 400fr (6v).

History of Aviation. *June.* 30, 50, 75, 100fr; airmail, 200, 400fr (6v). Airmail souvenir sheet, 500fr.
Peter Paul Rubens, 400th anniversary. *June.* 10, 25, 35, 50, 75fr; airmail, 500fr (6v). 3 airmail souvenir sheets, 400, 1000, 1500fr.
Rowland Hill. *Aug.* 20, 30, 40, 75fr; airmail, 200, 400fr (6v). Airmail souvenir sheet, 500fr.
World Cup Soccer. *Sept.* Overprinted "Rep. Fed. Islamique / des Comores / 1 Argentine / 2 Hollande / 3 Bresil." 30, 50, 75, 100fr; airmail 200, 400fr (6v). Airmail souvenir sheet, 500fr.
Europe-Africa. *Sept.* 10, 25, 35, 50fr; airmail, 100. 500fr (6v). Airmail souvenir sheet, 500fr.

CONGO PEOPLE'S REPUBLIC
1970
Paintings. *Feb.* 3, 40fr; airmail, 25fr (3v). (Fragonard, Boucher).
Olympic Games. *Feb.* 2, 5, 15, 50fr (4v). Airmail souvenir sheet, 100fr.
Kennedys, King and Space. *Feb.* 1, 10, 20, 30fr (4v).

1971
13th World Boy Scout Jamboree, Japan. *July 14.* Gold foil, airmail, 1000fr and silver foil souvenir sheet of 4 (90fr x 4).

1977
History of Aviation, famous fliers. 60, 75, 100, 200, 300fr (5v). Souvenir sheet, 500fr.
Peter Paul Rubens, 400th birth anniversary. **Mao Tse-tung,** 1st anniversary of death. *Sept.* Embossed gold foil, 400, 600fr (2v).
Famous Persons. *Dec.* 200, 200, 250, 300fr (4v) (Baudouin, de Gaulle, QEII Silver Jubilee (2)). Airmail souvenir sheet, 500fr (QEII and Royal Family).

DAHOMEY
1974
World Cup Soccer Championships, Munich. *July 16.* Airmail, 35, 40, 100, 200, 300fr (5v). Souvenir sheet, 500fr. Embossed gold foil, 1000fr, same souvenir sheet.
UPU centenary. *Aug. 5.* Airmail, 50, 100, 125, 150, 200fr (5v). Souvenir sheet, 500fr. 6 souvenir sheets with simulated perforations. Airmail gold foil 1000fr, same souvenir sheet.
Conquest of Solar System's Planets. *Oct. 31.* Perf., imperf. Airmail 50, 100, 150, 200fr (4v). 4 souvenir sheets with simulated perforations. Souvenir sheet; 500fr.
World Soccer Champions, Germany. *Nov.* Perf., imperf. Airmail 100, 125, 150, 300fr (4v). 4 souvenir sheets with simulated perforations. Souvenir sheet, 500fr. Embossed gold foil, perf., imperf., 1000fr and 4 souvenir sheets.

ECUADOR
1966
International Telecommunication Union, centenary *Jan. 27.* Perf., imperf. 10c x 2, 80c; airmail, 1.50, 3, 4s (6v). 2 souvenir sheets of 3 (10, 80c, 3s; 10c, 1.50, 4s).
Space Exploration. *Jan. 27.* 10c, 1s; airmail, 1.30, 2, 2.50, 3.50s (6v). Souvenir sheet of 3 (10c, 1.30, 3.50s) perf., imperf.
Dante and Galileo. 10, 80c; airmail, 2, 3s (4v). Souvenir sheet of 3 (10, 80c, 3s) perf., imperf.
Pope Paul VI. 10c; airmail, 1.30, 3.50s (3v). Souvenir sheet of 3 (10c, 1.30, 3.50s) perf., imperf.
Famous Men. *June 24.* 10c, 1s; airmail, 1.50, 2.50, 4s (5v). (Hammarskjold, Churchill, Schweitzer, J.F. Kennedy). Souvenir sheet of 3 (10c, 1.50, 4s).
Olympic Games. (Greek athletes, classic period). *June 27.* 10c x 2, 80c; airmail, 1.30, 3, 3.50s (6v). 2 souvenir sheets of 3 (10c, 1.30, 3.50s; 10, 80c, 3s) perf., imperf.
Winter Olympics, 1924-1968, 10c, 1s; airmail, 1.50, 2, 2.50, 4s (6v). Souvenir sheet of 3 (10c, 1.50, 4s) perf., imperf.
French-American Space Research. 10c; airmail, 1.50, 4s (3v). Souvenir sheet of 3 (10c, 1.50, 4s) perf., imperf.
Italian Space Research. 10c; airmail, 1.30, 3.50s (3v). Souvenir sheet of 3 (10c, 1.30, 3.50s) perf., imperf.
Moon Exploration. 10, 80c, 1s; airmail, 2, 2.50, 3s (6v). Souvenir sheet of 3 (10, 80c, 3s) perf., imperf.

1967
19th Summer Olympics, Mexico. *Mar. 13.* 10c, 1s; airmail, 1.30, 2, 2.50, 3.50s (6v). Souvenir sheet of 3 (10c, 1.30, 3.50s) perf., imperf. Diamond-shaped; 10c x 2, 80c; airmail, 1.50, 3, 4s (6v). 2 souvenir sheets of 3 (10c, 1.50, 4s; 10, 80c, 3s) perf., imperf.
National Eucharistic Congress, 4th. *May. 10.* 10, 60, 80c, 1s; airmail, 1.50, 2s (6v). souvenir sheet, 10s perf., imperf.
Madonnas, paintings. *May.* 10, 40, 50c; airmail, 1.30, 2.50, 3s (6v). (Reni, van Hemesen, Memling, Durer, Raphael, Murillo).
Women, paintings. *Sept. 9.* 10c, 1s; airmail, 1.50, 2, 2.50, 4s (6v). (van der Weyden, Rubens, Durer, Gainsborough, Manet, Raphael). Souvenir sheet of 3 (10c, 1.50, 4s) perf., imperf.
John F. Kennedy. 50th birth anniversary. *Sept. 11.* 10c x 2, 80c; airmail, 1.30, 3, 3.50s (6v). 2 souvenir sheets of 3 (10, 80c, 3s; 10c, 1.30, 3.50s) perf., imperf.
Christmas. *Dec. 29.* 10c x 2, 40, 50, 60c; airmail, 2.50s (6v).

1968
Christian Local Art. *Jan. 19.* 10, 80c, 1s; airmail, 1.30, 1.50, 2s (6v). Souvenir sheet of 3 (3, 3.50, 4s) perf., imperf.
Tourist Year (9th COTAL Congress) *Apr. 1.* 20, 30, 40, 50, 60, 80c, 1s; airmail, 1.30, 1.50, 2s (10v).

1969
Pope Paul VI, Latin America visit and **39th International Eucharistic Congress.** Bogota, 40, 60c, 1s; airmail, 1.30, 2s (5v). Souvenir sheets of 2 (1, 2s) and 3 (40, 60c, 1.30s); imperf.
Guayaquil University Centenary, religious paintings with university coat of arms ovptd. in silver. 40, 60c, 1s; airmail, 1.30, 2s (5v). (van der Weyden, Raphael, Veronese). Souvenir sheets of 3 (40, 60c, 2s) and 2 (1, 2s) imperf.

EQUATORIAL GUINEA
Most sets exist perf., imperf.
Most imperf. sets have surface colored paper

1972
Apollo 15. *Jan. 28.* 1, 3, 5, 8, 10p; airmail, 15, 25p (7v). 3 airmail semi-postal souvenir sheets 25p+200p, perf.; 50p+250p, imperf.; gold foil, 200p+25p, perf., 200p+50p, imperf.
11th Winter Olympics, Sapporo. *Feb. 3.* 1, 2, 3, 5, 8p; airmail, 15, 50p (7v). 2 airmail semi-postal souvenir sheets, 200p+25p, perf.; 250p+50p, imperf.; gold foil, 200p+25p, perf., 200p+50p, imperf., 2 each.
Christmas; paintings. *1971.* 1, 3, 5, 8, 10p; airmail, 15, 25p (7v). 2 airmail semi-postal souvenir sheets 25p+200p, perf.; 50p+200p, imperf. (Virgin and Child by da Vinci, Murillo, Raphael, Mabuse, van der Weyden, Durer), gold foil, 200p+25p, perf., 250p+50p., imperf.
Easter. *Apr. 28.* 1, 3, 5, 8, 10p; airmail, 15, 25p (7v). 2 souvenir sheets (25, 200p). perf., semi-postal 250p+50p, imperf., gold foil airmail semi-postal 200p+25p, perf., 250+50p, imperf., 2 each with designs by Velazquez and El Greco.
20th Summer Olympics, Munich (sports; inscribed "Augsburgo"). *May 5.* 1, 2, 3, 5, 8p; airmail, 15, 50p (7v). 2 airmail semi-postal souvenir sheets 200p+25p, perf.; 250p+50p, imperf. Presentation folder with gold foil airmail semi-postal 200p+25p, perf., 200p+50p, imperf.
Gold Medal Winners, Sapporo. *May 25.* 1, 2, 3, 5, 8p; airmail, 15, 50p (7v). Airmail souvenir sheet, 250p+50p, imperf.; souvenir sheet of 2 (25, 200p) perf. Gold foil, 200p+25p, perf., 250p+50p, imperf., 6 each.
Black Gold Medal Winners, Munich. *June 26.* 1, 2, 3, 5, 8p; airmail, 15, 50p (7v). 2 airmail semi-postal souvenir sheets

200p+25p, perf.; 250p+50p, imperf. Gold foil, 200p+25p, perf., 250p+50p, imperf., 9 each.
Olympic Games, Regatta in Kiel & Oberschleissheim. *July 25.* 1, 2, 3, 5, 8p; airmail, 15, 50p (7v). 2 airmail semi-postal souvenir sheets 200p+25p, perf.; 250p+50p, imperf. Gold foil, 200p+25p, perf., 250p+50p, imperf., 2 each.
1972 Munich Olympics. *Aug. 10.* 1, 2, 3, 5, 8p; airmail, 15, 50p (7v). 2 airmail semi-postal souvenir sheets 200p+25p, perf.; 250p+50p, imperf. *Aug. 17.* 10 gold foil sheets, 200p+25p each, perf. Same, 10 imperf. sheets, 250p+50p each.
Olympic Equestrian Events. *Aug. 24.* 1, 2, 3, 5, 8p; airmail, 15, 50, 50p (7v). 2 airmail semi-postal souvenir sheets 200p+25p, perf.; 250p+50p, imperf. Gold foil souvenir sheets, 200p+25p, perf. Same, imperf. sheets, 250p+50p, 8 each. 2 stamps, 200p+25p, perf., 250p+50p, imperf. 3 sheets of 2, 200p+25p (2 perf., 1 imperf.)
Japanese Railroad centenary (locomotives). *Sept. 21.* 1, 3, 5, 8, 10p; airmail, 15, 25p (7v). 2 airmail semi-postal souvenir sheets 200p+25p, perf.; 250p+50p, imperf. 11 gold foil souvenir sheets of 1; (200p+25p, perf. (9), 200p+25p, imperf. (2). 2 sheets of 2, each 200p+25p, perf., imperf.
Gold Medal Winners, Munich Games. *Oct. 30.* 1, 2, 3, 5, 8p; airmail, 15, 50p (7v). 2 airmail semi-postal souvenir sheets 200p+25p, perf.; 250p+50p, imperf. 4 gold foil souvenir sheets, 200p+25p, perf., 250p+50p, imperf., 2 each.
Christmas and 500th birth anniversary of Lucas Cranach. (Madonnas and Christmas seals). *Nov. 22.* 1, 3, 5, 8, 10p; airmail, 15, 25p (7v). (Giotto, Schongauer, Fouquet, de Morales, Fini, David, Sassetta). 2 airmail semi-postal souvenir sheets. 200p+25p, perf., 250+50p., imperf. Gold foil souvenir sheets, 200p+25p (6), perf., 250p+50p (6) imperf. Souvenir sheets of 2, 200p+25p, perf., imperf. Ovptd. stamp 200p+25p.
American and Russian astronaut memorial. *Dec. 14.* 1, 3, 5, 8, 10p; airmail, 15, 25p (7v). 2 airmail semi-postal souvenir sheets 200p+25p, perf.; 250p+50p, imperf. Gold foil ovptd. "Apollo 16 and 17" 200p+25p, perf., 250p+50p, imperf., 2 each.

1973
Trans-Atlantic Yacht Race. *Jan. 22,* 1, 2, 3, 5, 8p; airmail, 15, 50p (7v). 2 airmail semi-postal souvenir sheets 200p+25p, perf.; 250p+50p, imperf.
Renoir paintings. *Feb. 22.* 1, 2, 3, 5, 8p; airmail, 15, 50p (7v). 2 airmail semi-postal souvenir sheets 25p+200p, perf.; 50p+250p, imperf. Gold foil, 200p+25p, perf., 250p+50p, imperf.
Conquest of Venus (spacecraft). *Mar. 22.* 1, 3, 5, 8, 10p; airmail, 15, 25p (7v). 2 airmail semi-postal souvenir sheets 200p+25p, perf.; 250p+50p, imperf.
Apollo Flights 11-17. *Mar. 22.* 18 gold foil airmail semi-postal souvenir sheets: 14 sheets of 1 (7 x 200p+25p, perf.; 7 x 250p+50p, imperf.); 4 sheets of 2, 200p+25p, perf., 250p+50p, imperf. 2 each.
National Workers Party. *April* 1, 1.50, 2, 4, 5p (5v).
Independence, 4th anniversary. *April.* 1.50, 2, 3, 4, 5p (5v).
Easter, paintings. *Apr. 25.* 1, 3, 5, 8, 10p; airmail, 15, 25p (7v). (Verrocchio, Perugino, Tintoretto, Witz, Pontormo). 2 airmail semi-postal souvenir sheets 200p+25p, perf.; 250p+50p, imperf. Gold foil issue of 1972 ovptd. 4 sheets, 200p+25p, perf., 250p+50p, imperf. 2 each.
Copernicus. 500th birth anniversary (US and USSR space explorations). *May 15.* 4 gold foil airmail semi-postal souvenir sheets, 200p+25p, perf.; 250p+50p, imperf., 2 each.
Tour de France bicycle race. 59th. *May 22.* 1, 2, 3, 5, 8p; airmail, 15, 50p (7v). 2 airmail semi-postal souvenir sheets 200p+25p, perf.; 250p+50p, imperf.
Paintings. *June 29.* 1, 2, 3, 5, 8p; airmail, 15, 50p (7v). 2 airmail semi-postal souvenir sheets 200p+25p, perf.; 250p+50p, imperf.
World Cup Soccer Championships, Munich. 1974. *Aug. 30,* 5, 10, 15, 20, 25, 55, 60c; airmail, 5, 70p (9v). 2 airmail souvenir sheets, 130p, perf.; 200p, imperf.
Rubens paintings. *Sept. 23.* 1, 2, 3, 5, 8p; airmail, 15, 50p (7v). 2 souvenir sheets of 2 (200, 25p perf.; 250, 50p imperf).

New Currency: Ekuele
World Cup Soccer Championships, Munich, 1974. *Oct. 24.* 2 Gold foil souvenir sheets 130e x 2, perf.; 200e x 2, imperf. 2 souvenir sheets of 2, 130p, perf., 200p, imperf.
Christmas, paintings. *Oct. 30.* 1, 3, 5, 8, 10p; airmail, 15, 25p (7v). (Nativity by, van der Weyden, Bosco, de Carvajal, Mabuse, Lucas Jordon, P. Goecke, Maino, Fabriano, Lochner). 2 airmail semi-postal souvenir sheets 200p+25p, perf.; 250p+50p, imperf.
Apollo Program and J.F. Kennedy. *Nov. 10.* Gold foil airmail semi-postal 200p+25p, perf.; 250p+50p, imperf. and souvenir sheets (same).
World Cup Soccer (famous players). *Nov. 20.* 30, 35, 40, 45, 50, 65, 70c; airmail, 8, 60p (9v). 2 souvenir sheets, 130p, perf., 200p, imperf.
Princess Anne's Wedding. *Dec. 17.* Gold foil airmail souvenir sheets, 2 sheets of 1, 250e each; 1 sheet of 2, 250e x 2, perf., imperf.
Pablo Picasso Memorial (Blue Period paintings). *Dec. 20.* 30, 35, 40, 45, 50c; airmail, 8, 60e (7v). 2 souvenir sheets, 130e, perf.; 200e, imperf.

1974
Copernicus, 500th birth anniversary. *Feb. 8.* 5, 10, 15, 20c, 4e, airmail, 10, 70e (7v). 2 souvenir sheets 130e, perf.; 200e, imperf. *Apr. 10.* 8 gold foil souvenir sheets; 130e (3), perf.; 200e (3), imperf., 250e, perf., 300e, imperf. 4 souvenir sheets of 2, 250e, perf., 250e, imperf; 2 each.
World Cup Soccer Championships (final games) Munich. *Feb. 28.* 75, 80, 85, 90, 95c, 1, 1.25e; airmail, 10, 50e (9v). 2 souvenir sheets, 130e, perf.; 200e, imperf.
Easter, paintings. *Mar. 27.* 1, 3, 5, 8, 10p; airmail, 15, 25p (7v). (Fra Angelico, Castagno, Allori, Multscher, della Francesca, Pleydenwurff, Correggio). 2 airmail semi-postal souvenir sheets 200p+25p, perf.; 250p+50p, imperf.
Holy Year 1975 (famous churches). *Apr. 11,* 5 10, 15, 20c, 3.50e; airmail, 10, 70e (7v). 2 souvenir sheets 130e, perf., 200e, imperf.
World Cup Soccer (contemporary players). *Apr. 30.* 1.50, 1.75, 2, 2.25, 2.50, 3, 3.50e; airmail, 10, 60e (9v). 2 souvenir sheets of 2, 65e x 2, perf.; 100e x 2, imperf.
UPU centenary (transportation from messenger to rocket). *May 30.* 60, 70, 80c, 1, 1.50e; airmail, 30, 50e (7v). 2 souvenir sheets, 225e, perf.; 150e x 2, imperf. *June 8.* 2 airmail deluxe souvenir sheets, 130e. 1 sheet of 2, 130e, perf.
Picasso Memorial (Pink Period paintings). *June 28.* 55, 60, 65, 70, 75c; airmail, 10, 50e (7v), 2 souvenir sheets 130e, perf.; 200e, imperf.
World Cup Soccer Championships. *July 8.* 6 gold foil airmail souvenir sheets; 4 sheets of 1, 130e (2), 250e (2); 2 sheets of 2, 130e x 2, 250e x 2.
Aleksander Solzhenitsyn. *July 25.* Gold foil airmail souvenir sheets, 250e perf., 300e imperf.
Opening of American West. *July 30.* 30, 35, 40, 45, 50c; airmail, 8, 60p (7v). 2 souvenir sheets 130p, perf.; 200p, imperf.
Flowers. *Aug. 20.* 5, 10, 15, 20, 25c, 1, 3, 5, 8, 10p; airmail, 5, 15, 25, 70p (14v). 4 souvenir sheets: 130p, 200p; 2 semi-postal, 200p+25p, 250p+50p.
Christmas. *Sept. 16.* 60, 70, 80c, 1, 1.50e; airmail, 30, 50e (7v). 2 souvenir sheets. 225e, perf.; 300e, imperf.
Barcelona soccer team, 75th anniversary. *Sept. 25.* 1, 3, 5, 8, 10e; airmail, 15, 60e (7v, miniature sheet of 7 plus label). 2 souvenir sheets 200e, perf.; 300e, imperf. 4 gold foil airmail souvenir sheets, 200e each, perf. and imperf.
UPU centenary and ESPANA 75. *Oct. 9.* 1.25, 1.50, 1.75, 2, 2.25e; airmail, 35, 60e (7v). 2 airmail souvenir sheets 225e, perf., 300e, imperf. *Oct. 14.* Gold foil sheets, 250e, 300e, 250e x 2 perf., imperf.

Nature protection, Australian animals: *Oct. 25.* 80, 85, 90, 95c. 1e; airmail, 15, 40e (7v). 2 souvenir sheets 130e, perf., 200e, imperf. **African animals:** *Nov. 6.* 55, 60, 65, 70, 75c; airmail, 10, 70e (7v). 2 souvenir sheets 130e, perf.; 200e, imperf. **Australian and South American Birds:** *Nov. 26.* 1.25, 1.50, 1.75, 2, 2.25, 2.50, 2.75, 3, 3.50, 4p; airmail, 20, 25, 30, 35p (14v). 4 souvenir sheets 130p x 2, perf.; 200p x 2, imperf. **Endangered Species:** *Dec. 17,* 10, 15, 20, 25, 30, 35, 40, 45, 50, 55, 60c, 1, 2e; airmail, 10, 70e (15v se-tenant in sheet of 15).
Monkeys, various species. *Dec. 27.* Se-tenant in sheets of 16. 5, 10, 15, 20, 25, 30, 35, 40, 45, 50, 55, 60c, 1, 2e; airmail 10, 70e (16v).
Cats, various species. *Dec. 27.* Se-tenant in sheets of 16. 5, 10, 15, 20, 25, 30, 35, 40, 45, 50, 55, 60c, 1, 2e; airmail 10, 70e (16v).
Fish, various species. *Dec. 27.* Se-tenant in sheets of 16. 5, 10, 15, 20, 25, 30, 35, 40, 45, 50, 55, 60c, 1, 2e; airmail 10, 70e (16v).
Butterflies, various species. *Dec. 27.* Se-tenant in sheets of 16, 5, 10, 15, 20, 25, 30, 35, 40, 45, 50, 55, 60c, 1, 2e; airmail 10, 70e (16v).

1975
Picasso Memorial (Paintings from last period). *Jan. 27.* 5, 10, 15, 20, 25c; airmail, 5, 70e (7v). 2 souvenir sheets 130e, perf.; 200e, imperf.
ARPHILA 75 Philatelic Exhibition Paris. *Jan. 27.* 8 gold foil airmail souvenir sheets, 3 sheets of 1, 250e, 1 sheet of 2, 250e, perf.; 3 sheets of 1, 300e; 1 sheet of 2, 300e, imperf.
Easter and Holy Year 1975. *Feb. 15.* 60, 70, 80c, 1, 1.50e; airmail, 30, 50e (7v). 2 airmail souvenir sheets 225e, perf.; 300e, imperf.
12th Winter Olympics, Innsbruck, 1976. *Mar. 10.* 5, 10, 15, 20, 25, 30, 35, 40, 45c, 25, 70e (11v). 2 souvenir sheets 130e, perf.; 200e, imperf. 2 gold foil souvenir sheets, 1 sheet of 1, 250e, 1 sheet of 2, 250e x 2.
Don Quixote. *Apr. 4.* 30, 35, 40, 45, 50c; airmail, 25, 60e (7v). 2 souvenir sheets 130e, perf.; 200e, imperf.
American Bicentennial. *April 30.* (First Issue) 5, 20, 40, 75c, 2, 5, 8e; airmail 25, 30e (9v). Airmail souvenir sheets, 130e, perf., 200e, imperf.
April 30. (Second Issue) 10, 30, 50c, 1, 3, 6, 10e; airmail, 12, 40e (9v). 2 airmail souvenir sheets, 130e, perf., 200e, imperf.
July 4 (Presidents) 5, 10, 20, 30, 40, 50, 75c, 1, 2, 3, 5, 6, 8, 10e; airmail, 12, 25, 30, 40e (18v). 4 airmail souvenir sheets, 225e x 2, perf., 300e x 2, imperf. Embossed gold foil 6 souvenir sheets airmail 200e x 2, 200e (2) perf., 300e x 2, 300e (2) imperf.
Bull Fight. *May 26.* 80, 85, 90, 95c, 8e; airmail, 35, 40e (7v). 2 airmail souvenir sheets, 130e, perf., 200e, imperf.
Apollo-Soyuz Space Project. *June 20.* 1, 2, 3, 5, 5.50, 7, 7.50, 9, 15e; airmail, 20, 30e (11v). 2 airmail souvenir sheets, 225e, perf., 300e, imperf.
Apollo-Soyuz Space Project. *July 17.* Airmail souvenir sheet, 250e, perf.
Famous Painters, Nudes. *Aug. 10.* Se-tenant in sheets of 16. 5, 10, 15, 20, 25, 30, 35, 40, 45, 50, 55, 60c, 1, 2e; airmail 10, 70e (16v). (Egyptian, Greek, Roman, Indian art, Goes, Durer, Liss, Beniort, Renior, Gauguin, Stenlen, Picasso, Modigliani, Matisse, Padua). Airmail souvenir sheetlets embossed gold foil, 10 x 200p + 25p., perf., 10 x 250p+50p, imperf.
Conquerors of the Seas. *Sept. 5.* 30, 35, 40, 45, 50, 55, 60, 65, 70, 75c; airmail 8, 10, 50, 60p (14v). 4 airmail souvenir sheets, 130p, perf., 200p, imperf., 2 each.
Christmas and Holy Year 1975. *Oct.* 60, 70, 80c, 1, 1.50e; airmail 30, 50e (7v) (Jordan, Barocci, Vereycke, Rubens, Mengs, Del Castillo, Cavedone). 2 airmail souvenir sheets, 225e, perf., 300e, imperf. Embossed gold foil, 4 souvenir sheets, 200e, perf., 300e, imperf. 2 gold foil miniature sheets of 2, 200e+200e, perf., 300e+300e, imperf.
President Macias, I.W.Y. *Dec. 25.* 1.50, 3, 3.50, 5, 7, 10e; airmail 100, 300e (8v). 2 airmail souvenir sheets (world events), 100 (U.S., Yorktown 2c), 300e, imperf.

1976
Uniforms, Cavalry. *Feb. 2.* 5, 10, 15, 20, 25c; airmail, 5, 70p (7v). 2 airmail souvenir sheets, 130p, perf., 200p, imperf.
12th Winter Olympics, Innsbruck '76. *Feb.* 50, 55, 60, 65, 70, 75, 80, 85, 90e; airmail 35, 60e (11v). 2 airmail souvenir sheets, 130e, perf., 200e, imperf.
21st Summer Olympics Montreal '76. Ancient to Modern Games. *Feb.* 50, 60, 70, 80, 90c; airmail 35, 60e (7v). 2 souvenir sheets airmail, 225e, perf., 300e, imperf.
21st Summer Olympics Montreal '76 *Mar. 5.* 50, 60, 70, 80, 90c; airmail 30, 60e (7v). 2 airmail souvenir sheets 225e, perf., 300e, imperf. 4 embossed gold foil airmail souvenir sheets, 250e, perf., 300e, imperf. 2 miniature sheets of 2, 250ex2, perf., 300ex2, imperf.
U.N. 30th Anniversary. *June.* Airmail souvenir sheet, 250e, perf.
El Greco, paintings. *Apr. 5.* 1, 3, 5, 8, 10e; airmail, 15, 25e (7v). 2 airmail semipostal souvenir sheets, 200+25e, perf., 250+50e, imperf.
21st Summer Olympics, Montreal, modern games. *May 7.* 50, 55, 60, 65, 70, 75, 80, 85, 90c; airmail, 35, 60e (11v). 2 airmail souvenir sheets, 225e, perf., 300e, imperf. 4 embossed on gold foil souvenir sheets, 250e, perf., 300e, imperf. (2 each). 2 miniature sheets of 2, 250e x 2, perf., 300e x 2, imperf.
Contemporary Automobiles, *June 10.* 1, 3, 5, 8, 10p; airmail, 15, 25p (7v). 2 airmail semipostal souvenir sheets, 200+25p, perf., 250+50p, imperf.
Nature Protection, European Animals, *July 1.* 5, 10, 15, 20, 25c; airmail, 5, 70p (7v). 2 airmail souvenir sheets, 130p, perf., 200p, imperf. **Asian Animals.** *Sept. 20.* 30, 35, 40, 45c, 8p; airmail 50c, 60p (7v). 2 airmail souvenir sheets, 130p, perf., 200p, imperf.
Asian Birds. *Sept. 20.* 55, 60, 65, 70, 75c; airmail, 10, 50p (7v). 2 airmail souvenir sheets, 130p, perf., 200p, imperf. **European Birds.** *Sept. 20.* 5, 10, 15, 20, 25c; airmail, 5, 70p (7v). 2 airmail souvenir sheets, 130p, perf., 200p, imperf. **North American Birds.** *Sept. 20.* 80, 85, 90, 95c, 1p; airmail 15, 40p (7v). 2 airmail souvenir sheets, 130p, perf., 200p, imperf.
Motorcycle Aces. *July 22.* 1e x 2, 2e x 2, 3e x 2, 4e x 2, 5e x 2, 10e x 2, 30e x 2, 40e x 2 (16v) in setenant blocks of 8 different values.
21st Summer Olympics, Montreal. *Aug.* 7, 10, 25e setenant strip of 3; airmail, 200e (4v). Airmail souvenir sheet, 300e, imperf.
Flowers. *Aug. 16.* South America. 30, 35, 40, 45, 50c; airmail, 8, 60p (7v). 2 airmail souvenir sheets, 130p, perf., 200p, imperf.
Oceania. 80, 85, 90, 95c, 1p; airmail, 15, 40p (7v). 2 airmail souvenir sheets, 130p, perf., 200p, imperf.

1977
Butterflies. *Jan.* 80, 85, 90, 95c; 8c; airmail, 35, 40e (7v). 2 airmail souvenir sheets, 130e, perf., 200e, imperf.
Madrid Real, 75th anniversary. *Jan.* 2, 4, 5, 8, 10, 15e; airmail, 20, 35, 150e (9v).
Ancient Carriages. *Feb.* 5, 10, 15, 20, 25, 30, 35, 40, 45, 50, 55, 60c, 1, 2e; airmail, 10, 70e (16v).
Chinese Art. *Feb.* 60, 70, 80c, 1, 1.50e; airmail, 30, 50e (7v). 2 airmail souvenir sheets, 130e, perf., 200e, imperf.
African Masks. *Mar.* 5, 10, 15, 20, 25c; airmail, 5, 70e (7v). 2 airmail souvenir sheets, 130e, perf., 200e, imperf.
North American Animals, 1.25, 1.50, 1.75, 2, 2.25e; airmail, 20, 50e (7v). 2 airmail souvenir sheets, 130e, perf., 200e, imperf.
World Championship Soccer, Argentina '78. *July 25.* **Famous Players.** 2, 4, 5, 8, 10, 15e; airmail, 20, 35e (8v). 2 airmail souvenir sheets, 150e, perf., 250e, imperf.
Famous Teams. 2, 4, 5, 8, 10, 15e; airmail, 20, 35e (8v se-tenant). 2 gold foil embossed souvenir sheets, 500e (Amphilex '77, Cutty Sark, Concorde); airmail, 500e (World Cup).
Napoleon. *Aug. 20.*
Life and Battle Scenes. 5, 10, 15, 20, 25, 30, 35, 40, 45, 50, 55, 60c, 1, 2e; airmail, 10, 70e (setenant in sheet of 16).
Military Uniforms. 5, 10, 15, 20, 25, 30, 35, 40, 45, 50, 55, 60c, 1, 2e; airmail, 10, 70e (se-tenant in sheet of 16).

South American Animals. *Aug.* 2.50, 2.75, 3, 3.50, 4e; airmail, 25, 35e (7v). 2 airmail souvenir sheets, 130e, perf., 200e imperf.
U.S.S.R. Space Program, 20th anniversary. *Dec. 15.* 2, 4, 5, 8, 10, 15e; airmail, 20, 35e (8v). 2 airmail souvenir sheets, 150e, imperf., 250e, perf.

1978
Ancient Sailing Ships. *Jan. 6.* 5, 10, 15, 20, 25c; airmail, 5, 70e, also 5, 10, 20, 25, 70e (12v). 4 airmail souvenir sheets, 150, 225e, perf., 250, 300e, imperf. Gold foil embossed airmail souvenir sheets, 500e, perf., imperf.
Pre-Olympics '80. *Jan. 17.*
Winter Games, Lake Placid. 5, 10, 20, 25e; airmail, 70e (5v). 2 airmail souvenir sheets, 150e, perf., 250e, imperf. Gold foil embossed airmail souvenir sheet, 500e, perf., imperf.
Summer Games, Moscow. 2, 3, 5, 8, 10, 15e; airmail, 30, 50e (8v). 2 airmail souvenir sheets, 150e, perf., 250e, imperf. Gold foil embossed airmail souvenir sheet, 500e perf., imperf.
Summer Water Games, Talinn. 5, 10, 20, 25e; airmail, 70e (5v). 2 airmail souvenir sheets, 150e, perf., 250e, imperf. Gold foil embossed airmail souvenir sheet, 500e. perf., imperf.
QE II Coronation, 25th anniversary. *Apr. 25.* 2, 5, 8, 10, 12, 15e; airmail, 30, 50e (8v). 2 airmail souvenir sheets, 150e perf., 250e imperf.
English Knights of 1200-1350 A.D. *Apr. 25.* 5, 10, 15, 20, 25e; airmail, 15, 70e (7v). 2 airmail souvenir sheets, 130e perf., 250e imperf.
Old Locomotives. *Aug.* 1, 2, 3, 5, 10e; airmail, 25, 70e (7v). 2 airmail souvenir sheets, 150e perf., 250e imperf.
Prehistoric Animals. *Aug.* 30, 35, 40, 45, 50e; airmail, 25, 60e (7v). Airmail souvenir sheet, 130e.
Souvenir Sheets. *Aug.* Airmail: **Francisco Goya,** "Maja Vestida," 150e; **Per Paul Rubens — UNICEF,** 250e; **Europa—CEPT—Europhila, 78,** 250e; **30th International Stamp Fair, Riccione,** 150e; **1978 Events.** Sheet of 3, QE II Coronation, 150e; CEPT. 250e and World Cup Soccer, Argentina '78 and Spain '82, 150e; Christmas, Titian painting, "The Virgin." 150e.

NUMERICAL INDEX OF WATERMARK ILLUSTRATIONS (VOL. 2)

1989 NUMBER CHANGES (VOL. 2)

No. in 1988 Cat.	No. in 1989 Cat.
AFGHANISTAN	
252-261	deleted
O2	deleted
Q21-Q22	deleted
BELGIUM	
1083	1084
BRAZIL	
41	deleted
296a	deleted
2073A	2073C
COSTA RICA	
87a	deleted
O21a	deleted
332	334
334	332
335	337
337	335
345	349
346	354
347	359
348	364
DENMARK	
318a	494a
318b	688a
EGYPT	
155a-158a	deleted
ESTONIA	
35b	deleted
FINLAND	
11b	deleted
FRANCE	
Council of Europe	
1O29	1O33
1O31	1O34
1O32	1O31
1O33	1O35
1O34	1O29
1O35	1O32
UNESCO	
2O29	2O31
2O30	2O34
2O31	2O29
2O33	2O35
2O34	2O30
2O35	2O33

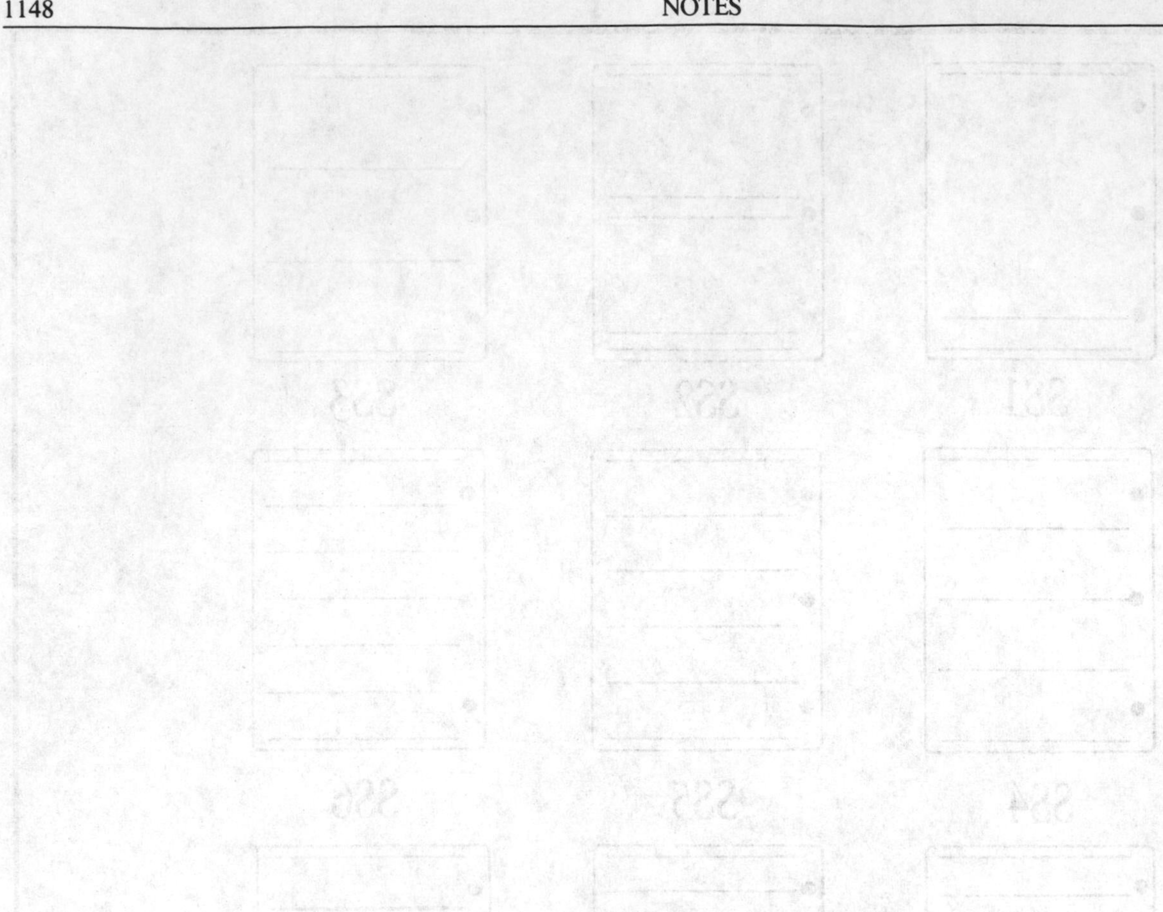

APPROVALS

FOR YOUR COLLECTING PLEASURE WRITE TO...
The Rideout Stamp Family - Manson, Wilma, Ronald

For over 30 years we have been mailing fine selections of General World and Topical groups Postpaid both ways on approval. Our vast stock and experience Guaranteed to please you. You may ask for any special groups you would like to inspect and with your first selection we have a nice set of stamps which we will include as a thank you for trying our service. You may cancel at anytime. You have up to 30 days to inspect the approvals without a reminder being sent. We Aim to please you. Try us soon. I, Manson Rideout, am a 26 year APS member, also long time ATA.

MANSON RIDEOUT PHILATELIST LTD.
P.O. Box 1009, Houlton, Maine 04730
Or In Canada RR #1, Upper Woodstock, N.B., Canada E0J 1Z0

SCOTT STAMP MONTHLY AND CATALOGUE UPDATE.
Write for advertising information
P.O. Box 828, Sidney, OH 45365

SCOTT PUBLISHING COMPANY
Are you interested in advertising in the 1990 Scott Catalogues?
Let us know and we'll send you information when it is available.
P.O. Box 828, Sidney, OH 45365

ACCESSORIES

30% DISCOUNT

ON . . . SCOTT, MINKUS, WHITE ACE, HARCO, ELBE, ENOR, SHOWGARD, LIGHTHOUSE, HAWID, CMC, GLASSINES, HARRIS, HAGNER, KABE, DAVO, SAFE, LINDNER, VPD, BOOKS, STANLEY GIBBONS, etc. Send $1.00 for catalog, refundable with $20.00 order.

Send SASE For Current List of Specials!

TERMS: ORDERS UNDER $20.00 add $3.00 SHIPPING. Add 15% shipping and handling under $50.00 net; 10% over $50.00 net; 5% over $100 net; FREE SHIPPING OVER $150.00 net. Alaska, Hawaii and outside continental U.S., add 25% shipping. VISA and MasterCard accepted on all orders.

GOPHER WHOLESALERS
Phone in your order: 612-731-6196 for fast UPS service
P.O. Box 25041-C, Woodbury, MN 55125

Showgard® Mounts

The time proven hingeless method for protecting stamp values!

• AT STAMP DEALERS EVERYWHERE •

Sample on request from:

VIDIFORMS COMPANY, INC.
110 Brenner Drive, Congers, NY 10920 U.S.A.
In Canada: Showgard Group Canada, 1110 Beaulac St., Ville St. Laurent, Quebec H4R 1R7

AUCTIONS

DO YOU COLLECT U.S. OR WORLDWIDE STAMPS AND POSTAL HISTORY? ARE YOU A SPECIALIST?

AN INVITATION TO CONSIGN

Individual stamps, covers or collections for Public Auctions or Private Treaty Sale.

WHAT IS A SCHIFF "ESPECIALLY FOR SPECIALISTS" AUCTION?

It's an auction designed with YOU in mind, whether you are a buyer or a seller of U.S. or Worldwide stamps.

WE ALSO PURCHASE OUTRIGHT

Contact us first, describing your material. Include your address and phone numbers.

IF YOU DO NOT GET OUR CATALOGS YOU ARE MISSING OUT!

SEND $8.50 ($12.50 overseas)
...for a year's subscription to catalogs and prices realized or send $1.50 for our next auction catalog and prices realized ($1.00 catalogs only).

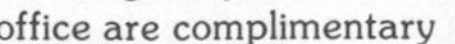

Catalogs picked up at our office are complimentary

JACQUES C. SCHIFF, JR., INC.
195 Main Street
Ridgefield Park, N.J. 07660 U.S.A.
201-641-5566 (from NYC 662-2777)

QUALIFIED AUCTIONEER

Especially For Specialists

(Established 1947)
Licensed and Bonded Auctioneers

STAMP STORES

OMEGA STAMP & COIN CO.
Brooklyn's Largest Buys & Sells U.S. & Foreign Collections.
2076 East 17th St., Brooklyn, NY 11229. Ph. 718-339-9191.

100 Years of Service & Experience

NATICK STAMPS & HOBBIES

Established 1887 Phone (213) 626-3339

"Downtown Los Angeles' ONLY Stamp & Hobby Shop"

ARCO PLAZA "C" LEVEL, DOWNTOWN HOBBY SHOP
505 SOUTH FLOWER STREET, LOS ANGELES, CALIFORNIA 90071

- First Day Cover Service • New Issue Service
- Supplies for all your philatelic needs
- World Wide Stock
- New and Larger Store To Better Serve You

P.F.

EVERYTHING FOR THE STAMP COLLECTOR

44734

TOPICALS

• TOPICALS •

For many years (first as Filatelia Pampa) we have been a leader in this field. ANY sub-topic is Not Strange for us!

LARGE WORLDWIDE STOCK
ALL TOPICS
...including varieties, cancels, covers, etc.

WANT LISTS WELCOME
...any Catalogue #, any main language.

ERCOLE GLORIA - Gregorio Zuskis
Piazza Pio Xi 1, 20123 Milan, ITALY

Do You Collect Any Of These?

Aircraft	Children & IYC	Hands	QE Jubilee & Coronation	Sports
Animals	Christmas	Horses	Red Cross	Sports, Winter
Antarctic	Coins	Insects	Religion	Stained Glass
Archeology	Costumes	ITU	Reptiles	Stamp on Stamp & Shows
Art Works	Churchill	Lighthouses	Rotary	Trains
Astronomy	Dogs & Cats	Maps	Roosevelt	Transportation
Bells	Energy	Medical	Royal Weddings	U.N. Related
Bicentennial	Europa	Minerals	Scientists	UPU 75th & 100th
Bicycles & Motorcycles	Fairy Tales	Military	Scouts	Waterfalls
Birds	Fire & Police	Music	Sea Shells	Windmills
Bridges	Fish	Mushrooms	Ships	Women
Butterflies	Flags	Nuclear	Soccer	Writers
Chess	Flowers	Olympics	Space	Zeppelins
	Food	Paintings		

TRY ARKSARBEN FOR ALL YOUR TOPICS!
We stock 105 DIFFERENT TOPICS. Send a #10 SASE for your favorite topical price list. We have stamps and covers, so ask for what you need. Want lists also filled.

● WE BUY TOPICAL AND WORLDWIDE COLLECTIONS ●

AKSARBEN "TOPICALS"
1917 Missouri Ave., Omaha, NE 68107
ATA Life Member #1578, Phone 492-734-1553

TOPICALS

TOPICALS • TOPICALS • TOPICALS • TOPICALS

CITY HALL STAMP CO.,INC.
The TOPICAL Market SPECIALIST

- Want lists filled on all topics.
- Always ready to buy topical collections.
- Absolute satisfaction guaranteed.

City Hall Stamp Co., Inc.
Wholesale-Retail

P.O. Box 52, East Station
Yonkers, N.Y. 10704
Phone 914-969-3554, 969-2023

Cable — Alkastamp, Yonkers, N.Y. • Telex #497 2032

TOPICALS • TOPICALS • TOPICALS • TOPICALS

SCOTT STAMP MONTHLY AND CATALOGUE UPDATE.
Write for advertising information
P.O. Box 828, Sidney, OH 45365

PLAN NOW TO FEATURE YOUR ADVERTISING MESSAGE IN THE SCOTT® 1990 CATALOGUES

Call 513-498-0802 or write to us and we'll place your name on our prospect list to receive full information, as soon as it is available, on advertising rates and copy deadlines. If you are interested in specific positions, place your name on our reservation list as soon as possible.

Scott Publishing Company
P.O. Box 828, Sidney, OH 45365